American Statistics Index 1991

Covering Publications Issued
January 1–December 31, 1991

A comprehensive guide to the statistical publications of the U.S. Government

Index

 Congressional Information Service

Editorial Advisory Board

Hon. Richard Bolling, Former Representative from Missouri

Edward DiRoma New York Public Library

William Kingsley, American Council of Life Insurance

John W. Lehman Washington, D.C.

Robert R. Nathan Robert R. Nathan Associates

Conrad Taeuber Washington, D.C.

Special Consultant

Ruth Fine Washington, D.C.

Staff

Editorial Director Susan I. Jover

Director of Statistical Services Darlene J. Montgomery

Managing Editor Daniel Coyle

Asst. Managing Editor, Index Lee McKee

Asst. Managing Editor, Abstracts Benjamin S. Pitkin

Asst. Managing Editor, Acquisitions Cheryl Waldman

Abstracting and Indexing Staff John Brodkin Thomas W. FitzHugh E. Q. Johnson, Jr. Shant Markarian, Jr.

Jane A. Lean Shelley W. Walker Betsy H. Witte

Accuracy Editor Maria M. Brown

Editorial Assistants Vanessa Belton Hubbard Luis R. Lugo

Acquisitions Editors Laura King Dean T. Lake Loretta Saltzman Robert Sellars

Production Staff Dorothy W. Rogers, Coordinator Stephanie Hines, Asst. Coordinator Helene Gaffney

Congressional Information Service

Systems Support Staff Nadine Benton Elizabeth Lane Pat Simons Melvin Turner

Computer Operators Nahid Heffernan Marc Balthrop

EDP Admin. Assistant Paola Schrage

Vice President/Controller Max E. Venegas

Accounting Staff Stuart Abramowitz Vivian Brenner Donald Hawkins Mark Peele David Sauer Regina Sheffield Susan Sinicropi Rita Skolnik-Crowley Paula Solorzano Gail Taylor Emmy Wong

Manager, Administrative Services Lee Mayer

Administrative Services Coordinator Bonnie Balzer

Personnel Director Rebecca Warwick

Vice President, Manufacturing William C. Smith

President Paul P. Massa

Vice President and Editorial Director Susan I. Jover

Exec. Vice President, CIS James F. Connolly

Vice President, Planning and Research Howard Goldstein

Vice President, Finance Carolyn J. Kull

Vice President, EDP & Technology E. Don Johnson

Senior Developer Jack Wolfire

Manager, Applications Programming Andrew Ross

Manager, Systems and Operations Mojtaba Anvari

Project Leader Robert Starbird

Programmer/Analysts Kambiz Ilchi Eugene Ryzhikov Bryan Zimmer

Plant Operations Manager William Idol

Micropublishing Production Staff Marjorie Abuan Zenaida Altherr Donna Barrick Catherine Bassford Lukman Bazarah Sandra Bohnke Margaret Bowles Karla Bradburn Zina Brown Abel David Parker Davis James Day Dorothy Faunce Margaret Fisher Janice Garcia Patricia Garrison Robert Goddard Michelle Goostree Teresa Graham Matilda Gregory Susan Harding Diane Harrison Diana Hawk Mildred Harrison Kimberly Hayes Sandra Heineman Joyce Herbert Mary Ann Hodges Faith Holmes Kathy Hutchinson Dianette Johnson Elizabeth Kennedy Jane Kiger Donna Lacey Ida Lamkin Ethel LeBeaux Edwin Legaspi Robin Long Betty Lyles Ruth Mattingly

Eric Merson Elaine Miles James Mowrer Sharon Norris Sonja Norris Edgar O'Bannon Scott Owen Marjorie Rickerson Gloria Robinson Barbara Schirmacher Nilza Silva Doris Stevens Maria Stewart Rose Thompson Mary Tippett Armando Vicente Shaun Woolcock Gertrude Young

Director, Research Alexander D. McRae

Electronic Publishing Projects Eric Massant Mark Vonderhaar

Research Staff Caryl Dikkers Elizabeth Daugharty Bonnie Lease William Wears

Documents on Demand Coordinator Sharon L. Schmedicke

National Sales Manager John P. Beil

Sales Representatives John Cox James Drummond Jane Edwards Scott Eller Donald Fitch Christine Hansen

Paul Hennrikus Jeffrey Strandberg

Customer Service Manager Katie Culliton

Marketing Services Assistants Maria Fanelli Toby Holtzman

Vice President, Marketing Richard K. Johnson

Director of Communications Jack Carey

Marketing Services Manager Raymond W. Crow, Jr.

Advertising, Publicity, and Promotion Staff Linda Brown Constance Cudjoe Courtenay Diederich Tom Felt Diane Keely Alix Stock Marcia Taylor Shanon Venegas

Secretary to the President Karen L. Grossnickle

Secretary to Editorial Director Xinia Smartt

Admin. Ass't Finance Susan Savage

Staff Assistants Curtis Brevard Scott Gundersen Jon Markus Lynn Pizzulli

---

ISSN 0091 - 1658 Key Title: American Statistics Index

The Library of Congress Cataloged the First Issue of This Title as Follows:

American Statistics Index, 1973- Washington. Congressional Information Service, annual.

"A comprehensive guide and index to the statistical publications of the U.S. Government."

1. United States-Statistics-Bibliography. 2. United States-Statistics-Abstracts. I. Congressional Information Service.

Z7554.U5A46 016.3173 73-82599 ISSN 0091 - 1658 MARC-S

International Standard Book Number For the Set: 0-88692-241-0 For Index Volume: 0-88692-242-9 For Abstract Volume: 0-88692-243-7

Published by Congressional Information Service, Inc. 4520 East-West Highway Bethesda, MD 20814 U.S.A.

♾™

The paper used in this publication meets the minimum requirements of American National Standard for Information Sciences-Permanence of Paper for Printed Library Materials, ANSI Z39.48-1984.

A privately organized reference service. Printed and Bound in the United States of America. Copyright © 1992 by Congressional Information Service All rights reserved.

CONTENTS

The American Statistics Index 1991 Annual
is published in two volumes, the contents
of which are summarized below.

Index

Detailed Table of Contents: Index Volume v

User Guide vii

Introduction to the American Statistics Index vii
Coverage of ASI Annual and Monthly Editions vii
Statistical Publications Covered by ASI viii
Organization of ASI Abstracts and Indexes ix
How ASI Abstracts Statistical Publications xi
How ASI Indexes Statistical Publications xii
Acquiring the Documents xx
Additional CIS Services xx
Sample Abstracts xxiii
Sample Search xxvi
Where To Write for Statistical Publications xxviii
Document Availability Symbols xxxii
Acronyms and Selected Abbreviations xxxiii
Issuing Agencies and ASI Accession Numbers xxxiv

Index by Subjects and Names 1

Index by Categories 841

Index by Titles 921

Index by Agency Report Numbers 989

**Index of Superintendent of
Documents Numbers** 1007

**Guide to Selected
Standard Classifications** 1023

Abstracts

Detailed Table of Contents: Abstracts Volume

Issuing Agencies and ASI Accession Numbers v

User Guide xvii

Abstracts of Statistical Publications 1

Index by Subjects and Names — 1

(This index contains references to subjects, to corporate authors, and to individual authors of articles and publications.)

Index by Categories — 841

(This index contains references to publications tables, and groups of tables that contain breakdowns of statistical data by State, by industry, by age, or by some other standard category.)

Geographic Breakdowns

By Census Division	841
By City	842
By County	846
By Foreign Country	847
By Outlying Area	854
By Region	857
By SMSA or MSA	864
By State	865
By Urban-Rural and Metro-Nonmetro	879

Economic Breakdowns

By Commodity	881
By Federal Agency	885
By Income	887
By Individual Company or Institution	888
By Industry	894
By Occupation	898

Demographic Breakdowns

By Age	900
By Disease	905
By Educational Attainment	906
By Marital Status	908
By Race and Ethnic Group	909
By Sex	914

Index by Titles — 921

(This index contains an alphabetical listing of all publication titles abstracted.)

Index by Agency Report Numbers — 989

(This index contains a listing of all publications abstracted for which there are agency report numbers available, arranged by issuing agency.)

Index of Superintendent of Documents Numbers — 1007

(This index contains a listing of Superintendent of Documents Classification Numbers for publications abstracted by ASI.)

Guide to Selected Standard Classifications — 1023

(This guide outlines the major standard classification systems used by various Federal agencies to arrange and present social and economic statistical data.)

Census Regions and Divisions	1023
Outlying Areas of the U.S.	1023
Standard Federal Administrative Regions	1023
Farm Production Regions	1023
Federal Reserve Districts	1024
Federal Home Loan Bank Districts	1024
Bureau of Labor Statistics Regions (and Regional Offices)	1024
Metropolitan Statistical Areas	1025
Consolidated Metropolitan Statistical Areas	1026
Cities with Population over 100,000	1027
Consumer Price Index Cities	1027
Standard Industrial Classification	1028
Standard Occupational Classification	1036
Standard International Trade Classification, Revision 3	1039

USER GUIDE

INTRODUCTION TO THE AMERICAN STATISTICS INDEX

The U.S. Government is the world's most important and prolific publisher of statistics. Federal agencies produce a continual flow of facts and figures on virtually every aspect of life in America and on most matters of worldwide concern.

Until the initiation of the American Statistics Index (ASI) and related services in 1972, use of Government statistics was hampered by the absence of adequate tools to identify relevant publications and pinpoint the data within them, as well as by the difficulty of locating and acquiring the publications themselves.

Major statistical agencies, such as the Census Bureau, index their own publications and disseminate them widely; other agencies issue publications lists and partial indexes; many agencies do neither. Nowhere in the Government is this wealth of data indexed, or even listed, completely. Many of these publications are not available through the Government Printing Office nor listed in its *Monthly Catalog;* and many are unavailable at depository libraries.

ASI aims to be a master guide and index to all the statistical publications of the U.S. Government. It was created to meet the need expressed in 1971 by the President's Commission on Federal Statistics, for "a central catalog of data available in government agencies . . . a single source in which one could locate all data currently collected by the Federal Government on a particular subject."

Specifically, the purpose of ASI is to perform the following functions, promptly and comprehensively:

- **Identify** the statistical data published by all branches and agencies of the Federal Government.
- **Catalog** the publications in which these data appear, providing full bibliographic information about each publication.
- **Announce** new publications as they appear.
- **Describe** the contents of these publications fully.
- **Index** this information in full subject detail.
- **Micropublish** virtually all the publications covered by ASI, thereby providing, on a continuing basis, reliable access to the statistics themselves.

To assure comprehensiveness, ASI staff members monitor all published document listings and regularly visit or contact over 500 Federal offices. In 1991, ASI collected, abstracted, and micropublished approximately 5,000 titles, including 600 periodicals. To assure prompt coverage during the year, full abstracts and indexing for all publications, including statistical articles within individual issues of periodicals, are published in an ASI Monthly Supplement issued 5 to 6 weeks after the month in which publications are obtained. The source documents themselves are issued on ASI microfiche about two weeks later.

This ASI 1991 Annual cumulates and enhances ASI Monthly Supplement coverage of Federal statistical publications issued during 1991. It is meant to be used in coordination with other ASI publications and services that provide comprehensive coverage of Federal statistical publications issued since the 1960s.

The following User's Guide discusses how the ASI system is organized; what kinds of statistical publications and statistics are issued by the Federal Government and accessible through ASI; how these publications are cataloged for retrieval through ASI; how their contents are abstracted and indexed in ASI; and where one can obtain the publications in hardcopy or on ASI microfiche.

COVERAGE OF ASI ANNUAL AND MONTHLY EDITIONS

ASI full coverage of U.S. Government statistical publications dates from the 1960s. This coverage is achieved through a base ASI Retrospective Edition, covering publications issued from 1960-73; Annual editions, each covering publications issued during a single year of coverage, 1974-91; and Monthly Supplement editions, issued throughout each year.

Each ASI edition is issued in 2 sections: an Abstracts Section that contains full descriptions of the content and format of each publication, organized by ASI accession number; and an Index Section that contains comprehensive subject and name, category, title, and report number indexes, with references keyed to abstract accession numbers.

The separate ASI editions are more fully described below.

ASI 1991 Annual

The ASI 1991 Annual, covering publications issued Jan. 1–Dec. 31, 1991, cumulates coverage of all publications originally abstracted and indexed in the ASI 1991 Monthly Supplements. It replaces and fully supersedes those Monthly Supplements.

In addition, the 1991 Annual contains full abstracts and indexing for all periodicals actively being published in 1991. In this respect, it is also designed to serve as the base reference source for all periodicals currently publishing in 1992, and to be used in conjunction with ASI 1992 Monthly Supplements for locating data contained in current periodicals. Abstracts of periodicals and other recurring publications in the 1991 Annual reflect the format and content of the latest issue received during the year, and include notations of any significant changes occurring during the year.

ASI 1992 Monthly Supplements

ASI 1992 Monthly Supplements provide current abstracts and indexing for all new publications issued during each month of 1992. These include wholly new publications, new items in series, and updates or new editions of annuals, semiannuals, or other publications covered in previous ASI editions.

Monthly Supplements may also include abstracts for some publications that were issued prior to 1992, but that only recently came to our attention. Such publications are covered, provided they are still current enough to be of general interest.

All statistical periodicals covered by ASI, whether quarterly, monthly, weekly, or daily, are reviewed by the ASI staff on a continuing basis, and the issues received are listed in each Monthly Supplement in the "Periodicals Received and Reviewed" section. However, Monthly Supplements do not re-abstract or re-index periodicals that have remained substantially unchanged since this 1991 Annual.

Only those periodicals that show significant changes in content or format since the basic description in this 1991 Annual are re-abstracted and indexed in the detail necessary to describe the change.

Periodical articles that contain statistical data are abstracted and indexed individually each month.

Monthly Supplements are issued 5 to 6 weeks after the end of the month covered, generally by the 10th-12th of each month.

ASI Retrospective Coverage

This ASI 1991 Annual is the eighteenth annual cumulation issued since the publication of ASI's base 1974 Annual Retrospective Edition. The Retrospective Edition covers statistical publications in print as of Jan. 1, 1974, as well as significant publications issued since the early 1960s.

In the case of repetitive or continuing publications, such as annuals or periodicals, which present continuing series of statistics over long periods of time, the Retrospective Edition does not describe each issuance published since 1960. Rather, it describes in full the format and contents of the most recent edition received at the time, and, where possible, characterizes major changes in format that occurred prior to 1974.

Subsequent annual cumulations, taken together, provide comprehensive coverage of statistical publications issued since Jan. 1, 1974. These annuals are published as hardcover abstracts and index volumes in the spring following the year of coverage.

ASI Multi-year Cumulative Indexes

ASI has published three multiple-year cumulative indexes to date. The 1974–79 Cumulative Index, published in May 1990, which revises and supersedes the separate Annual Index volumes issued for 1974 through 1979, is designed to be used in conjunction with ASI First through Sixth Annual Supplements as originally published. A cumulation covering ASI 1980 through 1984 Index volumes was published in 1985, and a cumulation covering ASI 1985 through 1988 Index volumes was published in 1989. Subsequent cumulations will be issued every four years. For more information about these multiple-year indexes, consult the most recent CIS catalog.

STATISTICAL PUBLICATIONS COVERED BY ASI

Publications included in ASI cover a wide range of subjects, reflecting the many concerns of hundreds of central and regional Federal agencies. These issuing agencies are listed in the detailed table of contents in each Abstracts volume and in the list of "Issuing Agencies and ASI Accession Numbers" in the Index volume. ASI abstracts and indexes all Federal agency publications that contain social, economic, demographic, or natural resources data, and a selection of publications with scientific and technical data.

ASI includes all Federal publications that contain primary data of research value or secondary data collected on a special subject, and also special studies and analyses or other statistics-related materials. All types of

publications are covered, whether published as periodicals, as special one-time reports, as items within a large continuing report series, or as annual or biennial reports.

For purposes of inclusion in ASI, the term "publication" is defined as all printed or duplicated materials that may be distributed by an agency to members of the public, whether on a broad or a limited basis. In a few cases, ASI has obtained single copies of materials that are not generally available for distribution, and has micropublished them for distribution. Press releases and other ephemera are included only if they contain basic data not readily available in another form.

In addition to printed reports, ASI covers CD-ROM releases, microfiche, and wall maps that present statistics. Coverage of CD-ROM products issued by Federal agencies began in 1990.

The sections below describe selected examples of the approximately 5,000 titles covered every year by ASI.

Basic Social and Economic Statistical Data

Since its early organization, and as required by the U.S. Constitution, the Federal Government has been responsible for gathering basic national social and economic data. Today, six large Federal statistical agencies, each in a specialized field, have as their major function the regular collection, analysis, and publication of such data. Data published by these agencies are broadly characterized below:

- **Agricultural Statistics Board, Department of Agriculture —** Monthly to annual reports on every important U.S. crop, with data on production, yield, prices, prospective plantings, and indicated production for the season.
- **Bureau of the Census —** Decennial census of population and housing; quinquennial economic and agricultural censuses; Census of Governments; Current Housing Reports, Current Industrial Reports, monthly foreign trade data, and reports from the monthly Current Population Survey; and methodological studies, indexes, and guides.
- **Bureau of Labor Statistics —** Monthly reports on the Consumer Price Index and unemployment rate; and other periodic, serial, and annual reports on prices, wages and hours, benefits, collective bargaining, work stoppages, and productivity.
- **Energy Information Administration —** Weekly to annual reports on U.S. production, consumption, stocks, trade, and prices of all major energy resources; finances and operations of oil companies, electric utilities, and other energy industries; and projections of energy supply and demand.
- **National Center for Education Statistics —** Annual and other collections of data on elementary, secondary, and higher education schools, staff, students, finances, curricula, and graduates.
- **National Center for Health Statistics —** Monthly and annual collections of vital statistics; and periodic surveys of the health condition of the population, and of health care, personnel, and facilities.

Many additional departments and agencies regularly compile primary data, both from required reports in their areas of responsibility and from special surveys; for example: Bureau of Mines' *Mineral Industry Surveys*, Justice Department's *Uniform Crime Reports* and victimization surveys, Treasury Department income tax statistics, Federal Reserve data on finances and banking, Department of Transportation data on highways and air traffic, and National Science Foundation's Surveys of Science Resources.

Program Related Statistics

Almost all executive departments and administrative or regulatory agencies publish statistics on their own funding and programs.

These data cover agency financial statements, personnel, processing efficiency, workloads, accidents, persons served, and payments made. Some of these data are of interest well beyond the functioning of the agency; for example, social security recipients and payments, food stamp recipients, aliens admitted, speed of handling court cases, nuclear power plant shutdowns and accidents, Federal civilian workforce, and military troop strengths.

ASI provides full coverage of these types of program statistics, but, where possible, selects agency-wide reports for inclusion, and excludes subagency reports that only repeat data in the reports of the larger unit.

For example, the basic financial publication for the entire Government, the *Budget of the U.S.*, is fully covered by ASI; but ASI does not also cover budget requests or justifications from individual agencies unless they present significant data not available elsewhere. ASI generally covers the annual report of each separate agency, but not those of sub-agencies unless they include unique data. Also, ASI covers data on grants, contracts, and procurements, as reported by a large agency as a whole (such as DOD *Prime Contract Awards),* but usually excludes reports by individual divisions.

Special Studies

Many agencies produce a steady stream of monographs, analyses, and studies on subjects within their areas of activity; these are covered by ASI whenever they include statistical data of probable research value. Some agencies also undertake large special studies from time to time; an example of this kind of study covered by ASI in 1991 is the Department of Health and Human Services' *Characteristics of Physicians* State report series, which presents detailed data on practicing physicians.

In some cases, special commissions are created specifically for the purpose of studying a problem of current concern. Studies of this nature have been covered by ASI beginning with those from the early 1960s. For instance, this 1991 Annual covers *Beyond Rhetoric: A New American Agenda for Children and Families,* the final report of the National Commission on Children, with data and recommendations on health, education, and welfare policies affecting children and families.

Some original studies are included which, although not primarily quantitative in nature, present statistics unavailable anywhere else; a number of reports by the General Accounting Office fall into this category. Other publications in ASI which are primarily non-statistical, may contain significant statistical sections. Congressional committee hearings and prints are prime examples.

Non-Tabular Statistics-Related Materials

Publications selected for inclusion in ASI generally contain statistical data in tabular form. However, maps, charts, listings, and narrative materials have also been covered if they provide aid in locating statistical data or in understanding statistical programs. Thus, we cover narrative discussions of statistical methodology, classification guides, directories, and bibliographies that include references to a significant body of statistical materials.

In general, we have attempted to cover all such material issued by the major statistical agencies, but we have applied somewhat more rigid standards for inclusion of material from other agencies.

Exclusions and Selective Coverage

The following kinds of material are either excluded from ASI or covered only on a selective basis:

- **Scientific and technical data —** Highly technical studies, scientific and experimental observations, engineering data, clinical medical studies, and animal laboratory studies are generally excluded from ASI. These data are disseminated through such information services as NTIS, NASA, ERIC, and the National Library of Medicine; ASI makes no attempt to duplicate this coverage.

  We do provide selective coverage of technical data with broad social or economic implications or particular current interest, as well as the less technical publications of technically oriented agencies. For instance, we do cover epidemiological studies; a large number of reports on energy resources, use, and conservation; EPA publications presenting monitoring data and pollution abatement measures and technologies; NOAA weather observations and forecasting techniques; and selected NASA publications.

- **Contract studies —** ASI coverage of contract studies by private organizations is typically limited to those that have been issued by a Federal agency as its own publication, either directly through the agency, through GPO, or through NTIS. In special cases, additional contract studies are covered that we would normally exclude but that have been recommended by an agency as being of particular importance.

- **Classified and confidential data —** These data are not included.

- **Congressional publications —** Congressional publications that contain substantial statistical information are included in ASI. However, ASI does not include any appropriations hearings, which contain primarily Federal program data, and which are abstracted and indexed in detail in the comprehensive *CIS/Index to Publications of the U.S. Congress.*

  When ASI covers a congressional publication also covered by the CIS/Index, it is completely re-abstracted and indexed to highlight the statistical data.

ORGANIZATION OF ASI ABSTRACTS AND INDEXES

ASI provides access to statistical data through companion volumes of indexes and abstracts. In making a subject search, you should consult this 1991 Annual for descriptions of publications issued during 1991, and for basic descriptions of periodicals that continue publication in 1992. The 1992 Monthly Supplements will cover new publications issued during 1992, including new editions of annual reports, and will change and update information regarding 1992 issues of periodicals. To search for material issued prior to 1991, you should consult the ASI Retrospective Edition and the subsequent Annuals, and all multi-year ASI cumulative indexes.

ASI Indexes

Ordinarily, research in ASI will begin with the Index volume. The ASI indexes are designed to lead you to the information you seek from a variety of starting points. The five basic ASI indexes are designed to answer the following types of questions:

- **Subject and Name Index —** "What publications provide statistical data on cost of living and related matters?" and "What publications were issued by the Office of Management and Budget?"
- **Category Index —** "What publications provide cost of living data broken down by city, or some other geographic category?"
- **Title Index —** "What statistical data are included in a periodical entitled *Monthly Labor Review*?"
- **Agency Report Number Index —** "Where in ASI will I find reports in the BLS Bulletin 3050 series?"
- **SuDoc Number Index —** "Does ASI cover the report with the Superintendent of Documents number E3.49:989?"

Each ASI index reference will lead you to an abstract. Descriptive abstracts are provided for every publication; they are designed to tell you enough about the information content of the publication to enable you to decide whether or not it is likely to contain the specific data for which you are looking.

This system depends upon a basic key — the ASI accession number — which identifies publications (or specific parts of publications) in both the index and the abstract volumes.

ASI Accession Numbers

Each ASI abstract carries a unique accession number, which identifies not only the individual publication, but also the issuing agency and the publication type (see Sample Abstracts on p. xxiii-xxv for an illustration of how accession numbers appear on abstracts). The accession number has four basic components, the form and functions of which are described below.

- **Issuing Agency —** In the accession number for any one publication's abstract, the first two to four digits (up to the digit before the hyphen) are keyed to an overall coding scheme and represent the agency that issued the publication. (Coding for large agencies may be broken down by subagency or subject matter area.)
- **Publication type —** The last digit before the

hyphen is keyed to the document's publication type, as follows:

2 =	Current periodicals, daily through semi-annual
4 =	annuals and biennials
6 =	publications in series
8 =	special and irregular publications
1, 3, 5, 7, 9 =	special series and special groups of publications (such as census reports or crop reports) that do not fall into one of the four basic types or which are most clearly represented if kept together under a special heading.

- **Sequential ASI serial number —** The digits after the hyphen form a unique serial number, sequentially assigned, basically in order of ASI acquisition, so that every publication has its own unique number that can be easily found in the Abstracts volumes of ASI.
- **Analytic number —** In many cases, ASI describes publications by using a main abstract in coordination with subordinate abstracts called "analytics," which are printed after the main abstract and are identified and sequenced by decimal numbers (.1, .2, or .3, etc.) following the main abstract accession number.

Analytics are frequently used to describe and individually index distinct parts of a large publication. They are also used to abstract and separately index the individual publications comprising a series, or the statistical articles appearing in individual issues of periodicals.

To use the ASI indexes and abstracts effectively, you do not need to know the ASI agency-coding or publication-type coding schemes, which are incorporated into accession numbers, but familiarity with codes can speed interpretation of entries in the indexes.

Arrangement of Abstracts by Accession Number

All abstracts are arranged by accession number in ascending order. This system automatically catalogs all publications, first by issuing agency, then by publication type, and then by individual publication serial number. All index references are made to these accession numbers. For ease in referring from index to abstract, every page of

Sample: ASI Accession Numbers

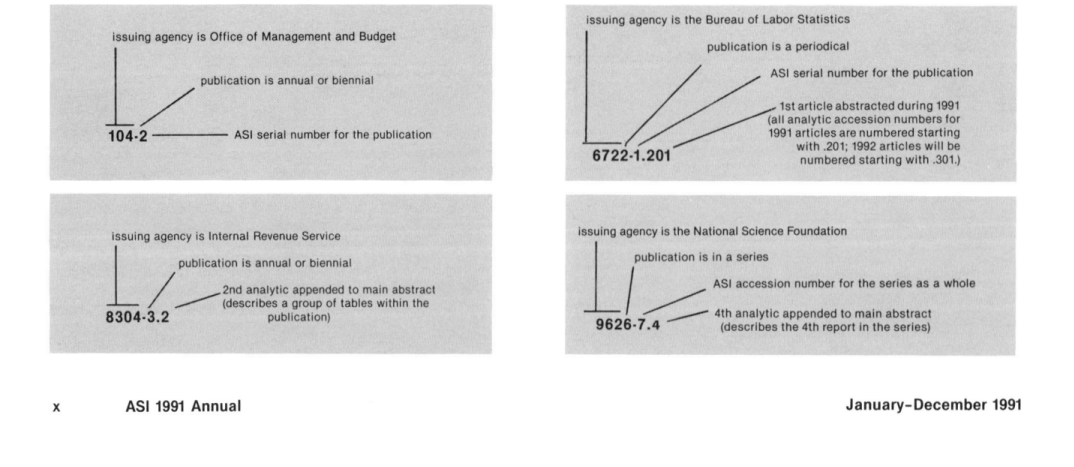

abstracts in the Abstracts volume carries a locator number in the upper right or left corner.

Continuity of Accession Numbers

Generally, once ASI has assigned an accession number to a publication, all successive issues or updates of that publication will receive the same accession number. If the number is changed, cross-references between the old and new numbers are included in the abstracts. The accession number will change if, for example, the periodicity of the publication changes from quarterly to annual, or if the issuing agency of the publication changes.

- List individual titles of all tables in publications that present continuing time series data or data from basic censuses (handling of table listings is further discussed below).
- Review continuity and length of time series data, providing references to ASI abstracts of earlier publications in the series (with the exception of semiannual or annual reports bearing the same accession number) and any breaks in publishing continuity since ASI coverage began.
- Indicate whether a serial publication has been temporarily suspended, discontinued, or transferred to another agency.
- Provide references to known related publications that present similar or identical source data in different analytical or publication formats.

In all cases, the aim is to specify as precisely as possible the actual data to be found in a publication. Particular pains are taken to distinguish among publications providing different data on similar subject matter.

HOW ASI ABSTRACTS STATISTICAL PUBLICATIONS

All ASI abstracts are original and are based upon examination of the entire document. Abstracts differ substantially in degree of detail, depending on the type of publications and the kind of data being described. However, all abstracts are written to fulfill certain objectives.

These objectives are to describe a publication fully enough to allow you to determine if it is likely to contain the specific statistical data you seek; to provide the bibliographic data you need to identify and locate the publication if you wish to borrow or acquire it; and to tell you where in the publication you can find the data, often with specific page ranges.

Guidelines for Describing Statistical Contents

In describing the basic subject matter or statistical data of a publication, ASI does not attempt to summarize observations or conclusions. Rather, we attempt to state consistently what a publication is about; what specific data are presented, from what source, and at what level of detail; and what relationship the publication has to other statistical series. In describing a publication, ASI abstractors observe the following guidelines:

- State the subject matter and purpose of the publication as a whole.
- Identify sources of data presented, whether primary (based on original collection) or whether selected or reprinted from other published sources.
- Describe, if data are primary, the sample type and size, the survey methodology, or the information reporting requirement by which the data were gathered.
- Specify time span and geographic coverage of the data (special methods, discussed below, are used to describe time coverage and currency of data in periodicals).
- State periodicity of data collection and publication.
- Indicate breakdowns of the data and the level of detail they provide.
- Outline physical contents of the publication, such as number of charts and tables, and presence of narrative discussion, appendices, bibliographies, and index. Include page ranges to indicate the quantity and location of each type of material.

Listing of Table Titles

For every publication, ASI attempts to identify, mention, and index the subjects and categories for which significant amounts of statistical data are presented. Often, the best way to describe in detail the data in a statistical publication is to list the titles of the tables it contains.

In general, ASI lists individual titles of tables that carry forward a continuing time series of data in biennial, annual or periodical publications. We also list table titles for publications presenting data from basic surveys and censuses. We usually list the titles exactly as they appear in the original publication. Where necessary for clarity or additional detail, these titles are augmented by material in brackets. Pagination for each table, or group of tables, is given.

Abstracts of special or irregular publications generally do not list tables, but describe the tables in varying degrees of detail, depending upon their number and complexity. If listing table titles is the clearest and briefest way to indicate the exact data present, it is done for any type of publication.

Special Aspects of Abstracts Describing Periodicals

This 1991 Annual contains full descriptions of all statistical periodicals that published any issues during 1991. Since most statistical periodicals retain constant format, features, and tables, it would be redundant to provide full abstracts for each issue. Therefore, abstracts of periodicals indicate the features common to all issues and list tables that appear in each issue or at regular intervals. Periodicals that were discontinued during 1991 are so annotated in this 1991 Annual; All others may be presumed to be continuing publication in 1992.

Statistical articles in periodicals are individually abstracted and indexed each month, and special tables that appear only in certain issues are listed. All such articles and special tables appearing in periodical issues during 1991 are included in this 1991 Annual.

In listing tables for periodicals, we do not give the time coverage of the data as a specific month or year, but describe it in a way that will apply to all issues. The abstracts do not include page ranges, which may change from issue to issue.

All abstracts of periodicals in this annual include a notation of issues received, reviewed, and microfilmed during 1991. The cover dates of the issues are labeled (P) if they approximate the publication date: or (D) if they represent the period covered by the data presented. The body of the abstract usually indicates the time lag between the data date and the publication date.

Periodical abstracts in the 1991 Annual serve as the base abstracts for continuing periodicals, to be used in conjunction with the 1992 Monthly Supplements. Issues of those periodicals received during 1992 will be listed in the Monthly Supplements "Periodicals Received and Reviewed" section as they are received, but will not be re-abstracted of re-indexed unless their contents change significantly.

Provision of Bibliographic Data

ASI abstracts for each publication provide, at a minimum, primary bibliographic information, such as title, date, collation, agency report number (if any), and periodicity. In addition, we include, whenever possible, the Superintendent of Documents classification number, the Library of Congress card number, the Government Printing Office (GPO) *Monthly Catalog* entry number, the GPO stock number, and the depository Item Number.

However, many Government publications covered in ASI have not been assigned all, or in some cases any, identification or classification numbers. Many of the publications we cover are not cataloged either in the GPO *Monthly Catalog* or in the issuing agency's own catalog or publication list, if one exists.

Each document abstract provides as much specific information on hardcopy availability as we are able to obtain at time of publication, and includes information on ASI microfiche availability and price. (For more information about the availability of documents or microfiche, see below "Acquiring the Documents.")

Usually, all bibliographic information for a publication is given at the head of the main abstract, following the title (see Sample Abstracts on p. xxiii-xxv for detailed labeling of bibliographic information provided). When analytic abstracts are being used to describe separate documents in a series, however (see sample abstract for publications in series), only bibliographic data common to the entire series are included in the main abstract, and information individual to each document is shown in its respective analytic abstract.

Frequently, a publication that is going to be cataloged by the GPO *Monthly Catalog* will not have been cataloged by the time ASI monthly abstracts are published. If such *Monthly Catalog* entries appear prior to the ASI Annual, information from them is included in the published Annual. Occasionally, items have not yet been covered in the *Monthly Catalog*, but are documents within continuing series for which established classification data exist; in such cases, we will publish classification data, based on precedent, in the absence of *Monthly Catalog* verification. In addition, ASI publishes bibliographic data revisions and additions in a special section at the end of each quarterly Monthly Supplement index volume. These revisions and additions are then cumulated annually and issued as separate pamphlets to supplement the bibliographic data in each past ASI Annual.

References to Publication Dates

When a date is included in the title of a publication, ASI prints it as part of the title; this date usually represents the period covered by the data or, sometimes, the year the report was prepared. When a date is given anywhere within a publication to indicate date of transmittal, final preparation, or printing, ASI lists this date in the bibliographic data. The user should remember, however, that schedules are often delayed and the publication may not actually have become available until later.

Some publications contain no date at all, and, for these, ASI lists in the bibliographic data the closest approximation it can determine of the year of actual release.

Uses of Main Abstracts and Analytic Abstracts

To handle the broad variety of materials it includes, ASI developed a flexible approach to document accessioning and abstracting. As described earlier in the section on the ASI accession number, we use a structured abstract system that provides for main abstracts and subordinate abstracts (analytics).

ASI uses analytics for the following purposes:

- To single out part of a publication for more detailed abstracting, or to divide the publication into parts, generally into groups of tables, which are then listed. Analytics may also be used for sections or chapters of a publication, each of which is then further described.
- To abstract individual publications in a series. The title and bibliographic data unique to the publication are given in the analytic; data common to the series as a whole are given in the main abstract.
- To abstract articles in periodicals. Article abstracts are identified by 3-digit analytics, beginning with .201 for the first article abstracted in 1991. Thus, article abstracts always follow table listings, which begin with .1.

ASI provides for each individual publication the descriptive information outlined in the above sections. For periodicals, annuals, or one-time publications, the basic information is usually given in the main abstract (see the Sample Abstracts on p. xxiii and xxiv).

For publications in series, information common to the series as a whole is given in the main abstract, and that peculiar to each individual publication in the series is given in its respective analytic (see Sample Abstract on p. xxv). This system allows complete descriptions of individual, related publications without extensive repetition of common characteristics.

The use of analytics also allows ASI to index to specific parts or even single tables in publications. Any index terms may be assigned to an analytic to indicate data specific only to that analytic, and the ASI accession number, with a decimal, will lead the user to it.

For example, the accession number 6224-2.2, under a given index term means that the second analytic, not the publication as a whole, contains data on that topic. The main abstract, however, will contain the basic information on the subject, data type and source, and overall contents of the publication.

When index terms apply to the entire publication or to many of the analytics used, these terms are assigned to the main abstract only and are not repeated for the individual analytics to which they apply.

HOW ASI INDEXES STATISTICAL PUBLICATIONS

ASI indexes are designed to serve a wide range of needs and search approaches for locating statistical materials.

To accomplish this, the following five separate indexes have been provided:

- **Index by Subjects and Names,** which contains references to specific subject areas, places, and personal and corporate authors.
- **Index by Categories** (and accompanying Guide to Selected Standard Classifications), which contains references to tabular data breakdowns by twenty-one common geographic, demographic, and economic categories (e.g., by State, by sex, or by specific industry).
- **Index by Titles**
- **Index by Agency Report Numbers**
- **Index of Superintendent of Documents Numbers**

This section reviews basic ASI objectives and policies in building these five indexes; provides instructions and suggestions for using each of them; and gives specific hints on which indexes to use for answers to a number of different types of questions.

INDEX BY SUBJECTS AND NAMES

The Index by Subjects and Names provides access to:

- **Subjects** of publications and of specific data within publications.
- **Place names,** including names of cities, counties, States, and foreign countries to which data relate.
- **Government agency names,** including the Federal national or regional agencies, commissions, or congressional committees that issue publications or that are the subjects of data contained in publications.
- **Major Government programs or proposals** to which data relate (e.g., Work Incentive Program, Medicare).
- **Special classes of publications or data** (e.g., publications under the terms "Opinion and attitude surveys," "Statistical programs and activities," "Projections," "Directories," and "Bibliographies").
- **Individual personal names, companies, and institutions,** both as authors and as subjects of publications.
- **Major surveys** through which significant bodies of data have been collected (e.g., Current Population Survey).

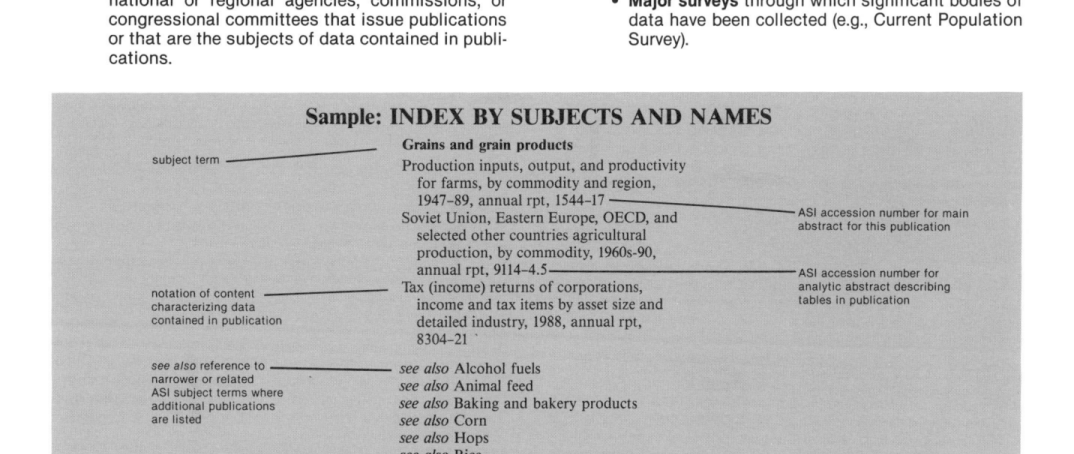

As illustrated in the above sample, this index consists of the following four basic structural elements:

- Subject and author terms (subject terms are based upon a controlled vocabulary).
- *See* and *see also* cross references directing the user to the appropriate index term or to terms under which additional related data may be found.
- Notations of content, which summarize the relevant data content and time coverage of each publication indexed to a particular term. Under an author's name the title is used as a notation of content.
- ASI accession numbers, which refer the user to the full ASI abstract for that publication.

ASI Subject Terms

Subject terms and cross references in the Index by Subjects and Names are based on a controlled vocabulary developed by ASI to meet the particular needs of ASI data coverage. This vocabulary is constantly reviewed and enlarged to respond to the ever expanding range of subjects receiving attention in Government publications.

Publications abstracted in ASI cover an extremely wide variety of subjects, and the data presented range from the very general to the very specific. In selecting subject index terms for the ASI controlled vocabulary, we have strived to maintain a middle level of specificity, which allows for adequate flexibility in indexing to specific subjects, but avoids too great a fragmentation and scattering of subject references. For example, in dealing with data on commodities, the ASI controlled vocabulary generally contains terms for commodity groups, such as the terms "Grains and grain products," "Animal feed," and "Baking and bakery products," found in the preceding sample. However, in the case of selected specific commodities, which are frequently dealt with in publications covered by ASI, we have established separate index terms (e.g., "Wheat," "Corn," "Rice," and "Soybeans" in the preceding sample).

ASI policy is to index to subject terms that reflect the principal subject matters and data contents of each publication abstracted. In addition, unusual items or items of special interest that occur in the body of a report or article, or in individual tables or groups of tables, will be indexed whether or not they relate to the primary focus of the publication at hand.

When indexing a publication to which a hierarchy of vocabulary terms might apply, we select the most specific applicable term or terms in the controlled vocabulary, and do not also index to broader or narrower terms that do not reflect so well its particular focus. But when the focus of the document is equally upon the more general and the more particular subject term, we place index entries under both terms.

For example, when indexing large compendia that present major data on commodities, we index both to the terms for commodity groups and also to those terms for specific commodities that have been established in the controlled vocabulary. Publications primarily focusing on a single commodity, such as wheat, corn, or rice, will be indexed only to the specific commodity terms and not to the more general term "Grains and grain products." Publications that focus on the general subject of grains, but contain a considerable amount of data on one or more of these specific commodities, will be indexed both to the specific commodity terms and to "Grains and grain products." Finally, publications that include some data on the specific commodities, but have a main focus that is on grains will be indexed only to "Grains and grain products."

Cross References

The *see also* references provided by ASI, such as those shown in the preceding sample, are designed to guide you to additional material to be found under the related or narrower terms cited, and to remind you of the need to check the Index by Categories where additional data may be available.

ASI also provides *see* references to aid in locating the specific form of phraseology of subject terms used by ASI. ("Great Plains," for example, is not a term used by ASI, but relevant entries will be found under the term "North Central States.")

Notations of Content

Each index entry under a subject or category term contains an ASI accession number and a "notation of content," a brief description of a report's subject matter or data content. These notations assist you in selecting relevant entries under any particular term and restricting the number of abstracts to which you need refer.

Notations of content are individually written for each publication indexed by ASI. They include, at a minimum, the main subject or subjects of the publication as they relate to the specific index term, and the data date. Additional information that may be noted, as relevant, includes geographic area of coverage, major data breakdowns, and periodicity of publication. Under an author term, the publication title is used as the notation of content.

In selecting the first words for notations of content, we have attempted to choose key words that will automatically group index entries according to their prime subject content. The key words perform some of the functions of a "second-level" index term (e.g., the word "Production" used in the preceding sample to group entries relating to grain farming). Although the informal type of grouping thus achieved can be helpful to you, these groups will not always bring together all related material. A complete search should include examination of all notations of content under a given term.

In general, only one notation of content for any one publication appears under a specific index term. This entry must reflect the full scope of the publication being indexed as it relates to that subject term. As a result, in many cases, the notation of content must be quite general, subsuming coverage of a great deal of specific data. In those cases, however, when the material relating to an index term is too diverse to be covered by a single notation of content, a second notation may be used under that term.

As stated above, usually only one notation of content for any one publication will appear under a specific index term. However, the wording of the notation of content for a single publication may be different for each of the index terms under which it appears. In such cases, the differences reflect an effort to relate the wording and initial key word of the notation of content to the specific index term under which it appears.

For example, the publication in the above index sample with the notation of content, "Soviet Union, Eastern Europe, OECD, and selected other countries agricultural production, by commodity, 1960s–90, annual rpt," contains data on a wide variety of additional economic subjects relating to Eastern Europe and other countries. Under the index term "Eastern Europe", to reflect this broad scope, the notation of content reads "Economic conditions in USSR, Eastern Europe, OECD, and selected other countries, 1960s–90, annual rpt."

In all cases, it must be remembered that notations of content are brief and highly condensed guides, and cannot be used as substitutes for the abstracts. The full abstracts will further describe the extent and limitations of the data indicated in the index entry, and will often note the existence of related data that could not be indicated in the brief space occupied by the index entry.

Other Indexing Conventions

* **Alphabetization** — Following Library of Congress practice, ASI alphabetizes on a word-by-word basis. For example, "New Jersey" and "New York" precede "Newark," and "Fire departments" precedes

"Firearms." It is important to know if there is a word break in a term, since a compound word like "Airlines" will follow all terms beginning with the word "Air" (i.e., "Air pollution"). Hyphenated words are alphabetized as if they were two separate words.

- **Proper Names —** These have been entered in natural word order. Thus, you will find "Department of Labor" rather than "Labor Department," and "Bureau of Labor Statistics" rather than "Labor Statistics Bureau." However, names of individuals always have last name first, such as "Boyd, Gayle M."
- **References to the United States —** Because of the nature and scope of most U.S. Government statistical publications, "U.S." is an implied prefix for many of the subjects in the ASI Subject Index. Thus, you will find "Army" rather than "U.S. Army," and "Foreign relations" rather than "U.S. Government-foreign relations." In agency titles, the prefix "U.S." has been dropped whenever possible, except where necessary to conform to *U.S. Government Manual* usage (e.g., U.S. Postal Service). In notations of content, "U.S." is always implied unless "foreign," "world," or "by country" is specified.

Making a Subject Index Search

If you are seeking a specific piece of information in ASI, you will often find it quickly by referring to the obvious subject term or terms, locating the relevant group of notations of content, and selecting the one or ones most pertinent to your search. You should then consult the abstract for a full description of the publication and its availability.

If such a search does not yield the information required, or if you desire a more complete survey of possible data on the subject, additional steps should be taken. As previously noted, your first step should be to consult the more specific and related *see also* terms listed under the relevant subject terms in order to obtain additional leads.

Your next step should be to consult more general terms that encompass the subject matter sought. Despite our efforts to index to the most specific available term, some statistical publications are so wide-ranging or so detailed in their subject coverage that it is impractical to include references to all the specific topics they mention. It is wise, therefore, when checking the specific subject term in which you are interested, also to check the more general terms related to it.

Searching the subject terms, however, is only part of making a successful subject search in ASI. For instance, a publication that contains data on agriculture may break down these data by hundreds of different commodities, one of which is likely to be grains. The existence of these breakdowns by category adds a new dimension to statistical data retrieval. To help the researcher locate this kind of information quickly, ASI has provided an Index by Categories, which is discussed in detail below.

A limited amount of overlapping (or "double posting") occurs between the Index by Subjects and Names and the Index by Categories. Detailed data subject matter shown in tabular breakdowns (e.g., occupational breakdowns) are always indexed in the Index by Categories. In selected cases, where tabular breakdowns or cross-tabulations provide an extensive or particularly significant body of data on a given subject, references to these data have been included in both the Index of Subjects and Names (e.g., indexed to the subject terms "Clerical workers," "Nurses and nursing," "Blue-collar workers," etc.) and the Index by Categories (e.g., "By Occupation"). The existence of this limited overlap should not mislead the user with respect to the large amount of additional data available through the Index by Categories.

INDEX BY CATEGORIES

As mentioned above, to provide a ready access to the multiplicity of detailed statistical data in tabular breakdowns and cross-classifications, ASI has created a special type of supplementary index: the Index by Categories. This index includes references to all publications that contain comparative tabular data broken down in any or several of the following twenty-one standard categories:

- **Geographic Categories —** By census division; By city; By county; By foreign country; By outlying area (territories of the U.S.); By region; By SMSA or MSA; By State; and By urban-rural and metro-nonmetro.
- **Economic Categories —** By commodity; By Federal agency; By income; By individual company or institution; By industry; and By occupation.
- **Demographic Categories —** By age; By disease; By educational attainment; By marital status; By race and ethnic group; and By sex.

For easier use, index entries within each of the categories are grouped according to subject matter, under one of the following nineteen subheadings:

Agriculture and Food
Banking, Finance, and Insurance
Communications and Transportation
Education
Energy Resources and Demand
Geography and Climate
Government and Defense
Health and Vital Statistics
Housing and Construction
Industry and Commerce
Labor and Employment
Law Enforcement
Natural Resources, Environment, and Pollution
Population
Prices and Cost of Living
Public Welfare and Social Security
Recreation and Leisure
Science and Technology
Veterans Affairs

In those instances where a reference might logically fit under two or more of the subheadings, we have tried to select the most obvious one and to place it there. A brief listing of the kinds of material referenced under each subheading is given at the beginning of the Index by Categories.

Sample: INDEX BY CATEGORIES

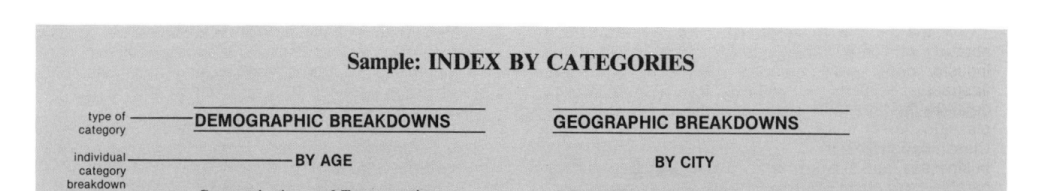

As illustrated in the above sample, this index consists of the following four basic structural elements:

- Category terms, for the twenty-one categories listed above.
- Subject subheadings, to group entries within each category by subject matter. These are listed above.
- Notations of content, which are used just as in the Index by Subjects and Names to characterize further the data indexed to the category.
- ASI accession numbers, which refer the user to the full ASI abstract for that publication.

In the Index by Categories, data in the specified categories can be identified with greater detail and specificity than in the Index by Subjects and Names. This index also provides the best and most complete source for locating comparative data on a wide variety of subjects.

Breakdowns in individual tables, to which references are made in the Index by Categories, may vary considerably in the detail provided. Breakdowns "By sex" are, by definition, complete. Breakdowns "By State" are usually, but not always, for all 50 States. However, detail in breakdowns of such categories as "By city," "By SMSA," "By Federal agency," "By industry," "By commodity," and "By occupation," varies widely. In the abstracts of publications containing such breakdowns, we have, when possible, tried to include an indication of the degree of detail provided (i.e., "by detailed industries," "by major cause of death," "for 20 large cities," etc.).

In searching the Index by Categories for very detailed data, such as those on a small city, minor industry, or other specific entity, you are likely to find several entries referring to publications that could possibly contain the information you want. You will usually find it necessary to go back to the abstract to ascertain which publication has or is most likely to have that information. In some cases, where a high degree of specificity is desired, an examination of the Index by Categories and the abstracts will help to narrow the field of possibilities, but it may still be necessary actually to examine the text of two or three publications to be certain the exact information needed is there.

Examples and further instructions for making various types of Category Index searches follow.

Making a Search by Geographic Categories

Much data on Chicago can be located under the term "Chicago, Ill." in the Index by Subjects and Names. These entries represent instances where Chicago is the principal subject of a publication or where a significant body of information relating to Chicago can be found. There are considerable additional data, however, to be found in individual tables that have a breakdown by city, including Chicago. These data are located in the Index by Categories under the term "By city."

Similarly, you can find data on individual States, counties, SMSAs, MSAs, or foreign countries in the Index by Categories. The number of places included in reports indexed to these categories may vary considerably. Breakdowns by State or county are usually complete, unless the notation of content indicates that data are limited to a specific part of the country, or to "large counties" or "selected counties." In the case of cities or foreign countries, there may be wider variation; when practical, the notation of content indicates the degree of detail provided (e.g., "40 cities" in the sample above).

Data on the regions of the U.S. can be found under the category "By region." Since, however, the different Federal agencies use a variety of regional delineations, such data may not be comparable from one report to another. To assist the user, ASI has provided lists of six major regional structures in the Guide to Selected Standard Classifications, further described below.

Making a Search by Economic Categories

The Index by Categories term "By Industry" will lead to reports and to individual tables which present a wealth of detailed data on both major and minor industries. These data can often be found only through the Index by Categories, since the Subject Index would become unwieldy if ASI attempted to index each column of every table.

In the same way as for cities, explained above, the notation of content will generally indicate the level of industry detail provided in each publication, and the abstract will specify further. In some cases, the degree of detail in the breakdowns may be based upon a standard classification system, such as the Standard Industrial Classification (SIC) which classifies all types of industries, businesses, and services for purposes of developing comparable statistical data. Whenever such a standard classification is used, this fact is noted in the abstract and frequently in the notation of content as well. Several of the most frequently used classifications, including the SIC, are listed in ASI's Guide to Standard Statistical Classifications, further described below.

The use of the SIC listing to find data on a specific industry is illustrated in the sample below. For example, if you want data on the typesetting industry, an industry for which there is no separate entry in the Subject Index, you can refer to the SIC listing to determine at what SIC level the typesetting service industry is specified. Since it is specified at the 4-digit level, you can then examine the entries under "By Industry" in the Category Index, and check the abstracts of likely references, to find reports and specific tables that present data broken down to the SIC 4-digit level.

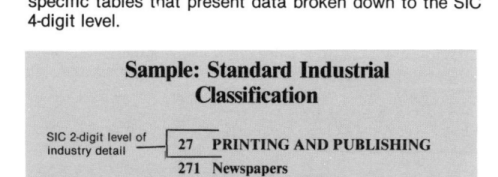

Very detailed data on commodities can be found in the same way, using the category term "By Commodity." The industry and commodity categories only partially overlap, since many firms produce a wide range of commodities but are classified only in the industry of their major activity. ASI policy is to follow the classification— industry-based or commodity-based—used by the publication. To make a complete search for such economic data, you will probably want to examine both categories.

Data shown for individual entities of all kinds, including companies or their brand name products, universities, hospitals, foundations, and government projects may be found under "By Individual Company or Institution." Category indexing is also provided for data "By Federal Agency," "By Occupation," and "By Income," including both salary levels and total family income.

Making a Search by Demographic Categories

When you want data about specific groups of the population, the Category Index is a versatile tool to augment the Subject Index. For example, the following subjects can be thoroughly searched using this two-pronged approach:

- **Women —** Data may be found under the subject terms "Women," "Women's employment," or "Maternity." Quantities of additional data may be found under the category term "By Sex."
- **Age groups —** Look under subject terms "Children," "Youth," or "Aged and aging." Look also under the category term "By Age."
- **Blacks —** Look under such subject terms as "Black Americans," "Black students," or "Racial discrimination." More data can be found under the category term "By Race."
- **The poor —** The subject term "Poverty" will lead to reports dealing specifically with the poor. Additional data can be extracted from reports with breakdowns "By Income," found in the Category Index.
- **Divorced persons —** The subject term "Marriage and divorce" will lead to reports specifically on this subject. The category term "By Marital Status" will lead to additional data.

In a similar way you can find data on demographic groups under the categories "By Occupation," "By Industry," "By Educational Attainment," or "By Disease."

Making a Search for Comparative Data

A major advantage of the Index by Categories is the ease with which it enables you to locate comparative data on a subject. This index is the logical starting point for such search questions as: "Which cities have the highest unemployment rate?" "Which States have the lowest taxes?" "Which are the largest industries in the U.S. in specified States?" "Do people with more education really earn more money?" (These last two questions each combine two category terms: "By Industry" and "By State," and "By Income" and "By Educational Attainment.") Data pertinent to these questions will also be found under the subject terms "Employment and unemployment, general," "State and local taxes," etc. However, the most efficient search for such comparative data will begin with the Index by Categories.

ASI's Guide to Selected Standard Classifications

As stated above, Federal statistical data breakdowns are frequently presented in terms of several standard classification systems, and ASI abstracts generally make note of their use. To provide an easily accessible reference for the user, we have printed a number of major classification systems or lists in the "Guide to Selected Standard Classifications." The Guide, which appears at the end of the Index volume, includes the following listings:

- Census regions and divisions; outlying areas of the U.S.; Standard Federal Administrative Regions; farm production regions; Federal Reserve Districts; Federal Home Loan Bank Districts; and Bureau of Labor Statistics Regions.
- Metropolitan Statistical Areas (MSAs); Consolidated Metropolitan Statistical Areas; cities with population over 100,000 (based on the 1990 Census of Population) and Consumer Price Index cities.
- Standard Industrial Classification (SIC), providing 1- to 4-digit codes for industry divisions through individual industries.
- Standard Occupational Classification, providing 1- to 3-digit codes for major and minor occupational groups.
- Standard International Trade Classification (SITC), a system of 3-digit codes for commodities in world trade, developed by the United Nations, used for foreign trade data, and consistent with the 7-digit codes used for U.S. import-export data.

Even when data breakdowns do not correspond with one of these standard classification systems, these listings can still serve as useful guides to what may be included in breakdowns at varying levels of detail (i.e., "by major industry group" will approximate the 2-digit SIC level, and "by detailed industries" will approximate the 4-digit level).

Government publications that describe these and

other standard classification systems, survey methods, glossaries, and directories are abstracted and microfilmed by ASI, and can usually also be obtained in hardcopy by the user. Such publications are generally indexed to "Methodology" or "Classifications" as well as to their respective subjects.

INDEX BY TITLES

This index lists titles of all publications covered by ASI in the 1991 Annual. It also lists titles of periodical articles, conference papers, and reports within larger publications when these are separately abstracted.

This index lists all main titles and also analytic titles of individual monographs within a series, except when series reports are essentially identical, e.g., a series of State reports or country reports. In these cases, the name of each State or country can be found in the Index by Subjects and Names; the reports will also be listed, usually in alphabetical order, in the Abstracts volume under the ASI accession number for the series. Series reports on individual commodities or industries are listed in the Index by Titles under the name of the commodity, followed by the name of the series, e.g., "Footwear, Current Industrial Report."

Titles are listed alphabetically in natural word order, as they appear in the abstract. ASI routinely omits initial articles (a, an, the) in titles, both in the abstracts and in this index. Titles that begin with Arabic numbers (e.g., "1991 Joint Economic Report") appear at the end of the index.

To assist users in locating a publication, we provide in certain cases alternate word orders for titles, including all of those beginning with Arabic numerals. For example, census reports are generally listed under the overall title of the census and under the title of the individual report as well.

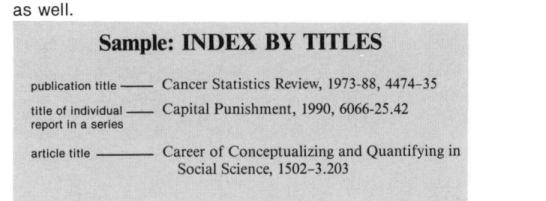

Each title is followed by the ASI accession number, which directs the user to the abstract of the publication.

Anyone knowing the title of the publication desired can locate it most quickly in this index. Users should keep in mind that notations of content in the Index by Subjects and Names and in the Index by Categories bear no necessary relationship to a publication's title and should not be confused with it.

INDEX BY AGENCY REPORT NUMBERS

This index lists the report numbers assigned to publications by the issuing agency. It can be useful both for identifying one specific document and for locating an entire series of numbered publications.

We have grouped numbers in this index under the names of each issuing executive department, independent agency or commission, or congressional body, but generally have not attempted to group them by bureau, office, or committee within a department or independent agency. (Frequently, the alphabetical prefixes of the numbers themselves serve to identify agencies.)

Exceptions to this general rule are Census Bureau publication numbers, which are preceded with the word "Census" so that they group together and are not inter-

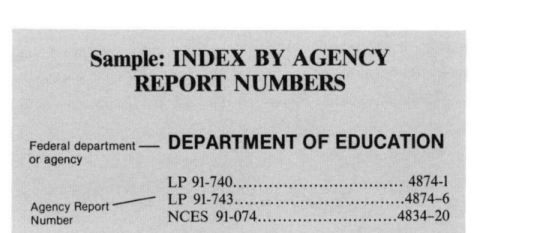

mixed with other Commerce Department reports. Also, the "DHHS" prefix in the Department of Health and Human Services report numbers has been omitted so that numbers will group more meaningfully.

INDEX OF SUPERINTENDENT OF DOCUMENTS NUMBERS

This index presents, in shelf list order, the Superintendent of Documents (SuDocs) Classification Numbers of publications abstracted by ASI during 1991, and provides references from the SuDocs numbers to ASI accession numbers.

The index enables a user who has obtained a SuDocs number from the Monthly Catalog or some other source to quickly locate the ASI abstract and then obtain the document.

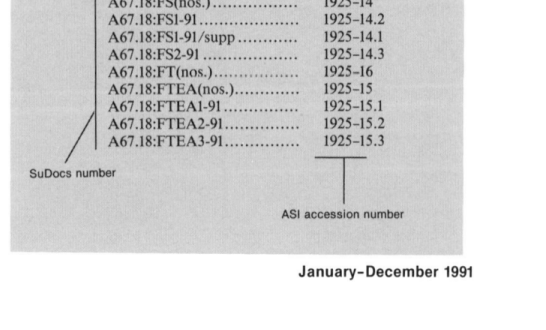

Suggestions for Making Information Searches

The "best" information search technique to use with ASI abstracts and indexes depends upon the type of information needed and upon the amount and type of information with which the search begins. Listed below are some examples of the types of information you can obtain through ASI, together with suggested routes for searching.

IN ORDER TO . . .	YOU SHOULD . . .		
Pinpoint specific statistical data on any subject treated in Federal Government publications.	Use the subject index.		
		Locate continuing monthly or quarterly reports on a particular subject.	Look in the subject index. The notations of content include the periodicity of the reports.
Locate broad analyses of comprehensive studies.	Use the subject index; concentrate on the more general subject terms.	Determine the availability of comparable historical data.	Look in the Abstracts Section of each ASI edition, under the same accession number. The abstract will state whether the report is part of a continuing time series; e.g., "Twentieth annual report." Also, look in the abstract for references to earlier publications, changes in ASI accession numbers, or breaks in continuity.
Determine whether data are available for specific parts of the U.S., such as States, cities, or counties; for specific industries or commodities; or for specific groups of people, such as races, men and women, or age, income, or occupational groups.	Use both the subject and category indexes.		
Find comparative data for States, cities, foreign countries, Government agencies, commodities, industries, or groups of people.	Use the category index.	Locate the report of a specific Board or Commission.	Look in the subject index under the name of the issuing agency.
		Locate an agency publication list.	Look in the subject index under "Government publications lists."
Find out what Federal Reserve district Florida is in.	Look in the Guide to Selected Standard Classifications.	Review the entire statistical output of any particular Federal Government agency or office.	Look in the detailed table of contents for the ASI accession number and page of the agency that interests you. Look in the Abstracts Section for all publications under this accession number.
Determine whether a large report, with a breakdown by industry, will include data on the dog food industry.	Look at the Standard Industrial Classification Codes listed in the Guide to Selected Standard Classifications to determine that the industry you are looking for has a 4-digit code. Look in the indexes for notations of content specifying detailed industry breakdowns. Look at the table listing in the abstract for tables specifying 4-digit detail.	Find out how many Federal Government agencies publish data on the same subject.	Look in the subject index, at the ASI accession numbers following the notations of content. The first two to four digits (minus the digit before the hyphen) indicate the issuing agency of the publication.
Find data on Minneapolis.	Look in the subject index under "Minneapolis, Minn." Look also in the category index under "By city."	Locate a specific statistical article in a periodical.	Look in the title index or in the subject index under the author's name.
Be confident that you have found the latest data available.	Look at the dates in the notations of content that interest you in the ASI 1991 Annual. Check ASI 1992 Monthly Supplements under the same index terms to see if there are similar notations with later dates. ASI is current to 6-10 weeks after publication of the reports covered. If the notations of content indicate a periodical, locate the latest issue in the "Periodicals Received and Reviewed" section.	Determine the content of a specific publication when you know the title or agency report number.	Use the title index or the agency report number index to locate the pertinent abstract.
		Locate all the reports in a specific series.	Look in the title index of each edition of ASI under the title of the series. If it is a numbered series, use the agency report number index.
		Find a report you remember hearing about in the 1970s.	Start out by checking the ASI Retrospective Edition Index and 1974-79 Cumulative Index.
Find the latest issue of a periodical carrying forward a statistical time series.	Look in ASI 1991 Annual for description of the periodical. Look for the title in the "Periodicals Received and Reviewed" section of the latest	Locate reports describing specific statistical methods; locate reports containing projected data.	Look in the subject index under "Methodology;" look in the subject index under "Projections."

ACQUIRING THE DOCUMENTS

Once you have identified a publication that appears to contain the data you seek, you may wish to borrow or acquire the publication itself, either in its original hardcopy form or in microform.

Acquiring Documents From a Library

Although there are no complete collections in existence, Government documents can be found in many libraries, particularly those that have been designated as U.S. Government depository libraries. There are usually at least two depositories in each congressional district, approximately 1,300 throughout the country.

The publication abstracts that contain a bullet (•) and an Item Number indicate publications that have been made available to depository libraries by the Government Printing Office. However, fewer than 50 depositories receive *all* the publications that are theoretically available to them, and even these libraries receive only about three-quarters of all the publications covered by ASI.

Libraries that subscribe to the ASI Microfiche Library will have complete collections of the materials abstracted and indexed in ASI.

Requesting or Purchasing Publications From the Government

Whether or not they are sent to depositories, many Government publications can be purchased while the supply lasts, either from the Government Printing Office, or, in certain cases, from the National Technical Information Service, or the issuing agency.

If a publication listed in ASI is available for sale, the price and source, when known, are listed in the abstract. It should be noted that the prices of Government publications are subject to frequent change. The price listed is that printed on the publication or in the GPO *Monthly Catalog,* or is based on firm information about a later price from another source.

When the publication abstract contains a single dagger (†), inquiries should be addressed directly to the issuing agency in order to determine whether copies are available for distribution. Principal agency addresses are listed in each Annual Abstracts volume in the section labeled "Where to Write for Statistical Publications."

Some publications intended for internal or official use only have been printed in small editions, and copies generally are not available for distribution. In some cases, the agency will honor a written request for a copy of one of these publications, but this will be decided by the agency on a case-by-case basis. Abstracts of publications in this category carry a double dagger (‡).

In some cases, we have been informed by the agency that there are absolutely no copies available for distribution outside the agency. Abstracts of publications in this category carry a diamond symbol (♦). In most of these cases, the agencies have cooperated with our attempt to make the data available to the public by permitting ASI to microfilm the publications for inclusion in the ASI Microfiche Library. The agency itself will not honor requests for publications that carry this symbol.

The ASI Microfiche Program

Because of the enormous difficulty of acquiring, cataloging, and maintaining a collection of all the publications covered by ASI, no complete hardcopy collection of these publications now exists in any library. For this reason, CIS has undertaken to make these publications available in American Standard microfiche on a continuing basis.

Our microfiche sheets measure 105 × 149 mm (approximately 4" × 6"), and contain up to 98 document pages. Each has an eye-readable "title header" that conclusively identifies the accession number, series title (if any), dates of periodical issues, and document title of each publication filmed. Documents are separated from each other, and they are plainly sequenced for file integrity and quick retrieval according to ASI accession number.

Researchers may view microfiche with the aid of a simple reader, such as those found in most libraries and offices. Individual pages from a microfiche can be reproduced in full size with the aid of a reader-printer; these machines are becoming increasingly available in libraries and offices.

With a few specific exclusions, all publications abstracted and indexed in ASI are available on ASI microfiche. The microfiche availability and unit count for a given publication are indicated by the notation "ASI/MF" in the publication's abstract. We have systematically excluded only publications that reprint other items in the ASI Microfiche Library, large or colored maps that are unsuitable for reproduction in standard microfiche, and large appendix volumes that are non-statistical (such as public hearing testimony) or highly technical.

Automatically updated collections of current publications, on silver-halide, archival-quality microfiche, are available on a subscription basis. Retrospective collections, shipped in their entirety and ready for use, may also be purchased. Collections may be ordered to contain the entire range of ASI publications, may be limited to "non-depository" publications (i.e., those not included in Government documents classes sent to depository libraries), or may be limited to publications of a single Government agency. For details, please write: CIS Library Services Manager.

ASI Documents on Demand

Since June 1, 1975, individual publications covered in ASI have been available on diazo microfiche or paper copy for purchase through our ASI DOCUMENTS ON DEMAND service. The price of any document is based on the "unit count" data indicated for the document, e.g. ASI/MF/3. (Note that a unit count of 3 is the minimum order for any document, regardless of size; each additional 100 pages or less equals 1 additional unit.) Please ask your librarian for additional ordering information; or write CIS Documents on Demand, P.O. Box 30056, Bethesda, MD 20814.

ADDITIONAL CIS SERVICES

Index to International Statistics and Statistical Reference Index

Beginning in January 1983, Congressional Information Service initiated publication of the Index to International Statistics (IIS), a comprehensive monthly index and abstracting service, covering the statistical publications of international intergovernmental organizations, including UN, OECD, EC, OAS, and approximately 90 other important organizations.

Since 1980, Congressional Information Service has published the Statistical Reference Index (SRI), a monthly abstract and index publication with annual cumulations, covering statistical reports from a broad range of U.S. sources other than the Federal Government. These sources include trade, professional, and other nonprofit associations; business organizations; commercial publishers; independent research centers; State government agencies; and university research centers. SRI has selected from these sources a cross-section of documents presenting basic national and State data on business, industry, finance, economic and social conditions, the environment, and the population.

SRI and IIS complement ASI's coverage of statistical materials by providing access to data not collected by the Federal Government and to alternative sources and analyses of data. Because the abstracting and indexing styles of the two publications are quite similar, researchers can use ASI, SRI, and IIS without significantly changing their search methods.

Most of the documents covered in SRI and IIS are included in their respective Microfiche Libraries, available on a subscription basis. For more information about SRI, IIS, and their microfiche programs, contact the CIS Marketing Department.

Statistical Masterfile

In 1989, CIS introduced a new CD-ROM product, the Statistical Masterfile, which allows users to search simultaneously the abstracts and indexing from ASI, SRI, and IIS. The three component data bases may be purchased separately or in any combination. Both current year service and retrospective coverage are available for each data base. Current service subscribers receive quarterly CD-ROM disk updates.

For additional information, contact the CIS Marketing Department.

CIS On-Line Services

Through cooperative arrangements with on-line computer services, the CIS data base is made available to the public. This service makes possible direct on-line computer searching of the abstracts and indexing contained in all American Statistics Indexes and all CIS/Indexes, from our first publication to the present.

CIS/Indexes to Publications of the U.S. Congress

Since 1970, Congressional Information Service has published the CIS/Index, a monthly abstract and index publication with annual cumulations, which covers all publications of the U.S. Congress. Selected congressional publications containing statistical data are covered in ASI as well as CIS. Those covered by ASI are re-abstracted and re-indexed to focus on their statistical contents.

However, ASI does not repeat CIS/Index coverage of the wide range of congressional publications that contain no substantial statistical data. Nor does ASI abstract or index the publications of the Senate and House Appropriations Committees. Since CIS/Indexes provide detailed access to the extensive program statistics and background information contained in publications of these committees, we believe that reabstracting them for ASI would be a duplication of effort and service.

The CIS/Microfiche Library and CIS Documents on Demand services provide full-text availability of CIS/ Index publications in a manner paralleling ASI microfiche services.

Other Services

In early 1992 Congressional Information Service will publish a *Guide to 1990 U.S. Decennial Census Publications* covering all decennial census publications issued in 1990 and 1991 as well as some key background reports on possible undercounts and other methodological issues. A cumulative edition of the Guide will be issued each spring to include coverage of reports issued within the past year. The abstracts and indexing in the Guide will be substantially reprinted from ASI annual editions and combined in a single volume for the convenience of researchers. A companion microfiche collection is also available. CIS issued a similar Guide and microfiche collection for the 1980 Census.

The Census Guides and other CIS publications and microform collections are fully described in the CIS catalog, available on request.

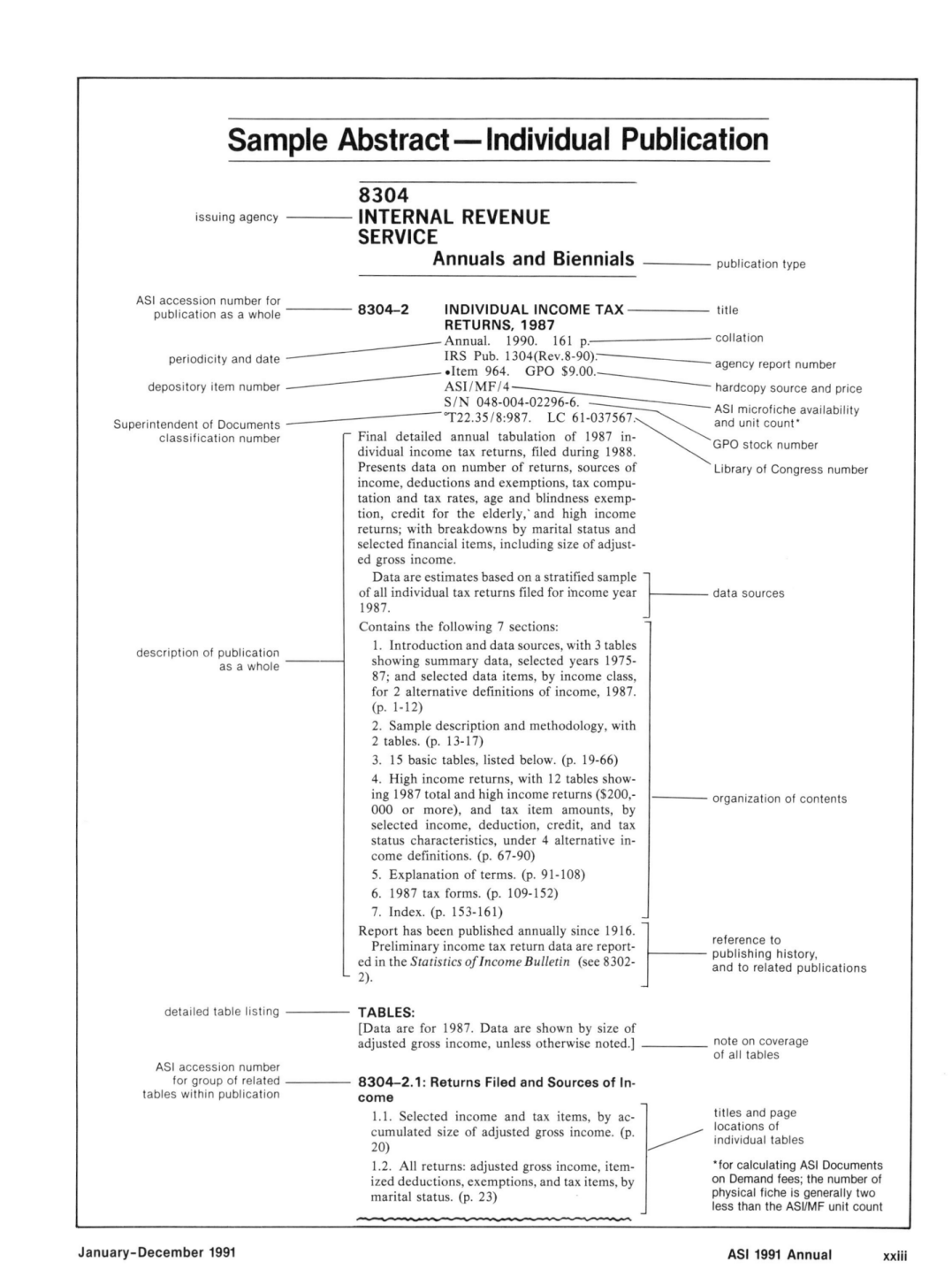

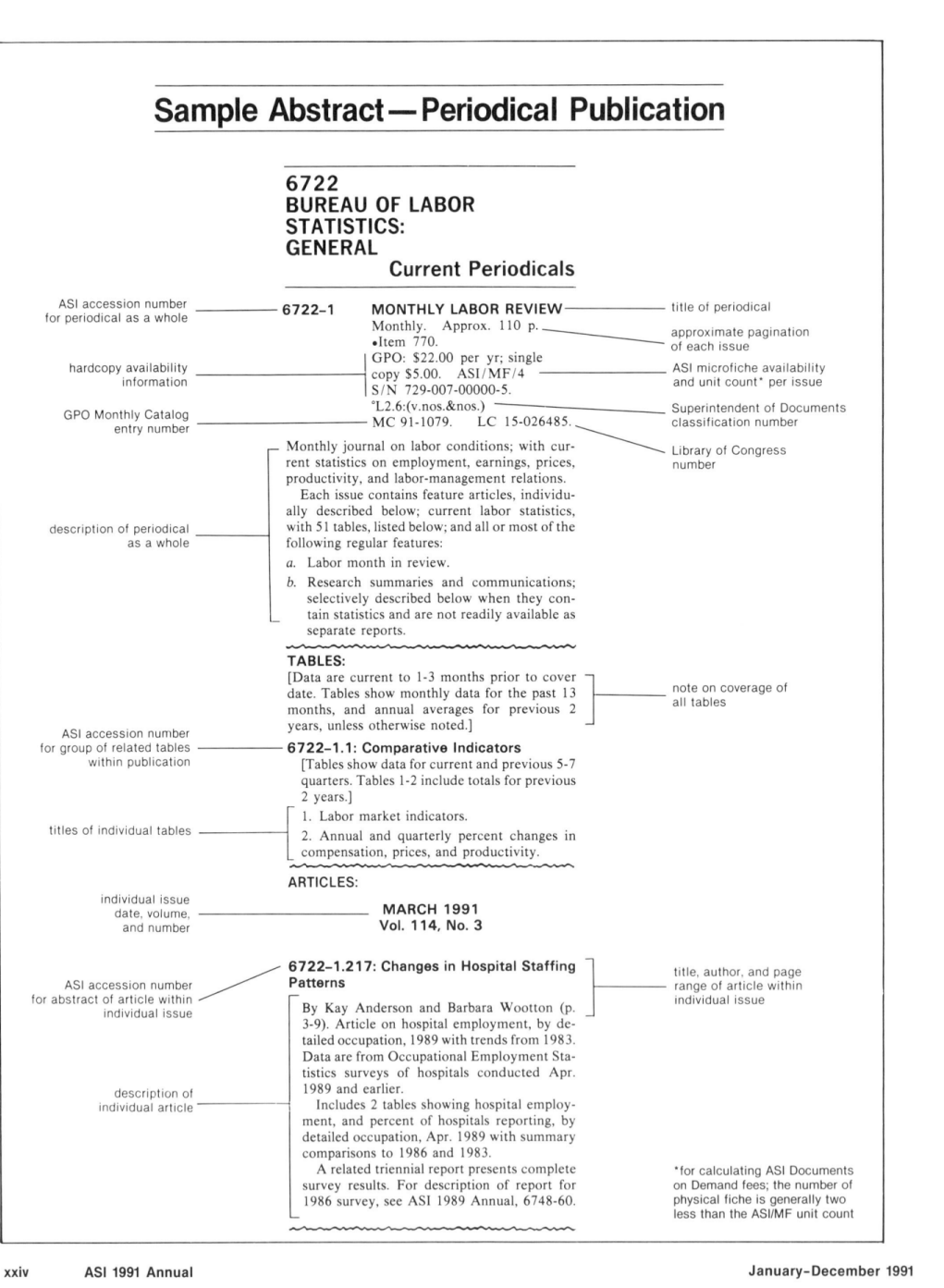

Sample Abstract — Publications in Series

**2546
BUREAU OF CENSUS:
POPULATION**

**Publications
in Series**

ASI accession number for series as a whole ——— **2546–1** **CURRENT POPULATION REPORTS. Series P-20: Population Characteristics** ——— title of series

•Item 142-C-1. ——— depository item number for all publications in series

hardcopy availability for all publications in series ——— GPO: subscription with series P-23, and -60, $96.00 per yr; single copy prices vary. For individual bibliographic data, see below. P-20, (nos.)

GPO Stock number ——— S/N 803-005-00000-1.

LC 52-002169. ——— Library of Congress number

description of series as a whole ——— Continuing series of reports presenting current data on selected characteristics of persons, families, and households, with some historical trends. Subjects covered include education and enrollment, fertility, mobility, voting, marital status and living arrangements, ethnic origin, and rural population. ——— major subjects

Data are from Current Population Surveys conducted in the month or months indicated in the title, with comparisons to previous surveys. ——— data sources

Series contains recurring and special reports, and, for some topics, both advance data and final reports.

Reports are described below in order of receipt.

ASI accession number for individual report in series ——— **2546–1.448: Hispanic Population in the U.S.: March 1990** ——— agency report number date

[No. 449. Mar. 1991. iii + 34 p. + errata. ——— collation

*C3.186/14-2:990. S/N 803-005-00048-6. ——— Superintendent of Documents classification number

$2.25. ASI/MF/3] ——— GPO stock number price ASI microfiche availability and unit count*

description of report subject matter ——— By Jesus M. Garcia and Patricia A. Montgomery. Report presenting summary data on socioeconomic characteristics of the Hispanic origin population, 1990. Data are from the Mar. 1990 Current Population Survey (CPS).

Contents: introduction, with 4 charts and 1 summary table (p. 1-5); 4 detailed tables, listed below (p. 6-15); and appendices, with definitions, notes on data source and reliability, 5 standard error tables, and facsimile questionnaire (p. 17-34). ——— organization of contents

Previous report, for Mar. 1989, is described in ASI 1990 Annual under 2546-1.443. ——— reference to previous annual report

titles and page locations of individual tables ——— **TABLES:**

1. Selected social characteristics of all persons and Hispanic persons [age, sex, marital status, and years of school completed]. (p. 6)

2. Selected economic characteristics of all persons and Hispanic persons [labor force status, occupational group, percent distribution by earnings, and median earnings, by sex;

*for calculating ASI Documents on Demand fees; the number of physical fiche is generally two less than the ASI/MF unit count

Sample ASI Search

"How much did the chemicals industry invest in pollution control equipment in New Jersey?"

Step 1

Check the ASI Index Volume

Start with a "subject" approach where extensive cross-references will lead to the proper index reference from almost any likely point of entry.

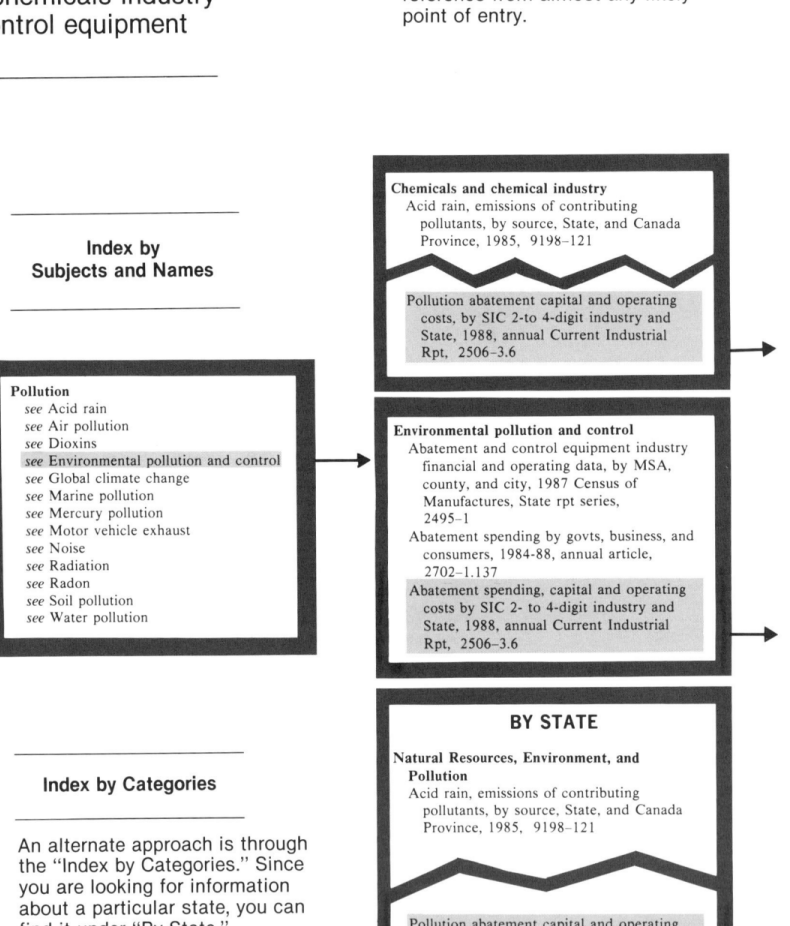

Step 2

Go from the index to the data description in the appropriate Abstracts volume

The ASI accession number in the index will lead to a publication entry that fully describes the document and pinpoints the tables containing the statistics you need.

2506 BUREAU OF CENSUS: MANUFACTURING Publications in series

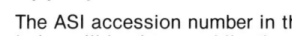

2506-3.6: Manufacturers' Pollution Abatement Capital Expenditures and Operating Costs, Final Report for 1988

[Annual. Sept. 1990. 55 p. MA200(88)-1. °C3.158:MA200(88)-1/990. LC 77-646295. Price not given. ASI/MF/3]

Annual report for 1988 on pollution abatement control capital expenditures and operating costs, for U.S. by SIC 4-digit industry, and for States by 2-digit industry. Data are from a sample survey of approximately 20,000 establishments with 20 or more employees, in industries with abatement capital expenditures or annual operating costs of at least $1 million.

Contents: introduction (p. 1); and 6 tables, listed below (p. 2-55).

Advance annual report for 1988 was received in Apr. 1990 and is also available on ASI microfiche under this number [Apr. 1990. 2 p. MA200(88)-1. C3.158:MA200(88)-1. Price not given. ASI/MF/3]. No advance or final reports were issued for 1987. Final report for 1986, titled *Pollution Abatement Costs and Expenditures,* is described in ASI 1989 Annual under this number.

TABLES:

[Data are for 1988. Tables show data for U.S. by SIC 2- to 4-digit industry ("a" tables) and for States by SIC 2-digit major industry groups ("b" tables). Tables 1-2 show hazardous and nonhazardous solid waste pollutants.]

1a-1b. Pollution abatement capital expenditures [for air and solid waste pollution, by pollutant type; and for air and water pollution, by abatement technique (end-of-line, production process change)]. (p. 2-21)

2a-2b. Pollution abatement operating costs by form of abatement [payments for public sewage services and solid waste collection and disposal; and for pollutants abated from air, water, and solid waste]. (p. 22-38)

3a-3b. Pollution abatement operating costs by kind of cost [depreciation; labor; materials and supplies; and services, equipment leasing, and other costs] and cost recovered by form of pollutants [air, water, solid waste]. (p. 39-55)

Step 3

Retrieve the publication

The ASI abstract contains the bibliographic information you need to locate the publication in a library's hardcopy collection or to obtain it from the issuing source, if copies are available.

Alternatively, if you have access to an ASI Microfiche Library collection, the ASI number will lead you directly to the correct microfiche. Or, individual publications abstracted in any ASI Monthly or Annual Supplement are available for purchase on microfiche directly from Congressional Information Service through our CIS & ASI Documents on Demand Service.

Order kits supplied to all ASI subscribers provide the necessary information about costs and how to place microfiche orders. Details are also available by writing CIS Documents on Demand.

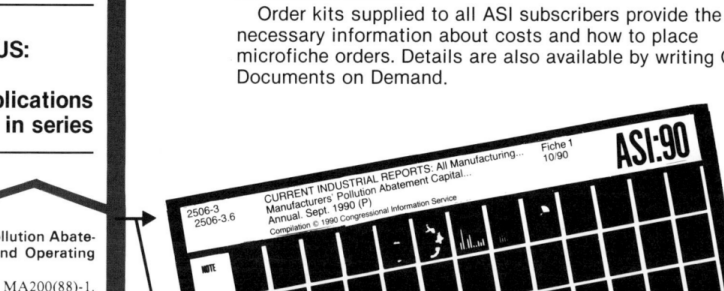

Where to Write for Statistical Publications

Publications abstracted in ASI are frequently available to the public from the Government Printing Office, the National Technical Information Service, or the issuing agency. In addition, a complete collection of abstracted publications is available in the ASI Microfiche Library.

Information about the source and availability of specific publications is given in each ASI abstract. (For illustrations, see the Sample Abstracts; for background information, see the section headed "Acquiring the Documents" on p. xx.)

The mailing addresses of GPO, NTIS, and principal issuing agency sources of publications are listed below.

When ordering publications from the issuing agency, requests should be directed to the specific subagency, Information Division, c/o the parent agency. Where the subagency has a separate mailing address, it is given.

There has been no attempt to list regional or field offices for every agency and subagency. Listings and addresses of these offices can be found in most agency catalogs, and in local telephone directories for the cities in which they are located.

Addresses have been provided for the sources of publications, periodicals, and/or specials and irregulars, which may be available only, or more conveniently, from offices in other locations than the central information office for an agency. Identification of other unusual sources will appear with the abstract of a publication.

GOVERNMENT PRINTING OFFICE (GPO)
Superintendent of Documents
Washington, DC 20402

NATIONAL TECHNICAL INFORMATION SERVICE (NTIS)
5285 Port Royal Rd
Springfield, VA 22161

EXECUTIVE OFFICE OF THE PRESIDENT
Publications Unit, Rm G236
New Executive Office Bldg
Washington, DC 20503

COUNCIL OF ECONOMIC ADVISERS
New Executive Office Bldg
Washington, DC 20506

COUNCIL ON ENVIRONMENTAL QUALITY
722 Jackson Pl., N.W.
Washington, DC 20006

OFFICE OF MANAGEMENT & BUDGET
Publications Unit, Rm G236
New Executive Office Bldg
Washington, DC 20503

OFFICE OF SCIENCE AND TECHNOLOGY POLICY
New Executive Office Building
Washington, DC 20506

OFFICE OF THE U.S. TRADE REPRESENTATIVE
600 17th St., N.W.
Washington, DC 20506

DEPARTMENT OF AGRICULTURE
(Subagency Name)
Information Division
Washington, DC 20250

AGRICULTURAL MARKETING SERVICE
Information Staff Rm 3068-S
Washington, DC 20250

Cotton Division
4841 Summer Ave.
Memphis, TN 38122

AGRICULTURAL STATISTICS
5820 S. Building
Washington, DC 20250

ECONOMIC RESEARCH SERVICE
ERS-NASS Publications
P.O. Box 1608
Rockville, MD 20850

FOREST SERVICE—Forest
Experiment Stations

Intermountain (INT)
324 25th St.
Ogden, UT 84401

North Central (NC)
1992 Folwell Ave.
St. Paul, MN 55108

Northeastern (NE)
370 Reed Rd
Broomall, PA 19008

Pacific Northwest (PNW)
P.O. Box 3890
Portland, OR 97208

Pacific Southwest (PSW)
1960 Addison St.
P.O. Box 245
Berkeley, CA 94701

Rocky Mountain (RM)
240 West Prospect St.
Fort Collins, CO 80526

Southeastern (SE)
P.O. Box 2680
Asheville NC 28802

Southern (SO)
T-10210 Postal Services Bldg
701 Loyola Ave.
New Orleans, LA 70113

SOIL CONSERVATION SERVICE
(Western U.S.)
West Technical Service Center, Rm 510
511 N.W. Broadway
Portland, OR 97209

DEPARTMENT OF COMMERCE
(Subagency Name)
Office of Public Affairs
Washington, DC 20230

BUREAU OF ECONOMIC ANALYSIS
Information Services Division
1401 K St., N.W.
Washington, DC 20235

BUREAU OF THE CENSUS
Customer Services
Data User Services Division
Washington, DC 20233

NATIONAL INSTITUTE OF STANDARDS AND TECHNOLOGY
Office of Information Activities
Rm 640, Administration Bldg
Washington, DC 20234

NATIONAL OCEANIC AND ATMOSPHERIC ADMINISTRATION
Office of Public Affairs
WSC-5
Rockville, MD 20852

Environmental Satellite, Data, and Information Service
Library and Information Services Division
Rockville, MD 20852

Environmental Research Laboratories
Public Information Office
Boulder, CO 80302

National Climatic Data Center
EDIS
Federal Building
Asheville, NC 28801

National Marine Fisheries Service
Public Affairs
Rm 6268, 1335 East-West Highway
Silver Spring, MD 20910

National Ocean Service
Public Information Office
WSC-1
Rockville, MD 20852

National Weather Service
Rm 400, Gramax Bldg
8060 13th St.
Silver Spring, MD 20910

PATENT AND TRADEMARK OFFICE
Office of Public Affairs
2021 Jefferson Davis Highway
Arlington, VA 20231

DEPARTMENT OF COMMERCE DISTRICT OFFICES— INTERNATIONAL TRADE ADMINISTRATION

319 World Trade Center Alaska
4201 Tudor Center Dr.
Anchorage, AK 99508

4360 Chamblee-Dunwoody Rd.
Atlanta, GA 30341

Rm 415, U.S. Customhouse
Baltimore, MD 21202

Berry Bldg., 2015 2nd Ave. N.,
Birmingham, AL 35203

Suite 307, World Trade Center
Commonwealth Pier Area
Boston, MA 02210

Rm 1312, 111 W. Huron St.
Buffalo, NY 14202

Suite 809, 405 Capitol St.
Charleston, WV 25301

55 E. Monroe St.
Chicago, IL 60603

550 Main St.
Cincinnati, OH 45202

Rm 600, 666 Euclid Ave.
Cleveland, OH 44114

Suite 172, 1835 Assembly St.
Columbia, SC 29201

Rm 7A5, 1100 Commerce St.
Dallas, TX 75242

Suite 600, 1625 Broadway
Denver, CO 80202

Rm 817, 210 Walnut St.
Des Moines, IA 50309

1140 McNamara Bldg, 477 Michigan Ave.
Detroit, MI 48226

Rm 203, 324 W. Market St.
Greensboro, NC 27402

Rm 610-B, 450 Main St.
Hartford, CT 06103

P.O. Box 50026, 400 Ala Moana Blvd.
Honolulu, HI 96850

Rm 2625, 515 Rusk Ave.
Houston, TX 77002

Suite 520, One N. Capitol St.
Indianapolis, IN 46204

328 Jackson Mall Office Center
Jackson, MS 39213

Rm 635, 601 E. 12th St.
Kansas City, MO 64106

Suite 635, 320 W. Capitol Ave.
Little Rock, AR 72201

Rm 9200, 11000 Wilshire Blvd.
Los Angeles, CA 90024

Rm 636B, 601 W. Broadway
Louisville, KY 40202

Suite 224, 51 SW 1st Ave.
Miami, FL 33130

517 E. Wisconsin Ave.
Milwaukee, WI 53202

Rm 108, 110 S. 4th St.
Minneapolis, MN 55401

Suite 1114, Parkway Towers
Nashville, TN 37219

2 Canal St.
New Orleans, LA 70130

Rm 3718, Federal Office Bldg
New York, NY 10278

6601 Broadway Extension
Oklahoma City, OK 73116

11133 O St.
Omaha, NE 68137

Suite 202, 475 Allendale Rd.
King of Prussia, PA 19406

Rm 3412, Federal Bldg and U.S. Courthouse
Phoenix, AZ 85025

Rm 2002, 1000 Liberty Ave.
Pittsburgh, PA 15222

Suite 242, 1 World Trade Center
121 SW Salmon St.
Portland, OR 9204

1755 E. Plumb La., No. 152
Reno, NV 89502

Rm 8010, 400 N. 8th St.
Richmond, VA 23240

Rm 105, 324 S. State St.
Salt Lake City, UT 84111

6363 Greenwich Dr.
San Diego, CA 92122

Box 36013, 450 Golden Gate Ave.
San Francisco, CA 94102

Rm G-55, Federal Bldg, Chardon Ave.
San Juan, PR 00918

120 Barnard St., A-107
Savannah, GA 31401

Suite 290, 3131 Elliott Ave.
Seattle, WA 98121

Suite 610, 7911 Forsyth Blvd.
St. Louis, MO 63105

Suite 100, Bldg 6, 3131 Princeton Pike
Trenton, NJ 08648

DEPARTMENT OF DEFENSE

Office of the Assistant Secretary of Defense (Public Affairs)
The Pentagon
Washington, DC 20301

Directorate for Information Operations and Reports (DIOR)
Suite 1204, 1215 Jefferson Davis Hwy.
Arlington, VA 22202-4302

DEFENSE LOGISTICS AGENCY
Defense Fuel Supply Center
Public Affairs
Bldg 8, Cameron Station
Alexandria, VA 22314

U.S. AIR FORCE PUBLICATIONS
Office of the Secretary of the Air Force
Office of Information
Public Information Division
Headquarters, USAF
Washington, DC 20330

U.S. ARMY PUBLICATIONS
Public Information Office
Office of the Chief of Information
Headquarters, Department of the Army
Washington, DC 20310

U.S. ARMY CORPS OF ENGINEERS
Public Affairs Office
Forrestal Bldg
Washington, DC 20314

U.S. ARMY CORPS OF ENGINEERS REGIONAL OFFICES

Alaska District
P.O. Box 7002
Anchorage, AK 99510

Detroit District
P.O. Box 1027
Detroit, MI 48231

Louisville District
P.O. Box 59
Louisville, KY 40201

Lower Mississippi Valley Division
P.O. Box 60
Vicksburg, MS 39180

Missouri River Division
Downtown Station, P.O. Box 103
Omaha, NE 68101

Mobile District
P.O. Box 2288
Mobile, AL 36828

Nashville District
P.O. Box 1070
Nashville, TN 37202

New England Division
424 Trapelo Rd
Waltham, MA 02154

New Orleans District
P.O. Box 60267
New Orleans, LA 70160

North Atlantic Division
90 Church St.
New York, NY 10007

North Central Division
536 S. Clark St.
Chicago, IL 60605

Ohio River Division
P.O. Box 1159
Cincinnati, OH 45201

South Atlantic Division
510 Title Bldg
30 Pryor St., S.W.
Atlanta, GA 30303

South Pacific Division
630 Sansome St.
San Francisco, CA 94111

Southwest Division
1114 Commerce St.
Dallas, TX 75242

U.S. NAVY PUBLICATIONS
Public Information Division
Office of Information
Department of the Navy
Washington, DC 20350

DEPARTMENT OF EDUCATION
(Specified Office)
400 Maryland Ave., S.W.
Washington, DC 20202

NATIONAL CENTER FOR EDUCATION STATISTICS
OERI
555 New Jersey Ave., N.W.
Washington, DC 20208

NATIONAL ASSESSMENT OF EDUCATIONAL PROGRESS (NAEP)
CN6710
Princeton, NJ 08541-6710

DEPARTMENT OF ENERGY
(Subagency Name)
Washington, DC 20585

BONNEVILLE POWER ADMINISTRATION
Public Involvement
P.O. Box 12999
Portland, OR 97212

ENERGY INFORMATION ADMINISTRATION
National Energy Information Center
EI-20, Mail Station 1F048
1000 Independence Ave., S.W.
Washington, DC 20585

FEDERAL ENERGY REGULATORY COMMISSION
Public Information Office, Rm 1000
825 North Capitol St., N.E.
Washington, DC 20426

OAK RIDGE NATIONAL LABORATORY
Technical Information Center
P.O. Box 62
Oak Ridge, TN 37831

DEPARTMENT OF HEALTH AND HUMAN SERVICES
Office of Public Affairs
Rm 647-D, HHH Bldg
200 Independence Ave., S.W.
Washington, DC 20201

CENTERS FOR DISEASE CONTROL
1600 Clifton Rd, N.E.
Atlanta, GA 30333

FOOD AND DRUG ADMINISTRATION
HFE 88
5600 Fishers La.
Rockville, MD 20857

HEALTH CARE FINANCING ADMINISTRATION
648 East High Rise Bldg
6401 Security Blvd
Baltimore, MD 21235

HEALTH RESOURCES AND SERVICES ADMINISTRATION
(Subagency Name)
14-43 Parklawn Bldg
5600 Fishers La.
Rockville, MD 20857

National Maternal and Child Health Clearinghouse
38th & R Sts., N.W.
Washington, DC 20057

Clearinghouse for Primary Care Information
8201 Greensboro Dr., Suite 600
McLean, VA 22102

NATIONAL CENTER FOR HEALTH STATISTICS
Rm 1-57, Federal Center Bldg #2
3700 East-West Hwy
Hyattsville, MD 20782

NATIONAL CLEARINGHOUSE FOR ALCOHOL AND DRUG INFORMATION
P.O. Box 2345
Rockville, MD 20852

NATIONAL INSTITUTES OF HEALTH
Office of Information
Rm 307, Bldg 1
9000 Rockville Pike
Bethesda, MD 20205

NATIONAL INSTITUTE OF MENTAL HEALTH
Public Inquiries
Rm 11A-21, 5600 Fishers La.
Rockville, MD 20857

NATIONAL INSTITUTE FOR OCCUPATIONAL SAFETY AND HEALTH
Publications, DTS
4676 Columbia Parkway
Cincinnati, OH 45226

OFFICE OF HUMAN DEVELOPMENT SERVICES
Rm 339D, HHH Bldg
200 Independence Ave., S.W.
Washington, DC 20201

OFFICE ON SMOKING AND HEALTH
Rm 158, 5600 Fishers La.
Rockville, MD 20857

PUBLIC HEALTH SERVICE
Office of Public Affairs
Rm 740-G, HHH Bldg
200 Independence Ave., S.W.
Washington, DC 20201

OHIC/ODPHP
P.O. Box 1133
Washington, DC 20013-1133

SOCIAL SECURITY ADMINISTRATION
Printing and Records Management Branch
1121 Operations Bldg
6401 Security Blvd
Baltimore, MD 21235

DEPARTMENT OF HOUSING AND URBAN DEVELOPMENT
Publication Service Center
Rm B-258
Washington, DC 20410

OFFICE OF POLICY DEVELOPMENT AND RESEARCH
HUD USER
PO. Box 6091
Rockville, MD 20850

DEPARTMENT OF THE INTERIOR
(Subagency Name)
Office of Information
Washington, DC 20240

BUREAU OF MINES
Publication Distribution Section
4800 Forbes Ave.
Pittsburgh, PA 15213

FISH AND WILDLIFE SERVICE
Natl Coastal Ecosystems Team
NASA Slidell Computer Complex
1010 Gause Blvd.
Slidell, LA 709458

U.S. GEOLOGICAL SURVEY
USGS Books and Open-File Rpts. Section
Box 25425, Federal Center
Denver, CO 80225

DEPARTMENT OF JUSTICE
Office of Public Information
10th and Constitution Ave., N.W.
Washington, DC 20530

BUREAU OF PRISONS
320 1st St., N.W.
Washington, DC 20534

DRUG ENFORCEMENT ADMINISTRATION
1405 I St., N.W.
Washington, DC 20537

FEDERAL BUREAU OF INVESTIGATION
9th and Pennsylvania Ave., N.W.
Washington, DC 20535

FOREIGN CLAIMS SETTLEMENT COMMISSION OF THE U.S.
Vanguard Building
1111 20th St., N.W.
Washington, DC 20579

IMMIGRATION AND NATURALIZATION SERVICE
425 I St., N.W.
Attn: Tariff Rm 235
Washington, DC 20536

NATIONAL CRIMINAL JUSTICE REFERENCE SERVICE (NCJRS)
Box 6000
Rockville, MD 20850

OFFICE OF JUSTICE PROGRAMS
633 Indiana Ave., N.W.
Washington, DC 20531

DEPARTMENT OF LABOR
Office of Information, Publications, and Reports
200 Constitution Ave., N.W.
Washington, DC 20210

BUREAU OF LABOR STATISTICS
Information Office
GAO Bldg
441 G St., N.W.
Washington, DC 20212

BUREAU OF LABOR STATISTICS REGIONAL OFFICES
Region I
Rm 1603, JFK Federal Bldg
Government Center
Boston, MA 02203

Region II
201 Varick St.
New York, NY 10014

Region III
3535 Market St.
P.O. Box 13309
Philadelphia, PA 19104

Region IV
1371 Peachtree St., N.E.
Atlanta, GA 30367

Region V
Federal Office Bldg
230 S. Dearborn St.
Chicago, IL 60604

Region VI
555 Griffin St., Rm 221
Dallas, TX 75202

Regions VII and VIII
911 Walnut St.
Kansas City, MO 64106

Regions IX and X
71 Stevenson St.
San Francisco, CA 94119-3766

EMPLOYMENT AND TRAINING ADMINISTRATION
Rm 10426, 601 D St., N.W.
Washington, DC 20213

MINE SAFETY AND HEALTH ADMINISTRATION
Office of Information
Ballston Tower #3, Rm 902
4015 Wilson Blvd
Arlington, VA 22203

DEPARTMENT OF STATE
(Subagency Name)
Bureau of Public Affairs
Washington, DC 20520

DEPARTMENT OF TRANSPORTATION
Office of Public & Consumer Affairs (S-81)
400 7th St., S.W.
Washington, DC 20590

Transportation Systems Center
Kendall Sq.
Cambridge, MA 02142

FEDERAL AVIATION ADMINISTRATION
Public Inquiry Center (APA-420)
800 Independence Ave., S.W.
Washington, DC 20590

FEDERAL HIGHWAY ADMINISTRATION
Office of Public Affairs (HPA-1)
400 7th St., S.W.
Washington, DC 20590

FEDERAL RAILROAD ADMINISTRATION
Office of Public Affairs (ROA-30)
400 7th St., S.W.
Washington, DC 20590

MARITIME ADMINISTRATION
Office of Public Affairs (MAR-240)
400 7th St., S.W.
Washington, DC 20590

NATIONAL HIGHWAY TRAFFIC SAFETY ADMINISTRATION
400 7th St., S.W.
Washington, DC 20590

SAINT LAWRENCE SEAWAY DEVELOPMENT CORPORATION
P.O. Box 44090
Washington, DC 20026-4090

URBAN MASS TRANSPORTATION ADMINISTRATION
Office of Public Affairs (UPA-1)
400 7th St., S.W.
Washington, DC 20590

U.S. COAST GUARD
Public Affairs Division (G-BPA)
2100 2nd St., S.W.
Washington, DC 20593

DEPARTMENT OF THE TREASURY
Public Affairs Office
15th and Pennsylvania Ave., N.W.
Washington, DC 20220

BUREAU OF ALCOHOL, TOBACCO AND FIREARMS
Office of Public Affairs
1200 Pennsylvania Ave., N.W.
Washington, DC 20226

BUREAU OF ENGRAVING AND PRINTING
Public Affairs Section, Rm 602-11A
14th and C Sts., S.W.
Washington, DC 20228

BUREAU OF THE PUBLIC DEBT
Washington, DC 20226

COMPTROLLER OF THE CURRENCY
Communications Division
490 L'Enfant Plaza East, S.W.
Washington, DC 20219

FINANCIAL MANAGEMENT SERVICE
Pennsylvania Ave. and Madison Pl., N.W.
Washington, DC 20226

INTERNAL REVENUE SERVICE
Office of Public Affairs
1111 Constitution Ave., N.W.
Washington, DC 20224

OFFICE OF REVENUE SHARING
Office of Public Affairs
2401 E St., N.W.
Washington, DC 20226

OFFICE OF THRIFT SUPERVISION
1700 G St., N.W.
Washington, DC 20552

U.S. CUSTOMS SERVICE
Office of Public Affairs
1301 Constitution Ave., N.W.
Washington, DC 20229

U.S. MINT
Assistant to the Director for Public Affairs
501 13th St., N.W.
Washington, DC 20220

U.S. SAVINGS BOND DIVISION
Washington, DC 20226

U.S. SECRET SERVICE
Office of Public Affairs
1800 G St., N.W.
Washington, DC 20223

DEPARTMENT OF VETERANS AFFAIRS
Office of Public Affairs
810 Vermont Ave., N.W.
Washington, DC 20420

INDEPENDENT AGENCIES

ACTION
Office of Public Affairs
1100 Vermont Ave., N.W.
Washington, DC 20525

AMERICAN BATTLE MONUMENTS COMMISSION
20 Massachusetts Ave., N.W.
Washington, DC 20314

APPALACHIAN REGIONAL COMMISSION
Archivist
1666 Connecticut Ave., N.W.
Washington, DC 20235

CENTRAL INTELLIGENCE AGENCY
Photoduplication Service
Library of Congress
Washington, DC 20540

CONSUMER PRODUCT SAFETY COMMISSION
Bureau of Information and Education
Product Safety Information Division
5401 Westbard Ave.
Bethesda, MD 20207

ENVIRONMENTAL PROTECTION AGENCY
(Subagency Name)
401 M St., S.W.
Washington, DC 20460

Documents Distribution Division
1901 Ross Ave.
Cincinnati, OH 45212

Office of Air Quality Planning and Standards
Research Triangle Park, NC 27711

ENVIRONMENTAL PROTECTION AGENCY REGIONAL OFFICES
Region I
Rm 2203, JFK Federal Bldg
Boston, MA 02203

Region II
Rm 1009, 26 Federal Plaza
New York, NY 10278

Region III
841 Chestnut St.
Philadelphia, PA 19107

Region IV
345 Courtland St., N.E.
Atlanta, GA 30365

Region V
230 South Dearborn St.
Chicago, IL 60604

Region VI
1445 Ross Ave.
Dallas, TX 75202

Region VII
726 Minnesota Ave.
Kansas City, KS 66101

Region VIII
999 18th St., Suite 500
Denver, CO 80202-2405

Region IX
1235 Mission St.
San Francisco, CA 94103

Region X
1200 6th Ave.
Seattle, WA 98101

EQUAL EMPLOYMENT OPPORTUNITY COMMISSION
1801 L St., N.W.
Washington, DC 20507

EXPORT-IMPORT BANK OF THE UNITED STATES
Public Affairs Office
811 Vermont Ave., N.W.
Washington, DC 20571

FARM CREDIT ADMINISTRATION
Information Division
1501 Farm Credit Dr.
McLean, VA 22102

FEDERAL COMMUNICATIONS COMMISSION
Public Information Office
1919 M St., N.W.
Washington, DC 20554

FEDERAL DEPOSIT INSURANCE CORPORATION
Information Office
550 17th St., N.W.
Washington, DC 20429

FEDERAL ELECTION COMMISSION
999 E St., N.W.
Washington, DC 20463

FEDERAL EMERGENCY MANAGEMENT AGENCY
Office of Public Affairs
500 C St., S.W.
Washington, DC 20472

FEDERAL HOME LOAN BANKS
Federal Home Loan Bank of Atlanta
Peachtree Center Station
P.O. Box 56527
Atlanta, GA 30343

Federal Home Loan Bank of Boston
P.O. Box 2196
Boston, MA 02106

Federal Home Loan Bank of Chicago
111 E. Wacker Dr.
Chicago, IL 60601

Federal Home Loan Bank of Cincinnati
2500 DuBois Tower
P.O. Box 598
Cincinnati, OH 45201

Federal Home Loan Bank of Dallas
500 E. John Carpenter Freeway
P.O. Box 619026
Dallas/Ft. Worth, TX 75261

Federal Home Loan Bank of Des Moines
907 Walnut St.
Des Moines, IA 50309

Federal Home Loan Bank of Indianapolis
1350 Merchants Plaza, South Tower
115 W. Washington St.
P.O. Box 60
Indianapolis, IN 46206

Federal Home Loan Bank of New York
One World Trade Center
New York, NY 10048

Federal Home Loan Bank of Pittsburgh
11 Stanwix St.
Gateway Center
Pittsburgh, PA 15222

Federal Home Loan Bank of San Francisco
600 California St.
P.O. Box 7948
San Francisco, CA 94120

Federal Home Loan Bank of Seattle
600 Stewart St.
Seattle, WA 98101

Federal Home Loan Bank of Topeka
3 Townsite Plaza
P.O. Box 176 120 East 6th St.
Topeka, KS 66601

FEDERAL HOME LOAN MORTGAGE CORPORATION
1770 G St., N.W.
Washington, DC 20552

FEDERAL HOUSING FINANCE BOARD
1777 F St., N.W.
Washington, DC 20066

FEDERAL MARITIME COMMISSION
Public Information Office
1100 L St., N.W.
Washington, DC 20573

FEDERAL MEDIATION AND CONCILIATION SERVICE
2100 K St., N.W.
Washington, DC 20427

FEDERAL RESERVE SYSTEM
Board of Governors
Publications Section
Division of Administrative Services
Washington, DC 20551

Federal Reserve Bank of Atlanta
Research Department
P.O. Box 1731
Atlanta, GA 30301

Federal Reserve Bank of Boston
Bank & Public Information Center
600 Atlantic Ave.
Boston, MA 02106

Federal Reserve Bank of Chicago
Publications Division
P.O. Box 834
Chicago, IL 60690

Federal Reserve Bank of Cleveland
Research Department
P.O. Box 6387
Cleveland, OH 44101

Federal Reserve Bank of Dallas
Research Department
Station K
Dallas, TX 75222

Federal Reserve Bank of Kansas City
Research Department
925 Grand Ave.
Kansas City, MO 64198

Federal Reserve Bank of Minneapolis
Office of Public Information
Minneapolis, MN 55480

Federal Reserve Bank of New York
Public Information Department
33 Liberty St.
New York, NY 10045

Federal Reserve Bank of Philadelphia
Public Information Department
PO Box 66
Philadelphia, PA 19105

Federal Reserve Bank of Richmond
Bank and Public Relations Department
P.O. Box 27622
Richmond, VA 23261

Federal Reserve Bank of St. Louis
Research Department
Box 442
St. Louis, MO 63166

Federal Reserve Bank of San Francisco
Research Information Center
P.O. Box 7702
San Francisco, CA 94120

FEDERAL TRADE COMMISSION
Public Reference Room
Pennsylvania Ave. at 6th St., N.W.
Rm 130
Washington, DC 20580

GENERAL SERVICES ADMINISTRATION
Director of Information
18th & F Sts., N.W.
Washington, DC 20405

INTERSTATE COMMERCE COMMISSION
Public Information Office
12th St. and Constitution Ave., N.W.
Washington, DC 20423

MERIT SYSTEMS PROTECTION BOARD
1120 Vermont Ave., N.W.
Washington, DC 20419

NATIONAL AERONAUTICS AND SPACE ADMINISTRATION
Headquarters, Information Center
Washington, DC 20546

NATIONAL ARCHIVES AND RECORDS ADMINISTRATION
Publications Services
Washington, DC 20408

NATIONAL CREDIT UNION ADMINISTRATION
Office of Public Information
1776 G St., N.W.
Washington, DC 20456

NATIONAL FOUNDATION ON THE ARTS AND HUMANITIES
1100 Pennsylvania, Ave., N.W.
Washington, DC 20506

NATIONAL LABOR RELATIONS BOARD
1717 Pennsylvania Ave., N.W.
Washington, DC 20570

NATIONAL MEDIATION BOARD
1425 K St., N.W.
Washington, DC 20572

NATIONAL SCIENCE FOUNDATION
Public Information Branch, Rm 531
1800 G St., N.W.
Washington, DC 20550

NATIONAL TRANSPORTATION SAFETY BOARD
Publications Unit
800 Independence Ave., S.W.
Washington, DC 20594

OFFICE OF PERSONNEL MANAGEMENT
Office of Public Affairs
1900 E St., N.W.
Washington, DC 20415

PANAMA CANAL COMMISSION
2000 L St., N.W.
Washington, DC 20036

PEACE CORPS
1990 K St., N.W.
Washington, DC 20526

PENSION BENEFIT GUARANTY CORPORATION
2020 K St., N.W.
Washington, DC 20006

RAILROAD RETIREMENT BOARD
Division of Information Service
844 Rush St.
Chicago, IL 60611

RESOLUTION TRUST CORPORATION
Corporate Communications Office
Washington, DC 20434

SECURITIES AND EXCHANGE COMMISSION
Office of Public Information
450 5th St., N.W.
Washington, DC 20549

SELECTIVE SERVICE SYSTEM
600 E St., N.W.
Washington, DC 20435

SMALL BUSINESS ADMINISTRATION
Office of Public Communications
409 Third St., S.W.
Washington, DC 20416

SMITHSONIAN INSTITUTION
Office of Public Affairs
Washington, DC 20560

TENNESSEE VALLEY AUTHORITY
Suite 300, 412 First St., S.E.
Washington, DC 20444

Public Affairs Office
400 W. Summit Hill Dr.
Knoxville, TN 37902-1499

Division of Energy Use and Distributor Relations
721 Power Building
Chattanooga, TN 37401

Division of Land and Forest Resources
Norris, TN 37828

National Fertilizer Development Center
Muscle Shoals, AL 35660

Technical Library
NFD 1A 100E
Muscle Shoals, AL 35660-1010

U.S. ARMS CONTROL AND DISARMAMENT AGENCY
Office of Public Affairs
320 21st St., N.W.
Washington, DC 20451

U.S. INFORMATION AGENCY
Office of Public Liaison
301 Fourth St., S.W.
Washington, DC 20547

U.S. INTERNATIONAL DEVELOPMENT COOPERATION AGENCY
Office of Public Affairs
Washington, DC 20523-0001

Agency for International Development
Director, Office of Public Affairs
Washington, DC 20523-0001

AID Document and Information Handling Facility
1500 Wilson Blvd., Suite 1010
Arlington, VA 22209-2404

Overseas Private Investment Corporation
1615 M St., N.W.
Washington, DC 20527

U.S. INTERNATIONAL TRADE COMMISSION
Office of the Secretary
500 E St., S.W.
Washington, DC 20436

U.S. OFFICE OF SPECIAL COUNSEL
Suite 1100, 1120 Vermont Ave., N.W.
Washington, DC 20005

U.S. POSTAL SERVICE
475 L'Enfant Plaza West, S.W.
Washington, DC 20260

SPECIAL BOARDS, COMMITTEES, AND COMMISSIONS

ADVISORY COMMISSION ON INTERGOVERNMENTAL RELATIONS
800 K St., N.W.
South Building, Suite 450
Washington, DC 20575

ARCHITECTURAL AND TRANSPORTATION BARRIERS COMPLIANCE BOARD
Suite 501, 1111 18th St., N.W.
Washington, DC 20036

BOARD FOR INTERNATIONAL BROADCASTING
Suite 400, 1201 Connecticut Ave., N.W.
Washington, DC 20036

BOARD OF FOREIGN SCHOLARSHIPS
U.S. Information Agency
Rm 247, 301 4th St., S.W.
Washington, DC 20547

COMMISSION ON CIVIL RIGHTS
1121 Vermont Ave., N.W.
Washington, DC 20425

COMMODITY FUTURES TRADING COMMISSION
Office of Public Information
2033 K St., N.W.
Washington, DC 20581
Suite 4600, 233 S. Wacker Dr.
Chicago, IL 60606
Rm 400, 4901 Main St.
Kansas City, MO 64112
510 Grain Exchange Building
Minneapolis, MN 55415
Suite 4747, One World Trade Center
New York, NY 10048

FEDERAL FINANCIAL INSTITUTIONS EXAMINATION COUNCIL
Suite 8508, 1776 G St., N.W.
Washington, DC 20006

FEDERAL LABOR RELATIONS AUTHORITY
500 C St., S.W.
Washington, DC 20424

HARRY S. TRUMAN SCHOLARSHIP FOUNDATION
712 Jackson Place, N.W.
Washington, DC 20006

INTER-AMERICAN FOUNDATION
1515 Wilson Blvd, 5th Fl.
Rosslyn, VA 22209

INTERNATIONAL JOINT COMMISSION, U.S. AND CANADA
United States Section
2001 S St., N.W.
Washington, DC 20440

JAPAN-U.S. FRIENDSHIP COMMISSION
Rm 3416, 1200 Pennsylvania Ave., N.W.
Washington, DC 20004

MARINE MAMMAL COMMISSION
Rm 512, 1825 Connecticut Ave., N.W.
Washington, DC 20009

MIGRATORY BIRD CONSERVATION COMMISSION
18th & C Sts., N.W., 622 ARL SQ
Washington, DC 20240

NATIONAL ADVISORY COUNCIL ON ADULT EDUCATION
Rm 323, 425 13th St., N.W.
Washington, DC 20004

NATIONAL ADVISORY COUNCIL ON INDIAN EDUCATION
330 C St., S.W., Room 4072
Switzer Bldg, Mail Stop 2419
Washington, DC 20202-7556

NATIONAL ADVISORY COUNCIL ON INTERNATIONAL MONETARY AND FINANCIAL POLICIES
Rm 5410
Department of the Treasury
Washington, DC 20220

NATIONAL CAPITAL PLANNING COMMISSION
Suite 301, 801 Pennsylvania Ave., N.W.
Washington, DC 20576

NATIONAL COMMISSION FOR EMPLOYMENT POLICY
1522 K St., N.W., Rm 300
Washington, DC 20005

NATIONAL COMMISSION ON LIBRARIES AND INFORMATION SCIENCE
1111 18th St., N.W., Suite 310
Washington, DC 20036

OFFICE OF NAVAJO AND HOPI INDIAN RELOCATION
P.O. Box KK
Flagstaff, AZ 86002

PRESIDENT'S COMMITTEE ON EMPLOYMENT OF PEOPLE WITH DISABILITIES
1111 20th St., N.W., Suite 636
Washington, DC 20036

PROSPECTIVE PAYMENT ASSESSMENT COMMISSION
300 7th St., S.W.
Washington, DC 20024

U.S. ADVISORY COMMISSION ON PUBLIC DIPLOMACY
Rm 1008, 1750 Pennsylvania Ave., N.W.
Washington, DC 20547

JUDICIAL BRANCH

ADMINISTRATIVE OFFICE OF U.S. COURTS
Washington, DC 20544

FEDERAL JUDICIAL CENTER
1520 H St., N.W.
Washington, DC 20005

SPECIAL COURTS
U.S. Court of International Trade
1 Federal Plaza
New York, NY 10007

U.S. Court of Claims
717 Madison Pl., N.W.
Washington, DC 20005

U.S. Tax Court
400 2nd St., N.W.
Washington, DC 20217

UNITED STATES CONGRESS
(House Committee Name)
U.S. House of Representatives
Washington, DC 20515
(Senate Committee Name)
U.S. Senate
Washington, DC 20510
(Joint Committee Name)
U.S. Congress
Washington, DC 20510

CONGRESSIONAL BUDGET OFFICE
Office of Intergovernmental Relations
2nd and D Sts., S.W.
Washington, DC 20515

LIBRARY OF CONGRESS
Publications Officer
Washington, DC 20540

OFFICE OF TECHNOLOGY ASSESSMENT
Office of Public Affairs
Washington, DC 20510

U.S. GENERAL ACCOUNTING OFFICE
Document Handling and Information
Services Facility
P.O. Box 6015
Gaithersburg, MD 20877

QUASI-OFFICIAL AGENCIES

AMERICAN NATIONAL RED CROSS
Office of Public Affairs and
Financial Development
17th and D Sts., N.W.
Washington, DC 20006

NATIONAL RAILROAD PASSENGER CORPORATION (AMTRAK)
Public Affairs Department
60 Massachusetts Ave., N.E.
Washington, DC 20002

U.S. INSTITUTE OF PEACE
1550 M St., N.W.
Washington, DC 20005-1708

Document Availability Symbols

The following abbreviations and symbols are used to indicate the availability of documents abstracted by ASI. The symbols are provided in the bibliographic data section given at the head of each abstract.

GPO For sale by Government Printing Office, Washington, D.C., 20402.

The GPO stock number (S/N) is also given. The price is given if it has been announced at the time ASI goes to press; GPO prices change frequently, however.

NTIS For sale by National Technical Information Service, 5285 Port Royal Rd., Springfield, Va., 22161.

Order number and price are also given if available.

† or ‡ Inquire of the issuing agency.

† Copies are available at the time the document is issued, often free of charge, but supplies may be limited.

‡ Limited or restricted distribution has been specified by the agency. In some cases a request for a copy will be honored.

Addresses of major issuing agency offices are given in the Abstracts Volume, p. xxxvii; Index Volume, p. xxviii. If documents are available from another office, the name and address will be given in the bibliographic data section of the abstract.

♦ No distribution. Issuing agency has specified it should not be contacted.

ASI/MF Available on ASI microfiche. Microfiche collections are available in many libraries. The number following this notation indicates the unit count for ordering individual documents on microfiche through ASI "Documents on Demand." For information, see p. xxx.

● **Item** Depository item number, assigned to classes of documents issued to depository libraries.

ACRONYMS AND SELECTED ABBREVIATIONS

The following acronyms and abbreviations may be used without further identification:

Abbreviation	Full Form
ADAMHA	Alcohol, Drug Abuse and Mental Health Administration
Admin	Administration
AFDC	Aid to Families with Dependent Children
AID	Agency for International Development
Amtrak	National Railroad Passenger Corporation
Assn	Association
BEA	Bureau of Economic Analysis
Bibl	Bibliography
BLS	Bureau of Labor Statistics
Bull	Bulletin
Bur	Bureau
CAB	Civil Aeronautics Board
CBO	Congressional Budget Office
CCC	Commodity Credit Corporation
CDC	Centers for Disease Control
CES	Center for Educ Statistics
CETA	Comprehensive Employment and Training Act
CIA	Central Intelligence Agency
Conf	Conference
CPI	Consumer Price Index
CRS	Congressional Research Service
CY	Calendar year
DEA	Drug Enforcement Administration
Dept	Department
Dev	Development
Div	Division
DOD	Department of Defense
DOE	Department of Energy
DOT	Department of Transportation
EC	European Community (formerly European Economic Community, EEC)
EDA	Economic Development Administration
EIA	Energy Information Administration
EPA	Environmental Protection Agency
ERS	Economic Research Service
ESEA	Elementary and Secondary Education Act
Eximbank	Export-Import Bank
FAA	Federal Aviation Administration
FAO	Food and Agriculture Organization (UN)
FAS	Foreign Agricultural Service
FBI	Federal Bureau of Investigation
FCC	Federal Communications Commission
FDA	Food and Drug Administration
FDIC	Federal Deposit Insurance Corporation
Fed	Federal
FERC	Federal Energy Regulatory Commission
FHA	Federal Housing Administration
FHLB	Federal Home Loan Bank
FHLBB	Federal Home Loan Bank Board
FmHA	Farmers Home Administration
FSLIC	Federal Savings and Loan Insurance Corporation
FTC	Federal Trade Commission
FY	Fiscal year
GAO	General Accounting Office
GATT	General Agreement on Tariffs and Trade
GDP	Gross Domestic Product
GNP	Gross National Product
Govtl	Governmental
GPO	Government Printing Office
GSA	General Services Administration
GS	General Schedule
HCFA	Health Care Financing Administration
HHS	Department of Health and Human Services
HMO	Health maintenance organization
HRSA	Health Resources and Services Administration
HUD	Department of Housing and Urban Development
Hwy	Highway
ICC	Interstate Commerce Commission
IMF	International Monetary Fund
Info	Information
Inst	Institute
Instn	Institution
Intl	International
IRA	Individual retirement arrangement
IRS	Internal Revenue Service
ITA	International Trade Administration
LC	Library of Congress
MarAd	Maritime Administration
Mgmt	Management
MSA	Metropolitan Statistical Area (formerly SMSA)
NASA	National Aeronautics and Space Administration
NASS	National Agricultural Statistics Service
Natl	National
NATO	North Atlantic Treaty Organization
NCHS	National Center for Health Statistics
NIH	National Institutes of Health
NIMH	National Institute of Mental Health
NLRB	National Labor Relations Board
NOAA	National Oceanic and Atmospheric Administration
NOW	Negotiable orders of withdrawal
NRC	Nuclear Regulatory Commission
NSF	National Science Foundation
NTIS	National Technical Information Services
OAS	Organization of American States
OASDHI	Old-Age, Survivors, Disability, and Health Insurance Program
OCS	Outer continental shelf
OECD	Organization for Economic Cooperation and Development
OHDS	Office of Human Development Services
OMB	Office of Management and Budget
OPEC	Organization of Petroleum Exporting Countries
OPM	Office of Personnel Management
OSHA	Occupational Safety and Health Administration
PAD	Petroleum Administration for Defense (abolished in 1954 but acronym still in use)
PHS	Public Health Service
PPI	Producer Price Index
PRC	People's Republic of China
Pub	Publication
R&D	Research and Development
REA	Rural Electrification Administration
Res	Research
Rpt	Report
S&L	Savings and Loan Association
SALT	Strategic Arms Limitation Talks
SBA	Small Business Administration
SEC	Securities and Exchange Commission
SIC	Standard Industrial Classification
SITC	Standard International Trade Classification
SMSA	Standard Metropolitan Statistical Area (see MSA)
SRS	Statistical Reporting Service
SSA	Social Security Administration
SSI	Supplemental Security Income
TSUSA	Tariff Schedules of the U.S., Annotated
TTPI	Trust Territory of the Pacific Islands
TVA	Tennessee Valley Authority
USDA	Department of Agriculture
USGS	U.S. Geological Survey
USIA	U.S. Information Agency
USITC	U.S. International Trade Commission
USPS	U.S. Postal Service
VA	Veterans Administration

Issuing Agencies and ASI Accession Numbers

Listed below are issuing agencies for all publications abstracted in this Annual. Agencies are arranged to reflect current departmental organizations.

EXECUTIVE OFFICE OF THE PRESIDENT

- 100 Office of Management and Budget
- 200 Council of Economic Advisers
- 230 Office of National Drug Control Policy
- 440 Office of the U.S. Trade Representative
- 480 Council on Environmental Quality

DEPARTMENT OF AGRICULTURE

- 1000 General
- 1120 Agricultural Cooperative Service
- 1180 Farmers Home Administration
- 1200 Forest Service
- 1240 Rural Electrification Administration
- 1260 Soil Conservation Service
- 1270 Office of Transportation
- 1290 Federal Grain Inspection Service
- Agricultural Marketing Service
  - 1300 General
  - 1309–
  - 1319 Commodity Reports
- 1350 Human Nutrition Information Service
- 1360 Food and Nutrition Service
- 1370 Food Safety and Inspection Service
- 1380 Packers and Stockyards Administration
- 1390 Animal and Plant Health Inspection Service
- Economic Research Service
  - 1500 General
  - 1520 International
  - 1540 National Economics
  - 1560 National Economics, Commodities
  - 1580 Natural Resources
  - 1590 Economic Development
- National Agricultural Statistics Service
  - 1610–
  - 1631 Agricultural Statistics Board
- 1700 Agricultural Research Service
- 1740 Cooperative State Research Service
- 1760 Office of Grants and Program Systems
- Agricultural Stabilization and Conservation Service
  - 1800 General
  - 1820 Commodity Credit Corp.
- 1920 Foreign Agricultural Service
- 1950 Office of International Cooperation and Development

DEPARTMENT OF COMMERCE

- 2000 General
- 2020 Bureau of Export Administration
- 2040 International Trade Administration
- 2060 Economic Development Administration
- 2100 Minority Business Development Agency
- National Oceanic and Atmospheric Administration
  - 2140 General
  - 2150 National Environmental Satellite, Data, and Information Service
  - 2160 National Marine Fisheries Service
  - 2170 National Ocean Service
  - 2180 National Weather Service
- 2210 National Institute of Standards and Technology
- 2220 National Technical Information Service
- 2240 Patent and Trademark Office
- Bureau of Census
  - 2300 Bibliographies and Guides
  - 2320 General
  - 2329 1987 Enterprise Statistics
  - 2331 1987 Census of Agriculture
  - 2340 Agriculture
  - 2373 1987 Census of Construction Industries
  - 2380 Construction
  - 2393 1987 Census of Service Industries
  - 2399 1987 Census of Retail Trade
  - 2407 1987 Census of Wholesale Trade
  - 2410 Business
  - 2420 Foreign Trade
  - 2455 1987 Census of Governments
  - 2460 Governments
  - 2480 Housing
  - 2497 1987 Census of Manufactures
  - 2500 Manufacturing
  - 2515 1987 Census of Mineral Industries
  - 2540 Population
  - 2551 1990 Census of Population and Housing
  - 2579 1987 Census of Transportation
  - 2591 1987 Economic Censuses of Outlying Areas
  - 2620 Methodology
- 2700 Bureau of Economic Analysis
- 2800 National Telecommunications and Information Administration
- 2900 U.S. Travel and Tourism Administration

DEPARTMENT OF ENERGY

- 3000 General
- 3020 Office of the Secretary of Energy
- 3080 Federal Energy Regulatory Commission
- 3160 Energy Information Administration
- 3220 Bonneville Power Administration
- 3230 Southeastern Power Administration
- 3240 Southwestern Power Administration
- 3250 Western Area Power Administration
- 3300 Conservation and Renewable Energy
- 3320 Environment, Safety, and Health
- 3330 Fossil Energy
- 3340 Defense Programs
- 3350 Nuclear Energy

3360 Civilian Radioactive Waste Management
3400 International Affairs and Energy Emergencies

DEPARTMENT OF DEFENSE

3500 General
3540 Office of the Secretary of Defense
3600 Department of Air Force
3700 Department of Army
3750 Army Corps of Engineers
3800 Department of Navy
3900 Defense Agencies

DEPARTMENT OF HEALTH AND HUMAN SERVICES

4000 General

Public Health Service

4040 General
4060 Food and Drug Administration
4070 Agency for Toxic Substances and Disease Registry
4080 Indian Health Service Health Resources and Services Administration
- 4100 General
- 4110 Bureau of Health Professions

National Center for Health Statistics

- 4120 Bibliographies and Guides
- 4140 General
- 4160 Methodology

4180 Agency for Health Care Policy and Research

Centers for Disease Control

- 4200 General
- 4240 National Institute for Occupational Safety and Health

National Institutes of Health

- 4430 General
- 4460 National Library of Medicine
- 4470 NIH Research Institutes

Alcohol, Drug Abuse and Mental Health Administration

- 4480 National Institute on Alcohol Abuse and Alcoholism
- 4490 National Institute on Drug Abuse
- 4500 National Institute of Mental Health

4600 Office of Human Development Services

4650 Health Care Financing Administration
4690 Family Support Administration

Social Security Administration

- 4700 General
- 4740 Office of Policy

DEPARTMENT OF EDUCATION

4800 General

Office of Educational Research and Improvement

- 4810 General National Center for Education Statistics
- 4820 General
- 4830 Elementary and Secondary Education
- 4840 Postsecondary Education
- 4860 Information Services
- 4870 Library Programs

4880 Office of Research
4890 National Assessment of Educational Progress
4940 Office of Special Education and Rehabilitative Services

DEPARTMENT OF HOUSING AND URBAN DEVELOPMENT

5000 General
5120 Community Planning and Development
5140 Housing (FHA)
5180 Policy Development and Research

DEPARTMENT OF INTERIOR

5300 General
5500 Fish and Wildlife Service
5540 National Park Service

Bureau of Mines

- 5600 General
- 5610 Mineral Industry Surveys

5640 Office of Surface Mining Reclamation and Enforcement
5660 Geological Survey
5700 Bureau of Indian Affairs
5720 Bureau of Land Management
5730 Minerals Management Service
5820 Bureau of Reclamation

DEPARTMENT OF JUSTICE

6000 General
6060 Office of Justice Programs
6220 Federal Bureau of Investigation
6240 Bureau of Prisons
6260 Immigration and Naturalization Service
6280 Drug Enforcement Administration
6290 U.S. Marshals Service

DEPARTMENT OF LABOR

6300 General
6360 Bureau of International Labor Affairs
6400 Employment and Training Administration
6460 Office of Labor— Management Standards
6500 Employment Standards Administration
6560 Women's Bureau
6600 Occupational Safety and Health Administration
6660 Mine Safety and Health Administration
6680 Pension and Welfare Benefits Administration

Bureau of Labor Statistics

- 6720 General
- 6740 Employment Analysis and Trends
- 6760 Prices and Living Conditions
- 6780 Wages and Industrial Relations
- 6820 Productivity and Technology
- 6840 Occupational Safety and Health
- 6860 Foreign Labor Conditions
- 6880 Methodology
- 6940 Regional Office 4, Atlanta
- 6960 Regional Office 6, Dallas

DEPARTMENT OF STATE

7000 General
7140 Bureau of Intelligence and Research
7180 Bureau of Consular Affairs

DEPARTMENT OF TRANSPORTATION

Code	Agency
7300	General
7400	Coast Guard
7500	Federal Aviation Administration
7550	Federal Highway Administration
7600	Federal Railroad Administration
7700	Maritime Administration
7740	Saint Lawrence Seaway Development Corp.
7760	National Highway Traffic Safety Administration
7880	Urban Mass Transportation Administration

DEPARTMENT OF TREASURY

Code	Agency
8000	General
8100	Financial Management Service
8140	U.S. Customs Service
8200	U.S. Mint
8240	Bureau of the Public Debt
8300	Internal Revenue Service
8400	Office of the Comptroller of Currency
8430	Office of Thrift Supervision
8440	U.S. Savings Bonds Division
8460	U.S. Secret Service
8480	Bureau of Alcohol, Tobacco and Firearms

DEPARTMENT OF VETERANS AFFAIRS

Code	Agency
8600	General
8650	Veterans Benefits Administration
8700	Veterans Health Services and Research Administration

INDEPENDENT AGENCIES

Code	Agency
9020	ACTION
9080	Appalachian Regional Commission
9110	Central Intelligence Agency
9160	Consumer Product Safety Commission
	Environmental Protection Agency
9180	General
9190	Air and Radiation
9200	Water
9210	Solid Waste and Emergency Response
9240	Equal Employment Opportunity Commission
9250	Export-Import Bank
9260	Farm Credit Administration
9270	Federal Election Commission
9280	Federal Communications Commission
9290	Federal Deposit Insurance Corp.
9300	Federal Home Loan Banks
9330	Federal Maritime Commission
9360	Federal Reserve Board of Governors
	Federal Reserve Banks
9371	Federal Reserve Bank of Atlanta
9373	Federal Reserve Bank of Boston
9375	Federal Reserve Bank of Chicago
9377	Federal Reserve Bank of Cleveland
9379	Federal Reserve Bank of Dallas
9381	Federal Reserve Bank of Kansas City
9383	Federal Reserve Bank of Minneapolis
9385	Federal Reserve Bank of New York
9387	Federal Reserve Bank of Philadelphia
9389	Federal Reserve Bank of Richmond
9391	Federal Reserve Bank of St. Louis
9393	Federal Reserve Bank of San Francisco
9400	Federal Trade Commission
9410	Federal Home Loan Mortgage Corp.
9430	Federal Emergency Management Agency
9440	Federal Housing Finance Board
9450	General Services Administration
9480	Interstate Commerce Commission
9490	Merit Systems Protection Board
9500	National Aeronautics and Space Administration
9510	National Archives and Records Administration
9530	National Credit Union Administration
9560	National Foundation on the Arts and the Humanities
9580	National Labor Relations Board
9610	National Transportation Safety Board
9620	National Science Foundation
9630	Nuclear Regulatory Commission
9650	Peace Corps
9660	Panama Canal Commission
9670	Pension Benefit Guaranty Corp.
9680	Postal Rate Commission
9700	Railroad Retirement Board
9720	Resolution Trust Corp.
9730	Securities and Exchange Commission
9740	Selective Service System
9760	Small Business Administration
9800	Tennessee Valley Authority
9840	Office of Personnel Management
9850	U.S. Information Agency
9860	U.S. Postal Service
9880	U.S. International Trade Commission
9890	U.S. Office of Special Counsel
	U.S. International Development Cooperation Agency
9900	General
9910	Agency for International Development
9920	Veterans Administration (transferred to Dept of Veterans Affairs)

SPECIAL BOARDS, COMMITTEES, AND COMMISSIONS

Code	Agency
10040	Advisory Commission on Intergovernmental Relations
10310	Board for International Broadcasting
10320	Board of Foreign Scholarships
11040	Commission on Civil Rights
11710	Committee for Purchase from the Blind and Other Severely Handicapped
11920	Commodity Futures Trading Commission
12800	Federal Financing Bank
13000	Federal Financial Institutions Examination Council
13360	Federal Labor Relations Authority
14310	Harry S. Truman Scholarship Foundation
14350	Interagency Task Force on Acid Precipitation
14420	Inter-American Foundation
14640	International Joint Commission, U.S. and Canada
14730	Marine Mammal Commission
14810	Monitored Retrievable Storage Commission
14850	National Advisory Council on Child Nutrition
14870	National Advisory Council on Indian Education

15340 National Advisory Council on International Monetary and Financial Policies
15450 National Capital Planning Commission
15490 National Commission for Employment Policy
15520 National Commission on Children
15630 National Commission on Libraries and Information Science
15910 National Education Goals Panel
16000 Office of Navajo and Hopi Indian Relocation
17200 Prospective Payment Assessment Commission
17260 Physician Payment Review Commission
17590 U.S. Advisory Commission on Public Diplomacy
17610 U.S. Architectural and Transportation Barriers Compliance Board
17660 U.S. Sentencing Commission

UNITED STATES COURTS

18200 Administrative Office of the U.S. Courts
18220 Special Courts
18400 Federal Judicial Center

UNITED STATES CONGRESS

House Committees
21140 House Aging Committee, Select
21160 House Agriculture Committee
21200 House Armed Services Committee
21240 House Banking, Finance and Urban Affairs Committee
21260 House Budget Committee
21300 House District of Columbia Committee
21340 House Education and Labor Committee
21360 House Energy and Commerce Committee
21380 House Foreign Affairs Committee
21400 House Government Operations Committee
21420 House Administration Committee
21440 House Interior and Insular Affairs Committee
21520 House Judiciary Committee
21560 House Merchant Marine and Fisheries Committee
21620 House Post Office and Civil Service Committee
21640 House Public Works and Transportation Committee
21700 House Science, Space, and Technology Committee
21720 House Small Business Committee
21780 House Ways and Means Committee
21940 House Special Publications
21960 House Temporary Committees

Joint Committees
23840 Joint Economic Committee
23870 Joint Printing Committee
23890 Joint Commissions and Special Committees

Senate Committees
25160 Senate Agriculture, Nutrition, and Forestry Committee
25240 Senate Banking, Housing, and Urban Affairs Committee
25250 Senate Budget Committee
25260 Senate Commerce, Science and Transportation Committee
25310 Senate Energy and Natural Resources Committee
25320 Senate Environment and Public Works Committee
25360 Senate Finance Committee
25380 Senate Foreign Relations Committee
25400 Senate Governmental Affairs Committee
25410 Senate Indian Affairs Committee, Select
25520 Senate Judiciary Committee
25540 Senate Labor and Human Resources Committee
25920 Senate Documents
25940 Senate Special Publications

General Accounting Office
26102-
26106 General
26111 Accounting and Financial Management
26113 Resources, Community and Economic Development
26119 General Government
26121 Human Resources
26123 National Security and International Affairs
26125 Information Management and Technology
26131 Program Evaluation and Methodology
26200 Government Printing Office
26300 Congressional Budget Office
26350 Office of Technology Assessment
26400 Library of Congress

QUASI-OFFICIAL AGENCIES

29250 American National Red Cross
29520 National Railroad Passenger Corp. (AMTRAK)
29570 Smithsonian Institution

Index by Subjects and Names

Index by Subjects and Names

This index contains references to subjects, to corporate authors, and to individual authors. References to individual items within a tabular breakdown (e.g. data about a particular State in a table that is broken down State-by-State) have been included only on a very selective basis. For complete references to information of this kind, please use the Index by Categories.

For information on how to make best use of both indexes, please consult the User Guide.

Abandoned property
see Vacant and abandoned property

Abel, Andrew B.
"Equity Premium Puzzle", 9387–1.204

Abilene, Tex.
see also under By City and By SMSA or MSA in the "Index by Categories"

Abken, Peter A.
"Beyond Plain Vanilla: A Taxonomy of Swaps", 9371–1.205
"Globalization of Stock, Futures, and Options Markets", 9371–1.209
"Valuation of Default-Risky Interest-Rate Swaps", 9371–10.62

Abnormalities
see Birth defects

Abortion
Cancer (breast) precursor hormonal changes risk relation to selected reproductive factors, 1983-89 study, article, 4472–1.227
Certificates of birth, death, marriage, and divorce, and fetal death and abortion rpts, 1989 natl standard revisions, 4147–4.27
Deaths related to pregnancy, and rates, by detailed cause and demographic characteristics, 1988, US Vital Statistics annual rpt, 4144–2
Deaths related to pregnancy, rates, and risk, by pregnancy outcome, cause, and maternal characteristics, 1979-86, article, 4202–7.206
Health condition and health care resources, use, and spending, 1950s-89, annual data compilation, 4144–11
Homeless teens pregnancy prevalence and outcomes, services availability, health condition, and drug abuse, 1989 conf, 4108–55
Minority group health condition, services use, costs, and indicators of services need, 1950s-88, 4118–55
Performance of abortions, by method, patient characteristics, and State, 1972-88, article, 4202–7.207
Performance of abortions, by method, pregnancy history, and other characteristics of woman, 1988 US Vital Statistics annual rpt, 4146–5.120
Poor women's pregnancies, by whether intended, outcome, contraceptives use, marital status, and race, 1985-86 local area study, article, 4042–3.241
Public opinion on abortion, by respondent characteristics, data compilation, 1991 annual rpt, 6064–6.2

State and Metro Area Data Book, 1991 data compilation, 2328–54
Statistical Abstract of US, 1991 annual data compilation, 2324–1.2
Vital and Health Statistics series: reprints of monthly rpt supplements, 4147–24
Youth and children social, economic, and demographic characteristics, 1950s-90, 4818–5

Abrasive materials
Employment, earnings, and hours, by SIC 1- to 4-digit industry, monthly and annual averages, selected years 1909-90, annual rpt, 6744–4
Exports and imports of US, by country and detailed commodity, monthly rpt, 2422–12
Exports and imports of US, by Harmonized System 6-digit commodity and country, 1990, annual rpt, 2424–13
Exports and imports of US, by transport mode, country, and SITC 1- to 3-digit commodity, 1990, annual rpt, 2424–12
Exports of US, detailed Schedule B commodities with countries of destination, 1990, annual rpt, 2424–10
Manufacturing annual survey, 1989: finances and operations, by SIC 2- to 4-digit industry, series, 2506–15
Manufacturing census, 1987: finances and operations, by SIC 2- to 4-digit industry, State, and MSA, with trends from 1849, 2497–1
Manufacturing census, 1987: finances and operations, by type of organization and SIC 2- to 4-digit industry, subject rpt, 2497–5
Mineral Industry Surveys, commodity review of production, trade, stocks, and use, quarterly rpt, 5612–2.19
Mineral Industry Surveys, commodity reviews of production, trade, stocks, and use, monthly rpt series, 5612–1
Mineral Industry Surveys, commodity reviews of production, trade, use, and industry operations, advance annual rpt series, 5614–5
Mineral Industry Surveys, State reviews of production, 1990, preliminary annual rpt, 5614–6
Minerals Yearbook, 1988, Vol 3: foreign country reviews of production, trade, and policy, by commodity, annual rpt series, 5604–17
Minerals Yearbook, 1989, Vol 1: commodity reviews of production, reserves, supply, use, and trade, annual rpt series, 5604–15
Minerals Yearbook, 1989, Vol 2: State reviews of production and sales by commodity, and business activity, annual rpt series, 5604–16
Minerals Yearbook, 1989, Vol 2: State reviews of production, sales, and firms, by commodity, and business activity, annual rpt, 5604–34

Minerals Yearbook, 1990, Vol 1: commodity reviews of production, reserves, supply, use, and trade, annual rpt series, 5604–20
Occupational injuries and incidence, employment, and hours in nonmetallic minerals mines and related operations, 1989, annual rpt, 6664–1
Occupational injury and illness rates, by SIC 2- to 4-digit industry, 1988-89, annual rpt, 6844–7
Occupational injury and illness rates, by SIC 2- to 4-digit industry, 1989, annual rpt, 6844–1
Price indexes (producer), by stage of processing and detailed commodity, monthly rpt, 6762–6
Price indexes (producer), by stage of processing and detailed commodity, monthly 1990, annual rpt, 6764–2
Production, prices, trade, use, employment, tariffs, and stockpiles, by mineral, with foreign comparisons, 1986-90, annual rpt, 5604–18
Production, reserves, and use of industrial minerals, and characteristics of individual deposits, State rpt series, 5606–10
Stockpiling of strategic material by Fed Govt, activity, and inventory by commodity, as of Mar 1991, semiannual rpt, 3542–22
Stockpiling of strategic material, inventories and needs, by commodity, as of Jan 1991, annual rpt, 3544–37

Absenteeism
Child care arrangements, costs, and impacts on mothers labor force status, by selected characteristics, 1983 and 1988, article, 6722–1.246
Crime victimization rates, by victim and offender characteristics, circumstances, and offense, 1988 survey, annual rpt, 6066–3.42
Crime victimization rates, by victim and offender characteristics, circumstances, and offense, 1989 survey, annual rpt, 6066–3.44
Disability, acute and chronic health conditions, absenteeism, and health services use, by selected characteristics, 1987, CD-ROM, 4147–10.177
Education data compilation, 1991 annual rpt, 4824–2
High school dropout rates, and subsequent completion, by student and school characteristics, alternative estimates, 1990, annual rpt, 4834–23
Labor force not at work, and hours lost, for illness and other reasons, by worker characteristics and industry div, monthly rpt, periodic data, 6742–2
Labor force not at work, unemployed, and working less than 35 hours, by reason, sex, race, region, and State, 1990, annual rpt, 6744–7.1; 6744–7.2
Longshore workers injuries resulting in lost time, FY76-90, annual rpt, 6504–10

Absenteeism

Mines (coal) and related operations occupational injuries and incidence, employment, and hours, 1989, annual rpt, 6664–4

Mines (metal) and related operations occupational injuries and incidence, employment, and hours, 1989, annual rpt, 6664–3

Mines (nonmetallic minerals) and related operations occupational injuries and incidence, employment, and hours, 1989, annual rpt, 6664–1

Mines (sand and gravel) and related operations occupational injuries and incidence, employment, and hours, 1989, annual rpt, 6664–2

Mines (stone) and related operations occupational injuries and incidence, employment, and hours, 1989, annual rpt, 6664–5

Mines (underground coal) back injuries, by circumstances, victim characteristics, and treatment, mid 1980s, 5608–166

Minority group and women health condition, services use, payment sources, and health care labor force, by poverty status, 1940s-89, chartbook, 4118–56

Minority group health condition, services use, costs, and indicators of services need, 1950s-88, 4118–55

Occupational injuries, by circumstances, body site, equipment type, and industry, with safety measures, series, 6846–1

Occupational injuries, illnesses, and workdays lost, by SIC 2-digit industry, 1989-90, annual press release, 6844–3

Occupational injury and illness rates, by SIC 2- to 4-digit industry, 1988-89, annual rpt, 6844–7

Occupational injury and illness rates, by SIC 2- to 4-digit industry, 1989, annual rpt, 6844–1

Railroad accidents, casualties, and damage, by cause, railroad, and State, 1990, annual rpt, 7604–1

Restaurant and drinking place occupational injury and illness rates, and workdays lost by State, 1989, article, 6722–1.231

Statistical Abstract of US, 1991 annual data compilation, 2324–1.3; 2324–1.13

Abt Associates, Inc.

"Recipient Housing in the Housing Voucher and Certificate Programs", 5186–14.4

"Update on AIDS in Prisons and Jails", 6066–28.1

"What America's Users Spend on Illegal Drugs", 236–2.1

Abu Dhabi

see United Arab Emirates

Accident insurance

see Automobile insurance

see Property and casualty insurance

Accidental deaths

Aircraft (general aviation) accidents, by circumstances, characteristics of persons and aircraft involved, and type of flying, 1988, annual rpt, 9614–3

Aircraft accidents and circumstances, for US operations of domestic and foreign airlines and general aviation, periodic rpt, 9612–1

Aircraft accidents, casualties, and damage, for commercial operations by detailed circumstances, 1987, annual rpt, 9614–2

Index by Subjects and Names

Aircraft accidents, deaths, and circumstances, by carrier and carrier type, preliminary 1990, annual press release, 9614–9

Aircraft accidents, deaths, and rates, for airlines and general aviation by type of service, 1980-89, annual rpt, 7504–1.9

Aircraft accidents victims compensation, legal costs, and time to disposition, under intl agreements and US liability system, aggregate 1970-84, GAO rpt, 26113–501

Aircraft hijackings, on-board explosions, and other crime, US and foreign incidents, 1985-89, annual rpt, 7504–31

Bombing incidents, casualties, and damage, by target, circumstances, and State, 1990, annual rpt, 6224–5

Child accident deaths and death rates, by cause, age, sex, race, and State, 1980-85, 4108–54

Child accident deaths and injuries by cause, and victimization, rates by race, sex, and age, 1979-88, chartbook, 4108–56

Coast Guard search and rescue missions, and lives and property lost and saved, by district and assisting unit, FY90, annual rpt, 7404–2

Construction industry occupational deaths, by cause, age, industry, and region, 1985-89, 6608–4

Consumer Product Safety Commission activities, recalls by brand, and casualties and medical costs, by product type, FY89, annual rpt, 9164–2

Deaths and rates, by cause and age, preliminary 1989-90, US Vital Statistics annual rpt, 4144–7

Deaths and rates, by cause, provisional data, monthly rpt, 4142–1.2

Deaths and rates, by detailed cause and demographic characteristics, 1988 and trends from 1900, US Vital Statistics annual rpt, 4144–2

Disasters and natl security incidents and mgmt, with data by major event and State, 1991 annual rpt, 9434–6

Diving (underwater sport and occupational) deaths, by circumstances, diver characteristics, and location, 1970-89, annual rpt, 2144–5

Earthquake intensity, time, location, damage, and seismic characteristics, for US and foreign earthquakes, 1985, annual rpt, 5664–13

Firearm accident deaths and injuries by selected city, and effects of gun design modifications, 1988-89, GAO rpt, 26131–80

Firearms-related deaths and death rates, by motive, age, sex, and race, for persons aged 1-34, 1979-88, 4146–5.119

Foreign countries disasters, casualties, damage, and aid by US and others, FY90 and trends from FY64, annual rpt, 9914–12

Grain handling facility explosions and casualties, by firm, FY90, annual rpt, 1294–1

Hazardous material transport accidents, casualties, and damage, by mode of transport, with DOT control activities, 1989, annual rpt, 7304–4

Hurricanes and tropical storms frequency, intensity, deaths, and damage, by State and selected city, 1886-1989, 2188–15

Indian and Alaska Native disease and disorder cases, deaths, and health services use, by tribe, reservation, and Indian Health Service area, late 1950s-86, 4088–2

Indian Health Service facilities and use, and Indian health and other characteristics, by IHS region, 1980s-89, annual chartbook, 4084–7

Indian Health Service facilities, funding, operations, and Indian health and other characteristics, 1950s-90, annual chartbook, 4084–1

Infant death rate, by cause, region, and race, 1980-87, article, 4202–7.208

Insurance (life) coverage and claims by age, by type, for Federal civilian employees, FY89 with trends from FY84, annual rpt, 9844–35.3

Investigations of deaths, US and Canada systems, jurisdictions, medical officers qualifications, types of deaths covered, and related statutes, 1990 listing, 4208–34

Law enforcement officer assaults and deaths by circumstances, agency, victim and offender characteristics, and location, 1990, annual rpt, 6224–3

Mental illness and drug and alcohol abuse direct and indirect costs, by age and sex, 1985, 4048–35

Military deaths by cause, age, race, and rank, and personnel captured and missing, by service branch, FY90, annual rpt, 3544–40

Military personnel deaths by service branch and age group, and veterans death rates, 1966-90, annual rpt, 8654–1

Mines (coal) and related operations occupational injuries and incidence, employment, and hours, 1989, annual rpt, 6664–4

Mines (metal) and related operations occupational injuries and incidence, employment, and hours, 1989, annual rpt, 6664–3

Mines (nonmetallic minerals) and related operations occupational injuries and incidence, employment, and hours, 1989, annual rpt, 6664–1

Mines (sand and gravel) and related operations occupational injuries and incidence, employment, and hours, 1989, annual rpt, 6664–2

Mines (stone) and related operations occupational injuries and incidence, employment, and hours, 1989, annual rpt, 6664–5

Mines and mills injuries by circumstances, employment, and hours, by type of operation and State, quarterly rpt, 6662–1

Mines occupational deaths, by circumstances and selected victim characteristics, semiannual rpt series, 6662–3

Mines safety and health enforcement, training, and funding, with casualties, by type of mine and State, FY89, annual rpt, 6664–6

Minority group health condition, services use, costs, and indicators of services need, 1950s-88, 4118–55

Mobile home fires, casualties, damage, and impacts of safety standards, with data on Michigan trailer parks, 1980s, hearing, 21248–145

Index by Subjects and Names

Morbidity and Mortality Weekly Report, infectious notifiable disease cases by State, and public health issues, 4202–1

Occupational deaths, by equipment type, circumstances, and OSHA standards violated, series, 6606–2

Occupational deaths data collection and processing by States, Natl Inst for Occupational Safety and Health guidelines, 1990 rpt, 4248–89

Occupational injury and illness rates by SIC 2- to 4-digit industry, and deaths by cause and industry div, 1989, annual rpt, 6844–1

Park natl system visitor deaths, by cause, victim age, region, and park, 1980-90, annual rpt, 5544–6

Pipeline accidents, casualties, safety enforcement activity, and Federal funding, by State, 1989, annual rpt, 7304–5

Preventive disease and health improvement goals and recommended activities for 2000, with trends 1970s-80s, 4048–10

Prisoners and movements, by offense, location, and selected other characteristics, data compilation, 1991 annual rpt, 6064–6.6

Prisoners in Federal and State instns, deaths by cause, sex, and State, 1989, annual rpt, 6064–26.4

Railroad accidents, casualties, and damage, by cause, railroad, and State, 1990, annual rpt, 7604–1

Railroad accidents, casualties, and damage, Fed Railroad Admin activities, and safety inspectors by State, 1989, annual rpt, 7604–12

Ships accidents and casualties, by circumstances and characteristics of persons and vessels involved, 1988, annual rpt, 7404–11

Ships and marine facilities accidents, casualties, and circumstances, Coast Guard investigation results, periodic rpt, 9612–4

State and Metro Area Data Book, 1991 data compilation, 2328–54

Statistical Abstract of US, 1991 annual data compilation, 2324–1.2

Subway accidents, casualties, and damage, by circumstances and system, 1989, annual rpt, 7884–5

Terrorism incidents in US, related activity, and casualties, by attack type, target, group, and location, 1990, annual rpt, 6224–6

Transit systems finances and operations, by mode of transport, size of fleet, and for 468 systems, 1989, annual rpt, 7884–4

Transportation accident deaths, by mode, 1989-90, annual press release, 9614–6

Transportation safety programs, and accidents, casualties, and damage, by mode of transport, 1989, annual rpt, 7304–19

Vital statistics provisional data, monthly rpt, 4142–1

Weather forecasts of severe storms, Natl Weather Service forecast accuracy and storm characteristics, series, 2186–6

Weather phenomena and storm characteristics, casualties, and property damage, by State, monthly listing, 2152–3

see also Drowning
see also Homicide
see also Poisoning and drug reaction
see also Suicide
see also Traffic accident fatalities
see also War casualties
see also under By Disease in the "Index by Categories"

Accidents and accident prevention

Child accident deaths and injuries by cause, and victimization, rates by race, sex, and age, 1979-88, chartbook, 4108–56

Child health, behavioral, emotional, and school problems relation to family structure, by selected characteristics, 1988, 4147–10.178

Child health condition and services use, 1990 chartbook, 4108–49

Child injury rates, by presence of injury prevention education program for preschoolers, local area study, 1979-82, article, 4042–3.236

Disability, acute and chronic health conditions, absenteeism, and health services use, by selected characteristics, 1987, CD-ROM, 4147–10.177

Disability Insurance beneficiaries costs to Medicare until age 64 under alternative coverage assumptions, model results, 1989, article, 4742–1.208

Firearm accident deaths and injuries by selected city, and effects of gun design modifications, 1988-89, GAO rpt, 26131–80

Health condition and health care resources, use, and spending, 1950s-89, annual data compilation, 4144–11

HHS financial aid, by program, recipient, State, and city, FY90, annual regional listings, 4004–3

Hospital discharges and length of stay, by diagnosis, patient and instn characteristics, procedure performed, and payment source, 1988, annual rpt, 4147–13.107

Hospital discharges and length of stay by region and diagnosis, and procedures performed, by age and sex, 1989, annual rpt, 4146–8.198

Hospital discharges by detailed diagnostic and procedure category, primary diagnosis, and length of stay, by age, sex, and region, 1988, annual rpt, 4147–13.105; 4147–13.108

Hospital trauma units, and other characteristics of Medicare hospital providers, by instn, 1989, annual regional rpt series, 4654–14

Hunter safety funding by Fish and Wildlife Service, by State, FY89, annual rpt, 5504–1

Hunter safety funding by Fish and Wildlife Service, by State, FY90, annual rpt, 5504–13

Hunter safety funding by Fish and Wildlife Service, by State, FY92, semiannual press release, 5502–1

Indian and Alaska Native disease and disorder cases, deaths, and health services use, by tribe, reservation, and Indian Health Service area, late 1950s-86, 4088–2

Indian Health Service outpatient services provided, by reason for visit and age, FY88-89, annual rpt, 4084–2

Accounting and auditing

Indian Health Service, tribal, and contract facilities hospitalization, by diagnosis, age, sex, and service area, FY89, annual rpt, 4084–5

Injuries, by type, circumstances, and victim characteristics, and related activity limitations, 1985-87, 4147–10.176

Injuries, related impairments, and activity limitations, by circumstances and victim characteristics, 1985-87, 4147–10.179

Minority group health condition, services use, costs, and indicators of services need, 1950s-88, 4118–55

Morbidity and Mortality Weekly Report, infectious notifiable disease cases by State, and public health issues, 4202–1

Park natl system accidents, crimes, hazardous waste sites, and funding, 1970s-91, GAO rpt, 26113–545

Postal Service employment and related expenses, FY90, annual rpt, 9864–5.1

Preventive disease and health improvement goals and recommended activities for 2000, with trends 1970s-80s, 4048–10

Statistical Abstract of US, 1991 annual data compilation, 2324–1.3

see also Accidental deaths
see also Agricultural accidents and safety
see also Aviation accidents and safety
see also Disasters
see also Driving while intoxicated
see also Drowning
see also Fires and fire prevention
see also Marine accidents and safety
see also Mine accidents and safety
see also Motor vehicle safety devices
see also Nuclear accidents and safety
see also Occupational health and safety
see also Poisoning and drug reaction
see also Product safety
see also Property damage and loss
see also Railroad accidents and safety
see also Space program accidents and safety
see also Spinal cord injuries
see also Traffic accident fatalities
see also Traffic accidents and safety
see also Traffic engineering
see also Transportation accidents and safety
see also Workers compensation
see also under By Disease in the "Index by Categories"

Accounting and auditing

Air Force fiscal mgmt system operations and techniques, quarterly rpt, 3602–1

Banking industry structure and deposit insurance reform, findings and recommendations, with background data, 1989-90, 8008–147

Banks financial performance relation to deposit insurance value and other financial and accounting measures, 1986-87, technical paper, 9366–6.264

Banks market value calculation method to expose undercapitalization, with model results and background data for selected failed banks, 1960s-89, working paper, 9377–9.112

Computer use at home, school, and work, by purpose and selected user characteristics, 1989, Current Population Rpt, 2546–2.158

County Business Patterns, 1988: employment, establishments, and payroll, by SIC 2- to 4-digit industry and county, annual State rpt series, 2326–6

Accounting and auditing

County Business Patterns, 1989: employment, establishments, and payroll, by SIC 2- to 4-digit industry and county, annual State rpt series, 2326–8

Deposit insurance accounting in Federal budget, outlays by instn type, and Bank Insurance Fund finances, late 1970s-96, 26308–100

Depreciable assets class lives measurement, investment, and industry operations, industry rpt series, 8006–5

Employee (temporary) supply establishments by occupation supplied, receipts by source, and payroll, by MSA, 1987 Census of Service Industries, 2393–4.8

Employment, earnings, and hours, by SIC 1- to 4-digit industry, monthly and annual averages, selected years 1909-90, annual rpt, 6744–4

Employment, unemployment, and labor force characteristics, by region and census div, 1990, annual rpt, 6744–7.1

Enterprise Statistics, 1987: finances and operations for companies, by size, level of diversification, form of organization, and industry group, 2329–8

Fed Govt consolidated financial statements based on business accounting methods, FY89-90, annual rpt, 8104–5

Fed Govt labor productivity, indexes of output and labor costs by function, FY67-89, annual rpt, 6824–1.6

Finances and operations, by SIC 2- to 4-digit industry, forecast 1991, annual rpt, 2044–28

GAO activities, operations, and resulting cost savings to Fed Govt, FY90, annual rpt, 26104–1

HUD programs fraud and abuse, financial and program mgmt improvement activities, 1990, annual rpt, 5004–9

Insurance (property and casualty) industry solvency monitoring by States, firms designated for increased attention, and views on monitoring system effectiveness, 1980s, GAO rpt, 26119–316

Manufacturing employment, by detailed occupation and SIC 2-digit industry, 1989 survey, triennial rpt, 6748–52

Medicare Cost Report reviews, revisions ratio to initially reported costs, by category, FY84, article, 4652–1.233

Minority Business Dev Centers mgmt and financial aid, and characteristics of businesses, by region and State, FY90, annual rpt, 2104–6

NASA activities and funding, 1990, annual compilation of papers, 21704–1

OASDHI future cost estimates, actuarial study series, 4706–1

Occupational injury and illness rates, by SIC 2- to 4-digit industry, 1988-89, annual rpt, 6844–7

Occupational injury and illness rates, by SIC 2- to 4-digit industry, 1989, annual rpt, 6844–1

Pension plans (defined benefit) impacts of Omnibus Budget Reconciliation Act contribution deductibility limit, 1984-89, tax, 8008–152

Pension plans funding status under 1987 accounting standards, for defined benefit plans, 1987-89, technical paper, 9366–6.259

Puerto Rico economic censuses, 1987: wholesale and retail trade and service industry finances and operations, by SIC 2- to 4-digit industry and municipio, 2591–1

Railroad retirement system actuarial evaluation, 1989 and projected to 2064, annual rpt, 9704–1

Railroad retirement system funding and benefits findings and recommendations, with background industry data, 1960s-90 and projected to 2060, 9708–1

Receipts for services, by SIC 2- to 4-digit kind of business, 1990, annual rpt, 2413–8

Recordkeeping Practices Survey, 1989: data coverage, methodology, businesses views, and applications for 1992 economic censuses, 2328–67

Service industries census, 1987: depreciable assets, capital and operating expenses, and receipts, by SIC 2- to 4-digit kind of business, 2393–2

Service industries census, 1987: establishments, receipts by source, payroll, and employment, by SIC 2- to 4-digit kind of business, State, and MSA, 2393–4

State and local govts receiving Federal funds, compliance with Federal audit requirements, 1991 article, 10042–1.204

Tax (income) returns computer matching program to indentify underreported income, effectiveness, 1987, GAO rpt, 26119–325

Tax (income) returns of corporations, income and tax items by asset size and detailed industry, 1987, annual rpt, 8304–4

Tax (income) returns of corporations, income and tax items by asset size and detailed industry, 1988, annual rpt, 8304–21

Tax (income) returns of high income individuals not filed, by selected characteristics, 1987, and assessments under alternative IRS enforcement programs, 1990, GAO rpt, 26119–322

Tax (income) returns of partnerships, income statement and balance sheet items, by industry group, 1989, annual article, 8302–2.216; 8304–18

Tax (income) returns of sole proprietorships, income statement items, by industry group, 1989, annual article, 8302–2.214

Tax collection, enforcement, and litigation activity of IRS, with data by type of tax, region, and State, FY90, annual rpt, 8304–3

Tax preparation services establishments, receipts by source, payroll, and employment, by State and MSA, 1987 Census of Service Industries, 2393–4

Tax preparation services negligence and fraud, IRS civil penalty cases and examiners views of program admin, 1989, GAO rpt, 26119–315

Tax return audit rates of IRS, by type of tax, FY64-89, hearing, 21408–125

Taxpayer opinions about quality of IRS income tax return audits and delinquent tax collection activity, 1989, article, 8304–8.1

see also Federal Inspectors General reports

Index by Subjects and Names

see also Financial disclosure

Achievement tests

see Educational tests

Acid rain

Coal trade of US effects of acid rain laws, alternative projections to 2000, annual rpt, 3164–77.1

EC sulfur dioxide emissions reduction levels, by country, 1980 and projected to 2003, annual rpt, 3164–77.1

Electric power plants coal and oil deliveries by sulfur content and location, and sulfur removal capacity use by plant, 1989-90, annual rpt, 3164–42

Energy natl strategy plans for conservation and pollution reduction, impacts on electric power supply, costs, and emissions, projected under alternative assumptions, 1995-2030, 3166–6.49

Environmental impacts of acid rain and air pollution, and methods of neutralizing acidified water bodies, summary research rpt series, 5506–5

Maine streams water quality, acidity, and fish effects of acid rain, 1986-87, 9208–130

Research on acid rain, activities of Natl Acid Precipitation Assessment Program, 1990 annual rpt, 14354–1

Research on acid rain, data quality and accuracy for 2 natl field and lab data collection programs, 1989, annual rpt, 5664–17

Research on acid rain, data quality and accuracy for 2 natl field data collection programs, 1978-89, 5668–124

Water supply and quality in streams and lakes, and groundwater levels in wells, by drainage basin, 1988, annual State rpt series, 5666–16

Water supply and quality in streams and lakes, and groundwater levels in wells, by drainage basin, 1989, annual State rpt series, 5666–12

Water supply and quality in streams and lakes, and groundwater levels in wells, by drainage basin, 1990, annual State rpt series, 5666–10

Water supply in US and southern Canada, streamflow, surface and groundwater conditions, and reservoir levels, by location, monthly rpt, 5662–3

Acquired immune deficiency syndrome

Africa (sub-Saharan) AIDS epidemic impacts on population size and components of change, model description and results, 1990-2015, working paper, 2326–18.57

Black Americans AIDS knowledge, attitudes, info sources, and testing, 1990 survey, 4146–8.208

Cancer cases, deaths, and survival rates, by sex, race, age, and body site, 1973-88, annual rpt, 4474–35

Cases of AIDS by race, sex, and risk category, deaths and survivors, projected 1989-93, 4206–2.34

Cases of AIDS by risk group, race, sex, age, State, and SMSA, and deaths, monthly rpt, 4202–9

Child health condition and services use, 1990 chartbook, 4108–49

Classification codes for AIDS virus and related conditions, *Intl Classification of Diseases*, 9th revision, 1991 rpt, 4206–2.45

Index by Subjects and Names

Adamache, Killard W.

Criminal justice system AIDS cases and policies, series, 6066–28
Deaths and rates, by detailed cause and demographic characteristics, 1988 and trends from 1900, US Vital Statistics annual rpt, 4144–2
Deaths from AIDS, and AIDS virus infection rates, by age, race, and sex, preliminary 1989, annual rpt, 4144–7
Deaths from AIDS, by age, race, and sex, monthly rpt, annual table, 4142–1.2
Developing countries AIDS virus infection prevalence, by sex, city, urban-rural location, and country, 1991, semiannual rpt, 2322–4
Developing countries economic and social conditions from 1960s, and Intl Dev Cooperation Agency and AID activities and funding, FY90-92, annual rpt, 9904–4
Drug abuse and treatment, research on biological and behavioral factors and addiction potential of new drugs, 1990 annual conf, 4494–11
Drug abuse indicators for selected metro areas, research results, data collection, and policy issues, 1991 semiannual conf, 4492–5
Drug abuse prevalence among minorities, related health effects and crime, treatment, and research status and needs, mid 1970s-90, 4498–72
Drug abuse, prevention, treatment, and health research results, as of 1990, triennial rpt, 4498–68
Drug abusers AIDS cases, by drug use, sexual behavior, and other characteristics, 1984-88 local area study, article, 4042–3.206
Drug abusers AIDS risk behavior and other characteristics, for persons in methadone maintenance programs, 1985-87, hearing, 21968–55
Drug abusers with positive AIDS virus tests in 1971-72, AIDS symptoms and deaths as of 1988, article, 4042–3.237
Drug and alcohol abuse treatment services, funding, staffing, and client load, characteristics, and outcomes, by setting, 1989 conf, 4498–73
Education and info activities and funding of CDC, public users, and donated media ads, 1987-91, articles, 4042–3.256
Fed Govt financial and nonfinancial domestic aid, 1991 base edition with supplements, annual listing, 104–5
Fed Govt personnel action appeals, decisions of Merit Systems Protection Board by agency and region, FY90, annual rpt, 9494–2
Health care settings transmission of AIDS and hepatitis viruses, occupational exposure, prevention policies, and OSHA regulation, 1990 hearings, 21348–119
Health care settings transmission of AIDS virus to patients during invasive procedures, CDC prevention guidelines, 1991 rpt, 4206–2.44
Health condition and health care resources, use, and spending, 1950s-89, annual data compilation, 4144–11
HHS financial aid, by program, recipient, State, and city, FY90, annual regional listings, 4004–3

Hispanic Americans AIDS knowledge, attitudes, info sources, and testing, 1990 survey, 4146–8.209
Homeless persons alcohol abuse, by sex, age, race, and additional diagnoses, aggregate 1985-87, 4488–14
Hospitalization and charges for AIDS patients, by hospital and patient characteristics, and payment source, 1986-87, 4186–6.15
Labor laws enacted, by State, 1990, annual article, 6722–1.209
Medicaid home and community services for AIDS patients, under waiver program in 6 States, 1988-89, article, 4652–1.216
Medicaid services use and costs for AIDS and AIDS virus infection patients, 1991, article, 4652–1.215
Minority group AIDS knowledge and info sources, 1987 local area survey, article, 4042–3.210
Minority group and women health condition, services use, payment sources, and health care labor force, by poverty status, 1940s-89, chartbook, 4118–56
Minority group health condition, services use, costs, and indicators of services need, 1950s-88, 4118–55
Morbidity and Mortality Weekly Report, infectious notifiable disease cases by age, race, and State, and deaths, 1930s-90, annual rpt, 4204–1
Morbidity and Mortality Weekly Report, infectious notifiable disease cases by State, and public health issues, 4202–1
Natl Cancer Inst activities, grants by recipient, and cancer deaths and cases, FY90 and trends, annual rpt, 4474–13
Natl Household Seroprevalence Survey on AIDS virus infection and risk factor prevalence, methodology and pretest results, 1989, 4148–30
Natl Inst of Allergy and Infectious Diseases activities, grants by recipient and location, and disease cases, FY83-90, annual rpt, 4474–30
Natl Inst of Neurological Disorders and Stroke activities, and disorder cases, FY90, annual rpt, 4474–25
NIH activities, funding by program and recipient type, staff, and clinic patients, by inst, FY90, annual rpt, 4434–3
Non-Hodgkin's lymphoma risk among men with AIDS virus infection, 1981-88 and projected to 1992, article, 4472–1.212
North Dakota AIDS public knowledge, 1987-89 surveys, article, 4042–3.211
Nursing home reimbursement by Medicaid, States payment ratesetting methods, limits, and allowances, 1988, article, 4652–1.253
Opportunistic diseases diagnosed in AIDS patients, by age group, monthly rpt, annual data, 4202–9
Physicians and RNs AIDS knowledge, attitudes, and transmission prevention practices, 1990-91, 4186–9.11
Pneumonia (*pneumocystis carinii*) in child AIDS patients, prevention and control, CDC guidelines, 1991 rpt, 4206–2.38
Preventive disease and health improvement goals and recommended activities for 2000, with trends 1970s-80s, 4048–10
Prison testing programs by jail size, and State inmates with AIDS, by region, data compilation, 1991 annual rpt, 6064–6.1; 6064–6.6

Prisoners AIDS cases, and testing and control policies, 1989 survey, 6066–28.1
Prisoners in jails, AIDS deaths by county and facility, and testing policies, by State, 1988, regional rpt series, 6068–144
Prisoners in jails, deaths by cause, 1989-90, annual rpt, 6066–25.38
Public knowledge, attitudes, info sources, and testing for AIDS, 1990 survey, 4146–8.195; 4146–8.201; 4146–8.205
State and Metro Area Data Book, 1991 data compilation, 2328–54
Statistical Abstract of US, 1991 annual data compilation, 2324–1.2; 2324–1.3
Testing for AIDS virus antibodies and counseling sessions by setting, and CDC funding and funds uncommitted by State, 1989-90, GAO rpt, 26121–428
Testing for AIDS virus antibodies, public opinion on mandatory testing, data compilation, 1991 annual rpt, 6064–6.2
Tuberculosis testing and treatment for persons with AIDS virus infection, CDC guidelines, 1991 rpt, 4206–2.41
Tuberculosis transmission in health care settings, prevention and screening methods, CDC guidelines, 1990 rpt, 4206–2.35
Veterans health care centers AIDS cases by sex, race, risk factor, and facility, and AIDS prevention and treatment issues, quarterly rpt, 8702–1
Waste (medical) generation, sources, health worker exposure and risk, and incineration emissions, 1980s, 4078–1
Women in methadone maintenance programs, AIDS knowledge, attitudes, and risk behavior, effects of life skills training, 1988 local area study, article, 4042–3.221
Women's AIDS knowledge, attitudes, and risk behavior, 1988 survey, 4146–8.200

Acquisitions, business

see Business acquisitions and mergers

Acrylics

see Plastics and plastics industry

ACTION

Activities and funding of ACTION, by program, FY90, annual rpt, 9024–2
Budget of US, authoritative financial statements with appropriations, outlays, and receipts, by category and agency, FY90, annual rpt, 8104–2.1
Budget of US, obligations and authority by function, agency, and program, with summaries, analyses, and historical tables, FY92, annual rpt, 104–2
Education funding by Federal agency, program, and recipient type, and instn spending, FY80-90, annual rpt, 4824–8
Expenditures of Fed Govt in States, by type, program, agency, and State, FY90, annual rpt, 2464–2
see also Foster Grandparent Program
see also Retired Senior Volunteer Program
see also Senior Companion Program
see also Student Community Service Program
see also VISTA

Adamache, Killard W.

"Nationwide Evaluation of Medicaid Competition Demonstrations. Volume 8. Enrollment Choice and Biased Selection", 4658–45.8

Adamache, Killard W.

"Payment to Health Maintenance Organizations and the Geographic Factor", 4652–1.203

Adams, Diane

"Reassessment of External Insulin Infusion Pumps. Health Technology Assessment Report, 1990", 4186–10.4

Adams, E. Kathleen

"Medicaid Mysteries: Transitional Benefits, Medicaid Coverage, and Welfare Exits", 4652–1.217

Adams, Patricia F.

"AIDS Knowledge and Attitudes. Provisional Data from the National Health Interview Survey", 4146–8.201

Adelman, Clifford

"College Course Map, Taxonomy and Transcript Data Based on the Postsecondary Records, 1972-84, of the High School Class of 1972", 4888–4

"Light and Shadows on College Athletes, College Transcripts and Labor Market History", 4888–5

"Women at Thirtysomething: Paradoxes of Attainment", 4888–6

Aden

see Yemen, South

Adhesives

- Exports and imports of US, by Harmonized System 6-digit commodity and country, 1990, annual rpt, 2424–13
- Exports of US, detailed Schedule B commodities with countries of destination, 1990, annual rpt, 2424–10
- Injuries from use of consumer products, by severity, victim age, and detailed product, 1990, annual rpt, 9164–6
- Manufacturing census, 1987: finances and operations, by SIC 2- to 4-digit industry, State, and MSA, with trends from 1849, 2497–1
- Manufacturing census, 1987: finances and operations, by type of organization and SIC 2- to 4-digit industry, subject rpt, 2497–5
- Manufacturing finances and operations, by SIC 2- to 4-digit industry, forecast 1991, annual rpt, 2044–28
- Pollution (air) emissions factors, by detailed pollutant and source, data compilation, 1990 rpt, 9198–120
- Price indexes (producer), by stage of processing and detailed commodity, monthly rpt, 6762–6
- Price indexes (producer), by stage of processing and detailed commodity, monthly 1990, annual rpt, 6764–2

Adirim, Terry

"National Survey of State Maternal and Newborn Drug Testing and Reporting Policies", 4042–3.220

Adkins, Daniel C.

"U.S. Petroleum Supply", 3164–2.1

Administration

see Administration of justice

see Administrative law and procedure

see Business management

see Executives and managers

see Health facilities administration

see Public administration

see School administration and staff

Administration for Children, Youth, and Families

Head Start enrollment and operations, by North Central State, annual chartbook, discontinued, 4604–12

Head Start enrollment, funding, and staff, FY90, annual rpt, 4604–8

Head Start handicapped enrollment, by handicap, State, and for Indian and migrant programs, 1987/88, annual rpt, 4604–1

Homeless and runaway youth programs, funding, activities, and participant characteristics, FY90, annual rpt, 4604–3

Research and evaluation programs of HHS, 1970-90, annual listing, 4004–30

Administration for Native Americans

Research and evaluation programs of HHS, 1970-90, annual listing, 4004–30

Administration of justice

- Budget of US, obligations and authority by function, agency, and program, with summaries, analyses, and historical tables, FY92, annual rpt, 104–2
- Data on crime, criminal justice admin and enforcement, and public opinion, data compilation, 1991 annual rpt, 6064–6
- Employment and payroll, by function and level of govt, 1990, annual rpt series, 2466–1
- Employment, payroll, and spending for criminal justice, by level of govt, State, and selected city and county, FY71-88, annual rpt, 6064–9
- Employment, payroll, and spending for criminal justice, by level of govt, State, and selected city and county, 1984-86, biennial rpt, 6064–4
- Energy use in commercial buildings, costs, and conservation, by building characteristics, survey rpt series, 3166–8
- Foreign countries human rights conditions in 170 countries, 1990, annual rpt, 21384–3
- Govt census, 1987: employment, payroll, and average earnings, by function, level of govt, State, county, and population size, 2455–2
- Govt census, 1987: local govt employment by function, payroll, and average earnings, for individual counties, cities, and school and special districts, 2455–1
- Govt finances, by level of govt, State, and for large cities and counties, annual rpt series, 2466–2
- Judicial Conf proceedings and findings, spring 1991, semiannual rpt, 18202–2
- Justice Natl Inst rpts, 1983-89, listing, 6068–240
- State and local govt employment of minorities and women, by occupation, function, and pay level, 1990, annual rpt, 9244–6.4

see also Administrative law and procedure

see also Arrest

see also Civil procedure

see also Correctional institutions

see also Courts

see also Crime and criminals

see also Crime victim compensation

see also Criminal procedure

see also Due process of law

see also Evidence

see also Extradition

see also Federal aid to law enforcement

see also Fines and settlements

see also Judges

see also Judicial reform

see also Juries

see also Law enforcement

see also Lawyers and legal services

see also Legal aid

see also Legal arbitration and mediation

see also Military law

see also Pardons

see also Parole and probation

see also Pretrial detention and release

see also Sentences, criminal procedure

see also Trials

see also Witnesses

see also under names of specific types of courts (listed under Courts)

Administration on Aging

Research and evaluation programs of HHS, 1970-90, annual listing, 4004–30

Administration on Developmental Disabilities

Research and evaluation programs of HHS, 1970-90, annual listing, 4004–30

Administrative agencies

see under Executive Office of the President

see under Federal boards, committees, and commissions

see under Federal executive departments

see under Federal independent agencies

Administrative Conference of the U.S.

- Budget of US, authoritative financial statements with appropriations, outlays, and receipts, by category and agency, FY90, annual rpt, 8104–2.1
- Budget of US, obligations and authority by function, agency, and program, with summaries, analyses, and historical tables, FY92, annual rpt, 104–2

Administrative law and procedure

- Advisory committees of Fed Govt, and members, staff, meetings, and costs by agency, FY90, annual rpt, 9454–18
- Airport security operations to prevent hijacking, screening results, enforcement actions, and hijacking attempts, 2nd half 1989, semiannual rpt, 7502–5
- Criminal case processing in Federal district courts, and dispositions, by offense, district, and offender characteristics, 1986, annual rpt, 6064–29
- Criminal case processing in Federal district courts, and dispositions, by offense, 1980-89, annual rpt, 6064–31
- Fed Govt labor productivity, indexes of output and labor costs by function, FY67-89, annual rpt, 6824–1.6
- Fed Govt regulatory programs evaluation, review process, and actions taken, by agency, 1980s-90, annual rpt, 104–28
- Jail population by sex, race, and for 25 jurisdictions, and instn conditions, 1988-90, annual rpt, 6066–25.38
- Jails under court order to reduce overcrowding and to improve conditions, by State, 1989, annual rpt, 6064–26.1
- Jails under court order to reduce overcrowding and to improve conditions, 1988, regional rpt series, 6068–144
- Medicare Hospital Insurance appeals backlog reduction actions of SSA Chicago administrative law judges, effectiveness, FY89, GAO rpt, 26121–398
- Older persons discrimination in Federal aid programs, Age Discrimination Act enforcement by agency, FY90, annual rpt, 4004–27
- SSA activities, litigation, finances, and staff, FY90, annual rpt, 4704–6
- Unemployment insurance programs of States, quality appraisal results, FY90, annual rpt, 6404–16

Index by Subjects and Names

US attorneys case processing and collections, by case type and Federal district, FY90, annual rpt, 6004–2
see also Antitrust law
see also Civil procedure
see also Commercial law
see also Consumer protection
see also Environmental impact statements
see also Environmental regulation
see also Federal Inspectors General reports
see also Financial institutions regulation
see also Fines and settlements
see also Freedom of information
see also Government and business
see also Government forms and paperwork
see also Labor law
see also Licenses and permits
see also Maritime law
see also Price regulation
see also Tax laws and courts
see also Tax protests and appeals
see also under names of individual regulatory commissions (listed under Federal independent agencies)

Administrative Office of the U.S. Courts
Activities of Administrative Office, 1990, annual rpt, 18204–16
Activities of Administrative Office, 1991, annual rpt, 18204–2.2
Budget of US, authoritative financial statements with appropriations, outlays, and receipts, by category and agency, FY90, annual rpt, 8104–2.1
Budget of US, obligations and authority by function, agency, and program, with summaries, analyses, and historical tables, FY92, annual rpt, 104–2
Caseloads (civil and criminal) for Federal district, appeals, and bankruptcy courts, by offense, circuit, and district, 1990, annual rpt, 18204–11
Caseloads (civil and criminal) for Federal district, appeals, and special courts, by offense, circuit, and district, 1990, annual rpt, 18204–8
Caseloads (civil and criminal) for Federal district, appeals, and special courts, 1991, annual rpt, 18204–2
Caseloads (criminal) in Federal district courts, by offense, disposition, and district, 1980-90, last issue of annual rpt, 18204–1
Caseloads, actions, procedure duration, judges, and jurors, by Federal district and appeals court, 1986-91, annual rpt, 18204–3
Drug testing of criminal defendants, demonstration program operations, offender characteristics, and judges views, 1987-90, 18208–11
Judicial Conf proceedings and findings, spring 1991, semiannual rpt, 18202–2
Wiretaps authorized, costs, arrests, trials, and convictions, by offense and jurisdiction, 1990, annual rpt, 18204–7

Administrators
see Business management
see Executives and managers

Adolescents
see Youth

Adoption
Alien orphans admissions, FY89-90, fact sheet, 6266–2.4; 6266–2.8
Assistance programs under Ways and Means Committee jurisdiction, finances, operations, and participant characteristics, FY70s-90, annual rpt, 21784–11

Families with adopted members, by selected characteristics, 1987, CD-ROM, 4147–10.177
Foster care programs cases, problems, and operations for selected States, 1970s-90, hearings, 21788–202
Foster care programs operations, funding sources, and client characteristics, for selected States, 1960s-95, 25368–169
HHS financial aid, by program, recipient, State, and city, FY90, annual regional listings, 4004–3
Immigrant and nonimmigrant visas of US issued and refused, by class, issuing office, and nationality, FY89, annual rpt, 7184–1
State and Metro Area Data Book, 1991 data compilation, 2328–54
Statistical Abstract of US, 1991 annual data compilation, 2324–1.12

Adult day care
Disability (functional) of aged, long-term care sources, and health and other characteristics, 1984-85, 4147–13.104
Employee leave for illness, disability, and dependent care, coverage, provisions, terminations, costs, and methods of covering for absent worker, by firm size, 1988 survey, 9768–21
Fed Govt employee family-related and work schedule benefits, availability, admin, and personnel directors views, 1990 survey, 9496–2.7
Finances of adult day care centers, revenue by source and expenses by type, by agency type, FY86, article, 4652–1.234
Health maintenance organizations financial performance and services use, demonstration project results, 1985-89, article, 4652–1.235
Long-term care institutional and community services, spending and use by type and payment source, FY88, and Medicaid growth since FY75, 26306–6.156

Adult education
Bilingual education programs enrollment, funding, and services, by State, FY85-89, series, 4808–20
Education Dept programs funding, operations, and effectiveness, FY90, annual rpt, 4804–5
Enrollment and other data for adult and vocational education programs, by student characteristics, 1980s-90, annual rpt, 4824–2.26
Homeless adults educational services, funding, participation, and staff, by State, 1989, annual rpt series, 4804–39
Homeless persons aid programs of Fed Govt, program descriptions and funding, by agency and State, FY87-90, annual GAO rpt, 26104–21
Indian education funding of Fed Govt, and enrollment, degrees, and program grants and fellowships by State, late 1960s-FY89, annual rpt, 14874–1
Natl Education Goals progress indicators, by State, 1991, annual rpt, 15914–1
see also Correspondence courses

Advertising
AIDS info and education activities and funding of CDC, and donation of media ads, 1987-92, articles, 4042–3.256
Airline consumer complaints to DOT about service by US and foreign carrier, and for travel and cargo service, by reason, monthly rpt, 7302–11

Advertising

Business statistics, detailed data for major industries and economic indicators, *Survey of Current Business*, monthly rpt, 2702–1.7
County Business Patterns, 1988: employment, establishments, and payroll, by SIC 2- to 4-digit industry and county, annual State rpt series, 2326–6
County Business Patterns, 1989: employment, establishments, and payroll, by SIC 2- to 4-digit industry and county, annual State rpt series, 2326–8
DOD competitive and formally advertised awards, by contractor type and service branch, various periods FY81-90, semiannual rpt, 3542–1.2
Drug (prescription) advertising direct to consumer, benefits and problems, review of studies published 1984-91, GAO rpt, 26131–86
Electric utilities privately owned, finances and operations, detailed data, 1989, annual rpt, 3164–23
Employment, earnings, and hours, by SIC 1- to 4-digit industry, monthly and annual averages, selected years 1909-90, annual rpt, 6744–4
Enterprise Statistics, 1987: finances and operations for companies, by size, level of diversification, form of organization, and industry group, 2329–8
Exports and imports of services, direct and among multinatl firms affiliates, by industry and world area, 1986-90, article, 2702–1.223
Finances and operations, by SIC 2- to 4-digit industry, forecast 1991, annual rpt, 2044–28
Food marketing cost indexes, by expense category, monthly rpt with articles, 1502–4
Help-wanted ads in New England States, Fed Reserve 1st District, monthly rpt, 9373–2.2
Help-wanted ads index and ratio to unemployment, *Survey of Current Business*, cyclical indicators, monthly rpt, 2702–1.1
Manufacturing annual survey, 1989: value of shipments, by SIC 4- to 5-digit product class, 2506–15.2
Manufacturing census, 1987: finances and operations, by SIC 2- to 4-digit industry, State, and MSA, with trends from 1849, 2497–1
Manufacturing census, 1987: finances and operations, by type of organization and SIC 2- to 4-digit industry, subject rpt, 2497–5
Milk order advertising and promotion finances, and producer participation, by region, 1990, annual article, 1317–4.204
Multinatl US firms and foreign affiliates finances and operations, by industry and world area of parent firm, 1989 benchmark survey, preliminary annual rpt, 2704–5
Natural gas interstate pipeline company detailed financial and operating data, by firm, 1989, annual rpt, 3164–38
Occupational injury and illness rates, by SIC 2- to 4-digit industry, 1988-89, annual rpt, 6844–7
Price indexes (producer), by stage of processing and detailed commodity, monthly rpt, 6762–6

Advertising

Price indexes (producer), by stage of processing and detailed commodity, monthly 1990, annual rpt, 6764–2

Puerto Rico economic censuses, 1987: wholesale and retail trade and service industry finances and operations, by SIC 2- to 4-digit industry and municipio, 2591–1

Puerto Rico economic censuses, 1987: wholesale, retail, and service industries finances and operations, by establishment characteristics and SIC 2- and 3-digit industry, subject rpts, 2591–2

Retail trade census, 1987: depreciable assets, capital and operating expenses, sales, value added, and inventories, by SIC 2- to 4-digit kind of business, 2399–2

Securities industry self-regulatory organizations oversight by SEC, violations, and complaints, FY86-89, GAO rpt, 26119–336

Service industries census, 1987: depreciable assets, capital and operating expenses, and receipts, by SIC 2- to 4-digit kind of business, 2393–2

Service industries census, 1987: establishments, receipts by source, payroll, and employment, by SIC 2- to 4-digit kind of business, State, and MSA, 2393–4

Service industries receipts, by SIC 2- to 4-digit kind of business, 1990, annual rpt, 2413–8

Statistical Abstract of US, 1991 annual data compilation, 2324–1.18

Tax (income) returns filed by type of filer, selected income items, quarterly rpt, 8302–2.1

Tax (income) returns of corporations, income and tax items by asset size and detailed industry, 1987, annual rpt, 8304–4

Tax (income) returns of corporations, income and tax items by asset size and detailed industry, 1988, annual rpt, 8304–21

Tax (income) returns of sole proprietorships, income statement items, by industry group, 1989, annual article, 8302–2.214

Telephone and telegraph firms detailed finances and operations, 1989, annual rpt, 9284–6.2

Travel to US, trade shows and other promotional activities, with magazine ad costs and circulation, for selected countries, 1991-92, annual rpt, 2904–11

Wholesale trade census, 1987: depreciable assets, capital and operating expenses, sales, value added, and inventories, by SIC 2- to 3-digit kind of business, 2407–2

see also Direct marketing
see also Labeling
see also Sales promotion

Advisory Commission on Intergovernmental Relations

Activities and finances of ACIR, 1990, annual rpt, 10044–3

Budget of US, authoritative financial statements with appropriations, outlays, and receipts, by category and agency, FY90, annual rpt, 8104–2.1

Budget of US, obligations and authority by function, agency, and program, with summaries, analyses, and historical tables, FY92, annual rpt, 104–2

Education (public elementary and secondary) financing issues, and indicators of school districts fiscal independence, 1960s-80s, 10048–78

Govt finances, tax systems and revenue, and fiscal structure, by level of govt and State, 1991 with historical trends, annual rpt, 10044–1

Intergovernmental Perspective, quarterly journal, 10042–1

R&D funding by Fed Govt, by field, performer type, agency, and State, FY89-91, annual rpt, 9627–20

State and local govt competition in taxes, services, regulation, and dev incentives, 1970-89, 10048–79

State and local govt spending measures using indicators of service costs and demand, with comparisons to fiscal capacity and actual outlays, by State, 1986-87, 10048–77

State-local relations advisory organizations activities, staff, and funding, 1990, 10048–80

Taxes, spending, and govt efficiency, public opinion by respondent characteristics, 1991 survey, annual rpt, 10044–2

Technology dev programs of govts, info sources and funding, 1990 rpt, 10048–81

Advisory Committee on Federal Pay

Budget of US, authoritative financial statements with appropriations, outlays, and receipts, by category and agency, FY90, annual rpt, 8104–2.1

Advisory Committee on the Future of the U.S. Space Program

Recommendations of committee, 1990 rpt, 9508–38

Advisory Council on Historic Preservation

Budget of US, authoritative financial statements with appropriations, outlays, and receipts, by category and agency, FY90, annual rpt, 8104–2.1

Budget of US, obligations and authority by function, agency, and program, with summaries, analyses, and historical tables, FY92, annual rpt, 104–2

Aerial surveys

Environmental and natural resource data sources, and aerial survey R&D rpts, quarterly listing, 9502–7

Oceanographic research ships, fleet condition, funding, voyages, and modernization costs, for NOAA, 1980s-90 and projected to 2020, 2148–60

Whales (bowhead) population in Beaufort Sea, and fall aerial survey operations, 1979-90, annual rpt, 5734–10

Aeronautical engineering
see Aviation sciences

Aeronautical navigation

Airport capacity improvement projects and funding, traffic, and delays, by major airport, 1987-90 and forecast to 1998, annual rpt, 7504–43

Exports and imports of US, by Harmonized System 6-digit commodity and country, 1990, annual rpt, 2424–13

Exports of US, detailed Schedule B commodities with countries of destination, 1990, annual rpt, 2424–10

FAA air traffic control and airway facilities and services, finances and operations, FY85-89, annual rpt, 7504–37

Index by Subjects and Names

FAA air traffic control and airway facilities improvement under Aviation System Capital Investment Plan, 1981-90 and projected to 2005, annual rpt, 7504–12

FAA air traffic control facility traffic levels, including instrument operations, by airport and State, FY90, annual rpt, 7504–27

FAA certifications for pilots and nonpilots by type, age, sex, region, and State, 1990, annual rpt, 7504–2

General aviation activity, 1990, triennial survey rpt, 7508–3

General aviation aircraft, flight hours, and equipment, by type, use, and model of aircraft, region, and State, 1990, annual rpt, 7504–29

Instrument flight rule aircraft handled, by user type, FAA traffic control center, and region, FY85-90 and projected to FY2005, annual rpt, 7504–15

Instruments and related products shipments, trade, use, and firms, by detailed type, 1989, annual Current Industrial Rpt, 2506–12.26

Manufacturing census, 1987: finances and operations, by SIC 2- to 4-digit industry, State, and MSA, with trends from 1849, 2497–1

Natl Ocean Service Charting and Geodetic Service activities and funding, by State, FY91-92, biennial rpt, 2174–10

Traffic, aircraft, pilots, airports, and fuel use, forecast FY91-2002 and trends from FY81, annual rpt, 7504–6

see also Radar

Aerospace industry

Business statistics, detailed data for major industries and economic indicators, *Survey of Current Business,* monthly rpt, 2702–1.23

Capital expenditures for plant and equipment, by major industry group, quarterly rpt, 2502–2

County Business Patterns, 1988: employment, establishments, and payroll, by SIC 2- to 4-digit industry and county, annual State rpt series, 2326–6

County Business Patterns, 1989: employment, establishments, and payroll, by SIC 2- to 4-digit industry and county, annual State rpt series, 2326–8

Employment and Earnings, detailed data, monthly rpt, 6742–2.6

Employment Cost Index and percent change by occupational group, industry div, region, and metro-nonmetro area, quarterly press release, 6782–5

Employment Cost Index in aerospace manufacturing, by occupational group and industry, monthly rpt, 6782–1.1

Employment, earnings, and hours, by SIC 1- to 4-digit industry, monthly and annual averages, selected years 1909-90, annual rpt, 6744–4

Enterprise Statistics, 1987: finances and operations for companies, by size, level of diversification, form of organization, and industry group, 2329–8

Imports of US given duty-free treatment for value of US material sent abroad, by commodity and country, 1989, annual rpt, 9884–14

Input-output structure of US economy, detailed interindustry transactions for 84 industries, and components of final demand, 1986, annual article, 2702–1.206

Index by Subjects and Names

Input-output structure of US economy, detailed interindustry transactions for 85 industries, 1982 benchmark data, 2702–1.213

Manufacturing annual survey, 1989: finances and operations, by SIC 2- to 4-digit industry, series, 2506–15

Manufacturing census, 1987: employment and shipments under Fed Govt contracts, by SIC 4-digit industry, 2497–7

Manufacturing census, 1987: finances and operations, by SIC 2- to 4-digit industry, State, and MSA, with trends from 1849, 2497–1

Manufacturing census, 1987: finances and operations, by type of organization and SIC 2- to 4-digit industry, subject rpt, 2497–5

Manufacturing corporations financial statements, by selected SIC 2- to 3-digit industry, quarterly rpt, 2502–1

Manufacturing finances and operations, by SIC 2- to 4-digit industry, forecast 1991, annual rpt, 2044–28

Occupational injury and illness rates, by SIC 2- to 4-digit industry, 1988-89, annual rpt, 6844–7

Occupational injury and illness rates, by SIC 2- to 4-digit industry, 1989, annual rpt, 6844–1

Pollution (water) industrial releases in wastewater, levels, treatment, costs, and regulation, with background financial and operating data, 1989 industry rpt, 9206–4.13

Price indexes (producer), by stage of processing and detailed commodity, monthly rpt, 6762–6

R&D funding, and scientists and engineers education and employment, for US and selected foreign countries, 1991 annual rpt, 9627–35.1

Sales, orders, backlog, and firms, by product for govt, military, and other customers, 1990, annual Current Industrial Rpt, 2506–12.22

Shipments, trade, use, and firms, by type of craft and engine, monthly Current Industrial Rpt, 2506–12.24

Statistical Abstract of US, 1991 annual data compilation, 2324–1.22

Tax (income) returns of corporations, income and tax items by asset size and detailed industry, 1987, annual rpt, 8304–4

Tax (income) returns of corporations, income and tax items by asset size and detailed industry, 1988, annual rpt, 8304–21

see also Aircraft

see also Missiles and rockets

see also Spacecraft

Aetna Life Insurance Co.

Fed Govt civilian employees health insurance coverage, by plan, FY89, annual rpt, 9844–35.1

AFDC

see Aid to Families with Dependent Children

Affirmative action

see Discrimination in employment

see Minority employment

Afghanistan

Agricultural exports of high-value commodities, indexes and sales by commodity, world area, and country, 1960s-86, 1528–323

Agricultural trade of US, by detailed commodity and country, 1989, annual rpt, 1524–8

Agricultural trade of US, by detailed commodity and country, 1990, semiannual rpt, 1522–4

AID economic aid to developing countries, obligations and disbursements by country, quarterly rpt, 9912–4

AID loans repayment status and terms by program and country, and status of predecessor agency loans, quarterly rpt, 9912–3

Economic and military aid and loans from US and intl agencies, by program and country, FY46-90, annual rpt, 9914–5

Economic and social conditions of developing countries from 1960s, and Intl Dev Cooperation Agency and AID activities and funding, FY90-92, annual rpt, 9904–4

Economic, social, political, and geographic summary data, by country, 1991, annual factbook, 9114–2

Exports and imports of US, by transport mode, country, and SITC 1- to 3-digit commodity, 1990, annual rpt, 2424–12

Exports and imports of US with Communist countries, by detailed commodity and country, quarterly rpt with articles, 9882–2

Exports of US, detailed Schedule B commodities with countries of destination, 1990, annual rpt, 2424–10

Human rights conditions in 170 countries, and US economic and military aid, 1990, annual rpt, 21384–3

Military aid of US, arms sales, and training programs costs and budget requests, by program, world region, and country, FY90-92, annual rpt, 7144–13

Refugee resettlement programs and funding, arrivals by country of origin, and indicators of adjustment, by State, FY90, annual rpt, 4694–5

UN voting record and share of votes in agreement with US, by issue, country, and world area, 1990, annual rpt, 7004–18

see also under By Foreign Country in the "Index by Categories"

Africa

Agricultural conditions in sub-Saharan Africa by country, with Ethiopia grain production and use, and dev aid by major donor, 1960s-80s, hearing, 23848–216

Agricultural exports of high-value commodities, indexes and sales by commodity, world area, and country, 1960s-86, 1528–323

Agricultural exports of US, for grains, oilseed products, hides, skins, and cotton, by country, weekly rpt, 1922–3

Agricultural production, prices, and trade, by country, 1960s-90, annual world area rpt, 1524–4.2

Agricultural trade of US, by commodity and country, bimonthly rpt, 1522–1

Agricultural trade of US, by detailed commodity and country, 1989, annual rpt, 1524–8

Agricultural trade of US, by detailed commodity and country, 1990, semiannual rpt, 1522–4

AID economic aid to developing countries, obligations and disbursements by country, quarterly rpt, 9912–4

AID economic and dev aid fund for Africa, funding by project, 1980s-90, GAO rpt, 26123–333

AID housing and urban dev program financial statements, FY90, annual rpt, 9914–4

AID loans repayment status and terms by program and country, and status of predecessor agency loans, quarterly rpt, 9912–3

AIDS epidemic impacts on population size and components of change, for sub-Saharan Africa, model description and results, 1990-2015, working paper, 2326–18.57

AIDS virus infection prevalence in developing countries, by sex, selected city, urban-rural location, and country, 1991, semiannual rpt, 2322–4

Air traffic and passengers, for intl routes over north Atlantic, by aviation type and route, alternative forecasts 1991-2010 and trends from 1980, annual rpt, 7504–44

Alien workers (unauthorized) and Fair Labor Standards Act employer compliance, hiring impacts, and aliens overstaying visas by country and State, 1986-90, annual rpt, 6264–6

Aliens (illegal) overstaying visas, by class of admission, mode of arrival, age, country, and State, FY85-88, annual rpt, 6264–5

Capital intl market financial data by firm, and Intl Finance Corp finances, by country, 1990 hearing, 21248–149

Child health and welfare indicators, and economic conditions, for developing countries, 1950s-80s, hearing, 25388–57

Construction contract awards and billings, by country of contractor and world area of award, 1989, annual article, 2042–1.201

Corporations in US under foreign control, income tax returns, assets and income statement items by industry div, country, and world area, 1988, article, 8302–2.219

Dairy imports, consumption, and market conditions, by sub-Saharan Africa country, 1961-88, 1528–321

Deforestation, and OECD imports of tropical wood, by country, 1980s, annual rpt, 9114–4.10

Developing countries economic, population, and agricultural data, US and other aid sources, and AID activity, 1989 world area rpt, 9916–12.32

Economic and military aid and loans from US and intl agencies, by program and country, FY46-90, annual rpt, 9914–5

Economic and military aid from US and intl agencies, and US defense spending, for Middle East and East Africa, FY80-90, GAO rpt, 26123–360

Economic and social conditions of developing countries from 1960s, and Intl Dev Cooperation Agency and AID activities and funding, FY90-92, annual rpt, 9904–4

Energy producers finances and operations, by energy type for US firms domestic and foreign operations, 1989, annual rpt, 3164–44.2

Africa

Energy production by type, and oil trade, and use, by country group and selected country, monthly rpt, 9112–2

Energy use and production, by fuel type, country, and country group, projected 1995-2010 and trends from 1970, annual rpt, 3164–84

Energy use in developing countries, and economic and environmental impacts, by fuel type, world area, and country, 1980s-90, 26358–232

English language program of USIA, enrollment and staff, by country and world region, FY90, annual rpt, 9854–2

Exchange and training programs of Federal agencies, participants by world area, and funding, by program, FY89, annual rpt, 9854–8

Exports and imports (waterborne) of US, by type of service, commodity, country, route, and US port, 1988, annual rpt, 7704–2

Exports and imports (waterborne) of US, by type of service, customs district, port, and world area, monthly rpt, 2422–7

Exports and imports of OECD, total and for 4 major countries, and US trade by country, by commodity, 1970-89, world area rpt, 9116–1.6

Exports and imports of US, by Harmonized System 6-digit commodity and country, 1990, annual rpt, 2424–13

Exports and imports of US, by selected country, country group, and commodity group, 1990, annual rpt, 2044–37

Exports and imports of US, by transport mode, country, and SITC 1- to 3-digit commodity, 1990, annual rpt, 2424–12

Family planning and population activities of AID, grants by project and recipient, and contraceptive shipments, by country, FY90, annual rpt series, 9914–13

Food supply, needs, and aid for developing countries, status and alternative forecasts, 1991 world area rpt, 1526–8.1

Grain production and needs, and related economic outlook, by world area and selected country, forecast 1990/91-1991/92, 1528–313

Grain production, use, imports, and stocks, for Sahel region by country, 1989/90, 9918–18

Immigrant and nonimmigrant visas of US issued and refused, by class, issuing office, and nationality, FY89, annual rpt, 7184–1

Immigrants admitted to US, by country of birth, FY81-90, annual rpt, 6264–4

Immigrants admitted to US, by occupational group and country of birth, preliminary FY90, annual table, 6264–1

Immigrants in US, population characteristics and fertility, by birthplace and compared to native born, 1980s, Current Population rpt, 2546–2.162

Investment (foreign direct) of US, by industry group and world area, 1987-90, annual article, 2702–1.220

Loans of US banks to foreigners at all US and foreign offices, by country group and country, quarterly rpt, 13002–1

Military aid of US, arms sales, and training, by country, FY50-90, annual rpt, 3904–3

Military spending and imports of developing countries, measures to determine eligibility for US economic aid, by country, 1986-87, annual rpt, 9914–1

Multinatl firms US affiliates, finances, and operations, by industry, world area of parent firm, and State, 1988-89, annual rpt, 2704–4

Multinatl US firms and foreign affiliates finances and operations, by industry and world area of parent firm, 1989 benchmark survey, preliminary annual rpt, 2704–5

Multinatl US firms foreign affiliates, income statement items by country and world area, 1986, biennial article, 8302–2.212

Oil and gas reserves and discoveries, by country and country group, quarterly rpt, 3162–43

Oils, oilseeds, and meal imports, by commodity, world area of destination, and major producer, 1960s-88, 1528–314

Peace Corps activities, funding by program, and volunteers, by country, FY92, annual rpt, 9654–1

R&D funding by Fed Govt, by field, performer type, agency, and State, FY89-91, annual rpt, 9627–20

Refugee arrivals in US by world area and country of origin, and quotas, monthly rpt, 7002–4

Refugee arrivals in US by world area of origin and State of settlement, and Federal aid, FY90-91 and proposed FY92 allocations, annual rpt, 7004–16

Refugee resettlement programs and funding, arrivals by country of origin, and indicators of adjustment, by State, FY90, annual rpt, 4694–5

Tax (income) returns of corporations with foreign tax credit, income, and tax items, by country and world region of credit, 1986, biennial article, 8302–2.207

Terrorism (intl) incidents, casualties, and attacks on US targets, by attack type and country, 1990, annual rpt, 7004–22

Terrorism (intl) incidents, casualties, and attacks on US targets, by attack type and world area, 1990, annual rpt, 7004–13

Tide height and time daily at coastal points, forecast 1992, annual rpt, 2174–2.4; 2174–2.5

Travel to and from US on US and foreign flag air carriers, by country, world area, and US port, monthly rpt, 7302–2

Travel to and from US on US and foreign flag air carriers, by world area, 1990, annual rpt, 2904–13

Travel to US, by characteristics of visit and traveler, country, port city, and State of destination, quarterly rpt, 2902–1

UN voting record and share of votes in agreement with US, by issue, country, and world area, 1990, annual rpt, 7004–18

US military and civilian personnel and dependents, by service branch, world area, and country, quarterly rpt, 3542–20

USIA library holdings, use, and staff, by country and city, FY90, annual rpt, 9854–4

Weather conditions and effect on agriculture, by US region, State, and city, and world area, weekly rpt, 2182–7

Weather events and anomalies, precipitation and temperature for US and foreign locations, weekly rpt, 2182–6

see also African Development Bank

see also African Development Fund

Index by Subjects and Names

see also Algeria

see also Angola

see also Benin

see also Botswana

see also Burkina Faso

see also Burundi

see also Cameroon

see also Cape Verde

see also Central African Republic

see also Chad

see also Comoros

see also Congo

see also Djibouti

see also Egypt

see also Equatorial Guinea

see also Ethiopia

see also Gabon

see also Gambia

see also Ghana

see also Guinea

see also Guinea-Bissau

see also Ivory Coast

see also Kenya

see also Lesotho

see also Liberia

see also Libya

see also Madagascar

see also Malawi

see also Mali

see also Mauritania

see also Mauritius

see also Morocco

see also Mozambique

see also Namibia

see also Niger

see also Nigeria

see also Reunion

see also Rwanda

see also Sao Tome and Principe

see also Senegal

see also Seychelles

see also Sierra Leone

see also Somalia

see also South Africa

see also Sudan

see also Swaziland

see also Tanzania

see also Togo

see also Tunisia

see also Uganda

see also Western Sahara

see also Zaire

see also Zambia

see also Zimbabwe

see also under By Foreign Country in the "Index by Categories"

African Americans

see Black Americans

African Development Bank

AID loans repayment status and terms by program and country, and status of predecessor agency loans, quarterly rpt, 9912–3

Loan activity by purpose and country, FY89, annual rpt, 15344–1.9

Loans and grants for economic and military aid from US and intl agencies, by program and country, FY46-90, annual rpt, 9914–5

African Development Fund

Loan activity by purpose and country, FY89, annual rpt, 15344–1.9

Index by Subjects and Names

Age

see Age discrimination
see Aged and aging
see Children
see Life expectancy
see Population characteristics
see Youth
see under By Age in the "Index by Categories"

Age discrimination

Fed Govt aid programs discrimination against aged, Age Discrimination Act enforcement by agency, FY90, annual rpt, 4004–27

Fed Govt personnel action appeals, decisions of Merit Systems Protection Board by agency and region, FY90, annual rpt, 9494–2

Labor laws enacted, by State, 1990, annual article, 6722–1.209

Age Discrimination Act

Enforcement of Act, by Federal agency, FY90, annual rpt, 4004–27

Aged and aging

Abuse and neglect of aged by circumstances and characteristics of abuser and victim, and States protective services budgets and staff, by location, 1980s, hearing, 21148–62

Abuse of aged, State agency reporting and investigation procedures, 1989 survey, article, 4042–3.213

Assets of households, by type of holding and selected characteristics, 1988, Current Population Rpt, 2546–20.16

Black Americans social and economic characteristics, for South and total US, 1989-90 and trends from 1969, Current Population Rpt, 2546–1.450

Board and care homes regulation and rules enforcement by States, 1988, 4008–112

Cancer cases, deaths, and survival rates, by sex, race, age, and body site, 1973-88, annual rpt, 4474–35

Census of Population and Housing, 1990: population and housing characteristics, households, and land area, by county, subdiv, and place, State rpt series, 2551–1

Census of Population and Housing, 1990: population and housing selected characteristics, by region, press release, 2328–74

Clothing expenses of aged, by selected characteristics, 1987, 1702–1.202

Consumer Expenditure Survey, household income by source, and itemized spending, by selected characteristics and region, 1988-89, annual rpt, 6764–5

Consumer Income, socioeconomic characteristics of persons, families, and households, detailed cross-tabulations, Current Population Rpt series, 2546–6

Crimes against aged and handicapped, State laws, data compilation, 1991 annual rpt, 6064–6.1

Deaths and rates, by detailed cause and demographic characteristics, 1988 and trends from 1900, US Vital Statistics annual rpt, 4144–2

Deaths of aged in hospitals, nursing homes, and own home, by cause, age, marital status, and region, 1986, article, 4652–1.201

Developing countries aged population and selected characteristics, 1980s and projected to 2020, country rpt series, 2326–19

Disability (functional) of aged, long-term care sources, and health and other characteristics, 1984-85, 4147–13.104

Disability (functional), persons needing aid with activities of daily living, by age and household income, 1986, fact sheet, 2326–17.22

Disabled aged long-term care needs and costs, late 1980s and projected 2018-60, GAO rpt, 26121–433

Drug (prescription) spending by aged, and manufacturer and retail price changes, by drug type, 1981-88, 4658–56

Drug and alcohol abuse treatment facilities, services, use, funding, staff, and client characteristics, 1989, biennial rpt, 4494–10

Foreign countries family composition, poverty status, labor conditions, and welfare indicators and needs, by country, 1960s-88, hearing, 23846–4.30

Germany (West) health condition of children and aged, health care costs, and natl health insurance payroll tax rates, 1985-88, 23898–5

Health care (primary) research, methodology and findings, 1991 annual conf, 4184–4

Health care centers federally funded, aged persons use, targeted programs offered, and funding sources, 1987, article, 4042–3.229

Health care services and long term care for aged, series, 4186–7

Health care services use of aged, by service type, discharge destination, and prior care source, 1986, 4188–72

Health care spending by type and payment source, with background data and foreign comparisons, 1960s-80s and projected to 2000, 26308–98

Health condition and care of aged, data availability and collection methodology, for US and selected countries, 1988 conf, 4147–5.6

Health condition and health care resources, use, and spending, 1950s-89, annual data compilation, 4144–11

Health condition improvement and disease prevention goals and recommended activities for 2000, with trends 1970s-80s, 4048–10

Hispanic Americans social and economic characteristics, by detailed origin, 1991, Current Population Rpt, 2546–1.448; 2546–1.451

Households and family characteristics, by location, 1990, annual Current Population Rpt, 2546–1.447

Households and housing characteristics, MSA surveys, fact sheet series, 2485–11

Households and housing characteristics, unit and neighborhood quality, and journey to work by MSA location, for 11 MSAs, 1984 survey, supplement, 2485–8

Households and housing detailed characteristics, and unit and neighborhood quality, by location, 1987, biennial rpt supplement, 2485–13

Households and housing detailed characteristics, and unit and neighborhood quality, by location, 1989, biennial rpt, 2485–12

Households and housing detailed characteristics, and unit and neighborhood quality, MSA surveys, series, 2485–6

Households by tenure and population size, by age group, State, and county, 1980 and 1985, 2546–3.169

Households composition, income, benefits, and labor force status, Survey of Income and Program Participation methodology, working paper series, 2626–10

Housing inventory change from 1973, by reason, unit and household characteristics, and location, 1983 survey, biennial rpt, 2485–14

Housing worst case problems prevalence and households characteristics, for poor households with high rent, and substandard units, 1970s-84, annual rpt, 5184–10

Income (household) and poverty status under alternative income definitions, by recipient characteristics, 1990, annual Current Population Rpt, 2546–6.69

Income of aged householders by source, and spending by type, 1987, article, 1702–1.204

Injuries from use of consumer products, by severity, victim age, and detailed product, 1990, annual rpt, 9164–6

Labor force status of older men by urban-rural location, and distribution of men by age and occupation, 1860s-1980, article, 9371–1.202

Living arrangements, family relationships, and marital status, by selected characteristics, 1990, annual Current Population Rpt, 2546–1.449

Living arrangements of aged, by poverty status, 1989, annual rpt, 4744–3.1

Migration of aged to southern coastal areas, household finances, services needs, and local economic impacts, for selected counties, 1990, 2068–38

Minority group health condition, services use, costs, and indicators of services need, 1950s-88, 4118–55

Population size and characteristics, historical index to *Current Population Rpts*, 1991 listing, 2546–2.160

Poverty status of aged by health and other characteristics, and Medicaid income and asset eligibility limits by State, 1984-90, 23898–5

Poverty status of population and families, by detailed characteristics, 1988-89, annual Current Population Rpt, 2546–6.67

Poverty status of population and families, by detailed characteristics, 1990, annual Current Population Rpt, 2546–6.71

Puerto Rico population and housing characteristics, 1990 Census of Population and Housing, press release, 2328–78

Rural areas aged household income sources, and poverty status, 1983-84, 1598–268

State and Metro Area Data Book, 1991 data compilation, 2328–54

Statistical Abstract of US, 1991 annual data compilation, 2324–1

Survey of Income and Program Participation, data collection, methodology, and use, 1990 annual conf papers, 2624–1

Unemployment of groups with historically high rates, 1985-89, biennial rpt, 6504–2.2

Aged and aging

Virgin Islands population and housing characteristics, 1990 Census of Population and Housing, press release, 2328–81

Vision of aged and glaucoma patients, effects of altitude, 1991 technical rpt, 7506–10.80

Voting and registration, by socioeconomic and demographic characteristics, 1990 congressional election, biennial Current Population Rpt, 2546–1.454

Women (older) household income by source, and expenses by type, by living arrangement and other characteristics, 1988, article, 1702–1.210

see also Adult day care
see also Age discrimination
see also Alzheimer's disease
see also Civil service pensions
see also Foster Grandparent Program
see also Geriatrics
see also Individual retirement arrangements
see also Medicare
see also Military benefits and pensions
see also Nursing homes
see also Old age assistance
see also Old-Age, Survivors, Disability, and Health Insurance
see also Pensions and pension funds
see also Retired Senior Volunteer Program
see also Retirement
see also Retirement communities
see also Senior Companion Program
see also Social security
see also Supplemental Security Income
see also Veterans benefits and pensions
see also under By Age in the "Index by Categories"

Agency for Health Care Policy and Research

Activities and funding of AHCPR for health care services outcome research and practice guidelines dev, FY88-89, 4188–70

Budget of US, obligations and authority by function, agency, and program, with summaries, analyses, and historical tables, FY92, annual rpt, 104–2

Health care services needs, delivery, and costs, series, 4186–9

Health care services use and costs, methodology and findings of natl survey, series, 4186–8

Hospital costs and use, data compilation project analyses, series, 4186–6

Hospital inpatient case-mix specialization level related to industry structure and market characteristics, 1980-85, 4188–71

Info on health care treatments effectiveness, feasibility of linking Federal and other databases, 1991 narrative rpt, 4188–73

Medicare coverage of new health care technologies, risks and benefit evaluations, series, 4186–10

Natl Medical Expenditure Survey data accuracy and response rates, for 2 organizations conducting screenings, 1986, 4188–68

Older persons health care services and long term care, series, 4186–7

Older persons health care services use, by service type, discharge destination, and prior care source, 1986, 4188–72

Primary health care research, methodology and findings, 1991 annual conf, 4184–4

Primary health care research, provider role, Federal funding, and provision to minority groups, 1990 conf papers, 4188–69

Research and evaluation programs of HHS, 1970-90, annual listing, 4004–30

Agency for International Development

Activities and funding of Intl Dev Cooperation Agency and AID, FY90-92, and developing countries economic and social conditions from 1960s, annual rpt, 9904–4

Africa (Sahel) grain production, use, imports, and stocks, by country, 1989/90, 9918–18

Africa economic and dev aid fund of AID, funding by project, 1980s-90, GAO rpt, 26123–333

Budget of US, authoritative financial statements with appropriations, outlays, and receipts, by category and agency, FY90, annual rpt, 8104–2.1

Budget of US, obligations and authority by function, agency, and program, with summaries, analyses, and historical tables, FY92, annual rpt, 104–2

Contracts for AID dev project procurement awarded by host countries, oversight issues with background data, 1991 GAO rpt, 26123–342

Counterpart funds impacts on US aid programs effectiveness and developing countries economic and fiscal condition, literature review, 1991 rpt, 9918–21

Currency (foreign) accounts owned by US under AID admin and by foreign govts with joint AID control, status by program and country, quarterly rpt, 9912–1

Dev funds of AID obligated but unspent by country, and impacts of alternative allocation formulas, FY87-90, GAO rpt, 26123–327

Dev projects of AID, and socioeconomic impacts, evaluation rpt series, 9916–1

Dev projects of AID, special study series, 9916–3

Disabled persons in developing countries aid program activities and funding, for UN, AID, and Intl Labor Organization, late 1970s-90, GAO rpt, 26123–321

Disasters, casualties, damage, and aid by US and others, by country, FY90 and trends from FY64, annual rpt, 9914–12

Eastern Europe energy production, trade, use, and AID dev assistance, for 3 countries, 1980s-91, 25318–81

Economic aid to developing countries, obligations and disbursements by country, quarterly rpt, 9912–4

Economic, population, and agricultural data, US and other aid sources, and AID activity, country rpt series, 9916–12

Education funding by Federal agency, program, and recipient type, and instn spending, FY80-90, annual rpt, 4824–8

Energy assistance to developing countries, and global warming reduction activities, for AID, 1980s-FY92, GAO rpt, 26123–352

Exchange and training programs of Federal agencies, participants by world area, and funding, by program, FY89, annual rpt, 9854–8

Family planning and population activities of AID, grants by project and recipient, and contraceptive shipments, by country, FY90, annual rpt series, 9914–13

Higher education instns and AID collaboration on aid projects, and funding, by purpose and world region, 1960s-89, 26358–247

Housing and urban dev program of AID, financial statements, FY90, annual rpt, 9914–4

Latin America energy use and trade, by selected country, 1970s-80s and projected to 2000, 3408–1

Liabilities (contingent) and claims paid by Fed Govt on federally insured and guaranteed contracts with foreign obligors, by country and program, periodic rpt, 8002–12

Loan activity, terms, and purpose, by country, FY89, annual rpt, 15344–1.10

Loan repayment status and terms by program and country, AID and predecessor agencies, quarterly rpt, 9912–3

Loans and grants for economic and military aid from US and intl agencies, by program and country, FY46-90, annual rpt, 9914–5

Military spending and imports of developing countries, measures to determine eligibility for US economic aid, by country, 1986-87, annual rpt, 9914–1

Panama economic aid after US sanctions and military invasion, AID funding by program, as of 1991, GAO rpt, 26123–330

Peru cocaine production, acreage, and economic impacts of crop eradication and conversion to legitimate agricultural use, 1960s-87, 9918–19

PL 480 food aid impacts on developing countries economic dev, literature review, 1979-88, 9918–20

R&D and related funding of Fed Govt to higher education and nonprofit instns, by field, instn, agency, and State, FY89, annual rpt, 9627–17

R&D funding by Fed Govt, by field, performer type, agency, and State, FY89-91, annual rpt, 9627–20

Agency for Toxic Substances and Disease Registry

Waste (medical) generation, sources, health worker exposure and risk, and incineration emissions, 1980s, 4078–1

Agent Orange

see Dioxins

Agrarian reform

see Land reform

Agricultural accidents and safety

Aircraft (general aviation) accidents, by circumstances, characteristics of persons and aircraft involved, and type of flying, 1988, annual rpt, 9614–3

Child accident deaths and death rates, by cause, age, sex, race, and State, 1980-85, 4108–54

Deaths and rates, by cause, age, sex, race, and State, 1988, US Vital Statistics annual rpt, 4144–2.5

Grain handling facility explosions and casualties, by firm, FY90, annual rpt, 1294–1

Injuries from use of consumer products, by severity, victim age, and detailed product, 1990, annual rpt, 9164–6

Injuries, illnesses, and workdays lost, by SIC 2-digit industry, 1989-90, annual press release, 6844–3

Injuries, related impairments, and activity limitations, by circumstances and victim characteristics, 1985-87, 4147–10.179

Index by Subjects and Names

Agricultural credit

Injury and illness rates by SIC 2- to 4-digit industry, and deaths by cause and industry div, 1989, annual rpt, 6844–1

Injury and illness rates, by SIC 2- to 4-digit industry, 1988-89, annual rpt, 6844–7

Workers compensation laws of States and Fed Govt, 1991 semiannual rpt, 6502–1

Agricultural chemicals

see Fertilizers

see Pesticides

Agricultural commodities

Industrial uses of new and traditional agricultural crops, replacement of imports and nonrenewable resources, R&D funding, and economic impacts, 1970s-90, 26358–239

see also Agricultural exports and imports

see also Agricultural marketing

see also Agricultural prices

see also Agricultural production

see also Agricultural production costs

see also Agricultural production quotas and price supports

see also Agricultural stocks

see also Agricultural subsidies

see also Animal feed

see also Animals

see also Census of Agriculture

see also Citrus fruits

see also Cocoa and chocolate

see also Coffee

see also Corn

see also Cotton

see also Dairy industry and products

see also Flowers and nursery products

see also Food and food industry

see also Food consumption

see also Food prices

see also Food supply

see also Fruit and fruit products

see also Grains and grain products

see also Gum and wood chemicals

see also Hides and skins

see also Honey and beekeeping

see also Hops

see also Livestock and livestock industry

see also Lumber industry and products

see also Meat and meat products

see also Natural fibers

see also Nuts

see also Oils, oilseeds, and fats

see also Peanuts

see also Poultry industry and products

see also Rice

see also Seeds

see also Soybeans

see also Spices and herbs

see also Sugar industry and products

see also Tea

see also Tobacco industry and products

see also Vegetables and vegetable products

see also Wheat

see also Wool and wool trade

see also under By Commodity in the "Index by Categories"

Agricultural Cooperative Service

Budget of US, obligations and authority by function, agency, and program, with summaries, analyses, and historical tables, FY92, annual rpt, 104–2

Cooperatives finances, aggregate for top 100 assns by commodity group, 1989, annual rpt, 1124–3

Cooperatives, finances, and membership, by type of service, commodity, and State, 1989, annual rpt, 1124–1

Cooperatives finances, operations, activities, and current issues, monthly journal, 1122–1

Cooperatives, finances, operations, activities, and membership, commodity rpt series, 1126–1

Cooperatives, membership, farms, and income, historical review, 1913-81, 1128–66

Dairy exports market conditions, with background data by country, 1986-89, 1128–65

Grain cooperatives finances and operations, by grain handled and selected characteristics, 1983-85, series, 1128–44

Agricultural cooperatives

see Rural cooperatives

Agricultural credit

Agricultural Outlook, production, prices, marketing, and trade, by commodity, forecast and current situation, monthly rpt with articles, 1502–4

Agricultural Statistics, 1990, annual rpt, 1004–1

Assets and debts of private sector, balance sheets by segment, 1945-90, semiannual rpt, 9365–4.1

Banks (commercial) and farm loans, by ratio of farm to total loans, 1985 and 1990, article, 9362–1.207

Banks (insured commercial and savings) finances, for foreign and domestic offices, by asset size, 1989, annual rpt, 9294–4.2

Banks (natl) charters, mergers, liquidations, enforcement cases, and financial performance, with data by instn and State, quarterly rpt, 8402–3

Banks agricultural loans share of all loans, impact of State branching laws, bank urban-rural location, and other factors, 1981-86, article, 9393–8.202

Banks finances and operations, by metro-nonmetro location, 1987-89, annual rpt, 1544–29

Banks financial performance in Fed Reserve 10th District, by urban-rural location and State, 1989-90, article, 9381–16.201

CCC certificate exchange activity, by commodity, biweekly press release, 1802–16

CCC loan activities by commodity, and agency operating results, monthly press release, 1802–7

CCC price support and other program outlays, with production and marketing outlook, by commodity, projected 1990-96, 26306–6.160

Census of Agriculture, 1987: farms, farmland, production, finances, and operator characteristics, by county, final State rpt series, 2331–1

Corn farms, finances, acreage, and production, by size, region, and State, 1987, 1568–304

Costs of production, itemized by farm sales size and region, 1990, annual rpt, 1614–3

Cotton loan rates, and micronaire differentials of CCC, monthly rpt, annual tables, 1309–12

Cotton prices at selected spot markets, NYC futures prices, and CCC loan rates, 1990/91 and trends from 1943, annual rpt, 1309–2

Data on agriculture, compilation, 1990 and trends from 1920, annual rpt, 1004–14

Debt outstanding, by sector and type of debt and holder, monthly rpt, 9362–1.1

Delinquent borrowers aid services of Farm Credit System and FmHA, activities, with background data, 1989 hearings, 25168–74

Economic Indicators of the Farm Sector, balance sheets, and receipts by detailed commodity, by State, 1985-89, annual rpt, 1544–18

Economic Indicators of the Farm Sector, income, expenses, receipts by commodity, assets, and liabilities, 1990 and trends from 1945, annual rpt, 1544–16

Employment related to agriculture, by industry, region, and metro-nonmetro location, 1987, 1598–271

Fed Govt farm subsidy rates under 1985 and 1990 farm bills, by selected program and commodity, 1990 rpt, 1008–54

Fed Govt finances, cash and debt transactions, daily tables, 8102–4

Financial and marketing conditions of farms, forecast 1991, annual chartbook, 1504–8

Financial and marketing conditions of farms, forecast 1991, annual conf, 1004–16

Flow-of-funds accounts, savings, investments, and credit statements, quarterly rpt, 9365–3.3

FmHA activities, and loans and grants by program and State, FY90 and trends from FY70, annual rpt, 1184–17

FmHA farm and rural housing program loan appeals filed in 3 States, by disposition, 1988-90, GAO rpt, 26113–516

FmHA guaranteed and direct loan program costs under alternative assumptions, 1981-89, 1598–273

FmHA loan servicing eligibility, use, and effects on borrowers solvency, 1988-89, GAO rpt, 26113–497

FmHA loans and borrower supervision activities in farm and housing programs, by type and State, monthly rpt, 1182–1

FmHA loans, by type, borrower characteristics, and State, quarterly rpt, 1182–8

FmHA loans, by type, borrower race, and State, quarterly rpt, 1182–5

FmHA property acquired through foreclosure, value, acreage, and sales, for farm and nonfarm property by State, monthly rpt, 1182–6

Govt-sponsored enterprises financial condition and capital adequacy, with data by enterprise, 1970s-90 and projected to 1996, 26308–99

Govt-sponsored enterprises financial condition, capital adequacy, and impacts on Federal borrowing, with data by enterprise, 1980s-90, last issue of annual rpt, 8004–15

Grain price support and loan programs operations of USDA, with farmers views on Federal programs, by region and State, 1990 hearings, 21168–43

Grain storage facility and equipment loans to farmers under CCC program, by State, FY68-91, annual table, 1804–14

Grain support loan programs of USDA, activity and status by grain and State, monthly rpt, 1802–3

Honey production, prices, trade, stocks, marketing, and CCC honey loan and distribution activities, monthly rpt, 1311–2

Agricultural credit

Iraq agricultural imports under CCC export credit guarantee programs, FY81-90, GAO rpt, 26123–314

Land transfers, by source of credit financing and region, 1982-91, article, 1561–16.202

Loans (farm) outstanding, and lenders financial condition, quarterly rpt with articles, 1541–1

Loans (farm) outstanding, by lender, and farm and nonfarm banks and assets held, 1990 conf papers, 9368–90

Loans (farm), terms, delinquency, agricultural bank failures, and credit conditions by Fed Reserve District, quarterly rpt, 9365–3.10

Lumber and wood products exports, imports, and export promotion of US by country, and trade balance, by commodity, FAS quarterly circular, 1925–36

Mortgage loan activity, by type of lender, loan, and mortgaged property, monthly press release, 5142–18

Mortgage loan activity, by type of lender, loan, and mortgaged property, quarterly press release, 5142–30

North Central States business and economic conditions, Fed Reserve 9th District, quarterly journal, 9383–19

North Central States farm credit conditions and economic devs, Fed Reserve 7th District, monthly rpt, 9375–10

North Central States farm credit conditions, earnings, and expenses, Fed Reserve 9th District, quarterly rpt, 9383–11

Small farms loans, defaults, income, and financial condition, 1980-89, article, 1502–7.202

South Central States agricultural banks financial ratios, and farm receipts by commodity, 1980s-90, annual article, 9391–16.209

Southeastern States, Fed Reserve 5th District insured commercial banks financial statements, by State, quarterly rpt, 9389–18

Southeastern States, Fed Reserve 8th District banking and economic conditions, quarterly rpt with articles, 9391–16

Southwestern States farm credit conditions and real estate values, Fed Reserve 11th District, quarterly rpt, 9379–11

Specialized farm financial condition, by commodity, 1987, series, 1566–8

State and Metro Area Data Book, 1991 data compilation, 2328–54

Storage facility and equipment loans to farmers under CCC grain program, by State, monthly table, 1802–9

West Central States farm real estate values, farm loan trends, and regional farm price index, Fed Reserve 10th District, quarterly rpt, 9381–16.1

see also Agricultural production quotas and price supports

see also Farm Credit System

Agricultural education

Course completions, by detailed program, sex, race, and instn type, for 1972 high school class, as of 1984, 4888–4

Degrees (PhD) in science and engineering, by field, instn, employment prospects, sex, race, and other characteristics, 1960s-90, annual rpt, 9627–30

Degrees awarded in higher education, by level, field, race, and sex, 1988/89 with trends from 1978/79, biennial rpt, 4844–17

Degrees awarded in science and engineering, by field, level, and sex, 1966-89, 9627–33

Digest of Education Statistics, 1991 annual data compilation, 4824–2

Enrollment in science and engineering grad programs, by field, source of funds, and characteristics of student and instn, 1975-89, annual rpt, 9627–7

Expenditures and staffing for agricultural research by USDA, State agencies, and other instns, by topic, FY90, annual rpt, 1744–2

Expenditures for research and education, USDA appropriations by program and subagency, FY82-90, annual rpt, 1004–19

Expenditures for research and education, USDA competitive awards by program and recipient, FY90, annual listing, 1764–1

Foreign countries education and training programs of USDA, participants by program, sponsor, and country, annual rpt, discontinued, 1954–1

Teachers in higher education instns, employment and other characteristics, by instn type and control, 1987/88 survey, 4846–4.4

Veterans education aid under GI Bill and other programs, and participation by period of service and State, FY89, annual rpt, 8604–9

Yearbook of Agriculture, special topics, 1990 annual compilation of papers, 1004–18

see also Agricultural extension work

Agricultural energy use

Bonneville Power Admin energy conservation and resource planning activities, FY89-90, 3228–11

Census of Agriculture, 1987: farms, farmland, production, finances, and operator characteristics, by county, final State rpt series, 2331–1

Census of Agriculture, 1987: horticultural specialties producers, finances, and operations, by crop and State, 1988 survey, 2337–1

Conservation of energy, State programs aid from Fed Govt, and energy savings, by State, 1989, annual rpt, 3304–1

Developing countries energy use, and economic and environmental impacts, by fuel type, world area, and country, 1980s-90, 26358–232

Diesel and other fuel costs, impacts of oil price increases on farms, 1989, article, 1541–1.203

Economic Indicators of the Farm Sector, income, expenses, receipts by commodity, assets, and liabilities, 1990 and trends from 1945, annual rpt, 1544–16

Economic Indicators of the Farm Sector, itemized production costs, receipts, and returns, by commodity and region, 1987-89, annual rpt, 1544–20

Energy use by mode of transport, fuel supply, and demographic and economic factors of vehicle use, 1970s-89, annual rpt, 3304–5

Index by Subjects and Names

Financial and marketing conditions of farms, forecast 1991, annual conf, 1004–16

Fuel oil and kerosene sales and deliveries, by end-use, PAD district, and State, 1989, annual rpt, 3164–94

Gasoline and other motor fuel use, by consuming sector and State, 1990, annual rpt, 7554–1.1

Prices received and paid by farmers, by commodity and State, 1990, annual rpt, 1629–5

Prices received by farmers for major products, and paid for farm inputs and living items, by State, monthly rpt, 1629–1

Production inputs, finances, mgmt, and land value and transfers, periodic situation rpt with articles, 1561–16

Production itemized costs, by farm sales size and region, 1990, annual rpt, 1614–3

Agricultural exports and imports

Agricultural Outlook, production, prices, marketing, and trade, by commodity, forecast and current situation, monthly rpt with articles, 1502–4

Agricultural Stabilization and Conservation Service programs, annual commodity fact sheet series, 1806–4

Agricultural Statistics, 1990, annual rpt, 1004–1

Australia agricultural input and output indexes, and freight rates, 1950s-80s, 1528–311

Business statistics, detailed data for major industries and economic indicators, *Survey of Current Business*, monthly rpt, 2702–1.14

Caribbean Basin Initiative investment incentives, economic impacts, with finances and employment by country, 1984-90, 2048–141

Central America agricultural export promotion of nontraditional crops, impacts on income export stability, late 1970s-80s, 1528–312

Communist countries trade with US, by detailed commodity and country, quarterly rpt with articles, 9882–2

Data on agriculture, compilation, 1990 and trends from 1920, annual rpt, 1004–14

Developing countries agricultural and economic conditions, and US agricultural exports, effects of US aid, 1989 conf papers, 1548–372

Developing countries agricultural exports of high-value commodities to OECD, 1970s-87, 1528–316

Developing countries agricultural supply, demand, and market for US exports, with socioeconomic conditions, country rpt series, 1526–6

Developing countries economic, population, and agricultural data, US and other aid sources, and AID activity, country rpt series, 9916–12

Developing countries food supply, needs, and aid, status and alternative forecasts, world area rpt series, 1526–8

Developing countries grains production and needs, and related economic outlook, by world area and selected country, forecast 1990/91-1991/92, 1528–313

Eastern Europe agricultural production, trade, and land reform, with selected economic indicators, by country, 1960s-90, article, 1522–3.202

Index by Subjects and Names

Agricultural exports and imports

EC trade with US by country, and total agricultural trade, selected years 1958-90, country and commodity, annual rpt, 7144–7

Employment, land use, and capital required for agricultural exports, by commodity and country of destination, and comparisons to imports, 1977-87, 1548–373

Environmental regulation impacts on agricultural trade, with indicators of pollution and fertilizer use intensity by crop, 1991 article, 1522–3.203

Export credit sales agreement terms, by commodity and country, FY89, annual rpt, 15344–1.11

Export licensing, monitoring, and enforcement activities, FY90, annual rpt, 2024–1

Export promotion and foreign food aid programs budget of USDA, with trade by commodity and country, FY85-91 and projected to FY2000, 21168–44

Exports and imports (agricultural), by selected commodity, 1940-90, annual rpt, 204–1.8

Exports and imports (agricultural) commodity and country, prices, and world market devs, monthly rpt, 1922–12

Exports and imports (agricultural) of US, by commodity and country, bimonthly rpt, 1522–1

Exports and imports (agricultural) of US, by commodity, country, and US port, 1950s-91, annual rpt, 1924–9

Exports and imports (agricultural) of US, by detailed commodity and country, 1989, annual rpt, 1524–8

Exports and imports (agricultural) of US, by detailed commodity and country, 1990, semiannual rpt, 1522–4

Exports and imports (agricultural) of US, outlook and current situation, quarterly rpt, 1542–4

Exports and imports between US and outlying areas, by detailed commodity and mode of transport, 1990, annual rpt, 2424–11

Exports and imports of US, by country and detailed commodity, monthly rpt, 2422–12

Exports and imports of US by country, and trade shifts by commodity, 1990, semiannual rpt, 9882–9

Exports and imports of US, by Harmonized System 6-digit commodity and country, 1990, annual rpt, 2424–13

Exports and imports of US, by selected country, country group, and commodity group, 1990, annual rpt, 2044–37

Exports and imports of US, by transport mode, country, and SITC 1- to 3-digit commodity, 1990, annual rpt, 2424–12

Exports and imports of US shipped through Canada, by detailed commodity, customs district, and country, 1989, annual rpt, 7704–11

Exports, imports, and balances of US, by selected country, country group, and commodity group, preliminary data, monthly rpt, 2042–34

Exports, imports, and balances of US with major trading partners, by product category, 1986-90, annual chartbook, 9884–21

Exports, imports, and trade flows, by country and commodity, with background economic indicators, data compilation, monthly CD-ROM, 2002–6

Exports, imports, supply, consumption, prices, spending, and indexes, by food commodity, 1989, annual rpt, 1544–4

Exports of agricultural products and nonelectrical machinery, *Survey of Current Business*, monthly rpt, 2702–1.2

Exports of grains, oilseed products, hides, skins, and cotton, by country, weekly rpt, 1922–3

Exports of US, detailed commodities by country, monthly CD-ROM, 2422–13

Exports of US, detailed Schedule B commodities with countries of destination, 1990, annual rpt, 2424–10

Farmers views on Federal agricultural support, trade, and fiscal policies, by region and State, 1989 survey, hearings, 21168–43

Farmline, agricultural situation and related topics, monthly rpt, 1502–6

FDA activities, funding, facilities, and staff, findings and recommendations, 1980s-91, 4008–115

FDA detention of imports, by reason, product, shipper, brand, and country, monthly listing, 4062–2

Foreign and US agricultural production, prices, trade, and use, periodic rpt with articles, 1522–3

Foreign and US agricultural supply and demand indicators, by selected crop, monthly rpt, 1522–5

Foreign and US fresh and processed fruit, vegetable, and nut production and trade, FAS monthly circular with articles, 1925–34

Foreign countries agricultural and trade policy impacts on US exports, with data by commodity and country, 1989, annual rpt, 1924–8

Foreign countries agricultural production, consumption, and policies, and US export dev and promotion, monthly journal, 1922–2

Foreign countries agricultural production, prices, and trade, by country, 1980-90 and forecast 1991, annual world area rpt series, 1524–4

Foreign countries agricultural production, trade, and policies, summary data by country, 1989-90, annual factbook, 1924–12

High-value agricultural exports, indexes and sales value by commodity, world area, and country, 1960s-86, 1528–323

Immigration restrictions effects on US agricultural labor costs and trade competitiveness, 1980s, 1598–276

Imports, exports, and employment impacts, by SIC 2- to 4-digit industry and commodity, quarterly rpt, 2322–2

Imports injury to price-supported US agricultural industry, investigations with background financial and operating data, series, 9886–10

Imports of US, detailed commodities by country, monthly CD-ROM, 2422–14

Imports of US given duty-free treatment for value of US material sent abroad, by commodity and country, 1989, annual rpt, 9884–14

Intl transactions summary, 1980s-90, annual article, 9362–1.202

Iraq agricultural imports under CCC export credit guarantee programs, FY81-90, GAO rpt, 26123–314

Japan economic conditions, financial and intl policies, and trade devs, 1950s-80s and projected to 2050, compilation of papers, 23848–220

Market research and promotion for agricultural exports, USDA activities, with background data, 1991 GAO rpt, 26113–504

Marketing and financial conditions of farms, forecast 1991, annual conf, 1004–16

Mexico agricultural trade with US by commodity, and trade restrictions, 1980s, GAO rpt, 26123–335

Mexico imports from US, by industry and State, 1987-90, 2048–154

Middle East export controls of US, with trade, dual-use commodity licenses, and arms sales, by country, 1980s-90, GAO rpt, 26123–339

North Central States farm credit conditions and economic devs, Fed Reserve 7th District, monthly rpt, 9375–10

OECD intl trade position for US and 4 countries, and factors affecting US competition, periodic pamphlet, 2042–25

OECD trade, total and for 4 major countries, and US trade by country, by commodity, 1970-89, world area rpt series, 9116–1

Panama Canal traffic and tolls, by commodity, flag of vessel, and trade route, FY90, annual rpt, 9664–3.1

Price indexes for exports and imports, by selected end-use category, monthly press release, 6762–15

Price indexes for exports and imports of goods and services, and dollar exchange rate indexes, quarterly press release, 6762–13

Price support program changes and other effects on farm income and production, for livestock and program and nonprogram crop producers, model results, 1988, 1548–375

Processed food production and stocks by State, shipments, exports, ingredients, and use, periodic Current Industrial Rpt series, 2506–4

Quarantined fruits and vegetable imports, by crop, country, and port of entry, FY88, annual rpt, 1524–7

Soviet Union agricultural conditions and factors affecting US grain exports and CCC credit guarantees, 1990 hearings, 21168–49

Soviet Union agricultural trade, by commodity and country, 1955-90, 1528–322

Statistical Abstract of US, 1991 annual data compilation, 2324–1.23

Tariff Schedule of US, classifications and rates of duty by detailed imported commodity, 1992 base edition, 9886–13

West Central States economic indicators, Fed Reserve 10th District, quarterly rpt, 9381–16.2

see also Public Law 480

see also under names of specific commodities or commodity groups (listed under Agricultural commodities)

Agricultural extension work

Agricultural extension work

Expenditures for research and education, USDA appropriations by program and subagency, FY82-90, annual rpt, 1004–19

Expenditures of Fed Govt in States, by type, program, agency, and State, FY90, annual rpt, 2464–2

Foreign countries agricultural research grants of USDA, by program, subagency, and country, FY90, annual listing, 1954–3

Pest control integrated mgmt programs for vegetables, acreage, costs, savings, and funding sources and recipients, by State, 1980s, 1568–298

Agricultural finance

Agricultural Economics Research, quarterly journal, 1502–3

Agricultural Statistics, 1990, annual rpt, 1004–1

Assets and debts of private sector, balance sheets by segment, 1945-90, semiannual rpt, 9365–4.1

Capital gains preferential tax treatment impacts on agricultural finances and operations, 1991 article, 1561–16.202

Census of Agriculture, 1987: farms, farmland, production, finances, and operator characteristics, by county, final State rpt series, 2331–1

Census of Agriculture, 1987: horticultural specialties producers, finances, and operations, by crop and State, 1988 survey, 2337–1

Conservation programs under Food Security Act, farm finances and environmental benefits of alternative policies, projected 1991-2005, 1588–153

Dairy farms financial statement, by size and region, 1985-89, annual article, 1561–2.201

Dairy industry biotechnology devs, and bST impacts on farm finances and Federal support programs, 1980s and projected to 1998, 26358–237

Data on agriculture, compilation, 1990 and trends from 1920, annual rpt, 1004–14

Economic Indicators of the Farm Sector, balance sheets, and receipts by detailed commodity, by State, 1985-89, annual rpt, 1544–18

Economic Indicators of the Farm Sector, income, expenses, receipts by commodity, assets, and liabilities, 1990 and trends from 1945, annual rpt, 1544–16

Expenditures for farm inputs and living items, and prices received for major products, by commodity and State, monthly rpt, 1629–1

Finances of farms, debts, assets, and receipts, and lenders financial condition, quarterly rpt with articles, 1541–1

Financial and marketing conditions of farms, forecast 1991, annual chartbook, 1504–8

Financial and marketing conditions of farms, forecast 1991, annual conf, 1004–16

Financial condition of farm sector, and prices, supply, and demand by commodity, 1988-90 and forecast 1991, annual article, 9381–1.203

Financial condition of farms, by commodity, 1987, series, 1566–8

Financial condition of farms, 1920s-90, annual rpt, 204–1.8

Financial stress indicators for farms, operator quits, and loan problems and mediation, 1970s-90, 1598–272

Flow-of-funds accounts, savings, investments, and credit statements, quarterly rpt, 9365–3.3

Foreign direct investment in US, major transactions by type, industry, country, and US location, 1989, annual rpt, 2044–20

Multinatl US firms and foreign affiliates finances and operations, by industry and world area of parent firm, 1989 benchmark survey, preliminary annual rpt, 2704–5

North Central States farm credit conditions and economic devs, Fed Reserve 7th District, monthly rpt, 9375–10

North Central States farm credit conditions, earnings, and expenses, Fed Reserve 9th District, quarterly rpt, 9383–11

SEC registration, firms required to file annual rpts, as of Sept 1990, annual listing, 9734–5

State and Metro Area Data Book, 1991 data compilation, 2328–54

Statistical Abstract of US, 1991 annual data compilation, 2324–1.23

Tax (income) returns filed by type of filer, selected income items, quarterly rpt, 8302–2.1

Tax (income) returns for foreign corporate activity in US, assets, and income statement items, by industry div and selected country, 1986-87, article, 8302–2.205

Tax (income) returns of corporations, income and tax items by asset size and detailed industry, 1987, annual rpt, 8304–4

Tax (income) returns of corporations, income and tax items by asset size and detailed industry, 1988, annual rpt, 8304–21

Tax (income) returns of corporations with foreign tax credit, income and tax items by industry group, 1986, biennial article, 8302–2.203

Tax (income) returns of multinatl US firms foreign affiliates, income statement items, by asset size and industry, 1986, biennial article, 8302–2.212

Tax (income) returns of partnerships, income statement and balance sheet items, by industry group, 1989, annual article, 8302–2.216; 8304–18

Tax (income) returns of US corporations under foreign control, assets and income statement items by industry div and country, 1988, article, 8302–2.219

Tax returns filed, by type of tax and IRS region and service center, projected 1990-97 and trends from 1978, annual rpt, 8304–9

West Central States economic indicators, Fed Reserve 10th District, quarterly rpt, 9381–16.2

see also Agricultural credit
see also Agricultural insurance
see also Agricultural prices
see also Agricultural production costs
see also Agricultural production quotas and price supports
see also Agricultural subsidies

Index by Subjects and Names

see also Farm Credit System
see also Farm income
see also Rural cooperatives

Agricultural forecasts

Agricultural Economics Research, quarterly journal, 1502–3

Agricultural Outlook, production, prices, marketing, and trade, by commodity, forecast and current situation, monthly rpt with articles, 1502–4

Carbon dioxide in atmosphere, measurement, methodology, and research results, series, 3006–11

Carbon dioxide in atmosphere, North Central States economic and agricultural impacts, model descriptions and results, 1980s and projected to 2030, 3006–11.15

Coffee production, trade and quotas, and use, by country, with US and intl prices, FAS periodic circular, 1925–5

Conservation programs under Food Security Act, farm finances and environmental benefits of alternative policies, projected 1991-2005, 1588–153

Corn season average price forecasts using futures settlement prices, 1986-92, article, 1561–4.201

Cotton export forecasts using season shipment data, 1990/91, article, 1561–1.204

Cotton production, trade, and use, for selected countries, FAS monthly circular, 1925–4.2

Dairy industry biotechnology devs, and bST impacts on farm finances and Federal support programs, 1980s and projected to 1998, 26358–237

Dairy production, trade, use, and prices, for US and selected countries, forecast 1992 and trends from 1987, FAS semiannual circular, 1925–10

Developing countries food supply, needs, and aid, status and alternative forecasts, world area rpt series, 1526–8

Developing countries grains production and needs, and related economic outlook, by world area and selected country, forecast 1990/91-1991/92, 1528–313

Exports and imports (agricultural) commodity and country, prices, and world market devs, monthly rpt, 1922–12

Exports and imports (agricultural) of US, outlook and current situation, quarterly rpt, 1542–4

Fertilizer production capacity by firm, for US and Canada, 1986-91 and projected to 1997, triennial rpt, 9808–66

Financial and marketing conditions of farms, forecast 1991, annual chartbook, 1504–8

Fish and shellfish catch and stocks in northwest Atlantic, by species and location, 1887-1991 and forecast to 1993, semiannual conf, 2162–9

Foreign and US agricultural supply and demand indicators, by selected crop, monthly rpt, 1522–5

Foreign countries agricultural production, prices, and trade, by country, 1980-90 and forecast 1991, annual world area rpt series, 1524–4

Grain production, supply, trade, and use, by country and world region, forecasts and trends, FAS monthly circular, 1925–2.1

Lumber and pulp products supply and use, and timber resources, detailed data, prices, 1950s-87 and alternative projections to 2040, 1208–24.20

Index by Subjects and Names

Agricultural machinery and equipment

Marketing and financial conditions of farms, forecast 1991, annual conf, 1004–16

Molasses (feed) production forecasts, weekly rpt, supplement, 1311–16

Pesticide and fertilizer use reduction, environmental and economic impacts by commodity and region, alternative forecasts 1989-94, hearing, 23848–222

Production, acreage, and yield for selected crops, forecasts by selected world region and country, FAS monthly circular, 1925–28

Production inputs, finances, mgmt, and land value and transfers, periodic situation rpt with articles, 1561–16

Timber acreage, by ownership, forest type, and State, 1950s-87 and projected to 2040, 1208–357

Timber in Alaska, production, trade, and Pacific basin market demand, 1960s-2010, 1208–365; 1208–367

Wheat production and trade, by country, 1989-92, article, 1502–4.202

Agricultural income

see Farm income

Agricultural industries

see Agricultural finance

see Agricultural labor

see Agricultural marketing

see Agricultural production

see Agricultural services

see Agricultural wages

see Agriculture

see Dairy industry and products

see Farms and farmland

see Flowers and nursery products

see Food and food industry

see Fruit and fruit products

see Grains and grain products

see Honey and beekeeping

see Livestock and livestock industry

see Meat and meat products

see Poultry industry and products

see Rural cooperatives

see Sugar industry and products

see Tobacco industry and products

see Vegetables and vegetable products

see Veterinary medicine

Agricultural insurance

Agricultural Statistics, 1990, annual rpt, 1004–1

Budget of US, obligations and authority by function, agency, and program, with summaries, analyses, and historical tables, FY92, annual rpt, 104–2

Costs of production, itemized by farm sales size and region, 1990, annual rpt, 1614–3

Economic Indicators of the Farm Sector, balance sheets, and receipts by detailed commodity, by State, 1985-89, annual rpt, 1544–18

Expenditures of Fed Govt in States, by type, program, agency, and State, FY90, annual rpt, 2464–2

Farmers views on Federal agricultural support, trade, and fiscal policies, by region and State, 1989 survey, hearings, 21168–43

Agricultural labor

Agricultural Statistics, 1990, annual rpt, 1004–1

Alien workers legal residence applications, by crop and country of origin, periodic rpt, 6262–3

Census of Agriculture, 1987: horticultural specialties producers, finances, and operations, by crop and State, 1988 survey, 2337–1

Corn farms, finances, acreage, and production, by size, region, and State, 1987, 1568–304

County Business Patterns, 1988: employment, establishments, and payroll, by SIC 2- to 4-digit industry and county, annual State rpt series, 2326–6

County Business Patterns, 1989: employment, establishments, and payroll, by SIC 2- to 4-digit industry and county, annual State rpt series, 2326–8

Data on agriculture, compilation, 1990 and trends from 1920, annual rpt, 1004–14

Economic and employment conditions, alternative BLS projections to 2005 and trends 1970s-90, biennial article, 6722–1.253

Economic indicators and components, current data and annual trends, monthly rpt, 23842–1.2

Economic Indicators of the Farm Sector, itemized production costs, receipts, and returns, by commodity and region, 1987-89, annual rpt, 1544–20

Economic Indicators of the Farm Sector, production inputs, output, and productivity, by commodity and region, 1947-89, annual rpt, 1544–17

Educational attainment, by sociodemographic characteristics and location, 1989 and trends from 1940, biennial Current Population Rpt, 2546–1.452

Employment and Earnings, detailed data, monthly rpt, 6742–2

Employment and labor productivity, 1947-89 annual rpt, 204–1.8

Employment, earnings, and days worked, for farm workers by selected characteristics and region, biennial rpt, discontinued, 1594–2

Employment, earnings, and hours, monthly press release, 6742–5

Employment on farms, wages, and hours, by payment method, worker type, region, and State, 1910-90, 1618–21

Employment on farms, wages, hours, and perquisites, by State, monthly rpt, 1631–1

Employment related to agriculture, by industry, region, and metro-nonmetro location, 1987, 1598–271

Employment situation, earnings, hours, and other BLS economic indicators, transcripts of BLS Commissioner's monthly testimony, periodic rpt, 23846–4

Employment, unemployment, and labor force characteristics, by region and State, 1990, annual rpt, 6744–7.1; 6744–7.2

Employment, wages, hours, and payroll costs, by major industry group and demographic characteristics, *Survey of Current Business,* monthly rpt, 2702–1.8

Farmline, agricultural situation and related topics, monthly rpt, 1502–6

Food stamp recipient household size, composition, income, and income and deductions allowed, summer 1988, annual rpt, 1364–8

Hispanic Americans social and economic characteristics, by detailed origin, 1991, Current Population Rpt, 2546–1.448; 2546–1.451

Immigrant and nonimmigrant visas of US issued and refused, by class, issuing office, and nationality, FY89, annual rpt, 7184–1

Immigrants admitted to US, by class of admission and for top 15 countries of birth, FY89-90, fact sheet, 6266–2.8

Immigrants admitted to US, by occupational group and country of birth, preliminary FY90, annual table, 6264–1

Immigration restrictions effects on US agricultural labor costs and trade competitiveness, 1980s, 1598–276

Industrial uses of new and traditional agricultural crops, replacement of imports and nonrenewable resources, R&D funding, and economic impacts, 1970s-90, 26358–239

Labor laws enacted, by State, 1990, annual article, 6722–1.209

Manufacturing employment, by detailed occupation and SIC 2-digit industry, 1989 survey, triennial rpt, 6748–52

Minimum wage rates, 1938-91, annual rpt, 4744–3.1

Moonlighting employment, by reason, and characteristics of workers and primary and secondary jobs, 1991, press release, 6726–1.40

Soviet Union, Eastern Europe, OECD, and selected other countries economic conditions, 1960s-90, annual rpt, 9114–4.2

Statistical Abstract of US, 1991 annual data compilation, 2324–1.23

Temporary help supply establishments by occupation supplied, receipts by source, and payroll, by MSA, 1987 Census of Service Industries, 2393–4.8

Unemployment insurance laws of States, comparison of provisions, 1991, base edition with semiannual revisions, 6402–2

Voting and registration, by socioeconomic and demographic characteristics, 1990 congressional election, biennial Current Population Rpt, 2546–1.454

Youth labor force status, by sex, race, and industry div, summer 1987-91, annual press release, 6744–14

see also Agricultural accidents and safety

see also Agricultural wages

see also Farm operators

see also Migrant workers

see also under By Occupation in the "Index by Categories"

Agricultural land

see Farms and farmland

Agricultural machinery and equipment

Accidents (fatal), deaths, and rates, by circumstances, characteristics of persons and vehicles involved, and location, 1989, annual rpt, 7764–10

Agricultural Outlook, production, prices, marketing, and trade, by commodity, forecast and current situation, monthly rpt with articles, 1502–4

Agriculture census, 1987: farms, farmland, production, finances, and operator characteristics, by county, final State rpt series, 2331–1

County Business Patterns, 1988: employment, establishments, and payroll, by SIC 2- to 4-digit industry and county, annual State rpt series, 2326–6

Agricultural machinery and equipment

County Business Patterns, 1989: employment, establishments, and payroll, by SIC 2- to 4-digit industry and county, annual State rpt series, 2326–8

DOD prime contract awards, by detailed procurement category, FY87-90, annual rpt, 3544–18

Drivers licenses issued and in force by age and sex, fees, and renewal, by license class and State, 1989, annual rpt, 7554–16

Employment, earnings, and hours, by SIC 1- to 4-digit industry, monthly and annual averages, selected years 1909-90, annual rpt, 6744–4

Employment related to agriculture, by industry, region, and metro-nonmetro location, 1987, 1598–271

Enterprise Statistics, 1987: finances and operations for companies, by size, level of diversification, form of organization, and industry group, 2329–8

Exports and imports (agricultural) of US, by commodity and country, bimonthly rpt, 1522–1

Exports and imports (agricultural) of US, by detailed commodity and country, 1989, annual rpt, 1524–8

Exports and imports (agricultural) of US, by detailed commodity and country, 1990, semiannual rpt, 1522–4

Exports and imports of US, by country and detailed commodity, monthly rpt, 2422–12

Exports and imports of US, by Harmonized System 6-digit commodity and country, 1990, annual rpt, 2424–13

Exports and imports of US, by transport mode, country, and SITC 1- to 3-digit commodity, 1990, annual rpt, 2424–12

Exports of US, detailed Schedule B commodities with countries of destination, 1990, annual rpt, 2424–10

Farm credit, terms, delinquency, agricultural bank failures, and credit conditions by Fed Reserve District, quarterly rpt, 9365–3.10

Farm income, expenses, receipts by commodity, assets, liabilities, and ratios, 1990 and trends from 1945, annual rpt, 1544–16

Farm production inputs, finances, mgmt, and land value and transfers, periodic situation rpt with articles, 1561–16

Farm production inputs, output, and productivity, by commodity and region, 1947-89, annual rpt, 1544–17

Farm production itemized costs, by farm sales size and region, 1990, annual rpt, 1614–3

Farm sector balance sheet, and marketing receipts by detailed commodity, by State, 1985-89, annual rpt, 1544–18

Grain storage facility and equipment loans to farmers under CCC program, by State, FY68-91, annual table, 1804–14

Grain storage facility and equipment loans to farmers under CCC program, by State, monthly table, 1802–9

Horticultural specialties census, 1988: producers, finances, and operations, by crop and State, 1987 Census of Agriculture, 2337–1

Injuries from use of consumer products, by severity, victim age, and detailed product, 1990, annual rpt, 9164–6

Input-output structure of US economy, detailed interindustry transactions for 84 industries, and components of final demand, 1986, annual article, 2702–1.206

Input-output structure of US economy, detailed interindustry transactions for 85 industries, 1982 benchmark data, 2702–1.213

Labor productivity, indexes of output, hours, and employment by SIC 2- to 4-digit industry, 1967-89, annual rpt, 6824–1.3

Manufacturing annual survey, 1989: finances and operations, by SIC 2- to 4-digit industry, series, 2506–15

Manufacturing census, 1987: finances and operations, by SIC 2- to 4-digit industry, State, and MSA, with trends from 1849, 2497–1

Manufacturing census, 1987: finances and operations, by type of organization and SIC 2- to 4-digit industry, subject rpt, 2497–5

Manufacturing finances and operations, by SIC 2- to 4-digit industry, forecast 1991, annual rpt, 2044–28

Multinatl US firms and foreign affiliates finances and operations, by industry and world area of parent firm, 1989 benchmark survey, preliminary annual rpt, 2704–5

North Central States farm credit conditions and economic devs, Fed Reserve 7th District, monthly rpt, 9375–10

Occupational injury and illness rates, by SIC 2- to 4-digit industry, 1988-89, annual rpt, 6844–7

Occupational injury and illness rates, by SIC 2- to 4-digit industry, 1989, annual rpt, 6844–1

OECD trade, total and for 4 major countries, and US trade by country, by commodity, 1970-89, world area rpt series, 9116–1

Pollution (air) levels for 6 pollutants, by source, 1970-89 and trends from 1940, annual rpt, 9194–13

Price indexes (producer), by stage of processing and detailed commodity, monthly rpt, 6762–6

Price indexes (producer), by stage of processing and detailed commodity, monthly 1990, annual rpt, 6764–2

Prices received and paid by farmers, by commodity and State, 1990, annual rpt, 1629–5

Prices received by farmers for major products, and paid for farm inputs and living items, by State, monthly rpt, 1629–1

Productivity measures for farm and garden equipment industry, 1958-88, article, 6722–1.232

Productivity of labor and capital, and indexes of output, hours, and employment, 1967-89, annual rpt, 6824–1.5

Puerto Rico economic censuses, 1987: wholesale and retail trade and service industry finances and operations, by SIC 2- to 4-digit industry and municipio, 2591–1

Shipments, trade, use, and firms, for farm and garden equipment by product, 1990, annual Current Industrial Rpt, 2506–12.1

Index by Subjects and Names

Soviet Union agricultural reform issues, with background data for USSR and US, 1970s-90, article, 9381–1.210

Statistical Abstract of US, 1991 annual data compilation, 2324–1.23

Tax (income) returns of corporations, income and tax items by asset size and detailed industry, 1987, annual rpt, 8304–4

Tax (income) returns of corporations, income and tax items by asset size and detailed industry, 1988, annual rpt, 8304–21

Wholesale trade census, 1987: establishments, sales by customer class, employment, inventories, and expenses, by SIC 2- to 4-digit kind of business, 2407–4

see also Lawn and garden equipment

Agricultural marketing

Agricultural Outlook, production, prices, marketing, and trade, by commodity, forecast and current situation, monthly rpt with articles, 1502–4

Agricultural Statistics, 1990, annual rpt, 1004–1

Australia agricultural input and output indexes, and freight rates, 1950s-80s, 1528–311

Census of Agriculture, 1987: horticultural specialties producers, finances, and operations, by crop and State, 1988 survey, 2337–1

Consumer research, food marketing, legislation, and regulation devs, and consumption and price trends, quarterly journal, 1541–7

Costs of food marketing by component, farm-retail food prices, and industry finances and productivity, 1920s-90, annual rpt, 1544–9

Costs of production, itemized by farm sales size and region, 1990, annual rpt, 1614–3

County Business Patterns, 1988: employment, establishments, and payroll, by SIC 2- to 4-digit industry and county, annual State rpt series, 2326–6

County Business Patterns, 1989: employment, establishments, and payroll, by SIC 2- to 4-digit industry and county, annual State rpt series, 2326–8

Data on agriculture, compilation, 1990 and trends from 1920, annual rpt, 1004–14

DOD prime contract awards, by detailed procurement category, FY87-90, annual rpt, 3544–18

Economic indicators and components, current data and annual trends, monthly rpt, 23842–1.1

Economic Indicators of the Farm Sector, balance sheets, and receipts by detailed commodity, by State, 1985-89, annual rpt, 1544–18

Economic Indicators of the Farm Sector, income, expenses, receipts by commodity, assets, and liabilities, 1990 and trends from 1945, annual rpt, 1544–16

Economic Indicators of the Farm Sector, itemized production costs, receipts, and returns, by commodity and region, 1987-89, annual rpt, 1544–20

Employment, earnings, and hours, by SIC 1- to 4-digit industry, monthly and annual averages, selected years 1909-90, annual rpt, 6744–4

Index by Subjects and Names

Agricultural Marketing Service

Employment related to agriculture, by industry, region, and metro-nonmetro location, 1987, 1598–271

Enterprise Statistics, 1987: auxiliaries of multi-establishment firms, finances and operations by function, industry, and State, 2329–6

Enterprise Statistics, 1987: finances and operations for companies, by size, level of diversification, form of organization, and industry group, 2329–8

Fed Govt financial and nonfinancial domestic aid, 1991 base edition with supplements, annual listing, 104–5

Food stamp use at farmers markets, costs and participation, demonstration project results for 14 States, 1989, hearing, 21168–46

Foreign countries agricultural research grants of USDA, by program, subagency, and country, FY90, annual listing, 1954–3

Great Lakes area economic conditions and outlook, for US and Canada, 1970s-90, 9375–15

Input-output structure of US economy, detailed interindustry transactions for 84 industries, and components of final demand, 1986, annual article, 2702–1.206

Input-output structure of US economy, detailed interindustry transactions for 85 industries, 1982 benchmark data, 2702–1.213

Marketing and financial conditions of farms, forecast 1991, annual chartbook, 1504–8

Marketing and financial conditions of farms, forecast 1991, annual conf, 1004–16

Occupational injury and illness rates, by SIC 2- to 4-digit industry, 1988-89, annual rpt, 6844–7

Occupational injury and illness rates, by SIC 2- to 4-digit industry, 1989, annual rpt, 6844–1

Puerto Rico economic censuses, 1987: wholesale and retail trade and service industry finances and operations, by SIC 2- to 4-digit industry and municipio, 2591–1

Puerto Rico economic censuses, 1987: wholesale, retail, and service industries finances and operations, by establishment characteristics and SIC 2- and 3-digit industry, subject rpts, 2591–2

Research (agricultural) funding and staffing for USDA, State agencies, and other instns, by topic, FY90, annual rpt, 1744–2

Research and education grants, USDA competitive awards by program and recipient, FY90, annual listing, 1764–1

State and Metro Area Data Book, 1991 data compilation, 2328–54

Tax (income) returns of corporations, income and tax items by asset size and detailed industry, 1987, annual rpt, 8304–4

Tax (income) returns of corporations, income and tax items by asset size and detailed industry, 1988, annual rpt, 8304–21

Transportation census, 1987: finances and operations by size, ownership, and State, and revenues by MSA, by SIC 2- to 4-digit industry, 2579–1

Truck and warehouse services finances and inventory, by SIC 2- to 4-digit industry, 1989 survey, annual rpt, 2413–14

Truck rates for fruit and vegetables weekly by growing area and market, and shipments monthly by State and country of origin, 1990, annual rpt, 1311–15

Vertically integrated markets, and farm products produced under contract, 1960s-90, article, 9381–1.205

Wholesale trade census, 1987: depreciable assets, capital and operating expenses, sales, value added, and inventories, by SIC 2- to 3-digit kind of business, 2407–2

Wholesale trade census, 1987: establishments, sales by customer class, employment, inventories, and expenses, by SIC 2- to 4-digit kind of business, 2407–4

Wholesale trade sales and inventories, by SIC 2- to 3-digit kind of business, monthly rpt, 2413–7

Wholesale trade sales, inventories, purchases, and gross margins, by SIC 2- to 3-digit kind of business, 1990, annual rpt, 2413–13

see also Agricultural exports and imports

see also Agricultural prices

see also Agricultural production quotas and price supports

see also Agricultural stocks

see also Agricultural surpluses

see also Food inspection

see also Food prices

see also Food stores

see also Rural cooperatives

see also under names of specific commodities or commodity groups (listed under Agricultural commodities)

Agricultural Marketing Service

Activities, funding, and staff of Federal food safety and quality regulation agencies, 1980s, GAO rpt, 26113–503

Apple production, marketing, and prices, for Appalachia and compared to other States, 1988-91, annual rpt, 1311–13

Bean (dried) prices by State, market activity, and foreign and US production, use, stocks, and trade, weekly rpt, 1311–17

Bean (dried) production and prices by State, exports and foreign production by country, and USDA food aid purchases, by bean type, 1984-90, annual rpt, 1311–18

Budget of US, obligations and authority by function, agency, and program, with summaries, analyses, and historical tables, FY92, annual rpt, 104–2

Cotton (long staple) production, prices, exports, stocks, and mill use, monthly rpt, 1309–12

Cotton acreage planted by State and county, and fiber quality, by variety, 1991, annual rpt, 1309–6

Cotton fiber and processing test results, by variety, region, State, and production area, 1990, annual rpt, 1309–16

Cotton fiber grade, staple, and mike, for upland and American pima cotton by State, monthly rpt, 1309–11

Cotton fiber grade, staple, mike, and other quality indicators, for upland cotton by classing office, weekly rpt, 1309–15

Cotton linters production, stocks, use, and prices, monthly rpt, 1309–10

Cotton prices at selected spot markets, NYC futures prices, and CCC loan rates, 1990/91 and trends from 1943, annual rpt, 1309–2

Cotton prices in 8 spot markets, futures prices at NYC exchange, farm prices, and CCC loan stocks, monthly rpt, 1309–1

Cotton quality, by State, 1990, annual rpt, 1309–7

Cotton quality, supply, and carryover, 1989-90, annual rpt, 1309–8

Cottonseed prices and quality, by State, seasonal weekly rpt, 1309–14

Cottonseed quality factors, by State, 1990 crop, annual rpt, 1309–5

Dairy prices, by product and selected area, with related marketing data, 1990, annual rpt, 1317–1

Expenditures of Fed Govt in States, by type, program, agency, and State, FY90, annual rpt, 2464–2

Food aid programs purchases, by commodity, firm, and shipping point or destination, weekly rpt, 1302–3

Fruit and vegetable shipments, and arrivals in US and Canada cities, by mode of transport and State and country of origin, 1990, annual rpt series, 1311–4

Fruit and vegetable shipments by mode of transport, arrivals, and imports, by commodity and State and country of origin, weekly rpt, 1311–3

Fruit and vegetable wholesale prices in NYC by State, and shipments and arrivals by mode of transport, by commodity, weekly rpt, 1311–20

Fruit and vegetable wholesale prices in NYC, Chicago, and selected shipping points, by crop, 1990, annual rpt, 1311–8

Grain production, prices, trade, and export inspections by US port and country of destination, by grain type, weekly rpt, 1313–2

Grain stocks by region and market city, and grain inspected for export, by type, weekly rpt, 1313–4

Hay (alfalfa and prairie) prices, for selected areas, weekly rpt, 1313–5

Honey production, prices, trade, stocks, marketing, and CCC honey loan and distribution activities, monthly rpt, 1311–2

Hops production, stocks, use, and US trade by country, monthly rpt, 1313–7

Livestock, meat, and wool, market news summary data by animal type and market, weekly rpt, 1315–1

Milk order market prices and detailed operations, by State and market area, 1989-90, annual rpt, 1317–3

Milk order market prices and detailed operations, monthly rpt with articles, 1317–4

Milk order market sales, by container size and type, outlet type, and market area, 1989, biennial rpt, 1317–6

Molasses (feed) wholesale prices by market area, and trade, weekly rpt, 1311–16

Molasses supply, use, wholesale prices by market, and imports by country, 1985-90, annual rpt, 1311–19

Peaches production, marketing, and prices in 3 southeastern States and Appalachia, 1990, annual rpt, 1311–12

Agricultural Marketing Service

Peanut production and US exports by country, prices, and stocks, weekly rpt, 1311–1

Peanut production, prices, stocks, exports, use, inspection, and quality, by region and State, 1980-90, annual rpt, 1311–5

Poultry and egg prices and marketing, by selected region, State, and city, monthly and weekly 1990, annual rpt, 1317–2

Rice market activities, prices, inspections, sales, trade, supply, and use, for US and selected foreign markets, weekly rpt, 1313–8

Tobacco leaf stocks, production, sales, and import inspections by country, by product, quarterly rpt, 1319–3

Tobacco marketing activity, prices, and sales, by grade, type, market, and State, 1989-90, annual rpt series, 1319–5

Tobacco production, prices, stocks, taxes by State, and trade and production by country, 1990, annual rpt, 1319–1

Truck rates for fruit and vegetables weekly by growing area and market, and shipments monthly by State and country of origin, 1990, annual rpt, 1311–15

Wheat (durum) acreage, production, prices, stocks, use, and US and Canada exports by country, quarterly rpt, suspended, 1313–6

Wool prices, sales, trade, and stocks, and sheep inventory, weekly and biweekly rpt, 1315–2

Agricultural pests

see Pesticides

see Pests and pest control

Agricultural policy

Agricultural Economics Research, quarterly journal, 1502–3

Agricultural Outlook, production, prices, marketing, and trade, by commodity, forecast and current situation, monthly rpt with articles, 1502–4

Court criminal case processing in Federal district courts, and dispositions, by offense, 1980-89, annual rpt, 6064–31

Farm financial and marketing conditions, forecast 1991, annual conf, 1004–16

Fed Govt farm subsidy rates under 1985 and 1990 farm bills, by selected program and commodity, 1990 rpt, 1008–54

Fed Govt policy issues and effects on agricultural production, prices, income, and trade, and crop support levels by program, semiannual rpt, discontinued, 1542–6

Foreign countries agricultural and trade policy impacts on US exports, with data by commodity and country, 1989, annual rpt, 1924–8

Foreign countries agricultural production, consumption, and policies, and US export dev and promotion, monthly journal, 1922–2

Foreign countries agricultural production, trade, and policies, summary data by country, 1989-90, annual factbook, 1924–12

Price support program changes and other effects on farm income and production, for livestock and program and nonprogram crop producers, model results, 1988, 1548–375

see also Agricultural credit

see also Agricultural finance

see also Agricultural marketing

see also Agricultural prices

see also Agricultural production quotas and price supports

see also Agricultural subsidies

see also Food prices

see also Land reform

Agricultural prices

Agricultural Economics Research, quarterly journal, 1502–3

Agricultural Outlook, production, prices, marketing, and trade, by commodity, forecast and current situation, monthly rpt with articles, 1502–4

Agricultural Statistics, 1990, annual rpt, 1004–1

CCC commodities for sale, and prices, monthly press release, 1802–4

Central America agricultural export promotion of nontraditional crops, impacts on income export stability, late 1970s-80s, 1528–312

Data on agriculture, compilation, 1990 and trends from 1920, annual rpt, 1004–14

Developing countries agricultural supply, demand, and market for US exports, with socioeconomic conditions, country rpt series, 1526–6

Eastern Europe agricultural production, trade, and land reform, with selected economic indicators, by country, 1960s-90, article, 1522–3.202

Economic indicators and components, current data and annual trends, monthly rpt, 23842–1.4

Export and import price indexes, by selected end-use category, monthly press release, 6762–15

Farmline, agricultural situation and related topics, monthly rpt, 1502–6

Finances and operations of farm sector, 1970s-91, article, 9362–1.207

Financial and marketing conditions of farms, forecast 1991, annual conf, 1004–16

Financial condition of farm sector, and prices, supply, and demand by commodity, 1988-90 and forecast 1991, annual article, 9381–1.203

Financial condition of farms, 1920s-90, annual rpt, 204–1.8

Foreign and US agricultural prices and US import prices, for selected commodities, bimonthly rpt, 1522–1.3

Foreign and US agricultural production, prices, trade, and use, periodic rpt with articles, 1522–3

Foreign and US agricultural supply and demand indicators, by selected crop, monthly rpt, 1522–5

Foreign and US economic conditions, for major industrial countries, biweekly rpt, 9112–1

Foreign countries agricultural production, prices, and trade, by country, 1980-90 and forecast 1991, annual world area rpt series, 1524–4

Imports injury to price-supported US agricultural industry, investigations with background financial and operating data, series, 9886–10

Monetary policy impact on farm prices, alternative model results, 1976-90, article, 9391–1.217

Index by Subjects and Names

North Central States farm credit conditions and economic devs, Fed Reserve 7th District, monthly rpt, 9375–10

Prices (farm-retail) for food, marketing cost components, and industry finances and productivity, 1920s-90, annual rpt, 1544–9

Prices received and paid by farmers, by commodity and State, 1990, annual rpt, 1629–5

Prices received by farmers and production value, by detailed crop and State, 1988-90, annual rpt, 1621–2

Prices received by farmers for major products, and paid for farm inputs and living items, by State, monthly rpt, 1629–1

Producer Price Index, by major commodity group and subgroup, and processing stage, monthly press release, 6762–5

Producer price indexes, by stage of processing and detailed commodity, monthly rpt, 6762–6

Producer price indexes, by stage of processing and detailed commodity, monthly 1990, annual rpt, 6764–2

Southeastern States, Fed Reserve 8th District banking and economic conditions, quarterly rpt with articles, 9391–16

Soviet Union, Eastern Europe, OECD, and selected other countries economic conditions, 1960s-90, annual rpt, 9114–4.2

Statistical Abstract of US, 1991 annual data compilation, 2324–1.23

Survey of Current Business, detailed data for major industries and economic indicators, monthly rpt, 2702–1.5

West Central States economic indicators, Fed Reserve 10th District, quarterly rpt, 9381–16.2

West Central States farm real estate values, farm loan trends, and regional farm price index, Fed Reserve 10th District, quarterly rpt, 9381–16.1

see also Agricultural production quotas and price supports

see also Food prices

see also under names of specific commodities or commodity groups (listed under Agricultural commodities)

Agricultural production

Acreage planted and harvested, by crop and State, 1989-90 and planned as of June 1991, annual rpt, 1621–23

Aerial survey R&D rpts, and sources of natural resource and environmental data, quarterly listing, 9502–7

Agricultural Economics Research, quarterly journal, 1502–3

Agricultural Outlook, production, prices, marketing, and trade, by commodity, forecast and current situation, monthly rpt with articles, 1502–4

Agricultural Stabilization and Conservation Service programs, annual commodity fact sheet series, 1806–4

Agricultural Statistics, 1990, annual rpt, 1004–1

Business statistics, detailed data for major industries and economic indicators, *Survey of Current Business*, monthly rpt, 2702–1.14

Census of Agriculture, 1987: farms, farmland, production, finances, and operator characteristics, by county, final State rpt series, 2331–1

Index by Subjects and Names

Agricultural production quotas and price supports

Conservation Reserve Program acreage, plantings, and impacts on farm production, soil erosion, water quality, and wildlife habitat, 1991 conf, 1208–360

Data on agriculture, compilation, 1990 and trends from 1920, annual rpt, 1004–14

Farmline, agricultural situation and related topics, monthly rpt, 1502–6

Finances and operations of farm sector, 1970s-91, article, 9362–1.207

Financial and marketing conditions of farms, forecast 1991, annual chartbook, 1504–8

Global climate change environmental, infrastructure, and health impacts, with model results and background data, 1850s-2100, 9188–113

Imports injury to price-supported US agricultural industry, investigations with background financial and operating data, series, 9886–10

Income (personal) per capita disparity among States, with data by industrial base, 1979, 1989, and projected to 1995, 1548–379

Input-output structure of US economy, detailed interindustry transactions for 84 industries, and components of final demand, 1986, annual article, 2702–1.206

Input-output structure of US economy, detailed interindustry transactions for 85 industries, 1982 benchmark data, 2702–1.213

Irrigation projects of Reclamation Bur in western US, crop production and acreage by commodity, State, and project, 1989, annual rpt, 5824–12

Natl income and product accounts and components, *Survey of Current Business*, monthly rpt, 2702–1.24

Occupational injury and illness rates, by SIC 2- to 4-digit industry, 1988-89, annual rpt, 6844–7

Occupational injury and illness rates, by SIC 2- to 4-digit industry, 1989, annual rpt, 6844–1

Palau admin, and social, economic, and govtl data, FY90, annual rpt, 7004–6

Pollution (air) emissions factors, by detailed pollutant and source, data compilation, 1990 rpt, 9198–120

Production, farms, acreage, and related data, by selected crop and State, monthly rpt, 1621–1

Production indicators for farms, 1947-90, annual rpt, 204–1.8

Production, prices, trade, and use, for foreign and US agriculture, periodic rpt with articles, 1522–3

State and Metro Area Data Book, 1991 data compilation, 2328–54

Statistical Abstract of US, 1991 annual data compilation, 2324–1.23

Weather conditions and effect on agriculture, by US region, State, and city, and world area, weekly rpt, 2182–7

Weather phenomena and storm characteristics, casualties, and property damage, by State, monthly listing, 2152–3

see also Agricultural forecasts

see also Agricultural production costs

see also Agricultural production quotas and price supports

---

see also Agricultural productivity

see also Agricultural stocks

see also Agricultural surpluses

see also Aquaculture

see also Fertilizers

see also Food supply

see also Foreign agriculture

see also under names of specific commodities or commodity groups (listed under Agricultural commodities)

Agricultural production costs

Agricultural Outlook, production, prices, marketing, and trade, by commodity, forecast and current situation, monthly rpt with articles, 1502–4

Business statistics, detailed data for major industries and economic indicators, *Survey of Current Business*, monthly rpt, 2702–1.14

Census of Agriculture, 1987: farms, farmland, production, finances, and operator characteristics, by county, final State rpt series, 2331–1

Census of Agriculture, 1987: horticultural specialties producers, finances, and operations, by crop and State, 1988 survey, 2337–1

Costs of food marketing by component, farm-retail food prices, and industry finances and productivity, 1920s-90, annual rpt, 1544–9

Costs of production, itemized by farm sales size and region, 1990, annual rpt, 1614–3

Data on agriculture, compilation, 1990 and trends from 1920, annual rpt, 1004–14

Economic indicators and components, current data and annual trends, monthly rpt, 23842–1.1; 23842–1.4

Economic Indicators of the Farm Sector, balance sheets, and receipts by detailed commodity, by State, 1985-89, annual rpt, 1544–18

Economic Indicators of the Farm Sector, income, expenses, receipts by commodity, assets, and liabilities, 1990 and trends from 1945, annual rpt, 1544–16

Economic Indicators of the Farm Sector, itemized production costs, receipts, and returns, by commodity and region, 1987-89, annual rpt, 1544–20

Farmline, agricultural situation and related topics, monthly rpt, 1502–6

Fertilizer use and costs by type, and acreage harvested, by State, 1970s-90, biennial rpt, 9804–5

Finances of farms, debts, assets, and receipts, and lenders financial condition, quarterly rpt with articles, 1541–1

Finances of farms, production inputs, mgmt, and land value and transfers, periodic situation rpt with articles, 1561–16

Financial and marketing conditions of farms, forecast 1991, annual chartbook, 1504–8

Financial condition of farms, 1920s-90, annual rpt, 204–1.8

Imports injury to price-supported US agricultural industry, investigations with background financial and operating data, series, 9886–10

North Central States farm credit conditions, earnings, and expenses, Fed Reserve 9th District, quarterly rpt, 9383–11

Prices received and paid by farmers, by commodity and State, 1990, annual rpt, 1629–5

Prices received by farmers for major products, and paid for farm inputs and living items, by State, monthly rpt, 1629–1

State and Metro Area Data Book, 1991 data compilation, 2328–54

Tax (income) returns of corporations, income and tax items by asset size and detailed industry, 1987, annual rpt, 8304–4

Tax (income) returns of corporations, income and tax items by asset size and detailed industry, 1988, annual rpt, 8304–21

see also Agricultural marketing

see also under names of specific commodities or commodity groups (listed under Agricultural commodities)

Agricultural production quotas and price supports

Acreage reduction program compliance, enrollment, and yield on planted acreage, by commodity and State, annual press release series, 1004–20

Acreage under Agricultural Stabilization and Conservation Service programs, rankings by commodity and congressional district, 1989, biennial rpt, 1804–17

Agricultural Outlook, production, prices, marketing, and trade, by commodity, forecast and current situation, monthly rpt with articles, 1502–4

Agricultural Stabilization and Conservation Service producer payments and certificate value, by program, monthly rpt, 1802–10

Agricultural Stabilization and Conservation Service producer payments, by program and State, 1990, annual table, 1804–12

Agricultural Stabilization and Conservation Service programs, annual commodity fact sheet series, 1806–4

Agricultural Statistics, 1990, annual rpt, 1004–1

Budget of US, CBO analysis of revenue and spending alternatives and projections of economic indicators, FY92-96, annual rpt, 26304–3

Budget of US, CBO analysis of savings and revenues under alternative spending cuts and tax changes, projected FY92-97, 26306–3.118

CCC financial condition and major commodity program operations, FY62-87, annual chartbook, 1824–2

CCC loan activities by commodity, and agency operating results, monthly press release, 1802–7

CCC price support and other program outlays, with production and marketing outlook, by commodity, projected 1990-96, 26306–6.160

Certificate exchange activity of CCC, by commodity, biweekly press release, 1802–16

Conservation programs under Food Security Act, farm finances and environmental benefits of alternative policies, projected 1991-2005, 1588–153

Crop subsidies of USDA, farmers reorganizations to remain under payment limits, effectiveness of laws to prevent abuse, 1989, GAO rpt, 26113–546

Dairy cooperatives exemption from antitrust laws, impacts on industry structure and pricing, with background data, 1930s-80s, GAO rpt, 26113–499

Agricultural production quotas and price supports

Index by Subjects and Names

Dairy industry biotechnology devs, and bST impacts on farm finances and Federal support programs, 1980s and projected to 1998, 26358–237

Dairy production by State, stocks, prices, and CCC price support activities, by product type, monthly rpt, 1627–3

Dairy production, prices, trade, and use, periodic situation rpt with articles, 1561–2

Dairy products price support purchases, sales, donations, and inventories of CCC, monthly rpt, 1802–2

Dairy storage holdings and purchases of USDA by product, and milk order deliveries and prices by market area, 1990, annual rpt, 1317–1.1; 1317–1.5

Data on agriculture, compilation, 1990 and trends from 1920, annual rpt, 1004–14

Economic Indicators of the Farm Sector, balance sheets, and receipts by detailed commodity, by State, 1985-89, annual rpt, 1544–18

Economic Indicators of the Farm Sector, income, expenses, receipts by commodity, assets, and liabilities, 1990 and trends from 1945, annual rpt, 1544–16

Expenditures of Fed Govt in States, by type, program, agency, and State, FY90, annual rpt, 2464–2

Farmers views on Federal agricultural support, trade, and fiscal policies, by region and State, 1989 survey, hearings, 21168–43

Fed Govt farm subsidy rates under 1985 and 1990 farm bills, by selected program and commodity, 1990 rpt, 1008–54

Feed production, acreage, stocks, use, trade, prices, and price supports, periodic situation rpt with articles, 1561–4

Grain and feed trade, and export and support prices, for US and major producer countries, FAS monthly circular, 1925–2.4

Grain production, prices, trade, and export inspections by US port and country of destination, by grain type, weekly rpt, 1313–2

Grain support loan programs of USDA, activity and status by grain and State, monthly rpt, 1802–3

Imports injury to price-supported US agricultural industry, investigations with background financial and operating data, series, 9886–10

Milk order market policy alternatives impacts on supply, interregional marketings, and pricing, by region, 1988, 1568–294

Milk order market prices and detailed operations, by State and market area, 1989-90, annual rpt, 1317–3

Milk order market prices and detailed operations, monthly rpt with articles, 1317–4

Milk order market sales, by container size and type, outlet type, and market area, 1989, biennial rpt, 1317–6

Oilseed price support programs eligibility requirements, and market loan and repayment rates, 1990-92, article, 1561–3.202

Peanut production and US exports by country, prices, and stocks, weekly rpt, 1311–1

Price support program changes and other effects on farm income and production, for livestock and program and nonprogram crop producers, model results, 1988, 1548–375

Price support program provisions, for selected commodities, 1961-90, 1568–302; 1568–303

Rice foreign and US production, prices, trade, stocks, and use, periodic situation rpt, 1561–8

Statistical Abstract of US, 1991 annual data compilation, 2324–1.23

Sugar and sweeteners production, prices, trade, supply, and use, quarterly situation rpt with articles, 1561–14

Tobacco marketing activity, prices, and sales, by grade, type, market, and State, 1989-90, annual rpt series, 1319–5

Tobacco production, marketing, use, price supports, and trade, quarterly situation rpt with articles, 1561–10

Tobacco quotas, support levels, and loan receipts, by type of tobacco, 1983-91, annual rpt, 1319–1.2

Wheat and rye price supports and loan rates, quarterly situation rpt with articles, 1561–12

Wheat deficiency program payments freeze in 1985, impacts on participation, production, costs, exports, and returns, model results, 1990 rpt, 1548–376

Agricultural productivity

Agricultural Statistics, 1990, annual rpt, 1004–1

Data on agriculture, compilation, 1990 and trends from 1920, annual rpt, 1004–14

Economic Indicators of the Farm Sector, itemized production costs, receipts, and returns, by commodity and region, 1987-89, annual rpt, 1544–20

Economic Indicators of the Farm Sector, production inputs, output, and productivity, by commodity and region, 1947-89, annual rpt, 1544–17

Feed production, acreage, stocks, use, trade, prices, and price supports, periodic situation rpt with articles, 1561–4

Fertilizer use, and effects on agricultural productivity, for selected US regions and PRC, 1989 hearing, 25168–76

Foreign and US agricultural production, acreage, and yield for selected crops, forecasts by selected world region and country, FAS monthly circular, 1925–28

Foreign and US agricultural supply and demand indicators, by selected crop, monthly rpt, 1522–5

Foreign countries agricultural production, prices, and trade, by country, 1980-90 and forecast 1991, annual world area rpt series, 1524–4

Global climate change economic impacts, projected to 2100 with background data for 1980s, 3028–5

Irrigation projects of Reclamation Bur in western US, crop production and acreage by commodity, State, and project, 1989, annual rpt, 5824–12

Production, farms, acreage, and related data, by selected crop and State, monthly rpt, 1621–1

Production indicators for farms, 1947-90, annual rpt, 204–1.8

Research (agricultural) funding and staffing for USDA, State agencies, and other instns, by topic, FY90, annual rpt, 1744–2

Research (agricultural) investment impacts on productivity, indicators for developed and developing countries, late 1960s-80, 1528–318

Soviet Union agricultural reform issues, with background data for USSR and US, 1970s-90, article, 9381–1.210

Vegetable production, prices, trade, stocks, and use, for selected fresh and processing crops, periodic situation rpt with articles, 1561–11

Wheat and rye foreign and US production, prices, trade, stocks, and use, quarterly situation rpt with articles, 1561–12

see also under names of specific commodities or commodity groups (listed under Agricultural commodities)

Agricultural Reconciliation Act

Subsidy rates of Fed Govt under 1985 and 1990 farm bills, by selected program and commodity, 1990 rpt, 1008–54

Agricultural Research Service

Budget of US, obligations and authority by function, agency, and program, with summaries, analyses, and historical tables, FY92, annual rpt, 104–2

Child rearing costs of married couple households, by expenditure type, child's age, income, and region, 1990 and projected to 2007, 1708–87

Family Economics Review, consumer goods prices and supply, and home economics, quarterly journal, 1702–1

Sugarcane clones yields, stability, and fungi resistance, 1990/91, annual rpt, 1704–2

see also Cooperative State Research Service

Agricultural sciences and research

Acid rain research activities of Natl Acid Precipitation Assessment Program, 1990 annual rpt, 14354–1

Agricultural Economics Research, quarterly journal, 1502–3

Biotechnology commercial applications, industry finances and capitalization, patents, and govt support, for US, Japan, and EC, late 1970s-91, 26358–248

Budget of US, obligations and authority by function, agency, and program, with summaries, analyses, and historical tables, FY92, annual rpt, 104–2

Carbon dioxide in atmosphere, measurement, methodology, and research results, series, 3006–11

Dairy industry biotechnology devs, and bST impacts on farm finances and Federal support programs, 1980s and projected to 1998, 26358–237

Developing countries aid projects collaboration of AID and US higher education instns, and funding, by purpose and world region, 1960s-89, 26358–247

Employment and other characteristics of science and engineering PhDs, by field and State, 1989, biennial rpt, 9627–18

Expenditures and staffing for agricultural research by USDA, State agencies, and other instns, by topic, FY90, annual rpt, 1744–2

Expenditures for R&D and related activities of higher education and nonprofit instns by Fed Govt, by field, instn, agency, and State, FY89, annual rpt, 9627–17

Index by Subjects and Names

Expenditures for R&D by Fed Govt, by field, performer type, agency, and State, FY89-91, annual rpt, 9627-20

Expenditures for R&D by higher education instns and federally funded centers, by field, instn, and State, FY89, annual rpt, 9627-13

Expenditures for research and education, USDA appropriations by program and subagency, FY82-90, annual rpt, 1004-19

Expenditures for research and education, USDA competitive awards by program and recipient, FY90, annual listing, 1764-1

Facilities for R&D of higher education instns, equipment acquisition and service costs, condition, and financing, by field and subfield, 1988-90, triennial survey series, 9627-27

Farm financial and marketing conditions, forecast 1991, annual chartbook, 1504-8

Foreign and US funding for R&D, and scientists and engineering employment and education, 1991 annual rpt, 9627-35.1

Foreign countries agricultural research grants of USDA, by program, subagency, and country, FY90, annual listing, 1954-3

Higher education instn agricultural scientists, by field and source of Federal support, 1987, 26358-231

Industrial uses of new and traditional agricultural crops, replacement of imports and nonrenewable resources, R&D funding, and economic impacts, 1970s-90, 26358-239

Productivity impacts of agricultural research investment, indicators for developed and developing countries, late 1960s-80, 1528-318

Sugarcane clones yields, stability, and fungi resistance, 1990/91, annual rpt, 1704-2

Weather services activities and funding, by Federal agency, planned FY91-92, annual rpt, 2144-2

Yearbook of Agriculture, special topics, 1991 annual compilation of papers, 1004-18

see also Agricultural education

Agricultural services

Aircraft (general aviation), flight hours, and equipment, by type, use, and model of aircraft, region, and State, 1990, annual rpt, 7504-29

Census of Agriculture, 1987: farms, farmland, production, finances, and operator characteristics, by county, final State rpt series, 2331-1

Cooperatives, finances, and membership, by type of service, commodity, and State, 1989, annual rpt, 1124-1

Cotton ginning activity and charges, by State, 1990/91, annual rpt, 1564-3

County Business Patterns, 1988: employment, establishments, and payroll, by SIC 2- to 4-digit industry and county, annual State rpt series, 2326-6

County Business Patterns, 1989: employment, establishments, and payroll, by SIC 2- to 4-digit industry and county, annual State rpt series, 2326-8

Economic Indicators of the Farm Sector, income, expenses, receipts by commodity, assets, and liabilities, 1990 and trends from 1945, annual rpt, 1544-16

Economic Indicators of the Farm Sector, itemized production costs, receipts, and returns, by commodity and region, 1987-89, annual rpt, 1544-20

Employment related to agriculture, by industry, region, and metro-nonmetro location, 1987, 1598-271

Farm production itemized costs, by farm sales size and region, 1990, annual rpt, 1614-3

Helicopters, use, and landing facilities, by craft type, region, and State, 1989, 7508-75

Occupational injury and illness rates, by SIC 2- to 4-digit industry, 1988-89, annual rpt, 6844-7

Occupational injury and illness rates, by SIC 2- to 4-digit industry, 1989, annual rpt, 6844-1

Tax (income) returns of corporations, income and tax items by asset size and detailed industry, 1987, annual rpt, 8304-4

Tax (income) returns of sole proprietorships, income statement items, by industry group, 1989, annual article, 8302-2.214

Yearbook of Agriculture, special topics, 1990 annual compilation of papers, 1004-18

see also Veterinary medicine

see also under By Industry in the "Index by Categories"

Agricultural Stabilization and Conservation Service

Acreage under ASCS programs, rankings by commodity and congressional district, 1989, biennial rpt, 1804-17

Activities of ASCS, annual commodity fact sheet series, 1806-4

Budget of US, obligations and authority by function, agency, and program, with summaries, analyses, and historical tables, FY92, annual rpt, 104-2

CCC commodities for sale, and prices, monthly press release, 1802-4

CCC loan activities by commodity, and agency operating results, monthly press release, 1802-7

Colorado River Salinity Control Program participation and payments, FY87-90, annual rpt, 1804-23

Conservation program of USDA, funding by practice, region and State, monthly rpt, 1802-15

Conservation program of USDA, participation and payments by practice and State, FY90, annual rpt, 1804-7

Conservation programs of USDA, benefits denied for noncompliance, and appeals disposition, by State, periodic rpt, discontinued, 1802-18

Dairy products price support purchases, sales, donations, and inventories of CCC, monthly rpt, 1802-2

Emergency Conservation Program for farmland damaged by natural disaster, aid and participation by State, FY90, annual rpt, 1804-22

Emergency Conservation Program for farmland damaged by natural disaster, funding by region and State, monthly rpt, 1802-13

Field offices, funding, and staff of USDA subagencies responsible for farm programs, FY89, GAO rpt, 26113-507

Agricultural Statistics Board

Grain storage facility and equipment loans to farmers under CCC program, by State, FY68-91, annual table, 1804-14

Grain support loan programs of USDA, activity and status by grain and State, monthly rpt, 1802-3

Pesticide production, trade, and additives, by type, with manufacturers listing, 1987-89, annual rpt, 1804-5

Producer payments and certificate value, by program, monthly rpt, 1802-10

Producer payments, by program and State, 1990, annual table, 1804-12

Rural Clean Water Program funding for control of pollution from farming, by region and State, monthly rpt, 1802-14

Storage facility and equipment loans to farmers under CCC grain program, by State, monthly table, 1802-9

Timber and orchard damage from natural disaster, USDA restoration aid and program participation by practice and State, FY89-90, annual rpt, 1824-24

Timber improvement program for private land, Fed Govt cost-sharing funds by region and State, monthly rpt, 1802-11

Timber improvement program for private land, participation and payments by State, FY90, annual rpt, 1804-20

Water Bank Program agreements, payments to farmers, and wetlands acreage, by State, 1972-91, annual rpt, 1804-21

Wetlands preservation under Water Bank Program, acreage, agreements, and payments, by State, monthly rpt, 1802-5

see also Commodity Credit Corp.

Agricultural Statistics Board

Acreage of farmland, and operations, by sales size, region, and State, 1989-91, annual rpt, 1614-4

Acreage planted and harvested, by crop and State, 1989-90 and planned as of June 1991, annual rpt, 1621-23

Acreage planted, by selected crop and State, 1982-90 and planned 1991, annual rpt, 1621-22

Cattle and calves for beef and milk, by State, as of July 1991, semiannual press release, 1623-1

Cattle and calves on feed, inventory and marketings by State, monthly release, 1623-2

Celery acreage planted and growing, by growing area, monthly rpt, 1621-14

Cold storage food stocks by commodity and census div, and warehouse space use, by State, monthly rpt, 1631-5

Cold storage food stocks by commodity, and warehouse space use, by census div, 1990, annual rpt, 1631-11

Cotton ginnings, by State and county, seasonal biweekly rpt, 1631-19

Dairy cattle, milk production, and grain and other concentrates fed, by State, monthly rpt, 1627-1

Dairy production by commodity, and plants, by State, 1990, annual rpt, 1627-5

Dairy production by State, stocks, prices, and CCC price support activities, by product type, monthly rpt, 1627-3

Egg production and layer inventory, by State, 1989-90, annual rpt, 1625-7

Egg production by type of product, and eggs broken under Federal inspection by region, monthly rpt, 1625-2

Agricultural Statistics Board

Employment on farms, wages, and hours, by payment method, worker type, region, and State, 1910-90, 1618–21

Employment on farms, wages, hours, and perquisites, by State, monthly rpt, 1631–1

Fertilizer and pesticide use and application rates, by type, crop, and State, series, 1616–1

Fish (catfish) raised on farms, inventory, stocks, and production, by major producer State, quarterly rpt, 1631–18

Fish (catfish) raised on farms, production, inventory, imports, and prices, by State, as of Feb 1991, last issue of semiannual rpt, 1631–17

Fish (catfish) raised on farms, production, inventory, sales, prices, and imports, monthly release, 1631–14

Fish (trout) raised on farms, production, sales, prices, and losses, 1990-91, annual rpt, 1631–16

Flower and foliage plant production, sales, prices, and growers, by crop and State, 1989-90 and planting planned 1991, annual rpt, 1631–8

Fruit and nut production, prices, and use, 1988-91, annual rpt series, 1621–18

Grain stocks on and off farms, by crop, quarterly rpt, 1621–4

Hogs inventory, value, farrowings, and farms, by State, quarterly release, 1623–3

Honey production, prices, stocks, and bee colonies, by State, 1989-90, annual rpt, 1631–6

Hops stocks held by growers, dealers, and brewers, 1989-91, semiannual press release, 1621–8

Livestock slaughter and meat production, by livestock type and State, monthly rpt, 1623–9

Livestock slaughter, meat production, and slaughter plants, by species and State, 1990, annual rpt, 1623–10

Meat animal production, prices, receipts, and disposition, by species and State, 1988-90, annual rpt, 1623–8

Milk of manufacturing grade, fat content and prices received by farmers in Minnesota and Wisconsin, monthly rpt, 1629–6

Milk of manufacturing grade, fat content and prices received by farmers in Minnesota and Wisconsin, 1988-90, annual rpt, 1629–2

Milk production, use, and receipts, and milk cow inventory, by State, 1988-90, annual rpt, 1627–4

Mink and pelt production, prices, and farms, selected years 1969-91, annual rpt, 1631–7

Mushroom production, sales, and prices, by State, 1966/67-1990/91 and planned 1991/92, annual rpt, 1631–9

Peanut stocks, millings, and use, by grade and type, monthly rpt, 1621–6

Potato production, prices, stocks, and use, by State, 1981-90, annual rpt, 1621–11

Potato production, stocks, processing, yields, and harvest losses, by State, periodic rpt, 1621–10

Poultry (broiler) hatcheries eggs set and chicks placed, by State, weekly rpt, 1625–11

Poultry (chicken and turkey) hatchery production, 1989-90, annual rpt, 1625–8

Poultry (chicken, egg, and turkey) production and inventories, monthly rpt, 1625–1

Poultry (chicken, egg, and turkey) production and prices, by State, 1989-90, annual rpt, 1625–5

Poultry slaughtered under Fed Govt inspection, pounds certified, and condemnations by cause, by State, monthly rpt, 1625–3

Prices received and paid by farmers, by commodity and State, 1990, annual rpt, 1629–5

Prices received by farmers and production value, by detailed crop and State, 1988-90, annual rpt, 1621–2

Prices received by farmers for major products, and paid for farm inputs and living items, by State, monthly rpt, 1629–1

Production, farms, acreage, and related data, by selected crop and State, monthly rpt, 1621–1

Production itemized costs, by farm sales size and region, 1990, annual rpt, 1614–3

Publications of ASB, releases planned 1991, annual listing, 1614–1

Rice stocks on and off farms and total in all positions, periodic rpt, 1621–7

Sheep, lamb, and goat inventory, by State, 1989-91, annual press release, 1623–4

Sheep, lamb, and goat loss to predators and other causes, by region and State, 1990, 1618–20

Sugar production, trade, and use, quarterly rpt, 1621–28

Turkey hatcheries egg inventory and poult placements, by region, monthly rpt, 1625–10

Turkey production by State, and losses by region, 1989-90, and hatchery plans, 1991, annual rpt, 1625–6

Vegetable production, acreage, and yield, current and forecast for selected fresh and processing crops by State, periodic rpt, 1621–12

Vegetable production, value, and acreage, for selected fresh and processing crops by State, 1988-90, annual rpts, 1621–25

Wheat and rye acreage seeded, by State, 1989-91, annual rpt, 1621–30

Wool and mohair production and prices, by State, 1989-90, annual press release, 1623–6

Agricultural stocks

Africa (Sahel) grain production, use, imports, and stocks, by country, 1989/90, 9918–18

Agricultural Outlook, production, prices, marketing, and trade, by commodity, forecast and current situation, monthly rpt with articles, 1502–4

Agricultural Stabilization and Conservation Service programs, annual commodity fact sheet series, 1806–4

Agricultural Statistics, 1990, annual rpt, 1004–1

Apple production, marketing, and prices, for Appalachia and compared to other States, 1988-91, annual rpt, 1311–13

Bean (dried) prices by State, market activity, and foreign and US production, use, stocks, and trade, weekly rpt, 1311–17

Index by Subjects and Names

Business statistics, detailed data for major industries and economic indicators, *Survey of Current Business*, monthly rpt, 2702–1.14

Cattle and calves for beef and milk, by State, as of July 1991, semiannual press release, 1623–1

Cattle and calves on feed, inventory and marketings by State, monthly release, 1623–2

Census of Agriculture, 1987: farms, farmland, production, finances, and operator characteristics, by county, final State rpt series, 2331–1

Cocoa and cocoa products foreign and US production, prices, and trade, 1980s-92, FAS semiannual circular, 1925–9

Coffee production, trade and quotas, and use, by country, with US and intl prices, FAS periodic circular, 1925–5

Cold storage food stocks by commodity and census div, and warehouse space use, by State, monthly rpt, 1631–5

Cold storage food stocks by commodity, and warehouse space use, by census div, 1990, annual rpt, 1631–11

Cotton (long staple) production, prices, exports, stocks, and mill use, monthly rpt, 1309–12

Cotton linters production, stocks, use, and prices, monthly rpt, 1309–10

Cotton production and trade for US and selected countries, FAS periodic circular series, 1925–4

Cotton quality, supply, and carryover, 1989-90, annual rpt, 1309–8

Dairy production by State, stocks, prices, and CCC price support activities, by product type, monthly rpt, 1627–3

Dairy production, prices, trade, and use, periodic situation rpt with articles, 1561–2

Dairy production, trade, use, and prices, for US and selected countries, forecast 1992 and trends from 1987, FAS semiannual circular, 1925–10

Dairy products, commercial and Fed Govt storage holdings of butter, cheese, and nonfat dry milk, monthly rpt, 1317–4.2

Dairy storage holdings, total and for USDA by product, 1990, annual rpt, 1317–1.1

Developing countries food supply, needs, and aid, status and alternative forecasts, world area rpt series, 1526–8

Developing countries grains production and needs, and related economic outlook, by world area and selected country, forecast 1990/91-1991/92, 1528–313

Economic Indicators of the Farm Sector, balance sheets, and receipts by detailed commodity, by State, 1985-89, annual rpt, 1544–18

Economic Indicators of the Farm Sector, income, expenses, receipts by commodity, assets, and liabilities, 1990 and trends from 1945, annual rpt, 1544–16

Feed production, acreage, stocks, use, trade, prices, and price supports, periodic situation rpt with articles, 1561–4

Finances and operations of farm sector, 1970s-91, article, 9362–1.207

Fish (catfish) raised on farms, inventory, stocks, and production, by major producer State, quarterly rpt, 1631–18

Index by Subjects and Names

Agricultural subsidies

Fish (catfish) raised on farms, production, inventory, imports, and prices, by State, as of Feb 1991, last issue of semiannual rpt, 1631–17

Fish (catfish) raised on farms, production, inventory, sales, prices, and imports, monthly release, 1631–14

Fish hatcheries and farms, production, costs, prices, and sales, for catfish and trout, 1970s-91, semiannual situation rpt, 1561–15

Foreign and US agricultural supply and demand indicators, by selected crop, monthly rpt, 1522–5

Foreign countries agricultural production, prices, and trade, by country, 1980-90 and forecast 1991, annual world area rpt series, 1524–4

Fruit and nut production, prices, trade, stocks, and use, by selected crop, periodic situation rpt with articles, 1561–6

Grain production, prices, trade, and export inspections by US port and country of destination, by grain type, weekly rpt, 1313–2

Honey production, prices, stocks, and bee colonies, by State, 1989-90, annual rpt, 1631–6

Honey production, prices, trade, stocks, marketing, and CCC honey loan and distribution activities, monthly rpt, 1311–2

Hops production, stocks, use, and US trade by country, monthly rpt, 1313–7

Imports injury to price-supported US agricultural industry, investigations with background financial and operating data, series, 9886–10

Livestock, meat, poultry, and egg production, prices, trade, and stocks, monthly rpt, 1561–17

Livestock, meat, poultry, and egg production, prices, trade, stocks, and use, periodic situation rpt with articles, 1561–7

Oils, oilseeds, and fats foreign and US production and trade, FAS periodic circular series, 1925–1

Onions in summer storage, shrinkage and loss, 1988-90, annual rpts, 1621–25

Peanut production and US exports by country, prices, and stocks, weekly rpt, 1311–1

Peanut production, prices, stocks, exports, use, inspection, and quality, by region and State, 1980-90, annual rpt, 1311–5

Peanut stocks, millings, and use, by grade and type, monthly rpt, 1621–6

Potato production, acreage, disposition, prices, and trade, by State and country, 1949-90, 1568–305

Potato production, prices, stocks, and use, by State, 1981-90, annual rpt, 1621–11

Potato production, stocks, processing, yields, and harvest losses, by State, periodic rpt, 1621–10

Rice foreign and US production, prices, trade, stocks, and use, periodic situation rpt, 1561–8

Rice market activities, prices, inspections, sales, trade, supply, and use, for US and selected foreign markets, weekly rpt, 1313–8

Soviet Union GNP by detailed income and outlay component, 1985, 2326–18.59

Sugar and sweeteners production, prices, trade, supply, and use, quarterly situation rpt with articles, 1561–14

Sugar production, acreage, yield, stocks, deliveries, and price by State, and trade by country, 1950s-90, 1568–306

Tax (income) returns of corporations, income and tax items by asset size and detailed industry, 1987, annual rpt, 8304–4

Tobacco leaf stocks, production, sales, and import inspections by country, by product, quarterly rpt, 1319–3

Tobacco production, prices, stocks, taxes by State, and trade and production by country, 1990, annual rpt, 1319–1

Transportation census, 1987: finances and operations by size, ownership, and State, and revenues by MSA, by SIC 2- to 4-digit industry, 2579–1

Vegetable production, prices, trade, stocks, and use, for selected fresh and processing crops, periodic situation rpt with articles, 1561–11

Wheat and rye foreign and US production, prices, trade, stocks, and use, quarterly situation rpt with articles, 1561–12

Wool prices, sales, trade, and stocks, and sheep inventory, weekly and biweekly rpt, 1315–2

see also Agricultural surpluses

see also Grain storage and facilities

Agricultural subsidies

Agricultural Stabilization and Conservation Service producer payments and certificate value, by program, monthly rpt, 1802–10

Agricultural Stabilization and Conservation Service producer payments, by program and State, 1990, annual table, 1804–12

Assistance (financial and nonfinancial) of Fed Govt, 1991 base edition with supplements, annual listing, 104–5

Budget of US, balances of budget authority obligated and unobligated, by function and agency, FY90-92, annual rpt, 104–8

Budget of US, CBO analysis and review of FY92 budget by function, annual rpt, 26304–2

Budget of US, formula grant program obligations to State and local govts, by agency, program, and State, FY92, annual rpt, 104–30

Budget of US, House concurrent resolution, with spending and revenue targets, FY92 and projected to FY96, annual rpt, 21264–2

Budget of US, midsession review of FY92 budget, by function, annual rpt, 104–7

Budget of US, obligations and authority by function, agency, and program, with summaries, analyses, and historical tables, FY92, annual rpt, 104–2

Budget of US, receipts by source, outlays by agency and program, and balances, monthly rpt, 8102–3

Budget of US, Senate concurrent resolution, with spending and revenue targets, FY92, annual rpt, 25254–1

Canada wheat producer subsidy costs and returns, 1990-92, article, 1561–12.202

Census of Agriculture, 1987: farms, farmland, production, finances, and operator characteristics, by county, final State rpt series, 2331–1

China agricultural prices and govt subsidies, by selected commodity, 1979-89, article, 1524–4.3

China economic indicators and reform issues, with background data, 1950s-90, compilation of papers, 23848–155

Colorado River Salinity Control Program participation and payments, FY87-90, annual rpt, 1804–23

Conservation program of USDA, funding by practice, region and State, monthly rpt, 1802–15

Conservation program of USDA, participation and payments by practice and State, FY90, annual rpt, 1804–7

Conservation programs of USDA, benefits denied for noncompliance, and appeals disposition, by State, periodic rpt, discontinued, 1802–18

Corn farms, finances, acreage, and production, by size, region, and State, 1987, 1568–304

Disaster aid of USDA for producers of crops ineligible for price supports by State, and methodology, 1988-89, GAO rpt, 26113–533

EC dairy product export subsidies, by commodity, 1991, FAS semiannual circular, 1925–10

EC export subsidies by commodity, FAS monthly circular, 1925–32

Economic Indicators of the Farm Sector, balance sheets, and receipts by detailed commodity, by State, 1985-89, annual rpt, 1544–18

Economic Indicators of the Farm Sector, income, expenses, receipts by commodity, assets, and liabilities, 1990 and trends from 1945, annual rpt, 1544–16

Emergency Conservation Program for farmland damaged by natural disaster, aid and participation by State, FY90, annual rpt, 1804–22

Emergency Conservation Program for farmland damaged by natural disaster, funding by region and State, monthly rpt, 1802–13

Expenditures of Fed Govt in States, by type, program, agency, and State, FY90, annual rpt, 2464–2

Exports (agricultural) under federally financed programs, by commodity and country, bimonthly rpt, periodic data, 1522–1

Fed Govt farm subsidy rates under 1985 and 1990 farm bills, by selected program and commodity, 1990 rpt, 1008–54

Foreign and US agricultural production, prices, trade, and use, periodic rpt with articles, 1522–3

Foreign and US agricultural subsidies for producers and consumers, production and trade impacts, model description, 1991 rpt, 1528–315

Foreign countries agricultural and trade policy impacts on US exports, with data by commodity and country, 1989, annual rpt, 1924–8

Foreign countries agricultural production, prices, and trade, by country, 1980-90 and forecast 1991, annual world area rpt series, 1524–4

Fraud and abuse in USDA programs, audits and investigations, 1st half FY91, semiannual rpt, 1002–4

Agricultural subsidies

Grain price support and loan programs operations of USDA, with farmers views on Federal programs, by region and State, 1990 hearings, 21168–43

Great Lakes area economic conditions and outlook, for US and Canada, 1970s-90, 9375–15

Korea (South) agricultural subsidies to producers and consumers, by commodity, 1987-89, article, 1522–3.205

Latin America agricultural subsidies to producers and consumers, by selected commodity for 6 countries, 1982-87, 1528–324

Loans and loan guarantees of Fed Govt, outstanding amounts by agency and program, *Treasury Bulletin*, quarterly rpt, 8002–4.9

Pest control integrated mgmt programs for vegetables, acreage, costs, savings, and funding sources and recipients, by State, 1980s, 1568–298

Rice market activities, prices, inspections, sales, trade, supply, and use, for US and selected foreign markets, weekly rpt, 1313–8

Soviet Union agricultural reform issues, with background data for USSR and US, 1970s-90, article, 9381–1.210

Soviet Union agricultural subsidies to producers and consumers, by selected commodity, 1986, 1528–320

State and Metro Area Data Book, 1991 data compilation, 2328–54

Statistical Abstract of US, 1991 annual data compilation, 2324–1.23

Tax expenditures, Federal revenues forgone through income tax deductions and exclusions by type, FY92-96, annual rpt, 21784–10

Timber and orchard damage from natural disaster, USDA restoration aid and program participation by practice and State, FY89-90, annual rpt, 1804–24

Water Bank Program agreements, payments to farmers, and wetlands acreage, by State, 1972-91, annual rpt, 1804–21

Wheat and corn stocks, demand impacts of storage subsidy programs, model description and results, 1972-87, 1548–378

Zimbabwe agricultural conditions impacts of economic policies, 1980s, 1528–319

see also Agricultural credit

see also Agricultural production quotas and price supports

Agricultural surpluses

Agricultural Stabilization and Conservation Service programs, annual commodity fact sheet series, 1806–4

CCC commodities for sale, and prices, monthly press release, 1802–4

CCC financial condition and major commodity program operations, FY62-87, annual chartbook, 1824–2

CCC loan activities by commodity, and agency operating results, monthly press release, 1802–7

Cotton prices in 8 spot markets, futures prices at NYC exchange, farm prices, and CCC loan stocks, monthly rpt, 1309–1

Dairy products price support purchases, sales, donations, and inventories of CCC, monthly rpt, 1802–2

Grain stocks on and off farms, by crop, quarterly rpt, 1621–4

Grain support loan programs of USDA, activity and status by grain and State, monthly rpt, 1802–3

see also Agricultural production quotas and price supports

see also Agricultural stocks

see also Food assistance

see also Public Law 480

Agricultural Trade Development and Assistance Act

see Public Law 480

Agricultural transportation

see Agricultural marketing

Agricultural wages

Agricultural Outlook, production, prices, marketing, and trade, by commodity, forecast and current situation, monthly rpt with articles, 1502–4

Census of Agriculture, 1987: farms, farmland, production, finances, and operator characteristics, by county, final State rpt series, 2331–1

Census of Agriculture, 1987: horticultural specialties producers, finances, and operations, by crop and State, 1988 survey, 2337–1

Earnings by industry div, and personal income per capita and by source, by State, MSA, and county, 1984-89, annual regional rpts, 2704–2

Earnings, employment, and hours on farms, by payment method, worker type, region, and State, 1910-90, 1618–21

Economic Indicators of the Farm Sector, balance sheets, and receipts by detailed commodity, by State, 1985-89, annual rpt, 1544–18

Economic Indicators of the Farm Sector, income, expenses, receipts by commodity, assets, and liabilities, 1990 and trends from 1945, annual rpt, 1544–16

Immigration restrictions effects on US agricultural labor costs and trade competitiveness, 1980s, 1598–276

Income (household, family, and personal), by source, detailed characteristics, and region, 1988-89, annual Current Population Rpt, 2546–6.68

Income (household, family, and personal), by source, detailed characteristics, and region, 1990, annual Current Population Rpt, 2546–6.70

Production itemized costs, by farm sales size and region, 1990, annual rpt, 1614–3

Social security earnings records errors and rates, by employment type, late 1930s-87, GAO rpt, 26121–422

State and Metro Area Data Book, 1991 data compilation, 2328–54

Statistical Abstract of US, 1991 annual data compilation, 2324–1.23

Wages, employment, hours, and perquisites, for farm labor by State, monthly rpt, 1631–1

Agriculture

Agricultural Statistics, 1990, annual rpt, 1004–1

Classification codes concordance of Canada and US SICs, for 1- to 4-digit levels, 1991 rpt, 2628–31

Data coverage and availability of Census Bur rpts and data files, 1991 annual listing, 2304–2

Index by Subjects and Names

Data on agriculture, compilation, 1990 and trends from 1920, annual rpt, 1004–14

Data on agriculture, young readers pamphlet series, 2346–1

Statistical Abstract of US, 1991 annual data compilation, 2324–1.23

see also Agricultural accidents and safety

see also Agricultural commodities

see also Agricultural credit

see also Agricultural education

see also Agricultural energy use

see also Agricultural exports and imports

see also Agricultural extension work

see also Agricultural finance

see also Agricultural forecasts

see also Agricultural insurance

see also Agricultural labor

see also Agricultural machinery and equipment

see also Agricultural marketing

see also Agricultural policy

see also Agricultural prices

see also Agricultural production

see also Agricultural production costs

see also Agricultural production quotas and price supports

see also Agricultural productivity

see also Agricultural sciences and research

see also Agricultural services

see also Agricultural stocks

see also Agricultural subsidies

see also Agricultural surpluses

see also Agricultural wages

see also Botany

see also Census of Agriculture

see also Drought

see also Farm income

see also Farm operators

see also Farms and farmland

see also Fertilizers

see also Food and food industry

see also Foreign agriculture

see also Forests and forestry

see also Horticulture

see also Irrigation

see also Pesticides

see also Pests and pest control

see also Rural areas

see also Soils and soil conservation

see also Wildlife and wildlife conservation

see also under By Industry in the "Index by Categories"

Agriculture Department

see Department of Agriculture

Aguadilla, P.R.

see also under By SMSA or MSA in the "Index by Categories"

Aguilar, Linda M.

"Going Gets Tough: State and Local Governments Confront the Nineties", 9375–1.207

Aguirre International

"Final Report: Longitudinal Study of Structured English Immersion Strategy, Early-Exit and Late-Exit Transitional Bilingual Education Programs for Language-Minority Children", 4808–27

Ahearn, Mary C.

"Farm Wealth: Its Distribution and Comparison to the Wealth of U.S. Households", 1541–1.207

AID

see Agency for International Development

Index by Subjects and Names

Aid to blind

Library of Congress activities, acquisitions, services, and financial statements, FY90, annual rpt, 26404–1

Medicaid and SSI recipients, by eligibility type, from 1970s, and by State, 1989, annual rpt, 4744–3.6; 4744–3.8

Vending facilities run by blind on Federal and non-Federal property, finances and operations by agency and State, FY90, annual rpt, 4944–2

Vocational rehabilitation cases of State agencies by disposition and applicant characteristics, and closures by reason, FY84-88, annual rpt, 4944–6

Vocational rehabilitation cases of State agencies, by disposition and State, FY90 and trends from FY21, annual rpt, 4944–5

Vocational rehabilitation programs of Fed Govt and States, activities and funding, FY90, annual rpt, 4944–1

see also Supplemental Security Income

Aid to disabled and handicapped persons

Budget of US, formula grant program obligations to State and local govts, by agency, program, and State, FY92, annual rpt, 104–30

Developing countries disabled persons aid program activities and funding, for UN, AID, and Intl Labor Organization, late 1970s-90, GAO rpt, 26123–321

Education funding by Federal agency, program, and recipient type, and instn spending, FY80-90, annual rpt, 4824–8

Energy aid for low income households, funding sources, costs, and participation, by State, FY89, annual rpt, 4694–8

Energy aid for low income households, program characteristics by State, FY90, annual rpt, 4694–9

Fed Govt financial and nonfinancial domestic aid, 1991 base edition with supplements, annual listing, 104–5

Food stamp recipient household size, composition, income, and income and deductions allowed, summer 1988, annual rpt, 1364–8

HHS financial aid, by program, recipient, State, and city, FY90, annual regional listings, 4004–3

Library of Congress activities, acquisitions, services, and financial statements, FY90, annual rpt, 26404–1

Mail (free) for blind and handicapped, volume and costs, FY90, annual rpt, 9864–2

Mail (free) for blind and handicapped, volume and weight, quarterly rpt, 9862–1

Mail (free) revenue and subsidy for revenue forgone, FY90, and volume from FY86, annual rpt, 9864–1

Mail volume, revenues, and subsidies for revenue forgone, by class of mail, FY90, annual rpt, 9864–5.2; 9864–5.3

Medicaid and SSI recipients, by eligibility type, from 1970s, and by State, 1989, annual rpt, 4744–3.8

Railroad employee benefits program finances and beneficiaries, FY90, annual rpt, 9704–1

Recreation (outdoor) facilities of Fed Govt, Golden Access Passports issued, FY88-90, annual rpt, 5544–14

see also Aid to blind

see also Disability benefits and insurance

see also Old-Age, Survivors, Disability, and Health Insurance

see also Sheltered workshops

see also Special education

see also Supplemental Security Income

see also Vocational rehabilitation

see also Workers compensation

Aid to Families with Dependent Children

Beneficiaries families and children, and total and average payments, by public assistance program and State, since 1940, monthly rpt, 4742–1.5

Beneficiaries of AFDC, demographic and financial characteristics by State, FY89, annual rpt, 4694–1

Benefits and beneficiaries, from 1936, and by State, 1988, annual rpt, 4744–3.9

Budget of US, obligations and authority by function, agency, and program, with summaries, analyses, and historical tables, FY92, annual rpt, 104–2

Child and family health, education, and welfare condition, findings and recommendations, 1991 rpt, 15528–1

Child Support Enforcement Program finances and operations, by State, FY85-89, annual rpt, 4694–6

Children and youth social, economic, and demographic characteristics, 1950s-90, 4818–5

Computer records matching of welfare data, Federal and State agencies compliance with recipient protection provisions before benefits reduction, 1990, GAO rpt, 26121–404

Expenditures, coverage, and benefits for social welfare programs, late 1930s-89, annual rpt, 4744–3.1

Expenditures of Fed Govt in States, by type, program, agency, and State, FY90, annual rpt, 2464–2

Finances and operations of programs under Ways and Means Committee jurisdiction, FY70s-90, annual rpt, 21784–11

Food stamp eligibility and payment errors, by type, recipient characteristics, and State, FY89, annual rpt, 1364–15

Food stamp recipient household size, composition, income, and income and deductions allowed, summer 1988, annual rpt, 1364–8

Indian (Cherokee) Agency activities in North Carolina, FY91, annual rpt, 5704–4

Medicaid beneficiaries services use and costs, by service type and eligibility, 1975-89, article, 4652–1.209

Medicaid eligibility expansion provisions, adoption by States, and impacts on service use and costs, 1984-89, GAO rpt, 26121–429

Medicaid hospital discharges, by eligibility and instn characteristics, for 2 States, 1984, article, 4652–1.249

Medicaid reimbursement of hospitals under Federal and State provisions, with services use, costs, and profits, by State, 1980s, 17206–1.11

Medicaid services use and costs in alternative treatment settings, model description and results, FY87, article, 4652–1.211

Air cargo

Medicaid transitional benefits for families leaving AFDC, operations and subsequent medical costs, for 2 States, 1980s, article, 4652–1.217

Medicare and Medicaid eligibility, participation, coverage, and program finances, various periods 1966-91, biennial rpt, 4654–1

Parents departure, absence, and presence, family economic impacts, 1983-86, Current Population Rpt, 2546–20.17

Single mothers earnings, employment and welfare benefits, and poverty status, 1989, GAO rpt, 26121–413

State and Metro Area Data Book, 1991 data compilation, 2328–54

Statistical Abstract of US, 1991 annual data compilation, 2324–1.12

Teenage mothers child support awards, payment status, health insurance inclusion, and govt aid for collection, by selected characteristics, 1987, 4698–5

see also Work incentive programs

Aid to Permanently and Totally Disabled

see Aid to disabled and handicapped persons

AIDS

see Acquired immune deficiency syndrome

Aiken County, S.C.

Wages by occupation, for office and plant workers, 1991 survey, periodic MSA rpt, 6785–12.4

Air bases

see Military bases, posts, and reservations

Air cargo

Accidents and circumstances, for US operations of domestic and foreign airlines and general aviation, periodic rpt, 9612–1

Aircraft registered with FAA, by type and characteristics of aircraft, make, carrier, State, and county, 1989, annual rpt, 7504–3

Business statistics, detailed data for major industries and economic indicators, *Survey of Current Business*, monthly rpt, 2702–1.11

Collective bargaining agreements expiring during year, and workers covered, by firm, union, industry group, and State, 1991, annual rpt, 6784–9

Consumer complaints against air carriers, agents, and cargo handlers, monthly rpt, 7302–11

Exports and imports between US and outlying areas, by detailed commodity and mode of transport, 1990, annual rpt, 2424–11

Exports and imports of US, by transport mode, country, and SITC 1- to 3-digit commodity, 1990, annual rpt, 2424–12

Exports of US, detailed commodities by country, monthly CD-ROM, 2422–13

Finances of airlines, by carrier, carrier group, and for total certificated system, quarterly rpt, 7302–7

Fruit and vegetable shipments, and arrivals in US and Canada cities, by mode of transport and State and country of origin, 1990, annual rpt series, 1311–4

Fruit and vegetable shipments by mode of transport, arrivals, and imports, by commodity and State and country of origin, weekly rpt, 1311–3

Fruit and vegetable wholesale prices in NYC by State, and shipments and arrivals by mode of transport, by commodity, weekly rpt, 1311–20

Air cargo

Hazardous cargo inspections at airports, compliance and enforcement actions, 2nd half 1989, semiannual rpt, 7502–5

Hazardous material transport accidents, casualties, and damage, by mode of transport, with DOT control activities, 1989, annual rpt, 7304–4

Imports of US, detailed commodities by country, monthly CD-ROM, 2422–14

Mail (air) carried by US certificated carriers, by airport and carrier, 1990, annual rpt, 7504–35

Mail (express parcel) shipments and revenues of private air and surface carriers, and impact of State regulation, 1976-89, 7308–201

Mail operating costs of USPS, itemized by class of mail, FY90, annual rpt, 9864–4

Mail revenue, costs, and volume, by class of mail, FY90, annual rpt, 9864–2

Military and personal property shipments, passenger traffic, and costs, by service branch and mode of transport, quarterly rpt, 3702–1

Natl transportation system planning, use, condition, accidents, and needs, by mode of transport, 1940s-90 and projected to 2020, 7308–202

Price indexes (producer), by stage of processing and detailed commodity, monthly rpt, 6762–6

Price indexes for exports and imports of manufactured goods and services, quarterly press release, 6762–13

Publications and data files of Census Bur on foreign trade, 1991 guide, 2428–11

Tax (excise) collections of IRS, by source, quarterly rpt, 8302–1

Traffic (passenger and cargo), and departures by aircraft type, by carrier and airport, 1990, annual rpt, 7504–35

Traffic (passenger and cargo), carrier enplanement shares, and FAA airport improvement program grants, by airport and State, 1989, annual rpt, 7504–48

Traffic, aircraft, carriers, airports, and FAA activities, detailed data, 1980-89, annual rpt, 7504–1

Traffic, aircraft, pilots, airports, and fuel use, forecast FY91-2002 and trends from FY81, annual rpt, 7504–6

Traffic and passenger and freight enplanements, by airport, 1960s-90 and projected to 2010, hub area rpt series, 7506–7

Traffic, capacity, and performance, by carrier and type of operation, monthly rpt, 7302–6

Traffic, capacity, and performance for medium regional airlines, by carrier, quarterly rpt, 7302–8

see also Military airlift

Air conditioning

Apartment completions by region and metro-nonmetro location, and absorption rate, by size and rent class, preliminary 1990, annual Current Housing Rpt, 2484–3

Apartment market absorption rates and characteristics for nonsubsidized furnished and unfurnished units, 1989, annual Current Housing Rpt, 2484–2

Commercial buildings energy use, costs, and conservation, by building characteristics, survey rpt series, 3166–8

Energy conservation measures impacts on consumption, by component and end-use sector, 1970s-88 and projected under alternative oil prices to 1995, 3308–93

Energy supply, demand, and prices, by fuel type and end-use sector, projections and underlying assumptions, 1990-2010, annual rpt, 3164–90

Equipment shipments, trade, use, and firms, by product, 1990, annual Current Industrial Rpt, 2506–12.7

Exports and imports of US, by country and detailed commodity, monthly rpt, 2422–12

Exports and imports of US, by Harmonized System 6-digit commodity and country, 1990, annual rpt, 2424–13

Exports and imports of US, by transport mode, country, and SITC 1- to 3-digit commodity, 1990, annual rpt, 2424–12

Exports of US, detailed Schedule B commodities with countries of destination, 1990, annual rpt, 2424–10

Home mortgages FHA-insured, financial, property, and mortgagor characteristics, by metro area, 1990, annual rpt, 5144–24

Home mortgages FHA-insured, financial, property, and mortgagor characteristics, by State, 1990, annual rpt, 5144–1

Home mortgages FHA-insured, financial, property, and mortgagor characteristics, total and by State and outlying area, 1990, annual rpt, 5144–25

Home mortgages FHA-insured, financial, property, and mortgagor characteristics, 1990, annual rpt, 5144–17; 5144–23

Housing (low income) energy aid, funding sources, costs, and participation, by State, FY89, annual rpt, 4694–8

Housing alteration and repair spending, by property and job characteristics, and region, quarterly rpt, annual tables, 2382–7.2

Housing and households detailed characteristics, and unit and neighborhood quality, by location, 1989, biennial rpt, 2485–12

Housing and households detailed characteristics, and unit and neighborhood quality, MSA surveys, series, 2485–6

Housing attic insulation radiant barriers performance impacts of ventilation and dust, 1990 rpt, 3308–97

Housing energy use, and availability of appliances by type, selected years 1978-87, annual rpt, 3164–74.1

Housing inventory change from 1973, by reason, unit and household characteristics, and location, 1983 survey, biennial rpt, 2485–14

Housing units (1-family) by selected structural characteristics, sales, and prices, 1970s-90, article, 1702–1.205

Housing units completed, single and multifamily units by structural and financial characteristics, inside-outside MSAs, and region, 1986-90, annual rpt, 2384–1

Housing units completed, single and multifamily units by structural characteristics, monthly rpt, quarterly tables, 2382–2.2

Injuries from use of consumer products, by severity, victim age, and detailed product, 1990, annual rpt, 9164–6

Index by Subjects and Names

Manufacturing finances and operations, by SIC 2- to 4-digit industry, forecast 1991, annual rpt, 2044–28

Pollution (air) indoor levels in workplace, and health impacts, for Library of Congress Madison building, 1989 study, series, 4248–92

Price indexes (producer), by stage of processing and detailed commodity, monthly rpt, 6762–6

Price indexes (producer), by stage of processing and detailed commodity, monthly 1990, annual rpt, 6764–2

Puerto Rico economic censuses, 1987: wholesale and retail trade and service industry finances and operations, by SIC 2- to 4-digit industry and municipio, 2591–1

R&D facilities for biological and medical sciences, space and equipment adequacy, needs, and funding by source, by instn type, 1990, biennial rpt, 4434–17

Shipments and PPI for building materials, by type, bimonthly rpt, 2042–1.5; 2042–1.6

Solar collector and photovoltaic module shipments by end-use sector and State, and trade, 1989, annual rpt, 3164–62

TVA electric power purchases of municipal and cooperative distributors, and prices and use by distributor and consumer sector, monthly rpt, 9802–1

Wholesale trade census, 1987: establishments, sales by customer class, employment, inventories, and expenses, by SIC 2- to 4-digit kind of business, 2407–4

Air Force

Criminal case processing in military courts, and prisoners by facility, by service branch, data compilation, 1991 annual rpt, 6064–6.5

Deaths by cause, age, race, and rank, and personnel captured and missing, by service branch, FY90, annual rpt, 3544–40

Health care facilities of DOD in US and abroad, beds, admissions, outpatient visits, and births, by service branch, quarterly rpt, 3542–15

Pacific basin US military personnel, dependents, aircraft, ships, and costs, by service branch and location, 1990, GAO rpt, 26123–357

Persian Gulf War costs to US by category and service branch, and offsetting contributions by allied country, monthly rpt, 102–3

Persian Gulf War costs to US by category and service branch, and offsetting contributions by allied country, various periods FY90-91, annual rpt, 104–7

Personnel (civilian and military) of DOD, by service branch, major installation, and State, as of Sept 1990, annual rpt, 3544–7

Personnel active duty and recruit social, economic, and parents characteristics, by service branch and State, FY89, annual rpt, 3544–41

Personnel active duty strength, recruits, and reenlistment, by race, sex, and service branch, quarterly press release, 3542–7

Personnel, contracts, and payroll, by service branch and location, with top 5 contractors and maps, by State and country, FY90, annual rpt, 3544–29

Index by Subjects and Names

Air pollution

Personnel needs, costs, and force readiness, by service branch, FY92, annual rpt, 3504–1

Personnel of DOD, and organization, budget, weapons, and property, by service branch, State, and country, 1991 annual summary rpt, 3504–13

Personnel strengths, for active duty, civilians, and dependents, by service branch and US and foreign location, quarterly rpt, 3542–20

Personnel strengths, for active duty, civilians, and reserves, by service branch, FY90 and trends, annual rpt, 3544–1

Personnel strengths, for active duty, civilians, and reserves, by service branch, quarterly rpt, 3542–14

Personnel strengths, for active duty enlisted and officers, by sex and race, 1970s-90, GAO rpt, 26123–325

Personnel strengths in US and abroad, by service branch, world area, and country, quarterly press release, 3542–9

Personnel strengths, summary by service branch, monthly press release, 3542–2

Recruiting compliance of Air Force with gender-neutral selection, with aptitude test results by sex, FY86-90, GAO rpt, 26123–359

Reserve forces personnel strengths and characteristics, by component, FY90, annual rpt, 3544–38

Reserve forces personnel strengths and characteristics, by component, quarterly rpt, 3542–4

ROTC programs enrollment, grads, staff, scholarships, and costs, by service branch, FY86-89, GAO rpt, 26123–337

Training and education programs of DOD, funding, staff, students, and facilities, by service branch, FY92, annual rpt, 3504–5

Women military personnel on active and reserve duty, by demographic and service characteristics and service branch, FY89, annual chartbook, 3544–26

see also Department of Air Force

Air freight

see Air cargo

Air National Guard

see National Guard

Air navigation

see Aeronautical navigation

Air piracy

Airport security operations to prevent hijacking, screening results, enforcement actions, and hijacking attempts, 2nd half 1989, semiannual rpt, 7502–5

Hijacking attempts on US and foreign aircraft, summary data 1978-88, annual rpt, 7304–1

Hijackings, on-board explosions, and other crime, US and foreign incidents, 1985-89, annual rpt, 7504–31

Hijackings, other crimes against aviation, and airport screening results, data compilation, 1991 annual rpt, 6064–6.3

Sentences for Federal offenses, guidelines by offense and circumstances, series, 17668–1

Terrorism (intl) incidents, casualties, and attacks on US targets, by attack type and country, 1990, annual rpt, 7004–22

Air pollution

Abatement equipment shipments by industry, and new and backlog orders, by product, 1990, annual Current Industrial Rpt, 2506–12.5

Abatement equipment US industry intl competitiveness, with selected foreign and US operating data, 1970s-92, 2046–12.45

Abatement spending by govts, business, and consumers, 1987-89, annual article, 2702–1.229

Abatement spending, capital and operating costs by SIC 2-digit industry, 1989, advance annual Current Industrial Rpt, 2506–3.6

Assistance (financial and nonfinancial) of Fed Govt, 1991 base edition with supplements, annual listing, 104–5

Carbon dioxide in atmosphere, DOE R&D programs and funding at natl labs, universities, and other instns, FY91, annual summary rpt, 3004–18.1; 3004–18.7

Carbon dioxide in atmosphere, measurement, methodology, and research results, series, 3006–11

Coastal areas environmental and socioeconomic conditions, and potential impact of oil and gas OCS leases, final statement series, 5736–1

Costs of environmental protection programs to govts and households, by program type and city size, 1960s-88 and projected to 2000, 9188–114

Detroit metro area air pollution emissions and levels, by pollutant, 1980-90, 14648–25

Developing countries energy use, and economic and environmental impacts, by fuel type, world area, and country, 1980s-90, 26358–232

Electric power plants production and capacity by fuel type, prices, demand, and air pollution law impacts, by region, 1989-90 and projected to 2010, annual rpt, 3164–81

Electric utilities privately owned, air pollution emissions and abatement equipment by fuel type and State, 1985-89, annual rpt, 3164–11.5

Electric utilities privately owned, pollution abatement outlays by type of pollutant and equipment, and firm, 1989, annual rpt, 3164–23

Emissions factors, by detailed pollutant and source, data compilation, 1990 rpt, 9198–120

Emissions levels for 3 pollutants, and capacity of electric plants with abatement equipment, by type, 1985-89, annual rpt, 3164–74.5

Emissions levels for 5 pollutants, by detailed source and State, annual rpt, discontinued, 9194–7

Emissions levels for 6 pollutants, by source and selected MSA, 1980-89, annual rpt, 9194–1

Emissions levels for 6 pollutants, by source, 1970-89 and trends from 1940, annual rpt, 9194–13

Energy natl strategy plans for conservation and pollution reduction, impacts of technology and regulation proposals, projected 1990-2030, 3166–6.47

Energy natl strategy plans for conservation and pollution reduction, impacts on electric power supply, costs, and emissions, projected under alternative assumptions, 1995-2030, 3166–6.49

Energy natl strategy plans for conservation, impacts on energy use and pollution under alternative technology investment assumptions, projected 1990-2030, 3166–6.48

Energy supply, demand, and prices, by fuel type and end-use sector, projections and underlying assumptions, 1990-2010, annual rpt, 3164–90

Environmental impacts of acid rain and air pollution, and methods of neutralizing acidified water bodies, summary research rpt series, 5506–5

EPA pollution control grant program activities, monthly rpt, 9182–8

Foreign and US environmental and wildlife conservation agreements provisions, status, and signatories, as of 1991, listing, 9886–4.169

Health condition and health care resources, use, and spending, 1950s-89, annual data compilation, 4144–11

Health condition improvement and disease prevention goals and recommended activities for 2000, with trends 1970s-80s, 4048–10

Health effects of selected pollutants on animals by species and on humans, and environmental levels, series, 5506–14

Indoor air pollution levels and emissions rates, by pollutant type and source, 1991 handbook, 3326–1.2

Indoor air pollution levels in workplace, and health impacts, for Library of Congress Madison building, 1989 study, 4248–92

Lead levels in environment, sources of emissions and exposure, and health effects, literature review, 1990 rpt, 9198–84

Medical waste generation, sources, health workers exposure and risk, and incineration emissions, 1980s, 4078–1

Mines safety and health enforcement, training, and funding, with casualties, by type of mine and State, FY89, annual rpt, 6664–6

Neighborhood and housing quality, indicators and attitudes, by householder type and location, 1985, biennial rpt supplement, 2485–13

North Carolina environmental and socioeconomic conditions, and impacts of proposed OCS oil and gas exploration, 1970s-90 and projected to 2020, 5738–22

Ozone in stratosphere, levels, depletion rates and climate impacts, and properties of chlorofluorocarbons and substitutes, 1990 rpt, 9508–37

Ozone levels reductions from alternative motor fuels use, series, 9196–5

Respiratory diseases related to occupational hazards, epidemiology, diagnosis, and treatment, for selected industries and work settings, 1988 conf, 4248–90

Soviet Union, Eastern Europe, OECD, and selected other countries pollution and deforestation indicators, 1960s-90, annual rpt, 9114–4.10

Statistical Abstract of US, 1991 annual data compilation, 2324–1.6

Air pollution

Sulfur dioxide emissions reduction levels, by EC member, 1980 and projected to 2003, annual rpt, 3164–77.1

Timber wastes burning, air pollution emissions, 1982, 1208–343

Waste (hazardous) incinerators health and safety violations, by type of violation, 1991 rpt, 6608–5

Yearbook of Agriculture, special topics, 1991 annual compilation of papers, 1004–18

see also Acid rain

see also Global climate change

see also Motor vehicle exhaust

see also Radiation

see also Radon

Air safety

see Aviation accidents and safety

Air traffic control

Airport capacity improvement projects and funding, traffic, and delays, by major airport, 1987-90 and forecast to 1998, annual rpt, 7504–43

Certificates for pilots and nonpilots held, by type of certificate, age, sex, region, and State, 1990, annual rpt, 7504–2

Employment levels at ATC facilities, by selected characteristics of staff, FY89, annual rpt, 7504–41

Employment levels, by job level and selected ATC facility, FY88-90, GAO rpt, 26113–522

Employment of DOT, by subagency, occupation, and selected personnel characteristics, FY90, annual rpt, 7304–18

FAA tower, instrument, flight center, and flight services operations, quarterly rpt, 7502–16

Instrument flight rule aircraft handled, by user type, FAA traffic control center, and region, FY85-90 and projected to FY2005, annual rpt, 7504–15

Medical research and test results for aviation, technical rpt series, 7506–10

Operational errors, and other incidents, monthly rpt, 7502–15

Operations and finances of FAA, and staff by region, FY89-90, annual rpt, 7504–10

Operations and finances of FAA ATC and airway facilities and services, FY85-89, annual rpt, 7504–37

Operations of FAA ATC facilities, by service and aviation type, and facility, 1980-89, annual rpt, 7504–1.2

Operations of FAA ATC facilities, improvement under Aviation System Capital Investment Plan, 1981-90 and projected to 2005, annual rpt, 7504–12

Traffic, aircraft, pilots, airports, and fuel use, forecast FY91-2002 and trends from FY81, annual rpt, 7504–6

Traffic and other aviation activity forecasts of FAA, 1991 annual conf, 7504–28

Traffic and passenger and freight enplanements, by airport, 1960s-90 and projected to 2010, hub area rpt series, 7506–7

Traffic and passenger enplanements, by airport, region, and State, projected FY91-2005 and trends from FY83, annual rpt, 7504–7

Traffic levels at FAA ATC facilities, by airport and State, FY90, annual rpt, 7504–27

see also Aviation accidents and safety

Air transportation

see Air cargo

see Air travel

see Airlines

see Airports and airways

see Military aviation

Air travel

Aliens (illegal) overstaying visas, by class of admission, mode of arrival, age, country, and State, FY85-88, annual rpt, 6264–5

Atlantic Ocean intl air traffic and passengers, by aviation type and route, alternative forecasts 1991-2010 and trends from 1980, annual rpt, 7504–44

Child fare proposal impacts on family airline travel and industry revenue, with costs and accidents compared to auto travel, 1990 hearing, 21648–61

Consumer complaints against air carriers, agents, and cargo handlers, monthly rpt, 7302–11

Energy use by mode of transport, fuel supply, and demographic and economic factors of vehicle use, 1970s-89, annual rpt, 3304–5

Fed Govt financial and nonfinancial domestic aid, 1991 base edition with supplements, annual listing, 104–5

Foreign travel from US, characteristics of visit and traveler, and world area of destination, 1990 in-flight survey, annual rpt, 2904–14

Foreign travel to and from US on US and foreign flag air carriers, by country, world area, and US port, monthly rpt, 7302–2

Foreign travel to and from US on US and foreign flag air carriers, by world area, 1990, annual rpt, 2904–13

Foreign travel to US, by characteristics of visit and traveler, country, port city, and State of destination, monthly rpt, 2902–1

Foreign travel to US, by characteristics of visit and traveler, world area of origin, and US destination, 1990 survey, annual rpt, 2904–12

Import restraint elimination impacts on US economy and selected service industries, 1970s-90, 9886–4.173

Natl transportation system planning, use, condition, accidents, and needs, by mode of transport, 1940s-90 and projected to 2020, 7308–202

Passenger enplanements and traffic, by airport, region, and State, projected FY91-2005 and trends from FY83, annual rpt, 7504–7

Passenger traffic, aircraft, pilots, airports, and fuel use, forecast FY91-2002 and trends from FY81, annual rpt, 7504–6

Passenger traffic, capacity, and performance, by carrier and type of operation, monthly rpt, 7302–6

Passenger traffic, capacity, and performance for medium regional airlines, by carrier, quarterly rpt, 7302–8

Price indexes for exports and imports of manufactured goods and services, quarterly press release, 6762–13

Southeastern States, Fed Reserve 6th District, economic indicators by State and MSA, quarterly rpt, 9371–14

State and Metro Area Data Book, 1991 data compilation, 2328–54

Tax (excise) collections of IRS, by source, quarterly rpt, 8302–1; 8302–2.1

Traffic (passenger and cargo), and departures by aircraft type, by carrier and airport, 1990, annual rpt, 7504–35

Traffic (passenger, cargo, and mail), and airline operations, by type of service, air carrier, State, and country, 1980-89, annual rpt, 7504–1.4; 7504–1.6

Traffic and passenger and freight enplanements, by airport, 1960s-90 and projected to 2010, hub area rpt series, 7506–7

see also Aeronautical navigation

see also Aircraft

see also Airlines

see also Airports and airways

see also Aviation accidents and safety

see also Civil aviation

see also General aviation

see also Military aviation

see also Pilots

Aircraft

Airline market entry impacts of carrier control of airports, facility and aircraft availability, noise regulation, and other barriers, late 1980s and projected to 1997, 7308–199.8

Business statistics, detailed data for major industries and economic indicators, *Survey of Current Business*, monthly rpt, 2702–1.23

Costs of operating privately owned small planes by component, and Fed Govt mileage reimbursement rates, 1989, annual rpt, 9454–13.2

Customs Service activities, collections, entries processed by mode of transport, and seizures, FY86-90, annual rpt, 8144–1

Exports and imports between US and outlying areas, by detailed commodity and mode of transport, 1990, annual rpt, 2424–11

Exports and imports of US, by country and detailed commodity, monthly rpt, 2422–12

Exports and imports of US, by Harmonized System 6-digit commodity and country, 1990, annual rpt, 2424–13

Exports and imports of US, by selected country, country group, and commodity group, 1990, annual rpt, 2044–37

Exports and imports of US, by transport mode, country, and SITC 1- to 3-digit commodity, 1990, annual rpt, 2424–12

Exports of US, detailed Schedule B commodities with countries of destination, 1990, annual rpt, 2424–10

Flight and engine hours, and shutdown rates, by aircraft and engine model, and air carrier, monthly rpt, 7502–13

Foreign countries economic, social, political, and geographic summary data, by country, 1991, annual factbook, 9114–2

Gear production for selected uses under alternative production requirements, and industry finances and operations, late 1940s-89, 2028–1

General aviation activity, 1990, triennial survey rpt, 7508–3

General aviation aircraft, flight hours, and equipment, by type, use, and model of aircraft, region, and State, 1990, annual rpt, 7504–29

Index by Subjects and Names — Airlines

Maintenance of aircraft by independent repair stations, airlines use and costs, 1980s-90, GAO rpt, 26113–492

Maintenance requirements of FAA for aging craft, airlines compliance and repair facilities operations, 1989-91, GAO rpt, 26113–527

Manufacturing annual survey, 1989: value of shipments, by SIC 4- to 5-digit product class, 2506–15.2

Manufacturing census, 1987: employment and shipments under Fed Govt contracts, by SIC 4-digit industry, 2497–7

Natl transportation system planning, use, condition, accidents, and needs, by mode of transport, 1940s-90 and projected to 2020, 7308–202

OECD trade, total and for 4 major countries, and US trade by country, by commodity, 1970-89, world area rpt series, 9116–1

Pollution (air) contributing to global warming, emissions factors and control costs, by pollutant and source, 1990 rpt, 9198–124

Pollution (air) emissions factors, by detailed pollutant and source, data compilation, 1990 rpt, 9198–120

Pollution (air) levels for 6 pollutants, by source, 1970-89 and trends from 1940, annual rpt, 9194–13

Price indexes (producer), by stage of processing and detailed commodity, monthly rpt, 6762–6

Price indexes (producer), by stage of processing and detailed commodity, monthly 1990, annual rpt, 6764–2

Registrations of aircraft with FAA, by type and characteristics of aircraft, make, carrier, State, and county, 1989, annual rpt, 7504–3

Rental establishments, and receipts by type of equipment rented, by State, 1987 Census of Service Industries, 2393–4.7

Shipments of general aviation aircraft, and commercial carriers orders and deliveries, by aircraft type, quarterly rpt, 7502–16

Shipments, trade, use, and firms, by type of craft and engine, monthly Current Industrial Rpt, 2506–12.24

State and Metro Area Data Book, 1991 data compilation, 2328–54

Statistical Abstract of US, 1991 annual data compilation, 2324–1.22

Traffic (passenger and cargo), and departures by aircraft type, by carrier and airport, 1990, annual rpt, 7504–35

Traffic, aircraft, carriers, airports, and FAA activities, detailed data, 1980-89, annual rpt, 7504–1

Traffic, aircraft, pilots, airports, and fuel use, forecast FY91-2002 and trends from FY81, annual rpt, 7504–6

Traffic and other aviation activity forecasts of FAA, 1991 annual conf, 7504–28

Wholesale trade census, 1987: establishments, sales by customer class, employment, inventories, and expenses, by SIC 2- to 4-digit kind of business, 2407–4

see also Aerial surveys
see also Aeronautical navigation
see also Aerospace industry
see also Aircraft noise

see also Aviation accidents and safety
see also Aviation fuels
see also Helicopters
see also Military aircraft
see also under By Commodity in the "Index by Categories"

Aircraft accidents

see Aviation accidents and safety

Aircraft carriers

see Naval vessels

Aircraft noise

Abatement measures for aircraft noise, and industry compliance costs, aggregate FY90-2000, GAO rpt, 26113–534

Airline market entry impacts of carrier control of airports, facility and aircraft availability, noise regulation, and other barriers, late 1980s and projected to 1997, 7308–199.8

Birds (geese) pre-migration feeding behavior impacts of aircraft disturbance, for 3 species at Izembek Lagoon, Alaska, 1970s-88, 5738–23

Health effects of aircraft noise, noise level policies, and aircraft replacement schedules and costs, 1960s-90 and projected to 2006, hearing, 21648–64

Whales (bowhead) population in Arctic areas, impacts of subsistence whaling, shipping, noise, and other human activity, mid 1970s-80s, 5738–30

Whales (bowhead and white) migration through Beaufort Sea, behavior impacts of oil drilling and aircraft noise, spring 1989, 5738–27

Airlines

Aircraft registered with FAA, by type and characteristics of aircraft, make, carrier, State, and county, 1989, annual rpt, 7504–3

Airport finances, operations by carrier, and capacity improvement and dev funding, by airport, 1977-87 and projected to 2020, hearing, 21648–59

Business statistics, detailed data for major industries and economic indicators, *Survey of Current Business*, monthly rpt, 2702–1.11

Capital expenditures for plant and equipment, by major industry group, quarterly rpt, 2502–2

Collective bargaining agreements expiring during year, and workers covered, by firm, union, industry group, and State, 1991, annual rpt, 6784–9

Commuter carrier and air taxi aircraft, hours flown, and equipment, by type and model of aircraft, region, and State, 1990, annual rpt, 7504–29

Consumer complaints by reason, passengers denied boarding, and late flights, by reporting carrier and airport, monthly rpt, 7302–11

Consumer complaints, passengers denied boarding, and late flights, by carrier, 1985-91, GAO rpt, 26113–542

County Business Patterns, 1988: employment, establishments, and payroll, by SIC 2- to 4-digit industry and county, annual State rpt series, 2326–6

County Business Patterns, 1989: employment, establishments, and payroll, by SIC 2- to 4-digit industry and county, annual State rpt series, 2326–8

CPI by component for US city average, and by region, population size, and for 27 metro areas, monthly rpt, 6762–2

Deregulation of airlines in 1978, impacts on industry structure, competition, fares, finances, operations, and intl service, with data by carrier and airport, 1980s, series, 7308–199

Employment, earnings, and hours, by SIC 1- to 4-digit industry, monthly and annual averages, selected years 1909-90, annual rpt, 6744–4

Finances and operations, by SIC 2- to 4-digit industry, forecast 1991, annual rpt, 2044–28

Finances of airlines, by carrier, carrier group, and for total certificated system, quarterly rpt, 7302–7

Financial and operating summary data for airlines, quarterly rpt, 7502–16

Flight and engine hours, and shutdown rates, by aircraft and engine model, and air carrier, monthly rpt, 7502–13

Fuel use and efficiency under alternative technological improvements and load factors, by model, projected 1995-2010, 3028–6

Hijackings, on-board explosions, and other crime, US and foreign incidents, 1985-89, annual rpt, 7504–31

Labor productivity, indexes of output, hours, and employment by SIC 2- to 4-digit industry, 1967-89, annual rpt, 6824–1.4

Maintenance of aircraft by independent repair stations, airlines use and costs, 1980s-90, GAO rpt, 26113–492

Maintenance requirements of FAA for aging craft, airlines compliance and repair facilities operations, 1989-91, GAO rpt, 26113–527

Military and personal property shipments, passenger traffic, and costs, by service branch and mode of transport, quarterly rpt, 3702–1

Noise abatement measures for airports and aircraft, and industry compliance costs, aggregate FY90-2000, GAO rpt, 26113–534

Price indexes (producer), by stage of processing and detailed commodity, monthly rpt, 6762–6

Reservation system (computerized) operations, travel agency revenues by firm, and frequent flyer awards schedules by carrier, 1988, 7308–199.9

Statistical Abstract of US, 1991 annual data compilation, 2324–1.22

Tax (income) returns of corporations, income and tax items by asset size and detailed industry, 1987, annual rpt, 8304–4

Tax (income) returns of corporations, income and tax items by asset size and detailed industry, 1988, annual rpt, 8304–21

Tax (income) returns of sole proprietorships, income statement items, by industry group, 1989, annual article, 8302–2.214

Traffic (passenger and cargo), and departures by aircraft type, by carrier and airport, 1990, annual rpt, 7504–35

Traffic (passenger and cargo), carrier enplanement shares, and FAA airport improvement program grants, by airport and State, 1989, annual rpt, 7504–48

Airlines

Traffic, aircraft, carriers, airports, and FAA activities, detailed data, 1980-89, annual rpt, 7504–1

Traffic, aircraft, pilots, airports, and fuel use, forecast FY91-2002 and trends from FY81, annual rpt, 7504–6

Traffic and other aviation activity forecasts of FAA, 1991 annual conf, 7504–28

Traffic and passenger and freight enplanements, by airport, 1960s-90 and projected to 2010, hub area rpt series, 7506–7

Traffic and passenger enplanements, by airport, region, and State, projected FY91-2005 and trends from FY83, annual rpt, 7504–7

Traffic, capacity, and performance, by carrier and type of operation, monthly rpt, 7302–6

Traffic, capacity, and performance for medium regional airlines, by carrier, quarterly rpt, 7302–8

Traffic levels at FAA air traffic control facilities, by airport and State, FY90, annual rpt, 7504–27

see also Aviation accidents and safety

see also under By Individual Company or Institution in the "Index by Categories"

see also under By Industry in the "Index by Categories"

Airports and airways

Acreage of land, by use, ownership, and State, 1987 and trends from 1910, 1588–48

Atlantic Ocean intl air traffic and passengers, by aviation type and route, alternative forecasts 1991-2010 and trends from 1980, annual rpt, 7504–44

Budget of US, formula grant program obligations to State and local govts, by agency, program, and State, FY92, annual rpt, 104–30

Budget of US, obligations and authority by function, agency, and program, with summaries, analyses, and historical tables, FY92, annual rpt, 104–2

Capacity expansion and improvement funding sources, alternative methods, late 1980s and projected to 2000, hearing, 21648–63

Capacity improvement projects and funding, traffic, and delays, by major airport, 1987-90 and forecast to 1998, annual rpt, 7504–43

Condition, mgmt, R&D, and funding, for transportation and environmental public works, 1986-91, 26358–235

Construction industries census, 1987: establishments, employment, receipts, and expenditures, by SIC 4-digit industry and State, final industry rpt series, 2373–1

Crimes against civil aviation, and circumstances, US and worldwide, 1985-89, annual rpt, 7504–31

Deregulation of airlines in 1978, impacts on industry structure, competition, fares, finances, operations, and intl service, with data by carrier and airport, 1980s, series, 7308–199

Engineering and architectural establishments, receipts by type of client and project, payroll, and employment, by State, 1987 Census of Service Industries, 2393–4.16

FAA activities and finances, and staff by region, FY89-90, annual rpt, 7504–10

FAA airport improvement program activities and grants, by State and airport, FY90, annual rpt, 7504–38

FAA airport improvement program activities, funding, and airport operations, by location, projected 1990-99, biennial rpt, 7504–42

FAA airport planning and dev project grants, by airport and location, quarterly press release, 7502–14

Fed Govt Airport and Airway Trust Fund financial condition, monthly rpt, 8102–9.5

Fed Govt-owned real property inventory and costs, worldwide summary by purpose, agency, and location, 1989, annual rpt, 9454–5

Fed Govt spending in States, by type, program, agency, and State, FY90, annual rpt, 2464–2

Fed Govt surplus personal property donations to govt and nonprofit agencies, with data by State, FY88-90, biennial rpt, 9454–22

Finances, operations by carrier, and capacity improvement and dev funding, by airport, 1977-87 and projected to 2020, hearing, 21648–59

Foreign countries economic, social, political, and geographic summary data, by country, 1991, annual factbook, 9114–2

General aviation activity, 1990, triennial survey rpt, 7508–3

Govt census, 1987: employment, payroll, and average earnings, by function, level of govt, State, county, and population size, 2455–2

Govt employment and payroll, by function, level of govt, and jurisdiction, 1990, annual rpt series, 2466–1

Govt finances, by level of govt, State, and for large cities and counties, annual rpt series, 2466–2

Helicopters, use, and landing facilities, by craft type, region, and State, 1989, 7508–75

Hub airports air carrier operations, by airport, quarterly rpt, 7502–16

Military airfields joint use by civil aircraft, and effectiveness in reducing airport congestion, FY85-89, GAO rpt, 26113–524

Natl Ocean Service Charting and Geodetic Service activities and funding, by State, FY91-92, biennial rpt, 2174–10

Natl transportation system planning, use, condition, accidents, and needs, by mode of transport, 1940s-90 and projected to 2020, 7308–202

Passenger complaints, boarding denials, and late flights, by reporting carrier and airport, monthly rpt, 7302–11

Passenger travel to and from US on US and foreign flag air carriers, by country, world area, and US port, monthly rpt, 7302–2

Security operations of airports to prevent hijacking, screening results, enforcement actions, and hijacking attempts, 2nd half 1989, semiannual rpt, 7502–5

State and Metro Area Data Book, 1991 data compilation, 2328–54

Statistical Abstract of US, 1991 annual data compilation, 2324–1.22

Index by Subjects and Names

Traffic (passenger and cargo), and departures by aircraft type, by carrier and airport, 1990, annual rpt, 7504–35

Traffic (passenger and cargo), carrier enplanement shares, and FAA airport improvement program grants, by airport and State, 1989, annual rpt, 7504–48

Traffic, aircraft, carriers, airports, and FAA activities, detailed data, 1980-89, annual rpt, 7504–1

Traffic, aircraft, pilots, and fuel use, forecast FY91-2002 and trends from FY81, annual rpt, 7504–6

Traffic and other aviation activity forecasts of FAA, 1991 annual conf, 7504–28

Traffic and passenger and freight enplanements, by airport, 1960s-90 and projected to 2010, hub area rpt series, 7506–7

Traffic and passenger enplanements, by airport, region, and State, projected FY91-2005 and trends from FY83, annual rpt, 7504–7

Traffic levels at FAA air traffic control facilities, by airport and State, FY90, annual rpt, 7504–27

Weather stations of Natl Weather Service, locations and types of observations made, 1990 annual listing, 2184–5

see also Air traffic control

see also Aircraft noise

see also Aviation accidents and safety

Aitken, Sherrie S.

"National Study of Guardian *Ad Litem* Representation", 4608–28

Aizcorbe, Ana M.

"Note on Empirical Tests of Separability and the 'Approximation' View of Functional Form", 6886–6.77

"Procyclical Labor Productivity, Increasing Returns to Labor, and Labor Hoarding in U.S. Auto Assembly Plant Employment", 6886–6.72

Ajman

see United Arab Emirates

Akhtar, M. A.

"Political and Institutional Independence of U.S. Monetary Policy", 9385–8.106

"U.S. Financial System: A Status Report and a Structural Perspective", 9385–8.84

Akron, Ohio

CPI by component for US city average, and by region, population size, and for 15 metro areas, monthly rpt, 6762–1

CPI by component for US city average, and by region, population size, and for 27 metro areas, monthly rpt, 6762–2

see also under By City and By SMSA or MSA in the "Index by Categories"

Alabama

Appalachian Regional Commission funding, by project and State, planned FY91, annual rpt, 9084–3

Banks (insured commercial and savings) deposits by instn, State, MSA, and county, as of June 1990, annual regional rpt, 9295–3.4

Coal production and mines by county, prices, productivity, miners, and reserves, by mining method and State, 1989-90, annual rpt, 3164–25

County Business Patterns, 1989: employment, establishments, and payroll, by SIC 2- to 4-digit industry and county, annual State rpt, 2326–8.2

Index by Subjects and Names

Alaska

DOD prime contract awards, by contractor, service branch, State, and city, FY90, annual rpt, 3544–22

Economic indicators by State and MSA, Fed Reserve 6th District, quarterly rpt, 9371–14

Education system in Appalachia, improvement initiatives, and indicators of success, by State, 1960s-89, 9088–36

Employment and housing and mortgage market indicators by State, FHLB 4th District, quarterly rpt, 9302–36

Employment and unemployment, for 8 southeastern States, 1989-90, annual rpt, 6944–2

Employment by industry div, earnings, and hours, for 8 southeastern States, quarterly press release, 6942–7

Fed Govt spending in States and local areas, by type, State, county, and city, FY90, annual rpt, 2464–3

Fed Govt spending in States, by type, program, agency, and State, FY90, annual rpt, 2464–2

Fish (catfish) raised on farms, inventory, stocks, and production, by major producer State, quarterly rpt, 1631–18

Fish and shellfish catch, wholesale receipts, prices, trade, and other market activities, weekly regional rpt, 2162–6.3

HHS financial aid, by program, recipient, State, and city, FY90, annual regional listing, 4004–3.4

Hospital deaths of Medicare patients, actual and expected rates by diagnosis, and hospital characteristics, by instn, FY87-89, annual regional rpt, 4654–14.4

Housing census, 1990: inventory, occupancy, and costs, State fact sheet, 2326–21.2

Hunter characteristics and expenditures, 1990 conf papers, annual rpt, 1204–38

Income (personal) per capita and by source, and earnings by industry div, by State, MSA, and county, 1984-89, annual regional rpt, 2704–2.4

Jail adult and juvenile population, employment, spending, instn conditions, and inmate programs, by county and facility, 1988, regional rpt series, 6068–144.4

Marriages, divorces, and rates, by characteristics of spouses, State, and county, 1987 and trends from 1920, US Vital Statistics annual rpt, 4144–4

Methane production in coal fields by basin, and resources remaining, 1970s-89, article, 3162–4.201

Mineral Industry Surveys, State reviews of production, 1990, preliminary annual rpt, 5614–6

Minerals Yearbook, 1989, Vol 2: State review of production and sales by commodity, and business activity, annual rpt, 5604–16.2

Minerals Yearbook, 1989, Vol 2: State reviews of production, sales, and firms, by commodity, and business activity, annual rpt, 5604–34

Physicians, by specialty, age, sex, and location of training and practice, 1989, State rpt, 4116–6.1

Population and housing census, 1990: population and housing characteristics, households, and land area, by county, subdiv, and place, State rpt, 2551–1.2

Population and housing census, 1990: voting age and total population by race, and housing units, by block, redistricting counts required under PL 94-171, State CD-ROM release, 2551–6.1

Population and housing census, 1990: voting age and total population by race, and housing units, by county and city, redistricting counts required under PL 94-171, State summary rpt, 2551–5.1

Statistical Abstract of US, 1991 annual data compilation, 2324–1

Supplemental Security Income payments and beneficiaries, by type of eligibility, State, and county, Dec 1989, annual rpt, 4744–27.4

Textile mill employment, earnings, and hours, for 8 Southeastern States, quarterly press release, 6942–1

Timber in Alabama, acreage and volume by species, forest type, ownership, and county, 1990, series, 1206–30

Water supply and quality in streams and lakes, and groundwater levels in wells, by drainage basin, 1990, annual State rpt, 5666–10.1

see also Birmingham, Ala.

see also Huntsville, Ala.

see also Jefferson County, Ala.

see also Walker County, Ala.

see also under By State in the "Index by Categories"

Alameddine, Fadi

"Some Problems of Infinite Regress in Social-Choice Models: A Category Theory Solution", 9377–9.106

Alamogordo, N.Mex.

Wages by occupation, and benefits for office and plant workers, 1991 survey, periodic MSA rpt, 6785–3.5

Alamprese, Judith A.

"No Gift Wasted: Effective Strategies for Educating Highly Able, Disadvantaged Students in Mathematics and Science. Volume I: Findings", 4808–34.1

"No Gift Wasted: Effective Strategies for Educating Highly Able, Disadvantaged Students in Mathematics and Science. Volume II: Case Studies", 4808–34.2

Alaska

Agricultural Statistics, 1990, annual rpt, 1004–1

Banks (insured commercial and savings) deposits by instn, State, MSA, and county, as of June 1990, annual regional rpt, 9295–3.6

Birds (geese) pre-migration feeding behavior impacts of aircraft disturbance, for 3 species at Izembek Lagoon, Alaska, 1970s-88, 5738–23

Birds (waterfowl) coastal population and breeding success, for murre and kittiwake in Bering Sea colonies, 1979-89, 5738–31

Coal production and mines by county, prices, productivity, miners, and reserves, by mining method and State, 1989-90, annual rpt, 3164–25

Coastal areas pollutant concentrations in fish and sediments, by contaminant, fish species, and Pacific coast site, 1984-86, 2168–121

County Business Patterns, 1989: employment, establishments, and payroll, by SIC 2- to 4-digit industry and county, annual State rpt, 2326–8.3

DOD civilian and military personnel and dependents, by service branch and US and foreign location, quarterly rpt, 3542–20

DOD prime contract awards, by contractor, service branch, State, and city, FY90, annual rpt, 3544–22

Environmental conditions and oil dev impacts for Alaska OCS, compilation of papers, series, 2176–1

Fed Govt spending in States and local areas, by type, State, county, and city, FY90, annual rpt, 2464–3

Fed Govt spending in States, by type, program, agency, and State, FY90, annual rpt, 2464–2

Fish and shellfish catch, wholesale receipts, prices, trade, and other market activities, weekly regional rpt, 2162–6.5

Fish catch and habitat impacts of Arctic Ocean oil and gas dev, and assessment methods, 1988 conf, 5738–24

Fishing for subsistence, role in Alaska communities economies, with indicators for Yakutat, 1980s, 1208–350

HHS financial aid, by program, recipient, State, and city, FY90, annual regional listing, 4004–3.10

Hospital deaths of Medicare patients, actual and expected rates by diagnosis, and hospital characteristics, by instn, FY87-89, annual regional rpt, 4654–14.10

Ice conditions of Bering Sea and Alaska north coast, monthly rpt, 2182–5

Income (personal) per capita and by source, and earnings by industry div, by State, MSA, and county, 1984-89, annual regional rpt, 2704–2.5

Jail adult and juvenile population, employment, spending, instn conditions, and inmate programs, by county and facility, 1988, regional rpt series, 6068–144.5

Land (submerged) grant holdings of Alaska Natives, exchange for upland acreage, impacts on conservation acreage and acquisition, 1989-90, 5728–38

Land area in Alaska by ownership, and availability for mineral exploration and dev, 1984-86, 5608–152

Marine mammals and birds population and distribution, by species and northeast Pacific Ocean location, literature and data base review, 1950s-88, 5738–28

Marine mammals protection activities and funding, populations, and harvests, by species, 1989, annual rpt, 5504–12

Marriages, divorces, and rates, by characteristics of spouses, State, and county, 1987 and trends from 1920, US Vital Statistics annual rpt, 4144–4

Military presence of US in Pacific basin, personnel, dependents, aircraft, ships, and costs, by service branch and location, 1990, GAO rpt, 26123–357

Mineral Industry Surveys, State reviews of production, 1990, preliminary annual rpt, 5614–6

Minerals resources and production of Juneau region, by mineral and site, 1987-88, 5608–169

Minerals resources of Alaska, and geologic characteristics, compilation of papers, 1989, annual rpt, 5664–15

Minerals resources of Alaska, production, oil and gas leases, reserves, and exploratory wells, with maps and bibl, 1989, annual rpt, 5664–11

Alaska

Minerals Yearbook, 1989, Vol 2: State review of production and sales by commodity, and business activity, annual rpt, 5604–16.3

Minerals Yearbook, 1989, Vol 2: State reviews of production, sales, and firms, by commodity, and business activity, annual rpt, 5604–34

Oil and gas OCS leases environmental and socioeconomic impact and coastal area description, 1990 final statement, 5736–1.22

Oil and gas OCS leases environmental and socioeconomic impact and coastal area description, 1991 final statement, 5736–1.24

Oil and gas OCS leases suspended for environmental reasons and repurchased by Fed Govt, costs of cancellation for 3 States, 1990, GAO rpt, 26113–509

Oil and gas OCS reserves, and leasing and dev activity, 1990 periodic regional rpt, 5736–3.1

Oil and gas OCS reserves of Fed Govt, leasing and exploration activity, production, revenue, and costs, by ocean area, FY90, annual rpt, 5734–4

Oil and gas reserves, 1988 and projected under alternative technology and policy assumptions to 2030, Natl Energy Strategy, 3166–6.51

Oil and gas supply, demand, and prices, alternative projections 1989-2010, annual rpt, 3164–89

Oil and lease condensate production on Alaska North Slope and other US areas, 1949-90, annual rpt, 3164–74.2

Oil crude, gas liquids, and refined products supply, demand, and movement, by PAD district and State, 1990, annual rpt, 3164–2

Oil production on North Slope, and impacts of lifting export controls on US oil trade, West Coast prices, and shipping industry, 1988 and forecast 1995, GAO rpt, 26113–496

Otters (sea) population and behavior, for Pacific Ocean, 1914-90, 5508–109

Physicians, by specialty, age, sex, and location of training and practice, 1989, State rpt, 4116–6.2

Population and housing census, 1990: population and housing characteristics, households, and land area, by county, subdiv, and place, State rpt, 2551–1.3

Population and housing census, 1990: voting age and total population by race, and housing units, by block, redistricting counts required under PL 94-171, State CD-ROM release, 2551–6.2

Population and housing census, 1990: voting age and total population by race, and housing units, by county and city, redistricting counts required under PL 94-171, State summary rpt, 2551–5.2

Rural areas in Alaska, population characteristics and energy resources dev effects, series, 5736–5

Seals (harbor) population at selected southern Alaska coastal sites, 1976-88, 14738–6

Ships freight rates for lumber from Alaska and Puget Sound to Asian markets, by product and port, 1988, 1208–358

Statistical Abstract of US, 1991 annual data compilation, 2324–1

Supplemental Security Income payments and beneficiaries, by type of eligibility, State, and county, Dec 1989, annual rpt, 4744–27.10

Telecommunications domestic and intl rates, by type of service and area served, 1989, annual rpt, 9284–6.6

Tide height and time daily at coastal points, forecast 1992, annual rpt, 2174–2.1

Timber in Alaska, production, trade, and Pacific basin market demand, 1960s-2010, 1208–365; 1208–367

Timber in northwestern US and British Columbia, production, prices, trade, and employment, quarterly rpt, 1202–3

Wages by occupation, and benefits for office and plant workers, 1991 survey, periodic MSA rpt, 6785–3.8

Walrus population, habitat mgmt, and intl conservation needs, by world region, 1990 conf, 14738–9

Water resources data collection and analysis activities of USGS Water Resources Div District, with project descriptions, 1990 rpt, 5666–26.13

Water resources dev projects of Army Corps of Engineers, characteristics, and costs, 1950s-89, biennial State rpt, 3756–1.2

Water supply, and snow survey results, monthly State rpt, 1266–2.1

Water supply, and snow survey results, 1990, annual State rpt, 1264–14.4

Wetlands (riparian) acreage, and Bur of Land Mgmt activities, mgmt plans, and scientific staff, 1990 State rpt, 5726–8.3

Wetlands acreage, resources, soil and water properties, and conservation efforts, by wetland type, 1988 State rpt, 5506–11.5

Whales (humpback) population and sightings off southeastern Alaska, 1979-86, 14738–10

see also Alaska Natives
see also Aleutian Islands
see also Anchorage, Alaska
see also Cook Inlet, Alaska
see also Gulf of Alaska
see also Ketchikan, Alaska
see also Nikishka, Alaska
see also Prince William Sound, Alaska
see also Seldovia, Alaska
see also Valdez, Alaska
see also Yakutat, Alaska
see also under By State in the "Index by Categories"

Alaska Natives

Census of Population and Housing, 1990: voting age and total population by race, and housing units, by block, redistricting counts required under PL 94-171, State CD-ROM series, 2551–6

Census of Population and Housing, 1990: voting age and total population by race, and housing units, by county and city, redistricting counts required under PL 94-171, State summary rpt series, 2551–5

Census of Population, 1990: Indian and Alaska Native population on reservations and in other designated areas, by selected site, press release, 2328–76

Census of Population, 1990: population by detailed Native American, Asian, and Pacific Islander group, race, region, and State, with data for 1980, press release, 2328–72

Index by Subjects and Names

Census of Population, 1990: population by race and detailed Hipanic origin, region, and State, with data for 1980, press release, 2328–73

Census of Population, 1990: population by race, Hispanic origin, region, census div, and State, with data for 1980, fact sheet, 2326–20.2

Disease and disorder cases among Indians and Alaska Natives, deaths, and health services use, by tribe, reservation, and Indian Health Service area, late 1950s-86, 4088–2

Education data compilation, 1991 annual rpt, 4824–2

Education funding of Fed Govt, and enrollment, degrees, and program grants and fellowships by State, for Indians, late 1960s-FY89, annual rpt, 14874–1

Health condition and other characteristics of Indians, and Indian Health Service facilities and use, by IHS region, 1980s-89, annual chartbook, 4084–7

Health condition and other characteristics of Indians, and Indian Health Service facilities, funding, and operations, 1950s-90, annual chartbook, 4084–1

Hospitalization in Indian Health Service, tribal, and contract facilities, by diagnosis, age, sex, and IHS service area, FY89, annual rpt, 4084–5

Land (submerged) grant holdings of Alaska Natives, exchange for upland acreage, impacts on conservation acreage and acquisition, 1989-90, 5728–38

Land area in Alaska by ownership, and availability for mineral exploration and dev, 1984-86, 5608–152

Rural areas in Alaska, population characteristics and energy resources dev effects, series, 5736–5

Timber in Alaska, production, trade, and Pacific basin market demand, 1960s-2010, 1208–365

Walrus and polar bear harvest by Alaska Natives, by village, 1988/89, annual rpt, 5504–12

Whales (bowhead) catch and quota for Eskimos, and other marine mammals harvest, 1970s-91, annual rpt, 14734–1

Whales (bowhead) population in Arctic areas, impacts of subsistence whaling, shipping, noise, and other human activity, mid 1970s-80s, 5738–30

Alaska Power Administration

Finances and operations of Federal power admins and electric utilities, 1989, annual rpt, 3164–24.2

Financial statements, and DOE audit, for APA, FY89-90, 3006–5.22

Albania

Agricultural exports of high-value commodities, indexes and sales by commodity, world area, and country, 1960s-86, 1528–323

Agricultural trade of US, by detailed commodity and country, 1989, annual rpt, 1524–8

Agricultural trade of US, by detailed commodity and country, 1990, semiannual rpt, 1522–4

Economic and military aid and loans from US and intl agencies, by program and country, FY46-90, annual rpt, 9914–5

Index by Subjects and Names

Alcohol abuse and treatment

Economic, social, political, and geographic summary data, by country, 1991, annual factbook, 9114–2

Export licensing, monitoring, and enforcement activities, FY90, annual rpt, 2024–1

Exports and imports of US, by commodity and country, 1970-89, world area rpt, 9116–1.3

Exports and imports of US, by transport mode, country, and SITC 1- to 3-digit commodity, 1990, annual rpt, 2424–12

Exports and imports of US with Communist countries, by detailed commodity and country, quarterly rpt with articles, 9882–2

Human rights conditions in 170 countries, and US economic and military aid, 1990, annual rpt, 21384–3

Market economy transition of Eastern Europe countries, energy production and use, by fuel, 1985-90, 9118–13

UN voting record and share of votes in agreement with US, by issue, country, and world area, 1990, annual rpt, 7004–18

see also under By Foreign Country in the "Index by Categories"

Albany, Ga.

see also under By SMSA or MSA in the "Index by Categories"

Albany, N.Y.

Wages by occupation, and benefits for office and plant workers, 1990 survey, periodic MSA rpt, 6785–3.1; 6785–3.2

see also under By City and By SMSA or MSA in the "Index by Categories"

Albuquerque, N.Mex.

see also under By City and By SMSA or MSA in the "Index by Categories"

Alcohol abuse and treatment

Abuse of alcohol, related injury and illness, series, 4486–1

Abuse of drugs and alcohol, by selected characteristics, 1990 survey, biennial rpt, 4494–5

Assistance (financial and nonfinancial) of Fed Govt, 1991 base edition with supplements, annual listing, 104–5

Child health condition and services use, 1990 chartbook, 4108–49

Children and youth social, economic, and demographic characteristics, 1950s-90, 4818–5

Cocaine-related emergency room admissions, by user and use characteristics, for major metro areas, 1987-89, article, 4042–3.204

Costs (direct and indirect) of drug and alcohol abuse and mental illness, by type, 1970s-88, article, 4042–3.219

Costs (direct and indirect) of mental illness and drug and alcohol abuse, by type and patient age and sex, 1985 with 1980 and 1988 comparisons, 4048–35

Crime, criminal justice admin and enforcement, and public opinion, data compilation, 1991 annual rpt, 6064–6

Deaths and rates, by detailed cause and demographic characteristics, 1988 and trends from 1900, US Vital Statistics annual rpt, 4144–2

Drug abuse in combination with alcohol, emergency room admissions and deaths, by sex, race, age, and major metro area, 1990, annual rpt, 4494–8

Drug abuse in combination with alcohol, indicators for selected metro areas, research results, data collection, and policy issues, 1991 semiannual conf, 4492–5

Drug abusers characteristics, for persons in methadone maintenance and inpatient treatment programs, 1970s-87, hearing, 21968–55

Education data compilation, 1991 annual rpt, 4824–2

Employee drug and alcohol use, and drinkers reporting adverse effects, for young adults by selected characteristics, 1984, article, 6722–1.237

Family members and spouses alcohol abuse, population exposure by selected characteristics, 1988, 4146–8.207

Fetal alcohol syndrome prevention program for Indians, evaluation, 1988-89 local area study, article, 4042–3.239

Health condition and health care resources, use, and spending, 1950s-89, annual data compilation, 4144–11

HHS financial aid, by program, recipient, State, and city, FY90, annual regional listings, 4004–3

Homeless persons aid programs of Fed Govt, program descriptions and funding, by agency and State, FY87-90, annual GAO rpt, 26104–21

Homeless persons alcohol abuse, by sex, age, race, and additional diagnoses, aggregate 1985-87, 4488–14

Hospitals for mental health care of States and counties, patients and admissions by age, diagnosis, and State, FY89, annual rpt, 4504–2

Indian and Alaska Native disease and disorder cases, deaths, and health services use, by tribe, reservation, and Indian Health Service area, late 1950s-86, 4088–2

Indian Health Service facilities and use, and Indian health and other characteristics, by IHS region, 1980s-89, annual chartbook, 4084–7

Indian Health Service facilities, funding, operations, and Indian health and other characteristics, 1950s-90, annual chartbook, 4084–1

Insurance (health) coverage and provisions of small business employee benefit plans, by plan type and occupational group, 1990, biennial rpt, 6784–20

Insurance (health) plans for employees, drug and alcohol abuse treatment coverage and provisions, by plan type, 1989, article, 6722–1.221

Jail population, by criminal, correctional, drug use, and family history, and selected other characteristics, 1989, 6066–19.62

Jail population, by sociodemographic characteristics, criminal and drug use history, whether convicted, offense, and sentencing, 1989, annual rpt, 6064–26.3

Minority group and women health condition, services use, payment sources, and health care labor force, by poverty status, 1940s-89, chartbook, 4118–56

Minority group drug abuse prevalence, related health effects and crime, treatment, and research status and needs, mid 1970s-90, 4498–72

Minority group health condition, services use, costs, and indicators of services need, 1950s-88, 4118–55

Neurological, cognitive, and behavioral residual effects of long-term drug abuse, 1989 conf, 4498–69

Palau admin, and social, economic, and govtl data, FY90, annual rpt, 7004–6

Parole and probation clients in program for drug- and alcohol-dependent Federal offenders, as of various dates 1987-91, annual rpt, 18204–2.1; 18204–8.7

Preventive disease and health improvement goals and recommended activities for 2000, with trends 1970s-80s, 4048–10

Prison treatment units, and clients by age, sex, and race, by State, data compilation, 1991 annual rpt, 6064–6.6

Public opinion on drinking and alcoholism, by respondent characteristics, data compilation, 1991 annual rpt, 6064–6.3

Research grants and awards of ADAMHA, by recipient, FY90, annual listing, 4044–13

Research on alcoholism, treatment programs, and patient characteristics, quarterly journal, 4482–1

Research on drug abuse and treatment, biological and behavioral factors, and addiction potential of new drugs, 1990 annual conf, 4494–11

Rural areas drug and alcohol abuse, related crime, and treatment, by substance and State, 1988-90, GAO rpt, 26131–79

Statistical Abstract of US, 1991 annual data compilation, 2324–1.3

Treatment and prevention programs of States for drug and alcohol abuse, funding, facilities, and patient characteristics, FY89, 4488–15

Treatment facilities for drug and alcohol abuse, services, use, funding, staff, and client characteristics, 1989, biennial rpt, 4494–10

Treatment services for drug and alcohol abuse, funding, staffing, and client load, characteristics, and outcomes, by setting, 1989 conf, 4498–73

VA mental health care services, staff, research, and training programs, 1991 biennial listing, 8704–2

Veterans (homeless) with mental illness, VA program services, costs, staff, client characteristics, and outcome, 1990, annual rpt, 8604–11

Veterans alcohol abuse prevalence, screening results by age and race, for 5 VA medical centers, 1990, GAO rpt, 26121–416

Violent and criminal behavior relation to drug abuse, with data on street gang activity and selected population groups, 1989 conf, 4498–70

Vocational rehabilitation cases of State agencies by disposition and applicant characteristics, and closures by reason, FY84-88, annual rpt, 4944–6

Women's alcohol use and abuse related to race, employment status, and other characteristics, 1981 local area study, article, 4042–3.212

Youth alcohol use, knowledge, attitudes, and info sources, series, 4006–10

Youth drug, alcohol, and cigarette use and attitudes, by substance type and selected characteristics, 1975-90 surveys, annual rpt, 4494–4

Alcohol abuse and treatment

see also Driving while intoxicated
see also Drug and alcohol testing

Alcohol, Drug Abuse, and Mental Health Administration

Budget of US, obligations and authority by function, agency, and program, with summaries, analyses, and historical tables, FY92, annual rpt, 104–2

Expenditures of Fed Govt in States, by type, program, agency, and State, FY90, annual rpt, 2464–2

Financial aid of HHS, by program, recipient, State, and city, FY90, annual regional listings, 4004–3

Mental illness and drug and alcohol abuse direct and indirect costs, by age and sex, 1985, 4048–35

Research and evaluation programs of HHS, 1970-90, annual listing, 4004–30

Research grants and awards of ADAMHA, by recipient, FY90, annual listing, 4044–13

States drug and alcohol abuse treatment and prevention programs, funding, facilities, and patient characteristics, FY89, 4488–15

see also National Institute of Mental Health
see also National Institute on Alcohol Abuse and Alcoholism
see also National Institute on Drug Abuse

Alcohol fuels

Auto alternative fuels costs, emissions, health impacts, and characteristics, 1990 rpt, 9196–5.1; 9196–5.4

Consumption of wood, waste, and alcohol fuels, by region, 1980-88, annual rpt, 3164–74.7

Economic, environmental, and health impacts of methanol fuel substitution for gasoline, projected 2000-2010, article, 9379–1.208

Electric power plants and capacity, by fuel used, owner, location, and operating status, 1990 and for units planned 1991-2000, annual listing, 3164–36

Hwy Trust Fund finances, unobligated balances by State, and receipt losses from increased ethanol use, 1980s-90, hearing, 25328–31

Methanol use in autos, oil price and economic impacts, 1990 technical paper, 9379–12.62

Natl Energy Strategy plans for conservation and pollution reduction, impacts of technology and regulation proposals, projected 1990-2030, 3166–6.47

Production of denatured alcohol for fuel use, monthly rpt, 8486–1.3

Research and education grants, USDA competitive awards by program and recipient, FY90, annual listing, 1764–1

Supply, demand, and movement of crude oil, gas liquids, and refined products, by PAD district and State, 1990, annual rpt, 3164–2

Tax (income) returns filed by type of filer, selected income items, quarterly rpt, 8302–2.1

Tax (income) returns of corporations, income and tax items by asset size and detailed industry, 1988, annual rpt, 8304–21

Tax expenditures, Federal revenues forgone through income tax deductions and exclusions by type, FY92-96, annual rpt, 21784–10

see also Biomass energy
see also Gasohol

Alcohol use

Agent Orange exposure of Vietnam veterans, and other factors relation to dev of rare cancers, 1984-88, 4208–33

Beer trade compared to domestic consumption and production, for 26 countries, mid 1970s-87, article, 9391–1.201

Boat accidents, casualties, and damage, by cause, vessel and operator characteristics, and State, 1990, annual rpt, 7404–1.2

Cancer (hepatocellular) risk relation to hepatitis infection, race, smoking, drinking, and oral contraceptives and estrogen use, 1984-90 local area study, article, 4472–1.237

Consumer Expenditure Survey, food spending by item, household composition, income, age, race, and region, 1980-88, biennial rpt, 1544–30

Consumer Expenditure Survey, household income by source, and itemized spending, by selected characteristics and region, 1988-89, annual rpt, 6764–5

Consumer Expenditure Survey, spending by category, and income, by selected household characteristics and location, 1990, annual press release, 6726–1.42

Consumption of alcohol, by selected characteristics, 1990 survey, biennial rpt, 4494–5

Consumption of food, dietary composition, and nutrient intake, 1987/88 natl survey, preliminary rpt series, 1356–1

Consumption per capita of selected beverages, 1970s-90, FAS annual circular, 1925–15.3

Consumption, supply, trade, prices, spending, and indexes, by food commodity, 1989, annual rpt, 1544–4

CPI components relative importance, by selected MSA, region, population size, and for US city average, 1990, annual rpt, 6884–1

Deaths and rates, by detailed cause and demographic characteristics, 1988 and trends from 1900, US Vital Statistics annual rpt, 4144–2

Diabetics health-related behaviors, weight, and body mass, by level of exercise, 1991 article, 4042–3.246

Health condition and health care resources, use, and spending, 1950s-89, annual data compilation, 4144–11

Hypertensive persons monitoring own blood pressure at home, health condition and risk behavior, local area study, 1991 article, 4042–3.207

Minority group drug abuse prevalence, related health effects and crime, treatment, and research status and needs, mid 1970s-90, 4498–72

Minority group health condition, services use, costs, and indicators of services need, 1950s-88, 4118–55

Women's alcohol use and abuse related to race, employment status, and other characteristics, 1981 local area study, article, 4042–3.212

see also Alcohol abuse and treatment
see also Driving while intoxicated

Alcoholic beverages

see Alcohol use
see Alcoholic beverages control laws
see Beer and breweries
see Liquor and liquor industry
see Wine and winemaking

Alcoholic beverages control laws

Arrests, by offense, offender characteristics, and location, 1990, annual rpt, 6224–2.2

Bur of Alcohol, Tobacco, and Firearms regulatory activities, staff, and funding, and tax revenues and rates, 1980s-91, GAO rpt, 26119–335

Court civil and criminal caseloads for Federal district, appeals, and bankruptcy courts, by type of suit and offense, circuit, and district, 1990, annual rpt, 18204–11

Court civil and criminal caseloads for Federal district, appeals, and special courts, 1990, annual rpt, 18204–8

Court civil and criminal caseloads for Federal district courts, 1991, annual rpt, 18204–2.1

Court criminal case processing in Federal district courts, and dispositions, by offense, district, and offender characteristics, 1986, annual rpt, 6064–29

Court criminal case processing in Federal district courts, and dispositions, by offense, 1980-89, annual rpt, 6064–31

Court criminal cases in Federal district courts, by offense, disposition, and district, 1980-90, last issue of annual rpt, 18204–1

Juvenile courts delinquency cases, by offense, referral source, disposition, age, sex, race, State, and county, 1988, annual rpt, 6064–12

Sentences for Federal offenses, guidelines by offense and circumstances, series, 17668–1

Traffic accidents deaths impacts of drinking age laws, 1982-90, annual fact sheet, 7766–15.3; 7766–15.4

Traffic deaths by circumstances and State, drunk drivers involved in fatal accidents, and impacts of minimum age drinking laws, 1982-89, annual fact sheet, 7766–15.1

US attorneys civil and criminal cases by type and disposition, and collections, by Federal district, FY90, annual rpt, 6004–2.1

Youth alcohol purchase, consumption, and age misrepresentation laws and penalties, by State, 1991 listing, 4006–10.3

Alcoholism

see Alcohol abuse and treatment

Alerich, Carol

"Forest Statistics for Kentucky, 1975 and 1988", 1206–12.15

Aleutian Islands

Environmental conditions and oil dev impacts for Alaska OCS, compilation of papers, series, 2176–1

Alexandria, La.

Wages by occupation, and benefits for office and plant workers, 1991 survey, periodic MSA rpt, 6785–3.6

see also under By SMSA or MSA in the "Index by Categories"

Index by Subjects and Names

Alexandria, Va.

Fed Govt land acquisition and dev projects in DC metro area, characteristics and funding by agency and project, FY91-95, annual rpt, 15454–1

see also under By City in the "Index by Categories"

Alfalfa

see Animal feed

Algal blooms

see Eutrophication

Algeria

- Agricultural exports of high-value commodities, indexes and sales by commodity, world area, and country, 1960s-86, 1528–323
- Agricultural exports of US, impacts of foreign agricultural and trade policy, with data by commodity and country, 1989, annual rpt, 1924–8
- Agricultural production, prices, and trade, by country, 1960s-90, annual world area rpt, 1524–4.2
- Agricultural production, trade, and policies in foreign countries, summary data by country, 1989-90, annual factbook, 1924–12
- Agricultural trade of US, by detailed commodity and country, 1989, annual rpt, 1524–8
- Agricultural trade of US, by detailed commodity and country, 1990, semiannual rpt, 1522–4
- Economic and military aid and loans from US and intl agencies, by program and country, FY46-90, annual rpt, 9914–5
- Economic conditions, income, production, prices, employment, and trade, 1991 periodic country rpt, 2046–4.22
- Economic conditions, policy, and trade practices, by country, 1988-90, annual rpt, 21384–5
- Economic, social, political, and geographic summary data, by country, 1991, annual factbook, 9114–2
- Exports and imports of US, by commodity and country, 1970-89, world area rpt, 9116–1.1
- Exports and imports of US, by Harmonized System 6-digit commodity and country, 1990, annual rpt, 2424–13
- Exports and imports of US, by selected country, country group, and commodity group, 1990, annual rpt, 2044–37
- Exports and imports of US, by transport mode, country, and SITC 1- to 3-digit commodity, 1990, annual rpt, 2424–12
- Exports of US, detailed Schedule B commodities with countries of destination, 1990, annual rpt, 2424–10
- Food supply, needs, and aid for developing countries, status and alternative forecasts, 1991 world area rpt, 1526–8.1
- Human rights conditions in 170 countries, and US economic and military aid, 1990, annual rpt, 21384–3
- Military aid of US, arms sales, and training programs costs and budget requests, by program, world region, and country, FY90-92, annual rpt, 7144–13
- Natural gas and liquefied gas trade of US with 5 countries, by US firm, 1955-90, annual article, 3162–4.208
- Oil production, and exports and prices for US, by major exporting country, detailed data, monthly rpt with articles, 3162–24

Oil production, trade, use, and stocks, by selected country and country group, monthly rpt, 3162–42

- UN voting record and share of votes in agreement with US, by issue, country, and world area, 1990, annual rpt, 7004–18
- *see also* under By Foreign Country in the "Index by Categories"

Alien workers

- Admissions to US of aliens, by class of admission, impact of Immigration Reform and Control Act, FY84-89, 6266–1.1
- Admissions to US of immigrants, by occupational group and country of birth, preliminary FY90, annual table, 6264–1
- Certification of alien workers, Labor Dept grants to States for application processing automation, 1991, press release, 6406–2.32
- Economic and labor force impacts of immigration, alien workers, amnesty programs, and employer sanctions, series, 6366–5
- Farm labor costs and trade of US, effects of immigration restrictions on selected industries, 1980s, 1598–276
- Fed Govt civilian employees work-years, pay rates, and benefits use and costs, by agency, FY89, annual rpt, 9844–31
- Illegal alien worker and Fair Labor Standards Act employer compliance, hiring impacts, and aliens overstaying visas by country and State, 1986-90, annual rpt, 6264–6
- Illegal aliens applications for legal residence under Immigration Reform and Control Act, by selected characteristics, State, and country, periodic rpt, 6262–3
- Illegal aliens overstaying visas, by class of admission, mode of arrival, age, country, and State, FY85-88, annual rpt, 6264–5
- Iraq invasion of Kuwait, alien worker refugees fleeing from Iraq and Kuwait, intl aid by source, and costs to host and native countries, 1990-91, GAO rpt, 26123–326
- Palau admin, and social, economic, and govtl data, FY90, annual rpt, 7004–6
- Visas of US issued and refused to immigrants and nonimmigrants, by class, issuing office, and nationality, FY89, annual rpt, 7184–1

Aliens

- Abortions in US, by place of woman's residence and State of occurrence, 1988, US Vital Statistics annual rpt, 4146–5.120
- Admissions to US of aliens, by class of admission and selected port and country, FY89-90, fact sheet, 6266–2.7
- Admissions to US of aliens, by class of admission, impact of Immigration Reform and Control Act, FY84-89, 6266–1.1
- Admissions to US of aliens, by class of admission, port, country, and State of destination, quarterly rpt, discontinued, 6262–2
- Admissions to US of aliens on parole status, by world region, type of admission, and State, FY89, fact sheet, 6266–2.6
- AFDC beneficiaries demographic and financial characteristics, by State, FY89, annual rpt, 4694–1
- AIDS cases in US among persons from countries with predominantly heterosexual transmission patterns, and among their sexual contacts, monthly rpt, 4202–9

Aliens

- Air travel to and from US on US and foreign flag carriers, by world area, 1990, annual rpt, 2904–13
- Assistance (financial and nonfinancial) of Fed Govt, 1991 base edition with supplements, annual listing, 104–5
- Criminal defendants for Federal offenses pretrial processing, detention, and release, by defendant characteristics and district, 1988, hearing, 25528–114
- Deaths in US, by State of occurrence and birthplace abroad, 1988, US Vital Statistics annual rpt, 4144–2.1
- Education (bilingual) enrollment, and Education Dept activities and funding by program, by State, FY88-90, biennial rpt, 4804–14
- Fetal deaths and rates, by characteristics of mother and birth, 1988, US Vital Statistics annual rpt, 4144–2.3
- Food stamp eligibility and payment errors, by type, recipient characteristics, and State, FY89, annual rpt, 1364–15
- Food stamp recipient household size, composition, income, and income and deductions allowed, summer 1988, annual rpt, 1364–8
- Illegal alien worker and Fair Labor Standards Act employer compliance, hiring impacts, and aliens overstaying visas by country and State, 1986-90, annual rpt, 6264–6
- Illegal aliens applications for legal residence under Immigration Reform and Control Act, by selected characteristics, State, and country, periodic rpt, 6262–3
- Illegal aliens apprehended and officer hours, for Border Patrol by location, 1980s, fact sheet, 6266–2.2
- Illegal aliens enforcement activity of Coast Guard, by nationality, 2nd half FY91, semiannual rpt, 7402–4
- Illegal aliens overstaying visas, by class of admission, mode of arrival, age, country, and State, FY85-88, annual rpt, 6264–5
- Illegal aliens overstaying visas, by State of sojourn and world area of origin, 1985-88, fact sheet, 6266–2.1
- Illegal entry and smuggling of aliens, Federal sentencing guidelines by offense and circumstances, series, 17668–1
- Income from US sources and tax withheld for foreign natls not residing in US, by country and tax treaty status, 1988, annual article, 8302–2.206
- Malaria cases in US, for military personnel and US and foreign natls, and by country of infection, 1966-89, annual rpt, 4205–4
- OASDI benefits for nonresident aliens, payments and withholdings, 1984-90 and projections to 2000, actuarial rpt, 4706–1.105
- Population not registered to vote, total and without US citizenship, by selected characteristics, 1990 congressional election, biennial Current Population Rpt, 2546–1.454
- Science and engineering PhDs employment and other characteristics, by field and State, 1989, biennial rpt, 9627–18
- Supplemental Security Income alien recipients, by legal status, for applications made 1974-89, annual rpt, 4744–3.8
- Supplemental Security Income beneficiaries income from OASI and other sources, and work history, 1988, article, 4742–1.216

Aliens

Supplemental Security Income benefit award rate by applicant characteristics and eligibility class, 1987, article, 4742–1.213

Tuberculosis cases and deaths, by patient characteristics, State, and city, 1989 and trends from 1953, annual rpt, 4204–10

Tuberculosis prevention and screening methods among aliens, CDC guidelines, 1990 rpt, 4206–2.36

see also Alien workers

see also Citizenship

see also Deportation

see also Foreign medical graduates

see also Foreign students

see also Immigration and emigration

see also Mexicans in the U.S.

see also Refugees

Alig, Ralph J.

"Changes in Area of Timberland in the U.S., 1952-2040, By Ownership, Forest Type, Region and State", 1208–357

Alimony

see Child support and alimony

Allegheny County, Pa.

AIDS virus infection and risk factor prevalence, natl survey methodology and pretest results, 1989, 4148–30

Allen, Edward W.

"Food Grain Outlook", 1004–16.1

"Summer Quarter Feed and Residual Use of Wheat", 1561–12.203

Allen-Hagen, Barbara

"Public Juvenile Facilities, 1989: Children in Custody", 6064–5.1

Allen, Joseph

"Teen Outreach: The Fifth Year of National Replication", 25548–104

Allen, W. Bruce

"Impact of State Economic Regulation of Motor Carriage on Intrastate and Interstate Commerce", 7308–200

Allentown, Pa.

see also under By City and By SMSA or MSA in the "Index by Categories"

Allergies

Cases of acute and chronic conditions, disability, absenteeism, and health services use, by selected characteristics, 1987, CD-ROM, 4147–10.177

Deaths and rates, by detailed cause and demographic characteristics, 1988 and trends from 1900, US Vital Statistics annual rpt, 4144–2

Natl Inst of Allergy and Infectious Diseases activities, grants by recipient and location, and disease cases, FY83-90, annual rpt, 4474–30

Pollution (air) indoor levels in workplace, and health impacts, for Library of Congress Madison building, 1989 study, series, 4248–92

Allied health personnel

Medicare reimbursement of hospitals under prospective payment system, and effect on services, finances, and beneficiary payments, 1979-90, annual rpt, 17204–2

Military health care personnel, and accessions by training source, by occupation, specialty, and service branch, FY89, annual rpt, 3544–24

VA Medicine and Surgery Dept trainees, by detailed program and city, FY90, annual rpt, 8704–4

see also Clinical laboratory technicians

see also Dietitians and nutritionists

see also Midwives

Allied Stores Corp.

Leveraged buyouts impacts on financial performance, for 4 transactions, 1980s-90, GAO rpt, 26119–355

Allshouse, Jane E.

"Food Consumption, Prices, and Expenditures, 1968-89", 1544–4

Alpena, Mich.

Wages by occupation, and benefits for office and plant workers, 1991 survey, periodic MSA rpt, 6785–3.8

Alpert, William T.

"Leave Policies in Small Business: Findings from the U.S. Small Business Administration Employee Leave Survey", 9768–21

Altig, David

"Bracket Creep in the Age of Indexing: Have We Solved the Problem?", 9377–9.117

"Case of the Missing Interest Deductions: Will Tax Reform Increase U.S. Saving Rates?", 9377–1.202

"Inflation, Personal Taxes, and Real Output: A Dynamic Analysis", 9377–9.110

Alton, Ill.

see also under By SMSA or MSA in the "Index by Categories"

Altoona, Pa.

see also under By SMSA or MSA in the "Index by Categories"

Altus, Okla.

Wages by occupation, for office and plant workers, 1991 survey, periodic MSA rpt, 6785–3.5

Aluminum and aluminum industry

Building materials PPI, by type, bimonthly rpt, 2042–1.5

Business statistics, detailed data for major industries and economic indicators, *Survey of Current Business*, monthly rpt, 2702–1.17

Castings (nonferrous) shipments, by metal type, 1990, annual Current Industrial Rpt, 2506–10.5

County Business Patterns, 1988: employment, establishments, and payroll, by SIC 2- to 4-digit industry and county, annual State rpt series, 2326–6

County Business Patterns, 1989: employment, establishments, and payroll, by SIC 2- to 4-digit industry and county, annual State rpt series, 2326–8

Employment, earnings, and hours, by SIC 1- to 4-digit industry, monthly and annual averages, selected years 1909-90, annual rpt, 6744–4

Energy conservation and resource planning activities of Bonneville Power Admin, FY89-90, 3228–11

Energy use and prices for manufacturing industries, 1988 survey, series, 3166–13

Exports and imports between US and outlying areas, by detailed commodity and mode of transport, 1990, annual rpt, 2424–11

Exports and imports of building materials, by commodity and country, 1989-90, article, 2042–1.204

Exports and imports of US, by country and detailed commodity, monthly rpt, 2422–12

Exports and imports of US, by Harmonized System 6-digit commodity and country, 1990, annual rpt, 2424–13

Exports and imports of US, by selected country, country group, and commodity group, 1990, annual rpt, 2044–37

Exports and imports of US, by transport mode, country, and SITC 1- to 3-digit commodity, 1990, annual rpt, 2424–12

Exports and imports of US shipped through Canada, by detailed commodity, customs district, and country, 1989, annual rpt, 7704–11

Exports of US, detailed Schedule B commodities with countries of destination, 1990, annual rpt, 2424–10

Furniture (office) shipments by product, and metals used by type, 1990, annual Current Industrial Rpt, 2506–7.8

Futures and options trading volume, by commodity and exchange, FY90, annual rpt, 11924–2

Imports of US given duty-free treatment for value of US material sent abroad, by commodity and country, 1989, annual rpt, 9884–14

Injuries from use of consumer products, by severity, victim age, and detailed product, 1990, annual rpt, 9164–6

Labor productivity, indexes of output, hours, and employment by SIC 2- to 4-digit industry, 1967-89, annual rpt, 6824–1.3

Manufacturing annual survey, 1989: finances and operations, by SIC 2- to 4-digit industry, series, 2506–15

Manufacturing census, 1987: employment and shipments under Fed Govt contracts, by SIC 4-digit industry, 2497–7

Manufacturing census, 1987: finances and operations, by SIC 2- to 4-digit industry, State, and MSA, with trends from 1849, 2497–1

Manufacturing census, 1987: finances and operations, by type of organization and SIC 2- to 4-digit industry, subject rpt, 2497–5

Manufacturing finances and operations, by SIC 2- to 4-digit industry, forecast 1991, annual rpt, 2044–28

Mineral industries census, 1987: energy use and costs, by fuel type, SIC 2- to 4-digit industry, and State, subject rpt, 2517–2

Mineral industries census, 1987: finances and operations, by establishment characteristics, SIC 2- to 4-digit industry, and State, subject rpt, 2517–1

Mineral Industry Surveys, commodity review of production, trade, stocks, and use, monthly rpt, 5612–1.1

Mineral Industry Surveys, commodity review of production, trade, stocks, and use, quarterly rpt, 5612–2.2

Minerals Yearbook, 1988, Vol 3: foreign country reviews of production, trade, and policy, by commodity, annual rpt series, 5604–17

Minerals Yearbook, 1989, Vol 1: commodity review of production, reserves, supply, use, and trade, annual rpt, 5604–15.8

Minerals Yearbook, 1989, Vol 2: State reviews of production and sales by commodity, and business activity, annual rpt series, 5604–16

Minerals Yearbook, 1989, Vol 2: State reviews of production, sales, and firms, by commodity, and business activity, annual rpt, 5604–34

Index by Subjects and Names

Mines (metal) and related operations occupational injuries and incidence, employment, and hours, 1989, annual rpt, 6664–3

Occupational injury and illness rates, by SIC 2- to 4-digit industry, 1988-89, annual rpt, 6844–7

Occupational injury and illness rates, by SIC 2- to 4-digit industry, 1989, annual rpt, 6844–1

OECD trade, total and for 4 major countries, and US trade by country, by commodity, 1970-89, world area rpt series, 9116–1

Pacific Northwest aluminum industry electricity purchased from Bonneville Power Admin, by customer, FY90, annual rpt, 3224–1

Pacific Northwest aluminum industry electricity purchased from Bonneville Power Admin, by customer, 1990, semiannual rpt, 3222–1

Pollution (air) emissions factors, by detailed pollutant and source, data compilation, 1990 rpt, 9198–120

Price indexes (producer), by stage of processing and detailed commodity, monthly rpt, 6762–6

Price indexes (producer), by stage of processing and detailed commodity, monthly 1990, annual rpt, 6764–2

Production, prices, trade, and foreign and US industry devs, by commodity, bimonthly rpt with articles, 5602–4

Production, prices, trade, use, employment, tariffs, and stockpiles, by mineral, with foreign comparisons, 1986-90, annual rpt, 5604–18

Shipments (defense and total), trade, use, and inventories of aluminum ingots and mill products, monthly Current Industrial Rpt, 2506–10.9

Soviet Union, Eastern Europe, OECD, and selected other countries minerals production, by commodity, 1960s-90, annual rpt, 9114–4.6

Statistical Abstract of US, 1991 annual data compilation, 2324–1.25

Stockpiling of strategic material by Fed Govt, activity, and inventory by commodity, as of Mar 1991, semiannual rpt, 3542–22

Stockpiling of strategic material, inventories and needs, by commodity, as of Jan 1991, annual rpt, 3544–37

Wire and cable (insulated) shipments, trade, use, and firms, by product, 1990, annual Current Industrial Rpt, 2506–10.8

see also under By Commodity in the "Index by Categories"

Aluminum Co. of America

Tennessee Valley river control activities, and hydroelectric power generation and capacity, 1989, annual rpt, 9804–7

Alzheimer's disease

Deaths and rates, by detailed cause and demographic characteristics, 1988 and trends from 1900, US Vital Statistics annual rpt, 4144–2

Natl Inst of Neurological Disorders and Stroke activities, and disorder cases, FY90, annual rpt, 4474–25

Nursing home Alzheimer's disease units, and beds, by facility characteristics, 1987, 4186–8.12

Nursing home residents with mental disorders, by disorder type and resident and instn characteristics, 1985, 4147–13.106

Amarillo, Tex.

see also under By City and By SMSA or MSA in the "Index by Categories"

Ambrose, Michael P.

"Federal Civilian Work Years and Personnel Costs in the Executive Branch for FY90", 9842–1.204

Ambulatory aids

see Prosthetics and orthotics

American Battle Monuments Commission

Budget of US, authoritative financial statements with appropriations, outlays, and receipts, by category and agency, FY90, annual rpt, 8104–2.1

Budget of US, obligations and authority by function, agency, and program, with summaries, analyses, and historical tables, FY92, annual rpt, 104–2

American Forces Information Service

"Defense '91: Almanac", 3504–13

American Historical Association

Financial statements of AHA, and membership by State, 1989, annual rpt, 29574–2

American Hospital Assocation

"Comparative Analysis of Annual Survey and Medicare Cost Report Margin Data", 17206–2.25

American Housing Survey

Current Housing Reports, unit and household characteristics, subject rpt series, 2486–1

Data coverage and availability of Census Bur rpts and data files, 1991 annual listing, 2304–2

Data coverage and availability, 1991 pamphlet, 2326–7.77

Housing and households characteristics, MSA surveys, fact sheet series, 2485–11

Housing and households characteristics, unit and neighborhood quality, and journey to work by MSA location, for 11 MSAs, 1984 survey, supplement, 2485–8

Housing and households detailed characteristics, and unit and neighborhood quality, by location, 1987, biennial rpt supplement, 2485–13

Housing and households detailed characteristics, and unit and neighborhood quality, by location, 1989, biennial rpt, 2485–12

Housing and households detailed characteristics, and unit and neighborhood quality, MSA surveys, series, 2485–6

Housing inventory change from 1973, by reason, unit and household characteristics, and location, 1983 survey, biennial rpt, 2485–14

American Indians

see Indians

American Medical Association

"Characteristics of Physicians, Jan. 1, 1989", 4116–6

American National Red Cross

Activities and finances of Red Cross, FY90, annual rpt, 29254–1

AIDS info and education activities and funding of CDC, and donation of media ads, 1987-92, articles, 4042–3.256

American Telephone and Telegraph Co.

American Samoa

Agriculture census, 1987: farms, farmland, production, finances, and operator characteristics, by island and island group, 1990, final outlying area rpt, 2331–1.55

Banks (insured commercial and savings) deposits by instn, State, MSA, and county, as of June 1990, annual regional rpt, 9295–3.6

Economic, social, political, and geographic summary data, by country, 1991, annual factbook, 9114–2

Employment, earnings, and minimum wage, by establishment and industry, for American Samoa, 1989, biennial rpt, 6504–6

Exports and imports between US and outlying areas, by detailed commodity and mode of transport, 1990, annual rpt, 2424–11

Fed Govt spending in States and local areas, by type, State, county, and city, FY90, annual rpt, 2464–3

Fed Govt spending in States, by type, program, agency, and State, FY90, annual rpt, 2464–2

HHS financial aid, by program, recipient, State, and city, FY90, annual regional listing, 4004–3.9

Hospital deaths of Medicare patients, actual and expected rates by diagnosis, and hospital characteristics, by instn, FY87-89, annual regional rpt, 4654–14.9

Minerals Yearbook, 1989, Vol 2: State reviews of production, sales, and firms, by commodity, and business activity, annual rpt, 5604–34

Physicians, by specialty, age, sex, and location of training and practice, 1989, State rpt, 4116–6.53

see also under By Outlying Area in the "Index by Categories"

American Schools and Hospitals Abroad

AID economic aid to developing countries, obligations and disbursements by country, quarterly rpt, 9912–4

Developing countries economic and social conditions from 1960s, and Intl Dev Cooperation Agency and AID activities and funding, FY90-92, annual rpt, 9904–4

American Stock Exchange

Trading volume on American Stock Exchange, monthly rpt, 9362–1.1

Trading volume, securities listed by type, and finances, by exchange, selected years 1938-89, annual rpt, 9734–2.1; 9734–2.2

American Telephone and Telegraph Co.

Fiber optics and copper wire mileage and access lines, and fiber systems investment, by telecommunications firm, 1985-90, annual rpt, 9284–18

Finances and operations, detail for telephone firms, 1989, annual rpt, 9284–6

Finances and operations of local and long distance firms, subscribership, and charges, late 1970s-91, semiannual rpt, 9282–7

Intl telecommunications operations of US carriers, finances, rates, and traffic by service type, firm, and country, 1975-89, annual rpt, 9284–17

Americans for Nonsmokers' Rights

"Major Local Smoking Ordinances in the U.S. A Detailed Matrix of the Provisions of Workplace, Restaurant, and Public Places Smoking Ordinances", 4478–196

Ames Laboratory

see also Department of Energy National Laboratories

Amman, Gene D.

"Insect Infestation of Fire-Injured Trees in the Greater Yellowstone Area", 1208–379

Ammonia

see Chemicals and chemical industry

Ammunition

- County Business Patterns, 1988: employment, establishments, and payroll, by SIC 2- to 4-digit industry and county, annual State rpt series, 2326–6
- County Business Patterns, 1989: employment, establishments, and payroll, by SIC 2- to 4-digit industry and county, annual State rpt series, 2326–8
- Criminal cases by type and disposition, and collections, for US attorneys, by Federal district, FY90, annual rpt, 6004–2.1
- DOD budget, procurement appropriations by item, service branch, and defense agency, FY90-93, annual rpt, 3544–32
- DOD outlays and obligations, by function and service branch, quarterly rpt, 3542–3
- DOD prime contract awards, by category, contract and contractor type, and service branch, FY81-1st half FY91, semiannual rpt, 3542–1
- DOD prime contract awards, by category, contractor type, and State, FY88-90, annual rpt, 3544–11
- DOD prime contract awards, by detailed procurement category, FY87-90, annual rpt, 3544–18
- Employment, earnings, and hours, by SIC 1- to 4-digit industry, monthly and annual averages, selected years 1909-90, annual rpt, 6744–4
- Enterprise Statistics, 1987: finances and operations for companies, by size, level of diversification, form of organization, and industry group, 2329–8
- Exports and imports of US, by country and detailed commodity, monthly rpt, 2422–12
- Exports and imports of US, by Harmonized System 6-digit commodity and country, 1990, annual rpt, 2424–13
- Exports of US, detailed Schedule B commodities with countries of destination, 1990, annual rpt, 2424–10
- Imports of US given duty-free treatment for value of US material sent abroad, by commodity and country, 1989, annual rpt, 9884–14
- Manufacturing annual survey, 1989: finances and operations, by SIC 2- to 4-digit industry, series, 2506–15
- Manufacturing census, 1987: employment and shipments under Fed Govt contracts, by SIC 4-digit industry, 2497–7
- Manufacturing census, 1987: finances and operations, by SIC 2- to 4-digit industry, State, and MSA, with trends from 1849, 2497–1
- Manufacturing census, 1987: finances and operations, by type of organization and SIC 2- to 4-digit industry, subject rpt, 2497–5

Military and personal property shipments, passenger traffic, and costs, by service branch and mode of transport, quarterly rpt, 3702–1

- Occupational injury and illness rates, by SIC 2- to 4-digit industry, 1988-89, annual rpt, 6844–7
- Occupational injury and illness rates, by SIC 2- to 4-digit industry, 1989, annual rpt, 6844–1
- OECD trade, total and for 4 major countries, and US trade by country, by commodity, 1970-89, world area rpt series, 9116–1
- Price indexes (producer), by stage of processing and detailed commodity, monthly rpt, 6762–6
- Price indexes (producer), by stage of processing and detailed commodity, monthly 1990, annual rpt, 6764–2
- Tax (excise) collections of IRS, by source, quarterly rpt, 8302–1
- Tax (income) returns of corporations, income and tax items by asset size and detailed industry, 1987, annual rpt, 8304–4
- Tax (income) returns of corporations, income and tax items by asset size and detailed industry, 1988, annual rpt, 8304–21

Amnesties

see Pardons

Amtrak

see National Railroad Passenger Corp.

Amusement parks

Service industries census, 1987: establishments, receipts by source, payroll, and employment, by SIC 2- to 4-digit kind of business, State, and MSA, 2393–4

Anaheim, Calif.

- CPI by component for US city average, and by region, population size, and for 15 metro areas, monthly rpt, 6762–1
- CPI by component for US city average, and by region, population size, and for 27 metro areas, monthly rpt, 6762–2
- Housing starts and completions authorized by building permits in 40 MSAs, quarterly rpt, 2382–9
- Wages by occupation, for office and plant workers, 1990 survey, periodic MSA rpt, 6785–11.2
- *see also* under By City and By SMSA or MSA in the "Index by Categories"

Anchorage, Alaska

- CPI by component for US city average, and by region, population size, and for 27 metro areas, monthly rpt, 6762–2
- CPI in Anchorage, impacts of OCS oil resources dev, 1980-87 and projected to 2015, 5736–5.11
- Tide height and time daily at coastal points, forecast 1992, annual rpt, 2174–2.1
- *see also* under By City and By SMSA or MSA in the "Index by Categories"

Anderson, Ind.

see also under By SMSA or MSA in the "Index by Categories"

Anderson, Kay

"Changes in Hospital Staffing Patterns", 6722–1.217

Anderson, Keith B.

"Petroleum Tariffs as a Source of Government Revenue", 9406–1.61

Anderson, Patricia

"New Jersey Unemployment Insurance Reemployment Demonstration Project Follow-Up Report", 6406–6.32

Anderson, R. E., Jr.

"Agricultural Trade Outlook", 1004–16.1

Anderson, S.C.

see also under By SMSA or MSA in the "Index by Categories"

Andorra

- Economic, social, political, and geographic summary data, by country, 1991, annual factbook, 9114–2
- Exports and imports of US, by transport mode, country, and SITC 1- to 3-digit commodity, 1990, annual rpt, 2424–12

Andrews, Elizabeth J.

"Increasing the Use of Underutilized Fish and Fishing Opportunities by California Anglers: The Use of Onboard Refrigeration and New Marketing Strategies", 2168–125

Andrews, Roxanne

"Access to Hospital Care for California and Michigan Medicaid Recipients", 4652–1.249

Anemia

see Blood diseases and disorders

see Nutrition and malnutrition

see Sickle cell anemia

Anesthesiology

- HHS financial aid, by program, recipient, State, and city, FY90, annual regional listings, 4004–3
- Labor supply of physicians, by specialty, age, sex, and location of training and practice, 1989, State rpt series, 4116–6
- Medicare payments to physicians, charges by specialty and treatment setting, and assignment rate by State, 1970s-88, article, 4652–1.240
- Medicare reimbursement of anesthesiologists, charges, and time billed, 1987, GAO rpt, 26121–417
- Medicare Supplementary Medical Insurance physicians fee schedule, methodology with data by procedure and specialty, 1991, annual rpt, 17264–1
- Military health care personnel, and accessions by training source, by occupation, specialty, and service branch, FY89, annual rpt, 3544–24
- VA health care facilities physicians, dentists, and nurses, by selected employment characteristics and VA district, quarterly rpt, 8602–6
- VA health care staff and turnover, by occupation, physician specialty, and location, 1990, annual rpt, 8604–8

Anetzberger, Georgia

"Survey of State Public Health Departments on Procedures for Reporting Elder Abuse", 4042–3.213

Angelo, Luigi

"U.S. Sugar Statistical Compendium", 1568–306

Angola

Agricultural exports of high-value commodities, indexes and sales by commodity, world area, and country, 1960s-86, 1528–323

Index by Subjects and Names

Animal feed

Agricultural trade of US, by detailed commodity and country, 1989, annual rpt, 1524–8

Agricultural trade of US, by detailed commodity and country, 1990, semiannual rpt, 1522–4

Dairy imports, consumption, and market conditions, by sub-Saharan Africa country, 1961-88, 1528–321

Economic and military aid and loans from US and intl agencies, by program and country, FY46-90, annual rpt, 9914–5

Economic conditions, policy, and trade practices, by country, 1988-90, annual rpt, 21384–5

Economic, population, and agricultural data, US and other aid sources, and AID activity, 1989 country rpt, 9916–12.32

Economic, social, political, and geographic summary data, by country, 1991, annual factbook, 9114–2

Exports and imports of US, by commodity and country, 1970-89, world area rpt, 9116–1.6

Exports and imports of US, by Harmonized System 6-digit commodity and country, 1990, annual rpt, 2424–13

Exports and imports of US, by selected country, country group, and commodity group, 1990, annual rpt, 2044–37

Exports and imports of US, by transport mode, country, and SITC 1- to 3-digit commodity, 1990, annual rpt, 2424–12

Exports of US, detailed Schedule B commodities with countries of destination, 1990, annual rpt, 2424–10

Food supply, needs, and aid for developing countries, status and alternative forecasts, 1991 world area rpt, 1526–8.1

Human rights conditions in 170 countries, and US economic and military aid, 1990, annual rpt, 21384–3

Oil exports to US by OPEC and non-OPEC countries, monthly rpt, 3162–24.3

UN voting record and share of votes in agreement with US, by issue, country, and world area, 1990, annual rpt, 7004–18

see also under By Foreign Country in the "Index by Categories"

Anguilla

Agricultural trade of US, by detailed commodity and country, 1990, semiannual rpt, 1522–4

Economic, social, political, and geographic summary data, by country, 1991, annual factbook, 9114–2

Exports and imports of US, by transport mode, country, and SITC 1- to 3-digit commodity, 1990, annual rpt, 2424–12

Angwin, Peter A.

"Forest Pest Conditions in the Rocky Mountain Region, 1989", 1206–11.1

Animal and Plant Health Inspection Service

Animal protection, licensing, and inspection activities of USDA, and animals used in research, by State, FY89, annual rpt, 1394–10

Budget of US, obligations and authority by function, agency, and program, with summaries, analyses, and historical tables, FY92, annual rpt, 104–2

Cattle tuberculosis cases and cooperative Federal-State eradication activities, by State, FY89-90, annual rpt, 1394–13

Foreign and US animal disease outbreaks, quarterly rpt, 1392–3

Natl Veterinary Services Labs activities, biologic drug products evaluation and disease testing, FY90, annual rpt, 1394–17

Poultry Natl Improvement Plan participating hatcheries and birds, by species and disease program, 1991, annual listing, 1394–15

Animal diseases and zoonoses

Cattle tuberculosis cases and cooperative Federal-State eradication activities, by State, FY89-90, annual rpt, 1394–13

Deaths and rates, by detailed cause and demographic characteristics, 1988 and trends from 1900, US Vital Statistics annual rpt, 4144–2

Fish and sediments pollutant concentrations, by contaminant, fish species, and Pacific coast site, 1984-86, 2168–121

Fish and shellfish aquaculture in US and Japan, mgmt, methods, and biological data for selected species, 1988 conf, annual rpt, 2164–15

Fish kills in coastal areas related to pollution and natural causes, by land use, State, and county, 1980s, 2178–32

Fish population and disease, and pollutant levels, near New York Bight sewage sludge dumpsite, 1986-90, last issue of annual rpt, 2164–19

Fishery mgmt and R&D, Fed Govt grants by project and State, and rpts, 1990, annual listing, 2164–3

Fishery research of State fish and wildlife agencies, federally funded projects and costs by species and State, 1990, annual listing, 5504–23

Foreign and US animal disease outbreaks, quarterly rpt, 1392–3

Marine mammals strandings, research results, 1987 conf, 2168–127

Morbidity and Mortality Weekly Report, infectious notifiable disease cases by age, race, and State, and deaths, 1930s-90, annual rpt, 4204–1

Morbidity and Mortality Weekly Report, infectious notifiable disease cases by State, and public health issues, 4202–1

Natl Veterinary Services Labs activities, biologic drug products evaluation and disease testing, FY90, annual rpt, 1394–17

New York Bight pollution levels, sources, treatment costs, economic losses, and environmental and health effects, 1990 conf, 9208–131

Poultry Natl Improvement Plan participating hatcheries and birds, by species and disease program, 1991, annual listing, 1394–15

Poultry slaughtered under Fed Govt inspection, pounds certified, and condemnations by cause, by State, monthly rpt, 1625–3

Research (agricultural) funding and staffing for USDA, State agencies, and other instns, by topic, FY90, annual rpt, 1744–2

Seals (harbor) population and physical characteristics at selected Washington State coastal sites, 1975-80, 14738–7

Wildlife research of State fish and wildlife agencies, federally funded projects and costs by species and State, 1990, annual listing, 5504–24

see also Rabies

see also Veterinary medicine

Animal experimentation

Brain wound research of Army, usefulness of Louisiana State University animal experiments, with results, 1980s, GAO rpt, 26121–396

HHS financial aid, by program, recipient, State, and city, FY90, annual regional listings, 4004–3

Licensing and inspection of facilities, and other animal protection activities of USDA, with animals used in research, by State, FY89, annual rpt, 1394–10

NIH activities, funding by program and recipient type, staff, and clinic patients, by inst, FY90, annual rpt, 4434–3

NIH Research Resources Center activities and funding, by program, FY90, annual rpt, 4434–12

Reproduction and population research, Fed Govt funding by project, FY89, annual listing, 4474–9

Respiratory diseases related to occupational hazards, epidemiology, diagnosis, and treatment, for selected industries and work settings, 1988 conf, 4248–90

Animal feed

Acreage planted and harvested, by crop and State, 1989-90 and planned as of June 1991, annual rpt, 1621–23

Acreage planted, by selected crop and State, 1982-90 and planned 1991, annual rpt, 1621–22

Acreage reduction program compliance, enrollment, and yield on planted acreage, by commodity and State, annual press release series, 1004–20

Agricultural data compilation, 1990 and trends from 1920, annual rpt, 1004–14

Agricultural production, prices, and trade, for PRC, 1960s-90, annual rpt, 1524–4.3

Agricultural Stabilization and Conservation Service feed grains program, 1955-91, annual fact sheet, 1806–4.8

Agricultural Stabilization and Conservation Service producer payments and certificate value, by program, monthly rpt, 1802–10

Agricultural Stabilization and Conservation Service producer payments, by program and State, 1990, annual table, 1804–12

Agricultural Statistics, 1990, annual rpt, 1004–1

Agriculture census, 1987: farms, farmland, production, finances, and operator characteristics, by county, final State rpt series, 2331–1

Cattle and calves on feed, inventory and marketings by State, monthly release, 1623–2

Cattle feedlots and marketing, by lot size and State, selected years 1955-89, 1568–300

Chemicals (inorganic) production by State, shipments, trade, and use, by product, 1990, annual Current Industrial Rpt, 2506–8.14

Costs of feeding livestock in selected locations, periodic situation rpt with articles, 1561–7

County Business Patterns, 1988: employment, establishments, and payroll, by SIC 2- to 4-digit industry and county, annual State rpt series, 2326–6

Animal feed

Index by Subjects and Names

County Business Patterns, 1989: employment, establishments, and payroll, by SIC 2- to 4-digit industry and county, annual State rpt series, 2326–8

Dairy cattle, milk production, and grain and other concentrates fed, by State, monthly rpt, 1627–1

Dairy herd feed prices, by selected State, 1990, annual rpt, 1317–1.4

Dairy production by State, stocks, prices, and CCC price support activities, by product type, monthly rpt, 1627–3

Developing countries agricultural supply, demand, and market for US exports, with socioeconomic conditions, country rpt series, 1526–6

Employment, earnings, and hours, by SIC 1- to 4-digit industry, monthly and annual averages, selected years 1909-90, annual rpt, 6744–4

Exports (agricultural) of high-value commodities, indexes and sales value by commodity, world area, and country, 1960s-86, 1528–323

Exports and imports (agricultural) commodity and country, prices, and world market devs, monthly rpt, 1922–12

Exports and imports (agricultural) of US, by commodity and country, bimonthly rpt, 1522–1

Exports and imports (agricultural) of US, by detailed commodity and country, 1989, annual rpt, 1524–8

Exports and imports (agricultural) of US, by detailed commodity and country, 1990, semiannual rpt, 1522–4

Exports and imports between US and outlying areas, by detailed commodity and mode of transport, 1990, annual rpt, 2424–11

Exports and imports of US, by country and detailed commodity, monthly rpt, 2422–12

Exports and imports of US, by Harmonized System 6-digit commodity and country, 1990, annual rpt, 2424–13

Exports and imports of US, by selected country, country group, and commodity group, 1990, annual rpt, 2044–37

Exports and imports of US, by transport mode, country, and SITC 1- to 3-digit commodity, 1990, annual rpt, 2424–12

Exports and imports of US shipped through Canada, by detailed commodity, customs district, and country, 1989, annual rpt, 7704–11

Exports of grains, oilseed products, hides, skins, and cotton, by country, weekly rpt, 1922–3

Exports of US, detailed Schedule B commodities with countries of destination, 1990, annual rpt, 2424–10

Farm financial and marketing conditions, forecast 1991, annual chartbook, 1504–8

Farm financial and marketing conditions, forecast 1991, annual conf, 1004–16

Farm income, expenses, receipts by commodity, assets, liabilities, and ratios, 1990 and trends from 1945, annual rpt, 1544–16

Farm production inputs, output, and productivity, by commodity and region, 1947-89, annual rpt, 1544–17

Farm production itemized costs, by farm sales size and region, 1990, annual rpt, 1614–3

Farm production itemized costs, receipts, and returns, by commodity and region, 1987-89, annual rpt, 1544–20

Farm sector balance sheet, and receipts by detailed commodity, by State, 1985-89, annual rpt, 1544–18

Fish (processed) production by location, and trade, by species and product, 1987-90, annual rpts, 2166–6

Fish (trout) raised on farms, production, sales, prices, and losses, 1990-91, annual rpt, 1631–16

Fish and shellfish cold storage holdings, by product and species, preliminary data, monthly press release, 2162–2

Fish catch, trade, use, and fishery operations, with selected foreign data, by species, 1980s-90, annual rpt, 2164–1

Foreign and US agricultural supply and demand indicators, by selected crop, monthly rpt, 1522–5

Foreign and US grain production, prices, trade, stocks, and use, FAS periodic circular series, 1925–2

Foreign countries agricultural production, prices, and trade, by country, 1980-90 and forecast 1991, annual world area rpt series, 1524–4

Foreign countries agricultural production, trade, and policies, summary data by country, 1989-90, annual factbook, 1924–12

Hay (alfalfa and prairie) prices, for selected areas, weekly rpt, 1313–5

Imports and quotas of dairy products, by commodity and country of origin, FAS monthly rpt, 1925–31

Irrigation projects of Reclamation Bur in western US, crop production and acreage by commodity, State, and project, 1989, annual rpt, 5824–12

Labor productivity, indexes of output, hours, and employment by SIC 2- to 4-digit industry, 1967-89, annual rpt, 6824–1.3

Livestock, meat, poultry, and egg production, prices, trade, and stocks, monthly rpt, 1561–17

Manufacturing annual survey, 1989: finances and operations, by SIC 2- to 4-digit industry, series, 2506–15

Manufacturing census, 1987: finances and operations, by SIC 2- to 4-digit industry, State, and MSA, with trends from 1849, 2497–1

Manufacturing census, 1987: finances and operations, by type of organization and SIC 2- to 4-digit industry, subject rpt, 2497–5

Milk (nonfat) and whey feed prices in central States, 1990, annual rpt, 1317–1.4

Molasses (feed) wholesale prices by market area, and trade, weekly rpt, 1311–16

Molasses supply, use, wholesale prices by market, and imports by country, 1985-90, annual rpt, 1311–19

Occupational injury and illness rates, by SIC 2- to 4-digit industry, 1988-89, annual rpt, 6844–7

Occupational injury and illness rates, by SIC 2- to 4-digit industry, 1989, annual rpt, 6844–1

OECD trade, total and for 4 major countries, and US trade by country, by commodity, 1970-89, world area rpt series, 9116–1

Oil and fat production, consumption by end use, and stocks, by type, quarterly Current Industrial Rpt, 2506–4.4

Oilseed production and exports, and nutrient value for feed, 1987-92, article, 1561–3.203

Packers feeding and marketing of livestock, by animal type and State, 1989, annual rpt, 1384–1.2

Pesticide and fertilizer use reduction, environmental and economic impacts by commodity and region, alternative forecasts 1989-94, hearing, 23848–222

PL 480 long-term credit sales allocations, by commodity and country, periodic press release, 1922–7

Potato production, acreage, disposition, prices, and trade, by State and country, 1949-90, 1568–305

Potato production, prices, stocks, and use, by State, 1981-90, annual rpt, 1621–11

Price indexes (producer), by stage of processing and detailed commodity, monthly rpt, 6762–6

Price indexes (producer), by stage of processing and detailed commodity, monthly 1990, annual rpt, 6764–2

Price support and other CCC program outlays, with production and marketing outlook, by commodity, projected 1990-96, 26306–6.160

Price support program provisions, for selected commodities, 1961-90, 1568–302

Prices (producer and retail) of meat and fish, 1981-91, semiannual situation rpt, 1561–15.3

Prices received and paid by farmers, by commodity and State, 1990, annual rpt, 1629–5

Prices received by farmers and production value, by detailed crop and State, 1988-90, annual rpt, 1621–2

Prices received by farmers for major products, and paid for farm inputs and living items, by State, monthly rpt, 1629–1

Production, acreage, stocks, use, trade, prices, and price supports, periodic situation rpt with articles, 1561–4

Production, farms, acreage, and related data, by selected crop and State, monthly rpt, 1621–1

Production, prices, trade, and marketing, by commodity, current situation and forecast, monthly rpt with articles, 1502–4

Production, prices, trade, and stocks, for feedstuffs and feed grains by type, weekly rpt, 1313–2

Rice market activities, prices, inspections, sales, trade, supply, and use, for US and selected foreign markets, weekly rpt, 1313–8

Seed exports, by type, world region, and country, FAS quarterly rpt, 1925–13

Wheat and rye foreign and US production, prices, trade, stocks, and use, quarterly situation rpt with articles, 1561–12

see also Pasture and rangeland

see also Pet food and supplies

see also under By Commodity in the "Index by Categories"

Index by Subjects and Names

Animal oils
see Oils, oilseeds, and fats

Animals

Accidents involving animals, deaths and rates by cause, age, sex, race, and State, 1988, US Vital Statistics annual rpt, 4144–2

Exports and imports of US, by country and detailed commodity, monthly rpt, 2422–12

Exports and imports of US, by Harmonized System 6-digit commodity and country, 1990, annual rpt, 2424–13

Exports and imports of US, by transport mode, country, and SITC 1- to 3-digit commodity, 1990, annual rpt, 2424–12

Exports of US, detailed Schedule B commodities with countries of destination, 1990, annual rpt, 2424–10

Licensing and inspection of facilities, and other animal protection activities of USDA, with animals used in research, by State, FY89, annual rpt, 1394–10

see also Animal diseases and zoonoses
see also Animal experimentation
see also Animal feed
see also Birds and bird conservation
see also Endangered species
see also Fish and fishing industry
see also Fishing, sport
see also Hunting and trapping
see also Livestock and livestock industry
see also Marine mammals
see also Pasture and rangeland
see also Pet food and supplies
see also Pets
see also Poultry industry and products
see also Rabies
see also Veterinary medicine
see also Wildlife and wildlife conservation
see also Wildlife refuges
see also Zoological parks

Ann Arbor, Mich.

CPI by component for US city average, and by region, population size, and for 15 metro areas, monthly rpt, 6762–1

CPI by component for US city average, and by region, population size, and for 27 metro areas, monthly rpt, 6762–2

Wages by occupation, and benefits for office and plant workers, 1990 survey, periodic MSA rpt, 6785–3.1

see also under By City and By SMSA or MSA in the "Index by Categories"

Anniston, Ala.

see also under By SMSA or MSA in the "Index by Categories"

Annual Housing Survey
see American Housing Survey

Annual Survey of Manufactures

Data coverage and availability of Census Bur rpts and data files, 1991 annual listing, 2304–2

Finances and operations, by SIC 2- to 4-digit industry, 1989 survey, series, 2506–15

Operations and performance of manufacturing industries, analytical rpt series, 2506–16

Antarctica

Environmental summary data, and intl claims and disputes, 1991 annual factbook, 9114–2

NSF activities, finances, and funding by program, FY90, annual rpt, 9624–6

US military and civilian personnel and dependents, by service branch, world area, and country, quarterly rpt, 3542–20

Anthropology

Employment and other characteristics of science and engineering PhDs, by field and State, 1989, biennial rpt, 9627–18

Fed Govt aid to higher education and nonprofit instns for R&D and related activities, by field, instn, agency, and State, FY89, annual rpt, 9627–17

Higher education grad programs enrollment in science and engineering, by field, source of funds, and characteristics of student and instn, 1975-89, annual rpt, 9627–7

R&D funding by Fed Govt, by field, performer type, agency, and State, FY89-91, annual rpt, 9627–20

Anthropometry
see Body measurements

Antigua and Barbuda

Agricultural trade of US, by detailed commodity and country, 1990, semiannual rpt, 1522–4

AID loans repayment status and terms by program and country, and status of predecessor agency loans, quarterly rpt, 9912–3

Economic, social, political, and geographic summary data, by country, 1991, annual factbook, 9114–2

Exports and imports of US, by transport mode, country, and SITC 1- to 3-digit commodity, 1990, annual rpt, 2424–12

Human rights conditions in 170 countries, and US economic and military aid, 1990, annual rpt, 21384–3

Investment (direct) incentives of Caribbean Basin Initiative, economic impacts, with finances and employment by country, 1984-90, 2048–141

Labor conditions, union coverage, and work accidents, 1991 annual regional rpt, 6366–4.56

Military aid of US, arms sales, and training programs costs and budget requests, by program, world region, and country, FY90-92, annual rpt, 7144–13

UN voting record and share of votes in agreement with US, by issue, country, and world area, 1990, annual rpt, 7004–18

see also under By Foreign Country in the "Index by Categories"

Antimony
see Metals and metal industries

Antiques

Exports and imports of US, by country and detailed commodity, monthly rpt, 2422–12

Exports and imports of US, by Harmonized System 6-digit commodity and country, 1990, annual rpt, 2424–13

Exports of US, detailed Schedule B commodities with countries of destination, 1990, annual rpt, 2424–10

Antitrust law

Banks (natl) charters, mergers, liquidations, enforcement cases, and financial performance, with data by instn and State, quarterly rpt, 8402–3

Cases filed under antitrust law, by Fed Govt and private parties, data compilation, 1991 annual rpt, 6064–6.5

Apartment houses

Court civil and criminal caseloads for Federal district, appeals, and bankruptcy courts, by type of suit and offense, circuit, and district, 1990, annual rpt, 18204–11

Court civil and criminal caseloads for Federal district, appeals, and special courts, 1990, annual rpt, 18204–8

Court civil and criminal caseloads for Federal district courts, 1991, annual rpt, 18204–2.1

Court criminal case processing in Federal district courts, and dispositions, by offense, district, and offender characteristics, 1986, annual rpt, 6064–29

Court criminal case processing in Federal district courts, and dispositions, by offense, 1980-89, annual rpt, 6064–31

Court criminal cases in Federal district courts, by offense, disposition, and district, 1980-90, last issue of annual rpt, 18204–1

Dairy cooperatives exemption from antitrust laws, impacts on industry structure and pricing, with background data, 1930s-80s, GAO rpt, 26113–499

Debt delinquent on Federal accounts, cases and collections of Justice Dept and private law firms, pilot project results, FY90, annual rpt, 6004–20

Sentences for Federal offenses, guidelines by offense and circumstances, series, 17668–1

US attorneys civil and criminal cases by type and disposition, and collections, by Federal district, FY90, annual rpt, 6004–2.1; 6004–2.7

Antrobius, William L.

"Montana Forest Pest Conditions and Program Highlights, 1989", 1206–49.2

Apartment houses

Alteration and repair spending, by property and job characteristics, and region, quarterly rpt, annual tables, 2382–7.2

American Housing Survey: inventory change from 1973, by reason, unit and household characteristics, and location, 1983, biennial rpt, 2485–14

American Housing Survey: unit and households characteristics, unit and neighborhood quality, and journey to work by MSA location, for 11 MSAs, 1984 survey, supplement, 2485–8

American Housing Survey: unit and households detailed characteristics, and unit and neighborhood quality, MSA rpt series, 2485–6

American Housing Survey: unit and households detailed characteristics, and unit and neighborhood quality, 1987, biennial rpt, 2485–12; 2485–13

Arson incidents by whether structure occupied, property value, and arrest rate, by property type, 1990, annual rpt, 6224–2.1

Assets and debts of private sector, balance sheets by segment, 1945-90, semiannual rpt, 9365–4.1

Census of Housing, 1990: inventory, occupancy, and costs, State fact sheet series, 2326–21

Construction industries census, 1987: establishments, employment, receipts, and expenditures, by SIC 4-digit industry and State, final industry rpt series, 2373–1

Apartment houses

Construction put in place, permits, housing sales, costs, material prices, and employment, bimonthly rpt with articles, 2042–1

Construction put in place, value of new public and private structures, by type, monthly rpt, 2382–4

Fed Govt financial and nonfinancial domestic aid, 1991 base edition with supplements, annual listing, 104–5

Households and family characteristics, by location, 1990, annual Current Population Rpt, 2546–1.447

HUD multifamily housing stock and mortgage foreclosures, by region, 1990, GAO rpt, 26131–84

Market absorption rates and characteristics for nonsubsidized furnished and unfurnished units, 1989, annual Current Housing Rpt, 2484–2

Market absorption rates for apartments and condominiums, and completions by rent class and sales price, quarterly rpt, 2482–2

Mortgage loan activity, by type of lender, loan, and mortgaged property, monthly press release, 5142–18

Mortgage loan activity, by type of lender, loan, and mortgaged property, quarterly press release, 5142–30

Mortgage loan activity of insured savings instns, by purpose and State, various periods 1984-89, annual rpt, 8434–3

New apartment units completed by region and metro-nonmetro location, and absorption rates, by size and price class, preliminary 1990, annual Current Housing Rpt, 2484–3

New housing starts, by units per structure and metro-nonmetro location, and mobile home placements and prices, by region, monthly rpt, 2382–1

New housing units authorized, by region, State, selected MSA, and permit-issuing place, monthly rpt, 2382–5

New housing units authorized, by State, MSA, and permit-issuing place, 1990, annual rpt, 2384–2

New housing units completed and under construction, by units per structure, region, and inside-outside MSAs, monthly rpt, 2382–2

New single and multifamily units, by structural and financial characteristics, inside-outside MSAs, and region, 1986-90, annual rpt, 2384–1

North Central States, FHLB 7th District housing vacancy rates for single and multifamily units and mobile homes, by ZIP code, annual MSA rpt series, 9304–18

Savings instns failures, inventory of real estate assets available from Resolution Trust Corp, 1989, semiannual listing, 9722–2.1

Savings instns failures, inventory of real estate assets available from Resolution Trust Corp, 1990, semiannual listing, 9722–2.2; 9722–2.3; 9722–2.7

Savings instns failures, inventory of real estate assets available from Resolution Trust Corp, 1991, semiannual listing, 9722–2.13

Southeastern States, Fed Reserve 6th District, economic indicators by State and MSA, quarterly rpt, 9371–14

State and Metro Area Data Book, 1991 data compilation, 2328–54

Statistical Abstract of US, 1991 annual data compilation, 2324–1.26

Vacant housing characteristics and costs, and occupancy and vacancy rates, by region and metro-nonmetro location, quarterly rpt, 2482–1

Vacant housing characteristics, and occupancy and vacancy rates, by tenure and location, 1960s-90, annual rpt, 2484–1

West Central States, FHLB 10th District housing vacancy rates for single and multifamily units and mobile homes, by ZIP code, annual MSA rpt series, 9304–22

Western States, FHLB 12th District housing vacancy rates for single and multifamily units and mobile homes, by ZIP code, annual MSA rpt series, 9304–21

Wiretaps authorized, costs, arrests, trials, and convictions, by offense and jurisdiction, 1990, annual rpt, 18204–7

see also Condominiums and cooperatives

see also Rooming and boarding houses

Appalachia

Agricultural Stabilization and Conservation Service producer payments and certificate value, by program, monthly rpt, 1802–10

Apple production, marketing, and prices, for Appalachia and compared to other States, 1988-91, annual rpt, 1311–13

Assistance dev project funding by Appalachian Regional Commission, by project and State, planned FY91, annual rpt, 9084–3

Coal production and mines by county, prices, productivity, miners, and reserves, by mining method and State, 1989-90, annual rpt, 3164–25

Dev projects in Appalachia, and funding by source, by program and State, FY90, annual rpt, 9084–1

Education system in Appalachia, improvement initiatives, and indicators of success, by State, 1960s-89, 9088–36

Fed Govt spending in States, by type, program, agency, and State, FY90, annual rpt, 2464–2

Great Smoky Mountain region visitor activities and opinions, 1990 conf papers, annual rpt, 1204–38

HHS financial aid, by program, recipient, State, and city, FY90, annual regional listings, 4004–3

Hwy system and access roads funding and completion status, by State, quarterly tables, 9082–1

Peaches production, marketing, and prices in 3 southeastern States and Appalachia, 1990, annual rpt, 1311–12

Population of Appalachia, by State and county, 1980 and 1990, annual rpt, 9084–1

see also under By Region in the "Index by Categories"

see also under names of individual States

Appalachian Regional Commission

Activities of ARC, local dev projects, and funding by source, by program and State, FY90, annual rpt, 9084–1

Budget of US, authoritative financial statements with appropriations, outlays, and receipts, by category and agency, FY90, annual rpt, 8104–2.1

Budget of US, obligations and authority by function, agency, and program, with summaries, analyses, and historical tables, FY92, annual rpt, 104–2

Education funding by Federal agency, program, and recipient type, and instn spending, FY80-90, annual rpt, 4824–8

Education system in Appalachia, improvement initiatives, and indicators of success, by State, 1960s-89, 9088–36

Expenditures of ARC, by project and State, planned FY91, annual rpt, 9084–3

Hwy system and access roads funding and completion status, by State, quarterly tables, 9082–1

R&D funding by Fed Govt, by field, performer type, agency, and State, FY89-91, annual rpt, 9627–20

Apparel

see Clothing and clothing industry

Appeals

see Court of Military Appeals

see Federal courts of appeals

see Supreme Court

see Tax protests and appeals

see U.S. Court of Appeals for the Federal Circuit

Appel, D. H.

"Water Resources Activities of the USGS in West Virginia, 1989", 5666–26.12

Applebee, Arthur N.

"Learning To Write in Our Nation's Schools. National Assessment of Educational Progress, 1988", 4896–7.1

Apples

see Fruit and fruit products

Appleton, Wis.

see also under By SMSA or MSA in the "Index by Categories"

Appliances

see Household appliances and equipment

Apportionment

see Congressional apportionment

Apprenticeship

Minimum wage exemption certificates and employment under Fair Labor Standards Act, FY88-89, annual rpt, 6504–2.1

Veterans education aid under GI Bill and other programs, and participation by period of service and State, FY89, annual rpt, 8604–9

Women's employment in skilled manual occupations, and apprenticeships, 1978-89, 6564–1.1

Appropriations

see Budget of the U.S.

see Defense budgets and appropriations

Aptitude tests

see Educational tests

Aquaculture

Agriculture census, 1987: farms, farmland, production, finances, and operator characteristics, by county, final State rpt series, 2331–1

Bass (striped) stocks status on Atlantic coast, and sport and commercial catch by State, 1972-89, annual rpt, 5504–29

Canada salmon aquaculture production by species, and farms, by region, 1976-90, article, 2162–1.203

Catfish and trout hatcheries and farms, production, costs, prices, and sales, 1970s-91, semiannual situation rpt, 1561–15

Index by Subjects and Names

Catfish raised on farms, inventory, stocks, and production, by producer State, quarterly rpt, 1631–18

Catfish raised on farms, production, inventory, imports, and prices, by State, as of Feb 1991, last issue of semiannual rpt, 1631–17

Catfish raised on farms, production, inventory, sales, prices, and imports, monthly release, 1631–14

Chile salmon aquaculture production, and exports by market, by species, 1980-89 and projected to 1993, article, 2162–1.204

China shrimp production and exports, 1982-90, article, 1524–4.3

Denmark aquaculture production by species, 1985-88, article, 2162–1.202

Farm financial and marketing conditions, forecast 1991, annual chartbook, 1504–8

Farm financial and marketing conditions, forecast 1991, annual conf, 1004–16

Farm income, expenses, receipts by commodity, assets, liabilities, and ratios, 1990 and trends from 1945, annual rpt, 1544–16

Faroe Islands salmon farms, production, and exports, 1980-86 with projections to 1990, 2162–1.201

Hatcheries and research stations under Fish and Wildlife Service mgmt, acreage by site and State, as of Sept 1991, annual rpt, 5504–8

Japan and US aquaculture mgmt, methods, and biological data for selected species, 1988 conf, annual rpt, 2164–15

Natl Fish Hatchery System activities and deliveries, by species, hatchery, and jurisdiction of waters stocked, FY90, annual rpt, 5504–10

Norway salmon aquaculture production, farms, and exports, 1971-88 with projections to 1990, article, 2162–1.204

R&D and mgmt of fisheries, Fed Govt grants by project and State, and rpts, 1990, annual listing, 2164–3

Research and education grants, USDA competitive awards by program and recipient, FY90, annual listing, 1764–1

Research of State fish and wildlife agencies, federally funded fishery projects and costs by species and State, 1990, annual listing, 5504–23

Salmon and trout wild and hatchery juvenile population and characteristics, for Pacific Northwest, 1981-85, 2168–123

Southeast Asia shrimp aquaculture harvest by country, and Thailand revenues and costs, 1984-89, article, 2162–1.203

Statistical Abstract of US, 1991 annual data compilation, 2324–1.24

Trout raised on farms, production, sales, and prices, 1990-91, annual rpt, 1631–16

Arab Republic of Egypt

see Egypt

Arabian Peninsula

see Oman

see Qatar

see Saudi Arabia

see United Arab Emirates

see Yemen

see Yemen, North

see Yemen, South

Arbitration

see Civil procedure

see Labor-management relations, general

see Labor-management relations in government

see Legal arbitration and mediation

Arboretums

see Botanical gardens

Architect of the Capitol

Activities of Capitol Architect, funding, costs, and contracts, FY88, annual rpt, 25944–1

Budget of US, obligations and authority by function, agency, and program, with summaries, analyses, and historical tables, FY92, annual rpt, 104–2

Expenditures for salaries, supplies, and services, itemized by payee and function, 1st half FY91, semiannual rpt, 25922–2

Architectural and Transportation Barriers Compliance Board

see U.S. Architectural and Transportation Barriers Compliance Board

Architectural barriers to the handicapped

Building access for disabled to Federal and federally funded facilities, complaints by disposition, FY90, annual rpt, 17614–1

Election polling places accessibility to aged and disabled, precincts by barrier type and State, 1990 natl elections, biennial rpt, 9274–6

Public housing renovation costs and alternative funding methods, by project type and region, 1990 rpt, 5188–127

Architecture

County Business Patterns, 1988: employment, establishments, and payroll, by SIC 2- to 4-digit industry and county, annual State rpt series, 2326–6

County Business Patterns, 1989: employment, establishments, and payroll, by SIC 2- to 4-digit industry and county, annual State rpt series, 2326–8

Degrees awarded in higher education, by level, field, race, and sex, 1988/89 with trends from 1978/79, biennial rpt, 4844–17

Earthquake preparedness costs and benefits, with data for California events and effects of 1989 Loma Prieta quake, 1980s, hearings, 21248–154

Higher education course completions, by detailed program, sex, race, and instn type, for 1972 high school class, as of 1984, 4888–4

Puerto Rico economic censuses, 1987: wholesale and retail trade and service industry finances and operations, by SIC 2- to 4-digit industry and municipio, 2591–1

Service industries census, 1987: establishments, receipts by source, payroll, and employment, by SIC 2- to 4-digit kind of business, State, and MSA, 2393–4

see also Architectural barriers to the handicapped

Arctic

see also Arctic Ocean

Arctic Ocean

Environmental conditions and oil dev impacts for Alaska OCS, compilation of papers, series, 2176–1

Environmental summary data, and intl claims and disputes, 1991 annual factbook, 9114–2

Fish catch and habitat impacts of Arctic Ocean oil and gas dev, and assessment methods, 1988 conf, 5738–24

Tide height and time daily at coastal points, forecast 1992, annual rpt, 2174–2.5

Whales (bowhead) population in Arctic areas, behavioral differences by location, 1970s-80s, 5738–29

Whales (bowhead) population in Arctic areas, impacts of subsistence whaling, shipping, noise, and other human activity, mid 1970s-80s, 5738–30

see also Beaufort Sea

see also Chukchi Sea

Area studies

Arts Natl Endowment activities and grants, FY90, annual rpt, 9564–3

Degrees awarded in higher education, by level, field, race, and sex, 1988/89 with trends from 1978/79, biennial rpt, 4844–17

Exchange and training programs of Federal agencies, participants by world area, and funding, by program, FY89, annual rpt, 9854–8

Higher education course completions, by detailed program, sex, race, and instn type, for 1972 high school class, as of 1984, 4888–4

Latin America dev grants of Inter-American Foundation by program area, and fellowships by field and instn, by country, FY72-90, annual rpt, 14424–2

Latin America dev grants of Inter-American Foundation by recipient, and fellowships, by country, FY90, annual rpt, 14424–1

Student aid funding and participation, by Federal program, instn type and control, and State, various periods 1959-89, annual rpt, 4804–28

Area wage surveys

Southeastern US wages of office and plant workers, for 27 MSAs, 1990, press release, 6946–3.21

Wages by occupation, and benefits for office and plant workers in selected MSAs, 1990, annual rpt, 6785–1

Wages by occupation, and benefits for office and plant workers, periodic MSA survey rpt series, 6785–3; 6785–11; 6785–12

Wages by occupation, for office and plant workers in metro areas, by industry div and region, Aug 1990, annual rpt, 6785–9

Wages by occupation, for office and plant workers in selected MSAs, 1991 surveys, annual rpt, 6785–5

Wages by occupation, for office and plant workers in selected MSAs, 1991 surveys, annual summary rpts, 6785–6

Wages for 4 occupational groups, relative pay levels in 60 MSAs, 1990, annual rpt, 6785–8

Wages for 4 occupational groups, relative pay levels in 75 labor market areas, 1990, annual rpt, 6785–13

see also Industry wage surveys

Arecibo, P.R.

see also under By SMSA or MSA in the "Index by Categories"

Argentina

Agricultural exports of high-value commodities, indexes and sales by commodity, world area, and country, 1960s-86, 1528–323

Argentina

Agricultural exports of US, impacts of foreign agricultural and trade policy, with data by commodity and country, 1989, annual rpt, 1924–8

Agricultural production, prices, and trade, by country, 1960s-90, annual world area rpt, 1524–4.2

Agricultural production, trade, and policies in foreign countries, summary data by country, 1989-90, annual factbook, 1924–12

Agricultural subsidies to producers and consumers in 6 Latin America countries, by selected commodity, 1982-87, 1528–324

Agricultural trade of US, by detailed commodity and country, 1989, annual rpt, 1524–8

Agricultural trade of US, by detailed commodity and country, 1990, semiannual rpt, 1522–4

AID loans repayment status and terms by program and country, and status of predecessor agency loans, quarterly rpt, 9912–3

Background Notes, summary social, political, and economic data, 1990 rpt, 7006–2.7

Bearings (ball) from 14 countries, injury to US industry from foreign subsidized and less than fair value imports, investigation with background financial and operating data, 1991 rpt, 9886–19.74

Dollar exchange rate (black-market) in Argentina, relationship with official rate and other economic indicators, model description and results, 1991 technical paper, 9366–7.261

Economic and military aid and loans from US and intl agencies, by program and country, FY46-90, annual rpt, 9914–5

Economic conditions in USSR, Eastern Europe, OECD, and selected other countries, 1960s-90, annual rpt, 9114–4

Economic conditions, policy, and trade practices, by country, 1988-90, annual rpt, 21384–5

Economic, social, political, and geographic summary data, by country, 1991, annual factbook, 9114–2

Exports and imports of US, by commodity and country, 1970-89, world area rpt, 9116–1.4

Exports and imports of US, by Harmonized System 6-digit commodity and country, 1990, annual rpt, 2424–13

Exports and imports of US, by selected country, country group, and commodity group, 1990, annual rpt, 2044–37

Exports and imports of US, by transport mode, country, and SITC 1- to 3-digit commodity, 1990, annual rpt, 2424–12

Exports, imports, and balances of US with major trading partners, by product category, 1986-90, annual chartbook, 9884–21

Exports of US, detailed Schedule B commodities with countries of destination, 1990, annual rpt, 2424–10

Human rights conditions in 170 countries, and US economic and military aid, 1990, annual rpt, 21384–3

Imports of goods, services, and investment from US, trade barriers, impacts, and US actions, by country, 1990, annual rpt, 444–2

Imports of US given duty-free treatment for value of US material sent abroad, by commodity and country, 1989, annual rpt, 9884–14

Inflation rates and public debt burden in Argentina and Brazil, 1980s-91, technical paper, 9379–12.69

Inflation relation to money supply and public debt in Argentina and Brazil, model description and results, 1980s-90, technical paper, 9379–12.75

Labor conditions, union coverage, and work accidents, 1991 annual country rpt, 6366–4.29

Military aid of US, arms sales, and training programs costs and budget requests, by program, world region, and country, FY90-92, annual rpt, 7144–13

Multinatl US firms and foreign affiliates finances and operations, by industry and world area of parent firm, 1989 benchmark survey, preliminary annual rpt, 2704–5

Multinatl US firms foreign affiliates, income statement items by country and world area, 1986, biennial article, 8302–2.212

Nuclear power generation in US and 20 countries, monthly rpt, 3162–24.10

Nuclear power plant capacity, generation, and operating status, by plant and foreign and US location, 1990 and projected to 2030, annual rpt, 3164–57

Silicon metal from Argentina at less than fair value, injury to US industry, investigation with background financial and operating data, 1991 rpt, 9886–14.330

Spacecraft and satellite launches since 1957, quarterly listing, 9502–2

Steel wire rope from 2 countries at less than fair value, injury to US industry, investigation with background financial and operating data, 1991 rpt, 9886–14.324

Steel wire rope from 8 countries, injury to US industry from foreign subsidized and less than fair value imports, investigation with background financial and operating data, 1990 rpt, 9886–19.73

UN voting record and share of votes in agreement with US, by issue, country, and world area, 1990, annual rpt, 7004–18

see also under By Foreign Country in the "Index by Categories"

Argon

see Gases

Argonne National Laboratory

see also Department of Energy National Laboratories

Arid zones

Selenium levels in Western States arid areas, and plant and animal exposure effects, 1990 conf, 5668–121

Arizona

Banks (insured commercial and savings) deposits by instn, State, MSA, and county, as of June 1990, annual regional rpt, 9295–3.6

Coal production and mines by county, prices, productivity, miners, and reserves, by mining method and State, 1989-90, annual rpt, 3164–25

Colorado River sand deposit characteristics, and density of campsites, 1920s-80s, 5668–122

Index by Subjects and Names

County Business Patterns, 1989: employment, establishments, and payroll, by SIC 2- to 4-digit industry and county, annual State rpt, 2326–8.4

DOD prime contract awards, by contractor, service branch, State, and city, FY90, annual rpt, 3544–22

Fed Govt spending in States and local areas, by type, State, county, and city, FY90, annual rpt, 2464–3

Fed Govt spending in States, by type, program, agency, and State, FY90, annual rpt, 2464–2

Fertilizer and pesticide use and application rates, by type, crop, and State, 1990, 1616–1.2

Gemstone production in selected States, Mineral Industry Surveys, 1988-90, advance annual rpt, 5614–5.10

Health maintenance organizations and other prepaid managed care plans Medicaid enrollment and use, for 20 States, 1985-89, chartbook, 4108–29

HHS financial aid, by program, recipient, State, and city, FY90, annual regional listing, 4004–3.9

Hispanic Americans in counties bordering Mexico, by selected characteristics, 1980, Current Population Rpt, 2546–2.159

Hospital deaths of Medicare patients, actual and expected rates by diagnosis, and hospital characteristics, by instn, FY87-89, annual regional rpt, 4654–14.9

Income (personal) per capita and by source, and earnings by industry div, by State, MSA, and county, 1984-89, annual regional rpt, 2704–2.5

Indian (Navajo and Hopi) relocation program activities and caseloads, 1975-90, 16008–5

Jail adult and juvenile population, employment, spending, instn conditions, and inmate programs, by county and facility, 1988, regional rpt series, 6068–144.5

Marriages, divorces, and rates, by characteristics of spouses, State, and county, 1987 and trends from 1920, US Vital Statistics annual rpt, 4144–4

Mineral industries census, 1987: finances and operations, by SIC 2- to 4-digit industry, State, and county, census div rpt, 2515–1.8

Mineral Industry Surveys, State reviews of production, 1990, preliminary annual rpt, 5614–6

Minerals Yearbook, 1989, Vol 2: State review of production and sales by commodity, and business activity, annual rpt, 5604–16.4

Minerals Yearbook, 1989, Vol 2: State reviews of production, sales, and firms, by commodity, and business activity, annual rpt, 5604–34

Oranges (fresh) exports of US, demand indicators for 4 countries, with production, trade, and use, 1960s-90, 1528–317

Physicians, by specialty, age, sex, and location of training and practice, 1989, State rpt, 4116–6.3

Population and housing census, 1990: population and housing characteristics, households, and land area, by county, subdiv, and place, State rpt, 2551–1.4

Index by Subjects and Names

Population and housing census, 1990: voting age and total population by race, and housing units, by block, redistricting counts required under PL 94-171, State CD-ROM release, 2551–6.3

Population and housing census, 1990: voting age and total population by race, and housing units, by county and city, redistricting counts required under PL 94-171, State summary rpt, 2551–5.3

Statistical Abstract of US, 1991 annual data compilation, 2324–1

Supplemental Security Income payments and beneficiaries, by type of eligibility, State, and county, Dec 1989, annual rpt, 4744–27.9

Timber in Arizona, resources by species, forest and tree characteristics, ownership, and county, 1984-85, 1208–374

Water (groundwater) supply, quality, chemistry, other characteristics, and use, 1991 regional rpt, 5666–25.13

Water quality, chemistry, hydrology, and other characteristics, 1989 local area study, 5666–27.17

Water resources dev projects of Army Corps of Engineers, characteristics, and costs, 1950s-89, biennial State rpt, 3756–1.3

Water supply, and snow survey results, monthly State rpt, 1266–2.2

Water supply, and snow survey results, 1990, annual State rpt, 1264–14.8

Wetlands (riparian) acreage, and Bur of Land Mgmt activities, mgmt plans, and scientific staff, 1990 State rpt, 5726–8.4

see also Phoenix, Ariz.

see also Tucson, Ariz.

see also under By State in the "Index by Categories"

Arkansas

Banks (insured commercial and savings) deposits by instn, State, MSA, and county, as of June 1990, annual regional rpt, 9295–3.4

Coal production and mines by county, prices, productivity, miners, and reserves, by mining method and State, 1989-90, annual rpt, 3164–25

County Business Patterns, 1989: employment, establishments, and payroll, by SIC 2- to 4-digit industry and county, annual State rpt, 2326–8.5

DOD prime contract awards, by contractor, service branch, State, and city, FY90, annual rpt, 3544–22

Economic and banking conditions, for Fed Reserve 8th District, quarterly rpt with articles, 9391–16

Employment by industry div, earnings, and hours, by southwestern State, monthly rpt, 6962–2

Fed Govt spending in States and local areas, by type, State, county, and city, FY90, annual rpt, 2464–3

Fed Govt spending in States, by type, program, agency, and State, FY90, annual rpt, 2464–2

Fish (catfish) raised on farms, inventory, stocks, and production, by major producer State, quarterly rpt, 1631–18

Floods on Arkansas, Red, and Trinity Rivers, storm characteristics, and Natl Weather Service forecast accuracy, 1990, 2186–6.4

FmHA farm and rural housing program loan appeals filed in 3 States, by disposition, 1988-90, GAO rpt, 26113–516

HHS financial aid, by program, recipient, State, and city, FY90, annual regional listing, 4004–3.6

Hospital deaths of Medicare patients, actual and expected rates by diagnosis, and hospital characteristics, by instn, FY87-89, annual regional rpt, 4654–14.6

Income (personal) per capita and by source, and earnings by industry div, by State, MSA, and county, 1984-89, annual regional rpt, 2704–2.4

Jail adult and juvenile population, employment, spending, instn conditions, and inmate programs, by county and facility, 1988, regional rpt series, 6068–144.4

Marriages, divorces, and rates, by characteristics of spouses, State, and county, 1987 and trends from 1920, US Vital Statistics annual rpt, 4144–4

Mineral Industry Surveys, State reviews of production, 1990, preliminary annual rpt, 5614–6

Minerals Yearbook, 1989, Vol 2: State review of production and sales by commodity, and business activity, annual rpt, 5604–16.5

Minerals Yearbook, 1989, Vol 2: State reviews of production, sales, and firms, by commodity, and business activity, annual rpt, 5604–34

Older persons aid programs funding, and long term care ombudsman funding and visits by State, 1988-90, 25248–126

Physicians, by specialty, age, sex, and location of training and practice, 1989, State rpt, 4116–6.4

Population and housing census, 1990: population and housing characteristics, households, and land area, by county, subdiv, and place, State rpt, 2551–1.5

Population and housing census, 1990: voting age and total population by race, and housing units, by block, redistricting counts required under PL 94-171, State CD-ROM release, 2551–6.4

Population and housing census, 1990: voting age and total population by race, and housing units, by county and city, redistricting counts required under PL 94-171, State summary rpt, 2551–5.4

Rice market activities, prices, inspections, sales, trade, supply, and use, for US and selected foreign markets, weekly rpt, 1313–8

Rice stocks on and off farms and total in all positions, periodic rpt, 1621–7

Statistical Abstract of US, 1991 annual data compilation, 2324–1

Supplemental Security Income payments and beneficiaries, by type of eligibility, State, and county, Dec 1989, annual rpt, 4744–27.6

Water (groundwater) supply, quality, chemistry, and use, 1987, State rpt, 5666–28.6

Water (groundwater) supply, quality, chemistry, and use, 1990, State rpt, 5666–28.12

Water supply and quality in streams and lakes, and groundwater levels in wells, by drainage basin, 1990, annual State rpt, 5666–10.4

Armed services reserves

see also Fort Smith, Ark.

see also Little Rock, Ark.

see also North Little Rock, Ark.

see also under By State in the "Index by Categories"

Arkansas River

Floods on Arkansas, Red, and Trinity Rivers, storm characteristics, and Natl Weather Service forecast accuracy, 1990, 2186–6.4

Water supply and quality in streams and lakes, and groundwater levels in wells, by drainage basin, 1988, annual State rpt series, 5666–16

Water supply and quality in streams and lakes, and groundwater levels in wells, by drainage basin, 1989, annual State rpt series, 5666–12

Water supply and quality in streams and lakes, and groundwater levels in wells, by drainage basin, 1990, annual State rpt series, 5666–10

Arlington, Tex.

Employment, earnings, and hours, for Fort Worth-Arlington metro area, late 1970s-90, annual rpt, 6964–2

Wages by occupation, and benefits for office and plant workers, 1991 survey, periodic labor market rpt, 6785–3.10

see also under By City and By SMSA or MSA in the "Index by Categories"

Arlington, Va.

Fed Govt land acquisition and dev projects in DC metro area, characteristics and funding by agency and project, FY91-95, annual rpt, 15454–1

Armbruster, Michael J.

"Characterization of Habitat Used by Whooping Cranes During Migration", 5508–111

Armed Forces Institute of Pathology

Death investigation systems of US and Canada, jurisdictions, medical officers qualifications, types of deaths covered, and related statutes, 1990 listing, 4208–34

Armed services

see also Air Force

see also Armed services reserves

see also Army

see also Coast Guard

see also Department of Defense

see also Marine Corps

see also Military personnel

see also Navy

see also Selective service

see also Voluntary military service

Armed services reserves

Army Dept activities, personnel, discipline, budget, and assistance, FY83 summary data, annual rpt, 3704–11

Army Reserve and National Guard wartime preparedness, for general support maintenance units, as of May 1990, GAO rpt, 26123–354

Army strategic capability, force strengths, budget, and mgmt, FY74-93, annual rpt, 3704–13

Base construction, renovation, and land acquisition, DOD budget requests by project, service branch, State, and country, FY92-93, annual rpt, 3544–15

Base support costs by function, and personnel and acreage by installation, by service branch, FY91, annual rpt, 3504–11

Armed services reserves

Budget of DOD, base construction and family housing appropriations by facility, service branch, and location, FY90-93, annual rpt, 3544–39

Budget of DOD, procurement appropriations by item, service branch, and defense agency, FY90-93, annual rpt, 3544–32

Budget of DOD, R&D appropriations by item, service branch, and defense agency, FY90-93, annual rpt, 3544–33

Budget of US, obligations and authority by function, agency, and program, with summaries, analyses, and historical tables, FY92, annual rpt, 104–2

Foreign and US reserve forces structure and training, for US and 5 European countries, as of 1990, GAO rpt, 26123–358

Health care personnel and turnover, by specialty for reserves, FY89, annual rpt, 3544–24.8

Navy personnel strengths, accessions, and attrition, detailed statistics, quarterly rpt, 3802–4

Pay and benefits for active duty personnel, reserves, retirees, and survivors, 1940s-80s and projected to 2049, 21208–34

Persian Gulf War costs to US by category and service branch, and offsetting contributions by allied country, monthly rpt, 102–3

Persian Gulf War Navy and Marine Corps reserves mobilized, 1990-91, GAO rpt, 26123–351

Persian Gulf War Operation Desert Shield and Desert Storm deployment and deaths by selected personnel characteristics, 1990-91, annual rpt supplement, 3544–41.2

Persian Gulf War Operation Desert Storm deployment by personnel characteristics, and offsetting contributions by allied countries, 1990-91, annual rpt supplement, 3504–13

Personnel active duty strength, recruits, and reenlistment, by race, sex, and service branch, quarterly press release, 3542–7

Personnel and equipment strengths, and readiness, by reserve component, FY90, annual rpt, 3544–31

Personnel and payroll for reserve units, by service branch, by State and country, FY90, annual rpt, 3544–29

Personnel attrition in reserves, by reason, personnel characteristics, reserve component, and State, FY88, GAO rpt, 26123–329

Personnel needs, costs, and force readiness, by service branch, FY92, annual rpt, 3504–1

Personnel of DOD, and organization, budget, weapons, and property, by service branch, State, and country, 1991 annual summary rpt, 3504–13

Personnel strengths and characteristics, by reserve component, FY90, annual rpt, 3544–38

Personnel strengths and characteristics, by reserve component, quarterly rpt, 3542–4

Personnel strengths for active duty, civilians, and reserves, by service branch, FY90, annual rpt, 3544–2

Personnel strengths, for active duty, civilians, and reserves, by service branch, quarterly rpt, 3542–14

Personnel strengths for reserve components, by selected characteristics, FY90, annual rpt, 3544–1.5

Statistical Abstract of US, 1991 annual data compilation, 2324–1.11

Training and education programs of DOD, funding, staff, students, and facilities, by service branch, FY92, annual rpt, 3504–5

Women military personnel on active and reserve duty, by demographic and service characteristics and service branch, FY89, annual chartbook, 3544–26

see also Coast Guard Reserve

see also Marine Reserve

see also National Guard

Arms and munitions

see Ammunition

see Arms control and disarmament

see Arms trade

see Bombs

see Chemical and biological warfare agents

see Defense contracts and procurement

see Defense expenditures

see Explosives

see Firearms

see Military assistance

see Military weapons

see Missiles and rockets

see Nuclear weapons

Arms control and disarmament

Nuclear weapons labs and DOE screening of contractors for foreign ownership, control, or influence, compliance by lab, FY88-90, GAO rpt, 26113–520

Nuclear weapons systems of US and USSR, costs, and military forces survival after attack, projected under alternative arms control proposals, FY92-2006, 26306–6.161

Treaties and other bilateral and multilateral agreements of US in force, by country, as of Jan 1991, annual listing, 7004–1

see also Intermediate-Range Nuclear Forces Treaty

see also Strategic Arms Reduction Talks

Arms Control and Disarmament Agency

see U.S. Arms Control and Disarmament Agency

Arms trade

China economic indicators and reform issues, with background data, 1950s-90, compilation of papers, 23848–155

Criminal cases by type and disposition, and collections, for US attorneys, by Federal district, FY90, annual rpt, 6004–2.1

Criminal sentences for Federal offenses, guidelines by offense and circumstances, series, 17668–1

Debt to US of foreign govts and private obligors, by country and program, periodic rpt, 8002–6

Developing countries economic aid from US, military spending and imports measures to determine aid eligibility, by country, 1986-87, annual rpt, 9914–1

Exports and imports of arms and share of GNP by country, and US customs seizures and defense industry employment, 1980s-90, article, 9373–1.221

Exports and imports of US, by Harmonized System 6-digit commodity and country, 1990, annual rpt, 2424–13

Exports of US, detailed Schedule B commodities with countries of destination, 1990, annual rpt, 2424–10

Index by Subjects and Names

Finances of Fed Govt, cash and debt transactions, daily tables, 8102–4

Foreign and US military weapons trade, production, and defense industry finances, with data by firm and country, 1980s-91, 26358–241

Foreign countries human rights conditions in 170 countries, and US economic and military aid, 1990, annual rpt, 21384–3

Foreign countries military aid of US, arms sales, and training, by country, FY50-90, annual rpt, 3904–3

Foreign countries military aid of US, arms sales, and training programs costs and budget requests, by program, world region, and country, FY90-92, annual rpt, 7144–13

Liabilities (contingent) and claims paid by Fed Govt on federally insured and guaranteed contracts with foreign obligors, by country and program, periodic rpt, 8002–12

Middle East export controls of US, with trade, dual-use commodity licenses, and arms sales, by country, 1980s-90, GAO rpt, 26123–339

Navy procurement, by contractor and location, FY90, annual rpt, 3804–13

Soviet Union, China, OECD, and selected other countries economic and military aid, by recipient, 1960s-90, annual rpt, 9114–4.9

Statistical Abstract of US, 1991 annual data compilation, 2324–1.11

see also Military assistance

Army

Activities, personnel, discipline, budget, and assistance, FY83 summary data, annual rpt, 3704–11

Base closings, costs and savings for 71 Army and Navy bases, FY92-97, GAO rpt, 26123–341

Computer simulations use in large military exercises, costs and effectiveness in Army Germany deployment exercise, 1969-90, GAO rpt, 26123–318

Criminal case processing in military courts, and prisoners by facility, by service branch, data compilation, 1991 annual rpt, 6064–6.5

Deaths by cause, age, race, and rank, and personnel captured and missing, by service branch, FY90, annual rpt, 3544–40

Health care facilities of DOD in US and abroad, beds, admissions, outpatient visits, and births, by service branch, quarterly rpt, 3542–15

NATO and Warsaw Pact military forces reductions under proposed treaty, and US budget savings, 1990 rpt, 26306–3.114

Pacific basin US military personnel, dependents, aircraft, ships, and costs, by service branch and location, 1990, GAO rpt, 26123–357

Persian Gulf War costs to US by category and service branch, and offsetting contributions by allied country, monthly rpt, 102–3

Persian Gulf War costs to US by category and service branch, and offsetting contributions by allied country, various periods FY90-91, annual rpt, 104–7

Personnel (civilian and military) of DOD, by service branch, major installation, and State, as of Sept 1990, annual rpt, 3544–7

Index by Subjects and Names

Arrest

Personnel active duty and recruit social, economic, and parents characteristics, by service branch and State, FY89, annual rpt, 3544–41

Personnel active duty strength, recruits, and reenlistment, by race, sex, and service branch, quarterly press release, 3542–7

Personnel, contracts, and payroll, by service branch and location, with top 5 contractors and maps, by State and country, FY90, annual rpt, 3544–29

Personnel needs, costs, and force readiness, by service branch, FY92, annual rpt, 3504–1

Personnel of DOD, and organization, budget, weapons, and property, by service branch, State, and country, 1991 annual summary rpt, 3504–13

Personnel strengths, for active duty, civilians, and dependents, by service branch and US and foreign location, quarterly rpt, 3542–20

Personnel strengths, for active duty, civilians, and reserves, by service branch, FY90 and trends, annual rpt, 3544–1

Personnel strengths, for active duty, civilians, and reserves, by service branch, quarterly rpt, 3542–14

Personnel strengths, for active duty enlisted and officers, by sex and race, 1970s-90, GAO rpt, 26123–325

Personnel strengths in US and abroad, by service branch, world area, and country, quarterly press release, 3542–9

Personnel strengths, summary by service branch, monthly press release, 3542–2

Reserve forces and National Guard wartime preparedness, for general support maintenance units, as of May 1990, GAO rpt, 26123–354

Reserve forces personnel strengths and characteristics, by component, FY90, annual rpt, 3544–38

Reserve forces personnel strengths and characteristics, by component, quarterly rpt, 3542–4

ROTC programs enrollment, grads, staff, scholarships, and costs, by service branch, FY86-89, GAO rpt, 26123–337

Strategic capability of Army, force strengths, budget, and mgmt, FY74-93, annual rpt, 3704–13

Training and education programs of DOD, funding, staff, students, and facilities, by service branch, FY92, annual rpt, 3504–5

Women military personnel on active and reserve duty, by demographic and service characteristics and service branch, FY89, annual chartbook, 3544–26

see also Army Corps of Engineers
see also Department of Army
see also National Guard

Army Corps of Engineers

Activities of Corps, FY88, annual rpt, 3754–1

Activities, personnel, discipline, budget, and assistance, FY83 summary data, annual rpt, 3704–11

Budget of US, obligations and authority by function, agency, and program, with summaries, analyses, and historical tables, FY92, annual rpt, 104–2

Columbia River Power System projects, plant investment allocation schedule, FY90, annual rpt, 3224–1

Expenditures of Fed Govt in States, by type, program, agency, and State, FY90, annual rpt, 2464–2

Finances and operations of Federal power admins and electric utilities, 1989, annual rpt, 3164–24.2

Fish and shellfish catch, life cycles, and environmental needs, for selected coastal species and regions, series, 5506–8

Freight (waterborne domestic and foreign), by port and State, 1989, annual rpt series, 3754–7

Great Lakes and connecting channels water levels, and forecasts, semimonthly rpt, 3752–2

Great Lakes water levels and forecasts, and Corps flood prevention activities, monthly rpt and supplements, 3752–1

Hydroelectric power plants capacity and other characteristics, for western US, FY90, annual rpt, 3254–1

Kuwait reconstruction after Persian Gulf War, Army Corps of Engineers contract awards by firm and purpose, 1st qtr 1991, article, 2042–1.203

Procurement, DOD prime contract awards by contractor, service branch, State, and city, FY90, annual rpt, 3544–22

Procurement, DOD prime contract awards in labor surplus areas, by service branch, State, and area, 1st half FY91, semiannual rpt, 3542–19

Recreation (outdoor) facilities of Fed Govt, fees and visits by managing agency, FY88-90, annual rpt, 5544–14

Southeastern Fed Power Program financial statements, FY90, annual rpt, 3234–1

Water resources dev projects of Corps, characteristics, and costs, 1950s-89, biennial State rpt series, 3756–1

Water resources dev projects of Corps, characteristics, and costs, 1950s-91, biennial State rpt series, 3756–2

Arnade, Carlos A.

"Export Demand for U.S. Corn, Soybeans, and Wheat", 1568–297

"Risk Aversion Through Nontraditional Export Promotion Programs in Central America", 1528–312

Arnold, Bruce

"Trade Restraints and the Competitive Status of the Textile, Apparel, and Nonrubber-Footwear Industries", 26306–6.162

Arrest

Airport security operations to prevent hijacking, screening results, enforcement actions, and hijacking attempts, 2nd half 1989, semiannual rpt, 7502–5

Arrest rates, by offense, sex, age, and race, 1965-89, annual rpt, 6224–7

Arrests and criminal case processing, by offense, offender characteristics, and location, data compilation, 1991 annual rpt, 6064–6.4; 6064–6.5

Arrests and rates, by offense, offender characteristics, population size, and jurisdiction, 1990, annual rpt, 6224–2.1; 6224–2.2

Children and youth social, economic, and demographic characteristics, 1950s-90, 4818–5

Coast Guard drug, immigration, and fisheries enforcement activities, 2nd half FY91, semiannual rpt, 7402–4

Cocaine abuse, user characteristics, and related crime and violence, 1988 conf, 4498–74

Counterfeiting and other Secret Service investigations and arrests by type, and dispositions, FY90 and trends from FY81, annual rpt, 8464–1

Drug (illegal) production, eradication, and seizures, by substance, with US aid, by country, 1987-91, annual rpt, 7004–17

Drug (illegal) spending, by user group and substance, 1988-90, 236–2.1

Drug abuse and trafficking reduction programs activities, funding, staff, and Bush Admin budget request, by Federal agency and program area, FY90-92, 238–2

Drug abuse indicators for selected metro areas, research results, data collection, and policy issues, 1991 semiannual conf, 4492–5

Drug and alcohol abuse in rural areas, related crime, and treatment, with comparisons to nonrural areas, by substance and State, 1988-90, GAO rpt, 26131–79

Drug control task forces enforcement activities by drug type and State, and organization, staff, and spending, 1988, 6068–244

Drug test results at arrest, by drug type, offense, and sex, for selected urban areas, quarterly rpt, 6062–3

Felony arrests, prosecutions, convictions, and sentencing, by offender characteristics and offense, 1988, 6066–25.33; 6066–25.39

Foreign countries human rights conditions in 170 countries, 1990, annual rpt, 21384–3

Jail population, by sociodemographic characteristics, criminal and drug use history, whether convicted, offense, and sentencing, 1989, annual rpt, 6064–26.3

Law enforcement officer assaults and deaths by circumstances, agency, victim and offender characteristics, and location, 1990, annual rpt, 6224–3

Marijuana crop eradication activities of DEA and local agencies by State, and drug potency and prices, 1982-90, annual rpt, 6284–4

Marshals Service activities, FY89, annual rpt, 6294–1

Postal Service inspection activities, 2nd half FY91, semiannual rpt, 9862–2

Pretrial processing, detention, and release, for Federal offenders, by defendant characteristics and district, 1988, hearing, 25528–114

Records (criminal) repository characteristics, holdings, use, and reporting requirements, by State, 1989, 6068–241

State and Metro Area Data Book, 1991 data compilation, 2328–54

Statistical Abstract of US, 1991 annual data compilation, 2324–1.5

Violent crime victimizations, circumstances, victim characteristics, arrest, recidivism, sentences, and prisoners, 1980s, 6068–148

Warrants issued for search and arrest, caseloads of Federal district courts, by circuit and district, 1990, annual rpt, 18204–8.27

Arrest

Wiretaps authorized, costs, arrests, trials, and convictions, by offense and jurisdiction, 1990, annual rpt, 18204–7

Women prisoners in State instns, by offense, drug use history, whether abused, and other characteristics, 1986, 6066–19.61

see also Pretrial detention and release

Arsenic

see Hazardous substances

see Metals and metal industries

see Trace metals

Arson

- Arrest rates, by offense, sex, age, and race, 1965-89, annual rpt, 6224–7
- Arrests, prosecutions, convictions, and sentencing, for felony offenders, by offender characteristics and offense, 1988, 6066–25.33; 6066–25.39
- Bombing incidents, casualties, and damage, by target, circumstances, and State, 1990, annual rpt, 6224–5
- Court criminal case processing in Federal district courts, and dispositions, by offense, district, and offender characteristics, 1986, annual rpt, 6064–29
- Court criminal case processing in Federal district courts, and dispositions, by offense, 1980-89, annual rpt, 6064–31
- Crime, criminal justice admin and enforcement, and public opinion, data compilation, 1991 annual rpt, 6064–6
- Crime Index by population size and region, and offenses by large city, Jan-June 1991, semiannual rpt, 6222–1
- Crimes, arrests, and rates, by offense, offender characteristics, population size, and jurisdiction, 1990, annual rpt, 6224–2.1; 6224–2.2
- Drug and alcohol abuse and mental illness direct and indirect costs, by type and patient age and sex, 1985 with 1980 and 1988 comparisons, 4048–35
- Forest fires and acres burned on Forest Service land, by cause, forest, and State, 1989, annual rpt, 1204–6
- Homicides, by circumstance, victim and offender relationship, and type of weapon, 1990, annual rpt, 6224–2.1
- Jail population, by criminal, correctional, drug use, and family history, and selected other characteristics, 1989, 6066–19.62
- Jail population, by sociodemographic characteristics, criminal and drug use history, whether convicted, offense, and sentencing, 1989, annual rpt, 6064–26.3
- Juvenile courts delinquency cases, by offense, referral source, disposition, age, sex, race, State, and county, 1988, annual rpt, 6064–12
- Prison and parole admissions and releases, sentence length, and time served, by offense and offender characteristics, 1985, annual rpt, 6064–33
- Sentences for Federal offenses, guidelines by offense and circumstances, series, 17668–1
- *Statistical Abstract of US*, 1991 annual data compilation, 2324–1.5
- Terrorism (intl) incidents, casualties, and attacks on US targets, by attack type and country, 1990, annual rpt, 7004–22
- Terrorism (intl) incidents, casualties, and attacks on US targets, by attack type and world area, 1990, annual rpt, 7004–13

Terrorism incidents in US, related activity, and casualties, by attack type, target group, and location, 1990, annual rpt, 6224–6

Wiretaps authorized, costs, arrests, trials, and convictions, by offense and jurisdiction, 1990, annual rpt, 18204–7

Women prisoners in State instns, by offense, drug use history, whether abused, and other characteristics, 1986, 6066–19.61

Art

- Copyrights Register activities, registrations by material type, and fees, FY90 and trends from 1790, annual rpt, 26404–2
- Exports and imports of US, by country and detailed commodity, monthly rpt, 2422–12
- Exports and imports of US, by Harmonized System 6-digit commodity and country, 1990, annual rpt, 2424–13
- Exports and imports of US, by selected country, country group, and commodity group, 1990, annual rpt, 2044–37
- Exports of US, detailed Schedule B commodities with countries of destination, 1990, annual rpt, 2424–10
- Franchise business opportunities by firm and kind of business, and sources of aid and info, 1990 annual listing, 2104–7
- Injuries from use of consumer products, by severity, victim age, and detailed product, 1990, annual rpt, 9164–6
- Library of Congress activities, acquisitions, services, and financial statements, FY90, annual rpt, 26404–1
- Natl Endowment for Arts activities and grants, FY90, annual rpt, 9564–3
- OECD trade, total and for 4 major countries, and US trade by country, by commodity, 1970-89, world area rpt series, 9116–1
- Service industries census, 1987: establishments, receipts by source, payroll, and employment, by SIC 2- to 4-digit kind of business, State, and MSA, 2393–4
- Service industries receipts, by SIC 2- to 4-digit kind of business, 1990, annual rpt, 2413–8
- *Statistical Abstract of US*, 1991 annual data compilation, 2324–1.7
- Tariff Schedule of US, classifications and rates of duty by detailed imported commodity, 1992 base edition, 9886–13

see also Antiques

Arteriosclerosis

see Circulatory diseases

Arthritis

see Musculoskeletal diseases

Artificial fibers

see Synthetic fibers and fabrics

Artificial foods

see Synthetic food products

Artificial satellites

see Communications satellites

see Meteorological satellites

see Satellites

Artificial sweeteners

see Syrups and sweeteners

Arts and the humanities

Degrees awarded in higher education, by level, field, race, and sex, 1988/89 with trends from 1978/79, biennial rpt, 4844–17

Index by Subjects and Names

- Education data compilation, 1991 annual rpt, 4824–2
- Education natl goals progress indicators, by State, 1991, annual rpt, 15914–1
- High school advanced placement for college credit, programs by selected characteristics and school control, 1984-86, 4838–46
- Higher education course completions, by detailed program, sex, race, and instn type, for 1972 high school class, as of 1984, 4888–4
- Japan-US Friendship Commission educational and cultural exchange activities, grants, and trust fund status, FY89-90, biennial report, 14694–1
- Student loan debt burden of 1986 college grads, by selected student characteristics and instn control, 1987, 4808–26
- Teachers in higher education instns, employment and other characteristics, by instn type and control, 1987/88 survey, 4846–4.4

see also Architecture

see also Art

see also Cultural activities

see also Dance

see also Federal aid to arts and humanities

see also Foreign languages

see also Language arts

see also Motion pictures

see also Museums

see also Music

see also Performing arts

see also Photography and photographic equipment

see also Social sciences

see also Theater

Aruba

- Agricultural trade of US, by detailed commodity and country, 1990, semiannual rpt, 1522–4
- Economic, social, political, and geographic summary data, by country, 1991, annual factbook, 9114–2
- Exports and imports of US, by transport mode, country, and SITC 1- to 3-digit commodity, 1990, annual rpt, 2424–12
- Investment (direct) incentives of Caribbean Basin Initiative, economic impacts, with finances and employment by country, 1984-90, 2048–141

Aruffo, John F.

"AIDS Knowledge in Low-Income and Minority Populations", 4042–3.210

Arvin, Donald V.

"Statistical Summary of Streamflow Data for Indiana", 5666–27.15

Asbestos

see Asbestos contamination

see Nonmetallic minerals and mines

Asbestos contamination

- Air pollution emissions factors, by detailed pollutant and source, data compilation, 1990 rpt, 9198–120
- Building asbestos removal aid from EPA, occupational asbestos exposure cancer cases and deaths, and Catholic schools abatement costs, 1985-90, hearing, 25328–32
- Cancer (colorectal) and polyps risk relation to occupational asbestos exposure, 1986-88 local area study, article, 4472–1.238

Index by Subjects and Names

Commercial buildings with asbestos, and remedial action, 1989, survey rpt, 3166–8.9

Deaths and rates, by detailed cause and demographic characteristics, 1988 and trends from 1900, US Vital Statistics annual rpt, 4144–2

Fed Govt asbestos trust fund financial condition, monthly rpt, 8102–9.13

Respiratory diseases related to occupational hazards, epidemiology, diagnosis, and treatment, for selected industries and work settings, 1988 conf, 4248–90

Torts for product liability, asbestos-related personal injury caseload in Federal district courts, 1990, annual rpt, 18204–8.13; 18204–8.18; 18204–11

Torts for product liability, asbestos-related personal injury caseload in Federal district courts, 1991, annual rpt, 18204–2.1

ASEAN

see Association of Southeast Asian Nations

Ash, Mark

"Corn Cleaning Practices of U.S. Commercial Elevators", 1561–4.202

Asheville, N.C.

Wages by occupation, and benefits for office and plant workers, 1991 survey, periodic MSA rpt, 6785–3.5

see also Under By SMSA or MSA in the "Index by Categories"

Ashland, Ky.

see also Under By SMSA or MSA in the "Index by Categories"

Asia

- Agricultural exports of high-value commodities, indexes and sales by commodity, world area, and country, 1960s-86, 1528–323
- Agricultural exports of US, for grains, oilseed products, hides, skins, and cotton, by country, weekly rpt, 1922–3
- Agricultural production, prices, and trade, by country, 1960s-90, annual world area rpt, 1524–4.2
- Agricultural trade of US, by commodity and country, bimonthly rpt, 1522–1
- Agricultural trade of US, by detailed commodity and country, 1989, annual rpt, 1524–8
- Agricultural trade of US, by detailed commodity and country, 1990, semiannual rpt, 1522–4
- AID economic aid to developing countries, obligations and disbursements by country, quarterly rpt, 9912–4
- AID housing and urban dev program financial statements, FY90, annual rpt, 9914–4
- AID loans repayment status and terms by program and country, and status of predecessor agency loans, quarterly rpt, 9912–3
- AIDS virus infection prevalence in developing countries, by sex, selected city, urban-rural location, and country, 1991, semiannual rpt, 2322–4
- Alien workers (unauthorized) and Fair Labor Standards Act employer compliance, hiring impacts, and aliens overstaying visas by country and State, 1986-90, annual rpt, 6264–6
- Aliens (illegal) overstaying visas, by class of admission, mode of arrival, age, country, and State, FY85-88, annual rpt, 6264–5

Child health and welfare indicators, and economic conditions, for developing countries, 1950s-80s, hearing, 25388–57

Coal trade flows and reserves, by country, 1980-89 and projected to 2010, annual rpt, 3164–77

Construction contract awards and billings, by country of contractor and world area of award, 1989, annual article, 2042–1.201

Corporations in US under foreign control, income tax returns, assets and income statement items by industry div, country, and world area, 1988, article, 8302–2.219

Deforestation, and OECD imports of tropical wood, by country, 1980s, annual rpt, 9114–4.10

Dollar exchange rate trade-weighted index of Fed Reserve Bank of Atlanta, by world area, quarterly rpt, 9371–15

Dollar exchange rate trade-weighted index of Fed Reserve Bank of Dallas, by world area, monthly rpt, 9379–13

Economic and military aid and loans from US and intl agencies, by program and country, FY46-90, annual rpt, 9914–5

Economic and social conditions of developing countries from 1960s, and Intl Dev Cooperation Agency and AID activities and funding, FY90-92, annual rpt, 9904–4

Energy use in developing countries, and economic and environmental impacts, by fuel type, world area, and country, 1980s-90, 26358–232

English language program of USIA, enrollment and staff, by country and world region, FY90, annual rpt, 9854–2

Exchange and training programs of Federal agencies, participants by world area, and funding, by program, FY89, annual rpt, 9854–8

Export and import balances of US, and dollar exchange rates, with 5 Asian countries, 1991 semiannual rpt, 8002–14

Exports and imports (waterborne) of US, by type of service, commodity, country, route, and US port, 1988, annual rpt, 7704–2

Exports and imports (waterborne) of US, by type of service, customs district, port, and world area, monthly rpt, 2422–7

Exports and imports of OECD, total and for 4 major countries, and US trade by country, by commodity, 1970-89, world area rpt, 9116–1.7

Exports and imports of US, by Harmonized System 6-digit commodity and country, 1990, annual rpt, 2424–13

Exports and imports of US, by selected country, country group, and commodity group, 1990, annual rpt, 2044–37

Exports and imports of US, by transport mode, country, and SITC 1- to 3-digit commodity, 1990, annual rpt, 2424–12

Exports, imports, and balances of US, by selected country, country group, and commodity group, preliminary data, monthly rpt, 2042–34

Exports, imports, and balances of US with major trading partners, by product category, 1986-90, annual chartbook, 9884–21

Family planning and population activities of AID, grants by project and recipient, and contraceptive shipments, by country, FY90, annual rpt series, 9914–13

Grain production and needs, and related economic outlook, by world area and selected country, forecast 1990/91-1991/92, 1528–313

Immigrant and nonimmigrant visas of US issued and refused, by class, issuing office, and nationality, FY89, annual rpt, 7184–1

Immigrants admitted to US, by country of birth, FY81-90, annual rpt, 6264–4

Immigrants admitted to US, by occupational group and country of birth, preliminary FY90, annual table, 6264–1

Immigrants in US, population characteristics and fertility, by birthplace and compared to native born, 1980s, Current Population rpt, 2546–2.162

Investment (foreign direct) of US, by industry group and world area, 1987-90, annual article, 2702–1.220

Labor costs and indexes, by selected country, 1990, semiannual rpt, 6822–3

Labor shortages, for Japan and 4 east Asia countries, 1991 rpt, 6366–4.17

Loans of US banks to foreigners at all US and foreign offices, by country group and country, quarterly rpt, 13002–1

Lumber (hardwood) exports of US to Europe and Asia, by species and country, 1981-89, 1208–373

Military aid of US, arms sales, and training, by country, FY50-90, annual rpt, 3904–3

Military aid of US, arms sales, and training programs costs and budget requests, by program, world region, and country, FY90-92, annual rpt, 7144–13

Military spending and imports of developing countries, measures to determine eligibility for US economic aid, by country, 1986-87, annual rpt, 9914–1

Multinatl firms US affiliates, finances, and operations, by industry, world area of parent firm, and State, 1988-89, annual rpt, 2704–4

Multinatl US firms and foreign affiliates finances and operations, by industry and world area of parent firm, 1989 benchmark survey, preliminary annual rpt, 2704–5

Multinatl US firms foreign affiliates, income statement items by country and world area, 1986, biennial article, 8302–2.212

Nuclear power plant capacity, generation, and operating status, by plant and foreign and US location, 1990 and projected to 2030, annual rpt, 3164–57

Nuclear power plant spent fuel and demand for uranium and enrichment services, for US and other country groups, projected 1991-2040, annual rpt, 3164–72

Oil and gas reserves and discoveries, by country and country group, quarterly rpt, 3162–43

Oils, oilseeds, and meal imports, by commodity, world area of destination, and major producer, 1960s-88, 1528–314

Peace Corps activities, funding by program, and volunteers, by country, FY92, annual rpt, 9654–1

R&D funding by Fed Govt, by field, performer type, agency, and State, FY89-91, annual rpt, 9627–20

Refugee arrivals in US by world area and country of origin, and quotas, monthly rpt, 7002–4

Asia

Refugee arrivals in US by world area of origin and State of settlement, and Federal aid, FY90-91 and proposed FY92 allocations, annual rpt, 7004–16

Refugee resettlement programs and funding, arrivals by country of origin, and indicators of adjustment, by State, FY90, annual rpt, 4694–5

Tax (income) returns of corporations with foreign tax credit, income, and tax items, by country and world region of credit, 1986, biennial article, 8302–2.207

Terrorism (intl) incidents, casualties, and attacks on US targets, by attack type and country, 1990, annual rpt, 7004–22

Terrorism (intl) incidents, casualties, and attacks on US targets, by attack type and world area, 1990, annual rpt, 7004–13

Tidal currents, daily time and velocity by station for North America and Asia coasts, forecast 1992, annual rpt, 2174–1.2

Tide height and time daily at coastal points, forecast 1992, annual rpt, 2174–2.5

Timber market demand for Alaska products, and imports transport costs from Alaska and Puget Sound, by Pacific basin country, 1970s-2010, 1208–367

Travel to and from US on US and foreign flag air carriers, by country, world area, and US port, monthly rpt, 7302–2

Travel to and from US on US and foreign flag air carriers, by world area, 1990, annual rpt, 2904–13

Travel to US, by characteristics of visit and traveler, country, port city, and State of destination, quarterly rpt, 2902–1

UN voting record and share of votes in agreement with US, by issue, country, and world area, 1990, annual rpt, 7004–18

US military and civilian personnel and dependents, by service branch, world area, and country, quarterly rpt, 3542–20

USIA library holdings, use, and staff, by country and city, FY90, annual rpt, 9854–4

Weather conditions and effect on agriculture, by US region, State, and city, and world area, weekly rpt, 2182–7

Weather events and anomalies, precipitation and temperature for US and foreign locations, weekly rpt, 2182–6

Weather forecasts for US and Northern Hemisphere, precipitation and temperature by location, semimonthly rpt, 2182–1

see also Afghanistan
see also Asian Development Bank
see also Bahrain
see also Bangladesh
see also Bhutan
see also Brunei
see also Burma
see also Cambodia
see also China, Peoples Republic
see also Hong Kong
see also India
see also Indonesia
see also Iran
see also Iraq
see also Israel
see also Japan
see also Jordan
see also Korea, North
see also Korea, South
see also Kuwait
see also Laos
see also Lebanon
see also Macao
see also Malaysia
see also Maldives
see also Middle East
see also Mongolia
see also Myanmar
see also Nepal
see also Oman
see also Pakistan
see also Philippines
see also Qatar
see also Saudi Arabia
see also Singapore
see also Southeast Asia
see also Sri Lanka
see also Syria
see also Taiwan
see also Thailand
see also Turkey
see also United Arab Emirates
see also Vietnam
see also Yemen
see also Yemen, North
see also Yemen, South
see also under By Foreign Country in the "Index by Categories"

Asian Americans

Agriculture census, 1987: farms, farmland, production, finances, and operator characteristics, by county, final State rpt series, 2331–1

AIDS cases by risk group, race, sex, age, State, and MSA, and deaths, monthly rpt, 4202–9

Alien workers (unauthorized) and Fair Labor Standards Act employer compliance, hiring impacts, and aliens overstaying visas by country and State, 1986-90, annual rpt, 6264–6

Arrests and prisoners, by offense, offender characteristics, and location, data compilation, 1991 annual rpt, 6064–6.4; 6064–6.6

Arrests, by offense, offender characteristics, and location, 1990, annual rpt, 6224–2.2

Births and rates, by characteristics of birth, infant, and parents, 1989 and trends from 1940, US Vital Statistics advance annual rpt, 4146–5.123

Business mgmt and financial aid from Minority Business Dev Centers, and characteristics of businesses, by region and State, FY90, annual rpt, 2104–6

Cancer (colorectal) risk related to intake of fat, fiber, and carbohydrates, for Sha Giao, PRC, and San Francisco Chinese, 1991 article, 4472–1.201

Cancer death rates of minorities, by body site, age, sex, and substate area, 1950s-80, atlas, 4478–78

Census of Population and Housing, 1990: population and housing characteristics, households, and land area, by county, subdiv, and place, State rpt series, 2551–1

Census of Population and Housing, 1990: voting age and total population by race, and housing units, by block, redistricting counts required under PL 94-171, State CD-ROM series, 2551–6

Census of Population and Housing, 1990: voting age and total population by race,

Index by Subjects and Names

and housing units, by county and city, redistricting counts required under PL 94-171, State summary rpt series, 2551–5

Census of Population, 1990: metro area population by race, Hispanic origin, and MSA, press release, 2328–75

Census of Population, 1990: population by detailed Native American, Asian, and Pacific Islander group, race, region, and State, with data for 1980, press release, 2328–72

Census of Population, 1990: population by race and detailed Hipanic origin, region, and State, with data for 1980, press release, 2328–73

Census of Population, 1990: population by race, Hispanic origin, region, census div, and State, with data for 1980, fact sheet, 2326–20.2

Census of Population, 1990: post-enumeration survey results compared to census counts, by race, sex, city, county, and State, press release, 2328–69

Child accident deaths and death rates, by cause, age, sex, race, and State, 1980-85, 4108–54

Deaths and rates, by detailed cause and demographic characteristics, 1988 and trends from 1900, US Vital Statistics annual rpt, 4144–2

Drug abuse prevalence among minorities, related health effects and crime, treatment, and research status and needs, mid 1970s-90, 4498–72

Education data compilation, 1991 annual rpt, 4824–2

Educational performance and conditions, characteristics, attitudes, activities, and plans, 1988 8th grade class, natl longitudinal survey, series, 4826–9

Educational performance of elementary and secondary students, and factors affecting proficiency, by selected characteristics, 1990 natl assessments, subject rpt series, 4896–8

Educational service delivery and discipline, and discrimination indicators by State, 1988, biennial rpt, 4804–33

Fed Equal Opportunity Recruitment Program activity, and employment by sex, race, pay grade, and occupational group, FY90, annual rpt, 9844–33

Fed Govt employment of minorities and women, and compliance with EEOC standards, by occupation and agency, FY88-92, GAO rpt, 26119–342

FmHA loans, by type, borrower characteristics, and State, quarterly rpt, 1182–8

FmHA loans, by type, borrower race, and State, quarterly rpt, 1182–5

Food aid program of USDA for women, infants, and children, participants by race, State, and Indian agency, Apr 1990, annual rpt, 1364–16

Health condition improvement and disease prevention goals and recommended activities for 2000, with trends 1970s-80s, 4048–10

Health condition indicators and health occupations school enrollment, 1950s-89, annual data compilation, 4144–11

Health condition of minorities, services use, costs, and indicators of services need, 1950s-88, 4118–55

Index by Subjects and Names

Assault

Health condition, services use, payment sources, and health care labor force, for minorities and women by poverty status, 1940s-89, chartbook, 4118–56

Heart disease screening program for persons of Southeast Asians origin, effectiveness, 1989 local area study, article, 4042–3.222

Higher education degrees awarded, by level, field, race, and sex, 1988/89 with trends from 1978/79, biennial rpt, 4844–17

Higher education enrollment of minorities, degrees, factors affecting participation, and earnings, by race, 1960s-88, 4808–29

Immigrants in US, population characteristics and fertility, by birthplace and compared to native born, 1980s, Current Population rpt, 2546–2.162

Nuclear engineering enrollment and degrees granted by instn and State, and grad placement, by student characteristics, 1990, annual rpt, 3004–5

Prisoners, characteristics, and movements, by State, 1989, annual rpt, 6064–26

Radiation protection and health physics enrollment and degrees granted by instn and State, and grad placement, by student characteristics, 1990, annual rpt, 3004–7

Science and engineering grad enrollment, by field, source of funds, and characteristics of student and instn, 1975-89, annual rpt, 9627–7

Science and engineering PhDs, by field, instn, employment prospects, sex, race, and other characteristics, 1960s-90, annual rpt, 9627–30

Science and engineering PhDs employment and other characteristics, by field and State, 1989, biennial rpt, 9627–18

State and local govt employment of minorities and women, by occupation, function, pay level, and State, 1990, annual rpt, 9244–6

State and Metro Area Data Book, 1991 data compilation, 2328–54

Statistical Abstract of US, 1991 annual data compilation, 2324–1

see also Pacific Islands Americans

see also under By Race and Ethnic Group in the "Index by Categories"

Asian Development Bank

Financial statements, financial ratios, and loan commitments by country, 1984-89, hearing, 21248–149

Loan activity by purpose and country, and funds by source, FY89, annual rpt, 15344–1.8

Loans and grants for economic and military aid from US and intl agencies, by program and country, FY46-90, annual rpt, 9914–5

Asikoglu, Yaman

"Critical Evaluation of Exchange Rate Policy in Turkey", 9385–8.112

Asphalt and tar

Consumption of energy, by detailed fuel type, end-use sector, and State, 1960-89, State Energy Data System annual rpt, 3164–39

County Business Patterns, 1988: employment, establishments, and payroll, by SIC 2- to 4-digit industry and county, annual State rpt series, 2326–6

County Business Patterns, 1989: employment, establishments, and payroll, by SIC 2- to 4-digit industry and county, annual State rpt series, 2326–8

Employment, earnings, and hours, by SIC 1- to 4-digit industry, monthly and annual averages, selected years 1909-90, annual rpt, 6744–4

Exports and imports of US, by Harmonized System 6-digit commodity and country, 1990, annual rpt, 2424–13

Exports of US, detailed Schedule B commodities with countries of destination, 1990, annual rpt, 2424–10

Hwy construction material use by type, and spending, by State, various periods 1944-90, annual rpt, 7554–29

Manufacturing census, 1987: finances and operations, by type of organization and SIC 2- to 4-digit industry, subject rpt, 2497–5

Occupational injury and illness rates, by SIC 2- to 4-digit industry, 1988-89, annual rpt, 6844–7

Occupational injury and illness rates, by SIC 2- to 4-digit industry, 1989, annual rpt, 6844–1

Pollution (air) emissions factors, by detailed pollutant and source, data compilation, 1990 rpt, 9198–120

Price indexes (producer), by stage of processing and detailed commodity, monthly rpt, 6762–6

Price indexes (producer), by stage of processing and detailed commodity, monthly 1990, annual rpt, 6764–2

Price indexes (producer) for building materials, by type, bimonthly rpt, 2042–1.5

Prices and spending for fuel, by type, end-use sector, and State, 1989, annual rpt, 3164–64

Supply, demand, and movement of crude oil, gas liquids, and refined products, by PAD district and State, 1990, annual rpt, 3164–2

Supply, demand, and prices of crude oil and refined products, and refinery capacity and stocks, by State, 1960-91, annual rpt, 3164–95

Supply, demand, trade, stocks, and refining of oil and gas liquids, by detailed product, State, and PAD district, monthly rpt with articles, 3162–6

Aspirin

see Drugs

Assassination

Terrorism (intl) incidents, casualties, and attacks on US targets, by attack type and country, 1990, annual rpt, 7004–22

Terrorism (intl) incidents, casualties, and attacks on US targets, by attack type and world area, 1990, annual rpt, 7004–13

Terrorism incidents in US, related activity, and casualties, by attack type, target, group, and location, 1990, annual rpt, 6224–6

Assault

Arrest rates, by offense, sex, age, and race, 1965-89, annual rpt, 6224–7

Arrests, prosecutions, convictions, and sentencing, for felony offenders, by offender characteristics and offense, 1988, 6066–25.33; 6066–25.39

Child accident deaths and injuries by cause, and victimization, rates by race, sex, and age, 1979-88, chartbook, 4108–56

Court civil and criminal caseloads for Federal district, appeals, and bankruptcy courts, by type of suit and offense, circuit, and district, 1990, annual rpt, 18204–11

Court civil and criminal caseloads for Federal district, appeals, and special courts, 1990, annual rpt, 18204–8

Court civil and criminal caseloads for Federal district courts, 1991, annual rpt, 18204–2.1

Court criminal case processing in Federal district courts, and dispositions, by offense, district, and offender characteristics, 1986, annual rpt, 6064–29

Court criminal case processing in Federal district courts, and dispositions, by offense, 1980-89, annual rpt, 6064–31

Court criminal cases in Federal district courts, by offense, disposition, and district, 1980-90, last issue of annual rpt, 18204–1

Crime, criminal justice admin and enforcement, and public opinion, data compilation, 1991 annual rpt, 6064–6

Crime Index by population size and region, and offenses by large city, Jan-June 1991, semiannual rpt, 6222–1

Crimes, arrests by offender characteristics, and rates, by offense, and law enforcement employees, by population size and jurisdiction, 1990, annual rpt, 6224–2

Deaths and rates, by detailed cause and demographic characteristics, 1988 and trends from 1900, US Vital Statistics annual rpt, 4144–2

Drug abuse history of jail population, by offense, conviction status, criminal and family history, and selected other characteristics, 1989, 6066–19.63

Drug abuse relation to violent and criminal behavior, with data on street gang activity and selected population groups, 1989 conf, 4498–70

Drug test results at arrest, by drug type, offense, and sex, for selected urban areas, quarterly rpt, 6062–3

Jail population, by criminal, correctional, drug use, and family history, and selected other characteristics, 1989, 6066–19.62

Jail population, by sociodemographic characteristics, criminal and drug use history, whether convicted, offense, and sentencing, 1989, annual rpt, 6064–26.3

Juvenile courts delinquency cases, by offense, referral source, disposition, age, sex, race, State, and county, 1988, annual rpt, 6064–12

Minority group health condition, services use, costs, and indicators of services need, 1950s-88, 4118–55

Occupational deaths, by cause and industry div, 1989, annual rpt, 6844–1

Older persons abuse, State agency reporting and investigation procedures, 1989 survey, article, 4042–3.213

Pretrial processing, detention, and release, for Federal offenders, by defendant characteristics and district, 1988, hearing, 25528–114

Prison and parole admissions and releases, sentence length, and time served, by offense and offender characteristics, 1985, annual rpt, 6064–33

Probation and split sentences by State courts for felony offenses, sentence lengths, case processing time, and felon characteristics, by offense, 1986, 6068–242

Assault

Railroad accidents, casualties, and damage, by cause, railroad, and State, 1990, annual rpt, 7604–1

Sentences for Federal crimes, guidelines use and results by offense and district, and Sentencing Commission activities, 1990, annual rpt, 17664–1

Sentences for Federal offenses, guidelines by offense and circumstances, series, 17668–1

State and Metro Area Data Book, 1991 data compilation, 2328–54

Teenagers crime victimization, by victim and offender characteristics, circumstances, and offense, 1985-88 surveys, 6066–3.43

Terrorism (intl) incidents, casualties, and attacks on US targets, by attack type and country, 1990, annual rpt, 7004–22

Terrorism (intl) incidents, casualties, and attacks on US targets, by attack type and world area, 1990, annual rpt, 7004–13

Victimization rates, by victim and offender characteristics, circumstances, and offense, survey rpt series, 6066–3

Victimizations by region and victim characteristics, and rpts to police, by offense, 1973-90, annual rpt, 6066–25.35; 6066–25.41

Victimizations by violent crime, circumstances, victim characteristics, arrest, recidivism, sentences, and prisoners, 1980s, 6068–148

Victimizations of households, by offense, household characteristics, and location, 1975-90, annual rpt, 6066–25.40

Women prisoners in State instns, by offense, drug use history, whether abused, and other characteristics, 1986, 6066–19.61

Women's rape and other violent crime victimization, by relation to offender, circumstances, and victim characteristics, 1973-87, 6068–243

see also Assaults on police

see also Domestic violence

Assaults on police

Assaults and deaths of law enforcement officers, by circumstances, agency, victim and offender characteristics, and location, 1990, annual rpt, 6224–3

Assaults and deaths of law enforcement officers, by circumstances, and offender characteristics, data compilation, 1991 annual rpt, 6064–6.3

Statistical Abstract of US, 1991 annual data compilation, 2324–1.5

Assets and liabilities

see Business assets and liabilities, general

see Business assets and liabilities, specific industry

see Business inventories

see Foreign debts

see Government assets and liabilities

see International reserves

see Personal debt

see Wealth

Association for Commuter Transportation

"National Commuter Transportation Survey, People and Programs", 7888–81

Association of Southeast Asian Nations

Exports and imports of US by country, and trade shifts by commodity, 1990, semiannual rpt, 9882–9

UN voting record and share of votes in agreement with US, by issue, country, and world area, 1990, annual rpt, 7004–18

Associations

Construction and building materials trade and professional assns, and labor unions, 1991 listing, article, 2042–1.202

County Business Patterns, 1988: employment, establishments, and payroll, by SIC 2- to 4-digit industry and county, annual State rpt series, 2326–6

County Business Patterns, 1989: employment, establishments, and payroll, by SIC 2- to 4-digit industry and county, annual State rpt series, 2326–8

Education and library assns staff and membership, by assn, 1991 GAO rpt, 26121–414

Employment, earnings, and hours, by SIC 1- to 4-digit industry, monthly and annual averages, selected years 1909-90, annual rpt, 6744–4

Lumber and wood products export market dev, assn listing, FAS quarterly circular, supplement, 1925–36

Service industries census, 1987: establishments, receipts by source, payroll, and employment, by SIC 2- to 4-digit kind of business, State, and MSA, 2393–4

Tax (income) returns of corporations, income and tax items by asset size and detailed industry, 1987, annual rpt, 8304–4

Tax (income) returns of corporations, income and tax items by asset size and detailed industry, 1988, annual rpt, 8304–21

see also Consumer cooperatives

see also Cooperatives

see also Credit unions

see also Labor unions

see also Membership organizations

see also Nonprofit organizations and foundations

see also Political action committees

see also Rural cooperatives

see also Tax exempt organizations

see also under By Industry in the "Index by Categories"

Asthma

see Respiratory diseases

Astronautics

see Astronauts

see Communications satellites

see Meteorological satellites

see Satellites

see Space program accidents and safety

see Space programs

see Space sciences

Astronauts

Foreign and US space program activities, missions, launchings, payloads, and flight duration, 1957-90, annual rpt, 21704–4

NASA project launch schedules and technical descriptions, press release series, 9506–2

Spacecraft launches and other activities of NASA and USSR, with flight data, 1957-90, annual rpt, 9504–6.1

Astronomy

Data sources and availability for space sciences and related topics, 1991 annual listing, 9504–10

Data sources for space sciences and related topics, use by format and user type, FY90, annual rpt, 9504–11

Index by Subjects and Names

Degrees (PhD) in science and engineering, by field, instn, employment prospects, sex, race, and other characteristics, 1960s-90, annual rpt, 9627–30

Degrees awarded in science and engineering, by field, level, and sex, 1966-89, 9627–33

Employment and other characteristics of science and engineering PhDs, by field and State, 1989, biennial rpt, 9627–18

Fed Govt aid to higher education and nonprofit instns for R&D and related activities, by field, instn, agency, and State, FY89, annual rpt, 9627–17

Higher education grad programs enrollment in science and engineering, by field, source of funds, and characteristics of student and instn, 1975-89, annual rpt, 9627–7

NASA project launch schedules and technical descriptions, press release series, 9506–2

NASA R&D funding to higher education instns, by field, instn, and State, FY90, annual listing, 9504–7

Planetary space probe findings, and NASA activities and finances, 1957-90, annual rpt, 9504–6.1

R&D funding by Fed Govt, by field, performer type, agency, and State, FY89-91, annual rpt, 9627–20

R&D funding by higher education instns and federally funded centers, by field, instn, and State, FY89, annual rpt, 9627–13

Star position tables, planet coordinates, time conversion factors, and listing of observatories worldwide, 1992, annual rpt, 3804–7

Sunspots frequency, monthly 1971-80, decennial rpt, 2156–4.1

AT&T

see American Telephone and Telegraph Co.

Athens, Ga.

see also under By SMSA or MSA in the "Index by Categories"

Athletics

see Physical education and training

see Sporting goods

see Sports and athletics

Atkins, John T.

"Simulation of Rainfall-Runoff Response in Mined and Unmined Watersheds in Coal Areas of West Virginia", 5666–27.1

Atlanta, Ga.

Cancer cases, by race, income, education, and area population density, for 3 metro areas, 1978-82, article, 4472–1.210

CPI by component for US city average, and by region, population size, and for 27 metro areas, monthly rpt, 6762–2

Drug abuse indicators for selected metro areas, research results, data collection, and policy issues, 1991 semiannual conf, 4492–5

Drug test results at arrest, by drug type, offense, and sex, for selected urban areas, quarterly rpt, 6062–3

Financial instns location relation to ZIP code area income and minority population, by instn type for 5 cities, 1977-89, article, 9377–1.208

Fruit and vegetable shipments, and arrivals in US and Canada cities, by mode of transport and State and country of origin, 1990, annual rpt, 1311–4.1

Index by Subjects and Names

Housing mortgage secondary market underwriting guidelines, and indicators of discrimination, for Atlanta metro area, 1989, GAO rpt, 26113–500

Housing starts and completions authorized by building permits in 40 MSAs, quarterly rpt, 2382–9

Wages by occupation, and benefits for office and plant workers, 1991 survey, periodic MSA rpt, 6785–12.3

see also under By City and By SMSA or MSA in the "Index by Categories"

Atlantic City, N.J.

see also under By SMSA or MSA in the "Index by Categories"

Atlantic Ocean

Air traffic and passengers, for intl routes over north Atlantic, by aviation type and route, alternative forecasts 1991-2010 and trends from 1980, annual rpt, 7504–44

Coastal areas environmental conditions, fish, wildlife, use, and mgmt, 1990 rpt, 5506–9.42

Coastal currents, temperatures, and salinity, for Atlantic Ocean from Florida straits to northern Brazil, series, 2146–7

Environmental summary data, and intl claims and disputes, 1991 annual factbook, 9114–2

Estuary environmental and fishery conditions, research results and methodology, 1991 rpt, 2176–7.25

Estuary environmental conditions, and fish and shellfish catch by species and region, 1980s, 2178–27

Exports and imports (waterborne) of US, by type of service, commodity, country, route, and US port, 1988, annual rpt, 7704–2

Fish (groundfish) juvenile population distribution by species, for New England area, 1968-86, 2168–122

Fish (striped bass) stocks status on Atlantic coast, and sport and commercial catch by State, 1979-88, annual rpt, 5504–29

Fish and shellfish catch and stocks in northwest Atlantic, by species and location, 1887-1991 and forecast to 1993, semiannual conf, 2162–9

Fish and shellfish catch, life cycles, and environmental needs, for selected coastal species and regions, series, 5506–8

Fish and shellfish distribution in Atlantic Ocean, bottom trawl survey results by species and location, periodic rpt series, 2164–18

Fish catch, trade, use, and fishery operations, with selected foreign data, by species, 1980s-90, annual rpt, 2164–1

Fish larvae abundance, distribution, and growth, for selected Western Hemisphere sites, 1989 conf, 2168–126

Fishing (ocean sport) activities, and catch by species, by angler characteristics and State, 1987-89, annual coastal area rpt, 2166–17.1

Fishing (ocean sport and commercial) catch and quotas for US and Canada, by species for North Atlantic Ocean, 1990, annual rpt, 2164–14

Hurricanes and tropical storms in north Atlantic Ocean, characteristics, 1990, annual article, 2152–8.202

Marine Fisheries Review, US and foreign fisheries resources, dev, mgmt, and research, quarterly journal, 2162–1

Marine mammals strandings on land, physical characteristics and tests performed, for New England, 1970s, 14738–8

Mariners Weather Log, quarterly journal, 2152–8

Mineral industries census, 1987: finances and operations, by establishment characteristics, SIC 2- to 4-digit industry, and State, subject rpt, 2517–1

Oil and gas dev impacts on Atlantic OCS, and environmental conditions, series, discontinued, 5736–6

Oil and gas OCS reserves, and leasing and dev activity, 1990 periodic regional rpt, 5736–3.1

Oil and gas OCS reserves of Fed Govt, leasing and exploration activity, production, revenue, and costs, by ocean area, FY90, annual rpt, 5734–4

Oil and gas proposed exploration off North Carolina, environmental and socioeconomic impacts, 1970s-90 and projected to 2020, 5738–22

Oil, gas, and minerals production, revenue, and leasing activity, for Federal OCS lands by ocean region and State, 1950s-90, annual rpt, 5734–3

Pollutant concentrations in coastal and estuarine sediments, by contaminant and selected site, 1984-89, 2176–3.13

Recreation (outdoor) coastal facilities of Fed Govt and States, visitor and site characteristics, 1987-90 survey, regional rpt, 2176–9.1; 2176–9.2; 2176–9.4; 2176–9.7

Research activities of Atlantic Oceanographic and Meteorological Lab, and bibl, FY90, annual rpt, 2144–19

Sewage sludge discharges and water properties at Atlantic Ocean deepwater dumpsite, 1990, annual rpt, 2164–20

Sharks and other fish tagged and recovered, by species, 1990, annual rpt, 2164–21

Temperature of sea surface by ocean and for US coastal areas, and Bering Sea ice conditions, monthly rpt, 2182–5

Tidal currents, daily time and velocity by station for North America coasts, forecast 1992, annual rpt, 2174–1.1

Tide height and time daily at coastal points, forecast 1992, annual rpt, 2174–2.3; 2174–2.4

Walrus population, habitat mgmt, and intl conservation needs, by world region, 1990 conf, 14738–9

Wetlands in coastal areas, acreage by wetland type, estuarine basin, and county, 1989, 2178–31

see also Caribbean area

see also New York Bight

Atlantic Oceanographic and Meteorological Laboratory

see National Oceanic and Atmospheric Administration

Atmospheric sciences

Acid rain research activities of Natl Acid Precipitation Assessment Program, 1990 annual rpt, 14354–1

Atlantic Oceanographic and Meteorological Lab research activities and bibl, FY90, annual rpt, 2144–19

Carbon dioxide in atmosphere, DOE R&D programs and funding at natl labs, universities, and other instns, FY91, annual summary rpt, 3004–18.1; 3004–18.7

Carbon dioxide in atmosphere, measurement, methodology, and research results, series, 3006–11

Degrees (PhD) in science and engineering, by field, instn, employment prospects, sex, race, and other characteristics, 1960s-90, annual rpt, 9627–30

Degrees awarded in science and engineering, by field, level, and sex, 1966-89, 9627–33

Employment and other characteristics of science and engineering PhDs, by field and State, 1989, biennial rpt, 9627–18

Fed Govt aid to higher education and nonprofit instns for R&D and related activities, by field, instn, agency, and State, FY89, annual rpt, 9627–17

Global climate change environmental, infrastructure, and health impacts, with model results and background data, 1850s-2100, 9188–113

Global climate change research, Federal budget by agency, and alternative estimates of contributing gases levels and impacts, late 1980s-90, GAO rpt, 26113–495

Global climate change trends and contributing gases levels, Federal and intl data collection activities, mgmt, and inventory, 1990 rpt, 3028–4

Great Lakes Environmental Research Lab activities, FY90 annual rpt, 2144–26

Higher education grad programs enrollment in science and engineering, by field, source of funds, and characteristics of student and instn, 1975-89, annual rpt, 9627–7

NASA R&D funding to higher education instns, by field, instn, and State, FY90, annual listing, 9504–7

Pacific Marine Environmental Lab research activities and bibl, FY90, annual rpt, 2144–21

R&D funding by Fed Govt, by field, performer type, agency, and State, FY89-91, annual rpt, 9627–20

R&D funding by higher education instns and federally funded centers, by field, instn, and State, FY89, annual rpt, 9627–13

see also Meteorology

ATMs

see Automated tellers

Atomic bombs

see Nuclear explosives and explosions

see Nuclear weapons

Atomic energy

see Nuclear power

Atomic Energy Commission

Radioactivity levels at former AEC and Manhattan Project research and storage sites and nearby areas, test results series, 3006–9

Atomic explosives

see Nuclear explosives and explosions

Atomic weapons

see Nuclear weapons

Attitudes

see Opinion and attitude surveys

Attleboro, Mass.

Wages by occupation, for office and plant workers, 1991 survey, periodic MSA rpt, 6785–12.6

see also under By SMSA or MSA in the "Index by Categories"

Attorneys-at-law

Attorneys-at-law
see Lawyers and legal services

Auburn, Maine
see also under By SMSA or MSA in the "Index by Categories"

Audiology
see Ear diseases and infections
see Hearing and hearing disorders
see Speech pathology and audiology

Audiovisual education
see Educational broadcasting
see Educational technology

Auditing
see Accounting and auditing

Auerbach, Alan J.
"Generational Accounting: A New Approach for Understanding the Effects of Fiscal Policy on Saving", 9377–9.116
"Generational Accounts: A Meaningful Alternative to Deficit Accounting", 9377–9.111

Augusta, Ga.
Wages by occupation, for office and plant workers, 1991 survey, periodic MSA rpt, 6785–12.4
see also under By SMSA or MSA in the "Index by Categories"

Aurora, Colo.
see also under By City in the "Index by Categories"

Aurora, Ill.
see also under By SMSA or MSA in the "Index by Categories"

Ausman, La Verne
"Credit Outlook at FmHA", 1004–16.1

Austin, Tex.
see also under By City and By SMSA or MSA in the "Index by Categories"

Australia
Agricultural exports of high-value commodities, indexes and sales by commodity, world area, and country, 1960s-86, 1528–323
Agricultural exports of US, impacts of foreign agricultural and trade policy, with data by commodity and country, 1989, annual rpt, 1924–8
Agricultural input and output indexes, and freight rates, for Australia, 1950s-80s, 1528–311
Agricultural production, prices, and trade, by country, 1980s and forecast 1991, annual world region rpt, 1524–4.5
Agricultural production, trade, and policies in foreign countries, summary data by country, 1989-90, annual factbook, 1924–12
Agricultural trade of US, by detailed commodity and country, 1989, annual rpt, 1524–8
Agricultural trade of US, by detailed commodity and country, 1990, semiannual rpt, 1522–4
Background Notes, summary social, political, and economic data, 1991 rpt, 7006–2.38
Economic and military aid and loans from US and intl agencies, by program and country, FY46-90, annual rpt, 9914–5
Economic conditions in Communist and OECD countries, 1989, annual rpt, 7144–11
Economic conditions in USSR, Eastern Europe, OECD, and selected other countries, 1960s-90, annual rpt, 9114–4

Economic conditions, income, production, prices, employment, and trade, 1991 periodic country rpt, 2046–4.18
Economic conditions, policy, and trade practices, by country, 1988-90, annual rpt, 21384–5
Economic, social, political, and geographic summary data, by country, 1991, annual factbook, 9114–2
Energy prices, by fuel type and end use, for 10 countries, 1980-89 annual rpt, 3164–50.6
Exports and imports (waterborne) of US, by type of service, commodity, country, route, and US port, 1988, annual rpt, 7704–2
Exports and imports (waterborne) of US, by type of service, customs district, port, and world area, monthly rpt, 2422–7
Exports and imports of OECD members, by country, 1989, annual rpt, 7144–10
Exports and imports of US, by Harmonized System 6-digit commodity and country, 1990, annual rpt, 2424–13
Exports and imports of US, by selected country, country group, and commodity group, 1990, annual rpt, 2044–37
Exports and imports of US, by transport mode, country, and SITC 1- to 3-digit commodity, 1990, annual rpt, 2424–12
Exports of US, detailed Schedule B commodities with countries of destination, 1990, annual rpt, 2424–10
GNP and GNP growth for OECD members, by country, 1980-90, annual rpt, 7144–8
Human rights conditions in 170 countries, and US economic and military aid, 1990, annual rpt, 21384–3
Imports of goods, services, and investment from US, trade barriers, impacts, and US actions, by country, 1990, annual rpt, 444–2
Lamb meat from Australia and New Zealand, US industry intl competitiveness, investigation with background financial and operating data and foreign comparisons, 1990 rpt, 9886–4.166
Multinatl firms US affiliates, finances, and operations, by industry, world area of parent firm, and State, 1988-89, annual rpt, 2704–4
Multinatl US firms and foreign affiliates finances and operations, by industry and world area of parent firm, 1989 benchmark survey, preliminary annual rpt, 2704–5
Multinatl US firms foreign affiliates, income statement items by country and world area, 1986, biennial article, 8302–2.212
Oil exports to US by OPEC and non-OPEC countries, monthly rpt, 3162–24.3
Oil production, trade, use, and stocks, by selected country and country group, monthly rpt, 3162–42
Oil supply, demand, and stock forecasts, by world area, quarterly rpt, 3162–34
Older persons health condition and care research, data availability and collection methodology, for US and selected countries, 1988 conf, 4147–5.6
R&D funding by Fed Govt, by field, performer type, agency, and State, FY89-91, annual rpt, 9627–20
Space programs activities, missions, launchings, payloads, and flight duration, for foreign and US programs, 1957-90, annual rpt, 21704–4

Spacecraft and satellite launches since 1957, quarterly listing, 9502–2
Steel imports of US under voluntary restraint agreement, by product, customs district, and country, with US industry operating data, quarterly rpt, 9882–13
Tax revenue, by level of govt and type of tax, for OECD countries, mid 1960s-89, annual rpt, 10044–1.2
Timber in Pacific basin, sandalwood resources, habitat, harvest, exports, and uses, 1990 conf, 1208–366
UN voting record and share of votes in agreement with US, by issue, country, and world area, 1990, annual rpt, 7004–18
Weather conditions and effect on agriculture, by US region, State, and city, and world area, weekly rpt, 2182–7
see also under By Foreign Country in the "Index by Categories"

Austria
Agricultural exports of high-value commodities, indexes and sales by commodity, world area, and country, 1960s-86, 1528–323
Agricultural production, prices, and trade, by country, 1970s-90, and forecast 1991, annual world region rpt, 1524–4.4
Agricultural production, trade, and policies in foreign countries, summary data by country, 1989-90, annual factbook, 1924–12
Agricultural trade of US, by detailed commodity and country, 1989, annual rpt, 1524–8
Agricultural trade of US, by detailed commodity and country, 1990, semiannual rpt, 1522–4
AID loans repayment status and terms by program and country, and status of predecessor agency loans, quarterly rpt, 9912–3
Bearings (ball) from 14 countries, injury to US industry from foreign subsidized and less than fair value imports, investigation with background financial and operating data, 1991 rpt, 9886–19.74
Economic and military aid and loans from US and intl agencies, by program and country, FY46-90, annual rpt, 9914–5
Economic conditions, income, production, prices, employment, and trade, 1991 periodic country rpt, 2046–4.44
Economic conditions, investment and export opportunities, and trade practices, 1991 country market research rpt, 2046–6.7
Economic conditions, policy, and trade practices, by country, 1988-90, annual rpt, 21384–5
Economic, social, political, and geographic summary data, by country, 1991, annual factbook, 9114–2
Exports and imports of OECD members, by country, 1989, annual rpt, 7144–10
Exports and imports of US, by Harmonized System 6-digit commodity and country, 1990, annual rpt, 2424–13
Exports and imports of US, by selected country, country group, and commodity group, 1990, annual rpt, 2044–37
Exports and imports of US, by transport mode, country, and SITC 1- to 3-digit commodity, 1990, annual rpt, 2424–12
Exports of US, detailed Schedule B commodities with countries of destination, 1990, annual rpt, 2424–10

Index by Subjects and Names

Automobiles

GNP and GNP growth for OECD members, by country, 1980-90, annual rpt, 7144–8

Human rights conditions in 170 countries, and US economic and military aid, 1990, annual rpt, 21384–3

Labor conditions, union coverage, and work accidents, 1990 annual country rpt, 6366–4.10

Multinatl US firms and foreign affiliates finances and operations, by industry and world area of parent firm, 1989 benchmark survey, preliminary annual rpt, 2704–5

Multinatl US firms foreign affiliates, income statement items by country and world area, 1986, biennial article, 8302–2.212

Oil production, trade, use, and stocks, by selected country and country group, monthly rpt, 3162–42

Paper (coated groundwood) from 9 countries at less than fair value, injury to US industry, investigation with background financial and operating data, 1991 rpt, 9886–14.306

Steel imports of US under voluntary restraint agreement, by product, customs district, and country, with US industry operating data, quarterly rpt, 9882–13

Tax revenue, by level of govt and type of tax, for OECD countries, mid 1960s-89, annual rpt, 10044–1.2

UN voting record and share of votes in agreement with US, by issue, country, and world area, 1990, annual rpt, 7004–18

see also under By Foreign Country in the "Index by Categories"

Authors

see Writers and writing

Automated data processing

see Computer industry and products

see Computer use

see Information storage and retrieval systems

Automated tellers

Transactions on regional and natl shared ATM networks, and debit cards in circulation, 1978-90, article, 9387–1.203

Automation

Air traffic control and airway facilities improvement activities under Aviation System Capital Investment Plan, 1981-90 and projected to 2005, annual rpt, 7504–12

Alien labor certification processing by States, Labor Dept grants for automation, 1991, press release, 6406–2.32

Manufacturing high technology use, by type and selected industry, 1988 survey, fact sheet, 2326–17.23

NSF R&D grant awards, by div and program, FY89, periodic rpt, 9626–7.3

Postal Service productivity, indexes of output and labor, capital, and other inputs, alternative model descriptions and results, 1960s-89, 9688–6

Securities trading activity and automation, with data by country, exchange, security type, and individual contract, 1980s-90, article, 9371–1.209

see also Automated tellers

see also Computer industry and products

see also Computer networks

see also Computer use

see also Electronic funds transfer

see also Industrial robots

see also Information storage and retrieval systems

Automobile exhaust

see Motor vehicle exhaust

Automobile industry

see Motor vehicle industry

Automobile insurance

Consumer Expenditure Survey, household income by source, and itemized spending, by selected characteristics and region, 1988-89, annual rpt, 6764–5

Cost differentials for auto insurance among cities, premiums and cost factors for selected cities, mid 1980s, working paper, 9383–20.9

Costs of operating autos and motorcycles by component, and Fed Govt mileage reimbursement rates, 1989, annual rpt, 9454–13

CPI by component for US city average, and by region, population size, and for 27 metro areas, monthly rpt, 6762–2

Automobile parking

see Parking facilities

Automobile rental

see Motor vehicle rental

Automobile repair and maintenance

Collective bargaining agreements expiring during year, and workers covered, by firm, union, industry group, and State, 1991, annual rpt, 6784–9

Consumer Expenditure Survey, household income by source, and itemized spending, by selected characteristics and region, 1988-89, annual rpt, 6764–5

Costs of operating autos and motorcycles by component, and Fed Govt mileage reimbursement rates, 1989, annual rpt, 9454–13

County Business Patterns, 1988: employment, establishments, and payroll, by SIC 2- to 4-digit industry and county, annual State rpt series, 2326–6

County Business Patterns, 1989: employment, establishments, and payroll, by SIC 2- to 4-digit industry and county, annual State rpt series, 2326–8

CPI by component for US city average, and by region, population size, and for 27 metro areas, monthly rpt, 6762–2

CPI components relative importance, by selected MSA, region, population size, and for US city average, 1990, annual rpt, 6884–1

Employment, earnings, and hours, by SIC 1- to 4-digit industry, monthly and annual averages, selected years 1909-90, annual rpt, 6744–4

Enterprise Statistics, 1987: auxiliaries of multi-establishment firms, finances and operations by function, industry, and State, 2329–6

Enterprise Statistics, 1987: finances and operations for companies, by size, level of diversification, form of organization, and industry group, 2329–8

Equipment for auto repair PPI, monthly 1990, annual rpt, 6764–2

Franchise business opportunities by firm and kind of business, and sources of aid and info, 1990 annual listing, 2104–7

Input-output structure of US economy, detailed interindustry transactions for 84 industries, and components of final demand, 1986, annual article, 2702–1.206

Input-output structure of US economy, detailed interindustry transactions for 85 industries, 1982 benchmark data, 2702–1.213

Labor productivity, indexes of output, hours, and employment by SIC 2- to 4-digit industry, 1967-89, annual rpt, 6824–1.4

Occupational injury and illness rates, by SIC 2- to 4-digit industry, 1988-89, annual rpt, 6844–7

Occupational injury and illness rates, by SIC 2- to 4-digit industry, 1989, annual rpt, 6844–1

Pollution (water) industrial releases in wastewater, levels, treatment, costs, and regulation, with background financial and operating data, 1989 industry rpt, 9206–4.13

Postal Service operating costs, itemized by class of mail, FY90, annual rpt, 9864–4

Puerto Rico economic censuses, 1987: wholesale and retail trade and service industry finances and operations, by SIC 2- to 4-digit industry and municipio, 2591–1

Puerto Rico economic censuses, 1987: wholesale, retail, and service industries finances and operations, by establishment characteristics and SIC 2- and 3-digit industry, subject rpts, 2591–2

Service industries census, 1987: depreciable assets, capital and operating expenses, and receipts, by SIC 2- to 4-digit kind of business, 2393–2

Service industries census, 1987: establishments, receipts by source, payroll, and employment, by SIC 2- to 4-digit kind of business, State, and MSA, 2393–4

Service industries receipts, by SIC 2- to 4-digit kind of business, 1990, annual rpt, 2413–8

Tax (income) returns of corporations, income and tax items by asset size and detailed industry, 1987, annual rpt, 8304–4

Tax (income) returns of corporations, income and tax items by asset size and detailed industry, 1988, annual rpt, 8304–21

Tax (income) returns of partnerships, income statement and balance sheet items, by industry group, 1989, annual article, 8302–2.216; 8304–18

Tax (income) returns of sole proprietorships, income statement items, by industry group, 1989, annual article, 8302–2.214

Automobile safety devices

see Motor vehicle safety devices

Automobile theft

see Motor vehicle theft

Automobiles

AFDC beneficiaries demographic and financial characteristics, by State, FY89, annual rpt, 4694–1

Agriculture census, 1987: farms, farmland, production, finances, and operator characteristics, by island and island group, 1990, final outlying area rpt, 2331–1.55; 2331–1.56

Arson incidents by whether structure occupied, property value, and arrest rate, by property type, 1990, annual rpt, 6224–2.1

Automobiles

Bombing incidents, casualties, and damage, by target, circumstances, and State, 1990, annual rpt, 6224–5

Business statistics, detailed data for major industries and economic indicators, *Survey of Current Business*, monthly rpt, 2702–1.23

Commuting accessibility impact on auto ownership, employment location, and housing values, for Philadelphia metro area census tracts, 1980, working paper, 9387–8.231

Consumer Expenditure Survey, household income by source, and itemized spending, by selected characteristics and region, 1988-89, annual rpt, 6764–5

Consumer Expenditure Survey, spending by category, and income, by selected household characteristics and location, 1990, annual press release, 6726–1.42

Costs of operating autos by component, and Fed Govt mileage reimbursement rates, 1989, annual rpt, 9454–13.1

CPI by component for US city average, and by region, population size, and for 27 metro areas, monthly rpt, 6762–2

CPI components relative importance, by selected MSA, region, population size, and for US city average, 1990, annual rpt, 6884–1

Electric-powered autos, R&D activity and DOE funding shares, FY90, annual rpt, 3304–2

Energy conservation measures impacts on consumption, by component and end-use sector, 1970s-88 and projected under alternative oil prices to 1995, 3308–93

Energy economy and miles traveled per car, monthly rpt, annual data, 3162–24.1

Energy economy performance of autos and light trucks by make, standards, and enforcement, 1978-91 model years, annual rpt, 7764–9

Energy economy, sales, and market shares, by size and model for domestic and foreign makes, 1991 model year, semiannual rpt, 3302–4

Energy economy test results for US and foreign makes, 1992 model year, annual rpt, 3304–11

Energy use and vehicle registrations, by vehicle type, 1960-90, annual rpt, 3164–74.1

Energy use by mode of transport, fuel supply, and demographic and economic factors of vehicle use, 1970s-89, annual rpt, 3304–5

Farm income, expenses, receipts by commodity, assets, liabilities, and ratios, 1990 and trends from 1945, annual rpt, 1544–16

Farm prices received for major products and paid for farm inputs and living items, by commodity and State, monthly rpt, 1629–1

Farm production itemized costs, by farm sales size and region, 1990, annual rpt, 1614–3

Households assets, by type of holding and selected characteristics, 1988, Current Population Rpt, 2546–20.16

Households with autos and trucks available, by location, 1989, biennial rpt, 2485–12

Households with autos and trucks available, MSA surveys, series, 2485–6

Hwy Statistics, detailed data by State, 1990, annual rpt, 7554–1

Hwy Statistics, summary data by State, 1989-90, annual rpt, 7554–24

Hwy traffic volume on rural roads and city streets, monthly rpt, 7552–8

Loans for autos, monthly rpt, 23842–1.5

Loans for autos outstanding, *Survey of Current Business*, monthly rpt, 2702–1.9

Loans for students and other financial services, banks profitability indicators, 1985-89, 4808–36

Loans of banks and finance companies, rates, terms, and related data, monthly rpt series, 9365–2

Manufacturing census, 1987: finances and operations, by SIC 2- to 4-digit industry, State, and MSA, with trends from 1849, 2497–1

Natl income and product accounts and components, *Survey of Current Business*, monthly rpt, 2702–1.24

Natl transportation system planning, use, condition, accidents, and needs, by mode of transport, 1940s-90 and projected to 2020, 7308–202

Price indexes (producer), by stage of processing and detailed commodity, monthly rpt, 6762–6

Price indexes (producer), by stage of processing and detailed commodity, monthly 1990, annual rpt, 6764–2

Prices received and paid by farmers, by commodity and State, 1990, annual rpt, 1629–5

Puerto Rico economic censuses, 1987: wholesale and retail trade and service industry finances and operations, by SIC 2- to 4-digit industry and municipio, 2591–1

Quality changes in autos since last model year, factory and retail value, 1991 model year, annual press release, 6764–3

Recalls of motor vehicles and equipment with safety-related defects, by make, monthly listing, 7762–12

Recalls of motor vehicles and equipment with safety-related defects, by make, quarterly listing, 7762–2

Retail trade census, 1987: finances and employment, for establishments with and without payroll, by SIC 2- to 4-digit kind of business, State, and MSA, 2401–1

Retail trade sales and inventories, by kind of business, region, and selected State, MSA, and city, monthly rpt, 2413–3

Retail trade sales, by kind of business, advance monthly rpt, 2413–2

Retail trade sales, inventories, purchases, gross margin, and accounts receivable, by SIC 2- to 4-digit kind of business and form of ownership, 1989, annual rpt, 2413–5

Sales and prices for domestic and import autos and trucks, and auto production and inventories, 1991 model year, annual article, 2702–1.228

Sales of domestic and imported cars, monthly rpt, quarterly data, 23842–1.1

Soviet Union, Eastern Europe, OECD, and selected other countries consumer and producer goods and services production and sales, 1960s-90, annual rpt, 9114–4.7

Soviet Union GNP by detailed income and outlay component, 1985, 2326–18.59

Index by Subjects and Names

State and Metro Area Data Book, 1991 data compilation, 2328–54

Statistical Abstract of US, 1991 annual data compilation, 2324–1.21

Tax (excise) collections of IRS, by source, quarterly rpt, 8302–1; 8302–2.1

Travel patterns, personal and household characteristics, and auto and public transport use, 1990 survey, series, 7556–6

Weight of autos, by component material, 1975-90, article, 5602–4.202

Weight of autos, impacts on fatal traffic accident rates, with data for young drivers, 1976-78 and 1986-88, GAO rpt, 26131–89

Wholesale trade sales and inventories, by SIC 2- to 3-digit kind of business, monthly rpt, 2413–7

see also Automobile insurance

see also Automobile repair and maintenance

see also Drivers licenses

see also Gasoline

see also Gasoline service stations

see also Motor vehicle exhaust

see also Motor vehicle exports and imports

see also Motor vehicle fleets

see also Motor vehicle industry

see also Motor vehicle parts and supplies

see also Motor vehicle registrations

see also Motor vehicle rental

see also Motor vehicle safety devices

see also Motor vehicle theft

see also Traffic accident fatalities

see also Traffic accidents and safety

see also under By Commodity in the "Index by Categories"

Autopsies

Aviation medicine research and test results, technical rpt series, 7506–10

Death investigation systems of US and Canada, jurisdictions, medical officers qualifications, types of deaths covered, and related statutes, 1990 listing, 4208–34

Diving (underwater sport and occupational) deaths, by circumstances, diver characteristics, and location, 1970-89, annual rpt, 2144–5

Drug abuse emergency room admissions and deaths, by drug type and source, sex, race, age, and major metro area, 1990, annual rpt, 4494–8

Drug abuse indicators for selected metro areas, research results, data collection, and policy issues, 1991 semiannual conf, 4492–5

Infant death rate from sudden infant death syndrome and share autopsied, by race and region, 1980 and 1987, article, 4202–7.208

Performance of autopsies, by cause of death, age, race, and sex, 1988, US Vital Statistics annual rpt, 4144–2.1

Tuberculosis cases diagnosed at time of death, by State and city, 1989, annual rpt, 4204–10

Avalanches

Incidents and mgmt of disasters and natl security threats, with data by major event and State, 1991 annual rpt, 9434–6

Ave, Eunice

"Early Estimates. National Postsecondary Statistics, Collegiate and Noncollegiate: Fall 1990", 4844–16

Index by Subjects and Names

Aviation medicine

Avery, Robert B.

"Deregulation and the Location of Financial Institution Offices", 9377–1.208

"Loan Commitments and Bank Risk Exposure", 9377–9.105

"Risk-Based Capital and Deposit Insurance Reform", 9377–9.109

Aviation

see Aeronautical navigation
see Aerospace industry
see Air traffic control
see Air travel
see Aircraft
see Airlines
see Airports and airways
see Astronauts
see Aviation accidents and safety
see Aviation fuels
see Aviation medicine
see Aviation sciences
see Civil aviation
see General aviation
see Military aviation
see Space program accidents and safety
see Space programs
see Space sciences
see Spacecraft

Aviation accidents and safety

- Accidents and circumstances, for US operations of domestic and foreign airlines and general aviation, periodic rpt, 9612–1
- Accidents by type of aviation, near collisions, air traffic control and pilot errors, and runway incursions, monthly rpt, 7502–15
- Accidents, casualties, and damage for air carriers, by detailed circumstances, 1987, annual rpt, 9614–2
- Accidents, deaths, and circumstances, by carrier and carrier type, preliminary 1990, annual press release, 9614–9
- Accidents, deaths, and rates, by type of air service, 1980-89, annual rpt, 7504–1.9
- Air taxi and commuter airlines operating certificates, FAA revocations for safety violations, 1987-91, GAO rpt, 26113–547
- Airport improvement program of FAA, activities, funding, and airport operations, by location, projected 1990-99, biennial rpt, 7504–42
- Child accident deaths and death rates, by cause, age, sex, race, and State, 1980-85, 4108–54
- Child fare proposal impacts on family airline travel and industry revenue, with costs and accidents compared to auto travel, 1990 hearing, 21648–61
- Deaths and rates, by detailed cause and demographic characteristics, 1988 and trends from 1900, US Vital Statistics annual rpt, 4144–2
- DOT activities by subagency, budget, and summary accident data, FY88, annual rpt, 7304–1
- General aviation accidents, by circumstances, characteristics of persons and aircraft involved, and type of flying, 1988, annual rpt, 9614–3
- Hazardous material transport accidents, casualties, and damage, by mode of transport, with DOT control activities, 1989, annual rpt, 7304–4

Injury and illness rates by SIC 2- to 4-digit industry, and deaths by cause and industry div, 1989, annual rpt, 6844–1

- Injury and illness rates, by SIC 2- to 4-digit industry, 1988-89, annual rpt, 6844–7
- Medical research and test results for aviation, technical rpt series, 7506–10
- Safety programs, and accidents, casualties, and damage, by mode of transport, 1989, annual rpt, 7304–19
- *Statistical Abstract of US,* 1991 annual data compilation, 2324–1.22
- Victims compensation for aircraft accidents, legal costs, and time to disposition, under intl agreements and US liability system, aggregate 1970-84, GAO rpt, 26113–501
- Weather services activities and funding, by Federal agency, planned FY91-92, annual rpt, 2144–2

see also Air piracy

see also Air traffic control

see also Space program accidents and safety

Aviation fuels

- Business statistics, detailed data for major industries and economic indicators, *Survey of Current Business,* monthly rpt, 2702–1.18
- Conservation measures impacts on energy consumption, by component and end-use sector, 1970s-88 and projected under alternative oil prices to 1995, 3308–93
- Consumption and fuel efficiency under alternative aircraft technological improvements and load factors, by model, projected 1995-2010, 3028–6
- Consumption of aviation fuels, forecast FY91-2002 and trends from FY81, annual rpt, 7504–6
- Consumption of energy, by detailed fuel type, end-use sector, and State, 1960-89, State Energy Data System annual rpt, 3164–39
- Consumption of energy by mode of transport, fuel supply, and demographic and economic factors of vehicle use, 1970s-89, annual rpt, 3304–5
- Consumption of fuel, total and per hour, by grade and aircraft type, 1990, annual rpt, 7504–29.3
- Costs of fuel, role in airline fare-setting, 1990 rpt, 7308–199.7
- Costs of operating privately owned small planes by component, and Fed Govt mileage reimbursement rates, 1989, annual rpt, 9454–13.2
- Exports and imports of US, by Harmonized System 6-digit commodity and country, 1990, annual rpt, 2424–13
- Exports of US, detailed Schedule B commodities with countries of destination, 1990, annual rpt, 2424–10
- Fed Govt energy use and efficiency, by agency and fuel type, FY90, annual rpt, 3304–22
- Foreign and US oil production, trade, and stocks, by product and country, 1986-89, annual rpt, 3164–50.2
- General aviation activity, 1990, triennial survey rpt, 7508–3
- Iraq invasion of Kuwait, impacts on oil prices and industry profits, as of 4th qtr 1990, 3166–6.46
- Manufacturing annual survey, 1989: finances and operations, by SIC 2- to 4-digit industry, series, 2506–15

Minerals Yearbook, 1988, Vol 3: foreign country reviews of production, trade, and policy, by commodity, annual rpt series, 5604–17

- Price indexes (producer), by stage of processing and detailed commodity, monthly rpt, 6762–6
- Price indexes (producer), by stage of processing and detailed commodity, monthly 1990, annual rpt, 6764–2
- Prices and spending for fuel, by type, end-use sector, and State, 1989, annual rpt, 3164–64
- Prices and volume of oil products sold and purchased by refiners, processors, and distributors, by product, end-use sector, PAD district, and State, monthly rpt with articles, 3162–11
- Prices of jet fuel for domestic and intl operations, quarterly rpt, 7502–16
- Supply and demand of oil and refined products, refinery capacity and use, and prices, weekly rpt, 3162–32
- Supply, demand, and movement of crude oil, gas liquids, and refined products, by PAD district and State, 1990, annual rpt, 3164–2
- Supply, demand, and prices, by fuel type and end-use sector, alternative projections 1989-2010, annual rpt, 3164–75
- Supply, demand, and prices, by fuel type and end-use sector, with foreign comparisons, 1990 and trends from 1949, annual rpt, 3164–74.1; 3164–74.2
- Supply, demand, and prices, by fuel type, end-use sector, and country, detailed data, monthly rpt with articles, 3162–24
- Supply, demand, and prices of crude oil and refined products, and refinery capacity and stocks, by State, 1960-91, annual rpt, 3164–95
- Supply, demand, and prices of energy, forecasts by resource type, quarterly rpt, 3162–34
- Supply, demand, and prices of oil and gas, alternative projections 1989-2010, annual rpt, 3164–89
- Supply, demand, trade, stocks, and refining of oil and gas liquids, by detailed product, State, and PAD district, monthly rpt with articles, 3162–6
- Tax (excise) collections of IRS, by source, quarterly rpt, 8302–1
- Tax provisions of States for motor fuel, auto registration fees, and disposition of receipts, by State, as of Jan 1991, biennial rpt, 7554–37
- Wholesale trade census, 1987: oil bulk stations, sales and storage capacity by product, inventories, expenses, employment, and modes of transport, 2407–4.2

Aviation industry

see Aerospace industry

see Aircraft

see Airlines

see Aviation accidents and safety

Aviation medicine

- Military health care personnel, and accessions by training source, by occupation, specialty, and service branch, FY89, annual rpt, 3544–24
- Research and test results for aviation medicine, technical rpt series, 7506–10

Aviation sciences

Aviation sciences

Environmental and natural resource data sources, and aerial survey R&D rpts, quarterly listing, 9502–7

Fed Govt aeronautics and space activities and budgets, by agency, and foreign programs, 1957-FY90, annual rpt, 9504–9

NASA R&D funding to higher education instns, by field, instn, and State, FY90, annual listing, 9504–7

R&D funding by Fed Govt, by field, performer type, agency, and State, FY89-91, annual rpt, 9627–20

R&D funding by higher education instns and federally funded centers, by field, instn, and State, FY89, annual rpt, 9627–13

see also Space sciences

Avila, Lixion

"Eastern North Pacific Hurricanes—1990", 2152–8.202

Awards, medals, and prizes

Mint (US) activities, finances, coin and medals production and holdings, and gold and silver transactions, by facility, FY90, annual rpt, 8204–1

see also Employee bonuses and work incentives

see also Military awards, decorations, and medals

Babula, Ronald A.

"Agricultural Interest Rates and Inflationary Expectations: A Regional Analysis", 1502–3.201

Bachu, Amara

"Fertility of American Women: June 1990", 2546–1.455

"Profile of the Foreign-Born Population in the U.S.", 2546–2.162

Backus, David K.

"International Evidence on the Historical Properties of Business Cycles", 9383–20.15

Badlands National Park

Birds in Badlands Natl Park juniper forest and mixed grass rangeland habitats, population and species diversity by season, 1991 rpt, 1208–364

Bags

see Packaging and containers

Bahamas

Agricultural exports of high-value commodities, indexes and sales by commodity, world area, and country, 1960s-86, 1528–323

Agricultural exports of US, impacts of foreign agricultural and trade policy, with data by commodity and country, 1989, annual rpt, 1924–8

Agricultural trade of US, by detailed commodity and country, 1989, annual rpt, 1524–8

Agricultural trade of US, by detailed commodity and country, 1990, semiannual rpt, 1522–4

Economic and military aid and loans from US and intl agencies, by program and country, FY46-90, annual rpt, 9914–5

Economic conditions, policy, and trade practices, by country, 1988-90, annual rpt, 21384–5

Economic, social, political, and geographic summary data, by country, 1991, annual factbook, 9114–2

Exports and imports of US, by commodity and country, 1970-89, world area rpt, 9116–1.5

Exports and imports of US, by Harmonized System 6-digit commodity and country, 1990, annual rpt, 2424–13

Exports and imports of US, by selected country, country group, and commodity group, 1990, annual rpt, 2044–37

Exports and imports of US, by transport mode, country, and SITC 1- to 3-digit commodity, 1990, annual rpt, 2424–12

Exports of US, detailed Schedule B commodities with countries of destination, 1990, annual rpt, 2424–10

Human rights conditions in 170 countries, and US economic and military aid, 1990, annual rpt, 21384–3

Investment (direct) incentives of Caribbean Basin Initiative, economic impacts, with finances and employment by country, 1984-90, 2048–141

Military aid of US, arms sales, and training programs costs and budget requests, by program, world region, and country, FY90-92, annual rpt, 7144–13

Multinatl US firms and foreign affiliates finances and operations, by industry and world area of parent firm, 1989 benchmark survey, preliminary annual rpt, 2704–5

Multinatl US firms foreign affiliates, income statement items by country and world area, 1986, biennial article, 8302–2.212

Oil exports to US by OPEC and non-OPEC countries, monthly rpt, 3162–24.3

Ships in world merchant fleet, tonnage, and new ship construction and deliveries, by vessel type and country, as of Jan 1990, annual rpt, 7704–3

UN voting record and share of votes in agreement with US, by issue, country, and world area, 1990, annual rpt, 7004–18

see also under By Foreign Country in the "Index by Categories"

Bahrain

Agricultural exports of high-value commodities, indexes and sales by commodity, world area, and country, 1960s-86, 1528–323

Agricultural trade of US, by detailed commodity and country, 1989, annual rpt, 1524–8

Agricultural trade of US, by detailed commodity and country, 1990, semiannual rpt, 1522–4

AID economic aid to developing countries, obligations and disbursements by country, quarterly rpt, 9912–4

Economic and military aid and loans from US and intl agencies, by program and country, FY46-90, annual rpt, 9914–5

Economic conditions, income, production, prices, employment, and trade, 1991 periodic country rpt, 2046–4.77

Economic conditions, policy, and trade practices, by country, 1988-90, annual rpt, 21384–5

Economic, social, political, and geographic summary data, by country, 1991, annual factbook, 9114–2

Exports and imports of US, by commodity and country, 1970-89, world area rpt, 9116–1.1

Exports and imports of US, by selected country, country group, and commodity group, 1990, annual rpt, 2044–37

Exports and imports of US, by transport mode, country, and SITC 1- to 3-digit commodity, 1990, annual rpt, 2424–12

Exports of US, detailed Schedule B commodities with countries of destination, 1990, annual rpt, 2424–10

Human rights conditions in 170 countries, and US economic and military aid, 1990, annual rpt, 21384–3

Oil production, trade, use, and stocks, by selected country and country group, monthly rpt, 3162–42

UN voting record and share of votes in agreement with US, by issue, country, and world area, 1990, annual rpt, 7004–18

Bail

see Pretrial detention and release

Bailey, James F.

"Estimation of Flood-Frequency Characteristics and the Effects of Urbanization for Streams in the Philadelphia, Pa. Area", 5666–27.9

Bailey, Laura

"Development Impact of U.S. Program Food Assistance: Evidence from the AID Evaluation Literature", 9918–20

Baillie, Richard T.

"Risk Premium in Forward Foreign Exchange Markets and G-3 Central Bank Intervention: Evidence of Daily Effects, 1985-90", 9377–9.118

Baily, Mary Ann

"Economic Consequences for Medicaid of Human Immunodeficiency Virus Infection", 4652–1.215

Baj, John

"Feasibility Study of the Use of Unemployment Insurance Wage-Record Data as an Evaluation Tool for JTPA", 15496–1.13

Baker, C. Scott

"Population Characteristics of Humpback Whales in Southeastern Alaska: Summer and Late Season, 1986", 14738–10

Baker, Cathy

"Employer-Sponsored Prescription Drug Benefits", 6722–1.215

Baker, Samuel L.

"Medicaid Prospective Payment: Case-Mix Increase", 4652–1.206

Baker, Susan P.

"Childhood Injury: State-by-State Mortality Facts", 4108–54

Bakersfield, Calif.

see also under By City and By SMSA or MSA in the "Index by Categories"

Baking and bakery products

Confectionery shipments, trade, use, and ingredients used, by product, 1990, annual Current Industrial Rpt, 2506–4.5

Consumer Expenditure Survey, food spending by item, household composition, income, age, race, and region, 1980-88, biennial rpt, 1544–30

Consumer Expenditure Survey, household income by source, and itemized spending, by selected characteristics and region, 1988-89, annual rpt, 6764–5

Index by Subjects and Names

Balance of payments

Consumption of food, dietary composition, and nutrient intake, 1987/88 natl survey, preliminary rpt series, 1356–1

Consumption, supply, trade, prices, spending, and indexes, by food commodity, 1989, annual rpt, 1544–4

County Business Patterns, 1988: employment, establishments, and payroll, by SIC 2- to 4-digit industry and county, annual State rpt series, 2326–6

County Business Patterns, 1989: employment, establishments, and payroll, by SIC 2- to 4-digit industry and county, annual State rpt series, 2326–8

CPI by component for US city average, and by region, population size, and for 27 metro areas, monthly rpt, 6762–2

Employment, earnings, and hours, by SIC 1- to 4-digit industry, monthly and annual averages, selected years 1909-90, annual rpt, 6744–4

Enterprise Statistics, 1987: finances and operations for companies, by size, level of diversification, form of organization, and industry group, 2329–8

Exports and imports (agricultural) of US, by detailed commodity and country, 1989, annual rpt, 1524–8

Exports and imports (agricultural) of US, by detailed commodity and country, 1990, semiannual rpt, 1522–4

Exports and imports of US, by country and detailed commodity, monthly rpt, 2422–12

Exports and imports of US, by Harmonized System 6-digit commodity and country, 1990, annual rpt, 2424–13

Exports and imports of US, by transport mode, country, and SITC 1- to 3-digit commodity, 1990, annual rpt, 2424–12

Exports of US, detailed Schedule B commodities with countries of destination, 1990, annual rpt, 2424–10

Labor productivity, indexes of output, hours, and employment by SIC 2- to 4-digit industry, 1967-89, annual rpt, 6824–1.3

Manufacturing annual survey, 1989: finances and operations, by SIC 2- to 4-digit industry, series, 2506–15

Manufacturing census, 1987: finances and operations, by SIC 2- to 4-digit industry, State, and MSA, with trends from 1849, 2497–1

Manufacturing census, 1987: finances and operations, by type of organization and SIC 2- to 4-digit industry, subject rpt, 2497–5

Manufacturing finances and operations, by SIC 2- to 4-digit industry, forecast 1991, annual rpt, 2044–28

Occupational injury and illness rates, by SIC 2- to 4-digit industry, 1988-89, annual rpt, 6844–7

Occupational injury and illness rates, by SIC 2- to 4-digit industry, 1989, annual rpt, 6844–1

Pollution (air) emissions factors, by detailed pollutant and source, data compilation, 1990 rpt, 9198–120

Price indexes (producer), by stage of processing and detailed commodity, monthly rpt, 6762–6

Price indexes (producer), by stage of processing and detailed commodity, monthly 1990, annual rpt, 6764–2

Prices (farm-retail) for food, marketing cost components, and industry finances and productivity, 1920s-90, annual rpt, 1544–9

Puerto Rico economic censuses, 1987: wholesale and retail trade and service industry finances and operations, by SIC 2- to 4-digit industry and municipio, 2591–1

Retail trade census, 1987: finances and employment, for establishments with and without payroll, by SIC 2- to 4-digit kind of business, State, and MSA, 2401–1

Retail trade sales and inventories, by kind of business, region, and selected State, MSA, and city, monthly rpt, 2413–3

Retail trade sales, inventories, purchases, gross margin, and accounts receivable, by SIC 2- to 4-digit kind of business and form of ownership, 1989, annual rpt, 2413–5

Tax (income) returns of corporations, income and tax items by asset size and detailed industry, 1987, annual rpt, 8304–4

Tax (income) returns of corporations, income and tax items by asset size and detailed industry, 1988, annual rpt, 8304–21

Wheat flour bakery cost, quarterly situation rpt with articles, 1561–12

Balance of payments

Agricultural Outlook, production, prices, marketing, and trade, by commodity, forecast and current situation, monthly rpt with articles, 1502–4

Agricultural trade, outlook and current situation, quarterly rpt, 1542–4

Argentina black-market dollar exchange rate relationship with official rate and other economic indicators, model description and results, 1991 technical paper, 9366–7.261

Budget deficits impact on trade deficit, model description and results, 1960s-89, working paper, 9371–10.60

Budget deficits impact on trade deficit, model description and results, 1970s-89, article, 9371–1.207

Capital movements between US and foreign countries, *Treasury Bulletin*, quarterly rpt, 8002–4.11

China economic indicators and reform issues, with background data, 1950s-90, compilation of papers, 23848–155

Communist and OECD countries economic conditions, 1989, annual rpt, 7144–11

Data series on trade, methodology, use, and sources, 1991 article, 9389–1.206

Developing countries economic and social conditions from 1960s, and Intl Dev Cooperation Agency and AID activities and funding, FY90-92, annual rpt, 9904–4

Developing countries economic, population, and agricultural data, US and other aid sources, and AID activity, country rpt series, 9916–12

Eastern Europe foreign debt components, trade, balances, and other economic indicators, by country, 1985-89, hearing, 21248–148

EC economic integration economic impacts, with background data by country, 1988-90, article, 9379–1.201

Economic indicators and components, current data and annual trends, monthly rpt, 23842–1.7

Energy producers finances and operations, by energy type for US firms domestic and foreign operations, 1989, annual rpt, 3164–44

Exports and imports of US by country, and trade shifts by commodity, 1990, semiannual rpt, 9882–9

Exports and imports of US, by selected country, country group, and commodity group, annual rpt, suspended, 2044–38

Exports and imports of US, by selected country, country group, and commodity group, 1990, annual rpt, 2044–37

Exports, imports, and balances of US by commodity group, world area, and country, and related employment, annual rpt, discontinued, 2044–26

Exports, imports, and balances of US, by selected country, country group, and commodity group, preliminary data, monthly rpt, 2042–34

Exports, imports, and balances of US with major trading partners, by product category, 1986-90, annual chartbook, 9884–21

Exports, imports, and trade flows, by country and commodity, with background economic indicators, data compilation, monthly CD-ROM, 2002–6

Fed Govt financial operations, detailed data, *Treasury Bulletin*, quarterly rpt, 8002–4

Fed Reserve Board and Reserve banks finances, staff, and review of monetary policy and economic devs, 1990, annual rpt, 9364–1

Financial instns (intl) funds by source and disbursements by purpose, by country, with US policy review, FY89, annual rpt, 15344–1

Flows of trade and investment, and economic indicators, for selected countries and country groups, selected years 1946-90, annual rpt, 204–1.9

Foreign and US economic conditions, and trade devs and balances, with data by selected country and country group, monthly rpt, 9882–14

Foreign and US economic conditions, for major industrial countries, biweekly rpt, 9112–1

Foreign and US economic conditions, trade balances, and exchange rates, for selected OECD and Asian countries, 1991 semiannual rpt, 8002–14

Foreign countries economic conditions and implications for US, periodic country rpt series, 2046–4

Foreign direct investment in US manufacturing, impacts on trade balances, with data by industry, 1980s-93, technical paper, 9385–8.91

GDP and GNP as measures of production, factor income components, and receipts from and payments to foreigners, 1980s-91, article, 2702–1.215

Intl transactions accounts statistical discrepancy assessment, with data for services component, and alternative regression results, 1970s-90, technical paper, 9366–7.258

Intl transactions of US, and economic and monetary trends for US and 7 major industrialized countries, quarterly rpt, 9391–7

Balance of payments

Intl transactions summary, monthly rpt, 9362–1.3

Intl transactions summary, 1980s-90, annual article, 9362–1.202

Intl transactions, *Survey of Current Business*, monthly rpt, quarterly tables, 2702–1.26

Investment (foreign direct) impact on manufacturing trade balance, with background data, late 1960s-90 and auto forecasts to 1993, article, 9385–1.210

Investment (foreign direct) in US, by industry group of US affiliate and country of parent firm, 1980-86, 2708–41

Investment (intl) position of US, by component, industry, world region, and country, 1989-90, annual article, 2702–1.212

Investment (intl) position of US under alternative valuation methods, 1982-89, article, 2702–1.211

Japan and US bilateral trade balances, indicators of surplus and deficit persistence for detailed commodity groups, 1962-88, technical paper, 9366–7.264

Japan balance of payments by component, and foreign securities purchases by country, 1980s-90, article, 9393–8.204

Japan balance of trade with US and other countries, mid 1960s-88, article, 9391–1.209

Japan economic conditions, financial and intl policies, and trade devs, 1950s-80s and projected to 2050, compilation of papers, 23848–220

Lumber and wood products exports, imports, and export promotion of US by country, and trade balance, by commodity, FAS quarterly circular, 1925–36

Multinatl firms US affiliates, finances, and operations, by industry, world area of parent firm, and State, 1988-89, annual rpt, 2704–4

Multinatl firms US affiliates, investment trends and impact on US economy, 1991 annual rpt, 2004–9

Natl income and product accounts and components, *Survey of Current Business*, monthly rpt, 2702–1.24; 2702–1.25

OECD intl trade position for US and 4 countries, and factors affecting US competition, periodic pamphlet, 2042–25

Overseas Business Reports: economic conditions, investment and export opportunities, and trade practices, country market research rpt series, 2046–6

Savings rates impacts on GNP and balance of payments, 1950s-89 and projected to 2009, article, 9385–1.201

Soviet Union, China, OECD, and selected other countries trade and balances, 1960s-90, annual rpt, 9114–4.8

Soviet Union, Eastern Europe, OECD, and selected other countries economic conditions, 1960s-90, annual rpt, 9114–4

Soviet Union economic conditions under General Secretary Gorbachev, 1990 and trends from 1975, annual rpt, 9114–6

Statistical Abstract of US, 1991 annual data compilation, 2324–1.29; 2324–1.31

Telecommunications finances, rates, and traffic for US carriers intl operations, by service type, firm, and country, 1975-89, annual rpt, 9284–17

Telecommunications industry intl competitiveness, with financial and operating data by product or service, firm, and country, 1990 rpt, 2008–30

see also Foreign debts

see also Foreign exchange

see also Foreign investments

see also Foreign trade

Balance of trade

see Balance of payments

Balance sheets

see Business assets and liabilities, general

see Business assets and liabilities, specific industry

see Business income and expenses, general

see Business income and expenses, specific industry

see Government assets and liabilities

Balanced Budget and Emergency Deficit Control Act

Budget of US, House concurrent resolution, with spending and revenue targets, FY92 and projected to FY96, annual rpt, 21264–2

Budget of US, Senate concurrent resolution, with spending and revenue targets, FY92, annual rpt, 25254–1

Balcazar, Hector

"Interpretive Views on Hispanics' Perinatal Problems of Low Birth Weight and Prenatal Care", 4042–3.234

Baldwin, Jennifer

"Medicaid Hospital Payment", 17206–1.11

Balke, Nathan S.

"Algebra of Price Stability", 9379–12.79

"Detecting Level Shifts in Time Series: Misspecification and a Proposed Solution", 9379–12.71

"Large Shocks, Small Shocks, and Economic Fluctuations: Outliers in Macroeconomic Times Series", 9379–12.63

"Modeling Trends in Macroeconomic Time Series", 9379–1.205

Ball, Judy K.

"AIDS in U.S. Hospitals, 1986-87: A National Perspective", 4186–6.15

Ballenger, Louella

"Sole Proprietorship Returns, 1989", 8302–2.214

Ballistic missiles

see Intermediate-Range Nuclear Forces Treaty

see Missiles and rockets

see Nuclear weapons

Baltic States

see Estonia

see Latvia

see Lithuania

Baltic, Tony

"Forest and Rangeland Resource Interactions: A Supporting Technical Document for the 1989 RPA Assessment", 1208–24.19

Baltimore, Md.

CPI by component for US city average, and by region, population size, and for 15 metro areas, monthly rpt, 6762–1

CPI by component for US city average, and by region, population size, and for 27 metro areas, monthly rpt, 6762–2

Fruit and vegetable shipments, and arrivals in US and Canada cities, by mode of transport and State and country of origin, 1990, annual rpt, 1311–4.1

Housing starts and completions authorized by building permits in 40 MSAs, quarterly rpt, 2382–9

see also under By City and By SMSA or MSA in the "Index by Categories"

Bananas

see Fruit and fruit products

Bangladesh

Agricultural exports of high-value commodities, indexes and sales by commodity, world area, and country, 1960s-86, 1528–323

Agricultural exports of US, impacts of foreign agricultural and trade policy, with data by commodity and country, 1989, annual rpt, 1924–8

Agricultural production, subsidies, and input prices, for Bangladesh, 1991 article, 1502–3.203

Agricultural production, trade, and policies in foreign countries, summary data by country, 1989-90, annual factbook, 1924–12

Agricultural trade of US, by detailed commodity and country, 1989, annual rpt, 1524–8

Agricultural trade of US, by detailed commodity and country, 1990, semiannual rpt, 1522–4

AID economic aid to developing countries, obligations and disbursements by country, quarterly rpt, 9912–4

AID loans repayment status and terms by program and country, and status of predecessor agency loans, quarterly rpt, 9912–3

Background Notes, summary social, political, and economic data, 1990 rpt, 7006–2.8

Economic and military aid and loans from US and intl agencies, by program and country, FY46-90, annual rpt, 9914–5

Economic and social conditions of developing countries from 1960s, and Intl Dev Cooperation Agency and AID activities and funding, FY90-92, annual rpt, 9904–4

Economic conditions, income, production, prices, employment, and trade, 1991 periodic country rpt, 2046–4.73

Economic conditions, policy, and trade practices, by country, 1988-90, annual rpt, 21384–5

Economic, population, and agricultural data, US and other aid sources, and AID activity, 1990 country rpt, 9916–12.43

Economic, social, political, and geographic summary data, by country, 1991, annual factbook, 9114–2

Exports and imports of US, by selected country, country group, and commodity group, 1990, annual rpt, 2044–37

Exports and imports of US, by transport mode, country, and SITC 1- to 3-digit commodity, 1990, annual rpt, 2424–12

Exports of US, detailed Schedule B commodities with countries of destination, 1990, annual rpt, 2424–10

Grain production and needs, and related economic outlook, by world area and selected country, forecast 1990/91-1991/92, 1528–313

Human rights conditions in 170 countries, and US economic and military aid, 1990, annual rpt, 21384–3

Index by Subjects and Names

Military aid of US, arms sales, and training programs costs and budget requests, by program, world region, and country, FY90-92, annual rpt, 7144–13

Towels (shop) from Bangladesh at less than fair value, injury to US industry, investigation with background financial and operating data, 1991 rpt, 9886–14.310

UN voting record and share of votes in agreement with US, by issue, country, and world area, 1990, annual rpt, 7004–18

see also under By Foreign Country in the "Index by Categories"

Bangor, Maine

see also under By SMSA or MSA in the "Index by Categories"

Bank deposits

Assets and debts of private sector, balance sheets by segment, 1945-90, semiannual rpt, 9365–4.1

Banking industry structure and deposit insurance reform, findings and recommendations, with background data, 1989-90, 8008–147

Banks balance sheets, by Fed Reserve District, for major banks in NYC, and for US branches and agencies of foreign banks, weekly rpt, 9365–1.3

Banks production costs relation to output, core deposits, and branches, by bank asset size, alternative model results, 1985-87, working paper, 9371–10.54

Business statistics, detailed data for major industries and economic indicators, *Survey of Current Business*, monthly rpt, 2702–1.9

Commercial and savings banks (insured) finances, by State, 1989, annual rpt, 9294–4

Commercial and savings banks insured by FDIC, financial condition and performance, by asset size and region, quarterly rpt, 9292–1

Commercial banks (insured) domestic and foreign office consolidated financial statements, monthly rpt, quarterly data, 9362–1.4

Commercial banks profitability, balance sheet and income statement items, and financial ratios, by asset size, 1985-90, annual article, 9362–1.204

Credit unions federally insured, finances by instn characteristics and State, as of June 1991, semiannual rpt, 9532–6

Credit unions federally insured, finances, 1989-90, annual rpt, 9534–1

Debits and turnover of demand and savings deposits, monthly rpt, 9362–1.1

Debits, deposits, and deposit turnover, for commercial banks by type of account, monthly rpt, 9365–2.5

Deposits in insured commercial and savings banks, by instn, State, MSA, and county, as of June 1990, annual regional rpt series, 9295–3

Economic indicators and components, current data and annual trends, monthly rpt, 23842–1.5

Economic indicators compounded annual rates of change, 1971-90, annual rpt, 9391–9.1

Failures of banks, deposits by whether federally insured, 1930s-80s, working paper, 9377–9.112

Farm income, expenses, receipts by commodity, assets, liabilities, and ratios, 1990 and trends from 1945, annual rpt, 1544–16

Fed Reserve banks finances and staff, 1990, annual rpt, 9364–1.1

Financial and monetary conditions, selected US summary data, weekly rpt, 9391–4

Financial, banking, and mortgage market activity, weekly rpt series, 9365–1

Flow-of-funds accounts, savings, investments, and credit statements, quarterly rpt, 9365–3.3

Foreign and domestic deposits in US banks, and for 30 largest commercial banks, 1990 hearings, 25248–121

Foreign countries banks deposits, for 7 heavily indebted developing countries, 1982-89, technical paper, 9385–8.109

Households assets, by type of holding and selected characteristics, 1988, Current Population Rpt, 2546–20.16

Interest rates on bank deposits, relation to bank market concentration indicators and Treasury security rates, 1980s, technical paper, 9366–6.261

Interest rates on bank loans and deposits, relation to market concentration indicators, 1985-90, technical paper, 9366–6.283

Intl transactions, *Survey of Current Business*, monthly rpt, quarterly tables, 2702–1.26

Mail volume to and from households, use and views, by class, source, content, and household characteristics, 1987-88, annual rpt, 9864–10

Merger applications approved, and assets and offices involved, by bank, 1989, annual rpt, 9294–5

Metro and nonmetro areas banks finances and operations, 1987-89, annual rpt, 1544–29

Mexico banks deregulation impacts on finances, with data by bank, 1960s-90, technical paper, 9385–8.121

Monetary trends, Fed Reserve Bank of St Louis monthly rpt, 9391–2

New England States, FHLB 1st District thrifts financial operations compared to banks, and housing industry indicators, bimonthly rpt with articles, 9302–4

Nonprofit charitable organizations finances, and revenue and investments of top 10 instns, 1986-87, article, 8302–2.210

North Central States business and economic conditions, Fed Reserve 9th District, quarterly journal, 9383–19

North Central States, FHLB 6th District insured S&Ls financial condition and operations by State, quarterly rpt, 9302–23

North Central States, FHLB 8th District S&Ls, locations, assets, and savings, 1991, annual listing, 9304–9

Northeast States bank financial performance compared to rest of US, 1970s-90, article, 9373–1.220

Savings banks insured by Bank Insurance Fund, financial condition and performance, by asset size and region, quarterly rpt, 9292–5

Savings instns failure resolution activity and finances of Resolution Trust Corp, with data by asset type, State, region, and instn, monthly rpt, 9722–3

Bank holding companies

Savings instns failure resolution activity of Resolution Trust Corp, assets, deposits, and assets availability and sales, periodic press release, 9722–1

Savings instns failure resolution activity of Resolution Trust Corp, with data by State and instn, and RTC financial statements, 1989, annual rpt, 9724–1

Savings instns finances and operations by district and State, mortgage loan activity and terms by MSA, and FHLB finances, 1989 and trends from 1900, annual rpt, 8434–3

Savings instns insured by Savings Assn Insurance Fund, assets, liabilities, and deposit and loan activity, by conservatorship status, monthly rpt, 8432–1

Savings instns insured by Savings Assn Insurance Fund, finances by profitability group, district, and State, quarterly rpt, 8432–4

Southeastern States, Fed Reserve 5th District, economic indicators by State, quarterly rpt, 9389–16

Southeastern States, Fed Reserve 5th District insured commercial banks financial statements, by State, quarterly rpt, 9389–18

Southeastern States, Fed Reserve 8th District banking and economic conditions, quarterly rpt with articles, 9391–16

State and Metro Area Data Book, 1991 data compilation, 2328–54

Statistical Abstract of US, 1991 annual data compilation, 2324–1.16

West Central States economic indicators, Fed Reserve 10th District, quarterly rpt, 9381–16.2

West Central States, Fed Reserve 10th District banking industry structure, performance, and financial devs, 1990, annual rpt, 9381–14

West Central States, FHLB 10th District thrifts, locations, assets, and deposits, 1991, annual listing, 9304–17

Western States, FHLB 11th District S&Ls, offices, and financial condition, 1991 annual listing, 9304–23

see also Certificates of deposit

see also Checking accounts

see also Deposit insurance

see also International reserves

see also Negotiable orders of withdrawal accounts

see also Savings

Bank holding companies

Capital aid receipt of problem banks, relation to BHC affiliation and other factors, with data for Texas, 1985-88, article, 9391–1.205

Equity capital costs of BHCs and impact on ability to raise capital, 1960s-80s, technical paper, 9366–6.274

Fed Reserve Board and Reserve banks finances, staff, and review of monetary policy and economic devs, 1990, annual rpt, 9364–1

Finances of financial instns by type and selected instn, and deposit insurance reform issues, 1970s-90, GAO rpt, 26119–320

Financial and economic analysis, technical paper series, 9393–10

Bank holding companies

Financial condition of banks and deposit insurance funds, potential losses, and regulatory issues, 1980s-90 and projected to 1995, 21248–147

Financial ratios of large BHCs, by asset size, 1971-87, article, 9383–6.203

Merger applications approved, and assets and offices involved, by bank, 1989, annual rpt, 9294–5

Metro and nonmetro areas banks finances and operations, 1987-89, annual rpt, 1544–29

Reform of banking system and deposit insurance, findings and recommendations, with background data, 1989-90, 8008–147

Securities (bank-ineligible) dealing by BHC subsidiaries, subsidiary and parent firm finances, 1989-91, GAO rpt, 26119–280

Tax (income) returns of corporations, income and tax items by asset size and detailed industry, 1987, annual rpt, 8304–4

Tax (income) returns of corporations, income and tax items by asset size and detailed industry, 1988, annual rpt, 8304–21

West Central States, Fed Reserve 10th District banking industry structure, performance, and financial devs, 1990, annual rpt, 9381–14.1

Bank Insurance Fund

Budget of US, midsession review of FY92 budget, by function, annual rpt, 104–7

Commercial and savings banks insured by BIF, financial condition and performance, by asset size and region, quarterly rpt, 9292–1

Deposits in FDIC BIF-insured commercial and savings banks, by instn, State, MSA, and county, as of June 1990, annual regional rpt series, 9295–3

Finances and potential losses of BIF, 1990 hearings, 25248–125

Finances of BIF, FY89-92, 26308–100

Finances of BIF, with assessments of large banks, 1990 hearings, 25248–121

Financial condition of banks and deposit insurance funds, potential losses, and regulatory issues, 1980s-90 and projected to 1995, 21248–147

New England States thrifts loan delinquency rates by loan type, time past due, thrift charter type, and State, 1990, annual article, 9302–4.202

Reform of banking system and deposit insurance, findings and recommendations, with background data, 1989-90, 8008–147

Savings banks insured by BIF, financial condition and performance, by asset size and region, quarterly rpt, 9292–5

Bank reserve requirements

see Financial institutions regulation

Bank reserves

see Banks and banking

Banker, David

"What Do Farmers Consider Important When Making Management Decisions?", 1541–1.206

Bankruptcy

Airline financial and operating summary data, quarterly rpt, 7502–16

Business bankruptcy filings with SEC participation, by firm, FY90, annual rpt, 9734–2.4

Farm finances, debts, assets, and receipts, and lenders financial condition, quarterly rpt with articles, 1541–1

Farm financial stress indicators, operator quits, and loan problems and mediation, 1970s-90, 1598–272

FmHA loans and borrower supervision activities in farm and housing programs, by type and State, monthly rpt, 1182–1

Statistical Abstract of US, 1991 annual data compilation, 2324–1.17

US attorneys civil and criminal cases by type and disposition, and collections, by Federal district, FY90, annual rpt, 6004–2.1

see also Business failures and closings

see also Federal bankruptcy courts

Banks and banking

Acquisitions and mergers of banks in Southeastern States, assets and major institutions involved, by State, 1984-89, article, 9371–1.203

Acquisitions of banks, purchase price relation to target and acquiring banks earnings variability and other factors, 1980s, working paper, 9371–10.57

Assets and liabilities of Fed Reserve member and nonmember banks, 1989-90, annual rpt, 9364–1.2

Assets, branches, holding company status, and charter class, by insured commercial bank, quarterly listing, suspended, 9362–7

Assets, firms, and financial performance of banks, by asset size, 1970s-90, article, 9383–6.203

Assets, income, and financial ratios of insured commercial banks, by asset size and State, quarterly rpt, 13002–3

Assets, liabilities, loans, investments, and deposits for commercial banks, total and in and outside NYC, monthly rpt, 9362–1.1

Banks failures, survival probability model forecasting performance, 1986-90, article, 9377–1.204

Boycotts (intl) invitations received by US firms, by country, FY90, annual rpt, 2024–1

Business formations impacts of local bank market structure and economic conditions, 1980s, working paper, 9377–9.123

Business statistics, detailed data for major industries and economic indicators, *Survey of Current Business*, monthly rpt, 2702–1.9

Capital of banks by component, and capital/asset ratios compared to other industry groups, 1900s-80s, working paper, 9375–13.61

Competitive performance in duopoly banking market, model description and results, 1970s-86 local area study, working paper, 9387–8.251

County Business Patterns, 1988: employment, establishments, and payroll, by SIC 2- to 4-digit industry and county, annual State rpt series, 2326–6

County Business Patterns, 1989: employment, establishments, and payroll, by SIC 2- to 4-digit industry and county, annual State rpt series, 2326–8

Criminal cases by type and disposition, and collections, for US attorneys, by Federal district, FY90, annual rpt, 6004–2.1

Index by Subjects and Names

Debits, deposits and turnover, consumer credit, interest rates, and status changes, monthly rpt series, 9365–2

Developing countries debt burden and related indicators, by country and for 9 US money-center banks, 1960s-89, article, 9292–4.201

Economies and inefficiencies of scale, model description and results for large banks, 1987, working paper, 9375–13.66

Economies of scale and other efficiency measures for banking, alternative estimates, 1991 article, 9375–1.209

Economies of scale and scope, impacts of regulation for large banks, alternative model results, 1972-87, working paper, 9375–13.50

Economies of scale in banking, alternative model results for large banks, by asset size, 1985-87, article, 9371–1.208

Economies of scope for large banks, alternative model results, 1988, working paper, 9389–19.28

Employment, earnings, and hours, by SIC 1- to 4-digit industry, monthly and annual averages, selected years 1909-90, annual rpt, 6744–4

Failures of banks, forecasting performance of bank financial ratios and local market economic conditions, 1980s-89, article, 9377–1.203

Failures of banks, forecasting performance of measures using alternative capital/asset ratio requirements, 1982-89, working paper, 9377–9.109

Failures of banks, interbank exposure risk indicators by bank size, 1980s-90, working paper, 9377–9.107

Failures of State-chartered Fed Reserve member banks, assets and losses to FDIC, by instn, 1984-90, hearing, 21242–1

Fed Reserve discount window borrowing of banks, relation to interest rate spreads and banks financial performance indicators, 1980s-90, technical paper, 9385–8.111

Fed Reserve discount window borrowing of banks, relation to interest rate spreads and discount borrowing outstanding, by bank asset size, 1981-90, article, 9385–1.209

Fed Reserve discount window borrowing of banks, relation to interest rate spreads, 1980s-90, technical paper, 9385–8.110

Finances and operations, by SIC 2- to 4-digit industry, forecast 1991, annual rpt, 2044–28

Finances of banks and thrifts, by instn type, 1990, annual rpt, 13004–2

Finances of insured commercial and savings banks, by State, 1989, annual rpt, 9294–4

Financial and economic devs, Fed Reserve Bank of Boston bimonthly journal, 9373–1

Financial and economic devs, Fed Reserve Bank of Chicago bimonthly journal, 9375–1

Financial and economic devs, Fed Reserve Bank of New York quarterly journal, 9385–1

Financial and economic devs, Fed Reserve Bank of Philadelphia bimonthly journal, 9387–1

Financial, banking, and mortgage market activity, weekly rpt series, 9365–1

Financial condition and performance of insured commercial and savings banks, by asset size and region, quarterly rpt, 9292–1

Index by Subjects and Names

Banks and banking

Financial condition of banks and deposit insurance funds, potential losses, and regulatory issues, 1980s-90 and projected to 1995, 21248–147

Financial performance of banks in Fed Reserve 10th District, by urban-rural location and State, 1989-90, article, 9381–16.201

Financial performance of banks, risk assessment, and regulation, 1990 annual conf papers, 9375–7

Financial ratios of real estate lenders compared to other US and Texas banks, and bank deposit insurance fund finances and potential losses, 1990 hearings, 25248–125

Foreign and US banks capital costs, operating ratios, and intl market shares, for US and 4 countries, 1980s-90, article, 9385–1.203

Foreign branches of US banks, assets and liabilities by world region and country, quarterly rpt, 9365–3.7

Foreign branches of US banks, balance sheets, monthly rpt, 9362–1.3

Foreign direct investment in US, by industry group and world area, 1987-90, annual article, 2702–1.219

Foreign direct investment of US, by industry group and world area, 1987-90, annual article, 2702–1.220

Foreign-owned banks in US, assets relation to foreign and domestic economic and financial indicators, by type of banking instn, 1970s-89, technical paper, 9385–8.108

Foreign-owned banks US subsidiaries, assets, and regulatory issues, with data by State and firm, 1989-90, hearing, 21248–155

Fraud and abuse in banks and thrifts, Federal criminal enforcement activities, case dispositions, and settlements, with data by district, 1982-90, hearing, 21248–142

Great Lakes area economic conditions and outlook, for US and Canada, 1970s-90, 9375–15

Intl banking and securities instns assets by selected firm, and financial performance indicators by selected country, late 1980s-90, article, 9385–1.206

Intl banking competition and deposit insurance reform issues, with background data, 1990 hearings, 25248–121; 25248–122; 25248–123

Intl banking competition issues, with background data, 1980s, 21248–153

Intl transactions of US, and economic and monetary trends for US and 10 major trading partners, quarterly rpt, 9391–7

Intl transactions, *Survey of Current Business*, monthly rpt, quarterly tables, 2702–1.26

Investments and loans of commercial banks, monthly rpt, 23842–1.5

Investments and loans of commercial banks, 1972-90, annual rpt, 204–1.5

Japan financial instns and stock market conditions, and other economic indicators, with intl comparisons, 1980s-90, hearing, 21248–152

Labor productivity, indexes of output, hours, and employment by SIC 2- to 4-digit industry, 1967-89, annual rpt, 6824–1.4

Mail volume to and from households, use, and views, by class, source, content, and household characteristics, 1987-88, annual rpt, 9864–10

Market concentration indicators and Treasury security rates relation to bank deposit interest rates, 1980s, technical paper, 9366–6.261

Market value calculation method to expose bank undercapitalization, with model results and background data for selected failed banks, 1960s-89, working paper, 9377–9.112

Merger applications approved, and assets and offices involved, by bank, 1989, annual rpt, 9294–5

Metro and nonmetro areas banks finances and operations, 1987-89, annual rpt, 1544–29

Mexico banks deregulation impacts on finances, with data by bank, 1960s-90, technical paper, 9385–8.121

Multinatl firms US affiliates, finances, and operations, by industry, world area of parent firm, and State, 1988-89, annual rpt, 2704–4

Multinatl firms US affiliates, investment trends and impact on US economy, 1991 annual rpt, 2004–9

Natl banks charters, mergers, liquidations, enforcement cases, and financial performance, with data by instn and State, quarterly rpt, 8402–3

New England States, FHLB 1st District thrifts financial operations compared to banks, and housing industry indicators, bimonthly rpt with articles, 9302–4

North Central States business and economic conditions, Fed Reserve 9th District, quarterly journal, 9383–19

Northeast States bank financial performance compared to rest of US, 1970s-90, article, 9373–1.220

Occupational injury and illness rates, by SIC 2- to 4-digit industry, 1988-89, annual rpt, 6844–7

Occupational injury and illness rates, by SIC 2- to 4-digit industry, 1989, annual rpt, 6844–1

Production costs of banks, relation to output, core deposits, and branches, by bank asset size, alternative model results, 1985-87, working paper, 9371–10.54

Productivity of banks, relation to costs, technological devs, deregulation, and other factors, alternative measures, 1980s, technical paper, 9366–6.265

Profitability of banks, balance sheet and income statement items, and financial ratios, by asset size, 1985-90, annual article, 9362–1.204

Profitability of banks, indicators for student loans and other financial services, 1985-89, 4808–36

Robberies, by type of premises, population size, and region, 1990, annual rpt, 6224–2.1

Robbery of banks and related crimes by State, casualties, and hostages, data compilation, 1991 annual rpt, 6064–6.3

Robbery of banks, Federal district court caseloads by disposition and district, 1980-90, last issue of annual rpt, 18204–1

Robbery of banks, US attorneys cases by disposition, FY90, annual rpt, 6004–2.1; 6004–2.7

Small Business Investment Companies capital holdings, SBA obligation, and ownership, as of July 1991, semiannual listing, 9762–4

South Central States agricultural banks financial ratios, and farm receipts by commodity, 1980s-90, annual article, 9391–16.209

South Central States bank performance indicators by asset size, Fed Reserve 8th District, 1987-90, annual article, 9391–16.208

Southeastern States, Fed Reserve 6th District banks financial ratios, by asset size and State, 1986-90, annual article, 9371–1.211

Southeastern States, Fed Reserve 8th District banking and economic conditions, quarterly rpt with articles, 9391–16

Southwestern States bank performance indicators by asset size and FDIC assistance receipt, Fed Reserve 11th District, 1987-90, article, 9379–1.206

State and Metro Area Data Book, 1991 data compilation, 2328–54

State gross product growth, impact of State bank credit conditions, 1980-86, article, 9377–1.206

Statistical Abstract of US, 1991 annual data compilation, 2324–1.16

Tax (income) returns for foreign corporate activity in US, assets, and income statement items, by industry div and selected country, 1986-87, article, 8302–2.205

Tax (income) returns of corporations, income and tax items by asset size and detailed industry, 1987, annual rpt, 8304–4

Tax (income) returns of corporations, income and tax items by asset size and detailed industry, 1988, annual rpt, 8304–21

Tax (income) returns of corporations with foreign tax credit, income and tax items by industry group, 1986, biennial article, 8302–2.203

Tax (income) returns of multinatl US firms foreign affiliates, income statement items, by asset size and industry, 1986, biennial article, 8302–2.212

Tax expenditures, Federal revenues forgone through income tax deductions and exclusions by type, FY92-96, annual rpt, 21784–10

Tax rates and revenue of State and local govts, by source and State, 1991 and historical trends, annual rpt, 10044–1

Texas banks and thrifts profitability and solvency indicators, and problem assets by type, 1980s, working paper, 9379–14.11

Texas banks failures relation to portfolio risk indicators and year of establishment, 1980s, working paper, 9379–14.10

Texas economic and housing conditions, bank failures, and thrift and Federal regulators real estate holdings, 1980s-90, hearings, 21248–146

Undercapitalized banks financial performance, by State and inside-outside Texas, aggregate 1985-89, article, 9391–1.212

West Central States economic indicators, Fed Reserve 10th District, quarterly rpt, 9381–16.2

West Central States, Fed Reserve 10th District banking industry structure, performance, and financial devs, 1990, annual rpt, 9381–14

Banks and banking

see also Agricultural credit
see also Automated tellers
see also Bank deposits
see also Bank holding companies
see also Checking accounts
see also Commercial credit
see also Consumer credit
see also Credit
see also Credit cards
see also Credit unions
see also Deposit insurance
see also Discrimination in credit
see also Electronic funds transfer
see also Eurocurrency
see also Export-Import Bank
see also Farm Credit System
see also Federal Financing Bank
see also Federal Home Loan Banks
see also Federal Reserve System
see also Financial institutions regulation
see also Flow-of-funds accounts
see also Foreign exchange
see also Interest rates
see also International reserves
see also Loans
see also Money supply
see also Mortgages
see also Negotiable orders of withdrawal accounts
see also Savings
see also Savings institutions
see also under By Industry in the "Index by Categories"

Banks for Cooperatives
see Farm Credit System

Baquet, Claudia R.
"Socioeconomic Factors and Cancer Incidence Among Blacks and Whites", 4472–1.210

Barbados
Agricultural exports of high-value commodities, indexes and sales by commodity, world area, and country, 1960s-86, 1528–323
Agricultural trade of US, by detailed commodity and country, 1989, annual rpt, 1524–8
Agricultural trade of US, by detailed commodity and country, 1990, semiannual rpt, 1522–4
AID economic aid to developing countries, obligations and disbursements by country, quarterly rpt, 9912–4
Economic and military aid and loans from US and intl agencies, by program and country, FY46-90, annual rpt, 9914–5
Economic conditions, policy, and trade practices, by country, 1988-90, annual rpt, 21384–5
Economic, social, political, and geographic summary data, by country, 1991, annual factbook, 9114–2
Exports and imports of US, by transport mode, country, and SITC 1- to 3-digit commodity, 1990, annual rpt, 2424–12
Exports of US, detailed Schedule B commodities with countries of destination, 1990, annual rpt, 2424–10
Human rights conditions in 170 countries, and US economic and military aid, 1990, annual rpt, 21384–3
Investment (direct) incentives of Caribbean Basin Initiative, economic impacts, with finances and employment by country, 1984-90, 2048–141

Labor conditions, union coverage, and work accidents, 1991 annual regional rpt, 6366–4.56
Military aid of US, arms sales, and training programs costs and budget requests, by program, world region, and country, FY90-92, annual rpt, 7144–13
Multinatl US firms and foreign affiliates finances and operations, by industry and world area of parent firm, 1989 benchmark survey, preliminary annual rpt, 2704–5
Rum imports (duty-free) of US under Caribbean Basin Initiative, by country, 1989-90, annual rpt, 9884–15
UN voting record and share of votes in agreement with US, by issue, country, and world area, 1990, annual rpt, 7004–18

Barbagallo, Mary B.
"Federal Offshore Statistics: 1990, Leasing, Exploration, Production, and Revenues", 5734–3

Barber and beauty shops
County Business Patterns, 1988: employment, establishments, and payroll, by SIC 2- to 4-digit industry and county, annual State rpt series, 2326–6
County Business Patterns, 1989: employment, establishments, and payroll, by SIC 2- to 4-digit industry and county, annual State rpt series, 2326–8
CPI by component for US city average, and by region, population size, and for 27 metro areas, monthly rpt, 6762–2
Employment, earnings, and hours, by SIC 1- to 4-digit industry, monthly and annual averages, selected years 1909-90, annual rpt, 6744–4
Enterprise Statistics, 1987: finances and operations for companies, by size, level of diversification, form of organization, and industry group, 2329–8
Franchise business opportunities by firm and kind of business, and sources of aid and info, 1990 annual listing, 2104–7
Labor productivity, indexes of output, hours, and employment by SIC 2- to 4-digit industry, 1967-89, annual rpt, 6824–1.4
Occupational injury and illness rates, by SIC 2- to 4-digit industry, 1988-89, annual rpt, 6844–7
Occupational injury and illness rates, by SIC 2- to 4-digit industry, 1989, annual rpt, 6844–1
Puerto Rico economic censuses, 1987: wholesale and retail trade and service industry finances and operations, by SIC 2- to 4-digit industry and municipio, 2591–1
Puerto Rico economic censuses, 1987: wholesale, retail, and service industries finances and operations, by establishment characteristics and SIC 2- and 3-digit industry, subject rpts, 2591–2
Receipts for services, by SIC 2- to 4-digit kind of business, 1990, annual rpt, 2413–8
Senate receipts, itemized expenses by payee, and balances, 1st half FY91, semiannual listing, 25922–1
Service industries census, 1987: depreciable assets, capital and operating expenses, and receipts, by SIC 2- to 4-digit kind of business, 2393–2

Service industries census, 1987: establishments, receipts by source, payroll, and employment, by SIC 2- to 4-digit kind of business, State, and MSA, 2393–4
Tax (income) returns of partnerships, income statement and balance sheet items, by industry group, 1989, annual article, 8302–2.216; 8304–18
Tax (income) returns of sole proprietorships, income statement items, by industry group, 1989, annual article, 8302–2.214

Barbett, Samuel F.
"State Higher Education Profiles, Third Edition: A Comparison of State Higher Education Data for FY87", 4844–13

Barges
Accidents involving merchant ships, and casualties, by circumstances and characteristics of persons and vessels involved, 1988, annual rpt, 7404–11
Accidents involving ships and marine facilities, casualties, and circumstances, Coast Guard investigation results, periodic rpt, 9612–4
Coal shipments to electric utilities under contract, and rates, by firm, transport mode, and region, 1979-87, 3168–121
Construction and operating subsidies of MarAd by firm, and ship deliveries and fleet by country, by vessel type, FY90, annual rpt, 7704–14.1
Containers (intermodal) and equipment owned by shipping and leasing companies, inventory by type and size, 1990, annual rpt, 7704–10
Foreign and US merchant ships, tonnage, and new ship construction and deliveries, by vessel type and country, as of Jan 1990, annual rpt, 7704–3
Grain shipments and rates for barge and rail loadings, periodic situation rpt with articles, 1561–4
Mississippi River system freight traffic by commodity and waterway, 1988 and projected to 2000, article, 9391–16.202
Natl transportation system planning, use, condition, accidents, and needs, by mode of transport, 1940s-90 and projected to 2020, 7308–202
Oil and refined products stocks, and interdistrict shipments by mode of transport, monthly rpt, 3162–6.3
Oil bulk stations, sales and storage capacity by product, inventories, expenses, employment, and modes of transport, 1987 Census of Wholesale Trade, 2407–4.2
Oil import traffic by US port and vessel type, marine oil pollution sources, and costs and operations of proposed offshore terminals, late 1980s, 5738–25
Oil refinery crude received, by mode of transport and PAD district, 1990, annual rpt, 3164–2.1
St Lawrence Seaway ship, cargo, and passenger traffic, and toll revenue, 1990 and trends from 1959, annual rpt, 7744–2

Barite
see Nonmetallic minerals and mines

Barium
see Metals and metal industries

Index by Subjects and Names

Barkema, Alan D.
"Crossroads for the Cattle Industry", 9381–1.201
"How Will Reform of the Soviet Farm Economy Affect U.S. Agriculture?", 9381–1.210
"Outlook for Agricultural Lenders and Policymakers in the 1990s", 9368–90
"Quiet Revolution in the U.S. Food Market", 9381–1.205
"Turning Point in the Farm Recovery?", 9381–1.203

Barley
see Animal feed
see Grains and grain products

Barnard, Charles H.
"Measuring the Contribution of Farm Dwellings to Operator Income and Asset Values", 1541–1.211

Barnes, Richard L.
"Intra-North American Trade and Other Trade Issues", 1004–16.1

Bartelsman, Eric J.
"Sourcing Externalities", 9366–6.267

Barth, James R.
"Banking Industry in Turmoil: A Report on the Condition of the U.S. Banking Industry and the Bank Insurance Fund", 21248–147

Baseball
Service industries census, 1987: establishments, receipts by source, payroll, and employment, by SIC 2- to 4-digit kind of business, State, and MSA, 2393–4

Basic Educational Opportunity Grant
see Student aid

Baskerville, Valerie G.
"Supplemental Security Income: State and County Data, December 1989", 4744–27

Basketball
Educational and employment performance of college athletes compared to other students, for 1972 high school class, as of 1986, 4888–5
Injuries from use of consumer products, by severity, victim age, and detailed product, 1990, annual rpt, 9164–6

Bass, Joel L.
"Childhood Injury Prevention in a Suburban Massachusetts Population", 4042–3.236

Bassoff, Betty Z.
"Requiring Formal Training in Preventive Health Practices for Child Day Care Providers", 4042–3.243

Bastian, Lisa D.
"Criminal Victimization, 1990", 6066–25.41
"Teenage Victims", 6066–3.43

Baton Rouge, La.
see also under By City and By SMSA or MSA in the "Index by Categories"

Battelle Human Affairs Research Centers
"Cost and Outcome Analysis of Kidney Transplantation. The Implications of Initial Immunosuppressive Protocol and Diabetes", 4658–59
"Evaluation of the Impacts of the Washington Alternative Work Search Experiment", 6406–6.35

Battelle Memorial Institute
see also Department of Energy National Laboratories

Batteries
Auto (electric-powered) R&D activity and DOE funding shares, FY90, annual rpt, 3304–2
Business statistics, detailed data for major industries and economic indicators, *Survey of Current Business*, monthly rpt, 2702–1.17
County Business Patterns, 1988: employment, establishments, and payroll, by SIC 2- to 4-digit industry and county, annual State rpt series, 2326–6
County Business Patterns, 1989: employment, establishments, and payroll, by SIC 2- to 4-digit industry and county, annual State rpt series, 2326–8
Exports and imports of US, by country and detailed commodity, monthly rpt, 2422–12
Exports and imports of US, by Harmonized System 6-digit commodity and country, 1990, annual rpt, 2424–13
Exports of US, detailed Schedule B commodities with countries of destination, 1990, annual rpt, 2424–10
Injuries from use of consumer products, by severity, victim age, and detailed product, 1990, annual rpt, 9164–6
Manufacturing census, 1987: employment and shipments under Fed Govt contracts, by SIC 4-digit industry, 2497–7
Manufacturing census, 1987: finances and operations, by SIC 2- to 4-digit industry, State, and MSA, with trends from 1849, 2497–1
Manufacturing census, 1987: finances and operations, by type of organization and SIC 2- to 4-digit industry, subject rpt, 2497–5
OECD trade, total and for 4 major countries, and US trade by country, by commodity, 1970-89, world area rpt series, 9116–1
Pollution (air) emissions factors, by detailed pollutant and source, data compilation, 1990 rpt, 9198–120
Price indexes (producer), by stage of processing and detailed commodity, monthly rpt, 6762–6
Price indexes (producer), by stage of processing and detailed commodity, monthly 1990, annual rpt, 6764–2

Battle Creek, Mich.
Wages by occupation, and benefits for office and plant workers, 1991 survey, periodic labor market rpt, 6785–3.9
see also under By SMSA or MSA in the "Index by Categories"

Battleships
see Naval vessels

Bauer, Paul W.
"Local Banking Markets and Firm Location", 9377–9.123

Baugher, Eleanor F.
"Poverty in the U.S., 1988-89", 2546–6.67
"Poverty in the U.S.: 1990", 2546–6.71

Bauman, Alvin
"Wages and Compensation: 1990 Negotiated Adjustments", 6722–1.227

Bauxite
see Aluminum and aluminum industry

Bay City, Mich.
see also under By SMSA or MSA in the "Index by Categories"

BEA
see Bureau of Economic Analysis

Beaches
see Lakes and lakeshores
see Seashores

Beans
see Vegetables and vegetable products

Bearings
see Machines and machinery industry

Bears
see Wildlife and wildlife conservation

Beaufort Sea
Environmental conditions and oil dev impacts for Alaska OCS, compilation of papers, series, 2176–1
Fish catch and habitat impacts of Arctic Ocean oil and gas dev, and assessment methods, 1988 conf, 5738–24
Oil and gas OCS leases environmental and socioeconomic impact and coastal area description, 1990 final statement, 5736–1.22
Whales (bowhead) population in Beaufort Sea, and fall aerial survey operations, 1979-90, annual rpt, 5734–10
Whales (bowhead and white) migration through Beaufort Sea, behavior impacts of oil drilling and aircraft noise, spring 1989, 5738–27

Beaumont, Tex.
Ships in Natl Defense Reserve Fleet at Beaumont harbor, as of Jan 1991, semiannual listing, 7702–2
Wages by occupation, and benefits for office and plant workers, 1991 survey, periodic MSA rpt, 6785–3.6
see also under By City and By SMSA or MSA in the "Index by Categories"

Beauregard, Karen M.
"Access to Health Care: Findings from the Survey of American Indians and Alaska Natives. National Medical Expenditure Survey ", 4186–8.18

Beauty aids
see Cosmetics and toiletries

Beauty parlors
see Barber and beauty shops

Beaver County, Pa.
see also under By SMSA or MSA in the "Index by Categories"

Becher, Albert E.
"Geohydrology and Water Quality in the Vicinity of the Gettysburg National Military Park and Eisenhower Historic Site, Pennsylvania", 5666–28.8

Bechter, Dan M.
"Total Production Index for Washington, D.C.", 9389–1.203

Bechtold, William A.
"Longleaf Pine Resource", 1208–355

Beck, Allen J.
"Profile of Jail Inmates, 1989", 6066–19.62

Becketti, Sean
"Can Losses of Federal Financial Programs Be Reduced?", 9381–1.207

Bednarzik, Robert W.
"Helping Poland Cope with Unemployment", 6722–1.203
"Trade-Sensitive U.S. Industries: Employment Trends and Worker Characteristics", 6366–3.27

Beeman, Robert
"Affirmative Employment Statistics for Executive Branch (Non-Postal) Agencies, as of Sept. 30, 1990", 9842–1.202

Beer and breweries

Index by Subjects and Names

Beer and breweries

Business statistics, detailed data for major industries and economic indicators, *Survey of Current Business*, monthly rpt, 2702–1.14

Consumer Expenditure Survey, food spending by item, household composition, income, age, race, and region, 1980-88, biennial rpt, 1544–30

Consumption of food, dietary composition, and nutrient intake, 1987/88 natl survey, preliminary rpt series, 1356–1

Consumption per capita of selected beverages, 1970s-90, FAS annual circular, 1925–15.3

Consumption, supply, trade, prices, spending, and indexes, by food commodity, 1989, annual rpt, 1544–4

County Business Patterns, 1988: employment, establishments, and payroll, by SIC 2- to 4-digit industry and county, annual State rpt series, 2326–6

County Business Patterns, 1989: employment, establishments, and payroll, by SIC 2- to 4-digit industry and county, annual State rpt series, 2326–8

CPI by component for US city average, and by region, population size, and for 27 metro areas, monthly rpt, 6762–2

Employment, earnings, and hours, by SIC 1- to 4-digit industry, monthly and annual averages, selected years 1909-90, annual rpt, 6744–4

Exports (agricultural) of US, impacts of foreign agricultural and trade policy, with data by commodity and country, 1989, annual rpt, 1924–8

Exports and imports (agricultural) of US, by commodity and country, bimonthly rpt, 1522–1

Exports and imports (agricultural) of US, by detailed commodity and country, 1989, annual rpt, 1524–8

Exports and imports (agricultural) of US, by detailed commodity and country, 1990, semiannual rpt, 1522–4

Exports and imports of beer compared to domestic production and consumption, for 26 countries, mid 1970s-87, article, 9391–1.201

Exports and imports of US, by country and detailed commodity, monthly rpt, 2422–12

Exports and imports of US, by Harmonized System 6-digit commodity and country, 1990, annual rpt, 2424–13

Exports of US, detailed Schedule B commodities with countries of destination, 1990, annual rpt, 2424–10

Grain (feed) consumption, by end use, periodic situation rpt with articles, 1561–4

Grain prices for brewers, rice and corn grits, periodic situation rpt, 1561–8

Grain production, prices, trade, and export inspections by US port and country of destination, by grain type, weekly rpt, 1313–2

Hops production, stocks, use, and US trade by country, monthly rpt, 1313–7

Hops stocks held by growers, dealers, and brewers, 1989-91, semiannual press release, 1621–8

Labor productivity, indexes of output, hours, and employment by SIC 2- to 4-digit industry, 1967-89, annual rpt, 6824–1.3

Manufacturing annual survey, 1989: finances and operations, by SIC 2- to 4-digit industry, series, 2506–15

Manufacturing census, 1987: finances and operations, by SIC 2- to 4-digit industry, State, and MSA, with trends from 1849, 2497–1

Manufacturing census, 1987: finances and operations, by type of organization and SIC 2- to 4-digit industry, subject rpt, 2497–5

Occupational injury and illness rates, by SIC 2- to 4-digit industry, 1988-89, annual rpt, 6844–7

Occupational injury and illness rates, by SIC 2- to 4-digit industry, 1989, annual rpt, 6844–1

Pollution (air) emissions factors, by detailed pollutant and source, data compilation, 1990 rpt, 9198–120

Price indexes (producer), by stage of processing and detailed commodity, monthly rpt, 6762–6

Price indexes (producer), by stage of processing and detailed commodity, monthly 1990, annual rpt, 6764–2

Production of beer, monthly rpt, 1313–7

Production, stocks, materials used, and tax-free and taxable removals by State, for beer, monthly rpt, 8486–1.1

Tax (income) returns of corporations, income and tax items by asset size and detailed industry, 1987, annual rpt, 8304–4

Tax (income) returns of corporations, income and tax items by asset size and detailed industry, 1988, annual rpt, 8304–21

Tax rates and revenue of State and local govts, by source and State, 1991 and historical trends, annual rpt, 10044–1

Wholesale trade census, 1987: establishments, sales by customer class, employment, inventories, and expenses, by SIC 2- to 4-digit kind of business, 2407–4

Youth alcohol use, knowledge, attitudes, and info sources, series, 4006–10

Bees and beeswax

see Honey and beekeeping

Behavior

see Intelligence levels

see Mental health and illness

see Sexual behavior

see Social sciences

Behavioral sciences

see Anthropology

see Psychology

see Social sciences

see Sociology

Behrens, John O.

"Singular Fact: The Single Audit Program Works", 10042–1.204

Beier, Ken R.

"Predicting Employment Tax Compliance: Further Analysis of the SVC-i Employer Survey", 8304–8.1

Belgium

Agricultural exports of high-value commodities, indexes and sales by commodity, world area, and country, 1960s-86, 1528–323

Agricultural production, prices, and trade, by country, 1970s-90, and forecast 1991, annual world region rpt, 1524–4.4

Agricultural production, trade, and policies in foreign countries, summary data by country, 1989-90, annual factbook, 1924–12

Agricultural trade of US, by detailed commodity and country, 1989, annual rpt, 1524–8

Agricultural trade of US, by detailed commodity and country, 1990, semiannual rpt, 1522–4

AID loans repayment status and terms by program and country, and status of predecessor agency loans, quarterly rpt, 9912–3

Businesses (foreign) activity in US, income tax returns, assets, and income statement items, by industry div and selected country, 1986-87, article, 8302–2.205

Dollar exchange rates of selected foreign countries, weekly chartbook, 9365–1.5

Economic and military aid and loans from US and intl agencies, by program and country, FY46-90, annual rpt, 9914–5

Economic and monetary trends, compounded annual rates of change for US and 10 major trading partners, quarterly rpt, 9391–7

Economic conditions in USSR, Eastern Europe, OECD, and selected other countries, 1960s-90, annual rpt, 9114–4

Economic conditions, income, production, prices, employment, and trade, 1991 periodic country rpt, 2046–4.59

Economic conditions, policy, and trade practices, by country, 1988-90, annual rpt, 21384–5

Economic, social, political, and geographic summary data, by country, 1991, annual factbook, 9114–2

Exports and imports of NATO members with PRC, by country, 1987-90, annual rpt, 7144–14

Exports and imports of OECD members, by country, 1989, annual rpt, 7144–10

Exports and imports of US, by Harmonized System 6-digit commodity and country, 1990, annual rpt, 2424–13

Exports and imports of US, by selected country, country group, and commodity group, 1990, annual rpt, 2044–37

Exports and imports of US, by transport mode, country, and SITC 1- to 3-digit commodity, 1990, annual rpt, 2424–12

Exports and imports of US with EC by country, and total agricultural trade, selected years 1958-90, annual rpt, 7144–7

Exports of US, detailed Schedule B commodities with countries of destination, 1990, annual rpt, 2424–10

GNP and GNP growth for OECD members, by country, 1980-90, annual rpt, 7144–8

Human rights conditions in 170 countries, and US economic and military aid, 1990, annual rpt, 21384–3

Intl transactions of US with 9 countries, 1986-88, *Survey of Current Business*, monthly rpt, annual table, 2702–1.26

Labor conditions, union coverage, and work accidents, 1991 annual country rpt, 6366–4.18

Multinatl US firms and foreign affiliates finances and operations, by industry and world area of parent firm, 1989 benchmark survey, preliminary annual rpt, 2704–5

Index by Subjects and Names

Multinatl US firms foreign affiliates, income statement items by country and world area, 1986, biennial article, 8302–2.212

Nuclear power generation in US and 20 countries, monthly rpt, 3162–24.10

Nuclear power plant capacity, generation, and operating status, by plant and foreign and US location, 1990 and projected to 2030, annual rpt, 3164–57

Oil production, trade, use, and stocks, by selected country and country group, monthly rpt, 3162–42

Paper (coated groundwood) from 5 countries at less than fair value, injury to US industry, investigation with background financial and operating data, 1991 rpt, 9886–14.336

Paper (coated groundwood) from 9 countries at less than fair value, injury to US industry, investigation with background financial and operating data, 1991 rpt, 9886–14.306

Tax revenue, by level of govt and type of tax, for OECD countries, mid 1960s-89, annual rpt, 10044–1.2

UN voting record and share of votes in agreement with US, by issue, country, and world area, 1990, annual rpt, 7004–18

see also under By Foreign Country in the "Index by Categories"

Belize

Agricultural exports of high-value commodities, indexes and sales by commodity, world area, and country, 1960s-86, 1528–323

Agricultural trade of US, by detailed commodity and country, 1989, annual rpt, 1524–8

Agricultural trade of US, by detailed commodity and country, 1990, semiannual rpt, 1522–4

AID economic aid to developing countries, obligations and disbursements by country, quarterly rpt, 9912–4

AID loans repayment status and terms by program and country, and status of predecessor agency loans, quarterly rpt, 9912–3

Economic and military aid and loans from US and intl agencies, by program and country, FY46-90, annual rpt, 9914–5

Economic and social conditions of developing countries from 1960s, and Intl Dev Cooperation Agency and AID activities and funding, FY90-92, annual rpt, 9904–4

Economic, social, political, and geographic summary data, by country, 1991, annual factbook, 9114–2

Exports and imports of US, by transport mode, country, and SITC 1- to 3-digit commodity, 1990, annual rpt, 2424–12

Exports of US, detailed Schedule B commodities with countries of destination, 1990, annual rpt, 2424–10

Human rights conditions in 170 countries, and US economic and military aid, 1990, annual rpt, 21384–3

Investment (direct) incentives of Caribbean Basin Initiative, economic impacts, with finances and employment by country, 1984-90, 2048–141

Military aid of US, arms sales, and training programs costs and budget requests, by program, world region, and country, FY90-92, annual rpt, 7144–13

UN voting record and share of votes in agreement with US, by issue, country, and world area, 1990, annual rpt, 7004–18

Belkindas, Misha

"USSR: Gross National Products Accounts, 1985", 2326–18.59

Bell Operating Companies

Fiber optics and copper wire mileage and access lines, and fiber systems investment, by telecommunications firm, 1985-90, annual rpt, 9284–18

Finances and operations, detail for telephone firms, 1989, annual rpt, 9284–6

Finances and operations of local and long distance firms, subscribership, and charges, late 1970s-91, semiannual rpt, 9282–7

Local telephone rates and low-income subsidies, by region, company, and city, 1980s-90, semiannual rpt, 9282–8

Belleville, Ill.

see also under By SMSA or MSA in the "Index by Categories"

Bellingham, Wash.

Housing vacancy rates for single and multifamily units and mobile homes, by city and ZIP code, 1991, annual MSA rpt, 9304–21.3

see also under By SMSA or MSA in the "Index by Categories"

Beloit, Wis.

see also under By SMSA or MSA in the "Index by Categories"

Belongia, Michael T.

"Alternative Measures of Money as Indicators of Inflation: A Survey and Some New Evidence", 9391–1.202

"Monetary Policy and the Farm/Nonfarm Price Ratio: A Comparison of Effects in Alternative Models", 9391–1.217

Benedict, M. Beth

"Accessibility and Effectiveness of Care Under Medicaid", 4652–1.210

Benhabib, Jess

"Homework in Macroeconomics: Household Production and Aggregate Fluctuations", 9383–20.5

Benin

Agricultural exports of high-value commodities, indexes and sales by commodity, world area, and country, 1960s-86, 1528–323

Agricultural trade of US, by detailed commodity and country, 1989, annual rpt, 1524–8

Agricultural trade of US, by detailed commodity and country, 1990, semiannual rpt, 1522–4

AID economic aid to developing countries, obligations and disbursements by country, quarterly rpt, 9912–4

AID loans repayment status and terms by program and country, and status of predecessor agency loans, quarterly rpt, 9912–3

Dairy imports, consumption, and market conditions, by sub-Saharan Africa country, 1961-88, 1528–321

Economic and military aid and loans from US and intl agencies, by program and country, FY46-90, annual rpt, 9914–5

Economic and social conditions of developing countries from 1960s, and Intl Dev Cooperation Agency and AID activities and funding, FY90-92, annual rpt, 9904–4

Berger, Louis, International, Inc.

Economic conditions, income, production, prices, employment, and trade, 1990 periodic country rpt, 2046–4.7

Economic, social, political, and geographic summary data, by country, 1991, annual factbook, 9114–2

Exports and imports of US, by commodity and country, 1970-89, world area rpt, 9116–1.6

Exports and imports of US, by transport mode, country, and SITC 1- to 3-digit commodity, 1990, annual rpt, 2424–12

Exports of US, detailed Schedule B commodities with countries of destination, 1990, annual rpt, 2424–10

Human rights conditions in 170 countries, and US economic and military aid, 1990, annual rpt, 21384–3

Military aid of US, arms sales, and training programs costs and budget requests, by program, world region, and country, FY90-92, annual rpt, 7144–13

UN voting record and share of votes in agreement with US, by issue, country, and world area, 1990, annual rpt, 7004–18

see also under By Foreign Country in the "Index by Categories"

Bennett, Claudette E.

"Black Population in the U.S.: March 1989-90", 2546–1.450

Bennett, D. Gordon

"Impact of Elderly In-Migration on Private and Public Economic Development Efforts in Predominantly Rural Areas Along the South Atlantic Coast", 2068–38

Bennett, Paul

"Evidence on the Influence of Financial Changes on Interest Rates and Monetary Policy", 9385–8.73

Benson, Peter

"Diversity of Private Schools. Schools and Staffing Survey", 4836–3.7

"Private Schools in the U.S.: A Statistical Profile, with Comparisons to Public Schools", 4838–47

Benston, George J.

"Potential Diversification and Bank Acquisition Prices", 9371–10.57

Benton Harbor, Mich.

see also under By SMSA or MSA in the "Index by Categories"

Benzyl paraben

see Chemicals and chemical industry

Bergen County, N.J.

Wages by occupation, for office and plant workers, 1990 survey, periodic MSA rpt, 6785–11.1

see also under By SMSA or MSA in the "Index by Categories"

Berger, Allen N.

"Loan Commitments and Bank Risk Exposure", 9377–9.105

"Measurement and Efficiency Issues in Commercial Banking", 9366–6.265

"Risk-Based Capital and Deposit Insurance Reform", 9377–9.109

Berger, Louis, International, Inc.

"Promoting Trade and Investment in Constrained Environments: AID Experience in Latin America and the Caribbean", 9916–3.63

Bering Sea

Bering Sea

Birds (waterfowl) coastal population and breeding success, for murre and kittiwake in Bering Sea colonies, 1979-89, 5738–31

Environmental conditions and oil dev impacts for Alaska OCS, compilation of papers, series, 2176–1

Fish catch in excess of domestic processor needs, and use of estimates for Alaska fishing rights allocation, 1984-90, GAO rpt, 26113–523

Ice conditions of Bering Sea and Alaska north coast, monthly rpt, 2182–5

Oil and gas OCS leases environmental and socioeconomic impact and coastal area description, 1991 final statement, 5736–1.24

Research activities of Pacific Marine Environmental Lab, and bibl, FY90, annual rpt, 2144–21

Tide height and time daily at coastal points, forecast 1992, annual rpt, 2174–2.5

Berkeley, Calif.

see also under By City in the "Index by Categories"

Berkeley Planning Associates

"Improving the Quality of Training Under JTPA", 6406–10.1

"JTPA Staffing and Staff Training at the State and SDA Levels", 6406–10.2

Berkovec, James A.

"Changes in the Cost of Equity Capital for Bank Holding Companies and the Effects on Raising Capital", 9366–6.274

Berkowitz, Monroe

"U.S. Worker Rehabilitation in International Perspective", 6722–1.242

Berman, Matthew

"Alaska Statewide and Regional Economic and Demographic Systems: Effects of OCS Exploration and Development, 1990", 5736–5.11

Bermuda

Agricultural exports of US, impacts of foreign agricultural and trade policy, with data by commodity and country, 1989, annual rpt, 1924–8

Agricultural trade of US, by detailed commodity and country, 1989, annual rpt, 1524–8

Agricultural trade of US, by detailed commodity and country, 1990, semiannual rpt, 1522–4

Businesses (foreign) activity in US, income tax returns, assets, and income statement items, by industry div and selected country, 1986-87, article, 8302–2.205

Economic and military aid and loans from US and intl agencies, by program and country, FY46-90, annual rpt, 9914–5

Economic, social, political, and geographic summary data, by country, 1991, annual factbook, 9114–2

Exports and imports of US, by transport mode, country, and SITC 1- to 3-digit commodity, 1990, annual rpt, 2424–12

Exports of US, detailed Schedule B commodities with countries of destination, 1990, annual rpt, 2424–10

Multinatl US firms and foreign affiliates finances and operations, by industry and world area of parent firm, 1989 benchmark survey, preliminary annual rpt, 2704–5

Multinatl US firms foreign affiliates, income statement items by country and world area, 1986, biennial article, 8302–2.212

Berries

see Fruit and fruit products

Berry, Janice T.

"Fertilizer Summary Data, 1990", 9804–5

Bertelson, Daniel F.

"Forest Statistics for East Oklahoma Counties, 1986", 1206–39.4

Beryllium

see Metals and metal industries

Beske, Alan E.

"Distribution and Abundance of Golden Eagles and Other Raptors in Campbell and Converse Counties, Wyoming", 5506–12.1

Best, G. Ronnie

"Soil-Vegetation Correlations in Selected Wetlands and Uplands of North-central Florida", 5506–10.11

Bethlehem, Pa.

see also under By SMSA or MSA in the "Index by Categories"

Betting

see Gambling

see Pari-mutuel wagering

Beverages

Cherry juice and concentrate from 2 countries at less than fair value, injury to US industry, investigation with background financial and operating data, 1991 rpt, 9886–14.308

Consumer Expenditure Survey, food spending by item, household composition, income, age, race, and region, 1980-88, biennial rpt, 1544–30

Consumer Expenditure Survey, household income by source, and itemized spending, by selected characteristics and region, 1988-89, annual rpt, 6764–5

Consumption of food, dietary composition, and nutrient intake, 1987/88 natl survey, preliminary rpt series, 1356–1

Consumption per capita of selected beverages, 1970s-90, FAS annual circular, 1925–15.3

Consumption, supply, trade, prices, spending, and indexes, by food commodity, 1989, annual rpt, 1544–4

Containers (beverage) natl deposit law proposal, public views, with State deposit laws effectiveness, 1970s-89, GAO rpt, 26113–494

County Business Patterns, 1988: employment, establishments, and payroll, by SIC 2- to 4-digit industry and county, annual State rpt series, 2326–6

County Business Patterns, 1989: employment, establishments, and payroll, by SIC 2- to 4-digit industry and county, annual State rpt series, 2326–8

CPI by component for US city average, and by region, population size, and for 27 metro areas, monthly rpt, 6762–2

Employment, earnings, and hours, by SIC 1- to 4-digit industry, monthly and annual averages, selected years 1909-90, annual rpt, 6744–4

Exports (agricultural) of high-value commodities, indexes and sales value by commodity, world area, and country, 1960s-86, 1528–323

Exports and imports (agricultural) of US, by commodity and country, bimonthly rpt, 1522–1

Index by Subjects and Names

Exports and imports (agricultural) of US, by detailed commodity and country, 1989, annual rpt, 1524–8

Exports and imports (agricultural) of US, by detailed commodity and country, 1990, semiannual rpt, 1522–4

Exports and imports between US and outlying areas, by detailed commodity and mode of transport, 1990, annual rpt, 2424–11

Exports and imports of US, by country and detailed commodity, monthly rpt, 2422–12

Exports and imports of US, by Harmonized System 6-digit commodity and country, 1990, annual rpt, 2424–13

Exports and imports of US, by selected country, country group, and commodity group, 1990, annual rpt, 2044–37

Exports and imports of US, by transport mode, country, and SITC 1- to 3-digit commodity, 1990, annual rpt, 2424–12

Exports of US, detailed Schedule B commodities with countries of destination, 1990, annual rpt, 2424–10

Foreign and US fresh and processed fruit, vegetable, and nut production and trade, FAS monthly circular with articles, 1925–34

Households food and beverage spending and per capita consumption, by food and beverage type, 1980s-90, article, 1702–1.212

Manufacturing census, 1987: finances and operations, by SIC 2- to 4-digit industry, State, and MSA, with trends from 1849, 2497–1

Manufacturing census, 1987: finances and operations, by type of organization and SIC 2- to 4-digit industry, subject rpt, 2497–5

Multinatl US firms and foreign affiliates finances and operations, by industry and world area of parent firm, 1989 benchmark survey, preliminary annual rpt, 2704–5

Nutrient, caloric, and waste composition, detailed data for raw, processed, and prepared foods, 1991 rpt, 1356–3.15

Occupational injury and illness rates, by SIC 2- to 4-digit industry, 1988-89, annual rpt, 6844–7

Occupational injury and illness rates, by SIC 2- to 4-digit industry, 1989, annual rpt, 6844–1

OECD trade, total and for 4 major countries, and US trade by country, by commodity, 1970-89, world area rpt series, 9116–1

Orange juice (frozen) cold storage stocks, by census div, 1990, annual rpt, 1631–11

Orange juice processing plants evaporating capacity, for Mexico by plant and location, 1991, article, 1925–34.214

Orange juice production, use, exports, and stocks, by country, 1985-91, article, 1925–34.231

Pineapple (canned fruit and juice) production and exports, by country, 1988-91, annual article, 1925–34.216

Pineapple (canned fruit and juice) production and exports, for 2 countries, forecast 1991, semiannual article, 1925–34.243

Index by Subjects and Names

Bibliographies

Price indexes (producer), by stage of processing and detailed commodity, monthly rpt, 6762–6

Price indexes (producer), by stage of processing and detailed commodity, monthly 1990, annual rpt, 6764–2

Soviet Union GNP by component and industry sector, and CIA estimation methods, 1950s-87, 23848–223

Statistical Abstract of US, 1991 annual data compilation, 2324–1.3; 2324–1.27

Tax (income) returns of corporations, income and tax items by asset size and detailed industry, 1987, annual rpt, 8304–4

Youth ability to distinguish among beverages with and without alcoholic content, 1991 survey, 4006–10.2

see also Beer and breweries

see also Coffee

see also Liquor and liquor industry

see also Soft drink industry and products

see also Tea

see also Wine and winemaking

Bezirganian, Steve D.

"U.S. Affiliates of Foreign Companies: Operations in 1989", 2702–1.214

Bhutan

Agricultural exports of high-value commodities, indexes and sales by commodity, world area, and country, 1960s-86, 1528–323

Background Notes, summary social, political, and economic data, 1990 rpt, 7006–2.42

Economic and military aid and loans from US and intl agencies, by program and country, FY46-90, annual rpt, 9914–5

Economic, social, political, and geographic summary data, by country, 1991, annual factbook, 9114–2

Exports and imports of US, by transport mode, country, and SITC 1- to 3-digit commodity, 1990, annual rpt, 2424–12

Human rights conditions in 170 countries, and US economic and military aid, 1990, annual rpt, 21384–3

UN voting record and share of votes in agreement with US, by issue, country, and world area, 1990, annual rpt, 7004–18

see also under By Foreign Country in the "Index by Categories"

Bianchi, Suzanne

"Family Disruption and Economic Hardship: The Short-Run Picture for Children", 2546–20.17

Bibliographies

Accident deaths and injuries of children by cause, and victimization, rates by race, sex, and age, 1979-88, chartbook, 4108–56

Acid rain and air pollution environmental impacts, and methods of neutralizing acidified water bodies, summary research rpt series, 5506–5

Acid rain research activities of Natl Acid Precipitation Assessment Program, 1990 annual rpt, 14354–1

AIDS virus infection prevalence in developing countries, by sex, selected city, urban-rural location, and country, 1991, semiannual rpt, 2322–4

Airline market entry impacts of carrier control of airports, facility and aircraft availability, noise regulation, and other barriers, late 1980s and projected to 1997, 7308–199.8

Alaska OCS environmental conditions and oil dev impacts, compilation of papers, series, 2176–1

Alcohol abuse research, treatment programs, and patient characteristics and health effects, quarterly journal, 4482–1

Atlantic Oceanographic and Meteorological Lab research activities and bibl, FY90, annual rpt, 2144–19

Auto (electric-powered) R&D activity and DOE funding shares, FY90, annual rpt, 3304–2

Birds (migratory forest dwellers) population status, literature review, 1940s-80s, 1208–382

Cancer cases, deaths, and survival rates, by sex, race, age, and body site, 1973-88, annual rpt, 4474–35

China urbanization, bibl, 1991 working paper, 2326–18.60

Coastal and estuarine pollutant concentrations in fish, shellfish, and environment, series, 2176–3

Coastal and riparian areas environmental conditions, fish, wildlife, use, and mgmt, for individual ecosystems, series, 5506–9

Crime, criminal justice admin and enforcement, and public opinion, data compilation, 1991 annual rpt, 6064–6

Criminal justice issues, series, 6066–25

Developing countries counterpart funds impacts on US aid programs effectiveness and domestic economic and fiscal condition, literature review, 1991 rpt, 9918–21

Developing countries economic, population, and agricultural data, US and other aid sources, and AID activity, country rpt series, 9916–12

Disasters and natl security incidents and mgmt, with data by major event and State, 1991 annual rpt, 9434–6

Drug (prescription) advertising direct to consumer, benefits and problems, review of studies published 1984-91, GAO rpt, 26131–86

Drug abuse and treatment, research on biological and behavioral factors and addiction potential of new drugs, 1990 annual conf, 4494–11

Drug abuse, prevention, treatment, and health research results, as of 1990, triennial rpt, 4498–68

Earthquakes of San Andreas Fault system, location and seismic characteristics, by event, 1769-1989, 5668–123

Economic indicators relation to interest rates and financial market regulatory and structural changes, 1950s-80s, technical paper, 9385–8.73

Employment and unemployment current statistics and articles, Monthly Labor Review, 6722–1

Environmental and natural resource data sources, and aerial survey R&D rpts, quarterly listing, 9502–7

Fish and shellfish catch, life cycles, and environmental needs, for selected coastal species and regions, series, 5506–8

Fishery mgmt and R&D, Fed Govt grants by project and State, and rpts, 1990, annual listing, 2164–3

Foreign countries *Background Notes,* summary social, political, and economic data, series, 7006–2

Foreign countries economic and social conditions, working paper series, 2326–18

Foreign countries statistical abstracts and rpts, 1991 annual listing, 2324–1

Forest Service mgmt of public lands and resources dev, environmental, economic, and social impacts of alternative programs, projected to 2040, 1208–24

Franchise business opportunities by firm and kind of business, and sources of aid and info, 1990 annual listing, 2104–7

Geothermal resources, power plant capacity and operating status, leases, and wells, by location, 1960s-94, 3308–87

Global climate change economic impacts, projected to 2100 with background data for 1980s, 3028–5

Global climate change trends and contributing gases levels, Federal and intl data collection activities, mgmt, and inventory, 1990 rpt, 3028–4

Great Lakes Environmental Research Lab activities, FY90 annual rpt, 2144–26

Hazardous substances and conditions occupational exposure and health effects, literature review, series, 4246–4

Hazardous substances and conditions occupational exposure, measurement, and proposed standards, series, 4246–1

Health care cost control measures and insurance provisions, for Germany, France, and Japan, 1960s-91, GAO rpt, 26121–437

Health condition and quality of life measurement, rpts and other info sources, quarterly listing, 4122–1

Homelessness issues, population at risk, contributing factors, and Federal funding for services and prevention, with bibl, 1991 compilation of papers, 25928–9

Households composition, income, benefits, and labor force status, Survey of Income and Program Participation methodology, working paper series, 2626–10

Import restraint elimination impacts on US economy by selected sector, model description and results, 1988, 9886–4.174

Indian (Navajo and Hopi) relocation program activities and caseloads, 1975-90, 16008–5

Insurance (health) natl coverage alternative proposals and indicators of need, 1989, 4658–54

Lead levels in environment, sources of emissions and exposure, and health effects, literature review, 1990 rpt, 9198–84

Lumber production, prices by region and State, trade by country, and use, by species and product, 1960-88, annual rpt, 1204–29

Marine Fisheries Review, US and foreign fisheries resources, dev, mgmt, and research, quarterly journal, 2162–1

Marine mammals and birds population and distribution, by species and northeast Pacific Ocean location, literature and data base review, 1950s-88, 5738–28

Marine mammals protection, Federal and intl regulatory and research activities, 1990, annual rpt, 14734–1

Materials (advanced structural) devs, use, and R&D funding, for ceramics, metal alloys, polymers, and composites, 1960s-80s and projected to 2000, 5608–162

Bibliographies

Medicaid demonstration projects evaluation, for 6 States, 1988 rpt, 4658–45

Minerals (strategic) supply and characteristics of individual deposits, by country, commodity rpt series, 5666–21

Minerals resources of Alaska, and geologic characteristics, compilation of papers, 1989, annual rpt, 5664–15

Minerals resources of Alaska, production, oil and gas leases, reserves, and exploratory wells, with maps and bibl, 1989, annual rpt, 5664–11

Morbidity and Mortality Weekly Report, infectious notifiable disease cases by age, race, and State, and deaths, 1930s-90, annual rpt, 4204–1

Motorcycle helmet use and mandatory use laws impacts on accident casualties and costs, literature review, 1956-89, GAO rpt, 26113–537

NOAA Environmental Research Labs rpts, FY90, annual listing, 2144–25

Occupational deaths data collection and processing by States, Natl Inst for Occupational Safety and Health guidelines, 1990 rpt, 4248–89

Occupational safety and health research and demonstration grants by State, and project listing, FY90, annual rpt, 4244–2

Oil and gas OCS reserves, and leasing and dev activity, periodic regional rpt series, 5736–3

Oil enhanced recovery research contracts of DOE, project summaries, funding, and bibl, quarterly rpt, 3002–14

Pacific Marine Environmental Lab research activities and bibl, FY90, annual rpt, 2144–21

PL 480 food aid impacts on developing countries economic dev, literature review, 1979-88, 9918–20

Pollutants contributing to climate change, atmospheric concentrations by monitoring site, 1989, annual rpt, 2144–28

Radiation exposure of population near Hanford, Wash, nuclear plant, with methodology, 1944-66, series, 3356–5

Radiation from electronic devices, incidents by type of device, and FDA control activities, 1990, annual rpt, 4064–13

Radioactive waste from nuclear power plants, storage pending opening of permanent repository, safety and costs of alternative methods, projected 1991-2050, 14818–1

Smoking and smokeless tobacco use, attitudes, and smoking intervention research spending and results, with bibl, 1960s-90, 4478–195

Solar photovoltaic R&D sponsored by DOE, projects, funding, and rpts, FY90, annual listing, 3304–20

States statistical abstracts and rpts, 1991 annual listing, 2324–1

Storms (severe) natl lab research activities and bibl, FY90, annual rpt, 2144–20

Tax (income) returns processing, IRS workload forecasts, compliance, and enforcement, data compilation, 1991 annual rpt, 8304–8

Telecommunications and Info Natl Admin rpts, FY90, annual listing, 2804–3

see also CD-ROM catalogs and guides

see also Computer data file guides

see also Government publications lists

Bicycles

Accident deaths and injuries of children by cause, and victimization, rates by race, sex, and age, 1979-88, chartbook, 4108–56

Accident deaths and rates, by cause, age, sex, race, and State, 1988, US Vital Statistics annual rpt, 4144–2

Accidents (fatal), circumstances, and characteristics of persons and vehicles involved, 1990, semiannual rpt, 7762–11

Accidents (fatal), deaths, and rates, by circumstances, characteristics of persons and vehicles involved, and location, 1989, annual rpt, 7764–10

Accidents and deaths of pedestrians and bicyclists involving autos, 1980-90, annual fact sheet, 7766–15.5

Accidents, casualties, circumstances, and characteristics of persons and vehicles involved, 1989, annual rpt, 7764–18

Accidents involving consumer products, injuries by severity, victim age, and detailed product, 1990, annual rpt, 9164–6

Child accident deaths and death rates, by cause, age, sex, race, and State, 1980-85, 4108–54

Exports and imports of US, by country and detailed commodity, monthly rpt, 2422–12

Exports and imports of US, by Harmonized System 6-digit commodity and country, 1990, annual rpt, 2424–13

Exports of US, detailed Schedule B commodities with countries of destination, 1990, annual rpt, 2424–10

Housing and households characteristics, unit and neighborhood quality, and journey to work by MSA location, for 11 MSAs, 1984 survey, supplement, 2485–8

Housing and households detailed characteristics, and unit and neighborhood quality, by location, 1985, biennial rpt supplement, 2485–13

Manufacturing annual survey, 1989: finances and operations, by SIC 2- to 4-digit industry, series, 2506–15

Manufacturing finances and operations, by SIC 2- to 4-digit industry, forecast 1991, annual rpt, 2044–28

Price indexes (producer), by stage of processing and detailed commodity, monthly rpt, 6762–6

Price indexes (producer), by stage of processing and detailed commodity, monthly 1990, annual rpt, 6764–2

Safety programs, and accidents, casualties, and damage, by mode of transport, 1989, annual rpt, 7304–19

Thefts, and value of property stolen and recovered, by property type, 1990, annual rpt, 6224–2.1

Travel patterns, personal and household characteristics, and auto and public transport use, 1990 survey, series, 7556–6

Biddlecom, Ann E.

"AIDS Knowledge and Attitudes of Black Americans: U.S., 1990. Provisional Data from the National Health Interview Survey", 4146–8.208

"AIDS Knowledge and Attitudes of Hispanic Americans: U.S. 1990. Provisional Data from the National Health Interview Survey", 4146–8.209

Index by Subjects and Names

Bilingual education

Activities, structure, and effectiveness of bilingual education and English immersion programs, 1984-88 longitudinal study, 4808–27

Digest of Education Statistics, 1991 annual data compilation, 4824–2

Discrimination in education, indicators for service delivery and discipline, by State, 1988, biennial rpt, 4804–33

Education Dept programs funding, operations, and effectiveness, FY90, annual rpt, 4804–5

Enrollment, funding, and services of bilingual education programs, by State, FY85-89, series, 4808–20

Enrollment in bilingual education, and Education Dept activities and funding by program, by State, FY88-90, biennial rpt, 4804–14

Libraries (public) English as second language programs and services, project descriptions and funding, by State, FY87, annual rpt, 4874–10

Billheimer, John W.

"HOV Lane Violation Study", 7308–203

Billings, Mont.

see also under By SMSA or MSA in the "Index by Categories"

Biloxi, Miss.

see also under By SMSA or MSA in the "Index by Categories"

Binghamton, N.Y.

see also under By SMSA or MSA in the "Index by Categories"

Biologic drug products

Biotechnology commercial applications, industry finances and capitalization, patents, and govt support, for US, Japan, and EC, late 1970s-91, 26358–248

County Business Patterns, 1988: employment, establishments, and payroll, by SIC 2- to 4-digit industry and county, annual State rpt series, 2326–6

County Business Patterns, 1989: employment, establishments, and payroll, by SIC 2- to 4-digit industry and county, annual State rpt series, 2326–8

Epoetin alfa treatment for anemia in kidney dialysis patients, dosages, costs, Medicare reimbursement, and facility income effects, 1989, 4008–113

Exports and imports (agricultural) of US, by detailed commodity and country, 1989, annual rpt, 1524–8

Exports and imports (agricultural) of US, by detailed commodity and country, 1990, semiannual rpt, 1522–4

Exports and imports of US, by Harmonized System 6-digit commodity and country, 1990, annual rpt, 2424–13

Exports of US, detailed Schedule B commodities with countries of destination, 1990, annual rpt, 2424–10

Manufacturing annual survey, 1989: value of shipments, by SIC 4- to 5-digit product class, 2506–15.2

Manufacturing census, 1987: finances and operations, by SIC 2- to 4-digit industry, State, and MSA, with trends from 1849, 2497–1

Manufacturing census, 1987: finances and operations, by type of organization and SIC 2- to 4-digit industry, subject rpt, 2497–5

Index by Subjects and Names

Manufacturing finances and operations, by SIC 2- to 4-digit industry, forecast 1991, annual rpt, 2044–28

Occupational injury and illness rates, by SIC 2- to 4-digit industry, 1988-89, annual rpt, 6844–7

Occupational injury and illness rates, by SIC 2- to 4-digit industry, 1989, annual rpt, 6844–1

Prescriptions for drugs, by drug type and brand, and for new drugs, 1989, annual rpt, 4064–12

Price indexes (producer), by stage of processing and detailed commodity, monthly rpt, 6762–6

Price indexes (producer), by stage of processing and detailed commodity, monthly 1990, annual rpt, 6764–2

Veterinary Services Natl Labs activities, biologic drug products evaluation and disease testing, FY90, annual rpt, 1394–17

see also Vaccination and vaccines

Biological sciences

- Alaska OCS environmental conditions and oil dev impacts, compilation of papers, series, 2176–1
- Carbon dioxide in atmosphere, measurement, methodology, and research results, series, 3006–11
- Degrees (PhD) in science and engineering, by field, instn, employment prospects, sex, race, and other characteristics, 1960s-90, annual rpt, 9627–30
- Degrees awarded in higher education, by level, field, race, and sex, 1988/89 with trends from 1978/79, biennial rpt, 4844–17
- Degrees awarded in science and engineering, by field, level, and sex, 1966-89, 9627–33
- DOE R&D projects and funding at natl labs, universities, and other instns, FY91, annual summary rpt, 3004–18.4
- Employment and other characteristics of science and engineering PhDs, by field and State, 1989, biennial rpt, 9627–18
- Fed Govt aid to higher education and nonprofit instns for R&D and related activities, by field, instn, agency, and State, FY89, annual rpt, 9627–17
- High school advanced placement for college credit, programs by selected characteristics and school control, 1984-86, 4838–46
- Higher education course completions, by detailed program, sex, race, and instn type, for 1972 high school class, as of 1984, 4888–4
- Higher education grad programs enrollment in science and engineering, by field, source of funds, and characteristics of student and instn, 1975-89, annual rpt, 9627–7
- Land Mgmt Bur wildlife mgmt activities and funding, acreage by habitat type, and scientific staff, State rpt series, 5726–7
- Land Mgmt Bur wildlife mgmt activities and funding, acreage, staff, and plans, habitat study series, 5726–6
- Lead levels in environment, sources of emissions and exposure, and health effects, literature review, 1990 rpt, 9198–84

NASA R&D funding to higher education instns, by field, instn, and State, FY90, annual listing, 9504–7

NIH grants for R&D, training, construction, and medical libraries, by location and recipient, FY90, annual listings, 4434–7

Oceanographic research and distribution activities of World Data Center A by country, and cruises by ship, 1989, annual rpt, 2144–15

R&D equipment of higher education instns, acquisition and service costs, condition, and financing, by field and subfield, 1988-90, triennial survey series, 9627–27

R&D facilities for biological and medical sciences, space and equipment adequacy, needs, and funding by source, by instn type, 1990, biennial rpt, 4434–17

R&D funding by Fed Govt, by field, performer type, agency, and State, FY89-91, annual rpt, 9627–20

R&D funding by higher education instns and federally funded centers, by field, instn, and State, FY89, annual rpt, 9627–13

Research on population and reproduction, Federal funding by project, FY89, annual listing, 4474–9

Research on population and reproduction, Natl Inst of Child Health and Human Dev funding and activities, 1990, annual rpt, 4474–33

Research on wildlife and plants, habitat study series, 5506–13

Wetlands (riparian) acreage, and Bur of Land Mgmt activities, mgmt plans, and scientific staff, State rpt series, 5726–8

see also Biotechnology

see also Botany

see also Genetics

see also Physiology

see also Zoology

Biological warfare agents

see Chemical and biological warfare agents

Biomass energy

Consumption of wood, waste, and alcohol fuels, by end-use sector and region, 1989, 3166–6.56

Consumption of wood, waste, and alcohol fuels, by region, 1980-88, annual rpt, 3164–74.7

Developing countries energy use, and economic and environmental impacts, by fuel type, world area, and country, 1980s-90, 26358–232

DOE R&D projects and funding at natl labs, universities, and other instns, FY91, annual summary rpt, 3004–18.4

Electric power plants certification applications filed with FERC, for small production and cogeneration facilities, FY80-90, annual listing, 3084–13

Natl Energy Strategy plans for conservation and pollution reduction, impacts of technology and regulation proposals, projected 1990-2030, 3166–6.47

Natl Energy Strategy plans for renewable energy dev, supply projected under alternative cost and capacity use assumptions, 1990-2030, 3166–6.50

Pollution (air) contributing to global warming, emissions factors and control costs, by pollutant and source, 1990 rpt, 9198–124

Birds and bird conservation

Prices and spending for fuel, by type, end-use sector, and State, 1989, annual rpt, 3164–64

Supply, demand, and prices, by fuel type and end-use sector, alternative projections 1989-2010, annual rpt, 3164–75

Supply, demand, and prices, by fuel type and end-use sector, projections and underlying assumptions, 1990-2010, annual rpt, 3164–90

see also Alcohol fuels

see also Gasohol

see also Wood fuel

Biotechnology

- Agricultural research and education grants, USDA competitive awards by program and recipient, FY90, annual listing, 1764–1
- Budget of US, obligations and authority by function, agency, and program, with summaries, analyses, and historical tables, FY92, annual rpt, 104–2
- Cell cultures with genetic abnormalities, availability and cultures shipped, 1990-91, biennial listing, 4474–23
- Commercial applications of biotechnology, industry finances and capitalization, patents, and govt support, for US, Japan, and EC, late 1970s-91, 26358–248
- Dairy industry biotechnology devs, and bST impacts on farm finances and Federal support programs, 1980s and projected to 1998, 26358–237
- DOE R&D projects and funding at natl labs, universities, and other instns, FY91, annual summary rpt, 3004–18.4
- Farm financial and marketing conditions, forecast 1991, annual conf, 1004–16
- Fed Govt financial and nonfinancial domestic aid, 1991 base edition with supplements, annual listing, 104–5
- Gene amplification thermal cyclers and subassemblies from UK at less than fair value, injury to US industry, investigation with background financial and operating data, 1990 rpt, 9886–14.301; 9886–14.327
- HHS financial aid, by program, recipient, State, and city, FY90, annual regional listings, 4004–3
- Manufacturing finances and operations, by SIC 2- to 4-digit industry, forecast 1991, annual rpt, 2044–28
- NIH activities, funding by program and recipient type, staff, and clinic patients, by inst, FY90, annual rpt, 4434–3
- Reproduction and population research, Fed Govt funding by project, FY89, annual listing, 4474–9
- Sugarcane clones yields, stability, and fungi resistance, 1990/91, annual rpt, 1704–2

Birch and Davis Associates, Inc.

"Prepaid Medicaid Chartbook: Selected Enrollment and Utilization Data", 4108–29

Bird, Alan R.

"Status of the Nonmetro Labor Force, 1987", 1598–264

Birds and bird conservation

Acid rain and air pollution environmental impacts, and methods of neutralizing acidified water bodies, summary research rpt series, 5506–5

Alaska coastal waterfowl population and breeding success, for murre and kittiwake in Bering Sea colonies, 1979-89, 5738–31

Birds and bird conservation

Alaska OCS environmental conditions and oil dev impacts, compilation of papers, series, 2176–1

Alaska rural areas population characteristics, and energy resources dev effects, series, 5736–5

Badlands Natl Park juniper forest and mixed grass rangeland habitats, bird population and species diversity by season, 1991 rpt, 1208–364

Coastal and riparian areas environmental conditions, fish, wildlife, use, and mgmt, for individual ecosystems, series, 5506–9

Coastal areas environmental and socioeconomic conditions, and potential impact of oil and gas OCS leases, final statement series, 5736–1

Crane (sandhill) hunting activity and permits, by State and county, 1989/90-1990/91, annual rpt, 5504–31

Crane (whooping) migration roosting sites and population, by wetland type, 1990 rpt, 5508–111

Criminal case processing in Federal district courts, and dispositions, by offense, 1980-89, annual rpt, 6064–31

Duck breeding population, by species, State, and Canada Province, 1990-91 with trends from 1955, annual rpt, 5504–30

Duck hunting stamps philatelic and sales info, 1991/92, annual supplement, 5504–25

Eagles (bald) Great Lakes population, breeding, and research status, 1990 conf, 14648–26

Endangered animals and plants conservation spending of Federal agencies and States, by species, FY90, annual rpt, 5504–33

Endangered animals and plants population status and mgmt activity, by species, 1990, biennial rpt, 5504–35

Environmental Quality, status of problems, protection programs, research, and intl issues, 1991 annual rpt, 484–1

Fish and Wildlife Service restoration programs funding, land purchases, and project listing, by State, FY89, annual rpt, 5504–1

Forest Service mgmt of public lands and resources dev, environmental, economic, and social impacts of alternative programs, projected to 2040, 1208–24

Geese pre-migration feeding behavior impacts of aircraft disturbance, for 3 species at Izembek Lagoon, Alaska, 1970s-88, 5738–23

Idaho Snake River area birds of prey, rodent, and vegetation distribution and characteristics, research results, 1990, annual rpt, 5724–14

Land Mgmt Bur wildlife mgmt activities and funding, acreage, staff, and plans, habitat study series, 5726–6

Migratory Bird Conservation Commission wetlands habitat acquisition, funding by State, FY92, press release, 5306–4.11

Migratory forest-dwelling birds population status, literature review, 1940s-80s, 1208–382

Migratory waterfowl refuge and breeding area acreage under Fish and Wildlife Service mgmt, by site and State, as of Sept 1991, annual rpt, 5504–8

Mourning dove population, by hunting and nonhunting State, 1966-91, annual rpt, 5504–15

North Carolina environmental and socioeconomic conditions, and impacts of proposed OCS oil and gas exploration, 1970s-90 and projected to 2020, 5738–22

Owl (northern spotted) conservation impacts on Pacific Northwest timber industry, 1980s and alternative projections to 2000, hearing, 21168–45

Owl (northern spotted) conservation impacts on Pacific Northwest timber sales of Forest Service, 1990 hearing, 21168–47

Owl (northern spotted) population and reproduction rate on lands open and closed to logging, estimation methodology, 1987, 1208–342

Pacific Ocean marine mammal and bird population density and distribution, by species and selected northeast location, literature and data base review, 1950s-88, 5738–28

Pollutants health effects for animals by species and for humans, and environmental levels, for selected substances, series, 5506–14

Population of birds, surveys design and trend analysis methodology, 1988 conf, 5508–108

Public lands acreage, grants, use, revenues, and allocations, by State, FY90, annual rpt, 5724–1.2

Research of State fish and wildlife agencies, federally funded wildlife projects and costs by species and State, 1990, annual listing, 5504–24

Research on fish and wildlife population, habitat, and mgmt, technical rpt series, 5506–12

Research on wildlife and plants, habitat study series, 5506–13

Timber in Montana, harvest methods impacts on bird population by species, 1989-90, 1208–372

Washington State marine sanctuaries proposal, environmental and economic impacts, with background data, 1984-89, 2178–30

Waterfowl (migratory) hunter harvest, age and sex ratios by species, State, and flyway, 1986-90, annual rpt, 5504–32

Waterfowl (migratory) hunter harvest and unretrieved kills, and duck stamps sold, by species, State, Canada Province, and flyway, 1989-90, annual rpt, 5504–28

Waterfowl (migratory) population, habitat conditions, and flight forecasts, for Canada and US by region, 1991 and trends from 1955, annual rpt, 5504–27

Waterfowl (migratory) refuge and breeding area acreage, and agreements and payments to farmers under Water Bank Program, by State, 1972-91, annual rpt, 1804–21

Waterfowl (migratory) wetlands acreage, and agreements and payments to farmers under Water Bank Program, monthly rpt, 1802–5

Wetlands acreage, resources, soil and water properties, and conservation efforts, by wetland type, State rpt series, 5506–11

Wetlands wildlife and migratory bird habitat acquisition, funding by State, FY92, press release, 5306–4.8

Woodcock population from 1968, and hunter harvest, by State, 1991, annual rpt, 5504–11

Index by Subjects and Names

see also Poultry industry and products

Birdsey, Richard A.

"Impacts of U.S. Forest Management Policies on the Carbon Cycle", 1004–16.1

Birkhead, Guthrie S.

"New York State's Two-Dose Schedule for Measles Immunization", 4042–3.227

Birmingham, Ala.

Drug test results at arrest, by drug type, offense, and sex, for selected urban areas, quarterly rpt, 6062–3

Housing and households characteristics, unit and neighborhood quality, and journey to work by MSA location, for 11 MSAs, 1984 survey, supplement, 2485–8

Housing and households characteristics, 1988 survey, MSA fact sheet, 2485–11.4

see also under By City and By SMSA or MSA in the "Index by Categories"

Birnbaum, Howard

"Savings Estimate for a Medicare Insured Group", 4652–1.244

Birth control

see Abortion

see Contraceptives

see Family planning

see Sexual sterilization

Birth defects

Cancer (childhood) survivors risk of miscarriage, stillbirth, and birth defects, by chemotherapy and radiotherapy exposure, study, 1991 article, 4472–1.233

Cases and rates for birth defects, by type, 1979-80 and 1986-87, article, 4202–7.203

Child health condition and services use, 1990 chartbook, 4108–49

Deaths and rates, by cause and age, preliminary 1989-90, US Vital Statistics annual rpt, 4144–7

Deaths and rates, by cause, provisional data, monthly rpt, 4142–1.2

Deaths and rates, by detailed cause and demographic characteristics, 1988 and trends from 1900, US Vital Statistics annual rpt, 4144–2

Fetal alcohol syndrome medical care and research costs, 1985, 4048–35

Fetal alcohol syndrome prevention program for Indians, evaluation, 1988-89 local area study, article, 4042–3.239

Food aid program of USDA for women, infants, and children, health services need of participants, for Rhode Island, 1983-84, article, 4042–3.247

Head Start handicapped enrollment, by handicap, State, and for Indian and migrant programs, 1987/88, annual rpt, 4604–1

Hospital discharges and length of stay, by diagnosis, patient and instn characteristics, procedure performed, and payment source, 1988, annual rpt, 4147–13.107

Hospital discharges and length of stay by region and diagnosis, and procedures performed, by age and sex, 1989, annual rpt, 4146–8.198

Hospital discharges by detailed diagnostic and procedure category, primary diagnosis, and length of stay, by age, sex, and region, 1988, annual rpt, 4147–13.105; 4147–13.108

Indian Health Service facilities and use, and Indian health and other characteristics, by IHS region, 1980s-89, annual chartbook, 4084–7

Index by Subjects and Names

Indian Health Service, tribal, and contract facilities hospitalization, by diagnosis, age, sex, and service area, FY89, annual rpt, 4084–5

Infant death rate, by cause, region, and race, 1980-87, article, 4202–7.208

Lead levels in environment, sources of emissions and exposure, and health effects, literature review, 1990 rpt, 9198–84

Medicaid coverage effects on prenatal care use and birth outcomes, charges, and Medicaid payments, for California, 1983, article, 4652–1.241

Minority group health condition, services use, costs, and indicators of services need, 1950s-88, 4118–55

Pollutants health effects for animals by species and for humans, and environmental levels, for selected substances, series, 5506–14

Pollutants reproductive health and fetal dev effects, with production, trade, and Federal regulatory activities by selected substance, 1980s-90, GAO rpt, 26131–90

Syphilis (congenital) cases, by region, State, and selected city, 1978-90 and trends from FY41, 4205–42

see also under By Disease in the "Index by Categories"

Birthplace

- Deaths in US, by State of occurrence and birth, and birthplace abroad, 1988, US Vital Statistics annual rpt, 4144–2.1
- Hispanic Americans in counties bordering Mexico, by selected characteristics, 1980, Current Population Rpt, 2546–2.159
- Immigrant and nonimmigrant visas of US issued and refused, by class, issuing office, and nationality, FY89, annual rpt, 7184–1
- Immigrants admitted to US, by country of birth, FY81-90, annual rpt, 6264–4
- Immigrants admitted to US, by occupational group and country of birth, preliminary FY90, annual table, 6264–1
- Immigrants in US, population characteristics and fertility, by birthplace and compared to native born, 1980s, Current Population rpt, 2546–2.162
- Refugee arrivals and resettlement in US, by age, sex, sponsoring agency, State, and country, monthly rpt, 4692–2
- Refugee arrivals in US by world area of origin and State of settlement, and Federal aid, FY90-91 and proposed FY92 allocations, annual rpt, 7004–16
- *Statistical Abstract of US*, 1991 annual data compilation, 2324–1.1

Births

- Alaska rural areas population characteristics, and energy resources dev effects, series, 5736–5
- Births and rates, by characteristics of birth, infant, and parents, 1989 and trends from 1940, US Vital Statistics advance annual rpt, 4146–5.123
- Births and rates by mother's age, and fertility rates, by mother's education, child's race, census div, and State, 1980 and 1985, 4147–21.49
- Births and rates, by State, preliminary 1989-90, US Vital Statistics annual rpt, 4144–7

Births, fertility rates, and childless women, by selected characteristics, 1990, annual Current Population Rpt, 2546–1.455

Certificates of birth, death, marriage, and divorce, and fetal death and abortion rpts, 1989 natl standard revisions, 4147–4.27

China economic indicators and reform issues, with background data, 1950s-90, compilation of papers, 23848–155

Health condition and health care resources, use, and spending, 1950s-89, annual data compilation, 4144–11

Hospital discharges and length of stay by region and diagnosis, and procedures performed, by age and sex, 1989, annual rpt, 4146–8.198

Indian Health Service and tribal hospital admissions, length of stay, beds, and births, by facility and service area, FY70-89, annual rpt, 4084–4

Indian Health Service and tribal hospital capacity, use, and births, by area and facility, quarterly rpt, 4082–1

Indian Health Service facilities and use, and Indian health and other characteristics, by IHS region, 1980s-89, annual chartbook, 4084–7

Indian Health Service facilities, funding, operations, and Indian health and other characteristics, 1950s-90, annual chartbook, 4084–1

Medicaid coverage effects on prenatal care use and birth outcomes, charges, and Medicaid payments, for California, 1983, article, 4652–1.241

Medicaid reimbursement of hospitals under prospective payment system, effect on maternity case-mix for South Carolina, various periods 1985-87, article, 4652–1.206

Military health care facilities of DOD in US and abroad, admissions, beds, outpatient visits, and births, by service branch, quarterly rpt, 3542–15

Minority group and women health condition, services use, payment sources, and health care labor force, by poverty status, 1940s-89, chartbook, 4118–56

Minority group health condition, services use, costs, and indicators of services need, 1950s-88, 4118–55

Poor women's pregnancies, by whether intended, outcome, contraceptives use, marital status, and race, 1985-86 local area study, article, 4042–3.241

Population size and characteristics, 1969-88, Current Population Rpt, biennial rpt, 2546–2.161

State and Metro Area Data Book, 1991 data compilation, 2328–54

Statistical Abstract of US, 1991 annual data compilation, 2324–1.2

Vital and Health Statistics series: reprints of monthly rpt supplements, 4147–24

Vital statistics provisional data, monthly rpt, 4142–1

see also Abortion

see also Birth defects

see also Birthplace

see also Births out of wedlock

see also Birthweight

see also Fertility

see also Fetal deaths

see also Infant mortality

Birthweight

see also Maternity

see also Maternity benefits

see also Obstetrics and gynecology

see also Prenatal care

see also Teenage pregnancy

Births out of wedlock

- Abortions, by method, patient characteristics, and State, 1972-88, article, 4202–7.207
- Abortions, by method, pregnancy history, and other characteristics of woman, 1988, US Vital Statistics annual rpt, 4146–5.120
- Births and rates, by characteristics of birth, infant, and parents, 1989 and trends from 1940, US Vital Statistics advance annual rpt, 4146–5.123
- Births, fertility rates, and childless women, by selected characteristics, 1990, annual Current Population Rpt, 2546–1.455
- Families with children by householder marital status, and birth rates for all and unmarried women, 1950s-90, 4818–5
- Fetal deaths and rates, by characteristics of mother and birth, 1988, US Vital Statistics annual rpt, 4144–2.3
- Foreign countries family composition, poverty status, labor conditions, and welfare indicators and needs, by country, 1960s-88, hearing, 23846–4.30
- Income (household) and poverty status under alternative income definitions, by recipient characteristics, 1990, annual Current Population Rpt, 2546–6.69
- Minority group health condition, services use, costs, and indicators of services need, 1950s-88, 4118–55
- Poor women's pregnancies, by whether intended, outcome, contraceptives use, marital status, and race, 1985-86 local area study, article, 4042–3.241
- Population size and characteristics, 1969-88, Current Population Rpt, biennial rpt, 2546–2.161
- Smoking during pregnancy, by age, race, education, marital status, and birth order, 1970s-80s, article, 4042–3.203
- *State and Metro Area Data Book*, 1991 data compilation, 2328–54
- *Statistical Abstract of US*, 1991 annual data compilation, 2324–1.2
- Teenage mothers child support awards, payment status, health insurance inclusion, and govt aid for collection, by selected characteristics, 1987, 4698–5

Birthweight

- Births and rates, by characteristics of birth, infant, and parents, 1989 and trends from 1940, US Vital Statistics advance annual rpt, 4146–5.123
- Chlamydia infection among pregnant women, and pregnancy outcomes, 1986-88 local area study, article, 4042–3.240
- Deaths and rates, by cause and age, preliminary 1989-90, US Vital Statistics annual rpt, 4144–7
- Deaths and rates, by cause, provisional data, monthly rpt, 4142–1.2
- Deaths and rates, by detailed cause and demographic characteristics, 1988 and trends from 1900, US Vital Statistics annual rpt, 4144–2
- Education natl goals progress indicators, by State, 1991, annual rpt, 15914–1

Birthweight

Food aid program of USDA for women, infants, and children, enrollment of children at high risk of poor nutrition, for Tennessee, 1982-84, article, 4042–3.216

Food aid program of USDA for women, infants, and children, health services need of participants, for Rhode Island, 1983-84, article, 4042–3.247

Food aid program of USDA for women, infants, and children, prenatal participation effect on Medicaid costs and birth outcomes, for 5 States, 1987-88, 1368–2

Health condition and health care resources, use, and spending, 1950s-89, annual data compilation, 4144–11

Health condition and services use, for children, 1990 chartbook, 4108–49

Hispanic Americans low birthweight cases and inadequate prenatal care, 1980s, article, 4042–3.234

Indian Health Service facilities and use, and Indian health and other characteristics, by IHS region, 1980s-89, annual chartbook, 4084–7

Indian Health Service facilities, funding, operations, and Indian health and other characteristics, 1950s-90, annual chartbook, 4084–1

Low birthweight prevention and other health improvement goals and recommended activities for 2000, with trends 1970s-80s, 4048–10

Medicaid coverage effects on prenatal care use and birth outcomes, charges, and Medicaid payments, for California, 1983, article, 4652–1.241

Minority group health condition, services use, costs, and indicators of services need, 1950s-88, 4118–55

Montana health care access indicators, 1989 hearing, 23898–6

Prenatal care nutritional and educational programs for women at risk of preterm delivery, and rate of anemia and low-weight births, 1985-86, article, 4042–3.235

State and Metro Area Data Book, 1991 data compilation, 2328–54

Statistical Abstract of US, 1991 annual data compilation, 2324–1.2

Bismarck, N.Dak.

see also under By SMSA or MSA in the "Index by Categories"

Bismuth

see Metals and metal industries

Bixby, Ann K.

"Benefits and Beneficiaries Under Public Employee Retirement Systems, FY88", 4742–1.212

"Overview of Public Social Welfare Expenditures, FY88", 4742–1.202

"Public Social Welfare Expenditures, FY88", 4742–1.209

Black Americans

Abortions, by method, pregnancy history, and other characteristics of woman, 1988, US Vital Statistics annual rpt, 4146–5.120

Agriculture census, 1987: farms, farmland, production, finances, and operator characteristics, by county, final State rpt series, 2331–1

AIDS cases by risk group, race, sex, age, State, and MSA, and deaths, monthly rpt, 4202–9

AIDS public knowledge, attitudes, info sources, and testing, for blacks, 1990 survey, 4146–8.208

Alcohol use and abuse by women related to race, employment status, and other characteristics, 1981 local area study, article, 4042–3.212

Births and rates, by characteristics of birth, infant, and parents, 1989 and trends from 1940, US Vital Statistics advance annual rpt, 4146–5.123

Cancer cases, by race, income, education, and area population density, for 3 metro areas, 1978-82, article, 4472–1.210

Cancer cases, deaths, and survival rates, by sex, race, age, and body site, 1973-88, annual rpt, 4474–35

Cancer death rates of minorities, by body site, age, sex, and substate area, 1950s-80, atlas, 4478–78

Census of Population and Housing, 1990: population and housing characteristics, households, and land area, by county, subdiv, and place, State rpt series, 2551–1

Census of Population and Housing, 1990: population and housing selected characteristics, by region, press release, 2328–74

Census of Population and Housing, 1990: voting age and total population by race, and housing units, by block, redistricting counts required under PL 94-171, State CD-ROM series, 2551–6

Census of Population and Housing, 1990: voting age and total population by race, and housing units, by county and city, redistricting counts required under PL 94-171, State summary rpt series, 2551–5

Census of Population, 1990: metro area population by race, Hispanic origin, and MSA, press release, 2328–75

Census of Population, 1990: population by detailed Native American, Asian, and Pacific Islander group, race, region, and State, with data for 1980, press release, 2328–72

Census of Population, 1990: population by race and detailed Hipanic origin, region, and State, with data for 1980, press release, 2328–73

Census of Population, 1990: population by race, Hispanic origin, region, census div, and State, with data for 1980, fact sheet, 2326–20.2

Census of Population, 1990: post-enumeration survey results compared to census counts, by race, sex, city, county, and State, press release, 2328–69

Child accident deaths and death rates, by cause, age, sex, race, and State, 1980-85, 4108–54

Child mineral levels in hair, serum, and urine, for healthy and anemic black children, local area study, 1991 article, 4042–3.248

Consumer Income, socioeconomic characteristics of persons, families, and households, detailed cross-tabulations, Current Population Rpt series, 2546–6

Crime, criminal justice admin and enforcement, and public opinion, data compilation, 1991 annual rpt, 6064–6

Crimes, arrests, and rates, by offense, offender characteristics, population size, and jurisdiction, 1990, annual rpt, 6224–2.1; 6224–2.2

Index by Subjects and Names

Deaths and rates, by detailed cause and demographic characteristics, 1988 and trends from 1900, US Vital Statistics annual rpt, 4144–2

Drug abuse prevalence among minorities, related health effects and crime, treatment, and research status and needs, mid 1970s-90, 4498–72

Drug, alcohol, and cigarette use, by selected characteristics, 1990 survey, biennial rpt, 4494–5

Drug and alcohol abuse treatment facilities, services, use, funding, staff, and client characteristics, 1989, biennial rpt, 4494–10

Education data compilation, 1991 annual rpt, 4824–2

Educational attainment, by sociodemographic characteristics and location, 1989 and trends from 1940, biennial Current Population Rpt, 2546–1.452

Employment, unemployment, and labor force characteristics, by region, State, and selected metro area, 1990, annual rpt, 6744–7

Fed Equal Opportunity Recruitment Program activity, and employment by sex, race, pay grade, and occupational group, FY90, annual rpt, 9844–33

Fed Govt employment of minorities and women, and compliance with EEOC standards, by occupation and agency, FY88-92, GAO rpt, 26119–342

Financial instns location relation to ZIP code area income and minority population, by instn type for 5 cities, 1977-89, article, 9377–1.208

FmHA loans, by type, borrower characteristics, and State, quarterly rpt, 1182–8

FmHA loans, by type, borrower, race, and State, quarterly rpt, 1182–5

Food aid program of USDA for women, infants, and children, participants by race, State, and Indian agency, Apr 1990, annual rpt, 1364–16

Foster care placement of black children whose parents abuse drugs, by placement reason and outcome, and household and parent characteristics, 1986-90, 4008–114

Health condition and health care resources, use, and spending, 1950s-89, annual data compilation, 4144–11

Health condition improvement and disease prevention goals and recommended activities for 2000, with trends 1970s-80s, 4048–10

Health condition of minorities, services use, costs, and indicators of services need, 1950s-88, 4118–55

Health condition, services use, payment sources, and health care labor force, for minorities and women by poverty status, 1940s-89, chartbook, 4118–56

Households and family characteristics, by location, 1990, annual Current Population Rpt, 2546–1.447

Households and housing characteristics, unit and neighborhood quality, and journey to work by MSA location, for 11 MSAs, 1984 survey, supplement, 2485–8

Households and housing detailed characteristics, and unit and neighborhood quality, by location, 1987, biennial rpt supplement, 2485–13

Index by Subjects and Names

Black students

Households and housing detailed characteristics, and unit and neighborhood quality, by location, 1989, biennial rpt, 2485–12

Households and housing detailed characteristics, and unit and neighborhood quality, MSA surveys, series, 2485–6

Households composition, income, benefits, and labor force status, Survey of Income and Program Participation methodology, working paper series, 2626–10

Housing inventory change from 1973, by reason, unit and household characteristics, and location, 1983 survey, biennial rpt, 2485–14

Hypertension risk for women, by age and race, aggregate 1976-80, article, 4042–3.231

Immigrants in US, population characteristics and fertility, by birthplace and compared to native born, 1980s, Current Population rpt, 2546–2.162

Income (household) and poverty status under alternative income definitions, by recipient characteristics, 1990, annual Current Population Rpt, 2546–6.69

Jail adult and juvenile population, employment, spending, instn conditions, and inmate programs, by county and facility, 1988, regional rpt series, 6068–144

Labor force status, by race, detailed Hispanic origin, and sex, quarterly rpt, 6742–18

Labor force status of black women, employment by age and education, and women's and families earnings, 1980-90, fact sheet, 6564–1.2

Labor force, wages, hours, and payroll costs, by major industry group and demographic characteristics, *Survey of Current Business*, monthly rpt, 2702–1.8

Living arrangements, family relationships, and marital status, by selected characteristics, 1990, annual Current Population Rpt, 2546–1.449

Marriages, divorces, and rates, by characteristics of spouses, State, and county, 1987 and trends from 1920, US Vital Statistics annual rpt, 4144–4

Military personnel strengths, for active duty enlisted and officers, by sex and race, 1970s-90, GAO rpt, 26123–325

Poor black men's drug and condom use and sexual behavior, local area study, 1991 article, 4042–3.254

Population size and characteristics, historical index to *Current Population Rpts,* 1991 listing, 2546–2.160

Population social and economic characteristics, for Black Americans, for South and total US, 1989-90 and trends from 1969, Current Population Rpt, 2546–1.450

Prisoner admissions by State and for Federal instns, by race, 1926-86, 6068–245

Prisoners, characteristics, and movements, by State, 1989, annual rpt, 6064–26

Science and engineering PhDs, by field, instn, employment prospects, sex, race, and other characteristics, 1960s-90, annual rpt, 9627–30

Science and engineering PhDs employment and other characteristics, by field and State, 1989, biennial rpt, 9627–18

State and local govt employment of minorities and women, by occupation, function, pay level, and State, 1990, annual rpt, 9244–6

State and Metro Area Data Book, 1991 data compilation, 2328–54

Statistical Abstract of US, 1991 annual data compilation, 2324–1

Unemployed displaced black workers, by demographic and current and former employment characteristics, and compared to whites, 1978-86, article, 6722–1.234

Voting and registration, by socioeconomic and demographic characteristics, 1990 congressional election, biennial Current Population Rpt, 2546–1.454

see also Black colleges

see also Black students

see also Racial discrimination

see also Sickle cell anemia

see also under By Race and Ethnic Group in the "Index by Categories"

Black colleges

Agricultural research funding and staffing for USDA, State agencies, and other instns, by topic, FY90, annual rpt, 1744–2

Enrollment, degrees awarded, and finances of predominantly black instns, 1976-89, annual rpt, 4824–2.17

Enrollment of minorities in higher education, degrees, factors affecting participation, and earnings, by race, 1960s-88, 4808–29

Finances, funding sources, enrollment, and student characteristics, for black colleges, with data for Louisiana instns, 1970s-90, hearing, 25258–24

Medical and biological R&D facilities, space and equipment adequacy, needs, and funding by source, by instn type, 1990, biennial rpt, 4434–17

Navy research grants, by recipient type, FY90, annual rpt, 3804–13.3

R&D and related funding of Fed Govt to higher education and nonprofit instns, by field, instn, agency, and State, FY89, annual rpt, 9627–17

R&D funding by higher education instns and federally funded centers, by field, instn, and State, FY89, annual rpt, 9627–13

Science and engineering grad enrollment, by field, source of funds, and characteristics of student and instn, 1975-89, annual rpt, 9627–7

Student aid funding and participation, by Federal program, instn type and control, and State, various periods 1959-89, annual rpt, 4804–28

Black, Herbert T.

"Update on U.S. Coalbed Methane Production", 3162–4.201

Black lung disease

Assistance of Fed Govt, by type, program, agency, and State, FY90, annual rpt, 2464–2

Beneficiaries deaths, erroneous benefit payments, and use of SSA and other sources of death info, by agency, 1990, GAO rpt, 26121–406

Benefits and beneficiaries by recipient type, from 1970, and by State, 1989, annual rpt, 4744–3.7

Benefits and coverage under workers compensation, by type of program and insurer, and State, 1987-88, annual article, 4742–1.207

Benefits by county, FY90, annual regional listings, 4004–3

Benefits to miners, widows, and dependents, with data by State reported quarterly, monthly rpt, 4742–1.6; 4742–1.13

Compensation benefits and claims by State, trust fund receipts by source, and disbursements, 1990, annual rpt, 6504–3

Deaths and rates, by detailed cause and demographic characteristics, 1988 and trends from 1900, US Vital Statistics annual rpt, 4144–2

Epidemiology, diagnosis, and treatment of occupational respiratory diseases, for selected industries and work settings, 1988 conf, 4248–90

Statistical Abstract of US, 1991 annual data compilation, 2324–1.12

Tax (excise) collections of IRS, by source, quarterly rpt, 8302–2.1

Tax (excise) collections of IRS for black lung benefits, quarterly rpt, 8302–1

Trust funds financial condition, for black lung, monthly rpt, 8102–9.10

Black market

see Black market currency

see Underground economy

Black market currency

Argentina black-market dollar exchange rate relationship with official rate and other economic indicators, model description and results, 1991 technical paper, 9366–7.261

Black students

Computer use at home, school, and work, by purpose and selected user characteristics, 1989, Current Population Rpt, 2546–2.158

Condition of Education, detail for elementary, secondary, and higher education, 1920s-90 and projected to 2001, annual rpt, 4824–1

Digest of Education Statistics, 1991 annual data compilation, 4824–2

Discrimination in education, indicators for service delivery and discipline, by State, 1988, biennial rpt, 4804–33

Eighth grade class of 1988: educational performance and conditions, characteristics, attitudes, activities, and plans, natl longitudinal survey, series, 4826–9

Elementary and secondary students educational performance, and factors affecting proficiency, by selected characteristics, 1988 natl assessments, subject rpt series, 4896–7

Elementary and secondary students educational performance, and factors affecting proficiency, by selected characteristics, 1990 natl assessments, subject rpt series, 4896–8

Enrollment, by grade, instn type and control, and student characteristics, 1989 and trends from 1947, annual Current Population Rpt, 2546–1.453

High school class of 1972: education, employment, and family characteristics, activities, and attitudes, natl longitudinal study, series, 4836–1

Black students

Higher education degrees awarded, by level, field, race, and sex, 1988/89 with trends from 1978/79, biennial rpt, 4844–17

Higher education enrollment of minorities, degrees, factors affecting participation, and earnings, by race, 1960s-88, 4808–29

Nuclear engineering enrollment and degrees granted by instn and State, and grad placement, by student characteristics, 1990, annual rpt, 3004–5

Radiation protection and health physics enrollment and degrees granted by instn and State, and grad placement, by student characteristics, 1990, annual rpt, 3004–7

Science and engineering grad enrollment, by field, source of funds, and characteristics of student and instn, 1975-89, annual rpt, 9627–7

Student aid funding and participation, by Federal program, instn type and control, and State, various periods 1959-89, annual rpt, 4804–28

see also under By Race and Ethnic Group in the "Index by Categories"

Black, T. N.

"National Urban Mass Transportation Statistics: 1989 Section 15 Annual Report", 7884–4

Blalock, Joseph B.

"Resolution Costs of Thrift Failures", 9292–4.202

Blase, Melvin G.

"Edible and Industrial Rapeseed Oils", 1004–16.1

Blaylock, James R.

"Construction of True Cost of Food Indexes from Estimated Engel Curves", 1598–275

Bleiwas, Donald I.

"Availability of Primary Nickel in Market-Economy Countries. A Minerals Availability Appraisal", 5606–4.28

"Cobalt Availability: A Minerals Availability Appraisal", 5606–4.29

Blind

Education (special) enrollment by age, staff, funding, and needs, by type of handicap and State, 1989/90, annual rpt, 4944–4

Educational service delivery and discipline, and discrimination indicators by State, 1988, biennial rpt, 4804–33

Head Start handicapped enrollment, by handicap, State, and for Indian and migrant programs, 1987/88, annual rpt, 4604–1

Libraries for blind and handicapped, readership, circulation, staff, funding, and holdings, FY90, annual listing, 26404–3

Vending facilities run by blind on Federal and non-Federal property, finances and operations by agency and State, FY90, annual rpt, 4944–2

Veterans health care, patients, visits, costs, and operating beds, by VA and contract facility, and region, quarterly rpt, 8602–4

see also Aid to blind

see also Supplemental Security Income

Blisard, William N.

"Construction of True Cost of Food Indexes from Estimated Engel Curves", 1598–275

Blocks, city

Census Bur geographic levels of data coverage, maps, and reference products, 1991 pamphlet, 2326–7.79

Census of Population and Housing, 1990: voting age and total population by race, and housing units, by block, redistricting counts required under PL 94-171, State CD-ROM series, 2551–6

Blood

AIDS cases at VA health care centers by sex, race, risk factor, and facility, and AIDS prevention and treatment issues, quarterly rpt, 8702–1

Exports and imports of US, by Harmonized System 6-digit commodity and country, 1990, annual rpt, 2424–13

Hepatitis B and C screening of blood donors, PHS guidelines, 1991 rpt, 4206–2.40

Iron levels in blood, indicators for Hispanics by detailed origin, 1970s-88, 4147–2.111

Lead levels in environment, sources of emissions and exposure, and health effects, literature review, 1990 rpt, 9198–84

Shipments of blood and blood products, 1989 Annual Survey of Manufactures, 2506–15.2

Transfusion recipients AIDS cases, by age group, sex, race, and presence of other risk factors, monthly rpt, 4202–9

Transfusion recipients hepatitis cases, by strain, 1988 and trends from 1966, 4205–2

see also Blood diseases and disorders

see also Blood pressure

see also Septicemia

Blood diseases and disorders

Agent Orange exposure of Vietnam veterans, and other factors relation to dev of rare cancers, 1984-88, 4208–33

Anemia incidence and low-weight birth rates, for women at risk of preterm delivery, in prenatal care nutritional and educational programs, 1985-86, article, 4042–3.235

Anemia treatment of kidney dialysis patients with Epoetin alfa, dosages, costs, Medicare reimbursement, and facility income effects, 1989, 4008–113

Black children's mineral levels in hair, serum, and urine, for healthy and anemic children, local area study, 1991 article, 4042–3.248

Cancer death rates of minorities, by body site, age, sex, and substate area, 1950s-80, atlas, 4478–78

Cancer death, survival, and incidence rates, by type and body site, 1974 and 1986, article, 4472–1.232

Canine lymphoma risk relation to herbicide exposure and other factors, and implications for humans, 1984-88, article, 4472–1.220

Cases of acute and chronic conditions, disability, absenteeism, and health services use, by selected characteristics, 1987, CD-ROM, 4147–10.177

Deaths and rates, by cause, provisional data, monthly rpt, 4142–1.2

Deaths and rates, by detailed cause and demographic characteristics, 1988 and trends from 1900, US Vital Statistics annual rpt, 4144–2

Hemophiliac and blood transfusion AIDS virus infection prevalence, natl survey methodology and pretest results, 1989, 4148–30

Hemophiliac and coagulation disorder AIDS cases, by age group, sex, race, and presence of other risk factors, monthly rpt, 4202–9

Hemophiliacs blood clotting products costs, and Medicare reimbursement under prospective payment system, FY91-92, 17206–1.10

HHS financial aid, by program, recipient, State, and city, FY90, annual regional listings, 4004–3

Hodgkin's disease and other cancers cases, deaths, and survival rates, by sex, race, and age, 1973-88, annual rpt, 4474–35

Hospital discharges and length of stay, by diagnosis, patient and instn characteristics, procedure performed, and payment source, 1988, annual rpt, 4147–13.107

Hospital discharges and length of stay by region and diagnosis, and procedures performed, by age and sex, 1989, annual rpt, 4146–8.198

Hospital discharges by detailed diagnostic and procedure category, primary diagnosis, and length of stay, by age, sex, and region, 1988, annual rpt, 4147–13.105; 4147–13.108

Indian Health Service, tribal, and contract facilities hospitalization, by diagnosis, age, sex, and service area, FY89, annual rpt, 4084–5

Lead levels in environment, sources of emissions and exposure, and health effects, literature review, 1990 rpt, 9198–84

Leukemia and other cancers cases, deaths, and survival rates, by sex, race, and age, 1973-88, annual rpt, 4474–35

Lymphoma deaths and rates, for Hodgkin's disease and other types, provisional data, monthly rpt, 4142–1.2

Natl Heart, Lung, and Blood Inst activities, and grants by recipient and location, FY90 and disease trends from 1940, annual rpt, 4474–15

Non-Hodgkin's lymphoma and other cancers cases, deaths, and survival rates, by sex, race, and age, 1973-88, annual rpt, 4474–35

Non-Hodgkin's lymphoma cases in areas using phenoxy herbicides, local area study, 1985-88, article, 4472–1.207

Non-Hodgkin's lymphoma risk among men with AIDS virus infection, 1981-88 and projected to 1992, article, 4472–1.212

see also Septicemia

see also Sickle cell anemia

see also under By Disease in the "Index by Categories"

Blood poisoning

see Septicemia

Blood pressure

Child heart rate relationship to elevated blood pressure and mothers heart rate, 1971-73, article, 4042–3.232

Heart disease deaths and risk factors, for PRC, Finland, and US, 1980s, article, 4042–3.202

Indians and Alaska Natives preventive health practices, exams by type, and smoking and overweight status, by selected characteristics, 1987, 4186–8.19

see also Hypertension

Index by Subjects and Names

Bloom, Barbara

"Health Insurance and Medical Care: Health of Our Nation's Children, U.S., 1988", 4146–8.192

"Long-Term Care for the Functionally Dependent Elderly. Vital and Health Statistics Series 13", 4147–13.104

Bloomington, Ill.

see also under By SMSA or MSA in the "Index by Categories"

Bloomington, Ind.

see also under By SMSA or MSA in the "Index by Categories"

Blostein, Joel

"Shigellosis from Swimming in a Park Pond in Michigan", 4042–3.224

Blue collar workers

- Earnings, annual average percent changes for selected occupational groups, selected MSAs, monthly rpt, 6782–1.1
- Educational attainment, by sociodemographic characteristics and location, 1989 and trends from 1940, biennial Current Population Rpt, 2546–1.452
- Employment, earnings, and hours, by SIC 1- to 4-digit industry, monthly and annual averages, selected years 1909-90, annual rpt, 6744–4
- Employment, earnings, and hours, monthly press release, 6742–5
- Employment situation, earnings, hours, and other BLS economic indicators, transcripts of BLS Commissioner's monthly testimony, periodic rpt, 23846–4
- Employment, unemployment, and labor force characteristics, by region, State, and selected metro area, 1990, annual rpt, 6744–7
- Fed Govt civilian employees work-years, pay rates, and benefits use and costs, by agency, FY89, annual rpt, 9844–31
- Fed Govt civilian employment and payroll, by occupation, pay grade, sex, agency, and location, 1989, biennial rpt, 9844–4
- Immigrants admitted to US, by occupational group and country of birth, preliminary FY90, annual table, 6264–1
- Income (household, family, and personal), by source, detailed characteristics, and region, 1988-89, annual Current Population Rpt, 2546–6.68
- Income (household, family, and personal), by source, detailed characteristics, and region, 1990, annual Current Population Rpt, 2546–6.70
- Labor hourly costs, by component, industry sector, worker class, and firm size, 1990, annual rpt, 6744–22
- Mineral industries census, 1987: finances and operations, by establishment characteristics, SIC 2- to 4-digit industry, and State, subject rpt, 2517–1
- Puerto Rico economic censuses, 1987: wholesale and retail trade sales by customer class, and employment, by SIC 2- and 3-digit kind of business, subject rpt, 2591–2.2
- State and local govt employment of minorities and women, by occupation, function, pay level, and State, 1990, annual rpt, 9244–6
- Wages, hourly and weekly averages by industry div, monthly press release, 6742–3

Wholesale trade census, 1987: establishments, sales by customer class, employment, inventories, and expenses, by SIC 2- to 4-digit kind of business, 2407–4

Women's employment in skilled manual occupations, and apprenticeships, 1978-89, 6564–1.1

see also Area wage surveys

see also Industry wage surveys

see also Production workers

see also Service workers

see also under By Occupation in the "Index by Categories"

see also under names of specific industries or industry groups

Blue Cross-Blue Shield

- Fed Govt civilian employees and retirees health insurance coverage, by plan, FY89, annual rpt, 9844–35.1; 9844–35.2
- Medicare supplemental private insurance premiums, costs, claims, and benefit provisions, with data by firm, 1988-90, hearing, 21788–198
- Transplant patients immunosuppressive drug coverage under Medicare and other insurance sources, costs, and procedures, 1991 rpt, 26358–246

Blumenthal, Rona M.

"OASDI Beneficiaries by State and County, December 1990", 4744–28

Blumenthal, Sally

"Tax Incentives for Rehabilitating Historic Buildings: FY90 Analysis", 5544–17

Board for International Broadcasting

- Budget of US, authoritative financial statements with appropriations, outlays, and receipts, by category and agency, FY90, annual rpt, 8104–2.1
- Budget of US, obligations and authority by function, agency, and program, with summaries, analyses, and historical tables, FY92, annual rpt, 104–2
- Radio Free Europe and Radio Liberty broadcast and financial data, FY90, annual rpt, 10314–1

Board of Foreign Scholarships

Fulbright-Hays academic exchanges, grants by purpose, and foreign govt share of costs, by country, FY90, annual rpt, 10324–1

Boarding houses

see Rooming and boarding houses

Boards of education

see School boards

Boats and boating

- Coastal areas recreation facilities of Fed Govt and States, visitor and site characteristics, 1987-90 survey, regional rpt series, 2176–9
- County Business Patterns, 1988: employment, establishments, and payroll, by SIC 2- to 4-digit industry and county, annual State rpt series, 2326–6
- County Business Patterns, 1989: employment, establishments, and payroll, by SIC 2- to 4-digit industry and county, annual State rpt series, 2326–8
- Drug, immigration, and fisheries enforcement activities of Coast Guard, 2nd half FY91, semiannual rpt, 7402–4
- Employment, earnings, and hours, by SIC 1- to 4-digit industry, monthly and annual averages, selected years 1909-90, annual rpt, 6744–4

Boats and boating

- Energy use by mode of transport, fuel supply, and demographic and economic factors of vehicle use, 1970s-89, annual rpt, 3304–5
- Exports and imports of US, by country and detailed commodity, monthly rpt, 2422–12
- Exports and imports of US, by Harmonized System 6-digit commodity and country, 1990, annual rpt, 2424–13
- Exports of US, detailed Schedule B commodities with countries of destination, 1990, annual rpt, 2424–10
- Fishery employment, vessels, plants, and cooperatives, by State, 1989 and trends from 1970, annual rpt, 2164–1.10
- Fishing (ocean sport) activities, and catch by species, by angler characteristics and State, annual coastal area rpt series, 2166–17
- Fishing (ocean sport) catch, by species, mode of fishing, and coastal region, 1990, annual rpt, 2164–1.2
- Florida environmental, social, and economic conditions, and impacts of proposed OCS oil and gas leases in southern coastal areas, 1990 compilation of papers, 5738–19
- Great Lakes area economic conditions and outlook, for US and Canada, 1970s-90, 9375–15
- Manatees killed in Florida and other US waters, by cause, 1978-90, annual rpt, 14734–1
- Manufacturing annual survey, 1989: finances and operations, by SIC 2- to 4-digit industry, series, 2506–15
- Manufacturing census, 1987: finances and operations, by SIC 2- to 4-digit industry, State, and MSA, with trends from 1849, 2497–1
- Manufacturing census, 1987: finances and operations, by type of organization and SIC 2- to 4-digit industry, subject rpt, 2497–5
- Manufacturing finances and operations, by SIC 2- to 4-digit industry, forecast 1991, annual rpt, 2044–28
- New York and New Jersey Raritan Bay commercial and sport fishing activity, 1885-1989, article, 2162–1.205
- Northeastern US recreation areas use, mgmt, and tourism dev issues, 1990 conf, 1208–356
- Occupational injury and illness rates, by SIC 2- to 4-digit industry, 1988-89, annual rpt, 6844–7
- Occupational injury and illness rates, by SIC 2- to 4-digit industry, 1989, annual rpt, 6844–1
- Price indexes (producer), by stage of processing and detailed commodity, monthly rpt, 6762–6
- Price indexes (producer), by stage of processing and detailed commodity, monthly 1990, annual rpt, 6764–2
- Public lands acreage, grants, use, revenues, and allocations, by State, FY90, annual rpt, 5724–1.2
- Public lands recreation facilities and use, and Land Mgmt Bur mgmt activities, funding, and plans, State rpt series, 5726–5
- Recalls of recreational boats and engines with safety-related defects, by make, periodic listing, 7402–5

Boats and boating

Recreation (outdoor) coastal facilities, by State, county, estuary, and level of govt, 1972-84, 2178–29

Registrations of boats, and accidents, casualties, and damage by cause, by vessel characteristics and State, 1990, annual rpt, 7404–1

Retail trade census, 1987: finances and employment, for establishments with and without payroll, by SIC 2- to 4-digit kind of business, State, and MSA, 2401–1

Virgin Islands population and housing characteristics, 1990 Census of Population and Housing, press release, 2328–81

see also Barges
see also Ferries
see also Inland water transportation
see also Marine accidents and safety
see also Ships and shipping

Bobbitt, Sharon A.

"Characteristics of Stayers, Movers, and Leavers: Results from the Teacher Followup Survey, 1988-89. Schools and Staffing Survey", 4836–3.5

"Early Estimates. Key Statistics for Public and Private Elementary and Secondary Education, School Year 1990-91", 4834–19

Boca Raton, Fla.

Housing starts and completions authorized by building permits in 40 MSAs, quarterly rpt, 2382–9

see also under By SMSA or MSA in the "Index by Categories"

Body measurements

Colon polyps cases and risk, effects of body mass, 1986-88 local area study, article, 4472–1.206

Lead levels in environment, sources of emissions and exposure, and health effects, literature review, 1990 rpt, 9198–84

see also Birthweight
see also Obesity

Boerstler, Heidi

"Analysis of Nursing Home Capital Reimbursement Systems", 4652–1.236

Bogart, William T.

"Property Taxes, Homeownership Capitalization Rates, and Housing Consumption", 9387–8.252

Bogs

see Wetlands

Boise, Idaho

see also under By City and By SMSA or MSA in the "Index by Categories"

Boldin, Michael D.

"Characterizing Business Cycles with a Markov Switching Model: Evidence of Multiple Equilibria", 9385–8.96

"Sunspots, Asset Bubbles, and the Store of Value Motive in Overlapping Generations Models", 9385–8.90

Bolivia

Agricultural exports of high-value commodities, indexes and sales by commodity, world area, and country, 1960s-86, 1528–323

Agricultural production, trade, and policies in foreign countries, summary data by country, 1989-90, annual factbook, 1924–12

Agricultural trade of US, by detailed commodity and country, 1989, annual rpt, 1524–8

Agricultural trade of US, by detailed commodity and country, 1990, semiannual rpt, 1522–4

AID economic aid to developing countries, obligations and disbursements by country, quarterly rpt, 9912–4

AID loans repayment status and terms by program and country, and status of predecessor agency loans, quarterly rpt, 9912–3

Background Notes, summary social, political, and economic data, 1991 rpt, 7006–2.52

Cocaine and alternative crop production in Andean countries, and impacts on US agricultural exports, with data for Bolivia, 1980s-91, GAO rpt, 26123–366

Cocaine production, eradication, and legal use, worldwide and for South America, 1970s-80s, conf, 4498–74

Economic and military aid and loans from US and intl agencies, by program and country, FY46-90, annual rpt, 9914–5

Economic and social conditions of developing countries from 1960s, and Intl Dev Cooperation Agency and AID activities and funding, FY90-92, annual rpt, 9904–4

Economic conditions, policy, and trade practices, by country, 1988-90, annual rpt, 21384–5

Economic, social, political, and geographic summary data, by country, 1991, annual factbook, 9114–2

Exports and imports of US, by commodity and country, 1970-89, world area rpt, 9116–1.4

Exports and imports of US, by selected country, country group, and commodity group, 1990, annual rpt, 2044–37

Exports and imports of US, by transport mode, country, and SITC 1- to 3-digit commodity, 1990, annual rpt, 2424–12

Exports of US, detailed Schedule B commodities with countries of destination, 1990, annual rpt, 2424–10

Human rights conditions in 170 countries, and US economic and military aid, 1990, annual rpt, 21384–3

Military aid of US, arms sales, and training programs costs and budget requests, by program, world region, and country, FY90-92, annual rpt, 7144–13

Multinatl US firms foreign affiliates, income statement items by country and world area, 1986, biennial article, 8302–2.212

UN voting record and share of votes in agreement with US, by issue, country, and world area, 1990, annual rpt, 7004–18

see also under By Foreign Country in the "Index by Categories"

Bolling, H. Christine

"Peru: An Export Market Profile", 1526–6.14

Bolts

see Hardware

Bombs

Aircraft hijackings, on-board explosions, and other crime, US and foreign incidents, 1985-89, annual rpt, 7504–31

Airport security operations to prevent hijacking, screening results, enforcement actions, and hijacking attempts, 2nd half 1989, semiannual rpt, 7502–5

Homicides, by circumstance, victim and offender relationship, and type of weapon, 1990, annual rpt, 6224–2.1

Incidents of bombing, casualties, and damage, by target, data compilation, 1991 annual rpt, 6064–6.3

Incidents of bombing, damage, and casualties, by target, circumstances, and State, 1990, annual rpt, 6224–5

Law enforcement officer assaults and deaths by circumstances, agency, victim and offender characteristics, and location, 1990, annual rpt, 6224–3

Terrorism (intl) incidents, casualties, and attacks on US targets, by attack type and country, 1990, annual rpt, 7004–22

Terrorism (intl) incidents, casualties, and attacks on US targets, by attack type and world area, 1990, annual rpt, 7004–13

Terrorism incidents in US, related activity, and casualties, by attack type, target, group, and location, 1990, annual rpt, 6224–6

see also Military weapons
see also Nuclear explosives and explosions

Bonds

see Government securities
see Municipal bonds
see Securities
see Surety bonds
see Tax exempt securities

Bonneville Power Administration

Activities of BPA, operations, maintenance, and environmental protection plans, FY90-99, 3228–14

Bonneville Power Admin mgmt of Fed Columbia River Power System, finances, operations, and sales by customer, FY90, annual rpt, 3224–1

Building codes for energy efficiency, effect on house construction practices in BPA service areas, 1987, 3228–15

Electric power capacity and use in Pacific Northwest, by energy source, projected under alternative load and demand cases, 1991-2011, annual rpt, 3224–3

Electric power wholesale purchases of REA borrowers, by borrower, supplier, and State, 1940-89, annual rpt, 1244–5

Energy conservation (housing) program of BPA, activities, cost effectiveness, and participation, series, 3226–1

Energy conservation and resource planning activities of Bonneville Power Admin, FY89-90, 3228–11

Finances and operations of Federal power admins and electric utilities, 1989, annual rpt, 3164–24.2

Finances and sales for Fed Columbia River Power System, summary data, quarterly rpt, 3222–2

Radon indoor air pollution levels in Pacific Northwest, with geological and soil characteristics, by township, 1989 rpt, 5668–114

Sales, revenue, and rates of BPA, by customer and customer type, 1990, semiannual rpt, 3222–1

Bonuses

see Employee bonuses and work incentives

Books and bookselling

Copyrights Register activities, registrations by material type, and fees, FY90 and trends from 1790, annual rpt, 26404–2

County Business Patterns, 1988: employment, establishments, and payroll, by SIC 2- to 4-digit industry and county, annual State rpt series, 2326–6

Index by Subjects and Names

County Business Patterns, 1989: employment, establishments, and payroll, by SIC 2- to 4-digit industry and county, annual State rpt series, 2326–8

Employment, earnings, and hours, by SIC 1- to 4-digit industry, monthly and annual averages, selected years 1909-90, annual rpt, 6744–4

Enterprise Statistics, 1987: finances and operations for companies, by size, level of diversification, form of organization, and industry group, 2329–8

Exports and imports of US, by country and detailed commodity, monthly rpt, 2422–12

Exports and imports of US, by Harmonized System 6-digit commodity and country, 1990, annual rpt, 2424–13

Exports of US, detailed Schedule B commodities with countries of destination, 1990, annual rpt, 2424–10

GPO bookstores, 1991 annual listing, 2304–2

GPO pricing and marketing policies, findings and recommendations, 1990 rpt, 26208–3

Manufacturing annual survey, 1989: finances and operations, by SIC 2- to 4-digit industry, series, 2506–15

Manufacturing census, 1987: finances and operations, by SIC 2- to 4-digit industry, State, and MSA, with trends from 1849, 2497–1

Manufacturing census, 1987: finances and operations, by type of organization and SIC 2- to 4-digit industry, subject rpt, 2497–5

Manufacturing finances and operations, by SIC 2- to 4-digit industry, forecast 1991, annual rpt, 2044–28

Occupational injury and illness rates, by SIC 2- to 4-digit industry, 1988-89, annual rpt, 6844–7

Occupational injury and illness rates, by SIC 2- to 4-digit industry, 1989, annual rpt, 6844–1

OECD trade, total and for 4 major countries, and US trade by country, by commodity, 1970-89, world area rpt series, 9116–1

Price indexes (producer), by stage of processing and detailed commodity, monthly rpt, 6762–6

Price indexes (producer), by stage of processing and detailed commodity, monthly 1990, annual rpt, 6764–2

Puerto Rico economic censuses, 1987: wholesale and retail trade and service industry finances and operations, by SIC 2- to 4-digit industry and municipio, 2591–1

Retail trade census, 1987: finances and employment, for establishments with and without payroll, by SIC 2- to 4-digit kind of business, State, and MSA, 2401–1

Retail trade sales and inventories, by kind of business, region, and selected State, MSA, and city, monthly rpt, 2413–3

Retail trade sales, inventories, purchases, gross margin, and accounts receivable, by SIC 2- to 4-digit kind of business and form of ownership, 1989, annual rpt, 2413–5

Statistical Abstract of US, 1991 annual data compilation, 2324–1.7

Tax (income) returns of sole proprietorships, income statement items, by industry group, 1989, annual article, 8302–2.214

see also Libraries

Booz-Allen and Hamilton, Inc.

"Veterans Housing Loan Program Evaluation, Final Report", 8608–7

Border Patrol

see U.S. Border Patrol

Borland, Ron

"Adults' Accounts of Onset of Regular Smoking: Influences of School, Work, and Other Settings", 4042–3.217

Boron

see Gases

Boss, Leslie

"Cancer", 4088–2

Boston, Mass.

CPI by component for US city average, and by region, population size, and for 15 metro areas, monthly rpt, 6762–1

CPI by component for US city average, and by region, population size, and for 27 metro areas, monthly rpt, 6762–2

Drug abuse indicators for selected metro areas, research results, data collection, and policy issues, 1991 semiannual conf, 4492–5

Financial instns location relation to ZIP code area income and minority population, by instn type for 5 cities, 1977-89, article, 9377–1.208

Firearm purchasers criminal records checks, and firearms use in crime, with data by State, 1987-90, 26358–244

Fish and shellfish catch, wholesale receipts, prices, trade, and other market activities, weekly regional rpt, 2162–6.5

Fruit and vegetable shipments, and arrivals in US and Canada cities, by mode of transport and State and country of origin, 1990, annual rpt, 1311–4.1

Housing vacancy and property value appreciation rates for 4 metro areas, 1991 GAO rpt, 26131–84

Interest rates on conventional fixed-rate mortgages, monthly rpt, 9373–2.7

Pumpkin farms, production costs, shipments, and sales by State, prices, and imports by country, 1978-90, article, 1561–11.203

Wages by occupation, for office and plant workers, 1990 survey, periodic MSA rpt, 6785–11.1

see also under By City and By SMSA or MSA in the "Index by Categories"

Botanical gardens

Service industries census, 1987: establishments, receipts by source, payroll, and employment, by SIC 2- to 4-digit kind of business, State, and MSA, 2393–4

Botany

Carbon dioxide in atmosphere, DOE R&D programs and funding at natl labs, universities, and other instns, FY91, annual summary rpt, 3004–18.1; 3004–18.7

Carbon dioxide in atmosphere, measurement, methodology, and research results, series, 3006–11

DOE R&D projects and funding at natl labs, universities, and other instns, FY91, annual summary rpt, 3004–18.4

Higher education grad programs enrollment in science and engineering, by field,

Botswana

source of funds, and characteristics of student and instn, 1975-89, annual rpt, 9627–7

Research (agricultural) funding and staffing for USDA, State agencies, and other instns, by topic, FY90, annual rpt, 1744–2

Research and education grants, USDA competitive awards by program and recipient, FY90, annual listing, 1764–1

Research on wildlife and plants, habitat study series, 5506–13

Shrublands in western US, ecology, biology, and cheatgrass invasion and related fire threat, 1989 conf papers, 1208–351

see also Botanical gardens

see also Flowers and nursery products

see also Forests and forestry

see also Fruit and fruit products

see also Horticulture

see also Plants and vegetation

see also Vegetables and vegetable products

Botswana

Agricultural exports of high-value commodities, indexes and sales by commodity, world area, and country, 1960s-86, 1528–323

Agricultural trade of US, by detailed commodity and country, 1989, annual rpt, 1524–8

Agricultural trade of US, by detailed commodity and country, 1990, semiannual rpt, 1522–4

AID economic aid to developing countries, obligations and disbursements by country, quarterly rpt, 9912–4

AID loans repayment status and terms by program and country, and status of predecessor agency loans, quarterly rpt, 9912–3

Background Notes, summary social, political, and economic data, 1990 rpt, 7006–2.16

Dairy imports, consumption, and market conditions, by sub-Saharan Africa country, 1961-88, 1528–321

Economic and military aid and loans from US and intl agencies, by program and country, FY46-90, annual rpt, 9914–5

Economic and social conditions of developing countries from 1960s, and Intl Dev Cooperation Agency and AID activities and funding, FY90-92, annual rpt, 9904–4

Economic, population, and agricultural data, US and other aid sources, and AID activity, 1989 country rpt, 9916–12.32; 9916–12.38

Economic, social, political, and geographic summary data, by country, 1991, annual factbook, 9114–2

Exports and imports of US, by transport mode, country, and SITC 1- to 3-digit commodity, 1990, annual rpt, 2424–12

Exports of US, detailed Schedule B commodities with countries of destination, 1990, annual rpt, 2424–10

Human rights conditions in 170 countries, and US economic and military aid, 1990, annual rpt, 21384–3

Military aid of US, arms sales, and training programs costs and budget requests, by program, world region, and country, FY90-92, annual rpt, 7144–13

UN voting record and share of votes in agreement with US, by issue, country, and world area, 1990, annual rpt, 7004–18

Botswana

see also under By Foreign Country in the "Index by Categories"

Bottles
see Packaging and containers

Botulism
see Food and waterborne diseases

Boucher, Janice L.
"Europe 1992: A Closer Look", 9371–1.210
"Stationary Representations, Cointegration, and Rational Expectations with an Application to the Forward Foreign Exchange Market", 9371–10.64

Boulder, Colo.
CPI by component for US city average, and by region, population size, and for 27 metro areas, monthly rpt, 6762–2
Housing starts and completions authorized by building permits in 40 MSAs, quarterly rpt, 2382–9
see also under By SMSA or MSA in the "Index by Categories"

Bourque, Mary L.
"Levels of Mathematics Achievement: Initial Performance Standards for the 1990 NAEP Mathematics Assessment", 4896–8.2

Boutwell, Robert C.
"Physician Consultative Services Under Medicare: Final Report", 4658–47

Bovine somatotropin
see Hormones

Boxes
see Packaging and containers

Boy Scouts of America
Statistical Abstract of US, 1991 annual data compilation, 2324–1.7

Boycotts
Exporters (US) antiboycott law violations and fines by firm, and invitations to boycott by country, FY90, annual rpt, 2024–1
Intl boycotts by OPEC and other countries, US firms and shareholders cooperation and tax benefits denied, 1986, annual rpt, 8004–13
Intl boycotts by OPEC and other countries, US taxpayers IRS filings, cooperation, and tax benefits denied, 1976-86, GAO rpt, 26119–349
Tax (income) returns of corporations with foreign tax credit, income, and tax items, by country and world region of credit, 1986, biennial article, 8302–2.207
Tax (income) returns of corporations with foreign tax credit, income and tax items by industry group, 1986, biennial article, 8302–2.203

Boyd, John H.
"Investigating the Banking Consolidation Trend", 9383–6.203

Bradbury, Katharine L.
"Can Local Governments Give Citizens What They Want? Referendum Outcomes in Massachusetts", 9373–1.208

Bradenton, Fla.
see also under By SMSA or MSA in the "Index by Categories"

Bradford, Charles H.
"Market Cycles and Their Effect on Real Estate Lending by Credit Unions: Case Study of Region I", 9536–1.6

Bradford, John J.
"Foreign Recipients of U.S. Income, 1988", 8302–2.206
"U.S. Possessions Corporation Returns, 1987", 8302–2.213

Brain diseases
see Cerebrovascular diseases
see Neurological disorders

Brainich, Eric
"Exporting: An Avenue for Dairy Cooperatives", 1128–65

Branch, Laurence G.
"Concordance Between Planned and Approved Visits During Initial Home Care", 4652–1.254

Brand, Liesel E.
"Child Day Care Services: An Industry at a Crossroads", 6722–1.202

Brand names
see Trademarks
see under By Individual Company or Institution in the "Index by Categories"

Brass
see Metals and metal industries

Brauer, David A.
"Effect of Import Competition on Manufacturing Wages", **9385**–8.89
"Effect of Imports on U.S. Manufacturing Wages", **9385**–1.204

Braund, Stephen R., and Associates
"North Slope Subsistence Study: Barrow, 1988. Alaska Social and Economic Study", 5736–5.12

Brazil
Agricultural exports of high-value commodities from developing countries to OECD, 1970s-87, 1528–316
Agricultural exports of high-value commodities, indexes and sales by commodity, world area, and country, 1960s-86, 1528–323
Agricultural exports of US, impacts of foreign agricultural and trade policy, with data by commodity and country, 1989, annual rpt, 1924–8
Agricultural production, prices, and trade, by country, 1960s-90, annual world area rpt, 1524–4.2
Agricultural production, trade, and policies in foreign countries, summary data by country, 1989-90, annual factbook, 1924–12
Agricultural subsidies to producers and consumers in 6 Latin America countries, by selected commodity, 1982-87, 1528–324
Agricultural trade of US, by detailed commodity and country, 1989, annual rpt, 1524–8
Agricultural trade of US, by detailed commodity and country, 1990, semiannual rpt, 1522–4
AID economic aid to developing countries, obligations and disbursements by country, quarterly rpt, 9912–4
AID loans repayment status and terms by program and country, and status of predecessor agency loans, quarterly rpt, 9912–3
Background Notes, summary social, political, and economic data, 1990 rpt, 7006–2.4
Bearings (ball) from 14 countries, injury to US industry from foreign subsidized and less than fair value imports, investigation with background financial and operating data, 1991 rpt, 9886–19.74

Index by Subjects and Names

Economic and military aid and loans from US and intl agencies, by program and country, FY46-90, annual rpt, 9914–5
Economic and monetary trends, compounded annual rates of change for US and 13 trading partners, quarterly rpt annual supplement, 9391–7
Economic conditions in USSR, Eastern Europe, OECD, and selected other countries, 1960s-90, annual rpt, 9114–4
Economic conditions, policy, and trade practices, by country, 1988-90, annual rpt, 21384–5
Economic, social, political, and geographic summary data, by country, 1991, annual factbook, 9114–2
Energy use in developing countries, and economic and environmental impacts, by fuel type, world area, and country, 1980s-90, 26358–232
Exports and imports of US, by commodity and country, 1970-89, world area rpt, 9116–1.4
Exports and imports of US, by Harmonized System 6-digit commodity and country, 1990, annual rpt, 2424–13
Exports and imports of US, by selected country, country group, and commodity group, 1990, annual rpt, 2044–37
Exports and imports of US, by transport mode, country, and SITC 1- to 3-digit commodity, 1990, annual rpt, 2424–12
Exports and imports, trade agreements and relations, and USITC investigations, 1990, annual rpt, 9884–5
Exports, imports, and balances of US with major trading partners, by product category, 1986-90, annual chartbook, 9884–21
Exports of US, detailed Schedule B commodities with countries of destination, 1990, annual rpt, 2424–10
Human rights conditions in 170 countries, and US economic and military aid, 1990, annual rpt, 21384–3
Imports of goods, services, and investment from US, trade barriers, impacts, and US actions, by country, 1990, annual rpt, 444–2
Inflation rates and public debt burden in Brazil and Argentina, 1980s-91, technical paper, 9379–12.69
Inflation relation to money supply and public debt in Argentina and Brazil, model description and results, 1980s-90, technical paper, 9379–12.75
Military aid of US, arms sales, and training programs costs and budget requests, by program, world region, and country, FY90-92, annual rpt, 7144–13
Military weapons trade, production, and defense industry finances, with data by firm and country, 1980s-91, 26358–241
Multinatl US firms and foreign affiliates finances and operations, by industry and world area of parent firm, 1989 benchmark survey, preliminary annual rpt, 2704–5
Multinatl US firms foreign affiliates, income statement items by country and world area, 1986, biennial article, 8302–2.212
Nuclear power generation in US and 20 countries, monthly rpt, 3162–24.10
Nuclear power plant capacity, generation, and operating status, by plant and foreign and US location, 1990 and projected to 2030, annual rpt, 3164–57

Oil exports to US by OPEC and non-OPEC countries, monthly rpt, 3162–24.3

Pipes and tubes (welded nonalloy steel) from 6 countries, injury to US industry from foreign subsidized and less than fair value imports, investigation with background financial and operating data, 1991 rpt, 9886–19.81

Poultry products exports of US, EC, and 3 leading countries, by world area, 1986-90, semiannual rpt, 1925–33.1

Price variability among products and cities, relation to inflation, for Brazil, alternative model results for 1980s, working paper, 9379–14.14

Silicon metal from Brazil at less than fair value, injury to US industry, investigation with background financial and operating data, 1991 rpt, 9886–14.321

Spacecraft and satellite launches since 1957, quarterly listing, 9502–2

Steel disc wheels from Brazil at less than fair value, injury to US industry, investigation supplement, 1991 rpt, 9886–14.333

Steel imports of US under voluntary restraint agreement, by product, customs district, and country, with US industry operating data, quarterly rpt, 9882–13

Sugar production, use, and exports, for Brazil, 1970s-91, FAS periodic circular, 1925–14.2

Telecommunications industry intl competitiveness, with financial and operating data by product or service, firm, and country, 1990 rpt, 2008–30

UN voting record and share of votes in agreement with US, by issue, country, and world area, 1990, annual rpt, 7004–18

see also under By Foreign Country in the "Index by Categories"

Brazoria, Tex.

CPI by component for US city average, and by region, population size, and for 15 metro areas, monthly rpt, 6762–1

CPI by component for US city average, and by region, population size, and for 27 metro areas, monthly rpt, 6762–2

Housing starts and completions authorized by building permits in 40 MSAs, quarterly rpt, 2382–9

see also under By SMSA or MSA in the "Index by Categories"

Bread

see Baking and bakery products

Breast-feeding

Child health condition and services use, 1990 chartbook, 4108–49

Health condition improvement and disease prevention goals and recommended activities for 2000, with trends 1970s-80s, 4048–10

Breidenbaugh, M. Zermain

"Medicare End Stage Renal Disease Population, 1982-87", 4652–1.208

Bremer-Fox, Jennifer

"Development Impact of U.S. Program Food Assistance: Evidence from the AID Evaluation Literature", 9918–20

Bremerton, Wash.

Wages by occupation, and benefits for office and plant workers, 1991 survey, periodic MSA rpt, 6785–3.4

see also under By SMSA or MSA in the "Index by Categories"

Bribery

see Corruption and bribery

Bridgeport, Conn.

see also under By City and By SMSA or MSA in the "Index by Categories"

Bridges and tunnels

Condition of bridges, repair and replacement needs under alternative assessment methods, 1990 and projected to 1996, GAO rpt, 26113–539

Condition of hwys and bridges, share with deficiencies, by State, 1980s, article, 9373–1.207

Construction industries census, 1987: establishments, employment, receipts, and expenditures, by SIC 4-digit industry and State, final industry rpt series, 2373–1

Fed Govt and State surface transportation funding and regulation, FY91 with projections to FY96, 26358–242

Forest Service activities and finances, by region and State, FY90, annual rpt, 1204–1.1

Hwy Statistics, detailed data by State, 1990, annual rpt, 7554–1

Natl transportation system planning, use, condition, accidents, and needs, by mode of transport, 1940s-90 and projected to 2020, 7308–202

Public lands acreage and use, and Land Mgmt Bur activities and finances, annual State rpt series, 5724–11

Ships and marine facilities accidents, casualties, and circumstances, Coast Guard investigation results, periodic rpt, 9612–4

State and Metro Area Data Book, 1991 data compilation, 2328–54

Toll facilities, mileage, and operating status, by type of system, as of Jan 1990, biennial listing, 7554–39

Bridges, Clay

"Waterfowl Habitat Management on Public Lands: A Strategy for the Future", 5726–6.2

Bridgeton, N.J.

see also under By SMSA or MSA in the "Index by Categories"

Briscoe, William W.

"Within DRG Case Complexity: Change Update and Distributional Differences", 17206–2.21

Brislin, Patricia

"De Novo Banking in the Third District", 9387–1.201

Bristol, Conn.

see also under By SMSA or MSA in the "Index by Categories"

Bristol, Tenn.

see also under By SMSA or MSA in the "Index by Categories"

Britain, Gerald

"Improving the Collection and Use of Program Performance Data", 9916–12.45

British Columbia Province, Canada

Marine mammals and birds population and distribution, by species and northeast Pacific Ocean location, literature and data base review, 1950s-88, 5738–28

Tidal currents, daily time and velocity by station for North America and Asia coasts, forecast 1992, annual rpt, 2174–1.2

Timber in northwestern US and British Columbia, production, prices, trade, and employment, quarterly rpt, 1202–3

Water quality, chemistry, hydrology, and other characteristics, 1989 local area study, 5666–27.16

British Virgin Islands

Agricultural trade of US, by detailed commodity and country, 1990, semiannual rpt, 1522–4

Economic, social, political, and geographic summary data, by country, 1991, annual factbook, 9114–2

Exports and imports of US, by transport mode, country, and SITC 1- to 3-digit commodity, 1990, annual rpt, 2424–12

Investment (direct) incentives of Caribbean Basin Initiative, economic impacts, with finances and employment by country, 1984-90, 2048–141

Rum imports (duty-free) of US under Caribbean Basin Initiative, by country, 1989-90, annual rpt, 9884–15

Broach, Dana

"Exchange Ideology as a Moderator of the Procedural Justice-Satisfaction Relationship", 7506–10.90

"Flight Service Specialist Initial Qualifications Course: Content Validation of FAA Academy Course 50232", 7506–10.83

Broadcasting

see Educational broadcasting

see Political broadcasting

see Public broadcasting

see Radio

see Television

Brock, K. E.

"Serum Selenium Level in Relation to In Situ Cervical Cancer in Australia", 4472–1.203

Brockton, Mass.

see also under By SMSA or MSA in the "Index by Categories"

Brokers

see Futures trading

see Real estate business

see Stockbrokers

Bromine

see Nonmetallic minerals and mines

Brookhaven National Laboratory

"Indoor Air Quality Environmental Information Handbook: Combustion Sources, 1989 Update", 3326–1.2

"Radioactive Materials Released from Nuclear Power Plants, Annual Report, 1988", 9634–1

see also Department of Energy National Laboratories

Brooks, Barbara G.

"Occupational Radiation Exposure at Commercial Nuclear Power Reactors and Other Facilities, 1987", 9634–3

Brooks, David J.

"Analysis of the Timber Situation in Alaska: 1970-2010", 1208–367

"Timber Products Output and Timber Harvests in Alaska: Projections for 1989-2010", 1208–365

Brooks, Robert T.

"Forest Wildlife Habitat Statistics for Maryland and Delaware, 1986", 1206–44.5

Brooms

see Household supplies and utensils

Brothers, Stephen L., Jr.

Brothers, Stephen L., Jr.
"Energy Management Annual Report, FY90", 9804–26

Brown, E. Richard
"Loss of Medicaid and Access to Health Services", 4652–1.242

Brown, Marilyn A.
"Electricity Savings Among Participants Three Years After Weatherization in Bonneville's 1986 Residential Weatherization Program", 3226–1.7
"Energy-Related Inventions Program: Commercial Progress of Participants Through 1988", 3308–91
"Impact of Bonneville's Model Conservation Standards on the Energy Efficiency of New Home Construction", 3228–15

Brown, Mark J.
"Forest Statistics for the Piedmont of North Carolina, 1990", 1206–4.14

Brown, Patricia Q.
"Salaries of Full-Time Instructional Faculty on 9- and 10-Month Contracts in Institutions of Higher Education, 1979-80 Through 1989-90", 4844–8

Brown, Richard N., Jr.
"U.S. Markets for Caribbean Basin Fruits and Vegetables: Selected Characteristics for 17 Fresh and Frozen Imports, 1975-87", 1568–299

Brown, Scott
"Disability and Health: Characteristics of Persons by Limitation of Activity and Assessed Health Status, U.S., 1984-88", 4146–8.202

Browne, Lynn E.
"Massachusetts in the 1990s: The Role of State Government. Overview", 9373–1.202; 9373–4.27
"Role of Services in New England's Rise and Fall: Engine of Growth or Along for the Ride?", 9373–1.212

Brownsville, Tex.
see also under By SMSA or MSA in the "Index by Categories"

Brucellosis
see Animal diseases and zoonoses

Brunei
Agricultural exports of high-value commodities, indexes and sales by commodity, world area, and country, 1960s-86, 1528–323
Agricultural trade of US, by detailed commodity and country, 1989, annual rpt, 1524–8
Agricultural trade of US, by detailed commodity and country, 1990, semiannual rpt, 1522–4
Background Notes, summary social, political, and economic data, 1991 rpt, 7006–2.39
Economic and military aid and loans from US and intl agencies, by program and country, FY46-90, annual rpt, 9914–5
Economic, social, political, and geographic summary data, by country, 1991, annual factbook, 9114–2
Exports and imports of US, by transport mode, country, and SITC 1- to 3-digit commodity, 1990, annual rpt, 2424–12
Exports of US, detailed Schedule B commodities with countries of destination, 1990, annual rpt, 2424–10
Human rights conditions in 170 countries, and US economic and military aid, 1990, annual rpt, 21384–3

UN voting record and share of votes in agreement with US, by issue, country, and world area, 1990, annual rpt, 7004–18

Brunner, Allan D.
"Recent Developments Affecting the Profitability of Commercial Banks", 9362–1.204

Bruton, Henry
"Development Impact of Counterpart Funds: A Review of the Literature", 9918–21

Bryan, Tex.
see also under By SMSA or MSA in the "Index by Categories"

bST
see Hormones

Bucci, Michael
"Growth of Employer-Sponsored Group Life Insurance", 6722–1.248
"Health Maintenance Organizations: Plan Offerings and Enrollments", 6722–1.222

Buchanan, Robert J.
"Medicaid Payment Policies for Nursing Home Care: A National Survey", 4652–1.253

Buck, Jeffrey A.
"Medicaid Support of Alcohol, Drug Abuse, and Mental Health Services", 4652–1.256

Buckley, John E.
"Area Wage Surveys, Selected Metropolitan Areas, 1990", 6785–1

Buckley, Katharine C.
"1991 Outlook for Fruit and Tree Nuts", 1004–16.1

Budget Enforcement Act
Budget of US, CBO analysis of revenue and spending alternatives and projections of economic indicators, FY92-96, annual rpt, 26304–3
Budget of US, obligations and authority by function, agency, and program, with summaries, analyses, and historical tables, FY92, annual rpt, 104–2
Budget of US, Senate concurrent resolution, with spending and revenue targets, FY92, annual rpt, 25254–1

Budget of the U.S.
Budget of US, authoritative financial statements with appropriations, outlays, and receipts, by agency, FY90, annual rpt, 8104–2
Budget of US, balances of budget authority obligated and unobligated, by function and agency, FY90-92, annual rpt, 104–8
Budget of US, CBO analysis and review of FY92 budget by function, annual rpt, 26304–2
Budget of US, CBO analysis of revenue and spending alternatives and projections of economic indicators, FY92-96, annual rpt, 26304–3
Budget of US, compilation of background material on fiscal and tax policy, 1960s-96, 21788–203
Budget of US, formula grant program obligations to State and local govts, by agency, program, and State, FY92, annual rpt, 104–30
Budget of US, historical data, selected years FY34-90 and projected to FY96, annual rpt, 104–22
Budget of US, House Budget Committee analysis of Bush Admin proposals and economic assumptions, FY92, 21268–42

Index by Subjects and Names

Budget of US, House concurrent resolution, with spending and revenue targets, FY92 and projected to FY96, annual rpt, 21264–2
Budget of US, legislative process overview with summary projections and glossary, FY90-95, 21268–43
Budget of US, midsession review of FY92 budget, by function, annual rpt, 104–7
Budget of US, object class analysis of obligations, by agency, FY92, annual rpt, 104–9
Budget of US, obligations and authority by function, agency, and program, with summaries, analyses, and historical tables, FY92, annual rpt, 104–2
Budget of US, receipts and outlays on natl income and product basis, FY92, annual article, 2702–1.204
Budget of US, Senate concurrent resolution, with spending and revenue targets, FY92, annual rpt, 25254–1
Census of Population and Housing, 1990: Budget of US constraints impacts on census operations, hearing, 21628–88
Child and family health, education, and welfare condition, findings and recommendations, 1991 rpt, 15528–1
Deficits under Reagan Admin, impact on capital stock, foreign debt, and other economic indicators, with background data, 1950s-88, article, 9393–8.201
Deposit insurance accounting in Federal budget, outlays by instn type, and Bank Insurance Fund finances, late 1970s-96, 26308–100
Economic Report of the President for 1991, Joint Economic Committee critique and policy recommendations, annual rpt, 23844–2
Energy taxes impacts on GNP and budget deficit, for alternative taxation methods, projected 1991-2000, 3166–6.57
Fed Govt agencies budget requests and program costs and characteristics, series, 26306–3
Fuel tax revenue use for budget deficit reduction, projected FY91-95, GAO rpt, 26113–544
OASDI trust funds finances, effects of inclusion in budget deficit figures, and social security tax reduction proposals, 1990 hearing, 25368–171
Receipts by source and outlays by agency, final statements compared to OMB forecasts, FY91, press release, 8008–153
Receipts by source and outlays by agency, *Treasury Bulletin*, quarterly rpt, 8002–4.1
Receipts by source and outlays by function, monthly rpt, quarterly and annual data, 23842–1.6
Receipts by source, outlays by agency and program, and balances, monthly rpt, 8102–3
Receipts, outlays, and debt, Fed Reserve Bank of St Louis monthly rpt, 9391–2; 9391–3
Statistical Abstract of US, 1991 annual data compilation, 2324–1.10
see also Defense budgets and appropriations
see also Executive impoundment of appropriated funds
see also Fiscal policy

Index by Subjects and Names

see also Nonappropriated funds
see also Public debt

Budgets
see Budget of the U.S.
see Defense budgets and appropriations
see Family budgets
see Foreign budgets

Budzeika, George
"Determinants of the Growth of Foreign Banking Assets in the U.S.", 9385–8.108

Buechner, Jay S.
"WIC Program Participation—A Marketing Approach", 4042–3.247

Buescher, Paul A.
"Problems in Estimating the Number of Women in Need of Subsidized Prenatal Care", 4042–3.226

Buffalo, N.Y.
- CPI by component for US city average, and by region, population size, and for 27 metro areas, monthly rpt, 6762–2
- Fruit and vegetable shipments, and arrivals in US and Canada cities, by mode of transport and State and country of origin, 1990, annual rpt, 1311–4.1
- Housing and households characteristics, unit and neighborhood quality, and journey to work by MSA location, for 11 MSAs, 1984 survey, supplement, 2485–8
- Housing and households characteristics, 1988 survey, MSA fact sheet, 2485–11.6
- Wages by occupation, for office and plant workers, 1990 survey, periodic MSA rpt, 6785–11.3
- Wages by occupation, for office and plant workers, 1991 survey, periodic MSA rpt, 6785–12.6
- *see also* under By City and By SMSA or MSA in the "Index by Categories"

Building abandonment
see Vacant and abandoned property

Building and loan associations
see Savings institutions

Building codes
- Earthquake preparedness costs and benefits, with data for California events and effects of 1989 Loma Prieta quake, 1980s, hearings, 21248–154
- Energy conservation and resource planning activities of Bonneville Power Admin, FY89-90, 3228–11
- Energy-efficiency building codes, effect on house construction practices in Bonneville Power Admin service areas, 1987, 3228–15
- Public housing renovation costs and alternative funding methods, by project type and region, 1990 rpt, 5188–127

Building laws
see Building codes
see Building permits
see Zoning and zoning laws

Building maintenance services
see Janitorial and maintenance services

Building materials
- Acid rain research activities of Natl Acid Precipitation Assessment Program, 1990 annual rpt, 14354–1
- Assns (trade and professional) and labor unions, for construction and building materials industries, 1991 listing, article, 2042–1.202
- Business statistics, detailed data for major industries and economic indicators, *Survey of Current Business*, monthly rpt, 2702–1.19; 2702–1.21

Clay (construction) production and shipments by region and State, trade, and use, by product, quarterly Current Industrial Rpt, 2506–9.2

Construction industries census, 1987: establishments, employment, receipts, and expenditures, by SIC 4-digit industry and State, final industry rpt series, 2373–1

County Business Patterns, 1988: employment, establishments, and payroll, by SIC 2- to 4-digit industry and county, annual State rpt series, 2326–6

County Business Patterns, 1989: employment, establishments, and payroll, by SIC 2- to 4-digit industry and county, annual State rpt series, 2326–8

DOD prime contract awards, by category, contract and contractor type, and service branch, FY81-1st half FY91, semiannual rpt, 3542–1

DOD prime contract awards, by category, contractor type, and State, FY88-90, annual rpt, 3544–11

DOD prime contract awards, by detailed procurement category, FY87-90, annual rpt, 3544–18

Employment, earnings, and hours, by SIC 1- to 4-digit industry, monthly and annual averages, selected years 1909-90, annual rpt, 6744–4

Energy use in commercial buildings, costs, and conservation, by building characteristics, survey rpt series, 3166–8

Exports and imports of building materials, by commodity and country, 1989-90, article, 2042–1.204

Exports and imports of US, by country and detailed commodity, monthly rpt, 2422–12

Exports and imports of US, by Harmonized System 6-digit commodity and country, 1990, annual rpt, 2424–13

Exports and imports of US, by transport mode, country, and SITC 1- to 3-digit commodity, 1990, annual rpt, 2424–12

Exports of US, detailed Schedule B commodities with countries of destination, 1990, annual rpt, 2424–10

Farm prices received and paid, by commodity and State, 1990, annual rpt, 1629–5

Farm prices received for major products and paid for farm inputs and living items, by commodity and State, monthly rpt, 1629–1

Farm production itemized costs, by farm sales size and region, 1990, annual rpt, 1614–3

Franchise business opportunities by firm and kind of business, and sources of aid and info, 1990 annual listing, 2104–7

Glass (flat) production, shipments, inventories, and trade, quarterly Current Industrial Rpt, 2506–9.6

Home mortgages FHA-insured, financial, property, and mortgagor characteristics, by metro area, 1990, annual rpt, 5144–24

Home mortgages FHA-insured, financial, property, and mortgagor characteristics, by State, 1990, annual rpt, 5144–1

Home mortgages FHA-insured, financial, property, and mortgagor characteristics, total and by State and outlying area, 1990, annual rpt, 5144–25

Building materials

Home mortgages FHA-insured, financial, property, and mortgagor characteristics, 1990, annual rpt, 5144–17; 5144–23

Housing alteration and repair spending for homeowner and contracted jobs, quarterly rpt, 2382–7.1

Housing and households detailed characteristics, and unit and neighborhood quality, by location, 1989, biennial rpt, 2485–12

Housing units completed, single and multifamily units by structural and financial characteristics, inside-outside MSAs, and region, 1986-90, annual rpt, 2384–1

Hwy construction material prices and indexes for Federal-aid system, by type of material and urban-rural location, quarterly rpt, 7552–7

Hwy construction material prices and indexes for Federal-aid system, by type of material, quarterly press release, 7552–16

Hwy construction material use by type, and spending, by State, various periods 1944-90, annual rpt, 7554–29

Hwy receipts by source, and spending by function, by level of govt and State, 1990, annual rpt, 7554–1.3

Injuries from use of consumer products, by severity, victim age, and detailed product, 1990, annual rpt, 9164–6

Injuries from use of consumer products, related deaths and costs, and recalls by brand, by product type, FY89, annual rpt, 9164–2

Labor productivity, indexes of output, hours, and employment by SIC 2- to 4-digit industry, 1967-89, annual rpt, 6824–1.3

Manufacturing census, 1987: employment and shipments under Fed Govt contracts, by SIC 4-digit industry, 2497–7

Manufacturing census, 1987: finances and operations, by SIC 2- to 4-digit industry, State, and MSA, with trends from 1849, 2497–1

Manufacturing census, 1987: finances and operations, by type of organization and SIC 2- to 4-digit industry, subject rpt, 2497–5

Manufacturing finances and operations, by SIC 2- to 4-digit industry, forecast 1991, annual rpt, 2044–28

Mexico construction value and trade, and import duties on materials and equipment by type, 1991 article, 2042–1.207

Minerals Yearbook, 1989, Vol 2: State reviews of production, sales, and firms, by commodity, and business activity, annual rpt, 5604–34

Occupational injury and illness rates, by SIC 2- to 4-digit industry, 1988-89, annual rpt, 6844–7

Occupational injury and illness rates, by SIC 2- to 4-digit industry, 1989, annual rpt, 6844–1

Pollution (air) emissions factors, by detailed pollutant and source, data compilation, 1990 rpt, 9198–120

Price indexes (producer), by stage of processing and detailed commodity, monthly rpt, 6762–6

Price indexes (producer), by stage of processing and detailed commodity, monthly 1990, annual rpt, 6764–2

Building materials

Price indexes (producer) for material inputs, by construction industry, monthly rpt, 6762–6

Production, shipments, PPI, and stocks of building materials, by type, bimonthly rpt, 2042–1.5; 2042–1.6

Puerto Rico economic censuses, 1987: wholesale and retail trade and service industry finances and operations, by SIC 2- to 4-digit industry and municipio, 2591–1

Retail trade census, 1987: finances and employment, for establishments with and without payroll, by SIC 2- to 4-digit kind of business, State, and MSA, 2401–1

Retail trade sales and inventories, by kind of business, region, and selected State, MSA, and city, monthly rpt, 2413–3

Retail trade sales, by kind of business, advance monthly rpt, 2413–2

Retail trade sales, inventories, purchases, gross margin, and accounts receivable, by SIC 2- to 4-digit kind of business and form of ownership, 1989, annual rpt, 2413–5

Soviet Union GNP by component and industry sector, and CIA estimation methods, 1950s-87, 23848–223

Soviet Union GNP by detailed income and outlay component, 1985, 2326–18.59

Statistical Abstract of US, 1991 annual data compilation, 2324–1.26

Taiwan imports of building materials, and share from US, by commodity, 1989-90, article, 2042–1.205

Tax (income) returns of corporations, income and tax items by asset size and detailed industry, 1987, annual rpt, 8304–4

Tax (income) returns of corporations, income and tax items by asset size and detailed industry, 1988, annual rpt, 8304–21

Wholesale trade census, 1987: depreciable assets, capital and operating expenses, sales, value added, and inventories, by SIC 2- to 3-digit kind of business, 2407–2

Wholesale trade census, 1987: establishments, sales by customer class, employment, inventories, and expenses, by SIC 2- to 4-digit kind of business, 2407–4

Wholesale trade sales, inventories, purchases, and gross margins, by SIC 2- to 3-digit kind of business, 1990, annual rpt, 2413–13

see also Asbestos contamination
see also Cement and concrete
see also Clay industry and products
see also Floor coverings
see also Insulation
see also Lumber industry and products
see also Paints and varnishes
see also Stone products and quarries
see also Wall coverings

Building permits

Business statistics, detailed data for major industries and economic indicators, *Survey of Current Business*, monthly rpt, 2702–1.6

Construction authorized by building permits, by type of construction, region, State, and MSA, bimonthly rpt, 2042–1.3

Housing starts and completions authorized by building permits in 40 MSAs, quarterly rpt, 2382–9

New England States economic indicators, Fed Reserve 1st District, monthly rpt, 9373–2.6

New housing units authorized, by region, State, selected MSA, and permit-issuing place, monthly rpt, 2382–5

New housing units authorized, by State, MSA, and permit-issuing place, 1990, annual rpt, 2384–2

North Central States business and economic conditions, Fed Reserve 9th District, quarterly journal, 9383–19

Nuclear power plant operating licenses, and construction permits granted and pending, monthly rpt, 3162–24.8

Southeastern States, Fed Reserve 5th District, economic indicators by State, quarterly rpt, 9389–16

Southeastern States, Fed Reserve 6th District, economic indicators by State and MSA, quarterly rpt, 9371–14

Southeastern States, FHLB 4th District, employment and housing and mortgage market indicators by State, quarterly rpt, 9302–36

State and Metro Area Data Book, 1991 data compilation, 2328–54

Statistical Abstract of US, 1991 annual data compilation, 2324–1.26

West Central States economic indicators, Fed Reserve 10th District, quarterly rpt, 9381–16.2

see also Zoning and zoning laws

Buildings

see Apartment houses
see Architectural barriers to the handicapped
see Architecture
see Building codes
see Building materials
see Building permits
see Commercial buildings
see Condominiums and cooperatives
see Construction industry
see Elevators
see Housing condition and occupancy
see Housing construction
see Housing maintenance and repair
see Housing sales
see Housing supply and requirements
see Industrial plants and equipment
see Mobile homes
see Prefabricated buildings
see Public buildings
see Vacant and abandoned property

Bulgaria

Agricultural exports of high-value commodities, indexes and sales by commodity, world area, and country, 1960s-86, 1528–323

Agricultural exports of US, impacts of foreign agricultural and trade policy, with data by commodity and country, 1989, annual rpt, 1924–8

Agricultural production, trade, and policies in foreign countries, summary data by country, 1989-90, annual factbook, 1924–12

Agricultural trade of US, by detailed commodity and country, 1989, annual rpt, 1524–8

Agricultural trade of US, by detailed commodity and country, 1990, semiannual rpt, 1522–4

Index by Subjects and Names

Debt to foreign lenders by component, trade, balances, and other economic indicators, by Eastern Europe country, 1985-89, hearing, 21248–148

Economic conditions in USSR, Eastern Europe, OECD, and selected other countries, 1960s-90, annual rpt, 9114–4

Economic conditions, policy, and trade practices, by country, 1988-90, annual rpt, 21384–5

Economic, social, political, and geographic summary data, by country, 1991, annual factbook, 9114–2

Export licensing, monitoring, and enforcement activities, FY90, annual rpt, 2024–1

Exports and imports of Bulgaria with US, US tariffs, and impacts of US granting most favored nation status, 1987-90, GAO rpt, 26123–323

Exports and imports of US, by commodity and country, 1970-89, world area rpt, 9116–1.3

Exports and imports of US, by selected country, country group, and commodity group, 1990, annual rpt, 2044–37

Exports and imports of US, by transport mode, country, and SITC 1- to 3-digit commodity, 1990, annual rpt, 2424–12

Exports and imports of US with Communist countries, by detailed commodity and country, quarterly rpt with articles, 9882–2

Exports of US, detailed Schedule B commodities with countries of destination, 1990, annual rpt, 2424–10

Human rights conditions in 170 countries, and US economic and military aid, 1990, annual rpt, 21384–3

Market economy transition of Eastern Europe countries, economic conditions and energy balance, by country, 1985-90, 9118–13

Market economy transition of Eastern Europe countries, with trade agreements and bilateral US trade data by country, late 1980s-90, annual rpt, 444–2

Nuclear power plant capacity and operating status, by plant and communist and regulated market country, as of Dec 1990, annual rpt, 3164–57.2

UN voting record and share of votes in agreement with US, by issue, country, and world area, 1990, annual rpt, 7004–18

see also under By Foreign Country in the "Index by Categories"

Bulger, Arthur J.

"Proposed Estuarine Classification: Analysis of Species Salinity Ranges", 2176–7.20

Bull, Len

"Pesticide Use by Tillage System, 1988 and 1989 Corn Production", 1561–16.201

Bullard, James B.

"FOMC in 1990: Onset of Recession", 9391–1.213

Bureau for Refugee Programs, State Department

Arrivals in US by world area of origin and State of settlement, and Federal aid, FY90-91 and proposed FY92 allocations, annual rpt, 7004–16

Arrivals in US, by world area of origin, processing, and nationality, monthly rpt, 7002–4

Index by Subjects and Names

Bureau of Alcohol, Tobacco and Firearms

Alcoholic beverages and tobacco production, removals, stocks, and material used, by State, monthly rpt series, 8486–1

Budget of US, obligations and authority by function, agency, and program, with summaries, analyses, and historical tables, FY92, annual rpt, 104–2

Regulatory activities, staff, and funding of BATF, and tax revenues and rates, 1980s-91, GAO rpt, 26119–335

Bureau of Census

Activities, rpts, and user services of Census Bur, monthly rpt, 2302–3

Agricultural summary data, young readers pamphlet series, 2346–1

AIDS virus infection prevalence in developing countries, by sex, selected city, urban-rural location, and country, 1991, semiannual rpt, 2322–4

American Housing Survey: inventory change from 1973, by reason, unit and household characteristics, and location, 1983, biennial rpt, 2485–14

American Housing Survey: unit and households characteristics, MSA fact sheet series, 2485–11

American Housing Survey: unit and households characteristics, unit and neighborhood quality, and journey to work by MSA location, for 11 MSAs, 1984 survey, supplement, 2485–8

American Housing Survey: unit and households detailed characteristics, and unit and neighborhood quality, MSA rpt series, 2485–6

American Housing Survey: unit and households detailed characteristics, and unit and neighborhood quality, 1987, biennial rpt, 2485–12; 2485–13

Annual Survey of Manufactures, 1989: finances and operations, by SIC 2- to 4-digit industry, series, 2506–15

Apartment and condominium completions and absorption rates, by size and price class, preliminary 1990, annual Current Housing Rpt, 2484–3

Apartment and condominium completions by rent class and sales price, and market absorption rates, quarterly rpt, 2482–2

Apartment market absorption rates and characteristics for nonsubsidized furnished and unfurnished units, 1989, annual Current Housing Rpt, 2484–2

Assistance (formula grants) of Fed Govt, use of Census of Population data for allocation, and effects of data errors on funding, with data by program and State, FY91, GAO rpt, 26119–361

Budget of US, obligations and authority by function, agency, and program, with summaries, analyses, and historical tables, FY92, annual rpt, 104–2

Capital expenditures for plant and equipment, by major industry group, quarterly rpt, 2502–2

Census of Agriculture, 1987: farms, farmland, production, finances, and operator characteristics, by county, final State rpt series, 2331–1

Census of Agriculture, 1987: horticultural specialties producers, finances, and operations, by crop and State, 1988 survey, 2337–1

Census of Construction Industries, 1987: finances and operations, by SIC 4-digit industry and State, final rpt series, 2373–1

Census of Govts, 1987: data coverage of final rpts, 2460–1

Census of Govts, 1987: employment, payroll, and average earnings, by function, level of govt, State, county, and population size, 2455–2

Census of Govts, 1987: local govt employment by function, payroll, and average earnings, for individual counties, cities, and school and special districts, 2455–1

Census of Govts, 1987: State and local govt employment, payroll, OASDHI coverage, and employee benefits costs, by level of govt and State, 2455–4

Census of Govts, 1987: State and local labor-mgmt policies, agreements, and coverage and bargaining units, by function, level of govt, and State, 2455–3

Census of Housing, 1990: inventory, occupancy, and costs, State fact sheet series, 2326–21

Census of Manufactures, 1987: employment and shipments under Fed Govt contracts, by SIC 4-digit industry, 2497–7

Census of Manufactures, 1987: finances and operations, by SIC 2- to 4-digit industry, State, and MSA, with trends from 1849, 2497–1

Census of Manufactures, 1987: finances and operations, by type of organization and SIC 2- to 4-digit industry, subject rpt, 2497–5

Census of Mineral Industries, 1987: energy use and costs, by fuel type, SIC 2- to 4-digit industry, and State, subject rpt, 2517–2

Census of Mineral Industries, 1987: finances and operations, by establishment characteristics, SIC 2- to 4-digit industry, and State, subject rpt, 2517–1

Census of Mineral Industries, 1987: finances and operations, by SIC 2- to 4-digit industry, State, and county, census div rpt series, 2515–1

Census of Population and Housing, data concordance of 1990 and 1980 census rpts, pamphlet, 2308–61

Census of Population and Housing, 1990: Budget of US constraints impacts on census operations, hearing, 21628–88

Census of Population and Housing, 1990: data accuracy and quality issues, hearing, 21628–91

Census of Population and Housing, 1990: data collection progress, hearing, 21628–86

Census of Population and Housing, 1990: data coverage and release schedules for rpts, 1991, 2308–62

Census of Population and Housing, 1990: data item selection, questionnaire dev, and testing, series, 2626–11

Census of Population and Housing, 1990: housing units occupied and vacant, persons in group quarters, and household size, by region, census div, and State, press release, 2328–71

Census of Population and Housing, 1990: local govt review of preliminary results, issues, hearing, 21628–93

Bureau of Census

Census of Population and Housing, 1990: New York State and NYC data collection activities and status, hearing, 21628–90

Census of Population and Housing, 1990: Pennsylvania data collection activities and status, hearing, 21628–89

Census of Population and Housing, 1990: Pennsylvania preparations for count, hearing, 21628–87

Census of Population and Housing, 1990: population and housing characteristics, households, and land area, by county, subdiv, and place, State rpt series, 2551–1

Census of Population and Housing, 1990: population and housing selected characteristics, by region, press release, 2328–74

Census of Population and Housing, 1990: population counts for congressional districts and change from 1980, by State, press release, 2328–32

Census of Population and Housing, 1990: population size and characteristics, summary results and trends, fact sheet series, 2326–20

Census of Population and Housing, 1990: Puerto Rico population and housing characteristics, press release, 2328–78

Census of Population and Housing, 1990: Texas data collection activities and status, hearing, 21628–92

Census of Population and Housing, 1990: Virgin Islands population and housing characteristics, press release, 2328–81

Census of Population and Housing, 1990: voting age and total population by race, and housing units, by block, redistricting counts required under PL 94-171, State CD-ROM series, 2551–6

Census of Population and Housing, 1990: voting age and total population by race, and housing units, redistricting counts required under PL 94-171, State CD-ROM user guide, 2308–63

Census of Population and Housing, 1990: voting age and total population by race, and housing units, by county and city, redistricting counts required under PL 94-171, State summary rpt series, 2551–5

Census of Population, 1990: cities population and undercounts, and related Federal aid losses, 1990 mayoral survey, hearing, 25408–113

Census of Population, 1990: congressional apportionment and official population counts, by State, 2328–22

Census of Population, 1990: congressional redistricting data coverage and availability, guide, 2308–59

Census of Population, 1990: data adjustment for undercounts, final decision, 2008–31

Census of Population, 1990: data coverage evaluation and improvement activities, and post-census sample use, hearing, 21628–96

Census of Population, 1990: data coverage evaluation and improvement activities, and revised counts for 1970-90 censuses, hearing, 21628–95

Census of Population, 1990: data enumeration errors under alternative definitions, and compared to 1980, GAO rpt, 26119–353

Bureau of Census

Census of Population, 1990: Guam population by district, press release, 2328–79

Census of Population, 1990: Hispanic population by detailed origin, region, and State, with data for 1980, press release, 2328–73

Census of Population, 1990: homeless shelter and on-street population, by State and for 200 cities, press release, 2328–70

Census of Population, 1990: Indian and Alaska Native population on reservations and in other designated areas, by selected site, press release, 2328–76

Census of Population, 1990: metro area population by race, Hispanic origin, and MSA, press release, 2328–75

Census of Population, 1990: population by detailed Native American, Asian, and Pacific Islander group, race, region, and State, with data for 1980, press release, 2328–72

Census of Population, 1990: population by State and region, with Federal and military personnel abroad by State of residence and agency, press release, 2328–66

Census of Population, 1990: post-enumeration survey results compared to census counts, by race, sex, city, county, and State, press release, 2328–69

Census of Population, 1990: post-enumeration survey use for adjusting census counts, with estimates of undercount by race, 1950-80, GAO rpt, 26119–327

Census of Population, 1990: urban areas land area, housing units, and population, by State and compared to rural areas, press release, 2328–39

Census of Population, 1990: urban areas population, for 396 areas, press release, 2328–37

Census of Population, 1990: Virgin Islands population by location, press release, 2328–77

Census of Retail Trade, 1987: depreciable assets, capital and operating expenses, sales, value added, and inventories, by SIC 2- to 4-digit kind of business, 2399–2

Census of Retail Trade, 1987: finances and employment, for establishments with and without payroll, by SIC 2- to 4-digit kind of business, State, and MSA, 2401–1

Census of Service Industries, 1987: depreciable assets, capital and operating expenses, and receipts, by SIC 2- to 4-digit kind of business, 2393–2

Census of Service Industries, 1987: establishments, receipts by source, payroll, and employment, by SIC 2- to 4-digit kind of business, State, and MSA, 2393–4

Census of Service Industries, 1987: hotels and other lodging places, receipts, payroll, employment, ownership, and rooms, by State and MSA, subject rpt, 2393–3

Census of Transportation, 1987: finances and operations by size, ownership, and State, and revenues by MSA, by SIC 2- to 4-digit industry, 2579–1

Census of Wholesale Trade, 1987: depreciable assets, capital and operating expenses, sales, value added, and inventories, by SIC 2- to 3-digit kind of business, 2407–2

Census of Wholesale Trade, 1987: finances and operations by SIC 2- to 4-digit kind of business, and oil bulk station operations by State, 2407–4

Chemical and oil products shipments, firms, trade, and use, by product, periodic Current Industrial Rpt series, 2506–8

City population size for cities with population over 100,000, as of Apr 1990, biennial press release, 2324–7

Clay and glass production, shipments, trade, and stocks, by product, periodic Current Industrial Rpt series, 2506–9

Clothing and shoe production, shipments, trade, and use, by product, periodic Current Industrial Rpt series, 2506–6

Construction put in place, value of new public and private structures, by type, monthly rpt, 2382–4

Consumer Expenditure Survey, spending for selected categories, 1991 semiannual pamphlet, 2322–3

Corporations financial statements for manufacturing, mining, and trade, by selected SIC 2- to 3-digit industry, quarterly rpt, 2502–1

Cotton ginnings and production, by State and county, 1990, annual rpt, 2344–1

Cotton ginnings, by State and county, seasonal monthly rpt, 2342–2

Cotton ginnings, by State, seasonal semimonthly rpt, 2342–1

County Business Patterns, 1988: employment, establishments, and payroll, by SIC 2- to 4-digit industry and county, annual State rpt series, 2326–6

County Business Patterns, 1989: employment, establishments, and payroll, by SIC 2- to 4-digit industry and county, annual State rpt series, 2326–8

County population size for counties with population over 100,000, as of Apr 1990, press release, 2328–68

Current Housing Reports, unit and household characteristics, subject rpt series, 2486–1

Current Population Reports, demographic, social, and economic characteristics, series, 2546–1

Current Population Reports, demographic subjects, special study series, 2546–2

Current Population Reports, income and socioeconomic characteristics of persons, families, and households, detailed cross-tabulations, series, 2546–6

Current Population Reports, population estimates and projections, by region and State, series, 2546–3

Current Population Reports, population estimates for civilian, resident, and total population, monthly rpt, 2542–1

Data collection and publication operations of Bur, US Code Title 13 text, 1991 rpt, 21628–94

Data collection, methodology, and related issues, 1991 annual conf, 2624–2

Data collection using tax and other govt admin records, methodological and disclosure issues, 1988-89 annual conf papers, 8304–17

Data coverage and availability of Census Bur rpts and data files, 1991 annual listing, 2304–2

Data coverage, availability, and use, for Census Bur rpts and products, series, 2326–7

Index by Subjects and Names

Data files and rpts of Census Bur, monthly listing, 2302–6

Developing countries aged population and selected characteristics, 1980s and projected to 2020, country rpt series, 2326–19

Economic Censuses of Puerto Rico, 1987: wholesale and retail trade and service industry finances and operations, by SIC 2- to 4-digit industry and municipio, 2591–1

Economic Censuses of Puerto Rico, 1987: wholesale, retail, and service industries finances and operations, by establishment characteristics and SIC 2- and 3-digit industry, subject rpts, 2591–2

Employment (temporary) for 1990 census, impact on natl employment trends, 1990, article, 6742–2.202

Enterprise Statistics, 1987: auxiliaries of multi-establishment firms, finances and operations by function, industry, and State, 2329–6

Enterprise Statistics, 1987: finances and operations for companies, by size, level of diversification, form of organization, and industry group, 2329–8

Export and import statistics, Census Bur publications and data files, 1991 guide, 2428–11

Export and import statistics classification codes of Census Bur for countries, 1991 edition, 2428–3

Export and import statistics classification codes of Census Bur for foreign ports, 1991, 2428–12

Export statistics classification codes of Census Bur for countries, commodities, and customs districts, 1990 base edition supplement, 2428–5

Exports and imports (waterborne) of US, by type of service, customs district, port, and world area, monthly rpt, 2422–7

Exports and imports between US and outlying areas, by detailed commodity and mode of transport, 1990, annual rpt, 2424–11

Exports and imports of US, by country and detailed commodity, monthly rpt, 2422–12

Exports and imports of US, by Harmonized System 6-digit commodity and country, 1990, annual rpt, 2424–13

Exports and imports of US, by transport mode, country, and SITC 1- to 3-digit commodity, 1990, annual rpt, 2424–12

Exports, imports, and trade flows, by country and commodity, with background economic indicators, data compilation, monthly CD-ROM, 2002–6

Exports of US, detailed commodities by country, monthly CD-ROM, 2422–13

Exports of US, detailed Schedule B commodities with countries of destination, 1990, annual rpt, 2424–10

Exports of US, detailed Schedule E commodities by mode of transport, world area, and country, annual rpts, discontinued, 2424–5

Fed Govt spending in States and local areas, by type, State, county, and city, FY90, annual rpt, 2464–3

Fed Govt spending in States, by type, program, agency, and State, FY90, annual rpt, 2464–2

Index by Subjects and Names

Food (processed) production and stocks by State, shipments, exports, ingredients, and use, periodic Current Industrial Rpt series, 2506–4

Foreign countries economic and social conditions, working paper series, 2326–18

Govt employment and payroll, by function, level of govt, and jurisdiction, 1990, annual rpt series, 2466–1

Govt finances, by level of govt, State, and for large cities and counties, annual rpt series, 2466–2

Govt retirement systems of States and local areas, cash and security holdings and finances, quarterly rpt, 2462–2

Housing alteration and repair spending, by characteristics of property and region, annual rpt, discontinued, 2384–4

Housing alteration and repair spending, by type, tenure, region, and other characteristics, quarterly rpt, 2382–7

Housing starts and completions authorized by building permits in 40 MSAs, quarterly rpt, 2382–9

Housing starts, by units per structure and metro-nonmetro location, and mobile home placements and prices, by region, monthly rpt, 2382–1

Housing units (1-family) sold and for sale by price, stage of construction, months on market, and region, monthly rpt, 2382–3

Housing units (1-family) sold, prices and price index by region, quarterly rpt, 2382–8

Housing units authorized, by region, State, selected MSA, and permit-issuing place, monthly rpt, 2382–5

Housing units authorized, by State, MSA, and permit-issuing place, 1990, annual rpt, 2384–2

Housing units completed and under construction, by region and units per structure, monthly rpt, 2382–2

Housing units completed, single and multifamily units by structural and financial characteristics, inside-outside MSAs, and region, 1986-90, annual rpt, 2384–1

Housing vacancy and occupancy rates, and vacant unit characteristics, by tenure and location, 1960s-90, annual rpt, 2484–1

Housing vacant unit characteristics and costs, and occupancy and vacancy rates, by region and metro-nonmetro location, quarterly rpt, 2482–1

Imports, exports, and employment impacts, by SIC 2- to 4-digit industry and commodity, quarterly rpt, 2322–2

Imports of US, detailed commodities by country, monthly CD-ROM, 2422–14

Imports of US, detailed Schedule A commodities by mode of transport, world area, and country, annual rpts, discontinued, 2424–2

Imports of US, detailed TSUSA commodities with countries of origin, annual rpt, discontinued, 2424–4

Industry classification codes concordance of Canada and US SICs, for 1- to 4-digit levels, 1991 rpt, 2628–31

Input-output tables construction of BEA, comparison to Census Bur source data, 1972 and 1977, working paper, 9375–13.53

Lumber, paper, and related products shipments, trade, stocks, and use, periodic Current Industrial Rpt series, 2506–7

Machinery and equipment production, shipments, trade, stocks, orders, use, and firms, by product, periodic Current Industrial Rpt series, 2506–12

Manufacturing industries operations and performance, analytical rpt series, 2506–16

Manufacturing production, shipments, inventories, orders, and pollution control costs, periodic Current Industrial Rpt series, 2506–3

Map and geographic computer-readable database of Census Bur, TIGER files availability and use, 1990 rpt, 2628–30

Metals (intermediate product) shipments, trade, and inventories, by product, periodic Current Industrial Rpt series, 2506–11

Metals (primary) production, shipments, trade, stocks, and material used, by product, periodic Current Industrial Rpt series, 2506–10

MSA population size, by area, as of Apr 1990, annual press release, 2324–8

Population and housing data, and policy issues, fact sheet series, 2326–17

Population size, July 1981-89 and compared to 1980 and 1990, annual press release, 2324–10

Poverty rate under alternative measurement methods, and public opinion on definition, 1988-89, hearing, 21968–56

Poverty threshold and rates under alternative threshold adjustment methodologies, 1980s-90, hearing, 23848–221

Recordkeeping Practices Survey, 1989: data coverage, methodology, businesses views, and applications for 1992 economic censuses, 2328–67

Retail trade sales and inventories, by kind of business, region, and selected State, MSA, and city, monthly rpt, 2413–3

Retail trade sales, by kind of business, advance monthly rpt, 2413–2

Retail trade sales, inventories, purchases, gross margin, and accounts receivable, by SIC 2- to 4-digit kind of business and form of ownership, 1989, annual rpt, 2413–5

Service industries receipts, by SIC 2- to 4-digit kind of business, 1990, annual rpt, 2413–8

State and local govts receiving Federal funds, compliance with Federal audit requirements, 1991 article, 10042–1.204

State and Metro Area Data Book, 1991 data compilation, 2328–54

Statistical Abstract of US, 1991 annual data compilation, 2324–1

Statistical programs of Fed Govt, index of spending for 4 agencies, 1976-88, hearing, 23848–218

Survey of Income and Program Participation, data collection, methodology, and comparisons to other data bases, working paper series, 2626–10

Survey of Income and Program Participation, data collection, methodology, and use, 1990 annual conf papers, 2624–1

Bureau of Export Administration

Survey of Income and Program Participation, household income and socioeconomic characteristics, special study series, 2546–20

Tax revenue, by level of govt, type of tax, State, and selected large county, quarterly rpt, 2462–3

Textile mill production, trade, sales, stocks, and material used, by product, region, and State, periodic Current Industrial Rpt series, 2506–5

Truck and warehouse services finances and inventory, by SIC 2- to 4-digit industry, 1989 survey, annual rpt, 2413–14

Wholesale trade sales and inventories, by SIC 2- to 3-digit kind of business, monthly rpt, 2413–7

Wholesale trade sales, inventories, purchases, and gross margins, by SIC 2- to 3-digit kind of business, 1990, annual rpt, 2413–13

Bureau of Consular Affairs, State Department

Visas of US issued and refused to immigrants and nonimmigrants, by class, issuing office, and nationality, FY89, annual rpt, 7184–1

Bureau of Economic Analysis

Data coverage and availability of BEA rpts, 1991 rpt, 2708–45

Foreign direct investment in US, by industry group of US affiliate and country of parent firm, 1980-86, 2708–41

Income (personal) per capita and by source, and earnings by industry div, by State, MSA, and county, 1984-89, annual regional rpts, 2704–2

Input-output tables construction of BEA, comparison to Census Bur source data, 1972 and 1977, working paper, 9375–13.53

Multinatl firms US affiliates, finances, and operations, by industry, world area of parent firm, and State, 1988-89, annual rpt, 2704–4

Multinatl US firms and foreign affiliates finances and operations, by industry and world area of parent firm, 1989 benchmark survey, preliminary annual rpt, 2704–5

Statistical programs of Fed Govt, index of spending for 4 agencies, 1976-88, hearing, 23848–218

Survey of Current Business, detailed data for major industries and economic indicators, monthly rpt, 2702–1

Bureau of Engraving and Printing

Budget of US, obligations and authority by function, agency, and program, with summaries, analyses, and historical tables, FY92, annual rpt, 104–2

Bureau of Export Administration

Budget of US, obligations and authority by function, agency, and program, with summaries, analyses, and historical tables, FY92, annual rpt, 104–2

Gear production for selected uses under alternative production requirements, and industry finances and operations, late 1940s-89, 2028–1

Licensing of exports, monitoring, and enforcement activities, FY90, annual rpt, 2024–1

Bureau of Health Care Delivery and Assistance

Bureau of Health Care Delivery and Assistance
Migrant workers and dependents by county, and health centers use and programs funding, by State, 1986-89, 4108–53

Bureau of Health Professions
Minority group and women health condition, services use, payment sources, and health care labor force, by poverty status, 1940s-89, chartbook, 4118–56
Minority group health condition, services use, costs, and indicators of services need, 1950s-88, 4118–55
Physicians, by specialty, age, sex, and location of training and practice, 1989, State rpt series, 4116–6

Bureau of Indian Affairs
Budget of US, obligations and authority by function, agency, and program, with summaries, analyses, and historical tables, FY92, annual rpt, 104–2
Cherokee Indian Agency activities in North Carolina, FY91, annual rpt, 5704–4
Education (special) enrollment by age, staff, funding, and needs, by type of handicap and State, 1989/90, annual rpt, 4944–4
Education funding of Fed Govt, and enrollment, degrees, and program grants and fellowships by State, for Indians, late 1960s-FY89, annual rpt, 14874–1
Expenditures of Fed Govt in States, by type, program, agency, and State, FY90, annual rpt, 2464–2
Finances and operations of Federal power admins and electric utilities, 1989, annual rpt, 3164–24.2
Timber mgmt programs of Bur of Indian Affairs, funding, acreage, harvest, and tribal investment, by tribe and location, FY77-89 and projected to FY96, hearing, 25418–4
Tribal govt increased authority over BIA funds, with data by program, tribe, and region, FY78-90, GAO rpt, 26113–508

Bureau of Intelligence and Research, State Department
Communist and OECD countries economic conditions, 1989, annual rpt, 7144–11
EC trade with US by country, and total agricultural trade, selected years 1958-90, annual rpt, 7144–7
Foreign countries *Geographic Notes*, boundaries, claims, nomenclature, and other devs, periodic rpt, 7142–3
Military aid of US, arms sales, and training programs costs and budget requests, by program, world region, and country, FY90-92, annual rpt, 7144–13
NATO members trade with PRC, by country, 1987-90, annual rpt, 7144–14
OECD members GNP and GNP growth, by country, 1980-90, annual rpt, 7144–8
OECD trade, by country, 1989, annual rpt, 7144–10

Bureau of International Labor Affairs
Caribbean area duty-free exports to US, and imports from US, by country, and impact on US employment, by commodity, 1990, annual rpt, 6364–2
Developing countries labor standards impacts on social and economic dev, 1988 conf papers, 6368–9
Exports and imports impacts on US industries and employment, series, 6366–3

Foreign countries labor conditions, union coverage, and work accidents, annual country rpt series, 6366–4
Immigration, alien workers, amnesty programs, and employer sanctions impacts on US economy and labor force, series, 6366–5

Bureau of Justice Assistance
Drug control task forces enforcement activities by drug type and State, and organization, staff, and spending, 1988, 6068–244
Jail drug treatment programs finances and operations, FY89-90, 21408–120

Bureau of Justice Statistics
Activities of BJS and States for criminal justice data collection, annual rpt, discontinued, 6064–21
Court criminal case processing in Federal district courts, and dispositions, by offense, district, and offender characteristics, 1986, annual rpt, 6064–29
Court criminal case processing in Federal district courts, and dispositions, by offense, 1980-89, annual rpt, 6064–31
Crime and criminal justice data collection programs and rpts, 1989, annual listing, 6064–25
Crime, criminal justice admin and enforcement, and public opinion, data compilation, 1991 annual rpt, 6064–6
Crime victimization rates, by victim and offender characteristics, circumstances, and offense, survey rpt series, 6066–3
Criminal justice issues, series, 6066–19; 6066–25
Criminal justice spending, employment, and payroll, by level of govt, State, and selected city and county, FY71-88, biennial rpt, 6064–9
Criminal justice spending, employment, and payroll, by level of govt, State, and selected city and county, 1984-86, biennial rpt, 6064–4
Criminal records repository characteristics, holdings, use, and reporting requirements, by State, 1989, 6068–241
Drug enforcement, offenses, and public opinion, BJS rpts, 1975-89, annual pamphlet, 6064–30
Jail adult and juvenile population, employment, spending, instn conditions, and inmate programs, by county and facility, 1988, regional rpt series, 6068–144
Juvenile correctional and detention public and private instns, inmates, and expenses, by instn and resident characteristics and State, 1987, biennial rpt, 6064–13
Prison and parole admissions and releases, sentence length, and time served, by offense and offender characteristics, 1985, annual rpt, 6064–33
Prisoner admissions by State and for Federal instns, by race, 1926-86, 6068–245
Prisoners, characteristics, and movements, by State, 1989, annual rpt, 6064–26
Prisoners in Federal and State instns, by sex and State, June 1991, semiannual rpt, 6062–4
Probation and split sentences by State courts for felony offenses, sentence lengths, case processing time, and felon characteristics, by offense, 1986, 6068–242

Index by Subjects and Names

Violent crime victimizations, circumstances, victim characteristics, arrest, recidivism, sentences, and prisoners, 1980s, 6068–148
Women's rape and other violent crime victimization, by relation to offender, circumstances, and victim characteristics, 1973-87, 6068–243

Bureau of Labor Statistics
Auto quality changes since last model year, factory and retail value, 1991 model year, annual press release, 6764–3
Budget of US, obligations and authority by function, agency, and program, with summaries, analyses, and historical tables, FY92, annual rpt, 104–2
Collective bargaining agreements expiring during year, and workers covered, by firm, union, industry group, and State, 1991, annual rpt, 6784–9
Collective bargaining wage and benefit changes, quarterly press release, 6782–2
Consumer Expenditure Survey, household income by source, and itemized spending, by selected characteristics and region, 1988-89, annual rpt, 6764–5
Consumer Expenditure Survey, spending by category, selected household characteristics, and region, quarterly rpt, 6762–14
CPI by component for US city average, and by region, population size, and for 15 metro areas, monthly rpt, 6762–1
CPI by component for US city average, and by region, population size, and for 27 metro areas, monthly rpt, 6762–2
CPI components relative importance, by selected MSA, region, population size, and for US city average, 1990, annual rpt, 6884–1
CPI use in escalator clauses of collective bargaining agreements and other contracts, with conversion factors for index rebasing, 1991 guide, 6888–34
Dallas-Fort Worth-Arlington metro area employment, earnings, hours, and CPI changes, late 1970s-90, annual rpt, 6964–2
Data programs and publications of BLS, as of Feb 1991, listing, 6728–35
Department store inventory price indexes, by class of item, monthly table, 6762–7
Economic indicators, prices, labor costs, and productivity, BLS econometric analyses and methodology, working paper series, 6886–6
Employer Cost Index by region, quarterly press release, 6942–8
Employment and Earnings, detailed data, monthly rpt, 6742–2
Employment Cost Index and percent change by occupational group, industry div, region, and metro-nonmetro area, quarterly press release, 6782–5
Employment, earnings, and hours, by SIC 1- to 4-digit industry, monthly and annual averages, selected years 1909-90, annual rpt, 6744–4
Employment, earnings, and hours, monthly press release, 6742–5
Employment, unemployment, and labor force characteristics, by region, State, and selected metro area, 1990, annual rpt, 6744–7

Index by Subjects and Names

Export and import price indexes, by selected end-use category, monthly press release, 6762–15

Export and import price indexes for goods and services, and dollar exchange rate indexes, quarterly press release, 6762–13

Family members labor force status and earnings, by family composition and race, quarterly press release, 6742–21

Fed Govt labor productivity, indexes of output and labor costs, by function, FY67-89, 6824–4

Foreign and US manufacturing labor costs and indexes, by selected country, 1990, semiannual rpt, 6822–3

Houston metro area employment, earnings, hours, and CPI changes, 1970s-90, annual rpt, 6964–1

Injuries at workplace, by circumstances, body site, equipment type, and industry, with safety measures, series, 6846–1

Injury and illness rates by SIC 2- to 4-digit industry, and deaths by cause and industry div, 1989, annual rpt, 6844–1

Injury and illness rates, by SIC 2- to 4-digit industry, 1988-89, annual rpt, 6844–7

Labor force characteristics, press release series, 6726–1

Labor hourly costs, by component, industry sector, worker class, and firm size, 1990, annual rpt, 6744–22

Living costs abroad, State Dept indexes, housing allowances, and hardship differentials by country and major city, quarterly rpt, issuing agency change, 6862–1

Lumber industry workers and wages by occupation, annual State survey rpt series, 6787–7

Manufacturing employment, by detailed occupation and SIC 2-digit industry, 1989 survey, triennial rpt, 6748–52

Minority group labor force status, by race, detailed Hispanic origin, and sex, quarterly rpt, 6742–18

Monthly Labor Review, current statistics and articles, 6722–1

Occupational injuries, illnesses, and workdays lost, by SIC 2-digit industry, 1989-90, annual press release, 6844–3

Occupational Outlook Quarterly, journal, 6742–1

Producer Price Index, by major commodity group and subgroup, and processing stage, monthly press release, 6762–5

Producer price indexes, by stage of processing and detailed commodity, monthly rpt, 6762–6

Producer price indexes, by stage of processing and detailed commodity, monthly 1990, annual rpt, 6764–2

Productivity and costs of labor for private, nonfarm business, and manufacturing sectors, revised data, quarterly rpt, 6822–2

Productivity and costs of labor, indexes, preliminary data, quarterly rpt, 6822–1

Productivity of labor and capital, indexes and percent change, 1948-90, annual press release, 6824–2

Productivity of labor, indexes of output, hours, and employment by SIC 2- to 4-digit industry, 1967-89, annual rpt, 6824–1

Small business employees benefit plan coverage and provisions, by plan type and occupational group, 1990, biennial rpt, 6784–20

Southeastern US employment by industry div, earnings, and hours, for 8 States, quarterly press release, 6942–7

Southeastern US employment by industry div, unemployment, and CPI, for 8 States, 1989-90, annual rpt, 6944–2

Southeastern US employment conditions, suspended series, 6946–1

Southeastern US employment conditions, with comparisons to other regions, press release series, 6946–3

Southeastern US textile mill employment, earnings, and hours, for 8 States, quarterly press release, 6942–1

Southern US textile mill employment, 1951-90, annual rpt, 6944–1

Southwestern US employment by industry div, earnings, and hours, by State, with CPI by major component for 2 Texas MSAs, monthly rpt, 6962–2

State and local govt collective bargaining, wage and benefit changes and coverage, 1st half 1991, semiannual press release, 6782–6

State and local govt employment and payroll, monthly rpt, 6742–4

Statistical programs of Fed Govt, index of spending for 4 agencies, 1976-88, hearing, 23848–218

Unemployment, by State and metro area, monthly press release, 6742–12

Unemployment, employment, and labor force, by State, MSA, and city, monthly rpt, 6742–22

Unemployment insurance coverage of establishments, employment, and wages, by SIC 4-digit industry and State, 1990, annual rpt, 6744–16

Wage and benefit changes from collective bargaining and mgmt decisions, by industry div, monthly rpt, 6782–1

Wages by occupation, and benefits for office and plant workers in selected MSAs, 1990, annual rpt, 6785–1

Wages by occupation, and benefits for office and plant workers, periodic MSA survey rpt series, 6785–3; 6785–11; 6785–12

Wages by occupation, for office and plant workers in metro areas, by industry div and region, Aug 1990, annual rpt, 6785–9

Wages by occupation, for office and plant workers in selected MSAs, 1991 surveys, annual rpt, 6785–5

Wages by occupation, for office and plant workers in selected MSAs, 1991 surveys, annual summary rpts, 6785–6

Wages for 4 occupational groups, relative pay levels in 60 MSAs, 1990, annual rpt, 6785–8

Wages for 4 occupational groups, relative pay levels in 75 labor market areas, 1990, annual rpt, 6785–13

Wages, hourly and weekly averages by industry div, monthly press release, 6742–3

Wages, hours, and employment by occupation, and benefits, for selected locations, industry survey rpt series, 6787–6

Bureau of Land Management

Wages of full- and part-time workers, by selected characteristics, quarterly press release, 6742–20

Wages of workers covered by unemployment insurance, by industry div, State, and MSA, 1989-90, annual press releases, 6784–17

Women's labor force status, by age, race, and family status, quarterly rpt, 6742–17

Work stoppages, workers involved, and days idle, 1990 and trends from 1947, annual press release, 6784–12

Youth labor force status by age, Apr and July 1991 and change from 1990, annual press release, 6744–13

Youth labor force status, by sex, race, and industry div, summer 1987-91, annual press release, 6744–14

Bureau of Land Management

Acreage, grants, use, revenues, and allocations, for public lands by State, FY90 and trends, annual rpt, 5724–1

Activities and finances of BLM, and public land acreage and use, annual State rpt series, 5724–11

Activities and finances of BLM, by State, FY89, annual rpt, 5724–13

Activities of BLM in Southwestern US, FY90, annual rpt, 5724–15

Alaska submerged land grant holdings of Alaska Natives, exchange for upland acreage, impacts on conservation acreage and acquisition, 1989-90, 5728–38

Budget of US, obligations and authority by function, agency, and program, with summaries, analyses, and historical tables, FY92, annual rpt, 104–2

Coal leasing activity on Federal land, acreage, production, and reserves, by coal region and State, FY90, annual rpt, 5724–10

Expenditures of Fed Govt in States, by type, program, agency, and State, FY90, annual rpt, 2464–2

Horse and burro wild herd areas in western States, population, adoption, and mgmt costs, as of FY89, biennial rpt, 5724–8

Idaho Snake River area birds of prey, rodent, and vegetation distribution and characteristics, research results, 1990, annual rpt, 5724–14

Public lands, Fed Govt payments to local govts in lieu of property taxes, by State and county, FY91, annual rpt, 5724–9

Public lands, Fed Govt payments to local govts in lieu of property taxes, by State, FY91, annual press release, 5306–4.10

Recreation (outdoor) facilities of Fed Govt, fees and visits by managing agency, FY88-90, annual rpt, 5544–14

Recreation (outdoor) facilities on public land, use, and Land Mgmt Bur mgmt activities, funding, and plans, State rpt series, 5726–5

Sheep (desert bighorn) population and mgmt on public land, by State, 1989 rpt, 5728–36

Wetlands (riparian) acreage, and Bur of Land Mgmt activities, mgmt plans, and scientific staff, State rpt series, 5726–8

Wildlife mgmt activities and funding, acreage by habitat type, and scientific staff, for Bur of Land Mgmt, State rpt series, 5726–7

Bureau of Land Management

Wildlife mgmt activities and funding, acreage, staff, and plans of Bur of Land Mgmt, habitat study series, 5726–6

Wildlife mgmt on public lands, endangered species, and BLM activities and funding, FY80-90, 5728–37

Bureau of Mines

- Alaska land area by ownership, and availability for mineral exploration and dev, 1984-86, 5608–152
- Alaska minerals resources and production, by mineral and site, for Juneau region, 1987-88, 5608–169
- Back injuries in underground coal mines, by circumstances, victim characteristics, and treatment, mid 1980s, 5608–166
- Budget of US, obligations and authority by function, agency, and program, with summaries, analyses, and historical tables, FY92, annual rpt, 104–2
- China minerals production and trade, by commodity, 1988-89, annual rpt, 5604–38
- Explosives and blasting agents use, by type, industry, and State, 1990, Mineral Industry Surveys, annual rpt, 5614–22
- Foreign and US minerals supply under alternative market conditions, reserves, and background industry data, series, 5606–4
- Helium market demand and Bur production, sales, and financial statements, FY90, annual rpt, 5604–32
- Helium resources in storage and natural gas reserves, by State, 1950-89 and projected to 2020, biennial rpt, 5604–44
- Mineral Industry Surveys, commodity reviews of production, trade, stocks, and use, monthly rpt series, 5612–1
- Mineral Industry Surveys, commodity reviews of production, trade, stocks, and use, quarterly rpt series, 5612–2
- Mineral Industry Surveys, commodity reviews of production, trade, use, and industry operations, advance annual rpt series, 5614–5
- Mineral Industry Surveys, State reviews of production, 1990, preliminary annual rpt, 5614–6
- Minerals (industrial) reserves, production, and use, and characteristics of individual deposits, State rpt series, 5606–10
- Minerals production, prices, trade, and foreign and US industry devs, by commodity, bimonthly rpt with articles, 5602–4
- Minerals production, prices, trade, use, employment, tariffs, and stockpiles, by mineral, with foreign comparisons, 1986-90, annual rpt, 5604–18
- *Minerals Yearbook, 1988,* data collection and availability, annual rpt, 5604–48
- *Minerals Yearbook, 1988,* Vol 3: foreign country reviews of production, trade, and policy, by commodity, annual rpt series, 5604–17
- *Minerals Yearbook, 1989,* Vol 1: commodity reviews of production, reserves, supply, use, and trade, annual rpt series, 5604–15
- *Minerals Yearbook, 1989,* Vol 2: State reviews of production and sales by commodity, and business activity, annual rpt series, 5604–16

Index by Subjects and Names

- *Minerals Yearbook, 1989,* Vol 2: State reviews of production, sales, and firms, by commodity, and business activity, annual rpt, 5604–34
- *Minerals Yearbook, 1990,* Vol 1: commodity reviews of production, reserves, supply, use, and trade, annual rpt series, 5604–20
- Natural gas composition and helium levels, analyses of individual wells and pipelines, by selected State and county, 1917-90, annual rpt, 5604–2
- Phosphate rock production, prices, sales, trade, and use, 1991, Mineral Industry Surveys, annual rpt, 5614–20
- Potash production, prices, trade, use, and sales, 1990 crop year, Mineral Industry Surveys, annual rpt, 5614–19
- Public lands minerals resources and availability, State rpt series, 5606–7
- Publications and patents of Mines Bur, monthly listing, 5602–2
- Publications and patents of Mines Bur, 1985-89, quinquennial listing, 5608–168
- Publications of Bur of Mines, annual listing, periodicity change, 5604–40
- Salt production capacity, by firm and facility, 1990, annual listing, 5614–30
- Soviet Union minerals production and trade, by commodity, 1985-89 and projected to 2005, annual rpt, 5604–39
- Technologically advanced structural materials devs and data needs, 1989 conf, 5608–167
- Technologically advanced structural materials devs, use, and R&D funding, for ceramics, metal alloys, polymers, and composites, 1960s-80s and projected to 2000, 5608–162

Bureau of Prisons

- Activities of Bur, and inmate and staff characteristics, 1990, annual rpt, 6244–2
- Budget of US, obligations and authority by function, agency, and program, with summaries, analyses, and historical tables, FY92, annual rpt, 104–2
- Costs of construction and operation, capacity, and inmates, for Federal and State prisons, 1985-89, GAO rpt, 26119–341
- Crime, criminal justice admin and enforcement, and public opinion, data compilation, 1991 annual rpt, 6064–6
- Debt delinquent on Federal accounts, cases and collections of Justice Dept and private law firms, pilot project results, FY90, annual rpt, 6004–20
- Facilities characteristics for Bur admin offices and correctional instns, 1991, annual listing, 6244–4
- Fed Prison Industries finances and operations, FY90, annual rpt, 6244–3
- Fed Prison Industries sales, by commodity and Federal agency, FY90, annual rpt, 6244–5
- Halfway house placements of Federal prisoners, duration, and employment, and house capacity, 1990-91, GAO rpt, 26119–347
- Prisoners in Federal instns, by sex, prison, security level, contract facility type, and region, monthly rpt series, 6242–1

Bureau of Reclamation

- Activities and finances of Bur, FY90, annual rpt, 5824–1
- Budget of US, obligations and authority by function, agency, and program, with summaries, analyses, and historical tables, FY92, annual rpt, 104–2
- Colorado River Basin Federal reservoir and power operations and revenues, 1990-91, annual rpt, 5824–6
- Columbia River Power System projects, plant investment allocation schedule, FY90, annual rpt, 3224–1
- Hydroelectric power plants capacity and other characteristics, for western US, FY90, annual rpt, 3254–1
- Irrigation projects of Bur, acreage limits monitoring activities by region, 1988-90, annual rpt, 5824–13
- Irrigation projects of Reclamation Bur in western US, crop production and acreage by commodity, State, and project, 1989, annual rpt, 5824–12
- Recreation (outdoor) facilities of Fed Govt, fees and visits by managing agency, FY88-90, annual rpt, 5544–14

Bureau of Security and Consular Affairs *see* Bureau of Consular Affairs, State Department

Bureau of the Mint *see* U.S. Mint

Bureau of the Public Debt

- Budget of US, obligations and authority by function, agency, and program, with summaries, analyses, and historical tables, FY92, annual rpt, 104–2
- Public debt issued, redeemed, and outstanding, by series and source, and gifts to reduce debt, monthly rpt, 8242–2
- Savings bonds issued, redeemed, and outstanding, by series, monthly table, 8242–1

Bureaucracy

- *see* Civil service system
- *see* Government efficiency
- *see* Government employees
- *see* International employees
- *see* Political science
- *see* Public administration

Burfisher, Mary E.

"Less Developed Countries' Performance in High-Value Agricultural Trade", 1528–316

Burgdorf, Kenneth

- "Academic Research Equipment and Equipment Needs in Selected Science and Engineering Fields, 1989-90", 9627–27.2
- "Academic Research Equipment and Equipment Needs in the Physical Sciences, 1989", 9627–27.3
- "Academic Research Equipment in Computer Science, Central Computer Facilities and Engineering, 1989", 9627–27.1
- "Characteristics of Science/Engineering Equipment in Academic Settings: 1989-90", 9627–27.4

Burglary

- *see* Motor vehicle theft
- *see* Robbery and theft
- *see* Security devices

Burial and burial laws

- *see* Cemeteries and funerals
- *see* Military cemeteries and funerals

Index by Subjects and Names

Buses

Burke, Laurie B.

"Drug Utilization in the U.S., 1989: Eleventh Annual Review", 4064–12

Burke, Thomas P.

"How Firm Size and Industry Affect Employee Benefits", 6722–1.204

"Trends in Employer-Provided Health Care Benefits", 6722–1.214

Burkina Faso

- Agricultural exports of high-value commodities, indexes and sales by commodity, world area, and country, 1960s-86, 1528–323
- Agricultural trade of US, by detailed commodity and country, 1989, annual rpt, 1524–8
- Agricultural trade of US, by detailed commodity and country, 1990, semiannual rpt, 1522–4
- AID economic aid to developing countries, obligations and disbursements by country, quarterly rpt, 9912–4
- Dairy imports, consumption, and market conditions, by sub-Saharan Africa country, 1961-88, 1528–321
- Economic and military aid and loans from US and intl agencies, by program and country, FY46-90, annual rpt, 9914–5
- Economic and social conditions of developing countries from 1960s, and Intl Dev Cooperation Agency and AID activities and funding, FY90-92, annual rpt, 9904–4
- Economic conditions, income, production, prices, employment, and trade, 1990 periodic country rpt, 2046–4.5
- Economic, social, political, and geographic summary data, by country, 1991, annual factbook, 9114–2
- Exports and imports of US, by transport mode, country, and SITC 1- to 3-digit commodity, 1990, annual rpt, 2424–12
- Exports of US, detailed Schedule B commodities with countries of destination, 1990, annual rpt, 2424–10
- Grain production, use, imports, and stocks, for Sahel region by country, 1989/90, 9918–18
- Human rights conditions in 170 countries, and US economic and military aid, 1990, annual rpt, 21384–3
- Military aid of US, arms sales, and training programs costs and budget requests, by program, world region, and country, FY90-92, annual rpt, 7144–13
- UN voting record and share of votes in agreement with US, by issue, country, and world area, 1990, annual rpt, 7004–18
- *see also* under By Foreign Country in the "Index by Categories"

Burlington, N.C.

see also under By SMSA or MSA in the "Index by Categories"

Burlington, Vt.

see also under By SMSA or MSA in the "Index by Categories"

Burma

- Agricultural exports of high-value commodities, indexes and sales by commodity, world area, and country, 1960s-86, 1528–323
- Agricultural trade of US, by detailed commodity and country, 1989, annual rpt, 1524–8

- Agricultural trade of US, by detailed commodity and country, 1990, semiannual rpt, 1522–4
- AID economic aid to developing countries, obligations and disbursements by country, quarterly rpt, 9912–4
- AID loans repayment status and terms by program and country, and status of predecessor agency loans, quarterly rpt, 9912–3
- Economic and military aid and loans from US and intl agencies, by program and country, FY46-90, annual rpt, 9914–5
- Economic and social conditions of developing countries from 1960s, and Intl Dev Cooperation Agency and AID activities and funding, FY90-92, annual rpt, 9904–4
- Economic conditions, income, production, prices, employment, and trade, 1991 periodic country rpt, 2046–4.14
- Economic, social, political, and geographic summary data, by country, 1991, annual factbook, 9114–2
- Exports and imports of US, by transport mode, country, and SITC 1- to 3-digit commodity, 1990, annual rpt, 2424–12
- Exports of US, detailed Schedule B commodities with countries of destination, 1990, annual rpt, 2424–10
- Human rights conditions in 170 countries, and US economic and military aid, 1990, annual rpt, 21384–3
- UN voting record and share of votes in agreement with US, by issue, country, and world area, 1990, annual rpt, 7004–18
- *see also* Myanmar
- *see also* under By Foreign Country in the "Index by Categories"

Burn injuries

see Fires and fire prevention

Burns, Barbara J.

"Mental Illness in Nursing Homes: U.S., 1985. Vital and Health Statistics Series 13", 4147–13.106

Burns, Eugene M.

"Commercial Buildings Characteristics, 1989. Commercial Buildings Energy Consumption Survey", 3166–8.9

Burr, Jeffrey A.

- "Household and Nonhousehold Living Arrangements in Later Life: A Longitudinal Analysis of a Social Process", 2626–10.134
- "Racial Differences in Health and Health Care Service Utilization: The Effect of Socioeconomic Status", 2626–10.127

Burundi

- Agricultural exports of high-value commodities, indexes and sales by commodity, world area, and country, 1960s-86, 1528–323
- Agricultural trade of US, by detailed commodity and country, 1989, annual rpt, 1524–8
- Agricultural trade of US, by detailed commodity and country, 1990, semiannual rpt, 1522–4
- AID economic aid to developing countries, obligations and disbursements by country, quarterly rpt, 9912–4
- *Background Notes*, summary social, political, and economic data, 1991 rpt, 7006–2.45
- Dairy imports, consumption, and market conditions, by sub-Saharan Africa country, 1961-88, 1528–321

- Economic and military aid and loans from US and intl agencies, by program and country, FY46-90, annual rpt, 9914–5
- Economic and social conditions of developing countries from 1960s, and Intl Dev Cooperation Agency and AID activities and funding, FY90-92, annual rpt, 9904–4
- Economic conditions, income, production, prices, employment, and trade, 1991 periodic country rpt, 2046–4.32
- Economic, population, and agricultural data, US and other aid sources, and AID activity, 1989 country rpt, 9916–12.31
- Economic, social, political, and geographic summary data, by country, 1991, annual factbook, 9114–2
- Exports and imports of US, by transport mode, country, and SITC 1- to 3-digit commodity, 1990, annual rpt, 2424–12
- Exports of US, detailed Schedule B commodities with countries of destination, 1990, annual rpt, 2424–10
- Human rights conditions in 170 countries, and US economic and military aid, 1990, annual rpt, 21384–3
- Military aid of US, arms sales, and training programs costs and budget requests, by program, world region, and country, FY90-92, annual rpt, 7144–13
- *Minerals Yearbook, 1988*, Vol 3: foreign country review of production, trade, and policy, by commodity, annual rpt, 5604–17.80
- UN voting record and share of votes in agreement with US, by issue, country, and world area, 1990, annual rpt, 7004–18
- *see also* under By Foreign Country in the "Index by Categories"

Burwell, Brian

"Access to Medicaid and Medicare by the Low-Income Disabled", 4652–1.218

Buses

- Accidents (fatal), circumstances, and characteristics of persons and vehicles involved, 1990, semiannual rpt, 7762–11
- Accidents (fatal), deaths, and rates, by circumstances, characteristics of persons and vehicles involved, and location, 1989, annual rpt, 7764–10
- Accidents at hwy-railroad grade-crossings, detailed data by State and railroad, 1989, annual rpt, 7604–2
- Accidents, casualties, circumstances, and characteristics of persons and vehicles involved, 1989, annual rpt, 7764–18
- County Business Patterns, 1988: employment, establishments, and payroll, by SIC 2- to 4-digit industry and county, annual State rpt series, 2326–6
- County Business Patterns, 1989: employment, establishments, and payroll, by SIC 2- to 4-digit industry and county, annual State rpt series, 2326–8
- Customs Service activities, collections, entries processed by mode of transport, and seizures, FY86-90, annual rpt, 8144–1
- DOT activities by subagency, budget, and summary accident data, FY88, annual rpt, 7304–1
- Drivers licenses issued and in force by age and sex, fees, and renewal, by license class and State, 1989, annual rpt, 7554–16

Buses

Employment, earnings, and hours, by SIC 1- to 4-digit industry, monthly and annual averages, selected years 1909-90, annual rpt, 6744–4

Energy economy, sales, and market shares, by size and model for domestic and foreign makes, 1991 model year, semiannual rpt, 3302–4

Energy use and vehicle registrations, by vehicle type, 1960-90, annual rpt, 3164–74.1

Energy use by mode of transport, fuel supply, and demographic and economic factors of vehicle use, 1970s-89, annual rpt, 3304–5

Exports and imports of US, by country and detailed commodity, monthly rpt, 2422–12

Exports and imports of US, by Harmonized System 6-digit commodity and country, 1990, annual rpt, 2424–13

Finances and operations of interstate carriers, by carrier, 1989, annual rpt, 9486–6.3

Finances and operations of transit systems, by mode of transport, size of fleet, and for 468 systems, 1989, annual rpt, 7884–4

Finances, costs, and needs of transit systems, by selected system, 1987-89, biennial rpt, 7884–8

High occupancy vehicle lanes for carpools and buses, use, design, and enforcement, for US and Canada, 1989, 7888–80

Hwy Statistics, detailed data by State, 1990, annual rpt, 7554–1

Hwy Statistics, summary data by State, 1989-90, annual rpt, 7554–24

Labor productivity, indexes of output, hours, and employment by SIC 2- to 4-digit industry, 1967-89, annual rpt, 6824–1.4

Manufacturing annual survey, 1989: finances and operations, by SIC 2- to 4-digit industry, series, 2506–15

Military and personal property shipments, passenger traffic, and costs, by service branch and mode of transport, quarterly rpt, 3702–1

Natl park system visits and overnight stays, by park and State, monthly rpt, 5542–4

Natl transportation system planning, use, condition, accidents, and needs, by mode of transport, 1940s-90 and projected to 2020, 7308–202

Occupational injury and illness rates, by SIC 2- to 4-digit industry, 1988-89, annual rpt, 6844–7

Occupational injury and illness rates, by SIC 2- to 4-digit industry, 1989, annual rpt, 6844–1

Price indexes (producer), by stage of processing and detailed commodity, monthly rpt, 6762–6

Price indexes (producer), by stage of processing and detailed commodity, monthly 1990, annual rpt, 6764–2

Recalls of motor vehicles and equipment with safety-related defects, by make, monthly listing, 7762–12

Ridership and selected revenue data, for individual large Class I bus carriers, quarterly rpt, 9482–13

Rural areas bus connector service to Greyhound intercity routes, finances and operations by system, 1987-90, 7888–79

Safety inspections of trucks and buses, fines, and vehicles and drivers ordered out of service, by State, with program funding, FY89, 25268–78

Safety programs, and accidents, casualties, and damage, by mode of transport, 1989, annual rpt, 7304–19

Statistical Abstract of US, 1991 annual data compilation, 2324–1.21

Tax provisions of States for motor fuel, auto registration fees, and disposition of receipts, by State, as of Jan 1991, biennial rpt, 7554–37

Travel from US, characteristics of visit and traveler, and country of destination, 1990 in-flight survey, annual rpt, 2904–14

Travel patterns, personal and household characteristics, and auto and public transport use, 1990 survey, series, 7556–6

Travel to US, by characteristics of visit and traveler, world area of origin, and US destination, 1990 survey, annual rpt, 2904–12

Urban Mass Transportation Admin grants for transit systems, by city and State, FY90, annual rpt, 7884–10

see also School busing

Business acquisitions and mergers

Acquisitions and mergers by type, with data for large transactions by payment method and firm, late 1960s-90, working paper, 9366–1.161

Airline deregulation in 1978, and regional and major carriers agreements, impacts on service to small communities, late 1980s, 7308–199.10

Airline financial and operating summary data, quarterly rpt, 7502–16

Banking industry structure and deposit insurance reform, findings and recommendations, with background data, 1989-90, 8008–147

Banks (agricultural) financial performance, before and after Farm Credit System mergers, by district, 1986-89, article, 1541–1.205

Banks (insured commercial and savings) finances, and changes in status, by State, 1989, annual rpt, 9294–4.1

Banks (natl) charters, mergers, liquidations, enforcement cases, and financial performance, with data by instn and State, quarterly rpt, 8402–3

Banks acquisitions purchase price relation to target and acquiring banks earnings variability and other factors, 1980s, working paper, 9371–10.57

Banks in southeastern States, mergers and acquisitions, assets and major institutions involved, by State, 1984-89, article, 9371–1.203

Banks mergers approved, and assets and offices involved, by instn, 1989, annual rpt, 9294–5

Credit unions federally insured, finances, mergers, closings, and insurance fund losses and financial statements, FY90, annual rpt, 9534–7

Energy producers finances and operations, by energy type for US firms domestic and foreign operations, 1989, annual rpt, 3164–44

Energy resources of US, foreign direct investment by energy type and firm, US affiliates operations, and acquisitions, as of 1989, annual rpt, 3164–80

Index by Subjects and Names

European Community economic integration issues, with intracountry mergers and acquisitions, late 1980s, 21248–153

Farm Credit System financial condition, impacts of instn mergers, by district, 1982-89, 1548–381

Fed Reserve Board and Reserve banks finances, staff, and review of monetary policy and economic devs, 1990, annual rpt, 9364–1

Foreign direct investment in US by country, and finances, employment, and acreage owned, by industry group of business acquired or established, 1984-90, annual article, 2702–1.210

Foreign direct investment in US, major transactions by type, industry, country, and US location, 1989, annual rpt, 2044–20

Foreign direct investment in US, new and established affiliates assets, and acquisitions, by industry div, 1980s, technical paper, 9366–7.255

Leveraged buyouts impacts on financial performance, for 4 transactions, 1980s-90, GAO rpt, 26119–355

Leveraged buyouts in manufacturing, relation to industry size, concentration ratios, and financial indicators, 1988, technical paper, 9385–8.86

Multinatl firms US affiliates, investment trends and impact on US economy, 1991 annual rpt, 2004–9

Oil refinery capacity, closings, and acquisitions by plant, and fuel used, by PAD district, 1973-89, annual rpt, 3164–2.1

Oil refinery operations and finances, with ownership changes, shutdowns, and reactivations, by firm, 1970s-90, 3168–119

Pension plans of firms acquired in leveraged buyouts, finances, participation, terminations, and replacements, 1982-87, GAO rpt, 26121–408

Savings and loan assns, FHLB 11th District members, offices, and financial condition, 1991 annual listing, 9304–23

Savings instns failure resolution activity and finances of Resolution Trust Corp, with data by asset type, State, region, and instn, monthly rpt, 9722–3

Savings instns failure resolution activity of Resolution Trust Corp, assets, deposits, and assets availability and sales, periodic press release, 9722–1

Savings instns failure resolution activity of Resolution Trust Corp, with data by State and instn, and RTC financial statements, 1989, annual rpt, 9724–1

Savings instns voluntary, supervisory, and SAIF-assisted mergers and FHLB membership changes, selected years 1970-89, annual rpt, 8434–3.1

Statistical Abstract of US, 1991 annual data compilation, 2324–1.17

UK firms acquisition of US firms, financing, sources, and rates of return, with data by firm, 1980s, technical paper, 9385–8.82

Business and industry

Business America, foreign and domestic commerce, and US investment and trade opportunities, biweekly journal, 2042–24

Foreign countries economic and social conditions, working paper series, 2326–18

Index by Subjects and Names

Health care R&D funding, by type of source and performer, 1981-90, annual rpt, 4434–3

R&D funding by higher education instns and federally funded centers, by field, instn, and State, FY89, annual rpt, 9627–13

Rural areas economic conditions and dev, quarterly journal, 1502–8

Science and engineering PhDs, by field, instn, employment prospects, sex, race, and other characteristics, 1960s-90, annual rpt, 9627–30

Science and engineering PhDs employment and other characteristics, by field and State, 1989, biennial rpt, 9627–18

Survey of Current Business, detailed data for major industries and economic indicators, monthly rpt, 2702–1

see also Agriculture

see also Area wage surveys

see also Automation

see also Banks and banking

see also Business acquisitions and mergers

see also Business assets and liabilities, general

see also Business assets and liabilities, specific industry

see also Business cycles

see also Business education

see also Business ethics

see also Business failures and closings

see also Business firms and establishments, number

see also Business formations

see also Business income and expenses, general

see also Business income and expenses, specific industry

see also Business inventories

see also Business management

see also Business orders

see also Business outlook and attitude surveys

see also Capital investments, general

see also Capital investments, specific industry

see also Commercial buildings

see also Commercial credit

see also Commercial law

see also Communications industries

see also Competition

see also Construction industry

see also Consultants

see also Conversion of industry

see also Corporations

see also Credit

see also Defense industries

see also Depreciation

see also Divestiture

see also Earnings, general

see also Earnings, local and regional

see also Earnings, specific industry

see also Economic concentration and diversification

see also Electric power plants and equipment

see also Employee benefits

see also Employee performance and appraisal

see also Employment and unemployment, general

see also Employment and unemployment, local and regional

see also Employment and unemployment, specific industry

see also Executives and managers

see also Export processing zones

see also Financial institutions

see also Fish and fishing industry

see also Foreign corporations

see also Forests and forestry

see also Franchises

see also Government and business

see also Home-based offices and workers

see also Hours of labor

see also Industrial and commercial energy use

see also Industrial arts

see also Industrial capacity and utilization

see also Industrial plants and equipment

see also Industrial production

see also Industrial production indexes

see also Industrial purchasing

see also Industrial robots

see also Industrial siting

see also Industrial standards

see also Industry wage surveys

see also Input-output analysis

see also Insurance and insurance industry

see also Labor law

see also Labor-management relations, general

see also Labor mobility

see also Labor productivity

see also Labor supply and demand

see also Labor turnover

see also Labor unions

see also Manufacturing

see also Marketing

see also Mines and mineral resources

see also Minority businesses

see also Multinational corporations

see also Occupational health and safety

see also Occupations

see also Ownership of enterprise

see also Partnerships

see also Payroll

see also Personnel management

see also Printing and publishing industry

see also Production costs

see also Productivity

see also Proprietorships

see also Public administration

see also Public utilities

see also Real estate business

see also Repair industries

see also Retail trade

see also Service industries

see also Small business

see also Standard Industrial Classification

see also Trade adjustment assistance

see also Trademarks

see also Transportation and transportation equipment

see also Value added tax

see also Wholesale trade

see also Women-owned businesses

see also under By Individual Company or Institution in the "Index by Categories"

see also under By Industry in the "Index by Categories"

see also under names of specific industries or industry groups

Business assets and liabilities, general

Acquisitions and mergers by type, with data for large transactions by payment method and firm, late 1960s-90, working paper, 9366–1.161

Assets and debts of private sector, balance sheets by segment, 1945-90, semiannual rpt, 9365–4.1

Business assets and liabilities, general

Assets and liabilities of US, and impacts of inflation, 1990 and trends from 1948, article, 9391–1.220

Caribbean Basin Initiative investment incentives, economic impacts, with finances and employment by country, 1984-90, 2048–141

Corporations financial statements for manufacturing, mining, and trade, by selected SIC 2- to 3-digit industry, quarterly rpt, 2502–1

Debt and business cycle sensitivity of major industry sectors, with intl comparisons, 1970s-88, technical paper, 9385–8.103

Debt impacts on financial performance during recessions, with data by industry group, 1970s-80s, technical paper, 9385–8.78

Debt outstanding, by sector and type of debt and holder, monthly rpt, 9362–1.1

Debt/asset ratios impact on investment and employment, 1971-87, technical paper, 9385–8.77

Economic indicators and components, current data and annual trends, monthly rpt, 23842–1.5

Enterprise Statistics, 1987: auxiliaries of multi-establishment firms, finances and operations by function, industry, and State, 2329–6

Flow-of-funds accounts, savings, investments, and credit statements, quarterly rpt, 9365–3.3

Foreign-controlled US corporations income tax returns, assets and income statement items by industry div and country, 1988, article, 8302–2.219

Foreign countries tax credits on corporate income tax returns, income, and tax items, by country and world region of credit, 1986, biennial article, 8302–2.207

Foreign countries tax credits on corporate income tax returns, with income and tax items by industry group, 1986, biennial article, 8302–2.203

Foreign-owned corporate activity in US, income tax returns, assets, and income statement items, by industry div and selected country, 1986-87, article, 8302–2.205

Households assets, by type of holding and selected characteristics, 1988, Current Population Rpt, 2546–20.16

Imports and tariff provisions effect on US industries and products, investigations with background financial and operating data, series, 9886–4

Manufacturing annual survey, 1989: finances and operations, by SIC 2- and 3-digit industry and State, 2506–15.3

Manufacturing census, 1987: finances and operations, by SIC 2- to 4-digit industry, State, and MSA, with trends from 1849, 2497–1

Multinatl firms US affiliates finances and operations, by industry div, country of parent firm, and State, 1988-89, annual article, 2702–1.214

Multinatl firms US affiliates, finances, and operations, by industry, world area of parent firm, and State, 1988-89, annual rpt, 2704–4

Multinatl firms US affiliates, investment trends and impact on US economy, 1991 annual rpt, 2004–9

Business assets and liabilities, general

Multinatl US firms and foreign affiliates finances and operations, by industry and world area of parent firm, 1989 benchmark survey, preliminary annual rpt, 2704–5

Multinatl US firms and foreign affiliates finances and operations, by industry of parent firm and affiliate, world area, and selected country, 1989, annual article, 2702–1.225

Multinatl US firms foreign affiliates income tax returns, income statement items, by asset size, industry, and country, 1986, biennial article, 8302–2.212

Partnership income tax returns, income statement and balance sheet items by industry group, 1989, annual article, 8302–2.216; 8304–18

Productivity of labor and capital, indexes and percent change, 1948-90, annual press release, 6824–2

Puerto Rico and other US possessions corporations income tax returns, income and tax items, and employment, by selected industry, 1987, article, 8302–2.213

Retail trade census, 1987: depreciable assets, capital and operating expenses, sales, value added, and inventories, by SIC 2- to 4-digit kind of business, 2399–2

Securities (medium-term) outstanding, issuers, and borrowings size, by industry group, 1983-90, technical paper, 9366–6.276

Service industries census, 1987: depreciable assets, capital and operating expenses, and receipts, by SIC 2- to 4-digit kind of business, 2393–2

Small business capital formation sources and issues, 1990 annual conf, 9734–4

Statistical Abstract of US, 1991 annual data compilation, 2324–1.16; 2324–1.17

Tax (income) returns filed by type of filer, selected income items, quarterly rpt, 8302–2.1

Tax (income) returns of corporations, income and tax items by asset size and detailed industry, 1987, annual rpt, 8304–4

Tax (income) returns of corporations, income and tax items by asset size and detailed industry, 1988, annual rpt, 8304–21

Tax (income) returns of corporations, summary data by asset size and industry div, 1987, annual article, 8302–2.204

Tax (income) returns of corporations, summary data by asset size and industry div, 1988, annual article, 8302–2.215; 8302–2.217

Wholesale trade census, 1987: depreciable assets, capital and operating expenses, sales, value added, and inventories, by SIC 2- to 3-digit kind of business, 2407–2

see also Agricultural finance
see also Bankruptcy
see also Business assets and liabilities, specific industry
see also Business income and expenses, general
see also Business inventories
see also Capital investments, general
see also Depreciation

see also Divestiture
see also Foreign investments
see also Government assets and liabilities
see also Industrial plants and equipment
see also Investments
see also Mortgages
see also Operating ratios

Business assets and liabilities, specific industry

Agricultural cooperatives finances, aggregate for top 100 assns by commodity group, 1989, annual rpt, 1124–3

Agricultural cooperatives, finances, and membership, by type of service, commodity, and State, 1989, annual rpt, 1124–1

Agricultural cooperatives finances, operations, activities, and current issues, monthly journal, 1122–1

Agricultural cooperatives, finances, operations, activities, and membership, commodity rpt series, 1126–1

Airline finances, by carrier, carrier group, and for total certificated system, quarterly rpt, 7302–7

American Historical Assn financial statements, and membership by State, 1989, annual rpt, 29574–2

Bank deposit insurance system reform issues, with background industry financial data, 1970s-90, GAO rpt, 26119–320

Bank holding company subsidiaries dealing in bank-ineligible securities, subsidiary and parent firm finances, 1989-91, GAO rpt, 26119–280

Banking and economic conditions, for Fed Reserve 8th District, quarterly rpt with articles, 9391–16

Banking industry structure and deposit insurance reform, findings and recommendations, with background data, 1989-90, 8008–147

Banking intl competition and deposit insurance reform issues, with background data, 1990 hearings, 25248–123

Banking intl competition issues, with background data, 1980s, 21248–153

Banks (foreign-owned) assets in US, relation to foreign and domestic economic and financial indicators, by instn type, 1970s-89, technical paper, 9385–8.108

Banks (insured commercial) and offices, and summary assets and liabilities, 1989-90, annual rpt, 9364–1.2

Banks (insured commercial) assets, income, and financial ratios, by asset size and State, quarterly rpt, 13002–3

Banks (insured commercial) domestic and foreign office consolidated financial statements, monthly rpt, quarterly data, 9362–1.4

Banks (insured commercial), Fed Reserve 5th District members financial statements, by State, quarterly rpt, 9389–18

Banks (insured commercial and savings) finances, by State, 1989, annual rpt, 9294–4

Banks (insured commercial and savings) financial condition and performance, by asset size and region, quarterly rpt, 9292–1

Banks (natl) charters, mergers, liquidations, enforcement cases, and financial performance, with data by instn and State, quarterly rpt, 8402–3

Index by Subjects and Names

Banks (US) foreign branches assets and liabilities, by world region and country, quarterly rpt, 9365–3.7

Banks (US) foreign branches, balance sheets, monthly rpt, 9362–1.3

Banks agricultural loans share of all loans, impact of State branching laws, bank urban-rural location, and other factors, 1981-86, article, 9393–8.202

Banks and deposit insurance funds financial condition, potential losses, and regulatory issues, 1980s-90 and projected to 1995, 21248–147

Banks and thrifts finances by instn type, and Fed Financial Instns Exam Council financial statements, 1990, annual rpt, 13004–2

Banks and thrifts in Texas, profitability and solvency indicators, and problem assets by type, 1980s, working paper, 9379–14.11

Banks, assets, and financial performance, by asset size, 1970s-90, article, 9383–6.203

Banks assets and market share, compared to other financial instns by detailed industry group, 1950s-90, working paper, 9375–13.62

Banks balance sheets, by Fed Reserve District, for major banks in NYC, and for US branches and agencies of foreign banks, weekly rpt, 9365–1.3

Banks capital aid receipt relation to bank holding company affiliation and other factors, with data for Texas, 1985-88, article, 9391–1.205

Banks capital by component, and capital/asset ratios compared to other industry groups, 1900s-80s, working paper, 9375–13.61

Banks commercial loan growth, by bank financial and district employment characteristics, 1989-90, article, 9385–1.208

Banks failures forecasting performance of measures using alternative capital/asset ratio requirements, 1982-89, working paper, 9377–9.109

Banks failures, interbank exposure risk indicators by bank size, 1980s-90, working paper, 9377–9.107

Banks failures involving assets over $90 million, listing by instn, 1973-89, working paper, 9377–9.115

Banks finances and operations, by metro-nonmetro location, 1987-89, annual rpt, 1544–29

Banks financial performance, risk assessment, and regulation, 1990 annual conf papers, 9375–7

Banks in Fed Reserve 1st District, selected assets, monthly rpt, 9373–2.7

Banks in Fed Reserve 3rd District, assets, income, and rates of return, by major instn, quarterly rpt, annual table, 9387–10

Banks in Fed Reserve 3rd District established since 1985, assets by firm, as of Jan 1990, article, 9387–1.201

Banks in Fed Reserve 8th District, financial performance indicators by asset size, 1987-90, annual article, 9391–16.208

Banks in Fed Reserve 9th District, finances and performance ratios, by State, quarterly journal, 9383–19

Banks in Fed Reserve 11th District, financial performance indicators by asset size and FDIC assistance receipt, 1987-90, article, 9379–1.206

Index by Subjects and Names

Business assets and liabilities, specific industry

Banks in Mexico, deregulation impacts on finances, with data by bank, 1960s-90, technical paper, 9385–8.121

Banks in southeastern States, mergers and acquisitions, assets and major institutions involved, by State, 1984-89, article, 9371–1.203

Banks in Texas, failures relation to portfolio risk indicators and year of establishment, 1980s, working paper, 9379–14.10

Banks market value calculation method to expose undercapitalization, with model results and background data for selected failed banks, 1960s-89, working paper, 9377–9.112

Banks mergers approved, and assets and offices involved, by instn, 1989, annual rpt, 9294–5

Banks owned by foreigners, US subsidiaries, assets, and regulatory issues, with data by State and firm, 1989-90, hearing, 21248–155

Banks profitability, balance sheet and income statement items, and financial ratios, by asset size, 1985-90, annual article, 9362–1.204

Construction industries census, 1987: establishments, employment, receipts, and expenditures, by SIC 4-digit industry and State, final industry rpt series, 2373–1

Credit unions (federally-insured) financial performance, by charter type and region, 1st half 1991, semiannual rpt, 9532–7

Credit unions, assets, and members, for US, 12 countries, and 5 regional confederations, 1986 and 1989, release, 9538–9

Credit unions assets, members, and location, 1991 annual listing, 9534–6

Credit unions federally insured, finances by instn characteristics and State, as of June 1991, semiannual rpt, 9532–6

Credit unions federally insured, finances, mergers, closings, and insurance fund losses and financial statements, FY90, annual rpt, 9534–7

Credit unions federally insured, finances, 1989-90, annual rpt, 9534–1

Credit unions finances, operations, and regulation, series, 9536–1

Credit unions in Fed Reserve 8th District, finances and members by State, 1984 and 1990, article, 9391–16.210

Electric power distribution loans from REA, and borrower operating and financial data, by firm and State, 1990, annual rpt, 1244–1

Electric power sales by customer, plants, and capacity of Southeastern Power Admin, FY90, annual rpt, 3234–1

Electric utilities finances and operations, detailed data for public and privately owned firms, 1989, annual rpt, 3164–11.4

Electric utilities finances and operations, detailed data for publicly owned firms, 1989, annual rpt, 3164–24

Electric utilities privately owned, finances and operations, detailed data, 1989, annual rpt, 3164–23

Energy producers finances and operations, by energy type for US firms domestic and foreign operations, 1989, annual rpt, 3164–44

Energy resources of US, foreign direct investment by energy type and firm, and US affiliates operations, as of 1989, annual rpt, 3164–80

Finance companies credit outstanding and leasing activities, by credit type, monthly rpt, 9365–2.7

Financial instns and assets by type, nonfinancial sector debt outstanding, and banks profitability trends, 1970s-89, technical paper, 9385–8.84

Financial instns holdings, for banks in and outside NYC, and for thrift instns, monthly rpt, 9362–1.1

Financial instns with intl operations, assets by selected banking and securities instn, and financial performance indicators by selected country, late 1980s-90, article, 9385–1.206

Grain cooperatives finances and operations, by grain handled and selected characteristics, 1983-85, series, 1128–44

Insurance (life) companies finances, performance ratios, and problem holdings, by firm, 1989-90, hearing, 21368–133

Insurance industry finances, underwriting activities, and investment plan mgmt, 1960s-90, 21248–159

Labor unions reporting to Labor Dept, parent bodies and locals by location, 1990 listing, 6468–17

Natural gas interstate pipeline company detailed financial and operating data, by firm, 1989, annual rpt, 3164–38

Nonprofit charitable organizations finances, and revenue and investments of top 10 instns, 1986-87, article, 8302–2.210

Nonprofit charitable organizations finances, by asset size and State, 1987, article, 8302–2.218

Nonprofit charitable organizations finances, 1988, table, 8302–2.220

Oil company production and imports by type, and financial data, 1977-89, annual rpt, 3164–74.1

Pension plans funding status under 1987 accounting standards, for defined benefit plans, 1987-89, technical paper, 9366–6.259

Pension plans of firms acquired in leveraged buyouts, finances, participation, terminations, and replacements, 1982-87, GAO rpt, 26121–408

Railroad (Class I) finances and operations, detailed data by firm, class of service, and district, 1989, annual rpt, 9486–6.1

Savings and loan assns, FHLB 6th District insured members financial condition and operations by State, quarterly rpt, 9302–23

Savings and loan assns, FHLB 8th District members, locations, assets, and savings, 1991, annual listing, 9304–9

Savings and loan assns, FHLB 11th District members, offices, and financial condition, 1991 annual listing, 9304–23

Savings banks insured by Bank Insurance Fund, financial condition and performance, by asset size and region, quarterly rpt, 9292–5

Savings instns facing insolvency, financial performance by whether recovered, 1980s, working paper, 9377–9.121

Savings instns failure resolution activity and finances of Resolution Trust Corp, with data by asset type, State, region, and instn, monthly rpt, 9722–3

Savings instns failure resolution activity of Resolution Trust Corp, assets, deposits, and assets availability and sales, periodic press release, 9722–1

Savings instns failure resolution activity of Resolution Trust Corp, with assets and retained senior executives compensation, by instn, 1988-90, hearing, 21248–144

Savings instns failure resolution activity of Resolution Trust Corp, with data by State and instn, and RTC financial statements, 1989, annual rpt, 9724–1

Savings instns failure resolution activity of Resolution Trust Corp, with instns assets and senior executive compensation, 1990, hearing, 21248–157

Savings instns failure resolution activity of Resolution Trust Corp, 1991 semiannual hearing, 21242–1

Savings instns failure resolution costs to FSLIC, relation to asset quality indicators and tax benefit grants, 1984-87, article, 9292–4.202

Savings instns, FHLB 1st District members financial operations compared to banks, and related economic and housing indicators, bimonthly rpt with articles, 9302–4

Savings instns, FHLB 6th District members financial condition and operations by State, monthly rpt, 9302–11

Savings instns, FHLB 10th District members, locations, assets, and deposits, 1991, annual listing, 9304–17

Savings instns finances and operations by district and State, mortgage loan activity and terms by MSA, and FHLB finances, 1989 and trends from 1900, annual rpt, 8434–3

Savings instns financial condition and devs, working paper series, 9379–14

Savings instns insured by Savings Assn Insurance Fund, assets, liabilities, and deposit and loan activity, by conservatorship status, monthly rpt, 8432–1

Savings instns insured by Savings Assn Insurance Fund, finances by profitability group, district, and State, quarterly rpt, 8432–4

Savings instns mortgage debt holdings and other assets, returns on assets, and impacts of qualified lender regulations, 1970s-89, GAO rpt, 26119–337

Securities industry finances, for broker-dealers and individual stock exchanges and clearing agencies, 1985-89, annual rpt, 9734–2.1

Shipping firms combined financial statements, FY88-89, annual rpt, 7704–14.5

Small Business Investment Companies capital holdings, SBA obligation, and ownership, as of July 1991, semiannual listing, 9762–4

Space station commercial dev and operating costs and income under alternative financing options, projected 1989-2000, 21708–129

Stockbrokers issuing securities credit, balance sheet, as of June 1990, annual rpt, 9365–5.1

Telecommunications industry intl competitiveness, with financial and operating data by product or service, firm, and country, 1990 rpt, 2008–30

Business assets and liabilities, specific industry

Telephone and telegraph firms detailed finances and operations, 1989, annual rpt, 9284–6

Telephone firms borrowing under Rural Telephone Program, and financial and operating data, by State, 1990, annual rpt, 1244–2

Transit systems finances and operations, by mode of transport, size of fleet, and for 468 systems, 1989, annual rpt, 7884–4

Truck interstate carriers finances and operations, by district, 1989, annual rpt, 9486–6.2

see also Agricultural finance
see also Business income and expenses, specific industry
see also Business inventories
see also Capital investments, specific industry
see also Depreciation
see also Educational finance
see also Government assets and liabilities
see also under By Industry in the "Index by Categories"

Business assistance

see Government and business
see Subsidies
see Trade adjustment assistance

Business cycles

- Banking panics severity and Federal regulatory policy, 1873-1934, technical paper, 9385–8.99
- Banks and deposit insurance funds financial condition, potential losses, and regulatory issues, 1980s-90 and projected to 1995, 21248–147
- Corporations debt impacts on financial performance during recessions, with data by industry group, 1970s-80s, technical paper, 9385–8.78
- Debt and business cycle sensitivity of major industry sectors, with intl comparisons, 1970s-88, technical paper, 9385–8.103
- Economic indicators and cyclical devs and outlook, by Fed Reserve Bank District, periodic rpt, 9362–8
- Employment over business cycles, by census div and State, 1988-92, release, 9538–8
- Employment situation, earnings, hours, and other BLS economic indicators, transcripts of BLS Commissioner's monthly testimony, periodic rpt, 23846–4
- Forecasts of cycle expansion and contraction phases for 4 countries, model description and results, 1850s-1982, working paper, 9387–8.250
- Forecasts of industrial production growth and business cycle turning points, performance of diffusion indexes, 1960s-90, technical paper, 9366–6.277
- Forecasts of recessions, performance of experimental indicators indexes and interest rate spreads, with data for 1940s-91, article, 9375–1.212
- GNP and components, inflation, and money supply variability and growth rates over business cycles, for 10 industrial countries, 1850s-1980s, working paper, 9383–20.15
- GNP and industrial production correlation with selected price indexes over business cycles, 1957-89, article, 9383–6.204
- GNP and other economic indicators variability over the business cycle, model description and results, 1947-90, technical paper, 9366–6.275

GNP growth and unemployment rate over the business cycle, alternative models descriptions and results, 1950s-80s, technical paper, 9385–8.96

GNP variability, and correlation between wages and hours, impact of energy use and prices, model description and results, 1940s-87, working paper, 9375–13.57

GNP variability, real business cycle model assessment, with results for 1950s-84, article, 9375–1.205

Intl transmission of business cycles among 7 OECD countries, model description and results, 1960s-88, working paper, 9377–9.113

Manufacturing activity index of Natl Assn of Purchasing Managers, economic indicator forecasting performance, various periods 1948-91, article, 9385–1.215; 9385–8.120

Massachusetts housing prices economic impacts over business cycle expansion, 1984-87, article, 9373–1.216

Money supply impact on economic indicators, incorporation by real business cycle models, assessment of alternative models, 1991 articles, 9383–6.202

North Central States industry diversification, and employment and output relation to natl economic conditions, by industry and State, 1950s-89, working paper, 9375–13.63

Statistical Abstract of US, 1991 annual data compilation, 2324–1.17

Survey of Current Business, detailed financial and business data, and economic indicators, monthly rpt, 2702–1.1; 2702–1.3

Unemployment insurance alternative policies impacts on employment and hours worked, with data for selected countries, 1970s, article, 9383–6.205

Unemployment insurance programs impacts on business cycles and economic indicators, regression results, 1950s-89, 6406–6.34

Unemployment insurance programs of States, finances, operations, tax provisions, and vulnerability to recessions, 1970s-90s, hearing, 21788–201

see also Economic indicators

Business diversification

see Economic concentration and diversification

Business education

Construction (hwy) minority contractor training, funding by region, FY91, annual release, 7554–40

Course completions, by detailed program, sex, race, and instn type, for 1972 high school class, as of 1984, 4888–4

Degrees awarded in higher education, by level, field, race, and sex, 1988/89 with trends from 1978/79, biennial rpt, 4844–17

Digest of Education Statistics, 1991 annual data compilation, 4824–2

Service industries census, 1987: establishments, receipts by source, payroll, and employment, by SIC 2- to 4-digit kind of business, State, and MSA, 2393–4

Student aid funding and participation, by Federal program, instn type and control, and State, various periods 1959-89, annual rpt, 4804–28

Index by Subjects and Names

Student loan debt burden of 1986 college grads, by selected student characteristics and instn control, 1987, 4808–26

Teachers in higher education instns, employment and other characteristics, by instn type and control, 1987/88 survey, 4846–4.4

Business efficiency

see Business management
see Consultants
see Labor productivity
see Operating ratios
see Productivity

Business energy use

see Agricultural energy use
see Industrial and commercial energy use
see Transportation energy use

Business ethics

- Banks and thrifts fraud and abuse, Federal agencies enforcement activities and staff, with data by instn and location, 1988-90, hearing, 21408–119
- Futures trading oversight of CFTC and individual exchanges, foreign activity, and customer views, late 1980s, hearing, 25168–77
- Health condition screening and monitoring of employees, businesses practices and views, 1989 survey, 26358–250
- Securities industry self-regulatory organizations oversight by SEC, violations, and complaints, FY86-89, GAO rpt, 26119–336
- Stock short selling activity indicators, and regulatory issues, 1980s-89 and trends from 1940, hearings, 21408–122

Business failures and closings

- Airline deregulation in 1978, impacts on industry structure, competition, fares, finances, operations, and intl service, with data by carrier and airport, 1980s, series, 7308–199
- Bank deposit insurance fund finances, potential losses, and real estate lenders financial ratios compared to other US and Texas banks, 1990 hearings, 25248–125
- Bank deposit insurance system reform issues, with background industry financial data, 1970s-90, GAO rpt, 26119–320
- Banking industry structure and deposit insurance reform, findings and recommendations, with background data, 1989-90, 8008–147
- Banking panics severity and Federal regulatory policy, 1873-1934, technical paper, 9385–8.99
- Banks (agricultural) failures, quarterly rpt, 9365–3.10
- Banks (insured commercial and savings) finances, and changes in status, by State, 1989, annual rpt, 9294–4.1
- Banks (insured commercial and savings) financial condition and performance, by asset size and region, quarterly rpt, 9292–1
- Banks (natl) charters, mergers, liquidations, enforcement cases, and financial performance, with data by instn and State, quarterly rpt, 8402–3
- Banks and deposit insurance funds financial condition, potential losses, and regulatory issues, 1980s-90 and projected to 1995, 21248–147
- Banks and thrifts fraud and abuse, Federal agencies enforcement activities and staff, with data by instn and location, 1988-90, hearing, 21408–119

Index by Subjects and Names

Business firms

Banks and thrifts fraud and abuse, Federal criminal enforcement activities, case dispositions, and settlements, with data by district, 1982-90, hearing, 21248–142

Banks and thrifts in Texas, profitability and solvency indicators, and problem assets by type, 1980s, working paper, 9379–14.11

Banks, assets, and financial performance, by asset size, 1970s-90, article, 9383–6.203

Banks capital aid receipt relation to bank holding company affiliation and other factors, with data for Texas, 1985-88, article, 9391–1.205

Banks failures, assets and losses to FDIC, for State-chartered Fed Reserve members by instn, 1984-90, hearing, 21242–1

Banks failures declarations relation to selected regulatory activity indicators, 1960s-89, working paper, 9377–9.115

Banks failures forecasting performance of bank financial ratios and local market economic conditions, 1980s-89, article, 9377–1.203

Banks failures forecasting performance of measures using alternative capital/asset ratio requirements, 1982-89, working paper, 9377–9.109

Banks failures, interbank exposure risk indicators by bank size, 1980s-90, working paper, 9377–9.107

Banks failures, survival probability model forecasting performance, 1986-90, article, 9377–1.204

Banks in Texas, failures relation to portfolio risk indicators and year of establishment, 1980s, working paper, 9379–14.10

Banks market value calculation method to expose undercapitalization, with model results and background data for selected failed banks, 1960s-89, working paper, 9377–9.112

Banks mergers approved, and assets and offices involved, by instn, 1989, annual rpt, 9294–5

Corporations debt impacts on financial performance during recessions, with data by industry group, 1970s-80s, technical paper, 9385–8.78

Credit unions federally insured, finances, mergers, closings, and insurance fund losses and financial statements, FY90, annual rpt, 9534–7

Credit unions federally insured, finances, 1989-90, annual rpt, 9534–1

Electric power plants and capacity, by fuel used, owner, location, and operating status, 1990 and for units planned 1991-2000, annual listing, 3164–36

Electric power plants summer capacity and fuel source, for new and retired units, 1989, annual rpt, 3164–11.1

Failures and formation of business, selected years 1946-90, annual rpt, 204–1.7

Farm credit conditions, earnings, and expenses, Fed Reserve 9th District, quarterly rpt, 9383–11

Farm finances, debts, assets, and receipts, and lenders financial condition, quarterly rpt with articles, 1541–1

Farm financial stress indicators, operator quits, and loan problems and mediation, 1970s-90, 1598–272

Farm operators entries and exits, by State, late 1970s-87, 1598–269

Financial instns failures, by instn type, US and Fed Reserve 10th District, 1989-90, annual rpt, 9381–14.1

FmHA loans and borrower supervision activities in farm and housing programs, by type and State, monthly rpt, 1182–1

Hazardous waste treatment facility closures, by EPA review status and waste disposal method, 1991, GAO rpt, 26113–528

Hospital closures and rates, with financial, operating, and market characteristics, by location, late 1980s, GAO rpt, 26121–392

Hospital reimbursement by Medicare under prospective payment system, and effect on services, finances, and beneficiary payments, 1979-90, annual rpt, 17204–2

Hospital trauma centers unreimbursed costs and other factors contributing to closure, and views on nontrauma care impacts, 1989-90, GAO rpt, 26121–419

Hospitals in rural areas, closures related to selected factors, 1980s, GAO rpt, 26121–409

Hospitals in rural areas, financial and operating performance impacts of Medicare prospective payment reimbursement system, 1980s-87, 4658–51

Insurance (property and casualty) industry solvency monitoring by States, firms designated for increased attention, and views on monitoring system effectiveness, 1980s, GAO rpt, 26119–316

Labor laws enacted, by State, 1990, annual article, 6722–1.209

North Central States business and economic conditions, Fed Reserve 9th District, quarterly journal, 9383–19

Nuclear power plant capacity, generation, and operating status, by plant and foreign and US location, 1990 and projected to 2030, annual rpt, 3164–57

Nuclear reactors for domestic use and export by function and operating status, with owner, operating characteristics, and location, 1990 annual listing, 3354–15

Oil refinery capacity, closings, and acquisitions by plant, and fuel used, by PAD district, 1973-89, annual rpt, 3164–2.1

Oil refinery operations and finances, with ownership changes, shutdowns, and reactivations, by firm, 1970s-90, 3168–119

Oil supply and industry of OPEC and US, impacts of oil embargo imposed after Iraq invasion of Kuwait, 1989-91, hearing, 21368–132

Railroad retirement system funding and benefits findings and recommendations, with background industry data, 1960s-90 and projected to 2060, 9708–1

Savings banks insured by Bank Insurance Fund, financial condition and performance, by asset size and region, quarterly rpt, 9292–5

Savings instns facing insolvency, financial performance by whether recovered, 1980s, working paper, 9377–9.121

Savings instns failure resolution activity and finances of Resolution Trust Corp, with data by asset type, State, region, and instn, monthly rpt, 9722–3

Savings instns failure resolution activity of Resolution Trust Corp, assets, deposits, and assets availability and sales, periodic press release, 9722–1

Savings instns failure resolution activity of Resolution Trust Corp, with assets and retained senior executives compensation, by instn, 1988-90, hearing, 21248–144

Savings instns failure resolution activity of Resolution Trust Corp, with data by State and instn, and RTC financial statements, 1989, annual rpt, 9724–1

Savings instns failure resolution activity of Resolution Trust Corp, with instns assets and senior executive compensation, 1990, hearing, 21248–157

Savings instns failure resolution activity of Resolution Trust Corp, 1991 semiannual hearing, 21242–1

Savings instns failure resolution costs to FSLIC, relation to asset quality indicators and tax benefit grants, 1984-87, article, 9292–4.202

Savings instns failures, financial performance of instns under Resolution Trust Corp conservatorship, quarterly rpt, 9722–5

Savings instns failures, inventory of real estate assets available from Resolution Trust Corp, semiannual listing series, 9722–2

Savings instns failures, low-grade junk bonds holdings of Resolution Trust Corp, quarterly press release, 9722–4

Savings instns insured by Savings Assn Insurance Fund, assets, liabilities, and deposit and loan activity, by conservatorship status, monthly rpt, 8432–1

Schools of higher education closing, by instn type and control, 1960/61-1989/90, annual rpt, 4824–2.19

State and Metro Area Data Book, 1991 data compilation, 2328–54

Statistical Abstract of US, 1991 annual data compilation, 2324–1.17

Survey of Current Business, detailed data for major industries and economic indicators, monthly rpt, 2702–1.4

Survey of Current Business, detailed financial and business data, and economic indicators, monthly rpt, 2702–1.1

Texas economic and housing conditions, bank failures, and thrift and Federal regulators real estate holdings, 1980s-90, hearings, 21248–146

Unemployed displaced workers losing job 1985-90, by demographic and current and former employment characteristics, as of Jan 1990, article, 6722–1.225

Uranium mill capacity by plant, and production, by operating status, 1986-90, annual rpt, 3164–65.1

West Central States economic indicators, Fed Reserve 10th District, quarterly rpt, 9381–16.2

see also Bankruptcy

Business firms

see Bank holding companies

see Business acquisitions and mergers

see Business failures and closings

see Business firms and establishments, number

see Business formations

see Corporations

Business firms

see Foreign corporations
see Franchises
see Government corporations and enterprises
see Holding companies
see Home-based offices and workers
see Industrial plants and equipment
see Industrial siting
see Minority businesses
see Multinational corporations
see Partnerships
see Proprietorships
see Public utilities
see Small business
see Small Business Investment Companies
see Women-owned businesses
see under By Individual Company or Institution in the "Index by Categories"

Business firms and establishments, number

- Agricultural cooperatives, finances, and membership, by type of service, commodity, and State, 1989, annual rpt, 1124–1
- Agricultural cooperatives, finances, operations, activities, and membership, commodity rpt series, 1126–1
- American Samoa employment, earnings, and minimum wage, by establishment and industry, 1989, biennial rpt, 6504–6
- Banking industry structure, performance, and financial devs, for Fed Reserve 10th District, 1990, annual rpt, 9381–14.1
- Banks (insured commercial) and offices, and summary assets and liabilities, 1989-90, annual rpt, 9364–1.2
- Banks (insured commercial) assets, income, and financial ratios, by asset size and State, quarterly rpt, 13002–3
- Banks (insured commercial and savings) deposits by instn, State, MSA, and county, as of June 1990, annual regional rpt series, 9295–3
- Banks (insured commercial and savings) finances, and changes in status, by State, 1989, annual rpt, 9294–4.1
- Banks (natl) charters, mergers, liquidations, enforcement cases, and financial performance, with data by instn and State, quarterly rpt, 8402–3
- Banks, assets, and financial performance, by asset size, 1970s-90, article, 9383–6.203
- Building (commercial) energy use, costs, and conservation, by building characteristics, survey rpt series, 3166–8
- Chemical and oil products shipments, firms, trade, and use, by product, periodic Current Industrial Rpt series, 2506–8
- Construction industries census, 1987: establishments, employment, receipts, and expenditures, by SIC 4-digit industry and State, final industry rpt series, 2373–1
- Corporations income tax returns, income and tax items by asset size and detailed industry, 1987, annual rpt, 8304–4
- Corporations income tax returns, income and tax items by asset size and detailed industry, 1988, annual rpt, 8304–21
- County Business Patterns, 1988: employment, establishments, and payroll, by SIC 2- to 4-digit industry and county, annual State rpt series, 2326–6
- County Business Patterns, 1989: employment, establishments, and payroll, by SIC 2- to 4-digit industry and county, annual State rpt series, 2326–8
- Credit unions federally insured, finances by instn characteristics and State, as of June 1991, semiannual rpt, 9532–6
- Credit unions federally insured, finances, mergers, closings, and insurance fund losses and financial statements, FY90, annual rpt, 9534–7
- Credit unions federally insured, finances, 1989-90, annual rpt, 9534–1
- Dairy production by commodity, and plants, by State, 1990, annual rpt, 1627–5
- Electric power distribution loans from REA, and borrower operating and financial data, by firm and State, 1990, annual rpt, 1244–1
- Enterprise Statistics, 1987: auxiliaries of multi-establishment firms, finances and operations by function, industry, and State, 2329–6
- Enterprise Statistics, 1987: finances and operations for companies, by size, level of diversification, form of organization, and industry group, 2329–8
- Exports, imports, balances, US consumption, and operations of industries affected, by industry, 1986-90, semiannual rpt, 9882–9
- Fertilizer (inorganic) shipments, trade, use, and firms, by product and State, with stocks, 1990, annual Current Industrial Rpt, 2506–8.13
- Fish (processed) production by location, and trade, by species and product, 1987-90, annual rpts, 2166–6
- Fishery employment, vessels, plants, and cooperatives, by State, 1989 and trends from 1970, annual rpt, 2164–1.10
- Foreign-controlled US corporations income tax returns, assets and income statement items by industry div and country, 1988, article, 8302–2.219
- Foreign-owned corporate activity in US, income tax returns, assets, and income statement items, by industry div and selected country, 1986-87, article, 8302–2.205
- Franchise business opportunities by firm and kind of business, and sources of aid and info, 1990 annual listing, 2104–7
- Gear production for selected uses under alternative production requirements, and industry finances and operations, late 1940s-89, 2028–1
- Glassware shipments, trade, use, and firms, by product, 1990, annual Current Industrial Rpt, 2506–9.3
- Great Lakes area economic conditions and outlook, for US and Canada, 1970s-90, 9375–15
- Hazardous substances industrial releases, accuracy of EPA reporting, and nonreporting facilities by State and industry, 1987-90, GAO rpt, 26113–532
- Hazardous waste generation and disposal taxes, rates, and firms filing returns, by substance type, 1988, annual article, 8302–2.202
- Horticultural specialties census, 1988: producers, finances, and operations, by crop and State, 1987 Census of Agriculture, 2337–1
- Hotels and other lodging places, receipts, payroll, employment, ownership, and rooms, by State and MSA, 1987 Census of Service Industries, subject rpt, 2393–3

Index by Subjects and Names

- Imports under Generalized System of Preferences, status, and US tariffs, with trade by country and US economic impacts, for selected commodities, 1986-90, annual rpt, 9884–23
- Industry (US) intl competitiveness, with selected foreign and US operating data by major firm and product, series, 2046–12
- Livestock packers purchases and feeding, and livestock markets, dealers, and sales, by State, 1989, annual rpt, 1384–1
- Log home manufacturers in Montana, sales, production, and timber use, 1960s-88, 1208–370
- Lumber industry firms, employment, and payroll in northeast States, by industry, 1982-86, 1208–375
- Machinery and equipment production, shipments, trade, stocks, orders, use, and firms, by product, periodic Current Industrial Rpt series, 2506–12
- Manufacturing annual survey, 1989: establishments, employment, finances, inventories, and energy use, by SIC 2- to 4-digit industry, 2506–15.1
- Manufacturing annual survey, 1989: finances and operations, by SIC 2- and 3-digit industry and State, 2506–15.3
- Manufacturing census, 1987: finances and operations, by SIC 2- to 4-digit industry, State, and MSA, with trends from 1849, 2497–1
- Manufacturing census, 1987: finances and operations, by type of organization and SIC 2- to 4-digit industry, subject rpt, 2497–5
- Metals (intermediate product) shipments, trade, and inventories, by product, periodic Current Industrial Rpt series, 2506–11
- Mineral industries census, 1987: finances and operations, by establishment characteristics, SIC 2- to 4-digit industry, and State, subject rpt, 2517–1
- Mineral industries census, 1987: finances and operations, by SIC 2- to 4-digit industry, State, and county, census div rpt series, 2515–1
- *Minerals Yearbook, 1989,* Vol 2: State reviews of production, sales, and firms, by commodity, and business activity, annual rpt, 5604–34
- Minority Business Dev Centers mgmt and financial aid, and characteristics of businesses, by region and State, FY90, annual rpt, 2104–6
- Multinatl US firms and foreign affiliates finances and operations, by industry and world area of parent firm, 1989 benchmark survey, preliminary annual rpt, 2704–5
- Multinatl US firms foreign affiliates income tax returns, income statement items, by asset size, industry, and country, 1986, biennial article, 8302–2.212
- Oil bulk stations, sales and storage capacity by product, inventories, expenses, employment, and modes of transport, 1987 Census of Wholesale Trade, 2407–4.2
- Partnership income tax returns, income statement and balance sheet items by industry group, 1989, annual article, 8302–2.216; 8304–18

Index by Subjects and Names

Business income and expenses, general

Potato chip plants and potatoes processed, by region, 1989-90, annual rpt, 1621–11

Puerto Rico and other US possessions corporations income tax returns, income and tax items, and employment, by selected industry, 1987, article, 8302–2.213

Puerto Rico economic censuses, 1987: wholesale and retail trade and service industry finances and operations, by SIC 2- to 4-digit industry and municipio, 2591–1

Puerto Rico economic censuses, 1987: wholesale, retail, and service industries finances and operations, by establishment characteristics and SIC 2- and 3-digit industry, subject rpts, 2591–2

Retail trade census, 1987: finances and employment, for establishments with and without payroll, by SIC 2- to 4-digit kind of business, State, and MSA, 2401–1

Savings instns, FHLB 1st District members by type and State, 1990, annual rpt, 9304–2

Savings instns finances and operations by district and State, mortgage loan activity and terms by MSA, and FHLB finances, 1989 and trends from 1900, annual rpt, 8434–3

Savings instns insured by Savings Assn Insurance Fund, assets, liabilities, and deposit and loan activity, by conservatorship status, monthly rpt, 8432–1

Savings instns insured by Savings Assn Insurance Fund, finances by profitability group, district, and State, quarterly rpt, 8432–4

Securities industry finances, for broker-dealers and individual stock exchanges and clearing agencies, 1985-89, annual rpt, 9734–2.1

Service industries census, 1987: establishments, receipts by source, payroll, and employment, by SIC 2- to 4-digit kind of business, State, and MSA, 2393–4

Solar collector and photovoltaic module shipments by end-use sector and State, and trade, 1989, annual rpt, 3164–62

Sole proprietorship income tax returns, income statement items by industry group, 1989, annual article, 8302–2.214

State and Metro Area Data Book, 1991 data compilation, 2328–54

Statistical Abstract of US, 1991 annual data compilation, 2324–1.17

Survey of Current Business, detailed data for major industries and economic indicators, monthly rpt, 2702–1.4

Telecommunications industry intl competitiveness, with financial and operating data by product or service, firm, and country, 1990 rpt, 2008–30

Telephone and telegraph firms detailed finances and operations, 1989, annual rpt, 9284–6

Telephone firms borrowing under Rural Telephone Program, and financial and operating data, by State, 1990, annual rpt, 1244–2

Telephone service subscribership, charges, and local and long distance firm finances and operations, late 1970s-91, semiannual rpt, 9282–7

Transit systems finances and operations, by mode of transport, size of fleet, and for 468 systems, 1989, annual rpt, 7884–4

Transportation census, 1987: finances and operations by size, ownership, and State, and revenues by MSA, by SIC 2- to 4-digit industry, 2579–1

Truck and bus interstate carriers finances and operations, by district, 1989, annual rpt, 9486–6.3

Truck interstate carriers finances and operations, by district, 1989, annual rpt, 9486–6.2

TV and radio stations on the air, by class of operation, monthly press release, 9282–4

Unemployment insurance coverage of establishments, employment, and wages, by SIC 4-digit industry and State, 1990, annual rpt, 6744–16

Uranium supply and industry operations, various periods 1947-90 and projected to 2000, annual rpt, 3164–65

Vending facilities run by blind on Federal and non-Federal property, finances and operations by agency and State, FY90, annual rpt, 4944–2

Wholesale trade census, 1987: establishments, sales by customer class, employment, inventories, and expenses, by SIC 2- to 4-digit kind of business, 2407–4

Wire and cable (insulated) shipments, trade, use, and firms, by product, 1990, annual Current Industrial Rpt, 2506–10.8

Women-owned businesses and sales, by industry div and ownership type, and data needs and availability, 1987, 9768–22

see also Business acquisitions and mergers

see also Business failures and closings

see also Business formations

see also Farms and farmland

see also Industrial plants and equipment

see also under By Industry in the "Index by Categories"

Business formations

Banks (insured commercial and savings) finances, and changes in status, by State, 1989, annual rpt, 9294–4.1

Banks in Fed Reserve 3rd District established since 1985, assets by firm, as of Jan 1990, article, 9387–1.201

Banks market structure and local economic conditions, impacts on business formations, 1980s, working paper, 9377–9.123

Credit unions federally insured, finances, mergers, closings, and insurance fund losses and financial statements, FY90, annual rpt, 9534–7

Credit unions federally insured, finances, 1989-90, annual rpt, 9534–1

Electric power plants summer capacity and fuel source, for new and retired units, 1989, annual rpt, 3164–11.1

Farm operators entries and exits, by State, late 1970s-87, 1598–269

Formation and failures of business, selected years 1946-90, annual rpt, 204–1.7

Minority Business Dev Centers mgmt and financial aid, and characteristics of businesses, by region and State, FY90, annual rpt, 2104–6

Multinatl US firms foreign affiliates, income statement items by asset size, industry, and country, 1986, biennial article, 8302–2.212

New England States economic indicators, Fed Reserve 1st District, monthly rpt, 9373–2.3

North Central States business and economic conditions, Fed Reserve 9th District, quarterly journal, 9383–19

State and Metro Area Data Book, 1991 data compilation, 2328–54

Statistical Abstract of US, 1991 annual data compilation, 2324–1.17

Survey of Current Business, detailed data for major industries and economic indicators, monthly rpt, 2702–1.4

Survey of Current Business, detailed financial and business data, and economic indicators, monthly rpt, 2702–1.1

Tennessee Valley industrial dev and employment, by SIC 2-digit industry, firm, and location, 1990, annual rpt, 9804–3

West Central States economic indicators, Fed Reserve 10th District, quarterly rpt, 9381–16.2

Business income and expenses, general

Alien nonresidents income from US sources and tax withheld by country and US tax treaty status, 1988, annual article, 8302–2.206

Caribbean Basin Initiative investment incentives, economic impacts, with finances and employment by country, 1984-90, 2048–141

Corporations debt impacts on financial performance during recessions, with data by industry group, 1970s-80s, technical paper, 9385–8.78

Corporations finances, monthly rpt, 9362–1.1

Corporations financial statements for manufacturing, mining, and trade, by selected SIC 2- to 3-digit industry, quarterly rpt, 2502–1

Economic indicators and components, current data and annual trends, monthly rpt, 23842–1.1; 23842–1.3; 23842–1.5

Economic indicators compounded annual rates of change, monthly rpt, 9391–3

Economic indicators compounded annual rates of change, 1971-90, annual rpt, 9391–9.2

Enterprise Statistics, 1987: auxiliaries of multi-establishment firms, finances and operations by function, industry, and State, 2329–6

Enterprise Statistics, 1987: finances and operations for companies, by size, level of diversification, form of organization, and industry group, 2329–8

Foreign-controlled US corporations income tax returns, assets and income statement items by industry div and country, 1988, article, 8302–2.219

Foreign countries tax credits on corporate income tax returns, income, and tax items, by country and world region of credit, 1986, biennial article, 8302–2.207

Foreign countries tax credits on corporate income tax returns, with income and tax items by industry group, 1986, biennial article, 8302–2.203

Foreign direct investment in US by country, and finances, employment, and acreage owned, by industry group of business acquired or established, 1984-90, annual article, 2702–1.210

Business income and expenses, general

Index by Subjects and Names

Foreign direct investment in US, by industry group and world area, 1987-90, annual article, 2702–1.219

Foreign direct investment in US, by industry group of US affiliate and country of parent firm, 1980-86, 2708–41

Foreign direct investment of US, by industry group and world area, 1987-90, annual article, 2702–1.220

Foreign-owned corporate activity in US, income tax returns, assets, and income statement items, by industry div and selected country, 1986-87, article, 8302–2.205

Health care spending by businesses, households, and govts, 1965-89, article, 4652–1.230

Imports and tariff provisions effect on US industries and products, investigations with background financial and operating data, series, 9886–4

Imports injury to US industries from foreign subsidized products and sales at less than fair value, investigations with background financial and operating data, series, 9886–19

Imports injury to US industries from foreign subsidized products, investigations with background financial and operating data, series, 9886–15

Imports injury to US industries from sales at less than fair value, investigations with background financial and operating data, series, 9886–14

Imports of US given duty-free treatment for value of US material sent abroad, by commodity and country, 1989, annual rpt, 9884–14

Income (personal) per capita and by source, and earnings by industry div, by State, MSA, and county, 1984-89, annual regional rpts, 2704–2

Industry (US) intl competitiveness, with selected foreign and US operating data by major firm and product, series, 2046–12

Industry finances and operations, by SIC 2- to 4-digit industry, forecast 1991, annual rpt, 2044–28

Investment spending relation to cash flow, by SIC 2-digit manufacturing industry, 1958-86, article, 9375–1.202

Investments rate of return under alternative valuation methods, for US business and for direct foreign investment in and of US, 1982-90, article, 2702–1.217

Manufacturing and trade inventories, sales, and inventory/sales ratios, quarterly article, 2702–1.28

Manufacturing annual survey, 1989: establishments, employment, finances, inventories, and energy use, by SIC 2- to 4-digit industry, 2506–15.1

Manufacturing census, 1987: finances and operations, by SIC 2- to 4-digit industry, State, and MSA, with trends from 1849, 2497–1

Manufacturing census, 1987: finances and operations, by type of organization and SIC 2- to 4-digit industry, subject rpt, 2497–5

Minority Business Dev Centers mgmt and financial aid, and characteristics of businesses, by region and State, FY90, annual rpt, 2104–6

Multinatl firms US affiliates finances and operations, by industry div, country of parent firm, and State, 1988-89, annual article, 2702–1.214

Multinatl firms US affiliates, finances, and operations, by industry, world area of parent firm, and State, 1988-89, annual rpt, 2704–4

Multinatl firms US affiliates, investment trends and impact on US economy, 1991 annual rpt, 2004–9

Multinatl US firms and foreign affiliates finances and operations, by industry and world area of parent firm, 1989 benchmark survey, preliminary annual rpt, 2704–5

Multinatl US firms and foreign affiliates finances and operations, by industry of parent firm and affiliate, world area, and selected country, 1989, annual article, 2702–1.225

Multinatl US firms foreign affiliates income tax returns, income statement items, by asset size, industry, and country, 1986, biennial article, 8302–2.212

Natl income and product accounts and components, *Survey of Current Business*, monthly rpt, 2702–1.24

Partnership income tax returns, income statement and balance sheet items by industry group, 1989, annual article, 8302–2.216; 8304–18

Pollution (water) industrial releases in wastewater, levels, treatment, costs, and regulation, with background financial and operating data, industry rpt series, 9206–4

Pollution abatement spending by govts, business, and consumers, 1987-89, annual article, 2702–1.229

Productivity and costs of labor for private, nonfarm business, and manufacturing sectors, revised data, quarterly rpt, 6822–2

Puerto Rico and other US possessions corporations income tax returns, income and tax items, and employment, by selected industry, 1987, article, 8302–2.213

Puerto Rico economic censuses, 1987: wholesale and retail trade and service industry finances and operations, by SIC 2- to 4-digit industry and municipio, 2591–1

Puerto Rico economic censuses, 1987: wholesale, retail, and service industries finances and operations, by establishment characteristics and SIC 2- and 3-digit industry, subject rpts, 2591–2

Retail trade census, 1987: depreciable assets, capital and operating expenses, sales, value added, and inventories, by SIC 2- to 4-digit kind of business, 2399–2

Retail trade census, 1987: finances and employment, for establishments with and without payroll, by SIC 2- to 4-digit kind of business, State, and MSA, 2401–1

Retail trade sales and inventories, by kind of business, region, and selected State, MSA, and city, monthly rpt, 2413–3

Retail trade sales, by kind of business, advance monthly rpt, 2413–2

Retail trade sales, inventories, purchases, gross margin, and accounts receivable, by SIC 2- to 4-digit kind of business and form of ownership, 1989, annual rpt, 2413–5

Sales and ratio to inventories, by industry div, 1947-90, annual rpt, 204–1.1; 204–1.3; 204–1.7

Service industries census, 1987: depreciable assets, capital and operating expenses, and receipts, by SIC 2- to 4-digit kind of business, 2393–2

Service industries census, 1987: establishments, receipts by source, payroll, and employment, by SIC 2- to 4-digit kind of business, State, and MSA, 2393–4

Service industries exports and imports of US, direct and among multinatl firms affiliates, by industry and world area, 1986-90, article, 2702–1.223

Service industries receipts, by SIC 2- to 4-digit kind of business, 1990, annual rpt, 2413–8

Small business dev centers mgmt and technical aid activities, funding, and client satisfaction and performance, 1980s, hearing, 25728–43

Sole proprietorship income tax returns, income statement items by industry group, 1989, annual article, 8302–2.214

Soviet Union GNP by detailed income and outlay component, 1985, 2326–18.59

State and Metro Area Data Book, 1991 data compilation, 2328–54

Statistical Abstract of US, 1991 annual data compilation, 2324–1.17

Survey of Current Business, detailed data for major industries and economic indicators, monthly rpt, 2702–1

Tax (income) returns filed by type of filer, selected income items, quarterly rpt, 8302–2.1

Tax (income) returns of corporations, income and tax items by asset size and detailed industry, 1987, annual rpt, 8304–4

Tax (income) returns of corporations, income and tax items by asset size and detailed industry, 1988, annual rpt, 8304–21

Tax (income) returns of corporations, summary data by asset size and industry div, 1987, annual article, 8302–2.204

Tax (income) returns of corporations, summary data by asset size and industry div, 1988, annual article, 8302–2.215; 8302–2.217

Tax (income) returns of individuals, selected income and tax items by income level, preliminary 1989, annual article, 8302–2.209

Wholesale trade census, 1987: depreciable assets, capital and operating expenses, sales, value added, and inventories, by SIC 2- to 3-digit kind of business, 2407–2

Wholesale trade census, 1987: establishments, sales by customer class, employment, inventories, and expenses, by SIC 2- to 4-digit kind of business, 2407–4

Wholesale trade sales and inventories, by SIC 2- to 3-digit kind of business, monthly rpt, 2413–7

Wholesale trade sales, inventories, purchases, and gross margins, by SIC 2- to 3-digit kind of business, 1990, annual rpt, 2413–13

Index by Subjects and Names

Women-owned businesses and sales, by industry div and ownership type, and data needs and availability, 1987, 9768–22

see also Agricultural finance
see also Agricultural marketing
see also Agricultural production costs
see also Business assets and liabilities, general
see also Business income and expenses, specific industry
see also Capital investments, general
see also Depreciation
see also Economic indicators
see also Employee benefits
see also Energy production costs
see also Farm income
see also Industrial and commercial energy use
see also Industrial purchasing
see also Labor costs and cost indexes
see also Operating ratios
see also Payroll
see also Production costs
see also Professionals' fees
see also Royalties
see also Value added tax

Business income and expenses, specific industry

Adult day care centers revenue by source, and expenses by type, by agency type, FY86, article, 4652–1.234

Aerospace industry sales, orders, backlog, and firms, by product for govt, military, and other customers, 1990, annual Current Industrial Rpt, 2506–12.22

Agricultural cooperatives finances, aggregate for top 100 assns by commodity group, 1989, annual rpt, 1124–3

Agricultural cooperatives, finances, and membership, by type of service, commodity, and State, 1989, annual rpt, 1124–1

Agricultural cooperatives finances, operations, activities, and current issues, monthly journal, 1122–1

Agricultural cooperatives, finances, operations, activities, and membership, commodity rpt series, 1126–1

Agricultural cooperatives, membership, farms, and income, historical review, 1913-81, 1128–66

AID housing and urban dev program financial statements, FY90, annual rpt, 9914–4

Air travel of families and industry revenue impacts of proposed child fares, with costs and accidents compared to auto travel, 1990 hearing, 21648–61

Aircraft noise abatement measures, and industry compliance costs, aggregate FY90-2000, GAO rpt, 26113–534

Airline computer reservation system operations, travel agency revenues by firm, and frequent flyer awards by carrier, 1988, 7308–199.9

Airline deregulation in 1978, impacts on industry structure, competition, fares, finances, operations, and intl service, with data by carrier and airport, 1980s, series, 7308–199

Airline finances, by carrier, carrier group, and for total certificated system, quarterly rpt, 7302–7

Airline financial and operating summary data, quarterly rpt, 7502–16

Business income and expenses, specific industry

Airline operations and passenger, cargo, and mail traffic, by type of service, air carrier, State, and country, 1980-89, annual rpt, 7504–1.6

Alaska Power Admin financial statements, and DOE audit, 1989-90, 3006–5.22

American Historical Assn financial statements, and membership by State, 1989, annual rpt, 29574–2

Army and Air Force Exchange Service financial statements, FY88-89, annual rpt, 3504–21

Auto industry finances and operations, trade by country, and prices of selected US and foreign models, monthly rpt, 9882–8

Banks (insured commercial) assets, income, and financial ratios, by asset size and State, quarterly rpt, 13002–3

Banks (insured commercial), Fed Reserve 5th District members financial statements, by State, quarterly rpt, 9389–18

Banks (insured commercial and savings) finances, by State, 1989, annual rpt, 9294–4

Banks (insured commercial and savings) financial condition and performance, by asset size and region, quarterly rpt, 9292–1

Banks (natl) charters, mergers, liquidations, enforcement cases, and financial performance, with data by instn and State, quarterly rpt, 8402–3

Banks and deposit insurance funds financial condition, potential losses, and regulatory issues, 1980s-90 and projected to 1995, 21248–147

Banks and thrifts finances by instn type, and Fed Financial Instns Exam Council financial statements, 1990, annual rpt, 13004–2

Banks economies and inefficiencies of scale, model description and results for large banks, 1987, working paper, 9375–13.66

Banks economies of scale, alternative model results for large banks, by asset size, 1985-87, article, 9371–1.208

Banks economies of scale and other efficiency measures, alternative estimates, 1991 article, 9375–1.209

Banks economies of scale and scope, impacts of regulation for large banks, alternative model results, 1972-87, working paper, 9375–13.50

Banks economies of scope, for large banks, alternative model results, 1988, working paper, 9389–19.28

Banks finances and operations, by metro-nonmetro location, 1987-89, annual rpt, 1544–29

Banks in Fed Reserve 3rd District, assets, income, and rates of return, by major instn, quarterly rpt, annual table, 9387–10

Banks production costs relation to output, core deposits, and branches, by bank asset size, alternative model results, 1985-87, working paper, 9371–10.54

Banks profitability, balance sheet and income statement items, and financial ratios, by asset size, 1985-90, annual article, 9362–1.204

Banks profitability indicators for student loans and other financial services, 1985-89, 4808–36

Biotechnology commercial applications, industry finances and capitalization, patents, and govt support, for US, Japan, and EC, late 1970s-91, 26358–248

Bus (Class I) passengers and selected revenue data, for individual large carriers, quarterly rpt, 9482–13

Bus connector service between rural areas and Greyhound intercity routes, finances and operations by system, 1987-90, 7888–79

CCC loan activities by commodity, and agency operating results, monthly press release, 1802–7

Construction industries census, 1987: establishments, employment, receipts, and expenditures, by SIC 4-digit industry and State, final industry rpt series, 2373–1

Cotton ginning activity and charges, by State, 1990/91, annual rpt, 1564–3

Credit Union Natl Admin Central Liquidity Facility, financial statements, FY90, annual rpt, 9534–5

Credit unions federally insured, finances by instn characteristics and State, as of June 1991, semiannual rpt, 9532–6

Credit unions federally insured, finances, mergers, closings, and insurance fund losses and financial statements, FY90, annual rpt, 9534–7

Credit unions federally insured, finances, 1989-90, annual rpt, 9534–1

Drug (prescription) mail service industry structure, finances, and operations, 1989 survey, 4658–60

Electric power distribution loans from REA, and borrower operating and financial data, by firm and State, 1990, annual rpt, 1244–1

Electric power plants production, fuel use, stocks, and costs by fuel type, and sales, by State, monthly rpt with articles, 3162–35

Electric power purchases of municipal and cooperative distributors, and prices and use by distributor and consumer sector, for TVA, monthly rpt, 9802–1

Electric power sales and finances, for Bonneville Power Admin mgmt of Fed Columbia River Power System, summary data, quarterly rpt, 3222–2

Electric power sales and finances of TVA, FY90, annual rpt, 9804–1

Electric power sales and revenue, by end-use sector, consumption level, and utility, 1989, annual rpt, 3164–91

Electric power sales by customer, activities by plant, and financial statements of Western Area Power Admin, FY90, annual rpt, 3254–1

Electric power sales by customer, financial statements, and operations and costs by project, for Southwestern Fed Power System, FY90, annual rpt, 3244–1

Electric power sales by customer, plants, and capacity of Southeastern Power Admin, FY90, annual rpt, 3234–1

Electric power sales, finances, and operations, for Fed Columbia River Power System, FY90, annual rpt, 3224–1

Electric power sales, revenue, and rates of Bonneville Power Admin, by customer and customer type, 1990, semiannual rpt, 3222–1

Business income and expenses, specific industry

Index by Subjects and Names

Electric power wholesale trade, by utility, type of ownership, and region, 1988, biennial rpt, 3164–92

Electric utilities conservation programs impacts on prices and supply costs, alternative estimates, 1991 rpt, 3308–99

Electric utilities finances and operations, detailed data for public and privately owned firms, 1989, annual rpt, 3164–11.4

Electric utilities finances and operations, detailed data for publicly owned firms, 1989, annual rpt, 3164–24

Electric utilities privately owned, finances and operations, detailed data, 1989, annual rpt, 3164–23

Energy producers finances and operations, by energy type for US firms domestic and foreign operations, 1989, annual rpt, 3164–44

Energy production, dev, and distribution firms revenues and income, quarterly rpt, 3162–38

Energy-related inventions supported by DOE, sales, jobs created, and inventor financing, 1980-88, 3308–91

Energy resources of US, foreign direct investment by energy type and firm, and US affiliates operations, as of 1989, annual rpt, 3164–80

Farm Credit System banks financial statements, 1990, annual rpt, 9264–5

Farm Credit System financial condition, quarterly rpt, 9262–2

Farm Credit System financial statements and loan activity by lender type, and borrower characteristics, 1990, annual rpt, 9264–2

Fed Home Loan Bank of Atlanta financial statements, quarterly rpt, 9302–37

Fed Home Loan Bank of Atlanta financial statements, 1989-90, annual rpt, 9304–1

Fed Home Loan Bank of Boston financial statements, quarterly rpt, 9302–35

Fed Home Loan Bank of Boston financial statements, 1989-90, annual rpt, 9304–2

Fed Home Loan Bank of Chicago financial statements, 1988-90, annual rpt, 9304–4

Fed Home Loan Bank of Cincinnati financial statements, 1989-90, annual rpt, 9304–6

Fed Home Loan Bank of Dallas financial statements, 1989-90, annual rpt, 9304–11

Fed Home Loan Bank of Des Moines financial statements, 1988-90, annual rpt, 9304–7

Fed Home Loan Bank of Indianapolis financial statements, 1988-90, annual rpt, 9304–10

Fed Home Loan Bank of New York financial statements, 1988-90, annual rpt, 9304–12

Fed Home Loan Bank of Pittsburgh financial statements, 1988-90, annual rpt, 9304–13

Fed Home Loan Bank of San Francisco financial statements, 1989-90, annual rpt, 9304–14

Fed Home Loan Bank of Seattle financial statements, 1988-90, annual rpt, 9304–15

Fed Home Loan Bank of Topeka financial statements, 1988-90, annual rpt, 9304–16

Fed Home Loan Banks financial statements, monthly tables, 9442–1

Fed Home Loan Banks financial statements, 1988-90, annual rpt, 9444–1

Fed Home Loan Mortgage Corp activities and financial statements, 1990, annual rpt, 9414–1

Fed Natl Mortgage Assn activities and finances, 1988-89, annual rpt, 5184–9

Fed Reserve Bank of Atlanta financial statements, 1989-90 annual rpt, 9371–4

Fed Reserve Bank of Boston financial statements, 1989-90, annual rpt, 9373–26

Fed Reserve Bank of Chicago financial statements, 1989-90, annual rpt, 9375–5

Fed Reserve Bank of Cleveland financial statements, 1989-90, annual rpt, 9377–5

Fed Reserve Bank of Dallas financial statements, 1989-90, annual rpt, 9379–2

Fed Reserve Bank of Kansas City financial statements, 1989-90, annual rpt, 9381–3

Fed Reserve Bank of Minneapolis financial statements, 1989-90, annual rpt, 9383–2

Fed Reserve Bank of New York financial statements, 1989-90, annual rpt, 9385–2

Fed Reserve Bank of Philadelphia financial statements, 1989-90, annual rpt, 9387–3

Fed Reserve Bank of Richmond financial statements, 1989-90, annual rpt, 9389–2

Fed Reserve Bank of San Francisco financial statements, 1989-90, annual rpt, 9393–2

Fed Reserve Bank of St Louis financial statements, 1989-90, annual rpt, 9391–17

Fed Reserve Board and Reserve banks finances, staff, and review of monetary policy and economic devs, 1990, annual rpt, 9364–1

Fed Reserve System, Board of Governors, and district banks financial statements, performance, and fiscal services, 1990-91, annual rpt, 9364–10

Food marketing cost indexes, by expense category, monthly rpt with articles, 1502–4

Food prices (farm-retail), marketing cost components, and industry finances and productivity, 1920s-90, annual rpt, 1544–9

Gear production for selected uses under alternative production requirements, and industry finances and operations, late 1940s-89, 2028–1

Govt Natl Mortgage Assn finances, and mortgage-backed securities program, FY90, annual rpt, 5144–6

GPO activities, finances, and production, FY90, annual rpt, 26204–1

Grain cooperatives finances and operations, by grain handled and selected characteristics, 1983-85, series, 1128–44

Health Care Financing Review, provider prices, price inputs and indexes, and labor, quarterly journal, 4652–1.1

Health maintenance organizations financial performance, and hospital use, demonstration project results, 1985-88, article, 4652–1.202

Health maintenance organizations financial performance and services use, demonstration project results, 1985-89, article, 4652–1.235

Helium market demand and Bur of Mines production, sales, and financial statements, FY90, annual rpt, 5604–32

Hospices operations, services, costs, and patient characteristics, for instns without Medicare certification, FY85-86, 4658–52

Hospital cost control through revenue and reimbursement caps, demonstration project results with background data, 1980s, 4658–48

Hospital reimbursement by Medicaid, impacts of Federal and State provisions, with services use, costs, and profits, by State, 1980s, 17206–1.11

Hospital reimbursement by Medicare under prospective payment system, analyses of alternative payment plans, series, 17206–1

Hospital reimbursement by Medicare under prospective payment system, diagnosis related group code assignment and effects on care and instn finances, 1984/85, series, 4006–7

Hospital reimbursement by Medicare under prospective payment system, impacts on costs, industry structure and operations, and quality of care, series, 17206–2

Hospital reimbursement by Medicare under prospective payment system, methodology, inputs, and data by diagnostic group, 1991 annual rpt, 17204–1

Hospital trauma centers unreimbursed costs and other factors contributing to closure, and views on nontrauma care impacts, 1989-90, GAO rpt, 26121–419

Hospitals in rural areas, financial and operating performance impacts of Medicare prospective payment reimbursement system, 1980s-87, 4658–51

Hotels and other lodging places, receipts, payroll, employment, ownership, and rooms, by State and MSA, 1987 Census of Service Industries, subject rpt, 2393–3

Insurance (health) private plans to supplement Medicare, loss ratio performance, sales abuse cases, and State enforcement, late 1980s, GAO rpt, 26121–410

Insurance (property and casualty) companies tax and income impacts of tax reform, with background financial data, 1970s-91, 8008–151

Juvenile correctional and detention public and private instns, inmates, and expenses, by instn and resident characteristics and State, 1987, biennial rpt, 6064–13

Kidney dialysis patients anemia treatment with Epoetin alfa, dosages, costs, Medicare reimbursement, and facility income effects, 1989, 4008–113

Labor unions reporting to Labor Dept, parent bodies and locals by location, 1990 listing, 6468–17

Labs (independent clinical) profitability and cost indexes by customer type, and impacts of Medicare fee caps, 1988-89, GAO rpt, 26121–425

Log home manufacturers in Montana, sales, production, and timber use, 1960s-88, 1208–370

Mental health care facilities, finances, caseload, staff, and characteristics of instn and patients, 1988, 4506–4.14

Mental health care facilities outlays, by function, instn type, funding source, and State, 1988, 4506–3.45

Metals (primary) production, shipments, trade, stocks, and material used, by product, periodic Current Industrial Rpt series, 2506–10

Index by Subjects and Names

Business income and expenses, specific industry

Military post exchange operations, and sales by commodity, by facility and location worldwide, FY89, annual rpt, 3504–10

Mineral industries census, 1987: finances and operations, by establishment characteristics, SIC 2- to 4-digit industry, and State, subject rpt, 2517–1

Mineral industries census, 1987: finances and operations, by SIC 2- to 4-digit industry, State, and county, census div rpt series, 2515–1

Minerals production, prices, trade, and foreign and US industry devs, by commodity, bimonthly rpt with articles, 5602–4

Mint (US) activities, finances, coin and medals production and holdings, and gold and silver transactions, by facility, FY90, annual rpt, 8204–1

Natural and supplemental gas production, prices, trade, use, reserves, and pipeline company finances, by firm and State, monthly rpt with articles, 3162–4

Natural gas interstate pipeline company detailed financial and operating data, by firm, 1989, annual rpt, 3164–38

Nonprofit charitable organizations finances, and revenue and investments of top 10 instns, 1986-87, article, 8302–2.210

Nonprofit charitable organizations finances, by asset size and State, 1987, article, 8302–2.218

Nonprofit charitable organizations finances, 1988, table, 8302–2.220

Nuclear power plant safety standards and research, design, licensing, construction, operation, and finances, with data by reactor, quarterly journal, 3352–4

Nursing home reimbursement by Medicaid, States payment ratesetting methods, analysis for 7 States, 1980s, article, 4652–1.255

Nursing home reimbursement by Medicaid, States payment ratesetting methods, limits, and allowances, 1988, article, 4652–1.253

Oil bulk stations, sales and storage capacity by product, inventories, expenses, employment, and modes of transport, 1987 Census of Wholesale Trade, 2407–4.2

Oil company production and imports by type, and financial data, 1977-89, annual rpt, 3164–74.1

Oil company profits, by product, line of business, and for independent firms, 1989-90, article, 3162–44

Oil price and industry profit impacts of Iraq invasion of Kuwait, as of 4th qtr 1990, 3166–6.46

Oil refinery operations and finances, with ownership changes, shutdowns, and reactivations, by firm, 1970s-90, 3168–119

Oil supply and industry of OPEC and US, impacts of oil embargo imposed after Iraq invasion of Kuwait, 1989-91, hearing, 21368–132

Overseas Private Investment Corp finances and activities, with list of insured projects and firms, FY90, annual rpt, 9904–2

Panama Canal Commission finances and activities, with Canal traffic and local govt operations, FY90, annual rpt, 9664–3

Pension Benefit Guaranty Corp activities and finances, FY90, annual rpt, 9674–1

Physicians fee schedule under Medicare Supplementary Medical Insurance, analyses of costs and other issues, series, 17266–1

Physicians fee schedule under Medicare Supplementary Medical Insurance, methodology with data by procedure and specialty, 1991, annual rpt, 17264–1

Physicians practice cost indexes and components, by State, MSA, and for rural areas, 1989 rpt, 4658–50

Postal Service activities, finances, and mail volume and subsidies, FY90, annual rpt, 9864–5.3

Postal Service activities, financial statements, and employment, FY86-90, annual rpt, 9864–1

Postal Service operating costs, itemized by class of mail, FY90, annual rpt, 9864–4

Postal Service revenue and mail volume by class, and special service transactions, quarterly rpt, 9862–1

Postal Service revenue, costs, and volume, by service type and class of mail, FY90, annual rpt, 9864–2

Prison Industries (Federal) finances and operations, FY90, annual rpt, 6244–3

Prison Industries (Federal) sales, by commodity and Federal agency, FY90, annual rpt, 6244–5

Prisons and jails operated under private contract, costs and characteristics of instns, by facility and State, 1990, GAO rpt, 26119–321

Radio Free Europe and Radio Liberty broadcast and financial data, FY90, annual rpt, 10314–1

Railroad (Amtrak) finances and operations, FY90, annual rpt, 29524–1

Railroad (Class I) finances and operations, detailed data by firm, class of service, and district, 1989, annual rpt, 9486–6.1

Railroad Retirement Accounts financial statements, FY89, annual rpt, 9704–1

Railroad retirement system funding and benefits findings and recommendations, with background industry data, 1960s-90 and projected to 2060, 9708–1

Railroad revenue, income, freight, and rate of return, by Class I freight railroad and district, quarterly rpt, 9482–2

Reclamation Bur irrigation activities, finances, and project impacts in western US, 1989, annual rpt, 5824–12

Recreation (outdoor) coastal facilities of Fed Govt and States, visitor and site characteristics, 1987-90 survey, regional rpt series, 2176–9

Red Cross financial statements, FY89-90, annual rpt, 29254–1

Resolution Trust Corp financial statements and activities, with data on savings instns conservatorships by State and instn, 1989, annual rpt, 9724–1

Savings and loan assns, FHLB 6th District insured members financial condition and operations by State, quarterly rpt, 9302–23

Savings banks insured by Bank Insurance Fund, financial condition and performance, by asset size and region, quarterly rpt, 9292–5

Savings instns failures, financial performance of instns under Resolution Trust Corp conservatorship, quarterly rpt, 9722–5

Savings instns, FHLB 1st District members financial operations compared to banks, and related economic and housing indicators, bimonthly rpt with articles, 9302–4

Savings instns, FHLB 6th and 11th District and natl cost of funds indexes, and mortgage and Treasury bill rates, monthly rpt, 9302–38

Savings instns, FHLB 6th District members financial condition and operations by State, monthly rpt, 9302–11

Savings instns, FHLB 7th District and natl cost of funds indexes, and mortgage rates, monthly rpt, 9302–30

Savings instns finances and operations by district and State, mortgage loan activity and terms by MSA, and FHLB finances, 1989 and trends from 1900, annual rpt, 8434–3

Savings instns insured by Savings Assn Insurance Fund, finances by profitability group, district, and State, quarterly rpt, 8432–4

Securities industry finances, for broker-dealers and individual stock exchanges and clearing agencies, 1985-89, annual rpt, 9734–2.1

Semiconductor and fiber optics industries quality control spending, effectiveness, and views, survey results, 1980s, 2218–84

Shipping firms combined financial statements, FY88-89, annual rpt, 7704–14.5

Space programs involvement by private sector, govt contracts, costs, revenue, and R&D spending, 1970s-80s and projected to 2000, 26306–6.154

Space station commercial dev and operating costs and income under alternative financing options, projected 1989-2000, 21708–129

St Lawrence Seaway Dev Corp finances and activities, and Seaway cargo tonnage, 1989, annual rpt, 7744–1

Steel imports of US under voluntary restraint agreement, by product, customs district, and country, with US industry operating data, quarterly rpt, 9882–13

Steel industry finances, operations, and modernization efforts, with data on major companies and foreign industry, 1968-91, last issue of annual rpt, 9884–24

Telecommunications finances, rates, and traffic for US carriers intl operations, by service type, firm, and country, 1975-89, annual rpt, 9284–17

Telecommunications industry intl competitiveness, with financial and operating data by product or service, firm, and country, 1990 rpt, 2008–30

Telephone and telegraph firms detailed finances and operations, 1989, annual rpt, 9284–6

Telephone firms borrowing under Rural Telephone Program, and financial and operating data, by State, 1990, annual rpt, 1244–2

Telephone local service charges and low-income subsidies, by region, company, and city, 1980s-90, semiannual rpt, 9282–8

Business income and expenses, specific industry

Telephone rural cooperative bank financial statements, FY89, annual rpt, 1244–4

Telephone service subscribership, charges, and local and long distance firm finances and operations, late 1970s-91, semiannual rpt, 9282–7

Textile mill production, trade, sales, stocks, and material used, by product, region, and State, periodic Current Industrial Rpt series, 2506–5

Timber sales of Forest Service, expenses, and operations, by region, State, and natl forest, FY90, annual rpts, 1204–36

Transit systems finances and operations, by mode of transport, size of fleet, and for 468 systems, 1989, annual rpt, 7884–4

Transit systems finances, costs, and needs, by selected system, 1987-89, biennial rpt, 7884–8

Transit systems under private, public, and nonprofit ownership, funding, staff, and service and area characteristics, 1990 rpt, 7888–81

Transportation census, 1987: finances and operations by size, ownership, and State, and revenues by MSA, by SIC 2- to 4-digit industry, 2579–1

Truck and bus interstate carriers finances and operations, by district, 1989, annual rpt, 9486–6.3

Truck and warehouse services finances and inventory, by SIC 2- to 4-digit industry, 1989 survey, annual rpt, 2413–14

Truck interstate carriers finances and operations, by district, 1989, annual rpt, 9486–6.2

Truck itemized costs per mile, finances, and operations, for agricultural carriers, 1990, annual rpt, 1311–15

Truck transport of household goods, financial and operating data by firm, quarterly rpt, 9482–14

Truck transport of property, financial and operating data by region and firm, quarterly rpt, 9482–5

TV (cable) deregulation in 1986, impacts on prices and services, 1986-91, GAO rpt, 26113–431

TVA finances and operations by program and facility, FY90, annual rpt, 9804–32

Uranium enrichment facilities of DOE, financial statements, FY89-90, annual rpt, 3354–7

Vending facilities run by blind on Federal and non-Federal property, finances and operations by agency and State, FY90, annual rpt, 4944–2

Warehouse services finances, by SIC 3- to 4-digit industry, 1989 survey, annual rpt, 2413–14

Workers compensation programs under Federal admin, finances and operations, FY90, annual rpt, 6504–10

see also Agricultural finance

see also Agricultural marketing

see also Agricultural production costs

see also Business assets and liabilities, specific industry

see also Capital investments, specific industry

see also Depreciation

see also Educational finance

see also Energy production costs

see also Farm income

see also Operating ratios

see also Payroll

see also Production costs

see also under By Industry in the "Index by Categories"

Business inventories

Alcoholic beverages and tobacco production, removals, stocks, and material used, by State, monthly rpt series, 8486–1

Assets and debts of private sector, balance sheets by segment, 1945-90, semiannual rpt, 9365–4.1

Auto industry finances and operations, trade by country, and prices of selected US and foreign models, monthly rpt, 9882–8

Auto production, inventories, and inventory/sales ratio, 1991 model year, annual article, 2702–1.228

Budget deficits under Reagan Admin, impact on capital stock, foreign debt, and other economic indicators, with background data, 1950s-88, article, 9393–8.201

Building materials production, shipments, and stocks, by type, bimonthly rpt, 2042–1.6

Business statistics, detailed data for major industries and economic indicators, *Survey of Current Business*, monthly rpt, 2702–1

Chemical and oil products shipments, firms, trade, and use, by product, periodic Current Industrial Rpt series, 2506–8

Clay and glass production, shipments, trade, and stocks, by product, periodic Current Industrial Rpt series, 2506–9

Construction industries census, 1987: establishments, employment, receipts, and expenditures, by SIC 4-digit industry and State, final industry rpt series, 2373–1

Cotton (long staple) production, prices, exports, stocks, and mill use, monthly rpt, 1309–12

Cotton linters production, stocks, use, and prices, monthly rpt, 1309–10

Cotton, wool, and synthetic fiber production, prices, trade, and use, periodic situation rpt with articles, 1561–1

Department store inventory price indexes, by class of item, monthly table, 6762–7

Economic indicators and components, and Fed Reserve 4th District business and financial conditions, monthly chartbook, 9377–10

Economic indicators and components, current data and annual trends, monthly rpt, 23842–1.1; 23842–1.3

Economic indicators compounded annual rates of change, monthly rpt, 9391–3

Economic indicators impacts of commercial paper-bank loan firm financing mix and selected interest rate spreads, model description and results, 1960s-89, technical paper, 9366–6.268

Enterprise Statistics, 1987: auxiliaries of multi-establishment firms, finances and operations by function, industry, and State, 2329–6

Fertilizer (inorganic) shipments, trade, use, and firms, by product and State, with stocks, 1990, annual Current Industrial Rpt, 2506–8.13

Flow-of-funds accounts, savings, investments, and credit statements, quarterly rpt, 9365–3.3

Index by Subjects and Names

Food (processed) production and stocks by State, shipments, exports, ingredients, and use, periodic Current Industrial Rpt series, 2506–4

Imports and tariff provisions effect on US industries and products, investigations with background financial and operating data, series, 9886–4

Imports injury to US industries from foreign subsidized products and sales at less than fair value, investigations with background financial and operating data, series, 9886–19

Imports injury to US industries from foreign subsidized products, investigations with background financial and operating data, series, 9886–15

Imports injury to US industries from sales at less than fair value, investigations with background financial and operating data, series, 9886–14

Input-output structure of US economy, detailed interindustry transactions for 84 industries, and components of final demand, 1986, annual article, 2702–1.206

Input-output structure of US economy, detailed interindustry transactions for 85 industries, 1982 benchmark data, 2702–1.213

Inventories and ratio to sales, by industry div, 1947-90, annual rpt, 204–1.1; 204–1.3

Lumber, paper, and related products shipments, trade, stocks, and use, periodic Current Industrial Rpt series, 2506–7

Machinery and equipment production, shipments, trade, stocks, orders, use, and firms, by product, periodic Current Industrial Rpt series, 2506–12

Manufacturing and trade inventories, sales, and inventory/sales ratios, quarterly article, 2702–1.28

Manufacturing annual survey, 1989: establishments, employment, finances, inventories, and energy use, by SIC 2- to 4-digit industry, 2506–15.1

Manufacturing annual survey, 1989: finances and operations, by SIC 2- and 3-digit industry and State, 2506–15.3

Manufacturing census, 1987: finances and operations, by SIC 2- to 4-digit industry, State, and MSA, with trends from 1849, 2497–1

Manufacturing census, 1987: finances and operations, by type of organization and SIC 2- to 4-digit industry, subject rpt, 2497–5

Manufacturing shipments, inventories, and orders, by SIC 2- to 3-digit industry, monthly Current Industrial Rpt, 2506–3.1

Metals (intermediate product) shipments, trade, and inventories, by product, periodic Current Industrial Rpt series, 2506–11

Metals (primary) production, shipments, trade, stocks, and material used, by product, periodic Current Industrial Rpt series, 2506–10

Middle Atlantic States manufacturing business outlook, monthly survey rpt, 9387–11

Mineral industries census, 1987: finances and operations, by establishment characteristics, SIC 2- to 4-digit industry, and State, subject rpt, 2517–1

Index by Subjects and Names

Business machines and equipment

Mineral industries census, 1987: finances and operations, by SIC 2- to 4-digit industry, State, and county, census div rpt series, 2515–1

Mineral Industry Surveys, commodity reviews of production, trade, stocks, and use, monthly rpt series, 5612–1

Mineral Industry Surveys, commodity reviews of production, trade, stocks, and use, quarterly rpt series, 5612–2

Mobile home placements and prices by State, and dealer inventories, by region, monthly rpt, 2382–1

Multinatl firms US affiliates, finances, and operations, by industry, world area of parent firm, and State, 1988-89, annual rpt, 2704–4

Multinatl US firms and foreign affiliates finances and operations, by industry and world area of parent firm, 1989 benchmark survey, preliminary annual rpt, 2704–5

Natl income and product accounts and components, *Survey of Current Business*, monthly rpt, 2702–1.24

Nonprofit charitable organizations finances, and revenue and investments of top 10 instns, 1986-87, article, 8302–2.210

Nonprofit charitable organizations finances, by asset size and State, 1987, article, 8302–2.218

Productivity of labor and capital, indexes and percent change, 1948-90, annual press release, 6824–2

Puerto Rico economic censuses, 1987: wholesale and retail trade and service industry finances and operations, by SIC 2- to 4-digit industry and municipio, 2591–1

Puerto Rico economic censuses, 1987: wholesale, retail, and service industries finances and operations, by establishment characteristics and SIC 2- and 3-digit industry, subject rpts, 2591–2

Retail trade census, 1987: depreciable assets, capital and operating expenses, sales, value added, and inventories, by SIC 2- to 4-digit kind of business, 2399–2

Retail trade sales and inventories, by kind of business, region, and selected State, MSA, and city, monthly rpt, 2413–3

Retail trade sales, inventories, purchases, gross margin, and accounts receivable, by SIC 2- to 4-digit kind of business and form of ownership, 1989, annual rpt, 2413–5

Soviet Union GNP by detailed income and outlay component, 1985, 2326–18.59

State and Metro Area Data Book, 1991 data compilation, 2328–54

Statistical Abstract of US, 1991 annual data compilation, 2324–1.27; 2324–1.28

Tax (income) returns filed by type of filer, selected income items, quarterly rpt, 8302–2.1

Tax (income) returns of corporations, income and tax items by asset size and detailed industry, 1987, annual rpt, 8304–4

Tax (income) returns of corporations, income and tax items by asset size and detailed industry, 1988, annual rpt, 8304–21

Tax (income) returns of partnerships, income statement and balance sheet items, by industry group, 1989, annual article, 8302–2.216; 8304–18

Textile mill production, trade, sales, stocks, and material used, by product, region, and State, periodic Current Industrial Rpt series, 2506–5

Truck and warehouse services finances and inventory, by SIC 2- to 4-digit industry, 1989 survey, annual rpt, 2413–14

Wholesale trade census, 1987: depreciable assets, capital and operating expenses, sales, value added, and inventories, by SIC 2- to 3-digit kind of business, 2407–2

Wholesale trade census, 1987: establishments, sales by customer class, employment, inventories, and expenses, by SIC 2- to 4-digit kind of business, 2407–4

Wholesale trade sales and inventories, by SIC 2- to 3-digit kind of business, monthly rpt, 2413–7

Wholesale trade sales, inventories, purchases, and gross margins, by SIC 2- to 3-digit kind of business, 1990, annual rpt, 2413–13

see also Agricultural stocks

see also Business orders

see also Coal stocks

see also Energy stocks and inventories

see also Petroleum stocks

Business loans

see Commercial credit

Business machines and equipment

County Business Patterns, 1988: employment, establishments, and payroll, by SIC 2- to 4-digit industry and county, annual State rpt series, 2326–6

County Business Patterns, 1989: employment, establishments, and payroll, by SIC 2- to 4-digit industry and county, annual State rpt series, 2326–8

DOD prime contract awards, by detailed procurement category, FY87-90, annual rpt, 3544–18

Electric utilities privately owned, finances and operations, detailed data, 1989, annual rpt, 3164–23

Employment, earnings, and hours, by SIC 1- to 4-digit industry, monthly and annual averages, selected years 1909-90, annual rpt, 6744–4

Enterprise Statistics, 1987: finances and operations for companies, by size, level of diversification, form of organization, and industry group, 2329–8

Exports and imports between US and outlying areas, by detailed commodity and mode of transport, 1990, annual rpt, 2424–11

Exports and imports of US, by country and detailed commodity, monthly rpt, 2422–12

Exports and imports of US, by Harmonized System 6-digit commodity and country, 1990, annual rpt, 2424–13

Exports and imports of US, by selected country, country group, and commodity group, 1990, annual rpt, 2044–37

Exports and imports of US, by transport mode, country, and SITC 1- to 3-digit commodity, 1990, annual rpt, 2424–12

Exports of US, detailed Schedule B commodities with countries of destination, 1990, annual rpt, 2424–10

Furniture (office) shipments by product, and metals used by type, 1990, annual Current Industrial Rpt, 2506–7.8

House of Representatives salaries, expenses, and contingent fund disbursement, detailed listings, quarterly rpt, 21942–1

Imports of US given duty-free treatment for value of US material sent abroad, by commodity and country, 1989, annual rpt, 9884–14

Injuries from use of consumer products, by severity, victim age, and detailed product, 1990, annual rpt, 9164–6

Input-output structure of US economy, detailed interindustry transactions for 84 industries, and components of final demand, 1986, annual article, 2702–1.206

Input-output structure of US economy, detailed interindustry transactions for 85 industries, 1982 benchmark data, 2702–1.213

Manufacturing annual survey, 1989: finances and operations, by SIC 2- to 4-digit industry, series, 2506–15

Manufacturing census, 1987: finances and operations, by SIC 2- to 4-digit industry, State, and MSA, with trends from 1849, 2497–1

Manufacturing census, 1987: finances and operations, by type of organization and SIC 2- to 4-digit industry, subject rpt, 2497–5

Multinatl US firms and foreign affiliates finances and operations, by industry and world area of parent firm, 1989 benchmark survey, preliminary annual rpt, 2704–5

Natural gas interstate pipeline company detailed financial and operating data, by firm, 1989, annual rpt, 3164–38

Occupational injury and illness rates, by SIC 2- to 4-digit industry, 1988-89, annual rpt, 6844–7

Occupational injury and illness rates, by SIC 2- to 4-digit industry, 1989, annual rpt, 6844–1

OECD trade, total and for 4 major countries, and US trade by country, by commodity, 1970-89, world area rpt series, 9116–1

Pollution (water) industrial releases in wastewater, levels, treatment, costs, and regulation, with background financial and operating data, 1989 industry rpt, 9206–4.13

Price indexes (producer), by stage of processing and detailed commodity, monthly rpt, 6762–6

Price indexes (producer), by stage of processing and detailed commodity, monthly 1990, annual rpt, 6764–2

Puerto Rico economic censuses, 1987: wholesale and retail trade and service industry finances and operations, by SIC 2- to 4-digit industry and municipio, 2591–1

Retail trade census, 1987: finances and employment, for establishments with and without payroll, by SIC 2- to 4-digit kind of business, State, and MSA, 2401–1

Tax (income) returns of corporations, income and tax items by asset size and detailed industry, 1987, annual rpt, 8304–4

Tax (income) returns of corporations, income and tax items by asset size and detailed industry, 1988, annual rpt, 8304–21

Business machines and equipment

Thefts, and value of property stolen and recovered, by property type, 1990, annual rpt, 6224–2.1

Typewriters (portable electric) from Singapore at less than fair value, injury to US industry, investigation with background financial and operating data, 1991 rpt, 9886–14.312

Wholesale trade census, 1987: establishments, sales by customer class, employment, inventories, and expenses, by SIC 2- to 4-digit kind of business, 2407–4

see also Computer industry and products
see also Office supplies
see also under By Commodity in the "Index by Categories"

Business management

- Asset allocation funds performance relative to stock index and Treasury bill rates, model description and alternative results, 1980s-90, technical paper, 9385–8.87
- Bank deposit insurance system reform issues, with background industry financial data, 1970s-90, GAO rpt, 26119–320
- Banks financial performance, risk assessment, and regulation, 1990 annual conf papers, 9375–7
- Banks in Texas, failures relation to portfolio risk indicators and year of establishment, 1980s, working paper, 9379–14.10
- Banks regulatory enforcement activities of Federal agencies, effectiveness, with data on capital-deficient banks, late 1980s-90, GAO rpt, 26119–334
- County Business Patterns, 1988: employment, establishments, and payroll, by SIC 2- to 4-digit industry and county, annual State rpt series, 2326–6
- County Business Patterns, 1989: employment, establishments, and payroll, by SIC 2- to 4-digit industry and county, annual State rpt series, 2326–8
- Enterprise Statistics, 1987: auxiliaries of multi-establishment firms, finances and operations by function, industry, and State, 2329–6
- Exports and imports of services, direct and among multinatl firms affiliates, by industry and world area, 1986-90, article, 2702–1.223
- Insurance industry finances, underwriting activities, and investment plan mgmt, 1960s-90, 21248–159
- Minority Business Dev Centers mgmt and financial aid, and characteristics of businesses, by region and State, FY90, annual rpt, 2104–6
- Multinatl US firms and foreign affiliates finances and operations, by industry and world area of parent firm, 1989 benchmark survey, preliminary annual rpt, 2704–5
- Mutual funds financial performance impacts of selected mgmt decisions, model results, late 1970s-84, technical paper, 9385–8.80
- Natural gas interstate pipeline company detailed financial and operating data, by firm, 1989, annual rpt, 3164–38
- Quality mgmt practices of corporations, effects on employee and customer relations, operations, and finances, 1988-89, GAO rpt, 26123–345
- Securities intl markets computer use and risk mgmt methods, 1991 GAO rpt, 26125–44

Service industries census, 1987: establishments, receipts by source, payroll, and employment, by SIC 2- to 4-digit kind of business, State, and MSA, 2393–4

see also Business outlook and attitude surveys
see also Consultants
see also Employee performance and appraisal
see also Executives and managers
see also Industrial purchasing
see also Industrial siting
see also Labor-management relations, general
see also Personnel management

Business orders

- Aircraft orders and deliveries of commercial carriers, by aircraft type, quarterly rpt, 7502–16
- Business statistics, detailed data for major industries and economic indicators, *Survey of Current Business*, monthly rpt, 2702–1
- Economic indicators and components, current data and annual trends, monthly rpt, 23842–1.3
- Gear production for selected uses under alternative production requirements, and industry finances and operations, late 1940s-89, 2028–1
- Machinery and equipment production, shipments, trade, stocks, orders, use, and firms, by product, periodic Current Industrial Rpt series, 2506–12
- Manufacturing shipments and new and unfilled orders, 1947-90, annual rpt, 204–1.3
- Manufacturing shipments, inventories, and orders, by SIC 2- to 3-digit industry, monthly Current Industrial Rpt, 2506–3.1
- Middle Atlantic States manufacturing business outlook, monthly survey rpt, 9387–11
- Minority Business Dev Centers mgmt and financial aid, and characteristics of businesses, by region and State, FY90, annual rpt, 2104–6
- Semiconductors and related equipment import dependency of US firms, and sales from Japan firms delayed and denied, 1988-91, GAO rpt, 26123–361
- Ships under foreign flag owned by US firms and foreign affiliates, by type, owner, and country of registry and construction, as of Jan 1991, semiannual rpt, 7702–3
- *Statistical Abstract of US*, 1991 annual data compilation, 2324–1.27
- Textile mill production, trade, sales, stocks, and material used, by product, region, and State, periodic Current Industrial Rpt series, 2506–5
- Uranium marketing, contracts, prices, utility shipments, and trade, 1982-90 and projected to 2000, annual rpt, 3164–65.2

Business outlook and attitude surveys

- Aircraft noise abatement measures, and industry compliance costs, aggregate FY90-2000, GAO rpt, 26113–534
- Copyright infringement and copying issues for prerecorded training videos, businesses views, 1987 survey, hearing, 21528–82
- Data collection activities of Fed Govt, and quality and privacy issues, 1990 conf, 106–4.14

Index by Subjects and Names

- Depreciable assets class lives measurement, investment, and industry operations, industry rpt series, 8006–5
- Drug (prescription) mail service industry structure, finances, and operations, 1989 survey, 4658–60
- Farm chemicals use sources of groundwater pollution, with background data and farmers views, 1970s-80s, hearing, 25168–76
- Farm credit conditions and real estate values, Fed Reserve 11th District, quarterly rpt, 9379–11
- Farm credit conditions, earnings, and expenses, Fed Reserve 9th District, quarterly rpt, 9383–11
- Farm operators mgmt and production decisions, and opinions on agricultural practices, 1988 survey, article, 1541–1.206
- Farmers views on Federal agricultural support, trade, and fiscal policies, by region and State, 1989 survey, hearings, 21168–43
- Genetic damage and trait monitoring and screening of employees, use, costs, benefits, and procedures, 1980s, 26358–230
- Health condition screening and monitoring of employees, businesses practices and views, 1989 survey, 26358–250
- Hospices operations, services, costs, and patient characteristics, for instns without Medicare certification, FY85-86, 4658–52
- Hospital trauma centers unreimbursed costs and other factors contributing to closure, and views on nontrauma care impacts, 1989-90, GAO rpt, 26121–419
- Insurance (health) provided by employers, small business and restaurant owners views, 1989 hearings, 23898–7
- Middle Atlantic States manufacturing business outlook, monthly survey rpt, 9387–11
- North Central States business and economic conditions, Fed Reserve 9th District, quarterly journal, 9383–19
- North Central States farm credit conditions and economic devs, Fed Reserve 7th District, monthly rpt, 9375–10
- Quality mgmt practices of corporations, effects on employee and customer relations, operations, and finances, 1988-89, GAO rpt, 26123–345
- Recordkeeping Practices Survey, 1989: data coverage, methodology, businesses views, and applications for 1992 economic censuses, 2328–67
- Recruitment, hiring, compensation, and other employment practices of large firms, 1989 survey, GAO rpt, 26119–324
- Semiconductor and fiber optics industries quality control spending, effectiveness, and views, survey results, 1980s, 2218–84
- Small business dev centers mgmt and technical aid activities, funding, and client satisfaction and performance, 1980s, hearing, 25728–43
- Telecommunications industry intl competitiveness, with financial and operating data by product or service, firm, and country, 1990 rpt, 2008–30

Index by Subjects and Names

West Central States farm real estate values, farm loan trends, and regional farm price index, Fed Reserve 10th District, quarterly rpt, 9381–16.1

Business services

see Accounting and auditing
see Advertising
see Computer use
see Consultants
see Courier services
see Credit bureaus and agencies
see Direct marketing
see Employment services
see Janitorial and maintenance services
see Public relations
see Service industries

Busing

see School busing

Butler, Alison

- "Trade Imbalances and Economic Theory: The Case for a U.S.-Japan Trade Deficit", 9391–1.209
- "Trade-Related Aspects of Intellectual Property Rights: What Is at Stake?", 9391–1.203

Butler, Gertrude S.

"Foreign Ownership of U.S. Agricultural Land Through Dec. 31, 1990: County-Level Data", 1584–3

Butter

see Dairy industry and products

Butynski, William

- "Drug Treatment Services: Funding and Admissions", 4498–73
- "State Resources and Services Related to Alcohol and Other Drug Abuse Problems, FY89: An Analysis of State Alcohol and Drug Abuse Profile Data", 4488–15

Buxton, Boyd M.

"Costs of Producing Oranges and Grapefruit, 1988/89", 1561–6.201

Buzzanell, Peter J.

- "California's Sweetener Industries—Recent Developments and Prospects", 1561–14.206
- "Mexico's Sugar Industry in Transition—Implications for Sweetener Trade with the U.S.", 1561–14.204
- "Thailand: Emergence of a Sugar Superpower", 1561–14.201
- "Trends in U.S. Soft Drink Consumption—Demand Implications for Low-Calorie and Other Sweeteners", 1561–14.210
- "World and U.S. Outlook for Sweeteners", 1004–16.1

Buzzard, Kenneth

"Medicaid and Third-Party Liability: Using Information To Achieve Program Goals", 4652–1.212

Bye, Barry V.

"Medicare Costs Prior to Retirement for Disabled-Worker Beneficiaries", 4742–1.208

Byrne, Daniel J.

"Comparison of Alternative Weight Recalibration Methods for Diagnosis-Related Groups", 4652–1.227

Cable Communications Policy Act

Deregulation of CATV in 1986, impacts on prices and services, 1986-91, GAO rpt, 26113–431

Cable television

- Consumer Expenditure Survey, spending for selected categories, 1991 semiannual pamphlet, 2322–3
- Copyright royalty fees from CATV, and funds available for distribution, 1989-90, annual rpt, 26404–2
- County Business Patterns, 1988: employment, establishments, and payroll, by SIC 2- to 4-digit industry and county, annual State rpt series, 2326–6
- County Business Patterns, 1989: employment, establishments, and payroll, by SIC 2- to 4-digit industry and county, annual State rpt series, 2326–8
- CPI by component for US city average, and by region, population size, and for 27 metro areas, monthly rpt, 6762–2
- Deregulation of CATV in 1986, impacts on prices and services, 1986-91, GAO rpt, 26113–431
- Equipment shipments, trade, use, and firms, for electronic communications systems and related products, 1990, annual Current Industrial Rpt, 2506–12.35
- Mail volume to and from households, use, and views, by class, source, content, and household characteristics, 1987-88, annual rpt, 9864–10
- Manufacturing finances and operations, by SIC 2- to 4-digit industry, forecast 1991, annual rpt, 2044–28
- Price indexes (producer), by stage of processing and detailed commodity, monthly rpt, 6762–6
- Price indexes (producer), by stage of processing and detailed commodity, monthly 1990, annual rpt, 6764–2
- *State and Metro Area Data Book*, 1991 data compilation, 2328–54
- *Statistical Abstract of US*, 1991 annual data compilation, 2324–1.18

Cadmium

see Metals and metal industries

Caggiano, John

"Survey of Payers and Payees with IRS-Identified Invalid TINs", 8304–8.1

Caguas, P.R.

see also under By SMSA or MSA in the "Index by Categories"

Calcium

see Nonmetallic minerals and mines
see Vitamins and nutrients

Calder, Nigel

"View from Another Bridge", 2152–8.201

Calem, Paul S.

- "Financing Constraints and Investment: New Evidence from the U.S. Hospital Industry", 9387–8.243
- "Reputation Acquisition, Collateral, and Moral Hazard in Debt Markets", 9387–8.244

Calhoun, Samuel D.

"World Oilseed and Products Trade, 1962-88", 1528–314

California

- AIDS patient home and community services under Medicaid waiver in 6 States, 1988-89, article, 4652–1.216
- Banks (insured commercial and savings) deposits by instn, State, MSA, and county, as of June 1990, annual regional rpt, 9295–3.6
- Banks (multinatl) US branches assets and liabilities, total and for 3 States, monthly rpt, quarterly data, 9362–1.4

California

- Bean (dried) prices by State, market activity, and foreign and US production, use, stocks, and trade, weekly rpt, 1311–17
- Birth outcomes and prenatal care use effects of Medicaid coverage, charges, and Medicaid payments, for California, 1983, article, 4652–1.241
- Carpool high occupancy vehicle lanes use, design, enforcement, and drivers views, for California, 1988-89, 7308–203
- Celery acreage planted and growing, by growing area, monthly rpt, 1621–14
- Child day care providers health and safety training, by facility size, for California, 1987 survey, article, 4042–3.243
- Child welfare programs funding by source, and foster care program operations and client characteristics, for selected States, 1960s-95, 25368–169
- Coal production and mines by county, prices, productivity, miners, and reserves, by mining method and State, 1989-90, annual rpt, 3164–25
- Coastal areas pollutant concentrations in fish and sediments, by contaminant, fish species, and Pacific coast site, 1984-86, 2168–121
- County Business Patterns, 1989: employment, establishments, and payroll, by SIC 2- to 4-digit industry and county, annual State rpt, 2326–8.6
- Dairy prices, by product and selected area, with related marketing data, 1990, annual rpt, 1317–1
- DOD prime contract awards, by contractor, service branch, State, and city, FY90, annual rpt, 3544–22
- Drought impacts in California, Central Valley reservoir storage and capacity, and Kern County crop production and irrigation, 1989-91, article, 1561–6.202
- Earthquake (Loma Prieta) relief funding and response by FEMA, 1989-90, GAO rpt, 26113–511
- Earthquake preparedness costs and benefits, with data for California events and effects of 1989 Loma Prieta quake, 1980s, hearings, 21248–154
- Earthquakes of San Andreas Fault system, location and seismic characteristics, by event, 1769-1989, 5668–123
- Farm employment, wages, and hours, by payment method, worker type, region, and State, 1910-90, 1618–21
- Fed Govt spending in States and local areas, by type, State, county, and city, FY90, annual rpt, 2464–3
- Fed Govt spending in States, by type, program, agency, and State, FY90, annual rpt, 2464–2
- Fish (grenadier) catch off California, physical characteristics, and palatability, 1965-85, article, 2162–1.204
- Fish and shellfish sport and commercial landings for California, permits issued, and harbor facilities, 1916-86, 5738–20
- Fishing (sport) from California commercial passenger boats with refrigeration equipment, anglers views, 1989 survey, 2168–125
- Fishing (sport) from California commercial passenger vessels, angler and boat owner characteristics and opinions, 1987-88, article, 2162–1.202

California

Global climate change environmental, infrastructure, and health impacts, with model results and background data, 1850s-2100, 9188–113

HHS financial aid, by program, recipient, State, and city, FY90, annual regional listing, 4004–3.9

Hispanic Americans in counties bordering Mexico, by selected characteristics, 1980, Current Population Rpt, 2546–2.159

Hospital deaths of Medicare patients, actual and expected rates by diagnosis, and hospital characteristics, by instn, FY87-89, annual regional rpt, 4654–14.9

Housing census, 1990: inventory, occupancy, and costs, State fact sheet, 2326–21.6

Hwy funds pooled by States from FHwA funds for specific projects, demonstration project results, FY88-90, GAO rpt, 26113–471

Income (personal) per capita and by source, and earnings by industry div, by State, MSA, and county, 1984-89, annual regional rpt, 2704–2.5

Jail adult and juvenile population, employment, spending, instn conditions, and inmate programs, by county and facility, 1988, regional rpt series, 6068–144.5

Marine mammals and birds population and distribution, by species and northeast Pacific Ocean location, literature and data base review, 1950s-88, 5738–28

Marriages, divorces, and rates, by characteristics of spouses, State, and county, 1987 and trends from 1920, US Vital Statistics annual rpt, 4144–4

Medicaid child preventive health care visits, exams, and immunizations, for California, 1981-84, article, 4652–1.214

Medicaid demonstration projects evaluation, for 6 States, 1988 rpt, 4658–45

Medicaid hospital discharges, by eligibility and instn characteristics, for 2 States, 1984, article, 4652–1.249

Medicaid prepaid plans for physician services, characteristics of selected plans in 4 States, various periods 1983-89, article, 4652–1.228

Medicaid transitional benefits for families leaving AFDC, operations and subsequent medical costs, for 2 States, 1980s, article, 4652–1.217

Mental health and substance abuse treatment services outlays by Medicaid, by service type, diagnosis, and eligibility, for 2 states, 1984, article, 4652–1.256

Mineral Industry Surveys, State reviews of production, 1990, preliminary annual rpt, 5614–6

Minerals production by commodity, shipments, and liquefied petroleum gas transport by mode, for California, 1986-87, conf, 5668–119

Minerals Yearbook, 1989, Vol 2: State review of production and sales by commodity, and business activity, annual rpt, 5604–16.6

Minerals Yearbook, 1989, Vol 2: State reviews of production, sales, and firms, by commodity, and business activity, annual rpt, 5604–34

Natural gas production and wellhead capacity, by production area, 1980-89 and alternative forecasts 1990-91, biennial rpt, 3164–93

Oil and gas dev impacts on California OCS water quality, marine life, and sediments, by site, 1986-89, annual rpt, 5734–11

Oil production on Alaska North Slope, and impacts of lifting export controls on US oil trade, West Coast prices, and shipping industry, 1988 and forecast 1995, GAO rpt, 26113–496

Onion farm acreage, pesticide use, operators, and other characteristics, for 6 producer States, 1989, article, 1561–11.201

Oranges (fresh) exports of US, demand indicators for 4 countries, with production, trade, and use, 1960s-90, 1528–317

Oranges and grapefruit production costs for California and Florida, 1988/89, article, 1561–6.201

Otters (sea) population and behavior, for Pacific Ocean, 1914-90, 5508–109

Otters (sea) population, and relocation project results, for California, 1982-89, annual rpt, 5504–12

Otters (sea) population off California coast, 1982-90, annual rpt, 14734–1

Peppers (dried chili and paprika) acreage and production in California, 1971-90, FAS annual circular, 1925–15.1

Physicians, by specialty, age, sex, and location of training and practice, 1989, State rpt, 4116–6.5

Pistachio production, 1989-91, annual rpt, 1621–18.6

Population and housing census, 1990: population and housing characteristics, households, and land area, by county, subdiv, and place, State rpt, 2551–1.6

Population and housing census, 1990: voting age and total population by race, and housing units, by block, redistricting counts required under PL 94-171, State CD-ROM release, 2551–6.5

Population and housing census, 1990: voting age and total population by race, and housing units, by county and city, redistricting counts required under PL 94-171, State summary rpt, 2551–5.5

Pumpkin farms, production costs, shipments, and sales by State, prices, and imports by country, 1978-90, article, 1561–11.203

Recreation (outdoor) coastal facilities of California, visitor spending by purpose at 5 coastal sites, 1989, 2176–9.6

Recreation (outdoor) facilities on public land, use, and Land Mgmt Bur mgmt activities, funding, and plans, 1990 State rpt, 5726–5.2

Refugee aid funding of Fed Govt and States, impacts of reductions, with data by selected State and California county, late 1980s, GAO rpt, 26121–402

Rice market activities, prices, inspections, sales, trade, supply, and use, for US and selected foreign markets, weekly rpt, 1313–8

Rice stocks on and off farms and total in all positions, periodic rpt, 1621–7

Statistical Abstract of US, 1991 annual data compilation, 2324–1

Sugar acreage, production, and use, for California, by county, 1970s-91, article, 1561–14.206

Supplemental Security Income payments and beneficiaries, by type of eligibility, State, and county, Dec 1989, annual rpt, 4744–27.9

Index by Subjects and Names

Timber in northwestern US and British Columbia, production, prices, trade, and employment, quarterly rpt, 1202–3

Timber industry impacts of northern spotted owl conservation in Pacific Northwest, and local govts Federal payments and severance taxes, 1980s and projected to 2000, hearing, 21168–50

Timber industry impacts of northern spotted owl conservation in Pacific Northwest, and worker aid programs, 1980s and projected to 2000, hearing, 21728–76

Timber industry impacts of northern spotted owl conservation in Pacific Northwest, 1980s and alternative projections to 2000, hearings, 21168–45

Walnut production and use, 1989-91, annual rpt, 1621–18.8

Water (groundwater) supply, quality, chemistry, and use, 1987-89, local area rpt, 5666–28.14

Water (groundwater) supply, quality, chemistry, other characteristics, and use, 1991 regional rpt, 5666–25.9; 5666–25.11; 5666–25.12; 5666–25.13

Water quality, chemistry, hydrology, and other characteristics, 1989 local area study, 5666–27.5; 5666–27.6

Water quality, chemistry, hydrology, and other characteristics, 1990 local area study, 5666–27.4; 5666–27.10; 5666–27.12

Water quality, chemistry, hydrology, and other characteristics, 1991 local area study, 5666–27.21

Water supply and quality in streams and lakes, and groundwater levels in wells, by drainage basin, 1990, annual State rpt, 5666–10.5

Water supply in Nevada and eastern California, streamflow, precipitation, and reservoir storage, 1991 water year, annual rpt, 1264–8

see also Anaheim, Calif.
see also Fresno, Calif.
see also Kern County, Calif.
see also Lompoc, Calif.
see also Long Beach, Calif.
see also Los Angeles, Calif.
see also Los Angeles County, Calif.
see also Mono County, Calif.
see also Oakland, Calif.
see also Orange County, Calif.
see also Riverside, Calif.
see also Sacramento, Calif.
see also San Bernardino, Calif.
see also San Diego, Calif.
see also San Francisco, Calif.
see also San Jose, Calif.
see also Santa Ana, Calif.
see also Santa Barbara, Calif.
see also Santa Clara County, Calif.
see also Santa Maria, Calif.
see also Stockton, Calif.
see also Sunnyvale, Calif.
see also under By State in the "Index by Categories"

Callis, Robert R.

"Current Housing Reports, Series H-111. Housing Vacancies and Homeownership, Annual Statistics: 1990", 2484–1

Calomiris, Charles W.

"Optimal Contingent Bank Liquidation Under Moral Hazard", 9375–13.64

Index by Subjects and Names

Cambodia

Agricultural trade of US, by detailed commodity and country, 1989, annual rpt, 1524–8

Agricultural trade of US, by detailed commodity and country, 1990, semiannual rpt, 1522–4

AID economic aid to developing countries, obligations and disbursements by country, quarterly rpt, 9912–4

Background Notes, summary social, political, and economic data, 1990 rpt, 7006–2.21

Economic and military aid and loans from US and intl agencies, by program and country, FY46-90, annual rpt, 9914–5

Economic and social conditions of developing countries from 1960s, and Intl Dev Cooperation Agency and AID activities and funding, FY90-92, annual rpt, 9904–4

Economic, social, political, and geographic summary data, by country, 1991, annual factbook, 9114–2

Exports and imports of US, by transport mode, country, and SITC 1- to 3-digit commodity, 1990, annual rpt, 2424–12

Exports and imports of US with Communist countries, by detailed commodity and country, quarterly rpt with articles, 9882–2

Human rights conditions in 170 countries, and US economic and military aid, 1990, annual rpt, 21384–3

Military aid of US, arms sales, and training programs costs and budget requests, by program, world region, and country, FY90-92, annual rpt, 7144–13

Refugee resettlement programs and funding, arrivals by country of origin, and indicators of adjustment, by State, FY90, annual rpt, 4694–5

Refugees from Cambodia in Thailand border camps by site, and UN aid by donor country, 1980s, GAO rpt, 26123–313

Refugees from Indochina, arrivals, and departures, by country of origin and resettlement, camp, and ethnicity, monthly rpt, 7002–4

UN voting record and share of votes in agreement with US, by issue, country, and world area, 1990, annual rpt, 7004–18

see also under By Foreign Country in the "Index by Categories"

Cameroon

Agricultural exports of high-value commodities, indexes and sales by commodity, world area, and country, 1960s-86, 1528–323

Agricultural trade of US, by detailed commodity and country, 1989, annual rpt, 1524–8

Agricultural trade of US, by detailed commodity and country, 1990, semiannual rpt, 1522–4

AID economic aid to developing countries, obligations and disbursements by country, quarterly rpt, 9912–4

AID loans repayment status and terms by program and country, and status of predecessor agency loans, quarterly rpt, 9912–3

Dairy imports, consumption, and market conditions, by sub-Saharan Africa country, 1961-88, 1528–321

Economic and military aid and loans from US and intl agencies, by program and country, FY46-90, annual rpt, 9914–5

Economic and social conditions of developing countries from 1960s, and Intl Dev Cooperation Agency and AID activities and funding, FY90-92, annual rpt, 9904–4

Economic conditions, income, production, prices, employment, and trade, 1991 periodic country rpt, 2046–4.57

Economic, social, political, and geographic summary data, by country, 1991, annual factbook, 9114–2

Exports and imports of US, by commodity and country, 1970-89, world area rpt, 9116–1.6

Exports and imports of US, by selected country, country group, and commodity group, 1990, annual rpt, 2044–37

Exports and imports of US, by transport mode, country, and SITC 1- to 3-digit commodity, 1990, annual rpt, 2424–12

Exports of US, detailed Schedule B commodities with countries of destination, 1990, annual rpt, 2424–10

Human rights conditions in 170 countries, and US economic and military aid, 1990, annual rpt, 21384–3

Military aid of US, arms sales, and training programs costs and budget requests, by program, world region, and country, FY90-92, annual rpt, 7144–13

Minerals Yearbook, 1988, Vol 3: foreign country review of production, trade, and policy, by commodity, annual rpt, 5604–17.80

UN voting record and share of votes in agreement with US, by issue, country, and world area, 1990, annual rpt, 7004–18

see also under By Foreign Country in the "Index by Categories"

Campaign funds

Consumer spending for cash contributions, by charity type and selected characteristics, 1988/89, article, 1702–1.214

Election campaign funds raised and spent by party committees, by State and party, 1989-90, press release, 9276–1.88

Fed Election Commission activities, and campaign finances, various periods 1975-90, annual rpt, 9274–1

Fed Election Commission activities, campaign finances, elections, and procedures, press release series, 9276–1

Statistical Abstract of US, 1991 annual data compilation, 2324–1.8

Tax returns with presidential election campaign fund designation, and amounts involved, FY90 with trends from FY72, annual rpt, 8304–3.1

see also Political action committees

Campbell, G. Ricardo

"European Court of Justice Orders Equal Treatment in Awarding Pensions to Men and Women", 4742–1.205

Campbell, John

"How Long Will It Last?", 9373–25.201

Camping

Census of Service Industries, 1987: hotels and other lodging places, receipts, payroll, employment, ownership, and rooms, by State and MSA, subject rpt, 2393–3

Campos-Outcalt, Doug

Coastal areas recreation facilities, by State, county, estuary, and level of govt, 1972-84, 2178–29

Coastal areas recreation facilities of Fed Govt and States, visitor and site characteristics, 1987-90 survey, regional rpt series, 2176–9

Colorado River sand deposit characteristics, and density of campsites, 1920s-80s, 5668–122

County Business Patterns, 1988: employment, establishments, and payroll, by SIC 2 to 4-digit industry and county, annual State rpt series, 2326–6

County Business Patterns, 1989: employment, establishments, and payroll, by SIC 2- to 4-digit industry and county, annual State rpt series, 2326–8

Fires on Forest Service land and acres burned, by cause, forest, and State, 1989, annual rpt, 1204–6

Forest Service activities and finances, by region and State, FY90, annual rpt, 1204–1.1

Forests (natl) recreational use, by type of activity and State, 1990, annual rpt, 1204–17

Franchise business opportunities by firm and kind of business, and sources of aid and info, 1990 annual listing, 2104–7

Injuries from use of consumer products, by severity, victim age, and detailed product, 1990, annual rpt, 9164–6

Natl park system visits and overnight stays, by park and State, monthly rpt, 5542–4

Natl park system visits and overnight stays, by park and State, 1990, annual rpt, 5544–12

Public lands acreage, grants, use, revenues, and allocations, by State, FY90, annual rpt, 5724–1.2

Public lands recreation facilities and use, and Land Mgmt Bur mgmt activities, funding, and plans, State rpt series, 5726–5

Puerto Rico economic censuses, 1987: wholesale and retail trade and service industry finances and operations, by SIC 2- to 4-digit industry and municipio, 2591–1

Puerto Rico economic censuses, 1987: wholesale, retail, and service industries finances and operations, by establishment characteristics and SIC 2- and 3-digit industry, subject rpts, 2591–2

Service industries census, 1987: establishments, receipts by source, payroll, and employment, by SIC 2- to 4-digit kind of business, State, and MSA, 2393–4

Tax (income) returns of sole proprietorships, income statement items, by industry group, 1989, annual article, 8302–2.214

Travel from US, characteristics of visit and traveler, and country of destination, 1990 in-flight survey, annual rpt, 2904–14

Travel to US, by characteristics of visit and traveler, world area of origin, and US destination, 1990 survey, annual rpt, 2904–12

Campos-Outcalt, Doug

"Reporting of Communicable Diseases by University Physicians", 4042–3.252

Campus security

Campus security

Bombing incidents, casualties, and damage, by target, circumstances, and State, 1990, annual rpt, 6224–5

Crime victimization of teens, by victim and offender characteristics, circumstances, and offense, 1985-88 surveys, 6066–3.43

Crime victimization of women, by relation to offender, circumstances, and victim characteristics, for rape and other violent offenses, 1973-87, 6068–243

Crime victimization rates, by victim and offender characteristics, circumstances, and offense, 1988 survey, annual rpt, 6066–3.42

Crime victimization rates, by victim and offender characteristics, circumstances, and offense, 1989 survey, annual rpt, 6066–3.44

Law enforcement personnel, and crimes by offense, by higher education instn, 1990, annual rpt, 6224–2.1; 6224–2.3

Natl Education Goals progress indicators, by State, 1991, annual rpt, 15914–1

Teachers views on safety, discipline, and student drug use, for elementary and secondary schools, 1991 survey, 4826–1.31

Terrorism incidents in US, related activity, and casualties, by attack type, target, group, and location, 1990, annual rpt, 6224–6

Canada

Abortions in US, by place of woman's residence and State of occurrence, 1988, US Vital Statistics annual rpt, 4146–5.120

Agricultural exports of high-value commodities from developing countries to OECD, 1970s-87, 1528–316

Agricultural exports of high-value commodities, indexes and sales by commodity, world area, and country, 1960s-86, 1528–323

Agricultural exports of US, impacts of foreign agricultural and trade policy, with data by commodity and country, 1989, annual rpt, 1924–8

Agricultural production, prices, and trade, by country, 1980s and forecast 1991, annual world region rpt, 1524–4.5

Agricultural production, trade, and policies in foreign countries, summary data by country, 1989-90, annual factbook, 1924–12

Agricultural trade by commodity and country, prices, and world market devs, monthly rpt, 1922–12

Agricultural trade of US, by detailed commodity and country, 1989, annual rpt, 1524–8

Agricultural trade of US, by detailed commodity and country, 1990, semiannual rpt, 1522–4

AIDS and hepatitis viruses transmission in health care settings, occupational exposure, prevention policies, and OSHA regulation, 1990 hearings, 21348–119

AIDS cases in prisons and jails, and testing and control policies, 1989 survey, 6066–28.1

Apple import demand in 4 countries, 1960s-83, 1568–296

Apple industry competitiveness of US and Canada, investigation with background financial and operating data, 1991 rpt, 9886–4.172

Auto imports duties and origin preference eligibility rules under proposed North American Free Trade Agreement, 1978-91, 9886–4.178

Auto industry finances and operations, trade by country, and prices of selected US and foreign models, monthly rpt, 9882–8

Auto trade of Canada and US, and production, sales, prices, and employment, selected years 1965-88, annual rpt, 2044–35

Background Notes, summary social, political, and economic data, 1991 rpt, 7006–2.24

Banks capital costs, operating ratios, and intl market shares, for US and 5 OECD countries, 1980s-90, article, 9385–1.203

Bearings (ball) from 14 countries, injury to US industry from foreign subsidized and less than fair value imports, investigation with background financial and operating data, 1991 rpt, 9886–19.74

Birds (duck) breeding population, by species, State, and Canada Province, 1990-91 and trends from 1955, annual rpt, 5504–30

Birds (waterfowl) hunter harvest and unretrieved kills, and duck stamps sold, by species, State, Canada Province, and flyway, 1989-90, annual rpt, 5504–28

Birds (waterfowl) population, habitat conditions, and migratory flight forecasts, for Canada and US by region, 1991 and trends from 1955, annual rpt, 5504–27

Birds (woodcock) population in US and Canada from 1968, and hunter harvest, by State, 1991, annual rpt, 5504–11

Businesses (foreign) activity in US, income tax returns, assets, and income statement items, by industry div and selected country, 1986-87, article, 8302–2.205

Cancer (breast) risk relation to dietary fat and nutrient intake, for Canada, 1982-87, article, 4472–1.204

Carpool and bus high occupancy vehicle lanes use, design, and enforcement, for US and Canada, 1989, 7888–80

Coal exports of US to Canada by mode of transport, and overseas, by State of origin, quarterly rpt, 3162–8

Cocaine abuse, user characteristics, and related crime and violence, 1988 conf, 4498–74

Construction contract awards and billings, by country of contractor and world area of award, 1989, annual article, 2042–1.201

Corporations in US under foreign control, income tax returns, assets and income statement items by industry div, country, and world area, 1988, article, 8302–2.219

Death investigation systems of US and Canada, jurisdictions, medical officers qualifications, types of deaths covered, and related statutes, 1990 listing, 4208–34

Deaths in US, by State of occurrence and birthplace abroad, 1988, US Vital Statistics annual rpt, 4144–2.1

Dollar exchange rate trade-weighted index of Fed Reserve Bank of Atlanta, by world area, quarterly rpt, 9371–15

Dollar exchange rate trade-weighted index of Fed Reserve Bank of Dallas, by world area, monthly rpt, 9379–13

Dollar exchange rates of Mexico peso and Canada dollar, relation to domestic and

Index by Subjects and Names

US prices and nominal exchange rate, model description and results, 1991 technical paper, 9379–12.77

Economic aid of US and other donor countries by type and recipient, and role in advancing economic interests, 1980s-90, 2048–152

Economic and military aid and loans from US and intl agencies, by program and country, FY46-90, annual rpt, 9914–5

Economic and monetary trends, compounded annual rates of change and quarterly indicators for US and 7 major industrialized countries, quarterly rpt, 9391–7

Economic conditions, and oil supply and demand, for major industrial countries, biweekly rpt, 9112–1

Economic conditions and outlook, for US and Canada Great Lakes area, 1970s-90, 9375–15

Economic conditions, consumer and stock prices and production indexes, 6 OECD countries and US, *Business Conditions Digest*, monthly rpt, 2702–1.2

Economic conditions in Communist and OECD countries, 1989, annual rpt, 7144–11

Economic conditions in USSR, Eastern Europe, OECD, and selected other countries, 1960s-90, annual rpt, 9114–4

Economic conditions, policy, and trade practices, by country, 1988-90, annual rpt, 21384–5

Economic indicators, and dollar exchange rates, for selected OECD countries, 1991 semiannual rpt, 8002–14

Economic, social, political, and geographic summary data, by country, 1991, annual factbook, 9114–2

Electric power generation projects on Columbia River, returns to Canada, projected 1991-2011, annual rpt, 3224–3.2

Electric power trade of US with Canada by Province, and with Mexico, by US region, 1988, annual rpt, 3164–92.1

Energy conservation measures impacts on consumption, by component and end-use sector, 1970s-88 and projected under alternative oil prices to 1995, 3308–93

Energy prices, by fuel type and end use, for 10 countries, 1980-89 annual rpt, 3164–50.6

Energy producers finances and operations, by energy type for US firms domestic and foreign operations, 1989, annual rpt, 3164–44.2

Energy production by type, and oil trade, and use, by country group and selected country, monthly rpt, 9112–2

Energy use and production, by fuel type, country, and country group, projected 1995-2010 and trends from 1970, annual rpt, 3164–84

Exports and imports (waterborne) of US, by type of service, customs district, port, and world area, monthly rpt, 2422–7

Exports and imports of NATO members with PRC, by country, 1987-90, annual rpt, 7144–14

Exports and imports of OECD members, by country, 1989, annual rpt, 7144–10

Exports and imports of US by country, and trade shifts by commodity, 1990, semiannual rpt, 9882–9

Index by Subjects and Names

Canada

Exports and imports of US, by Harmonized System 6-digit commodity and country, 1990, annual rpt, 2424–13

Exports and imports of US, by selected country, country group, and commodity group, 1990, annual rpt, 2044–37

Exports and imports of US, by transport mode, country, and SITC 1- to 3-digit commodity, 1990, annual rpt, 2424–12

Exports and imports of US, Canada, and Mexico, and outlook for North America free trade area proposal, 1990, 2048–153

Exports and imports of US shipped through Canada, by detailed commodity, customs district, and country, 1989, annual rpt, 7704–11

Exports and imports, trade agreements and relations, and USITC investigations, 1990, annual rpt, 9884–5

Exports, imports, and balances of US, by selected country, country group, and commodity group, preliminary data, monthly rpt, 2042–34

Exports, imports, and balances of US with major trading partners, by product category, 1986-90, annual chartbook, 9884–21

Exports of US, detailed Schedule B commodities with countries of destination, 1990, annual rpt, 2424–10

Farmland in US owned by foreigners, holdings, acreage, and value by land use, owner country, State, and county, 1990, annual rpt, 1584–3

Fertilizer production capacity by firm, for US and Canada, 1986-91 and projected to 1997, triennial rpt, 9808–66

Fish (sablefish) catch, and exports to Japan, 1984-89, 2162–1.201

Fish (salmon) aquaculture production by species, and farms, by Canada region, 1976-90, article, 2162–1.203

Fishing (ocean sport and commercial) catch and quotas for US and Canada, by species for North Atlantic Ocean, 1990, annual rpt, 2164–14

Fruit and vegetable shipments, and arrivals in US and Canada cities, by mode of transport and State and country of origin, 1990, annual rpt series, 1311–4

GNP and GNP growth for OECD members, by country, 1980-90, annual rpt, 7144–8

Health care universal system in Canada, operations and costs, and implications for US, 1987-91, GAO rpt, 26121–424

Human rights conditions in 170 countries, and US economic and military aid, 1990, annual rpt, 21384–3

Immigrants admitted to US, by country of birth, FY81-90, annual rpt, 6264–4

Immigrants in US, population characteristics and fertility, by birthplace and compared to native born, 1980s, Current Population rpt, 2546–2.162

Immigration impacts on Canada and US trade, with background data, 1960s-86, technical paper, 9379–12.64

Imports of goods, services, and investment from US, trade barriers, impacts, and US actions, by country, 1990, annual rpt, 444–2

Imports of US given duty-free treatment for value of US material sent abroad, by commodity and country, 1989, annual rpt, 9884–14

Industry classification codes concordance of Canada and US SICs, for 1- to 4-digit levels, 1991 rpt, 2628–31

Interest and exchange rates, security yields, and stock indexes, for selected foreign countries, weekly chartbook, 9365–1.5

Investment (foreign direct) in US, by country and world area, 1987-90, annual article, 2702–1.219

Investment (foreign direct) in US, by industry group of US affiliate and country of parent firm, 1980-86, 2708–41

Investment (foreign direct) in US, major transactions by type, industry, country, and US location, 1989, annual rpt, 2044–20

Investment (foreign direct) in US manufacturing, impacts on trade balances, with data by industry, 1980s-93, technical paper, 9385–8.91

Investment (foreign direct) of US, by industry group and world area, 1987-90, annual article, 2702–1.220

Labor conditions, union coverage, and work accidents, 1991 annual country rpt, 6366–4.37

Labor costs and indexes, by selected country, 1990, semiannual rpt, 6822–3

Libraries of higher education instns, holdings, outlays, staff, and instn characteristics, 1969-88, 4468–4

Lumber (softwood) from Canada, injury to US industry from foreign subsidized imports, investigation with background financial and operating data, 1991 rpt, 9886–15.78

Lumber exports from northwestern US ports by selected country, and US imports from Canada, quarterly rpt, 1202–3

Magnesium from Canada and Norway, injury to US industry from foreign subsidized and less than fair value imports, investigation with background financial and operating data, 1991 rpt, 9886–19.80

Military aid of US, arms sales, and training, by country, FY50-90, annual rpt, 3904–3

Minerals trade between Canada and US, by commodity, 1987-89, article, 5602–4.201

Multinatl firms US affiliates, finances, and operations, by industry, world area of parent firm, and State, 1988-89, annual rpt, 2704–4

Multinatl firms US affiliates, investment trends and impact on US economy, 1991 annual rpt, 2004–9

Multinatl US firms and foreign affiliates finances and operations, by industry and world area of parent firm, 1989 benchmark survey, preliminary annual rpt, 2704–5

Multinatl US firms foreign affiliates, income statement items by country and world area, 1986, biennial article, 8302–2.212

Natural gas and liquefied gas trade of US with 5 countries, by US firm, 1955-90, annual article, 3162–4.208

Natural gas imports of US by country, 1988 and projected to 2030, Natl Energy Strategy, 3166–6.52

Natural gas imports of US from Canada under long-term contracts by region, with contract provisions, 1986-90, article, 3162–4.206

Nepheline syenite from Canada at less than fair value, injury to US industry, investigation with background financial and operating data, 1991 rpt, 9886–14.326

Nuclear power generation in US and 20 countries, monthly rpt, 3162–24.10

Nuclear power plant capacity, generation, and operating status, by plant and foreign and US location, 1990 and projected to 2030, annual rpt, 3164–57

Nuclear power plant spent fuel and demand for uranium and enrichment services, for US and other country groups, projected 1991-2040, annual rpt, 3164–72

Oil production, trade, use, and stocks, by selected country and country group, monthly rpt, 3162–42

Oil production, use, stocks, and exports and prices for US, by country, detailed data, monthly rpt with articles, 3162–24

Oil supply, demand, and stock forecasts, by world area, quarterly rpt, 3162–34

Older persons health condition and care research, data availability and collection methodology, for US and selected countries, 1988 conf, 4147–5.6

Oranges (fresh) exports of US, demand indicators for 4 countries, with production, trade, and use, 1960s-90, 1528–317

Peaches production, marketing, and prices in 3 southeastern States and Appalachia, 1990, annual rpt, 1311–12

Physicians trained in Canada and practicing in US, by activity, sex, and county, 1989, State rpt series, 4116–6

Pork from Canada, injury to US industry from foreign subsidized imports, investigation supplement, 1991 rpt, 9886–15.77

Potash production, prices, trade, use, and sales, 1990 crop year, Mineral Industry Surveys, annual rpt, 5614–19

R&D funding by Fed Govt, by field, performer type, agency, and State, FY89-91, annual rpt, 9627–20

Radiation and radionuclide concentrations, monitoring results of intl and foreign agencies, quarterly rpt, 9192–5

Recreation (outdoor) facilities of Fed Govt and States in coastal areas, out-of-State visitors by location of residence, 1987-90 survey, regional rpt series, 2176–9

Savings rates impacts of income tax deduction for interest payments, with indicators for US, Canada, and other OECD countries, 1990 article, 9377–1.202

Science and engineering employment, by professional characteristics, age, and sex, for selected countries, 1991 working paper, 2326–18.63

Spacecraft and satellite launches since 1957, quarterly listing, 9502–2

St Lawrence Seaway ship, cargo, and passenger traffic, and toll revenue, 1990 and trends from 1959, annual rpt, 7744–2

Steel sheet piling imports from Canada at less than fair value, injury to US industry, investigation with background financial and operating data, 1991 rpt, 9886–14.311

Canada

Steel wire rope from Canada at less than fair value, injury to US industry, investigation with background financial and operating data, 1991 rpt, 9886–14.323

Sugar production, acreage, use, and trade with US, for Canada, 1950s-98, article, 1561–14.203

Tax (income) returns of corporations with foreign tax credit, income, and tax items, by country and world region of credit, 1986, biennial article, 8302–2.207

Tax revenue, by level of govt and type of tax, for OECD countries, mid 1960s-89, annual rpt, 10044–1.2

Telecommunications domestic and intl rates, by type of service and area served, 1989, annual rpt, 9284–6.6

Telecommunications industry intl competitiveness, with financial and operating data by product or service, firm, and country, 1990 rpt, 2008–30

Tide height and time daily at coastal points, forecast 1992, annual rpt, 2174–2.3

Timber in western US and Canada, lodgepole pine spiral grain defect incidence and severity, 1991 rpt, 1208–380

Tobacco and cigarette production, use, and trade, for Canada, 1985-91, article, 1925–16.201

Tomato arrivals in US and Canada cities from Mexico, 1970s-90, article, 1561–11.202

Trade agreements of US with Canada and Mexico, economic impacts, business leaders views in North Central States, 1991 survey, article, 9383–19.204

Transportation energy use, fuel prices, vehicle registrations, and mileage, by selected country, 1970s-89, annual rpt, 3304–5.1

Travel to and from US, by world area, forecast 1991-92, annual rpt, 2904–9

Travel to and from US on US and foreign flag air carriers, by country, world area, and US port, monthly rpt, 7302–2

Travel to US, trade shows and other promotional activities, with magazine ad costs and circulation, for selected countries, 1991-92, annual rpt, 2904–11

UN voting record and share of votes in agreement with US, by issue, country, and world area, 1990, annual rpt, 7004–18

US military industrial base restructuring following relaxation of East-West tensions, with top US and foreign DOD contract awards, FY87-93, 26358–245

Walrus population, habitat mgmt, and intl conservation needs, by world region, 1990 conf, 14738–9

Water supply in US and southern Canada, streamflow, surface and groundwater conditions, and reservoir levels, by location, monthly rpt, 5662–3

Weather conditions and effect on agriculture, by US region, State, and city, and world area, weekly rpt, 2182–7

Wheat producer subsidy costs and returns, for Canada, 1990-92, article, 1561–12.202

Wheat quality indicators, for US exports and foreign wheat production, 1960s-90, hearing, 25168–75

see also British Columbia Province, Canada

see also Montreal, Canada
see also Ontario Province, Canada
see also Toronto, Canada
see also Vancouver, Canada
see also Winnipeg, Canada
see also under By Foreign Country in the "Index by Categories"

Canal Zone

see Panama Canal

Canals

Reclamation Bur irrigation activities, finances, and project impacts in western US, 1989, annual rpt, 5824–12

St Lawrence Seaway ship, cargo, and passenger traffic, and toll revenue, 1990 and trends from 1959, annual rpt, 7744–2

see also Panama Canal

Cancer

see Carcinogens
see Neoplasms

Candy and confectionery products

Consumer Expenditure Survey, food spending by item, household composition, income, age, race, and region, 1980-88, biennial rpt, 1544–30

Consumption of food, dietary composition, and nutrient intake, 1987/88 natl survey, preliminary rpt series, 1356–1

Consumption, supply, trade, prices, spending, and indexes, by food commodity, 1989, annual rpt, 1544–4

County Business Patterns, 1988: employment, establishments, and payroll, by SIC 2- to 4-digit industry and county, annual State rpt series, 2326–6

County Business Patterns, 1989: employment, establishments, and payroll, by SIC 2- to 4-digit industry and county, annual State rpt series, 2326–8

CPI by component for US city average, and by region, population size, and for 27 metro areas, monthly rpt, 6762–2

Employment, earnings, and hours, by SIC 1- to 4-digit industry, monthly and annual averages, selected years 1909-90, annual rpt, 6744–4

Exports (agricultural) of US, impacts of foreign agricultural and trade policy, with data by commodity and country, 1989, annual rpt, 1924–8

Exports and imports (agricultural) of US, by commodity and country, bimonthly rpt, 1522–1

Exports and imports (agricultural) of US, by detailed commodity and country, 1989, annual rpt, 1524–8

Exports and imports (agricultural) of US, by detailed commodity and country, 1990, semiannual rpt, 1522–4

Exports and imports of US, by country and detailed commodity, monthly rpt, 2422–12

Exports and imports of US, by Harmonized System 6-digit commodity and country, 1990, annual rpt, 2424–13

Exports and imports of US, by transport mode, country, and SITC 1- to 3-digit commodity, 1990, annual rpt, 2424–12

Exports of US, detailed Schedule B commodities with countries of destination, 1990, annual rpt, 2424–10

Manufacturing annual survey, 1989: finances and operations, by SIC 2- to 4-digit industry, series, 2506–15

Manufacturing census, 1987: finances and operations, by SIC 2- to 4-digit industry, State, and MSA, with trends from 1849, 2497–1

Manufacturing census, 1987: finances and operations, by type of organization and SIC 2- to 4-digit industry, subject rpt, 2497–5

Manufacturing finances and operations, by SIC 2- to 4-digit industry, forecast 1991, annual rpt, 2044–28

Nutrient, caloric, and waste composition, detailed data for raw, processed, and prepared snacks and sweets, 1991 rpt, 1356–3.16

Occupational injury and illness rates, by SIC 2- to 4-digit industry, 1988-89, annual rpt, 6844–7

Occupational injury and illness rates, by SIC 2- to 4-digit industry, 1989, annual rpt, 6844–1

Price indexes (producer), by stage of processing and detailed commodity, monthly rpt, 6762–6

Price indexes (producer), by stage of processing and detailed commodity, monthly 1990, annual rpt, 6764–2

Puerto Rico economic censuses, 1987: wholesale and retail trade and service industry finances and operations, by SIC 2- to 4-digit industry and municipio, 2591–1

Retail trade census, 1987: finances and employment, for establishments with and without payroll, by SIC 2- to 4-digit kind of business, State, and MSA, 2401–1

Retail trade sales and inventories, by kind of business, region, and selected State, MSA, and city, monthly rpt, 2413–3

Shipments, trade, use, and ingredients, by confectionery product, 1990, annual Current Industrial Rpt, 2506–4.5

Wholesale trade census, 1987: establishments, sales by customer class, employment, inventories, and expenses, by SIC 2- to 4-digit kind of business, 2407–4

see also Cocoa and chocolate

Canner, Glenn B.

"Home Mortgage Disclosure Act: Expanded Data on Residential Lending", 9362–1.206

"Payment of Household Debts", 9362–1.201

Canning, Patrick

"Estimating Producer Welfare Effects of the Conservation Reserve Program", 1502–3.202

Cans

see Packaging and containers

Canton, Ohio

see also under By SMSA or MSA in the "Index by Categories"

Cantor, Richard

"Panel Study of the Effects of Leverage on Investment and Employment", 9385–8.77

Capacity utilization, industrial

see Industrial capacity and utilization

Cape Coral, Fla.

see also under By SMSA or MSA in the "Index by Categories"

Index by Subjects and Names

Cape Verde

Agricultural exports of high-value commodities, indexes and sales by commodity, world area, and country, 1960s-86, 1528–323

Agricultural trade of US, by detailed commodity and country, 1990, semiannual rpt, 1522–4

AID economic aid to developing countries, obligations and disbursements by country, quarterly rpt, 9912–4

AID loans repayment status and terms by program and country, and status of predecessor agency loans, quarterly rpt, 9912–3

Dairy imports, consumption, and market conditions, by sub-Saharan Africa country, 1961-88, 1528–321

Economic and military aid and loans from US and intl agencies, by program and country, FY46-90, annual rpt, 9914–5

Economic and social conditions of developing countries from 1960s, and Intl Dev Cooperation Agency and AID activities and funding, FY90-92, annual rpt, 9904–4

Economic conditions, income, production, prices, employment, and trade, 1990 periodic country rpt, 2046–4.10

Economic, social, political, and geographic summary data, by country, 1991, annual factbook, 9114–2

Exports and imports of US, by transport mode, country, and SITC 1- to 3-digit commodity, 1990, annual rpt, 2424–12

Human rights conditions in 170 countries, and US economic and military aid, 1990, annual rpt, 21384–3

Military aid of US, arms sales, and training programs costs and budget requests, by program, world region, and country, FY90-92, annual rpt, 7144–13

UN voting record and share of votes in agreement with US, by issue, country, and world area, 1990, annual rpt, 7004–18

Capehart, Thomas

"Characteristics of Flue-Cured and Burley Farms Compared", 1561–10.204

"Financial Characteristics of Burley Tobacco Farms", 1561–10.202

Capital gains

see Investments

Capital investments, general

Agricultural export-related employment, land, and capital inputs, by commodity and country of destination, and compared to imports, 1977-87, 1548–373

Assets (depreciable) class lives measurement, investment, and industry operations, industry rpt series, 8006–5

Assets and debts of private sector, balance sheets by segment, 1945-90, semiannual rpt, 9365–4.1

Banks capital costs, operating ratios, and intl market shares, for US and 5 OECD countries, 1980s-90, article, 9385–1.203

Capital stock measures, by type and industry, 1950s-80s, technical paper, 9385–8.92

China economic indicators and reform issues, with background data, 1950s-90, compilation of papers, 23848–155

Corporations debt/asset ratios impact on investment and employment, 1971-87, technical paper, 9385–8.77

Eastern Europe foreign debt components, trade, balances, and other economic indicators, by country, 1985-89, hearing, 21248–148

Eastern Europe transition to market economies, economic conditions, intl aid, and energy balance, by country, 1985-90, 9118–13

Economic and employment conditions, alternative BLS projections to 2005 and trends 1970s-90, biennial article, 6722–1.251

Economic indicators and components, current data and annual trends, monthly rpt, 23842–1.1; 23842–1.5

Economic indicators compounded annual rates of change, monthly rpt, 9391–3

Economic indicators impacts of commercial paper-bank loan firm financing mix and selected interest rate spreads, model description and results, 1960s-89, technical paper, 9366–6.268

Enterprise Statistics, 1987: auxiliaries of multi-establishment firms, finances and operations by function, industry, and State, 2329–6

Expenditures for new plants and equipment, by industry div, 1947-2nd qtr 1991, annual rpt, 204–1.3

Expenditures for new plants and equipment, monthly rpt, 9362–1.1

Expenditures for plant and equipment, by industry div, bimonthly rpt, 2042–1.4

Expenditures for plant and equipment, by major industry group, quarterly rpt, 2502–2

Flow-of-funds accounts, savings, investments, and credit statements, quarterly rpt, 9365–3.3

Foreign countries economic conditions and implications for US, periodic country rpt series, 2046–4

Franchise business opportunities by firm and kind of business, and sources of aid and info, 1990 annual listing, 2104–7

Gross private fixed investment, 1929-90, annual rpt, 204–1.1

Imports and tariff provisions effect on US industries and products, investigations with background financial and operating data, series, 9886–4

Imports injury to US industries from foreign subsidized products and sales at less than fair value, investigations with background financial and operating data, series, 9886–19

Imports injury to US industries from sales at less than fair value, investigations with background financial and operating data, series, 9886–14

Industry (US) intl competitiveness, with selected foreign and US operating data by major firm and product, series, 2046–12

Interest rates impact on GNP and components, alternative regression results, late 1950s-80s, technical paper, 9385–8.79

Japan and US capital costs and contributing factors, 1920s-90, article, 9385–1.202

Manufacturing annual survey, 1989: establishments, employment, finances, inventories, and energy use, by SIC 2- to 4-digit industry, 2506–15.1

Manufacturing annual survey, 1989: finances and operations, by SIC 2- and 3-digit industry and State, 2506–15.3

Capital investments, general

Manufacturing capital investment spending, relation to cash flow, working capital, and other factors, 1970s, working paper, 9375–13.49

Manufacturing census, 1987: finances and operations, by SIC 2- to 4-digit industry, State, and MSA, with trends from 1849, 2497–1

Manufacturing census, 1987: finances and operations, by type of organization and SIC 2- to 4-digit industry, subject rpt, 2497–5

Manufacturing industry group investment spending relation to concentration ratios and other factors, 1960s-82, technical paper, 9385–8.81

Manufacturing investment spending relation to cash flow, by SIC 2-digit industry, 1958-86, article, 9375–1.202

Manufacturing investment spending relation to dollar exchange rate, by SIC 2-digit industry, 1963-86, article, 9375–1.208

Middle Atlantic States manufacturing business outlook, monthly survey rpt, 9387–11

Multinatl firms US affiliates finances and operations, by industry div, country of parent firm, and State, 1988-89, annual article, 2702–1.214; 2702–1.218

Multinatl firms US affiliates, finances, and operations, by industry, world area of parent firm, and State, 1988-89, annual rpt, 2704–4

Multinatl firms US affiliates, investment trends and impact on US economy, 1991 annual rpt, 2004–9

Multinatl US firms and foreign affiliates finances and operations, by industry and world area of parent firm, 1989 benchmark survey, preliminary annual rpt, 2704–5

Multinatl US firms and foreign affiliates finances and operations, by industry of parent firm and affiliate, world area, and selected country, 1989, annual article, 2702–1.225

Multinatl US firms foreign affiliates capital expenditures, by major industry group, world area, and country, 1986-91, semiannual article, 2702–1.207

Multinatl US firms foreign affiliates capital expenditures, by major industry group, world area, and country, 1987-91, semiannual article, 2702–1.222

Natl income and product accounts and components, *Survey of Current Business*, monthly rpt, 2702–1.24; 2702–1.25

Pollution abatement capital and operating costs, by SIC 2-digit industry, 1989, advance annual Current Industrial Rpt, 2506–3.6

Pollution abatement spending by govts, business, and consumers, 1987-89, annual article, 2702–1.229

Productivity of labor and capital, indexes and percent change, 1948-90, annual press release, 6824–2

Retail trade census, 1987: depreciable assets, capital and operating expenses, sales, value added, and inventories, by SIC 2- to 4-digit kind of business, 2399–2

Service industries census, 1987: depreciable assets, capital and operating expenses, and receipts, by SIC 2- to 4-digit kind of business, 2393–2

Capital investments, general

Small businesses investment spending, impacts of bank loan commitments, 1980-84, article, 9381–1.211

Soviet Union GNP by component and industry sector, and CIA estimation methods, 1950s-87, 23848–223

Soviet Union GNP by detailed income and outlay component, 1985, 2326–18.59

State and Metro Area Data Book, 1991 data compilation, 2328–54

Statistical Abstract of US, 1991 annual data compilation, 2324–1.17; 2324–1.27

Tax (income) returns of corporations, income and tax items by asset size and detailed industry, 1987, annual rpt, 8304–4

Tax reform and investment stimulation proposals, with background data, 1990 hearings, 25368–170

Tennessee Valley industrial dev and employment, by SIC 2-digit industry, firm, and location, 1990, annual rpt, 9804–3

Wholesale trade census, 1987: depreciable assets, capital and operating expenses, sales, value added, and inventories, by SIC 2- to 3-digit kind of business, 2407–2

see also Capital investments, specific industry

see also Depreciation

see also Foreign investments

see also Industrial plants and equipment

see also Venture capital

Capital investments, specific industry

Agricultural cooperatives finances, aggregate for top 100 assns by commodity group, 1989, annual rpt, 1124–3

Agricultural investment spending in Soviet Union, by purpose and compared to total, 1970s-89, article, 9381–1.210

Airline finances, by carrier, carrier group, and for total certificated system, quarterly rpt, 7302–7

Airport capacity expansion and improvement funding sources, alternative methods, late 1980s and projected to 2000, hearing, 21648–63

Airport capacity improvement projects and funding, traffic, and delays, by major airport, 1987-90 and forecast to 1998, annual rpt, 7504–43

Airport finances, operations by carrier, and capacity improvement and dev funding, by airport, 1977-87 and projected to 2020, hearing, 21648–59

Bank holding company equity capital costs and impact on ability to raise capital, 1960s-80s, technical paper, 9366–6.274

Construction industries census, 1987: establishments, employment, receipts, and expenditures, by SIC 4-digit industry and State, final industry rpt series, 2373–1

Electric power distribution loans from REA, and borrower operating and financial data, by firm and State, 1990, annual rpt, 1244–1

Electric power plants production and capital costs, operations, and fuel use, by fuel type, plant, utility, and location, 1989, annual rpt, 3164–9

Electric power sales by customer, activities by plant, and financial statements of Western Area Power Admin, FY90, annual rpt, 3254–1

Electric power sales by customer, financial statements, and operations and costs by project, for Southwestern Fed Power System, FY90, annual rpt, 3244–1

Electric power sales by customer, plants, and capacity of Southeastern Power Admin, FY90, annual rpt, 3234–1

Electric power sales, finances, and operations, for Fed Columbia River Power System, FY90, annual rpt, 3224–1

Electric utilities finances and operations, detailed data for public and privately owned firms, 1989, annual rpt, 3164–11.4

Electric utilities finances and operations, detailed data for publicly owned firms, 1989, annual rpt, 3164–24

Electric utilities privately owned, finances and operations, detailed data, 1989, annual rpt, 3164–23

Energy producers finances and operations, by energy type for US firms domestic and foreign operations, 1989, annual rpt, 3164–44

Farm Credit System financial condition, quarterly rpt, 9262–2

Farm income, expenses, receipts by commodity, assets, liabilities, and ratios, 1990 and trends from 1945, annual rpt, 1544–16

Farm production itemized costs, receipts, and returns, by commodity and region, 1987-89, annual rpt, 1544–20

Farm sector balance sheet, and marketing receipts by detailed commodity, by State, 1985-89, annual rpt, 1544–18

Fed Reserve System, Board of Governors, and district banks financial statements, performance, and fiscal services, 1990-91, annual rpt, 9364–10

Gear production for selected uses under alternative production requirements, and industry finances and operations, late 1940s-89, 2028–1

Grain cooperatives finances and operations, by grain handled and selected characteristics, 1983-85, series, 1128–44

Helium market demand and Bur of Mines production, sales, and financial statements, FY90, annual rpt, 5604–32

Hospital investment spending relation to instn interest costs, cash flow, size, and chain membership, 1981-85, working paper, 9387–8.243

Hospital reimbursement by Medicare under prospective payment system, capital costs and cost ratios, by selected characteristics, 1988 with trends from 1981, 17206–1.9

Hospital reimbursement by Medicare under prospective payment system, effect of including moveable equipment costs, with results for Maryland, FY89, 17206–2.24

Medicaid nursing home capital investment reimbursement under alternative methodologies, 30-year financial results, 1991 article, 4652–1.236

Mental health care facilities outlays, by function, instn type, funding source, and State, 1988, 4506–3.45

Mineral industries census, 1987: finances and operations, by establishment characteristics, SIC 2- to 4-digit industry, and State, subject rpt, 2517–1

Mineral industries census, 1987: finances and operations, by SIC 2- to 4-digit industry, State, and county, census div rpt series, 2515–1

Minerals production, prices, trade, use, employment, tariffs, and stockpiles, by mineral, with foreign comparisons, 1986-90, annual rpt, 5604–18

Natural gas interstate pipeline company detailed financial and operating data, by firm, 1989, annual rpt, 3164–38

Nonprofit charitable organizations finances, by asset size and State, 1987, article, 8302–2.218

Nuclear power plant operating, maintenance, and capital additions costs, relation to plant characteristics and regulation, 1974-89, 3168–108

Oil production of USSR, exports, and investments, 1980s and projected to 1994, GAO rpt, 26123–349

Panama Canal Commission finances and activities, with Canal traffic and local govt operations, FY90, annual rpt, 9664–3

Pipeline and compressor station construction costs, 1984-87, annual rpt, 3084–3

Postal Service activities, finances, and mail volume and subsidies, FY90, annual rpt, 9864–5.3

Railroad (Amtrak) finances and operations, FY90, annual rpt, 29524–1

Reclamation Bur irrigation activities, finances, and project impacts in western US, 1989, annual rpt, 5824–12

Red Cross financial statements, FY89-90, annual rpt, 29254–1

Securities firms equity capital costs and financial ratios, with data by firm, for US and Japan, 1980s-91, article, 9385–1.212

St Lawrence Seaway Dev Corp finances and activities, and Seaway cargo tonnage, 1989, annual rpt, 7744–1

Steel industry finances, operations, and modernization efforts, with data on major companies and foreign industry, 1968-91, last issue of annual rpt, 9884–24

Telecommunications fiber optics and copper wire mileage and access lines, and fiber systems investment, by firm, 1985-90, annual rpt, 9284–18

Telephone and telegraph firms detailed finances and operations, 1989, annual rpt, 9284–6

Telephone firms borrowing under Rural Telephone Program, and financial and operating data, by State, 1990, annual rpt, 1244–2

Transit systems finances and operations, by mode of transport, size of fleet, and for 468 systems, 1989, annual rpt, 7884–4

Transportation natl system planning, use, condition, accidents, and needs, by mode of transport, 1940s-90 and projected to 2020, 7308–202

Truck and bus interstate carriers finances and operations, by district, 1989, annual rpt, 9486–6.3

Truck interstate carriers finances and operations, by district, 1989, annual rpt, 9486–6.2

TVA finances and operations by program and facility, FY90, annual rpt, 9804–32

see also Depreciation

see also Foreign investments

see also Industrial plants and equipment

Capital punishment

Federal criminal sentencing, guidelines by offense and circumstances, series, 17668–1

Index by Subjects and Names

Caribbean area

Prisoners and movements, by offense, location, and selected other characteristics, data compilation, 1991 annual rpt, 6064–6.6

Prisoners under death sentence, and executions from 1930, by offense, prisoner characteristics, and State, 1989, annual rpt, 6064–26.6

Prisoners under death sentence by prison control and prisoner characteristics, and executions from 1930, by State, 1973-90, annual rpt, 6066–25.42

Public opinion on crime and crime-related issues, by respondent characteristics, data compilation, 1991 annual rpt, 6064–6.2

State and Metro Area Data Book, 1991 data compilation, 2328–54

Statistical Abstract of US, 1991 annual data compilation, 2324–1.5

Caplan, Lois A.

"Hong Kong's Role in Pacific Rim Agricultural Trade", 1524–4.5

Capper-Volstead Act

Dairy cooperatives exemption from antitrust laws, impacts on industry structure and pricing, with background data, 1930s-80s, GAO rpt, 26113–499

Carbon black

see Chemicals and chemical industry

Carbon dioxide

see Air pollution

see Global climate change

Carbon monoxide

see Air pollution

Carcinogens

Beryllium occupational exposure and lung cancer death risk, 1952-88, article, 4472–1.224

Cancer (bladder) cases and risk among chemical plant workers, 1973-88, local area study, article, 4472–1.209

Cigarette smoke tar, nicotine, and carbon monoxide content, by brand, 1989, 9408–53

Detroit metro area air pollution emissions and levels, by pollutant, 1980-90, 14648–25

Natl Cancer Inst epidemiology and biometry activities, FY90, annual rpt, 4474–29

Occupational exposure to hazardous substances and conditions, and health effects, literature review, series, 4246–4

Pesticide use, economic effects of revised EPA regulations, with data for tomatoes, 1988 conf papers, 1588–154

Pollutants health effects assessment, methodology and data needs, series, 9186–9

Pollutants health effects for animals by species and for humans, and environmental levels, for selected substances, series, 5506–14

Research and testing activities under Natl Toxicology Program, FY89 and planned FY90, annual rpt, 4044–16

see also Asbestos contamination

see also Dioxins

see also Radiation

see also Radon

Cardinell, Alex P.

"Hydrologic Environments and Water-Quality Characteristics at Four Landfills in Mecklenburg County, N.C., 1980-86", 5666–27.11

Cardiovascular diseases

Asian Americans heart disease screening program effectiveness, for persons of Southeast Asian origin, 1989 local area study, article, 4042–3.222

Cases of acute and chronic conditions, disability, absenteeism, and health services use, by selected characteristics, 1987, CD-ROM, 4147–10.177

Child heart rate relationship to elevated blood pressure and mothers heart rate, 1971-73, article, 4042–3.232

Deaths and rates, by cause and age, preliminary 1989-90, US Vital Statistics annual rpt, 4144–7

Deaths and rates, by cause, provisional data, monthly rpt, 4142–1.2

Deaths and rates, by detailed cause and demographic characteristics, 1988 and trends from 1900, US Vital Statistics annual rpt, 4144–2

Deaths and risk factors for heart disease, for PRC, Finland, and US, 1980s, article, 4042–3.202

Deaths from heart disease, stroke, and chronic obstructive lung disease, by country and sex, 1987, annual rpt, 4474–6

Diabetes and complications cases, deaths, and hospitalization, by age, sex, race, State, and region, 1980-86, annual rpt, 4205–41

Electronic defibrillator device implants in cardiac patients, risks and benefit evaluation for Medicare coverage, 1991 rpt, 4186–10.5

Health condition and health care resources, use, and spending, 1950s-89, annual data compilation, 4144–11

Health maintenance organizations Medicare enrollees quality of care indicators compared to fee-for-service, demonstration projects results, mid 1980s, 4658–46

HHS financial aid, by program, recipient, State, and city, FY90, annual regional listings, 4004–3

Hospital charges and length of stay for heart and lung patients with selected nonsurgical procedures, for Maryland, FY84, article, 4652–1.204

Hospital deaths of Medicare patients, actual and expected rates by diagnosis, with hospital characteristics, by instn, FY87-89, annual regional rpt series, 4654–14

Indian and Alaska Native disease and disorder cases, deaths, and health services use, by tribe, reservation, and Indian Health Service area, late 1950s-86, 4088–2

Indian Health Service facilities and use, and Indian health and other characteristics, by IHS region, 1980s-89, annual chartbook, 4084–7

Indians and Alaska Natives chronic disease prevalence, for 8 conditions by age and sex, 1987, 4186–8.20

Minority group health condition, services use, costs, and indicators of services need, 1950s-88, 4118–55

Natl Heart, Lung, and Blood Inst activities, and grants by recipient and location, FY90 and disease trends from 1940, annual rpt, 4474–15

Occupational deaths, by cause and industry div, 1989, annual rpt, 6844–1

Older persons deaths in hospitals, nursing homes, and own home, by cause, age, marital status, and region, 1986, article, 4652–1.201

Physicians consultations requested by attending physician, Medicare reimbursement issues, with use by diagnosis, specialty, location, and other characteristics, 1986, 4658–47

Preventive disease and health improvement goals and recommended activities for 2000, with trends 1970s-80s, 4048–10

Smoking involuntary exposure, health effects, and toxic substance levels of sidestream smoke, literature review, 1970s-90, 4248–91

Smoking-related cancer and other diseases, death risk by body site and sex, 1960s-91, article, 4472–1.219

South Carolina heart disease risk assessment program activities and costs, 1987-88 study, article, 4042–3.245

State and Metro Area Data Book, 1991 data compilation, 2328–54

Statistical Abstract of US, 1991 annual data compilation, 2324–1.2

Surgery-related deaths and complications, by procedure and VA facility, and compared to non-VA instns, FY84-89, last issue of biennial rpt, 8704–1

see also Hypertension

see also under By Disease in the "Index by Categories"

Carey, Max L.

"Industry Output and Job Growth Continues Slow into Next Century", 6722–1.253

Carey, Timothy S.

"Nationwide Evaluation of Medicaid Competition Demonstrations. Volume 4. Quality of Care Study", 4658–45.4

Cargo

see Air cargo

see Freight

Caribbean area

Agricultural exports of high-value commodities, indexes and sales by commodity, world area, and country, 1960s-86, 1528–323

Agricultural exports to US, by whether duty levied, commodity, and Caribbean country, 1990-91, annual article, 1925–34.239

Agricultural trade of Caribbean basin with US, by whether duty levied, commodity, and country, 1983-90, annual article, 1925–34.230

Agricultural trade of US, by commodity and country, bimonthly rpt, 1522–1

Agricultural trade of US, by detailed commodity and country, 1989, annual rpt, 1524–8

Agricultural trade of US, by detailed commodity and country, 1990, semiannual rpt, 1522–4

AID dev funds obligated but unspent by country, and impacts of alternative allocation formulas, FY87-90, GAO rpt, 26123–327

AID economic aid to developing countries, obligations and disbursements by country, quarterly rpt, 9912–4

Caribbean area

AID housing and urban dev program financial statements, FY90, annual rpt, 9914–4

AID loans repayment status and terms by program and country, and status of predecessor agency loans, quarterly rpt, 9912–3

AIDS virus infection prevalence in developing countries, by sex, selected city, urban-rural location, and country, 1991, semiannual rpt, 2322–4

Air traffic and passengers, for intl routes over north Atlantic, by aviation type and route, alternative forecasts 1991-2010 and trends from 1980, annual rpt, 7504–44

Coastal currents, temperatures, and salinity, for Atlantic Ocean from Florida straits to northern Brazil, series, 2146–7

Corporations in US under foreign control, income tax returns, assets and income statement items by industry div, country, and world area, 1988, article, 8302–2.219

Economic and social conditions of developing countries from 1960s, and Intl Dev Cooperation Agency and AID activities and funding, FY90-92, annual rpt, 9904–4

Export and investment promotion projects of AID in Latin America and Caribbean, effectiveness, 1974-89, 9916–3.63

Exports (duty-free) of Caribbean area to US, and imports from US, by country, and impact on US employment, by commodity, 1990, annual rpt, 6364–2

Exports (duty-free) of Caribbean area to US, by commodity and country, with consumer and industry impacts, 1984-90, annual rpt, 9884–20

Exports (duty-free) to US under Caribbean Basin Initiative which are ineligible under Generalized System of Preferences, by commodity, 1989, 9886–4.171

Exports and imports (waterborne) of US, by type of service, commodity, country, route, and US port, 1988, annual rpt, 7704–2

Exports and imports (waterborne) of US, by type of service, customs district, port, and world area, monthly rpt, 2422–7

Exports and imports of OECD, total and for 4 major countries, and US trade by country, by commodity, 1970-89, world area rpt, 9116–1.5

Exports and imports of US by country, and trade shifts by commodity, 1990, semiannual rpt, 9882–9

Exports and imports of US, by Harmonized System 6-digit commodity and country, 1990, annual rpt, 2424–13

Exports and imports of US, by selected country, country group, and commodity group, 1990, annual rpt, 2044–37

Exports and imports of US, by transport mode, country, and SITC 1- to 3-digit commodity, 1990, annual rpt, 2424–12

Exports of US, detailed Schedule B commodities with countries of destination, 1990, annual rpt, 2424–10

Family planning and population activities of AID, grants by project and recipient, and contraceptive shipments, by country, FY90, annual rpt series, 9914–13

Fruit and vegetable exports to US, by commodity, country, and port of entry, 1975-87, 1568–299

Grain production and needs, and related economic outlook, by world area and selected country, forecast 1990/91-1991/92, 1528–313

Immigrants admitted to US, by country of birth, FY81-90, annual rpt, 6264–4

Immigrants admitted to US, by occupational group and country of birth, preliminary FY90, annual table, 6264–1

Immigration, alien workers, amnesty programs, and employer sanctions impacts on US economy and labor force, series, 6366–5

Inter-American Foundation activities, grants by recipient, and fellowships, by country, FY90, annual rpt, 14424–1

Inter-American Foundation dev grants by program area, and fellowships by field and instn, by country, FY72-90, annual rpt, 14424–2

Investment (direct) incentives of Caribbean Basin Initiative, economic impacts, with finances and employment by country, 1984-90, 2048–141

Investment (foreign direct) in US, by industry group and world area, 1987-90, annual article, 2702–1.219

Labor conditions, union coverage, and work accidents, 1991 annual regional rpt, 6366–4.56

Loans of US banks to foreigners at all US and foreign offices, by country group and country, quarterly rpt, 13002–1

Military aid of US, arms sales, and training programs costs and budget requests, by program, world region, and country, FY90-92, annual rpt, 7144–13

Multinatl US firms and foreign affiliates finances and operations, by industry and world area of parent firm, 1989 benchmark survey, preliminary annual rpt, 2704–5

Multinatl US firms foreign affiliates, income statement items by country and world area, 1986, biennial article, 8302–2.212

Oil exports to US by OPEC and non-OPEC countries, monthly rpt, 3162–24.3

Oils, oilseeds, and meal imports, by commodity, world area of destination, and major producer, 1960s-88, 1528–314

Peace Corps activities, funding by program, and volunteers, by country, FY92, annual rpt, 9654–1

Refugee arrivals in US by world area and country of origin, and quotas, monthly rpt, 7002–4

Rum imports (duty-free) of US under Caribbean Basin Initiative, by country, 1989-90, annual rpt, 9884–15

Sharks and other fish tagged and recovered, by species, 1990, annual rpt, 2164–21

Tax (income) returns of corporations with foreign tax credit, income, and tax items, by country and world region of credit, 1986, biennial article, 8302–2.207

Textile imports under Multifiber Arrangement by product and country, and status of bilateral agreements, 1987-90, annual rpt, 9884–18

Travel to and from US on US and foreign flag air carriers, by world area, 1990, annual rpt, 2904–13

Travel to US, by characteristics of visit and traveler, country, port city, and State of destination, quarterly rpt, 2902–1

Index by Subjects and Names

Weather stations of Natl Weather Service, locations and types of observations made, 1990 annual listing, 2184–5

see also Anguilla

see also Antigua and Barbuda

see also Aruba

see also Bahamas

see also Barbados

see also Bermuda

see also British Virgin Islands

see also Cayman Islands

see also Cuba

see also Dominica

see also Dominican Republic

see also Grenada

see also Haiti

see also Jamaica

see also Netherlands Antilles

see also Puerto Rico

see also St. Christopher and Nevis

see also St. Lucia

see also St. Vincent and The Grenadines

see also Trinidad and Tobago

see also U.S. Virgin Islands

see also under By Foreign Country in the "Index by Categories"

Caribbean Basin Initiative

see Trade agreements

Carlin, Thomas A.

"Changes in Farm Structure", 1004–16.1

Carlino, Gerald

"Effects of Exchange Rate and Productivity Changes on U.S. Industrial Output at the State Level", 9387–8.255

"Persistence and Convergence in Relative Regional Incomes", 9387–8.232

Carlisle, Pa.

see also under By SMSA or MSA in the "Index by Categories"

Carlson, Keith M.

"Future of Social Security: An Update", 9391–1.207

"U.S. Balance Sheet: What Is It and What Does It Tell Us?", 9391–1.220

Carlson, Mary

"Outlook for Natural Gas, 1991", 3162–4.207

"Take-or-Pay Settlements", 3162–4.202

Carlstrom, Charles T.

"Bracket Creep in the Age of Indexing: Have We Solved the Problem?", 9377–9.117

"Inflation, Personal Taxes, and Real Output: A Dynamic Analysis", 9377–9.110

"Magnification Effects and Acyclical Real Wages", 9377–9.114

"Zero Inflation: Transition Costs and Shoe-Leather Benefits", 9377–9.122

Carnes, Richard B.

"Productivity in Industry and Government, 1989", 6722–1.228

Carpets and rugs

Business statistics, detailed data for major industries and economic indicators, *Survey of Current Business*, monthly rpt, 2702–1.22

County Business Patterns, 1988: employment, establishments, and payroll, by SIC 2- to 4-digit industry and county, annual State rpt series, 2326–6

County Business Patterns, 1989: employment, establishments, and payroll, by SIC 2- to 4-digit industry and county, annual State rpt series, 2326–8

Index by Subjects and Names

Exports and imports of US, by Harmonized System 6-digit commodity and country, 1990, annual rpt, 2424–13

Injuries from use of consumer products, by severity, victim age, and detailed product, 1990, annual rpt, 9164–6

Manufacturing census, 1987: finances and operations, by type of organization and SIC 2- to 4-digit industry, subject rpt, 2497–5

Manufacturing finances and operations, by SIC 2- to 4-digit industry, forecast 1991, annual rpt, 2044–28

Price indexes (producer), by stage of processing and detailed commodity, monthly rpt, 6762–6

Price indexes (producer), by stage of processing and detailed commodity, monthly 1990, annual rpt, 6764–2

Puerto Rico economic censuses, 1987: wholesale and retail trade and service industry finances and operations, by SIC 2- to 4-digit industry and municipio, 2591–1

Retail trade census, 1987: finances and employment, for establishments with and without payroll, by SIC 2- to 4-digit kind of business, State, and MSA, 2401–1

Shipments, trade, and use, for carpets and rugs by product, 1990, annual Current Industrial Rpt, 2506–5.9

Carpools

see Commuting

Carrington, Natalie R.

"Offshore Scientific and Technical Publications, 1988 Annual", 5734–5

Carroll, Christopher D.

"Does Consumer Sentiment Affect Household Spending? If So, Why?", 9366–6.282

Cartels

see Monopolies and cartels

see Organization of Petroleum Exporting Countries

Carter, Carol

"Rural Hospitals Under Medicare's Prospective Payment System", 17206–1.12

Carter, Grace M.

"How Services and Costs Vary by Day of Stay for Medicare Hospital Stays", 17208–2

"Methodology for Measuring Case-Mix Change: How Much Change in the Case Mix Index Is DRG Creep?", 17206–2.23

Carter, Patricia W.

"U.S. Civil Airmen Statistics, 1990", 7504–2

Cartography

Aerial survey R&D rpts, and sources of natural resource and environmental data, quarterly listing, 9502–7

Census Bur geographic levels of data coverage, maps, and reference products, 1991 pamphlet, 2326–7.79

Census Bur TIGER computer-readable map and geographic data base, files availability and use, 1990 rpt, 2628–30

Copyrights Register activities, registrations by material type, and fees, FY90 and trends from 1790, annual rpt, 26404–2

Geological Survey activities and funding, FY90, annual rpt, 5664–8

Library of Congress activities, acquisitions, services, and financial statements, FY90, annual rpt, 26404–1

Natl Ocean Service Charting and Geodetic Service activities and funding, by State, FY91-92, biennial rpt, 2174–10

see also Maps

Cary, Lawrence E.

"Trends in Selected Water-Quality Characteristics, Flathead River at Flathead, British Columbia, and at Columbia Falls, Montana, Water Years 1975-86", 5666–27.16

Case, Karl E.

"Real Estate Cycle and the Economy: Consequences of the Massachusetts Boom of 1984-87", 9373–1.216

Case, Robert A.

"Deadliest, Costliest, and Most Intense U.S. Hurricanes of This Century (and Other Frequently Requested Hurricane Facts)", 2188–15

Casey, J.

"Shark Tagger, 1990 Summary", 2164–21

Caskets

see Cemeteries and funerals

Casper, Wyo.

see also under By SMSA or MSA in the "Index by Categories"

Castor oil

see Oils, oilseeds, and fats

Casualty insurance

see Property and casualty insurance

Catalogs

see Bibliographies

see CD-ROM catalogs and guides

see Computer data file guides

see Directories

see Government publications lists

Catfish

see Aquaculture

Cathey, Henry M.

"Alternative Garden Crops for the 21st Century", 1004–16.1

Cattan, Peter

"Child-Care Problems: An Obstacle to Work", 6722–1.245

Cattle

see Dairy industry and products

see Livestock and livestock industry

CATV

see Cable television

Cayman Islands

Agricultural trade of US, by detailed commodity and country, 1989, annual rpt, 1524–8

Agricultural trade of US, by detailed commodity and country, 1990, semiannual rpt, 1522–4

Economic, social, political, and geographic summary data, by country, 1991, annual factbook, 9114–2

Exports and imports of US, by transport mode, country, and SITC 1- to 3-digit commodity, 1990, annual rpt, 2424–12

Multinatl US firms foreign affiliates, income statement items by country and world area, 1986, biennial article, 8302–2.212

CD audio recordings and equipment

see Home video and audio equipment

see Recording industry

CD-ROM catalogs and guides

Census Bur activities, rpts, and user services, monthly rpt, 2302–3

Census Bur rpts and data files, coverage and availability, 1991 annual listing, 2304–2

Census Bur rpts and data files, coverage, availability, and use, series, 2326–7

Cement and concrete

Census Bur rpts and data files, monthly listing, 2302–6

Census of Population and Housing, 1990: voting age and total population by race, and housing units, redistricting counts required under PL 94-171, State CD-ROM user guide, 2308–63

Export and import statistics, Census Bur publications and data files, 1991 guide, 2428–11

Library of Congress rpts and products, 1990, annual listing, 26404–6

Map and geographic computer-readable database of Census Bur, TIGER files availability and use, 1990 rpt, 2628–30

Space science and related data sources and availability, 1991 annual listing, 9504–10

CD-ROM releases

Census of Population and Housing, 1990: voting age and total population by race, and housing units, by block, redistricting counts required under PL 94-171, State CD-ROM series, 2551–6

Disability, acute and chronic health conditions, absenteeism, and health services use, by selected characteristics, 1987, CD-ROM, 4147–10.177

Exports, imports, and trade flows, by country and commodity, with background economic indicators, data compilation, monthly CD-ROM, 2002–6

Exports of US, detailed commodities by country, monthly CD-ROM, 2422–13

Imports of US, detailed commodities by country, monthly CD-ROM, 2422–14

see also CD-ROM catalogs and guides

see also CD-ROM technology and use

CD-ROM technology and use

Libraries technological aid, project descriptions and funding, FY89, annual listing, 4874–6

Library of Congress activities, acquisitions, services, and financial statements, FY90, annual rpt, 26404–1

Space science and related data sources, use by format and user type, FY90, annual rpt, 9504–11

see also CD-ROM catalogs and guides

see also CD-ROM releases

Cedar Falls, Iowa

Wages by occupation, and benefits for office and plant workers, 1991 survey, periodic MSA rpt, 6785–3.7

see also under By SMSA or MSA in the "Index by Categories"

Cedar Rapids, Iowa

Wages by occupation, and benefits for office and plant workers, 1991 survey, periodic MSA rpt, 6785–3.7

see also under By City and By SMSA or MSA in the "Index by Categories"

Celery

see Vegetables and vegetable products

Cell cultures

see Genetics

Cellular telephones

see Mobile radio

Cement and concrete

Business statistics, detailed data for major industries and economic indicators, *Survey of Current Business*, monthly rpt, 2702–1.21

County Business Patterns, 1988: employment, establishments, and payroll, by SIC 2- to 4-digit industry and county, annual State rpt series, 2326–6

Cement and concrete

County Business Patterns, 1989: employment, establishments, and payroll, by SIC 2- to 4-digit industry and county, annual State rpt series, 2326–8

Employment, earnings, and hours, by SIC 1- to 4-digit industry, monthly and annual averages, selected years 1909-90, annual rpt, 6744–4

Energy use and prices for manufacturing industries, 1988 survey, series, 3166–13

Exports and imports of building materials, by commodity and country, 1989-90, article, 2042–1.204

Exports and imports of US, by country and detailed commodity, monthly rpt, 2422–12

Exports and imports of US, by Harmonized System 6-digit commodity and country, 1990, annual rpt, 2424–13

Exports and imports of US, by transport mode, country, and SITC 1- to 3-digit commodity, 1990, annual rpt, 2424–12

Exports of US, detailed Schedule B commodities with countries of destination, 1990, annual rpt, 2424–10

Hwy construction material prices and indexes for Federal-aid system, by type of material and urban-rural location, quarterly rpt, 7552–7

Hwy construction material prices and indexes for Federal-aid system, by type of material, quarterly press release, 7552–16

Hwy construction material use by type, and spending, by State, various periods 1944-90, annual rpt, 7554–29

Imports of gray portland cement and clinker from Venezuela, injury to US industry from foreign subsidized and less than fair value imports, investigation with background financial and operating data, 1991 rpt, 9886–19.76

Imports of portland cement and clinker from Japan at less than fair value, injury to US industry, investigation with background financial and operating data, 1991 rpt, 9886–14.309

Labor productivity, indexes of output, hours, and employment by SIC 2- to 4-digit industry, 1967-89, annual rpt, 6824–1.3

Manufacturing annual survey, 1989: finances and operations, by SIC 2- to 4-digit industry, series, 2506–15

Manufacturing census, 1987: finances and operations, by SIC 2- to 4-digit industry, State, and MSA, with trends from 1849, 2497–1

Manufacturing census, 1987: finances and operations, by type of organization and SIC 2- to 4-digit industry, subject rpt, 2497–5

Manufacturing finances and operations, by SIC 2- to 4-digit industry, forecast 1991, annual rpt, 2044–28

Mineral Industry Surveys, commodity review of production, trade, and use, 1990, advance annual rpt, 5614–5.21

Mineral Industry Surveys, commodity review of production, trade, stocks, and use, monthly rpt, 5612–1.2

Mineral Industry Surveys, State reviews of production, 1990, preliminary annual rpt, 5614–6

Minerals Yearbook, 1988, Vol 3: foreign country reviews of production, trade, and policy, by commodity, annual rpt series, 5604–17

Minerals Yearbook, 1989, Vol 1: commodity review of production, reserves, supply, use, and trade, annual rpt, 5604–15.15

Minerals Yearbook, 1989, Vol 2: State reviews of production and sales by commodity, and business activity, annual rpt series, 5604–16

Minerals Yearbook, 1989, Vol 2: State reviews of production, sales, and firms, by commodity, and business activity, annual rpt, 5604–34

Occupational injuries and incidence, employment, and hours in stone mines and related operations, 1989, annual rpt, 6664–5

Occupational injury and illness rates, by SIC 2- to 4-digit industry, 1988-89, annual rpt, 6844–7

Occupational injury and illness rates, by SIC 2- to 4-digit industry, 1989, annual rpt, 6844–1

OECD trade, total and for 4 major countries, and US trade by country, by commodity, 1970-89, world area rpt series, 9116–1

Pollution (air) abatement equipment shipments by industry, and new and backlog orders, by product, 1990, annual Current Industrial Rpt, 2506–12.5

Pollution (air) contributing to global warming, emissions factors and control costs, by pollutant and source, 1990 rpt, 9198–124

Pollution (air) emissions factors, by detailed pollutant and source, data compilation, 1990 rpt, 9198–120

Price indexes (producer), by stage of processing and detailed commodity, monthly rpt, 6762–6

Price indexes (producer), by stage of processing and detailed commodity, monthly 1990, annual rpt, 6764–2

Production and PPI for building materials, and cement shipments to census divs, Puerto Rico, and foreign countries, bimonthly rpt, 2042–1.5; 2042–1.6

Production, prices, trade, and foreign and US industry devs, by commodity, bimonthly rpt with articles, 5602–4

Production, prices, trade, use, employment, tariffs, and stockpiles, by mineral, with foreign comparisons, 1986-90, annual rpt, 5604–18

Statistical Abstract of US, 1991 annual data compilation, 2324–1.25

Taiwan imports of building materials, and share from US, by commodity, 1989-90, article, 2042–1.205

Tax (income) returns of corporations, income and tax items by asset size and detailed industry, 1987, annual rpt, 8304–4

Tax (income) returns of corporations, income and tax items by asset size and detailed industry, 1988, annual rpt, 8304–21

Cemeteries and funerals

Casket manufacturers finances and operations, by type of organization, 1987 Census of Manufactures, subject rpt, 2497–5

Casket manufacturers finances and operations, 1987 Census of Manufactures, 2497–1

Index by Subjects and Names

Casket manufacturers financial and operating data, 1989 Annual Survey of Manufactures, series, 2506–15

Casket manufacturers price indexes, monthly rpt, 6762–6

Casket manufacturers price indexes, monthly 1990, annual rpt, 6764–2

County Business Patterns, 1988: employment, establishments, and payroll, by SIC 2- to 4-digit industry and county, annual State rpt series, 2326–6

County Business Patterns, 1989: employment, establishments, and payroll, by SIC 2- to 4-digit industry and county, annual State rpt series, 2326–8

CPI by component for US city average, and by region, population size, and for 27 metro areas, monthly rpt, 6762–2

Employee paid leave days for funerals, by occupational group, for small businesses, 1990, biennial rpt, 6784–20

Employment, earnings, and hours, by SIC 1- to 4-digit industry, monthly and annual averages, selected years 1909-90, annual rpt, 6744–4

Puerto Rico economic censuses, 1987: wholesale and retail trade and service industry finances and operations, by SIC 2- to 4-digit industry and municipio, 2591–1

Puerto Rico economic censuses, 1987: wholesale, retail, and service industries finances and operations, by establishment characteristics and SIC 2- and 3-digit industry, subject rpts, 2591–2

Service industries census, 1987: depreciable assets, capital and operating expenses, and receipts, by SIC 2- to 4-digit kind of business, 2393–2

Service industries census, 1987: establishments, receipts by source, payroll, and employment, by SIC 2- to 4-digit kind of business, State, and MSA, 2393–4

Service industries receipts, by SIC 2- to 4-digit kind of business, 1990, annual rpt, 2413–8

Tax (income) returns of sole proprietorships, income statement items, by industry group, 1989, annual article, 8302–2.214

Workers compensation laws of States and Fed Govt, 1991 semiannual rpt, 6502–1

see also Military cemeteries and funerals

Censorship

Foreign countries human rights conditions in 170 countries, 1990, annual rpt, 21384–3

see also Freedom of the press

Census Bureau

see Bureau of Census

Census divisions

see under By Census Division in the "Index by Categories"

Census of Agriculture

Data coverage and availability of Census Bur rpts and data files, 1991 annual listing, 2304–2

Data on agriculture, young readers pamphlet series, 2346–1

Farms, farmland, production, finances, and operator characteristics, by county, 1987 census, final State rpt series, 2331–1

Horticultural specialties census, 1988: producers, finances, and operations, by crop and State, 1987 Census of Agriculture, 2337–1

Index by Subjects and Names

Census of Construction Industries
Finances and operations, by SIC 4-digit industry and State, 1987 census, final rpt series, 2373–1

Census of Governments
Data coverage and availability of Census Bur rpts and data files, 1991 annual listing, 2304–2
Data coverage of final rpts, 1987 census, 2460–1
Employment, payroll, and average earnings, by function, level of govt, State, county, and population size, 1987 census, 2455–2
Labor-mgmt policies, agreements, and coverage and bargaining units, by function, level of govt, and State, 1987 census, 2455–3
Local govt employment by function, payroll, and average earnings, for individual counties, cities, and school and special districts, 1987 census, 2455–1
State and local govt employment, payroll, OASDHI coverage, and employee benefits costs, by level of govt and State, 1987 census, 2455–4

Census of Housing
Data coverage and availability of Census Bur rpts and data files, 1991 annual listing, 2304–2
Data coverage and availability, 1991 pamphlet, 2326–7.77
Housing inventory, occupancy, and costs, 1990 census, State fact sheet series, 2326–21
see also Census of Population and Housing

Census of Manufactures
Employment and shipments under Fed Govt contracts, by SIC 4-digit industry, 1987 census, 2497–7
Finances and operations, by SIC 2- to 4-digit industry, State, and MSA, 1987 with trends from 1849, 2497–1
Finances and operations, by type of organization and SIC 2- to 4-digit industry, 1987 census, subject rpt, 2497–5
Operations and performance of manufacturing industries, analytical rpt series, 2506–16

Census of Mineral Industries
Energy use and costs, by fuel type, SIC 2- to 4-digit industry, and State, 1987 census, subject rpt, 2517–2
Finances and operations, by establishment characteristics, SIC 2- to 4-digit industry, and State, 1987 census, subject rpt, 2517–1
Finances and operations, by SIC 2- to 4-digit industry, State, and county, 1987 census, census div rpt series, 2515–1

Census of Outlying Areas
Puerto Rico wholesale and retail trade and service industry finances and operations, by SIC 2- to 4-digit industry and municipio, 1987 census, 2591–1
Puerto Rico wholesale, retail, and service industries finances and operations, by establishment characteristics and SIC 2- and 3-digit industry, 1987 census, subject rpts, 2591–2

Census of Population
Assistance (formula grants) of Fed Govt, use of Census of Population data for allocation, and effects of data errors on funding, with data by program and State, FY91, GAO rpt, 26119–361

Cities population and undercounts in 1990 census, and related Federal aid losses, 1990 mayoral survey, hearing, 25408–113
Congressional apportionment and official population counts, by State, 1990 census, 2328–22
Congressional redistricting data coverage and availability, 1990 census, guide, 2308–59
Data adjustment for undercounts, final decision, 1990 census, 2008–31
Data coverage and availability of Census Bur rpts and data files, 1991 annual listing, 2304–2
Data coverage evaluation and improvement activities, and post-census sample use, 1990 census, hearing, 21628–96
Data coverage evaluation and improvement activities for 1990 census, and revised counts for 1970-90 censuses, hearing, 21628–95
Data enumeration errors under alternative definitions, for 1990 census and compared to 1980, GAO rpt, 26119–353
Data on individuals, public availability for 1790-1990 censuses, pamphlet, 2326–7.81
Guam population by district, 1990 census, press release, 2328–79
Hispanic Americans population by detailed origin, region, and State, 1990 census with data for 1980, press release, 2328–73
Homeless shelter and on-street population, by State and for 200 cities, 1990 census, press release, 2328–70
Indian and Alaska Native population on reservations and in other designated areas, by selected site, 1990 census, press release, 2328–76
Metro area population by race, Hispanic origin, and MSA, 1990 census, press release, 2328–75
Population by detailed Native American, Asian, and Pacific Islander group, region, and State, 1990 census with data for 1980, press release, 2328–72
Population by State and region, with Federal and military personnel abroad by State of residence and agency, 1990 census, press release, 2328–66
Post-enumeration survey results compared to census counts, by race, sex, city, county, and State, 1990 census, press release, 2328–69
Post-enumeration survey use for adjusting 1990 census counts, with estimates of undercount by race, 1950-90, GAO rpt, 26119–327
Urban areas land area, housing units, and population, by State and compared to rural areas, 1990 census, press release, 2328–39
Urban areas population, for 396 areas, 1990 census, press release, 2328–37
Virgin Islands population by location, 1990 census, press release, 2328–77
see also Census of Population and Housing

Census of Population and Housing
Budget of US constraints impacts on 1990 census operations, hearing, 21628–88
Congressional districts population, 1990 census counts and change from 1980, by State, press release, 2328–32

Census of Population and Housing

Data accuracy and quality issues, 1990 census, hearing, 21628–91
Data collection progress, 1990 census, hearing, 21628–86
Data concordance of rpts from 1990 and 1980 censuses, pamphlet, 2308–61
Data coverage and availability of Census Bur population statistics, 1991 pamphlet, 2326–7.78
Data coverage and availability of Census Bur rpts and data files, 1991 annual listing, 2304–2
Data coverage and release schedules for 1990 census rpts, pamphlet, 2308–62
Data coverage by geographic level, maps, and reference products from Census Bur, 1991 pamphlet, 2326–7.79
Data item selection, questionnaire dev, and testing, 1990 census, series, 2626–11
Employment (temporary) for 1990 census, impact on natl employment trends, 1990, article, 6742–2.202
Housing occupied and vacant units, persons in group quarters, and household size, by region, census div, and State, 1990 census, press release, 2328–71
Local govt review of preliminary results, issues, 1990 census, hearing, 21628–93
Map and geographic computer-readable database of Census Bur, TIGER files availability and use, 1990 rpt, 2628–30
Minority group data coverage and availability from Census Bur, 1991 pamphlet, 2326–7.80
New York State and NYC data collection activities and status, 1990 census, hearing, 21628–90
Pennsylvania data collection activities and status, 1990 census, hearing, 21628–89
Pennsylvania preparations for count, 1990 census, hearing, 21628–87
Population (voting age and total) by race, and housing units, by block, redistricting counts required under PL 94-171, 1990 census, State CD-ROM series, 2551–6
Population (voting age and total) by race, and housing units, redistricting counts required under PL 94-171, 1990 census, State CD-ROM user guide, 2308–63
Population (voting age and total) by race, and housing units, by county and city, redistricting counts required under PL 94-171, 1990 census, State summary rpt series, 2551–5
Population and housing characteristics, households, and land area, by county, subdiv, and place, 1990 census, State rpt series, 2551–1
Population and housing selected characteristics, by region, 1990 census, press release, 2328–74
Population size and characteristics, summary results and trends, 1990, fact sheet series, 2326–20
Puerto Rico population and housing characteristics, 1990 census, press release, 2328–78
Texas data collection activities and status, 1990 census, hearing, 21628–92
Virgin Islands population and housing characteristics, 1990 Census of Population and Housing, press release, 2328–81
see also Census of Housing
see also Census of Population

Census of Retail Trade

Census of Retail Trade

Finances and employment, for establishments with and without payroll, by SIC 2- to 4-digit kind of business, State, and MSA, 1987 census, 2401–1

Finances, depreciable assets, capital and operating expenses, sales, value added, and inventories, by SIC 2- to 4-digit kind of business, 1987 census, 2399–2

Census of Service Industries

Establishments, receipts by source, payroll, and employment, by SIC 2- to 4-digit kind of business, and MSA, 1987 census, 2393–4

Finances, depreciable assets, capital and operating expenses, and receipts, by SIC 2- to 4-digit kind of business, 1987 census, 2393–2

Hotels and other lodging places, receipts, payroll, employment, ownership, and rooms, by State and MSA, 1987 census, subject rpt, 2393–3

Census of Transportation

Finances and operations by size, ownership, and State, and revenues by MSA, by SIC 2- to 4-digit industry, 1987 census, 2579–1

Census of Wholesale Trade

Finances and operations by SIC 2- to 4-digit kind of business, and oil bulk station operations by State, 1987 census, 2407–4

Finances, depreciable assets, capital and operating expenses, sales, value added, and inventories, by SIC 2- to 3-digit kind of business, 1987 census, 2407–2

Census tracts

Census of Population and Housing, 1990: voting age and total population by race, and housing units, by block, redistricting counts required under PL 94-171, State CD-ROM series, 2551–6

Center for Health Economics Research

"Physician Consultative Services Under Medicare: Final Report", 4658–47

"Prospective Payments System's Impacts on Rural Hospitals", 4658–51

Center for Health Policy Studies

"Hospital Cost Variations Under PPS", 17206–2.26

Center for Population Research

Activities and funding of Demographic and Behavioral Sciences Branch, 1960s-89, 4478–194

Centers for Disease Control

Agent Orange exposure of Vietnam veterans, and other factors relation to dev of rare cancers, 1984-88, 4208–33

AIDS cases by risk group, race, sex, age, State, and MSA, and deaths, monthly rpt, 4202–9

AIDS info and education activities and funding of CDC, and donation of media ads, 1987-92, articles, 4042–3.256

AIDS virus antibody tests and counseling sessions by setting, and CDC funding and funds uncommitted by State, 1989-90, GAO rpt, 26121–428

Budget of US, obligations and authority by function, agency, and program, with summaries, analyses, and historical tables, FY92, annual rpt, 104–2

Death investigation systems of US and Canada, jurisdictions, medical officers qualifications, types of deaths covered, and related statutes, 1990 listing, 4208–34

Diabetes and complications cases, deaths, and hospitalization, by age, sex, race, State, and region, 1980-86, annual rpt, 4205–41

Expenditures of Fed Govt in States, by type, program, agency, and State, FY90, annual rpt, 2464–2

Financial aid of HHS, by program, recipient, State, and city, FY90, annual regional listings, 4004–3

Hepatitis cases by infection source, age, sex, race, and State, and deaths, by strain, 1988 and trends from 1966, 4205–2

Malaria cases in US, for military personnel and US and foreign natls, and by country of infection, 1966-89, annual rpt, 4205–4

Morbidity and Mortality Weekly Report, infectious notifiable disease cases and deaths, and other public health issues, periodic journal, 4202–7

Morbidity and Mortality Weekly Report, infectious notifiable disease cases by age, race, and State, and deaths, 1930s-90, annual rpt, 4204–1

Morbidity and Mortality Weekly Report, infectious notifiable disease cases by State, and public health issues, 4202–1

Morbidity and Mortality Weekly Report, special supplements, series, 4206–2

Research and evaluation programs of HHS, 1970-90, annual listing, 4004–30

Sexually transmitted disease cases and control activity, by strain, State, and selected city, issuing agency transfer, 4204–14

Sexually transmitted disease cases and control activity, by strain, State, and selected city, 1940s-90, 4205–42

Ship (passenger) sanitary inspection scores, biweekly rpt, 4202–10

Tuberculosis cases and deaths, by patient characteristics, State, and city, 1989 and trends from 1953, annual rpt, 4204–10

Vaccination needs for intl travel by country, and disease prevention recommendations, 1991 annual rpt, 4204–11

see also National Institute for Occupational Safety and Health

CENTO

see Central Treaty Organization

Central African Republic

Agricultural exports of high-value commodities, indexes and sales by commodity, world area, and country, 1960s-86, 1528–323

Agricultural trade of US, by detailed commodity and country, 1989, annual rpt, 1524–8

Agricultural trade of US, by detailed commodity and country, 1990, semiannual rpt, 1522–4

AID economic aid to developing countries, obligations and disbursements by country, quarterly rpt, 9912–4

Economic and military aid and loans from US and intl agencies, by program and country, FY46-90, annual rpt, 9914–5

Economic and social conditions of developing countries from 1960s, and Intl Dev Cooperation Agency and AID activities and funding, FY90-92, annual rpt, 9904–4

Economic, social, political, and geographic summary data, by country, 1991, annual factbook, 9114–2

Index by Subjects and Names

Exports and imports of US, by transport mode, country, and SITC 1- to 3-digit commodity, 1990, annual rpt, 2424–12

Exports of US, detailed Schedule B commodities with countries of destination, 1990, annual rpt, 2424–10

Human rights conditions in 170 countries, and US economic and military aid, 1990, annual rpt, 21384–3

Military aid of US, arms sales, and training programs costs and budget requests, by program, world region, and country, FY90-92, annual rpt, 7144–13

Minerals Yearbook, 1988, Vol 3: foreign country review of production, trade, and policy, by commodity, annual rpt, 5604–17.80

UN voting record and share of votes in agreement with US, by issue, country, and world area, 1990, annual rpt, 7004–18

see also under By Foreign Country in the "Index by Categories"

Central America

Agricultural export promotion of nontraditional crops, impacts on Central America income export stability, late 1970s-80s, 1528–312

Agricultural exports of high-value commodities, indexes and sales by commodity, world area, and country, 1960s-86, 1528–323

Agricultural exports of US, for grains, oilseed products, hides, skins, and cotton, by country, weekly rpt, 1922–3

Agricultural trade of US, by detailed commodity and country, 1989, annual rpt, 1524–8

Agricultural trade of US, by detailed commodity and country, 1990, semiannual rpt, 1522–4

Aliens (illegal) legal residence applications under Immigration Reform and Control Act, by selected characteristics, State, and country, periodic rpt, 6262–3

Aliens (illegal) overstaying visas, by class of admission, mode of arrival, age, country, and State, FY85-88, annual rpt, 6264–5

Corporations in US under foreign control, income tax returns, assets and income statement items by industry div, country, and world area, 1988, article, 8302–2.219

Deforestation, and OECD imports of tropical wood, by country, 1980s, annual rpt, 9114–4.10

Economic and military aid and loans from US and intl agencies, by program and country, FY46-90, annual rpt, 9914–5

Economic and social conditions of developing countries from 1960s, and Intl Dev Cooperation Agency and AID activities and funding, FY90-92, annual rpt, 9904–4

Exports (duty-free) of Caribbean area to US, and imports from US, by country, and impact on US employment, by commodity, 1990, annual rpt, 6364–2

Exports (duty-free) of Caribbean area to US, by commodity and country, with consumer and industry impacts, 1984-90, annual rpt, 9884–20

Exports and imports (waterborne) of US, by type of service, commodity, country, route, and US port, 1988, annual rpt, 7704–2

Index by Subjects and Names

Exports and imports (waterborne) of US, by type of service, customs district, port, and world area, monthly rpt, 2422–7

Exports and imports of OECD, total and for 4 major countries, and US trade by country, by commodity, 1970-89, world area rpt, 9116–1.2

Fish larvae abundance, distribution, and growth, for selected Western Hemisphere sites, 1989 conf, 2168–126

Grain production and needs, and related economic outlook, by world area and selected country, forecast 1990/91-1991/92, 1528–313

Immigrants admitted to US, by country of birth, FY81-90, annual rpt, 6264–4

Immigrants admitted to US, by occupational group and country of birth, preliminary FY90, annual table, 6264–1

Immigration, alien workers, amnesty programs, and employer sanctions impacts on US economy and labor force, series, 6366–5

Inter-American Foundation activities, grants by recipient, and fellowships, by country, FY90, annual rpt, 14424–1

Inter-American Foundation dev grants by program area, and fellowships by field and instn, by country, FY72-90, annual rpt, 14424–2

Investment (direct) incentives of Caribbean Basin Initiative, economic impacts, with finances and employment by country, 1984-90, 2048–141

Investment (foreign direct) of US, by industry group and world area, 1987-90, annual article, 2702–1.220

Military aid of US, arms sales, and training programs costs and budget requests, by program, world region, and country, FY90-92, annual rpt, 7144–13

Multinatl US firms and foreign affiliates finances and operations, by industry and world area of parent firm, 1989 benchmark survey, preliminary annual rpt, 2704–5

Multinatl US firms foreign affiliates, income statement items by country and world area, 1986, biennial article, 8302–2.212

Oils, oilseeds, and meal imports, by commodity, world area of destination, and major producer, 1960s-88, 1528–314

Peace Corps activities, funding by program, and volunteers, by country, FY92, annual rpt, 9654–1

R&D funding by Fed Govt, by field, performer type, agency, and State, FY89-91, annual rpt, 9627–20

Tax (income) returns of corporations with foreign tax credit, income, and tax items, by country and world region of credit, 1986, biennial article, 8302–2.207

Terrorism (intl) incidents, casualties, and attacks on US targets, by attack type and country, 1990, annual rpt, 7004–22

Travel to and from US on US and foreign flag air carriers, by world area, 1990, annual rpt, 2904–13

Travel to US, by characteristics of visit and traveler, country, port city, and State of destination, quarterly rpt, 2902–1

Weather events and anomalies, precipitation and temperature for US and foreign locations, weekly rpt, 2182–6

Weather stations of Natl Weather Service, locations and types of observations made, 1990 annual listing, 2184–5

see also Belize

see also Caribbean area

see also Costa Rica

see also El Salvador

see also Guatemala

see also Honduras

see also Inter-American Development Bank

see also Nicaragua

see also Organization of American States

see also Panama

see also under By Foreign Country in the "Index by Categories"

Central cities

Births, fertility rates, and childless women, by selected characteristics, 1990, annual Current Population Rpt, 2546–1.455

Black Americans social and economic characteristics, for South and total US, 1989-90 and trends from 1969, Current Population Rpt, 2546–1.450

Census of Population, 1990: top 39 MSAs and 40 cities population, with trends from 1900, fact sheet, 2326–20.3

Community Dev Block Grant allocation, by State, county, and city, FY84-91, 5128–17

Consumer Income, socioeconomic characteristics of persons, families, and households, detailed cross-tabulations, Current Population Rpt series, 2546–6

Educational enrollment, by grade, instn type and control, and student characteristics, 1989 and trends from 1947, annual Current Population Rpt, 2546–1.453

Employment and unemployment in metro and nonmetro areas, monthly rpt, quarterly data, 6742–2.9

Households and family characteristics, by location, 1990, annual Current Population Rpt, 2546–1.447

Housing and households detailed characteristics, and unit and neighborhood quality, by location, 1987, biennial rpt supplement, 2485–13

Housing and households detailed characteristics, and unit and neighborhood quality, by location, 1989, biennial rpt, 2485–12

Housing and households detailed characteristics, and unit and neighborhood quality, MSA surveys, series, 2485–6

Housing inventory change from 1973, by reason, unit and household characteristics, and location, 1983 survey, biennial rpt, 2485–14

Housing vacancy and occupancy rates, and vacant unit characteristics and costs, by region and metro-nonmetro location, quarterly rpt, 2482–1

Income (household) and poverty status under alternative income definitions, by recipient characteristics, 1990, annual Current Population Rpt, 2546–6.69

Retail trade census, 1987: finances and employment, for establishments with and without payroll, by SIC 2- to 4-digit kind of business, State, and MSA, 2401–1

State and Metro Area Data Book, 1991 data compilation, 2328–54

Voting and registration, by socioeconomic and demographic characteristics, 1990 congressional election, biennial Current Population Rpt, 2546–1.454

Centrally planned economies

see also Urban renewal

Central Intelligence Agency

Budget of US, authoritative financial statements with appropriations, outlays, and receipts, by category and agency, FY90, annual rpt, 8104–2.1

Budget of US, obligations and authority by function, agency, and program, with summaries, analyses, and historical tables, FY92, annual rpt, 104–2

Chiefs of State and Cabinet members, by country, bimonthly listing, 9112–4

China economic conditions after 1988 austerity program, with background data, 1978-90, 9118–9

Developing countries foreign debt, and IMF credit outstanding, by country, 1984-90, 9118–11

Eastern Europe economic and political conditions, and impacts of geographic factors, by country, 1990 conf, 9118–18

Eastern Europe transition to market economies, economic conditions, intl aid, and energy balance, by country, 1985-90, 9118–13

Economic conditions, and oil supply and demand, for major industrial countries, biweekly rpt, 9112–1

Economic, social, political, and geographic summary data, by country, 1991, annual factbook, 9114–2

Energy production by type, and oil trade, and use, by country group and selected country, monthly rpt, 9112–2

OECD trade, total and for 4 major countries, and US trade by country, by commodity, 1970-89, world area rpt series, 9116–1

Soviet Union, Eastern Europe, OECD, and selected other countries economic conditions, 1960s-90, annual rpt, 9114–4

Soviet Union economic conditions, CIA GNP estimation methods assessment, 1989, GAO rpt, 26123–365

Soviet Union economic conditions under General Secretary Gorbachev, 1990 and trends from 1975, annual rpt, 9114–6

Soviet Union GNP by component and industry sector, and CIA estimation methods, 1950s-87, 23848–223

Youth population declines relative to other age groups, by selected country, 1985 and projected to 2010, 9118–17

Central Treaty Organization

Economic and military aid and loans from US and intl agencies, by program and country, FY46-90, annual rpt, 9914–5

Centrally planned economies

Agricultural and economic conditions in developing countries, and agricultural exports of US, effects of US aid, 1989 conf papers, 1548–372

Agricultural Outlook, production, prices, marketing, and trade, by commodity, forecast and current situation, monthly rpt with articles, 1502–4

Agricultural trade of US, by commodity and country, bimonthly rpt, 1522–1

Agricultural trade of US, by detailed commodity and country, 1989, annual rpt, 1524–8

Economic and social conditions of foreign countries, working paper series, 2326–18

Economic conditions in USSR, Eastern Europe, OECD, and selected other countries, 1960s-90, annual rpt, 9114–4

Centrally planned economies

Energy use and production, by fuel type, country, and country group, projected 1995-2010 and trends from 1970, annual rpt, 3164–84

Global climate change economic impacts, projected to 2100 with background data for 1980s, 3028–5

Nuclear power plant capacity and operating status, by plant and communist and regulated market country, as of Dec 1990, annual rpt, 3164–57.2

Oil and gas production and trade by country, and use, for centrally planned economy countries, monthly rpt, 9112–2

Oil and gas reserves and discoveries, by country and country group, quarterly rpt, 3162–43

Oils, oilseeds, and meal imports, by commodity, world area of destination, and major producer, 1960s-88, 1528–314

see also Albania
see also Bulgaria
see also Cambodia
see also China, Peoples Republic
see also Council for Mutual Economic Assistance
see also Cuba
see also Czechoslovakia
see also East-West trade
see also Eastern Europe
see also Germany, East
see also Hungary
see also Korea, North
see also Poland
see also Romania
see also Soviet Union
see also Vietnam
see also Yugoslavia
see also under By Foreign Country in the "Index by Categories"

Ceramic products

see Clay industry and products
see Pottery and porcelain products

Cereals

see Grains and grain products

Cerebrovascular diseases

Cases of acute and chronic conditions, disability, absenteeism, and health services use, by selected characteristics, 1987, CD-ROM, 4147–10.177

Deaths and rates, by cause and age, preliminary 1989-90, US Vital Statistics annual rpt, 4144–7

Deaths and rates, by cause, provisional data, monthly rpt, 4142–1.2

Deaths and rates, by detailed cause and demographic characteristics, 1988 and trends from 1900, US Vital Statistics annual rpt, 4144–2

Deaths from heart disease, stroke, and chronic obstructive lung disease, by country and sex, 1987, annual rpt, 4474–6

Diabetes and complications cases, deaths, and hospitalization, by age, sex, race, State, and region, 1980-86, annual rpt, 4205–41

Health condition and health care resources, use, and spending, 1950s-89, annual data compilation, 4144–11

HHS financial aid, by program, recipient, State, and city, FY90, annual regional listings, 4004–3

Hospital deaths of Medicare patients, actual and expected rates by diagnosis, with hospital characteristics, by instn, FY87-89, annual regional rpt series, 4654–14

Hospital post-discharge service use, by type, for Medicare pneumonia, stroke, and hip replacement cases, 1981-86, article, 4652–1.223

Indian Health Service facilities and use, and Indian health and other characteristics, by IHS region, 1980s-89, annual chartbook, 4084–7

Minority group health condition, services use, costs, and indicators of services need, 1950s-88, 4118–55

Natl Heart, Lung, and Blood Inst activities, and grants by recipient and location, FY90 and disease trends from 1940, annual rpt, 4474–15

Natl Inst of Neurological Disorders and Stroke activities, and disorder cases, FY90, annual rpt, 4474–25

Older persons deaths in hospitals, nursing homes, and own home, by cause, age, marital status, and region, 1986, article, 4652–1.201

Preventive disease and health improvement goals and recommended activities for 2000, with trends 1970s-80s, 4048–10

Smoking-related cancer and other diseases, death risk by body site and sex, 1960s-91, article, 4472–1.219

State and Metro Area Data Book, 1991 data compilation, 2328–54

Surgical procedures for carotid endarterectomy, risks and benefit evaluation for Medicare coverage, 1990 rpt, 4186–10.2

Surgical procedures for cerebral artery bypass to reduce stroke risk, risks and benefit evaluation for Medicare coverage, 1991 rpt, 4186–10.3

see also under By Disease in the "Index by Categories"

Cerrelli, Ezio C.

"1990 Traffic Fatalities, Preliminary Report", 7762–11

Certificates of deposit

Banks (insured commercial) domestic and foreign office consolidated financial statements, monthly rpt, quarterly data, 9362–1.4

Banks (insured commercial and savings) finances, for foreign and domestic offices, by asset size, 1989, annual rpt, 9294–4.2

Economic indicators and components, current data and annual trends, monthly rpt, 23842–1.5

Foreign and US economic conditions, and trade devs and balances, with data by selected country and country group, monthly rpt, 9882–14

Foreign and US industrial stock indexes and long-term govt bond yields, for selected countries, weekly chartbook, 9365–1.5

Households assets, by type of holding and selected characteristics, 1988, Current Population Rpt, 2546–20.16

Interest rates for commercial paper, govt securities, other financial instruments, and home mortgages, monthly rpt, 9365–2.14

Interest rates forecasting performance of Treasury bill and other security yields at alternative maturities, 1950s-80s, article, 9389–1.201

Interest rates on bank deposits, relation to bank market concentration indicators and Treasury security rates, 1980s, technical paper, 9366–6.261

North Central States, FHLB 6th District insured S&Ls financial condition and operations by State, quarterly rpt, 9302–23

Savings instns insured by Savings Assn Insurance Fund, assets, liabilities, and deposit and loan activity, by conservatorship status, monthly rpt, 8432–1

Southeastern States, Fed Reserve 5th District insured commercial banks financial statements, by State, quarterly rpt, 9389–18

Southeastern States, Fed Reserve 8th District banking and economic conditions, quarterly rpt with articles, 9391–16

Yields on govt and private issues, weekly rpt, 9391–4

Certification

see Licenses and permits
see Occupational testing and certification

Cesium

see Metals and metal industries

Ceylon

see Sri Lanka

CFE treaty

see Treaty on Conventional Armed Forces in Europe

Chad

Agricultural exports of high-value commodities, indexes and sales by commodity, world area, and country, 1960s-86, 1528–323

Agricultural trade of US, by detailed commodity and country, 1989, annual rpt, 1524–8

Agricultural trade of US, by detailed commodity and country, 1990, semiannual rpt, 1522–4

AID economic aid to developing countries, obligations and disbursements by country, quarterly rpt, 9912–4

Dairy imports, consumption, and market conditions, by sub-Saharan Africa country, 1961-88, 1528–321

Economic and military aid and loans from US and intl agencies, by program and country, FY46-90, annual rpt, 9914–5

Economic and social conditions of developing countries from 1960s, and Intl Dev Cooperation Agency and AID activities and funding, FY90-92, annual rpt, 9904–4

Economic conditions, income, production, prices, employment, and trade, 1991 periodic country rpt, 2046–4.13

Economic, social, political, and geographic summary data, by country, 1991, annual factbook, 9114–2

Exports and imports of US, by transport mode, country, and SITC 1- to 3-digit commodity, 1990, annual rpt, 2424–12

Exports of US, detailed Schedule B commodities with countries of destination, 1990, annual rpt, 2424–10

Grain production, use, imports, and stocks, for Sahel region by country, 1989/90, 9918–18

Human rights conditions in 170 countries, and US economic and military aid, 1990, annual rpt, 21384–3

Military aid of US, arms sales, and training programs costs and budget requests, by program, world region, and country, FY90-92, annual rpt, 7144–13

Index by Subjects and Names

Minerals Yearbook, 1988, Vol 3: foreign country review of production, trade, and policy, by commodity, annual rpt, 5604–17.80

UN voting record and share of votes in agreement with US, by issue, country, and world area, 1990, annual rpt, 7004–18

see also under By Foreign Country in the "Index by Categories"

Chalfant, James A.

"Alternative Measures of Money as Indicators of Inflation: A Survey and Some New Evidence", 9391–1.202

Champaign, Ill.

see also under By SMSA or MSA in the "Index by Categories"

CHAMPUS

see Civilian Health and Medical Program of the Uniformed Services

Chan, Anthony

- "Are the Preliminary Announcements of Some Macroeconomic Variables Rational?", 9385–8.94
- "Empirical Examination of Government Expenditures and the Ex Ante Crowding Out Effect for the British Economy", 9385–8.83
- "How Well Do Asset Allocation Managers Allocate Assets?", 9385–8.87

Chance, Don M.

"Effect of Margins on the Volatility of Stock and Derivative Markets: A Review of the Evidence", 11924–4.2

Chaney, Bradford

"Academic Research Equipment in Computer Science, Central Computer Facilities and Engineering, 1989", 9627–27.1

Chari, V. V.

"Playing By the Rules: A Proposal for Federal Budget Reform", 9383–2

"Reconsideration of the Problem of Social Cost: Free Riders and Monopolists", 9383–20.12

Charity

see Gifts and private contributions

see Nonprofit organizations and foundations

Charleston, S.C.

Wages by occupation, for office and plant workers, 1990 survey, periodic MSA rpt, 6785–11.2

see also under By SMSA or MSA in the "Index by Categories"

Charleston, W.Va.

see also under By SMSA or MSA in the "Index by Categories"

Charlotte Amalie, V.I.

Census of Population, 1990: Virgin Islands population by location, press release, 2328–77

Charlotte, N.C.

- Housing starts and completions authorized by building permits in 40 MSAs, quarterly rpt, 2382–9
- Wages by occupation, and benefits for office and plant workers, 1991 survey, periodic MSA rpt, 6785–12.7

see also under By City and By SMSA or MSA in the "Index by Categories"

Charlottesville, Va.

see also under By SMSA or MSA in the "Index by Categories"

Charrette, Susan M.

"Theoretical Analysis of Capital Flight from Debtor Nations", 9385–8.109

Chartbooks

- CCC financial condition and major commodity program operations, FY62-87, annual chartbook, 1824–2
- Child accident deaths and injuries by cause, and victimization, rates by race, sex, and age, 1979-88, chartbook, 4108–56
- Child health condition and services use, 1990 chartbook, 4108–49
- Economic indicators and components, and Fed Reserve 4th District business and financial conditions, monthly chartbook, 9377–10
- Exports, imports, and balances of US with major trading partners, by product category, 1986-90, annual chartbook, 9884–21
- Farm financial and marketing conditions, forecast 1991, annual chartbook, 1504–8
- Farm production, marketing, trade, food consumption, and nutrition programs, annual chartbook, discontinued, 1504–3
- Financial data for US and selected foreign countries, including exchange rates, interest rates, gold prices, and security yields, weekly chartbook, 9365–1.5
- Health maintenance organizations and other prepaid managed care plans Medicaid enrollment and use, for 20 States, 1985-89, chartbook, 4108–29
- Indian Health Service facilities and use, and Indian health and other characteristics, by IHS region, 1980s-89, annual chartbook, 4084–7
- Indian Health Service facilities, funding, operations, and Indian health and other characteristics, 1950s-90, annual chartbook, 4084–1
- Military women personnel on active and reserve duty, by demographic and service characteristics and service branch, FY89, annual chartbook, 3544–26
- Minority group and women health condition, services use, payment sources, and health care labor force, by poverty status, 1940s-89, chartbook, 4118–56
- Pollution (air) levels for 6 pollutants, by source and selected MSA, 1980-89, annual rpt, 9194–1
- Science and engineering academic research system status, R&D performance, and Fed Govt support, 1950s-88 with trends and projections, 9628–83
- Travel to and from US, by world area, forecast 1991-92, annual rpt, 2904–9
- Weather trends and deviations, by world region, 1880s-1990, annual chartbook, 2184–9

see also Maps

Chattanooga, Tenn.

Wages by occupation, for office and plant workers, 1991 survey, periodic MSA rpt, 6785–3.10

see also under By City and By SMSA or MSA in the "Index by Categories"

Cheatgrass

see Pests and pest control

Checking accounts

Assets and debts of private sector, balance sheets by segment, 1945-90, semiannual rpt, 9365–4.1

Chemicals and chemical industry

- Budget of US, authoritative financial statements with appropriations, outlays, and receipts, by category and agency, FY90, annual rpt, 8104–2.1
- Commercial banks finances, for foreign and domestic offices, by asset size, 1989, annual rpt, 9294–4.2
- Commercial banks holdings of demand deposits of individuals, partnerships, and corporations, monthly rpt, 9362–1.1
- Deposits in insured commercial and savings banks, by instn, State, MSA, and county, as of June 1990, annual regional rpt series, 9295–3
- Economic indicators and components, current data and annual trends, monthly rpt, 23842–1.5
- Economic indicators compounded annual rates of change, 1971-90, annual rpt, 9391–9.1
- Farm sector assets by type, 1990, annual rpt, 1544–16.2
- Financial and monetary conditions, selected US summary data, weekly rpt, 9391–4
- Flow-of-funds accounts, savings, investments, and credit statements, quarterly rpt, 9365–3.3
- Forgery of checks and bonds, Secret Service investigations and arrests, FY90 and trends from FY81, annual rpt, 8464–1
- Households assets, by type of holding and selected characteristics, 1988, Current Population Rpt, 2546–20.16
- Households bill payment transactions, by method, 1987-88, annual rpt, 9864–10
- Monetary trends, Fed Reserve Bank of St Louis monthly rpt, 9391–2
- Southeastern States, Fed Reserve 5th District insured commercial banks financial statements, by State, quarterly rpt, 9389–18
- West Central States economic indicators, Fed Reserve 10th District, quarterly rpt, 9381–16.2

see also Negotiable orders of withdrawal accounts

Cheese

see Dairy industry and products

Chelius, James R.

"Role of Workers' Compensation in Developing Safer Workplaces", 6722–1.243

Chemical and biological warfare agents

- Agent Orange exposure of Vietnam veterans, and other factors relation to dev of rare cancers, 1984-88, 4208–33
- Disasters and natl security incidents and mgmt, with data by major event and State, 1991 annual rpt, 9434–6
- Disposal of chemical weapons, DOD budget appropriations, FY90-93, annual rpt, 3544–32
- Security measures at chemical and biological weapons research labs, and govt and contractor staff, 1988-90, GAO rpt, 26123–356

Chemicals and chemical industry

- Agricultural crops (new and traditional) use in industry, replacement of imports and nonrenewable resources, R&D funding, and economic impacts, 1970s-90, 26358–239
- Antimony trioxide (refined) from PRC at less than fair value, injury to US industry, investigation with background financial and operating data, 1991 rpt, 9886–14.317

Chemicals and chemical industry

Benzyl paraben from Japan at less than fair value, injury to US industry, investigation with background financial and operating data, 1991 rpt, 9886–14.303

Business statistics, detailed data for major industries and economic indicators, *Survey of Current Business*, monthly rpt, 2702–1.12

Cancer (bladder) cases and risk among chemical plant workers, 1973-88, local area study, article, 4472–1.209

Capital expenditures for plant and equipment, by major industry group, quarterly rpt, 2502–2

Chlorine production capacity and salt feedstocks needs, by firm and facility, 1989, annual listing, 5614–30

Chlorofluorocarbons and substitutes properties and impacts on stratospheric ozone, 1990 rpt, 9508–37

Collective bargaining agreements expiring during year, and workers covered, by firm, union, industry group, and State, 1991, annual rpt, 6784–9

Communist countries trade with US, by detailed commodity and country, quarterly rpt with articles, 9882–2

County Business Patterns, 1988: employment, establishments, and payroll, by SIC 2- to 4-digit industry and county, annual State rpt series, 2326–6

County Business Patterns, 1989: employment, establishments, and payroll, by SIC 2- to 4-digit industry and county, annual State rpt series, 2326–8

DOD prime contract awards, by detailed procurement category, FY87-90, annual rpt, 3544–18

EC economic integration impacts on domestic economic conditions and US trade, 1985-90, 9886–4.170

Employment, earnings, and hours, by SIC 1- to 4-digit industry, monthly and annual averages, selected years 1909-90, annual rpt, 6744–4

Employment in manufacturing, by detailed occupation and SIC 2-digit industry, 1989 survey, triennial rpt, 6748–52

Employment, unemployment, and labor force characteristics, by region and census div, 1990, annual rpt, 6744–7.1

Energy producers finances and operations, by energy type for US firms domestic and foreign operations, 1989, annual rpt, 3164–44.1

Energy use and prices for manufacturing industries, 1988 survey, series, 3166–13

Enterprise Statistics, 1987: auxiliaries of multi-establishment firms, finances and operations by function, industry, and State, 2329–6

Enterprise Statistics, 1987: finances and operations for companies, by size, level of diversification, form of organization, and industry group, 2329–8

Environmental Quality, status of problems, protection programs, research, and intl issues, 1991 annual rpt, 484–1

Export and import price indexes for chemicals, by commodity, 1985-90, article, 6722–1.229

Exports and imports between US and outlying areas, by detailed commodity and mode of transport, 1990, annual rpt, 2424–11

Exports and imports of US, by country and detailed commodity, monthly rpt, 2422–12

Exports and imports of US by country, and trade shifts by commodity, 1990, semiannual rpt, 9882–9

Exports and imports of US, by Harmonized System 6-digit commodity and country, 1990, annual rpt, 2424–13

Exports and imports of US, by leading country, and shipments by leading State, 1987-90, fact sheet, 2326–17.32

Exports and imports of US, by selected country, country group, and commodity group, 1990, annual rpt, 2044–37

Exports and imports of US, by transport mode, country, and SITC 1- to 3-digit commodity, 1990, annual rpt, 2424–12

Exports and imports of US shipped through Canada, by detailed commodity, customs district, and country, 1989, annual rpt, 7704–11

Exports of US, detailed commodities by country, monthly CD-ROM, 2422–13

Exports of US, detailed Schedule B commodities with countries of destination, 1990, annual rpt, 2424–10

Foreign direct investment impact on trade balance, with background data, late 1960s-90 and auto forecasts to 1993, article, 9385–1.210

Foreign direct investment in US, by industry group and world area, 1987-90, annual article, 2702–1.219

Foreign direct investment in US, by industry group of US affiliate and country of parent firm, 1980-86, 2708–41

Foreign direct investment in US manufacturing, impacts on trade balances, with data by industry, 1980s-93, technical paper, 9385–8.91

Foreign direct investment of US, by industry group and world area, 1987-90, annual article, 2702–1.220

Imports, exports, and employment impacts, by SIC 2- to 4-digit industry and commodity, quarterly rpt, 2322–2

Imports of US, detailed commodities by country, monthly CD-ROM, 2422–14

Imports of US given duty-free treatment for value of US material sent abroad, by commodity and country, 1989, annual rpt, 9884–14

Injuries from use of consumer products, by severity, victim age, and detailed product, 1990, annual rpt, 9164–6

Input-output structure of US economy, detailed interindustry transactions for 84 industries, and components of final demand, 1986, annual article, 2702–1.206

Input-output structure of US economy, detailed interindustry transactions for 85 industries, 1982 benchmark data, 2702–1.213

Labor productivity, indexes of output, hours, and employment by SIC 2- to 4-digit industry, 1967-89, annual rpt, 6824–1.3

Manufacturing annual survey, 1989: finances and operations, by SIC 2- to 4-digit industry, series, 2506–15

Manufacturing census, 1987: employment and shipments under Fed Govt contracts, by SIC 4-digit industry, 2497–7

Index by Subjects and Names

Manufacturing census, 1987: finances and operations, by SIC 2- to 4-digit industry, State, and MSA, with trends from 1849, 2497–1

Manufacturing census, 1987: finances and operations, by type of organization and SIC 2- to 4-digit industry, subject rpt, 2497–5

Manufacturing corporations financial statements, by selected SIC 2- to 3-digit industry, quarterly rpt, 2502–1

Manufacturing finances and operations, by SIC 2- to 4-digit industry, forecast 1991, annual rpt, 2044–28

Manufacturing industries operations and performance, analytical rpt series, 2506–16

Manufacturing production, shipments, inventories, orders, and pollution control costs, periodic Current Industrial Rpt series, 2506–3

Mexico imports from US, by industry and State, 1987-90, 2048–154

Multinatl firms US affiliates, finances, and operations, by industry, world area of parent firm, and State, 1988-89, annual rpt, 2704–4

Multinatl firms US affiliates, investment trends and impact on US economy, 1991 annual rpt, 2004–9

Multinatl US firms and foreign affiliates finances and operations, by industry and world area of parent firm, 1989 benchmark survey, preliminary annual rpt, 2704–5

Nepheline syenite from Canada at less than fair value, injury to US industry, investigation with background financial and operating data, 1991 rpt, 9886–14.326

Occupational injury and illness rates, by SIC 2- to 4-digit industry, 1988-89, annual rpt, 6844–7

Occupational injury and illness rates, by SIC 2- to 4-digit industry, 1989, annual rpt, 6844–1

OECD trade, total and for 4 major countries, and US trade by country, by commodity, 1970-89, world area rpt series, 9116–1

Pollution (air) abatement equipment shipments by industry, and new and backlog orders, by product, 1990, annual Current Industrial Rpt, 2506–12.5

Pollution (air) emissions factors, by detailed pollutant and source, data compilation, 1990 rpt, 9198–120

Pollution abatement capital and operating costs, by SIC 2-digit industry, 1989, advance annual Current Industrial Rpt, 2506–3.6

Price indexes (producer), by stage of processing and detailed commodity, monthly rpt, 6762–6

Price indexes (producer), by stage of processing and detailed commodity, monthly 1990, annual rpt, 6764–2

Production, shipments, firms, trade, and use, by product, periodic Current Industrial Rpt series, 2506–8

Puerto Rico and other US possessions corporations income tax returns, income and tax items, and employment, by selected industry, 1987, article, 8302–2.213

Puerto Rico economic censuses, 1987: wholesale and retail trade and service industry finances and operations, by SIC 2- to 4-digit industry and municipio, 2591–1

Puerto Rico economic censuses, 1987: wholesale, retail, and service industries finances and operations, by establishment characteristics and SIC 2- and 3-digit industry, subject rpts, 2591–2

R&D funding, and scientists and engineers education and employment, for US and selected foreign countries, 1991 annual rpt, 9627–35.1

Sodium sulfur compounds from 4 countries at less than fair value, injury to US industry, investigation with background financial and operating data, 1991 rpt, 9886–14.305

Soviet Union, Eastern Europe, OECD, and selected other countries consumer and producer goods and services production and sales, 1960s-90, annual rpt, 9114–4.7

Soviet Union GNP by component and industry sector, and CIA estimation methods, 1950s-87, 23848–223

Soviet Union GNP by detailed income and outlay component, 1985, 2326–18.59

Statistical Abstract of US, 1991 annual data compilation, 2324–1.27

Sulfanilic acid from PRC at less than fair value, injury to US industry, investigation with background financial and operating data, 1991 rpt, 9886–14.334

Synthetic organic chemical production, by detailed product, quarterly rpt, 9882–1

Tariff Schedule of US, classifications and rates of duty by detailed imported commodity, 1992 base edition, 9886–13

Tax (excise) collections of IRS, by source, quarterly rpt, 8302–1

Tax (excise) on hazardous waste generation and disposal, rates, and firms filing returns, by substance type, 1988, annual article, 8302–2.202

Tax (income) returns of corporations, income and tax items by asset size and detailed industry, 1987, annual rpt, 8304–4

Tax (income) returns of corporations, income and tax items by asset size and detailed industry, 1988, annual rpt, 8304–21

Tax (income) returns of corporations with foreign tax credit, income and tax items by industry group, 1986, biennial article, 8302–2.203

Tax (income) returns of multinatl US firms foreign affiliates, income statement items, by asset size and industry, 1986, biennial article, 8302–2.212

Underground storage of oil and other hazardous substances, systems and facilities subject to EPA regulation, as of 1988, article, 3162–6.203

Wholesale trade census, 1987: depreciable assets, capital and operating expenses, sales, value added, and inventories, by SIC 2- to 3-digit kind of business, 2407–2

Wholesale trade census, 1987: establishments, sales by customer class, employment, inventories, and expenses, by SIC 2- to 4-digit kind of business, 2407–4

Wholesale trade sales and inventories, by SIC 2- to 3-digit kind of business, monthly rpt, 2413–7

Wholesale trade sales, inventories, purchases, and gross margins, by SIC 2- to 3-digit kind of business, 1990, annual rpt, 2413–13

see also Adhesives

see also Chemical and biological warfare agents

see also Dioxins

see also Drugs

see also Explosives

see also Fertilizers

see also Food ingredients and additives

see also Gases

see also Gum and wood chemicals

see also Hazardous substances

see also Hazardous waste and disposal

see also Paints and varnishes

see also Pesticides

see also Petrochemicals

see also Pharmaceutical industry

see also Plastics and plastics industry

see also Soap and detergent industry

see also Synthetic fibers and fabrics

see also under By Commodity in the "Index by Categories"

see also under By Industry in the "Index by Categories"

Chemistry

Degrees (PhD) in science and engineering, by field, instn, employment prospects, sex, race, and other characteristics, 1960s-90, annual rpt, 9627–30

Degrees awarded in science and engineering, by field, level, and sex, 1966-89, 9627–33

DOE R&D projects and funding at natl labs, universities, and other instns, FY91, annual summary rpt, 3004–18.5

Employment and other characteristics of science and engineering PhDs, by field and State, 1989, biennial rpt, 9627–18

Fed Govt aid to higher education and nonprofit instns for R&D and related activities, by field, instn, agency, and State, FY89, annual rpt, 9627–17

Higher education course completions, by detailed program, sex, race, and instn type, for 1972 high school class, as of 1984, 4888–4

Higher education grad programs enrollment in science and engineering, by field, source of funds, and characteristics of student and instn, 1975-89, annual rpt, 9627–7

NASA R&D funding to higher education instns, by field, instn, and State, FY90, annual listing, 9504–7

R&D equipment of higher education instns, acquisition and service costs, condition, and financing, by field and subfield, 1988-90, triennial survey series, 9627–27

R&D funding by Fed Govt, by field, performer type, agency, and State, FY89-91, annual rpt, 9627–20

R&D funding by higher education instns and federally funded centers, by field, instn, and State, FY89, annual rpt, 9627–13

Water quality, chemistry, hydrology, and other characteristics, local area studies, series, 5666–27

see also Chemicals and chemical industry

Chemotherapy

Cancer treatments using chemotherapy drugs for indications not listed on drug label, costs, and insurance reimbursement problems, 1990 physicians survey, GAO rpt, 26131–81

Childhood cancer survivors risk of miscarriage, stillbirth, and birth defects, by chemotherapy and radiotherapy exposure, study, 1991 article, 4472–1.233

Chen, Carl R.

"Cross-Sectional Analysis of Mutual Funds' Market Timing and Security Selection Skill", 9385–8.80

"How Well Do Asset Allocation Managers Allocate Assets?", 9385–8.87

Chen, Moon S., Jr.

"Promoting Heart Health for Southeast Asians: A Database for Planning Interventions", 4042–3.222

Chernobyl, USSR

Nuclear reactor accident in Chernobyl, monitoring results for strontium-90 fallout at 53 sites worldwide, May 1986, annual rpt, 3004–29

Nuclear reactor accident in Chernobyl, radionuclide releases and concentrations in food and water, by selected Soviet Republic, 1986-87 article, 4042–3.201

Cherries

see Fruit and fruit products

Chesapeake Bay

Army Corps of Engineers water resources dev projects, characteristics, and costs, 1950s-89, biennial State rpt series, 3756–1

Army Corps of Engineers water resources dev projects, characteristics, and costs, 1950s-91, biennial State rpt series, 3756–2

Fish (striped bass) stocks status on Atlantic coast, and sport and commercial catch by State, 1979-88, annual rpt, 5504–29

Fish and shellfish catch, by species and Middle Atlantic and Chesapeake State and port, 1988-89, article, 2162–1.204

Pollutant concentrations in coastal and estuarine sediments, by contaminant and selected site, 1984-89, 2176–3.13

Tidal currents, daily time and velocity by station for North America coasts, forecast 1992, annual rpt, 2174–1.1

Tide height and tidal current velocity daily at Middle Atlantic coastal stations, forecast 1992, annual rpt, 2174–11

Water supply and quality in streams and lakes, and groundwater levels in wells, by drainage basin, 1988, annual State rpt series, 5666–16

Water supply and quality in streams and lakes, and groundwater levels in wells, by drainage basin, 1989, annual State rpt series, 5666–12

Water supply and quality in streams and lakes, and groundwater levels in wells, by drainage basin, 1990, annual State rpt series, 5666–10

Chesapeake, Va.

see also under By City in the "Index by Categories"

Cheyenne, Wyo.

see also under By SMSA or MSA in the "Index by Categories"

Chicago Board of Trade

Chicago Board of Trade
Futures trading oversight of CFTC and individual exchanges, foreign activity, and customer views, late 1980s, hearing, 25168–77

Chicago, Ill.
Airline market entry impacts of carrier control of airports, facility and aircraft availability, noise regulation, and other barriers, late 1980s and projected to 1997, 7308–199.8
Auto and auto parts manufacturing wages, employment, and benefits, by occupation, region, and selected labor market area, 1989 survey, 6787–6.252
CPI by component for US city average, and by region, population size, and for 15 metro areas, monthly rpt, 6762–1
CPI by component for US city average, and by region, population size, and for 27 metro areas, monthly rpt, 6762–2
Drug abuse indicators for selected metro areas, research results, data collection, and policy issues, 1991 semiannual conf, 4492–5
Drug test results at arrest, by drug type, offense, and sex, for selected urban areas, quarterly rpt, 6062–3
Employment growth in Chicago service, manufacturing, and other industries, analysis of contributing factors, 1970s-87, article, 9375–1.204
Fruit and vegetable shipments, and arrivals in US and Canada cities, by mode of transport and State and country of origin, 1990, annual rpt, 1311–4.2
Fruit and vegetable wholesale prices in NYC, Chicago, and selected shipping points, by crop, 1990, annual rpt, 1311–8
Govt fiscal capacity, for Chicago area municipalities, 1987, article, 10042–1.203
Homeless persons social services spending and client characteristics, and youth programs cases, for Michigan, 1980s, hearing, 25418–5
Housing starts and completions authorized by building permits in 40 MSAs, quarterly rpt, 2382–9
Medicaid HMO enrollees, payments, terminations, services use, and State oversight, for Chicago, Ill, late 1980s, GAO rpt, 26121–399
Oil prices by product, for 4 cities, seasonal weekly rpt, 3162–45
see also under By City and By SMSA or MSA in the "Index by Categories"

Chicanos
see Hispanic Americans
see Mexicans in the U.S.

Chickens
see Poultry industry and products

Chico, Calif.
see also under By SMSA or MSA in the "Index by Categories"

Child abuse and neglect
Assistance for child abuse and neglect prevention, State funding and funding sources, FY89, GAO rpt, 26121–423
Cases of abuse and neglect reported, and victim characteristics, data compilation, 1991 annual rpt, 6064–6.2
Cases of abuse reported, and related deaths, by State, late 1980s, hearing, 25548–102
Court delinquency and neglect case dispositions, by State and county, 1988, annual rpt, 6064–12

Deaths and injuries of children in accidents by cause, and victimization, rates by race, sex, and age, 1979-88, chartbook, 4108–56
Deaths and rates, by detailed cause and demographic characteristics, 1988 and trends from 1900, US Vital Statistics annual rpt, 4144–2
Facilities for juvenile correction and detention, inmates, and expenses, by instn and resident characteristics and State, for public and private instns, 1987, biennial rpt, 6064–13
Facilities for juveniles, population, and costs, by facility and resident characteristics, region, and State, 1985-89, biennial rpt, 6064–5
Foster care placement of black children whose parents abuse drugs, by placement reason and outcome, and household and parent characteristics, 1986-90, 4008–114
Foster care placements, discharges, and returns to care, by selected characteristics of children, and length of stay factors, 1985-86, GAO rpt, 26121–432
Foster care programs cases, problems, and operations for selected States, 1970s-90, hearings, 21788–202
Foster care programs operations, funding sources, and client characteristics, for selected States, 1960s-95, 25368–169
Health condition and services use, for children, 1990 chartbook, 4108–49
HHS financial aid, by program, recipient, State, and city, FY90, annual regional listings, 4004–3
Homeless and runaway youth programs, funding, activities, and participant characteristics, FY90, annual rpt, 4604–3
Labor laws enacted, by State, 1990, annual article, 6722–1.209
Legal proceedings representation of child abuse and neglect victims, caseloads, State requirements, and compensation, by State and county, 1989, 4608–28
Preventive disease and health improvement goals and recommended activities for 2000, with trends 1970s-80s, 4048–10
Sentences for Federal offenses, guidelines by offense and circumstances, series, 17668–1
Statistical Abstract of US, 1991 annual data compilation, 2324–1.5
US attorneys civil and criminal cases by type and disposition, and collections, by Federal district, FY90, annual rpt, 6004–2.1
Victimizations of women, by relation to offender, circumstances, and victim characteristics, for rape and other violent offenses, 1973-87, 6068–243

Child day care
AFDC beneficiaries demographic and financial characteristics, by State, FY89, annual rpt, 4694–1
AFDC Job Opportunities and Basic Skills Training Program Federal and State funding by State, and administrators views, 1989-91, GAO rpt, 26121–435
Appalachian States child day care workload limits, 1988, 9088–36
Arrangements for child care, costs, and impacts on mothers labor force status, by selected characteristics, 1983 and 1988, article, 6722–1.246

Consumer Expenditure Survey, spending for selected categories, 1991 semiannual pamphlet, 2322–3
Cost of living and quality of life indicators for 14 MSAs, 1980s, GAO rpt, 26123–346
County Business Patterns, 1988: employment, establishments, and payroll, by SIC 2- to 4-digit industry and county, annual State rpt series, 2326–6
County Business Patterns, 1989: employment, establishments, and payroll, by SIC 2- to 4-digit industry and county, annual State rpt series, 2326–8
Employee benefit plan coverage, by benefit type and worker characteristics, late 1970s-80s, 15496–1.11
Employee leave for illness, disability, and dependent care, coverage, provisions, terminations, costs, and methods of covering for absent worker, by firm size, 1988 survey, 9768–21
Employer-provided child care aid activities, North Central States employers views, 1990 survey, article, 9383–19.201
Employer-provided day care, share of firms reporting positive effects, 1982 survey, 15496–1.12
Employment, earnings, and hours, by SIC 1- to 4-digit industry, monthly and annual averages, selected years 1909-90, annual rpt, 6744–4
Employment in day care by occupation, and mothers in labor force, 1976-88 with day care employment projected to 2000, article, 6722–1.202
Fed Govt employee family-related and work schedule benefits, availability, admin, and personnel directors views, 1990 survey, 9496–2.7
Food aid programs of USDA, costs and participation by program, FY69-89, annual rpt, 1364–9
Health and safety training of child care providers, by health area and center size, for California, 1987 survey, article, 4042–3.243
Health condition and services use, for children, 1990 chartbook, 4108–49
Hepatitis cases by infection source, age, sex, race, and State, and deaths, by strain, 1988 and trends from 1966, 4205–2
Labor force status of mothers, impacts of child care needs, and unemployed mothers characteristics, 1986, article, 6722–1.245
Labor laws enacted, by State, 1990, annual article, 6722–1.209
Occupational injury and illness rates, by SIC 2- to 4-digit industry, 1988-89, annual rpt, 6844–7
Occupational injury and illness rates, by SIC 2- to 4-digit industry, 1989, annual rpt, 6844–1
Receipts for services, by SIC 2- to 4-digit kind of business, 1990, annual rpt, 2413–8
Service industries census, 1987: establishments, receipts by source, payroll, and employment, by SIC 2- to 4-digit kind of business, State, and MSA, 2393–4
Single mothers earnings, employment and welfare benefits, and poverty status, 1989, GAO rpt, 26121–413

Index by Subjects and Names

Child welfare

Special education programs, enrollment by age, staff, funding, and needs, by type of handicap and State, 1989/90, annual rpt, 4944–4

State and Metro Area Data Book, 1991 data compilation, 2328–54

Statistical Abstract of US, 1991 annual data compilation, 2324–1.12

Tax (income) returns child care credits claimed, noncompliance indicators, and returns with child care provider income, 1970s-90, article, 8304–8.1

Tax (income) returns filed by type of filer, selected income items, quarterly rpt, 8302–2.1

Tax (income) returns of partnerships, income statement and balance sheet items, by industry group, 1989, annual article, 8302–2.216

Tax (income) returns of sole proprietorships, income statement items, by industry group, 1989, annual article, 8302–2.214

Tax expenditures, Federal revenues forgone through income tax deductions and exclusions by type, FY92-96, annual rpt, 21784–10

Women's employment interruption to provide child care, and impacts on social security benefits, 1990 working paper, 2626–10.138

Child labor

Employer illegal alien worker and Fair Labor Standards Act compliance, hiring impacts, and aliens overstaying visas by country and State, 1986-90, annual rpt, 6264–6

Fair Labor Standards Act admin, with coverage under minimum wage and overtime provisions, and illegal employment of minors, by industry div, FY89, annual rpt, 6504–2.1

Illegal employment of minors and injuries by industry group, and selected characteristics of working youths, 1983-90, GAO rpt, 26121–426

Labor laws enacted, by State, 1990, annual article, 6722–1.209

Child mortality

Abuse-related deaths, by State, late 1980s, hearing, 25548–102

Accident deaths and injuries of children by cause, and victimization, rates by race, sex, and age, 1979-88, chartbook, 4108–56

Accident deaths of children, by cause, age, sex, race, and State, 1980-85, 4108–54

AIDS cases by risk group, race, sex, age, State, and MSA, and deaths, monthly rpt, 4202–9

Air travel of families and industry revenue impacts of proposed child fares, with costs and accidents compared to auto travel, 1990 hearing, 21648–61

Children and youth social, economic, and demographic characteristics, 1950s-90, 4818–5

Deaths and rates, by cause, age, sex, race, and State, preliminary 1989-90 and trends from 1960, US Vital Statistics annual rpt, 4144–7

Deaths and rates, by detailed cause and demographic characteristics, 1988 and trends from 1900, US Vital Statistics annual rpt, 4144–2

Developing countries child health and welfare indicators, and economic conditions, 1950s-80s, hearing, 25388–57

Developing countries economic and social conditions from 1960s, and Intl Dev Cooperation Agency and AID activities and funding, FY90-92, annual rpt, 9904–4

Firearms-related deaths and death rates, by motive, age, sex, and race, for persons aged 1-34, 1979-88, 4146–5.119

Health condition and health care resources, use, and spending, 1950s-89, annual data compilation, 4144–11

Health condition and services use, for children, 1990 chartbook, 4108–49

Hispanic Americans deaths and rates, by cause, age, sex, and detailed origin, average 1979-81, 4147–20.18

Indonesia child and infant survival programs of AID, effectiveness with background data, 1970s-87, 9916–1.73

see also Infant mortality

Child support and alimony

Assistance programs under Ways and Means Committee jurisdiction, finances, operations, and participant characteristics, FY70s-90, annual rpt, 21784–11

Awards and payment status of child support and alimony, by selected characteristics of woman, 1989, biennial Current Population Rpt, 2546–6.72

Awards of child support, receipt, and reasons for nonsupport, 1989-90, fact sheet, 2326–17.37

Child Support Enforcement Program finances and operations, by State, FY85-89, annual rpt, 4694–6

Children and youth social, economic, and demographic characteristics, 1950s-90, 4818–5

Family economic impacts of departure, absence, and presence of parents, 1983-86, Current Population Rpt, 2546–20.17

HHS financial aid, by program, recipient, State, and city, FY90, annual regional listings, 4004–3

Income (household, family, and personal), by source, detailed characteristics, and region, 1988-89, annual Current Population Rpt, 2546–6.68

Income (household, family, and personal), by source, detailed characteristics, and region, 1990, annual Current Population Rpt, 2546–6.70

Paternity determination through genetic testing, labs, services, and costs, 1991 listing, 4698–4

Single mothers earnings, employment and welfare benefits, and poverty status, 1989, GAO rpt, 26121–413

State and Metro Area Data Book, 1991 data compilation, 2328–54

Statistical Abstract of US, 1991 annual data compilation, 2324–1.12

Tax (income) returns of individuals, selected income and tax items by income level, preliminary 1989, annual article, 8302–2.209

Teenage mothers child support awards, payment status, health insurance inclusion, and govt aid for collection, by selected characteristics, 1987, 4698–5

Child Support Enforcement Program

Finances and operations for program, FY85-89, annual rpt, 4694–6

Child Trends, Inc.

"Developmental, Learning, and Emotional Problems: Health of Our Nation's Children, U.S., 1988", 4146–8.193

Child welfare

AIDS patient home and community services under Medicaid waiver in 6 States, 1988-89, article, 4652–1.216

Appalachia local dev projects, and funding by source, by program and State, FY90, annual rpt, 9084–1

Assistance (financial and nonfinancial) of Fed Govt, 1991 base edition with supplements, annual listing, 104–5

Assistance programs under Ways and Means Committee jurisdiction, finances, operations, and participant characteristics, FY70s-90, annual rpt, 21784–11

Benefits, beneficiary characteristics, and trust funds of OASDHI, Medicaid, SSI, and related programs, selected years 1937-89, annual rpt, 4744–3

Budget of US, formula grant program obligations to State and local govts, by agency, program, and State, FY92, annual rpt, 104–30

Budget of US, House concurrent resolution, with spending and revenue targets, FY92 and projected to FY96, annual rpt, 21264–2

Developing countries child health and welfare indicators, and economic conditions, 1950s-80s, hearing, 25388–57

Expenditures for child welfare programs by source, and foster care cases, problems, and program operations for selected States, 1970s-90, hearings, 21788–202

Expenditures for child welfare programs by type and source, and foster care program operations and client characteristics, for selected States, 1960s-95, 25368–169

Expenditures for public welfare by program, FY50s-88, annual article, 4742–1.209

Food aid program for children during summer vacation, nonprofit sponsors compliance with USDA regulations, 1989-90, GAO rpt, 26113–541

Food aid program of USDA for women, infants, and children, enrollment of children at high risk of poor nutrition, for Tennessee, 1982-84, article, 4042–3.216

Food aid program of USDA for women, infants, and children, participants and costs by State and Indian agency, FY88, annual tables, 1364–12

Food aid program of USDA for women, infants, and children, participants by race, State, and Indian agency, Apr 1990, annual rpt, 1364–16

Food aid program of USDA for women, infants, and children, participants, clinics, and costs, by State and Indian agency, monthly tables, 1362–16

Food aid programs of USDA, costs and participation by program, FY69-89, annual rpt, 1364–9

Food aid programs of USDA for children, evaluation, biennial narrative rpt, discontinued, 14854–1

Food stamp eligibility and payment errors, by type, recipient characteristics, and State, FY89, annual rpt, 1364–15

Child welfare

Food stamp recipient household size, composition, income, and income and deductions allowed, summer 1988, annual rpt, 1364–8

Health care programs in urban areas for mothers and children, activities and budgets, 1990, listing, 4108–51

Health, education, and welfare condition of children and families, findings and recommendations, 1991 rpt, 15528–1

HHS financial aid, by program, recipient, State, and city, FY90, annual regional listings, 4004–3

Homeless and runaway youth programs, funding, activities, and participant characteristics, FY90, annual rpt, 4604–3

Homeless persons aid programs of Fed Govt, program descriptions and funding, by agency and State, FY87-90, annual GAO rpt, 26104–21

Indochina Amerasian children arriving in US and refugee camps under Orderly Departure Program, monthly rpt, 7002–4

Insurance (health) coverage of children, by source, family composition, income, and parent employment status, 1977 and 1987, 4186–8.14

Medicaid child preventive health care visits, exams, and immunizations, for California, 1981-84, article, 4652–1.214

OASDI benefit payments, trust fund finances, and economic and demographic assumptions, 1970-90 and alternative projections to 2000, actuarial rpt, 4706–1.105

PL 480 exports by commodity, and recipients, by program, sponsor, and country, FY88 and cumulative from FY55, annual rpt, 1924–7

Railroad retirement, survivors, unemployment, and health insurance programs, monthly rpt, 9702–2

Refugee resettlement programs and funding, arrivals by country of origin, and indicators of adjustment, by State, FY90, annual rpt, 4694–5

Rural areas children in poverty by selected family characteristics, and compared to urban areas, 1987-88, 1598–270

State and Metro Area Data Book, 1991 data compilation, 2328–54

Supplemental Security Income and Medicaid eligibility and payment provisions, and beneficiaries living arrangements, by State, 1991, annual rpt, 4704–13

Supplemental Security Income payments and beneficiaries, by type of eligibility, State, and county, Dec 1989, annual rpt, 4744–27

Veterans compensation and pension recipients, for each US war, 1775-1990, annual rpt, 8604–2

Veterans disability and death compensation and pension cases, by type of entitlement and period of service, monthly rpt, 8602–5

Veterans disability and death compensation cases of VA, by entitlement type, period of service, sex, age, and State, FY89, annual rpt, 8604–7

Veterans education aid under GI Bill and other programs, and participation by period of service and State, FY89, annual rpt, 8604–9

Workers compensation laws of States and Fed Govt, 1991 semiannual rpt, 6502–1

see also Adoption

see also Aid to Families with Dependent Children

see also Child abuse and neglect

see also Child day care

see also Child support and alimony

see also Foster home care

see also Head Start Project

see also School lunch and breakfast programs

Childbirth

see Births

see Birthweight

see Infant mortality

see Maternity

see Midwives

see Obstetrics and gynecology

Children

AIDS cases by risk group, race, sex, age, State, and MSA, and deaths, monthly rpt, 4202–9

AIDS child patients *pneumocystis carinii* pneumonia prevention and control, CDC guidelines, 1991 rpt, 4206–2.38

Black Americans social and economic characteristics, for South and total US, 1989-90 and trends from 1969, Current Population Rpt, 2546–1.450

Black children's mineral levels in hair, serum, and urine, for healthy and anemic children, local area study, 1991 article, 4042–3.248

Budget of US, House Budget Committee analysis of Bush Admin proposals and economic assumptions, FY92, 21268–42

Cancer cases, deaths, and survival rates, by sex, race, age, and body site, 1973-88, annual rpt, 4474–35

Census of Population and Housing, 1990: population and housing characteristics, households, and land area, by county, subdiv, and place, State rpt series, 2551–1

Census of Population and Housing, 1990: population and housing selected characteristics, by region, press release, 2328–74

Consumer Expenditure Survey, household income by source, and itemized spending, by selected characteristics and region, 1988-89, annual rpt, 6764–5

Consumer Income, socioeconomic characteristics of persons, families, and households, detailed cross-tabulations, Current Population Rpt series, 2546–6

Costs of rearing children, by expense type and urban-rural location, 1981 and 1989, 4818–5

Costs of rearing children for married couple households, by expenditure type, child's age, income, and region, 1990 and projected to 2007, 1708–87

Diphtheria, tetanus, and pertussis vaccination schedules, dosages, and precautions, CDC recommendations, 1991 rpt, 4206–2.46

Divorces and children involved, by marriage duration, race and age of spouses, and State, 1987 and trends from 1950, US Vital Statistics annual rpt, 4144–4.2

Divorces by age of spouses and duration of marriage, and children involved, by State, 1988 and trends from 1940, US Vital Statistics advance annual rpt, 4146–5.121

Fires on Forest Service land and acres burned, by cause, forest, and State, 1989, annual rpt, 1204–6

Fluoride exposure by source, and health risks and benefits, with research results, 1930s-89, 4048–36

Food spending, by item, household composition, income, age, race, and region, 1980-88, Consumer Expenditure Survey biennial rpt, 1544–30

Foreign countries family composition, poverty status, labor conditions, and welfare indicators and needs, by country, 1960s-88, hearing, 23846–4.30

Health, behavioral, emotional, and school problems of children relation to family structure, by selected characteristics, 1988, 4147–10.178

Health care (primary) research, methodology and findings, 1991 annual conf, 4184–4

Health condition and health care resources, use, and spending, 1950s-89, annual data compilation, 4144–11

Health condition and services use, for children, 1990 chartbook, 4108–49

Health condition improvement and disease prevention goals and recommended activities for 2000, with trends 1970s-80s, 4048–10

Health insurance coverage of children, and children with a regular source of care, by selected characteristics, 1988, 4146–8.192

Heart rate in children relationship to elevated blood pressure and mothers heart rate, 1971-73, article, 4042–3.232

Hispanic Americans social and economic characteristics, by detailed origin, 1991, Current Population Rpt, 2546–1.448; 2546–1.451

Homeless children educational projects, activities, and funding, FY90, annual rpt, 4804–35

Households and family characteristics, by location, 1990, annual Current Population Rpt, 2546–1.447

Households and housing characteristics, unit and neighborhood quality, and journey to work by MSA location, for 11 MSAs, 1984 survey, supplement, 2485–8

Households and housing detailed characteristics, and unit and neighborhood quality, by location, 1987, biennial rpt supplement, 2485–13

Households and housing detailed characteristics, and unit and neighborhood quality, by location, 1989, biennial rpt, 2485–12

Households and housing detailed characteristics, and unit and neighborhood quality, MSA surveys, series, 2485–6

Households composition, income, benefits, and labor force status, Survey of Income and Program Participation methodology, working paper series, 2626–10

Housing inventory change from 1973, by reason, unit and household characteristics, and location, 1983 survey, biennial rpt, 2485–14

Immigrant and nonimmigrant visas of US issued and refused, by class, issuing office, and nationality, FY89, annual rpt, 7184–1

Immigrants admitted to US, by class of admission and for top 15 countries of birth, FY89-90, fact sheet, 6266–2.4; 6266–2.8

Index by Subjects and Names

Chile

Income (household) and poverty status under alternative income definitions, by recipient characteristics, 1990, annual Current Population Rpt, 2546–6.69

Influenza vaccine for *Haemophilus influenza* type b, child dosages and schedules, CDC guidelines, 1991 rpt, 4206–2.37

Injuries and accident deaths of children by cause, and victimization, rates by race, sex, and age, 1979-88, chartbook, 4108–56

Injuries from use of consumer products, by severity, victim age, and detailed product, 1990, annual rpt, 9164–6

Injury rates by presence of injury prevention education program for preschoolers, local area study, 1979-82, article, 4042–3.236

Insurance (health) coverage, uninsured population under age 65 by selected characteristics, 1987, 4186–8.13

Lead levels in environment, sources of emissions and exposure, and health effects, literature review, 1990 rpt, 9198–84

Lead paint in privately owned housing, levels, exposure, and testing and abatement costs, 1990 rpt, 5188–128

Lead poisoning among children, cases and rates by race, and screening tests conducted, for NYC, 1988, article, 4202–7.201

Living arrangements, family relationships, and marital status, by selected characteristics, 1990, annual Current Population Rpt, 2546–1.449

Married couple families income and expenses, and wife's employment status, before and after having children, 1987-89, article, 1702–1.211

Minority group and women health condition, services use, payment sources, and health care labor force, by poverty status, 1940s-89, chartbook, 4118–56

Minority group health condition, services use, costs, and indicators of services need, 1950s-88, 4118–55

Population of children and youth, social, economic, and demographic characteristics, 1950s-90, 4818–5

Population of children from age 10 and from birth, by county, 1988, annual rpt, 6064–12

Population size and characteristics, historical index to *Current Population Rpts,* 1991 listing, 2546–2.160

Poverty status of population and families, by detailed characteristics, 1988-89, annual Current Population Rpt, 2546–6.67

Poverty status of population and families, by detailed characteristics, 1990, annual Current Population Rpt, 2546–6.71

Puerto Rico population and housing characteristics, 1990 Census of Population and Housing, press release, 2328–78

Radiation exposure of population near Hanford, Wash, nuclear plant, with methodology, 1944-66, series, 3356–5

Railroad accidents, casualties, and damage, by cause, railroad, and State, 1990, annual rpt, 7604–1

Research contracts and grants of Natl Inst of Child Health and Human Dev, annual listing, discontinued, 4474–36

Rubella vaccination of children and women of childbearing age, and surveillance, CDC guidelines, 1990 rpt, 4206–2.33

Rural areas children in poverty by selected family characteristics, and compared to urban areas, 1987-88, 1598–270

Smoking exposure of children before and after birth, by source and degree of exposure and family characteristics, 1988, 4146–8.204

State and Metro Area Data Book, 1991 data compilation, 2328–54

Statistical Abstract of US, 1991 annual data compilation, 2324–1

Tax (income) returns for dependents taxed at parents' rate, taxable income, and tax generated, by tax rate and income level, 1987, annual article, 8302–2.211

Virgin Islands population and housing characteristics, 1990 Census of Population and Housing, press release, 2328–81

see also Adoption

see also Aid to Families with Dependent Children

see also Birth defects

see also Births

see also Births out of wedlock

see also Breast-feeding

see also Child abuse and neglect

see also Child day care

see also Child labor

see also Child mortality

see also Child support and alimony

see also Child welfare

see also Compensatory education

see also Educational enrollment

see also Elementary and secondary education

see also Foster home care

see also Handicapped children

see also Head Start Project

see also Infant mortality

see also Juvenile courts and cases

see also Juvenile delinquency

see also Juvenile detention and correctional institutions

see also Old-Age, Survivors, Disability, and Health Insurance

see also Parents

see also Pediatrics

see also Preschool education

see also Remedial education

see also School lunch and breakfast programs

see also Single parents

see also Special education

see also Students

see also Youth

see also Youth employment

see also under By Age in the "Index by Categories"

Children's Safety Network

"Data Book of Child and Adolescent Injury", 4108–56

Childs, Nathan W.

"Domestic Rice Consumption Patterns, 1988/89", 1561–8.204

Chile

Agricultural exports of high-value commodities, indexes and sales by commodity, world area, and country, 1960s-86, 1528–323

Agricultural exports of US, impacts of foreign agricultural and trade policy, with data by commodity and country, 1989, annual rpt, 1924–8

Agricultural production, prices, and trade, by country, 1960s-90, annual world area rpt, 1524–4.2

Agricultural production, trade, and policies in foreign countries, summary data by country, 1989-90, annual factbook, 1924–12

Agricultural subsidies to producers and consumers in 6 Latin America countries, by selected commodity, 1982-87, 1528–324

Agricultural trade of US, by detailed commodity and country, 1989, annual rpt, 1524–8

Agricultural trade of US, by detailed commodity and country, 1990, semiannual rpt, 1522–4

AID economic aid to developing countries, obligations and disbursements by country, quarterly rpt, 9912–4

AID loans repayment status and terms by program and country, and status of predecessor agency loans, quarterly rpt, 9912–3

Background Notes, summary social, political, and economic data, 1990 rpt, 7006–2.14

Economic and military aid and loans from US and intl agencies, by program and country, FY46-90, annual rpt, 9914–5

Economic and social conditions of developing countries from 1960s, and Intl Dev Cooperation Agency and AID activities and funding, FY90-92, annual rpt, 9904–4

Economic conditions, policy, and trade practices, by country, 1988-90, annual rpt, 21384–5

Economic, social, political, and geographic summary data, by country, 1991, annual factbook, 9114–2

Exports and imports of US, by commodity and country, 1970-89, world area rpt, 9116–1.4

Exports and imports of US, by Harmonized System 6-digit commodity and country, 1990, annual rpt, 2424–13

Exports and imports of US, by selected country, country group, and commodity group, 1990, annual rpt, 2044–37

Exports and imports of US, by transport mode, country, and SITC 1- to 3-digit commodity, 1990, annual rpt, 2424–12

Exports of US, detailed Schedule B commodities with countries of destination, 1990, annual rpt, 2424–10

Fish (salmon) aquaculture production of Chile, and exports by market, by species, 1980-89 and projected to 1993, article, 2162–1.204

Grapes (table) and other fruit, acreage, production, and trade, and use, for Chile, selected years 1970-91, article, 1925–34.222

Human rights conditions in 170 countries, and US economic and military aid, 1990, annual rpt, 21384–3

Imports of goods, services, and investment from US, trade barriers, impacts, and US actions, by country, 1990, annual rpt, 444–2

Labor conditions, union coverage, and work accidents, 1991 annual country rpt, 6366–4.47

Military aid of US, arms sales, and training programs costs and budget requests, by program, world region, and country, FY90-92, annual rpt, 7144–13

Chile

Multinatl US firms and foreign affiliates finances and operations, by industry and world area of parent firm, 1989 benchmark survey, preliminary annual rpt, 2704–5

Multinatl US firms foreign affiliates, income statement items by country and world area, 1986, biennial article, 8302–2.212

Steel wire rope from 8 countries, injury to US industry from foreign subsidized and less than fair value imports, investigation with background financial and operating data, 1990 rpt, 9886–19.73

Strawberry trade of US and Mexico, and Mexico and Chile supply and use, 1986-91, annual article, 1925–34.218

Tomato (paste and canned) imports of US, and Chile paste exports, by country, 1986-90, article, 1925–34.211

UN voting record and share of votes in agreement with US, by issue, country, and world area, 1990, annual rpt, 7004–18 *see also* under By Foreign Country in the "Index by Categories"

Chillicothe, Ohio

Wages by occupation, and benefits for office and plant workers, 1991 survey, periodic MSA rpt, 6785–3.5

Chin, E.

"Mineral Industries of China, 1989", 5604–38

Chin, Ko-lin

"Violence as Regulation and Social Control in the Distribution of Crack", 4498–70

China, Nationalist

see Taiwan

China, Peoples Republic

- Agricultural exports of high-value commodities, indexes and sales by commodity, world area, and country, 1960s-86, 1528–323
- Agricultural exports of US, for grains, oilseed products, hides, skins, and cotton, by country, weekly rpt, 1922–3
- Agricultural exports of US, impacts of foreign agricultural and trade policy, with data by commodity and country, 1989, annual rpt, 1924–8
- Agricultural production, prices, and trade, for PRC, 1960s-90, annual rpt, 1524–4.3
- Agricultural production, trade, and policies in foreign countries, summary data by country, 1989-90, annual factbook, 1924–12
- Agricultural trade by commodity and country, prices, and world market devs, monthly rpt, 1922–12
- Agricultural trade of US, by detailed commodity and country, 1989, annual rpt, 1524–8
- Agricultural trade of US, by detailed commodity and country, 1990, semiannual rpt, 1522–4
- Antimony trioxide (refined) from PRC at less than fair value, injury to US industry, investigation with background financial and operating data, 1991 rpt, 9886–14.317
- Bearings (ball) from 14 countries, injury to US industry from foreign subsidized and less than fair value imports, investigation with background financial and operating data, 1991 rpt, 9886–19.74
- Cancer (colorectal) risk related to intake of fat, fiber, and carbohydrates, for Sha Giao, PRC, and San Francisco Chinese, 1991 article, 4472–1.201

Cotton production, trade, and use, for selected countries, FAS monthly circular, 1925–4.2

Drug abuse indicators, for selected countries, 1991 semiannual conf, 4492–5.2

Economic and military aid and loans from US and intl agencies, by program and country, FY46-90, annual rpt, 9914–5

Economic conditions in Communist and OECD countries, 1989, annual rpt, 7144–11

Economic conditions in PRC after 1988 austerity program, with background data, 1978-90, 9118–9

Economic conditions, policy, and trade practices, by country, 1988-90, annual rpt, 21384–5

Economic indicators and reform in PRC, with data for 1950s-90, compilation of papers, 23848–155

Economic indicators, trade balances, and dollar exchange rates, 1991 semiannual rpt, 8002–14

Economic, social, political, and geographic summary data, by country, 1991, annual factbook, 9114–2

Energy use and production, by fuel type, country, and country group, projected 1995-2010 and trends from 1970, annual rpt, 3164–84

Energy use in developing countries, and economic and environmental impacts, by fuel type, world area, and country, 1980s-90, 26358–232

Export licensing, monitoring, and enforcement activities, FY90, annual rpt, 2024–1

Exports and imports, by commodity, 1985-90, annual rpt, 9114–4.8

Exports and imports of NATO members with PRC, by country, 1987-90, annual rpt, 7144–14

Exports and imports of OECD members, by country, 1989, annual rpt, 7144–10

Exports and imports of PRC with US and through Hong Kong, and impacts of revoking most favored nation status, 1987-90, hearing, 25368–174

Exports and imports of US, by commodity and country, 1970-89, world area rpt, 9116–1.7

Exports and imports of US by country, and trade shifts by commodity, 1990, semiannual rpt, 9882–9

Exports and imports of US, by Harmonized System 6-digit commodity and country, 1990, annual rpt, 2424–13

Exports and imports of US, by selected country, country group, and commodity group, 1990, annual rpt, 2044–37

Exports and imports of US, by transport mode, country, and SITC 1- to 3-digit commodity, 1990, annual rpt, 2424–12

Exports and imports of US with Communist countries, by detailed commodity and country, quarterly rpt with articles, 9882–2

Exports, imports, and balances of US with major trading partners, by product category, 1986-90, annual chartbook, 9884–21

Exports of clothing, footwear, luggage, games, toys, and sporting goods to US from PRC and other countries, 1985-90, article, 9882–2.201

Exports of US, detailed Schedule B commodities with countries of destination, 1990, annual rpt, 2424–10

Fans (electric) from PRC at less than fair value, injury to US industry, investigation with background financial and operating data, 1991 rpt, 9886–14.335

Fertilizer use, and effects on agricultural productivity, for selected US regions and PRC, 1989 hearing, 25168–76

Fireworks (sparklers) from PRC at less than fair value, injury to US industry, investigation with background financial and operating data, 1991 rpt, 9886–14.315

GNP estimation methodology and results, 1978-89, with yuan-dollar prices by commodity, 1981, working paper, 2326–18.58

Heart disease deaths and risk factors, for PRC, Finland, and US, 1980s, article, 4042–3.202

Human rights conditions in 170 countries, and US economic and military aid, 1990, annual rpt, 21384–3

Imports of goods, services, and investment from US, trade barriers, impacts, and US actions, by country, 1990, annual rpt, 444–2

Labor conditions and work accidents, 1991 annual country rpt, 6366–4.25

Lug nuts (chrome-plated) from PRC and Taiwan at less than fair value, injury to US industry, investigation with background financial and operating data, 1991 rpt, 9886–14.329

Minerals production and trade of PRC, by commodity, 1988-89, annual rpt, 5604–38

Multinatl US firms and foreign affiliates finances and operations, by industry and world area of parent firm, 1989 benchmark survey, preliminary annual rpt, 2704–5

Nuclear power plant capacity and operating status, by plant and communist and regulated market country, as of Dec 1990, annual rpt, 3164–57.2

Oil production, and exports by country, for PRC, monthly rpt, 9112–2

Oil production and exports to US, by major exporting country, detailed data, monthly rpt with articles, 3162–24

Oil production, trade, use, and stocks, by selected country and country group, monthly rpt, 3162–42

Oil supply, demand, and stock forecasts, by world area, quarterly rpt, 3162–34

Pipe fittings (carbon steel) from 2 countries at less than fair value, injury to US industry, investigation with background financial and operating data, 1991 rpt, 9886–14.319

Ships in world merchant fleet, tonnage, and new ship construction and deliveries, by vessel type and country, as of Jan 1990, annual rpt, 7704–3

Silicon metal from PRC at less than fair value, injury to US industry, investigation with background financial and operating data, 1991 rpt, 9886–14.314

Sodium sulfur compounds from 4 countries at less than fair value, injury to US industry, investigation with background financial and operating data, 1991 rpt, 9886–14.305

Index by Subjects and Names

Chronologies

Soviet Union, China, OECD, and selected other countries economic and military aid, by recipient, 1960s-90, annual rpt, 9114–4.9

Space programs activities, missions, launchings, payloads, and flight duration, for foreign and US programs, 1957-90, annual rpt, 21704–4

Space programs involvement by private sector, govt contracts, costs, revenue, and R&D spending, 1970s-80s and projected to 2000, 26306–6.154

Spacecraft and satellite launches since 1957, quarterly listing, 9502–2

Steel imports of US under voluntary restraint agreement, by product, customs district, and country, with US industry operating data, quarterly rpt, 9882–13

Steel wire rope from 4 countries, injury to US industry from foreign subsidized and less than fair value imports, investigation with background financial and operating data, 1991 rpt, 9886–19.79

Steel wire rope from 8 countries, injury to US industry from foreign subsidized and less than fair value imports, investigation with background financial and operating data, 1990 rpt, 9886–19.73

Sulfanilic acid from PRC at less than fair value, injury to US industry, investigation with background financial and operating data, 1991 rpt, 9886–14.334

Tidal currents, daily time and velocity by station for North America and Asia coasts, forecast 1992, annual rpt, 2174–1.2

Timber in northwestern US and British Columbia, production, prices, trade, and employment, quarterly rpt, 1202–3

Tools from PRC at less than fair value, injury to US industry, investigation with background financial and operating data, 1991 rpt, 9886–14.304

Tungsten ore from PRC at less than fair value, injury to US industry, investigation with background financial and operating data, 1991 rpt, 9886–14.307; 9886–14.332

UN voting record and share of votes in agreement with US, by issue, country, and world area, 1990, annual rpt, 7004–18

Urbanization in PRC, bibl, 1991 working paper, 2326–18.60

see also under By Foreign Country in the "Index by Categories"

Chinese Americans

see Asian Americans

Chiropractic and naturopathy

County Business Patterns, 1988: employment, establishments, and payroll, by SIC 2- to 4-digit industry and county, annual State rpt series, 2326–6

County Business Patterns, 1989: employment, establishments, and payroll, by SIC 2- to 4-digit industry and county, annual State rpt series, 2326–8

Degrees awarded in higher education, by level, field, race, and sex, 1988/89 with trends from 1978/79, biennial rpt, 4844–17

Health condition and health care resources, use, and spending, 1950s-89, annual data compilation, 4144–11

Service industries census, 1987: establishments, receipts by source, payroll, and employment, by SIC 2- to 4-digit kind of business, State, and MSA, 2393–4

Service industries receipts, by SIC 2- to 4-digit kind of business, 1990, annual rpt, 2413–8

Tax (income) returns of sole proprietorships, income statement items, by industry group, 1989, annual article, 8302–2.214

Chlamydia

see Sexually transmitted diseases

Chlorine

see Gases

Chlorofluorocarbons

see Chemicals and chemical industry

Cho, Byung I.

"Trends and Patterns of Methamphetamine Abuse in the Republic of Korea", 4498–75

Chocolate

see Cocoa and chocolate

Choi, Jai

"Sociodemographic and Health Characteristics of Persons by Private Health Insurance Coverage and Type of Plan: U.S., 1975", 4147–16.4

Choi, Won S.

"State Tobacco Prevention and Control Activities: Results of the 1989-90 Association of State and Territorial Health Officials (ASTHO) Survey, Final Report", 4206–2.47

Cholesterol

Cancer (colon) risk relation to serum cholesterol levels, 1965-89 local area study, article, 4472–1.226

Consumption of food, dietary composition, and nutrient intake, 1987/88 natl survey, preliminary rpt series, 1356–1

Deaths and rates, by detailed cause and demographic characteristics, 1988 and trends from 1900, US Vital Statistics annual rpt, 4144–2

Food composition, detailed data on nutrients, calories, and waste, for raw, processed, and prepared foods, series, 1356–3

Health condition and health care resources, use, and spending, 1950s-89, annual data compilation, 4144–11

Health condition improvement and disease prevention goals and recommended activities for 2000, with trends 1970s-80s, 4048–10

Heart disease deaths and risk factors, for PRC, Finland, and US, 1980s, article, 4042–3.202

Minority group and women health condition, services use, payment sources, and health care labor force, by poverty status, 1940s-89, chartbook, 4118–56

Minority group health condition, services use, costs, and indicators of services need, 1950s-88, 4118–55

Navy personnel serum cholesterol levels, by sex, 1989 study, article, 4042–3.215

Christensen, Lee A.

"Outlook for Poultry and Eggs", 1004–16.1

"Overview of International Egg Production and Trade", 1561–7.204

"U.S. Broiler Exports to the USSR: Temporary Phenomena or Emerging Trend?", 1561–7.205

Christensen, Sandra

"Restructuring Health Insurance for Medicare Enrollees", 26306–6.159

Christiano, Lawrence J.

"Modeling the Liquidity Effect of a Money Shock", 9383–6.202

Christiansted, V.I.

Census of Population, 1990: Virgin Islands population by location, press release, 2328–77

Christmas Island

Economic, social, political, and geographic summary data, by country, 1991, annual factbook, 9114–2

Exports and imports of US, by transport mode, country, and SITC 1- to 3-digit commodity, 1990, annual rpt, 2424–12

Chriszt, Michael J.

"European Monetary Union: How Close Is It?", 9371–1.212

Chromium

see Metals and metal industries

Chronic health conditions

see Diseases and disorders

see Health condition

Chronologies

Agricultural cooperatives, membership, farms, and income, historical review, 1913-81, 1128–66

Aircraft accidents, casualties, and damage, for commercial operations by detailed circumstances, 1987, annual rpt, 9614–2

Aircraft accidents, deaths, and circumstances, by carrier and carrier type, preliminary 1990, annual press release, 9614–9

Aircraft hijackings and attempts, persons involved, and location, for US and foreign carriers, 2nd half 1989, semiannual rpt, 7502–5

Aircraft hijackings, on-board explosions, and other crime, US and foreign incidents, 1985-89, annual rpt, 7504–31

Bank deposit insurance programs of OECD members, operations by country, 1970s-80s, technical paper, 9385–8.93

Banks in southeastern States, mergers and acquisitions, assets and major institutions involved, by State, 1984-89, article, 9371–1.203

Banks mergers approved, and assets and offices involved, by instn, 1989, annual rpt, 9294–5

Budget of US, legislative process overview with summary projections and glossary, FY90-95, 21268–43

Capitol Architect outlays for salaries, supplies, and services, itemized by payee and function, 1st half FY91, semiannual rpt, 25922–2

China trade policy changes, Jan 1988-Jan 1991, 9118–9

Consumer Product Safety Commission activities, recalls by brand, and casualties and medical costs, by product type, FY89, annual rpt, 9164–2

Earthquake intensity, time, location, damage, and seismic characteristics, for US and foreign earthquakes, 1985, annual rpt, 5664–13

Earthquakes and other ground motion, intensity by station, 1988, annual rpt, 5664–14

Electric power disturbances, utility, location, customers affected, power losses, cause, and restoration time involved, listing, monthly rpt, 3162–35

Chronologies

Electric power disturbances, utility, location, customers affected, power losses, cause, and restoration time involved, listing, 1989, annual rpt, 3164–11

Environmental and wildlife conservation intl agreements provisions, status, and signatories, as of 1991, listing, 9886–4.169

Exporters (US) antiboycott law violations and fines by firm, and invitations to boycott by country, FY90, annual rpt, 2024–1

Fed Govt civilian pay legislation, 1945-90, annual rpt, 9844–6.7

Fed Govt debt subject to statutory limits, and legislative history, FY40-90 and projected to FY96, annual rpt, 104–2.9

Fed Govt financial and nonfinancial domestic aid programs and changes since 1965, by agency, 1991 base edition with supplements, annual listing, 104–5

Futures and options trading volume, by commodity and exchange, FY90, annual rpt, 11924–2

GATT trade negotiations, objectives and results of each round from 1947, 1991 technical paper, 9385–8.115

House of Representatives salaries, expenses, and contingent fund disbursement, detailed listings, quarterly rpt, 21942–1

Iraq agricultural imports under CCC export credit guarantee programs, FY81-90, GAO rpt, 26123–314

Labor-mgmt collective bargaining agreements expiring during year, and workers covered, by firm, union, industry group, and State, 1991, annual rpt, 6784–9

Medicare provision changes, 1966-95, as of 1991, 26306–6.159

OASDHI, Medicaid, SSI, and related programs benefits, beneficiary characteristics, and trust funds, selected years 1937-89, annual rpt, 4744–3

Persian Gulf War events and UN Security Council resolutions, listing, 1990-91, annual rpt supplement, 3504–13

Senate receipts, itemized expenses by payee, and balances, 1st half FY91, semiannual listing, 25922–1

Space programs activities, missions, launchings, payloads, and flight duration, for foreign and US programs, 1957-90, annual rpt, 21704–4

Spacecraft launches and other activities of NASA and USSR, with flight data, 1957-90, annual rpt, 9504–6.1

Spaceflights (manned) of US and USSR, 1961-90, annual rpt, 9504–9.1

Star position tables, planet coordinates, time conversion factors, and listing of observatories worldwide, 1992, annual rpt, 3804–7

State Dept officers, ambassadors, and Chiefs of US overseas missions, by country and intl agency, 1778-1990, 7008–1

Terrorism (intl) incidents, casualties, and attacks on US targets, by attack type and country, 1990, annual rpt, 7004–22

Terrorism (intl) incidents, casualties, and attacks on US targets, by attack type and world area, 1990, annual rpt, 7004–13

Terrorism incidents in US, related activity, and casualties, by attack type, target, group, and location, 1990, annual rpt, 6224–6

Index by Subjects and Names

Water supply, hydrologic events, and end use, by State, 1988-89, annual rpt, 5664–12

Chrysler Corp.

Energy economy, sales, and market shares, by size and model for domestic and foreign makes, 1991 model year, semiannual rpt, 3302–4

Energy economy test results, 1992 model year, annual rpt, 3304–11

Safety of domestic and foreign autos, crash test results by model, press release series, 7766–7

Chu, Kenneth C.

"Analysis of the Role of Cancer Prevention and Control Measures in Reducing Cancer Mortality", 4472–1.232

Chukchi Sea

Environmental conditions and oil dev impacts for Alaska OCS, compilation of papers, series, 2176–1

Fish catch and habitat impacts of Arctic Ocean oil and gas dev, and assessment methods, 1988 conf, 5738–24

Chula Vista, Calif.

see also under By City in the "Index by Categories"

Church and state

see also Religious liberty

Churches

see Religious organizations

CIA

see Central Intelligence Agency

Cichon, Deborah R.

"International Science and Technology Data Update: 1991", 9627–35

Cigarettes and cigars

see Smoking

see Tobacco industry and products

Cimini, Michael

"Collective Bargaining in 1990: Search for Solutions Continues", 6722–1.207

Cincinnati, Ohio

CPI by component for US city average, and by region, population size, and for 27 metro areas, monthly rpt, 6762–2

Fruit and vegetable shipments, and arrivals in US and Canada cities, by mode of transport and State and country of origin, 1990, annual rpt, 1311–4.1

Wages by occupation, for office and plant workers, 1991 survey, periodic MSA rpt, 6785–12.5

see also under By City and By SMSA or MSA in the "Index by Categories"

Cinema

see Motion pictures

Circulatory diseases

Cases of acute and chronic conditions, disability, absenteeism, and health services use, by selected characteristics, 1987, CD-ROM, 4147–10.177

Deaths and rates, by cause and age, preliminary 1989-90, US Vital Statistics annual rpt, 4144–7

Deaths and rates, by detailed cause and demographic characteristics, 1988 and trends from 1900, US Vital Statistics annual rpt, 4144–2

Hospital discharges and length of stay, by diagnosis, patient and instn characteristics, procedure performed, and payment source, 1988, annual rpt, 4147–13.107

Hospital discharges and length of stay by region and diagnosis, and procedures performed, by age and sex, 1989, annual rpt, 4146–8.198

Hospital discharges by detailed diagnostic and procedure category, primary diagnosis, and length of stay, by age, sex, and region, 1988, annual rpt, 4147–13.105; 4147–13.108

Indian Health Service, tribal, and contract facilities hospitalization, by diagnosis, age, sex, and service area, FY89, annual rpt, 4084–5

see also Blood diseases and disorders

see also Cardiovascular diseases

see also Cerebrovascular diseases

see also Hypertension

see also under By Disease in the "Index by Categories"

Cirrhosis of liver

see Digestive diseases

Cities

Auto insurance cost differentials among cities, premiums and cost factors for selected cities, mid 1980s, working paper, 9383–20.9

Census of Population and Housing, 1990: population and housing characteristics, households, and land area, by county, subdiv, and place, State rpt series, 2551–1

Census of Population, 1990: cities population and undercounts, and related Federal aid losses, 1990 mayoral survey, hearing, 25408–113

Census of Population, 1990: post-enumeration survey results compared to census counts, by race, sex, city, county, and State, press release, 2328–69

Community Dev Block Grant allocation, by State, county, and city, FY84-91, 5128–17

Crimes, arrests by offender characteristics, and rates, by offense, and law enforcement employees, by population size and jurisdiction, 1990, annual rpt, 6224–2

Criminal justice spending, employment, and payroll, by level of govt, State, and selected city and county, FY71-88, biennial rpt, 6064–9

Fed Govt spending in States and local areas, by type, State, county, and city, FY90, annual rpt, 2464–3.2

Gazetteer of US places, mountains, bodies of water, and other political and physical features, 1990 rpt, 5668–117

Govt census, 1987: State and local govt employment, payroll, OASDHI coverage, and employee benefits costs, by level of govt and State, 2455–4

Govt census, 1987: State and local labor-mgmt policies, agreements, and coverage and bargaining units, by function, level of govt, and State, 2455–3

Govt employment and payroll, by function, for 295 largest cities, 1990, annual rpt, 2466–1.2

Govt employment and payroll, by function, level of govt, and State, 1990, annual rpt, 2466–1.1

Govt employment of minorities and women, by occupation, function, pay grade, and level of govt, 1990, annual rpt, 9244–6.3

Govt finances, by level of govt, State, and for large cities and counties, annual rpt series, 2466–2

Govt finances, tax systems and revenue, and fiscal structure, by level of govt and State, 1991 with historical trends, annual rpt, 10044–1

Index by Subjects and Names

Civil aviation

Govt revenue and spending declines, share of cities by region, late 1980s, article, 9375–1.207

Labor surplus areas eligible for preferential Fed Govt contracts, monthly listing, 6402–1

Population size of cities with population over 100,000, as of Apr 1990, biennial press release, 2324–7

Quality of life ratings, for 130 cites, 1979/80, article, 9387–1.202

State and Metro Area Data Book, 1991 data compilation, 2328–54

Statistical Abstract of US, 1991 annual data compilation, 2324–1

see also Blocks, city

see also Census tracts

see also Central cities

see also City and town planning

see also Harbors and ports

see also Metropolitan Statistical Areas

see also Neighborhoods

see also Suburbs

see also Urban areas

see also Wards, city

see also ZIP codes

see also under By City and By SMSA or MSA in the "Index by Categories"

see also under names of individual cities

Citizen-government relations

see Government-citizen relations

Citizen lawsuits

see Government-citizen lawsuits

Citizenship

Criminal cases by type and disposition, and collections, for US attorneys, by Federal district, FY90, annual rpt, 6004–2.1

Criminal defendants for Federal offenses pretrial processing, detention, and release, by defendant characteristics and district, 1988, hearing, 25528–114

Criminal sentences for Federal offenses, guidelines by offense and circumstances, series, 17668–1

DOD civilian employment, by service branch and defense agency, with summary military employment data, quarterly rpt, 3542–16

DOD civilian employment, by US citizenship, service branch, and country, quarterly rpt, 3542–20

Education natl goals progress indicators, by State, 1991, annual rpt, 15914–1

Fed Govt civilian employment, by citizenship status and location, bimonthly rpt, 9842–1

Foreign countries human rights conditions in 170 countries, 1990, annual rpt, 21384–3

Immigrants in US, population characteristics and fertility, by birthplace and compared to native born, 1980s, Current Population rpt, 2546–2.162

Naturalization petitions filed and granted, by Federal district court, 1990, annual rpt, 18204–8.28

Refugee arrivals and resettlement in US, by age, sex, sponsoring agency, State, and country, monthly rpt, 4692–2

see also Alien workers

see also Aliens

see also Foreign medical graduates

see also Foreign students

Citrus fruits

Agricultural Statistics, 1990, annual rpt, 1004–1

Agriculture census, 1987: farms, farmland, production, finances, and operator characteristics, by county, final State rpt series, 2331–1

Agriculture census, 1987: horticultural specialties producers, finances, and operations, by crop and State, 1988 survey, 2337–1

Consumer Expenditure Survey, food spending by item, household composition, income, age, race, and region, 1980-88, biennial rpt, 1544–30

Consumption of food, dietary composition, and nutrient intake, 1987/88 natl survey, preliminary rpt series, 1356–1

Consumption, supply, trade, prices, spending, and indexes, by food commodity, 1989, annual rpt, 1544–4

CPI by component for US city average, and by region, population size, and for 27 metro areas, monthly rpt, 6762–2

Exports and imports (agricultural) of US, by commodity and country, bimonthly rpt, 1522–1

Exports and imports (agricultural) of US, by detailed commodity and country, 1989, annual rpt, 1524–8

Exports and imports (agricultural) of US, by detailed commodity and country, 1990, semiannual rpt, 1522–4

Exports and imports between US and outlying areas, by detailed commodity and mode of transport, 1990, annual rpt, 2424–11

Exports and imports of US, by country and detailed commodity, monthly rpt, 2422–12

Exports and imports of US, by Harmonized System 6-digit commodity and country, 1990, annual rpt, 2424–13

Exports of US, detailed Schedule B commodities with countries of destination, 1990, annual rpt, 2424–10

Farm income, expenses, receipts by commodity, assets, liabilities, and ratios, 1990 and trends from 1945, annual rpt, 1544–16

Farm sector balance sheet, and receipts by detailed commodity, by State, 1985-89, annual rpt, 1544–18

Foreign and US fresh and processed fruit, vegetable, and nut production and trade, FAS monthly circular with articles, 1925–34

Foreign countries agricultural production, prices, and trade, by country, 1980-90 and forecast 1991, annual world area rpt series, 1524–4

Foreign countries agricultural production, trade, and policies, summary data by country, 1989-90, annual factbook, 1924–12

Futures and options trading volume, by commodity and exchange, FY90, annual rpt, 11924–2

Futures trading in selected commodities and financial instruments and indexes, NYC, Chicago, and other markets activity, semimonthly rpt, 11922–5

Imports of fruits and vegetables under quarantine, by crop, country, and port of entry, FY88 annual rpt, 1524–7

Orange juice (frozen) cold storage stocks, by census div, 1990, annual rpt, 1631–11

Orange juice processing plants evaporating capacity, for Mexico by plant and location, 1991, article, 1925–34.214

Orange juice production, use, exports, and stocks, by country, 1985-91, article, 1925–34.231

Oranges (fresh) exports of US, demand indicators for 4 countries, with production, trade, and use, 1960s-90, 1528–317

Oranges and grapefruit production costs for California and Florida, 1988/89, article, 1561–6.201

Price indexes (producer), by stage of processing and detailed commodity, monthly rpt, 6762–6

Price indexes (producer), by stage of processing and detailed commodity, monthly 1990, annual rpt, 6764–2

Prices (farm-retail) for food, marketing cost components, and industry finances and productivity, 1920s-90, annual rpt, 1544–9

Prices (wholesale) for fresh fruit and vegetables in NYC, Chicago, and selected shipping points, by crop, 1990, annual rpt, 1311–8

Prices (wholesale) of fruit and vegetables in NYC by State, and shipments and arrivals by mode of transport, by commodity, weekly rpt, 1311–20

Prices received and paid by farmers, by commodity and State, 1990, annual rpt, 1629–5

Prices received by farmers and production value, by detailed crop and State, 1988-90, annual rpt, 1621–2

Prices received by farmers for major products, and paid for farm inputs and living items, by State, monthly rpt, 1629–1

Production, farms, acreage, and related data, by selected crop and State, monthly rpt, 1621–1

Production, prices, and use of fruit and nuts, 1988-91, annual rpt series, 1621–18

Production, prices, trade, stocks, and use, by selected crop, periodic situation rpt with articles, 1561–6

Shipments by mode of transport, arrivals, and imports, for fruit and vegetables by commodity and State and country of origin, weekly rpt, 1311–3

Shipments of fruit and vegetables, and arrivals in US and Canada cities, by mode of transport and State and country of origin, 1990, annual rpt series, 1311–4

see also under By Commodity in the "Index by Categories"

City and town planning

Community Dev Block Grant activities and funding, by program, FY75-90, annual rpt, 5124–8

Economic Dev Admin activities, and funding by program, recipient, State, and county, FY90 and cumulative from FY66, annual rpt, 2064–2

City taxation

see State and local taxes

Civil aviation

Military airfields joint use by civil aircraft, and effectiveness in reducing airport congestion, FY85-89, GAO rpt, 26113–524

Civil aviation

Pilots and nonpilots certified by FAA, by certificate type, age, sex, region, and State, 1990, annual rpt, 7504–2

Statistical Abstract of US, 1991 annual data compilation, 2324–1.22

Traffic, aircraft, carriers, airports, and FAA activities, detailed data, 1980-89, annual rpt, 7504–1

see also Aerospace industry
see also Air cargo
see also Air piracy
see also Air traffic control
see also Aircraft
see also Airlines
see also Airports and airways
see also Aviation accidents and safety
see also General aviation
see also Pilots

Civil defense

Assistance (financial and nonfinancial) of Fed Govt, 1991 base edition with supplements, annual listing, 104–5

Expenditures of Fed Govt in States, by type, program, agency, and State, FY90, annual rpt, 2464–2

Mgmt of disasters and natl security threats, with data by major event and State, 1991 annual rpt, 9434–6

see also National Guard

Civil engineering

see Bridges and tunnels
see Canals
see Dams
see Harbors and ports
see Highways, streets, and roads
see Irrigation
see Public works
see Reclamation of land
see Rivers and waterways
see Traffic engineering

Civil liberties

see Civil rights
see Due process of law
see Electronic surveillance
see Habeas corpus
see Right of privacy
see Searches and seizures

Civil-military relations

see also Defense contracts and procurement
see also Defense industries
see also Impacted areas

Civil procedure

Appellate court pre-argument conferences impacts on case processing, disposition, and duration, for Federal 6th circuit, 1985-86, 18408–45

DC appeals and superior courts civil and criminal caseloads, 1971-88, hearing, 21308–27

Federal district and appeals court caseloads, actions, procedure duration, judges, and jurors, by court, 1986-91, annual rpt, 18204–3

Federal district, appeals, and bankruptcy courts, civil cases terminated by circuit and district, 1990, annual rpt, 18204–11

Federal district, appeals, and special courts civil and criminal caseloads, by offense, circuit, and district, 1990, annual rpt, 18204–8

Federal district, appeals, and special courts civil and criminal caseloads, 1991, annual rpt, 18204–2

Judicial Conf proceedings and findings, spring 1991, semiannual rpt, 18202–2

Patent and trademark litigation, by court, FY90, annual rpt, 2244–1.5

Securities law enforcement activities of SEC, FY90, annual rpt, 9734–2.3

SSA activities, litigation, finances, and staff, FY90, annual rpt, 4704–6

Statistical Abstract of US, 1991 annual data compilation, 2324–1.5

US attorneys case processing and collections, by case type and Federal district, FY90, annual rpt, 6004–2

US attorneys staffing disparities among district offices, and caseload by litigation type, FY87-90, GAO rpt, 26119–323

see also Administrative law and procedure
see also Adoption
see also Bankruptcy
see also Child support and alimony
see also Claims
see also Contempt of court
see also Contracts
see also Divestiture
see also Evidence
see also Extradition
see also Fines and settlements
see also Government-citizen lawsuits
see also Guardianship
see also Habeas corpus
see also Indian claims
see also Judgments, civil procedure
see also Juries
see also Legal arbitration and mediation
see also Marriage and divorce
see also Tax protests and appeals
see also Torts
see also Trials

Civil rights

Commission on Civil Rights rpts, 1991 listing, 11048–188

Court civil and criminal caseloads for Federal district, appeals, and bankruptcy courts, by type of suit and offense, circuit, and district, 1990, annual rpt, 18204–11

Court civil and criminal caseloads for Federal district, appeals, and special courts, 1990, annual rpt, 18204–8

Court civil and criminal caseloads for Federal district courts, 1991, annual rpt, 18204–2.1

Court criminal cases in Federal district courts, by offense, disposition, and district, 1980-90, last issue of annual rpt, 18204–1

Criminal sentences for Federal offenses, guidelines by offense and circumstances, series, 17668–1

Fed Govt accounts receivable, delinquent debt cases and collections of Justice Dept and private law firms, pilot project results, FY90, annual rpt, 6004–20

Foreign countries human rights conditions in 170 countries, 1990, annual rpt, 21384–3

Helsinki Final Act implementation by NATO and Warsaw Pact, Apr 1990-Mar 1991, last issue of semiannual rpt, 7002–1

UN voting record and share of votes in agreement with US, by issue, country, and world area, 1990, annual rpt, 7004–18

US attorneys case processing and collections, by case type and Federal district, FY90, annual rpt, 6004–2

see also Age discrimination
see also Discrimination against the handicapped

see also Discrimination in credit
see also Discrimination in education
see also Discrimination in employment
see also Discrimination in housing
see also Due process of law
see also Freedom of information
see also Racial discrimination
see also Religious liberty
see also Right of assembly
see also Right of privacy
see also Sex discrimination

Civil Rights Commission

see Commission on Civil Rights

Civil service pensions

Beneficiaries and taxes collected for social insurance programs since 1940, monthly rpt, 4742–1.1

Benefits and beneficiaries of govt pension plans, by type of plan and eligibility, and level of govt, selected years 1954-88, annual article, 4742–1.212

Budget of US, CBO analysis of revenue and spending alternatives and projections of economic indicators, FY92-96, annual rpt, 26304–3

Budget of US, object class analysis of obligations, by agency, FY92, annual rpt, 104–9

Budget of US, obligations and authority by function, agency, and program, with summaries, analyses, and historical tables, FY92, annual rpt, 104–2

Budget of US, receipts by source, outlays by agency and program, and balances, monthly rpt, 8102–3

Census of Govts, 1987: State and local govt employment, payroll, OASDHI coverage, and employee benefits costs, by level of govt and State, 2455–4

Coverage under pension plans by industry, vestment, and recipient income, by participant characteristics, 1987, Current Population Rpt, 2546–20.18

Deaths of beneficiaries, erroneous benefit payments, and use of SSA and other sources of death info, by agency, 1990, GAO rpt, 26121–406

Expenditures, coverage, and benefits for social welfare programs, late 1930s-89, annual rpt, 4744–3.1; 4744–3.3

Expenditures for public welfare by program, FY50s-88, annual article, 4742–1.209

Expenditures of Fed Govt in States, by type, program, agency, and State, FY90, annual rpt, 2464–2

Fed Govt civil service retirement system actuarial valuation, FY79-90 and projected to FY2065, annual rpt, 9844–34

Fed Govt civilian employees demographic and employment characteristics, as of Sept 1990, annual article, 9842–1.201

Fed Govt civilian employees work-years, pay rates, and benefits use and costs, by agency, FY89, annual rpt, 9844–31

Finances of govts, by level of govt, State, and for large cities and counties, annual rpt series, 2466–2

Finances of govts, tax systems and revenue, and fiscal structure, by level of govt and State, 1991 and historical trends, annual rpt, 10044–1

Flow-of-funds accounts, savings, investments, and credit statements, quarterly rpt, 9365–3.3

Index by Subjects and Names

Income (household, family, and personal), by source, detailed characteristics, and region, 1988-89, annual Current Population Rpt, 2546–6.68

Income (household, family, and personal), by source, detailed characteristics, and region, 1990, annual Current Population Rpt, 2546–6.70

Indian Health Service employment of Indians and non-Indians, training, hires, and quits, by occupation, FY89, annual rpt, 4084–6

Judicial Survivors Annuity Fund financial condition and annuitants, June 1982-90, annual rpt, 18204–8.11

Judicial Survivors Annuity Fund financial condition and annuitants, June 1987-91, annual rpt, 18204–2.1

Massachusetts State govt spending and employment by program, revenues by source, debt, and public works financing, compared to other States, 1990 compilation of papers, 9373–4.27

Mortgage loan activity, by type of lender, loan, and mortgaged property, monthly press release, 5142–18

Mortgage loan activity, by type of lender, loan, and mortgaged property, quarterly press release, 5142–30

Postal Service employment and related expenses, FY90, annual rpt, 9864–5.3

Rural areas aged household income sources, and poverty status, 1983-84, 1598–268

Senior Executive Service membership characteristics, entries, exits, and awards, FY79-90, annual rpt, 9844–36

State and local govt retirement systems, cash and security holdings and finances, quarterly rpt, 2462–2

Statistical Abstract of US, 1991 annual data compilation, 2324–1.12

Transit systems finances and operations, by mode of transport, size of fleet, and for 468 systems, 1989, annual rpt, 7884–4

Civil service system

Equal Opportunity Recruitment Program activity, and Fed Govt employment by sex, race, pay grade, and occupational group, FY90, annual rpt, 9844–33

Merit system oversight and enforcement activities of OPM, series, 9496–2

Merit Systems Protection Board decisions on appeals of Fed Govt personnel actions, by agency and region, FY90, annual rpt, 9494–2

Senior Executive Service membership characteristics, entries, exits, and awards, FY79-90, annual rpt, 9844–36

Violations and prohibited political activity reported by Federal employees, cases by type, FY90, annual rpt, 9894–1

see also Civil service pensions

see also Federal employees

see also Labor-management relations in government

see also State and local employees

Civil works

see Public works

Civilian Health and Medical Program of the Uniformed Services

Costs, workload, and enrollment in managed health care demonstration projects for military dependents and retirees, 1988-90, 26306–3.117

Claims

AID economic aid to developing countries, obligations and disbursements by country, quarterly rpt, 9912–4

Aircraft accidents victims compensation, legal costs, and time to disposition, under intl agreements and US liability system, aggregate 1970-84, GAO rpt, 26113–501

Banks (US) and nonbanking firms claims on foreigners, by type and country, *Treasury Bulletin,* quarterly rpt, 8002–4.11

Crime victim compensation and support service applications by disposition, and grant funding by State, 1986-91, GAO rpt, 26119–348

Debt delinquent on Federal accounts, cases and collections of Justice Dept and private law firms, pilot project results, FY90, annual rpt, 6004–20

Fed Govt contingent liabilities and claims paid on insured and guaranteed contracts with foreign obligors, by country and program, periodic rpt, 8002–12

Foreign govt claims of US natls, by claim type and country, 1990, annual rpt, 6004–16

Medical malpractice claims resolution through arbitration and litigation, Michigan program cases, awards, duration, and costs, late 1970s-80s, GAO rpt, 26121–394

Mining claims on public lands, cumulative FY76-90, annual rpt, 5724–1.2

Public lands acreage and use, and Land Mgmt Bur activities and finances, annual State rpt series, 5724–11

Radiation exposure of Navy personnel on nuclear-powered vessels and at support facilities, and injury claims, 1950s-90, annual rpt, 3804–10

Railroad safety violation claims settled, by carrier, FY90, annual rpt, 7604–10

Truck transport of household goods, performance and disposition of damage claims, for selected carriers, 1990, annual rpt, 9484–11

US attorneys civil cases, by type and disposition, FY90, annual rpt, 6004–2.5

see also Crime victim compensation

see also Fines and settlements

see also Indian claims

see also Insurance and insurance industry

see also under specific types of insurance (listed under Insurance and insurance industry)

Clair, Robert T.

"Learning from One Another: The U.S. and European Banking Experience", 9379–12.70

Clark, Donald R., Jr.

"Dicofol (Kelthane) as an Environmental Contaminant: A Review", 5506–12.2

Clark, Michelle A.

"Banking at Credit Unions: An Industry Profile", 9391–16.210

"District Banks in 1990: Bruised, but Not Broken", 9391–16.208

"Government-Sponsored Enterprises: Safe and Sound?", 9391–16.201

"Home Equity Loans: Flexible Enough To Withstand a Real Estate Downturn?", 9391–16.206

Classifications

Clark, Robert L.

"Employee Benefits for American Workers", 15496–1.11

Clarke, Raymond P.

"Application of the Leslie Model to Commercial Catch and Effort of the Slipper Lobster, *Scyllarides squammosus,* Fishery in the Northwestern Hawaiian Islands", 2162–1.203

Clarksville, Tenn.

Water quality, chemistry, hydrology, and other characteristics, 1990 local area study, 5666–27.23

see also under By SMSA or MSA in the "Index by Categories"

Clary, Warren P.

"Small Mammals of a Beaver Pond Ecosystem and Adjacent Riparian Habitat in Idaho", 1208–377

Class actions

see Government-citizen lawsuits

Classifications

AIDS virus and related conditions codes in *Intl Classification of Diseases,* 9th revision, 1991 rpt, 4206–2.45

Census Bur geographic levels of data coverage, maps, and reference products, 1991 pamphlet, 2326–7.79

Census of Population and Housing, 1990: voting age and total population by race, and housing units, redistricting counts required under PL 94-171, State CD-ROM user guide, 2308–63

Computer systems purchase and use, and data recording, processing, and transfer, Fed Govt standards, series, 2216–2

Congressional districts classification codes for Fed Govt use, 1990 listing, 2216–2.193

Education (postsecondary) course completions, by detailed program, sex, race, and instn type, for 1972 high school class, as of 1984, 4888–4

Education curricula classification codes and descriptions, by program area, 1990, rpt, 4828–29

Export and import statistics, Census Bur publications and data files, 1991 guide, 2428–11

Export and import statistics classification codes of Census Bur for countries, 1991 edition, 2428–3

Export and import statistics classification codes of Census Bur for foreign ports, 1991, 2428–12

Export statistics classification codes of Census Bur for countries, commodities, and customs districts, 1990 base edition supplement, 2428–5

Hospital prospective payment system use of diagnostic related groups reflecting case severity and complexity to reduce payment variation, model results, 1986, article, 4652–1.245

Library of Congress activities, acquisitions, services, and financial statements, FY90, annual rpt, 26404–1

Library of Congress rpts and products, 1990, annual listing, 26404–6

Medicare reimbursement of hospitals under prospective payment system, diagnostic group classification evaluations, 1990 rpt, 17206–2.18

Natl income and product accounts benchmark revisions, definition and classification changes, 1929-87, article, 2702–1.221

Classifications

Natl income and product accounts benchmark revisions, new, dropped, and revised tables, 1991 article, 2702–1.224

Nursing home reimbursement by Medicaid, resident classification using patient and care characteristics, New York State, 1990 article, 4652–1.205

Occupational deaths data collection and processing by States, Natl Inst for Occupational Safety and Health guidelines, 1990 rpt, 4248–89

Occupational titles dictionary and classification codes, 1991 base edition and supplements, 6406–1

Oil and gas field codes and locations, 1990, annual listing, 3164–70

Poverty area definitions, and population, by metro-nonmetro location, 1972-89, article, 6722–1.219

Tariff Schedule of US, classifications and rates of duty by detailed imported commodity, 1992 base edition, 9886–13

Textile Agreement Category System import classification codes, correlation with TSUSA, 1992 annual rpt, 2044–31

Wetlands acreage, resources, soil and water properties, and conservation efforts, by wetland type, State rpt series, 5506–11

see also Standard Industrial Classification

see also "Guide to Selected Standard Classifications" section in the back of this Index

Classified information

see Internal security

Clauson, Annette L.

"Costs of Producing and Selling Burley Tobacco: 1989 and Preliminary 1990", 1561–10.201

"Costs of Producing and Selling Flue-Cured Tobacco: 1989, 1990, and Preliminary 1991", 1561–10.205

"Tobacco Cost of Production", 1004–16.1

"1989 and Preliminary 1990 Cost of Production Estimates for Sugarbeet and Sugarcane Operations", 1561–14.202

"1989 Crop Sugarbeet and Sugarcane Production and Processing Costs", 1561–14.205

"1990 and Preliminary 1991 Cost of Production Estimates for Sugarbeet and Sugarcane Operations", 1561–14.208

Clay industry and products

Business statistics, detailed data for major industries and economic indicators, *Survey of Current Business*, monthly rpt, 2702–1.21

County Business Patterns, 1988: employment, establishments, and payroll, by SIC 2- to 4-digit industry and county, annual State rpt series, 2326–6

County Business Patterns, 1989: employment, establishments, and payroll, by SIC 2- to 4-digit industry and county, annual State rpt series, 2326–8

Employment, earnings, and hours, by SIC 1- to 4-digit industry, monthly and annual averages, selected years 1909-90, annual rpt, 6744–4

Exports and imports between US and outlying areas, by detailed commodity and mode of transport, 1990, annual rpt, 2424–11

Exports and imports of building materials, by commodity and country, 1989-90, article, 2042–1.204

Index by Subjects and Names

Exports and imports of US, by country and detailed commodity, monthly rpt, 2422–12

Exports and imports of US, by Harmonized System 6-digit commodity and country, 1990, annual rpt, 2424–13

Exports and imports of US, by transport mode, country, and SITC 1- to 3-digit commodity, 1990, annual rpt, 2424–12

Exports and imports of US shipped through Canada, by detailed commodity, customs district, and country, 1989, annual rpt, 7704–11

Exports of US, detailed commodities by country, monthly CD-ROM, 2422–13

Exports of US, detailed Schedule B commodities with countries of destination, 1990, annual rpt, 2424–10

Hwy construction material use by type, and spending, by State, various periods 1944-90, annual rpt, 7554–29

Imports, exports, and employment impacts, by SIC 2- to 4-digit industry and commodity, quarterly rpt, 2322–2

Imports of US, detailed commodities by country, monthly CD-ROM, 2422–14

Labor productivity, indexes of output, hours, and employment by SIC 2- to 4-digit industry, 1967-89, annual rpt, 6824–1.3

Manufacturing annual survey, 1989: finances and operations, by SIC 2- to 4-digit industry, series, 2506–15

Manufacturing census, 1987: finances and operations, by SIC 2- to 4-digit industry, State, and MSA, with trends from 1849, 2497–1

Manufacturing census, 1987: finances and operations, by type of organization and SIC 2- to 4-digit industry, subject rpt, 2497–5

Manufacturing finances and operations, by SIC 2- to 4-digit industry, forecast 1991, annual rpt, 2044–28

Mineral industries census, 1987: energy use and costs, by fuel type, SIC 2- to 4-digit industry, and State, subject rpt, 2517–2

Mineral industries census, 1987: finances and operations, by establishment characteristics, SIC 2- to 4-digit industry, and State, subject rpt, 2517–1

Mineral industries census, 1987: finances and operations, by SIC 2- to 4-digit industry, State, and county, census div rpt series, 2515–1

Mineral Industry Surveys, commodity review of production, trade, and use, 1989, advance annual rpt, 5614–5.3

Mineral Industry Surveys, State reviews of production, 1990, preliminary annual rpt, 5614–6

Minerals Yearbook, 1988, Vol 3: foreign country reviews of production, trade, and policy, by commodity, annual rpt series, 5604–17

Minerals Yearbook, 1989, Vol 1: commodity review of production, reserves, supply, use, and trade, annual rpt, 5604–15.17

Minerals Yearbook, 1989, Vol 2: State reviews of production and sales by commodity, and business activity, annual rpt series, 5604–16

Minerals Yearbook, 1989, Vol 2: State reviews of production, sales, and firms, by commodity, and business activity, annual rpt, 5604–34

Occupational injuries and incidence, employment, and hours in nonmetallic minerals mines and related operations, 1989, annual rpt, 6664–1

Occupational injury and illness rates, by SIC 2- to 4-digit industry, 1988-89, annual rpt, 6844–7

Occupational injury and illness rates, by SIC 2- to 4-digit industry, 1989, annual rpt, 6844–1

Pollution (air) emissions factors, by detailed pollutant and source, data compilation, 1990 rpt, 9198–120

Price indexes (producer), by stage of processing and detailed commodity, monthly rpt, 6762–6

Price indexes (producer), by stage of processing and detailed commodity, monthly 1990, annual rpt, 6764–2

Production, prices, trade, use, employment, tariffs, and stockpiles, by mineral, with foreign comparisons, 1986-90, annual rpt, 5604–18

Production, reserves, and use of industrial minerals, and characteristics of individual deposits, State rpt series, 5606–10

Production, shipments, and PPI for building materials, by type, bimonthly rpt, 2042–1.5; 2042–1.6

Production, shipments, trade, and stocks, by clay product, periodic Current Industrial Rpt series, 2506–9

Taiwan imports of building materials, and share from US, by commodity, 1989-90, article, 2042–1.205

Technologically advanced structural materials devs, use, and R&D funding, for ceramics, metal alloys, polymers, and composites, 1960s-80s and projected to 2000, 5608–162

see also Pottery and porcelain products

see also under By Commodity in the "Index by Categories"

see also under By Industry in the "Index by Categories"

Clean Air Act

Coal production and mining employment effects of Clean Air Act, by region, projected 2000-2010, annual rpt, 3164–68

Electric power plants production and capacity by fuel type, prices, demand, and air pollution law impacts, by region, 1989-90 and projected to 2010, annual rpt, 3164–81

Energy natl strategy plans for conservation and pollution reduction, impacts on electric power supply, costs, and emissions, projected under alternative assumptions, 1995-2030, 3166–6.49

Enforcement of environmental legislation by EPA and State govts, activities, FY90, annual rpt, 9184–21

Clean Water Act

Enforcement of environmental legislation by EPA and State govts, activities, FY90, annual rpt, 9184–21

EPA and State govt identification of polluted water locations and sources, activities, 1991, GAO rpt, 26113–536

Wastewater treatment facilities in small communities, construction and repair needs to meet Clean Water Act standards, by State and region, 1988 and 2008, 1588–155

Index by Subjects and Names

Clinics

Cleaning services
see Domestic workers and services
see Janitorial and maintenance services
see Laundry and cleaning services

Clearwater, Fla.
Housing starts and completions authorized by building permits in 40 MSAs, quarterly rpt, 2382–9
see also under By SMSA or MSA in the "Index by Categories"

Clemency
Criminal case processing in Federal courts, by offense, disposition, and jurisdiction, data compilation, 1991 annual rpt, 6064–6.5
Executions, commutations of sentence, and other removals of inmates from death row, data compilation, 1991 annual rpt, 6064–6.6
Prison and parole admissions and releases, sentence length, and time served, by offense and offender characteristics, 1985, annual rpt, 6064–33
Prisoners released from sentences and death row, by reason and State, 1989, annual rpt, 6064–26.4; 6064–26.6
Prisoners removed from death row, by reason, 1973-90, annual rpt, 6066–25.42
see also Pardons

Clergy
Health care facilities of VA, Medicine and Surgery Dept chaplaincy trainees by city, FY90, annual rpt, 8704–4
Prisons Bur admin offices and correctional instns, facility characteristics, 1991, annual listing, 6244–4
see also Missions and missionaries

Clerical workers
Air traffic control and airway facilities staff, by employment and other characteristics, FY89, annual rpt, 7504–41
DOT employment, by subagency, occupation, and selected personnel characteristics, FY90, annual rpt, 7304–18
Earnings, annual average percent changes for selected occupational groups, selected MSAs, monthly rpt, 6782–1.1
Employee benefit plan coverage and provisions in small businesses, by plan type and occupational group, 1990, biennial rpt, 6784–20
Employment, earnings, and hours, monthly press release, 6742–5
Employment situation, earnings, hours, and other BLS economic indicators, transcripts of BLS Commissioner's monthly testimony, periodic rpt, 23846–4
Employment, unemployment, and labor force characteristics, by region, State, and selected metro area, 1990, annual rpt, 6744–7
Health maintenance organizations enrollment and availability for production and office workers, by industry div, selected metro area, and region, 1984-89, article, 6722–1.222
Immigrants admitted to US, by occupational group and country of birth, preliminary FY90, annual table, 6264–1
Income (household, family, and personal), by source, detailed characteristics, and region, 1988-89, annual Current Population Rpt, 2546–6.68

Income (household, family, and personal), by source, detailed characteristics, and region, 1990, annual Current Population Rpt, 2546–6.70
Manufacturing employment, by detailed occupation and SIC 2-digit industry, 1989 survey, triennial rpt, 6748–52
Puerto Rico economic censuses, 1987: wholesale and retail trade sales by customer class, and employment, by SIC 2- and 3-digit kind of business, subject rpt, 2591–2.2
State and local govt employment of minorities and women, by occupation, function, pay level, and State, 1990, annual rpt, 9244–6
Temporary help supply establishments by occupation supplied, receipts by source, and payroll, by MSA, 1987 Census of Service Industries, 2393–4.8
Wholesale trade census, 1987: establishments, sales by customer class, employment, inventories, and expenses, by SIC 2- to 4-digit kind of business, 2407–4
see also Area wage surveys
see also Industry wage surveys
see also under By Occupation in the "Index by Categories"

Cleveland County, Okla.
Housing and households characteristics, unit and neighborhood quality, and journey to work by MSA location, for 11 MSAs, 1984 survey, supplement, 2485–8
Housing and households detailed characteristics, and unit and neighborhood quality, by location, 1988 survey, MSA rpt, 2485–6.6

Cleveland, Linda E.
"Report on the Diet and Health Knowledge Survey", 1004–16.1

Cleveland, Ohio
Auto and auto parts manufacturing wages, employment, and benefits, by occupation, region, and selected labor market area, 1989 survey, 6787–6.252
CPI by component for US city average, and by region, population size, and for 15 metro areas, monthly rpt, 6762–1
CPI by component for US city average, and by region, population size, and for 27 metro areas, monthly rpt, 6762–2
Drug test results at arrest, by drug type, offense, and sex, for selected urban areas, quarterly rpt, 6062–3
Financial instns location relation to ZIP code area income and minority population, by instn type for 5 cities, 1977-89, article, 9377–1.208
Housing and households characteristics, unit and neighborhood quality, and journey to work by MSA location, for 11 MSAs, 1984 survey, supplement, 2485–8
Housing and households characteristics, 1988 survey, MSA fact sheet, 2485–11.5
Housing and households detailed characteristics, and unit and neighborhood quality, by location, 1988 survey, MSA rpt, 2485–6.3
Wages by occupation, for office and plant workers, 1991 survey, periodic MSA rpt, 6785–12.7
see also under By City and By SMSA or MSA in the "Index by Categories"

Clifton, Daphne G.
"Sources and Concentrations of Dissolved Solids and Selenium in the San Joaquin River and Its Tributaries, California, October 1985-March 1987", 5666–27.5

Climate
see Global climate change
see Meteorology
see Weather

Clinical laboratory technicians
AIDS virus antibody testing lab staff, by type of test, Aug 1991, article, 4042–3.256
Employment, earnings, and hours, by SIC 1- to 4-digit industry, monthly and annual averages, selected years 1909-90, annual rpt, 6744–4
Employment of medical and dental labs, by State, 1987 Census of Service Industries, 2393–4.12
Hepatitis B cases, exposure, and vaccination policies for students in nursing and lab technician training programs, 1989, article, 4042–3.244
Military health care personnel, and accessions by training source, by occupation, specialty, and service branch, FY89, annual rpt, 3544–24
VA health care staff and turnover, by occupation, physician specialty, and location, 1990, annual rpt, 8604–8
VA Medicine and Surgery Dept trainees, by detailed program and city, FY90, annual rpt, 8704–4

Clinics
County Business Patterns, 1988: employment, establishments, and payroll, by SIC 2- to 4-digit industry and county, annual State rpt series, 2326–6
County Business Patterns, 1989: employment, establishments, and payroll, by SIC 2- to 4-digit industry and county, annual State rpt series, 2326–8
Drug abuse prevalence among minorities, related health effects and crime, treatment, and research status and needs, mid 1970s-90, 4498–72
Drug and alcohol abuse treatment and prevention programs of States, funding, facilities, and patient characteristics, FY89, 4488–15
Drug and alcohol abuse treatment facilities, services, use, funding, staff, and client characteristics, 1989, biennial rpt, 4494–10
Food aid program of USDA for women, infants, and children, participants and costs by State and Indian agency, FY88, annual tables, 1364–12
Food aid program of USDA for women, infants, and children, participants by race, State, and Indian agency, Apr 1990, annual rpt, 1364–16
Food aid program of USDA for women, infants, and children, participants, clinics, and costs, by State and Indian agency, monthly tables, 1362–16
Indian Health Service facilities and use, and Indian health and other characteristics, by IHS region, 1980s-89, annual chartbook, 4084–7
Indian Health Service facilities, funding, operations, and Indian health and other characteristics, 1950s-90, annual chartbook, 4084–1

Clinics

Indian Health Service outpatient visits, by facility and IHS service area, FY89-90, annual rpt, 4084–8

Medicaid beneficiaries and payments, by service type, FY72-89, annual rpt, 4744–3.6

Medicaid beneficiaries emergency room visits relation to availability of other sources of care, for upstate New York, 1985-87, article, 4652–1.232

Medicaid demonstration projects evaluation, for 6 States, 1988 rpt, 4658–45

Medicaid services use and costs in alternative treatment settings, model description and results, FY87, article, 4652–1.211

Medicare and Medicaid beneficiaries and program operations, 1991, annual fact book, 4654–18

Medicare and Medicaid eligibility, participation, coverage, and program finances, various periods 1966-91, biennial rpt, 4654–1

Mental health care facilities, finances, caseload, staff, and characteristics of instn and patients, 1988, 4506–4.14

Mental health care facilities, staff, and patient characteristics, *Statistical Notes* series, 4506–3

Military health care facilities of DOD in US and abroad, admissions, beds, outpatient visits, and births, by service branch, quarterly rpt, 3542–15

NIH activities, funding by program and recipient type, staff, and clinic patients, by inst, FY90, annual rpt, 4434–3

Occupational injury and illness rates, by SIC 2- to 4-digit industry, 1988-89, annual rpt, 6844–7

Physicians payments, charges by specialty and treatment setting, and assignment rate by State, for Medicare, 1970s-88, article, 4652–1.240

Receipts for services, by SIC 2- to 4-digit kind of business, 1990, annual rpt, 2413–8

Service industries census, 1987: establishments, receipts by source, payroll, and employment, by SIC 2- to 4-digit kind of business, State, and MSA, 2393–4

VA mental health care services, staff, research, and training programs, 1991 biennial listing, 8704–2

Veterans health care, patients, visits, costs, and operating beds, by VA and contract facility, and region, quarterly rpt, 8602–4

Waste (medical) generation, sources, health worker exposure and risk, and incineration emissions, 1980s, 4078–1

see also Clinical laboratory technicians

see also Hospitals

see also Medical examinations and tests

Clocks

see Watches and clocks

Clothing and clothing industry

Business statistics, detailed data for major industries and economic indicators, *Survey of Current Business*, monthly rpt, 2702–1.22

Caribbean Basin Initiative investment incentives, economic impacts, with finances and employment by country, 1984-90, 2048–141

Child rearing costs of married couple households, by expenditure type, child's age, income, and region, 1990 and projected to 2007, 1708–87

Collective bargaining agreements expiring during year, and workers covered, by firm, union, industry group, and State, 1991, annual rpt, 6784–9

Consumer Expenditure Survey, household income by source, and itemized spending, by selected characteristics and region, 1988-89, annual rpt, 6764–5

Consumer Expenditure Survey, spending by category, and income, by selected household characteristics and location, 1990, annual press release, 6726–1.42

Consumer Expenditure Survey, spending by category, selected household characteristics, and region, quarterly rpt, 6762–14

Consumer spending, natl income and product accounts, *Survey of Current Business*, monthly rpt, 2702–1.25

County Business Patterns, 1988: employment, establishments, and payroll, by SIC 2- to 4-digit industry and county, annual State rpt series, 2326–6

County Business Patterns, 1989: employment, establishments, and payroll, by SIC 2- to 4-digit industry and county, annual State rpt series, 2326–8

CPI by component for US city average, and by region, population size, and for 27 metro areas, monthly rpt, 6762–2

CPI components relative importance, by selected MSA, region, population size, and for US city average, 1990, annual rpt, 6884–1

Employment, earnings, and hours, by SIC 1- to 4-digit industry, monthly and annual averages, selected years 1909-90, annual rpt, 6744–4

Employment in manufacturing, by detailed occupation and SIC 2-digit industry, 1989 survey, triennial rpt, 6748–52

Employment, unemployment, and labor force characteristics, by region and census div, 1990, annual rpt, 6744–7.1

Energy use and prices for manufacturing industries, 1988 survey, series, 3166–13

Enterprise Statistics, 1987: auxiliaries of multi-establishment firms, finances and operations by function, industry, and State, 2329–6

Enterprise Statistics, 1987: finances and operations for companies, by size, level of diversification, form of organization, and industry group, 2329–8

Expenditures for clothing, by type, 1982-90, article, 1702–1.209

Exports and imports between US and outlying areas, by detailed commodity and mode of transport, 1990, annual rpt, 2424–11

Exports and imports of US, by country and detailed commodity, monthly rpt, 2422–12

Exports and imports of US by country, and trade shifts by commodity, 1990, semiannual rpt, 9882–9

Exports and imports of US, by Harmonized System 6-digit commodity and country, 1990, annual rpt, 2424–13

Exports and imports of US, by selected country, country group, and commodity group, 1990, annual rpt, 2044–37

Exports and imports of US, by transport mode, country, and SITC 1- to 3-digit commodity, 1990, annual rpt, 2424–12

Exports of US, detailed commodities by country, monthly CD-ROM, 2422–13

Exports of US, detailed Schedule B commodities with countries of destination, 1990, annual rpt, 2424–10

Franchise business opportunities by firm and kind of business, and sources of aid and info, 1990 annual listing, 2104–7

Import restrictions proposed for textiles, apparel, and shoes, economic impacts, projected 1991-2000, with imports by country, 1989-90, 26306–6.162

Imports, exports, and employment impacts, by SIC 2- to 4-digit industry and commodity, quarterly rpt, 2322–2

Imports of clothing, footwear, luggage, toys, games, and sporting goods from PRC and other countries, 1985-90, article, 9882–2.201

Imports of textiles, by country of origin, monthly rpt, 2042–27

Imports of textiles, by product and country of origin, monthly rpt series, 2046–8; 2046–9

Imports of textiles, total and from US, by commodity and country, 1987-89, 2048–155

Imports of textiles under Multifiber Arrangement by product and country, and status of bilateral agreements, 1987-90, annual rpt, 9884–18

Imports of US, detailed commodities by country, monthly CD-ROM, 2422–14

Imports of US given duty-free treatment for value of US material sent abroad, by commodity and country, 1989, annual rpt, 9884–14

Injuries from use of consumer products, by severity, victim age, and detailed product, 1990, annual rpt, 9164–6

Input-output structure of US economy, detailed interindustry transactions for 84 industries, and components of final demand, 1986, annual article, 2702–1.206

Input-output structure of US economy, detailed interindustry transactions for 85 industries, 1982 benchmark data, 2702–1.213

Labor productivity, indexes of output, hours, and employment by SIC 2- to 4-digit industry, 1967-89, annual rpt, 6824–1.3

Manufacturing annual survey, 1989: finances and operations, by SIC 2- to 4-digit industry, series, 2506–15

Manufacturing census, 1987: finances and operations, by SIC 2- to 4-digit industry, State, and MSA, with trends from 1849, 2497–1

Manufacturing census, 1987: finances and operations, by type of organization and SIC 2- to 4-digit industry, subject rpt, 2497–5

Manufacturing finances and operations, by SIC 2- to 4-digit industry, forecast 1991, annual rpt, 2044–28

Manufacturing production, shipments, inventories, orders, and pollution control costs, periodic Current Industrial Rpt series, 2506–3

Mexico imports from US, by industry and State, 1987-90, 2048–154

Index by Subjects and Names

Natl income and product accounts and components, *Survey of Current Business*, monthly rpt, 2702–1.24

Occupational injury and illness rates, by SIC 2- to 4-digit industry, 1988-89, annual rpt, 6844–7

Occupational injury and illness rates, by SIC 2- to 4-digit industry, 1989, annual rpt, 6844–1

OECD trade, total and for 4 major countries, and US trade by country, by commodity, 1970-89, world area rpt series, 9116–1

Older persons clothing expenses, by selected characteristics, 1987, 1702–1.202

Price indexes (producer), by stage of processing and detailed commodity, monthly rpt, 6762–6

Price indexes (producer), by stage of processing and detailed commodity, monthly 1990, annual rpt, 6764–2

Production, shipments, trade, and use of clothes, by product, periodic Current Industrial Rpt series, 2506–6

Puerto Rico and other US possessions corporations income tax returns, income and tax items, and employment, by selected industry, 1987, article, 8302–2.213

Puerto Rico economic censuses, 1987: wholesale and retail trade and service industry finances and operations, by SIC 2- to 4-digit industry and municipio, 2591–1

Puerto Rico economic censuses, 1987: wholesale, retail, and service industries finances and operations, by establishment characteristics and SIC 2- and 3-digit industry, subject rpts, 2591–2

Retail trade census, 1987: depreciable assets, capital and operating expenses, sales, value added, and inventories, by SIC 2- to 4-digit kind of business, 2399–2

Retail trade census, 1987: finances and employment, for establishments with and without payroll, by SIC 2- to 4-digit kind of business, State, and MSA, 2401–1

Retail trade sales and inventories, by kind of business, region, and selected State, MSA, and city, monthly rpt, 2413–3

Retail trade sales, by kind of business, advance monthly rpt, 2413–2

Retail trade sales, inventories, purchases, gross margin, and accounts receivable, by SIC 2- to 4-digit kind of business and form of ownership, 1989, annual rpt, 2413–5

Soviet Union GNP by detailed income and outlay component, 1985, 2326–18.59

Statistical Abstract of US, 1991 annual data compilation, 2324–1.27

Tax (income) returns of corporations, income and tax items by asset size and detailed industry, 1987, annual rpt, 8304–4

Tax (income) returns of corporations, income and tax items by asset size and detailed industry, 1988, annual rpt, 8304–21

Tax (income) returns of corporations with foreign tax credit, income and tax items by industry group, 1986, biennial article, 8302–2.203

Tax (income) returns of sole proprietorships, income statement items, by industry group, 1989, annual article, 8302–2.214

Thefts, and value of property stolen and recovered, by property type, 1990, annual rpt, 6224–2.1

Wholesale trade census, 1987: depreciable assets, capital and operating expenses, sales, value added, and inventories, by SIC 2- to 3-digit kind of business, 2407–2

Wholesale trade census, 1987: establishments, sales by customer class, employment, inventories, and expenses, by SIC 2- to 4-digit kind of business, 2407–4

see also Shoes and shoe industry

see also under By Commodity in the "Index by Categories"

see also under By Industry in the "Index by Categories"

Clover

see Animal feed

see Pasture and rangeland

CMEA

see Council for Mutual Economic Assistance

Coady, Sean

"Government Policies and Programs Affecting Tobacco Production and Trade in Major Tobacco Trading Nations", 1561–10.206

Coal and coal mining

Alaska minerals resources, production, oil and gas leases, reserves, and exploratory wells, with maps and bibl, 1989, annual rpt, 5664–11

Back injuries in underground coal mines, by circumstances, victim characteristics, and treatment, mid 1980s, 5608–166

Birds (raptors) population, habitat, and reproductive success, for coal mining areas of Montana and Wyoming, 1970s-80s, technical rpt, 5506–12.1

Business statistics, detailed data for major industries and economic indicators, *Survey of Current Business*, monthly rpt, 2702–1.18

China economic indicators and reform issues, with background data, 1950s-90, compilation of papers, 23848–155

Consumption of energy, by air pollutant source, fuel type, and State, annual rpt, discontinued, 9194–14

Consumption of energy, by detailed fuel type, end-use sector, and State, 1960-89, State Energy Data System annual rpt, 3164–39

County Business Patterns, 1988: employment, establishments, and payroll, by SIC 2- to 4-digit industry and county, annual State rpt series, 2326–6

County Business Patterns, 1989: employment, establishments, and payroll, by SIC 2- to 4-digit industry and county, annual State rpt series, 2326–8

Developing countries energy use, and economic and environmental impacts, by fuel type, world area, and country, 1980s-90, 26358–232

Electric power and industrial plants prohibited from oil and gas primary use, and gas use by State, 1977-90, annual rpt, 3334–1

Electric power plants (steam) fuel receipts, costs, and quality, by fuel, plant, utility, and State, 1990, annual rpt, 3164–42

Electric power plants and capacity, by fuel used, owner, location, and operating status, 1990 and for units planned 1991-2000, annual listing, 3164–36

Coal and coal mining

Electric power plants production and capacity by fuel type, prices, demand, and air pollution law impacts, by region, 1989-90 and projected to 2010, annual rpt, 3164–81

Electric power plants production and capital costs, operations, and fuel use, by fuel type, plant, utility, and location, 1989, annual rpt, 3164–9

Electric power plants production, capacity, sales, and fuel stocks, use, and costs, by State, 1985-89, annual rpt, 3164–11

Electric power plants production, fuel use, stocks, and costs by fuel type, and sales, by State, monthly rpt with articles, 3162–35

Electric utilities coal shipments under contract and rates, by firm, transport mode, and region, 1979-87, 3168–121

Employment, earnings, and hours, by SIC 1- to 4-digit industry, monthly and annual averages, selected years 1909-90, annual rpt, 6744–4

Energy Info Admin and alternative estimates of coal production, labor hours, and production value, by State, with methodology, 1983-88, 3166–12.6

Enterprise Statistics, 1987: auxiliaries of multi-establishment firms, finances and operations by function, industry, and State, 2329–6

Enterprise Statistics, 1987: finances and operations for companies, by size, level of diversification, form of organization, and industry group, 2329–8

Environmental Quality, status of problems, protection programs, research, and intl issues, 1991 annual rpt, 484–1

Explosives and blasting agents use, by type, industry, and State, 1990, Mineral Industry Surveys, annual rpt, 5614–22

Exports and imports between US and outlying areas, by detailed commodity and mode of transport, 1990, annual rpt, 2424–11

Fed Govt and Indian land oil, gas, and minerals production and revenue, by State, 1990 and trends from 1920, annual rpt, 5734–2

Fed Govt and Indian land oil, gas, and minerals production, revenue, and leasing, by State, 1980s and trends from 1920, 5738–21

Fed Govt coal leasing activity, acreage, production, and reserves, by coal region and State, FY90, annual rpt, 5724–10

Fed Govt energy use and efficiency, by agency and fuel type, FY90, annual rpt, 3304–22

Finances and operations, by SIC 2- to 4-digit industry, forecast 1991, annual rpt, 2044–28

Finances and operations of energy producers, by energy type for US firms domestic and foreign operations, 1989, annual rpt, 3164–44

Foreign and US coal trade flows and reserves, by country, 1980-89 and projected to 2010, annual rpt, 3164–77

Foreign and US energy production, trade, use, and reserves, and oil and refined products supply and prices, by country, 1980-89, annual rpt, 3164–50

Foreign and US energy use and production, by fuel type, country, and country group, projected 1995-2010 and trends from 1970, annual rpt, 3164–84

Coal and coal mining

Foreign countries electric power generation by fuel type, and fuel switching from oil to coal capability, by country, 1973-89, article, 3162–37.201

Foreign direct investment in US energy sources by type and firm, and US affiliates operations, as of 1989, annual rpt, 3164–80

Great Lakes area economic conditions and outlook, for US and Canada, 1970s-90, 9375–15

Housing and households detailed characteristics, and unit and neighborhood quality, by location, 1989, biennial rpt, 2485–12

Housing and households detailed characteristics, and unit and neighborhood quality, MSA surveys, series, 2485–6

Housing inventory change from 1973, by reason, unit and household characteristics, and location, 1983 survey, biennial rpt, 2485–14

Injuries by circumstances, employment, and hours, for mining industries by type of operation and State, quarterly rpt, 6662–1

Input-output structure of US economy, detailed interindustry transactions for 84 industries, and components of final demand, 1986, annual article, 2702–1.206

Input-output structure of US economy, detailed interindustry transactions for 85 industries, 1982 benchmark data, 2702–1.213

Labor productivity, indexes of output, hours, and employment by SIC 2- to 4-digit industry, 1967-89, annual rpt, 6824–1.2

Manufacturing corporations financial statements, by selected SIC 2- to 3-digit industry, quarterly rpt, 2502–1

Manufacturing energy use and prices, 1988 survey, series, 3166–13

Methane production in coal fields, and proved reserves, by State, 1989-90, 3164–46.3

Methane production in coal fields by basin, and resources remaining, 1970s-89, article, 3162–4.201

Mineral industries census, 1987: energy use and costs, by fuel type, SIC 2- to 4-digit industry, and State, subject rpt, 2517–2

Mineral industries census, 1987: finances and operations, by establishment characteristics, SIC 2- to 4-digit industry, and State, subject rpt, 2517–1

Mineral industries census, 1987: finances and operations, by SIC 2- to 4-digit industry, State, and county, census div rpt series, 2515–1

Minerals Yearbook, 1988, Vol 3: foreign country reviews of production, trade, and policy, by commodity, annual rpt series, 5604–17

Natl Energy Strategy, coal liquids production under alternative oil price and technology assumptions, projected 2000-2030, 3166–6.53

Natl Energy Strategy plans for conservation and pollution reduction, impacts of technology and regulation proposals, projected 1990-2030, 3166–6.47

Natl Energy Strategy plans for conservation and pollution reduction, impacts on electric power supply, costs, and emissions, projected under alternative assumptions, 1995-2030, 3166–6.49

Occupational deaths in mining accidents, by circumstances and selected victim characteristics, semiannual rpt series, 6662–3

Occupational injuries and incidence, employment, and hours in coal mines and related operations, 1989, annual rpt, 6664–4

Occupational injuries and incidence, employment, and hours in metal mines and related operations, 1989, annual rpt, 6664–3

Occupational injury and illness rates, by SIC 2- to 4-digit industry, 1988-89, annual rpt, 6844–7

Occupational injury and illness rates, by SIC 2- to 4-digit industry, 1989, annual rpt, 6844–1

Occupational safety and health enforcement, training, and funding, with casualties, by type of mine and State, FY89, annual rpt, 6664–6

Pollution (air) abatement equipment shipments by industry, and new and backlog orders, by product, 1990, annual Current Industrial Rpt, 2506–12.5

Pollution (air) contributing to global warming, emissions factors and control costs, by pollutant and source, 1990 rpt, 9198–124

Pollution (air) emissions factors, by detailed pollutant and source, data compilation, 1990 rpt, 9198–120

Pollution (air) levels for 6 pollutants, by source, 1970-89 and trends from 1940, annual rpt, 9194–13

Production and mines by county, prices, productivity, miners, and reserves, by mining method and State, 1989-90, annual rpt, 3164–25

Production and reserves of oil and gas, and coal production, by major country and world area, late 1930s-90, article, 9371–1.213

Production by State and region, trade, use, and stocks, weekly rpt, 3162–1

Production, dev, and distribution firms revenues and income, quarterly rpt, 3162–38

Production, prices, exports, and use by sector, for coal, with data by region, projected 1995-2010 and trends from 1970, annual rpt, 3164–68

Production, reserves, and use of industrial minerals, and characteristics of individual deposits, 1991 State rpt, 5606–10.1

Production, stocks, and shipments of coal by State, end-use sector, and mode of transport, quarterly rpt, 3162–8

Public lands acreage, grants, use, revenues, and allocations, by State, FY90, annual rpt, 5724–1.2

Reclamation of coal mining land, Office of Surface Mining Reclamation and Enforcement activities and funding, by State and Indian tribe, FY77-90, annual rpt, 5644–1

Respiratory diseases related to occupational hazards, epidemiology, diagnosis, and treatment, for selected industries and work settings, 1988 conf, 4248–90

Soviet Union, Eastern Europe, OECD, and selected other countries energy reserves, production, and use, and oil trade and revenue, 1960s-90, annual rpt, 9114–4.4

Index by Subjects and Names

Soviet Union GNP by detailed income and outlay component, 1985, 2326–18.59

State and Metro Area Data Book, 1991 data compilation, 2328–54

Statistical Abstract of US, 1991 annual data compilation, 2324–1.19; 2324–1.25

Subsidence of land above coal mines, State property insurance program income and expenses in 6 States, 1990, GAO rpt, 26113–530

Supply, demand, and distribution of energy, and regulatory impacts, series, 3166–6

Supply, demand, and prices, by fuel type and end-use sector, alternative projections 1989-2010, annual rpt, 3164–75

Supply, demand, and prices, by fuel type and end-use sector, projections and underlying assumptions, 1990-2010, annual rpt, 3164–90

Supply, demand, and prices, by fuel type and end-use sector, with foreign comparisons, 1990 and trends from 1949, annual rpt, 3164–74

Supply, demand, and prices, by fuel type, end-use sector, and country, detailed data, monthly rpt with articles, 3162–24

Supply, demand, and prices of energy, forecasts by resource type, quarterly rpt, 3162–34

Supply, demand, prices, trade, and stocks of coal, coke, and breeze, by end-use sector and State, quarterly rpt with articles, 3162–37

Tax (excise) on coal and other black lung trust fund receipts, fund disbursements, and claims and benefits by State, 1990, annual rpt, 6504–3

Tax (income) returns of corporations, income and tax items by asset size and detailed industry, 1987, annual rpt, 8304–4

Tax (income) returns of corporations, income and tax items by asset size and detailed industry, 1988, annual rpt, 8304–21

Tax (income) returns of corporations with foreign tax credit, income and tax items by industry group, 1986, biennial article, 8302–2.203

Tax (income) returns of sole proprietorships, income statement items, by industry group, 1989, annual article, 8302–2.214

Water quality, chemistry, hydrology, and other characteristics, local area studies, series, 5666–27

Wholesale trade census, 1987: establishments, sales by customer class, employment, inventories, and expenses, by SIC 2- to 4-digit kind of business, 2407–4

see also Black lung disease

see also Coal exports and imports

see also Coal prices

see also Coal reserves

see also Coal stocks

see also under By Commodity in the "Index by Categories"

see also under By Industry in the "Index by Categories"

Coal exports and imports

Business statistics, detailed data for major industries and economic indicators, *Survey of Current Business*, monthly rpt, 2702–1.18

Index by Subjects and Names — Coal stocks

Electric utilities coal imports, by utility and country of origin, 1986-90, annual rpt, 3164–42

Exports and imports of coal, by country of origin and destination, 1988, annual rpt, 3164–50.4

Exports and imports of US, by country and detailed commodity, monthly rpt, 2422–12

Exports and imports of US, by Harmonized System 6-digit commodity and country, 1990, annual rpt, 2424–13

Exports and imports of US, by selected country, country group, and commodity group, 1990, annual rpt, 2044–37

Exports and imports of US, by transport mode, country, and SITC 1- to 3-digit commodity, 1990, annual rpt, 2424–12

Exports and imports of US shipped through Canada, by detailed commodity, customs district, and country, 1989, annual rpt, 7704–11

Exports, imports, and average price, by country of destination and origin, weekly rpt, monthly data, 3162–1.2

Exports of coal from US and other countries, by world area of destination, projected 1995-2010 and trends from 1970, annual rpt, 3164–68

Exports of coal to Canada by mode of transport, and overseas, by State of origin, quarterly rpt, 3162–8

Exports of US, detailed commodities by country, monthly CD-ROM, 2422–13

Exports of US, detailed Schedule B commodities with countries of destination, 1990, annual rpt, 2424–10

Foreign and US coal trade flows and reserves, by country, 1980-89 and projected to 2010, annual rpt, 3164–77

Imports, exports, and employment impacts, by SIC 2- to 4-digit industry and commodity, quarterly rpt, 2322–2

Imports of US, detailed commodities by country, monthly CD-ROM, 2422–14

Mexico imports from US, by industry and State, 1987-90, 2048–154

Minerals Yearbook, 1988, Vol 3: foreign country reviews of production, trade, and policy, by commodity, annual rpt series, 5604–17

Natl Energy Strategy, coal liquids production under alternative oil price and technology assumptions, projected 2000-2030, 3166–6.53

Natl Energy Strategy plans for conservation and pollution reduction, impacts of technology and regulation proposals, projected 1990-2030, 3166–6.47

OECD trade, total and for 4 major countries, and US trade by country, by commodity, 1970-89, world area rpt series, 9116–1

Statistical Abstract of US, 1991 annual data compilation, 2324–1.25

Supply, demand, and prices, by fuel type and end-use sector, alternative projections 1989-2010, annual rpt, 3164–75

Supply, demand, and prices, by fuel type and end-use sector, with foreign comparisons, 1990 and trends from 1949, annual rpt, 3164–74

Supply, demand, and prices, by fuel type, end-use sector, and country, detailed data, monthly rpt with articles, 3162–24

Supply, demand, and prices of energy, forecasts by resource type, quarterly rpt, 3162–34

Supply, demand, prices, trade, and stocks of coal, coke, and breeze, by end-use sector and State, quarterly rpt with articles, 3162–37

Coal prices

Business statistics, detailed data for major industries and economic indicators, *Survey of Current Business,* monthly rpt, 2702–1.18

Electric power plants (steam) fuel receipts, costs, and quality, by fuel, plant, utility, and State, 1990, annual rpt, 3164–42

Electric power plants production, capacity, sales, and fuel stocks, use, and costs, by State, 1985-89, annual rpt, 3164–11

Electric power plants production, fuel use, stocks, and costs by fuel type, and sales, by State, monthly rpt with articles, 3162–35

Electric utilities coal receipts, use, stocks, and delivered price, by State, and import and export prices, weekly rpt, monthly data, 3162–1.2

Energy Info Admin and alternative estimates of coal production, labor hours, and production value, by State, with methodology, 1983-88, 3166–12.6

Housing energy prices, by fuel and State, 1989 and forecast 1990-91, 3166–6.54

Natl Energy Strategy, coal liquids production under alternative oil price and technology assumptions, projected 2000-2030, 3166–6.53

Natl Energy Strategy plans for conservation and pollution reduction, impacts of technology and regulation proposals, projected 1990-2030, 3166–6.47

OECD energy prices, by fuel type and end use, for 10 countries, 1980-89 annual rpt, 3164–50.6

Prices and spending for fuel, by type, end-use sector, and State, 1989, annual rpt, 3164–64

Prices, production, exports, and use by sector, for coal, with data by region, projected 1995-2010 and trends from 1970, annual rpt, 3164–68

Prices, productivity, miners, reserves, and production and mines by county, by mining method and State, 1989-90, annual rpt, 3164–25

Prices, supply, and demand, by fuel type and end-use sector, alternative projections 1989-2010, annual rpt, 3164–75

Prices, supply, and demand, by fuel type and end-use sector, projections and underlying assumptions, 1990-2010, annual rpt, 3164–90

Prices, supply, and demand, by fuel type and end-use sector, with foreign comparisons, 1990 and trends from 1949, annual rpt, 3164–74

Prices, supply, and demand of energy, forecasts by resource type, quarterly rpt, 3162–34

Prices, supply, demand, trade, and stocks of coal, coke, and breeze, by end-use sector and State, quarterly rpt with articles, 3162–37

Producer price indexes, by stage of processing and detailed commodity, monthly rpt, 6762–6

Producer price indexes, by stage of processing and detailed commodity, monthly 1990, annual rpt, 6764–2

Coal reserves

Energy Info Admin and alternative estimates of coal production, labor hours, and production value, by State, with methodology, 1983-88, 3166–12.6

Fed Govt coal leasing activity, acreage, production, and reserves, by coal region and State, FY90, annual rpt, 5724–10

Foreign and US coal trade flows and reserves, by country, 1980-89 and projected to 2010, annual rpt, 3164–77

Foreign and US energy reserves, by type of fuel and country, as of Jan 1990, annual rpt, 3164–50.7

Minerals Yearbook, 1988, Vol 3: foreign country reviews of production, trade, and policy, by commodity, annual rpt series, 5604–17

Producers finances and operations, by energy type for US firms domestic and foreign operations, 1989, annual rpt, 3164–44.4

Public lands minerals resources and availability, State rpt series, 5606–7

Reserves, prices, productivity, miners, and production and mines by county, by mining method and State, 1989-90, annual rpt, 3164–25

Soviet Union, Eastern Europe, OECD, and selected other countries energy reserves, production, and use, and oil trade and revenue, 1960s-90, annual rpt, 9114–4.4

State and Metro Area Data Book, 1991 data compilation, 2328–54

Supply, demand, and prices, by fuel type and end-use sector, with foreign comparisons, 1990 and trends from 1949, annual rpt, 3164–74

Coal stocks

Business statistics, detailed data for major industries and economic indicators, *Survey of Current Business,* monthly rpt, 2702–1.18

Electric power plants production, capacity, sales, and fuel stocks, use, and costs, by State, 1985-89, annual rpt, 3164–11

Electric power plants production, fuel use, stocks, and costs by fuel type, and sales, by State, monthly rpt with articles, 3162–35

Electric utilities coal receipts, use, stocks, and delivered price, by State, weekly rpt, monthly data, 3162–1.2

Electric utilities, coke plants, and other industry stocks of coal, monthly rpt, 3162–24.6

Electric utilities, coke plants, other industrial, producer, and distributor coal stocks, and total coke and breeze stocks, quarterly rpt with articles, 3162–37

Stocks of coal, by State, quarterly rpt, 3162–8

Supply, demand, and prices, by fuel type and end-use sector, with foreign comparisons, 1990 and trends from 1949, annual rpt, 3164–74.4

Supply, demand, and prices, by fuel type, end-use sector, and country, detailed data, monthly rpt with articles, 3162–24

Supply, demand, and prices of energy, forecasts by resource type, quarterly rpt, 3162–34

Coast Guard

Coast Guard

Accidents involving merchant ships, and casualties, by circumstances and characteristics of persons and vessels involved, 1988, annual rpt, 7404–11

Accidents involving ships and marine facilities, casualties, and circumstances, Coast Guard investigation results, periodic rpt, 9612–4

Boat registrations, and accidents, casualties, and damage by cause, by vessel characteristics and State, 1990, annual rpt, 7404–1

Budget of US, obligations and authority by function, agency, and program, with summaries, analyses, and historical tables, FY92, annual rpt, 104–2

Courts (military) cases and actions, FY90, annual rpt, 3504–3

Criminal case processing in military courts, and prisoners by facility, by service branch, data compilation, 1991 annual rpt, 6064–6.5

Drug enforcement training of US for foreign govts, enrollment in US and host countries by program, 1989-90, annual rpt, 7004–17

Drug, immigration, and fisheries enforcement activities of USCG, 2nd half FY91, semiannual rpt, 7402–4

Employment of DOT, by subagency, occupation, and selected personnel characteristics, FY90, annual rpt, 7304–18

Expenditures of Fed Govt in States, by type, program, agency, and State, FY90, annual rpt, 2464–2

Oil spill from tanker Exxon Valdez, Federal cleanup and damage assessment costs, and reimbursement from Exxon, by agency, as of Sept 1990, GAO rpt, 26113–510

Oil spill from tanker Glacier Bay, cleanup costs and area economic benefits, with data by firm and agency, 1987, 5736–5.15

Recalls of recreational boats and engines with safety-related defects, by make, periodic listing, 7402–5

Search and rescue missions, and lives and property lost and saved, by USCG district and assisting unit, FY90, annual rpt, 7404–2

Statistical Abstract of US, 1991 annual data compilation, 2324–1.11

Women military personnel on active and reserve duty, by demographic and service characteristics and service branch, FY89, annual chartbook, 3544–26

see also Coast Guard Reserve

Coast Guard Reserve

Personnel and equipment strengths, and readiness, by reserve component, FY90, annual rpt, 3544–31

Personnel strengths and characteristics, by reserve component, FY90, annual rpt, 3544–38

Personnel strengths and characteristics, by reserve component, quarterly rpt, 3542–4

Personnel strengths for reserve components, by selected characteristics, FY90, annual rpt, 3544–1.5

Coastal areas

Alaska submerged land grant holdings of Alaska Natives, exchange for upland acreage, impacts on conservation acreage and acquisition, 1989-90, 5728–38

Birds (waterfowl) coastal population and breeding success, for murre and kittiwake in Bering Sea colonies, 1979-89, 5738–31

California OCS oil and gas dev impacts on water quality, marine life, and sediments, by site, 1986-89, annual rpt, 5734–11

Coast Guard search and rescue missions, and lives and property lost and saved, by district and assisting unit, FY90, annual rpt, 7404–2

Environmental and socioeconomic conditions, and potential impact of oil and gas OCS leases, final statement series, 5736–1

Environmental conditions, fish, wildlife, use, and mgmt, for individual coastal and riparian ecosystems, series, 5506–9

Environmental conditions of coastal areas and estuaries, research results and methodology, series, 2176–7

Environmental Quality, status of problems, protection programs, research, and intl issues, 1991 annual rpt, 484–1

Fish (groundfish) juvenile population distribution by species, for New England area, 1968-86, 2168–122

Fish and shellfish catch, life cycles, and environmental needs, for selected coastal species and regions, series, 5506–8

Fish catch, trade, use, and fishery operations, with selected foreign data, by species, 1980s-90, annual rpt, 2164–1

Fish kills in coastal areas related to pollution and natural causes, by land use, State, and county, 1980s, 2178–32

Fish larvae abundance, distribution, and growth, for selected Western Hemisphere sites, 1989 conf, 2168–126

Florida environmental, social, and economic conditions, and impacts of proposed OCS oil and gas leases in southern coastal areas, 1990 compilation of papers, 5738–19

Global climate change environmental, infrastructure, and health impacts, with model results and background data, 1850s-2100, 9188–113

Landfills distance from wetlands and water habitats, for 11 States, 1990 rpt, 9188–115

Manatees (West Indian) population off Puerto Rico, and sightings by coastal region, 1976-89, 14738–11

Manatees grazing effects on seagrass, by southeast Florida site, 1987-89, 14738–12

Marine Fisheries Review, US and foreign fisheries resources, dev, mgmt, and research, quarterly journal, 2162–1

Marine mammals and birds population and distribution, by species and northeast Pacific Ocean location, literature and data base review, 1950s-88, 5738–28

Marine mammals strandings on land, physical characteristics and tests performed, for New England, 1970s, 14738–8

Middle Atlantic States tide height and tidal current velocity daily at selected coastal stations, forecast 1992, annual rpt, 2174–11

New York Bight pollution levels, sources, treatment costs, economic losses, and environmental and health effects, 1990 conf, 9208–131

North Carolina environmental and socioeconomic conditions, and impacts of proposed OCS oil and gas exploration, 1970s-90 and projected to 2020, 5738–22

Ocean surface temperature by ocean and for US coastal areas, and Bering Sea ice conditions, monthly rpt, 2182–5

Older persons migration to southern coastal areas, household finances, services needs, and local economic impacts, for selected counties, 1990, 2068–38

Pacific Ocean coast pollutant concentrations in fish and sediments, by contaminant, fish species, and site, 1984-86, 2168–121

Pollutant concentrations in coastal and estuarine fish, shellfish, and environment, series, 2176–3

Pollution (water) fish kills, by pollution source, month, location, and State, 1977-87, last issue of annual rpt, 9204–3

Recreation (outdoor) coastal facilities and finances, by site and level of govt, State rpt series, discontinued, 2176–6

Recreation (outdoor) coastal facilities, by State, county, estuary, and level of govt, 1972-84, 2178–29

Recreation (outdoor) coastal facilities of Fed Govt and States, visitor and site characteristics, 1987-90 survey, regional rpt series, 2176–9

Seals (harbor) population and physical characteristics at selected Washington State coastal sites, 1975-80, 14738–7

Tidal currents, daily time and velocity by station for North America and Asia coasts, forecast 1992, annual rpts, 2174–1

Tide height and time daily at coastal points worldwide, forecast 1992, annual rpt series, 2174–2

Washington State marine sanctuaries proposal, environmental and economic impacts, with background data, 1984-89, 2178–30

Water (saline) withdrawal and use, for coastal areas, State rpt series, 5666–24

Wetlands acreage, resources, soil and water properties, and conservation efforts, by wetland type, State rpt series, 5506–11

see also Chesapeake Bay

see also Continental shelf

see also Estuaries

see also Harbors and ports

see also New York Bight

see also Offshore mineral resources

see also Offshore oil and gas

see also Puget Sound

see also Raritan Bay

see also San Francisco Bay

see also Seashores

see also Territorial waters

see also Wetlands

Coates, Edward M., III

"Profit Sharing Today: Plans and Provisions", 6722–1.223

Cobalt

see Metals and metal industries

Coble, R. W.

"Ground-Water Level Data for North Carolina, 1987", 5666–28.1

Cocaine

Abuse of cocaine and marijuana reported in household and telephone surveys, data accuracy, 1988, article, 4042–3.230

Index by Subjects and Names

Cocoa and chocolate

Abuse of cocaine, related emergency room admissions, by user and use characteristics, for major metro areas, 1987-89, article, 4042–3.204

Abuse of cocaine, user characteristics, and related crime and violence, 1988 conf, 4498–74

Abuse of drugs and alcohol, by selected characteristics, 1990 survey, biennial rpt, 4494–5

Abuse of drugs, emergency room admissions and deaths, by drug type and source, sex, race, age, and major metro area, 1990, annual rpt, 4494–8

Abuse of drugs, indicators for selected metro areas, research results, data collection, and policy issues, 1991 semiannual conf, 4492–5

Abuse of drugs, State treatment and prevention programs, funding, facilities, and patient characteristics, FY89, 4488–15

Abuse of drugs, treatment, biological and behavioral factors, and addiction potential of new drugs, research results, 1990 annual conf, 4494–11

Andean countries cocaine and alternative crop production and impacts on US agricultural exports, with data for Bolivia, 1980s-91, GAO rpt, 26123–366

Arrests for drug- and nondrug-related offenses, urine test results by drug type, offense, and sex, for selected urban areas, quarterly rpt, 6062–3

Coast Guard drug, immigration, and fisheries enforcement activities, 2nd half FY91, semiannual rpt, 7402–4

Customs Service activities, collections, entries processed by mode of transport, and seizures, FY86-90, annual rpt, 8144–1

Deaths and rates, by detailed cause and demographic characteristics, 1988 and trends from 1900, US Vital Statistics annual rpt, 4144–2

Enforcement activities of drug control task forces by drug type and State, and organization, staff, and spending, 1988, 6068–244

Expenditures of users for illegal drugs, by user group and substance, 1988-90, 236–2.1

Fed Govt drug abuse and trafficking reduction programs activities, funding, staff, and Bush Admin budget request, by Federal agency and program area, FY90-92, 238–2

Fed Govt drug smuggling interdiction programs, budget, and seizures, FY87-90, GAO rpt, 26119–318

Foreign countries drug production, eradication, and seizures, by illegal substance, with US aid, by country, 1987-91, annual rpt, 7004–17

Health condition and health care resources, use, and spending, 1950s-89, annual data compilation, 4144–11

Jail population, by sociodemographic characteristics, criminal and drug use history, whether convicted, offense, and sentencing, 1989, annual rpt, 6064–26.3

Labs for illegal drug manufacture, seizures by substance and location, 1989-90, annual rpt, 6284–3

Latin America cocaine production, eradication, and seizures, by country, 1988-90, 236–2.1

Minority group drug abuse prevalence, related health effects and crime, treatment, and research status and needs, mid 1970s-90, 4498–72

Minority group health condition, services use, costs, and indicators of services need, 1950s-88, 4118–55

Neurological, cognitive, and behavioral residual effects of long-term drug abuse, 1989 conf, 4498–69

Organized Crime Drug Enforcement Task Forces regional investigation activities by agency and region, FY83-90, biennial rpt, 6004–17

Peru cocaine production, acreage, and economic impacts of crop eradication and conversion to legitimate agricultural use, 1960s-87, 9918–19

Public opinion on crime and crime-related issues, by respondent characteristics, data compilation, 1991 annual rpt, 6064–6.2

Research on drug abuse and treatment, summaries of findings, resource materials, and grant listings, periodic rpt, 4492–4

Research on drug abuse, prevention, treatment, and health impacts, as of 1990, triennial rpt, 4498–68

Rural areas drug and alcohol abuse, related crime, and treatment, by substance and State, 1988-90, GAO rpt, 26131–79

Sentences for Federal offenses, guidelines by offense and circumstances, series, 17668–1

Supply of drugs in US by country of origin, abuse, prices, and seizures, by substance, 1990, annual rpt, 6284–2

Testing for drugs, urinalysis methods accuracy by drug type, 1991, 6066–26.6

Treatment facilities for drug and alcohol abuse, services, use, funding, staff, and client characteristics, 1989, biennial rpt, 4494–10

Treatment services for drug and alcohol abuse, funding, staffing, and client load, characteristics, and outcomes, by setting, 1989 conf, 4498–73

Violent and criminal behavior relation to drug abuse, with data on street gang activity and selected population groups, 1989 conf, 4498–70

Youth drug, alcohol, and cigarette use and attitudes, by substance type and selected characteristics, 1975-90 surveys, annual rpt, 4494–4

Cochrane, Nancy J.

"Agricultural Privatization and Land Reform in Central Europe", 1522–3.202

Cocoa and chocolate

Agricultural Statistics, 1990, annual rpt, 1004–1

Business statistics, detailed data for major industries and economic indicators, *Survey of Current Business,* monthly rpt, 2702–1.14

Consumption, supply, trade, prices, spending, and indexes, by food commodity, 1989, annual rpt, 1544–4

County Business Patterns, 1988: employment, establishments, and payroll, by SIC 2- to 4-digit industry and county, annual State rpt series, 2326–6

County Business Patterns, 1989: employment, establishments, and payroll, by SIC 2- to 4-digit industry and county, annual State rpt series, 2326–8

Exports (agricultural) of high-value commodities, indexes and sales value by commodity, world area, and country, 1960s-86, 1528–323

Exports and imports (agricultural) of US, by commodity and country, bimonthly rpt, 1522–1

Exports and imports (agricultural) of US, by detailed commodity and country, 1989, annual rpt, 1524–8

Exports and imports (agricultural) of US, by detailed commodity and country, 1990, semiannual rpt, 1522–4

Exports and imports of US, by country and detailed commodity, monthly rpt, 2422–12

Exports and imports of US, by Harmonized System 6-digit commodity and country, 1990, annual rpt, 2424–13

Exports and imports of US, by transport mode, country, and SITC 1- to 3-digit commodity, 1990, annual rpt, 2424–12

Exports of US, detailed Schedule B commodities with countries of destination, 1990, annual rpt, 2424–10

Foreign and US cocoa and cocoa products production, prices, and trade, 1980s-92, FAS semiannual circular, 1925–9

Foreign countries agricultural production, prices, and trade, by country, 1980-90 and forecast 1991, annual world area rpt series, 1524–4

Foreign countries agricultural production, trade, and policies, summary data by country, 1989-90, annual factbook, 1924–12

Futures and options trading volume, by commodity and exchange, FY90, annual rpt, 11924–2

Futures trading in selected commodities and financial instruments and indexes, NYC, Chicago, and other markets activity, semimonthly rpt, 11922–5

Imports and quotas of dairy products, by commodity and country of origin, FAS monthly rpt, 1925–31

Manufacturing annual survey, 1989: finances and operations, by SIC 2- to 4-digit industry, series, 2506–15

Manufacturing census, 1987: finances and operations, by SIC 2- to 4-digit industry, State, and MSA, with trends from 1849, 2497–1

Manufacturing census, 1987: finances and operations, by type of organization and SIC 2- to 4-digit industry, subject rpt, 2497–5

Nutrient, caloric, and waste composition, detailed data for raw, processed, and prepared snacks and sweets, 1991 rpt, 1356–3.16

Occupational injury and illness rates, by SIC 2- to 4-digit industry, 1988-89, annual rpt, 6844–7

Occupational injury and illness rates, by SIC 2- to 4-digit industry, 1989, annual rpt, 6844–1

OECD trade, total and for 4 major countries, and US trade by country, by commodity, 1970-89, world area rpt series, 9116–1

Cocoa and chocolate

Price indexes (producer), by stage of processing and detailed commodity, monthly rpt, 6762–6

Price indexes (producer), by stage of processing and detailed commodity, monthly 1990, annual rpt, 6764–2

Shipments, trade, use, and ingredients, by confectionery product, 1990, annual Current Industrial Rpt, 2506–4.5

Coconut oil

see Oils, oilseeds, and fats

Cody, Brian J.

"Monetary and Exchange Rate Policies in Anticipation of a European Central Bank", 9387–8.238

Coffee

Africa (sub-Saharan) agricultural conditions by country, with Ethiopia grain production and use, and dev aid by major donor, 1960s-80s, hearing, 23848–216

Agricultural Statistics, 1990, annual rpt, 1004–1

Business statistics, detailed data for major industries and economic indicators, *Survey of Current Business,* monthly rpt, 2702–1.14

Consumer Expenditure Survey, food spending by item, household composition, income, age, race, and region, 1980-88, biennial rpt, 1544–30

Consumption of food, dietary composition, and nutrient intake, 1987/88 natl survey, preliminary rpt series, 1356–1

Consumption per capita of selected beverages, 1970s-90, FAS annual circular, 1925–15.3

Consumption, supply, trade, prices, spending, and indexes, by food commodity, 1989, annual rpt, 1544–4

County Business Patterns, 1988: employment, establishments, and payroll, by SIC 2- to 4-digit industry and county, annual State rpt series, 2326–6

County Business Patterns, 1989: employment, establishments, and payroll, by SIC 2- to 4-digit industry and county, annual State rpt series, 2326–8

CPI by component for US city average, and by region, population size, and for 27 metro areas, monthly rpt, 6762–2

Exports and imports (agricultural) of US, by commodity and country, bimonthly rpt, 1522–1

Exports and imports (agricultural) of US, by detailed commodity and country, 1989, annual rpt, 1524–8

Exports and imports (agricultural) of US, by detailed commodity and country, 1990, semiannual rpt, 1522–4

Exports and imports of US, by country and detailed commodity, monthly rpt, 2422–12

Exports and imports of US, by Harmonized System 6-digit commodity and country, 1990, annual rpt, 2424–13

Exports and imports of US, by transport mode, country, and SITC 1- to 3-digit commodity, 1990, annual rpt, 2424–12

Exports of US, detailed Schedule B commodities with countries of destination, 1990, annual rpt, 2424–10

Farm income, expenses, receipts by commodity, assets, liabilities, and ratios, 1990 and trends from 1945, annual rpt, 1544–16

Foreign countries agricultural production, prices, and trade, by country, 1980-90 and forecast 1991, annual world area rpt series, 1524–4

Foreign countries agricultural production, trade, and policies, summary data by country, 1989-90, annual factbook, 1924–12

Futures and options trading volume, by commodity and exchange, FY90, annual rpt, 11924–2

Futures trading in selected commodities and financial instruments and indexes, NYC, Chicago, and other markets activity, semimonthly rpt, 11922–5

Hypertensive persons monitoring own blood pressure at home, health condition and risk behavior, local area study, 1991 article, 4042–3.207

Manufacturing annual survey, 1989: finances and operations, by SIC 2- to 4-digit industry, series, 2506–15

Manufacturing census, 1987: finances and operations, by SIC 2- to 4-digit industry, State, and MSA, with trends from 1849, 2497–1

Manufacturing census, 1987: finances and operations, by type of organization and SIC 2- to 4-digit industry, subject rpt, 2497–5

Occupational injury and illness rates, by SIC 2- to 4-digit industry, 1988-89, annual rpt, 6844–7

Occupational injury and illness rates, by SIC 2- to 4-digit industry, 1989, annual rpt, 6844–1

OECD trade, total and for 4 major countries, and US trade by country, by commodity, 1970-89, world area rpt series, 9116–1

Pollution (air) emissions factors, by detailed pollutant and source, data compilation, 1990 rpt, 9198–120

Price indexes (producer), by stage of processing and detailed commodity, monthly rpt, 6762–6

Price indexes (producer), by stage of processing and detailed commodity, monthly 1990, annual rpt, 6764–2

Prices received and paid by farmers, by commodity and State, 1990, annual rpt, 1629–5

Prices received by farmers and production value, by detailed crop and State, 1988-90, annual rpt, 1621–2

Production, farms, acreage, and related data, by selected crop and State, monthly rpt, 1621–1

Production, trade and quotas, and use, by country, with US and intl prices, FAS periodic circular, 1925–5

Research on drug abuse and treatment, biological and behavioral factors, and addiction potential of new drugs, 1990 annual conf, 4494–11

Soviet Union, Eastern Europe, OECD, and selected other countries agricultural production, by commodity, 1960s-90, annual rpt, 9114–4.5

Cogeneration of heat and electricity

see Electric power and heat cogeneration

Cohabitation

see Living arrangements

Index by Subjects and Names

Cohen, Robyn L.

"Prisoners in 1990", 6066–25.37

Cohen, Steven B.

"Data Collection Organization Effects in the National Medical Expenditure Survey", 4188–68

"Sample Design of the 1987 Household Survey. National Medical Expenditure Survey", 4186–8.21

Coins and coinage

Budget of US, receipts by source, outlays by agency and program, and balances, monthly rpt, 8102–3

Currency and coin outstanding and in circulation, by type and denomination, *Treasury Bulletin,* quarterly rpt, 8002–4.16

Exports and imports of US, by country and detailed commodity, monthly rpt, 2422–12

Exports and imports of US, by Harmonized System 6-digit commodity and country, 1990, annual rpt, 2424–13

Exports and imports of US, by transport mode, country, and SITC 1- to 3-digit commodity, 1990, annual rpt, 2424–12

Exports of US, detailed Schedule B commodities with countries of destination, 1990, annual rpt, 2424–10

Fed Reserve banks finances and staff, 1990, annual rpt, 9364–1.1

Injuries from use of consumer products, by severity, victim age, and detailed product, 1990, annual rpt, 9164–6

Production of coins, and use and holdings of monetary metals, by metal type and US Mint facility, FY90, annual rpt, 8204–1

Production of coins by US Mint, for US by denomination and mint, and for foreign countries, monthly table, 8202–1

Seignorage in Budget of US, classified as deficit financing, FY92, annual rpt, 104–2.2

Seignorage in Fed Govt authoritative financial statements, FY90, annual rpt, 8104–2.1

Seignorage in Fed Govt consolidated financial statements, FY89-90, annual rpt, 8104–5

Thefts, and value of property stolen and recovered, by property type, 1990, annual rpt, 6224–2.1

see also Counterfeiting and forgery

see also Money supply

Coke

see Coal and coal mining

Colby, W. Hunter

"China's Livestock Feed Industry", 1524–4.3

Cold storage and refrigeration

Agricultural Statistics, 1990, annual rpt, 1004–1

Business statistics, detailed data for major industries and economic indicators, *Survey of Current Business,* monthly rpt, 2702–1.14

Containers (intermodal) and equipment owned by shipping and leasing companies, inventory by type and size, 1990, annual rpt, 7704–10

County Business Patterns, 1988: employment, establishments, and payroll, by SIC 2- to 4-digit industry and county, annual State rpt series, 2326–6

Index by Subjects and Names

Colombia

County Business Patterns, 1989: employment, establishments, and payroll, by SIC 2- to 4-digit industry and county, annual State rpt series, 2326–8

Dairy storage holdings, total and for USDA by product, 1990, annual rpt, 1317–1.1

DOD prime contract awards, by detailed procurement category, FY87-90, annual rpt, 3544–18

Employment, earnings, and hours, by SIC 1- to 4-digit industry, monthly and annual averages, selected years 1909-90, annual rpt, 6744–4

Energy supply, demand, and prices, by fuel type and end-use sector, projections and underlying assumptions, 1990-2010, annual rpt, 3164–90

Energy use in commercial buildings, costs, and conservation, by building characteristics, survey rpt series, 3166–8

Energy use of households, and availability of appliances by type, selected years 1978-87, annual rpt, 3164–74.1

Equipment shipments, trade, use, and firms, by product, 1990, annual Current Industrial Rpt, 2506–12.7

Exports and imports of US, by country and detailed commodity, monthly rpt, 2422–12

Exports and imports of US, by Harmonized System 6-digit commodity and country, 1990, annual rpt, 2424–13

Exports and imports of US, by transport mode, country, and SITC 1- to 3-digit commodity, 1990, annual rpt, 2424–12

Exports of US, detailed Schedule B commodities with countries of destination, 1990, annual rpt, 2424–10

Fish (processed) production by location, and trade, by species and product, 1987-90, annual rpts, 2166–6

Fish (squid) catch, trade, consumption, and cold storage holdings, by country and species, 1963-90, 2166–19.10

Fish and shellfish catch, wholesale receipts, prices, trade, and other market activities, weekly regional rpts, 2162–6

Fish and shellfish cold storage holdings, by product and species, preliminary data, monthly press release, 2162–2

Fish catch, prices, trade by country, cold storage holdings, and market devs, for Japan, semimonthly press release, 2162–7

Fish catch, trade, use, and fishery operations, with selected foreign data, by species, 1980s-90, annual rpt, 2164–1

Fishing (sport) from California commercial passenger boats with refrigeration equipment, anglers views, 1989 survey, 2168–125

Food stocks in cold storage by commodity and census div, and warehouse space use, by State, monthly rpt, 1631–5

Food stocks in cold storage by commodity, and warehouse space use, by census div, 1990, annual rpt, 1631–11

Fruit and nut production, prices, and use, 1988-91, annual rpt series, 1621–18

Manufacturing annual survey, 1989: finances and operations, by SIC 2- to 4-digit industry, series, 2506–15

Manufacturing census, 1987: finances and operations, by SIC 2- to 4-digit industry, State, and MSA, with trends from 1849, 2497–1

Manufacturing finances and operations, by SIC 2- to 4-digit industry, forecast 1991, annual rpt, 2044–28

Meat, poultry, and egg production, prices, trade, and stocks, monthly rpt, 1561–17

Military Sealift Command shipping operations, finances, and personnel, FY90, annual rpt, 3804–14

Nut cold storage holdings, by type and region, weekly rpt, periodic data, 1311–1

Poultry and egg prices and marketing, by selected region, State, and city, monthly and weekly 1990, annual rpt, 1317–2

Price indexes (producer), by stage of processing and detailed commodity, monthly rpt, 6762–6

Price indexes (producer), by stage of processing and detailed commodity, monthly 1990, annual rpt, 6764–2

Puerto Rico economic censuses, 1987: wholesale and retail trade and service industry finances and operations, by SIC 2- to 4-digit industry and municipio, 2591–1

Ships under foreign flag owned by US firms and foreign affiliates, by type, owner, and country of registry and construction, as of Jan 1991, semiannual rpt, 7702–3

Transportation census, 1987: finances and operations by size, ownership, and State, and revenues by MSA, by SIC 2- to 4-digit industry, 2579–1

Vegetable production, prices, trade, stocks, and use, for selected fresh and processing crops, periodic situation rpt with articles, 1561–11

Warehouse services finances, by SIC 3- to 4-digit industry, 1989 survey, annual rpt, 2413–14

Wholesale trade census, 1987: establishments, sales by customer class, employment, inventories, and expenses, by SIC 2- to 4-digit kind of business, 2407–4

see also Ice, manufactured

Coldren, James R., Jr.

"Multi-Jurisdictional Drug Control Task Forces 1988: A Key Program of State Drug Control Strategies", 6068–244

Cole, Harold L.

"Reputation with Multiple Relationships: Reviving Reputation Models of Debt", 9383–20.7

Coleman, Wilbur J., II

"Precautionary Money Balances with Aggregate Uncertainty", 9366–7.253

Coliform bacteria

see Food and waterborne diseases

Collective bargaining

see Labor-management relations, general

see Labor unions

College Station, Tex.

see also under By SMSA or MSA in the "Index by Categories"

Colleges and universities

see Black colleges

see Federal aid to higher education

see Federal aid to medical education

see Higher education

see Junior colleges

see State funding for higher education

see under By Individual Company or Institution in the "Index by Categories"

Collender, Robert N.

"Analysis of Financial Performance of Federal Land Banks, Federal Intermediate Credit Banks, Farm Credit Banks, and Related Associations, 1986-89", 1548–381

"Have Mergers Improved the Financial Performance of Farm Credit Banks?", 1541–1.205

Collins, Carlyn L.

"HIV Safety Guidelines and Laboratory Training", 4042–3.256

Collins, Dennis C.

"Forest Statistics for Land Outside National Forests in Northwestern Montana, 1989", 1206–25.10

"Forest Statistics for Land Outside National Forests in West-Central Montana, 1989", 1206–25.9

Collins, John G.

"Impairments Due to Injuries: U.S., 1985-87. Vital and Health Statistics Series 10", 4147–10.179

"Types of Injuries by Selected Characteristics: U.S., 1985-87. Vital and Health Statistics Series 10", 4147–10.176

Collins, Keith

"Oilseed Provisions in the 1990 Farm Bill", 1004–16.1

Collins, Sean

"Prediction Techniques for Box-Cox Regression Models", 9366–6.262

Collins, William E.

"Some Personality Characteristics of Air Traffic Control Specialist Trainees: Interactions of Personality and Aptitude Test Scores with FAA Academy Success and Career Expectations", 7506–10.87

Colombia

Agricultural exports of high-value commodities, indexes and sales by commodity, world area, and country, 1960s-86, 1528–323

Agricultural exports of US, impacts of foreign agricultural and trade policy, with data by commodity and country, 1989, annual rpt, 1924–8

Agricultural production, prices, and trade, by country, 1960s-90, annual world area rpt, 1524–4.2

Agricultural production, trade, and policies in foreign countries, summary data by country, 1989-90, annual factbook, 1924–12

Agricultural subsidies to producers and consumers in 6 Latin America countries, by selected commodity, 1982-87, 1528–324

Agricultural trade of US, by detailed commodity and country, 1989, annual rpt, 1524–8

Agricultural trade of US, by detailed commodity and country, 1990, semiannual rpt, 1522–4

AID economic aid to developing countries, obligations and disbursements by country, quarterly rpt, 9912–4

AID loans repayment status and terms by program and country, and status of predecessor agency loans, quarterly rpt, 9912–3

Cocaine production, eradication, and legal use, worldwide and for South America, 1970s-80s, conf, 4498–74

Colombia

Economic and military aid and loans from US and intl agencies, by program and country, FY46-90, annual rpt, 9914–5

Economic and social conditions of developing countries from 1960s, and Intl Dev Cooperation Agency and AID activities and funding, FY90-92, annual rpt, 9904–4

Economic conditions, policy, and trade practices, by country, 1988-90, annual rpt, 21384–5

Economic, social, political, and geographic summary data, by country, 1991, annual factbook, 9114–2

Exports and imports of US, by commodity and country, 1970-89, world area rpt, 9116–1.4

Exports and imports of US, by Harmonized System 6-digit commodity and country, 1990, annual rpt, 2424–13

Exports and imports of US, by selected country, country group, and commodity group, 1990, annual rpt, 2044–37

Exports and imports of US, by transport mode, country, and SITC 1- to 3-digit commodity, 1990, annual rpt, 2424–12

Exports, imports, and balances of US with major trading partners, by product category, 1986-90, annual chartbook, 9884–21

Exports of US, detailed Schedule B commodities with countries of destination, 1990, annual rpt, 2424–10

Flower (fresh cut) production, trade, and wholesale prices, for Colombia and US, various periods 1986-91, 1925–34.210

Hostages kidnapped in Colombia, listing as of 1990, 7004–22

Human rights conditions in 170 countries, and US economic and military aid, 1990, annual rpt, 21384–3

Imports of goods, services, and investment from US, trade barriers, impacts, and US actions, by country, 1990, annual rpt, 444–2

Labor conditions, union coverage, and work accidents, 1991 annual country rpt, 6366–4.42

Military aid of US, arms sales, and training programs costs and budget requests, by program, world region, and country, FY90-92, annual rpt, 7144–13

Multinatl US firms and foreign affiliates finances and operations, by industry and world area of parent firm, 1989 benchmark survey, preliminary annual rpt, 2704–5

Multinatl US firms foreign affiliates, income statement items by country and world area, 1986, biennial article, 8302–2.212

Oil exports to US by OPEC and non-OPEC countries, monthly rpt, 3162–24.3

UN voting record and share of votes in agreement with US, by issue, country, and world area, 1990, annual rpt, 7004–18

see also under By Foreign Country in the "Index by Categories"

Colombotos, John

"Physicians, Nurses, and AIDS: Preliminary Findings from a National Study", 4186–9.11

Colony, Roger

"Markov Model for Nearshore Sea Ice Trajectories", 2176–1.38

Colorado

Air traffic and passenger and freight enplanements, by airport, 1960s-89 and projected to 2010, hub area rpt, 7506–7.39

Banks (insured commercial and savings) deposits by instn, State, MSA, and county, as of June 1990, annual regional rpt, 9295–3.6

Coal production and mines by county, prices, productivity, miners, and reserves, by mining method and State, 1989-90, annual rpt, 3164–25

County Business Patterns, 1989: employment, establishments, and payroll, by SIC 2- to 4-digit industry and county, annual State rpt, 2326–8.7

DOD prime contract awards, by contractor, service branch, State, and city, FY90, annual rpt, 3544–22

Drug abuse indicators for selected metro areas, research results, data collection, and policy issues, 1991 semiannual conf, 4492–5

Fed Govt spending in States and local areas, by type, State, county, and city, FY90, annual rpt, 2464–3

Fed Govt spending in States, by type, program, agency, and State, FY90, annual rpt, 2464–2

Financial and economic devs, Fed Reserve 10th District, quarterly rpt, 9381–16

Gemstone production in selected States, Mineral Industry Surveys, 1988-90, advance annual rpt, 5614–5.10

HHS financial aid, by program, recipient, State, and city, FY90, annual regional listing, 4004–3.8

Hospital deaths of Medicare patients, actual and expected rates by diagnosis, and hospital characteristics, by instn, FY87-89, annual regional rpt, 4654–14.8

Income (personal) per capita and by source, and earnings by industry div, by State, MSA, and county, 1984-89, annual regional rpt, 2704–2.5

Jail adult and juvenile population, employment, spending, instn conditions, and inmate programs, by county and facility, 1988, regional rpt series, 6068–144.5

Land subsidence above coal mines, State property insurance program income and expenses in 6 States, 1990, GAO rpt, 26113–530

Marriages, divorces, and rates, by characteristics of spouses, State, and county, 1987 and trends from 1920, US Vital Statistics annual rpt, 4144–4

Methane production in coal fields by basin, and resources remaining, 1970s-89, article, 3162–4.201

Mineral industries census, 1987: finances and operations, by SIC 2- to 4-digit industry, State, and county, census div rpt, 2515–1.8

Mineral Industry Surveys, State reviews of production, 1990, preliminary annual rpt, 5614–6

Minerals Yearbook, 1989, Vol 2: State review of production and sales by commodity, and business activity, annual rpt, 5604–16.7

Minerals Yearbook, 1989, Vol 2: State reviews of production, sales, and firms, by commodity, and business activity, annual rpt, 5604–34

Index by Subjects and Names

Nuclear power plant (helium-cooled) at Fort St Vrain, occupational radiation exposure, 1974-87, annual rpt, 9634–3

Nursing home reimbursement by Medicaid, States payment ratesetting methods, analysis for 7 States, 1980s, article, 4652–1.255

Occupational deaths data collection from multiple sources, BLS pilot study results for 2 States, 1990, article, 6722–1.249

Onion farm acreage, pesticide use, operators, and other characteristics, for 6 producer States, 1989, article, 1561–11.201

Physicians, by specialty, age, sex, and location of training and practice, 1989, State rpt, 4116–6.6

Population and housing census, 1990: population and housing characteristics, households, and land area, by county, subdiv, and place, State rpt, 2551–1.7

Population and housing census, 1990: voting age and total population by race, and housing units, by block, redistricting counts required under PL 94-171, State CD-ROM release, 2551–6.2

Population and housing census, 1990: voting age and total population by race, and housing units, by county and city, redistricting counts required under PL 94-171, State summary rpt, 2551–5.6

Recreation (outdoor) facilities on public land, use, and Land Mgmt Bur mgmt activities, funding, and plans, 1990 State rpt, 5726–5.1

Statistical Abstract of US, 1991 annual data compilation, 2324–1

Supplemental Security Income payments and beneficiaries, by type of eligibility, State, and county, Dec 1989, annual rpt, 4744–27.8

Tourism visits, by site, trip purpose, and State of origin, 1985-87, 5726–5.1

Water (groundwater) supply, quality, chemistry, and use, 1987-88, regional rpt, 5666–28.3

Water quality, chemistry, hydrology, and other characteristics, 1989 local area study, 5666–27.17

Water resources dev projects of Army Corps of Engineers, characteristics, and costs, 1950s-89, biennial State rpt, 3756–1.6

Water resources dev projects of Army Corps of Engineers, characteristics, and costs, 1950s-91, biennial State rpt, 3756–2.6

Water salinity control program for Colorado River, participation and payments, FY87-90, annual rpt, 1804–23

Water supply and quality in streams and lakes, and groundwater levels in wells, by drainage basin, 1990, annual State rpt, 5666–10.6

Water supply, and snow survey results, monthly State rpt, 1266–2.3

Water supply in Colorado, streamflow, precipitation, and reservoir storage, 1991 water year, annual rpt, 1264–13

Wetlands plant, soil, and water characteristics, for Big Meadows area in Rocky Mountain Natl Park, 1987-88, 5508–113

Wildlife mgmt activities and funding, acreage by habitat type, and scientific staff, for Bur of Land Mgmt, 1990 State rpt, 5726–7.3

Index by Subjects and Names

Commercial buildings

see also Boulder, Colo.
see also Colorado Springs, Colo.
see also Denver, Colo.
see also under By State in the "Index by Categories"

Colorado River

- Agricultural Stabilization and Conservation Service producer payments and certificate value, by program, monthly rpt, 1802–10
- Groundwater supply, quality, chemistry, other characteristics, and use, 1991 regional rpt, 5666–25.13
- Reservoir and power operations and revenues of Fed Govt, for Colorado River Basin, 1990-91, annual rpt, 5824–6
- Salinity control program for Colorado River, participation and payments, FY87-90, annual rpt, 1804–23
- Sand deposit characteristics, and density of campsites, for Colorado River, 1920s-80s, 5668–122
- Water quality, chemistry, hydrology, and other characteristics, 1989 local area study, 5666–27.17
- Water supply and quality in streams and lakes, and groundwater levels in wells, by drainage basin, 1988, annual State rpt series, 5666–16
- Water supply and quality in streams and lakes, and groundwater levels in wells, by drainage basin, 1989, annual State rpt series, 5666–12
- Water supply and quality in streams and lakes, and groundwater levels in wells, by drainage basin, 1990, annual State rpt series, 5666–10

Colorado Springs, Colo.

- Housing starts and completions authorized by building permits in 40 MSAs, quarterly rpt, 2382–9
- Wages by occupation, for office and plant workers, 1990 survey, periodic MSA rpt, 6785–3.3
- *see also* under By City and By SMSA or MSA in the "Index by Categories"

Columbia, Mo.

see also under By SMSA or MSA in the "Index by Categories"

Columbia River

- Bonneville Power Admin mgmt of Fed Columbia River Power System, finances, operations, and sales by customer, FY90, annual rpt, 3224–1
- Electric power capacity and use in Pacific Northwest, by energy source, projected under alternative load and demand cases, 1991-2011, annual rpt, 3224–3
- Fish and shellfish catch, wholesale receipts, prices, trade, and other market activities, weekly regional rpt, 2162–6.5
- Radiation exposure of population near Hanford, Wash, nuclear plant, with methodology, 1944-66, series, 3356–5
- Seals (harbor) population and physical characteristics at selected Washington State coastal sites, 1975-80, 14738–7
- Water supply and quality in streams and lakes, and groundwater levels in wells, by drainage basin, 1988, annual State rpt series, 5666–16
- Water supply and quality in streams and lakes, and groundwater levels in wells, by drainage basin, 1989, annual State rpt series, 5666–12

Water supply and quality in streams and lakes, and groundwater levels in wells, by drainage basin, 1990, annual State rpt series, 5666–10

Water supply in US and southern Canada, streamflow, surface and groundwater conditions, and reservoir levels, by location, monthly rpt, 5662–3

Columbia, S.C.

- Fruit and vegetable shipments, and arrivals in US and Canada cities, by mode of transport and State and country of origin, 1990, annual rpt, 1311–4.1
- *see also* under By SMSA or MSA in the "Index by Categories"

Columbia University School of Public Health

"Physicians, Nurses, and AIDS: Preliminary Findings from a National Study", 4186–9.11

Columbus, Ga.

see also under By City and By SMSA or MSA in the "Index by Categories"

Columbus, Ohio

see also under By City and By SMSA or MSA in the "Index by Categories"

Combs, Debra L.

"Death Investigation in the U.S. and Canada, 1990", 4208–34

Combs, Gerald F.

"Fifty Years of Progress in the Nutrition Field", 1004–16.1

Combs, L. J.

"Water Resources Activities of the USGS in Kansas, FY87-88", 5666–26.10

Commemorations and memorials

see Monuments and memorials

Commerce

see Foreign trade
see Interstate commerce

Commerce Department

see Department of Commerce

Commercial banking

see Banks and banking

Commercial buildings

- Assets and debts of private sector, balance sheets by segment, 1945-90, semiannual rpt, 9365–4.1
- Bombing incidents, casualties, and damage, by target, circumstances, and State, 1990, annual rpt, 6224–5
- Construction industries census, 1987: establishments, employment, receipts, and expenditures, by SIC 4-digit industry and State, final industry rpt series, 2373–1
- Construction put in place, permits, housing sales, costs, material prices, and employment, bimonthly rpt with articles, 2042–1
- Construction put in place, value of new public and private structures, by type, monthly rpt, 2382–4
- Crime victimization of women, by relation to offender, circumstances, and victim characteristics, for rape and other violent offenses, 1973-87, 6068–243
- Crime victimization rates, by victim and offender characteristics, circumstances, and offense, 1988 survey, annual rpt, 6066–3.42
- Crime victimization rates, by victim and offender characteristics, circumstances, and offense, 1989 survey, annual rpt, 6066–3.44
- Energy conservation and resource planning activities of Bonneville Power Admin, FY89-90, 3228–11

Energy conservation programs of States, Federal aid and savings, by State, 1989, annual rpt, 3304–1

Energy supply, demand, and prices, by fuel type and end-use sector, projections and underlying assumptions, 1990-2010, annual rpt, 3164–90

Energy use in commercial buildings, costs, and conservation, by building characteristics, survey rpt series, 3166–8

Engineering and architectural establishments, receipts by type of client and project, payroll, and employment, by State, 1987 Census of Service Industries, 2393–4.16

Fed Govt-owned real property inventory and costs, worldwide summary by purpose, agency, and location, 1989, annual rpt, 9454–5

Flow-of-funds accounts, savings, investments, and credit statements, quarterly rpt, 9365–3.3

Historic buildings rehabilitation tax incentives, projects, costs, ownership, and use, FY77-90, annual rpt, 5544–17

Mortgage loan activity, by type of lender, loan, and mortgaged property, monthly press release, 5142–18

Multinatl firms US affiliates finances and operations, by industry div, country of parent firm, and State, 1988-89, annual article, 2702–1.214

Multinatl firms US affiliates, finances, and operations, by industry, world area of parent firm, and State, 1988-89, annual rpt, 2704–4

Multinatl firms US affiliates, investment trends and impact on US economy, 1991 annual rpt, 2004–9

Neighborhood and housing quality, indicators and attitudes, by householder type and location, for 11 MSAs, 1984 survey, supplement, 2485–8

Neighborhood and housing quality, indicators and attitudes, by householder type and location, 1987, biennial rpt supplement, 2485–13

Neighborhood and housing quality, indicators and attitudes, by householder type and location, 1989, biennial rpt, 2485–12

Robberies, by type of premises, population size, and region, 1990, annual rpt, 6224–2.1

Savings instns failures, inventory of real estate assets available from Resolution Trust Corp, 1990, semiannual listing, 9722–2.4

Savings instns failures, inventory of real estate assets available from Resolution Trust Corp, 1991, semiannual listing, 9722–2.10

State and Metro Area Data Book, 1991 data compilation, 2328–54

Statistical Abstract of US, 1991 annual data compilation, 2324–1.26

Terrorism incidents in US, related activity, and casualties, by attack type, target, group, and location, 1990, annual rpt, 6224–6

Vacancy rates for offices, by selected city, 1980-90, 21248–147

Wiretaps authorized, costs, arrests, trials, and convictions, by offense and jurisdiction, 1990, annual rpt, 18204–7

Commercial credit

Commercial credit

Agricultural cooperatives finances, aggregate for top 100 assns by commodity group, 1989, annual rpt, 1124–3

Assets and debts of private sector, balance sheets by segment, 1945-90, semiannual rpt, 9365–4.1

Banks (commercial) business loans, and commercial paper of nonfinancial companies, weekly rpt, 9391–4

Banks commercial loan growth, by bank financial and district employment characteristics, 1989-90, article, 9385–1.208

Banks profitability indicators for student loans and other financial services, 1985-89, 4808–36

Credit reporting and collection establishments, and receipts by source and class of client, by MSA, 1987 Census of Service Industries, 2393–4.4

Economic indicators and components, current data and annual trends, monthly rpt, 23842–1.5

Financial and business detailed statistics, *Fed Reserve Bulletin*, monthly rpt with articles, 9362–1

Flow-of-funds accounts, savings, investments, and credit statements, quarterly rpt, 9365–3.3

Minority Business Dev Centers mgmt and financial aid, and characteristics of businesses, by region and State, FY90, annual rpt, 2104–6

Monetary trends, Fed Reserve Bank of St Louis monthly rpt, 9391–2

Mortage lending impacts on credit union financial performance, for northeast States and total US, 1980s-90, article, 9536–1.6

North Central States business and economic conditions, Fed Reserve 9th District, quarterly journal, 9383–19

Overseas Business Reports: economic conditions, investment and export opportunities, and trade practices, country market research rpt series, 2046–6

Savings instns insured by Savings Assn Insurance Fund, assets, liabilities, and deposit and loan activity, by conservatorship status, monthly rpt, 8432–1

Small businesses investment spending, impacts of bank loan commitments, 1980-84, article, 9381–1.211

Southeastern States, Fed Reserve 5th District insured commercial banks financial statements, by State, quarterly rpt, 9389–18

Survey of Current Business, detailed data for major industries and economic indicators, monthly rpt, 2702–1.9

Tax (income) returns of corporations, income and tax items by asset size and detailed industry, 1988, annual rpt, 8304–21

West Central States economic indicators, Fed Reserve 10th District, quarterly rpt, 9381–16.2

Commercial education

see Business education

Commercial finance companies

see Finance companies

Commercial law

Court civil and criminal caseloads for Federal district, appeals, and bankruptcy courts, by type of suit and offense, circuit, and district, 1990, annual rpt, 18204–11

Court civil and criminal caseloads for Federal district, appeals, and special courts, 1990, annual rpt, 18204–8

Court civil and criminal caseloads for Federal district courts, 1991, annual rpt, 18204–2.1

Industry structure, conduct, and govt regulation, effects on competition, series, 9406–1

Legal services establishments, lawyers by field, receipts by class of client, expenses, and employment, by MSA, 1987 Census of Service Industries, 2393–4.13

see also Antitrust law

see also Bankruptcy

see also Interstate commerce

see also Licenses and permits

see also Maritime law

see also Patents

see also Price regulation

see also Trademarks

Commercial treaties

see Trade agreements

Commissaries

see Military post exchanges and commissaries

Commission of Fine Arts

Budget of US, authoritative financial statements with appropriations, outlays, and receipts, by category and agency, FY90, annual rpt, 8104–2.1

Budget of US, obligations and authority by function, agency, and program, with summaries, analyses, and historical tables, FY92, annual rpt, 104–2

Commission on Civil Rights

Budget of US, authoritative financial statements with appropriations, outlays, and receipts, by category and agency, FY90, annual rpt, 8104–2.1

Budget of US, obligations and authority by function, agency, and program, with summaries, analyses, and historical tables, FY92, annual rpt, 104–2

Publications of Commission, 1991 listing, 11048–188

Commission on Railroad Retirement Reform

Findings and recommendations on retirement system funding and benefits, with background industry data, 1960s-90 and projected to 2060, 9708–1

Commissions of the Federal Government

see Federal boards, committees, and commissions

see Federal independent agencies

Committee for Purchase from the Blind and Other Severely Handicapped

Budget of US, authoritative financial statements with appropriations, outlays, and receipts, by category and agency, FY90, annual rpt, 8104–2.1

Budget of US, obligations and authority by function, agency, and program, with summaries, analyses, and historical tables, FY92, annual rpt, 104–2

Workshops for blind and handicapped, finances, operations, and Federal procurement, FY80-88, annual rpt, 11714–1

Committee on Problems of Drug Dependence, Inc.

"Problems of Drug Dependence, 1990: Proceeding of the 52nd Annual Scientific Meeting, The Committee on Problems of Drug Dependence, Inc.", 4494–11

Committees of Congress

see Congressional committees

see Congressional joint committees

Commodities

see Agricultural commodities

see Foreign trade

see Futures trading

see Manufacturing

see Mines and mineral resources

see Natural resources

see Stockpiling

see Strategic materials

see under By Commodity in the "Index by Categories"

see under names of specific commodities or commodity groups

Commodity Credit Corp.

Agricultural Stabilization and Conservation Service programs, annual commodity fact sheet series, 1806–4

Agricultural Statistics, 1990, annual rpt, 1004–1

Agriculture census, 1987: farms, farmland, production, finances, and operator characteristics, by county, final State rpt series, 2331–1

Budget of US, obligations and authority by function, agency, and program, with summaries, analyses, and historical tables, FY92, annual rpt, 104–2

Certificate exchange activity of CCC, by commodity, biweekly press release, 1802–16

Cotton loan rates, and micronaire differentials of CCC, monthly rpt, annual tables, 1309–12

Cotton prices at selected spot markets, NYC futures prices, and CCC loan rates, 1990/91 and trends from 1943, annual rpt, 1309–2

Cotton prices in 8 spot markets, futures prices at NYC exchange, farm prices, and CCC loan stocks, monthly rpt, 1309–1

Cotton production, trade, and use, for selected countries, FAS monthly circular, 1925–4.2

Dairy production by State, stocks, prices, and CCC price support activities, by product type, monthly rpt, 1627–3

Dairy products price support purchases, sales, donations, and inventories of CCC, monthly rpt, 1802–2

Dairy products uncommitted stocks, periodic situation rpt with articles, 1561–2

Economic Indicators of the Farm Sector, balance sheets, and receipts by detailed commodity, by State, 1985-89, annual rpt, 1544–18

Export credit sales agreement terms, by commodity and country, FY89, annual rpt, 15344–1.11

Exports (agricultural) under federally financed programs, by commodity and country, bimonthly rpt, periodic data, 1522–1

Exports (agricultural) under federally financed programs, FY60-90, annual rpt, 1924–9

Index by Subjects and Names

Financial condition and major commodity program operations of CCC, FY62-87, annual chartbook, 1824–2

Grain and feed trade, and export and support prices, for US and major producer countries, FAS monthly circular, 1925–2.4

Grain futures contracts, stocks in deliverable position by type, weekly tables, 11922–4

Grain production, prices, trade, and export inspections by US port and country of destination, by grain type, weekly rpt, 1313–2

Grain storage facility and equipment loans to farmers under CCC program, by State, FY68-91, annual table, 1804–14

Honey production, prices, trade, stocks, marketing, and CCC honey loan and distribution activities, monthly rpt, 1311–2

Iraq agricultural imports under CCC export credit guarantee programs, FY81-90, GAO rpt, 26123–314

Iraq purchases under CCC credit guarantee program, FY81-90, with contingent liabilities projected to FY97, hearing, 21248–155

Liabilities (contingent) and claims paid by Fed Govt on federally insured and guaranteed contracts with foreign obligors, by country and program, periodic rpt, 8002–12

Loans (farm) outstanding, and lenders financial condition, quarterly rpt with articles, 1541–1

Loans of CCC, activities and operating results, monthly release, 1802–7

Loans of CCC, and liquidations, by commodity, monthly 1986-90, annual rpt, 1544–16

Lumber and wood products exports, imports, and export promotion of US by country, and trade balance, by commodity, FAS quarterly circular, 1925–36

Oils, oilseeds, and fats foreign and US production and trade, FAS periodic circular series, 1925–1

PL 480 exports by commodity, and recipients, by program, sponsor, and country, FY88 and cumulative from FY55, annual rpt, 1924–7

Price support and other CCC program outlays, with production and marketing outlook, by commodity, projected 1990-96, 26306–6.160

Price support program provisions, for selected commodities, 1961-90, 1568–302; 1568–303

Rice foreign and US production, prices, trade, stocks, and use, periodic situation rpt, 1561–8

Rice market activities, prices, inspections, sales, trade, supply, and use, for US and selected foreign markets, weekly rpt, 1313–8

Sale offerings of CCC commodities, and prices, monthly press release, 1802–4

Seed exports, by type, world region, and country, FAS quarterly rpt, 1925–13

Statistical Abstract of US, 1991 annual data compilation, 2324–1.23

Storage facility and equipment loans to farmers under CCC grain program, by State, monthly table, 1802–9

Wheat stocks and prices estimated under alternative reserve storage assumptions, 1990-91, article, 1561–12.201

Commodity Exchange Authority *see* Commodity Futures Trading Commission

Commodity futures *see* Futures trading

Commodity Futures Trading Commission

Activities, funding, and staff of CFTC, and futures and options trading volume by commodity and exchange, FY90, annual rpt, 11924–2

Budget of US, authoritative financial statements with appropriations, outlays, and receipts, by category and agency, FY90, annual rpt, 8104–2.1

Budget of US, obligations and authority by function, agency, and program, with summaries, analyses, and historical tables, FY92, annual rpt, 104–2

Futures trading in selected commodities and financial instruments and indexes, NYC, Chicago, and other markets activity, semimonthly rpt, 11922–5

Grain futures contracts, stocks in deliverable position by type, weekly tables, 11922–4

Regulation of futures trading, CFTC and individual exchanges oversight, foreign activity, and customer views, late 1980s, hearing, 25168–77

Regulation of securities and commodity trading, activities and interagency coordination, FY91, annual rpt, 11924–4

Common carriers

see Airlines

see Buses

see Passenger ships

see Public utilities

see Railroads

see Ships and shipping

see Taxicabs

see Trucks and trucking industry

Common markets and free trade areas

Canada and US free trade agreement impacts on minerals industry, 1991 article, 5602–4.201

Export and import agreements, negotiations, and related legislation, 1990, annual rpt, 444–1

Exports and imports, trade agreements and relations, and USITC investigations, 1990, annual rpt, 9884–5

Loans of US banks to foreigners at all US and foreign offices, by country group and country, quarterly rpt, 13002–1

North America free trade area proposal for Canada, US, and Mexico, outlook with trade data, 1990, 2048–153

see also Council for Mutual Economic Assistance

see also European Community

see also Export processing zones

Communicable diseases

see Acquired immune deficiency syndrome

see Animal diseases and zoonoses

see Infective and parasitic diseases

see Pneumonia and influenza

see Rabies

see Sexually transmitted diseases

see Tuberculosis

Communications industries

Capital expenditures for plant and equipment, by major industry group, quarterly rpt, 2502–2

Communications industries

Collective bargaining agreements expiring during year, and workers covered, by firm, union, industry group, and State, 1991, annual rpt, 6784–9

County Business Patterns, 1988: employment, establishments, and payroll, by SIC 2- to 4-digit industry and county, annual State rpt series, 2326–6

County Business Patterns, 1989: employment, establishments, and payroll, by SIC 2- to 4-digit industry and county, annual State rpt series, 2326–8

Criminal cases by type and disposition, and collections, for US attorneys, by Federal district, FY90, annual rpt, 6004–2.1

DOD budget, manpower needs, costs, and force readiness by service branch, FY92, annual rpt, 3504–1

DOD budget, R&D appropriations by item, service branch, and defense agency, FY90-93, annual rpt, 3544–33

DOD prime contract awards, by detailed procurement category, FY87-90, annual rpt, 3544–18

Employment, earnings, and hours, by SIC 1- to 4-digit industry, monthly and annual averages, selected years 1909-90, annual rpt, 6744–4

Exports and imports of US, by Harmonized System 6-digit commodity and country, 1990, annual rpt, 2424–13

Exports of US, detailed Schedule B commodities with countries of destination, 1990, annual rpt, 2424–10

Foreign direct investment in US, major transactions by type, industry, country, and US location, 1989, annual rpt, 2044–20

Input-output structure of US economy, detailed interindustry transactions for 84 industries, and components of final demand, 1986, annual article, 2702–1.206

Input-output structure of US economy, detailed interindustry transactions for 85 industries, 1982 benchmark data, 2702–1.213

Manufacturing census, 1987: employment and shipments under Fed Govt contracts, by SIC 4-digit industry, 2497–7

Manufacturing census, 1987: finances and operations, by SIC 2- to 4-digit industry, State, and MSA, with trends from 1849, 2497–1

Mineral industries census, 1987: finances and operations, by establishment characteristics, SIC 2- to 4-digit industry, and State, subject rpt, 2517–1

Occupational injury and illness rates, by SIC 2- to 4-digit industry, 1988-89, annual rpt, 6844–7

Occupational injury and illness rates, by SIC 2- to 4-digit industry, 1989, annual rpt, 6844–1

SEC registration, firms required to file annual rpts, as of Sept 1990, annual listing, 9734–5

Senate receipts, itemized expenses by payee, and balances, 1st half FY91, semiannual listing, 25922–1

Service industries census, 1987: establishments, receipts by source, payroll, and employment, by SIC 2- to 4-digit kind of business, State, and MSA, 2393–4

Communications industries

Soviet Union GNP by component and industry sector, and CIA estimation methods, 1950s-87, 23848–223

Soviet Union GNP by detailed income and outlay component, 1985, 2326–18.59

Tax (income) returns of corporations, income and tax items by asset size and detailed industry, 1987, annual rpt, 8304–4

Tax (income) returns of corporations, income and tax items by asset size and detailed industry, 1988, annual rpt, 8304–21

Tax (income) returns of corporations with foreign tax credit, income and tax items by industry group, 1986, biennial article, 8302–2.203

Tax (income) returns of partnerships, income statement and balance sheet items, by industry group, 1989, annual article, 8302–2.216; 8304–18

Tax (income) returns of sole proprietorships, income statement items, by industry group, 1989, annual article, 8302–2.214

see also Books and bookselling

see also Cable television

see also Communications satellites

see also Educational broadcasting

see also Home video and audio equipment

see also Information services

see also Journalism

see also Mass media

see also Motion pictures

see also Newspapers

see also Periodicals

see also Political broadcasting

see also Printing and publishing industry

see also Public broadcasting

see also Radio

see also Recording industry

see also Telecommunication

see also Telegraph

see also Telephones and telephone industry

see also Television

see also under By Industry in the "Index by Categories"

Communications Satellite Corp.

Finances and operations of COMSAT, 1988-89, annual rpt, 9284–6.5

Finances, rates, and traffic for US telecommunications carriers intl operations, by service type, firm, and country, 1975-89, annual rpt, 9284–17

Communications satellites

Exports of US, detailed Schedule B commodities with countries of destination, 1990, annual rpt, 2424–10

Finances and operations, by SIC 2- to 4-digit industry, forecast 1991, annual rpt, 2044–28

Foreign countries economic, social, political, and geographic summary data, by country, 1991, annual factbook, 9114–2

Launchings and other activities of NASA and Soviet Union, with flight data, 1957-90, annual rpt, 9504–6.1

Price indexes (producer), by stage of processing and detailed commodity, monthly rpt, 6762–6

Price indexes (producer), by stage of processing and detailed commodity, monthly 1990, annual rpt, 6764–2

Shipments, trade, use, and firms, for electronic communications systems and related products, 1990, annual Current Industrial Rpt, 2506–12.35

Telephone and telegraph firms detailed finances and operations, 1989, annual rpt, 9284–6

TV (satellite) copyright royalty fees, and funds available for distribution, 1989-90, annual rpt, 26404–2

TV broadcasting operating budgets for US Govt overseas services, FY88 and FY91, annual rpt, 17594–1

Communism

see Centrally planned economies

see Communist parties

see Socialism

Communist countries

see Centrally planned economies

see East-West trade

Communist parties

Foreign countries economic, social, political, and geographic summary data, by country, 1991, annual factbook, 9114–2

Community-based correctional programs

Federal correctional instn inmates, by sex, prison, security level, contract facility type, and region, monthly rpt series, 6242–1

Juvenile correctional and detention public and private instns, inmates, and expenses, by instn and resident characteristics and State, 1987, biennial rpt, 6064–13

Prisoners from Federal instns, halfway house placements, duration, and employment, and house capacity, 1990-91, GAO rpt, 26119–347

Sentences for Federal offenses, guidelines by offense and circumstances, series, 17668–1

Sex offenders treatment programs for adults and juveniles, by program type and State, data compilation, 1991 annual rpt, 6064–6.1

Community colleges

see Junior colleges

Community development

Appalachia local dev projects, and funding by source, by program and State, FY90, annual rpt, 9084–1

Assistance (financial and nonfinancial) of Fed Govt, 1991 base edition with supplements, annual listing, 104–5

Budget of US, CBO analysis and review of FY92 budget by function, annual rpt, 26304–2

Budget of US, House concurrent resolution, with spending and revenue targets, FY92 and projected to FY96, annual rpt, 21264–2

Budget of US, obligations and authority by function, agency, and program, with summaries, analyses, and historical tables, FY92, annual rpt, 104–2

Budget of US, Senate concurrent resolution, with spending and revenue targets, FY92, annual rpt, 25254–1

Economic Dev Admin activities, and funding by program, recipient, State, and county, FY90 and cumulative from FY66, annual rpt, 2064–2

Expenditures of Fed Govt in States, by type, program, agency, and State, FY90, annual rpt, 2464–2

FmHA activities, and loans and grants by program and State, FY90 and trends from FY70, annual rpt, 1184–17

Govt census, 1987: employment, payroll, and average earnings, by function, level of govt, State, county, and population size, 2455–2

Govt employment and payroll, by function, level of govt, and jurisdiction, 1990, annual rpt series, 2466–1

HHS financial aid, by program, recipient, State, and city, FY90, annual regional listings, 4004–3

Indian (Navajo and Hopi) relocation program activities and caseloads, monthly rpt, 16002–1

Indian (Navajo and Hopi) relocation program activities and caseloads, 1975-90, 16008–5

State and local govt employment of minorities and women, by occupation, function, and pay level, 1990, annual rpt, 9244–6.4

see also City and town planning

see also Community Development Block Grants

see also Urban Development Action Grants

see also Urban renewal

Community Development Block Grants

Allocation of CDBGs, by State, county, and city, FY84-91, 5128–17

Budget of US, formula grant program obligations to State and local govts, by agency, program, and State, FY92, annual rpt, 104–30

Expenditures and activities under CDBG, by program, FY75-90, annual rpt, 5124–8

Expenditures of Fed Govt in States, by type, program, agency, and State, FY90, annual rpt, 2464–2

Housing (rental) rehabilitation funding and activities of HUD, by program and region, FY90, annual rpt, 5124–7

Southeastern States community dev grants from HUD, by purpose and location, quarterly rpt, 9389–16

Community health services

AIDS patient home and community services under Medicaid waiver in 6 States, 1988-89, article, 4652–1.216

Drug and alcohol abuse treatment facilities, services, use, funding, staff, and client characteristics, 1989, biennial rpt, 4494–10

Health promotion program availability and participation, by type of program and sponsor, 1986-87 local area study, article, 4042–3.223

HHS financial aid, by program, recipient, State, and city, FY90, annual regional listings, 4004–3

Hospices use by cancer patients, by service type, use of other facilities, patient and instn characteristics, and other indicators, local area study, 1980-85, 4658–53

Indian Health Service facilities and use, and Indian health and other characteristics, by IHS region, 1980s-89, annual chartbook, 4084–7

Indian Health Service facilities, funding, operations, and Indian health and other characteristics, 1950s-90, annual chartbook, 4084–1

Indian Health Service outpatient visits, by facility and IHS service area, FY89-90, annual rpt, 4084–8

Long-term care institutional and community services, spending and use by type and payment source, FY88, and Medicaid growth since FY75, 26306–6.156

Medicaid coverage loss impacts on health services use, California transfer of selected Medicaid groups to county care, 1991 article, 4652–1.242

Medicaid services use and costs in alternative treatment settings, model description and results, FY87, article, 4652–1.211

Mental health care facilities, staff, and patient characteristics, *Statistical Notes* series, 4506–3

Mentally retarded Medicaid beneficiaries instnl and community care services under waiver, late 1970s-80s, article, 4652–1.219

Migrant workers and dependents by county, and health centers use and programs funding, by State, 1986-89, 4108–53

Older frail persons community-based care demonstration projects, evaluation of case mgmt services admin, 1991 rpt, 4186–7.8

Older persons use of federally funded health centers, targeted programs offered, and funding sources, 1987, article, 4042–3.229

Physicians payments, charges by specialty and treatment setting, and assignment rate by State, for Medicare, 1970s-88, article, 4652–1.240

see also Group homes for the handicapped
see also Home health services
see also Respite care

Community mental health centers
see Community health services
see Mental health facilities and services

Community Planning and Development, HUD

Budget of US, obligations and authority by function, agency, and program, with summaries, analyses, and historical tables, FY92, annual rpt, 104–2

Community Dev Block Grant activities and funding, by program, FY75-90, annual rpt, 5124–8

Community Dev Block Grant allocation, by State, county, and city, FY84-91, 5128–17

Housing (rental) rehabilitation funding and activities of HUD, by program and region, FY90, annual rpt, 5124–7

Urban Dev Action Grants funding, activities, and jobs and taxes generated, annual rpt, discontinued, 5124–5

Community Relations Service

Activities of CRS, investigation and mediation of minority discrimination disputes, FY90, annual rpt, 6004–9

Community treatment centers
see Community-based correctional programs
see Community health services
see Group homes for the handicapped

Commuter air carriers
see Airlines

Commuter rail
see Urban transportation

Commuting

Accessibility of commuting, impacts on auto ownership, employment location, and housing values, for Philadelphia area census tracts, 1980, working paper, 9387–8.231

Carpool and bus high occupancy vehicle lanes use, design, and enforcement, for US and Canada, 1989, 7888–80

Carpool high occupancy vehicle lanes use, design, enforcement, and drivers views, for California, 1988-89, 7308–203

Energy use by mode of transport, fuel supply, and demographic and economic factors of vehicle use, 1970s-89, annual rpt, 3304–5

Housing and households characteristics, unit and neighborhood quality, and journey to work by MSA location, for 11 MSAs, 1984 survey, supplement, 2485–8

Housing and households detailed characteristics, and unit and neighborhood quality, by location, 1985, biennial rpt supplement, 2485–13

Hwy Statistics, summary data by State, 1989-90, annual rpt, 7554–24

Natl transportation system planning, use, condition, accidents, and needs, by mode of transport, 1940s-90 and projected to 2020, 7308–202

Population size and characteristics, historical index to *Current Population Rpts*, 1991 listing, 2546–2.160

Transit systems under private, public, and nonprofit ownership, funding, staff, and service and area characteristics, 1990 rpt, 7888–81

Travel patterns, personal and household characteristics, and auto and public transport use, 1990 survey, series, 7556–6

see also Buses
see also Pedestrians
see also Subways
see also Urban transportation

Comoros

Agricultural exports of high-value commodities, indexes and sales by commodity, world area, and country, 1960s-86, 1528–323

Agricultural trade of US, by detailed commodity and country, 1989, annual rpt, 1524–8

Agricultural trade of US, by detailed commodity and country, 1990, semiannual rpt, 1522–4

AID economic aid to developing countries, obligations and disbursements by country, quarterly rpt, 9912–4

Dairy imports, consumption, and market conditions, by sub-Saharan Africa country, 1961-88, 1528–321

Economic and military aid and loans from US and intl agencies, by program and country, FY46-90, annual rpt, 9914–5

Economic and social conditions of developing countries from 1960s, and Intl Dev Cooperation Agency and AID activities and funding, FY90-92, annual rpt, 9904–4

Economic, social, political, and geographic summary data, by country, 1991, annual factbook, 9114–2

Exports and imports of US, by transport mode, country, and SITC 1- to 3-digit commodity, 1990, annual rpt, 2424–12

Human rights conditions in 170 countries, and US economic and military aid, 1990, annual rpt, 21384–3

Military aid of US, arms sales, and training programs costs and budget requests, by program, world region, and country, FY90-92, annual rpt, 7144–13

UN voting record and share of votes in agreement with US, by issue, country, and world area, 1990, annual rpt, 7004–18

Compact disc audio recordings and equipment
see Home video and audio equipment
see Recording industry

Compact disc data storage
see CD-ROM catalogs and guides
see CD-ROM releases
see CD-ROM technology and use

Compact of Free Association Act

Economic conditions, population characteristics, and Federal aid, for Pacific territories, 1989 hearing, 21448–44

Companies
see Business acquisitions and mergers
see Business failures and closings
see Business firms and establishments, number
see Business formations
see Corporations
see Ownership of enterprise
see Partnerships
see Proprietorships
see under By Individual Company or Institution in the "Index by Categories"

Compensation
see Claims
see Crime victim compensation
see Earnings, general
see Earnings, local and regional
see Earnings, specific industry
see Employee benefits
see Federal pay
see Military pay
see Payroll
see State and local employees pay
see Torts

Compensatory education

Appalachia education system, improvement initiatives, and indicators of success, by State, 1960s-89, 9088–36

Discrimination within schools, Education Dept enforcement activities and adequacy, FY81-91, GAO rpt, 26121–427

Education Dept programs funding, operations, and effectiveness, FY90, annual rpt, 4804–5

Elementary and secondary education enrollment, staff, finances, operations, programs, and policies, 1987/88 biennial survey, series, 4836–3

Expenditures of Fed Govt in States, by type, program, agency, and State, FY90, annual rpt, 2464–2

Homeless children educational projects, activities, and funding, FY90, annual rpt, 4804–35

Immigrant children education programs funding by Fed Govt and school districts, and student characteristics, 1980s, GAO rpt, 26121–418

Migrant workers children education programs enrollment, staff, and effectiveness, by State, 1980s, 4808–30

Migrant workers children education programs enrollment, staff, finances, and outcomes, 1980s, 4808–22

Poverty area school districts compensatory education programs, Federal grant program activities, participation, and coordinators views, 1989/90, 4808–32

Science and math education programs for gifted minority students, participation and outcomes, 1981-88 study, 4808–34

Tutoring and mentoring of disadvantaged elementary and secondary students by college students, program and participant characteristics, 1989, 4808–23

see also Bilingual education

Compensatory education

see also Head Start Project
see also Remedial education
see also Special education

Competition

- Agricultural research and education grants, USDA competitive awards by program and recipient, FY90, annual listing, 1764–1
- Airline deregulation in 1978, impacts on industry structure, competition, fares, finances, operations, and intl service, with data by carrier and airport, 1980s, series, 7308–199
- DOD competitive and formally advertised awards, by contractor type and service branch, various periods FY81-90, semiannual rpt, 3542–1.2
- DOD prime contract awards, by size and type of contract, service branch, competitive status, category, and labor standard, FY90, annual rpt, 3544–19
- Electric utilities purchase contracts with nonutility generators, competitive bidding use, 1980s-90, GAO rpt, 26113–498
- Futures trading oversight of CFTC and individual exchanges, foreign activity, and customer views, late 1980s, hearing, 25168–77
- Industry structure, conduct, and govt regulation, effects on competition, series, 9406–1
- Investigations of GAO, 1989-91, listing, 26106–10.5
- Mail (express parcel) shipments and revenues of private air and surface carriers, and impact of State regulation, 1976-89, 7308–201
- NASA procurement contract awards, by type, contractor, State, and country, FY91 with trends from 1961, semiannual rpt, 9502–6
- Navy procurement, by contractor and location, FY90, annual rpt, 3804–13
- NIH activities, funding by program and recipient type, staff, and clinic patients, by inst, FY90, annual rpt, 4434–3
- Semiconductor and fiber optics industries quality control spending, effectiveness, and views, survey results, 1980s, 2218–84
- State and local govt competition in taxes, services, regulation, and dev incentives, 1970-89, 10048–79
- *see also* Antitrust law
- *see also* Dumping
- *see also* Economic concentration and diversification
- *see also* Foreign competition
- *see also* Monopolies and cartels

Comptroller General of the U.S.

see General Accounting Office

Compulsory military service

see Draft evasion and protest
see Selective service

Computer data file guides

- BEA rpts data coverage and availability, 1991 annual article, 2702–1.203
- BEA rpts data coverage and availability, 1991 rpt, 2708–45
- Census Bur activities, rpts, and user services, monthly rpt, 2302–3
- Census Bur rpts and data files, coverage and availability, 1991 annual listing, 2304–2
- Census Bur rpts and data files, coverage, availability, and use, series, 2326–7
- Census Bur rpts and data files, monthly listing, 2302–6
- Education data collection activities and programs of NCES, 1991, annual listing, 4824–7
- Education Research and Improvement Office computer data files, 1991 listing, 4868–10
- Educational performance and conditions, characteristics, attitudes, activities, and plans, 1988 8th grade class, natl longitudinal survey, series, 4826–9
- Energy Info Admin activities, 1990, annual rpt, 3164–29
- Energy Info Admin forecasting and data analysis models, 1991, annual listing, 3164–87
- Energy Info Admin rpts and data files, 1990, listing, 3168–117
- Export and import statistics, Census Bur publications and data files, 1991 guide, 2428–11
- Fed Govt standards for data recording, processing, and transfer, and for purchase and use of computer systems, series, 2216–2
- Global climate change trends and contributing gases levels, Federal and intl data collection activities, mgmt, and inventory, 1990 rpt, 3028–4
- Labor force data of BLS, major statistical and analytical programs and rpts, as of Feb 1991, listing, 6728–35
- Library of Congress rpts and products, 1990, annual listing, 26404–6
- Map and geographic computer-readable database of Census Bur, TIGER files availability and use, 1990 rpt, 2628–30
- NTIS computer data files, 1991 annual listing, 2224–3
- Social security research rpts and microdata files of SSA, 1991 biennial listing, 4744–12
- Space science and related data sources and availability, 1991 annual listing, 9504–10
- USDA rpts, computer data files, and visual aids, 1991 annual listing, 1004–13
- *see also* CD-ROM catalogs and guides

Computer industry and products

- Capital stock measures, by type and industry, 1950s-80s, technical paper, 9385–8.92
- Consumer Expenditure Survey, spending for selected categories, 1991 semiannual pamphlet, 2322–3
- County Business Patterns, 1988: employment, establishments, and payroll, by SIC 2- to 4-digit industry and county, annual State rpt series, 2326–6
- County Business Patterns, 1989: employment, establishments, and payroll, by SIC 2- to 4-digit industry and county, annual State rpt series, 2326–8
- Displays (high-info content flat panel) from Japan at less than fair value, injury to US industry, investigation with background financial and operating data, 1991 rpt, 9886–14.328
- DOD prime contract awards, by detailed procurement category, FY87-90, annual rpt, 3544–18
- Employment, earnings, and hours, by SIC 1- to 4-digit industry, monthly and annual averages, selected years 1909-90, annual rpt, 6744–4
- Enterprise Statistics, 1987: auxiliaries of multi-establishment firms, finances and operations by function, industry, and State, 2329–6
- Exports and imports between US and outlying areas, by detailed commodity and mode of transport, 1990, annual rpt, 2424–11
- Exports and imports of US, by country and detailed commodity, monthly rpt, 2422–12
- Exports and imports of US, by Harmonized System 6-digit commodity and country, 1990, annual rpt, 2424–13
- Exports and imports of US, by selected country, country group, and commodity group, 1990, annual rpt, 2044–37
- Exports and imports of US, by transport mode, country, and SITC 1- to 3-digit commodity, 1990, annual rpt, 2424–12
- Exports of US, detailed Schedule B commodities with countries of destination, 1990, annual rpt, 2424–10
- Fed Govt agencies computer mainframe and related equipment procurement and compatibility, FY86-89, GAO rpt series, 26125–41
- Fed Govt computer and telecommunication systems acquisition plans and obligations, by agency, FY89-91, last issue of annual rpt, 104–20
- Fed Govt computer and telecommunication systems acquisition plans and obligations, by agency, FY90-95, annual rpt, 104–33
- Fed Govt computer systems and equipment, by type, make, and agency, 2nd half FY90, semiannual listing, 9452–9
- Fed Govt info mgmt activities, technology spending, and paperwork burden, by agency, planned FY91-92, annual rpt, 104–19
- Fed Govt standards for data recording, processing, and transfer, and for purchase and use of computer systems, series, 2216–2
- Franchise business opportunities by firm and kind of business, and sources of aid and info, 1990 annual listing, 2104–7
- GSA activities and finances, FY90, annual rpt, 9454–1
- Higher education instn R&D equipment, acquisition and service costs, condition, and financing, by field and subfield, 1988-90, triennial survey series, 9627–27
- House of Representatives salaries, expenses, and contingent fund disbursement, detailed listings, quarterly rpt, 21942–1
- Households computer ownership, and year of purchase, by selected characteristics, 1989, Current Population Rpt, 2546–2.158
- Imports of US given duty-free treatment for value of US material sent abroad, by commodity and country, 1989, annual rpt, 9884–14
- Japan manufacturing firms US affiliates, employment, and wages, by selected industry and State, 1980s, 2048–151
- Mail volume to and from households, use, and views, by class, source, content, and household characteristics, 1987-88, annual rpt, 9864–10
- Manufacturing annual survey, 1989: finances and operations, by SIC 2- to 4-digit industry, series, 2506–15

Index by Subjects and Names

Manufacturing census, 1987: employment and shipments under Fed Govt contracts, by SIC 4-digit industry, 2497–7

Manufacturing census, 1987: finances and operations, by SIC 2- to 4-digit industry, State, and MSA, with trends from 1849, 2497–1

Manufacturing census, 1987: finances and operations, by type of organization and SIC 2- to 4-digit industry, subject rpt, 2497–5

Manufacturing finances and operations, by SIC 2- to 4-digit industry, forecast 1991, annual rpt, 2044–28

Military computer systems engineering and technical support contract costs, late 1980s, GAO rpt, 26125–45

Military exercises using computer simulations, costs and effectiveness in Army Germany deployment exercise, 1969-90, GAO rpt, 26123–318

Modem shipments, trade, use, and firms, 1990, annual Current Industrial Rpt, 2506–12.35

Occupational injury and illness rates, by SIC 2- to 4-digit industry, 1988-89, annual rpt, 6844–7

Occupational injury and illness rates, by SIC 2- to 4-digit industry, 1989, annual rpt, 6844–1

OECD trade, total and for 4 major countries, and US trade by country, by commodity, 1970-89, world area rpt series, 9116–1

Office buildings computer systems cooling and refrigeration equipment, by building characteristics, 1989, survey rpt, 3166–8.9

Price indexes (producer), by stage of processing and detailed commodity, monthly rpt, 6762–6

Price indexes (producer), by stage of processing and detailed commodity, monthly 1990, annual rpt, 6764–2

Puerto Rico economic censuses, 1987: wholesale and retail trade and service industry finances and operations, by SIC 2- to 4-digit industry and municipio, 2591–1

R&D funding, and scientists and engineers education and employment, for US and selected foreign countries, 1991 annual rpt, 9627–35.1

Retail trade census, 1987: depreciable assets, capital and operating expenses, sales, value added, and inventories, by SIC 2- to 4-digit kind of business, 2399–2

Retail trade census, 1987: finances and employment, for establishments with and without payroll, by SIC 2- to 4-digit kind of business, State, and MSA, 2401–1

Science, engineering, and math education grants of NSF, by recipient and level, FY89, biennial listing, 9624–27

Service industries census, 1987: depreciable assets, capital and operating expenses, and receipts, by SIC 2- to 4-digit kind of business, 2393–2

Service industries census, 1987: establishments, receipts by source, payroll, and employment, by SIC 2- to 4-digit kind of business, State, and MSA, 2393–4

Soviet Union, Eastern Europe, OECD, and selected other countries consumer and producer goods and services production and sales, 1960s-90, annual rpt, 9114–4.7

Statistical Abstract of US, 1991 annual data compilation, 2324–1.27

Wholesale trade census, 1987: depreciable assets, capital and operating expenses, sales, value added, and inventories, by SIC 2- to 3-digit kind of business, 2407–2

Wholesale trade census, 1987: establishments, sales by customer class, employment, inventories, and expenses, by SIC 2- to 4-digit kind of business, 2407–4

Word processors (personal) from Japan and Singapore at less than fair value, injury to US industry, investigation with background financial and operating data, 1990 rpt, 9886–14.302

Word processors from Japan at less than fair value, injury to US industry, investigation with background financial and operating data, 1991 rpt, 9886–14.325

see also CD-ROM catalogs and guides
see also CD-ROM releases
see also CD-ROM technology and use
see also Computer data file guides
see also Computer networks
see also Computer sciences
see also Computer use
see also Industrial robots
see also Information storage and retrieval systems
see also Semiconductors
see also under By Commodity in the "Index by Categories"

Computer Matching and Privacy Protection Act

Public welfare computer records matching, Federal and State agencies compliance with recipient protection provisions before benefits reduction, 1990, GAO rpt, 26121–404

Computer networks

Airline computer reservation system operations, travel agency revenues by firm, and frequent flyer awards by carrier, 1988, 7308–199.9

BEA rpts data coverage and availability, 1991 annual article, 2702–1.203

Fed Govt computer and telecommunication systems acquisition plans and obligations, by agency, FY90-95, annual rpt, 104–33

Fed Govt computer systems with sensitive unclassified data, security plans by characteristics of info and system, and agency, 1989, 2218–85

Fed Govt standards for data recording, processing, and transfer, and for purchase and use of computer systems, series, 2216–2

Households, school, and work computer use, by purpose and selected user characteristics, 1989, Current Population Rpt, 2546–2.158

Libraries technological aid, project descriptions and funding, FY89, annual listing, 4874–6

Space science and related data sources, use by format and user type, FY90, annual rpt, 9504–11

see also Automated tellers
see also Electronic funds transfer

Computer programmers

see Computer use

Computer software

Computer sciences

Asia science and engineering employment, by selected characteristics, for 3 countries, 1991 working paper, 2326–18.61

Degrees (PhD) in science and engineering, by field, instn, employment prospects, sex, race, and other characteristics, 1960s-90, annual rpt, 9627–30

Degrees awarded in higher education, by level, field, race, and sex, 1988/89 with trends from 1978/79, biennial rpt, 4844–17

Degrees awarded in science and engineering, by field, level, and sex, 1966-89, 9627–33

DOT employment, by subagency, occupation, and selected personnel characteristics, FY90, annual rpt, 7304–18

Employment and other characteristics of science and engineering PhDs, by field and State, 1989, biennial rpt, 9627–18

Fed Govt aid to higher education and nonprofit instns for R&D and related activities, by field, instn, agency, and State, FY89, annual rpt, 9627–17

Foreign and US funding for R&D, and scientists and engineering employment and education, 1991 annual rpt, 9627–35.1

Foreign countries science and engineering employment, by professional characteristics, age, and sex, for selected countries, 1991 working paper, 2326–18.62; 2326–18.63

High school advanced placement for college credit, programs by selected characteristics and school control, 1984-86, 4838–46

Higher education course completions, by detailed program, sex, race, and instn type, for 1972 high school class, as of 1984, 4888–4

Higher education grad programs enrollment in science and engineering, by field, source of funds, and characteristics of student and instn, 1975-89, annual rpt, 9627–7

NASA R&D funding to higher education instns, by field, instn, and State, FY90, annual listing, 9504–7

NSF activities, finances, and funding by program, FY90, annual rpt, 9624–6

NSF R&D grant awards, by div and program, periodic rpt series, 9626–7

R&D equipment of higher education instns, acquisition and service costs, condition, and financing, by field and subfield, 1988-90, triennial survey series, 9627–27

R&D funding by Fed Govt, by field, performer type, agency, and State, FY89-91, annual rpt, 9627–20

R&D funding by higher education instns and federally funded centers, by field, instn, and State, FY89, annual rpt, 9627–13

Computer Security Act

Fed Govt computer systems with sensitive unclassified data, security plans by characteristics of info and system, and agency, 1989, 2218–85

Computer software

see Computer industry and products

Computer use

Computer use

Air Force fiscal mgmt system operations and techniques, quarterly rpt, 3602–1

Air traffic control and airway facilities staff, by employment and other characteristics, FY89, annual rpt, 7504–41

County Business Patterns, 1988: employment, establishments, and payroll, by SIC 2- to 4-digit industry and county, annual State rpt series, 2326–6

County Business Patterns, 1989: employment, establishments, and payroll, by SIC 2- to 4-digit industry and county, annual State rpt series, 2326–8

Drug (prescription) mail service industry structure, finances, and operations, 1989 survey, 4658–60

Earnings, annual average percent changes for selected occupational groups, selected MSAs, monthly rpt, 6782–1.1

Education data compilation, 1991 annual rpt, 4824–2

Educational performance of elementary and secondary students, and factors affecting proficiency, by selected characteristics, 1990 natl assessments, subject rpt series, 4896–8

Employee (temporary) supply establishments by occupation supplied, receipts by source, and payroll, by MSA, 1987 Census of Service Industries, 2393–4.8

Employment, earnings, and hours, by SIC 1- to 4-digit industry, monthly and annual averages, selected years 1909-90, annual rpt, 6744–4

Employment, unemployment, and labor force characteristics, by region and census div, 1990, annual rpt, 6744–7.1

Enterprise Statistics, 1987: auxiliaries of multi-establishment firms, finances and operations by function, industry, and State, 2329–6

Enterprise Statistics, 1987: finances and operations for companies, by size, level of diversification, form of organization, and industry group, 2329–8

Exports and imports of services, direct and among multinatl firms affiliates, by industry and world area, 1986-90, article, 2702–1.223

Fed Govt computer and telecommunication systems acquisition plans and obligations, by agency, FY89-91, last issue of annual rpt, 104–20

Fed Govt computer and telecommunication systems acquisition plans and obligations, by agency, FY90-95, annual rpt, 104–33

Fed Govt computer systems with sensitive unclassified data, security plans by characteristics of info and system, and agency, 1989, 2218–85

Fed Govt data collection activities, and quality and privacy issues, 1990 conf, 106–4.14

Fed Govt standards for data recording, processing, and transfer, and for purchase and use of computer systems, series, 2216–2

Fed Reserve System, Board of Governors, and district banks financial statements, performance, and fiscal services, 1990-91, annual rpt, 9364–10

Households, school, and work computer use, by family income, 1989, fact sheet, 2326–17.30

Households, school, and work computer use, by purpose and selected user characteristics, 1989, Current Population Rpt, 2546–2.158

Industry finances and operations, by SIC 2- to 4-digit industry, forecast 1991, annual rpt, 2044–28

Manufacturing employment, by detailed occupation and SIC 2-digit industry, 1989 survey, triennial rpt, 6748–52

Multinatl US firms and foreign affiliates finances and operations, by industry and world area of parent firm, 1989 benchmark survey, preliminary annual rpt, 2704–5

Natl Agricultural Statistics Service minority group staff, promotion, and discrimination complaints, 1988-90, GAO rpt, 26119–326

Occupational injury and illness rates, by SIC 2- to 4-digit industry, 1988-89, annual rpt, 6844–7

Occupational injury and illness rates, by SIC 2- to 4-digit industry, 1989, annual rpt, 6844–1

Puerto Rico economic censuses, 1987: wholesale and retail trade and service industry finances and operations, by SIC 2- to 4-digit industry and municipio, 2591–1

Puerto Rico economic censuses, 1987: wholesale, retail, and service industries finances and operations, by establishment characteristics and SIC 2- and 3-digit industry, subject rpts, 2591–2

Schools (elementary and secondary) computer use, by grade level, 1991 edition, annual rpt, 4824–2.30

Securities intl markets computer use and risk mgmt methods, 1991 GAO rpt, 26125–44

Service industries census, 1987: depreciable assets, capital and operating expenses, and receipts, by SIC 2- to 4-digit kind of business, 2393–2

Service industries census, 1987: establishments, receipts by source, payroll, and employment, by SIC 2- to 4-digit kind of business, State, and MSA, 2393–4

Service industries receipts, by SIC 2- to 4-digit kind of business, 1990, annual rpt, 2413–8

Social security earnings records errors and rates, by employment type, late 1930s-87, GAO rpt, 26121–422

Space science and related data sources, use by format and user type, FY90, annual rpt, 9504–11

State and Metro Area Data Book, 1991 data compilation, 2328–54

Statistical Abstract of US, 1991 annual data compilation, 2324–1.4; 2324–1.13; 2324–1.28

Students computer use at home and school, by selected characteristics, 1991 edition, annual rpt, 4824–2.30

Tax (income) returns filed, by type, IRS service center, and whether full-paid, refund, and electronically filed, 1990 and projected to 1998, semiannual rpt, 8302–7

Tax (income) returns of individuals, IRS processing and taxpayer info activity, electronic filings, and refunds, periodic press release, 8302–6

Index by Subjects and Names

Tax (income) returns of sole proprietorships, income statement items, by industry group, 1989, annual article, 8302–2.214

Tax (income) returns processing, IRS workload forecasts, compliance, and enforcement, data compilation, 1991 annual rpt, 8304–8

Tax (income) withholding and related documents filed, by type and IRS service center, 1990 and projected 1991-98, annual rpt, 8304–22

Tax info returns on magnetic media, FY90, annual rpt, 8304–3.1

Tax returns filed, by type of tax, whether electronically filed, and IRS region and service center, projected 1990-97 and trends from 1978, annual rpt, 8304–9

Wages for 4 occupational groups, relative pay levels in 60 MSAs, 1990, annual rpt, 6785–8

Workplace computer use, by selected worker characteristics, 1991 edition, annual rpt, 4824–2.30

see also Automation

see also CD-ROM technology and use

see also Computer networks

see also Computer sciences

see also Economic and econometric models

see also Mathematic models and modeling

COMSAT

see Communications Satellite Corp.

COMSIS Corp.

"National Urban Mass Transportation Statistics: 1989 Section 15 Annual Report", 7884–4

Concentration, business

see Economic concentration and diversification

Concord, Calif.

see also under By City in the "Index by Categories"

Concrete

see Cement and concrete

Condemnation of property

see Property condemnation

Condominiums and cooperatives

American Housing Survey: inventory change from 1973, by reason, unit and household characteristics, and location, 1983, biennial rpt, 2485–14

American Housing Survey: unit and households detailed characteristics, and unit and neighborhood quality, MSA rpt series, 2485–6

American Housing Survey: unit and households detailed characteristics, and unit and neighborhood quality, 1987, biennial rpt, 2485–12

Market absorption rate and characteristics, 1989, annual Current Housing Rpt, 2484–2

Market absorption rates for condominiums, and completions by sales price, quarterly rpt, 2482–2

Mortgages FHA-insured for 1-family units, by loan type and mortgage characteristics, quarterly rpt, 5142–45

New condominium units completed and absorption rates, by size and price class, preliminary 1990, annual Current Housing Rpt, 2484–3

New condominium units completed, by size, price, and location, 1990, annual rpt, 2384–1.7

Index by Subjects and Names

Conferences

New condominiums, by intended use, units per structure, tenure, and region, monthly rpt, annual tables, 2382–1

Savings instns failures, inventory of real estate assets available from Resolution Trust Corp, 1990, semiannual listing, 9722–2.2; 9722–2.3; 9722–2.8

Savings instns failures, inventory of real estate assets available from Resolution Trust Corp, 1991, semiannual listing, 9722–2.14

Tax (income) returns filed, by type of return and IRS district, 1989 and projected 1990-97, annual rpt, 8304–24

Tax (income) returns filed, by type of tax and IRS region and service center, projected 1990-97 and trends from 1978, annual rpt, 8304–9

Tax (income) returns of corporations, income and tax items by asset size and detailed industry, 1987, annual rpt, 8304–4

Tax (income) returns of corporations, income and tax items by asset size and detailed industry, 1988, annual rpt, 8304–21

Confectionery products *see* Candy and confectionery products

Conferences

- Agricultural and economic conditions in developing countries, and agricultural exports of US, effects of US aid, 1989 conf papers, 1548–372
- Air traffic and other aviation activity forecasts of FAA, 1991 annual conf, 7504–28
- Arctic Ocean fish catch and habitat impacts of oil and gas dev, and assessment methods, 1988 conf, 5738–24
- Banks financial performance, risk assessment, and regulation, 1990 annual conf papers, 9375–7
- Birds (bald eagle) Great Lakes population, breeding, and research status, 1990 conf, 14648–26
- Birds population surveys design and trend analysis methodology, 1988 conf, 5508–108
- California minerals production by commodity, shipments, and liquefied petroleum gas transport by mode, 1986-87, conf, 5668–119
- Civil Rights Commission rpts, 1991 listing, 11048–188
- Communist countries debt to US and other Western banks, by country, 1980s, conf, 25388–56
- Conservation Reserve Program acreage, plantings, and impacts on farm production, soil erosion, water quality, and wildlife habitat, 1991 conf, 1208–360
- Developing countries labor standards impacts on social and economic dev, 1988 conf papers, 6368–9
- Drug (methamphetamine) abuse, availability, health effects, and treatment, 1990 conf papers, 4498–75
- Drug (steroid) use prevalence and health effects, 1989 conf papers, 4498–67
- Drug abuse and treatment, research on biological and behavioral factors and addiction potential of new drugs, 1990 annual conf, 4494–11
- Drug abuse indicators for selected metro areas, research results, data collection, and policy issues, 1991 semiannual conf, 4492–5
- Drug abuse psychotherapy and counseling outcomes, research results and methodology, 1990 conf, 4498–71
- Drug abuse relation to violent and criminal behavior, with data on street gang activity and selected population groups, 1989 conf, 4498–70
- Drug and alcohol abuse treatment services, funding, staffing, and client load, characteristics, and outcomes, by setting, 1989 conf, 4498–73
- Eastern Europe economic and political conditions, and impacts of geographic factors, by country, 1990 conf, 9118–18
- Estuary eutrophication and algal blooms, causes and environmental effects, 1991 conf, 2176–7.22
- Farm financial and marketing conditions, forecast 1991, annual conf, 1004–16
- Financial and monetary studies, Fed Reserve Bank of Boston conf series, 9373–3
- Fish (shark and ray) population, physical characteristics, landings, and fishery mgmt, 1987 conf, 2168–124
- Fish and shellfish aquaculture in US and Japan, mgmt, methods, and biological data for selected species, 1988 conf, annual rpt, 2164–15
- Fish and shellfish catch and stocks in northwest Atlantic, by species and location, 1887-1991 and forecast to 1993, semiannual conf, 2162–9
- Fish larvae abundance, distribution, and growth, for selected Western Hemisphere sites, 1989 conf, 2168–126
- Fishing (sport) warmwater resources mgmt in western US, 1991 conf, 1208–381
- Govt admin and tax records use in data collection, methodological and disclosure issues, 1988-89 annual conf papers, 8304–17
- Health care (primary) research, methodology and findings, 1991 annual conf, 4184–4
- Health care (primary) research, provider role, Federal funding, and provision to minority groups, 1990 conf papers, 4188–69
- Health condition and quality of life measurement, rpts and other info sources, quarterly listing, 4122–1
- Homeless teens pregnancy prevalence and outcomes, services availability, health condition, and drug abuse, 1989 conf, 4108–55
- Hwy safety improvement measures, costs, and accident and death reductions by type of accident and improvement, 1990 conf, 7558–110
- Industrial pollutant concentrations and costs by process and waste prevention or treatment method, 1990 biennial conf, 9184–22
- Judicial Conf proceedings and findings, spring 1991, semiannual rpt, 18202–2
- Library of Congress activities, acquisitions, services, and financial statements, FY90, annual rpt, 26404–1
- Marine mammals strandings, research results, 1987 conf, 2168–127
- Materials (advanced structural) devs and data needs, 1989 conf, 5608–167
- New York Bight pollution levels, sources, treatment costs, economic losses, and environmental and health effects, 1990 conf, 9208–131
- NIH intl program activities and funding, by inst and country, FY90, annual rpt, 4474–6
- Older persons health condition and care research, data availability and collection methodology, for US and selected countries, 1988 conf, 4147–5.6
- Otters (sea) conservation measures taken after Exxon Valdez oil spill in Alaska, 1990 conf, 5508–110
- Pesticide use, economic effects of revised EPA regulations, with data for tomatoes, 1988 conf papers, 1588–154
- Pollutants health effects assessment, methodology and data needs, series, 9186–9
- Radioactive low-level waste repository site design, characteristics, and monitoring techniques, 1987 conf, 5668–116
- Recreation (outdoor) mgmt, research methods, and public opinion, 1990 conf papers, annual rpt, 1204–38
- Recreation areas use in northeastern US, mgmt, and tourism dev issues, 1990 conf, 1208–356
- Respiratory diseases related to occupational hazards, epidemiology, diagnosis, and treatment, for selected industries and work settings, 1988 conf, 4248–90
- Selenium levels in Western States arid areas, and plant and animal exposure effects, 1990 conf, 5668–121
- Shrublands in western US, ecology, biology, and cheatgrass invasion and related fire threat, 1989 conf papers, 1208–351
- Soil mgmt and characteristics, for western mountain forest areas, 1990 conf, 1208–378
- Statistical data collection, methodology, and related issues, 1991 annual conf, 2624–2
- *Survey of Income and Program Participation*, data collection, methodology, and use, 1990 annual conf papers, 2624–1
- Surveys and other data collection activities of Fed Govt, and quality and privacy issues, 1990 conf, 106–4.14
- Telecommunications and Info Natl Admin rpts, FY90, annual listing, 2804–3
- Timber in Pacific basin, sandalwood resources, habitat, harvest, exports, and uses, 1990 conf, 1208–366
- Timber in southeastern US, longleaf pine mgmt and use, 1989 conf, 1208–355
- Timber in southeastern US, pine natural growth and plantation acreage, and lumber industries impacts of shift to plantation pine, 1989 conf papers, 1208–346
- Tree seedlings production techniques, and reforestry transplantation effectiveness, 1990 conf, 1208–376
- Violence among minority youth, prevention strategies, 1990 conf, 4042–3.218
- Vital and Health Statistics Natl Committee activities, FY90, annual narrative rpt, 4164–1
- Walrus population, habitat mgmt, and intl conservation needs, by world region, 1990 conf, 14738–9
- Weights, measures, and performance standards dev, proposals, and policies, 1991 annual conf, 2214–7
- Wilderness areas use, mental health and educational benefits, and leadership training programs effectiveness, 1990 conf papers, 1208–347

Conflict of interests

Conflict of interests

Sentences for Federal offenses, guidelines by offense and circumstances, series, 17668–1

US attorneys civil and criminal cases by type and disposition, and collections, by Federal district, FY90, annual rpt, 6004–2.1

USDA employees financial disclosure rpts filings, processing, errors, and conflicts of interest exposed, 1989, GAO rpt, 26119–314

Congenital malformations

see Birth defects

Conglomerates

see Business acquisitions and mergers

see Economic concentration and diversification

Congo

Agricultural exports of high-value commodities, indexes and sales by commodity, world area, and country, 1960s-86, 1528–323

Agricultural trade of US, by detailed commodity and country, 1989, annual rpt, 1524–8

Agricultural trade of US, by detailed commodity and country, 1990, semiannual rpt, 1522–4

AID economic aid to developing countries, obligations and disbursements by country, quarterly rpt, 9912–4

Dairy imports, consumption, and market conditions, by sub-Saharan Africa country, 1961-88, 1528–321

Economic and military aid and loans from US and intl agencies, by program and country, FY46-90, annual rpt, 9914–5

Economic and social conditions of developing countries from 1960s, and Intl Dev Cooperation Agency and AID activities and funding, FY90-92, annual rpt, 9904–4

Economic conditions, income, production, prices, employment, and trade, 1991 periodic country rpt, 2046–4.66

Economic, social, political, and geographic summary data, by country, 1991, annual factbook, 9114–2

Exports and imports of US, by commodity and country, 1970-89, world area rpt, 9116–1.6

Exports and imports of US, by selected country, country group, and commodity group, 1990, annual rpt, 2044–37

Exports and imports of US, by transport mode, country, and SITC 1- to 3-digit commodity, 1990, annual rpt, 2424–12

Exports of US, detailed Schedule B commodities with countries of destination, 1990, annual rpt, 2424–10

Human rights conditions in 170 countries, and US economic and military aid, 1990, annual rpt, 21384–3

Military aid of US, arms sales, and training programs costs and budget requests, by program, world region, and country, FY90-92, annual rpt, 7144–13

Minerals Yearbook, 1988, Vol 3: foreign country review of production, trade, and policy, by commodity, annual rpt, 5604–17.80

UN voting record and share of votes in agreement with US, by issue, country, and world area, 1990, annual rpt, 7004–18

Congress

Budget of US, authoritative financial statements with appropriations, outlays, and receipts, by agency, FY90, annual rpt, 8104–2

Budget of US, object class analysis of obligations, by agency, FY92, annual rpt, 104–9

Budget of US, obligations and authority by function, agency, and program, with summaries, analyses, and historical tables, FY92, annual rpt, 104–2

Budget of US, receipts by source, outlays by agency and program, and balances, monthly rpt, 8102–3

Congressional Directory, members of 102nd Congress, other officials, elections, and districts, 1991-92, biennial rpt, 23874–1

Election voter turnout and registration, by socioeconomic and demographic characteristics, 1990 congressional election, biennial Current Population Rpt, 2546–1.454

Financial consolidated statements of Fed Govt based on business accounting methods, FY89-90, annual rpt, 8104–5

Financial operations of Fed Govt, detailed data, *Treasury Bulletin,* quarterly rpt, 8002–4

Mail (franked) to households, by content, 1987-88, annual rpt, 9864–10

Statistical Abstract of US, 1991 annual data compilation, 2324–1.8

see also Architect of the Capitol

see also Congressional apportionment

see also Congressional Budget Office

see also Congressional committees

see also Congressional districts

see also Congressional employees

see also Congressional-executive relations

see also Congressional investigations

see also Congressional joint committees

see also Congressional powers

see also General Accounting Office

see also Government Printing Office

see also House of Representatives

see also Library of Congress

see also Office of Technology Assessment

see also Senate

Congressional apportionment

Census of Population, 1990: congressional apportionment and official population counts, by State, 2328–22

Census of Population, 1990: congressional redistricting data coverage and availability, guide, 2308–59

Census of Population, 1990: data adjustment for undercounts, final decision, 2008–31

Census of Population, 1990: population size, by State, census div, and region, and congressional seats apportioned by State, 1990 and trends from 1790, fact sheet, 2326–20.1

Congressional Budget Office

Budget of US, authoritative financial statements with appropriations, outlays, and receipts, by category and agency, FY90, annual rpt, 8104–2.1

Budget of US, CBO analysis and review of FY92 budget by function, annual rpt, 26304–2

Budget of US, CBO analysis of revenue and spending alternatives and projections of economic indicators, FY92-96, annual rpt, 26304–3

Budget of US, obligations and authority by function, agency, and program, with summaries, analyses, and historical tables, FY92, annual rpt, 104–2

Deposit insurance accounting in Federal budget, outlays by instn type, and Bank Insurance Fund finances, late 1970s-96, 26308–100

Fed Govt agencies budget requests and program costs and characteristics, series, 26306–3

Fed Govt programs of congressional interest, objectives, feasibility, benefits, and costs, series, 26306–6

Govt-sponsored enterprises financial condition and capital adequacy, with data by enterprise, 1970s-90 and projected to 1996, 26308–99

Health care spending by type and payment source, with background data and foreign comparisons, 1960s-80s and projected to 2000, 26308–98

HHS research and evaluation programs, 1970-90, annual listing, 4004–30

Congressional committees

Budget of US, House concurrent resolution, with spending and revenue targets, FY92 and projected to FY96, annual rpt, 21264–2

Budget of US, Senate concurrent resolution, with spending and revenue targets, FY92, annual rpt, 25254–1

Congressional Directory, members of 102nd Congress, other officials, elections, and districts, 1991-92, biennial rpt, 23874–1

House of Representatives salaries, expenses, and contingent fund disbursement, detailed listings, quarterly rpt, 21942–1

Public works condition, mgmt, R&D, and funding, for transportation and environmental projects, 1986-91, 26358–235

Senate receipts, itemized expenses by payee, and balances, 1st half FY91, semiannual listing, 25922–1

see also Congressional joint committees

see also House Administration Committee

see also House Aging Committee, Select

see also House Agriculture Committee

see also House Armed Services Committee

see also House Banking, Finance and Urban Affairs Committee

see also House Budget Committee

see also House District of Columbia Committee

see also House Education and Labor Committee

see also House Energy and Commerce Committee

see also House Foreign Affairs Committee

see also House Government Operations Committee

see also House Hunger Committee, Select

see also House Interior and Insular Affairs Committee

see also House Judiciary Committee

see also House Merchant Marine and Fisheries Committee

see also House Narcotics Abuse and Control Committee, Select

see also House Post Office and Civil Service Committee

see also House Public Works and Transportation Committee

Index by Subjects and Names

Connecticut

see also House Science, Space, and Technology Committee
see also House Small Business Committee
see also House Ways and Means Committee
see also Joint Economic Committee
see also Joint Printing Committee
see also Joint Taxation Committee
see also Senate Aging Committee, Special
see also Senate Agriculture, Nutrition, and Forestry Committee
see also Senate Banking, Housing, and Urban Affairs Committee
see also Senate Budget Committee
see also Senate Commerce, Science and Transportation Committee
see also Senate Energy and Natural Resources Committee
see also Senate Environment and Public Works Committee
see also Senate Finance Committee
see also Senate Foreign Relations Committee
see also Senate Governmental Affairs Committee
see also Senate Indian Affairs Committee, Select
see also Senate Judiciary Committee
see also Senate Labor and Human Resources Committee
see also Senate Small Business Committee
see also under names of individual subcommittees (starting with Subcommittee)

Congressional districts

- Agricultural Stabilization and Conservation Service programs acreage, rankings by commodity and congressional district, 1989, biennial rpt, 1804–17
- Census of Population and Housing, 1990: population counts for congressional districts and change from 1980, by State, press release, 2328–32
- Census of Population and Housing, 1990: voting age and total population by race, and housing units, by block, redistricting counts required under PL 94-171, State CD-ROM series, 2551–6
- Classification codes for congressional districts for Fed Govt use, 1990 listing, 2216–2.193
- *Congressional Directory*, members of 102nd Congress, other officials, elections, and districts, 1991-92, biennial rpt, 23874–1
- Energy conservation aid of Fed Govt to public and nonprofit private instns, by building type and State, 1990, annual rpt, 3304–15
- Fed Govt spending in States and local areas, by type, State, county, and city, FY90, annual rpt, 2464–3
- Forests (natl) and other lands under Forest Service mgmt, acreage by forest and location, 1990, annual rpt, 1204–2
- Forests (natl) revenue share paid to States, and acreage, by forest, region, county, and congressional district, FY90, annual rpt, 1204–33
- HHS financial aid, by program, recipient, State, and city, FY90, annual regional listings, 4004–3
- NSF grants and contracts, by field, instn, and State, FY89, annual rpt, 9624–26
- *Statistical Abstract of US*, 1991 annual data compilation, 2324–1.8
- VA programs spending, by State, county, and congressional district, FY90, annual rpt, 8604–6

Votes cast by party, candidate, and State, 1990 natl elections, biennial rpt, 9274–5
see also Congressional apportionment

Congressional employees

- Capitol Architect activities, funding, costs, and contracts, FY88, annual rpt, 25944–1
- Capitol Architect outlays for salaries, supplies, and services, itemized by payee and function, 1st half FY91, semiannual rpt, 25922–2
- *Congressional Directory*, members of 102nd Congress, other officials, elections, and districts, 1991-92, biennial rpt, 23874–1
- Employment and payroll (civilian) of Fed Govt, by pay system, agency, and location, 1990, annual rpt, 9844–6.1; 9844–6.2
- Employment, earnings, and hours, by SIC 1- to 4-digit industry, monthly and annual averages, selected years 1909-90, annual rpt, 6744–4
- House of Representatives salaries, expenses, and contingent fund disbursement, detailed listings, quarterly rpt, 21942–1
- Senate receipts, itemized expenses by payee, and balances, 1st half FY91, semiannual listing, 25922–1
- *Statistical Abstract of US*, 1991 annual data compilation, 2324–1.8

Congressional-executive relations

- Budget of US, CBO analysis and review of FY92 budget by function, annual rpt, 26304–2
- Budget of US, legislative process overview with summary projections and glossary, FY90-95, 21268–43
- HHS cost savings from legislative actions and proposals, 1st half FY91, semiannual rpt, 4002–6
- *see also* Executive impoundment of appropriated funds

Congressional investigations

- Senate receipts, itemized expenses by payee, and balances, 1st half FY91, semiannual listing, 25922–1
- *see also* General Accounting Office

Congressional joint committees

- Budget of US, authoritative financial statements with appropriations, outlays, and receipts, by category and agency, FY90, annual rpt, 8104–2.1
- *see also* Joint Economic Committee
- *see also* Joint Printing Committee
- *see also* Joint Taxation Committee

Congressional powers

- Budget of US, House concurrent resolution, with spending and revenue targets, FY92 and projected to FY96, annual rpt, 21264–2
- Budget of US, legislative process overview with summary projections and glossary, FY90-95, 21268–43
- Budget of US, Senate concurrent resolution, with spending and revenue targets, FY92, annual rpt, 25254–1
- *Congressional Directory*, members of 102nd Congress, other officials, elections, and districts, 1991-92, biennial rpt, 23874–1
- *see also* Congressional-executive relations

Congressional Research Service

"International Economic Competitiveness, Trade Performance and U.S. Living Standards", 21788–204

"Reauthorization of the Motor Carrier Safety Assistance Program (MCSAP): Options Intended To Improve Highway Safety", 25268–78

"Space Activities of the U.S., Soviet Union and Other Launching Countries/Organizations, 1957-90", 21704–4

"Workshop on U.S.-USSR Commercial Relations, Apr. 17, 1989", 25388–56
see also Library of Congress

Connecticut

- Banks (insured commercial and savings) deposits by instn, State, MSA, and county, as of June 1990, annual regional rpt, 9295–3.1
- Cancer (brain and central nervous system) cases and rates, by whether confirmed by radiography alone, for Connecticut, 1960s-88, article, 4472–1.234
- County Business Patterns, 1989: employment, establishments, and payroll, by SIC 2- to 4-digit industry and county, annual State rpt, 2326–8.8
- DOD prime contract awards, by contractor, service branch, State, and city, FY90, annual rpt, 3544–22
- Economic indicators for New England States, Fed Reserve 1st District, monthly rpt, 9373–2
- Employment variability in New England relation to service and financial industries employment, with data by selected industry group and State, 1970s-89, article, 9373–1.212
- Fed Govt spending in States and local areas, by type, State, county, and city, FY90, annual rpt, 2464–3
- Fed Govt spending in States, by type, program, agency, and State, FY90, annual rpt, 2464–2
- HHS financial aid, by program, recipient, State, and city, FY90, annual regional listing, 4004–3.1
- Hospital deaths of Medicare patients, actual and expected rates by diagnosis, and hospital characteristics, by instn, FY87-89, annual regional rpt, 4654–14.1
- Housing census, 1990: inventory, occupancy, and costs, State fact sheet, 2326–21.8
- Income (personal) per capita and by source, and earnings by industry div, by State, MSA, and county, 1984-89, annual regional rpt, 2704–2.2
- Marriages, divorces, and rates, by characteristics of spouses, State, and county, 1987 and trends from 1920, US Vital Statistics annual rpt, 4144–4
- Mineral Industry Surveys, State reviews of production, 1990, preliminary annual rpt, 5614–6
- *Minerals Yearbook, 1989*, Vol 2: State review of production and sales by commodity, and business activity, annual rpt, 5604–16.8
- *Minerals Yearbook, 1989*, Vol 2: State reviews of production, sales, and firms, by commodity, and business activity, annual rpt, 5604–34
- Physicians, by specialty, age, sex, and location of training and practice, 1989, State rpt, 4116–6.7
- Population and housing census, 1990: population and housing characteristics, households, and land area, by county, subdiv, and place, State rpt, 2551–1.8

Connecticut

Population and housing census, 1990: voting age and total population by race, and housing units, by block, redistricting counts required under PL 94-171, State CD-ROM release, 2551–6.6

Population and housing census, 1990: voting age and total population by race, and housing units, by county and city, redistricting counts required under PL 94-171, State summary rpt, 2551–5.7

Savings instns, FHLB 1st District members financial operations compared to banks, and related economic and housing indicators, bimonthly rpt with articles, 9302–4

Statistical Abstract of US, 1991 annual data compilation, 2324–1

Supplemental Security Income payments and beneficiaries, by type of eligibility, State, and county, Dec 1989, annual rpt, 4744–27.1

Water resources dev projects of Army Corps of Engineers, characteristics, and costs, 1950s-91, biennial State rpt, 3756–2.7

Water supply and quality in streams and lakes, and groundwater levels in wells, by drainage basin, 1990, annual State rpt, 5666–10.7

Water supply in northeastern US, precipitation and stream runoff by station, monthly rpt, 2182–3

Wetlands acreage, resources, soil and water properties, and conservation efforts, by wetland type, 1988 State rpt, 5506–11.4

see also under By State in the "Index by Categories"

Conner, Roger C.

"Forest Resources of Arizona", 1208–374

"Forest Statistics for Land Outside National Forests in Eastern Montana, 1989", 1206–25.8

"Forest Statistics for Land Outside National Forests in Northwestern Montana, 1989", 1206–25.10; 1206–25.11

Connor, John M.

"U.S. Beef Packing Industry: Changing Market Structure and Performance Implications", 1004–16.1

Conrad, Judy

"Hurricane Gold. Part I—The Loss", 2152–8.203

"Hurricane Gold. Part II—The Find", 2152–8.203

Conrail

see Consolidated Rail Corp.

Conscription

see Draft evasion and protest

see Selective service

Conservation of natural resources

Agricultural Conservation Program funding, by practice, region and State, monthly rpt, 1802–15

Agricultural Stabilization and Conservation Service producer payments and certificate value, by program, monthly rpt, 1802–10

Agricultural Stabilization and Conservation Service producer payments, by program and State, 1990, annual table, 1804–12

Agricultural Statistics, 1990, annual rpt, 1004–1

Appalachia local dev projects, and funding by source, by program and State, FY90, annual rpt, 9084–1

Assistance (financial and nonfinancial) of Fed Govt, 1991 base edition with supplements, annual listing, 104–5

Budget of US, balances of budget authority obligated and unobligated, by function and agency, FY90-92, annual rpt, 104–8

Budget of US, CBO analysis and review of FY92 budget by function, annual rpt, 26304–2

Budget of US, formula grant program obligations to State and local govts, by agency, program, and State, FY92, annual rpt, 104–30

Budget of US, House concurrent resolution, with spending and revenue targets, FY92 and projected to FY96, annual rpt, 21264–2

Budget of US, midsession review of FY92 budget, by function, annual rpt, 104–7

Budget of US, obligations and authority by function, agency, and program, with summaries, analyses, and historical tables, FY92, annual rpt, 104–2

Budget of US, receipts by source, outlays by agency and program, and balances, monthly rpt, 8102–3

Budget of US, Senate concurrent resolution, with spending and revenue targets, FY92, annual rpt, 25254–1

Coastal areas recreation facilities, by State, county, estuary, and level of govt, 1972-84, 2178–29

Coastal areas recreation facilities of Fed Govt and States, visitor and site characteristics, 1987-90 survey, regional rpt series, 2176–9

Construction industries census, 1987: establishments, employment, receipts, and expenditures, by SIC 4-digit industry and State, final industry rpt series, 2373–1

Construction put in place, permits, housing sales, costs, material prices, and employment, bimonthly rpt with articles, 2042–1

Construction put in place, value of new public and private structures, by type, monthly rpt, 2382–4

Court civil and criminal caseloads for Federal district courts, 1991, annual rpt, 18204–2.1

Developing countries economic, population, and agricultural data, US and other aid sources, and AID activity, country rpt series, 9916–12

DOD prime contract awards, by detailed procurement category, FY87-90, annual rpt, 3544–18

Environmental Quality, status of problems, protection programs, research, and intl issues, 1991 annual rpt, 484–1

Fed Govt accounts receivable, delinquent debt cases and collections of Justice Dept and private law firms, pilot project results, FY90, annual rpt, 6004–20

Fed Govt construction spending, by program and type of structure, FY85-92, annual article, 2042–1.206

Fed Govt labor productivity, indexes of output and labor costs by function, FY67-89, annual rpt, 6824–1.6

Fed Govt spending in States, by type, program, agency, and State, FY90, annual rpt, 2464–2

Fish and Wildlife Service restoration programs finances by State, and excise tax collections, FY90, annual rpt, 5504–13

Fish and Wildlife Service restoration programs funding, land purchases, and project listing, by State, FY89, annual rpt, 5504–1

Index by Subjects and Names

FmHA loans, by type, borrower race, and State, quarterly rpt, 1182–5

Forest Service activities and finances, by region and State, FY90, annual rpt, 1204–1

Govt census, 1987: employment, payroll, and average earnings, by function, level of govt, State, county, and population size, 2455–2

Govt employment and payroll, by function, level of govt, and jurisdiction, 1990, annual rpt series, 2466–1

Govt finances, by level of govt, State, and for large cities and counties, annual rpt series, 2466–2

Interior Dept programs fraud and abuse, audits and investigations, 2nd half FY91, semiannual rpt, 5302–2

Land and Water Conservation Fund grants, State matching funds, and balances, by State, FY90, annual rpt, 5544–18

Land Mgmt Bur activities and finances, and public land acreage and use, annual State rpt series, 5724–11

New Hampshire and Vermont public opinion on natural resources use and mgmt, 1991 rpt, 1208–371

State and local govt employment of minorities and women, by occupation, function, and pay level, 1990, annual rpt, 9244–6.4

Tax expenditures, Federal revenues forgone through income tax deductions and exclusions by type, FY92-96, annual rpt, 21784–10

TVA finances and operations by program and facility, FY90, annual rpt, 9804–32

Wetlands preservation under Water Bank Program, acreage, agreements, and payments, by State, monthly rpt, 1802–5

see also Birds and bird conservation

see also Endangered species

see also Energy conservation

see also Environmental pollution and control

see also Environmental regulation

see also Flood control

see also Forests and forestry

see also International cooperation in conservation

see also Land use

see also Marine resources conservation

see also National forests

see also National parks

see also Plants and vegetation

see also Reclamation of land

see also Recycling of waste materials

see also Severance taxes

see also Soils and soil conservation

see also State forests

see also State funding for natural resources and conservation

see also Water resources development

see also Wilderness areas

see also Wildlife and wildlife conservation

see also Wildlife refuges

Consolidated Metropolitan Statistical Areas

see Metropolitan Statistical Areas

see under By SMSA or MSA in the "Index by Categories"

Consolidated Rail Corp.

Finances and operations of Class I railroads, detailed data by firm, class of service, and district, 1989, annual rpt, 9486–6.1

Index by Subjects and Names

Construction industry

Constantine, J. Robert
"Eugene V. Debs: An American Paradox", 6722–1.240

Constitutional law

Court civil and criminal caseloads for Federal district, appeals, and bankruptcy courts, by type of suit and offense, circuit, and district, 1990, annual rpt, 18204–11

Court civil and criminal caseloads for Federal district, appeals, and special courts, 1990, annual rpt, 18204–8

Court civil and criminal caseloads for Federal district courts, 1991, annual rpt, 18204–2.1

US attorneys civil and criminal cases by type and disposition, and collections, by Federal district, FY90, annual rpt, 6004–2.1

see also Administrative law and procedure
see also Citizenship
see also Civil rights
see also Congressional-executive relations
see also Congressional powers
see also Due process of law
see also Federal-State relations
see also Habeas corpus
see also Interstate relations
see also Judicial powers
see also Right of assembly
see also Right of privacy

Construction industry

Airport improvement program of FAA, activities, funding, and airport operations, by location, projected 1990-99, biennial rpt, 7504–42

American Samoa employment, earnings, and minimum wage, by establishment and industry, 1989, biennial rpt, 6504–6

Appalachia hwy system and access roads funding and completion status, by State, quarterly tables, 9082–1

Assns (trade and professional) and labor unions, for construction and building materials industries, 1991 listing, article, 2042–1.202

Business statistics, detailed data for major industries and economic indicators, *Survey of Current Business*, monthly rpt, 2702–1.6

Census Bur rpts and data files, coverage and availability, 1991 annual listing, 2304–2

Classification codes concordance of Canada and US SICs, for 1- to 4-digit levels, 1991 rpt, 2628–31

Collective bargaining agreements expiring during year, and workers covered, by firm, union, industry group, and State, 1991, annual rpt, 6784–9

Collective bargaining wage and benefit changes, quarterly press release, 6782–2

Collective bargaining wage changes and coverage, by industry sector and whether contract includes escalator clause and lump sum payment, 1980-90, annual article, 6722–1.227

Contracts for industrial and commercial construction, *Survey of Current Business*, cyclical indicators, monthly rpt, 2702–1.1

County Business Patterns, 1988: employment, establishments, and payroll, by SIC 2- to 4-digit industry and county, annual State rpt series, 2326–6

County Business Patterns, 1989: employment, establishments, and payroll, by SIC 2- to 4-digit industry and county, annual State rpt series, 2326–8

DOD appropriations for base construction and family housing, by facility, service branch, and location, FY90-93, annual rpt, 3544–39

DOD budget requests for base construction, renovation, and land acquisition, by project, service branch, State, and country, FY92-93, annual rpt, 3544–15

DOD budget, weapons acquisition costs by system and service branch, FY91-93, annual rpt, 3504–2

DOD contracts, payroll, and personnel, by service branch and location, with top 5 contractors and maps, by State and country, FY90, annual rpt, 3544–29

DOD outlays and obligations, by function and service branch, quarterly rpt, 3542–3

DOD prime contract awards, by category, contract and contractor type, and service branch, FY81-1st half FY91, semiannual rpt, 3542–1

DOD prime contract awards, by category, contractor type, and State, FY88-90, annual rpt, 3544–11

DOD prime contract awards, by detailed procurement category, FY87-90, annual rpt, 3544–18

DOD prime contract awards, by size and type of contract, service branch, competitive status, category, and labor standard, FY90, annual rpt, 3544–19

DOD property, supply, and equipment inventory, by service branch, FY90, annual rpt, 3544–6

Earnings by industry div, and personal income per capita and by source, by State, MSA, and county, 1984-89, annual regional rpts, 2704–2

Earnings, weekly averages, monthly rpt, 23842–1.2

Education (postsecondary) course completions, by detailed program, sex, race, and instn type, for 1972 high school class, as of 1984, 4888–4

Electric utilities finances and operations, detailed data for public and privately owned firms, 1989, annual rpt, 3164–11.4

Electric utilities finances and operations, detailed data for publicly owned firms, 1989, annual rpt, 3164–24

Electric utilities privately owned, finances and operations, detailed data, 1989, annual rpt, 3164–23

Embassy and other US diplomatic facilities security improvement construction projects costs and activities, 1986-90, GAO rpt, 26123–322

Employment and Earnings, detailed data, monthly rpt, 6742–2.5

Employment, earnings, and hours, by SIC 1- to 4-digit industry, monthly and annual averages, selected years 1909-90, annual rpt, 6744–4

Employment, earnings, and hours, monthly press release, 6742–5

Employment situation, earnings, hours, and other BLS economic indicators, transcripts of BLS Commissioner's monthly testimony, periodic rpt, 23846–4

Employment, unemployment, and labor force characteristics, by region, State, and selected metro area, 1990, annual rpt, 6744–7

Energy use by mode of transport, fuel supply, and demographic and economic factors of vehicle use, 1970s-89, annual rpt, 3304–5

Engineering and architectural establishments, receipts by type of client and project, payroll, and employment, by State, 1987 Census of Service Industries, 2393–4.16

Enterprise Statistics, 1987: auxiliaries of multi-establishment firms, finances and operations by function, industry, and State, 2329–6

Enterprise Statistics, 1987: finances and operations for companies, by size, level of diversification, form of organization, and industry group, 2329–8

Explosives and blasting agents use, by type, industry, and State, 1990, Mineral Industry Surveys, annual rpt, 5614–22

Farm production itemized costs, by farm sales size and region, 1990, annual rpt, 1614–3

Fed Govt financial and nonfinancial domestic aid, 1991 base edition with supplements, annual listing, 104–5

Fed Govt land acquisition and dev projects in DC metro area, characteristics and funding by agency and project, FY91-95, annual rpt, 15454–1

Finances and operations, by SIC 2- to 4-digit industry, forecast 1991, annual rpt, 2044–28

Foreign direct investment in US, major transactions by type, industry, country, and US location, 1989, annual rpt, 2044–20

Franchise business opportunities by firm and kind of business, and sources of aid and info, 1990 annual listing, 2104–7

Health care R&D, training, construction, and medical library grants of NIH, by location and recipient, FY90, annual listings, 4434–7

Health care spending, by service type, payment source, and sector, projected 1990-2000 and trends from 1965, article, 4652–1.251

Health care spending, by service type, payment source, and sector, 1960s-90, annual article, 4652–1.221; 4652–1.252

Hospital reimbursement by Medicare under prospective payment system, construction cost indexes evaluation, 1991 article, 4652–1.247

Hwy construction and repair work involvement in fatal traffic accidents, 1989, annual rpt, 7764–10

Hwy construction bids and contracts for Federal-aid hwys, by State, 1st half 1991, semiannual rpt, 7552–12

Hwy construction material prices and indexes for Federal-aid system, by type of material and urban-rural location, quarterly rpt, 7552–7

Hwy construction minority contractor training, funding by region, FY91, annual release, 7554–40

Hwy funding, costs, and completion status of Federal-aid system, by State, as of June 1991, semiannual rpt, 7552–5

Hwy receipts by source, and spending by function, by level of govt and State, 1990, annual rpt, 7554–1.3

Construction industry

Import restraint elimination impacts on US economy and selected service industries, 1970s-90, 9886–4.173

Imports, exports, and employment impacts, by SIC 2- to 4-digit industry and commodity, quarterly rpt, 2322–2

Industry activity, construction put in place, permits, material prices, and employment, bimonthly rpt with articles, 2042–1

Input-output structure of US economy, detailed interindustry transactions for 84 industries, and components of final demand, 1986, annual article, 2702–1.206

Input-output structure of US economy, detailed interindustry transactions for 85 industries, 1982 benchmark data, 2702–1.213

Jail adult and juvenile population, employment, spending, instn conditions, and inmate programs, by county and facility, 1988, regional rpt series, 6068–144

Kuwait reconstruction after Persian Gulf War, Army Corps of Engineers contract awards by firm and purpose, 1st qtr 1991, article, 2042–1.203

Loan activity for mortgages, by type of lender, loan, and mortgaged property, monthly press release, 5142–18

Loan activity for mortgages, by type of lender, loan, and mortgaged property, quarterly press release, 5142–30

Machinery for construction, shipments, exports, and firms by product, 1990, annual Current Industrial Rpt, 2506–12.3

Mexico construction value and trade, and import duties on materials and equipment by type, 1991 article, 2042–1.207

Middle Atlantic States economic conditions, Fed Reserve 3rd District, quarterly rpt, 9387–10

Military aid of US, arms sales, and training, by country, FY50-90, annual rpt, 3904–3

Multinatl US firms and foreign affiliates finances and operations, by industry and world area of parent firm, 1989 benchmark survey, preliminary annual rpt, 2704–5

Natl Guard activities, personnel, and facilities, FY90, annual rpt, 3504–22

Natural gas interstate pipeline company detailed financial and operating data, by firm, 1989, annual rpt, 3164–38

New construction (public and private) activity, and new housing starts, 1929-90, annual rpt, 204–1.3

New construction (public and private) put in place, value by type, monthly rpt, 2382–4

New England States economic indicators, Fed Reserve 1st District, monthly rpt, 9373–2.6

NIH activities, funding by program and recipient type, staff, and clinic patients, by inst, FY90, annual rpt, 4434–3

NIH grants and contracts, quarterly listing, 4432–1

Nuclear power plant capacity, generation, and operating status, by plant and foreign and US location, 1990 and projected to 2030, annual rpt, 3164–57

Occupational deaths in construction industries, by cause, age, and region, 1985-89, 6608–4

Occupational injuries, illnesses, and workdays lost, by SIC 2-digit industry, 1989-90, annual press release, 6844–3

Occupational injury and illness rates, by SIC 2- to 4-digit industry, 1988-89, annual rpt, 6844–7

Occupational injury and illness rates, by SIC 2- to 4-digit industry, 1989, annual rpt, 6844–1

Persian Gulf War costs to US by category and service branch, and offsetting contributions by allied country, monthly rpt, 102–3

Persian Gulf War costs to US by category and service branch, and offsetting contributions by allied country, various periods FY90-91, annual rpt, 104–7

Pipeline and compressor station construction costs, 1984-87, annual rpt, 3084–3

Pollution (air) emissions factors, by detailed pollutant and source, data compilation, 1990 rpt, 9198–120

Price indexes (producer), by stage of processing and detailed commodity, monthly 1990, annual rpt, 6764–2

Price indexes (producer) for material inputs, by construction industry, monthly rpt, 6762–6

Prison construction and operating costs, capacity, and inmates, for Federal and State facilities, 1985-89, GAO rpt, 26119–341

Puerto Rico and other US possessions corporations income tax returns, income and tax items, and employment, by selected industry, 1987, article, 8302–2.213

Puerto Rico economic censuses, 1987: wholesale and retail trade sales by customer class, and employment, by SIC 2- and 3-digit kind of business, subject rpt, 2591–2.2

R&D facilities for biological and medical sciences, space and equipment adequacy, needs, and funding by source, by instn type, 1990, biennial rpt, 4434–17

Respiratory diseases related to occupational hazards, epidemiology, diagnosis, and treatment, for selected industries and work settings, 1988 conf, 4248–90

Science and engineering employment and education, and R&D spending, for US and selected foreign countries, 1991 annual rpt, 9627–35.2

SEC registration, firms required to file annual rpts, as of Sept 1990, annual listing, 9734–5

South Central States employment by industry div, income, and other economic indicators, for 4 States, 1989-90 and forecast 1991-92, annual article, 9391–16.207

Soviet Union GNP by component and industry sector, and CIA estimation methods, 1950s-87, 23848–223

Soviet Union GNP by detailed income and outlay component, 1985, 2326–18.59

State and Metro Area Data Book, 1991 data compilation, 2328–54

Statistical Abstract of US, 1991 annual data compilation, 2324–1.26

Tax (income) returns filed by type of filer, selected income items, quarterly rpt, 8302–2.1

Index by Subjects and Names

Tax (income) returns for foreign corporate activity in US, assets, and income statement items, by industry div and selected country, 1986-87, article, 8302–2.205

Tax (income) returns of corporations, income and tax items by asset size and detailed industry, 1987, annual rpt, 8304–4

Tax (income) returns of corporations, income and tax items by asset size and detailed industry, 1988, annual rpt, 8304–21

Tax (income) returns of corporations with foreign tax credit, income and tax items by industry group, 1986, biennial article, 8302–2.203

Tax (income) returns of multinatl US firms foreign affiliates, income statement items, by asset size and industry, 1986, biennial article, 8302–2.212

Tax (income) returns of partnerships, income statement and balance sheet items, by industry group, 1989, annual article, 8302–2.216; 8304–18

Tax (income) returns of sole proprietorships, income statement items, by industry group, 1989, annual article, 8302–2.214

Tax (income) returns of US corporations under foreign control, assets and income statement items by industry div and country, 1988, article, 8302–2.219

VA health care, nursing home, and other facilities construction projects, costs and completion status by site, FY90, annual rpt, 8604–3.5

VA programs spending, by State, county, and congressional district, FY90, annual rpt, 8604–6

Wage and benefit changes from collective bargaining and mgmt decisions, by industry div, monthly rpt, 6782–1

West Central States economic indicators, Fed Reserve 10th District, quarterly rpt, 9381–16.2

Wholesale trade census, 1987: establishments, sales by customer class, employment, inventories, and expenses, by SIC 2- to 4-digit kind of business, 2407–4

see also Building codes
see also Building materials
see also Building permits
see also Cement and concrete
see also Census of Construction Industries
see also Housing construction
see also Housing maintenance and repair
see also Plumbing and heating
see also Shipbuilding and repairing
see also Wrecking and demolition
see also under By Industry in the "Index by Categories"

Consultants

Agricultural technical consultants, by type, 1989, 26358–231

AID and Intl Dev Cooperation Agency activities and funding, FY90-92, with developing countries economic and social conditions from 1960s, annual rpt, 9904–4

Credit unions federally insured, finances by instn characteristics and State, as of June 1991, semiannual rpt, 9532–6

DOD prime contract awards, by detailed procurement category, FY87-90, annual rpt, 3544–18

Index by Subjects and Names

Employment, earnings, and hours, by SIC 1- to 4-digit industry, monthly and annual averages, selected years 1909-90, annual rpt, 6744–4

Enterprise Statistics, 1987: finances and operations for companies, by size, level of diversification, form of organization, and industry group, 2329–8

Fed Govt agencies appointments of consultants and experts for temporary employment, and rule violations, 1986-89, GAO rpt, 26119–354

Fed Govt contracts for consulting services, obligations by agency, FY87-89, GAO rpt, 26119–343

Finances and operations, by SIC 2- to 4-digit industry, forecast 1991, annual rpt, 2044–28

Mental health care services, staffing, research, and training programs in VA facilities, 1991 biennial listing, 8704–2

Minority Business Dev Centers mgmt and financial aid, and characteristics of businesses, by region and State, FY90, annual rpt, 2104–6

Nuclear Regulatory Commission budget, staff, and activities, by program, FY90-93, annual rpt, 9634–9

Pest control integrated mgmt programs for vegetables, acreage, costs, savings, and funding sources and recipients, by State, 1980s, 1568–298

Physicians consultations requested by attending physician, Medicare reimbursement issues, with use by diagnosis, specialty, location, and other characteristics, 1986, 4658–47

Physicians consulting and attending at VA facilities, by specialty, quarterly rpt, 8602–6

Puerto Rico economic censuses, 1987: wholesale and retail trade and service industry finances and operations, by SIC 2- to 4-digit industry and municipio, 2591–1

Puerto Rico economic censuses, 1987: wholesale, retail, and service industries finances and operations, by establishment characteristics and SIC 2- and 3-digit industry, subject rpts, 2591–2

Receipts for services, by SIC 2- to 4-digit kind of business, 1990, annual rpt, 2413–8

Science and engineering PhDs employment and other characteristics, by field and State, 1989, biennial rpt, 9627–18

Senate receipts, itemized expenses by payee, and balances, 1st half FY91, semiannual listing, 25922–1

Service industries census, 1987: establishments, receipts by source, payroll, and employment, by SIC 2- to 4-digit kind of business, State, and MSA, 2393–4

Tax (income) returns of sole proprietorships, income statement items, by industry group, 1989, annual article, 8302–2.214

Consumer complaints see Consumer protection

Consumer cooperatives *Statistical Abstract of US*, 1991 annual data compilation, 2324–1.17 *see also* Rural cooperatives

Consumer credit

Airline consumer complaints to DOT about service by US and foreign carrier, and for travel and cargo service, by reason, monthly rpt, 7302–11

Assets and debts of private sector, balance sheets by segment, 1945-90, semiannual rpt, 9365–4.1

Auto, mobile home, and other consumer installment credit loans, monthly rpt, 23842–1.5

Banks (insured commercial and savings) finances, for foreign and domestic offices, by asset size, 1989, annual rpt, 9294–4.2

Banks (natl) charters, mergers, liquidations, enforcement cases, and financial performance, with data by instn and State, quarterly rpt, 8402–3

Business statistics, detailed data for major industries and economic indicators, *Survey of Current Business*, monthly rpt, 2702–1.9

Credit reporting and collection establishments, and receipts by source and class of client, by MSA, 1987 Census of Service Industries, 2393–4.4

Debt outstanding for installment and noninstallment credit, monthly rpt series, 9365–2

Financial and business detailed statistics, *Fed Reserve Bulletin*, monthly rpt with articles, 9362–1

Flow-of-funds accounts, savings, investments, and credit statements, quarterly rpt, 9365–3.3

Households debt, and payment behavior and difficulties, by selected characteristics, 1980s-90, article, 9362–1.201

Households debt holdings impact of credit constraints and other factors, model description and results, 1980-83, technical paper, 9379–12.73

Installment credit outstanding, extensions, and liquidations, monthly rpt, 9362–1.1

New England States economic indicators, Fed Reserve 1st District, monthly rpt, 9373–2.7

North Central States business and economic conditions, Fed Reserve 9th District, quarterly journal, 9383–19

North Central States, FHLB 6th District insured savings instns financial condition and operations by State, monthly rpt, 9302–11

Outstanding installment credit by type, and noninstallment credit, 1950-90, annual rpt, 204–1.5

Retail trade sales, inventories, purchases, gross margin, and accounts receivable, by SIC 2- to 4-digit kind of business and form of ownership, 1989, annual rpt, 2413–5

Savings instns insured by Savings Assn Insurance Fund, assets, liabilities, and deposit and loan activity, by conservatorship status, monthly rpt, 8432–1

Southeastern States, Fed Reserve 5th District, economic indicators by State, quarterly rpt, 9389–16

Southeastern States, Fed Reserve 5th District insured commercial banks financial statements, by State, quarterly rpt, 9389–18

Consumer Expenditure Survey

Southeastern States, Fed Reserve 8th District banking and economic conditions, quarterly rpt with articles, 9391–16

Statistical Abstract of US, 1991 annual data compilation, 2324–1.16

Survey of Current Business, detailed financial and business data, and economic indicators, monthly rpt, 2702–1.1

West Central States economic indicators, Fed Reserve 10th District, quarterly rpt, 9381–16.2

see also Credit bureaus and agencies *see also* Credit cards *see also* Credit unions *see also* Discrimination in credit *see also* Finance companies *see also* Personal debt

Consumer Expenditure Survey

Charity cash contributions of consumers, by charity type and selected characteristics, 1988/89, article, 1702–1.214

Child rearing costs for single parent families, by expense type and age of child, 1990, article, 1702–1.203

Child rearing costs of married couple households, by expenditure type, child's age, income, and region, 1990 and projected to 2007, 1708–87

Economic indicators, prices, labor costs, and productivity, BLS econometric analyses and methodology, working paper series, 6886–6

Expenditures by category, and income, by selected household characteristics and location, 1990 survey, annual press release, 6726–1.42

Expenditures by category, selected household characteristics, and region, quarterly rpt, 6762–14

Expenditures by commodity, and household income by source, by selected characteristics and region, 1988-89 survey, annual rpt, 6764–5

Expenditures for selected categories, Consumer Expenditure Survey, 1991 semiannual pamphlet, 2322–3

Food spending, by item, household composition, income, age, race, and region, 1980-88, Consumer Expenditure Survey biennial rpt, 1544–30

Lower middle-class household income by source and spending by type, for 2-parent and single mother families by selected characteristics, 1987, article, 1702–1.207

Married couple families with one spouse working, and income by source and expenses by type, by selected characteristics, 1987, article, 1702–1.201

Men (never married) housing costs, by type and selected characteristics, 1987, article, 1702–1.208

Minority group household income by source, and spending by type, by householder characteristics, 1987, article, 1702–1.206

Older persons household income by source, and spending by type, 1987, article, 1702–1.204

Older women's household income by source, and expenses by type, by living arrangement and other characteristics, 1988, article, 1702–1.210

Youth employment impacts on family income, and expenses by type, with selected family characteristics, 1989, article, 1702–1.213

Consumer expenditures

Consumer expenditures
see Personal consumption

Consumer income
see Personal and household income

Consumer Price Index

Agricultural Outlook, production, prices, marketing, and trade, by commodity, forecast and current situation, monthly rpt with articles, 1502–4

Alaska socioeconomic impacts of OCS oil resources dev, 1980-89 and projected to 2020, 5736–5.11

Budget of US, CBO analysis of revenue and spending alternatives and projections of economic indicators, FY92-96, annual rpt, 26304–3

Canada and US auto trade, production, sales, prices, and employment, selected years 1965-88, annual rpt, 2044–35

CPI by component for US city average, and by region, population size, and for 15 metro areas, monthly rpt, 6762–1

CPI by component for US city average, and by region, population size, and for 27 metro areas, monthly rpt, 6762–2

CPI changes for selected items, 1981-June 1991, article, 6722–1.247

CPI changes for selected items, 1981-90, annual article, 6722–1.226

CPI components relative importance, by selected MSA, region, population size, and for US city average, 1990, annual rpt, 6884–1

CPI rounding errors impact on rebased index, 1991 article, 9375–1.206

Dairy products CPI for all urban consumers, US city average, monthly rpt, 1317–4.2

Dallas-Fort Worth-Arlington metro area employment, earnings, hours, and CPI changes, late 1970s-90, annual rpt, 6964–2

Developing countries economic and social conditions from 1960s, and Intl Dev Cooperation Agency and AID activities and funding, FY90-92, annual rpt, 9904–4

Eastern Europe transition to market economies, economic conditions, intl aid, and energy balance, by country, 1985-90, 9118–13

EC economic integration economic impacts, with background data by country, 1988-90, article, 9379–1.201

Economic conditions, consumer and stock prices and production indexes, 6 OECD countries and US, *Business Conditions Digest*, monthly rpt, 2702–1.2

Economic indicators and components, and Fed Reserve 4th District business and financial conditions, monthly chartbook, 9377–10

Economic indicators and components, current data and annual trends, monthly rpt, 23842–1.4

Economic indicators and relation to govt finances by level of govt, selected years 1929-90, annual rpt, 10044–1

Economic indicators compounded annual rates of change, monthly rpt, 9391–3

Economic indicators compounded annual rates of change, 1971-90, annual rpt, 9391–9.2

Economic indicators, monthly rpt, 9362–1.2

Economic indicators, prices, labor costs, and productivity, BLS econometric analyses and methodology, working paper series, 6886–6

Energy taxes economic and energy demand impacts, for alternative taxation methods, projected 1991-2000, 3166–6.57

Energy use by mode of transport, fuel supply, and demographic and economic factors of vehicle use, 1970s-89, annual rpt, 3304–5

Escalator clauses of collective bargaining agreements and other contracts, use of CPI, with conversion factors for index rebasing, 1991 guide, 6888–34

Family Economics Review, consumer goods prices and supply, and home economics, quarterly journal, 1702–1

Food consumption, supply, trade, prices, spending, and indexes, by commodity, 1989, annual rpt, 1544–4

Food spending, by item, household composition, income, age, race, and region, 1980-88, Consumer Expenditure Survey biennial rpt, 1544–30

Footwear production, employment, use, prices, and US trade by country, quarterly rpt, 9882–6

Foreign and US consumer price indexes, for 7 OECD countries, *Survey of Current Business*, monthly rpt, 2702–1.2

Foreign and US economic conditions, for major industrial countries, biweekly rpt, 9112–1

Foreign and US industrial production indexes and CPI, for US and 6 OECD countries, current data and annual trends, monthly rpt, 23842–1.7

Foreign countries economic and monetary trends, compounded annual rates of change and quarterly indicators for US and 7 major industrialized countries, quarterly rpt, 9391–7

Foreign countries economic conditions and implications for US, periodic country rpt series, 2046–4

Health care component of CPI, since 1940, monthly rpt, 4742–1.8

Health Care Financing Review, provider prices, price inputs and indexes, and labor, quarterly journal, 4652–1.1

Health care price changes impacts on inflation rate, with CPI components relative weights, 1986 and 1990, article, 9381–1.212

Health condition and health care resources, use, and spending, 1950s-89, annual data compilation, 4144–11

Higher education instn revenue by source and spending by function, by State and instn control, FY80-88, annual rpt, 4844–6

Households food and beverage spending and per capita consumption, by food and beverage type, 1980s-90, article, 1702–1.212

Housing units (1-family) by selected structural characteristics, sales, and prices, 1970s-90, article, 1702–1.205

Houston metro area employment, earnings, hours, and CPI changes, 1970s-90, annual rpt, 6964–1

Inflation actual and expected rates based on alternative price indexes, 1950s-87, article, 9377–1.201

Monthly Labor Review, CPI and PPI current statistics, 6722–1.4

New England States economic indicators, Fed Reserve 1st District, monthly rpt, 9373–2.3

North Central States business and economic conditions, Fed Reserve 9th District, quarterly journal, 9383–19

North Central States farm credit conditions and economic devs, Fed Reserve 7th District, monthly rpt, 9375–10

OASDI benefit payments, trust fund finances, and economic and demographic assumptions, 1970-90 and alternative projections to 2000, actuarial rpt, 4706–1.105

Persian Gulf War impacts on US economic conditions compared to previous oil shock periods, and Saudi Arabia oil production and prices, 1990-92, hearings, 21248–156

Price indexes (consumer and producer), by commodity group, selected years 1929-90, annual rpt, 204–1.4

Southeastern States, Fed Reserve 8th District banking and economic conditions, quarterly rpt with articles, 9391–16

Southeastern US employment by industry div, unemployment, and CPI, for 8 States, 1989-90, annual rpt, 6944–2

Soviet Union, Eastern Europe, OECD, and selected other countries economic conditions, 1960s-90, annual rpt, 9114–4.2

Statistical Abstract of US, 1991 annual data compilation, 2324–1.15

Survey of Current Business, detailed data for major industries and economic indicators, monthly rpt, 2702–1.5

Telephone local service charges and low-income subsidies, by region, company, and city, 1980s-90, semiannual rpt, 9282–8

Telephone service subscribership, charges, and local and long distance firm finances and operations, late 1970s-91, semiannual rpt, 9282–7

Texas, Dallas-Ft Worth and Houston MSAs, CPI by major component, monthly rpt, 6962–2

Consumer Product Safety Commission

Activities of CPSC, recalls by brand, and casualties and medical costs by product type, FY89, annual rpt, 9164–2

Budget of US, authoritative financial statements with appropriations, outlays, and receipts, by category and agency, FY90, annual rpt, 8104–2.1

Budget of US, obligations and authority by function, agency, and program, with summaries, analyses, and historical tables, FY92, annual rpt, 104–2

Injuries from use of consumer products, by severity, victim age, and detailed product, 1990, annual rpt, 9164–6

R&D funding by Fed Govt, by field, performer type, agency, and State, FY89-91, annual rpt, 9627–20

Consumer protection

Airline consumer complaints by reason, passengers denied boarding, and late flights, by reporting carrier and airport, monthly rpt, 7302–11

Airline consumer complaints, passengers denied boarding, and late flights, by carrier, 1985-91, GAO rpt, 26113–542

Index by Subjects and Names

Banks customer complaints received by Fed Reserve System, by type and disposition, 1990, annual rpt, 9364–1

Board and care homes regulation and rules enforcement by States, 1988, 4008–112

Building access for disabled to Federal and federally funded facilities, complaints by disposition, FY90, annual rpt, 17614–1

Consumer Product Safety Commission activities, recalls by brand, and casualties and medical costs, by product type, FY89, annual rpt, 9164–2

Criminal sentences for Federal offenses, guidelines by offense and circumstances, series, 17668–1

Drug (prescription) advertising direct to consumer, benefits and problems, review of studies published 1984-91, GAO rpt, 26131–86

Drug and alcohol abuse treatment services, funding, staffing, and client load, characteristics, and outcomes, by setting, 1989 conf, 4498–73

FDA activities, funding, facilities, and staff, findings and recommendations, 1980s-91, 4008–115

FDA investigations and regulatory activities, quarterly rpt, suspended, 4062–3

Fed Govt financial and nonfinancial domestic aid, 1991 base edition with supplements, annual listing, 104–5

Futures trading oversight of CFTC and individual exchanges, foreign activity, and customer views, late 1980s, hearing, 25168–77

Health Care Financing Admin research activities and grants, by program, FY90, annual listing, 4654–10

Health maintenance organizations Medicare enrollees quality of care indicators compared to fee-for-service, demonstration projects results, mid 1980s, 4658–46

HHS financial aid, by program, recipient, State, and city, FY90, annual regional listings, 4004–3

Higher education instn tuition costs relation to quality, indicators for private instns, regression results, 1985/86, 4888–3

Hospital deaths of Medicare patients, actual and expected rates by diagnosis, with hospital characteristics, by instn, FY87-89, annual regional rpt series, 4654–14

Hospital reimbursement by Medicare under prospective payment system, diagnosis related group code assignment and effects on care and instn finances, 1984/85, series, 4006–7

Hospital reimbursement by Medicare under prospective payment system, impacts on costs, industry structure and operations, and quality of care, series, 17206–2

Imports detained by FDA, by reason, product, shipper, brand, and country, monthly listing, 4062–2

Insurance (health) for long-term care, affordability and State regulation issues, 1986-90, hearing, 21368–130

Kidney end-stage disease treatment access and quality of care indicators, impacts of Medicare payment reductions, 1980s, 4658–44

Medicaid demonstration projects evaluation, for 6 States, 1988 rpt, 4658–45

Medicare supplemental private insurance loss ratio performance, sales abuse cases, and State enforcement, late 1980s, GAO rpt, 26121–410

Nursing home reimbursement by Medicaid, States payment ratesetting methods, limits, and allowances, 1988, article, 4652–1.253

Postal Service customer complaints received, by type, FY90, annual rpt, 9864–5.2

Postal Service inspection activities, 2nd half FY91, semiannual rpt, 9862–2

Securities industry self-regulatory organizations oversight by SEC, violations, and complaints, FY86-89, GAO rpt, 26119–336

State govt protective inspection and regulation funding, by State, FY89, 10044–1

Steel industry product quality and customer service improvements, producers and purchasers opinions, 1968-91, last issue of annual rpt, 9884–24

Truck transport of household goods, performance and disposition of damage claims, for selected carriers, 1990, annual rpt, 9484–11

US attorneys civil and criminal cases by type and disposition, and collections, by Federal district, FY90, annual rpt, 6004–2.1

Water (bottled) quality standards of FDA, EPA, and States, with use in 12 States, 1990, GAO rpt, 26113–519

see also Defective products

see also Food ingredients and additives

see also Food inspection

see also Hazardous substances

see also Labeling

see also Licenses and permits

see also Motor vehicle safety devices

see also Product safety

Consumer surveys

Consumer attitude indexes, *Survey of Current Business*, monthly rpt, 2702–1.1

Containers (beverage) natl deposit law proposal, public views, with State deposit laws effectiveness, 1970s-89, GAO rpt, 26113–494

Debt of households, and payment behavior and difficulties, by selected characteristics, 1980s-90, article, 9362–1.201

Fishing (sport) from California commercial passenger boats with refrigeration equipment, anglers views, 1989 survey, 2168–125

Food consumer research, marketing, legislation, and regulation devs, and consumption and price trends, quarterly journal, 1541–7

Forecasts of consumer spending, performance of consumer sentiment index, 1950s-90, technical paper, 9366–6.282

Forecasts of durable goods spending, performance of consumer confidence levels as indicators, 1970s-91, article, 9381–1.206

Futures trading oversight of CFTC and individual exchanges, foreign activity, and customer views, late 1980s, hearing, 25168–77

Imports purchasing decisions of consumers, importance of brand name, authenticity, origin, and other factors, 1984 survey, hearing, 25528–115

Containerization

Kidney end-stage disease treatment access and quality of care indicators, impacts of Medicare payment reductions, 1980s, 4658–44

Mail volume to and from households, use, and views, by class, source, content, and household characteristics, 1987-88, annual rpt, 9864–10

Medicaid demonstration projects evaluation, for 6 States, 1988 rpt, 4658–45

Older persons migration to southern coastal areas, household finances, services needs, and local economic impacts, for selected counties, 1990, 2068–38

Physicians accepting approved Medicare charges as full payment, Medicare beneficiaries willing to switch from regular physician, 1989 survey, article, 4652–1.248

Postal Service customer satisfaction, and on-time 1st class mail delivery, by region and city, 1991 survey, press release, 9868–1

Recreation (outdoor) coastal facilities of Fed Govt and States, visitor and site characteristics, 1987-90 survey, regional rpt series, 2176–9

Recreation (outdoor) mgmt, research methods, and public opinion, 1990 conf papers, annual rpt, 1204–38

Savings impact of proposed Federal deposit insurance limit changes, 1989 survey, hearings, 25248–121

Shellfish recreational harvesters selected characteristics, location of harvest and residence, and spending, 1985 survey, 2178–28

Travel from US, characteristics of visit and traveler, and country of destination, 1990 in-flight survey, annual rpt, 2904–14

Travel to US, by characteristics of visit and traveler, world area of origin, and US destination, 1990 survey, annual rpt, 2904–12

Wilderness areas use, mental health and educational benefits, and leadership training programs effectiveness, 1990 conf papers, 1208–347

see also American Housing Survey

see also Consumer Expenditure Survey

see also National Medical Expenditure Survey

see also Nationwide Food Consumption Survey

Consumers

see Boycotts

see Consumer cooperatives

see Consumer credit

see Consumer Price Index

see Consumer protection

see Consumer surveys

see Cost of living

see Personal and household income

see Personal consumption

Consumption

see Food consumption

see Personal consumption

see under names of specific commodities or commodity groups

Containerization

Fruit and vegetable shipments, and arrivals in US and Canada cities, by mode of transport and State and country of origin, 1990, annual rpt series, 1311–4

Containerization

Fruit and vegetable shipments by mode of transport, arrivals, and imports, by commodity and State and country of origin, weekly rpt, 1311–3

Intermodal containers and equipment owned by shipping and leasing companies, inventory by type and size, 1990, annual rpt, 7704–10

Military and personal property shipments, passenger traffic, and costs, by service branch and mode of transport, quarterly rpt, 3702–1

Military Sealift Command shipping operations, finances, and personnel, FY90, annual rpt, 3804–14

Oil refinery crude received, by mode of transport and PAD district, 1990, annual rpt, 3164–2.1

Railroad (Class I) finances and operations, detailed data by firm, class of service, and district, 1989, annual rpt, 9486–6.1

Shipborne trade of US, by type of service, customs district, port, and world area, monthly rpt, 2422–7

Shipbuilding and repair facilities, capacity, and employment, by shipyard, 1990, annual rpt, 7704–9

Ships, cargo, and passenger traffic, and toll revenue on St Lawrence Seaway, 1990 and trends from 1959, annual rpt, 7744–2

Ships in world merchant fleet, tonnage, and new ship construction and deliveries, by vessel type and country, as of Jan 1990, annual rpt, 7704–3

Ships under foreign flag owned by US firms and foreign affiliates, by type, owner, and country of registry and construction, as of Jan 1991, semiannual rpt, 7702–3

Truck trailer shipments, exports, and firms, by trailer type, monthly Current Industrial Rpt, 2506–12.25

Containers

see Containerization

see Packaging and containers

Contempt of court

Court civil and criminal caseloads for Federal district, appeals, and bankruptcy courts, by type of suit and offense, circuit, and district, 1990, annual rpt, 18204–11

Court civil and criminal caseloads for Federal district, appeals, and special courts, 1990, annual rpt, 18204–8

Court civil and criminal caseloads for Federal district courts, 1991, annual rpt, 18204–2.1

Court criminal cases in Federal district courts, by offense, disposition, and district, 1980-90, last issue of annual rpt, 18204–1

Sentences for Federal offenses, guidelines by offense and circumstances, series, 17668–1

US attorneys civil and criminal cases by type and disposition, and collections, by Federal district, FY90, annual rpt, 6004–2.1

Continental shelf

Alaska OCS environmental conditions and oil dev impacts, compilation of papers, series, 2176–1

California OCS oil and gas dev impacts on water quality, marine life, and sediments, by site, 1986-89, annual rpt, 5734–11

Earthquake intensity, time, location, damage, and seismic characteristics, for US and foreign earthquakes, 1985, annual rpt, 5664–13

Environmental conditions, fish, wildlife, use, and mgmt, for individual coastal and riparian ecosystems, series, 5506–9

Research on OCS, Minerals Mgmt Service rpts, 1988, annual listing, 5734–5

Workers compensation programs under Federal admin, finances and operations, FY90, annual rpt, 6504–10

see also Coastal areas

see also Offshore mineral resources

see also Offshore oil and gas

see also Territorial waters

Continental Shelf Associates, Inc.

"Synthesis of Available Biological, Geological, Chemical, Socioeconomic, and Cultural Resource Information for the South Florida Area", 5738–19

Continuing education

see Adult education

Continuous Work History Sample

Employment by industry and State, impacts of decline in employers voluntary reporting on CWHS, 1970s-86, article, 4742–1.203

Contraband

Customs Service activities, collections, entries processed by mode of transport, and seizures, FY86-90, annual rpt, 8144–1

Endangered animals and plants US trade and permits, by species, purpose, disposition, and country, 1989, annual rpt, 5504–19

see also Drug and narcotics offenses

Contraception

see Contraceptives

see Family planning

see Sexual sterilization

Contraceptives

AIDS public knowledge and info sources, for blacks and Hispanics, 1987 local area survey, article, 4042–3.210

AIDS public knowledge, attitudes, info sources, and testing, for blacks, 1990 survey, 4146–8.208

AIDS public knowledge, attitudes, info sources, and testing, for Hispanics, 1990 survey, 4146–8.209

AIDS public knowledge, attitudes, info sources, and testing, 1990 survey, 4146–8.195; 4146–8.201; 4146–8.205

AIDS virus infection and risk factor prevalence, natl survey methodology and pretest results, 1989, 4148–30

Cancer (breast) precursor hormonal changes risk relation to selected reproductive factors, 1983-89 study, article, 4472–1.227

Cancer (hepatocellular) risk relation to hepatitis infection, race, smoking, drinking, and oral contraceptives and estrogen use, 1984-90 local area study, article, 4472–1.237

Developing countries family planning and population activities of AID, grants by project and recipient, and contraceptive shipments, by country, FY90, annual rpt series, 9914–13

Exports and imports of US, by Harmonized System 6-digit commodity and country, 1990, annual rpt, 2424–13

Index by Subjects and Names

Exports of US, detailed Schedule B commodities with countries of destination, 1990, annual rpt, 2424–10

Genital human papillomavirus risk relation to presence of other cervical cancer risk factors, local area study, 1991 article, 4472–1.215

Health condition and health care resources, use, and spending, 1950s-89, annual data compilation, 4144–11

Minority group and women health condition, services use, payment sources, and health care labor force, by poverty status, 1940s-89, chartbook, 4118–56

Minority group health condition, services use, costs, and indicators of services need, 1950s-88, 4118–55

Oral contraceptives prescriptions, 1989, annual rpt, 4064–12

Poor black men's drug and condom use and sexual behavior, local area study, 1991 article, 4042–3.254

Poor women's pregnancies, by whether intended, outcome, contraceptives use, marital status, and race, 1985-86 local area study, article, 4042–3.241

Research on population and reproduction, Federal funding by project, FY89, annual listing, 4474–9

Research on population and reproduction, Natl Inst of Child Health and Human Dev funding and activities, 1990, annual rpt, 4474–33

Shipments, trade, and use of drugs, by product, 1990, annual Current Industrial Rpt, 2506–8.5

Statistical Abstract of US, 1991 annual data compilation, 2324–1.2

Contract labor

see Temporary and seasonal employment

Contracts

Aircraft maintenance by independent repair stations, airlines use and costs, 1980s-90, GAO rpt, 26113–492

Coal shipments to electric utilities under contract, and rates, by firm, transport mode, and region, 1979-87, 3168–121

Construction (industrial and commercial) contracts, *Survey of Current Business,* cyclical indicators, monthly rpt, 2702–1.1

Construction industries census, 1987: establishments, employment, receipts, and expenditures, by SIC 4-digit industry and State, final industry rpt series, 2373–1

Court civil and criminal caseloads for Federal district, appeals, and bankruptcy courts, by type of suit and offense, circuit, and district, 1990, annual rpt, 18204–11

Court civil and criminal caseloads for Federal district, appeals, and special courts, 1990, annual rpt, 18204–8

Court civil and criminal caseloads for Federal district courts, 1991, annual rpt, 18204–2.1

Electric utilities purchase contracts with nonutility generators, competitive bidding use, 1980s-90, GAO rpt, 26113–498

Escalator clauses of collective bargaining agreements and other contracts, use of CPI, with conversion factors for index rebasing, 1991 guide, 6888–34

Hospitals, receipts by source, contract services, expenses, and employment, by facility type and State, 1987 Census of Service Industries, 2393–4.12

Index by Subjects and Names

Housing alteration and repair spending, by job category and for work under contract, quarterly rpt, 2382–7

Labor laws enacted, by State, 1990, annual article, 6722–1.209

Natural gas imports of US from Canada under long-term contracts by region, with contract provisions, 1986-90, article, 3162–4.206

Natural gas interstate pipeline company sales and contract deliveries, by firm and State, 1984-89, annual article, 3162–4.204

Natural gas take-or-pay contracts, settlement costs under FERC Order 500 by interstate pipeline firm, as of Oct 1990, article, 3162–4.202

Swap contracts, by contract and counterparty type, and currency, late 1980s, article, 9371–1.205

Uranium marketing, contracts, prices, utility shipments, and trade, 1982-90 and projected to 2000, annual rpt, 3164–65.2

Western Area Power Admin activities by plant, financial statements, and sales by customer, FY90, annual rpt, 3254–1

see also Agricultural production quotas and price supports

see also Business orders

see also Defense contracts and procurement

see also Defense industries

see also Escalator clauses

see also Futures trading

see also Government contracts and procurement

see also Labor-management relations, general

see also Labor-management relations in government

Contributions

see Campaign funds

see Gifts and private contributions

Controlled substances

see Alcoholic beverages control laws

see Cocaine

see Drug abuse and treatment

see Drug and narcotics offenses

see Marijuana

Convalescent homes

see Nursing homes

Convenience stores

see Food stores

Conventions

see Treaties and conventions

Conversion of industry

Military forces, research, and manufacturing base restructuring following relaxation of East-West tensions, with background data, FY87-93, 26358–245

Convictions, criminal

see Sentences, criminal procedure

Cook, Edward C.

"Government Intervention in Soviet Agriculture: Estimates of Consumer and Producer Subsidy Equivalents", 1528–320

Cook Inlet, Alaska

Oil spill from tanker Glacier Bay, cleanup costs and area economic benefits, with data by firm and agency, 1987, 5736–5.15

Cook Islands

Economic, social, political, and geographic summary data, by country, 1991, annual factbook, 9114–2

Exports and imports of US, by transport mode, country, and SITC 1- to 3-digit commodity, 1990, annual rpt, 2424–12

Cook, Leah M.

"Financing Capital Expenditures in Massachusetts", 9373–1.207; 9373–4.27

Cook, Timothy

"Interest Rate Expectations and the Slope of the Money Market Yield Curve", 9389–1.201

"Reaction of Interest Rates to the Employment Report: The Role of Policy Anticipations", 9389–1.205

Cooking equipment

see Household appliances and equipment

Cooking utensils

see Household supplies and utensils

Coon, M. D.

"Performance and Compatibility Analysis of Oil Weathering and Transport-Related Models for Use in the Environmental Assessment Process", 2176–1.36

Cooper, David J.

"Ecology of Wetlands in Big Meadows, Rocky Mountain National Park, Colorado", 5508–113

Cooperative State Research Service

Budget of US, obligations and authority by function, agency, and program, with summaries, analyses, and historical tables, FY92, annual rpt, 104–2

Expenditures and staffing for agricultural research by USDA, State agencies, and other instns, by topic, FY90, annual rpt, 1744–2

Expenditures of Fed Govt in States, by type, program, agency, and State, FY90, annual rpt, 2464–2

Cooperatives

Political action committees, by type, 1974-91, semiannual press release, 9276–1.86; 9276–1.91

Political action committees contributions by party and finances, by PAC type, 1989-90, press release, 9276–1.89

Soviet Union GNP by detailed income and outlay component, 1985, 2326–18.59

Tax (income) withholding and related documents filed, by type and IRS service center, 1990 and projected 1991-98, annual rpt, 8304–22

see also Condominiums and cooperatives

see also Consumer cooperatives

see also Credit unions

see also Rural cooperatives

Copiers, office

see Business machines and equipment

Copper and copper industry

Building materials PPI, by type, bimonthly rpt, 2042–1.5

Business statistics, detailed data for major industries and economic indicators, *Survey of Current Business*, monthly rpt, 2702–1.17

Castings (nonferrous) shipments, by metal type, 1990, annual Current Industrial Rpt, 2506–10.5

Coin production and monetary metals use and holdings of US Mint, by metal type, FY90, annual rpt, 8204–1

County Business Patterns, 1988: employment, establishments, and payroll, by SIC 2- to 4-digit industry and county, annual State rpt series, 2326–6

Copper and copper industry

County Business Patterns, 1989: employment, establishments, and payroll, by SIC 2- to 4-digit industry and county, annual State rpt series, 2326–8

Employment, earnings, and hours, by SIC 1- to 4-digit industry, monthly and annual averages, selected years 1909-90, annual rpt, 6744–4

Exports and imports between US and outlying areas, by detailed commodity and mode of transport, 1990, annual rpt, 2424–11

Exports and imports of US, by country and detailed commodity, monthly rpt, 2422–12

Exports and imports of US, by Harmonized System 6-digit commodity and country, 1990, annual rpt, 2424–13

Exports and imports of US, by transport mode, country, and SITC 1- to 3-digit commodity, 1990, annual rpt, 2424–12

Exports of US, detailed Schedule B commodities with countries of destination, 1990, annual rpt, 2424–10

Furniture (office) shipments by product, and metals used by type, 1990, annual Current Industrial Rpt, 2506–7.8

Futures and options trading volume, by commodity and exchange, FY90, annual rpt, 11924–2

Futures trading in selected commodities and financial instruments and indexes, NYC, Chicago, and other markets activity, semimonthly rpt, 11922–5

Labor productivity, indexes of output, hours, and employment by SIC 2- to 4-digit industry, 1967-89, annual rpt, 6824–1.2; 6824–1.3

Manufacturing annual survey, 1989: finances and operations, by SIC 2- to 4-digit industry, series, 2506–15

Manufacturing census, 1987: finances and operations, by SIC 2- to 4-digit industry, State, and MSA, with trends from 1849, 2497–1

Manufacturing census, 1987: finances and operations, by type of organization and SIC 2- to 4-digit industry, subject rpt, 2497–5

Manufacturing finances and operations, by SIC 2- to 4-digit industry, forecast 1991, annual rpt, 2044–28

Mineral industries census, 1987: energy use and costs, by fuel type, SIC 2- to 4-digit industry, and State, subject rpt, 2517–2

Mineral industries census, 1987: finances and operations, by establishment characteristics, SIC 2- to 4-digit industry, and State, subject rpt, 2517–1

Mineral Industry Surveys, commodity review of production, trade, stocks, and use, monthly rpt, 5612–1.6

Mineral Industry Surveys, State reviews of production, 1990, preliminary annual rpt, 5614–6

Minerals Yearbook, 1988, Vol 3: foreign country reviews of production, trade, and policy, by commodity, annual rpt series, 5604–17

Minerals Yearbook, 1989, Vol 1: commodity review of production, reserves, supply, use, and trade, annual rpt, 5604–15.20

Minerals Yearbook, 1989, Vol 2: State reviews of production and sales by commodity, and business activity, annual rpt series, 5604–16

Copper and copper industry

Minerals Yearbook, 1989, Vol 2: State reviews of production, sales, and firms, by commodity, and business activity, annual rpt, 5604–34

Mines (metal) and related operations occupational injuries and incidence, employment, and hours, 1989, annual rpt, 6664–3

Occupational injury and illness rates, by SIC 2- to 4-digit industry, 1988-89, annual rpt, 6844–7

Occupational injury and illness rates, by SIC 2- to 4-digit industry, 1989, annual rpt, 6844–1

OECD trade, total and for 4 major countries, and US trade by country, by commodity, 1970-89, world area rpt series, 9116–1

Pollution (air) emissions factors, by detailed pollutant and source, data compilation, 1990 rpt, 9198–120

Price indexes (producer), by stage of processing and detailed commodity, monthly rpt, 6762–6

Price indexes (producer), by stage of processing and detailed commodity, monthly 1990, annual rpt, 6764–2

Production, prices, trade, and foreign and US industry devs, by commodity, bimonthly rpt with articles, 5602–4

Production, prices, trade, use, employment, tariffs, and stockpiles, by mineral, with foreign comparisons, 1986-90, annual rpt, 5604–18

Soviet Union, Eastern Europe, OECD, and selected other countries minerals production, by commodity, 1960s-90, annual rpt, 9114–4.6

Statistical Abstract of US, 1991 annual data compilation, 2324–1.25

Stockpiling of strategic material by Fed Govt, activity, and inventory by commodity, as of Mar 1991, semiannual rpt, 3542–22

Stockpiling of strategic material, inventories and needs, by commodity, as of Jan 1991, annual rpt, 3544–37

Telecommunications fiber optics and copper wire mileage and access lines, and fiber systems investment, by firm, 1985-90, annual rpt, 9284–18

Wire and cable (insulated) shipments, trade, use, and firms, by product, 1990, annual Current Industrial Rpt, 2506–10.8

see also under By Commodity in the "Index by Categories"

Copyright

Court civil and criminal caseloads for Federal district, appeals, and bankruptcy courts, by type of suit and offense, circuit, and district, 1990, annual rpt, 18204–11

Court civil and criminal caseloads for Federal district, appeals, and special courts, 1990, annual rpt, 18204–8

Court civil and criminal caseloads for Federal district courts, 1991, annual rpt, 18204–2.1

Criminal cases by type and disposition, and collections, for US attorneys, by Federal district, FY90, annual rpt, 6004–2.1

Criminal sentences for Federal offenses, guidelines by offense and circumstances, series, 17668–1

Exports of goods, services, and investment, trade barriers, impacts, and US actions, by country, 1989, annual rpt, 444–2

Foreign countries economic conditions, policy, and trade practices, by country, 1988-90, annual rpt, 21384–5

Infringement of copyright, lawsuit damages and legal fee awards, by case, 1930s-87, hearing, 21528–82

Intl agreements of US establishing copyright relations, by country, as of Jan 1991, annual listing, 7004–1

Intl and domestic patent and copyright protection, products excluded, and countries and agreements involved, 1990 article, 9391–1.203

Legal services establishments, lawyers by field, receipts by class of client, expenses, and employment, by MSA, 1987 Census of Service Industries, 2393–4.13

Register of Copyrights activities, registrations by material type, and fees, FY90 and trends from 1790, annual rpt, 26404–2

Registrations and claims and fees collected by type of material, claims and fees, and fee transfers, for Library of Congress Copyright Office, FY90, annual rpt, 26404–1

Statistical Abstract of US, 1991 annual data compilation, 2324–1.18

Videos for employee training, businesses views on copying and copyright infringement issues, 1987 survey, hearing, 21528–82

see also Patents

see also Trademarks

Copyright Act

Infringement of copyright, lawsuit damages and legal fee awards, by case, 1930s-87, hearing, 21528–82

Copyright Royalty Tribunal

Royalty fees from cable and satellite TV and jukeboxes available for distribution by Tribunal, 1989-90, annual rpt, 26404–2

Coral

see Marine resources

Coral reefs and islands

Alaska OCS environmental conditions and oil dev impacts, compilation of papers, series, 2176–1

Fish (baitfish) catch distribution by species and South Pacific country or territory, 1965-85, article, 2162–1.201

Gazetteer of US places, mountains, bodies of water, and other political and physical features, 1990 rpt, 5668–117

Recreation (outdoor) coastal facilities, by State, county, estuary, and level of govt, 1972-84, 2178–29

Recreation (outdoor) coastal facilities of Fed Govt and States, visitor and site characteristics, 1987-90 survey, regional rpt series, 2176–9

Corder, Larry S.

"Health Care Coverage: U.S., 1976", 4147–16.5

Corn

Acreage planted and harvested, by crop and State, 1989-90 and planned as of June 1991, annual rpt, 1621–23

Acreage planted, by selected crop and State, 1982-90 and planned 1991, annual rpt, 1621–22

Acreage reduction program compliance, enrollment, and yield on planted acreage, by commodity and State, annual press release series, 1004–20

Acreage under Agricultural Stabilization and Conservation Service programs, rankings by commodity and congressional district, 1989, biennial rpt, 1804–17

Agricultural data compilation, 1990 and trends from 1920, annual rpt, 1004–14

Agricultural Statistics, 1990, annual rpt, 1004–1

Agriculture census, 1987: farms, farmland, production, finances, and operator characteristics, by county, final State rpt series, 2331–1

Alcoholic beverages production, stocks, materials used, and taxable and tax-free removals, for beer and distilled spirits by State, monthly rpt, 8486–1.1; 8486–1.3

Business statistics, detailed data for major industries and economic indicators, *Survey of Current Business,* monthly rpt, 2702–1.14

CCC certificate exchange activity, by commodity, biweekly press release, 1802–16

CCC financial condition and major commodity program operations, FY62-87, annual chartbook, 1824–2

Consumption, supply, trade, prices, spending, and indexes, by food commodity, 1989, annual rpt, 1544–4

Cooperatives finances and operations, by grain handled and selected characteristics, 1983-85, series, 1128–44

County Business Patterns, 1988: employment, establishments, and payroll, by SIC 2- to 4-digit industry and county, annual State rpt series, 2326–6

County Business Patterns, 1989: employment, establishments, and payroll, by SIC 2- to 4-digit industry and county, annual State rpt series, 2326–8

Export demand for US corn, wheat, and soybeans, by selected country, 1960s-83, 1568–297

Exports (agricultural) of high-value commodities, indexes and sales value by commodity, world area, and country, 1960s-86, 1528–323

Exports and imports (agricultural) commodity and country, prices, and world market devs, monthly rpt, 1922–12

Exports and imports (agricultural) of US, by commodity and country, bimonthly rpt, 1522–1

Exports and imports (agricultural) of US, by detailed commodity and country, 1989, annual rpt, 1524–8

Exports and imports (agricultural) of US, by detailed commodity and country, 1990, semiannual rpt, 1522–4

Exports and imports between US and outlying areas, by detailed commodity and mode of transport, 1990, annual rpt, 2424–11

Exports and imports of US, by country and detailed commodity, monthly rpt, 2422–12

Exports and imports of US, by Harmonized System 6-digit commodity and country, 1990, annual rpt, 2424–13

Exports and imports of US, by selected country, country group, and commodity group, 1990, annual rpt, 2044–37

Exports and imports of US, by transport mode, country, and SITC 1- to 3-digit commodity, 1990, annual rpt, 2424–12

Index by Subjects and Names

Corporations

Exports of grains, oilseed products, hides, skins, and cotton, by country, weekly rpt, 1922–3

Exports of US, detailed Schedule B commodities with countries of destination, 1990, annual rpt, 2424–10

Farm financial condition, 1987, commodity rpt, 1566–8.7

Farm income, expenses, receipts by commodity, assets, liabilities, and ratios, 1990 and trends from 1945, annual rpt, 1544–16

Farm sector balance sheet, and receipts by detailed commodity, by State, 1985-89, annual rpt, 1544–18

Farms, finances, acreage, and production, for corn by size of farm and sales, region, and State, 1987, 1568–304

Fertilizer and pesticide use and application rates, by type, crop, and State, 1990, 1616–1.1; 1616–1.2

Foreign and US agricultural production, acreage, and yield for selected crops, forecasts by selected world region and country, FAS monthly circular, 1925–28

Foreign and US agricultural supply and demand indicators, by selected crop, monthly rpt, 1522–5

Foreign and US grain production, prices, trade, stocks, and use, FAS periodic circular series, 1925–2

Foreign and US oils, oilseeds, and fats production and trade, FAS periodic circular series, 1925–1

Foreign countries agricultural production, prices, and trade, by country, 1980-90 and forecast 1991, annual world area rpt series, 1524–4

Futures and options trading volume, by commodity and exchange, FY90, annual rpt, 11924–2

Futures contracts, stocks in deliverable position by type, weekly table, 11922–4.3

Futures trading in selected commodities and financial instruments and indexes, NYC, Chicago, and other markets activity, semimonthly rpt, 11922–5

Inspection of grain for domestic use and export, and foreign buyers complaints, FY90, annual rpt, 1294–1

Inspection of grain for export, test results by commodity and port region, 1988-90, annual rpt series, 1294–2

Irrigation projects of Reclamation Bur in western US, crop production and acreage by commodity, State, and project, 1989, annual rpt, 5824–12

Labor productivity, indexes of output, hours, and employment by SIC 2- to 4-digit industry, 1967-89, annual rpt, 6824–1.3

Loan support programs of USDA for grains, activity and status by grain and State, monthly rpt, 1802–3

Manufacturing annual survey, 1989: finances and operations, by SIC 2- to 4-digit industry, series, 2506–15

Manufacturing census, 1987: finances and operations, by type of organization and SIC 2- to 4-digit industry, subject rpt, 2497–5

OECD trade, total and for 4 major countries, and US trade by country, by commodity, 1970-89, world area rpt series, 9116–1

Pesticide and fertilizer use reduction, environmental and economic impacts by commodity and region, alternative forecasts 1989-94, hearing, 23848–222

Pesticide use on corn by tilling method, 1988-89, article, 1561–16.201

Price (season average) forecasts for corn using futures settlement prices, 1986-92, article, 1561–4.201

Price indexes (producer), by stage of processing and detailed commodity, monthly rpt, 6762–6

Price indexes (producer), by stage of processing and detailed commodity, monthly 1990, annual rpt, 6764–2

Price support and other CCC program outlays, with production and marketing outlook, by commodity, projected 1990-96, 26306–6.160

Price support program provisions, for selected commodities, 1961-90, 1568–302

Prices received and paid by farmers, by commodity and State, 1990, annual rpt, 1629–5

Prices received by farmers and production value, by detailed crop and State, 1988-90, annual rpt, 1621–2

Prices received by farmers for major products, and paid for farm inputs and living items, by State, monthly rpt, 1629–1

Production, acreage, stocks, use, trade, prices, and price supports, periodic situation rpt with articles, 1561–4

Production costs for corn, wheat, and soybeans in current and constant dollars, 1975-79, article, 1541–1.208

Production, farms, acreage, and related data, by selected crop and State, monthly rpt, 1621–1

Production itemized costs, receipts, and returns, by commodity and region, 1987-89, annual rpt, 1544–20

Production of oil and fat, consumption by end use, and stocks, by type, quarterly Current Industrial Rpt, 2506–4.4

Production of oil, crushings, and stocks, by oilseed type and State, quarterly Current Industrial Rpt, 2506–4.3

Production, prices, trade, and export inspections by US port and country of destination, by grain type, weekly rpt, 1313–2

Production, prices, trade, and marketing, by commodity, current situation and forecast, monthly rpt with articles, 1502–4

Production, prices, trade, and use of oils and fats, periodic situation rpt with articles, 1561–3

Soviet Union agricultural trade, by commodity and country, 1955-90, 1528–322

State and Metro Area Data Book, 1991 data compilation, 2328–54

Statistical Abstract of US, 1991 annual data compilation, 2324–1.23

Stocks of grain by region and market city, and grain inspected for export, by type, weekly rpt, 1313–4

Stocks of grain on and off farms, by crop, quarterly rpt, 1621–4

Stocks of wheat and corn, demand impacts of storage subsidy programs, model description and results, 1972-87, 1548–378

Sweeteners (refined corn) trade, use, and wholesale prices, by commodity, quarterly situation rpt with articles, 1561–14

Weather conditions and effect on agriculture, by US region, State, and city, and world area, weekly rpt, 2182–7

Zimbabwe agricultural conditions impacts of economic policies, 1980s, 1528–319

see also under By Commodity in the "Index by Categories"

Cornelius, Llewellyn

"Usual Sources of Medical Care and Their Characteristics. National Medical Expenditure Survey", 4186–8.22

Coroners

Death investigation systems of US and Canada, jurisdictions, medical officers qualifications, types of deaths covered, and related statutes, 1990 listing, 4208–34

Corporate profits

see Business income and expenses, general

see Business income and expenses, specific industry

see Operating ratios

Corporation for Public Broadcasting

Budget of US, authoritative financial statements with appropriations, outlays, and receipts, by category and agency, FY90, annual rpt, 8104–2.1

Budget of US, obligations and authority by function, agency, and program, with summaries, analyses, and historical tables, FY92, annual rpt, 104–2

Expenditures of Fed Govt in States, by type, program, agency, and State, FY90, annual rpt, 2464–2

Corporations

Agriculture census, 1987: farms, farmland, production, finances, and operator characteristics, by county, final State rpt series, 2331–1

Agriculture census, 1987: horticultural specialties producers, finances, and operations, by crop and State, 1988 survey, 2337–1

Aircraft (general aviation), flight hours, and equipment, by type, use, and model of aircraft, region, and State, 1990, annual rpt, 7504–29

Assets and debts of private sector, balance sheets by segment, 1945-90, semiannual rpt, 9365–4.1

Boycotts (intl) by OPEC and other countries, US firms and shareholders cooperation and tax benefits denied, 1986, annual rpt, 8004–13

Boycotts (intl) by OPEC and other countries, US taxpayers IRS filings, cooperation, and tax benefits denied, 1976-86, GAO rpt, 26119–349

Enterprise Statistics, 1987: finances and operations for companies, by size, level of diversification, form of organization, and industry group, 2329–8

Financial data, security issues, profits, taxes, and dividends, monthly rpt, 9362–1.1

Financial statements for manufacturing, mining, and trade corporations, by selected SIC 2- to 3-digit industry, quarterly rpt, 2502–1

Flow-of-funds accounts, savings, investments, and credit statements, quarterly rpt, 9365–3.3

Corporations

Helicopters, use, and landing facilities, by craft type, region, and State, 1989, 7508–75

Historic buildings rehabilitation tax incentives, projects, costs, ownership, and use, FY77-90, annual rpt, 5544–17

Income tax and other govt finances, by level of govt and State, 1991 and historical trends, annual rpt, 10044–1

Manufacturing census, 1987: finances and operations, by type of organization and SIC 2- to 4-digit industry, subject rpt, 2497–5

Mineral industries census, 1987: finances and operations, by establishment characteristics, SIC 2- to 4-digit industry, and State, subject rpt, 2517–1

Navy procurement, by contractor and location, FY90, annual rpt, 3804–13

Partnerships (limited) conversion to corporations, and impacts on share values, with data by firm, 1980s-91, hearing, 25248–124

Political action committees, by type, 1974-91, semiannual press release, 9276–1.86; 9276–1.91

Political action committees contributions by party and finances, by PAC type, 1989-90, press release, 9276–1.89

Productivity and costs of labor for private, nonfarm business, and manufacturing sectors, revised data, quarterly rpt, 6822–2

Profits by industry div, profit tax liability, and dividends, monthly rpt, quarterly data, 23842–1.1

Profits by industry div, stockholders equity, and costs per unit of output, 1929-90, annual rpt, 204–1.1; 204–1.7

Puerto Rico and other US possessions corporations income tax returns, income and tax items, and employment, by selected industry, 1987, article, 8302–2.213

Puerto Rico economic censuses, 1987: wholesale, retail, and service industries finances and operations, by size, form of organization, and SIC 2- and 3-digit industry, subject rpt, 2591–2.1

Puerto Rico statehood referendum proposal, impacts on Federal tax revenue and aid outlays, corporations tax-favored status, and economic conditions, projected FY91-2000, hearing, 25368–168; 26306–3.112

Retail trade census, 1987: depreciable assets, capital and operating expenses, sales, value added, and inventories, by SIC 2- to 4-digit kind of business, 2399–2

Retail trade sales, inventories, purchases, gross margin, and accounts receivable, by SIC 2- to 4-digit kind of business and form of ownership, 1989, annual rpt, 2413–5

SEC registration, firms required to file annual rpts, as of Sept 1990, annual listing, 9734–5

Service industries census, 1987: depreciable assets, capital and operating expenses, and receipts, by SIC 2- to 4-digit kind of business, 2393–2

Statistical Abstract of US, 1991 annual data compilation, 2324–1.17

Survey of Current Business, detailed data for major industries and economic indicators, monthly rpt, 2702–1

Index by Subjects and Names

Tax (income) collection, enforcement, and litigation activity of IRS, with data by type of tax, region, and State, FY90, annual rpt, 8304–3

Tax (income) returns and supplemental documents filed, by type, FY90 and projected to FY99, semiannual rpt, 8302–4

Tax (income) returns filed by type of filer, selected income items, quarterly rpt, 8302–2.1

Tax (income) returns filed, by type of return and IRS district, 1989 and projected 1990-97, annual rpt, 8304–24

Tax (income) returns filed, by type of tax and IRS region and service center, projected 1990-97 and trends from 1978, annual rpt, 8304–9

Tax (income) returns of corporations, income and tax items by asset size and detailed industry, 1987, annual rpt, 8304–4

Tax (income) returns of corporations, income and tax items by asset size and detailed industry, 1988, annual rpt, 8304–21

Tax (income) returns of corporations, summary data by asset size and industry div, 1987, annual article, 8302–2.204

Tax (income) returns of corporations, summary data by asset size and industry div, 1988, annual article, 8302–2.215; 8302–2.217

Tax (income) returns of corporations with foreign tax credit, income, and tax items, by country and world region of credit, 1986, biennial article, 8302–2.207

Tax (income) returns of corporations with foreign tax credit, income and tax items by industry group, 1986, biennial article, 8302–2.203

Tax (income) returns processing, IRS workload forecasts, compliance, and enforcement, data compilation, 1991 annual rpt, 8304–8

Tax (income) revenue from corporations, impacts of tax reform and other factors, 1990 hearing, 25368–173

Tax collections of State govts by detailed type of tax, and tax rates, by State, FY90, annual rpt, 2466–2.7

Tax expenditures, Federal revenues forgone through income tax deductions and exclusions by type, FY92-96, annual rpt, 21784–10

Tax returns and supplemental documents filed, by type, FY89 and projected to FY98, annual article, 8302–2.208

Tax revenue, by level of govt, type of tax, State, and selected large county, quarterly rpt, 2462–3

Terrorism (intl) incidents, casualties, and attacks on US targets, by attack type and country, 1990, annual rpt, 7004–22

Terrorism (intl) incidents, casualties, and attacks on US targets, by attack type and world area, 1990, annual rpt, 7004–13

Transportation census, 1987: finances and operations by size, ownership, and State, and revenues by MSA, by SIC 2- to 4-digit industry, 2579–1

Truck and warehouse services finances and inventory, by SIC 2- to 4-digit industry, 1989 survey, annual rpt, 2413–14

Wholesale trade census, 1987: depreciable assets, capital and operating expenses, sales, value added, and inventories, by SIC 2- to 3-digit kind of business, 2407–2

Wholesale trade sales, inventories, purchases, and gross margins, by SIC 2- to 3-digit kind of business, 1990, annual rpt, 2413–13

see also Bank holding companies

see also Business acquisitions and mergers

see also Economic concentration and diversification

see also Foreign corporations

see also Government corporations and enterprises

see also Holding companies

see also Monopolies and cartels

see also Multinational corporations

see also Public utilities

see also under By Individual Company or Institution in the "Index by Categories"

Corps of Engineers

see Army Corps of Engineers

Corpus Christi, Tex.

see also under By City and By SMSA or MSA in the "Index by Categories"

Correctional institutions

AIDS cases in prisons and jails, and testing and control policies, 1989 survey, 6066–28.1

Budget of US, obligations and authority by function, agency, and program, with summaries, analyses, and historical tables, FY92, annual rpt, 104–2

Costs of construction and operation, capacity, and inmates, for Federal and State prisons, 1985-89, GAO rpt, 26119–341

Data on crime, criminal justice admin and enforcement, and public opinion, data compilation, 1991 annual rpt, 6064–6

Drug abuse and trafficking reduction programs activities, funding, staff, and Bush Admin budget request, by Federal agency and program area, FY90-92, 238–2

Drug and alcohol abuse and mental illness direct and indirect costs, by type and patient age and sex, 1985 with 1980 and 1988 comparisons, 4048–35

Employment, earnings, facilities, and inmates of State and local correctional instns, by level of govt, facility characteristics, and State, data compilation, 1991 annual rpt, 6064–6.1; 6064–6.6

Employment, payroll, and spending for criminal justice, by level of govt, State, and selected city and county, FY71-88, annual rpt, 6064–9

Employment, payroll, and spending for criminal justice, by level of govt, State, and selected city and county, 1984-86, biennial rpt, 6064–4

Fed Bur of Prisons activities, and inmate and staff characteristics, 1990, annual rpt, 6244–2

Fed Bur of Prisons admin offices and correctional instns, facility characteristics, 1991, annual listing, 6244–4

Fed Govt-owned real property inventory and costs, worldwide summary by purpose, agency, and location, 1989, annual rpt, 9454–5

Index by Subjects and Names

Cost of living

Fed Govt spending in States, by type, program, agency, and State, FY90, annual rpt, 2464–2

Federal and State correctional instns population by sex, admissions, and instn capacity and overcrowding, by State, 1980s-90, annual rpt, 6066–25.37

Foreign countries human rights conditions in 170 countries, 1990, annual rpt, 21384–3

Govt census, 1987: employment, payroll, and average earnings, by function, level of govt, State, county, and population size, 2455–2

Govt census, 1987: local govt employment by function, payroll, and average earnings, for individual counties, cities, and school and special districts, 2455–1

Govt employment and payroll, by function, level of govt, and jurisdiction, 1990, annual rpt series, 2466–1

Govt finances, tax systems and revenue, and fiscal structure, by level of govt and State, 1991 with historical trends, annual rpt, 10044–1

Jail adult and juvenile population, employment, spending, instn conditions, and inmate programs, by county and facility, 1988, regional rpt series, 6068–144

Jail population by sex, race, and for 25 jurisdictions, and instn conditions, 1988-90, annual rpt, 6066–25.38

Jail population, capacity, and instns under court order to reduce overcrowding and improve conditions, by State, 1989, annual rpt, 6064–26.1

Palau admin, and social, economic, and govtl data, FY90, annual rpt, 7004–6

Privately operated prisons and jails, costs and characteristics of instns, by facility and State, 1990, GAO rpt, 26119–321

State and Metro Area Data Book, 1991 data compilation, 2328–54

Statistical Abstract of US, 1991 annual data compilation, 2324–1.5

see also Community-based correctional programs

see also Juvenile detention and correctional institutions

see also Military prisons

see also Parole and probation

see also Prison work programs

see also Prisoners

see also Rehabilitation of criminals

Correspondence courses

Service industries census, 1987: establishments, receipts by source, payroll, and employment, by SIC 2- to 4-digit kind of business, State, and MSA, 2393–4

Veterans education aid under GI Bill and other programs, and participation by period of service and State, FY89, annual rpt, 8604–9

Corrigan, E. Gerald

"Immediate Challenges for Public Policy", 9385–2

Corruption and bribery

Court civil and criminal caseloads for Federal district, appeals, and bankruptcy courts, by type of suit and offense, circuit, and district, 1990, annual rpt, 18204–11

Court civil and criminal caseloads for Federal district, appeals, and special courts, 1990, annual rpt, 18204–8

Court civil and criminal caseloads for Federal district courts, 1991, annual rpt, 18204–2.1

Court criminal case processing in Federal district courts, and dispositions, by offense, district, and offender characteristics, 1986, annual rpt, 6064–29

Court criminal case processing in Federal district courts, and dispositions, by offense, 1980-89, annual rpt, 6064–31

Court criminal cases in Federal district courts, by offense, disposition, and district, 1980-90, last issue of annual rpt, 18204–1

Drug enforcement regional task forces investigation of organized crime, activities by agency and region, FY83-90, biennial rpt, 6004–17

Govt officials prosecuted and convicted for corruption, by level of govt, data compilation, 1991 annual rpt, 6064–6.5

Sentences for Federal crimes, guidelines use and results by offense and district, and Sentencing Commission activities, 1990, annual rpt, 17664–1

Sentences for Federal offenses, guidelines by offense and circumstances, series, 17668–1

Statistical Abstract of US, 1991 annual data compilation, 2324–1.5

US attorneys civil and criminal cases by type and disposition, and collections, by Federal district, FY90, annual rpt, 6004–2.1; 6004–2.7

Wiretaps authorized, costs, arrests, trials, and convictions, by offense and jurisdiction, 1990, annual rpt, 18204–7

see also Federal Inspectors General reports

Corundum

see Abrasive materials

Cosmetics and toiletries

County Business Patterns, 1988: employment, establishments, and payroll, by SIC 2- to 4-digit industry and county, annual State rpt series, 2326–6

County Business Patterns, 1989: employment, establishments, and payroll, by SIC 2- to 4-digit industry and county, annual State rpt series, 2326–8

CPI by component for US city average, and by region, population size, and for 27 metro areas, monthly rpt, 6762–2

Exports and imports of US, by country and detailed commodity, monthly rpt, 2422–12

Exports and imports of US, by Harmonized System 6-digit commodity and country, 1990, annual rpt, 2424–13

Exports and imports of US, by transport mode, country, and SITC 1- to 3-digit commodity, 1990, annual rpt, 2424–12

Exports of US, detailed Schedule B commodities with countries of destination, 1990, annual rpt, 2424–10

Franchise business opportunities by firm and kind of business, and sources of aid and info, 1990 annual listing, 2104–7

Imports detained by FDA, by reason, product, shipper, brand, and country, monthly listing, 4062–2

Imports purchasing decisions of consumers, importance of brand name, authenticity, origin, and other factors, 1984 survey, hearing, 25528–115

Injuries from use of consumer products, by severity, victim age, and detailed product, 1990, annual rpt, 9164–6

Labor productivity, indexes of output, hours, and employment by SIC 2- to 4-digit industry, 1967-89, annual rpt, 6824–1.3

Manufacturing annual survey, 1989: finances and operations, by SIC 2- to 4-digit industry, series, 2506–15

Manufacturing census, 1987: finances and operations, by SIC 2- to 4-digit industry, State, and MSA, with trends from 1849, 2497–1

Manufacturing census, 1987: finances and operations, by type of organization and SIC 2- to 4-digit industry, subject rpt, 2497–5

Manufacturing finances and operations, by SIC 2- to 4-digit industry, forecast 1991, annual rpt, 2044–28

Occupational injury and illness rates, by SIC 2- to 4-digit industry, 1988-89, annual rpt, 6844–7

Occupational injury and illness rates, by SIC 2- to 4-digit industry, 1989, annual rpt, 6844–1

OECD trade, total and for 4 major countries, and US trade by country, by commodity, 1970-89, world area rpt series, 9116–1

Price indexes (producer), by stage of processing and detailed commodity, monthly rpt, 6762–6

Price indexes (producer), by stage of processing and detailed commodity, monthly 1990, annual rpt, 6764–2

Toothpaste and other sources of fluoride exposure, and health risks and benefits, 1930s-89, 4048–36

Toxicology Natl Program research and testing activities, FY89 and planned FY90, annual rpt, 4044–16

COSMOS Corp.

"No Gift Wasted: Effective Strategies for Educating Highly Able, Disadvantaged Students in Mathematics and Science", 4808–34

Cost of living

Cost of living and quality of life indicators for 14 MSAs, 1980s, GAO rpt, 26123–346

Economic indicators, prices, labor costs, and productivity, BLS econometric analyses and methodology, working paper series, 6886–6

Energy use by mode of transport, fuel supply, and demographic and economic factors of vehicle use, 1970s-89, annual rpt, 3304–5

Farm prices received for major products and paid for farm inputs and living items, by commodity and State, monthly rpt, 1629–1

Foreign countries living costs, State Dept indexes, housing allowances, and hardship differentials by country and major city, quarterly rpt, 7002–7

Higher education instn tuition relation to other instn financial indicators, by instn control, 1960s-88, 4808–24

Statistical Abstract of US, 1991 annual data compilation, 2324–1.15

see also Consumer Price Index

see also Energy prices

Cost of living

see also Family budgets
see also Food prices
see also Housing costs and financing
see also Inflation
see also Medical costs
see also Prices
see also Producer Price Index
see also Rent

Cost of living adjustments
see Escalator clauses

Cost of production
see Agricultural production costs
see Business income and expenses, general
see Business income and expenses, specific industry
see Energy production costs
see Producer Price Index
see Production costs

Costa Rica

- Agricultural exports of high-value commodities, indexes and sales by commodity, world area, and country, 1960s-86, 1528–323
- Agricultural exports of US, impacts of foreign agricultural and trade policy, with data by commodity and country, 1989, annual rpt, 1924–8
- Agricultural production, trade, and policies in foreign countries, summary data by country, 1989-90, annual factbook, 1924–12
- Agricultural trade of US, by detailed commodity and country, 1989, annual rpt, 1524–8
- Agricultural trade of US, by detailed commodity and country, 1990, semiannual rpt, 1522–4
- AID economic aid to developing countries, obligations and disbursements by country, quarterly rpt, 9912–4
- AID loans repayment status and terms by program and country, and status of predecessor agency loans, quarterly rpt, 9912–3
- Borders (maritime) of Costa Rica, geographic coordinates, as of Oct 1988, 7006–8.6
- Economic and military aid and loans from US and intl agencies, by program and country, FY46-90, annual rpt, 9914–5
- Economic and social conditions of developing countries from 1960s, and Intl Dev Cooperation Agency and AID activities and funding, FY90-92, annual rpt, 9904–4
- Economic conditions, policy, and trade practices, by country, 1988-90, annual rpt, 21384–5
- Economic, social, political, and geographic summary data, by country, 1991, annual factbook, 9114–2
- Exports and imports of US, by commodity and country, 1970-89, world area rpt, 9116–1.2
- Exports and imports of US, by Harmonized System 6-digit commodity and country, 1990, annual rpt, 2424–13
- Exports and imports of US, by selected country, country group, and commodity group, 1990, annual rpt, 2044–37
- Exports and imports of US, by transport mode, country, and SITC 1- to 3-digit commodity, 1990, annual rpt, 2424–12
- Exports of US, detailed Schedule B commodities with countries of destination, 1990, annual rpt, 2424–10

Fruit (fresh) imports from US by type, for Costa Rica, FY86-90, article, 1925–34.203

- Human rights conditions in 170 countries, and US economic and military aid, 1990, annual rpt, 21384–3
- Investment (direct) incentives of Caribbean Basin Initiative, economic impacts, with finances and employment by country, 1984-90, 2048–141
- Labor conditions, union coverage, and work accidents, 1991 annual country rpt, 6366–4.33
- Military aid of US, arms sales, and training programs costs and budget requests, by program, world region, and country, FY90-92, annual rpt, 7144–13
- Multinatl US firms and foreign affiliates finances and operations, by industry and world area of parent firm, 1989 benchmark survey, preliminary annual rpt, 2704–5
- Multinatl US firms foreign affiliates, income statement items by country and world area, 1986, biennial article, 8302–2.212
- UN voting record and share of votes in agreement with US, by issue, country, and world area, 1990, annual rpt, 7004–18

see also under By Foreign Country in the "Index by Categories"

Cote d'Ivoire
see Ivory Coast

Cotton

- Acreage of upland cotton estimated under alternative program planting assumptions, by region, 1988-91, article, 1561–1.205
- Acreage planted and harvested, by crop and State, 1989-90 and planned as of June 1991, annual rpt, 1621–23
- Acreage planted, by selected crop and State, 1982-90 and planned 1991, annual rpt, 1621–22
- Acreage planted by State and county, and fiber quality, by cotton variety, 1991, annual rpt, 1309–6
- Acreage reduction program compliance, enrollment, and yield on planted acreage, by commodity and State, annual press release series, 1004–20
- Acreage under Agricultural Stabilization and Conservation Service programs, rankings by commodity and congressional district, 1989, biennial rpt, 1804–17
- Africa (sub-Saharan) agricultural conditions by country, with Ethiopia grain production and use, and dev aid by major donor, 1960s-80s, hearing, 23848–216
- Agricultural data compilation, 1990 and trends from 1920, annual rpt, 1004–14
- Agricultural Stabilization and Conservation Service cotton programs, 1955-91, annual fact sheet, 1806–4.9; 1806–4.10
- Agricultural Stabilization and Conservation Service producer payments and certificate value, by program, monthly rpt, 1802–10
- Agricultural Stabilization and Conservation Service producer payments, by program and State, 1990, annual table, 1804–12
- *Agricultural Statistics, 1990*, annual rpt, 1004–1
- Agriculture census, 1987: farms, farmland, production, finances, and operator characteristics, by county, final State rpt series, 2331–1

Index by Subjects and Names

- Business statistics, detailed data for major industries and economic indicators, *Survey of Current Business*, monthly rpt, 2702–1.22
- CCC certificate exchange activity, by commodity, biweekly press release, 1802–16
- CCC cotton and grain loan activity, by commodity, weekly rpt, 1313–2
- CCC financial condition and major commodity program operations, FY62-87, annual chartbook, 1824–2
- Clothing and shoe production, shipments, trade, and use, by product, periodic Current Industrial Rpt series, 2506–6
- County Business Patterns, 1988: employment, establishments, and payroll, by SIC 2- to 4-digit industry and county, annual State rpt series, 2326–6
- County Business Patterns, 1989: employment, establishments, and payroll, by SIC 2- to 4-digit industry and county, annual State rpt series, 2326–8
- Employment, earnings, and hours, by SIC 1- to 4-digit industry, monthly and annual averages, selected years 1909-90, annual rpt, 6744–4
- Exports (agricultural) of US, impacts of foreign agricultural and trade policy, with data by commodity and country, 1989, annual rpt, 1924–8
- Exports and imports (agricultural) commodity and country, prices, and world market devs, monthly rpt, 1922–12
- Exports and imports (agricultural) of US, by commodity and country, bimonthly rpt, 1522–1
- Exports and imports (agricultural) of US, by detailed commodity and country, 1989, annual rpt, 1524–8
- Exports and imports (agricultural) of US, by detailed commodity and country, 1990, semiannual rpt, 1522–4
- Exports and imports between US and outlying areas, by detailed commodity and mode of transport, 1990, annual rpt, 2424–11
- Exports and imports of US, by country and detailed commodity, monthly rpt, 2422–12
- Exports and imports of US, by Harmonized System 6-digit commodity and country, 1990, annual rpt, 2424–13
- Exports and imports of US, by selected country, country group, and commodity group, 1990, annual rpt, 2044–37
- Exports and imports of US, by transport mode, country, and SITC 1- to 3-digit commodity, 1990, annual rpt, 2424–12
- Exports of cotton, forecasts using season shipment data, 1990/91, article, 1561–1.204
- Exports of grains, oilseed products, hides, skins, and cotton, by country, weekly rpt, 1922–3
- Exports of US, detailed Schedule B commodities with countries of destination, 1990, annual rpt, 2424–10
- Farm financial and marketing conditions, forecast 1991, annual chartbook, 1504–8
- Farm financial and marketing conditions, forecast 1991, annual conf, 1004–16
- Farm income, expenses, receipts by commodity, assets, liabilities, and ratios, 1990 and trends from 1945, annual rpt, 1544–16

Index by Subjects and Names

Farm sector balance sheet, and receipts by detailed commodity, by State, 1985-89, annual rpt, 1544–18

Fertilizer and pesticide use and application rates, by type, crop, and State, 1990, 1616–1.1

Fiber and processing test results, by cotton staple, region, State, and production area, 1990, annual rpt, 1309–16

Fiber grade, staple, and mike, for upland and American pima cotton by State, monthly rpt, 1309–11

Fiber grade, staple, mike, and other quality indicators, for upland cotton by classing office, weekly rpt, 1309–15

Fiber quality, by State, 1990, annual rpt, 1309–7

Fiber quality, supply, and carryover, 1989-90, annual rpt, 1309–8

Foreign and US agricultural production, acreage, and yield for selected crops, forecasts by selected world region and country, FAS monthly circular, 1925–28

Foreign and US agricultural supply and demand indicators, by selected crop, monthly rpt, 1522–5

Foreign and US cotton production and trade, FAS periodic circular series, 1925–4

Foreign countries agricultural production, prices, and trade, by country, 1980-90 and forecast 1991, annual world area rpt series, 1524–4

Foreign countries agricultural production, trade, and policies, summary data by country, 1989-90, annual factbook, 1924–12

Futures and options trading volume, by commodity and exchange, FY90, annual rpt, 11924–2

Futures trading in selected commodities and financial instruments and indexes, NYC, Chicago, and other markets activity, semimonthly rpt, 11922–5

Ginning activity and charges, by State, 1990/91, annual rpt, 1564–3

Ginnings and production, by State and county, 1990, annual rpt, 2344–1

Ginnings, by State and county, seasonal monthly rpt, 2342–2

Ginnings, by State, seasonal semimonthly rpt, 2342–1

Ginnings of cotton, by State and county, seasonal biweekly rpt, 1631–19

Imports of textiles, by country of origin, monthly rpt, 2042–27

Imports of textiles, by product and country of origin, monthly rpt series, 2046–8; 2046–9

Imports of textiles under Multifiber Arrangement by product and country, and status of bilateral agreements, 1987-90, annual rpt, 9884–18

Irrigation projects of Reclamation Bur in western US, crop production and acreage by commodity, State, and project, 1989, annual rpt, 5824–12

Linters production, stocks, use, and prices, monthly rpt, 1309–10

Manufacturing annual survey, 1989: finances and operations, by SIC 2- to 4-digit industry, series, 2506–15

Manufacturing census, 1987: finances and operations, by SIC 2- to 4-digit industry, State, and MSA, with trends from 1849, 2497–1

Manufacturing census, 1987: finances and operations, by type of organization and SIC 2- to 4-digit industry, subject rpt, 2497–5

Occupational injury and illness rates, by SIC 2- to 4-digit industry, 1988-89, annual rpt, 6844–7

Occupational injury and illness rates, by SIC 2- to 4-digit industry, 1989, annual rpt, 6844–1

OECD trade, total and for 4 major countries, and US trade by country, by commodity, 1970-89, world area rpt series, 9116–1

Pesticide and fertilizer use reduction, environmental and economic impacts by commodity and region, alternative forecasts 1989-94, hearing, 23848–222

PL 480 long-term credit sales allocations, by commodity and country, periodic press release, 1922–7

Pollution (air) emissions factors, by detailed pollutant and source, data compilation, 1990 rpt, 9198–120

Price indexes (producer), by stage of processing and detailed commodity, monthly rpt, 6762–6

Price indexes (producer), by stage of processing and detailed commodity, monthly 1990, annual rpt, 6764–2

Price support and other CCC program outlays, with production and marketing outlook, by commodity, projected 1990-96, 26306–6.160

Price support program provisions, for selected commodities, 1961-90, 1568–302

Prices in selected spot markets, futures prices at NYC exchange, farm prices, and CCC loan stocks, monthly rpt, 1309–1

Prices of cotton at selected spot markets, NYC futures prices, and CCC loan rates, 1990/91 and trends from 1943, annual rpt, 1309–2

Prices received and paid by farmers, by commodity and State, 1990, annual rpt, 1629–5

Prices received by farmers and production value, by detailed crop and State, 1988-90, annual rpt, 1621–2

Prices received by farmers for major products, and paid for farm inputs and living items, by State, monthly rpt, 1629–1

Production, farms, acreage, and related data, by selected crop and State, monthly rpt, 1621–1

Production inputs, output, and productivity for farms, by commodity and region, 1947-89, annual rpt, 1544–17

Production itemized costs, receipts, and returns, by commodity and region, 1987-89, annual rpt, 1544–20

Production, prices, exports, stocks, and mill use of long staple cotton, monthly rpt, 1309–12

Production, prices, trade, and marketing, by commodity, current situation and forecast, monthly rpt with articles, 1502–4

Production, prices, trade, and use of cotton, wool, and synthetic fibers, periodic situation rpt with articles, 1561–1

Production, trade, sales, stocks, and material used, by product, region, and State, periodic Current Industrial Rpt series, 2506–5

Counselors and counseling

Soviet Union agricultural trade, by commodity and country, 1955-90, 1528–322

Statistical Abstract of US, 1991 annual data compilation, 2324–1.23

Water quality impacts of cotton farms fertilizer, pesticide and irrigation use and soil conservation practices, 1989, 1588–151

Zimbabwe agricultural conditions impacts of economic policies, 1980s, 1528–319

see also under By Commodity in the "Index by Categories"

Cottonseed

see Oils, oilseeds, and fats

Cottrell, David W.

"U.S.-Mexican Vegetable Trade", 1561–11.202

Couch, David

"Olympia Oyster. Species Profiles: Life Histories and Environmental Requirements of Coastal Fishes and Invertebrates (Pacific Northwest)", 5506–8.131

Coughlin, Cletus C.

"Consumer's Guide to Regional Economic Multipliers", 9391–1.206

"Measuring State Exports: Is There a Better Way?", 9391–1.219

"U.S. Trade Remedy Laws: Do They Facilitate or Hinder Free Trade?", 9391–1.215

Coulehan, John L.

"Cardiovascular Disease", 4088–2

Council for Mutual Economic Assistance

Economic conditions in Communist and OECD countries, 1989, annual rpt, 7144–11

Exports and imports of OECD members, by country, 1989, annual rpt, 7144–10

Council of Economic Advisers

Budget of US, authoritative financial statements with appropriations, outlays, and receipts, by category and agency, FY90, annual rpt, 8104–2.1

Budget of US, obligations and authority by function, agency, and program, with summaries, analyses, and historical tables, FY92, annual rpt, 104–2

Economic indicators and components, current data and annual trends, monthly rpt, 23842–1

Economic Report of the President for 1991, with economic trends from 1929, annual rpt, 204–1

Council on Environmental Quality

Budget of US, authoritative financial statements with appropriations, outlays, and receipts, by category and agency, FY90, annual rpt, 8104–2.1

Budget of US, obligations and authority by function, agency, and program, with summaries, analyses, and historical tables, FY92, annual rpt, 104–2

Environmental Quality, status of problems, protection programs, research, and intl issues, 1991 annual rpt, 484–1

Counselors and counseling

AIDS info and education activities and funding of CDC, and donation of media ads, 1987-92, articles, 4042–3.256

AIDS virus antibody tests and counseling sessions by setting, and CDC funding and funds uncommitted by State, 1989-90, GAO rpt, 26121–428

Counselors and counseling

Drug abuse psychotherapy and counseling outcomes, research results and methodology, 1990 conf, 4498–71

Drug and alcohol abuse treatment facilities, services, use, funding, staff, and client characteristics, 1989, biennial rpt, 4494–10

Drug and alcohol abuse treatment services, funding, staffing, and client load, characteristics, and outcomes, by setting, 1989 conf, 4498–73

Education (special) enrollment by age, staff, funding, and needs, by type of handicap and State, 1989/90, annual rpt, 4944–4

Education data compilation, 1991 annual rpt, 4824–2

Education Dept enforcement activities to eliminate discrimination within schools, and adequacy, FY81-91, GAO rpt, 26121–427

Education services for homeless adults, funding, participation, and staff, by State, 1989, annual rpt series, 4804–39

Educational enrollment, finances, staff, and high school grads, for elementary and secondary public school systems by State, FY88-89, annual rpt, 4834–6

Genetic damage and trait monitoring and screening of employees, use, costs, benefits, and procedures, 1980s, 26358–230

Health condition improvement and disease prevention goals and recommended activities for 2000, with trends 1970s-80s, 4048–10

Homeless and runaway youth programs, funding, activities, and participant characteristics, FY90, annual rpt, 4604–3

Hospices operations, services, costs, and patient characteristics, for instns without Medicare certification, FY85-86, 4658–52

Juvenile correctional and detention public and private instns, inmates, and expenses, by instn and resident characteristics and State, 1987, biennial rpt, 6064–13

Physicians visits, by patient and practice characteristics, diagnosis, and services provided, 1989, 4146–8.206

School guidance counselors, by region and State, 1988/89, annual rpt, 4834–20

VA Medicine and Surgery Dept trainees, by detailed program and city, FY90, annual rpt, 8704–4

VA mental health care services, staff, research, and training programs, 1991 biennial listing, 8704–2

Youth counseling program based at schools, client risk behaviors and outcomes, 1988/89 study, hearing, 25548–104

see also Clergy

see also Psychiatry

see also Social work

see also Vocational guidance

Counterfeiting and forgery

Arrest rates, by offense, sex, age, and race, 1965-89, annual rpt, 6224–7

Arrests, by offense, offender characteristics, and location, 1990, annual rpt, 6224–2.2

Court civil and criminal caseloads for Federal district, appeals, and bankruptcy courts, by type of suit and offense, circuit, and district, 1990, annual rpt, 18204–11

Court civil and criminal caseloads for Federal district, appeals, and special courts, 1990, annual rpt, 18204–8

Court civil and criminal caseloads for Federal district courts, 1991, annual rpt, 18204–2.1

Court criminal case processing in Federal district courts, and dispositions, by offense, district, and offender characteristics, 1986, annual rpt, 6064–29

Court criminal case processing in Federal district courts, and dispositions, by offense, 1980-89, annual rpt, 6064–31

Court criminal cases in Federal district courts, by offense, disposition, and district, 1980-90, last issue of annual rpt, 18204–1

Crime, criminal justice admin and enforcement, and public opinion, data compilation, 1991 annual rpt, 6064–6

Currency (counterfeit) seized and in circulation, and operations suppressed by Secret Service, data compilation, 1991 annual rpt, 6064–6.4

Postal Service inspection activities, 2nd half FY91, semiannual rpt, 9862–2

Pretrial processing, detention, and release, for Federal offenders, by defendant characteristics and district, 1988, hearing, 25528–114

Secret Service counterfeiting and other investigations and arrests by type, and disposition, FY90 and trends from FY81, annual rpt, 8464–1

Sentences for Federal crimes, guidelines use and results by offense and district, and Sentencing Commission activities, 1990, annual rpt, 17664–1

Sentences for Federal offenses, guidelines by offense and circumstances, series, 17668–1

US attorneys civil and criminal cases by type and disposition, and collections, by Federal district, FY90, annual rpt, 6004–2.1

Counties

Agricultural Conservation Program, counties served by State, FY90, annual rpt, 1804–7

Census of Population and Housing, 1990: population and housing characteristics, households, and land area, by county, subdiv, and place, State rpt series, 2551–1

Census of Population, 1990: post-enumeration survey results compared to census counts, by race, sex, city, county, and State, press release, 2328–69

Community Dev Block Grant allocation, by State, county, and city, FY84-91, 5128–17

Crimes, arrests by offender characteristics, and rates, by offense, and law enforcement employees, by population size and jurisdiction, 1990, annual rpt, 6224–2

Criminal justice spending, employment, and payroll, by level of govt, State, and selected city and county, FY71-88, biennial rpt, 6064–9

Farmland damaged by natural disaster, Emergency Conservation Program aid and participation by State, FY90, annual rpt, 1804–22

Gazetteer of US places, mountains, bodies of water, and other political and physical features, 1990 rpt, 5668–117

Govt census, 1987: State and local govt employment, payroll, OASDHI coverage, and employee benefits costs, by level of govt and State, 2455–4

Govt census, 1987: State and local labor-mgmt policies, agreements, and coverage and bargaining units, by function, level of govt, and State, 2455–3

Govt employment and payroll, by function and population size, for 398 largest counties, 1990, annual rpt, 2466–1.3

Govt employment and payroll, by function, level of govt, and State, 1990, annual rpt, 2466–1.1

Govt employment of minorities and women, by occupation, function, pay grade, and level of govt, 1990, annual rpt, 9244–6.3

Govt finances, by level of govt, State, and for large cities and counties, annual rpt series, 2466–2

Govt finances, tax systems and revenue, and fiscal structure, by level of govt and State, 1991 with historical trends, annual rpt, 10044–1

Households by tenure and population size, by age group, State, and county, 1980 and 1985, 2546–3.169

Income (personal) per capita and by source, and earnings by industry div, by State, MSA, and county, 1984-89, annual regional rpts, 2704–2

Labor surplus areas eligible for preferential Fed Govt contracts, monthly listing, 6402–1

Population size of counties with population over 100,000, as of Apr 1990, press release, 2328–68

Rural areas economic and social conditions, dev, and problems, periodic journal, 1502–7

Soil surveys and maps for counties, 1899-1990, annual listing, 1264–11

State and Metro Area Data Book, 1991 data compilation, 2328–54

Statistical Abstract of US, 1991 annual data compilation, 2324–1

see also County Business Patterns

see also under By County in the "Index by Categories"

County Business Patterns

Employment, establishments, and payroll, by SIC 2- to 4-digit industry and county, 1988, annual State rpt series, 2326–6

Employment, establishments, and payroll, by SIC 2- to 4-digit industry and county, 1989, annual State rpt series, 2326–8

Courier services

Census of Transportation, 1987: finances and operations by size, ownership, and State, and revenues by MSA, by SIC 2- to 4-digit industry, 2579–1

Employment, earnings, and hours, by SIC 1- to 4-digit industry, monthly and annual averages, selected years 1909-90, annual rpt, 6744–4

Tax (income) returns of sole proprietorships, income statement items, by industry group, 1989, annual article, 8302–2.214

Truck accidents, casualties, and damage, by circumstances and characteristics of persons and vehicles involved, 1988, annual rpt, 7554–9

Index by Subjects and Names

Court of International Trade

Budget of US, authoritative financial statements with appropriations, outlays, and receipts, by category and agency, FY90, annual rpt, 8104–2.1

Budget of US, obligations and authority by function, agency, and program, with summaries, analyses, and historical tables, FY92, annual rpt, 104–2

Caseloads of Court of Intl Trade, decisions, and appeals, FY90-91, annual rpt, 18224–2

Cases filed and terminated, 1989-90, annual rpt, 18204–8.21

Court of Military Appeals

Cases and actions of military courts, FY90, annual rpt, 3504–3

Courtless, Joan C.

"Clothing Expenditures of Single-Parent Households", 1004–16.1

"Developments in Apparel, Textiles, and Fibers Affecting the Consumer", 1702–1.209

"Trends in Savings", 1702–1.215

Courts

Budget of US, authoritative financial statements with appropriations, outlays, and receipts, by agency, FY90, annual rpt, 8104–2

Budget of US, object class analysis of obligations, by agency, FY92, annual rpt, 104–9

Budget of US, obligations and authority by function, agency, and program, with summaries, analyses, and historical tables, FY92, annual rpt, 104–2

Budget of US, receipts by source, outlays by agency and program, and balances, monthly rpt, 8102–3

Congressional Directory, members of 102nd Congress, other officials, elections, and districts, 1991-92, biennial rpt, 23874–1

Employment, earnings, and hours, by SIC 1- to 4-digit industry, monthly and annual averages, selected years 1909-90, annual rpt, 6744–4

Employment, payroll, and spending for criminal justice, by level of govt, State, and selected city and county, FY71-88, annual rpt, 6064–9

Employment, payroll, and spending for criminal justice, by level of govt, State, and selected city and county, 1984-86, biennial rpt, 6064–4

Fed Govt consolidated financial statements based on business accounting methods, FY89-90, annual rpt, 8104–5

Fed Govt labor productivity, indexes of output and labor costs by function, FY67-89, annual rpt, 6824–1.6

GSA mgmt of court buildings, spending, and rental income, 1980s-91, hearing, 21648–60

Judicial Conf proceedings and findings, spring 1991, semiannual rpt, 18202–2

Statistical Abstract of US, 1991 annual data compilation, 2324–1.5

see also Administrative Office of the U.S. Courts

see also Civil procedure

see also Contempt of court

see also Court of International Trade

see also Court of Military Appeals

see also Courts-martial and courts of inquiry

see also Criminal procedure

see also D.C. courts

see also Federal bankruptcy courts

see also Federal courts of appeals

see also Federal district courts

see also Federal Judicial Center

see also Judges

see also Judicial Conference of the U.S.

see also Judicial powers

see also Judicial reform

see also Juries

see also Juvenile courts and cases

see also Parole and probation

see also Sentences, criminal procedure

see also State courts

see also Supreme Court

see also Tax Court of the U.S.

see also Tax laws and courts

see also Traffic laws and courts

see also Trials

see also U.S. Claims Court

see also U.S. Court of Appeals for the Federal Circuit

see also Witnesses

Courts martial and courts of inquiry

Army Dept activities, personnel, discipline, budget, and assistance, FY83 summary data, annual rpt, 3704–11

Cases and actions of military courts, FY90, annual rpt, 3504–3

Criminal case processing in military courts, and prisoners by facility, by service branch, data compilation, 1991 annual rpt, 6064–6.5; 6064–6.6

Cousineau, Michael R.

"Loss of Medicaid and Access to Health Services", 4652–1.242

Covey, Ted

"Agricultural Interest Rates and Inflationary Expectations: A Regional Analysis", 1502–3.201

Cowan, Cathy A.

"Burden of Health Care Costs: Business, Households, and Governments", 4652–1.230

Cowles, C. McKeen

"Review Effect on Cost Reports: Impact Smaller than Anticipated", 4652–1.233

Cows

see Dairy industry and products

see Livestock and livestock industry

Coyle, William T.

"Prospects for Japan's Livestock Sector", 1524–4.5

CPI

see Consumer Price Index

Crabbe, Leland

"Callable Corporate Bonds: A Vanishing Breed", 9366–6.269

"Corporate Medium-Term Notes", 9366–6.276

Crabs

see Shellfish

Crabtree, Norman

"Domestic Natural Gas Reserves and Production Dedicated to Interstate Pipeline Companies, 1990", 3162–4.209

Craig, R. Sean

"EMS Interest Rate Differentials and Fiscal Policy: A Model with an Empirical Application to Italy", 9366–7.259

Cranberries

see Fruit and fruit products

Credit

Crandell, W. Dean

"Availability of Federally Owned Minerals for Exploration and Development in Western States: Nevada, 1985", 5606–7.6

Cranston, R.I.

Housing and households characteristics, unit and neighborhood quality, and journey to work by MSA location, for 11 MSAs, 1984 survey, supplement, 2485–8

Housing and households detailed characteristics, and unit and neighborhood quality, by location, 1988 survey, MSA rpt, 2485–6.7

Craven, Jill

"Dollar's Fall Boosts U.S. Machinery Exports, 1985-90", 6722–1.233

Credit

Assets and debts of private sector, balance sheets by segment, 1945-90, semiannual rpt, 9365–4.1

Banks Fed Reserve discount window borrowing, relation to interest rate spreads and banks financial performance indicators, 1980s-90, technical paper, 9385–8.111

Banks Fed Reserve discount window borrowing, relation to interest rate spreads and discount borrowing outstanding, by bank asset size, 1981-90, article, 9385–1.209

Banks Fed Reserve discount window borrowing, relation to interest rate spreads, 1980s-90, technical paper, 9385–8.110

Budget of US, CBO analysis of revenue and spending alternatives and projections of economic indicators, FY92-96, annual rpt, 26304–3

Budget of US, House concurrent resolution, with spending and revenue targets, FY92 and projected to FY96, annual rpt, 21264–2

Budget of US, obligations and authority by function, agency, and program, with summaries, analyses, and historical tables, FY92, annual rpt, 104–2

Budget of US, Senate concurrent resolution, with spending and revenue targets, FY92, annual rpt, 25254–1

Corporations short-term credit market debt, by type of debt, 1950s-89, working paper, 9375–13.62

Demand for credit, activity indicators, 1981-90, annual rpt, 204–1.5

Economic indicators and components, current data and annual trends, monthly rpt, 23842–1.5

Economic indicators performance, and Fed Reserve monetary policy objectives, as of July 1991, semiannual rpt, 9362–4

Financial and business detailed statistics, *Fed Reserve Bulletin*, monthly rpt with articles, 9362–1

Home equity lines of credit share of all loans, and delinquency compared to other loans, by southeastern State, 1988-90, article, 9391–16.206

Italy interest rates and spread relation to regional income and debt, and outside borrowing, model description and results, 1981-84, technical paper, 9366–7.248

Statistical Abstract of US, 1991 annual data compilation, 2324–1.16

Credit

see also Agricultural credit
see also Business assets and liabilities, general
see also Business assets and liabilities, specific industry
see also Commercial credit
see also Commodity Credit Corp.
see also Consumer credit
see also Credit bureaus and agencies
see also Credit cards
see also Credit unions
see also Discrimination in credit
see also Finance companies
see also Foreign debts
see also Government assets and liabilities
see also Interest payments
see also International finance
see also Loan delinquency and default
see also Loans
see also Mortgages
see also Public debt

Credit bureaus and agencies

County Business Patterns, 1988: employment, establishments, and payroll, by SIC 2- to 4-digit industry and county, annual State rpt series, 2326–6

County Business Patterns, 1989: employment, establishments, and payroll, by SIC 2- to 4-digit industry and county, annual State rpt series, 2326–8

Mortgage loan activity, by type of lender, loan, and mortgaged property, monthly press release, 5142–18

Mortgage loan activity, by type of lender, loan, and mortgaged property, quarterly press release, 5142–30

Occupational injury and illness rates, by SIC 2- to 4-digit industry, 1988-89, annual rpt, 6844–7

Puerto Rico economic censuses, 1987: wholesale and retail trade and service industry finances and operations, by SIC 2- to 4-digit industry and municipio, 2591–1

Puerto Rico economic censuses, 1987: wholesale, retail, and service industries finances and operations, by establishment characteristics and SIC 2- and 3-digit industry, subject rpts, 2591–2

Service industries census, 1987: depreciable assets, capital and operating expenses, and receipts, by SIC 2- to 4-digit kind of business, 2393–2

Service industries census, 1987: establishments, receipts by source, payroll, and employment, by SIC 2- to 4-digit kind of business, State, and MSA, 2393–4

Service industries receipts, by SIC 2- to 4-digit kind of business, 1990, annual rpt, 2413–8

Tax (income) returns of corporations, income and tax items by asset size and detailed industry, 1987, annual rpt, 8304–4

Tax (income) returns of corporations, income and tax items by asset size and detailed industry, 1988, annual rpt, 8304–21

Tax (income) returns of sole proprietorships, income statement items, by industry group, 1989, annual article, 8302–2.214

Credit cards

Banks (natl) charters, mergers, liquidations, enforcement cases, and financial performance, with data by instn and State, quarterly rpt, 8402–3

Banks profitability indicators for student loans and other financial services, 1985-89, 4808–36

Economic indicators and components, current data and annual trends, monthly rpt, 23842–1.5

Mail volume to and from households, use, and views, by class, source, content, and household characteristics, 1987-88, annual rpt, 9864–10

Money supply components impact of credit card ownership, model description and results, 1983, working paper, 9379–12.74

Statistical Abstract of US, 1991 annual data compilation, 2324–1.16

Credit unions

Assets and liabilities of depository instns, monthly rpt, 9362–1.1

Assets, members, and location of credit unions, 1991 annual listing, 9534–6

Budget of US, CBO analysis of savings and revenues under alternative spending cuts and tax changes, projected FY92-97, 26306–3.118

County Business Patterns, 1988: employment, establishments, and payroll, by SIC 2- to 4-digit industry and county, annual State rpt series, 2326–6

County Business Patterns, 1989: employment, establishments, and payroll, by SIC 2- to 4-digit industry and county, annual State rpt series, 2326–8

Employment, earnings, and hours, by SIC 1- to 4-digit industry, monthly and annual averages, selected years 1909-90, annual rpt, 6744–4

Finances, mergers, and closings of federally insured credit unions, and insurance fund losses and financial statements, FY90, annual rpt, 9534–7

Finances of banks and thrifts, by instn type, 1990, annual rpt, 13004–2

Finances of federally insured credit unions, by instn characteristics and State, as of June 1991, semiannual rpt, 9532–6

Finances of federally insured credit unions, 1989-90, annual rpt, 9534–1

Finances, operations, and regulation of credit unions, series, 9536–1

Financial performance of credit unions, 1989-90, release, 9538–8

Financial performance of federally-insured credit unions, by charter type and region, 1st half 1991, semiannual rpt, 9532–7

Flow-of-funds accounts, savings, investments, and credit statements, quarterly rpt, 9365–3.3

Foreign and US credit unions, assets, and members, for 13 countries and 5 regional confederations, 1986 and 1989, release, 9538–9

Installment credit outstanding, and terms, by lender and credit type, monthly rpt, 9365–2.6

Installment credit outstanding, by type of holder, *Survey of Current Business*, monthly rpt, 2702–1.9

Mortage lending impacts on credit union financial performance, for northeast States and total US, 1980s-90, article, 9536–1.6

Index by Subjects and Names

Rural Credit Unions cooperatives, memberships, and loans, by State, 1989, annual rpt, 1124–1

Southeastern States, Fed Reserve 8th District credit unions finances and members by State, 1984 and 1990, article, 9391–16.210

State and Metro Area Data Book, 1991 data compilation, 2328–54

Statistical Abstract of US, 1991 annual data compilation, 2324–1.16

Tax (income) returns of corporations, income and tax items by asset size and detailed industry, 1987, annual rpt, 8304–4

Tax expenditures, Federal revenues forgone through income tax deductions and exclusions by type, FY92-96, annual rpt, 21784–10

West Central States economic indicators, Fed Reserve 10th District, quarterly rpt, 9381–16.2

Crime and criminals

AIDS cases and policies in criminal justice system, series, 6066–28

Cocaine abuse, user characteristics, and related crime and violence, 1988 conf, 4498–74

Crimes, arrests by offender characteristics, and rates, by offense, and law enforcement employees, by population size and jurisdiction, 1990, annual rpt, 6224–2

Data on crime and criminal justice, activities of Bur of Justice Statistics and States, annual rpt, discontinued, 6064–21

Data on crime and criminal justice, programs and rpts, 1989, annual listing, 6064–25

Data on crime and criminal justice, research results, series, 6066–26

Data on crime, criminal justice admin and enforcement, and public opinion, data compilation, 1991 annual rpt, 6064–6

Data on criminal justice issues, series, 6066–19; 6066–25

Drug abuse relation to violent and criminal behavior, with data on street gang activity and selected population groups, 1989 conf, 4498–70

Drug and alcohol abuse and mental illness direct and indirect costs, by type and patient age and sex, 1985 with 1980 and 1988 comparisons, 4048–35

Drug and alcohol abuse and mental illness direct and indirect costs, by type, 1970s-88, article, 4042–3.219

Index of crime by population size and region, and offenses by large city, Jan.-June 1991, semiannual rpt, 6222–1

Index of crime, victimizations and arrest by offense, circumstances, and location, data compilation, 1991 annual rpt, 6064–6.3; 6064–6.4

Justice Natl Inst rpts, 1983-89, listing, 6068–240

Neighborhood and housing quality, indicators and attitudes, by householder type and location, for 11 MSAs, 1984 survey, supplement, 2485–8

Neighborhood and housing quality, indicators and attitudes, by householder type and location, 1987, biennial rpt supplement, 2485–13

Index by Subjects and Names

Neighborhood and housing quality, indicators and attitudes, by householder type and location, 1989, biennial rpt, 2485–12

Neighborhood and housing quality, indicators and attitudes, MSA surveys, series, 2485–6

Palau admin, and social, economic, and govtl data, FY90, annual rpt, 7004–6

Park natl system accidents, crimes, hazardous waste sites, and funding, 1970s-91, GAO rpt, 26113–545

Records (criminal) repository characteristics, holdings, use, and reporting requirements, by State, 1989, 6068–241

State and Metro Area Data Book, 1991 data compilation, 2328–54

Statistical Abstract of US, 1991 annual data compilation, 2324–1.5

Veterans (homeless) domiciliary program of VA, participant characteristics and outcomes, 1990 annual rpt, 8604–10

Victimization rates, by victim and offender characteristics, circumstances, and offense, survey rpt series, 6066–3

Violent crime victimizations, circumstances, victim characteristics, arrest, recidivism, sentences, and prisoners, 1980s, 6068–148

Wiretaps authorized, costs, arrests, trials, and convictions, by offense and jurisdiction, 1990, annual rpt, 18204–7

see also Air piracy
see also Arrest
see also Arson
see also Assassination
see also Assault
see also Assaults on police
see also Black market currency
see also Bombs
see also Child abuse and neglect
see also Contraband
see also Correctional institutions
see also Corruption and bribery
see also Counterfeiting and forgery
see also Courts
see also Crime victim compensation
see also Criminal investigations
see also Criminal procedure
see also Detective and protective services
see also Domestic violence
see also Driving while intoxicated
see also Drug and narcotics offenses
see also Fraud
see also Gambling
see also Homicide
see also Hostages
see also Juvenile delinquency
see also Kidnapping
see also Law enforcement
see also Motor vehicle theft
see also Organized crime
see also Parole and probation
see also Pretrial detention and release
see also Prisoners
see also Prostitution
see also Rape
see also Recidivism
see also Rehabilitation of criminals
see also Robbery and theft
see also Sentences, criminal procedure
see also Sex crimes
see also Smuggling
see also Tax delinquency and evasion

see also Terrorism
see also Trials
see also Vandalism
see also Violence

Crime Index

see Crime and criminals

Crime victim compensation

Banks and thrifts fraud and abuse, Federal agencies enforcement activities and staff, with data by instn and location, 1988-90, hearing, 21408–119

Banks and thrifts fraud and abuse, Federal criminal enforcement activities, case dispositions, and settlements, with data by district, 1982-90, hearing, 21248–142

Expenditures for crime victim compensation and support services by State, and applications by disposition, 1986-91, GAO rpt, 26119–348

Savings instns fraud and abuse, Federal indictments and case dispositions, FY89-91, press release, 6008–33

Criminal investigations

Banks and thrifts fraud and abuse, Federal agencies enforcement activities and staff, with data by instn and location, 1988-90, hearing, 21408–119

Banks and thrifts fraud and abuse, Federal criminal enforcement activities, case dispositions, and settlements, with data by district, 1982-90, hearing, 21248–142

Data on crime, criminal justice admin and enforcement, and public opinion, data compilation, 1991 annual rpt, 6064–6

Drug abuse and trafficking reduction programs activities, funding, staff, and Bush Admin budget request, by Federal agency and program area, FY90-92, 238–2

Drug enforcement regional task forces investigation of organized crime, activities by agency and region, FY83-90, biennial rpt, 6004–17

Marijuana crop eradication activities of DEA and local agencies by State, and drug potency and prices, 1982-90, annual rpt, 6284–4

Money laundering enforcement activities of IRS, staff, and funding, abatement, 1985-90, GAO rpt, 26123–338

Money laundering investigation network of Treasury Dept, funding, and staff detailed from other agencies, 1990-91, GAO rpt, 26119–330

Money laundering investigations of Fed Govt using IRS large cash transaction rpts, and rpts filed and penalties for nonfiling by region, 1989-91, GAO rpt, 26119–356

Postal Service inspection activities, FY90, annual rpt, 9864–9

Postal Service inspection activities, 2nd half FY91, semiannual rpt, 9862–2

Savings instns fraud and abuse, Federal indictments and case dispositions, FY89-91, press release, 6008–33

Secret Service counterfeiting and other investigations and arrests by type, and disposition, FY90 and trends from FY81, annual rpt, 8464–1

Securities law enforcement activities of SEC, FY90, annual rpt, 9734–2.3

Tax litigation and enforcement activity of IRS, FY90, annual rpt, 8304–3.1

Criminal procedure

Terrorism incidents in US, related activity, and casualties, by attack type, target, group, and location, 1990, annual rpt, 6224–6

Wiretaps authorized, costs, arrests, trials, and convictions, by offense and jurisdiction, 1990, annual rpt, 18204–7

see also Police
see also Searches and seizures

Criminal Justice Statistics Association

"Multi-Jurisdictional Drug Control Task Forces 1988: A Key Program of State Drug Control Strategies", 6068–244

Criminal procedure

Banks and thrifts fraud and abuse, Federal criminal enforcement activities, case dispositions, and settlements, with data by district, 1982-90, hearing, 21248–142

Court civil and criminal caseloads for Federal district, appeals, and bankruptcy courts, by type of suit and offense, circuit, and district, 1990, annual rpt, 18204–11

Data on crime and criminal justice, programs and rpts, 1989, annual listing, 6064–25

Data on crime and criminal justice, research results, series, 6066–26

Data on crime, criminal justice admin and enforcement, and public opinion, data compilation, 1991 annual rpt, 6064–6

Data on criminal justice issues, series, 6066–19; 6066–25

DC appeals and superior courts civil and criminal caseloads, 1971-88, hearing, 21308–27

Drug abuse and enforcement issues, series, 236–2

Drug abuse and trafficking reduction programs activities, funding, staff, and Bush Admin budget request, by Federal agency and program area, FY90-92, 238–2

Drug abuse, treatment, and enforcement policy issues, series, 236–1

Drug control task forces enforcement activities by drug type and State, and organization, staff, and spending, 1988, 6068–244

Drug enforcement regional task forces investigation of organized crime, activities by agency and region, FY83-90, biennial rpt, 6004–17

Drug testing of criminal defendants, demonstration program operations, offender characteristics, and judges views, 1987-90, 18208–11

Environmental legislation enforcement activities of EPA and State govts, FY90, annual rpt, 9184–21

Fed Govt budgetary changes impacts on criminal justice system workload, model description, 1991 GAO rpt, 26119–340

Federal district and appeals court caseloads, actions, procedure duration, judges, and jurors, by court, 1986-91, annual rpt, 18204–3

Federal district, appeals, and special courts civil and criminal caseloads, by offense, circuit, and district, 1990, annual rpt, 18204–8

Federal district, appeals, and special courts civil and criminal caseloads, 1991, annual rpt, 18204–2

Federal district court criminal case processing and dispositions, by offense, 1980-89, annual rpt, 6064–31

Criminal procedure

Federal district court criminal caseloads, by offense, disposition, and district, 1980-90, last issue of annual rpt, 18204–1

Judicial Conf proceedings and findings, spring 1991, semiannual rpt, 18202–2

Juvenile arrests, by disposition and population size, 1990, annual rpt, 6224–2.2

Lawyers for defense, subpoenas by Federal prosecutors, and public and private indigent defense lawyers pay by State, 1986-90, hearing, 21408–123

Legal services establishments, lawyers by field, receipts by class of client, expenses, and employment, by MSA, 1987 Census of Service Industries, 2393–4.13

Pension laws admin and enforcement under Employee Retirement Income Security Act (ERISA), 1990, annual rpt, 6684–1

Records (criminal) repository characteristics, holdings, use, and reporting requirements, by State, 1989, 6068–241

Secret Service counterfeiting and other investigations and arrests by type, and disposition, FY90 and trends from FY81, annual rpt, 8464–1

Statistical Abstract of US, 1991 annual data compilation, 2324–1.5

US attorneys case processing and collections, by case type and Federal district, FY90, annual rpt, 6004–2

US attorneys staffing disparities among district offices, and caseload by litigation type, FY87-90, GAO rpt, 26119–323

see also Arrest

see also Capital punishment

see also Crime victim compensation

see also Evidence

see also Extradition

see also Fines and settlements

see also Habeas corpus

see also Juries

see also Pardons

see also Parole and probation

see also Pretrial detention and release

see also Searches and seizures

see also Sentences, criminal procedure

see also Trials

Cromwell, Brian A.

"Local Banking Markets and Firm Location", 9377–9.123

"Prointegrative Subsidies and Their Effect on Housing Markets: Do Race-Based Loans Work?", 9377–9.108

Crook, Frederick W.

"China's Grain Production Economy: A Review by Regions", 1524–4.3

Crop insurance

see Agricultural insurance

Crop yields

see Agricultural productivity

Crops

see Agricultural commodities

Cross, Stephen

"Do Capital Markets Predict Problems in Large Commercial Banks?", 9373–1.210

Crosswhite, William M.

"Trends in Resource Protection Policies in Agriculture", 1561–16.203

Croushore, Dean D.

"Measure of Federal Reserve Credibility", 9387–8.240

"Short-Run Costs of Disinflation", 9387–8.247

Crutcher, J. W.

"Results of the Preliminary Radiological Survey at the Former Diamond Magnesium Company Site, Luckey, Ohio (DML001)", 3006–9.8

Crutchfield, Stephen R.

"Cotton Production and Water Quality: An Initial Assessment", 1588–151

CSR, Inc.

"National Study of Guardian *Ad Litem* Representation", 4608–28

Cuba

Abortions in US, by place of woman's residence and State of occurrence, 1988, US Vital Statistics annual rpt, 4146–5.120

Agricultural exports of high-value commodities, indexes and sales by commodity, world area, and country, 1960s-86, 1528–323

Agricultural trade of US, by detailed commodity and country, 1990, semiannual rpt, 1522–4

Aliens (illegal) enforcement activity of Coast Guard, by nationality, 2nd half FY91, semiannual rpt, 7402–4

Background Notes, summary social, political, and economic data, 1990 rpt, 7006–2.5

Cancer deaths in Cuba and among Cuban-born Americans, by body site, 1970s-83, article, 4042–3.205

Deaths in US, by State of occurrence and birthplace abroad, 1988, US Vital Statistics annual rpt, 4144–2.1

Debt of Communist countries to US and other Western banks, by country, 1980s, conf, 25388–56

Economic and military aid and loans from US and intl agencies, by program and country, FY46-90, annual rpt, 9914–5

Economic, social, political, and geographic summary data, by country, 1991, annual factbook, 9114–2

Exports and imports, by commodity, 1970-90, annual rpt, 9114–4.8

Exports and imports of US, by transport mode, country, and SITC 1- to 3-digit commodity, 1990, annual rpt, 2424–12

Exports and imports of US with Communist countries, by detailed commodity and country, quarterly rpt with articles, 9882–2

Human rights conditions in 170 countries, and US economic and military aid, 1990, annual rpt, 21384–3

Nuclear power plant capacity and operating status, by plant and communist and regulated market country, as of Dec 1990, annual rpt, 3164–57.2

Refugee resettlement programs and funding, arrivals by country of origin, and indicators of adjustment, by State, FY90, annual rpt, 4694–5

Soviet Union, China, OECD, and selected other countries economic and military aid, by recipient, 1960s-90, annual rpt, 9114–4.9

UN voting record and share of votes in agreement with US, by issue, country, and world area, 1990, annual rpt, 7004–18

see also under By Foreign Country in the "Index by Categories"

Cuban Americans

see Hispanic Americans

Cultural activities

Education natl goals progress indicators, by State, 1991, annual rpt, 15914–1

see also Anthropology

see also Area studies

see also Art

see also Arts and the humanities

see also Dance

see also Educational exchanges

see also Ethnic studies

see also Exchange of persons programs

see also Federal aid to arts and humanities

see also International cooperation in cultural activities

see also Language arts

see also Motion pictures

see also Museums

see also Music

see also Performing arts

see also Theater

Cumberland, Md.

see also under By SMSA or MSA in the "Index by Categories"

Cummings, K. Michael

"Tobacco Advertising in Retail Stores", 4042–3.250

Cummings, T. Ray

"Natural Ground-Water Quality in Michigan, 1974-87", 5666–28.10

Cummins, David E.

"Changes in Financial Profile of Cooperatives Handling Grain: First-Handlers with $5 Million or More in Sales, 1983 and 1985", 1128–44.4

"Patronage Refunds Boost Income of Local Grain Cooperatives", 1122–1.208

Cunningham, Charles V.

"New Provisions for Upland Cotton Farm Programs", 1561–1.203

Cunningham, Peter J.

"Health Care Coverage: Findings from the Survey of American Indians and Alaska Natives. National Medical Expenditure Survey", 4186–8.17

"Insuring the Children: A Decade of Change. National Medical Expenditure Survey", 4186–8.14

Cunningham, Richard A.

"Twenty-two Year Results of a Scots Pine (*Pinus sylvestris* L.) Provenance Test in North Dakota", 1208–383

Cunningham, Rosemary T.

"Behavior of Real Rates of Interest in a Small, Opening Economy", 9371–10.56

Cunningham, Thomas J.

"Behavior of Real Rates of Interest in a Small, Opening Economy", 9371–10.56

Cuperas, Gerrit W.

"Integrated Pest Management (IPM) in the Vegetable Industry During the 1980's", 1568–298

Curran, Thomas C.

"National Air Quality and Emissions Trends Report, 1989", 9194–1

Currency

see Black market currency

see Coins and coinage

see Flow-of-funds accounts

see Foreign exchange

see Money supply

see Special foreign currency programs

Index by Subjects and Names

Current Employment Survey

Employment and Earnings, detailed data, monthly rpt, 6742–2

Current Population Reports

see Current Population Survey

see Survey of Income and Program Participation

Current Population Survey

Consumer Income, socioeconomic characteristics of persons, families, and households, detailed cross-tabulations, series, 2546–6

Data collection, methodology, and comparisons to other data bases, Survey of Income and Program Participation, working paper series, 2626–10

Data coverage and availability of Census Bur population statistics, 1991 pamphlet, 2326–7.78

Data coverage and availability of Census Bur rpts and data files, 1991 annual listing, 2304–2

Employment and Earnings, detailed data, monthly rpt, 6742–2

Employment, unemployment, and labor force characteristics, by region, State, and selected metro area, 1990, annual rpt, 6744–7

Housing and household characteristics, subject rpt series, 2486–1

Income data from Survey of Income and Program Participation compared to CPS, 1984, technical paper, 4746–26.8

Labor force characteristics, press release series, 6726–1

Minority group data coverage and availability from Census Bur, 1991 pamphlet, 2326–7.80

Population and housing data, and policy issues, fact sheet series, 2326–17

Population demographic, social, and economic characteristics, series, 2546–1

Population demographic subjects, special study series, 2546–2

Population estimates and projections, by region and State, series, 2546–3

Population estimates for civilian, resident, and total population, monthly rpt, 2542–1

Unemployment, by State and metro area, monthly press release, 6742–12

Curricula

Athletes in college, educational and employment performance compared to other students, for 1972 high school class, as of 1986, 4888–5

Classification codes and descriptions for curricula, by program area, 1990, rpt, 4828–29

Condition of Education, detail for elementary, secondary, and higher education, 1920s-90 and projected to 2001, annual rpt, 4824–1

Digest of Education Statistics, 1991 annual data compilation, 4824–2

Eighth grade class of 1988: educational performance and conditions, characteristics, attitudes, activities, and plans, natl longitudinal survey, series, 4826–9

High school advanced placement for college credit, programs by selected characteristics and school control, 1984-86, 4838–46

High school class of 1972: education, employment, and family characteristics, activities, and attitudes, natl longitudinal study, series, 4836–1

Higher education course completions, by detailed program, sex, race, and instn type, for 1972 high school class, as of 1984, 4888–4

Higher education enrollment, faculty, finances, and degrees, by instn level and control, and State, FY87, annual rpt, 4844–13

Natl Education Goals progress indicators, by State, 1991, annual rpt, 15914–1

Private elementary and secondary schools, students, and staff characteristics, various periods 1979-88, 4838–47

Statistical Abstract of US, 1991 annual data compilation, 2324–1.4

Women's employment and educational experiences compared to men, for high school class of 1972, natl longitudinal study, as of 1986, 4888–6

see also Agricultural education

see also Area studies

see also Arts and the humanities

see also Astronomy

see also Biological sciences

see also Business education

see also Chemistry

see also Earth sciences

see also Economics

see also Educational reform

see also Environmental sciences

see also Ethnic studies

see also Foreign languages

see also Geography

see also Health education

see also History

see also Home economics

see also Industrial arts

see also Information sciences

see also Journalism

see also Language arts

see also Legal education

see also Mathematics

see also Medical education

see also Military education

see also Physical education and training

see also Physical sciences

see also Physics

see also Political science

see also Psychology

see also Scientific education

see also Sex education

see also Social sciences

see also Social work

see also Sociology

see also Teacher education

see also Vocational education and training

Customs administration

Court civil and criminal caseloads for Federal district courts, 1991, annual rpt, 18204–2.1

Court of Intl Trade caseloads, decisions, and appeals, FY90-91, annual rpt, 18224–2

Criminal cases by type and disposition, and collections, for US attorneys, by Federal district, FY90, annual rpt, 6004–2.1

Criminal cases in Federal district courts, by offense, disposition, and district, 1980-90, last issue of annual rpt, 18204–1

Customs Service activities, collections, entries processed by mode of transport, and seizures, FY86-90, annual rpt, 8144–1

Cyprus

FDA detention of imports, by reason, product, shipper, brand, and country, monthly listing, 4062–2

Fruit and vegetable imports under quarantine, by crop, country, and port of entry, FY88, annual rpt, 1524–7

Grain inspected for domestic use and export, foreign buyers complaints, and handling facilities explosions, FY90, annual rpt, 1294–1

Grain inspected for export, test results by commodity and port region, 1988-90, annual rpt, 1294–2

Meat and poultry inspection activities and staff of Federal, State, and foreign govts, FY90, annual rpt, 1374–1

Meat plants inspected and certified for exporting to US, by country, 1990, annual listing, 1374–2

Tea imports inspected by FDA, by type and country, 1985-90, FAS annual circular, 1925–15.3

Tobacco leaf stocks, production, sales, and import inspections by country, by product, quarterly rpt, 1319–3

see also Smuggling

Customs duties

see Tariffs and foreign trade controls

Customs Service

see U.S. Customs Service

Cutlery

see Household supplies and utensils

see Tools

Cutrufelli, Rena

"Composition of Foods. Snacks and Sweets: Raw, Processed, Prepared", 1356–3.16

Cuyahoga County, Ohio

Housing and households characteristics, unit and neighborhood quality, and journey to work by MSA location, for 11 MSAs, 1984 survey, supplement, 2485–8

Housing and households detailed characteristics, and unit and neighborhood quality, by location, 1988 survey, MSA rpt, 2485–6.3

Cyclones

see Storms

Cynamon, Marcie

"AIDS Knowledge and Attitudes. Provisional Data from the National Health Interview Survey", 4146–8.195

Cypress, Beulah K.

"Office Visits for Family Planning, National Ambulatory Medical Care Survey: U.S., 1977", 4147–16.5

"Office Visits for Respiratory Conditions, National Ambulatory Medical Care Survey: U.S., 1975-76", 4147–16.5

"Office Visits to Psychiatrists: National Ambulatory Medical Care Survey, U.S., 1975-76", 4147–16.4

Cyprus

Agricultural exports of high-value commodities, indexes and sales by commodity, world area, and country, 1960s-86, 1528–323

Agricultural trade of US, by detailed commodity and country, 1989, annual rpt, 1524–8

Agricultural trade of US, by detailed commodity and country, 1990, semiannual rpt, 1522–4

AID loans repayment status and terms by program and country, and status of predecessor agency loans, quarterly rpt, 9912–3

Cyprus

Economic and military aid and loans from US and intl agencies, by program and country, FY46-90, annual rpt, 9914–5

Economic and social conditions of developing countries from 1960s, and Intl Dev Cooperation Agency and AID activities and funding, FY90-92, annual rpt, 9904–4

Economic, social, political, and geographic summary data, by country, 1991, annual factbook, 9114–2

Exports and imports of US, by transport mode, country, and SITC 1- to 3-digit commodity, 1990, annual rpt, 2424–12

Exports of US, detailed Schedule B commodities with countries of destination, 1990, annual rpt, 2424–10

Human rights conditions in 170 countries, and US economic and military aid, 1990, annual rpt, 21384–3

Military aid of US, arms sales, and training programs costs and budget requests, by program, world region, and country, FY90-92, annual rpt, 7144–13

Ships in world merchant fleet, tonnage, and new ship construction and deliveries, by vessel type and country, as of Jan 1990, annual rpt, 7704–3

UN voting record and share of votes in agreement with US, by issue, country, and world area, 1990, annual rpt, 7004–18

see also under By Foreign Country in the "Index by Categories"

Czapla, Thomas E.

"Distribution and Abundance of Fishes and Invertebrates in Central Gulf of Mexico Estuaries", 2176–7.23

Czechoslovakia

Agricultural exports of high-value commodities, indexes and sales by commodity, world area, and country, 1960s-86, 1528–323

Agricultural production, trade, and policies in foreign countries, summary data by country, 1989-90, annual factbook, 1924–12

Agricultural trade of US, by detailed commodity and country, 1989, annual rpt, 1524–8

Agricultural trade of US, by detailed commodity and country, 1990, semiannual rpt, 1522–4

Debt to foreign lenders by component, trade, balances, and other economic indicators, by Eastern Europe country, 1985-89, hearing, 21248–148

Economic and military aid and loans from US and intl agencies, by program and country, FY46-90, annual rpt, 9914–5

Economic conditions in USSR, Eastern Europe, OECD, and selected other countries, 1960s-90, annual rpt, 9114–4

Economic conditions, income, production, prices, employment, and trade, 1991 periodic country rpt, 2046–4.53

Economic conditions, policy, and trade practices, by country, 1988-90, annual rpt, 21384–5

Economic, social, political, and geographic summary data, by country, 1991, annual factbook, 9114–2

Energy production, trade, use, and AID dev assistance, for 3 Eastern Europe countries, 1980s-91, 25318–81

Export licensing, monitoring, and enforcement activities, FY90, annual rpt, 2024–1

Exports and imports of US, by commodity and country, 1970-89, world area rpt, 9116–1.3

Exports and imports of US, by selected country, country group, and commodity group, 1990, annual rpt, 2044–37

Exports and imports of US, by transport mode, country, and SITC 1- to 3-digit commodity, 1990, annual rpt, 2424–12

Exports and imports of US with Communist countries, by detailed commodity and country, quarterly rpt with articles, 9882–2

Exports of US, detailed Schedule B commodities with countries of destination, 1990, annual rpt, 2424–10

Human rights conditions in 170 countries, and US economic and military aid, 1990, annual rpt, 21384–3

Labor conditions, union coverage, and work accidents, 1991 annual country rpt, 6366–4.35

Market economy transition of Eastern Europe countries, economic conditions and energy balance, by country, 1985-90, 9118–13

Market economy transition of Eastern Europe countries, with trade agreements and bilateral US trade data by country, late 1980s-90, annual rpt, 444–2

Military aid of US, arms sales, and training programs costs and budget requests, by program, world region, and country, FY90-92, annual rpt, 7144–13

Nuclear power plant capacity and operating status, by plant and communist and regulated market country, as of Dec 1990, annual rpt, 3164–57.2

Spacecraft and satellite launches since 1957, quarterly listing, 9502–2

Steel imports of US under voluntary restraint agreement, by product, customs district, and country, with US industry operating data, quarterly rpt, 9882–13

UN voting record and share of votes in agreement with US, by issue, country, and world area, 1990, annual rpt, 7004–18

see also under By Foreign Country in the "Index by Categories"

Daberkow, Stan G.

"Crop Sequences Among 1990 Major Field Crops and Associated Farm Program Participation", 1561–16.204

"Cropping Pattern Comparisons Between 1989 and 1988", 1561–16.201

"Outlook for Farm Inputs", 1004–16.1

Dahl, Carol

"What Motivates Oil Producers?: Testing Alternative Hypotheses", 9379–12.68

Dahl, David S.

"Both Public and Private Efforts Needed To Reform Health Care, Respondents Say", 9383–19.202

"Energy Policy: Emphasize Conservation, Say District Business Leaders", 9383–19.203

"Free Trade Agreement Bolsters Border Communities", 9383–19.204

"Gap Exists Between Need and Provision of Child Care Services", 9383–19.201

Index by Subjects and Names

Dahl, Thomas E.

"Wetlands Losses in the U.S. 1780's to 1980's", 5508–107

Dahomey

see Benin

Dairy industry and products

Acreage under Agricultural Stabilization and Conservation Service programs, rankings by commodity and congressional district, 1989, biennial rpt, 1804–17

Africa (sub-Saharan) dairy imports, consumption, and market conditions, by country, 1961-88, 1528–321

Agricultural data compilation, 1990 and trends from 1920, annual rpt, 1004–14

Agricultural Stabilization and Conservation Service dairy programs, 1949-91, annual fact sheet, 1806–4.5

Agricultural Stabilization and Conservation Service producer payments and certificate value, by program, monthly rpt, 1802–10

Agricultural Stabilization and Conservation Service producer payments, by program and State, 1990, annual table, 1804–12

Agricultural Statistics, 1990, annual rpt, 1004–1

Agriculture census, 1987: farms, farmland, production, finances, and operator characteristics, by county, final State rpt series, 2331–1

Biotechnology devs in dairy industry, and bST impacts on farm finances and Federal support programs, 1980s and projected to 1998, 26358–237

Business statistics, detailed data for major industries and economic indicators, *Survey of Current Business*, monthly rpt, 2702–1.14

Cattle and calves for beef and milk, by State, as of July 1991, semiannual press release, 1623–1

Cattle, milk production, and grain and other concentrates fed, by State, monthly rpt, 1627–1

CCC financial condition and major commodity program operations, FY62-87, annual chartbook, 1824–2

Cold storage food stocks by commodity and census div, and warehouse space use, by State, monthly rpt, 1631–5

Cold storage food stocks by commodity, and warehouse space use, by census div, 1990, annual rpt, 1631–11

Confectionery shipments, trade, use, and ingredients used, by product, 1990, annual Current Industrial Rpt, 2506–4.5

Consumer Expenditure Survey, food spending by item, household composition, income, age, race, and region, 1980-88, biennial rpt, 1544–30

Consumer Expenditure Survey, household income by source, and itemized spending, by selected characteristics and region, 1988-89, annual rpt, 6764–5

Consumption of food, dietary composition, and nutrient intake, 1987/88 natl survey, preliminary rpt series, 1356–1

Consumption per capita of selected beverages, 1970s-90, FAS annual circular, 1925–15.3

Consumption, supply, trade, prices, spending, and indexes, by food commodity, 1989, annual rpt, 1544–4

Cooperatives (dairy) exemption from antitrust laws, impacts on industry structure and pricing, with background data, 1930s-80s, GAO rpt, 26113–499

Index by Subjects and Names

Dairy industry and products

County Business Patterns, 1988: employment, establishments, and payroll, by SIC 2- to 4-digit industry and county, annual State rpt series, 2326–6

County Business Patterns, 1989: employment, establishments, and payroll, by SIC 2- to 4-digit industry and county, annual State rpt series, 2326–8

CPI by component for US city average, and by region, population size, and for 27 metro areas, monthly rpt, 6762–2

Employment, earnings, and hours, by SIC 1- to 4-digit industry, monthly and annual averages, selected years 1909-90, annual rpt, 6744–4

Enterprise Statistics, 1987: finances and operations for companies, by size, level of diversification, form of organization, and industry group, 2329–8

Exports (agricultural) of high-value commodities, indexes and sales value by commodity, world area, and country, 1960s-86, 1528–323

Exports (agricultural) of US, impacts of foreign agricultural and trade policy, with data by commodity and country, 1989, annual rpt, 1924–8

Exports and imports (agricultural) commodity and country, prices, and world market devs, monthly rpt, 1922–12

Exports and imports (agricultural) of US, by commodity and country, bimonthly rpt, 1522–1

Exports and imports (agricultural) of US, by detailed commodity and country, 1989, annual rpt, 1524–8

Exports and imports (agricultural) of US, by detailed commodity and country, 1990, semiannual rpt, 1522–4

Exports and imports between US and outlying areas, by detailed commodity and mode of transport, 1990, annual rpt, 2424–11

Exports and imports of dairy, livestock, and poultry products, by commodity and country, FAS monthly circular, 1925–32

Exports and imports of US, by country and detailed commodity, monthly rpt, 2422–12

Exports and imports of US, by Harmonized System 6-digit commodity and country, 1990, annual rpt, 2424–13

Exports and imports of US, by transport mode, country, and SITC 1- to 3-digit commodity, 1990, annual rpt, 2424–12

Exports of dairy products, market conditions with background data by country, 1986-89, 1128–65

Exports of US, detailed Schedule B commodities with countries of destination, 1990, annual rpt, 2424–10

Farm credit, terms, delinquency, agricultural bank failures, and credit conditions by Fed Reserve District, quarterly rpt, 9365–3.10

Farm financial and marketing conditions, forecast 1991, annual chartbook, 1504–8

Farm financial and marketing conditions, forecast 1991, annual conf, 1004–16

Farm income, expenses, receipts by commodity, assets, liabilities, and ratios, 1990 and trends from 1945, annual rpt, 1544–16

Farm sector balance sheet, and receipts by detailed commodity, by State, 1985-89, annual rpt, 1544–18

Farms (dairy) financial statements, by size and region, 1985-89, annual article, 1561–2.201

Food aid programs of USDA, costs and participation by program, FY69-89, annual rpt, 1364–9

Foreign and US dairy production, trade, use, and prices, forecast 1992 and trends from 1987, FAS semiannual circular, 1925–10

Foreign countries agricultural production, prices, and trade, by country, 1980-90 and forecast 1991, annual world area rpt series, 1524–4

Herd Improvement Program cooperatives and cows tested, by State, 1989, annual rpt, 1124–1

Imports and quotas of dairy products, by commodity and country of origin, FAS monthly rpt, 1925–31

Labor productivity, indexes of output, hours, and employment by SIC 2- to 4-digit industry, 1967-89, annual rpt, 6824–1.3

Manufacturing annual survey, 1989: finances and operations, by SIC 2- to 4-digit industry, series, 2506–15

Manufacturing census, 1987: finances and operations, by SIC 2- to 4-digit industry, State, and MSA, with trends from 1849, 2497–1

Manufacturing census, 1987: finances and operations, by type of organization and SIC 2- to 4-digit industry, subject rpt, 2497–5

Manufacturing finances and operations, by SIC 2- to 4-digit industry, forecast 1991, annual rpt, 2044–28

Milk farm, processor, and retail prices in 29 cities, 1980s-91, GAO rpt, 26113–540

Milk of manufacturing grade, fat content and prices received by farmers in Minnesota and Wisconsin, monthly rpt, 1629–6

Milk of manufacturing grade, fat content and prices received by farmers in Minnesota and Wisconsin, 1988-90, annual rpt, 1629–2

Milk order market policy alternatives impacts on supply, interregional marketings, and pricing, by region, 1988, 1568–294

Milk order market prices and detailed operations, by State and market area, 1989-90, annual rpt, 1317–3

Milk order market prices and detailed operations, monthly rpt with articles, 1317–4

Milk order market sales, by container size and type, outlet type, and market area, 1989, biennial rpt, 1317–6

Nutrient, caloric, and waste composition, detailed data for raw, processed, and prepared foods, 1991 rpt, 1356–3.15

Occupational injury and illness rates, by SIC 2- to 4-digit industry, 1988-89, annual rpt, 6844–7

Occupational injury and illness rates, by SIC 2- to 4-digit industry, 1989, annual rpt, 6844–1

OECD trade, total and for 4 major countries, and US trade by country, by commodity, 1970-89, world area rpt series, 9116–1

Pesticide and fertilizer use reduction, environmental and economic impacts by commodity and region, alternative forecasts 1989-94, hearing, 23848–222

Price indexes (producer), by stage of processing and detailed commodity, monthly rpt, 6762–6

Price indexes (producer), by stage of processing and detailed commodity, monthly 1990, annual rpt, 6764–2

Price support and other CCC program outlays, with production and marketing outlook, by commodity, projected 1990-96, 26306–6.160

Price support program provisions, for selected commodities, 1961-90, 1568–303

Price support purchases, sales, donations, and inventories of CCC, for dairy products, monthly rpt, 1802–2

Prices (farm-retail) for food, marketing cost components, and industry finances and productivity, 1920s-90, annual rpt, 1544–9

Prices of dairy products, by type and selected area, with related marketing data, 1990, annual rpt, 1317–1

Prices received and paid by farmers, by commodity and State, 1990, annual rpt, 1629–5

Prices received by farmers for major products, and paid for farm inputs and living items, by State, monthly rpt, 1629–1

Production inputs, output, and productivity for farms, by commodity and region, 1947-89, annual rpt, 1544–17

Production itemized costs, receipts, and returns, by commodity and region, 1987-89, annual rpt, 1544–20

Production of dairy products by type, and plants, by State, 1990, annual rpt, 1627–5

Production of manufactured dairy products by State, stocks, prices, and CCC price support activities, by product type, monthly rpt, 1627–3

Production, prices, trade, and marketing, by commodity, current situation and forecast, monthly rpt with articles, 1502–4

Production, prices, trade, and use for dairy products, periodic situation rpt with articles, 1561–2

Production, prices, trade, and use of oils and fats, periodic situation rpt with articles, 1561–3

Production, use, and receipts, and milk cow inventory, by State, 1988-90, annual rpt, 1627–4

Puerto Rico economic censuses, 1987: wholesale and retail trade and service industry finances and operations, by SIC 2- to 4-digit industry and municipio, 2591–1

Radiation and radionuclide concentrations in air, water, and milk, monitoring results by State and site, quarterly rpt, 9192–5

Radiation exposure of population near Hanford, Wash, nuclear plant, with methodology, 1944-66, series, 3356–5

Radionuclide releases and concentrations in water, milk, and other food products after Chernobyl, USSR, reactor accident, for selected Republics, 1986-87, 4042–3.201

Retail trade census, 1987: finances and employment, for establishments with and without payroll, by SIC 2- to 4-digit kind of business, State, and MSA, 2401–1

Dairy industry and products

Southern US dairy farm characteristics, by type of milk handler used, 1991 article, 1122–1.206

State and Metro Area Data Book, 1991 data compilation, 2328–54

Statistical Abstract of US, 1991 annual data compilation, 2324–1.23

Supply and demand indicators for livestock and dairy products, and for selected foreign and US crops, monthly rpt, 1522–5

Tax (income) returns of corporations, income and tax items by asset size and detailed industry, 1987, annual rpt, 8304–4

Tax (income) returns of corporations, income and tax items by asset size and detailed industry, 1988, annual rpt, 8304–21

Tax (income) returns of partnerships, income statement and balance sheet items, by industry group, 1989, annual article, 8302–2.216; 8304–18

Wholesale trade census, 1987: establishments, sales by customer class, employment, inventories, and expenses, by SIC 2- to 4-digit kind of business, 2407–4

see also under By Commodity in the "Index by Categories"

Dale, Charles

"Economics of Energy Futures Markets", 3162–11.201

Dale, Martin E.

"Tree Value Conversion Standards Revisited", 1208–361

Dallas County, Tex.

AIDS virus infection and risk factor prevalence, natl survey methodology and pretest results, 1989, 4148–30

Dallas, Tex.

- CPI by component for US city average, and by region, population size, and for 15 metro areas, monthly rpt, 6762–1
- CPI by component for US city average, and by region, population size, and for 27 metro areas, monthly rpt, 6762–2
- CPI by major component for 2 Texas MSAs, monthly rpt, 6962–2
- Drug test results at arrest, by drug type, offense, and sex, for selected urban areas, quarterly rpt, 6062–3
- Employment, earnings, hours, and CPI changes, for Dallas-Fort Worth metro area, late 1970s-90, annual rpt, 6964–2
- Fruit and vegetable shipments, and arrivals in US and Canada cities, by mode of transport and State and country of origin, 1990, annual rpt, 1311–4.2
- Housing starts and completions authorized by building permits in 40 MSAs, quarterly rpt, 2382–9
- Wages by occupation, and benefits for office and plant workers, 1990 survey, periodic MSA rpt, 6785–11.3

see also under By City and By SMSA or MSA in the "Index by Categories"

Dalton, Donald H.

"Japanese Direct Investment in U.S. Manufacturing", 2048–151

Dalzell, P.

"Review of the South Pacific Tuna Baitfisheries: Small Pelagic Fisheries Associated with Coral Reefs", 2162–1.201

Dams

- Army Corps of Engineers water resources dev projects, characteristics, and costs, 1950s-89, biennial State rpt series, 3756–1
- Army Corps of Engineers water resources dev projects, characteristics, and costs, 1950s-91, biennial State rpt series, 3756–2
- Failures of dams, deaths, and unsafe dams by State, 1874-1982, 9434–6
- Tennessee Valley river control activities, and hydroelectric power generation and capacity, 1989, annual rpt, 9804–7
- TVA finances and operations by program and facility, FY90, annual rpt, 9804–32

see also Reservoirs

Danbury, Conn.

see also under By SMSA or MSA in the "Index by Categories"

Dance

- County Business Patterns, 1988: employment, establishments, and payroll, by SIC 2- to 4-digit industry and county, annual State rpt series, 2326–6
- County Business Patterns, 1989: employment, establishments, and payroll, by SIC 2- to 4-digit industry and county, annual State rpt series, 2326–8
- Injuries from use of consumer products, by severity, victim age, and detailed product, 1990, annual rpt, 9164–6
- Natl Endowment for Arts activities and grants, FY90, annual rpt, 9564–3
- Puerto Rico economic censuses, 1987: wholesale and retail trade and service industry finances and operations, by SIC 2- to 4-digit industry and municipio, 2591–1
- Puerto Rico economic censuses, 1987: wholesale, retail, and service industries finances and operations, by establishment characteristics and SIC 2- and 3-digit industry, subject rpts, 2591–2
- Service industries census, 1987: establishments, receipts by source, payroll, and employment, by SIC 2- to 4-digit kind of business, State, and MSA, 2393–4

Danville, Va.

see also under By SMSA or MSA in the "Index by Categories"

Daronco, Karla M.

"1986 Corporation Foreign Tax Credit, A Geographic Focus", 8302–2.207

Das Gupta, Prithwis

"Estimates of Households by Age of Householder and Tenure for Counties: July 1, 1985", 2546–3.169

Data processing

- *see* Computer industry and products
- *see* Computer networks
- *see* Computer sciences
- *see* Computer use
- *see* Information storage and retrieval systems

Dates

see Chronologies

Daugherty, Arthur B.

"Major Uses of Land in the U.S.: 1987", 1588–48

Davenport, Edgar L.

"Changes in Florida's Industrial Roundwood Products Output, 1977-87", 1208–352

"Changes in South Carolina's Industrial Timber Products Output, 1988", 1208–359

Index by Subjects and Names

"Pulpwood Prices in the Southeast, 1989", 1204–22

Davenport, Iowa

Wages by occupation, for office and plant workers, 1991 survey, periodic MSA rpt, 6785–12.1

see also under By SMSA or MSA in the "Index by Categories"

Davidson, Christine

"Comparison of Alien Admissions Before and After IRCA", 6266–1.1

Davies, Sally M.

"Effects of Closure Policies on Bank Risk-Taking", 9366–6.272

Davis County, Utah

- Housing and households characteristics, unit and neighborhood quality, and journey to work by MSA location, for 11 MSAs, 1984 survey, supplement, 2485–8
- Housing and households detailed characteristics, and unit and neighborhood quality, by location, 1988 survey, MSA rpt, 2485–6.5

Davis, Donald

"Explaining the Volume of Intraindustry Trade: Are Increasing Returns Necessary?", 9366–7.265

Davis, Jo Ann

"Key Statistics on Public Elementary and Secondary Education Reported by State and by Regional, Locale, and Wealth Clusters, 1988-89", 4834–20

Davis, Richard G.

"Inflation: Measurement and Policy Issues", 9385–1.207

Davis, Stacy C.

"Transportation Energy Data Book: Edition 11", 3304–5

Davis, Steve J.

"Gross Job Creation, Gross Job Destruction and Employment Reallocation", 9375–13.56

Davison, Cecil W.

"Export Demand for U.S. Corn, Soybeans, and Wheat", 1568–297

DAWN

see Drug Abuse Warning Network

Dawson, Deborah A.

"Family Structure and Children's Health: U.S., 1988. Vital and Health Statistics Series 10", 4147–10.178

Dawson, John M.

"Felons Sentenced to Probation in State Courts, 1986", 6068–242

Day care programs

see Adult day care

see Child day care

Day, Charles

"Individual Income Tax Rates, 1987", 8302–2.211

Day, Kelly

"Economic Implications of a Ban on EBDC Disease Control Uses in Vegetable Production", 1561–11.204

Daylight hours

see Time of day

Dayton, Ohio

Wages by occupation, and benefits for office and plant workers, 1990 survey, periodic MSA rpt, 6785–3.3

see also under By City and By SMSA or MSA in the "Index by Categories"

Index by Subjects and Names

Deaths

Daytona Beach, Fla.

Wages by occupation, and benefits for office and plant workers, 1991 survey, periodic labor market rpt, 6785–3.9

see also under By SMSA or MSA in the "Index by Categories"

D.C.

- Banks (insured commercial), Fed Reserve 5th District members financial statements, by State, quarterly rpt, 9389–18
- Banks (insured commercial and savings) deposits by instn, State, MSA, and county, as of June 1990, annual regional rpt, 9295–3.2
- Budget of US, authoritative financial statements with appropriations, outlays, and receipts, by category and agency, FY90, annual rpt, 8104–2.1
- Budget of US, obligations and authority by function, agency, and program, with summaries, analyses, and historical tables, FY92, annual rpt, 104–2
- Budget of US, Senate concurrent resolution, with spending and revenue targets, FY92, annual rpt, 25254–1
- *Congressional Directory*, members of 102nd Congress, other officials, elections, and districts, 1991-92, biennial rpt, 23874–1
- County Business Patterns, 1989: employment, establishments, and payroll, by SIC 2- to 4-digit industry and county, annual State rpt, 2326–8.10
- CPI by component for US city average, and by region, population size, and for 15 metro areas, monthly rpt, 6762–1
- CPI by component for US city average, and by region, population size, and for 27 metro areas, monthly rpt, 6762–2
- DOD civilian and military personnel in DC metro area, FY90, and in Pentagon from 1945, annual rpt, 3544–1.1
- DOD prime contract awards, by contractor, service branch, State, and city, FY90, annual rpt, 3544–22
- Drug abuse indicators for selected metro areas, research results, data collection, and policy issues, 1991 semiannual conf, 4492–5
- Drug, alcohol, and cigarette use, by selected characteristics, and for DC, 1990 survey, biennial rpt, 4494–5.3
- Drug test results at arrest, by drug type, offense, and sex, for selected urban areas, quarterly rpt, 6062–3
- Economic indicators by State, Fed Reserve 5th District, quarterly rpt, 9389–16
- Education funding by Federal agency, program, and recipient type, and instn spending, FY80-90, annual rpt, 4824–8
- Employment and housing and mortgage market indicators by State, FHLB 4th District, quarterly rpt, 9302–36
- Fed Govt civilian employment and payroll, by agency in DC metro area, total US, and abroad, bimonthly rpt, 9842–1
- Fed Govt civilian employment and payroll, by occupation, pay grade, sex, agency, and location, 1989, biennial rpt, 9844–4
- Fed Govt civilian employment and payroll, by pay system, agency, and location, 1990, annual rpt, 9844–6
- Fed Govt land acquisition and dev projects in DC metro area, characteristics and funding by agency and project, FY91-95, annual rpt, 15454–1

Fed Govt spending in States and local areas, by type, State, county, and city, FY90, annual rpt, 2464–3

- Fed Govt spending in States, by type, program, agency, and State, FY90, annual rpt, 2464–2
- Fruit and vegetable shipments, and arrivals in US and Canada cities, by mode of transport and State and country of origin, 1990, annual rpt, 1311–4.1
- HHS financial aid, by program, recipient, State, and city, FY90, annual regional listing, 4004–3.3
- Hospital deaths of Medicare patients, actual and expected rates by diagnosis, and hospital characteristics, by instn, FY87-89, annual regional rpt, 4654–14.3
- Housing census, 1990: inventory, occupancy, and costs, State fact sheet, 2326–21.10
- Housing starts and completions authorized by building permits in 40 MSAs, quarterly rpt, 2382–9
- Income (personal) per capita and by source, and earnings by industry div, by State, MSA, and county, 1984-89, annual regional rpt, 2704–2.2
- Jail adult and juvenile population, employment, spending, instn conditions, and inmate programs, by county and facility, 1988, regional rpt series, 6068–144.4
- Marriages, divorces, and rates, by characteristics of spouses, State, and county, 1987 and trends from 1920, US Vital Statistics annual rpt, 4144–4
- Navy command proposed decentralization and relocation from DC area, savings, and cost of living indicators for 14 MSAs, 1980s, GAO rpt, 26123–346
- Physicians, by specialty, age, sex, and location of training and practice, 1989, State rpt, 4116–6.9
- Population and housing census, 1990: population and housing characteristics, households, and land area, by county, subdiv, and place, State rpt, 2551–1.10
- Population and housing census, 1990: voting age and total population by race, and housing units, by block, redistricting counts required under PL 94-171, State CD-ROM release, 2551–6.6
- Population and housing census, 1990: voting age and total population by race, and housing units, by county and city, redistricting counts required under PL 94-171, State summary rpt, 2551–5.9
- Production index for DC, by component, 1987-91, article, 9389–1.203
- *Statistical Abstract of US*, 1991 annual data compilation, 2324–1
- Supplemental Security Income payments and beneficiaries, by type of eligibility, State, and county, Dec 1989, annual rpt, 4744–27.3
- Transportation natl system planning, use, condition, accidents, and needs, by mode of transport, 1940s-90 and projected to 2020, 7308–202
- Wages by occupation, for office and plant workers, 1991 survey, periodic MSA rpt, 6785–12.3
- Water quality, chemistry, hydrology, and other characteristics, 1990 local area study, 5666–27.22

Workers compensation programs under Federal admin, finances and operations, FY90, annual rpt, 6504–10

see also D.C. courts

see also under By City, By SMSA or MSA, and By State in the "Index by Categories"

D.C. courts

- Caseloads (civil and criminal) for Federal district, appeals, and bankruptcy courts, by offense, circuit, and district, 1990, annual rpt, 18204–11
- Caseloads (civil and criminal) for Federal district, appeals, and special courts, 1990, annual rpt, 18204–8
- Caseloads (civil and criminal) for Federal district, appeals, and special courts, 1991, annual rpt, 18204–2
- Caseloads (civil and criminal) of DC appeals and superior courts, 1971-88, hearing, 21308–27

De Alteriis, Martin

"Public Health Model of Medicaid Emergency Room Use", 4652–1.232

De Kock, Gabriel

"Expected Inflation and Real Interest Rates Based on Index-Linked Bond Prices: The UK Experience", 9385–1.214

de Leeuw, Frank

"Gross Product by Industry, 1977-88: Progress Report on Improving the Estimates", 2702–1.201

De Soto County, Miss.

- Housing and households characteristics, unit and neighborhood quality, and journey to work by MSA location, for 11 MSAs, 1984 survey, supplement, 2485–8
- Housing and households detailed characteristics, and unit and neighborhood quality, by location, 1988 survey, MSA rpt, 2485–6.1

Deaf

- Education (special) enrollment by age, staff, funding, and needs, by type of handicap and State, 1989/90, annual rpt, 4944–4
- Educational service delivery and discipline, and discrimination indicators by State, 1988, biennial rpt, 4804–33
- Head Start handicapped enrollment, by handicap, State, and for Indian and migrant programs, 1987/88, annual rpt, 4604–1
- Vocational rehabilitation cases of State agencies by disposition and applicant characteristics, and closures by reason, FY84-88, annual rpt, 4944–6

Deapen, Roger E.

"Differences Between Oklahoma Indian Infant Mortality and Other Races", 4042–3.209

Death penalty

see Capital punishment

Deaths

- AFDC beneficiaries demographic and financial characteristics, by State, FY89, annual rpt, 4694–1
- Africa (sub-Saharan) AIDS epidemic impacts on population size and components of change, model description and results, 1990-2015, working paper, 2326–18.57
- AIDS cases by race, sex, and risk category, and deaths and survivors, projected 1989-93, 4206–2.34
- AIDS deaths and rates, by age group, monthly rpt, 4202–9

Deaths

Index by Subjects and Names

Alaska rural areas population characteristics, and energy resources dev effects, series, 5736–5

Alcohol users by consumption level, and abstainers, deaths by cause, age, and sex, 1986-87, article, 4482–1.201

Cancer cases, deaths, and survival rates, by sex, race, age, and body site, 1973-88, annual rpt, 4474–35

Cancer death rates of minorities, by body site, age, sex, and substate area, 1950s-80, atlas, 4478–78

Cancer death, survival, and incidence rates, by type and body site, 1974 and 1986, article, 4472–1.232

Cancer deaths by age, and cases, by sex, 1985 and 1990, annual rpt, 4474–13

Cancer deaths in Cuba and among Cuban-born Americans, by body site, 1970s-83, article, 4042–3.205

Certificates of birth, death, marriage, and divorce, and fetal death and abortion rpts, 1989 natl standard revisions, 4147–4.27

Cirrhosis of liver deaths, by age, sex, race, and whether alcohol involved, 1987 and trends from 1910, 4486–1.10

Deaths and rates, by cause, age, sex, race, and State, preliminary 1989-90 and trends from 1960, US Vital Statistics annual rpt, 4144–7

Deaths and rates, by detailed cause and demographic characteristics, 1988 and trends from 1900, US Vital Statistics annual rpt, 4144–2

Deaths recorded in 121 cities, weekly rpt, 4202–1

Developing countries aged population and selected characteristics, 1980s and projected to 2020, country rpt series, 2326–19

Diabetes and complications cases, deaths, and hospitalization, by age, sex, race, State, and region, 1980-86, annual rpt, 4205–41

Diseases (chronic) causing death, rates by cause, weekly rpt, monthly feature, 4202–1

Drug and alcohol abuse and mental illness direct and indirect costs, by type, 1970s-88, article, 4042–3.219

Global climate change environmental, infrastructure, and health impacts, with model results and background data, 1850s-2100, 9188–113

Health condition and health care resources, use, and spending, 1950s-89, annual data compilation, 4144–11

Health condition improvement and disease prevention goals and recommended activities for 2000, with trends 1970s-80s, 4048–10

Heart disease deaths and risk factors, for PRC, Finland, and US, 1980s, article, 4042–3.202

Heart, Lung, and Blood Natl Inst activities, and grants by recipient and location, FY90 and disease trends from 1940, annual rpt, 4474–15

Hepatitis cases by infection source, age, sex, race, and State, and deaths, by strain, 1988 and trends from 1966, 4205–2

Hispanic Americans deaths and rates, by cause, age, sex, and detailed origin, average 1979-81, 4147–20.18

Hospices operations, services, costs, and patient characteristics, for instns without Medicare certification, FY85-86, 4658–52

Hospices use by cancer patients, by service type, use of other facilities, patient and instn characteristics, and other indicators, local area study, 1980-85, 4658–53

Hospital deaths of Medicare patients, actual and expected rates by diagnosis, with hospital characteristics, by instn, FY87-89, annual regional rpt series, 4654–14

Hospitalization costs relation to services timing, by selected patient and hospital characteristics, for Medicare discharges, 1987-88, 17208–2

Indian and Alaska Native disease and disorder cases, deaths, and health services use, by tribe, reservation, and Indian Health Service area, late 1950s-86, 4088–2

Indian Health Service facilities and use, and Indian health and other characteristics, by IHS region, 1980s-89, annual chartbook, 4084–7

Indian Health Service facilities, funding, operations, and Indian health and other characteristics, 1950s-90, annual chartbook, 4084–1

Kidney end-stage disease cases, treatment, outcomes, and characteristics of patients, organ donors, and facilities, late 1970s-88, annual rpt, 4474–37

Kidney end-stage disease treatment access and quality of care indicators, impacts of Medicare payment reductions, 1980s, 4658–44

Kidney end-stage disease treatment facilities, Medicare enrollment and reimbursement, survival, and patient characteristics, 1983-89, annual rpt, 4654–16

Medicare coverage of new health care technologies, risks and benefit evaluations, series, 4186–10

Medicare reimbursement of hospitals under prospective payment system, impacts on instns and beneficiaries, 1988, annual rpt, 4654–13

Military deaths by cause, age, race, and rank, and personnel captured and missing, by service branch, FY90, annual rpt, 3544–40

Military personnel deaths by service branch and age group, and veterans death rates, 1966-90, annual rpt, 8654–1

Military reserve forces attrition, by reason, personnel characteristics, reserve component, and State, FY88, GAO rpt, 26123–329

Minority group and women health condition, services use, payment sources, and health care labor force, by poverty status, 1940s-89, chartbook, 4118–56

Minority group health condition, services use, costs, and indicators of services need, 1950s-88, 4118–55

Morbidity and Mortality Weekly Report, infectious notifiable disease cases by age, race, and State, and deaths, 1930s-90, annual rpt, 4204–1

Nursing home and other long term care services under Medicare hospital use reduction demonstration, results for Rochester, NY, 1980s, 4658–43

OASDI benefit payments, trust fund finances, and economic and demographic assumptions, 1970-90 and alternative projections to 2000, actuarial rpt, 4706–1.105

Older persons deaths in hospitals, nursing homes, and own home, by cause, age, marital status, and region, 1986, article, 4652–1.201

Older persons health care services use, by service type, discharge destination, and prior care source, 1986, 4188–72

Older persons health condition and care research, data availability and collection methodology, for US and selected countries, 1988 conf, 4147–5.6

Population size and characteristics, 1969-88, Current Population Rpt, biennial rpt, 2546–2.161

Pregnancies (ectopic) and related deaths, by race, age, and region, 1970-87, article, 4202–7.202

Pregnancy-related deaths, rates, and risk, by pregnancy outcome, cause, and maternal characteristics, 1979-86, article, 4202–7.206

Prison and parole admissions and releases, sentence length, and time served, by offense and offender characteristics, 1985, annual rpt, 6064–33

Prisoners and movements, by offense, location, and selected other characteristics, data compilation, 1991 annual rpt, 6064–6.6

Prisoners, characteristics, and movements, by State, 1989, annual rpt, 6064–26

Prisoners in jails, deaths by cause, by county and facility, 1988, regional rpt series, 6068–144

Prisoners in jails, deaths by cause, 1989-90, annual rpt, 6066–25.38

Radiation exposure of uranium miners and risk of death from cancer and lung diseases, for Indians and compared to whites and foreign countries, 1950s-84, hearing, 25548–101

Research on population and reproduction, Federal funding by project, FY89, annual listing, 4474–9

Research on population, family, and sexual behavior, activities and funding, 1960s-89, 4478–194

Respiratory diseases related to occupational hazards, epidemiology, diagnosis, and treatment, for selected industries and work settings, 1988 conf, 4248–90

Retirees deaths within 8 years of retirement, by health and other characteristics, 1982-88, article, 4742–1.206

SSA and other sources of beneficiary death info, use and erroneous benefit payments by agency, 1990, GAO rpt, 26121–406

State and Metro Area Data Book, 1991 data compilation, 2328–54

Statistical Abstract of US, 1991 annual data compilation, 2324–1.2

Surgery-related deaths and complications, by procedure and VA facility, and compared to non-VA instns, FY84-89, last issue of biennial rpt, 8704–1

Tuberculosis cases and deaths, by patient characteristics, State, and city, 1989 and trends from 1953, annual rpt, 4204–10

Veterans and servicepersons life insurance, actuarial analyses of VA programs, 1990, annual rpt, 8604–1

Index by Subjects and Names

Veterans disability and death compensation and pension cases, by type of entitlement and period of service, monthly rpt, 8602–5

Veterans disability and death compensation cases of VA, by entitlement type, period of service, sex, age, and State, FY89, annual rpt, 8604–7

Veterans disability by type, and deaths, by period of service, and VA activities, FY90, annual rpt, 8604–3.6

Vital and Health Statistics series: death rates for selected causes and population groups, 4147–20

Vital and Health Statistics series: reprints of monthly rpt supplements, 4147–24

Vital statistics provisional data, monthly rpt, 4142–1

Vocational rehabilitation cases of State agencies by disposition and applicant characteristics, and closures by reason, FY84-88, annual rpt, 4944–6

see also Accidental deaths
see also Autopsies
see also Capital punishment
see also Cemeteries and funerals
see also Child mortality
see also Coroners
see also Drowning
see also Fetal deaths
see also Homicide
see also Infant mortality
see also Poisoning and drug reaction
see also Suicide
see also Traffic accident fatalities
see also War casualties

DeBald, Paul S.
"Tree Value Conversion Standards Revisited", 1208–361

DeBerry, Marshall M., Jr.
"Criminal Victimization, 1989", 6066–25.35
"Criminal Victimization, 1990", 6066–25.41

DeBraal, J. Peter
"Foreign Ownership of U.S. Agricultural Land Through Dec. 31, 1990", 1584–2
"Foreign Ownership of U.S. Agricultural Land Through Dec. 31, 1990: County-Level Data", 1584–3

Debt

see Agricultural credit
see Business assets and liabilities, general
see Business assets and liabilities, specific industry
see Commercial credit
see Consumer credit
see Credit
see Credit bureaus and agencies
see Foreign debts
see Government assets and liabilities
see Government securities
see Loans
see Mortgages
see Municipal bonds
see Personal debt
see Public debt
see U.S. savings bonds

Decatur, Ala.
see also under By SMSA or MSA in the "Index by Categories"

Decatur, Ill.
see also under By SMSA or MSA in the "Index by Categories"

Decision Resources Corp.
"Debt Burden Facing College Graduates", 4808–26
"Summary of State Chapter 1 Migrant Education Program Participation and Achievement Information, 1987-88", 4808–30

Decontrol of prices
see Price regulation

Default
see Bankruptcy
see Loan delinquency and default

Defective products

Aircraft (general aviation) accidents, by circumstances, characteristics of persons and aircraft involved, and type of flying, 1988, annual rpt, 9614–3

Aircraft accidents, casualties, and damage, for commercial operations by detailed circumstances, 1987, annual rpt, 9614–2

Auto and auto equipment recalls for safety-related defects, by make, monthly listing, 7762–12

Auto and auto equipment recalls for safety-related defects, by make, quarterly listing, 7762–2

Boats (recreational) and engines recalls for safety-related defects, by make, periodic listing, 7402–5

Consumer Product Safety Commission activities, recalls by brand, and casualties and medical costs, by product type, FY89, annual rpt, 9164–2

Imports detained by FDA, by reason, product, shipper, brand, and country, monthly listing, 4062–2

Railroad accidents, casualties, and damage, by cause, railroad, and State, 1990, annual rpt, 7604–1

Defense
see Civil defense
see Department of Defense
see Military intervention
see Military invasion and occupation
see National defense
see War

Defense agencies

Base construction, renovation, and land acquisition, DOD budget requests by project, service branch, State, and country, FY92-93, annual rpt, 3544–15

Budget of DOD, base construction and family housing appropriations by facility, service branch, and location, FY90-93, annual rpt, 3544–39

Budget of DOD, manpower needs, costs, and force readiness by service branch, FY92, annual rpt, 3504–1

Budget of DOD, procurement appropriations by item, service branch, and defense agency, FY90-93, annual rpt, 3544–32

Budget of DOD, R&D appropriations by item, service branch, and defense agency, FY90-93, annual rpt, 3544–33

Expenditures and obligations of DOD, by function and service branch, quarterly rpt, 3542–3

Pacific basin US military personnel, dependents, aircraft, ships, and costs, by service branch and location, 1990, GAO rpt, 26123–357

Personnel (civilian) of DOD, by service branch and defense agency, with summary military employment data, quarterly rpt, 3542–16

Defense budgets and appropriations

Personnel (civilian and military) of DOD, by service branch and defense agency, quarterly rpt, 3542–14.1

Property, supply, and equipment inventory of DOD, by service branch, FY90, annual rpt, 3544–6

see also Defense Communications Agency
see also Defense Contract Audit Agency
see also Defense Intelligence Agency
see also Defense Investigative Service
see also Defense Logistics Agency
see also Defense Mapping Agency
see also Defense Nuclear Agency
see also Defense Security Assistance Agency
see also On-Site Inspection Agency

Defense budgets and appropriations

Air Force fiscal mgmt system operations and techniques, quarterly rpt, 3602–1

Army Dept activities, personnel, discipline, budget, and assistance, FY83 summary data, annual rpt, 3704–11

Army strategic capability, force strengths, budget, and mgmt, FY74-93, annual rpt, 3704–13

Base construction, renovation, and land acquisition, DOD budget requests by project, service branch, State, and country, FY92-93, annual rpt, 3544–15

Budget of DOD, organization, personnel, weapons, and property, by service branch, State, and country, 1991 annual summary rpt, 3504–13

Budget of DOD, programs, policies, and operations, FY90, annual rpt, 3544–2

Budget of US, authoritative financial statements with appropriations, outlays, and receipts, by category and agency, FY90, annual rpt, 8104–2.1

Budget of US, balances of budget authority obligated and unobligated, by function and agency, FY90-92, annual rpt, 104–8

Budget of US, CBO analysis and review of FY92 budget by function, annual rpt, 26304–2

Budget of US, CBO analysis of revenue and spending alternatives and projections of economic indicators, FY92-96, annual rpt, 26304–3

Budget of US, CBO analysis of savings and revenues under alternative spending cuts and tax changes, projected FY92-97, 26306–3.118

Budget of US, House Budget Committee analysis of Bush Admin proposals and economic assumptions, FY92, 21268–42

Budget of US, House concurrent resolution, with spending and revenue targets, FY92 and projected to FY96, annual rpt, 21264–2

Budget of US, midsession review of FY92 budget, by function, annual rpt, 104–7

Budget of US, object class analysis of obligations, by agency, FY92, annual rpt, 104–9

Budget of US, obligations and authority by function, agency, and program, with summaries, analyses, and historical tables, FY92, annual rpt, 104–2

Budget of US, receipts by source, outlays by agency and program, and balances, monthly rpt, 8102–3

Budget of US, Senate concurrent resolution, with spending and revenue targets, FY92, annual rpt, 25254–1

Defense budgets and appropriations

Index by Subjects and Names

Construction of military bases and family housing, DOD appropriations by facility, service branch, and location, FY90-93, annual rpt, 3544–39

Foreign countries military aid of US, arms sales, and training programs costs and budget requests, by program, world region, and country, FY90-92, annual rpt, 7144–13

Investigations of Federal agency and program operations, summaries of findings, 1981-90, annual GAO rpt, 26104–5

Natl Guard activities, personnel, and facilities, FY90, annual rpt, 3504–22

NATO and Warsaw Pact military forces reductions under proposed treaty, and US budget savings, 1990 rpt, 26306–3.114

Navy budget, personnel, procurement, and equipment, planned FY91-93, annual fact sheet, 3804–16

Navy ship modernization program costs and admin, FY87, GAO rpt, 26123–320

Pacific basin US military personnel, dependents, aircraft, ships, and costs, by service branch and location, 1990, GAO rpt, 26123–357

Persian Gulf War costs to US, and weapons budget requests, CBO analysis and review of FY92 Federal budget, annual rpt, 26304–2

Persian Gulf War costs to US by category and service branch, and offsetting contributions by allied country, monthly rpt, 102–3

Persian Gulf War costs to US by category and service branch, and offsetting contributions by allied country, various periods FY90-91, annual rpt, 104–7

Personnel needs, costs, and force readiness, by service branch, FY92, annual rpt, 3504–1

Procurement appropriations, by item, service branch, and defense agency, FY90-93, annual rpt, 3544–32

R&D funding by item, service branch, and defense agency, FY90-93, annual rpt, 3544–33

Reserve forces personnel and equipment strengths, and readiness, by reserve component, FY90, annual rpt, 3544–31

Statistical Abstract of US, 1991 annual data compilation, 2324–1.11

Training and education programs of DOD, funding, staff, students, and facilities, by service branch, FY92, annual rpt, 3504–5

Weapons acquisition costs by system and service branch, DOD budget, FY91-93, annual rpt, 3504–2

see also Defense expenditures

Defense Communications Agency

Personnel (civilian and military) of DOD, by service branch and defense agency, quarterly rpt, 3542–14.1

Defense Contract Audit Agency

Personnel (civilian and military) of DOD, by service branch and defense agency, quarterly rpt, 3542–14.1

Defense contracts and procurement

Aerospace industry sales, orders, backlog, and firms, by product for govt, military, and other customers, 1990, annual Current Industrial Rpt, 2506–12.22

Army Dept activities, personnel, discipline, budget, and assistance, FY83 summary data, annual rpt, 3704–11

Army equipment unserviceable inventories, and repair and replacement costs, late 1980s, GAO rpt, 26123–312

Budget of DOD, organization, personnel, weapons, and property, by service branch, State, and country, 1991 annual summary rpt, 3504–13

Budget of DOD, procurement appropriations by item, service branch, and defense agency, FY90-93, annual rpt, 3544–32

Budget of DOD, programs, policies, and operations, FY90, annual rpt, 3544–2

Budget of US, authoritative financial statements with appropriations, outlays, and receipts, by category and agency, FY90, annual rpt, 8104–2.1

Budget of US, object class analysis of obligations, by agency, FY92, annual rpt, 104–9

Chemical and biological weapons research labs security measures, and govt and contractor staff, 1988-90, GAO rpt, 26123–356

Computer systems engineering and technical support contract costs of DOD, late 1980s, GAO rpt, 26125–45

Employment impacts of military spending reductions and base closings, by region and State, 1988-89 and projected FY91-95, article, 9371–1.206

Expenditures and obligations of DOD, by function and service branch, quarterly rpt, 3542–3

Expenditures of Fed Govt in States and local areas, by type, State, county, and city, FY90, annual rpt, 2464–3

Expenditures of Fed Govt in States, by type, program, agency, and State, FY90, annual rpt, 2464–2

Fraud and abuse in DOD programs, audits and investigations, 1st half FY91, semiannual rpt, 3542–18

Fuel oil and kerosene sales and deliveries, by end-use, PAD district, and State, 1989, annual rpt, 3164–94

Input-output structure of US economy, detailed interindustry transactions for 84 industries, and components of final demand, 1986, annual article, 2702–1.206

Input-output structure of US economy, detailed interindustry transactions for 85 industries, 1982 benchmark data, 2702–1.213

Investigations of Federal agency and program operations, summaries of findings, 1981-90, annual GAO rpt, 26104–5

Leasing of military equipment by equipment type and service branch and feasibility of lease refinancing, 1988, GAO rpt, 26111–75

Machine tool procurement by DOD of foreign-made tools, use of restriction waivers by service branch and country, FY86-89, GAO rpt, 26123–324

Manufacturing census, 1987: employment and shipments under Fed Govt contracts, and SIC 4-digit industry, 2497–7

Milk order market sales, by container size and type, outlet type, and market area, 1989, biennial rpt, 1317–6

Natl Guard activities, personnel, and facilities, FY90, annual rpt, 3504–22

Natl income and product accounts and components, *Survey of Current Business,* monthly rpt, 2702–1.24

Navy budget, personnel, procurement, and equipment, planned FY91-93, annual fact sheet, 3804–16

Navy procurement, by contractor and location, FY90, annual rpt, 3804–13

Navy small and disadvantaged business procurement office locations, and supply and service codes, 1990 biennial listing, 3804–5

Pacific basin US military personnel, dependents, aircraft, ships, and costs, by service branch and location, 1990, GAO rpt, 26123–357

Persian Gulf War costs to US by category and service branch, and offsetting contributions by allied country, monthly rpt, 102–3

Persian Gulf War costs to US by category and service branch, and offsetting contributions by allied country, various periods FY90-91, annual rpt, 104–7

Post exchange operations, and sales by commodity, by facility and location worldwide, FY89, annual rpt, 3504–10

Prime contract awards of DOD, by category, contract and contractor type, and service branch, FY81-1st half FY91, semiannual rpt, 3542–1

Prime contract awards of DOD, by category, contractor type, and State, FY88-90, annual rpt, 3544–11

Prime contract awards of DOD, by contractor, service branch, State, and city, FY90, annual rpt, 3544–22

Prime contract awards of DOD, by detailed procurement category, FY87-90, annual rpt, 3544–18

Prime contract awards of DOD, by service branch and State, 1st half FY91, semiannual rpt, 3542–5

Prime contract awards of DOD, by size and type of contract, service branch, competitive status, category, and labor standard, FY90, annual rpt, 3544–19

Prime contract awards of DOD, for top 100 contractors, FY90, annual listing, 3544–5

Prime contract awards of DOD in labor surplus areas, by service branch, State, and area, 1st half FY91, semiannual rpt, 3542–19

Prime contracts, payroll, and personnel, by service branch and location, with top 5 contractors and maps, by State and country, FY90, annual rpt, 3544–29

R&D prime contract awards of DOD, for top 500 contractors, FY90, annual listing, 3544–4

R&D prime contract awards of DOD to US and foreign nonprofit instns and govt agencies, by instn and location, FY90, annual listing, 3544–17

Reserve forces personnel and equipment strengths, and readiness, by reserve component, FY90, annual rpt, 3544–31

Restructuring of military forces, research, and manufacturing base following relaxation of East-West tensions, with background data, FY87-93, 26358–245

Space programs involvement by private sector, govt contracts, costs, revenue, and R&D spending, 1970s-80s and projected to 2000, 26306–6.154

Index by Subjects and Names

Statistical Abstract of US, 1991 annual data compilation, 2324–1.11

Subcontract awards by DOD contractors to small and disadvantaged business, by firm and service branch, quarterly rpt, 3542–17

Survey of Current Business, defense activity indicators, monthly rpt, 2702–1.2

Wages impacts of military procurement and other factors, 1940s-90, technical paper, 9379–12.65

Weapons acquisition costs by system and service branch, DOD budget, FY91-93, annual rpt, 3504–2

Workers compensation programs under Federal admin, finances and operations, FY90, annual rpt, 6504–10

Defense Department

see Department of Defense

Defense expenditures

Air Force fiscal mgmt system operations and techniques, quarterly rpt, 3602–1

Autos and light trucks owned and leased by service branch, and costs and savings from GSA leases, FY89, GAO rpt, 26123–344

Base closings, costs and savings for 71 Army and Navy bases, FY92-97, GAO rpt, 26123–341

Base support costs by function, and personnel and acreage by installation, by service branch, FY91, annual rpt, 3504–11

Communist and OECD countries economic conditions, 1989, annual rpt, 7144–11

Developing countries economic aid from US, military spending and imports measures to determine aid eligibility, by country, 1986-87, annual rpt, 9914–1

Developing countries economic and social conditions from 1960s, and Intl Dev Cooperation Agency and AID activities and funding, FY90-92, annual rpt, 9904–4

Economic indicators compounded annual rates of change, monthly rpt, 9391–3

Economic indicators compounded annual rates of change, 1971-90, annual rpt, 9391–9.2

Employment impacts of military spending reductions and base closings, by region and State, 1988-89 and projected FY91-95, article, 9371–1.206

Energy use and efficiency of Fed Govt, by agency and fuel type, FY90, annual rpt, 3304–22

Expenditures and obligations of DOD, by function and service branch, quarterly rpt, 3542–3

Expenditures for contracts and payroll, and personnel, by service branch and location, with top 5 contractors and maps, by State and country, FY90, annual rpt, 3544–29

Expenditures for defense, and share of GNP, 1940s-80s, article, 9391–1.204

Expenditures of Fed Govt, by function, FY89, annual rpt, 2466–2.2

Expenditures of Fed Govt by type, and other finances, selected years 1952-89, annual rpt, 10044–1

Expenditures of Fed Govt in States and local areas, by type, State, county, and city, FY90, annual rpt, 2464–3

Expenditures of Fed Govt in States, by type, program, agency, and State, FY90, annual rpt, 2464–2

Financial consolidated statements of Fed Govt based on business accounting methods, FY89-90, annual rpt, 8104–5

Foreign countries economic, social, political, and geographic summary data, by country, 1991, annual factbook, 9114–2

Hazardous waste site remedial action at military installations, activities and funding by site and State, FY90, annual rpt, 3544–36

Investigations of Federal agency and program operations, summaries of findings, 1981-90, annual GAO rpt, 26104–5

Japan economic conditions, financial and intl policies, and trade devs, 1950s-80s and projected to 2050, compilation of papers, 23848–220

Loans and loan guarantees of Fed Govt, outstanding amounts by agency and program, *Treasury Bulletin*, quarterly rpt, 8002–4.9

Middle East and East Africa economic and military aid from US and intl agencies, and US defense spending, FY80-90, GAO rpt, 26123–360

Natl Guard activities, personnel, and facilities, FY90, annual rpt, 3504–22

Natl income and product accounts and components, *Survey of Current Business*, monthly rpt, 2702–1.24

NATO and Japan military spending and indicators of ability to support common defense, by country, 1970s-89, annual rpt, 3544–28

Navy command proposed decentralization and relocation from DC area, savings, and cost of living indicators for 14 MSAs, 1980s, GAO rpt, 26123–346

Nuclear weapons elimination under Intermediate-Range Nuclear Forces Treaty, US and USSR on site inspections, and US costs and staffing, FY89-91, GAO rpt, 26123–364

Nuclear weapons systems of US and USSR, costs, and military forces survival after attack, projected under alternative arms control proposals, FY92-2006, 26306–6.161

Persian Gulf War costs to US by category and service branch, and offsetting contributions by allied country, monthly rpt, 102–3

Persian Gulf War costs to US by category and service branch, and offsetting contributions by allied country, various periods FY90-91, annual rpt, 104–7

Science and engineering academic research system status, R&D performance, and Fed Govt support, 1950s-88 with trends and projections, 9628–83

Sealift Military Command shipping operations, finances, and personnel, FY90, annual rpt, 3804–14

Service academy costs by type, staff, and grad advancement in military, FY88-90, GAO rpt, 26123–355

Soviet Union, Eastern Europe, OECD, and selected other countries economic conditions, 1960s-90, annual rpt, 9114–4.2

State and Metro Area Data Book, 1991 data compilation, 2328–54

Statistical Abstract of US, 1991 annual data compilation, 2324–1.11

Defense Logistics Agency

Survey of Current Business, defense activity indicators, monthly rpt, 2702–1.2

Training and education programs of DOD, funding, staff, students, and facilities, by service branch, FY92, annual rpt, 3504–5

see also Budget of the U.S.

see also Defense budgets and appropriations

see also Defense contracts and procurement

see also Defense research

see also Military pay

Defense industries

Aluminum ingot and mill product defense and total shipments, trade, use, and inventories, monthly Current Industrial Rpt, 2506–10.9

Employment impacts of military spending reductions and base closings, by region and State, 1988-89 and projected FY91-95, article, 9371–1.206

Foreign and US military weapons trade, production, and defense industry finances, with data by firm and country, 1980s-91, 26358–241

Manufacturing census, 1987: employment and shipments under Fed Govt contracts, by SIC 4-digit industry, 2497–7

Restructuring of military forces, research, and manufacturing base following relaxation of East-West tensions, with background data, FY87-93, 26358–245

Survey of Current Business, defense activity indicators, monthly rpt, 2702–1.2

see also Arms trade

see also Conversion of industry

see also Defense contracts and procurement

Defense Intelligence Agency

Persian Gulf War costs to US by category and service branch, and offsetting contributions by allied country, monthly rpt, 102–3

Persian Gulf War costs to US by category and service branch, and offsetting contributions by allied country, various periods FY90-91, annual rpt, 104–7

Soviet Union economic conditions under General Secretary Gorbachev, 1990 and trends from 1975, annual rpt, 9114–6

Defense Investigative Service

Personnel (civilian and military) of DOD, by service branch and defense agency, quarterly rpt, 3542–14.1

Defense Logistics Agency

DOD prime contract awards, by detailed procurement category, FY87-90, annual rpt, 3544–18

Fishery products purchases of DLA, by base of destination, weekly regional rpt, 2162–6.5

Hazardous waste site remedial action at military installations, activities and funding by site and State, FY90, annual rpt, 3544–36

Persian Gulf War costs to US by category and service branch, and offsetting contributions by allied country, monthly rpt, 102–3

Persian Gulf War costs to US by category and service branch, and offsetting contributions by allied country, various periods FY90-91, annual rpt, 104–7

Personnel (civilian and military) of DOD, by service branch and defense agency, quarterly rpt, 3542–14.1

Procurement, DOD prime contract awards by category, contract and contractor type, and service branch, FY81-1st half FY91, semiannual rpt, 3542–1

Defense Logistics Agency

Procurement, DOD prime contract awards by contractor, service branch, State, and city, FY90, annual rpt, 3544–22

Procurement, DOD prime contract awards by service branch and State, 1st half FY91, semiannual rpt, 3542–5

Procurement, DOD prime contract awards by size and type of contract, service branch, competitive status, category, and labor standard, FY90, annual rpt, 3544–19

Procurement, DOD prime contract awards in labor surplus areas, by service branch, State, and area, 1st half FY91, semiannual rpt, 3542–19

Procurement, subcontract awards by DOD contractors to small and disadvantaged business, by firm and service branch, quarterly rpt, 3542–17

Property, supply, and equipment inventory of DOD, by service branch, FY90, annual rpt, 3544–6

Requisitions of supplies from DLA, processing time and efficiency, FY89, GAO rpt, 26123–331

Shipments by DOD of military and personal property, passenger traffic, and costs, by service branch and mode of transport, quarterly rpt, 3702–1

Stockpiling of strategic material by Fed Govt, activity, and inventory by commodity, semiannual rpt, discontinued, 3902–2

Stockpiling of strategic material, inventories and needs, by commodity, as of Jan 1991, annual rpt, 3544–37

Stockpiling of strategic material, inventories, costs, and goals by commodity, semiannual rpt, discontinued, 3902–3

Defense Mapping Agency

Persian Gulf War costs to US by category and service branch, and offsetting contributions by allied country, monthly rpt, 102–3

Persian Gulf War costs to US by category and service branch, and offsetting contributions by allied country, various periods FY90-91, annual rpt, 104–7

Personnel (civilian and military) of DOD, by service branch and defense agency, quarterly rpt, 3542–14.1

Defense Nuclear Agency

Personnel (civilian and military) of DOD, by service branch and defense agency, quarterly rpt, 3542–14.1

Defense research

Animals use in Army brain wound research, usefulness of Louisiana State University experiments, with results, 1980s, GAO rpt, 26121–396

Budget of DOD, manpower needs, costs, and force readiness by service branch, FY92, annual rpt, 3504–1

Budget of DOD, organization, personnel, weapons, and property, by service branch, State, and country, 1991 annual summary rpt, 3504–13

Budget of DOD, programs, policies, and operations, FY90, annual rpt, 3544–2

Budget of DOD, R&D appropriations by item, service branch, and defense agency, FY90-93, annual rpt, 3544–33

Budget of DOD, weapons acquisition costs by system and service branch, FY91-93, annual rpt, 3504–2

Budget of US, obligations and authority by function, agency, and program, with summaries, analyses, and historical tables, FY92, annual rpt, 104–2

Chemical and biological weapons research labs security measures, and govt and contractor staff, 1988-90, GAO rpt, 26123–356

Expenditures and obligations of DOD, by function and service branch, quarterly rpt, 3542–3

Expenditures for DOD base support by function, and personnel and acreage by installation, by service branch, FY91, annual rpt, 3504–11

Expenditures for R&D, and scientists and engineers education and employment, for US and selected foreign countries, 1991 annual rpt, 9627–35

Expenditures for R&D by Fed Govt, by field, performer type, agency, and State, FY89-91, annual rpt, 9627–20

Manufacturing census, 1987: employment and shipments under Fed Govt contracts, by SIC 4-digit industry, 2497–7

Navy procurement, by contractor and location, FY90, annual rpt, 3804–13

Nuclear reactors for domestic use and export by function and operating status, with owner, operating characteristics, and location, 1990 annual listing, 3354–15

Prime contract awards of DOD, by category, contract and contractor type, and service branch, FY81-1st half FY91, semiannual rpt, 3542–1

Prime contract awards of DOD, by category, contractor type, and State, FY88-90, annual rpt, 3544–11

Prime contract awards of DOD, by detailed procurement category, FY87-90, annual rpt, 3544–18

Prime contract awards of DOD for R&D, for top 500 contractors, FY90, annual listing, 3544–4

Prime contract awards of DOD for R&D to US and foreign nonprofit instns and govt agencies, by instn and location, FY90, annual listing, 3544–17

Prime contracts, payroll, and personnel, by service branch and location, with top 5 contractors and maps, by State and country, FY90, annual rpt, 3544–29

Radioactive waste and spent fuel generation, inventory, and disposal, 1960s-89 and projected to 2020, annual rpt, 3364–2

Restructuring of military forces, research, and manufacturing base following relaxation of East-West tensions, with background data, FY87-93, 26358–245

Soviet Union military weapons systems, presence, and force strengths, and compared to US, 1991 annual rpt, 3504–20

Weather services activities and funding, by Federal agency, planned FY91-92, annual rpt, 2144–2

see also Military science

see also Strategic Defense Initiative

Defense Security Assistance Agency

Foreign countries military aid of US, arms sales, and training, by country, FY50-90, annual rpt, 3904–3

Liabilities (contingent) and claims paid by Fed Govt on federally insured and guaranteed contracts with foreign obligors, by country and program, periodic rpt, 8002–12

DeGennaro, Ramon P.

"Troubled Savings and Loan Institutions: Voluntary Restructuring Under Insolvency", 9377–9.121

Degrees, educational

see Degrees, higher education

see Educational attainment

see under By Educational Attainment in the "Index by Categories"

Degrees, higher education

Athletes in college, educational and employment performance compared to other students, for 1972 high school class, as of 1986, 4888–5

Black higher education instns finances, funding sources, enrollment, and student characteristics, with data for Louisiana instns, 1970s-90, hearing, 25258–24

Condition of Education, detail for higher education, 1960s-90, annual rpt, 4824–1.2

Data on education, selected trends and projections 1978-2001, pamphlet, 4828–27

Degrees awarded and enrollment in higher education, by sex, full- and part-time status, and instn level and control, fall 1990, annual rpt, 4844–16

Degrees awarded in higher education, by level, field, race, and sex, 1988/89 with trends from 1978/79, biennial rpt, 4844–17

Degrees awarded in higher education, by level, 1980s-92, annual press release, 4804–19

Degrees awarded in higher education, by sex, degree level, and instn control, 1990-91, annual rpt, 4844–14

Degrees, faculty, finances, and enrollment in higher education, by instn level and control, and State, FY87, annual rpt, 4844–13

Digest of Education Statistics, 1991 annual data compilation, 4824–2

Fed Govt civilian employees demographic and employment characteristics, as of Sept 1990, annual article, 9842–1.201

Health condition, services use, payment sources, and health care labor force, for minorities and women by poverty status, 1940s-89, chartbook, 4118–56

High school class of 1972: education, employment, and family characteristics, activities, and attitudes, natl longitudinal study, series, 4836–1

Indian education funding of Fed Govt, and enrollment, degrees, and program grants and fellowships by State, late 1960s-FY89, annual rpt, 14874–1

Minority group higher education enrollment, degrees, factors affecting participation, and earnings, 1960s-88, 4808–29

Natl Education Goals progress indicators, by State, 1991, annual rpt, 15914–1

Nuclear engineering and science educational facilities, student aid, and degrees granted, by instn, 1990, 3008–126

Nuclear engineering enrollment and degrees by instn and State, and women grads plans and employment, 1990, annual rpt, 3006–8.14

Nuclear engineering enrollment and degrees granted by instn and State, and grad placement, by student characteristics, 1990, annual rpt, 3004–5

Poland labor force status by education level, sex, and sector, college enrollment, and grads by field, 1960s-88, article, 6722–1.203

Radiation protection and health physics enrollment and degrees granted by instn and State, and female grads plans and employment, 1990, annual rpt, 3006–8.15

Radiation protection and health physics enrollment and degrees granted by instn and State, and grad placement, by student characteristics, 1990, annual rpt, 3004–7

Science and engineering academic research system status, R&D performance, and Fed Govt support, 1950s-88 with trends and projections, 9628–83

Science and engineering degrees, by field, level, and sex, 1966-89, 9627–33

Science and engineering employment and education, and R&D spending, for US and selected foreign countries, 1991 annual rpt, 9627–35.2

Science and engineering PhDs, by field, instn, employment prospects, sex, race, and other characteristics, 1960s-90, annual rpt, 9627–30

Science and engineering PhDs employment and other characteristics, by field and State, 1989, biennial rpt, 9627–18

Statistical Abstract of US, 1991 annual data compilation, 2324–1.4

Teachers and other special education staff, training, degrees, and certification, by field and State, FY89, annual rpt, 4944–4

Teachers in higher education instns, employment and other characteristics, by instn type and control, 1987/88 survey, 4846–4.4

Telecommunications industry intl competitiveness, with financial and operating data by product or service, firm, and country, 1990 rpt, 2008–30

Women's employment and educational experiences compared to men, for high school class of 1972, natl longitudinal study, as of 1986, 4888–6

see also under By Educational Attainment in the "Index by Categories"

Deich, Michael

"Federal Infrastructure Subsidies: Grants or Credits?", 26306–3.113

Delaware

Banks (insured commercial and savings) deposits by instn, State, MSA, and county, as of June 1990, annual regional rpt, 9295–3.2

County Business Patterns, 1989: employment, establishments, and payroll, by SIC 2- to 4-digit industry and county, annual State rpt, 2326–8.9

DOD prime contract awards, by contractor, service branch, State, and city, FY90, annual rpt, 3544–22

Employment growth and unemployment rates, Fed Reserve 3rd District, quarterly rpt, 9387–10

Fed Govt spending in States and local areas, by type, State, county, and city, FY90, annual rpt, 2464–3

Fed Govt spending in States, by type, program, agency, and State, FY90, annual rpt, 2464–2

Forest wildlife habitat characteristics, by location, 1986, State rpt, 1206–44.5

HHS financial aid, by program, recipient, State, and city, FY90, annual regional listing, 4004–3.3

Hospital deaths of Medicare patients, actual and expected rates by diagnosis, and hospital characteristics, by instn, FY87-89, annual regional rpt, 4654–14.3

Housing census, 1990: inventory, occupancy, and costs, State fact sheet, 2326–21.9

Income (personal) per capita and by source, and earnings by industry div, by State, MSA, and county, 1984-89, annual regional rpt, 2704–2.2

Marriages, divorces, and rates, by characteristics of spouses, State, and county, 1987 and trends from 1920, US Vital Statistics annual rpt, 4144–4

Mineral Industry Surveys, State reviews of production, 1990, preliminary annual rpt, 5614–6

Minerals Yearbook, 1989, Vol 2: State review of production and sales by commodity, and business activity, annual rpt, 5604–16.9

Minerals Yearbook, 1989, Vol 2: State reviews of production, sales, and firms, by commodity, and business activity, annual rpt, 5604–34

Physicians, by specialty, age, sex, and location of training and practice, 1989, State rpt, 4116–6.8

Population and housing census, 1990: population and housing characteristics, households, and land area, by county, subdiv, and place, State rpt, 2551–1.9

Population and housing census, 1990: voting age and total population by race, and housing units, by block, redistricting counts required under PL 94-171, State CD-ROM release, 2551–6.1

Population and housing census, 1990: voting age and total population by race, and housing units, by county and city, redistricting counts required under PL 94-171, State summary rpt, 2551–5.8

Statistical Abstract of US, 1991 annual data compilation, 2324–1

Supplemental Security Income payments and beneficiaries, by type of eligibility, State, and county, Dec 1989, annual rpt, 4744–27.3

Timber and pulpwood production, by product, 1950s-85, State rpt, 1206–15.10

Water supply and quality in streams and lakes, and groundwater levels in wells, by drainage basin, 1990, annual State rpt, 5666–10.19

Wetlands acreage, resources, soil and water properties, and conservation efforts, by wetland type, 1985 State rpt, 5506–11.2

see also Wilmington, Del.

see also under By State in the "Index by Categories"

Delaware River

Army Corps of Engineers water resources dev projects, characteristics, and costs, 1950s-89, biennial State rpt series, 3756–1

Army Corps of Engineers water resources dev projects, characteristics, and costs, 1950s-91, biennial State rpt series, 3756–2

Tidal currents, daily time and velocity by station for North America coasts, forecast 1992, annual rpt, 2174–1.1

Water supply and quality in streams and lakes, and groundwater levels in wells, by drainage basin, 1988, annual State rpt series, 5666–16

Water supply and quality in streams and lakes, and groundwater levels in wells, by drainage basin, 1989, annual State rpt series, 5666–12

Water supply and quality in streams and lakes, and groundwater levels in wells, by drainage basin, 1990, annual State rpt series, 5666–10

Water supply in northeastern US, precipitation and stream runoff by station, monthly rpt, 2182–3

Water supply in US and southern Canada, streamflow, surface and groundwater conditions, and reservoir levels, by location, monthly rpt, 5662–3

Delaware River Basin Commission

Budget of US, authoritative financial statements with appropriations, outlays, and receipts, by category and agency, FY90, annual rpt, 8104–2.1

Budget of US, obligations and authority by function, agency, and program, with summaries, analyses, and historical tables, FY92, annual rpt, 104–2

Delivery services

see Courier services

Della Rocco, Pamela S.

"Selection of Air Traffic Controllers for Automated Systems: Applications from Current Research", 7506–10.79

DeLozier, James E.

"National Ambulatory Medical Care Survey: 1989 Summary", 4146–8.206

Delray Beach, Fla.

see also under By SMSA or MSA in the "Index by Categories"

Demand deposits

see Checking accounts

see Negotiable orders of withdrawal accounts

Demirguc-Kunt, Asli

"On the Valuation of Deposit Institutions", 9377–9.112

"Principal-Agent Problems in Commercial-Bank Failure Decisions", 9377–9.115

Democratic Party

Campaign finances, elections, procedures, and Fed Election Commission activities, press release series, 9276–1

Congressional Directory, members of 102nd Congress, other officials, elections, and districts, 1991-92, biennial rpt, 23874–1

Election campaign funds raised and spent by party committees, by State and party, 1989-90, press release, 9276–1.88

State and Metro Area Data Book, 1991 data compilation, 2328–54

Statistical Abstract of US, 1991 annual data compilation, 2324–1.8

Votes cast by party, candidate, and State, 1990 natl elections, biennial rpt, 9274–5

Democratic Peoples Republic of Korea

see Korea, North

Demography

see Population characteristics

see Population size

see Vital statistics

see under Demographic Breakdowns in the "Index by Categories"

Demolition

Demolition

see Wrecking and demolition

Demonstration and pilot projects

- Assistance (financial and nonfinancial) of Fed Govt, 1991 base edition with supplements, annual listing, 104–5
- Court-annexed arbitration for civil cases, pilot program evaluation, 1984-86, 18408–46
- Debt delinquent on Federal accounts, cases and collections of Justice Dept and private law firms, pilot project results, FY90, annual rpt, 6004–20
- Developing countries population and economic data, and AID dev projects, special study series, 9916–3
- Disabled persons rehabilitation, Federal and State activities and funding, FY90, annual rpt, 4944–1
- Drug testing of criminal defendants, demonstration program operations, offender characteristics, and judges views, 1987-90, 18208–11
- Economic Dev Admin activities, and funding by program, recipient, State, and county, FY90 and cumulative from FY66, annual rpt, 2064–2
- Education (bilingual) programs enrollment, funding, and services, by State, FY85-89, series, 4808–20
- Education (early childhood) for handicapped children, project descriptions, 1990/91, annual listing, 4944–10
- Employee leave transfer to other employees, Federal pilot programs operations and costs by agency, FY89, 9848–40
- Energy conservation and resource planning activities of Bonneville Power Admin, FY89-90, 3228–11
- Energy-efficiency building codes, effect on house construction practices in Bonneville Power Admin service areas, 1987, 3228–15
- EPA pollution control grant program activities, monthly rpt, 9182–8
- Food stamp use at farmers markets, costs and participation, demonstration project results for 14 States, 1989, hearing, 21168–46
- Health Care Financing Admin research activities and grants, by program, FY90, annual listing, 4654–10
- *Health Care Financing Review*, quarterly journal, 4652–1
- Health maintenance organizations Medicare enrollees quality of care indicators compared to fee-for-service, demonstration projects results, mid 1980s, 4658–46
- Heart, Lung, and Blood Natl Inst activities, and grants by recipient and location, FY90 and disease trends from 1940, annual rpt, 4474–15
- HHS research and evaluation programs, 1970-90, annual listing, 4004–30
- Home health care services Medicare claim filings under prior and concurrent authorization, demonstration project results, 1987, 4658–57
- Homeless and runaway youth programs, funding, activities, and participant characteristics, FY90, annual rpt, 4604–3
- Homeless children educational projects, activities, and funding, FY90, annual rpt, 4804–35
- Homeless persons aid programs of Fed Govt, program descriptions and funding, by agency and State, FY87-90, annual GAO rpt, 26104–21
- Homeless persons employment and training services, demonstration project results, FY88, 6406–10.5
- Hospital cost control through revenue and reimbursement caps, demonstration project results with background data, 1980s, 4658–48
- Housing loan programs of FmHA in rural areas, and housing voucher demonstration program results, 1980s, hearing, 21248–143
- Hwy funds pooled by States from FHwA funds for specific projects, demonstration project results, FY88-90, GAO rpt, 26113–471
- Indian education funding of Fed Govt, and enrollment, degrees, and program grants and fellowships by State, late 1960s-FY89, annual rpt, 14874–1
- Kidney end-stage disease research of CDC and HCFA, project listing, 1990, annual rpt, 4654–16
- Libraries technological aid, project descriptions and funding, FY89, annual listing, 4874–6
- Literacy programs in workplaces, demonstration projects funding and participant characteristics, FY88, 4808–37
- Literacy programs in workplaces, Education Dept funding and project descriptions, FY90, annual listing, 4804–40
- Medicaid demonstration projects evaluation, for 6 States, 1988 rpt, 4658–45
- Military dependents and retirees managed health care demonstration projects, enrollment, workload, and costs, 1988-90, 26306–3.117
- Nursing home and other long term care services under Medicare hospital use reduction demonstration, results for Rochester, NY, 1980s, 4658–43
- Occupational safety and health research and demonstration grants by State, and project listing, FY90, annual rpt, 4244–2
- Oil enhanced recovery research contracts of DOE, project summaries, funding, and bibl, quarterly rpt, 3002–14
- Older and handicapped persons cash aid in place of food stamps, pilot project results by area, as of July 1990, semiannual rpt, 1362–6
- Older frail persons community-based care demonstration projects, evaluation of case mgmt services admin, 1991 rpt, 4186–7.8
- *Public Health Reports*, bimonthly journal, 4042–3
- Rent supplement programs evaluation, housing vouchers compared to Section 8 certificates, 1985-88, series, 5186–14
- Traffic accidents impacts of speed limits, with accident circumstances and speed averages, for States with 55 and 65 mph limit, 1986-89, annual rpt, 7764–15
- Unemployment insurance job search services, impacts on UI claims activity and reemployment, and claimant characteristics, for Tacoma, Wash, 1986-87, 6406–6.35
- Unemployment insurance reemployment and training services, and bonus for early reemployment, New Jersey demonstration project results, 1986-90, 6406–6.32

DeNavas, Carmen

- "Money Income of Households, Families, and Persons in the U.S.: 1988-89", 2546–6.68
- "Money Income of Households, Families, and Persons in the U.S.: 1990", 2546–6.70

Denison, Tex.

see also under By SMSA or MSA in the "Index by Categories"

Denmark

- Agricultural production, prices, and trade, by country, 1970s-90, and forecast 1991, annual world region rpt, 1524–4.4
- Agricultural production, trade, and policies in foreign countries, summary data by country, 1989-90, annual factbook, 1924–12
- Agricultural trade of US, by detailed commodity and country, 1989, annual rpt, 1524–8
- Agricultural trade of US, by detailed commodity and country, 1990, semiannual rpt, 1522–4
- AID loans repayment status and terms by program and country, and status of predecessor agency loans, quarterly rpt, 9912–3
- Cancer (renal) risk relation to obesity, by age and sex, for Denmark, 1977-87, article, 4472–1.230
- Economic and military aid and loans from US and intl agencies, by program and country, FY46-90, annual rpt, 9914–5
- Economic conditions, income, production, prices, employment, and trade, 1991 periodic country rpt, 2046–4.23
- Economic conditions, policy, and trade practices, by country, 1988-90, annual rpt, 21384–5
- Economic, social, political, and geographic summary data, by country, 1991, annual factbook, 9114–2
- Exports and imports of NATO members with PRC, by country, 1987-90, annual rpt, 7144–14
- Exports and imports of OECD members, by country, 1989, annual rpt, 7144–10
- Exports and imports of US, by Harmonized System 6-digit commodity and country, 1990, annual rpt, 2424–13
- Exports and imports of US, by selected country, country group, and commodity group, 1990, annual rpt, 2044–37
- Exports and imports of US, by transport mode, country, and SITC 1- to 3-digit commodity, 1990, annual rpt, 2424–12
- Exports and imports of US with EC by country, and total agricultural trade, selected years 1958-90, annual rpt, 7144–7
- Exports of US, detailed Schedule B commodities with countries of destination, 1990, annual rpt, 2424–10
- Fish catch and aquaculture production for Denmark, by species, 1985-88, article, 2162–1.202
- GNP and GNP growth for OECD members, by country, 1980-90, annual rpt, 7144–8
- Human rights conditions in 170 countries, and US economic and military aid, 1990, annual rpt, 21384–3
- Labor conditions, union coverage, and work accidents, 1990 annual country rpt, 6366–4.5

Index by Subjects and Names

Multinatl US firms and foreign affiliates finances and operations, by industry and world area of parent firm, 1989 benchmark survey, preliminary annual rpt, 2704–5

Multinatl US firms foreign affiliates, income statement items by country and world area, 1986, biennial article, 8302–2.212

Oil production, trade, use, and stocks, by selected country and country group, monthly rpt, 3162–42

Tax revenue, by level of govt and type of tax, for OECD countries, mid 1960s-89, annual rpt, 10044–1.2

UN voting record and share of votes in agreement with US, by issue, country, and world area, 1990, annual rpt, 7004–18

see also under By Foreign Country in the "Index by Categories"

Densen, Paul M.

"Tracing the Elderly Through the Health Care System: An Update", 4188–72

Dental condition

- Acute and chronic health conditions, disability, absenteeism, and health services use, by selected characteristics, 1987, CD-ROM, 4147–10.177
- Child health condition and services use, 1990 chartbook, 4108–49
- Deaths and rates, by detailed cause and demographic characteristics, 1988 and trends from 1900, US Vital Statistics annual rpt, 4144–2
- Fluoride exposure by source, and health risks and benefits, with research results, 1930s-89, 4048–36
- HHS financial aid, by program, recipient, State, and city, FY90, annual regional listings, 4004–3
- Indian and Alaska Native disease and disorder cases, deaths, and health services use, by tribe, reservation, and Indian Health Service area, late 1950s-86, 4088–2
- Minority group health condition, services use, costs, and indicators of services need, 1950s-88, 4118–55
- Preventive disease and health improvement goals and recommended activities for 2000, with trends 1970s-80s, 4048–10
- Research and training grants of Natl Inst of Dental Research, by recipient instn, FY89, annual listing, 4474–19

Dentists and dentistry

- AIDS virus transmission from health care workers to patients during invasive procedures, CDC prevention guidelines, 1991 rpt, 4206–2.44
- County Business Patterns, 1988: employment, establishments, and payroll, by SIC 2- to 4-digit industry and county, annual State rpt series, 2326–6
- County Business Patterns, 1989: employment, establishments, and payroll, by SIC 2- to 4-digit industry and county, annual State rpt series, 2326–8
- CPI by component for US city average, and by region, population size, and for 27 metro areas, monthly rpt, 6762–2
- Degrees awarded in higher education, by level, field, race, and sex, 1988/89 with trends from 1978/79, biennial rpt, 4844–17
- Education in science and engineering, grad programs enrollment by field, source of funds, and characteristics of student and instn, 1975-89, annual rpt, 9627–7

Employment, earnings, and hours, by SIC 1- to 4-digit industry, monthly and annual averages, selected years 1909-90, annual rpt, 6744–4

Enterprise Statistics, 1987: auxiliaries of multi-establishment firms, finances and operations by function, industry, and State, 2329–6

Enterprise Statistics, 1987: finances and operations for companies, by size, level of diversification, form of organization, and industry group, 2329–8

Expenditures for health care, by service type, payment source, and sector, projected 1990-2000 and trends from 1965, article, 4652–1.251

Expenditures for health care, by service type, payment source, and sector, 1960s-90, annual article, 4652–1.221; 4652–1.252

Fed Govt financial and nonfinancial domestic aid, 1991 base edition with supplements, annual listing, 104–5

Franchise business opportunities by firm and kind of business, and sources of aid and info, 1990 annual listing, 2104–7

Germany (West) health care spending, by funding source and service type, and resource growth, 1970-89, article, 4652–1.238

Health Care Financing Review, provider prices, price inputs and indexes, and labor, quarterly journal, 4652–1.1

Health condition and health care resources, use, and spending, 1950s-89, annual data compilation, 4144–11

Health maintenance organizations and other prepaid managed care plans Medicaid enrollment and use, for 20 States, 1985-89, chartbook, 4108–29

Hepatitis cases by infection source, age, sex, race, and State, and deaths, by strain, 1988 and trends from 1966, 4205–2

HHS financial aid, by program, recipient, State, and city, FY90, annual regional listings, 4004–3

Implants of medical devices, by type, reason, duration, and user characteristics, 1988, 4146–8.197

Indian and Alaska Native disease and disorder cases, deaths, and health services use, by tribe, reservation, and Indian Health Service area, late 1950s-86, 4088–2

Indian Health Service facilities and use, and Indian health and other characteristics, by IHS region, 1980s-89, annual chartbook, 4084–7

Indian Health Service facilities, funding, operations, and Indian health and other characteristics, 1950s-90, annual chartbook, 4084–1

Insurance (health) coverage and provisions of employee benefit plans, by plan type, firm size, and industry sector, 1988, article, 6722–1.204

Insurance (health) coverage and provisions of small business employee benefit plans, by plan type and occupational group, 1990, biennial rpt, 6784–20

Medicaid beneficiaries and payments, by service type, FY72-89, annual rpt, 4744–3.6

Medicare and Medicaid beneficiaries and program operations, 1991, annual fact book, 4654–18

Medicare and Medicaid eligibility, participation, coverage, and program finances, various periods 1966-91, biennial rpt, 4654–1

Military health care personnel, and accessions by training source, by occupation, specialty, and service branch, FY89, annual rpt, 3544–24

Minority group and women health condition, services use, payment sources, and health care labor force, by poverty status, 1940s-89, chartbook, 4118–56

Minority group health condition, services use, costs, and indicators of services need, 1950s-88, 4118–55

Navy personnel strengths, accessions, and attrition, detailed statistics, quarterly rpt, 3802–4

Older persons health care services use, by service type, discharge destination, and prior care source, 1986, 4188–72

Puerto Rico economic censuses, 1987: wholesale, retail, and service industries finances and operations, by establishment characteristics and SIC 2- and 3-digit industry, subject rpts, 2591–2

Receipts for services, by SIC 2- to 4-digit kind of business, 1990, annual rpt, 2413–8

Research and training grants of Natl Inst of Dental Research, by recipient instn, FY89, annual listing, 4474–19

Service industries census, 1987: depreciable assets, capital and operating expenses, and receipts, by SIC 2- to 4-digit kind of business, 2393–2

Service industries census, 1987: establishments, receipts by source, payroll, and employment, by SIC 2- to 4-digit kind of business, State, and MSA, 2393–4

State and Metro Area Data Book, 1991 data compilation, 2328–54

Statistical Abstract of US, 1991 annual data compilation, 2324–1.3

Tax (income) returns of corporations, income and tax items by asset size and detailed industry, 1987, annual rpt, 8304–4

Tax (income) returns of corporations, income and tax items by asset size and detailed industry, 1988, annual rpt, 8304–21

Tax (income) returns of sole proprietorships, income statement items, by industry group, 1989, annual article, 8302–2.214

VA health care facilities physicians, dentists, and nurses, by selected employment characteristics and VA district, quarterly rpt, 8602–6

VA health care professionals employment, by district and facility, quarterly rpt, 8602–4

VA health care staff and turnover, by occupation, physician specialty, and location, 1990, annual rpt, 8604–8

VA Medicine and Surgery Dept trainees, by detailed program and city, FY90, annual rpt, 8704–4

see also Dental condition

Denver, Colo.

Air traffic and passenger and freight enplanements, by airport, 1960s-89 and projected to 2010, hub area rpt, 7506–7.39

Denver, Colo.

CPI by component for US city average, and by region, population size, and for 27 metro areas, monthly rpt, 6762–2

Drug abuse indicators for selected metro areas, research results, data collection, and policy issues, 1991 semiannual conf, 4492–5

Drug test results at arrest, by drug type, offense, and sex, for selected urban areas, quarterly rpt, 6062–3

Housing starts and completions authorized by building permits in 40 MSAs, quarterly rpt, 2382–9

Housing vacancy and property value appreciation rates for 4 metro areas, 1991 GAO rpt, 26131–84

Housing vacancy rates for single and multifamily units and mobile homes, by city and ZIP code, 1991, annual MSA rpt, 9304–22.2

Wages by occupation, for office and plant workers, 1990 survey, periodic MSA rpt, 6785–11.4

see also under By City and By SMSA or MSA in the "Index by Categories"

Department of Agriculture

Acreage reduction program compliance, enrollment, and yield on planted acreage, by commodity and State, annual press release series, 1004–20

Activities and programs of USDA, by subagency, FY90, annual rpt, 1004–3

Agricultural data compilation, 1990 and trends from 1920, annual rpt, 1004–14

Agricultural Statistics, 1990, annual rpt, 1004–1

Budget of US, authoritative financial statements with appropriations, outlays, and receipts, by category and agency, FY90, annual rpt, 8104–2.1

Budget of US, formula grant program obligations to State and local govts, by agency, program, and State, FY92, annual rpt, 104–30

Budget of US, obligations and authority by function, agency, and program, with summaries, analyses, and historical tables, FY92, annual rpt, 104–2

Credit sales agreement terms, by commodity and country, FY89, annual rpt, 15344–1.11

Disaster aid of USDA for producers of crops ineligible for price supports by State, and methodology, 1988-89, GAO rpt, 26113–533

Education funding by Federal agency, program, and recipient type, and instn spending, FY80-90, annual rpt, 4824–8

Employee financial disclosure rpts filings, processing, errors, and conflicts of interest exposed, for USDA, 1989, GAO rpt, 26119–314

Expenditures of Fed Govt in States, by type, program, agency, and State, FY90, annual rpt, 2464–2

Export market research and promotion activities of USDA, with background data, 1991 GAO rpt, 26113–504

Export promotion and foreign food aid programs budget of USDA, with trade by commodity and country, FY85-91 and projected to FY2000, 21168–44

Farm financial and marketing conditions, forecast 1991, annual conf, 1004–16

Field offices, funding, and staff of USDA subagencies responsible for farm programs, FY89, GAO rpt, 26113–507

Fraud and abuse in USDA programs, audits and investigations, 1st half FY91, semiannual rpt, 1002–4

Publications, computer data files, and visual aids of USDA, 1991 annual listing, 1004–13

R&D and related funding of Fed Govt to higher education and nonprofit instns, by field, instn, agency, and State, FY89, annual rpt, 9627–17

R&D funding by Fed Govt, by field, performer type, agency, and State, FY89-91, annual rpt, 9627–20

Research and education appropriations of USDA, by program and subagency, FY82-90, annual rpt, 1004–19

Science and engineering grad enrollment, by field, source of funds, and characteristics of student and instn, 1975-89, annual rpt, 9627–7

Subsidy rates of Fed Govt under 1985 and 1990 farm bills, by selected program and commodity, 1990 rpt, 1008–54

Yearbook of Agriculture, special topics, 1991 annual compilation of papers, 1004–18

see also Agricultural Cooperative Service

see also Agricultural Marketing Service

see also Agricultural Research Service

see also Agricultural Stabilization and Conservation Service

see also Agricultural Statistics Board

see also Animal and Plant Health Inspection Service

see also Commodity Credit Corp.

see also Cooperative State Research Service

see also Economic Research Service

see also Farmers Home Administration

see also Federal Crop Insurance Corp.

see also Federal Grain Inspection Service

see also Food and Nutrition Service

see also Food Safety and Inspection Service

see also Foreign Agricultural Service

see also Forest Service

see also Human Nutrition Information Service

see also National Agricultural Statistics Service

see also Office of Grants and Program Systems, USDA

see also Office of International Cooperation and Development, USDA

see also Office of Transportation, USDA

see also Packers and Stockyards Administration

see also Rural Electrification Administration

see also Soil Conservation Service

see also under By Federal Agency in the "Index by Categories"

Department of Air Force

Base closings in Europe, by service branch and location, FY91, GAO rpt, 26123–336

Base construction, renovation, and land acquisition, DOD budget requests by project, service branch, State, and country, FY92-93, annual rpt, 3544–15

Base support costs by function, and personnel and acreage by installation, by service branch, FY91, annual rpt, 3504–11

Budget of DOD, base construction and family housing appropriations by facility, service branch, and location, FY90-93, annual rpt, 3544–39

Budget of DOD, procurement appropriations by item, service branch, and defense agency, FY90-93, annual rpt, 3544–32

Budget of DOD, programs, policies, and operations, FY90, annual rpt, 3544–2

Budget of DOD, R&D appropriations by item, service branch, and defense agency, FY90-93, annual rpt, 3544–33

Budget of DOD, weapons acquisition costs by system and service branch, FY91-93, annual rpt, 3504–2

Budget of US, obligations and authority by function, agency, and program, with summaries, analyses, and historical tables, FY92, annual rpt, 104–2

Courts (military) cases and actions, FY90, annual rpt, 3504–3

DOD prime contract awards, by detailed procurement category, FY87-90, annual rpt, 3544–18

Expenditures and obligations of DOD, by function and service branch, quarterly rpt, 3542–3

Fiscal mgmt system operations and techniques of Air Force, quarterly rpt, 3602–1

Hazardous waste site remedial action at military installations, activities and funding by site and State, FY90, annual rpt, 3544–36

Health care personnel, and accessions by training source, by occupation, specialty, and service branch, FY89, annual rpt, 3544–24

Personnel (civilian) of DOD, by service branch and defense agency, with summary military employment data, quarterly rpt, 3542–16

Personnel (civilian and military) of DOD, by service branch, major installation, and State, as of Sept 1990, annual rpt, 3544–7

Physicians, by specialty, age, sex, and location of training and practice, 1989, State rpt series, 4116–6

Procurement, DOD prime contract awards by category, contract and contractor type, and service branch, FY81-1st half FY91, semiannual rpt, 3542–1

Procurement, DOD prime contract awards by contractor, service branch, State, and city, FY90, annual rpt, 3544–22

Procurement, DOD prime contract awards by service branch and State, 1st half FY91, semiannual rpt, 3542–5

Procurement, DOD prime contract awards by size and type of contract, service branch, competitive status, category, and labor standard, FY90, annual rpt, 3544–19

Procurement, DOD prime contract awards in labor surplus areas, by service branch, State, and area, 1st half FY91, semiannual rpt, 3542–19

Procurement, subcontract awards by DOD contractors to small and disadvantaged business, by firm and service branch, quarterly rpt, 3542–17

Property, supply, and equipment inventory of DOD, by service branch, FY90, annual rpt, 3544–6

Shipments by DOD of military and personal property, passenger traffic, and costs, by service branch and mode of transport, quarterly rpt, 3702–1

Index by Subjects and Names

Department of Defense

see also Air Force
see also terms beginning with Defense and with Military

Department of Army

Activities, personnel, discipline, budget, and assistance, FY83 summary data, annual rpt, 3704–11

Animals use in Army brain wound research, usefulness of Louisiana State University experiments, with results, 1980s, GAO rpt, 26121–396

Base closings in Europe, by service branch and location, FY91, GAO rpt, 26123–336

Base construction, renovation, and land acquisition, DOD budget requests by project, service branch, State, and country, FY92-93, annual rpt, 3544–15

Base support costs by function, and personnel and acreage by installation, by service branch, FY91, annual rpt, 3504–11

Budget of DOD, base construction and family housing appropriations by facility, service branch, and location, FY90-93, annual rpt, 3544–39

Budget of DOD, procurement appropriations by item, service branch, and defense agency, FY90-93, annual rpt, 3544–32

Budget of DOD, programs, policies, and operations, FY90, annual rpt, 3544–2

Budget of DOD, R&D appropriations by item, service branch, and defense agency, FY90-93, annual rpt, 3544–33

Budget of DOD, weapons acquisition costs by system and service branch, FY91-93, annual rpt, 3504–2

Budget of US, obligations and authority by function, agency, and program, with summaries, analyses, and historical tables, FY92, annual rpt, 104–2

Chemical and biological weapons research labs security measures, and govt and contractor staff, 1988-90, GAO rpt, 26123–356

Courts (military) cases and actions, FY90, annual rpt, 3504–3

DOD prime contract awards, by detailed procurement category, FY87-90, annual rpt, 3544–18

Equipment unserviceable inventories, and repair and replacement costs, for Army, late 1980s, GAO rpt, 26123–312

Expenditures and obligations of DOD, by function and service branch, quarterly rpt, 3542–3

Expenditures of Fed Govt in States, by type, program, agency, and State, FY90, annual rpt, 2464–2

Hazardous waste site remedial action at military installations, activities and funding by site and State, FY90, annual rpt, 3544–36

Health care personnel, and accessions by training source, by occupation, specialty, and service branch, FY89, annual rpt, 3544–24

Personnel (civilian) of DOD, by service branch and defense agency, with summary military employment data, quarterly rpt, 3542–16

Personnel (civilian and military) of DOD, by service branch, major installation, and State, as of Sept 1990, annual rpt, 3544–7

Physicians, by specialty, age, sex, and location of training and practice, 1989, State rpt series, 4116–6

Procurement, DOD prime contract awards by category, contract and contractor type, and service branch, FY81-1st half FY91, semiannual rpt, 3542–1

Procurement, DOD prime contract awards by contractor, service branch, State, and city, FY90, annual rpt, 3544–22

Procurement, DOD prime contract awards by service branch and State, 1st half FY91, semiannual rpt, 3542–5

Procurement, DOD prime contract awards by size and type of contract, service branch, competitive status, category, and labor standard, FY90, annual rpt, 3544–19

Procurement, DOD prime contract awards in labor surplus areas, by service branch, State, and area, 1st half FY91, semiannual rpt, 3542–19

Procurement, subcontract awards by DOD contractors to small and disadvantaged business, by firm and service branch, quarterly rpt, 3542–17

Property, supply, and equipment inventory of DOD, by service branch, FY90, annual rpt, 3544–6

Shipments by DOD of military and personal property, passenger traffic, and costs, by service branch and mode of transport, quarterly rpt, 3702–1

Strategic capability of Army, force strengths, budget, and mgmt, FY74-93, annual rpt, 3704–13

see also Army

see also Army Corps of Engineers

see also National Guard

see also Reserve Officers Training Corps

see also terms beginning with Defense and with Military

Department of Commerce

Activities, funding, and staff of Commerce Dept, by subagency, FY90, annual rpt, 2004–1

Budget appropriations and staff for Commerce Dept, by subagency, FY90-92, annual rpt, 2004–6

Budget of US, authoritative financial statements with appropriations, outlays, and receipts, by category and agency, FY90, annual rpt, 8104–2.1

Budget of US, obligations and authority by function, agency, and program, with summaries, analyses, and historical tables, FY92, annual rpt, 104–2

Census of Population, 1990: data adjustment for undercounts, final decision, 2008–31

Education funding by Federal agency, program, and recipient type, and instn spending, FY80-90, annual rpt, 4824–8

Expenditures of Fed Govt in States, by type, program, agency, and State, FY90, annual rpt, 2464–2

Exports, imports, and trade flows, by country and commodity, with background economic indicators, data compilation, monthly CD-ROM, 2002–6

Fraud and abuse in Commerce Dept programs, audits and investigations, 2nd half FY91, semiannual rpt, 2002–5

Multinatl firms US affiliates, investment trends and impact on US economy, 1991 annual rpt, 2004–9

Publications of Commerce Dept, with economic indicator performance from 1961, biweekly listing, 2002–1

R&D and related funding of Fed Govt to higher education and nonprofit instns, by field, instn, agency, and State, FY89, annual rpt, 9627–17

R&D funding by Fed Govt, by field, performer type, agency, and State, FY89-91, annual rpt, 9627–20

Telecommunications industry intl competitiveness, with financial and operating data by product or service, firm, and country, 1990 rpt, 2008–30

see also Bureau of Census

see also Bureau of Economic Analysis

see also Bureau of Export Administration

see also Economic Development Administration

see also Foreign Trade Zones Board

see also International Trade Administration

see also Minority Business Development Agency

see also National Environmental Satellite, Data, and Information Service

see also National Institute of Standards and Technology

see also National Marine Fisheries Service

see also National Ocean Service

see also National Oceanic and Atmospheric Administration

see also National Technical Information Service

see also National Telecommunications and Information Administration

see also National Weather Service

see also Patent and Trademark Office

see also U.S. Travel and Tourism Administration

see also under By Federal Agency in the "Index by Categories"

Department of Defense

Base support costs by function, and personnel and acreage by installation, by service branch, FY91, annual rpt, 3504–11

Budget of DOD, manpower needs, costs, and force readiness by service branch, FY92, annual rpt, 3504–1

Budget of DOD, organization, personnel, weapons, and property, by service branch, State, and country, 1991 annual summary rpt, 3504–13

Budget of DOD, programs, policies, and operations, FY90, annual rpt, 3544–2

Budget of DOD, weapons acquisition costs by system and service branch, FY91-93, annual rpt, 3504–2

Budget of US, authoritative financial statements with appropriations, outlays, and receipts, by category and agency, FY90, annual rpt, 8104–2.1

Budget of US, obligations and authority by function, agency, and program, with summaries, analyses, and historical tables, FY92, annual rpt, 104–2

Computer systems of Fed Govt with sensitive unclassified data, security plans by characteristics of info and system, and agency, 1989, 2218–85

Courts (military) cases and actions, FY90, annual rpt, 3504–3

Dependents Schools basic skills and college entrance test scores, 1990-91, annual rpt, 3504–16

Department of Defense

Education funding by Federal agency, program, and recipient type, and instn spending, FY80-90, annual rpt, 4824–8

Employment (civilian) of Fed Govt, by work schedule, selected agency, State, and MSA, as of Dec 1990, biennial article, 9842–1.203

Employment, earnings, and hours, by SIC 1- to 4-digit industry, monthly and annual averages, selected years 1909-90, annual rpt, 6744–4

Exchange service financial statements, FY88-89, annual rpt, 3504–21

Expenditures of Fed Govt in States and local areas, by type, State, county, and city, FY90, annual rpt, 2464–3

Expenditures of Fed Govt in States, by type, program, agency, and State, FY90, annual rpt, 2464–2

Foreign countries military aid of US, arms sales, and training programs costs and budget requests, by program, world region, and country, FY90-92, annual rpt, 7144–13

Fraud and abuse in DOD programs, audits and investigations, 1st half FY91, semiannual rpt, 3542–18

Intl exchange and training programs of Federal agencies, participants by world area, and funding, by program, FY89, annual rpt, 9854–8

Manufacturing census, 1987: employment and shipments under Fed Govt contracts, by SIC 4-digit industry, 2497–7

Natl Guard activities, personnel, and facilities, FY90, annual rpt, 3504–22

Officers assigned to multiservice organizations, designation of critical positions for qualified joint specialty officers, 1987-90 and projected to 1994, GAO rpt, 26123–317

Pay grade reclassification for Federal employees, budget impacts and demonstration project results, 1990, 26306–3.119

Personnel (civilian) of DOD, by service branch and defense agency, with summary military employment data, quarterly rpt, 3542–16

Personnel (civilian and military) of DOD, by service branch, major installation, and State, as of Sept 1990, annual rpt, 3544–7

Personnel strengths, for active duty, civilians, and reserves, by service branch, FY90 and trends, annual rpt, 3544–1

Personnel strengths, for active duty, civilians, and reserves, by service branch, quarterly rpt, 3542–14

Post exchange operations, and sales by commodity, by facility and location worldwide, FY89, annual rpt, 3504–10

Procurement, DOD prime contract awards by category, contract and contractor type, and service branch, FY81-1st half FY91, semiannual rpt, 3542–1

Procurement, DOD prime contract awards by contractor, service branch, State, and city, FY90, annual rpt, 3544–22

Procurement, DOD prime contract awards by service branch and State, 1st half FY91, semiannual rpt, 3542–5

Procurement, DOD prime contract awards in labor surplus areas, by service branch, State, and area, 1st half FY91, semiannual rpt, 3542–19

Property (real) of Fed Govt, inventory and costs, worldwide summary by location, agency, and use, 1989, annual rpt, 9454–5

Property (real) of Fed Govt, leased inventory and rental costs, worldwide summary by location and agency, 1989, annual rpt, 9454–10

Property, supply, and equipment inventory of DOD, by service branch, FY90, annual rpt, 3544–6

R&D and related funding of Fed Govt to higher education and nonprofit instns, by field, instn, agency, and State, FY89, annual rpt, 9627–17

R&D funding by Fed Govt, by field, performer type, agency, and State, FY89-91, annual rpt, 9627–20

Science and engineering grad enrollment, by field, source of funds, and characteristics of student and instn, 1975-89, annual rpt, 9627–7

Service academy costs by type, staff, and grad advancement in military, FY88-90, GAO rpt, 26123–355

Soviet Union military weapons systems, presence, and force strengths, and compared to US, 1991 annual rpt, 3504–20

Spacecraft launches and other activities of NASA and USSR, with flight data, 1957-90, annual rpt, 9504–6.1

Survey of Current Business, defense activity indicators, monthly rpt, 2702–1.2

Training and education programs of DOD, funding, staff, students, and facilities, by service branch, FY92, annual rpt, 3504–5

see also Armed Forces Institute of Pathology

see also Army Corps of Engineers

see also Court of Military Appeals

see also Defense agencies

see also Defense Communications Agency

see also Defense Contract Audit Agency

see also Defense Intelligence Agency

see also Defense Investigative Service

see also Defense Logistics Agency

see also Defense Mapping Agency

see also Defense Nuclear Agency

see also Defense Security Assistance Agency

see also Department of Air Force

see also Department of Army

see also Department of Navy

see also Marine Corps

see also Office of the Secretary of Defense

see also On-Site Inspection Agency

see also terms beginning with Defense and with Military

see also under By Federal Agency in the "Index by Categories"

Department of Education

Activities of Education Dept, FY89-90, annual rpt, 4804–6

Banks profitability indicators for student loans and other financial services, 1985-89, 4808–36

Bilingual education and English immersion programs activities, structure, and effectiveness, 1984-88 longitudinal study, 4808–27

Bilingual education enrollment, and Education Dept activities and funding by program, by State, FY88-90, biennial rpt, 4804–14

Budget of US, authoritative financial statements with appropriations, outlays, and receipts, by category and agency, FY90, annual rpt, 8104–2.1

Budget of US, formula grant program obligations to State and local govts, by agency, program, and State, FY92, annual rpt, 104–30

Budget of US, obligations and authority by function, agency, and program, with summaries, analyses, and historical tables, FY92, annual rpt, 104–2

Compensatory education programs in high poverty school districts, Federal grant program activities, participation, and coordinators views, 1989/90, 4808–32

Discrimination in education, indicators for service delivery and discipline, by State, 1988, biennial rpt, 4804–33

Discrimination within schools, Education Dept enforcement activities and adequacy, FY81-91, GAO rpt, 26121–427

Education data, selected performance and financial indicators by State, annual table with supplements, discontinued, 4804–32

Enrollment, staff, and spending, by instn level and control, and teacher salaries, 1980s-92, annual press release, 4804–19

Expenditures for education by Federal agency, program, and recipient type, and instn spending, FY80-90, annual rpt, 4824–8

Expenditures of Fed Govt in States, by type, program, agency, and State, FY90, annual rpt, 2464–2

Expenditures, operations, and effectiveness of Education Dept programs, FY90, annual rpt, 4804–5

Financial aid programs of Education Dept, 1991 annual listing, 4804–3

Fraud and abuse in Education Dept programs, audits and investigations, 2nd half FY91, semiannual rpt, 4802–1

Fulbright-Hays academic exchanges, grants by purpose, and foreign govt share of costs, by country, FY90, annual rpt, 10324–1

Handicapped children early education project descriptions, 1990/91, annual listing, 4944–10

Higher education instn tuition and other costs, govt aid, impacts on enrollment, and cost containment methods, 1970s-90 and projected to 2001, 4808–25

Higher education instn tuition relation to other instn financial indicators, by instn control, 1960s-88, 4808–24

Homeless adults educational services, funding, participation, and staff, by State, 1989, annual rpt series, 4804–39

Homeless children educational projects, activities, and funding, FY90, annual rpt, 4804–35

Intl exchange and training programs of Federal agencies, participants by world area, and funding, by program, FY89, annual rpt, 9854–8

Literacy programs in workplaces, demonstration projects funding and participant characteristics, FY88, 4808–37

Literacy programs in workplaces, Education Dept funding and project descriptions, FY90, annual listing, 4804–40

Migrant workers children education programs enrollment, staff, and effectiveness, by State, 1980s, 4808–30

Migrant workers children education programs enrollment, staff, finances, and outcomes, 1980s, 4808–22

Index by Subjects and Names

Minority group higher education enrollment, degrees, factors affecting participation, and earnings, 1960s-88, 4808–29

Pell grants and applicants, by tuition, family and student income, instn type and control, and State, 1989/90, annual rpt, 4804–1

Poverty area schools academic environment and teaching methods impacts on student performance, 1989/90 study, 4808–28

R&D and related funding of Fed Govt to higher education and nonprofit instns, by field, instn, agency, and State, FY89, annual rpt, 9627–17

R&D funding by Fed Govt, by field, performer type, agency, and State, FY89-91, annual rpt, 9627–20

Science and math education programs for gifted minority students, participation and outcomes, 1981-88 study, 4808–34

Science and math teacher dev project funding of Fed Govt, participation, operations, and effectiveness, 1985-90, 4808–31

Student aid funding and participation, by Federal program, instn type and control, and State, various periods 1959-89, annual rpt, 4804–28

Student guaranteed loan activity, by program, guarantee agency, and State, quarterly rpt, 4802–2

Student guaranteed loan default rate, causes, defaulter characteristics, and preventive recommendations, FY81-90, 4808–35

Student guaranteed loans, defaults, and collections, by type of loan, lender, and guarantee agency, with data by State and top lender, FY90, annual rpt, 4804–38

Student loan debt burden of 1986 college grads, by selected student characteristics and instn control, 1987, 4808–26

Student loans of Fed Govt in default, losses, and rates, by instn and State, as of June 1990, annual rpt, 4804–18

Student supplemental grants, loans, and work-study awards, Federal share by instn and State, 1991/92, annual listing, 4804–17

Tutoring and mentoring of disadvantaged elementary and secondary students by college students, program and participant characteristics, 1989, 4808–23

Vocational education in postsecondary instns, States performance measurement activities and related legislation, 1989/90, 4808–33

see also National Assessment of Educational Progress

see also Office of Bilingual Education and Minority Language Affairs

see also Office of Educational Research and Improvement

see also Office of Special Education and Rehabilitative Services

see also under By Federal Agency in the "Index by Categories"

Department of Energy

Budget of US, authoritative financial statements with appropriations, outlays, and receipts, by category and agency, FY90, annual rpt, 8104–2.1

Budget of US, formula grant program obligations to State and local govts, by agency, program, and State, FY92, annual rpt, 104–30

Department of Energy: Conservation and Renewable Energy

Budget of US, obligations and authority by function, agency, and program, with summaries, analyses, and historical tables, FY92, annual rpt, 104–2

Carbon dioxide in atmosphere, measurement, methodology, and research results, series, 3006–11

Contracts and grants of DOE, by category, State, and for top contractors, FY90, annual rpt, 3004–21

Data collection forms of DOE and related rpts, 1990, annual listing, 3164–86

Education funding by Federal agency, program, and recipient type, and instn spending, FY80-90, annual rpt, 4824–8

Employment in energy-related fields, manpower studies and devs, series, 3006–8

Energy use, costs, and conservation, for DOE, by end use, fuel type, and field office, FY90, annual rpt, 3004–27

Expenditures of Fed Govt in States, by type, program, agency, and State, FY90, annual rpt, 2464–2

Finances and mgmt of DOE programs, audits and investigations, series, 3006–5

Fraud and abuse in DOE programs, audit resolution activities, 2nd half FY91, semiannual rpt, 3002–15

Fraud and abuse in DOE programs, audits and investigations, 2nd half FY91, semiannual rpt, 3002–12

Inventions recommended by Natl Inst of Standards and Technology for DOE support, awards, and evaluation status, 1990, annual listing, 2214–5

Manufacturing census, 1987: employment and shipments under Fed Govt contracts, by SIC 4-digit industry, 2497–7

Natl Energy Strategy plans for conservation, R&D, security, and pollution reduction, with background data, 1991 biennial rpt, 3004–34

Nuclear engineering and science educational facilities, student aid, and degrees granted, by instn, 1990, 3008–126

Nuclear engineering enrollment and degrees granted by instn and State, and grad placement, by student characteristics, 1990, annual rpt, 3004–5

Nuclear material inventory discrepancies at DOE and contractor facilities, annual rpt, issuing agency transfer, 3004–32

Nuclear weapons facilities of DOE, contract security forces skill deficiencies, and costs compared to Federal security, late 1980s, GAO rpt, 26113–493

Nuclear weapons labs and DOE screening of contractors for foreign ownership, control, or influence, compliance by lab, FY88-90, GAO rpt, 26113–520

Oil enhanced recovery research contracts of DOE, project summaries, funding, and bibl, quarterly rpt, 3002–14

R&D and related funding of Fed Govt to higher education and nonprofit instns, by field, instn, agency, and State, FY89, annual rpt, 9627–17

R&D funding by Fed Govt, by field, performer type, agency, and State, FY89-91, annual rpt, 9627–20

R&D projects and funding of DOE at natl labs, universities, and other instns, periodic summary rpt series, 3004–18

Radiation and radionuclide concentrations in surface air at selected monitoring sites worldwide, and effects of nuclear tests and accidents, 1989, annual rpt, 3004–31

Radiation protection and health physics enrollment and degrees granted by instn and State, and grad placement, by student characteristics, 1990, annual rpt, 3004–7

Radioactive strontium fallout, monitoring results for 65 sites worldwide, quarterly 1986 and trends from 1958, annual rpt, 3004–29

Radioactivity levels at former AEC and Manhattan Project research and storage sites and nearby areas, test results series, 3006–9

Strategic Petroleum Reserve capacity, inventory, fill rate, and finances, quarterly rpt, 3002–13

Toxicology Natl Program research and testing activities, FY89 and planned FY90, annual rpt, 4044–16

see also Alaska Power Administration

see also Bonneville Power Administration

see also Department of Energy: Civilian Radioactive Waste Management

see also Department of Energy: Conservation and Renewable Energy

see also Department of Energy: Defense Programs

see also Department of Energy: Environment, Safety, and Health

see also Department of Energy: Fossil Energy

see also Department of Energy: International Affairs and Energy Emergencies

see also Department of Energy National Laboratories

see also Department of Energy: Nuclear Energy

see also Energy Information Administration

see also Federal Energy Regulatory Commission

see also Office of the Secretary of Energy

see also Southeastern Power Administration

see also Southwestern Power Administration

see also Western Area Power Administration

see also under By Federal Agency in the "Index by Categories"

Department of Energy: Civilian Radioactive Waste Management

Nuclear Waste Fund finances and CRWM activities, quarterly GAO rpt, 26102–4

Nuclear Waste Fund finances, and CRWM Program costs, quarterly rpt, 3362–1

Nuclear Waste Fund finances, and CRWM R&D costs, FY88-89, annual rpt, 3364–1

Spent fuel and radioactive waste generation, inventory, and disposal, 1960s-89 and projected to 2020, annual rpt, 3364–2

Storage and transport needs, disposal site characteristics, and costs, for proposed radioactive waste mgmt plan, 1991 rpt, 3368–1

Department of Energy: Conservation and Renewable Energy

Auto (electric-powered) R&D activity and DOE funding shares, FY90, annual rpt, 3304–2

Auto and light truck fuel economy, sales, and market shares, by size and model for US and foreign makes, 1991 model year, semiannual rpt, 3302–4

Auto engine and power train R&D projects, DOE contracts and funding by recipient, FY90, annual rpt, 3304–17

Department of Energy: Conservation and Renewable Energy

Auto fuel economy test results for US and foreign makes, 1992 model year, annual rpt, 3304–11

Conservation aid of DOE, activities, funding, and grants by State, by program, annual rpt, discontinued, 3304–21

Conservation aid of Fed Govt to public and nonprofit private instns, by building type and State, 1990, annual rpt, 3304–15

Consumption of energy, impacts of conservation measures by component and end-use sector, 1970s-88 and projected under alternative oil prices to 1995, 3308–93

Electric utilities conservation programs energy savings, under alternative participation rates, projected 1990-2010, 3308–98

Electric utilities conservation programs impacts on prices and supply costs, alternative estimates, 1991 rpt, 3308–99

Energy use and efficiency in Federal buildings, by agency, annual rpt, discontinued, 3304–25

Energy use and efficiency of Fed Govt, by agency and fuel type, FY90, annual rpt, 3304–22

Gasohol sales, and tax rates on all motor fuels, by State, 1983-90, annual rpt, 3304–9

Geothermal resources, power plant capacity and operating status, leases, and wells, by location, 1960s-94, 3308–87

Housing attic insulation radiant barriers performance impacts of ventilation and dust, 1990 rpt, 3308–97

Hydrogen energy R&D activity and funding of DOE, and project listing, FY90, annual rpt, 3304–18

Inventions supported by DOE, sales, jobs created, and inventor financing, 1980-88, 3308–91

Solar photovoltaic R&D sponsored by DOE, projects, funding, and rpts, FY90, annual listing, 3304–20

State govt energy conservation programs, Federal aid and savings, by State, 1989, annual rpt, 3304–1

Transportation energy use by mode, fuel supply, and demographic and economic factors of vehicle use, 1970s-89, annual rpt, 3304–5

Department of Energy: Defense Programs

Nuclear material inventory discrepancies at DOE and contractor facilities, 1989/90, annual rpt, 3344–2

Department of Energy: Environment, Safety, and Health

Environmental impacts of energy technologies, issues and control measures, handbook series, 3326–1

Radiation exposure at DOE and DOE-contractor sites, by facility type and contractor, dose type, and worker age, sex, and occupation, 1988, annual rpt, 3324–1

Department of Energy: Fossil Energy

Electric power and industrial plants prohibited from oil and gas primary use, and gas use by State, 1977-90, annual rpt, 3334–1

Naval Petroleum and Oil Shale Reserves production and revenue by fuel type, sales by purchaser, and wells, by reserve, FY90, annual rpt, 3334–3

Department of Energy: International Affairs and Energy Emergencies

Latin America energy use and trade, by selected country, 1970s-80s and projected to 2000, 3408–1

Department of Energy National Laboratories

Contracts and grants of DOE, by category, State, and for top contractors, FY90, annual rpt, 3004–21

Environmental samples from DOE facilities, DOE natl labs quality control performance, late 1980s, 3006–5.21

Environmental samples from DOE facilities, DOE natl labs testing costs compared to commercial labs, FY87-89, 3006–5.23

Expenditures for R&D and related activities of higher education and nonprofit instns by Fed Govt, by field, instn, agency, and State, FY89, annual rpt, 9627–17.1

Expenditures for R&D by higher education instns and federally funded centers, by field, instn, and State, FY89, annual rpt, 9627–13

Hydrogen energy R&D activity and funding of DOE, and project listing, FY90, annual rpt, 3304–18

Idaho Natl Engineering Lab radiation monitoring results, for facilities and nearby areas, 1990, annual rpt, 3354–10

Los Alamos Natl Lab contract security strike, reasons and temporary replacement workers skill deficiencies, 1989, GAO rpt, 26113–493

Nuclear material inventory discrepancies at DOE and contractor facilities, 1989/90, annual rpt, 3344–2

Nuclear reactors for domestic use and export by function and operating status, with owner, operating characteristics, and location, 1990 annual listing, 3354–15

Nuclear weapons labs and DOE screening of contractors for foreign ownership, control, or influence, compliance by lab, FY88-90, GAO rpt, 26113–520

Oil enhanced recovery research contracts of DOE, project summaries, funding, and bibl, quarterly rpt, 3002–14

R&D projects and funding of DOE at natl labs, universities, and other instns, periodic summary rpt series, 3004–18

Radiation exposure at DOE and DOE-contractor sites, by facility type and contractor, dose type, and worker age, sex, and occupation, 1988, annual rpt, 3324–1

Radioactive and hazardous waste at DOE facilities, disposal and remediation activities and funding, planned FY91-97, annual rpt, 3024–7

Radioactive waste and spent fuel generation, inventory, and disposal, 1960s-89 and projected to 2020, annual rpt, 3364–2

Radioactive waste at DOE nuclear weapons facilities, storage plans, and mgmt issues, 1988, 26358–236

Security forces under contract at DOE nuclear weapons facilities, skill deficiencies, and costs compared to Federal security, late 1980s, GAO rpt, 26113–493

Solar photovoltaic R&D sponsored by DOE, projects, funding, and rpts, FY90, annual listing, 3304–20

Index by Subjects and Names

Department of Energy: Nuclear Energy

Hanford, Wash nuclear plant, nearby population radiation exposure, with methodology, 1944-66, series, 3356–5

Idaho Natl Engineering Lab radiation monitoring results, for facilities and nearby areas, 1990, annual rpt, 3354–10

Radioactive low-level waste disposal activities of States and interstate compacts, with data by disposal facility and reactor, 1989, annual rpt, 3354–14

Reactors for domestic use and export by function and operating status, with owner, operating characteristics, and location, 1990, annual listing, 3354–15

Safety standards and research, design, licensing, construction, operation, and finances, for nuclear power plants with data by reactor, quarterly journal, 3352–4

Spent fuel from nuclear power plants and additional storage capacity needed, by reactor, projected 1990-2040, annual rpt, 3354–2

Uranium enrichment facilities of DOE, financial statements, FY89-90, annual rpt, 3354–7

Uranium tailings at inactive mills, remedial action activities by site, and funding, FY90, annual rpt, 3354–9

Department of Health and Human Services

Alcohol use, knowledge, attitudes, and info sources of youth, series, 4006–10

Board and care homes regulation and rules enforcement by States, 1988, 4008–112

Budget of US, authoritative financial statements with appropriations, outlays, and receipts, by category and agency, FY90, annual rpt, 8104–2.1

Budget of US, formula grant program obligations to State and local govts, by agency, program, and State, FY92, annual rpt, 104–30

Budget of US, obligations and authority by function, agency, and program, with summaries, analyses, and historical tables, FY92, annual rpt, 104–2

Drug abuse, prevention, treatment, and health research results, triennial rpt, issuing agency change, 4008–66

Education funding by Federal agency, program, and recipient type, and instn spending, FY80-90, annual rpt, 4824–8

Expenditures of Fed Govt in States and local areas, by type, State, county, and city, FY90, annual rpt, 2464–3.2

Expenditures of Fed Govt in States, by type, program, agency, and State, FY90, annual rpt, 2464–2

FDA activities, funding, facilities, and staff, findings and recommendations, 1980s-91, 4008–115

Financial aid of HHS, by program, recipient, State, and city, FY90, annual regional listings, 4004–3

Foster care placement of black children whose parents abuse drugs, by placement reason and outcome, and household and parent characteristics, 1986-90, 4008–114

Fraud and abuse in HHS programs, audits and investigations, 1st half FY91, semiannual rpt, 4002–6

Freedom of Info Act requests, disposition, costs, and fees, for HHS, 1990, annual rpt, 4004–21

Index by Subjects and Names

Health care professionals licensing and disciplinary actions of State medical boards, 1950s-87, series, 4006–8

Hispanic Americans employment of HHS in Mountain region, hiring and promotion practices, 1980s, GAO rpt, 26121–393

Intl exchange and training programs of Federal agencies, participants by world area, and funding, by program, FY89, annual rpt, 9854–8

Kidney dialysis patients anemia treatment with Epoetin alfa, dosages, costs, Medicare reimbursement, and facility income effects, 1989, 4008–113

Medicare reimbursement of hospitals under prospective payment system, diagnosis related group code assignment and effects on care and instn finances, 1984/85, series, 4006–7

Older persons discrimination in Federal aid programs, Age Discrimination Act enforcement by agency, FY90, annual rpt, 4004–27

Physicians licensing and disciplinary activities of State medical boards, investigative staff, and licensing fees, by State, 1985-90, 4008–83

R&D and related funding of Fed Govt to higher education and nonprofit instns, by field, instn, agency, and State, FY89, annual rpt, 9627–17

R&D funding by Fed Govt, by field, performer type, agency, and State, FY89-91, annual rpt, 9627–20

Research and evaluation programs of HHS, 1970-90, annual listing, 4004–30

Science and engineering grad enrollment, by field, source of funds, and characteristics of student and instn, 1975-89, annual rpt, 9627–7

see also Agency for Health Care Policy and Research

see also Agency for Toxic Substances and Disease Registry

see also Alcohol, Drug Abuse and Mental Health Administration

see also Bureau of Health Care Delivery and Assistance

see also Bureau of Health Professions

see also Centers for Disease Control

see also Division of Research Grants, NIH

see also Family Support Administration

see also Food and Drug Administration

see also Health Care Financing Administration

see also Health Resources and Services Administration

see also Indian Health Service

see also National Cancer Institute

see also National Center for Health Statistics

see also National Center for Nursing Research

see also National Center for Research Resources, NIH

see also National Eye Institute

see also National Heart, Lung, and Blood Institute

see also National Institute for Occupational Safety and Health

see also National Institute of Allergy and Infectious Diseases

see also National Institute of Arthritis and Musculoskeletal and Skin Diseases

see also National Institute of Child Health and Human Development

see also National Institute of Diabetes and Digestive and Kidney Diseases

see also National Institute of Environmental Health Sciences

see also National Institute of General Medical Sciences

see also National Institute of Mental Health

see also National Institute on Alcohol Abuse and Alcoholism

see also National Institute on Deafness and Other Communication Disorders

see also National Institute on Drug Abuse

see also National Institutes of Health

see also National Library of Medicine

see also Office of Human Development Services

see also Office of Policy, SSA

see also Public Health Service

see also Social Security Administration

see also under By Federal Agency in the "Index by Categories"

Department of Housing and Urban Development

Activities and staff of HUD, by region, FY89, 5008–37

Activities of HUD, and housing programs operations and funding, 1989, annual rpt, 5004–10

Apartment and condominium completions by rent class and sales price, and market absorption rates, quarterly rpt, 2482–2

Budget of US, authoritative financial statements with appropriations, outlays, and receipts, by category and agency, FY90, annual rpt, 8104–2.1

Budget of US, formula grant program obligations to State and local govts, by agency, program, and State, FY92, annual rpt, 104–30

Budget of US, obligations and authority by function, agency, and program, with summaries, analyses, and historical tables, FY92, annual rpt, 104–2

Education funding by Federal agency, program, and recipient type, and instn spending, FY80-90, annual rpt, 4824–8

Expenditures of Fed Govt in States, by type, program, agency, and State, FY90, annual rpt, 2464–2

Fraud and abuse in HUD programs, audits and investigations, FY91, semiannual rpt, 5002–8; 5002–11

Fraud and abuse in HUD programs, financial and program mgmt improvement activities, 1990, annual rpt, 5004–9

Low income housing construction and repair loans of HUD to nonprofit organizations, project delays, and starts, 1980s, GAO rpt, 26113–506

Low income housing supply impacts of HUD programs to maintain supply and to deter insured mortgage prepayment, 1986-90 and projected to 2005, GAO rpt, 26131–84

R&D and related funding of Fed Govt to higher education and nonprofit instns, by field, instn, agency, and State, FY89, annual rpt, 9627–17

R&D funding by Fed Govt, by field, performer type, agency, and State, FY89-91, annual rpt, 9627–20

Securities backed by mortgages, investments by major financial instns, quarterly press release, discontinued, 5002–12

Department of Justice

Utility allowances used in HUD public housing and rent assistance programs, coverage and adequacy, 1985-89, GAO rpt, 26113–512

see also Community Planning and Development, HUD

see also Government National Mortgage Association

see also Housing (FHA), HUD

see also Policy Development and Research, HUD

see also under By Federal Agency in the "Index by Categories"

Department of Interior

Activities of Interior Dept, press release series, 5306–4

Budget of US, authoritative financial statements with appropriations, outlays, and receipts, by category and agency, FY90, annual rpt, 8104–2.1

Budget of US, formula grant program obligations to State and local govts, by agency, program, and State, FY92, annual rpt, 104–30

Budget of US, obligations and authority by function, agency, and program, with summaries, analyses, and historical tables, FY92, annual rpt, 104–2

Education funding by Federal agency, program, and recipient type, and instn spending, FY80-90, annual rpt, 4824–8

Expenditures of Fed Govt in States, by type, program, agency, and State, FY90, annual rpt, 2464–2

Fraud and abuse in DOI programs, audits and investigations, 2nd half FY91, semiannual rpt, 5302–2

R&D and related funding of Fed Govt to higher education and nonprofit instns, by field, instn, agency, and State, FY89, annual rpt, 9627–17

R&D funding by Fed Govt, by field, performer type, agency, and State, FY89-91, annual rpt, 9627–20

see also Bureau of Indian Affairs

see also Bureau of Land Management

see also Bureau of Mines

see also Bureau of Reclamation

see also Fish and Wildlife Service

see also Geological Survey

see also Minerals Management Service

see also National Park Service

see also Office of Surface Mining Reclamation and Enforcement

see also Office of Territorial and International Affairs

see also under By Federal Agency in the "Index by Categories"

Department of Justice

Asset Forfeiture Program of Justice Dept, seizures, finances, and disbursements, FY86-90, annual rpt, 6004–21

Asset forfeiture programs of Justice Dept and Customs Service, finances, and disbursements by State and judicial district, FY85-90, hearing, 25408–112

Budget of US, authoritative financial statements with appropriations, outlays, and receipts, by category and agency, FY90, annual rpt, 8104–2.1

Budget of US, formula grant program obligations to State and local govts, by agency, program, and State, FY92, annual rpt, 104–30

Department of Justice

Budget of US, obligations and authority by function, agency, and program, with summaries, analyses, and historical tables, FY92, annual rpt, 104–2

Debt delinquent on Federal accounts, cases and collections of DOJ and private law firms, pilot project results, FY90, annual rpt, 6004–20

Drug enforcement regional task forces investigation of organized crime, activities by agency and region, FY83-90, biennial rpt, 6004–17

Education funding by Federal agency, program, and recipient type, and instn spending, FY80-90, annual rpt, 4824–8

Environmental legislation enforcement activities of EPA and State govts, FY90, annual rpt, 9184–21

Expenditures of Fed Govt in States, by type, program, agency, and State, FY90, annual rpt, 2464–2

Money laundering investigation network of Treasury Dept, funding, and staff detailed from other agencies, 1990-91, GAO rpt, 26119–330

R&D funding by Fed Govt, by field, performer type, agency, and State, FY89-91, annual rpt, 9627–20

Savings instns fraud and abuse, Federal indictments and case dispositions, FY89-91, press release, 6008–33

US attorneys case processing and collections, by case type and Federal district, FY90, annual rpt, 6004–2

Victims of crime, compensation and support service applications by disposition, and grant funding by State, 1986-91, GAO rpt, 26119–348

see also Bureau of Justice Assistance

see also Bureau of Justice Statistics

see also Bureau of Prisons

see also Community Relations Service

see also Drug Enforcement Administration

see also Federal Bureau of Investigation

see also Foreign Claims Settlement Commission

see also Immigration and Naturalization Service

see also National Institute of Justice

see also Office of Justice Programs

see also Office of Juvenile Justice and Delinquency Prevention

see also U.S. Marshals Service

see also U.S. Parole Commission

see also under By Federal Agency in the "Index by Categories"

Department of Labor

Activities and funding of DOL, by program and State, FY90, annual rpt, 6304–1

Budget of US, authoritative financial statements with appropriations, outlays, and receipts, by category and agency, FY90, annual rpt, 8104–2.1

Budget of US, formula grant program obligations to State and local govts, by agency, program, and State, FY92, annual rpt, 104–30

Budget of US, obligations and authority by function, agency, and program, with summaries, analyses, and historical tables, FY92, annual rpt, 104–2

Education funding by Federal agency, program, and recipient type, and instn spending, FY80-90, annual rpt, 4824–8

Expenditures of Fed Govt in States, by type, program, agency, and State, FY90, annual rpt, 2464–2

Fraud and abuse in DOL programs, audits and investigations activity, and racketeering cases by type and disposition, FY88-89, GAO rpt, 26111–74

Fraud and abuse in DOL programs, audits and investigations, 2nd half FY91, semiannual rpt, 6302–2

HHS research and evaluation programs, 1970-90, annual listing, 4004–30

Job Training Partnership Act State and local admin, funding, effectiveness, and participants, GAO rpt series, 26106–8

R&D and related funding of Fed Govt to higher education and nonprofit instns, by field, instn, agency, and State, FY89, annual rpt, 9627–17

R&D funding by Fed Govt, by field, performer type, agency, and State, FY89-91, annual rpt, 9627–20

see also Bureau of International Labor Affairs

see also Bureau of Labor Statistics

see also Employment and Training Administration

see also Employment Standards Administration

see also Mine Safety and Health Administration

see also Occupational Safety and Health Administration

see also Office of Labor-Management Standards

see also Pension and Welfare Benefits Administration

see also Women's Bureau

see also under By Federal Agency in the "Index by Categories"

Department of Navy

Base closings in Europe, by service branch and location, FY91, GAO rpt, 26123–336

Base construction, renovation, and land acquisition, DOD budget requests by project, service branch, State, and country, FY92-93, annual rpt, 3544–15

Base support costs by function, and personnel and acreage by installation, by service branch, FY91, annual rpt, 3504–11

Budget of DOD, base construction and family housing appropriations by facility, service branch, and location, FY90-93, annual rpt, 3544–39

Budget of DOD, procurement appropriations by item, service branch, and defense agency, FY90-93, annual rpt, 3544–32

Budget of DOD, programs, policies, and operations, FY90, annual rpt, 3544–2

Budget of DOD, R&D appropriations by item, service branch, and defense agency, FY90-93, annual rpt, 3544–33

Budget of DOD, weapons acquisition costs by system and service branch, FY91-93, annual rpt, 3504–2

Budget of Navy, personnel, procurement, and equipment, planned FY91-93, annual fact sheet, 3804–16

Budget of US, obligations and authority by function, agency, and program, with summaries, analyses, and historical tables, FY92, annual rpt, 104–2

Index by Subjects and Names

Courts (military) cases and actions, FY90, annual rpt, 3504–3

Decentralization of Navy command and relocation from DC area, savings, and cost of living indicators for 14 MSAs, 1980s, GAO rpt, 26123–346

DOD prime contract awards, by detailed procurement category, FY87-90, annual rpt, 3544–18

Drug and alcohol abuse education and treatment programs activity of Navy, semiannual tables, discontinued, 3802–6

Expenditures and obligations of DOD, by function and service branch, quarterly rpt, 3542–3

Hazardous waste site remedial action at military installations, activities and funding by site and State, FY90, annual rpt, 3544–36

Health care personnel, and accessions by training source, by occupation, specialty, and service branch, FY89, annual rpt, 3544–24

Homeport construction proposals of Navy, assignments and costs compared to existing ports, 1990s, GAO rpt, 26123–347

Military Sealift Command shipping operations, finances, and personnel, FY90, annual rpt, 3804–14

Personnel (civilian) of DOD, by service branch and defense agency, with summary military employment data, quarterly rpt, 3542–16

Personnel (civilian and military) of DOD, by service branch, major installation, and State, as of Sept 1990, annual rpt, 3544–7

Personnel strengths, accessions, and attrition, detailed statistics for Navy and Naval Reserve, quarterly rpt, 3802–4

Physicians, by specialty, age, sex, and location of training and practice, 1989, State rpt series, 4116–6

Procurement, DOD prime contract awards by category, contract and contractor type, and service branch, FY81-1st half FY91, semiannual rpt, 3542–1

Procurement, DOD prime contract awards by contractor, service branch, State, and city, FY90, annual rpt, 3544–22

Procurement, DOD prime contract awards by service branch and State, 1st half FY91, semiannual rpt, 3542–5

Procurement, DOD prime contract awards by size and type of contract, service branch, competitive status, category, and labor standard, FY90, annual rpt, 3544–19

Procurement, DOD prime contract awards in labor surplus areas, by service branch, State, and area, 1st half FY91, semiannual rpt, 3542–19

Procurement of Navy, by contractor and location, FY90, annual rpt, 3804–13

Procurement, subcontract awards by DOD contractors to small and disadvantaged business, by firm and service branch, quarterly rpt, 3542–17

Property, supply, and equipment inventory of DOD, by service branch, FY90, annual rpt, 3544–6

Radiation exposure of Navy personnel on nuclear-powered vessels and at support facilities, and injury claims, 1950s-90, annual rpt, 3804–10

Index by Subjects and Names

Radioactive waste from Navy nuclear-powered vessels and support facilities, releases in harbors, and public exposure, 1970s-90, annual rpt, 3804–11

Shipments by DOD of military and personal property, passenger traffic, and costs, by service branch and mode of transport, quarterly rpt, 3702–1

Small and disadvantaged business procurement office locations, and supply and service codes, 1990 biennial listing, 3804–5

see also Marine Corps
see also Marine Reserve
see also Naval Oceanography Command
see also Navy
see also U.S. Naval Observatory
see also terms beginning with Defense and with Military

Department of State

Budget of US, authoritative financial statements with appropriations, outlays, and receipts, by category and agency, FY90, annual rpt, 8104–2.1

Budget of US, obligations and authority by function, agency, and program, with summaries, analyses, and historical tables, FY92, annual rpt, 104–2

Drug (illegal) production, eradication, and seizures, by substance, with US aid, by country, 1987-91, annual rpt, 7004–17

Economic conditions, policy, and trade practices, by country, 1988-90, annual rpt, 21384–5

Education funding by Federal agency, program, and recipient type, and instn spending, FY80-90, annual rpt, 4824–8

Embassy and other US diplomatic facilities security improvement construction projects costs and activities, 1986-90, GAO rpt, 26123–322

Foreign countries *Background Notes*, summary social, political, and economic data, series, 7006–2

Fraud and abuse in State Dept programs, audits and investigations, 2nd half FY91, semiannual rpt, 7002–6

Helsinki Final Act implementation by NATO and Warsaw Pact, Apr 1990-Mar 1991, last issue of semiannual rpt, 7002–1

Human rights conditions in 170 countries, and US economic and military aid, 1990, annual rpt, 21384–3

Intl organizations funding by US and other countries, by organization and program, FY90, annual rpt, 7004–9

Living costs abroad, State Dept indexes, housing allowances, and hardship differentials by country and major city, quarterly rpt, 7002–7

Loan repayment status and terms by program and country, AID and predecessor agencies, quarterly rpt, 9912–3

Maritime claims and boundary agreements of coastal countries, series, 7006–8

Minority group and women employment in State Dept and Foreign Service, and hiring goals, FY89-90, biennial rpt, 7004–21

Officers of State Dept, ambassadors at large, and Chiefs of US overseas missions, by country and intl agency, 1778-1990, 7008–1

Pacific territories admin, and Palau social, economic, and govtl data, FY90, annual rpt, 7004–6

R&D funding by Fed Govt, by field, performer type, agency, and State, FY89-91, annual rpt, 9627–20

Refugee aid funding of US by program, agency, and intl organization, and admissions to US, 1980s-90, GAO rpt, 26123–334

Terrorism (intl) incidents, casualties, and attacks on US targets, by attack type and country, 1990, 7004–22

Terrorism (intl) incidents, casualties, and attacks on US targets, by attack type and world area, 1990, annual rpt, 7004–13

Treaties and other bilateral and multilateral agreements of US in force, by country, as of Jan 1991, annual listing, 7004–1

UN participation of US, and member and nonmember shares of UN budget by country, FY89-91, annual rpt, 7004–5

UN voting record and share of votes in agreement with US, by issue, country, and world area, 1990, annual rpt, 7004–18

see also Bureau for Refugee Programs, State Department

see also Bureau of Consular Affairs, State Department

see also Bureau of Intelligence and Research, State Department

see also under By Federal Agency in the "Index by Categories"

Department of Transportation

Activities of DOT by subagency, budget, and summary accident data, FY88, annual rpt, 7304–1

Air traffic, capacity, and performance, by carrier and type of operation, monthly rpt, 7302–6

Air traffic, capacity, and performance for medium regionals, by carrier, quarterly rpt, 7302–8

Air travel to and from US on US and foreign flag carriers, by country, world area, and US port, monthly rpt, 7302–2

Airline consumer complaints by reason, passengers denied boarding, and late flights, by reporting carrier and airport, monthly rpt, 7302–11

Airline deregulation in 1978, impacts on industry structure, competition, fares, finances, operations, and intl service, with data by carrier and airport, 1980s, series, 7308–199

Airline finances, by carrier, carrier group, and for total certificated system, quarterly rpt, 7302–7

Bridges repair and replacement needs under alternative assessment methods, 1990 and projected to 1996, GAO rpt, 26113–539

Budget of US, authoritative financial statements with appropriations, outlays, and receipts, by category and agency, FY90, annual rpt, 8104–2.1

Budget of US, formula grant program obligations to State and local govts, by agency, program, and State, FY92, annual rpt, 104–30

Budget of US, obligations and authority by function, agency, and program, with summaries, analyses, and historical tables, FY92, annual rpt, 104–2

Carpool high occupancy vehicle lanes use, design, enforcement, and drivers views, for California, 1988-89, 7308–203

Department of Treasury

Education funding by Federal agency, program, and recipient type, and instn spending, FY80-90, annual rpt, 4824–8

Employment of DOT, by subagency, occupation, and selected personnel characteristics, FY90, annual rpt, 7304–18

Expenditures of Fed Govt in States and local areas, by type, State, county, and city, FY90, annual rpt, 2464–3.2

Expenditures of Fed Govt in States, by type, program, agency, and State, FY90, annual rpt, 2464–2

Finances and staff of DOT, by subagency, FY90-92, annual rpt, 7304–10

Fraud and abuse in DOT programs, audits and investigations, 1st half FY91, semiannual rpt, 7302–4

Hazardous material transport accidents, casualties, and damage, by mode of transport, with DOT control activities, 1989, annual rpt, 7304–4

Mail (express parcel) shipments and revenues of private air and surface carriers, and impact of State regulation, 1976-89, 7308–201

Natl transportation system planning, use, condition, accidents, and needs, by mode of transport, 1940s-90 and projected to 2020, 7308–202

Pipeline accidents, casualties, safety enforcement activity, and Federal funding, by State, 1989, annual rpt, 7304–5

Public works condition, mgmt, R&D, and funding, for transportation and environmental projects, 1986-91, 26358–235

R&D and related funding of Fed Govt to higher education and nonprofit instns, by field, instn, agency, and State, FY89, annual rpt, 9627–17

R&D funding by Fed Govt, by field, performer type, agency, and State, FY89-91, annual rpt, 9627–20

Safety programs, and accidents, casualties, and damage, by mode of transport, 1989, annual rpt, 7304–19

Trucking industry deregulation by States, potential economic and market impacts, with background data, mid 1970s-80s, 7308–200

see also Coast Guard
see also Coast Guard Reserve
see also Federal Aviation Administration
see also Federal Highway Administration
see also Federal Railroad Administration
see also Maritime Administration
see also National Highway Traffic Safety Administration
see also St. Lawrence Seaway Development Corp.
see also Urban Mass Transportation Administration
see also under By Federal Agency in the "Index by Categories"

Department of Treasury

Banking industry structure and deposit insurance reform, findings and recommendations, with background data, 1989-90, 8008–147

Bill offerings, auction results by Fed Reserve District, and terms, periodic press release series, 8002–7

Boycotts (intl) by OPEC and other countries, US firms and shareholders cooperation and tax benefits denied, 1986, annual rpt, 8004–13

Department of Treasury

Budget of US, authoritative financial statements with appropriations, outlays, and receipts, by category and agency, FY90, annual rpt, 8104–2.1

Budget of US, obligations and authority by function, agency, and program, with summaries, analyses, and historical tables, FY92, annual rpt, 104–2

Budget of US, receipts by source and outlays by agency, final statements compared to OMB forecasts, FY91, press release, 8008–153

Competitiveness (intl) and taxation issues, with comparisons of US and foreign tax rates and revenue, 1988-91, press release, 8008–150

Depreciable assets class lives measurement, investment, and industry operations, industry rpt series, 8006–5

Education funding by Federal agency, program, and recipient type, and instn spending, FY80-90, annual rpt, 4824–8

Expenditures of Fed Govt in States, by type, program, agency, and State, FY90, annual rpt, 2464–2

Fed Govt contingent liabilities and claims paid on insured and guaranteed contracts with foreign obligors, by country and program, periodic rpt, 8002–12

Fed Govt financial operations, detailed data, *Treasury Bulletin*, quarterly rpt, 8002–4

Foreign and US economic indicators, trade balances, and exchange rates, for selected OECD and Asian countries, 1991 semiannual rpt, 8002–14

Foreign govt and private obligors debt to US, by country and program, periodic rpt, 8002–6

Govt-sponsored enterprises financial condition, capital adequacy, and impacts on Federal borrowing, with data by enterprise, 1980s-90, last issue of annual rpt, 8004–15

Hospital tax exempt status dependent on acceptance of charity, Medicare, and Medicaid cases, proposal and issues with background data, 1989, press release, 8008–149

Insurance (property and casualty) companies tax and income impacts of tax reform, with background financial data, 1970s-91, 8008–151

Money laundering investigation network of Treasury Dept, funding, and staff detailed from other agencies, 1990-91, GAO rpt, 26119–330

Pension plans (defined benefit) impacts of Omnibus Budget Reconciliation Act contribution deductibility limit, 1984-89, 8008–152

R&D funding by Fed Govt, by field, performer type, agency, and State, FY89-91, annual rpt, 9627–20

Securities (govt) purchases and holdings of individuals and households, terms, and purchase methods, 1980s-90, 8008–148

Securities and commodity trading regulatory activities and interagency coordination, FY91, annual rpt, 11924–4

Tax expenditures, Federal revenues forgone through income tax deductions and exclusions by type, FY92-96, annual rpt, 21784–10

see also Bureau of Alcohol, Tobacco and Firearms

see also Bureau of Engraving and Printing

see also Bureau of the Public Debt

see also Federal Open Market Committee

see also Financial Management Service

see also Internal Revenue Service

see also Office of the Comptroller of the Currency

see also Office of Thrift Supervision

see also U.S. Customs Service

see also U.S. Mint

see also U.S. Savings Bonds Division

see also U.S. Secret Service

see also under By Federal Agency in the "Index by Categories"

Department of Veterans Affairs

Activities and programs of VA, and veterans characteristics, FY90, annual rpt, 8604–3

Activities and programs of VA, monthly rpt, discontinued, 8602–3

Budget of US, authoritative financial statements with appropriations, outlays, and receipts, by category and agency, FY90, annual rpt, 8104–2.1

Budget of US, obligations and authority by function, agency, and program, with summaries, analyses, and historical tables, FY92, annual rpt, 104–2

Compensation and pension cases of VA, by type of entitlement and period of service, monthly rpt, 8602–5

Disability and death compensation cases of VA, by entitlement type, period of service, sex, age, and State, FY89, annual rpt, 8604–7

Education aid under GI Bill and other programs, and participation by period of service and State, FY89, annual rpt, 8604–9

Education funding by Federal agency, program, and recipient type, and instn spending, FY80-90, annual rpt, 4824–8

Employment (civilian) of Fed Govt, by work schedule, selected agency, State, and MSA, as of Dec 1990, biennial article, 9842–1.203

Expenditures for VA programs, by State, county, and congressional district, FY90, annual rpt, 8604–6

Fraud and abuse in VA programs, audits and investigations, 2nd half FY91, semiannual rpt, 8602–1

Health care for veterans, patients, visits, costs, and operating beds, by VA and contract facility, and region, quarterly rpt, 8602–4

Health care professionals of VA, by selected employment characteristics and VA district, quarterly rpt, 8602–6

Health care staff of VA, and turnover, by occupation and location, 1990, annual rpt, 8604–8

Health care staff of VA, work-years, pay rates, and benefits use and costs, by agency, FY89, annual rpt, 9844–31

Homeless veterans domiciliary program of VA, participant characteristics and outcomes, 1990 annual rpt, 8604–10

Homeless veterans with mental illness, VA program services, costs, staff, client characteristics, and outcome, 1990, annual rpt, 8604–11

Housing programs of VA, costs, terms, and user characteristics, 1985-89, 8608–7

Insurance (life) for veterans and servicepersons, actuarial analyses of VA programs, 1990, annual rpt, 8604–1

Index by Subjects and Names

Insurance (life) for veterans and servicepersons, finances and coverage by program and State, 1990, annual rpt, 8604–4

Loan guarantee operations of VA, quarterly rpt, discontinued, 8602–2

Physicians, by specialty, age, sex, and location of training and practice, 1989, State rpt series, 4116–6

Population of veterans, by period of service, age, and State, as of Mar 1991, annual rpt, 8604–12

Property acquired by Fed Govt through foreclosure and savings instn failure, 1-family homes inventory by State, acquisition costs, and sales, for 4 agencies, 1986-90, GAO rpt, 26113–513

R&D funding by Fed Govt, by field, performer type, agency, and State, FY89-91, annual rpt, 9627–20

War participants, deaths, veterans living, and compensation and pension recipients, for each US war, 1775-1990, annual rpt, 8604–2

see also Veterans Administration

see also Veterans Benefits Administration

see also Veterans Health Services and Research Administration

see also under By Federal Agency in the "Index by Categories"

Department stores

Census of Retail Trade, 1987: depreciable assets, capital and operating expenses, sales, value added, and inventories, by SIC 2- to 4-digit kind of business, 2399–2

Census of Retail Trade, 1987: finances and employment, for establishments with and without payroll, by SIC 2- to 4-digit kind of business, State, and MSA, 2401–1

Collective bargaining agreements expiring during year, and workers covered, by firm, union, industry group, and State, 1991, annual rpt, 6784–9

Construction authorized by building permits, by type of construction, region, State, and MSA, bimonthly rpt, 2042–1.3

County Business Patterns, 1988: employment, establishments, and payroll, by SIC 2- to 4-digit industry and county, annual State rpt series, 2326–6

County Business Patterns, 1989: employment, establishments, and payroll, by SIC 2- to 4-digit industry and county, annual State rpt series, 2326–8

Employment, earnings, and hours, by SIC 1- to 4-digit industry, monthly and annual averages, selected years 1909-90, annual rpt, 6744–4

Enterprise Statistics, 1987: auxiliaries of multi-establishment firms, finances and operations by function, industry, and State, 2329–6

Enterprise Statistics, 1987: finances and operations for companies, by size, level of diversification, form of organization, and industry group, 2329–8

Finances and operations, by SIC 2- to 4-digit industry, forecast 1991, annual rpt, 2044–28

Financial statements for manufacturing, mining, and trade corporations, by selected SIC 2- to 3-digit industry, quarterly rpt, 2502–1

Index by Subjects and Names

Inventory price indexes for department stores, by class of item, monthly table, 6762–7

Labor productivity, indexes of output, hours, and employment by SIC 2- to 4-digit industry, 1967-89, annual rpt, 6824–1.4

Mail volume to and from households, use, and views, by class, source, content, and household characteristics, 1987-88, annual rpt, 9864–10

Military post exchange operations, and sales by commodity, by facility and location worldwide, FY89, annual rpt, 3504–10

Occupational injury and illness rates, by SIC 2- to 4-digit industry, 1988-89, annual rpt, 6844–7

Occupational injury and illness rates, by SIC 2- to 4-digit industry, 1989, annual rpt, 6844–1

Older persons migration to southern coastal areas, household finances, services needs, and local economic impacts, for selected counties, 1990, 2068–38

Puerto Rico economic censuses, 1987: wholesale and retail trade and service industry finances and operations, by SIC 2- to 4-digit industry and municipio, 2591–1

Puerto Rico economic censuses, 1987: wholesale, retail, and service industries finances and operations, by establishment characteristics and SIC 2- and 3-digit industry, subject rpts, 2591–2

Sales and inventories, by kind of retail business, region, and selected State, MSA, and city, monthly rpt, 2413–3

Sales, inventories, purchases, gross margin, and accounts receivable, by SIC 2- to 4-digit kind of business and form of ownership, 1989, annual rpt, 2413–5

Sales of retailers, by kind of business, advance monthly rpt, 2413–2

State and Metro Area Data Book, 1991 data compilation, 2328–54

Tax (income) returns of corporations, income and tax items by asset size and detailed industry, 1987, annual rpt, 8304–4

Tax (income) returns of corporations, income and tax items by asset size and detailed industry, 1988, annual rpt, 8304–21

Tax (income) returns of corporations with foreign tax credit, income and tax items by industry group, 1986, biennial article, 8302–2.203

Tax (income) returns of partnerships, income statement and balance sheet items, by industry group, 1989, annual article, 8302–2.216; 8304–18

Tax (income) returns of sole proprietorships, income statement items, by industry group, 1989, annual article, 8302–2.214

Deportation

Cases and reviews in Federal district courts, 1990, annual rpt, 18204–8.18

Cases and reviews in Federal district courts, 1991, annual rpt, 18204–2.1

Cases of deportation, by reason, data compilation, 1991 annual rpt, 6064–6.4

Deposit insurance

Budget of US, CBO analysis and review of FY92 budget by function, annual rpt, 26304–2

Budget of US, CBO analysis of revenue and spending alternatives and projections of economic indicators, FY92-96, annual rpt, 26304–3

Budget of US, compilation of background material on fiscal and tax policy, 1960s-96, 21788–203

Budget of US, deposit insurance accounting, insurance outlays by instn type, and Bank Insurance Fund finances, late 1970s-96, 26308–100

Budget of US, House concurrent resolution, with spending and revenue targets, FY92 and projected to FY96, annual rpt, 21264–2

Budget of US, midsession review of FY92 budget, by function, annual rpt, 104–7

Budget of US, obligations and authority by function, agency, and program, with summaries, analyses, and historical tables, FY92, annual rpt, 104–2

Budget of US, Senate concurrent resolution, with spending and revenue targets, FY92, annual rpt, 25254–1

Coverage of deposits, for commercial and savings banks by State, 1989, annual rpt, 9294–4

Coverage of deposits in insured commercial and savings banks, by instn, State, MSA, and county, as of June 1990, annual regional rpt series, 9295–3

Credit unions federally insured, finances by instn characteristics and State, as of June 1991, semiannual rpt, 9532–6

Credit unions federally insured, finances, mergers, closings, and insurance fund losses and financial statements, FY90, annual rpt, 9534–7

Credit unions federally insured, finances, 1989-90, annual rpt, 9534–1

Fed Govt loans, loan guarantees, and insurance programs outstanding amounts, by agency and program, FY88-90, GAO rpt, 26111–65

Finances and potential losses of Bank Insurance Fund, 1990 hearings, 25248–125

Financial condition of banks and deposit insurance funds, potential losses, and regulatory issues, 1980s-90 and projected to 1995, 21248–147

Financial performance of banks, relation to deposit insurance value and other financial and accounting measures, 1986-87, technical paper, 9366–6.264

Intl banking competition and deposit insurance reform issues, with background data, 1990 hearings, 25248–122

OECD members bank deposit insurance programs operations, by country, 1970s-80s, technical paper, 9385–8.93

Reform of bank deposit insurance system, issues, with background industry financial data, 1970s-90, GAO rpt, 26119–320

Reform of banking system and deposit insurance, findings and recommendations, with background data, 1989-90, 8008–147

Regulation of banks and related issues, quarterly journal, 9292–4

Savings impact of proposed Federal deposit insurance limit changes, 1989 survey, hearings, 25248–121

Savings instns deposits, by SAIF insurance coverage status, 1939-89, annual rpt, 8434–3.1

Savings instns failure resolution activity of Resolution Trust Corp, assets, deposits, and assets availability and sales, periodic press release, 9722–1

Statistical Abstract of US, 1991 annual data compilation, 2324–1.16

Depository libraries

see Libraries

Deposits

see Bank deposits

see Certificates of deposit

see Negotiable orders of withdrawal accounts

see Savings

Depreciation

Airline finances, by carrier, carrier group, and for total certificated system, quarterly rpt, 7302–7

Airline operations and passenger, cargo, and mail traffic, by type of service, air carrier, State, and country, 1980-89, annual rpt, 7504–1.6

Assets (depreciable) class lives measurement, investment, and industry operations, industry rpt series, 8006–5

Assets and debts of private sector, balance sheets by segment, 1945-90, semiannual rpt, 9365–4.1

Auto, private airplane, and motorcycle operating costs by component, and Fed Govt mileage reimbursement rates, 1989, annual rpt, 9454–13

Budget of US, obligations and authority by function, agency, and program, with summaries, analyses, and historical tables, FY92, annual rpt, 104–2

Construction industries census, 1987: establishments, employment, receipts, and expenditures, by SIC 4-digit industry and State, final industry rpt series, 2373–1

Electric power plants production and capital costs, operations, and fuel use, by fuel type, plant, utility, and location, 1989, annual rpt, 3164–9

Electric utilities finances and operations, detailed data for public and privately owned firms, 1989, annual rpt, 3164–11.4

Electric utilities finances and operations, detailed data for publicly owned firms, 1989, annual rpt, 3164–24

Electric utilities privately owned, finances and operations, detailed data, 1989, annual rpt, 3164–23

Energy producers finances and operations, by energy type for US firms domestic and foreign operations, 1989, annual rpt, 3164–44.1

Enterprise Statistics, 1987: auxiliaries of multi-establishment firms, finances and operations by function, industry, and State, 2329–6

Farm income, expenses, receipts by commodity, assets, liabilities, and ratios, 1990 and trends from 1945, annual rpt, 1544–16

Fed Govt consolidated financial statements based on business accounting methods, FY89-90, annual rpt, 8104–5

Manufacturing census, 1987: finances and operations, by SIC 2- to 4-digit industry, State, and MSA, with trends from 1849, 2497–1

Multinatl firms US affiliates, finances, and operations, by industry, world area of parent firm, and State, 1988-89, annual rpt, 2704–4

Depreciation

Index by Subjects and Names

Multinatl US firms and foreign affiliates finances and operations, by industry and world area of parent firm, 1989 benchmark survey, preliminary annual rpt, 2704–5

Natl income and product accounts and components, *Survey of Current Business,* monthly rpt, 2702–1.24

Natural gas interstate pipeline company detailed financial and operating data, by firm, 1989, annual rpt, 3164–38

Nonprofit charitable organizations finances, and revenue and investments of top 10 instns, 1986-87, article, 8302–2.210

Nonprofit charitable organizations finances, by size of contributions received, 1987, article, 8302–2.218

Nursing home reimbursement by Medicaid, States payment ratesetting methods, limits, and allowances, 1988, article, 4652–1.253

Railroad (Class I) finances and operations, detailed data by firm, class of service, and district, 1989, annual rpt, 9486–6.1

Retail trade census, 1987: depreciable assets, capital and operating expenses, sales, value added, and inventories, by SIC 2- to 4-digit kind of business, 2399–2

Service industries census, 1987: depreciable assets, capital and operating expenses, and receipts, by SIC 2- to 4-digit kind of business, 2393–2

Soviet Union GNP by detailed income and outlay component, 1985, 2326–18.59

Tax (income) returns filed by type of filer, selected income items, quarterly rpt, 8302–2.1

Tax (income) returns of corporations, income and tax items by asset size and detailed industry, 1987, annual rpt, 8304–4

Tax (income) returns of corporations, income and tax items by asset size and detailed industry, 1988, annual rpt, 8304–21

Tax (income) returns of corporations, summary data by asset size and industry div, 1987, annual article, 8302–2.204

Tax (income) returns of corporations, summary data by asset size and industry div, 1988, annual article, 8302–2.215; 8302–2.217

Tax (income) returns of corporations with foreign tax credit, income and tax items by industry group, 1986, biennial article, 8302–2.203

Tax (income) returns of partnerships, income statement and balance sheet items, by industry group, 1989, annual article, 8302–2.216; 8304–18

Tax (income) returns of sole proprietorships, income statement items, by industry group, 1989, annual article, 8302–2.214

Tax expenditures, Federal revenues forgone through income tax deductions and exclusions by type, FY92-96, annual rpt, 21784–10

Telephone and telegraph firms detailed finances and operations, 1989, annual rpt, 9284–6

Telephone firms borrowing under Rural Telephone Program, and financial and operating data, by State, 1990, annual rpt, 1244–2

Truck and warehouse services finances and inventory, by SIC 2- to 4-digit industry, 1989 survey, annual rpt, 2413–14

Truck interstate carriers finances and operations, by district, 1989, annual rpt, 9486–6.2

Truck itemized costs per mile, finances, and operations, for agricultural carriers, 1990, annual rpt, 1311–15

Truck transport of fruit and vegetables, itemized costs per mile by item for fleets and owner-operator trucks, monthly table, 1272–1

TVA finances and operations by program and facility, FY90, annual rpt, 9804–32

Wholesale trade census, 1987: depreciable assets, capital and operating expenses, sales, value added, and inventories, by SIC 2- to 3-digit kind of business, 2407–2

Depressions see Business cycles

Deregulation see Government and business see Price regulation

Des Moines, Iowa Wages by occupation, for office and plant workers, 1991 survey, periodic MSA rpt, 6785–3.8 *see also* under By City and By SMSA or MSA in the "Index by Categories"

Desegregation of schools *see* Discrimination in education

Deserts and desertification *see* Arid zones

Desmarchelier, John A. "Changing Structure and Cycles in the World Sugar Industry", 1004–16.1

DeStefano, Frank "Diabetes Surveillance, 1980-87", 4205–41

Destroyers see Naval vessels

Detective and protective services Child welfare programs funding by source, and foster care program operations and client characteristics, for selected States, 1960s-95, 25368–169

County Business Patterns, 1988: employment, establishments, and payroll, by SIC 2- to 4-digit industry and county, annual State rpt series, 2326–6

County Business Patterns, 1989: employment, establishments, and payroll, by SIC 2- to 4-digit industry and county, annual State rpt series, 2326–8

Education (postsecondary) course completions, by detailed program, sex, race, and instn type, for 1972 high school class, as of 1984, 4888–4

Employee (temporary) supply establishments by occupation supplied, receipts by source, and payroll, by MSA, 1987 Census of Service Industries, 2393–4.8

Employment, earnings, and hours, by SIC 1- to 4-digit industry, monthly and annual averages, selected years 1909-90, annual rpt, 6744–4

Employment, unemployment, and labor force characteristics, by region and census div, 1990, annual rpt, 6744–7.1

Franchise business opportunities by firm and kind of business, and sources of aid and info, 1990 annual listing, 2104–7

Manufacturing employment, by detailed occupation and SIC 2-digit industry, 1989 survey, triennial rpt, 6748–52

Marshals Service activities, FY89, annual rpt, 6294–1

Nuclear weapons facilities of DOE, contract security forces skill deficiencies, and costs compared to Federal security, late 1980s, GAO rpt, 26113–493

Older persons abuse and neglect by circumstances and characteristics of abuser and victim, and States protective services budgets and staff, by location, 1980s, hearing, 21148–62

Puerto Rico economic censuses, 1987: wholesale and retail trade and service industry finances and operations, by SIC 2- to 4-digit industry and municipio, 2591–1

Receipts for services, by SIC 2- to 4-digit kind of business, 1990, annual rpt, 2413–8

Senate receipts, itemized expenses by payee, and balances, 1st half FY91, semiannual listing, 25922–1

Service industries census, 1987: establishments, receipts by source, payroll, and employment, by SIC 2- to 4-digit kind of business, State, and MSA, 2393–4

Soviet Union GNP by detailed income and outlay component, 1985, 2326–18.59

State and local govt employment of minorities and women, by occupation, function, pay level, and State, 1990, annual rpt, 9244–6

see also Campus security

see also Security devices

Detention

see Arrest

see Correctional institutions

see Habeas corpus

see Juvenile detention and correctional institutions

see Pretrial detention and release

see Prisoners

Detergent industry *see* Soap and detergent industry

Detroit, Mich.

Auto and auto parts manufacturing wages, employment, and benefits, by occupation, region, and selected labor market area, 1989 survey, 6787–6.252

Cancer cases, by race, income, education, and area population density, for 3 metro areas, 1978-82, article, 4472–1.210

CPI by component for US city average, and by region, population size, and for 15 metro areas, monthly rpt, 6762–1

CPI by component for US city average, and by region, population size, and for 27 metro areas, monthly rpt, 6762–2

Drug abuse indicators for selected metro areas, research results, data collection, and policy issues, 1991 semiannual conf, 4492–5

Drug test results at arrest, by drug type, offense, and sex, for selected urban areas, quarterly rpt, 6062–3

Financial instns location relation to ZIP code area income and minority population, by instn type for 5 cities, 1977-89, article, 9377–1.208

Fruit and vegetable shipments, and arrivals in US and Canada cities, by mode of transport and State and country of origin, 1990, annual rpt, 1311–4.1

Index by Subjects and Names

Diabetes

Pollution (air) emissions and levels in Detroit area, by pollutant, 1980-90, 14648–25

Runaway and other youth services programs cases, and school dropouts, for Detroit, 1980s, hearing, 25418–5

Wages by occupation, for office and plant workers, 1990 survey, periodic MSA rpt, 6785–11.4

see also under By City and By SMSA or MSA in the "Index by Categories"

Deutsch, Melinda

"Comments on the Evaluation of Policy Models", 9366–7.267

Devaney, Barbara

"Savings in Medicaid Costs for Newborns and Their Mothers from Prenatal Participation in the WIC Program", rpt, 9904–4 1368–2

Developing countries

- Agricultural and economic conditions in developing countries, and agricultural exports of US, effects of US aid, 1989 conf papers, 1548–372
- Agricultural exports of high-value commodities from developing countries to OECD, 1970s-87, 1528–316
- Agricultural exports of high-value commodities, indexes and sales by commodity, world area, and country, 1960s-86, 1528–323
- Agricultural production, prices, and trade, by country, 1960s-90, annual world area rpt, 1524–4.2
- Agricultural research investment impacts on productivity, indicators for developed and developing countries, late 1960s-80, 1528–318
- Agricultural supply, demand, and market for US exports, with socioeconomic conditions, country rpt series, 1526–6
- Agricultural trade of US, by commodity and country, bimonthly rpt, 1522–1
- Agricultural trade of US, by detailed commodity and country, 1989, annual rpt, 1524–8
- Agricultural trade of US, by detailed commodity and country, 1990, semiannual rpt, 1522–4
- AID dev projects and socioeconomic impacts, evaluation rpt series, 9916–1
- AID dev projects, special study series, 9916–3
- AID economic aid to developing countries, obligations and disbursements by country, quarterly rpt, 9912–4
- AID loans repayment status and terms by program and country, and status of predecessor agency loans, quarterly rpt, 9912–3
- AIDS virus infection prevalence in developing countries, by sex, selected city, urban-rural location, and country, 1991, semiannual rpt, 2322–4
- Bank deposits in foreign banks, for 7 heavily indebted developing countries, 1982-89, technical paper, 9385–8.109
- Capital intl market financial data by firm, and Intl Finance Corp finances, by country, 1990 hearing, 21248–149
- Child health and welfare indicators, and economic conditions, for developing countries, 1950s-80s, hearing, 25388–57
- Debt burden and related indicators for developing countries, by country and for 9 US money-center banks, 1960s-89, article, 9292–4.201

Debt of developing countries, and IMF credit outstanding, by world area and country, 1984-90, 9118–11

- Economic aid of US, bilateral and through intl dev banks, by program and world region, 1990 annual rpt, 9904–1
- Economic aid programs of US, and developing countries economic and fiscal condition, impacts of counterpart funds, literature review, 1991 rpt, 9918–21
- Economic and military aid and loans from US and intl agencies, by program and country, FY46-90, annual rpt, 9914–5
- Economic and social conditions of developing countries from 1960s, and Intl Dev Cooperation Agency and AID activities and funding, FY90-92, annual rpt, 9904–4
- Economic conditions in USSR, Eastern Europe, OECD, and selected other countries, 1960s-90, annual rpt, 9114–4
- Economic, population, and agricultural data, US and other aid sources, and AID activity, country rpt series, 9916–12
- Energy use in developing countries, and economic and environmental impacts, by fuel type, world area, and country, 1980s-90, 26358–232
- Exports and imports of US, by selected country, country group, and commodity group, 1990, annual rpt, 2044–37
- Exports and imports of US, by world area, periodic pamphlet, 2042–25
- Family planning and population activities of AID, grants by project and recipient, and contraceptive shipments, by country, FY90, annual rpt series, 9914–13
- Food supply, needs, and aid for developing countries, status and alternative forecasts, world area rpt series, 1526–8
- Global climate change economic impacts, projected to 2100 with background data for 1980s, 3028–5
- Global warming contributing air pollutants, US and foreign emissions and control measures, 1980s and projected to 2020, 26358–233
- Grain production and needs, and related economic outlook, by world area and selected country, forecast 1990/91-1991/92, 1528–313
- Imports of US given duty-free treatment for value of US material sent abroad, by commodity and country, 1989, annual rpt, 9884–14
- Inflation control programs of developing countries using exchange rate policies, evaluation, 1980s-91, technical paper, 9366–7.256
- Investment (foreign direct) of US, by industry group and world area, 1987-90, annual article, 2702–1.220
- Labor standards in developing countries, impacts on social and economic dev, 1988 conf papers, 6368–9
- Loans and other funding from intl financial instns by source and disbursements by purpose, by country, with US policy review, FY89, annual rpt, 15344–1
- Loans of US banks to foreigners at all US and foreign offices, by country group and country, quarterly rpt, 13002–1
- Military spending and imports of developing countries, measures to determine eligibility for US economic aid, by country, 1986-87, annual rpt, 9914–1

Multinatl US firms and foreign affiliates finances and operations, by industry and world area of parent firm, 1989 benchmark survey, preliminary annual rpt, 2704–5

- Multinatl US firms and foreign affiliates finances and operations, by industry of parent firm and affiliate, world area, and selected country, 1989, annual article, 2702–1.225
- Oils, oilseeds, and meal imports, by commodity, world area of destination, and major producer, 1960s-88, 1528–314
- Older persons in developing countries, population and selected characteristics, 1980s and projected to 2020, country rpt series, 2326–19
- Overseas Private Investment Corp finances and activities, with list of insured projects and firms, FY90, annual rpt, 9904–2
- Peace Corps activities, funding by program, and volunteers, by country, FY92, annual rpt, 9654–1
- PL 480 food aid impacts on developing countries economic dev, literature review, 1979-88, 9918–20
- Rice production, trade, stocks, and use, by world region, country, and country group, 1966/67-1989/90, FAS circular, 1925–2.6
- *Statistical Abstract of US*, 1991 annual data compilation, 2324–1.31
- *see also* under By Foreign Country in the "Index by Categories"
- *see also* under names of individual countries

Development Associates, Inc.

"Handbook of Effective Migrant Education Practices", 4808–22

DeVilbiss, John M.

"Draft Economic Diversity and Dependency Assessment, Rocky Mountain Region", 1208–362

Dewees, Christopher M.

- "Competing for the Recreational Dollar: An Analysis of the California Commercial Passenger-Carrying Fishing Vessel Industry", 2162–1.202
- "Increasing the Use of Underutilized Fish and Fishing Opportunities by California Anglers: The Use of Onboard Refrigeration and New Marketing Strategies", 2168–125

Diabetes

- Cases, deaths, and hospitalization, for diabetes and complications, by age, sex, race, State, and region, 1980-86, annual rpt, 4205–41
- Deaths and rates, by cause and age, preliminary 1989-90, US Vital Statistics annual rpt, 4144–7
- Deaths and rates, by cause, provisional data, monthly rpt, 4142–1.2
- Deaths and rates, by detailed cause and demographic characteristics, 1988 and trends from 1900, US Vital Statistics annual rpt, 4144–2
- Glucose blood levels home monitoring by diabetics, and factors affecting results, 1990 rpt, 4068–71
- Health condition and health care resources, use, and spending, 1950s-89, annual data compilation, 4144–11
- Health maintenance organizations Medicare enrollees quality of care indicators compared to fee-for-service, demonstration projects results, mid 1980s, 4658–46

Diabetes

Health-related behaviors, weight, and body mass, for diabetics, by level of physical exercise, 1991 article, 4042–3.246

Indian and Alaska Native disease and disorder cases, deaths, and health services use, by tribe, reservation, and Indian Health Service area, late 1950s-86, 4088–2

Indian Health Service facilities and use, and Indian health and other characteristics, by IHS region, 1980s-89, annual chartbook, 4084–7

Indian Health Service facilities, funding, operations, and Indian health and other characteristics, 1950s-90, annual chartbook, 4084–1

Indians and Alaska Natives chronic disease prevalence, for 8 conditions by age and sex, 1987, 4186–8.20

Insulin infusion pumps for continuous therapy, risks and benefit evaluation for Medicare coverage, 1991 rpt, 4186–10.4

Ketoacidosis cases among diabetics, deaths, and hospitalization, by age, sex, race, State, and region, 1980-86, annual rpt, 4205–41

Kidney end-stage disease cases, treatment, outcomes, and characteristics of patients, organ donors, and facilities, late 1970s-88, annual rpt, 4474–37

Kidney end-stage disease treatment facilities, Medicare enrollment and reimbursement, survival, and patient characteristics, 1983-89, annual rpt, 4654–16

Kidney transplants, needs, costs, payment sources, and impact of immunosuppressive drugs on outcome, 1950s-87 and projected to 1995, 4658–59

Minority group health condition, services use, costs, and indicators of services need, 1950s-88, 4118–55

Preventive disease and health improvement goals and recommended activities for 2000, with trends 1970s-80s, 4048–10

Research and care services for diabetes, programs and funding by Federal agency and NIH inst, FY90, annual rpt, 4474–34

State and Metro Area Data Book, 1991 data compilation, 2328–54

see also under By Disease in the "Index by Categories"

Diamonds

see Gemstones

Diamonds, industrial

see Abrasive materials

Diatomite

see Nonmetallic minerals and mines

Dichter, Phyllis

"Child Survival in Indonesia", 9916–1.73

Dicker, Marvin

"Determinants of Total Family Charges for Health Care: U.S., 1980", 4146–12.27

Dickey, David A.

"Primer on Cointegration with an Application to Money and Income", 9391 1.210

Dickey, Lynn E.

"Composition of Foods. 1990 Supplement: Raw, Processed, Prepared", 1356–3.15

Dicofol

see Pesticides

Dictionaries

see Glossaries

Diebold, Francis X.

"Further Evidence on Business Cycle Duration Dependence", 9387–8.250

Diesel fuel

Agriculture census, 1987: farms, farmland, production, finances, and operator characteristics, by county, final State rpt series, 2331–1

Auto fuel economy test results for US and foreign makes, 1992 model year, annual rpt, 3304–11

Consumption and tax rates for motor fuel, by fuel type and State, monthly rpt, quarterly data, 7552–1

Farm diesel and other fuel costs, impacts of oil price increases, 1989, article, 1541–1.203

Farm prices received and paid, by commodity and State, 1990, annual rpt, 1629–5

Farm prices received for major products and paid for farm inputs and living items, by commodity and State, monthly rpt, 1629–1

Farm production inputs supply, demand, and prices, 1970s-90 and projected to 1995, article, 1561–16.201

Farm production inputs supply, demand, and prices, 1980s-91 and forecast 1992, article, 1561–16.204

Farm production itemized costs, by farm sales size and region, 1990, annual rpt, 1614–3

Fed Govt energy use and efficiency, by agency and fuel type, FY90, annual rpt, 3304–22

Foreign and US oil prices, by refined product and country, 1980-89, annual rpt, 3164–50.6

Injuries from use of consumer products, by severity, victim age, and detailed product, 1990, annual rpt, 9164–6

Pollution (air) contributing to global warming, emissions factors and control costs, by pollutant and source, 1990 rpt, 9198–124

Pollution (air) levels for 6 pollutants, by source, 1970-89 and trends from 1940, annual rpt, 9194–13

Price indexes (producer), by stage of processing and detailed commodity, monthly rpt, 6762–6

Price indexes (producer), by stage of processing and detailed commodity, monthly 1990, annual rpt, 6764–2

Prices and spending for fuel, by type, end-use sector, and State, 1989, annual rpt, 3164–64

Prices and volume of oil products sold and purchased by refiners, processors, and distributors, by product, end-use sector, PAD district, and State, monthly rpt with articles, 3162–11

Prices of wholesale and retail No 2 diesel oil, monthly rpt, 3162–24.9

Sales and deliveries of fuel oil and kerosene, by end-use, PAD district, and State, 1989, annual rpt, 3164–94

Tax (excise) collections of IRS, by source, quarterly rpt, 8302–1

Tax (excise) rates for motor fuels, by State, 1980-89, annual table, 7554–32

Index by Subjects and Names

Tax provisions of States for motor fuel, auto registration fees, and disposition of receipts, by State, as of Jan 1991, biennial rpt, 7554–37

Taxes on energy, economic and energy demand impacts of alternative taxation methods, projected 1991-2000, 3166–6.57

Transit systems finances and operations, by mode of transport, size of fleet, and for 468 systems, 1989, annual rpt, 7884–4

Transportation energy use by mode, fuel supply, and demographic and economic factors of vehicle use, 1970s-89, annual rpt, 3304–5

Diet

see Food consumption

see Nutrition and malnutrition

see Vitamins and nutrients

Dietitians and nutritionists

Education in science and engineering, grad programs enrollment by field, source of funds, and characteristics of student and instn, 1975-89, annual rpt, 9627–7

Hospices operations, services, costs, and patient characteristics, for instns without Medicare certification, FY85-86, 4658–52

Indian Health Service facilities, funding, operations, and Indian health and other characteristics, 1950s-90, annual chartbook, 4084–1

Military health care personnel, and accessions by training source, by occupation, specialty, and service branch, FY89, annual rpt, 3544–24

VA health care staff and turnover, by occupation, physician specialty, and location, 1990, annual rpt, 8604–8

VA Medicine and Surgery Dept trainees, by detailed program and city, FY90, annual rpt, 8704–4

Digestive diseases

Agent Orange exposure of Vietnam veterans, and other factors relation to dev of rare cancers, 1984-88, 4208–33

Cancer (colon) risk relation to serum cholesterol levels, 1965-89 local area study, article, 4472–1.226

Cancer (colorectal) and polyps risk relation to occupational asbestos exposure, 1986-88 local area study, article, 4472–1.238

Cancer (colorectal) risk related to intake of fat, fiber, and carbohydrates, for Sha Giao, PRC, and San Francisco Chinese, 1991 article, 4472–1.201

Cancer (colorectal) risk relation to physical activity level, 1960s-88, article, 4472–1.222

Cancer (gastric) risk by presence of *Helicobacter pylori* bacteria in digestive tract, 1985-89 local area study, article, 4472–1.211

Cancer (gastric) risk relation to *Helicobacter pylori* infection, 1982-89 study, article, 4472–1.236

Cancer (hepatic) among steroids users, cases and deaths, 1960s-88, conf papers, 4498–67

Cancer (hepatocellular) risk relation to hepatitis infection, race, smoking, drinking, and oral contraceptives and estrogen use, 1984-90 local area study, article, 4472–1.237

Index by Subjects and Names

Cancer (large-bowel) risk related to nonsteroidal anti-inflammatory drug use, 1977-88 local area study, article, 4472–1.205

Cancer cases, deaths, and survival rates, by sex, race, age, and body site, 1973-88, annual rpt, 4474–35

Cancer death rates of minorities, by body site, age, sex, and substate area, 1950s-80, atlas, 4478–78

Cancer death risk relation to smoking by body site, and compared to other smoking-related diseases, by sex, 1960s-91, article, 4472–1.219

Cancer death, survival, and incidence rates, by type and body site, 1974 and 1986, article, 4472–1.232

Cancer deaths and rates, by body site, provisional data, monthly rpt, 4142–1.2

Cases of acute and chronic conditions, disability, absenteeism, and health services use, by selected characteristics, 1987, CD-ROM, 4147–10.177

Cirrhosis of liver deaths, by age, sex, race, and whether alcohol involved, 1987 and trends from 1910, 4486–1.10

Colon polyps cases and risk, effects of body mass, 1986-88 local area study, article, 4472–1.206

Deaths and rates, by cause and age, preliminary 1989-90, US Vital Statistics annual rpt, 4144–7

Deaths and rates, by cause, provisional data, monthly rpt, 4142–1.2

Deaths and rates, by detailed cause and demographic characteristics, 1988 and trends from 1900, US Vital Statistics annual rpt, 4144–2

Gastroenteritis outbreaks, specimen collection and diagnosis procedures, CDC guidelines, 1990 rpt, 4206–2.32

Health condition and health care resources, use, and spending, 1950s-89, annual data compilation, 4144–11

HHS financial aid, by program, recipient, State, and city, FY90, annual regional listings, 4004–3

Hospital deaths of Medicare patients, actual and expected rates by diagnosis, with hospital characteristics, by instn, FY87-89, annual regional rpt series, 4654–14

Hospital discharges and length of stay, by diagnosis, patient and instn characteristics, procedure performed, and payment source, 1988, annual rpt, 4147–13.107

Hospital discharges and length of stay by region and diagnosis, and procedures performed, by age and sex, 1989, annual rpt, 4146–8.198

Hospital discharges by detailed diagnostic and procedure category, primary diagnosis, and length of stay, by age, sex, and region, 1988, annual rpt, 4147–13.105; 4147–13.108

Incontinence among nursing home residents, by age and sex, 1987, 4186–8.11

Incontinence among nursing home residents with mental disorders, by resident and instn characteristics, 1985, 4147–13.106

Indian and Alaska Native disease and disorder cases, deaths, and health services use, by tribe, reservation, and Indian Health Service area, late 1950s-86, 4088–2

Indian Health Service facilities and use, and Indian health and other characteristics, by IHS region, 1980s-89, annual chartbook, 4084–7

Indian Health Service facilities, funding, operations, and Indian health and other characteristics, 1950s-90, annual chartbook, 4084–1

Indian Health Service, tribal, and contract facilities hospitalization, by diagnosis, age, sex, and service area, FY89, annual rpt, 4084–5

Indians and Alaska Natives chronic disease prevalence, for 8 conditions by age and sex, 1987, 4186–8.20

Minority group health condition, services use, costs, and indicators of services need, 1950s-88, 4118–55

State and Metro Area Data Book, 1991 data compilation, 2328–54

Ulcer treatment drug (ranitidine hydrochloride), impact of temporary import duty suspension on US competition, 1991 rpt, 9886–4.167

see also under By Disease in the "Index by Categories"

DiGiovanni, Dawn M.

"Biomass Statistics for Maryland, 1986", 1206–43.3

"Forest Statistics for New Jersey, 1987", 1206–12.14

"Forest Statistics for West Virginia, 1975 and 1989", 1206–12.13

"Forest Wildlife Habitat Statistics for Maryland and Delaware, 1986", 1206–44.5

Dill, Linda M.

"Decline in Establishment Reporting: Impact on CWHS Industrial and Geographic Data", 4742–1.203

Dillard, Fay B.

"U.S. Natural Gas Imports and Exports, 1990", 3162–4.208

DiLullo, Anthony J.

"U.S. International Sales and Purchases of Services: U.S. Cross-Border Transactions, 1987-90, and Sales by Affiliates, 1988-89", 2702–1.223

Dinkins, Julia M.

"Housing Expenditures for Never-Married Men: A Focus on One-Person Consumer Units", 1702–1.208

"Money Contributions to Religion, Charity, Education, and Politics", 1702–1.214

Dioxins

Agent Orange exposure of Vietnam veterans, and other factors relation to dev of rare cancers, 1984-88, 4208–33

Air pollution emissions factors, by detailed pollutant and source, data compilation, 1990 rpt, 9198–120

Detroit metro area air pollution emissions and levels, by pollutant, 1980-90, 14648–25

Industrial wastewater pollution releases, levels, treatment, costs, and regulation, with background financial and operating data, industry rpt series, 9206–4

Diphtheria

see Infective and parasitic diseases

Diplomacy

see Diplomatic and consular service

see Foreign relations

Direct marketing

Diplomatic and consular service

Congressional Directory, members of 102nd Congress, other officials, elections, and districts, 1991-92, biennial rpt, 23874–1

Developing countries economic and social conditions from 1960s, and Intl Dev Cooperation Agency and AID activities and funding, FY90-92, annual rpt, 9904–4

Embassy and other US diplomatic facilities security improvement construction projects costs and activities, 1986-90, GAO rpt, 26123–322

Employment (civilian) of Fed Govt, work-years, pay rates, and benefits use and costs, by agency, FY89, annual rpt, 9844–31

Employment and payroll (civilian) of Fed Govt, by pay system, agency, and location, 1990, annual rpt, 9844–6

Living costs abroad, State Dept indexes, housing allowances, and hardship differentials by country and major city, quarterly rpt, 7002–7

Minority group and women employment in State Dept and Foreign Service, and hiring goals, FY89-90, biennial rpt, 7004–21

Officers of State Dept, ambassadors at large, and Chiefs of US overseas missions, by country and intl agency, 1778-1990, 7008–1

Terrorism (intl) incidents, casualties, and attacks on US targets, by attack type and country, 1990, annual rpt, 7004–22

Terrorism (intl) incidents, casualties, and attacks on US targets, by attack type and world area, 1990, annual rpt, 7004–13

UN participation of US, and member and nonmember shares of UN budget by country, FY89-91, annual rpt, 7004–5

Visas of US issued and refused to immigrants and nonimmigrants, by class, issuing office, and nationality, FY89, annual rpt, 7184–1

Direct marketing

Census of Retail Trade, 1987: finances and employment, for establishments with and without payroll, by SIC 2- to 4-digit kind of business, State, and MSA, 2401–1

Computer use at home, school, and work, by purpose and selected user characteristics, 1989, Current Population Rpt, 2546–2.158

County Business Patterns, 1988: employment, establishments, and payroll, by SIC 2- to 4-digit industry and county, annual State rpt series, 2326–6

County Business Patterns, 1989: employment, establishments, and payroll, by SIC 2- to 4-digit industry and county, annual State rpt series, 2326–8

Drug (prescription) mail service industry structure, finances, and operations, 1989 survey, 4658–60

Employment, earnings, and hours, by SIC 1- to 4-digit industry, monthly and annual averages, selected years 1909-90, annual rpt, 6744–4

Mail volume to and from households, use, and views, by class, source, content, and household characteristics, 1987-88, annual rpt, 9864–10

Military post exchange operations, and sales by commodity, by facility and location worldwide, FY89, annual rpt, 3504–10

Direct marketing

Puerto Rico economic censuses, 1987: wholesale and retail trade and service industry finances and operations, by SIC 2- to 4-digit industry and municipio, 2591–1

Sales and inventories, by kind of retail business, region, and selected State, MSA, and city, monthly rpt, 2413–3

Sales, inventories, purchases, gross margin, and accounts receivable, by SIC 2- to 4-digit kind of business and form of ownership, 1989, annual rpt, 2413–5

Sales of retailers, by kind of business, advance monthly rpt, 2413–2

Service industries census, 1987: establishments, receipts by source, payroll, and employment, by SIC 2- to 4-digit kind of business, State, and MSA, 2393–4

Service industries receipts, by SIC 2- to 4-digit kind of business, 1990, annual rpt, 2413–8

Tax (income) returns of sole proprietorships, income statement items, by industry group, 1989, annual article, 8302–2.214

Directories

- Advisory committees of Fed Govt, and members, staff, meetings, and costs by agency, FY90, annual rpt, 9454–18
- Agricultural production, trade, and policies in foreign countries, summary data by country, 1989-90, annual factbook, 1924–12
- Agricultural research and education grants, USDA competitive awards by program and recipient, FY90, annual listing, 1764–1
- Agricultural research grants of USDA, by program, subagency, and country, FY90, annual listing, 1954–3
- Airport planning and dev project grants of FAA, by airport and location, quarterly press release, 7502–14
- Alcohol, Drug Abuse and Mental Health Admin research grants and awards, by recipient, FY90, annual listing, 4044–13
- Allergy and Infectious Diseases Natl Inst activities, grants by recipient and location, and disease cases, FY83-90, annual rpt, 4474–30
- Appalachia local dev projects, and funding by source, by program and State, FY90, annual rpt, 9084–1
- Arts Natl Endowment activities and grants, FY90, annual rpt, 9564–3
- Assistance (financial and nonfinancial) of Fed Govt, and agency regional and local offices, 1991 base edition with supplements, annual listing, 104–5
- Astronomical tables, time conversion factors, and listing of observatories worldwide, 1992, annual rpt, 3804–7
- Attorneys general of US and Canada, 1990 listing, 4208–34
- Auto and auto equipment recalls for safety-related defects, by make, monthly listing, 7762–12
- Auto and auto equipment recalls for safety-related defects, by make, quarterly listing, 7762–2
- Boats (recreational) and engines recalls for safety-related defects, by make, periodic listing, 7402–5
- Cell cultures with genetic abnormalities, availability and cultures shipped, 1990-91, biennial listing, 4474–23

Census Bur State data centers and support agencies, 1991 annual listing, 2304–2

Child and maternal health programs of major urban health depts, activities and budgets, 1990, listing, 4108–51

Coal distribution firms and producing districts served, quarterly rpt, annual listing, 3162–8

Congressional Directory, members of 102nd Congress, other officials, elections, and districts, 1991-92, biennial rpt, 23874–1

Construction and building materials trade and professional assns, and labor unions, 1991 listing, article, 2042–1.202

Consumer Product Safety Commission activities, by brand, and casualties and medical costs, by product type, FY89, annual rpt, 9164–2

Containers (intermodal) and equipment owned by shipping and leasing companies, inventory by type and size, 1990, annual rpt, 7704–10

Credit unions assets, members, and location, 1991 annual listing, 9534–6

DC metro area land acquisition and dev projects of Fed Govt, characteristics and funding by agency and project, FY91-95, annual rpt, 15454–1

Death investigation systems of US and Canada, jurisdictions, medical officers qualifications, types of deaths covered, and related statutes, 1990 listing, 4208–34

Dental Research Natl Inst research and training grants, by recipient, FY89, annual listing, 4474–19

DOD budget, organization, personnel, weapons, and property, by service branch, State, and country, 1991 annual summary rpt, 3504–13

DOD contractor subcontract awards to small and disadvantaged business, by firm and service branch, quarterly rpt, 3542–17

DOD prime contract awards for R&D, for top 500 contractors, FY90, annual listing, 3544–4

DOD prime contract awards for R&D to US and foreign nonprofit instns and govt agencies, by instn and location, FY90, annual listing, 3544–17

DOE R&D projects and funding at natl labs, universities, and other instns, periodic summary rpt series, 3004–18

Drug (prescription) mail service industry structure, finances, and operations, 1989 survey, 4658–60

Drug abuse and trafficking reduction grant programs and funding, by Federal agency and State, FY90-92, 236–1.5

Economic Dev Admin activities, and funding by program, recipient, State, and county, FY90 and cumulative from FY66, annual rpt, 2064–2

Education (early childhood) for handicapped children, project descriptions, 1990/91, annual listing, 4944–10

Education (special) programs and funding of States, project listing, 1989/90, annual rpt, 4944–4

Education data collection activities and programs of NCES, 1991, annual listing, 4824–7

Education Dept financial aid programs, 1991 annual listing, 4804–3

Index by Subjects and Names

Education Dept programs funding, operations, and effectiveness, FY90, annual rpt, 4804–5

Education funding of Fed Govt, and enrollment, degrees, and program grants and fellowships by State, for Indians, late 1960s-FY89, annual rpt, 14874–1

Educational projects, activities, and funding for homeless children, FY90, annual rpt, 4804–35

Electric power plants and capacity, by fuel used, owner, location, and operating status, 1990 and for units planned 1991-2000, annual listing, 3164–36

Electric power plants financed by REA, with location, capacity, and owner, as of Jan 1991, annual listing, 1244–6

Electric power plants production and capital costs, operations, and fuel use, by fuel type, plant, utility, and location, 1989, annual rpt, 3164–9

Energy (hydrogen) R&D activity and funding of DOE, and project listing, FY90, annual rpt, 3304–18

Energy conservation aid of Fed Govt to public and nonprofit private instns, by building type and State, 1990, annual rpt, 3304–15

Energy-related inventions recommended by Natl Inst of Standards and Technology for DOE support, awards, and evaluation status, 1990, annual listing, 2214–5

Engineering research and education grants of NSF, FY90, annual listing, 9624–24

Environmental and wildlife conservation intl agreements provisions, status, and signatories, as of 1991, listing, 9886–4.169

EPA R&D programs and funding, FY90, annual listing, 9184–18

Exchange and training programs of Federal agencies, participants by world area, and funding, by program, FY89, annual rpt, 9854–8

Exports and imports of US, by Harmonized System 6-digit commodity and country, 1990, annual rpt, 2424–13

Exports of US, detailed Schedule B commodities with countries of destination, 1990, annual rpt, 2424–10

Fertilizer production capacity by firm, for US and Canada, 1986-91 and projected to 1997, triennial rpt, 9808–66

Fish and shellfish foreign market conditions for US products, country rpt series, 2166–19

Fish and Wildlife Service restoration programs funding, land purchases, and project listing, by State, FY89, annual rpt, 5504–1

Fish Hatchery Natl System activities and deliveries, by species, hatchery, and jurisdiction of waters stocked, FY90, annual rpt, 5504–10

Fishery mgmt and R&D, Fed Govt grants by project and State, and rpts, 1990, annual listing, 2164–3

Fishery research of State fish and wildlife agencies, federally funded projects and costs by species and State, 1990, annual listing, 5504–23

Foreign govt Chiefs of State and Cabinet members, by country, bimonthly listing, 9112–4

Index by Subjects and Names

Directories

Foreign trade zones (US) operations and movement of goods, by zone and commodity, FY88, annual rpt, 2044–30

Franchise business opportunities by firm and kind of business, and sources of aid and info, 1990 annual listing, 2104–7

Geographic gazetteer of US places, mountains, bodies of water, and other political and physical features, 1990 rpt, 5668–117

Global climate change trends and contributing gases levels, Federal and intl data collection activities, mgmt, and inventory, 1990 rpt, 3028–4

Hazardous waste site remedial action under Superfund, current and proposed sites descriptions and status, periodic listings, series, 9216–3

Hazardous waste site remedial action under Superfund, current and proposed sites priority ranking and status by location, series, 9216–5

Hazardous waste site remedial action under Superfund, EPA records of decision by site, FY89, annual rpt, 9214–5

Health Care Financing Admin research activities and grants, by program, FY90, annual listing, 4654–10

Health Care Policy and Research Agency grants, by recipient and location, FY90, 4186–9.10

Heart, Lung, and Blood Natl Inst activities, and grants by recipient and location, FY90 and disease trends from 1940, annual rpt, 4474–15

HHS financial aid, by program, recipient, State, and city, FY90, annual regional listings, 4004–3

HHS research and evaluation programs, 1970-90, annual listing, 4004–30

Homeless adults educational services, funding, participation, and staff, by State, 1989, annual rpt series, 4804–39

Humanities Natl Endowment activities and grants, FY90, annual rpt, 9564–2

Hydroelectric power plants licensed by FERC, characteristics and location, as of Oct 1991, annual listing, 3084–11

Kidney end-stage disease research of CDC and HCFA, project listing, 1990, annual rpt, 4654–16

Labor surplus areas eligible for preferential Fed Govt contracts, monthly listing, 6402–1

Labor unions and employer organizations in foreign countries, listing, annual country rpt series, 6366–4

Labor unions reporting to Labor Dept, parent bodies and locals by location, 1990 listing, 6468–17

Libraries (depository) for Federal publications, 1991 annual listing, 2214–1

Libraries (major urban resource centers) dev projects and funding, by city and State, FY84-88, listing, 4878–4

Libraries (public) English as second language programs and services, project descriptions and funding, by State, FY87, annual rpt, 4874–10

Libraries for blind and handicapped, readership, circulation, staff, funding, and holdings, FY90, annual listing, 26404–3

Libraries technological aid, project descriptions and funding, FY89, annual listing, 4874–6

Library science training grants for disadvantaged students, by instn and State, FY90, annual listing, 4874–1

Lumber and wood products export market dev, assn listing, FAS quarterly circular, supplement, 1925–36

Marine mammals research, Federal funding by topic, recipient, and agency, FY90, annual rpt, 14734–2

Meat plants inspected and certified for exporting to US, by country, 1990, annual listing, 1374–2

Medicare and Medicaid carriers and State offices, listing, 1990 biennial rpt, 4654–1

Mental health care services, staffing, research, and training programs in VA facilities, 1991 biennial listing, 8704–2

Military post exchange operations, and sales by commodity, by facility and location worldwide, FY89, annual rpt, 3504–10

Mineral Industry Surveys, commodity reviews of production, trade, use, and industry operations, advance annual rpt series, 5614–5

Museum Services Inst activities and finances, and grants by recipient, FY90, annual rpt, 9564–7

NASA R&D funding to higher education instns, by field, instn, and State, FY90, annual listing, 9504–7

Navy small and disadvantaged business procurement office locations, and supply and service codes, 1990 biennial listing, 3804–5

NIH grants for R&D, training, construction, and medical libraries, by location and recipient, FY90, annual listings, 4434–7

NSF grants and contracts, by field, instn, and State, FY89, annual rpt, 9624–26

NSF R&D grant awards, by div and program, periodic rpt series, 9626–7

Nuclear engineering and science educational facilities, student aid, and degrees granted, by instn, 1990, 3008–126

Nuclear reactors for domestic use and export by function and operating status, with owner, operating characteristics, and location, 1990 annual listing, 3354–15

Occupational safety and health research and demonstration grants by State, and project listing, FY90, annual rpt, 4244–2

Oil and gas field codes and locations, 1990, annual listing, 3164–70

Oil and gas OCS reserves, and leasing and dev activity, periodic regional rpt series, 5736–3

Oil enhanced recovery research contracts of DOE, project summaries, funding, and bibl, quarterly rpt, 3002–14

Overseas Business Reports: economic conditions, investment and export opportunities, and trade practices, country market research rpt series, 2046–6

Paternity determination through genetic testing, labs, services, and costs, 1991 listing, 4698–4

Pesticide manufacturers, and State regulatory agencies, 1989 annual listing, 1804–5

Population and reproduction research, Fed Govt funding by project, FY89, annual listing, 4474–9

Poultry Natl Improvement Plan participating hatcheries and birds, by species and disease program, 1991, annual listing, 1394–15

Prisons Bur admin offices and correctional instns, facility characteristics, 1991, annual listing, 6244–4

Real estate assets of failed thrifts, inventory of properties available from Resolution Trust Corp, semiannual listing series, 9722–2

Refugee resettlement programs and funding, arrivals by country of origin, and indicators of adjustment, by State, FY90, annual rpt, 4694–5

Salt production capacity, by firm and facility, 1990, annual listing, 5614–30

Savings and loan assns, FHLB 8th District members, locations, assets, and savings, 1991, annual listing, 9304–9

Savings and loan assns, FHLB 11th District members, offices, and financial condition, 1991 annual listing, 9304–23

Savings instns, FHLB 10th District members, locations, assets, and deposits, 1991, annual listing, 9304–17

School agencies (public elementary and secondary), by enrollment size and location, fall 1989, annual listing, 4834–1

Science, engineering, and math education grants of NSF, by recipient and level, FY89, biennial listing, 9624–27

SEC registration, firms required to file annual rpts, as of Sept 1990, annual listing, 9734–5

Shipbuilding and repair facilities, capacity, and employment, by shipyard, 1990, annual rpt, 7704–9

Ships in US merchant fleet and Natl Defense Reserve Fleet, vessels, tonnage, and owner, as of Jan 1991, semiannual listing, 7702–2

Ships in world bulk carrier fleet, characteristics by country of registry, annual listing, discontinued, 7704–13

Ships in world tanker fleet, characteristics by country of registry, annual listing, discontinued, 7704–17

Ships under foreign flag owned by US firms and foreign affiliates, by type, owner, and country of registry and construction, as of Jan 1991, semiannual rpt, 7702–3

Small Business Investment Companies capital holdings, SBA obligation, and ownership, as of July 1991, semiannual listing, 9762–4

Solar photovoltaic R&D sponsored by DOE, projects, funding, and rpts, FY90, annual listing, 3304–20

State Dept officers, ambassadors, and Chiefs of US overseas missions, by country and intl agency, 1778-1990, 7008–1

State-local relations advisory organizations activities, staff, and funding, 1990, 10048–80

Student aid funding and participation, by Federal program, instn type and control, and State, various periods 1959-89, annual rpt, 4804–28

Student supplemental grants, loans, and work-study awards, Federal share by instn and State, 1991/92, annual listing, 4804–17

Technology dev programs of govts, info sources and funding, 1990 rpt, 10048–81

Toll facilities, mileage, and operating status, by type of system, as of Jan 1990, biennial listing, 7554–39

Directories

Transit systems finances and operations, by mode of transport, size of fleet, and for 468 systems, 1989, annual rpt, 7884–4

Treaties and other bilateral and multilateral agreements of US in force, by country, as of Jan 1991, annual listing, 7004–1

Urban Mass Transportation Admin R&D projects and funding, FY90, annual listing, 7884–1

Urban Mass Transportation Admin research and training grants to higher education instns, by project, FY90, annual listing, 7884–7

Vital statistics records offices in US and Canada, 1990 listing, 4208–34

Wastewater treatment facilities construction grants of EPA to State and local govts, by project, monthly listing, 9202–3

Water resources data collection and analysis activities of USGS Water Resources Div Districts, with project descriptions, series, 5666–26

Weather stations of Natl Weather Service, locations and types of observations made, 1990 annual listing, 2184–5

Wildlife research of State fish and wildlife agencies, federally funded projects and costs by species and State, 1990, annual listing, 5504–24

Workers compensation advisory and study commissions, and functions, by State, 1991 semiannual rpt, 6502–1

see also Bibliographies

see also CD-ROM catalogs and guides

see also Chronologies

see also Computer data file guides

see also Demonstration and pilot projects

see also Government publications lists

Disability benefits and insurance

Employee benefit plan coverage and provisions, by plan type, firm size, and industry sector, 1988, article, 6722–1.204

Employee leave for illness, disability, and dependent care, coverage, provisions, terminations, costs, and methods of covering for absent worker, by firm size, 1988 survey, 9768–21

Expenditures (private) for social welfare, by category, 1970s-88, annual article, 4742–1.204

Expenditures, coverage, and benefits for social welfare programs, late 1930s-89, annual rpt, 4744–3.1

Expenditures for public welfare by program, FY50s-88, annual article, 4742–1.209

Govt census, 1987: State and local govt employment, payroll, OASDHI coverage, and employee benefits costs, by level of govt and State, 2455–4

Govt pension plan benefits and beneficiaries, by type of plan and eligibility, and level of govt, selected years 1954-88, annual article, 4742–1.212

HHS financial aid, by program, recipient, State, and city, FY90, annual regional listings, 4004–3

Households composition, income, benefits, and labor force status, Survey of Income and Program Participation methodology, working paper series, 2626–10

Kidney transplants, needs, costs, payment sources, and impact of immunosuppressive drugs on outcome, 1950s-87 and projected to 1995, 4658–59

Leave transfer to other employees, Federal pilot programs operations and costs by agency, FY89, 9848–40

Short-term disability insurance laws of States, comparison of provisions, 1991, base edition with semiannual revisions, 6402–2

Small business employees benefit plan coverage and provisions, by plan type and occupational group, 1990, biennial rpt, 6784–20

State and local govt employees benefit plan coverage, by benefit type, 1990, press release, 6726–1.41

Statistical Abstract of US, 1991 annual data compilation, 2324–1.12

Survivor benefits of employer-sponsored plans, coverage by plan type and payment method, 1989, article, 6722–1.230

Veterans and servicepersons life insurance, actuarial analyses of VA programs, 1990, annual rpt, 8604–1

Veterans disability and death compensation and pension cases, by type of entitlement and period of service, monthly rpt, 8602–5

Veterans disability and death compensation cases of VA, by entitlement type, period of service, sex, age, and State, FY89, annual rpt, 8604–7

Veterans health care, patients, visits, costs, and operating beds, by VA and contract facility, and region, quarterly rpt, 8602–4

see also Maternity benefits

see also Old-Age, Survivors, Disability, and Health Insurance

see also Workers compensation

Disabled and handicapped persons

Crimes against aged and handicapped, State laws, data compilation, 1991 annual rpt, 6064–6.1

DOT employment, by subagency, occupation, and selected personnel characteristics, FY90, annual rpt, 7304–18

Education data compilation, 1991 annual rpt, 4824–2

Employment and minimum wage exemption certificates under Fair Labor Standards Act, FY88-89, annual rpt, 6504–2.1

Employment and other characteristics of disabled persons, 1989 hearing, 23898–7

Fed Govt civilian employees demographic and employment characteristics, as of Sept 1990, annual article, 9842–1.201

Fed Govt civilian employment of minorities, women, veterans, and disabled persons, as of Sept 1988 and 1990, biennial article, 9842–1.202

Fed Govt employment of minorities, women, and disabled, by agency and occupation, FY89, annual rpt, 9244–10

Health care (primary) research, methodology and findings, 1991 annual conf, 4184–4

Health condition improvement and disease prevention goals and recommended activities for 2000, with trends 1970s-80s, 4048–10

Households composition, income, benefits, and labor force status, Survey of Income and Program Participation methodology, working paper series, 2626–10

Injuries, related impairments, and activity limitations, by circumstances and victim characteristics, 1985-87, 4147–10.179

Index by Subjects and Names

Libraries for blind and handicapped, readership, circulation, staff, funding, and holdings, FY90, annual listing, 26404–3

Nursing home reimbursement by Medicaid, resident classification using patient and care characteristics, New York State, 1990 article, 4652–1.205

Older persons health condition and care research, data availability and collection methodology, for US and selected countries, 1988 conf, 4147–5.6

Older persons long-term care needs and costs, late 1980s and projected 2018-60, GAO rpt, 26121–433

Population of disabled persons and related activity limitation days and health services use, by health status, disability type, and other characteristics, 1984-88, 4146–8.202

Population with acute and chronic conditions, disability, absenteeism, and health services use, by selected characteristics, 1987, CD-ROM, 4147–10.177

Poverty status of population and families, by detailed characteristics, 1988-89, annual Current Population Rpt, 2546–6.67

Poverty status of population and families, by detailed characteristics, 1990, annual Current Population Rpt, 2546–6.71

Respiratory diseases related to occupational hazards, epidemiology, diagnosis, and treatment, for selected industries and work settings, 1988 conf, 4248–90

SSA minority, handicapped, and women employees, by pay grade, FY90, annual rpt, 4704–6

Statistical Abstract of US, 1991 annual data compilation, 2324–1.12

Survey of Income and Program Participation, data collection, methodology, and use, 1990 annual conf papers, 2624–1

VA employment characteristics and activities, FY90, annual rpt, 8604–3.8

Veterans disability by type, and deaths, by period of service, and VA activities, FY90, annual rpt, 8604–3.6

see also Adult day care

see also Aid to blind

see also Aid to disabled and handicapped persons

see also Architectural barriers to the handicapped

see also Blind

see also Deaf

see also Disability benefits and insurance

see also Discrimination against the handicapped

see also Group homes for the handicapped

see also Handicapped children

see also Learning disabilities

see also Medicare

see also Mental retardation

see also Mobility limitations

see also Old-Age, Survivors, Disability, and Health Insurance

see also Rehabilitation of the disabled

see also Sheltered workshops

see also Special education

see also Supplemental Security Income

see also Vocational rehabilitation

Index by Subjects and Names

Disadvantaged

see Compensatory education
see Disabled and handicapped persons
see Discrimination against the handicapped
see Discrimination in credit
see Discrimination in education
see Discrimination in employment
see Discrimination in housing
see Handicapped children
see Minority businesses
see Minority employment
see Minority groups
see Poverty
see Racial discrimination
see Sex discrimination

DiSalvo, James

"Conduct in a Banking Duopoly", 9387–8.251

Disarmament

see Arms control and disarmament

Disaster relief

- Agricultural Stabilization and Conservation Service producer payments and certificate value, by program, monthly rpt, 1802–10
- Agricultural Stabilization and Conservation Service producer payments, by program and State, 1990, annual table, 1804–12
- AID economic aid to developing countries, obligations and disbursements by country, quarterly rpt, 9912–4
- Army Corps of Engineers water resources dev projects, characteristics, and costs, 1950s-89, biennial State rpt series, 3756–1
- Army Corps of Engineers water resources dev projects, characteristics, and costs, 1950s-91, biennial State rpt series, 3756–2
- Assistance (financial and nonfinancial) of Fed Govt, 1991 base edition with supplements, annual listing, 104–5
- Budget of US, formula grant program obligations to State and local govts, by agency, program, and State, FY92, annual rpt, 104–30
- Budget of US, obligations and authority by function, agency, and program, with summaries, analyses, and historical tables, FY92, annual rpt, 104–2
- Developing countries economic and social conditions from 1960s, and Intl Dev Cooperation Agency and AID activities and funding, FY90-92, annual rpt, 9904–4
- Economic Dev Admin activities, and funding by program, recipient, State, and county, FY90 and cumulative from FY66, annual rpt, 2064–2
- Expenditures of Fed Govt in States, by type, program, agency, and State, FY90, annual rpt, 2464–2
- Farmland damaged by natural disaster, Emergency Conservation Program aid and participation by State, FY90, annual rpt, 1804–22
- Farmland damaged by natural disaster, Emergency Conservation Program funding by region and State, monthly rpt, 1802–13
- Fed Emergency Mgmt Agency activities and funding, annual rpt, discontinued, 9434–2
- Fed Emergency Mgmt Agency disaster relief funding and response, for Loma Prieta earthquake and Hurricane Hugo, 1989-90, GAO rpt, 26113–511
- FmHA activities, and loans and grants by program and State, FY90 and trends from FY70, annual rpt, 1184–17
- FmHA loans, by type, borrower characteristics, and State, quarterly rpt, 1182–8
- FmHA loans, by type, borrower race, and State, quarterly rpt, 1182–5
- Foreign countries disasters, casualties, damage, and aid by US and others, FY90 and trends from FY64, annual rpt, 9914–12
- HHS financial aid, by program, recipient, State, and city, FY90, annual regional listings, 4004–3
- Land Mgmt Bur activities and funding by State, FY89, annual rpt, 5724–13
- Natl Guard activities, personnel, and facilities, FY90, annual rpt, 3504–22
- PL 480 exports by commodity, and recipients, by program, sponsor, and country, FY88 and cumulative from FY55, annual rpt, 1924–7
- Price support program provisions, for selected commodities, 1961-90, 1568–302
- Red Cross activities and finances, FY90, annual rpt, 29254–1
- Timber and orchard damage from natural disaster, USDA restoration aid and program participation by practice and State, FY89-90, annual rpt, 1804–24
- Unemployment insurance laws of States, comparison of provisions, 1991, base edition with semiannual revisions, 6402–2
- USDA disaster aid for producers of crops ineligible for price supports by State, and methodology, 1988-89, GAO rpt, 26113–533

see also Agricultural insurance
see also War relief

Disasters

- Foreign countries disasters, casualties, damage, and aid by US and others, FY90 and trends from FY64, annual rpt, 9914–12
- Incidents and mgmt of disasters and natl security threats, with data by major event and State, 1991 annual rpt, 9434–6
- Presidential declarations of natl disasters, by event type, aggregate 1967-90, annual rpt, 9434–6

see also Accidents and accident prevention
see also Avalanches
see also Disaster relief
see also Drought
see also Earthquakes
see also Fires and fire prevention
see also Floods
see also Forest fires
see also Nuclear accidents and safety
see also Storms
see also Tsunamis
see also Volcanoes

Discrimination

see Age discrimination
see Civil rights
see Discrimination against the handicapped
see Discrimination in credit
see Discrimination in education
see Discrimination in employment
see Discrimination in housing
see Racial discrimination

Discrimination in employment

see Sex discrimination

Discrimination against the handicapped

- Educational service delivery and discipline, and discrimination indicators by State, 1988, biennial rpt, 4804–33
- Fed Govt and State rehabilitation activities and funding, FY90, annual rpt, 4944–1
- Fed Govt personnel action appeals, decisions of Merit Systems Protection Board by agency and region, FY90, annual rpt, 9494–2
- HHS financial aid, by program, recipient, State, and city, FY90, annual regional listings, 4004–3
- Labor laws enacted, by State, 1990, annual article, 6722–1.209
- *see also* Architectural barriers to the handicapped

Discrimination in credit

- Financial instns location relation to ZIP code area income and minority population, by instn type for 5 cities, 1977-89, article, 9377–1.208
- Mortgage applications by disposition, and secondary loan market sales by purchaser type, by applicant and neighborhood characteristics, 1990, article, 9362–1.206
- Mortgage subsidy programs to promote neighborhood racial integration, effectiveness and impacts on housing prices, 1983-89, working paper, 9377–9.108

Discrimination in education

- *Digest of Education Statistics,* 1991 annual data compilation, 4824–2
- Education Dept activities, FY89-90, annual rpt, 4804–6
- Education Dept enforcement activities to eliminate discrimination within schools, and adequacy, FY81-91, GAO rpt, 26121–427
- Education Dept programs funding, operations, and effectiveness, FY90, annual rpt, 4804–5
- Minority group and sexual discrimination in education, indicators for service delivery and discipline, by State, 1988, biennial rpt, 4804–33

Discrimination in employment

- Air Force recruiting compliance with gender-neutral selection, with aptitude test results by sex, FY86-90, GAO rpt, 26123–359
- Alien workers (unauthorized) and Fair Labor Standards Act employer compliance, hiring impacts, and aliens overstaying visas by country and State, 1986-90, annual rpt, 6264–6
- Assistance (financial and nonfinancial) of Fed Govt, 1991 base edition with supplements, annual listing, 104–5
- Court civil and criminal caseloads for Federal district, appeals, and special courts, 1990, annual rpt, 18204–8
- Court civil and criminal caseloads for Federal district courts, 1991, annual rpt, 18204–2.1
- Disabled persons rehabilitation, Federal and State activities and funding, FY90, annual rpt, 4944–1
- DOE employment discrimination complaints and processing, FY85-90, 3006–5.25
- Fed Equal Opportunity Recruitment Program activity, and employment by sex, race, pay grade, and occupational group, FY90, annual rpt, 9844–33

Discrimination in employment

Fed Govt contractor compliance with equal employment laws, FY90, 6508–36

Fed Govt employment discrimination complaints, processing, and disposition, by complaint type and agency, FY89, annual rpt, 9244–11

Fed Govt employment of minorities and women, and compliance with EEOC standards, by occupation and agency, FY88-92, GAO rpt, 26119–342

Fed Govt personnel action appeals, decisions of Merit Systems Protection Board by agency and region, FY90, annual rpt, 9494–2

Fed Govt spending in States, by type, program, agency, and State, FY90, annual rpt, 2464–2

Fed Govt violations of personnel practices, cases by type, FY90, annual rpt, 9894–1

HHS employment of Hispanics in Mountain region, hiring and promotion practices, 1980s, GAO rpt, 26121–393

Labor laws enacted, by State, 1990, annual article, 6722–1.209

Library of Congress employment by race, Hispanic origin, and sex, and affirmative action needs, 1989, hearing, 21428–9

Marshals Service activities, FY89, annual rpt, 6294–1

Natl Agricultural Statistics Service minority group staff, promotion, and discrimination complaints, 1988-90, GAO rpt, 26119–326

Natl Labor Relations Board cases, backlog, and processing time, 1960s-89, GAO rpt, 26121–395

Pension benefits disparity between men and women in small business plans by selected participant and plan characteristics, impacts of 1986 Tax Reform Act, 1984-85, GAO rpt, 26121–412

State Dept and Foreign Service minority and women employment, and hiring goals, FY89-90, biennial rpt, 7004–21

Discrimination in housing

Assistance (financial and nonfinancial) of Fed Govt, 1991 base edition with supplements, annual listing, 104–5

Atlanta metro area secondary mortgage market underwriting guidelines, and indicators of discrimination, 1989, GAO rpt, 26113–500

Court civil and criminal caseloads for Federal district courts, 1991, annual rpt, 18204–2.1

Fed Govt spending in States, by type, program, agency, and State, FY90, annual rpt, 2464–2

Racial integration promotion through mortgage subsidy programs, effectiveness and impacts on housing prices, 1983-89, working paper, 9377–9.108

Diseases and disorders

Cases of acute and chronic conditions, disability, absenteeism, and health services use, by selected characteristics, 1987, CD-ROM, 4147–10.177

Chronic diseases causing death, rates by cause, weekly rpt, monthly feature, 4202–1

Deaths and rates, by detailed cause and demographic characteristics, 1988 and trends from 1900, US Vital Statistics annual rpt, 4144–2

Foreign countries disasters, casualties, damage, and aid by US and others, FY90 and trends from FY64, annual rpt, 9914–12

HHS financial aid, by program, recipient, State, and city, FY90, annual regional listings, 4004–3

Homeless persons alcohol abuse, by sex, age, race, and additional diagnoses, aggregate 1985-87, 4488–14

Hospital discharges by detailed diagnostic and procedure category, primary diagnosis, and length of stay, by age, sex, and region, 1988, annual rpt, 4147–13.105; 4147–13.108

Indian and Alaska Native disease and disorder cases, deaths, and health services use, by tribe, reservation, and Indian Health Service area, late 1950s-86, 4088–2

Indian Health Service facilities and use, and Indian health and other characteristics, by IHS region, 1980s-89, annual chartbook, 4084–7

Indian Health Service facilities, funding, operations, and Indian health and other characteristics, 1950s-90, annual chartbook, 4084–1

Indian Health Service outpatient services provided, by reason for visit and age, FY88-89, annual rpt, 4084–2

Military deaths by cause, age, race, and rank, and personnel captured and missing, by service branch, FY90, annual rpt, 3544–40

Minority group health condition, services use, costs, and indicators of services need, 1950s-88, 4118–55

Morbidity and Mortality Weekly Report, infectious notifiable disease cases by State, and public health issues, 4202–1

NIH rpts, 1991 annual listing, 4434–2

Nursing home reimbursement by Medicaid, resident classification using patient and care characteristics, New York State, 1990 article, 4652–1.205

Older persons health condition and care research, data availability and collection methodology, for US and selected countries, 1988 conf, 4147–5.6

Palau admin, and social, economic, and govtl data, FY90, annual rpt, 7004–6

Pollutants health effects for animals by species and for humans, and environmental levels, for selected substances, series, 5506–14

State and Metro Area Data Book, 1991 data compilation, 2328–54

Statistical Abstract of US, 1991 annual data compilation, 2324–1.3

see also Accidents and accident prevention

see also Acquired immune deficiency syndrome

see also Alcohol abuse and treatment

see also Allergies

see also Alzheimer's disease

see also Animal diseases and zoonoses

see also Birth defects

see also Black lung disease

see also Blood diseases and disorders

see also Cardiovascular diseases

see also Cerebrovascular diseases

see also Circulatory diseases

see also Diabetes

see also Digestive diseases

see also Drug abuse and treatment

see also Ear diseases and infections

see also Epidemiology and epidemiologists

see also Eye diseases and defects

see also Food and waterborne diseases

see also Health condition

see also Hearing and hearing disorders

see also Hereditary diseases

see also Hypertension

see also Immunity disorders

see also Infective and parasitic diseases

see also Learning disabilities

see also Mental health and illness

see also Mental retardation

see also Metabolic and endocrine diseases

see also Mobility limitations

see also Musculoskeletal diseases

see also Neoplasms

see also Neurological disorders

see also Nose and throat disorders

see also Nutrition and malnutrition

see also Obesity

see also Occupational health and safety

see also Pathology

see also Pneumonia and influenza

see also Poisoning and drug reaction

see also Rabies

see also Respiratory diseases

see also Septicemia

see also Sexually transmitted diseases

see also Sickle cell anemia

see also Skin diseases

see also Spinal cord injuries

see also Tuberculosis

see also Urogenital diseases

see also Vaccination and vaccines

see also under By Disease in the "Index by Categories"

Dismukes, Robert

"Trends in Costs of Production of Corn, Wheat, and Soybeans, 1975-89", 1541–1.208

Displaced workers

see Labor turnover

Disposable income

see Personal and household income

Distillate fuels

see Diesel fuel

see Fuel oil

see Kerosene

Distribution of income

see Business income and expenses, general

see Earnings, general

see National income and product accounts

see Personal and household income

see Poverty

see Wealth

District courts

see Federal district courts

District of Columbia

see D.C.

Districts

see Common markets and free trade areas

see Congressional districts

see Export processing zones

see School districts

see Special districts

see Wards, city

Diversification of business

see Economic concentration and diversification

Index by Subjects and Names

Divestiture

Acquisitions and mergers by type, with data for large transactions by payment method and firm, late 1960s-90, working paper, 9366–1.161

Energy producers finances and operations, by energy type for US firms domestic and foreign operations, 1989, annual rpt, 3164–44

Diving

see Marine accidents and safety

Division of Research Grants, NIH

Grants and contracts of NIH, by inst and type of recipient, FY81-90, annual rpt, 4434–9

Grants of NIH for R&D, training, construction, and medical libraries, by location and recipient, FY90, annual listings, 4434–7

Division of Research Resources, NIH

see also National Center for Research Resources, NIH

Divorce

see Marriage and divorce

Djibouti

Agricultural exports of high-value commodities, indexes and sales by commodity, world area, and country, 1960s-86, 1528–323

Agricultural trade of US, by detailed commodity and country, 1989, annual rpt, 1524–8

Agricultural trade of US, by detailed commodity and country, 1990, semiannual rpt, 1522–4

AID economic aid to developing countries, obligations and disbursements by country, quarterly rpt, 9912–4

Economic and military aid and loans from US and intl agencies, by program and country, FY46-90, annual rpt, 9914–5

Economic and social conditions of developing countries from 1960s, and Intl Dev Cooperation Agency and AID activities and funding, FY90-92, annual rpt, 9904–4

Economic, social, political, and geographic summary data, by country, 1991, annual factbook, 9114–2

Exports and imports of US, by transport mode, country, and SITC 1- to 3-digit commodity, 1990, annual rpt, 2424–12

Exports of US, detailed Schedule B commodities with countries of destination, 1990, annual rpt, 2424–10

Human rights conditions in 170 countries, and US economic and military aid, 1990, annual rpt, 21384–3

Military aid of US, arms sales, and training programs costs and budget requests, by program, world region, and country, FY90-92, annual rpt, 7144–13

UN voting record and share of votes in agreement with US, by issue, country, and world area, 1990, annual rpt, 7004–18

Doane, William M.

"Promising New Products and Processes from Corn", 1004–16.1

Doctors

see Physicians

Documents

see Bibliographies

see Environmental impact statements

see Government documents

see Government forms and paperwork

see Government publications lists

DOD

see Department of Defense

DOE

see Department of Energy

Doering, Otto

"Changing Chemical Use: The Impact on Producers and Consumers", 1004–16.1

"Looking Back While Going Forward: An Essential for Policy Economists", 1502–3.202

Dolton, David D.

"Mourning Dove Breeding Population Status, 1991", 5504–15

Domagalski, Joseph L.

"Regional Assessment of Nonpoint-Source Pesticide Residues in Ground Water, San Joaquin Valley, Calif. Regional Aquifer-System Analysis", 5666–25.12

Domestic International Sales Corporations

Boycotts (intl) by OPEC and other countries, US firms and shareholders cooperation and tax benefits denied, 1986, annual rpt, 8004–13

Boycotts (intl) by OPEC and other countries, US taxpayers IRS filings, cooperation, and tax benefits denied, 1976-86, GAO rpt, 26119–349

Tax (income) returns filed by type of filer, selected income items, quarterly rpt, 8302–2.1

Tax (income) returns of corporations, income and tax items by asset size and detailed industry, 1987, annual rpt, 8304–4

Tax (income) returns of corporations, income and tax items by asset size and detailed industry, 1988, annual rpt, 8304–21

Tax (income) returns of corporations with foreign tax credit, income, and tax items, by country and world region of credit, 1986, biennial article, 8302–2.207

Tax (income) returns of corporations with foreign tax credit, income and tax items by industry group, 1986, biennial article, 8302–2.203

Tax collection activity of IRS, by type of tax, FY90, annual rpt, 8304–3.1

see also Foreign Sales Corporations

Domestic relations

see Child abuse and neglect

see Domestic violence

see Families and households

see Marriage and divorce

Domestic violence

Arrests, by offense, offender characteristics, and location, 1990, annual rpt, 6224–2.2

Crimes, arrests, and rates, by offense, offender characteristics, population size, and jurisdiction, 1990, annual rpt, 6224–2.1; 6224–2.2

Drug abuse relation to violent and criminal behavior, with data on street gang activity and selected population groups, 1989 conf, 4498–70

Fed Govt financial and nonfinancial domestic aid, 1991 base edition with supplements, annual listing, 104–5

Homeless and runaway youth programs, funding, activities, and participant characteristics, FY90, annual rpt, 4604–3

Homicides, by circumstance, victim and offender relationship, and type of weapon, 1990, annual rpt, 6224–2.1

Domestic workers and services

Jail population, by criminal, correctional, drug use, and family history, and selected other characteristics, 1989, 6066–19.62

Jail population, by sociodemographic characteristics, criminal and drug use history, whether convicted, offense, and sentencing, 1989, annual rpt, 6064–26.3

Jail population drug abuse history, by offense, conviction status, criminal and family history, and selected other characteristics, 1989, 6066–19.63

Older persons abuse and neglect by circumstances and characteristics of abuser and victim, and States protective services budgets and staff, by location, 1980s, hearing, 21148–62

Police response to disturbances, officers assaulted and killed, by circumstances, 1990, annual rpt, 6224–3

Preventive disease and health improvement goals and recommended activities for 2000, with trends 1970s-80s, 4048–10

Teenagers crime victimization, by victim and offender characteristics, circumstances, and offense, 1985-88 surveys, 6066–3.43

Victimization rates, by victim and offender · characteristics, circumstances, and offense, 1988 survey, annual rpt, 6066–3.42

Victimization rates, by victim and offender characteristics, circumstances, and offense, 1989 survey, annual rpt, 6066–3.44

Victimizations and arrest, by offense, circumstances, and location, data compilation, 1991 annual rpt, 6064–6.3; 6064–6.4

Victimizations by violent crime, circumstances, victim characteristics, arrest, recidivism, sentences, and prisoners, 1980s, 6068–148

Women abused by partners, interval between incident and seeking help, by type of abuse, 1987 local area study, article, 4042–3.228

Women prisoners in State instns, by number of children, whether abused, and other characteristics, data compilation, 1991 annual rpt, 6064–6.6

Women prisoners in State instns, by offense, drug use history, whether abused, and other characteristics, 1986, 6066–19.61

Women's rape and other violent crime victimization, by relation to offender, circumstances, and victim characteristics, 1973-87, 6068–243

see also Child abuse and neglect

Domestic workers and services

CPI by component for US city average, and by region, population size, and for 27 metro areas, monthly rpt, 6762–2

Educational attainment, by sociodemographic characteristics and location, 1989 and trends from 1940, biennial Current Population Rpt, 2546–1.452

Employment and Earnings, detailed data, monthly rpt, 6742–2

Employment, earnings, and hours, monthly press release, 6742–5

Employment, unemployment, and labor force characteristics, by region and census div, 1990, annual rpt, 6744–7.1

Franchise business opportunities by firm and kind of business, and sources of aid and info, 1990 annual listing, 2104–7

Domestic workers and services

Social security earnings records errors and rates, by employment type, late 1930s-87, GAO rpt, 26121–422

Unemployment insurance laws of States, comparison of provisions, 1991, base edition with semiannual revisions, 6402–2

Workers compensation laws of States and Fed Govt, 1991 semiannual rpt, 6502–1

see also Homemaker services

Domiciliary care

see Group homes for the handicapped

see Home health services

see Homemaker services

see Nursing homes

see Respite care

see Veterans health facilities and services

Dominica

- Agricultural trade of US, by detailed commodity and country, 1990, semiannual rpt, 1522–4
- Economic, social, political, and geographic summary data, by country, 1991, annual factbook, 9114–2
- Exports and imports of US, by transport mode, country, and SITC 1- to 3-digit commodity, 1990, annual rpt, 2424–12
- Human rights conditions in 170 countries, and US economic and military aid, 1990, annual rpt, 21384–3
- Investment (direct) incentives of Caribbean Basin Initiative, economic impacts, with finances and employment by country, 1984-90, 2048–141
- Labor conditions, union coverage, and work accidents, 1991 annual regional rpt, 6366–4.56
- Military aid of US, arms sales, and training programs costs and budget requests, by program, world region, and country, FY90-92, annual rpt, 7144–13
- UN voting record and share of votes in agreement with US, by issue, country, and world area, 1990, annual rpt, 7004–18

see also under By Foreign Country in the "Index by Categories"

Dominican Republic

- Agricultural exports of high-value commodities, indexes and sales by commodity, world area, and country, 1960s-86, 1528–323
- Agricultural exports of US, impacts of foreign agricultural and trade policy, with data by commodity and country, 1989, annual rpt, 1924–8
- Agricultural production, trade, and policies in foreign countries, summary data by country, 1989-90, annual factbook, 1924–12
- Agricultural trade of US, by detailed commodity and country, 1989, annual rpt, 1524–8
- Agricultural trade of US, by detailed commodity and country, 1990, semiannual rpt, 1522–4
- AID economic aid to developing countries, obligations and disbursements by country, quarterly rpt, 9912–4
- AID loans repayment status and terms by program and country, and status of predecessor agency loans, quarterly rpt, 9912–3
- Aliens (illegal) enforcement activity of Coast Guard, by nationality, 2nd half FY91, semiannual rpt, 7402–4

Economic and military aid and loans from US and intl agencies, by program and country, FY46-90, annual rpt, 9914–5

- Economic and social conditions of developing countries from 1960s, and Intl Dev Cooperation Agency and AID activities and funding, FY90-92, annual rpt, 9904–4
- Economic conditions, policy, and trade practices, by country, 1988-90, annual rpt, 21384–5
- Economic, social, political, and geographic summary data, by country, 1991, annual factbook, 9114–2
- Exports and imports of US, by commodity and country, 1970-89, world area rpt, 9116–1.5
- Exports and imports of US, by Harmonized System 6-digit commodity and country, 1990, annual rpt, 2424–13
- Exports and imports of US, by selected country, country group, and commodity group, 1990, annual rpt, 2044–37
- Exports and imports of US, by transport mode, country, and SITC 1- to 3-digit commodity, 1990, annual rpt, 2424–12
- Exports of US, detailed Schedule B commodities with countries of destination, 1990, annual rpt, 2424–10
- Human rights conditions in 170 countries, and US economic and military aid, 1990, annual rpt, 21384–3
- Imports of US given duty-free treatment for value of US material sent abroad, by commodity and country, 1989, annual rpt, 9884–14
- Investment (direct) incentives of Caribbean Basin Initiative, economic impacts, with finances and employment by country, 1984-90, 2048–141
- Labor conditions, union coverage, and work accidents, 1991 annual country rpt, 6366–4.55
- Military aid of US, arms sales, and training programs costs and budget requests, by program, world region, and country, FY90-92, annual rpt, 7144–13
- Multinatl US firms and foreign affiliates finances and operations, by industry and world area of parent firm, 1989 benchmark survey, preliminary annual rpt, 2704–5
- Multinatl US firms foreign affiliates, income statement items by country and world area, 1986, biennial article, 8302–2.212
- Rum imports (duty-free) of US under Caribbean Basin Initiative, by country, 1989-90, annual rpt, 9884–15
- UN voting record and share of votes in agreement with US, by issue, country, and world area, 1990, annual rpt, 7004–18

see also under By Foreign Country in the "Index by Categories"

Donald, James R.

"World and U.S. Agricultural Outlook", 1004–16.1

Dong, Joani

"U.S.-Mexico Fruit Trade", 1561–6.203

Donovan, Robert J.

"Paid Advertising for AIDS Prevention—Would the Ends Justify the Means?", 4042–3.256

Index by Subjects and Names

Dooley, Samuel W., Jr.

"Guidelines for Preventing the Transmission of Tuberculosis in Health-Care Settings, with Special Focus on HIV-Related Issues", 4206–2.35

Dormitories

see Group quarters

Dorohow, Debbie

"1989 Examination Customer Satisfaction Survey", 8304–8.1

DOT

see Department of Transportation

Dothan, Ala.

see also under By SMSA or MSA in the "Index by Categories"

Dover, N.H.

see also under By SMSA or MSA in the "Index by Categories"

Downs, Michael A.

- "Northern Institutional Profile Analysis: Beaufort Sea. Alaska Social and Economic Study", 5736–5.10
- "Northern Institutional Profile Analysis: Chukchi Sea. Alaska Social and Economic Study", 5736–5.9

Doyle, Herbert A., Jr.

"Sound Medical Evidence: Key to FECA Claims", 6722–1.244

Drabenstott, Mark R.

- "Crossroads for the Cattle Industry", 9381–1.201
- "Outlook for Agricultural Lenders and Policymakers in the 1990s", 9368–90
- "Turning Point in the Farm Recovery?", 9381–1.203

Draft

see Draft evasion and protest

see Selective service

Draft evasion and protest

- Criminal cases in Federal district courts, by offense, disposition, and district, 1980-90, last issue of annual rpt, 18204–1
- Sentences for Federal offenses, guidelines by offense and circumstances, series, 17668–1
- US attorneys civil and criminal cases by type and disposition, and collections, by Federal district, FY90, annual rpt, 6004–2.1

Dragos, Stefanie L.

"Water Resources Activities in Utah by the USGS, Oct. 1, 1988-Sept. 30, 1989", 5666–26.15

Drain, Mary C.

"Heavy Rail Transit Safety, 1989 Annual Report", 7884–5

Dredging

- Army Corps of Engineers water resources dev projects, characteristics, and costs, 1950s-89, biennial State rpt series, 3756–1
- Army Corps of Engineers water resources dev projects, characteristics, and costs, 1950s-91, biennial State rpt series, 3756–2
- Coastal areas environmental and socioeconomic conditions, and potential impact of oil and gas OCS leases, final statement series, 5736–1
- Panama Canal dredging operations, FY90, annual rpt, 9664–3.2
- Wetlands acreage conserved and disturbed in southeastern US, by habitat and disturbance type and State, 1988, article, 2162–1.202

Wetlands acreage, resources, soil and water properties, and conservation efforts, by wetland type, State rpt series, 5506–11

Drew, Craig P.

"Energy Management Annual Report, FY90", 9804–26

Drinking places

see Restaurants and drinking places

Drinking water

see Water fluoridation

see Water supply and use

Drivers licenses

Accidents (fatal), deaths, and rates, by circumstances, characteristics of persons and vehicles involved, and location, 1989, annual rpt, 7764–10

Govt finances, tax systems and revenue, and fiscal structure, by level of govt and State, 1991 with historical trends, annual rpt, 10044–1

Hwy Statistics, detailed data by State, 1990, annual rpt, 7554–1

Hwy Statistics, summary data by State, 1989-90, annual rpt, 7554–24

Licenses issued and in force by age and sex, fees, and renewal, by license class and State, 1989, annual rpt, 7554–16

Revenue, by level of govt, type of tax, State, and selected large county, quarterly rpt, 2462–3

Revenue of State govts by detailed source, and tax rates, by State, FY90, annual rpt, 2466–2.7

State and Metro Area Data Book, 1991 data compilation, 2328–54

State govt revenue by source, spending and debt by function, and holdings, FY90, annual rpt, 2466–2.6

Statistical Abstract of US, 1991 annual data compilation, 2324–1.21

Travel patterns, personal and household characteristics, and auto and public transport use, 1990 survey, series, 7556–6

Driving while intoxicated

Accident deaths involving alcohol, by drive and victim age and blood alcohol levels, weekly rpt, quarterly table, 4202–1

Accidents (fatal), alcohol levels of drivers and others involved, by circumstances and characteristics of persons and vehicles, 1989, annual rpt, 7764–16

Accidents (fatal), alcohol levels of drivers and others involved, 1982-90, annual fact sheet, 7766–15.3

Accidents (fatal), deaths, and rates, by circumstances, characteristics of persons and vehicles involved, and location, 1989, annual rpt, 7764–10

Accidents (fatal) involvement of drunk drivers, and impacts of minimum age drinking laws, 1982-89, annual fact sheet, 7766–15.1

Accidents (fatal) involvement of drunk drivers, and impacts of minimum age drinking laws, 1982-90, annual fact sheet, 7766–15.4

Accidents, casualties, circumstances, and characteristics of persons and vehicles involved, 1989, annual rpt, 7764–18

Arrests, by offense, offender characteristics, and location, 1990, annual rpt, 6224–2.2

Boating while intoxicated enforcement cases of Coast Guard, 2nd half FY91, semiannual rpt, 7402–4

Court civil and criminal caseloads for Federal district, appeals, and bankruptcy courts, by type of suit and offense, circuit, and district, 1990, annual rpt, 18204–11

Court civil and criminal caseloads for Federal district, appeals, and special courts, 1990, annual rpt, 18204–8

Court civil and criminal caseloads for Federal district courts, 1991, annual rpt, 18204–2.1

Court criminal cases in Federal district courts, by offense, disposition, and district, 1980-90, last issue of annual rpt, 18204–1

Crime, criminal justice admin and enforcement, and public opinion, data compilation, 1991 annual rpt, 6064–6

Drug abuse history of jail population, by offense, conviction status, criminal and family history, and selected other characteristics, 1989, 6066–19.63

Drunk driving accidents, deaths, and injuries, by alcohol level, data compilation, 1991 annual rpt, 6064–6.3

Jail population, by criminal, correctional, drug use, and family history, and selected other characteristics, 1989, 6066–19.62

Jail population, by sociodemographic characteristics, criminal and drug use history, whether convicted, offense, and sentencing, 1989, annual rpt, 6064–26.3

Natl Hwy Traffic Safety Admin activities and grants, and fatal traffic accident data, 1989, annual rpt, 7764–1

Preventive disease and health improvement goals and recommended activities for 2000, with trends 1970s-80s, 4048–10

Prisoners on probation by offense, and prisoner characteristics, 1989, annual rpt, 6064–26.2

Sentences for Federal offenses, guidelines by offense and circumstances, series, 17668–1

Statistical Abstract of US, 1991 annual data compilation, 2324–1.21

Truck accidents, casualties, and damage, by circumstances and characteristics of persons and vehicles involved, 1988, annual rpt, 7554–9

Truck accidents, circumstances, severity, and characteristics of drivers and vehicles, 1989, annual rpt, 7764–20

Youth alcohol use, knowledge, attitudes, and info sources, series, 4006–10

Dropouts

see School dropouts

Drought

California drought impacts, Central Valley reservoir storage and capacity, and Kern County crop production and irrigation, 1989-91, article, 1561–6.202

Farm water supply, crop moisture, and drought indexes, weekly rpt, seasonal data, 2182–7

Farmland damaged by natural disaster, Emergency Conservation Program aid and participation by State, FY90, annual rpt, 1804–22

Foreign countries disasters, casualties, damage, and aid by US and others, FY90 and trends from FY64, annual rpt, 9914–12

Incidents and mgmt of disasters and natl security threats, with data by major event and State, 1991 annual rpt, 9434–6

Timber and orchard damage from natural disaster, USDA restoration aid and program participation by practice and State, FY89-90, annual rpt, 1804–24

Water supply, hydrologic events, and end use, by State, 1988-89, annual rpt, 5664–12

Weather events and anomalies, precipitation and temperature for US and foreign locations, weekly rpt, 2182–6

Drowning

Boat registrations, and accidents, casualties, and damage by cause, by vessel characteristics and State, 1990, annual rpt, 7404–1

Child accident deaths and death rates, by cause, age, sex, race, and State, 1980-85, 4108–54

Child accident deaths and injuries by cause, and victimization, rates by race, sex, and age, 1979-88, chartbook, 4108–56

Deaths and rates, by detailed cause and demographic characteristics, 1988 and trends from 1900, US Vital Statistics annual rpt, 4144–2

Diving (underwater sport and occupational) deaths, by circumstances, diver characteristics, and location, 1970-89, annual rpt, 2144–5

Foreign countries disasters, casualties, damage, and aid by US and others, FY90 and trends from FY64, annual rpt, 9914–12

Homicides, by circumstance, victim and offender relationship, and type of weapon, 1990, annual rpt, 6224–2.1

Infant death rate, by cause, region, and race, 1980-87, article, 4202–7.208

Minority group health condition, services use, costs, and indicators of services need, 1950s-88, 4118–55

Park natl system visitor deaths, by cause, victim age, region, and park, 1980-90, annual rpt, 5544–6

Preventive disease and health improvement goals and recommended activities for 2000, with trends 1970s-80s, 4048–10

Safety programs, and accidents, casualties, and damage, by mode of transport, 1989, annual rpt, 7304–19

Drug abuse and treatment

Abuse and enforcement issues, series, 236–2

Abuse of drugs and alcohol, by selected characteristics, 1990 survey, biennial rpt, 4494–5

Abuse of drugs, emergency room admissions and deaths by drug type and major metro area, semiannual rpt, discontinued, 4492–3

Abuse of drugs, emergency room admissions and deaths, by drug type and source, sex, race, age, and major metro area, 1990, annual rpt, 4494–8

Abuse of drugs, indicators for selected metro areas, research results, data collection, and policy issues, 1991 semiannual conf, 4492–5

Abuse of drugs, prices, seizures, and supply by country of origin, by substance, 1990, annual rpt, 6284–2

Abuse, treatment, and enforcement policy issues, series, 236–1

ACTION activities and funding, by program, FY90, annual rpt, 9024–2

Drug abuse and treatment

Index by Subjects and Names

AIDS and AIDS virus infection patients service use and costs under Medicaid, 1991, article, 4652–1.215

AIDS cases among drug abusers, by drug use, sexual behavior, and other characteristics, 1984-88 local area study, article, 4042–3.206

AIDS cases at VA health care centers by sex, race, risk factor, and facility, and AIDS prevention and treatment issues, quarterly rpt, 8702–1

AIDS cases by race, sex, and risk category, and deaths and survivors, projected 1989-93, 4206–2.34

AIDS cases by risk group, race, sex, age, State, and MSA, and deaths, monthly rpt, 4202–9

AIDS knowledge, attitudes, and risk behaviors of women in methadone maintenance programs, effects of life skills training, 1988 local area study, article, 4042–3.221

AIDS patient home and community services under Medicaid waiver in 6 States, 1988-89, article, 4652–1.216

AIDS patient hospital use and charges, by hospital and patient characteristics, and payment source, 1986-87, 4186–6.15

AIDS public knowledge, attitudes, and risk behaviors, for women, 1988 survey, 4146–8.200

AIDS symptoms and deaths among drug abusers with positive AIDS virus tests in 1971-72, as of 1988, article, 4042–3.237

AIDS virus infection and risk factor prevalence, natl survey methodology and pretest results, 1989, 4148–30

Assistance (financial and nonfinancial) of Fed Govt, 1991 base edition with supplements, annual listing, 104–5

Budget of US, obligations and authority by function, agency, and program, with summaries, analyses, and historical tables, FY92, annual rpt, 104–2

Child health condition and services use, 1990 chartbook, 4108–49

Children (emotionally disturbed) residential facilities, use, funding, and characteristics of patients, staff, and instn, 1988, 4506–3.44

Children and youth social, economic, and demographic characteristics, 1950s-90, 4818–5

Costs (direct and indirect) of drug and alcohol abuse and mental illness, by type, 1970s-88, article, 4042–3.219

Costs (direct and indirect) of mental illness and drug and alcohol abuse, by type and patient age and sex, 1985 with 1980 and 1988 comparisons, 4048–35

Crime, criminal justice admin and enforcement, and public opinion, data compilation, 1991 annual rpt, 6064–6

Crime victimization of teens, by victim and offender characteristics, circumstances, and offense, 1985-88 surveys, 6066–3.43

Criminal case processing in Federal district courts, and dispositions, by offense, district, and offender characteristics, 1986, annual rpt, 6064–29

Criminal defendants for Federal offenses pretrial processing, detention, and release, by defendant characteristics and district, 1988, hearing, 25528–114

Criminal sentences for Federal offenses, guidelines by offense and circumstances, series, 17668–1

Deaths and rates, by detailed cause and demographic characteristics, 1988 and trends from 1900, US Vital Statistics annual rpt, 4144–2

Education data compilation, 1991 annual rpt, 4824–2

Education data, detail for elementary and secondary education, 1920s-90 and projected to 2001, annual rpt, 4824–1.1

Education Dept programs funding, operations, and effectiveness, FY90, annual rpt, 4804–5

Education natl goals progress indicators, by State, 1991, annual rpt, 15914–1

Employee drug abuse prevention programs and policies, by firm size, 1988 and 1990, article, 6722–1.224

Employee drug and alcohol use, and drinkers reporting adverse effects, for young adults by selected characteristics, 1984, article, 6722–1.237

Expenditures of users for illegal drugs, by user group and substance, 1988-90, 236–2.1

Facilities for mental health care, outpatient programs, use, and client characteristics, by instn type and State, 1988, 4506–3.40; 4506–3.46

Fed Govt drug abuse and trafficking reduction programs activities, funding, staff, and Bush Admin budget request, by Federal agency and program area, FY90-92, 238–2

Fed Govt drug abuse and trafficking reduction programs funding, and Bush Admin budget request, by agency and program area, FY90-92, 238–1

Food stamp recipient household size, composition, income, and income and deductions allowed, summer 1988, annual rpt, 1364–8

Foreign countries drug use and enforcement activities, by country, 1987-91, annual rpt, 7004–17

Foster care placement of black children whose parents abuse drugs, by placement reason and outcome, and household and parent characteristics, 1986-90, 4008–114

Health condition and health care resources, use, and spending, 1950s-89, annual data compilation, 4144–11

Hepatitis cases by infection source, age, sex, race, and State, and deaths, by strain, 1988 and trends from 1966, 4205–2

HHS financial aid, by program, recipient, State, and city, FY90, annual regional listings, 4004–3

Homeless and runaway youth programs, funding, activities, and participant characteristics, FY90, annual rpt, 4604–3

Homeless persons aid programs of Fed Govt, program descriptions and funding, by agency and State, FY87-90, annual GAO rpt, 26104–21

Homeless persons alcohol abuse, by sex, age, race, and additional diagnoses, aggregate 1985-87, 4488–14

Homeless teens pregnancy prevalence and outcomes, services availability, health condition, and drug abuse, 1989 conf, 4108–55

Hospital services and facilities availability, by selected instn characteristics, 1980, 1983, and 1987, 17206–2.22

Hospitals for mental health care of States and counties, patients and admissions by age, diagnosis, and State, FY89, annual rpt, 4504–2

Hospitals for mental health care, private instns patients characteristics, 1986, 4506–3.47

Indian and Alaska Native disease and disorder cases, deaths, and health services use, by tribe, reservation, and Indian Health Service area, late 1950s-86, 4088–2

Indian Health Service facilities, funding, operations, and Indian health and other characteristics, 1950s-90, annual chartbook, 4084–1

Insurance (health) coverage and provisions of small business employee benefit plans, by plan type and occupational group, 1990, biennial rpt, 6784–20

Insurance (health) plans for employees, drug and alcohol abuse treatment coverage and provisions, by plan type, 1989, article, 6722–1.221

Jail adult and juvenile population, employment, spending, instn conditions, and inmate programs, by county and facility, 1988, regional rpt series, 6068–144

Jail drug treatment programs finances and operations, FY89-90, 21408–120

Jail population, by criminal, correctional, drug use, and family history, and selected other characteristics, 1989, 6066–19.62

Jail population, by sociodemographic characteristics, criminal and drug use history, whether convicted, offense, and sentencing, 1989, annual rpt, 6064–26.3

Jail population drug abuse history, by offense, conviction status, criminal and family history, and selected other characteristics, 1989, 6066–19.63

Juvenile correctional and detention public and private instns, inmates, and expenses, by instn and resident characteristics and State, 1987, biennial rpt, 6064–13

Medicaid spending for mental health and substance abuse treatment services, by service type, diagnosis, and eligibility, for 2 states, 1984, article, 4652–1.256

Methadone maintenance programs client characteristics and treatment outcomes, compared to inpatient programs, 1970s-87, hearing, 21968–55

Methamphetamine abuse, availability, health effects, and treatment, 1990 conf papers, 4498–75

Minority group and women health condition, services use, payment sources, and health care labor force, by poverty status, 1940s-89, chartbook, 4118–56

Minority group drug abuse prevalence, related health effects and crime, treatment, and research status and needs, mid 1970s-90, 4498–72

Minority group health condition, services use, costs, and indicators of services need, 1950s-88, 4118–55

Navy drug and alcohol abuse education and treatment program activity, semiannual tables, discontinued, 3802–6

Index by Subjects and Names

Drug and narcotics offenses

Neurological, cognitive, and behavioral residual effects of long-term drug abuse, 1989 conf, 4498–69

Nursing home residents with mental disorders, by disorder type and resident and instn characteristics, 1985, 4147–13.106

Parole and probation clients in program for drug- and alcohol-dependent Federal offenders, as of various dates 1987-91, annual rpt, 18204–2.1; 18204–8.7

Poor black men's drug and condom use and sexual behavior, local area study, 1991 article, 4042–3.254

Pregnant women's drug abuse, States reporting policies and status of treatment funding, 1990, article, 4042–3.220

Preventive disease and health improvement goals and recommended activities for 2000, with trends 1970s-80s, 4048–10

Prison treatment units, and clients by age, sex, and race, by State, data compilation, 1991 annual rpt, 6064–6.6

Psychotherapy and counseling drug abuse treatment outcomes, research results and methodology, 1990 conf, 4498–71

Research grants and awards of ADAMHA, by recipient, FY90, annual listing, 4044–13

Research on drug abuse and treatment, biological and behavioral factors, and addiction potential of new drugs, 1990 annual conf, 4494–11

Research on drug abuse and treatment, summaries of findings, resource materials, and grant listings, periodic rpt, 4492–4

Research on drug abuse, prevention, treatment, and health impacts, as of 1990, triennial rpt, 4498–68

Rural areas drug and alcohol abuse, related crime, and treatment, by substance and State, 1988-90, GAO rpt, 26131–79

Statistical Abstract of US, 1991 annual data compilation, 2324–1.3; 2324–1.5

Steroids use and and health effects, 1989 conf papers, 4498–67

Student aid funding and participation, by Federal program, instn type and control, and State, various periods 1959-89, annual rpt, 4804–28

Teachers views on safety, discipline, and student drug use, for elementary and secondary schools, 1991 survey, 4826–1.31

Treatment and prevention programs of States for drug and alcohol abuse, funding, facilities, and patient characteristics, FY89, 4488–15

Treatment facilities for drug and alcohol abuse, services, use, funding, staff, and client characteristics, 1989, biennial rpt, 4494–10

Treatment services for drug and alcohol abuse, funding, staffing, and client load, characteristics, and outcomes, by setting, 1989 conf, 4498–73

VA health care facilities physicians, dentists, and nurses, by selected employment characteristics and VA district, quarterly rpt, 8602–6

VA mental health care services, staff, research, and training programs, 1991 biennial listing, 8704–2

Veterans (homeless) domiciliary program of VA, participant characteristics and outcomes, 1990 annual rpt, 8604–10

Veterans (homeless) with mental illness, VA program services, costs, staff, client characteristics, and outcome, 1990, annual rpt, 8604–11

Violent and criminal behavior relation to drug abuse, with data on street gang activity and selected population groups, 1989 conf, 4498–70

Violent crime victimizations, circumstances, victim characteristics, arrest, recidivism, sentences, and prisoners, 1980s, 6068–148

Vocational rehabilitation cases of State agencies by disposition and applicant characteristics, and closures by reason, FY84-88, annual rpt, 4944–6

Women prisoners in State instns, by offense, drug use history, whether abused, and other characteristics, 1986, 6066–19.61

Youth drug, alcohol, and cigarette use and attitudes, by substance type and selected characteristics, 1975-90 surveys, annual rpt, 4494–4

see also Alcohol abuse and treatment
see also Cocaine
see also Drug and alcohol testing
see also Drug and narcotics offenses
see also Marijuana

Drug Abuse Warning Network

Cocaine-related emergency room admissions, by user and use characteristics, for major metro areas, 1987-89, article, 4042–3.204

Emergency room admissions and deaths, by drug type and major metro area, semiannual rpt, discontinued, 4492–3

Emergency room admissions and deaths, by drug type and source, sex, race, age, and major metro area, 1990, annual rpt, 4494–8

Emergency room admissions, for selected metro areas, 1991 semiannual conf, 4492–5

Drug and alcohol testing

Arrests, by offense, offender characteristics, and location, data compilation, 1991 annual rpt, 6064–6.4

Arrests for drug- and nondrug-related offenses, urine test results by drug type, offense, and sex, for selected urban areas, quarterly rpt, 6062–3

Criminal defendants drug testing demonstration program operations, offender characteristics, and judges views, 1987-90, 18208–11

Employee drug abuse prevention programs and policies, by firm size, 1988 and 1990, article, 6722–1.224

Fed Govt drug abuse and trafficking reduction programs activities, funding, staff, and Bush Admin budget request, by Federal agency and program area, FY90-92, 238–2

Fed Govt employee drug testing, results, and costs, by agency, FY87-92, GAO rpt, 26119–344

Fed Govt personnel action appeals, decisions of Merit Systems Protection Board by agency and region, FY90, annual rpt, 9494–2

Labor laws enacted, by State, 1990, annual article, 6722–1.209

Navy battleship *USS Iowa* explosion, safety and personnel mgmt issues, with technical analysis, FY89, GAO rpt, 26123–315

Public opinion on employer drug testing, by sex, data compilation, 1991 annual rpt, 6064–6.2

Tanker Exxon Valdez oil spill, safety issues, with oil lost and crew alcohol and drug test results, 1989, 9618–17

Traffic accidents, deaths, and injuries, alcohol levels of drivers, data compilation, 1991 annual rpt, 6064–6.3

Traffic fatal accidents, alcohol levels of drivers and others, by circumstances and characteristics of persons and vehicles, 1989, annual rpt, 7764–16

Urinalysis methods accuracy, by drug type, 1991, 6066–26.6

Drug and narcotics offenses

Abuse of drugs, indicators for selected metro areas, research results, data collection, and policy issues, 1991 semiannual conf, 4492–5

Arrest rates, by offense, sex, age, and race, 1965-89, annual rpt, 6224–7

Arrests, by offense, offender characteristics, and location, data compilation, 1991 annual rpt, 6064–6.4

Arrests, by offense, offender characteristics, and location, 1990, annual rpt, 6224–2.2

Arrests for drug- and nondrug-related offenses, urine test results by drug type, offense, and sex, for selected urban areas, quarterly rpt, 6062–3

Arrests for drug trafficking and possession, 1985-89, annual rpt, 6066–25.37

Arrests, prosecutions, convictions, and sentencing, for felony offenders, by offender characteristics and offense, 1988, 6066–25.33; 6066–25.39

Assaults and deaths of law enforcement officers, by circumstances, agency, victim and offender characteristics, and location, 1990, annual rpt, 6224–3

Coast Guard drug, immigration, and fisheries enforcement activities, 2nd half FY91, semiannual rpt, 7402–4

Cocaine abuse, user characteristics, and related crime and violence, 1988 conf, 4498–74

Costs (direct and indirect) of mental illness and drug and alcohol abuse, by type and patient age and sex, 1985 with 1980 and 1988 comparisons, 4048–35

Court civil and criminal caseloads for Federal district, appeals, and bankruptcy courts, by type of suit and offense, circuit, and district, 1990, annual rpt, 18204–11

Court civil and criminal caseloads for Federal district, appeals, and special courts, 1990, annual rpt, 18204–8

Court civil and criminal caseloads for Federal district courts, 1991, annual rpt, 18204–2.1

Court criminal case processing in Federal district courts, and dispositions, by offense, district, and offender characteristics, 1986, annual rpt, 6064–29

Court criminal case processing in Federal district courts, and dispositions, by offense, 1980-89, annual rpt, 6064–31

Court criminal cases in Federal district courts, by offense, disposition, and district, 1980-90, last issue of annual rpt, 18204–1

Crime, criminal justice admin and enforcement, and public opinion, data compilation, 1991 annual rpt, 6064–6

Drug and narcotics offenses

Crimes, arrests, and rates, by offense, offender characteristics, population size, and jurisdiction, 1990, annual rpt, 6224–2.1; 6224–2.2

Customs Service activities, collections, entries processed by mode of transport, and seizures, FY86-90, annual rpt, 8144–1

Data on drug offenses, enforcement, and public opinion, BJS rpts, 1975-89, annual pamphlet, 6064–30

Drug testing of criminal defendants, demonstration program operations, offender characteristics, and judges views, 1987-90, 18208–11

Enforcement, abuse, and treatment policy issues, series, 236–1

Enforcement activities of drug control task forces by drug type and State, and organization, staff, and spending, 1988, 6068–244

Enforcement and abuse issues, series, 236–2

Fed Govt drug abuse and trafficking reduction programs activities, funding, staff, and Bush Admin budget request, by Federal agency and program area, FY90-92, 238–2

Fed Govt drug abuse and trafficking reduction programs funding, and Bush Admin budget request, by agency and program area, FY90-92, 238–1

Fed Govt drug smuggling interdiction programs, budget, and seizures, FY87-90, GAO rpt, 26119–318

Fed Govt financial and nonfinancial domestic aid, 1991 base edition with supplements, annual listing, 104–5

Foreign countries drug production, eradication, and seizures, by illegal substance, with US aid, by country, 1987-91, annual rpt, 7004–17

Foreign countries economic and military aid loans and grants from US and intl agencies, by program and country, FY46-90, annual rpt, 9914–5

Homicides, by circumstance, victim and offender relationship, and type of weapon, 1990, annual rpt, 6224–2.1

Immigration and Naturalization Service drug and property seizures, FY89, fact sheet, 6266–2.3

Jail population, by criminal, correctional, drug use, and family history, and selected other characteristics, 1989, 6066–19.62

Jail population, by sociodemographic characteristics, criminal and drug use history, whether convicted, offense, and sentencing, 1989, annual rpt, 6064–26.3

Jail population drug abuse history, by offense, conviction status, criminal and family history, and selected other characteristics, 1989, 6066–19.63

Juvenile correctional and detention public and private instns, inmates, and expenses, by instn and resident characteristics and State, 1987, biennial rpt, 6064–13

Juvenile courts delinquency cases, by offense, referral source, disposition, age, sex, race, State, and county, 1988, annual rpt, 6064–12

Juvenile facilities, population, and costs, by facility and resident characteristics, region, and State, 1985-89, biennial rpt, 6064–5

Labs for illegal drug manufacture, seizures by substance and location, 1989-90, annual rpt, 6284–3

Land Mgmt Bur activities and funding by State, FY89, annual rpt, 5724–13

Marijuana crop eradication activities of DEA and local agencies by State, and drug potency and prices, 1982-90, annual rpt, 6284–4

Marshals Service activities, FY89, annual rpt, 6294–1

Methamphetamine abuse, availability, health effects, and treatment, 1990 conf papers, 4498–75

Natl Guard drug enforcement support activities spending and needs, by State, FY89-91, GAO rpt, 26123–343

Natl Guard drug enforcement support, strengths by mission, FY90, annual rpt, 3504–22

New York City drug enforcement personnel, arrests, and seizures, 1985-90, hearing, 25528–117

Organized Crime Drug Enforcement Task Forces regional investigation activities by agency and region, FY83-90, biennial rpt, 6004–17

Peru cocaine production, acreage, and economic impacts of crop eradication and conversion to legitimate agricultural use, 1960s-87, 9918–19

Postal Service inspection activities, 2nd half FY91, semiannual rpt, 9862–2

Pretrial processing, detention, and release, for Federal offenders, by defendant characteristics and district, 1988, hearing, 25528–114

Pretrial release of felony defendants and rearrests, by offense type and selected characteristics, 1988, 6066–25.36

Prison and parole admissions and releases, sentence length, and time served, by offense and offender characteristics, 1985, annual rpt, 6064–33

Probation and split sentences by State courts for felony offenses, sentence lengths, case processing time, and felon characteristics, by offense, 1986, 6068–242

Rural areas drug and alcohol abuse, related crime, and treatment, by substance and State, 1988-90, GAO rpt, 26131–79

Seizures of criminal assets, Justice Dept and Customs Service forfeiture programs finances, and disbursements by State and judicial district, FY85-90, hearing, 25408–112

Seizures of criminal assets, Justice Dept program holdings, finances, and disbursements, FY86-90, annual rpt, 6004–21

Sentences for Federal crimes, guidelines use and results by offense and district, and Sentencing Commission activities, 1990, annual rpt, 17664–1

Sentences for Federal offenses, guidelines by offense and circumstances, series, 17668–1

State and local drug enforcement programs, FY90, annual rpt, 6064–32

Statistical Abstract of US, 1991 annual data compilation, 2324–1.5

Supply of drugs in US by country of origin, abuse, prices, and seizures, by substance, 1990, annual rpt, 6284–2

Index by Subjects and Names

Tax litigation and enforcement activity of IRS, FY90, annual rpt, 8304–3.1

US attorneys civil and criminal cases by type and disposition, and collections, by Federal district, FY90, annual rpt, 6004–2.1; 6004–2.7

US attorneys staffing disparities among district offices, and caseload by litigation type, FY87-90, GAO rpt, 26119–323

Violent and criminal behavior relation to drug abuse, with data on street gang activity and selected population groups, 1989 conf, 4498–70

Wiretaps authorized, costs, arrests, trials, and convictions, by offense and jurisdiction, 1990, annual rpt, 18204–7

Women prisoners in State instns, by offense, drug use history, whether abused, and other characteristics, 1986, 6066–19.61

Drug Enforcement Administration

Budget of US, obligations and authority by function, agency, and program, with summaries, analyses, and historical tables, FY92, annual rpt, 104–2

Foreign countries drug enforcement personnel training of US, enrollment in US and host countries by program, 1989-90, annual rpt, 7004–17

Labs for illegal drug manufacture, seizures by substance and location, 1989-90, annual rpt, 6284–3

Marijuana crop eradication activities of DEA and local agencies by State, and drug potency and prices, 1982-90, annual rpt, 6284–4

Supply of drugs in US by country of origin, abuse, prices, and seizures, by substance, 1990, annual rpt, 6284–2

Drug industry
see Pharmaceutical industry

Drug Use Forecasting System

Drug test results at arrest, by drug type, offense, and sex, for selected urban areas, quarterly rpt, 6062–3

Drugs

Advertising of prescription drugs direct to consumer, benefits and problems, review of studies published 1984-91, GAO rpt, 26131–86

Allergy and Infectious Diseases Natl Inst activities, grants by recipient and location, and disease cases, FY83-90, annual rpt, 4474–30

Cancer (large-bowel) risk related to nonsteroidal anti-inflammatory drug use, 1977-88 local area study, article, 4472–1.205

Consumer Expenditure Survey, household income by source, and itemized spending, by selected characteristics and region, 1988-89, annual rpt, 6764–5

CPI by component for US city average, and by region, population size, and for 27 metro areas, monthly rpt, 6762–2

Cyclosporine use in kidney transplants, effectiveness and costs, with comparison to other immunosuppressive protocols, 1985-87 study, 1989 rpt, 4658–59

Diet pills (nonprescription) and analgesics sales and adverse reactions, and diet and drug effects on hypertension, 1980s-90, hearing, 21728–77

Expenditures for health care, by service type, payment source, and sector, projected 1990-2000 and trends from 1965, article, 4652–1.251

Index by Subjects and Names

Drugstores

Expenditures for health care, by service type, payment source, and sector, 1960s-90, annual article, 4652–1.221; 4652–1.252

Exports and imports (agricultural) of US, by commodity and country, bimonthly rpt, 1522–1

Exports and imports (agricultural) of US, by detailed commodity and country, 1990, semiannual rpt, 1522–4

Exports and imports between US and outlying areas, by detailed commodity and mode of transport, 1990, annual rpt, 2424–11

Exports and imports of US, by Harmonized System 6-digit commodity and country, 1990, annual rpt, 2424–13

Exports and imports of US, by selected country, country group, and commodity group, 1990, annual rpt, 2044–37

Exports and imports of US, by transport mode, country, and SITC 1- to 3-digit commodity, 1990, annual rpt, 2424–12

Exports of US, detailed Schedule B commodities with countries of destination, 1990, annual rpt, 2424–10

Health Care Financing Review, provider prices, price inputs and indexes, and labor, quarterly journal, 4652–1.1

Health maintenance organizations and other prepaid managed care plans Medicaid enrollment and use, for 20 States, 1985-89, chartbook, 4108–29

Hospices operations, services, costs, and patient characteristics, for instns without Medicare certification, FY85-86, 4658–52

Ibuprofen from India, injury to US industry from foreign subsidized and less than fair value imports, investigation with background financial and operating data, 1991 rpt, 9886–19.77

Immunosuppressive drugs for transplant patients, coverage under Medicare and other insurance sources, costs, and procedures, 1991 rpt, 26358–246

Imports detained by FDA, by reason, product, shipper, brand, and country, monthly listing, 4062–2

Input-output structure of US economy, detailed interindustry transactions for 84 industries, and components of final demand, 1986, annual article, 2702–1.206

Input-output structure of US economy, detailed interindustry transactions for 85 industries, 1982 benchmark data, 2702–1.213

Insurance (health) coverage and provisions of small business employee benefit plans, by plan type and occupational group, 1990, biennial rpt, 6784–20

Insurance (health) plans for employees, coverage of prescription drugs by plan type, and copayments required, 1989, article, 6722–1.215

Mail service pharmacy industry structure, finances, and operations, 1989 survey, 4658–60

Malaria treatment with parenteral quinidine gluconate, CDC recommendations, 1991 rpt, 4206–2.40

Manufacturing annual survey, 1989: value of shipments, by SIC 4- to 5-digit product class, 2506–15.2

Manufacturing census, 1987: finances and operations, by SIC 2- to 4-digit industry, State, and MSA, with trends from 1849, 2497–1

Marketing applications for drugs, FDA processing by drug, purpose, and producer, 1990, annual rpt, 4064–14

Marketing of prescription drugs, practices, spending by selected firm, and physicians views, 1990 hearings, 25548–103

Medicaid beneficiaries and payments, by service type, FY72-89, annual rpt, 4744–3.6

Medicaid beneficiaries services use and costs, by service type and eligibility, 1975-89, article, 4652–1.209

Medicare and Medicaid beneficiaries and program operations, 1991, annual fact book, 4654–18

Medicare and Medicaid eligibility, participation, coverage, and program finances, various periods 1966-91, biennial rpt, 4654–1

Medicare beneficiaries copayment limits, alternative proposals, 1991, 26306–6.159

Mental health care in private hospitals, patients characteristics, 1986, 4506–3.47

Mental illness and drug and alcohol abuse direct and indirect costs, by age and sex, 1985, 4048–35

OECD trade, total and for 4 major countries, and US trade by country, by commodity, 1970-89, world area rpt series, 9116–1

Older persons spending for prescription drugs, and manufacturer and retail price changes, by drug type, 1981-88, 4658–56

Opium and poppy straw concentrate imports of US, and morphine use, 1985-88, annual rpt, 3544–37

Opium legal production and US imports by country, and analgesics opium content, 1980s, hearing, 21528–81

Orphan drug tax credit, corporate income tax returns by asset size and detailed industry, 1987, annual rpt, 8304–4

Orphan drug tax credit, corporate income tax returns by asset size and detailed industry, 1988, annual rpt, 8304–21

Orphan drug tax credit, corporate income tax returns, quarterly rpt, 8302–2.1

Pennsylvania aid to aged for prescription drugs, program enrollment, use, and costs, FY85-87, article, 4652–1.237

Physicians visits, by patient and practice characteristics, diagnosis, and services provided, 1989, 4146–8.206

Prescription drug abuse, emergency room admissions by drug type and major metro area, 1990, annual rpt, 4494–8

Prescriptions for drugs, by drug type and brand, and for new drugs, 1989, annual rpt, 4064–12

Price indexes (producer), by stage of processing and detailed commodity, monthly rpt, 6762–6

Price indexes (producer), by stage of processing and detailed commodity, monthly 1990, annual rpt, 6764–2

Production of synthetic organic chemicals, by detailed product, quarterly rpt, 9882–1

Regulatory and investigation activities of FDA, quarterly rpt, suspended, 4062–3

Reproduction and population research, Fed Govt funding by project, FY89, annual listing, 4474–9

Shipments, trade, and use of drugs, by product, 1990, annual Current Industrial Rpt, 2506–8.5

Stockpiling of strategic material by Fed Govt, activity, and inventory by commodity, as of Mar 1991, semiannual rpt, 3542–22

Stockpiling of strategic material, inventories and needs, by commodity, as of Jan 1991, annual rpt, 3544–37

Teenagers physicians office visits, by reason and characteristics of physicians, patients, and visit, 1985, 4146–8.199

Ulcer treatment drug (ranitidine hydrochloride), impact of temporary import duty suspension on US competition, 1991 rpt, 9886–4.167

see also Biologic drug products

see also Chemotherapy

see also Cocaine

see also Drug abuse and treatment

see also Drug and alcohol testing

see also Drug and narcotics offenses

see also Drugstores

see also Hormones

see also Marijuana

see also Pharmaceutical industry

see also Poisoning and drug reaction

see also Vaccination and vaccines

see also under By Commodity in the "Index by Categories"

Drugstores

Census of Retail Trade, 1987: depreciable assets, capital and operating expenses, sales, value added, and inventories, by SIC 2- to 4-digit kind of business, 2399–2

Census of Retail Trade, 1987: finances and employment, for establishments with and without payroll, by SIC 2- to 4-digit kind of business, State, and MSA, 2401–1

County Business Patterns, 1988: employment, establishments, and payroll, by SIC 2- to 4-digit industry and county, annual State rpt series, 2326–6

County Business Patterns, 1989: employment, establishments, and payroll, by SIC 2- to 4-digit industry and county, annual State rpt series, 2326–8

Employment, earnings, and hours, by SIC 1- to 4-digit industry, monthly and annual averages, selected years 1909-90, annual rpt, 6744–4

Enterprise Statistics, 1987: auxiliaries of multi-establishment firms, finances and operations by function, industry, and State, 2329–6

Enterprise Statistics, 1987: finances and operations for companies, by size, level of diversification, form of organization, and industry group, 2329–8

Finances and operations, by SIC 2- to 4-digit industry, forecast 1991, annual rpt, 2044–28

Franchise business opportunities by firm and kind of business, and sources of aid and info, 1990 annual listing, 2104–7

Labor productivity, indexes of output, hours, and employment by SIC 2- to 4-digit industry, 1967-89, annual rpt, 6824–1.4

Occupational injury and illness rates, by SIC 2- to 4-digit industry, 1988-89, annual rpt, 6844–7

Drugstores

Occupational injury and illness rates, by SIC 2- to 4-digit industry, 1989, annual rpt, 6844–1

Puerto Rico economic censuses, 1987: wholesale and retail trade and service industry finances and operations, by SIC 2- to 4-digit industry and municipio, 2591–1

Puerto Rico economic censuses, 1987: wholesale, retail, and service industries finances and operations, by establishment characteristics and SIC 2- and 3-digit industry, subject rpts, 2591–2

Sales and inventories, by kind of retail business, region, and selected State, MSA, and city, monthly rpt, 2413–3

Sales, inventories, purchases, gross margin, and accounts receivable, by SIC 2- to 4-digit kind of business and form of ownership, 1989, annual rpt, 2413–5

Sales of retailers, by kind of business, advance monthly rpt, 2413–2

State and Metro Area Data Book, 1991 data compilation, 2328–54

Tax (income) returns of corporations, income and tax items by asset size and detailed industry, 1987, annual rpt, 8304–4

Tax (income) returns of corporations, income and tax items by asset size and detailed industry, 1988, annual rpt, 8304–21

Tobacco ads in food and drug stores, prevalence and characteristics, 1987 local area study, article, 4042–3.250

Drunk drivers
see Driving while intoxicated

Drunkenness
see Alcohol abuse and treatment

Drury, David
"Workers with Disabilities in Large and Small Firms: Profiles from the SIPP", 2626–10.130

Dubai
see United Arab Emirates

Dubay, Lisa C.
"Changes in Medicare Skilled Nursing Facility Benefit Admissions", 4652–1.222

Dubman, Robert
"Financial Performance of Specialized Corn-Soybean Farms, 1987", 1566–8.7
"Financial Performance of Specialized Hog Farms, 1987", 1566–8.6
"Which Farmers Will Be Most Affected by Increasing Oil Prices?", 1541–1.203

Dubrovsky, Neil M.
"Geochemical Relations and Distribution of Selected Trace Elements in Ground Water of the Northern Part of the Western San Joaquin Valley, Calif. Regional Aquifer-System Analysis", 5666–25.11
"Regional Assessment of Nonpoint-Source Pesticide Residues in Ground Water, San Joaquin Valley, Calif. Regional Aquifer-System Analysis", 5666–25.12

Dubuque, Iowa
see also under By SMSA or MSA in the "Index by Categories"

Duca, John V.
"Credit Cards and Money Demand: A Cross-Sectional Study", 9379–12.74
"Econometric Analysis of Borrowing Constraints and Household Debt", 9379–12.73

Duck stamps
see Hunting and fishing licenses

Due process of law
Court caseloads, actions, procedure duration, judges, and jurors, by Federal district and appeals court, 1986-91, annual rpt, 18204–3

Court civil and criminal caseloads for Federal district, appeals, and special courts, 1990, annual rpt, 18204–8

Court civil and criminal caseloads for Federal district, appeals, and special courts, 1991, annual rpt, 18204–2

Foreign countries human rights conditions in 170 countries, 1990, annual rpt, 21384–3

US attorneys civil and criminal cases by type and disposition, and collections, by Federal district, FY90, annual rpt, 6004–2.1; 6004–2.7

see also Civil procedure
see also Criminal procedure

Duewer, Lawrence A.
"Beefpacking and Processing Plants: Computer-Assisted Cost Analysis", 1568–301
"Revisions in Conversion Factors for Pork Consumption Series", 1561–7.201

Duffee, Gregory R.
"New Test for Mean Reversion in Stock Prices", 9366–6.266

Duffield, James A.
"Will Immigration Reform Affect the Economic Competitiveness of Labor-Intensive Crops?", 1598–276

Duffy, Louise K.
"Petroleum: An Energy Profile", 3164–95
"Regulation of Underground Petroleum Storage", 3162–6.203

Duluth, Minn.
see also under By SMSA or MSA in the "Index by Categories"

Dummit, Laura A.
"Case Mix, Financial Status, and Capital Investments", 17206–2.19

Dumping
Communist countries imports of US, status of dumping investigations by product, quarterly rpt with articles, 9882–2

Export and import agreements, negotiations, and related legislation, 1990, annual rpt, 444–1

Imports injury to US industries from foreign subsidized products and sales at less than fair value, investigations with background financial and operating data, series, 9886–19

Imports injury to US industries from foreign subsidized products, investigations with background financial and operating data, series, 9886–15

Imports injury to US industries from sales at less than fair value, investigations with background financial and operating data, series, 9886–14

USITC activities, investigations, and rpts, FY90, annual rpt, 9884–1

see also Trade adjustment assistance

Dumps
see Hazardous waste and disposal
see Landfills
see Radioactive waste and disposal

Dunham, Denis
"Food Cost Review, 1990", 1544–9

Index by Subjects and Names

Dunkirk, N.Y.
see also under By SMSA or MSA in the "Index by Categories"

Dunson, Bruce H.
"Cyclical Effects of the Unemployment Insurance (UI) Program: Final Report", 6406–6.34

Durham, N.C.
Wages by occupation, for office and plant workers, 1991 survey, periodic MSA rpt, 6785–3.7
see also under By City and By SMSA or MSA in the "Index by Categories"

Dursthoff, Clay
"Significant Features of Fiscal Federalism, 1991 Edition. Volume 1. Budget Processes and Tax Systems", 10044–1.1

Duties
see Tariffs and foreign trade controls

Duval, Joseph S.
"Radium Distribution Map and Radon Potential in the Bonneville Power Administration Service Area", 5668–114

Dyes
see Paints and varnishes

Eaglin, James B.
"Pre-Argument Conference Program in the Sixth Circuit Court of Appeals", 18408–45

Ear diseases and infections
Cases of acute and chronic conditions, disability, absenteeism, and health services use, by selected characteristics, 1987, CD-ROM, 4147–10.177

Deaths and rates, by detailed cause and demographic characteristics, 1988 and trends from 1900, US Vital Statistics annual rpt, 4144–2

see also under By Disease in the "Index by Categories"

Eargle, Judith
"Household Wealth and Asset Ownership: 1988", 2546–20.16

Earl, Robert
"Nutrition Labeling: Current Status and Comparison of Various Proposals", 1004–16.1

Earnings, general
AFDC beneficiaries demographic and financial characteristics, by State, FY89, annual rpt, 4694–1

Alien workers (unauthorized) and Fair Labor Standards Act employer compliance, hiring impacts, and aliens overstaying visas by country and State, 1986-90, annual rpt, 6264–6

Athletes in college, educational and employment performance compared to other students, for 1972 high school class, as of 1986, 4888–5

Black American displaced workers, by demographic and current and former employment characteristics, and compared to whites, 1978-86, article, 6722–1.234

Collective bargaining contract expirations, wage increases, and coverage, by major industry group, 1991, annual article, 6722–1.206

Collective bargaining wage and benefit changes, by industry div, monthly rpt, 6782–1

Collective bargaining wage and benefit changes, quarterly press release, 6782–2

Index by Subjects and Names

Earnings, general

Collective bargaining wage changes and coverage, by industry sector and whether contract includes escalator clause and lump sum payment, 1980-90, annual article, 6722–1.227

College grads of 1986, student loan debt burden by selected student characteristics and instn control, 1987, 4808–26

Data on personal income and earnings, estimates by State, data sources and reliability, 1980-87, article, 2702–1.202

Disabled persons rehabilitation, Federal and State activities and funding, FY90, annual rpt, 4944–1

Displaced workers losing job 1985-90, by demographic and former and current employment characteristics, as of Jan 1990, article, 6722–1.225

Distribution of earnings, by sex, race, industry div, and occupation, 1960-89, article, 6722–1.201

Drug and alcohol abuse and mental illness direct and indirect costs, by type, 1970s-88, article, 4042–3.219

Earnings and hours of production or nonsupervisory workers on nonagricultural payrolls, monthly rpt, 6742–2.6

Earnings by industry div, and personal income per capita and by source, by State, MSA, and county, 1984-89, annual regional rpts, 2704–2

Earnings by industry group, region, and State, 1988-90, annual article, 2702–1.216

Earnings, employment, and hours, and other BLS economic indicators, transcripts of BLS Commissioner's monthly testimony, periodic rpt, 23846–4

Earnings, employment, and hours, by SIC 1- to 4-digit industry, monthly and annual averages, selected years 1909-90, annual rpt, 6744–4

Earnings, employment, and hours, monthly press release, 6742–5

Earnings, employment, hours, and productivity, by industry div, selected years 1929-90, annual rpt, 204–1.2

Economic and employment conditions, alternative BLS projections to 2005 and trends 1970s-90, biennial article, 6722–1.251

Economic indicators and components, and Fed Reserve 4th District business and financial conditions, monthly chartbook, 9377–10

Economic indicators and components, current data and annual trends, monthly rpt, 23842–1.2

Economic indicators compounded annual rates of change, 1971-90, annual rpt, 9391–9.2

Economic indicators, prices, labor costs, and productivity, BLS econometric analyses and methodology, working paper series, 6886–6

Education data, detail for elementary, secondary, and higher education, 1920s-90 and projected to 2001, annual rpt, 4824–1

Educational attainment and work experience impact on earnings, model description and results for men, by census div, 1979-88, article, 9373–1.213

Educational attainment, by sociodemographic characteristics and

location, 1989 and trends from 1940, biennial Current Population Rpt, 2546–1.452

Family members labor force status and earnings, by family composition and race, quarterly press release, 6742–21

Farm operators age and off-farm employment, sales, and land value changes relationship to farm sales size, model description and results, 1974-78, 1548–374

Food stamp eligibility and payment errors, by type, recipient characteristics, and State, FY89, annual rpt, 1364–15

Food stamp recipient household size, composition, income, and income and deductions allowed, summer 1988, annual rpt, 1364–8

Forecasts of employment conditions, alternative BLS projections to 2005 and trends 1970s-90, biennial article, 6722–1.254

Higher education grads and advanced degree recipients, average salaries by field, 1991 edition, annual rpt, 4824–2.28

Hispanic Americans social and economic characteristics, by detailed origin, 1991, Current Population Rpt, 2546–1.448; 2546–1.451

Households composition, income, benefits, and labor force status, Survey of Income and Program Participation methodology, working paper series, 2626–10

Immigrants earnings compared to native-born, relation to social and demographic characteristics, model description and results, 1970 and 1980, technical paper, 9385–8.100; 9385–8.101

Imports and tariff provisions effect on US industries and products, investigations with background financial and operating data, series, 9886–4

Imports competition impacts on manufacturing wages, regression results, late 1950s-85, technical paper, 9385–8.89

Imports injury to US industries from foreign subsidized products and sales at less than fair value, investigations with background financial and operating data, series, 9886–19

Imports injury to US industries from foreign subsidized products, investigations with background financial and operating data, series, 9886–15

Imports injury to US industries from sales at less than fair value, investigations with background financial and operating data, series, 9886–14

Income (household) by source, and itemized spending, by selected characteristics and region, 1988-89 Consumer Expenditure Survey, annual rpt, 6764–5

Income (household, family, and personal), by source, detailed characteristics, and region, 1988-89, annual Current Population Rpt, 2546–6.68

Income (household, family, and personal), by source, detailed characteristics, and region, 1990, annual Current Population Rpt, 2546–6.70

Income (personal) per capita, by region compared to total US, alternative model results, 1929-87, working paper, 9387–8.232

Income (personal) per capita disparity between metro and nonmetro areas, and causal factors, by State, 1979-88, 1548–380

Income disparity between wealthiest and other families, and income sources, 1980s and trends from 1949, 23848–219

Indians and Alaska Natives health care coverage, by type, employment status, and other characteristics, 1987, 4186–8.17

Industry finances and operations, by SIC 2- to 4-digit industry, forecast 1991, annual rpt, 2044–28

Japan manufacturing firms US affiliates, employment, and wages, by selected industry and State, 1980s, 2048–151

Job Training Partnership Act participation by selected characteristics and State, and outcomes, by urban-rural location, 1987-88, 1598–267

Labor force, wages, hours, and payroll costs, by major industry group and demographic characteristics, *Survey of Current Business*, monthly rpt, 2702–1.8

Labor laws enacted, by State, 1990, annual article, 6722–1.209

Manufacturing annual survey, 1989: establishments, employment, finances, inventories, and energy use, by SIC 2- to 4-digit industry, 2506–15.1

Manufacturing census, 1987: finances and operations, by SIC 2- to 4-digit industry, State, and MSA, with trends from 1849, 2497–1

Manufacturing census, 1987: finances and operations, by type of organization and SIC 2- to 4-digit industry, subject rpt, 2497–5

Manufacturing wages impacts of foreign competition and other factors, late 1950s-89, article, 9385–1.204

Military procurement and other factors impacts on wages, 1940s-90, technical paper, 9379–12.65

Minority group higher education enrollment, degrees, factors affecting participation, and earnings, 1960s-88, 4808–29

Monthly Labor Review, current statistics and articles, 6722–1

Multinatl firms US affiliates, investment trends and impact on US economy, 1991 annual rpt, 2004–9

Multinatl US firms and foreign affiliates finances and operations, by industry and world area of parent firm, 1989 benchmark survey, preliminary annual rpt, 2704–5

Natl income and product accounts and components, *Survey of Current Business*, monthly rpt, 2702–1.24

Natl income and product accounts benchmark revisions of GDP and natl income, various periods 1959-80, tables, 2702–1.227

OASDHI admin, and SSA activities, 1930s-90 and projected to 2064, annual data compilation, 4704–12

OASDHI coverage of employment and earnings, late 1930s-89, annual rpt, 4744–3.1; 4744–3.2; 4744–3.3

OASDI coverage of wages, 1970-90 and alternative projections to 2000, actuarial rpt, 4706–1.105

Occupational Outlook Quarterly, journal, 6742–1

Earnings, general

Older persons in rural areas, household income sources, and poverty status, 1983-84, 1598–268

Pay comparability of Fed Govt with private industry, by occupation for 22 MSAs, 1989, GAO rpt, 26119–332

Pension benefits disparity between men and women in small business plans by selected participant and plan characteristics, impacts of 1986 Tax Reform Act, 1984-85, GAO rpt, 26121–412

Pension coverage by industry, vestment, and recipient income, by participant characteristics, 1987, Current Population Rpt, 2546–20.18

Pension plans and OASI benefits, earnings replacement rates, by age, salary, years of participation, and occupational group, 1989, article, 6722–1.238

Population size and characteristics, 1969-88, Current Population Rpt, biennial rpt, 2546–2.161

Poverty rate among workers in metro and nonmetro areas, relation to employment and other characteristics, 1987, 1598–274

Poverty status of population and families, by detailed characteristics, 1988-89, annual Current Population Rpt, 2546–6.67

Poverty status of population and families, by detailed characteristics, 1990, annual Current Population Rpt, 2546–6.71

Recruitment, hiring, compensation, and other employment practices of large firms, 1989 survey, GAO rpt, 26119–324

Refugee resettlement programs and funding, arrivals by country of origin, and indicators of adjustment, by State, FY90, annual rpt, 4694–5

Rural areas economic and social conditions, dev, and problems, periodic journal, 1502–7

Rural areas economic conditions and dev, quarterly journal, 1502–8

Rural areas labor force characteristics, with comparisons to urban areas, 1987, 1598–264

Science and engineering PhDs employment and other characteristics, by field and State, 1989, biennial rpt, 9627–18

Social security earnings records errors and rates, by employment type, late 1930s-87, GAO rpt, 26121–422

State and Metro Area Data Book, 1991 data compilation, 2328–54

Statistical Abstract of US, 1991 annual data compilation, 2324–1.13; 2324–1.27

Student aid Pell grants and applicants, by tuition, income level, instn type and control, and State, 1989/90, annual rpt, 4804–1

Survey of Current Business, detailed financial and business data, and economic indicators, monthly rpt, 2702–1.4

Survey of Current Business, earnings and compensation indexes, monthly rpt, 2702–1.2

Tax (income) returns filed by type of filer, selected income items, quarterly rpt, 8302–2.1

Tax (income) returns of individuals, selected income and tax items, by adjusted gross income and State, 1986-88, article, 8302–2.201

Tax (income) returns of individuals, selected income and tax items by income level, preliminary 1989, annual article, 8302–2.209

Tax credit for hiring from groups with high unemployment rates, participation by State, and effectiveness, FY88, GAO rpt, 26121–407

Unemployed displaced and economically disadvantaged workers, training program operations and performance, series, 6406–10

Unemployment insurance coverage of establishments, employment, and wages, by SIC 4-digit industry and State, 1990, annual rpt, 6744–16

Unemployment insurance coverage of wages, by industry div, State, and MSA, 1989-90, annual press releases, 6784–17

Unemployment insurance programs of States and Fed Govt, benefits adequacy, and work disincentives, series, 6406–6

Union coverage of workers and earnings, by age, sex, race, occupational group, and industry div, 1989-90, press release, 6726–1.36

Vocational rehabilitation cases of State agencies by disposition and applicant characteristics, and closures by reason, FY84-88, annual rpt, 4944–6

Wage differentials among industries, by industry and country, and correlation of differentials between countries, for US and West Germany, 1979-87, technical paper, 9366–6.281

Wages, hourly and weekly averages by industry div, monthly press release, 6742–3

Wages of full- and part-time workers, by selected characteristics, quarterly press release, 6742–20

Women awarded child support and alimony, award amount, and payment status, by selected characteristics of woman, 1989, biennial Current Population Rpt, 2546–6.72

Women's employment and educational experiences compared to men, for high school class of 1972, natl longitudinal study, as of 1986, 4888–6

Women's labor force status, earnings, and other characteristics, with comparisons to men, fact sheet series, 6564–1

see also Agricultural wages
see also Area wage surveys
see also Earnings, local and regional
see also Earnings, specific industry
see also Educational employees pay
see also Employee benefits
see also Employee bonuses and work incentives
see also Escalator clauses
see also Farm income
see also Federal pay
see also Foreign labor conditions
see also Government pay
see also Industry wage surveys
see also Labor costs and cost indexes
see also Military pay
see also Minimum wage
see also Payroll
see also Professionals' fees
see also State and local employees pay
see also Wage deductions

Index by Subjects and Names

Earnings, local and regional

American Samoa employment, earnings, and minimum wage, by establishment and industry, 1989, biennial rpt, 6504–6

Dallas-Fort Worth-Arlington metro area employment, earnings, hours, and CPI changes, late 1970s-90, annual rpt, 6964–2

Houston metro area employment, earnings, hours, and CPI changes, 1970s-90, annual rpt, 6964–1

New England States economic indicators, Fed Reserve 1st District, monthly rpt, 9373–2.2

North Central States business and economic conditions, Fed Reserve 9th District, quarterly journal, 9383–19

Southeastern US manufacturing hours and earnings, for 8 States, quarterly press release, 6942–7

Southeastern US services and manufacturing sectors, earnings and earnings distribution by State, 1989, article, 9391–16.205

Southeastern US wages covered under unemployment insurance, by industry div, State, and metro area, 1989-90, annual press release, 6946–3.22

Southwestern US employment by industry div, earnings, and hours, by State, monthly rpt, 6962–2

Tennessee Valley industrial dev and employment, by SIC 2-digit industry, firm, and location, 1990, annual rpt, 9804–3

Texas and Louisiana per capita income, impacts of industry mix and other factors, for 36 MSAs, 1969-88, article, 9379–1.209

Texas services sector growth impact on wages, with data by industry and sector, late 1970s-89, article, 9379–1.210

see also Area wage surveys
see also under By Census Division, By City, By County, By Region, By SMSA or MSA, and By State in the "Index by Categories"

Earnings, specific industry

Construction employment, earnings, and hours, by selected SIC 2- to 3-digit industry, bimonthly rpt, 2042–1.7

Food prices (farm-retail), marketing cost components, and industry finances and productivity, 1960s-90, annual rpt, 1544–9.3

Gear production for selected uses under alternative production requirements, and industry finances and operations, late 1940s-89, 2028–1

Health Care Financing Review, provider prices, price inputs and indexes, and labor, quarterly journal, 4652–1.1

Manufacturing employment by selected characteristics, wages, and import and export penetration rates, by SIC 2- to 4-digit industry, 1982-89, 6366–3.27

Mineral industries census, 1987: finances and operations, by establishment characteristics, SIC 2- to 4-digit industry, and State, subject rpt, 2517–1

Mineral industries census, 1987: finances and operations, by SIC 2- to 4-digit industry, State, and county, census div rpt series, 2515–1

Minerals production, prices, trade, use, employment, tariffs, and stockpiles, by mineral, with foreign comparisons, 1986-90, annual rpt, 5604–18

Railroad employment, earnings, and hours, by occupation for Class I railroads, 1990, annual table, 9484–5

Railroad retirement system funding and benefits findings and recommendations, with background industry data, 1960s-90 and projected to 2060, 9708–1

Steel industry finances, operations, and modernization efforts, with data on major companies and foreign industry, 1968-91, last issue of annual rpt, 9884–24

Textile mill employment, earnings, and hours, for 8 Southeastern States, quarterly press release, 6942–1

Timber-based industry hourly earnings, by major industry and selected State, 1972-88, annual rpt, 1204–29

Timber industry impacts of northern spotted owl conservation in Pacific Northwest, 1980s and alternative projections to 2000, hearings, 21168–45

Vending facilities run by blind on Federal and non-Federal property, finances and operations by agency and State, FY90, annual rpt, 4944–2

see also Agricultural wages

see also Educational employees pay

see also Farm income

see also Federal pay

see also Government pay

see also Industry wage surveys

see also Military pay

see also Payroll

see also State and local employees pay

see also under By Industry in the "Index by Categories"

Earth sciences

Data sources for space sciences and related topics, use by format and user type, FY90, annual rpt, 9504–11

Degrees (PhD) in science and engineering, by field, instn, employment prospects, sex, race, and other characteristics, 1960s-90, annual rpt, 9627–30

Degrees awarded in science and engineering, by field, level, and sex, 1966-89, 9627–33

DOD budget, manpower needs, costs, and force readiness by service branch, FY92, annual rpt, 3504–1

DOE R&D projects and funding at natl labs, universities, and other instns, FY90, annual summary rpt, 3004–18.2

Employment and other characteristics of science and engineering PhDs, by field and State, 1989, biennial rpt, 9627–18

Fed Govt aid to higher education and nonprofit instns for R&D and related activities, by field, instn, agency, and State, FY89, annual rpt, 9627–17

Higher education course completions, by detailed program, sex, race, and instn type, for 1972 high school class, as of 1984, 4888–4

Higher education grad programs enrollment in science and engineering, by field, source of funds, and characteristics of student and instn, 1975-89, annual rpt, 9627–7

NASA project launch schedules and technical descriptions, press release series, 9506–2

NASA R&D funding to higher education instns, by field, instn, and State, FY90, annual listing, 9504–7

R&D funding by higher education instns and federally funded centers, by field, instn, and State, FY89, annual rpt, 9627–13

Space science and related data sources and availability, 1991 annual listing, 9504–10

see also Geography

see also Geology

see also Hydrology

see also Oceanography

Earthquakes

Alaska minerals resources and geologic characteristics, compilation of papers, 1989, annual rpt, 5664–15

Alaska OCS environmental conditions and oil dev impacts, compilation of papers, series, 2176–1

California Loma Prieta earthquake relief funding and response by FEMA, 1989-90, GAO rpt, 26113–511

Foreign countries disasters, casualties, damage, and aid by US and others, FY90 and trends from FY64, annual rpt, 9914–12

Incidents and mgmt of disasters and natl security threats, with data by major event and State, 1991 annual rpt, 9434–6

Intensity of ground motion by station, 1988, annual rpt, 5664–14

Intensity, time, location, damage, and seismic characteristics of US and foreign earthquakes, 1985, annual rpt, 5664–13

Midwestern States earthquakes intensity, time, and seismograph locations, 1977-90, annual rpt, 9634–10

Preparedness for earthquakes, costs and benefits, with data for California events and effects of 1989 Loma Prieta quake, 1980s, hearings, 21248–154

San Andreas fault system earthquakes location and seismic characteristics, by event, 1769-1989, 5668–123

East Pakistan

see Bangladesh

East-West trade

Agricultural trade of US, by detailed commodity and country, 1989, annual rpt, 1524–8

Agricultural trade of US, by detailed commodity and country, 1990, semiannual rpt, 1522–4

Bulgaria trade with US, US tariffs, and impacts of US granting most favored nation status, 1987-90, GAO rpt, 26123–323

China trade with NATO members, by country, 1987-90, annual rpt, 7144–14

China trade with US and through Hong Kong, and impacts of revoking most favored nation status, 1987-90, hearing, 25368–174

Eastern Europe imports from US, and trade opportunities, periodic rpt, 2042–33

Eastern Europe transition to market economies, US trade prospects, with background data by country, 1980s, hearing, 25728–42

Export licensing, monitoring, and enforcement activities, FY90, annual rpt, 2024–1

Exports and imports of US, by Harmonized System 6-digit commodity and country, 1990, annual rpt, 2424–13

Exports and imports of US, by selected country, country group, and commodity group, 1990, annual rpt, 2044–37

Eastern Europe

Exports and imports of US, by transport mode, country, and SITC 1- to 3-digit commodity, 1990, annual rpt, 2424–12

Exports and imports of US, by world area, periodic pamphlet, 2042–25

Exports and imports of US with Communist countries, by detailed commodity and country, quarterly rpt with articles, 9882–2

Exports, imports, and balances of US with major trading partners, by product category, 1986-90, annual chartbook, 9884–21

Imports of goods, services, and investment from US, trade barriers, impacts, and US actions, by country, 1990, annual rpt, 444–2

Oil exports to centrally planned economies from market economy countries, monthly rpt, 3162–42.2

Oils, oilseeds, and meal imports, by commodity, world area of destination, and major producer, 1960s-88, 1528–314

Service industries exports and imports of US, direct and among multinatl firms affiliates, by industry and world area, 1986-90, article, 2702–1.223

Soviet Union economic conditions under General Secretary Gorbachev, 1990 and trends from 1975, annual rpt, 9114–6

Soviet Union hard currency trade by commodity, and balance of payments, 1960s-90, annual rpt, 9114–4.3

Eastern Europe

Agricultural exports of high-value commodities, indexes and sales by commodity, world area, and country, 1960s-86, 1528–323

Agricultural exports of US, for grains, oilseed products, hides, skins, and cotton, by country, weekly rpt, 1922–3

Agricultural production, trade, and land reform in Eastern Europe, with selected economic indicators, by country, 1960s-90, article, 1522–3.202

Agricultural trade of US, by commodity and country, bimonthly rpt, 1522–1

Agricultural trade of US, by detailed commodity and country, 1989, annual rpt, 1524–8

Agricultural trade of US, by detailed commodity and country, 1990, semiannual rpt, 1522–4

AID housing and urban dev program financial statements, FY90, annual rpt, 9914–4

Coal trade flows and reserves, by country, 1980-89 and projected to 2010, annual rpt, 3164–77

Debt of Communist countries to US and other Western banks, by country, 1980s, conf, 25388–56

Debt to foreign lenders by component, trade, balances, and other economic indicators, by Eastern Europe country, 1985-89, hearing, 21248–148

Economic aid to Eastern Europe from US, by agency and country, FY90-92, GAO rpt, 26123–319

Economic and military aid and loans from US and intl agencies, by program and country, FY46-90, annual rpt, 9914–5

Economic and political conditions in Eastern Europe, and impacts of geographic factors, by country, 1990 conf, 9118–18

Eastern Europe

Economic and social conditions of developing countries from 1960s, and Intl Dev Cooperation Agency and AID activities and funding, FY90-92, annual rpt, 9904–4

Economic conditions in Communist and OECD countries, 1989, annual rpt, 7144–11

Economic conditions in USSR, Eastern Europe, OECD, and selected other countries, 1960s-90, annual rpt, 9114–4

Export licensing, monitoring, and enforcement activities, FY90, annual rpt, 2024–1

Exports and imports (waterborne) of US, by type of service, customs district, port, and world area, monthly rpt, 2422–7

Exports and imports of OECD members, by country, 1989, annual rpt, 7144–10

Exports and imports of OECD, total and for 4 major countries, and US trade by country, by commodity, 1970-89, world area rpt, 9116–1.3

Exports and imports of US by country, and trade shifts by commodity, 1990, semiannual rpt, 9882–9

Exports and imports of US, by Harmonized System 6-digit commodity and country, 1990, annual rpt, 2424–13

Exports and imports of US, by selected country, country group, and commodity group, 1990, annual rpt, 2044–37

Exports and imports of US, by transport mode, country, and SITC 1- to 3-digit commodity, 1990, annual rpt, 2424–12

Exports and imports of US with Communist countries, by detailed commodity and country, quarterly rpt with articles, 9882–2

Exports, imports, and balances of US with major trading partners, by product category, 1986-90, annual chartbook, 9884–21

Imports from US, and trade opportunities in Eastern Europe, periodic rpt, 2042–33

Livestock (cattle and hog) stocks and slaughter, and meat production, trade, and use, for Eastern Europe by country, 1989-91, semiannual rpt, 1925–33.2

Loans of US banks to foreigners at all US and foreign offices, by country group and country, quarterly rpt, 13002–1

Market economy transition of Eastern Europe countries, economic conditions, intl aid, and energy balance, by country, 1985-90, 9118–13

Market economy transition of Eastern Europe countries, US trade prospects, with background data by country, 1980s, hearing, 25728–42

Market economy transition of Eastern Europe countries, with trade agreements and bilateral US trade data by country, late 1980s-90, annual rpt, 444–2

Multinatl US firms and foreign affiliates finances and operations, by industry and world area of parent firm, 1989 benchmark survey, preliminary annual rpt, 2704–5

NATO members and Japan economic aid to developing countries and Eastern Europe, 1980-89, annual rpt, 3544–28

Oil and gas production, use, and trade by country, centrally planned economy countries, monthly rpt, 9112–2

Oils, oilseeds, and meal imports, by commodity, world area of destination, and major producer, 1960s-88, 1528–314

Peace Corps activities, funding by program, and volunteers, by country, FY92, annual rpt, 9654–1

Radio Free Europe and Radio Liberty broadcast and financial data, FY90, annual rpt, 10314–1

Refugee arrivals in US by world area and country of origin, and quotas, monthly rpt, 7002–4

Refugee arrivals in US by world area of origin and State of settlement, and Federal aid, FY90-91 and proposed FY92 allocations, annual rpt, 7004–16

Refugee resettlement programs and funding, arrivals by country of origin, and indicators of adjustment, by State, FY90, annual rpt, 4694–5

Service industries exports and imports of US, direct and among multinatl firms affiliates, by industry and world area, 1986-90, article, 2702–1.223

Terrorism (intl) incidents, casualties, and attacks on US targets, by attack type and world area, 1990, annual rpt, 7004–13

Travel to US, by characteristics of visit and traveler, country, port city, and State of destination, quarterly rpt, 2902–1

UN voting record and share of votes in agreement with US, by issue, country, and world area, 1990, annual rpt, 7004–18

US military and civilian personnel and dependents, by service branch, world area, and country, quarterly rpt, 3542–20

USIA library holdings, use, and staff, by country and city, FY90, annual rpt, 9854–4

see also Albania
see also Bulgaria
see also Council for Mutual Economic Assistance
see also Czechoslovakia
see also Germany, East
see also Hungary
see also Poland
see also Romania
see also Soviet Union
see also Warsaw Pact
see also Yugoslavia
see also under By Foreign Country in the "Index by Categories"

Easton, Pa.

see also under By SMSA or MSA in the "Index by Categories"

Eau Claire, Wis.

see also under By SMSA or MSA in the "Index by Categories"

Eavesdropping

see Electronic surveillance

Echelberger, Herbert E.

"Northern Forest Lands: Resident Attitudes and Resource Use", 1208–371

Ecology

see Conservation of natural resources
see Environmental pollution and control
see Environmental sciences
see Marine pollution
see Marine resources conservation
see State funding for natural resources and conservation
see Wildlife and wildlife conservation

Index by Subjects and Names

Economic and econometric models

Agricultural Economics Research, quarterly journal, 1502–3

Agricultural subsidies for producers and consumers of US and foreign govts, production and trade impacts, model description, 1991 rpt, 1528–315

Auto assembly plant productivity and relation to labor reserves, model description and results, 1990 working paper, 6886–6.72

Banks failures, survival probability model forecasting performance, 1986-90, article, 9377–1.204

Banks financial performance, risk assessment, and regulation, 1990 annual conf papers, 9375–7

BLS econometric analyses and methodology, for economic indicators, prices, labor costs, and productivity, working paper series, 6886–6

Business cycle models incorporating money supply impact on economic indicators, assessment of alternative models, 1991 articles, 9383–6.202

Energy Info Admin forecasting and data analysis models, 1991, annual listing, 3164–87

Energy natl strategy plans for conservation and pollution reduction, impacts on electric power supply, costs, and emissions, projected under alternative assumptions, 1995-2030, 3166–6.49

Energy natl strategy plans for conservation, impacts on energy use and pollution under alternative technology investment assumptions, projected 1990-2030, 3166–6.48

Energy natl strategy plans for renewable energy dev, supply projected under alternative cost and capacity use assumptions, 1990-2030, 3166–6.50

Energy supply, demand, and prices, by fuel type and end-use sector, alternative projections 1989-2010, annual rpt, 3164–75

Energy supply, demand, distribution, and regulatory impacts, series, 3166–6

Farm income and production effects of changes in support programs and other factors, for livestock and program and nonprogram crop producers, model results, 1988, 1548–375

Farm prices impact of monetary policy, alternative model results, 1976-90, article, 9391–1.217

Finance (intl) and financial policy, and external factors affecting US economy, technical paper series, 9366–7

Financial and banking devs in Southeastern States, working paper series, 9371–10

Financial and economic analysis, and economic issues affecting North Central States, working paper series, 9375–13

Financial and economic analysis and forecasting methodology, technical paper series, 9366–6; 9377–9

Financial and economic analysis of banking and nonbanking sectors, working paper series, 9381–10

Financial and economic analysis, technical paper series, 9379–12; 9383–20; 9385–8; 9389–19; 9393–10

Financial and economic devs, Fed Reserve Bank of Richmond bimonthly journal, 9389–1

Index by Subjects and Names

Financial and monetary research and econometric analyses, working paper series, 9387–8

Foreign countries economic and social conditions, working paper series, 2326–18

GNP and employment forecasting performance of alternative models, with results, 1958-88, article, 9371–1.201

GNP and GNP deflator variability, alternative models assessment and results, 1869-1988, article, 9379–1.205

GNP changes related to labor force composition and changes in participation, model description and results, 1940s-2000, article, 9373–1.201

GNP variability, real business cycle model assessment, with results for 1950s-84, article, 9375–1.205

Hospital reimbursement by Medicare under prospective payment system, marginal cost and labor demand by metro-nonmetro location, model description and results, 1980s, 17206–2.26

Import restraint elimination impacts on US economy by selected sector, model description and results, 1988, 9886–4.174

Louisiana economic indicators and oil rig growth forecasts, model description and results, 1991, article, 9379–1.202

Manufacturing industries operations and performance, analytical rpt series, 2506–16

Money supply relation to GNP and interest rates, alternative models description and results, 1953-88, article, 9391–1.210

New England States employment growth rates, and performance of alternative forecasts, 1950s-91, article, 9373–1.211

Oil import tariff and excise tax economic impacts, model description and results, 1991 paper, 9406–1.61

Postal Service productivity, indexes of output and labor, capital, and other inputs, alternative model descriptions and results, 1960s-89, 9688–6

Regional multipliers derived from input-output models, use in estimating economic impacts of spending changes, 1991 article, 9391–1.206

Rice prices under alternative stock and loan assumptions, model description and results, 1976-89, article, 1561–8.202

Savings instns financial condition and devs, working paper series, 9379–14

Stock market pricing efficiency, model description and results, late 1920s-90, article, 9373–1.206

Survey of Income and Program Participation, household composition, income, benefits, and labor force status, methodology, working paper series, 2626–10

see also Input-output analysis

see also Mathematic models and modeling

Economic assistance

see Economic policy

see International assistance

see Military assistance

see State funding for economic development

Economic censuses

Data coverage and availability of Census Bur rpts and data files, 1991 annual listing, 2304–2

see also Census of Construction Industries

see also Census of Manufactures

see also Census of Mineral Industries

see also Census of Outlying Areas

see also Census of Retail Trade

see also Census of Service Industries

see also Census of Transportation

see also Census of Wholesale Trade

see also Enterprise Statistics Program

see also Recordkeeping Practices Survey

Economic concentration and diversification

Acquisitions (leveraged buyout) in manufacturing, relation to industry size, concentration ratios, and financial indicators, 1988, technical paper, 9385–8.86

Agriculture census, 1987: farms, farmland, production, finances, and operator characteristics, by county, final State rpt series, 2331–1

Airline deregulation in 1978, impacts on industry structure, competition, fares, finances, operations, and intl service, with data by carrier and airport, 1980s, series, 7308–199

Auto and light truck fuel economy, sales, and market shares, by size and model for US and foreign makes, 1991 model year, semiannual rpt, 3302–4

Bank holding company subsidiaries dealing in bank-ineligible securities, subsidiary and parent firm finances, 1989-91, GAO rpt, 26119–280

Banking industry structure, performance, and financial devs, for Fed Reserve 10th District, 1990, annual rpt, 9381–14.1

Banking intl competition issues, with background data, 1980s, 21248–153

Banks (natl) charters, mergers, liquidations, enforcement cases, and financial performance, with data by instn and State, quarterly rpt, 8402–3

Banks, assets, and financial performance, by asset size, 1970s-90, article, 9383–6.203

Banks assets and market share, compared to other financial instns by detailed industry group, 1950s-90, working paper, 9375–13.62

Banks competitive performance in duopoly market, model description and results, 1970s-86 local area study, working paper, 9387–8.251

Banks financial performance, risk assessment, and regulation, 1990 annual conf papers, 9375–7

Banks in OECD countries, asset shares of 3-5 largest firms, 1984, technical paper, 9385–8.93

Banks interest rates on loans and deposits, relation to market concentration indicators, 1985-90, technical paper, 9366–6.283

Banks market concentration indicators and Treasury security rates relation to bank deposit interest rates, 1980s, technical paper, 9366–6.261

Banks market structure and local economic conditions, impacts on business formations, 1980s, working paper, 9377–9.123

Construction industries census, 1987: establishments, employment, receipts, and expenditures, by SIC 4-digit industry and State, final industry rpt series, 2373–1

Economic crises and depressions

Enterprise Statistics, 1987: finances and operations for companies, by size, level of diversification, form of organization, and industry group, 2329–8

Farms, farmland, and sales distribution, by sales size, various periods 1969-84, 1588–150

Food industry vertically integrated markets, and farm products produced under contract, 1960s-90, article, 9381–1.205

Hospital reimbursement by Medicare under prospective payment system, impacts on costs, industry structure and operations, and quality of care, series, 17206–2

Import prices relation to dollar exchange rate for 32 industries, and impacts of domestic market concentration, 1990 working paper, 9387–8.234

Imports from Communist countries, market share by selected commodity, quarterly rpt, 9882–2

Imports injury to US industries from sales at less than fair value, investigations with background financial and operating data, series, 9886–14

Investment spending of manufacturing industry groups, relation to concentration ratios and other factors, 1960s-82, technical paper, 9385–8.81

Japan corporations finances, for firms affiliated with integrated conglomerates and independent firms, 1976-89, article, 9375–1.203

Livestock industry regional concentration impacts on water pollution, 1991 article, 1522–3.204

Manufacturing census, 1987: finances and operations, by SIC 2- to 4-digit industry, State, and MSA, with trends from 1849, 2497–1

Oil and gas OCS lease bidding under alternative leasing systems, activity, royalty rates, and production, by sale, lessee type, and ocean area, FY79-89, annual rpt, 5734–12

Semiconductor and fiber optics industries quality control spending, effectiveness, and views, survey results, 1980s, 2218–84

Telecommunications finances, rates, and traffic for US carriers intl operations, by service type, firm, and country, 1975-89, annual rpt, 9284–17

Telecommunications industry intl competitiveness, with financial and operating data by product or service, firm, and country, 1990 rpt, 2008–30

Texas and Louisiana per capita income, impacts of industry mix and other factors, for 36 MSAs, 1969-88, article, 9379–1.209

Transportation census, 1987: finances and operations by size, ownership, and State, and revenues by MSA, by SIC 2- to 4-digit industry, 2579–1

see also Antitrust law

see also Business acquisitions and mergers

see also Competition

see also Holding companies

see also Monopolies and cartels

see also Ownership of enterprise

Economic crises and depressions

see Business cycles

Economic development

Economic development

Budget of US, House concurrent resolution, with spending and revenue targets, FY92 and projected to FY96, annual rpt, 21264–2

Budget of US, obligations and authority by function, agency, and program, with summaries, analyses, and historical tables, FY92, annual rpt, 104–2

Coastal areas environmental and socioeconomic conditions, and potential impact of oil and gas OCS leases, final statement series, 5736–1

Economic Dev Admin activities, and funding by program, recipient, State, and county, FY90 and cumulative from FY66, annual rpt, 2064–2

Economic Dev Admin rpts, 1988-90, annual listing, 2064–9

Expenditures of Fed Govt in States, by type, program, agency, and State, FY90, annual listing, 2464–2

Fed Govt financial and nonfinancial domestic aid, 1991 base edition with supplements, annual listing, 104–5

Forest Service mgmt of public lands and resources dev, environmental, economic, and social impacts of alternative programs, projected to 2040, 1208–24

Labor laws enacted, by State, 1990, annual article, 6722–1.209

New Hampshire and Vermont public opinion on natural resources use and mgmt, 1991 rpt, 1208–371

Older persons migration to southern coastal areas, household finances, services needs, and local economic impacts, for selected counties, 1990, 2068–38

Rural areas economic and social conditions, dev, and problems, periodic journal, 1502–7

Rural areas economic conditions and dev, quarterly journal, 1502–8

Tax expenditures, Federal revenues forgone through income tax deductions and exclusions by type, FY92-96, annual rpt, 21784–10

Tennessee Valley industrial dev and employment, by SIC 2-digit industry, firm, and location, 1990, annual rpt, 9804–3

TVA finances and operations by program and facility, FY90, annual rpt, 9804–32

Wetlands acreage, resources, soil and water properties, and conservation efforts, by wetland type, State rpt series, 5506–11

see also Business cycles

see also Community development

see also Community Development Block Grants

see also Developing countries

see also Economic indicators

see also Job creation

see also Regional planning

see also State funding for economic development

see also Urban Development Action Grants

see also Urban renewal

Economic Development Administration

Activities of EDA, and funding by program, recipient, State, and county, FY90 and cumulative from FY66, annual rpt, 2064–2

Budget of US, obligations and authority by function, agency, and program, with summaries, analyses, and historical tables, FY92, annual rpt, 104–2

Expenditures of Fed Govt in States, by type, program, agency, and State, FY90, annual rpt, 2464–2

Older persons migration to southern coastal areas, household finances, services needs, and local economic impacts, for selected counties, 1990, 2068–38

Publications of EDA, 1988-90, annual listing, 2064–9

Economic indicators

Agricultural Outlook, production, prices, marketing, and trade, by commodity, forecast and current situation, monthly rpt with articles, 1502–4

Argentina black-market dollar exchange rate relationship with official rate and other economic indicators, model description and results, 1991 technical paper, 9366–7.261

BEA rpts data coverage and availability, 1991 rpt, 2708–45

Budget deficits under Reagan Admin, impact on capital stock, foreign debt, and other economic indicators, with background data, 1950s-88, article, 9393–8.201

Budget of US, CBO analysis and review of FY92 budget by function, annual rpt, 26304–2

Budget of US, CBO analysis of revenue and spending alternatives and projections of economic indicators, FY92-96, annual rpt, 26304–3

Budget of US, compilation of background material on fiscal and tax policy, 1960s-96, 21788–203

Budget of US, House Budget Committee analysis of Bush Admin proposals and economic assumptions, FY92, 21268–42

Budget of US, House concurrent resolution, with spending and revenue targets, FY92 and projected to FY96, annual rpt, 21264–2

Budget of US, midsession review of FY92 budget, by function, annual rpt, 104–7

Budget of US, obligations and authority by function, agency, and program, with summaries, analyses, and historical tables, FY92, annual rpt, 104–2

Budget of US, Senate concurrent resolution, with spending and revenue targets, FY92, annual rpt, 25254–1

Business America, foreign and domestic commerce, and US investment and trade opportunities, biweekly journal, 2042–24

Business formations impacts of local bank market structure and economic conditions, 1980s, working paper, 9377–9.123

Caribbean Basin Initiative investment incentives, economic impacts, with finances and employment by country, 1984-90, 2048–141

China economic indicators and reform issues, with background data, 1950s-90, compilation of papers, 23848–155

Communist and OECD countries economic conditions, 1989, annual rpt, 7144–11

Credit (commercial paper-bank loan) financing mix and selected interest rate spreads, impact on economic indicators, model description and results, 1960s-89, technical paper, 9366–6.268

Developing countries agricultural supply, demand, and market for US exports, with socioeconomic conditions, country rpt series, 1526–6

Developing countries child health and welfare indicators, and economic conditions, 1950s-80s, hearing, 25388–57

Developing countries economic and social conditions from 1960s, and Intl Dev Cooperation Agency and AID activities and funding, FY90-92, annual rpt, 9904–4

Developing countries economic, population, and agricultural data, US and other aid sources, and AID activity, country rpt series, 9916–12

Developing countries labor standards impacts on social and economic dev, 1988 conf papers, 6368–9

Developing countries population and economic data, and AID dev projects, special study series, 9916–3

Eastern Europe agricultural production, trade, and land reform, with selected economic indicators, by country, 1960s-90, article, 1522–3.202

Eastern Europe economic and political conditions, and impacts of geographic factors, by country, 1990 conf, 9118–18

Eastern Europe foreign debt components, trade, balances, and other economic indicators, by country, 1985-89, hearing, 21248–148

Eastern Europe transition to market economies, economic conditions, intl aid, and energy balance, by country, 1985-90, 9118–13

EC economic integration economic impacts, with background data by country, 1988-90, article, 9379–1.201

EC economic integration issues, with economic indicators and trade by country, 1985-89, article, 9371–1.210

Economic and financial devs, Fed Reserve Bank of Boston quarterly journal, 9373–25

Economic indicators and components, and Fed Reserve 4th District business and financial conditions, monthly chartbook, 9377–10

Economic indicators and components, current data and annual trends, monthly rpt, 23842–1

Economic indicators and cyclical devs and outlook, by Fed Reserve Bank District, periodic rpt, 9362–8

Economic indicators compounded annual rates of change, monthly rpt, 9391–3

Economic indicators compounded annual rates of change, 1971-90, annual rpt, 9391–9

Economic indicators performance, and Fed Reserve monetary policy objectives, as of July 1991, semiannual rpt, 9362–4

Economic indicators performance from 1961, and Commerce Dept rpts, biweekly listing, 2002–1

Economic indicators summary, monthly rpt, 2302–3

Economic Report of the President for 1991, Joint Economic Committee critique and policy recommendations, annual rpt, 23844–2

Economic Report of the President for 1991, with economic trends from 1929, annual rpt, 204–1

Energy supply, demand, and price forecasts, economic and weather assumptions, quarterly rpt, 3162–34

Index by Subjects and Names

Economic policy

Energy supply, demand, and prices, by fuel type and end-use sector, projections and underlying assumptions, 1990-2010, annual rpt, 3164–90

Energy supply, demand, distribution, and regulatory impacts, series, 3166–6

Exports and imports of US, relation to domestic and foreign economic indicators, model description and results, 1967-88, technical paper, 9385–8.117

Fed Reserve Board and Reserve banks finances, staff, and review of monetary policy and economic devs, 1990, annual rpt, 9364–1

Financial and business detailed statistics, *Fed Reserve Bulletin*, monthly rpt with articles, 9362–1

Financial and economic analysis, technical paper series, 9379–12; 9383–20; 9385–8; 9389–19; 9393–10

Financial and economic devs, Fed Reserve Bank of New York quarterly journal, 9385–1

Financial and monetary conditions, selected US summary data, weekly rpt, 9391–4

Financial market regulatory and structural changes impacts on interest rates, 1950s-80s, technical paper, 9385–8.73

Forecasts of economic and employment conditions, alternative BLS projections to 2005 and trends 1970s-90, biennial article, 6722–1.251

Forecasts of economic indicators, performance of manufacturing activity index of Natl Assn of Purchasing Managers, various periods 1948-91, article, 9385–1.215

Forecasts of economic indicators, performance of preliminary estimates, 1966-90, technical paper, 9385–8.94

Forecasts of economic indicators, 1991-92 with trends from 1948, annual article, 9383–6.201

Foreign and US economic conditions and competitiveness issues, with data by country, 1960s-90, 21788–204

Foreign and US economic conditions, and trade devs and balances, with data by selected country and country group, monthly rpt, 9882–14

Foreign and US economic conditions, for major industrial countries, biweekly rpt, 9112–1

Foreign and US economic indicators, trade balances, and exchange rates, for selected OECD and Asian countries, 1991 semiannual rpt, 8002–14

Foreign countries agricultural production, trade, and policies, summary data by country, 1989-90, annual factbook, 1924–12

Foreign countries *Background Notes*, summary social, political, and economic data, series, 7006–2

Foreign countries economic and monetary trends, compounded annual rates of change and quarterly indicators for US and 7 major industrialized countries, quarterly rpt, 9391–7

Foreign countries economic conditions and implications for US, periodic country rpt series, 2046–4

Foreign countries economic conditions, policy, and trade practices, by country, 1988-90, annual rpt, 21384–5

Foreign countries economic indicators, and trade and investment flows, for selected countries and country groups, selected years 1946-90, annual rpt, 204–1.9

Foreign countries economic indicators, and trade and trade flows by commodity, by country, data compilation, monthly CD-ROM, 2002–6

Foreign countries economic, social, political, and geographic summary data, by country, 1991, annual factbook, 9114–2

Great Lakes area economic conditions and outlook, for US and Canada, 1970s-90, 9375–15

Israel and Egypt govt budgets, foreign debt, and economic indicators, 1980s, hearing, 21388–58

Japan economic conditions, financial and intl policies, and trade devs, 1950s-80s and projected to 2050, compilation of papers, 23848–220

Japan financial instns and stock market conditions, and other economic indicators, with intl comparisons, 1980s-90, hearing, 21248–152

Japan interest rates relation to monetary policy and financial instn regulation, with background data and model results, 1960s-91, article, 9385–1.213; 9385–8.116

Louisiana economic indicators and oil rig growth forecasts, model description and results, 1991, article, 9379–1.202

Manufacturing activity index of Natl Assn of Purchasing Managers, economic indicator forecasting performance, various periods 1948-91, article, 9385–8.120

Mexico banks deregulation impacts on finances, with data by bank, 1960s-90, technical paper, 9385–8.121

New England States economic indicators, Fed Reserve 1st District, monthly rpt, 9373–2

North Carolina environmental and socioeconomic conditions, and impacts of proposed OCS oil and gas exploration, 1970s-90 and projected to 2020, 5738–22

North Central States business and economic conditions, Fed Reserve 9th District, quarterly journal, 9383–19

Overseas Business Reports: economic conditions, investment and export opportunities, and trade practices, country market research rpt series, 2046–6

Persian Gulf War impacts on US economic conditions compared to previous oil shock periods, and Saudi Arabia oil production and prices, 1990-92, hearings, 21248–156

Public works capital stock and investment spending economic impacts, with data by type of stock and region, 1950s-88, conf, 9373–3.34

Puerto Rico statehood referendum proposal, impacts on Federal tax revenue and aid outlays, corporations tax-favored status, and economic conditions, projected FY91-2000, hearing, 25368–168; 26306–3.112

Rocky Mountain region employment and income, and economic dependence on shipments outside area, by industry and county group, 1980s, 1208–362

Rural areas economic conditions and dev, quarterly journal, 1502–8

Southeastern States, Fed Reserve 5th District, economic indicators by State, quarterly rpt, 9389–16

Southeastern States, Fed Reserve 8th District banking and economic conditions, quarterly rpt with articles, 9391–16

Soviet Union, Eastern Europe, OECD, and selected other countries economic conditions, 1960s-90, annual rpt, 9114–4

Soviet Union economic conditions under General Secretary Gorbachev, 1990 and trends from 1975, annual rpt, 9114–6

Survey of Current Business, detailed data for major industries and economic indicators, monthly rpt, 2702–1

Texas economic and housing conditions, bank failures, and thrift and Federal regulators real estate holdings, 1980s-90, hearings, 21248–146

Unemployment insurance programs impacts on business cycles and economic indicators, regression results, 1950s-89, 6406–6.34

West Central States financial and economic devs, Fed Reserve 10th District, quarterly rpt, 9381–16

Zimbabwe agricultural conditions impacts of economic policies, 1980s, 1528–319

see also Business and industry

see also Business assets and liabilities, general

see also Business cycles

see also Business income and expenses, general

see also Business inventories

see also Capital investments, general

see also Consumer Price Index

see also Credit

see also Earnings, general

see also Economic and econometric models

see also Employment and unemployment, general

see also Flow-of-funds accounts

see also Gross Domestic Product

see also Gross National Product

see also Housing costs and financing

see also Housing sales

see also Industrial capacity and utilization

see also Industrial production

see also Industrial production indexes

see also Inflation

see also Job creation

see also Job vacancy

see also Labor productivity

see also Labor turnover

see also Money supply

see also National income and product accounts

see also Personal and household income

see also Personal consumption

see also Prices

see also Producer Price Index

Economic policy

Budget of US, CBO analysis of revenue and spending alternatives and projections of economic indicators, FY92-96, annual rpt, 26304–3

Budget of US, midsession review of FY92 budget, by function, annual rpt, 104–7

Dollar exchange rate forecasting performance of central bank policy intervention indicators, with model results for 2 currencies, 1985-90, working paper, 9377–9.118

Economic policy

Dollar exchange rates of yen and mark, impact of Fed Reserve policy interventions and other economic indicators, 1985-89, technical paper, 9385–8.114

EC economic integration issues, with economic indicators and trade by country, 1985-89, article, 9371–1.210

Economic Report of the President for 1991, Joint Economic Committee critique and policy recommendations, annual rpt, 23844–2

Economic Report of the President for 1991, with economic trends from 1929, annual rpt, 204–1

Financial and economic analysis, technical paper series, 9379–12; 9389–19

Financial and economic devs, Fed Reserve Bank of Atlanta bimonthly rpt with articles, 9371–1

Financial and economic devs, Fed Reserve Bank of Chicago bimonthly journal, 9375–1

Financial and economic devs, Fed Reserve Bank of Dallas bimonthly journal, 9379–1

Financial and economic devs, Fed Reserve Bank of Kansas City bimonthly journal, 9381–1

Financial and economic devs, Fed Reserve Bank of Minneapolis quarterly journal, 9383–6

Financial and economic devs, Fed Reserve Bank of New York quarterly journal, 9385–1

Financial and economic devs, Fed Reserve Bank of Philadelphia bimonthly journal, 9387–1

Financial and economic devs, Fed Reserve Bank of Richmond bimonthly journal, 9389–1

Financial and economic devs, Fed Reserve Bank of San Francisco quarterly journal, 9393–8

Financial and economic devs, Fed Reserve Bank of St Louis bimonthly journal, 9391–1

Foreign countries economic conditions and implications for US, periodic country rpt series, 2046–4

Foreign countries economic conditions, policy, and trade practices, by country, 1988-90, annual rpt, 21384–5

Overseas Business Reports: economic conditions, investment and export opportunities, and trade practices, country market research rpt series, 2046–6

Soviet Union economic conditions under General Secretary Gorbachev, 1990 and trends from 1975, annual rpt, 9114–6

Zimbabwe agricultural conditions impacts of economic policies, 1980s, 1528–319

see also Business cycles

see also Conversion of industry

see also Defense expenditures

see also Economic development

see also Employment and unemployment, general

see also Fiscal policy

see also Foreign economic relations

see also Foreign trade

see also Foreign trade promotion

see also Government spending

see also Inflation

see also Interest rates

see also International assistance

see also International sanctions

see also Land reform

see also Military assistance

see also Monetary policy

see also Price regulation

see also Prices

see also State funding for economic development

see also Subsidies

see also Tariffs and foreign trade controls

see also terms beginning with Federal aid

Economic relations

see Foreign economic relations

Economic Research Service

Activities, funding, and staff of ERS, by branch, planned FY91, annual rpt, 1504–6

Africa (sub-Saharan) dairy imports, consumption, and market conditions, by country, 1961-88, 1528–321

Agricultural Economics Research, quarterly journal, 1502–3

Agricultural Outlook, production, prices, marketing, and trade, by commodity, forecast and current situation, monthly rpt with articles, 1502–4

Apple import demand in 4 countries, 1960s-83, 1568–296

Australia agricultural input and output indexes, and freight rates, 1950s-80s, 1528–311

Banks finances and operations, by metro-nonmetro location, 1987-89, annual rpt, 1544–29

Beef (choice) price and price spread data series revisions, with methodology, 1970s-90, 1568–295

Beef packing and processing plant operating costs, model methodology and results, 1988, 1568–301

Budget of US, obligations and authority by function, agency, and program, with summaries, analyses, and historical tables, FY92, annual rpt, 104–2

Cattle feedlots and marketing, by lot size and State, selected years 1955-89, 1568–300

Central America agricultural export promotion of nontraditional crops, impacts on income export stability, late 1970s-80s, 1528–312

Children in poverty by selected family characteristics, for rural areas compared to urban areas, 1987-88, 1598–270

Conservation programs under Food Security Act, farm finances and environmental benefits of alternative policies, projected 1991-2005, 1588–153

Corn farms, finances, acreage, and production, by size, region, and State, 1987, 1568–304

Cotton farms fertilizer, pesticide and irrigation use, soil conservation practices, and water quality impacts, 1989, 1588–151

Cotton ginning activity and charges, by State, 1990/91, annual rpt, 1564–3

Cotton, wool, and synthetic fiber production, prices, trade, and use, periodic situation rpt with articles, 1561–1

Dairy production, prices, trade, and use, periodic situation rpt with articles, 1561–2

Index by Subjects and Names

Developing countries agricultural and economic conditions, and US agricultural exports, effects of US aid, 1989 conf papers, 1548–372

Developing countries agricultural exports of high-value commodities to OECD, 1970s-87, 1528–316

Developing countries agricultural supply, demand, and market for US exports, with socioeconomic conditions, country rpt series, 1526–6

Developing countries food supply, needs, and aid, status and alternative forecasts, world area rpt series, 1526–8

Developing countries grains production and needs, and related economic outlook, by world area and selected country, forecast 1990/91-1991/92, 1528–313

Economic Indicators of the Farm Sector, balance sheets, and receipts by detailed commodity, by State, 1985-89, annual rpt, 1544–18

Economic Indicators of the Farm Sector, income, expenses, receipts by commodity, assets, and liabilities, 1990 and trends from 1945, annual rpt, 1544–16

Economic Indicators of the Farm Sector, itemized production costs, receipts, and returns, by commodity and region, 1987-89, annual rpt, 1544–20

Economic Indicators of the Farm Sector, production inputs, output, and productivity, by commodity and region, 1947-89, annual rpt, 1544–17

Employment, earnings, and days worked, for farm workers by selected characteristics and region, biennial rpt, discontinued, 1594–2

Employment related to agriculture, by industry, region, and metro-nonmetro location, 1987, 1598–271

Export demand for US corn, wheat, and soybeans, by selected country, 1960s-83, 1568–297

Exports (agricultural) of high-value commodities, indexes and sales value by commodity, world area, and country, 1960s-86, 1528–323

Exports (agricultural) related employment, land, and capital inputs, by commodity and country of destination, and compared to imports, 1977-87, 1548–373

Exports and imports (agricultural) of US, by commodity and country, bimonthly rpt, 1522–1

Exports and imports (agricultural) of US, by detailed commodity and country, 1989, annual rpt, 1524–8

Exports and imports (agricultural) of US, by detailed commodity and country, 1990, semiannual rpt, 1522–4

Exports and imports (agricultural) of US, outlook and current situation, quarterly rpt, 1542–4

Farm Credit System financial condition, impacts of instn mergers, by district, 1982-89, 1548–381

Farmland in US owned by foreigners, holdings, acquisitions, and disposals by land use, owner type and country, and State, 1990, annual rpt, 1584–2

Farmland in US owned by foreigners, holdings, acreage, and value by land use, owner country, State, and county, 1990, annual rpt, 1584–3

Index by Subjects and Names

Economics

Farmland rental by assessment method, and rent receipts per acre and as share of land value by land type and State, 1960s-80s, 1548–377

Farmline, agricultural situation and related topics, monthly rpt, 1502–6

Farms, farmland, and sales distribution, by sales size, various periods 1969-84, 1588–150

Fed Govt policy issues and effects on agricultural production, prices, income, and trade, and crop support levels by program, semiannual rpt, discontinued, 1542–6

Feed production, acreage, stocks, use, trade, prices, and price supports, periodic situation rpt with articles, 1561–4

Fertilizer and cropland demand impacts of proposed environmental regulation, model description and inputs, 1964-89, 1588–152

Finances of farms, debts, assets, and receipts, and lenders financial condition, quarterly rpt with articles, 1541–1

Finances, production, marketing, trade, food consumption, and nutrition programs, annual chartbook, discontinued, 1504–3

Financial and marketing conditions of farms, forecast 1991, annual chartbook, 1504–8

Financial condition of farms, by commodity, 1987, series, 1566–8

Financial stress indicators for farms, operator quits, and loan problems and mediation, 1970s-90, 1598–272

Fish hatcheries and farms, production, costs, prices, and sales, for catfish and trout, 1970s-91, semiannual situation rpt, 1561–15

Flower and foliage plant production, marketing, and trade by country, by State, 1960s-88, 1568–293

FmHA guaranteed and direct loan program costs under alternative assumptions, 1981-89, 1598–273

Food consumer research, marketing, legislation, and regulation devs, and consumption and price trends, quarterly journal, 1541–7

Food consumption, supply, trade, prices, spending, and indexes, by commodity, 1989, annual rpt, 1544–4

Food cost index alternative to CPI, by category, region, and household income, size, race, and food budget level, 1980-85, 1598–275

Food prices (farm-retail), marketing cost components, and industry finances and productivity, 1920s-90, annual rpt, 1544–9

Food spending, by item, household composition, income, age, race, and region, 1980-88, Consumer Expenditure Survey biennial rpt, 1544–30

Foreign and US agricultural production, prices, trade, and use, periodic rpt with articles, 1522–3

Foreign and US agricultural subsidies for producers and consumers, production and trade impacts, model description, 1991 rpt, 1528–315

Foreign and US agricultural supply and demand indicators, by selected crop, monthly rpt, 1522–5

Foreign countries agricultural production, prices, and trade, by country, 1980-90 and forecast 1991, annual world area rpt series, 1524–4

Fruit and nut production, prices, trade, stocks, and use, by selected crop, periodic situation rpt with articles, 1561–6

Fruit and vegetable imports under quarantine, by crop, country, and port of entry, FY88, annual rpt, 1524–7

Fruit and vegetable production, imports by country, use, exports, and prices, by commodity, 1975-87, 1568–299

Immigration restrictions effects on US agricultural labor costs and trade competitiveness, 1980s, 1598–276

Income (personal) per capita disparity among States, with data by industrial base, 1979, 1989, and projected to 1995, 1548–379

Income (personal) per capita disparity between metro and nonmetro areas, and causal factors, by State, 1979-88, 1548–380

Job Training Partnership Act funding and performance indicators in service delivery areas, by urban-rural location, 1987-88, 1598–266

Job Training Partnership Act participation by selected characteristics and State, and outcomes, by urban-rural location, 1987-88, 1598–267

Land acreage, by use, ownership, and State, 1987 and trends from 1910, 1588–48

Latin America agricultural subsidies to producers and consumers, by selected commodity for 6 countries, 1982-87, 1528–324

Livestock, meat, poultry, and egg production, prices, trade, and stocks, monthly rpt, 1561–17

Livestock, meat, poultry, and egg production, prices, trade, stocks, and use, periodic situation rpt with articles, 1561–7

Milk order market policy alternatives impacts on supply, interregional marketings, and pricing, by region, 1988, 1568–294

Oils, oilseeds, and fats production, prices, trade, and use, periodic situation rpt with articles, 1561–3

Oils, oilseeds, and meal imports, by commodity, world area of destination, and major producer, 1960s-88, 1528–314

Older persons in rural areas, household income sources, and poverty status, 1983-84, 1598–268

Operators entries and exits, by region and State, late 1970s-87, 1598–269

Oranges (fresh) exports of US, demand indicators for 4 countries, with production, trade, and use, 1960s-90, 1528–317

Pest control integrated mgmt programs for vegetables, acreage, costs, savings, and funding sources and recipients, by State, 1980s, 1568–298

Pesticide use, economic effects of revised EPA regulations, with data for tomatoes, 1988 conf papers, 1588–154

Potato production, acreage, disposition, prices, and trade, by State and country, 1949-90, 1568–305

Poverty rate among workers in metro and nonmetro areas, relation to employment and other characteristics, 1987, 1598–274

Price support program changes and other effects on farm income and production, for livestock and program and nonprogram crop producers, model results, 1988, 1548–375

Price support program provisions, for selected commodities, 1961-90, 1568–302; 1568–303

Production inputs, finances, mgmt, and land value and transfers, periodic situation rpt with articles, 1561–16

Research (agricultural) investment impacts on productivity, indicators for developed and developing countries, late 1960s-80, 1528–318

Rice foreign and US production, prices, trade, stocks, and use, periodic situation rpt, 1561–8

Rural areas economic and social conditions, dev, and problems, periodic journal, 1502–7

Rural areas economic and social indicators used to determine Federal aid need, late 1960s-86, 1598–265

Rural areas economic conditions and dev, quarterly journal, 1502–8

Rural areas labor force characteristics, with comparisons to urban areas, 1987, 1598–264

Sales class relation to farm operator age and off-farm employment, sales, and land value changes, model description and results, 1974-78, 1548–374

Soviet Union agricultural subsidies to producers and consumers, by selected commodity, 1986, 1528–320

Soviet Union agricultural trade, by commodity and country, 1955-90, 1528–322

Sugar and sweeteners production, prices, trade, supply, and use, quarterly situation rpt with articles, 1561–14

Sugar production, acreage, yield, stocks, deliveries, and price by State, and trade by country, 1950s-90, 1568–306

Tobacco production, marketing, use, price supports, and trade, quarterly situation rpt with articles, 1561–10

Vegetable production, prices, trade, stocks, and use, for selected fresh and processing crops, periodic situation rpt with articles, 1561–11

Wastewater treatment facilities in small communities, construction and repair needs to meet Clean Water Act standards, by State and region, 1988 and 2008, 1588–155

Wheat and corn stocks, demand impacts of storage subsidy programs, model description and results, 1972-87, 1548–378

Wheat and rye foreign and US production, prices, trade, stocks, and use, quarterly situation rpt with articles, 1561–12

Wheat deficiency program payments freeze in 1985, impacts on participation, production, costs, exports, and returns, model results, 1990 rpt, 1548–376

Zimbabwe agricultural conditions impacts of economic policies, 1980s, 1528–319

Economics

Agricultural Economics Research, quarterly journal, 1502–3

Agricultural research funding and staffing for USDA, State agencies, and other instns, by topic, FY90, annual rpt, 1744–2

Economics

Degrees awarded in science and engineering, by field, level, and sex, 1966-89, 9627–33

Education data compilation, 1991 annual rpt, 4824–2

Employment and other characteristics of science and engineering PhDs, by field and State, 1989, biennial rpt, 9627–18

Fed Govt aid to higher education and nonprofit instns for R&D and related activities, by field, instn, agency, and State, FY89, annual rpt, 9627–17

Higher education course completions, by detailed program, sex, race, and instn type, for 1972 high school class, as of 1984, 4888–4

Higher education grad programs enrollment in science and engineering, by field, source of funds, and characteristics of student and instn, 1975-89, annual rpt, 9627–7

R&D funding by Fed Govt, by field, performer type, agency, and State, FY89-91, annual rpt, 9627–20

R&D funding by higher education instns and federally funded centers, by field, instn, and State, FY89, annual rpt, 9627–13

see also Economic and econometric models *see also* Economic policy

Econometrics, Inc.

"Intercity Bus Feeder Project Program Analysis", 7888–79

Ectopic pregnancy

see Maternity

Ecuador

- Agricultural exports of high-value commodities, indexes and sales by commodity, world area, and country, 1960s-86, 1528–323
- Agricultural exports of US, impacts of foreign agricultural and trade policy, with data by commodity and country, 1989, annual rpt, 1924–8
- Agricultural production, trade, and policies in foreign countries, summary data by country, 1989-90, annual factbook, 1924–12
- Agricultural trade of US, by detailed commodity and country, 1989, annual rpt, 1524–8
- Agricultural trade of US, by detailed commodity and country, 1990, semiannual rpt, 1522–4
- AID economic aid to developing countries, obligations and disbursements by country, quarterly rpt, 9912–4
- AID loans repayment status and terms by program and country, and status of predecessor agency loans, quarterly rpt, 9912–3
- *Background Notes*, summary social, political, and economic data, 1991 rpt, 7006–2.35
- Economic and military aid and loans from US and intl agencies, by program and country, FY46-90, annual rpt, 9914–5
- Economic and social conditions of developing countries from 1960s, and Intl Dev Cooperation Agency and AID activities and funding, FY90-92, annual rpt, 9904–4
- Economic conditions, policy, and trade practices, by country, 1988-90, annual rpt, 21384–5

Economic, population, and agricultural data, US and other aid sources, and AID activity, 1989 country rpt, 9916–12.42

Economic, social, political, and geographic summary data, by country, 1991, annual factbook, 9114–2

Exports and imports of US, by commodity and country, 1970-89, world area rpt, 9116–1.4

Exports and imports of US, by Harmonized System 6-digit commodity and country, 1990, annual rpt, 2424–13

Exports and imports of US, by selected country, country group, and commodity group, 1990, annual rpt, 2044–37

Exports and imports of US, by transport mode, country, and SITC 1- to 3-digit commodity, 1990, annual rpt, 2424–12

Exports of US, detailed Schedule B commodities with countries of destination, 1990, annual rpt, 2424–10

Human rights conditions in 170 countries, and US economic and military aid, 1990, annual rpt, 21384–3

Labor conditions, union coverage, and work accidents, 1991 annual country rpt, 6366–4.49

Military aid of US, arms sales, and training programs costs and budget requests, by program, world region, and country, FY90-92, annual rpt, 7144–13

Multinatl US firms and foreign affiliates finances and operations, by industry and world area of parent firm, 1989 benchmark survey, preliminary annual rpt, 2704–5

Multinatl US firms foreign affiliates, income statement items by country and world area, 1986, biennial article, 8302–2.212

Oil exports to US by OPEC and non-OPEC countries, monthly rpt, 3162–24.3

Oil production, trade, use, and stocks, by selected country and country group, monthly rpt, 3162–42

UN voting record and share of votes in agreement with US, by issue, country, and world area, 1990, annual rpt, 7004–18

see also under By Foreign Country in the "Index by Categories"

Edinburg, Tex.

see also under By SMSA or MSA in the "Index by Categories"

Edison, Hali J.

"Re-Assessment of the Relationship Between Real Exchange Rates and Real Interest Rates: 1974-90", 9366–7.262

Editorial occupations

see Journalism

see Writers and writing

Edmonds, Larry D.

"Temporal Trends in the Prevalence of Congenital Malformations at Birth Based on the Birth Defects Monitoring Program, U.S., 1979-87", 4202–7.203

Education

Condition of Education, detail for elementary, secondary, and higher education, 1920s-90 and projected to 2001, annual rpt, 4824–1

Data on education, computer files from Office of Educational Research and Improvement, 1991 listing, 4868–10

Digest of Education Statistics, 1991 annual data compilation, 4824–2

Index by Subjects and Names

Foreign countries *Background Notes*, summary social, political, and economic data, series, 7006–2

Statistical Abstract of US, 1991 annual data compilation, 2324–1.4

see also Adult education

see also Agricultural education

see also American Schools and Hospitals Abroad

see also Area studies

see also Bilingual education

see also Black colleges

see also Black students

see also Business education

see also Campus security

see also Compensatory education

see also Correspondence courses

see also Curricula

see also Degrees, higher education

see also Discrimination in education

see also Educational attainment

see also Educational broadcasting

see also Educational employees pay

see also Educational enrollment

see also Educational exchanges

see also Educational facilities

see also Educational finance

see also Educational materials

see also Educational reform

see also Educational research

see also Educational retention rates

see also Educational technology

see also Educational tests

see also Elementary and secondary education

see also Ethnic studies

see also Federal aid to education

see also Federal aid to higher education

see also Federal aid to medical education

see also Federal aid to vocational education

see also Head Start Project

see also Health education

see also Higher education

see also Learning disabilities

see also Legal education

see also Libraries

see also Medical education

see also Military education

see also National Assessment of Educational Progress

see also Physical education and training

see also Preschool education

see also Private schools

see also Remedial education

see also School administration and staff

see also School boards

see also School busing

see also School districts

see also School dropouts

see also School lunch and breakfast programs

see also Scientific education

see also Sex education

see also Special education

see also Student aid

see also Student discipline

see also Students

see also Teacher education

see also Teachers

see also Tuition and fees

see also Veterans education

see also Vocational education and training

see also Work-study programs

see also under By Industry in the "Index by Categories"

Index by Subjects and Names

Education Commission of the States
see National Assessment of Educational Progress

Education of handicapped children
see Special education

Educational attainment

Athletes in college, educational and employment performance compared to other students, for 1972 high school class, as of 1986, 4888–5

Births, fertility rates, and childless women, by selected characteristics, 1990, annual Current Population Rpt, 2546–1.455

Black Americans social and economic characteristics, for South and total US, 1989-90 and trends from 1969, Current Population Rpt, 2546–1.450

Condition of Education, detail for elementary, secondary, and higher education, 1920s-90 and projected to 2001, annual rpt, 4824–1

Consumer Income, socioeconomic characteristics of persons, families, and households, detailed cross-tabulations, Current Population Rpt series, 2546–6

Data on education, 1960s-89, pamphlet, 4828–26

Digest of Education Statistics, 1991 annual data compilation, 4824–2

Earnings impact of educational attainment and work experience, model description and results for men, by census div, 1979-88, article, 9373–1.213

High school class of 1972: education, employment, and family characteristics, activities, and attitudes, natl longitudinal study, series, 4836–1

Hispanic Americans social and economic characteristics, by detailed origin, 1991, Current Population Rpt, 2546–1.448; 2546–1.451

Households and family characteristics, by location, 1990, annual Current Population Rpt, 2546–1.447

Income (household) and poverty status under alternative income definitions, by recipient characteristics, 1990, annual Current Population Rpt, 2546–6.69

Income relation to educational attainment, by sex, 1987, fact sheet, 2326–17.25

Military recruits, percent high school grads by sex and service branch, quarterly press release, 3542–7

Natl Education Goals progress indicators, by State, 1991, annual rpt, 15914–1

Population educational attainment, by sociodemographic characteristics and location, 1989 and trends from 1940, biennial Current Population Rpt, 2546–1.452

Population educational enrollment status and attainment, by selected characteristics, 1989 and trends from 1947, annual Current Population Rpt, 2546–1.453

Population size and characteristics, historical index to *Current Population Rpts*, 1991 listing, 2546–2.160

Population size and characteristics, 1969-88, Current Population Rpt, biennial rpt, 2546–2.161

Rural areas economic and social indicators used to determine Federal aid need, late 1960s-86, 1598–265

State and Metro Area Data Book, 1991 data compilation, 2328–54

Statistical Abstract of US, 1991 annual data compilation, 2324–1.4

Taiwan labor force educational attainment index relation to GDP growth, 1960s-86, working paper, 9371–10.55

Women's labor force status, earnings, and other characteristics, with comparisons to men, fact sheet series, 6564–1

see also Degrees, higher education

see also Educational retention rates

see also National Assessment of Educational Progress

see also School dropouts

see also under By Educational Attainment in the "Index by Categories"

Educational broadcasting

Humanities Natl Endowment activities and grants, FY90, annual rpt, 9564–2

State and Metro Area Data Book, 1991 data compilation, 2328–54

TV and radio stations on the air, by class of operation, monthly press release, 9282–4

Educational development
see Educational reform

Educational employees pay

Benefit plan coverage of State and local employees, by benefit type, 1987, 6726–1.41

Collective bargaining wage and benefit changes and coverage, monthly rpt, 6782–1

Condition of Education, detail for elementary, secondary, and higher education, 1920s-90 and projected to 2001, annual rpt, 4824–1

County Business Patterns, 1988: employment, establishments, and payroll, by SIC 2- to 4-digit industry and county, annual State rpt series, 2326–6

County Business Patterns, 1989: employment, establishments, and payroll, by SIC 2- to 4-digit industry and county, annual State rpt series, 2326–8

Digest of Education Statistics, 1991 annual data compilation, 4824–2

Elementary and secondary education enrollment, staff, finances, operations, programs, and policies, 1987/88 biennial survey, series, 4836–3

Elementary and secondary public school systems enrollment, finances, staff, and high school grads, by State, FY88-89, annual rpt, 4834–6

Govt employment and payroll, by function, level of govt, and jurisdiction, 1990, annual rpt series, 2466–1

High school class of 1972: teaching employment experience by selected characteristics, natl longitudinal study, 1976-86, 4836–1.13

Higher education enrollment, faculty, finances, and degrees, by instn level and control, and State, FY87, annual rpt, 4844–13

Higher education faculty employment and other characteristics, by instn type and control, 1987/88 survey, 4846–4.4

Higher education faculty salaries, by instn type and State, by rank and sex, 1989/90, annual rpt, 4844–8

Higher education instn tuition and other costs, govt aid, impacts on enrollment, and cost containment methods, 1970s-90 and projected to 2001, 4808–25

Educational enrollment

Higher education instn tuition relation to other instn financial indicators, by instn control, 1960s-88, 4808–24

Payroll and employment of State and local govts, monthly rpt, 6742–4

Pension systems of State and local govts, finances, coverage, and benefits, by system, FY88, annual rpt, 2466–2.1

Pension systems of State and local govts, finances, coverage, and benefits, by system, FY89, annual rpt, 2466–2.8

Private elementary and secondary schools, students, and staff characteristics, various periods 1979-88, 4838–47

Science and engineering PhDs employment and other characteristics, by field and State, 1989, biennial rpt, 9627–18

Service industries census, 1987: depreciable assets, capital and operating expenses, and receipts, by SIC 2- to 4-digit kind of business, 2393–2

State and Metro Area Data Book, 1991 data compilation, 2328–54

Statistical Abstract of US, 1991 annual data compilation, 2324–1.4

Teachers salaries, 1980s-92, annual press release, 4804–19

Educational enrollment

Appalachia education system, improvement initiatives, and indicators of success, by State, 1960s-89, 9088–36

Bilingual education enrollment, and Education Dept activities and funding by program, by State, FY88-90, biennial rpt, 4804–14

Bilingual education programs enrollment, funding, and services, by State, FY85-89, series, 4808–20

Black higher education instns finances, funding sources, enrollment, and student characteristics, with data for Louisiana instns, 1970s-90, hearing, 25258–24

Children and youth social, economic, and demographic characteristics, 1950s-90, 4818–5

Compulsory school attendance laws enacted, by State, 1990, annual article, 6722–1.209

Condition of Education, detail for elementary, secondary, and higher education, 1920s-90 and projected to 2001, annual rpt, 4824–1

Data on education, selected trends and projections 1978-2001, pamphlet, 4828–27

Data on education, 1960s-89, pamphlet, 4828–26

Developing countries child health and welfare indicators, and economic conditions, 1950s-80s, hearing, 25388–57

Developing countries economic and social conditions from 1960s, and Intl Dev Cooperation Agency and AID activities and funding, FY90-92, annual rpt, 9904–4.1

Digest of Education Statistics, 1991 annual data compilation, 4824–2

Discrimination in education, indicators for service delivery and discipline, by State, 1988, biennial rpt, 4804–33

Eighth grade class of 1988: characteristics of schools attended, natl longitudinal survey, 1991 rpt, 4826–9.10

Elementary and secondary education enrollment, staff, finances, operations, programs, and policies, 1987/88 biennial survey, series, 4836–3

Educational enrollment

Elementary and secondary education enrollment, teachers, high school grads, and spending, by instn control and State, 1990/91, annual rpt, 4834–19

Elementary and secondary public school systems enrollment, finances, staff, and high school grads, by State, FY88-89, annual rpt, 4834–6

Elementary and secondary public schools and enrollment, by State, 1989/90, annual rpt, 4834–17

Elementary and secondary public schools, enrollment and other characteristics, for top 100 districts, 1988/89, annual rpt, 4834–22

Elementary and secondary public schools, enrollment, teachers, funding, and other characteristics, by region and State, 1988/89, annual rpt, 4834–20

Elementary and secondary public schools enrollment, under alternative average daily attendance computation methods, by State, 1985-86, 4838–48

Enrollment, by grade, instn type and control, and student characteristics, 1989 and trends from 1947, annual Current Population Rpt, 2546–1.453

Enrollment, staff, and spending, by instn level and control, and teacher salaries, 1980s-92, annual press release, 4804–19

Govt census, 1987: school system total and instructional employment, payroll, and average earnings, by enrollment size and State, 2455–2

Head Start enrollment, funding, and staff, FY90, annual rpt, 4604–8

Head Start handicapped enrollment, by handicap, State, and for Indian and migrant programs, 1987/88, annual rpt, 4604–1

Health condition, services use, payment sources, and health care labor force, for minorities and women by poverty status, 1940s-89, chartbook, 4118–56

High school advanced placement for college credit, programs by selected characteristics and school control, 1984-86, 4838–46

High school class of 1972: education, employment, and family characteristics, activities, and attitudes, natl longitudinal study, series, 4836–1

High school class of 1990: college enrollment, and labor force participation of grads and dropouts, by race and sex, press release, 6726–1.38

Higher education enrollment and degrees awarded by sex, and instn finances, by instn level and control, 1990-91, annual rpt, 4844–14

Higher education enrollment and degrees awarded, by sex, full- and part-time status, and instn level and control, fall 1990, annual rpt, 4844–16

Higher education enrollment, by student and instn characteristics, fall 1989, biennial rpt, 4844–2

Higher education enrollment, faculty, finances, and degrees, by instn level and control, and State, FY87, annual rpt, 4844–13

Higher education instn student aid and other sources of support, with student expenses and characteristics, by instn type and control, 1990 triennial study, series, 4846–5

Index by Subjects and Names

Higher education instn tuition and other costs, govt aid, impacts on enrollment, and cost containment methods, 1970s-90 and projected to 2001, 4808–25

Higher education instn tuition costs relation to quality, indicators for private instns, regression results, 1985/86, 4888–3

Higher education instn tuition relation to other instn financial indicators, by instn control, 1960s-88, 4808–24

Hispanic Americans in counties bordering Mexico, by selected characteristics, 1980, Current Population Rpt, 2546–2.159

Homeless and runaway youth programs, funding, activities, and participant characteristics, FY90, annual rpt, 4604–3

Homeless children educational projects, activities, and funding, FY90, annual rpt, 4804–35

Housing and households detailed characteristics, and unit and neighborhood quality, by location, 1987, biennial rpt supplement, 2485–13

Indian education funding of Fed Govt, and enrollment, degrees, and program grants and fellowships by State, late 1960s-FY89, annual rpt, 14874–1

Migrant workers children education programs enrollment, staff, and effectiveness, by State, 1980s, 4808–30

Migrant workers children education programs enrollment, staff, finances, and outcomes, 1980s, 4808–22

Minority group higher education enrollment, degrees, factors affecting participation, and earnings, 1960s-88, 4808–29

Natl Education Goals progress indicators, by State, 1991, annual rpt, 15914–1

Nuclear engineering and science educational facilities, student aid, and degrees granted, by instn, 1990, 3008–126

Nuclear engineering enrollment and degrees granted by instn and State, and grad placement, by student characteristics, 1990, annual rpt, 3004–5

Pacific territories economic conditions, population characteristics, and Federal aid, 1989 hearing, 21448–44

Palau admin, and social, economic, and govtl data, FY90, annual rpt, 7004–6

Pell grants and applicants, by tuition, family and student income, instn type and control, and State, 1989/90, annual rpt, 4804–1

Poland labor force status by education level, sex, and sector, college enrollment, and grads by field, 1960s-88, article, 6722–1.203

Population size and characteristics, historical index to *Current Population Rpts,* 1991 listing, 2546–2.160

Population size and characteristics, 1969-88, Current Population Rpt, biennial rpt, 2546–2.161

Private elementary and secondary schools, students, and staff characteristics, various periods 1979-88, 4838–47

Radiation protection and health physics enrollment and degrees granted by instn and State, and female grads plans and employment, 1990, annual rpt, 3006–8.15

Radiation protection and health physics enrollment and degrees granted by instn and State, and grad placement, by student characteristics, 1990, annual rpt, 3004–7

Refugee resettlement programs and funding, arrivals by country of origin, and indicators of adjustment, by State, FY90, annual rpt, 4694–5

Science and engineering academic research system status, R&D performance, and Fed Govt support, 1950s-88 with trends and projections, 9628–83

Science and engineering grad enrollment, by field, source of funds, and characteristics of student and instn, 1975-89, annual rpt, 9627–7

Science and math education programs for gifted minority students, participation and outcomes, 1981-88 study, 4808–34

Special education programs, enrollment by age, staff, funding, and needs, by type of handicap and State, 1989/90, annual rpt, 4944–4

State and Metro Area Data Book, 1991 data compilation, 2328–54

Statistical Abstract of US, 1991 annual data compilation, 2324–1.4

USIA English language program enrollment and staff, by country and world region, FY90, annual rpt, 9854–2

Voting and registration, by socioeconomic and demographic characteristics, 1990 congressional election, biennial Current Population Rpt, 2546–1.454

Women's employment and educational experiences compared to men, for high school class of 1972, natl longitudinal study, as of 1986, 4888–6

see also Black students

see also Educational retention rates

see also Foreign students

see also School dropouts

see also Students

Educational exchanges

Education Dept programs funding, operations, and effectiveness, FY90, annual rpt, 4804–5

Fulbright-Hays academic exchanges, grants by purpose, and foreign govt share of costs, by country, FY90, annual rpt, 10324–1

Japan-US Friendship Commission educational and cultural exchange activities, grants, and trust fund status, FY89-90, biennial report, 14694–1

NIH intl program activities and funding, by inst and country, FY90, annual rpt, 4474–6

Participation in intl exchange and training programs, by world region, and funding, by Federal agency, FY89, annual rpt, 9854–8

Student aid funding and participation, by Federal program, instn type and control, and State, various periods 1959-89, annual rpt, 4804–28

Educational facilities

Appalachia education system, improvement initiatives, and indicators of success, by State, 1960s-89, 9088–36

Asbestos in buildings, EPA aid for removal, occupational asbestos exposure cancer cases and deaths, and Catholic schools abatement costs, 1985-90, hearing, 25328–32

Assistance (financial and nonfinancial) of Fed Govt, 1991 base edition with supplements, annual listing, 104–5

Index by Subjects and Names

Educational finance

Construction industries census, 1987: establishments, employment, receipts, and expenditures, by SIC 4-digit industry and State, final industry rpt series, 2373–1

Construction put in place, permits, housing sales, costs, material prices, and employment, bimonthly rpt with articles, 2042–1

Construction put in place, value of new public and private structures, by type, monthly rpt, 2382–4

County Business Patterns, 1988: employment, establishments, and payroll, by SIC 2- to 4-digit industry and county, annual State rpt series, 2326–6

County Business Patterns, 1989: employment, establishments, and payroll, by SIC 2- to 4-digit industry and county, annual State rpt series, 2326–8

Digest of Education Statistics, 1991 annual data compilation, 4824–2

DOD prime contract awards, by category, contract and contractor type, and service branch, FY81-1st half FY91, semiannual rpt, 3542–1

Education Dept programs funding, operations, and effectiveness, FY90, annual rpt, 4804–5

Elementary and secondary education enrollment, staff, finances, operations, programs, and policies, 1987/88 biennial survey, series, 4836–3

Elementary and secondary public schools and enrollment, by State, 1989/90, annual rpt, 4834–17

Elementary and secondary public schools, enrollment and other characteristics, for top 100 districts, 1988/89, annual rpt, 4834–22

Elementary and secondary public schools, enrollment, teachers, funding, and other characteristics, by region and State, 1988/89, annual rpt, 4834–20

Energy conservation aid of Fed Govt to public and nonprofit private instns, by building type and State, 1990, annual rpt, 3304–15

Energy supply, demand, and prices, by fuel type and end-use sector, projections and underlying assumptions, 1990-2010, annual rpt, 3164–90

Energy use in commercial buildings, costs, and conservation, by building characteristics, survey rpt series, 3166–8

Enterprise Statistics, 1987: finances and operations for companies, by size, level of diversification, form of organization, and industry group, 2329–8

Expenditures for public welfare by program, FY50s-88, annual article, 4742–1.209

Fed Govt-owned real property inventory and costs, worldwide summary by purpose, agency, and location, 1989, annual rpt, 9454–5

Food and alcoholic beverage spending, by place of purchase, 1968-90, annual rpt, 1544–4.5

Franchise business opportunities by firm and kind of business, and sources of aid and info, 1990 annual listing, 2104–7

Head Start enrollment, funding, and staff, FY90, annual rpt, 4604–8

Health promotion program availability and participation, by type of program and sponsor, 1986-87 local area study, article, 4042–3.223

Higher education instn revenue by source and spending by function, by State and instn control, FY80-88, annual rpt, 4844–6

Higher education instn tuition costs relation to quality, indicators for private instns, regression results, 1985/86, 4888–3

Housing and households detailed characteristics, and unit and neighborhood quality, by location, 1987, biennial rpt supplement, 2485–13

Injuries, by type, circumstances, and victim characteristics, and related activity limitations, 1985-87, 4147–10.176

Injuries, related impairments, and activity limitations, by circumstances and victim characteristics, 1985-87, 4147–10.179

Juvenile correctional and detention public and private instns, inmates, and expenses, by instn and resident characteristics and State, 1987, biennial rpt, 6064–13

Medical and biological R&D facilities, space and equipment adequacy, needs, and funding by source, by instn type, 1990, biennial rpt, 4434–17

Migrant workers children education programs enrollment, staff, finances, and outcomes, 1980s, 4808–22

Military training and education programs funding, staff, students, and facilities, by service branch, FY92, annual rpt, 3504–5

Milk home delivery, and sales by wholesale outlet type, by region, 1989 survey, biennial article, 1317–4.201

Nuclear engineering and science educational facilities, student aid, and degrees granted, by instn, 1990, 3008–126

Nuclear reactors for domestic use and export by function and operating status, with owner, operating characteristics, and location, 1990 annual listing, 3354–15

R&D equipment of higher education instns, acquisition and service costs, condition, and financing, by field and subfield, 1988-90, triennial survey series, 9627–27

R&D funding by higher education instns and federally funded centers, by field, instn, and State, FY89, annual rpt, 9627–13

Service industries census, 1987: establishments, receipts by source, payroll, and employment, by SIC 2- to 4-digit kind of business, State, and MSA, 2393–4

Ships for oceanographic research, fleet condition, funding, voyages, and modernization costs, for NOAA, 1980s-90 and projected to 2020, 2148–60

Smoking bans in public places, local ordinances provisions, as of 1989, 4478–196

State and Metro Area Data Book, 1991 data compilation, 2328–54

Statistical Abstract of US, 1991 annual data compilation, 2324–1.4

see also Campus security

see also Libraries

see also under By Individual Company or Institution in the "Index by Categories"

Educational finance

Appalachia education system, improvement initiatives, and indicators of success, by State, 1960s-89, 9088–36

Asbestos in buildings, EPA aid for removal, occupational asbestos exposure cancer

cases and deaths, and Catholic schools abatement costs, 1985-90, hearing, 25328–32

Black higher education instns finances, funding sources, enrollment, and student characteristics, with data for Louisiana instns, 1970s-90, hearing, 25258–24

Children and youth social, economic, and demographic characteristics, 1950s-90, 4818–5

Condition of Education, detail for elementary, secondary, and higher education, 1920s-90 and projected to 2001, annual rpt, 4824–1

Consumer Expenditure Survey, household income by source, and itemized spending, by selected characteristics and region, 1988-89, annual rpt, 6764–5

Consumer Expenditure Survey, spending by category, and income, by selected household characteristics and location, 1990, annual press release, 6726–1.42

Consumer spending for cash contributions, by charity type and selected characteristics, 1988/89, article, 1702–1.214

CPI components relative importance, by selected MSA, region, population size, and for US city average, 1990, annual rpt, 6884–1

Data on education, selected trends and projections 1978-2001, pamphlet, 4828–27

Data on education, 1960s-89, pamphlet, 4828–26

Developing countries economic and social conditions from 1960s, and Intl Dev Cooperation Agency and AID activities and funding, FY90-92, annual rpt, 9904–4

Digest of Education Statistics, 1991 annual data compilation, 4824–2

Elementary and secondary education enrollment, teachers, high school grads, and spending, by instn control and State, 1990/91, annual rpt, 4834–19

Elementary and secondary public school systems enrollment, finances, staff, and high school grads, by State, FY88-89, annual rpt, 4834–6

Elementary and secondary public school systems financing issues, and indicators of school districts fiscal independence, 1960s-80s, 10048–78

Elementary and secondary public schools, enrollment, teachers, funding, and other characteristics, by region and State, 1988/89, annual rpt, 4834–20

Enterprise Statistics, 1987: auxiliaries of multi-establishment firms, finances and operations by function, industry, and State, 2329–6

Enterprise Statistics, 1987: finances and operations for companies, by size, level of diversification, form of organization, and industry group, 2329–8

Expenditures (private) for social welfare, by category, 1970s-88, annual article, 4742–1.204

Expenditures, coverage, and benefits for social welfare programs, late 1930s-89, annual rpt, 4744–3.1

Expenditures, enrollment, and spending, by instn level and control, and teachers salaries, 1980s-92, annual press release, 4804–19

Educational finance

Expenditures for public welfare by program, FY50s-88, annual article, 4742–1.209

Expenditures for public welfare programs, by program type and level of govt, FY65-88, annual article, 4742–1.202

Exports and imports of services, direct and among multinatl firms affiliates, by industry and world area, 1986-90, article, 2702–1.223

Govt census, 1987: employment, payroll, and average earnings, by function, level of govt, State, county, and population size, 2455–2

Govt finances, by level of govt, State, and for large cities and counties, annual rpt series, 2466–2

Govt spending measures using indicators of service costs and demand, with comparisons to fiscal capacity and actual outlays, by State, for State and local govts, 1986-87, 10048–77

Higher education enrollment and degrees awarded by sex, and instn finances, by instn level and control, 1990-91, annual rpt, 4844–14

Higher education enrollment, faculty, finances, and degrees, by instn level and control, and State, FY87, annual rpt, 4844–13

Higher education instn revenue by source and spending by function, by State and instn control, FY80-88, annual rpt, 4844–6

Higher education instn tuition and other costs, govt aid, impacts on enrollment, and cost containment methods, 1970s-90 and projected to 2001, 4808–25

Higher education instn tuition costs relation to quality, indicators for private instns, regression results, 1985/86, 4888–3

Higher education instn tuition relation to other instn financial indicators, by instn control, 1960s-88, 4808–24

Immigrant children education programs funding by Fed Govt and school districts, and student characteristics, 1980s, GAO rpt, 26121–418

Input-output structure of US economy, detailed interindustry transactions for 84 industries, and components of final demand, 1986, annual article, 2702–1.206

Input-output structure of US economy, detailed interindustry transactions for 85 industries, 1982 benchmark data, 2702–1.213

Japan-US Friendship Commission educational and cultural exchange activities, grants, and trust fund status, FY89-90, biennial report, 14694–1

Libraries (public) finances, staff, and operations, by State and population size, 1989, annual rpt, 4824–6

Libraries of higher education instns, holdings, outlays, staff, and instn characteristics, 1969-88, 4468–4

Migrant workers children education programs enrollment, staff, finances, and outcomes, 1980s, 4808–22

Natl Education Goals progress indicators, by State, 1991, annual rpt, 15914–1

New England States govt revenue and spending issues, with data by State, 1970s-80s, article, 9373–25.202

Nonprofit charitable organizations finances, by asset size and State, 1987, article, 8302–2.218

Private elementary and secondary schools, students, and staff characteristics, various periods 1979-88, 4838–47

R&D equipment of higher education instns, acquisition and service costs, condition, and financing, by field and subfield, 1988-90, triennial survey series, 9627–27

R&D facilities for biological and medical sciences, space and equipment adequacy, needs, and funding by source, by instn type, 1990, biennial rpt, 4434–17

R&D funding by higher education instns and federally funded centers, by field, instn, and State, FY89, annual rpt, 9627–13

Rural areas education spending per student, by State, 1920s-87, article, 1502–7.201

Service industries census, 1987: depreciable assets, capital and operating expenses, and receipts, by SIC 2- to 4-digit kind of business, 2393–2

Service industries census, 1987: establishments, receipts by source, payroll, and employment, by SIC 2- to 4-digit kind of business, State, and MSA, 2393–4

Service industries receipts, by SIC 2- to 4-digit kind of business, 1990, annual rpt, 2413–8

Soviet Union GNP by component and industry sector, and CIA estimation methods, 1950s-87, 23848–223

Soviet Union GNP by detailed income and outlay component, 1985, 2326–18.59

Special education programs, enrollment by age, staff, funding, and needs, by type of handicap and State, 1989/90, annual rpt, 4944–4

State and Metro Area Data Book, 1991 data compilation, 2328–54

Statistical Abstract of US, 1991 annual data compilation, 2324–1.4

Tax (income) returns of corporations, income and tax items by asset size and detailed industry, 1987, annual rpt, 8304–4

Tax (income) returns of corporations, income and tax items by asset size and detailed industry, 1988, annual rpt, 8304–21

Tax (income) returns of sole proprietorships, income statement items, by industry group, 1989, annual article, 8302–2.214

see also Educational employees pay

see also Federal aid to education

see also Federal aid to higher education

see also Federal aid to medical education

see also Federal aid to vocational education

see also State funding for education

see also State funding for higher education

see also Student aid

see also Tuition and fees

Educational materials

Agricultural summary data, young readers pamphlet series, 2346–1

Assistance (financial and nonfinancial) of Fed Govt, 1991 base edition with supplements, annual listing, 104–5

Bilingual education and English immersion programs activities, structure, and effectiveness, 1984-88 longitudinal study, 4808–27

Index by Subjects and Names

CPI by component for US city average, and by region, population size, and for 27 metro areas, monthly rpt, 6762–2

Drug abuse and treatment research summaries, resource materials and grant listings, periodic rpt, 4492–4

Education Dept programs funding, operations, and effectiveness, FY90, annual rpt, 4804–5

Elementary and secondary students educational performance, and factors affecting proficiency, by selected characteristics, 1988 natl assessments, subject rpt series, 4896–7

Elementary and secondary students educational performance, and factors affecting proficiency, by selected characteristics, 1990 natl assessments, subject rpt series, 4896–8

Exports and imports of US, by Harmonized System 6-digit commodity and country, 1990, annual rpt, 2424–13

Exports of US, detailed Schedule B commodities with countries of destination, 1990, annual rpt, 2424–10

Franchise business opportunities by firm and kind of business, and sources of aid and info, 1990 annual listing, 2104–7

Humanities Natl Endowment activities and grants, FY90, annual rpt, 9564–2

Mail revenue and subsidy for revenue forgone, by class of mail, FY90, and volume from FY86, annual rpt, 9864–1

Mail revenue, costs, and volume, by class of mail, FY90, annual rpt, 9864–2

Mail volume, revenues, and subsidies for revenue forgone, by class of mail, FY90, annual rpt, 9864–5.3

Mail volume to and from households, use, and views, by class, source, content, and household characteristics, 1987-88, annual rpt, 9864–10

Poverty area schools academic environment and teaching methods impacts on student performance, 1989/90 study, 4808–28

Price indexes (producer), by stage of processing and detailed commodity, monthly rpt, 6762–6

Science, engineering, and math education grants of NSF, by recipient and level, FY89, biennial listing, 9624–27

Educational reform

Appalachia education system, improvement initiatives, and indicators of success, by State, 1960s-89, 9088–36

Bilingual education programs enrollment, funding, and services, by State, FY85-89, series, 4808–20

Compensatory education programs in high poverty school districts, Federal grant program activities, participation, and coordinators views, 1989/90, 4808–32

Digest of Education Statistics, 1991 annual data compilation, 4824–2

Elementary and secondary students educational performance, and factors affecting proficiency, by selected characteristics, 1990 natl assessments, subject rpt series, 4896–8

Natl Education Goals progress indicators, by State, 1991, annual rpt, 15914–1

Poverty area schools academic environment and teaching methods impacts on student performance, 1989/90 study, 4808–28

Index by Subjects and Names

Science and math teacher dev project funding of Fed Govt, participation, operations, and effectiveness, 1985-90, 4808–31

Educational research

- Assistance (financial and nonfinancial) of Fed Govt, 1991 base edition with supplements, annual listing, 104–5
- Bilingual education and English immersion programs activities, structure, and effectiveness, 1984-88 longitudinal study, 4808–27
- Bilingual education enrollment, and Education Dept activities and funding by program, by State, FY88-90, biennial rpt, 4804–14
- Bilingual education programs enrollment, funding, and services, by State, FY85-89, series, 4808–20
- Data collection and reporting improvement, and performance indicators dev, recommendations, 1991 rpt, 4828–40
- Data collection and reporting improvement for Federal and State educational agencies, recommendations, 1991 rpt, 4828–39
- Education Dept programs funding, operations, and effectiveness, FY90, annual rpt, 4804–5
- Educational Resources Info Center (ERIC) activities, 1990-91, annual rpt, 4814–3
- Fast Response Survey System, estimates for education data, series, 4826–1
- Handicapped children early education project descriptions, 1990/91, annual listing, 4944–10
- Office of Educational Research and Improvement activities, FY90, annual narrative rpt, 4814–1
- Science, engineering, and math education grants of NSF, by recipient and level, FY89, biennial listing, 9624–27
- Tax (income) returns of corporations, income and tax items by asset size and detailed industry, 1987, annual rpt, 8304–4
- Vocational education in postsecondary instns, States performance measurement activities and related legislation, 1989/90, 4808–33
- *see also* National Assessment of Educational Progress

Educational Resources Information Center "ERIC Annual Report, 1991", 4814–3

Educational retention rates

- Appalachia education system, improvement initiatives, and indicators of success, by State, 1960s-89, 9088–36
- Bilingual education and English immersion programs activities, structure, and effectiveness, 1984-88 longitudinal study, 4808–27
- *Condition of Education*, detail for elementary, secondary, and higher education, 1920s-90 and projected to 2001, annual rpt, 4824–1
- Data on education, selected trends and projections 1978-2001, pamphlet, 4828–27
- *Digest of Education Statistics*, 1991 annual data compilation, 4824–2
- Discrimination in education, indicators for service delivery and discipline, by State, 1988, biennial rpt, 4804–33

Educational tests

Eighth grade class of 1988: educational performance and conditions, characteristics, attitudes, activities, and plans, natl longitudinal survey, series, 4826–9

- Elementary and secondary education enrollment, staff, finances, operations, programs, and policies, 1987/88 biennial survey, series, 4836–3
- Elementary and secondary education enrollment, teachers, high school grads, and spending, by instn control and State, 1990/91, annual rpt, 4834–19
- Elementary and secondary public schools, enrollment, teachers, funding, and other characteristics, by region and State, 1988/89, annual rpt, 4834–20
- Gifted minority students science and math education programs, participation and outcomes, 1981-88 study, 4808–34
- High school advanced placement for college credit, students later applying to college, by school control, 1984-86, 4838–46
- High school dropout rates, and subsequent completion, by student and school characteristics, alternative estimates, 1990, annual rpt, 4834–23
- High school grads by instn control, and higher education completions by level, 1980s-92, annual press release, 4804–19
- High school grads, other completions, and 12th and 9th grade enrollment, by State, classes of FY88 and FY89, annual rpt, 4834–6
- Higher education instn tuition costs relation to quality, indicators for private instns, regression results, 1985/86, 4888–3
- Migrant workers children education programs enrollment, staff, finances, and outcomes, 1980s, 4808–22
- Minority group higher education enrollment, degrees, factors affecting participation, and earnings, 1960s-88, 4808–29
- Natl Education Goals progress indicators, by State, 1991, annual rpt, 15914–1
- New England States high school grad rates, 1988, article, 9373–25.202
- Pacific territories economic conditions, population characteristics, and Federal aid, 1989 hearing, 21448–44
- Remedial education programs in higher education instns, and enrollment, courses, and faculty, by instn characteristics, 1989/90, 4826–1.30
- Special education programs, enrollment by age, staff, funding, and needs, by type of handicap and State, 1989/90, annual rpt, 4944–4
- *Statistical Abstract of US*, 1991 annual data compilation, 2324–1.4
- Women's employment and educational experiences compared to men, for high school class of 1972, natl longitudinal study, as of 1986, 4888–6
- *see also* School dropouts

Educational technology

- Bilingual education and English immersion programs activities, structure, and effectiveness, 1984-88 longitudinal study, 4808–27
- Computer use at home, school, and work, by purpose and selected user characteristics, 1989, Current Population Rpt, 2546–2.158

Computer use in elementary and secondary schools, by grade level, 1991 edition, annual rpt, 4824–2.30

see also Educational broadcasting

Educational television

see Educational broadcasting

Educational tests

- Appalachia education system, improvement initiatives, and indicators of success, by State, 1960s-89, 9088–36
- Athletes in college, educational and employment performance compared to other students, for 1972 high school class, as of 1986, 4888–5
- Bilingual education and English immersion programs activities, structure, and effectiveness, 1984-88 longitudinal study, 4808–27
- Bilingual education programs enrollment, funding, and services, by State, FY85-89, series, 4808–20
- Black higher education instns finances, funding sources, enrollment, and student characteristics, with data for Louisiana instns, 1970s-90, hearing, 25258–24
- Children and youth social, economic, and demographic characteristics, 1950s-90, 4818–5
- *Condition of Education*, detail for elementary and secondary education, 1920s-90 and projected to 2001, annual rpt, 4824–1.1
- *Digest of Education Statistics*, 1991 annual data compilation, 4824–2
- DOD Dependents Schools basic skills and college entrance test scores, 1990-91, annual rpt, 3504–16
- Eighth grade class of 1988: educational performance and conditions, characteristics, attitudes, activities, and plans, natl longitudinal survey, series, 4826–9
- Higher education instn tuition costs relation to quality, indicators for private instns, regression results, 1985/86, 4888–3
- Indian education funding of Fed Govt, and enrollment, degrees, and program grants and fellowships by State, late 1960s-FY89, annual rpt, 14874–1
- Migrant workers children education programs enrollment, staff, and effectiveness, by State, 1980s, 4808–30
- Migrant workers children education programs enrollment, staff, finances, and outcomes, 1980s, 4808–22
- Minority group higher education enrollment, degrees, factors affecting participation, and earnings, 1960s-88, 4808–29
- Poverty area schools academic environment and teaching methods impacts on student performance, 1989/90 study, 4808–28
- Private elementary and secondary schools, students, and staff characteristics, various periods 1979-88, 4838–47
- Science and math education programs for gifted minority students, participation and outcomes, 1981-88 study, 4808–34
- *Statistical Abstract of US*, 1991 annual data compilation, 2324–1.4
- Texas school district quality indicators, model description and results by district and county, 1989, technical paper, 9379–12.67
- Women's employment and educational experiences compared to men, for high school class of 1972, natl longitudinal study, as of 1986, 4888–6

Educational tests

see also National Assessment of Educational Progress

Edwards, Clark
"Doing Agricultural Economics", 1502–3.201

Edwards, John H.
"Relative Price Variability and Inflation: Inter and Intracity Evidence from Brazil in the 1980's", 9379–14.14

Edwards, Mark L.
"Summary of Selected Nationwide School Bus Crash Statistics in 1989", 7764–22

EG&G Idaho, Inc.
"Environmental Monitoring for EG&G Idaho Facilities at the Idaho National Engineering Laboratory, Annual Report, 1990", 3354–10

Eggert, Gerald M.
"ACCESS: Medicare Program: Reducing Hospital Use Among Medicare Beneficiaries", 4658–43

Eggs
see Poultry industry and products

Egypt
- Agricultural exports of high-value commodities, indexes and sales by commodity, world area, and country, 1960s-86, 1528–323
- Agricultural exports of US, impacts of foreign agricultural and trade policy, with data by commodity and country, 1989, annual rpt, 1924–8
- Agricultural production, prices, and trade, by country, 1960s-90, annual world area rpt, 1524–4.2
- Agricultural production, trade, and policies in foreign countries, summary data by country, 1989-90, annual factbook, 1924–12
- Agricultural trade by commodity and country, prices, and world market devs, monthly rpt, 1922–12
- Agricultural trade of US, by detailed commodity and country, 1989, annual rpt, 1524–8
- Agricultural trade of US, by detailed commodity and country, 1990, semiannual rpt, 1522–4
- AID economic aid to developing countries, obligations and disbursements by country, quarterly rpt, 9912–4
- AID loans repayment status and terms by program and country, and status of predecessor agency loans, quarterly rpt, 9912–3
- *Background Notes*, summary social, political, and economic data, 1990 rpt, 7006–2.19
- Cotton production, trade, and prices, for Egypt, 1980-91, article, 1561–1.201
- Economic and military aid and loans from US and intl agencies, by program and country, FY46-90, annual rpt, 9914–5
- Economic and social conditions of developing countries from 1960s, and Intl Dev Cooperation Agency and AID activities and funding, FY90-92, annual rpt, 9904–4
- Economic conditions in USSR, Eastern Europe, OECD, and selected other countries, 1960s-90, annual rpt, 9114–4
- Economic conditions, income, production, prices, employment, and trade, 1991 periodic country rpt, 2046–4.75
- Economic conditions, policy, and trade practices, by country, 1988-90, annual rpt, 21384–5

Economic, population, and agricultural data, US and other aid sources, and AID activity, 1989 country rpt, 9916–12.37

Economic, social, political, and geographic summary data, by country, 1991, annual factbook, 9114–2

Export controls and trade of US with Middle East countries, with dual-use commodity licenses and arms sales, 1980s-90, GAO rpt, 26123–339

Exports and imports of US, by commodity and country, 1970-89, world area rpt, 9116–1.1

Exports and imports of US, by Harmonized System 6-digit commodity and country, 1990, annual rpt, 2424–13

Exports and imports of US, by selected country, country group, and commodity group, 1990, annual rpt, 2044–37

Exports and imports of US, by transport mode, country, and SITC 1- to 3-digit commodity, 1990, annual rpt, 2424–12

Exports of US, detailed Schedule B commodities with countries of destination, 1990, annual rpt, 2424–10

Food supply, needs, and aid for developing countries, status and alternative forecasts, 1991 world area rpt, 1526–8.1

Govt budgets, foreign debt, and economic indicators of Israel and Egypt, 1980s, hearing, 21388–58

Grain production and needs, and related economic outlook, by world area and selected country, forecast 1990/91-1991/92, 1528–313

Human rights conditions in 170 countries, and US economic and military aid, 1990, annual rpt, 21384–3

Imports of goods, services, and investment from US, trade barriers, impacts, and US actions, by country, 1990, annual rpt, 444–2

Labor conditions, union coverage, and work accidents, 1991 annual country rpt, 6366–4.23

Military aid of US, arms sales, and training programs costs and budget requests, by program, world region, and country, FY90-92, annual rpt, 7144–13

Multinatl US firms and foreign affiliates finances and operations, by industry and world area of parent firm, 1989 benchmark survey, preliminary annual rpt, 2704–5

Multinatl US firms foreign affiliates, income statement items by country and world area, 1986, biennial article, 8302–2.212

Nuclear power plant capacity, generation, and operating status, by plant and foreign and US location, 1990 and projected to 2030, annual rpt, 3164–57

UN voting record and share of votes in agreement with US, by issue, country, and world area, 1990, annual rpt, 7004–18

see also under By Foreign Country in the "Index by Categories"

Ehrlich, Phyllis
"Survey of State Public Health Departments on Procedures for Reporting Elder Abuse", 4042–3.213

Eichenbaum, Martin
"Technology Shocks and the Business Cycle", 9375–1.205

Eischeid, Jon K.
"Comprehensive Precipitation Data Set for Global Land Areas", 3006–11.14

Eisler, Ronald
- "Boron Hazards to Fish, Wildlife, and Invertebrates: A Synoptic Review", 5506–14.3
- "Chlordane Hazards to Fish, Wildlife, and Invertebrates: A Synoptic Review", 5506–14.1
- "Paraquat Hazards to Fish, Wildlife, and Invertebrates: A Synoptic Review", 5506–14.2

Eisner, Robert
"Infrastructure and Regional Economic Performance: Comment", 9373–1.217

El-Bassel, Nabila
"Drug Use and Sexual Behavior of Indigent African American Men", 4042–3.254

El Bilassi, Assma
"Background on Egypt's Cotton Sector", 1561–1.201

El Monte, Calif.
see also under By City in the "Index by Categories"

El-Osta, Hisham S.
"Farm Wealth: Its Distribution and Comparison to the Wealth of U.S. Households", 1541–1.207

El Paso, Tex.
- Wages by occupation, and benefits for office and plant workers, 1991 survey, periodic MSA rpt, 6785–3.5
- *see also* under By City and By SMSA or MSA in the "Index by Categories"

El Salvador
- Agricultural exports of high-value commodities, indexes and sales by commodity, world area, and country, 1960s-86, 1528–323
- Agricultural exports of US, impacts of foreign agricultural and trade policy, with data by commodity and country, 1989, annual rpt, 1924–8
- Agricultural production, trade, and policies in foreign countries, summary data by country, 1989-90, annual factbook, 1924–12
- Agricultural trade of US, by detailed commodity and country, 1989, annual rpt, 1524–8
- Agricultural trade of US, by detailed commodity and country, 1990, semiannual rpt, 1522–4
- AID economic aid to developing countries, obligations and disbursements by country, quarterly rpt, 9912–4
- AID loans repayment status and terms by program and country, and status of predecessor agency loans, quarterly rpt, 9912–3
- Economic and military aid and loans from US and intl agencies, by program and country, FY46-90, annual rpt, 9914–5
- Economic and social conditions of developing countries from 1960s, and Intl Dev Cooperation Agency and AID activities and funding, FY90-92, annual rpt, 9904–4
- Economic conditions, policy, and trade practices, by country, 1988-90, annual rpt, 21384–5
- Economic, population, and agricultural data, US and other aid sources, and AID activity, 1989 country rpt, 9916–12.35

Index by Subjects and Names

Electric power

Economic, social, political, and geographic summary data, by country, 1991, annual factbook, 9114–2

Exports and imports of US, by commodity and country, 1970-89, world area rpt, 9116–1.2

Exports and imports of US, by selected country, country group, and commodity group, 1990, annual rpt, 2044–37

Exports and imports of US, by transport mode, country, and SITC 1- to 3-digit commodity, 1990, annual rpt, 2424–12

Exports of US, detailed Schedule B commodities with countries of destination, 1990, annual rpt, 2424–10

Human rights conditions in 170 countries, and US economic and military aid, 1990, annual rpt, 21384–3

Investment (direct) incentives of Caribbean Basin Initiative, economic impacts, with finances and employment by country, 1984-90, 2048–141

Labor conditions, union coverage, and work accidents, 1990 annual country rpt, 6366–4.11

Military aid of US, arms sales, and training programs costs and budget requests, by program, world region, and country, FY90-92, annual rpt, 7144–13

Multinatl US firms foreign affiliates, income statement items by country and world area, 1986, biennial article, 8302–2.212

UN voting record and share of votes in agreement with US, by issue, country, and world area, 1990, annual rpt, 7004–18

see also under By Foreign Country in the "Index by Categories"

Elderly

see Aged and aging

Eldridge, Dan P.

"British Invasion: Explaining the Strength of UK Acquisitions of U.S. Firms in the Late 1980's", 9385–8.82

Elections

Census of Population and Housing, 1990: voting age and total population by race, and housing units, by block, redistricting counts required under PL 94-171, State CD-ROM series, 2551–6

Census of Population and Housing, 1990: voting age and total population by race, and housing units, by county and city, redistricting counts required under PL 94-171, State summary rpt series, 2551–5

Congressional Directory, members of 102nd Congress, other officials, elections, and districts, 1991-92, biennial rpt, 23874–1

Criminal cases by type and disposition, and collections, for US attorneys, by Federal district, FY90, annual rpt, 6004–2.1

Criminal sentences for Federal offenses, guidelines by offense and circumstances, series, 17668–1

Fed Election Commission activities, campaign finances, elections, and procedures, press release series, 9276–1

Foreign countries economic, social, political, and geographic summary data, by country, 1991, annual factbook, 9114–2

Foreign countries voting record in UN and share of votes in agreement with US, by issue, country, and world area, 1990, annual rpt, 7004–18

Labor Relations Natl Board-conducted representation elections, by major industry group and location, FY89, annual rpt, 9584–1.2

Labor unions representation elections conducted by NLRB, results, monthly rpt, 9582–2

Mail volume to and from households, use, and views, by class, source, content, and household characteristics, 1987-88, annual rpt, 9864–10

Massachusetts property tax increase referenda and outcomes, and relation to community characteristics, FY81-91, article, 9373–1.208

Polling places accessibility to aged and handicapped, precincts by barrier type and State, 1990 natl elections, biennial rpt, 9274–6

Population size and characteristics, historical index to *Current Population Rpts*, 1991 listing, 2546–2.160

Puerto Rico statehood referendum proposal, impacts on Federal tax revenue and aid outlays, corporations tax-favored status, and economic conditions, projected FY91-2000, hearing, 25368–168; 26306–3.112

State and Metro Area Data Book, 1991 data compilation, 2328–54

Statistical Abstract of US, 1991 annual data compilation, 2324–1.8

Votes cast by party, candidate, and State, 1990 natl elections, biennial rpt, 9274–5

Voting and registration, by socioeconomic and demographic characteristics, 1990 congressional election, biennial Current Population Rpt, 2546–1.454

Youth and children social, economic, and demographic characteristics, 1950s-90, 4818–5

see also Campaign funds

see also Political action committees

see also Political broadcasting

Electric power

Agriculture census, 1987: farms, farmland, production, finances, and operator characteristics, by county, final State rpt series, 2331–1

Auto (electric-powered) R&D activity and DOE funding shares, FY90, annual rpt, 3304–2

Bonneville Power Admin energy conservation and resource planning activities, FY89-90, 3228–11

Bonneville Power Admin housing energy conservation program activities, cost effectiveness, and participation, series, 3226–1

Bonneville Power Admin mgmt of Fed Columbia River Power System, finances and sales, summary data, quarterly rpt, 3222–2

Bonneville Power Admin mgmt of Fed Columbia River Power System, finances, operations, and sales by customer, FY90, annual rpt, 3224–1

Bonneville Power Admin sales, revenues, and rates, by customer and customer type, 1990, semiannual rpt, 3222–1

Building codes for energy efficiency, effect on house construction practices in BPA service areas, 1987, 3228–15

Business statistics, detailed data for major industries and economic indicators, *Survey of Current Business*, monthly rpt, 2702–1.13

Capital expenditures for plant and equipment, by major industry group, quarterly rpt, 2502–2

China economic indicators and reform issues, with background data, 1950s-90, compilation of papers, 23848–155

Commercial buildings energy use, costs, and conservation, by building characteristics, survey rpt series, 3166–8

Conservation programs of utilities, energy savings under alternative participation rates, projected 1990-2010, 3308–98

Conservation programs of utilities, impacts on electric power prices and supply costs, alternative estimates, 1991 rpt, 3308–99

Construction industries census, 1987: establishments, employment, receipts, and expenditures, by SIC 4-digit industry and State, final industry rpt series, 2373–1

Consumer Expenditure Survey, household income by source, and itemized spending, by selected characteristics and region, 1988-89, annual rpt, 6764–5

Consumption of energy, by detailed fuel type, end-use sector, and State, 1960-89, State Energy Data System annual rpt, 3164–39

County Business Patterns, 1988: employment, establishments, and payroll, by SIC 2- to 4-digit industry and county, annual State rpt series, 2326–6

County Business Patterns, 1989: employment, establishments, and payroll, by SIC 2- to 4-digit industry and county, annual State rpt series, 2326–8

Developing countries energy use, and economic and environmental impacts, by fuel type, world area, and country, 1980s-90, 26358–232

Employment, earnings, and hours, by SIC 1- to 4-digit industry, monthly and annual averages, selected years 1909-90, annual rpt, 6744–4

Enterprise Statistics, 1987: auxiliaries of multi-establishment firms, finances and operations by function, industry, and State, 2329–6

Exports and imports of US, by country and detailed commodity, monthly rpt, 2422–12

Exports and imports of US, by Harmonized System 6-digit commodity and country, 1990, annual rpt, 2424–13

Exports and imports of US, by transport mode, country, and SITC 1- to 3-digit commodity, 1990, annual rpt, 2424–12

Exports of US, detailed Schedule B commodities with countries of destination, 1990, annual rpt, 2424–10

Farm income, expenses, receipts by commodity, assets, liabilities, and ratios, 1990 and trends from 1945, annual rpt, 1544–16

Farm production inputs supply, demand, and prices, 1970s-90 and projected to 1995, article, 1561–16.201

Farm production inputs supply, demand, and prices, 1980s-91 and forecast 1992, article, 1561–16.204

Farm production itemized costs, by farm sales size and region, 1990, annual rpt, 1614–3

Fed Govt energy use and efficiency, by agency and fuel type, FY90, annual rpt, 3304–22

Foreign and US energy production and use, by energy type and country, 1980-89, annual rpt, 3164–50.5

Electric power

Foreign and US energy production, trade, use, and reserves, and oil and refined products supply and prices, by country, 1980-89, annual rpt, 3164–50

Foreign countries economic conditions and implications for US, periodic country rpt series, 2046–4

Foreign countries economic, social, political, and geographic summary data, by country, 1991, annual factbook, 9114–2

Foreign countries electric current characteristics, by country and selected city, 1991 rpt, 2048–1

Foreign countries electric power generation by fuel type, and fuel switching from oil to coal capability, by country, 1973-89, article, 3162–37.201

Global climate change environmental, infrastructure, and health impacts, with model results and background data, 1850s-2100, 9188–113

Govt census, 1987: employment, payroll, and average earnings, by function, level of govt, State, county, and population size, 2455–2

Govt census, 1987: local govt employment by function, payroll, and average earnings, for individual counties, cities, and school and special districts, 2455–1

Govt employment and payroll, by function, level of govt, and jurisdiction, 1990, annual rpt series, 2466–1

Govt labor productivity, indexes of output and labor costs by function, FY67-89, annual rpt, 6824–1.6

Housing (low income) energy aid, funding sources, costs, and participation, by State, FY89, annual rpt, 4694–8

Housing (rental) market absorption rates, by whether utilities included in rent, 1989, annual Current Housing Rpt, 2484–2

Housing and households characteristics, unit and neighborhood quality, and journey to work by MSA location, for 11 MSAs, 1984 survey, supplement, 2485–8

Housing and households detailed characteristics, and unit and neighborhood quality, by location, 1987, biennial rpt supplement, 2485–13

Housing and households detailed characteristics, and unit and neighborhood quality, by location, 1989, biennial rpt, 2485–12

Housing and households detailed characteristics, and unit and neighborhood quality, MSA surveys, series, 2485–6

Housing attic insulation radiant barriers performance impacts of ventilation and dust, 1990 rpt, 3308–97

Housing heating and air conditioning equipment shipments by type of fuel used, bimonthly rpt, 2042–1.6

Housing inventory change from 1973, by reason, unit and household characteristics, and location, 1983 survey, biennial rpt, 2485–14

Housing units (1-family) by selected structural characteristics, sales, and prices, 1970s-90, article, 1702–1.205

Housing units completed, single and multifamily units by structural and financial characteristics, inside-outside MSAs, and region, 1986-90, annual rpt, 2384–1

Industrial electricity use indexes, by SIC 2- to 4-digit industry, monthly rpt, 9365–2.24

Labor productivity, indexes of output, hours, and employment by SIC 2- to 4-digit industry, 1967-89, annual rpt, 6824–1.4

Latin America energy use and trade, by selected country, 1970s-80s and projected to 2000, 3408–1

Manufacturing annual survey, 1989: establishments, employment, finances, inventories, and energy use, by SIC 2- to 4-digit industry, 2506–15.1

Manufacturing annual survey, 1989: finances and operations, by SIC 2- and 3-digit industry and State, 2506–15.3

Manufacturing census, 1987: finances and operations, by SIC 2- to 4-digit industry, State, and MSA, with trends from 1849, 2497–1

Manufacturing energy use and prices, 1988 survey, series, 3166–13

Mineral industries census, 1987: energy use and costs, by fuel type, SIC 2- to 4-digit industry, and State, subject rpt, 2517–2

Mineral industries census, 1987: finances and operations, by SIC 2- to 4-digit industry, State, and county, census div rpt series, 2515–1

Natl Energy Strategy plans for conservation and pollution reduction, impacts of technology and regulation proposals, projected 1990-2030, 3166–6.47

Natl Energy Strategy plans for conservation and pollution reduction, impacts on electric power supply, costs, and emissions, projected under alternative assumptions, 1995-2030, 3166–6.49

Natl Energy Strategy plans for conservation, R&D, security, and pollution reduction, with background data, 1991 biennial rpt, 3004–34

Natl Energy Strategy plans for renewable energy dev, supply projected under alternative cost and capacity use assumptions, 1990-2030, 3166–6.50

New England States electric power sales, Fed Reserve 1st District, monthly rpt, 9373–2.4

Occupational injury and illness rates, by SIC 2- to 4-digit industry, 1988-89, annual rpt, 6844–7

Occupational injury and illness rates, by SIC 2- to 4-digit industry, 1989, annual rpt, 6844–1

Pacific Northwest electric power capacity and use, by energy source, projected under alternative load and demand cases, 1991-2011, annual rpt, 3224–3

Panama Canal electric power generated, purchased, and sold, FY89-90, annual rpt, 9664–3.2

Production, dev, and distribution firms revenues and income, quarterly rpt, 3162–38

Production of electric power, and utility fuel use, stocks, and costs by fuel type, and sales, by State, monthly rpt with articles, 3162–35

Production, sales, plant capacity, and fuel stocks, use, and costs, by State, 1985-89, annual rpt, 3164–11

Retail trade census, 1987: depreciable assets, capital and operating expenses, sales, value added, and inventories, by SIC 2- to 4-digit kind of business, 2399–2

Index by Subjects and Names

Service industries census, 1987: depreciable assets, capital and operating expenses, and receipts, by SIC 2- to 4-digit kind of business, 2393–2

Southeastern Power Admin sales by customer, plants, capacity, and Southeastern Fed Power Program financial statements, FY90, annual rpt, 3234–1

Southwestern Fed Power System financial statements, sales by customer, and operations and costs by project, FY90, annual rpt, 3244–1

Soviet Union, Eastern Europe, OECD, and selected other countries energy reserves, production, and use, and oil trade and revenue, 1960s-90, annual rpt, 9114–4.4

Soviet Union GNP by component and industry sector, and CIA estimation methods, 1950s-87, 23848–223

Soviet Union GNP by detailed income and outlay component, 1985, 2326–18.59

State and Metro Area Data Book, 1991 data compilation, 2328–54

Statistical Abstract of US, 1991 annual data compilation, 2324–1.19

Supply, demand, and distribution of energy, and regulatory impacts, series, 3166–6

Supply, demand, and prices, by fuel type and end-use sector, alternative projections 1989-2010, annual rpt, 3164–75

Supply, demand, and prices, by fuel type and end-use sector, projections and underlying assumptions, 1990-2010, annual rpt, 3164–90

Supply, demand, and prices, by fuel type and end-use sector, with foreign comparisons, 1990 and trends from 1949, annual rpt, 3164–74

Supply, demand, and prices, by fuel type, end-use sector, and country, detailed data, monthly rpt with articles, 3162–24

Supply, demand, and prices of energy, forecasts by resource type, quarterly rpt, 3162–34

Supply of electric power, production and capacity by fuel type, prices, demand, and air pollution law impacts, by region, 1989-90 and projected to 2010, annual rpt, 3164–81

Tax (income) returns of corporations, income and tax items by asset size and detailed industry, 1987, annual rpt, 8304–4

Tax (income) returns of corporations, income and tax items by asset size and detailed industry, 1988, annual rpt, 8304–21

Transit systems finances and operations, by mode of transport, size of fleet, and for 468 systems, 1989, annual rpt, 7884–4

Transportation energy use by mode, fuel supply, and demographic and economic factors of vehicle use, 1970s-89, annual rpt, 3304–5

TVA electric power distributors finances and operations, by firm, annual rpt, discontinued, 9804–19

TVA electric power purchases and resales, with electricity use, average bills, and rates by customer class, by distributor, 1990, annual tables, 9804–14

TVA electric power purchases of municipal and cooperative distributors, and prices and use by distributor and consumer sector, monthly rpt, 9802–1

Index by Subjects and Names

TVA finances and electric power sales, FY90, annual rpt, 9804–1

TVA finances and operations by program and facility, FY90, annual rpt, 9804–32

Utilities finances and operations, detailed data for privately owned firms, 1989, annual rpt, 3164–23

Utilities finances and operations, detailed data for public and privately owned firms, 1989, annual rpt, 3164–11.4

Utilities finances and operations, detailed data for publicly owned firms, 1989, annual rpt, 3164–24

Utilities purchase contracts with nonutility generators, competitive bidding use, 1980s-90, GAO rpt, 26113–498

Western Area Power Admin activities by plant, financial statements, and sales by customer, FY90, annual rpt, 3254–1

Wholesale trade census, 1987: depreciable assets, capital and operating expenses, sales, value added, and inventories, by SIC 2- to 3-digit kind of business, 2407–2

Wholesale trade of electric power, by type of ownership and North American Electric Reliability Council region, 1989, article, 3162–24.201; 3162–35.201

Wholesale trade of electric power, by utility, type of ownership, and region, 1988, biennial rpt, 3164–92

see also Electric power and heat cogeneration

see also Electric power plants and equipment

see also Electric power prices

see also Electrical machinery and equipment

see also Hydroelectric power

see also Nuclear power

see also Rural electrification

see also Solar energy

see also Wind energy

Electric power and heat cogeneration

Certification applications filed with FERC, for small power production and cogeneration facilities, FY80-90, annual listing, 3084–13

Consumption of electric power, indexes by SIC 2- to 4-digit industry, monthly rpt, 9365–2.24

Manufacturing annual survey, 1989: establishments, employment, finances, inventories, and energy use, by SIC 2- to 4-digit industry, 2506–15.1

Manufacturing annual survey, 1989: finances and operations, by SIC 2- to 4-digit industry and State, 2506–15.3

Manufacturing census, 1987: finances and operations, by SIC 2- to 4-digit industry, State, and MSA, with trends from 1849, 2497–1

Manufacturing energy use and prices, 1988 survey, series, 3166–13

Mineral industries census, 1987: energy use and costs, by fuel type, SIC 2- to 4-digit industry, and State, subject rpt, 2517–2

Mineral industries census, 1987: finances and operations, by establishment characteristics, SIC 2- to 4-digit industry, and State, subject rpt, 2517–1

Mineral industries census, 1987: finances and operations, by SIC 2- to 4-digit industry, State, and county, census div rpt series, 2515–1

Pollution (air) emissions factors, by detailed pollutant and source, data compilation, 1990 rpt, 9198–120

Electric power plants and equipment

Birds of prey, rodent, and vegetation distribution and characteristics, for Idaho Snake River area, research results, 1990, annual rpt, 5724–14

Bonneville Power Admin mgmt of Fed Columbia River Power System, finances, operations, and sales by customer, FY90, annual rpt, 3224–1

Bonneville Power Admin operations, maintenance, and environmental protection plans, FY90-99, 3228–14

Business statistics, detailed data for major industries and economic indicators, *Survey of Current Business*, monthly rpt, 2702–1.13; 2702–1.18

Capacity and plants, by fuel used, owner, location, and operating status, 1990, and for units planned 1991-2000, annual listing, 3164–36

Capacity and production of electric power by fuel type, prices, demand, and air pollution law impacts, by region, 1989-90 and projected to 2010, annual rpt, 3164–81

Capacity of power plants, production, sales, and fuel stocks, use, and costs, by State, 1985-89, annual rpt, 3164–11

Capital and production costs, operations, and fuel use, by fuel type, plant, utility, and location, 1989, annual rpt, 3164–9

Certification applications filed with FERC, for small power production and cogeneration facilities, FY80-90, annual listing, 3084–13

Coal, coke, and breeze supply, demand, prices, trade, and stocks, by end-use sector and State, quarterly rpt with articles, 3162–37

Coal production and mines by county, prices, productivity, miners, and reserves, by mining method and State, 1989-90, annual rpt, 3164–25

Coal production, prices, exports, and use by sector, with data by region, projected 1995-2010 and trends from 1970, annual rpt, 3164–68

Coal production, stocks, and shipments, by State of origin and destination, end-use sector, and mode of transport, quarterly rpt, 3162–8

Coal receipts, use, stocks, and delivered price to electric utilities, by State, weekly rpt, monthly data, 3162–1.2

Coal shipments to electric utilities under contract, and rates, by firm, transport mode, and region, 1979-87, 3168–121

Colorado River Basin Federal reservoir and power operations and revenues, 1990-91, annual rpt, 5824–6

Construction industries census, 1987: establishments, employment, receipts, and expenditures, by SIC 4-digit industry and State, final industry rpt series, 2373–1

Construction put in place, permits, housing sales, costs, material prices, and employment, bimonthly rpt with articles, 2042–1

Construction put in place, private and public, by type and region, monthly rpt, annual tables, 2382–4

Construction put in place, value of new public and private structures, by type, monthly rpt, 2382–4

Electric power plants and equipment

County Business Patterns, 1988: employment, establishments, and payroll, by SIC 2- to 4-digit industry and county, annual State rpt series, 2326–6

County Business Patterns, 1989: employment, establishments, and payroll, by SIC 2- to 4-digit industry and county, annual State rpt series, 2326–8

Eastern Europe energy production, trade, use, and AID dev assistance, for 3 countries, 1980s-91, 25318–81

Employment, earnings, and hours, by SIC 1- to 4-digit industry, monthly and annual averages, selected years 1909-90, annual rpt, 6744–4

Energy prices and spending, by fuel type, end-use sector, and State, 1989, annual rpt, 3164–64

Energy supply, demand, and prices, by fuel type and end-use sector, alternative projections 1989-2010, annual rpt, 3164–75

Energy supply, demand, and prices, by fuel type and end-use sector, projections and underlying assumptions, 1990-2010, annual rpt, 3164–90

Energy supply, demand, and prices, by fuel type and end-use sector, with foreign comparisons, 1990 and trends from 1949, annual rpt, 3164–74

Energy supply, demand, and prices, by fuel type, end-use sector, and country, detailed data, monthly rpt with articles, 3162–24

Energy supply, demand, and prices, forecasts by resource type, quarterly rpt, 3162–34

Energy use, by detailed fuel type, end-use sector, and State, 1960-89, State Energy Data System annual rpt, 3164–39

Energy use in transportation and other sectors, by fuel type, 1970s-89, annual rpt, 3304–5

Energy use of power plants, production, stocks, and costs by fuel type, and sales, by State, monthly rpt with articles, 3162–35

Engineering and architectural establishments, receipts by type of client and project, payroll, and employment, by State, 1987 Census of Service Industries, 2393–4.16

Environmental Quality, status of problems, protection programs, research, and intl issues, 1991 annual rpt, 484–1

Exports and imports of US, by country and detailed commodity, monthly rpt, 2422–12

Exports and imports of US, by Harmonized System 6-digit commodity and country, 1990, annual rpt, 2424–13

Exports and imports of US, by selected country, country group, and commodity group, 1990, annual rpt, 2044–37

Exports and imports of US, by transport mode, country, and SITC 1- to 3-digit commodity, 1990, annual rpt, 2424–12

Exports of US, detailed Schedule B commodities with countries of destination, 1990, annual rpt, 2424–10

Fed Govt-owned real property inventory and costs, worldwide summary by purpose, agency, and location, 1989, annual rpt, 9454–5

Fuel oil and kerosene sales and deliveries, by end-use, PAD district, and State, 1989, annual rpt, 3164–94

Electric power plants and equipment

Hydroelectric power generation and capacity, for TVA projects, 1989, annual rpt, 9804–7

Hydroelectric power plants licensed by FERC, characteristics and location, as of Oct 1991, annual listing, 3084–11

Imports of US given duty-free treatment for value of US material sent abroad, by commodity and country, 1989, annual rpt, 9884–14

Labor productivity, indexes of output, hours, and employment by SIC 2- to 4-digit industry, 1967-89, annual rpt, 6824–1.3

Manufacturing annual survey, 1989: finances and operations, by SIC 2- to 4-digit industry, series, 2506–15

Manufacturing census, 1987: finances and operations, by SIC 2- to 4-digit industry, State, and MSA, with trends from 1849, 2497–1

Manufacturing census, 1987: finances and operations, by type of organization and SIC 2- to 4-digit industry, subject rpt, 2497–5

Manufacturing finances and operations, by SIC 2- to 4-digit industry, forecast 1991, annual rpt, 2044–28

Natl Energy Strategy plans for conservation and pollution reduction, impacts on electric power supply, costs, and emissions, projected under alternative assumptions, 1995-2030, 3166–6.49

Natl forests revenue, by source, forest, and State, FY90, annual rpt, 1204–34

Natural and supplemental gas production, prices, trade, use, reserves, and pipeline company finances, by firm and State, monthly rpt with articles, 3162–4

Natural gas interstate pipeline company sales and contract deliveries, by firm and State, 1984-89, annual article, 3162–4.204

Natural gas use, by end-use sector and PAD district, seasonal weekly rpt, 3162–45

Nuclear power plant capacity, generation, and operating status, by plant and foreign and US location, 1990 and projected to 2030, annual rpt, 3164–57

Nuclear power plant operating, maintenance, and capital additions costs, relation to plant characteristics and regulation, 1974-89, 3168–108

Nuclear power plant radioactive waste, releases and waste composition by plant, 1988, annual rpt, 9634–1

Nuclear power plant safety standards and research, design, licensing, construction, operation, and finances, with data by reactor, quarterly journal, 3352–4

Nuclear power plant spent fuel and demand for uranium and enrichment services, for US and other country groups, projected 1991-2040, annual rpt, 3164–72

Nuclear power plant spent fuel and waste generation, inventory, and disposal, 1960s-89 and projected to 2020, annual rpt, 3364–2

Nuclear power plant spent fuel discharges and additional storage capacity needed, by reactor, projected 1990-2040, annual rpt, 3354–2

Nuclear power plant spent fuel discharges, storage capacity, and inventories, by reactor, 1968-89, 3166–6.55

Nuclear power plant spent fuel storage pending opening of permanent repository, safety and costs of alternative methods, projected 1991-2050, 14818–1

Nuclear reactor and other low-level radioactive disposal activities of States and interstate compacts, with data by disposal facility and reactor, 1989, annual rpt, 3354–14

Nuclear reactors for domestic use and export by function and operating status, with owner, operating characteristics, and location, 1990 annual listing, 3354–15

Nuclear reactors operations, by commercial facility, 1990, annual rpt, 9634–12

Nuclear reactors trade of OECD, total and for 4 major countries, and US trade by country, 1980-90, world area rpt series, 9116–1

Nuclear Regulatory Commission activities, finances, and staff, with data for individual power plants, FY90, annual rpt, 9634–2

Occupational injury and illness rates, by SIC 2- to 4-digit industry, 1988-89, annual rpt, 6844–7

Occupational injury and illness rates, by SIC 2- to 4-digit industry, 1989, annual rpt, 6844–1

OECD trade, total and for 4 major countries, and US trade by country, by commodity, 1970-89, world area rpt series, 9116–1

Oil and gas primary use prohibited for power and industrial plants, and gas use by State, 1977-90, annual rpt, 3334–1

Oil and gas supply, demand, and prices, alternative projections 1989-2010, annual rpt, 3164–89

Oil and refined products supply, demand, prices, and refinery capacity and stocks, by State, 1960-91, annual rpt, 3164–95

Pacific Northwest electric power capacity and use, by energy source, projected under alternative load and demand cases, 1991-2011, annual rpt, 3224–3

Pollution (air) abatement equipment shipments by industry, and new and backlog orders, by product, 1990, annual Current Industrial Rpt, 2506–12.5

Pollution (air) contributing to global warming, emissions factors and control costs, by pollutant and source, 1990 rpt, 9198–124

Pollution (air) contributing to global warming, US and foreign emissions and control measures, 1980s and projected to 2020, 26358–233

Pollution (air) emissions and abatement equipment, for privately owned electric utilities by fuel type and State, 1985-89, annual rpt, 3164–11.5

Pollution (air) emissions factors, by detailed pollutant and source, data compilation, 1990 rpt, 9198–120

Pollution (air) levels for 3 pollutants, and capacity of plants with abatement equipment, by type, 1985-89, annual rpt, 3164–74.5

Pollution (air) levels for 6 pollutants, by source, 1970-89 and trends from 1940, annual rpt, 9194–13

Price indexes (producer), by stage of processing and detailed commodity, monthly rpt, 6762–6

Index by Subjects and Names

Production and capacity use indexes, by SIC 2- to 4-digit industry, monthly rpt, 9365–2.24

R&D facilities for biological and medical sciences, space and equipment adequacy, needs, and funding by source, by instn type, 1990, biennial rpt, 4434–17

Reclamation Bur irrigation activities, finances, and project impacts in western US, 1989, annual rpt, 5824–12

Rural Electrification Admin financed electric power plants, with location, capacity, and owner, as of Jan 1991, annual listing, 1244–6

Rural Electrification Admin loans, and borrower operating and financial data, by distribution firm and State, 1990, annual rpt, 1244–1

Southeastern Power Admin sales by customer, plants, capacity, and Southeastern Fed Power Program financial statements, FY90, annual rpt, 3234–1

Southwestern Fed Power System financial statements, sales by customer, and operations and costs by project, FY90, annual rpt, 3244–1

State and Metro Area Data Book, 1991 data compilation, 2328–54

Steam-driven power plants fuel receipts, costs, and quality, by fuel, plant, utility, and State, 1990, annual rpt, 3164–42

TVA finances and operations by program and facility, FY90, annual rpt, 9804–32

Utilities finances and operations, detailed data for privately owned firms, 1989, annual rpt, 3164–23

Utilities finances and operations, detailed data for public and privately owned firms, 1989, annual rpt, 3164–11.4

Utilities finances and operations, detailed data for publicly owned firms, 1989, annual rpt, 3164–24

Utilities purchase contracts with nonutility generators, competitive bidding use, 1980s-90, GAO rpt, 26113–498

Water use by end use, well withdrawals, and public supply deliveries, by county, State rpt series, 5666–24

Western Area Power Admin activities by plant, financial statements, and sales by customer, FY90, annual rpt, 3254–1

Wood, waste, and alcohol fuel use, by end-use sector and region, 1989, 3166–6.56

see also Electric power and heat cogeneration

see also Nuclear accidents and safety

Electric power prices

Bonneville Power Admin sales, revenues, and rates, by customer and customer type, 1990, semiannual rpt, 3222–1

Conservation programs of utilities, impacts on electric power prices and supply costs, alternative estimates, 1991 rpt, 3308–99

CPI by component for US city average, and by region, population size, and for 27 metro areas, monthly rpt, 6762–2

Farm electric power use and average monthly bill, monthly rpt, annual table, 1629–1

Food marketing cost indexes, by expense category, monthly rpt with articles, 1502–4

Housing electric power bills, and rankings, by State, as of Jan 1990, annual rpt, 1244–1.6

Index by Subjects and Names

Electrical machinery and equipment

Housing energy prices, by fuel and State, 1989 and forecast 1990-91, 3166–6.54

Import price indexes for electric power, quarterly press release, 6762–13

Natl Energy Strategy plans for conservation and pollution reduction, impacts of technology and regulation proposals, projected 1990-2030, 3166–6.47

OECD energy prices, by fuel type and end use, for 10 countries, 1980-89 annual rpt, 3164–50.6

Prices and spending for fuel, by type, end-use sector, and State, 1989, annual rpt, 3164–64

Prices, production and capacity by fuel type, demand, and air pollution law impacts, for electric power by region, 1989-90 and projected to 2010, annual rpt, 3164–81

Prices, supply, and demand, by fuel type and end-use sector, alternative projections 1989-2010, annual rpt, 3164–75

Prices, supply, and demand, by fuel type and end-use sector, projections and underlying assumptions, 1990-2010, annual rpt, 3164–90

Prices, supply, and demand, by fuel type and end-use sector, with foreign comparisons, 1990 and trends from 1949, annual rpt, 3164–74

Prices, supply, and demand of energy, forecasts by resource type, quarterly rpt, 3162–34

Producer price indexes, by stage of processing and detailed commodity, monthly rpt, 6762–6

Producer price indexes, by stage of processing and detailed commodity, monthly 1990, annual rpt, 6764–2

Retail electric power prices, by end-use sector, monthly rpt, 3162–24.9; 3162–35

Retail electric power sales and revenue, by end-use sector, 1985-89, annual rpt, 3164–11.3

Rural Electrification Admin borrowers wholesale purchases, by borrower, supplier, and State, 1940-89, annual rpt, 1244–5

Statistical Abstract of US, 1991 annual data compilation, 2324–1.15

TVA electric power purchases and resales, with electricity use, average bills, and rates by customer class, by distributor, 1990, annual tables, 9804–14

TVA electric power purchases of municipal and cooperative distributors, and prices and use by distributor and consumer sector, monthly rpt, 9802–1

Wholesale trade of electric power, by utility, type of ownership, and region, 1988, biennial rpt, 3164–92

Electric utilities

see Electric power

see Electric power plants and equipment

see Electric power prices

see Rural electrification

Electrical machinery and equipment

Building materials PPI, by type, bimonthly rpt, 2042–1.5

Business statistics, detailed data for major industries and economic indicators, *Survey of Current Business,* monthly rpt, 2702–1.17

Capital expenditures for plant and equipment, by major industry group, quarterly rpt, 2502–2

Child accident deaths and death rates, by cause, age, sex, race, and State, 1980-85, 4108–54

Collective bargaining agreements expiring during year, and workers covered, by firm, union, industry group, and State, 1991, annual rpt, 6784–9

Construction industries census, 1987: finances and operations, by SIC 4-digit industry and State, final rpt, 2373–1.12

County Business Patterns, 1988: employment, establishments, and payroll, by SIC 2- to 4-digit industry and county, annual State rpt series, 2326–6

County Business Patterns, 1989: employment, establishments, and payroll, by SIC 2- to 4-digit industry and county, annual State rpt series, 2326–8

DOD prime contract awards, by detailed procurement category, FY87-90, annual rpt, 3544–18

Employment, earnings, and hours, by SIC 1- to 4-digit industry, monthly and annual averages, selected years 1909-90, annual rpt, 6744–4

Employment in manufacturing, by detailed occupation and SIC 2-digit industry, 1989 survey, triennial rpt, 6748–52

Employment, unemployment, and labor force characteristics, by region and census div, 1990, annual rpt, 6744–7.1

Energy use and prices for manufacturing industries, 1988 survey, series, 3166–13

Enterprise Statistics, 1987: auxiliaries of multi-establishment firms, finances and operations by function, industry, and State, 2329–6

Enterprise Statistics, 1987: finances and operations for companies, by size, level of diversification, form of organization, and industry group, 2329–8

Exports and imports between US and outlying areas, by detailed commodity and mode of transport, 1990, annual rpt, 2424–11

Exports and imports of US, by country and detailed commodity, monthly rpt, 2422–12

Exports and imports of US, by Harmonized System 6-digit commodity and country, 1990, annual rpt, 2424–13

Exports and imports of US, by selected country, country group, and commodity group, 1990, annual rpt, 2044–37

Exports and imports of US, by transport mode, country, and SITC 1- to 3-digit commodity, 1990, annual rpt, 2424–12

Exports of US, detailed commodities by country, monthly CD-ROM, 2422–13

Exports of US, detailed Schedule B commodities with countries of destination, 1990, annual rpt, 2424–10

Foreign countries electric current characteristics, by country and selected city, 1991 rpt, 2048–1

Foreign direct investment of US, by industry group and world area, 1987-90, annual article, 2702–1.220

Imports, exports, and employment impacts, by SIC 2- to 4-digit industry and commodity, quarterly rpt, 2322–2

Imports of US, detailed commodities by country, monthly CD-ROM, 2422–14

Imports of US given duty-free treatment for value of US material sent abroad, by commodity and country, 1989, annual rpt, 9884–14

Injuries from use of consumer products, by severity, victim age, and detailed product, 1990, annual rpt, 9164–6

Input-output structure of US economy, detailed interindustry transactions for 84 industries, and components of final demand, 1986, annual article, 2702–1.206

Input-output structure of US economy, detailed interindustry transactions for 85 industries, 1982 benchmark data, 2702–1.213

Labor productivity, indexes of output, hours, and employment by SIC 2- to 4-digit industry, 1967-89, annual rpt, 6824–1.3

Manufacturing annual survey, 1989: finances and operations, by SIC 2- to 4-digit industry, series, 2506–15

Manufacturing census, 1987: employment and shipments under Fed Govt contracts, by SIC 4-digit industry, 2497–7

Manufacturing census, 1987: finances and operations, by SIC 2- to 4-digit industry, State, and MSA, with trends from 1849, 2497–1

Manufacturing census, 1987: finances and operations, by type of organization and SIC 2- to 4-digit industry, subject rpt, 2497–5

Manufacturing corporations financial statements, by selected SIC 2- to 3-digit industry, quarterly rpt, 2502–1

Manufacturing finances and operations, by SIC 2- to 4-digit industry, forecast 1991, annual rpt, 2044–28

Manufacturing industries operations and performance, analytical rpt series, 2506–16

Manufacturing production, shipments, inventories, orders, and pollution control costs, periodic Current Industrial Rpt series, 2506–3

Mexico imports from US, by industry and State, 1987-90, 2048–154

Military and personal property shipments, passenger traffic, and costs, by service branch and mode of transport, quarterly rpt, 3702–1

Multinatl firms US affiliates, finances, and operations, by industry, world area of parent firm, and State, 1988-89, annual rpt, 2704–4

Multinatl US firms and foreign affiliates finances and operations, by industry and world area of parent firm, 1989 benchmark survey, preliminary annual rpt, 2704–5

Occupational injury and illness rates, by SIC 2- to 4-digit industry, 1988-89, annual rpt, 6844–7

Occupational injury and illness rates, by SIC 2- to 4-digit industry, 1989, annual rpt, 6844–1

OECD trade, total and for 4 major countries, and US trade by country, by commodity, 1970-89, world area rpt series, 9116–1

Pollution (air) emissions factors, by detailed pollutant and source, data compilation, 1990 rpt, 9198–120

Pollution abatement capital and operating costs, by SIC 2-digit industry, 1989, advance annual Current Industrial Rpt, 2506–3.6

Electrical machinery and equipment

Price indexes (producer), by stage of processing and detailed commodity, monthly rpt, 6762–6

Price indexes (producer), by stage of processing and detailed commodity, monthly 1990, annual rpt, 6764–2

Puerto Rico and other US possessions corporations income tax returns, income and tax items, and employment, by selected industry, 1987, article, 8302–2.213

Puerto Rico economic censuses, 1987: wholesale and retail trade and service industry finances and operations, by SIC 2- to 4-digit industry and municipio, 2591–1

Puerto Rico economic censuses, 1987: wholesale, retail, and service industries finances and operations, by establishment characteristics and SIC 2- and 3-digit industry, subject rpts, 2591–2

Statistical Abstract of US, 1991 annual data compilation, 2324–1.27

Switchgear, switchboard apparatus, relays, and other equipment shipments, trade, use, and firms, by product, 1990, annual Current Industrial Rpt, 2506–12.11

Taiwan imports of building materials, and share from US, by commodity, 1989-90, article, 2042–1.205

Tax (income) returns of corporations, income and tax items by asset size and detailed industry, 1987, annual rpt, 8304–4

Tax (income) returns of corporations, income and tax items by asset size and detailed industry, 1988, annual rpt, 8304–21

Tax (income) returns of corporations with foreign tax credit, income and tax items by industry group, 1986, biennial article, 8302–2.203

Tax (income) returns of multinatl US firms foreign affiliates, income statement items, by asset size and industry, 1986, biennial article, 8302–2.212

Tax (income) returns of sole proprietorships, income statement items, by industry group, 1989, annual article, 8302–2.214

Wholesale trade census, 1987: depreciable assets, capital and operating expenses, sales, value added, and inventories, by SIC 2- to 3-digit kind of business, 2407–2

Wholesale trade census, 1987: establishments, sales by customer class, employment, inventories, and expenses, by SIC 2- to 4-digit kind of business, 2407–4

Wholesale trade sales and inventories, by SIC 2- to 3-digit kind of business, monthly rpt, 2413–7

Wholesale trade sales, inventories, purchases, and gross margins, by SIC 2- to 3-digit kind of business, 1990, annual rpt, 2413–13

Wire and cable (insulated) shipments, trade, use, and firms, by product, 1990, annual Current Industrial Rpt, 2506–10.8

see also Batteries

see also Electric power plants and equipment

see also Electronics industry and products

see also Engines and motors

see also Household appliances and equipment

see also Lighting equipment

see also under By Commodity in the "Index by Categories"

see also under By Industry in the "Index by Categories"

Electromagnetic radiation

see Nuclear medicine and radiology

see Radiation

see X-rays

Electronic data processing

see Computer industry and products

see Computer sciences

see Computer use

see Electronic funds transfer

see Information storage and retrieval systems

Electronic funds transfer

Bank deposits, account debits, and deposit turnover, for commercial banks by type of account, monthly rpt, 9365–2.5

Budget of US, authoritative financial statements with appropriations, outlays, and receipts, by category and agency, FY90, annual rpt, 8104–2.1

Fed Govt finances, cash and debt transactions, daily tables, 8102–4

Fed Reserve System, Board of Governors, and district banks financial statements, performance, and fiscal services, 1990-91, annual rpt, 9364–10

Households bill payment transactions, by method, 1987-88, annual rpt, 9864–10

OASDI beneficiaries using direct deposit, and benefits, by State, 1989, annual rpt, 4744–3.3

Telegraph firms money order operations and revenue, 1989, annual rpt, 9284–6.3

see also Automated tellers

Electronic mail

see Computer networks

see Postal service

Electronic surveillance

Criminal releases electronically monitored, by offense and State, data compilation, 1991 annual rpt, 6064–6.6

Criminal releases electronically monitored, by region and State, 1989, annual rpt, 6064–26.2; 6064–26.5

Criminal sentences for Federal offenses, guidelines by offense and circumstances, series, 17668–1

Equipment shipments, trade, use, and firms, for electronic communications systems and related products, 1990, annual Current Industrial Rpt, 2506–12.35

Space programs activities, missions, launchings, payloads, and flight duration, for foreign and US programs, 1957-90, annual rpt, 21704–4

Statistical Abstract of US, 1991 annual data compilation, 2324–1.5

Wiretaps and results by offense and location, and public opinion, data compilation, 1991 annual rpt, 6064–6.2; 6064–6.5

Wiretaps authorized, costs, arrests, trials, and convictions, by offense and jurisdiction, 1990, annual rpt, 18204–7

see also Radar

Electronics industry and products

Communications and related electronic equipment shipments, trade, use, and firms, 1990, annual Current Industrial Rpt, 2506–12.35

Competitiveness (intl) of US telecommunications industry, with financial and operating data by product or service, firm, and country, 1990 rpt, 2008–30

Index by Subjects and Names

County Business Patterns, 1988: employment, establishments, and payroll, by SIC 2- to 4-digit industry and county, annual State rpt series, 2326–6

County Business Patterns, 1989: employment, establishments, and payroll, by SIC 2- to 4-digit industry and county, annual State rpt series, 2326–8

DOD prime contract awards, by category, contract and contractor type, and service branch, FY81-1st half FY91, semiannual rpt, 3542–1

DOD prime contract awards, by category, contractor type, and State, FY88-90, annual rpt, 3544–11

DOD prime contract awards, by detailed procurement category, FY87-90, annual rpt, 3544–18

DOD prime contract awards, by size and type of contract, service branch, competitive status, category, and labor standard, FY90, annual rpt, 3544–19

Employment, earnings, and hours, by SIC 1- to 4-digit industry, monthly and annual averages, selected years 1909-90, annual rpt, 6744–4

Enterprise Statistics, 1987: finances and operations for companies, by size, level of diversification, form of organization, and industry group, 2329–8

Exports and imports between US and outlying areas, by detailed commodity and mode of transport, 1990, annual rpt, 2424–11

Exports and imports of US, by country and detailed commodity, monthly rpt, 2422–12

Exports and imports of US, by Harmonized System 6-digit commodity and country, 1990, annual rpt, 2424–13

Exports and imports of US, by transport mode, country, and SITC 1- to 3-digit commodity, 1990, annual rpt, 2424–12

Exports of US, detailed commodities by country, monthly CD-ROM, 2422–13

Exports of US, detailed Schedule B commodities with countries of destination, 1990, annual rpt, 2424–10

Foreign direct investment impact on trade balance, with background data, late 1960s-90 and auto forecasts to 1993, article, 9385–1.210

Foreign direct investment in US manufacturing, impacts on trade balances, with data by industry, 1980s-93, technical paper, 9385–8.91

Foreign direct investment of US, by industry group and world area, 1987-90, annual article, 2702–1.220

Health care electronic equipment shipments, trade, use, and firms, by product, 1990, annual Current Industrial Rpt, 2506–12.34

Imports detained by FDA, by reason, product, shipper, brand, and country, monthly listing, 4062–2

Imports of US, detailed commodities by country, monthly CD-ROM, 2422–14

Imports of US given duty-free treatment for value of US material sent abroad, by commodity and country, 1989, annual rpt, 9884–14

Input-output structure of US economy, detailed interindustry transactions for 84 industries, and components of final demand, 1986, annual article, 2702–1.206

Index by Subjects and Names

Input-output structure of US economy, detailed interindustry transactions for 85 industries, 1982 benchmark data, 2702–1.213

Japan manufacturing firms US affiliates, employment, and wages, by selected industry and State, 1980s, 2048–151

Labor productivity, indexes of output, hours, and employment by SIC 2- to 4-digit industry, 1967-89, annual rpt, 6824–1.3

Manufacturing annual survey, 1989: finances and operations, by SIC 2- to 4-digit industry, series, 2506–15

Manufacturing census, 1987: employment and shipments under Fed Govt contracts, by SIC 4-digit industry, 2497–7

Manufacturing census, 1987: finances and operations, by SIC 2- to 4-digit industry, State, and MSA, with trends from 1849, 2497–1

Manufacturing census, 1987: finances and operations, by type of organization and SIC 2- to 4-digit industry, subject rpt, 2497–5

Manufacturing corporations financial statements, by selected SIC 2- to 3-digit industry, quarterly rpt, 2502–1

Manufacturing finances and operations, by SIC 2- to 4-digit industry, forecast 1991, annual rpt, 2044–28

Materials (advanced structural) devs and data needs, 1989 conf, 5608–167

Multinatl firms US affiliates, investment trends and impact on US economy, 1991 annual rpt, 2004–9

Multinatl US firms and foreign affiliates finances and operations, by industry and world area of parent firm, 1989 benchmark survey, preliminary annual rpt, 2704–5

Occupational injury and illness rates, by SIC 2- to 4-digit industry, 1988-89, annual rpt, 6844–7

Occupational injury and illness rates, by SIC 2- to 4-digit industry, 1989, annual rpt, 6844–1

OECD trade, total and for 4 major countries, and US trade by country, by commodity, 1970-89, world area rpt series, 9116–1

Pollution (air) emissions factors, by detailed pollutant and source, data compilation, 1990 rpt, 9198–120

Price indexes (producer), by stage of processing and detailed commodity, monthly rpt, 6762–6

Price indexes (producer), by stage of processing and detailed commodity, monthly 1990, annual rpt, 6764–2

Puerto Rico and other US possessions corporations income tax returns, income and tax items, and employment, by selected industry, 1987, article, 8302–2.213

Puerto Rico economic censuses, 1987: wholesale and retail trade and service industry finances and operations, by SIC 2- to 4-digit industry and municipio, 2591–1

Radiation from electronic devices, incidents by type of device, and FDA control activities, 1990, annual rpt, 4064–13

Retail trade census, 1987: finances and employment, for establishments with and without payroll, by SIC 2- to 4-digit kind of business, State, and MSA, 2401–1

Shipments, trade, use, and firms, for consumer electronics by product, 1990, annual Current Industrial Rpt, 2506–12.20

Statistical Abstract of US, 1991 annual data compilation, 2324–1.18; 2324–1.27

Switchgear, switchboard apparatus, relays, and other equipment shipments, trade, use, and firms, by product, 1990, annual Current Industrial Rpt, 2506–12.11

Tariff Schedule of US, classifications and rates of duty by detailed imported commodity, 1992 base edition, 9886–13

Tax (income) returns of corporations, income and tax items by asset size and detailed industry, 1987, annual rpt, 8304–4

Tax (income) returns of corporations, income and tax items by asset size and detailed industry, 1988, annual rpt, 8304–21

Wholesale trade census, 1987: establishments, sales by customer class, employment, inventories, and expenses, by SIC 2- to 4-digit kind of business, 2407–4

see also Automated tellers

see also CD-ROM technology and use

see also Computer industry and products

see also Electronic funds transfer

see also Electronic surveillance

see also Home video and audio equipment

see also Lasers

see also Radio

see also Semiconductors

see also Television

see also Video recordings and equipment

see also under By Commodity in the "Index by Categories"

see also under By Industry in the "Index by Categories"

Elementary and secondary education

Appalachia education system, improvement initiatives, and indicators of success, by State, 1960s-89, 9088–36

Assistance (financial and nonfinancial) of Fed Govt, 1991 base edition with supplements, annual listing, 104–5

Condition of Education, detail for elementary and secondary education, 1920s-90 and projected to 2001, annual rpt, 4824–1.1

Data collection activities and programs of NCES, 1991, annual listing, 4824–7

Data on education, estimates from Fast Response Survey System, series, 4826–1

Data on education, selected performance and financial indicators by State, annual table with supplements, discontinued, 4804–32

Data on education, selected trends and projections 1978-2001, pamphlet, 4828–27

Data on education, 1960s-89, pamphlet, 4828–26

Data on elementary and secondary education, enrollment, staff, finances, operations, programs, and policies, 1987/88 biennial survey, series, 4836–3

Data on elementary and secondary public schools, enrollment and other characteristics, for top 100 districts, 1988/89, annual rpt, 4834–22

Data on public elementary and secondary education, schools, enrollment, teachers,

Elevators

funding, and other characteristics, by region and State, 1988/89, annual rpt, 4834–20

Digest of Education Statistics, 1991 annual data compilation, 4824–2

Eighth grade class of 1988: educational performance and conditions, characteristics, attitudes, activities, and plans, natl longitudinal survey, series, 4826–9

Natl Education Goals progress indicators, by State, 1991, annual rpt, 15914–1

State and Metro Area Data Book, 1991 data compilation, 2328–54

Statistical Abstract of US, 1991 annual data compilation, 2324–1.4

see also Bilingual education

see also Compensatory education

see also Curricula

see also Discrimination in education

see also Educational attainment

see also Educational broadcasting

see also Educational enrollment

see also Educational exchanges

see also Educational facilities

see also Educational finance

see also Educational materials

see also Educational reform

see also Educational research

see also Educational technology

see also Educational tests

see also Federal aid to education

see also Head Start Project

see also National Assessment of Educational Progress

see also Preschool education

see also Private schools

see also Remedial education

see also School administration and staff

see also School districts

see also School lunch and breakfast programs

see also Special education

see also State funding for education

see also Students

see also Teacher education

see also Teachers

see also Vocational education and training

Elevators

County Business Patterns, 1988: employment, establishments, and payroll, by SIC 2- to 4-digit industry and county, annual State rpt series, 2326–6

County Business Patterns, 1989: employment, establishments, and payroll, by SIC 2- to 4-digit industry and county, annual State rpt series, 2326–8

Exports and imports of US, by country and detailed commodity, monthly rpt, 2422–12

Exports and imports of US, by Harmonized System 6-digit commodity and country, 1990, annual rpt, 2424–13

Exports and imports of US, by transport mode, country, and SITC 1- to 3-digit commodity, 1990, annual rpt, 2424–12

Exports of US, detailed Schedule B commodities with countries of destination, 1990, annual rpt, 2424–10

Housing and households detailed characteristics, and unit and neighborhood quality, by location, 1989, biennial rpt, 2485–12

Housing and households detailed characteristics, and unit and neighborhood quality, MSA surveys, series, 2485–6

Elevators

Housing inventory change from 1973, by reason, unit and household characteristics, and location, 1983 survey, biennial rpt, 2485–14

Injuries from use of consumer products, by severity, victim age, and detailed product, 1990, annual rpt, 9164–6

Manufacturing annual survey, 1989: finances and operations, by SIC 2- to 4-digit industry, series, 2506–15

Manufacturing census, 1987: finances and operations, by SIC 2- to 4-digit industry, State, and MSA, with trends from 1849, 2497–1

Manufacturing census, 1987: finances and operations, by type of organization and SIC 2- to 4-digit industry, subject rpt, 2497–5

Occupational deaths involving vehicle-mounted elevating platforms, circumstances, and OSHA standards violated, 1991 rpt, 6606–2.17

Occupational injury and illness rates, by SIC 2- to 4-digit industry, 1988-89, annual rpt, 6844–7

Occupational injury and illness rates, by SIC 2- to 4-digit industry, 1989, annual rpt, 6844–1

Price indexes (producer), by stage of processing and detailed commodity, monthly rpt, 6762–6

Price indexes (producer), by stage of processing and detailed commodity, monthly 1990, annual rpt, 6764–2

Smoking bans in public places, local ordinances provisions, as of 1989, 4478–196

see also Grain storage and facilities

Elgin, Ill.

see also under By SMSA or MSA in the "Index by Categories"

Elizabeth, N.J.

see also under By City in the "Index by Categories"

Elkhart, Ind.

see also under By SMSA or MSA in the "Index by Categories"

Ellice Islands

see Tuvalu

Ellwood, David T.

"Medicaid Mysteries: Transitional Benefits, Medicaid Coverage, and Welfare Exits", 4652–1.217

Ellwood, Marilyn R.

"Access to Medicaid and Medicare by the Low-Income Disabled", 4652–1.218

Elmira, N.Y.

see also under By SMSA or MSA in the "Index by Categories"

Ely, David P.

"Stock Returns and Inflation: Further Tests of the Role of the Central Bank", 9379–14.12

Elyria, Ohio

see also under By SMSA or MSA in the "Index by Categories"

Emami, Ali

"Note on the Value of the Right Data", 1502–3.203

Embargo

see International sanctions

Embezzlement

see Fraud

Emblom, Edward F.

"Tax Amnesty, Improving Compliance?", 8304–8.1

Emergency medical service

Airline emergency medical kit items use, occupation of person administering aid, and patient symptoms, 1986-87, technical rpt, 7506–10.82

Airline emergency medical kit items use, 1986-88, technical rpt, 7506–10.81

Cocaine-related emergency room admissions, by user and use characteristics, for major metro areas, 1987-89, article, 4042–3.204

Cocaine-related emergency room episodes, by age, sex, race, and Hispanic origin, 1985-89, annual data compilation, 4144–11

Consumer Product Safety Commission activities, recalls by brand, and casualties and medical costs, by product type, FY89, annual rpt, 9164–2

Consumer products use, injuries by severity, victim age, and detailed product, 1990, annual rpt, 9164–6

Crime victimization of women, by relation to offender, circumstances, and victim characteristics, for rape and other violent offenses, 1973-87, 6068–243

Crime victimization rates, by victim and offender characteristics, circumstances, and offense, 1988 survey, annual rpt, 6066–3.42

Crime victimization rates, by victim and offender characteristics, circumstances, and offense, 1989 survey, annual rpt, 6066–3.44

Drug abuse emergency room admissions and deaths, by drug type and major metro area, semiannual rpt, discontinued, 4492–3

Drug abuse emergency room admissions and deaths, by drug type and source, sex, race, age, and major metro area, 1990, annual rpt, 4494–8

Drug abuse indicators for selected metro areas, research results, data collection, and policy issues, 1991 semiannual conf, 4492–5

Drug abuse prevalence among minorities, related health effects and crime, treatment, and research status and needs, mid 1970s-90, 4498–72

Fed Govt financial and nonfinancial domestic aid, 1991 base edition with supplements, annual listing, 104–5

Health maintenance organizations and other prepaid managed care plans Medicaid enrollment and use, for 20 States, 1985-89, chartbook, 4108–29

Helicopters, use, and landing facilities, by craft type, region, and State, 1989, 7508–75

Hospital services and facilities availability, by selected instn characteristics, 1980, 1983, and 1987, 17206–2.22

Hospital trauma centers unreimbursed costs and other factors contributing to closure, and views on nontrauma care impacts, 1989-90, GAO rpt, 26121–419

Hospitals, receipts by source, contract services, expenses, and employment, by facility type and State, 1987 Census of Service Industries, 2393–4.12

Medicaid beneficiaries emergency room visits relation to availability of other sources of care, for upstate New York, 1985-87, article, 4652–1.232

Index by Subjects and Names

Medicaid services use and costs in alternative treatment settings, model description and results, FY87, article, 4652–1.211

Military health care personnel, and accessions by training source, by occupation, specialty, and service branch, FY89, annual rpt, 3544–24

Physicians, by specialty, age, sex, and location of training and practice, 1989, State rpt series, 4116–6

Traffic accidents in urban and rural areas, emergency medical service response times, 1989, annual rpt, 7764–10

Emergency relief

see Disaster relief

Emery

see Abrasive materials

Emery, Kenneth M.

"Algebra of Price Stability", 9379–12.79

"Modeling the Effects of Inflation on the Demand for Money", 9379–1.203

Emigration

see Immigration and emigration

see Refugees

Eminent domain

see Property condemnation

Emissions

see Air pollution

see Global climate change

see Motor vehicle exhaust

Emmett, Robert L.

"Distribution and Abundance of Fishes and Invertebrates in West Coast Estuaries, Volume II: Species Life History Summaries", 2176–7.24

Emphysema

see Respiratory diseases

Employee benefits

AFDC beneficiaries demographic and financial characteristics, by State, FY89, annual rpt, 4694–1

Alien nonresidents income from US sources and tax withheld by country and US tax treaty status, 1988, annual article, 8302–2.206

Budget of US, obligations and authority by function, agency, and program, with summaries, analyses, and historical tables, FY92, annual rpt, 104–2

Child care aid provided by employers, North Central States employers activities and views, 1991 survey, article, 9383–19.201

Collective bargaining wage and benefit changes, quarterly press release, 6782–2

Collective bargaining wage changes and coverage, by industry sector and whether contract includes escalator clause and lump sum payment, 1980-90, annual article, 6722–1.227

Construction industries census, 1987: establishments, employment, receipts, and expenditures, by SIC 4-digit industry and State, final industry rpt series, 2373–1

Costs (hourly) of labor, by component, industry sector, worker class, and firm size, 1990, annual rpt, 6744–22

Coverage and provisions of employee benefit plans, by plan type, firm size, and industry sector, 1988, article, 6722–1.204

Coverage under employee benefit plans, by benefit type and worker characteristics, late 1970s-80s, 15496–1.11

Employee benefits

Criminal sentences for Federal offenses, guidelines by offense and circumstances, series, 17668–1

Educational enrollment, finances, staff, and high school grads, for elementary and secondary public school systems by State, FY88-89, annual rpt, 4834–6

Electric utilities privately owned, finances and operations, detailed data, 1989, annual rpt, 3164–23

Enterprise Statistics, 1987: auxiliaries of multi-establishment firms, finances and operations by function, industry, and State, 2329–6

Expenditures (private) for social welfare, by category, 1970s-88, annual article, 4742–1.204

Farm employment, wages, and hours, by payment method, worker type, region, and State, 1910-90, 1618–21

Farm income, expenses, receipts by commodity, assets, liabilities, and ratios, 1990 and trends from 1945, annual rpt, 1544–16

Farm labor, wages, hours, and perquisites, by State, monthly rpt, 1631–1

Farm production itemized costs, by farm sales size and region, 1990, annual rpt, 1614–3

Fed Govt civilian employees work-years by schedule, overtime, holidays, and personnel cost components, FY89-90, annual article, 9842–1.204

Fed Govt civilian employees work-years, pay rates, and benefits use and costs, by agency, FY89, annual rpt, 9844–31

Fed Govt consolidated financial statements based on business accounting methods, FY89-90, annual rpt, 8104–5

Fed Govt employee family-related and work schedule benefits, availability, admin, and personnel directors views, 1990 survey, 9496–2.7

Fed Govt obligations object class analysis, by agency, Budget of US, FY92, annual rpt, 104–9

Fed Govt spending in States, by type, program, agency, and State, FY90, annual rpt, 2464–2

Govt census, 1987: State and local govt employment, payroll, OASDHI coverage, and employee benefits costs, by level of govt and State, 2455–4

Govt finances, by level of govt, State, and for large cities and counties, annual rpt series, 2466–2

Health Care Financing Review, provider prices, price inputs and indexes, and labor, quarterly journal, 4652–1.1

Health promotion program availability and participation, by type of program and sponsor, 1986-87 local area study, article, 4042–3.223

Labor Dept programs fraud and abuse, audits and investigations activity, and racketeering cases by type and disposition, FY88-89, GAO rpt, 26111–74

Labor laws enacted, by State, 1990, annual article, 6722–1.209

Leave for illness, disability, and dependent care, coverage, provisions, terminations, costs, and methods of covering for absent worker, by firm size, 1988 survey, 9768–21

Leave transfer to other employees, Federal pilot programs operations and costs by agency, FY89, 9848–40

Manufacturing annual survey, 1989: establishments, employment, finances, inventories, and energy use, by SIC 2- to 4-digit industry, 2506–15.1

Manufacturing annual survey, 1989: finances and operations, by SIC 2- and 3-digit industry and State, 2506–15.3

Manufacturing census, 1987: finances and operations, by SIC 2- to 4-digit industry, State, and MSA, with trends from 1849, 2497–1

Mineral industries census, 1987: finances and operations, by establishment characteristics, SIC 2- to 4-digit industry, and State, subject rpt, 2517–1

Mineral industries census, 1987: finances and operations, by SIC 2- to 4-digit industry, State, and county, census div rpt series, 2515–1

Multinatl firms US affiliates, finances, and operations, by industry, world area of parent firm, and State, 1988-89, annual rpt, 2704–4

Multinatl US firms and foreign affiliates finances and operations, by industry and world area of parent firm, 1989 benchmark survey, preliminary annual rpt, 2704–5

Natural gas interstate pipeline company detailed financial and operating data, by firm, 1989, annual rpt, 3164–38

Nonprofit charitable organizations finances, and revenue and investments of top 10 instns, 1986-87, article, 8302–2.210

Nonprofit charitable organizations finances, by size of contributions received, 1987, article, 8302–2.218

Part-time employment by health insurance coverage and worker characteristics, and temporary and contract employment, 1979-89, GAO rpt, 26121–411

Postal Service employment and related expenses, FY90, annual rpt, 9864–5.3

Postal Service operating costs, itemized by class of mail, FY90, annual rpt, 9864–4

Postal Service productivity, indexes of output and labor, capital, and other inputs, alternative model descriptions and results, 1960s-89, 9688–6

Railroad employee benefits program finances and beneficiaries, FY90, annual rpt, 9704–1

Railroad employment, earnings, and hours, by occupation for Class I railroads, 1990, annual table, 9484–5

Railroad retirement, survivors, unemployment, and health insurance programs, monthly rpt, 9702–2

Recruitment, hiring, compensation, and other employment practices of large firms, 1989 survey, GAO rpt, 26119–324

Retail trade census, 1987: depreciable assets, capital and operating expenses, sales, value added, and inventories, by SIC 2- to 4-digit kind of business, 2399–2

Senate receipts, itemized expenses by payee, and balances, 1st half FY91, semiannual listing, 25922–1

Service industries census, 1987: depreciable assets, capital and operating expenses, and receipts, by SIC 2- to 4-digit kind of business, 2393–2

Single mothers earnings, employment and welfare benefits, and poverty status, 1989, GAO rpt, 26121–413

Small business employees benefit plan coverage and provisions, by plan type and occupational group, 1990, biennial rpt, 6784–20

State and local govt employees benefit plan coverage, by benefit type, 1990, press release, 6726–1.41

Statistical Abstract of US, 1991 annual data compilation, 2324–1.13

Tax (excise) collections of IRS, by source, quarterly rpt, 8302–1

Tax (income) returns and supplemental documents filed, by type, FY90 and projected to FY99, semiannual rpt, 8302–4

Tax (income) returns filed by type of filer, selected income items, quarterly rpt, 8302–2.1

Tax (income) returns of corporations, income and tax items by asset size and detailed industry, 1987, annual rpt, 8304–4

Tax (income) returns of corporations, income and tax items by asset size and detailed industry, 1988, annual rpt, 8304–21

Tax (income) returns of partnerships, income statement and balance sheet items, by industry group, 1989, annual article, 8302–2.216; 8304–18

Tax collection, enforcement, and litigation activity of IRS, with data by type of tax, region, and State, FY90, annual rpt, 8304–3

Tax deferred employee savings plans, by type of investment and investment manager, 1988, 21248–159

Tax deferred salary reduction 401(k) plan and IRA participation, and pension coverage by industry, 1987, fact sheet, 2326–17.35

Tax deferred salary reduction 401(k) plan participation, by pension coverage, earnings level, and sex, 1987, Current Population Rpt, 2546–20.18

Tax expenditures, Federal revenues forgone through income tax deductions and exclusions by type, FY92-96, annual rpt, 21784–10

Tax returns and supplemental documents filed, by type, FY89 and projected to FY98, annual article, 8302–2.208

Tax returns filed, by type of tax and IRS district, 1989 and projected 1990-97, annual rpt, 8304–24

Tax returns filed, by type of tax and IRS region and service center, projected 1990-97 and trends from 1978, annual rpt, 8304–9

Teachers in higher education instns, employment and other characteristics, by instn type and control, 1987/88 survey, 4846–4.4

Telephone and telegraph firms detailed finances and operations, 1989, annual rpt, 9284–6.2; 9284–6.3

Transit systems finances and operations, by mode of transport, size of fleet, and for 468 systems, 1989, annual rpt, 7884–4

Truck and warehouse services finances and inventory, by SIC 2- to 4-digit industry, 1989 survey, annual rpt, 2413–14

Employee benefits

Truck interstate carriers finances and operations, by district, 1989, annual rpt, 9486–6.2

VA health care facilities nonveteran outpatient visits, by eligibility type, facility, and region, quarterly rpt, 8602–4

Wage and benefit changes from collective bargaining and mgmt decisions, by industry div, monthly rpt, 6782–1

Wholesale trade census, 1987: depreciable assets, capital and operating expenses, sales, value added, and inventories, by SIC 2- to 3-digit kind of business, 2407–2

see also Area wage surveys
see also Civil service pensions
see also Disability benefits and insurance
see also Employee bonuses and work incentives
see also Health insurance
see also Industry wage surveys
see also Labor costs and cost indexes
see also Life insurance
see also Military benefits and pensions
see also Pensions and pension funds
see also Vacations and holidays
see also Wage deductions

Employee bonuses and work incentives

Costs (hourly) of labor, by component, industry sector, worker class, and firm size, 1990, annual rpt, 6744–22

Fed Govt civilian employees work-years by schedule, overtime, holidays, and personnel cost components, FY89-90, annual article, 9842–1.204

Fed Govt employee incentive awards, costs, and benefits, by award type and agency, FY89, annual rpt, 9844–20

Fed Govt R&D labs technology transfer cooperative agreements, patents, royalties, and incentive payments to employees, by agency, FY89, GAO rpt, 26131–85

Fed Govt Senior Executive Service membership characteristics, entries, exits, and awards, FY79-90, annual rpt, 9844–36

Govt census, 1987: State and local govt employment, payroll, OASDHI coverage, and employee benefits costs, by level of govt and State, 2455–4

NASA staff characteristics and personnel actions, FY90, annual rpt, 9504–1

Profit-sharing plan employee participation, by type of plan and selected provision, 1985-89, article, 6722–1.223

Small business employees benefit plan coverage and provisions, by plan type and occupational group, 1990, biennial rpt, 6784–20

Teacher employment, vacancies, and pay, by State, region, and school enrollment size, 1987/88, 4836–3.6

Employee development

Air Force fiscal mgmt system operations and techniques, quarterly rpt, 3602–1

Air traffic control staffing levels, by job level and selected facility, FY88-90, GAO rpt, 26113–522

Bonneville Power Admin operations, maintenance, and environmental protection plans, FY90-99, 3228–14

Drug abuse and trafficking reduction programs activities, funding, staff, and Bush Admin budget request, by Federal agency and program area, FY90-92, 238–2

Fed Govt Senior Executive Service membership characteristics, entries, exits, and awards, FY79-90, annual rpt, 9844–36

Hazardous material transport accidents, casualties, and damage, by mode of transport, with DOT control activities, 1989, annual rpt, 7304–4

HHS employment of Hispanics in Mountain region, hiring and promotion practices, 1980s, GAO rpt, 26121–393

Indian Health Service employment of Indians and non-Indians, training, hires, and quits, by occupation, FY89, annual rpt, 4084–6

Law enforcement spending and employment, by activity and level of govt, data compilation, 1991 annual rpt, 6064–6.1

Literacy programs in workplaces, demonstration projects funding and participant characteristics, FY88, 4808–37

Literacy programs in workplaces, Education Dept funding and project descriptions, FY90, annual listing, 4804–40

Marshals Service activities, FY89, annual rpt, 6294–1

Military training and education programs funding, staff, students, and facilities, by service branch, FY92, annual rpt, 3504–5

Mines (underground coal) back injuries, by circumstances, victim characteristics, and treatment, mid 1980s, 5608–166

Mines safety and health enforcement, training, and funding, with casualties, by type of mine and State, FY89, annual rpt, 6664–6

NASA staff characteristics and personnel actions, FY90, annual rpt, 9504–1

Occupational Safety and Health admin standards, enforcement, and training activities, inspectors views, 1989-90, GAO rpt, 26121–391

Teachers of science and math, professional dev project funding of Fed Govt, participation, operations, and effectiveness, 1985-90, 4808–31

Training provided by employer, share of employees by type of training and firm size, 1987, 15496–1.12

Veterans education aid under GI Bill and other programs, and participation by period of service and State, FY89, annual rpt, 8604–9

Videos for employee training, businesses views on copying and copyright infringement issues, 1987 survey, hearing, 21528–82

Employee-management relations

see Labor-management relations, general
see Labor-management relations in government

Employee performance and appraisal

Fed Govt Senior Executive Service membership characteristics, entries, exits, and awards, FY79-90, annual rpt, 9844–36

Fed Govt violations of personnel practices, cases by type, FY90, annual rpt, 9894–1

see also Employee bonuses and work incentives

Employee Retirement Income Security Act

Admin and enforcement of Act, 1990, annual rpt, 6684–1

Index by Subjects and Names

Employment and Training Administration

Budget of US, obligations and authority by function, agency, and program, with summaries, analyses, and historical tables, FY92, annual rpt, 104–2

Employment programs, training, and unemployment compensation, current devs and grants to States, press release series, 6406–2

Employment services local offices operations, State and Federal oversight, staff, and costs, 1983-91, GAO rpt, 26121–430

Expenditures of Fed Govt in States, by type, program, agency, and State, FY90, annual rpt, 2464–2

Labor surplus areas eligible for preferential Fed Govt contracts, monthly listing, 6402–1

Occupational titles dictionary and classification codes, 1991 base edition and supplements, 6406–1

Trade adjustment aid for workers, petitions by disposition, selected industry, union, and State, monthly rpt, 6402–13

Unemployed displaced and economically disadvantaged workers, training program operations and performance, series, 6406–10

Unemployment insurance claims and covered unemployment by program, and extended benefit triggers, by State, weekly rpt, 6402–15

Unemployment insurance claims, by program, weekly press release, 6402–14

Unemployment insurance laws of States, comparison of provisions, 1991, base edition with semiannual revisions, 6402–2

Unemployment insurance programs of States and Fed Govt, benefits adequacy, and work disincentives, series, 6406–6

Unemployment insurance programs of States, benefits, coverage, and tax provisions, as of Jan 1991, semiannual listing, 6402–7

Unemployment insurance programs of States, quality appraisal results, FY90, annual rpt, 6404–16

Employment and unemployment, general

AFDC beneficiaries demographic and financial characteristics, by State, FY89, annual rpt, 4694–1

Agricultural export-related employment, land, and capital inputs, by commodity and country of destination, and compared to imports, 1977-87, 1548–373

Agriculture-related employment, by industry, region, and metro-nonmetro location, 1987, 1598–271

Assets of households, by type of holding and selected characteristics, 1988, Current Population Rpt, 2546–20.16

Athletes in college, educational and employment performance compared to other students, for 1972 high school class, as of 1986, 4888–5

BLS labor force data, major statistical and analytical programs and rpts, as of Feb 1991, listing, 6728–35

Budget of US, CBO analysis of revenue and spending alternatives and projections of economic indicators, FY92-96, annual rpt, 26304–3

Index by Subjects and Names

Employment and unemployment, general

Business cycle patterns of GNP growth and unemployment rate, alternative models descriptions and results, 1950s-80s, technical paper, 9385–8.96

Coastal areas environmental and socioeconomic conditions, and potential impact of oil and gas OCS leases, final statement series, 5736–1

Computer use at home, school, and work, by family income, 1989, fact sheet, 2326–17.30

Computer use at home, school, and work, by purpose and selected user characteristics, 1989, Current Population Rpt, 2546–2.158

Consumer Expenditure Survey, household income by source, and itemized spending, by selected characteristics and region, 1988-89, annual rpt, 6764–5

Consumer Income, socioeconomic characteristics of persons, families, and households, detailed cross-tabulations, Current Population Rpt series, 2546–6

Corporations debt/asset ratios impact on investment and employment, 1971-87, technical paper, 9385–8.77

County Business Patterns, 1988: employment, establishments, and payroll, by SIC 2- to 4-digit industry and county, annual State rpt series, 2326–6

County Business Patterns, 1989: employment, establishments, and payroll, by SIC 2- to 4-digit industry and county, annual State rpt series, 2326–8

Criminal case processing in Federal district courts, and dispositions, by offense, district, and offender characteristics, 1986, annual rpt, 6064–29

Criminal defendants for Federal offenses pretrial processing, detention, and release, by defendant characteristics and district, 1988, hearing, 25528–114

Disabled persons employment and other characteristics, 1989 hearing, 23898–7

Disabled persons rehabilitation, Federal and State activities and funding, FY90, annual rpt, 4944–1

DOD prime contract awards in labor surplus areas, by service branch, State, and area, 1st half FY91, semiannual rpt, 3542–19

Drug, alcohol, and cigarette use, by selected characteristics, 1990 survey, biennial rpt, 4494–5

Drug testing of criminal defendants, demonstration program operations, offender characteristics, and judges views, 1987-90, 18208–11

Economic and monetary trends, compounded annual rates of change and quarterly indicators for US and 7 major industrialized countries, quarterly rpt, 9391–7

Economic conditions, and oil supply and demand, for major industrial countries, biweekly rpt, 9112–1

Economic indicators and components, and Fed Reserve 4th District business and financial conditions, monthly chartbook, 9377–10

Economic indicators and components, current data and annual trends, monthly rpt, 23842–1.2

Economic indicators compounded annual rates of change, monthly rpt, 9391–3

Economic indicators compounded annual rates of change, 1971-90, annual rpt, 9391–9.2

Economic indicators, monthly rpt, 9362–1.2

Economic indicators performance, and Fed Reserve monetary policy objectives, as of July 1991, semiannual rpt, 9362–4

Education data, detail for elementary, secondary, and higher education, 1920s-90 and projected to 2001, annual rpt, 4824–1

Educational attainment, by sociodemographic characteristics and location, 1989 and trends from 1940, biennial Current Population Rpt, 2546–1.452

Educational enrollment, by grade, instn type and control, and student characteristics, 1989 and trends from 1947, annual Current Population Rpt, 2546–1.453

Employment and Earnings, detailed data, monthly rpt, 6742–2

Employment by industry and State, impacts of decline in employers voluntary reporting on Continuous Work History Sample, 1970s-86, article, 4742–1.203

Employment, earnings, and hours, by SIC 1- to 4-digit industry, monthly and annual averages, selected years 1909-90, annual rpt, 6744–4

Employment, earnings, and hours, monthly press release, 6742–5

Employment in manufacturing and nonagricultural industries, by MSA, 1989-90, annual press release, 6946–3.20

Employment situation, earnings, hours, and other BLS economic indicators, transcripts of BLS Commissioner's monthly testimony, periodic rpt, 23846–4

Employment, unemployment, and labor force characteristics, by region, State, and selected metro area, 1990, annual rpt, 6744–7

Enterprise Statistics, 1987: auxiliaries of multi-establishment firms, finances and operations by function, industry, and State, 2329–6

Enterprise Statistics, 1987: finances and operations for companies, by size, level of diversification, form of organization, and industry group, 2329–8

Exports and export-related employment, by SIC 3-digit industry and State, model results, 1987, annual rpt, 2506–16.1

Exports and imports impacts on US industries and employment, series, 6366–3

Exports, imports, balances, US consumption, and operations of industries affected, by industry, 1986-90, semiannual rpt, 9882–9

Family economic impacts of departure, absence, and presence of parents, 1983-86, Current Population Rpt, 2546–20.17

Family members labor force status and earnings, by family composition and race, quarterly press release, 6742–21

Farm operators age and off-farm employment, sales, and land value changes relationship to farm sales size, model description and results, 1974-78, 1548–374

Food stamp eligibility and payment errors, by type, recipient characteristics, and State, FY89, annual rpt, 1364–15

Food stamp recipient household size, composition, income, and income and deductions allowed, summer 1988, annual rpt, 1364–8

Forecasts of economic and employment conditions, alternative BLS projections to 2005 and trends 1970s-90, biennial article, 6722–1.251

Forecasts of employment conditions, alternative BLS projections to 2005 and trends 1970s-90, biennial article, 6722–1.252; 6722–1.253; 6722–1.254

Forecasts of GNP and employment, performance of alternative models, with results, 1958-88, article, 9371–1.201

·Foreign direct investment in US by country, and finances, employment, and acreage owned, by industry group of business acquired or established, 1984-90, annual article, 2702–1.210

GNP changes related to labor force composition and changes in participation, model description and results, 1940s-2000, article, 9373–1.201

High school and college grads and dropouts employment status and income, 1991 edition, annual rpt, 4824–2.28

High school class of 1972: education, employment, and family characteristics, activities, and attitudes, natl longitudinal study, series, 4836–1

High school class of 1972: women's employment and educational experiences compared to men, natl longitudinal study, as of 1986, 4888–6

High school class of 1990: college enrollment, and labor force participation of grads and dropouts, by race and sex, press release, 6726–1.38

Households and family characteristics, by location, 1990, annual Current Population Rpt, 2546–1.447

Households composition, income, benefits, and labor force status, Survey of Income and Program Participation methodology, working paper series, 2626–10

Immigrants in US, population characteristics and fertility, by birthplace and compared to native born, 1980s, Current Population rpt, 2546–2.162

Immigration, alien workers, amnesty programs, and employer sanctions impacts on US economy and labor force, series, 6366–5

Imports (duty-free) from Caribbean area, impact on US employment by industry, 1990, annual rpt, 6364–2

Imports and tariff provisions effect on US industries and products, investigations with background financial and operating data, series, 9886–4

Imports, exports, and employment impacts, by SIC 2- to 4-digit industry and commodity, quarterly rpt, 2322–2

Imports injury to US industries from foreign subsidized products and sales at less than fair value, investigations with background financial and operating data, series, 9886–19

Imports under Generalized System of Preferences, status, and US tariffs, with trade by country and US economic impacts, for selected commodities, 1986-90, annual rpt, 9884–23

Employment and unemployment, general

Index by Subjects and Names

Income (household) and poverty status under alternative income definitions, by recipient characteristics, 1990, annual Current Population Rpt, 2546–6.69

Income (personal) and poverty status changes, by selected characteristics, 1987-88, Current Population Rpt, 2546–20.19

Income and consumer spending of households, for selected population groups, quarterly journal, 1702–1

Industry (US) intl competitiveness, with selected foreign and US operating data by major firm and product, series, 2046–12

Industry finances and operations, by SIC 2- to 4-digit industry, forecast 1991, annual rpt, 2044–28

Inflation forecasting performance of money supply, unemployment, and other monetary and economic indicators, 1959-88, article, 9379–1.204

Inflation relation to unemployment and Fed Reserve inflation forecast accuracy indicators, 1960s-83, working paper, 9387–8.240

Injuries, related impairments, and activity limitations, by circumstances and victim characteristics, 1985-87, 4147–10.179

Insurance (health) coverage, by insurance type and selected characteristics, 1989, 4146–8.203

Insurance (health) coverage of children, by source, family composition, income, and parent employment status, 1977 and 1987, 4186–8.14

Insurance (health) coverage, uninsured persons by employment and other characteristics and State, 1988, GAO rpt, 26121–403

Insurance (health) provided by employer, coverage offered to and chosen by families with 2 working spouses, 1977 and 1987, 4186–8.16

Interest rates and Fed Reserve monetary policy targets, relation to unexpected employment news, 1970s-91, article, 9389–1.205

Jail population, by criminal, correctional, drug use, and family history, and selected other characteristics, 1989, 6066–19.62

Jail population drug abuse history, by offense, conviction status, criminal and family history, and selected other characteristics, 1989, 6066–19.63

Japan manufacturing firms US affiliates, employment, and wages, by selected industry and State, 1980s, 2048–151

Labor force characteristics, press release series, 6726–1

Labor force status by race and sex, employment by industry div, and unemployment duration and reason, selected years 1929-90, annual rpt, 204–1.2

Labor force, wages, hours, and payroll costs, by major industry group and demographic characteristics, *Survey of Current Business*, monthly rpt, 2702–1.8

Living arrangements, family relationships, and marital status, by selected characteristics, 1990, annual Current Population Rpt, 2546–1.449

Local areas with labor surplus and eligible for preferential Fed Govt contracts, monthly listing, 6402–1

Manufacturing annual survey, 1989: establishments, employment, finances, inventories, and energy use, by SIC 2- to 4-digit industry, 2506–15.1

Manufacturing annual survey, 1989: finances and operations, by SIC 2- and 3-digit industry and State, 2506–15.3

Manufacturing census, 1987: employment and shipments under Fed Govt contracts, by SIC 4-digit industry, 2497–7

Manufacturing census, 1987: finances and operations, by SIC 2- to 4-digit industry, State, and MSA, with trends from 1849, 2497–1

Manufacturing census, 1987: finances and operations, by type of organization and SIC 2- to 4-digit industry, subject rpt, 2497–5

Manufacturing employment, by detailed occupation and SIC 2-digit industry, 1989 survey, triennial rpt, 6748–52

Military spending reductions and base closings employment impacts, by region and State, 1988-89 and projected FY91-95, article, 9371–1.206

Minority Business Dev Centers mgmt and financial aid, and characteristics of businesses, by region and State, FY90, annual rpt, 2104–6

Monthly Labor Review, current statistics and articles, 6722–1

Multinatl firms US affiliates finances and operations, by industry div, country of parent firm, and State, 1988-89, annual article, 2702–1.214

Multinatl firms US affiliates, finances, and operations, by industry, world area of parent firm, and State, 1988-89, annual rpt, 2704–4

Multinatl firms US affiliates, investment trends and impact on US economy, 1991 annual rpt, 2004–9

Multinatl US firms and foreign affiliates finances and operations, by industry and world area of parent firm, 1989 benchmark survey, preliminary annual rpt, 2704–5

Multinatl US firms and foreign affiliates finances and operations, by industry of parent firm and affiliate, world area, and selected country, 1989, annual article, 2702–1.225

Natl Commission for Employment Policy activities and rpts, 1990 annual rpt, 15494–1

OASDHI admin, and SSA activities, 1930s-90 and projected to 2064, annual data compilation, 4704–12

OASDHI coverage of employment and earnings, late 1930s-89, annual rpt, 4744–3.1; 4744–3.2

OASDI benefit payments, trust fund finances, and economic and demographic assumptions, 1970-90 and alternative projections to 2000, actuarial rpt, 4706–1.105

Occupational Outlook Quarterly, journal, 6742–1

Older men's labor force status by urban-rural location, and distribution of men by age and occupation, 1860s-1980, article, 9371–1.202

Persian Gulf War impacts on US economic conditions compared to previous oil shock periods, and Saudi Arabia oil production and prices, 1990-92, hearings, 21248–156

Population size and characteristics, 1969-88, Current Population Rpt, biennial rpt, 2546–2.161

Poverty rate among workers in metro and nonmetro areas, relation to employment and other characteristics, 1987, 1598–274

Poverty status of population and families, by detailed characteristics, 1988-89, annual Current Population Rpt, 2546–6.67

Poverty status of population and families, by detailed characteristics, 1990, annual Current Population Rpt, 2546–6.71

Prisoners and movements, by offense, location, and selected other characteristics, data compilation, 1991 annual rpt, 6064–6.6

Recession impacts on employment, by census div and State, 1988-92, release, 9538–8

Refugee resettlement programs and funding, arrivals by country of origin, and indicators of adjustment, by State, FY90, annual rpt, 4694–5

Retail trade census, 1987: finances and employment, for establishments with and without payroll, by SIC 2- to 4-digit kind of business, State, and MSA, 2401–1

Retired pension recipients income, by selected characteristics, 1986, Current Population Rpt, 2546–20.18

Rural areas economic and social conditions, dev, and problems, periodic journal, 1502–7

Rural areas economic and social indicators used to determine Federal aid need, late 1960s-86, 1598–265

Rural areas economic conditions and dev, quarterly journal, 1502–8

Rural areas labor force characteristics, with comparisons to urban areas, 1987, 1598–264

Service industries census, 1987: establishments, receipts by source, payroll, and employment, by SIC 2- to 4-digit kind of business, State, and MSA, 2393–4

Small business dev centers mgmt and technical aid activities, funding, and client satisfaction and performance, 1980s, hearing, 25728–43

State and Metro Area Data Book, 1991 data compilation, 2328–54

Statistical Abstract of US, 1991 annual data compilation, 2324–1

Survey of Income and Program Participation, data collection, methodology, and use, 1990 annual conf papers, 2624–1

Taxes, spending, and govt efficiency, public opinion by respondent characteristics, 1991 survey, annual rpt, 10044–2

Trade adjustment aid for workers, petitions by disposition, selected industry, union, and State, monthly rpt, 6402–13

Travel patterns, personal and household characteristics, and auto and public transport use, 1990 survey, series, 7556–6

Unemployed workers methods of seeking jobs, by sex, age, and race, monthly rpt, 6742–2.2

Unemployment, by State and metro area, monthly press release, 6742–12

Index by Subjects and Names

Employment and unemployment, local and regional

Unemployment, employment, and labor force, by region and State, 1989-90, press release, 6726–1.37

Unemployment, employment, and labor force, by State, MSA, and city, monthly rpt, 6742–22

Unemployment insurance coverage of establishments, employment, and wages, by SIC 4-digit industry and State, 1990, annual rpt, 6744–16

Unemployment of groups with historically high rates, 1985-89, biennial rpt, 6504–2.2

Union coverage of workers and earnings, by age, sex, race, occupational group, and industry div, 1989-90, press release, 6726–1.36

Voting and registration, by socioeconomic and demographic characteristics, 1990 congressional election, biennial Current Population Rpt, 2546–1.454

Wholesale trade census, 1987: establishments, sales by customer class, employment, inventories, and expenses, by SIC 2- to 4-digit kind of business, 2407–4

see also Absenteeism
see also Agricultural labor
see also Alien workers
see also Apprenticeship
see also Area wage surveys
see also Blue collar workers
see also Child labor
see also Clerical workers
see also Discrimination in employment
see also Domestic workers and services
see also Earnings, general
see also Employee benefits
see also Employee development
see also Employee performance and appraisal
see also Employment and unemployment, local and regional
see also Employment and unemployment, specific industry
see also Employment services
see also Engineers and engineering
see also Executives and managers
see also Foreign labor conditions
see also Government employees
see also Health occupations
see also Home-based offices and workers
see also Hours of labor
see also Industry wage surveys
see also Job creation
see also Job tenure
see also Job vacancy
see also Labor costs and cost indexes
see also Labor law
see also Labor-management relations, general
see also Labor-management relations in government
see also Labor productivity
see also Labor supply and demand
see also Labor turnover
see also Manpower training programs
see also Migrant workers
see also Military personnel
see also Minority employment
see also Moonlighting
see also Occupational health and safety
see also Occupational testing and certification

see also Occupations
see also Overtime
see also Paraprofessionals
see also Part-time employment
see also Payroll
see also Pensions and pension funds
see also Personnel management
see also Prison work programs
see also Production workers
see also Professional and technical workers
see also Public service employment
see also Retirement
see also Scientists and technicians
see also Self-employment
see also Sheltered workshops
see also Temporary and seasonal employment
see also Underemployment
see also Unemployment insurance
see also Unpaid family workers
see also Vacations and holidays
see also Veterans employment
see also Vocational rehabilitation
see also Volunteers
see also Wage deductions
see also Women's employment
see also Work conditions
see also Work incentive programs
see also Work stoppages
see also Workers compensation
see also Worksharing
see also Youth employment

Employment and unemployment, local and regional

Alaska rural areas population characteristics, and energy resources dev effects, series, 5736–5

Alaska subsistence fishing role in local economies, with indicators for Yakutat, 1980s, 1208–350

American Samoa employment, earnings, and minimum wage, by establishment and industry, 1989, biennial rpt, 6504–6

Chicago employment growth in service, manufacturing, and other industries, analysis of contributing factors, 1970s-87, article, 9375–1.204

Dallas-Fort Worth-Arlington metro area employment, earnings, hours, and CPI changes, late 1970s-90, annual rpt, 6964–2

Florida environmental, social, and economic conditions, and impacts of proposed OCS oil and gas leases in southern coastal areas, 1990 compilation of papers, 5738–19

Great Lakes area economic conditions and outlook, for US and Canada, 1970s-90, 9375–15

Houston metro area employment, earnings, hours, and CPI changes, 1970s-90, annual rpt, 6964–1

Louisiana economic indicators and oil rig growth forecasts, model description and results, 1991, article, 9379–1.202

Massachusetts housing prices economic impacts over business cycle expansion, 1984-87, article, 9373–1.216

Middle Atlantic States economic conditions, Fed Reserve 3rd District, quarterly rpt, 9387–10

Middle Atlantic States manufacturing business outlook, monthly survey rpt, 9387–11

New England employment growth rates by selected industry, projected 1990s with background data for 1980s, article, 9373–25.201

New England States economic indicators, Fed Reserve 1st District, monthly rpt, 9373–2.2

New England States employment and personal income growth rates, and unemployment, by State, 1989-90 and projected to 1993, semiannual article, 9302–4.201; 9302–4.203

New England States employment growth rates, and performance of alternative forecasts, 1950s-91, article, 9373–1.211

New England States employment variability relation to service and financial industries employment, with data by selected industry group and State, 1970s-89, article, 9373–1.212

North Carolina environmental and socioeconomic conditions, and impacts of proposed OCS oil and gas exploration, 1970s-90 and projected to 2020, 5738–22

North Central States business and economic conditions, Fed Reserve 9th District, quarterly journal, 9383–19

North Central States industry diversification, and employment and output relation to natl economic conditions, by industry and State, 1950s-89, working paper, 9375–13.63

northeastern US timber resources, and related manufacturing industries employment and finances, by State, 1977-87, 1208–375

Northwestern US and British Columbia forest industry production, prices, trade, and employment, quarterly rpt, 1202–3

Pacific territories economic conditions, population characteristics, and Federal aid, 1989 hearing, 21448–44

Palau admin, and social, economic, and govtl data, FY90, annual rpt, 7004–6

Puerto Rico and other US possessions corporations income tax returns, income and tax items, and employment, by selected industry, 1987, article, 8302–2.213

Puerto Rico economic censuses, 1987: wholesale and retail trade and service industry finances and operations, by SIC 2- to 4-digit industry and municipio, 2591–1

Puerto Rico economic censuses, 1987: wholesale, retail, and service industries finances and operations, by establishment characteristics and SIC 2- and 3-digit industry, subject rpts, 2591–2

Rocky Mountain region employment and income, and economic dependence on shipments outside area, by industry and county group, 1980s, 1208–362

South Central States employment by industry div, income, and other economic indicators, for 4 States, 1989-90 and forecast 1991-92, annual article, 9391–16.207

Southeastern States, Fed Reserve 5th District, economic indicators by State, quarterly rpt, 9389–16

Southeastern States, Fed Reserve 6th District, economic indicators by State and MSA, quarterly rpt, 9371–14

Employment and unemployment, local and regional

Southeastern States, Fed Reserve 8th District banking and economic conditions, quarterly rpt with articles, 9391–16

Southeastern States, FHLB 4th District, employment and housing and mortgage market indicators by State, quarterly rpt, 9302–36

Southeastern US employment by industry div, earnings, and hours, for 8 States, quarterly press release, 6942–7

Southeastern US employment by industry div, unemployment, and CPI, for 8 States, 1989-90, annual rpt, 6944–2

Southeastern US employment conditions, with comparisons to other regions, press release series, 6946–3

Southeastern US textile mill employment, earnings, and hours, for 8 States, quarterly press release, 6942–1

Southeastern US timber resources, and industry employment and output, by State, 1980s, article, 9391–16.204

Southern US textile mill employment, 1951-90, annual rpt, 6944–1

Southwestern US employment by industry div, earnings, and hours, by State, monthly rpt, 6962–2

Southwestern US Hispanic population in counties bordering Mexico, by selected characteristics, 1980, Current Population Rpt, 2546–2.159

Tennessee Valley industrial dev and employment, by SIC 2-digit industry, firm, and location, 1990, annual rpt, 9804–3

Texas and Louisiana per capita income, impacts of industry mix and other factors, for 36 MSAs, 1969-88, article, 9379–1.209

West Central States economic indicators, Fed Reserve 10th District, quarterly rpt, 9381–16.2

West Central States population, income, and employment growth, by MSA, metro-nonmetro location, and State, for Fed Reserve 10th District, 1970s-90s, article, 9381–1.209

Western US employment growth by industry div and manufacturing group, Fed Reserve 10th District, 1989-90, annual article, 9381–1.202

see also Area wage surveys

see also Earnings, local and regional

see also under By Census Division, By City, By County, By Region, By SMSA or MSA, and By State in the "Index by Categories"

Employment and unemployment, specific industry

Arms trade and share of GNP by country, and US customs seizures and defense industry employment, 1980s-90, article, 9373–1.221

Auto assembly plant productivity and relation to labor reserves, model description and results, 1990 working paper, 6886–6.72

Auto industry finances and operations, trade by country, and prices of selected US and foreign models, monthly rpt, 9882–8

Auto trade of Canada and US, and production, sales, prices, and employment, selected years 1965-88, annual rpt, 2044–35

Banks (Fed Reserve) and branch officers, staff, and salary, 1990, annual rpt, 9364–1.1

Index by Subjects and Names

Banks (insured commercial) employment, by asset size and State, 1989, annual rpt, 9294–4

Banks (insured commercial), Fed Reserve 5th District members financial statements, by State, quarterly rpt, 9389–18

Banks (insured commercial) financial condition and performance, by asset size and region, quarterly rpt, 9292–1.1

Child day care employment by occupation, and mothers in labor force, 1976-88 with day care employment projected to 2000, article, 6722–1.202

Coal miners working daily, mines, and labor productivity, quarterly rpt, 3162–37.4

Coal production and mines by county, prices, productivity, miners, and reserves, by mining method and State, 1989-90, annual rpt, 3164–25

Construction employment, earnings, and hours, by selected SIC 2- to 3-digit industry, bimonthly rpt, 2042–1.7

Construction industries census, 1987: establishments, employment, receipts, and expenditures, by SIC 4-digit industry and State, final industry rpt series, 2373–1

Credit unions federally insured, finances by instn characteristics and State, as of June 1991, semiannual rpt, 9532–6

Electric power distribution loans from REA, and borrower operating and financial data, by firm and State, 1990, annual rpt, 1244–1

Electric power plants production and capital costs, operations, and fuel use, by fuel type, plant, utility, and location, 1989, annual rpt, 3164–9

Electric utilities privately owned, finances and operations, detailed data, 1989, annual rpt, 3164–23

Energy-related fields manpower studies and devs, series, 3006–8

Fed Reserve System, Board of Governors, and district banks financial statements, performance, and fiscal services, 1990-91, annual rpt, 9364–10

Fish processing and wholesale plants and employment, by region, 1987, annual rpt, 2166–6.2

Fishery employment, vessels, plants, and cooperatives, by State, 1989 and trends from 1970, annual rpt, 2164–1.10

Fishing (ocean sport and commercial) catch and quotas for US and Canada, by species for North Atlantic Ocean, 1990, annual rpt, 2164–14

Footwear production, employment, use, prices, and US trade by country, quarterly rpt, 9882–6

Gear production for selected uses under alternative production requirements, and industry finances and operations, late 1940s-89, 2028–1

Health Care Financing Review, provider prices, price inputs and indexes, and labor, quarterly journal, 4652–1.1

Hospital employment, by detailed occupation, 1989, article, 6722–1.217

Hotels and other lodging places, receipts, payroll, employment, ownership, and rooms, by State and MSA, 1987 Census of Service Industries, subject rpt, 2393–3

Juvenile correctional and detention public and private instns, inmates, and expenses, by instn and resident characteristics and State, 1987, biennial rpt, 6064–13

Lumber (hardwood) production, prices, employment, and trade, quarterly rpt, 1202–4

Lumber and pulp products supply and use, and timber resources, detailed data, 1950s-87 and alternative projections to 2040, 1208–24.20

Lumber industry firms, employment, and payroll in northeast States, by industry, 1982-86, 1208–375

Manufacturing employment by selected characteristics, wages, and import and export penetration rates, by SIC 2- to 4-digit industry, 1982-89, 6366–3.27

Mineral industries census, 1987: finances and operations, by establishment characteristics, SIC 2- to 4-digit industry, and State, subject rpt, 2517–1

Mineral industries census, 1987: finances and operations, by SIC 2- to 4-digit industry, State, and county, census div rpt series, 2515–1

Mineral Industry Surveys, commodity reviews of production, trade, use, and industry operations, advance annual rpt series, 5614–5

Minerals production, prices, trade, use, employment, tariffs, and stockpiles, by mineral, with foreign comparisons, 1986-90, annual rpt, 5604–18

Mines (coal) and related operations occupational injuries and incidence, employment, and hours, 1989, annual rpt, 6664–4

Mines (metal) and related operations occupational injuries and incidence, employment, and hours, 1989, annual rpt, 6664–3

Mines (nonmetallic minerals) and related operations occupational injuries and incidence, employment, and hours, 1989, annual rpt, 6664–1

Mines (sand and gravel) and related operations occupational injuries and incidence, employment, and hours, 1989, annual rpt, 6664–2

Mines (stone) and related operations occupational injuries and incidence, employment, and hours, 1989, annual rpt, 6664–5

Mines and mills injuries by circumstances, employment, and hours, by type of operation and State, quarterly rpt, 6662–1

Natural gas interstate pipeline company detailed financial and operating data, by firm, 1989, annual rpt, 3164–38

Oil and gas exploratory rigs in operation, wells and footage drilled, and seismic exploration crews, monthly rpt, 3162–24.5

Oil bulk stations, sales and storage capacity by product, inventories, expenses, employment, and modes of transport, 1987 Census of Wholesale Trade, 2407–4.2

Railroad employee benefits program finances and beneficiaries, FY90, annual rpt, 9704–1

Railroad employment by occupational group, for Class I line-haul railroads, monthly rpt, 9482–3

Railroad employment, earnings, and hours, by occupation for Class I railroads, 1990, annual table, 9484–5

Index by Subjects and Names

Railroad retirement system funding and benefits findings and recommendations, with background industry data, 1960s-90 and projected to 2060, 9708–1

Ship-related employment, FY89-90, annual rpt, 7704–14.3

Shipbuilding and repair facilities, capacity, and employment, by shipyard, 1990, annual rpt, 7704–9

Ships in US merchant fleet, operating subsidies, construction, and ship-related employment, monthly rpt, 7702–1

Steel imports of US under voluntary restraint agreement, by product, customs district, and country, with US industry operating data, quarterly rpt, 9882–13

Steel industry finances, operations, and modernization efforts, with data on major companies and foreign industry, 1968-91, last issue of annual rpt, 9884–24

Telecommunications industry intl competitiveness, with financial and operating data by product or service, firm, and country, 1990 rpt, 2008–30

Telephone and telegraph firms detailed finances and operations, 1989, annual rpt, 9284–6

Telephone firms borrowing under Rural Telephone Program, and financial and operating data, by State, 1990, annual rpt, 1244–2

Textile, apparel, and shoe import restriction proposals economic impacts, projected 1991-2000, with imports by country, 1989-90, 26306–6.162

Textile mill employment, earnings, and hours, for 8 Southeastern States, quarterly press release, 6942–1

Textile mill employment in southern US, 1951-90, annual rpt, 6944–1

Timber in northwestern US and British Columbia, production, prices, trade, and employment, quarterly rpt, 1202–3

Timber industry impacts of northern spotted owl conservation in Pacific Northwest, and local govts Federal payments and severance taxes, 1980s and projected to 2000, hearing, 21168–50

Timber industry impacts of northern spotted owl conservation in Pacific Northwest, and worker aid programs, 1980s and projected to 2000, hearing, 21728–76

Timber industry impacts of northern spotted owl conservation in Pacific Northwest, 1980s and alternative projections to 2000, hearings, 21168–45

Timber sales of Forest Service, expenses, and operations, by region, State, and natl forest, FY90, annual rpts, 1204–36

Transportation census, 1987: finances and operations by size, ownership, and State, and revenues by MSA, by SIC 2- to 4-digit industry, 2579–1

Truck and bus interstate carriers finances and operations, by district, 1989, annual rpt, 9486–6.3

Truck interstate carriers finances and operations, by district, 1989, annual rpt, 9486–6.2

Uranium reserves and industry operations, by region and State, various periods 1966-90, annual rpt, 3164–65.1

see also Agricultural labor

see also Earnings, specific industry

Employment Standards Administration

see also Federal employees

see also Government employees

see also Health occupations

see also Industry wage surveys

see also Military personnel

see also State and local employees

see also Teachers

see also under By Industry in the "Index by Categories"

see also under By Occupation in the "Index by Categories"

Employment Cost Index

see Labor costs and cost indexes

Employment services

Assistance (financial and nonfinancial) of Fed Govt, 1991 base edition with supplements, annual listing, 104–5

Budget of US, formula grant program obligations to State and local govts, by agency, program, and State, FY92, annual rpt, 104–30

Budget of US, obligations and authority by function, agency, and program, with summaries, analyses, and historical tables, FY92, annual rpt, 104–2

County Business Patterns, 1988: employment, establishments, and payroll, by SIC 2- to 4-digit industry and county, annual State rpt series, 2326–6

County Business Patterns, 1989: employment, establishments, and payroll, by SIC 2- to 4-digit industry and county, annual State rpt series, 2326–8

Disabled persons workshops finances, operations, and Federal procurement, FY80-90, annual rpt, 11714–1

Employment, earnings, and hours, by SIC 1- to 4-digit industry, monthly and annual averages, selected years 1909-90, annual rpt, 6744–4

Finances and operations, by SIC 2- to 4-digit industry, forecast 1991, annual rpt, 2044–28

Franchise business opportunities by firm and kind of business, and sources of aid and info, 1990 annual listing, 2104–7

Labor Dept activities and funding, by program and State, FY90, annual rpt, 6304–1

Labor Dept employment programs, training, and unemployment compensation, current devs and grants to States, press release series, 6406–2

Labor laws enacted, by State, 1990, annual article, 6722–1.209

Occupational injury and illness rates, by SIC 2- to 4-digit industry, 1988-89, annual rpt, 6844–7

Occupational injury and illness rates, by SIC 2- to 4-digit industry, 1989, annual rpt, 6844–1

Puerto Rico economic censuses, 1987: wholesale and retail trade and service industry finances and operations, by SIC 2- to 4-digit industry and municipio, 2591–1

Puerto Rico economic censuses, 1987: wholesale, retail, and service industries finances and operations, by establishment characteristics and SIC 2- and 3-digit industry, subject rpts, 2591–2

Receipts for services, by SIC 2- to 4-digit kind of business, 1990, annual rpt, 2413–8

Service industries census, 1987: establishments, receipts by source, payroll, and employment, by SIC 2- to 4-digit kind of business, State, and MSA, 2393–4

State and local govt employment of minorities and women, by occupation, function, and pay level, 1990, annual rpt, 9244–6.4

Temporary help supply agencies depreciable assets, capital and operating expenses, and receipts, 1987 Census of Service Industries, 2393–2

Temporary help supply agencies finances and operations, by size, level of diversification, and form of organization, 1987 Enterprise Statistics survey, 2329–8

Temporary help supply agencies receipts, 1990, annual rpt, 2413–8

Temporary help supply services establishments, receipts by source, payroll, and employment, by State and MSA, 1987 Census of Service Industries, 2393–4

Unemployment insurance employment services local offices operations, State and Federal oversight, staff, and costs, 1983-91, GAO rpt, 26121–430

Unemployment insurance job search services, impacts on UI claims activity and reemployment, and claimant characteristics, for Tacoma, Wash, 1986-87, 6406–6.35

Unemployment insurance reemployment and training services, and bonus for early reemployment, New Jersey demonstration project results, 1986-90, 6406–6.32

Employment Standards Administration

Alien workers (unauthorized) and Fair Labor Standards Act employer compliance, hiring impacts, and aliens overstaying visas by country and State, 1986-90, annual rpt, 6264–6

American Samoa employment, earnings, and minimum wage, by establishment and industry, 1989, biennial rpt, 6504–6

Black lung benefits and claims by State, trust fund receipts by source, and disbursements, 1990, annual rpt, 6504–3

Budget of US, obligations and authority by function, agency, and program, with summaries, analyses, and historical tables, FY92, annual rpt, 104–2

Child labor law violations and injuries by industry group, and employment of minors by selected characteristics, 1983-90, GAO rpt, 26121–426

Fair Labor Standards Act admin, enforcement, and coverage, FY89, annual rpt, 6504–2

Fed Govt contractor compliance with equal employment laws, FY90, 6508–36

Unemployment of groups with historically high rates, biennial rpt, coverage transfer, 6504–4

Workers compensation laws of States and Fed Govt, 1991 semiannual rpt, 6502–1

Workers compensation programs of States, admin, coverage, benefits, finances, processing, and staff, 1987-90, annual rpt, 6504–9

Workers compensation programs under Federal admin, finances and operations, FY90, annual rpt, 6504–10

Employment Standards Administration

see also Women's Bureau

Encephalitis

see Infective and parasitic diseases

Endangered species

Coastal and riparian areas environmental conditions, fish, wildlife, use, and mgmt, for individual ecosystems, series, 5506–9

Coastal areas environmental and socioeconomic conditions, and potential impact of oil and gas OCS leases, final statement series, 5736–1

Conservation activities for endangered plants and animals, and population status, by species, 1990, biennial rpt, 5504–35

Conservation spending of Federal agencies and States for endangered animals and plants, by species, FY90, annual rpt, 5504–33

Environmental Quality, status of problems, protection programs, research, and intl issues, 1991 annual rpt, 484–1

Exports, imports, and permits for endangered animals and plants, by species, purpose, disposition, and country, 1989, annual rpt, 5504–19

Fish and Wildlife Service conservation and habitat mgmt activities, and endangered species by group, FY90, biennial rpt, 5504–20

Fish Hatchery Natl System activities and deliveries, by species, hatchery, and jurisdiction of waters stocked, FY90, annual rpt, 5504–10

Foreign and US environmental and wildlife conservation agreements provisions, status, and signatories, as of 1991, listing, 9886–4.169

Forest Service acreage, staff, finances, and mgmt activities in Pacific Northwest, with data by forest, 1970s-89, annual rpt, 1204–37

Forest Service mgmt of public lands and resources dev, environmental, economic, and social impacts of alternative programs, projected to 2040, 1208–24

Land Mgmt Bur wildlife mgmt activities and funding, acreage by habitat type, and scientific staff, State rpt series, 5726–7

Land Mgmt Bur wildlife mgmt activities and funding, acreage, staff, and plans, habitat study series, 5726–6

Manatees (West Indian) population off Puerto Rico, and sightings by coastal region, 1976-89, 14738–11

Manatees grazing effects on seagrass, by southeast Florida site, 1987-89, 14738–12

Marine mammals protection activities and funding, populations, and harvests, by species, 1989, annual rpt, 5504–12

Marine mammals protection, Federal and intl regulatory and research activities, 1990, annual rpt, 14734–1

Marine mammals strandings on land, physical characteristics and tests performed, for New England, 1970s, 14738–8

Otters (sea) conservation measures taken after Exxon Valdez oil spill in Alaska, 1990 conf, 5508–110

Otters (sea) population and behavior, for Pacific Ocean, 1914-90, 5508–109

Owl (northern spotted) conservation impacts on Pacific Northwest timber industry, and local govts Federal payments and severance taxes, 1980s and projected to 2000, hearing, 21168–50

Owl (northern spotted) conservation impacts on Pacific Northwest timber industry, and worker aid programs, 1980s and projected to 2000, hearing, 21728–76

Owl (northern spotted) conservation impacts on Pacific Northwest timber industry, 1980s and alternative projections to 2000, hearing, 21168–45

Owl (northern spotted) conservation impacts on Pacific Northwest timber sales of Forest Service, 1990 hearing, 21168–47

Owl (northern spotted) population and reproduction rate on lands open and closed to logging, estimation methodology, 1987, 1208–342

Pacific Ocean marine mammal and bird population density and distribution, by species and selected northeast location, literature and data base review, 1950s-88, 5738–28

Public lands acreage, grants, use, revenues, and allocations, by State, FY90, annual rpt, 5724–1.2

Public lands wildlife mgmt, endangered species, and activities and funding, FY80-90, 5728–37

Research of State fish and wildlife agencies, federally funded fishery projects and costs by species and State, 1990, annual listing, 5504–23

Research of State fish and wildlife agencies, federally funded wildlife projects and costs by species and State, 1990, annual listing, 5504–24

Research on fish and wildlife population, habitat, and mgmt, technical rpt series, 5506–12

Research on wildlife and plants, habitat study series, 5506–13

Sheep (desert bighorn) population and mgmt on public land, by State, 1989 rpt, 5728–36

Statistical Abstract of US, 1991 annual data compilation, 2324–1.6

Turtles (sea) population near oil drilling rigs, and habitat characteristics, 1988-90, 5738–26

Walrus population, habitat mgmt, and intl conservation needs, by world region, 1990 conf, 14738–9

Wetlands acreage, resources, soil and water properties, and conservation efforts, by wetland type, State rpt series, 5506–11

Whales (bowhead) population in Arctic areas, behavioral differences by location, 1970s-80s, 5738–29

Whales (bowhead) population in Arctic areas, impacts of subsistence whaling, shipping, noise, and other human activity, mid 1970s-80s, 5738–30

Whales (bowhead) population in Beaufort Sea, and fall aerial survey operations, 1979-90, annual rpt, 5734–10

Whales (humpback) population and sightings off southeastern Alaska, 1979-86, 14738–10

Whooping crane migration roosting sites and population, by wetland type, 1990 rpt, 5508–111

Endocrine diseases

see Metabolic and endocrine diseases

Energy

see terms listed under Energy resources and consumption

Index by Subjects and Names

Energy assistance

see Low-income energy assistance

Energy conservation

Aircraft fuel use and efficiency under alternative technological improvements and load factors, by model, projected 1995-2010, 3028–6

Auto and light truck fuel economy performance by make, standards, and enforcement, 1978-91 model years, annual rpt, 7764–9

Auto engine and power train R&D projects, DOE contracts and funding by recipient, FY90, annual rpt, 3304–17

Auto fuel consumption, miles traveled, and mileage, 1967-88, 3168–120

Auto fuel economy test results for US and foreign makes, 1992 model year, annual rpt, 3304–11

Bonneville Power Admin energy conservation and resource planning activities, FY89-90, 3228–11

Bonneville Power Admin housing energy conservation program activities, cost effectiveness, and participation, series, 3226–1

Building codes for energy efficiency, effect on house construction practices in BPA service areas, 1987, 3228–15

Commercial buildings energy use, costs, and conservation, by building characteristics, survey rpt series, 3166–8

Consumption of energy, impacts of conservation measures by component and end-use sector, 1970s-88 and projected under alternative oil prices to 1995, 3308–93

DOE energy conservation aid activities, funding, and grants by State, by program, annual rpt, discontinued, 3304–21

DOE energy use, costs, and conservation, by end use, fuel type, and field office, FY90, annual rpt, 3004–27

Electric utilities conservation programs energy savings, under alternative participation rates, projected 1990-2010, 3308–98

Electric utilities conservation programs impacts on prices and supply costs, alternative estimates, 1991 rpt, 3308–99

Expenditures of Fed Govt in States, by type, program, agency, and State, FY90, annual rpt, 2464–2

Fed Govt building energy spending, and conservation retrofit costs and savings, 1988-90, 26358–240

Fed Govt building energy use and efficiency, by agency, annual rpt, discontinued, 3304–25

Fed Govt energy use and efficiency, by agency and fuel type, FY90, annual rpt, 3304–22

Fed Govt financial and nonfinancial domestic aid, 1991 base edition with supplements, annual listing, 104–5

Foreign and US oil dependency, energy demand, and efficiency measures, for 6 OECD countries, 1970s-88, article, 9375–1.210

Housing (low income) energy aid, funding sources, costs, and participation, by State, FY89, annual rpt, 4694–8

Housing (public) renovation costs and alternative funding methods, by project type and region, 1990 rpt, 5188–127

Index by Subjects and Names

Manufacturing energy use and prices, 1988 survey, series, 3166–13

Natl Energy Strategy plans for conservation and pollution reduction, impacts of technology and regulation proposals, projected 1990-2030, 3166–6.47

Natl Energy Strategy plans for conservation and pollution reduction, impacts on electric power supply, costs, and emissions, projected under alternative assumptions, 1995-2030, 3166–6.49

Natl Energy Strategy plans for conservation, impacts on energy use and pollution under alternative technology investment assumptions, projected 1990-2030, 3166–6.48

Natl Energy Strategy plans for conservation, R&D, security, and pollution reduction, with background data, 1991 biennial rpt, 3004–34

Natl Energy Strategy plans for renewable energy dev, supply projected under alternative cost and capacity use assumptions, 1990-2030, 3166–6.50

Natl Energy Strategy plans, North Central States business leaders views, 1991 survey, article, 9383–19.203

Oil and gas primary use prohibited for power and industrial plants, and gas use by State, 1977-90, annual rpt, 3334–1

Production and demand for energy, impacts of alternative Federal policies and new technologies, 1970s-89 and projected to 2015, 26358–243

Public and nonprofit private instns conservation grants of Fed Govt, by building type and State, 1990, annual rpt, 3304–15

State govt energy conservation programs, Federal aid and savings, by State, 1989, annual rpt, 3304–1

Supply, demand, and distribution of energy, and regulatory impacts, series, 3166–6

Supply, demand, and prices, by fuel type and end-use sector, projections and underlying assumptions, 1990-2010, annual rpt, 3164–90

Tax expenditures, Federal revenues forgone through income tax deductions and exclusions by type, FY92-96, annual rpt, 21784–10

Transportation energy use by mode, fuel supply, and demographic and economic factors of vehicle use, 1970s-89, annual rpt, 3304–5

TVA energy use by fuel type, and conservation costs and savings, FY90, annual rpt, 9804–26

see also Alcohol fuels
see also Biomass energy
see also Electric power and heat cogeneration
see also Geothermal resources
see also Insulation
see also Solar energy
see also Synthetic fuels
see also Wind energy

Energy consumption

see Agricultural energy use
see Energy conservation
see Energy resources and consumption
see Government energy use
see Housing energy use
see Industrial and commercial energy use

see Transportation energy use
see under names of specific types of energy (listed under Energy resources and consumption)

Energy exploration and drilling

Aerial survey R&D rpts, and sources of natural resource and environmental data, quarterly listing, 9502–7

Alaska minerals resources and geologic characteristics, compilation of papers, 1989, annual rpt, 5664–15

Alaska minerals resources, production, oil and gas leases, reserves, and exploratory wells, with maps and bibl, 1989, annual rpt, 5664–11

Alaska OCS environmental conditions and oil dev impacts, compilation of papers, series, 2176–1

Alaska rural areas population characteristics, and energy resources dev effects, series, 5736–5

Arctic Ocean fish catch and habitat impacts of oil and gas dev, and assessment methods, 1988 conf, 5738–24

Coastal and riparian areas environmental conditions, fish, wildlife, use, and mgmt, for individual ecosystems, series, 5506–9

County Business Patterns, 1988: employment, establishments, and payroll, by SIC 2- to 4-digit industry and county, annual State rpt series, 2326–6

County Business Patterns, 1989: employment, establishments, and payroll, by SIC 2- to 4-digit industry and county, annual State rpt series, 2326–8

Employment, earnings, and hours, by SIC 1- to 4-digit industry, monthly and annual averages, selected years 1909-90, annual rpt, 6744–4

Enterprise Statistics, 1987: auxiliaries of multi-establishment firms, finances and operations by function, industry, and State, 2329–6

Enterprise Statistics, 1987: finances and operations for companies, by size, level of diversification, form of organization, and industry group, 2329–8

Equipment for drilling and transport, exports of US by country, 1990, annual rpt, 2424–10

Foreign countries oil and gas reserves and discoveries, by country and country group, quarterly rpt, 3162–43

Geothermal resources, power plant capacity and operating status, leases, and wells, by location, 1960s-94, 3308–87

Gulf of Mexico oil and gas reserves, production, and leasing status, by location, 1989, annual rpt, 5734–6

Imports, exports, and employment impacts, by SIC 2- to 4-digit industry and commodity, quarterly rpt, 2322–2

Income (personal) per capita disparity among States, with data by industrial base, 1979, 1989, and projected to 1995, 1548–379

Income and revenue of oil drilling firms, quarterly rpt, 3162–38

Louisiana economic indicators and oil rig growth forecasts, model description and results, 1991, article, 9379–1.202

Middle East and East Africa economic and military aid from US and intl agencies, and US defense spending, FY80-90, GAO rpt, 26123–360

Mineral industries census, 1987: energy use and costs, by fuel type, SIC 2- to 4-digit industry, and State, subject rpt, 2517–2

Mineral industries census, 1987: finances and operations, by establishment characteristics, SIC 2- to 4-digit industry, and State, subject rpt, 2517–1

Mineral industries census, 1987: finances and operations, by SIC 2- to 4-digit industry, State, and county, census div rpt series, 2515–1

Minerals Yearbook, 1988, Vol 3: foreign country reviews of production, trade, and policy, by commodity, annual rpt series, 5604–17

Multinatl firms US affiliates, finances, and operations, by industry, world area of parent firm, and State, 1988-89, annual rpt, 2704–4

Multinatl US firms and foreign affiliates finances and operations, by industry and world area of parent firm, 1989 benchmark survey, preliminary annual rpt, 2704–5

Natl Energy Strategy, oil and gas reserves, 1988 and projected under alternative technology and policy assumptions to 2030, 3166–6.51

Natural gas interstate pipeline company detailed financial and operating data, by firm, 1989, annual rpt, 3164–38

Naval Petroleum and Oil Shale Reserves production and revenue by fuel type, sales by purchaser, and wells, by reserve, FY90, annual rpt, 3334–3

North Carolina environmental and socioeconomic conditions, and impacts of proposed OCS oil and gas exploration, 1970s-90 and projected to 2020, 5738–22

North Central States business and economic conditions, Fed Reserve 9th District, quarterly journal, 9383–19

Occupational injury and illness rates, by SIC 2- to 4-digit industry, 1989, annual rpt, 6844–1

Offshore oil and gas exploration and drilling activity on Federal leases, by ocean area and State, 1950s-90, annual rpt, 5734–3.3

Offshore oil and gas reserves, and leasing and dev activity, periodic regional rpt series, 5736–3

Offshore oil and gas reserves of Fed Govt, production, leasing and exploration activity, revenue, and costs, by ocean area, FY90, annual rpt, 5734–4

Oil and gas exploratory rigs in operation, wells and footage drilled, and seismic exploration crews, monthly rpt, 3162–24.5

Oil enhanced recovery research contracts of DOE, project summaries, funding, and bibl, quarterly rpt, 3002–14

Oil fields construction, finances and operations by SIC 4-digit industry and State, 1987 Census of Construction Industries, final rpt series, 2373–1

Oil, gas, and gas liquids reserves and production, by State and substate area, 1990, annual rpt, 3164–46

Pacific Ocean OCS oil and gas production, and wells, by drilling platform under Federal lease, 1960s-89, annual rpt, 5734–9

Energy exploration and drilling

Pacific Ocean oil and gas production, reserves, and wells drilled by location, 1989, annual rpt, 5734–7

Partnerships (limited) conversion to corporations, and impacts on share values, with data by firm, 1980s-91, hearing, 25248–124

Pollution (water) industrial releases in wastewater, levels, treatment, costs, and regulation, with background financial and operating data, 1989 industry rpt, 9206–4.12

Price indexes (producer), by stage of processing and detailed commodity, monthly 1990, annual rpt, 6764–2

Price indexes for producers of oil and gas drilling and production machinery and equipment, by detailed type, monthly rpt, 6762–6

Producers finances and operations, by energy type for US firms domestic and foreign operations, 1989, annual rpt, 3164–44.2

Public lands acreage and use, and Land Mgmt Bur activities and finances, annual State rpt series, 5724–11

Public lands acreage, grants, use, revenues, and allocations, by State, FY90, annual rpt, 5724–1.2

Public lands minerals resources and availability, State rpt series, 5606–7

State and Metro Area Data Book, 1991 data compilation, 2328–54

Statistical Abstract of US, 1991 annual data compilation, 2324–1.25

Supply, demand, and prices, by fuel type and end-use sector, with foreign comparisons, 1990 and trends from 1949, annual rpt, 3164–74

Tax (income) returns of corporations, income and tax items by asset size and detailed industry, 1987, annual rpt, 8304–4

Tax (income) returns of corporations, income and tax items by asset size and detailed industry, 1988, annual rpt, 8304–21

Tax (income) returns of corporations with foreign tax credit, income and tax items by industry group, 1986, biennial article, 8302–2.203

Tax (income) returns of multinatl US firms foreign affiliates, income statement items, by asset size and industry, 1986, biennial article, 8302–2.212

Tax (income) returns of partnerships, income statement and balance sheet items, by industry group, 1989, annual article, 8302–2.216; 8304–18

Tax (income) returns of sole proprietorships, income statement items, by industry group, 1989, annual article, 8302–2.214

Tax expenditures, Federal revenues forgone through income tax deductions and exclusions by type, FY92-96, annual rpt, 21784–10

Uranium reserves and industry operations, by region and State, various periods 1966-90, annual rpt, 3164–65.1

West Central States economic indicators, Fed Reserve 10th District, quarterly rpt, 9381–16.2

Whales (bowhead) population in Arctic areas, impacts of subsistence whaling, shipping, noise, and other human activity, mid 1970s-80s, 5738–30

Whales (bowhead and white) migration through Beaufort Sea, behavior impacts of oil drilling and aircraft noise, spring 1989, 5738–27

see also under By Industry in the "Index by Categories"

Energy exports and imports

China economic indicators and reform issues, with background data, 1950s-90, compilation of papers, 23848–155

China minerals production and trade, by commodity, 1988-89, annual rpt, 5604–38

Developing countries energy use, and economic and environmental impacts, by fuel type, world area, and country, 1980s-90, 26358–232

Eastern Europe energy production, trade, use, and AID dev assistance, for 3 countries, 1980s-91, 25318–81

Electric power capacity and use in Pacific Northwest, by energy source, projected under alternative load and demand cases, 1991-2011, annual rpt, 3224–3

Electric power import price indexes, quarterly press release, 6762–13

Electric power imports of US, by region, 1987-89, annual rpt, 3164–11.6

Electric power trade of US with Canada by Province, and with Mexico, by US region, 1988, annual rpt, 3164–92.1

Electric power wholesale trade, by type of ownership and North American Electric Reliability Council region, 1989, article, 3162–24.201; 3162–35.201

Exports and imports of US, by country and detailed commodity, monthly rpt, 2422–12

Exports and imports of US by country, and trade shifts by commodity, 1990, semiannual rpt, 9882–9

Exports and imports of US, by selected country, country group, and commodity group, 1990, annual rpt, 2044–37

Exports and imports of US, by transport mode, country, and SITC 1- to 3-digit commodity, 1990, annual rpt, 2424–12

Exports, imports, and balances of US, by selected country, country group, and commodity group, preliminary data, monthly rpt, 2042–34

Exports, imports, and trade flows, by country and commodity, with background economic indicators, data compilation, monthly CD-ROM, 2002–6

Exports of US, detailed commodities by country, monthly CD-ROM, 2422–13

Foreign and US energy production, trade, use, and reserves, and oil and refined products supply and prices, by country, 1980-89, annual rpt, 3164–50

Imports of US, detailed commodities by country, monthly CD-ROM, 2422–14

Latin America energy use and trade, by selected country, 1970s-80s and projected to 2000, 3408–1

Mexico imports from US, by industry and State, 1987-90, 2048–154

Middle East export controls of US, with trade, dual-use commodity licenses, and arms sales, by country, 1980s-90, GAO rpt, 26123–339

Minerals Yearbook, 1988, Vol 3: foreign country reviews of production, trade, and policy, by commodity, annual rpt series, 5604–17

Index by Subjects and Names

Natl Energy Strategy plans for conservation, impacts on energy use and pollution under alternative technology investment assumptions, projected 1990-2030, 3166–6.48

Natural gas imports of US from Canada under long-term contracts by region, with contract provisions, 1986-90, article, 3162–4.206

OECD trade, total and for 4 major countries, and US trade by country, by commodity, 1970-89, world area rpt series, 9116–1

Soviet Union minerals production and trade, by commodity, 1985-89 and projected to 2005, annual rpt, 5604–39

Statistical Abstract of US, 1991 annual data compilation, 2324–1.19

Supply, demand, and prices, by fuel type and end-use sector, alternative projections 1989-2010, annual rpt, 3164–75

Supply, demand, and prices, by fuel type and end-use sector, projections and underlying assumptions, 1990-2010, annual rpt, 3164–90

Supply, demand, and prices, by fuel type and end-use sector, with foreign comparisons, 1990 and trends from 1949, annual rpt, 3164–74

Supply, demand, and prices of energy, forecasts by resource type, quarterly rpt, 3162–34

Uranium marketing, contracts, prices, utility shipments, and trade, 1982-90 and projected to 2000, annual rpt, 3164–65.2

see also Coal exports and imports

see also Natural gas exports and imports

see also Petroleum exports and imports

Energy Information Administration

Activities of EIA, 1990, annual rpt, 3164–29

Building (commercial) energy use, costs, and conservation, by building characteristics, survey rpt series, 3166–8

Coal, coke, and breeze supply, demand, prices, trade, and stocks, by end-use sector and State, quarterly rpt with articles, 3162–37

Coal production and mines by county, prices, productivity, miners, and reserves, by mining method and State, 1989-90, annual rpt, 3164–25

Coal production by State and region, trade, use, and stocks, weekly rpt, 3162–1

Coal production, prices, exports, and use by sector, with data by region, projected 1995-2010 and trends from 1970, annual rpt, 3164–68

Coal production, stocks, and shipments, by State of origin and destination, end-use sector, and mode of transport, quarterly rpt, 3162–8

Coal shipments to electric utilities under contract, and rates, by firm, transport mode, and region, 1979-87, 3168–121

Coal trade flows and reserves, by country, 1980-89 and projected to 2010, annual rpt, 3164–77

Data analysis and forecasting models of EIA, 1991, annual listing, 3164–87

Data collection and analysis activities of EIA, 1987-90, annual narrative rpt, 26104–14

Data collection forms of DOE and related rpts, 1990, annual listing, 3164–86

Index by Subjects and Names

Energy prices

Data on energy resources, EIA rpts and data files, 1990, listing, 3168–117

Electric power plants (steam) fuel receipts, costs, and quality, by fuel, plant, utility, and State, 1990, annual rpt, 3164–42

Electric power plants and capacity, by fuel used, owner, location, and operating status, 1990 and for units planned 1991-2000, annual listing, 3164–36

Electric power plants production and capacity by fuel type, prices, demand, and air pollution law impacts, by region, 1989-90 and projected to 2010, annual rpt, 3164–81

Electric power plants production and capital costs, operations, and fuel use, by fuel type, plant, utility, and location, 1989, annual rpt, 3164–9

Electric power plants production, capacity, sales, and fuel stocks, use, and costs, by State, 1985-89, annual rpt, 3164–11

Electric power plants production, fuel use, stocks, and costs by fuel type, and sales, by State, monthly rpt with articles, 3162–35

Electric power sales and revenue, by end-use sector, consumption level, and utility, 1989, annual rpt, 3164–91

Electric power wholesale trade, by utility, type of ownership, and region, 1988, biennial rpt, 3164–92

Electric utilities finances and operations, detailed data for publicly owned firms, 1989, annual rpt, 3164–24

Electric utilities privately owned, finances and operations, detailed data, 1989, annual rpt, 3164–23

Energy producers finances and operations, by energy type for US firms domestic and foreign operations, 1989, annual rpt, 3164–44

Energy production, dev, and distribution firms revenues and income, quarterly rpt, 3162–38

Energy supply, demand, and prices, by fuel type and end-use sector, alternative projections 1989-2010, annual rpt, 3164–75

Energy supply, demand, and prices, by fuel type and end-use sector, projections and underlying assumptions, 1990-2010, annual rpt, 3164–90

Energy supply, demand, and prices, by fuel type and end-use sector, with foreign comparisons, 1990 and trends from 1949, annual rpt, 3164–74

Energy supply, demand, and prices, by fuel type, end-use sector, and country, detailed data, monthly rpt with articles, 3162–24

Energy supply, demand, and prices, forecasts by resource type, quarterly rpt, 3162–34

Energy supply, demand, distribution, and regulatory impacts, series, 3166–6

Energy supply, demand, prices, and trade, EIA and alternative estimates, with methodology, series, 3166–12

Energy use, by detailed fuel type, end-use sector, and State, 1960-89, State Energy Data System annual rpt, 3164–39

Foreign and US energy production, trade, use, and reserves, and oil and refined products supply and prices, by country, 1980-89, annual rpt, 3164–50

Foreign and US energy use and production, by fuel type, country, and country group, projected 1995-2010 and trends from 1970, annual rpt, 3164–84

Foreign countries oil and gas reserves and discoveries, by country and country group, quarterly rpt, 3162–43

Foreign direct investment in US energy sources by type and firm, and US affiliates operations, as of 1989, annual rpt, 3164–80

Fuel oil and kerosene sales and deliveries, by end-use, PAD district, and State, 1989, annual rpt, 3164–94

Gasoline supply, demand, prices, taxes, and auto registrations and mileage, 1900s-89, 3168–120

Heating fuels production, imports, stocks, and prices, by selected PAD district and State, seasonal weekly rpt, 3162–45

Iraq invasion of Kuwait, impacts on oil supply and prices, selected indicators, daily press release, 3162–44

Manufacturing energy use and prices, 1988 survey, series, 3166–13

Natural and supplemental gas production, prices, trade, use, reserves, and pipeline company finances, by firm and State, monthly rpt with articles, 3162–4

Natural gas deliverability and flow capacity from large gas fields in selected States, projections and production trends, discontinued series, 3166–10

Natural gas interstate pipeline company detailed financial and operating data, by firm, 1989, annual rpt, 3164–38

Natural gas production and wellhead capacity, by production area, 1980-89 and alternative forecasts 1990-91, biennial rpt, 3164–93

Nuclear power plant capacity, generation, and operating status, by plant and foreign and US location, 1990 and projected to 2030, annual rpt, 3164–57

Nuclear power plant operating, maintenance, and capital additions costs, relation to plant characteristics and regulation, 1974-89, 3168–108

Nuclear power plant spent fuel and demand for uranium and enrichment services, for US and other country groups, projected 1991-2040, annual rpt, 3164–72

Oil and gas field codes and locations, 1990, annual listing, 3164–70

Oil and gas supply, demand, and prices, alternative projections 1989-2010, annual rpt, 3164–89

Oil and refined products supply and demand, refinery capacity and use, and prices, weekly rpt, 3162–32

Oil and refined products supply, demand, prices, and refinery capacity and stocks, by State, 1960-91, annual rpt, 3164–95

Oil crude, gas liquids, and refined products supply, demand, and movement, by PAD district and State, 1990, annual rpt, 3164–2

Oil, gas, and gas liquids reserves and production, by State and substate area, 1990, annual rpt, 3164–46

Oil production, trade, use, and stocks, by selected country and country group, monthly rpt, 3162–42

Oil products sales and purchases of refiners, processors, and distributors, by product, end-use sector, PAD district, and State, monthly rpt with articles, 3162–11

Oil, refined products, and gas liquids supply, demand, trade, stocks, and refining, by detailed product, State, and PAD district, monthly rpt with articles, 3162–6

Oil refinery operations and finances, with ownership changes, shutdowns, and reactivations, by firm, 1970s-90, 3168–119

Prices and spending for fuel, by type, end-use sector, and State, 1989, annual rpt, 3164–64

Solar collector and photovoltaic module shipments by end-use sector and State, and trade, 1989, annual rpt, 3164–62

Uranium supply and industry operations, various periods 1947-90 and projected to 2000, annual rpt, 3164–65

Energy prices

Alternative motor fuels costs, emissions, health impacts, and characteristics, series, 9196–5

Commercial buildings energy use, costs, and conservation, by building characteristics, survey rpt series, 3166–8

CPI by component for US city average, and by region, population size, and for 27 metro areas, monthly rpt, 6762–2

CPI changes for selected items, 1981-90, annual article, 6722–1.226

CPI components relative importance, by selected MSA, region, population size, and for US city average, 1990, annual rpt, 6884–1

Economic indicators and components, current data and annual trends, monthly rpt, 23842–1.4

Economic indicators compounded annual rates of change, monthly rpt, 9391–3

Farm prices received for major products and paid for farm inputs and living items, by commodity and State, monthly rpt, 1629–1

Food prices (farm-retail), marketing cost components, and industry finances and productivity, 1920s-90, annual rpt, 1544–9

GNP variability, and correlation between wages and hours, impact of energy use and prices, model description and results, 1940s-87, working paper, 9375–13.57

Housing energy prices, by fuel and State, 1989 and forecast 1990-91, 3166–6.54

Manufacturing energy use and prices, 1988 survey, series, 3166–13

Minerals Yearbook, 1988, Vol 3: foreign country reviews of production, trade, and policy, by commodity, annual rpt series, 5604–17

Natl Energy Strategy plans for conservation and pollution reduction, impacts of technology and regulation proposals, projected 1990-2030, 3166–6.47

Natl Energy Strategy plans for conservation, impacts on energy use and pollution under alternative technology investment assumptions, projected 1990-2030, 3166–6.48

OECD energy prices, by fuel type and end use, for 10 countries, 1980-89 annual rpt, 3164–50.6

Prices and spending for fuel, by type, end-use sector, and State, 1989, annual rpt, 3164–64

Prices, supply, and demand, by fuel type and end-use sector, alternative projections 1989-2010, annual rpt, 3164–75

Energy prices

Prices, supply, and demand, by fuel type and end-use sector, projections and underlying assumptions, 1990-2010, annual rpt, 3164–90

Prices, supply, and demand, by fuel type and end-use sector, with foreign comparisons, 1990 and trends from 1949, annual rpt, 3164–74

Prices, supply, and demand of energy, forecasts by resource type, quarterly rpt, 3162–34

Producer Price Index, by major commodity group and subgroup, and processing stage, monthly press release, 6762–5

Producer price indexes, by stage of processing and detailed commodity, monthly rpt, 6762–6

Producer price indexes, by stage of processing and detailed commodity, monthly 1990, annual rpt, 6764–2

Productivity related to public capital stock, effects on model of energy prices and technological change, 1950-89, article, 9391–1.211

State and Metro Area Data Book, 1991 data compilation, 2328–54

State gross product impact of foreign labor productivity and dollar exchange rate, by industry sector and State, 1972-86, working paper, 9387–8.255

Statistical Abstract of US, 1991 annual data compilation, 2324–1.15; 2324–1.19

Uranium marketing, contracts, prices, utility shipments, and trade, 1982-90 and projected to 2000, annual rpt, 3164–65.2

see also Coal prices

see also Electric power prices

see also Natural gas prices

see also Petroleum prices

Energy production

see Energy production costs

see under Energy resources and consumption (for data on total production)

see under names of specific types of energy

Energy production costs

Alternative motor fuels costs, emissions, health impacts, and characteristics, series, 9196–5

China economic indicators and reform issues, with background data, 1950s-90, compilation of papers, 23848–155

Electric power distribution loans from REA, and borrower operating and financial data, by firm and State, 1990, annual rpt, 1244–1

Electric power plants (steam), delivered cost of coal, residual oil, and natural gas, monthly rpt, 3162–24.9

Electric power plants production and capital costs, operations, and fuel use, by fuel type, plant, utility, and location, 1989, annual rpt, 3164–9

Electric power plants production, capacity, sales, and fuel stocks, use, and costs, by State, 1985-89, annual rpt, 3164–11

Electric power plants production, fuel use, stocks, and costs by fuel type, and sales, by State, monthly rpt with articles, 3162–35

Electric utilities coal receipts, use, stocks, and delivered price, by State, weekly rpt, monthly data, 3162–1.2

Electric utilities conservation programs impacts on prices and supply costs, alternative estimates, 1991 rpt, 3308–99

Electric utilities finances and operations, detailed data for public and privately owned firms, 1989, annual rpt, 3164–11.4

Electric utilities finances and operations, detailed data for publicly owned firms, 1989, annual rpt, 3164–24

Electric utilities privately owned, finances and operations, detailed data, 1989, annual rpt, 3164–23

Energy supply, demand, and prices, by fuel type and end-use sector, with foreign comparisons, 1990 and trends from 1949, annual rpt, 3164–74

Natl Energy Strategy plans for conservation and pollution reduction, impacts on electric power supply, costs, and emissions, projected under alternative assumptions, 1995-2030, 3166–6.49

Natl Energy Strategy plans for renewable energy dev, supply projected under alternative cost and capacity use assumptions, 1990-2030, 3166–6.50

Natural gas interstate pipeline company detailed financial and operating data, by firm, 1989, annual rpt, 3164–38

Nuclear power plant operating, maintenance, and capital additions costs, relation to plant characteristics and regulation, 1974-89, 3168–108

Pipeline and compressor station construction costs, 1984-87, annual rpt, 3084–3

Pollution (air) contributing to global warming, emissions factors and control costs, by pollutant and source, 1990 rpt, 9198–124

Producers finances and operations, by energy type for US firms domestic and foreign operations, 1989, annual rpt, 3164–44

Southwestern Fed Power System financial statements, sales by customer, and operations and costs by project, FY90, annual rpt, 3244–1

Tax (income) returns of corporations, income and tax items by asset size and detailed industry, 1987, annual rpt, 8304–4

Tax (income) returns of corporations, income and tax items by asset size and detailed industry, 1988, annual rpt, 8304–21

Uranium enrichment facilities of DOE, financial statements, FY89-90, annual rpt, 3354–7

Uranium reserves and industry operations, by region and State, various periods 1966-90, annual rpt, 3164–65.1

Energy projections

Aircraft fuel use and efficiency under alternative technological improvements and load factors, by model, projected 1995-2010, 3028–6

Alaska North Slope oil production, and impacts of lifting export controls on US oil trade, West Coast prices, and shipping industry, 1988 and forecast 1995, GAO rpt, 26113–496

Alaska socioeconomic impacts of OCS oil resources dev, 1980-89 and projected to 2020, 5736–5.11

Alcohol (methanol) fuel substitution for gasoline, economic, environmental, and health impacts, projected 2000-2010, article, 9379–1.208

Index by Subjects and Names

Carbon dioxide in atmosphere, North Central States economic and agricultural impacts, model descriptions and results, 1980s and projected to 2030, 3006–11.15

Coal production, prices, exports, and use by sector, with data by region, projected 1995-2010 and trends from 1970, annual rpt, 3164–68

Coal trade flows and reserves, by country, 1980-89 and projected to 2010, annual rpt, 3164–77

Conservation measures impacts on energy consumption, by component and end-use sector, 1970s-88 and projected under alternative oil prices to 1995, 3308–93

Data analysis and forecasting models of EIA, 1991, annual listing, 3164–87

Electric power capacity and use in Pacific Northwest, by energy source, projected under alternative load and demand cases, 1991-2011, annual rpt, 3224–3

Electric power plants and capacity, by fuel used, owner, location, and operating status, 1990 and for units planned 1991-2000, annual listing, 3164–36

Electric power plants production and capacity by fuel type, prices, demand, and air pollution law impacts, by region, 1989-90 and projected to 2010, annual rpt, 3164–81

Electric power plants sales, imports, nonutility purchases, capacity, production, fuel use and costs, and prices, 1995-2010, annual rpt, 3164–11

Electric utilities conservation programs energy savings, under alternative participation rates, projected 1990-2010, 3308–98

Electric utilities conservation programs impacts on prices and supply costs, alternative estimates, 1991 rpt, 3308–99

Foreign and US energy use and production, by fuel type, country, and country group, projected 1995-2010 and trends from 1970, annual rpt, 3164–84

Global warming contributing air pollutants, US and foreign emissions and control measures, 1980s and projected to 2020, 26358–233

Natl Energy Strategy, coal liquids production under alternative oil price and technology assumptions, projected 2000-2030, 3166–6.53

Natl Energy Strategy, oil and gas reserves, 1988 and projected under alternative technology and policy assumptions to 2030, 3166–6.51

Natl Energy Strategy plans for conservation and pollution reduction, impacts of technology and regulation proposals, projected 1990-2030, 3166–6.47

Natl Energy Strategy plans for conservation and pollution reduction, impacts on electric power supply, costs, and emissions, projected under alternative assumptions, 1995-2030, 3166–6.49

Natl Energy Strategy plans for conservation, impacts on energy use and pollution under alternative technology investment assumptions, projected 1990-2030, 3166–6.48

Natl Energy Strategy plans for conservation, R&D, security, and pollution reduction, with background data, 1991 biennial rpt, 3004–34

Index by Subjects and Names

Energy resources and consumption

Natl Energy Strategy plans for renewable energy dev, supply projected under alternative cost and capacity use assumptions, 1990-2030, 3166–6.50

Natural gas production and wellhead capacity, by production area, 1980-89 and alternative forecasts 1990-91, biennial rpt, 3164–93

Natural gas production, use, prices, and trade, 1989-90 and projected to 2010, article, 3162–4.207

Natural gas reserves, by State, 1950-89 and projected to 2020, biennial rpt, 5604–44

Nuclear power plant capacity, generation, and operating status, by plant and foreign and US location, 1990 and projected to 2030, annual rpt, 3164–57

Nuclear power plant spent fuel and demand for uranium and enrichment services, for US and other country groups, projected 1991-2040, annual rpt, 3164–72

Nuclear power plant spent fuel and waste generation, inventory, and disposal, 1960s-89 and projected to 2020, annual rpt, 3364–2

Nuclear power plant spent fuel discharges and additional storage capacity needed, by reactor, projected 1990-2040, annual rpt, 3354–2

Nuclear power plant spent fuel storage pending opening of permanent repository, safety and costs of alternative methods, projected 1991-2050, 14818–1

Oil and gas supply, demand, and prices, alternative projections 1989-2010, annual rpt, 3164–89

Pacific Northwest energy conservation and resource planning activities of Bonneville Power Admin, FY89-90, 3228–11

Production and demand for energy, impacts of alternative Federal policies and new technologies, 1970s-89 and projected to 2015, 26358–243

Soviet Union minerals production and trade, by commodity, 1985-89 and projected to 2005, annual rpt, 5604–39

Strategic Petroleum Reserve capacity, inventory, fill rate, and finances, quarterly rpt, 3002–13

Supply, demand, and distribution of energy, and regulatory impacts, series, 3166–6

Supply, demand, and prices, by fuel type and end-use sector, alternative projections 1989-2010, annual rpt, 3164–75

Supply, demand, and prices, by fuel type and end-use sector, projections and underlying assumptions, 1990-2010, annual rpt, 3164–90

Supply, demand, and prices of energy, forecasts by resource type, quarterly rpt, 3162–34

Taxes on energy, economic and energy demand impacts of alternative taxation methods, projected 1991-2000, 3166–6.57

Uranium marketing, contracts, prices, utility shipments, and trade, 1982-90 and projected to 2000, annual rpt, 3164–65.2

Energy research and development

Aircraft fuel use and efficiency under alternative technological improvements and load factors, by model, projected 1995-2010, 3028–6

Auto (electric-powered) R&D activity and DOE funding shares, FY90, annual rpt, 3304–2

Bonneville Power Admin energy conservation and resource planning activities, FY89-90, 3228–11

Carbon dioxide in atmosphere, measurement, methodology, and research results, series, 3006–11

Electric utilities privately owned, finances and operations, detailed data, 1989, annual rpt, 3164–23

Employment of scientists and engineers related to energy, for PhDs by field and work activity, mid 1970s-80s, biennial rpt, 3006–8.17

Foreign and US funding for R&D, and scientists and engineering employment and education, 1991 annual rpt, 9627–35.1

Global warming contributing air pollutants, US and foreign emissions and control measures, 1980s and projected to 2020, 26358–233

Inventions recommended by Natl Inst of Standards and Technology for DOE support, awards, and evaluation status, 1990, annual listing, 2214–5

Inventions supported by DOE, sales, jobs created, and inventor financing, 1980-88, 3308–91

Minerals Yearbook, 1988, Vol 3: foreign country reviews of production, trade, and policy, by commodity, annual rpt series, 5604–17

Natl Energy Strategy, coal liquids production under alternative oil price and technology assumptions, projected 2000-2030, 3166–6.53

Natl Energy Strategy, oil and gas reserves, 1988 and projected under alternative technology and policy assumptions to 2030, 3166–6.51

Natl Energy Strategy plans for conservation and pollution reduction, impacts of technology and regulation proposals, projected 1990-2030, 3166–6.47

Natl Energy Strategy plans for conservation and pollution reduction, impacts on electric power supply, costs, and emissions, projected under alternative assumptions, 1995-2030, 3166–6.49

Natl Energy Strategy plans for conservation, impacts on energy use and pollution under alternative technology investment assumptions, projected 1990-2030, 3166–6.48

Natl Energy Strategy plans for conservation, R&D, security, and pollution reduction, with background data, 1991 biennial rpt, 3004–34

Natural gas interstate pipeline company detailed financial and operating data, by firm, 1989, annual rpt, 3164–38

Nuclear engineering and science educational facilities, student aid, and degrees granted, by instn, 1990, 3008–126

Nuclear power plant safety standards and research, design, licensing, construction, operation, and finances, with data by reactor, quarterly journal, 3352–4

Nuclear reactors for domestic use and export by function and operating status, with owner, operating characteristics, and location, 1990 annual listing, 3354–15

Producers finances and operations, by energy type for US firms domestic and foreign operations, 1989, annual rpt, 3164–44.5

Production and demand for energy, impacts of alternative Federal policies and new technologies, 1970s-89 and projected to 2015, 26358–243

Radioactive waste and spent fuel generation, inventory, and disposal, 1960s-89 and projected to 2020, annual rpt, 3364–2

Science and engineering employment related to energy, by field and industry segment, projected 1990 and 1996., 3006–8.16

Solar collector and photovoltaic module shipments by end-use sector and State, and trade, 1989, annual rpt, 3164–62

Tax (income) returns of corporations, income and tax items by asset size and detailed industry, 1987, annual rpt, 8304–4

Tax (income) returns of corporations, income and tax items by asset size and detailed industry, 1988, annual rpt, 8304–21

see also Department of Energy National Laboratories

see also Energy exploration and drilling

see also Federal funding for energy programs

Energy reserves

Minerals Yearbook, 1988, Vol 3: foreign country reviews of production, trade, and policy, by commodity, annual rpt series, 5604–17

Uranium reserves and industry operations, by region and State, various periods 1966-90, annual rpt, 3164–65.1

see also Coal reserves

see also Natural gas reserves

see also Petroleum reserves

Energy resources and consumption

China economic indicators and reform issues, with background data, 1950s-90, compilation of papers, 23848–155

China minerals production and trade, by commodity, 1988-89, annual rpt, 5604–38

Consumption of energy, by detailed fuel type, end-use sector, and State, 1960-89, State Energy Data System annual rpt, 3164–39

Data analysis and forecasting models of EIA, 1991, annual listing, 3164–87

Data on energy resources, EIA rpts and data files, 1990, listing, 3168–117

Developing countries economic and social conditions from 1960s, and Intl Dev Cooperation Agency and AID activities and funding, FY90-92, annual rpt, 9904–4

Developing countries energy use, and economic and environmental impacts, by fuel type, world area, and country, 1980s-90, 26358–232

Eastern Europe economic and political conditions, and impacts of geographic factors, by country, 1990 conf, 9118–18

Eastern Europe energy production, trade, use, and AID dev assistance, for 3 countries, 1980s-91, 25318–81

Eastern Europe transition to market economies, economic conditions, intl aid, and energy balance, by country, 1985-90, 9118–13

Employment in energy-related fields, manpower studies and devs, series, 3006–8

Environmental impacts of energy technologies, issues and control measures, handbook series, 3326–1

Energy resources and consumption

Environmental Quality, status of problems, protection programs, research, and intl issues, 1991 annual rpt, 484–1

Foreign and US energy production, trade, use, and reserves, and oil and refined products supply and prices, by country, 1980-89, annual rpt, 3164–50

Foreign and US energy use and production, by fuel type, country, and country group, projected 1995-2010 and trends from 1970, annual rpt, 3164–84

Foreign and US oil dependency, energy demand, and efficiency measures, for 6 OECD countries, 1970s-88, article, 9375–1.210

Foreign countries economic indicators, and trade and trade flows by commodity, by country, data compilation, monthly CD-ROM, 2002–6

Global warming contributing air pollutants, US and foreign emissions and control measures, 1980s and projected to 2020, 26358–233

GNP variability, and correlation between wages and hours, impact of energy use and prices, model description and results, 1940s-87, working paper, 9375–13.57

Great Lakes area economic conditions and outlook, for US and Canada, 1970s-90, 9375–15

Input-output structure of US economy, detailed interindustry transactions for 84 industries, and components of final demand, 1986, annual article, 2702–1.206

Input-output structure of US economy, detailed interindustry transactions for 85 industries, 1982 benchmark data, 2702–1.213

Latin America energy use and trade, by selected country, 1970s-80s and projected to 2000, 3408–1

Natl Energy Strategy plans for conservation and pollution reduction, impacts of technology and regulation proposals, projected 1990-2030, 3166–6.47

Natl Energy Strategy plans for conservation and pollution reduction, impacts on electric power supply, costs, and emissions, projected under alternative assumptions, 1995-2030, 3166–6.49

Natl Energy Strategy plans for conservation, impacts on energy use and pollution under alternative technology investment assumptions, projected 1990-2030, 3166–6.48

Natl Energy Strategy plans for conservation, R&D, security, and pollution reduction, with background data, 1991 biennial rpt, 3004–34

Natl Energy Strategy plans, North Central States business leaders views, 1991 survey, article, 9383–19.203

Natl income and product accounts and components, *Survey of Current Business*, monthly rpt, 2702–1.24

Production and capacity use indexes, by SIC 2- to 4-digit industry, monthly rpt, 9365–2.24

Soviet Union, Eastern Europe, OECD, and selected other countries energy reserves, production, and use, and oil trade and revenue, 1960s-90, annual rpt, 9114–4.4

Soviet Union GNP by component and industry sector, and CIA estimation methods, 1950s-87, 23848–223

Soviet Union GNP by detailed income and outlay component, 1985, 2326–18.59

Soviet Union minerals production and trade, by commodity, 1985-89 and projected to 2005, annual rpt, 5604–39

State and Metro Area Data Book, 1991 data compilation, 2328–54

Statistical Abstract of US, 1991 annual data compilation, 2324–1.19

Supply, demand, and distribution of energy, and regulatory impacts, series, 3166–6

Supply, demand, and prices, by fuel type and end-use sector, with foreign comparisons, 1990 and trends from 1949, annual rpt, 3164–74

Supply, demand, prices, and trade, EIA and alternative estimates, with methodology, series, 3166–12

see also Agricultural energy use
see also Alcohol fuels
see also Aviation fuels
see also Biomass energy
see also Coal and coal mining
see also Coal exports and imports
see also Coal prices
see also Coal reserves
see also Coal stocks
see also Department of Energy National Laboratories
see also Diesel fuel
see also Electric power
see also Electric power and heat cogeneration
see also Electric power plants and equipment
see also Electric power prices
see also Energy conservation
see also Energy exploration and drilling
see also Energy exports and imports
see also Energy prices
see also Energy production costs
see also Energy projections
see also Energy research and development
see also Energy reserves
see also Energy stocks and inventories
see also Energy supply disruptions
see also Federal funding for energy programs
see also Fuel oil
see also Fuel tax
see also Gasohol
see also Gasoline
see also Geothermal resources
see also Government energy use
see also Housing energy use
see also Hydroelectric power
see also Industrial and commercial energy use
see also Kerosene
see also Liquefied petroleum gas
see also Low-income energy assistance
see also Motor fuels
see also Natural gas and gas industry
see also Natural gas exports and imports
see also Natural gas liquids
see also Natural gas prices
see also Natural gas reserves
see also Nuclear power
see also Offshore oil and gas
see also Oil shale
see also Oil spills
see also Petrochemicals
see also Petroleum and petroleum industry
see also Petroleum exports and imports
see also Petroleum prices
see also Petroleum reserves

see also Petroleum stocks
see also Solar energy
see also Synthetic fuels
see also Tar sands
see also Transportation energy use
see also Uranium
see also Water power
see also Wind energy
see also Wood fuel

Energy stocks and inventories

Electric utilities fuel use and end of month stocks, by prime mover and energy resource, monthly rpt, 3162–24.7

Natural and supplemental gas production, prices, trade, use, reserves, and pipeline company finances, by firm and State, monthly rpt with articles, 3162–4

Natural gas interstate pipeline company detailed financial and operating data, by firm, 1989, annual rpt, 3164–38

Natural gas liquids supply, demand, and movement, by PAD district and State, 1990, annual rpt, 3164–2

Natural gas liquids supply, demand, trade, stocks, and refining, by detailed product and PAD district, monthly rpt with articles, 3162–6

Supply, demand, and prices, by fuel type and end-use sector, with foreign comparisons, 1990 and trends from 1949, annual rpt, 3164–74

Supply, demand, and prices of energy, forecasts by resource type, quarterly rpt, 3162–34

Tax (income) returns of corporations, income and tax items by asset size and detailed industry, 1987, annual rpt, 8304–4

Uranium enrichment facilities of DOE, financial statements, FY89-90, annual rpt, 3354–7

Uranium marketing, contracts, prices, utility shipments, and trade, 1982-90 and projected to 2000, annual rpt, 3164–65.2

see also Coal stocks
see also Naval Petroleum Reserves
see also Petroleum stocks
see also Strategic Petroleum Reserve

Energy supply disruptions

Electric power disturbances, utility, location, customers affected, power losses, cause, and restoration time involved, listing, monthly rpt, 3162–35

Electric power disturbances, utility, location, customers affected, power losses, cause, and restoration time involved, listing, 1989, annual rpt, 3164–11

Iraq invasion of Kuwait, impacts on oil prices and industry profits, as of 4th qtr 1990, 3166–6.46

Iraq invasion of Kuwait, impacts on oil supply and prices, selected indicators, daily press release, 3162–44

Iraq invasion of Kuwait, oil embargo impacts on OPEC and US oil supply and industry, 1989-91, hearing, 21368–132

Mgmt of disasters and natl security threats, with data by major event and State, 1991 annual rpt, 9434–6

Natl Energy Strategy plans for conservation and pollution reduction, impacts on electric power supply, costs, and emissions, projected under alternative assumptions, 1995-2030, 3166–6.49

Index by Subjects and Names

Persian Gulf War impacts on US economic conditions compared to previous oil shock periods, and Saudi Arabia oil production and prices, 1990-92, hearings, 21248–156 Supply, demand, and prices of energy, forecasts by resource type, quarterly rpt, 3162–34

Energy use

see Agricultural energy use
see Energy conservation
see Energy resources and consumption
see Government energy use
see Housing energy use
see Industrial and commercial energy use
see Transportation energy use
see under names of specific types of energy (listed under Energy resources and consumption)

Engel, Charles

"On the Foreign Exchange Risk Premium in a General Equilibrium Model", 9381–10.117

"Risk Premium and the Liquidity Premium in Foreign Exchange Markets", 9381–10.118

"Tests of Mean-Variance Efficiency of International Equity Markets", 9381–10.116

Engineers and engineering

Air traffic control and airway facilities staff, by employment and other characteristics, FY89, annual rpt, 7504–41

Army Corps of Engineers activities, FY88, annual rpt, 3754–1

Asia science and engineering employment, by selected characteristics, for 3 countries, 1991 working paper, 2326–18.61

China economic indicators and reform issues, with background data, 1950s-90, compilation of papers, 23848–155

County Business Patterns, 1988: employment, establishments, and payroll, by SIC 2- to 4-digit industry and county, annual State rpt series, 2326–6

County Business Patterns, 1989: employment, establishments, and payroll, by SIC 2- to 4-digit industry and county, annual State rpt series, 2326–8

Degrees (PhD) in science and engineering, by field, instn, employment prospects, sex, race, and other characteristics, 1960s-90, annual rpt, 9627–30

Degrees awarded in higher education, by level, field, race, and sex, 1988/89 with trends from 1978/79, biennial rpt, 4844–17

Degrees awarded in science and engineering, by field, level, and sex, 1966-89, 9627–33

DOD budget, R&D appropriations by item, service branch, and defense agency, FY90-93, annual rpt, 3544–33

DOE R&D projects and funding at natl labs, universities, and other instns, FY90, annual summary rpt, 3004–18.3

DOT employment, by subagency, occupation, and selected personnel characteristics, FY90, annual rpt, 7304–18

Education (postsecondary) course completions, by detailed program, sex, race, and instn type, for 1972 high school class, as of 1984, 4888–4

Education data compilation, 1991 annual rpt, 4824–2

Education in science and engineering, grad programs enrollment by field, source of funds, and characteristics of student and instn, 1975-89, annual rpt, 9627–7

Education in science, engineering, and math, NSF grants by recipient and level, FY89, biennial listing, 9624–27

Employee (temporary) supply establishments by occupation supplied, receipts by source, and payroll, by MSA, 1987 Census of Service Industries, 2393–4.8

Employment and education of scientists and engineers, and R&D spending, for US and selected foreign countries, 1991 annual rpt, 9627–35.2

Employment and other characteristics of science and engineering PhDs, by field and State, 1989, biennial rpt, 9627–18

Employment, earnings, and hours, by SIC 1- to 4-digit industry, monthly and annual averages, selected years 1909-90, annual rpt, 6744–4

Employment of scientists and engineers, and related topics, fact sheet series, discontinued, 9626–2

Employment, unemployment, and labor force characteristics, by region and census div, 1990, annual rpt, 6744–7.1

Energy-related employment of science and engineering PhDs, by field and work activity, mid 1970s-80s, biennial rpt, 3006–8.17

Energy-related employment of scientists and engineers, by field and industry segment, projected 1990 and 1996, 3006–8.16

Enterprise Statistics, 1987: auxiliaries of multi-establishment firms, finances and operations by function, industry, and State, 2329–6

Enterprise Statistics, 1987: finances and operations for companies, by size, level of diversification, form of organization, and industry group, 2329–8

Exports and imports of services, direct and among multinatl firms affiliates, by industry and world area, 1986-90, article, 2702–1.223

Fed Govt aid to higher education and nonprofit instns for R&D and related activities, by field, instn, agency, and State, FY89, annual rpt, 9627–17

Flight engineers certified by FAA, by age, sex, region, and State, 1990, annual rpt, 7504–2

Foreign countries science and engineering employment, by professional characteristics, age, and sex, for selected countries, 1991 working paper, 2326–18.62; 2326–18.63

Manufacturing employment, by detailed occupation and SIC 2-digit industry, 1989 survey, triennial rpt, 6748–52

Multinatl US firms and foreign affiliates finances and operations, by industry and world area of parent firm, 1989 benchmark survey, preliminary annual rpt, 2704–5

NASA R&D funding to higher education instns, by field, instn, and State, FY90, annual listing, 9504–7

NASA science and engineering staff retirement rates, projected 1991-95, GAO rpt, 26123–348

Navy personnel strengths, accessions, and attrition, detailed statistics, quarterly rpt, 3802–4

Engineers and engineering

NSF activities, finances, and funding by program, FY90, annual rpt, 9624–6

NSF R&D grant awards, by div and program, periodic rpt series, 9626–7

NSF science and engineering staff, and outside investigator research grant proposals and awards, 1980s-90, 9628–84

Nuclear engineering and science educational facilities, student aid, and degrees granted, by instn, 1990, 3008–126

Nuclear engineering enrollment and degrees by instn and State, and women grads plans and employment, 1990, annual rpt, 3006–8.14

Nuclear engineering enrollment and degrees granted by instn and State, and grad placement, by student characteristics, 1990, annual rpt, 3004–5

Occupational injury and illness rates, by SIC 2- to 4-digit industry, 1988-89, annual rpt, 6844–7

Occupational injury and illness rates, by SIC 2- to 4-digit industry, 1989, annual rpt, 6844–1

Puerto Rico economic censuses, 1987: wholesale and retail trade and service industry finances and operations, by SIC 2- to 4-digit industry and municipio, 2591–1

Puerto Rico economic censuses, 1987: wholesale, retail, and service industries finances and operations, by establishment characteristics and SIC 2- and 3-digit industry, subject rpts, 2591–2

R&D equipment of higher education instns, acquisition and service costs, condition, and financing, by field and subfield, 1988-90, triennial survey series, 9627–27

R&D funding by Fed Govt, by field, performer type, agency, and State, FY89-91, annual rpt, 9627–20

R&D funding by higher education instns and federally funded centers, by field, instn, and State, FY89, annual rpt, 9627–13

Receipts for services, by SIC 2- to 4-digit kind of business, 1990, annual rpt, 2413–8

Research and education grants of NSF for engineering, FY90, annual listing, 9624–24

Service industries census, 1987: depreciable assets, capital and operating expenses, and receipts, by SIC 2- to 4-digit kind of business, 2393–2

Service industries census, 1987: establishments, receipts by source, payroll, and employment, by SIC 2- to 4-digit kind of business, State, and MSA, 2393–4

Statistical Abstract of US, 1991 annual data compilation, 2324–1.20

Tax (income) returns of corporations, income and tax items by asset size and detailed industry, 1987, annual rpt, 8304–4

Tax (income) returns of corporations, income and tax items by asset size and detailed industry, 1988, annual rpt, 8304–21

Tax (income) returns of partnerships, income statement and balance sheet items, by industry group, 1989, annual article, 8302–2.216; 8304–18

Engineers and engineering

Tax (income) returns of sole proprietorships, income statement items, by industry group, 1989, annual article, 8302-2.214

Teachers in higher education instns, employment and other characteristics, by instn type and control, 1987/88 survey, 4846-4.4

Telecommunications and Info Natl Admin rpts, FY90, annual listing, 2804-3

Telecommunications industry intl competitiveness, with financial and operating data by product or service, firm, and country, 1990 rpt, 2008-30

see also Architecture

see also Biotechnology

see also Technological innovations

see also Traffic engineering

Engines and motors

Aircraft engine shipments, trade, use, and firms, by type, monthly Current Industrial Rpt, 2506-12.24

Airline flight and engine hours, and shutdown rates, by aircraft and engine model, and air carrier, monthly rpt, 7502-13

Auto (electric-powered) R&D activity and DOE funding shares, FY90, annual rpt, 3304-2

Auto and light truck fuel economy, sales, and market shares, by size and model for US and foreign makes, 1991 model year, semiannual rpt, 3302-4

Auto engine and power train R&D projects, DOE contracts and funding by recipient, FY90, annual rpt, 3304-17

County Business Patterns, 1988: employment, establishments, and payroll, by SIC 2- to 4-digit industry and county, annual State rpt series, 2326-6

County Business Patterns, 1989: employment, establishments, and payroll, by SIC 2- to 4-digit industry and county, annual State rpt series, 2326-8

Employment, earnings, and hours, by SIC 1- to 4-digit industry, monthly and annual averages, selected years 1909-90, annual rpt, 6744-4

Enterprise Statistics, 1987: finances and operations for companies, by size, level of diversification, form of organization, and industry group, 2329-8

Exports and imports of US, by country and detailed commodity, monthly rpt, 2422-12

Exports and imports of US, by Harmonized System 6-digit commodity and country, 1990, annual rpt, 2424-13

Exports and imports of US, by selected country, country group, and commodity group, 1990, annual rpt, 2044-37

Exports and imports of US, by transport mode, country, and SITC 1- to 3-digit commodity, 1990, annual rpt, 2424-12

Exports and imports of US shipped through Canada, by detailed commodity, customs district, and country, 1989, annual rpt, 7704-11

Exports of US, detailed Schedule B commodities with countries of destination, 1990, annual rpt, 2424-10

Fluid power products shipments and firms, by product, 1990, annual Current Industrial Rpt, 2506-12.31

Imports of US given duty-free treatment for value of US material sent abroad, by commodity and country, 1989, annual rpt, 9884-14

Injuries from use of consumer products, by severity, victim age, and detailed product, 1990, annual rpt, 9164-6

Labor productivity, indexes of output, hours, and employment by SIC 2- to 4-digit industry, 1967-89, annual rpt, 6824-1.3

Manufacturing census, 1987: employment and shipments under Fed Govt contracts, by SIC 4-digit industry, 2497-7

Manufacturing census, 1987: finances and operations, by SIC 2 to 4-digit industry, State, and MSA, with trends from 1849, 2497-1

Manufacturing census, 1987: finances and operations, by type of organization and SIC 2- to 4-digit industry, subject rpt, 2497-5

Manufacturing finances and operations, by SIC 2- to 4-digit industry, forecast 1991, annual rpt, 2044-28

OECD trade, total and for 4 major countries, and US trade by country, by commodity, 1970-89, world area rpt series, 9116-1

Price indexes (producer), by stage of processing and detailed commodity, monthly rpt, 6762-6

Price indexes (producer), by stage of processing and detailed commodity, monthly 1990, annual rpt, 6764-2

Recalls of motor vehicles and equipment with safety-related defects, by make, monthly listing, 7762-12

Recalls of motor vehicles and equipment with safety-related defects, by make, quarterly listing, 7762-2

Recalls of recreational boats and engines with safety-related defects, by make, periodic listing, 7402-5

Shipments, trade, use, and firms, for internal combustion engines by product, 1990, annual Current Industrial Rpt, 2506-12.6

see also Electric power plants and equipment

England

see United Kingdom

Englander, A. Steven

"Optimal Monetary Policy Design: Rules vs. Discretion Again", 9385-8.85

English language

see Language arts

see Language use and ability

Enid, Okla.

see also under By SMSA or MSA in the "Index by Categories"

Enlistment

see Voluntary military service

Enrollment

see Educational enrollment

Enterovirus infections

see Infective and parasitic diseases

Enterprise Statistics Program

Auxiliaries of multi-establishment firms, finances and operations by function, industry, and State, 1987 survey, 2329-6

Finances and operations for companies, by size, level of diversification, form of organization, and industry group, 1987 survey, 2329-8

Enterprise zones

see Export processing zones

Enterprises for New Directions, Inc.

"Building Better Communities with Student Volunteers: An Evaluation Report on the Student Community Service Program", 9028-14

Entertainment

see Performing arts

see Recreation

Entry level jobs

see Occupations

Enuresis

see Urogenital diseases

Environmental assessments

see Environmental impact statements

Environmental Data and Information Service

see National Environmental Satellite, Data, and Information Service

Environmental impact statements

Alaska OCS environmental conditions and oil dev impacts, compilation of papers, series, 2176-1

Birds (whooping crane) migration roosting sites and population by wetland type, 1990 rpt, 5508-111

California OCS oil and gas dev impacts on water quality, marine life, and sediments, by site, 1986-89, annual rpt, 5734-11

Coal Surface Mining Reclamation and Enforcement Office activities and funding, by State and Indian tribe, FY90, annual rpt, 5644-1

Environmental Quality, status of problems, protection programs, research, and intl issues, 1991 annual rpt, 484-1

Fish (brown trout) population, habitat quality, and streamflow, for Douglas Creek, Wyo, 1970s-89, 5508-112

Florida environmental, social, and economic conditions, and impacts of proposed OCS oil and gas leases in southern coastal areas, 1990 compilation of papers, 5738-19

Forest Service activities and finances, by region and State, FY90, annual rpt, 1204-1.1

Forest Service mgmt of public lands and resources dev, environmental, economic, and social impacts of alternative programs, projected to 2040, 1208-24

North Carolina environmental and socioeconomic conditions, and impacts of proposed OCS oil and gas exploration, 1970s-90 and projected to 2020, 5738-22

Offshore OCS rpts of Minerals Mgmt Service, 1988, annual listing, 5734-5

Oil and gas OCS leases environmental and socioeconomic impact and coastal area description, final statement series, 5736-1

Public lands acreage and use, and Land Mgmt Bur activities and finances, annual State rpt series, 5724-11

Environmental pollution and control

Abatement and control equipment industry finances and operations, by type of organization, 1987 Census of Manufactures, subject rpt, 2497-5

Abatement and control equipment industry finances and operations, 1987 Census of Manufactures, 2497-1

Abatement spending by govts, business, and consumers, 1987-89, annual article, 2702-1.229

Abatement spending, capital and operating costs by SIC 2-digit industry, 1989, advance annual Current Industrial Rpt, 2506-3.6

Agricultural Conservation Program participation and payments, by practice and State, FY90, annual rpt, 1804-7

Index by Subjects and Names

Alaska OCS environmental conditions and oil dev impacts, compilation of papers, series, 2176–1

Assistance (financial and nonfinancial) of Fed Govt, 1991 base edition with supplements, annual listing, 104–5

Bonneville Power Admin operations, maintenance, and environmental protection plans, FY90-99, 3228–14

Budget of US, formula grant program obligations to State and local govts, by agency, program, and State, FY92, annual rpt, 104–30

Budget of US, obligations and authority by function, agency, and program, with summaries, analyses, and historical tables, FY92, annual rpt, 104–2

Costs of environmental protection programs to govts and households, by program type and city size, 1960s-88 and projected to 2000, 9188–114

Disasters and natl security incidents and mgmt, with data by major event and State, 1991 annual rpt, 9434–6

DOE labs testing of environmental samples from DOE facilities, costs compared to commercial labs, FY87-89, 3006–5.23

DOE labs testing of environmental samples from DOE facilities, quality control performance, late 1980s, 3006–5.21

Electric utilities privately owned, pollution abatement outlays by type of pollutant and equipment, and firm, 1989, annual rpt, 3164–23

Environmental Quality, status of problems, protection programs, research, and intl issues, 1991 annual rpt, 484–1

EPA pollution control grant program activities, monthly rpt, 9182–8

EPA R&D programs and funding, FY90, annual listing, 9184–18

EPA rpts in NTIS collection, quarterly listing, 9182–5

Fed Govt spending in States, by type, program, agency, and State, FY90, annual rpt, 2464–2

Forest Service mgmt of public lands and resources dev, environmental, economic, and social impacts of alternative programs, projected to 2040, 1208–24

Health condition and health care resources, use, and spending, 1950s-89, annual data compilation, 4144–11

Health condition improvement and disease prevention goals and recommended activities for 2000, with trends 1970s-80s, 4048–10

Health effects of hazardous pollutants, assessment methodology and data needs, series, 9186–9

Health effects of selected pollutants on animals by species and on humans, and environmental levels, series, 5506–14

HHS financial aid, by program, recipient, State, and city, FY90, annual regional listings, 4004–3

State and Metro Area Data Book, 1991 data compilation, 2328–54

Statistical Abstract of US, 1991 annual data compilation, 2324–1.6

see also Acid rain

see also Air pollution

see also Asbestos contamination

see also Dioxins

Environmental Protection Agency

see also Environmental impact statements

see also Environmental regulation

see also Global climate change

see also Hazardous waste and disposal

see also International cooperation in environmental sciences

see also Landfills

see also Lead poisoning and pollution

see also Marine pollution

see also Mercury pollution

see also Motor vehicle exhaust

see also Noise

see also Oil spills

see also Pesticides

see also Radiation

see also Radioactive waste and disposal

see also Radon

see also Reclamation of land

see also Recycling of waste materials

see also Refuse and refuse disposal

see also Soil pollution

see also State funding for natural resources and conservation

see also Trace metals

see also Water pollution

Environmental Protection Agency

Acid rain effects on Maine streams water quality, acidity, and fish, 1986-87, 9208–130

Activities and progress for EPA regulatory and protection programs operations and mgmt goals, by office, quarterly rpt, 9182–11

Activities, funding, and staff of Federal food safety and quality regulation agencies, 1980s, GAO rpt, 26113–503

Air pollution emissions factors, by detailed pollutant and source, data compilation, 1990 rpt, 9198–120

Air pollution indoor levels in workplace, and health impacts, for Library of Congress Madison Building, 1989 study, series, 4248–92

Air pollution levels for 5 pollutants, by detailed source and State, annual rpt, discontinued, 9194–7

Air pollution levels for 6 pollutants, by source and selected MSA, 1980-89, annual rpt, 9194–1

Air pollution levels for 6 pollutants, by source, 1970-89 and trends from 1940, annual rpt, 9194–13

Asbestos in buildings, EPA aid for removal, occupational asbestos exposure cancer cases and deaths, and Catholic schools abatement costs, 1985-90, hearing, 25328–32

Auto alternative fuels costs, emissions, health impacts, and characteristics, series, 9196–5

Auto fuel economy test results for US and foreign makes, 1992 model year, annual rpt, 3304–11

Budget of US, authoritative financial statements with appropriations, outlays, and receipts, by category and agency, FY90, annual rpt, 8104–2.1

Budget of US, formula grant program obligations to State and local govts, by agency, program, and State, FY92, annual rpt, 104–30

Budget of US, obligations and authority by function, agency, and program, with summaries, analyses, and historical tables, FY92, annual rpt, 104–2

Costs of environmental protection programs to govts and households, by program type and city size, 1960s-88 and projected to 2000, 9188–114

Education funding by Federal agency, program, and recipient type, and instn spending, FY80-90, annual rpt, 4824–8

Energy use, by fuel pollutant source, fuel type, and State, annual rpt, discontinued, 9194–14

Environmental legislation enforcement activities of EPA and State govts, FY90, annual rpt, 9184–21

Environmental Quality, status of problems, protection programs, research, and intl issues, 1991 annual rpt, 484–1

Expenditures of Fed Govt in States, by type, program, agency, and State, FY90, annual rpt, 2464–2

Fraud and abuse in EPA programs, audits and investigations, 2nd half FY91, semiannual rpt, 9182–10

Global climate change environmental, infrastructure, and health impacts, with model results and background data, 1850s-2100, 9188–113

Global warming contributing pollutants emissions factors and control costs, by pollutant and source, 1990 rpt, 9198–124

Grants for pollution control, EPA program activities, monthly rpt, 9182–8

Hazardous substances industrial releases, accuracy of EPA reporting, and nonreporting facilities by State and industry, 1987-90, GAO rpt, 26113–532

Hazardous waste incinerators health and safety violations, by type of violation, 1991 rpt, 6608–5

Hazardous waste treatment facility closures, by EPA review status and waste disposal method, 1991, GAO rpt, 26113–528

Health effects of hazardous pollutants, assessment methodology and data needs, series, 9186–9

Industrial pollutant concentrations and costs by process and waste prevention or treatment method, 1990 biennial conf, 9184–22

Industrial wastewater pollution releases, levels, treatment, costs, and regulation, with background financial and operating data, industry rpt series, 9206–4

Landfills distance from wetlands and water habitats, for 11 States, 1990 rpt, 9188–115

Lead levels in environment, sources of emissions and exposure, and health effects, literature review, 1990 rpt, 9198–84

Lead paint in privately owned housing, levels, exposure, and testing and abatement costs, 1990 rpt, 5188–128

New York Bight pollution levels, sources, treatment costs, economic losses, and environmental and health effects, 1990 conf, 9208–131

Oil and other hazardous substances underground storage systems and facilities subject to EPA regulation, as of 1988, article, 3162–6.203

Pesticide use, economic effects of revised EPA regulations, with data for tomatoes, 1988 conf papers, 1588–154

Public works condition, mgmt, R&D, and funding, for transportation and environmental projects, 1986-91, 26358–235

Environmental Protection Agency

Publications of EPA in NTIS collection, quarterly listing, 9182–5

R&D and related funding of Fed Govt to higher education and nonprofit instns, by field, instn, agency, and State, FY89, annual rpt, 9627–17

R&D funding by Fed Govt, by field, performer type, agency, and State, FY89-91, annual rpt, 9627–20

R&D programs and funding of EPA, FY90, annual listing, 9184–18

Radiation and radionuclide concentrations in air, water, and milk, monitoring results by State and site, quarterly rpt, 9192–5

Superfund hazardous waste site remedial action, current and proposed sites descriptions and status, periodic listings, series, 9216–3

Superfund hazardous waste site remedial action, current and proposed sites priority ranking and status by location, series, 9216–5

Superfund hazardous waste site remedial action, EPA records of decision by site, FY89, annual rpt, 9214–5

Toxicology Natl Program research and testing activities, FY89 and planned FY90, annual rpt, 4044–16

Wastewater treatment facilities construction grants of EPA to State and local govts, by project, monthly listing, 9202–3

Water (bottled) quality standards of FDA, EPA, and States, with use in 12 States, 1990, GAO rpt, 26113–519

Water pollution areas and sources identification activities of EPA and State, 1991, GAO rpt, 26113–536

Water pollution fish kills, by pollution source, month, location, and State, 1977-87, last issue of annual rpt, 9204–3

Environmental regulation

Agricultural Conservation Program participation and payments, by practice and State, FY90, annual rpt, 1804–7

Beach closings due to contamination and medical waste, and bacterial levels, for New York and New Jersey, 1987-89, hearing, 21568–50

Coal production and mining employment effects of Clean Air Act, by region, projected 2000-2010, annual rpt, 3164–68

Coal Surface Mining Reclamation and Enforcement Office activities and funding, by State and Indian tribe, FY90, annual rpt, 5644–1

Costs of environmental protection programs to govts and households, by program type and city size, 1960s-88 and projected to 2000, 9188–114

Court civil and criminal caseloads for Federal district, appeals, and bankruptcy courts, by type of suit and offense, circuit, and district, 1990, annual rpt, 18204–11

Court civil and criminal caseloads for Federal district, appeals, and special courts, 1990, annual rpt, 18204–8

Court civil and criminal caseloads for Federal district courts, 1991, annual rpt, 18204–2.1

Criminal sentences for Federal offenses, guidelines by offense and circumstances, series, 17668–1

DOE facilities radioactive and hazardous waste disposal and remediation activities and funding, planned FY91-97, annual rpt, 3024–7

Electric power plants production and capacity by fuel type, prices, demand, and air pollution law impacts, by region, 1989-90 and projected to 2010, annual rpt, 3164–81

Energy natl strategy plans for conservation and pollution reduction, impacts of technology and regulation proposals, projected 1990-2030, 3166–6.47

Energy natl strategy plans for conservation and pollution reduction, impacts on electric power supply, costs, and emissions, projected under alternative assumptions, 1995-2030, 3166–6.49

Energy supply, demand, distribution, and regulatory impacts, series, 3166–6

Energy technologies environmental impacts, issues and control measures, handbook series, 3326–1

Environmental Quality, status of problems, protection programs, research, and intl issues, 1991 annual rpt, 484–1

EPA and State govt enforcement of environmental legislation, activities, FY90, annual rpt, 9184–21

EPA programs fraud and abuse, audits and investigations, 2nd half FY91, semiannual rpt, 9182–10

EPA regulatory and protection programs operations and mgmt goals, progress and activities, by office, quarterly rpt, 9182–11

Farmers views on Federal agricultural support, trade, and fiscal policies, by region and State, 1989 survey, hearings, 21168–43

Fertilizer and cropland demand impacts of proposed environmental regulation, model description and inputs, 1964-89, 1588–152

Great Lakes wastewater treatment by municipal and industrial facilities, releases, methods, effectiveness, pollutant limits, and enforcement, 1985-88, 14648–24

Hazardous material transport accidents, casualties, and damage, by mode of transport, with DOT control activities, 1989, annual rpt, 7304–4

Hazardous substances industrial releases, accuracy of EPA reporting, and nonreporting facilities by State and industry, 1987-90, GAO rpt, 26113–532

Hazardous waste incinerators health and safety violations, by type of violation, 1991 rpt, 6608–5

Hazardous waste site remedial action under Superfund, current and proposed sites priority ranking and status by location, series, 9216–5

Hazardous waste treatment facility closures, by EPA review status and waste disposal method, 1991, GAO rpt, 26113–528

Oil and other hazardous substances underground storage systems and facilities subject to EPA regulation, as of 1988, article, 3162–6.203

Oil underground storage, Federal trust fund for leaking tanks, financial condition, monthly rpt, 8102–9.11

Pesticide (EBDC) use on vegetable crops, consumer and producer cost impacts of proposed ban, 1985-89, article, 1561–11.204

Pesticide and fertilizer use reduction, environmental and economic impacts by commodity and region, alternative forecasts 1989-94, hearing, 23848–222

Pesticide use, economic effects of revised EPA regulations, with data for tomatoes, 1988 conf papers, 1588–154

Pollution abatement spending by govts, business, and consumers, 1987-89, annual article, 2702–1.229

Public lands acreage, grants, use, revenues, and allocations, by State, FY90 and trends, annual rpt, 5724–1

Public opinion on taxes, spending, and govt efficiency, by respondent characteristics, 1991 survey, annual rpt, 10044–2

Public works condition, mgmt, R&D, and funding, for transportation and environmental projects, 1986-91, 26358–235

Reproductive health and fetal dev effects of selected pollutants, with production, trade, and Federal regulatory activities by substance, 1980s-90, GAO rpt, 26131–90

Tax (excise) collections of IRS, by source, quarterly rpt, 8302–1

Tax (excise) on hazardous waste generation and disposal, rates, and firms filing returns, by substance type, 1988, annual article, 8302–2.202

US attorneys civil and criminal cases by type and disposition, and collections, by Federal district, FY90, annual rpt, 6004–2.1

Wastewater industrial releases pollution levels, treatment, costs, and regulation, with background financial and operating data, industry rpt series, 9206–4

Wastewater treatment facilities in small communities, construction and repair needs to meet Clean Water Act standards, by State and region, 1988 and 2008, 1588–155

Water (bottled) quality standards of FDA, EPA, and States, with use in 12 States, 1990, GAO rpt, 26113–519

Water pollution areas and sources identification activities of EPA and State, 1991, GAO rpt, 26113–536

Wetlands acreage, resources, soil and water properties, and conservation efforts, by wetland type, State rpt series, 5506–11

see also Environmental impact statements

Environmental sciences

Acid rain research activities of Natl Acid Precipitation Assessment Program, 1990 annual rpt, 14354–1

Alaska OCS environmental conditions and oil dev impacts, compilation of papers, series, 2176–1

Carbon dioxide in atmosphere, measurement, methodology, and research results, series, 3006–11

Degrees (PhD) in science and engineering, by field, instn, employment prospects, sex, race, and other characteristics, 1960s-90, annual rpt, 9627–30

Employment and other characteristics of science and engineering PhDs, by field and State, 1989, biennial rpt, 9627–18

Environmental Quality, status of problems, protection programs, research, and intl issues, 1991 annual rpt, 484–1

Fed Govt aid to higher education and nonprofit instns for R&D and related activities, by field, instn, agency, and State, FY89, annual rpt, 9627–17

Foreign and US funding for R&D, and scientists and engineering employment and education, 1991 annual rpt, 9627–35.1

Higher education course completions, by detailed program, sex, race, and instn type, for 1972 high school class, as of 1984, 4888–4

Higher education grad programs enrollment in science and engineering, by field, source of funds, and characteristics of student and instn, 1975-89, annual rpt, 9627–7

NASA R&D funding to higher education instns, by field, instn, and State, FY90, annual listing, 9504–7

NOAA Environmental Research Labs rpts, FY90, annual listing, 2144–25

NSF activities, finances, and funding by program, FY90, annual rpt, 9624–6

R&D equipment of higher education instns, acquisition and service costs, condition, and financing, by field and subfield, 1988-90, triennial survey series, 9627–27

R&D funding by Fed Govt, by field, performer type, agency, and State, FY89-91, annual rpt, 9627–20

R&D funding by higher education instns and federally funded centers, by field, instn, and State, FY89, annual rpt, 9627–13

see also Astronomy

see also Atmospheric sciences

see also Earth sciences

see also Energy research and development

see also International cooperation in environmental sciences

see also Meteorology

see also Oceanography

Epidemiology and epidemiologists

Animal disease outbreaks in US and foreign countries, quarterly rpt, 1392–3

Cancer Natl Inst epidemiology and biometry activities, FY90, annual rpt, 4474–29

Education in science and engineering, grad programs enrollment by field, source of funds, and characteristics of student and instn, 1975-89, annual rpt, 9627–7

Health condition improvement and disease prevention goals and recommended activities for 2000, with trends 1970s-80s, 4048–10

HHS financial aid, by program, recipient, State, and city, FY90, annual regional listings, 4004–3

Morbidity and Mortality Weekly Report, infectious notifiable disease cases by age, race, and State, and deaths, 1930s-90, annual rpt, 4204–1

Morbidity and Mortality Weekly Report, infectious notifiable disease cases by State, and public health issues, 4202–1

Morbidity and Mortality Weekly Report, special supplements, series, 4206–2

Occupational deaths data collection and processing by States, Natl Inst for Occupational Safety and Health guidelines, 1990 rpt, 4248–89

Occupational exposure to hazardous substances and conditions, and health effects, literature review, series, 4246–4

Public Health Reports, bimonthly journal, 4042–3

Respiratory diseases related to occupational hazards, epidemiology, diagnosis, and treatment, for selected industries and work settings, 1988 conf, 4248–90

Southern US epidemiologists, education, specialties, and State govt employment, 1989, article, 4042–3.253

Vermont health dept infectious notifiable disease cases reported, by source, and reasons for nonreporting, 1986-87, article, 4042–3.208

see also Diseases and disorders

see also Public health

Epilepsy

see Neurological disorders

Equal employment opportunity

see Discrimination in employment

Equal Employment Opportunity Commission

Budget of US, authoritative financial statements with appropriations, outlays, and receipts, by category and agency, FY90, annual rpt, 8104–2.1

Budget of US, obligations and authority by function, agency, and program, with summaries, analyses, and historical tables, FY92, annual rpt, 104–2

Expenditures of Fed Govt in States, by type, program, agency, and State, FY90, annual rpt, 2464–2

Fed Govt employment discrimination complaints, processing, and disposition, by complaint type and agency, FY89, annual rpt, 9244–11

Fed Govt employment of minorities, women, and disabled, by agency and occupation, FY89, annual rpt, 9244–10

State and local govt employment of minorities and women, by occupation, function, pay level, and State, 1990, annual rpt, 9244–6

Equatorial Guinea

Agricultural exports of high-value commodities, indexes and sales by commodity, world area, and country, 1960s-86, 1528–323

Agricultural trade of US, by detailed commodity and country, 1989, annual rpt, 1524–8

Agricultural trade of US, by detailed commodity and country, 1990, semiannual rpt, 1522–4

AID economic aid to developing countries, obligations and disbursements by country, quarterly rpt, 9912–4

Economic and military aid and loans from US and intl agencies, by program and country, FY46-90, annual rpt, 9914–5

Economic and social conditions of developing countries from 1960s, and Intl Dev Cooperation Agency and AID activities and funding, FY90-92, annual rpt, 9904–4

Economic, social, political, and geographic summary data, by country, 1991, annual factbook, 9114–2

Exports and imports of US, by transport mode, country, and SITC 1- to 3-digit commodity, 1990, annual rpt, 2424–12

Human rights conditions in 170 countries, and US economic and military aid, 1990, annual rpt, 21384–3

Military aid of US, arms sales, and training programs costs and budget requests, by program, world region, and country, FY90-92, annual rpt, 7144–13

Minerals Yearbook, 1988, Vol 3: foreign country review of production, trade, and policy, by commodity, annual rpt, 5604–17.80

UN voting record and share of votes in agreement with US, by issue, country, and world area, 1990, annual rpt, 7004–18

Ergonomics

see Biotechnology

see Body measurements

see Occupational health and safety

Ericsson, Neil R.

"Cointegration, Exogeneity, and Policy Analysis: An Overview", 9366–7.269

"Parameter Constancy, Mean Square Forecast Errors, and Measuring Forecast Performance: An Exposition, Extensions, and Illustration", 9366–7.266

"PC-GIVE and David Hendry's Econometric Methodology", 9366–7.260

Erie County, N.Y.

Housing and households characteristics, unit and neighborhood quality, and journey to work by MSA location, for 11 MSAs, 1984 survey, supplement, 2485–8

Erie, Pa.

see also under By City and By SMSA or MSA in the "Index by Categories"

Erlanger, Wendy J.

"No Gift Wasted: Effective Strategies for Educating Highly Able, Disadvantaged Students in Mathematics and Science. Volume I: Findings", 4808–34.1

Erosion

see Soils and soil conservation

Ervin, David

"Conservation and Environmental Issues in Agriculture: An Economic Evaluation of Policy Options", 1588–153

Escalator clauses

Budget of US, obligations and authority by function, agency, and program, with summaries, analyses, and historical tables, FY92, annual rpt, 104–2

Collective bargaining contract expirations, wage increases, and coverage, by major industry group, 1991, annual article, 6722–1.206

Collective bargaining wage and benefit changes, quarterly press release, 6782–2

Collective bargaining wage changes and coverage, by industry sector and whether contract includes escalator clause and lump sum payment, 1980-90, annual article, 6722–1.227

CPI use in escalator clauses of collective bargaining agreements and other contracts, with conversion factors for index rebasing, 1991 guide, 6888–34

Pension coverage by industry, vestment, and recipient income, by participant characteristics, 1987, Current Population Rpt, 2546–20.18

State and local govt collective bargaining, wage and benefit changes and coverage, 1st half 1991, semiannual press release, 6782–6

Supplemental Security Income and Medicaid eligibility and payment provisions, and beneficiaries living arrangements, by State, 1991, annual rpt, 4704–13

Wage adjustments in collective bargaining, Monthly Labor Review, 6722–1.3

Wage and benefit changes from collective bargaining and mgmt decisions, by industry div, monthly rpt, 6782–1

Escondido, Calif.

see also under By City in the "Index by Categories"

Eskimos

Eskimos
see Alaska Natives

Espinosa, Marco
"Inflationary Implications of Reducing Market Interest Rates via Alternative Monetary Policy Instruments", 9371–10.59
"On the Sustainability of International Coordination", 9371–10.61

Espionage
Sentences for Federal offenses, guidelines by offense and circumstances, series, 17668–1

Essential oils
see Spices and herbs

Essey, Mitchell A.
"Status of the State-Federal Bovine Tuberculosis Eradication Program, FY90", 1394–13.2

Estate tax
Budget of US, authoritative financial statements with appropriations, outlays, and receipts, by category and agency, FY90, annual rpt, 8104–2.1
Budget of US, CBO analysis of revenue and spending alternatives and projections of economic indicators, FY92-96, annual rpt, 26304–3
Budget of US, CBO analysis of savings and revenues under alternative spending cuts and tax changes, projected FY92-97, 26306–3.118
Budget of US, midsession review of FY92 budget, by function, annual rpt, 104–7
Budget of US, obligations and authority by function, agency, and program, with summaries, analyses, and historical tables, FY92, annual rpt, 104–2
Budget of US, receipts by source, outlays by agency and program, and balances, monthly rpt, 8102–3
Collections, enforcement, and litigation activity of IRS, with data by type of tax, region, and State, FY90, annual rpt, 8304–3
Fed Govt consolidated financial statements based on business accounting methods, FY89-90, annual rpt, 8104–5
Fed Govt finances, cash and debt transactions, daily tables, 8102–4
Fed Govt internal revenue and refunds, by type of tax, quarterly rpt, 8302–2.1
Fed Govt receipts by source and outlays by agency, *Treasury Bulletin*, quarterly rpt, 8002–4.1
Fed Govt tax provisions and receipts overview, by tax type, with background data, 1900s-91 and projected to 2000, 21788–197
Finances of govts, tax systems and revenue, and fiscal structure, by level of govt and State, 1991 and historical trends, annual rpt, 10044–1
Returns and supplemental documents filed, by type, FY89 and projected to FY98, annual article, 8302–2.208
Returns and supplemental documents filed, by type, FY90 and projected to FY99, semiannual rpt, 8302–4
Returns filed, accuracy of projections by return type, various periods 1983-90, article, 8304–8.1
Returns filed, by type of tax and IRS district, 1989 and projected 1990-97, annual rpt, 8304–24

Returns filed, by type of tax, region, and IRS service center, projected 1990-97 and trends from 1978, annual rpt, 8304–9
State govt revenue by source, spending and debt by function, and holdings, FY90, annual rpt, 2466–2.6
State govt tax collections by detailed type of tax, and tax rates, by State, FY90, annual rpt, 2466–2.7
see also Gift tax

Estes, James A.
"Sea Otter (Enhydra lutris): Behavior, Ecology, and Natural History", 5508–109

Estonia
Human rights conditions in 170 countries, and US economic and military aid, 1990, annual rpt, 21384–3

Estrella, Arturo
"Corporate Leverage and Taxes in the U.S. Economy", 9385–8.88

Estuaries
Alaska OCS environmental conditions and oil dev impacts, compilation of papers, series, 2176–1
Environmental conditions by estuary, and fish and shellfish landings by species and region, 1980s, 2178–27
Environmental conditions, fish, wildlife, use, and mgmt, for individual coastal and riparian ecosystems, series, 5506–9
Environmental conditions of coastal areas and estuaries, research results and methodology, series, 2176–7
Fishery research of State fish and wildlife agencies, federally funded projects and costs by species and State, 1990, annual listing, 5504–23
North Carolina environmental and socioeconomic conditions, and impacts of proposed OCS oil and gas exploration, 1970s-90 and projected to 2020, 5738–22
Pollutant concentrations in coastal and estuarine fish, shellfish, and environment, series, 2176–3
Recreation (outdoor) coastal facilities, by State, county, estuary, and level of govt, 1972-84, 2178–29
Recreation (outdoor) coastal facilities of Fed Govt and States, visitor and site characteristics, 1987-90 survey, regional rpt series, 2176–9
Water quality, chemistry, hydrology, and other characteristics, local area studies, series, 5666–27
Wetlands acreage, resources, soil and water properties, and conservation efforts, by wetland type, State rpt series, 5506–11
Wildlife and plant research results, habitat study series, 5506–13
Wildlife mgmt activities and funding, acreage, staff, and plans of Bur of Land Mgmt, habitat study series, 5726–6
see also Wetlands

Ethanol
see Alcohol fuels

Ethics and morality
Tax (income) admin and compliance issues, and taxpayer views, 1990 conf, 8304–25
see also Business ethics
see also Conflict of interests
see also Financial disclosure
see also Judicial ethics
see also Legal ethics

see also Medical ethics
see also Political ethics

Ethiopia
Agricultural conditions, grain production and use, and dev aid by major donor, for Ethiopia, 1960s-80s, hearing, 23848–216
Agricultural exports of high-value commodities, indexes and sales by commodity, world area, and country, 1960s-86, 1528–323
Agricultural trade of US, by detailed commodity and country, 1989, annual rpt, 1524–8
Agricultural trade of US, by detailed commodity and country, 1990, semiannual rpt, 1522–4
AID economic aid to developing countries, obligations and disbursements by country, quarterly rpt, 9912–4
AID loans repayment status and terms by program and country, and status of predecessor agency loans, quarterly rpt, 9912–3
Dairy imports, consumption, and market conditions, by sub-Saharan Africa country, 1961-88, 1528–321
Economic and military aid and loans from US and intl agencies, by program and country, FY46-90, annual rpt, 9914–5
Economic, social, political, and geographic summary data, by country, 1991, annual factbook, 9114–2
Exports and imports of US, by commodity and country, 1970-89, world area rpt, 9116–1.6
Exports and imports of US, by transport mode, country, and SITC 1- to 3-digit commodity, 1990, annual rpt, 2424–12
Exports of US, detailed Schedule B commodities with countries of destination, 1990, annual rpt, 2424–10
Food supply, needs, and aid for developing countries, status and alternative forecasts, 1991 world area rpt, 1526–8.1
Grain production and needs, and related economic outlook, by world area and selected country, forecast 1990/91-1991/92, 1528–313
Grain production, use, imports, and stocks, for Sahel region by country, 1989/90, 9918–18
Human rights conditions in 170 countries, and US economic and military aid, 1990, annual rpt, 21384–3
Refugee resettlement programs and funding, arrivals by country of origin, and indicators of adjustment, by State, FY90, annual rpt, 4694–5
UN voting record and share of votes in agreement with US, by issue, country, and world area, 1990, annual rpt, 7004–18
see also under By Foreign Country in the "Index by Categories"

Ethnic groups
see Ethnic studies
see Hispanic Americans
see Minority employment
see Minority groups
see under By Race and Ethnic Group in the "Index by Categories"

Ethnic studies
Higher education course completions, by detailed program, sex, race, and instn type, for 1972 high school class, as of 1984, 4888–4

Index by Subjects and Names

Europe

Eugene, Oreg.

Wages by occupation, for office and plant workers, 1991 survey, periodic MSA rpt, 6785–3.6

see also under By City and By SMSA or MSA in the "Index by Categories"

Eurocurrency

Economic integration of EC, European Currency Unit weights, and dollar and ECU exchange rates for each currency, 1991 article, 9371–1.212

Eurodollar and total market liabilities, US bank foreign branches market share, and Eurodollar deposit rates, quarterly rpt, 9391–7

Eurodollar deposit rates, weekly chartbook, 9365–1.5

Futures and options trading volume, by commodity and exchange, FY90, annual rpt, 11924–2

Futures trading in selected commodities and financial instruments and indexes, NYC, Chicago, and other markets activity, semimonthly rpt, 11922–5

Interest rates for commercial paper, govt securities, other financial instruments, and home mortgages, monthly rpt, 9365–2.14

Interest rates forecasting performance of Treasury bill and other security yields at alternative maturities, 1950s-80s, article, 9389–1.201

Europe

Agricultural exports of high-value commodities, indexes and sales by commodity, world area, and country, 1960s-86, 1528–323

Agricultural exports of US, for grains, oilseed products, hides, skins, and cotton, by country, weekly rpt, 1922–3

Agricultural production, prices, and trade, by country, 1970s-90, and forecast 1991, annual world region rpt, 1524–4.4

Agricultural trade of US, by commodity and country, bimonthly rpt, 1522–1

Agricultural trade of US, by detailed commodity and country, 1989, annual rpt, 1524–8

Agricultural trade of US, by detailed commodity and country, 1990, semiannual rpt, 1522–4

AID economic aid to developing countries, obligations and disbursements by country, quarterly rpt, 9912–4

Air traffic and passengers, for intl routes over north Atlantic, by aviation type and route, alternative forecasts 1991-2010 and trends from 1980, annual rpt, 7504–44

Alien workers (unauthorized) and Fair Labor Standards Act employer compliance, hiring impacts, and aliens overstaying visas by country and State, 1986-90, annual rpt, 6264–6

Aliens (illegal) overstaying visas, by class of admission, mode of arrival, age, country, and State, FY85-88, annual rpt, 6264–5

Coal trade flows and reserves, by country, 1980-89 and projected to 2010, annual rpt, 3164–77

Construction contract awards and billings, by country of contractor and world area of award, 1989, annual article, 2042–1.201

Corporations in US under foreign control, income tax returns, assets and income statement items by industry div, country, and world area, 1988, article, 8302–2.219

Dollar exchange rate trade-weighted index of Fed Reserve Bank of Atlanta, by world area, quarterly rpt, 9371–15

Dollar exchange rate trade-weighted index of Fed Reserve Bank of Dallas, by world area, monthly rpt, 9379–13

Drug abuse indicators, by world region and selected country, 1990 semiannual conf, 4492–5.1

Economic and military aid and loans from US and intl agencies, by program and country, FY46-90, annual rpt, 9914–5

Energy producers finances and operations, by energy type for US firms domestic and foreign operations, 1989, annual rpt, 3164–44.2

Energy production by type, and oil trade, and use, by country group and selected country, monthly rpt, 9112–2

Energy use and production, by fuel type, country, and country group, projected 1995-2010 and trends from 1970, annual rpt, 3164–84

English language program of USIA, enrollment and staff, by country and world region, FY90, annual rpt, 9854–2

Exchange and training programs of Federal agencies, participants by world area, and funding, by program, FY89, annual rpt, 9854–8

Exports and imports (waterborne) of US, by type of service, commodity, country, route, and US port, 1988, annual rpt, 7704–2

Exports and imports (waterborne) of US, by type of service, customs district, port, and world area, monthly rpt, 2422–7

Exports and imports of OECD members, by country, 1989, annual rpt, 7144–10

Exports and imports of US, by Harmonized System 6-digit commodity and country, 1990, annual rpt, 2424–13

Exports and imports of US, by selected country, country group, and commodity group, 1990, annual rpt, 2044–37

Exports and imports of US, by transport mode, country, and SITC 1- to 3-digit commodity, 1990, annual rpt, 2424–12

Immigrant and nonimmigrant visas of US issued and refused, by class, issuing office, and nationality, FY89, annual rpt, 7184–1

Immigrants admitted to US, by country of birth, FY81-90, annual rpt, 6264–4

Immigrants admitted to US, by occupational group and country of birth, preliminary FY90, annual table, 6264–1

Immigrants in US, population characteristics and fertility, by birthplace and compared to native born, 1980s, Current Population rpt, 2546–2.162

Investment (foreign direct) in US, by industry group and world area, 1987-90, annual article, 2702–1.219

Investment (foreign direct) in US, by industry group of US affiliate and country of parent firm, 1980-86, 2708–41

Investment (foreign direct) of US, by industry group and world area, 1987-90, annual article, 2702–1.220

Labor costs and indexes, by selected country, 1990, semiannual rpt, 6822–3

Loans of US banks to foreigners at all US and foreign offices, by country group and country, quarterly rpt, 13002–1

Lumber (hardwood) exports of US to Europe and Asia, by species and country, 1981-89, 1208–373

Military aid of US, arms sales, and training, by country, FY50-90, annual rpt, 3904–3

Military aid of US, arms sales, and training programs costs and budget requests, by program, world region, and country, FY90-92, annual rpt, 7144–13

Military weapons trade, production, and defense industry finances, with data by firm and country, 1980s-91, 26358–241

Multinatl firms US affiliates, finances, and operations, by industry, world area of parent firm, and State, 1988-89, annual rpt, 2704–4

Multinatl firms US affiliates, investment trends and impact on US economy, 1991 annual rpt, 2004–9

Multinatl US firms and foreign affiliates finances and operations, by industry and world area of parent firm, 1989 benchmark survey, preliminary annual rpt, 2704–5

Multinatl US firms foreign affiliates, income statement items by country and world area, 1986, biennial article, 8302–2.212

NATO and Warsaw Pact military forces reductions under proposed treaty, and US budget savings, 1990 rpt, 26306–3.114

Nuclear power plant capacity, generation, and operating status, by plant and foreign and US location, 1990 and projected to 2030, annual rpt, 3164–57

Nuclear power plant spent fuel demand for uranium and enrichment services, for US and other country groups, projected 1991-2040, annual rpt, 3164–72

Oil and gas reserves and discoveries, by country and country group, quarterly rpt, 3162–43

Oil supply, demand, and stock forecasts, by world area, quarterly rpt, 3162–34

Oils, oilseeds, and meal imports, by commodity, world area of destination, and major producer, 1960s-88, 1528–314

R&D funding by Fed Govt, by field, performer type, agency, and State, FY89-91, annual rpt, 9627–20

Tax (income) returns of corporations with foreign tax credit, income, and tax items, by country and world region of credit, 1986, biennial article, 8302–2.207

Terrorism (intl) incidents, casualties, and attacks on US targets, by attack type and country, 1990, annual rpt, 7004–22

Terrorism (intl) incidents, casualties, and attacks on US targets, by attack type and world area, 1990, annual rpt, 7004–13

Tide height and time daily at coastal points, forecast 1992, annual rpt, 2174–2.4

Timber in northwestern US and British Columbia, production, prices, trade, and employment, quarterly rpt, 1202–3

Travel to and from US, by world area, forecast 1991-92, annual rpt, 2904–9

Travel to and from US on US and foreign flag air carriers, by country, world area, and US port, monthly rpt, 7302–2

Travel to and from US on US and foreign flag air carriers, by world area, 1990, annual rpt, 2904–13

Travel to US, by characteristics of visit and traveler, country, port city, and State of destination, quarterly rpt, 2902–1

Europe

UN voting record and share of votes in agreement with US, by issue, country, and world area, 1990, annual rpt, 7004–18

US military and civilian personnel and dependents, by service branch, world area, and country, quarterly rpt, 3542–20

US military base closings in Europe, by service branch and location, FY91, GAO rpt, 26123–336

US military base support costs by function, and personnel and acreage by installation, by service branch, FY91, annual rpt, 3504–11

USIA library holdings, use, and staff, by country and city, FY90, annual rpt, 9854–4

Weather, air pressure, temperature, and precipitation data for US and foreign locations, monthly 1971-80, decennial rpt, 2156–4.2

Weather conditions and effect on agriculture, by US region, State, and city, and world area, weekly rpt, 2182–7

Weather events and anomalies, precipitation and temperature for US and foreign locations, weekly rpt, 2182–6

Weather forecasts accuracy evaluations, for US, UK, and European systems, quarterly rpt, 2182–8

Weather forecasts for US and Northern Hemisphere, precipitation and temperature by location, semimonthly rpt, 2182–1

Wheat quality indicators, for US exports and foreign wheat production, 1960s-90, hearing, 25168–75

see also Albania
see also Andorra
see also Austria
see also Belgium
see also Bulgaria
see also Central Treaty Organization
see also Cyprus
see also Czechoslovakia
see also Denmark
see also Eastern Europe
see also Estonia
see also Eurocurrency
see also European Community
see also European Space Agency
see also Finland
see also France
see also Germany
see also Germany, East
see also Germany, West
see also Gibraltar
see also Greece
see also Hungary
see also Iceland
see also Ireland
see also Italy
see also Latvia
see also Liechtenstein
see also Lithuania
see also Luxembourg
see also Malta
see also Monaco
see also Netherlands
see also North Atlantic Treaty Organization
see also Norway
see also Organization for Economic Cooperation and Development
see also Poland
see also Portugal
see also Romania

see also San Marino
see also Soviet Union
see also Spain
see also Sweden
see also Switzerland
see also United Kingdom
see also Yugoslavia
see also under By Foreign Country in the "Index by Categories"

European Community

Agricultural export subsidies of EC by commodity and destination, FAS monthly circular, 1925–32

Agricultural exports of high-value commodities from developing countries to OECD, 1970s-87, 1528–316

Agricultural exports of US, for grains, oilseed products, hides, skins, and cotton, by country, weekly rpt, 1922–3

Agricultural exports of US, impacts of foreign agricultural and trade policy, with data by commodity and country, 1989, annual rpt, 1924–8

Agricultural production, acreage, and yield for selected crops, forecasts by selected world region and country, FAS monthly circular, 1925–28

Agricultural production, prices, and trade, by country, 1970s-90, and forecast 1991, annual world region rpt, 1524–4.4

Agricultural production, trade, and policies in foreign countries, summary data by country, 1989-90, annual factbook, 1924–12

Agricultural trade by commodity and country, prices, and world market devs, monthly rpt, 1922–12

Agricultural trade of US, by commodity and country, bimonthly rpt, 1522–1

Agricultural trade of US, by detailed commodity and country, 1989, annual rpt, 1524–8

Agricultural trade of US, by detailed commodity and country, 1990, semiannual rpt, 1522–4

AID loans repayment status and terms by program and country, and status of predecessor agency loans, quarterly rpt, 9912–3

Air pollutant sulfur dioxide emissions reduction levels, by EC member, 1980 and projected to 2003, annual rpt, 3164–77.1

Almond production, trade, use, and stocks, for 6 countries and US, 1987-92, article, 1925–34.240

Banks financial performance, risk assessment, and regulation, 1990 annual conf papers, 9375–7

Biotechnology commercial applications, industry finances and capitalization, patents, and govt support, for US, Japan, and EC, late 1970s-91, 26358–248

Corporations in US under foreign control, income tax returns, assets and income statement items by industry div, country, and world area, 1988, article, 8302–2.219

Dairy imports under quota by commodity, by country of origin, FAS monthly rpt, 1925–31

Dairy product export subsidies of EC, by commodity, 1991, FAS semiannual circular, 1925–10

Economic conditions in Communist and OECD countries, 1989, annual rpt, 7144–11

Index by Subjects and Names

Economic conditions in USSR, Eastern Europe, OECD, and selected other countries, 1960s-90, annual rpt, 9114–4

Economic conditions, policy, and trade practices, by country, 1988-90, annual rpt, 21384–5

Economic integration of EC, economic impacts, with background data by country, 1988-90, article, 9379–1.201

Economic integration of EC, European Currency Unit weights, and dollar and ECU exchange rates for each currency, 1991 article, 9371–1.212

Economic integration of EC impacts on domestic economic conditions and US trade, 1985-90, 9886–4.170

Economic integration of EC, issues, with economic and trade indicators by country and trading partner group, 1985-89, article, 9371–1.210

Economic integration of EC, issues, with intracountry mergers and acquisitions, late 1980s, 21248–153

Exports and imports of OECD members, by country, 1989, annual rpt, 7144–10

Exports and imports of US by country, and trade shifts by commodity, 1990, semiannual rpt, 9882–9

Exports and imports of US, by selected country, country group, and commodity group, 1990, annual rpt, 2044–37

Exports and imports of US with EC by country, and total agricultural trade, selected years 1958-90, annual rpt, 7144–7

Exports and imports, trade agreements and relations, and USITC investigations, 1990, annual rpt, 9884–5

Exports, imports, and balances of US, by selected country, country group, and commodity group, preliminary data, monthly rpt, 2042–34

Exports, imports, and balances of US with major trading partners, by product category, 1986-90, annual chartbook, 9884–21

GNP and GNP growth for OECD members, by country, 1980-90, annual rpt, 7144–8

Gold and silver fineness standards of US and EC, 1990 hearing, 25388–58

Grain production, supply, trade, and use, by country and world region, forecasts and trends, FAS monthly circular, 1925–2.1

Imports of goods, services, and investment from US, trade barriers, impacts, and US actions, by country, 1990, annual rpt, 444–2

Imports of US given duty-free treatment for value of US material sent abroad, by commodity and country, 1989, annual rpt, 9884–14

Investment (foreign direct) in US, by industry group and world area, 1987-90, annual article, 2702–1.219

Investment (foreign direct) in US, by industry group of US affiliate and country of parent firm, 1980-86, 2708–41

Investment (foreign direct) of US, by industry group and world area, 1987-90, annual article, 2702–1.220

Iraq invasion of Kuwait, alien worker refugees fleeing from Iraq and Kuwait, intl aid by source, and costs to host and native countries, 1990-91, GAO rpt, 26123–326

Index by Subjects and Names

Excise tax

Loans and grants for economic and military aid from US and intl agencies, by program and country, FY46-90, annual rpt, 9914–5

Multinatl firms US affiliates, finances, and operations, by industry, world area of parent firm, and State, 1988-89, annual rpt, 2704–4

Multinatl US firms and foreign affiliates finances and operations, by industry and world area of parent firm, 1989 benchmark survey, preliminary annual rpt, 2704–5

Multinatl US firms foreign affiliates capital expenditures, by major industry group, world area, and country, 1986-91, semiannual article, 2702–1.207

Multinatl US firms foreign affiliates capital expenditures, by major industry group, world area, and country, 1987-91, semiannual article, 2702–1.222

Multinatl US firms foreign affiliates, income statement items by country and world area, 1986, biennial article, 8302–2.212

Oils, oilseeds, and meal imports, by commodity, world area of destination, and major producer, 1960s-88, 1528–314

Oranges (fresh) exports of US, demand indicators for 4 countries, with production, trade, and use, 1960s-90, 1528–317

Poultry products exports of US, EC, and 3 leading countries, by world area, 1986-90, semiannual rpt, 1925–33.1

Raisin and dried prune imports of EC, by country of origin and destination, 1989-90, tables, 1925–34.234

Raisin and prune production, trade, use, and stocks for EC and other countries, Turkey price supports, and Mexico production costs, 1985-91, annual article, 1925–34.250

Retirement age in EC under statutory social security programs, by sex and country, 1989, article, 4742–1.205

Rice production, trade, stocks, and use, by world region, country, and country group, 1966/67-1989/90, FAS circular, 1925–2.6

Science and engineering employment and education, and R&D spending, for US and selected foreign countries, 1991 annual rpt, 9627–35

Seed exports, by type, world region, and country, FAS quarterly rpt, 1925–13

Seignorage use for financing fiscal deficits in EC, with background data for EC, 1970s-88, working paper, 9387–8.238

Service industries exports and imports of US, direct and among multinatl firms affiliates, by industry and world area, 1986-90, article, 2702–1.223

Steel imports of US under voluntary restraint agreement, by product, customs district, and country, with US industry operating data, quarterly rpt, 9882–13

Tax (income) returns of corporations with foreign tax credit, income, and tax items, by country and world region of credit, 1986, biennial article, 8302–2.207

Telecommunications industry intl competitiveness, with financial and operating data by product or service, firm, and country, 1990 rpt, 2008–30

Textile imports under Multifiber Arrangement by product and country, and status of bilateral agreements, 1987-90, annual rpt, 9884–18

Tobacco trade of EC members, by country of origin and destination, 1989-90, annual article, 1925–16.215

European Space Agency

Activities, missions, launchings, payloads, and flight duration, for foreign and US space programs, 1957-90, annual rpt, 21704–4

Launchings of satellites and other space objects since 1957, quarterly listing, 9502 2

Private sector involvement in space programs, govt contracts, costs, revenue, and R&D spending, 1970s-80s and projected to 2000, 26306–6.154

Eutrophication

Coastal and estuarine environmental conditions, research results and methodology, series, 2176–7

Fish kills in coastal areas related to pollution and natural causes, by land use, State, and county, 1980s, 2178–32

Evanoff, Douglas D.

"Deregulation, Cost Economies and Allocative Efficiency of Large Commercial Banks", 9375–13.50

"Productive Efficiency in Banking", 9375–1.209

"Scale Elasticity and Efficiency for U.S. Banks", 9375–13.66

Evans, J. Albert

"Government Intervention in South Korean Agriculture", 1522–3.205

Evans, Roger W.

"Cost and Outcome Analysis of Kidney Transplantation. The Implications of Initial Immunosuppressive Protocol and Diabetes", 4658–59

Evansville, Ind.

see also under By City and By SMSA or MSA in the "Index by Categories"

Everett, Wash.

Housing vacancy rates for single and multifamily units and mobile homes, by city and ZIP code, 1991, annual MSA rpt, 9304–21.2

Evidence

Fingerprint files and other holdings of criminal record repositories, by State, 1989, 6068–241

Wiretaps authorized, costs, arrests, trials, and convictions, by offense and jurisdiction, 1990, annual rpt, 18204–7

Exceptional children

see Handicapped children

see Special education

Exchange of persons programs

Japan-US Friendship Commission educational and cultural exchange activities, grants, and trust fund status, FY89-90, biennial report, 14694–1

NIH intl program activities and funding, by inst and country, FY90, annual rpt, 4474–6

Participation in intl exchange and training programs, by world region, and funding, by Federal agency, FY89, annual rpt, 9854–8

see also Educational exchanges

Exchange rates

see Foreign exchange

Excise tax

Alcohol, Tobacco, and Firearms Bur regulatory activities, staff, and funding, and tax revenues and rates, 1980s-91, GAO rpt, 26119–335

Alcoholic beverages and tobacco production, removals, stocks, and material used, by State, monthly rpt series, 8486–1

Auto equipment excise taxes of Fed Govt and States, 1990, annual rpt, 7554–1

Autos with low gas mileage, Federal excise tax rates by model, and revenues, 1980s-90, annual rpt, 3304–5.3

Budget of US, authoritative financial statements with appropriations, outlays, and receipts, by category and agency, FY90, annual rpt, 8104–2.1

Budget of US, CBO analysis and review of FY92 budget by function, annual rpt, 26304–2

Budget of US, CBO analysis of revenue and spending alternatives and projections of economic indicators, FY92-96, annual rpt, 26304–3

Budget of US, CBO analysis of savings and revenues under alternative spending cuts and tax changes, projected FY92-97, 26306–3.118

Budget of US, midsession review of FY92 budget, by function, annual rpt, 104–7

Budget of US, obligations and authority by function, agency, and program, with summaries, analyses, and historical tables, FY92, annual rpt, 104–2

Budget of US, receipts by source, outlays by agency and program, and balances, monthly rpt, 8102–3

Coal excise tax and other black lung trust fund receipts, fund disbursements, and claims and benefits by State, 1990, annual rpt, 6504–3

Coal Surface Mining Reclamation and Enforcement Office activities and funding, by State and Indian tribe, FY90, annual rpt, 5644–1

Collections, enforcement, and litigation activity of IRS, with data by type of tax, region, and State, FY90, annual rpt, 8304–3

Competitiveness (intl) and taxation issues, with comparisons of US and foreign tax rates and revenue, 1988-91, press release, 8008–150

Energy producers finances and operations, by energy type for US firms domestic and foreign operations, 1989, annual rpt, 3164–44.1

Fed Govt consolidated financial statements based on business accounting methods, FY89-90, annual rpt, 8104–5

Fed Govt finances, cash and debt transactions, daily tables, 8102–4

Fed Govt internal revenue and refunds, by type of tax, quarterly rpt, 8302–2.1

Fed Govt receipts by source and outlays by agency, *Treasury Bulletin*, quarterly rpt, 8002–4.1

Fed Govt tax provisions and receipts overview, by tax type, with background data, 1900s-91 and projected to 2000, 21788–197

Fed Govt trust fund receipts, by source and fund, Budget of US, FY92, annual rpt, 104–9

Excise tax

Finances of govts, by level of govt, State, and for large cities and counties, annual rpt series, 2466–2

Finances of govts, tax systems and revenue, and fiscal structure, by level of govt and State, 1991 and historical trends, annual rpt, 10044–1

Fish and Wildlife Service restoration programs finances by State, and excise tax collections, FY90, annual rpt, 5504–13

Govt revenues by source, natl income and product accounts, *Survey of Current Business*, monthly rpt, 2702–1.25

Hazardous waste generation and disposal taxes, rates, and firms filing returns, by substance type, 1988, annual article, 8302–2.202

IRS collections, by excise tax source, quarterly rpt, 8302–1

Motorcycle operating costs by component, for 4 makes, and Fed Govt mileage reimbursement rates, 1989, annual rpt, 9454–13.3

Natl income and product accounts and components, *Survey of Current Business*, monthly rpt, 2702–1.24

New England States economic indicators, Fed Reserve 1st District, monthly rpt, 9373–2.5

Nonprofit charitable organizations finances, and revenue and investments of top 10 instns, 1986-87, article, 8302–2.210

Nonprofit charitable organizations finances, 1988, table, 8302–2.220

Oil import tariff and excise tax economic impacts, model description and results, 1991 paper, 9406–1.61

Railroad retirement system funding and benefits findings and recommendations, with background industry data, 1960s-90 and projected to 2060, 9708–1

Returns and supplemental documents filed, by type, FY89 and projected to FY98, annual article, 8302–2.208

Returns and supplemental documents filed, by type, FY90 and projected to FY99, semiannual rpt, 8302–4

Returns filed, accuracy of projections by return type, various periods 1983-90, article, 8304–8.1

Returns filed, by type of tax and IRS district, 1989 and projected 1990-97, annual rpt, 8304–24

Returns filed, by type of tax, region, and IRS service center, projected 1990-97 and trends from 1978, annual rpt, 8304–9

State and Metro Area Data Book, 1991 data compilation, 2328–54

Statistical Abstract of US, 1991 annual data compilation, 2324–1.9

Tobacco production, marketing, use, price supports, and trade, quarterly situation rpt with articles, 1561–10

Tobacco tariff and tax rates, and antismoking restrictions, by country, as of Jan 1991, article, 1925–16.207

Tobacco tax rates and receipts of Fed Govt and States, FY85-91, annual rpt, 1319–1.4

Transit systems finances and operations, by mode of transport, size of fleet, and for 468 systems, 1989, annual rpt, 7884–4

see also Fuel tax

see also Sales tax

see also Tolls

see also Windfall profit tax

Executive agreements

Bilateral and multilateral treaties and other agreements in force, by country, as of Jan 1991, annual listing, 7004–1

Executive clemency

see Pardons

Executive-congressional relations

see Congressional-executive relations

Executive departments

see Federal executive departments

Executive impoundment of appropriated funds

Rescissions and deferrals of budget authority, monthly rpt, 102–2

Executive Office of the President

Budget of US, authoritative financial statements with appropriations, outlays, and receipts, by category and agency, FY90, annual rpt, 8104–2.1

Budget of US, obligations and authority by function, agency, and program, with summaries, analyses, and historical tables, FY92, annual rpt, 104–2

Budget of US, receipts by source, outlays by agency and program, and balances, monthly rpt, 8102–3

see also Council of Economic Advisers

see also Council on Environmental Quality

see also National Security Council

see also Office of Management and Budget

see also Office of National Drug Control Policy

see also Office of Policy Development

see also Office of Science and Technology Policy

see also Office of the U.S. Trade Representative

see also Office of the Vice President

see also under names of individual Presidential commissions (starting with Presidential or President's)

Executives and managers

Aircraft (general aviation), flight hours, and equipment, by type, use, and model of aircraft, region, and State, 1990, annual rpt, 7504–29

Banks (Fed Reserve) and branch officers, staff, and salary, 1990, annual rpt, 9364–1.1

Educational attainment, by sociodemographic characteristics and location, 1989 and trends from 1940, biennial Current Population Rpt, 2546–1.452

Employment, unemployment, and labor force characteristics, by region, State, and selected metro area, 1990, annual rpt, 6744–7

Fed Govt civilian employment and payroll, by pay system, agency, and location, 1990, annual rpt, 9844–6

Fed Govt Senior Executive Service membership characteristics, entries, exits, and awards, FY79-90, annual rpt, 9844–36

Immigrants admitted to US, by occupational group and country of birth, preliminary FY90, annual table, 6264–1

Income (household, family, and personal), by source, detailed characteristics, and region, 1988-89, annual Current Population Rpt, 2546–6.68

Income (household, family, and personal), by source, detailed characteristics, and region, 1990, annual Current Population Rpt, 2546–6.70

Index by Subjects and Names

Leave for illness, disability, and dependent care, coverage, provisions, terminations, costs, and methods of covering for absent worker, by firm size, 1988 survey, 9768–21

Manufacturing employment, by detailed occupation and SIC 2-digit industry, 1989 survey, triennial rpt, 6748–52

Recruitment, hiring, compensation, and other employment practices of large firms, 1989 survey, GAO rpt, 26119–324

Savings instns failure resolution activity of Resolution Trust Corp, with assets and retained senior executives compensation, by instn, 1988-90, hearing, 21248–144

Savings instns failure resolution activity of Resolution Trust Corp, with instns assets and senior executive compensation, 1990, hearing, 21248–157

Savings instns fraud and abuse, Federal indictments and case dispositions, FY89-91, press release, 6008–33

Science and engineering PhDs employment and other characteristics, by field and State, 1989, biennial rpt, 9627–18

State Dept and Foreign Service minority and women employment, and hiring goals, FY89-90, biennial rpt, 7004–21

Steel industry finances, operations, and modernization efforts, with data on major companies and foreign industry, 1968-91, last issue of annual rpt, 9884–24

Unemployment insurance laws of States, comparison of provisions, 1991, base edition with semiannual revisions, 6402–2

see also Business management

see also Officials

Exercise

see Physical exercise

see Sports and athletics

Exhibitions and trade fairs

Business America, foreign and domestic commerce, and US investment and trade opportunities, biweekly journal, 2042–24

Travel to US, trade shows and other promotional activities, with magazine ad costs and circulation, for selected countries, 1991-92, annual rpt, 2904–11

Eximbank

see Export-Import Bank

Exploration, natural resources

see Energy exploration and drilling

see Mines and mineral resources

Explosives

Accident deaths and rates, by cause, age, sex, race, and State, 1988, US Vital Statistics annual rpt, 4144–2

Accidents (occupational) injury and illness rates by SIC 2- to 4-digit industry, and deaths by cause and industry div, 1989, annual rpt, 6844–1

Accidents involving consumer products, injuries by severity, victim age, and detailed product, 1990, annual rpt, 9164–6

Consumption of explosives and blasting agents, by type, industry, and State, 1990, Mineral Industry Surveys, annual rpt, 5614–22

County Business Patterns, 1988: employment, establishments, and payroll, by SIC 2- to 4-digit industry and county, annual State rpt series, 2326–6

County Business Patterns, 1989: employment, establishments, and payroll, by SIC 2- to 4-digit industry and county, annual State rpt series, 2326–8

Criminal sentences for Federal offenses, guidelines by offense and circumstances, series, 17668–1

Exports and imports of US, by country and detailed commodity, monthly rpt, 2422–12

Exports and imports of US, by Harmonized System 6-digit commodity and country, 1990, annual rpt, 2424–13

Exports and imports of US, by transport mode, country, and SITC 1- to 3-digit commodity, 1990, annual rpt, 2424–12

Exports of US, detailed Schedule B commodities with countries of destination, 1990, annual rpt, 2424–10

Fireworks (sparklers) from PRC at less than fair value, injury to US industry, investigation with background financial and operating data, 1991 rpt, 9886–14.315

Manufacturing annual survey, 1989: finances and operations, by SIC 2- to 4-digit industry, series, 2506–15

Manufacturing census, 1987: employment and shipments under Fed Govt contracts, by SIC 4-digit industry, 2497–7

Manufacturing census, 1987: finances and operations, by SIC 2- to 4-digit industry, State, and MSA, with trends from 1849, 2497–1

Manufacturing census, 1987: finances and operations, by type of organization and SIC 2- to 4-digit industry, subject rpt, 2497–5

OECD trade, total and for 4 major countries, and US trade by country, by commodity, 1970-89, world area rpt series, 9116–1

Price indexes (producer), by stage of processing and detailed commodity, monthly rpt, 6762–6

Price indexes (producer), by stage of processing and detailed commodity, monthly 1990, annual rpt, 6764–2

Regulatory activities, staff, and funding of Bur of Alcohol, Tobacco, and Firearms, and tax revenues and rates, 1980s-91, GAO rpt, 26119–335

Transport of hazardous material, accidents, casualties, and damage, by mode of transport, with DOT control activities, 1989, annual rpt, 7304–4

see also Ammunition

see also Bombs

see also Nuclear explosives and explosions

Export controls

see Tariffs and foreign trade controls

Export-Import Bank

Budget of US, authoritative financial statements with appropriations, outlays, and receipts, by category and agency, FY90, annual rpt, 8104–2.1

Budget of US, obligations and authority by function, agency, and program, with summaries, analyses, and historical tables, FY92, annual rpt, 104–2

Debt to US of foreign govts and private obligors, by country and program, periodic rpt, 8002–6

Financial condition of Eximbank, with credit and insurance authorizations and loan activity by country, FY90, annual rpt, 9254–1

Liabilities (contingent) and claims paid by Fed Govt on federally insured and guaranteed contracts with foreign obligors, by country and program, periodic rpt, 8002–12

Loans and grants for economic and military aid from US and intl agencies, by program and country, FY46-90, annual rpt, 9914–5

Loans of Eximbank, guarantees, and insurance authorizations, by country, FY89, annual rpt, 15344–1.12

Export processing zones

Mexico maquiladora plants impacts on trade with US, and outlook for North America free trade area proposal, 1990, 2048–153

US foreign trade zone operations and movement of goods, by zone and commodity, FY88, annual rpt, 2044–30

Export promotion

see Foreign trade promotion

Exports and imports

see Agricultural exports and imports

see Balance of payments

see Coal exports and imports

see East-West trade

see Energy exports and imports

see Foreign trade

see Motor vehicle exports and imports

see Natural gas exports and imports

see Petroleum exports and imports

see under names of specific commodities or commodity groups

Expositions

see Exhibitions and trade fairs

Expropriation of alien property

Claims against foreign govts by US natls, by claim type and country, 1990, annual rpt, 6004–16

Extension work

see Agricultural extension work

Exterminator services

see Pests and pest control

Extradition

Criminal cases by type and disposition, and collections, for US attorneys, by Federal district, FY90, annual rpt, 6004–2.1

Drug enforcement regional task forces investigation of organized crime, activities by agency and region, FY83-90, biennial rpt, 6004–17

Marshals Service activities, FY89, annual rpt, 6294–1

Exxon Corp.

Alaska oil spill from tanker Exxon Valdez, Federal cleanup and damage assessment costs, and reimbursement from Exxon, by agency, as of Sept 1990, GAO rpt, 26113–510

Alaska oil spill from tanker Exxon Valdez, impacts on marine mammals, and resulting legislation, 1990 annual rpt, 14734–1

Alaska oil spill from tanker Exxon Valdez, safety issues, with oil lost and crew alcohol and drug test results, 1989, 9618–17

Alaska oil spill from tanker Exxon Valdez, sea otter conservation measures, 1990 conf, 5508–110

Eye diseases and defects

Altitude effects on vision of aged and of glaucoma patients, 1991 technical rpt, 7506–10.80

Fair employment practices

Cancer cases, deaths, and survival rates, by sex, race, age, and body site, 1973-88, annual rpt, 4474–35

Cancer death rates of minorities, by body site, age, sex, and substate area, 1950s-80, atlas, 4478–78

Cases of acute and chronic conditions, disability, absenteeism, and health services use, by selected characteristics, 1987, CD-ROM, 4147–10.177

Deaths and rates, by detailed cause and demographic characteristics, 1988 and trends from 1900, US Vital Statistics annual rpt, 4144–2

Disabled persons and related activity limitation days and health services use, by health status, disability type, and other characteristics, 1984-88, 4146–8.202

Head Start handicapped enrollment, by handicap, State, and for Indian and migrant programs, 1987/88, annual rpt, 4604–1

HHS financial aid, by program, recipient, State, and city, FY90, annual regional listings, 4004–3

Injuries, related impairments, and activity limitations, by circumstances and victim characteristics, 1985-87, 4147–10.179

Pilots with aphakia and artificial lens implants, by sex, 1982-85, technical rpt, 7506–10.93

see also Blind

see also Optometry

see also under By Disease in the "Index by Categories"

Ezzati, Trena

"Office Visits to Dermatologists: National Ambulatory Medical Care Survey, U.S., 1975-76", 4147–16.4

"Office Visits to Ophthalmologists: National Ambulatory Medical Care Survey, U.S., 1976", 4147–16.4

"1977 Summary: National Ambulatory Medical Care Survey", 4147–16.5

FAA

see Federal Aviation Administration

Fabrics

see Synthetic fibers and fabrics

see Textile industry and fabrics

Factories

see Industrial plants and equipment

Factory closings

see Business failures and closings

Factory workers

see Production workers

Faculty

see Educational employees pay

see School administration and staff

see Teachers

Fagan, Jeffrey

"Violence as Regulation and Social Control in the Distribution of Crack", 4498–70

Fahim-Nader, Mahnaz

"Capital Expenditures by Majority-Owned Foreign Affiliates of U.S. Companies, Revised Estimates for 1991", 2702–1.222

"U.S. Business Enterprises Acquired or Established by Foreign Direct Investors in 1990", 2702–1.210

Fair employment practices

see Discrimination in employment

Fair housing

Fair housing
see Discrimination in housing

Fair Labor Standards Act
Admin of Act, with coverage under minimum wage and overtime provisions, and illegal employment of minors, by industry div, FY89, annual rpt, 6504–2.1
Minimum wage rates, 1938-91, annual rpt, 4744–3.1

Fairfax County, Va.
Fed Govt land acquisition and dev projects in DC metro area, characteristics and funding by agency and project, FY91-95, annual rpt, 15454–1

Fairfield, Calif.
see also under By SMSA or MSA in the "Index by Categories"

Fairlie, Gregory W.
"Donning Times and Flotation Characteristics of Infant Life Preservers: Four Representative Types", 7506–10.85

Fairs
see Exhibitions and trade fairs

Faith
see Clergy
see Missions and missionaries
see Religion
see Religious liberty
see Religious organizations

Falk, Edna
"Multifactor Productivity in Farm and Garden Equipment", 6722–1.232

Fall River, Mass.
see also under By SMSA or MSA in the "Index by Categories"

Fallout
see Nuclear explosives and explosions
see Radiation

Families and households
Alcohol abuse by family members and spouses, population exposure by selected characteristics, 1988, 4146–8.207
Alcohol use, knowledge, attitudes, and info sources of youth, series, 4006–10
American Housing Survey: inventory change from 1973, by reason, unit and household characteristics, and location, 1983, biennial rpt, 2485–14
American Housing Survey: unit and households characteristics, MSA fact sheet series, 2485–11
American Housing Survey: unit and households characteristics, unit and neighborhood quality, and journey to work by MSA location, for 11 MSAs, 1984 survey, supplement, 2485–8
American Housing Survey: unit and households detailed characteristics, and unit and neighborhood quality, MSA rpt series, 2485–6
American Housing Survey: unit and households detailed characteristics, and unit and neighborhood quality, 1987, biennial rpt, 2485–12; 2485–13
Births, fertility rates, and childless women, by selected characteristics, 1990, annual Current Population Rpt, 2546–1.455
Black Americans social and economic characteristics, for South and total US, 1989-90 and trends from 1969, Current Population Rpt, 2546–1.450
Black women's labor force status, employment by age and education, and women's and families earnings, 1980-90, fact sheet, 6564–1.2

Census of Population and Housing, 1990: housing units occupied and vacant, persons in group quarters, and household size, by region, census div, and State, press release, 2328–71
Census of Population and Housing, 1990: population and housing characteristics, households, and land area, by county, subdiv, and place, State rpt series, 2551–1
Census of Population and Housing, 1990: population and housing selected characteristics, by region, press release, 2328–74
Child health condition and services use, 1990 chartbook, 4108–49
Children and youth social, economic, and demographic characteristics, 1950s-90, 4818–5
Computer use at home, school, and work, by family income, 1989, fact sheet, 2326–17.30
Computer use at home, school, and work, by purpose and selected user characteristics, 1989, Current Population Rpt, 2546–2.158
Consumer Income, socioeconomic characteristics of persons, families, and households, detailed cross-tabulations, Current Population Rpt series, 2546–6
Court domestic relations caseloads for Federal district courts, 1990, annual rpt, 18204–8.13; 18204–8.18; 18204–11
Court domestic relations caseloads for Federal district courts, 1991, annual rpt, 18204–2.1
Crime victimization of households, by offense, household characteristics, and location, 1975-90, annual rpt, 6066–25.40
Crime victimization rates, by victim and offender characteristics, circumstances, and offense, 1988 survey, annual rpt, 6066–3.42
Crime victimization rates, by victim and offender characteristics, circumstances, and offense, 1989 survey, annual rpt, 6066–3.44
Current Housing Reports, unit and household characteristics, subject rpt series, 2486–1
Current Population Reports, historical index, 1991 listing, 2546–2.160
Disability, acute and chronic health conditions, absenteeism, and health services use, by selected characteristics, 1987, CD-ROM, 4147–10.177
Educational attainment, by sociodemographic characteristics and location, 1989 and trends from 1940, biennial Current Population Rpt, 2546–1.452
Educational performance and conditions, characteristics, attitudes, activities, and plans, 1988 8th grade class, natl longitudinal survey, series, 4826–9
Employment and Earnings, detailed data, monthly rpt, 6742–2.9
Employment and unemployment, by age, sex, race, marital and family status, industry div, and State, Monthly Labor Review, 6722–1.2
Enrollment, by grade, instn type and control, and student characteristics, 1989 and trends from 1947, annual Current Population Rpt, 2546–1.453

Family Economics Review, consumer goods prices and supply, and home economics, quarterly journal, 1702–1
Family relationships, living arrangements, and marital status, by selected characteristics, 1990, annual Current Population Rpt, 2546–1.449
Flow-of-funds accounts, savings, investments, and credit statements, quarterly rpt, 9365–3.3
Food aid programs of USDA, costs and participation by program, FY69-89, annual rpt, 1364–9
Food stamp eligibility and payment errors, by type, recipient characteristics, and State, FY89, annual rpt, 1364–15
Food stamp recipient household size, composition, income, and income and deductions allowed, summer 1988, annual rpt, 1364–8
Foreign countries family composition, poverty status, labor conditions, and welfare indicators and needs, by country, 1960s-88, hearing, 23846–4.30
Health care spending by businesses, households, and govts, 1965-89, article, 4652–1.230
Health, education, and welfare condition of children and families, findings and recommendations, 1991 rpt, 15528–1
High school class of 1972: education, employment, and family characteristics, activities, and attitudes, natl longitudinal study, series, 4836–1
Hispanic Americans in counties bordering Mexico, by selected characteristics, 1980, Current Population Rpt, 2546–2.159
Hispanic Americans social and economic characteristics, by detailed origin, 1991, Current Population Rpt, 2546–1.448; 2546–1.451
Home mortgages FHA-insured, financial, property, and mortgagor characteristics, by metro area, 1990, annual rpt, 5144–24
Home mortgages FHA-insured, financial, property, and mortgagor characteristics, by State, 1990, annual rpt, 5144–1
Home mortgages FHA-insured, financial, property, and mortgagor characteristics, total and by State and outlying area, 1990, annual rpt, 5144–25
Home mortgages FHA-insured, financial, property, and mortgagor characteristics, 1990, annual rpt, 5144–17; 5144–23
Homeless and runaway youth programs, funding, activities, and participant characteristics, FY90, annual rpt, 4604–3
Homeownership rates, by household type, householder age and sex, and location, 1960s-90, annual rpt, 2484–1.3
Hospices operations, services, costs, and patient characteristics, for instns without Medicare certification, FY85-86, 4658–52
Households and family characteristics, by location, 1990, annual Current Population Rpt, 2546–1.447
Households by tenure and population size, by age group, State, and county, 1980 and 1985, 2546–3.169
Housing affordability indicators, by household composition, income, and current tenure, 1988, 2486–1.11
Housing worst case problems prevalence and households characteristics, for poor

households with high rent, and substandard units, 1970s-84, annual rpt, 5184–10

Immigrant and nonimmigrant visas of US issued and refused, by class, issuing office, and nationality, FY89, annual rpt, 7184–1

Immigrants admitted to US, by class of admission and for top 15 countries of birth, FY89-90, fact sheet, 6266–2.4; 6266–2.8

Indian (Navajo and Hopi) relocation program activities and caseloads, 1975-90, 16008–5

Insurance (health) coverage of children, by source, family composition, income, and parent employment status, 1977 and 1987, 4186–8.14

Jail population, by criminal, correctional, drug use, and family history, and selected other characteristics, 1989, 6066–19.62

Jail population, by sociodemographic characteristics, criminal and drug use history, whether convicted, offense, and sentencing, 1989, annual rpt, 6064–26.3

Jail population drug abuse history, by offense, conviction status, criminal and family history, and selected other characteristics, 1989, 6066–19.63

Labor force status of family members and earnings, by family composition and race, quarterly press release, 6742–21

Labor force status of family members, monthly rpt, 6742–2.1

Mail volume to and from households, use, and views, by class, source, content, and household characteristics, 1987-88, annual rpt, 9864–10

Migrant workers and dependents by county, and health centers use and programs funding, by State, 1986-89, 4108–53

Older persons with functional limitations, long-term care sources, and health and other characteristics, 1984-85, 4147–13.104

Part-time employment by health insurance coverage and worker characteristics, and temporary and contract employment, 1979-89, GAO rpt, 26121–411

Population size and characteristics, 1969-88, Current Population Rpt, biennial rpt, 2546–2.161

Poverty rate among workers in metro and nonmetro areas, relation to employment and other characteristics, 1987, 1598–274

Poverty status by age group and living arrangements, and family poverty threshold, late 1930s-91, annual rpt, 4744–3.1

Poverty status of population and families, by detailed characteristics, 1988-89, annual Current Population Rpt, 2546–6.67

Poverty status of population and families, by detailed characteristics, 1990, annual Current Population Rpt, 2546–6.71

Puerto Rico population and housing characteristics, 1990 Census of Population and Housing, press release, 2328–78

Research on population and reproduction, Federal funding by project, FY89, annual listing, 4474–9

Research on population, family, and sexual behavior, activities and funding, 1960s-89, 4478–194

State and Metro Area Data Book, 1991 data compilation, 2328–54

Statistical Abstract of US, 1991 annual data compilation, 2324–1.1

Survey of Income and Program Participation, data collection, methodology, and use, 1990 annual conf papers, 2624–1

Survey of Income and Program Participation, household composition, income, benefits, and labor force status, methodology, working paper series, 2626–10

Survey of Income and Program Participation, household income and socioeconomic characteristics, special study series, 2546–20

Telephone service subscribership, charges, and local and long distance firm finances and operations, late 1970s-91, semiannual rpt, 9282–7

Travel patterns, personal and household characteristics, and auto and public transport use, 1990 survey, series, 7556–6

Travel patterns, personal and household characteristics, and auto use, 1990 survey, annual rpt, 7554–1.6

Virgin Islands population and housing characteristics, 1990 Census of Population and Housing, press release, 2328–81

Vocational rehabilitation cases of State agencies by disposition and applicant characteristics, and closures by reason, FY84-88, annual rpt, 4944–6

Wages of full- and part-time workers, by selected characteristics, quarterly press release, 6742–20

Women's labor force status, by age, race, and family status, quarterly rpt, 6742–17

Women's labor force status, earnings, and other characteristics, with comparisons to men, fact sheet series, 6564–1

see also Adoption

see also Aid to Families with Dependent Children

see also Child abuse and neglect

see also Child support and alimony

see also Child welfare

see also Children

see also Domestic violence

see also Family budgets

see also Family planning

see also Group quarters

see also Housing energy use

see also Living arrangements

see also Marriage and divorce

see also Maternity benefits

see also Military dependents

see also Parents

see also Personal and household income

see also Single parents

see also Unpaid family workers

see also Widows and widowers

Family budgets

Assets and debts of private sector, balance sheets by segment, 1945-90, semiannual rpt, 9365–4.1

Assets of households by type, and personal savings rate, 1970s-90, article, 1702–1.215

Assets of households, by type of holding and selected characteristics, 1988, Current Population Rpt, 2546–20.16

Child rearing costs of married couple households, by expenditure type, child's age, income, and region, 1990 and projected to 2007, 1708–87

Consumer Expenditure Survey, household income by source, and itemized spending, by selected characteristics and region, 1988-89, annual rpt, 6764–5

Economic indicators, prices, labor costs, and productivity, BLS econometric analyses and methodology, working paper series, 6886–6

Environmental protection programs costs to govts and households, by program type and city size, 1960s-88 and projected to 2000, 9188–114

Family Economics Review, consumer goods prices and supply, and home economics, quarterly journal, 1702–1

Food cost index alternative to CPI, by category, region, and household income, size, race, and food budget level, 1980-85, 1598–275

Food spending, by item, household composition, income, age, race, and region, 1980-88, Consumer Expenditure Survey biennial rpt, 1544–30

Health care charges relation to family health and sociodemographic characteristics, regression results, 1980, 4146–12.27

Higher education instn student aid and other sources of support, with student expenses and characteristics, by instn type and control, 1990 triennial study, series, 4846–5

Housing affordability and family income relation to housing costs, 1989 survey, fact sheet, 2326–17.33

Lower middle-class household income by source and spending by type, for 2-parent and single mother families by selected characteristics, 1987, article, 1702–1.207

Married couple families income and expenses, and wife's employment status, before and after having children, 1987-89, article, 1702–1.211

Married couple families with one spouse working, and income by source and expenses by type, by selected characteristics, 1987, article, 1702–1.201

Older persons migration to southern coastal areas, household finances, services needs, and local economic impacts, for selected counties, 1990, 2068–38

Older women's household income by source, and expenses by type, by living arrangement and other characteristics, 1988, article, 1702–1.210

Savings and Investment Incentive Act issues, with IRA participation and other background data, 1980s, 25368–175

Securities (govt) purchases and holdings of individuals and households, terms, and purchase methods, 1980s-90, 8008–148

Single parent families child rearing costs, by expense type and age of child, 1990, article, 1702–1.203

Student aid, costs, and income factors affecting access to undergrad education, 1990 rpt, 26306–6.153

Telephone local service charges and low-income subsidies, by region, company, and city, 1980s-90, semiannual rpt, 9282–8

Family budgets

Telephone service subscribership, charges, and local and long distance firm finances and operations, late 1970s-91, semiannual rpt, 9282–7

Youth employment impacts on family income, and expenses by type, with selected family characteristics, 1989, article, 1702–1.213

see also Personal consumption

Family income

see Personal and household income

see under By Income in the "Index by Categories"

Family planning

- Developing countries economic and social conditions from 1960s, and Intl Dev Cooperation Agency and AID activities and funding, FY90-92, annual rpt, 9904–4
- Developing countries family planning and population activities of AID, grants by project and recipient, and contraceptive shipments, by country, FY90, annual rpt series, 9914–13
- Health condition and health care resources, use, and spending, 1950s-89, annual data compilation, 4144–11
- Health condition improvement and disease prevention goals and recommended activities for 2000, with trends 1970s-80s, 4048–10
- HHS financial aid, by program, recipient, State, and city, FY90, annual regional listings, 4004–3
- Medicaid beneficiaries and payments, by service type, FY72-89, annual rpt, 4744–3.6
- Medicare and Medicaid beneficiaries and program operations, 1991, annual fact book, 4654–18
- Medicare and Medicaid eligibility, participation, coverage, and program finances, various periods 1966-91, biennial rpt, 4654–1
- Poor women's pregnancies, by whether intended, outcome, contraceptives use, marital status, and race, 1985-86 local area study, article, 4042–3.241
- Research on population and reproduction, Federal funding by project, FY89, annual listing, 4474–9
- Research on population and reproduction, Natl Inst of Child Health and Human Dev funding and activities, 1990, annual rpt, 4474–33
- Research on population, family, and sexual behavior, activities and funding, 1960s-89, 4478–194

see also Abortion

see also Contraceptives

see also Sex education

see also Sexual sterilization

Family Support Administration

- AFDC beneficiaries demographic and financial characteristics, by State, FY89, annual rpt, 4694–1
- Budget of US, obligations and authority by function, agency, and program, with summaries, analyses, and historical tables, FY92, annual rpt, 104–2
- Child Support Enforcement Program finances and operations, by State, FY85-89, annual rpt, 4694–6
- Energy aid for low income households, funding sources, costs, and participation, by State, FY89, annual rpt, 4694–8

Energy aid for low income households, program characteristics by State, FY90, annual rpt, 4694–9

- Expenditures of Fed Govt in States, by type, program, agency, and State, FY90, annual rpt, 2464–2
- Paternity determination through genetic testing, labs, services, and costs, 1991 listing, 4698–4
- Refugee aid funding of Fed Govt and States, impacts of reductions, with data by selected State and California county, late 1980s, GAO rpt, 26121–402
- Refugee arrivals and resettlement in US, by age, sex, sponsoring agency, State, and country, monthly rpt, 4692–2
- Refugee resettlement programs and funding, arrivals by country of origin, and indicators of adjustment, by State, FY90, annual rpt, 4694–5
- Research and evaluation programs of HHS, 1970-90, annual listing, 4004–30
- Teenage mothers child support awards, payment status, health insurance inclusion, and govt aid for collection, by selected characteristics, 1987, 4698–5

Famine

see Disasters

see Food supply

Fanning, Thomas

"Public Health Model of Medicaid Emergency Room Use", 4652–1.232

Fanning, William C.

"Singular Fact: The Single Audit Program Works", 10042–1.204

Fant, Mary L.

"Foreign Agricultural Trade of the U.S., 1989: Supplementary Tables", 1524–8

Fargo, N.Dak.

see also under By SMSA or MSA in the "Index by Categories"

Farley, Dean E.

"Case-Mix Specialization in the Market for Hospital Services", 4188–71

Farm costs

see Agricultural finance

see Agricultural production costs

Farm Costs and Returns Survey

- *Economic Indicators of the Farm Sector*, itemized production costs, receipts, and returns, by commodity and region, 1987-89, annual rpt, 1544–20
- Financial condition of farms, by commodity, 1987, series, 1566–8

Farm Credit Administration

- Budget of US, authoritative financial statements with appropriations, outlays, and receipts, by category and agency, FY90, annual rpt, 8104–2.1
- Budget of US, obligations and authority by function, agency, and program, with summaries, analyses, and historical tables, FY92, annual rpt, 104–2
- Farm Credit System financial statements and loan activity by lender type, and borrower characteristics, 1990, annual rpt, 9264–2
- Financial condition of Farm Credit System, quarterly rpt, 9262–2
- Financial statements of Farm Credit System banks, 1990, annual rpt, 9264–5

Farm Credit Banks

see Farm Credit System

Farm Credit System

- Budget of US, financial statements of federally sponsored enterprises, FY92, annual rpt, 104–2.5
- Business statistics, detailed data for major industries and economic indicators, *Survey of Current Business*, monthly rpt, 2702–1.9
- Cooperatives loans, assets, net worth, and assns, for FCS by district, 1989, annual rpt, 1124–1
- Delinquent borrowers aid services of Farm Credit System and FmHA, activities, with background data, 1989 hearings, 25168–74
- *Economic Indicators of the Farm Sector*, balance sheets, and receipts by detailed commodity, by State, 1985-89, annual rpt, 1544–18
- Financial condition and capital adequacy of govt-sponsored enterprises, with data by enterprise, 1970s-90 and projected to 1996, 26308–99
- Financial condition and capital adequacy of govt-sponsored enterprises, with impacts on Federal borrowing and data by enterprise, 1980s-90, last issue of annual rpt, 8004–15
- Financial condition and capital adequacy of govt-sponsored enterprises, with regulatory recommendations and data by enterprise, 1985-95, GAO rpt, 26119–296
- Financial condition of FCS, impacts of instn mergers, by district, 1982-89, 1548–381
- Financial condition of FCS, quarterly rpt, 9262–2
- Financial performance of FCS banks, before and after mergers, by district, 1986-89, article, 1541–1.205
- Financial statements and loan activity by lender type, and borrower characteristics, 1990, annual rpt, 9264–2
- Financial statements of FCS banks, 1990, annual rpt, 9264–5
- Flow-of-funds accounts, savings, investments, and credit statements, quarterly rpt, 9365–3.3
- Land transfers, by source of credit financing and region, 1982-91, article, 1561–16.202
- Loans (farm) by purpose and source, quarterly rpt, 9365–3.10
- Loans (farm) outstanding, and lenders financial condition, quarterly rpt with articles, 1541–1
- Loans (farm) outstanding, by lender, and farm and nonfarm banks and assets held, 1990 conf papers, 9368–90
- Loans (farm) outstanding, by lender type, 1990, annual rpt, 1544–16.2
- North Central States farm credit conditions and economic devs, Fed Reserve 7th District, monthly rpt, 9375–10

Farm debt

see Agricultural credit

see Agricultural finance

Farm income

- Acreage of farmland, and operations, by sales size, region, and State, 1989-91, annual rpt, 1614–4
- *Agricultural Outlook*, production, prices, marketing, and trade, by commodity, forecast and current situation, monthly rpt with articles, 1502–4

Index by Subjects and Names

Farm operators

Agricultural Statistics, 1990, annual rpt, 1004–1

Business statistics, detailed data for major industries and economic indicators, *Survey of Current Business*, monthly rpt, 2702–1.4

Census of Agriculture, 1987: farms, farmland, production, finances, and operator characteristics, by county, final State rpt series, 2331–1

Census of Agriculture, 1987: horticultural specialties producers, finances, and operations, by crop and State, 1988 survey, 2337–1

Corn farms, finances, acreage, and production, by size, region, and State, 1987, 1568–304

Data on agriculture, compilation, 1990 and trends from 1920, annual rpt, 1004–14

Data sources and adjustment factors of USDA for farm income estimates, with income by source, 1983-89, article, 1541–1.202

Distribution of farms, farmland, and sales, by sales size, various periods 1969-84, 1588–150

Economic and social conditions, dev, and problems in rural areas, periodic journal, 1502–7

Economic Indicators of the Farm Sector, balance sheets, and receipts by detailed commodity, by State, 1985-89, annual rpt, 1544–18

Economic Indicators of the Farm Sector, income, expenses, receipts by commodity, assets, and liabilities, 1990 and trends from 1945, annual rpt, 1544–16

Economic.Indicators of the Farm Sector, itemized production costs, receipts, and returns, by commodity and region, 1987-89, annual rpt, 1544–20

Farmline, agricultural situation and related topics, monthly rpt, 1502–6

Finances and operations of farm sector, 1970s-91, article, 9362–1.207

Finances of farms, debts, assets, and receipts, and lenders financial condition, quarterly rpt with articles, 1541–1

Financial and marketing conditions of farms, forecast 1991, annual chartbook, 1504–8

Financial and marketing conditions of farms, forecast 1991, annual conf, 1004–16

Financial condition of farms, by commodity, 1987, series, 1566–8

Financial condition of farms, 1920s-90, annual rpt, 204–1.8

Fish (catfish) raised on farms, production, inventory, imports, and prices, by State, as of Feb 1991, last issue of semiannual rpt, 1631–17

Fish (catfish) raised on farms, production, inventory, sales, prices, and imports, monthly release, 1631–14

Fish (trout) raised on farms, production, sales, prices, and losses, 1990-91, annual rpt, 1631–16

Fish hatcheries and farms, production, costs, prices, and sales, for catfish and trout, 1970s-91, semiannual situation rpt, 1561–15

Flower and foliage plant production, marketing, and trade by country, by State, 1960s-88, 1568–293

Flower and foliage plant production, sales, prices, and growers, by crop and State, 1989-90 and planting planned 1991, annual rpt, 1631–8

Flower and foliage plant production, trade, farms, acreage, and sales, for US by crop, with spending by country, 1987-90, article, 1502–4.201

Households (farm) income, by selected characteristics, 1988, article, 1541–1.207

Income (household, family, and personal), by source, detailed characteristics, and region, 1988-89, annual Current Population Rpt, 2546–6.68

Income (household, family, and personal), by source, detailed characteristics, and region, 1990, annual Current Population Rpt, 2546–6.70

Income (personal) per capita and by source, and earnings by industry div, by State, MSA, and county, 1984-89, annual regional rpts, 2704–2

Meat animal production, prices, receipts, and disposition, by species and State, 1988-90, annual rpt, 1623–8

Milk of manufacturing grade, fat content and prices received by farmers in Minnesota and Wisconsin, 1988-90, annual rpt, 1629–2

Milk production, use, and receipts, and milk cow inventory, by State, 1988-90, annual rpt, 1627–4

Mint oil production, yield, and farm prices by State, and NYC spot prices, various periods 1988-91, FAS annual circular, 1925–15.2

Mushroom production, sales, and prices, by State, 1966/67-1990/91 and planned 1991/92, annual rpt, 1631–9

Natl income and product accounts and components, *Survey of Current Business*, monthly rpt, 2702–1.24; 2702–1.25

North Central States farm credit conditions and economic devs, Fed Reserve 7th District, monthly rpt, 9375–10

North Central States farm credit conditions, earnings, and expenses, Fed Reserve 9th District, quarterly rpt, 9383–11

Potato production, acreage, disposition, prices, and trade, by State and country, 1949-90, 1568–305

Potato production, prices, stocks, and use, by State, 1981-90, annual rpt, 1621–11

Poultry (chicken, egg, and turkey) production and prices, by State, 1989-90, annual rpt, 1625–5

Poultry and egg prices and marketing, by selected region, State, and city, monthly and weekly 1990, annual rpt, 1317–2

Poverty status of population and families, by detailed characteristics, 1988-89, annual Current Population Rpt, 2546–6.67

Poverty status of population and families, by detailed characteristics, 1990, annual Current Population Rpt, 2546–6.71

Price support program changes and other effects on farm income and production, for livestock and program and nonprogram crop producers, model results, 1988, 1548–375

Prices (farm-retail) for food, marketing cost components, and industry finances and productivity, 1920s-90, annual rpt, 1544–9

Prices received and paid by farmers, by commodity and State, 1990, annual rpt, 1629–5

Prices received by farmers for major products, and paid for farm inputs and living items, by State, monthly rpt, 1629–1

Rice foreign and US production, prices, trade, stocks, and use, periodic situation rpt, 1561–8

Sales class relation to farm operator age and off-farm employment, sales, and land value changes, model description and results, 1974-78, 1548–374

Small farms loans, defaults, income, and financial condition, 1980-89, article, 1502–7.202

South Central States agricultural banks financial ratios, and farm receipts by commodity, 1980s-90, annual article, 9391–16.209

Southeastern States, Fed Reserve 5th District, economic indicators by State, quarterly rpt, 9389–16

Soviet Union GNP by detailed income and outlay component, 1985, 2326–18.59

State and Metro Area Data Book, 1991 data compilation, 2328–54

Statistical Abstract of US, 1991 annual data compilation, 2324–1.23

Survey of Current Business, detailed data for major industries and economic indicators, monthly rpt, 2702–1.5

Tax (income) returns filed by type of filer, selected income items, quarterly rpt, 8302–2.1

Tax (income) returns of corporations, income and tax items by asset size and detailed industry, 1987, annual rpt, 8304–4

Tax (income) returns of corporations, income and tax items by asset size and detailed industry, 1988, annual rpt, 8304–21

Tax (income) returns of individuals, selected income and tax items by income level, preliminary 1989, annual article, 8302–2.209

Tax (income) returns of partnerships, income statement and balance sheet items, by industry group, 1989, annual article, 8302–2.216; 8304–18

Tobacco marketing activity, prices, and sales, by grade, type, market, and State, 1989-90, annual rpt series, 1319–5

Tobacco production, prices, stocks, taxes by State, and trade and production by country, 1990, annual rpt, 1319–1

Vegetable production, prices, trade, stocks, and use, for selected fresh and processing crops, periodic situation rpt with articles, 1561–11

West Central States economic indicators, Fed Reserve 10th District, quarterly rpt, 9381–16.2

see also Agricultural production quotas and price supports

see also Agricultural subsidies

see also Agricultural wages

Farm labor

see Agricultural labor

see Agricultural wages

see Farm operators

see Migrant workers

Farm machinery

see Agricultural machinery and equipment

Farm operators

Census of Agriculture, 1987: farms, farmland, production, finances, and operator characteristics, by county, final State rpt series, 2331–1

Farm operators

Crop subsidies of USDA, farmers reorganizations to remain under payment limits, effectiveness of laws to prevent abuse, 1989, GAO rpt, 26113–546

Employment on farms, wages, and hours, by payment method, worker type, region, and State, 1910-90, 1618–21

Entries and exits of farm operators, by State, late 1970s-87, 1598–269

Financial stress indicators for farms, operator quits, and loan problems and mediation, 1970s-90, 1598–272

Great Lakes area economic conditions and outlook, for US and Canada, 1970s-90, 9375–15

Onion farm acreage, pesticide use, operators, and other characteristics, for 6 producer States, 1989, article, 1561–11.201

Part-time farming, selected characteristics of operation, 1987, young readers pamphlet, 2346–1.4

Pollution (groundwater) from farm chemicals use, with background data and farmers views, 1970s-80s, hearing, 25168–76

Sales class relation to farm operator age and off-farm employment, sales, and land value changes, model description and results, 1974-78, 1548–374

State and Metro Area Data Book, 1991 data compilation, 2328–54

Statistical Abstract of US, 1991 annual data compilation, 2324–1.23

Yearbook of Agriculture, special topics, 1990 annual compilation of papers, 1004–18

Farm population

Agricultural Statistics, 1990, annual rpt, 1004–1

Births, fertility rates, and childless women, by selected characteristics, 1990, annual Current Population Rpt, 2546–1.455

Black Americans social and economic characteristics, for South and total US, 1989-90 and trends from 1969, Current Population Rpt, 2546–1.450

Data on agriculture, compilation, 1990 and trends from 1920, annual rpt, 1004–14

Data on agriculture, young readers pamphlet series, 2346–1

Hispanic Americans social and economic characteristics, by detailed origin, 1991, Current Population Rpt, 2546–1.448; 2546–1.451

Housing and households detailed characteristics, and unit and neighborhood quality, by location, 1987, biennial rpt supplement, 2485–13

Housing and households detailed characteristics, and unit and neighborhood quality, by location, 1989, biennial rpt, 2485–12

Population on farms, employment, and labor productivity, 1947-89, annual rpt, 204–1.8

Population size and characteristics, historical index to *Current Population Rpts*, 1991 listing, 2546–2.160

Population size and characteristics, 1969-88, Current Population Rpt, biennial rpt, 2546–2.161

Rural areas economic and social conditions, dev, and problems, periodic journal, 1502–7

Statistical Abstract of US, 1991 annual data compilation, 2324–1.23

Western US activities of Reclamation Bur, land and population served, and recreation areas, by location, 1989, annual rpt, 5824–12

see also Farm operators

Farm prices

see Agricultural prices

see Food prices

Farmers Home Administration

Activities of FmHA, and loans and grants by program and State, FY90 and trends from FY70, annual rpt, 1184–17

American Housing Survey: unit and households detailed characteristics, and unit and neighborhood quality, MSA rpt series, 2485–6

American Housing Survey: unit and households detailed characteristics, and unit and neighborhood quality, 1987, biennial rpt, 2485–12

Borrowers, by loan type, borrower characteristics, and State, quarterly rpt, 1182–8

Borrowers, by loan type, race, and State, quarterly rpt, 1182–5

Budget of US, obligations and authority by function, agency, and program, with summaries, analyses, and historical tables, FY92, annual rpt, 104–2

Delinquent borrowers aid services of Farm Credit System and FmHA, activities, with background data, 1989 hearings, 25168–74

Economic Indicators of the Farm Sector, balance sheets, and receipts by detailed commodity, by State, 1985-89, annual rpt, 1544–18

Expenditures of Fed Govt in States, by type, program, agency, and State, FY90, annual rpt, 2464–2

Field offices, funding, and staff of USDA subagencies responsible for farm programs, FY89, GAO rpt, 26113–507

Housing loan programs of FmHA in rural areas, and housing voucher demonstration program results, 1980s, hearing, 21248–143

Housing units (1-family) sold and sales price by type of financing, monthly rpt, quarterly tables, 2382–3.2

Housing units completed, single and multifamily units by structural and financial characteristics, inside-outside MSAs, and region, 1986-90, annual rpt, 2384–1

Loan appeals for FmHA farm and rural housing programs in 3 States, 1988-90, GAO rpt, 26113–516

Loan servicing for FmHA loans, eligibility, use, and effects on borrowers solvency, 1988-89, GAO rpt, 26113–497

Loans (farm) by purpose and source, quarterly rpt, 9365–3.10

Loans (farm) outstanding, and lenders financial condition, quarterly rpt with articles, 1541–1

Loans (farm) outstanding, by lender, and farm and nonfarm banks and assets held, 1990 conf papers, 9368–90

Loans (farm) outstanding, by lender type, 1990, annual rpt, 1544–16.2

Loans (farm and home) and borrower supervision activities, for FmHA programs, by State, monthly rpt, 1182–1

Loans of FmHA, guaranteed and direct program costs under alternative assumptions, 1981-89, 1598–273

Mortgage applications by disposition, and secondary loan market sales by purchaser type, by applicant and neighborhood characteristics, 1990, article, 9362–1.206

Property acquired by Fed Govt through foreclosure and savings instn failure, 1-family homes inventory by State, acquisition costs, and sales, for 4 agencies, 1986-90, GAO rpt, 26113–513

Property acquired by FmHA through foreclosure, value, acreage, and sales, for farm and nonfarm property by State, monthly rpt, 1182–6

Property acquired by FmHA through foreclosure, value, and acreage under conservation easements by State, 1989-90, GAO rpt, 26113–514

Property acquired by FmHA through foreclosure, 1-family homes, value, sales, and leases, by State, monthly rpt, 1182–7

Farming

see Farm income

see Farm operators

see Farm population

see Farms and farmland

see under Agriculture and terms beginning with Agricultural

see under By Industry in the "Index by Categories"

see under By Occupation in the "Index by Categories"

Farms and farmland

Acreage of farmland, and operations, by sales size, region, and State, 1989-91, annual rpt, 1614–4

Acreage of farmland used for export crops, 1972-89, annual rpt, 1924–9

Acreage of land, by use, ownership, and State, 1987 and trends from 1910, 1588–48

Acreage of non-Federal land by use, soil and water conditions, and conservation needs, 1987, State rpt series, 1266–5

Acreage planted and harvested, by crop and State, 1989-90 and planned as of June 1991, annual rpt, 1621–23

Acreage planted, by selected crop and State, 1982-90 and planned 1991, annual rpt, 1621–22

Acreage, production, and related data, by selected crop and State, monthly rpt, 1621–1

Agricultural Economics Research, quarterly journal, 1502–3

Agricultural Outlook, production, prices, marketing, and trade, by commodity, forecast and current situation, monthly rpt with articles, 1502–4

Agricultural Statistics, 1990, annual rpt, 1004–1

Australia agricultural input and output indexes, and freight rates, 1950s-80s, 1528–311

Census of Agriculture, 1987: farms, farmland, production, finances, and operator characteristics, by county, final State rpt series, 2331–1

Coastal and riparian areas environmental conditions, fish, wildlife, use, and mgmt, for individual ecosystems, series, 5506–9

Conservation program of USDA, participation and payments by practice and State, FY90, annual rpt, 1804–7

Index by Subjects and Names

Fast food

Construction industries census, 1987: establishments, employment, receipts, and expenditures, by SIC 4-digit industry and State, final industry rpt series, 2373–1

Construction put in place (public and private), by type, bimonthly rpt, 2042–1.1

Construction put in place, value of new public and private structures, by type, monthly rpt, 2382–4

Corn farms, finances, acreage, and production, by size, region, and State, 1987, 1568–304

Data on agriculture, compilation, 1990 and trends from 1920, annual rpt, 1004–14

Data on agriculture, young readers pamphlet series, 2346–1

Developing countries agricultural supply, demand, and market for US exports, with socioeconomic conditions, country rpt series, 1526–6

Distribution of farms, farmland, and sales, by sales size, various periods 1969-84, 1588–150

Economic and social conditions, dev, and problems in rural areas, periodic journal, 1502–7

Economic Indicators of the Farm Sector, balance sheets, and receipts by detailed commodity, by State, 1985-89, annual rpt, 1544–18

Economic Indicators of the Farm Sector, income, expenses, receipts by commodity, assets, and liabilities, 1990 and trends from 1945, annual rpt, 1544–16

Economic Indicators of the Farm Sector, production inputs, output, and productivity, by commodity and region, 1947-89, annual rpt, 1544–17

Environmental Quality, status of problems, protection programs, research, and intl issues, 1991 annual rpt, 484–1

Environmental regulation proposals impacts on fertilizer and cropland demand, model description and inputs, 1964-89, 1588–152

Farm production, marketing, trade, food consumption, and nutrition programs, annual chartbook, discontinued, 1504–3

Fed Govt-owned real property inventory and costs, worldwide summary by purpose, agency, and location, 1989, annual rpt, 9454–5

Flower and foliage plant production, marketing, and trade by country, by State, 1960s-88, 1568–293

Flower and foliage plant production, sales, prices, and growers, by crop and State, 1989-90 and planting planned 1991, annual rpt, 1631–8

Flower and foliage plant production, trade, farms, acreage, and sales, for US by crop, with spending by country, 1987-90, article, 1502–4.201

Foreign countries agricultural production, prices, and trade, by country, 1980-90 and forecast 1991, annual world area rpt series, 1524–4

Foreign countries agricultural production, trade, and policies, summary data by country, 1989-90, annual factbook, 1924–12

Foreign countries economic, social, political, and geographic summary data, by country, 1991, annual factbook, 9114–2

Foreign ownership of US farmland, holdings, acquisitions, and disposals by land use, owner type and country, and State, 1990, annual rpt, 1584–2

Foreign ownership of US farmland, holdings, acreage, and value by land use, owner country, State, and county, 1990, annual rpt, 1584–3

Forest Service mgmt of public lands and resources dev, environmental, economic, and social impacts of alternative programs, projected to 2040, 1208–24

Grain storage facility and equipment loans to farmers under CCC program, by State, FY68-91, annual table, 1804–14

Great Lakes area economic conditions and outlook, for US and Canada, 1970s-90, 9375–15

Hogs inventory, value, farrowings, and farms, by State, quarterly release, 1623–3

Mink and pelt production, prices, and farms, selected years 1969-91, annual rpt, 1631–7

North Carolina timber acreage, resources, and removals, by species, ownership class, and county, 1989/90, series, 1206–4

North Central States farm credit conditions and farmland market values, Fed Reserve 9th District, quarterly rpt, 9383–11

Pollution (groundwater) from farm chemicals use and animal wastes, and reduction strategies, 1960s-90, 26358–231

Potato production, acreage, disposition, prices, and trade, by State and country, 1949-90, 1568–305

Puerto Rico economic censuses, 1987: wholesale and retail trade sales by customer class, and employment, by SIC 2- and 3-digit kind of business, subject rpt, 2591–2.2

Pumpkin farms, production costs, shipments, and sales by State, prices, and imports by country, 1978-90, article, 1561–11.203

Real estate assets of failed thrifts, inventory of properties available from Resolution Trust Corp, 1990, semiannual listing, 9722–2.9

Real estate assets of failed thrifts, inventory of properties available from Resolution Trust Corp, 1991, semiannual listing, 9722–2.15

Rental of farmland by assessment method, and rent receipts per acre and as share of land value by land type and State, 1960s-80s, 1548–377

Research (agricultural) funding and staffing for USDA, State agencies, and other instns, by topic, FY90, annual rpt, 1744–2

Rice farms, by size and full-time status of operator, for US and major producer State, 1982 and 1987, article, 1561–8.205

Sheep, lamb, and goat inventory, by State, 1989-91, annual press release, 1623–4

Southwestern States farm credit conditions and real estate values, Fed Reserve 11th District, quarterly rpt, 9379–11

Soviet Union agricultural reform issues, with background data for USSR and US, 1970s-90, article, 9381–1.210

State and Metro Area Data Book, 1991 data compilation, 2328–54

Statistical Abstract of US, 1991 annual data compilation, 2324–1.23

Storage facility and equipment loans to farmers under CCC grain program, by State, monthly table, 1802–9

Value and transfers of farmland, production inputs, finances, and mgmt, periodic situation rpt with articles, 1561–16

Value of farmland, relation to farm sales class, model description and results, 1974-78, 1548–374

Water pollution from farming, funding for control under Rural Clean Water Program by region and State, monthly rpt, 1802–14

West Central States farm real estate values, farm loan trends, and regional farm price index, Fed Reserve 10th District, quarterly rpt, 9381–16.1

Wetlands acreage, resources, soil and water properties, and conservation efforts, by wetland type, State rpt series, 5506–11

Wholesale trade census, 1987: establishments, sales by customer class, employment, inventories, and expenses, by SIC 2- to 4-digit kind of business, 2407–4

see also Agricultural accidents and safety
see also Agricultural commodities
see also Agricultural credit
see also Agricultural education
see also Agricultural energy use
see also Agricultural exports and imports
see also Agricultural extension work
see also Agricultural finance
see also Agricultural forecasts
see also Agricultural insurance
see also Agricultural labor
see also Agricultural machinery and equipment
see also Agricultural marketing
see also Agricultural policy
see also Agricultural prices
see also Agricultural production
see also Agricultural production costs
see also Agricultural production quotas and price supports
see also Agricultural productivity
see also Agricultural sciences and research
see also Agricultural stocks
see also Agricultural subsidies
see also Agricultural surpluses
see also Agricultural wages
see also Farm income
see also Farm operators
see also Farm population
see also Farmers Home Administration
see also Fertilizers
see also Irrigation
see also Pasture and rangeland
see also Pesticides
see also Soil pollution
see also Soils and soil conservation
see also under By Industry in the "Index by Categories"

Faroe Islands

Fish (salmon) farms, production, and exports of Faroe Islands, 1980-86 with projections to 1990, 2162–1.201

Farrar, C. D.

"Hydrologic and Geochemical Monitoring in Long Valley Caldera, Mono County, Calif., 1986", 5666–27.7

Fast food

see Restaurants and drinking places

Fast Response Survey System

Fast Response Survey System
Data collection activities and programs of NCES, 1991, annual listing, 4824–7

Fats and oils
see Oils, oilseeds, and fats

Fayette County, Ky.
Wages by occupation, for office and plant workers, 1991 survey, periodic MSA rpt, 6785–3.10
see also under By SMSA or MSA in the "Index by Categories"

Fayetteville, Ark.
see also under By SMSA or MSA in the "Index by Categories"

Fayetteville, N.C.
Wages by occupation, and benefits for office and plant workers, 1991 survey, periodic labor market rpt, 6785–3.9
see also under By SMSA or MSA in the "Index by Categories"

Fazzari, Steven
"Investment Smoothing with Working Capital: New Evidence on the Impact of Financial Constraints", 9375–13.49

FBI
see Federal Bureau of Investigation

FCC
see Federal Communications Commission

FDA
see Food and Drug Administration

Federal advisory bodies
see Federal boards, committees, and commissions

Federal agencies
see Federal boards, committees, and commissions
see Federal executive departments
see Federal independent agencies
see under By Federal Agency in the "Index by Categories"

Federal agencies fraud, waste, and abuse investigations
see Federal Inspectors General reports

Federal aid programs
Assistance (financial and nonfinancial) of Fed Govt, 1991 base edition with supplements, annual listing, 104–5
Budget of US, authoritative financial statements with appropriations, outlays, and receipts, by category and agency, FY90, annual rpt, 8104–2.1
Budget of US, balances of budget authority obligated and unobligated, by function and agency, FY90-92, annual rpt, 104–8
Budget of US, CBO analysis and review of FY92 budget by function, annual rpt, 26304–2
Budget of US, CBO analysis of revenue and spending alternatives and projections of economic indicators, FY92-96, annual rpt, 26304–3
Budget of US, CBO analysis of savings and revenues under alternative spending cuts and tax changes, projected FY92-97, 26306–3.118
Budget of US, House Budget Committee analysis of Bush Admin proposals and economic assumptions, FY92, 21268–42
Budget of US, House concurrent resolution, with spending and revenue targets, FY92 and projected to FY96, annual rpt, 21264–2
Budget of US, midsession review of FY92 budget, by function, annual rpt, 104–7

Budget of US, object class analysis of obligations, by agency, FY92, annual rpt, 104–9
Budget of US, obligations and authority by function, agency, and program, with summaries, analyses, and historical tables, FY92, annual rpt, 104–2
Budget of US, receipts by source, outlays by agency and program, and balances, monthly rpt, 8102–3
Budget of US, Senate concurrent resolution, with spending and revenue targets, FY92, annual rpt, 25254–1
Criminal cases by type and disposition, and collections, for US attorneys, by Federal district, FY90, annual rpt, 6004–2.1
Expenditures of Fed Govt, by function, FY89, annual rpt, 2466–2.2
Expenditures of Fed Govt in States and local areas, by type, State, county, and city, FY90, annual rpt, 2464–3
Expenditures of Fed Govt in States, by type, program, agency, and State, FY90, annual rpt, 2464–2
Finances of Fed Govt, cash and debt transactions, daily tables, 8102–4
Financial consolidated statements of Fed Govt based on business accounting methods, FY89-90, annual rpt, 8104–5
Insurance and credit programs actual and potential losses, by program, 1991 article, 9381–1.207
Investigations of Federal agency and program operations, summaries of findings, 1981-90, annual GAO rpt, 26104–5
Labor productivity of Federal employees, indexes of output and labor costs by function, 1967-89, annual rpt, 6824–1.6
Loans and loan guarantees of Fed Govt, outstanding amounts by agency and program, *Treasury Bulletin*, quarterly rpt, 8002–4.9
Loans, loan guarantees, and insurance programs of Fed Govt, outstanding amounts by agency and program, FY88-90, GAO rpt, 26111–65
State and Metro Area Data Book, 1991 data compilation, 2328–54
Statistical Abstract of US, 1991 annual data compilation, 2324–1.9
see also Agricultural credit
see also Agricultural production quotas and price supports
see also Agricultural subsidies
see also Agricultural surpluses
see also Aid to Families with Dependent Children
see also Child welfare
see also Community Development Block Grants
see also Federal aid to arts and humanities
see also Federal aid to education
see also Federal aid to higher education
see also Federal aid to highways
see also Federal aid to housing
see also Federal aid to law enforcement
see also Federal aid to libraries
see also Federal aid to local areas
see also Federal aid to medical education
see also Federal aid to medicine
see also Federal aid to railroads
see also Federal aid to rural areas
see also Federal aid to States

see also Federal aid to transportation
see also Federal aid to vocational education
see also Federal funding for energy programs
see also Federal funding for research and development
see also Federally Funded R&D Centers
see also Food assistance
see also Food stamp programs
see also Government and business
see also Head Start Project
see also Income maintenance
see also Legal aid
see also Manpower training programs
see also Medicaid
see also Medical assistance
see also Medicare
see also Old-Age, Survivors, Disability, and Health Insurance
see also Public housing
see also Public service employment
see also Public welfare programs
see also Rent supplements
see also Revenue sharing
see also School lunch and breakfast programs
see also Shipbuilding and operating subsidies
see also Social security
see also Student aid
see also Subsidies
see also Supplemental Security Income
see also Tax expenditures
see also Unemployment insurance
see also Urban Development Action Grants
see also Veterans benefits and pensions
see also Veterans health facilities and services
see also Veterans housing

Federal aid to agriculture
see Agricultural credit
see Agricultural production quotas and price supports
see Agricultural subsidies
see Agricultural surpluses
see Federal aid to rural areas

Federal aid to arts and humanities
Assistance (financial and nonfinancial) of Fed Govt, 1991 base edition with supplements, annual listing, 104–5
Budget of US, obligations and authority by function, agency, and program, with summaries, analyses, and historical tables, FY92, annual rpt, 104–2
Education Dept programs funding, operations, and effectiveness, FY90, annual rpt, 4804–5
Expenditures of Fed Govt in States, by type, program, agency, and State, FY90, annual rpt, 2464–2
Kennedy Center for Performing Arts and Natl Symphony Orchestra financial statements, and capital and maintenance costs and needs, 1970s-90, hearing, 21648–62
Museum Services Inst activities and finances, and grants by recipient, FY90, annual rpt, 9564–7
Natl Endowment for Arts activities and grants, FY90, annual rpt, 9564–3
Natl Endowment for Humanities activities and grants, FY90, annual rpt, 9564–2
Statistical Abstract of US, 1991 annual data compilation, 2324–1.7

Index by Subjects and Names

Federal aid to business
see Government and business
see Subsidies

Federal aid to cities
see Federal aid to local areas

Federal aid to education

Appalachia local dev projects, and funding by source, by program and State, FY90, annual rpt, 9084–1

Arts Natl Endowment activities and grants, FY90, annual rpt, 9564–3

Asbestos in buildings, EPA aid for removal, occupational asbestos exposure cancer cases and deaths, and Catholic schools abatement costs, 1985-90, hearing, 25328–32

Assistance (financial and nonfinancial) of Fed Govt, 1991 base edition with supplements, annual listing, 104–5

Bilingual education enrollment, and Education Dept activities and funding by program, by State, FY88-90, biennial rpt, 4804–14

Bilingual education programs enrollment, funding, and services, by State, FY85-89, series, 4808–20

Budget of US, balances of budget authority obligated and unobligated, by function and agency, FY90-92, annual rpt, 104–8

Budget of US, CBO analysis and review of FY92 budget by function, annual rpt, 26304–2

Budget of US, formula grant program obligations to State and local govts, by agency, program, and State, FY92, annual rpt, 104–30

Budget of US, House concurrent resolution, with spending and revenue targets, FY92 and projected to FY96, annual rpt, 21264–2

Budget of US, obligations and authority by function, agency, and program, with summaries, analyses, and historical tables, FY92, annual rpt, 104–2

Budget of US, receipts by source, outlays by agency and program, and balances, monthly rpt, 8102–3

Child and family health, education, and welfare condition, findings and recommendations, 1991 rpt, 15528–1

Compensatory education programs in high poverty school districts, Federal grant program activities, participation, and coordinators views, 1989/90, 4808–32

Construction put in place, by type of construction, bimonthly rpt, 2042–1.1

Digest of Education Statistics, 1991 annual data compilation, 4824–2

Drug abuse and trafficking reduction programs activities, funding, staff, and Bush Admin budget request, by Federal agency and program area, FY90-92, 238–2

Drug abuse and trafficking reduction programs funding, and Bush Admin budget request, by Federal agency and program area, FY90-92, 238–1

Education Dept financial aid programs, 1991 annual listing, 4804–3

Education Dept programs funding, operations, and effectiveness, FY90, annual rpt, 4804–5

Elementary and secondary public school systems enrollment, finances, staff, and high school grads, by State, FY88-89, annual rpt, 4834–6

Elementary and secondary public schools, enrollment, teachers, funding, and other characteristics, by region and State, 1988/89, annual rpt, 4834–20

Expenditures for education by Federal agency, program, and recipient type, and instn spending, FY80-90, annual rpt, 4824–8

Expenditures for public welfare by program, FY50s-88, annual article, 4742–1.209

Expenditures for public welfare programs, by program type and level of govt, FY65-88, annual article, 4742–1.202

Expenditures of Fed Govt in States, by type, program, agency, and State, FY90, annual rpt, 2464–2

Finances of Fed Govt, cash and debt transactions, daily tables, 8102–4

Finances of govts, by level of govt, State, and for large cities and counties, annual rpt series, 2466–2

Finances of govts, tax systems and revenue, and fiscal structure, by level of govt and State, 1991 and historical trends, annual rpt, 10044–1

Fraud and abuse in Education Dept programs, audits and investigations, 2nd half FY91, semiannual rpt, 4802–1

Handicapped children early education project descriptions, 1990/91, annual listing, 4944–10

Homeless adults educational services, funding, participation, and staff, by State, 1989, annual rpt series, 4804–39

Homeless children educational projects, activities, and funding, FY90, annual rpt, 4804–35

Homeless persons aid programs of Fed Govt, program descriptions and funding, by agency and State, FY87-90, annual GAO rpt, 26104–21

Humanities Natl Endowment activities and grants, FY90, annual rpt, 9564–2

Immigrant children education programs funding by Fed Govt and school districts, and student characteristics, 1980s, GAO rpt, 26121–418

Indian education funding of Fed Govt, and enrollment, degrees, and program grants and fellowships by State, late 1960s-FY89, annual rpt, 14874–1

Labor productivity of Federal employees, indexes of output and labor costs by function, 1967-89, annual rpt, 6824–1.6

Lands (public) acreage and grants, by State, FY90 and trends, annual rpt, 5724–1.1

Literacy programs in workplaces, demonstration projects funding and participant characteristics, FY88, 4808–37

Literacy programs in workplaces, Education Dept funding and project descriptions, FY90, annual listing, 4804–40

Mail operating costs of USPS, itemized by class of mail, FY90, annual rpt, 9864–4

Mail revenue, costs, and volume, by class of mail, FY90, annual rpt, 9864–2

Mail volume, revenues, and subsidies for revenue forgone, by class of mail, FY90, annual rpt, 9864–5.3

Natl Education Goals progress indicators, by State, 1991, annual rpt, 15914–1

NSF activities, finances, and funding by program, FY90, annual rpt, 9624–6

Pacific territories economic conditions, population characteristics, and Federal aid, 1989 hearing, 21448–44

Refugee resettlement programs and funding, arrivals by country of origin, and indicators of adjustment, by State, FY90, annual rpt, 4694–5

Science and math teacher dev project funding of Fed Govt, participation, operations, and effectiveness, 1985-90, 4808–31

Science, engineering, and math education grants of NSF, by recipient and level, FY89, biennial listing, 9624–27

Special education programs, enrollment by age, staff, funding, and needs, by type of handicap and State, 1989/90, annual rpt, 4944–4

State and Metro Area Data Book, 1991 data compilation, 2328–54

Statistical Abstract of US, 1991 annual data compilation, 2324–1.4

Surplus personal property of Fed Govt donated to govt and nonprofit agencies, with data by State, FY88-90, biennial rpt, 9454–22

Tax expenditures, Federal revenues forgone through income tax deductions and exclusions by type, FY92-96, annual rpt, 21784–10

see also Federal aid to higher education
see also Federal aid to medical education
see also Federal aid to vocational education
see also Head Start Project
see also School lunch and breakfast programs
see also Student aid
see also Veterans education

Federal aid to energy programs
see Federal funding for energy programs

Federal aid to higher education

Agricultural research funding and staffing for USDA, State agencies, and other instns, by topic, FY90, annual rpt, 1744–2

AID and higher education instns collaboration on aid projects, and funding, by purpose and world region, 1960s-89, 26358–247

Alcohol, Drug Abuse and Mental Health Admin research grants and awards, by recipient, FY90, annual listing, 4044–13

Assistance (financial and nonfinancial) of Fed Govt, 1991 base edition with supplements, annual listing, 104–5

Assistance for higher education instns and students, tuition and other costs, impacts on enrollment, and cost containment methods, 1970s-90 and projected to 2001, 4808–25

Black higher education instns finances, funding sources, enrollment, and student characteristics, with data for Louisiana instns, 1970s-90, hearing, 25258–24

Budget of US, obligations and authority by function, agency, and program, with summaries, analyses, and historical tables, FY92, annual rpt, 104–2

Digest of Education Statistics, 1991 annual data compilation, 4824–2

DOD prime contract awards, by category, contractor type, and State, FY88-90, annual rpt, 3544–11

DOD prime contract awards for R&D, for top 500 contractors, FY90, annual listing, 3544–4

Federal aid to higher education

DOD prime contract awards for R&D to US and foreign nonprofit instns and govt agencies, by instn and location, FY90, annual listing, 3544–17

DOE contracts and grants, by category, State, and for top contractors, FY90, annual rpt, 3004–21

DOE R&D projects and funding at natl labs, universities, and other instns, periodic summary rpt series, 3004–18

Education Dept programs funding, operations, and effectiveness, FY90, annual rpt, 4804–5

Engineering research and education grants of NSF, FY90, annual listing, 9624–24

Expenditures for education by Federal agency, program, and recipient type, and instn spending, FY80-90, annual rpt, 4824–8

Expenditures for higher education instn support, by Federal program and instn type and control, FY86-89, annual rpt, 4804–28

Expenditures of Fed Govt in States, by type, program, agency, and State, FY90, annual rpt, 2464–2

Finances, enrollment, faculty, and degrees in higher education, by instn level and control, and State, FY87, annual rpt, 4844–13

Finances of higher education instns, revenue by source and spending by function, by State and instn control, FY80-88, annual rpt, 4844–6

Govt-sponsored enterprises financial condition and capital adequacy, with data by enterprise, 1970s-90 and projected to 1996, 26308–99

Govt-sponsored enterprises financial condition, capital adequacy, and impacts on Federal borrowing, with data by enterprise, 1980s-90, last issue of annual rpt, 8004–15

HHS financial aid, by program, recipient, State, and city, FY90, annual regional listings, 4004–3

Higher education instn tuition relation to other instn financial indicators, by instn control, 1960s-88, 4808–24

Humanities Natl Endowment activities and grants, FY90, annual rpt, 9564–2

Libraries technological aid, project descriptions and funding, FY89, annual listing, 4874–6

NASA funding by program and type of performer, and contract awards by State, FY90, annual rpt, 9504–6.2

NASA procurement contract awards, by type, contractor, State, and country, FY91 with trends from 1961, semiannual rpt, 9502–6

NASA R&D funding to higher education instns, by field, instn, and State, FY90, annual listing, 9504–7

Navy research grants, by recipient type, FY90, annual rpt, 3804–13.3

NIH activities, funding by program and recipient type, staff, and clinic patients, by inst, FY90, annual rpt, 4434–3

NIH grants and contracts, by inst and type of recipient, FY81-90, annual rpt, 4434–9

NSF grants and contracts, by field, instn, and State, FY89, annual rpt, 9624–26

NSF R&D grant awards, by div and program, periodic rpt series, 9626–7

NSF research grants to predominantly undergrad instns, by NSF div, and principal investigator sex and race, FY88, 9628–85

Oil enhanced recovery research contracts of DOE, project summaries, funding, and bibl, quarterly rpt, 3002–14

R&D and related funding of Fed Govt to higher education and nonprofit instns, by field, instn, agency, and State, FY89, annual rpt, 9627–17

R&D equipment of higher education instns, acquisition and service costs, condition, and financing, by field and subfield, 1988-90, triennial survey series, 9627–27

R&D facilities for biological and medical sciences, space and equipment adequacy, needs, and funding by source, by instn type, 1990, biennial rpt, 4434–17

R&D funding by Fed Govt, by field, performer type, agency, and State, FY89-91, annual rpt, 9627–20

R&D funding by higher education instns and federally funded centers, by field, instn, and State, FY89, annual rpt, 9627–13

Science and engineering academic research system status, R&D performance, and Fed Govt support, 1950s-88 with trends and projections, 9628–83

Science, engineering, and math education grants of NSF, by recipient and level, FY89, biennial listing, 9624–27

State and Metro Area Data Book, 1991 data compilation, 2328–54

Urban Mass Transportation Admin research and training grants to higher education instns, by project, FY90, annual listing, 7884–7

see also Federal aid to medical education

see also Student aid

see also Veterans education

see also Work-study programs

Federal aid to highways

Allocation of Federal hwy funds, provisions by agency and program, as of Jan 1991, biennial rpt, 7554–37

Appalachia hwy system and access roads funding and completion status, by State, quarterly tables, 9082–1

Appalachia local dev projects, and funding by source, by program and State, FY90, annual rpt, 9084–1

Assistance (financial and nonfinancial) of Fed Govt, 1991 base edition with supplements, annual listing, 104–5

Bridges repair and replacement needs under alternative assessment methods, 1990 and projected to 1996, GAO rpt, 26113–539

Census of Population data use in Federal formula grant allocation, and effects of data errors on funding, with data by program and State, FY91, GAO rpt, 26119–361

Construction (hwy) minority contractor training, funding by region, FY91, annual release, 7554–40

Construction bids and contracts for Federal-aid hwys, by State, 1st half 1991, semiannual rpt, 7552–12

Construction material prices and indexes for Federal-aid hwy system, by type of material and urban-rural location, quarterly rpt, 7552–7

Index by Subjects and Names

Construction material prices and indexes for Federal-aid hwy system, by type of material, quarterly press release, 7552–16

Construction material use by type, and spending for hwys, by State, various periods 1944-90, annual rpt, 7554–29

Construction put in place, by type of construction, bimonthly rpt, 2042–1.1

Construction spending by Fed Govt, by program and type of structure, FY85-92, annual article, 2042–1.206

Credit subsidies for public works, proposed replacement for direct Federal grants, with background data by project type, FY88, 26306–3.113

Expenditures and regulation for surface transportation by Fed Govt and States, FY91 with projections to FY96, 26358–242

Expenditures, condition, mgmt, and R&D for transportation and environmental public works, 1986-91, 26358–235

Expenditures, costs, and completion status of Federal-aid hwy system, by State, as of June 1991, semiannual rpt, 7552–5

Expenditures of Fed Govt, by function, FY89, annual rpt, 2466–2.2

Expenditures of Fed Govt in States, by type, program, agency, and State, FY90, annual rpt, 2464–2

FHwA funding and inspection activity, FY88, annual rpt, 7304–1

Finances of govts, tax systems and revenue, and fiscal structure, by level of govt and State, 1991 and historical trends, annual rpt, 10044–1

Forest Service acreage, staff, finances, and mgmt activities in Pacific Northwest, with data by forest, 1970s-89, annual rpt, 1204–37

Forest Service activities and finances, by region and State, FY90, annual rpt, 1204–1.1

Forest Service timber sales, expenses, and operations, by region, State, and natl forest, FY90, annual rpts, 1204–36

Hwy Statistics, detailed data by State, 1990, annual rpt, 7554–1

Hwy Statistics, summary data by State, 1989-90, annual rpt, 7554–24

Hwy Trust Fund finances, unobligated balances by State, and receipt losses from increased ethanol use, 1980s-90, hearing, 25328–31

Hwy Trust Fund revenues, tax rates, and spending, FY87-91 with projections to FY95, GAO rpt, 26113–544

R&D for hwy design and construction, quarterly journal, 7552–3

Safety program funding by State, and accident and death reductions, FY90, annual rpt, 7554–26

State and Metro Area Data Book, 1991 data compilation, 2328–54

State govt revenue by source, spending and debt by function, and holdings, FY90, annual rpt, 2466–2.6

States hwy projects involving FHwA funds, demonstration project results, FY88-90, GAO rpt, 26113–471

Traffic safety grants and activities of Natl Hwy Traffic Safety Admin, and fatal traffic accident data, 1989, annual rpt, 7764–1

Index by Subjects and Names

Trust funds financial condition, for hwys, monthly rpt, 8102–9.7

Federal aid to housing

- Apartment units completed, by type and for units under Federal subsidy, 1970-89, annual rpt, 2484–2
- Apartment units completed under Federal subsidy, 1970-90, annual rpt, 2484–3
- Appalachia local dev projects, and funding by source, by program and State, FY90, annual rpt, 9084–1
- Assistance (financial and nonfinancial) of Fed Govt, 1991 base edition with supplements, annual listing, 104–5
- Assistance programs under Ways and Means Committee jurisdiction, finances, operations, and participant characteristics, FY70s-90, annual rpt, 21784–11
- Budget of US, balances of budget authority obligated and unobligated, by function and agency, FY90-92, annual rpt, 104–8
- Budget of US, CBO analysis and review of FY92 budget by function, annual rpt, 26304–2
- Budget of US, formula grant program obligations to State and local govts, by agency, program, and State, FY92, annual rpt, 104–30
- Budget of US, House concurrent resolution, with spending and revenue targets, FY92 and projected to FY96, annual rpt, 21264–2
- Budget of US, midsession review of FY92 budget, by function, annual rpt, 104–7
- Budget of US, obligations and authority by function, agency, and program, with summaries, analyses, and historical tables, FY92, annual rpt, 104–2
- Budget of US, Senate concurrent resolution, with spending and revenue targets, FY92, annual rpt, 25254–1
- Community Dev Block Grant activities and funding, by program, FY75-90, annual rpt, 5124–8
- Construction put in place, by type of construction, bimonthly rpt, 2042–1.1
- Construction spending by Fed Govt, by program and type of structure, FY85-92, annual article, 2042–1.206
- Expenditures for public welfare by program, FY50s-88, annual article, 4742–1.209
- Expenditures for public welfare programs, by program type and level of govt, FY65-88, annual article, 4742–1.202
- Expenditures of Fed Govt in States, by type, program, agency, and State, FY90, annual rpt, 2464–2
- Finances of govts, by level of govt, State, and for large cities and counties, annual rpt series, 2466–2
- FmHA farm and rural housing program loan appeals filed in 3 States, by disposition, 1988-90, GAO rpt, 26113–516
- Fraud and abuse in HUD programs, audits and investigations, FY91, semiannual rpt, 5002–8; 5002–11
- Fraud and abuse in HUD programs, financial and program mgmt improvement activities, 1990, annual rpt, 5004–9
- Govt Natl Mortgage Assn finances, and mortgage-backed securities program, FY90, annual rpt, 5144–6
- Govt-sponsored enterprises financial condition and capital adequacy, with data by enterprise, 1970s-90 and projected to 1996, 26308–99

Govt-sponsored enterprises financial condition, capital adequacy, and impacts on Federal borrowing, with data by enterprise, 1980s-90, last issue of annual rpt, 8004–15

- Homeless aid organizations donations of surplus Federal property by State, and compared to other recipients, FY87-80, GAO rpt, 26113–538
- Homeless persons aid programs of Fed Govt, program descriptions and funding, by agency and State, FY87-90, annual GAO rpt, 26104–21
- Homeless persons housing and food aid of Fed Govt, funding and operations, with data by State and county, FY89, hearing, 25408–111
- Homelessness issues, population at risk, contributing factors, and Federal funding for services and prevention, with bibl, 1991 compilation of papers, 25928–9
- HUD activities, and housing programs operations and funding, 1989, annual rpt, 5004–10
- Indian (Navajo and Hopi) relocation program activities and caseloads, monthly rpt, 16002–1
- Indian (Navajo and Hopi) relocation program activities and caseloads, 1975-90, 16008–5
- Loans and loan guarantees of Fed Govt, outstanding amounts by agency and program, *Treasury Bulletin*, quarterly rpt, 8002–4.9
- Low income housing construction and repair loans of HUD to nonprofit organizations, project delays, and starts, 1980s, GAO rpt, 26113–506
- Poor households with high rent, and substandard units, worst case problems prevalence and households characteristics, 1970s-84, annual rpt, 5184–10
- Rehabilitation of rental housing, HUD funding and activities by program and region, FY90, annual rpt, 5124–7
- Repossession of housing units under Federal programs, inventory by agency, 1989, 8608–7
- Rural areas housing loan programs of FmHA, and housing voucher demonstration program results, 1980s, hearing, 21248–143
- Tax credits for low income housing dev, and units constructed, by selected project and State, 1987-89, hearings, 25248–120
- Tax expenditures, Federal revenues forgone through income tax deductions and exclusions by type, FY92-96, annual rpt, 21784–10

see also Farmers Home Administration
see also Housing (FHA), HUD
see also Mortgages
see also Public housing
see also Rent supplements
see also Veterans housing

Federal aid to law enforcement

- Alcohol, Tobacco, and Firearms Bur regulatory activities, staff, and funding, and tax revenues and rates, 1980s-91, GAO rpt, 26119–335
- Asset Forfeiture Program of Justice Dept, seizures, finances, and disbursements, FY86-90, annual rpt, 6004–21
- Asset forfeiture programs of Justice Dept and Customs Service, finances, and disbursements by State and judicial district, FY85-90, hearing, 25408–112

Assistance (financial and nonfinancial) of Fed Govt, 1991 base edition with supplements, annual listing, 104–5

- Budget of US, CBO analysis and review of FY92 budget by function, annual rpt, 26304–2
- Budget of US, formula grant program obligations to State and local govts, by agency, program, and State, FY92, annual rpt, 104–30
- Budget of US, House concurrent resolution, with spending and revenue targets, FY92 and projected to FY96, annual rpt, 21264–2
- Budget of US, midsession review of FY92 budget, by function, annual rpt, 104–7
- Budget of US, obligations and authority by function, agency, and program, with summaries, analyses, and historical tables, FY92, annual rpt, 104–2
- Budget of US, receipts by source, outlays by agency and program, and balances, monthly rpt, 8102–3
- Budget of US, Senate concurrent resolution, with spending and revenue targets, FY92, annual rpt, 25254–1
- Criminal justice system workload impacts of budgetary changes, model description, 1991 GAO rpt, 26119–340
- Drug abuse and trafficking reduction grant programs and funding, by Federal agency and State, FY90-92, 236–1.5
- Drug abuse and trafficking reduction programs activities, funding, staff, and Bush Admin budget request, by Federal agency and program area, FY90-92, 238–2
- Drug abuse and trafficking reduction programs funding, and Bush Admin budget request, by Federal agency and program area, FY90-92, 238–1
- Drug abuse treatment, prevention, and enforcement grants to States, by Federal agency and State, FY87-91, 236–1.4
- Drug control task forces enforcement activities by drug type and State, and organization, staff, and spending, 1988, 6068–244
- Drug enforcement regional task forces investigation of organized crime, activities by agency and region, FY83-90, biennial rpt, 6004–17
- Drug enforcement support activities of Natl Guard, spending and needs by State, FY89-91, GAO rpt, 26123–343
- Drug smuggling interdiction programs, budget, and seizures of Fed govt, FY87-90, GAO rpt, 26119–318
- Employment, payroll, and spending for criminal justice, by level of govt, State, and selected city and county, FY71-88, annual rpt, 6064–9
- Employment, payroll, and spending for criminal justice, by level of govt, State, and selected city and county, 1984-86, biennial rpt, 6064–4
- Expenditures and employment for law enforcement, by activity and level of govt, data compilation, 1991 annual rpt, 6064–6.1
- Expenditures of Fed Govt in States, by type, program, agency, and State, FY90, annual rpt, 2464–2
- Juvenile delinquency prevention funding, by program and Federal agency, annual rpt, discontinued, 6064–11

Federal aid to law enforcement

Marijuana crop eradication activities of DEA and local agencies by State, and drug potency and prices, 1982-90, annual rpt, 6284–4

Marine mammals protection activities and funding, populations, and harvests, by species, 1989, annual rpt, 5504–12

Marshals Service activities, FY89, annual rpt, 6294–1

Money laundering enforcement activities of IRS, staff, and funding, abatement, 1985-90, GAO rpt, 26123–338

Money laundering investigation network of Treasury Dept, funding, and staff detailed from other agencies, 1990-91, GAO rpt, 26119–330

Office of Justice Programs activities and funding, FY90, annual rpt, 6064–18

Prison construction and operating costs, capacity, and inmates, for Federal and State facilities, 1985-89, GAO rpt, 26119–341

Surplus personal property of Fed Govt donated to govt and nonprofit agencies, with data by State, FY88-90, biennial rpt, 9454–22

Victims of crime, compensation and support service applications by disposition, and grant funding by State, 1986-91, GAO rpt, 26119–348

Wildlife protection enforcement activities, funding, costs, and staff of Fish and Wildlife Service, late 1970s-90, GAO rpt, 26113–525

Federal aid to libraries

Agricultural research and education appropriations of USDA, by program and subagency, FY82-90, annual rpt, 1004–19

Assistance (financial and nonfinancial) of Fed Govt, 1991 base edition with supplements, annual listing, 104–5

Blind and disabled persons library services, readership, circulation, staff, funding, and holdings, FY90, annual listing, 26404–3

Budget of US, formula grant program obligations to State and local govts, by agency, program, and State, FY92, annual rpt, 104–30

Education Dept programs funding, operations, and effectiveness, FY90, annual rpt, 4804–5

English as second language programs and services of public libraries, project descriptions and funding, by State, FY87, annual rpt, 4874–10

Expenditures for education by Federal agency, program, and recipient type, and instn spending, FY80-90, annual rpt, 4824–8

HHS financial aid, by program, recipient, State, and city, FY90, annual regional listings, 4004–3

Humanities Natl Endowment activities and grants, FY90, annual rpt, 9564–2

Libraries (public) finances, staff, and operations, by State and population size, 1989, annual rpt, 4824–6

Mail operating costs of USPS, itemized by class of mail, FY90, annual rpt, 9864–4

Mail revenue and subsidy for revenue forgone, by class of mail, FY90, and volume from FY86, annual rpt, 9864–1

Mail revenue, costs, and volume, by class of mail, FY90, annual rpt, 9864–2

Mail volume, revenues, and subsidies for revenue forgone, by class of mail, FY90, annual rpt, 9864–5.2; 9864–5.3

Natl Archives and Records Admin activities, finances, holdings, and staff, FY90, annual rpt, 9514–2

Natl Commission on Libraries and Info Science activities, FY90, annual rpt, 15634–1

NIH grants and contracts, quarterly listing, 4432–1

NIH grants for R&D, training, construction, and medical libraries, by location and recipient, FY90, annual listings, 4434–7

NIH Natl Library of Medicine activities, holdings, and grants, FY88-90, annual rpt, 4464–1

NIH Research Resources Center activities and funding, by program, FY90, annual rpt, 4434–12

Technological aid to libraries, project descriptions and funding, FY89, annual listing, 4874–6

Training in library science, grants for disadvantaged students, by instn and State, FY90, annual listing, 4874–1

Urban resource libraries dev projects and funding, by city and State, FY84-88, listing, 4878–4

Federal aid to local areas

Appalachian Regional Commission funding, by project and State, planned FY91, annual rpt, 9084–3

Arts Natl Endowment activities and grants, FY90, annual rpt, 9564–3

Asbestos in buildings, EPA aid for removal, occupational asbestos exposure cancer cases and deaths, and Catholic schools abatement costs, 1985-90, hearing, 25328–32

Assistance (financial) of Fed Govt to State and local govts, by program, budget function, and agency, FY90, GAO rpt, 26121–421

Assistance (financial and nonfinancial) of Fed Govt, 1991 base edition with supplements, annual listing, 104–5

Budget of US, House Budget Committee analysis of Bush Admin proposals and economic assumptions, FY92, 21268–42

Budget of US, midsession review of FY92 budget, by function, annual rpt, 104–7

Budget of US, obligations and authority by function, agency, and program, with summaries, analyses, and historical tables, FY92, annual rpt, 104–2

Census of Population, 1990: cities population and undercounts, and related Federal aid losses, 1990 mayoral survey, hearing, 25408–113

Drug abuse and trafficking reduction programs activities, funding, staff, and Bush Admin budget request, by Federal agency and program area, FY90-92, 238–2

Economic Dev Admin activities, and funding by program, recipient, State, and county, FY90 and cumulative from FY66, annual rpt, 2064–2

Economic indicators and components, current data and annual trends, monthly rpt, 23842–1.6

Education Dept programs funding, operations, and effectiveness, FY90, annual rpt, 4804–5

Index by Subjects and Names

Education funding by Federal agency, program, and recipient type, and instn spending, FY80-90, annual rpt, 4824–8

Environmental protection programs costs to govts and households, by program type and city size, 1960s-88 and projected to 2000, 9188–114

EPA pollution control grant program activities, monthly rpt, 9182–8

Expenditures of Fed Govt in States and local areas, by type, State, county, and city, FY90, annual rpt, 2464–3

Expenditures of Fed Govt in States, by type, program, agency, and State, FY90, annual rpt, 2464–2

Finances of govts, by level of govt, State, and for large cities and counties, annual rpt series, 2466–2

HHS financial aid, by program, recipient, State, and city, FY90, annual regional listings, 4004–3

Homeless persons aid programs of Fed Govt, program descriptions and funding, by agency and State, FY87-90, annual GAO rpt, 26104–21

Homeless persons housing and food aid of Fed Govt, funding and operations, with data by State and county, FY89, hearing, 25408–111

Housing (rental) rehabilitation funding and activities of HUD, by program and region, FY90, annual rpt, 5124–7

Indian (Navajo and Hopi) relocation program activities and caseloads, monthly rpt, 16002–1

Indian (Navajo and Hopi) relocation program activities and caseloads, 1975-90, 16008–5

Indian education funding of Fed Govt, and enrollment, degrees, and program grants and fellowships by State, late 1960s-FY89, annual rpt, 14874–1

Labor surplus areas eligible for preferential Fed Govt contracts, monthly listing, 6402–1

Land and Water Conservation Fund allocations for outdoor recreation area dev, by State, FY91, annual table, 5544–15

Lands (public) acreage, grants, use, revenues, and allocations, by State, FY90, annual rpt, 5724–1.3

Lands (public), Fed Govt payments to local govts in lieu of property taxes, by State and county, FY91, annual rpt, 5724–9

Loans and loan guarantees of Fed Govt, outstanding amounts by agency and program, *Treasury Bulletin*, quarterly rpt, 8002–4.9

R&D funding by Fed Govt, by field, performer type, agency, and State, FY89-91, annual rpt, 9627–20

State and Metro Area Data Book, 1991 data compilation, 2328–54

Surplus personal property of Fed Govt donated to govt and nonprofit agencies, with data by State, FY88-90, biennial rpt, 9454–22

Timber industry impacts of northern spotted owl conservation in Pacific Northwest, and local govts Federal payments and severance taxes, 1980s and projected to 2000, hearing, 21168–50

Transit systems finances and operations, by mode of transport, size of fleet, and for 468 systems, 1989, annual rpt, 7884–4

Index by Subjects and Names

Transit systems grants of Urban Mass Transportation Admin, by city and State, FY90, annual rpt, 7884–10

Urban areas park and recreation facilities rehabilitation funding, by city and State, FY91, press release, 5306–4.7

Wastewater treatment facilities construction grants of EPA to State and local govts, by project, monthly listing, 9202–3

see also Community Development Block Grants

see also Federal aid to rural areas

see also Revenue sharing

see also Urban Development Action Grants

Federal aid to medical education

- Alcohol, Drug Abuse and Mental Health Admin research grants and awards, by recipient, FY90, annual listing, 4044–13
- Allergy and Infectious Diseases Natl Inst activities, grants by recipient and location, and disease cases, FY83-90, annual rpt, 4474–30
- Assistance (financial and nonfinancial) of Fed Govt, 1991 base edition with supplements, annual listing, 104–5
- Budget of US, obligations and authority by function, agency, and program, with summaries, analyses, and historical tables, FY92, annual rpt, 104–2
- Dental Research Natl Inst research and training grants, by recipient, FY89, annual listing, 4474–19
- Health Care Policy and Research Agency grants, by recipient and location, FY90, 4186–9.10
- Heart, Lung, and Blood Natl Inst activities, and grants by recipient and location, FY90 and disease trends from 1940, annual rpt, 4474–15
- HHS financial aid, by program, recipient, State, and city, FY90, annual regional listings, 4004–3
- Military health care personnel, and accessions by training source, by occupation, specialty, and service branch, FY89, annual rpt, 3544–24
- Neurological Disorders and Stroke Natl Inst activities, and disorder cases, FY90, annual rpt, 4474–25
- NIH activities, funding by program and recipient type, staff, and clinic patients, by inst, FY90, annual rpt, 4434–3
- NIH grants and contracts, by inst and type of recipient, FY81-90, annual rpt, 4434–9
- NIH grants for R&D, training, construction, and medical libraries, by location and recipient, FY90, annual listings, 4434–7
- R&D and related funding of Fed Govt to higher education and nonprofit instns, by field, instn, agency, and State, FY89, annual rpt, 9627–17
- Science and engineering grad enrollment, by field, source of funds, and characteristics of student and instn, 1975-89, annual rpt, 9627–7

Federal aid to medicine

- AIDS virus antibody tests and counseling sessions by setting, and CDC funding and funds uncommitted by State, 1989-90, GAO rpt, 26121–428
- Alcohol abuse research, treatment programs, and patient characteristics and health effects, quarterly journal, 4482–1

Alcohol, Drug Abuse and Mental Health Admin research grants and awards, by recipient, FY90, annual listing, 4044–13

- Allergy and Infectious Diseases Natl Inst activities, grants by recipient and location, and disease cases, FY83-90, annual rpt, 4474–30
- Assistance (financial and nonfinancial) of Fed Govt, 1991 base edition with supplements, annual listing, 104–5
- Budget of US, CBO analysis and review of FY92 budget by function, annual rpt, 26304–2
- Budget of US, CBO analysis of savings and revenues under alternative spending cuts and tax changes, projected FY92-97, 26306–3.118
- Budget of US, House concurrent resolution, with spending and revenue targets, FY92 and projected to FY96, annual rpt, 21264–2
- Budget of US, obligations and authority by function, agency, and program, with summaries, analyses, and historical tables, FY92, annual rpt, 104–2
- Budget of US, receipts by source, outlays by agency and program, and balances, monthly rpt, 8102–3
- Cancer Natl Inst activities, grants by recipient, and cancer deaths and cases, FY90 and trends, annual rpt, 4474–13
- Cancer Natl Inst epidemiology and biometry activities, FY90, annual rpt, 4474–29
- Child and family health, education, and welfare condition, findings and recommendations, 1991 rpt, 15528–1
- Child Health and Human Dev Natl Inst contracts and grants, annual listing, discontinued, 4474–36
- Construction put in place, by type of construction, bimonthly rpt, 2042–1.1
- Construction spending by Fed Govt, by program and type of structure, FY85-92, annual article, 2042–1.206
- Dental Research Natl Inst research and training grants, by recipient, FY89, annual listing, 4474–19
- Developing countries family planning and population activities of AID, grants by project and recipient, and contraceptive shipments, by country, FY90, annual rpt series, 9914–13
- Diabetes research and care services programs and funding, by Federal agency and NIH inst, FY90, annual rpt, 4474–34
- Disabled persons rehabilitation, Federal and State activities and funding, FY90, annual rpt, 4944–1
- Drug abuse and treatment research summaries, and resource materials and grant listings, periodic rpt, 4492–4
- Drug abuse treatment, prevention, and enforcement grants to States, by Federal agency and State, FY87-91, 236–1.4
- Drug and alcohol abuse treatment and prevention programs of States, funding, facilities, and patient characteristics, FY89, 4488–15
- Drug and alcohol abuse treatment facilities, services, use, funding, staff, and client characteristics, 1989, biennial rpt, 4494–10
- Drug and alcohol abuse treatment services, funding, staffing, and client load, characteristics, and outcomes, by setting, 1989 conf, 4498–73

Federal aid to medicine

- Expenditures for health care by businesses, households, and govts, 1965-89, article, 4652–1.230
- Expenditures for health care, by service type, payment source, and sector, projected 1990-2000 and trends from 1965, article, 4652–1.251
- Expenditures for health care, by service type, payment source, and sector, 1960s-90, annual article, 4652–1.221; 4652–1.252
- Expenditures for health care by type and payment source, with background data and foreign comparisons, 1960s-80s and projected to 2000, 26308–98
- Expenditures for health care, cost containment methods, and insurance coverage issues, with background data, 1991 rpt, 26306–6.155
- Expenditures for public welfare by program, FY50s-88, annual article, 4742–1.209
- Expenditures of Fed Govt in States, by type, program, agency, and State, FY90, annual rpt, 2464–2
- FDA activities, funding, facilities, and staff, findings and recommendations, 1980s-91, 4008–115
- Finances of govts, by level of govt, State, and for large cities and counties, annual rpt series, 2466–2
- Fraud and abuse in HHS programs, audits and investigations, 1st half FY91, semiannual rpt, 4002–6
- Health Care Financing Admin research activities and grants, by program, FY90, annual listing, 4654–10
- Health Care Policy and Research Agency grants, by recipient and location, FY90, 4186–9.10
- Health condition and health care resources, use, and spending, 1950s-89, annual data compilation, 4144–11
- Heart, Lung, and Blood Natl Inst activities, and grants by recipient and location, FY90 and disease trends from 1940, annual rpt, 4474–15
- HHS financial aid, by program, recipient, State, and city, FY90, annual regional listings, 4004–3
- Kidney end-stage disease research of CDC and HCFA, project listing, 1990, annual rpt, 4654–16
- Library of Medicine of NIH, activities, holdings, and grants, FY88-90, annual rpt, 4464–1
- Loans and loan guarantees of Fed Govt, outstanding amounts by agency and program, *Treasury Bulletin*, quarterly rpt, 8002–4.9
- Mental health care facilities, finances, caseload, staff, and characteristics of instn and patients, 1988, 4506–4.14
- Mental health care facilities for emotionally disturbed children, use, funding, and characteristics of patients, staff, and instn, 1988, 4506–3.44
- Mental health care facilities outlays, by function, instn type, funding source, and State, 1988, 4506–3.45
- Mental illness and drug and alcohol abuse direct and indirect costs, by age and sex, 1985, 4048–35
- Migrant workers and dependents by county, and health centers use and programs funding, by State, 1986-89, 4108–53

Federal aid to medicine

NASA R&D funding to higher education instns, by field, instn, and State, FY90, annual listing, 9504–7

Neurological Disorders and Stroke Natl Inst activities, and disorder cases, FY90, annual rpt, 4474–25

Neurosciences research and public policy issues, series, 26356–9

NIH activities and funding, by inst, FY89-90, biennial rpt, 4434–16

NIH activities, funding by program and recipient type, staff, and clinic patients, by inst, FY90, annual rpt, 4434–3

NIH grants and contracts, by inst and type of recipient, FY81-90, annual rpt, 4434–9

NIH grants and contracts, quarterly listing, 4432–1

NIH grants for R&D, training, construction, and medical libraries, by location and recipient, FY90, annual listings, 4434–7

NIH intl program activities and funding, by inst and country, FY90, annual rpt, 4474–6

NIH Research Resources Center activities and funding, by program, FY90, annual rpt, 4434–12

Older persons use of federally funded health centers, targeted programs offered, and funding sources, 1987, article, 4042–3.229

Population, family, and sexual behavior research activities and funding, 1960s-89, 4478–194

Primary health care research, provider role, Federal funding, and provision to minority groups, 1990 conf papers, 4188–69

R&D and related funding of Fed Govt to higher education and nonprofit instns, by field, instn, agency, and State, FY89, annual rpt, 9627–17

R&D funding by Fed Govt, by field, performer type, agency, and State, FY89-91, annual rpt, 9627–20

Radiation from electronic devices, and FDA control activities and R&D grants, contracts, and interagency agreements, 1990, annual rpt, 4064–13

Reproduction and population research, Fed Govt funding by project, FY89, annual listing, 4474–9

Reproduction and population research, Natl Inst of Child Health and Human Dev funding and activities, 1990, annual rpt, 4474–33

Rural areas hospitals closures related to selected factors, 1980s, GAO rpt, 26121–409

Rural areas hospitals HCFA grants for improving financial stability, by program area, recipient, and State, FY89, 4658–58

Surplus personal property of Fed Govt donated to govt and nonprofit agencies, with data by State, FY88-90, biennial rpt, 9454–22

Tax expenditures, Federal revenues forgone through income tax deductions and exclusions by type, FY92-96, annual rpt, 21784–10

Toxicology Natl Program research and testing activities, FY89 and planned FY90, annual rpt, 4044–16

Universal coverage for health care and long term care financing, background data, 1990 rpt, 23898–5

Universal coverage under natl health insurance, alternative proposals and indicators of need, 1989, 4658–54

see also Civilian Health and Medical Program of the Uniformed Services

see also Federal aid to medical education

see also Medicaid

see also Medicare

see also Military health facilities and services

see also Supplemental Security Income

see also Veterans health facilities and services

Federal aid to railroads

Amtrak finances and operations, FY90, annual rpt, 29524–1

Assistance (financial and nonfinancial) of Fed Govt, 1991 base edition with supplements, annual listing, 104–5

Budget of US, obligations and authority by function, agency, and program, with summaries, analyses, and historical tables, FY92, annual rpt, 104–2

Expenditures, condition, mgmt, and R&D for transportation and environmental public works, 1986-91, 26358–235

Expenditures of Fed Govt in States, by type, program, agency, and State, FY90, annual rpt, 2464–2

Lands (public) acreage and grants, by State, FY90 and trends, annual rpt, 5724–1.1

Urban Mass Transportation Admin grants for transit systems, by city and State, FY90, annual rpt, 7884–10

Federal aid to research and development

see Federal funding for research and development

Federal aid to rural areas

Agricultural Stabilization and Conservation Service producer payments and certificate value, by program, monthly rpt, 1802–10

Appalachia hwy system and access roads funding and completion status, by State, quarterly tables, 9082–1

Appalachia local dev projects, and funding by source, by program and State, FY90, annual rpt, 9084–1

Appalachian Regional Commission funding, by project and State, planned FY91, annual rpt, 9084–3

Assistance (financial and nonfinancial) of Fed Govt, 1991 base edition with supplements, annual listing, 104–5

Budget of US, House Budget Committee analysis of Bush Admin proposals and economic assumptions, FY92, 21268–42

Colorado River Salinity Control Program participation and payments, FY87-90, annual rpt, 1804–23

Conservation program of USDA, funding by practice, region and State, monthly rpt, 1802–15

Conservation program of USDA, participation and payments by practice and State, FY90, annual rpt, 1804–7

Economic and social conditions, dev, and problems in rural areas, periodic journal, 1502–7

Economic and social indicators used to determine Federal aid need for rural areas, late 1960s-86, 1598–265

Expenditures of Fed Govt in States, by type, program, agency, and State, FY90, annual rpt, 2464–2

Index by Subjects and Names

Hospitals in rural areas, HCFA grants for improving financial stability, by program area, recipient, and State, FY89, 4658–58

Housing loan programs of FmHA in rural areas, and housing voucher demonstration program results, 1980s, hearing, 21248–143

Migrant workers and dependents by county, and health centers use and programs funding, by State, 1986-89, 4108–53

Timber improvement program for private land, Fed Govt cost-sharing funds by region and State, monthly rpt, 1802–11

Timber industry impacts of northern spotted owl conservation in Pacific Northwest, and worker aid programs, 1980s and projected to 2000, hearing, 21728–76

Water pollution from farming, funding for control under Rural Clean Water Program by region and State, monthly rpt, 1802–14

see also Agricultural production quotas and price supports

see also Agricultural subsidies

see also Farm Credit Administration

see also Farm Credit System

see also Farmers Home Administration

see also Rural Electrification Administration

see also Rural Telephone Bank

Federal aid to States

Agricultural research funding and staffing for USDA, State agencies, and other instns, by topic, FY90, annual rpt, 1744–2

AIDS virus antibody tests and counseling sessions by setting, and CDC funding and funds uncommitted by State, 1989-90, GAO rpt, 26121–428

Arts Natl Endowment activities and grants, FY90, annual rpt, 9564–3

Assistance (financial) of Fed Govt to State and local govts, by program, budget function, and agency, FY90, GAO rpt, 26121–421

Assistance (financial and nonfinancial) of Fed Govt, 1991 base edition with supplements, annual listing, 104–5

Audit requirement compliance of State and local govts receiving Federal funds, 1991 article, 10042–1.204

Block grant restructuring proposals, with grants by program area, FY91, article, 10042–1.202

Budget of US, House Budget Committee analysis of Bush Admin proposals and economic assumptions, FY92, 21268–42

Budget of US, obligations and authority by function, agency, and program, with summaries, analyses, and historical tables, FY92, annual rpt, 104–2

Child abuse and neglect prevention funding by States, and funding sources, FY89, GAO rpt, 26121–423

Child Support Enforcement Program admin, Fed Govt incentive payments to States, FY85-89, annual rpt, 4694–6

Child welfare programs funding by source, and foster care cases, problems, and program operations for selected States, 1970s-90, hearings, 21788–202

Child welfare programs funding by source, and foster care program operations and client characteristics, for selected States, 1960s-95, 25368–169

Index by Subjects and Names

Federal aid to States

Coal Surface Mining Reclamation and Enforcement Office activities and funding, by State and Indian tribe, FY90, annual rpt, 5644–1

Community Dev Block Grant activities and funding, by program, FY75-90, annual rpt, 5124–8

Consumer Product Safety Commission activities, recalls by brand, and casualties and medical costs, by product type, FY89, annual rpt, 9164–2

Disabled persons rehabilitation, Federal and State activities and funding, FY90, annual rpt, 4944–1

Disasters and natl security incidents and mgmt, with data by major event and State, 1991 annual rpt, 9434–6

Drug abuse and trafficking reduction grant programs and funding, by Federal agency and State, FY90-92, 236–1.5

Drug abuse and trafficking reduction programs activities, funding, staff, and Bush Admin budget request, by Federal agency and program area, FY90-92, 238–2

Drug abuse treatment, prevention, and enforcement grants to States, by Federal agency and State, FY87-91, 236–1.4

Drug and alcohol abuse treatment and prevention programs of States, funding, facilities, and patient characteristics, FY89, 4488–15

Drug and alcohol abuse treatment services, funding, staffing, and client load, characteristics, and outcomes, by setting, 1989 conf, 4498–73

Drug enforcement support activities of Natl Guard, spending and needs by State, FY89-91, GAO rpt, 26123–343

Economic Dev Admin activities, and funding by program, recipient, State, and county, FY90 and cumulative from FY66, annual rpt, 2064–2

Economic indicators and components, current data and annual trends, monthly rpt, 23842–1.6

Education (bilingual) enrollment, and Education Dept activities and funding by program, by State, FY88-90, biennial rpt, 4804–14

Education (bilingual) programs enrollment, funding, and services, by State, FY85-89, series, 4808–20

Education (early childhood) for handicapped children, project descriptions, 1990/91, annual listing, 4944–10

Education (public elementary and secondary), schools, enrollment, teachers, funding, and other characteristics, by region and State, 1988/89, annual rpt, 4834–20

Education Dept programs funding, operations, and effectiveness, FY90, annual rpt, 4804–5

Education funding by Federal agency, program, and recipient type, and instn spending, FY80-90, annual rpt, 4824–8

Education in science and math, teacher dev project funding of Fed Govt, participation, operations, and effectiveness, 1985-90, 4808–31

Employment programs, training, and unemployment compensation, current devs and grants to States, press release series, 6406–2

Employment services local offices operations, State and Federal oversight, staff, and costs, 1983-91, GAO rpt, 26121–430

Energy conservation programs of States, Federal aid and savings, by State, 1989, annual rpt, 3304–1

Environmental protection programs costs to govts and households, by program type and city size, 1960s-88 and projected to 2000, 9188–114

EPA pollution control grant program activities, monthly rpt, 9182–8

Expenditures of Fed Govt in States and local areas, by type, State, county, and city, FY90, annual rpt, 2464–3

Expenditures of Fed Govt in States, by type, program, agency, and State, FY90, annual rpt, 2464–2

Finances of govts, by level of govt, State, and for large cities and counties, annual rpt series, 2466–2

Finances of govts, tax systems and revenue, and fiscal structure, by level of govt and State, 1991 and historical trends, annual rpt, 10044–1

Fish and Wildlife Service restoration and hunter safety funding, by State, FY92, semiannual press release, 5502–1

Fish and Wildlife Service restoration programs funding, land purchases, and project listing, by State, FY89, annual rpt, 5504–1

Fish Hatchery Natl System activities and deliveries, by species, hatchery, and jurisdiction of waters stocked, FY90, annual rpt, 5504–10

Fishery mgmt and R&D, Fed Govt grants by project and State, and rpts, 1990, annual listing, 2164–3

Fishery research of State fish and wildlife agencies, federally funded projects and costs by species and State, 1990, annual listing, 5504–23

Forest Service activities and finances, by region and State, FY90, annual rpt, 1204–1

Forest Service timber sales, expenses, and operations, by region, State, and natl forest, FY90, annual rpts, 1204–36

Formula grant budget obligations to State and local govts, by agency, program, and State, FY92, annual rpt, 104–30

Formula grants of Fed Govt, use of Census of Population data for allocation, and effects of data errors on funding, with data by program and State, FY91, GAO rpt, 26119–361

HHS financial aid, by program, recipient, State, and city, FY90, annual regional listings, 4004–3

Historic Preservation Fund grants, by State, FY92, annual table, 5544–9

Homeless adults educational services, funding, participation, and staff, by State, 1989, annual rpt series, 4804–39

Homeless children educational projects, activities, and funding, FY90, annual rpt, 4804–35

Homeless persons aid programs of Fed Govt, program descriptions and funding, by agency and State, FY87-90, annual GAO rpt, 26104–21

Homeless persons housing and food aid of Fed Govt, funding and operations, with data by State and county, FY89, hearing, 25408–111

Housing (rental) rehabilitation funding and activities of HUD, by program and region, FY90, annual rpt, 5124–7

Humanities Natl Endowment activities and grants, FY90, annual rpt, 9564–2

Hwy funds pooled by States from FHwA funds for specific projects, demonstration project results, FY88-90, GAO rpt, 26113–471

Hwy Statistics, detailed data by State, 1990, annual rpt, 7554–1

Land and Water Conservation Fund allocations for outdoor recreation area dev, by State, FY91, annual table, 5544–15

Land and Water Conservation Fund grants, State matching funds, and balances, by State, FY90, annual rpt, 5544–18

Land Mgmt Bur activities and funding by State, FY89, annual rpt, 5724–13

Land subsidence above coal mines, State property insurance program income and expenses in 6 States, 1990, GAO rpt, 26113–530

Lands (public) acreage, grants, use, revenues, and allocations, by State, FY90 and trends, annual rpt, 5724–1

Marine mammals protection activities and funding, populations, and harvests, by species, 1989, annual rpt, 5504–12

Massachusetts public works funding, financing sources, and employment, by function and authority, 1980s and projected to 2000, article, 9373–1.207

Massachusetts State govt spending and employment by program, revenues by source, debt, and public works financing, compared to other States, 1990 compilation of papers, 9373–4.27

Medicare and Medicaid eligibility, participation, coverage, and program finances, various periods 1966-91, biennial rpt, 4654–1

Military surplus property donations to intl and State relief programs, FY86-90, GAO rpt, 26123–316

Mines safety and health enforcement, training, and funding, with casualties, by type of mine and State, FY89, annual rpt, 6664–6

Pacific territories economic conditions, population characteristics, and Federal aid, 1989 hearing, 21448–44

Pipeline accidents, casualties, safety enforcement activity, and Federal funding, by State, 1989, annual rpt, 7304–5

Puerto Rico statehood referendum proposal, impacts on Federal tax revenue and aid outlays, corporations tax-favored status, and economic conditions, projected FY91-2000, hearing, 25368–168; 26306–3.112

R&D funding by Fed Govt, by field, performer type, agency, and State, FY89-91, annual rpt, 9627–20

Refugee aid funding of Fed Govt and States, impacts of reductions, with data by selected State and California county, late 1980s, GAO rpt, 26121–402

Refugee resettlement programs and funding, arrivals by country of origin, and indicators of adjustment, by State, FY90, annual rpt, 4694–5

State and local govt competition in taxes, services, regulation, and dev incentives, 1970-89, 10048–79

Federal aid to States

State and Metro Area Data Book, 1991 data compilation, 2328–54

Surplus personal property of Fed Govt donated to govt and nonprofit agencies, with data by State, FY88-90, biennial rpt, 9454–22

Wastewater treatment facilities construction grants of EPA to State and local govts, by project, monthly listing, 9202–3

Wastewater treatment facilities construction loan funds for local govts, Federal and State funding by State, 1990, GAO rpt, 26113–521

Water resources data collection and analysis activities of USGS Water Resources Div Districts, with project descriptions, series, 5666–26

Wildlife research of State fish and wildlife agencies, federally funded projects and costs by species and State, 1990, annual listing, 5504–24

see also Medicaid

see also Revenue sharing

see also Supplemental Security Income

see also Unemployment insurance

Federal aid to transportation

- Air traffic control and airway facilities and services, finances and operations, FY85-89, annual rpt, 7504–37
- Air traffic control and airway facilities improvement activities under Aviation System Capital Investment Plan, 1981-90 and projected to 2005, annual rpt, 7504–12
- Airport and Airway Trust Fund financial condition, monthly rpt, 8102–9.5
- Airport and Airway Trust Fund improvement spending, by airport and State, FY91, annual rpt, 7504–48
- Airport capacity expansion and improvement funding sources, alternative methods, late 1980s and projected to 2000, hearing, 21648–63
- Airport capacity improvement projects and funding, traffic, and delays, by major airport, 1987-90 and forecast to 1998, annual rpt, 7504–43
- Airport dev program grants and projects, by FAA region and State, FY89, annual rpt, 7504–1.3
- Airport finances, operations by carrier, and capacity improvement and dev funding, by airport, 1977-87 and projected to 2020, hearing, 21648–59
- Airport improvement program of FAA, activities and grants by State and airport, FY90, annual rpt, 7504–38
- Airport improvement program of FAA, activities, funding, and airport operations, by location, projected 1990-99, biennial rpt, 7504–42
- Airport planning and dev project grants of FAA, by airport and location, quarterly press release, 7502–14
- Assistance (financial and nonfinancial) of Fed Govt, 1991 base edition with supplements, annual listing, 104–5
- Budget of US, balances of budget authority obligated and unobligated, by function and agency, FY90-92, annual rpt, 104–8
- Budget of US, CBO analysis and review of FY92 budget by function, annual rpt, 26304–2
- Budget of US, CBO analysis of savings and revenues under alternative spending cuts and tax changes, projected FY92-97, 26306–3.118

Budget of US, formula grant program obligations to State and local govts, by agency, program, and State, FY92, annual rpt, 104–30

Budget of US, House concurrent resolution, with spending and revenue targets, FY92 and projected to FY96, annual rpt, 21264–2

Budget of US, midsession review of FY92 budget, by function, annual rpt, 104–7

Budget of US, obligations and authority by function, agency, and program, with summaries, analyses, and historical tables, FY92, annual rpt, 104–2

Budget of US, receipts by source, outlays by agency and program, and balances, monthly rpt, 8102–3

Budget of US, Senate concurrent resolution, with spending and revenue targets, FY92, annual rpt, 25254–1

Credit subsidies for public works, proposed replacement for direct Federal grants, with background data by project type, FY88, 26306–3.113

DOT activities by subagency, budget, and summary accident data, FY88, annual rpt, 7304–1

DOT finances and staff, by subagency, FY90-92, annual rpt, 7304–10

Electric-powered autos, R&D activity and DOE funding shares, FY90, annual rpt, 3304–2

Expenditures and regulation for surface transportation by Fed Govt and States, FY91 with projections to FY96, 26358–242

Expenditures, condition, mgmt, and R&D for transportation and environmental public works, 1986-91, 26358–235

Expenditures of Fed Govt in States, by type, program, agency, and State, FY90, annual rpt, 2464–2

FAA activities and finances, and staff by region, FY89-90, annual rpt, 7504–10

Fraud and abuse in DOT programs, audits and investigations, 1st half FY91, semiannual rpt, 7302–4

Inland waterways trust funds financial condition, monthly rpt, 8102–9.8

Lands (public) acreage and grants, by State, FY90 and trends, annual rpt, 5724–1.1

Loans and loan guarantees of Fed Govt, outstanding amounts by agency and program, *Treasury Bulletin*, quarterly rpt, 8002–4.9

Natl transportation system planning, use, condition, accidents, and needs, by mode of transport, 1940s-90 and projected to 2020, 7308–202

Pipeline accidents, casualties, safety enforcement activity, and Federal funding, by State, 1989, annual rpt, 7304–5

Statistical Abstract of US, 1991 annual data compilation, 2324–1.21

Tax expenditures, Federal revenues forgone through income tax deductions and exclusions by type, FY92-96, annual rpt, 21784–10

Transit systems finances and operations, by mode of transport, size of fleet, and for 468 systems, 1989, annual rpt, 7884–4

Transit systems finances, costs, and needs, by selected system, 1987-89, biennial rpt, 7884–8

Urban Mass Transportation Admin grants for transit systems, by city and State, FY90, annual rpt, 7884–10

Urban Mass Transportation Admin R&D projects and funding, FY90, annual listing, 7884–1

Urban Mass Transportation Admin research and training grants to higher education instns, by project, FY90, annual listing, 7884–7

see also Federal aid to highways

see also Federal aid to railroads

see also Shipbuilding and operating subsidies

Federal aid to vocational education

- Assistance (financial and nonfinancial) of Fed Govt, 1991 base edition with supplements, annual listing, 104–5
- Budget of US, formula grant program obligations to State and local govts, by agency, program, and State, FY92, annual rpt, 104–30
- Education Dept programs funding, operations, and effectiveness, FY90, annual rpt, 4804–5
- Expenditures for education by Federal agency, program, and recipient type, and instn spending, FY80-90, annual rpt, 4824–8
- Expenditures for education, by Federal agency, program, and State, FY80-90, annual rpt, 4824–2.27
- Expenditures of Fed Govt in States, by type, program, agency, and State, FY90, annual rpt, 2464–2
- HHS financial aid, by program, recipient, State, and city, FY90, annual regional listings, 4004–3
- Student aid funding and participation, by Federal program, instn type and control, and State, various periods 1959-89, annual rpt, 4804–28
- Veterans education aid under GI Bill and other programs, and participation by period of service and State, FY89, annual rpt, 8604–9

Federal Aviation Administration

- Accidents by type of aviation, near collisions, air traffic control and pilot errors, and runway incursions, monthly rpt, 7502–15
- Activities and finances of FAA, and staff by region, FY89-90, annual rpt, 7504–10
- Activities of FAA, and detailed data on aircraft, traffic, carriers, and airports, 1980-89, annual rpt, 7504–1
- Air taxi and commuter airlines operating certificates, FAA revocations for safety violations, 1987-91, GAO rpt, 26113–547
- Air traffic control and airway facilities and services, finances and operations, FY85-89, annual rpt, 7504–37
- Air traffic control and airway facilities improvement activities under Aviation System Capital Investment Plan, 1981-90 and projected to 2005, annual rpt, 7504–12
- Air traffic control and airway facilities staff, by employment and other characteristics, FY89, annual rpt, 7504–41
- Air traffic control staffing levels, by job level and selected facility, FY88-90, GAO rpt, 26113–522
- Aircraft (general aviation), flight hours, and equipment, by type, use, and model of aircraft, region, and State, 1990, annual rpt, 7504–29

Index by Subjects and Names — Federal budget

Aircraft maintenance requirements of FAA for aging craft, airlines compliance and repair facilities operations, 1989-91, GAO rpt, 26113-527

Aircraft registered with FAA, by type and characteristics of aircraft, make, carrier, State, and county, 1989, annual rpt, 7504-3

Airline financial and operating summary data, quarterly rpt, 7502-16

Airport capacity improvement projects and funding, traffic, and delays, by major airport, 1987-90 and forecast to 1998, annual rpt, 7504-43

Airport improvement program of FAA, activities and grants by State and airport, FY90, annual rpt, 7504-38

Airport improvement program of FAA, activities, funding, and airport operations, by location, projected 1990-99, biennial rpt, 7504-42

Airport planning and dev project grants of FAA, by airport and location, quarterly press release, 7502-14

Airport security operations to prevent hijacking, screening results, enforcement actions, and hijacking attempts, 2nd half 1989, semiannual rpt, 7502-5

Atlantic Ocean intl air traffic and passengers, by aviation type and route, alternative forecasts 1991-2010 and trends from 1980, annual rpt, 7504-44

Budget of US, obligations and authority by function, agency, and program, with summaries, analyses, and historical tables, FY92, annual rpt, 104-2

Employment of DOT, by subagency, occupation, and selected personnel characteristics, FY90, annual rpt, 7304-18

Expenditures of Fed Govt in States, by type, program, agency, and State, FY90, annual rpt, 2464-2

Flight and engine hours, and shutdown rates, by aircraft and engine model, and air carrier, monthly rpt, 7502-13

General aviation activity, 1990, triennial survey rpt, 7508-3

Helicopters, use, and landing facilities, by craft type, region, and State, 1989, 7508-75

Hijackings, on-board explosions, and other crime, US and foreign incidents, 1985-89, annual rpt, 7504-31

Instrument flight rule aircraft handled, by user type, FAA traffic control center, and region, FY85-90 and projected to FY2005, annual rpt, 7504-15

Medical research and test results for aviation, technical rpt series, 7506-10

Noise policies, aircraft replacement schedules and costs, and health impacts, 1960s-90 and projected to 2006, hearing, 21648-64

Pilots and nonpilots certified by FAA, by certificate type, age, sex, region, and State, 1990, annual rpt, 7504-2

Traffic (passenger and cargo), and departures by aircraft type, by carrier and airport, 1990, annual rpt, 7504-35

Traffic (passenger and cargo), carrier enplanement shares, and FAA airport improvement program grants, by airport and State, 1989, annual rpt, 7504-48

Traffic, aircraft, pilots, airports, and fuel use, forecast FY91-2002 and trends from FY81, annual rpt, 7504-6

Traffic and other aviation activity forecasts of FAA, 1991 annual conf, 7504-28

Traffic and passenger and freight enplanements, by airport, 1960s-90 and projected to 2010, hub area rpt series, 7506-7

Traffic and passenger enplanements, by airport, region, and State, projected FY91-2005 and trends from FY83, annual rpt, 7504-7

Traffic levels at FAA air traffic control facilities, by airport and State, FY90, annual rpt, 7504-27

Federal bankruptcy courts

Caseloads (civil and criminal) for Federal district, appeals, and bankruptcy courts, by offense, circuit, and district, 1990, annual rpt, 18204-11

Caseloads (civil and criminal) for Federal district, appeals, and special courts, by offense, circuit, and district, 1990, annual rpt, 18204-8

Caseloads (civil and criminal) for Federal district, appeals, and special courts, 1991, annual rpt, 18204-2

Judicial Conf proceedings and findings, spring 1991, semiannual rpt, 18202-2

US attorneys work hours, by type of court and Federal district, FY90, annual rpt, 6004-2.6

Federal boards, committees, and commissions

Advisory committees of Fed Govt, and members, staff, meetings, and costs by agency, FY90, annual rpt, 9454-18

Budget of US, authoritative financial statements with appropriations, outlays, and receipts, by category and agency, FY90, annual rpt, 8104-2.1

Budget of US, obligations and authority by function, agency, and program, with summaries, analyses, and historical tables, FY92, annual rpt, 104-2

Budget of US, receipts by source, outlays by agency and program, and balances, monthly rpt, 8102-3

Education funding by Federal agency, program, and recipient type, and instn spending, FY80-90, annual rpt, 4824-8

Employment and payroll (civilian) of Fed Govt, by agency in DC metro area, total US, and abroad, bimonthly rpt, 9842-1

Financial operations of Fed Govt, detailed data, *Treasury Bulletin*, quarterly rpt, 8002-4

see also Advisory Commission on Intergovernmental Relations

see also Advisory Committee on Federal Pay

see also Atomic Energy Commission

see also Board for International Broadcasting

see also Board of Foreign Scholarships

see also Commission on Civil Rights

see also Commission on Railroad Retirement Reform

see also Committee for Purchase from the Blind and Other Severely Handicapped

see also Commodity Futures Trading Commission

see also Delaware River Basin Commission

see also Federal Committee on Statistical Methodology

see also Federal Election Commission

see also Federal Financial Institutions Examination Council

see also Federal Financing Bank

see also Federal independent agencies

see also Federal Labor Relations Authority

see also Federal Mine Safety and Health Review Commission

see also Interagency Task Force on Acid Precipitation

see also Interdepartment Radio Advisory Committee

see also International Boundary and Water Commission, U.S. and Mexico

see also International Joint Commission, U.S. and Canada

see also Interstate Commission on the Potomac River Basin

see also Japan-U.S. Friendship Commission

see also Marine Mammal Commission

see also Migratory Bird Conservation Commission

see also Monitored Retrievable Storage Commission

see also National Advisory Council on Child Nutrition

see also National Advisory Council on Educational Research and Improvement

see also National Advisory Council on Indian Education

see also National Advisory Council on International Monetary and Financial Policies

see also National Capital Planning Commission

see also National Commission for Employment Policy

see also National Commission on Children

see also National Commission on Libraries and Information Science

see also National Committee on Vital and Health Statistics

see also National Education Goals Panel

see also National Narcotics Intelligence Consumers Committee

see also Navajo and Hopi Indian Relocation Commission

see also Office of Navajo and Hopi Indian Relocation

see also Organized Crime Drug Enforcement Task Forces

see also Physician Payment Review Commission

see also Prospective Payment Assessment Commission

see also Susquehanna River Basin Commission

see also Truman, Harry S., Scholarship Foundation

see also U.S. Advisory Commission on Public Diplomacy

see also U.S. Architectural and Transportation Barriers Compliance Board

see also U.S. Holocaust Memorial Council

see also U.S. Sentencing Commission

see also Water Resources Council

see also under By Federal Agency in the "Index by Categories"

see also under names of individual Presidential commissions (starting with Presidential or President's)

Federal budget

see Budget of the U.S.

Federal buildings

Federal buildings
see Public buildings

Federal Bureau of Investigation
Arrest rates, by offense, sex, age, and race, 1965-89, annual rpt, 6224–7
Assaults and deaths of law enforcement officers, by circumstances, agency, victim and offender characteristics, and location, 1990, annual rpt, 6224–3
Banks and thrifts fraud and abuse, Federal agencies enforcement activities and staff, with data by instn and location, 1988-90, hearing, 21408–119
Bombing incidents, casualties, and damage, by target, circumstances, and State, 1990, annual rpt, 6224–5
Budget of US, obligations and authority by function, agency, and program, with summaries, analyses, and historical tables, FY92, annual rpt, 104–2
Crime Index by population size and region, and offenses by large city, Jan-June 1991, semiannual rpt, 6222–1
Crimes, arrests by offender characteristics, and rates, by offense, and law enforcement employees, by population size and jurisdiction, 1990, annual rpt, 6224–2
Jail inmates held for Federal authorities, by county and State, 1988, regional rpt series, 6068–144
Terrorism incidents in US, related activity, and casualties, by attack type, target, group, and location, 1990, annual rpt, 6224–6

Federal Bureau of Prisons
see Bureau of Prisons

Federal Committee on Statistical Methodology
Fed Govt policies relating to statistical programs technical operation, methodology, and use of data, working paper series, 106–4

Federal Communications Commission
Budget of US, authoritative financial statements with appropriations, outlays, and receipts, by category and agency, FY90, annual rpt, 8104–2.1
Budget of US, obligations and authority by function, agency, and program, with summaries, analyses, and historical tables, FY92, annual rpt, 104–2
Fiber optics and copper wire mileage and access lines, and fiber systems investment, by telecommunications firm, 1985-90, annual rpt, 9284–18
Intl telecommunications operations of US carriers, finances, rates, and traffic by service type, firm, and country, 1975-89, annual rpt, 9284–17
R&D funding by Fed Govt, by field, performer type, agency, and State, FY89-91, annual rpt, 9627–20
Telephone and telegraph firms detailed finances and operations, 1989, annual rpt, 9284–6
Telephone local service charges and low-income subsidies, by region, company, and city, 1980s-90, semiannual rpt, 9282–8
Telephone service subscribership, by household characteristics and State, periodic rpt, suspended, 9282–9
Telephone service subscribership, charges, and local and long distance firm finances and operations, late 1970s-91, semiannual rpt, 9282–7

TV and radio stations on the air, by class of operation, monthly press release, 9282–4
TV channel allocation and license status, for commercial and noncommercial UHF and VHF stations by market, as of June 30, 1991, semiannual rpt, 9282–6

Federal contracts
see Government contracts and procurement

Federal corporations
see Government corporations and enterprises

Federal courts
see Administrative Office of the U.S. Courts
see Court of International Trade
see Court of Military Appeals
see Courts
see Federal bankruptcy courts
see Federal courts of appeals
see Federal district courts
see Supreme Court
see Tax Court of the U.S.
see U.S. Claims Court
see U.S. Court of Appeals for the Federal Circuit

Federal courts of appeals
Budget of US, authoritative financial statements with appropriations, outlays, and receipts, by category and agency, FY90, annual rpt, 8104–2.1
Budget of US, obligations and authority by function, agency, and program, with summaries, analyses, and historical tables, FY92, annual rpt, 104–2
Caseloads (civil and criminal) for Federal district, appeals, and bankruptcy courts, by offense, circuit, and district, 1990, annual rpt, 18204–11
Caseloads (civil and criminal), for Federal district, appeals, and special courts, by offense, circuit, and district, 1990, annual rpt, 18204–8
Caseloads (civil and criminal) for Federal district, appeals, and special courts, 1991, annual rpt, 18204–2
Caseloads, actions, procedure duration, judges, and jurors, by Federal district and appeals court, 1986-91, annual rpt, 18204–3
Criminal case processing in Federal courts, by offense, disposition, and jurisdiction, data compilation, 1991 annual rpt, 6064–6.5
Judicial Conf proceedings and findings, spring 1991, semiannual rpt, 18202–2
Labor Relations Natl Board activities, cases, elections conducted, and litigation, FY89, annual rpt, 9584–1
Pre-argument conferences impacts on case processing, disposition, and duration, for 6th Circuit Court of Appeals, 1985-86, 18408–45
Statistical Abstract of US, 1991 annual data compilation, 2324–1.5
Tax litigation, prosecutions, and interpretive law decisions, FY90, annual rpt, 8304–3.3
US attorneys work hours, by type of court and Federal district, FY90, annual rpt, 6004–2.6
see also U.S. Court of Appeals for the Federal Circuit

Federal Crop Insurance Corp.
Budget of US, obligations and authority by function, agency, and program, with summaries, analyses, and historical tables, FY92, annual rpt, 104–2

Federal Deposit Insurance Corp.
Banks (insured commercial and savings) finances, by State, 1989, annual rpt, 9294–4
Banks (insured commercial and savings) financial condition and performance, by asset size and region, quarterly rpt, 9292–1
Banks in Fed Reserve 11th District, financial performance indicators by asset size and FDIC assistance receipt, 1987-90, article, 9379–1.206
Banks regulatory enforcement activities of Federal agencies, effectiveness, with data on capital-deficient banks, late 1980s-90, GAO rpt, 26119–334
Budget of US, authoritative financial statements with appropriations, outlays, and receipts, by category and agency, FY90, annual rpt, 8104–2.1
Budget of US, obligations and authority by function, agency, and program, with summaries, analyses, and historical tables, FY92, annual rpt, 104–2
Deposits in insured commercial and savings banks, by instn, State, MSA, and county, as of June 1990, annual regional rpt series, 9295–3
Merger applications approved, and assets and offices involved, by bank, 1989, annual rpt, 9294–5
Reform of banking system and deposit insurance, findings and recommendations, with background data, 1989-90, 8008–147
Regulation of banks and related issues, quarterly journal, 9292–4
Savings banks insured by Bank Insurance Fund, financial condition and performance, by asset size and region, quarterly rpt, 9292–5

Federal district courts
Budget of US, obligations and authority by function, agency, and program, with summaries, analyses, and historical tables, FY92, annual rpt, 104–2
Caseloads (civil and criminal) for Federal district, appeals, and bankruptcy courts, by offense, circuit, and district, 1990, annual rpt, 18204–11
Caseloads (civil and criminal), for Federal district, appeals, and special courts, by offense, circuit, and district, 1990, annual rpt, 18204–8
Caseloads (civil and criminal) for Federal district, appeals, and special courts, 1991, annual rpt, 18204–2
Caseloads, actions, procedure duration, judges, and jurors, by Federal district and appeals court, 1986-91, annual rpt, 18204–3
Civil cases court-annexed arbitration, pilot program evaluation, 1984-86, 18408–46
Criminal case processing in Federal district courts, and dispositions, by offense, district, and offender characteristics, 1986, annual rpt, 6064–29
Criminal case processing in Federal district courts, and dispositions, by offense, 1980-89, annual rpt, 6064–31
Criminal caseload of Federal district courts, by district, data compilation, 1991 annual rpt, 6064–6.1; 6064–6.5
Criminal cases in Federal district courts, by offense, disposition, and district, 1980-90, last issue of annual rpt, 18204–1

Index by Subjects and Names

Drug testing of criminal defendants, demonstration program operations, offender characteristics, and judges views, 1987-90, 18208–11

Judicial Conf proceedings and findings, spring 1991, semiannual rpt, 18202–2

Sentences for Federal crimes, guidelines use and results by offense and district, and Sentencing Commission activities, 1990, annual rpt, 17664–1

Statistical Abstract of US, 1991 annual data compilation, 2324–1.5

Tax litigation, prosecutions, and interpretive law decisions, FY90, annual rpt, 8304–3.3

US attorneys case processing and collections, by case type and Federal district, FY90, annual rpt, 6004–2

Wiretaps authorized, costs, arrests, trials, and convictions, by offense and jurisdiction, 1990, annual rpt, 18204–7

see also Federal bankruptcy courts

Federal Election Commission

Activities of FEC, and election campaign finances, various periods 1975-90, annual rpt, 9274–1

Activities of FEC, elections, procedures, and campaign finances, press release series, 9276–1

Budget of US, authoritative financial statements with appropriations, outlays, and receipts, by category and agency, FY90, annual rpt, 8104–2.1

Budget of US, obligations and authority by function, agency, and program, with summaries, analyses, and historical tables, FY92, annual rpt, 104–2

Polling places accessibility to aged and handicapped, precincts by barrier type and State, 1990 natl elections, biennial rpt, 9274–6

Votes cast by party, candidate, and State, 1990 natl elections, biennial rpt, 9274–5

Federal Emergency Management Agency

Activities and funding of FEMA, annual rpt, discontinued, 9434–2

Budget of US, authoritative financial statements with appropriations, outlays, and receipts, by category and agency, FY90, annual rpt, 8104–2.1

Budget of US, formula grant program obligations to State and local govts, by agency, program, and State, FY92, annual rpt, 104–30

Budget of US, obligations and authority by function, agency, and program, with summaries, analyses, and historical tables, FY92, annual rpt, 104–2

Disaster relief funding and response by FEMA, for Loma Prieta earthquake and Hurricane Hugo, 1989-90, GAO rpt, 26113–511

Disasters and natl security incidents and mgmt, with data by major event and State, 1991 annual rpt, 9434–6

Education funding by Federal agency, program, and recipient type, and instn spending, FY80-90, annual rpt, 4824–8

Expenditures of Fed Govt in States, by type, program, agency, and State, FY90, annual rpt, 2464–2

Homeless persons housing and food aid of Fed Govt, funding and operations, with data by State and county, FY89, hearing, 25408–111

Federal employees

Advisory committees of Fed Govt, and members, staff, meetings, and costs by agency, FY90, annual rpt, 9454–18

Air traffic control and airway facilities staff, by employment and other characteristics, FY89, annual rpt, 7504–41

Air traffic control and airway facilities supervisors task priorities, skills needed, and other characteristics, 1990 survey, technical rpt, 7506–10.84

Air traffic control staffing levels, by job level and selected facility, FY88-90, GAO rpt, 26113–522

Assaults and deaths of law enforcement officers, by circumstances, agency, victim and offender characteristics, and location, 1990, annual rpt, 6224–3

Census of Govts, 1987: employment, payroll, and average earnings, by function, level of govt, State, county, and population size, 2455–2

Census of Population, 1990: population by State and region, with Federal and military personnel abroad by State of residence and agency, press release, 2328–66

Consultants and experts appointed for temporary employment in Federal agencies, and rule violations, 1986-89, GAO rpt, 26119–354

Criminal justice spending, employment, and payroll, by level of govt, State, and selected city and county, FY71-88, biennial rpt, 6064–9

Criminal justice spending, employment, and payroll, by level of govt, State, and selected city and county, 1984-86, biennial rpt, 6064–4

Drug testing of Federal employees, results, and costs, by agency, FY87-92, GAO rpt, 26119–344

Employment (civilian) of Fed Govt, work-years, pay rates, and benefits use and costs, by agency, FY89, annual rpt, 9844–31

Employment and payroll (civilian) of Fed Govt, by agency in DC metro area, total US, and abroad, bimonthly rpt, 9842–1

Employment and payroll (civilian) of Fed Govt, by occupation, pay grade, sex, agency, and location, 1989, biennial rpt, 9844–4

Employment and payroll (civilian) of Fed Govt, by pay system, agency, and location, 1990, annual rpt, 9844–6

Employment and payroll, by function, level of govt, and State, 1990, annual rpt, 2466–1.1

Employment and payroll, by level of govt and State, 1991 and historical trends, annual rpt, 10044–1

Employment, earnings, and hours, by SIC 1- to 4-digit industry, monthly and annual averages, selected years 1909-90, annual rpt, 6744–4

Employment of Fed Govt, by pay system, agency, and location, biennial rpt, discontinued, 9844–8

Employment services local offices operations, State and Federal oversight, staff, and costs, 1983-91, GAO rpt, 26121–430

Employment situation, earnings, hours, and other BLS economic indicators, transcripts of BLS Commissioner's monthly testimony, periodic rpt, 23846–4

Federal employees

Health Care Financing Review, provider prices, price inputs and indexes, and labor, quarterly journal, 4652–1.1

Insurance (health and life) programs of Fed Govt, coverage and finances, FY89 with trends from FY84, annual rpt, 9844–35

Judicial personnel, by position, June 1989-90, annual rpt, 18204–8.10

Judicial personnel, by position, 1990-91, annual rpt, 18204–2.1

Labor productivity of Federal employees, indexes of output and labor costs by function, 1967-89, annual rpt, 6824–1.6

Law enforcement spending and employment, by activity and level of govt, data compilation, 1991 annual rpt, 6064–6.1

Leave transfer to other employees, Federal pilot programs operations and costs by agency, FY89, 9848–40

Minority group and women employment by Fed Govt, and compliance with EEOC standards, by occupation and agency, FY88-92, GAO rpt, 26119–342

Minority group, women, and disabled employment of Fed Govt, by agency and occupation, FY89, annual rpt, 9244–10

Pay grade reclassification for Federal employees, budget impacts and demonstration project results, 1990, 26306–3.119

Physicians, by specialty, age, sex, and location of training and practice, 1989, State rpt series, 4116–6

Recreation (outdoor) coastal facilities of Fed Govt and States, visitor and site characteristics, 1987-90 survey, regional rpt series, 2176–9

Royalties and incentive payments to Fed Govt R&D lab employees, by agency, FY89, GAO rpt, 26131–85

Science and engineering PhDs employment and other characteristics, by field and State, 1989, biennial rpt, 9627–18

Security of info, nondisclosure agreements for Federal and contractor employees, prepublication reviews, and costs, 1988-90, GAO rpt, 26123–328

Senior Executive Service membership characteristics, entries, exits, and awards, FY79-90, annual rpt, 9844–36

Shutdown of Fed Govt over Columbus Day holiday, employees affected, costs, and savings, Oct 1990, GAO rpt, 26119–311

Southwestern US employment by industry div, earnings, and hours, by State, monthly rpt, 6962–2

State and Metro Area Data Book, 1991 data compilation, 2328–54

Statistical Abstract of US, 1991 annual data compilation, 2324–1.10

Travel expenses of Fed Govt employees, operating costs for private autos, airplanes, and motorcycles, and reimbursement rates for business use, 1989, annual rpt, 9454–13

Unemployment insurance claims and covered unemployment by program, and extended benefit triggers, by State, weekly rpt, 6402–15

Unemployment insurance claims, by program, weekly press release, 6402–14

Unemployment insurance coverage of establishments, employment, and wages, by SIC 4-digit industry and State, 1990, annual rpt, 6744–16

Federal employees

Unemployment insurance laws of States, comparison of provisions, 1991, base edition with semiannual revisions, 6402–2

US attorneys staffing disparities among district offices, and caseload by litigation type, FY87-90, GAO rpt, 26119–323

VA health care facilities nonveteran outpatient visits, by eligibility type, facility, and region, quarterly rpt, 8602–4

Vietnam Orderly Departure Program, former Fed Govt employees arrivals in US and refugee camps, monthly rpt, 7002–4

Weather services activities and funding, by Federal agency, planned FY91-92, annual rpt, 2144–2

Workers compensation coverage and benefits, by type of program and insurer, and State, 1987-88, annual article, 4742–1.207

Workers compensation laws of States and Fed Govt, 1991 semiannual rpt, 6502–1

see also Civil service pensions

see also Civil service system

see also Congressional employees

see also Diplomatic and consular service

see also Federal pay

see also Labor-management relations in government

see also Military personnel

see also Postal employees

see also Presidential appointments

see also under names of individual Federal departments and agencies

Federal Energy Administration

see Department of Energy

Federal Energy Regulatory Commission

Activities of FERC, hydroelectric project licensing, and rate regulation, FY90, annual rpt, 3084–9

Electric power plants certification applications filed with FERC, for small production and cogeneration facilities, FY80-90, annual listing, 3084–13

Hydroelectric power plants licensed by FERC, characteristics and location, as of Oct 1991, annual listing, 3084–11

Natural gas pipelines and owners, and fields, as of Sept 1989, map, 3088–21

Pipeline and compressor station construction costs, 1984-87, annual rpt, 3084–3

Federal executive departments

Budget of US, object class analysis of obligations, by agency, FY92, annual rpt, 104–9

Budget of US, obligations and authority by function, agency, and program, with summaries, analyses, and historical tables, FY92, annual rpt, 104–2

Budget of US, receipts by source, outlays by agency and program, and balances, monthly rpt, 8102–3

Congressional Directory, members of 102nd Congress, other officials, elections, and districts, 1991-92, biennial rpt, 23874–1

Employment (civilian) of Fed Govt, work-years, pay rates, and benefits use and costs, by agency, FY89, annual rpt, 9844–31

Employment and payroll (civilian) of Fed Govt, by agency in DC metro area, total US, and abroad, bimonthly rpt, 9842–1

Employment, earnings, and hours, by SIC 1- to 4-digit industry, monthly and annual averages, selected years 1909-90, annual rpt, 6744–4

Financial consolidated statements of Fed Govt based on business accounting methods, FY89-90, annual rpt, 8104–5

Financial operations of Fed Govt, detailed data, *Treasury Bulletin*, quarterly rpt, 8002–4

Investigations of Federal agency and program operations, summaries of findings, 1981-90, annual GAO rpt, 26104–5

Regulatory programs of Fed Govt, evaluation, review process, and actions taken, by agency, 1980s-90, annual rpt, 104–28

see also Federal boards, committees, and commissions

see also Federal independent agencies

see also under By Federal Agency in the "Index by Categories"

see also under names of individual Federal departments and agencies

Federal expenditures

see Budget of the U.S.

see Defense expenditures

see Government contracts and procurement

see Government spending

see terms beginning with Federal aid and Federal funding

Federal Financial Institutions Examination Council

Banks (insured commercial) assets, income, and financial ratios, by asset size and State, quarterly rpt, 13002–3

Budget of US, obligations and authority by function, agency, and program, with summaries, analyses, and historical tables, FY92, annual rpt, 104–2

Financial statements of FFIEC, and bank and thrift finances by instn type, 1990, annual rpt, 13004–2

Loans of US banks to foreigners at all US and foreign offices, by country group and country, quarterly rpt, 13002–1

Federal Financing Bank

Budget of US, obligations and authority by function, agency, and program, with summaries, analyses, and historical tables, FY92, annual rpt, 104–2

Holdings and transactions of Fed Financing Bank, by borrower, monthly press release, 12802–1

Liabilities (contingent) and claims paid by Fed Govt on federally insured and guaranteed contracts with foreign obligors, by country and program, periodic rpt, 8002–12

Federal funding for energy programs

Agricultural research and education grants, USDA competitive awards by program and recipient, FY90, annual listing, 1764–1

AID energy assistance to developing countries, and global warming reduction activities, 1980s-FY92, GAO rpt, 26123–352

Assistance (financial and nonfinancial) of Fed Govt, 1991 base edition with supplements, annual listing, 104–5

Assistance programs under Ways and Means Committee jurisdiction, finances, operations, and participant characteristics, FY70s-90, annual rpt, 21784–11

Auto (electric-powered) R&D activity and DOE funding shares, FY90, annual rpt, 3304–2

Auto engine and power train R&D projects, DOE contracts and funding by recipient, FY90, annual rpt, 3304–17

Budget of US, balances of budget authority obligated and unobligated, by function and agency, FY90-92, annual rpt, 104–8

Budget of US, CBO analysis and review of FY92 budget by function, annual rpt, 26304–2

Budget of US, CBO analysis of savings and revenues under alternative spending cuts and tax changes, projected FY92-97, 26306–3.118

Budget of US, formula grant program obligations to State and local govts, by agency, program, and State, FY92, annual rpt, 104–30

Budget of US, House concurrent resolution, with spending and revenue targets, FY92 and projected to FY96, annual rpt, 21264–2

Budget of US, midsession review of FY92 budget, by function, annual rpt, 104–7

Budget of US, obligations and authority by function, agency, and program, with summaries, analyses, and historical tables, FY92, annual rpt, 104–2

Budget of US, receipts by source, outlays by agency and program, and balances, monthly rpt, 8102–3

Budget of US, Senate concurrent resolution, with spending and revenue targets, FY92, annual rpt, 25254–1

Conservation aid of DOE, activities, funding, and grants by State, by program, annual rpt, discontinued, 3304–21

Conservation aid of Fed Govt to public and nonprofit private instns, by building type and State, 1990, annual rpt, 3304–15

Conservation of energy, State programs aid from Fed Govt, and energy savings, by State, 1989, annual rpt, 3304–1

DOE budget authority, by program and subagency, FY91, annual rpt, 3024–5

DOE contracts and grants, by category, State, and for top contractors, FY90, annual rpt, 3004–21

DOE facilities radioactive and hazardous waste disposal and remediation activities and funding, planned FY91-97, annual rpt, 3024–7

DOE programs finances and mgmt, audits and investigations, series, 3006–5

Expenditures of Fed Govt in States, by type, program, agency, and State, FY90, annual rpt, 2464–2

Finances of Fed Govt, cash and debt transactions, daily tables, 8102–4

Fraud and abuse in DOE programs, audit resolution activities, 2nd half FY91, semiannual rpt, 3002–15

Fraud and abuse in DOE programs, audits and investigations, 2nd half FY91, semiannual rpt, 3002–12

HHS financial aid, by program, recipient, State, and city, FY90, annual regional listings, 4004–3

Hydrogen energy R&D activity and funding of DOE, and project listing, FY90, annual rpt, 3304–18

Inventions recommended by Natl Inst of Standards and Technology for DOE support, awards, and evaluation status, 1990, annual listing, 2214–5

Index by Subjects and Names

Inventions supported by DOE, sales, jobs created, and inventor financing, 1980-88, 3308–91

Loans and loan guarantees of Fed Govt, outstanding amounts by agency and program, *Treasury Bulletin*, quarterly rpt, 8002–4.9

Natl Energy Strategy plans for conservation and pollution reduction, impacts on electric power supply, costs, and emissions, projected under alternative assumptions, 1995-2030, 3166–6.49

Natl Energy Strategy plans for conservation, impacts on energy use and pollution under alternative technology investment assumptions, projected 1990-2030, 3166–6.48

Nuclear power plant safety standards and research, design, licensing, construction, operation, and finances, with data by reactor, quarterly journal, 3352–4

Nuclear radiation exposure at DOE and DOE-contractor sites, by facility type and contractor, 1987, annual rpt, 3324–1

Nuclear Regulatory Commission budget, staff, and activities, by program, FY90-93, annual rpt, 9634–9

Nuclear Waste Fund finances, and DOE Civilian Radioactive Waste Mgmt Office activities, quarterly GAO rpt, 26102–4

Nuclear Waste Fund finances, and DOE Civilian Radioactive Waste Mgmt Office R&D costs, FY88-89, annual rpt, 3364–1

Nuclear Waste Fund finances, and DOE Civilian Radioactive Waste Mgmt Program costs, quarterly rpt, 3362–1

Oil enhanced recovery research contracts of DOE, project summaries, funding, and bibl, quarterly rpt, 3002–14

R&D funding by Fed Govt, by field, performer type, agency, and State, FY89-91, annual rpt, 9627–20

R&D projects and funding of DOE at natl labs, universities, and other instns, periodic summary rpt series, 3004–18

Rural Electrification Admin loans, and borrower operating and financial data, by distribution firm and State, 1990, annual rpt, 1244–1

Rural Electrification Program lending, by State, FY90, annual rpt, 1244–7

Solar photovoltaic R&D sponsored by DOE, projects, funding, and rpts, FY90, annual listing, 3304–20

Southeastern Power Admin sales by customer, plants, capacity, and Southeastern Fed Power Program financial statements, FY90, annual rpt, 3234–1

Strategic Petroleum Reserve capacity, inventory, fill rate, and finances, quarterly rpt, 3002–13

Tax expenditures, Federal revenues forgone through income tax deductions and exclusions by type, FY92-96, annual rpt, 21784–10

TVA energy use by fuel type, and conservation costs and savings, FY90, annual rpt, 9804–26

TVA finances and operations by program and facility, FY90, annual rpt, 9804–32

Uranium enrichment facilities of DOE, financial statements, FY89-90, annual rpt, 3354–7

see also Department of Energy National Laboratories

see also Low-income energy assistance

Federal funding for research and development

Agricultural crops (new and traditional) use in industry, replacement of imports and nonrenewable resources, R&D funding, and economic impacts, 1970s-90, 26358–239

Agricultural research and education appropriations of USDA, by program and subagency, FY82-90, annual rpt, 1004–19

Agricultural research and education grants, USDA competitive awards by program and recipient, FY90, annual listing, 1764–1

Agricultural research funding and staffing for USDA, State agencies, and other instns, by topic, FY90, annual rpt, 1744–2

Agricultural research grants of USDA, by program, subagency, and country, FY90, annual listing, 1954–3

AID and higher education instns collaboration on aid projects, and funding, by purpose and world region, 1960s-89, 26358–247

Air traffic control and airway facilities improvement activities under Aviation System Capital Investment Plan, 1981-90 and projected to 2005, annual rpt, 7504–12

Assistance (financial and nonfinancial) of Fed Govt, 1991 base edition with supplements, annual listing, 104–5

Biological and medical R&D facilities, space and equipment adequacy, needs, and funding by source, by instn type, 1990, biennial rpt, 4434–17

Biotechnology commercial applications, industry finances and capitalization, patents, and govt support, for US, Japan, and EC, late 1970s-91, 26358–248

Budget of US, CBO analysis of savings and revenues under alternative spending cuts and tax changes, projected FY92-97, 26306–3.118

Budget of US, House Budget Committee analysis of Bush Admin proposals and economic assumptions, FY92, 21268–42

Budget of US, House concurrent resolution, with spending and revenue targets, FY92 and projected to FY96, annual rpt, 21264–2

Budget of US, midsession review of FY92 budget, by function, annual rpt, 104–7

Budget of US, obligations and authority by function, agency, and program, with summaries, analyses, and historical tables, FY92, annual rpt, 104–2

Budget of US, receipts by source, outlays by agency and program, and balances, monthly rpt, 8102–3

Budget of US, Senate concurrent resolution, with spending and revenue targets, FY92, annual rpt, 25254–1

Coal Surface Mining Reclamation and Enforcement Office activities and funding, by State and Indian tribe, FY90, annual rpt, 5644–1

Drug abuse and trafficking reduction programs activities, funding, staff, and Bush Admin budget request, by Federal agency and program area, FY90-92, 238–2

Drug abuse and trafficking reduction programs funding, and Bush Admin budget request, by Federal agency and program area, FY90-92, 238–1

Economic Dev Admin activities, and funding by program, recipient, State, and county, FY90 and cumulative from FY66, annual rpt, 2064–2

Engineering research and education grants of NSF, FY90, annual listing, 9624–24

Enterprise Statistics, 1987: auxiliaries of multi-establishment firms, finances and operations by function, industry, and State, 2329–6

EPA pollution control grant program activities, monthly rpt, 9182–8

EPA R&D programs and funding, FY90, annual listing, 9184–18

Expenditures for education by Federal agency, program, and recipient type, and instn spending, FY80-90, annual rpt, 4824–8

Expenditures for education, by Federal agency, program, and State, FY80-90, annual rpt, 4824–2.27

Expenditures for large nondefense R&D projects, by field, budget function, and Federal agency, FY80-91 and projected to FY96, 26306–3.116

Expenditures for R&D, and scientists and engineers education and employment, for US and selected foreign countries, 1991 annual rpt, 9627–35

Expenditures for R&D by Fed Govt, and policy issues, 1950s-91, 26358–238

Expenditures for R&D by Fed Govt, by field, performer type, agency, and State, FY89-91, annual rpt, 9627–20

Expenditures of Fed Govt in States, by type, program, agency, and State, FY90, annual rpt, 2464–2

Fish and Wildlife Service restoration programs funding, land purchases, and project listing, by State, FY89, annual rpt, 5504–1

Fishery mgmt and R&D, Fed Govt grants by project and State, and rpts, 1990, annual listing, 2164–3

Fishery research of State fish and wildlife agencies, federally funded projects and costs by species and State, 1990, annual listing, 5504–23

Forest Service activities and finances, by region and State, FY90, annual rpt, 1204–1

Geological Survey activities and funding, FY90, annual rpt, 5664–8

Great Lakes area economic conditions and outlook, for US and Canada, 1970s-90, 9375–15

Higher education and nonprofit instns R&D and related activities funding by Fed Govt, by field, instn, agency, and State, FY89, annual rpt, 9627–17

Higher education instn and federally funded center R&D funding, by field, instn, and State, FY89, annual rpt, 9627–13

Higher education instn R&D equipment, acquisition and service costs, condition, and financing, by field and subfield, 1988-90, triennial survey series, 9627–27

Higher education instn science and engineering research system status, R&D performance, and Federal support, 1950s-88, 9628–83

Federal funding for research and development

Hwy construction and design R&D, quarterly journal, 7552–3

Industry (US) intl competitiveness, with selected foreign and US operating data by major firm and product, series, 2046–12

MarAd activities, finances, subsidies, and world merchant fleet operations, FY90, annual rpt, 7704–14

Marine mammals protection activities and funding, populations, and harvests, by species, 1989, annual rpt, 5504–12

Materials (advanced structural) devs, use, and R&D funding, for ceramics, metal alloys, polymers, and composites, 1960s-80s and projected to 2000, 5608–162

NASA funding by program and type of performer, and contract awards by State, FY90, annual rpt, 9504–6.2

NASA procurement contract awards, by type, contractor, State, and country, FY91 with trends from 1961, semiannual rpt, 9502–6

NASA R&D funding to higher education instns, by field, instn, and State, FY90, annual listing, 9504–7

NSF activities, finances, and funding by program, FY90, annual rpt, 9624–6

NSF grants and contracts, by field, instn, and State, FY89, annual rpt, 9624–26

NSF programs fraud and abuse, audits and investigations, 2nd half FY91, semiannual rpt, 9622–1

NSF R&D grant awards, by div and program, periodic rpt series, 9626–7

NSF research grants to predominantly undergrad instns, by NSF div, and principal investigator sex and race, FY88, 9628–85

NSF science and engineering staff, and outside investigator research grant proposals and awards, 1980s-90, 9628–84

Occupational safety and health research and demonstration grants by State, and project listing, FY90, annual rpt, 4244–2

Oceanographic research ships, fleet condition, funding, voyages, and modernization costs, for NOAA, 1980s-90 and projected to 2020, 2148–60

Population and reproduction research, Fed Govt funding by project, FY89, annual listing, 4474–9

Property (real) of Fed Govt, inventory and costs, worldwide summary by location, agency, and use, 1989, annual rpt, 9454–5

Public works condition, mgmt, R&D, and funding, for transportation and environmental projects, 1986-91, 26358–235

Science and engineering grad enrollment, by field, source of funds, and characteristics of student and instn, 1975-89, annual rpt, 9627–7

Science and engineering PhDs employment and other characteristics, by field and State, 1989, biennial rpt, 9627–18

Space and aeronautics activities and budgets, by Federal agency, FY59-91, annual rpt, 9504–9.2

Space station commercial dev and operating costs and income under alternative financing options, projected 1989-2000, 21708–129

Index by Subjects and Names

State and Metro Area Data Book, 1991 data compilation, 2328–54

Statistical Abstract of US, 1991 annual data compilation, 2324–1.20

Tax expenditures, Federal revenues forgone through income tax deductions and exclusions by type, FY92-96, annual rpt, 21784–10

Technology Assessment Office activities and rpts, FY90, annual rpt, 26354–3

Technology transfer by Fed Govt R&D labs, cooperative agreements, patents, royalties, and incentive payments to employees, by agency, FY89, GAO rpt, 26131–85

Telecommunications and Info Natl Admin rpts, FY90, annual listing, 2804–3

Traffic safety grants and activities of Natl Hwy Traffic Safety Admin, and fatal traffic accident data, 1989, annual rpt, 7764–1

Urban Mass Transportation Admin R&D projects and funding, FY90, annual listing, 7884–1

Urban Mass Transportation Admin research and training grants to higher education instns, by project, FY90, annual listing, 7884–7

Weather services activities and funding, by Federal agency, planned FY91-92, annual rpt, 2144–2

Wildlife research of State fish and wildlife agencies, federally funded projects and costs by species and State, 1990, annual listing, 5504–24

Women scientists and engineers seeking 1st Federal grant and reentering career, NSF support program proposal submissions, grant awards, and applicants views, FY85-89, 9628–82

see also Defense research

see also Department of Energy National Laboratories

see also Federal aid to medicine

see also Federal funding for energy programs

see also Federally Funded R&D Centers

Federal Grain Inspection Service

Activities and finances of FGIS, domestic and export inspections, foreign buyers complaints, and handling facilities explosions, FY90, annual rpt, 1294–1

Activities, funding, and staff of Federal food safety and quality regulation agencies, 1980s, GAO rpt, 26113–503

Budget of US, obligations and authority by function, agency, and program, with summaries, analyses, and historical tables, FY92, annual rpt, 104–2

Exports of grains, inspection results by commodity and port region, 1988-90, annual rpt, 1294–2

Federal grants

see terms beginning with Federal aid and Federal funding

Federal Highway Administration

Activities of FHwA, funding, and inspections, FY88, annual rpt, 7304–1

Budget of US, obligations and authority by function, agency, and program, with summaries, analyses, and historical tables, FY92, annual rpt, 104–2

Construction (hwy) minority contractor training, funding by region, FY91, annual release, 7554–40

Construction bids and contracts for Federal-aid hwys, by State, 1st half 1991, semiannual rpt, 7552–12

Construction material prices and indexes for Federal-aid hwy system, by type of material and urban-rural location, quarterly rpt, 7552–7

Construction material prices and indexes for Federal-aid hwy system, by type of material, quarterly press release, 7552–16

Construction material use by type, and spending for hwys, by State, various periods 1944-90, annual rpt, 7554–29

Drivers licenses issued and in force by age and sex, fees, and renewal, by license class and State, 1989, annual rpt, 7554–16

Employment of DOT, by subagency, occupation, and selected personnel characteristics, FY90, annual rpt, 7304–18

Expenditures, costs, and completion status of Federal-aid hwy system, by State, as of June 1991, semiannual rpt, 7552–5

Expenditures for traffic safety programs of FHwA, by State, FY89, annual rpt, 7764–1.1

Expenditures of Fed Govt in States, by type, program, agency, and State, FY90, annual rpt, 2464–2

Gasoline and other motor fuel tax provisions, auto registration fees, and disposition of receipts, by State, as of Jan 1991, biennial rpt, 7554–37

Gasoline and other motor fuel tax rates, by State, 1980-89, annual table, 7554–32

Gasoline and other motor fuel use and tax rates, by State, monthly rpt, 7552–1

Hwy Statistics, detailed data by State, 1990, annual rpt, 7554–1

Hwy Statistics, summary data by State, 1989-90, annual rpt, 7554–24

Hwy Trust Fund revenues, tax rates, and spending, FY87-91 with projections to FY95, GAO rpt, 26113–544

R&D for hwy design and construction, quarterly journal, 7552–3

Safety improvement measures, costs, and accident and death reductions by type of accident and improvement, 1990 conf, 7558–110

Safety program funding by State, and accident and death reductions, FY90, annual rpt, 7554–26

Speed averages and vehicles exceeding 55 mph, by State, quarterly rpt, 7552–14

States hwy projects involving FHwA funds, demonstration project results, FY88-90, GAO rpt, 26113–471

Toll facilities, mileage, and operating status, by type of system, as of Jan 1990, biennial listing, 7554–39

Traffic volume on rural roads and city streets, monthly rpt, 7552–8

Travel patterns, personal and household characteristics, and auto and public transport use, 1990 survey, series, 7556–6

Truck accidents, casualties, and damage, by circumstances and characteristics of persons and vehicles involved, 1988, annual rpt, 7554–9

Truck safety inspections of FHwA conducted FY87-88, compliance review status as of 1990, GAO rpt, 26113–505

Index by Subjects and Names

Federal independent agencies

Federal Home Loan Bank Board

Budget of US, authoritative financial statements with appropriations, outlays, and receipts, by category and agency, FY90, annual rpt, 8104–2.1

R&D funding by Fed Govt, by field, performer type, agency, and State, FY89-91, annual rpt, 9627–20

see also Office of Thrift Supervision

Federal Home Loan Bank of Atlanta

Financial statements of Bank, quarterly rpt, 9302–37

Financial statements of Bank, 1989-90, annual rpt, 9304–1

Savings instns in southeastern States, industry review, periodic journal, suspended, 9302–2

Southeastern States, FHLB 4th District, employment and housing and mortgage market indicators by State, quarterly rpt, 9302–36

Federal Home Loan Bank of Boston

Financial statements of Bank, and members by type of instn and State, 1989-90, annual rpt, 9304–2

Financial statements of Bank, quarterly rpt, 9302–35

Savings instns, FHLB 1st District members financial operations compared to banks, and related economic and housing indicators, bimonthly rpt with articles, 9302–4

Federal Home Loan Bank of Chicago

Financial statements of Bank, 1988-90, annual rpt, 9304–4

Housing vacancy rates for single and multifamily units and mobile homes in FHLB 7th District, by ZIP code, annual MSA rpt series, 9304–18

Mortgage interest fixed and adjustable rates and fees offered by Illinois S&Ls, monthly rpt, 9302–6

Mortgage interest fixed and adjustable rates and fees offered by Wisconsin S&Ls, monthly rpt, 9302–7

Savings instns, FHLB 7th District and natl cost of funds indexes, and mortgage rates, monthly rpt, 9302–30

Federal Home Loan Bank of Cincinnati

Financial statements of Bank, 1989-90, annual rpt, 9304–6

Federal Home Loan Bank of Dallas

Financial statements of Bank, 1988-90, annual rpt, 9304–11

Savings instns, FHLB 9th District members finances and operations by State, quarterly rpt, discontinued, 9302–31

Federal Home Loan Bank of Des Moines

Financial statements of Bank, 1988-90, annual rpt, 9304–7

Savings and loan assns, FHLB 8th District members, locations, assets, and savings, 1991, annual listing, 9304–9

Savings instns, FHLB 8th District members financial operations by State and SMSA, quarterly rpt, discontinued, 9302–9

Federal Home Loan Bank of Indianapolis

Financial statements of Bank, 1988-90, annual rpt, 9304–10

Savings and loan assns, FHLB 6th District insured members financial condition and operations by State, quarterly rpt, 9302–23

Savings instns, FHLB 6th and 11th District and natl cost of funds indexes, and mortgage and Treasury bill rates, monthly rpt, 9302–38

Savings instns, FHLB 6th District members financial condition and operations by State, monthly rpt, 9302–11

Federal Home Loan Bank of New York

Financial statements of Bank, 1988-90, annual rpt, 9304–12

Federal Home Loan Bank of Pittsburgh

Financial statements of Bank, 1988-90, annual rpt, 9304–13

Federal Home Loan Bank of San Francisco

Financial statements of Bank, 1989-90, annual rpt, 9304–14

Savings and loan assns, FHLB 11th District members, offices, and financial condition, 1991 annual listing, 9304–23

Federal Home Loan Bank of Seattle

Financial statements of Bank, 1988-90, annual rpt, 9304–15

Housing vacancy rates for single and multifamily units and mobile homes in FHLB 12th District, by ZIP code, annual MSA rpt series, 9304–21

Federal Home Loan Bank of Topeka

Financial statements of Bank, 1988-90, annual rpt, 9304–16

Housing vacancy rates for single and multifamily units and mobile homes in FHLB 10th District, by ZIP code, annual MSA rpt series, 9304–22

Savings instns, FHLB 10th District members, locations, assets, and deposits, 1991, annual listing, 9304–17

Federal Home Loan Banks

Budget of US, financial statements of federally sponsored enterprises, FY92, annual rpt, 104–2.5

Finances and lending activity of FHLBs, 1935-89, annual rpt, 8434–3.4

Financial condition and capital adequacy of govt-sponsored enterprises, with data by enterprise, 1970s-90 and projected to 1996, 26308–99

Financial condition and capital adequacy of govt-sponsored enterprises, with impacts on Federal borrowing and data by enterprise, 1980s-90, last issue of annual rpt, 8004–15

Financial condition and capital adequacy of govt-sponsored enterprises, with regulatory recommendations and data by enterprise, 1985-95, GAO rpt, 26119–296

Financial statements of FHLBs, monthly rpt, 9442–1

Financial statements of FHLBs, 1988-90, annual rpt, 9444–1

see also Federal Home Loan Bank Board

see also Federal Home Loan Bank of Atlanta

see also Federal Home Loan Bank of Boston

see also Federal Home Loan Bank of Chicago

see also Federal Home Loan Bank of Cincinnati

see also Federal Home Loan Bank of Dallas

see also Federal Home Loan Bank of Des Moines

see also Federal Home Loan Bank of Indianapolis

see also Federal Home Loan Bank of New York

see also Federal Home Loan Bank of Pittsburgh

see also Federal Home Loan Bank of San Francisco

see also Federal Home Loan Bank of Seattle

see also Federal Home Loan Bank of Topeka

Federal Home Loan Mortgage Corp.

Budget of US, financial statements of federally sponsored enterprises, FY92, annual rpt, 104–2.5

Financial condition and capital adequacy of Freddie Mac, 1989, annual rpt, 5184–8

Financial condition and capital adequacy of govt-sponsored enterprises, with data by enterprise, 1970s-90 and projected to 1996, 26308–99

Financial condition and capital adequacy of govt-sponsored enterprises, with impacts on Federal borrowing and data by enterprise, 1980s-90, last issue of annual rpt, 8004–15

Financial condition and capital adequacy of govt-sponsored enterprises, with regulatory recommendations and data by enterprise, 1985-95, GAO rpt, 26119–296

Financial statements and activities of FHLMC, 1990, annual rpt, 9414–1

Mortgage applications by disposition, and secondary loan market sales by purchaser type, by applicant and neighborhood characteristics, 1990, article, 9362–1.206

Mortgage debt outstanding by purpose and holder type, 1978-89, annual rpt, 8434–3.3

Federal Housing Administration

see Housing (FHA), HUD

Federal Housing Finance Board

Budget of US, authoritative financial statements with appropriations, outlays, and receipts, by category and agency, FY90, annual rpt, 8104–2.1

Budget of US, obligations and authority by function, agency, and program, with summaries, analyses, and historical tables, FY92, annual rpt, 104–2

Fed Home Loan Banks financial statements, 1988-90, annual rpt, 9444–1

Financial statements of FHLBs, monthly rpt, 9442–1

Home mortgages (conventional) terms on loans closed, by lender type, with quarterly data for 32 MSAs, monthly rpt, 9442–2

Federal independent agencies

Budget of US, authoritative financial statements with appropriations, outlays, and receipts, by category and agency, FY90, annual rpt, 8104–2.1

Budget of US, object class analysis of obligations, by agency, FY92, annual rpt, 104–9

Budget of US, obligations and authority by function, agency, and program, with summaries, analyses, and historical tables, FY92, annual rpt, 104–2

Budget of US, receipts by source, outlays by agency and program, and balances, monthly rpt, 8102–3

Congressional Directory, members of 102nd Congress, other officials, elections, and districts, 1991-92, biennial rpt, 23874–1

Education funding by Federal agency, program, and recipient type, and instn spending, FY80-90, annual rpt, 4824–8

Employment (civilian) of Fed Govt, work-years, pay rates, and benefits use and costs, by agency, FY89, annual rpt, 9844–31

Federal independent agencies

Employment and payroll (civilian) of Fed Govt, by agency in DC metro area, total US, and abroad, bimonthly rpt, 9842–1

Financial consolidated statements of Fed Govt based on business accounting methods, FY89-90, annual rpt, 8104–5

Financial operations of Fed Govt, detailed data, *Treasury Bulletin*, quarterly rpt, 8002–4

Flow-of-funds accounts, savings, investments, and credit statements, quarterly rpt, 9365–3.3

Investigations of Federal agency and program operations, summaries of findings, 1981-90, annual GAO rpt, 26104–5

Regulatory programs of Fed Govt, evaluation, review process, and actions taken, by agency, 1980s-90, annual rpt, 104–28

see also ACTION

see also Administrative Conference of the U.S.

see also Advisory Council on Historic Preservation

see also American Battle Monuments Commission

see also Appalachian Regional Commission

see also Central Intelligence Agency

see also Commission of Fine Arts

see also Consumer Product Safety Commission

see also Environmental Protection Agency

see also Equal Employment Opportunity Commission

see also Export-Import Bank

see also Farm Credit Administration

see also Federal boards, committees, and commissions

see also Federal Communications Commission

see also Federal Deposit Insurance Corp.

see also Federal Emergency Management Agency

see also Federal Home Loan Bank Board

see also Federal Housing Finance Board

see also Federal Maritime Commission

see also Federal Mediation and Conciliation Service

see also Federal Reserve System

see also Federal Trade Commission

see also General Services Administration

see also Government corporations and enterprises

see also Interstate Commerce Commission

see also Merit Systems Protection Board

see also National Aeronautics and Space Administration

see also National Archives and Records Administration

see also National Credit Union Administration

see also National Foundation on the Arts and the Humanities

see also National Labor Relations Board

see also National Mediation Board

see also National Science Foundation

see also National Transportation Safety Board

see also Neighborhood Reinvestment Corp.

see also Nuclear Regulatory Commission

see also Occupational Safety and Health Review Commission

see also Office of Government Ethics

see also Office of Personnel Management

see also Office of Special Counsel

see also Panama Canal Commission

see also Peace Corps

see also Postal Rate Commission

see also Railroad Retirement Board

see also Resolution Trust Corp.

see also Securities and Exchange Commission

see also Selective Service System

see also Small Business Administration

see also Tennessee Valley Authority

see also U.S. Arms Control and Disarmament Agency

see also U.S. Information Agency

see also U.S. International Development Cooperation Agency

see also U.S. International Trade Commission

see also U.S. Postal Service

see also Veterans Administration

see also under By Federal Agency in the "Index by Categories"

Federal Inspectors General reports

Activities of Inspectors General, and fraud and abuse audits and investigations by agency, FY90, annual rpt, 104–29

Alcohol use, knowledge, attitudes, and info sources of youth, series, 4006–10

Board and care homes regulation and rules enforcement by States, 1988, 4008–112

Commerce Dept programs fraud and abuse, audits and investigations, 2nd half FY91, semiannual rpt, 2002–5

DOD programs fraud and abuse, audits and investigations, 1st half FY91, semiannual rpt, 3542–18

DOE programs finances and mgmt, audits and investigations, series, 3006–5

DOE programs fraud and abuse, audit resolution activities, 2nd half FY91, semiannual rpt, 3002–15

DOE programs fraud and abuse, audits and investigations, 2nd half FY91, semiannual rpt, 3002–12

DOT programs fraud and abuse, audits and investigations, FY79-88, annual rpt, 7304–1

DOT programs fraud and abuse, audits and investigations, 1st half FY91, semiannual rpt, 7302–4

Education Dept programs fraud and abuse, audits and investigations, 2nd half FY91, semiannual rpt, 4802–1

EPA programs fraud and abuse, audits and investigations, 2nd half FY91, semiannual rpt, 9182–10

GSA programs fraud and abuse, audits and investigations, semiannual rpt, 9452–8

Health care professionals licensing and disciplinary actions of State medical boards, 1950s-87, series, 4006–8

HHS programs fraud and abuse, audits and investigations, 1st half FY91, semiannual rpt, 4002–6

HUD programs fraud and abuse, audits and investigations, FY91, semiannual rpt, 5002–8; 5002–11

Interior Dept programs fraud and abuse, audits and investigations, 2nd half FY91, semiannual rpt, 5302–2

Kidney dialysis patients anemia treatment with Epoetin alfa, dosages, costs, Medicare reimbursement, and facility income effects, 1989, 4008–113

Index by Subjects and Names

Labor Dept programs fraud and abuse, audits and investigations activity, and racketeering cases by type and disposition, FY88-89, GAO rpt, 26111–74

Labor Dept programs fraud and abuse, audits and investigations, 2nd half FY91, semiannual rpt, 6302–2

Medicare reimbursement of hospitals under prospective payment system, diagnosis related group code assignment and effects on care and instn finances, 1984/85, series, 4006–7

NASA programs fraud and abuse, audits and investigations, 2nd half FY91, semiannual rpt, 9502–9

NSF programs fraud and abuse, audits and investigations, 2nd half FY91, semiannual rpt, 9622–1

Physicians licensing and disciplinary activities of State medical boards, investigative staff, and licensing fees, by State, 1985-90, 4008–83

Resolution Trust Corp programs fraud and abuse, audits and investigations, 2nd half FY91, semiannual rpt, 9722–6

Small Business Admin programs fraud and abuse, audits and investigations, 1st half FY91, semiannual rpt, 9762–5

State Dept programs fraud and abuse, audits and investigations, 2nd half FY91, semiannual rpt, 7002–6

USDA programs fraud and abuse, audits and investigations, 1st half FY91, semiannual rpt, 1002–4

VA programs fraud and abuse, audits and investigations, 2nd half FY90, semiannual rpt, 8602–1

Federal Intermediate Credit Banks

see Farm Credit System

Federal Judicial Center

Appellate court pre-argument conferences impacts on case processing, disposition, and duration, for Federal 6th circuit, 1985-86, 18408–45

Budget of US, authoritative financial statements with appropriations, outlays, and receipts, by category and agency, FY90, annual rpt, 8104–2.1

Budget of US, obligations and authority by function, agency, and program, with summaries, analyses, and historical tables, FY92, annual rpt, 104–2

Civil cases court-annexed arbitration, pilot program evaluation, 1984-86, 18408–46

Federal Labor Relations Authority

Activities of FLRA and Fed Services Impasses Panel, and cases by union, agency, and disposition, FY85-90, annual rpt, 13364–1

Budget of US, authoritative financial statements with appropriations, outlays, and receipts, by category and agency, FY90, annual rpt, 8104–2.1

Budget of US, obligations and authority by function, agency, and program, with summaries, analyses, and historical tables, FY92, annual rpt, 104–2

Federal land banks

see Farm Credit System

Federal lands

see Government supplies and property

see Military bases, posts, and reservations

see Public lands

Index by Subjects and Names

Federal-local relations

Army Corps of Engineers water resources dev projects, characteristics, and costs, 1950s-89, biennial State rpt series, 3756–1

Army Corps of Engineers water resources dev projects, characteristics, and costs, 1950s-91, biennial State rpt series, 3756–2

Census of Population and Housing, 1990: local govt review of preliminary results, issues, hearing, 21628–93

Census of Population, 1990: data adjustment for undercounts, final decision, 2008–31

see also Federal aid to local areas

see also Indian claims

see also Revenue sharing

Federal Maritime Commission

Activities of FMC, case filings by type and disposition, and civil penalties by shipper, FY90, annual rpt, 9334–1

Budget of US, authoritative financial statements with appropriations, outlays, and receipts, by category and agency, FY90, annual rpt, 8104–2.1

Budget of US, obligations and authority by function, agency, and program, with summaries, analyses, and historical tables, FY92, annual rpt, 104–2

Federal Mediation and Conciliation Service

Activities of FMCS, and cases by issue, region, and State, FY84-89, annual rpt, 9344–1

Budget of US, authoritative financial statements with appropriations, outlays, and receipts, by category and agency, FY90, annual rpt, 8104–2.1

Budget of US, obligations and authority by function, agency, and program, with summaries, analyses, and historical tables, FY92, annual rpt, 104–2

Federal Mine Safety and Health Act

Enforcement of mine safety and health, training, and funding, with casualties, by type of mine and State, FY89, annual rpt, 6664–6

Federal Mine Safety and Health Review Commission

Budget of US, authoritative financial statements with appropriations, outlays, and receipts, by category and agency, FY90, annual rpt, 8104–2.1

Budget of US, obligations and authority by function, agency, and program, with summaries, analyses, and historical tables, FY92, annual rpt, 104–2

Federal National Mortgage Association

Activities and finances of FNMA, 1988-89, annual rpt, 5184–9

Budget of US, financial statements of federally sponsored enterprises, FY92, annual rpt, 104–2.5

Financial condition and capital adequacy of govt-sponsored enterprises, with data by enterprise, 1970s-90 and projected to 1996, 26308–99

Financial condition and capital adequacy of govt-sponsored enterprises, with impacts on Federal borrowing and data by enterprise, 1980s-90, last issue of annual rpt, 8004–15

Financial condition and capital adequacy of govt-sponsored enterprises, with regulatory recommendations and data by enterprise, 1985-95, GAO rpt, 26119–296

Mortgage applications by disposition, and secondary loan market sales by purchaser type, by applicant and neighborhood characteristics, 1990, article, 9362–1.206

Mortgage debt outstanding by purpose and holder type, 1978-89, annual rpt, 8434–3.3

Federal officials

see Officials

Federal Open Market Committee

Chronology of FOMC decisions, 1990, annual article, 9391–1.213

Fed Reserve Board and Reserve banks finances, staff, and review of monetary policy and economic devs, 1990, annual rpt, 9364–1

Monetary aggregates growth and related devs, and FOMC activity, annual article, 9385–1

Monetary policy votes of Fed Reserve Bank District presidents and Board governors relative to inflation and GNP growth forecasts, 1965-85, article, 9373–1.214

Monetary policy votes of FOMC members, relation to regional employment conditions, 1965-85, article, 9373–1.205

Policies and transactions, *Fed Reserve Bulletin,* monthly rpt with articles, 9362–1

Federal Parent Locator Service

Child Support Enforcement Program finances and operations, by State, FY85-89, annual rpt, 4694–6

Federal pay

Advisory committees of Fed Govt, and members, staff, meetings, and costs by agency, FY90, annual rpt, 9454–18

Budget of US, authoritative financial statements with appropriations, outlays, and receipts, by category and agency, FY90, annual rpt, 8104–2.1

Budget of US, object class analysis of obligations, by agency, FY92, annual rpt, 104–9

Budget of US, obligations and authority by function, agency, and program, with summaries, analyses, and historical tables, FY92, annual rpt, 104–2

Census of Govts, 1987: employment, payroll, and average earnings, by function, level of govt, State, county, and population size, 2455–2

Criminal justice spending, employment, and payroll, by level of govt, State, and selected city and county, FY71-88, biennial rpt, 6064–9

Criminal justice spending, employment, and payroll, by level of govt, State, and selected city and county, 1984-86, biennial rpt, 6064–4

Earnings by industry div, and personal income per capita and by source, by State, MSA, and county, 1984-89, annual regional rpts, 2704–2

Employment, earnings, and hours, by SIC 1- to 4-digit industry, monthly and annual averages, selected years 1909-90, annual rpt, 6744–4

Family-related and work schedule benefits for Federal employees, availability, admin, and personnel directors views, 1990 survey, 9496–2.7

Finances of Fed Govt, cash and debt transactions, daily tables, 8102–4

Financial consolidated statements of Fed Govt based on business accounting methods, FY89-90, annual rpt, 8104–5

House of Representatives salaries, expenses, and contingent fund disbursement, detailed listings, quarterly rpt, 21942–1

Incentive awards to Federal employees, costs, and benefits, by award type and agency, FY89, annual rpt, 9844–20

Income (household, family, and personal), by source, detailed characteristics, and region, 1988-89, annual Current Population Rpt, 2546–6.68

Income (household, family, and personal), by source, detailed characteristics, and region, 1990, annual Current Population Rpt, 2546–6.70

Law enforcement spending and employment, by activity and level of govt, data compilation, 1991 annual rpt, 6064–6.1

Merit system oversight and enforcement activities of OPM, series, 9496–2

Natl income and product accounts and components, *Survey of Current Business,* monthly rpt, 2702–1.24

Pay comparability of Fed Govt with private industry, by occupation for 22 MSAs, 1989, GAO rpt, 26119–332

Pay rates, employment, work-years, and benefits use and costs, by agency, FY89, annual rpt, 9844–31

Payroll and employment (civilian) of Fed Govt, by agency in DC metro area, total US, and abroad, bimonthly rpt, 9842–1

Payroll and employment (civilian) of Fed Govt, by occupation, pay grade, sex, agency, and location, 1989, biennial rpt, 9844–4

Payroll and employment (civilian) of Fed Govt, by pay system, agency, and location, 1990, annual rpt, 9844–6

Payroll and employment, by function, level of govt, and State, 1990, annual rpt, 2466–1.1

Payroll and employment, by level of govt and State, 1991 and historical trends, annual rpt, 10044–1

Payroll of Fed Govt, by State and county, FY90, annual rpt, 2464–3.1

Payroll of Fed Govt, spending for civilian, military, and postal workers by State, FY90, annual rpt, 2464–2

Postal Service employment and related expenses, FY90, annual rpt, 9864–5.1; 9864–5.3

Postal Service operating costs, itemized by class of mail, FY90, annual rpt, 9864–4

Postal Service productivity, indexes of output and labor, capital, and other inputs, alternative model descriptions and results, 1960s-89, 9688–6

Postal Service revenue, costs, and volume, by service type and class of mail, FY90, annual rpt, 9864–2

R&D personnel costs for intramural programs, by agency, FY89-91, annual rpt, 9627–20

Science and engineering PhDs employment and other characteristics, by field and State, 1989, biennial rpt, 9627–18

Senate receipts, itemized expenses by payee, and balances, 1st half FY91, semiannual listing, 25922–1

Senior Executive Service membership characteristics, entries, exits, and awards, FY79-90, annual rpt, 9844–36

Federal pay

Shutdown of Fed Govt over Columbus Day holiday, employees affected, costs, and savings, Oct 1990, GAO rpt, 26119-311

State and Metro Area Data Book, 1991 data compilation, 2328-54

Statistical Abstract of US, 1991 annual data compilation, 2324-1.10

Travel expenses of Fed Govt employees, operating costs for private autos, airplanes, and motorcycles, and reimbursement rates for business use, 1989, annual rpt, 9454-13

Unemployment insurance coverage of establishments, employment, and wages, by SIC 4-digit industry and State, 1990, annual rpt, 6744-16

VA health care facilities physicians, dentists, and nurses, by selected employment characteristics and VA district, quarterly rpt, 8602-6

see also Civil service pensions

see also Military benefits and pensions

see also Military pay

Federal Power Marketing Administrations

see Alaska Power Administration

see Bonneville Power Administration

see Southeastern Power Administration

see Southwestern Power Administration

see Western Area Power Administration

Federal Prison Industries

Employment in UNICOR and other work programs, by instn, 1991, annual listing, 6244-4

Finances and operations, FY90, annual rpt, 6244-3

Sales, by commodity and Federal agency, FY90, annual rpt, 6244-5

Federal prisons

see Correctional institutions

see Federal Prison Industries

see Prisoners

Federal publications lists

see Government publications lists

Federal Railroad Administration

Accidents, casualties, and damage, by cause, railroad, and State, 1990, annual rpt, 7604-1

Activities of FRA, safety inspectors by State, and accidents, casualties, and damage, 1989, annual rpt, 7604-12

Budget of US, obligations and authority by function, agency, and program, with summaries, analyses, and historical tables, FY92, annual rpt, 104-2

Employment of DOT, by subagency, occupation, and selected personnel characteristics, FY90, annual rpt, 7304-18

Expenditures of Fed Govt in States, by type, program, agency, and State, FY90, annual rpt, 2464-2

Hwy-railroad grade-crossing accidents, detailed data by State and railroad, 1989, annual rpt, 7604-2

Inspections by Fed Railroad Admin, safety defects and violations reported, by type, 1985-89, GAO rpt, 26113-515

Safety violation claims settled, by rail carrier, FY90, annual rpt, 7604-10

Federal Republic of Germany

see Germany

see Germany, West

Federal Reserve Bank of Atlanta

Dollar exchange rate trade-weighted index of Bank, by world area, quarterly rpt, 9371-15

Economic indicators by State and MSA, Fed Reserve 6th District, quarterly rpt, 9371-14

Financial and banking devs in southeastern States, working paper series, 9371-10

Financial and economic devs, bimonthly journal, 9371-1

Financial statements of Bank, 1989-90, annual rpt, 9371-4

Federal Reserve Bank of Boston

Economic and financial devs, quarterly journal, 9373-25

Economic indicators for New England States, Fed Reserve 1st District, monthly rpt, 9373-2

Financial and banking devs, research rpt series, 9373-4

Financial and economic devs, bimonthly journal, 9373-1

Financial and monetary studies, conf series, 9373-3

Financial statements of Bank, 1989-90, annual rpt, 9373-26

Federal Reserve Bank of Chicago

Banks financial performance, risk assessment, and regulation, 1990 annual conf papers, 9375-7

Farm credit conditions and economic devs, Fed Reserve 7th District, monthly rpt, 9375-10

Financial and economic analysis, and economic issues affecting North Central States, working paper series, 9375-13

Financial and economic devs, bimonthly journal, 9375-1

Financial statements of Bank, 1989-90, annual rpt, 9375-5

Great Lakes area economic conditions and outlook, for US and Canada, 1970s-90, 9375-15

Federal Reserve Bank of Cleveland

Economic indicators and components, and Fed Reserve 4th District business and financial conditions, monthly chartbook, 9377-10

Financial and economic analysis and forecasting methodology, technical paper series, 9377-9

Financial and economic devs, quarterly journal, 9377-1

Financial statements of Bank, 1989-90, annual rpt, 9377-5

Federal Reserve Bank of Dallas

Dollar exchange rate trade-weighted index of Bank, by world area, monthly rpt, 9379-13

Farm credit conditions and real estate values, Fed Reserve 11th District, quarterly rpt, 9379-11

Financial and economic analysis, technical paper series, 9379-12

Financial and economic devs, bimonthly journal, 9379-1

Financial statements of Bank, 1989-90, annual rpt, 9379-2

Savings instns financial condition and devs, working paper series, 9379-14

Federal Reserve Bank of Kansas City

Banking industry structure, performance, and financial devs, for Fed Reserve 10th District, 1990, annual rpt, 9381-14

Financial and economic analysis of banking and nonbanking sectors, working paper series, 9381-10

Financial and economic devs, bimonthly journal, 9381-1

Financial and economic devs, Fed Reserve 10th District, quarterly rpt, 9381-16

Financial statements of Bank, 1989-90, annual rpt, 9381-3

Federal Reserve Bank of Minneapolis

Business and economic conditions, Fed Reserve 9th District, quarterly journal, 9383-19

Farm credit conditions, earnings, and expenses, Fed Reserve 9th District, quarterly rpt, 9383-11

Financial and economic analysis, technical paper series, 9383-20

Financial and economic devs, quarterly journal, 9383-6

Financial statements of Bank, 1989-90, annual rpt, 9383-2

Federal Reserve Bank of New York

Financial and economic analysis, technical paper series, 9385-8

Financial and economic devs, quarterly journal, 9385-1

Financial statements of Bank, 1989-90, annual rpt, 9385-2

Federal Reserve Bank of Philadelphia

Economic conditions, Fed Reserve 3rd District, quarterly rpt, 9387-10

Financial and economic devs, bimonthly journal, 9387-1

Financial and monetary research and econometric analyses, working paper series, 9387-8

Financial statements of Bank, 1989-90, annual rpt, 9387-3

Manufacturing business outlook, for Fed Reserve 3rd District, monthly survey rpt, 9387-11

Middle Atlantic States manufacturing output index, monthly rpt, 9387-12

Federal Reserve Bank of Richmond

Banks (insured commercial), Fed Reserve 5th District members financial statements, by State, quarterly rpt, 9389-18

Economic indicators by State, Fed Reserve 5th District, quarterly rpt, 9389-16

Financial and economic analysis, technical paper series, 9389-19

Financial and economic devs, bimonthly journal, 9389-1

Financial statements of Bank, 1989-90, annual rpt, 9389-2

Federal Reserve Bank of San Francisco

Financial and economic analysis, technical paper series, 9393-10

Financial and economic devs, quarterly journal, 9393-8

Financial statements of Bank, 1989-90, annual rpt, 9393-2

Federal Reserve Bank of St. Louis

Economic and banking conditions, for Fed Reserve 8th District, quarterly rpt with articles, 9391-16

Economic indicators compounded annual rates of change, monthly rpt, 9391-3

Economic indicators compounded annual rates of change, 1971-90, annual rpt, 9391-9

Financial and economic devs, bimonthly journal, 9391-1

Index by Subjects and Names

Financial and monetary conditions, selected US summary data, weekly rpt, 9391–4

Financial statements of Bank, 1989-90, annual rpt, 9391–17

Intl transactions of US, and economic and monetary trends for US and 7 major industrialized countries, quarterly rpt, 9391–7

Monetary trends, monthly rpt, 9391–2

Federal Reserve Board of Governors

Assets and debts of private sector, balance sheets by segment, 1945-90, semiannual rpt series, 9365–4

Banks (insured commercial) assets, branches, holding company status, and charter class, by bank, quarterly listing, suspended, 9362–7

Budget of US, financial statements of federally sponsored enterprises, FY92, annual rpt, 104–2.5

Credit, interest rates, banking activity, and industrial production, monthly rpt series, 9365–2

Economic indicators and cyclical devs and outlook, by Fed Reserve Bank District, periodic rpt, 9362–8

Economic policy and banking practices, technical paper series, 9366–1

Finance (intl) and financial policy, and external factors affecting US economy, technical paper series, 9366–7

Finances and staff of Fed Reserve Board and Reserve banks, and review of monetary policy and economic devs, 1990, annual rpt, 9364–1

Financial and business detailed statistics, *Fed Reserve Bulletin*, monthly rpt with articles, 9362–1

Financial and economic analysis and forecasting methodology, technical paper series, 9366–6

Financial, banking, and mortgage market activity, weekly rpt series, 9365–1

Financial statements, performance, and fiscal services, for Fed Reserve System, Board of Governors, and district banks, 1989-91, annual rpt, 9364–10

Flow-of-funds accounts, US banks foreign branches assets and liabilities, and agricultural credit, quarterly rpt series, 9365–3

Loans (farm) outstanding, by lender, and farm and nonfarm banks and assets held, 1990 conf papers, 9368–90

Monetary aggregates and velocities, monthly rpt, discontinued, 9362–6

Monetary policy objectives of Fed Reserve, and performance of major economic indicators, as of July 1991, semiannual rpt, 9362–4

Securities credit issues of stockbrokers and other nonbank lenders, as of June 1990, annual rpt series, 9365–5

Federal Reserve System

Banks regulatory enforcement activities of Federal agencies, effectiveness, with data on capital-deficient banks, late 1980s-90, GAO rpt, 26119–334

Budget of US, obligations and authority by function, agency, and program, with summaries, analyses, and historical tables, FY92, annual rpt, 104–2

Business statistics, detailed data for major industries and economic indicators, *Survey of Current Business*, monthly rpt, 2702–1.9

County Business Patterns, 1988: employment, establishments, and payroll, by SIC 2- to 4-digit industry and county, annual State rpt series, 2326–6

County Business Patterns, 1989: employment, establishments, and payroll, by SIC 2- to 4-digit industry and county, annual State rpt series, 2326–8

Credit and reserves of depository instns, 1959-90, annual rpt, 204–1.5

Finances and staff of Fed Reserve Board and Reserve banks, and review of monetary policy and economic devs, 1990, annual rpt, 9364–1

Financial, banking, and mortgage market activity, weekly rpt series, 9365–1

Financial operations of Fed Govt, detailed data, *Treasury Bulletin*, quarterly rpt, 8002–4

Financial statements for Fed Reserve services, monthly rpt, periodic data, 9362–1.4

Financial statements, performance, and fiscal services, for Fed Reserve System, Board of Governors, and district banks, 1989-91, annual rpt, 9364–10

Foreign countries currency transactions of Fed Reserve and impact on receipts, profits, and Treasury payments, 1975-89, article, 9377–1.205

Monetary policy objectives of Fed Reserve, and performance of major economic indicators, as of July 1991, semiannual rpt, 9362–4

Monetary policy of Fed Reserve, political independence issues, with proposed restructuring legislation, 1970s-90, technical paper, 9385–8.106

Monetary policy votes of Fed Reserve Bank District presidents and Board governors relative to inflation and GNP growth forecasts, 1965-85, article, 9373–1.214

Reserve requirements for financial instns, and coverage, 1991 article, 9377–1.207

Reserves and borrowings of all member banks, monthly rpt, 23842–1.5

Reserves of depository instns, reserve and margin requirements, and borrowings from Fed Reserve, monthly rpt, 9362–1.1

Securities and commodity trading regulatory activities and interagency coordination, FY91, annual rpt, 11924–4

Transactions of US Treasury with Fed Reserve Banks, daily tables, 8102–4

see also Federal Open Market Committee

see also Federal Reserve Bank of Atlanta

see also Federal Reserve Bank of Boston

see also Federal Reserve Bank of Chicago

see also Federal Reserve Bank of Cleveland

see also Federal Reserve Bank of Dallas

see also Federal Reserve Bank of Kansas City

see also Federal Reserve Bank of Minneapolis

see also Federal Reserve Bank of New York

see also Federal Reserve Bank of Philadelphia

see also Federal Reserve Bank of Richmond

see also Federal Reserve Bank of San Francisco

see also Federal Reserve Bank of St. Louis

see also Federal Reserve Board of Governors

Federally Funded R&D Centers

Federal Savings and Loan Insurance Corp.

Savings instns failure resolution costs to FSLIC, relation to asset quality indicators and tax benefit grants, 1984-87, article, 9292–4.202

Federal Service Impasses Panel

see Federal Labor Relations Authority

Federal-State relations

Cattle tuberculosis cases and cooperative Federal-State eradication activities, by State, FY89-90, annual rpt, 1394–13

Coal Surface Mining Reclamation and Enforcement Office activities and funding, by State and Indian tribe, FY90, annual rpt, 5644–1

EPA regulatory and protection programs operations and mgmt goals, progress and activities, by office, quarterly rpt, 9182–11

Geological Survey activities and funding, FY90, annual rpt, 5664–8

Meat and poultry inspection activities and staff of Federal, State, and foreign govts, FY90, annual rpt, 1374–1

Unemployment insurance programs of States and Fed Govt, benefits adequacy, and work disincentives, series, 6406–6

see also Federal aid to States

Federal stockpiles

see Stockpiling

Federal Technology Transfer Act

Labs of Fed Govt, technology transfer cooperative agreements, patents, royalties, and incentive payments to employees, by agency, FY89, GAO rpt, 26131–85

Federal Trade Commission

Activities of FTC, FY89, annual narrative rpt, 9404–1

Budget of US, authoritative financial statements with appropriations, outlays, and receipts, by category and agency, FY90, annual rpt, 8104–2.1

Budget of US, obligations and authority by function, agency, and program, with summaries, analyses, and historical tables, FY92, annual rpt, 104–2

Cigarette smoke tar, nicotine, and carbon monoxide content, by brand, 1989, 9408–53

Industry structure, conduct, and govt regulation, effects on competition, series, 9406–1

R&D funding by Fed Govt, by field, performer type, agency, and State, FY89-91, annual rpt, 9627–20

Federal Transit Administration

see Urban Mass Transportation Administration

Federally Funded R&D Centers

Expenditures for R&D and related activities of higher education and nonprofit instns by Fed Govt, by field, instn, agency, and State, FY89, annual rpt, 9627–17.1

Expenditures for R&D by Fed Govt, by field, performer type, agency, and State, FY89-91, annual rpt, 9627–20

Expenditures for R&D by higher education instns and federally funded centers, by field, instn, and State, FY89, annual rpt, 9627–13

NASA procurement contract awards, by type, contractor, State, and country, FY91 with trends from 1961, semiannual rpt, 9502–6

Federally Funded R&D Centers

see also Department of Energy National Laboratories

Federally impacted areas
see Impacted areas

Federated Department Stores, Inc.
Leveraged buyouts impacts on financial performance, for 4 transactions, 1980s-90, GAO rpt, 26119–355

Federated States of Micronesia
see Micronesia Federated States

Feeds
see Animal feed

Feedstocks, petrochemical
see Petrochemicals

Feldspar
see Nonmetallic minerals and mines

Fellowships
see Student aid

Fenn, George
"Debt Maturity and the Back-to-the-Wall Theory of Corporate Finance", 9366–6.285
"Prudential Margin Policy in a Futures-Style Settlement System", 9366–6.278

Ferguson, George E.
"History of the Water Resources Division, USGS: Volume V, July 1, 1947-Apr. 30, 1957", 5668–118.1

Ferguson, Walter L.
"Welfare Implications of EPA's New Registration Standard: The Case of Fresh Market Tomatoes", 1588–154

Fernandez, Edward W.
"Hispanic Population of the U.S. Southwest Borderland", 2546–2.159

Ferries
Census of Transportation, 1987: finances and operations by size, ownership, and State, and revenues by MSA, by SIC 2- to 4-digit industry, 2579–1
County Business Patterns, 1988: employment, establishments, and payroll, by SIC 2- to 4-digit industry and county, annual State rpt series, 2326–6
County Business Patterns, 1989: employment, establishments, and payroll, by SIC 2- to 4-digit industry and county, annual State rpt series, 2326–8
Customs Service activities, collections, entries processed by mode of transport, and seizures, FY86-90, annual rpt, 8144–1
Finances and operations of transit systems, by mode of transport, size of fleet, and for 468 systems, 1989, annual rpt, 7884–4
Natl transportation system planning, use, condition, accidents, and needs, by mode of transport, 1940s-90 and projected to 2020, 7308–202
Toll facilities, mileage, and operating status, by type of system, as of Jan 1990, biennial listing, 7554–39
Urban Mass Transportation Admin grants for transit systems, by city and State, FY90, annual rpt, 7884–10

Ferroalloys
see Iron and steel industry

Fertility
Africa (sub-Saharan) AIDS epidemic impacts on population size and components of change, model description and results, 1990-2015, working paper, 2326–18.57
Birth expectations, childbearing delay, and childlessness among women born late

1930s-72, by age, education, and marital and employment status, late 1970s-90, Current Population Rpt, 2546–2.162
Births and rates, by characteristics of birth, infant, and parents, 1989 and trends from 1940, US Vital Statistics advance annual rpt, 4146–5.123
Births and rates by mother's age, and fertility rates, by mother's education, child's race, census div, and State, 1980 and 1985, 4147–21.49
Births, fertility rates, and childless women, by selected characteristics, 1990, annual Current Population Rpt, 2546–1.455
Developing countries economic and social conditions from 1960s, and Intl Dev Cooperation Agency and AID activities and funding, FY90-92, annual rpt, 9904–4
Developing countries family planning and population activities of AID, grants by project and recipient, and contraceptive shipments, by country, FY90, annual rpt series, 9914–13
Health condition and health care resources, use, and spending, 1950s-89, annual data compilation, 4144–11
Hispanic Americans in counties bordering Mexico, by selected characteristics, 1980, Current Population Rpt, 2546–2.159
Immigrants in US, population characteristics and fertility, by birthplace and compared to native born, 1980s, Current Population rpt, 2546–2.162
Indian and Alaska Native disease and disorder cases, deaths, and health services use, by tribe, reservation, and Indian Health Service area, late 1950s-86, 4088–2
Minority group health condition, services use, costs, and indicators of services need, 1950s-88, 4118–55
OASDI benefit payments, trust fund finances, and economic and demographic assumptions, 1970-90 and alternative projections to 2000, actuarial rpt, 4706–1.105
Population size and characteristics, historical index to *Current Population Rpts,* 1991 listing, 2546–2.160
Population size and characteristics, 1969-88, Current Population Rpt, biennial rpt, 2546–2.161
Research on population and reproduction, Federal funding by project, FY89, annual listing, 4474–9
Research on population and reproduction, Natl Inst of Child Health and Human Dev funding and activities, 1990, annual rpt, 4474–33
Research on population, family, and sexual behavior, activities and funding, 1960s-89, 4478–194
Statistical Abstract of US, 1991 annual data compilation, 2324–1.2
see also Abortion
see also Births
see also Family planning
see also Population size

Fertilizers
Africa (sub-Saharan) agricultural conditions by country, with Ethiopia grain production and use, and dev aid by major donor, 1960s-80s, hearing, 23848–216

Index by Subjects and Names

Agricultural cooperatives, finances, operations, activities, and membership, 1950s-88, commodity rpt, 1126–1.6
Agricultural Outlook, production, prices, marketing, and trade, by commodity, forecast and current situation, monthly rpt with articles, 1502–4
Agriculture census, 1987: farms, farmland, production, finances, and operator characteristics, by county, final State rpt series, 2331–1
Agriculture census, 1987: horticultural specialties producers, finances, and operations, by crop and State, 1988 survey, 2337–1
Business statistics, detailed data for major industries and economic indicators, *Survey of Current Business,* monthly rpt, 2702–1.12
Consumption and costs for fertilizer by type, and harvested acreage, by State, 1970s-90, biennial rpt, 9804–5
Consumption of fertilizer, by type and region, 1947-89, annual rpt, 1544–17.2
Consumption of fertilizer, by type and State, 1989-90, annual rpt, 9804–30
Cotton farms fertilizer, pesticide and irrigation use, soil conservation practices, and water quality impacts, 1989, 1588–151
County Business Patterns, 1988: employment, establishments, and payroll, by SIC 2- to 4-digit industry and county, annual State rpt series, 2326–6
County Business Patterns, 1989: employment, establishments, and payroll, by SIC 2- to 4-digit industry and county, annual State rpt series, 2326–8
Developing countries agricultural supply, demand, and market for US exports, with socioeconomic conditions, country rpt series, 1526–6
Employment, earnings, and hours, by SIC 1- to 4-digit industry, monthly and annual averages, selected years 1909-90, annual rpt, 6744–4
Employment related to agriculture, by industry, region, and metro-nonmetro location, 1987, 1598–271
Energy use and prices for manufacturing industries, 1988 survey, series, 3166–13
Environmental Quality, status of problems, protection programs, research, and intl issues, 1991 annual rpt, 484–1
Environmental regulation impacts on agricultural trade, with indicators of pollution and fertilizer use intensity by crop, 1991 article, 1522–3.203
Environmental regulation proposals impacts on fertilizer and cropland demand, model description and inputs, 1964-89, 1588–152
Exports and imports (agricultural) of US, by commodity and country, bimonthly rpt, 1522–1
Exports and imports (agricultural) of US, by detailed commodity and country, 1989, annual rpt, 1524–8
Exports and imports (agricultural) of US, by detailed commodity and country, 1990, semiannual rpt, 1522–4
Exports and imports of US, by country and detailed commodity, monthly rpt, 2422–12

Index by Subjects and Names

Exports and imports of US, by Harmonized System 6-digit commodity and country, 1990, annual rpt, 2424–13

Exports and imports of US, by transport mode, country, and SITC 1- to 3-digit commodity, 1990, annual rpt, 2424–12

Exports of US, detailed Schedule B commodities with countries of destination, 1990, annual rpt, 2424–10

Farm fertilizer and pesticide use, and application rates, by type, crop, and State, series, 1616–1

Farm finances and environmental benefits of alternative policies to Food Security Act conservation programs, projected 1991-2005, 1588–153

Farm income, expenses, receipts by commodity, assets, liabilities, and ratios, 1990 and trends from 1945, annual rpt, 1544–16

Farm pesticide and fertilizer use reduction, environmental and economic impacts by commodity and region, alternative forecasts 1989-94, hearing, 23848–222

Farm prices received for major products and paid for farm inputs and living items, by commodity and State, monthly rpt, 1629–1

Farm production inputs, finances, mgmt, and land value and transfers, periodic situation rpt with articles, 1561–16

Farm production itemized costs, by farm sales size and region, 1990, annual rpt, 1614–3

Farm production itemized costs, receipts, and returns, by commodity and region, 1987-89, annual rpt, 1544–20

Farm sector balance sheet, and marketing receipts by detailed commodity, by State, 1985-89, annual rpt, 1544–18

Foreign countries agricultural production, prices, and trade, by country, 1980-90 and forecast 1991, annual world area rpt series, 1524–4

Futures trading in selected commodities and financial instruments and indexes, NYC, Chicago, and other markets activity, semimonthly rpt, 11922–5

Injuries from use of consumer products, by severity, victim age, and detailed product, 1990, annual rpt, 9164–6

Labor productivity, indexes of output, hours, and employment by SIC 2- to 4-digit industry, 1967-89, annual rpt, 6824–1.3

Manufacturing annual survey, 1989: finances and operations, by SIC 2- to 4-digit industry, series, 2506–15

Manufacturing census, 1987: finances and operations, by SIC 2- to 4-digit industry, State, and MSA, with trends from 1849, 2497–1

Manufacturing census, 1987: finances and operations, by type of organization and SIC 2- to 4-digit industry, subject rpt, 2497–5

Manufacturing finances and operations, by SIC 2- to 4-digit industry, forecast 1991, annual rpt, 2044–28

Minerals Yearbook, 1988, Vol 3: foreign country reviews of production, trade, and policy, by commodity, annual rpt series, 5604–17

Minerals Yearbook, 1989, Vol 2: State reviews of production and sales by commodity, and business activity, annual rpt series, 5604–16

Occupational injury and illness rates, by SIC 2- to 4-digit industry, 1988-89, annual rpt, 6844–7

Occupational injury and illness rates, by SIC 2- to 4-digit industry, 1989, annual rpt, 6844–1

OECD trade, total and for 4 major countries, and US trade by country, by commodity, 1970-89, world area rpt series, 9116–1

Pollution (air) emissions factors, by detailed pollutant and source, data compilation, 1990 rpt, 9198–120

Pollution (groundwater) from farm chemicals use and animal wastes, and reduction strategies, 1960s-90, 26358–231

Pollution (groundwater) from farm chemicals use, with background data and farmers views, 1970s-80s, hearing, 25168–76

Price indexes (producer), by stage of processing and detailed commodity, monthly rpt, 6762–6

Price indexes (producer), by stage of processing and detailed commodity, monthly 1990, annual rpt, 6764–2

Prices received and paid by farmers, by commodity and State, 1990, annual rpt, 1629–5

Production capacity of fertilizer firms, for US and Canada, 1986-91 and projected to 1997, triennial rpt, 9808–66

Production of inorganic fertilizer by State, stocks, trade, and use, by product, quarterly Current Industrial Rpt, 2506–8.2

Shipments, trade, use, and firms, by product and State, with stocks, for inorganic fertilizers, 1990, annual Current Industrial Rpt, 2506–8.13; 2506–8.14

Soviet Union, Eastern Europe, OECD, and selected other countries consumer and producer goods and services production and sales, 1960s-90, annual rpt, 9114–4.7

Statistical Abstract of US, 1991 annual data compilation, 2324–1.23

TVA finances and operations by program and facility, FY90, annual rpt, 9804–32

Water (groundwater) supply, quality, chemistry, and use, State and local area rpt series, 5666–28

Water pollution fish kills, by pollution source, month, location, and State, 1977-87, last issue of annual rpt, 9204–3

Water supply and quality in streams and lakes, and groundwater levels in wells, by drainage basin, 1989, annual State rpt series, 5666–12

Water supply and quality in streams and lakes, and groundwater levels in wells, by drainage basin, 1990, annual State rpt series, 5666–10

Fescue

see Animal feed

see Pasture and rangeland

Fetal deaths

Cancer (childhood) survivors risk of miscarriage, stillbirth, and birth defects, by chemotherapy and radiotherapy exposure, study, 1991 article, 4472–1.233

Certificates of birth, death, marriage, and divorce, and fetal death and abortion rpts, 1989 natl standard revisions, 4147–4.27

Fiber optics

Deaths and rates, by detailed cause and demographic characteristics, 1988 and trends from 1900, US Vital Statistics annual rpt, 4144–2

Health condition and health care resources, use, and spending, 1950s-89, annual data compilation, 4144–11

Homeless teens pregnancy prevalence and outcomes, services availability, health condition, and drug abuse, 1989 conf, 4108–55

Lead levels in environment, sources of emissions and exposure, and health effects, literature review, 1990 rpt, 9198 84

Maternal deaths, rates, and risk, by pregnancy outcome, cause, and maternal characteristics, 1979-86, article, 4202–7.206

Pollutants reproductive health and fetal dev effects, with production, trade, and Federal regulatory activities by selected substance, 1980s-90, GAO rpt, 26131–90

Poor women's pregnancies, by whether intended, outcome, contraceptives use, marital status, and race, 1985-86 local area study, article, 4042–3.241

Preventive disease and health improvement goals and recommended activities for 2000, with trends 1970s-80s, 4048–10

Statistical Abstract of US, 1991 annual data compilation, 2324–1.2

see also Abortion

see also Infant mortality

FHA

see Housing (FHA), HUD

FHwA

see Federal Highway Administration

Fiber optics

DOD prime contract awards, by detailed procurement category, FY87-90, annual rpt, 3544–18

Exports and imports of US, by country and detailed commodity, monthly rpt, 2422–12

Exports and imports of US, by Harmonized System 6-digit commodity and country, 1990, annual rpt, 2424–13

Exports of US, detailed Schedule B commodities with countries of destination, 1990, annual rpt, 2424–10

Fed Govt standards for data recording, processing, and transfer, and for purchase and use of computer systems, 1990 rpt, 2216–2.196

Manufacturing finances and operations, by SIC 2- to 4-digit industry, forecast 1991, annual rpt, 2044–28

Quality control spending in semiconductor and fiber optics industries, effectiveness, and views, survey results, 1980s, 2218–84

Shipments, trade, use, and firms, for electronic communications systems and related products, 1990, annual Current Industrial Rpt, 2506–12.35

Telecommunications fiber optics and copper wire mileage and access lines, and fiber systems investment, by firm, 1985-90, annual rpt, 9284–18

Wire and cable (insulated) shipments, trade, use, and firms, by product, 1990, annual Current Industrial Rpt, 2506–10.8

Fibers

Fibers
see Cotton
see Natural fibers
see Silk
see Synthetic fibers and fabrics
see Wool and wool trade

FICA
see Social security tax

Field, Donald W.
"Coastal Wetlands of the U.S.: An Accounting of a Valuable National Resource", 2178–31

Field seeds
see Seeds

Fielding, William G.
"Meat Industry Competition and Consolidation in the 1990s", 1004–16.1

Fieleke, Norman S.
"Primer on the Arms Trade", 9373–1.221

Fiji
- Agricultural exports of high-value commodities, indexes and sales by commodity, world area, and country, 1960s-86, 1528–323
- AID economic aid to developing countries, obligations and disbursements by country, quarterly rpt, 9912–4
- Economic and social conditions of developing countries from 1960s, and Intl Dev Cooperation Agency and AID activities and funding, FY90-92, annual rpt, 9904–4
- Economic conditions, income, production, prices, employment, and trade, 1991 periodic country rpt, 2046–4.67
- Economic, social, and agricultural data, US and other aid sources, and AID activity, 1988 country rpt, 9916–12.28
- Economic, social, political, and geographic summary data, by country, 1991, annual factbook, 9114–2
- Exports and imports of US, by transport mode, country, and SITC 1- to 3-digit commodity, 1990, annual rpt, 2424–12
- Human rights conditions in 170 countries, and US economic and military aid, 1990, annual rpt, 21384–3
- Military aid of US, arms sales, and training programs costs and budget requests, by program, world region, and country, FY90-92, annual rpt, 7144–13
- UN voting record and share of votes in agreement with US, by issue, country, and world area, 1990, annual rpt, 7004–18

Filipino Americans
see Pacific Islands Americans

Films
see Motion pictures

Finance
- Fed Govt financial operations, detailed data, *Treasury Bulletin*, quarterly rpt, 8002–4
- *Federal Reserve Bulletin*, detailed financial statistics, monthly rpt with articles, 9362–1
- Financial and banking devs, Federal Reserve Bank of Boston research rpt series, 9373–4
- Financial and banking devs in southeastern States, working paper series, 9371–10
- Financial and economic analysis, and economic issues affecting North Central States, working paper series, 9375–13
- Financial and economic analysis and forecasting methodology, technical paper series, 9377–9

Financial and economic analysis of banking and nonbanking sectors, working paper series, 9381–10

Financial and economic analysis, technical paper series, 9379–12; 9383–20; 9385–8; 9389–19; 9393–10

Financial and economic devs, Fed Reserve Bank of Atlanta bimonthly journal, 9371–1

Financial and economic devs, Fed Reserve Bank of Chicago bimonthly journal, 9375–1

Financial and economic devs, Fed Reserve Bank of Cleveland quarterly journal, 9377–1

Financial and economic devs, Fed Reserve Bank of Dallas bimonthly journal, 9379–1

Financial and economic devs, Fed Reserve Bank of Kansas City bimonthly journal, 9381–1

Financial and economic devs, Fed Reserve Bank of Minneapolis quarterly journal, 9383–6

Financial and economic devs, Fed Reserve Bank of New York quarterly journal, 9385–1

Financial and economic devs, Fed Reserve Bank of Philadelphia bimonthly journal, 9387–1

Financial and economic devs, Fed Reserve Bank of Richmond bimonthly journal, 9389–1

Financial and economic devs, Fed Reserve Bank of San Francisco quarterly journal, 9393–8

Financial and economic devs, Fed Reserve Bank of St Louis bimonthly journal, 9391–1

Financial and monetary research and econometric analyses, working paper series, 9387–8

Financial and monetary studies, Fed Reserve Bank of Boston conf series, 9373–3

Japan economic conditions, financial and intl policies, and trade devs, 1950s-80s and projected to 2050, compilation of papers, 23848–220

see also Agricultural credit
see also Agricultural finance
see also Bankruptcy
see also Banks and banking
see also Certificates of deposit
see also Commercial credit
see also Consumer credit
see also Credit
see also Educational finance
see also Financial institutions
see also Financial institutions regulation
see also Fiscal policy
see also Flow-of-funds accounts
see also Foreign exchange
see also Futures trading
see also Government securities
see also Gross Domestic Product
see also Gross National Product
see also Housing costs and financing
see also Individual retirement arrangements
see also Inflation
see also Input-output analysis
see also Insurance and insurance industry
see also Interest rates
see also International finance

see also International reserves
see also Investments
see also Loans
see also Monetary policy
see also Money supply
see also Municipal bonds
see also National income and product accounts
see also New York Stock Exchange
see also Prices
see also Securities
see also Stock exchanges

Finance companies
- Assets, liabilities, and business loans of finance companies, monthly rpt, 9362–1.1
- Assets, liabilities, and credit activities, monthly rpt series, 9365–2
- Credit (installment) outstanding, and terms, by lender and credit type, monthly rpt, 9365–2.6
- Credit outstanding and leasing activities of finance companies, by credit type, monthly rpt, 9365–2.7
- Employment, earnings, and hours, by SIC 1- to 4-digit industry, monthly and annual averages, selected years 1909-90, annual rpt, 6744–4
- Finances of financial instns by type and selected instn, and deposit insurance reform issues, 1970s-90, GAO rpt, 26119–320
- Flow-of-funds accounts, savings, investments, and credit statements, quarterly rpt, 9365–3.3
- Home mortgages (conventional) terms on loans closed, by lender type, with quarterly data for 32 MSAs, monthly rpt, 9442–2
- Mortgage loan activity, by type of lender, loan, and mortgaged property, monthly press release, 5142–18
- Mortgage loan activity, by type of lender, loan, and mortgaged property, quarterly press release, 5142–30
- Occupational injury and illness rates, by SIC 2- to 4-digit industry, 1988-89, annual rpt, 6844–7
- Tax (income) returns of corporations, income and tax items by asset size and detailed industry, 1987, annual rpt, 8304–4

Financial crises and depressions
see Business cycles

Financial disclosure
- Election campaign finances and FEC activities, various periods 1975-90, annual rpt, 9274–1
- Elections, procedures, campaign finances, and Fed Election Commission activities, press release series, 9276–1
- SEC registration, firms required to file annual rpts, as of Sept 1990, annual listing, 9734–5
- Unemployment insurance programs of States, quality appraisal results, FY90, annual rpt, 6404–16
- USDA employees financial disclosure rpts filings, processing, errors, and conflicts of interest exposed, 1989, GAO rpt, 26119–314

Financial institutions
- AID loans repayment status and terms by program and country, and status of predecessor agency loans, quarterly rpt, 9912–3

Index by Subjects and Names

Financial Institutions Reform, Recovery, and Enforcement Act

American Samoa employment, earnings, and minimum wage, by establishment and industry, 1989, biennial rpt, 6504–6

Assets and debts of private sector, balance sheets by segment, 1945-90, semiannual rpt, 9365–4.1

Assets and instns by type, nonfinancial sector debt by type, and banks profitability, 1970s-89, technical paper, 9385–8.84

Assets, by type of financial instn and country, 1985, hearing, 21248–149

Bombing incidents, casualties, and damage, by target, circumstances, and State, 1990, annual rpt, 6224–5

Business statistics, detailed data for major industries and economic indicators, *Survey of Current Business*, monthly rpt, 2702–1.9

Capital expenditures for plant and equipment, by major industry group, quarterly rpt, 2502–2

Classification codes concordance of Canada and US SICs, for 1- to 4-digit levels, 1991 rpt, 2628–31

Collective bargaining agreements expiring during year, and workers covered, by firm, union, industry group, and State, 1991, annual rpt, 6784–9

County Business Patterns, 1988: employment, establishments, and payroll, by SIC 2- to 4-digit industry and county, annual State rpt series, 2326–6

County Business Patterns, 1989: employment, establishments, and payroll, by SIC 2- to 4-digit industry and county, annual State rpt series, 2326–8

Credit reporting and collection establishments, and receipts by source and class of client, by MSA, 1987 Census of Service Industries, 2393–4.4

Earnings by industry div, and personal income per capita and by source, by State, MSA, and county, 1984-89, annual regional rpts, 2704–2

Economic Report of the President for 1991, with economic trends from 1929, annual rpt, 204–1

Employment and Earnings, detailed data, monthly rpt, 6742–2.5

Employment, earnings, and hours, by SIC 1- to 4-digit industry, monthly and annual averages, selected years 1909-90, annual rpt, 6744–4

Employment, earnings, and hours, monthly press release, 6742–5

Employment situation, earnings, hours, and other BLS economic indicators, transcripts of BLS Commissioner's monthly testimony, periodic rpt, 23846–4

Employment, unemployment, and labor force characteristics, by region, State, and selected metro area, 1990, annual rpt, 6744–7

Federal Reserve Bulletin, detailed financial statistics, monthly rpt with articles, 9362–1

Financial and economic analysis of banking and nonbanking sectors, working paper series, 9381–10

Foreign direct investment in US, by industry group and world area, 1987-90, annual article, 2702–1.219

Foreign direct investment in US, by industry group of US affiliate and country of parent firm, 1980-86, 2708–41

Foreign direct investment in US, major transactions by type, industry, country, and US location, 1989, annual rpt, 2044–20

Foreign direct investment of US, by industry group and world area, 1987-90, annual article, 2702–1.220

Input-output structure of US economy, detailed interindustry transactions for 84 industries, and components of final demand, 1986, annual article, 2702–1.206

Input-output structure of US economy, detailed interindustry transactions for 85 industries, 1982 benchmark data, 2702–1.213

Intl banking and securities instns assets by selected firm, and financial performance indicators by selected country, late 1980s-90, article, 9385–1.206

Investment banking firms stock performance relation to returns on underwritten stock issues, late 1970s-87, technical paper, 9366–6.260

Japan financial instns and stock market conditions, and other economic indicators, with intl comparisons, 1980s-90, hearing, 21248–152

Location of financial instns, relation to ZIP code area income and minority population, by instn type for 5 cities, 1977-89, article, 9377–1.208

Mail volume to and from households, use, and views, by class, source, content, and household characteristics, 1987-88, annual rpt, 9864–10

Mortgage market regulatory and structural changes impacts on residential investment, with mortgage originations by financial instn type, 1970s-80s, technical paper, 9385–8.74

Multinatl firms US affiliates, finances, and operations, by industry, world area of parent firm, and State, 1988-89, annual rpt, 2704–4

Multinatl US firms and foreign affiliates finances and operations, by industry and world area of parent firm, 1989 benchmark survey, preliminary annual rpt, 2704–5

New England States economic indicators, Fed Reserve 1st District, monthly rpt, 9373–2.7

New England States employment variability relation to service and financial industries employment, with data by selected industry group and State, 1970s-89, article, 9373–1.212

Occupational injuries, illnesses, and workdays lost, by SIC 2-digit industry, 1989-90, annual press release, 6844–3

Occupational injury and illness rates, by SIC 2- to 4-digit industry, 1988-89, annual rpt, 6844–7

Occupational injury and illness rates, by SIC 2- to 4-digit industry, 1989, annual rpt, 6844–1

Puerto Rico and other US possessions corporations income tax returns, income and tax items, and employment, by selected industry, 1987, article, 8302–2.213

Securities (medium-term) outstanding, issuers, and borrowings size, by industry group, 1983-90, technical paper, 9366–6.276

State and Metro Area Data Book, 1991 data compilation, 2328–54

Statistical Abstract of US, 1991 annual data compilation, 2324–1.16

Tax (income) returns filed by type of filer, selected income items, quarterly rpt, 8302–2.1

Tax (income) returns for foreign corporate activity in US, assets, and income statement items, by industry div and selected country, 1986-87, article, 8302–2.205

Tax (income) returns of corporations, income and tax items by asset size and detailed industry, 1987, annual rpt, 8304–4

Tax (income) returns of corporations, income and tax items by asset size and detailed industry, 1988, annual rpt, 8304–21

Tax (income) returns of corporations with foreign tax credit, income and tax items by industry group, 1986, biennial article, 8302–2.203

Tax (income) returns of multinatl US firms foreign affiliates, income statement items, by asset size and industry, 1986, biennial article, 8302–2.212

Tax (income) returns of partnerships, income statement and balance sheet items, by industry group, 1989, annual article, 8302–2.216; 8304–18

Tax (income) returns of sole proprietorships, income statement items, by industry group, 1989, annual article, 8302–2.214

Tax (income) returns of US corporations under foreign control, assets and income statement items by industry div and country, 1988, article, 8302–2.219

Tax expenditures, Federal revenues forgone through income tax deductions and exclusions by type, FY92-96, annual rpt, 21784–10

Wage and benefit changes from collective bargaining and mgmt decisions, by industry div, monthly rpt, 6782–1

Wages by occupation, and benefits for office and plant workers, periodic MSA survey rpt series, 6785–11; 6785–12

see also Automated tellers

see also Bank holding companies

see also Banks and banking

see also Credit unions

see also Deposit insurance

see also Farm Credit System

see also Federal Reserve System

see also Finance companies

see also Financial institutions regulation

see also Insurance and insurance industry

see also Mutual funds

see also Savings institutions

see also Stockbrokers

see also under By Industry in the "Index by Categories"

Financial Institutions Reform, Recovery, and Enforcement Act

Banks and thrifts fraud and abuse, Federal agencies enforcement activities and staff, with data by instn and location, 1988-90, hearing, 21408–119

Savings instns mortgage debt holdings and other assets, returns on assets, and impacts of qualified lender regulations, 1970s-89, GAO rpt, 26119–337

Financial institutions regulation

Financial institutions regulation

Bank deposit insurance system reform issues, with background industry financial data, 1970s-90, GAO rpt, 26119–320

Bank holding company subsidiaries dealing in bank-ineligible securities, subsidiary and parent firm finances, 1989-91, GAO rpt, 26119–280

Banking panics severity and Federal regulatory policy, 1873-1934, technical paper, 9385–8.99

Banks (natl) charters, mergers, liquidations, enforcement cases, and financial performance, with data by instn and State, quarterly rpt, 8402–3

Banks agricultural loans share of all loans, impact of State branching laws, bank urban-rural location, and other factors, 1981-86, article, 9393–8.202

Banks and deposit insurance funds financial condition, potential losses, and regulatory issues, 1980s-90 and projected to 1995, 21248–147

Banks economies of scale and scope, impacts of regulation for large banks, alternative model results, 1972-87, working paper, 9375–13.50

Banks failures declarations relation to selected regulatory activity indicators, 1960s-89, working paper, 9377–9.115

Banks failures forecasting performance of measures using alternative capital/asset ratio requirements, 1982-89, working paper, 9377–9.109

Banks financial performance, for undercapitalized instns by State and inside-outside Texas, aggregate 1985-89, article, 9391–1.212

Banks financial performance, risk assessment, and regulation, 1990 annual conf papers, 9375–7

Banks market value calculation method to expose undercapitalization, with model results and background data for selected failed banks, 1960s-89, working paper, 9377–9.112

Banks output relation to costs, technological devs, deregulation, and other factors, alternative measures, 1980s, technical paper, 9366–6.265

Banks regulation and related issues, quarterly journal, 9292–4

Banks regulatory enforcement activities of Federal agencies, effectiveness, with data on capital-deficient banks, late 1980s-90, GAO rpt, 26119–334

Banks restrictions on business equity ownership, issues, with data for venture capital financing and comparisons to West Germany and Japan, 1970s-90, article, 9393–8.206

Banks stock price changes relation to regulatory exam results, 1980s, article, 9373–1.210

Banks stock returns impact of interstate and intrastate banking regulation, 1960s-89, article, 9393–8.205

Budget of US, obligations and authority by function, agency, and program, with summaries, analyses, and historical tables, FY92, annual rpt, 104–2

Capital aid receipt of problem banks, relation to bank holding company affiliation and other factors, with data for Texas, 1985-88, article, 9391–1.205

Court civil and criminal caseloads for Federal district courts, 1991, annual rpt, 18204–2.1

Credit unions federally insured, finances, 1989-90, annual rpt, 9534–1

Credit unions finances, operations, and regulation, series, 9536–1

Crimes, by characteristics of victim and offender, circumstances, and location, data compilation, 1991 annual rpt, 6064–6.3

Economic indicators relation to interest rates and financial market regulatory and structural changes, 1950s-80s, technical paper, 9385–8.73

Exports of goods, services, and investment, trade barriers, impacts, and US actions, by country, 1989, annual rpt, 444–2

Fed Home Loan Mortgage Corp financial condition and capital adequacy, 1989, annual rpt, 5184–8

Fed Reserve Board and Reserve banks finances, staff, and review of monetary policy and economic devs, 1990, annual rpt, 9364–1

Fed Reserve political independence issues, with proposed restructuring legislation, 1970s-90, technical paper, 9385–8.106

Fed Reserve System, Board of Governors, and district banks financial statements, performance, and fiscal services, 1990-91, annual rpt, 9364–10

Foreign countries currency assets held by banks, alternative measures of exchange rate risk, 1991 technical paper, 9366–7.254

Foreign-owned banks US subsidiaries, assets, and regulatory issues, with data by State and firm, 1989-90, hearing, 21248–155

Fraud and abuse in banks and thrifts, Federal agencies enforcement activities and staff, with data by instn and location, 1988-90, hearing, 21408–119

Fraud and abuse in thrifts, Federal indictments and case dispositions, FY89-91, press release, 6008–33

Futures margin requirements and settlement activity relation to price volatility, for 3 stock index contracts, 1980s-90, technical paper, 9366–6.278

Futures margin requirements impacts on contract price and trading activity, 1974-89, working paper, 9375–13.51

Futures trading oversight of CFTC and individual exchanges, foreign activity, and customer views, late 1980s, hearing, 25168–77

Govt-sponsored enterprises financial condition and capital adequacy, with data by enterprise, 1970s-90 and projected to 1996, 26308–99

Govt-sponsored enterprises financial condition and capital adequacy, with regulatory recommendations and data by enterprise, 1985-95, GAO rpt, 26119–296

Govt-sponsored enterprises financial condition, capital adequacy, and impacts on Federal borrowing, with data by enterprise, 1980s-90, last issue of annual rpt, 8004–15

Insurance (health) for long-term care, affordability and State regulation issues, 1986-90, hearing, 21368–130

Insurance (health) private plans to supplement Medicare, loss ratio

performance, sales abuse cases, and State enforcement, late 1980s, GAO rpt, 26121–410

Insurance (property and casualty) industry solvency monitoring by States, firms designated for increased attention, and views on monitoring system effectiveness, 1980s, GAO rpt, 26119–316

Intl banking competition and deposit insurance reform issues, with background data, 1990 hearings, 25248–122

Japan interest rates relation to monetary policy and financial instn regulation, with background data and model results, 1960s-91, article, 9385–1.213; 9385–8.116

Japan stock margin requirements impact on stock prices, volatility, and trading activity, 1951-88, technical paper, 9385–8.72

Merger applications approved, and assets and offices involved, by bank, 1989, annual rpt, 9294–5

Mexico banks deregulation impacts on finances, with data by bank, 1960s-90, technical paper, 9385–8.121

Mortgage loan activity rpts filed under Home Mortgage Disclosure Act, and instns covered, 1981-90, article, 9362–1.206

Mortgage market regulatory and structural changes impacts on residential investment, with mortgage originations by financial instn type, 1970s-80s, technical paper, 9385–8.74

Reform of banking system and deposit insurance, findings and recommendations, with background data, 1989-90, 8008–147

Reserve requirements for financial instns, and coverage, 1991 article, 9377–1.207

Resolution Trust Corp obligation limits compliance, and balance sheet, quarterly GAO rpt, 26102–6

Resolution Trust Corp programs fraud and abuse, audits and investigations, 2nd half FY91, semiannual rpt, 9722–6

Savings instns failure resolution activity and finances of Resolution Trust Corp, with data by asset type, State, region, and instn, monthly rpt, 9722–3

Savings instns failure resolution activity of Resolution Trust Corp, assets, deposits, and assets availability and sales, periodic press release, 9722–1

Savings instns failure resolution activity of Resolution Trust Corp, with data by State and instn, and RTC financial statements, 1989, annual rpt, 9724–1

Savings instns failure resolution activity of Resolution Trust Corp, with instns assets and senior executive compensation, 1990, hearing, 21248–157

Savings instns failure resolution activity of Resolution Trust Corp, 1991 semiannual hearing, 21242–1

Savings instns failures, financial performance of instns under Resolution Trust Corp conservatorship, quarterly rpt, 9722–5

Savings instns insured by Savings Assn Insurance Fund, assets, liabilities, and deposit and loan activity, by conservatorship status, monthly rpt, 8432–1

Savings instns mortgage debt holdings and other assets, returns on assets, and impacts of qualified lender regulations, 1970s-89, GAO rpt, 26119–337

SEC activities, securities industry finances, and exchange activity, selected years 1938-FY90, annual rpt, 9734–2

SEC registration, firms required to file annual rpts, as of Sept 1990, annual listing, 9734–5

Securities and commodity trading regulatory activities and interagency coordination, FY91, annual rpt, 11924–4

Securities industry self-regulatory organizations oversight by SEC, violations, and complaints, FY86-89, GAO rpt, 26119–336

Securities intl markets computer use and risk mgmt methods, 1991 GAO rpt, 26125–44

Stock short selling activity indicators, and regulatory issues, 1980s-89 and trends from 1940, hearings, 21408–122

Texas economic and housing conditions, bank failures, and thrift and Federal regulators real estate holdings, 1980s-90, hearings, 21248–146

see also Deposit insurance

Financial Management Service

Budget of US, authoritative financial statements with appropriations, outlays, and receipts, by agency, FY90, annual rpt, 8104–2

Budget of US, obligations and authority by function, agency, and program, with summaries, analyses, and historical tables, FY92, annual rpt, 104–2

Budget of US, receipts by source, outlays by agency and program, and balances, monthly rpt, 8102–3

Currency (foreign) holdings of US, transactions and balances by program and country, 1st half FY91, semiannual rpt, 8102–7

Currency (foreign) purchases of US with dollars, by country, 1st half FY91, semiannual rpt, 8102–5

Finances of Fed Govt, cash and debt transactions, daily tables, 8102–4

Financial consolidated statements of Fed Govt based on business accounting methods, FY89-90, annual rpt, 8104–5

Foreign countries currency exchange rates offered by US disbursing offices, by country, quarterly rpt, 8102–6

Trust funds of Fed Govt, financial condition, periodic rpt series, 8102–9

Financial ratios

see Operating ratios

Financial statements

see Business assets and liabilities, general

see Business assets and liabilities, specific industry

see Business income and expenses, general

see Business income and expenses, specific industry

see Government assets and liabilities

see Operating ratios

Financing Corp.

Budget of US, financial statements of federally sponsored enterprises, FY92, annual rpt, 104–2.5

Finch, Deborah M.

"Population Ecology, Habitat Requirements, and Conservation of Neotropical Migratory Birds", 1208–382

Fine arts

see Art

see Arts and the humanities

Fines and settlements

Airport security operations to prevent hijacking, screening results, enforcement actions, and hijacking attempts, 2nd half 1989, semiannual rpt, 7502–5

Auto and light truck fuel economy performance by make, standards, and enforcement, 1978-91 model years, annual rpt, 7764–9

Banks and thrifts fraud and abuse, Federal criminal enforcement activities, case dispositions, and settlements, with data by district, 1982-90, hearing, 21248–142

Budget of US, authoritative financial statements with appropriations, outlays, and receipts, by category and agency, FY90, annual rpt, 8104–2.1

Drug enforcement regional task forces investigation of organized crime, activities by agency and region, FY83-90, biennial rpt, 6004–17

Exporters (US) antiboycott law violations and fines by firm, and invitations to boycott by country, FY90, annual rpt, 2024–1

Fair Labor Standards Act admin, with coverage under minimum wage and overtime provisions, and illegal employment of minors, by industry div, FY89, annual rpt, 6504–2.1

Fed Govt accounts receivable, delinquent debt cases and collections of Justice Dept and private law firms, pilot project results, FY90, annual rpt, 6004–20

Fed Govt agencies civil fines imposed, and proposed inflation adjustments, FY87, hearing, 21408–124

Fed Govt agencies fraud cases involving small dollar amounts, investigations, dispositions, losses, and collections, 1986-90, GAO rpt, 26111–76

Federal criminal sentencing, guidelines by offense and circumstances, series, 17668–1

Federal criminal sentencing, guidelines use and results by offense and district, and Sentencing Commission activities, 1990, annual rpt, 17664–1

FTC activities, FY89, annual narrative rpt, 9404–1

Futures trading oversight of CFTC and individual exchanges, foreign activity, and customer views, late 1980s, hearing, 25168–77

Gasoline and other motor fuel tax provisions, auto registration fees, and disposition of receipts, by State, as of Jan 1991, biennial rpt, 7554–37

GSA programs fraud and abuse, audits and investigations, 2nd half FY91, semiannual rpt, 9452–8

IRS large cash transaction rpts filed and penalties for nonfiling by region, and Federal money laundering investigations use of rpts, 1989-91, GAO rpt, 26119–356

Maritime Commission activities, case filings by type and disposition, and civil penalties by shipper, FY90, annual rpt, 9334–1

Mines safety and health enforcement, training, and funding, with casualties, by type of mine and State, FY89, annual rpt, 6664–6

Oil industry overcharge settlements, use in low income energy assistance, by State, FY89, annual rpt, 4694–8

Pipeline accidents, casualties, safety enforcement activity, and Federal funding, by State, 1989, annual rpt, 7304–5

Railroad safety violation claims settled, by carrier, FY90, annual rpt, 7604–10

Savings instns fraud and abuse, Federal indictments and case dispositions, FY89-91, press release, 6008–33

Tax preparation services negligence and fraud, IRS civil penalty cases and examiners views of program admin, 1989, GAO rpt, 26119–315

Truck and bus safety inspections, fines, and vehicles and drivers ordered out of service, by State, with program funding, FY89, 25268–78

VA programs fraud and abuse, audits and investigations, 2nd half FY90, semiannual rpt, 8602–1

see also Crime victim compensation

see also Judgments, civil procedure

see also Torts

Fingerhut, Lois A.

"Firearm Mortality Among Children, Youth, and Young Adults 1-34 Years of Age, Trends and Current Status: U.S., 1979-88", 4146–5.119

Finland

Agricultural exports of high-value commodities, indexes and sales by commodity, world area, and country, 1960s-86, 1528–323

Agricultural exports of US, impacts of foreign agricultural and trade policy, with data by commodity and country, 1989, annual rpt, 1924–8

Agricultural production, prices, and trade, by country, 1970s-90, and forecast 1991, annual world region rpt, 1524–4.4

Agricultural production, trade, and policies in foreign countries, summary data by country, 1989-90, annual factbook, 1924–12

Agricultural trade of US, by detailed commodity and country, 1989, annual rpt, 1524–8

Agricultural trade of US, by detailed commodity and country, 1990, semiannual rpt, 1522–4

AID loans repayment status and terms by program and country, and status of predecessor agency loans, quarterly rpt, 9912–3

Background Notes, summary social, political, and economic data, 1990 rpt, 7006–2.1

Economic and military aid and loans from US and intl agencies, by program and country, FY46-90, annual rpt, 9914–5

Economic conditions, income, production, prices, employment, and trade, 1991 periodic country rpt, 2046–4.46

Economic conditions, policy, and trade practices, by country, 1988-90, annual rpt, 21384 5

Economic, social, political, and geographic summary data, by country, 1991, annual factbook, 9114–2

Finland

Exports and imports of OECD members, by country, 1989, annual rpt, 7144–10

Exports and imports of US, by Harmonized System 6-digit commodity and country, 1990, annual rpt, 2424–13

Exports and imports of US, by selected country, country group, and commodity group, 1990, annual rpt, 2044–37

Exports and imports of US, by transport mode, country, and SITC 1- to 3-digit commodity, 1990, annual rpt, 2424–12

Exports of US, detailed Schedule B commodities with countries of destination, 1990, annual rpt, 2424–10

GNP and GNP growth for OECD members, by country, 1980-90, annual rpt, 7144–8

Heart disease deaths and risk factors, for PRC, Finland, and US, 1980s, article, 4042–3.202

Human rights conditions in 170 countries, and US economic and military aid, 1990, annual rpt, 21384–3

Imports of goods, services, and investment from US, trade barriers, impacts, and US actions, by country, 1990, annual rpt, 444–2

Multinatl US firms and foreign affiliates finances and operations, by industry and world area of parent firm, 1989 benchmark survey, preliminary annual rpt, 2704–5

Multinatl US firms foreign affiliates, income statement items by country and world area, 1986, biennial article, 8302–2.212

Nuclear power generation in US and 20 countries, monthly rpt, 3162–24.10

Nuclear power plant capacity, generation, and operating status, by plant and foreign and US location, 1990 and projected to 2030, annual rpt, 3164–57

Oil production, trade, use, and stocks, by selected country and country group, monthly rpt, 3162–42

Paper (coated groundwood) from 5 countries at less than fair value, injury to US industry, investigation with background financial and operating data, 1991 rpt, 9886–14.336

Paper (coated groundwood) from 9 countries at less than fair value, injury to US industry, investigation with background financial and operating data, 1991 rpt, 9886–14.306

Steel imports of US under voluntary restraint agreement, by product, customs district, and country, with US industry operating data, quarterly rpt, 9882–13

Tax revenue, by level of govt and type of tax, for OECD countries, mid 1960s-89, annual rpt, 10044–1.2

UN voting record and share of votes in agreement with US, by issue, country, and world area, 1990, annual rpt, 7004–18

see also under By Foreign Country in the "Index by Categories"

Finley, Kerwin J.

"Comparison of Behavior of Bowhead Whales of the Davis Strait and Bering/Beaufort Stocks", 5738–29

Finucane, Fanchon F.

"Plan and Operation of the NHANES I Epidemiologic Followup Study, 1986. Vital and Health Statistics Series 1", 4147–1.26

Fire departments

Employee benefit plan coverage in State and local govts, by benefit type, 1987, 6726–1.41

Employment and payroll, by function and level of govt, 1990, annual rpt series, 2466–1

Finances of govts, by level of govt, State, and for large cities and counties, annual rpt series, 2466–2

Finances of govts, tax systems and revenue, and fiscal structure, by level of govt and State, 1991 and historical trends, annual rpt, 10044–1

Govt census, 1987: employment, payroll, and average earnings, by function, level of govt, State, county, and population size, 2455–2

Govt census, 1987: local govt employment by function, payroll, and average earnings, for individual counties, cities, and school and special districts, 2455–1

Govt census, 1987: State and local labor-mgmt policies, agreements, and coverage and bargaining units, by function, level of govt, and State, 2455–3

State and local govt employment of minorities and women, by occupation, function, and pay level, 1990, annual rpt, 9244–6.4

Fire extinguishers

see Fires and fire prevention

Firearms

Aircraft hijackings, on-board explosions, and other crime, US and foreign incidents, 1985-89, annual rpt, 7504–31

Airport security operations to prevent hijacking, screening results, enforcement actions, and hijacking attempts, 2nd half 1989, semiannual rpt, 7502–5

Child accident deaths and death rates, by cause, age, sex, race, and State, 1980-85, 4108–54

Child accident deaths and injuries by cause, and victimization, rates by race, sex, and age, 1979-88, chartbook, 4108–56

County Business Patterns, 1988: employment, establishments, and payroll, by SIC 2- to 4-digit industry and county, annual State rpt series, 2326–6

County Business Patterns, 1989: employment, establishments, and payroll, by SIC 2- to 4-digit industry and county, annual State rpt series, 2326–8

Court civil and criminal caseloads for Federal district, appeals, and bankruptcy courts, by type of suit and offense, circuit, and district, 1990, annual rpt, 18204–11

Court civil and criminal caseloads for Federal district, appeals, and special courts, 1990, annual rpt, 18204–8

Court civil and criminal caseloads for Federal district courts, 1991, annual rpt, 18204–2.1

Crime, criminal justice admin and enforcement, and public opinion, data compilation, 1991 annual rpt, 6064–6

Crime victimization rates, by victim and offender characteristics, circumstances, and offense, 1988 survey, annual rpt, 6066–3.42

Crime victimization rates, by victim and offender characteristics, circumstances, and offense, 1989 survey, annual rpt, 6066–3.44

Index by Subjects and Names

Crimes of violence, victimizations, circumstances, victim characteristics, arrest, recidivism, sentences, and prisoners, 1980s, 6068–148

Criminal cases by type and disposition, and collections, for US attorneys, by Federal district, FY90, annual rpt, 6004–2.1

Criminal records checks of firearm purchasers, and firearms use in crime, with data by State, 1987-90, 26358–244

Criminal records repository characteristics, holdings, use, and reporting requirements, by State, 1989, 6068–241

Criminal sentences for Federal offenses, guidelines by offense and circumstances, series, 17668–1

Deaths and injuries from firearm accidents by selected city, and effects of gun design modification, 1988-89, GAO rpt, 26131–80

Deaths and rates, by detailed cause and demographic characteristics, 1988 and trends from 1900, US Vital Statistics annual rpt, 4144–2

Deaths and rates from firearms, by motive, age, sex, and race, for persons aged 1-34, 1979-88, 4146–5.119

Exports and imports of US, by country and detailed commodity, monthly rpt, 2422–12

Exports and imports of US, by Harmonized System 6-digit commodity and country, 1990, annual rpt, 2424–13

Exports and imports of US, by transport mode, country, and SITC 1- to 3-digit commodity, 1990, annual rpt, 2424–12

Exports of US, detailed Schedule B commodities with countries of destination, 1990, annual rpt, 2424–10

Health condition improvement and disease prevention goals and recommended activities for 2000, with trends 1970s-80s, 4048–10

Homicides, by circumstance, victim and offender relationship, and type of weapon, 1990, annual rpt, 6224–2.1

Imports of US given duty-free treatment for value of US material sent abroad, by commodity and country, 1989, annual rpt, 9884–14

Injuries from use of consumer products, by severity, victim age, and detailed product, 1990, annual rpt, 9164–6

Law enforcement officer assaults and deaths by circumstances, agency, victim and offender characteristics, and location, 1990, annual rpt, 6224–3

Manufacturing annual survey, 1989: finances and operations, by SIC 2- to 4-digit industry, series, 2506–15

Manufacturing census, 1987: employment and shipments under Fed Govt contracts, by SIC 4-digit industry, 2497–7

Occupational injury and illness rates, by SIC 2- to 4-digit industry, 1988-89, annual rpt, 6844–7

Occupational injury and illness rates, by SIC 2- to 4-digit industry, 1989, annual rpt, 6844–1

OECD trade, total and for 4 major countries, and US trade by country, by commodity, 1970-89, world area rpt series, 9116–1

Price indexes (producer), by stage of processing and detailed commodity, monthly rpt, 6762–6

Index by Subjects and Names

Price indexes (producer), by stage of processing and detailed commodity, monthly 1990, annual rpt, 6764–2

Public opinion on crime and crime-related issues, by respondent characteristics, data compilation, 1991 annual rpt, 6064–6.2

Regulatory activities, staff, and funding of Bur of Alcohol, Tobacco, and Firearms, and tax revenues and rates, 1980s-91, GAO rpt, 26119–335

Sentences for Federal crimes, guidelines use and results by offense and district, and Sentencing Commission activities, 1990, annual rpt, 17664–1

Tariff Schedule of US, classifications and rates of duty by detailed imported commodity, 1992 base edition, 9886–13

Tax (excise) collections of IRS, by source, quarterly rpt, 8302–1

Tax (excise) on hunting and fishing equipment, revenue of Fish and Wildlife Service restoration programs, FY90, annual rpt, 5504–13

see also Ammunition

see also Military weapons

Fires and fire prevention

- Aircraft (general aviation) accidents, by circumstances, characteristics of persons and aircraft involved, and type of flying, 1988, annual rpt, 9614–3
- Aircraft accidents and circumstances, for US operations of domestic and foreign airlines and general aviation, periodic rpt, 9612–1
- Aircraft accidents, casualties, and damage, for commercial operations by detailed circumstances, 1987, annual rpt, 9614–2
- Boat registrations, and accidents, casualties, and damage by cause, by vessel characteristics and State, 1990, annual rpt, 7404–1
- Burn injuries, by circumstances and victim characteristics, and related activity limitation, 1985-87, 4147–10.176
- Burn occupational injuries, by body site, circumstances, and characteristics of persons and equipment involved, 1985 survey, 6846–1.20
- Burn units, and other characteristics of Medicare hospital providers, by instn, 1989, annual regional rpt series, 4654–14
- Bus (school) accidents, circumstances, victim characteristics, and vehicle type, 1989, annual rpt, 7764–22
- Child accident deaths and death rates, by cause, age, sex, race, and State, 1980-85, 4108–54
- Child accident deaths and injuries by cause, and victimization, rates by race, sex, and age, 1979-88, chartbook, 4108–56
- Deaths and rates, by detailed cause and demographic characteristics, 1988 and trends from 1900, US Vital Statistics annual rpt, 4144–2
- DOD prime contract awards, by detailed procurement category, FY87-90, annual rpt, 3544–18
- Extinguishers and smoke detectors, exports and imports of US by country, 1990, annual rpt, 2424–13
- Extinguishers and smoke detectors, exports of US by country, 1990, annual rpt, 2424–10
- Extinguishers PPI, monthly rpt, 6762–6

Extinguishers PPI, monthly 1990, annual rpt, 6764–2

- Fed Govt financial and nonfinancial domestic aid, 1991 base edition with supplements, annual listing, 104–5
- Foreign countries disasters, casualties, damage, and aid by US and others, FY90 and trends from FY64, annual rpt, 9914–12
- Hazardous waste incinerators health and safety violations, by type of violation, 1991 rpt, 6608–5
- Incidents and mgmt of disasters and natl security threats, with data by major event and State, 1991 annual rpt, 9434–6
- Infant death rate, by cause, region, and race, 1980-87, article, 4202–7.208
- Mines safety and health enforcement, training, and funding, with casualties, by type of mine and State, FY89, annual rpt, 6664–6
- Minority group health condition, services use, costs, and indicators of services need, 1950s-88, 4118–55
- Mobile home fires, casualties, damage, and impacts of safety standards, with data on Michigan trailer parks, 1980s, hearing, 21248–145
- Occupational deaths, by cause and industry div, 1989, annual rpt, 6844–1
- Panama Canal fires, and related property loss, FY89-90, annual rpt, 9664–3.2
- Pollution (air) emissions factors, by detailed pollutant and source, data compilation, 1990 rpt, 9198–120
- Pollution (air) emissions from burning of logging waste, 1982, 1208–343
- Pollution (air) levels for 6 pollutants, by source, 1970-89 and trends from 1940, annual rpt, 9194–13
- Preventive disease and health improvement goals and recommended activities for 2000, with trends 1970s-80s, 4048–10
- Public lands acreage, grants, use, revenues, and allocations, by State, FY90, annual rpt, 5724–1.3
- Railroad accidents, casualties, and damage, by cause, railroad, and State, 1990, annual rpt, 7604–1
- Ships accidents and casualties, by circumstances and characteristics of persons and vessels involved, 1988, annual rpt, 7404–11
- Ships and marine facilities accidents, casualties, and circumstances, Coast Guard investigation results, periodic rpt, 9612–4
- Shrublands in western US, ecology, biology, and cheatgrass invasion and related fire threat, 1989 conf papers, 1208–351
- *Statistical Abstract of US*, 1991 annual data compilation, 2324–1.5
- Subway accidents, casualties, and damage, by circumstances and system, 1989, annual rpt, 7884–5
- Traffic fatal accidents, deaths, and rates, by circumstances, characteristics of persons and vehicles involved, and location, 1989, annual rpt, 7764–10

see also Arson

see also Fire departments

see also Forest fires

see also Inflammable materials

Fiscal policy

- Budget of US, CBO analysis of revenue and spending alternatives and projections of economic indicators, FY92-96, annual rpt, 26304–3
- Budget of US, CBO analysis of savings and revenues under alternative spending cuts and tax changes, projected FY92-97, 26306–3.118
- Economic policy and banking practices, technical paper series, 9366–1
- *Economic Report of the President* for 1991, Joint Economic Committee critique and policy recommendations, annual rpt, 23844–2
- *Economic Report of the President* for 1991, with economic trends from 1929, annual rpt, 204–1
- European Monetary System countries interest rate differentials with Germany, relation to fiscal policy, with model results for Italy, 1979-90, technical paper, 9366–7.259
- Fed Govt financial operations, detailed data, *Treasury Bulletin*, quarterly rpt, 8002–4
- Financial and economic analysis, technical paper series, 9379–12
- Gambia cash transfers from AID linked to fiscal and govt reforms, effectiveness, 1987-89, 9916–1.74
- Govt finances, by level of govt, State, and for large cities and counties, annual rpt series, 2466–2
- Govt finances, tax systems and revenue, and fiscal structure, by level of govt and State, 1991 with historical trends, annual rpt, 10044–1
- Japan economic conditions, financial and intl policies, and trade devs, 1950s-80s and projected to 2050, compilation of papers, 23848–220
- OASDI trust funds finances, effects of inclusion in budget deficit figures, and social security tax reduction proposals, 1990 hearing, 25368–171
- Public debt burden on future generations forecast under alternative economic and fiscal policy assumptions, 1991 working paper, 9377–9.111
- Public debt burden on future generations forecast under alternative fiscal policies, and ratio of consumption to lifetime income, by sex and age, 1991 working paper, 9377–9.116
- Senegal cash transfers from AID linked to fiscal and govt reforms, effectiveness, 1980s, 9916–1.75
- State and local govt spending measures using indicators of service costs and demand, with comparisons to fiscal capacity and actual outlays, by State, 1986-87, 10048–77

see also Budget of the U.S.

see also Economic policy

see also Government assets and liabilities

see also Government spending

see also Income taxes

see also Monetary policy

see also Public debt

see also Subsidies

see also Tax expenditures

see also Tax incentives and shelters

see also Tax laws and courts

see also Tax reform

Fiscal policy

see also Taxation
see also terms beginning with Federal aid

Fish and fishing industry

Acid rain and air pollution environmental impacts, and methods of neutralizing acidified water bodies, summary research rpt series, 5506–5

Acid rain effects on Maine streams water quality, acidity, and fish, 1986-87, 9208–130

Agricultural Statistics, 1990, annual rpt, 1004–1

Alaska fish catch in excess of domestic processor needs, and use of estimates for fishing rights allocation, 1984-90, GAO rpt, 26113–523

Alaska OCS environmental conditions and oil dev impacts, compilation of papers, series, 2176–1

Alaska rural areas population characteristics, and energy resources dev effects, series, 5736–5

Alaska subsistence fishing role in local economies, with indicators for Yakutat, 1980s, 1208–350

American Samoa employment, earnings, and minimum wage, by establishment and industry, 1989, biennial rpt, 6504–6

Arctic Ocean fish catch and habitat impacts of oil and gas dev, and assessment methods, 1988 conf, 5738–24

Atlantic Ocean fish and shellfish catch and stocks, by species and northwest location, 1887-1991 and forecast to 1993, semiannual conf, 2162–9

Atlantic Ocean fish and shellfish distribution, bottom trawl survey results by species and location, periodic rpt series, 2164–18

Atlantic Ocean sport and commercial fishing catch and quotas for US and Canada, by species, 1990, annual rpt, 2164–14

Bass (striped) stocks status on Atlantic coast, and sport and commercial catch by State, 1972-89, annual rpt, 5504–29

Business statistics, detailed data for major industries and economic indicators, *Survey of Current Business,* monthly rpt, 2702–1.14

California sport and commercial fish and shellfish landings, permits issued, and harbor facilities, 1916-86, 5738–20

Coast Guard drug, immigration, and fisheries enforcement activities, 2nd half FY91, semiannual rpt, 7402–4

Coastal and estuarine environmental conditions, research results and methodology, series, 2176–7

Coastal and riparian areas environmental conditions, fish, wildlife, use, and mgmt, for individual ecosystems, series, 5506–9

Coastal areas environmental and socioeconomic conditions, and potential impact of oil and gas OCS leases, final statement series, 5736–1

Coastal areas fish and shellfish catch, life cycles, and environmental needs, for selected species and regions, series, 5506–8

Coastal areas fish kills related to pollution and natural causes, by land use, State, and county, 1980s, 2178–32

Cold storage holdings of fish and shellfish, by product and species, preliminary data, monthly press release, 2162–2

Consumer Expenditure Survey, food spending by item, household composition, income, age, race, and region, 1980-88, biennial rpt, 1544–30

Consumer Expenditure Survey, household income by source, and itemized spending, by selected characteristics and region, 1988-89, annual rpt, 6764–5

Consumption of food, dietary composition, and nutrient intake, 1987/88 natl survey, preliminary rpt series, 1356–1

Consumption, supply, trade, prices, spending, and indexes, by food commodity, 1989, annual rpt, 1544–4

County Business Patterns, 1988: employment, establishments, and payroll, by SIC 2- to 4-digit industry and county, annual State rpt series, 2326–6

County Business Patterns, 1989: employment, establishments, and payroll, by SIC 2- to 4-digit industry and county, annual State rpt series, 2326–8

CPI by component for US city average, and by region, population size, and for 27 metro areas, monthly rpt, 6762–2

Developing countries agricultural supply, demand, and market for US exports, with socioeconomic conditions, country rpt series, 1526–6

Endangered animals and plants conservation spending of Federal agencies and States, by species, FY90, annual rpt, 5504–33

Endangered animals and plants population status and mgmt activity, by species, 1990, biennial rpt, 5504–35

Environmental Quality, status of problems, protection programs, research, and intl issues, 1991 annual rpt, 484–1

Estuary environmental conditions, and fish and shellfish catch by species and region, 1980s, 2178–27

Exports and imports (agricultural) of US, by commodity and country, bimonthly rpt, 1522–1

Exports and imports (agricultural) of US, by detailed commodity and country, 1989, annual rpt, 1524–8

Exports and imports (agricultural) of US, by detailed commodity and country, 1990, semiannual rpt, 1522–4

Exports and imports between US and outlying areas, by detailed commodity and mode of transport, 1990, annual rpt, 2424–11

Exports and imports of US, by country and detailed commodity, monthly rpt, 2422–12

Exports and imports of US, by Harmonized System 6-digit commodity and country, 1990, annual rpt, 2424–13

Exports and imports of US, by transport mode, country, and SITC 1- to 3-digit commodity, 1990, annual rpt, 2424–12

Exports of US, detailed commodities by country, monthly CD-ROM, 2422–13

Exports of US, detailed Schedule B commodities with countries of destination, 1990, annual rpt, 2424–10

Fed Govt financial and nonfinancial domestic aid, 1991 base edition with supplements, annual listing, 104–5

Florida environmental, social, and economic conditions, and impacts of proposed OCS oil and gas leases in southern coastal areas, 1990 compilation of papers, 5738–19

Foreign and US environmental and wildlife conservation agreements provisions, status, and signatories, as of 1991, listing, 9886–4.169

Foreign and US oils, oilseeds, and fats production and trade, FAS periodic circular series, 1925–1

Foreign countries economic, social, political, and geographic summary data, by country, 1991, annual factbook, 9114–2

Foreign countries maritime claims and boundary agreements, series, 7006–8

Foreign countries market conditions for US fish and shellfish products, country rpt series, 2166–19

Forest Service acreage, staff, finances, and mgmt activities in Pacific Northwest, with data by forest, 1970s-89, annual rpt, 1204–37

Groundfish juvenile population distribution by species, for New England area, 1968-86, 2168–122

Hatcheries and research stations under Fish and Wildlife Service mgmt, acreage by site and State, as of Sept 1991, annual rpt, 5504–8

Imports of US, detailed commodities by country, monthly CD-ROM, 2422–14

Japan fish catch, prices, trade by country, cold storage holdings, import quotas, and market devs, semimonthly press release, 2162–7

Land Mgmt Bur wildlife mgmt activities and funding, acreage by habitat type, and scientific staff, State rpt series, 5726–7

Land Mgmt Bur wildlife mgmt activities and funding, acreage, staff, and plans, habitat study series, 5726–6

Landings and trade of commercial fisheries, by species, 1980-90, semiannual rpt, 1561–15.1

Landings, trade, use, and fishery operations, with selected foreign data, by species, 1980s-90, annual rpt, 2164–1

Landings, wholesale receipts, prices, trade, and other market activities, by region, weekly regional rpts, 2162–6

Larvae abundance, distribution, and growth, for fish at selected Western Hemisphere sites, 1989 conf papers, 2168–126

Manufacturing annual survey, 1989: finances and operations, by SIC 2- to 4-digit industry, series, 2506–15

Manufacturing census, 1987: finances and operations, by SIC 2- to 4-digit industry, State, and MSA, with trends from 1849, 2497–1

Manufacturing census, 1987: finances and operations, by type of organization and SIC 2- to 4-digit industry, subject rpt, 2497–5

Manufacturing finances and operations, by SIC 2- to 4-digit industry, forecast 1991, annual rpt, 2044–28

Marine Fisheries Review, US and foreign fisheries resources, dev, mgmt, and research, quarterly journal, 2162–1

Natl forests fish and wildlife activities funding, by source, FY88-90, GAO rpt, 26113–529

New York and New Jersey Raritan Bay commercial and sport fishing activity, 1885-1989, article, 2162–1.205

New York Bight fish population and disease, and pollutant levels, near sewage sludge dumpsite, 1986-90, last issue of annual rpt, 2164–19

Index by Subjects and Names

New York Bight pollution levels, sources, treatment costs, economic losses, and environmental and health effects, 1990 conf, 9208–131

North Carolina environmental and socioeconomic conditions, and impacts of proposed OCS oil and gas exploration, 1970s-90 and projected to 2020, 5738–22

Nutrient, caloric, and waste composition, detailed data for raw, processed, and prepared foods, 1991 rpt, 1356–3.15

Occupational injury and illness rates, by SIC 2- to 4-digit industry, 1988-89, annual rpt, 6844–7

Occupational injury and illness rates, by SIC 2- to 4-digit industry, 1989, annual rpt, 6844–1

OECD trade, total and for 4 major countries, and US trade by country, by commodity, 1970-89, world area rpt series, 9116–1

Oil and fat production, consumption by end use, and stocks, by type, quarterly Current Industrial Rpt, 2506–4.4

Oil and meal (fish) production and trade, quarterly tables, 2162–3

Palau admin, and social, economic, and govtl data, FY90, annual rpt, 7004–6

Pollutant concentrations in coastal and estuarine fish, shellfish, and environment, series, 2176–3

Pollutant concentrations in fish and sediments, by contaminant, fish species, and Pacific coast site, 1984-86, 2168–121

Pollutants health effects for animals by species and for humans, and environmental levels, for selected substances, series, 5506–14

Pollution (air) emissions factors, by detailed pollutant and source, data compilation, 1990 rpt, 9198–120

Pollution (water) fish kills, by pollution source, month, location, and State, 1977-87, last issue of annual rpt, 9204–3

Price indexes (producer), by stage of processing and detailed commodity, monthly rpt, 6762–6

Price indexes (producer), by stage of processing and detailed commodity, monthly 1990, annual rpt, 6764–2

Production of processed fish by location, and trade, by species and product, 1987-90, annual rpts, 2166–6

R&D and mgmt of fisheries, Fed Govt grants by project and State, and rpts, 1990, annual listing, 2164–3

R&D funding, and scientists and engineers education and employment, for US and selected foreign countries, 1991 annual rpt, 9627–35.1

Radiation exposure of population near Hanford, Wash, nuclear plant, with methodology, 1944-66, series, 3356–5

Research of State fish and wildlife agencies, federally funded fishery projects and costs by species and State, 1990, annual listing, 5504–23

Research on fish and wildlife population, habitat, and mgmt, technical rpt series, 5506–12

Research on wildlife and plants, habitat study series, 5506–13

Restoration programs of Fish and Wildlife Service, funding, land purchases, and project listing, by State, FY89, annual rpt, 5504–1

Fish and Wildlife Service

Salmon and trout wild and hatchery juvenile population and characteristics, for Pacific Northwest, 1981-85, 2168–123

Salmon from Norway, injury to US industry from foreign subsidized and less than fair value imports, investigation with background financial and operating data, 1991 rpt, 9886–19.75

Salmon landings by species, and trade of US by country, 1980-89, article, 1561–15.201

Sharks and other fish tagged and recovered, by species, 1990, annual rpt, 2164–21

Sharks and rays population, physical characteristics, landings, and fishery mgmt, 1987 conf, 2168–124

Ships accidents and casualties, by circumstances and characteristics of persons and vessels involved, 1988, annual rpt, 7404–11

Ships and marine facilities accidents, casualties, and circumstances, Coast Guard investigation results, periodic rpt, 9612–4

Ships for oceanographic research, fleet condition, funding, voyages, and modernization costs, for NOAA, 1980s-90 and projected to 2020, 2148–60

Soviet Union GNP by detailed income and outlay component, 1985, 2326–18.59

State and Metro Area Data Book, 1991 data compilation, 2328–54

Statistical Abstract of US, 1991 annual data compilation, 2324–1.24

Tax (income) returns of sole proprietorships, income statement items, by industry group, 1989, annual article, 8302–2.214

Trout (brown) population, habitat quality, and streamflow, for Douglas Creek, Wyo, 1970s-89, 5508–112

Tuna fishery porpoise kill, and Federal and intl marine mammal protection activity, with bibl, 1990, annual rpt, 14734–1

Washington State marine sanctuaries proposal, environmental and economic impacts, with background data, 1984-89, 2178–30

Wetlands acreage, resources, soil and water properties, and conservation efforts, by wetland type, State rpt series, 5506–11

Wholesale trade census, 1987: establishments, sales by customer class, employment, inventories, and expenses, by SIC 2- to 4-digit kind of business, 2407–4

see also Aquaculture

see also Fishing, sport

see also Marine mammals

see also Marine resources conservation

see also Shellfish

see also under By Commodity in the "Index by Categories"

see also under By Industry in the "Index by Categories"

Fish and Wildlife Service

Acid rain and air pollution environmental impacts, and methods of neutralizing acidified water bodies, summary research rpt series, 5506–5

Acreage of refuges and other land under FWS mgmt, by site and State, as of Sept 1991, annual rpt, 5504–8

Activities of FWS in conservation and habitat mgmt, and endangered species by group, FY90, biennial rpt, 5504–20

Alaska submerged land grant holdings of Alaska Natives, exchange for upland acreage, impacts on conservation acreage and acquisition, 1989-90, 5728–38

Bass (striped) stocks status on Atlantic coast, and sport and commercial catch by State, 1972-89, annual rpt, 5504–29

Birds population surveys design and trend analysis methodology, 1988 conf, 5508–108

Budget of US, obligations and authority by function, agency, and program, with summaries, analyses, and historical tables, FY92, annual rpt, 104–2

Coastal and riparian areas environmental conditions, fish, wildlife, use, and mgmt, for individual ecosystems, series, 5506–9

Coastal areas fish and shellfish catch, life cycles, and environmental needs, for selected species and regions, series, 5506–8

Crane (sandhill) hunting activity and permits, by State and county, 1989/90-1990/91, annual rpt, 5504–31

Duck breeding population, by species, State, and Canada Province, 1990-91 with trends from 1955, annual rpt, 5504–30

Duck hunting stamps philatelic and sales info, 1991/92, annual supplement, 5504–25

Endangered animals and plants conservation spending of Federal agencies and States, by species, FY90, annual rpt, 5504–33

Endangered animals and plants population status and mgmt activity, by species, 1990, biennial rpt, 5504–35

Endangered animals and plants US trade and permits, by species, purpose, disposition, and country, 1989, annual rpt, 5504–19

Enforcement of wildlife protection laws, FWS activities, funding, costs, and staff, late 1970s-90, GAO rpt, 26113–525

Expenditures of Fed Govt in States, by type, program, agency, and State, FY90, annual rpt, 2464–2

Fishery research of State fish and wildlife agencies, federally funded projects and costs by species and State, 1990, annual listing, 5504–23

Geese pre-migration feeding behavior impacts of aircraft disturbance, for 3 species at Izembek Lagoon, Alaska, 1970s-88, 5738–23

Hatchery Natl System activities and deliveries, by species, hatchery, and jurisdiction of waters stocked, FY90, annual rpt, 5504–10

Licenses for fishing and hunting issued, and costs, by State, FY90, annual tables, 5504–16

Marine mammals protection activities and funding, populations, and harvests, by species, 1989, annual rpt, 5504–12

Mourning dove population, by hunting and nonhunting State, 1966-91, annual rpt, 5504–15

Otters (sea) conservation measures taken after Exxon Valdez oil spill in Alaska, 1990 conf, 5508–110

Otters (sea) population and behavior, for Pacific Ocean, 1914-90, 5508–109

Pollutants health effects for animals by species and for humans, and environmental levels, for selected substances, series, 5506–14

Fish and Wildlife Service

Recreation (outdoor) facilities of Fed Govt, fees and visits by managing agency, FY88-90, annual rpt, 5544–14

Research on fish and wildlife population, habitat, and mgmt, technical rpt series, 5506–12

Research on wildlife and plants, habitat study series, 5506–13

Restoration and hunter safety funding of FWS, by State, FY92, semiannual press release, 5502–1

Restoration programs of FWS, finances by State, and excise tax collections, FY90, annual rpt, 5504–13

Restoration programs of FWS, funding, land purchases, and project listing, by State, FY89, annual rpt, 5504–1

Shellfish recreational harvesters selected characteristics, location of harvest and residence, and spending, 1985 survey, 2178–28

Trout (brown) population, habitat quality, and streamflow, for Douglas Creek, Wyo, 1970s-89, 5508–112

Waterfowl (migratory) hunter harvest, age and sex ratios by species, State, and flyway, 1986-90, annual rpt, 5504–32

Waterfowl (migratory) hunter harvest and unretrieved kills, and duck stamps sold, by species, State, Canada Province, and flyway, 1989-90, annual rpt, 5504–28

Waterfowl (migratory) population, habitat conditions, and flight forecasts, for Canada and US by region, 1991 and trends from 1955, annual rpt, 5504–27

Wetlands acreage, resources, soil and water properties, and conservation efforts, by wetland type, State rpt series, 5506–11

Wetlands and riparian soil and plant characteristics, series, 5506–10

Wetlands plant, soil, and water characteristics, for Big Meadows area in Rocky Mountain Natl Park, 1987-88, 5508–113

Wetlands, water, and land acreage, by State, 1780s and 1980s, 5508–107

Wetlands wildlife and migratory bird habitat acquisition, funding by State, FY92, press release, 5306–4.11

Whooping crane migration roosting sites and population, by wetland type, 1990 rpt, 5508–111

Wildlife research of State fish and wildlife agencies, federally funded projects and costs by species and State, 1990, annual listing, 5504–24

Woodcock population from 1968, and hunter harvest, by State, 1991, annual rpt, 5504–11

Fisher, Brian

"Competitor's View of U.S. Farm Programs", 1004–16.1

Fisher, Joseph P.

"Distribution and Abundance of Juvenile Salmonids off Oregon and Washington, 1981-85", 2168–123

Fisher, Linda J.

"Scientific Solutions to Food Safety Dilemmas: A Progress Report", 1004–16.1

Fisheries

see Fish and fishing industry

Fishing, sport

Atlantic Ocean fish and shellfish catch and stocks, by species and northwest location, 1887-1991 and forecast to 1993, semiannual conf, 2162–9

Atlantic Ocean sport and commercial fishing catch and quotas for US and Canada, by species, 1990, annual rpt, 2164–14

Bass (striped) stocks status on Atlantic coast, and sport and commercial catch by State, 1972-89, annual rpt, 5504–29

California commercial passenger fishing, angler and boat owner characteristics and opinions, 1987-88, article, 2162–1.202

California commercial passenger fishing boats with refrigeration equipment, anglers views, 1989 survey, 2168–125

California sport and commercial fish and shellfish landings, permits issued, and harbor facilities, 1916-86, 5738–20

Coastal areas fish and shellfish catch, life cycles, and environmental needs, for selected species and regions, series, 5506–8

Coastal areas recreation facilities of Fed Govt and States, visitor and site characteristics, 1987-90 survey, regional rpt series, 2176–9

Forest Service activities and finances, by region and State, FY90, annual rpt, 1204–1.1

Forest Service mgmt of public lands and resources dev, environmental, economic, and social impacts of alternative programs, projected to 2040, 1208–24

Forests (natl) recreational use, by type of activity and State, 1990, annual rpt, 1204–17

Great Lakes area economic conditions and outlook, for US and Canada, 1970s-90, 9375–15

Hatcheries and research stations under Fish and Wildlife Service mgmt, acreage by site and State, as of Sept 1991, annual rpt, 5504–8

Hatchery Natl System activities and deliveries, by species, hatchery, and jurisdiction of waters stocked, FY90, annual rpt, 5504–10

Injuries from use of consumer products, by severity, victim age, and detailed product, 1990, annual rpt, 9164–6

New York and New Jersey Raritan Bay commercial and sport fishing activity, 1885-1989, article, 2162–1.205

New York Bight pollution levels, sources, treatment costs, economic losses, and environmental and health effects, 1990 conf, 9208–131

Northeastern US recreation areas use, mgmt, and tourism dev issues, 1990 conf, 1208–356

Ocean sport anglers, fishing activities, and catch by species, by angler characteristics and State, annual coastal area rpt series, 2166–17

Ocean sport fishing catch, by species, mode of fishing, and coastal region, 1990, annual rpt, 2164–1.2

Public lands acreage and use, and Land Mgmt Bur activities and finances, annual State rpt series, 5724–11

Public lands acreage, grants, use, revenues, and allocations, by State, FY90, annual rpt, 5724–1.2

Public lands recreation facilities and use, and Land Mgmt Bur mgmt activities, funding, and plans, State rpt series, 5726–5

Recreation (outdoor) coastal facilities, by State, county, estuary, and level of govt, 1972-84, 2178–29

Research of State fish and wildlife agencies, federally funded fishery projects and costs by species and State, 1990, annual listing, 5504–23

Restoration and hunter safety funding of Fish and Wildlife Service, by State, FY92, semiannual press release, 5502–1

Restoration programs of Fish and Wildlife Service, finances by State, and excise tax collections, FY90, annual rpt, 5504–13

Restoration programs of Fish and Wildlife Service, funding, land purchases, and project listing, by State, FY89, annual rpt, 5504–1

Sharks and rays population, physical characteristics, landings, and fishery mgmt, 1987 conf, 2168–124

Water value estimates for sport fishing and irrigation, by river basin, 1991 article, 1502–7.203

Western US sport fishing warmwater resources mgmt, 1991 conf, 1208–381

see also Hunting and fishing licenses

Fissel, Gary S.

"Anatomy of the International Debt Crisis", 9292–4.201

Fissionable materials

see Radioactive materials

see Uranium

Fitchburg, Mass.

see also under By SMSA or MSA in the "Index by Categories"

Fitti, Joseph E.

"AIDS Knowledge and Attitudes. Provisional Data from the National Health Interview Survey", 4146–8.195

Fixed investment

see Capital investments, general

see Capital investments, specific industry

Flammable materials

see Inflammable materials

Flax

see Natural fibers

Flaxseed

see Oils, oilseeds, and fats

Fleming, Gretchen V.

"Preventive Health Care for Medicaid Children", 4652–1.214

Fleshman, J. Kenneth

"Infant Mortality", 4088–2

Flint, Mich.

see also under By City and By SMSA or MSA in the "Index by Categories"

Flood control

Army Corps of Engineers water resources dev projects, characteristics, and costs, 1950s-89, biennial State rpt series, 3756–1

Army Corps of Engineers water resources dev projects, characteristics, and costs, 1950s-91, biennial State rpt series, 3756–2

Assistance (financial and nonfinancial) of Fed Govt, 1991 base edition with supplements, annual listing, 104–5

Expenditures of Fed Govt in States, by type, program, agency, and State, FY90, annual rpt, 2464–2

Index by Subjects and Names

Florida

Fed Govt-owned real property inventory and costs, worldwide summary by purpose, agency, and location, 1989, annual rpt, 9454–5

FmHA activities, and loans and grants by program and State, FY90 and trends from FY70, annual rpt, 1184–17

Forest Service activities and finances, by region and State, FY90, annual rpt, 1204–1

Great Lakes flood prevention activities of Army Corps of Engineers and Intl Joint Commission, monthly rpt and supplements, 3752–1

Research on water resources, data collection and analysis activities of USGS Water Resources Div Districts, with project descriptions, series, 5666–26

Tennessee Valley river control activities, and hydroelectric power generation and capacity, 1989, annual rpt, 9804–7

TVA finances and operations by program and facility, FY90, annual rpt, 9804–32

Water quality, chemistry, hydrology, and other characteristics, local area studies, series, 5666–27

Water supply and quality in streams and lakes, and groundwater levels in wells, by drainage basin, 1988, annual State rpt series, 5666–16

Water supply and quality in streams and lakes, and groundwater levels in wells, by drainage basin, 1989, annual State rpt series, 5666–12

Water supply and quality in streams and lakes, and groundwater levels in wells, by drainage basin, 1990, annual State rpt series, 5666–10

Water supply in US and southern Canada, streamflow, surface and groundwater conditions, and reservoir levels, by location, monthly rpt, 5662–3

see also Dams

see also Dredging

see also Reservoirs

see also Watershed projects

Floods

Army Corps of Engineers water resources dev projects, characteristics, and costs, 1950s-89, biennial State rpt series, 3756–1

Army Corps of Engineers water resources dev projects, characteristics, and costs, 1950s-91, biennial State rpt series, 3756–2

Farm water supply, crop moisture, and drought indexes, weekly rpt, seasonal data, 2182–7

Farmland damaged by natural disaster, Emergency Conservation Program aid and participation by State, FY90, annual rpt, 1804–22

Forecasts of severe storms, Natl Weather Service forecast accuracy and storm characteristics, series, 2186–6

Foreign countries disasters, casualties, damage, and aid by US and others, FY90 and trends from FY64, annual rpt, 9914–12

Incidents and mgmt of disasters and natl security threats, with data by major event and State, 1991 annual rpt, 9434–6

Research on water resources, data collection and analysis activities of USGS Water Resources Div Districts, with project descriptions, series, 5666–26

Statistical Abstract of US, 1991 annual data compilation, 2324–1.6

Water supply, hydrologic events, and end use, by State, 1988-89, annual rpt, 5664–12

Water supply in US and southern Canada, streamflow, surface and groundwater conditions, and reservoir levels, by location, monthly rpt, 5662–3

Weather events and anomalies, precipitation and temperature for US and foreign locations, weekly rpt, 2182–6

Weather trends and deviations, by world region, 1880s-1990, annual chartbook, 2184–9

Wetlands acreage, resources, soil and water properties, and conservation efforts, by wetland type, State rpt series, 5506–11

see also Flood control

see also Tsunamis

Floor coverings

Exports and imports of US, by country and detailed commodity, monthly rpt, 2422–12

Exports and imports of US, by Harmonized System 6-digit commodity and country, 1990, annual rpt, 2424–13

Exports and imports of US, by transport mode, country, and SITC 1- to 3-digit commodity, 1990, annual rpt, 2424–12

Exports of US, detailed Schedule B commodities with countries of destination, 1990, annual rpt, 2424–10

Price indexes (producer), by stage of processing and detailed commodity, monthly 1990, annual rpt, 6764–2

Price indexes (producer) for building materials, by type, bimonthly rpt, 2042–1.5

Retail trade sales and inventories, by kind of business, region, and selected State, MSA, and city, monthly rpt, 2413–3

see also Carpets and rugs

Florence, Ala.

see also under By SMSA or MSA in the "Index by Categories"

Florence, S.C.

see also under By SMSA or MSA in the "Index by Categories"

Florida

Banks (insured commercial and savings) deposits by instn, State, MSA, and county, as of June 1990, annual regional rpt, 9295–3.2

Celery acreage planted and growing, by growing area, monthly rpt, 1621–14

Coastal currents, temperatures, and salinity, for Atlantic Ocean from Florida straits to northern Brazil, series, 2146–7

County Business Patterns, 1989: employment, establishments, and payroll, by SIC 2- to 4-digit industry and county, annual State rpt, 2326–8.11

DOD prime contract awards, by contractor, service branch, State, and city, FY90, annual rpt, 3544–22

Economic indicators by State and MSA, Fed Reserve 6th District, quarterly rpt, 9371–14

Employment and housing and mortgage market indicators by State, FHLB 4th District, quarterly rpt, 9302–36

Employment and unemployment, for 8 southeastern States, 1989-90, annual rpt, 6944–2

Employment by industry div, earnings, and hours, for 8 southeastern States, quarterly press release, 6942–7

Estuary environmental and fishery conditions, research results and methodology, 1991 rpt, 2176–7.25

Farm employment, wages, and hours, by payment method, worker type, region, and State, 1910-90, 1618–21

Fed Govt spending in States and local areas, by type, State, county, and city, FY90, annual rpt, 2464–3

Fed Govt spending in States, by type, program, agency, and State, FY90, annual rpt, 2464–2

Fertilizer and pesticide use and application rates, by type, crop, and State, 1990, 1616–1.2

Fish and shellfish catch, wholesale receipts, prices, trade, and other market activities, weekly regional rpt, 2162–6.3

Food aid program of USDA for women, infants, and children, prenatal participation effect on Medicaid costs and birth outcomes, for 5 States, 1987-88, 1368–2

HHS financial aid, by program, recipient, State, and city, FY90, annual regional listing, 4004–3.4

Hospital deaths of Medicare patients, actual and expected rates by diagnosis, and hospital characteristics, by instn, FY87-89, annual regional rpt, 4654–14.4

Housing census, 1990: inventory, occupancy, and costs, State fact sheet, 2326–21.11

Income (personal) per capita and by source, and earnings by industry div, by State, MSA, and county, 1984-89, annual regional rpt, 2704–2.4

Jail adult and juvenile population, employment, spending, instn conditions, and inmate programs, by county and facility, 1988, regional rpt series, 6068–144.4

Manatees grazing effects on seagrass, by southeast Florida site, 1987-89, 14738–12

Manatees killed in Florida and other US waters, by cause, 1978-90, annual rpt, 14734–1

Marriages, divorces, and rates, by characteristics of spouses, State, and county, 1987 and trends from 1920, US Vital Statistics annual rpt, 4144–4

Medicaid demonstration projects evaluation, for 6 States, 1988 rpt, 4658–45

Mineral Industry Surveys, State reviews of production, 1990, preliminary annual rpt, 5614–6

Minerals Yearbook, 1989, Vol 2: State review of production and sales by commodity, and business activity, annual rpt, 5604–16.10

Minerals Yearbook, 1989, Vol 2: State reviews of production, sales, and firms, by commodity, and business activity, annual rpt, 5604–34

Nursing home reimbursement by Medicaid, States payment ratesetting methods, analysis for 7 States, 1980s, article, 4652–1.255

Oil and gas OCS lease proposals, impacts on south Florida environmental, social, and economic conditions, 1990 compilation of papers, 5738–19

Florida

Oil and gas OCS leases suspended for environmental reasons and repurchased by Fed Govt, costs of cancellation for 3 States, 1990, GAO rpt, 26113–509

Oranges (fresh) exports of US, demand indicators for 4 countries, with production, trade, and use, 1960s-90, 1528–317

Oranges and grapefruit production costs for California and Florida, 1988/89, article, 1561–6.201

Peaches production, marketing, and prices in 3 southeastern States and Appalachia, 1990, annual rpt, 1311–12

Physicians, by specialty, age, sex, and location of training and practice, 1989, State rpt, 4116–6.10

Population and housing census, 1990: population and housing characteristics, households, and land area, by county, subdiv, and place, State rpt, 2551–1.11

Population and housing census, 1990: voting age and total population by race, and housing units, by block, redistricting counts required under PL 94-171, State CD-ROM release, 2551–6.7

Population and housing census, 1990: voting age and total population by race, and housing units, by county and city, redistricting counts required under PL 94-171, State summary rpt, 2551–5.10

Statistical Abstract of US, 1991 annual data compilation, 2324–1

Supplemental Security Income payments and beneficiaries, by type of eligibility, State, and county, Dec 1989, annual rpt, 4744–27.4

Textile mill employment, earnings, and hours, for 8 Southeastern States, quarterly press release, 6942–1

Timber in Florida, industrial roundwood production, by product and county, 1977-87, 1208–352

Timber in Florida, longleaf pine planting performance relation to seed source and site, 1968-83, 1208–345

Wages by occupation, and benefits for office and plant workers, 1991 survey, periodic labor market rpt, 6785–3.5

Water (groundwater) supply, quality, chemistry, other characteristics, and use, 1990 regional rpt, 5666–25.8

Water quality, chemistry, hydrology, and other characteristics, 1990 local area study, 5666–27.18

Water resources data collection and analysis activities of USGS Water Resources Div District, with project descriptions, 1990 rpt, 5666–26.14

Water supply and quality in streams and lakes, and groundwater levels in wells, by drainage basin, 1989, annual State rpt, 5666–12.8

Water supply and quality in streams and lakes, and groundwater levels in wells, by drainage basin, 1990, annual State rpt, 5666–10.8

Wetlands and riparian soil and plant characteristics, 1990 rpt, 5506–10.11

see also Boca Raton, Fla.

see also Clearwater, Fla.

see also Daytona Beach, Fla.

see also Fort Lauderdale, Fla.

see also Gainesville, Fla.

see also Hialeah, Fla.

see also Hollywood, Fla.

see also Jacksonville, Fla.

see also Melbourne, Fla.

see also Miami, Fla.

see also Orlando, Fla.

see also Palm Bay, Fla.

see also Pompano Beach, Fla.

see also St. Petersburg, Fla.

see also Tampa, Fla.

see also Titusville, Fla.

see also West Palm Beach, Fla.

see also under By State in the "Index by Categories"

Florists

see Flowers and nursery products

Flour

see Baking and bakery products

see Grains and grain products

Flow-of-funds accounts

Assets and debts of private sector, balance sheets by segment, 1945-90, semiannual rpt, 9365–4.1

Credit markets, direct and indirect sources of funds, monthly rpt, 9362–1.1

Flow-of-funds accounts, savings, investments, and credit statements, quarterly rpt, 9365–3.3

Foreign countries economic indicators, and trade and investment flows, for selected countries and country groups, selected years 1946-90, annual rpt, 204–1.9

Foreign direct investment of US, by industry group and world area, 1987-90, annual article, 2702–1.220

Intl investment position of US, by component, industry, world region, and country, 1989-90, annual article, 2702–1.212

Investment (intl) position of US under alternative valuation methods, 1982-89, article, 2702–1.211

Multinatl firms US affiliates, investment trends and impact on US economy, 1991 annual rpt, 2004–9

Statistical Abstract of US, 1991 annual data compilation, 2324–1.16

Flowers and nursery products

Agricultural Statistics, 1990, annual rpt, 1004–1

Agriculture census, 1987: farms, farmland, production, finances, and operator characteristics, by county, final State rpt series, 2331–1

Agriculture census, 1987: horticultural specialties producers, finances, and operations, by crop and State, 1988 survey, 2337–1

CPI by component for US city average, and by region, population size, and for 27 metro areas, monthly rpt, 6762–2

Endangered animals and plants US trade and permits, by species, purpose, disposition, and country, 1989, annual rpt, 5504–19

Exports and imports (agricultural) of US, by commodity and country, bimonthly rpt, 1522–1

Exports and imports (agricultural) of US, by detailed commodity and country, 1989, annual rpt, 1524–8

Exports and imports (agricultural) of US, by detailed commodity and country, 1990, semiannual rpt, 1522–4

Index by Subjects and Names

Exports and imports between US and outlying areas, by detailed commodity and mode of transport, 1990, annual rpt, 2424–11

Exports and imports of US, by country and detailed commodity, monthly rpt, 2422–12

Exports and imports of US, by Harmonized System 6-digit commodity and country, 1990, annual rpt, 2424–13

Exports of US, detailed Schedule B commodities with countries of destination, 1990, annual rpt, 2424–10

Farm financial and marketing conditions, forecast 1991, annual chartbook, 1504–8

Farm income, expenses, receipts by commodity, assets, liabilities, and ratios, 1990 and trends from 1945, annual rpt, 1544–16

Farm sector balance sheet, and receipts by detailed commodity, by State, 1985-89, annual rpt, 1544–18

Franchise business opportunities by firm and kind of business, and sources of aid and info, 1990 annual listing, 2104–7

Imports of cut flowers, by type and country, FAS monthly circular with articles, 1925–34

Injuries from use of consumer products, by severity, victim age, and detailed product, 1990, annual rpt, 9164–6

Production, marketing, and trade by country, for flowers and foliage plants, by State, 1960s-88, 1568–293

Production, sales, prices, and growers, by flower and foliage crop and State, 1989-90 and planting planned 1991, annual rpt, 1631–8

Production, trade, farms, acreage, and sales of flowers and foliage, for US by crop, and spending by country, 1987-90, article, 1502–4.201

Puerto Rico economic censuses, 1987: wholesale and retail trade and service industry finances and operations, by SIC 2- to 4-digit industry and municipio, 2591–1

Retail trade census, 1987: finances and employment, for establishments with and without payroll, by SIC 2- to 4-digit kind of business, State, and MSA, 2401–1

Shipments of domestic and imported cut flowers and decorative greens, by State and country of origin, weekly rpt, 1311–3

Statistical Abstract of US, 1991 annual data compilation, 2324–1.7

Tree seedlings produced for forest and windbarrier planting, by nursery ownership and State, FY90, annual rpt, 1204–7.2

Tree seedlings production techniques, and reforestry transplantation effectiveness, 1990 conf, 1208–376

Wholesale trade census, 1987: establishments, sales by customer class, employment, inventories, and expenses, by SIC 2- to 4-digit kind of business, 2407–4

see also Seeds

see also under By Commodity in the "Index by Categories"

Index by Subjects and Names

Floyd, L. M.
"Results of the Radiological Survey at 79 Avenue B, Lodi, N.J. (LJ091)", 3006–9.9
"Results of the Radiological Survey at 90 C Avenue, Lodi, N.J. (LJ079)", 3006–9.14
"Results of the Radiological Survey at 113 Avenue E, Lodi, N.J. (LJ081)", 3006–9.12

Flu
see Pneumonia and influenza

Fluoridation
see Water fluoridation

Fluorine
see Gases

Fluorocarbons
see Chemicals and chemical industry

Fluorspar
see Nonmetallic minerals and mines

Fluri, Robert
"Divisia Monetary Services Indexes for Switzerland: Are They Useful for Monetary Targeting?", 9391–1.221

Flynn, Garry L.
"Estimated Oil and Gas Reserves: Pacific Outer Continental Shelf (as of Dec. 31, 1989)", 5734–7

FNMA
see Federal National Mortgage Association

Fogarty International Center for Advanced Study in the Health Sciences
Activities and funding of NIH, by inst, FY89-90, biennial rpt, 4434–16
Intl programs of NIH, activities and funding by inst and country, FY90, annual rpt, 4474–6

Fogelstrom, Clarence
"Library Programs: Five-Year Report of Library Services Through Major Urban Resource Libraries (MURLs) and Metropolitan Public Libraries Serving as National or Regional Resource Centers, FY84-88", 4878–4

Foley, R. D.
"Results of the Preliminary Radiological Survey at the Former Diamond Magnesium Company Site, Luckey, Ohio (DML001)", 3006–9.8
"Results of the Radiological Survey at 6 Hancock Street, Lodi, N.J. (LJ033)", 3006–9.13
"Results of the Radiological Survey at 79 Avenue B, Lodi, N.J. (LJ091)", 3006–9.9
"Results of the Radiological Survey at 90 C Avenue, Lodi, N.J. (LJ079)", 3006–9.14
"Results of the Radiological Survey at 113 Avenue E, Lodi, N.J. (LJ081)", 3006–9.12
"Results of the Radiological Survey at 160 Essex Street, Lodi, N.J. (LJ072)", 3006–9.11
"Results of the Radiological Survey at 174 Essex Street, Lodi, N.J. (LJ073)", 3006–9.10

Fomby, Thomas B.
"Large Shocks, Small Shocks, and Economic Fluctuations: Outliers in Macroeconomic Times Series", 9379–12.63

Food, Agriculture, Conservation, and Trade Act
Subsidy rates of Fed Govt under 1985 and 1990 farm bills, by selected program and commodity, 1990 rpt, 1008–54

Food and Drug Administration

Activities, funding, and staff of Federal food safety and quality regulation agencies, 1980s, GAO rpt, 26113–503
Activities, funding, facilities, and staff of FDA, findings and recommendations, 1980s-91, 4008–115
Activities of FDA, quarterly rpt, suspended, 4062–3
Budget of US, obligations and authority by function, agency, and program, with summaries, analyses, and historical tables, FY92, annual rpt, 104–2
Cancer treatments using chemotherapy drugs for indications not listed on drug label, costs, and insurance reimbursement problems, 1990 physicians survey, GAO rpt, 26131–81
Diabetics home monitoring of blood glucose, and factors affecting test accuracy, 1990 rpt, 4068–71
Drug marketing application processing of FDA, by drug, purpose, and producer, 1990, annual rpt, 4064–14
Drug prescriptions, by drug type and brand, and for new drugs, 1989, annual rpt, 4064–12
Financial aid of HHS, by program, recipient, State, and city, FY90, annual regional listings, 4004–3
Freedom of Info Act requests to FDA, and processing time, by office, 1986-89, GAO rpt, 26121–436
Imports detained by FDA, by reason, product, shipper, brand, and country, monthly listing, 4062–2
Radiation from electronic devices, incidents by type of device, and FDA control activities, 1990, annual rpt, 4064–13
Research and evaluation programs of HHS, 1970-90, annual listing, 4004–30
Toxicology Natl Program research and testing activities, FY89 and planned FY90, annual rpt, 4044–16
Water (bottled) quality standards of FDA, EPA, and States, with use in 12 States, 1990, GAO rpt, 26113–519

Food and food industry

Agricultural Statistics, 1990, annual rpt, 1004–1
Business statistics, detailed data for major industries and economic indicators, *Survey of Current Business*, monthly rpt, 2702–1.14
Capital expenditures for plant and equipment, by major industry group, quarterly rpt, 2502–2
Collective bargaining agreements expiring during year, and workers covered, by firm, union, industry group, and State, 1991, annual rpt, 6784–9
County Business Patterns, 1988: employment, establishments, and payroll, by SIC 2- to 4-digit industry and county, annual State rpt series, 2326–6
County Business Patterns, 1989: employment, establishments, and payroll, by SIC 2- to 4-digit industry and county, annual State rpt series, 2326–8
Employment, earnings, and hours, by SIC 1- to 4-digit industry, monthly and annual averages, selected years 1909-90, annual rpt, 6744–4
Employment in manufacturing, by detailed occupation and SIC 2-digit industry, 1989 survey, triennial rpt, 6748–52

Food and food industry

Employment related to agriculture, by industry, region, and metro-nonmetro location, 1987, 1598–271
Employment, unemployment, and labor force characteristics, by region and census div, 1990, annual rpt, 6744–7.1
Energy use and prices for manufacturing industries, 1988 survey, series, 3166–13
Enterprise Statistics, 1987: auxiliaries of multi-establishment firms, finances and operations by function, industry, and State, 2329–6
Enterprise Statistics, 1987: finances and operations for companies, by size, level of diversification, form of organization, and industry group, 2329–8
Exports and imports (agricultural) of US, by detailed commodity and country, 1989, annual rpt, 1524–8
Exports and imports (agricultural) of US, by detailed commodity and country, 1990, semiannual rpt, 1522–4
Exports and imports between US and outlying areas, by detailed commodity and mode of transport, 1990, annual rpt, 2424–11
Exports and imports of US, by country and detailed commodity, monthly rpt, 2422–12
Exports and imports of US, by Harmonized System 6-digit commodity and country, 1990, annual rpt, 2424–13
Exports and imports of US, by transport mode, country, and SITC 1- to 3-digit commodity, 1990, annual rpt, 2424–12
Exports of US, detailed commodities by country, monthly CD-ROM, 2422–13
Exports of US, detailed Schedule B commodities with countries of destination, 1990, annual rpt, 2424–10
Finances and productivity of food industry, marketing cost components, and farm-retail food prices, 1920s-90, annual rpt, 1544–9
Foreign countries agricultural production, consumption, and policies, and US export dev and promotion, monthly journal, 1922–2
Foreign direct investment in US, by industry group and world area, 1987-90, annual article, 2702–1.219
Foreign direct investment in US, by industry group of US affiliate and country of parent firm, 1980-86, 2708–41
Foreign direct investment of US, by industry group and world area, 1987-90, annual article, 2702–1.220
Imports detained by FDA, by reason, product, shipper, brand, and country, monthly listing, 4062–2
Imports, exports, and employment impacts, by SIC 2- to 4-digit industry and commodity, quarterly rpt, 2322–2
Imports of US, detailed commodities by country, monthly CD-ROM, 2422 14
Input-output structure of US economy, detailed interindustry transactions for 84 industries, and components of final demand, 1986, annual article, 2702–1.206
Input-output structure of US economy, detailed interindustry transactions for 85 industries, 1982 benchmark data, 2702–1.213

Food and food industry

Labor productivity, indexes of output, hours, and employment by SIC 2- to 4-digit industry, 1967-89, annual rpt, 6824–1.3

Low-fat and nonfat foods introduced, by product type, 1990, article, 1502–4.204

Manufacturing annual survey, 1989: finances and operations, by SIC 2- to 4-digit industry, series, 2506–15

Manufacturing census, 1987: finances and operations, by SIC 2- to 4-digit industry, State, and MSA, with trends from 1849, 2497–1

Manufacturing census, 1987: finances and operations, by type of organization and SIC 2- to 4-digit industry, subject rpt, 2497–5

Manufacturing corporations financial statements, by selected SIC 2- to 3-digit industry, quarterly rpt, 2502–1

Manufacturing finances and operations, by SIC 2- to 4-digit industry, forecast 1991, annual rpt, 2044–28

Manufacturing industries operations and performance, analytical rpt series, 2506–16

Manufacturing production, shipments, inventories, orders, and pollution control costs, periodic Current Industrial Rpt series, 2506–3

Marketing, consumer research, legislation, and regulation devs, and consumption and price trends, quarterly journal, 1541–7

Mexico imports from US, by industry and State, 1987-90, 2048–154

Multinatl firms US affiliates, finances, and operations, by industry, world area of parent firm, and State, 1988-89, annual rpt, 2704–4

Multinatl US firms and foreign affiliates finances and operations, by industry and world area of parent firm, 1989 benchmark survey, preliminary annual rpt, 2704–5

Nutrient, caloric, and waste composition of food, detailed data for raw, processed, and prepared foods, series, 1356–3

Occupational injury and illness rates, by SIC 2- to 4-digit industry, 1988-89, annual rpt, 6844–7

Occupational injury and illness rates, by SIC 2- to 4-digit industry, 1989, annual rpt, 6844–1

Pollution abatement capital and operating costs, by SIC 2-digit industry, 1989, advance annual Current Industrial Rpt, 2506–3.6

Processed food production and stocks by State, shipments, exports, ingredients, and use, periodic Current Industrial Rpt series, 2506–4

Puerto Rico and other US possessions corporations income tax returns, income and tax items, and employment, by selected industry, 1987, article, 8302–2.213

Puerto Rico economic censuses, 1987: wholesale and retail trade and service industry finances and operations, by SIC 2- to 4-digit industry and municipio, 2591–1

Puerto Rico economic censuses, 1987: wholesale, retail, and service industries finances and operations, by establishment characteristics and SIC 2- and 3-digit industry, subject rpts, 2591–2

Research (agricultural) funding and staffing for USDA, State agencies, and other instns, by topic, FY90, annual rpt, 1744–2

Snack foods and sweets nutrient, caloric, and waste composition, detailed data for raw, processed, and prepared products, 1991 rpt, 1356–3.16

Soviet Union GNP by component and industry sector, and CIA estimation methods, 1950s-87, 23848–223

Soviet Union GNP by detailed income and outlay component, 1985, 2326–18.59

Statistical Abstract of US, 1991 annual data compilation, 2324–1.23; 2324–1.27

Supply, consumption, trade, prices, spending, and indexes, by food commodity, 1989, annual rpt, 1544–4

Tax (income) returns of corporations, income and tax items by asset size and detailed industry, 1987, annual rpt, 8304–4

Tax (income) returns of corporations, income and tax items by asset size and detailed industry, 1988, annual rpt, 8304–21

Tax (income) returns of corporations with foreign tax credit, income and tax items by industry group, 1986, biennial article, 8302–2.203

Tax (income) returns of multinatl US firms foreign affiliates, income statement items, by asset size and industry, 1986, biennial article, 8302–2.212

Tax (income) returns of sole proprietorships, income statement items, by industry group, 1989, annual article, 8302–2.214

Vertically integrated markets, and farm products produced under contract, 1960s-90, article, 9381–1.205

Wholesale trade census, 1987: depreciable assets, capital and operating expenses, sales, value added, and inventories, by SIC 2- to 3-digit kind of business, 2407–2

Wholesale trade census, 1987: establishments, sales by customer class, employment, inventories, and expenses, by SIC 2- to 4-digit kind of business, 2407–4

Wholesale trade sales and inventories, by SIC 2- to 3-digit kind of business, monthly rpt, 2413–7

Wholesale trade sales, inventories, purchases, and gross margins, by SIC 2- to 3-digit kind of business, 1990, annual rpt, 2413–13

see also Animal feed

see also Aquaculture

see also Baking and bakery products

see also Beer and breweries

see also Beverages

see also Candy and confectionery products

see also Cocoa and chocolate

see also Coffee

see also Cold storage and refrigeration

see also Dairy industry and products

see also Fish and fishing industry

see also Food and waterborne diseases

see also Food assistance

see also Food consumption

see also Food ingredients and additives

see also Food inspection

see also Food prices

Index by Subjects and Names

see also Food stamp programs

see also Food stores

see also Food supply

see also Fruit and fruit products

see also Grains and grain products

see also Honey and beekeeping

see also Ice, manufactured

see also Liquor and liquor industry

see also Livestock and livestock industry

see also Meat and meat products

see also Nuts

see also Oils, oilseeds, and fats

see also Packaging and containers

see also Peanuts

see also Pet food and supplies

see also Poultry industry and products

see also Restaurants and drinking places

see also Shellfish

see also Soft drink industry and products

see also Spices and herbs

see also Sugar industry and products

see also Synthetic food products

see also Syrups and sweeteners

see also Tea

see also Vegetables and vegetable products

see also Wine and winemaking

see also under By Commodity in the "Index by Categories"

see also under By Industry in the "Index by Categories"

Food and Nutrition Service

Budget of US, obligations and authority by function, agency, and program, with summaries, analyses, and historical tables, FY92, annual rpt, 104–2

Child food aid program during summer vacation, nonprofit sponsors compliance with USDA regulations, 1989-90, GAO rpt, 26113–541

Expenditures of Fed Govt in States, by type, program, agency, and State, FY90, annual rpt, 2464–2

Food aid programs of USDA, costs and participation by program, FY69-89, annual rpt, 1364–9

Food stamp eligibility and payment errors, by type, recipient characteristics, and State, FY89, annual rpt, 1364–15

Food stamp issues and participation, by State and county, as of July 1990, semiannual rpt, 1362–6

Food stamp recipient household size, composition, income, and income and deductions allowed, summer 1988, annual rpt, 1364–8

Women, infants, and children food aid program of USDA, participants and costs by State and Indian agency, FY88, annual tables, 1364–12

Women, infants, and children food aid program of USDA, participants by race, State, and Indian agency, Apr 1990, annual rpt, 1364–16

Women, infants, and children food aid program of USDA, participants, clinics, and costs, by State and Indian agency, monthly tables, 1362–16

Women, infants, and children food aid program of USDA, prenatal participation effect on Medicaid costs and birth outcomes, for 5 States, 1987-88, 1368–2

Food and waterborne diseases

Beach closings due to contamination and medical waste, and bacterial levels, for New York and New Jersey, 1987-89, hearing, 21568–50

Index by Subjects and Names

Food assistance

Deaths and rates, by cause, provisional data, monthly rpt, 4142–1.2

Deaths and rates, by detailed cause and demographic characteristics, 1988 and trends from 1900, US Vital Statistics annual rpt, 4144–2

Diarrhea bacteria *Escherichia coli* testing by State labs, and isolates confirmed, 1988, 4202–7.204

Farm financial and marketing conditions, forecast 1991, annual conf, 1004–16

Foreign travel vaccination needs by country, and disease prevention recommendations, 1991 annual rpt, 4204–11

Gastroenteritis outbreaks, specimen collection and diagnosis procedures, CDC guidelines, 1990 rpt, 4206–2.32

Health condition and health care resources, use, and spending, 1950s-89, annual data compilation, 4144–11

Hepatitis cases by infection source, age, sex, race, and State, and deaths, by strain, 1988 and trends from 1966, 4205–2

HHS financial aid, by program, recipient, State, and city, FY90, annual regional listings, 4004–3

Morbidity and Mortality Weekly Report, infectious notifiable disease cases by age, race, and State, and deaths, 1930s-90, annual rpt, 4204–1

Morbidity and Mortality Weekly Report, infectious notifiable disease cases by State, and public health issues, 4202–1

New York Bight pollution levels, sources, treatment costs, economic losses, and environmental and health effects, 1990 conf, 9208–131

Preventive disease and health improvement goals and recommended activities for 2000, with trends 1970s-80s, 4048–10

Shigellosis risk from swimming in park pond, 1989 local area study, article, 4042–3.224

Water supply and quality in streams and lakes, and groundwater levels in wells, by drainage basin, 1988, annual State rpt series, 5666–16

Water supply and quality in streams and lakes, and groundwater levels in wells, by drainage basin, 1989, annual State rpt series, 5666–12

Water supply and quality in streams and lakes, and groundwater levels in wells, by drainage basin, 1990, annual State rpt series, 5666–10

Yearbook of Agriculture, special topics, 1991 annual compilation of papers, 1004–18

see also Food inspection

see also under By Disease in the "Index by Categories"

Food assistance

Africa (Sahel) grain production, use, imports, and stocks, by country, 1989/90, 9918–18

Africa (sub-Saharan) dairy imports, consumption, and market conditions, by country, 1961-88, 1528–321

Agricultural Statistics, 1990, annual rpt, 1004–1

Assistance (financial and nonfinancial) of Fed Govt, 1991 base edition with supplements, annual listing, 104–5

Assistance programs under Ways and Means Committee jurisdiction, finances, operations, and participant characteristics, FY70s-90, annual rpt, 21784–11

Bean (dried) prices by State, market activity, and foreign and US production, use, stocks, and trade, weekly rpt, 1311–17

Bean (dried) production and prices by State, exports and foreign production by country, and USDA food aid purchases, by bean type, 1984-90, annual rpt, 1311–18

Budget of US, formula grant program obligations to State and local govts, by agency, program, and State, FY92, annual rpt, 104–30

Budget of US, obligations and authority by function, agency, and program, with summaries, analyses, and historical tables, FY92, annual rpt, 104–2

CCC dairy price support program foreign donations and domestic donations to poor, schools, Prisons Bur, and VA, monthly rpt, 1802–2

Child food aid program during summer vacation, nonprofit sponsors compliance with USDA regulations, 1989-90, GAO rpt, 26113–541

Child nutrition programs of USDA, evaluation, biennial narrative rpt, discontinued, 14854–1

Child nutrition programs of USDA, funding by program and State, FY89-90, annual rpt, 4824–2.27

Consumer research, food marketing, legislation, and regulation devs, and consumption and price trends, quarterly journal, 1541–7

Debt to US of foreign govts and private obligors, by country and program, periodic rpt, 8002–6

Developing countries economic and social conditions from 1960s, and Intl Dev Cooperation Agency and AID activities and funding, FY90-92, annual rpt, 9904–4

Developing countries food supply, needs, and aid, status and alternative forecasts, world area rpt series, 1526–8

Developing countries grains production and needs, and related economic outlook, by world area and selected country, forecast 1990/91-1991/92, 1528–313

Expenditures for public welfare by program, FY50s-88, annual article, 4742–1.209

Expenditures of Fed Govt in States, by type, program, agency, and State, FY90, annual rpt, 2464–2

Export promotion and foreign food aid programs budget of USDA, with trade by commodity and country, FY85-91 and projected to FY2000, 21168–44

Exports and imports of US, by Harmonized System 6-digit commodity and country, 1990, annual rpt, 2424–13

Exports of US, detailed Schedule B commodities with countries of destination, 1990, annual rpt, 2424–10

Farmers views on Federal agricultural support, trade, and fiscal policies, by region and State, 1989 survey, hearings, 21168–43

Fed Govt finances, cash and debt transactions, daily tables, 8102–4

Foreign countries disasters, casualties, damage, and aid by US and others, FY90 and trends from FY64, annual rpt, 9914–12

Homeless persons aid programs of Fed Govt, program descriptions and funding, by agency and State, FY87-90, annual GAO rpt, 26104–21

Homeless persons housing and food aid of Fed Govt, funding and operations, with data by State and county, FY89, hearing, 25408–111

Homelessness issues, population at risk, contributing factors, and Federal funding for services and prevention, with bibl, 1991 compilation of papers, 25928–9

Honey production, prices, trade, stocks, marketing, and CCC honey loan and distribution activities, monthly rpt, 1311–2

Households composition, income, benefits, and labor force status, Survey of Income and Program Participation methodology, working paper series, 2626–10

Indian (Cherokee) Agency activities in North Carolina, FY91, annual rpt, 5704–4

Iraq invasion of Kuwait, alien worker refugees fleeing from Iraq and Kuwait, intl aid by source, and costs to host and native countries, 1990-91, GAO rpt, 26123–326

Older and handicapped persons cash aid in place of food stamps, pilot project results by area, as of July 1990, semiannual rpt, 1362–6

Older persons in rural areas, household income sources, and poverty status, 1983-84, 1598–268

Purchases by food aid programs, by commodity, firm, and shipping point or destination, weekly rpt, 1302–3

Rice exports under Federal programs, periodic situation rpt, 1561–8

State and Metro Area Data Book, 1991 data compilation, 2328–54

Statistical Abstract of US, 1991 annual data compilation, 2324–1.12

USDA food aid programs costs and participation, by program, FY69-89, annual rpt, 1364–9

Women, infants, and children food aid program of USDA, enrollment of children at high risk of poor nutrition, for Tennessee, 1982-84, article, 4042–3.216

Women, infants, and children food aid program of USDA, participants and costs by State and Indian agency, FY88, annual tables, 1364–12

Women, infants, and children food aid program of USDA, participants by race, State, and Indian agency, Apr 1990, annual rpt, 1364–16

Women, infants, and children food aid program of USDA, participants, clinics, and costs, by State and Indian agency, monthly tables, 1362–16

Women, infants, and children food aid program of USDA participation, health services need of participants, for Rhode Island, 1983-84, article, 4042–3.247

Women, infants, and children food aid program of USDA, prenatal participation effect on Medicaid costs and birth outcomes, for 5 States, 1987-88, 1368–2

see also Food stamp programs

see also Public Law 480

see also School lunch and breakfast programs

Food consumption

Food consumption

Agricultural Outlook, production, prices, marketing, and trade, by commodity, forecast and current situation, monthly rpt with articles, 1502–4

Agricultural Statistics, 1990, annual rpt, 1004–1

Banana production, trade, and per capita consumption, by country, and US prices, selected years 1985-90 and projected to 1994, article, 1925–34.228

Bean (dried) prices by State, market activity, and foreign and US production, use, stocks, and trade, weekly rpt, 1311–17

Cancer (colorectal) risk related to intake of fat, fiber, and carbohydrates, for Sha Giao, PRC, and San Francisco Chinese, 1991 article, 4472–1.201

Child rearing costs of married couple households, by expenditure type, child's age, income, and region, 1990 and projected to 2007, 1708–87

Consumption of food, dietary composition, and nutrient intake, 1987/88 natl survey, preliminary rpt series, 1356–1

Consumption per capita of selected beverages, 1970s-90, FAS annual circular, 1925–15.3

Consumption, supply, trade, prices, spending, and indexes, by food commodity, 1989, annual rpt, 1544–4

Dairy production, prices, trade, and use, periodic situation rpt with articles, 1561–2

Dairy production, trade, use, and prices, for US and selected countries, forecast 1992 and trends from 1987, FAS semiannual circular, 1925–10

Developing countries agricultural supply, demand, and market for US exports, with socioeconomic conditions, country rpt series, 1526–6

Developing countries food supply, needs, and aid, status and alternative forecasts, world area rpt series, 1526–8

Developing countries grains production and needs, and related economic outlook, by world area and selected country, forecast 1990/91-1991/92, 1528–313

Diabetics health-related behaviors, weight, and body mass, by level of exercise, 1991 article, 4042–3.246

Eastern Europe agricultural production, trade, and land reform, with selected economic indicators, by country, 1960s-90, article, 1522–3.202

Expenditures by category, and income, by selected household characteristics and location, Consumer Expenditure Survey, 1990, annual press release, 6726–1.42

Expenditures by category, selected household characteristics, and region, Consumer Expenditure Survey, quarterly rpt, 6762–14

Expenditures by detailed category, and household income by source, by selected characteristics and region, 1988-89 Consumer Expenditure Survey, annual rpt, 6764–5

Expenditures for food, 1975-90, annual rpt, 1544–9

Expenditures of consumers, natl income and product accounts, *Survey of Current Business*, monthly rpt, 2702–1.25

Farm financial and marketing conditions, forecast 1991, annual chartbook, 1504–8

Farm home consumption of crops and livestock, 1945-90, annual rpt, 1544–16

Farm home consumption of meat raised on premises, by species and State, 1988-90, annual rpt, 1623–8

Fish and fish products per capita use for US, 1909-90, and by country, average 1986-88, annual rpt, 2164–1.8

Food spending, by item, household composition, income, age, race, and region, 1980-88, Consumer Expenditure Survey biennial rpt, 1544–30

Foreign and US agricultural production, prices, trade, and use, periodic rpt with articles, 1522–3

Foreign and US agricultural supply and demand indicators, by selected crop, monthly rpt, 1522–5

Foreign countries agricultural production, prices, and trade, by country, 1980-90 and forecast 1991, annual world area rpt series, 1524–4

Fruit and nut production, prices, trade, stocks, and use, by selected crop, periodic situation rpt with articles, 1561–6

Fruit and vegetable production, imports by country, use, exports, and prices, by commodity, 1975-87, 1568–299

Households food and beverage spending and per capita consumption, by food and beverage type, 1980s-90, article, 1702–1.212

Meat and poultry foreign and US production, trade, and use, by selected country, FAS semiannual circular series, 1925–33

Meat, poultry, and egg consumption per capita, periodic situation rpt with articles, 1561–7

Natl income and product accounts and components, *Survey of Current Business*, monthly rpt, 2702–1.24

Oils, oilseeds, and fats foreign and US production and trade, FAS periodic circular series, 1925–1

Oils, oilseeds, and fats production, prices, trade, and use, periodic situation rpt with articles, 1561–3

Processed food production and stocks by State, shipments, exports, ingredients, and use, periodic Current Industrial Rpt series, 2506–4

Research (agricultural) funding and staffing for USDA, State agencies, and other instns, by topic, FY90, annual rpt, 1744–2

Research on food consumption, marketing, legislation, and regulation devs, and consumption and price trends, quarterly journal, 1541–7

Rice foreign and US production, prices, trade, stocks, and use, periodic situation rpt, 1561–8

Soviet Union agricultural reform issues, with background data for USSR and US, 1970s-90, article, 9381–1.210

Soviet Union GNP by component and industry sector, and CIA estimation methods, 1950s-87, 23848–223

Soviet Union GNP by detailed income and outlay component, 1985, 2326–18.59

Statistical Abstract of US, 1991 annual data compilation, 2324–1.3

Sugar and honey foreign and US production, prices, trade, and use, FAS periodic circular series, 1925–14

Sugar and sweeteners production, prices, trade, supply, and use, quarterly situation rpt with articles, 1561–14

Sugar production, acreage, yield, stocks, deliveries, and price by State, and trade by country, 1950s-90, 1568–306

Sugar production, trade, and use, quarterly rpt, 1621–28

Travel to US, by characteristics of visit and traveler, world area of origin, and US destination, 1990 survey, annual rpt, 2904–12

Vegetable production, prices, trade, stocks, and use, for selected fresh and processing crops, periodic situation rpt with articles, 1561–11

Wheat and rye foreign and US production, prices, trade, stocks, and use, quarterly situation rpt with articles, 1561–12

see also Alcohol use

see also Food assistance

see also Food stamp programs

see also Nutrition and malnutrition

see also Vitamins and nutrients

Food for Peace Program

see Public Law 480

Food ingredients and additives

Confectionery shipments, trade, use, and ingredients used, by product, 1990, annual Current Industrial Rpt, 2506–4.5

Consumption, supply, trade, prices, spending, and indexes, by food commodity, 1989, annual rpt, 1544–4

Egg production by type of product, and eggs broken under Federal inspection by region, monthly rpt, 1625–2

Exports and imports of US, by country and detailed commodity, monthly rpt, 2422–12

Exports and imports of US, by Harmonized System 6-digit commodity and country, 1990, annual rpt, 2424–13

Exports and imports of US, by transport mode, country, and SITC 1- to 3-digit commodity, 1990, annual rpt, 2424–12

Exports and imports of US shipped through Canada, by detailed commodity, customs district, and country, 1989, annual rpt, 7704–11

Exports of US, detailed Schedule B commodities with countries of destination, 1990, annual rpt, 2424–10

Manufacturing annual survey, 1989: value of shipments, by SIC 4- to 5-digit product class, 2506–15.2

Nutrient, caloric, and waste composition of food, detailed data for raw, processed, and prepared foods, series, 1356–3

Price indexes (producer), by stage of processing and detailed commodity, monthly rpt, 6762–6

Price indexes (producer), by stage of processing and detailed commodity, monthly 1990, annual rpt, 6764–2

Production of processed food and stocks by State, shipments, exports, ingredients, and use, periodic Current Industrial Rpt series, 2506–4

Production of synthetic organic chemicals, by detailed product, quarterly rpt, 9882–1

Index by Subjects and Names

Food prices

Toxicology Natl Program research and testing activities, FY89 and planned FY90, annual rpt, 4044–16

see also Cholesterol

see also Cocoa and chocolate

see also Spices and herbs

see also Sugar industry and products

see also Syrups and sweeteners

see also Vitamins and nutrients

Food inspection

- Assistance (financial and nonfinancial) of Fed Govt, 1991 base edition with supplements, annual listing, 104–5
- Cattle (dairy) slaughtered under Federal inspection, by region, 1990, annual rpt, 1317–1.6
- Egg production by type of product, and eggs broken under Federal inspection by region, monthly rpt, 1625–2
- Expenditures of Fed Govt in States, by type, program, agency, and State, FY90, annual rpt, 2464–2
- FDA activities, funding, facilities, and staff, findings and recommendations, 1980s-91, 4008–115
- FDA investigations and regulatory activities, quarterly rpt, suspended, 4062–3
- Fed Govt food safety and quality regulation activities, funding, and staff, by agency, 1980s, GAO rpt, 26113–503
- Fishery products and establishments inspected, 1990, annual rpt, 2164–1.10
- Grain inspected for domestic use and export, foreign buyers complaints, and handling facilities explosions, FY90, annual rpt, 1294–1
- Grain inspected for export, test results by commodity and port region, 1988-90, annual rpt, 1294–2
- Grain inspected for export, weekly rpt, 1313–4
- Grain production, prices, trade, and export inspections by US port and country of destination, by grain type, weekly rpt, 1313–2
- Imports detained by FDA, by reason, product, shipper, brand, and country, monthly listing, 4062–2
- Livestock inspected by Fed Govt, by type, weekly rpt, 1315–1
- Livestock slaughter, meat production, and slaughter plants, by species and State, 1990, annual rpt, 1623–10
- Livestock slaughter under Fed Govt inspection, by livestock type and region, monthly rpt, 1623–9
- Meat and poultry inspection activities and staff of Federal, State, and foreign govts, FY90, annual rpt, 1374–1
- Meat plants inspected and certified for exporting to US, by country, 1990, annual listing, 1374–2
- Peanut production, prices, stocks, exports, use, inspection, and quality, by region and State, 1980-90, annual rpt, 1311–5
- Pesticide levels in food, comparison of US and UN standards, 1988-90, GAO rpt, 26131–88
- Poultry and egg prices and marketing, by selected region, State, and city, monthly and weekly 1990, annual rpt, 1317–2
- Poultry Natl Improvement Plan participating hatcheries and birds, by species and disease program, 1991, annual listing, 1394–15

Poultry slaughtered under Fed Govt inspection, pounds certified, and condemnations by cause, by State, monthly rpt, 1625–3

- Rice market activities, prices, inspections, sales, trade, supply, and use, for US and selected foreign markets, weekly rpt, 1313–8
- Ship (passenger) sanitary inspection scores, biweekly rpt, 4202–10
- Tea imports inspected by FDA, by type and country, 1985-90, FAS annual circular, 1925–15.3
- Wheat quality indicators, for US exports and foreign wheat production, 1960s-90, hearing, 25168–75
- *Yearbook of Agriculture*, special topics, 1991 annual compilation of papers, 1004–18
- *see also* Food and waterborne diseases

Food poisoning

see Food and waterborne diseases

Food prices

- *Agricultural Outlook*, production, prices, marketing, and trade, by commodity, forecast and current situation, monthly rpt with articles, 1502–4
- *Agricultural Statistics, 1990*, annual rpt, 1004–1
- Assistance programs purchases of food, by commodity, firm, and shipping point or destination, weekly rpt, 1302–3
- Banana production, trade, and per capita consumption, by country, and US prices, selected years 1985-90 and projected to 1994, article, 1925–34.228
- Beef (choice) price and price spread data series revisions, with methodology, 1970s-90, 1568–295
- Business statistics, detailed data for major industries and economic indicators, *Survey of Current Business*, monthly rpt, 2702–1.14
- Consumer research, food marketing, legislation, and regulation devs, and consumption and price trends, quarterly journal, 1541–7
- Cost of living and quality of life indicators for 14 MSAs, 1980s, GAO rpt, 26123–346
- CPI by component for US city average, and by region, population size, and for 27 metro areas, monthly rpt, 6762–2
- CPI changes for selected items, 1981-90, annual article, 6722–1.226
- CPI components relative importance, by selected MSA, region, population size, and for US city average, 1990, annual rpt, 6884–1
- Dairy prices, by product and selected area, with related marketing data, 1990, annual rpt, 1317–1
- Dairy production by State, stocks, prices, and CCC price support activities, by product type, monthly rpt, 1627–3
- Dairy production, prices, trade, and use, periodic situation rpt with articles, 1561–2
- Dairy production, trade, use, and prices, for US and selected countries, forecast 1992 and trends from 1987, FAS semiannual circular, 1925–10
- Developing countries agricultural supply, demand, and market for US exports, with socioeconomic conditions, country rpt series, 1526–6

Developing countries food supply, needs, and aid, status and alternative forecasts, world area rpt series, 1526–8

- Developing countries grains production and needs, and related economic outlook, by world area and selected country, forecast 1990/91-1991/92, 1528–313
- Economic indicators and components, current data and annual trends, monthly rpt, 23842–1.4
- Economic indicators compounded annual rates of change, monthly rpt, 9391–3
- Export and import price indexes for goods and services, and dollar exchange rate indexes, quarterly press release, 6762–13
- *Family Economics Review*, consumer goods prices and supply, and home economics, quarterly journal, 1702–1
- Farm financial and marketing conditions, forecast 1991, annual chartbook, 1504–8
- Farm financial and marketing conditions, forecast 1991, annual conf, 1004–16
- Farm-retail food prices, marketing cost components, and industry finances and productivity, 1920s-90, annual rpt, 1544–9
- Fish and shellfish catch, wholesale receipts, prices, trade, and other market activities, weekly regional rpts, 2162–6
- Fish exvessel prices, value added, and consumer spending, 1984-90, annual rpt, 2164–1.9
- Foreign and US economic conditions, for major industrial countries, biweekly rpt, 9112–1
- Foreign and US food prices in selected world capitals, monthly rpt, semiannual data, 1922–12
- Fruit and nut production, prices, and use, 1988-91, annual rpt series, 1621–18
- Fruit and nut production, prices, trade, stocks, and use, by selected crop, periodic situation rpt with articles, 1561–6
- Fruit and vegetable production, imports by country, use, exports, and prices, by commodity, 1975-87, 1568–299
- Fruit and vegetable wholesale prices in NYC by State, and shipments and arrivals by mode of transport, by commodity, weekly rpt, 1311–20
- Fruit and vegetable wholesale prices in NYC, Chicago, and selected shipping points, by crop, 1990, annual rpt, 1311–8
- Inflation impacts on food price dispersion, by city, model results, 1981-82, working paper, 6886–6.79
- Meat and fish retail and producer prices, 1981-91, semiannual situation rpt, 1561–15.3
- Meat, poultry, and egg production, prices, trade, and stocks, monthly rpt, 1561–17
- Meat, poultry, and egg production, prices, trade, stocks, and use, periodic situation rpt with articles, 1561–7
- Milk farm, processor, and retail prices in 29 cities, 1980s-91, GAO rpt, 26113–540
- Milk order market policy alternatives impacts on supply, interregional marketings, and pricing, by region, 1988, 1568–294
- Milk order market prices and detailed operations, by State and market area, 1989-90, annual rpt, 1317–3
- Milk order market prices and detailed operations, monthly rpt with articles, 1317–4

Food prices

Mint oil production, yield, and farm prices by State, and NYC spot prices, various periods 1988-91, FAS annual circular, 1925–15.2

North Central States farm credit conditions and economic devs, Fed Reserve 7th District, monthly rpt, 9375–10

Poultry and egg prices and marketing, by selected region, State, and city, monthly and weekly 1990, annual rpt, 1317–2

Price indexes, alternative food cost index by category, region, and household income, size, race, and food budget level, 1980-85, 1598–275

Price indexes for food, by city, model results, 1988-89, article, 6722–1.236

Price indexes for food, by selected metro area and region, model results, 1988-89, working paper, 6886–6.78

Prices, supply, demand, trade, spending, and indexes, by food commodity, 1989, annual rpt, 1544–4

Producer Price Index, by major commodity group and subgroup, and processing stage, monthly press release, 6762–5

Producer price indexes, by stage of processing and detailed commodity, monthly rpt, 6762–6

Producer price indexes, by stage of processing and detailed commodity, monthly 1990, annual rpt, 6764–2

Spice and pepper spot prices in NYC, 1980s-91, FAS annual circular, 1925–15.1

Statistical Abstract of US, 1991 annual data compilation, 2324–1.15

Sugar and sweeteners production, prices, trade, supply, and use, quarterly situation rpt with articles, 1561–14

Sugar production, acreage, yield, stocks, deliveries, and price by State, and trade by country, 1950s-90, 1568–306

Vegetable production, prices, trade, stocks, and use, for selected fresh and processing crops, periodic situation rpt with articles, 1561–11

see also Agricultural prices

Food Safety and Inspection Service

Activities, funding, and staff of Federal food safety and quality regulation agencies, 1980s, GAO rpt, 26113–503

Budget of US, obligations and authority by function, agency, and program, with summaries, analyses, and historical tables, FY92, annual rpt, 104–2

Expenditures of Fed Govt in States, by type, program, agency, and State, FY90, annual rpt, 2464–2

Meat and poultry inspection activities and staff of Federal, State, and foreign govts, FY90, annual rpt, 1374–1

Meat plants inspected and certified for exporting to US, by country, 1990, annual listing, 1374–2

Food Security Act

Conservation programs under Act, farm finances and environmental benefits of alternative policies, projected 1991-2005, 1588–153

Subsidy rates of Fed Govt under 1985 and 1990 farm bills, by selected program and commodity, 1990 rpt, 1008–54

Food shortage

see Food supply

see Nutrition and malnutrition

Food stamp programs

Assistance (financial and nonfinancial) of Fed Govt, 1991 base edition with supplements, annual listing, 104–5

Assistance programs under Ways and Means Committee jurisdiction, finances, operations, and participant characteristics, FY70s-90, annual rpt, 21784–11

Beneficiaries of food stamps, household size, composition, income, and income and deductions allowed, summer 1988, annual rpt, 1364–8

Benefits payment and eligibility errors, by type, recipient characteristics, and State, FY89, annual rpt, 1364–15

Budget of US, midsession review of FY92 budget, by function, annual rpt, 104–7

Budget of US, obligations and authority by function, agency, and program, with summaries, analyses, and historical tables, FY92, annual rpt, 104–2

Computer records matching of welfare data, Federal and State agencies compliance with recipient protection provisions before benefits reduction, 1990, GAO rpt, 26121–404

Consumer research, food marketing, legislation, and regulation devs, and consumption and price trends, quarterly journal, 1541–7

Costs and participation of USDA food aid programs, by program, FY69-89, annual rpt, 1364–9

Criminal cases in Federal district courts, by offense, disposition, and district, 1980-90, last issue of annual rpt, 18204–1

Expenditures, coverage, and benefits for social welfare programs, late 1930s-89, annual rpt, 4744–3.1; 4744–3.3; 4744–3.9

Expenditures of Fed Govt in States, by type, program, agency, and State, FY90, annual rpt, 2464–2

Family economic impacts of departure, absence, and presence of parents, 1983-86, Current Population Rpt, 2546–20.17

Farmers markets use of food stamps, costs and participation, demonstration project results for 14 States, 1989, hearing, 21168–46

Fed Reserve banks finances and staff, 1990, annual rpt, 9364–1.1

Finances of Fed Govt, cash and debt transactions, daily tables, 8102–4

Households composition, income, benefits, and labor force status, Survey of Income and Program Participation methodology, working paper series, 2626–10

Housing and households detailed characteristics, and unit and neighborhood quality, by location, 1989, biennial rpt, 2485–12

Housing and households detailed characteristics, and unit and neighborhood quality, MSA surveys, series, 2485–6

Income (household) and poverty status under alternative income definitions, by recipient characteristics, 1990, annual Current Population Rpt, 2546–6.69

Participation and coupons issued, by State and county, as of July 1990, semiannual rpt, 1362–6

Poverty status of population and families, by detailed characteristics, 1988-89, annual Current Population Rpt, 2546–6.67

Poverty status of population and families, by detailed characteristics, 1990, annual Current Population Rpt, 2546–6.71

Single mothers earnings, employment and welfare benefits, and poverty status, 1989, GAO rpt, 26121–413

State and Metro Area Data Book, 1991 data compilation, 2328–54

Statistical Abstract of US, 1991 annual data compilation, 2324–1.12

Food stocks

see Agricultural stocks

see Food supply

Food stores

Census of Retail Trade, 1987: depreciable assets, capital and operating expenses, sales, value added, and inventories, by SIC 2- to 4-digit kind of business, 2399–2

Census of Retail Trade, 1987: finances and employment, for establishments with and without payroll, by SIC 2- to 4-digit kind of business, State, and MSA, 2401–1

Collective bargaining agreements expiring during year, and workers covered, by firm, union, industry group, and State, 1991, annual rpt, 6784–9

County Business Patterns, 1988: employment, establishments, and payroll, by SIC 2- to 4-digit industry and county, annual State rpt series, 2326–6

County Business Patterns, 1989: employment, establishments, and payroll, by SIC 2- to 4-digit industry and county, annual State rpt series, 2326–8

Employment, earnings, and hours, by SIC 1- to 4-digit industry, monthly and annual averages, selected years 1909-90, annual rpt, 6744–4

Energy use in commercial buildings, costs, and conservation, by building characteristics, survey rpt series, 3166–8

Enterprise Statistics, 1987: auxiliaries of multi-establishment firms, finances and operations by function, industry, and State, 2329–6

Enterprise Statistics, 1987: finances and operations for companies, by size, level of diversification, form of organization, and industry group, 2329–8

Expenditures for food and alcoholic beverages, by place of purchase, 1968-90, annual rpt, 1544–4.5

Finances and operations, by SIC 2- to 4-digit industry, forecast 1991, annual rpt, 2044–28

Financial statements for manufacturing, mining, and trade corporations, by selected SIC 2- to 3-digit industry, quarterly rpt, 2502–1

Franchise business opportunities by firm and kind of business, and sources of aid and info, 1990 annual listing, 2104–7

Labor productivity, indexes of output, hours, and employment by SIC 2- to 4-digit industry, 1967-89, annual rpt, 6824–1.4

Mail volume to and from households, use, and views, by class, source, content, and household characteristics, 1987-88, annual rpt, 9864–10

Milk home delivery, and sales by wholesale outlet type, by region, 1989 survey, biennial article, 1317–4.201

Milk order market sales, by container size and type, outlet type, and market area, 1989, biennial rpt, 1317–6

Occupational injury and illness rates, by SIC 2- to 4-digit industry, 1988-89, annual rpt, 6844–7

Occupational injury and illness rates, by SIC 2- to 4-digit industry, 1989, annual rpt, 6844–1

Older persons migration to southern coastal areas, household finances, services needs, and local economic impacts, for selected counties, 1990, 2068–38

Prices (farm-retail) for food, marketing cost components, and industry finances and productivity, 1920s-90, annual rpt, 1544–9

Puerto Rico economic censuses, 1987: wholesale and retail trade and service industry finances and operations, by SIC 2- to 4-digit industry and municipio, 2591–1

Puerto Rico economic censuses, 1987: wholesale, retail, and service industries finances and operations, by establishment characteristics and SIC 2- and 3-digit industry, subject rpts, 2591–2

Robberies, by type of premises, population size, and region, 1990, annual rpt, 6224–2.1

Sales and inventories, by kind of retail business, region, and selected State, MSA, and city, monthly rpt, 2413–3

Sales, inventories, purchases, gross margin, and accounts receivable, by SIC 2- to 4-digit kind of business and form of ownership, 1989, annual rpt, 2413–5

Sales of retailers, by kind of business, advance monthly rpt, 2413–2

Smoking bans in public places, local ordinances provisions, as of 1989, 4478–196

State and Metro Area Data Book, 1991 data compilation, 2328–54

Statistical Abstract of US, 1991 annual data compilation, 2324–1.28

Tax (income) returns of corporations, income and tax items by asset size and detailed industry, 1987, annual rpt, 8304–4

Tax (income) returns of corporations, income and tax items by asset size and detailed industry, 1988, annual rpt, 8304–21

Tax (income) returns of corporations with foreign tax credit, income and tax items by industry group, 1986, biennial article, 8302–2.203

Tax (income) returns of partnerships, income statement and balance sheet items, by industry group, 1989, annual article, 8302–2.216; 8304–18

Tax (income) returns of sole proprietorships, income statement items, by industry group, 1989, annual article, 8302–2.214

Tobacco ads in food and drug stores, prevalence and characteristics, 1987 local area study, article, 4042–3.250

see also under By Industry in the "Index by Categories"

Food supply

Africa (Sahel) grain production, use, imports, and stocks, by country, 1989/90, 9918–18

Agricultural Outlook, production, prices, marketing, and trade, by commodity, forecast and current situation, monthly rpt with articles, 1502–4

Agricultural Statistics, 1990, annual rpt, 1004–1

Business statistics, detailed data for major industries and economic indicators, *Survey of Current Business*, monthly rpt, 2702–1.14

Developing countries agricultural supply, demand, and market for US exports, with socioeconomic conditions, country rpt series, 1526–6

Developing countries economic, population, and agricultural data, US and other aid sources, and AID activity, country rpt series, 9916–12

Developing countries food supply, needs, and aid, status and alternative forecasts, world area rpt series, 1526–8

Developing countries grains production and needs, and related economic outlook, by world area and selected country, forecast 1990/91-1991/92, 1528–313

Foreign and US agricultural supply and demand indicators, by selected crop, monthly rpt, 1522–5

Foreign countries agricultural production, prices, and trade, by country, 1980-90 and forecast 1991, annual world area rpt series, 1524–4

Foreign countries food aid needs, and production, prices, trade, and use, for foreign and US agriculture, periodic rpt with articles, 1522–3

Marketing, consumer research, legislation, and regulation devs, and consumption and price trends, quarterly journal, 1541–7

Research (agricultural) funding and staffing for USDA, State agencies, and other instns, by topic, FY90, annual rpt, 1744–2

Supply, consumption, trade, prices, spending, and indexes, by food commodity, 1989, annual rpt, 1544–4

see also Agricultural production

see also Agricultural stocks

see also Nutrition and malnutrition

see also under names of specific agricultural commodities (for data on production and stocks)

Foot health and diseases

see Podiatry

Football

Educational and employment performance of college athletes compared to other students, for 1972 high school class, as of 1986, 4888–5

Injuries from use of consumer products, by severity, victim age, and detailed product, 1990, annual rpt, 9164–6

Service industries census, 1987: establishments, receipts by source, payroll, and employment, by SIC 2- to 4-digit kind of business, State, and MSA, 2393–4

Footwear

see Shoes and shoe industry

Forage

see Animal feed

see Pasture and rangeland

Forced labor

Foreign countries human rights conditions in 170 countries, 1990, annual rpt, 21384–3

Sentences for Federal offenses, guidelines by offense and circumstances, series, 17668–1

Ford, Kathleen

"Contraceptive Utilization Among Widowed, Divorced, and Separated Women in the U.S.: 1973 and 1976", 4147–16.4

"Contraceptive Utilization in the U.S.: 1973 and 1976", 4147–16.4

"Use of Intrauterine Contraceptive Devices in the U.S.", 4147–16.5

Ford Motor Co.

Energy economy, sales, and market shares, by size and model for domestic and foreign makes, 1991 model year, semiannual rpt, 3302–4

Energy economy test results, 1992 model year, annual rpt, 3304–11

Safety of domestic and foreign autos, crash test results by model, press release series, 7766–7

Forecasts

see Agricultural forecasts

see Energy projections

see Population projections

see Projections and forecasts

Foreign affairs

see Foreign relations

Foreign Agricultural Service

AgExporter, production, consumption, and policies for selected countries, and US export dev and promotion, monthly journal, 1922–2

Budget of US, obligations and authority by function, agency, and program, with summaries, analyses, and historical tables, FY92, annual rpt, 104–2

Cocoa and cocoa products foreign and US production, prices, and trade, 1980s-92, FAS semiannual circular, 1925–9

Coffee production, trade and quotas, and use, by country, with US and intl prices, FAS periodic circular, 1925–5

Cotton production and trade for US and selected countries, FAS periodic circular series, 1925–4

Dairy imports under quota by commodity, by country of origin, FAS monthly rpt, 1925–31

Dairy production, trade, use, and prices, for US and selected countries, forecast 1992 and trends from 1987, FAS semiannual circular, 1925–10

Exports (agricultural) of US, impacts of foreign agricultural and trade policy, with data by commodity and country, 1989, annual rpt, 1924–8

Exports and imports (agricultural) commodity and country, prices, and world market devs, monthly rpt, 1922–12

Exports and imports (agricultural) of US, by commodity, country, and US port, 1950s-91, annual rpt, 1924–9

Exports of grains, oilseed products, hides, skins, and cotton, by country, weekly rpt, 1922–3

Fruit, vegetable, and nut (fresh and processed) foreign and US production and trade, FAS monthly circular with articles, 1925–34

Foreign Agricultural Service

Grain foreign and US production, prices, trade, stocks, and use, FAS periodic circular series, 1925–2

Livestock, poultry, and dairy trade, by commodity and country, FAS monthly circular, 1925–32

Livestock, poultry, and products foreign and US production, trade, and use, by selected country, FAS semiannual circular series, 1925–33

Lumber and wood products exports, imports, and export promotion of US by country, and trade balance, by commodity, FAS quarterly circular, 1925–36

Oils, oilseeds, and fats foreign and US production and trade, FAS periodic circular series, 1925–1

PL 480 exports by commodity, and recipients, by program, sponsor, and country, FY88 and cumulative from FY55, annual rpt, 1924–7

PL 480 long-term credit sales allocations, by commodity and country, periodic press release, 1922–7

Production, acreage, and yield for selected crops, forecasts by selected world region and country, FAS monthly circular, 1925–28

Production, trade, and policies in foreign countries, summary data by country, 1989-90, annual factbook, 1924–12

Seed exports, by type, world region, and country, FAS quarterly rpt, 1925–13

Spice, essential oil, and tea foreign and US production, prices, and trade, FAS annual circular series, 1925–15

Sugar and honey foreign and US production, prices, trade, and use, FAS periodic circular series, 1925–14

Sugar and sugar product imports of US under quota, by country, periodic rpt, 1922–9

Tobacco and products foreign and US industry review, FAS monthly circular articles, 1925–16

Foreign agriculture

Africa (Sahel) grain production, use, imports, and stocks, by country, 1989/90, 9918–18

Africa (sub-Saharan) agricultural conditions by country, with Ethiopia grain production and use, and dev aid by major donor, 1960s-80s, hearing, 23848–216

AgExporter, production, consumption, and policies for selected countries, and US export dev and promotion, monthly journal, 1922–2

Agricultural Outlook, production, prices, marketing, and trade, by commodity, forecast and current situation, monthly rpt with articles, 1502–4

Agricultural Statistics, 1990, annual rpt, 1004–1

AID dev projects and socioeconomic impacts, evaluation rpt series, 9916–1

Andean countries cocaine and alternative crop production and impacts on US agricultural exports, with data for Bolivia, 1980s-91, GAO rpt, 26123–366

Animal disease outbreaks in US and foreign countries, quarterly rpt, 1392–3

Assistance (technical) of USDA, personnel and agreements by project, world area, and country, annual rpt, discontinued, 1954–2

Index by Subjects and Names

Australia agricultural input and output indexes, and freight rates, 1950s-80s, 1528–311

Background Notes, foreign countries summary social, political, and economic data, series, 7006–2

Bean (dried) prices by State, market activity, and foreign and US production, use, stocks, and trade, weekly rpt, 1311–17

Bean (dried) production and prices by State, exports and foreign production by country, and USDA food aid purchases, by bean type, 1984-90, annual rpt, 1311–18

Canada wheat producer subsidy costs and returns, 1990-92, article, 1561–12.202

Central America agricultural export promotion of nontraditional crops, impacts on income export stability, late 1970s-80s, 1528–312

China economic indicators and reform issues, with background data, 1950s-90, compilation of papers, 23848–155

Cocaine production, acreage, and economic impacts of crop eradication and conversion to legitimate agricultural use, 1960s-87, 9918–19

Cocoa and cocoa products foreign and US production, prices, and trade, 1980s-92, FAS semiannual circular, 1925–9

Coffee production, trade and quotas, and use, by country, with US and intl prices, FAS periodic circular, 1925–5

Cotton production and trade for US and selected countries, FAS periodic circular series, 1925–4

Cotton, wool, and synthetic fiber production, prices, trade, and use, periodic situation rpt with articles, 1561–1

Dairy exports market conditions, with background data by country, 1986-89, 1128–65

Dairy production, trade, use, and prices, for US and selected countries, forecast 1992 and trends from 1987, FAS semiannual circular, 1925–10

Developing countries agricultural and economic conditions, and US agricultural exports, effects of US aid, 1989 conf papers, 1548–372

Developing countries agricultural supply, demand, and market for US exports, with socioeconomic conditions, country rpt series, 1526–6

Developing countries economic and social conditions from 1960s, and Intl Dev Cooperation Agency and AID activities and funding, FY90-92, annual rpt, 9904–4

Developing countries economic, population, and agricultural data, US and other aid sources, and AID activity, country rpt series, 9916–12

Developing countries energy use, and economic and environmental impacts, by fuel type, world area, and country, 1980s-90, 26358–232

Developing countries food supply, needs, and aid, status and alternative forecasts, world area rpt series, 1526–8

Developing countries grains production and needs, and related economic outlook, by world area and selected country, forecast 1990/91-1991/92, 1528–313

Drug (illegal) production, eradication, and seizures, by substance, with US aid, by country, 1987-91, annual rpt, 7004–17

Drug (opium) legal production and US imports by country, and analgesics opium content, 1980s, hearing, 21528–81

Eastern Europe agricultural production, trade, and land reform, with selected economic indicators, by country, 1960s-90, article, 1522–3.202

Economic conditions in foreign countries and implications for US, periodic country rpt series, 2046–4

Economic indicators, and trade and trade flows by commodity, by country, data compilation, monthly CD-ROM, 2002–6

Economic, social, political, and geographic summary data, by country, 1991, annual factbook, 9114–2

Exports (agricultural) of high-value commodities, indexes and sales value by commodity, world area, and country, 1960s-86, 1528–323

Farm financial and marketing conditions, forecast 1991, annual chartbook, 1504–8

Farm financial and marketing conditions, forecast 1991, annual conf, 1004–16

Fish catch by world region, processing, and US trade, 1982-89, semiannual rpt, 1561–15.1

Fish catch, trade, use, and fishery operations, with selected foreign data, by species, 1980s-90, annual rpt, 2164–1

Fruit, vegetable, and nut (fresh and processed) foreign and US production and trade, FAS monthly circular with articles, 1925–34

Germany agricultural resources and yield, and effects of natl unification, 1980s, article, 1522–3.201

Grain foreign and US production, prices, trade, stocks, and use, FAS periodic circular series, 1925–2

Imports injury to price-supported US agricultural industry, investigations with background financial and operating data, series, 9886–10

Korea (South) agricultural subsidies to producers and consumers, by commodity, 1987-89, article, 1522–3.205

Latin America agricultural subsidies to producers and consumers, by selected commodity for 6 countries, 1982-87, 1528–324

Livestock, poultry, and products foreign and US production, trade, and use, by selected country, FAS semiannual circular series, 1925–33

Meat and poultry inspection activities and staff of Federal, State, and foreign govts, FY90, annual rpt, 1374–1

Molasses supply, use, wholesale prices by market, and imports by country, 1985-90, annual rpt, 1311–19

Oils, oilseeds, and fats foreign and US production and trade, FAS periodic circular series, 1925–1

Overseas Business Reports: economic conditions, investment and export opportunities, and trade practices, country market research rpt series, 2046–6

Peanut and peanut oil exports of US, and foreign production, by country, 1985-91 and forecast 1992, annual rpt, 1311–5.2

Index by Subjects and Names

Foreign competition

Potato production, acreage, disposition, prices, and trade, by State and country, 1949-90, 1568–305

Production, acreage, and yield for selected crops, forecasts by selected world region and country, FAS monthly circular, articles, 1925–28

Production inputs supply, demand, and prices, 1970s-90 and projected to 1995, article, 1561–16.201

Production inputs supply, demand, and prices, 1980s-91 and forecast 1992, article, 1561–16.204

Production, prices, and trade of agricultural commodities, by country, 1980-90 and forecast 1991, annual world area rpt series, 1524–4

Production, prices, trade, and use, for foreign and US agriculture, periodic rpt with articles, 1522–3

Production, trade, and policies in foreign countries, summary data by country, 1989-90, annual factbook, 1924–12

Research (agricultural) funding and staffing for USDA, State agencies, and other instns, by topic, FY90, annual rpt, 1744–2

Research (agricultural) investment impacts on productivity, indicators for developed and developing countries, late 1960s-80, 1528–318

Research grants of USDA, by program, subagency, and country, FY90, annual listing, 1954–3

Rice foreign and US production, prices, trade, stocks, and use, periodic situation rpt, 1561–8

Rice market activities, prices, inspections, sales, trade, supply, and use, for US and selected foreign markets, weekly rpt, 1313–8

Soviet Union agricultural conditions and factors affecting US grain exports and CCC credit guarantees, 1990 hearings, 21168–49

Soviet Union agricultural reform issues, with background data for USSR and US, 1970s-90, article, 9381–1.210

Soviet Union agricultural subsidies to producers and consumers, by selected commodity, 1986, 1528–320

Soviet Union agricultural trade, by commodity and country, 1955-90, 1528–322

Soviet Union, Eastern Europe, OECD, and selected other countries economic conditions, 1960s-90, annual rpt, 9114–4

Soviet Union GNP by component and industry sector, and CIA estimation methods, 1950s-87, 23848–223

Soviet Union GNP by detailed income and outlay component, 1985, 2326–18.59

Spice, essential oil, and tea foreign and US production, prices, and trade, FAS annual circular series, 1925–15

Statistical Abstract of US, 1991 annual data compilation, 2324–1.31

Subsidies for agricultural producers and consumers of US and foreign govts, production and trade impacts, model description, 1991 rpt, 1528–315

Sugar and honey foreign and US production, prices, trade, and use, FAS periodic circular series, 1925–14

Supply and demand indicators for selected foreign and US crops, monthly rpt, 1522–5

Tobacco and products foreign and US industry review, FAS monthly circular articles, 1925–16

Tobacco production, prices, stocks, taxes by State, and trade and production by country, 1990, annual rpt, 1319–1

Weather conditions and effect on agriculture, by US region, State, and city, and world area, weekly rpt, 2182–7

Wheat and rye foreign and US production, prices, trade, stocks, and use, quarterly situation rpt with articles, 1561–12

Wheat quality indicators, for US exports and foreign wheat production, 1960s-90, hearing, 25168–75

Zimbabwe agricultural conditions impacts of economic policies, 1980s, 1528–319

Foreign area studies see Area studies

Foreign assistance see International assistance

Foreign budgets

AID dev projects and socioeconomic impacts, evaluation rpt series, 9916–1

Argentina and Brazil inflation rates and public debt burden, 1980s-91, technical paper, 9379–12.69

Argentina and Brazil inflation relation to money supply and public debt, model description and results, 1980s-90, technical paper, 9379–12.75

China economic indicators and reform issues, with background data, 1950s-90, compilation of papers, 23848–155

Developing countries child health and welfare indicators, and economic conditions, 1950s-80s, hearing, 25388–57

Developing countries counterpart funds impacts on US aid programs effectiveness and domestic economic and fiscal condition, literature review, 1991 rpt, 9918–21

Developing countries economic aid from US, military spending and imports measures to determine aid eligibility, by country, 1986-87, annual rpt, 9914–1

Developing countries economic and social conditions from 1960s, and Intl Dev Cooperation Agency and AID activities and funding, FY90-92, annual rpt, 9904–4; 9904–4.1

Developing countries economic, population, and agricultural data, US and other aid sources, and AID activity, country rpt series, 9916–12

Economic conditions in foreign countries and implications for US, periodic country rpt series, 2046–4

Economic, social, political, and geographic summary data, by country, 1991, annual factbook, 9114–2

Israel and Egypt govt budgets, foreign debt, and economic indicators, 1980s, hearing, 21388–58

Japan economic conditions, financial and intl policies, and trade devs, 1950s-80s and projected to 2050, compilation of papers, 23848–220

Mexico govt debt relation to deficit, model assessment, 1986-90, technical paper, 9379–12.78

NATO and Japan military spending and indicators of ability to support common defense, by country, 1970s-89, annual rpt, 3544–28

Overseas Business Reports: economic conditions, investment and export opportunities, and trade practices, country market research rpt series, 2046–6

Seignorage use for financing fiscal deficits in EC, with background data for EC, 1970s-88, working paper, 9387–8.238

Soviet Union GNP by component and industry sector, and CIA estimation methods, 1950s-87, 23848–223

Soviet Union GNP by detailed income and outlay component, 1985, 2326–18.59

UK govt debt, by holder and type of financial instrument, 1985 and 1990, article, 9385–1.214

UN participation of US, and member and nonmember shares of UN budget by country, FY89-91, annual rpt, 7004–5

see also International reserves

Foreign Claims Settlement Commission

Claims against foreign govts by US natls, by claim type and country, 1990, annual rpt, 6004–16

Foreign competition

Agricultural export market research and promotion activities of USDA, with background data, 1991 GAO rpt, 26113–504

Agricultural imports of US, competitive and noncompetitive, by commodity and country, bimonthly rpt, 1522–1.2

Agricultural trade of US, by commodity, country, and US port, 1950s-91, annual rpt, 1924–9

Airline deregulation in 1978, impacts on US carriers intl services, operations, and market shares, late 1970s-80s, 7308–199.11

Banking intl competition and deposit insurance reform issues, with background data, 1990 hearings, 25248–121; 25248–122; 25248–123

Banking intl competition issues, with background data, 1980s, 21248–153

Budget of US, House concurrent resolution, with spending and revenue targets, FY92 and projected to FY96, annual rpt, 21264–2

Caribbean area duty-free exports to US, and imports from US, by country, and impact on US employment, by commodity, 1990, annual rpt, 6364–2

Construction contract awards and billings, by country of contractor and world area of award, 1989, annual article, 2042–1.201

Economic conditions in foreign countries and US, and competitiveness issues, 1960s-90, 21788–204

Employment and industry impacts of trade, series, 6366–3

Export and import agreements, negotiations, and related legislation, 1990, annual rpt, 444–1

Farm labor costs and trade of US, effects of immigration restrictions on selected industries, 1980s, 1598–276

Imports and tariff provisions effect on US industries and products, investigations with background financial and operating data, series, 9886–4

Foreign competition

Imports injury to price-supported US agricultural industry, investigations with background financial and operating data, series, 9886–10

Imports injury to US industries from foreign subsidized products and sales at less than fair value, investigations with background financial and operating data, series, 9886–19

Imports injury to US industries from foreign subsidized products, investigations with background financial and operating data, series, 9886–15

Imports injury to US industries from sales at less than fair value, investigations with background financial and operating data, series, 9886–14

Imports injury to US industries, trade-remedy law petitions brought, by provision, 1979-90, article, 9391–1.215

Imports under Generalized System of Preferences, status, and US tariffs, with trade by country and US economic impacts, for selected commodities, 1986-90, annual rpt, 9884–23

Industry (US) intl competitiveness, with selected foreign and US operating data by major firm and product, series, 2046–12

Japan economic conditions, financial and intl policies, and trade devs, 1950s-80s and projected to 2050, compilation of papers, 23848–220

Manufacturing wages impacts of foreign competition and other factors, late 1950s-89, article, 9385–1.204

OECD intl trade position for US and 4 countries, and factors affecting US competition, periodic pamphlet, 2042–25

Patent and copyright intl and domestic protection, products excluded, and countries and agreements involved, 1990 article, 9391–1.203

Semiconductor and fiber optics industries quality control spending, effectiveness, and views, survey results, 1980s, 2218–84

Semiconductors and related equipment import dependency of US firms, and sales from Japan firms delayed and denied, 1988-91, GAO rpt, 26123–361

State gross product impact of foreign labor productivity and dollar exchange rate, by industry sector and State, 1972-86, working paper, 9387–8.255

Steel imports of US under voluntary restraint agreement, by product, customs district, and country, with US industry operating data, quarterly rpt, 9882–13

Taxation and intl competitiveness issues, with comparisons of US and foreign tax rates and revenue, 1988-91, press release, 8008–150

Technology dev programs of govts, info sources and funding, 1990 rpt, 10048–81

Telecommunications industry intl competitiveness, with financial and operating data by product or service, firm, and country, 1990 rpt, 2008–30

Textile imports, total and from US, by commodity and country, 1987-89, 2048–155

USITC activities, investigations, and rpts, FY90, annual rpt, 9884–1

Wages impacts of foreign competition, regression results, late 1950s-85, technical paper, 9385–8.89

see also Dumping

see also Foreign trade

Foreign corporations

Airport security operations to prevent hijacking, screening results, enforcement actions, and hijacking attempts, 2nd half 1989, semiannual rpt, 7502–5

Background Notes, foreign countries summary social, political, and economic data, series, 7006–2

Banking intl competition and deposit insurance reform issues, with background data, 1990 hearings, 25248–121

Banks branches and agencies of foreign banks, assets and liabilities, monthly rpt, 9362–1.1

Banks branches and agencies of foreign banks, assets and liabilities, monthly rpt, quarterly data, 9362–1.4

Banks capital costs, operating ratios, and intl market shares, for US and 5 OECD countries, 1980s-90, article, 9385–1.203

Boycotts (intl) by OPEC and other countries, US firms and shareholders cooperation and tax benefits denied, 1986, annual rpt, 8004–13

Business America, foreign and domestic commerce, and US investment and trade opportunities, biweekly journal, 2042–24

Capital cost indicators and contributing factors, for US and Japan, 1920s-90, article, 9385–1.202

Competitiveness (intl) of US industries, with selected foreign and US operating data by major firm and product, series, 2046–12

DOD prime contract awards, by category, contract and contractor type, and service branch, FY81-1st half FY91, semiannual rpt, 3542–1

DOD prime contract awards for R&D, for top 500 contractors, FY90, annual listing, 3544–4

Farmland in US owned by foreigners, holdings, acquisitions, and disposals by land use, owner type and country, and State, 1990, annual rpt, 1584–2

Imports and tariff provisions effect on US industries and products, investigations with background financial and operating data, series, 9886–4

Imports injury to US industries from foreign subsidized products and sales at less than fair value, investigations with background financial and operating data, series, 9886–19

Income from US sources and tax withheld for foreign natls not residing in US, by country and tax treaty status, 1988, annual article, 8302–2.206

Minerals foreign and US supply under alternative market conditions, reserves, and background industry data, series, 5606–4

Navy procurement, by contractor and location, FY90, annual rpt, 3804–13

Nuclear power plant capacity, generation, and operating status, by plant and foreign and US location, 1990 and projected to 2030, annual rpt, 3164–57

Overseas Business Reports: economic conditions, investment and export opportunities, and trade practices, country market research rpt series, 2046–6

Securities firms equity capital costs and financial ratios, with data by firm, for US and Japan, 1980s-91, article, 9385–1.212

Index by Subjects and Names

Service industries exports and imports of US, direct and among multinatl firms affiliates, by industry and world area, 1986-90, article, 2702–1.223

Tax (income) returns filed, by type of return and IRS district, 1989 and projected 1990-97, annual rpt, 8304–24

Tax (income) returns filed, by type of tax and IRS region and service center, projected 1990-97 and trends from 1978, annual rpt, 8304–9

Tax (income) returns of corporations, income and tax items by asset size and detailed industry, 1987, annual rpt, 8304–4

Tax (income) returns of corporations, income and tax items by asset size and detailed industry, 1988, annual rpt, 8304–21

Tax expenditures, Federal revenues forgone through income tax deductions and exclusions by type, FY92-96, annual rpt, 21784–10

Telecommunications industry intl competitiveness, with financial and operating data by product or service, firm, and country, 1990 rpt, 2008–30

see also Multinational corporations

Foreign countries

Aircraft hijackings, on-board explosions, and other crime, US and foreign incidents, 1985-89, annual rpt, 7504–31

Airline deregulation in 1978, impacts on US carriers intl services, operations, and market shares, late 1970s-80s, 7308–199.11

Background Notes, foreign countries summary social, political, and economic data, series, 7006–2

Census Bur rpts and data files, coverage and availability, 1991 annual listing, 2304–2

Chiefs of State and Cabinet members, by country, bimonthly listing, 9112–4

Classification codes for countries and ports under Tariff Schedule of US, 1992 base edition, 9886–13

Classification codes for countries, commodities, and customs districts for Census Bur export statistics, 1990 base edition supplement, 2428–5

Classification codes for countries for Census Bur foreign trade statistics, 1991 edition, 2428–3

Earthquake intensity, time, location, damage, and seismic characteristics, for US and foreign earthquakes, 1985, annual rpt, 5664–13

Economic and monetary trends, compounded annual rates of change and quarterly indicators for US and 7 major industrialized countries, quarterly rpt, 9391–7

Economic and social conditions of foreign countries, working paper series, 2326–18

Economic conditions in USSR, Eastern Europe, OECD, and selected other countries, 1960s-90, annual rpt, 9114–4

Economic, social, political, and geographic summary data, by country, 1991, annual factbook, 9114–2

Education data, detail for elementary, secondary, and higher education, 1920s-90 and projected to 2001, annual rpt, 4824–1

Index by Subjects and Names — Foreign debts

Education data for foreign countries, and students enrolled in US higher education instns, 1991 edition, annual rpt, 4824–2.29

Geographic Notes, foreign countries boundaries, claims, nomenclature, and other devs, periodic rpt, 7142–3

Health condition and health care resources, use, and spending, 1950s-89, annual data compilation, 4144–11

Health, welfare, and research aid from HHS, by program, recipient, and country, FY90, annual listing, 4004–3.10

Living costs abroad, State Dept indexes, housing allowances, and hardship differentials by country and major city, quarterly rpt, 7002–7

Mail (US) revenue, FY90, and volume from FY86, annual rpt, 9864–1

Mail (US) to foreign countries, USPS itemized operating costs, FY90, annual rpt, 9864–4

Mail (US) to foreign countries, USPS revenue, and costs by class of mail, FY90, annual rpt, 9864–2

Mail (US) to foreign countries, USPS revenue and volume, quarterly rpt, 9862–1

Mail (US) to foreign countries, USPS revenues, and postal rates by country, FY90, annual rpt, 9864–5

Mail to and from US households, 1987-88, annual rpt, 9864–10

Minerals foreign and US supply under alternative market conditions, reserves, and background industry data, series, 5606–4

Minerals production, prices, trade, use, employment, tariffs, and stockpiles, by mineral, with foreign comparisons, 1986-90, annual rpt, 5604–18

Minerals Yearbook, 1988, Vol 3: foreign country reviews of production, trade, and policy, by commodity, annual rpt series, 5604–17

Minerals Yearbook, 1989, Vol 1: commodity reviews of production, reserves, supply, use, and trade, annual rpt series, 5604–15

Minerals Yearbook, 1990, Vol 1: commodity reviews of production, reserves, supply, use, and trade, annual rpt series, 5604–20

Radioactive strontium fallout, monitoring results for 65 sites worldwide, quarterly 1986 and trends from 1958, annual rpt, 3004–29

Space launchings and characteristics of craft and flight, by country, 1957-90, annual rpt, 9504–9.1

Statistical Abstract of US, 1991 annual data compilation, 2324–1; 2324–1.31

Steel industry finances, operations, and modernization efforts, with data on major companies and foreign industry, 1968-91, last issue of annual rpt, 9884–24

Travel from US, characteristics of visit and traveler, and country of destination, 1990 in-flight survey, annual rpt, 2904–14

Travel to and from US on US and foreign flag air carriers, by country, world area, and US port, monthly rpt, 7302–2

Travel to US, by characteristics of visit and traveler, world area of origin, and US destination, 1990 survey, annual rpt, 2904–12

US coastal areas recreation facilities out-of-State visitors by location of residence, 1987-90 survey, regional rpt series, 2176–9

US govt civilian employment and payroll abroad, by agency, bimonthly rpt, 9842–1

US govt civilian employment and payroll, by occupation, pay grade, sex, agency, and location, 1989, biennial rpt, 9844–4

US govt civilian employment and payroll, by pay system and location, 1990, annual rpt, 9844–6.1

US govt-leased real property inventory and rental costs, worldwide summary by location and agency, 1989, annual rpt, 9454–10

US govt-owned real property inventory and costs, worldwide summary by location, agency, and use, 1989, annual rpt, 9454–5

US military and civilian personnel and dependents, by service branch, world area, and country, quarterly rpt, 3542–20

US military base support costs by function, and personnel and acreage by installation, by service branch, FY91, annual rpt, 3504–11

US military draft registrants residing abroad, FY90, annual rpt, 9744–1

US military hospitals abroad, admissions, beds, outpatient visits, and births, by service branch, quarterly rpt, 3542–15

US military personnel abroad, by service branch, world area, and country, quarterly press release, 3542–9

US military prime contract awards for R&D to US and foreign nonprofit instns and govt agencies, by instn and location, FY90, annual listing, 3544–17

US personal transfer payments to foreigners, *Survey of Current Business*, monthly rpt, 2702–1.4; 2702–1.24

US veterans living abroad, VA expenses by type and location, FY90, annual rpt, 8604–3.9

US veterans programs spending, by US and foreign location, FY90, annual rpt, 8604–6

Vaccination needs for intl travel by country, and disease prevention recommendations, 1991 annual rpt, 4204–11

Vital and Health Statistics series: foreign and US comparative data, 4147–5

Weather data for surface and upper air, averages by foreign and US station, monthly rpt, 2152–4

Weather events and anomalies, precipitation and temperature for US and foreign locations, weekly rpt, 2182–6

see also Africa
see also Agricultural exports and imports
see also Alien workers
see also Aliens
see also Asia
see also Balance of payments
see also Caribbean area
see also Central America
see also Centrally planned economies
see also Citizenship
see also Deportation
see also Developing countries
see also Diplomatic and consular service
see also East-West trade

see also Eastern Europe
see also Educational exchanges
see also Europe
see also Foreign agriculture
see also Foreign budgets
see also Foreign competition
see also Foreign corporations
see also Foreign debts
see also Foreign economic relations
see also Foreign exchange
see also Foreign investments
see also Foreign labor conditions
see also Foreign languages
see also Foreign medical graduates
see also Foreign opinion of U.S.
see also Foreign relations
see also Foreign students
see also Foreign trade
see also Foreign trade promotion
see also Immigration and emigration
see also International assistance
see also International cooperation in conservation
see also International cooperation in cultural activities
see also International cooperation in environmental sciences
see also International cooperation in law enforcement
see also International cooperation in science and technology
see also International finance
see also International military forces
see also International reserves
see also International sanctions
see also Latin America
see also Middle East
see also Military assistance
see also North America
see also Oceania
see also Refugees
see also South America
see also Southeast Asia
see also Tariffs and foreign trade controls
see also Trade agreements
see also Treaties and conventions
see also under By Foreign Country in the "Index by Categories"
see also under names of individual countries

Foreign currency programs
see Special foreign currency programs

Foreign debts

AID loans repayment status and terms by program and country, and status of predecessor agency loans, quarterly rpt, 9912–3

Argentina and Brazil inflation rates and public debt burden, 1980s-91, technical paper, 9379–12.69

Assets and debts of private sector, balance sheets by segment, 1945-90, semiannual rpt, 9365–4.1

Assistance (financial and nonfinancial) of Fed Govt, 1991 base edition with supplements, annual listing, 104–5

Bank deposits in foreign banks, for 7 heavily indebted developing countries, 1982-89, technical paper, 9385–8.109

Banks (natl) charters, mergers, liquidations, enforcement cases, and financial performance, with data by instn and State, quarterly rpt, 8402–3

Banks (US) foreign lending at all US and foreign offices, by country group and country, quarterly rpt, 13002–1

Foreign debts

Banks and nonbank liabilities to and claims on foreigners, by type and world area, monthly rpt, 9362–1.3

Budget deficits under Reagan Admin, impact on capital stock, foreign debt, and other economic indicators, with background data, 1950s-88, article, 9393–8.201

Budget of US, analysis of Federal debt held by foreigners, FY65-90, annual rpt, 104–2.2

Communist countries debt to US and other Western banks, by country, 1980s, conf, 25388–56

Currency (foreign) positions of US firms and foreign branches or affiliates, *Treasury Bulletin*, quarterly rpt, 8002–4.12

Developing countries child health and welfare indicators, and economic conditions, 1950s-80s, hearing, 25388–57

Developing countries debt burden and related indicators, by country and for 9 US money-center banks, 1960s-89, article, 9292–4.201

Developing countries economic and social conditions from 1960s, and Intl Dev Cooperation Agency and AID activities and funding, FY90-92, annual rpt, 9904–4

Developing countries foreign debt, and IMF credit outstanding, by country, 1984-90, 9118–11

Eastern Europe agricultural production, trade, and land reform, with selected economic indicators, by country, 1960s-90, article, 1522–3.202

Eastern Europe debt by source, and developing country debt, 1970s-90, annual rpt, 9114–4.2

Eastern Europe foreign debt components, trade, balances, and other economic indicators, by country, 1985-89, hearing, 21248–148

Eastern Europe transition to market economies, economic conditions, intl aid, and energy balance, by country, 1985-90, 9118–13

Eastern Europe transition to market economies, US trade prospects, with background data by country, 1980s, hearing, 25728–42

Economic aid of US and other donor countries by type and recipient, and role in advancing economic interests, 1980s-90, 2048–152

Economic and military aid and loans from US and intl agencies, by program and country, FY46-90, annual rpt, 9914–5

Eximbank financial condition, with credit and insurance authorizations and loan activity by country, FY90, annual rpt, 9254–1

Fed Govt finances, cash and debt transactions, daily tables, 8102–4

Investment (foreign direct) in US, by industry group of US affiliate and country of parent firm, 1980-86, 2708–41

Investment (intl) position of US, by component, industry, world region, and country, 1989-90, annual article, 2702–1.212

Israel and Egypt govt budgets, foreign debt, and economic indicators, 1980s, hearing, 21388–58

Outstanding debt on US credit, by program, world area, and country, selected years 1940-88, annual rpt, 15344–1.1

Outstanding debt to US of foreign govts and private obligors, by country and program, periodic rpt, 8002–6

Soviet Union economic conditions under General Secretary Gorbachev, 1990 and trends from 1975, annual rpt, 9114–6

Soviet Union hard currency debt to western countries, and balance of payments 1960s-90, annual rpt, 9114–4.3

Statistical Abstract of US, 1991 annual data compilation, 2324–1.16; 2324–1.31

Survey of Current Business, monthly rpt, quarterly tables, 2702–1.26

US govt contingent liabilities and claims paid on federally insured and guaranteed contracts with foreign obligors, by country and program, periodic rpt, 8002–12

US govt liabilities to foreigners and foreign official instns, *Treasury Bulletin*, quarterly rpt, 8002–4.10

US natls claims against foreign govts, by claim type and country, 1990, annual rpt, 6004–16

see also Balance of payments
see also International reserves
see also Public debt

Foreign economic relations

Assistance (financial and nonfinancial) of Fed Govt, 1991 base edition with supplements, annual listing, 104–5

Background Notes, foreign countries summary social, political, and economic data, series, 7006–2

Economic conditions in foreign countries and implications for US, periodic country rpt series, 2046–4

Economic indicators, and trade and investment flows, for selected countries and country groups, selected years 1946-90, annual rpt, 204–1.9

Overseas Business Reports: economic conditions, investment and export opportunities, and trade practices, country market research rpt series, 2046–6

Soviet Union, Eastern Europe, OECD, and selected other countries economic conditions, 1960s-90, annual rpt, 9114–4

see also Agricultural exports and imports
see also Arms trade
see also Balance of payments
see also Dumping
see also East-West trade
see also Foreign competition
see also Foreign corporations
see also Foreign debts
see also Foreign exchange
see also Foreign investments
see also Foreign trade
see also Foreign trade promotion
see also International assistance
see also International finance
see also International sanctions
see also Military assistance
see also Multinational corporations
see also Tariffs and foreign trade controls
see also Trade agreements
see also Treaties and conventions

Foreign exchange

Argentina black-market dollar exchange rate relationship with official rate and other economic indicators, model description and results, 1991 technical paper, 9366–7.261

Index by Subjects and Names

Background Notes, foreign countries summary social, political, and economic data, series, 7006–2

Banks (insured commercial and savings) finances, for foreign and domestic offices, by asset size, 1989, annual rpt, 9294–4.2

Banks capital requirements for holding foreign currency assets, alternative measures of exchange rate risk, 1991 technical paper, 9366–7.254

Chemicals export and import price indexes, by commodity, 1985-90, article, 6722–1.229

Corn, wheat, and soybeans export demand, by selected country, 1960s-83, 1568–297

Counterpart funds impacts on US aid programs effectiveness and developing countries economic and fiscal condition, literature review, 1991 rpt, 9918–21

Currency (foreign) accounts owned by US under AID admin and by foreign govts with AID control, status by program and country, quarterly rpt, 9912–1

Currency (foreign) holdings of US, transactions and balances by program and country, 1st half FY91, semiannual rpt, 8102–7

Currency (foreign) positions of US firms and foreign branches or affiliates, *Treasury Bulletin*, quarterly rpt, 8002–4.12

Currency (foreign) purchases of US with dollars, by country, 1st half FY91, semiannual rpt, 8102–5

Developing countries inflation control programs using exchange rate policies, evaluation, 1980s-91, technical paper, 9366–7.256

Dollar exchange rate and domestic monetary policy impacts of foreign exchange intervention, for US and Germany, 1985-87, article, 9373–1.209

Dollar exchange rate forecasting performance, assessment of alternative forecasts for 5 currencies, 1985-91, working paper, 9371–10.63

Dollar exchange rate forecasting performance of central bank policy intervention indicators, with model results for 2 currencies, 1985-90, working paper, 9377–9.118

Dollar exchange rate relation to interest rate differentials and inflation, for selected currencies and trade-weighted index, model description and results, 1974-90, technical paper, 9366–7.262

Dollar exchange rate trade-weighted index, for agricultural commodities, monthly rpt with articles, 1502–4

Dollar exchange rate trade-weighted index of Fed Reserve Bank of Atlanta, by world area, quarterly rpt, 9371–15

Dollar exchange rate trade-weighted index of Fed Reserve Bank of Dallas, by world area, monthly rpt, 9379–13

Dollar exchange rate trade-weighted index of Fed Reserve, weekly rpt, 9391–4

Dollar exchange rate trade-weighted index, *Treasury Bulletin*, quarterly rpt, 8002–4.10

Dollar exchange rate variability relation to currency bid-ask price spread, model description and results, 1983-90, technical paper, 9366–7.263

Dollar exchange rates, and State Dept indexes of living costs abroad and allowances, by country and major city, quarterly rpt, 7002–7

Index by Subjects and Names

Foreign investments

Dollar exchange rates of Mexico peso and Canada dollar, relation to domestic and US prices and nominal exchange rate, model description and results, 1991 technical paper, 9379–12.77

Dollar exchange rates of OECD and Asian currencies, 1991 semiannual rpt, 8002–14

Dollar exchange rates of OECD countries, 1989, annual rpt, 7144–11

Dollar exchange rates of yen and mark, impact of Fed Reserve policy interventions and other economic indicators, 1985-89, technical paper, 9385–8.114

Dollar exchange rates of 5 OECD countries, bimonthly rpt, 1522–1.3

Dollar exchange rates of 9 countries, *Survey of Current Business*, monthly rpt, quarterly tables, 2702–1.26

Dollar exchange rates of 10 countries, 1967-90, annual rpt, 204–1.9

Dollar exchange rates of 29 countries, 1990, semiannual rpt, 6822–3

Dollar exchange rates of 31 countries, and trade-weighted US index, monthly rpt, 9362–1.3

Dollar exchange rates of 35 countries, weekly chartbook, 9365–1.5

Dollar exchange rates offered by US disbursing offices, by country, quarterly rpt, 8102–6

Eastern Europe foreign debt components, trade, balances, and other economic indicators, by country, 1985-89, hearing, 21248–148

Eastern Europe transition to market economies, US trade prospects, with background data by country, 1980s, hearing, 25728–42

Economic and monetary trends, compounded annual rates of change and quarterly indicators for US and 7 major industrialized countries, quarterly rpt, 9391–7

Economic conditions, and trade devs and balances, with data by selected country and country group, monthly rpt, 9882–14

Economic conditions in foreign countries and implications for US, periodic country rpt series, 2046–4

Economic conditions, policy, and trade practices, by country, 1988-90, annual rpt, 21384–5

Economic indicators and components, and Fed Reserve 4th District business and financial conditions, monthly chartbook, 9377–10

Economic, social, political, and geographic summary data, by country, 1991, annual factbook, 9114–2

Exchange Stabilization Fund balance sheet and income and expenses, *Treasury Bulletin*, quarterly rpt, 8002–4.13

Export and import price indexes for goods and services, and dollar exchange rate indexes, quarterly press release, 6762–13

Fed Reserve Board and Reserve banks finances, staff, and review of monetary policy and economic devs, 1990, annual rpt, 9364–1

Fed Reserve foreign currency transactions impact on Fed Reserve receipts, profits, and Treasury payments, 1975-89, article, 9377–1.205

Finance (intl) and financial policy, and external factors affecting US economy, technical paper series, 9366–7

Flow-of-funds accounts, savings, investments, and credit statements, quarterly rpt, 9365–3.3

Forward foreign exchange rate relation to spot rate, model description and results for 4 currencies, 1970s-90, working paper, 9371–10.64

France and West Germany exchange rate relation to interest rate differentials, model description and results, 1980s, technical paper, 9366–7.249

Futures and options trading volume, by commodity and exchange, FY90, annual rpt, 11924–2

Futures trading in selected commodities and financial instruments and indexes, NYC, Chicago, and other markets activity, semimonthly rpt, 11922–5

Import prices relation to dollar exchange rate for 32 industries, and impacts of domestic market concentration, 1990 working paper, 9387–8.234

Investment (intl) position of US, by component, industry, world region, and country, 1989-90, annual article, 2702–1.212

Investment spending relation to dollar exchange rate, by SIC 2-digit manufacturing industry, 1963-86, article, 9375–1.208

Machinery and transport equipment export and import prices, impacts of dollar depreciation, 1985-90, article, 6722–1.233

OECD intl trade position for US and 4 countries, and factors affecting US competition, periodic pamphlet, 2042–25

Soviet Union, Eastern Europe, OECD, and selected other countries economic conditions, 1960s-90, annual rpt, 9114–4

State gross product impact of foreign labor productivity and dollar exchange rate, by industry sector and State, 1972-86, working paper, 9387–8.255

Statistical Abstract of US, 1991 annual data compilation, 2324–1.31

Swap contracts, by contract and counterparty type, and currency, late 1980s, article, 9371–1.205

Treasury and Fed Reserve foreign exchange operations, *Fed Reserve Bulletin*, monthly rpt, quarterly article, 9362–1

Treasury and Fed Reserve foreign exchange operations, quarterly journal, 9385–1

Turkey GNP, trade, investment, and inflation following currency devaluation, 1970s-90, technical paper, 9385–8.112

Zimbabwe agricultural conditions impacts of economic policies, 1980s, 1528–319

see also Balance of payments

see also Eurocurrency

see also International reserves

Foreign investments

Acquisitions and mergers by type, with data for large transactions by payment method and firm, late 1960s-90, working paper, 9366–1.161

Assets and debts of private sector, balance sheets by segment, 1945-90, semiannual rpt, 9365–4.1

Assets and liabilities of US, and impacts of inflation, 1990 and trends from 1948, article, 9391–1.220

Bank deposit insurance system reform issues, with background industry financial data, 1970s-90, GAO rpt, 26119–320

Banking industry structure and deposit insurance reform, findings and recommendations, with background data, 1989-90, 8008–147

Banks (foreign-owned) assets in US, relation to foreign and domestic economic and financial indicators, by instn type, 1970s-89, technical paper, 9385–8.108

Banks (insured commercial and savings) finances, for foreign and domestic offices, by asset size, 1989, annual rpt, 9294–4.2

Banks capital requirements for holding foreign currency assets, alternative measures of exchange rate risk, 1991 technical paper, 9366–7.254

Beer brewing intl licensing agreements, by major firm, 1987, article, 9391–1.201

Business America, foreign and domestic commerce, and US investment and trade opportunities, biweekly journal, 2042–24

Caribbean area duty-free exports to US, by commodity and country, with consumer and industry impacts, 1984-90, annual rpt, 9884–20

Caribbean Basin Initiative investment incentives, economic impacts, with finances and employment by country, 1984-90, 2048–141

China economic indicators and reform issues, with background data, 1950s-90, compilation of papers, 23848–155

Commercial real estate investment by foreigners, by State and investor country, 1980s, GAO rpt, 26123–350

Corporations and govt securities of US, foreign transactions, monthly rpt, 9362–1.3

Currency (foreign) positions of US firms and foreign branches or affiliates, *Treasury Bulletin*, quarterly rpt, 8002–4.12

Current account balance and net capital flows, 1988-90, semiannual rpt, 8002–14

Developing countries child health and welfare indicators, and economic conditions, 1950s-80s, hearing, 25388–57

Developing countries debt burden and related indicators, by country and for 9 US money-center banks, 1960s-89, article, 9292–4.201

Developing countries economic aid from US, bilateral and through intl dev banks, by program and world region, 1991 annual rpt, 9904–1

Direct foreign investment and trade of US, barriers, impacts, and US actions, by country, 1988, annual rpt, 444–2

Direct foreign investment impact on trade balance, with background data, late 1960s-90 and auto forecasts to 1993, article, 9385–1.210

Direct foreign investment in US by country, and finances, employment, and acreage owned, by industry group of business acquired or established, 1984-90, annual article, 2702–1.210

Direct foreign investment in US, by industry group and world area, 1987-90, annual article, 2702–1.219

Direct foreign investment in US, by industry group of US affiliate and country of parent firm, 1980-86, 2708–41

Foreign investments

Direct foreign investment in US, major transactions by type, industry, country, and US location, 1989, annual rpt, 2044–20

Direct foreign investment in US manufacturing, impacts on trade balances, with data by industry, 1980s-93, technical paper, 9385–8.91

Direct foreign investment in US, new and established affiliates assets, and acquisitions, by industry div, 1980s, technical paper, 9366–7.255

Direct foreign investment of US, by industry group and world area, 1987-90, annual article, 2702–1.220

Economic conditions in foreign countries and US, and competitiveness issues, 1960s-90, 21788–204

Economic conditions, policy, and trade practices, by country, 1988-90, annual rpt, 21384–5

Economic indicators and components, current data and annual trends, monthly rpt, 23842–1.7

Economic Report of the President for 1991, with economic trends from 1929, annual rpt, 204–1

Energy producers finances and operations, by energy type for US firms domestic and foreign operations, 1989, annual rpt, 3164–44

Energy resources of US, foreign direct investment by energy type and firm, US affiliates operations, and acquisitions, as of 1989, annual rpt, 3164–80

Exports, imports, and trade flows, by country and commodity, with background economic indicators, data compilation, monthly CD-ROM, 2002–6

Farmland (US) owned by foreigners, by owner country and State, as of Dec 1990, article, 1561–16.202

Farmland in US owned by foreigners, holdings, acquisitions, and disposals by land use, owner type and country, and State, 1990, annual rpt, 1584–2

Farmland in US owned by foreigners, holdings, acreage, and value by land use, owner country, State, and county, 1990, annual rpt, 1584–3

Flow-of-funds accounts, savings, investments, and credit statements, quarterly rpt, 9365–3.3

Flows of trade and investment, and economic indicators, for selected countries and country groups, selected years 1946-90, annual rpt, 204–1.1; 204–1.9

Futures trading oversight of CFTC and individual exchanges, foreign activity, and customer views, late 1980s, hearing, 25168–77

Great Lakes area economic conditions and outlook, for US and Canada, 1970s-90, 9375–15

Income from US sources and tax withheld for foreign natls not residing in US, by country and tax treaty status, 1988, annual article, 8302–2.206

Intl investment position of US, by component, industry, world region, and country, 1989-90, annual article, 2702–1.212

Intl investment position of US under alternative valuation methods, 1982-89, article, 2702–1.211

Index by Subjects and Names

Intl transactions summary, 1980s-90, annual article, 9362–1.202

Japan balance of payments by component, and foreign securities purchases by country, 1980s-90, article, 9393–8.204

Japan bank affiliates in US, loans by borrower type, late 1984-89, technical paper, 9385–8.97

Japan economic conditions, financial and intl policies, and trade devs, 1950s-80s and projected to 2050, compilation of papers, 23848–220

Japan financial instns and stock market conditions, and other economic indicators, with intl comparisons, 1980s-90, hearing, 21248–152

Japan manufacturing firms US affiliates, employment, and wages, by selected industry and State, 1980s, 2048–151

Liabilities (contingent) and claims paid by Fed Govt on federally insured and guaranteed contracts with foreign obligors, by country and program, periodic rpt, 8002–12

Mexico-US trade agreement proposal, economic impacts with background trade and investment data, 1985-90, 9886–4.168

OECD intl trade position for US and 4 countries, and factors affecting US competition, periodic pamphlet, 2042–25

Overseas Business Reports: economic conditions, investment and export opportunities, and trade practices, country market research rpt series, 2046–6

Overseas Private Investment Corp finances and activities, with list of insured projects and firms, FY90, annual rpt, 9904–2

Return on investments under alternative valuation methods, for US business and for direct foreign investment in and of US, 1982-90, article, 2702–1.217

Savings and Investment Incentive Act issues, with IRA participation and other background data, 1980s, 25368–175

Securities intl markets computer use and risk mgmt methods, 1991 GAO rpt, 26125–44

Southeastern States, Fed Reserve 5th District insured commercial banks financial statements, by State, quarterly rpt, 9389–18

State and Metro Area Data Book, 1991 data compilation, 2328–54

Statistical Abstract of US, 1991 annual data compilation, 2324–1.16; 2324–1.27; 2324–1.29

Steel industry finances, operations, and modernization efforts, with data on major companies and foreign industry, 1968-91, last issue of annual rpt, 9884–24

Stock and bond returns for foreign and domestic instruments, relationship to selected economic indicators for US, UK, and Japan, 1970s-80s, article, 9385–1.211

Survey of Current Business, monthly rpt, quarterly tables, 2702–1.26

Tax (income) returns filed by type of filer, selected income items, quarterly rpt, 8302–2.1

Tax (income) returns for foreign corporate activity in US, assets, and income statement items, by industry div and selected country, 1986-87, article, 8302–2.205

Tax (income) returns of corporations, income and tax items by asset size and detailed industry, 1987, annual rpt, 8304–4

Tax (income) returns of corporations, income and tax items by asset size and detailed industry, 1988, annual rpt, 8304–21

Tax (income) returns of corporations with foreign tax credit, income, and tax items, by country and world region of credit, 1986, biennial article, 8302–2.207

Tax (income) returns of corporations with foreign tax credit, income and tax items by industry group, 1986, biennial article, 8302–2.203

Tax (income) returns of US corporations under foreign control, assets and income statement items by industry div and country, 1988, article, 8302–2.219

Tax (income) withholding and related documents filed, by type and IRS service center, 1990 and projected 1991-98, annual rpt, 8304–22

Tax expenditures, Federal revenues forgone through income tax deductions and exclusions by type, FY92-96, annual rpt, 21784–10

Treasury bill offerings, auction results by Fed Reserve District, and terms, periodic press release series, 8002–7

UK firms acquisition of US firms, financing, sources, and rates of return, with data by firm, 1980s, technical paper, 9385–8.82

Uranium reserves and industry operations, by region and State, various periods 1966-90, annual rpt, 3164–65.1

see also Expropriation of alien property

see also Foreign corporations

see also Multinational corporations

Foreign labor conditions

Asia labor shortages, for Japan and 4 eastern countries, 1991 rpt, 6366–4.17

Australia agricultural input and output indexes, and freight rates, 1950s-80s, 1528–311

Background Notes, foreign countries summary social, political, and economic data, series, 7006–2

Canada and US auto trade, production, sales, prices, and employment, selected years 1965-88, annual rpt, 2044–35

Canada and US Great Lakes area economic conditions and outlook, 1970s-90, 9375–15

Caribbean area duty-free exports to US, by commodity and country, with consumer and industry impacts, 1984-90, annual rpt, 9884–20

Caribbean Basin Initiative investment incentives, economic impacts, with finances and employment by country, 1984-90, 2048–141

China economic indicators and reform issues, with background data, 1950s-90, compilation of papers, 23848–155

Competitiveness (intl) of US industries, with selected foreign and US operating data by major firm and product, series, 2046–12

Developing countries aged population and selected characteristics, 1980s and projected to 2020, country rpt series, 2326–19

Developing countries agricultural and economic conditions, and US agricultural exports, effects of US aid, 1989 conf papers, 1548–372

Index by Subjects and Names

Foreign relations

Developing countries economic and social conditions from 1960s, and Intl Dev Cooperation Agency and AID activities and funding, FY90-92, annual rpt, 9904–4

Developing countries labor standards impacts on social and economic dev, 1988 conf papers, 6368–9

EC economic integration economic impacts, with background data by country, 1988-90, article, 9379–1.201

Economic and monetary trends, compounded annual rates of change and quarterly indicators for US and 7 major industrialized countries, quarterly rpt, 9391–7

Economic and social conditions of foreign countries, working paper series, 2326–18

Economic conditions, and oil supply and demand, for major industrial countries, biweekly rpt, 9112–1

Economic conditions, and trade devs and balances, with data by selected country and country group, monthly rpt, 9882–14

Economic conditions in foreign countries and implications for US, periodic country rpt series, 2046–4

Economic conditions in foreign countries and US, and competitiveness issues, 1960s-90, 21788–204

Economic conditions, policy, and trade practices, by country, 1988-90, annual rpt, 21384–5

Economic indicators, and trade and investment flows, for selected countries and country groups, selected years 1946-90, annual rpt, 204–1.9

Economic, social, political, and geographic summary data, by country, 1991, annual factbook, 9114–2

Employment and unemployment current statistics and articles, Monthly Labor Review, 6722–1

Employment, unemployment, and productivity indexes, for US and selected OECD countries, Monthly Labor Review, 6722–1.6

Exports and imports of finished goods and industrial supplies, with related indicators, by industry and country, mid 1970s-90, 9385–1.205

Family composition, poverty status, labor conditions, and welfare indicators and needs, by country, 1960s-88, hearing, 23846–4.30

Human rights conditions in 170 countries, and US economic and military aid, 1990, annual rpt, 21384–3

Inflation long-run costs, with background data on unemployment and GNP growth for high- and low-inflation countries, 1980s, article, 9385–1.207

Japan economic conditions, financial and intl policies, and trade devs, 1950s-80s and projected to 2050, compilation of papers, 23848–220

Labor conditions, union coverage, and work accidents in foreign countries, annual country rpt series, 6366–4

Manufacturing labor costs and indexes, by selected country, 1990, semiannual rpt, 6822–3

Multinatl US firms and foreign affiliates finances and operations, by industry and world area of parent firm, 1989 benchmark survey, preliminary annual rpt, 2704–5

Multinatl US firms and foreign affiliates finances and operations, by industry of parent firm and affiliate, world area, and selected country, 1989, annual article, 2702–1.225

NATO and Japan military spending and indicators of ability to support common defense, by country, 1970s-89, annual rpt, 3544–28

Overseas Business Reports: economic conditions, investment and export opportunities, and trade practices, country market research rpt series, 2046–6

Peru cocaine production, acreage, and economic impacts of crop eradication and conversion to legitimate agricultural use, 1960s-87, 9918–19

Poland labor force status by education level, sex, and sector, college enrollment, and grads by field, 1960s-88, article, 6722–1.203

Radiation exposure of uranium miners and risk of death from cancer and lung diseases, for Indians and compared to whites and foreign countries, 1950s-84, hearing, 25548–101

Shift rotation health and safety effects, and US and foreign regulation, by selected industry and occupation, 1970s-89, 26356–9.3

Soviet Union, Eastern Europe, OECD, and selected other countries economic conditions, 1960s-90, annual rpt, 9114–4.2

Soviet Union GNP by detailed income and outlay component, 1985, 2326–18.59

State gross product impact of foreign labor productivity and dollar exchange rate, by industry sector and State, 1972-86, working paper, 9387–8.255

Statistical Abstract of US, 1991 annual data compilation, 2324–1.31

Steel industry finances, operations, and modernization efforts, with data on major companies and foreign industry, 1968-91, last issue of annual rpt, 9884–24

Taiwan labor force educational attainment index relation to GDP growth, 1960s-86, working paper, 9371–10.55

Textile, apparel, and shoe import restriction proposals economic impacts, projected 1991-2000, with imports by country, 1989-90, 26306–6.162

UK unemployment impacts of monetary policy, industry structure, and unemployment benefits, 1920-38, working paper, 9375–13.52

Unemployment insurance alternative policies impacts on employment and hours worked, with data for selected countries, 1970s, article, 9383–6.205

Unions reporting to Labor Dept, parent bodies and locals by location, 1990 listing, 6468–17

Wage differentials among industries, by industry and country, and correlation of differentials between countries, for US and West Germany, 1979-87, technical paper, 9366–6.281

Foreign languages

Background Notes, foreign countries summary social, political, and economic data, series, 7006–2

Degrees awarded in higher education, by level, field, race, and sex, 1988/89 with trends from 1978/79, biennial rpt, 4844–17

Education (postsecondary) course completions, by detailed program, sex, race, and instn type, for 1972 high school class, as of 1984, 4888–4

Education data compilation, 1991 annual rpt, 4824–2

Foreign countries economic, social, political, and geographic summary data, by country, 1991, annual factbook, 9114–2

High school advanced placement for college credit, programs by selected characteristics and school control, 1984-86, 4838–46

Hispanic Americans in counties bordering Mexico, by selected characteristics, 1980, Current Population Rpt, 2546–2.159

Japan-US Friendship Commission educational and cultural exchange activities, grants, and trust fund status, FY89-90, biennial report, 14694–1

Natl Education Goals progress indicators, by State, 1991, annual rpt, 15914–1

Radio Free Europe and Radio Liberty broadcast and financial data, FY90, annual rpt, 10314–1

Refugee resettlement programs and funding, arrivals by country of origin, and indicators of adjustment, by State, FY90, annual rpt, 4694–5

Statistical Abstract of US, 1991 annual data compilation, 2324–1.4

Student aid funding and participation, by Federal program, instn type and control, and State, various periods 1959-89, annual rpt, 4804–28

see also Bilingual education

see also Language use and ability

Foreign loans

see Export-Import Bank

see Foreign debts

see International assistance

see Military assistance

Foreign medical graduates

Enrollment in science and engineering grad programs, by field, source of funds, and characteristics of student and instn, 1975-89, annual rpt, 9627–7

Health condition and health care resources, use, and spending, 1950s-89, annual data compilation, 4144–11

Military health care personnel, and accessions by training source, by occupation, specialty, and service branch, FY89, annual rpt, 3544–24

Physicians, by specialty, age, sex, and location of training and practice, 1989, State rpt series, 4116–6

Foreign military sales

see Arms trade

see Military assistance

Foreign opinion of U.S.

Germany deployment of US forces, population favoring US withdrawal, 1982-90, GAO rpt, 26123–318

Foreign relations

Background Notes, foreign countries summary social, political, and economic data, series, 7006–2

Budget of US, CBO analysis and review of FY92 budget by function, annual rpt, 26304–2

Budget of US, CBO analysis of revenue and spending alternatives and projections of economic indicators, FY92-96, annual rpt, 26304–3

Foreign relations

Budget of US, midsession review of FY92 budget, by function, annual rpt, 104–7
Budget of US, obligations and authority by function, agency, and program, with summaries, analyses, and historical tables, FY92, annual rpt, 104–2
Criminal cases by type and disposition, and collections, for US attorneys, by Federal district, FY90, annual rpt, 6004–2.1
Helsinki Final Act implementation by NATO and Warsaw Pact, Apr 1990-Mar 1991, last issue of semiannual rpt, 7002–1
Loans and loan guarantees of Fed Govt, outstanding amounts by agency and program, *Treasury Bulletin*, quarterly rpt, 8002–4.9
Nuclear weapons labs and DOE screening of contractors for foreign ownership, control, or influence, compliance by lab, FY88-90, GAO rpt, 26113–520
State Dept programs fraud and abuse, audits and investigations, 2nd half FY91, semiannual rpt, 7002–6
UN voting record and share of votes in agreement with US, by issue, country, and world area, 1990, annual rpt, 7004–18
USIA activities, finances, and info services, FY91, annual rpt, 17594–1
see also Arms trade
see also Diplomatic and consular service
see also East-West trade
see also Educational exchanges
see also Exchange of persons programs
see also Executive agreements
see also Foreign countries
see also Foreign debts
see also Foreign economic relations
see also Foreign opinion of U.S.
see also Foreign students
see also Foreign trade
see also Foreign trade promotion
see also International assistance
see also International cooperation in conservation
see also International cooperation in cultural activities
see also International cooperation in environmental sciences
see also International cooperation in law enforcement
see also International cooperation in science and technology
see also International reserves
see also International sanctions
see also Military assistance
see also Military intervention
see also Military invasion and occupation
see also Treaties and conventions
see also War

Foreign Sales Corporations

Boycotts (intl) by OPEC and other countries, US firms and shareholders cooperation and tax benefits denied, 1986, annual rpt, 8004–13
Boycotts (intl) by OPEC and other countries, US taxpayers IRS filings, cooperation, and tax benefits denied, 1976-86, GAO rpt, 26119–349
Tax (income) returns filed, by type of return and IRS district, 1989 and projected 1990-97, annual rpt, 8304–24
Tax (income) returns filed, by type of tax and IRS region and service center, projected 1990-97 and trends from 1978, annual rpt, 8304–9

Tax expenditures, Federal revenues forgone through income tax deductions and exclusions by type, FY92-96, annual rpt, 21784–10
see also Domestic International Sales Corporations

Foreign Service

see Diplomatic and consular service

Foreign students

Agricultural education and training programs of USDA, foreign participants by program, sponsor, and country, annual rpt, discontinued, 1954–1
China economic indicators and reform issues, with background data, 1950s-90, compilation of papers, 23848–155
Condition of Education, detail for higher education, 1960s-90, annual rpt, 4824–1.2
Degrees awarded in higher education, by level, field, race, and sex, 1988/89 with trends from 1978/79, biennial rpt, 4844–17
Digest of Education Statistics, 1991 annual data compilation, 4824–2
Latin America dev grants of Inter-American Foundation by program area, and fellowships by field and instn, by country, FY72-90, annual rpt, 14424–2
Latin America dev grants of Inter-American Foundation by recipient, and fellowships, by country, FY90, annual rpt, 14424–1
Nuclear engineering enrollment and degrees granted by instn and State, and grad placement, by student characteristics, 1990, annual rpt, 3004–5
Radiation protection and health physics enrollment and degrees granted by instn and State, and grad placement, by student characteristics, 1990, annual rpt, 3004–7
Science and engineering employment and education, and R&D spending, for US and selected foreign countries, 1991 annual rpt, 9627–35.2
Science and engineering grad enrollment, by field, source of funds, and characteristics of student and instn, 1975-89, annual rpt, 9627–7
Science and engineering PhDs, by field, instn, employment prospects, sex, race, and other characteristics, 1960s-90, annual rpt, 9627–30
Statistical Abstract of US, 1991 annual data compilation, 2324–1.4
Telecommunications industry intl competitiveness, with financial and operating data by product or service, firm, and country, 1990 rpt, 2008–30
Travel from US, characteristics of visit and traveler, and country of destination, 1990 in-flight survey, annual rpt, 2904–14
Travel to US, by characteristics of visit and traveler, country, port city, and State of destination, quarterly rpt, 2902–1
Travel to US, by characteristics of visit and traveler, world area of origin, and US destination, 1990 survey, annual rpt, 2904–12
see also Educational exchanges
see also Foreign medical graduates

Foreign trade

Background Notes, foreign countries summary social, political, and economic data, series, 7006–2

Index by Subjects and Names

Business America, foreign and domestic commerce, and US investment and trade opportunities, biweekly journal, 2042–24
Business statistics, detailed data for major industries and economic indicators, *Survey of Current Business*, monthly rpt, 2702–1
Caribbean area duty-free exports to US, and imports from US, by country, and impact on US employment, by commodity, 1990, annual rpt, 6364–2
Caribbean area duty-free exports to US, by commodity and country, with consumer and industry impacts, 1984-90, annual rpt, 9884–20
Caribbean Basin Initiative investment incentives, economic impacts, with finances and employment by country, 1984-90, 2048–141
Census Bur export and import statistics, publications and data files, 1991 guide, 2428–11
Census Bur rpts and data files, coverage and availability, 1991 annual listing, 2304–2
China economic indicators and reform issues, with background data, 1950s-90, compilation of papers, 23848–155
Classification codes for countries, commodities, and customs districts for Census Bur export statistics, 1990 base edition supplement, 2428–5
Classification codes for countries for Census Bur foreign trade statistics, 1991 edition, 2428–3
Classification codes for foreign ports for Census Bur export and import statistics, 1991, 2428–12
Communist and OECD countries economic conditions, 1989, annual rpt, 7144–11
Consumer imports purchasing decisions, importance of brand name, authenticity, origin, and other factors, 1984 survey, hearing, 25528–115
Data series on trade, methodology, use, and sources, 1991 article, 9389–1.206
Developing countries economic aid from US, military spending and imports measures to determine aid eligibility, by country, 1986-87, annual rpt, 9914–1
Developing countries economic and social conditions from 1960s, and Intl Dev Cooperation Agency and AID activities and funding, FY90-92, annual rpt, 9904–4
Developing countries economic, population, and agricultural data, US and other aid sources, and AID activity, country rpt series, 9916–12
Developing countries grains production and needs, and related economic outlook, by world area and selected country, forecast 1990/91-1991/92, 1528–313
Developing countries labor standards impacts on social and economic dev, 1988 conf papers, 6368–9
Dollar exchange rate trade-weighted index of Fed Reserve Bank of Atlanta, by world area, quarterly rpt, 9371–15
Dollar exchange rate trade-weighted index of Fed Reserve Bank of Dallas, by world area, monthly rpt, 9379–13
Eastern Europe foreign debt components, trade, balances, and other economic indicators, by country, 1985-89, hearing, 21248–148

Index by Subjects and Names

Foreign trade

Eastern Europe transition to market economies, economic conditions, intl aid, and energy balance, by country, 1985-90, 9118–13

EC economic integration economic impacts, with background data by country, 1988-90, article, 9379–1.201

EC economic integration impacts on domestic economic conditions and US trade, 1985-90, 9886–4.170

EC economic integration issues, with economic indicators and trade by country, 1985-89, article, 9371–1.210

EC trade with US by country, and total agricultural trade, selected years 1958-90, annual rpt, 7144–7

Economic and employment conditions, alternative BLS projections to 2005 and trends 1970s-90, biennial article, 6722–1.251

Economic and monetary trends, compounded annual rates of change and quarterly indicators for US and 7 major industrialized countries, quarterly rpt, 9391–7

Economic conditions, and oil supply and demand, for major industrial countries, biweekly rpt, 9112–1

Economic conditions, and trade devs and balances, with data by selected country and country group, monthly rpt, 9882–14

Economic conditions in foreign countries and implications for US, periodic country rpt series, 2046–4

Economic conditions in foreign countries and US, and competitiveness issues, 1960s-90, 21788–204

Economic conditions, policy, and trade practices, by country, 1988-90, annual rpt, 21384–5

Economic indicators and components, and Fed Reserve 4th District business and financial conditions, monthly chartbook, 9377–10

Economic indicators and components, current data and annual trends, monthly rpt, 23842–1.7

Economic indicators compounded annual rates of change, monthly rpt, 9391–3

Economic, social, political, and geographic summary data, by country, 1991, annual factbook, 9114–2

Employment and industry impacts of trade, series, 6366–3

Export and import balance, by component, 1987-90, semiannual rpt, 8002–14

Exports and export prices of US, impact of domestic and foreign price levels and other factors, 1970s-89, article, 9393–8.203

Exports and export-related employment, by SIC 3-digit industry and State, model results, 1987, annual rpt, 2506–16.1

Exports and imports of US, by country and detailed commodity, monthly rpt, 2422–12

Exports and imports of US by country, and trade shifts by commodity, 1990, semiannual rpt, 9882–9

Exports and imports of US, by Harmonized System 6-digit commodity and country, 1990, annual rpt, 2424–13

Exports and imports of US, by selected country, country group, and commodity group, annual rpt, suspended, 2044–38

Exports and imports of US, by selected country, country group, and commodity group, 1990, annual rpt, 2044–37

Exports and imports of US, by transport mode, country, and SITC 1- to 3-digit commodity, 1990, annual rpt, 2424–12

Exports and imports of US, relation to domestic and foreign economic indicators, model description and results, 1967-88, technical paper, 9385–8.117

Exports and imports of US shipped through Canada, by detailed commodity, customs district, and country, 1989, annual rpt, 7704–11

Exports and imports, trade agreements and relations, and USITC investigations, 1990, annual rpt, 9884–5

Exports, imports, and balances, monthly rpt, 9362–1.3

Exports, imports, and balances of US by commodity group, world area, and country, and related employment, annual rpt, discontinued, 2044–26

Exports, imports, and balances of US, by selected country, country group, and commodity group, preliminary data, monthly rpt, 2042–34

Exports, imports, and balances of US with major trading partners, by product category, 1986-90, annual chartbook, 9884–21

Exports, imports, and trade flows, by country and commodity, with background economic indicators, data compilation, monthly CD-ROM, 2002–6

Exports of US, detailed commodities by country, monthly CD-ROM, 2422–13

Exports of US, detailed Schedule B commodities with countries of destination, 1990, annual rpt, 2424–10

Exports of US, detailed Schedule E commodities by mode of transport, world area, and country, annual rpts, discontinued, 2424–5

FDA activities, funding, facilities, and staff, findings and recommendations, 1980s-91, 4008–115

Finance (intl) and financial policy, and external factors affecting US economy, technical paper series, 9366–7

Flows of trade and investment, and economic indicators, for selected countries and country groups, selected years 1946-90, annual rpt, 204–1.1; 204–1.9

Generalized System of Preferences status, and US tariffs, with trade by country and US economic impacts, for selected commodities, 1985-89, annual rpt, 9884–23

Great Lakes area economic conditions and outlook, for US and Canada, 1970s-90, 9375–15

Immigration impacts on Canada and US trade, with background data, 1960s-86, technical paper, 9379–12.64

Import prices relation to dollar exchange rate for 32 industries, and impacts of domestic market concentration, 1990 working paper, 9387–8.234

Imports and tariff provisions effect on US industries and products, investigations with background financial and operating data, series, 9886–4

Imports, exports, and employment impacts, by SIC 2- to 4-digit industry and commodity, quarterly rpt, 2322–2

Imports injury to US industries from foreign subsidized products, investigations with background financial and operating data, series, 9886–15

Imports injury to US industries from sales at less than fair value, investigations with background financial and operating data, series, 9886–14

Imports injury to US industries, USITC rpts, 1983-90, annual listing, 9884–12

Imports of US, demand elasticities, assessment of alternative models, 1991 technical paper, 9366–7.250

Imports of US, detailed commodities by country, monthly CD-ROM, 2422–14

Imports of US, detailed Schedule A commodities by mode of transport, world area, and country, annual rpts, discontinued, 2424–2

Imports of US, detailed TSUSA commodities with countries of origin, annual rpt, discontinued, 2424–4

Imports of US given duty-free treatment for value of US material sent abroad, by commodity and country, 1989, annual rpt, 9884–14

Industry finances and operations, by SIC 2- to 4-digit industry, forecast 1991, annual rpt, 2044–28

Input-output structure of US economy, detailed interindustry transactions for 84 industries, and components of final demand, 1986, annual article, 2702–1.206

Input-output structure of US economy, detailed interindustry transactions for 85 industries, 1982 benchmark data, 2702–1.213

Intl transactions summary, 1980s-90, annual article, 9362–1.202

Investment (foreign direct) impact on manufacturing trade balance, with background data, late 1960s-90 and auto forecasts to 1993, article, 9385–1.210

Israel and Egypt govt budgets, foreign debt, and economic indicators, 1980s, hearing, 21388–58

Japan balance of trade with US and other countries, mid 1960s-88, article, 9391–1.209

Japan economic conditions, financial and intl policies, and trade devs, 1950s-80s and projected to 2050, compilation of papers, 23848–220

Japan manufacturing firms US affiliates, employment, and wages, by selected industry and State, 1980s, 2048–151

Manufacturing census, 1987: finances and operations, by SIC 2- to 4-digit industry, State, and MSA, with trends from 1849, 2497–1

Manufacturing employment by selected characteristics, wages, and import and export penetration rates, by SIC 2- to 4-digit industry, 1982-89, 6366–3.27

Manufacturing exports, by State, alternative estimates, 1986-87, article, 9391–1.219

Manufacturing trade of finished goods and industrial supplies, with related indicators, by industry and country, mid 1970s-90, 9385–1.205; 9385–8.95

Mexico imports from US, by industry and State, 1987-90, 2048–154

Middle East export controls of US, with trade, dual-use commodity licenses, and arms sales, by country, 1980s-90, GAO rpt, 26123–339

Foreign trade

Multinatl firms US affiliates finances and operations, by industry div, country of parent firm, and State, 1988-89, annual article, 2702–1.214

Multinatl firms US affiliates, finances, and operations, by industry, world area of parent firm, and State, 1988-89, annual rpt, 2704–4

Multinatl firms US affiliates, investment trends and impact on US economy, 1991 annual rpt, 2004–9

Multinatl US firms and foreign affiliates finances and operations, by industry and world area of parent firm, 1989 benchmark survey, preliminary annual rpt, 2704–5

Multinatl US firms and foreign affiliates finances and operations, by industry of parent firm and affiliate, world area, and selected country, 1989, annual article, 2702–1.225

Multinatl US firms foreign affiliates, income statement items by asset size, industry, and country, 1986, biennial article, 8302–2.212

Natl income and product accounts and components, *Survey of Current Business*, monthly rpt, 2702–1.24

Natl income and product accounts benchmark revisions of GDP and natl income, various periods 1959-80, tables, 2702–1.227

North America free trade area proposal for Canada, US, and Mexico, outlook with trade data, 1990, 2048–153

OECD intl trade position for US and 4 countries, and factors affecting US competition, periodic pamphlet, 2042–25

OECD trade, by country, 1989, annual rpt, 7144–10

OECD trade, total and for 4 major countries, and US trade by country, by commodity, 1970-89, world area rpt series, 9116–1

Outlying areas trade with US, by detailed commodity and mode of transport, 1990, annual rpt, 2424–11

Overseas Business Reports: economic conditions, investment and export opportunities, and trade practices, country market research rpt series, 2046–6

Overseas Private Investment Corp projects, and exports and export-related employment generated, FY90, annual rpt, 9904–2

Palau admin, and social, economic, and govtl data, FY90, annual rpt, 7004–6

Price indexes for exports and imports, by selected end-use category, monthly press release, 6762–15

Price indexes for exports and imports of goods and services, and dollar exchange rate indexes, quarterly press release, 6762–13

Price indexes for exports and imports of US, by SITC commodity, end-use, and SIC industry, Monthly Labor Review, 6722–1.4

Puerto Rico economic censuses, 1987: wholesale and retail trade sales by customer class, and employment, by SIC 2- and 3-digit kind of business, subject rpt, 2591–2.2

Reserves/imports ratio, and money supply growth rates, by selected country, selected years 1951-71, article, 9391–1.214

Index by Subjects and Names

Service industries census, 1987: export establishments and receipts, by SIC 2- to 4-digit kind of business, 2393–4.20

Service industries exports and imports of US, direct and among multinatl firms affiliates, by industry and world area, 1986-90, article, 2702–1.223

Soviet Union, China, OECD, and selected other countries trade and balances, 1960s-90, annual rpt, 9114–4.8

Soviet Union economic conditions under General Secretary Gorbachev, 1990 and trends from 1975, annual rpt, 9114–6

Soviet Union GNP by detailed income and outlay component, 1985, 2326–18.59

State and Metro Area Data Book, 1991 data compilation, 2328–54

Statistical Abstract of US, 1991 annual data compilation, 2324–1.15; 2324–1.22; 2324–1.27; 2324–1.29; 2324–1.31

Transportation natl system planning, use, condition, accidents, and needs, by mode of transport, 1940s-90 and projected to 2020, 7308–202

Turkey GNP, trade, investment, and inflation following currency devaluation, 1970s-90, technical paper, 9385–8.112

USITC activities, investigations, and rpts, FY90, annual rpt, 9884–1

Wholesale trade census, 1987: establishments, sales by customer class, employment, inventories, and expenses, by SIC 2- to 4-digit kind of business, 2407–4

Zimbabwe agricultural conditions impacts of economic policies, 1980s, 1528–319

see also Agricultural exports and imports

see also Arms trade

see also Balance of payments

see also Coal exports and imports

see also Common markets and free trade areas

see also Contraband

see also Customs administration

see also Domestic International Sales Corporations

see also Dumping

see also East-West trade

see also Energy exports and imports

see also Export-Import Bank

see also Export processing zones

see also Foreign competition

see also Foreign exchange

see also Foreign investments

see also Foreign Sales Corporations

see also Foreign trade promotion

see also International assistance

see also Maritime law

see also Military assistance

see also Motor vehicle exports and imports

see also Natural gas exports and imports

see also Petroleum exports and imports

see also Ships and shipping

see also Tariffs and foreign trade controls

see also Technology transfer

see also Trade adjustment assistance

see also Trade agreements

see also under names of specific commodities or commodity groups

Foreign trade promotion

Agricultural export market research and promotion activities of USDA, with background data, 1991 GAO rpt, 26113–504

Agricultural export promotion and foreign food aid programs budget of USDA, with trade by commodity and country, FY85-91 and projected to FY2000, 21168–44

Agricultural export promotion funding, by trade assn and commodity, FY91, article, 1925–34.233

Agricultural exports under federally financed programs, by commodity and country, bimonthly rpt, periodic data, 1522–1

Agricultural production, consumption, and policies for selected countries, and US export dev and promotion, monthly journal, 1922–2

Agricultural supply, demand, and market for US exports, with socioeconomic conditions, country rpt series, 1526–6

Assistance (financial and nonfinancial) of Fed Govt, 1991 base edition with supplements, annual listing, 104–5

Budget of US, obligations and authority by function, agency, and program, with summaries, analyses, and historical tables, FY92, annual rpt, 104–2

Budget of US, Senate concurrent resolution, with spending and revenue targets, FY92, annual rpt, 25254–1

Business America, foreign and domestic commerce, and US investment and trade opportunities, biweekly journal, 2042–24

Caribbean area duty-free exports to US, by commodity and country, with consumer and industry impacts, 1984-90, annual rpt, 9884–20

Central America agricultural export promotion of nontraditional crops, impacts on income export stability, late 1970s-80s, 1528–312

Cotton production, trade, and use, for selected countries, FAS monthly circular, 1925–4.2

Credit sales agreement terms, by commodity and country, FY89, annual rpt, 15344–1.11

Developing countries economic and social conditions from 1960s, and Intl Dev Cooperation Agency and AID activities and funding, FY90-92, annual rpt, 9904–4

Eastern Europe imports from US, and trade opportunities, periodic rpt, 2042–33

Economic aid of US and other donor countries by type and recipient, and role in advancing economic interests, 1980s-90, 2048–152

Eximbank financial condition, with credit and insurance authorizations and loan activity by country, FY90, annual rpt, 9254–1

Exports, imports, and trade flows, by country and commodity, with background economic indicators, data compilation, monthly CD-ROM, 2002–6

Fed Govt contingent liabilities and claims paid on insured and guaranteed contracts with foreign obligors, by country and program, periodic rpt, 8002–12

Fish and shellfish foreign market conditions for US products, country rpt series, 2166–19

Foreign countries economic conditions, policy, and trade practices, by country, 1988-90, annual rpt, 21384–5

Index by Subjects and Names

Forest Service

Grain and feed trade, and export and support prices, for US and major producer countries, FAS monthly circular, 1925–2.4

Intl organizations funding by US and other countries, by organization and program, FY90, annual rpt, 7004–9

Iraq agricultural imports under CCC export credit guarantee programs, FY81-90, GAO rpt, 26123–314

Iraq purchases under CCC credit guarantee program, FY81-90, with contingent liabilities projected to FY97, hearing, 21248–155

Japan economic conditions, financial and intl policies, and trade devs, 1950s-80s and projected to 2050, compilation of papers, 23848–220

Latin America and Caribbean AID export and investment promotion projects effectiveness, 1974-89, 9916–3.63

Lumber and wood products exports, imports, and export promotion of US by country, and trade balance, by commodity, FAS quarterly circular, 1925–36

Minority Business Dev Centers mgmt and financial aid, and characteristics of businesses, by region and State, FY90, annual rpt, 2104–6

Oils, oilseeds, and fats foreign and US production and trade, FAS periodic circular series, 1925–1

Overseas Business Reports: economic conditions, investment and export opportunities, and trade practices, country market research rpt series, 2046–6

Poultry and products foreign and US production, trade, and use, by selected country, FAS semiannual circular series, 1925–33

Seed exports, by type, world region, and country, FAS quarterly rpt, 1925–13

State and local govt competition in taxes, services, regulation, and dev incentives, 1970-89, 10048–79

Travel to US, market research data available from US Travel and Tourism Admin, 1991, annual rpt, 2904–15

Travel to US, trade shows and other promotional activities, with magazine ad costs and circulation, for selected countries, 1991-92, annual rpt, 2904–11

see also Exhibitions and trade fairs

Foreign Trade Zones Board

Trade zones (US) operations and movement of goods, by zone and commodity, FY88, annual rpt, 2044–30

Forensic sciences

Physicians, by specialty, age, sex, and location of training and practice, 1989, State rpt series, 4116–6

Forest fires

Environmental Quality, status of problems, protection programs, research, and intl issues, 1991 annual rpt, 484–1

Foreign countries disasters, casualties, damage, and aid by US and others, FY90 and trends from FY64, annual rpt, 9914–12

Forest Service acreage, staff, finances, and mgmt activities in Pacific Northwest, with data by forest, 1970s-89, annual rpt, 1204–37

Forest Service activities and finances, by region and State, FY90, annual rpt, 1204–1

Forest Service land fires and acres burned, by cause, forest, and State, 1989, annual rpt, 1204–6

Forest Service mgmt of public lands and resources dev, environmental, economic, and social impacts of alternative programs, projected to 2040, 1208–24

Incidents and mgmt of disasters and natl security threats, with data by major event and State, 1991 annual rpt, 9434–6

Insect infestation and damage in Yellowstone Natl Park timber following 1988 forest fires, 1989-90, 1208–379

Oregon Cascade Range forest fires historical frequency and severity, 1150-1985, 1208–354

Pollution (air) levels for 6 pollutants, by source, 1970-89 and trends from 1940, annual rpt, 9194–13

Public lands acreage and use, and Land Mgmt Bur activities and finances, annual State rpt series, 5724–11

Public lands acreage, grants, use, revenues, and allocations, by State, FY90, annual rpt, 5724–1.3

Soil mgmt and characteristics, for western mountain forest areas, 1990 conf, 1208–378

Wildfires on State and private lands under Federal protection, acreage by State, 1988, annual rpt, 1204–1.2

Forest Service

Acreage of land under Forest Service mgmt, by forest and location, 1990, annual rpt, 1204–2

Acreage of timber, by ownership, forest type, and State, 1950s-87 and projected to 2040, 1208–357

Activities and finances of Forest Service, by region and State, FY90, annual rpt, 1204–1

Activities, budget, priorities, and employee reward criteria, Forest Service supervisor and staff views, 1989 survey, 1989, hearing, 21408–121

Alabama timber acreage and value, by species, forest type, ownership, and county, 1990, series, 1206–30

Alaska submerged land grant holdings of Alaska Natives, exchange for upland acreage, impacts on conservation acreage and acquisition, 1989-90, 5728–38

Alaska subsistence fishing role in local economies, with indicators for Yakutat, 1980s, 1208–350

Alaska timber production, trade, and Pacific basin market demand, 1960s-2010, 1208–365; 1208–367

Arizona timber resources by species, forest and tree characteristics, ownership, and county, 1984-85, 1208–374

Beaver pond area rodent and shrew population and diversity compared to riparian habitat, 1988-89 study, 1208–377

Birds (migratory forest dwellers) population status, literature review, 1940s-80s, 1208–382

Birds (northern spotted owl) population and reproduction rate on lands open and closed to logging, estimation methodology, 1987, 1208–342

Birds in Badlands Natl Park juniper forest and mixed grass rangeland habitats, population and species diversity by season, 1991 rpt, 1208–364

Birds population impacts of timber harvest methods, by species, for Montana, 1989-90, 1208–372

Budget of US, obligations and authority by function, agency, and program, with summaries, analyses, and historical tables, FY92, annual rpt, 104–2

Expenditures of Fed Govt in States, by type, program, agency, and State, FY90, annual rpt, 2464–2

Farm acreage enrolled in Conservation Reserve Program, plantings, and impacts on production, soil erosion, water quality, and wildlife habitat, 1991 conf, 1208–360

Fires in Oregon Cascade Range forest areas, historical frequency and severity, 1150-1985, 1208–354

Fires on Forest Service land and acres burned, by cause, forest, and State, 1989, annual rpt, 1204–6

Fish and wildlife activities funding, by source, FY88-90, GAO rpt, 26113–529

Fishing (sport) warmwater resources mgmt in western US, 1991 conf, 1208–381

Florida industrial roundwood lumber production, by product and county, 1977-87, 1208–352

Forest Service recreation programs funding, and cost sharing pledges, 1980s-91, GAO rpt, 26113–518

Grazing of livestock on natl forest lands, by region and State, 1990, annual rpt, 1204–5

Gypsy moth infestation in Tennessee, timber at risk, by county, 1989, 1208–344

Horse and burro wild herd areas in western States, population, adoption, and mgmt costs, as of FY89, biennial rpt, 5724–8

Indiana timber resources and removals, by species, forest characteristics, ownership, and county, 1985-86, 1208–368

Insect and disease incidence and damage in forests, and control activities, State rpt series, 1206–49

Insect and disease incidence and damage in forests, annual regional rpt series, 1206–11

Insect infestation and damage in Yellowstone Natl Park timber following 1988 forest fires, 1989-90, 1208–379

Log home manufacturers in Montana, sales, production, and timber use, 1960s-88, 1208–370

Lumber (hardwood) exports of US to Europe and Asia, by species and country, 1981-89, 1208–373

Lumber (hardwood) production, prices, employment, and trade, quarterly rpt, 1202–4

Lumber production, prices by region and State, trade by country, and use, by species and product, 1960-88, annual rpt, 1204–29

Mgmt of public lands and resources dev, environmental, economic, and social impacts of alternative Forest Service programs, projected to 2040, 1208–24

Montana timber outside natl forests, acreage, resources, and mortality, by species and ownership class, 1988-89, 1206–25

Forest Service

New England States timber growth and relationship to tree and site characteristics, 1900s-85, 1208–349

New England timber acreage and resources, by State, 1982-85, pamphlet, 1208–363

New Hampshire and Vermont public opinion on natural resources use and mgmt, 1991 rpt, 1208–371

North Carolina timber acreage, resources, and removals, by species, ownership class, and county, 1989/90, series, 1206–4

North Central States timber harvest and industrial roundwood production, by product and county, State rpt series, 1206–10

North Central States veneer log production, mill receipts, and use, 1988, quadrennial rpt, 1208–220

Northeastern US forest wildlife habitat characteristics, by location, State rpt series, 1206–44

Northeastern US industrial roundwood production by product, State rpt series, 1206–15

Northeastern US pulpwood production by species and county, and shipments, by State, 1989, annual rpt, 1204–18

Northeastern US recreation areas use, mgmt, and tourism dev issues, 1990 conf, 1208–356

Northeastern US timber biomass volume, by characteristics of tree and forest, and county, State rpt series, 1206–43

Northeastern US timber, change in value by species, with methodology, 1970s-85, 1208–348

Northeastern US timber resources, and related manufacturing industries employment and finances, by State, 1977-87, 1208–375

Northeastern US timber resources and removals, by species, ownership, and county, State rpt series, 1206–12

Northeastern US timber survival rates, by species, model description and results, 1990 rpt, 1208–369

Northwestern US and British Columbia forest industry production, prices, trade, and employment, quarterly rpt, 1202–3

Oklahoma timber resources, growth, and removals, by species, forest type, ownership, and county, 1986, regional rpt series, 1206–39

Oregon (western) timber resources, acreage by land use and ownership, 1961-86, 1208–353

Pacific basin sandalwood resources, habitat, harvest, exports, and uses, 1990 conf, 1208–366

Pacific Northwest acreage, staff, finances, and mgmt activities of Forest Service, with data by forest, 1970s-89, annual rpt, 1204–37

Pine (lodgepole) spiral grain defect incidence and severity, for western US and Canada, 1991 rpt, 1208–380

Pine (longleaf) in southeastern US, mgmt and use, 1989 conf, 1208–355

Pine (longleaf) planting performance relation to seed source and site, for Florida and Georgia, 1968-83, 1208–345

Pine (Scots) suitability for conservation plantings, 1960s-82 study, 1208–383

Planting and dev of forests, by State, FY90, annual rpt, 1204–7

Plantings for reforestation, effectiveness and seedling production techniques, 1990 conf, 1208–376

Pollution (air) emissions from burning of logging waste, 1982, 1208–343

Recreation (outdoor) facilities of Fed Govt, fees and visits by managing agency, FY88-90, annual rpt, 5544–14

Recreation (outdoor) mgmt, research methods, and public opinion, 1990 conf papers, annual rpt, 1204–38

Recreation sites in natl forests, capacity, funding, and maintenance needs, 1980s-90, GAO rpt, 26113–502

Recreation use of natl forests, by type of activity and State, 1990, annual rpt, 1204–17

Revenue of natl forest land, by source, forest, and State, FY90, annual rpt, 1204–34

Revenue of natl forest land, share paid to States, and acreage, by forest, region, county, and congressional district, FY90, annual rpt, 1204–33

Rocky Mountain region employment and income, and economic dependence on shipments outside area, by industry and county group, 1980s, 1208–362

Ships freight rates for lumber from Alaska and Puget Sound to Asian markets, by product and port, 1988, 1208–358

Shrublands in western US, ecology, biology, and cheatgrass invasion and related fire threat, 1989 conf papers, 1208–351

Soil mgmt and characteristics, for western mountain forest areas, 1990 conf, 1208–378

South Carolina lumber and mill residue production, by product and species group, 1987-88, 1208–359

Southeastern US pine natural growth and plantation acreage, and lumber industries impacts of shift to plantation pine, 1989 conf papers, 1208–346

Southeastern US pulpwood and residue prices, spending, and transport shares by mode, 1988-89, annual rpt, 1204–22

Southern US pulpwood production by county, and mill capacity by firm, by State, 1989, annual rpt, 1204–23

Southern US veneer log receipts, production, and shipments, by species and State, with residue use, 1988, 1208–43

Timber sales of Forest Service, expenses, and operations, by region, State, and natl forest, FY90, annual rpts, 1204–36

Timber sales of Forest Service, impacts of northern spotted owl conservation in Pacific Northwest, 1990 hearing, 21168–47

Timber value conversion standards, for hardwood species conversion to lumber, 1972 and 1984, 1208–361

Virginia timber resources, growth, and removals, by species, ownership, treatment, and county, 1990-91, series, 1206–6

Wilderness areas use, mental health and educational benefits, and leadership training programs effectiveness, 1990 conf papers, 1208–347

Forests and forestry

Acreage of land, by use, ownership, and State, 1987 and trends from 1910, 1588–48

Index by Subjects and Names

Acreage of non-Federal land by use, soil and water conditions, and conservation needs, 1987, State rpt series, 1266–5

Acreage of timber, by ownership, forest type, and State, 1950s-87 and projected to 2040, 1208–357

Aerial survey R&D rpts, and sources of natural resource and environmental data, quarterly listing, 9502–7

Agricultural Conservation Program participation and payments, by practice and State, FY90, annual rpt, 1804–7

Agricultural data compilation, 1990 and trends from 1920, annual rpt, 1004–14

Agricultural Stabilization and Conservation Service producer payments and certificate value, by program, monthly rpt, 1802–10

Agricultural Stabilization and Conservation Service producer payments, by program and State, 1990, annual table, 1804–12

Agricultural Statistics, 1990, annual rpt, 1004–1

Agriculture census, 1987: farms, farmland, production, finances, and operator characteristics, by county, final State rpt series, 2331–1

Alabama timber acreage and value, by species, forest type, ownership, and county, 1990, series, 1206–30

Arizona timber resources by species, forest and tree characteristics, ownership, and county, 1984-85, 1208–374

Birds (migratory forest dwellers) population status, literature review, 1940s-80s, 1208–382

Birds in Badlands Natl Park juniper forest and mixed grass rangeland habitats, population and species diversity by season, 1991 rpt, 1208–364

Birds population impacts of timber harvest methods, by species, for Montana, 1989-90, 1208–372

Carbon dioxide in atmosphere, North Central States economic and agricultural impacts, model descriptions and results, 1980s and projected to 2030, 3006–11.15

County Business Patterns, 1988: employment, establishments, and payroll, by SIC 2- to 4-digit industry and county, annual State rpt series, 2326–6

County Business Patterns, 1989: employment, establishments, and payroll, by SIC 2- to 4-digit industry and county, annual State rpt series, 2326–8

Deforestation, and OECD imports of tropical wood, by country, 1980s, annual rpt, 9114–4.10

Developing countries agricultural supply, demand, and market for US exports, with socioeconomic conditions, country rpt series, 1526–6

Disaster damage to timber and orchards, USDA restoration aid and program participation by practice and State, FY89-90, annual rpt, 1804–24

Environmental Quality, status of problems, protection programs, research, and intl issues, 1991 annual rpt, 484–1

Farmland value, rent, taxes, foreign ownership, and transfers by probable use and lender type, with data by region and State, 1980-91, article, 1561–16.202

Fed Govt financial and nonfinancial domestic aid, 1991 base edition with supplements, annual listing, 104–5

Index by Subjects and Names

Fed Govt spending in States, by type, program, agency, and State, FY90, annual rpt, 2464–2

Florida environmental, social, and economic conditions, and impacts of proposed OCS oil and gas leases in southern coastal areas, 1990 compilation of papers, 5738–19

Foreign countries agricultural research grants of USDA, by program, subagency, and country, FY90, annual listing, 1954–3

Foreign countries economic, social, political, and geographic summary data, by country, 1991, annual factbook, 9114–2

Foreign ownership of US farmland, holdings, acquisitions, and disposals by land use, owner type and country, and State, 1990, annual rpt, 1584–2

Foreign ownership of US farmland, holdings, acreage, and value by land use, owner country, State, and county, 1990, annual rpt, 1584–3

Forest Service activities and finances, by region and State, FY90, annual rpt, 1204–1

Global climate change environmental, infrastructure, and health impacts, with model results and background data, 1850s-2100, 9188–113

Global warming contributing air pollutants, US and foreign emissions and control measures, 1980s and projected to 2020, 26358–233

Great Lakes area economic conditions and outlook, for US and Canada, 1970s-90, 9375–15

Gypsy moth infestation in Tennessee, timber at risk, by county, 1989, 1208–344

Improvement program for private timberland, Fed Govt cost-sharing funds by region and State, monthly rpt, 1802–11

Improvement program for private timberland, participation and payments by State, FY90, annual rpt, 1804–20

Indian (Cherokee) Agency activities in North Carolina, FY91, annual rpt, 5704–4

Indian Affairs Bur timber mgmt programs funding, acreage, harvest, and tribal investment, by tribe and location, FY77-89 and projected to FY96, hearing, 25418–4

Indiana timber resources and removals, by species, forest characteristics, ownership, and county, 1985-86, 1208–368

Insect and disease incidence and damage in forests, and control activities, State rpt series, 1206–49

Insect and disease incidence and damage in forests, annual regional rpt series, 1206–11

Insect infestation and damage in Yellowstone Natl Park timber following 1988 forest fires, 1989-90, 1208–379

Montana timber outside natl forests, acreage, resources, and mortality, by species and ownership class, 1988-89, 1206–25

New England States timber growth and relationship to tree and site characteristics, 1900s-85, 1208–349

New England timber acreage and resources, by State, 1982-85, pamphlet, 1208–363

New Hampshire and Vermont public opinion on natural resources use and mgmt, 1991 rpt, 1208–371

North Carolina timber acreage, resources, and removals, by species, ownership class, and county, 1989/90, series, 1206–4

Northeastern US forest wildlife habitat characteristics, by location, State rpt series, 1206–44

Northeastern US timber biomass volume, by characteristics of tree and forest, and county, State rpt series, 1206–43

Northeastern US timber, change in value by species, with methodology, 1970s-85, 1208–348

Northeastern US timber resources, and related manufacturing industries employment and finances, by State, 1977-87, 1208–375

Northeastern US timber resources and removals, by species, ownership, and county, State rpt series, 1206–12

Northeastern US timber survival rates, by species, model description and results, 1990 rpt, 1208–369

Northwestern US and British Columbia forest industry production, prices, trade, and employment, quarterly rpt, 1202–3

Occupational injury and illness rates, by SIC 2- to 4-digit industry, 1988-89, annual rpt, 6844–7

Occupational injury and illness rates, by SIC 2- to 4-digit industry, 1989, annual rpt, 6844–1

Oklahoma timber resources, growth, and removals, by species, forest type, ownership, and county, 1986, regional rpt series, 1206–39

Oregon (western) timber resources, acreage by land use and ownership, 1961-86, 1208–353

Pacific basin sandalwood resources, habitat, harvest, exports, and uses, 1990 conf, 1208–366

Pine (lodgepole) spiral grain defect incidence and severity, for western US and Canada, 1991 rpt, 1208–380

Pine (longleaf) in southeastern US, mgmt and use, 1989 conf, 1208–355

Pine (longleaf) planting performance relation to seed source and site, for Florida and Georgia, 1968-83, 1208–345

Pine (Scots) suitability for conservation plantings, 1960s-82 study, 1208–383

Planting and dev of forests, by State, FY90, annual rpt, 1204–7

Plantings for reforestation, effectiveness and seedling production techniques, 1990 conf, 1208–376

Public lands acreage, grants, use, revenues, and allocations, by State, FY90, annual rpt, 5724–1.2

Public lands and resources dev mgmt, environmental, economic, and social impacts of alternative Forest Service programs, projected to 2040, 1208–24

R&D funding, and scientists and engineers education and employment, for US and selected foreign countries, 1991 annual rpt, 9627–35.1

Research (agricultural) funding and staffing for USDA, State agencies, and other instns, by topic, FY90, annual rpt, 1744–2

Research and education grants, USDA competitive awards by program and recipient, FY90, annual listing, 1764–1

Soil mgmt and characteristics, for western mountain forest areas, 1990 conf, 1208–378

Southeastern US pine natural growth and plantation acreage, and lumber industries impacts of shift to plantation pine, 1989 conf papers, 1208–346

Southeastern US timber resources, and industry employment and output, by State, 1980s, article, 9391–16.204

State and Metro Area Data Book, 1991 data compilation, 2328–54

Statistical Abstract of US, 1991 annual data compilation, 2324–1.24

Tax (income) returns of sole proprietorships, income statement items, by industry group, 1989, annual article, 8302–2.214

Value conversion standards, for hardwood timber species conversion to lumber, 1972 and 1984, 1208–361

Virginia timber resources, growth, and removals, by species, ownership, treatment, and county, 1990-91, series, 1206–6

Wages and production workers by occupation, for logging and forestry industries, annual State survey rpt series, 6787–7

Wildlife and plant research results, habitat study series, 5506–13

see also Forest fires

see also Gum and wood chemicals

see also Lumber industry and products

see also National forests

see also National parks

see also State forests

see also Wood fuel

see also under By Industry in the "Index by Categories"

Forgery

see Counterfeiting and forgery

Fort Collins, Colo.

see also under By SMSA or MSA in the "Index by Categories"

Fort Lauderdale, Fla.

Air traffic and passenger and freight enplanements, by airport, 1960s-89 and projected to 2010, hub area rpt, 7506–7.40

CPI by component for US city average, and by region, population size, and for 15 metro areas, monthly rpt, 6762–1

CPI by component for US city average, and by region, population size, and for 27 metro areas, monthly rpt, 6762–2

Drug test results at arrest, by drug type, offense, and sex, for selected urban areas, quarterly rpt, 6062–3

Housing starts and completions authorized by building permits in 40 MSAs, quarterly rpt, 2382–9

see also under By City and By SMSA or MSA in the "Index by Categories"

Fort Myers, Fla.

see also under By SMSA or MSA in the "Index by Categories"

Fort Pierce, Fla.

see also under By SMSA or MSA in the "Index by Categories"

Fort Smith, Ark.

Fort Smith, Ark.
Wages by occupation, and benefits for office and plant workers, 1991 survey, periodic labor market rpt, 6785–3.9
see also under By SMSA or MSA in the "Index by Categories"

Fort Walton Beach, Fla.
see also under By SMSA or MSA in the "Index by Categories"

Fort Wayne, Ind.
see also under By City and By SMSA or MSA in the "Index by Categories"

Fort Worth, Tex.
CPI by component for US city average, and by region, population size, and for 15 metro areas, monthly rpt, 6762–1
CPI by component for US city average, and by region, population size, and for 27 metro areas, monthly rpt, 6762–2
CPI by major component for 2 Texas MSAs, monthly rpt, 6962–2
Employment, earnings, hours, and CPI changes, for Dallas-Fort Worth metro area, late 1970s-90, annual rpt, 6964–2
Housing starts and completions authorized by building permits in 40 MSAs, quarterly rpt, 2382–9
Wages by occupation, and benefits for office and plant workers, 1991 survey, periodic labor market rpt, 6785–3.10
see also under By City and By SMSA or MSA in the "Index by Categories"

Fortune, Peter
"Municipal Bond Market, Part I: Politics, Taxes, and Yields", 9373–1.215
"Stock Market Efficiency: An Autopsy?", 9373–1.206

Foster Grandparent Program
Activities and funding of ACTION, by program, FY90, annual rpt, 9024–2

Foster home care
Assistance programs under Ways and Means Committee jurisdiction, finances, operations, and participant characteristics, FY70s-90, annual rpt, 21784–11
Caseloads, funding by source, operations, and client characteristics, for selected States, 1960s-95, 25368–169
Caseloads, funding by source, problems, and program operations for selected States, 1970s-90, hearings, 21788–202
Drug abuse by parents of black children placed in foster care, cases by placement reason and outcome, and household and parent characteristics, 1986-90, 4008–114
HHS financial aid, by program, recipient, State, and city, FY90, annual regional listings, 4004–3
Homeless and runaway youth programs, funding, activities, and participant characteristics, FY90, annual rpt, 4604–3
Living arrangements, family relationships, and marital status, by selected characteristics, 1990, annual Current Population Rpt, 2546–1.449
Placements in foster care, discharges, and returns to care, by selected characteristics of children, and length of stay factors, 1985-86, GAO rpt, 26121–432
Supplemental Security Income and Medicaid eligibility and payment provisions, and beneficiaries living arrangements, by State, 1991, annual rpt, 4704–13

Foundations
see Nonprofit organizations and foundations

Foundries
Capital expenditures for plant and equipment, by major industry group, quarterly rpt, 2502–2
County Business Patterns, 1988: employment, establishments, and payroll, by SIC 2- to 4-digit industry and county, annual State rpt series, 2326–6
County Business Patterns, 1989: employment, establishments, and payroll, by SIC 2- to 4-digit industry and county, annual State rpt series, 2326–8
Employment, earnings, and hours, by SIC 1- to 4-digit industry, monthly and annual averages, selected years 1909-90, annual rpt, 6744–4
Enterprise Statistics, 1987: finances and operations for companies, by size, level of diversification, form of organization, and industry group, 2329–8
Manufacturing annual survey, 1989: finances and operations, by SIC 2- to 4-digit industry, series, 2506–15
Manufacturing census, 1987: employment and shipments under Fed Govt contracts, by SIC 4-digit industry, 2497–7
Manufacturing census, 1987: finances and operations, by SIC 2- to 4-digit industry, State, and MSA, with trends from 1849, 2497–1
Manufacturing census, 1987: finances and operations, by type of organization and SIC 2- to 4-digit industry, subject rpt, 2497–5
Manufacturing finances and operations, by SIC 2- to 4-digit industry, forecast 1991, annual rpt, 2044–28
Manufacturing industries operations and performance, analytical rpt series, 2506–16
Occupational injury and illness rates, by SIC 2- to 4-digit industry, 1988-89, annual rpt, 6844–7
Occupational injury and illness rates, by SIC 2- to 4-digit industry, 1989, annual rpt, 6844–1
Pollution (air) abatement equipment shipments by industry, and new and backlog orders, by product, 1990, annual Current Industrial Rpt, 2506–12.5
Pollution (air) emissions factors, by detailed pollutant and source, data compilation, 1990 rpt, 9198–120
Pollution abatement capital and operating costs, by SIC 2-digit industry, 1989, advance annual Current Industrial Rpt, 2506–3.6
Statistical Abstract of US, 1991 annual data compilation, 2324–1.27
Steel industry finances, operations, and modernization efforts, with data on major companies and foreign industry, 1968-91, last issue of annual rpt, 9884–24

Fox, Beverly J.
"Variations in Texas School Quality", 9379–12.67

Fox, Karl A.
"Career of Conceptualizing and Quantifying in Social Science", 1502–3.203

Fraher, James S.
"Reaction to Dairy Situation and Outlook", 1004–16.1

Index by Subjects and Names

France
Agricultural exports of high-value commodities, indexes and sales by commodity, world area, and country, 1960s-86, 1528–323
Agricultural production, prices, and trade, by country, 1970s-90, and forecast 1991, annual world region rpt, 1524–4.4
Agricultural production, trade, and policies in foreign countries, summary data by country, 1989-90, annual factbook, 1924–12
Agricultural trade of US, by detailed commodity and country, 1989, annual rpt, 1524–8
Agricultural trade of US, by detailed commodity and country, 1990, semiannual rpt, 1522–4
AID loans repayment status and terms by program and country, and status of predecessor agency loans, quarterly rpt, 9912–3
Auto sales shares, by firm, 1988, article, 9371–1.210
Background Notes, summary social, political, and economic data, 1990 rpt, 7006–2.13
Businesses (foreign) activity in US, income tax returns, assets, and income statement items, by industry div and selected country, 1986-87, article, 8302–2.205
Corporations in US under foreign control, income tax returns, assets and income statement items by industry div, country, and world area, 1988, article, 8302–2.219
Drug abuse indicators, by world region and selected country, 1990 semiannual conf, 4492–5.1
Drug abuse indicators, for selected countries, 1991 semiannual conf, 4492–5.2
Economic aid of US and other donor countries by type and recipient, and role in advancing economic interests, 1980s-90, 2048–152
Economic and military aid and loans from US and intl agencies, by program and country, FY46-90, annual rpt, 9914–5
Economic and monetary trends, compounded annual rates of change and quarterly indicators for US and 7 major industrialized countries, quarterly rpt, 9391–7
Economic conditions, and oil supply and demand, for major industrial countries, biweekly rpt, 9112–1
Economic conditions, consumer and stock prices and production indexes, 6 OECD countries and US, *Business Conditions Digest*, monthly rpt, 2702–1.2
Economic conditions in USSR, Eastern Europe, OECD, and selected other countries, 1960s-90, annual rpt, 9114–4
Economic conditions, income, production, prices, employment, and trade, 1991 periodic country rpt, 2046–4.26; 2046–4.64
Economic conditions, policy, and trade practices, by country, 1988-90, annual rpt, 21384–5
Economic indicators, and dollar exchange rates, for selected OECD countries, 1991 semiannual rpt, 8002–14
Economic, social, political, and geographic summary data, by country, 1991, annual factbook, 9114–2

Index by Subjects and Names

Fraud

Energy prices, by fuel type and end use, for 10 countries, 1980-89 annual rpt, 3164–50.6

Energy production by type, and oil trade, and use, by country group and selected country, monthly rpt, 9112–2

Exchange rate relation to interest rate differentials for France and West Germany, model description and results, 1980s, technical paper, 9366–7.249

Exports and imports, intl position of US and 4 OECD countries, and factors affecting US competition, periodic pamphlet, 2042–25

Exports and imports of NATO members with PRC, by country, 1987-90, annual rpt, 7144–14

Exports and imports of OECD members, by country, 1989, annual rpt, 7144–10

Exports and imports of OECD, total and for 4 major countries, and US trade by country, by commodity, 1970-89, world area rpt series, 9116–1

Exports and imports of US by country, and trade shifts by commodity, 1990, semiannual rpt, 9882–9

Exports and imports of US, by Harmonized System 6-digit commodity and country, 1990, annual rpt, 2424–13

Exports and imports of US, by selected country, country group, and commodity group, 1990, annual rpt, 2044–37

Exports and imports of US, by transport mode, country, and SITC 1- to 3-digit commodity, 1990, annual rpt, 2424–12

Exports and imports of US with EC by country, and total agricultural trade, selected years 1958-90, annual rpt, 7144–7

Exports, imports, and balances of US with major trading partners, by product category, 1986-90, annual chartbook, 9884–21

Exports of US, detailed Schedule B commodities with countries of destination, 1990, annual rpt, 2424–10

GNP and GNP growth for OECD members, by country, 1980-90, annual rpt, 7144–8

Health care cost control measures and insurance provisions, for Germany, France, and Japan, 1960s-91, GAO rpt, 26121–437

Human rights conditions in 170 countries, and US economic and military aid, 1990, annual rpt, 21384–3

Imports of goods, services, and investment from US, trade barriers, impacts, and US actions, by country, 1990, annual rpt, 444–2

Imports of US given duty-free treatment for value of US material sent abroad, by commodity and country, 1989, annual rpt, 9884–14

Interest and exchange rates, security yields, and stock indexes, for selected foreign countries, weekly chartbook, 9365–1.5

Intl transactions of US with 9 countries, 1986-88, *Survey of Current Business*, monthly rpt, annual table, 2702–1.26

Investment (foreign direct) in US, by industry group of US affiliate and country of parent firm, 1980-86, 2708–41

Investment (foreign direct) in US, major transactions by type, industry, country, and US location, 1989, annual rpt, 2044–20

Labor conditions, union coverage, and work accidents, 1991 annual country rpt, 6366–4.40

Multinatl firms US affiliates, finances, and operations, by industry, world area of parent firm, and State, 1988-89, annual rpt, 2704–4

Multinatl US firms and foreign affiliates finances and operations, by industry and world area of parent firm, 1989 benchmark survey, preliminary annual rpt, 2704–5

Multinatl US firms foreign affiliates, income statement items by country and world area, 1986, biennial article, 8302–2.212

Nuclear power generation in US and 20 countries, monthly rpt, 3162–24.10

Nuclear power plant capacity, generation, and operating status, by plant and foreign and US location, 1990 and projected to 2030, annual rpt, 3164–57

Oil production, trade, use, and stocks, by selected country and country group, monthly rpt, 3162–42

Oil use and stocks for selected OECD countries, monthly rpt, 3162–24.10

Paper (coated groundwood) from 5 countries at less than fair value, injury to US industry, investigation with background financial and operating data, 1991 rpt, 9886–14.336

Paper (coated groundwood) from 9 countries at less than fair value, injury to US industry, investigation with background financial and operating data, 1991 rpt, 9886–14.306

Science and engineering employment and education, and R&D spending, for US and selected foreign countries, 1991 annual rpt, 9627–35

Science and engineering employment, by professional characteristics, age, and sex, for selected countries, 1991 working paper, 2326–18.62

Space programs activities, missions, launchings, payloads, and flight duration, for foreign and US programs, 1957-90, annual rpt, 21704–4

Spacecraft and satellite launches since 1957, quarterly listing, 9502–2

Tax revenue, by level of govt and type of tax, for OECD countries, mid 1960s-89, annual rpt, 10044–1.2

Telecommunications industry intl competitiveness, with financial and operating data by product or service, firm, and country, 1990 rpt, 2008–30

Transportation energy use, fuel prices, vehicle registrations, and mileage, by selected country, 1970s-89, annual rpt, 3304–5.1

Travel to US, trade shows and other promotional activities, with magazine ad costs and circulation, for selected countries, 1991-92, annual rpt, 2904–11

UN voting record and share of votes in agreement with US, by issue, country, and world area, 1990, annual rpt, 7004–18

see also French Guiana

see also Monaco

see also New Caledonia

see also under By Foreign Country in the "Index by Categories"

Franchises

Business opportunities for franchises by firm and kind of business, and sources of aid and info, 1990 annual listing, 2104–7

Hotels and other lodging places, receipts, payroll, employment, and ownership, by State and MSA, 1987 Census of Service Industries, subject rpt, 2393–3.2

Puerto Rico economic censuses, 1987: wholesale and retail trade sales by customer class, and employment, by SIC 2- and 3-digit kind of business, subject rpt, 2591–2.2

Statistical Abstract of US, 1991 annual data compilation, 2324–1.28

Frankel, Jeffrey A.

"Indicator of Future Inflation Extracted from the Steepness of the Interest Rate Yield Curve Along Its Entire Length", 9385–8.118

Franklin, James C.

"Industry Output and Job Growth Continues Slow into Next Century", 6722–1.253

Fraud

Arrest rates, by offense, sex, age, and race, 1965-89, annual rpt, 6224–7

Arrests, by offense, offender characteristics, and location, 1990, annual rpt, 6224–2.2

Arrests, prosecutions, convictions, and sentencing, for felony offenders, by offender characteristics and offense, 1988, 6066–25.33; 6066–25.39

Banks and thrifts fraud and abuse, Federal agencies enforcement activities and staff, with data by instn and location, 1988-90, hearing, 21408–119

Banks and thrifts fraud and abuse, Federal criminal enforcement activities, case dispositions, and settlements, with data by district, 1982-90, hearing, 21248–142

Court civil and criminal caseloads for Federal district, appeals, and bankruptcy courts, by type of suit and offense, circuit, and district, 1990, annual rpt, 18204–11

Court civil and criminal caseloads for Federal district, appeals, and special courts, 1990, annual rpt, 18204–8

Court civil and criminal caseloads for Federal district courts, 1991, annual rpt, 18204–2.1

Court criminal case processing in Federal district courts, and dispositions, by offense, district, and offender characteristics, 1986, annual rpt, 6064–29

Court criminal case processing in Federal district courts, and dispositions, by offense, 1980-89, annual rpt, 6064–31

Court criminal cases in Federal district courts, by offense, disposition, and district, 1980-90, last issue of annual rpt, 18204–1

Crime, criminal justice admin and enforcement, and public opinion, data compilation, 1991 annual rpt, 6064–6

Drug abuse history of jail population, by offense, conviction status, criminal and family history, and selected other characteristics, 1989, 6066–19.63

Drug test results at arrest, by drug type, offense, and sex, for selected urban areas, quarterly rpt, 6062–3

Fed Govt agencies fraud cases involving small dollar amounts, investigations, dispositions, losses, and collections, 1986-90, GAO rpt, 26111–76

Fraud

HUD programs fraud and abuse, financial and program mgmt improvement activities, 1990, annual rpt, 5004–9

Jail population, by criminal, correctional, drug use, and family history, and selected other characteristics, 1989, 6066–19.62

Jail population, by sociodemographic characteristics, criminal and drug use history, whether convicted, offense, and sentencing, 1989, annual rpt, 6064–26.3

Postal Service inspection activities, 2nd half FY91, semiannual rpt, 9862–2

Pretrial processing, detention, and release, for Federal offenders, by defendant characteristics and district, 1988, hearing, 25528–114

Prison and parole admissions and releases, sentence length, and time served, by offense and offender characteristics, 1985, annual rpt, 6064–33

Secret Service counterfeiting and other investigations and arrests by type, and disposition, FY90 and trends from FY81, annual rpt, 8464–1

Securities industry self-regulatory organizations oversight by SEC, violations, and complaints, FY86-89, GAO rpt, 26119–336

Securities law enforcement activities of SEC, FY90, annual rpt, 9734–2.3

Sentences for Federal crimes, guidelines use and results by offense and district, and Sentencing Commission activities, 1990, annual rpt, 17664–1

Sentences for Federal offenses, guidelines by offense and circumstances, series, 17668–1

Unemployment insurance laws of States, comparison of provisions, 1991, base edition with semiannual revisions, 6402–2

Unemployment insurance programs of States, quality appraisal results, FY90, annual rpt, 6404–16

US attorneys case processing and collections, by case type and Federal district, FY90, annual rpt, 6004–2

Wiretaps authorized, costs, arrests, trials, and convictions, by offense and jurisdiction, 1990, annual rpt, 18204–7

Women prisoners in State instns, by offense, drug use history, whether abused, and other characteristics, 1986, 6066–19.61

see also Counterfeiting and forgery

see also Federal Inspectors General reports

Fravel, Frederic D.

"Intercity Bus Feeder Project Program Analysis", 7888–79

Frederiksted, V.I.

Census of Population, 1990: Virgin Islands population by location, press release, 2328–77

Freedom of information

Court civil and criminal caseloads for Federal district, appeals, and bankruptcy courts, by type of suit and offense, circuit, and district, 1990, annual rpt, 18204–11

Court civil and criminal caseloads for Federal district, appeals, and special courts, 1990, annual rpt, 18204–8

Court civil and criminal caseloads for Federal district courts, 1991, annual rpt, 18204–2.1

FDA Freedom of Info Act requests and processing time, by office, 1986-89, GAO rpt, 26121–436

Fed Govt info security measures and classification actions monitored by Info Security Oversight Office, FY90, annual rpt, 9454–21

HHS Freedom of Info Act requests, disposition, costs, and fees, 1990, annual rpt, 4004–21

USDA programs fraud and abuse, audits and investigations, 1st half FY91, semiannual rpt, 1002–4

see also Censorship

see also Freedom of the press

Freedom of the press

Foreign countries human rights conditions in 170 countries, 1990, annual rpt, 21384–3

Freeland, Mark S.

"Measuring Hospital Input Price Increases: The Rebased Hospital Market Basket", 4652–1.231

"Measuring Input Prices for Physicians: The Revised Medicare Economic Index", 4652–1.246

Freeman, Byron J.

"Tidal Salt Marshes of the Southeast Atlantic Coast: A Community Profile", 5506–9.42

Freeman, Jerry

"Distribution of West Indian Manatees (Trichechus manatus) in Puerto Rico: 1988-89", 14738–11

Freeman, Scott

"Optimality of Nominal Contracts", 9379–12.76

"Underdevelopment and the Enforcement of Laws and Contracts", 9379–12.72

Freeways

see Federal aid to highways

see Highways, streets, and roads

Freight

Animal protection, licensing, and inspection activities of USDA, and animals used in research, by State, FY89, annual rpt, 1394–10

Apple production, marketing, and prices, for Appalachia and compared to other States, 1988-91, annual rpt, 1311–13

Australia agricultural input and output indexes, and freight rates, 1950s-80s, 1528–311

Business statistics, detailed data for major industries and economic indicators, *Survey of Current Business*, monthly rpt, 2702–1.11

Census of Transportation, 1987: finances and operations by size, ownership, and State, and revenues by MSA, by SIC 2- to 4-digit industry, 2579–1

Coal production, stocks, and shipments, by State of origin and destination, end-use sector, and mode of transport, quarterly rpt, 3162–8

County Business Patterns, 1988: employment, establishments, and payroll, by SIC 2- to 4-digit industry and county, annual State rpt series, 2326–6

County Business Patterns, 1989: employment, establishments, and payroll, by SIC 2- to 4-digit industry and county, annual State rpt series, 2326–8

Employment, earnings, and hours, by SIC 1- to 4-digit industry, monthly and annual averages, selected years 1909-90, annual rpt, 6744–4

Energy use by mode of transport, fuel supply, and demographic and economic factors of vehicle use, 1970s-89, annual rpt, 3304–5

Index by Subjects and Names

Enterprise Statistics, 1987: auxiliaries of multi-establishment firms, finances and operations by function, industry, and State, 2329–6

Exports and imports of US, by transport mode, country, and SITC 1- to 3-digit commodity, 1990, annual rpt, 2424–12

Farm, food, grain, and all products rail freight index, and selected shipments by mode, monthly rpt with articles, 1502–4

Farm production itemized costs, by farm sales size and region, 1990, annual rpt, 1614–3

Food marketing cost indexes, by expense category, monthly rpt with articles, 1502–4

Food prices (farm-retail), marketing cost components, and industry finances and productivity, 1920s-90, annual rpt, 1544–9

Foreign trade zones (US) operations and movement of goods, by zone and commodity, FY88, annual rpt, 2044–30

Fruit and vegetable shipments, and arrivals in US and Canada cities, by mode of transport and State and country of origin, 1990, annual rpt series, 1311–4

Fruit and vegetable shipments by mode of transport, arrivals, and imports, by commodity and State and country of origin, weekly rpt, 1311–3

Fruit and vegetable shipments by truck, monthly by State and country of origin, and rates weekly by growing area and market, 1990, annual rpt, 1311–15

Fruit and vegetable wholesale prices in NYC by State, and shipments and arrivals by mode of transport, by commodity, weekly rpt, 1311–20

Grain shipments and rates for barge and rail loadings, periodic situation rpt with articles, 1561–4

Household goods carriers financial and operating data by firm, quarterly rpt, 9482–14

Import restraint elimination impacts on US economy and selected service industries, 1970s-90, 9886–4.173

Lumber (pulpwood and residue) prices, spending, and transport shares by mode, for southeast US, 1988-89, annual rpt, 1204–22

Lumber freight rates for products shipped from Alaska and Puget Sound to Asian markets, by product and port, 1988, 1208–358

Mail (express parcel) shipments and revenues of private air and surface carriers, and impact of State regulation, 1976-89, 7308–201

Military and personal property shipments, passenger traffic, and costs, by service branch and mode of transport, quarterly rpt, 3702–1

Military Sealift Command shipping operations, finances, and personnel, FY90, annual rpt, 3804–14

Mississippi River system freight traffic by commodity and waterway, 1988 and projected to 2000, article, 9391–16.202

Natl transportation system planning, use, condition, accidents, and needs, by mode of transport, 1940s-90 and projected to 2020, 7308–202

Index by Subjects and Names

Occupational injury and illness rates, by SIC 2- to 4-digit industry, 1988-89, annual rpt, 6844–7

Occupational injury and illness rates, by SIC 2- to 4-digit industry, 1989, annual rpt, 6844–1

Price indexes (producer), by stage of processing and detailed commodity, monthly 1990, annual rpt, 6764–2

Publications and data files of Census Bur on foreign trade, 1991 guide, 2428–11

Railroad (Class I) finances and operations, detailed data by firm, class of service, and district, 1989, annual rpt, 9486–6.1

Railroad retirement system funding and benefits findings and recommendations, with background industry data, 1960s-90 and projected to 2060, 9708–1

Railroad revenue, income, freight, and rate of return, by Class I freight railroad and district, quarterly rpt, 9482–2

Shipborne commerce (domestic and foreign) of US, freight by port and State, 1989, annual rpt, 3754–7

Shipborne trade of US, and Fed Govt sponsored cargo by agency, total and US-flag share by vessel type, selected years 1980-89, annual rpt, 7704–14.2; 7704–14.3

Shipborne trade of US, by type of service, commodity, country, route, and US port, 1988, annual rpt, 7704–2

St Lawrence Seaway ship, cargo, and passenger traffic, and toll revenue, 1990 and trends from 1959, annual rpt, 7744–2

Statistical Abstract of US, 1991 annual data compilation, 2324–1.21

Timber transport costs from Alaska and Puget Sound to Asia markets, by country, 1988, 1208–367

Truck and bus interstate carriers finances and operations, by district, 1989, annual rpt, 9486–6.3

Truck and warehouse services finances and inventory, by SIC 2- to 4-digit industry, 1989 survey, annual rpt, 2413–14

Truck interstate carriers finances and operations, by district, 1989, annual rpt, 9486–6.2

Truck transport of property, financial and operating data by region and firm, quarterly rpt, 9482–5

Trucking industry deregulation by States, potential economic and market impacts, with background data, mid 1970s-80s, 7308–200

Vegetable truck rates, by crop, growing area, and market, periodic situation rpt with articles, 1561–11

see also Air cargo

see also Containerization

see also Hazardous substances transport

Fremont, Calif.

see also under By City in the "Index by Categories"

French Guiana

Agricultural trade of US, by detailed commodity and country, 1989, annual rpt, 1524–8

Agricultural trade of US, by detailed commodity and country, 1990, semiannual rpt, 1522–4

Economic, social, political, and geographic summary data, by country, 1991, annual factbook, 9114–2

Exports and imports of US, by transport mode, country, and SITC 1- to 3-digit commodity, 1990, annual rpt, 2424–12

Exports of US, detailed Schedule B commodities with countries of destination, 1990, annual rpt, 2424–10

French, Mark W.

"Cyclical Patterns in the Variance of Economic Activity", 9366–6.275

French West Indies

see Caribbean area

Fresno, Calif.

Water quality, chemistry, hydrology, and other characteristics, 1989 local area study, 5666–27.2

see also under By City and By SMSA or MSA in the "Index by Categories"

Freund, Deborah A.

"Nationwide Evaluation of Medicaid Competition Demonstrations. Volume 1. Integrative Final Report", 4658–45.1

"Nationwide Evaluation of Medicaid Competition Demonstrations. Volume 3. Utilization and Cost Analyses", 4658–45.3

Freund, William H.

"Race/Ethnicity Trends in Degrees Conferred by Institutions of Higher Education: 1978-79 Through 1988-89", 4844–17

Friedman, Bruce

"ACCESS: Medicare Program: Reducing Hospital Use Among Medicare Beneficiaries", 4658–43

Friedman, Joel

"Impact of Collection Enforcement Action on Individual Taxpayer Behavior", 8304–8.1

Frieswyk, Thomas S.

"Biomass Statistics for Maryland, 1986", 1206–43.3

Fringe benefits

see Employee benefits

Frisvold, George B.

"Differences in Agricultural Research and Productivity Among 26 Countries", 1528–318

Fronczek, Peter J.

"Who Can Afford To Buy a House?", 2486–1.11

Fruit and fruit products

Africa (sub-Saharan) agricultural conditions by country, with Ethiopia grain production and use, and dev aid by major donor, 1960s-80s, hearing, 23848–216

Agricultural Statistics, 1990, annual rpt, 1004–1

Agriculture census, 1987: farms, farmland, production, finances, and operator characteristics, by county, final State rpt series, 2331–1

Agriculture census, 1987: horticultural specialties producers, finances, and operations, by crop and State, 1988 survey, 2337–1

Apple exports by destination country, 1986/87-1990/91, article, 1925–34.236

Apple import demand in 4 countries, 1960s-83, 1568–296

Apple industry competitiveness of US and Canada, investigation with background financial and operating data, 1991 rpt, 9886–4.172

Apple production, marketing, and prices, for Appalachia and compared to other States, 1988-91, annual rpt, 1311–13

Fruit and fruit products

Banana production, trade, and per capita consumption, by country, and US prices, selected years 1985-90 and projected to 1994, article, 1925–34.228

Central America agricultural export promotion of nontraditional crops, impacts on income export stability, late 1970s-80s, 1528–312

Cherry juice and concentrate from 2 countries at less than fair value, injury to US industry, investigation with background financial and operating data, 1991 rpt, 9886–14.308

Cherry production, by State, 1989-91, annual rpt, 1621–18.2

Cold storage food stocks by commodity and census div, and warehouse space use, by State, monthly rpt, 1631–5

Cold storage food stocks by commodity, and warehouse space use, by census div, 1990, annual rpt, 1631–11

Consumer Expenditure Survey, food spending by item, household composition, income, age, race, and region, 1980-88, biennial rpt, 1544–30

Consumer Expenditure Survey, household income by source, and itemized spending, by selected characteristics and region, 1988-89, annual rpt, 6764–5

Consumption of food, dietary composition, and nutrient intake, 1987/88 natl survey, preliminary rpt series, 1356–1

Consumption, supply, trade, prices, spending, and indexes, by food commodity, 1989, annual rpt, 1544–4

Costa Rica imports of US fresh fruits by type, FY86-90, article, 1925–34.203

County Business Patterns, 1988: employment, establishments, and payroll, by SIC 2- to 4-digit industry and county, annual State rpt series, 2326–6

County Business Patterns, 1989: employment, establishments, and payroll, by SIC 2- to 4-digit industry and county, annual State rpt series, 2326–8

CPI by component for US city average, and by region, population size, and for 27 metro areas, monthly rpt, 6762–2

Cranberry production, prices, use, and acreage, for selected States, 1989-90 and forecast 1991, annual rpt, 1621–18.4

Disaster damage to timber and orchards, USDA restoration aid and program participation by practice and State, FY89-90, annual rpt, 1804–24

Employment, earnings, and hours, by SIC 1- to 4-digit industry, monthly and annual averages, selected years 1909-90, annual rpt, 6744–4

Enterprise Statistics, 1987: finances and operations for companies, by size, level of diversification, form of organization, and industry group, 2329–8

Exports (agricultural) of high-value commodities, indexes and sales value by commodity, world area, and country, 1960s-86, 1528–323

Exports (agricultural) of US, impacts of foreign agricultural and trade policy, with data by commodity and country, 1989, annual rpt, 1924–8

Exports and imports (agricultural) of US, by commodity and country, bimonthly rpt, 1522–1

Fruit and fruit products

Exports and imports (agricultural) of US, by detailed commodity and country, 1989, annual rpt, 1524–8

Exports and imports (agricultural) of US, by detailed commodity and country, 1990, semiannual rpt, 1522–4

Exports and imports between US and outlying areas, by detailed commodity and mode of transport, 1990, annual rpt, 2424–11

Exports and imports of US, by country and detailed commodity, monthly rpt, 2422–12

Exports and imports of US, by Harmonized System 6-digit commodity and country, 1990, annual rpt, 2424–13

Exports and imports of US, by transport mode, country, and SITC 1- to 3-digit commodity, 1990, annual rpt, 2424–12

Exports of US, detailed Schedule B commodities with countries of destination, 1990, annual rpt, 2424–10

Farm financial and marketing conditions, forecast 1991, annual chartbook, 1504–8

Farm financial and marketing conditions, forecast 1991, annual conf, 1004–16

Farm financial condition, for fruit and vegetable operations, 1989, article, 1541–1.209

Farm income, expenses, receipts by commodity, assets, liabilities, and ratios, 1990 and trends from 1945, annual rpt, 1544–16

Farm sector balance sheet, and receipts by detailed commodity, by State, 1985-89, annual rpt, 1544–18

Fertilizer and pesticide use and application rates, by type, crop, and State, 1990, 1616–1.2

Foreign and US fresh and processed fruit, vegetable, and nut production and trade, FAS monthly circular with articles, 1925–34

Foreign countries agricultural production, prices, and trade, by country, 1980-90 and forecast 1991, annual world area rpt series, 1524–4

Foreign countries agricultural production, trade, and policies, summary data by country, 1989-90, annual factbook, 1924–12

Grapes (table) and other fruit, acreage, production, and trade, and use, for Chile, selected years 1970-91, article, 1925–34.222

Immigration restrictions effects on US agricultural labor costs and trade competitiveness, 1980s, 1598–276

Imports of fruits and vegetables under quarantine, by crop, country, and port of entry, FY88 annual rpt, 1524–7

Irrigation projects of Reclamation Bur in western US, crop production and acreage by commodity, State, and project, 1989, annual rpt, 5824–12

Kiwifruit from New Zealand at less than fair value, injury to US industry, investigation with background financial and operating data, 1991 rpt, 9886–14.316

Labor productivity, indexes of output, hours, and employment by SIC 2- to 4-digit industry, 1967-89, annual rpt, 6824–1.3

Liquor production, stocks, materials used, and taxable and tax-free removals, by State, monthly rpt, 8486–1.3

Manufacturing annual survey, 1989: finances and operations, by SIC 2- to 4-digit industry, series, 2506–15

Manufacturing census, 1987: finances and operations, by SIC 2- to 4-digit industry, State, and MSA, with trends from 1849, 2497–1

Manufacturing census, 1987: finances and operations, by type of organization and SIC 2- to 4-digit industry, subject rpt, 2497–5

Manufacturing finances and operations, by SIC 2- to 4-digit industry, forecast 1991, annual rpt, 2044–28

Mexico fruit trade with US, and US import duties, by commodity, 1970s-90, article, 1561–6.203

Nutrient, caloric, and waste composition, detailed data for raw, processed, and prepared foods, 1991 rpt, 1356–3.15

Occupational injury and illness rates, by SIC 2- to 4-digit industry, 1988-89, annual rpt, 6844–7

Occupational injury and illness rates, by SIC 2- to 4-digit industry, 1989, annual rpt, 6844–1

OECD trade, total and for 4 major countries, and US trade by country, by commodity, 1970-89, world area rpt series, 9116–1

Peach (canned) trade of US and Greece, by country, 1987-89, article, 1925–34.223

Peaches production, marketing, and prices in 3 southeastern States and Appalachia, 1990, annual rpt, 1311–12

Pineapple (canned fruit and juice) production and exports, by country, 1988-91, annual article, 1925–34.216

Pineapple (canned fruit and juice) production and exports, for 2 countries, forecast 1991, semiannual article, 1925–34.243

Price indexes (producer), by stage of processing and detailed commodity, monthly rpt, 6762–6

Price indexes (producer), by stage of processing and detailed commodity, monthly 1990, annual rpt, 6764–2

Prices (farm-retail) for food, marketing cost components, and industry finances and productivity, 1920s-90, annual rpt, 1544–9

Prices (wholesale) for fresh fruit and vegetables in NYC, Chicago, and selected shipping points, by crop, 1990, annual rpt, 1311–8

Prices (wholesale) of fruit and vegetables in NYC by State, and shipments and arrivals by mode of transport, by commodity, weekly rpt, 1311–20

Prices received and paid by farmers, by commodity and State, 1990, annual rpt, 1629–5

Prices received by farmers and production value, by detailed crop and State, 1988-90, annual rpt, 1621–2

Prices received by farmers for major products, and paid for farm inputs and living items, by State, monthly rpt, 1629–1

Production, acreage, and yield, current and forecast for melons and strawberries by State, periodic rpt, 1621–12

Production, farms, acreage, and related data, by selected crop and State, monthly rpt, 1621–1

Index by Subjects and Names

Production inputs, output, and productivity for farms, by commodity and region, 1947-89, annual rpt, 1544–17

Production of fruit and vegetables, imports by country, use, exports, and prices, by commodity, 1975-87, 1568–299

Production, prices, and use of fruit and nuts, 1988-91, annual rpt series, 1621–18

Production, prices, trade, and marketing, by commodity, current situation and forecast, monthly rpt with articles, 1502–4

Production, prices, trade, stocks, and use, by selected crop, periodic situation rpt with articles, 1561–6

Production, value, and acreage, for melons and strawberries, by State, 1988-90, annual rpts, 1621–25

Prune production, trade, use, and stocks for selected countries, 1987-91, table, 1925–34.204

Prune production, trade, use, and stocks, for US and 6 countries, 1988/89-1990/91, article, 1925–34.225

Puerto Rico economic censuses, 1987: wholesale and retail trade and service industry finances and operations, by SIC 2- to 4-digit industry and municipio, 2591–1

Puerto Rico economic censuses, 1987: wholesale, retail, and service industries finances and operations, by establishment characteristics and SIC 2- and 3-digit industry, subject rpts, 2591–2

Radiation exposure of population near Hanford, Wash, nuclear plant, with methodology, 1944-66, series, 3356–5

Raisin and dried prune imports of EC, by country of origin and destination, 1989-90, tables, 1925–34.234

Raisin and prune production, trade, use, and stocks for EC and other countries, Turkey price supports, and Mexico production costs, 1985-91, annual article, 1925–34.250

Raisin production, trade, and use, by country, 1987-91, annual article, 1925–34.221

Retail trade census, 1987: finances and employment, for establishments with and without payroll, by SIC 2- to 4-digit kind of business, State, and MSA, 2401–1

Shipments by mode of transport, arrivals, and imports, for fruit and vegetables by commodity and State and country of origin, weekly rpt, 1311–3

Shipments of fruit and vegetables, and arrivals in US and Canada cities, by mode of transport and State and country of origin, 1990, annual rpt series, 1311–4

Statistical Abstract of US, 1991 annual data compilation, 2324–1.3; 2324–1.23

Strawberry trade of US and Mexico, and Mexico and Chile supply and use, 1986-91, annual article, 1925–34.218

Tax (income) returns of corporations, income and tax items by asset size and detailed industry, 1988, annual rpt, 8304–21

Tax (income) returns of partnerships, income statement and balance sheet items, by industry group, 1989, annual article, 8302–2.216; 8304–18

Truck rates for fruit and vegetables weekly by growing area and market, and shipments monthly by State and country of origin, 1990, annual rpt, 1311–15

Index by Subjects and Names — Fuel tax

Truck transport of fruit and vegetables, itemized costs per mile by item for fleets and owner-operator trucks, monthly table, 1272–1

Wholesale trade census, 1987: establishments, sales by customer class, employment, inventories, and expenses, by SIC 2- to 4-digit kind of business, 2407–4

see also Citrus fruits
see also Nuts
see also Vegetables and vegetable products
see also under By Commodity in the "Index by Categories"

Frydl, Edward J.

"Some Issues in Corporate Leveraging: An Overview Essay", 9385–8.88

FTC

see Federal Trade Commission

FTC Communications

Finances and operations, detail for telegraph firms, 1989, annual rpt, 9284–6.3

Finances, rates, and traffic for US telecommunications carriers intl operations, by service type, firm, and country, 1975-89, annual rpt, 9284–17

Fuel

see terms listed under Energy resources and consumption

Fuel oil

Business statistics, detailed data for major industries and economic indicators, *Survey of Current Business*, monthly rpt, 2702–1.18

Commercial buildings energy use, costs, and conservation, by building characteristics, survey rpt series, 3166–8

Consumer Expenditure Survey, household income by source, and itemized spending, by selected characteristics and region, 1988-89, annual rpt, 6764–5

Consumption of energy, by detailed fuel type, end-use sector, and State, 1960-89, State Energy Data System annual rpt, 3164–39

CPI by component for US city average, and by region, population size, and for 27 metro areas, monthly rpt, 6762–2

Electric power plants and capacity, by fuel used, owner, location, and operating status, 1990 and for units planned 1991-2000, annual listing, 3164–36

Exports and imports of US, by country and detailed commodity, monthly rpt, 2422–12

Exports and imports of US, by Harmonized System 6-digit commodity and country, 1990, annual rpt, 2424–13

Exports of US, detailed Schedule B commodities with countries of destination, 1990, annual rpt, 2424–10

Fed Govt energy use and efficiency, by agency and fuel type, FY90, annual rpt, 3304–22

Foreign and US oil prices, by refined product and country, 1980-89, annual rpt, 3164–50.6

Futures and options trading volume, by commodity and exchange, FY90, annual rpt, 11924–2

Futures trading in selected commodities and financial instruments and indexes, NYC, Chicago, and other markets activity, semimonthly rpt, 11922–5

Heating fuels production, imports, stocks, and prices, by selected PAD district and State, seasonal weekly rpt, 3162–45

Housing (low income) energy aid, funding sources, costs, and participation, by State, FY89, annual rpt, 4694–8

Housing and households detailed characteristics, and unit and neighborhood quality, by location, 1989, biennial rpt, 2485–12

Housing and households detailed characteristics, and unit and neighborhood quality, MSA surveys, series, 2485–6

Housing energy prices, by fuel and State, 1989 and forecast 1990-91, 3166–6.54

Housing heating and air conditioning equipment shipments by type of fuel used, bimonthly rpt, 2042–1.6

Housing inventory change from 1973, by reason, unit and household characteristics, and location, 1983 survey, biennial rpt, 2485–14

Housing units (1-family) by selected structural characteristics, sales, and prices, 1970s-90, article, 1702–1.205

Housing units completed, single and multifamily units by structural and financial characteristics, inside-outside MSAs, and region, 1986-90, annual rpt, 2384–1

Imports of oil, traffic by US port and vessel type, marine oil pollution sources, and costs and operations of proposed offshore terminals, late 1980s, 5738–25

Iraq invasion of Kuwait, impacts on oil prices and industry profits, as of 4th qtr 1990, 3166–6.46

Iraq invasion of Kuwait, impacts on oil supply and prices, selected indicators, daily press release, 3162–44

Mineral industries census, 1987: energy use and costs, by fuel type, SIC 2- to 4-digit industry, and State, subject rpt, 2517–2

Minerals Yearbook, 1988, Vol 3: foreign country reviews of production, trade, and policy, by commodity, annual rpt series, 5604–17

Pollution (air) levels for 6 pollutants, by source, 1970-89 and trends from 1940, annual rpt, 9194–13

Price indexes (producer), by stage of processing and detailed commodity, monthly 1990, annual rpt, 6764–2

Prices and spending for fuel, by type, end-use sector, and State, 1989, annual rpt, 3164–64

Prices and volume of oil products sold and purchased by refiners, processors, and distributors, by product, end-use sector, PAD district, and State, monthly rpt with articles, 3162–11

Retail trade census, 1987: finances and employment, for establishments with and without payroll, by SIC 2- to 4-digit kind of business, State, and MSA, 2401–1

Sales and deliveries of fuel oil and kerosene, by end-use, PAD district, and State, 1989, annual rpt, 3164–94

Supply and demand of oil and refined products, refinery capacity and use, and prices, weekly rpt, 3162–32

Supply, demand, and movement of crude oil, gas liquids, and refined products, by PAD district and State, 1990, annual rpt, 3164–2

Supply, demand, and prices, by fuel type and end-use sector, alternative projections 1989-2010, annual rpt, 3164–75

Supply, demand, and prices, by fuel type and end-use sector, projections and underlying assumptions, 1990-2010, annual rpt, 3164–90

Supply, demand, and prices, by fuel type and end-use sector, with foreign comparisons, 1990 and trends from 1949, annual rpt, 3164–74.2

Supply, demand, and prices, by fuel type, end-use sector, and country, detailed data, monthly rpt with articles, 3162–24

Supply, demand, and prices of crude oil and refined products, and refinery capacity and stocks, by State, 1960-91, annual rpt, 3164–95

Supply, demand, and prices of energy, forecasts by resource type, quarterly rpt, 3162–34

Supply, demand, and prices of oil and gas, alternative projections 1989-2010, annual rpt, 3164–89

Supply, demand, trade, stocks, and refining of oil and gas liquids, by detailed product, State, and PAD district, monthly rpt with articles, 3162–6

Tax provisions of States for motor fuel, auto registration fees, and disposition of receipts, by State, as of Jan 1991, biennial rpt, 7554–37

Transportation energy use by mode, fuel supply, and demographic and economic factors of vehicle use, 1970s-89, annual rpt, 3304–5

Wholesale trade census, 1987: oil bulk stations, sales and storage capacity by product, inventories, expenses, employment, and modes of transport, 2407–4.2

Fuel tax

Alternative motor fuels costs, emissions, health impacts, and characteristics, series, 9196–5

Budget of US, authoritative financial statements with appropriations, outlays, and receipts, by category and agency, FY90, annual rpt, 8104–2.1

Budget of US, CBO analysis of savings and revenues under alternative spending cuts and tax changes, projected FY92-97, 26306–3.118

Collections of taxes, by level of govt, type of tax, State, and selected counties, quarterly rpt, 2462–3

Economic and energy demand impacts of alternative energy taxation methods, projected 1991-2000, 3166–6.57

Energy use by mode of transport, fuel supply, and demographic and economic factors of vehicle use, 1970s-89, annual rpt, 3304–5

Finances of govts, tax systems and revenue, and fiscal structure, by level of govt and State, 1991 and historical trends, annual rpt, 10044–1

Gasohol sales, and tax rates on all motor fuels, by State, 1983-90, annual rpt, 3304–9

Gasoline and diesel fuel Federal and State tax rates, by State, monthly rpt, 3162–11

Gasoline supply, demand, prices, taxes, and auto registrations and mileage, 1900s-89, 3168–120

Fuel tax

Hwy Statistics, summary data by State, 1989-90, annual rpt, 7554–24

Hwy Trust Fund finances, unobligated balances by State, and receipt losses from increased ethanol use, 1980s-90, hearing, 25328–31

Hwy Trust Fund revenues, tax rates, and spending, FY87-91 with projections to FY95, GAO rpt, 26113–544

IRS collections, by excise tax source, quarterly rpt, 8302–1

Oil import tariff and excise tax economic impacts, model description and results, 1991 paper, 9406–1.61

State and Metro Area Data Book, 1991 data compilation, 2328–54

State govt tax collections by detailed type of tax, and tax rates, by State, FY90, annual rpt, 2466–2.7

State govt tax provisions on motor fuel, auto registration fees, and disposition of receipts, by State, as of Jan 1991, biennial rpt, 7554–37

State govt tax rates on motor fuel, and gallons taxed, by State, 1990, annual rpt, 7554–1

State govt tax rates on motor fuel, by fuel type and State, monthly rpt, 7552–1

State govt tax rates on motor fuel, by State, 1980-89, annual table, 7554–32

Statistical Abstract of US, 1991 annual data compilation, 2324–1.21

Tax (excise) collections of IRS, by source, quarterly rpt, 8302–2.1

Fujairah *see* United Arab Emirates

Fullerton, Calif. *see also under* By City in the "Index by Categories"

Fullerton, Howard N., Jr. "Labor Force Projections: The Baby Boom Moves On", 6722–1.252

Fulton, John P. "Study Guided by the Health Belief Model of the Predictors of Breast Cancer Screening of Women Ages 40 and Older", 4042–3.233

Functional limitations *see* Mobility limitations

Funerals *see* Cemeteries and funerals *see* Military cemeteries and funerals

Fungicides *see* Pesticides

Funkhouser, Gordon E. "Donning Times and Flotation Characteristics of Infant Life Preservers: Four Representative Types", 7506–10.85

Furniture and furnishings

Collective bargaining agreements expiring during year, and workers covered, by firm, union, industry group, and State, 1991, annual rpt, 6784–9

Consumer Expenditure Survey, household income by source, and itemized spending, by selected characteristics and region, 1988-89, annual rpt, 6764–5

Consumer Expenditure Survey, spending by category, and income, by selected household characteristics and location, 1990, annual press release, 6726–1.42

Consumer Expenditure Survey, spending by category, selected household characteristics, and region, quarterly rpt, 6762–14

County Business Patterns, 1988: employment, establishments, and payroll, by SIC 2- to 4-digit industry and county, annual State rpt series, 2326–6

County Business Patterns, 1989: employment, establishments, and payroll, by SIC 2- to 4-digit industry and county, annual State rpt series, 2326–8

CPI by component for US city average, and by region, population size, and for 27 metro areas, monthly rpt, 6762–2

CPI components relative importance, by selected MSA, region, population size, and for US city average, 1990, annual rpt, 6884–1

DOD prime contract awards, by detailed procurement category, FY87-90, annual rpt, 3544–18

Employment, earnings, and hours, by SIC 1- to 4-digit industry, monthly and annual averages, selected years 1909-90, annual rpt, 6744–4

Employment in manufacturing, by detailed occupation and SIC 2-digit industry, 1989 survey, triennial rpt, 6748–52

Employment, unemployment, and labor force characteristics, by region and census div, 1990, annual rpt, 6744–7.1

Energy use and prices for manufacturing industries, 1988 survey, series, 3166–13

Enterprise Statistics, 1987: auxiliaries of multi-establishment firms, finances and operations by function, industry, and State, 2329–6

Enterprise Statistics, 1987: finances and operations for companies, by size, level of diversification, form of organization, and industry group, 2329–8

Exports and imports between US and outlying areas, by detailed commodity and mode of transport, 1990, annual rpt, 2424–11

Exports and imports of US, by country and detailed commodity, monthly rpt, 2422–12

Exports and imports of US, by Harmonized System 6-digit commodity and country, 1990, annual rpt, 2424–13

Exports and imports of US, by selected country, country group, and commodity group, 1990, annual rpt, 2044–37

Exports and imports of US, by transport mode, country, and SITC 1- to 3-digit commodity, 1990, annual rpt, 2424–12

Exports of US, detailed commodities by country, monthly CD-ROM, 2422–13

Exports of US, detailed Schedule B commodities with countries of destination, 1990, annual rpt, 2424–10

Farm sector assets by type, 1990, annual rpt, 1544–16.2

Farm sector balance sheet, and marketing receipts by detailed commodity, by State, 1985-89, annual rpt, 1544–18

Franchise business opportunities by firm and kind of business, and sources of aid and info, 1990 annual listing, 2104–7

Imports, exports, and employment impacts, by SIC 2- to 4-digit industry and commodity, quarterly rpt, 2322–2

Imports of textiles under Multifiber Arrangement by product and country, and status of bilateral agreements, 1987-90, annual rpt, 9884–18

Index by Subjects and Names

Imports of US, detailed commodities by country, monthly CD-ROM, 2422–14

Imports of US given duty-free treatment for value of US material sent abroad, by commodity and country, 1989, annual rpt, 9884–14

Injuries from use of consumer products, by severity, victim age, and detailed product, 1990, annual rpt, 9164–6

Injuries from use of consumer products, related deaths and costs, and recalls by brand, by product type, FY89, annual rpt, 9164–2

Input-output structure of US economy, detailed interindustry transactions for 84 industries, and components of final demand, 1986, annual article, 2702–1.206

Input-output structure of US economy, detailed interindustry transactions for 85 industries, 1982 benchmark data, 2702–1.213

Labor productivity, indexes of output, hours, and employment by SIC 2- to 4-digit industry, 1967-89, annual rpt, 6824–1.3

Lumber and pulp products supply and use, and timber resources, detailed data, 1950s-87 and alternative projections to 2040, 1208–24.20

Manufacturing annual survey, 1989: finances and operations, by SIC 2- to 4-digit industry, series, 2506–15

Manufacturing census, 1987: finances and operations, by SIC 2- to 4-digit industry, State, and MSA, with trends from 1849, 2497–1

Manufacturing census, 1987: finances and operations, by type of organization and SIC 2- to 4-digit industry, subject rpt, 2497–5

Manufacturing finances and operations, by SIC 2- to 4-digit industry, forecast 1991, annual rpt, 2044–28

Manufacturing industries operations and performance, analytical rpt series, 2506–16

Manufacturing production, shipments, inventories, orders, and pollution control costs, periodic Current Industrial Rpt series, 2506–3

Mexico imports from US, by industry and State, 1987-90, 2048–154

Military and personal property shipments, passenger traffic, and costs, by service branch and mode of transport, quarterly rpt, 3702–1

Military Sealift Command shipping operations, finances, and personnel, FY90, annual rpt, 3804–14

Natl income and product accounts and components, *Survey of Current Business*, monthly rpt, 2702–1.24

Northeastern US timber resources, and related manufacturing industries employment and finances, by State, 1977-87, 1208–375

Occupational injury and illness rates, by SIC 2- to 4-digit industry, 1988-89, annual rpt, 6844–7

Occupational injury and illness rates, by SIC 2- to 4-digit industry, 1989, annual rpt, 6844–1

OECD trade, total and for 4 major countries, and US trade by country, by commodity, 1970-89, world area rpt series, 9116–1

Index by Subjects and Names — Futures trading

Pollution abatement capital and operating costs, by SIC 2-digit industry, 1989, advance annual Current Industrial Rpt, 2506–3.6

Price indexes (producer), by stage of processing and detailed commodity, monthly rpt, 6762–6

Price indexes (producer), by stage of processing and detailed commodity, monthly 1990, annual rpt, 6764–2

Price indexes for department store inventories, by class of item, monthly table, 6762–7

Production, prices, employment, and trade, for hardwood lumber and products, quarterly rpt, 1202–4

Puerto Rico economic censuses, 1987: wholesale and retail trade and service industry finances and operations, by SIC 2- to 4-digit industry and municipio, 2591–1

Puerto Rico economic censuses, 1987: wholesale, retail, and service industries finances and operations, by establishment characteristics and SIC 2- and 3-digit industry, subject rpts, 2591–2

Retail trade census, 1987: depreciable assets, capital and operating expenses, sales, value added, and inventories, by SIC 2- to 4-digit kind of business, 2399–2

Retail trade census, 1987: finances and employment, for establishments with and without payroll, by SIC 2- to 4-digit kind of business, State, and MSA, 2401–1

Retail trade sales and inventories, by kind of business, region, and selected State, MSA, and city, monthly rpt, 2413–3

Retail trade sales, by kind of business, advance monthly rpt, 2413–2

Retail trade sales, inventories, purchases, gross margin, and accounts receivable, by SIC 2- to 4-digit kind of business and form of ownership, 1989, annual rpt, 2413–5

Soviet Union GNP by detailed income and outlay component, 1985, 2326–18.59

Tax (income) returns of corporations, income and tax items by asset size and detailed industry, 1987, annual rpt, 8304–4

Tax (income) returns of corporations, income and tax items by asset size and detailed industry, 1988, annual rpt, 8304–21

Tax (income) returns of corporations with foreign tax credit, income and tax items by industry group, 1986, biennial article, 8302–2.203

Tax (income) returns of sole proprietorships, income statement items, by industry group, 1989, annual article, 8302–2.214

Transportation census, 1987: finances and operations by size, ownership, and State, and revenues by MSA, by SIC 2- to 4-digit industry, 2579–1

Truck transport of household goods, financial and operating data by firm, quarterly rpt, 9482–14

Truck transport of household goods, performance and disposition of damage claims, for selected carriers, 1990, annual rpt, 9484–11

Warehouse services finances, by SIC 3- to 4-digit industry, 1989 survey, annual rpt, 2413–14

Wholesale trade census, 1987: depreciable assets, capital and operating expenses, sales, value added, and inventories, by SIC 2- to 3-digit kind of business, 2407–2

Wholesale trade census, 1987: establishments, sales by customer class, employment, inventories, and expenses, by SIC 2- to 4-digit kind of business, 2407–4

Wholesale trade sales and inventories, by SIC 2- to 3-digit kind of business, monthly rpt, 2413–7

Wholesale trade sales, inventories, purchases, and gross margins, by SIC 2- to 3-digit kind of business, 1990, annual rpt, 2413–13

see also Antiques

see also Carpets and rugs

see also Floor coverings

see also Household appliances and equipment

see also Household supplies and utensils

see also Wall coverings

see also under By Commodity in the "Index by Categories"

see also under By Industry in the "Index by Categories"

Furs and fur industry

Agriculture census, 1987: farms, farmland, production, finances, and operator characteristics, by county, final State rpt series, 2331–1

County Business Patterns, 1988: employment, establishments, and payroll, by SIC 2- to 4-digit industry and county, annual State rpt series, 2326–6

County Business Patterns, 1989: employment, establishments, and payroll, by SIC 2- to 4-digit industry and county, annual State rpt series, 2326–8

Endangered animals and plants US trade and permits, by species, purpose, disposition, and country, 1989, annual rpt, 5504–19

Exports and imports (agricultural) of US, by commodity and country, bimonthly rpt, 1522–1

Exports and imports (agricultural) of US, by detailed commodity and country, 1989, annual rpt, 1524–8

Exports and imports (agricultural) of US, by detailed commodity and country, 1990, semiannual rpt, 1522–4

Exports and imports of dairy, livestock, and poultry products, by commodity and country, FAS monthly circular, 1925–32

Exports and imports of US, by country and detailed commodity, monthly rpt, 2422–12

Exports and imports of US, by Harmonized System 6-digit commodity and country, 1990, annual rpt, 2424–13

Exports and imports of US, by transport mode, country, and SITC 1- to 3-digit commodity, 1990, annual rpt, 2424–12

Exports of US, detailed Schedule B commodities with countries of destination, 1990, annual rpt, 2424–10

Manufacturing annual survey, 1989: finances and operations, by SIC 2- to 4-digit industry, series, 2506–15

Manufacturing census, 1987: finances and operations, by SIC 2- to 4-digit industry, State, and MSA, with trends from 1849, 2497–1

Manufacturing census, 1987: finances and operations, by type of organization and SIC 2- to 4-digit industry, subject rpt, 2497–5

Mink and pelt production, prices, and farms, selected years 1969-91, annual rpt, 1631–7

Price indexes (producer), by stage of processing and detailed commodity, monthly rpt, 6762–6

Price indexes (producer), by stage of processing and detailed commodity, monthly 1990, annual rpt, 6764–2

Retail trade census, 1987: finances and employment, for establishments with and without payroll, by SIC 2- to 4-digit kind of business, State, and MSA, 2401–1

see also Hides and skins

Futrell, Marvin

"National Urban Mass Transportation Statistics: 1989 Section 15 Annual Report", 7884–4

Future

see Projections and forecasts

Futures trading

Banks (insured commercial and savings) finances, for foreign and domestic offices, by asset size, 1989, annual rpt, 9294–4.2

Cocoa bean futures prices at NYC exchange, 1980s-92, FAS semiannual circular, 1925–9

Corn season average price forecasts using futures settlement prices, 1986-92, article, 1561–4.201

Cotton prices at selected spot markets, NYC futures prices, and CCC loan rates, 1990/91 and trends from 1943, annual rpt, 1309–2

Cotton prices in 8 spot markets, futures prices at NYC exchange, farm prices, and CCC loan stocks, monthly rpt, 1309–1

Dairy prices, by product and selected area, with related marketing data, 1990, annual rpt, 1317–1

Energy futures market dev, and crude oil contract activity, Aug 1990, article, 3162–11.201

Exchange activity in selected commodities and financial instruments and indexes, NYC, Chicago, and other markets, semimonthly rpt, 11922–5

Gold and silver futures trading, Mineral Industry Surveys, monthly rpt, 5612–1.10

Grain futures contracts, stocks in deliverable position by type, weekly tables, 11922–4

Grain futures settlement prices, by commodity and exchange, weekly rpt, 1313–2

Margin requirements and settlement activity relation to price volatility for 3 stock futures contracts, 1980s-90, technical paper, 9366–6.278

Margin requirements for futures contracts, impacts on price and trading activity, 1974-89, working paper, 9375–13.51

Natural gas spot and futures prices, daily press release, weekly data, 3162–44

Regulation of futures trading, CFTC and individual exchanges oversight, foreign activity, and customer views, late 1980s, hearing, 25168–77

Regulation of securities and commodity trading, activities and interagency coordination, FY91, annual rpt, 11924–4

Futures trading

Rice market activities, prices, inspections, sales, trade, supply, and use, for US and selected foreign markets, weekly rpt, 1313–8

Statistical Abstract of US, 1991 annual data compilation, 2324–1.15

Trading activity and system automation, with data by country, stock exchange, security type, and individual contract, 1980s-90, article, 9371–1.209

Trading activity by commodity and exchange, and Commodity Futures Trading Commission oversight, FY90, annual rpt, 11924–2

see also Chicago Board of Trade

see also Options trading

Gabon

- Agricultural exports of high-value commodities, indexes and sales by commodity, world area, and country, 1960s-86, 1528–323
- Agricultural trade of US, by detailed commodity and country, 1989, annual rpt, 1524–8
- Agricultural trade of US, by detailed commodity and country, 1990, semiannual rpt, 1522–4
- AID economic aid to developing countries, obligations and disbursements by country, quarterly rpt, 9912–4
- Dairy imports, consumption, and market conditions, by sub-Saharan Africa country, 1961-88, 1528–321
- Economic and military aid and loans from US and intl agencies, by program and country, FY46-90, annual rpt, 9914–5
- Economic conditions, income, production, prices, employment, and trade, 1991 periodic country rpt, 2046–4.42
- Economic conditions, investment and export opportunities, and trade practices, 1991 country market research rpt, 2046–6.6
- Economic, social, political, and geographic summary data, by country, 1991, annual factbook, 9114–2
- Exports and imports of US, by commodity and country, 1970-89, world area rpt, 9116–1.6
- Exports and imports of US, by selected country, country group, and commodity group, 1990, annual rpt, 2044–37
- Exports and imports of US, by transport mode, country, and SITC 1- to 3-digit commodity, 1990, annual rpt, 2424–12
- Exports of US, detailed Schedule B commodities with countries of destination, 1990, annual rpt, 2424–10
- Human rights conditions in 170 countries, and US economic and military aid, 1990, annual rpt, 21384–3
- Military aid of US, arms sales, and training programs costs and budget requests, by program, world region, and country, FY90-92, annual rpt, 7144–13
- *Minerals Yearbook, 1988,* Vol 3: foreign country review of production, trade, and policy, by commodity, annual rpt, 5604–17.80
- Oil exports to US by OPEC and non-OPEC countries, monthly rpt, 3162–24.3
- Oil production, trade, use, and stocks, by selected country and country group, monthly rpt, 3162–42

UN voting record and share of votes in agreement with US, by issue, country, and world area, 1990, annual rpt, 7004–18

see also under By Foreign Country in the "Index by Categories"

Gabriel, Wendy L.

"Distribution of Sexually Immature Components of 10 Northwest Atlantic Groundfish Species Based on Northeast Fisheries Center Bottom Trawl Surveys, 1968-86", 2168–122

Gadsden, Ala.

see also under By SMSA or MSA in the "Index by Categories"

Gagnon, Joseph E.

"How Pervasive Is the Product Cycle? The Empirical Dynamics of American and Japanese Trade Flows", 9366–7.264

Gagnon, Raymond O.

- "National Ambulatory Medical Care Survey: 1989 Summary", 4146–8.206
- "Office Visits by Black Patients, National Ambulatory Medical Care Survey: U.S., 1975-76", 4147–16.5

Gail, Mitchell H.

"Projections of the Incidence of Non-Hodgkin's Lymphoma Related to Acquired Immunodeficiency Syndrome", 4472–1.212

Gainesville, Fla.

Wages by occupation, for office and plant workers, 1991 survey, periodic MSA rpt, 6785–12.5

see also under By SMSA or MSA in the "Index by Categories"

Gale, Fred

"Estimating Entry and Exit of U.S. Farms", 1598–269

Galginaitis, Michael

"Point Lay Case Study. Alaska Social and Economic Study", 5736–5.8

Gallipolis, Ohio

Wages by occupation, and benefits for office and plant workers, 1991 survey, periodic MSA rpt, 6785–3.5

Gallium

see Metals and metal industries

Galveston, Tex.

- CPI by component for US city average, and by region, population size, and for 15 metro areas, monthly rpt, 6762–1
- CPI by component for US city average, and by region, population size, and for 27 metro areas, monthly rpt, 6762–2
- Housing starts and completions authorized by building permits in 40 MSAs, quarterly rpt, 2382–9

see also under By SMSA or MSA in the "Index by Categories"

Gamber, Edward N.

"Magnification Effects and Acyclical Real Wages", 9377–9.114

Gambia

- Agricultural exports of high-value commodities, indexes and sales by commodity, world area, and country, 1960s-86, 1528–323
- Agricultural trade of US, by detailed commodity and country, 1989, annual rpt, 1524–8
- Agricultural trade of US, by detailed commodity and country, 1990, semiannual rpt, 1522–4
- AID cash transfers to Gambia linked to fiscal and govt reforms, effectiveness, 1987-89, 9916–1.74

Index by Subjects and Names

- AID economic aid to developing countries, obligations and disbursements by country, quarterly rpt, 9912–4
- Dairy imports, consumption, and market conditions, by sub-Saharan Africa country, 1961-88, 1528–321
- Economic and military aid and loans from US and intl agencies, by program and country, FY46-90, annual rpt, 9914–5
- Economic and social conditions of developing countries from 1960s, and Intl Dev Cooperation Agency and AID activities and funding, FY90-92, annual rpt, 9904–4
- Economic, population, and agricultural data, US and other aid sources, and AID activity, 1989 country rpt, 9916–12.33
- Economic, social, political, and geographic summary data, by country, 1991, annual factbook, 9114–2
- Human rights conditions in 170 countries, and US economic and military aid, 1990, annual rpt, 21384–3
- Military aid of US, arms sales, and training programs costs and budget requests, by program, world region, and country, FY90-92, annual rpt, 7144–13
- UN voting record and share of votes in agreement with US, by issue, country, and world area, 1990, annual rpt, 7004–18

Gambling

- Arrest rates, by offense, sex, age, and race, 1965-89, annual rpt, 6224–7
- Arrests, by offense, offender characteristics, and location, data compilation, 1991 annual rpt, 6064–6.4
- Arrests, by offense, offender characteristics, and location, 1990, annual rpt, 6224–2.2
- Court civil and criminal caseloads for Federal district, appeals, and bankruptcy courts, by type of suit and offense, circuit, and district, 1990, annual rpt, 18204–11
- Court civil and criminal caseloads for Federal district, appeals, and special courts, 1990, annual rpt, 18204–8
- Court civil and criminal caseloads for Federal district courts, 1991, annual rpt, 18204–2.1
- Court criminal case processing in Federal district courts, and dispositions, by offense, district, and offender characteristics, 1986, annual rpt, 6064–29
- Court criminal case processing in Federal district courts, and dispositions, by offense, 1980-89, annual rpt, 6064–31
- Court criminal cases in Federal district courts, by offense, disposition, and district, 1980-90, last issue of annual rpt, 18204–1
- Public opinion on legalized betting, by respondent characteristics, data compilation, 1991 annual rpt, 6064–6.2
- Puerto Rico economic censuses, 1987: hotel and motel receipts by source, subject rpt, 2591–2.2
- Sentences for Federal crimes, guidelines use and results by offense and district, and Sentencing Commission activities, 1990, annual rpt, 17664–1
- Sentences for Federal offenses, guidelines by offense and circumstances, series, 17668–1
- Tax (excise) collections of IRS, by source, quarterly rpt, 8302–1

Index by Subjects and Names

Gasohol

Tax (excise) returns filed, by type of return and IRS district, 1989 and projected 1990-97, annual rpt, 8304–24

Tax (excise) returns filed, by type of tax and IRS region and service center, projected 1990-97 and trends from 1978, annual rpt, 8304–9

Tax (income) withholding and related documents filed, by type and IRS service center, 1990 and projected 1991-98, annual rpt, 8304–22

US attorneys civil and criminal cases by type and disposition, and collections, by Federal district, FY90, annual rpt, 6004–2.1

Wiretaps authorized, costs, arrests, trials, and convictions, by offense and jurisdiction, 1990, annual rpt, 18204–7

see also Horse racing

see also Lotteries

see also Pari-mutuel wagering

Game

see Birds and bird conservation

see Hunting and fishing licenses

see Hunting and trapping

see Wildlife and wildlife conservation

Games

see Toys and games

Gangs, criminal

see Organized crime

Gansner, David A.

"Timber Value Growth Rates in New England", 1208–348

GAO

see General Accounting Office

Garbage

see Landfills

see Refuse and refuse disposal

Garcia, Jesus M.

"Hispanic Population in the U.S.: March 1990", 2546–1.448

"Hispanic Population in the U.S.: March 1991", 2546–1.451

Garden Grove, Calif.

see also under By City in the "Index by Categories"

Gardening

see Flowers and nursery products

see Horticulture

see Lawn and garden equipment

Garfinkel, Michelle R.

"Economic Consequences of Reducing Military Spending", 9391–1.204

"Multiplier Approach to the Money Supply Process: A Precautionary Note", 9391–1.218

Garland, Tex.

see also under By City in the "Index by Categories"

Garment industry

see Clothing and clothing industry

Garner, C. Alan

"Forecasting Consumer Spending: Should Economists Pay Attention to Consumer Confidence Surveys?", 9381–1.206

Garner, Thesia I.

"Living Arrangements of Young Adults Living Independently: Evidence from the Luxembourg Income Study", 2546–2.157

Garnishment of wages

see Wage deductions

Garrison, Howard H.

"Levels of Mathematics Achievement: Initial Performance Standards for the 1990 NAEP Mathematics Assessment", 4896–8.2

Garrison, Louis P., Jr.

"Medicaid, the Uninsured, and National Health Spending: Federal Policy Implications", 4652–1.220

Gary, Ind.

CPI by component for US city average, and by region, population size, and for 15 metro areas, monthly rpt, 6762–1

CPI by component for US city average, and by region, population size, and for 27 metro areas, monthly rpt, 6762–2

Housing starts and completions authorized by building permits in 40 MSAs, quarterly rpt, 2382–9

see also under By City and By SMSA or MSA in the "Index by Categories"

Gas appliances

see Household appliances and equipment

Gas utilities

see Natural gas and gas industry

Gas wells

see Energy exploration and drilling

Gases

Accident deaths and rates, by cause, age, sex, race, and State, 1988, US Vital Statistics annual rpt, 4144–2

Accidents (occupational) injury and illness rates by SIC 2- to 4-digit industry, and deaths by cause and industry div, 1989, annual rpt, 6844–1

Business statistics, detailed data for major industries and economic indicators, *Survey of Current Business*, monthly rpt, 2702–1.12

County Business Patterns, 1988: employment, establishments, and payroll, by SIC 2- to 4-digit industry and county, annual State rpt series, 2326–6

County Business Patterns, 1989: employment, establishments, and payroll, by SIC 2- to 4-digit industry and county, annual State rpt series, 2326–8

Exports and imports between US and outlying areas, by detailed commodity and mode of transport, 1990, annual rpt, 2424–11

Exports and imports of US, by country and detailed commodity, monthly rpt, 2422–12

Exports and imports of US, by Harmonized System 6-digit commodity and country, 1990, annual rpt, 2424–13

Exports and imports of US, by transport mode, country, and SITC 1- to 3-digit commodity, 1990, annual rpt, 2424–12

Exports of US, detailed Schedule B commodities with countries of destination, 1990, annual rpt, 2424–10

Helium and other components of natural gas, analyses of individual wells and pipelines, 1917-90, annual rpt, 5604–2

Helium market demand and Bur of Mines production, sales, and financial statements, FY90, annual rpt, 5604–32

Helium resources in storage and natural gas reserves, by State, 1950-89 and projected to 2020, biennial rpt, 5604–44

Hydrogen energy R&D activity and funding of DOE, and project listing, FY90, annual rpt, 3304–18

Manufacturing annual survey, 1989: finances and operations, by SIC 2- to 4-digit industry, series, 2506–15

Manufacturing census, 1987: employment and shipments under Fed Govt contracts, by SIC 4-digit industry, 2497–7

Manufacturing census, 1987: finances and operations, by SIC 2- to 4-digit industry, State, and MSA, with trends from 1849, 2497–1

Manufacturing census, 1987: finances and operations, by type of organization and SIC 2- to 4-digit industry, subject rpt, 2497–5

Minerals Yearbook, 1988, Vol 3: foreign country reviews of production, trade, and policy, by commodity, annual rpt series, 5604–17

Minerals Yearbook, 1989, Vol 1: commodity reviews of production, reserves, supply, use, and trade, annual rpt series, 5604–15

Minerals Yearbook, 1989, Vol 2: State reviews of production and sales by commodity, and business activity, annual rpt series, 5604–16

Minerals Yearbook, 1989, Vol 2: State reviews of production, sales, and firms, by commodity, and business activity, annual rpt, 5604–34

Minerals Yearbook, 1990, Vol 1: commodity reviews of production, reserves, supply, use, and trade, annual rpt series, 5604–20

Price indexes (producer), by stage of processing and detailed commodity, monthly rpt, 6762–6

Price indexes (producer), by stage of processing and detailed commodity, monthly 1990, annual rpt, 6764–2

Production and shipments of industrial gases, by product and State, 1989, annual Current Industrial Rpt, 2506–8.15

Production by State, shipments, trade, and use, by product for inorganic chemicals, 1990, annual Current Industrial Rpt, 2506–8.14

Production of industrial gases, by product, quarterly Current Industrial Rpt, 2506–8.3

Production, prices, trade, use, employment, tariffs, and stockpiles, by mineral, with foreign comparisons, 1986-90, annual rpt, 5604–18

see also Air pollution

see also Liquefied petroleum gas

see also Natural gas and gas industry

see also Natural gas liquids

see also Radon

see also under By Commodity in the "Index by Categories"

Gaske, M. Ellen

"Sources of Fluctuations in Long-Term Expected Real Rates of Interest: Evidence from the UK Indexed Bond Market", 9385–8.119

Gasohol

Auto alternative fuels costs, emissions, health impacts, and characteristics, 1990 rpt, 9196–5.1

Consumption and tax rates for motor fuel, by fuel type and State, monthly rpt, 7552–1

Consumption of gasohol, by State, 1980-87, annual rpt, 3304–5.2

Consumption of gasohol, by State, 1990, annual rpt, 7554–1.1

Consumption of gasohol, prices, efficiency, trade, and specifications, by type, 1979-87, annual rpt, 3304–5.4

Gasohol

Consumption of gasohol, sales and tax rates by State, 1983-90, annual rpt, 3304–9

Consumption of wood, waste, and alcohol fuels, by end-use sector and region, 1989, 3166–6.56

Energy use by mode of transport, fuel supply, and demographic and economic factors of vehicle use, 1970s-89, annual rpt, 3304–5

Tax (excise) rates for motor fuels, by State, 1980-89, annual table, 7554–32

Tax provisions of States for motor fuel, auto registration fees, and disposition of receipts, by State, as of Jan 1991, biennial rpt, 7554–37

Gasoline

Agriculture census, 1987: farms, farmland, production, finances, and operator characteristics, by county, final State rpt series, 2331–1

Auto fuel economy test results for US and foreign makes, 1992 model year, annual rpt, 3304–11

Auto, private airplane, and motorcycle operating costs by component, and Fed Govt mileage reimbursement rates, 1989, annual rpt, 9454–13

Business statistics, detailed data for major industries and economic indicators, *Survey of Current Business*, monthly rpt, 2702–1.18

Consumption and tax rates for motor fuel, by fuel type and State, monthly rpt, 7552–1

Consumption of energy, by detailed fuel type, end-use sector, and State, 1960-89, State Energy Data System annual rpt, 3164–39

Consumption of gasoline, and taxes, by State, 1989-90, annual rpt, 7554–24

Consumption of motor fuel, by consuming sector and State, 1990, annual rpt, 7554–1.1

CPI by component for US city average, and by region, population size, and for 27 metro areas, monthly rpt, 6762–2

Exports and imports of US, by country and detailed commodity, monthly rpt, 2422–12

Exports and imports of US, by Harmonized System 6-digit commodity and country, 1990, annual rpt, 2424–13

Exports of US, detailed Schedule B commodities with countries of destination, 1990, annual rpt, 2424–10

Farm prices received and paid, by commodity and State, 1990, annual rpt, 1629–5

Farm prices received for major products and paid for farm inputs and living items, by commodity and State, monthly rpt, 1629–1

Farm production inputs supply, demand, and prices, 1970s-90 and projected to 1995, article, 1561–16.201

Farm production inputs supply, demand, and prices, 1980s-91 and forecast 1992, article, 1561–16.204

Farm production itemized costs, by farm sales size and region, 1990, annual rpt, 1614–3

Fed Govt energy use and efficiency, by agency and fuel type, FY90, annual rpt, 3304–22

Index by Subjects and Names

Foreign and US oil production, trade, stocks, and prices, by refined product and country, 1977-89, annual rpt, 3164–50.6

Foreign and US oil production, trade, stocks, and prices, by refined product and country, 1986-89, annual rpt, 3164–50.2

Foreign direct investment in US energy sources by type and firm, and US affiliates operations, as of 1989, annual rpt, 3164–80

Futures and options trading volume, by commodity and exchange, FY90, annual rpt, 11924–2

Futures trading in selected commodities and financial instruments and indexes, NYC, Chicago, and other markets activity, semimonthly rpt, 11922–5

Injuries from use of consumer products, by severity, victim age, and detailed product, 1990, annual rpt, 9164–6

Iraq invasion of Kuwait, impacts on oil prices and industry profits, as of 4th qtr 1990, 3166–6.46

Iraq invasion of Kuwait, impacts on oil supply and prices, selected indicators, daily press release, 3162–44

Manufacturing annual survey, 1989: finances and operations, by SIC 2- to 4-digit industry, series, 2506–15

Mineral industries census, 1987: energy use and costs, by fuel type, SIC 2- to 4-digit industry, and State, subject rpt, 2517–2

Naval Petroleum and Oil Shale Reserves production and revenue by fuel type, sales by purchaser, and wells, by reserve, FY90, annual rpt, 3334–3

Pollution (air) emissions factors, by detailed pollutant and source, data compilation, 1990 rpt, 9198–120

Pollution (air) levels for 6 pollutants, by source, 1970-89 and trends from 1940, annual rpt, 9194–13

Price indexes (producer), by stage of processing and detailed commodity, monthly rpt, 6762–6

Price indexes (producer), by stage of processing and detailed commodity, monthly 1990, annual rpt, 6764–2

Prices (retail) of gasoline, response to wholesale price changes, by grade, 1983-90, article, 9391–1.216

Prices and spending for fuel, by type, end-use sector, and State, 1989, annual rpt, 3164–64

Prices and volume of oil products sold and purchased by refiners, processors, and distributors, by product, end-use sector, PAD district, and State, monthly rpt with articles, 3162–11

State and Metro Area Data Book, 1991 data compilation, 2328–54

Statistical Abstract of US, 1991 annual data compilation, 2324–1.25

Supply and demand of oil and refined products, refinery capacity and use, and prices, weekly rpt, 3162–32

Supply, demand, and movement of crude oil, gas liquids, and refined products, by PAD district and State, 1990, annual rpt, 3164–2

Supply, demand, and prices, by fuel type and end-use sector, alternative projections 1989-2010, annual rpt, 3164–75

Supply, demand, and prices, by fuel type and end-use sector, projections and underlying assumptions, 1990-2010, annual rpt, 3164–90

Supply, demand, and prices, by fuel type and end-use sector, with foreign comparisons, 1990 and trends from 1949, annual rpt, 3164–74.1; 3164–74.2

Supply, demand, and prices, by fuel type, end-use sector, and country, detailed data, monthly rpt with articles, 3162–24

Supply, demand, and prices of crude oil and refined products, and refinery capacity and stocks, by State, 1960-91, annual rpt, 3164–95

Supply, demand, and prices of energy, forecasts by resource type, quarterly rpt, 3162–34

Supply, demand, and prices of oil and gas, alternative projections 1989-2010, annual rpt, 3164–89

Supply, demand, prices, and taxes for gasoline, and auto registrations and travel, 1900s-89, 3168–120

Supply, demand, trade, stocks, and refining of oil and gas liquids, by detailed product, State, and PAD district, monthly rpt with articles, 3162–6

Transit systems finances and operations, by mode of transport, size of fleet, and for 468 systems, 1989, annual rpt, 7884–4

Transportation energy use by mode, fuel supply, and demographic and economic factors of vehicle use, 1970s-89, annual rpt, 3304–5

Wholesale trade census, 1987: oil bulk stations, sales and storage capacity by product, inventories, expenses, employment, and modes of transport, 2407–4.2

see also Aviation fuels

see also Diesel fuel

see also Fuel tax

see also Gasohol

see also Gasoline service stations

Gasoline service stations

Alternative motor fuels costs, emissions, health impacts, and characteristics, series, 9196–5

Census of Retail Trade, 1987: depreciable assets, capital and operating expenses, sales, value added, and inventories, by SIC 2- to 4-digit kind of business, 2399–2

Census of Retail Trade, 1987: finances and employment, for establishments with and without payroll, by SIC 2- to 4-digit kind of business, State, and MSA, 2401–1

Construction authorized by building permits, by type of construction, region, State, and MSA, bimonthly rpt, 2042–1.3

County Business Patterns, 1988: employment, establishments, and payroll, by SIC 2- to 4-digit industry and county, annual State rpt series, 2326–6

County Business Patterns, 1989: employment, establishments, and payroll, by SIC 2- to 4-digit industry and county, annual State rpt series, 2326–8

Credit (installment) outstanding, and terms, by lender and credit type, monthly rpt, 9365–2.6

Employment, earnings, and hours, by SIC 1- to 4-digit industry, monthly and annual averages, selected years 1909-90, annual rpt, 6744–4

Enterprise Statistics, 1987: auxiliaries of multi-establishment firms, finances and operations by function, industry, and State, 2329–6

Index by Subjects and Names

Enterprise Statistics, 1987: finances and operations for companies, by size, level of diversification, form of organization, and industry group, 2329–8

Foreign direct investment in US energy sources by type and firm, and US affiliates operations, as of 1989, annual rpt, 3164–80

Labor productivity, indexes of output, hours, and employment by SIC 2- to 4-digit industry, 1967-89, annual rpt, 6824–1.4

Mail volume to and from households, use, and views, by class, source, content, and household characteristics, 1987-88, annual rpt, 9864–10

Occupational injury and illness rates, by SIC 2- to 4-digit industry, 1988-89, annual rpt, 6844–7

Occupational injury and illness rates, by SIC 2- to 4-digit industry, 1989, annual rpt, 6844–1

Pollution (air) emissions factors, by detailed pollutant and source, data compilation, 1990 rpt, 9198–120

Puerto Rico economic censuses, 1987: wholesale and retail trade and service industry finances and operations, by SIC 2- to 4-digit industry and municipio, 2591–1

Puerto Rico economic censuses, 1987: wholesale, retail, and service industries finances and operations, by establishment characteristics and SIC 2- and 3-digit industry, subject rpts, 2591–2

Robberies, by type of premises, population size, and region, 1990, annual rpt, 6224–2.1

Sales and inventories, by kind of retail business, region, and selected State, MSA, and city, monthly rpt, 2413–3

Sales, inventories, purchases, gross margin, and accounts receivable, by SIC 2- to 4-digit kind of business and form of ownership, 1989, annual rpt, 2413–5

Sales of retailers, by kind of business, advance monthly rpt, 2413–2

State and Metro Area Data Book, 1991 data compilation, 2328–54

Tax (income) returns of corporations, income and tax items by asset size and detailed industry, 1987, annual rpt, 8304–4

Tax (income) returns of corporations, income and tax items by asset size and detailed industry, 1988, annual rpt, 8304–21

Tax (income) returns of partnerships, income statement and balance sheet items, by industry group, 1989, annual article, 8302–2.216; 8304–18

Tax (income) returns of sole proprietorships, income statement items, by industry group, 1989, annual article, 8302–2.214

Tax provisions of States for motor fuel, auto registration fees, and disposition of receipts, by State, as of Jan 1991, biennial rpt, 7554–37

see also Automobile repair and maintenance

Gasoline tax

see Fuel tax

Gastonia, N.C.

Housing starts and completions authorized by building permits in 40 MSAs, quarterly rpt, 2382–9

Wages by occupation, and benefits for office and plant workers, 1991 survey, periodic MSA rpt, 6785–12.7

see also under By SMSA or MSA in the "Index by Categories"

Gastrointestinal diseases

see Digestive diseases

Gates, Joseph S.

"Water Resources Activities in Utah by the USGS, Oct. 1, 1988-Sept. 30, 1989", 5666–26.15

GATT

see Trade agreements

Gatton, David E.

"U.S. Petroleum Supply", 3164–2.1

Gavin, Michael

"Terms of Trade, the Trade Balance, and Stability: The Role of Savings Behavior", 9366–7.251

Gavin, William T.

"Zero Inflation: Transition Costs and Shoe-Leather Benefits", 9377–9.122

GDP

see Gross Domestic Product

Geiman, Russell R.

"How Are We Doing? An Analysis of Projection Accuracy", 8304–8.1

Gelardi, Robert C.

"Low Calorie Sweeteners Outlook", 1004–16.1

Gemstones

Exports and imports between US and outlying areas, by detailed commodity and mode of transport, 1990, annual rpt, 2424–11

Exports and imports of US, by country and detailed commodity, monthly rpt, 2422–12

Exports and imports of US, by Harmonized System 6-digit commodity and country, 1990, annual rpt, 2424–13

Exports and imports of US, by selected country, country group, and commodity group, 1990, annual rpt, 2044–37

Exports of US, detailed Schedule B commodities with countries of destination, 1990, annual rpt, 2424–10

Mineral Industry Surveys, commodity review of production, trade, and use, 1988-90, advance annual rpt, 5614–5.10

Mineral Industry Surveys, State reviews of production, 1990, preliminary annual rpt, 5614–6

Minerals Yearbook, 1988, Vol 3: foreign country reviews of production, trade, and policy, by commodity, annual rpt series, 5604–17

Minerals Yearbook, 1989, Vol 1: commodity review of production, reserves, supply, use, and trade, annual rpt, 5604–15.26

Minerals Yearbook, 1989, Vol 2: State reviews of production and sales by commodity, and business activity, annual rpt series, 5604–16

Minerals Yearbook, 1989, Vol 2: State reviews of production, sales, and firms, by commodity, and business activity, annual rpt, 5604–34

Minerals Yearbook, 1990, Vol 1: commodity review of production, reserves, supply, use, and trade, annual rpt, 5604–20.22

Occupational injuries and incidence, employment, and hours in nonmetallic minerals mines and related operations, 1989, annual rpt, 6664–1

General Accounting Office

Production, prices, trade, use, employment, tariffs, and stockpiles, by mineral, with foreign comparisons, 1986-90, annual rpt, 5604–18

Production, reserves, and use of industrial minerals, and characteristics of individual deposits, State rpt series, 5606–10

Stockpiling of strategic material by Fed Govt, activity, and inventory by commodity, as of Mar 1991, semiannual rpt, 3542–22

Stockpiling of strategic material, inventories and needs, by commodity, as of Jan 1991, annual rpt, 3544–37

see also Jewelry

see also under By Commodity in the "Index by Categories"

Genay, Hesna

"Japan's Corporate Groups", 9375–1.203

General Accounting Office

Acquisitions (leveraged buyout) impacts on financial performance, for 4 transactions, 1980s-90, GAO rpt, 26119–355

Activities and operations of GAO, and resulting cost savings to Fed Govt, FY90, annual rpt, 26104–1

AFDC Job Opportunities and Basic Skills Training Program Federal and State funding by State, and administrators views, 1989-91, GAO rpt, 26121–435

Africa economic and dev aid fund of AID, funding by project, 1980s-90, GAO rpt, 26123–333

Agricultural export market research and promotion activities of USDA, with background data, 1991 GAO rpt, 26113–504

AID dev funds obligated but unspent by country, and impacts of alternative allocation formulas, FY87-90, GAO rpt, 26123–327

AID dev project procurement under host country contracts, oversight issues with background data, 1991 GAO rpt, 26123–342

AID energy assistance to developing countries, and global warming reduction activities, 1980s-FY92, GAO rpt, 26123–352

AIDS virus antibody tests and counseling sessions by setting, and CDC funding and funds uncommitted by State, 1989-90, GAO rpt, 26121–428

Air Force recruiting compliance with gender-neutral selection, with aptitude test results by sex, FY86-90, GAO rpt, 26123–359

Air taxi and commuter airlines operating certificates, FAA revocations for safety violations, 1987-91, GAO rpt, 26113–547

Air traffic control staffing levels, by job level and selected facility, FY88-90, GAO rpt, 26113–522

Aircraft accidents victims compensation, legal costs, and time to disposition, under intl agreements and US liability system, aggregate 1970-84, GAO rpt, 26113–501

Aircraft maintenance by independent repair stations, airlines use and costs, 1980s-90, GAO rpt, 26113–492

Aircraft maintenance requirements of FAA for aging craft, airlines compliance and repair facilities operations, 1989-91, GAO rpt, 26113–527

General Accounting Office

Index by Subjects and Names

Aircraft noise abatement measures, and industry compliance costs, aggregate FY90-2000, GAO rpt, 26113–534

Airline consumer complaints, passengers denied boarding, and late flights, by carrier, 1985-91, GAO rpt, 26113–542

Alaska North Slope oil production, and impacts of lifting export controls on US oil trade, West Coast prices, and shipping industry, 1988 and forecast 1995, GAO rpt, 26113–496

Alcohol, Tobacco, and Firearms Bur regulatory activities, staff, and funding, and tax revenues and rates, 1980s-91, GAO rpt, 26119–335

Anesthesiologists reimbursement by Medicare, charges, and time billed, 1987, GAO rpt, 26121–417

Animals use in Army brain wound research, usefulness of Louisiana State University experiments, with results, 1980s, GAO rpt, 26121–396

Army equipment unserviceable inventories, and repair and replacement costs, late 1980s, GAO rpt, 26123–312

Army Reserve and National Guard wartime preparedness, for general support maintenance units, as of May 1990, GAO rpt, 26123–354

Assistance (formula grants) of Fed Govt, use of Census of Population data for allocation, and effects of data errors on funding, with data by program and State, FY91, GAO rpt, 26119–361

Bank deposit insurance system reform issues, with background industry financial data, 1970s-90, GAO rpt, 26119–320

Bank holding company subsidiaries dealing in bank-ineligible securities, subsidiary and parent firm finances, 1989-91, GAO rpt, 26119–280

Banks regulatory enforcement activities of Federal agencies, effectiveness, with data on capital-deficient banks, late 1980s-90, GAO rpt, 26119–334

Boycotts (intl) by OPEC and other countries, US taxpayers IRS filings, cooperation, and tax benefits denied, 1976-86, GAO rpt, 26119–349

Bridges repair and replacement needs under alternative assessment methods, 1990 and projected to 1996, GAO rpt, 26113–539

Budget of US, authoritative financial statements with appropriations, outlays, and receipts, by category and agency, FY90, annual rpt, 8104–2.1

Budget of US, obligations and authority by function, agency, and program, with summaries, analyses, and historical tables, FY92, annual rpt, 104–2

Bulgaria trade with US, US tariffs, and impacts of US granting most favored nation status, 1987-90, GAO rpt, 26123–323

Cambodia refugees in Thailand border camps by site, and UN aid by donor country, 1980s, GAO rpt, 26123–313

Canada universal health care system operations and costs, and implications for US, 1987-91, GAO rpt, 26121–424

Cancer treatments using chemotherapy drugs for indications not listed on drug label, costs, and insurance reimbursement problems, 1990 physicians survey, GAO rpt, 26131–81

Census of Population, 1990: data enumeration errors under alternative definitions, and compared to 1980, GAO rpt, 26119–353

Census of Population, 1990: post-enumeration survey use for adjusting census counts, with estimates of undercount by race, 1950-80, GAO rpt, 26119–327

Child abuse and neglect prevention funding by States, and funding sources, FY89, GAO rpt, 26121–423

Child labor law violations and injuries by industry group, and employment of minors by selected characteristics, 1983-90, GAO rpt, 26121–426

Cocaine and alternative crop production in Andean countries, and impacts on US agricultural exports, with data for Bolivia, 1980s-91, GAO rpt, 26123–366

Computer mainframe and related equipment procurement and compatibility, for Federal agencies, FY86-89, GAO rpt series, 26125–41

Computer records matching of welfare data, Federal and State agencies compliance with recipient protection provisions before benefits reduction, 1990, GAO rpt, 26121–404

Consultants and experts appointed for temporary employment in Federal agencies, and rule violations, 1986-89, GAO rpt, 26119–354

Consulting services contracts of Fed Govt, obligations by agency, FY87-89, GAO rpt, 26119–343

Containers (beverage) natl deposit law proposal, public views, with State deposit laws effectiveness, 1970s-89, GAO rpt, 26113–494

Crime victim compensation and support service applications by disposition, and grant funding by State, 1986-91, GAO rpt, 26119–348

Criminal justice system workload impacts of budgetary changes, model description, 1991 GAO rpt, 26119–340

Dairy cooperatives exemption from antitrust laws, impacts on industry structure and pricing, with background data, 1930s-80s, GAO rpt, 26113–499

Defense Logistics Agency processing of supply requisitions, duration and efficiency, FY89, GAO rpt, 26123–331

Developing countries disabled persons aid program activities and funding, for UN, AID, and Intl Labor Organization, late 1970s-90, GAO rpt, 26123–321

Disaster aid of USDA for producers of crops ineligible for price supports by State, and methodology, 1988-89, GAO rpt, 26113–533

Disaster relief funding and response by FEMA, for Loma Prieta earthquake and Hurricane Hugo, 1989-90, GAO rpt, 26113–511

Drug (prescription) advertising direct to consumer, benefits and problems, review of studies published 1984-91, GAO rpt, 26131–86

Drug and alcohol abuse in rural areas, related crime, and treatment, with comparisons to nonrural areas, by substance and State, 1988-90, GAO rpt, 26131–79

Drug enforcement support activities of Natl Guard, spending and needs by State, FY89-91, GAO rpt, 26123–343

Drug smuggling interdiction programs, budget, and seizures of Fed govt, FY87-90, GAO rpt, 26119–318

Drug testing of Federal employees, results, and costs, by agency, FY87-92, GAO rpt, 26119–344

Eastern Europe economic aid of US, by agency and country, FY90-92, GAO rpt, 26123–319

Education Dept enforcement activities to eliminate discrimination within schools, and adequacy, FY81-91, GAO rpt, 26121–427

Education Dept Research Library proposed services, educators and librarians views, 1990 survey, GAO rpt, 26121–414

EIA data collection and analysis activities, 1987-90, annual narrative rpt, 26104–14

Electric utilities purchase contracts with nonutility generators, competitive bidding use, 1980s-90, GAO rpt, 26113–498

Embassy and other US diplomatic facilities security improvement construction projects costs and activities, 1986-90, GAO rpt, 26123–322

Employee recruitment, hiring, compensation, and other employment practices of large firms, 1989 survey, GAO rpt, 26119–324

Employment of minorities and women by Fed Govt, and compliance with EEOC standards, by occupation and agency, FY88-92, GAO rpt, 26119–342

Employment services local offices operations, State and Federal oversight, staff, and costs, 1983-91, GAO rpt, 26121–430

Energy aid for low income households, State and Federal funding, FY86-89, GAO rpt, 26121–401

Farm operators reorganizations to remain under USDA crop subsidy payment limits, effectiveness of laws to prevent abuse, 1989, GAO rpt, 26113–546

FDA Freedom of Info Act requests and processing time, by office, 1986-89, GAO rpt, 26121–436

Fed Govt aid to State and local areas, programs and funding, FY90, GAO rpt, 26121–421

Fed Govt property acquired through foreclosure and savings instn failure, 1-family homes inventory by State, acquisition costs, and sales, for 4 agencies, 1986-90, GAO rpt, 26113–513

Fed Govt shutdown over Columbus Day holiday, employees affected, costs, and savings, Oct 1990, GAO rpt, 26119–311

Firearm accident deaths and injuries by selected city, and effects of gun design modifications, 1988-89, GAO rpt, 26131–80

Fish catch in excess of domestic processor needs, and use of estimates for Alaska fishing rights allocation, 1984-90, GAO rpt, 26113–523

FmHA farm and rural housing program loan appeals filed in 3 States, by disposition, 1988-90, GAO rpt, 26113–516

FmHA loan servicing eligibility, use, and effects on borrowers solvency, 1988-89, GAO rpt, 26113–497

Index by Subjects and Names

General Accounting Office

FmHA property acquired through foreclosure, value, and acreage under conservation easements by State, 1989-90, GAO rpt, 26113–514

Food aid program for children during summer vacation, nonprofit sponsors compliance with USDA regulations, 1989-90, GAO rpt, 26113–541

Food safety and quality regulation activities, funding, and staff, by Federal agency, 1980s, GAO rpt, 26113–503

Foreign countries health care cost control measures and insurance provisions, for Germany, France, and Japan, 1960s-91, GAO rpt, 26121–437

Foreign direct investment in US commercial real estate, by State and country, 1980s, GAO rpt, 26123–350

Forest Service recreation programs funding, and cost sharing pledges, 1980s-91, GAO rpt, 26113–518

Forests (natl) recreation sites, capacity, funding, and maintenance needs, 1980s-90, GAO rpt, 26113–502

Foster care placements, discharges, and returns to care, by selected characteristics of children, and length of stay factors, 1985-86, GAO rpt, 26121–432

Fraud cases of Federal agencies involving small dollar amounts, investigations, dispositions, losses, and collections, 1986-90, GAO rpt, 26111–76

Global climate change research, Federal budget by agency, and alternative estimates of contributing gases levels and impacts, late 1980s-90, GAO rpt, 26113–495

Govt-sponsored enterprises financial condition and capital adequacy, with regulatory recommendations and data by enterprise, 1985-95, GAO rpt, 26119–296

Hazardous substances industrial releases, accuracy of EPA reporting, and nonreporting facilities by State and industry, 1987-90, GAO rpt, 26113–532

Hazardous waste treatment facility closures, by EPA review status and waste disposal method, 1991, GAO rpt, 26113–528

HHS employment of Hispanics in Mountain region, hiring and promotion practices, 1980s, GAO rpt, 26121–393

HHS research and evaluation programs, 1970-90, annual listing, 4004–30

Homeless aid organizations donations of surplus Federal property by State, and compared to other recipients, FY87-80, GAO rpt, 26113–538

Homeless persons aid programs of Fed Govt, program descriptions and funding, by agency and State, FY87-90, annual GAO rpt, 26104–21

Hospital closures and rates, with financial, operating, and market characteristics, by location, late 1980s, GAO rpt, 26121–392

Hospital trauma centers unreimbursed costs and other factors contributing to closure, and views on nontrauma care impacts, 1989-90, GAO rpt, 26121–419

Hospitals in rural areas, closures related to selected factors, 1980s, GAO rpt, 26121–409

Housing (low income) construction and repair loans of HUD to nonprofit organizations, project delays, and starts, 1980s, GAO rpt, 26113–506

Housing (low income) supply impacts of HUD programs to maintain supply and to deter insured mortgage prepayment, 1986-90 and projected to 2005, GAO rpt, 26131–84

Housing (low income) utility allowances used in HUD public housing and rent assistance programs, coverage and adequacy, 1985-89, GAO rpt, 26113–512

Housing mortgage secondary market underwriting guidelines, and indicators of discrimination, for Atlanta metro area, 1989, GAO rpt, 26113–500

Hwy funds pooled by States from FHwA funds for specific projects, demonstration project results, FY88-90, GAO rpt, 26113–471

Hwy Trust Fund revenues, tax rates, and spending, FY87-91 with projections to FY95, GAO rpt, 26113–544

Immigrant children education programs funding by Fed Govt and school districts, and student characteristics, 1980s, GAO rpt, 26121–418

Immigration and Naturalization Service mgmt effectiveness, applications processing, inspections, staffing, and funding, FY85-90, GAO rpt, 26119–317

Indian Affairs Bur funding under increased tribal authority, by program, tribe, and region, FY78-90, GAO rpt, 26113–508

Info security nondisclosure agreements for Federal and contractor employees, prepublication reviews, and costs, 1988-90, GAO rpt, 26123–328

Insurance (health) coverage, uninsured persons by employment and other characteristics and State, 1988, GAO rpt, 26121–403

Insurance (property and casualty) industry solvency monitoring by States, firms designated for increased attention, and views on monitoring system effectiveness, 1980s, GAO rpt, 26119–316

Investigations of Federal agency and program operations, summaries of findings, 1981-90, annual GAO rpt, 26104–5

Iraq agricultural imports under CCC export credit guarantee programs, FY81-90, GAO rpt, 26123–314

Iraq invasion of Kuwait, alien worker refugees fleeing from Iraq and Kuwait, intl aid by source, and costs to host and native countries, 1990-91, GAO rpt, 26123–326

IRS correspondence regarding adjustments to taxpayer accounts, quality, and accuracy of returns processing, 1987-90, GAO rpt, 26119–329

IRS returns processing and info distribution effectiveness, 1988-90, GAO rpt, 26119–319

IRS revenue agent attrition, separations by reason, and hires, by region and district, FY87-90, GAO rpt, 26119–345

Job Training Partnership Act State and local admin, funding, effectiveness, and participants, GAO rpt series, 26106–8

Juvenile status offender detentions in secure facilities, and States compliance with Federal policies to reduce detentions, 1983-89, GAO rpt, 26119–333

Labor Dept programs fraud and abuse, audits and investigations activity, and racketeering cases by type and disposition, FY88-89, GAO rpt, 26111–74

Labor Relations Natl Board cases, backlog, and processing time, 1960s-89, GAO rpt, 26121–395

Labs (independent clinical) profitability and cost indexes by customer type, and impacts of Medicare fee caps, 1988-89, GAO rpt, 26121–425

Labs of Fed Govt, technology transfer cooperative agreements, patents, royalties, and incentive payments to employees, by agency, FY89, GAO rpt, 26131–85

Land subsidence above coal mines, State property insurance program income and expenses in 6 States, 1990, GAO rpt, 26113–530

Loans, loan guarantees, and insurance programs of Fed Govt, outstanding amounts by agency and program, FY88-90, GAO rpt, 26111–65

Machine tool procurement by DOD of foreign-made tools, use of restriction waivers by service branch and country, FY86-89, GAO rpt, 26123–324

Medicaid eligibility expansion provisions, adoption by States, and impacts on service use and costs, 1984-89, GAO rpt, 26121–429

Medicaid funding shares of Fed Govt under alternative formulas, by State, FY89, GAO rpt, 26121–420

Medicaid HMO enrollees, payments, terminations, services use, and State oversight, for Chicago, Ill, late 1980s, GAO rpt, 26121–399

Medical malpractice claims resolution through arbitration and litigation, Michigan program cases, awards, duration, and costs, late 1970s-80s, GAO rpt, 26121–394

Medicare Hospital Insurance appeals backlog reduction actions of SSA Chicago administrative law judges, effectiveness, FY89, GAO rpt, 26121–398

Medicare payment limits on home health services, impacts of alternative determination methods on agencies finances, with data by service type, 1984-89, GAO rpt, 26121–400

Medicare supplemental private insurance loss ratio performance, sales abuse cases, and State enforcement, late 1980s, GAO rpt, 26121–410

Mexico agricultural trade with US by commodity, and trade restrictions, 1980s, GAO rpt, 26123–335

Middle East and East Africa economic and military aid from US and intl agencies, and US defense spending, FY80-90, GAO rpt, 26123–360

Middle East export controls of US, with trade, dual-use commodity licenses, and arms sales, by country, 1980s-90, GAO rpt, 26123–339

Military airfields joint use by civil aircraft, and effectiveness in reducing airport congestion, FY85-89, GAO rpt, 26113–524

Military autos and light trucks owned and leased by service branch, and costs and savings from GSA leases, FY89, GAO rpt, 26123–344

Military base closings, costs and savings for 71 Army and Navy bases, FY92-97, GAO rpt, 26123–341

General Accounting Office

Index by Subjects and Names

Military base closings in Europe, by service branch and location, FY91, GAO rpt, 26123–336

Military chemical and biological weapons research labs security measures, and govt and contractor staff, 1988-90, GAO rpt, 26123–356

Military computer systems engineering and technical support contract costs, late 1980s, GAO rpt, 26125–45

Military equipment leases by equipment type and service branch and feasibility of lease refinancing, 1988, GAO rpt, 26111–75

Military exercises using computer simulations, costs and effectiveness in Army Germany deployment exercise, 1969-90, GAO rpt, 26123–318

Military officers assigned to multiservice organizations, designation of critical positions for qualified joint specialty officers, 1987-90 and projected to 1994, GAO rpt, 26123–317

Military officers ROTC training enrollment, grads, staff, scholarships, and costs, by service branch, FY86-89, GAO rpt, 26123–337

Military personnel strengths, for active duty enlisted and officers, by sex and race, 1970s-90, GAO rpt, 26123–325

Military presence of US in Pacific basin, personnel, dependents, aircraft, ships, and costs, by service branch and location, 1990, GAO rpt, 26123–357

Military rail equipment inventory, defects, and repair and inspection needs, 1990, GAO rpt, 26113–535

Military reserve forces attrition, by reason, personnel characteristics, reserve component, and State, FY88, GAO rpt, 26123–329

Military reserve forces structure and training, for US and 5 European countries, as of 1990, GAO rpt, 26123–358

Military service academy costs by type, staffing, and grad advancement, FY88-90, GAO rpt, 26123–355

Military surplus property donations to intl and State relief programs, FY86-90, GAO rpt, 26123–316

Milk farm, processor, and retail prices in 29 cities, 1980s-91, GAO rpt, 26113–540

Minority Business Dev Agency special projects funding and mgmt, FY85-90, GAO rpt, 26113–517

Money laundering enforcement activities of IRS, staff, and funding, abatement, 1985-90, GAO rpt, 26123–338

Money laundering investigation network of Treasury Dept, funding, and staff detailed from other agencies, 1990-91, GAO rpt, 26119–330

Money laundering investigations of Fed Govt using IRS large cash transaction rpts, and rpts filed and penalties for nonfiling by region, 1989-91, GAO rpt, 26119–356

Motorcycle helmet use and mandatory use laws impacts on accident casualties and costs, literature review, 1956-89, GAO rpt, 26113–537

NASA science and engineering staff retirement rates, projected 1991-95, GAO rpt, 26123–348

Natl Agricultural Statistics Service minority group staff, promotion, and discrimination complaints, 1988-90, GAO rpt, 26119–326

Natl forests fish and wildlife activities funding, by source, FY88-90, GAO rpt, 26113–529

Navy aircraft pilots hours flown, by pilot category, aircraft type, and flight purpose, late 1980s, GAO rpt, 26123–332

Navy battleship *USS Iowa* explosion, safety and personnel mgmt issues, with technical analysis, FY89, GAO rpt, 26123–315

Navy command proposed decentralization and relocation from DC area, savings, and cost of living indicators for 14 MSAs, 1980s, GAO rpt, 26123–346

Navy flag officers, captains awaiting promotion, and billets, by pay grade and rank, as of Feb 1991, GAO rpt, 26123–340

Navy homeport construction proposals, assignments and costs compared to existing ports, 1990s, GAO rpt, 26123–347

Navy ship modernization program costs and admin, FY87, GAO rpt, 26123–320

Nuclear Waste Fund finances, and DOE Civilian Radioactive Waste Mgmt Office activities, quarterly GAO rpt, 26102–4

Nuclear weapons elimination under Intermediate-Range Nuclear Forces Treaty, US and USSR on site inspections, and US costs and staffing, FY89-91, GAO rpt, 26123–364

Nuclear weapons facilities of DOE, contract security forces skill deficiencies, and costs compared to Federal security, late 1980s, GAO rpt, 26113–493

Nuclear weapons labs and DOE screening of contractors for foreign ownership, control, or influence, compliance by lab, FY88-90, GAO rpt, 26113–520

OASDI retired-worker benefits, effect of proposal to privatize excess trust funds into individual accounts, 1990 GAO rpt, 26121–397

Occupational Safety and Health admin standards, enforcement, and training activities, inspectors views, 1989-90, GAO rpt, 26121–391

Oil and gas OCS leases suspended for environmental reasons and repurchased by Fed Govt, costs of cancellation for 3 States, 1990, GAO rpt, 26113–509

Oil spill from tanker Exxon Valdez, Federal cleanup and damage assessment costs, and reimbursement from Exxon, by agency, as of Sept 1990, GAO rpt, 26113–510

Older persons long-term care needs and costs, late 1980s and projected 2018-60, GAO rpt, 26121–433

Panama economic aid after US sanctions and military invasion, AID funding by program, as of 1991, GAO rpt, 26123–330

Park natl system accidents, crimes, hazardous waste sites, and funding, 1970s-91, GAO rpt, 26113–545

Part-time employment by health insurance coverage and worker characteristics, and temporary and contract employment, 1979-89, GAO rpt, 26121–411

Patent and Trademark Office patent application, issuance, and protection fees

and revenues under alternative fee schedules, FY92-93, GAO rpt, 26113–543

Pay comparability of Fed Govt with private industry, by occupation for 22 MSAs, 1989, GAO rpt, 26119–332

Pension benefits disparity between men and women in small business plans by selected participant and plan characteristics, impacts of 1986 Tax Reform Act, 1984-85, GAO rpt, 26121–412

Pension plans of firms acquired in leveraged buyouts, finances, participation, terminations, and replacements, 1982-87, GAO rpt, 26121–408

Persian Gulf War Navy and Marine Corps reserves mobilized, 1990-91, GAO rpt, 26123–351

Pesticide levels in food, comparison of US and UN standards, 1988-90, GAO rpt, 26131–88

Pollutants reproductive health and fetal dev effects, with production, trade, and Federal regulatory activities by selected substance, 1980s-90, GAO rpt, 26131–90

Pollution (water) areas and sources identification activities of EPA and State, 1991, GAO rpt, 26113–536

Postal Service Marketing and Customer Service Group expenses by type, FY87-90, GAO rpt, 26119–338

Prison construction and operating costs, capacity, and inmates, for Federal and State facilities, 1985-89, GAO rpt, 26119–341

Prisoners from Federal instns, halfway house placements, duration, and employment, and house capacity, 1990-91, GAO rpt, 26119–347

Prisons and jails operated under private contract, costs and characteristics of instns, by facility and State, 1990, GAO rpt, 26119–321

Public lands concession operations, receipts, and fees, by Federal agency and for top 100 firms, 1989, GAO rpt, 26113–531

Publications of GAO, FY90, annual listing, 26104–17

Publications of GAO, topical listings, series, 26106–10

Quality mgmt practices of corporations, effects on employee and customer relations, operations, and finances, 1988-89, GAO rpt, 26123–345

Railroad safety inspections by Fed Railroad Admin, defects and violations reported by type, 1985-89, GAO rpt, 26113–515

Refugee aid funding of Fed Govt and States, impacts of reductions, with data by selected State and California county, late 1980s, GAO rpt, 26121–402

Refugee aid funding of US by program, agency, and intl organization, and admissions to US, 1980s-90, GAO rpt, 26123–334

Resolution Trust Corp obligation limits compliance, and balance sheet, quarterly GAO rpt, 26102–6

Retirement housing centers tax-exempt bond use and other financing, defaults, and facility and resident characteristics, 1991 GAO rpt, 26119–328

Savings instns mortgage debt holdings and other assets, returns on assets, and impacts of qualified lender regulations, 1970s-89, GAO rpt, 26119–337

Index by Subjects and Names

Securities industry self-regulatory organizations oversight by SEC, violations, and complaints, FY86-89, GAO rpt, 26119–336

Securities intl markets computer use and risk mgmt methods, 1991 GAO rpt, 26125–44

Semiconductors and related equipment import dependency of US firms, and sales from Japan firms delayed and denied, 1988-91, GAO rpt, 26123–361

Single mothers earnings, employment and welfare benefits, and poverty status, 1989, GAO rpt, 26121–413

Small Business Admin surety bond guarantee program finances, and contracts by contractor race, obligee type, and region, FY87-89, GAO rpt, 26113–526

Social security earnings records errors and rates, by employment type, late 1930s-87, GAO rpt, 26121–422

Soviet Union economic conditions, CIA GNP estimation methods assessment, 1989, GAO rpt, 26123–365

Soviet Union oil production, exports, and investments, 1980s and projected to 1994, GAO rpt, 26123–349

Space programs involvement by private sector, commercial dev centers funding sources and flight requests, 1986-90, GAO rpt, 26123–353

Space science missions data archival storage of NASA, holdings, and missions not archived, 1950s-91, 26125–43

SSA and other sources of beneficiary death info, use and erroneous benefit payments by agency, 1990, GAO rpt, 26121–406

SSA public access by telephone, local line availability and effects of nationwide 800 number, by State, 1989 and 1991, GAO rpt, 26121–434

SSA staff reductions impacts on client services, 1980s, GAO rpt, 26121–415

Strikes, workers affected, and mgmt use and threats to use permanent replacement workers, 1985 and 1989, GAO rpt, 26121–405

Tax (income) refunds applied by IRS to outstanding debts to Fed Govt, impacts on subsequent taxpayer compliance, 1984-87, GAO rpt, 26119–339

Tax (income) returns computer matching program to indentify underreported income, effectiveness, 1987, GAO rpt, 26119–325

Tax (income) returns of high income individuals not filed, by selected characteristics, 1987, and assessments under alternative IRS enforcement programs, 1990, GAO rpt, 26119–322

Tax (income) returns with IRS Service Center and taxpayer errors, by type of error, 1990-91, GAO rpt, 26119–346

Tax credit for hiring from groups with high unemployment rates, participation by State, and effectiveness, FY88, GAO rpt, 26121–407

Tax preparation services negligence and fraud, IRS civil penalty cases and examiners views of program admin, 1989, GAO rpt, 26119–315

Traffic fatal accident rates impacts of auto weight, with data for young drivers, 1976-78 and 1986-88, GAO rpt, 26131–89

Travel agencies contracts of GSA, by business size and recipient, FY88-90, GAO rpt, 26119–331

Truck accidents, by carrier financial and operating conditions and driver characteristics, 1980s, GAO rpt, 26131–82

Truck safety inspections of FHwA conducted FY87-88, compliance review status as of 1990, GAO rpt, 26113–505

TV (cable) deregulation in 1986, impacts on prices and services, 1986-91, GAO rpt, 26113–431

US attorneys staffing disparities among district offices, and caseload by litigation type, FY87-90, GAO rpt, 26119–323

USDA employees financial disclosure rpts filings, processing, errors, and conflicts of interest exposed, 1989, GAO rpt, 26119–314

USDA subagencies responsible for farm programs, field offices, funding, and staff, FY89, GAO rpt, 26113–507

Veterans alcohol abuse prevalence, screening results by age and race, for 5 VA medical centers, 1990, GAO rpt, 26121–416

Vocational rehabilitation programs of States, service provision based on severity of client disability, evaluation, FY88, GAO rpt, 26121–438

Vocational training and education programs effectiveness, benefits, and participant characteristics, 1980s, GAO rpt, 26121–431

Wastewater treatment facilities construction loan funds for local govts, Federal and State funding by State, 1990, GAO rpt, 26113–521

Water (bottled) quality standards of FDA, EPA, and States, with use in 12 States, 1990, GAO rpt, 26113–519

Wildlife protection enforcement activities, funding, costs, and staff of Fish and Wildlife Service, late 1970s-90, GAO rpt, 26113–525

General Agreement on Tariffs and Trade see Trade agreements

General aviation

Accidents and circumstances, for US operations of domestic and foreign airlines and general aviation, periodic rpt, 9612–1

Accidents by type of aviation, near collisions, air traffic control and pilot errors, and runway incursions, monthly rpt, 7502–15

Accidents, deaths, and circumstances, by carrier and carrier type, preliminary 1990, annual press release, 9614–9

Accidents in general aviation, by circumstances, characteristics of persons and aircraft involved, and type of flying, 1988, annual rpt, 9614–3

Air traffic control and airway facilities improvement activities under Aviation System Capital Investment Plan, 1981-90 and projected to 2005, annual rpt, 7504–12

Aircraft (general aviation), flight hours, and equipment, by type, use, and model of aircraft, region, and State, 1990, annual rpt, 7504–29

Aircraft registered with FAA, by type and characteristics of aircraft, make, carrier, State, and county, 1989, annual rpt, 7504–3

General Services Administration

Airport improvement program of FAA, activities, funding, and airport operations, by location, projected 1990-99, biennial rpt, 7504–42

Atlantic Ocean intl air traffic and passengers, by aviation type and route, alternative forecasts 1991-2010 and trends from 1980, annual rpt, 7504–44

Hijacking attempts and airport security oprations, screening results, and enforcement actions, 2nd half 1989, semiannual rpt, 7502–5

Hijackings, on-board explosions, and other crime, US and foreign incidents, 1985-89, annual rpt, 7504–31

Instrument flight rule aircraft handled, by user type, FAA traffic control center, and region, FY85-90 and projected to FY2005, annual rpt, 7504–15

Pilots and nonpilots certified by FAA, by certificate type, age, sex, region, and State, 1990, annual rpt, 7504–2

State and Metro Area Data Book, 1991 data compilation, 2328–54

Traffic, aircraft, carriers, airports, and FAA activities, detailed data, 1980-89, annual rpt, 7504–1

Traffic, aircraft, pilots, airports, and fuel use, forecast FY91-2002 and trends from FY81, annual rpt, 7504–6

Traffic and other aviation activity forecasts of FAA, 1991 annual conf, 7504–28

Traffic and other general aviation activity, 1990, triennial survey rpt, 7508–3

Traffic and passenger and freight enplanements, by airport, 1960s-90 and projected to 2010, hub area rpt series, 7506–7

Traffic and passenger enplanements, by airport, region, and State, projected FY91-2005 and trends from FY83, annual rpt, 7504–7

Traffic levels at FAA air traffic control facilities, by airport and State, FY90, annual rpt, 7504–27

General Aviation Pilot and Aircraft Activity Survey

Aviation activity, 1990, triennial survey rpt, 7508–3

General Motors Corp.

Energy economy, sales, and market shares, by size and model for domestic and foreign makes, 1991 model year, semiannual rpt, 3302–4

Energy economy test results, 1992 model year, annual rpt, 3304–11

Safety of domestic and foreign autos, crash test results by model, press release series, 7766–7

General Services Administration

Activities and finances of GSA, FY90, annual rpt, 9454–1

Advisory committees of Fed Govt, and members, staff, meetings, and costs by agency, FY90, annual rpt, 9454–18

Assistance (financial and nonfinancial) of Fed Govt, 1991 base edition with supplements, annual listing, 104–5

Auto, private airplane, and motorcycle operating costs by component, and Fed Govt mileage reimbursement rates, 1989, annual rpt, 9454–13

Budget of US, authoritative financial statements with appropriations, outlays, and receipts, by category and agency, FY90, annual rpt, 8104–2.1

General Services Administration

Budget of US, obligations and authority by function, agency, and program, with summaries, analyses, and historical tables, FY92, annual rpt, 104–2

Computer systems and equipment of Fed Govt, by type, make, and agency, 2nd half FY90, semiannual listing, 9452–9

Court buildings mgmt by GSA, spending, and rental income, 1980s-91, hearing, 21648–60

Education funding by Federal agency, program, and recipient type, and instn spending, FY80-90, annual rpt, 4824–8

Employment of minorities and women by Fed Govt, and compliance with EEOC standards, by occupation and agency, FY88-92, GAO rpt, 26119–342

Fraud and abuse in GSA programs, audits and investigations, 2nd half FY91, semiannual rpt, 9452–8

Info Security Oversight Office monitoring of Federal security measures and classification actions, FY90, annual rpt, 9454–21

Military autos and light trucks owned and leased by service branch, and costs and savings from GSA leases, FY89, GAO rpt, 26123–344

Property (real) of Fed Govt, inventory and costs, worldwide summary by location, agency, and use, 1989, annual rpt, 9454–5

Property (real) of Fed Govt, leased inventory and rental costs, worldwide summary by location and agency, 1989, annual rpt, 9454–10

R&D funding by Fed Govt, by field, performer type, agency, and State, FY89-91, annual rpt, 9627–20

Surplus personal property of Fed Govt donated to govt and nonprofit agencies, with data by State, FY88-90, biennial rpt, 9454–22

Travel agencies contracts of GSA, by business size and recipient, FY88-90, GAO rpt, 26119–331

Generalized System of Preferences *see* Tariffs and foreign trade controls

Generating plants *see* Electric power plants and equipment

Genetic engineering *see* Biotechnology

Genetics

Cancer (breast) risk for men relation to incidence among relatives, 1983-86, article, 4472–1.213

Cancer risk for relatives of children with Ewing's tumor, by relationship, 1965-88, article, 4472–1.214

Cell cultures with genetic abnormalities, availability and cultures shipped, 1990-91, biennial listing, 4474–23

HHS financial aid, by program, recipient, State, and city, FY90, annual regional listings, 4004–3

Higher education grad programs enrollment in science and engineering, by field, source of funds, and characteristics of student and instn, 1975-89, annual rpt, 9627–7

Occupational genetic damage and trait monitoring and screening, use, costs, benefits, and procedures, 1980s, 26358–230

Occupational health condition screening and monitoring, businesses practices and views, 1989 survey, 26358–250

Paternity determination through genetic testing, labs, services, and costs, 1991 listing, 4698–4

Research on population and reproduction, Natl Inst of Child Health and Human Dev funding and activities, 1990, annual rpt, 4474–33

see also Biotechnology

see also Hereditary diseases

Genito-urinary diseases *see* Sexually transmitted diseases *see* Urogenital diseases

Genther, Phyllis A.

"Japanese Direct Investment in U.S. Manufacturing", 2048–151

Gentry, Eileen M.

"Monitoring the Exposure of 'America Responds to AIDS' PSA Campaign", 4042–3.256

Geography

Alaska minerals resources and geologic characteristics, compilation of papers, 1989, annual rpt, 5664–15

Census Bur geographic levels of data coverage, maps, and reference products, 1991 pamphlet, 2326–7.79

Census Bur rpts and data files, coverage and availability, 1991 annual listing, 2304–2

Eastern Europe economic and political conditions, and impacts of geographic factors, by country, 1990 conf, 9118–18

Education data, detail for elementary and secondary education, 1920s-90 and projected to 2001, annual rpt, 4824–1.1

Education in science and engineering, grad programs enrollment by field, source of funds, and characteristics of student and instn, 1975-89, annual rpt, 9627–7

Educational performance by subject and selected student characteristics, standard test results and credits, 1991 edition, annual rpt, 4824–2.12

Foreign countries *Geographic Notes,* boundaries, claims, nomenclature, and other devs, periodic rpt, 7142–3

Gazetteer of US places, mountains, bodies of water, and other political and physical features, 1990 rpt, 5668–117

Higher education course completions, by detailed program, sex, race, and instn type, for 1972 high school class, as of 1984, 4888–4

Statistical Abstract of US, 1991 annual data compilation, 2324–1.6

see also Cartography

see also Topography

Geological phenomena *see* Earthquakes *see* Volcanoes

Geological Survey

Acid rain data quality and accuracy, for 2 natl field and lab data collection programs, 1989, annual rpt, 5664–17

Acid rain data quality and accuracy, for 2 natl field data collection programs, 1978-89, 5668–124

Activities and funding of USGS, FY90, annual rpt, 5664–8

Alaska minerals resources and geologic characteristics, compilation of papers, 1989, annual rpt, 5664–15

Index by Subjects and Names

Alaska minerals resources, production, oil and gas leases, reserves, and exploratory wells, with maps and bibl, 1989, annual rpt, 5664–11

Budget of US, obligations and authority by function, agency, and program, with summaries, analyses, and historical tables, FY92, annual rpt, 104–2

California minerals production by commodity, shipments, and liquefied petroleum gas transport by mode, 1986-87, conf, 5668–119

Colorado River sand deposit characteristics, and density of campsites, 1920s-80s, 5668–122

Earthquake intensity, time, location, damage, and seismic characteristics, for US and foreign earthquakes, 1985, annual rpt, 5664–13

Earthquakes and other ground motion, intensity by station, 1988, annual rpt, 5664–14

Earthquakes of San Andreas Fault system, location and seismic characteristics, by event, 1769-1989, 5668–123

Gazetteer of US places, mountains, bodies of water, and other political and physical features, 1990 rpt, 5668–117

Groundwater supply, quality, chemistry, and use, State and local area rpt series, 5666–28

Groundwater supply, quality, chemistry, other characteristics, and use, regional rpt series, 5666–25

Minerals (strategic) supply and characteristics of individual deposits, by country, commodity rpt series, 5666–21

Publications of USGS, monthly listing, 5662–1

Publications of USGS, 1990, annual listing, 5664–4

Radioactive low-level waste repository site design, characteristics, and monitoring techniques, 1987 conf, 5668–116

Radon indoor air pollution levels in Pacific Northwest, with geological and soil characteristics, by township, 1989 rpt, 5668–114

Reservoirs capacity and area, by reservoir and State, 1988, 5668–120

Selenium levels in Western States arid areas, and plant and animal exposure effects, 1990 conf, 5668–121

South Carolina, Myrtle Beach offshore mineral resources, 1989 rpt, 5668–115

Water quality, chemistry, hydrology, and other characteristics, local area studies, series, 5666–27

Water resources data collection and analysis activities of USGS Water Resources Div Districts, with project descriptions, series, 5666–26

Water Resources Div history, series, 5668–118

Water supply and quality in streams and lakes, and groundwater levels in wells, by drainage basin, 1988, annual State rpt series, 5666–16

Water supply and quality in streams and lakes, and groundwater levels in wells, by drainage basin, 1989, annual State rpt series, 5666–12

Water supply and quality in streams and lakes, and groundwater levels in wells, by drainage basin, 1990, annual State rpt series, 5666–10

Index by Subjects and Names

Geothermal resources

Water supply, hydrologic events, and end use, by State, 1988-89, annual rpt, 5664–12

Water supply in US and southern Canada, streamflow, surface and groundwater conditions, and reservoir levels, by location, monthly rpt, 5662–3

Water use by end use, well withdrawals, and public supply deliveries, by county, State rpt series, 5666–24

Geology

- Alaska land area by ownership, and availability for mineral exploration and dev, 1984-86, 5608–152
- Alaska minerals resources and geologic characteristics, compilation of papers, 1989, annual rpt, 5664–15
- Alaska OCS environmental conditions and oil dev impacts, compilation of papers, series, 2176–1
- Coastal and riparian areas environmental conditions, fish, wildlife, use, and mgmt, for individual ecosystems, series, 5506–9
- Coastal areas environmental and socioeconomic conditions, and potential impact of oil and gas OCS leases, final statement series, 5736–1
- DOE R&D projects and funding at natl labs, universities, and other instns, FY90, annual summary rpt, 3004–18.2
- Geological Survey activities and funding, FY90, annual rpt, 5664–8
- Geological Survey rpts, 1990, annual listing, 5664–4
- Groundwater supply, quality, chemistry, and use, State and local area rpt series, 5666–28
- Groundwater supply, quality, chemistry, other characteristics, and use, regional rpt series, 5666–25
- Higher education course completions, by detailed program, sex, race, and instn type, for 1972 high school class, as of 1984, 4888–4
- Oceanographic research and distribution activities of World Data Center A by country, and cruises by ship, 1989, annual rpt, 2144–15
- R&D funding by Fed Govt, by field, performer type, agency, and State, FY89-91, annual rpt, 9627–20
- Water quality, chemistry, hydrology, and other characteristics, local area studies, series, 5666–27
- Wetlands acreage, resources, soil and water properties, and conservation efforts, by wetland type, State rpt series, 5506–11

George, Mark H.

- "Response Capability During Civil Air Carrier Inflight Medical Emergencies", 7506–10.82
- "Utilization of Emergency Medical Kits by Air Carriers", 7506–10.81

Georgia

- Appalachian Regional Commission funding, by project and State, planned FY91, annual rpt, 9084–3
- Banks (insured commercial and savings) deposits by instn, State, MSA, and county, as of June 1990, annual regional rpt, 9295–3.2
- County Business Patterns, 1989: employment, establishments, and payroll, by SIC 2- to 4-digit industry and county, annual State rpt, 2326–8.12

DOD prime contract awards, by contractor, service branch, State, and city, FY90, annual rpt, 3544–22

- Economic indicators by State and MSA, Fed Reserve 6th District, quarterly rpt, 9371–14
- Education system in Appalachia, improvement initiatives, and indicators of success, by State, 1960s-89, 9088–36
- Employment and housing and mortgage market indicators by State, FHLB 4th District, quarterly rpt, 9302–36
- Employment and unemployment, for 8 southeastern States, 1989-90, annual rpt, 6944–2
- Employment by industry div, earnings, and hours, for 8 southeastern States, quarterly press release, 6942–7
- Estuary environmental and fishery conditions, research results and methodology, 1991 rpt, 2176–7.25
- Fed Govt spending in States and local areas, by type, State, county, and city, FY90, annual rpt, 2464–3
- Fed Govt spending in States, by type, program, agency, and State, FY90, annual rpt, 2464–2
- Fertilizer use in 2 States, by county, 1988-89, hearing, 25168–76
- Foster care placements, discharges, and returns to care, by selected characteristics of children, and length of stay factors, 1985-86, GAO rpt, 26121–432
- HHS financial aid, by program, recipient, State, and city, FY90, annual regional listing, 4004–3.4
- Hospital deaths of Medicare patients, actual and expected rates by diagnosis, and hospital characteristics, by instn, FY87-89, annual regional rpt, 4654–14.4
- Income (personal) per capita and by source, and earnings by industry div, by State, MSA, and county, 1984-89, annual regional rpt, 2704–2.4
- Jail adult and juvenile population, employment, spending, instn conditions, and inmate programs, by county and facility, 1988, regional rpt series, 6068–144.4
- Marriages, divorces, and rates, by characteristics of spouses, State, and county, 1987 and trends from 1920, US Vital Statistics annual rpt, 4144–4
- Medicaid transitional benefits for families leaving AFDC, operations and subsequent medical costs, for 2 States, 1980s, article, 4652–1.217
- Medicare claims processing issues in Georgia, with data on beneficiary satisfaction, payments, and subcontractor review activity and savings, 1989-90, hearing, 21728–75
- Mineral Industry Surveys, State reviews of production, 1990, preliminary annual rpt, 5614–6
- *Minerals Yearbook, 1989,* Vol 2: State review of production and sales by commodity, and business activity, annual rpt, 5604–16.11
- *Minerals Yearbook, 1989,* Vol 2: State reviews of production, sales, and firms, by commodity, and business activity, annual rpt, 5604–34
- Peaches production, marketing, and prices in 3 southeastern States and Appalachia, 1990, annual rpt, 1311–12

Physicians, by specialty, age, sex, and location of training and practice, 1989, State rpt, 4116–6.11

- Population and housing census, 1990: population and housing characteristics, households, and land area, by county, subdiv, and place, State rpt, 2551–1.12
- Population and housing census, 1990: voting age and total population by race, and housing units, by block, redistricting counts required under PL 94-171, State CD-ROM release, 2551–6.3
- Population and housing census, 1990: voting age and total population by race, and housing units, by county and city, redistricting counts required under PL 94-171, State summary rpt, 2551–5.11
- *Statistical Abstract of US,* 1991 annual data compilation, 2324–1
- Supplemental Security Income payments and beneficiaries, by type of eligibility, State, and county, Dec 1989, annual rpt, 4744–27.4
- Textile mill employment, earnings, and hours, for 8 Southeastern States, quarterly press release, 6942–1
- Textile production workers and wages by occupation, and benefits, by location, 1990 survey, 6787–6.251
- Timber in Georgia, longleaf pine planting performance relation to seed source and site, 1968-83, 1208–345
- Water supply and quality in streams and lakes, and groundwater levels in wells, by drainage basin, 1990, annual State rpt, 5666–10.9

see also Atlanta, Ga. *see also* Augusta, Ga. *see also* Macon, Ga. *see also* Warner Robins, Ga. *see also* under By State in the "Index by Categories"

Geothermal resources

- Consumption of energy, by detailed fuel type, end-use sector, and State, 1960-89, State Energy Data System annual rpt, 3164–39
- Electric power plants (geothermal) capacity and operating status, wells, and leases, by location, 1960s-94, 3308–87
- Electric power plants and capacity, by fuel used, owner, location, and operating status, 1990 and for units planned 1991-2000, annual listing, 3164–36
- Electric power plants certification applications filed with FERC, for small production and cogeneration facilities, FY80-90, annual listing, 3084–13
- Foreign and US energy production and use, by energy type and country, 1980-89, annual rpt, 3164–50.5
- Land Mgmt Bur activities and funding by State, FY89, annual rpt, 5724–13
- Natl Energy Strategy plans for conservation and pollution reduction, impacts of technology and regulation proposals, projected 1990-2030, 3166–6.47
- Natl Energy Strategy plans for renewable energy dev, supply projected under alternative cost and capacity use assumptions, 1990-2030, 3166–6.50
- Pacific Northwest electric power capacity and use, by energy source, projected under alternative load and demand cases, 1991-2011, annual rpt, 3224–3

Geothermal resources

Public lands acreage and use, and Land Mgmt Bur activities and finances, annual State rpt series, 5724–11

Public lands acreage, grants, use, revenues, and allocations, by State, FY90, annual rpt, 5724–1.2

Public lands minerals resources and availability, State rpt series, 5606–7

Supply, demand, and prices, by fuel type and end-use sector, alternative projections 1989-2010, annual rpt, 3164–75

Supply, demand, and prices, by fuel type and end-use sector, projections and underlying assumptions, 1990-2010, annual rpt, 3164–90

Supply, demand, and prices, by fuel type and end-use sector, with foreign comparisons, 1990 and trends from 1949, annual rpt, 3164–74

Gerald, Elizabeth

"Aspects of Teacher Supply and Demand in Public School Districts and Private Schools: 1987-88. Schools and Staffing Survey", 4836–3.6

Geriatrics

Fed Govt funding of health care centers, aged persons use, targeted programs offered, and funding sources, 1987, article, 4042–3.229

Health care services and long term care for aged, series, 4186–7

HHS financial aid, by program, recipient, State, and city, FY90, annual regional listings, 4004–3

Research on aged health condition and care, data availability and collection methodology, for US and selected countries, 1988 conf, 4147–5.6

VA health care facilities physicians, dentists, and nurses, by selected employment characteristics and VA district, quarterly rpt, 8602–6

VA health care staff and turnover, by occupation, physician specialty, and location, 1990, annual rpt, 8604–8

VA Medicine and Surgery Dept trainees, by detailed program and city, FY90, annual rpt, 8704–4

VA mental health care services, staff, research, and training programs, 1991 biennial listing, 8704–2

German Democratic Republic

see Germany, East

German, Edward R.

"Quantity and Quality of Stormwater Runoff Recharged to the Floridan Aquifer System Through Two Drainage Wells in the Orlando, Fla., Area", 5666–27.3

Germanium

see Metals and metal industries

Germany

Agricultural production, prices, and trade, by country, 1970s-90, and forecast 1991, annual world region rpt, 1524–4.4

Agricultural production, trade, and policies in foreign countries, summary data by country, 1989-90, annual factbook, 1924–12

Agricultural resources and yield in Germany, and effects of natl unification, 1980s, article, 1522–3.201

AID loans repayment status and terms by program and country, and status of predecessor agency loans, quarterly rpt, 9912–3

Background Notes, summary social, political, and economic data, 1991 rpt, 7006–2.36

Banks capital costs, operating ratios, and intl market shares, for US and 5 OECD countries, 1980s-90, article, 9385–1.203

Cherry juice and concentrate from 2 countries at less than fair value, injury to US industry, investigation with background financial and operating data, 1991 rpt, 9886–14.308

Drug abuse indicators, by world region and selected country, 1990 semiannual conf, 4492–5.1

Economic aid of US and other donor countries by type and recipient, and role in advancing economic interests, 1980s-90, 2048–152

Economic and monetary trends, compounded annual rates of change and quarterly indicators for US and 7 major industrialized countries, quarterly rpt, 9391–7

Economic conditions in USSR, Eastern Europe, OECD, and selected other countries, 1960s-90, annual rpt, 9114–4

Economic conditions, income, production, prices, employment, and trade, 1991 periodic country rpt, 2046–4.34; 2046–4.71

Economic conditions, policy, and trade practices, by country, 1988-90, annual rpt, 21384–5

Economic, social, political, and geographic summary data, by country, 1991, annual factbook, 9114–2

Energy production by type, and oil trade, and use, by country group and selected country, monthly rpt, 9112–2

European Monetary System countries interest rate differentials with Germany, relation to fiscal policy, with model results for Italy, 1979-90, technical paper, 9366–7.259

Exports and imports of US by country, and trade shifts by commodity, 1990, semiannual rpt, 9882–9

Exports and imports of US, by selected country, country group, and commodity group, 1990, annual rpt, 2044–37

Exports, imports, and balances of US, by selected country, country group, and commodity group, preliminary data, monthly rpt, 2042–34

Exports, imports, and balances of US with major trading partners, by product category, 1986-90, annual chartbook, 9884–21

Farmland in US owned by foreigners, holdings, acreage, and value by land use, owner country, State, and county, 1990, annual rpt, 1584–3

GNP and GNP growth for OECD members, by country, 1980-90, annual rpt, 7144–8

Health care cost control measures and insurance provisions, for Germany, France, and Japan, 1960s-91, GAO rpt, 26121–437

Human rights conditions in 170 countries, and US economic and military aid, 1990, annual rpt, 21384–3

Inflation forecasting performance of expected long run inflation rate and other models, for Japan and Germany, 1970s-89, technical paper, 9366–7.268

Interest and exchange rates, security yields, and stock indexes, for selected foreign countries, weekly chartbook, 9365–1.5

Intl transactions of US with 9 countries, 1986-88, *Survey of Current Business*, monthly rpt, annual table, 2702–1.26

Military reserve forces structure and training, for US and 5 European countries, as of 1990, GAO rpt, 26123–358

Money demand in Germany hyperinflation after WWI, impact of relative prices of investment and consumer goods, model description and results for 1921-23, working paper, 9371–10.66

Nuclear power generation in US and 20 countries, monthly rpt, 3162–24.10

Oil production, trade, use, and stocks, by selected country and country group, monthly rpt, 3162–42

Oil use and stocks for selected OECD countries, monthly rpt, 3162–24.10

Paper (coated groundwood) from 5 countries at less than fair value, injury to US industry, investigation with background financial and operating data, 1991 rpt, 9886–14.336

Rayon yarn (high-tenacity filament) from 2 countries at less than fair value, injury to US industry, investigation with background financial and operating data, 1991 rpt, 9886–14.331

Spacecraft and satellite launches since 1957, quarterly listing, 9502–2

Travel to US, trade shows and other promotional activities, with magazine ad costs and circulation, for selected countries, 1991-92, annual rpt, 2904–11

UN voting record and share of votes in agreement with US, by issue, country, and world area, 1990, annual rpt, 7004–18

US Army deployment exercise in Germany using computer simulations, costs and effectiveness, with Germans favoring US military withdrawal, 1969-90, GAO rpt, 26123–318

see also Germany, East

see also Germany, West

see also under By Foreign Country in the "Index by Categories"

Germany, East

Agricultural exports of high-value commodities, indexes and sales by commodity, world area, and country, 1960s-86, 1528–323

Agricultural exports of US, impacts of foreign agricultural and trade policy, with data by commodity and country, 1989, annual rpt, 1924–8

Agricultural trade of US, by detailed commodity and country, 1989, annual rpt, 1524–8

Agricultural trade of US, by detailed commodity and country, 1990, semiannual rpt, 1522–4

Debt to foreign lenders by component, trade, balances, and other economic indicators, by Eastern Europe country, 1985-89, hearing, 21248–148

Economic and military aid and loans from US and intl agencies, by program and country, FY46-90, annual rpt, 9914–5

Economic conditions in USSR, Eastern Europe, OECD, and selected other countries, 1960s-90, annual rpt, 9114–4

Index by Subjects and Names

Ghana

Export licensing, monitoring, and enforcement activities, FY90, annual rpt, 2024–1

Exports and imports of US, by commodity and country, 1970-89, world area rpt, 9116–1.3

Exports and imports of US, by transport mode, country, and SITC 1- to 3-digit commodity, 1990, annual rpt, 2424–12

Exports of US, detailed Schedule B commodities with countries of destination, 1990, annual rpt, 2424–10

Market economy transition of Eastern Europe countries, with trade agreements and bilateral US trade data by country, late 1980s-90, annual rpt, 444–2

Nuclear power plant capacity, generation, and operating status, by plant and foreign and US location, 1990 and projected to 2030, annual rpt, 3164–57

Steel imports of US under voluntary restraint agreement, by product, customs district, and country, with US industry operating data, quarterly rpt, 9882–13

Germany, West

Agricultural exports of high-value commodities, indexes and sales by commodity, world area, and country, 1960s-86, 1528–323

Agricultural trade of US, by detailed commodity and country, 1989, annual rpt, 1524–8

Agricultural trade of US, by detailed commodity and country, 1990, semiannual rpt, 1522–4

Auto sales shares, by firm, 1988, article, 9371–1.210

Banks restrictions on business equity ownership, issues, with data for venture capital financing and comparisons to West Germany and Japan, 1970s-90, article, 9393–8.206

Businesses (foreign) activity in US, income tax returns, assets, and income statement items, by industry div and selected country, 1986-87, article, 8302–2.205

Corporations in US under foreign control, income tax returns, assets and income statement items by industry div, country, and world area, 1988, article, 8302–2.219

Dollar exchange rate and domestic monetary policy impacts of foreign exchange intervention, for US and Germany, 1985-87, article, 9373–1.209

Dollar exchange rates of yen and mark, impact of Fed Reserve policy interventions and other economic indicators, 1985-89, technical paper, 9385–8.114

Economic and military aid and loans from US and intl agencies, by program and country, FY46-90, annual rpt, 9914–5

Economic conditions, and oil supply and demand, for major industrial countries, biweekly rpt, 9112–1

Economic conditions, consumer and stock prices and production indexes, 6 OECD countries and US, *Business Conditions Digest*, monthly rpt, 2702–1.2

Economic conditions in USSR, Eastern Europe, OECD, and selected other countries, 1960s-90, annual rpt, 9114–4

Economic conditions, investment and export opportunities, and trade practices, 1991 country market research rpt, 2046–6.2

Economic indicators, and dollar exchange rates, for selected OECD countries, 1991 semiannual rpt, 8002–14

Energy conservation measures impacts on consumption, by component and end-use sector, 1970s-88 and projected under alternative oil prices to 1995, 3308–93

Energy prices, by fuel type and end use, for 10 countries, 1980-89 annual rpt, 3164–50.6

Energy production by type, and oil trade, and use, by country group and selected country, monthly rpt, 9112–2

Exchange rate relation to interest rate differentials for France and West Germany, model description and results, 1980s, technical paper, 9366–7.249

Exports and imports, intl position of US and 4 OECD countries, and factors affecting US competition, periodic pamphlet, 2042–25

Exports and imports of NATO members with PRC, by country, 1987-90, annual rpt, 7144–14

Exports and imports of OECD members, by country, 1989, annual rpt, 7144–10

Exports and imports of OECD, total and for 4 major countries, and US trade by country, by commodity, 1970-89, world area rpt series, 9116–1

Exports and imports of US, by Harmonized System 6-digit commodity and country, 1990, annual rpt, 2424–13

Exports and imports of US, by transport mode, country, and SITC 1- to 3-digit commodity, 1990, annual rpt, 2424–12

Exports and imports of US with EC by country, and total agricultural trade, selected years 1958-90, annual rpt, 7144–7

Exports of US, detailed Schedule B commodities with countries of destination, 1990, annual rpt, 2424–10

Fish imports of West Germany, by species and country, 1985-88, article, 2162–1.204

Health care spending in West Germany, by funding source and service type, and resource growth, 1970-89, article, 4652–1.238

Health condition of children and aged, health care costs, and natl health insurance payroll tax rates, for West Germany, 1985-88, 23898–5

Imports of goods, services, and investment from US, trade barriers, impacts, and US actions, by country, 1990, annual rpt, 444–2

Imports of US given duty-free treatment for value of US material sent abroad, by commodity and country, 1989, annual rpt, 9884–14

Investment (foreign direct) in US, by industry group of US affiliate and country of parent firm, 1980-86, 2708–41

Investment (foreign direct) in US, major transactions by type, industry, country, and US location, 1989, annual rpt, 2044–20

Labor conditions, union coverage, and work accidents, 1990 annual country rpt, 6366–4.3

Marriage among young adults, relation to age, employment, and school enrollment, for US and West Germany, mid-1980s, working paper, 2626–10.143

Marriage, employment, and school completion timing among young adults, for US and West Germany, mid-1980s, working paper, 2626–10.131

Multinatl firms US affiliates, finances, and operations, by industry, world area of parent firm, and State, 1988-89, annual rpt, 2704–4

Multinatl firms US affiliates, investment trends and impact on US economy, 1991 annual rpt, 2004–9

Multinatl US firms and foreign affiliates finances and operations, by industry and world area of parent firm, 1989 benchmark survey, preliminary annual rpt, 2704–5

Multinatl US firms foreign affiliates, income statement items by country and world area, 1986, biennial article, 8302–2.212

Nuclear power generation in US and 20 countries, monthly rpt, 3162–24.10

Nuclear power plant capacity, generation, and operating status, by plant and foreign and US location, 1990 and projected to 2030, annual rpt, 3164–57

Oil use and stocks for selected OECD countries, monthly rpt, 3162–24.10

Paper (coated groundwood) from 9 countries at less than fair value, injury to US industry, investigation with background financial and operating data, 1991 rpt, 9886–14.306

Science and engineering employment and education, and R&D spending, for US and selected foreign countries, 1991 annual rpt, 9627–35

Science and engineering employment, by professional characteristics, age, and sex, for selected countries, 1991 working paper, 2326–18.62

Sodium sulfur compounds from 4 countries at less than fair value, injury to US industry, investigation with background financial and operating data, 1991 rpt, 9886–14.305

Tax revenue, by level of govt and type of tax, for OECD countries, mid 1960s-89, annual rpt, 10044–1.2

Telecommunications industry intl competitiveness, with financial and operating data by product or service, firm, and country, 1990 rpt, 2008–30

Transportation energy use, fuel prices, vehicle registrations, and mileage, by selected country, 1970s-89, annual rpt, 3304–5.1

Wage differentials among industries, by industry and country, and correlation of differentials between countries, for US and West Germany, 1979-87, technical paper, 9366–6.281

Geronimus, Arline T.

"Differences in Hypertension Prevalence Among U.S. Black and White Women of Childbearing Age", 4042–3.231

Gertel, Karl

"Returns to Cash Rented Farmland and Common Stock, 1940-90", 1561–16.202

Gfroerer, Joseph C.

"Feasibility of Collecting Drug Abuse Data by Telephone", 4042–3.230

Ghana

Agricultural exports of high-value commodities, indexes and sales by commodity, world area, and country, 1960s-86, 1528–323

Ghana

Agricultural production, trade, and policies in foreign countries, summary data by country, 1989-90, annual factbook, 1924–12

Agricultural trade of US, by detailed commodity and country, 1989, annual rpt, 1524–8

Agricultural trade of US, by detailed commodity and country, 1990, semiannual rpt, 1522–4

AID economic aid to developing countries, obligations and disbursements by country, quarterly rpt, 9912–4

AID loans repayment status and terms by program and country, and status of predecessor agency loans, quarterly rpt, 9912–3

Background Notes, summary social, political, and economic data, 1990 rpt, 7006–2.40

Dairy imports, consumption, and market conditions, by sub-Saharan Africa country, 1961-88, 1528–321

Economic and military aid and loans from US and intl agencies, by program and country, FY46-90, annual rpt, 9914–5

Economic and social conditions of developing countries from 1960s, and Intl Dev Cooperation Agency and AID activities and funding, FY90-92, annual rpt, 9904–4

Economic conditions, income, production, prices, employment, and trade, 1991 periodic country rpt, 2046–4.51

Economic conditions, policy, and trade practices, by country, 1988-90, annual rpt, 21384–5

Economic, social, political, and geographic summary data, by country, 1991, annual factbook, 9114–2

Exports and imports of US, by commodity and country, 1970-89, world area rpt, 9116–1.6

Exports and imports of US, by transport mode, country, and SITC 1- to 3-digit commodity, 1990, annual rpt, 2424–12

Exports of US, detailed Schedule B commodities with countries of destination, 1990, annual rpt, 2424–10

Food supply, needs, and aid for developing countries, status and alternative forecasts, 1991 world area rpt, 1526–8.1

Human rights conditions in 170 countries, and US economic and military aid, 1990, annual rpt, 21384–3

Labor conditions, union coverage, and work accidents, 1991 annual country rpt, 6366–4.44

Military aid of US, arms sales, and training programs costs and budget requests, by program, world region, and country, FY90-92, annual rpt, 7144–13

UN voting record and share of votes in agreement with US, by issue, country, and world area, 1990, annual rpt, 7004–18

see also under By Foreign Country in the "Index by Categories"

GI Bill

see Veterans education

Gianfrancesco, Frank D.

"Prospective Payment System and Other Effects on Post-Hospital Services", 4652–1.223

Gibbard, Kathy

"Spent Nuclear Fuel Discharges from U.S. Reactors, 1989", 3166–6.55

Gibraltar

Agricultural trade of US, by detailed commodity and country, 1989, annual rpt, 1524–8

Agricultural trade of US, by detailed commodity and country, 1990, semiannual rpt, 1522–4

Economic, social, political, and geographic summary data, by country, 1991, annual factbook, 9114–2

Exports and imports of US, by transport mode, country, and SITC 1- to 3-digit commodity, 1990, annual rpt, 2424–12

Gift tax

Budget of US, CBO analysis of revenue and spending alternatives and projections of economic indicators, FY92-96, annual rpt, 26304–3

Budget of US, CBO analysis of savings and revenues under alternative spending cuts and tax changes, projected FY92-97, 26306–3.118

Budget of US, receipts by source, outlays by agency and program, and balances, monthly rpt, 8102–3

Collections, enforcement, and litigation activity of IRS, with data by type of tax, region, and State, FY90, annual rpt, 8304–3

Fed Govt internal revenue and refunds, by type of tax, quarterly rpt, 8302–2.1

Fed Govt receipts by source and outlays by agency, *Treasury Bulletin*, quarterly rpt, 8002–4.1

Fed Govt tax provisions and receipts overview, by tax type, with background data, 1900s-91 and projected to 2000, 21788–197

Fed Govt tax revenues, by type of tax, quarterly rpt, 2462–3

Finances of govts, tax systems and revenue, and fiscal structure, by level of govt and State, 1991 and historical trends, annual rpt, 10044–1

Returns and supplemental documents filed, by type, FY89 and projected to FY98, annual article, 8302–2.208

Returns and supplemental documents filed, by type, FY90 and projected to FY99, semiannual rpt, 8302–4

Returns filed, accuracy of projections by return type, various periods 1983-90, article, 8304–8.1

Returns filed, by type of tax and IRS district, 1989 and projected 1990-97, annual rpt, 8304–24

Returns filed, by type of tax, region, and IRS service center, projected 1990-97 and trends from 1978, annual rpt, 8304–9

State govt revenue by source, spending and debt by function, and holdings, FY90, annual rpt, 2466–2.6

State govt tax collections by detailed type of tax, and tax rates, by State, FY90, annual rpt, 2466–2.7

Gifts and private contributions

Adult day care centers revenue by source, and expenses by type, by agency type, FY86, article, 4652–1.234

AIDS info and education activities and funding of CDC, and donation of media ads, 1987-92, articles, 4042–3.256

Index by Subjects and Names

Budget of US, authoritative financial statements with appropriations, outlays, and receipts, by category and agency, FY90, annual rpt, 8104–2.1

Consumer Expenditure Survey, household income by source, and itemized spending, by selected characteristics and region, 1988-89, annual rpt, 6764–5

Consumer Expenditure Survey, spending by category, and income, by selected household characteristics and location, 1990, annual press release, 6726–1.42

Consumer spending for cash contributions, by charity type and selected characteristics, 1988/89, article, 1702–1.214

Drug (prescription) marketing practices, spending by selected firm, and physicians views, 1990 hearings, 25548–103

Drug and alcohol abuse treatment facilities, services, use, funding, staff, and client characteristics, 1989, biennial rpt, 4494–10

Education data compilation, 1991 annual rpt, 4824–2

Employee leave transfer to other employees, Federal pilot programs operations and costs by agency, FY89, 9848–40

Exports and imports of US, by Harmonized System 6-digit commodity and country, 1990, annual rpt, 2424–13

Exports of US, detailed Schedule B commodities with countries of destination, 1990, annual rpt, 2424–10

Health care spending by businesses, households, and govts, 1965-89, article, 4652–1.230

Higher education enrollment, faculty, finances, and degrees, by instn level and control, and State, FY87, annual rpt, 4844–13

Higher education instn revenue by source and spending by function, by State and instn control, FY80-88, annual rpt, 4844–6

Higher education instn tuition relation to other instn financial indicators, by instn control, 1960s-88, 4808–24

Hospital operations, and services spending by type and payment source, with background data and foreign comparisons, 1960s-80s and projected to 2000, 26308–98

Library of Congress gift, trust, and service fee funds, FY90, annual rpt, 26404–1

Mail volume to and from households, use, and views, by class, source, content, and household characteristics, 1987-88, annual rpt, 9864–10

Nonprofit charitable organizations finances, and revenue and investments of top 10 instns, 1986-87, article, 8302–2.210

Nonprofit charitable organizations finances, by asset size and State, 1987, article, 8302–2.218

Nonprofit charitable organizations finances, 1988, table, 8302–2.220

Public debt issued, redeemed, and outstanding, by series and source, and gifts to reduce debt, monthly rpt, 8242–2

Public welfare payments impacts on charitable contributions, model description and results, 1990 working paper, 6886–6.76

Index by Subjects and Names

R&D facilities for biological and medical sciences, space and equipment adequacy, needs, and funding by source, by instn type, 1990, biennial rpt, 4434–17

Red Cross financial statements, FY89-90, annual rpt, 29254–1

Service industries census, 1987: establishments, receipts by source, payroll, and employment, by SIC 2- to 4-digit kind of business, State, and MSA, 2393–4

Statistical Abstract of US, 1991 annual data compilation, 2324–1.12

Tax (income) returns filed by type of filer, selected income items, quarterly rpt, 8302–2.1

Tax (income) returns of corporations, income and tax items by asset size and detailed industry, 1987, annual rpt, 8304–4

Tax (income) returns of corporations, income and tax items by asset size and detailed industry, 1988, annual rpt, 8304–21

Tax (income) returns of individuals, selected income and tax items by income level, preliminary 1989, annual article, 8302–2.209

Tax expenditures, Federal revenues forgone through income tax deductions and exclusions by type, FY92-96, annual rpt, 21784–10

Truman, Harry S, Scholarship Fund receipts by source, transfers, and investment holdings and transactions, monthly rpt, 14312–1

see also Campaign funds

see also Gift tax

Gilbert, Dennis M.

"1989 Computer Security and Privacy Plans (CSPP) Review Project: A First-Year Federal Response to the Computer Security Act of 1987 (Final Report)", 2218–85

Gilbert Islands

see Kiribati

Gilbert, R. Alton

"Do Bank Holding Companies Act as 'Sources of Strength' for Their Bank Subsidiaries?", 9391–1.205

"Supervision of Under-Capitalized Banks: Is There a Case for Change?", 9391–1.212

Gilding, Thomas J.

"Changing Technology: Pesticide Use and the Environment", 1004–16.1

Gill, Mohinder

"Crop Sequences Among 1990 Major Field Crops and Associated Farm Program Participation", 1561–16.204

"Cropping Pattern Comparisons Between 1989 and 1988", 1561–16.201

Gilligan, Peggy

"New England Outlook", 9302–4.203

Gilliom, Robert J.

"Sources and Concentrations of Dissolved Solids and Selenium in the San Joaquin River and Its Tributaries, California, October 1985-March 1987", 5666–27.5

Gillum, Richard F.

"Resting Pulse Rate of Children and Young Adults Associated with Blood Pressure and Other Cardiovascular Risk Factors", 4042–3.232

Gilman, Wayne K.

"Hospital Experimental Payments Program: 1980-87", 4658–48

Gilmer, Robert W.

"Income Growth in the Southwest: Implications for Long-Term Development", 9379–1.209

Gilmore, Jeffrey L.

"Price and Quality in Higher Education", 4888–3

Ginzburg, Harold M.

"Consequences of the Nuclear Power Plant Accident at Chernobyl", 4042–3.201

Ginzel, John

"Outlook for Red Meats", 1004–16.1

Girl Scouts of U.S.A.

Statistical Abstract of US, 1991 annual data compilation, 2324–1.7

Gittings, Thomas A.

"Rounding Errors and Index Numbers", 9375–1.206

Glaciers

Alaska minerals resources and geologic characteristics, compilation of papers, 1989, annual rpt, 5664–15

see also Ice conditions

Glade, Edward H., Jr.

"Cotton Ginning Charges, Harvesting Practices, and Selected Marketing Costs, 1990/91 Season", 1564–3

"Marketing Foreign Raw Cotton to U.S. Mills—Prospects and Costs", 1561–1.206

Glanz, Karen

"Survey of Newspaper Coverage of HCFA Hospital Mortality Data", 4042–3.242

Glanz, Milton P.

"Private Social Welfare Expenditures, 1972-88", 4742–1.204

Glass and glass industry

Auto weight, by component material, 1975-90, article, 5602–4.202

Business statistics, detailed data for major industries and economic indicators, *Survey of Current Business,* monthly rpt, 2702–1.21

County Business Patterns, 1988: employment, establishments, and payroll, by SIC 2- to 4-digit industry and county, annual State rpt series, 2326–6

County Business Patterns, 1989: employment, establishments, and payroll, by SIC 2- to 4-digit industry and county, annual State rpt series, 2326–8

Employment, earnings, and hours, by SIC 1- to 4-digit industry, monthly and annual averages, selected years 1909-90, annual rpt, 6744–4

Enterprise Statistics, 1987: finances and operations for companies, by size, level of diversification, form of organization, and industry group, 2329–8

Exports and imports between US and outlying areas, by detailed commodity and mode of transport, 1990, annual rpt, 2424–11

Exports and imports of building materials, by commodity and country, 1989-90, article, 2042–1.204

Exports and imports of US, by country and detailed commodity, monthly rpt, 2422–12

Exports and imports of US, by Harmonized System 6-digit commodity and country, 1990, annual rpt, 2424–13

Exports and imports of US, by transport mode, country, and SITC 1- to 3-digit commodity, 1990, annual rpt, 2424–12

Exports of US, detailed commodities by country, monthly CD-ROM, 2422–13

Exports of US, detailed Schedule B commodities with countries of destination, 1990, annual rpt, 2424–10

Imports, exports, and employment impacts, by SIC 2- to 4-digit industry and commodity, quarterly rpt, 2322–2

Imports of US, detailed commodities by country, monthly CD-ROM, 2422–14

Injuries from use of consumer products, by severity, victim age, and detailed product, 1990, annual rpt, 9164–6

Input-output structure of US economy, detailed interindustry transactions for 84 industries, and components of final demand, 1986, annual article, 2702–1.206

Input-output structure of US economy, detailed interindustry transactions for 85 industries, 1982 benchmark data, 2702–1.213

Labor productivity, indexes of output, hours, and employment by SIC 2- to 4-digit industry, 1967-89, annual rpt, 6824–1.3

Manufacturing annual survey, 1989: finances and operations, by SIC 2- to 4-digit industry, series, 2506–15

Manufacturing census, 1987: finances and operations, by SIC 2- to 4-digit industry, State, and MSA, with trends from 1849, 2497–1

Manufacturing census, 1987: finances and operations, by type of organization and SIC 2- to 4-digit industry, subject rpt, 2497–5

Manufacturing finances and operations, by SIC 2- to 4-digit industry, forecast 1991, annual rpt, 2044–28

Multinatl US firms and foreign affiliates finances and operations, by industry and world area of parent firm, 1989 benchmark survey, preliminary annual rpt, 2704–5

Occupational injury and illness rates, by SIC 2- to 4-digit industry, 1988-89, annual rpt, 6844–7

Occupational injury and illness rates, by SIC 2- to 4-digit industry, 1989, annual rpt, 6844–1

OECD trade, total and for 4 major countries, and US trade by country, by commodity, 1970-89, world area rpt series, 9116–1

Pollution (air) emissions factors, by detailed pollutant and source, data compilation, 1990 rpt, 9198–120

Price indexes (producer), by stage of processing and detailed commodity, monthly rpt, 6762–6

Price indexes (producer), by stage of processing and detailed commodity, monthly 1990, annual rpt, 6764–2

Production, shipments, trade, and stocks, by glass product, periodic Current Industrial Rpt series, 2506–9

Tax (income) returns of corporations, income and tax items by asset size and detailed industry, 1987, annual rpt, 8304–4

Tax (income) returns of corporations, income and tax items by asset size and detailed industry, 1988, annual rpt, 8304–21

Glass and glass industry

Wholesale trade census, 1987: establishments, sales by customer class, employment, inventories, and expenses, by SIC 2- to 4-digit kind of business, 2407–4

see also under By Commodity in the "Index by Categories"

Glass, Ronald J.

"Subsistence as a Component of the Mixed Economic Base in a Modernizing Community", 1208–350

Glaz, B.

"Evaluation of New Canal Point Sugarcane Clones, 1990-91 Harvest Season", 1704–2

Gleason, Philip M.

"Child Care: Arrangements and Costs", 6722–1.246

"Drug and Alcohol Use at Work: A Survey of Young Workers", 6722–1.237

Glendale, Ariz.

see also under By City in the "Index by Categories"

Glendale, Calif.

see also under By City in the "Index by Categories"

Glenn, Mildred E.

"Water Resources Activities in Florida, 1989-90", 5666–26.14

Glens Falls, N.Y.

see also under By SMSA or MSA in the "Index by Categories"

Glick, Reuven

"Japanese Capital Flows in the 1980s", 9393–8.204

Global climate change

- AID energy assistance to developing countries, and global warming reduction activities, 1980s-FY92, GAO rpt, 26123–352
- Auto alternative fuels costs, emissions, health impacts, and characteristics, series, 9196–5
- Carbon dioxide in atmosphere, DOE R&D programs and funding at natl labs, universities, and other instns, FY91, annual summary rpt, 3004–18.1; 3004–18.7
- Carbon dioxide in atmosphere, measurement, methodology, and research results, series, 3006–11
- Data collection activities, mgmt, and inventory of Federal and intl agencies on global climate change trends and contributing gases levels, 1990 rpt, 3028–4
- Economic impacts of global climate change, projected to 2100 with background data for 1980s, 3028–5
- Emissions and control of pollutants contributing to global warming, for US and foreign countries, 1980s and projected to 2020, 26358–233
- Emissions factors and control costs for pollutants contributing to global warming, by pollutant and source, 1990 rpt, 9198–124
- Emissions of pollutants contributing to climate change, atmospheric concentrations by monitoring site, 1989, annual rpt, 2144–28
- Energy natl strategy plans for conservation and pollution reduction, impacts of technology and regulation proposals, projected 1990-2030, 3166–6.47

Energy natl strategy plans for conservation, R&D, security, and pollution reduction, with background data, 1991 biennial rpt, 3004–34

Environmental, infrastructure, and health impacts of global climate change, with model results and background data, 1850s-2100, 9188–113

Environmental Quality, status of problems, protection programs, research, and intl issues, 1991 annual rpt, 484–1

North Central States economic and agricultural impacts of atmospheric carbon dioxide, model descriptions and results, 1980s and projected to 2030, 3006–11.15

Ozone in stratosphere, levels, depletion rates and climate impacts, and properties of chlorofluorocarbons and substitutes, 1990 rpt, 9508–37

Research on global climate change, Federal budget by agency, and alternative estimates of contributing gases levels and impacts, late 1980s-90, GAO rpt, 26113–495

Soviet Union, Eastern Europe, OECD, and selected other countries pollution and deforestation indicators, 1960s-90, annual rpt, 9114–4.10

Weather trends and deviations, by world region, 1880s-1990, annual chartbook, 2184–9

Glossaries

Agricultural data compilation, 1990 and trends from 1920, annual rpt, 1004–14

Astronomical tables, time conversion factors, and listing of observatories worldwide, 1992, annual rpt, 3804–7

Budget of US, legislative process overview with summary projections and glossary, FY90-95, 21268–43

Computer systems purchase and use, and data recording, processing, and transfer, Fed Govt standards, series, 2216–2

Consumption of energy, by detailed fuel type, end-use sector, and State, 1960-89, State Energy Data System annual rpt, 3164–39

Electric power plants production and capital costs, operations, and fuel use, by fuel type, plant, utility, and location, 1989, annual rpt, 3164–9

Electric power plants production, fuel use, stocks, and costs by fuel type, and sales, by State, monthly rpt with articles, 3162–35

Electric power wholesale trade, by utility, type of ownership, and region, 1988, biennial rpt, 3164–92

Electric utilities finances and operations, detailed data for publicly owned firms, 1989, annual rpt, 3164–24

Electric utilities privately owned, finances and operations, detailed data, 1989, annual rpt, 3164–23

Lead levels in environment, sources of emissions and exposure, and health effects, literature review, 1990 rpt, 9198–84

Materials (advanced structural) devs, use, and R&D funding, for ceramics, metal alloys, polymers, and composites, 1960s-80s and projected to 2000, 5608–162

Natural and supplemental gas production, prices, trade, use, reserves, and pipeline company finances, by firm and State, monthly rpt with articles, 3162–4

OASDI benefit payments, trust fund finances, and economic and demographic assumptions, 1970-90 and alternative projections to 2000, actuarial rpt, 4706–1.105

Occupational titles dictionary and classification codes, 1991 base edition and supplements, 6406–1

Oil and gas OCS reserves, and leasing and dev activity, periodic regional rpt series, 5736–3

Radioactive waste and spent fuel generation, inventory, and disposal, 1960s-89 and projected to 2020, annual rpt, 3364–2

Supply, demand, trade, stocks, and refining of oil and gas liquids, by detailed product, State, and PAD district, monthly rpt with articles, 3162–6

Tidal currents, daily time and velocity by station for North America and Asia coasts, forecast 1992, annual rpts, 2174–1

Transit systems finances and operations, by mode of transport, size of fleet, and for 468 systems, 1989, annual rpt, 7884–4

Water supply, hydrologic events, and end use, by State, 1988-89, annual rpt, 5664–12

Gloucester, Mass.

Fish and shellfish catch, wholesale receipts, prices, trade, and other market activities, weekly regional rpt, 2162–6.5

see also under By SMSA or MSA in the "Index by Categories"

Gloves and mittens

see Clothing and clothing industry

GNMA

see Government National Mortgage Association

GNP

see Gross National Product

Goats

see Livestock and livestock industry

Gochenour, Allan

"Dollar's Fall Boosts U.S. Machinery Exports, 1985-90", 6722–1.233

Goddard, Kimball E.

"Composition, Distribution, and Hydrologic Effects of Contaminated Sediments Resulting from the Discharge of Gold Milling Wastes to Whitewood Creek at Lead and Deadwood, South Dakota", 5666–27.13

Gohdes, Dorothy

"Diabetes", 4088–2

Gohmann, Stephan F.

"Medicaid Payment Rates for Nursing Homes, 1979-86", 4652–1.224

Gold

- Alaska minerals resources and production, by mineral and site, for Juneau region, 1987-88, 5608–169
- Budget of US, authoritative financial statements with appropriations, outlays, and receipts, by category and agency, FY90, annual rpt, 8104–2.1
- Business statistics, detailed data for major industries and economic indicators, *Survey of Current Business*, monthly rpt, 2702–1.9
- Coin production and monetary metals use and holdings of US Mint, by metal type, FY90, annual rpt, 8204–1
- County Business Patterns, 1988: employment, establishments, and payroll, by SIC 2- to 4-digit industry and county, annual State rpt series, 2326–6

Index by Subjects and Names

County Business Patterns, 1989: employment, establishments, and payroll, by SIC 2- to 4-digit industry and county, annual State rpt series, 2326–8

Eastern Europe foreign debt components, trade, balances, and other economic indicators, by country, 1985-89, hearing, 21248–148

Exports and imports of US, by country and detailed commodity, monthly rpt, 2422–12

Exports and imports of US, by Harmonized System 6-digit commodity and country, 1990, annual rpt, 2424–13

Exports and imports of US, by transport mode, country, and SITC 1- to 3-digit commodity, 1990, annual rpt, 2424–12

Exports of US, detailed Schedule B commodities with countries of destination, 1990, annual rpt, 2424–10

Fed Reserve banks finances and staff, 1990, annual rpt, 9364–1.1

Flow-of-funds accounts, savings, investments, and credit statements, quarterly rpt, 9365–3.3

Foreign countries economic conditions and implications for US, periodic country rpt series, 2046–4

Futures and options trading volume, by commodity and exchange, FY90, annual rpt, 11924–2

Futures trading in selected commodities and financial instruments and indexes, NYC, Chicago, and other markets activity, semimonthly rpt, 11922–5

Investment (intl) position of US, by component, industry, world region, and country, 1989-90, annual article, 2702–1.212

Investment (intl) position of US under alternative valuation methods, 1982-89, article, 2702–1.211

Jewelry trade of US, gold jewelry production and sales, and US and EC gold and silver fineness standards, by country, 1980s, hearing, 25388–58

Mineral industries census, 1987: energy use and costs, by fuel type, SIC 2- to 4-digit industry, and State, subject rpt, 2517–2

Mineral industries census, 1987: finances and operations, by establishment characteristics, SIC 2- to 4-digit industry, and State, subject rpt, 2517–1

Mineral Industry Surveys, commodity review of production, trade, stocks, and use, monthly rpt, 5612–1.10

Mineral Industry Surveys, State reviews of production, 1990, preliminary annual rpt, 5614–6

Minerals Yearbook, 1988, Vol 3: foreign country reviews of production, trade, and policy, by commodity, annual rpt series, 5604–17

Minerals Yearbook, 1989, Vol 1: commodity review of production, reserves, supply, use, and trade, annual rpt, 5604–15.27

Minerals Yearbook, 1989, Vol 2: State reviews of production and sales by commodity, and business activity, annual rpt series, 5604–16

Minerals Yearbook, 1989, Vol 2: State reviews of production, sales, and firms, by commodity, and business activity, annual rpt, 5604–34

Mines (metal) and related operations occupational injuries and incidence, employment, and hours, 1989, annual rpt, 6664–3

Price indexes (producer), by stage of processing and detailed commodity, monthly rpt, 6762–6

Price indexes (producer), by stage of processing and detailed commodity, monthly 1990, annual rpt, 6764–2

Prices in London, current and 4-year trends, weekly chartbook, 9365–1.5

Production, prices, trade, and foreign and US industry devs, by commodity, bimonthly rpt with articles, 5602–4

Production, prices, trade, use, employment, tariffs, and stockpiles, by mineral, with foreign comparisons, 1986-90, annual rpt, 5604–18

Reserve assets of US by type, *Treasury Bulletin,* quarterly rpt, 8002–4.10

Reserve assets of US, monthly rpt, 9362–1.3

Soviet Union, Eastern Europe, OECD, and selected other countries minerals production, by commodity, 1960s-90, annual rpt, 9114–4.6

Soviet Union production and reserves, 1965-90, annual rpt, 9114–4.3

Statistical Abstract of US, 1991 annual data compilation, 2324–1.25

Stock price volatility relation to interest rates, oil and gold prices, and US money supply, for 10 countries, model description and results, 1970s-88, working paper, 9381–10.116

Water quality, chemistry, hydrology, and other characteristics, 1989 local area study, 5666–27.13

Goldberg, Miriam L.

"Commercial Buildings Characteristics, 1989. Commercial Buildings Energy Consumption Survey", 3166–8.9

Goldfield, Herschel

"Costs of Providing Screening Mammography", 17266–1.1

Goldgar, D. E.

"Inheritance of Nevus Number and Size in Melanoma and Dysplastic Nevus Syndrome Kindreds", 4472–1.235

Goldsmith, Marta V.

"State Policies and Programs for Encouraging Innovation and Technology Development", 10048–81

Goldstein, Paul J.

"Frequency of Cocaine Use and Violence: A Comparison Between Men and Women", 4498–74

Golf

Coastal areas recreation facilities of Fed Govt and States, visitor and site characteristics, 1987-90 survey, regional rpt series, 2176–9

County Business Patterns, 1988: employment, establishments, and payroll, by SIC 2- to 4-digit industry and county, annual State rpt series, 2326–6

County Business Patterns, 1989: employment, establishments, and payroll, by SIC 2- to 4-digit industry and county, annual State rpt series, 2326–8

Northeastern US tennis and golf participation, by facility type and location, 1979-87, conf, 1208–356

Government and business

Older persons migration to southern coastal areas, household finances, services needs, and local economic impacts, for selected counties, 1990, 2068–38

Service industries census, 1987: establishments, receipts by source, payroll, and employment, by SIC 2- to 4-digit kind of business, State, and MSA, 2393–4

Gonorrhea

see Sexually transmitted diseases

Goodfriend, Marvin

"Information-Aggregation Bias", 9389–19.31

Goodman, Jack L., Jr.

"Characteristics of Home Mortgage Debt, 1970-89: Trends and Implications", 9366–6.263

Goodman, William C.

"Massive Census Hiring Affected Nonfarm Payroll Employment Picture in 1990", 6742–2.202

Goodrich, Donna

"Testing a Census Approach to Compiling Data on Fatal Work Injuries", 6722–1.205

Gordon, David B.

"In Search of the Liquidity Effect", 9366–7.257

Gordon, Henry A.

"Early Estimates. National Postsecondary Statistics, Collegiate and Noncollegiate: Fall 1990", 4844–16

Gordon, John D.

"Summary of the National Atmospheric Deposition Program/National Trends Network Intersite-Comparison Program, Nov. 1978-Nov. 1989", 5668–124

Goshen, Ind.

see also under By SMSA or MSA in the "Index by Categories"

Goudreau, Robert E.

"Commercial Bank Profitability: Hampered Again by Large Banks' Loan Problems", 9371–1.211

"Southeastern Interstate Banking and Consolidation: 1984-89", 9371–1.203

Gould, David M.

"Immigrant Links to the Home Country: Empirical Implications for U.S. and Canadian Bilateral Trade Flows", 9379–12.64

Gould, Gregory J.

"OCS National Compendium: Outer Continental Shelf Oil and Gas Information through October 1990", 5736–3.1

Government agencies

see Government corporations and enterprises

see Local government

see State government

see under By Federal Agency in the "Index by Categories"

see under Federal boards, committees, and commissions

see under Federal executive departments

see under Federal independent agencies

Government and business

Airline deregulation in 1978, impacts on industry structure, competition, fares, finances, operations, and intl service, with data by carrier and airport, 1980s, series, 7308–199

Appalachia local dev projects, and funding by source, by program and State, FY90, annual rpt, 9084–1

Government and business

Assistance (financial and nonfinancial) of Fed Govt, 1991 base edition with supplements, annual listing, 104–5

Blind-operated vending facilities on Federal and non-Federal property, finances and operations by agency and State, FY90, annual rpt, 4944–2

Budget of US, House concurrent resolution, with spending and revenue targets, FY92 and projected to FY96, annual rpt, 21264–2

Budget of US, midsession review of FY92 budget, by function, annual rpt, 104–7

Budget of US, obligations and authority by function, agency, and program, with summaries, analyses, and historical tables, FY92, annual rpt, 104–2

Budget of US, receipts by source, outlays by agency and program, and balances, monthly rpt, 8102–3

Budget of US, Senate concurrent resolution, with spending and revenue targets, FY92, annual rpt, 25254–1

China economic indicators and reform issues, with background data, 1950s-90, compilation of papers, 23848–155

Computer systems purchase and use, and data recording, processing, and transfer, Fed Govt standards, series, 2216–2

Construction spending by Fed Govt, by program and type of structure, FY85-92, annual article, 2042–1.206

Economic Dev Admin activities, and funding by program, recipient, State, and county, FY90 and cumulative from FY66, annual rpt, 2064–2

Export and import product standards under GATT, Natl Inst of Standards and Technology info activities, and proposed standards by agency and country, 1990, annual rpt, 2214–6

FmHA activities, and loans and grants by program and State, FY90 and trends from FY70, annual rpt, 1184–17

Food consumer research, marketing, legislation, and regulation devs, and consumption and price trends, quarterly journal, 1541–7

Franchise business opportunities by firm and kind of business, and sources of aid and info, 1990 annual listing, 2104–7

Industry structure, conduct, and govt regulation, effects on competition, series, 9406–1

Insurance (health) for long-term care, affordability and State regulation issues, 1986-90, hearing, 21368–130

Labs of Fed Govt, technology transfer cooperative agreements, patents, royalties, and incentive payments to employees, by agency, FY89, GAO rpt, 26131–85

Lands (public) acreage and grants, by State, FY90 and trends, annual rpt, 5724–1.1

Loans and loan guarantees of Fed Govt, outstanding amounts by agency and program, *Treasury Bulletin*, quarterly rpt, 8002–4.9

Mail (express parcel) shipments and revenues of private air and surface carriers, and impact of State regulation, 1976-89, 7308–201

Materials (advanced structural) devs and data needs, 1989 conf, 5608–167

Minority Business Dev Centers mgmt and financial aid, and characteristics of businesses, by region and State, FY90, annual rpt, 2104–6

Nuclear power plant operating, maintenance, and capital additions costs, relation to plant characteristics and regulation, 1974-89, 3168–108

Nuclear Regulatory Commission budget, staff, and activities, by program, FY90-93, annual rpt, 9634–9

Oil and gas primary use prohibited for power and industrial plants, and gas use by State, 1977-90, annual rpt, 3334–1

Overseas Business Reports: economic conditions, investment and export opportunities, and trade practices, country market research rpt series, 2046–6

Regulatory programs of Fed Govt, evaluation, review process, and actions taken, by agency, 1980s-90, annual rpt, 104–28

Small business capital formation sources and issues, 1990 annual conf, 9734–4

Space programs involvement by private sector, commercial dev centers funding sources and flight requests, 1986-90, GAO rpt, 26123–353

Space programs involvement by private sector, govt contracts, costs, revenue, and R&D spending, 1970s-80s and projected to 2000, 26306–6.154

Spacecraft launches and other activities of NASA and USSR, with flight data, 1957-90, annual rpt, 9504–6.1

State and local govt competition in taxes, services, regulation, and dev incentives, 1970-89, 10048–79

Technology dev programs of govts, info sources and funding, 1990 rpt, 10048–81

Telephone firms borrowing under Rural Telephone Program, loan activity by State, FY90, annual tables, 1244–8

Telephone revenue increases requested, ordered, and pending, 1984-89, annual rpt, 9284–6.8

Trucking industry deregulation by States, potential economic and market impacts, with background data, mid 1970s-80s, 7308–200

Weights, measures, and performance standards dev, proposals, and policies, 1991 annual conf, 2214–7

see also Administrative law and procedure

see also Agricultural production quotas and price supports

see also Agricultural subsidies

see also Commercial law

see also Consumer protection

see also Defense contracts and procurement

see also Defense industries

see also Environmental regulation

see also Federal aid to railroads

see also Federal funding for research and development

see also Financial institutions regulation

see also Food inspection

see also Government contracts and procurement

see also Government corporations and enterprises

see also Government inspections

see also Labor law

see also Lobbying and lobbying groups

see also Mineral leases

see also Oil and gas leases

see also Price regulation

see also Subsidies

see also Tax exempt securities

see also Tax expenditures

see also Tax incentives and shelters

see also Trade adjustment assistance

see also under names of individual Federal agencies and commissions

Government and the press

Congressional Directory, press members admitted to congressional and White House galleries, 1991-92, biennial rpt, 23874–1

see also Freedom of the press

Government assets and liabilities

AID housing and urban dev program financial statements, FY90, annual rpt, 9914–4

Alaska Power Admin financial statements, and DOE audit, 1989-90, 3006–5.22

Army and Air Force Exchange Service financial statements, FY88-89, annual rpt, 3504–21

Assets and liabilities of US, and impacts of inflation, 1990 and trends from 1948, article, 9391–1.220

Bank Insurance Fund finances, FY89-92, 26308–100

Banking industry structure and deposit insurance reform, findings and recommendations, with background data, 1989-90, 8008–147

Bond (junk) holdings of Resolution Trust Corp, quarterly press release, 9722–4

Bonneville Power Admin mgmt of Fed Columbia River Power System, finances and sales, summary data, quarterly rpt, 3222–2

Bonneville Power Admin mgmt of Fed Columbia River Power System, finances, operations, and sales by customer, FY90, annual rpt, 3224–1

Budget of US, authoritative financial statements with appropriations, outlays, and receipts, by category and agency, FY90, annual rpt, 8104–2.1

Budget of US, CBO analysis of revenue and spending alternatives and projections of economic indicators, FY92-96, annual rpt, 26304–3

Budget of US, House concurrent resolution, with spending and revenue targets, FY92 and projected to FY96, annual rpt, 21264–2

Budget of US, obligations and authority by function, agency, and program, with summaries, analyses, and historical tables, FY92, annual rpt, 104–2

Credit Union Natl Admin Central Liquidity Facility, financial statements, FY90, annual rpt, 9534–5

Enterprises sponsored by govt, capital adequacy and outstanding debt and mortgage pools, by enterprise, 1970s-89, article, 9391–16.201

Eximbank financial condition, with credit and insurance authorizations and loan activity by country, FY90, annual rpt, 9254–1

Farm Credit System banks financial statements, 1990, annual rpt, 9264–5

Farm Credit System financial condition, quarterly rpt, 9262–2

Farm Credit System financial statements and loan activity by lender type, and borrower characteristics, 1990, annual rpt, 9264–2

Index by Subjects and Names

Government census

Fed Govt consolidated financial statements based on business accounting methods, FY89-90, annual rpt, 8104–5

Fed Govt insurance and credit programs actual and potential losses, by program, 1991 article, 9381–1.207

Fed Govt receipts by source and outlays by agency, *Treasury Bulletin*, quarterly rpt, 8002–4.1

Fed Govt unfunded liabilities and govt-sponsored enterprise insured loans, by program, as of year-end FY89, article, 9389–1.204

Fed Home Loan Bank of Atlanta financial statements, quarterly rpt, 9302–37

Fed Home Loan Bank of Atlanta financial statements, 1989-90, annual rpt, 9304–1

Fed Home Loan Bank of Boston financial statements, quarterly rpt, 9302–35

Fed Home Loan Bank of Boston financial statements, 1989-90, annual rpt, 9304–2

Fed Home Loan Bank of Chicago financial statements, 1988-90, annual rpt, 9304–4

Fed Home Loan Bank of Cincinnati financial statements, 1989-90, annual rpt, 9304–6

Fed Home Loan Bank of Dallas financial statements, 1989-90, annual rpt, 9304–11

Fed Home Loan Bank of Des Moines financial statements, 1988-90, annual rpt, 9304–7

Fed Home Loan Bank of Indianapolis financial statements, 1988-90, annual rpt, 9304–10

Fed Home Loan Bank of New York financial statements, 1988-90, annual rpt, 9304–12

Fed Home Loan Bank of Pittsburgh financial statements, 1988-90, annual rpt, 9304–13

Fed Home Loan Bank of San Francisco financial statements, 1989-90, annual rpt, 9304–14

Fed Home Loan Bank of Seattle financial statements, 1988-90, annual rpt, 9304–15

Fed Home Loan Bank of Topeka financial statements, 1988-90, annual rpt, 9304–16

Fed Home Loan Banks financial statements, monthly tables, 9442–1

Fed Home Loan Banks financial statements, 1988-90, annual rpt, 9444–1

Fed Home Loan Mortgage Corp activities and financial statements, 1990, annual rpt, 9414–1

Fed Home Loan Mortgage Corp financial condition and capital adequacy, 1989, annual rpt, 5184–8

Fed Natl Mortgage Assn activities and finances, 1988-89, annual rpt, 5184–9

Fed Reserve Bank of Atlanta financial statements, 1989-90 annual rpt, 9371–4

Fed Reserve Bank of Boston financial statements, 1989-90, annual rpt, 9373–26

Fed Reserve Bank of Chicago financial statements, 1989-90, annual rpt, 9375–5

Fed Reserve Bank of Cleveland financial statements, 1989-90, annual rpt, 9377–5

Fed Reserve Bank of Dallas financial statements, 1989-90, annual rpt, 9379–2

Fed Reserve Bank of Kansas City financial statements, 1989-90, annual rpt, 9381–3

Fed Reserve Bank of Minneapolis financial statements, 1989-90, annual rpt, 9383–2

Fed Reserve Bank of New York financial statements, 1989-90, annual rpt, 9385–2

Fed Reserve Bank of Philadelphia financial statements, 1989-90, annual rpt, 9387–3

Fed Reserve Bank of Richmond financial statements, 1989-90, annual rpt, 9389–2

Fed Reserve Bank of San Francisco financial statements, 1989-90, annual rpt, 9393–2

Fed Reserve Bank of St Louis financial statements, 1989-90, annual rpt, 9391–17

Fed Reserve Board and Reserve banks finances, staff, and review of monetary policy and economic devs, 1990, annual rpt, 9364–1

Govt Natl Mortgage Assn finances, and mortgage-backed securities program, FY90, annual rpt, 5144–6

Govt-sponsored enterprises financial condition and capital adequacy, with data by enterprise, 1970s-90 and projected to 1996, 26308–99

Govt-sponsored enterprises financial condition and capital adequacy, with regulatory recommendations and data by enterprise, 1985-95, GAO rpt, 26119–296

Govt-sponsored enterprises financial condition, capital adequacy, and impacts on Federal borrowing, with data by enterprise, 1980s-90, last issue of annual rpt, 8004–15

GPO activities, finances, and production, FY90, annual rpt, 26204–1

GSA activities and finances, FY90, annual rpt, 9454–1

Helium market demand and Bur of Mines production, sales, and financial statements, FY90, annual rpt, 5604–32

Housing units (1-family) acquired by Fed Govt through foreclosure and savings instn failure, inventory by State, acquisition costs, and sales, for 4 agencies, 1986-90, GAO rpt, 26113–513

Justice Dept Asset Forfeiture Program seizures, finances, and disbursements, FY86-90, annual rpt, 6004–21

Mint (US) activities, finances, coin and medals production and holdings, and gold and silver transactions, by facility, FY90, annual rpt, 8204–1

Overseas Private Investment Corp finances and activities, with list of insured projects and firms, FY90, annual rpt, 9904–2

Panama Canal Commission finances and activities, with Canal traffic and local govt operations, FY90, annual rpt, 9664–3

Pension Benefit Guaranty Corp activities and finances, FY90, annual rpt, 9674–1

Postal Service activities, finances, and mail volume and subsidies, FY90, annual rpt, 9864–5.3

Postal Service activities, financial statements, and employment, FY86-90, annual rpt, 9864–1

Prison Industries (Federal) finances and operations, FY90, annual rpt, 6244–3

Radio Free Europe and Radio Liberty broadcast and financial data, FY90, annual rpt, 10314–1

Railroad (Amtrak) finances and operations, FY90, annual rpt, 29524–1

Railroad Retirement Accounts financial statements, FY89, annual rpt, 9704–1

Railroad retirement system funding and benefits findings and recommendations, with background industry data, 1960s-90 and projected to 2060, 9708–1

Red Cross financial statements, FY89-90, annual rpt, 29254–1

Resolution Trust Corp financial statements and activities, with data on savings instns conservatorships by State and instn, 1989, annual rpt, 9724–1

Resolution Trust Corp obligation limits compliance, and balance sheet, quarterly GAO rpt, 26102–6

Resolution Trust Corp real estate assets from failed thrifts, availability, semiannual listing series, 9722–2

Rural Telephone Bank financial statements, FY89, annual rpt, 1244–4

Savings instns failure resolution activity of Resolution Trust Corp, 1991 semiannual hearing, 21242–1

Savings instns failures, financial performance of instns under Resolution Trust Corp conservatorship, quarterly rpt, 9722–5

Southwestern Fed Power System financial statements, sales by customer, and operations and costs by project, FY90, annual rpt, 3244–1

SSA activities, litigation, finances, and staff, FY90, annual rpt, 4704–6

St Lawrence Seaway Dev Corp finances and activities, and Seaway cargo tonnage, 1989, annual rpt, 7744–1

State and local govt employees pension system cash and security holdings and finances, quarterly rpt, 2462–2

Tax (income) unpaid accounts receivable of IRS by collection status, and IRS budget and staff, with data by district, 1980s-91, hearing, 21788–200

TVA finances and electric power sales, FY90, annual rpt, 9804–1

TVA finances and operations by program and facility, FY90, annual rpt, 9804–32

Uranium enrichment facilities of DOE, financial statements, FY89-90, annual rpt, 3354–7

Western Area Power Admin activities by plant, financial statements, and sales by customer, FY90, annual rpt, 3254–1

Workers compensation programs under Federal admin, finances and operations, FY90, annual rpt, 6504–10

see also Defense budgets and appropriations

see also Foreign budgets

see also Foreign debts

see also Government revenues

see also Government securities

see also Government spending

see also Government supplies and property

see also Government trust funds

see also International reserves

see also Military supplies and property

see also Municipal bonds

see also Public debt

see also State government spending

see also U.S. savings bonds

Government bonds

see Government securities

see Municipal bonds

see Tax exempt securities

see U.S. savings bonds

Government buildings

see Public buildings

Government census

see Census of Governments

Government-citizen lawsuits

Government-citizen lawsuits

Court civil and criminal caseloads for Federal district, appeals, and bankruptcy courts, by type of suit and offense, circuit, and district, 1990, annual rpt, 18204–11

Court civil and criminal caseloads for Federal district, appeals, and special courts, 1990, annual rpt, 18204–8

Court civil and criminal caseloads for Federal district courts, 1991, annual rpt, 18204–2.1

US attorneys case processing and collections, by case type and Federal district, FY90, annual rpt, 6004–2

Government-citizen relations

- IRS collections, enforcement, and litigation activity, with data by type of tax, region, and State, FY90, annual rpt, 8304–3
- IRS correspondence regarding adjustments to taxpayer accounts, quality, and accuracy of returns processing, 1987-90, GAO rpt, 26119–329
- IRS individual income tax returns processing and taxpayer info activity, electronic filings, and refunds, periodic press release, 8302–6
- IRS telephone system for income tax aid, accuracy, 1988-89 annual conf papers, 8304–17
- Mail (penalty) to households, by content, 1987-88, annual rpt, 9864–10
- Public opinion on taxes, spending, and govt efficiency, by respondent characteristics, 1991 survey, annual rpt, 10044–2
- Returns processing and info distribution of IRS, effectiveness, 1988-90, GAO rpt, 26119–319
- SSA public access by telephone, local line availability and effects of nationwide 800 number, by State, 1989 and 1991, GAO rpt, 26121–434
- SSA telephone info service performance, 1989-90, hearing, 21788–199
- *see also* Civil rights
- *see also* Elections
- *see also* Government and business
- *see also* Government-citizen lawsuits
- *see also* Impacted areas
- *see also* Lobbying and lobbying groups
- *see also* Taxation

Government contracts and procurement

- Aerospace industry sales, orders, backlog, and firms, by product for govt, military, and other customers, 1990, annual Current Industrial Rpt, 2506–12.22
- AID and Intl Dev Cooperation Agency activities and funding, FY90-92, with developing countries economic and social conditions from 1960s, annual rpt, 9904–4
- AID dev project procurement under host country contracts, oversight issues with background data, 1991 GAO rpt, 26123–342
- Audiovisual activities and spending of Fed Govt, by whether performed in-house and agency, FY90, annual rpt, 9514–1
- Budget of US, authoritative financial statements with appropriations, outlays, and receipts, by category and agency, FY90, annual rpt, 8104–2.1
- Budget of US, object class analysis of obligations, by agency, FY92, annual rpt, 104–9

Capitol Architect activities, funding, costs, and contracts, FY88, annual rpt, 25944–1

- Capitol Architect outlays for salaries, supplies, and services, itemized by payee and function, 1st half FY91, semiannual rpt, 25922–2
- Commerce Dept programs fraud and abuse, audits and investigations, 2nd half FY91, semiannual rpt, 2002–5
- Computer and telecommunication systems acquisition plans and obligations of Fed Govt, by agency, FY89-91, last issue of annual rpt, 104–20
- Computer and telecommunication systems acquisition plans and obligations of Fed Govt, by agency, FY90-95, annual rpt, 104–33
- Computer mainframe and related equipment procurement and compatibility, for Federal agencies, FY86-89, GAO rpt series, 26125–41
- Consulting services contracts of Fed Govt, obligations by agency, FY87-89, GAO rpt, 26119–343
- DC metro area land acquisition and dev projects of Fed Govt, characteristics and funding by agency and project, FY91-95, annual rpt, 15454–1
- Disabled persons workshops finances, operations, and Federal procurement, FY80-90, annual rpt, 11714–1
- DOE headquarters support costs, for contractor services compared to in-house, 1989, 3006–5.24
- DOT programs fraud and abuse, audits and investigations, 1st half FY91, semiannual rpt, 7302–4
- Electric power capacity and use in Pacific Northwest, by energy source, projected under alternative load and demand cases, 1991-2011, annual rpt, 3224–3
- EPA programs fraud and abuse, audits and investigations, 2nd half FY91, semiannual rpt, 9182–10
- Equal employment laws compliance by Fed Govt contractors, FY90, 6508–36
- Expenditures of Fed Govt in States and local areas, by type, State, county, and city, FY90, annual rpt, 2464–3
- Expenditures of Fed Govt in States, by type, program, agency, and State, FY90, annual rpt, 2464–2
- Fed Govt consolidated financial statements based on business accounting methods, FY89-90, annual rpt, 8104–5
- Fed Govt contract awards per capita, by State, 1980s-91, fact sheet, 2326–17.36
- Fed Govt obligations by function and agency, *Treasury Bulletin*, quarterly rpt, 8002–4.2
- Finances of govts, tax systems and revenue, and fiscal structure, by level of govt and State, 1991 and historical trends, annual rpt, 10044–1
- Food aid programs purchases, by commodity, firm, and shipping point or destination, weekly rpt, 1302–3
- Forest Service acreage, staff, finances, and mgmt activities in Pacific Northwest, with data by forest, 1970s-89, annual rpt, 1204–37
- Fraud and abuse in Fed Govt, audits and investigations by agency, FY90, annual rpt, 104–29

GPO activities, finances, and production, FY90, annual rpt, 26204–1

- GSA programs fraud and abuse, audits and investigations, 2nd half FY91, semiannual rpt, 9452–8
- HHS financial aid, by program, recipient, State, and city, FY90, annual regional listings, 4004–3
- HHS programs fraud and abuse, audits and investigations, 1st half FY91, semiannual rpt, 4002–6
- Higher education enrollment, faculty, finances, and degrees, by instn level and control, and State, FY87, annual rpt, 4844–13
- HUD programs fraud and abuse, audits and investigations, FY91, semiannual rpt, 5002–8; 5002–11
- Hwy construction bids and contracts for Federal-aid hwys, by State, 1st half 1991, semiannual rpt, 7552–12
- Indian Health Service, tribal, and contract facilities hospitalization, by diagnosis, age, sex, and service area, FY89, annual rpt, 4084–5
- Input-output structure of US economy, detailed interindustry transactions for 84 industries, and components of final demand, 1986, annual article, 2702–1.206
- Input-output structure of US economy, detailed interindustry transactions for 85 industries, 1982 benchmark data, 2702–1.213
- Interior Dept programs fraud and abuse, audits and investigations, 2nd half FY91, semiannual rpt, 5302–2
- Investigations of Federal agency and program operations, summaries of findings, 1981-90, annual GAO rpt, 26104–5
- Job Training Partnership Act programs contract duration, costs, and overruns, by service delivery area, 1989-90, GAO rpt, 26106–8.13
- Kuwait reconstruction after Persian Gulf War, Army Corps of Engineers contract awards by firm and purpose, 1st qtr 1991, article, 2042–1.203
- Labor laws enacted, by State, 1990, annual article, 6722–1.209
- Labor productivity of Federal employees, indexes of output and labor costs by function, 1967-89, annual rpt, 6824–1.6
- Labor surplus areas eligible for preferential Fed Govt contracts, monthly listing, 6402–1
- Land Mgmt Bur activities and funding by State, FY89, annual rpt, 5724–13
- Manufacturing census, 1987: employment and shipments under Fed Govt contracts, by SIC 4-digit industry, 2497–7
- Minority Business Dev Centers mgmt and financial aid, and characteristics of businesses, by region and State, FY90, annual rpt, 2104–6
- NASA funding by program and type of performer, and contract awards by State, FY90, annual rpt, 9504–6.2
- NASA programs fraud and abuse, audits and investigations, 2nd half FY91, semiannual rpt, 9502–9
- Natl income and product accounts and components, *Survey of Current Business*, monthly rpt, 2702–1.24

Index by Subjects and Names

Natl income and product accounts benchmark revisions of GDP and natl income, various periods 1959-80, tables, 2702–1.227

NIH grants and contracts, by inst and type of recipient, FY81-90, annual rpt, 4434–9

NIH grants for R&D, training, construction, and medical libraries, by location and recipient, FY90, annual listings, 4434–7

NSF programs fraud and abuse, audits and investigations, 2nd half FY91, semiannual rpt, 9622–1

Nuclear weapons facilities of DOE, contract security forces skill deficiencies, and costs compared to Federal security, late 1980s, GAO rpt, 26113–493

Nuclear weapons labs and DOE screening of contractors for foreign ownership, control, or influence, compliance by lab, FY88-90, GAO rpt, 26113–520

Postal Service inspection activities, 2nd half FY91, semiannual rpt, 9862–2

Prison Industries (Federal) finances and operations, FY90, annual rpt, 6244–3

Prison Industries (Federal) sales, by commodity and Federal agency, FY90, annual rpt, 6244–5

Prisons and jails operated under private contract, costs and characteristics of instns, by facility and State, 1990, GAO rpt, 26119–321

Puerto Rico economic censuses, 1987: wholesale and retail trade sales by customer class, and employment, by SIC 2- and 3-digit kind of business, subject rpt, 2591–2.2

Savings instns failure resolution activity and finances of Resolution Trust Corp, with data by asset type, State, region, and instn, monthly rpt, 9722–3

Security of info, nondisclosure agreements for Federal and contractor employees, prepublication reviews, and costs, 1988-90, GAO rpt, 26123–328

Service industries census, 1987: establishments, receipts by source, payroll, and employment, by SIC 2- to 4-digit kind of business, State, and MSA, 2393–4

Small Business Admin programs fraud and abuse, audits and investigations, 1st half FY91, semiannual rpt, 9762–5

Small Business Admin surety bond guarantee program finances, and contracts by contractor race, obligee type, and region, FY87-89, GAO rpt, 26113–526

Space programs involvement by private sector, govt contracts, costs, revenue, and R&D spending, 1970s-80s and projected to 2000, 26306–6.154

Space programs procurement contract awards of NASA, by type, contractor, State, and country, FY91 with trends from 1961, semiannual rpt, 9502–6

State and Metro Area Data Book, 1991 data compilation, 2328–54

State Dept programs fraud and abuse, audits and investigations, 2nd half FY91, semiannual rpt, 7002–6

Statistical programs of Fed Govt, funding by agency, FY90-92, annual rpt, 104–10

Travel agencies contracts of GSA, by business size and recipient, FY88-90, GAO rpt, 26119–331

TVA finances and operations by program and facility, FY90, annual rpt, 9804–32

US attorneys civil and criminal cases by type and disposition, and collections, by Federal district, FY90, annual rpt, 6004–2.1; 6004–2.5

USDA programs fraud and abuse, audits and investigations, 1st half FY91, semiannual rpt, 1002–4

VA and non-VA facilities health services sharing contracts, by service type and region, FY90, annual rpt, 8704–5

VA programs fraud and abuse, audits and investigations, 2nd half FY90, semiannual rpt, 8602–1

Wholesale trade census, 1987: establishments, sales by customer class, employment, inventories, and expenses, by SIC 2- to 4-digit kind of business, 2407–4

see also Defense contracts and procurement

see also Federal funding for energy programs

see also Federal funding for research and development

Government corporations and enterprises

Budget of US, object class analysis of obligations, by agency, FY92, annual rpt, 104–9

Budget of US, obligations and authority by function, agency, and program, with summaries, analyses, and historical tables, FY92, annual rpt, 104–2

Budget of US, receipts by source, outlays by agency and program, and balances, monthly rpt, 8102–3

Capital adequacy of govt-sponsored enterprises, and outstanding debt and mortgage pools, by enterprise, 1970s-89, article, 9391–16.201

Financial condition and capital adequacy of govt-sponsored enterprises, with data by enterprise, 1970s-90 and projected to 1996, 26308–99

Financial condition and capital adequacy of govt-sponsored enterprises, with impacts on Federal borrowing and data by enterprise, 1980s-90, last issue of annual rpt, 8004–15

Financial condition and capital adequacy of govt-sponsored enterprises, with regulatory recommendations and data by enterprise, 1985-95, GAO rpt, 26119–296

Financial consolidated statements of Fed Govt based on business accounting methods, FY89-90, annual rpt, 8104–5

Financial operations of Fed Govt, detailed data, *Treasury Bulletin*, quarterly rpt, 8002–4

Input-output structure of US economy, detailed interindustry transactions for 84 industries, and components of final demand, 1986, annual article, 2702–1.206

Input-output structure of US economy, detailed interindustry transactions for 85 industries, 1982 benchmark data, 2702–1.213

Investigations of Federal agency and program operations, summaries of findings, 1981-90, annual GAO rpt, 26104–5

Loans (insured) of govt-sponsored enterprises, and Fed Govt unfunded liabilities, by program, as of year-end FY89, article, 9389–1.204

Government efficiency

Loans, loan guarantees, and insurance programs of Fed Govt, outstanding amounts by agency and program, FY88-90, GAO rpt, 26111–65

Mortgage loan activity, by type of lender, loan, and mortgaged property, monthly press release, 5142–18

Mortgage loan activity, by type of lender, loan, and mortgaged property, quarterly press release, 5142–30

see also Commodity Credit Corp.

see also Communications Satellite Corp.

see also Corporation for Public Broadcasting

see also Export-Import Bank

see also Federal Crop Insurance Corp.

see also Federal Deposit Insurance Corp.

see also Federal Home Loan Mortgage Corp.

see also Federal Housing Finance Board

see also Federal National Mortgage Association

see also Federal Prison Industries

see also Federal Savings and Loan Insurance Corp.

see also Financing Corp.

see also Government National Mortgage Association

see also Inter-American Foundation

see also Legal Services Corp.

see also National Railroad Passenger Corp.

see also Neighborhood Reinvestment Corp.

see also Overseas Private Investment Corp.

see also Pennsylvania Avenue Development Corp.

see also Pension Benefit Guaranty Corp.

see also Resolution Trust Corp.

see also Rural Telephone Bank

see also St. Lawrence Seaway Development Corp.

see also Student Loan Marketing Association

see also Tennessee Valley Authority

see also U.S. Postal Service

Government debt

see Public debt

Government documents

GPO activities, finances, and production, FY90, annual rpt, 26204–1

GPO pricing and marketing policies, findings and recommendations, 1990 rpt, 26208–3

Labor productivity of Federal employees, indexes of output and labor costs by function, 1967-89, annual rpt, 6824–1.6

Natl Archives and Records Admin activities, finances, holdings, and staff, FY90, annual rpt, 9514–2

Space science and related data sources, use by format and user type, FY90, annual rpt, 9504–11

see also CD-ROM catalogs and guides

see also CD-ROM releases

see also Environmental impact statements

see also Federal Inspectors General reports

see also Government forms and paperwork

see also Government publications lists

Government efficiency

Air Force fiscal mgmt system operations and techniques, quarterly rpt, 3602–1

Budget of US, Bush Admin mgmt proposals, by function, FY92, annual rpt, 104–2.2

Court caseloads, actions, procedure duration, judges, and jurors, by Federal district and appeals court, 1986-91, annual rpt, 18204–3

Government efficiency

Court civil and criminal case dispositions and trials, and time to trial and case disposition, for Federal district courts, 1990, annual rpt, 18204–8.18

DC production index, by component, 1987-91, article, 9389–1.203

Drug marketing application processing of FDA, by drug, purpose, and producer, 1990, annual rpt, 4064–14

Employment discrimination complaints, processing, and disposition, by complaint type and Federal agency, FY89, annual rpt, 9244–11

Energy use and efficiency of Fed Govt, by agency and fuel type, FY90, annual rpt, 3304–22

EPA regulatory and protection programs operations and mgmt goals, progress and activities, by office, quarterly rpt, 9182–11

Fed Govt agencies and program operations investigations, summaries of findings, 1981-90, annual GAO rpt, 26104–5

FmHA activities, and loans and grants by program and State, FY90 and trends from FY70, annual rpt, 1184–17

Food stamp eligibility and payment errors, by type, recipient characteristics, and State, FY89, annual rpt, 1364–15

GPO pricing and marketing policies, findings and recommendations, 1990 rpt, 26208–3

Incentive awards to Federal employees, costs, and benefits, by award type and agency, FY89, annual rpt, 9844–20

Info mgmt activities of Fed Govt, technology spending, and paperwork burden, by agency, planned FY91-92, annual rpt, 104–19

IRS individual income tax returns processing and taxpayer info activity, electronic filings, and refunds, periodic press release, 8302–6

IRS operating costs, collections, and ratios, FY90, annual rpt, 8304–3.2

Labor productivity and productivity for other inputs, indexes and changes for 2- to 4-digit industries and govt functions, 1984-89, annual article, 6722–1.228

Labor productivity of Fed Govt, indexes of output and labor costs, by function, FY67-89, annual rpt, 6824–4

Labor productivity of govt employees, indexes of output and labor costs by function, FY67-89, annual rpt, 6824–1.6

Merit system oversight and enforcement activities of OPM, series, 9496–2

Merit Systems Protection Board decisions on appeals of Fed Govt personnel actions, by agency and region, FY90, annual rpt, 9494–2

Postal Service activities, finances, and mail volume and subsidies, FY90, annual rpt, 9864–5

Postal Service activities, financial statements, and employment, FY86-90, annual rpt, 9864–1

Postal Service customer satisfaction, and on-time 1st class mail delivery, by region and city, 1991 survey, press release, 9868–1

Postal Service productivity, indexes of output and labor, capital, and other inputs, alternative model descriptions and results, 1960s-89, 9688–6

Public opinion on taxes, spending, and govt efficiency, by respondent characteristics, 1991 survey, annual rpt, 10044–2

Regulatory programs of Fed Govt, evaluation, review process, and actions taken, by agency, 1980s-90, annual rpt, 104–28

SSA activities, and OASDHI admin, 1930s-90 and projected to 2064, annual data compilation, 4704–12

SSA activities, litigation, finances, and staff, FY90, annual rpt, 4704–6

SSA telephone info service performance, 1989-90, hearing, 21788–199

Tax (income) returns processing, IRS workload forecasts, compliance, and enforcement, data compilation, 1991 annual rpt, 8304–8

Tax (income) unpaid accounts receivable of IRS by collection status, and IRS budget and staff, with data by district, 1980s-91, hearing, 21788–200

Unemployment insurance programs of States, quality appraisal results, FY90, annual rpt, 6404–16

see also Federal Inspectors General reports *see also* General Accounting Office

Government employees

Employment and Earnings, detailed data, monthly rpt, 6742–2.5

Employment and payroll, by function and level of govt, 1990, annual rpt series, 2466–1

Employment, earnings, and hours, monthly press release, 6742–5

Employment, unemployment, and labor force characteristics, by State, MSA, and selected city, 1990, annual rpt, 6744–7.2; 6744–7.3

New England States economic indicators, Fed Reserve 1st District, monthly rpt, 9373–2.2

Palau admin, and social, economic, and govtl data, FY90, annual rpt, 7004–6

Science and engineering employment and education, and R&D spending, for US and selected foreign countries, 1991 annual rpt, 9627–35.2

Science and engineering PhDs, by field, instn, employment prospects, sex, race, and other characteristics, 1960s-90, annual rpt, 9627–30

State and Metro Area Data Book, 1991 data compilation, 2328–54

Statistical Abstract of US, 1991 annual data compilation, 2324–1.9

Terrorism (intl) incidents, casualties, and attacks on US targets, by attack type and country, 1990, annual rpt, 7004–22

Terrorism (intl) incidents, casualties, and attacks on US targets, by attack type and world area, 1990, annual rpt, 7004–13

Voting and registration, by socioeconomic and demographic characteristics, 1990 congressional election, biennial Current Population Rpt, 2546–1.454

Youth labor force status, by sex, race, and industry div, summer 1987-91, annual press release, 6744–14

see also Civil service pensions
see also Civil service system
see also Congressional employees
see also Corruption and bribery
see also Federal employees

Index by Subjects and Names

see also Federal pay
see also Government pay
see also International employees
see also Labor-management relations in government
see also Military pay
see also Military personnel
see also Officials
see also Police
see also Political ethics
see also Postal employees
see also Public service employment
see also State and local employees
see also State and local employees pay
see also State police

Government energy use

Auto fleet size, trip characteristics, and energy use, by fleet type, 1970s-89, annual rpt, 3304–5.3

Bonneville Power Admin mgmt of Fed Columbia River Power System, finances, operations, and sales by customer, FY90, annual rpt, 3224–1

Bonneville Power Admin sales, revenues, and rates, by customer and customer type, 1990, semiannual rpt, 3222–1

Building (commercial) energy use, costs, and conservation, by building characteristics, survey rpt series, 3166–8

Business statistics, detailed data for major industries and economic indicators, *Survey of Current Business*, monthly rpt, 2702–1.13

Conservation aid of Fed Govt to public and nonprofit private instns, by building type and State, 1990, annual rpt, 3304–15

Conservation of energy, State programs aid from Fed Govt, and energy savings, by State, 1989, annual rpt, 3304–1

DOD prime contract awards, by category, contract and contractor type, and service branch, FY81-1st half FY91, semiannual rpt, 3542–1

DOD prime contract awards, by category, contractor type, and State, FY88-90, annual rpt, 3544–11

DOD prime contract awards, by detailed procurement category, FY87-90, annual rpt, 3544–18

DOE energy use, costs, and conservation, by end use, fuel type, and field office, FY90, annual rpt, 3004–27

Electric utilities privately owned, finances and operations, detailed data, 1989, annual rpt, 3164–23

Fed Govt building energy spending, and conservation retrofit costs and savings, 1988-90, 26358–240

Fed Govt building energy use and efficiency, by agency, annual rpt, discontinued, 3304–25

Fed Govt energy use and efficiency, by agency and fuel type, FY90, annual rpt, 3304–22

Fed Govt energy use, by agency and fuel type, FY76-89, annual rpt, 3164–74.1

Gasoline and other motor fuel use, by consuming sector and State, 1990, annual rpt, 7554–1.1

Natural gas interstate pipeline company detailed financial and operating data, by firm, 1989, annual rpt, 3164–38

Pacific Northwest electric power capacity and use, by energy source, projected under alternative load and demand cases, 1991-2011, annual rpt, 3224–3

Index by Subjects and Names

Persian Gulf War costs to US by category and service branch, and offsetting contributions by allied country, monthly rpt, 102–3

Persian Gulf War costs to US by category and service branch, and offsetting contributions by allied country, various periods FY90-91, annual rpt, 104–7

Persian Gulf War fuel demand of US military by source, alternative estimates, 1990-91, article, 3162–44

Rural Electrification Admin borrowers wholesale purchases, by borrower, supplier, and State, 1940-89, annual rpt, 1244–5

Southwestern Fed Power System financial statements, sales by customer, and operations and costs by project, FY90, annual rpt, 3244–1

TVA energy use by fuel type, and conservation costs and savings, FY90, annual rpt, 9804–26

Government forms and paperwork

Alien workers (unauthorized) and Fair Labor Standards Act employer compliance, hiring impacts, and aliens overstaying visas by country and State, 1986-90, annual rpt, 6264–6

Consultants and experts appointed for temporary employment in Federal agencies, and rule violations, 1986-89, GAO rpt, 26119–354

Criminal sentences for Federal offenses, guidelines by offense and circumstances, series, 17668–1

Data collection using tax and other govt admin records, methodological and disclosure issues, 1988-89 annual conf papers, 8304–17

Deaths of infants, rates and racial misclassification on death certificates, for Oklahoma Indians, 1975-88, article, 4042–3.209

DOE data collection forms and related rpts, 1990, annual listing, 3164–86

Employment by industry and State, impacts of decline in employers voluntary reporting on Continuous Work History Sample, 1970s-86, article, 4742–1.203

Energy Info Admin activities, 1990, annual rpt, 3164–29

Fed Govt data collection activities, and quality and privacy issues, 1990 conf, 106–4.14

Fed Govt info mgmt activities, technology spending, and paperwork burden, by agency, planned FY91-92, annual rpt, 104–19

Fed Govt regulatory programs evaluation, review process, and actions taken, by agency, 1980s-90, annual rpt, 104–28

Irrigation projects of Reclamation Bur, acreage limits monitoring activities by region, 1988-90, annual rpt, 5824–13

IRS correspondence regarding adjustments to taxpayer accounts, quality, and accuracy of returns processing, 1987-90, GAO rpt, 26119–329

IRS large cash transaction rpts filed and penalties for nonfiling by region, and Federal money laundering investigations use of rpts, 1989-91, GAO rpt, 26119–356

Mail volume to and from households, use, and views, by class, source, content, and household characteristics, 1987-88, annual rpt, 9864–10

Mortgage loan activity rpts filed under Home Mortgage Disclosure Act, and instns covered, 1981-90, article, 9362–1.206

Occupational deaths data collection from multiple sources, BLS pilot study results for 2 States, 1990, article, 6722–1.249

Occupational exposure to hazardous substances and conditions, measurement, and proposed standards, series, 4246–1

Occupational injury death data collection methods of BLS and Texas, with Texas data by accident type and industry div, 1986, article, 6722–1.205

Pension laws admin and enforcement under Employee Retirement Income Security Act (ERISA), 1990, annual rpt, 6684–1

Recordkeeping Practices Survey, 1989: data coverage, methodology, businesses views, and applications for 1992 economic censuses, 2328–67

Social security earnings records errors and rates, by employment type, late 1930s-87, GAO rpt, 26121–422

Social security number issues, 1937-89, annual rpt, 4744–3.2

SSA activities, and OASDHI admin, 1930s-90 and projected to 2064, annual data compilation, 4704–12

State and local govts receiving Federal funds, compliance with Federal audit requirements, 1991 article, 10042–1.204

Tax (income) returns and supplemental documents filed, by type, FY90 and projected to FY99, semiannual rpt, 8302–4

Tax (income) returns filed, by type, IRS service center, and whether full-paid, refund, and electronically filed, 1990 and projected to 1998, semiannual rpt, 8302–7

Tax (income) returns filed by type of filer, selected income items, quarterly rpt, 8302–2.1

Tax (income) returns of individuals, IRS processing and taxpayer info activity, electronic filings, and refunds, periodic press release, 8302–6

Tax (income) returns processing, IRS workload forecasts, compliance, and enforcement, data compilation, 1991 annual rpt, 8304–8

Tax (income) withholding and related documents filed, by type and IRS service center, 1990 and projected 1991-98, annual rpt, 8304–22

Tax collection, enforcement, and litigation activity of IRS, with data by type of tax, region, and State, FY90, annual rpt, 8304–3

Tax returns and supplemental documents filed, by type, FY89 and projected to FY98, annual article, 8302–2.208

Tax returns filed, by type of tax and IRS district, 1989 and projected 1990-97, annual rpt, 8304–24

Tax returns filed, by type of tax and IRS region and service center, projected 1990-97 and trends from 1978, annual rpt, 8304–9

Tax returns processing and info distribution of IRS, effectiveness, 1988-90, GAO rpt, 26119–319

Unemployment insurance wage records use in evaluating Job Training Partnership Act programs, 1986-87, 15496–1.13

Government information

Vital statistics reporting, natl standards revisions for birth, death, marriage, and divorce certificates, and for fetal death and abortion rpts, 1989, 4147–4.27

see also Licenses and permits

Government grants

see Community Development Block Grants

see Federal aid programs

see Federal funding for research and development

see Revenue sharing

see Urban Development Action Grants

see terms beginning with Federal aid

Government housing

see Public housing

Government information

Advisory committees of Fed Govt, and members, staff, meetings, and costs by agency, FY90, annual rpt, 9454–18

Assistance (financial and nonfinancial) of Fed Govt, 1991 base edition with supplements, annual listing, 104–5

BEA rpts data coverage and availability, 1991 annual article, 2702–1.203

Computer and telecommunication systems acquisition plans and obligations of Fed Govt, by agency, FY89-91, last issue of annual rpt, 104–20

Computer and telecommunication systems acquisition plans and obligations of Fed Govt, by agency, FY90-95, annual rpt, 104–33

Criminal records repository characteristics, holdings, use, and reporting requirements, by State, 1989, 6068–241

Deaths of beneficiaries, erroneous benefit payments, and use of SSA and other sources of death info, by agency, 1990, GAO rpt, 26121–406

Export and import product standards under GATT, Natl Inst of Standards and Technology info activities, and proposed standards by agency and country, 1990, annual rpt, 2214–6

Fed Govt info mgmt activities, technology spending, and paperwork burden, by agency, planned FY91-92, annual rpt, 104–19

Firearm purchasers criminal records checks, and firearms use in crime, with data by State, 1987-90, 26358–244

Fishery info and rpts of Natl Marine Fisheries Service, 1990, annual rpt, 2164–1

Franchise business opportunities by firm and kind of business, and sources of aid and info, 1990 annual listing, 2104–7

Geological Survey activities and funding, FY90, annual rpt, 5664–8

Geological Survey Water Resources Div history, series, 5668–118

Global climate change trends and contributing gases levels, Federal and intl data collection activities, mgmt, and inventory, 1990 rpt, 3028–4

Hazardous substances industrial releases, accuracy of EPA reporting, and nonreporting facilities by State and industry, 1987-90, GAO rpt, 26113–532

Health care services outcome research and practice guidelines dev activities and funding of Agency for Health Care Policy and Research, FY88-89, 4188–70

Health care treatments effectiveness info, feasibility of linking Federal and other databases, 1991 narrative rpt, 4188–73

Government information

Labor productivity of Federal employees, indexes of output and labor costs by function, 1967-89, annual rpt, 6824–1.6

Land Mgmt Bur activities and finances, and public land acreage and use, annual State rpt series, 5724–11

Oceanographic research and distribution activities of World Data Center A by country, and cruises by ship, 1989, annual rpt, 2144–15

Pension laws admin and enforcement under Employee Retirement Income Security Act (ERISA), 1990, annual rpt, 6684–1

Security measures and classification actions of Fed Govt monitored by Info Security Oversight Office, FY90, annual rpt, 9454–21

Security of Fed Govt computer systems with sensitive unclassified data, plans by characteristics of info and system, and agency, 1989, 2218–85

Security of info, nondisclosure agreements for Federal and contractor employees, prepublication reviews, and costs, 1988-90, GAO rpt, 26123–328

Space science and related data sources, use by format and user type, FY90, annual rpt, 9504–11

Space science missions data archival storage of NASA, holdings, and missions not archived, 1950s-91, 26125–43

Tax (income) returns computer matching program to indentify underreported income, effectiveness, 1987, GAO rpt, 26119–325

USIA activities, finances, and info services, FY91, annual rpt, 17594–1

Weather services activities and funding, by Federal agency, planned FY91-92, annual rpt, 2144–2

see also CD-ROM catalogs and guides

see also CD-ROM releases

see also Computer data file guides

see also Freedom of information

see also Government and the press

see also Government documents

see also Government forms and paperwork

see also Government publications lists

see also Statistical programs and activities

Government inspections

Air taxi and commuter airlines operating certificates, FAA revocations for safety violations, 1987-91, GAO rpt, 26113–547

Animal protection, licensing, and inspection activities of USDA, and animals used in research, by State, FY89, annual rpt, 1394–10

Assistance (financial and nonfinancial) of Fed Govt, 1991 base edition with supplements, annual listing, 104–5

Auto safety, crash test results by domestic and foreign model, press release series, 7766–7

Board and care homes regulation and rules enforcement by States, 1988, 4008–112

Coal Surface Mining Reclamation and Enforcement Office activities and funding, by State and Indian tribe, FY90, annual rpt, 5644–1

Customs Service activities, collections, entries processed by mode of transport, and seizures, FY86-90, annual rpt, 8144–1

DOT employment, by subagency, occupation, and selected personnel characteristics, FY90, annual rpt, 7304–18

Hazardous material transport accidents, casualties, and damage, by mode of transport, with DOT control activities, 1989, annual rpt, 7304–4

Hazardous waste incinerators health and safety violations, by type of violation, 1991 rpt, 6608–5

Hearing aid performance test results, by make and model, 1991 annual rpt, 8704–3

Hwy funding and inspection activity of FHwA, FY88, annual rpt, 7304–1

Immigration and Naturalization Service mgmt effectiveness, applications processing, inspections, staffing, and funding, FY85-90, GAO rpt, 26119–317

Imports detained by FDA, by reason, product, shipper, brand, and country, monthly listing, 4062–2

Info Security Oversight Office monitoring of Federal security measures and classification actions, FY90, annual rpt, 9454–21

Labor productivity of Federal employees, indexes of output and labor costs by function, 1967-89, annual rpt, 6824–1.6

Mines safety and health enforcement, training, and funding, with casualties, by type of mine and State, FY89, annual rpt, 6664–6

Natl Hwy Traffic Safety Admin activities and grants, and fatal traffic accident data, 1989, annual rpt, 7764–1

Nuclear Regulatory Commission activities, finances, and staff, with data for individual power plants, FY90, annual rpt, 9634–2

Nuclear Regulatory Commission budget, staff, and activities, by program, FY90-93, annual rpt, 9634–9

Nuclear weapons elimination under Intermediate-Range Nuclear Forces Treaty, US and USSR on site inspections, and US costs and staffing, FY89-91, GAO rpt, 26123–364

Occupational exposure to hazardous substances and conditions, measurement, and proposed standards, series, 4246–1

Occupational Safety and Health admin standards, enforcement, and training activities, inspectors views, 1989-90, GAO rpt, 26121–391

Pipeline accidents, casualties, safety enforcement activity, and Federal funding, by State, 1989, annual rpt, 7304–5

Postal Service inspection activities, FY90, annual rpt, 9864–9

Postal Service inspection activities, 2nd half FY91, semiannual rpt, 9862–2

Railroad accidents, casualties, and damage, Fed Railroad Admin activities, and safety inspectors by State, 1989, annual rpt, 7604–12

Railroad safety inspections by Fed Railroad Admin, defects and violations reported by type, 1985-89, GAO rpt, 26113–515

Truck and bus safety inspections, fines, and vehicles and drivers ordered out of service, by State, with program funding, FY89, 25268–78

Index by Subjects and Names

Truck safety inspections of FHwA conducted FY87-88, compliance review status as of 1990, GAO rpt, 26113–505

see also Federal Inspectors General reports

see also Food inspection

see also Government investigations

Government investigations

Airport security operations to prevent hijacking, screening results, enforcement actions, and hijacking attempts, 2nd half 1989, semiannual rpt, 7502–5

Alien workers (unauthorized) and Fair Labor Standards Act employer compliance, hiring impacts, and aliens overstaying visas by country and State, 1986-90, annual rpt, 6264–6

Assistance (financial and nonfinancial) of Fed Govt, 1991 base edition with supplements, annual listing, 104–5

Child labor law violations and injuries by industry group, and employment of minors by selected characteristics, 1983-90, GAO rpt, 26121–426

Communist countries trade with US, by detailed commodity and country, quarterly rpt with articles, 9882–2

Community Relations Service investigation and mediation of minority discrimination disputes, FY90, annual rpt, 6004–9

Election campaign finances and FEC activities, various periods 1975-90, annual rpt, 9274–1

Exports and imports, trade agreements and relations, and USITC investigations, 1990, annual rpt, 9884–5

HHS research and evaluation programs, 1970-90, annual listing, 4004–30

Imports and tariff provisions effect on US industries and products, investigations with background financial and operating data, series, 9886–4

Imports injury to price-supported US agricultural industry, investigations with background financial and operating data, series, 9886–10

Imports injury to US industries from foreign subsidized products and sales at less than fair value, investigations with background financial and operating data, series, 9886–19

Imports injury to US industries from foreign subsidized products, investigations with background financial and operating data, series, 9886–15

Imports injury to US industries from sales at less than fair value, investigations with background financial and operating data, series, 9886–14

Imports injury to US industries, trade-remedy law petitions brought, by provision, 1979-90, article, 9391–1.215

Imports injury to US industries, USITC activities, investigations, and rpts, FY90, annual rpt, 9884–1

Imports injury to US industries, USITC rpts, 1983-90, annual listing, 9884–12

Imports under Generalized System of Preferences, status, and US tariffs, with trade by country and US economic impacts, for selected commodities, 1986-90, annual rpt, 9884–23

Labor Standards Act admin, with coverage under minimum wage and overtime provisions, and illegal employment of minors, by industry div, FY89, annual rpt, 6504–2.1

Index by Subjects and Names

Maritime Commission activities, case filings by type and disposition, and civil penalties by shipper, FY90, annual rpt, 9334–1

Mines safety and health enforcement, training, and funding, with casualties, by type of mine and State, FY89, annual rpt, 6664–6

Nuclear material inventory discrepancies at DOE and contractor facilities, 1989/90, annual rpt, 3344–2

Occupational deaths, by equipment type, circumstances, and OSHA standards violated, series, 6606–2

Pension laws admin and enforcement under Employee Retirement Income Security Act (ERISA), 1990, annual rpt, 6684–1

Securities industry self-regulatory organizations oversight by SEC, violations, and complaints, FY86-89, GAO rpt, 26119–336

Securities law enforcement activities of SEC, FY90, annual rpt, 9734–2.3

Toxicology Natl Program research and testing activities, FY89 and planned FY90, annual rpt, 4044–16

see also Congressional investigations

see also Criminal investigations

see also Environmental impact statements

see also Federal Inspectors General reports

see also General Accounting Office

see also Government inspections

Government lands

see Public lands

Government loans and grants

see Federal aid programs

see Federal funding for research and development

see terms beginning with Federal aid

Government National Mortgage Association

Budget of US, obligations and authority by function, agency, and program, with summaries, analyses, and historical tables, FY92, annual rpt, 104–2

Finances and mortgage-backed securities program of GNMA, FY90, annual rpt, 5144–6

Mortgage applications by disposition, and secondary loan market sales by purchaser type, by applicant and neighborhood characteristics, 1990, article, 9362–1.206

Government ownership

Electric power wholesale purchases of REA borrowers, by borrower, supplier, and State, 1940-89, annual rpt, 1244–5

Electric power wholesale trade, by utility, type of ownership, and region, 1988, biennial rpt, 3164–92

Electric utilities publicly owned, finances and operations, 1989, annual rpt, 3164–24.1

Hospital deaths of Medicare patients, actual and expected rates by diagnosis, with hospital characteristics, by instn, FY87-89, annual regional rpt series, 4654–14

Hospital reimbursement by Medicare under prospective payment system, impacts on instns and beneficiaries, 1988, annual rpt, 4654–13

Hospitals, receipts by source, contract services, expenses, and employment, by facility type and State, 1987 Census of Service Industries, 2393–4.12

Mental health care facilities, staff, and patient characteristics, *Statistical Notes* series, 4506–3

Mentally retarded persons care facilities and residents by selected characteristics, and use of Medicaid services and waiver programs, by State, late 1970s-80s, 4658–49

Uranium supply and industry operations, various periods 1947-90 and projected to 2000, annual rpt, 3164–65

see also Expropriation of alien property

see also Government assets and liabilities

see also Government corporations and enterprises

see also Government supplies and property

see also Military bases, posts, and reservations

see also Military health facilities and services

see also Military supplies and property

see also Public buildings

see also Public lands

see also Public works

see also Socialism

see also Surplus government property

see also Veterans health facilities and services

Government pay

State and Metro Area Data Book, 1991 data compilation, 2328–54

Statistical Abstract of US, 1991 annual data compilation, 2324–1.9

see also Civil service pensions

see also Educational employees pay

see also Federal pay

see also Military benefits and pensions

see also Military pay

see also State and local employees pay

Government price control

see Price regulation

Government Printing Office

Activities, finances, and production of GPO, FY90, annual rpt, 26204–1

Bookstores of GPO, 1991 annual listing, 2304–2

Budget of US, authoritative financial statements with appropriations, outlays, and receipts, by category and agency, FY90, annual rpt, 8104–2.1

Budget of US, obligations and authority by function, agency, and program, with summaries, analyses, and historical tables, FY92, annual rpt, 104–2

Pricing and marketing policies of GPO, findings and recommendations, 1990 rpt, 26208–3

Government publications

see Government documents

see Government publications lists

Government publications lists

Acid rain and air pollution environmental impacts, bibl, 1989 listing, 5506–5.26

Acid rain research activities of Natl Acid Precipitation Assessment Program, 1990 annual rpt, 14354–1

Agricultural data compilation, 1990 and trends from 1920, annual rpt, 1004–14

Agricultural Statistics Board releases planned 1991, annual listing, 1614–1

BEA rpts data coverage and availability, 1991 annual article, 2702–1.203

BEA rpts data coverage and availability, 1991 rpt, 2708–45

BLS labor force data, major statistical and analytical programs and rpts, as of Feb 1991, listing, 6728–35

Government publications lists

Census Bur activities, rpts, and user services, monthly rpt, 2302–3

Census Bur rpts and data files, coverage and availability, 1991 annual listing, 2304–2

Census Bur rpts and data files, coverage, availability, and use, series, 2326–7

Census Bur rpts and data files, monthly listing, 2302–6

Census of Population and Housing, data concordance of 1990 and 1980 census rpts, pamphlet, 2308–61

Census of Population and Housing, 1990: data coverage and release schedules for rpts, 1991, 2308–62

Census of Population and Housing, 1990: voting age and total population by race, and housing units, redistricting counts required under PL 94-171, State CD-ROM user guide, 2308–63

Civil Rights Commission rpts, 1991 listing, 11048–188

Commerce Dept rpts, biweekly listing, 2002–1

Crime and criminal justice data collection programs and rpts, 1989, annual listing, 6064–25

Current Population Reports, historical index, 1991 listing, 2546–2.160

DOD Directorate for Info Operations and Rpts publications, 1989 listing, 3548–21

DOE data collection forms and related rpts, 1990, annual listing, 3164–86

Drug abuse and treatment research summaries, resource materials and grant listings, periodic rpt, 4492–4

Drug enforcement, offenses, and public opinion, BJS rpts, 1975-89, annual pamphlet, 6064–30

Economic Dev Admin rpts, 1988-90, annual listing, 2064–9

Education Dept rpts, quarterly listing, 4812–1

Education Statistics Natl Center rpts, periodic listing, 4822–1

Employment Policy Natl Commission activities and rpts, 1990 annual rpt, 15494–1

Energy Info Admin activities, 1990, annual rpt, 3164–29

Energy Info Admin rpts and data files, 1990, listing, 3168–117

EPA rpts in NTIS collection, quarterly listing, 9182–5

Export and import statistics, Census Bur publications and data files, 1991 guide, 2428–11

Fishery info and rpts of Natl Marine Fisheries Service, 1990, annual rpt, 2164–1

Foreign countries *Background Notes,* summary social, political, and economic data, 1991 listing, 7006–2.29; 7006–2.48; 7006–2.55

FTC activities, FY89, annual narrative rpt, 9404–1

GAO rpts, FY90, annual listing, 26104–17

GAO rpts, topical listings, series, 26106–10

Geological Survey rpts and research journal articles, monthly listing, 5662–1

Geological Survey rpts, 1990, annual listing, 5664–4

Govt census, 1987: data coverage of final rpts, 2460–1

Health Statistics Natl Center rpts, quarterly listing, 4122–2

Government publications lists

Index by Subjects and Names

HHS research and evaluation programs, 1970-90, annual listing, 4004–30

Homelessness issues, population at risk, contributing factors, and Federal funding for services and prevention, with bibl, 1991 compilation of papers, 25928–9

Hwy construction and design R&D, quarterly journal, 7552–3

Hwy Traffic Safety Natl Admin and Fed Hwy Admin activities, 1989, annual rpt, 7764–1

Intl Trade Admin rpts, biweekly rpt, annual listing, 2042–24

Justice Natl Inst rpts, 1983-89, listing, 6068–240

Libraries and Info Science Natl Commission activities, FY90, annual rpt, 15634–1

Library of Congress rpts and products, 1990, annual listing, 26404–6

Library of Congress rpts and recordings, 1991, biennial listing, 26404–5

MarAd activities, finances, subsidies, and world merchant fleet operations, FY90, annual rpt, 7704–14

Medicare reimbursement of hospitals under prospective payment system, methodology, inputs, and data by diagnostic group, 1991 annual rpt, 17204–1

Minerals Mgmt Service OCS rpts, 1988, annual listing, 5734–5

Minerals resources of Alaska, production, oil and gas leases, reserves, and exploratory wells, with maps and bibl, 1989, annual rpt, 5664–11

Mines Bur rpts and patents, monthly listing, 5602–2

Mines Bur rpts and patents, 1985-89, quinquennial listing, 5608–168

Mines Bur rpts, annual listing, periodicity change, 5604–40

Natl Archives and Records Admin activities, finances, holdings, and staff, FY90, annual rpt, 9514–2

Natl Inst of Standards and Technology rpts, 1990, annual listing, 2214–1

NIH Natl Library of Medicine activities, holdings, and grants, FY88-90, annual rpt, 4464–1

NIH rpts, 1991 annual listing, 4434–2

NOAA Environmental Research Labs rpts, FY90, annual listing, 2144–25

NSF activities, finances, and funding by program, FY90, annual rpt, 9624–6

NSF rpts, 1990 annual listing, 9624–16

NSF Science Resources Studies Div rpts, 1988-91, listing, 9627–22

Occupational safety and health research and demonstration grants by State, and project listing, FY90, annual rpt, 4244–2

Oil enhanced recovery research contracts of DOE, project summaries, funding, and bibl, quarterly rpt, 3002–14

Radiation exposure of population near Hanford, Wash, nuclear plant, with methodology, 1944-66, series, 3356–5

Soil survey rpt abstracts, for Pacific Northwest counties, 1989 rpt, 5668–114

Soil surveys and maps for counties, 1899-1990, annual listing, 1264–11

Space science and related data sources and availability, 1991 annual listing, 9504–10

Space science and related data sources, use by format and user type, FY90, annual rpt, 9504–11

SSA activities, litigation, finances, and staff, FY90, annual rpt, 4704–6

SSA research rpts and microdata files, 1991 biennial listing, 4744–12

Statistical Abstract of US, guide to sources, 1991 annual rpt, 2324–1

Technology Assessment Office activities and rpts, FY90, annual rpt, 26354–3

Telecommunications and Info Natl Admin rpts, FY90, annual listing, 2804–3

Toxicology Natl Program research and testing activities, FY89 and planned FY90, annual rpt, 4044–16

Travel to US, market research data available from US Travel and Tourism Admin, 1991, annual rpt, 2904–15

USDA rpts, computer data files, and visual aids, 1991 annual listing, 1004–13

USITC activities, investigations, and rpts, FY90, annual rpt, 9884–1

USITC rpts, 1983-90, annual listing, 9884–12

Vital and Health Statistics series and other NCHS rpts, 1990, annual listing, 4124–1

see also CD-ROM catalogs and guides

Government regulation

see Administrative law and procedure

see Antitrust law

see Environmental regulation

see Government and business

see Government forms and paperwork

see Government inspections

see Interstate commerce

see Licenses and permits

see Price regulation

Government reorganization

Budget of US, Bush Admin mgmt proposals, by function, FY92, annual rpt, 104–2.2

Military forces, research, and manufacturing base restructuring following relaxation of East-West tensions, with background data, FY87-93, 26358–245

Navy command proposed decentralization and relocation from DC area, savings, and cost of living indicators for 14 MSAs, 1980s, GAO rpt, 26123–346

SSA staff reductions impacts on client services, 1980s, GAO rpt, 26121–415

Government revenues

Economic and employment conditions, alternative BLS projections to 2005 and trends 1970s-90, biennial article, 6722–1.251

Fed Govt consolidated financial statements based on business accounting methods, FY89-90, annual rpt, 8104–5

Fed Govt finances, cash and debt transactions, daily tables, 8102–4

Fed Govt financial transactions, *Survey of Current Business*, monthly rpt, 2702–1.9

Fed Govt programs under Ways and Means Committee jurisdiction, finances, operations, and participant characteristics, FY70s-90, annual rpt, 21784–11

Fed Govt receipts by source and outlays by agency, *Treasury Bulletin*, quarterly rpt, 8002–4.1

Fed Reserve foreign currency transactions impact on Fed Reserve receipts, profits, and Treasury payments, 1975-89, article, 9377–1.205

Finances of govts, by level of govt, State, and for large cities and counties, annual rpt series, 2466–2

Finances of govts, revenue and spending by level of govt, natl income and product accounts, selected years 1929-92, annual rpt, 204–1.6

Finances of govts, revenues by source, natl income and product accounts, *Survey of Current Business*, monthly rpt, 2702–1.25

Finances of govts, tax systems and revenue, and fiscal structure, by level of govt and State, 1991 and historical trends, annual rpt, 10044–1

Hwy receipts by source, and spending by function, by level of govt and State, 1990, annual rpt, 7554–1.3

Natl income and product accounts and components, *Survey of Current Business*, monthly rpt, 2702–1.24

New England States govt revenue and spending issues, with data by State, 1970s-80s, article, 9373–25.202

North Central States public debt by State, and govt spending changes by purpose, 1980s, article, 9375–1.207

Palau admin, and social, economic, and govtl data, FY90, annual rpt, 7004–6

Public lands acreage and use, and Land Mgmt Bur activities and finances, annual State rpt series, 5724–11

Puerto Rico statehood referendum proposal, impacts on Federal tax revenue and aid outlays, corporations tax-favored status, and economic conditions, projected FY91-2000, 26306–3.112

State and local govt revenue by source and outlays by type, 1986-90, annual article, 2702–1.205

State and Metro Area Data Book, 1991 data compilation, 2328–54

Statistical Abstract of US, 1991 annual data compilation, 2324–1.9; 2324–1.10

Timber sales of Forest Service, expenses, and operations, by region, State, and natl forest, FY90, annual rpts, 1204–36

see also Budget of the U.S.

see also Estate tax

see also Excise tax

see also Foreign budgets

see also Gift tax

see also Government assets and liabilities

see also Income taxes

see also Mineral leases

see also Oil and gas leases

see also Property tax

see also Sales tax

see also Severance taxes

see also Social security tax

see also State and local taxes

see also Tariffs and foreign trade controls

see also Tax expenditures

see also Taxation

see also Tolls

see also Unemployment insurance tax

see also User fees

see also Value added tax

Government securities

Assets and debts of private sector, balance sheets by segment, 1945-90, semiannual rpt, 9365–4.1

Banks (insured commercial and savings) finances, for foreign and domestic offices, by asset size, 1989, annual rpt, 9294–4.2

Banks (natl) charters, mergers, liquidations, enforcement cases, and financial performance, with data by instn and State, quarterly rpt, 8402–3

Index by Subjects and Names

Government spending

Banks profitability indicators for student loans and other financial services, 1985-89, 4808–36

Budget of US, authoritative financial statements with appropriations, outlays, and receipts, by category and agency, FY90, annual rpt, 8104–2.1

Budget of US, CBO analysis of revenue and spending alternatives and projections of economic indicators, FY92-96, annual rpt, 26304–3

Budget of US, obligations and authority by function, agency, and program, with summaries, analyses, and historical tables, FY92, annual rpt, 104–2

Budget of US, receipts by source, outlays by agency and program, and balances, monthly rpt, 8102–3

Business statistics, detailed data for major industries and economic indicators, *Survey of Current Business*, monthly rpt, 2702–1.9

Credit unions federally insured, finances by instn characteristics and State, as of June 1991, semiannual rpt, 9532–6

Economic indicators and components, and Fed Reserve 4th District business and financial conditions, monthly chartbook, 9377–10

Enterprises sponsored by govt, capital adequacy and outstanding debt and mortgage pools, by enterprise, 1970s-89, article, 9391–16.201

Fed Govt consolidated financial statements based on business accounting methods, FY89-90, annual rpt, 8104–5

Fed Govt finances, cash and debt transactions, daily tables, 8102–4

Fed Govt programs under Ways and Means Committee jurisdiction, finances, operations, and participant characteristics, FY70s-90, annual rpt, 21784–11

Fed Govt trust funds financial condition, by fund, periodic rpt series, 8102–9

Fed Home Loan Mortgage Corp activities and financial statements, 1990, annual rpt, 9414–1

Fed Reserve banks finances and staff, 1990, annual rpt, 9364–1.1

Finances of govts, by level of govt, State, and for large cities and counties, annual rpt series, 2466–2

Finances of govts, tax systems and revenue, and fiscal structure, by level of govt and State, 1991 and historical trends, annual rpt, 10044–1

Financial and business detailed statistics, *Fed Reserve Bulletin*, monthly rpt with articles, 9362–1

Financial operations of Fed Govt, detailed data, *Treasury Bulletin*, quarterly rpt, 8002–4

Flow-of-funds accounts, savings, investments, and credit statements, quarterly rpt, 9365–3.3

Foreign and US industrial stock indexes and long-term govt bond yields, for selected countries, weekly chartbook, 9365–1.5

Foreign govt assets and liabilities, and transactions in securities, monthly rpt, 9362–1.3

Forgery of checks and bonds, Secret Service investigations and arrests, FY90 and trends from FY81, annual rpt, 8464–1

Futures and options trading volume, by commodity and exchange, FY90, annual rpt, 11924–2

Futures trading in selected commodities and financial instruments and indexes, NYC, Chicago, and other markets activity, semimonthly rpt, 11922–5

Govt Natl Mortgage Assn finances, and mortgage-backed securities program, FY90, annual rpt, 5144–6

Households and personal purchases and holdings of govt securities, terms, and purchase methods, 1980s-90, 8008–148

Households assets, by type of holding and selected characteristics, 1988, Current Population Rpt, 2546–20.16

Hwy receipts by source, and spending by function, by level of govt and State, 1990, annual rpt, 7554–1.3

Interest rates for commercial paper, govt securities, other financial instruments, and home mortgages, monthly rpt, 9365–2.14

Interest rates forecasting performance of Treasury bill and other security yields at alternative maturities, 1950s-80s, article, 9389–1.201

Intl investment position of US, by component, industry, world region, and country, 1989-90, annual article, 2702–1.212

Issues, redemptions, and bonds outstanding, monthly rpt, 8242–2

Japan economic conditions, financial and intl policies, and trade devs, 1950s-80s and projected to 2050, compilation of papers, 23848–220

Medicare Hospital Insurance trust fund finances, 1966-90 and alternative projections to 2065, annual rpt, 4654–11

Medicare Supplementary Medical Insurance trust fund finances, various periods 1966-90 and projected to 2001, annual rpt, 4654–12

Mortgage-backed securities investment by major financial instns, quarterly press release, discontinued, 5002–12

Mortgage-backed securities transactions, and other activity of Fed Natl Mortgage Assn, 1988-89, annual rpt, 5184–9

OASDI trust funds finances, 1937-FY90 and alternative projections to 2065, annual rpt, 4704–4

Ownership of govt securities, dealer transactions and financing sources, and new State and local issues, monthly rpt, 9362–1.1

Rural Telephone Bank financial statements, FY89, annual rpt, 1244–4

Savings instns security holdings, by type, as of various dates 1984-89, annual rpt, 8434–3.1

Southeastern States, Fed Reserve 5th District insured commercial banks financial statements, by State, quarterly rpt, 9389–18

Southeastern States, Fed Reserve 8th District banking and economic conditions, quarterly rpt with articles, 9391–16

State and local govt employees pension system cash and security holdings and finances, quarterly rpt, 2462–2

Statistical Abstract of US, 1991 annual data compilation, 2324–1.9; 2324–1.10

Tax (income) returns filed by type of filer, selected income items, quarterly rpt, 8302–2.1

Tax (income) returns of corporations, income and tax items by asset size and detailed industry, 1987, annual rpt, 8304–4

Tax (income) returns of corporations, income and tax items by asset size and detailed industry, 1988, annual rpt, 8304–21

Tax expenditures, Federal revenues forgone through income tax deductions and exclusions by type, FY92-96, annual rpt, 21784–10

Treasury bill offerings, auction results by Fed Reserve District, and terms, periodic press release series, 8002–7

Truman, Harry S, Scholarship Fund receipts by source, transfers, and investment holdings and transactions, monthly rpt, 14312–1

Yields and interest rates for Treasury bills and US and municipal bonds, monthly rpt, 23842–1.5

Yields and interest rates on govt issues, weekly rpt, 9391–4

Yields, interest rates, issues, offerings, and ownership of govt securities, by type, selected years 1929-90, annual rpt, 204–1.5; 204–1.6

Yields of municipal and Treasury bonds, relation to tax policies, 1970-89, article, 9373–1.215

Yields on corporate, Treasury, and municipal long-term bonds, *Treasury Bulletin*, quarterly rpt, 8002–4.8

Yields, *Survey of Current Business*, cyclical indicators, monthly rpt, 2702–1.1

see also Municipal bonds

see also Tax exempt securities

see also U.S. savings bonds

Government services

see Public services

Government spending

Advisory committees of Fed Govt, and members, staff, meetings, and costs by agency, FY90, annual rpt, 9454–18

Business statistics, detailed data for major industries and economic indicators, *Survey of Current Business*, monthly rpt, 2702–1.9

Chicago metro area local govts fiscal capacity, 1987, article, 10042–1.203

Construction spending by Fed Govt, by program and type of structure, FY85-92, annual article, 2042–1.206

Criminal justice spending, employment, and payroll, by level of govt, State, and selected city and county, 1984-86, biennial rpt, 6064–4

Economic and employment conditions, alternative BLS projections to 2005 and trends 1970s-90, biennial article, 6722–1.251

Economic indicators and components, current data and annual trends, monthly rpt, 23842–1.6

Economic indicators compounded annual rates of change, monthly rpt, 9391–3

Economic indicators compounded annual rates of change, 1971-90, annual rpt, 9391–9.2

Expenditures of State and local govts, measures using indicators of service costs and demand, with comparisons to fiscal capacity and actual outlays, by State, 1986-87, 10048–77

Government spending

Fed Govt consolidated financial statements based on business accounting methods, FY89-90, annual rpt, 8104–5

Fed Govt finances, cash and debt transactions, daily tables, 8102–4

Fed Govt financial operations, detailed data, *Treasury Bulletin*, quarterly rpt, 8002–4

Fed Govt financial transactions, *Survey of Current Business*, monthly rpt, 2702–1.9

Fed Govt shutdown over Columbus Day holiday, employees affected, costs, and savings, Oct 1990, GAO rpt, 26119–311

Finances of govts, by level of govt, State, and for large cities and counties, annual rpt series, 2466–2

Finances of State and local govts, revenue by source and outlays by type, 1986-90, annual article, 2702–1.205

Flow-of-funds accounts, savings, investments, and credit statements, quarterly rpt, 9365–3.3

Health condition and health care resources, use, and spending, 1950s-89, annual data compilation, 4144–11

Investigations of Federal agency and program operations, summaries of findings, 1981-90, annual GAO rpt, 26104–5

Mail (franked and penalty) revenue and volume, FY86-87, annual rpt, 9864–1

Mail (penalty) for Federal agencies, USPS itemized operating costs, FY90, annual rpt, 9864–4

Natl income and product accounts and components, *Survey of Current Business*, monthly rpt, 2702–1.24

New England States govt revenue and spending issues, with data by State, 1970s-80s, article, 9373–25.202

North Central States public debt by State, and govt spending changes by purpose, 1980s, article, 9375–1.207

Pollution abatement spending by govts, business, and consumers, 1987-89, annual article, 2702–1.229

Public opinion on taxes, spending, and govt efficiency, by respondent characteristics, 1991 survey, annual rpt, 10044–2

Puerto Rico statehood referendum proposal, impacts on Federal tax revenue and aid outlays, corporations tax-favored status, and economic conditions, projected FY91-2000, 26306–3.112

Service industries census, 1987: establishments, receipts by source, payroll, and employment, by SIC 2- to 4-digit kind of business, State, and MSA, 2393–4

Statistical Abstract of US, 1991 annual data compilation, 2324–1.9; 2324–1.10

Statistical programs of Fed Govt, funding by agency, FY90-92, annual rpt, 104–10

Statistical programs of Fed Govt, index of spending for 4 agencies, 1976-88, hearing, 23848–218

UK personal consumption impacts of govt spending, alternative model results, 1950s-86, technical paper, 9385–8.83

UN participation of US, and member and nonmember shares of UN budget by country, FY89-91, annual rpt, 7004–5

see also Agricultural production quotas and price supports

see also Agricultural subsidies

Index by Subjects and Names

see also Budget of the U.S.

see also Civil service pensions

see also Defense expenditures

see also Executive impoundment of appropriated funds

see also Federal aid programs

see also Federal aid to arts and humanities

see also Federal aid to education

see also Federal aid to higher education

see also Federal aid to highways

see also Federal aid to housing

see also Federal aid to law enforcement

see also Federal aid to libraries

see also Federal aid to local areas

see also Federal aid to medical education

see also Federal aid to medicine

see also Federal aid to railroads

see also Federal aid to rural areas

see also Federal aid to States

see also Federal aid to transportation

see also Federal aid to vocational education

see also Federal funding for energy programs

see also Federal funding for research and development

see also Federal pay

see also Foreign budgets

see also Government assets and liabilities

see also Government contracts and procurement

see also Government energy use

see also Government pay

see also Military benefits and pensions

see also Military pay

see also Nonappropriated funds

see also Public services

see also Public welfare programs

see also Revenue sharing

see also State and local employees pay

see also State funding for economic development

see also State funding for education

see also State funding for health and hospitals

see also State funding for higher education

see also State funding for local areas

see also State funding for natural resources and conservation

see also State funding for public safety

see also State funding for social welfare

see also State funding for transportation

see also State government spending

see also Subsidies

see also Veterans benefits and pensions

see also under names of individual Federal departments and agencies

Government supplies and property

Assistance (financial and nonfinancial) of Fed Govt, 1991 base edition with supplements, annual listing, 104–5

Auto fleet size, trip characteristics, and energy use, by fleet type, 1970s-89, annual rpt, 3304–5.3

Bombing incidents, casualties, and damage, by target, circumstances, and State, 1990, annual rpt, 6224–5

Budget of US, object class analysis of obligations, by agency, FY92, annual rpt, 104–9

Budget of US, obligations and authority by function, agency, and program, with summaries, analyses, and historical tables, FY92, annual rpt, 104–2

Capital stock, by type and level of govt, 1989, article, 9391–1.208

Coal leasing activity on Federal land, acreage, production, and reserves, by coal region and State, FY90, annual rpt, 5724–10

Computer systems and equipment of Fed Govt, by type, make, and agency, 2nd half FY90, semiannual listing, 9452–9

Computer systems of Fed Govt with sensitive unclassified data, security plans by characteristics of info and system, and agency, 1989, 2218–85

Construction put in place, value of new public and private structures, by type, monthly rpt, 2382–4

Criminal cases by type and disposition, and collections, for US attorneys, by Federal district, FY90, annual rpt, 6004–2.1; 6004–2.7

Criminal cases in Federal district courts, by offense, disposition, and district, 1980-90, last issue of annual rpt, 18204–1

DOE energy use, costs, and conservation, by end use, fuel type, and field office, FY90, annual rpt, 3004–27

Fed Govt consolidated financial statements based on business accounting methods, FY89-90, annual rpt, 8104–5

Fed Govt obligations by function and agency, *Treasury Bulletin*, quarterly rpt, 8002–4.2

FmHA property acquired through foreclosure, value, acreage, and sales, for farm and nonfarm property by State, monthly rpt, 1182–6

FmHA property acquired through foreclosure, value, and acreage under conservation easements by State, 1989-90, GAO rpt, 26113–514

FmHA property acquired through foreclosure, 1-family homes, value, sales, and leases, by State, monthly rpt, 1182–7

GSA activities and finances, FY90, annual rpt, 9454–1

GSA programs fraud and abuse, audits and investigations, 2nd half FY91, semiannual rpt, 9452–8

Hazardous waste site remedial action under Superfund, current and proposed sites priority ranking and status by location, series, 9216–5

Labor productivity of Federal employees, indexes of output and labor costs by function, 1967-89, annual rpt, 6824–1.6

Loans and loan guarantees of Fed Govt, outstanding amounts by agency and program, *Treasury Bulletin*, quarterly rpt, 8002–4.9

Motor vehicle registrations, by public and private ownership, vehicle type, and State, 1990, annual rpt, 7554–1.2

Patents granted to Federal agencies, FY81-90, annual rpt, 2244–1.2

Postal Service activities, finances, and mail volume and subsidies, FY90, annual rpt, 9864–5.2; 9864–5.3

Prison Industries (Federal) sales, by commodity and Federal agency, FY90, annual rpt, 6244–5

Radio frequency assignments for Federal use, by agency, 1st half 1990, semiannual rpt, 2802–1

Real property leased by Fed Govt, inventory and rental costs, worldwide summary by location and agency, 1989, annual rpt, 9454–10

Index by Subjects and Names

Government trust funds

Real property owned by Fed Govt, inventory and costs, worldwide summary by location, agency, and use, 1989, annual rpt, 9454–5

Ships for oceanographic research, fleet condition, funding, voyages, and modernization costs, for NOAA, 1980s-90 and projected to 2020, 2148–60

Ships in US merchant fleet, operating subsidies, construction, and ship-related employment, monthly rpt, 7702–1

Terrorism (intl) incidents, casualties, and attacks on US targets, by attack type and country, 1990, annual rpt, 7004–22

Terrorism (intl) incidents, casualties, and attacks on US targets, by attack type and world area, 1990, annual rpt, 7004–13

Terrorism incidents in US, related activity, and casualties, by attack type, target, group, and location, 1990, annual rpt, 6224–6

Truck transport of household goods, performance and disposition of damage claims, for selected carriers, 1990, annual rpt, 9484–11

see also Military bases, posts, and reservations

see also Military supplies and property

see also Public buildings

see also Public lands

see also Surplus government property

Government trust funds

Abandoned Mine Reclamation Fund financial status, FY90, annual rpt, 5644–1

Airport and Airway Trust Fund improvement spending, by airport and State, FY91, annual rpt, 7504–48

Airport and Airway Trust Fund receipts and outlays, FY89-90, annual rpt, 7504–10; 7504–37

Airport finances, operations by carrier, and capacity improvement and dev funding, by airport, 1977-87 and projected to 2020, hearing, 21648–59

Black lung benefits and claims by State, trust fund receipts by source, and disbursements, 1990, annual rpt, 6504–3

Budget of US, authoritative financial statements with appropriations, outlays, and receipts, by agency, FY90, annual rpt, 8104–2

Budget of US, balances of budget authority obligated and unobligated, by function and agency, FY90-92, annual rpt, 104–8

Budget of US, CBO analysis of revenue and spending alternatives and projections of economic indicators, FY92-96, annual rpt, 26304–3

Budget of US, CBO analysis of savings and revenues under alternative spending cuts and tax changes, projected FY92-97, 26306–3.118

Budget of US, compilation of background material on fiscal and tax policy, 1960s-96, 21788–203

Budget of US, object class analysis of obligations, by agency, FY92, annual rpt, 104–9

Budget of US, obligations and authority by function, agency, and program, with summaries, analyses, and historical tables, FY92, annual rpt, 104–2

Budget of US, receipts by source, outlays by agency and program, and balances, monthly rpt, 8102–3

Civil service health and life insurance programs of Fed Govt, coverage and finances, FY89 with trends from FY84, annual rpt, 9844–35

Civil service retirement system actuarial valuation, FY79-90 and projected to FY2065, annual rpt, 9844–34

Credit unions federally insured, finances, mergers, closings, and insurance fund losses and financial statements, FY90, annual rpt, 9534–7

Currency (foreign) accounts owned by US under AID admin and by foreign govts with joint AID control, status by program and country, quarterly rpt, 9912–1

Currency (foreign) holdings of US, transactions and balances by program and country, 1st half FY91, semiannual rpt, 8102–7

DOD outlays and obligations, by function and service branch, quarterly rpt, 3542–3

Education funding by Federal agency, program, and recipient type, and instn spending, FY80-90, annual rpt, 4824–8

EPA pollution control grant program activities, monthly rpt, 9182–8

Fed Govt spending in States, by type, program, agency, and State, FY90, annual rpt, 2464–2

Fed Govt tax provisions and receipts overview, by tax type, with background data, 1900s-91 and projected to 2000, 21788–197

Fed Govt trust funds financial condition, by fund, periodic rpt series, 8102–9

Finances and operations of programs under Ways and Means Committee jurisdiction, FY70s-90, annual rpt, 21784–11

Finances of govts, by level of govt, State, and for large cities and counties, annual rpt series, 2466–2

Finances of govts, tax systems and revenue, and fiscal structure, by level of govt and State, 1991 and historical trends, annual rpt, 10044–1

Fish and Wildlife Service restoration programs finances by State, and excise tax collections, FY90, annual rpt, 5504–13

Helium market demand and Bur of Mines production, sales, and financial statements, FY90, annual rpt, 5604–32

Historic Preservation Fund grants, by State, FY92, annual table, 5544–9

Hwy Trust Fund finances, unobligated balances by State, and receipt losses from increased ethanol use, 1980s-90, hearing, 25328–31

Hwy Trust Fund receipts by source, and apportionments, by State, 1990, annual rpt, 7554–1.3

Hwy Trust Fund revenues, tax rates, and spending, FY87-91 with projections to FY95, GAO rpt, 26113–544

Hwy Trust Fund status and net revenues, FY57-89, annual rpt, 7554–24

Inter-American Foundation dev grants by program area, and fellowships by field and instn, by country, FY72-90, annual rpt, 14424–2

Japan-US Friendship Commission educational and cultural exchange activities, grants, and trust fund status, FY89-90, biennial report, 14694–1

Judicial Survivors Annuity Fund financial condition and annuitants, June 1982-90, annual rpt, 18204–8.11

Judicial Survivors Annuity Fund financial condition and annuitants, June 1987-91, annual rpt, 18204–2.1

Labor Dept activities and funding, by program and State, FY90, annual rpt, 6304–1

Land and Water Conservation Fund allocations for outdoor recreation area dev, by State, FY91, annual table, 5544–15

Land and Water Conservation Fund grants, State matching funds, and balances, by State, FY90, annual rpt, 5544–18

Lands (public) acreage, grants, use, revenues, and allocations, by State, FY90, annual rpt, 5724–1.3

Library of Congress activities, acquisitions, services, and financial statements, FY90, annual rpt, 26404–1

Medicare and Medicaid beneficiaries and program operations, 1991, annual fact book, 4654–18

Medicare and Medicaid benefits, trust fund finances, and services use, 1966-89 and projected to 1995, 21148–61

Medicare and Medicaid eligibility, participation, coverage, and program finances, various periods 1966-91, biennial rpt, 4654–1

Medicare Hospital Insurance and Supplementary Medical Insurance trust funds finances, early 1990s and projected to 2060s, annual article, 4742–1.211

Medicare Hospital Insurance trust fund finances, 1966-90 and alternative projections to 2065, annual rpt, 4654–11

Medicare Supplementary Medical Insurance trust fund finances, various periods 1966-90 and projected to 2001, annual rpt, 4654–12

Medicare trust funds income by source, financing, and natl health expenditures, 1960s-90, annual article, 4652–1.221

Natl Archives and Records Admin activities, finances, holdings, and staff, FY90, annual rpt, 9514–2

Nuclear Waste Fund finances, and DOE Civilian Radioactive Waste Mgmt Office activities, quarterly GAO rpt, 26102–4

Nuclear Waste Fund finances, and DOE Civilian Radioactive Waste Mgmt Office R&D costs, FY88-89, annual rpt, 3364–1

Nuclear Waste Fund finances, and DOE Civilian Radioactive Waste Mgmt Program costs, quarterly rpt, 3362–1

OASDHI admin, and SSA activities, 1930s-90 and projected to 2064, annual data compilation, 4704–12

OASDHI, Medicaid, SSI, and related programs benefits, beneficiary characteristics, and trust funds, selected years 1937-89, annual rpt, 4744–3

OASDHI trust funds financial status forecasts, evaluation of demographic and economic assumptions, 1991 article, 9391–1.207

OASDHI trust funds receipts, outlays, and assets since 1940, monthly rpt, 4742–1.2

OASDI actuarial balance and contingency fund ratio projections under technical advisory panel economic assumptions, with accuracy of past forecasts, 1990 article, 4742–1.201

OASDI benefit payments, trust fund finances, and economic and demographic

Government trust funds

assumptions, 1970-90 and alternative projections to 2000, actuarial rpt, 4706–1.105

- OASDI retired-worker benefits, effect of proposal to privatize excess trust funds into individual accounts, 1990 GAO rpt, 26121–397
- OASDI trust funds finances, effects of inclusion in budget deficit figures, and social security tax reduction proposals, 1990 hearing, 25368–171
- OASDI trust funds finances, FY90 and projected to 2060s, annual article, 4742–1.210
- OASDI trust funds finances, 1937-FY90 and alternative projections to 2065, annual rpt, 4704–4
- OASDI trust funds income and outlays, FY90, annual rpt, 4704–6
- Pension Benefit Guaranty Corp activities and finances, FY90, annual rpt, 9674–1
- Public debt issued, redeemed, and outstanding, by series and source, and gifts to reduce debt, monthly rpt, 8242–2
- Railroad employee benefits program finances and beneficiaries, FY90, annual rpt, 9704–1
- Railroad retirement system funding and benefits findings and recommendations, with background industry data, 1960s-90 and projected to 2060, 9708–1
- Receipts, outlays, debt, and assets, by fund, *Treasury Bulletin*, quarterly rpt, 8002–4.1; 8002–4.4; 8002–4.15
- Red Cross financial statements, FY89-90, annual rpt, 29254–1
- State and local govt employees pension system cash and security holdings and finances, quarterly rpt, 2462–2
- *Statistical Abstract of US*, 1991 annual data compilation, 2324–1.10
- Truman, Harry S, Scholarship Fund receipts by source, transfers, and investment holdings and transactions, monthly rpt, 14312–1
- Veterans and servicepersons life insurance, actuarial analyses of VA programs, 1990, annual rpt, 8604–1
- Veterans and servicepersons life insurance of VA, finances and coverage by program and State, 1990, annual rpt, 8604–4
- Workers compensation programs under Federal admin, finances and operations, FY90, annual rpt, 6504–10
- *see also* Unemployment trust funds

Government workers

- *see* Congressional employees
- *see* Federal employees
- *see* Government employees
- *see* Government pay
- *see* Military personnel
- *see* Postal employees
- *see* State and local employees

Graboyes, Robert F.

"International Trade and Payments Data: An Introduction", 9389–1.206

Graduates

see Degrees, higher education

see Educational attainment

Graf, Julia B.

"Aggradation and Degradation of Alluvial Sand Deposits, 1965-86, Colorado River, Grand Canyon National Park, Ariz.", 5668–122

Graham, Stanley L.

"Investigating the Banking Consolidation Trend", 9383–6.203

Grain storage and facilities

- CCC loans to farmers for grain storage facilities and equipment, by State, FY68-91, annual table, 1804–14
- Corn storage in commercial elevators, foreign material removal methods and costs, 1991, article, 1561–4.202
- Explosions and casualties at grain handling facilities, by firm, FY90, annual rpt, 1294–1
- Feed production, acreage, stocks, use, trade, prices, and price supports, periodic situation rpt with articles, 1561–4
- Foreign and US grain production, prices, trade, stocks, and use, FAS periodic circular series, 1925–2
- Hops stocks held by growers, dealers, and brewers, 1989-91, semiannual press release, 1621–8
- Loan support programs of USDA for grains, activity and status by grain and State, monthly rpt, 1802–3
- Loans to farmers under CCC program for grain storage facilities and equipment, by State, monthly table, 1802–9
- Rice stocks on and off farms and total in all positions, periodic rpt, 1621–7
- Stocks of grain by region and market city, and grain inspected for export, by type, weekly rpt, 1313–4
- Stocks of grain on and off farms, by crop, quarterly rpt, 1621–4
- Wheat and corn stocks, demand impacts of storage subsidy programs, model description and results, 1972-87, 1548–378
- Wheat stocks and prices estimated under alternative reserve storage assumptions, 1990-91, article, 1561–12.201
- Wheat storage in commercial elevators, foreign material removal methods and costs, 1991, article, 1561–12.204

Grains and grain products

- Acreage planted and harvested, by crop and State, 1989-90 and planned as of June 1991, annual rpt, 1621–23
- Acreage planted, by selected crop and State, 1982-90 and planned 1991, annual rpt, 1621–22
- Acreage reduction program compliance, enrollment, and yield on planted acreage, by commodity and State, annual press release series, 1004–20
- Acreage under Agricultural Stabilization and Conservation Service programs, rankings by commodity and congressional district, 1989, biennial rpt, 1804–17
- Africa (Sahel) grain production, use, imports, and stocks, by country, 1989/90, 9918–18
- Africa (sub-Saharan) agricultural conditions by country, with Ethiopia grain production and use, and dev aid by major donor, 1960s-80s, hearing, 23848–216
- Agricultural Stabilization and Conservation Service rye programs, 1955-91, annual fact sheet, 1806–4.12
- *Agricultural Statistics, 1990*, annual rpt, 1004–1
- Agriculture census, 1987: farms, farmland, production, finances, and operator characteristics, by county, final State rpt series, 2331–1

Index by Subjects and Names

- Alcoholic beverages production, stocks, materials used, and taxable and tax-free removals, for beer and distilled spirits by State, monthly rpt, 8486–1.1; 8486–1.3
- Business statistics, detailed data for major industries and economic indicators, *Survey of Current Business*, monthly rpt, 2702–1.14
- CCC certificate exchange activity, by commodity, biweekly press release, 1802–16
- CCC financial condition and major commodity program operations, FY62-87, annual chartbook, 1824–2
- Consumer Expenditure Survey, food spending by item, household composition, income, age, race, and region, 1980-88, biennial rpt, 1544–30
- Consumer Expenditure Survey, household income by source, and itemized spending, by selected characteristics and region, 1988-89, annual rpt, 6764–5
- Consumption of food, dietary composition, and nutrient intake, 1987/88 natl survey, preliminary rpt series, 1356–1
- Consumption, supply, trade, prices, spending, and indexes, by food commodity, 1989, annual rpt, 1544–4
- Cooperatives (grain) patronage refunds, and impacts on financial position, 1989, article, 1122–1.208
- Cooperatives finances and operations, by grain handled and selected characteristics, 1983-85, series, 1128–44
- Cooperatives, finances, operations, activities, and membership, 1950s-88, commodity rpt, 1126–1.5
- County Business Patterns, 1988: employment, establishments, and payroll, by SIC 2- to 4-digit industry and county, annual State rpt series, 2326–6
- County Business Patterns, 1989: employment, establishments, and payroll, by SIC 2- to 4-digit industry and county, annual State rpt series, 2326–8
- CPI by component for US city average, and by region, population size, and for 27 metro areas, monthly rpt, 6762–2
- Developing countries agricultural and economic conditions, and US agricultural exports, effects of US aid, 1989 conf papers, 1548–372
- Developing countries food supply, needs, and aid, status and alternative forecasts, world area rpt series, 1526–8
- Developing countries grains production and needs, and related economic outlook, by world area and selected country, forecast 1990/91-1991/92, 1528–313
- Employment, earnings, and hours, by SIC 1- to 4-digit industry, monthly and annual averages, selected years 1909-90, annual rpt, 6744–4
- Enterprise Statistics, 1987: finances and operations for companies, by size, level of diversification, form of organization, and industry group, 2329–8
- Export licensing, monitoring, and enforcement activities, FY90, annual rpt, 2024–1
- Exports (agricultural) of high-value commodities, indexes and sales value by commodity, world area, and country, 1960s-86, 1528–323

Index by Subjects and Names

Grains and grain products

Exports (agricultural) of US, impacts of foreign agricultural and trade policy, with data by commodity and country, 1989, annual rpt, 1924–8

Exports and imports (agricultural) commodity and country, prices, and world market devs, monthly rpt, 1922–12

Exports and imports (agricultural) of US, by commodity and country, bimonthly rpt, 1522–1

Exports and imports (agricultural) of US, by detailed commodity and country, 1989, annual rpt, 1524–8

Exports and imports (agricultural) of US, by detailed commodity and country, 1990, semiannual rpt, 1522–4

Exports and imports between US and outlying areas, by detailed commodity and mode of transport, 1990, annual rpt, 2424–11

Exports and imports of US, by country and detailed commodity, monthly rpt, 2422–12

Exports and imports of US, by Harmonized System 6-digit commodity and country, 1990, annual rpt, 2424–13

Exports and imports of US, by transport mode, country, and SITC 1- to 3-digit commodity, 1990, annual rpt, 2424–12

Exports and imports of US shipped through Canada, by detailed commodity, customs district, and country, 1989, annual rpt, 7704–11

Exports of grains, oilseed products, hides, skins, and cotton, by country, weekly rpt, 1922–3

Exports of US, detailed Schedule B commodities with countries of destination, 1990, annual rpt, 2424–10

Farm financial and marketing conditions, forecast 1991, annual conf, 1004–16

Farm income, expenses, receipts by commodity, assets, liabilities, and ratios, 1990 and trends from 1945, annual rpt, 1544–16

Farm sector balance sheet, and receipts by detailed commodity, by State, 1985-89, annual rpt, 1544–18

Flour milling production by State, stocks, daily capacity, and exports by country, monthly Current Industrial Rpt, 2506–4.1

Foreign and US agricultural production, acreage, and yield for selected crops, forecasts by selected world region and country, FAS monthly circular, 1925–28

Foreign and US agricultural production, prices, trade, and use, periodic rpt with articles, 1522–3

Foreign and US agricultural supply and demand indicators, by selected crop, monthly rpt, 1522–5

Foreign and US grain production, prices, trade, stocks, and use, FAS periodic circular series, 1925–2

Foreign countries agricultural production, prices, and trade, by country, 1980-90 and forecast 1991, annual world area rpt series, 1524–4

Foreign countries agricultural production, trade, and policies, summary data by country, 1989-90, annual factbook, 1924–12

Futures and options trading volume, by commodity and exchange, FY90, annual rpt, 11924–2

Futures contracts, stocks in deliverable position by type, weekly tables, 11922–4

Futures trading in selected commodities and financial instruments and indexes, NYC, Chicago, and other markets activity, semimonthly rpt, 11922–5

Great Lakes area economic conditions and outlook, for US and Canada, 1970s-90, 9375–15

Inspection of grain for domestic use and export, foreign buyers complaints, and handling facilities explosions, FY90, annual rpt, 1294–1

Inspection of grain for export, test results by commodity and port region, 1988-90, annual rpt series, 1294–2

Irrigation projects of Reclamation Bur in western US, crop production and acreage by commodity, State, and project, 1989, annual rpt, 5824–12

Labor productivity, indexes of output, hours, and employment by SIC 2- to 4-digit industry, 1967-89, annual rpt, 6824–1.3

Loan support programs of USDA for grains, activity and status by grain and State, monthly rpt, 1802–3

Manufacturing annual survey, 1989: finances and operations, by SIC 2- to 4-digit industry, series, 2506–15

Manufacturing census, 1987: finances and operations, by SIC 2- to 4-digit industry, State, and MSA, with trends from 1849, 2497–1

Manufacturing census, 1987: finances and operations, by type of organization and SIC 2- to 4-digit industry, subject rpt, 2497–5

Manufacturing finances and operations, by SIC 2- to 4-digit industry, forecast 1991, annual rpt, 2044–28

Multinatl US firms and foreign affiliates finances and operations, by industry and world area of parent firm, 1989 benchmark survey, preliminary annual rpt, 2704–5

Nutrient, caloric, and waste composition, detailed data for raw, processed, and prepared foods, 1991 rpt, 1356–3.15

Occupational injury and illness rates, by SIC 2- to 4-digit industry, 1988-89, annual rpt, 6844–7

Occupational injury and illness rates, by SIC 2- to 4-digit industry, 1989, annual rpt, 6844–1

OECD trade, total and for 4 major countries, and US trade by country, by commodity, 1970-89, world area rpt series, 9116–1

Pollution (air) abatement equipment shipments by industry, and new and backlog orders, by product, 1990, annual Current Industrial Rpt, 2506–12.5

Price indexes (producer), by stage of processing and detailed commodity, monthly rpt, 6762–6

Price indexes (producer), by stage of processing and detailed commodity, monthly 1990, annual rpt, 6764–2

Price support and loan programs operations of USDA, with farmers views on Federal programs, by region and State, 1990 hearings, 21168–43

Price support program provisions, for selected commodities, 1961-90, 1568–302; 1568–303

Prices (farm-retail) for food, marketing cost components, and industry finances and productivity, 1920s-90, annual rpt, 1544–9

Prices received and paid by farmers, by commodity and State, 1990, annual rpt, 1629–5

Prices received by farmers and production value, by detailed crop and State, 1988-90, annual rpt, 1621–2

Prices received by farmers for major products, and paid for farm inputs and living items, by State, monthly rpt, 1629–1

Production, farms, acreage, and related data, by selected crop and State, monthly rpt, 1621–1

Production inputs, output, and productivity for farms, by commodity and region, 1947-89, annual rpt, 1544–17

Production itemized costs, receipts, and returns, by commodity and region, 1987-89, annual rpt, 1544–20

Production, prices, trade, and export inspections by US port and country of destination, by grain type, weekly rpt, 1313–2

Production, prices, trade, and marketing, by commodity, current situation and forecast, monthly rpt with articles, 1502–4

Rye and wheat acreage seeded, by State, 1989-91, annual rpt, 1621–30

Rye foreign and US production, prices, trade, stocks, and use, quarterly situation rpt with articles, 1561–12

Rye programs of Agricultural Stabilization and Conservation Service, 1955-90, annual fact sheet, 1806–4.1

Seed exports, by type, world region, and country, FAS quarterly rpt, 1925–13

Sorghum production costs, by whether farmer participates in govt programs, 1986, article, 1541–1.210

Soviet Union agricultural conditions and factors affecting US grain exports and CCC credit guarantees, 1990 hearings, 21168–49

Soviet Union agricultural reform issues, with background data for USSR and US, 1970s-90, article, 9381–1.210

Soviet Union agricultural trade, by commodity and country, 1955-90, 1528–322

Soviet Union, Eastern Europe, OECD, and selected other countries agricultural production, by commodity, 1960s-90, annual rpt, 9114–4.5

Stocks of grain on and off farms, by crop, quarterly rpt, 1621–4

Tax (income) returns of corporations, income and tax items by asset size and detailed industry, 1987, annual rpt, 8304–4

Tax (income) returns of corporations, income and tax items by asset size and detailed industry, 1988, annual rpt, 8304–21

Wholesale trade census, 1987: establishments, sales by customer class, employment, inventories, and expenses, by SIC 2- to 4-digit kind of business, 2407–4

Zimbabwe agricultural conditions impacts of economic policies, 1980s, 1528–319

Grains and grain products

see also Alcohol fuels
see also Animal feed
see also Baking and bakery products
see also Corn
see also Gasohol
see also Grain storage and facilities
see also Hops
see also Oils, oilseeds, and fats
see also Rice
see also Soybeans
see also Wheat
see also under By Commodity in the "Index by Categories"

Gramm-Rudman Act
see Balanced Budget and Emergency Deficit Control Act

Grand Forks, N.Dak.
see also under By SMSA or MSA in the "Index by Categories"

Grand Island, Nebr.
Wages by occupation, and benefits for office and plant workers, 1991 survey, periodic labor market rpt, 6785–3.10

Grand Rapids, Mich.
see also under By City and By SMSA or MSA in the "Index by Categories"

Grand Teton National Park
Goats (mountain) population in Yellowstone and Grand Teton Natl Parks, and habitat mgmt options, 1970s-89, 5548–19

Granger, Clive W.
"Comments on the Evaluation of Policy Models", 9366–7.267

Grant, Bridget F.
"Liver Cirrhosis Mortality in the U.S., 1973-87", 4486–1.10

Grants and grants-in-aid
see State funding for economic development
see State funding for education
see State funding for health and hospitals
see State funding for higher education
see State funding for local areas
see State funding for public safety
see State funding for social welfare
see State government spending
see terms beginning with Federal aid

Grants Pass, Oreg.
Wages by occupation, for office and plant workers, 1991 survey, periodic MSA rpt, 6785–3.6

Grapefruit
see Citrus fruits

Graphics
see Advertising
see Art
see Cartography
see Chartbooks
see Maps
see Photography and photographic equipment
see Printing and publishing industry

Graphite
see Nonmetallic minerals and mines

Grasses
see Animal feed
see National grasslands
see Pasture and rangeland
see Plants and vegetation

Gravel
see Sand and gravel

Graven, Stanley N.
"Association of Prenatal Nutrition and Educational Services with Low Birth Weight Rates in a Florida Program", 4042–3.235

Graves, Edmund J.
"Detailed Diagnoses and Procedures, National Hospital Discharge Survey, 1988. Vital and Health Statistics Series 13", 4147–13.105
"Detailed Diagnoses and Procedures, National Hospital Discharge Survey, 1989. Vital and Health Statistics Series 13", 4147–13.108
"National Hospital Discharge Survey: Annual Summary, 1988. Vital and Health Statistics Series 13", 4147–13.107
"1989 Summary: National Hospital Discharge Survey", 4146–8.198

Gray, Fred
"Trends in U.S. Production and Use of Glucose Syrup and Dextrose, 1965-90, and Prospects for the Future", 1561–14.209

Grazing
see Pasture and rangeland

Grease
see Oils, oilseeds, and fats
see Petroleum and petroleum industry

Great Britain
see United Kingdom

Great Falls, Mont.
see also under By SMSA or MSA in the "Index by Categories"

Great Lakes
Army Corps of Engineers water resources dev projects, characteristics, and costs, 1950s-89, biennial State rpt series, 3756–1
Army Corps of Engineers water resources dev projects, characteristics, and costs, 1950s-91, biennial State rpt series, 3756–2
Birds (bald eagle) Great Lakes population, breeding, and research status, 1990 conf, 14648–26
Coal production, stocks, and shipments, by State of origin and destination, end-use sector, and mode of transport, quarterly rpt, 3162–8
Economic conditions and outlook, for US and Canada Great Lakes area, 1970s-90, 9375–15
Environmental Quality, status of problems, protection programs, research, and intl issues, 1991 annual rpt, 484–1
Environmental research lab for Great Lakes, activities, FY90 annual rpt, 2144–26
Estuary eutrophication and algal blooms, causes and environmental effects, 1991 conf, 2176–7.22
Exports and imports (waterborne) of US, by type of service, commodity, country, route, and US port, 1988, annual rpt, 7704–2
Fish catch, trade, use, and fishery operations, with selected foreign data, by species, 1980s-90, annual rpt, 2164–1
Fish Hatchery Natl System activities and deliveries, by species, hatchery, and jurisdiction of waters stocked, FY90, annual rpt, 5504–10
Global climate change environmental, infrastructure, and health impacts, with model results and background data, 1850s-2100, 9188–113
Ships in Great Lakes fleet, and tonnage, by activity status and vessel type, FY90, annual rpt, 7704–14.2

Ships in US merchant fleet, operating subsidies, construction, and ship-related employment, monthly rpt, 7702–1
St Lawrence Seaway Dev Corp finances and activities, and Seaway cargo tonnage, 1989, annual rpt, 7744–1
Wastewater treatment by municipal and industrial facilities, releases, methods, effectiveness, pollutant limits, and enforcement, for Great Lakes, 1985-88, 14648–24
Water levels, monthly 1971-80, decennial rpt, 2156–4.1
Water levels of Great Lakes and connecting channels, and forecasts, semimonthly rpt, 3752–2
Water levels of Great Lakes, and forecasts, monthly rpt and supplements, 3752–1
Water levels of Great Lakes, daily and monthly averages by site, 1990 and cumulative from 1900, annual rpt, 2174–3
Water supply and quality in streams and lakes, and groundwater levels in wells, by drainage basin, 1988, annual State rpt series, 5666–16
Water supply and quality in streams and lakes, and groundwater levels in wells, by drainage basin, 1989, annual State rpt series, 5666–12
Water supply and quality in streams and lakes, and groundwater levels in wells, by drainage basin, 1990, annual State rpt series, 5666–10
Water supply in northeastern US, precipitation and stream runoff by station, monthly rpt, 2182–3

Great Lakes Commission
Economic conditions and outlook, for US and Canada Great Lakes area, 1970s-90, 9375–15

Great Lakes Environmental Research Laboratory
see National Oceanic and Atmospheric Administration

Great Plains
see North Central States
see under By Region in the "Index by Categories"

Greece
Agricultural exports of high-value commodities, indexes and sales by commodity, world area, and country, 1960s-86, 1528–323
Agricultural production, prices, and trade, by country, 1970s-90, and forecast 1991, annual world region rpt, 1524–4.4
Agricultural production, trade, and policies in foreign countries, summary data by country, 1989-90, annual factbook, 1924–12
Agricultural trade of US, by detailed commodity and country, 1989, annual rpt, 1524–8
Agricultural trade of US, by detailed commodity and country, 1990, semiannual rpt, 1522–4
AID loans repayment status and terms by program and country, and status of predecessor agency loans, quarterly rpt, 9912–3
Background Notes, summary social, political, and economic data, 1990 rpt, 7006–2.20
Drug abuse indicators, by world region and selected country, 1990 semiannual conf, 4492–5.1

Index by Subjects and Names

Economic and military aid and loans from US and intl agencies, by program and country, FY46-90, annual rpt, 9914–5

Economic conditions, income, production, prices, employment, and trade, 1991 periodic country rpt, 2046–4.48

Economic conditions, policy, and trade practices, by country, 1988-90, annual rpt, 21384–5

Economic, social, political, and geographic summary data, by country, 1991, annual factbook, 9114–2

Exports and imports of NATO members with PRC, by country, 1987-90, annual rpt, 7144–14

Exports and imports of OECD members, by country, 1989, annual rpt, 7144–10

Exports and imports of US, by selected country, country group, and commodity group, 1990, annual rpt, 2044–37

Exports and imports of US, by transport mode, country, and SITC 1- to 3-digit commodity, 1990, annual rpt, 2424–12

Exports and imports of US with EC by country, and total agricultural trade, selected years 1958-90, annual rpt, 7144–7

Exports of US, detailed Schedule B commodities with countries of destination, 1990, annual rpt, 2424–10

Fish (squid) catch, trade, consumption, and cold storage holdings, by country and species, 1963-90, 2166–19.10

GNP and GNP growth for OECD members, by country, 1980-90, annual rpt, 7144–8

Human rights conditions in 170 countries, and US economic and military aid, 1990, annual rpt, 21384–3

Imports of goods, services, and investment from US, trade barriers, impacts, and US actions, by country, 1990, annual rpt, 444–2

Military aid of US, arms sales, and training programs costs and budget requests, by program, world region, and country, FY90-92, annual rpt, 7144–13

Multinatl US firms and foreign affiliates finances and operations, by industry and world area of parent firm, 1989 benchmark survey, preliminary annual rpt, 2704–5

Multinatl US firms foreign affiliates, income statement items by country and world area, 1986, biennial article, 8302–2.212

Oil production, trade, use, and stocks, by selected country and country group, monthly rpt, 3162–42

Peach (canned) trade of US and Greece, by country, 1987-89, article, 1925–34.223

Raisin and prune production, trade, use, and stocks for EC and other countries, Turkey price supports, and Mexico production costs, 1985-91, annual article, 1925–34.250

Ships in world merchant fleet, tonnage, and new ship construction and deliveries, by vessel type and country, as of Jan 1990, annual rpt, 7704–3

Tax revenue, by level of govt and type of tax, for OECD countries, mid 1960s-89, annual rpt, 10044–1.2

UN voting record and share of votes in agreement with US, by issue, country, and world area, 1990, annual rpt, 7004–18

see also under By Foreign Country in the "Index by Categories"

Greeley, Colo.

see also under By SMSA or MSA in the "Index by Categories"

Green Bay, Wis.

see also under By SMSA or MSA in the "Index by Categories"

Green, Edward J.

"Contracts, Constraints, and Consumption", 9383–20.13

"Eliciting Traders' Knowledge in 'Frictionless' Asset Market", 9383–20.14

Green, James L.

"1990 Annual Statistics and Highlights Report, National Space Science Data Center", 9504–11

Green, Robert C.

"Program Provisions for Program Crops: A Database for 1961-90", 1568–302

"Program Provisions for Rye, Dry Edible Beans, Oil Crops, Tobacco, Sugar, Honey, Wool, Mohair, Gum Naval Stores, and Dairy Products: A Database for 1961-90", 1568–303

Green, Sharon L.

"Ground-Water Levels in Wyoming, 1980 Through September 1989", 5666–28.4

Greenberg, Brian

"Two Notes on Relating the Risk of Disclosure for Microdata and Geographic Area Size", 2626–10.137

Greenberg, David

"Wage Differentials and Job Changes", 2626–10.121

Greene, Catherine R.

"Characteristics of Onion Growers and Farms in 6 Major Onion States", 1561–11.201

"Integrated Pest Management (IPM) in the Vegetable Industry During the 1980's", 1568–298

"Outlook for Vegetables", 1004–16.1

Greene, David L.

"Energy Efficiency Improvement Potential of Commercial Aircraft to 2010", 3028–6

Greenfeld, Lawrence A.

"Capital Punishment, 1990", 6066–25.42

"Women in Prison", 6066–19.61

Greenhouse effect

see Global climate change

Greenland

Agricultural trade of US, by detailed commodity and country, 1989, annual rpt, 1524–8

Agricultural trade of US, by detailed commodity and country, 1990, semiannual rpt, 1522–4

Economic, social, political, and geographic summary data, by country, 1991, annual factbook, 9114–2

Exports and imports of US, by transport mode, country, and SITC 1- to 3-digit commodity, 1990, annual rpt, 2424–12

Tide height and time daily at coastal points, forecast 1992, annual rpt, 2174–2.3

Walrus population, habitat mgmt, and intl conservation needs, by world region, 1990 conf, 14738–9

Greensboro, N.C.

see also under By City and By SMSA or MSA in the "Index by Categories"

Greenville, S.C.

see also under By SMSA or MSA in the "Index by Categories"

Greenwood, Jeremy

"Tax Analysis in a Real Business Cycle Model: On Measuring Harberger Triangles and Okun Gaps", 9383–20.8

Greer, Thomas V.

"Market Structure Issues and the U.S. Sweetener Industry", 1004–16.1

Greeting cards

see Printing and publishing industry

Greisman, Paul

"Western Gulf of Alaska Tides and Circulation", 2176–1.36

Grenada

Agricultural trade of US, by detailed commodity and country, 1990, semiannual rpt, 1522–4

AID economic aid to developing countries, obligations and disbursements by country, quarterly rpt, 9912–4

Background Notes, summary social, political, and economic data, 1990 rpt, 7006–2.17

Economic and military aid and loans from US and intl agencies, by program and country, FY46-90, annual rpt, 9914–5

Economic, social, political, and geographic summary data, by country, 1991, annual factbook, 9114–2

Exports and imports of US, by transport mode, country, and SITC 1- to 3-digit commodity, 1990, annual rpt, 2424–12

Human rights conditions in 170 countries, and US economic and military aid, 1990, annual rpt, 21384–3

Investment (direct) incentives of Caribbean Basin Initiative, economic impacts, with finances and employment by country, 1984-90, 2048–141

Labor conditions, union coverage, and work accidents, 1991 annual regional rpt, 6366–4.56

Military aid of US, arms sales, and training programs costs and budget requests, by program, world region, and country, FY90-92, annual rpt, 7144–13

Nutmeg and mace production in Grenada, 1970s-90, FAS annual circular, 1925–15.1

UN voting record and share of votes in agreement with US, by issue, country, and world area, 1990, annual rpt, 7004–18

see also under By Foreign Country in the "Index by Categories"

Grendon, John H.

"Dientamoeba fragilis Detection Methods and Prevalence: A Survey of State Public Health Laboratories", 4042–3.225

Greyhound Lines, Inc.

Finances and operations of interstate carriers, 1989, annual rpt, 9486–6.3

Rural areas bus connector service to Greyhound intercity routes, finances and operations by system, 1987-90, 7888–79

Grise, Verner N.

"Costs of Producing and Selling Flue-Cured Tobacco: 1989, 1990, and Preliminary 1991", 1561–10.205

"Economic Importance of the U.S. Tobacco Industry", 1561–10.203

"Outlook for Tobacco", 1004–16.1

Grocery stores

Grocery stores
see Food stores

Gross Domestic Product

Business statistics, detailed data for major industries and economic indicators, *Survey of Current Business*, monthly rpt, 2702–1

Developing countries agricultural and economic conditions, and US agricultural exports, effects of US aid, 1989 conf papers, 1548–372

Developing countries economic and social conditions from 1960s, and Intl Dev Cooperation Agency and AID activities and funding, FY90-92, annual rpt, 9904–4

Eastern Europe foreign debt components, trade, balances, and other economic indicators, by country, 1985-89, hearing, 21248–148

EC economic integration economic impacts, with background data by country, 1988-90, article, 9379–1.201

Economic Report of the President for 1991, with economic trends from 1929, annual rpt, 204–1

Foreign and US energy use and production, by fuel type, country, and country group, projected 1995-2010 and trends from 1970, annual rpt, 3164–84

Foreign countries economic conditions and implications for US, periodic country rpt series, 2046–4

Foreign countries economic conditions, policy, and trade practices, by country, 1988-90, annual rpt, 21384–5

GDP and GNP as measures of production, factor income components, and receipts from and payments to foreigners, 1980s-91, article, 2702–1.215

Natl income and product accounts and components, *Survey of Current Business*, monthly rpt, 2702–1.24

Natl income and product accounts benchmark revisions, selected years 1977-90, article, 2702–1.226

NATO and Japan military spending and indicators of ability to support common defense, by country, 1970s-89, annual rpt, 3544–28

Regional gross product, by industry div, 1986, article, 9373–1.211

State gross product growth, impact of State bank credit conditions, 1980-86, article, 9377–1.206

State gross product impact of foreign labor productivity and dollar exchange rate, by industry sector and State, 1972-86, working paper, 9387–8.255

State gross product impacts of public works stock, by region, 1970s-86, article, 9373–1.217

Taiwan labor force educational attainment index relation to GDP growth, 1960s-86, working paper, 9371–10.55

see also Gross National Product

Gross National Product

Banks loan commitments, selected interest rates, and other factors relation to GNP, 1973-87, technical paper, 9385–8.75

Budget of US, CBO analysis of revenue and spending alternatives and projections of economic indicators, FY92-96, annual rpt, 26304–3

Budget of US, obligations and authority by function, agency, and program, with summaries, analyses, and historical tables, FY92, annual rpt, 104–2

Business cycle (real) model of GNP variability, assessment, with results for 1950s-84, article, 9375–1.205

Business cycle patterns of GNP growth and unemployment rate, alternative models descriptions and results, 1950s-80s, technical paper, 9385–8.96

Business cycle variation and growth rates of GNP and components, inflation, and money supply, for 10 industrial countries, 1850s-1980s, working paper, 9383–20.15

Business statistics, detailed data for major industries and economic indicators, *Survey of Current Business*, monthly rpt, 2702–1

China economic conditions after 1988 austerity program, with background data, 1978-90, 9118–9

China GNP estimation methodology and results, 1978-89, with yuan-dollar prices by commodity, 1981, working paper, 2326–18.58

Communist and OECD countries economic conditions, 1989, annual rpt, 7144–11

Data sources and reliability for GNP by industry, and constant dollar estimate revisions, 1977-88, article, 2702–1.201

Developing countries economic aid from US, military spending and imports measures to determine aid eligibility, by country, 1986-87, annual rpt, 9914–1

Developing countries economic and social conditions from 1960s, and Intl Dev Cooperation Agency and AID activities and funding, FY90-92, annual rpt, 9904–4

Eastern Europe transition to market economies, economic conditions, intl aid, and energy balance, by country, 1985-90, 9118–13

Economic and employment conditions, alternative BLS projections to 2005 and trends 1970s-90, biennial article, 6722–1.251; 6722–1.253

Economic indicators and components, and Fed Reserve 4th District business and financial conditions, monthly chartbook, 9377–10

Economic indicators and components, current data and annual trends, monthly rpt, 23842–1.1

Economic indicators and relation to govt finances by level of govt, selected years 1929-90, annual rpt, 10044–1

Economic indicators compounded annual rates of change, monthly rpt, 9391–3

Economic indicators compounded annual rates of change, 1971-90, annual rpt, 9391–9.2

Economic indicators, monthly rpt, 9362–1.2

Economic indicators performance, and Fed Reserve monetary policy objectives, as of July 1991, semiannual rpt, 9362–4

Economic indicators relation to potential GNP, model description and results, 1960-91, working paper, 9375–13.65

Economic Report of the President for 1991, with economic trends from 1929, annual rpt, 204–1

Energy taxes impacts on GNP and budget deficit, for alternative taxation methods, projected 1991-2000, 3166–6.57

Financial and economic analysis and forecasting methodology, technical paper series, 9366–6

Forecasts of GNP and employment, performance of alternative models, with results, 1958-88, article, 9371–1.201

Forecasts of GNP and inflation, performance of alternative monetary aggregates, model description and results, 1948-87, working paper, 9371–10.53

Forecasts of GNP and money supply, performance of alternative monetary policy rules, 1991 technical paper, 9379–12.66

Foreign and US economic conditions and competitiveness issues, with data by country, 1960s-90, 21788–204

Foreign and US economic conditions, for major industrial countries, biweekly rpt, 9112–1

Foreign and US economic indicators, trade balances, and exchange rates, for selected OECD and Asian countries, 1991 semiannual rpt, 8002–14

Foreign countries *Background Notes*, summary social, political, and economic data, series, 7006–2

Foreign countries economic and monetary trends, compounded annual rates of change and quarterly indicators for US and 7 major industrialized countries, quarterly rpt, 9391–7

Foreign countries economic conditions and implications for US, periodic country rpt series, 2046–4

Foreign countries economic indicators, and trade and investment flows, for selected countries and country groups, selected years 1946-90, annual rpt, 204–1.9

Foreign countries economic, social, political, and geographic summary data, by country, 1991, annual factbook, 9114–2

GDP and GNP as measures of production, factor income components, and receipts from and payments to foreigners, 1980s-91, article, 2702–1.215

GNP by industry group, 1986-89, article, 2702–1.208

Inflation long-run costs, with background data on unemployment and GNP growth for high- and low-inflation countries, 1980s, article, 9385–1.207

Interest rates impact on GNP and components, alternative regression results, late 1950s-80s, technical paper, 9385–8.79

Labor force composition and changes in participation related to GNP changes, model description and results, 1940s-2000, article, 9373–1.201

Military spending, and share of GNP, 1940s-80s, article, 9391–1.204

Money supply relation to GNP, alternative model results, 1960s-90, working paper, 9377–9.104

Money supply relation to GNP and interest rates, alternative models description and results, 1953-88, article, 9391–1.210

Natl income and product accounts and components, *Survey of Current Business*, monthly rpt, 2702–1.24

OASDI benefit payments, trust fund finances, and economic and demographic assumptions, 1970-90 and alternative projections to 2000, actuarial rpt, 4706–1.105

OECD members GNP and GNP growth, by country, 1980-90, annual rpt, 7144–8

Index by Subjects and Names

Overseas Business Reports: economic conditions, investment and export opportunities, and trade practices, country market research rpt series, 2046–6

Palau admin, and social, economic, and govtl data, FY90, annual rpt, 7004–6

Persian Gulf War impacts on US economic conditions compared to previous oil shock periods, and Saudi Arabia oil production and prices, 1990-92, hearings, 21248–156

PPI and components correlation with GNP and industrial production over business cycles, 1957-89, article, 9383–6.204

Public debt burden on future generations forecast under alternative economic and fiscal policy assumptions, 1991 working paper, 9377–9.111

Savings rates impacts on GNP and balance of payments, 1950s-89 and projected to 2009, article, 9385–1.201

Soviet Union, Eastern Europe, OECD, and selected other countries economic conditions, 1960s-90, annual rpt, 9114–4

Soviet Union economic conditions, CIA GNP estimation methods assessment, 1989, GAO rpt, 26123–365

Soviet Union GNP by component and industry sector, and CIA estimation methods, 1950s-87, 23848–223

Soviet Union GNP by detailed income and outlay component, 1985, 2326–18.59

State and Metro Area Data Book, 1991 data compilation, 2328–54

Statistical Abstract of US, 1991 annual data compilation, 2324–1.14

Stock price dispersion index impact on GNP, 1948-87, article, 9375–1.201

Transportation energy use by mode, fuel supply, and demographic and economic factors of vehicle use, 1970s-89, annual rpt, 3304–5.2

Turkey GNP, trade, investment, and inflation following currency devaluation, 1970s-90, technical paper, 9385–8.112

Variability of GNP and GNP deflator, alternative models assessment and results, 1869-1988, article, 9379–1.205

Zimbabwe agricultural conditions impacts of economic policies, 1980s, 1528–319

see also Gross Domestic Product

Grosz, Andrew E.

"Textural and Mineralogic Analyses of Surficial Sediments Offshore of Myrtle Beach, S.C.", 5668–115

Groundwater

see Hydrology

see Rivers and waterways

see Water supply and use

Group health

see Blue Cross-Blue Shield

see Health insurance

see Health maintenance organizations

Group homes for the handicapped

Child welfare programs funding by source, and foster care program operations and client characteristics, for selected States, 1960s-95, 25368–169

Drug abuse prevalence among minorities, related health effects and crime, treatment, and research status and needs, mid 1970s-90, 4498–72

Drug and alcohol abuse treatment facilities, services, use, funding, staff, and client characteristics, 1989, biennial rpt, 4494–10

Long-term care institutional and community services, spending and use by type and payment source, FY88, and Medicaid growth since FY75, 26306–6.156

Medicaid beneficiaries services use and costs, by service type and eligibility, 1975-89, article, 4652–1.209

Mentally retarded persons care facilities and residents by selected characteristics, and use of Medicaid services and waiver programs, by State, late 1970s-80s, 4658–49

Regulation and enforcement of board and care homes by States, 1988, 4008–112

Supplemental Security Income and Medicaid eligibility and payment provisions, and beneficiaries living arrangements, by State, 1991, annual rpt, 4704–13

Group quarters

Accident deaths and rates, by cause, age, sex, race, and State, 1988, US Vital Statistics annual rpt, 4144–2.5

AFDC beneficiaries demographic and financial characteristics, by State, FY89, annual rpt, 4694–1

Census of Population and Housing, 1990: housing units occupied and vacant, persons in group quarters, and household size, by region, census div, and State, press release, 2328–71

Census of Population and Housing, 1990: population and housing characteristics, households, and land area, by county, subdiv, and place, State rpt series, 2551–1

Census of Population and Housing, 1990: population and housing selected characteristics, by region, press release, 2328–74

County Business Patterns, 1988: employment, establishments, and payroll, by SIC 2- to 4-digit industry and county, annual State rpt series, 2326–6

County Business Patterns, 1989: employment, establishments, and payroll, by SIC 2- to 4-digit industry and county, annual State rpt series, 2326–8

Foster care placements, discharges, and returns to care, by selected characteristics of children, and length of stay factors, 1985-86, GAO rpt, 26121–432

Higher education instn student aid and other sources of support, with student expenses and characteristics, by instn type and control, 1990 triennial study, series, 4846–5

Homeless and runaway youth programs, funding, activities, and participant characteristics, FY90, annual rpt, 4604–3

Living arrangements, family relationships, and marital status, by selected characteristics, 1990, annual Current Population Rpt, 2546–1.449

Puerto Rico population and housing characteristics, 1990 Census of Population and Housing, press release, 2328–78

State and Metro Area Data Book, 1991 data compilation, 2328–54

Statistical Abstract of US, 1991 annual data compilation, 2324–1.1

Supplemental Security Income and Medicaid eligibility and payment provisions, and beneficiaries living arrangements, by State, 1991, annual rpt, 4704–13

Guam

Virgin Islands population and housing characteristics, 1990 Census of Population and Housing, press release, 2328–81

see also Group homes for the handicapped

see also Transient housing

Grubb, Charles T.

"Nationwide Evaluation of Medicaid Competition Demonstrations. Volume 5. Access and Satisfaction", 4658–45.5

Gruben, William C.

"Forecasting the Louisiana Economy", 9379–1.202

GSA

see General Services Administration

Guadagno, Mary Ann

"Comparison of Lower Middle Income Two-Parent and Single-Mother Families", 1702–1.207

"Economic Status of Two-Parent Families with Employed Teens and Young Adults", 1702–1.213

"Family Income and Expenditures of Married-Couple Families When One Spouse Is not Employed", 1702–1.201

"Income and Expenditures of Two-Parent Families When One Parent Is Not Employed", 1004–16.1

Guam

Banks (insured commercial and savings) deposits by instn, State, MSA, and county, as of June 1990, annual regional rpt, 9295–3.6

Census of Population, 1990: Guam population by district, press release, 2328–79

Economic conditions, population characteristics, and Federal aid, for Pacific territories, 1989 hearing, 21448–44

Economic, social, political, and geographic summary data, by country, 1991, annual factbook, 9114–2

Exports and imports between US and outlying areas, by detailed commodity and mode of transport, 1990, annual rpt, 2424–11

Fed Govt spending in States and local areas, by type, State, county, and city, FY90, annual rpt, 2464–3

Fed Govt spending in States, by type, program, agency, and State, FY90, annual rpt, 2464–2

HHS financial aid, by program, recipient, State, and city, FY90, annual regional listing, 4004–3.9

Hospital deaths of Medicare patients, actual and expected rates by diagnosis, and hospital characteristics, by instn, FY87-89, annual regional rpt, 4654–14.9

Military presence of US in Pacific basin, personnel, dependents, aircraft, ships, and costs, by service branch and location, 1990, GAO rpt, 26123–357

Minerals Yearbook, 1989, Vol 2: State reviews of production, sales, and firms, by commodity, and business activity, annual rpt, 5604–34

Physicians, by specialty, age, sex, and location of training and practice, 1989, State rpt, 4116–6.53

Statistical Abstract of US, 1991 annual data compilation, 2324–1.30

see also under By Outlying Area in the "Index by Categories"

Guaranteed income

Guaranteed income
see Income maintenance

Guaranteed student loans
see Student aid

Guarantees and warranties
see also Surety bonds

Guardia, Enrique J.
"Food Safety and the Environment", 1004–16.1

Guardianship
Child abuse and neglect victims representation in legal proceedings, caseloads, State requirements, and compensation, by State and county, 1989, 4608–28
OASDI and SSI recipients with representative payee, by beneficiary type, 1989, annual rpt, 4744–3.3; 4744–3.8
Supplemental Security Income and Medicaid eligibility and payment provisions, and beneficiaries living arrangements, by State, 1991, annual rpt, 4704–13
see also Foster home care
see also Parents

Guatemala
Agricultural exports of high-value commodities, indexes and sales by commodity, world area, and country, 1960s-86, 1528–323
Agricultural exports of US, impacts of foreign agricultural and trade policy, with data by commodity and country, 1989, annual rpt, 1924–8
Agricultural production, trade, and policies in foreign countries, summary data by country, 1989-90, annual factbook, 1924–12
Agricultural trade of US, by detailed commodity and country, 1989, annual rpt, 1524–8
Agricultural trade of US, by detailed commodity and country, 1990, semiannual rpt, 1522–4
AID economic aid to developing countries, obligations and disbursements by country, quarterly rpt, 9912–4
AID loans repayment status and terms by program and country, and status of predecessor agency loans, quarterly rpt, 9912–3
Economic and military aid and loans from US and intl agencies, by program and country, FY46-90, annual rpt, 9914–5
Economic and social conditions of developing countries from 1960s, and Intl Dev Cooperation Agency and AID activities and funding, FY90-92, annual rpt, 9904–4
Economic conditions, policy, and trade practices, by country, 1988-90, annual rpt, 21384–5
Economic, population, and agricultural data, US and other aid sources, and AID activity, 1988 country rpt, 9916–12.30
Economic, social, political, and geographic summary data, by country, 1991, annual factbook, 9114–2
Exports and imports of US, by commodity and country, 1970-89, world area rpt, 9116–1.2
Exports and imports of US, by selected country, country group, and commodity group, 1990, annual rpt, 2044–37
Exports and imports of US, by transport mode, country, and SITC 1- to 3-digit commodity, 1990, annual rpt, 2424–12

Exports of US, detailed Schedule B commodities with countries of destination, 1990, annual rpt, 2424–10
Human rights conditions in 170 countries, and US economic and military aid, 1990, annual rpt, 21384–3
Investment (direct) incentives of Caribbean Basin Initiative, economic impacts, with finances and employment by country, 1984-90, 2048–141
Labor conditions, union coverage, and work accidents, 1991 annual country rpt, 6366–4.32
Military aid of US, arms sales, and training programs costs and budget requests, by program, world region, and country, FY90-92, annual rpt, 7144–13
Multinatl US firms and foreign affiliates finances and operations, by industry and world area of parent firm, 1989 benchmark survey, preliminary annual rpt, 2704–5
Multinatl US firms foreign affiliates, income statement items by country and world area, 1986, biennial article, 8302–2.212
UN voting record and share of votes in agreement with US, by issue, country, and world area, 1990, annual rpt, 7004–18
see also under By Foreign Country in the "Index by Categories"

Guey-Lee, Louise
"Annual Prospects for World Coal Trade, 1991", 3164–77
"Higher World Oil Prices: The Potential for Oil-to-Coal Switching", 3162–37.201

Guinea
Agricultural exports of high-value commodities, indexes and sales by commodity, world area, and country, 1960s-86, 1528–323
Agricultural trade of US, by detailed commodity and country, 1989, annual rpt, 1524–8
Agricultural trade of US, by detailed commodity and country, 1990, semiannual rpt, 1522–4
AID economic aid to developing countries, obligations and disbursements by country, quarterly rpt, 9912–4
AID loans repayment status and terms by program and country, and status of predecessor agency loans, quarterly rpt, 9912–3
Dairy imports, consumption, and market conditions, by sub-Saharan Africa country, 1961-88, 1528–321
Economic and military aid and loans from US and intl agencies, by program and country, FY46-90, annual rpt, 9914–5
Economic and social conditions of developing countries from 1960s, and Intl Dev Cooperation Agency and AID activities and funding, FY90-92, annual rpt, 9904–4
Economic, population, and agricultural data, US and other aid sources, and AID activity, 1987 country rpt, 9916–12.24
Economic, social, political, and geographic summary data, by country, 1991, annual factbook, 9114–2
Exports and imports of US, by transport mode, country, and SITC 1- to 3-digit commodity, 1990, annual rpt, 2424–12
Exports of US, detailed Schedule B commodities with countries of destination, 1990, annual rpt, 2424–10

Human rights conditions in 170 countries, and US economic and military aid, 1990, annual rpt, 21384–3
Military aid of US, arms sales, and training programs costs and budget requests, by program, world region, and country, FY90-92, annual rpt, 7144–13
UN voting record and share of votes in agreement with US, by issue, country, and world area, 1990, annual rpt, 7004–18
see also under By Foreign Country in the "Index by Categories"

Guinea-Bissau
Agricultural exports of high-value commodities, indexes and sales by commodity, world area, and country, 1960s-86, 1528–323
Agricultural trade of US, by detailed commodity and country, 1989, annual rpt, 1524–8
Agricultural trade of US, by detailed commodity and country, 1990, semiannual rpt, 1522–4
AID economic aid to developing countries, obligations and disbursements by country, quarterly rpt, 9912–4
Dairy imports, consumption, and market conditions, by sub-Saharan Africa country, 1961-88, 1528–321
Economic and military aid and loans from US and intl agencies, by program and country, FY46-90, annual rpt, 9914–5
Economic and social conditions of developing countries from 1960s, and Intl Dev Cooperation Agency and AID activities and funding, FY90-92, annual rpt, 9904–4
Economic, population, and agricultural data, US and other aid sources, and AID activity, 1990 country rpt, 9916–12.47
Economic, social, political, and geographic summary data, by country, 1991, annual factbook, 9114–2
Exports and imports of US, by transport mode, country, and SITC 1- to 3-digit commodity, 1990, annual rpt, 2424–12
Human rights conditions in 170 countries, and US economic and military aid, 1990, annual rpt, 21384–3
Military aid of US, arms sales, and training programs costs and budget requests, by program, world region, and country, FY90-92, annual rpt, 7144–13
UN voting record and share of votes in agreement with US, by issue, country, and world area, 1990, annual rpt, 7004–18
see also under By Foreign Country in the "Index by Categories"

Gulf of Alaska
Army Corps of Engineers water resources dev projects, characteristics, and costs, 1950s-89, biennial State rpt series, 3756–1
Army Corps of Engineers water resources dev projects, characteristics, and costs, 1950s-91, biennial State rpt series, 3756–2
Environmental conditions and oil dev impacts for Alaska OCS, compilation of papers, series, 2176–1
Fish catch in excess of domestic processor needs, and use of estimates for Alaska fishing rights allocation, 1984-90, GAO rpt, 26113–523

Fish catch, trade, use, and fishery operations, with selected foreign data, by species, 1980s-90, annual rpt, 2164–1
see also Cook Inlet, Alaska
see also Prince William Sound, Alaska

Gulf of Mexico

Estuary environmental and fishery conditions, research results and methodology, 1991 rpt, 2176–7.23

Estuary environmental conditions, and fish and shellfish catch by species and region, 1980s, 2178–27

Fish and shellfish catch, life cycles, and environmental needs, for selected coastal species and regions, series, 5506–8

Fish and shellfish catch, wholesale receipts, prices, trade, and other market activities, weekly regional rpt, 2162–6.3

Fish catch, trade, use, and fishery operations, with selected foreign data, by species, 1980s-90, annual rpt, 2164–1

Fish larvae abundance, distribution, and growth, for selected Western Hemisphere sites, 1989 conf, 2168–126

Fishing (ocean sport) activities, and catch by species, by angler characteristics and State, 1987-89, annual coastal area rpt, 2166–17.1

Marine Fisheries Review, US and foreign fisheries resources, dev, mgmt, and research, quarterly journal, 2162–1

Mineral industries census, 1987: finances and operations, by establishment characteristics, SIC 2- to 4-digit industry, and State, subject rpt, 2517–1

Natural gas production and wellhead capacity, by production area, 1980-89 and alternative forecasts 1990-91, biennial rpt, 3164–93

Oil and gas OCS lease proposals, impacts on south Florida environmental, social, and economic conditions, 1990 compilation of papers, 5738–19

Oil and gas OCS leases environmental and socioeconomic impact and coastal area description, 1990 final statement, 5736–1.23

Oil and gas OCS reserves, and leasing and dev activity, 1990 periodic regional rpt, 5736–3.1

Oil and gas OCS reserves of Fed Govt, leasing and exploration activity, production, revenue, and costs, by ocean area, FY90, annual rpt, 5734–4

Oil and gas OCS reserves, production, and leasing status, for Gulf of Mexico by location, 1989, annual rpt, 5734–6

Oil, gas, and minerals production, revenue, and leasing activity, for Federal OCS lands by ocean region and State, 1950s-90, annual rpt, 5734–3

Pollutant concentrations in coastal and estuarine sediments, by contaminant and selected site, 1984-89, 2176–3.13

Recreation (outdoor) coastal facilities of Fed Govt and States, visitor and site characteristics, 1987-90 survey, regional rpt, 2176–9.1; 2176–9.3; 2176–9.4; 2176–9.7

Sharks and other fish tagged and recovered, by species, 1990, annual rpt, 2164–21

Temperature of sea surface by ocean and for US coastal areas, and Bering Sea ice conditions, monthly rpt, 2182–5

Tidal currents, daily time and velocity by station for North America coasts, forecast 1992, annual rpt, 2174–1.1

Tide height and time daily at coastal points, forecast 1992, annual rpt, 2174–2.3

Turtles (sea) population near oil drilling rigs, and habitat characteristics, 1988-90, 5738–26

Water supply and quality in streams and lakes, and groundwater levels in wells, by drainage basin, 1988, annual State rpt series, 5666–16

Water supply and quality in streams and lakes, and groundwater levels in wells, by drainage basin, 1989, annual State rpt series, 5666–12

Water supply and quality in streams and lakes, and groundwater levels in wells, by drainage basin, 1990, annual State rpt series, 5666–10

Wetlands in coastal areas, acreage by wetland type, estuarine basin, and county, 1989, 2178–31

Gulfport, Miss.

see also under By SMSA or MSA in the "Index by Categories"

Gum and wood chemicals

County Business Patterns, 1988: employment, establishments, and payroll, by SIC 2- to 4-digit industry and county, annual State rpt series, 2326–6

County Business Patterns, 1989: employment, establishments, and payroll, by SIC 2- to 4-digit industry and county, annual State rpt series, 2326–8

Employment, earnings, and hours, by SIC 1- to 4-digit industry, monthly and annual averages, selected years 1909-90, annual rpt, 6744–4

Exports and imports of US, by country and detailed commodity, monthly rpt, 2422–12

Exports and imports of US, by Harmonized System 6-digit commodity and country, 1990, annual rpt, 2424–13

Exports of US, detailed Schedule B commodities with countries of destination, 1990, annual rpt, 2424–10

Manufacturing annual survey, 1989: finances and operations, by SIC 2- to 4-digit industry, series, 2506–15

Manufacturing census, 1987: finances and operations, by SIC 2- to 4-digit industry, State, and MSA, with trends from 1849, 2497–1

Manufacturing census, 1987: finances and operations, by type of organization and SIC 2- to 4-digit industry, subject rpt, 2497–5

Occupational injury and illness rates, by SIC 2- to 4-digit industry, 1988-89, annual rpt, 6844–7

Occupational injury and illness rates, by SIC 2- to 4-digit industry, 1989, annual rpt, 6844–1

Price indexes (producer), by stage of processing and detailed commodity, monthly rpt, 6762–6

Price indexes (producer), by stage of processing and detailed commodity, monthly 1990, annual rpt, 6764–2

Price support program provisions, for selected commodities, 1961-90, 1568–303

Guns

see Firearms

see Military weapons

Gunter, Lewell

"Will Immigration Reform Affect the Economic Competitiveness of Labor-Intensive Crops?", 1598–276

Gunther, Jeffery W.

"Risk and Failure Among Newly Established Texas Banks", 9379–14.10

Gupta, Nandini S.

"National Survey of State Maternal and Newborn Drug Testing and Reporting Policies", 4042–3.220

Gustafson, Elizabeth

"Empirical Examination of Government Expenditures and the Ex Ante Crowding Out Effect for the British Economy", 9385–8.83

Gustman, Alan L.

"Pension Portability and Labor Mobility: Evidence from the Survey of Income and Program Participation", 2626–10.123

Guterman, Stuart

"Medicare-Dependent Hospitals Under PPS", 17206–2.16

Guyana

Agricultural exports of high-value commodities, indexes and sales by commodity, world area, and country, 1960s-86, 1528–323

Agricultural trade of US, by detailed commodity and country, 1989, annual rpt, 1524–8

Agricultural trade of US, by detailed commodity and country, 1990, semiannual rpt, 1522–4

AID economic aid to developing countries, obligations and disbursements by country, quarterly rpt, 9912–4

AID loans repayment status and terms by program and country, and status of predecessor agency loans, quarterly rpt, 9912–3

Economic and military aid and loans from US and intl agencies, by program and country, FY46-90, annual rpt, 9914–5

Economic and social conditions of developing countries from 1960s, and Intl Dev Cooperation Agency and AID activities and funding, FY90-92, annual rpt, 9904–4

Economic, social, political, and geographic summary data, by country, 1991, annual factbook, 9114–2

Exports and imports of US, by transport mode, country, and SITC 1- to 3-digit commodity, 1990, annual rpt, 2424–12

Exports of US, detailed Schedule B commodities with countries of destination, 1990, annual rpt, 2424–10

Human rights conditions in 170 countries, and US economic and military aid, 1990, annual rpt, 21384–3

Investment (direct) incentives of Caribbean Basin Initiative, economic impacts, with finances and employment by country, 1984-90, 2048–141

Labor conditions, union coverage, and work accidents, 1991 annual country rpt, 6366–4.38

Military aid of US, arms sales, and training programs costs and budget requests, by program, world region, and country, FY90-92, annual rpt, 7144–13

Guyana

UN voting record and share of votes in agreement with US, by issue, country, and world area, 1990, annual rpt, 7004–18

Guzda, Henry P.
"James P. Mitchell: Social Conscience of the Cabinet", 6722–1.239

Gyourko, Joseph
"How Accurate Are Quality-of-Life Rankings Across Cities?", 9387–1.202

Gypsum
see Nonmetallic minerals and mines

Gypsy moths
see Pests and pest control

Habeas corpus
Court civil and criminal caseloads for Federal district, appeals, and special courts, 1990, annual rpt, 18204–8
Court civil and criminal caseloads for Federal district courts, 1991, annual rpt, 18204–2.1
Prisoners petitions filed in Federal courts of appeals and district courts, by type of petition, circuit, and district, 1990, annual rpt, 18204–11
US attorneys case processing and collections, by case type and Federal district, FY90, annual rpt, 6004–2

Haber, Sheldon E.
"Estimates of Employer Contributions for Health Insurance by Worker Characteristics", 2626–10.136

Hackett, Ronald L.
"Veneer Industry and Timber Use, North Central Region, 1988", 1208–220

Haddy, Theresa B.
"Minerals in Hair, Serum, and Urine of Healthy and Anemic Black Children", 4042–3.248

Hadley, Jack
"Hospital Cost Variations Under PPS", 17206–2.26

Hadlock, Paul
"High Technology Employment: Another View", 6722–1.235

Hafer, R. W.
"Evaluating Monetary Base Targeting Rules", 9379–12.66

Haffner, William H.
"Maternal Health", 4088–2

Hafner, Anne
"Careers in Teaching: Following Members of the High School Class of 1972 In and Out of Teaching", 4836–1.13

Hafnium
see Metals and metal industries

Hagemeyer, D.
"Occupational Radiation Exposure at Commercial Nuclear Power Reactors and Other Facilities, 1987", 9634–3

Hagerstown, Md.
see also under By SMSA or MSA in the "Index by Categories"

Hahn, Thomas
"Interest Rate Expectations and the Slope of the Money Market Yield Curve", 9389–1.201

Hahn, William F.
"Price Transmission Asymmetry in Pork and Beef Markets", 1502–3.201

Haines, Terry A.
"Intensive Studies of Stream Fish Populations in Maine", 9208–130

Haiti

Agricultural exports of US, impacts of foreign agricultural and trade policy, with data by commodity and country, 1989, annual rpt, 1924–8
Agricultural trade of US, by detailed commodity and country, 1989, annual rpt, 1524–8
Agricultural trade of US, by detailed commodity and country, 1990, semiannual rpt, 1522–4
AID economic aid to developing countries, obligations and disbursements by country, quarterly rpt, 9912–4
AID loans repayment status and terms by program and country, and status of predecessor agency loans, quarterly rpt, 9912–3
Aliens (illegal) enforcement activity of Coast Guard, by nationality, 2nd half FY91, semiannual rpt, 7402–4
Economic and military aid and loans from US and intl agencies, by program and country, FY46-90, annual rpt, 9914–5
Economic and social conditions of developing countries from 1960s, and Intl Dev Cooperation Agency and AID activities and funding, FY90-92, annual rpt, 9904–4
Economic conditions, policy, and trade practices, by country, 1988-90, annual rpt, 21384–5
Economic, population, and agricultural data, US and other aid sources, and AID activity, 1989 country rpt, 9916–12.40
Economic, social, political, and geographic summary data, by country, 1991, annual factbook, 9114–2
Exports and imports of US, by commodity and country, 1970-89, world area rpt, 9116–1.5
Exports and imports of US, by selected country, country group, and commodity group, 1990, annual rpt, 2044–37
Exports and imports of US, by transport mode, country, and SITC 1- to 3-digit commodity, 1990, annual rpt, 2424–12
Exports of US, detailed Schedule B commodities with countries of destination, 1990, annual rpt, 2424–10
Human rights conditions in 170 countries, and US economic and military aid, 1990, annual rpt, 21384–3
Investment (direct) incentives of Caribbean Basin Initiative, economic impacts, with finances and employment by country, 1984-90, 2048–141
Labor conditions, union coverage, and work accidents, 1991 annual country rpt, 6366–4.13
Military aid of US, arms sales, and training programs costs and budget requests, by program, world region, and country, FY90-92, annual rpt, 7144–13
Rum imports (duty-free) of US under Caribbean Basin Initiative, by country, 1989-90, annual rpt, 9884–15
UN voting record and share of votes in agreement with US, by issue, country, and world area, 1990, annual rpt, 7004–18
see also under By Foreign Country in the "Index by Categories"

Index by Subjects and Names

Hakkio, Craig S.
"Cointegration: How Short Is the Long Run?", 9381–10.119

Halfway houses
see Community-based correctional programs
see Group homes for the handicapped
see Sheltered workshops

Hall, Jonathan V.
"National Wetlands Inventory. Alaska Coastal Wetlands Survey", 5506–11.5

Hall, Margaret J.
"Medicaid-Financed Residential Care for Persons with Mental Retardation", 4652–1.219

Hall, Peter
"AID Donor Coordination in Malawi", 9916–12.41

Hallman, Jeffrey J.
"Cointegration and Transformed Series", 9377–9.104

Halm, Glenn E.
"Labor Shortages: A Growing Dilemma in East Asia", 6366–4.17

Haltiwanger, John
"Gross Job Creation, Gross Job Destruction and Employment Reallocation", 9375–13.56

Hamak, John E.
"Analyses of Natural Gases, 1990", 5604–2
"Helium Resources of the U.S., 1989", 5604–44

Hamaker, J. W.
"NASA In-House Commercially Developed Space Facility (CDSF) Study Report: Cost Estimation and Economic Analysis", 21708–129

Hamdani, Kausar
"Comparative Analysis of Corporate Takeovers", 9385–8.88
"Disaggregate Analysis of Discount Window Borrowing", 9385–1.209

Hamilton County, Ind.
Housing and households characteristics, unit and neighborhood quality, and journey to work by MSA location, for 11 MSAs, 1984 survey, supplement, 2485–8
Housing and households detailed characteristics, and unit and neighborhood quality, by location, 1988 survey, MSA rpt, 2485–6.4

Hamilton, Michael M.
"Availability of Federally Owned Minerals for Exploration and Development in Western States: Nevada, 1985", 5606–7.6

Hamilton, Ohio
CPI by component for US city average, and by region, population size, and for 27 metro areas, monthly rpt, 6762–2
see also under By SMSA or MSA in the "Index by Categories"

Hamm, Larry G.
"Dairy Industry in the 1990's", 1004–16.1

Hammer, Charles H.
"Advanced Placement Programs in Public and Private Schools: Characteristics of Schools and Program Offerings, 1984-86", 4838–46
"Aspects of Teacher Supply and Demand in Public School Districts and Private Schools: 1987-88. Schools and Staffing Survey", 4836–3.6

Index by Subjects and Names

Harbors and ports

Hammett, K. M.
"Land Use, Water Use, Streamflow Characteristics, and Water-Quality Characteristics of the Charlotte Harbor Inflow Area, Florida", 5666–27.18

Hammett, Theodore M.
"Update on AIDS in Prisons and Jails", 6066–28.1

Hammock, Delia A.
"Consumer Perceptions on Scientific Solutions to Food Safety and Environmental Dilemmas", 1004–16.1

Hammond, Ind.
see also under By SMSA or MSA in the "Index by Categories"

Hammond, John
"End-Stage Renal Disease", 4088–2
"Infectious Diseases", 4088–2

Hampton, Va.
see also under By City in the "Index by Categories"

Hand tools
see Tools

Handbags
see Leather industry and products

Handelsman, Harry
"Carotid Endarterectomy. Health Technology Assessment Report, 1990", 4186–10.2
"Implantation of the Automatic Cardioverter-Defibrillator. Health Technology Assessment Report, 1990", 4186–10.5

Handicapped
see Aid to blind
see Aid to disabled and handicapped persons
see Architectural barriers to the handicapped
see Blind
see Deaf
see Disabled and handicapped persons
see Discrimination against the handicapped
see Group homes for the handicapped
see Handicapped children
see Learning disabilities
see Mental retardation
see Mobility limitations
see Rehabilitation of the disabled
see Supplemental Security Income

Handicapped children
Developmental, learning, and emotional problems in children, and share receiving special treatment and education, by selected characteristics, 1988, 4146–8.193

Education data compilation, 1991 annual rpt, 4824–2

Family structure relation to child health, behavioral, emotional, and school problems, by selected characteristics, 1988, 4147–10.178

Foster care programs cases, problems, and operations for selected States, 1970s-90, hearings, 21788–202

Head Start handicapped enrollment, by handicap, State, and for Indian and migrant programs, 1987/88, annual rpt, 4604–1

HHS financial aid, by program, recipient, State, and city, FY90, annual regional listings, 4004–3

Mental health care facilities, finances, caseload, staff, and characteristics of instn and patients, 1988, 4506–4.14

Mental health care facilities of States and counties, patients and admissions by age, diagnosis, and State, FY89, annual rpt, 4504–2

Mental health care facilities, staff, and patient characteristics, *Statistical Notes* series, 4506–3
see also Birth defects
see also Learning disabilities
see also Old-Age, Survivors, Disability, and Health Insurance
see also Special education
see also Supplemental Security Income

Handy, Matthew
"Sandhill Crane Harvest and Hunter Activity in the Central Flyway During the 1990-91 Hunting Season", 5504–31

Hanford Engineering Development Laboratory
see also Department of Energy National Laboratories

Hanford Environmental Dose Reconstruction Project
Radiation exposure of population near Hanford, Wash, nuclear plant, with methodology, 1944-66, series, 3356–5

Hanks, James W.
"Description of High-Occupancy Vehicle Facilities in North America", 7888–80

Hannan, Timothy H.
"Functional Relationship Between Prices and Market Concentration: The Case of the Banking Industry", 9366–6.283
"Inferring Market Power from Time-Series Data: The Case of the Banking Firm", 9366–6.261

Hanousek, Janet
"Thrift Delinquency Rates", 9302–4.202

Hansen, LeRoy
"Alternative Allocations of Water in Rural Areas", 1502–7.203

Hanson, Gregory D.
"Financial Performance of Specialized Corn-Soybean Farms, 1987", 1566–8.7
"Financial Performance of Specialized Hog Farms, 1987", 1566–8.6
"Small Farmers Weathered 1980's Financial Stress Better than Large Farmers", 1502–7.202

Hanzlick, Dennis J.
"Interpolation, Analysis, and Archival of Data on Sea Ice Trajectories and Ocean Currents Obtained from Satellite-Linked Instruments", 2176–1.38

Harber, Richard P., Jr.
"Can Zambia Grow Out of Its Debt Problem?", 9916–12.25
"Zambia Macroeconomic Background", 9916–12.25

Harbors and ports
Accidents involving ships and marine facilities, casualties, and circumstances, Coast Guard investigation results, periodic rpt, 9612–4

Army Corps of Engineers water resources dev projects, characteristics, and costs, 1950s-89, biennial State rpt series, 3756–1

Army Corps of Engineers water resources dev projects, characteristics, and costs, 1950s-91, biennial State rpt series, 3756–2

California sport and commercial fish and shellfish landings, permits issued, and harbor facilities, 1916-86, 5738–20

Classification codes for countries and ports under Tariff Schedule of US, 1992 base edition, 9886–13

Coal production, stocks, and shipments, by State of origin and destination, end-use sector, and mode of transport, quarterly rpt, 3162–8

Construction industries census, 1987: establishments, employment, receipts, and expenditures, by SIC 4-digit industry and State, final industry rpt series, 2373–1

Customs Service activities, and collections total and for selected ports, bimonthly journal, 8142–2

Export and import statistics classification codes of Census Bur for foreign ports, 1991, 2428–12

Export statistics classification codes of Census Bur for countries, commodities, and customs districts, 1990 base edition supplement, 2428–5

Exports and imports (agricultural) of US, by commodity, country, and US port, 1950s-91, annual rpt, 1924–9

Exports and imports (waterborne) of US, by type of service, commodity, country, route, and US port, 1988, annual rpt, 7704–2

Exports and imports (waterborne) of US, by type of service, customs district, port, and world area, monthly rpt, 2422–7

Exports of US, detailed commodities by country, monthly CD-ROM, 2422–13

Fed Govt Harbor Maintenance Trust Fund financial condition, monthly rpt, 8102–9.12

Fed Govt-owned real property inventory and costs, worldwide summary by purpose, agency, and location, 1989, annual rpt, 9454–5

Fish and shellfish catch, wholesale receipts, prices, trade, and other market activities, weekly regional rpts, 2162–6

Fish catch, by species, use, region, State, and major port, 1980s-90, annual rpt, 2164–1.1

Florida environmental, social, and economic conditions, and impacts of proposed OCS oil and gas leases in southern coastal areas, 1990 compilation of papers, 5738–19

Foreign countries economic, social, political, and geographic summary data, by country, 1991, annual factbook, 9114–2

Freight (waterborne domestic and foreign), by port and State, 1989, annual rpt series, 3754–7

Govt employment and payroll, by function, level of govt, and jurisdiction, 1990, annual rpt series, 2466–1

Imports of US, detailed commodities by country, monthly CD-ROM, 2422–14

Middle Atlantic States tide height and tidal current velocity daily at selected coastal stations, forecast 1992, annual rpt, 2174–11

Military and personal property shipments, passenger traffic, and costs, by service branch and mode of transport, quarterly rpt, 3702–1

Natl transportation system planning, use, condition, accidents, and needs, by mode of transport, 1940s-90 and projected to 2020, 7308–202

Navy homeport construction proposals, assignments and costs compared to existing ports, 1990s, GAO rpt, 26123–347

Harbors and ports

Navy nuclear-powered vessels and support facilities radioactive waste, releases in harbors, and public exposure, 1970s-90, annual rpt, 3804–11

Oil import traffic by US port and vessel type, marine oil pollution sources, and costs and operations of proposed offshore terminals, late 1980s, 5738–25

Pollutant concentrations in coastal and estuarine sediments, by contaminant and selected site, 1984-89, 2176–3.13

Publications and data files of Census Bur on foreign trade, 1991 guide, 2428–11

Seals (harbor) population and physical characteristics at selected Washington State coastal sites, 1975-80, 14738–7

St Lawrence Seaway ship, cargo, and passenger traffic, and toll revenue, 1990 and trends from 1959, annual rpt, 7744–2

Tidal currents, daily time and velocity by station for North America and Asia coasts, forecast 1992, annual rpts, 2174–1

Tide height and time daily at coastal points worldwide, forecast 1992, annual rpt series, 2174–2

Transportation census, 1987: finances and operations by size, ownership, and State, and revenues by MSA, by SIC 2- to 4-digit industry, 2579–1

Water quality, chemistry, hydrology, and other characteristics, local area studies, series, 5666–27

Workers compensation programs under Federal admin, finances and operations, FY90, annual rpt, 6504–10

see also Dredging

Hardouvelis, Gikas A.

"Margin Requirements, Speculative Trading and Stock Price Fluctuations: The Case of Japan", 9385–8.72

Hardware

County Business Patterns, 1988: employment, establishments, and payroll, by SIC 2- to 4-digit industry and county, annual State rpt series, 2326–6

County Business Patterns, 1989: employment, establishments, and payroll, by SIC 2- to 4-digit industry and county, annual State rpt series, 2326–8

CPI by component for US city average, and by region, population size, and for 27 metro areas, monthly rpt, 6762–2

DOD prime contract awards, by detailed procurement category, FY87-90, annual rpt, 3544–18

Employment, earnings, and hours, by SIC 1- to 4-digit industry, monthly and annual averages, selected years 1909-90, annual rpt, 6744–4

Enterprise Statistics, 1987: finances and operations for companies, by size, level of diversification, form of organization, and industry group, 2329–8

Exports and imports between US and outlying areas, by detailed commodity and mode of transport, 1990, annual rpt, 2424–11

Exports and imports of building materials, by commodity and country, 1989-90, article, 2042–1.204

Exports and imports of US, by country and detailed commodity, monthly rpt, 2422–12

Exports and imports of US, by Harmonized System 6-digit commodity and country, 1990, annual rpt, 2424–13

Exports and imports of US, by transport mode, country, and SITC 1- to 3-digit commodity, 1990, annual rpt, 2424–12

Exports of US, detailed Schedule B commodities with countries of destination, 1990, annual rpt, 2424–10

Franchise business opportunities by firm and kind of business, and sources of aid and info, 1990 annual listing, 2104–7

Injuries from use of consumer products, by severity, victim age, and detailed product, 1990, annual rpt, 9164–6

Manufacturing annual survey, 1989: finances and operations, by SIC 2- to 4-digit industry, series, 2506–15

Manufacturing census, 1987: employment and shipments under Fed Govt contracts, by SIC 4-digit industry, 2497–7

Manufacturing census, 1987: finances and operations, by SIC 2- to 4-digit industry, State, and MSA, with trends from 1849, 2497–1

Manufacturing census, 1987: finances and operations, by type of organization and SIC 2- to 4-digit industry, subject rpt, 2497–5

Manufacturing finances and operations, by SIC 2- to 4-digit industry, forecast 1991, annual rpt, 2044–28

Occupational injury and illness rates, by SIC 2- to 4-digit industry, 1988-89, annual rpt, 6844–7

Occupational injury and illness rates, by SIC 2- to 4-digit industry, 1989, annual rpt, 6844–1

Price indexes (producer), by stage of processing and detailed commodity, monthly rpt, 6762–6

Price indexes (producer), by stage of processing and detailed commodity, monthly 1990, annual rpt, 6764–2

Puerto Rico economic censuses, 1987: wholesale and retail trade and service industry finances and operations, by SIC 2- to 4-digit industry and municipio, 2591–1

Puerto Rico economic censuses, 1987: wholesale, retail, and service industries finances and operations, by establishment characteristics and SIC 2- and 3-digit industry, subject rpts, 2591–2

Retail trade census, 1987: finances and employment, for establishments with and without payroll, by SIC 2- to 4-digit kind of business, State, and MSA, 2401–1

Retail trade sales and inventories, by kind of business, region, and selected State, MSA, and city, monthly rpt, 2413–3

Retail trade sales, by kind of business, advance monthly rpt, 2413–2

Retail trade sales, inventories, purchases, gross margin, and accounts receivable, by SIC 2- to 4-digit kind of business and form of ownership, 1989, annual rpt, 2413–5

Shipments and PPI for building materials, by type, bimonthly rpt, 2042–1.5; 2042–1.6

Taiwan imports of building materials, and share from US, by commodity, 1989-90, article, 2042–1.205

Tax (income) returns of corporations, income and tax items by asset size and detailed industry, 1987, annual rpt, 8304–4

Wholesale trade census, 1987: depreciable assets, capital and operating expenses, sales, value added, and inventories, by SIC 2- to 3-digit kind of business, 2407–2

Wholesale trade census, 1987: establishments, sales by customer class, employment, inventories, and expenses, by SIC 2- to 4-digit kind of business, 2407–4

Wholesale trade sales and inventories, by SIC 2- to 3-digit kind of business, monthly rpt, 2413–7

Wholesale trade sales, inventories, purchases, and gross margins, by SIC 2- to 3-digit kind of business, 1990, annual rpt, 2413–13

see also Lawn and garden equipment

see also Tools

see also under By Commodity in the "Index by Categories"

Hardy, Ann M.

"AIDS Knowledge and Attitudes of Black Americans: U.S., 1990. Provisional Data from the National Health Interview Survey", 4146–8.208

"AIDS Knowledge and Attitudes of Hispanic Americans: U.S., 1990. Provisional Data from the National Health Interview Survey", 4146–8.209

"AIDS Knowledge and Attitudes. Provisional Data from the National Health Interview Survey", 4146–8.201; 4146–8.205

Hargett, Norman L.

"Fertilizer Summary Data, 1990", 9804–5

Harlingen, Tex.

see also under By SMSA or MSA in the "Index by Categories"

Harlow, Caroline W.

"Drugs and Jail Inmates, 1989", 6066–19.63

"Female Victims of Violent Crime", 6068–243

Harrington, Charlene

"Social Health Maintenance Organizations' Service Use and Costs, 1985-89", 4652–1.235

Harris, Ethan S.

"Decline in U.S. Saving and Its Implications for Economic Growth", 9385–1.201

"Tracking the Economy with the Purchasing Managers Index", 9385–1.215; 9385–8.120

Harris, Richard B.

"Tracking Wildlife by Satellite: Current Systems and Performance", 5506–12.3

Harrisburg, Pa.

see also under By SMSA or MSA in the "Index by Categories"

Harrison, W. D.

"Subsea Permafrost: Probing, Thermal Regime, and Data Analyses, 1975-81", 2176–1.39

Harry S. Truman Scholarship Foundation

see Truman, Harry S., Scholarship Foundation

Hartford, Conn.

see also under By City and By SMSA or MSA in the "Index by Categories"

Hartley, A. L.

"Cancer Incidence in the Families of Children with Ewing's Tumor", 4472–1.214

Index by Subjects and Names

Hazardous substances

Hartman, Sara E.
"Hospital Experimental Payments Program: 1980-87", 4658–48

Harvey, David J.
"Farm-Raised Salmon: Impacts on U.S. Seafood Trade", 1561–15.201
"Outlook for U.S. Aquaculture", 1004–16.1

Harvey, James
"Financial Institution Performance, 1990", 9381–14.1

Harwell, Debra
"Index of Bank Control Share Prices", 9381–14.1

Harwood, Joy L.
"Canada's GRIP Program: A Boon for Canada's Wheat Producers?", 1561–12.202
"Farmer-Owned Reserve—Old Name, New Game: An Analysis of New Rules and 1990 Wheat Crop Entry", 1561–12.201

Haslag, Joseph H.
"Money Growth, Supply Shocks, and Inflation", 9379–1.204

Hassler, Thomas J.
"Olympia Oyster. Species Profiles: Life Histories and Environmental Requirements of Coastal Fishes and Invertebrates (Pacific Northwest)", 5506–8.131

Hastings, Nebr.
Wages by occupation, and benefits for office and plant workers, 1991 survey, periodic labor market rpt, 6785–3.10

Haugen, Steven F.
"U.S. Labor Market Weakened in 1990", 6722–1.212

Haverhill, Mass.
see also under By SMSA or MSA in the "Index by Categories"

Hawaii
AIDS patient home and community services under Medicaid waiver in 6 States, 1988-89, article, 4652–1.216
Banks (insured commercial and savings) deposits by instn, State, MSA, and county, as of June 1990, annual regional rpt, 9295–3.6
County Business Patterns, 1989: employment, establishments, and payroll, by SIC 2- to 4-digit industry and county, annual State rpt, 2326–8.13
DOD civilian and military personnel and dependents, by service branch and US and foreign location, quarterly rpt, 3542–20
DOD prime contract awards, by contractor, service branch, State, and city, FY90, annual rpt, 3544–22
Fed Govt spending in States and local areas, by type, State, county, and city, FY90, annual rpt, 2464–3
Fed Govt spending in States, by type, program, agency, and State, FY90, annual rpt, 2464–2
Fish and shellfish catch, wholesale receipts, prices, trade, and other market activities, semiweekly regional rpt, 2162–6.4
Foreign direct investment in US commercial real estate, by State and country, 1980s, GAO rpt, 26123–350
Ginger acreage and production in Hawaii, 1977-90, FAS annual circular, 1925–15.1
HHS financial aid, by program, recipient, State, and city, FY90, annual regional listing, 4004–3.9

Hospital deaths of Medicare patients, actual and expected rates by diagnosis, and hospital characteristics, by instn, FY87-89, annual regional rpt, 4654–14.9
Housing census, 1990: inventory, occupancy, and costs, State fact sheet, 2326–21.13
Income (personal) per capita and by source, and earnings by industry div, by State, MSA, and county, 1984-89, annual regional rpt, 2704–2.5
Lobster (slipper) catch and effort, for northwest Hawaii sites, 1985-86, article, 2162–1.203
Marriages, divorces, and rates, by characteristics of spouses, State, and county, 1987 and trends from 1920, US Vital Statistics annual rpt, 4144–4
Military presence of US in Pacific basin, personnel, dependents, aircraft, ships, and costs, by service branch and location, 1990, GAO rpt, 26123–357
Mineral Industry Surveys, State reviews of production, 1990, preliminary annual rpt, 5614–6
Minerals Yearbook, 1989, Vol 2: State review of production and sales by commodity, and business activity, annual rpt, 5604–16.12
Minerals Yearbook, 1989, Vol 2: State reviews of production, sales, and firms, by commodity, and business activity, annual rpt, 5604–34
Physicians, by specialty, age, sex, and location of training and practice, 1989, State rpt, 4116–6.12
Population and housing census, 1990: population and housing characteristics, households, and land area, by county, subdiv, and place, State rpt, 2551–1.13
Population and housing census, 1990: voting age and total population by race, and housing units, by block, redistricting counts required under PL 94-171, State CD-ROM release, 2551–6.8
Population and housing census, 1990: voting age and total population by race, and housing units, by county and city, redistricting counts required under PL 94-171, State summary rpt, 2551–5.12
Statistical Abstract of US, 1991 annual data compilation, 2324–1
Supplemental Security Income payments and beneficiaries, by type of eligibility, State, and county, Dec 1989, annual rpt, 4744–27.9
Telecommunications domestic and intl rates, by type of service and area served, 1989, annual rpt, 9284–6.6
Tide height and time daily at coastal points, forecast 1992, annual rpt, 2174–2.2
Timber in Pacific basin, sandalwood resources, habitat, harvest, exports, and uses, 1990 conf, 1208–366
Water supply and quality in streams and lakes, and groundwater levels in wells, by drainage basin, 1989, annual State rpt, 5666–12.10
see also Honolulu, Hawaii
see also under By State in the "Index by Categories"

Hawaiian Telephone Co.
Finances, rates, and traffic for US telecommunications carriers intl operations, by service type, firm, and country, 1975-89, annual rpt, 9284–17

Hawkins, M. M.
"Is There Evidence of a Therapy-Related Increase in Germ Cell Mutation Among Childhood Cancer Survivors?", 4472–1.233

Hay
see Animal feed
see Pasture and rangeland

Hayes, Donald W.
"Forecasting the Louisiana Economy", 9379–1.202

Hayes, Howard M.
"Case-Control Study of Canine Malignant Lymphoma: Positive Association with Dog Owner's Use of 2,4-Dichlorophenoxyacetic Acid Herbicides", 4472–1.220

Hayghe, Howard V.
"Anti-Drug Programs in the Workplace: Are They Here To Stay?", 6722–1.224
"Volunteers in the U.S.: Who Donates the Time?", 6722–1.213

Haynes, Richard W.
"Analysis of the Timber Situation in Alaska: 1970-2010", 1208–367
"Analysis of the Timber Situation in the U.S.: 1989-2040", 1208–24.20
"Timber Products Output and Timber Harvests in Alaska: Projections for 1989-2010", 1208–365

Hayward, Calif.
see also under By City in the "Index by Categories"

Hazardous substances
Air pollution indoor levels in workplace, and health impacts, for Library of Congress Madison Building, 1989 study, series, 4248–92
Criminal cases by type and disposition, and collections, for US attorneys, by Federal district, FY90, annual rpt, 6004–2.1
Criminal sentences for Federal offenses, guidelines by offense and circumstances, series, 17668–1
Disasters and natl security incidents and mgmt, with data by major event and State, 1991 annual rpt, 9434–6
Fed Govt spending in States, by type, program, agency, and State, FY90, annual rpt, 2464–2
Genetic damage and trait monitoring and screening of employees, use, costs, benefits, and procedures, 1980s, 26358–230
Health effects of hazardous pollutants, assessment methodology and data needs, series, 9186–9
Health effects of selected pollutants on animals by species and on humans, and environmental levels, series, 5506–14
HHS financial aid, by program, recipient, State, and city, FY90, annual regional listings, 4004–3
Nicotine, tar, and carbon monoxide content of cigarettes, by brand, 1989, 9408–53
Occupational exposure to hazardous substances and conditions, and health effects, literature review, series, 4246–4
Occupational exposure to hazardous substances and conditions, measurement, and proposed standards, series, 4246–1
Occupational health condition screening and monitoring, businesses practices and views, 1989 survey, 26358–250

Hazardous substances

Occupational illness rates, by cause and SIC 2- to 3-digit industry, 1989, annual rpt, 6844–1

Reproductive health and fetal dev effects of selected pollutants, with production, trade, and Federal regulatory activities by substance, 1980s-90, GAO rpt, 26131–90

Research and testing activities under Natl Toxicology Program, FY89 and planned FY90, annual rpt, 4044–16

Smoking involuntary exposure, health effects, and toxic substance levels of sidestream smoke, literature review, 1970s-90, 4248–91

Tax (excise) collections of IRS, by source, quarterly rpt, 8302–1

see also Air pollution

see also Asbestos contamination

see also Carcinogens

see also Dioxins

see also Hazardous substances transport

see also Hazardous waste and disposal

see also Inflammable materials

see also Lead poisoning and pollution

see also Marine pollution

see also Mercury pollution

see also Motor vehicle exhaust

see also Pesticides

see also Poisoning and drug reaction

see also Product safety

see also Radiation

see also Radioactive materials

see also Radioactive waste and disposal

see also Radon

see also Soil pollution

see also Trace metals

see also Water pollution

Hazardous substances transport

Accidents, and mgmt of disasters and natl security threats, with data by major event and State, 1991 annual rpt, 9434–6

Accidents, casualties, and damage involving hazardous substances, by mode of transport, with DOT control activities, 1989, annual rpt, 7304–4

Airport security inspections of hazardous cargo, compliance and enforcement actions, 2nd half 1989, semiannual rpt, 7502–5

Census of Transportation, 1987: finances and operations by size, ownership, and State, and revenues by MSA, by SIC 2- to 4-digit industry, 2579–1

DOE facilities radioactive and hazardous waste disposal and remediation activities and funding, planned FY91-97, annual rpt, 3024–7

DOT activities by subagency, budget, and summary accident data, FY88, annual rpt, 7304–1

Natl transportation system planning, use, condition, accidents, and needs, by mode of transport, 1940s-90 and projected to 2020, 7308–202

Pipeline accidents, casualties, safety enforcement activity, and Federal funding, by State, 1989, annual rpt, 7304–5

Radioactive low-level waste disposal activities of States and interstate compacts, with data by disposal facility and reactor, 1989, annual rpt, 3354–14

Radioactive waste at DOE nuclear weapons facilities, storage plans, and mgmt issues, 1988, 26358–236

Radioactive waste from nuclear power plants, releases and waste composition by plant, 1988, annual rpt, 9634–1

Radioactive waste from nuclear power plants, storage pending opening of permanent repository, safety and costs of alternative methods, projected 1991-2050, 14818–1

Radioactive waste mgmt proposal, storage and transport needs, disposal site characteristics, and costs, 1991 rpt, 3368–1

Railroad accidents, casualties, and damage, Fed Railroad Admin activities, and safety inspectors by State, 1989, annual rpt, 7604–12

Railroad accidents involving hazardous materials, damage, and persons evacuated, by cause, railroad, and State, 1990, annual rpt, 7604–1

Railroad safety violation claims settled, by carrier, FY90, annual rpt, 7604–10

Safety programs, and accidents, casualties, and damage, by mode of transport, 1989, annual rpt, 7304–19

Truck accidents, casualties, and damage, by circumstances and characteristics of persons and vehicles involved, 1988, annual rpt, 7554–9

Truck accidents, circumstances, severity, and characteristics of drivers and vehicles, 1989, annual rpt, 7764–20

Truck and bus safety inspections, fines, and vehicles and drivers ordered out of service, by State, with program funding, FY89, 25268–78

Hazardous waste and disposal

Air pollution emissions factors, by detailed pollutant and source, data compilation, 1990 rpt, 9198–120

Bonneville Power Admin operations, maintenance, and environmental protection plans, FY90-99, 3228–14

Budget of US, formula grant program obligations to State and local govts, by agency, program, and State, FY92, annual rpt, 104–30

Budget of US, obligations and authority by function, agency, and program, with summaries, analyses, and historical tables, FY92, annual rpt, 104–2

Closings of treatment facilities, EPA reviews by status and waste disposal method, 1991, GAO rpt, 26113–528

Costs of environmental protection programs to govts and households, by program type and city size, 1960s-88 and projected to 2000, 9188–114

DOE facilities radioactive and hazardous waste disposal and remediation activities and funding, planned FY91-97, annual rpt, 3024–7

Environmental Quality, status of problems, protection programs, research, and intl issues, 1991 annual rpt, 484–1

EPA and State govt enforcement of environmental legislation, activities, FY90, annual rpt, 9184–21

EPA pollution control grant program activities, monthly rpt, 9182–8

Fed Govt financial and nonfinancial domestic aid, 1991 base edition with supplements, annual listing, 104–5

HHS financial aid, by program, recipient, State, and city, FY90, annual regional listings, 4004–3

Index by Subjects and Names

Incinerators of hazardous waste health and safety violations, by type of violation, 1991 rpt, 6608–5

Industrial hazardous substances releases, accuracy of EPA reporting, and nonreporting facilities by State and industry, 1987-90, GAO rpt, 26113–532

Industrial pollutant concentrations and costs by process and waste prevention or treatment method, 1990 biennial conf, 9184–22

Manufacturing pollution abatement capital and operating costs, by SIC 2-digit industry, 1989, advance annual Current Industrial Rpt, 2506–3.6

Medical waste generation, sources, health workers exposure and risk, and incineration emissions, 1980s, 4078–1

Military installations hazardous waste site remedial action, activities and funding by site and State, FY90, annual rpt, 3544–36

Park natl system accidents, crimes, hazardous waste sites, and funding, 1970s-91, GAO rpt, 26113–545

R&D facilities for biological and medical sciences, space and equipment adequacy, needs, and funding by source, by instn type, 1990, biennial rpt, 4434–17

State and Metro Area Data Book, 1991 data compilation, 2328–54

Statistical Abstract of US, 1991 annual data compilation, 2324–1.6

Superfund financial condition, monthly rpt, 8102–9.6

Superfund hazardous waste site remedial action, current and proposed sites descriptions and status, periodic listings, series, 9216–3

Superfund hazardous waste site remedial action, current and proposed sites priority ranking and status by location, series, 9216–5

Superfund hazardous waste site remedial action, EPA records of decision by site, FY89, annual rpt, 9214–5

Superfund R&D projects and funding, FY90, annual listing, 9184–18

Tax (excise) collections of IRS, by source, quarterly rpt, 8302–2.1

Tax (excise) on hazardous waste generation and disposal, rates, and firms filing returns, by substance type, 1988, annual article, 8302–2.202

Water pollution industrial releases in wastewater, levels, treatment, costs, and regulation, with background financial and operating data, 1989 industry rpt, 9206–4.5

see also Radioactive waste and disposal

Hazelnuts

see Nuts

Head Start Project

Appalachia education system, improvement initiatives, and indicators of success, by State, 1960s-89, 9088–36

Assistance programs under Ways and Means Committee jurisdiction, finances, operations, and participant characteristics, FY70s-90, annual rpt, 21784–11

Bilingual education programs enrollment, funding, and services, by State, FY85-89, series, 4808–20

Costs, benefits, and participation for Head Start and GI Bill education programs, 1950s-90, hearing, 23848–217

Index by Subjects and Names

Enrollment, funding, and staff for Head Start, FY90, annual rpt, 4604–8

Expenditures for program, by recipient agency and location, FY90, annual regional listings, 4004–3

Handicapped children enrollment in Head Start, by handicap, State, and for Indian and migrant programs, 1987/88, annual rpt, 4604–1

North Central States Head Start operations and enrollment, annual chartbook, discontinued, 4604–12

Health care costs

see Medical costs

Health Care Financing Administration

- Budget of US, obligations and authority by function, agency, and program, with summaries, analyses, and historical tables, FY92, annual rpt, 104–2
- Drug (prescription) mail service industry structure, finances, and operations, 1989 survey, 4658–60
- Drug (prescription) spending by aged, and manufacturer and retail price changes, by drug type, 1981-88, 4658–56
- Financial aid of HHS, by program, recipient, State, and city, FY90, annual regional listings, 4004–3
- *Health Care Financing Review,* quarterly journal, 4652–1
- Health care services use and costs, methodology and findings of natl survey and Medicare and Medicaid records, 1980, series, 4146–12
- Health maintenance organizations Medicare enrollees quality of care indicators compared to fee-for-service, demonstration projects results, mid 1980s, 4658–46
- Home health care services Medicare claim filings under prior and concurrent authorization, demonstration project results, 1987, 4658–57
- Hospices operations, services, costs, and patient characteristics, for instns without Medicare certification, FY85-86, 4658–52
- Hospices use by cancer patients, by service type, use of other facilities, patient and instn characteristics, and other indicators, local area study, 1980-85, 4658–53
- Hospital cost control through revenue and reimbursement caps, demonstration project results with background data, 1980s, 4658–48
- Hospital deaths, analysis of newspaper coverage of HCFA data releases, Dec 1987, article, 4042–3.242
- Hospital deaths of Medicare patients, actual and expected rates by diagnosis, with hospital characteristics, by instn, FY87-89, annual regional rpt series, 4654–14
- Hospitals in rural areas, financial and operating performance impacts of Medicare prospective payment reimbursement system, 1980s-87, 4658–51
- Hospitals in rural areas, HCFA grants for improving financial stability, by program area, recipient, and State, FY89, 4658–58
- Insurance (health) natl coverage alternative proposals and indicators of need, 1989, 4658–54
- Kidney end-stage disease treatment access and quality of care indicators, impacts of Medicare payment reductions, 1980s, 4658–44

Kidney end-stage disease treatment facilities, Medicare enrollment and reimbursement, survival, and patient characteristics, 1983-89, annual rpt, 4654–16

- Kidney transplants, needs, costs, payment sources, and impact of immunosuppressive drugs on outcome, 1950s-87 and projected to 1995, 4658–59
- Medicaid demonstration projects evaluation, for 6 States, 1988 rpt, 4658–45
- Medicare and Medicaid beneficiaries and program operations, 1991, annual fact book, 4654–18
- Medicare and Medicaid eligibility, participation, coverage, and program finances, various periods 1966-91, biennial rpt, 4654–1
- Medicare enrollment, and use by type of service, annual rpt, discontinued, 4657–5
- Medicare Hospital Insurance trust fund finances, 1966-90 and alternative projections to 2065, annual rpt, 4654–11
- Medicare reimbursement of hospitals under prospective payment system for discharge delays due to limited nursing home space, 1985, 4658–55
- Medicare reimbursement of hospitals under prospective payment system, impacts on instns and beneficiaries, 1988, annual rpt, 4654–13
- Medicare Supplementary Medical Insurance trust fund finances, various periods 1966-90 and projected to 2001, annual rpt, 4654–12
- Mentally retarded persons care facilities and residents by selected characteristics, and use of Medicaid services and waiver programs, by State, late 1970s-80s, 4658–49
- Nursing home and other long term care services under Medicare hospital use reduction demonstration, results for Rochester, NY, 1980s, 4658–43
- Physicians consultations requested by attending physician, Medicare reimbursement issues, with use by diagnosis, specialty, location, and other characteristics, 1986, 4658–47
- Physicians practice cost indexes and components, by State, MSA, and for rural areas, 1989 rpt, 4658–50
- Research activities and grants of HCFA, by program, FY90, annual listing, 4654–10
- Research and evaluation programs of HHS, 1970-90, annual listing, 4004–30

Health condition

- Accessibility of health care, persons with and without usual care source by selected characteristics, 1987, 4186–8.22
- Aircraft noise policies, health impacts, and aircraft replacement schedules and costs, 1960s-90 and projected to 2006, hearing, 21648–64
- Aviation medicine research and test results, technical rpt series, 7506–10
- Child health condition and services use, 1990 chartbook, 4108–49
- Child health insurance coverage, and children with a regular source of care, by selected characteristics, 1988, 4146–8.192
- Children and youth social, economic, and demographic characteristics, 1950s-90, 4818–5

Health condition

- Data on health care use and costs, methodology and findings of natl survey and Medicare and Medicaid records, 1980, series, 4146–12
- Data on health condition and health care resources, use, and spending, 1950s-89, annual data compilation, 4144–11
- Data on health condition and quality of life measures, rpts and other info sources, quarterly listing, 4122–1
- Developing countries aged population and selected characteristics, 1980s and projected to 2020, country rpt series, 2326–19
- Developing countries economic, population, and agricultural data, US and other aid sources, and AID activity, country rpt series, 9916–12
- Disabled persons and related activity limitation days and health services use, by health status, disability type, and other characteristics, 1984-88, 4146–8.202
- Drug (steroid) use prevalence and health effects, 1989 conf papers, 4498–67
- Foster care placements, discharges, and returns to care, by selected characteristics of children, and length of stay factors, 1985-86, GAO rpt, 26121–432
- Global climate change environmental, infrastructure, and health impacts, with model results and background data, 1850s-2100, 9188–113
- Health care services needs, delivery, and costs, series, 4186–9
- Health condition improvement and disease prevention goals and recommended activities for 2000, with trends 1970s-80s, 4048–10
- Homeless teens pregnancy prevalence and outcomes, services availability, health condition, and drug abuse, 1989 conf, 4108–55
- Indian Health Service facilities and use, and Indian health and other characteristics, by IHS region, 1980s-89, annual chartbook, 4084–7
- Indian Health Service facilities, funding, operations, and Indian health and other characteristics, 1950s-90, annual chartbook, 4084–1
- Injuries, related impairments, and activity limitations, by circumstances and victim characteristics, 1985-87, 4147–10.179
- Lead levels in environment, sources of emissions and exposure, and health effects, literature review, 1990 rpt, 9198–84
- Minority group and women health condition, services use, payment sources, and health care labor force, by poverty status, 1940s-89, chartbook, 4118–56
- Minority group health condition, services use, costs, and indicators of services need, 1950s-88, 4118–55
- Nursing home reimbursement by Medicaid, resident classification using patient and care characteristics, New York State, 1990 article, 4652–1.205
- Older persons with functional limitations, long-term care sources, and health and other characteristics, 1984-85, 4147–13.104
- Population size and characteristics, historical index to *Current Population Rpts,* 1991 listing, 2546–2.160

Health condition

Primary health care research, methodology and findings, 1991 annual conf, 4184–4

Public Health Reports, bimonthly journal, 4042–3

Retirees deaths within 8 years of retirement, by health and other characteristics, 1982-88, article, 4742–1.206

Statistical Abstract of US, 1991 annual data compilation, 2324–1.3

Survey of Income and Program Participation, data collection, methodology, and use, 1990 annual conf papers, 2624–1

Veterans (homeless) domiciliary program of VA, participant characteristics and outcomes, 1990 annual rpt, 8604–10

Veterans (homeless) with mental illness, VA program services, costs, staff, client characteristics, and outcome, 1990, annual rpt, 8604–11

Vital and Health Statistics series: advance data rpts, 4146–8

Vital and Health Statistics series and other NCHS rpts, 1990, annual listing, 4124–1

Vital and Health Statistics series: foreign and US comparative data, 4147–5

Vital and Health Statistics series: health condition, medical costs, and use of facilities and services, 4147–10

Vital and Health Statistics series: reprints of advance data rpts, 4147–16

Youth health condition, risk factors, and preventive and treatment services use and availability, 1970s-89, 26358–234

see also Absenteeism

see also Dental condition

see also Disabled and handicapped persons

see also Diseases and disorders

see also Handicapped children

see also Hospitalization

see also Medical examinations and tests

see also Mental health and illness

see also Mobility limitations

see also Nutrition and malnutrition

see also Obesity

see also Occupational health and safety

see also Vital statistics

Health education

AIDS cases in prisons and jails, and testing and control policies, 1989 survey, 6066–28.1

AIDS info and education activities and funding of CDC, and donation of media ads, 1987-92, articles, 4042–3.256

AIDS knowledge, attitudes, and risk behaviors of women in methadone maintenance programs, effects of life skills training, 1988 local area study, article, 4042–3.221

AIDS public knowledge, attitudes, and risk behaviors, for women, 1988 survey, 4146–8.200

AIDS public knowledge, attitudes, info sources, and testing, for blacks, 1990 survey, 4146–8.208

AIDS public knowledge, attitudes, info sources, and testing, for Hispanics, 1990 survey, 4146–8.209

AIDS public knowledge, attitudes, info sources, and testing, 1990 survey, 4146–8.195; 4146–8.201; 4146–8.205

Assistance (financial and nonfinancial) of Fed Govt, 1991 base edition with supplements, annual listing, 104–5

Child day care providers health and safety training, by facility size, for California, 1987 survey, article, 4042–3.243

Developing countries family planning and population activities of AID, grants by project and recipient, and contraceptive shipments, by country, FY90, annual rpt series, 9914–13

Diabetics home monitoring of blood glucose, and factors affecting test accuracy, 1990 rpt, 4068–71

Health promotion program availability and participation, by type of program and sponsor, 1986-87 local area study, article, 4042–3.223

Higher education course completions, by detailed program, sex, race, and instn type, for 1972 high school class, as of 1984, 4888–4

Kidney end-stage disease treatment facilities, Medicare enrollment and reimbursement, survival, and patient characteristics, 1983-89, annual rpt, 4654–16

Morbidity and Mortality Weekly Report, infectious notifiable disease cases by State, and public health issues, 4202–1

Prenatal care nutritional and educational programs for women at risk of preterm delivery, and rate of anemia and low-weight births, 1985-86, article, 4042–3.235

Preventive disease and health improvement goals and recommended activities for 2000, with trends 1970s-80s, 4048–10

Smoking cessation program in 11 communities, methods and effectiveness, 1983-88, article, 4472–1.231

Smoking cessation rates for Hispanics, effects of Spanish language self-help guide, 1987-88 local area study, article, 4042–3.249

Smoking prevention, control, and surveillance activities and funding of States, and tobacco farm receipts, by State, 1989-90, 4206–2.47

USDA food aid programs costs and participation, by program, FY69-89, annual rpt, 1364–9

VA Medicine and Surgery Dept trainees, by detailed program and city, FY90, annual rpt, 8704–4

see also Sex education

Health, Education and Welfare Department

see Department of Education

see Department of Health and Human Services

Health facilities administration

Child and maternal health programs of major urban health depts, activities and budgets, 1990, listing, 4108–51

Drug and alcohol abuse treatment facilities, services, use, funding, staff, and client characteristics, 1989, biennial rpt, 4494–10

Govt employment and payroll, by function, level of govt, and jurisdiction, 1990, annual rpt series, 2466–1

HHS financial aid, by program, recipient, State, and city, FY90, annual regional listings, 4004–3

Hospital costs and use, data compilation project analyses, series, 4186–6

Indian Health Service employment of Indians and non-Indians, training, hires, and quits, by occupation, FY89, annual rpt, 4084–6

Mental health care facilities, finances, caseload, staff, and characteristics of instn and patients, 1988, 4506–4.14

Mental health care facilities, staff, and patient characteristics, *Statistical Notes* series, 4506–3

Military health care personnel, and accessions by training source, by occupation, specialty, and service branch, FY89, annual rpt, 3544–24

Older frail persons community-based care demonstration projects, evaluation of case mgmt services admin, 1991 rpt, 4186–7.8

Physicians, by specialty, age, sex, and location of training and practice, 1989, State rpt series, 4116–6

VA health care facilities physicians, dentists, and nurses, by selected employment characteristics and VA district, quarterly rpt, 8602–6

VA health care staff and turnover, by occupation, physician specialty, and location, 1990, annual rpt, 8604–8

VA Medicine and Surgery Dept trainees, by detailed program and city, FY90, annual rpt, 8704–4

VA mental health care services, staff, research, and training programs, 1991 biennial listing, 8704–2

see also Health planning and evaluation

Health facilities and services

Accessibility of health care, persons with and without usual care source by selected characteristics, 1987, 4186–8.22

AIDS and hepatitis viruses transmission in health care settings, occupational exposure, prevention policies, and OSHA regulation, 1990 hearings, 21348–119

Assistance (financial and nonfinancial) of Fed Govt, 1991 base edition with supplements, annual listing, 104–5

Bombing incidents, casualties, and damage, by target, circumstances, and State, 1990, annual rpt, 6224–5

Child accident deaths and death rates, by cause, age, sex, race, and State, 1980-85, 4108–54

Construction industries census, 1987: establishments, employment, receipts, and expenditures, by SIC 4-digit industry and State, final industry rpt series, 2373–1

Contracts for sharing health services among VA and non-VA facilities, by service type and region, FY90, annual rpt, 8704–5

County Business Patterns, 1988: employment, establishments, and payroll, by SIC 2- to 4-digit industry and county, annual State rpt series, 2326–6

County Business Patterns, 1989: employment, establishments, and payroll, by SIC 2- to 4-digit industry and county, annual State rpt series, 2326–8

Credit reporting and collection establishments, and receipts by source and class of client, by MSA, 1987 Census of Service Industries, 2393–4.4

Crime victimization of teens, by victim and offender characteristics, circumstances, and offense, 1985-88 surveys, 6066–3.43

Data on health care use and costs, methodology and findings of natl survey and Medicare and Medicaid records, 1980, series, 4146–12

Data on health condition and health care resources, use, and spending, 1950s-89, annual data compilation, 4144–11

Index by Subjects and Names

Health facilities and services

Deaths in health facilities, by cause, age, and sex, 1988, US Vital Statistics annual rpt, 4144–2.1

Demand for health services, needs, delivery, and costs, series, 4186–9

Developing countries economic and social conditions from 1960s, and Intl Dev Cooperation Agency and AID activities and funding, FY90-92, annual rpt, 9904–4

Education natl goals progress indicators, by State, 1991, annual rpt, 15914–1

Energy use in commercial buildings, costs, and conservation, by building characteristics, survey rpt series, 3166–8

Enterprise Statistics, 1987: auxiliaries of multi-establishment firms, finances and operations by function, industry, and State, 2329–6

Enterprise Statistics, 1987: finances and operations for companies, by size, level of diversification, form of organization, and industry group, 2329–8

Expenditures for health care, by service type, payment source, and sector, projected 1990-2000 and trends from 1965, article, 4652–1.251

Expenditures for health care, by service type, payment source, and sector, 1960s-90, annual article, 4652–1.221; 4652–1.252

Fed Govt labor productivity, indexes of output and labor costs by function, FY67-89, annual rpt, 6824–1.6

Finances and operations, by SIC 2- to 4-digit industry, forecast 1991, annual rpt, 2044–28

Franchise business opportunities by firm and kind of business, and sources of aid and info, 1990 annual listing, 2104–7

Health Care Financing Review, quarterly journal, 4652–1

HHS financial aid, by program, recipient, State, and city, FY90, annual regional listings, 4004–3

Housing and households detailed characteristics, and unit and neighborhood quality, by location, 1985, biennial rpt supplement, 2485–13

Housing and households detailed characteristics, and unit and neighborhood quality, by location, 1989, biennial rpt, 2485–12

Indian and Alaska Native disease and disorder cases, deaths, and health services use, by tribe, reservation, and Indian Health Service area, late 1950s-86, 4088–2

Indian Health Service and tribal facility outpatient visits, by type of provider, selected hospital, and service area, FY90, annual rpt, 4084–3

Indian Health Service facilities and use, and Indian health and other characteristics, by IHS region, 1980s-89, annual chartbook, 4084–7

Indian Health Service facilities, funding, operations, and Indian health and other characteristics, 1950s-90, annual chartbook, 4084–1

Indian Health Service outpatient services provided, by reason for visit and age, FY88-89, annual rpt, 4084–2

Indian Health Service outpatient visits, by facility and IHS service area, FY89-90, annual rpt, 4084–8

Indians and Alaska Natives health care access indicators, by selected characteristics, 1987, 4186–8.18

Info on health care treatments effectiveness, feasibility of linking Federal and other databases, 1991 narrative rpt, 4188–73

Jail adult and juvenile population, employment, spending, instn conditions, and inmate programs, by county and facility, 1988, regional rpt series, 6068–144

Kidney end-stage disease treatment access and quality of care indicators, impacts of Medicare payment reductions, 1980s, 4658–44

Mail volume to and from households, use, and views, by class, source, content, and household characteristics, 1987-88, annual rpt, 9864–10

Medicare and Medicaid eligibility, participation, coverage, and program finances, various periods 1966-91, biennial rpt, 4654–1

Medicare coverage of new health care technologies, risks and benefit evaluations, series, 4186–10

Mines (underground coal) back injuries, by circumstances, victim characteristics, and treatment, mid 1980s, 5608–166

Multinatl US firms and foreign affiliates finances and operations, by industry and world area of parent firm, 1989 benchmark survey, preliminary annual rpt, 2704–5

NIH grants for R&D, training, construction, and medical libraries, by location and recipient, FY90, annual listings, 4434–7

Occupational injury and illness rates, by SIC 2- to 4-digit industry, 1988-89, annual rpt, 6844–7

Occupational injury and illness rates, by SIC 2- to 4-digit industry, 1989, annual rpt, 6844–1

Older persons migration to southern coastal areas, household finances, services needs, and local economic impacts, for selected counties, 1990, 2068–38

Palau admin, and social, economic, and govtl data, FY90, annual rpt, 7004–6

Preventive disease and health improvement goals and recommended activities for 2000, with trends 1970s-80s, 4048–10

Prisoners in Federal instns, by sex, prison, security level, contract facility type, and region, monthly rpt series, 6242–1

Prisons Bur admin offices and correctional instns, facility characteristics, 1991, annual listing, 6244–4

Receipts for services, by SIC 2- to 4-digit kind of business, 1990, annual rpt, 2413–8

Refugee resettlement programs and funding, arrivals by country of origin, and indicators of adjustment, by State, FY90, annual rpt, 4694–5

Research on health care services outcomes and practice guidelines dev activities and funding of Agency for Health Care Policy and Research, FY88-89, 4188–70

Retirement housing centers tax-exempt bond use and other financing, defaults, and facility and resident characteristics, 1991 GAO rpt, 26119–328

Science and engineering PhDs employment and other characteristics, by field and State, 1989, biennial rpt, 9627–18

Service industries census, 1987: depreciable assets, capital and operating expenses, and receipts, by SIC 2- to 4-digit kind of business, 2393–2

Service industries census, 1987: establishments, receipts by source, payroll, and employment, by SIC 2- to 4-digit kind of business, State, and MSA, 2393–4

Smoking bans in public places, local ordinances provisions, as of 1989, 4478–196

Soviet Union GNP by component and industry sector, and CIA estimation methods, 1950s-87, 23848–223

Soviet Union GNP by detailed income and outlay component, 1985, 2326–18.59

State and Metro Area Data Book, 1991 data compilation, 2328–54

Tax (income) returns of corporations, income and tax items by asset size and detailed industry, 1987, annual rpt, 8304–4

Tax (income) returns of corporations, income and tax items by asset size and detailed industry, 1988, annual rpt, 8304–21

Tax (income) returns of partnerships, income statement and balance sheet items, by industry group, 1989, annual article, 8302–2.216; 8304–18

Tax (income) returns of sole proprietorships, income statement items, by industry group, 1989, annual article, 8302–2.214

Tuberculosis transmission in health care settings, prevention and screening methods, CDC guidelines, 1990 rpt, 4206–2.35

Vital and Health Statistics series and other NCHS rpts, 1990, annual listing, 4124–1

Vital and Health Statistics series: foreign and US comparative data, 4147–5

Vital and Health Statistics series: health care facilities use and labor force, 4147–13

Vital and Health Statistics series: health condition, medical costs, and use of facilities and services, 4147–10

Youth health condition, risk factors, and preventive and treatment services use and availability, 1970s-89, 26358–234

see also Abortion

see also Alcohol abuse and treatment

see also Chemotherapy

see also Civilian Health and Medical Program of the Uniformed Services

see also Clinics

see also Community health services

see also Dentists and dentistry

see also Drug abuse and treatment

see also Emergency medical service

see also Family planning

see also Group homes for the handicapped

see also Health facilities administration

see also Health insurance

see also Health maintenance organizations

see also Health occupations

see also Health planning and evaluation

see also Home health services

see also Hospices

see also Hospitalization

see also Hospitals

see also Laboratories

see also Medical costs

see also Medical examinations and tests

Health facilities and services

see also Medical supplies and equipment
see also Medical transplants
see also Mental health facilities and services
see also Military health facilities and services
see also Nursing homes
see also Occupational therapy
see also Physical therapy
see also Public health
see also Regional medical programs
see also Rehabilitation of the disabled
see also Respiratory therapy
see also Respite care
see also Speech pathology and audiology
see also State funding for health and hospitals
see also Vaccination and vaccines
see also Veterans health facilities and services
see also terms listed under Health occupations
see also under By Industry in the "Index by Categories"
see also under Medicine and terms beginning with Medical

Health insurance

- Accessibility of health care, persons with and without usual care source by selected characteristics, 1987, 4186–8.22
- AIDS patient hospital use and charges, by hospital and patient characteristics, and payment source, 1986-87, 4186–6.15
- Assistance programs under Ways and Means Committee jurisdiction, finances, operations, and participant characteristics, FY70s-90, annual rpt, 21784–11
- Canada universal health care system operations and costs, and implications for US, 1987-91, GAO rpt, 26121–424
- Cancer treatments using chemotherapy drugs for indications not listed on drug label, costs, and insurance reimbursement problems, 1990 physicians survey, GAO rpt, 26131–81
- Child and family health, education, and welfare condition, findings and recommendations, 1991 rpt, 15528–1
- Child health condition and services use, 1990 chartbook, 4108–49
- Child health insurance coverage, and children with a regular source of care, by selected characteristics, 1988, 4146–8.192
- Child health insurance coverage, by source, family composition, income, and parent employment status, 1977 and 1987, 4186–8.14
- Child support and alimony awards, and payment status, by selected characteristics of woman, 1989, biennial Current Population Rpt, 2546–6.72
- Consumer Expenditure Survey, household income by source, and itemized spending, by selected characteristics and region, 1988-89, annual rpt, 6764–5
- County Business Patterns, 1988: employment, establishments, and payroll, by SIC 2- to 4-digit industry and county, annual State rpt series, 2326–6
- County Business Patterns, 1989: employment, establishments, and payroll, by SIC 2- to 4-digit industry and county, annual State rpt series, 2326–8
- Coverage (universal) under natl health insurance, alternative proposals and indicators of need, 1989, 4658–54

Coverage expansion for Medicaid and employer-provided insurance plans under alternative proposals, and uninsured population characteristics, 1991 rpt, 26306–6.157

- Coverage under health insurance, by insurance type and selected characteristics, 1989, 4146–8.203
- Coverage under health insurance by source, and services reimbursed by type, 1991 rpt, 26306–6.155
- Crime victimization rates, by victim and offender characteristics, circumstances, and offense, 1988 survey, annual rpt, 6066–3.42
- Crime victimization rates, by victim and offender characteristics, circumstances, and offense, 1989 survey, annual rpt, 6066–3.44
- Data on health care use and costs, methodology and findings of natl survey and Medicare and Medicaid records, 1980, series, 4146–12
- Disabled Medicare enrollees supplementary health insurance coverage, by enrollee characteristics, 1984, article, 4652–1.243
- Drug (prescription) coverage under employee health plans by plan type, and copayments required, 1989, article, 6722–1.215
- Drug (prescription) mail service industry structure, finances, and operations, 1989 survey, 4658–60
- Drug, alcohol, and cigarette use, by selected characteristics, and for DC, 1990 survey, biennial rpt, 4494–5.3
- Drug and alcohol abuse treatment coverage and provisions under employee health plans, by plan type, 1989, article, 6722–1.221
- Drug and alcohol abuse treatment facilities, services, use, funding, staff, and client characteristics, 1989, biennial rpt, 4494–10
- Employee benefit plan coverage and provisions, by plan type, firm size, and industry sector, 1988, article, 6722–1.204
- Employee benefit plan coverage, by benefit type and worker characteristics, late 1970s-80s, 15496–1.11
- Employer-provided health insurance and cost containment activities, North Central States employers views, 1991 survey, article, 9383–19.202
- Employer-provided health insurance, coverage offered to and chosen by families with 2 working spouses, 1977 and 1987, 4186–8.16
- Employer-provided health insurance coverage, under alternative plan types, 1990 rpt, 23898–5
- Employer-provided health insurance, small business and restaurant owners views, 1989 hearings, 23898–7
- Employer-sponsored HMO and fee-for-service health plans, coverage, provisions, and premiums, 1989, article, 6722–1.214
- Expenditures, coverage, and benefits for social welfare programs, late 1930s-89, annual rpt, 4744–3.1
- Expenditures for health care by businesses, households, and govts, 1965-89, article, 4652–1.230

Index by Subjects and Names

- Expenditures for health care, by service type, payment source, and sector, projected 1990-2000 and trends from 1965, article, 4652–1.251
- Expenditures for health care, by service type, payment source, and sector, 1960s-90, annual article, 4652–1.221; 4652–1.252
- Fed Govt civilian employees and retirees health insurance coverage by plan, and program finances, FY89, annual rpt, 9844–35.1; 9844–35.2
- Fed Govt civilian employees work-years, pay rates, and benefits use and costs, by agency, FY89, annual rpt, 9844–31
- Foreign countries health care cost control measures and insurance provisions, for Germany, France, and Japan, 1960s-91, GAO rpt, 26121–437
- Germany (West) health care spending, by funding source and service type, and resource growth, 1970-89, article, 4652–1.238
- Govt census, 1987: State and local govt employment, payroll, OASDHI coverage, and employee benefits costs, by level of govt and State, 2455–4
- Health condition and health care resources, use, and spending, 1950s-89, annual data compilation, 4144–11
- Hospices use by cancer patients, by service type, use of other facilities, patient and instn characteristics, and other indicators, local area study, 1980-85, 4658–53
- Hospital and physician use by uninsured persons as percent of insured persons use, 1977-86 surveys, article, 4652–1.220
- Hospital discharges and length of stay, by diagnosis, patient and instn characteristics, procedure performed, and payment source, 1988, annual rpt, 4147–13.107
- Hospital operations, and services spending by type and payment source, with background data and foreign comparisons, 1960s-80s and projected to 2000, 26308–98
- Households composition, income, benefits, and labor force status, Survey of Income and Program Participation methodology, working paper series, 2626–10
- Income (household) and poverty status under alternative income definitions, by recipient characteristics, 1990, annual Current Population Rpt, 2546–6.69
- Indians and Alaska Natives health care access indicators, by selected characteristics, 1987, 4186–8.18
- Indians and Alaska Natives health care coverage, by type, employment status, and other characteristics, 1987, 4186–8.17
- Kidney transplants, needs, costs, payment sources, and impact of immunosuppressive drugs on outcome, 1950s-87 and projected to 1995, 4658–59
- Labor hourly costs, by component, industry sector, worker class, and firm size, 1990, annual rpt, 6744–22
- Long-term care institutional and community services, spending and use by type and payment source, FY88, and Medicaid growth since FY75, 26306–6.156
- Long-term health care costs for aged, under alternative private insurance policy types, 1989 hearing, 23898–8

Index by Subjects and Names

Long-term health insurance policies, claims, affordability, and State regulation, 1986-89, hearing, 21368–130

Massachusetts State govt spending and employment by program, revenues by source, debt, and public works financing, compared to other States, 1990 compilation of papers, 9373–4.27

Medicaid programs detection and use of private health insurance, for New York State, 1984-89, article, 4652–1.212

Medicare supplemental private insurance loss ratio performance, sales abuse cases, and State enforcement, late 1980s, GAO rpt, 26121–410

Medicare supplemental private insurance premiums, costs, claims, and benefit provisions, with data by firm, 1988-90, hearing, 21788–198

Mental health care in private hospitals, patients characteristics, 1986, 4506–3.47

Minority group and women health condition, services use, payment sources, and health care labor force, by poverty status, 1940s-89, chartbook, 4118–56

Minority group health condition, services use, costs, and indicators of services need, 1950s-88, 4118–55

Montana health care access indicators, 1989 hearing, 23898–6

Occupational health condition screening and monitoring, businesses practices and views, 1989 survey, 26358–250

Occupational injury and illness rates, by SIC 2- to 4-digit industry, 1988-89, annual rpt, 6844–7

Occupational injury and illness rates, by SIC 2- to 4-digit industry, 1989, annual rpt, 6844–1

Older persons insurance coverage, by type and poverty status, 1988, annual rpt, 17204–2

Part-time employment by health insurance coverage and worker characteristics, and temporary and contract employment, 1979-89, GAO rpt, 26121–411

Poverty status of population and families, by detailed characteristics, 1988-89, annual Current Population Rpt, 2546–6.67

Poverty status of population and families, by detailed characteristics, 1990, annual Current Population Rpt, 2546–6.71

Preferred provider organizations marketing outlook under Medicare, with beneficiaries views on switching to Medicare-assignment physicians, 1989 survey, article, 4652–1.248

Prepaid managed care plans Medicaid enrollment and use, for 20 States, 1985-89, chartbook, 4108–29

Small business employees benefit plan coverage and provisions, by plan type and occupational group, 1990, biennial rpt, 6784–20

State and local govt employees benefit plan coverage, by benefit type, 1990, press release, 6726–1.41

Statistical Abstract of US, 1991 annual data compilation, 2324–1.3; 2324–1.16

Teenage mothers child support awards, payment status, health insurance inclusion, and govt aid for collection, by selected characteristics, 1987, 4698–5

Transplant patients immunosuppressive drug coverage under Medicare and other insurance sources, costs, and procedures, 1991 rpt, 26358–246

Unemployment insurance laws of States, comparison of provisions, 1991, base edition with semiannual revisions, 6402–2

Uninsured labor force, by selected characteristics and metro-nonmetro location, 1987, 1598–264

Uninsured population, by demographic and employment characteristics, model description and results, 1987, working paper, 6886–6.75

Uninsured population by employment and other characteristics and State, 1988, GAO rpt, 26121–403

Uninsured population under age 65, by selected characteristics, 1987, 4186–8.13

see also Area wage surveys

see also Blue Cross-Blue Shield

see also Civilian Health and Medical Program of the Uniformed Services

see also Disability benefits and insurance

see also Health maintenance organizations

see also Industry wage surveys

see also Medicaid

see also Medicare

see also Old-Age, Survivors, Disability, and Health Insurance

see also Workers compensation

Health maintenance organizations

Consumer Expenditure Survey, spending for selected categories, 1991 semiannual pamphlet, 2322–3

County Business Patterns, 1988: employment, establishments, and payroll, by SIC 2- to 4-digit industry and county, annual State rpt series, 2326–6

County Business Patterns, 1989: employment, establishments, and payroll, by SIC 2- to 4-digit industry and county, annual State rpt series, 2326–8

Drug (prescription) coverage under employee health plans by plan type, and copayments required, 1989, article, 6722–1.215

Drug and alcohol abuse treatment coverage and provisions under employee health plans, by plan type, 1989, article, 6722–1.221

Employee benefit plan coverage and provisions in small businesses, by plan type and occupational group, 1990, biennial rpt, 6784–20

Employer-sponsored HMO and fee-for-service health plans, coverage, provisions, and premiums, 1989, article, 6722–1.214

Employer-sponsored HMO availability and enrollment of production and office workers, by industry div, selected metro area, and region, 1984-89, article, 6722–1.222

Enrollment in HMOs, 1991, annual fact book, 4654–18

Fed Govt civilian employees health insurance coverage, by plan, FY89, annual rpt, 9844–35.1

Financial performance of social HMOs, and hospital use, demonstration project results, 1985-88, article, 4652–1.202

Financial performance of social HMOs, and services use by type, demonstration project results, 1985-89, article, 4652–1.235

Health Care Financing Admin research activities and grants, by program, FY90, annual listing, 4654–10

Health occupations

Health condition and health care resources, use, and spending, 1950s-89, annual data compilation, 4144–11

Hospices use by cancer patients, by service type, use of other facilities, patient and instn characteristics, and other indicators, local area study, 1980-85, 4658–53

Kidney transplants, needs, costs, payment sources, and impact of immunosuppressive drugs on outcome, 1950s-87 and projected to 1995, 4658–59

Medicaid demonstration projects evaluation, for 6 States, 1988 rpt, 4658–45

Medicaid enrollment and use for HMOs and other prepaid managed care plans, for 20 States, 1985-89, chartbook, 4108–29

Medicaid HMO enrollees, payments, terminations, services use, and State oversight, for Chicago, Ill, late 1980s, GAO rpt, 26121–399

Medicaid services use and costs in alternative treatment settings, model description and results, FY87, article, 4652–1.211

Medicare and Medicaid eligibility, participation, coverage, and program finances, various periods 1966-91, biennial rpt, 4654–1

Medicare beneficiaries risk-based HMO contracts, factors affecting participation, model description and results, 1984-86, article, 4652–1.226

Medicare HMO enrollees quality of care indicators compared to fee-for-service, demonstration projects results, mid 1980s, 4658–46

Medicare reimbursement of risk-based HMOs under alternative geographic adjustment factors, for selected counties, 1983-87, article, 4652–1.203

Primary health care research, methodology and findings, 1991 annual conf, 4184–4

Statistical Abstract of US, 1991 annual data compilation, 2324–1.3

Health occupations

AIDS and hepatitis viruses transmission in health care settings, occupational exposure, prevention policies, and OSHA regulation, 1990 hearings, 21348–119

AIDS virus transmission from health care workers to patients during invasive procedures, CDC prevention guidelines, 1991 rpt, 4206–2.44

Data on health condition and health care resources, use, and spending, 1950s-89, annual data compilation, 4144–11

DOD budget, manpower needs, costs, and force readiness by service branch, FY92, annual rpt, 3504–1

Drug and alcohol abuse treatment facilities, services, use, funding, staff, and client characteristics, 1989, biennial rpt, 4494–10

Drug and alcohol abuse treatment services, funding, staffing, and client load, characteristics, and outcomes, by setting, 1989 conf, 4498–73

Employment, earnings, and hours, by SIC 1- to 4-digit industry, monthly and annual averages, selected years 1909-90, annual rpt, 6744–4

Employment, unemployment, and labor force characteristics, by region and census div, 1990, annual rpt, 6744–7.1

Health occupations

Govt census, 1987: employment, payroll, and average earnings, by function, level of govt, State, county, and population size, 2455–2

Govt census, 1987: local govt employment by function, payroll, and average earnings, for individual counties, cities, and school and special districts, 2455–1

Hepatitis cases by infection source, age, sex, race, and State, and deaths, by strain, 1988 and trends from 1966, 4205–2

HHS financial aid, by program, recipient, State, and city, FY90, annual regional listings, 4004–3

Hospital employment, by detailed occupation, 1989, article, 6722–1.217

Hospital reimbursement by Medicare under prospective payment system, effect of adjusting wage index for occupational mix, 1990 rpt, 17206–2.17

Indian Health Service employment of Indians and non-Indians, training, hires, and quits, by occupation, FY89, annual rpt, 4084–6

Licensing and discipline of health professionals by State medical boards, 1950s-87, series, 4006–8

Manufacturing employment, by detailed occupation and SIC 2-digit industry, 1989 survey, triennial rpt, 6748–52

Medicare reimbursement of hospitals under prospective payment system, and effect on services, finances, and beneficiary payments, 1979-90, annual rpt, 17204–2

Mental health care facilities, staff, service, and patient characteristics, series, 4506–4

Military health care personnel, and accessions by training source, by occupation, specialty, and service branch, FY89, annual rpt, 3544–24

Minority group and women health condition, services use, payment sources, and health care labor force, by poverty status, 1940s-89, chartbook, 4118–56

State and Metro Area Data Book, 1991 data compilation, 2328–54

Temporary help supply establishments by occupation supplied, receipts by source, and payroll, by MSA, 1987 Census of Service Industries, 2393–4.8

VA health care staff and turnover, by occupation, physician specialty, and location, 1990, annual rpt, 8604–8

VA health care staff, work-years, pay rates, and benefits use and costs, by agency, FY89, annual rpt, 9844–31

VA Medicine and Surgery Dept trainees, by detailed program and city, FY90, annual rpt, 8704–4

Veterans (homeless) with mental illness, VA program services, costs, staff, client characteristics, and outcome, 1990, annual rpt, 8604–11

Veterans Health Services and Research Admin health care staff and salary, by pay system and occupational group, 1990, annual rpt, 9844–6.3

Vital and Health Statistics series: health care facilities use and labor force, 4147–13

Waste (medical) generation, sources, health worker exposure and risk, and incineration emissions, 1980s, 4078–1

see also Allied health personnel

see also Anesthesiology

see also Chiropractic and naturopathy

see also Clinical laboratory technicians

see also Coroners

see also Dentists and dentistry

see also Dietitians and nutritionists

see also Epidemiology and epidemiologists

see also Foreign medical graduates

see also Geriatrics

see also Health facilities administration

see also Medical education

see also Midwives

see also Nuclear medicine and radiology

see also Nurses and nursing

see also Obstetrics and gynecology

see also Occupational therapy

see also Optometry

see also Orthopedics

see also Osteopathy

see also Pathology

see also Pediatrics

see also Pharmacists and pharmacy

see also Physical therapy

see also Physicians

see also Podiatry

see also Psychiatry

see also Respiratory therapy

see also Social work

see also Speech pathology and audiology

see also Surgeons and surgery

see also Veterinary medicine

see also under Medicine and terms beginning with Medical

Health of workers

see Absenteeism

see Occupational health and safety

Health planning and evaluation

Assistance (financial and nonfinancial) of Fed Govt, 1991 base edition with supplements, annual listing, 104–5

Canada universal health care system operations and costs, and implications for US, 1987-91, GAO rpt, 26121–424

Data on health condition and health care resources, use, and spending, 1950s-89, annual data compilation, 4144–11

Demand for health services, needs, delivery, and costs, series, 4186–9

Drug abuse, prevention, treatment, and health research results, as of 1990, triennial rpt, 4498–68

Health maintenance organizations Medicare enrollees quality of care indicators compared to fee-for-service, demonstration projects results, mid 1980s, 4658–46

HHS financial aid, by program, recipient, State, and city, FY90, annual regional listings, 4004–3

HHS research and evaluation programs, 1970-90, annual listing, 4004–30

Hospices use by cancer patients, by service type, use of other facilities, patient and instn characteristics, and other indicators, local area study, 1980-85, 4658–53

Insurance (health) natl coverage alternative proposals and indicators of need, 1989, 4658–54

Medicaid demonstration projects evaluation, for 6 States, 1988 rpt, 4658–45

Nursing home and other long term care services under Medicare hospital use reduction demonstration, results for Rochester, NY, 1980s, 4658–43

Older frail persons community-based care demonstration projects, evaluation of case mgmt services admin, 1991 rpt, 4186–7.8

Preventive disease and health improvement goals and recommended activities for 2000, with trends 1970s-80s, 4048–10

Public Health Reports, bimonthly journal, 4042–3

Research activities and grants of HCFA, by program, FY90, annual listing, 4654–10

Rural areas hospitals HCFA grants for improving financial stability, by program area, recipient, and State, FY89, 4658–58

VA Medicine and Surgery Dept trainees, by detailed program and city, FY90, annual rpt, 8704–4

see also Regional medical programs

Health Resources and Services Administration

Budget of US, obligations and authority by function, agency, and program, with summaries, analyses, and historical tables, FY92, annual rpt, 104–2

Child accident deaths and death rates, by cause, age, sex, race, and State, 1980-85, 4108–54

Child accident deaths and injuries by cause, and victimization, rates by race, sex, and age, 1979-88, chartbook, 4108–56

Child and maternal health programs of major urban health depts, activities and budgets, 1990, listing, 4108–51

Child health condition and services use, 1990 chartbook, 4108–49

Expenditures of Fed Govt in States, by type, program, agency, and State, FY90, annual rpt, 2464–2

Financial aid of HHS, by program, recipient, State, and city, FY90, annual regional listings, 4004–3

Homeless teens pregnancy prevalence and outcomes, services availability, health condition, and drug abuse, 1989 conf, 4108–55

Medicaid enrollment and use for HMOs and other prepaid managed care plans, for 20 States, 1985-89, chartbook, 4108–29

Research and evaluation programs of HHS, 1970-90, annual listing, 4004–30

see also Bureau of Health Care Delivery and Assistance

see also Bureau of Health Professions

Health surveys

see under names of individual surveys (listed under Surveys)

Hearing aids

see Medical supplies and equipment

Hearing and hearing disorders

Disabled persons and related activity limitation days and health services use, by health status, disability type, and other characteristics, 1984-88, 4146–8.202

Head Start handicapped enrollment, by handicap, State, and for Indian and migrant programs, 1987/88, annual rpt, 4604–1

Hearing aid performance test results, by make and model, 1991 annual rpt, 8704–3

Injuries, related impairments, and activity limitations, by circumstances and victim characteristics, 1985-87, 4147–10.179

Insurance (health) coverage and provisions of small business employee benefit plans, by plan type and occupational group, 1990, biennial rpt, 6784–20

Workers compensation laws of States and Fed Govt, 1991 semiannual rpt, 6502–1

see also Deaf
see also Ear diseases and infections
see also Speech pathology and audiology

Heart diseases
see Cardiovascular diseases

Heating
see Plumbing and heating

Heating oil
see Fuel oil

Hebert, Paul J.
"Deadliest, Costliest, and Most Intense U.S. Hurricanes of This Century (and Other Frequently Requested Hurricane Facts)", 2188–15

Hedging
see Futures trading

Height
see Body measurements

Heinen, LuAnn
"Nationwide Evaluation of Medicaid Competition Demonstrations. Volume 2. Implementation and Operation Issues: Final Case Study Overview", 4658–45.2

Heinkel, Joan
"Analysis of Long-Term Contracts for Imports of Canadian Natural Gas", 3162–4.206

Heitmeyer, Mickey E.
"Water and Habitat Dynamics of the Mingo Swamp in Southeastern Missouri", 5506–13.2

Helbing, Charles
"Medicare Expenditures for Physician and Supplier Services, 1970-88", 4652–1.240
"Medicare Short-Stay Hospital Services by Diagnosis-Related Groups", 4652–1.250

Helicopters
Accidents and circumstances, for US operations of domestic and foreign airlines and general aviation, periodic rpt, 9612–1
Accidents in general aviation, by circumstances, characteristics of persons and aircraft involved, and type of flying, 1988, annual rpt, 9614–3
Air traffic control and airway facilities improvement activities under Aviation System Capital Investment Plan, 1981-90 and projected to 2005, annual rpt, 7504–12
Birds (geese) pre-migration feeding behavior impacts of aircraft disturbance, for 3 species at Izembek Lagoon, Alaska, 1970s-88, 5738–23
DOD budget, weapons acquisition costs by system and service branch, FY91-93, annual rpt, 3504–2
Exports and imports of US, by country and detailed commodity, monthly rpt, 2422–12
Exports and imports of US, by Harmonized System 6-digit commodity and country, 1990, annual rpt, 2424–13
Exports of US, detailed Schedule B commodities with countries of destination, 1990, annual rpt, 2424–10
Flight and engine hours, and shutdown rates, by aircraft and engine model, and air carrier, monthly rpt, 7502–13
Forest fires and acres burned on Forest Service land, by cause, forest, and State, 1989, annual rpt, 1204–6
General aviation aircraft, flight hours, and equipment, by type, use, and model of aircraft, region, and State, 1990, annual rpt, 7504–29

NATO and Warsaw Pact military forces reductions under proposed treaty, and US budget savings, 1990 rpt, 26306 3.114
Pilots and nonpilots certified by FAA, by certificate type, age, sex, region, and State, 1990, annual rpt, 7504–2
Price indexes (producer), by stage of processing and detailed commodity, monthly rpt, 6762–6
Price indexes (producer), by stage of processing and detailed commodity, monthly 1990, annual rpt, 6764–2
Registrations of aircraft with FAA, by type and characteristics of aircraft, make, carrier, State, and county, 1989, annual rpt, 7504–3
Shipments of general aviation aircraft, and commercial carriers orders and deliveries, by aircraft type, quarterly rpt, 7502–16
Shipments, trade, use, and firms, by type of craft and engine, monthly Current Industrial Rpt, 2506–12.24
Soviet Union military weapons systems, presence, and force strengths, and compared to US, 1991 annual rpt, 3504–20
Traffic, aircraft, carriers, airports, and FAA activities, detailed data, 1980-89, annual rpt, 7504–1
Traffic, aircraft, pilots, airports, and fuel use, forecast FY91-2002 and trends from FY81, annual rpt, 7504–6
Traffic, uses, craft, and landing facilities, by helicopter type, region, and State, 1989, 7508–75

Helium
see Gases

Hellman, Chan M.
"Cross-Level Inferences of Job Satisfaction in the Prediction of Intent To Leave", 7506–10.94

Helwege, Jean
"More on the International Similarity of Interindustry Wage Differentials: Evidence from the Federal Republic of Germany and the U.S.", 9366–6.281

Hemophilia
see Blood diseases and disorders

Hemp
see Natural fibers

Hendershot, Gerry E.
"Use of Family Planning Services by Currently Married Women 15-44 Years of Age: U.S., 1973 and 1976", 4147–16.5

Henderson, Allison
"Summary of State Chapter 1 Migrant Education Program Participation and Achievement Information, 1987-88", 4808–30

Henderson, David
"Estimating Entry and Exit of U.S. Farms", 1598–269

Hendricks, Ann
"Prospective Payments System's Impacts on Rural Hospitals", 4658–51

Henle, Peter
"Earnings Inequality Accelerates in the 1980's", 6722–1.201

Hepatitis
see Infective and parasitic diseases

Herbert, John H.
"Overview of Recent Developments in the Underground Storage Market", 3162–4.205

"Recent Trends and Regional Variability in Underground Storage Activities", 3162–4.203

Herbicides
see Pesticides

Herbs
see Spices and herbs

Herdendorf, Charles E.
"Hurricane Gold. Part I—The Loss", 2152–8.203
"Hurricane Gold. Part II—The Find", 2152–8.203

Hereditary diseases
Cancer (melanoma) precursor nevi genetic transmission risk, 1991 article, 4472–1.235
Cell cultures with genetic abnormalities, availability and cultures shipped, 1990-91, biennial listing, 4474–23
Deaths and rates, by detailed cause and demographic characteristics, 1988 and trends from 1900, US Vital Statistics annual rpt, 4144–2
HHS financial aid, by program, recipient, State, and city, FY90, annual regional listings, 4004–3
Occupational genetic damage and trait monitoring and screening, use, costs, benefits, and procedures, 1980s, 26358–230
see also Birth defects

Heroin
see Drug abuse and treatment
see Drug and narcotics offenses

Herr, William
"Toward an Analysis of the Farmers Home Administration's Direct and Guaranteed Farm Loan Programs", 1598–273

Hertel, Thomas W.
"Economic Assessment of the Freeze on Program Yields", 1548–376

Hervey, Jack L.
"Energy Dependence and Efficiency", 9375–1.210

Herz, Diane E.
"Worker Displacement Still Common in the Late 1980's", 6722–1.225

Hess, Charles E.
"Energy Issues for Agriculture: Challenges for Research", 1004–16.1

HEW
see Department of Education
see Department of Health and Human Services

Hexem, Roger W.
"Cash Rents for Farms, Cropland, and Pasture, 1960-89", 1548–377

Hialeah, Fla.
Housing starts and completions authorized by building permits in 40 MSAs, quarterly rpt, 2382–9
Wages by occupation, and benefits for office and plant workers, 1990 survey, periodic MSA rpt, 6785–11.3
see also under By City and By SMSA or MSA in the "Index by Categories"

Hickok, Susan A.
"Expanded, Cointegrated Model of U.S. Trade", 9385–8.117
"Factors Behind the Shifting Composition of U.S. Manufactured Goods Trade", 9385–8.95
"Shifting Composition of U.S. Manufactured Goods Trade", 9385–1.205

Hickok, Susan A.

"Uruguay Round of GATT Trade Negotiations", 9385–8.115

Hickory, N.C.

see also under By SMSA or MSA in the "Index by Categories"

Hides and skins

Agricultural Statistics, 1990, annual rpt, 1004–1

Agriculture census, 1987: farms, farmland, production, finances, and operator characteristics, by county, final State rpt series, 2331–1

Cold storage food stocks by commodity, and warehouse space use, by census div, 1990, annual rpt, 1631–11

Endangered animals and plants US trade and permits, by species, purpose, disposition, and country, 1989, annual rpt, 5504–19

Exports and imports (agricultural) of US, by commodity and country, bimonthly rpt, 1522–1

Exports and imports (agricultural) of US, by detailed commodity and country, 1989, annual rpt, 1524–8

Exports and imports (agricultural) of US, by detailed commodity and country, 1990, semiannual rpt, 1522–4

Exports and imports of dairy, livestock, and poultry products, by commodity and country, FAS monthly circular, 1925–32

Exports and imports of US, by country and detailed commodity, monthly rpt, 2422–12

Exports and imports of US, by Harmonized System 6-digit commodity and country, 1990, annual rpt, 2424–13

Exports and imports of US, by transport mode, country, and SITC 1- to 3-digit commodity, 1990, annual rpt, 2424–12

Exports of grains, oilseed products, hides, skins, and cotton, by country, weekly rpt, 1922–3

Exports of US, detailed Schedule B commodities with countries of destination, 1990, annual rpt, 2424–10

Farm sector balance sheet, and receipts by detailed commodity, by State, 1985-89, annual rpt, 1544–18

Foreign and US dairy production, trade, and use, by selected country, FAS semiannual circular series, 1925–33

Foreign countries agricultural production, prices, and trade, by country, 1980-90 and forecast 1991, annual world area rpt series, 1524–4

Manufacturing annual survey, 1989: finances and operations, by SIC 2- to 4-digit industry, series, 2506–15

Marketing data for livestock, meat, and wool, by species and market, weekly rpt, 1315–1

OECD trade, total and for 4 major countries, and US trade by country, by commodity, 1970-89, world area rpt series, 9116–1

Price indexes (producer), by stage of processing and detailed commodity, monthly rpt, 6762–6

Price indexes (producer), by stage of processing and detailed commodity, monthly 1990, annual rpt, 6764–2

see also Furs and fur industry

see also Leather industry and products

High Point, N.C.

see also under By SMSA or MSA in the "Index by Categories"

High School and Beyond Survey

Data collection activities and programs of NCES, 1991, annual listing, 4824–7

High school graduates

see Educational attainment

see Educational retention rates

see under By Educational Attainment in the "Index by Categories"

High School Transcript Study

Data collection activities and programs of NCES, 1991, annual listing, 4824–7

High schools

see Elementary and secondary education

Higher education

Appalachia education system, improvement initiatives, and indicators of success, by State, 1960s-89, 9088–36

Condition of Education, detail for higher education, 1960s-90, annual rpt, 4824–1.2

Data collection activities and programs of NCES, 1991, annual listing, 4824–7

Data on education, selected trends and projections 1978-2001, pamphlet, 4828–27

Data on education, 1960s-89, pamphlet, 4828–26

Data on higher education, enrollment, faculty, finances, and degrees, by instn level and control, and State, FY86, annual rpt, 4844–13

Digest of Education Statistics, 1991 annual data compilation, 4824–2

High school advanced placement for college credit, programs by selected characteristics and school control, 1984-86, 4838–46

High school class of 1972: education, employment, and family characteristics, activities, and attitudes, natl longitudinal study, series, 4836–1

Libraries of higher education instns, holdings, outlays, staff, and instn characteristics, 1969-88, 4468–4

Minority group higher education enrollment, degrees, factors affecting participation, and earnings, 1960s-88, 4808–29

R&D equipment of higher education instns, acquisition and service costs, condition, and financing, by field and subfield, 1988-90, triennial survey series, 9627–27

Remedial education programs in higher education instns, and enrollment, courses, and faculty, by instn characteristics, 1989/90, 4826–1.30

Science and engineering academic research system status, R&D performance, and Fed Govt support, 1950s-88 with trends and projections, 9628–83

State and Metro Area Data Book, 1991 data compilation, 2328–54

Statistical Abstract of US, 1991 annual data compilation, 2324–1.4

Vocational education in postsecondary instns, States performance measurement activities and related legislation, 1989/90, 4808–33

see also Adult education

see also Agricultural education

see also Area studies

see also Black colleges

see also Business education

see also Campus security

see also Curricula

see also Degrees, higher education

see also Educational attainment

see also Educational broadcasting

see also Educational enrollment

see also Educational exchanges

see also Educational facilities

see also Educational finance

see also Educational materials

see also Educational research

see also Educational technology

see also Educational tests

see also Ethnic studies

see also Federal aid to higher education

see also Federal aid to medical education

see also Junior colleges

see also Legal education

see also Medical education

see also Reserve Officers Training Corps

see also School administration and staff

see also Scientific education

see also Service academies

see also State funding for higher education

see also Student aid

see also Students

see also Teacher education

see also Teachers

see also Veterans education

see also Vocational education and training

see also Work-study programs

see also under By Individual Company or Institution in the "Index by Categories"

Higher Education General Information Survey

see Integrated Postsecondary Education Data System

Highway speed limit

see Traffic laws and courts

Highways, streets, and roads

Acreage of land, by use, ownership, and State, 1987 and trends from 1910, 1588–48

Appalachia hwy system and access roads funding and completion status, by State, quarterly tables, 9082–1

Appalachia local dev projects, and funding by source, by program and State, FY90, annual rpt, 9084–1

Census of Population, 1990: homeless shelter and on-street population, by State and for 200 cities, press release, 2328–70

Condition, mgmt, R&D, and funding, for transportation and environmental public works, 1986-91, 26358–235

Condition of hwys and bridges, share with deficiencies, by State, 1980s, article, 9373–1.207

Construction industries census, 1987: establishments, employment, receipts, and expenditures, by SIC 4-digit industry and State, final industry rpt series, 2373–1

Construction material PPI, by construction industry, monthly rpt, 6762–6

Construction material prices and indexes for Federal-aid hwy system, by type of material and urban-rural location, quarterly rpt, 7552–7

Construction material prices and indexes for Federal-aid hwy system, by type of material, quarterly press release, 7552–16

Construction material use by type, and spending for hwys, by State, various periods 1944-90, annual rpt, 7554–29

Index by Subjects and Names

Hispanic Americans

Construction put in place and cost indexes, by type of construction, bimonthly rpt, 2042–1.1; 2042–1.5

Construction put in place, value of new public and private structures, by type, monthly rpt, 2382–4

County Business Patterns, 1988: employment, establishments, and payroll, by SIC 2- to 4-digit industry and county, annual State rpt series, 2326–6

County Business Patterns, 1989: employment, establishments, and payroll, by SIC 2- to 4-digit industry and county, annual State rpt series, 2326–8

Crime victimization of women, by relation to offender, circumstances, and victim characteristics, for rape and other violent offenses, 1973-87, 6068–243

Crime victimization rates, by victim and offender characteristics, circumstances, and offense, 1988 survey, annual rpt, 6066–3.42

Crime victimization rates, by victim and offender characteristics, circumstances, and offense, 1989 survey, annual rpt, 6066–3.44

Energy use by mode of transport, fuel supply, and demographic and economic factors of vehicle use, 1970s-89, annual rpt, 3304–5

Foreign countries economic, social, political, and geographic summary data, by country, 1991, annual factbook, 9114–2

Forest Service mgmt of public lands and resources dev, environmental, economic, and social impacts of alternative programs, projected to 2040, 1208–24

Govt census, 1987: employment, payroll, and average earnings, by function, level of govt, State, county, and population size, 2455–2

Govt census, 1987: local govt employment by function, payroll, and average earnings, for individual counties, cities, and school and special districts, 2455–1

Govt census, 1987: State and local labor-mgmt policies, agreements, and coverage and bargaining units, by function, level of govt, and State, 2455–3

Govt employment and payroll, by function, level of govt, and jurisdiction, 1990, annual rpt series, 2466–1

Govt finances, by level of govt, State, and for large cities and counties, annual rpt series, 2466–2

Govt spending measures using indicators of service costs and demand, with comparisons to fiscal capacity and actual outlays, by State, for State and local govts, 1986-87, 10048–77

Hwy Statistics, detailed data by State, 1990, annual rpt, 7554–1

Hwy Statistics, summary data by State, 1989-90, annual rpt, 7554–24

Natl Hwy Traffic Safety Admin and Fed Hwy Admin activities and grants, 1989, annual rpt, 7764–1

Natl transportation system planning, use, condition, accidents, and needs, by mode of transport, 1940s-90 and projected to 2020, 7308–202

Neighborhood and housing quality, indicators and attitudes, by householder type and location, 1987, biennial rpt supplement, 2485–13

Neighborhood and housing quality, indicators and attitudes, by householder type and location, 1989, biennial rpt, 2485–12

Neighborhood and housing quality, indicators and attitudes, MSA surveys, series, 2485–6

Palau admin, and social, economic, and govtl data, FY90, annual rpt, 7004–6

Public lands acreage and use, and Land Mgmt Bur activities and finances, annual State rpt series, 5724–11

R&D for hwy design and construction, quarterly journal, 7552–3

Robberies, by type of premises, population size, and region, 1990, annual rpt, 6224–2.1

State and local govt employment of minorities and women, by occupation, function, and pay level, 1990, annual rpt, 9244–6.4

State and Metro Area Data Book, 1991 data compilation, 2328–54

State govt tax provisions on motor fuel, auto registration fees, and disposition of receipts, by State, as of Jan 1991, biennial rpt, 7554–37

Statistical Abstract of US, 1991 annual data compilation, 2324–1.21

Toll facilities, mileage, and operating status, by type of system, as of Jan 1990, biennial listing, 7554–39

Traffic volume on rural roads and city streets, monthly rpt, 7552–8

see also Bridges and tunnels

see also Federal aid to highways

see also Traffic accident fatalities

see also Traffic accidents and safety

see also Traffic engineering

see also Traffic laws and courts

Hijacking of aircraft

see Air piracy

Hildebrandt, Paula

"Rising Cost of Medical Care and Its Effect on Inflation", 9381–1.212

Hilgert, Cecelia

"Nonprofit Charitable Organizations, 1986 and 1987", 8302–2.218

Hill, Barry R.

"Sediment-Source Data for Four Basins Tributary to Lake Tahoe, California and Nevada, August 1983-June 1988", 5666–27.12

Hill, Catherine

"Development Impact of Counterpart Funds: A Review of the Literature", 9918–21

Hill, Daniel H.

"Response and Procedural Error Variance in Surveys: An Application of Poisson and Neyman Type A Regression", 2626–10.124

Hill, David

"Adults' Accounts of Onset of Regular Smoking: Influences of School, Work, and Other Settings", 4042–3.217

Hill, Ian T.

"Improving State Medicaid Programs for Pregnant Women and Children", 4652–1.213

Hill, Walter E.

"Building a Better Rural Policy: The President's Rural Development Initiative", 1004–16.1

Hilt, Donald E.

"Individual-Tree Probability of Survival Model for the Northeastern U.S.", 1208–369

Hilton, Margaret

"Shared Training: Learning from Germany", 6722–1.220

Hines, Franklin D.

"Forest Statistics for East Oklahoma Counties, 1986", 1206–39.4

Hing, Esther

"Long-Term Care for the Functionally Dependent Elderly. Vital and Health Statistics Series 13", 4147–13.104

Hinton, David

"U.S. Petroleum Developments: 1990", 3162–6.201

Hip fractures

see Musculoskeletal diseases

Hip replacement

see Prosthetics and orthotics

Hires

see Labor turnover

Hirst, Eric

"Effects of Utility DSM Programs on Electricity Costs and Prices", 3308–99

"Possible Effects of Electric-Utility DSM Programs, 1990-2010", 3308–98

Hirtle, Beverly

"Bank Loan Commitments and the Transmission of Monetary Policy", 9385–8.75

"Factors Affecting the Competitiveness of Internationally Active Financial Institutions", 9385–1.206

"Financial Market Evolution and the Interest Sensitivity of Output", 9385–8.79

"Simple Model of Bank Loan Commitments and Monetary Policy", 9385–8.76

Hispanic Americans

Agriculture census, 1987: farms, farmland, production, finances, and operator characteristics, by county, final State rpt series, 2331–1

AIDS cases by risk group, race, sex, age, State, and MSA, and deaths, monthly rpt, 4202–9

AIDS public knowledge, attitudes, info sources, and testing, for Hispanics, 1990 survey, 4146–8.209

Alien workers (unauthorized) and Fair Labor Standards Act employer compliance, hiring impacts, and aliens overstaying visas by country and State, 1986-90, annual rpt, 6264–6

Births and rates, by characteristics of birth, infant, and parents, 1989 and trends from 1940, US Vital Statistics advance annual rpt, 4146–5.123

Births of low birthweight to Hispanics, and inadequate prenatal care, 1980s, article, 4042–3.234

Blood iron levels indicators, for Hispanics by detailed origin, 1970s-88, 4147–2.111

Business mgmt and financial aid from Minority Business Dev Centers, and characteristics of businesses, by region and State, FY90, annual rpt, 2104–6

Cancer deaths in Cuba and among Cuban-born Americans, by body site, 1970s-83, article, 4042–3.205

Census of Population and Housing, 1990: population and housing characteristics, households, and land area, by county, subdiv, and place, State rpt series, 2551–1

Hispanic Americans

Index by Subjects and Names

Census of Population and Housing, 1990: population and housing selected characteristics, by region, press release, 2328–74

Census of Population and Housing, 1990: Texas data collection activities and status, hearing, 21628–92

Census of Population and Housing, 1990: voting age and total population by race, and housing units, by block, redistricting counts required under PL 94-171, State CD-ROM series, 2551–6

Census of Population and Housing, 1990: voting age and total population by race, and housing units, by county and city, redistricting counts required under PL 94-171, State summary rpt series, 2551–5

Census of Population, 1990: Hispanic population by detailed origin, region, and State, with data for 1980, press release, 2328–73

Census of Population, 1990: metro area population by race, Hispanic origin, and MSA, press release, 2328–75

Census of Population, 1990: population by detailed Native American, Asian, and Pacific Islander group, race, region, and State, with data for 1980, press release, 2328–72

Census of Population, 1990: population by race, Hispanic origin, region, census div, and State, with data for 1980, fact sheet, 2326–20.2

Census of Population, 1990: post-enumeration survey results compared to census counts, by race, sex, city, county, and State, press release, 2328–69

Consumer Income, socioeconomic characteristics of persons, families, and households, detailed cross-tabulations, Current Population Rpt series, 2546–6

Crime, criminal justice admin and enforcement, and public opinion, data compilation, 1991 annual rpt, 6064–6

Crimes, arrests, and rates, by offense, offender characteristics, population size, and jurisdiction, 1990, annual rpt, 6224–2.1; 6224–2.2

Deaths and rates, by detailed cause and demographic characteristics, 1988 and trends from 1900, US Vital Statistics annual rpt, 4144–2

Deaths and rates for Hispanics, by cause, age, sex, and detailed origin, average 1979-81, 4147–20.18

Drug abuse prevalence among minorities, related health effects and crime, treatment, and research status and needs, mid 1970s-90, 4498–72

Drug abuse relation to violent and criminal behavior, with data on street gang activity and selected population groups, 1989 conf, 4498–70

Drug, alcohol, and cigarette use, by selected characteristics, 1990 survey, biennial rpt, 4494–5

Drug and alcohol abuse treatment facilities, services, use, funding, staff, and client characteristics, 1989, biennial rpt, 4494–10

Education data compilation, 1991 annual rpt, 4824–2

Education data, detail for elementary, secondary, and higher education, 1920s-90 and projected to 2001, annual rpt, 4824–1

Educational attainment, by sociodemographic characteristics and location, 1989 and trends from 1940, biennial Current Population Rpt, 2546–1.452

Educational enrollment, by grade, instn type and control, and student characteristics, 1989 and trends from 1947, annual Current Population Rpt, 2546–1.453

Educational performance and conditions, characteristics, attitudes, activities, and plans, 1988 8th grade class, natl longitudinal survey, series, 4826–9

Educational performance of elementary and secondary students, and factors affecting proficiency, by selected characteristics, 1988 natl assessments, subject rpt series, 4896–7

Educational performance of elementary and secondary students, and factors affecting proficiency, by selected characteristics, 1990 natl assessments, subject rpt series, 4896–8

Educational service delivery and discipline, and discrimination indicators by State, 1988, biennial rpt, 4804–33

Employment and unemployment current statistics and articles, Monthly Labor Review, 6722–1

Employment, earnings, and hours, monthly press release, 6742–5

Employment, unemployment, and labor force characteristics, by region, State, and selected metro area, 1990, annual rpt, 6744–7

Fed Equal Opportunity Recruitment Program activity, and employment by sex, race, pay grade, and occupational group, FY90, annual rpt, 9844–33

Fed Govt employment of minorities and women, and compliance with EEOC standards, by occupation and agency, FY88-92, GAO rpt, 26119–342

FmHA loans, by type, borrower characteristics, and State, quarterly rpt, 1182–8

FmHA loans, by type, borrower race, and State, quarterly rpt, 1182–5

Food aid program of USDA for women, infants, and children, participants by race, State, and Indian agency, Apr 1990, annual rpt, 1364–16

Health condition improvement and disease prevention goals and recommended activities for 2000, with trends 1970s-80s, 4048–10

Health condition indicators and health occupations school enrollment, 1950s-89, annual data compilation, 4144–11

Health condition of minorities, services use, costs, and indicators of services need, 1950s-88, 4118–55

Health condition, services use, payment sources, and health care labor force, for minorities and women by poverty status, 1940s-89, chartbook, 4118–56

HHS employment of Hispanics in Mountain region, hiring and promotion practices, 1980s, GAO rpt, 26121–393

High school class of 1972: education, employment, and family characteristics, activities, and attitudes, natl longitudinal study, series, 4836–1

Higher education degrees awarded, by level, field, race, and sex, 1988/89 with trends from 1978/79, biennial rpt, 4844–17

Higher education enrollment of minorities, degrees, factors affecting participation, and earnings, by race, 1960s-88, 4808–29

Households and family characteristics, by location, 1990, annual Current Population Rpt, 2546–1.447

Households and housing characteristics, unit and neighborhood quality, and journey to work by MSA location, for 11 MSAs, 1984 survey, supplement, 2485–8

Households and housing detailed characteristics, and unit and neighborhood quality, by location, 1987, biennial rpt supplement, 2485–13

Households and housing detailed characteristics, and unit and neighborhood quality, by location, 1989, biennial rpt, 2485–12

Households and housing detailed characteristics, and unit and neighborhood quality, MSA surveys, series, 2485–6

Households composition, income, benefits, and labor force status, Survey of Income and Program Participation methodology, working paper series, 2626–10

Housing inventory change from 1973, by reason, unit and household characteristics, and location, 1983 survey, biennial rpt, 2485–14

Immigrants in US, population characteristics and fertility, by birthplace and compared to native born, 1980s, Current Population rpt, 2546–2.162

Income (household) and poverty status under alternative income definitions, by recipient characteristics, 1990, annual Current Population Rpt, 2546–6.69

Jail adult and juvenile population, employment, spending, instn conditions, and inmate programs, by county and facility, 1988, regional rpt series, 6068–144

Labor force status, by race, detailed Hispanic origin, and sex, quarterly rpt, 6742–18

Labor force, wages, hours, and payroll costs, by major industry group and demographic characteristics, *Survey of Current Business*, monthly rpt, 2702–1.8

Living arrangements, family relationships, and marital status, by selected characteristics, 1990, annual Current Population Rpt, 2546–1.449

Military personnel strengths, for active duty enlisted and officers, by sex and race, 1970s-90, GAO rpt, 26123–325

Nuclear engineering enrollment and degrees granted by instn and State, and grad placement, by student characteristics, 1990, annual rpt, 3004–5

Population of Hispanics in counties bordering Mexico, by selected characteristics, 1980, Current Population Rpt, 2546–2.159

Population size and characteristics, historical index to *Current Population Rpts*, 1991 listing, 2546–2.160

Population social and economic characteristics, for Hispanics by detailed origin, 1991, Current Population Rpt, 2546–1.448; 2546–1.451

Prisoners, characteristics, and movements, by State, 1989, annual rpt, 6064–26

Radiation protection and health physics enrollment and degrees granted by instn and State, and grad placement, by student characteristics, 1990, annual rpt, 3004–7

Index by Subjects and Names

Science and engineering grad enrollment, by field, source of funds, and characteristics of student and instn, 1975-89, annual rpt, 9627–7

Science and engineering PhDs, by field, instn, employment prospects, sex, race, and other characteristics, 1960s-90, annual rpt, 9627–30

Science and engineering PhDs employment and other characteristics, by field and State, 1989, biennial rpt, 9627–18

Smoking cessation rates for Hispanics, effects of Spanish language self-help guide, 1987-88 local area study, article, 4042–3.249

State and local govt employment of minorities and women, by occupation, function, pay level, and State, 1990, annual rpt, 9244–6

State and Metro Area Data Book, 1991 data compilation, 2328–54

Statistical Abstract of US, 1991 annual data compilation, 2324–1

Voting and registration, by socioeconomic and demographic characteristics, 1990 congressional election, biennial Current Population Rpt, 2546–1.454

see also under By Race and Ethnic Group in the "Index by Categories"

Hispanic Health and Nutrition Examination Survey

Blood iron levels indicators, for Hispanics by detailed origin, 1970s-88, 4147–2.111

Historic events

see Chronologies

Historic sites

- Acreage of land under Natl Park Service mgmt, by site, ownership, and region, FY91, semiannual rpt, 5542–1
- Assistance (financial and nonfinancial) of Fed Govt, 1991 base edition with supplements, annual listing, 104–5
- Coastal areas environmental and socioeconomic conditions, and potential impact of oil and gas OCS leases, final statement series, 5736–1
- Coastal areas recreation facilities of Fed Govt and States, visitor and site characteristics, 1987-90 survey, regional rpt series, 2176–9
- Criminal cases by type and disposition, and collections, for US attorneys, by Federal district, FY90, annual rpt, 6004–2.1
- DC metro area land acquisition and dev projects of Fed Govt, characteristics and funding by agency and project, FY91-95, annual rpt, 15454–1
- Fed Govt spending in States, by type, program, agency, and State, FY90, annual rpt, 2464–2
- Preservation Fund grants, by State, FY92, annual table, 5544–9
- Tax expenditures, Federal revenues forgone through income tax deductions and exclusions by type, FY92-96, annual rpt, 21784–10
- Tax incentives for historic buildings preservation, projects, costs, ownership, and use, FY77-90, annual rpt, 5544–17
- Visits in natl park system, by park and State, monthly rpt, 5542–4
- Visits in natl park system, by park and State, 1990, annual rpt, 5544–12

see also Monuments and memorials

History

- American Historical Assn financial statements, and membership by State, 1989, annual rpt, 29574–2
- Educational performance by subject and selected student characteristics, standard test results and credits, 1991 edition, annual rpt, 4824–2.12
- Fed Govt aid to higher education and nonprofit instns for R&D and related activities, by field, instn, agency, and State, FY89, annual rpt, 9627–17
- Higher education course completions, by detailed program, sex, race, and instn type, for 1972 high school class, as of 1984, 4888–4

Hitchner, Roger E.

"Outlook for Farm Commodity Program Spending, FY91-96", 26306–6.160

Hitt, Kerie J.

"Summary of Selected Characteristics of Large Reservoirs in the U.S. and Puerto Rico, 1988", 5668–120

HIV virus group

see Acquired immune deficiency syndrome

Hoachlander, E. Gareth

"Profile of Schools Attended by Eighth Graders in 1988. National Education Longitudinal Study of 1988", 4826–9.10

Hobbs, James R.

"Domestic Corporations Controlled by Foreign Persons, 1988", 8302–2.219

"Foreign Corporations with Income Effectively Connected with a U.S. Business, 1987", 8302–2.205

Hodgkin's disease

see Blood diseases and disorders

Hof, John

"Forest and Rangeland Resource Interactions: A Supporting Technical Document for the 1989 RPA Assessment", 1208–24.19

Hoff, Frederic L.

- "1989 and Preliminary 1990 Cost of Production Estimates for Sugarbeet and Sugarcane Operations", 1561–14.202
- "1990 and Preliminary 1991 Cost of Production Estimates for Sugarbeet and Sugarcane Operations", 1561–14.208

Hoffman, Charlene M.

"Federal Support for Education: FY80-90", 4824–8

Hoffman, Linwood A.

- "Forecasting Season-Average Corn Prices Using Current Futures Prices", 1561–4.201
- "Relationships Between Annual Farm Prices and Ending Stocks of Rough Rice", 1561–8.202

Hoffman, Ray J.

"Reconnaissance Investigation of Water Quality, Bottom Sediment, and Biota Associated with Irrigation Drainage in and near Stillwater Wildlife Management Area, Churchill County, Nevada, 1986-87", 5666–27.14

Hog cholera

see Animal diseases and zoonoses

Hogan, Christopher

"Case-Mix Specialization in the Market for Hospital Services", 4188–71

"Medicare Volume Performance Standard Rate of Increase for FY91", 17266–1.2

Holm, Lars-Erik

Hogs

see Livestock and livestock industry

Holahan, John

"Hospital Back-Up Days: Impact on Joint Medicare and Medicaid Beneficiaries", 4652–1.225

Holden, Thom

"Lake Superior's Wicked November Storms", 2152–8.204

Holding companies

- County Business Patterns, 1988: employment, establishments, and payroll, by SIC 2- to 4-digit industry and county, annual State rpt series, 2326–6
- County Business Patterns, 1989: employment, establishments, and payroll, by SIC 2- to 4-digit industry and county, annual State rpt series, 2326–8
- Employment, earnings, and hours, by SIC 1- to 4-digit industry, monthly and annual averages, selected years 1909-90, annual rpt, 6744–4
- Multinatl US firms and foreign affiliates finances and operations, by industry and world area of parent firm, 1989 benchmark survey, preliminary annual rpt, 2704–5
- Occupational injury and illness rates, by SIC 2- to 4-digit industry, 1988-89, annual rpt, 6844–7
- Occupational injury and illness rates, by SIC 2- to 4-digit industry, 1989, annual rpt, 6844–1
- Tax (income) returns filed, by type of return and IRS district, 1989 and projected 1990-97, annual rpt, 8304–24
- Tax (income) returns filed, by type of tax and IRS region and service center, projected 1990-97 and trends from 1978, annual rpt, 8304–9
- Tax (income) returns of corporations, income and tax items by asset size and detailed industry, 1987, annual rpt, 8304–4
- Tax (income) returns of corporations, income and tax items by asset size and detailed industry, 1988, annual rpt, 8304–21
- Tax (income) returns of corporations with foreign tax credit, income and tax items by industry group, 1986, biennial article, 8302–2.203
- Tax (income) returns of partnerships, income statement and balance sheet items, by industry group, 1989, annual article, 8302–2.216; 8304–18
- Telephone and telegraph corporate control and holding company finances and operations, 1989, annual rpt, 9284–6.1

see also Bank holding companies

Holidays

see Vacations and holidays

Holland

see Netherlands

Hollywood, Fla.

Housing starts and completions authorized by building permits in 40 MSAs, quarterly rpt, 2382–9

see also under By City and By SMSA or MSA in the "Index by Categories"

Holm, Lars-Erik

"Cancer Risk After Iodine-131 Therapy for Hyperthyroidism", 4472–1.218

Holohan, Thomas V.

Holohan, Thomas V.

"Extracranial-Intracranial Bypass To Reduce the Risk of Ischemic Stroke. Health Technology Assessment Report, 1990", 4186–10.3

Holthus, Kelly

"Outlook for Farm Credit", 1004–16.1

Holy See

see Vatican City

Home-based offices and workers

- American Housing Survey: unit and households characteristics, unit and neighborhood quality, and journey to work by MSA location, for 11 MSAs, 1984 survey, supplement, 2485–8
- American Housing Survey: unit and households detailed characteristics, and unit and neighborhood quality, 1987, biennial rpt, 2485–12; 2485–13
- Child care benefits for employees, work schedule and leave policies coverage by firm size and industry group, 1987, 15496–1.11
- Complaints about working at home, employees views, survey, 1991 rpt, 9496–2.7
- Computer use at home, school, and work, by purpose and selected user characteristics, 1989, Current Population Rpt, 2546–2.158
- Moonlighting employment, by reason, and characteristics of workers and primary and secondary jobs, 1991, press release, 6726–1.40

Home economics

- Degrees awarded in higher education, by level, field, race, and sex, 1988/89 with trends from 1978/79, biennial rpt, 4844–17
- Education data compilation, 1991 annual rpt, 4824–2
- Education Dept programs funding, operations, and effectiveness, FY90, annual rpt, 4804–5
- Enrollment in single-sex and mixed classes, and schools offering courses, by course, 1988, biennial rpt, 4804–33
- Farm financial and marketing conditions, forecast 1991, annual conf, 1004–16
- Higher education course completions, by detailed program, sex, race, and instn type, for 1972 high school class, as of 1984, 4888–4
- Teachers in higher education instns, employment and other characteristics, by instn type and control, 1987/88 survey, 4846–4.4

see also Family budgets

Home equity loans

see Credit

Home health services

- AIDS and AIDS virus infection patients service use and costs under Medicaid, 1991, article, 4652–1.215
- AIDS patient home and community services under Medicaid waiver in 6 States, 1988-89, article, 4652–1.216
- County Business Patterns, 1988: employment, establishments, and payroll, by SIC 2- to 4-digit industry and county, annual State rpt series, 2326–6
- County Business Patterns, 1989: employment, establishments, and payroll, by SIC 2- to 4-digit industry and county, annual State rpt series, 2326–8

Health Care Financing Review, provider prices, price inputs and indexes, and labor, quarterly journal, 4652–1.1

- Health maintenance organizations financial performance and services use, demonstration project results, 1985-89, article, 4652–1.235
- HHS financial aid, by program, recipient, State, and city, FY90, annual regional listings, 4004–3
- Hospices operations, services, costs, and patient characteristics, for instns without Medicare certification, FY85-86, 4658–52
- Hospices use by cancer patients, by service type, use of other facilities, patient and instn characteristics, and other indicators, local area study, 1980-85, 4658–53
- Hospital post-discharge service use, by type, for Medicare pneumonia, stroke, and hip replacement cases, 1981-86, article, 4652–1.223
- Hospital services and facilities availability, by selected instn characteristics, 1980, 1983, and 1987, 17206–2.22
- Insurance (health) coverage and provisions of small business employee benefit plans, by plan type and occupational group, 1990, biennial rpt, 6784–20
- Insurance (health) for long-term care, affordability and State regulation issues, 1986-90, hearing, 21368–130
- Kidney end-stage disease treatment access and quality of care indicators, impacts of Medicare payment reductions, 1980s, 4658–44
- Kidney end-stage disease treatment facilities, Medicare enrollment and reimbursement, survival, and patient characteristics, 1983-89, annual rpt, 4654–16
- Long-term care institutional and community services, spending and use by type and payment source, FY88, and Medicaid growth since FY75, 26306–6.156
- Medicaid beneficiaries services use and costs, by service type and eligibility, 1975-89, article, 4652–1.209
- Medicare and Medicaid beneficiaries and program operations, 1991, annual fact book, 4654–18
- Medicare and Medicaid eligibility, participation, coverage, and program finances, various periods 1966-91, biennial rpt, 4654–1
- Medicare and Medicaid enrollees, benefits, reimbursements, and services use, mid-1960s-89, annual rpt, 4744–3.5; 4744–3.6
- Medicare approval of home health care visits, planned and actual visits by service type, 1986, article, 4652–1.254
- Medicare beneficiaries home health care services use and costs, by agency and service type, patient characteristics, and State, 1988-89, article, 4652–1.229
- Medicare beneficiaries hospitalization length of stay and discharge destination related to insurance status and Medicaid nursing home reimbursement method, 1985, article, 4652–1.225
- Medicare claim filings for home health services under prior and concurrent authorization, demonstration project results, 1987, 4658–57

Medicare claims approved, charges, and reimbursements by type of service, from 1974, monthly rpt, quarterly data, 4742–1.11

- Medicare hospital use reduction demonstration providing nursing home and other long term care services, results for Rochester, NY, 1980s, 4658–43
- Medicare payment limits on home health services, impacts of alternative determination methods on agencies finances, with data by service type, 1984-89, GAO rpt, 26121–400
- Medicare reimbursement of hospitals under prospective payment system, and effect on services, finances, and beneficiary payments, 1979-90, annual rpt, 17204–2
- Medicare reimbursement of hospitals under prospective payment system, impacts on instns and beneficiaries, 1988, annual rpt, 4654–13
- Older persons health care services use, by service type, discharge destination, and prior care source, 1986, 4188–72
- Older persons long-term care needs and costs, late 1980s and projected 2018-60, GAO rpt, 26121–433
- Older persons with functional limitations, long-term care sources, and health and other characteristics, 1984-85, 4147–13.104
- Service industries census, 1987: establishments, receipts by source, payroll, and employment, by SIC 2- to 4-digit kind of business, State, and MSA, 2393–4
- Veterans disability and death compensation cases of VA, by entitlement type, period of service, sex, age, and State, FY89, annual rpt, 8604–7
- Veterans health care, patients, visits, costs, and operating beds, by VA and contract facility, and region, quarterly rpt, 8602–4

see also Respite care

Home Mortgage Disclosure Act

Lending activity rpts filed under Act, and instns covered, 1981-90, article, 9362–1.206

Home ownership

see Housing sales

see Housing tenure

Home video and audio equipment

- Business statistics, detailed data for major industries and economic indicators, *Survey of Current Business*, monthly rpt, 2702–1.17
- Consumer Expenditure Survey, household income by source, and itemized spending, by selected characteristics and region, 1988-89, annual rpt, 6764–5
- County Business Patterns, 1988: employment, establishments, and payroll, by SIC 2- to 4-digit industry and county, annual State rpt series, 2326–6
- County Business Patterns, 1989: employment, establishments, and payroll, by SIC 2- to 4-digit industry and county, annual State rpt series, 2326–8
- CPI by component for US city average, and by region, population size, and for 27 metro areas, monthly rpt, 6762–2
- Employment, earnings, and hours, by SIC 1- to 4-digit industry, monthly and annual averages, selected years 1909-90, annual rpt, 6744–4

Enterprise Statistics, 1987: finances and operations for companies, by size, level of diversification, form of organization, and industry group, 2329–8

Exports and imports of US, by country and detailed commodity, monthly rpt, 2422–12

Exports and imports of US, by Harmonized System 6-digit commodity and country, 1990, annual rpt, 2424–13

Exports and imports of US, by selected country, country group, and commodity group, 1990, annual rpt, 2044–37

Exports and imports of US, by transport mode, country, and SITC 1- to 3-digit commodity, 1990, annual rpt, 2424–12

Exports of US, detailed Schedule B commodities with countries of destination, 1990, annual rpt, 2424–10

Imports of US given duty-free treatment for value of US material sent abroad, by commodity and country, 1989, annual rpt, 9884–14

Injuries from use of consumer products, by severity, victim age, and detailed product, 1990, annual rpt, 9164–6

Manufacturing annual survey, 1989: value of shipments, by SIC 4- to 5-digit product class, 2506–15.2

Manufacturing census, 1987: finances and operations, by SIC 2- to 4-digit industry, State, and MSA, with trends from 1849, 2497–1

Manufacturing census, 1987: finances and operations, by type of organization and SIC 2- to 4-digit industry, subject rpt, 2497–5

Manufacturing finances and operations, by SIC 2- to 4-digit industry, forecast 1991, annual rpt, 2044–28

OECD trade, total and for 4 major countries, and US trade by country, by commodity, 1970-89, world area rpt series, 9116–1

Price indexes (producer), by stage of processing and detailed commodity, monthly rpt, 6762–6

Price indexes (producer), by stage of processing and detailed commodity, monthly 1990, annual rpt, 6764–2

Retail trade census, 1987: depreciable assets, capital and operating expenses, sales, value added, and inventories, by SIC 2- to 4-digit kind of business, 2399–2

Retail trade census, 1987: finances and employment, for establishments with and without payroll, by SIC 2- to 4-digit kind of business, State, and MSA, 2401–1

Retail trade sales and inventories, by kind of business, region, and selected State, MSA, and city, monthly rpt, 2413–3

Retail trade sales, inventories, purchases, gross margin, and accounts receivable, by SIC 2- to 4-digit kind of business and form of ownership, 1989, annual rpt, 2413–5

Shipments, trade, use, and firms, for consumer electronics by product, 1990, annual Current Industrial Rpt, 2506–12.20

Shipments, trade, use, and firms, for electronic communications systems and related products, 1990, annual Current Industrial Rpt, 2506–12.35

see also Video recordings and equipment

Homeless population

Alcohol abuse among homeless persons, by sex, age, race, and additional diagnoses, aggregate 1985-87, 4488–14

Assistance (financial and nonfinancial) of Fed Govt, 1991 base edition with supplements, annual listing, 104–5

Assistance for homeless of Fed Govt, program descriptions and funding, by agency and State, FY90, annual GAO rpt, 26104–21

Assistance for homeless persons, Federal housing and food programs funding and operations, FY89, hearing, 25408–111

Assistance programs under Ways and Means Committee jurisdiction, finances, operations, and participant characteristics, FY70s-90, annual rpt, 21784–11

Budget of US, House Budget Committee analysis of Bush Admin proposals and economic assumptions, FY92, 21268–42

Census of Population, 1990: homeless shelter and on-street population, by State and for 200 cities, press release, 2328–70

Education services for homeless adults, funding, participation, and staff, by State, 1989, annual rpt series, 4804–39

Educational projects, activities, and funding for homeless children, FY90, annual rpt, 4804–35

Employment and training services for homeless, demonstration project results, FY88, 6406–10.5

Fed Govt surplus property donated to homeless aid organizations by State, and compared to other recipients, FY87-90, GAO rpt, 26113–538

Foreign countries disasters, casualties, damage, and aid by US and others, FY90 and trends from FY64, annual rpt, 9914–12

HHS financial aid, by program, recipient, State, and city, FY90, annual regional listings, 4004–3

Mental illness and drug and alcohol abuse direct and indirect costs, by age and sex, 1985, 4048–35

Michigan homeless persons social services spending and client characteristics, and youth programs cases, 1980s, hearing, 25418–5

Population at risk of homelessness, contributing factors, and Federal funding for services and prevention, with bibl, 1991 compilation of papers, 25928–9

Teenage homeless girls pregnancy prevalence and outcomes, services availability, health condition, and drug abuse, 1989 conf, 4108–55

Veterans (homeless) domiciliary program of VA, participant characteristics and outcomes, 1990 annual rpt, 8604–10

Veterans (homeless) with mental illness, VA program services, costs, staff, client characteristics, and outcome, 1990, annual rpt, 8604–11

Youth (homeless and runaway) programs, funding, activities, and participant characteristics, FY90, annual rpt, 4604–3

Youths entering runaway and homeless centers, by selected characteristics, data compilation, 1991 annual rpt, 6064–6.6

Homemaker services

Employment, earnings, and hours, by SIC 1- to 4-digit industry, monthly and annual averages, selected years 1909-90, annual rpt, 6744–4

Hospices operations, services, costs, and patient characteristics, for instns without Medicare certification, FY85-86, 4658–52

Older persons with functional limitations, long-term care sources, and health and other characteristics, 1984-85, 4147–13.104

Homeowner's insurance

see Property and casualty insurance

Homesteads

Public lands acreage and grants, by State, FY90 and trends, annual rpt, 5724–1.1

Urban Homesteading Program properties, units, and rehabilitation costs by financing source, FY90, annual rpt, 5124–7

Homicide

Arrest rates, by offense, sex, age, and race, 1965-89, annual rpt, 6224–7

Arrests, prosecutions, convictions, and sentencing, for felony offenders, by offender characteristics and offense, 1988, 6066–25.33; 6066–25.39

Child accident deaths and death rates, by cause, age, sex, race, and State, 1980-85, 4108–54

Child accident deaths and injuries by cause, and victimization, rates by race, sex, and age, 1979-88, chartbook, 4108–56

Cocaine abuse, user characteristics, and related crime and violence, 1988 conf, 4498–74

Court civil and criminal caseloads for Federal district, appeals, and bankruptcy courts, by type of suit and offense, circuit, and district, 1990, annual rpt, 18204–11

Court civil and criminal caseloads for Federal district, appeals, and special courts, 1990, annual rpt, 18204–8

Court civil and criminal caseloads for Federal district courts, 1991, annual rpt, 18204–2.1

Court criminal case processing in Federal district courts, and dispositions, by offense, district, and offender characteristics, 1986, annual rpt, 6064–29

Court criminal case processing in Federal district courts, and dispositions, by offense, 1980-89, annual rpt, 6064–31

Court criminal cases in Federal district courts, by offense, disposition, and district, 1980-90, last issue of annual rpt, 18204–1

Crime, criminal justice admin and enforcement, and public opinion, data compilation, 1991 annual rpt, 6064–6

Crime Index by population size and region, and offenses by large city, Jan-June 1991, semiannual rpt, 6222–1

Crimes, arrests by offender characteristics, and rates, by offense, and law enforcement employees, by population size and jurisdiction, 1990, annual rpt, 6224–2

Deaths and rates, by cause and age, preliminary 1989-90, US Vital Statistics annual rpt, 4144–7

Deaths and rates, by cause, provisional data, monthly rpt, 4142–1.2

Homicide

Deaths and rates, by detailed cause and demographic characteristics, 1988 and trends from 1900, US Vital Statistics annual rpt, 4144–2

Deaths by cause, age, race, and sex, 1950s-89, annual rpt, 4144–11

Drug abuse history of jail population, by offense, conviction status, criminal and family history, and selected other characteristics, 1989, 6066–19.63

Drug test results at arrest, by drug type, offense, and sex, for selected urban areas, quarterly rpt, 6062–3

Executions of prisoners, by offense and race, 1930-89, annual rpt, 6064–26.6

Executions since 1930, and prisoners under death sentence by prison control and prisoner characteristics, by State, 1973-90, annual rpt, 6066–25.42

Firearm purchasers criminal records checks, and firearms use in crime, with data by State, 1987-90, 26358–244

Firearms-related deaths and death rates, by motive, age, sex, and race, for persons aged 1-34, 1979-88, 4146–5.119

Indian Health Service facilities and use, and Indian health and other characteristics, by IHS region, 1980s-89, annual chartbook, 4084–7

Indian Health Service facilities, funding, operations, and Indian health and other characteristics, 1950s-90, annual chartbook, 4084–1

Jail population, by criminal, correctional, drug use, and family history, and selected other characteristics, 1989, 6066–19.62

Jail population, by sociodemographic characteristics, criminal and drug use history, whether convicted, offense, and sentencing, 1989, annual rpt, 6064–26.3

Juvenile courts delinquency cases, by offense, referral source, disposition, age, sex, race, State, and county, 1988, annual rpt, 6064–12

Military deaths by cause, age, race, and rank, and personnel captured and missing, by service branch, FY90, annual rpt, 3544–40

Minority group health condition, services use, costs, and indicators of services need, 1950s-88, 4118–55

Pretrial processing, detention, and release, for Federal offenders, by defendant characteristics and district, 1988, hearing, 25528–114

Preventive disease and health improvement goals and recommended activities for 2000, with trends 1970s-80s, 4048–10

Prison and parole admissions and releases, sentence length, and time served, by offense and offender characteristics, 1985, annual rpt, 6064–33

Prisoners in Federal and State instns, deaths by cause, sex, and State, 1989, annual rpt, 6064–26.4

Prisoners in jails, deaths by cause, by county and facility, 1988, regional rpt series, 6068–144

Probation and split sentences by State courts for felony offenses, sentence lengths, case processing time, and felon characteristics, by offense, 1986, 6068–242

Sentences for Federal crimes, guidelines use and results by offense and district, and Sentencing Commission activities, 1990, annual rpt, 17664–1

Sentences for Federal offenses, guidelines by offense and circumstances, series, 17668–1

State and Metro Area Data Book, 1991 data compilation, 2328–54

Statistical Abstract of US, 1991 annual data compilation, 2324–1.5

Teenagers crime victimization, by victim and offender characteristics, circumstances, and offense, 1985-88 surveys, 6066–3.43

Terrorism (intl) incidents, casualties, and attacks on US targets, by attack type and country, 1990, annual rpt, 7004–22

Terrorism (intl) incidents, casualties, and attacks on US targets, by attack type and world area, 1990, annual rpt, 7004–13

Victimizations by violent crime, circumstances, victim characteristics, arrest, recidivism, sentences, and prisoners, 1980s, 6068–148

Wiretaps authorized, costs, arrests, trials, and convictions, by offense and jurisdiction, 1990, annual rpt, 18204–7

Women prisoners in State instns, by offense, drug use history, whether abused, and other characteristics, 1986, 6066–19.61

see also Assaults on police

Homosexuality

AIDS and AIDS virus infection patients service use and costs under Medicaid, 1991, article, 4652–1.215

AIDS cases among drug abusers, by drug use, sexual behavior, and other characteristics, 1984-88 local area study, article, 4042–3.206

AIDS cases and deaths, by whether intravenous drug user and sexual orientation, for selected metro areas, 1991 semiannual conf, 4492–5

AIDS cases at VA health care centers by sex, race, risk factor, and facility, and AIDS prevention and treatment issues, quarterly rpt, 8702–1

AIDS cases by race, sex, and risk category, and deaths and survivors, projected 1989-93, 4206–2.34

AIDS cases by risk group, race, sex, age, State, and MSA, and deaths, monthly rpt, 4202–9

AIDS patient home and community services under Medicaid waiver in 6 States, 1988-89, article, 4652–1.216

AIDS virus infection and risk factor prevalence, natl survey methodology and pretest results, 1989, 4148–30

Genital human papillomavirus risk relation to presence of other cervical cancer risk factors, local area study, 1991 article, 4472–1.215

Hepatitis cases by infection source, age, sex, race, and State, and deaths, by strain, 1988 and trends from 1966, 4205–2

Public opinion on homosexual relations legality, by respondent characteristics, data compilation, 1991 annual rpt, 6064–6.2

Honduras

Agricultural exports of high-value commodities, indexes and sales by commodity, world area, and country, 1960s-86, 1528–323

Agricultural exports of US, impacts of foreign agricultural and trade policy, with data by commodity and country, 1989, annual rpt, 1924–8

Index by Subjects and Names

Agricultural production, trade, and policies in foreign countries, summary data by country, 1989-90, annual factbook, 1924–12

Agricultural trade of US, by detailed commodity and country, 1989, annual rpt, 1524–8

Agricultural trade of US, by detailed commodity and country, 1990, semiannual rpt, 1522–4

AID economic aid to developing countries, obligations and disbursements by country, quarterly rpt, 9912–4

AID loans repayment status and terms by program and country, and status of predecessor agency loans, quarterly rpt, 9912–3

Economic and military aid and loans from US and intl agencies, by program and country, FY46-90, annual rpt, 9914–5

Economic and social conditions of developing countries from 1960s, and Intl Dev Cooperation Agency and AID activities and funding, FY90-92, annual rpt, 9904–4

Economic conditions, policy, and trade practices, by country, 1988-90, annual rpt, 21384–5

Economic, social, political, and geographic summary data, by country, 1991, annual factbook, 9114–2

Exports and imports of US, by commodity and country, 1970-89, world area rpt, 9116–1.2

Exports and imports of US, by selected country, country group, and commodity group, 1990, annual rpt, 2044–37

Exports and imports of US, by transport mode, country, and SITC 1- to 3-digit commodity, 1990, annual rpt, 2424–12

Exports of US, detailed Schedule B commodities with countries of destination, 1990, annual rpt, 2424–10

Human rights conditions in 170 countries, and US economic and military aid, 1990, annual rpt, 21384–3

Investment (direct) incentives of Caribbean Basin Initiative, economic impacts, with finances and employment by country, 1984-90, 2048–141

Labor conditions, union coverage, and work accidents, 1991 annual country rpt, 6366–4.14

Military aid of US, arms sales, and training programs costs and budget requests, by program, world region, and country, FY90-92, annual rpt, 7144–13

Multinatl US firms and foreign affiliates finances and operations, by industry and world area of parent firm, 1989 benchmark survey, preliminary annual rpt, 2704–5

Multinatl US firms foreign affiliates, income statement items by country and world area, 1986, biennial article, 8302–2.212

UN voting record and share of votes in agreement with US, by issue, country, and world area, 1990, annual rpt, 7004–18

see also under By Foreign Country in the "Index by Categories"

Honey and beekeeping

Acreage under Agricultural Stabilization and Conservation Service programs, rankings by commodity and congressional district, 1989, biennial rpt, 1804–17

Agricultural Statistics, 1990, annual rpt, 1004–1

Agriculture census, 1987: farms, farmland, production, finances, and operator characteristics, by county, final State rpt series, 2331–1

CCC certificate exchange activity, by commodity, biweekly press release, 1802–16

Exports and imports (agricultural) of US, by detailed commodity and country, 1990, semiannual rpt, 1522–4

Exports and imports of US, by country and detailed commodity, monthly rpt, 2422–12

Exports and imports of US, by Harmonized System 6-digit commodity and country, 1990, annual rpt, 2424–13

Exports of US, detailed Schedule B commodities with countries of destination, 1990, annual rpt, 2424–10

Farm sector balance sheet, and receipts by detailed commodity, by State, 1985-89, annual rpt, 1544–18

Foreign and US production, prices, trade, and use, FAS periodic circular series, 1925–14

Imports of honey, quarterly situation rpt, 1561–14.2

Price support program provisions, for selected commodities, 1961-90, 1568–303

Production, prices, and stocks of honey, and bee colonies, by State, 1989-90, annual rpt, 1631–6

Production, prices, trade, stocks, and marketing of honey, and CCC loan and distribution activities, monthly rpt, 1311–2

Hong Kong

Agricultural exports of high-value commodities, indexes and sales by commodity, world area, and country, 1960s-86, 1528–323

Agricultural exports of US, impacts of foreign agricultural and trade policy, with data by commodity and country, 1989, annual rpt, 1924–8

Agricultural production, prices, and trade, by country, 1980s and forecast 1991, annual world region rpt, 1524–4.5

Agricultural production, trade, and policies in foreign countries, summary data by country, 1989-90, annual factbook, 1924–12

Agricultural trade of US, by detailed commodity and country, 1989, annual rpt, 1524–8

Agricultural trade of US, by detailed commodity and country, 1990, semiannual rpt, 1522–4

Apple import demand in 4 countries, 1960s-83, 1568–296

Bearings (ball) from 14 countries, injury to US industry from foreign subsidized and less than fair value imports, investigation with background financial and operating data, 1991 rpt, 9886–19.74

China trade with US and through Hong Kong, and impacts of revoking most favored nation status, 1987-90, hearing, 25368–174

Economic and military aid and loans from US and intl agencies, by program and country, FY46-90, annual rpt, 9914–5

Economic conditions, income, production, prices, employment, and trade, 1991 periodic country rpt, 2046–4.37

Economic conditions, policy, and trade practices, by country, 1988-90, annual rpt, 21384–5

Economic, social, political, and geographic summary data, by country, 1991, annual factbook, 9114–2

Export and import balances of US, and dollar exchange rates, with 5 Asian countries, 1991 semiannual rpt, 8002–14

Exports and imports of US, by commodity and country, 1970-89, world area rpt, 9116–1.7

Exports and imports of US, by Harmonized System 6-digit commodity and country, 1990, annual rpt, 2424–13

Exports and imports of US, by selected country, country group, and commodity group, 1990, annual rpt, 2044–37

Exports and imports of US, by transport mode, country, and SITC 1- to 3-digit commodity, 1990, annual rpt, 2424–12

Exports of US, detailed Schedule B commodities with countries of destination, 1990, annual rpt, 2424–10

Fruit and vegetable exports of US to Hong Kong, by commodity, 1986-90, article, 1925–34.224

Human rights conditions in 170 countries, and US economic and military aid, 1990, annual rpt, 21384–3

Labor conditions and work accidents, 1990 annual country rpt, 6366–4.4

Multinatl US firms and foreign affiliates finances and operations, by industry and world area of parent firm, 1989 benchmark survey, preliminary annual rpt, 2704–5

Multinatl US firms foreign affiliates, income statement items by country and world area, 1986, biennial article, 8302–2.212

Older persons health condition and care research, data availability and collection methodology, for US and selected countries, 1988 conf, 4147–5.6

Oranges (fresh) exports of US, demand indicators for 4 countries, with production, trade, and use, 1960s-90, 1528–317

Ships freight rates for lumber from Alaska and Puget Sound to Asian markets, by product and port, 1988, 1208–358

Tobacco and cigarette production, use, and trade, for Hong Kong, 1980-91, article, 1925–16.210

Honolulu, Hawaii

CPI by component for US city average, and by region, population size, and for 27 metro areas, monthly rpt, 6762–2

Drug abuse indicators for selected metro areas, research results, data collection, and policy issues, 1991 semiannual conf, 4492–5

see also under By City and By SMSA or MSA in the "Index by Categories"

Hoos, Anne B.

"Effects of Storm-Water Runoff on Local Ground-Water Quality, Clarksville, Tenn.", 5666–27.23

Hopkinsville, Ky.

see also under By SMSA or MSA in the "Index by Categories"

Hoppe, Robert A.

"Role of the Elderly's Income in Rural Development", 1598–268

Hops

Agricultural Statistics, 1990, annual rpt, 1004–1

Agriculture census, 1987: farms, farmland, production, finances, and operator characteristics, by county, final State rpt series, 2331–1

Beer production, stocks, material used, tax-free removals, and taxable removals by State, monthly rpt, 8486–1.1

Exports and imports (agricultural) of US, by commodity and country, bimonthly rpt, 1522–1

Exports and imports (agricultural) of US, by detailed commodity and country, 1989, annual rpt, 1524–8

Exports and imports (agricultural) of US, by detailed commodity and country, 1990, semiannual rpt, 1522–4

Exports and imports of US, by Harmonized System 6-digit commodity and country, 1990, annual rpt, 2424–13

Exports of US, detailed Schedule B commodities with countries of destination, 1990, annual rpt, 2424–10

Farm income, expenses, receipts by commodity, assets, liabilities, and ratios, 1990 and trends from 1945, annual rpt, 1544–16

Farm sector balance sheet, and receipts by detailed commodity, by State, 1985-89, annual rpt, 1544–18

Foreign and US fresh and processed fruit, vegetable, and nut production and trade, FAS monthly circular with articles, 1925–34

Prices received and paid by farmers, by commodity and State, 1990, annual rpt, 1629–5

Prices received by farmers and production value, by detailed crop and State, 1988-90, annual rpt, 1621–2

Production, farms, acreage, and related data, by selected crop and State, monthly rpt, 1621–1

Production, stocks, and use of hops, and US trade by country, monthly rpt, 1313–7

Stocks held by growers, dealers, and brewers, 1989-91, semiannual press release, 1621–8

Hordinsky, J. R.

"Response Capability During Civil Air Carrier Inflight Medical Emergencies", 7506–10.82

"Utilization of Emergency Medical Kits by Air Carriers", 7506–10.81

Horgan, Constance

"Study To Evaluate the Use of Mail Service Pharmacies", 4658–60

Hormones

Bovine somatotropin (bST) use impacts on dairy farm finances and Federal support programs, 1980s and projected to 1998, 26358–237

Cancer (breast) precursor hormonal changes risk relation to selected reproductive factors, 1983-89 study, article, 4472–1.227

Cancer (hepatocellular) risk relation to hepatitis infection, race, smoking, drinking, and oral contraceptives and estrogen use, 1984-90 local area study, article, 4472–1.237

Hormones

Cancer treatments using chemotherapy drugs for indications not listed on drug label, costs, and insurance reimbursement problems, 1990 physicians survey, GAO rpt, 26131–81

Exports and imports of US, by country and detailed commodity, monthly rpt, 2422–12

Exports and imports of US, by Harmonized System 6-digit commodity and country, 1990, annual rpt, 2424–13

Insulin infusion pumps for continuous therapy, risks and benefit evaluation for Medicare coverage, 1991 rpt, 4186–10.4

Prescriptions for drugs, by drug type and brand, and for new drugs, 1989, annual rpt, 4064–12

Research on population and reproduction, Federal funding by project, FY89, annual listing, 4474–9

Shipments, trade, and use of drugs, by product, 1990, annual Current Industrial Rpt, 2506–8.5

Steroids use and attitudes of youth, by selected characteristics, 1975-90 surveys, annual rpt, 4494–4

Steroids use and health effects, 1989 conf papers, 4498–67

see also Metabolic and endocrine diseases

Horner, Rita A.

"Bering Sea Phytoplankton Studies", 2176–1.37

Horowitz, Richard

"NSSDC Data Listing", 9504–10

Horse racing

County Business Patterns, 1988: employment, establishments, and payroll, by SIC 2- to 4-digit industry and county, annual State rpt series, 2326–6

County Business Patterns, 1989: employment, establishments, and payroll, by SIC 2- to 4-digit industry and county, annual State rpt series, 2326–8

Puerto Rico economic censuses, 1987: wholesale and retail trade and service industry finances and operations, by SIC 2- to 4-digit industry and municipio, 2591–1

Service industries census, 1987: establishments, receipts by source, payroll, and employment, by SIC 2- to 4-digit kind of business, State, and MSA, 2393–4

Horses

see Horse racing

see Livestock and livestock industry

Horticulture

Census of Agriculture, 1987: horticultural specialties producers, finances, and operations, by crop and State, 1988 survey, 2337–1

see also Flowers and nursery products

Horton, Howard F.

"Dover and Rock Soles. Species Profiles: Life Histories and Environmental Requirements of Coastal Fishes and Invertebrates (Pacific Northwest)", 5506–8.130

Hosiery

see Clothing and clothing industry

Hosker, Ralph L.

"Status of the State-Federal Tuberculosis Eradication Program, FY89", 1394–13.2

Hoskin, Roger L.

"Canola: Prospects for an Emerging Market", 1561–3.203

"Oilseed Outlook", 1004–16.1

Hospices

Cancer patients hospices use, by service type, use of other facilities, patient and instn characteristics, and other indicators, local area study, 1980-85, 4658–53

Hospital deaths of Medicare patients, actual and expected rates by diagnosis, with hospital characteristics, by instn, FY87-89, annual regional rpt series, 4654–14

Hospital services and facilities availability, by selected instn characteristics, 1980, 1983, and 1987, 17206–2.22

Insurance (health) coverage and provisions of small business employee benefit plans, by plan type and occupational group, 1990, biennial rpt, 6784–20

Medicare and Medicaid beneficiaries and program operations, 1991, annual fact book, 4654–18

Minority group health condition, services use, costs, and indicators of services need, 1950s-88, 4118–55

Operations, services, costs, and patient characteristics, for hospices without Medicare certification, FY85-86, 4658–52

Hospital administration and staff

see Health facilities administration

Hospital Cost and Clinical Research Project

Costs and use of hospitals, data compilation project analyses, series, 4186–6

Hospital Cost and Utilization Project

Costs and use of hospitals, data compilation project analyses, series, 4186–6

Hospital insurance

see Health insurance

see Medicare

Hospitalization

Acute and chronic health conditions, disability, absenteeism, and health services use, by selected characteristics, 1987, CD-ROM, 4147–10.177

AIDS and AIDS virus infection patients service use and costs under Medicaid, 1991, article, 4652–1.215

AIDS patient hospital use and charges, by hospital and patient characteristics, and payment source, 1986-87, 4186–6.15

Births and rates, by characteristics of birth, infant, and parents, 1989 and trends from 1940, US Vital Statistics advance annual rpt, 4146–5.123

Child health condition and services use, 1990 chartbook, 4108–49

Consumer products use, injuries by severity, victim age, and detailed product, 1990, annual rpt, 9164–6

Cost control through hospital revenue and reimbursement caps, demonstration project results with background data, 1980s, 4658–48

Costs of hospitalization relation to services timing, by selected patient and hospital characteristics, for Medicare discharges, 1987-88, 17208–2

Crime victimization rates, by victim and offender characteristics, circumstances, and offense, 1988 survey, annual rpt, 6066–3.42

Crime victimization rates, by victim and offender characteristics, circumstances, and offense, 1989 survey, annual rpt, 6066–3.44

Index by Subjects and Names

Deaths in health facilities, by cause, age, and sex, 1988, US Vital Statistics annual rpt, 4144–2.1

Deaths of Medicare patients, actual and expected rates by diagnosis, with hospital characteristics, by instn, FY87-89, annual regional rpt series, 4654–14

Diabetes and complications cases, deaths, and hospitalization, by age, sex, race, State, and region, 1980-86, annual rpt, 4205–41

Disabled persons and related activity limitation days and health services use, by health status, disability type, and other characteristics, 1984-88, 4146–8.202

Discharges and length of stay, by diagnosis, patient and instn characteristics, procedure performed, and payment source, 1988, annual rpt, 4147–13.107

Discharges and length of stay by region and diagnosis, and procedures performed, by age and sex, 1989, annual rpt, 4146–8.198

Drug abuse indicators for selected metro areas, research results, data collection, and policy issues, 1991 semiannual conf, 4492–5

Drug abuse prevalence among minorities, related health effects and crime, treatment, and research status and needs, mid 1970s-90, 4498–72

Drug and alcohol abuse treatment and prevention programs of States, funding, facilities, and patient characteristics, FY89, 4488–15

Drug and alcohol abuse treatment facilities, services, use, funding, staff, and client characteristics, 1989, biennial rpt, 4494–10

Expenditures for health care by type and payment source, with background data and foreign comparisons, 1960s-80s and projected to 2000, 26308–98

Fetal deaths and rates, by characteristics of mother and birth, 1988, US Vital Statistics annual rpt, 4144–2.3

Health Care Financing Review, provider prices, price inputs and indexes, and labor, quarterly journal, 4652–1.1

Health condition and health care resources, use, and spending, 1950s-89, annual data compilation, 4144–11

Health maintenance organizations and other prepaid managed care plans Medicaid enrollment and use, for 20 States, 1985-89, chartbook, 4108–29

Health maintenance organizations financial performance, and hospital use, demonstration project results, 1985-88, article, 4652–1.202

Heart and lung patients nonsurgical procedures hospital charges and length of stay, for Maryland, FY84, article, 4652–1.204

Hepatitis cases by infection source, age, sex, race, and State, and deaths, by strain, 1988 and trends from 1966, 4205–2

Hospices use by cancer patients, by service type, use of other facilities, patient and instn characteristics, and other indicators, local area study, 1980-85, 4658–53

Indian and Alaska Native disease and disorder cases, deaths, and health services use, by tribe, reservation, and Indian Health Service area, late 1950s-86, 4088–2

Index by Subjects and Names

Hospitals

Indian Health Service and tribal hospital admissions, length of stay, beds, and births, by facility and service area, FY70-89, annual rpt, 4084–4

Indian Health Service and tribal hospital capacity, use, and births, by area and facility, quarterly rpt, 4082–1

Indian Health Service facilities and use, and Indian health and other.characteristics, by IHS region, 1980s-89, annual chartbook, 4084–7

Indian Health Service facilities, funding, operations, and Indian health and other characteristics, 1950s-90, annual chartbook, 4084–1

Indian Health Service, tribal, and contract facilities hospitalization, by diagnosis, age, sex, and service area, FY89, annual rpt, 4084–5

Insurance (health) coverage and provisions of small business employee benefit plans, by plan type and occupational group, 1990, biennial rpt, 6784–20

Insurance (health) coverage status relation to physician services use and hospitalization, 1984, working paper, 2626–10.120

Kidney end-stage disease cases, treatment, outcomes, and characteristics of patients, organ donors, and facilities, late 1970s-88, annual rpt, 4474–37

Kidney end-stage disease treatment access and quality of care indicators, impacts of Medicare payment reductions, 1980s, 4658–44

Kidney end-stage disease treatment facilities, Medicare enrollment and reimbursement, survival, and patient characteristics, 1983-89, annual rpt, 4654–16

Kidney transplants, needs, costs, payment sources, and impact of immunosuppressive drugs on outcome, 1950s-87 and projected to 1995, 4658–59

Medicaid beneficiaries services use and costs, by service type and eligibility, 1975-89, article, 4652–1.209

Medicaid coverage loss impacts on health services use, California transfer of selected Medicaid groups to county care, 1991 article, 4652–1.242

Medicaid hospital discharges, by eligibility and instn characteristics, for 2 States, 1984, article, 4652–1.249

Medicare and Medicaid beneficiaries and program operations, 1991, annual fact book, 4654–18

Medicare and Medicaid eligibility, participation, coverage, and program finances, various periods 1966-91, biennial rpt, 4654–1

Medicare and Medicaid enrollees, benefits, reimbursements, and services use, mid-1960s-89, annual rpt, 4744–3.5; 4744–3.6

Medicare beneficiaries hospital discharges, length of stay, and costs, by type of beneficiary and location, 1972-88, article, 4652–1.207

Medicare beneficiaries hospitalization length of stay and discharge destination related to insurance status and Medicaid nursing home reimbursement method, 1985, article, 4652–1.225

Medicare beneficiaries post-hospital service use, by type, for pneumonia, stroke, and hip replacement cases, 1981-86, article, 4652–1.223

Medicare claims approved, charges, and reimbursements by type of service, from 1974, monthly rpt, quarterly data, 4742–1.11

Medicare hospital discharges, length of stay, weights, and payments, by diagnosis, 1983-88, article, 4652–1.250

Medicare reimbursement of hospitals under prospective payment system, and effect on services, finances, and beneficiary payments, 1979-90, annual rpt, 17204–2

Medicare reimbursement of hospitals under prospective payment system, diagnosis related group code assignment and effects on care and instn finances, 1984/85, series, 4006–7

Medicare reimbursement of hospitals under prospective payment system for discharge delays due to limited nursing home space, 1985, 4658–55

Medicare reimbursement of hospitals under prospective payment system, impacts on costs, industry structure and operations, and quality of care, series, 17206–2

Medicare reimbursement of hospitals under prospective payment system, impacts on instns and beneficiaries, 1988, annual rpt, 4654–13

Mental health care facilities of States and counties, patients and admissions by age, diagnosis, and State, FY89, annual rpt, 4504–2

Mental health care facilities, staff, and patient characteristics, *Statistical Notes* series, 4506–3

Mental health care facilities, staff, service, and patient characteristics, series, 4506–4

Mental illness and drug and alcohol abuse direct and indirect costs, by age and sex, 1985, 4048–35

Military health care facilities of DOD in US and abroad, admissions, beds, outpatient visits, and births, by service branch, quarterly rpt, 3542–15

Minority group and women health condition, services use, payment sources, and health care labor force, by poverty status, 1940s-89, chartbook, 4118–56

Minority group health condition, services use, costs, and indicators of services need, 1950s-88, 4118–55

Montana health care access indicators, 1989 hearing, 23898–6

NIH activities, funding by program and recipient type, staff, and clinic patients, by inst, FY90, annual rpt, 4434–3

Nursing home admissions of Medicare patients, factors affecting change, 1983-85, article, 4652–1.222

Nursing home and other long term care services under Medicare hospital use reduction demonstration, results for Rochester, NY, 1980s, 4658–43

Nursing home residents length of stay, effects of data adjustment to reflect short-term hospital stays, model results, 1987, 4186–8.15

Occupational injuries, by circumstances, body site, equipment type, and industry, with safety measures, series, 6846–1

Older persons health care services use, by service type, discharge destination, and prior care source, 1986, 4188–72

Older persons hospital discharges and rates, for Medicare beneficiaries by diagnosis, age, sex, and race, 1988, article, 4202–7.205

Older persons with functional limitations, long-term care sources, and health and other characteristics, 1984-85, 4147–13.104

Physicians consultations requested by attending physician, Medicare reimbursement issues, with use by diagnosis, specialty, location, and other characteristics, 1986, 4658–47

State and Metro Area Data Book, 1991 data compilation, 2328–54

Statistical Abstract of US, 1991 annual data compilation, 2324–1.3

Use and costs of hospitals, data compilation project analyses, series, 4186–6

Use of hospitals by uninsured persons as percent of insured persons use, 1977-86 surveys, article, 4652–1.220

VA activities and programs, and veterans characteristics, FY90, annual rpt, 8604–3

Veterans (homeless) with mental illness, VA program services, costs, staff, client characteristics, and outcome, 1990, annual rpt, 8604–11

Veterans health care, patients, visits, costs, and operating beds, by VA and contract facility, and region, quarterly rpt, 8602–4

Vital and Health Statistics series: health care facilities use and labor force, 4147–13

Hospitalization insurance

see Health insurance

see Medicare

Hospitals

Accessibility of health care, persons with and without usual care source by selected characteristics, 1987, 4186–8.22

Adult day care centers revenue by source, and expenses by type, by agency type, FY86, article, 4652–1.234

Alcohol, Drug Abuse and Mental Health Admin research grants and awards, by recipient, FY90, annual listing, 4044–13

Allergy and Infectious Diseases Natl Inst activities, grants by recipient and location, and disease cases, FY83-90, annual rpt, 4474–30

Closings of hospitals, and rates, with financial, operating, and market characteristics, by location, late 1980s, GAO rpt, 26121–392

Construction put in place, permits, housing sales, costs, material prices, and employment, bimonthly rpt with articles, 2042–1

Construction put in place, value of new public and private structures, by type, monthly rpt, 2382–4

Cost control through hospital revenue and reimbursement caps, demonstration project results with background data, 1980s, 4658–48

Costs and use of hospitals, data compilation project analyses, series, 4186–6

County Business Patterns, 1988: employment, establishments, and payroll, by SIC 2- to 4-digit industry and county, annual State rpt series, 2326–6

County Business Patterns, 1989: employment, establishments, and payroll, by SIC 2- to 4-digit industry and county, annual State rpt series, 2326–8

CPI by component for US city average, and by region, population size, and for 27 metro areas, monthly rpt, 6762–2

Hospitals

Deaths of Medicare patients, actual and expected rates by diagnosis, with hospital characteristics, by instn, FY87-89, annual regional rpt series, 4654–14

Dental Research Natl Inst research and training grants, by recipient, FY89, annual listing, 4474–19

Employment, earnings, and hours, by SIC 1- to 4-digit industry, monthly and annual averages, selected years 1909-90, annual rpt, 6744–4

Employment in hospitals, by detailed occupation, 1989, article, 6722–1.217

Energy conservation aid of Fed Govt to public and nonprofit private instns, by building type and State, 1990, annual rpt, 3304–15

Energy use in commercial buildings, costs, and conservation, by building characteristics, survey rpt series, 3166–8

Enterprise Statistics, 1987: finances and operations for companies, by size, level of diversification, form of organization, and industry group, 2329–8

Expenditures for health care, by service type, payment source, and sector, projected 1990-2000 and trends from 1965, article, 4652–1.251

Expenditures for health care, by service type, payment source, and sector, 1960s-90, annual article, 4652–1.221; 4652–1.252

Expenditures for health care by type and payment source, with background data and foreign comparisons, 1960s-80s and projected to 2000, 26308–98

Expenditures for health care, cost containment methods, and insurance coverage issues, with background data, 1991 rpt, 26306–6.155

Fed Govt construction spending, by program and type of structure, FY85-92, annual article, 2042–1.206

Fed Govt-owned real property inventory and costs, worldwide summary by purpose, agency, and location, 1989, annual rpt, 9454–5

Germany (West) health care spending, by funding source and service type, and resource growth, 1970-89, article, 4652–1.238

Govt census, 1987: employment, payroll, and average earnings, by function, level of govt, State, county, and population size, 2455–2

Govt census, 1987: local govt employment by function, payroll, and average earnings, for individual counties, cities, and school and special districts, 2455–1

Govt census, 1987: State and local labor-mgmt policies, agreements, and coverage and bargaining units, by function, level of govt, and State, 2455–3

Govt employment and payroll, by function, level of govt, and jurisdiction, 1990, annual rpt series, 2466–1

Govt finances, by level of govt, State, and for large cities and counties, annual rpt series, 2466–2

Health Care Financing Review, provider prices, price inputs and indexes, and labor, quarterly journal, 4652–1.1

Health condition and health care resources, use, and spending, 1950s-89, annual data compilation, 4144–11

Heart and lung patients nonsurgical procedures hospital charges and length of stay, for Maryland, FY84, article, 4652–1.204

Higher education instn hospital operations, revenue and spending by State and instn control, FY80-88, annual rpt, 4844–6

Indian Health Service and tribal hospital admissions, length of stay, beds, and births, by facility and service area, FY70-89, annual rpt, 4084–4

Indian Health Service and tribal hospital capacity, use, and births, by area and facility, quarterly rpt, 4082–1

Indian Health Service facilities and use, and Indian health and other characteristics, by IHS region, 1980s-89, annual chartbook, 4084–7

Indian Health Service facilities, funding, operations, and Indian health and other characteristics, 1950s-90, annual chartbook, 4084–1

Indian Health Service outpatient visits, by facility and IHS service area, FY89-90, annual rpt, 4084–8

Inpatient case-mix specialization level related to industry structure and market characteristics, 1980-85, 4188–71

Investment spending of hospitals, relation to instn interest costs, cash flow, size, and chain membership, 1981-85, working paper, 9387–8.243

Kidney end-stage disease treatment facilities, Medicare enrollment and reimbursement, survival, and patient characteristics, 1983-89, annual rpt, 4654–16

Medicaid beneficiaries emergency room visits relation to availability of other sources of care, for upstate New York, 1985-87, article, 4652–1.232

Medicaid demonstration projects evaluation, for 6 States, 1988 rpt, 4658–45

Medicaid reimbursement of hospitals under Federal and State provisions, with services use, costs, and profits, by State, 1980s, 17206–1.11

Medicaid reimbursement of hospitals under prospective payment system, effect on maternity case-mix for South Carolina, various periods 1985-87, article, 4652–1.206

Medicaid services use and costs in alternative treatment settings, model description and results, FY87, article, 4652–1.211

Medicare and Medicaid beneficiaries and program operations, 1991, annual fact book, 4654–18

Medicare and Medicaid benefits, trust fund finances, and services use, 1966-89 and projected to 1995, 21148–61

Medicare Cost Report reviews, revisions ratio to initially reported costs, by category, FY84, article, 4652–1.233

Medicare facilities and beds, from 1967, and by State, 1989, annual rpt, 4744–3.5

Medicare hospital discharges, length of stay, weights, and payments, by diagnosis, 1983-88, article, 4652–1.250

Medicare input price index rebased to 1987, methodology and results, 1991, article, 4652–1.231

Medicare providers staffing, services available, and other characteristics, by hospital, FY87-89, annual regional rpt series, 4654–14

Index by Subjects and Names

Medicare reimbursement of hospitals under prospective payment and alternative systems, HCFA research activities and grants, FY90, annual listing, 4654–10

Medicare reimbursement of hospitals under prospective payment system, analyses of alternative payment plans, series, 17206–1

Medicare reimbursement of hospitals under prospective payment system, and effect on services, finances, and beneficiary payments, 1979-90, annual rpt, 17204–2

Medicare reimbursement of hospitals under prospective payment system, construction cost indexes evaluation, 1991 article, 4652–1.247

Medicare reimbursement of hospitals under prospective payment system, diagnosis related group code assignment and effects on care and instn finances, 1984/85, series, 4006–7

Medicare reimbursement of hospitals under prospective payment system, diagnostic group weight calibration alternative methods, FY84, article, 4652–1.227

Medicare reimbursement of hospitals under prospective payment system for discharge delays due to limited nursing home space, 1985, 4658–55

Medicare reimbursement of hospitals under prospective payment system, impacts on costs, industry structure and operations, and quality of care, series, 17206–2

Medicare reimbursement of hospitals under prospective payment system, impacts on instns and beneficiaries, 1988, annual rpt, 4654–13

Medicare reimbursement of hospitals under prospective payment system, methodology, inputs, and data by diagnostic group, 1991 annual rpt, 17204–1

NIH grants for R&D, training, construction, and medical libraries, by location and recipient, FY90, annual listings, 4434–7

Nonprofit charitable organizations finances, by asset size and State, 1987, article, 8302–2.218

Occupational injury and illness rates, by SIC 2- to 4-digit industry, 1988-89, annual rpt, 6844–7

Occupational injury and illness rates, by SIC 2- to 4-digit industry, 1989, annual rpt, 6844–1

Older persons deaths in hospitals, nursing homes, and own home, by cause, age, marital status, and region, 1986, article, 4652–1.201

Physicians, by specialty, age, sex, and location of training and practice, 1989, State rpt series, 4116–6

Physicians payments, charges by specialty and treatment setting, and assignment rate by State, for Medicare, 1970s-88, article, 4652–1.240

Pollution (air) emissions factors, by detailed pollutant and source, data compilation, 1990 rpt, 9198–120

Pollution (water) industrial releases in wastewater, levels, treatment, costs, and regulation, with background financial and operating data, 1989 industry rpt, 9206–4.3

Prospective payment system use of diagnostic related groups reflecting case severity and complexity to reduce hospital payment variation, model results, 1986, article, 4652–1.245

R&D and related funding of Fed Govt to higher education and nonprofit instns, by field, instn, agency, and State, FY89, annual rpt, 9627–17.1

R&D facilities for biological and medical sciences, space and equipment adequacy, needs, and funding by source, by instn type, 1990, biennial rpt, 4434–17

Receipts for services, by SIC 2- to 4-digit kind of business, 1990, annual rpt, 2413–8

Rural areas hospitals closures related to selected factors, 1980s, GAO rpt, 26121–409

Rural areas hospitals financial and operating performance impacts of Medicare prospective payment reimbursement system, 1980s-87, 4658–51

Rural areas hospitals HCFA grants for improving financial stability, by program area, recipient, and State, FY89, 4658–58

Service industries census, 1987: establishments, receipts by source, payroll, and employment, by SIC 2- to 4-digit kind of business, State, and MSA, 2393–4

Services and facilities availability, by selected hospital characteristics, survey results, 1980, 1983, and 1987, 17206–2.22

State and Metro Area Data Book, 1991 data compilation, 2328–54

Statistical Abstract of US, 1991 annual data compilation, 2324–1.3

Tax (income) returns of corporations, income and tax items by asset size and detailed industry, 1987, annual rpt, 8304–4

Tax (income) returns of corporations, income and tax items by asset size and detailed industry, 1988, annual rpt, 8304–21

Tax exempt status dependent on hospital acceptance of charity, Medicare, and Medicaid cases, proposal and issues with background data, 1989, press release, 8008–149

Waste (medical) generation, sources, health worker exposure and risk, and incineration emissions, 1980s, 4078–1

Workers compensation regulation of physician fees and hospital rates, provisions by State, 1991 semiannual rpt, 6502–1

see also American Schools and Hospitals Abroad

see also Clinics

see also Emergency medical service

see also Health facilities administration

see also Health maintenance organizations

see also Hospitalization

see also Mental health facilities and services

see also Military health facilities and services

see also Nursing homes

see also Veterans health facilities and services

Hostages

Aircraft hijackings, on-board explosions, and other crime, US and foreign incidents, 1985-89, annual rpt, 7504–31

Banks robberies and related crimes by State, casualties, and hostages, data compilation, 1991 annual rpt, 6064–6.3

Terrorism (intl) incidents, casualties, and attacks on US targets, by attack type and world area, 1990, annual rpt, 7004–13

US hostages kidnapped in Lebanon, Philippines, and Colombia, listing as of 1990, annual rpt, 7004–22

Hotels and motels

American Samoa employment, earnings, and minimum wage, by establishment and industry, 1989, biennial rpt, 6504–6

Business statistics, detailed data for major industries and economic indicators, *Survey of Current Business*, monthly rpt, 2702–1.11

Census of Service Industries, 1987: hotels and other lodging places, receipts, payroll, employment, ownership, and rooms, by State and MSA, subject rpt, 2393–3

Construction industries census, 1987: establishments, employment, receipts, and expenditures, by SIC 4-digit industry and State, final industry rpt series, 2373–1

Construction put in place, and authorized by region, by type, bimonthly rpt, 2042–1.1; 2042–1.3

Construction put in place, value of new public and private structures, by type, monthly rpt, 2382–4

County Business Patterns, 1988: employment, establishments, and payroll, by SIC 2- to 4-digit industry and county, annual State rpt series, 2326–6

County Business Patterns, 1989: employment, establishments, and payroll, by SIC 2- to 4-digit industry and county, annual State rpt series, 2326–8

CPI by component for US city average, and by region, population size, and for 27 metro areas, monthly rpt, 6762–2

Employment, earnings, and hours, by SIC 1- to 4-digit industry, monthly and annual averages, selected years 1909-90, annual rpt, 6744–4

Energy use in commercial buildings, costs, and conservation, by building characteristics, survey rpt series, 3166–8

Enterprise Statistics, 1987: auxiliaries of multi-establishment firms, finances and operations by function, industry, and State, 2329–6

Enterprise Statistics, 1987: finances and operations for companies, by size, level of diversification, form of organization, and industry group, 2329–8

Food and alcoholic beverage spending, by place of purchase, 1968-90, annual rpt, 1544–4.5

Franchise business opportunities by firm and kind of business, and sources of aid and info, 1990 annual listing, 2104–7

Labor productivity, indexes of output, hours, and employment by SIC 2- to 4-digit industry, 1967-89, annual rpt, 6824–1.4

Multinatl US firms and foreign affiliates finances and operations, by industry and world area of parent firm, 1989 benchmark survey, preliminary annual rpt, 2704–5

Occupational injury and illness rates, by SIC 2- to 4-digit industry, 1988-89, annual rpt, 6844–7

Occupational injury and illness rates, by SIC 2- to 4-digit industry, 1989, annual rpt, 6844–1

Palau admin, and social, economic, and govtl data, FY90, annual rpt, 7004–6

Park natl system visits and overnight stays, by park and State, monthly rpt, 5542–4

Park natl system visits and overnight stays, by park and State, 1990, annual rpt, 5544–12

Puerto Rico economic censuses, 1987: wholesale and retail trade and service industry finances and operations, by SIC 2- to 4-digit industry and municipio, 2591–1

Puerto Rico economic censuses, 1987: wholesale, retail, and service industries finances and operations, by establishment characteristics and SIC 2- and 3-digit industry, subject rpts, 2591–2

Receipts for services, by SIC 2- to 4-digit kind of business, 1990, annual rpt, 2413–8

Savings instns failures, inventory of real estate assets available from Resolution Trust Corp, 1990, semiannual listing, 9722–2.4

Savings instns failures, inventory of real estate assets available from Resolution Trust Corp, 1991, semiannual listing, 9722–2.10

Service industries census, 1987: depreciable assets, capital and operating expenses, and receipts, by SIC 2- to 4-digit kind of business, 2393–2

Service industries census, 1987: establishments, receipts by source, payroll, and employment, by SIC 2- to 4-digit kind of business, State, and MSA, 2393–4

State and Metro Area Data Book, 1991 data compilation, 2328–54

Tax (income) returns of corporations, income and tax items by asset size and detailed industry, 1987, annual rpt, 8304–4

Tax (income) returns of corporations, income and tax items by asset size and detailed industry, 1988, annual rpt, 8304–21

Tax (income) returns of corporations with foreign tax credit, income and tax items by industry group, 1986, biennial article, 8302–2.203

Tax (income) returns of partnerships, income statement and balance sheet items, by industry group, 1989, annual article, 8302–2.216; 8304–18

Tax (income) returns of sole proprietorships, income statement items, by industry group, 1989, annual article, 8302–2.214

Travel from US, characteristics of visit and traveler, and country of destination, 1990 in-flight survey, annual rpt, 2904–14

Travel to US, by characteristics of visit and traveler, world area of origin, and US destination, 1990 survey, annual rpt, 2904–12

Hotta, S. Steven

"Reassessment of External Insulin Infusion Pumps. Health Technology Assessment Report, 1990", 4186–10.4

Houchens, Robert L.

Houchens, Robert L.
"Within DRG Case Complexity: Change Update and Distributional Differences", 17206–2.21

Houck, James P.
"Agricultural Productivity and International Food Trade: A Cross-Section Approach", 1548–372

Houma, La.
see also under By SMSA or MSA in the "Index by Categories"

Hours of labor

- Agriculture census, 1987: farms, farmland, production, finances, and operator characteristics, by county, final State rpt series, 2331–1
- Border Patrol officer hours and alien apprehension rates, by location, 1980s, 6266–2.2
- Child care arrangements, costs, and impacts on mothers labor force status, by selected characteristics, 1983 and 1988, article, 6722–1.246
- Child labor law violations and injuries by industry group, and employment of minors by selected characteristics, 1983-90, GAO rpt, 26121–426
- Coal production, labor hours, and production value, by State, EIA and alternative estimates, with methodology, 1983-88, 3166–12.6
- Construction employment, earnings, and hours, by selected SIC 2- to 3-digit industry, bimonthly rpt, 2042–1.7
- Construction industries census, 1987: establishments, employment, receipts, and expenditures, by SIC 4-digit industry and State, final industry rpt series, 2373–1
- Dallas-Fort Worth-Arlington metro area employment, earnings, hours, and CPI changes, late 1970s-90, annual rpt, 6964–2
- Economic indicators and components, current data and annual trends, monthly rpt, 23842–1.2
- *Employment and Earnings*, detailed data, monthly rpt, 6742–2.3; 6742–2.6
- Employment and unemployment current statistics, Monthly Labor Review, 6722–1.1
- Employment, unemployment, and labor force characteristics, by region and State, 1990, annual rpt, 6744–7.1; 6744–7.2
- Farm and garden equipment industry productivity measures, 1958-88, article, 6722–1.232
- Farm employment, wages, and hours, by payment method, worker type, region, and State, 1910-90, 1618–21
- Farm labor, wages, hours, and perquisites, by State, monthly rpt, 1631–1
- Farm production inputs, output, and productivity, by commodity and region, 1947-89, annual rpt, 1544–17
- Fed Govt civilian employees work-years, pay rates, and benefits use and costs, by agency, FY89, annual rpt, 9844–31
- Foreign countries labor conditions, union coverage, and work accidents, annual country rpt series, 6366–4
- *Health Care Financing Review*, provider prices, price inputs and indexes, and labor, quarterly journal, 4652–1.1
- Hours and earnings, by industry div and major manufacturing group, Monthly Labor Review, 6722–1.2

Hours, employment, and earnings, and other BLS economic indicators, transcripts of BLS Commissioner's monthly testimony, periodic rpt, 23846–4

- Hours, employment, and earnings, by SIC 1- to 4-digit industry, monthly and annual averages, selected years 1909-90, annual rpt, 6744–4
- Hours, employment, and earnings, monthly press release, 6742–5
- Hours, employment, earnings, and productivity, by industry div, selected years 1929-90, annual rpt, 204–1.2
- Hours, labor force, wages, and payroll costs, by major industry group and demographic characteristics, *Survey of Current Business*, monthly rpt, 2702–1.8
- Houston metro area employment, earnings, hours, and CPI changes, 1970s-90, annual rpt, 6964–1
- Imports and tariff provisions effect on US industries and products, investigations with background financial and operating data, series, 9886–4
- Imports injury to US industries from foreign subsidized products and sales at less than fair value, investigations with background financial and operating data, series, 9886–19
- Imports injury to US industries from foreign subsidized products, investigations with background financial and operating data, series, 9886–15
- Imports injury to US industries from sales at less than fair value, investigations with background financial and operating data, series, 9886–14
- Labor laws enacted, by State, 1990, annual article, 6722–1.209
- Manufacturing annual survey, 1989: establishments, employment, finances, inventories, and energy use, by SIC 2- to 4-digit industry, 2506–15.1
- Manufacturing annual survey, 1989: finances and operations, by SIC 2- and 3-digit industry and State, 2506–15.3
- Manufacturing census, 1987: finances and operations, by SIC 2- to 4-digit industry, State, and MSA, with trends from 1849, 2497–1
- Manufacturing census, 1987: finances and operations, by type of organization and SIC 2- to 4-digit industry, subject rpt, 2497–5
- Middle Atlantic States manufacturing business outlook, monthly survey rpt, 9387–11
- Mineral industries census, 1987: finances and operations, by establishment characteristics, SIC 2- to 4-digit industry, and State, subject rpt, 2517–1
- Mineral industries census, 1987: finances and operations, by SIC 2- to 4-digit industry, State, and county, census div rpt series, 2515–1
- Mines (coal) and related operations occupational injuries and incidence, employment, and hours, 1989, annual rpt, 6664–4
- Mines (metal) and related operations occupational injuries and incidence, employment, and hours, 1989, annual rpt, 6664–3
- Mines (nonmetallic minerals) and related operations occupational injuries and incidence, employment, and hours, 1989, annual rpt, 6664–1

Index by Subjects and Names

- Mines (sand and gravel) and related operations occupational injuries and incidence, employment, and hours, 1989, annual rpt, 6664–2
- Mines (stone) and related operations occupational injuries and incidence, employment, and hours, 1989, annual rpt, 6664–5
- Mines (underground coal) back injuries, by circumstances, victim characteristics, and treatment, mid 1980s, 5608–166
- Mines and mills injuries by circumstances, employment, and hours, by type of operation and State, quarterly rpt, 6662–1
- New England States economic indicators, Fed Reserve 1st District, monthly rpt, 9373–2.2
- Railroad employment, earnings, and hours, by occupation for Class I railroads, 1990, annual table, 9484–5
- Shift rotation health and safety effects, and US and foreign regulation, by selected industry and occupation, 1970s-89, 26356–9.3
- Single mothers earnings, employment and welfare benefits, and poverty status, 1989, GAO rpt, 26121–413
- Southeastern US manufacturing hours and earnings, for 8 States, quarterly press release, 6942–7
- Southwestern US employment by industry div, earnings, and hours, by State, monthly rpt, 6962–2
- *State and Metro Area Data Book*, 1991 data compilation, 2328–54
- *Statistical Abstract of US*, 1991 annual data compilation, 2324–1.13
- *Survey of Current Business*, detailed financial and business data, and economic indicators, monthly rpt, 2702–1.1
- Teachers in higher education instns, employment and other characteristics, by instn type and control, 1987/88 survey, 4846–4.4
- Teachers in private schools, selected characteristics by instn level, size, and orientation, various periods 1979-88, 4838–47
- Teachers in public schools, demographic and employment characteristics, 1991 annual data compilation, 4824–2.9
- Textile mill employment, earnings, and hours, for 8 Southeastern States, quarterly press release, 6942–1
- Truck accidents, casualties, and damage, by circumstances and characteristics of persons and vehicles involved, 1988, annual rpt, 7554–9
- Truck interstate carriers finances and operations, by district, 1989, annual rpt, 9486–6.2
- Unemployment insurance alternative policies impacts on employment and hours worked, with data for selected countries, 1970s, article, 9383–6.205
- Unemployment insurance job search services, impacts on UI claims activity and reemployment, and claimant characteristics, for Tacoma, Wash, 1986-87, 6406–6.35
- US attorneys work hours, by type of court and Federal district, FY90, annual rpt, 6004–2.6

Volunteer workers by organization type, time served, whether otherwise employed, and other characteristics, 1989, article, 6722–1.213

Women's labor force status, earnings, and other characteristics, with comparisons to men, fact sheet series, 6564–1

Work stoppages, workers involved, and days idle, 1990 and trends from 1947, annual press release, 6784–12

see also Absenteeism
see also Area wage surveys
see also Earnings, general
see also Earnings, local and regional
see also Earnings, specific industry
see also Industry wage surveys
see also Labor productivity
see also Moonlighting
see also Overtime
see also Part-time employment
see also Temporary and seasonal employment
see also Underemployment
see also Worksharing

House Administration Committee

Library of Congress employment by race, Hispanic origin, and sex, and affirmative action needs, 1989, hearing, 21428–9

House Aging Committee, Select

Abuse and neglect of aged by circumstances and characteristics of abuser and victim, and States protective services budgets and staff, by location, 1980s, hearing, 21148–62

Medicare and Medicaid benefits, trust fund finances, and services use, 1966-89 and projected to 1995, 21148–61

House Agriculture Committee

Export promotion and foreign food aid programs budget of USDA, with trade by commodity and country, FY85-91 and projected to FY2000, 21168–44

Food stamp use at farmers markets, costs and participation, demonstration project results for 14 States, 1989, hearing, 21168–46

Grain price support and loan programs operations of USDA, with farmers views on Federal programs, by region and State, 1990 hearings, 21168–43

Soviet Union agricultural conditions and factors affecting US grain exports and CCC credit guarantees, 1990 hearings, 21168–49

Timber industry impacts of northern spotted owl conservation in Pacific Northwest, and local govts Federal payments and severance taxes, 1980s and projected to 2000, hearing, 21168–50

Timber industry impacts of northern spotted owl conservation in Pacific Northwest, 1980s and alternative projections to 2000, hearings, 21168–45

Timber sales of Forest Service, impacts of northern spotted owl conservation in Pacific Northwest, 1990 hearing, 21168–47

House Armed Services Committee

Pay and benefits for active duty personnel, reserves, retirees, and survivors, 1940s-80s and projected to 2049, 21208–34

House Banking, Finance and Urban Affairs Committee

Banks and deposit insurance funds financial condition, potential losses, and regulatory issues, 1980s-90 and projected to 1995, 21248–147

Banks and thrifts fraud and abuse, Federal criminal enforcement activities, case dispositions, and settlements, with data by district, 1982-90, hearing, 21248–142

Earthquake preparedness costs and benefits, with data for California events and effects of 1989 Loma Prieta quake, 1980s, hearings, 21248–154

Eastern Europe foreign debt components, trade, balances, and other economic indicators, by country, 1985-89, hearing, 21248–148

Foreign-owned banks US subsidiaries, assets, and regulatory issues, with data by State and firm, 1989-90, hearing, 21248–155

Insurance industry finances, underwriting activities, and investment plan mgmt, 1960s-90, 21248–159

Intl banking competition issues, with background data, 1980s, 21248–153

Intl Finance Corp finances, and intl capital market financial data by firm, by country, 1990 hearing, 21248–149

Japan financial instns and stock market conditions, and other economic indicators, with intl comparisons, 1980s-90, hearing, 21248–152

Mobile home fires, casualties, damage, and impacts of safety standards, with data on Michigan trailer parks, 1980s, hearing, 21248–145

Persian Gulf War impacts on US economic conditions compared to previous oil shock periods, and Saudi Arabia oil production and prices, 1990-92, hearings, 21248–156

Rural areas housing loan programs of FmHA, and housing voucher demonstration program results, 1980s, hearing, 21248–143

Savings instns failure resolution activity of Resolution Trust Corp, with assets and retained senior executives compensation, by instn, 1988-90, hearing, 21248–144

Savings instns failure resolution activity of Resolution Trust Corp, with instns assets and senior executive compensation, 1990, hearing, 21248–157

Savings instns failure resolution activity of Resolution Trust Corp, 1991 semiannual hearing, 21242–1

Texas economic and housing conditions, bank failures, and thrift and Federal regulators real estate holdings, 1980s-90, hearings, 21248–146

House Budget Committee

Budget of US, House Budget Committee analysis of Bush Admin proposals and economic assumptions, FY92, 21268–42

Budget of US, House concurrent resolution, with spending and revenue targets, FY92 and projected to FY96, annual rpt, 21264–2

Budget of US, legislative process overview with summary projections and glossary, FY90-95, 21268–43

House District of Columbia Committee

DC appeals and superior courts civil and criminal caseloads, 1971-88, hearing, 21308–27

House Education and Labor Committee

AIDS and hepatitis viruses transmission in health care settings, occupational exposure, prevention policies, and OSHA regulation, 1990 hearings, 21348–119

House Energy and Commerce Committee

Insurance (health) for long-term care, affordability and State regulation issues, 1986-90, hearing, 21368–130

Insurance company failures issues and contributing factors, with background data, 1988-90, hearing, 21368–133

Iraq invasion of Kuwait, oil embargo impacts on OPEC and US oil supply and industry, 1989-91, hearing, 21368–132

Medicare reimbursement for radiology services by location, and for home medical equipment under alternative proposals, 1990 hearing, 21368–131

House Foreign Affairs Committee

Economic conditions, policy, and trade practices, by country, 1988-90, annual rpt, 21384–5

Human rights conditions in 170 countries, and US economic and military aid, 1990, annual rpt, 21384–3

Israel and Egypt govt budgets, foreign debt, and economic indicators, 1980s, hearing, 21388–58

House Government Operations Committee

Banks and thrifts fraud and abuse, Federal agencies enforcement activities and staff, with data by instn and location, 1988-90, hearing, 21408–119

Fines (civil) imposed by Federal agencies, and proposed inflation adjustments, FY87, hearing, 21408–124

Forest Service mgmt activities, budget, priorities, and employee reward criteria, supervisor and staff views, 1989 survey, 1989, hearing, 21408–121

Jail drug treatment programs finances and operations, FY89-90, 21408–120

Lawyers for defense, subpoenas by Federal prosecutors, and public and private indigent defense lawyers pay by State, 1986-90, hearing, 21408–123

Stock short selling activity indicators, and regulatory issues, 1980s-89 and trends from 1940, hearings, 21408–122

Tax amnesty programs of States for delinquent taxpayers, participation, collections, and costs, by tax type and State, 1980s-90, hearing, 21408–125

House Hunger Committee, Select

Poverty rate under alternative measurement methods, and public opinion on definition, 1988-89, hearing, 21968–56

House Interior and Insular Affairs Committee

Pacific territories economic conditions, population characteristics, and Federal aid, 1989 hearing, 21448–44

Timber sales of Forest Service, impacts of northern spotted owl conservation in Pacific Northwest, 1990 hearing, 21168–47

House Judiciary Committee

Copyright infringement damage award and video screening issues, 1990 hearing, 21528–82

Drug (opium) legal production and US imports by country, and analgesics opium content, 1980s, hearing, 21528–81

House Merchant Marine and Fisheries Committee

Pollution (marine) bacterial levels, and beach closings due to contamination and medical waste, for New York and New Jersey, 1987-89, hearing, 21568–50

House Merchant Marine and Fisheries Committee

Timber sales of Forest Service, impacts of northern spotted owl conservation in Pacific Northwest, 1990 hearing, 21168–47

House Narcotics Abuse and Control Committee, Select

Methadone maintenance programs client characteristics and treatment outcomes, compared to inpatient programs, 1970s-87, hearing, 21968–55

House of Representatives

- Budget of US, authoritative financial statements with appropriations, outlays, and receipts, by category and agency, FY90, annual rpt, 8104–2.1
- Budget of US, obligations and authority by function, agency, and program, with summaries, analyses, and historical tables, FY92, annual rpt, 104–2
- Buildings and grounds under Capitol Architect supervision, itemized outlays by payee and function, 1st half FY91, semiannual rpt, 25922–2
- *Congressional Directory*, members of 102nd Congress, other officials, elections, and districts, 1991-92, biennial rpt, 23874–1
- Election campaign finances and FEC activities, various periods 1975-90, annual rpt, 9274–1
- Election campaign receipts and spending of congressional candidates, by candidate and State, 1989-Dec 1990, press release, 9276–1.87
- Salaries, expenses, and contingent fund disbursement, detailed listings, quarterly rpt, 21942–1
- *State and Metro Area Data Book*, 1991 data compilation, 2328–54
- *Statistical Abstract of US*, 1991 annual data compilation, 2324–1.8
- Votes cast by party, candidate, and State, 1990 natl elections, biennial rpt, 9274–5
- *see also* House Special Publications
- *see also* under names of individual committees (starting with House or Joint)
- *see also* under names of individual subcommittees (starting with Subcommittee)

House Post Office and Civil Service Committee

- Census Bur data collection and publication operations, US Code Title 13 text, 1991 rpt, 21628–94
- Census of Population and Housing, 1990: Budget of US constraints impacts on census operations, hearing, 21628–88
- Census of Population and Housing, 1990: data accuracy and quality issues, hearing, 21628–91
- Census of Population and Housing, 1990: data collection progress, hearing, 21628–86
- Census of Population and Housing, 1990: local govt review of preliminary results, issues, hearing, 21628–93
- Census of Population and Housing, 1990: New York State and NYC data collection activities and status, hearing, 21628–90
- Census of Population and Housing, 1990: Pennsylvania data collection activities and status, hearing, 21628–89
- Census of Population and Housing, 1990: Pennsylvania preparations for count, hearing, 21628–87
- Census of Population and Housing, 1990: Texas data collection activities and status, hearing, 21628–92
- Census of Population, 1990: data coverage evaluation and improvement activities, and post-census sample use, hearing, 21628–96
- Census of Population, 1990: data coverage evaluation and improvement activities, and revised counts for 1970-90 censuses, hearing, 21628–95

House Public Works and Transportation Committee

- Air travel of families and industry revenue impacts of proposed child fares, with costs and accidents compared to auto travel, 1990 hearing, 21648–61
- Aircraft noise policies, health impacts, and aircraft replacement schedules and costs, 1960s-90 and projected to 2006, hearing, 21648–64
- Airport capacity expansion and improvement funding sources, alternative methods, late 1980s and projected to 2000, hearing, 21648–63
- Airport finances, operations by carrier, and capacity improvement and dev funding, by airport, 1977-87 and projected to 2020, hearing, 21648–59
- Court buildings mgmt by GSA, spending, and rental income, 1980s-91, hearing, 21648–60
- Kennedy Center for Performing Arts and Natl Symphony Orchestra financial statements, and capital and maintenance costs and needs, 1970s-90, hearing, 21648–62

House Science, Space, and Technology Committee

- NASA activities and funding, 1990, annual compilation of papers, 21704–1
- Space programs activities, missions, launchings, payloads, and flight duration, for foreign and US programs, 1957-90, annual rpt, 21704–4
- Space station commercial dev and operating costs and income under alternative financing options, projected 1989-2000, 21708–129

House Small Business Committee

- Drug and diet effects on hypertension, and nonprescription diet pills and analgesics sales and adverse reactions, 1980s-90, hearing, 21728–77
- Medicare claims processing issues in Georgia, with data on beneficiary satisfaction, payments, and subcontractor review activity and savings, 1989-90, hearing, 21728–75
- Timber industry impacts of northern spotted owl conservation in Pacific Northwest, and worker aid programs, 1980s and projected to 2000, hearing, 21728–76

House Special Publications

House of Representatives salaries, expenses, and contingent fund disbursement, detailed listings, quarterly rpt, 21942–1

House trailers

see Mobile homes

House Ways and Means Committee

- Budget of US, compilation of background material on fiscal and tax policy, 1960s-96, 21788–203
- Child welfare programs funding by source, and foster care cases, problems, and program operations for selected States, 1970s-90, hearings, 21788–202

Index by Subjects and Names

- Fed Govt programs under Committee jurisdiction, finances, operations, and participant characteristics, FY70s-90, annual rpt, 21784–11
- Foreign countries economic conditions, policy, and trade practices, by country, 1988-90, annual rpt, 21384–5
- Medicare supplemental private insurance premiums, costs, claims, and benefit provisions, with data by firm, 1988-90, hearing, 21788–198
- SSA telephone info service performance, 1989-90, hearing, 21788–199
- Tax (income) unpaid accounts receivable of IRS by collection status, and IRS budget and staff, with data by district, 1980s-91, hearing, 21788–200
- Tax expenditures, Federal revenues forgone through income tax deductions and exclusions by type, FY92-96, annual rpt, 21784–10
- Tax provisions and receipts overview, by tax type, with background data, 1900s-90 and projected to 2000, 21788–197
- Unemployment insurance programs of States, finances, operations, tax provisions, and vulnerability to recessions, 1970s-90s, hearing, 21788–201

Household appliances and equipment

- American Housing Survey: inventory change from 1973, by reason, unit and household characteristics, and location, 1983, biennial rpt, 2485–14
- American Housing Survey: unit and households characteristics, unit and neighborhood quality, and journey to work by MSA location, for 11 MSAs, 1984 survey, supplement, 2485–8
- American Housing Survey: unit and households detailed characteristics, and unit and neighborhood quality, MSA rpt series, 2485–6
- American Housing Survey: unit and households detailed characteristics, and unit and neighborhood quality, 1987, biennial rpt, 2485–12; 2485–13
- Apartment completions by region and metro-nonmetro location, and absorption rate, by size and rent class, preliminary 1990, annual Current Housing Rpt, 2484–3
- Apartment market absorption rates and characteristics for nonsubsidized furnished and unfurnished units, 1989, annual Current Housing Rpt, 2484–2
- Business statistics, detailed data for major industries and economic indicators, *Survey of Current Business*, monthly rpt, 2702–1.17
- Consumer Expenditure Survey, household income by source, and itemized spending, by selected characteristics and region, 1988-89, annual rpt, 6764–5
- Consumer Expenditure Survey, spending by category, and income, by selected household characteristics and location, 1990, annual press release, 6726–1.42
- County Business Patterns, 1988: employment, establishments, and payroll, by SIC 2- to 4-digit industry and county, annual State rpt series, 2326–6
- County Business Patterns, 1989: employment, establishments, and payroll, by SIC 2- to 4-digit industry and county, annual State rpt series, 2326–8

Index by Subjects and Names

CPI by component for US city average, and by region, population size, and for 27 metro areas, monthly rpt, 6762–2

CPI components relative importance, by selected MSA, region, population size, and for US city average, 1990, annual rpt, 6884–1

Developing countries energy use, and economic and environmental impacts, by fuel type, world area, and country, 1980s-90, 26358–232

Employment, earnings, and hours, by SIC 1- to 4-digit industry, monthly and annual averages, selected years 1909-90, annual rpt, 6744–4

Energy conservation (housing) program of Bonneville Power Admin, activities, cost effectiveness, and participation, series, 3226–1

Energy conservation and resource planning activities of Bonneville Power Admin, FY89-90, 3228–11

Energy conservation measures impacts on consumption, by component and end-use sector, 1970s-88 and projected under alternative oil prices to 1995, 3308–93

Energy supply, demand, and prices, by fuel type and end-use sector, projections and underlying assumptions, 1990-2010, annual rpt, 3164–90

Energy use of households, and availability of appliances by type, selected years 1978-87, annual rpt, 3164–74.1

Enterprise Statistics, 1987: finances and operations for companies, by size, level of diversification, form of organization, and industry group, 2329–8

Environmental Quality, status of problems, protection programs, research, and intl issues, 1991 annual rpt, 484–1

Exports and imports between US and outlying areas, by detailed commodity and mode of transport, 1990, annual rpt, 2424–11

Exports and imports of US, by country and detailed commodity, monthly rpt, 2422–12

Exports and imports of US, by Harmonized System 6-digit commodity and country, 1990, annual rpt, 2424–13

Exports and imports of US, by transport mode, country, and SITC 1- to 3-digit commodity, 1990, annual rpt, 2424–12

Exports of US, detailed Schedule B commodities with countries of destination, 1990, annual rpt, 2424–10

Fans (electric) from PRC at less than fair value, injury to US industry, investigation with background financial and operating data, 1991 rpt, 9886–14.335

Home mortgages FHA-insured, financial, property, and mortgagor characteristics, by metro area, 1990, annual rpt, 5144–24

Home mortgages FHA-insured, financial, property, and mortgagor characteristics, by State, 1990, annual rpt, 5144–1

Home mortgages FHA-insured, financial, property, and mortgagor characteristics, 1990, annual rpt, 5144–17; 5144–23

Housing units completed, single and multifamily units by structural and financial characteristics, inside-outside MSAs, and region, 1986-90, annual rpt, 2384–1

Household supplies and utensils

Injuries from use of consumer products, by severity, victim age, and detailed product, 1990, annual rpt, 9164–6

Injuries from use of consumer products, related deaths and costs, and recalls by brand, by product type, FY89, annual rpt, 9164–2

Input-output structure of US economy, detailed interindustry transactions for 84 industries, and components of final demand, 1986, annual article, 2702–1.206

Input-output structure of US economy, detailed interindustry transactions for 85 industries, 1982 benchmark data, 2702–1.213

Labor productivity, indexes of output, hours, and employment by SIC 2- to 4-digit industry, 1967-89, annual rpt, 6824–1.3

Manufacturing annual survey, 1989: finances and operations, by SIC 2- to 4-digit industry, series, 2506–15

Manufacturing census, 1987: finances and operations, by SIC 2- to 4-digit industry, State, and MSA, with trends from 1849, 2497–1

Manufacturing census, 1987: finances and operations, by type of organization and SIC 2- to 4-digit industry, subject rpt, 2497–5

Manufacturing finances and operations, by SIC 2- to 4-digit industry, forecast 1991, annual rpt, 2044–28

Microwave oven and other consumer spending on selected durable goods and services, 1980, 1985, and 1989, semiannual pamphlet, feature, 2322–3

Microwave ovens (commercial) from Japan at less than fair value, injury to US industry, investigation with background financial and operating data, 1991 rpt, 9886–14.322

Multinatl US firms and foreign affiliates finances and operations, by industry and world area of parent firm, 1989 benchmark survey, preliminary annual rpt, 2704–5

Occupational injury and illness rates, by SIC 2- to 4-digit industry, 1988-89, annual rpt, 6844–7

Occupational injury and illness rates, by SIC 2- to 4-digit industry, 1989, annual rpt, 6844–1

Pollution (air) indoor levels and emissions rates, by pollutant type and source, 1990 handbook, 3326–1.2

Price indexes (producer), by stage of processing and detailed commodity, monthly rpt, 6762–6

Price indexes (producer), by stage of processing and detailed commodity, monthly 1990, annual rpt, 6764–2

Price indexes for department store inventories, by class of item, monthly table, 6762–7

Production of building materials, by type, bimonthly rpt, 2042–1.6

Puerto Rico economic censuses, 1987: wholesale and retail trade and service industry finances and operations, by SIC 2- to 4-digit industry and municipio, 2591–1

Puerto Rico economic censuses, 1987: wholesale, retail, and service industries finances and operations, by establishment characteristics and SIC 2- and 3-digit industry, subject rpts, 2591–2

Quality of housing and neighborhoods, and rents paid under housing voucher and Section 8 certificate programs, 1985-87 survey, 5186–14.4

Radiation from electronic devices, incidents by type of device, and FDA control activities, 1990, annual rpt, 4064–13

Retail trade census, 1987: depreciable assets, capital and operating expenses, sales, value added, and inventories, by SIC 2- to 4-digit kind of business, 2399–2

Retail trade census, 1987: finances and employment, for establishments with and without payroll, by SIC 2- to 4-digit kind of business, State, and MSA, 2401–1

Retail trade sales and inventories, by kind of business, region, and selected State, MSA, and city, monthly rpt, 2413–3

Retail trade sales, by kind of business, advance monthly rpt, 2413–2

Retail trade sales, inventories, purchases, gross margin, and accounts receivable, by SIC 2- to 4-digit kind of business and form of ownership, 1989, annual rpt, 2413–5

Shipments, trade, use, and firms, for appliances by product, 1990, annual Current Industrial Rpt, 2506–12.16

Shipments, trade, use, and firms, for electric housewares and fans by product, 1990, annual Current Industrial Rpt, 2506–12.15

Statistical Abstract of US, 1991 annual data compilation, 2324–1.26; 2324–1.27

Tax (income) returns of corporations, income and tax items by asset size and detailed industry, 1987, annual rpt, 8304–4

Tax (income) returns of corporations, income and tax items by asset size and detailed industry, 1988, annual rpt, 8304–21

Thefts, and value of property stolen and recovered, by property type, 1990, annual rpt, 6224–2.1

TVA electric power purchases of municipal and cooperative distributors, and prices and use by distributor and consumer sector, monthly rpt, 9802–1

Wholesale trade census, 1987: establishments, sales by customer class, employment, inventories, and expenses, by SIC 2- to 4-digit kind of business, 2407–4

see also Air conditioning

see also Furniture and furnishings

see also Hardware

see also Home video and audio equipment

see also Household supplies and utensils

see also Insulation

see also Lawn and garden equipment

see also Lighting equipment

see also Plumbing and heating

see also Security devices

see also Tools

see also Video recordings and equipment

see also Watches and clocks

see also under By Commodity in the "Index by Categories"

Household income

see Personal and household income

Household supplies and utensils

Chemicals (inorganic) production by State, shipments, trade, and use, by product, 1990, annual Current Industrial Rpt, 2506–8.14

Household supplies and utensils

Consumer Expenditure Survey, spending by category, and income, by selected household characteristics and location, 1990, annual press release, 6726–1.42

County Business Patterns, 1988: employment, establishments, and payroll, by SIC 2- to 4-digit industry and county, annual State rpt series, 2326–6

County Business Patterns, 1989: employment, establishments, and payroll, by SIC 2- to 4-digit industry and county, annual State rpt series, 2326–8

CPI by component for US city average, and by region, population size, and for 27 metro areas, monthly rpt, 6762–2

CPI components relative importance, by selected MSA, region, population size, and for US city average, 1990, annual rpt, 6884–1

Employment, earnings, and hours, by SIC 1- to 4-digit industry, monthly and annual averages, selected years 1909-90, annual rpt, 6744–4

Exports and imports between US and outlying areas, by detailed commodity and mode of transport, 1990, annual rpt, 2424–11

Exports and imports of US, by country and detailed commodity, monthly rpt, 2422–12

Exports and imports of US, by Harmonized System 6-digit commodity and country, 1990, annual rpt, 2424–13

Exports and imports of US, by transport mode, country, and SITC 1- to 3-digit commodity, 1990, annual rpt, 2424–12

Exports of US, detailed Schedule B commodities with countries of destination, 1990, annual rpt, 2424–10

Glassware shipments, trade, use, and firms, by product, 1990, annual Current Industrial Rpt, 2506–9.3

Imports detained by FDA, by reason, product, shipper, brand, and country, monthly listing, 4062–2

Injuries from use of consumer products, by severity, victim age, and detailed product, 1990, annual rpt, 9164–6

Injuries from use of consumer products, related deaths and costs, and recalls by brand, by product type, FY89, annual rpt, 9164–2

Light bulb production, shipments, stocks, trade, and firms, by type, monthly and quarterly Current Industrial Rpts, 2506–12.13; 2506–12.33

Linens production, shipments, trade, inventories, and use, quarterly Current Industrial Rpt, 2506–6.6

Manufacturing annual survey, 1989: finances and operations, by SIC 2- to 4-digit industry, series, 2506–15

Manufacturing census, 1987: finances and operations, by SIC 2- to 4-digit industry, State, and MSA, with trends from 1849, 2497–1

Manufacturing census, 1987: finances and operations, by type of organization and SIC 2- to 4-digit industry, subject rpt, 2497–5

Manufacturing finances and operations, by SIC 2- to 4-digit industry, forecast 1991, annual rpt, 2044–28

Occupational injury and illness rates, by SIC 2- to 4-digit industry, 1988-89, annual rpt, 6844–7

Occupational injury and illness rates, by SIC 2- to 4-digit industry, 1989, annual rpt, 6844–1

OECD trade, total and for 4 major countries, and US trade by country, by commodity, 1970-89, world area rpt series, 9116–1

Price indexes (producer), by stage of processing and detailed commodity, monthly rpt, 6762–6

Price indexes (producer), by stage of processing and detailed commodity, monthly 1990, annual rpt, 6764–2

Price indexes for department store inventories, by class of item, monthly table, 6762–7

Puerto Rico economic censuses, 1987: wholesale and retail trade and service industry finances and operations, by SIC 2- to 4-digit industry and municipio, 2591–1

Wholesale trade census, 1987: establishments, sales by customer class, employment, inventories, and expenses, by SIC 2- to 4-digit kind of business, 2407–4

see also Adhesives
see also Hardware
see also Personal care products
see also under By Commodity in the "Index by Categories"

Household workers

see Domestic workers and services

Households

see Families and households

Housewares

see Furniture and furnishings
see Household appliances and equipment
see Household supplies and utensils

Housing

see Apartment houses
see Building permits
see Census of Housing
see Community-based correctional programs
see Condominiums and cooperatives
see Discrimination in housing
see Federal aid to housing
see Foster home care
see Group homes for the handicapped
see Group quarters
see Home-based offices and workers
see Homesteads
see Hotels and motels
see Household appliances and equipment
see Housing (FHA), HUD
see Housing condition and occupancy
see Housing construction
see Housing costs and financing
see Housing energy use
see Housing maintenance and repair
see Housing sales
see Housing supply and requirements
see Housing tenure
see Insulation
see Living arrangements
see Low-income housing
see Military housing
see Mobile homes
see Mortgages
see Prefabricated buildings
see Public housing
see Real estate business
see Relocation
see Rent

see Rent control
see Rent supplements
see Retirement communities
see Rooming and boarding houses
see Transient housing
see Urban renewal
see Veterans housing
see Wrecking and demolition

Housing (FHA), HUD

Affordability indicators for housing, by household composition, income, and current tenure, 1988, 2486–1.11

American Housing Survey: unit and households detailed characteristics, and unit and neighborhood quality, MSA rpt series, 2485–6

American Housing Survey: unit and households detailed characteristics, and unit and neighborhood quality, 1987, biennial rpt, 2485–12

Applications to FHA for new and existing units, refinancings, and housing starts, monthly rpt, 5142–44

Govt Natl Mortgage Assn finances, and mortgage-backed securities program, FY90, annual rpt, 5144–6

Home mortgages FHA-insured, financial, property, and mortgagor characteristics, by metro area, quarterly rpt, periodicity change, 5142–2

Home mortgages FHA-insured, financial, property, and mortgagor characteristics, by State, 1990, annual rpt, 5144–1

Home mortgages FHA-insured, financial, property, and mortgagor characteristics, quarterly rpt, periodicity change, 5142–1

Home mortgages FHA-insured, financial, property, and mortgagor characteristics, total and for selected States, periodicity change, 5142–3

Home mortgages FHA-insured, financial, property, and mortgagor characteristics, 1990, annual rpt, 5144–17; 5144–23

Housing units (1-family) sold and sales price by type of financing, monthly rpt, quarterly tables, 2382–3.2

Housing units completed, single and multifamily units by structural and financial characteristics, inside-outside MSAs, and region, 1986-90, annual rpt, 2384–1

Insurance (private) on mortgages for 1-4 family units, monthly press release, 5142–38

Insured mortgages for 1-family units, by loan type and mortgage characteristics, quarterly rpt, 5142–45

Insured mortgages secondary market prices and yields, and interest rates on construction and conventional mortgage loans, by region, monthly press release, 5142–20

Lead paint in privately owned housing, levels, exposure, and testing and abatement costs, 1990 rpt, 5188–128

Mortgage loan activity, by type of lender, loan, and mortgaged property, monthly press release, 5142–18

Mortgage loan activity, by type of lender, loan, and mortgaged property, quarterly press release, 5142–30

Mortgages FHA-insured, financial, property, and mortgagor characteristics, by metro area, 1990, annual rpt, 5144–24

Index by Subjects and Names

Mortgages FHA-insured, financial, property, and mortgagor characteristics, total and by State and outlying area, 1990, annual rpt, 5144–25

Originations of mortgages, by State, 1978-89, annual press release, 5144–21

Property acquired by Fed Govt through foreclosure and savings instn failure, 1-family homes inventory by State, acquisition costs, and sales, for 4 agencies, 1986-90, GAO rpt, 26113–513

Housing and Urban Development Department *see* Department of Housing and Urban Development

Housing census

see Census of Housing

see Census of Population and Housing

Housing condition and occupancy

- American Housing Survey: inventory change from 1973, by reason, unit and household characteristics, and location, 1983, biennial rpt, 2485–14
- American Housing Survey: unit and households characteristics, MSA fact sheet series, 2485–11
- American Housing Survey: unit and households characteristics, unit and neighborhood quality, and journey to work by MSA location, for 11 MSAs, 1984 survey, supplement, 2485–8
- American Housing Survey: unit and households detailed characteristics, and unit and neighborhood quality, MSA rpt series, 2485–6
- American Housing Survey: unit and households detailed characteristics, and unit and neighborhood quality, 1987, biennial rpt, 2485–12; 2485–13
- Apartment and condominium completions and absorption rates, by size and price class, preliminary 1990, annual Current Housing Rpt, 2484–3
- Apartment market absorption rates and characteristics for nonsubsidized furnished and unfurnished units, 1989, annual Current Housing Rpt, 2484–2
- Arson incidents by whether structure occupied, property value, and arrest rate, by property type, 1990, annual rpt, 6224–2.1
- Bombing incidents, casualties, and damage, by target, circumstances, and State, 1990, annual rpt, 6224–5
- Census Bur data coverage and availability, 1991 pamphlet, 2326–7.77
- Census of Housing, 1990: inventory, occupancy, and costs, State fact sheet series, 2326–21
- Census of Population and Housing, 1990: housing units occupied and vacant, persons in group quarters, and household size, by region, census div, and State, press release, 2328–71
- Census of Population and Housing, 1990: population and housing characteristics, households, and land area, by county, subdiv, and place, State rpt series, 2551–1
- Census of Population and Housing, 1990: population and housing selected characteristics, by region, press release, 2328–74
- Crime victimization of women, by relation to offender, circumstances, and victim characteristics, for rape and other violent offenses, 1973-87, 6068–243

Crime victimization rates, by victim and offender characteristics, circumstances, and offense, 1988 survey, annual rpt, 6066–3.42

Crime victimization rates, by victim and offender characteristics, circumstances, and offense, 1989 survey, annual rpt, 6066–3.44

Criminal defendants for Federal offenses pretrial processing, detention, and release, by defendant characteristics and district, 1988, hearing, 25528–114

Data on population and housing, and policy issues, fact sheet series, 2326–17

Economic indicators and components, current data and annual trends, monthly rpt, 23842–1.3

- Foster care placement of black children whose parents abuse drugs, by placement reason and outcome, and household and parent characteristics, 1986-90, 4008–114
- Home mortgages FHA-insured, financial, property, and mortgagor characteristics, by metro area, 1990, annual rpt, 5144–24
- Home mortgages FHA-insured, financial, property, and mortgagor characteristics, by State, 1990, annual rpt, 5144–1
- Home mortgages FHA-insured, financial, property, and mortgagor characteristics, total and by State and outlying area, 1990, annual rpt, 5144–25
- Home mortgages FHA-insured, financial, property, and mortgagor characteristics, 1990, annual rpt, 5144–17; 5144–23
- Households and family characteristics, by location, 1990, annual Current Population Rpt, 2546–1.447
- Lead paint in privately owned housing, levels, exposure, and testing and abatement costs, 1990 rpt, 5188–128
- New single and multifamily units, by structural and financial characteristics, inside-outside MSAs, and region, 1986-90, annual rpt, 2384–1
- North Central States, FHLB 7th District housing vacancy rates for single and multifamily units and mobile homes, by ZIP code, annual MSA rpt series, 9304–18
- NYC rent control impacts on rental housing condition, late 1970s-87, working paper, 9387–8.246
- Pacific Northwest housing energy conservation program of Bonneville Power Admin, activities, cost effectiveness, and participation, series, 3226–1
- Pollution (air) indoor levels and emissions rates, by pollutant type and source, 1990 handbook, 3326–1.2
- Poor households with high rent, and substandard units, worst case problems prevalence and households characteristics, 1970s-84, annual rpt, 5184–10
- Puerto Rico population and housing characteristics, 1990 Census of Population and Housing, press release, 2328–78
- Quality of housing and neighborhoods, and rents paid under housing voucher and Section 8 certificate programs, 1985-87 survey, 5186–14.4
- Radon indoor air pollution levels in Pacific Northwest, with geological and soil characteristics, by township, 1989 rpt, 5668–114

Housing construction

- Retirement housing centers tax-exempt bond use and other financing, defaults, and facility and resident characteristics, 1991 GAO rpt, 26119–328
- Rural areas housing loan programs of FmHA, and housing voucher demonstration program results, 1980s, hearing, 21248–143
- Savings instns failures, inventory of real estate assets available from Resolution Trust Corp, 1989, semiannual listing, 9722–2.1
- Savings instns failures, inventory of real estate assets available from Resolution Trust Corp, 1990, semiannual listing, 9722–2.2; 9722–2.3; 9722–2.5; 9722–2.6; 9722–2.7; 9722–2.8
- Savings instns failures, inventory of real estate assets available from Resolution Trust Corp, 1991, semiannual listing, 9722–2.11; 9722–2.12; 9722–2.13; 9722–2.14
- *Statistical Abstract of US*, 1991 annual data compilation, 2324–1.26
- Terrorism incidents in US, related activity, and casualties, by attack type, target, group, and location, 1990, annual rpt, 6224–6
- Vacancy and property value appreciation rates for 4 metro areas, 1991 GAO rpt, 26131–84
- Vacant housing characteristics and costs, and occupancy and vacancy rates, by region and metro-nonmetro location, quarterly rpt, 2482–1
- Vacant housing characteristics, and occupancy and vacancy rates, by tenure and location, 1960s-90, annual rpt, 2484–1
- Virgin Islands population and housing characteristics, 1990 Census of Population and Housing, press release, 2328–81
- West Central States, FHLB 10th District housing vacancy rates for single and multifamily units and mobile homes, by ZIP code, annual MSA rpt series, 9304–22
- Western States, FHLB 12th District housing vacancy rates for single and multifamily units and mobile homes, by ZIP code, annual MSA rpt series, 9304–21
- Wiretaps authorized, costs, arrests, trials, and convictions, by offense and jurisdiction, 1990, annual rpt, 18204–7

see also Families and households

see also Furniture and furnishings

see also Household appliances and equipment

see also Housing maintenance and repair

see also Housing tenure

see also Insulation

see also Plumbing and heating

see also Rent

see also Rent supplements

see also Transient housing

Housing construction

- American Housing Survey: inventory change from 1973, by reason, unit and household characteristics, and location, 1983, biennial rpt, 2485–14
- Apartment and condominium completions and absorption rates, by size and price class, preliminary 1990, annual Current Housing Rpt, 2484–3

Housing construction

Apartment and condominium completions by rent class and sales price, and market absorption rates, quarterly rpt, 2482–2

Apartment units completed, by type and for units under Federal subsidy, 1970-89, annual rpt, 2484–2

Business statistics, detailed data for major industries and economic indicators, *Survey of Current Business*, monthly rpt, 2702–1.6

Census of Construction Industries, 1987: finances and operations, by SIC 4-digit industry and State, final rpt series, 2373–1

Earthquake preparedness costs and benefits, with data for California events and effects of 1989 Loma Prieta quake, 1980s, hearings, 21248–154

Economic indicators and components, and Fed Reserve 4th District business and financial conditions, monthly chartbook, 9377–10

Economic indicators and components, current data and annual trends, monthly rpt, 23842–1.3

Economic indicators, monthly rpt, 9362–1.2

Employment, earnings, and hours, by SIC 1- to 4-digit industry, monthly and annual averages, selected years 1909-90, annual rpt, 6744–4

Energy-efficiency building codes, effect on house construction practices in Bonneville Power Admin service areas, 1987, 3228–15

Engineering and architectural establishments, receipts by type of client and project, payroll, and employment, by State, 1987 Census of Service Industries, 2393–4.16

Farmland value, rent, taxes, foreign ownership, and transfers by probable use and lender type, with data by region and State, 1980-91, article, 1561–16.202

Fed Govt financial and nonfinancial domestic aid, 1991 base edition with supplements, annual listing, 104–5

Finances and operations, by SIC 2- to 4-digit industry, forecast 1991, annual rpt, 2044–28

Flow-of-funds accounts, savings, investments, and credit statements, quarterly rpt, 9365–3.3

Forecasts of housing starts by region, 1991-2000, with background data, 1973-87, article, 9387–1.205

Indian (Navajo and Hopi) relocation program activities and caseloads, monthly rpt, 16002–1

Indian (Navajo and Hopi) relocation program activities and caseloads, 1975-90, 16008–5

Loan rates for FHA and conventional construction loans by region, and builders with declining, stable, and advancing trends in new plans and unsold units, monthly press release, 5142–20

Low income housing construction and repair loans of HUD to nonprofit organizations, project delays, and starts, 1980s, GAO rpt, 26113–506

Lumber and pulp products supply and use, and timber resources, detailed data, 1950s-87 and alternative projections to 2040, 1208–24.20

Mortgage applications to FHA for new and existing units, refinancings, and housing starts, monthly rpt, 5142–44

Mortgage loan activity, by type of lender, loan, and mortgaged property, monthly press release, 5142–18

Mortgage loan activity, by type of lender, loan, and mortgaged property, quarterly press release, 5142–30

Mortgage loan activity of insured savings instns, by purpose and State, various periods 1984-89, annual rpt, 8434–3

New construction (public and private) put in place, value by type, monthly rpt, 2382–4

New England States economic indicators, Fed Reserve 1st District, monthly rpt, 9373–2.6

New England States, FHLB 1st District thrifts financial operations compared to banks, and housing industry indicators, bimonthly rpt with articles, 9302–4

New housing construction and sales by region, permits by State and MSA, costs, and material prices, bimonthly rpt with articles, 2042–1

New housing starts and authorizations, 1959-90 with trends from 1929, annual rpt, 204–1.3

New housing starts and completions authorized by building permits in 40 MSAs, quarterly rpt, 2382–9

New housing starts, by units per structure and metro-nonmetro location, and mobile home placements and prices, by region, monthly rpt, 2382–1

New housing units authorized, by region, State, selected MSA, and permit-issuing place, monthly rpt, 2382–5

New housing units authorized, by State, MSA, and permit-issuing place, 1990, annual rpt, 2384–2

New housing units completed and under construction, by units per structure, region, and inside-outside MSAs, monthly rpt, 2382–2

New single and multifamily units, by structural and financial characteristics, inside-outside MSAs, and region, 1986-90, annual rpt, 2384–1

New single-family houses sold and for sale, by price, stage of construction, months on market, and region, monthly rpt, 2382–3

New single-family housing units by selected structural characteristics, sales, and prices, 1970s-90, article, 1702–1.205

North Central States, FHLB 7th District housing vacancy rates for single and multifamily units and mobile homes, by ZIP code, annual MSA rpt series, 9304–18

Occupational deaths in construction industries, by cause, age, and region, 1985-89, 6608–4

Occupational injury and illness rates, by SIC 2- to 4-digit industry, 1988-89, annual rpt, 6844–7

Occupational injury and illness rates, by SIC 2- to 4-digit industry, 1989, annual rpt, 6844–1

Southeastern States, Fed Reserve 6th District, economic indicators by State and MSA, quarterly rpt, 9371–14

Southeastern States, FHLB 4th District, employment and housing and mortgage market indicators by State, quarterly rpt, 9302–36

Index by Subjects and Names

Soviet Union GNP by component and industry sector, and CIA estimation methods, 1950s-87, 23848–223

Soviet Union GNP by detailed income and outlay component, 1985, 2326–18.59

State and Metro Area Data Book, 1991 data compilation, 2328–54

Statistical Abstract of US, 1991 annual data compilation, 2324–1.26

Supply, demand, and financing of housing, and construction industry operations, biennial rpt, discontinued, 5184–5

West Central States, FHLB 10th District housing vacancy rates for single and multifamily units and mobile homes, by ZIP code, annual MSA rpt series, 9304–22

Western States, FHLB 12th District housing vacancy rates for single and multifamily units and mobile homes, by ZIP code, annual MSA rpt series, 9304–21

see also Building materials

see also Federal aid to housing

see also Housing condition and occupancy

see also Housing costs and financing

see also Housing maintenance and repair

see also Insulation

see also Prefabricated buildings

see also Property value

see also Public housing

see also Wrecking and demolition

Housing costs and financing

Affordability indicators for housing, by current tenure, 1988, fact sheet, 2326–17.31

Affordability indicators for housing, by household composition, income, and current tenure, 1988, 2486–1.11

Affordability of housing and family income relation to housing costs, 1989 survey, fact sheet, 2326–17.33

Alteration and repair spending for housing, by characteristics of property and region, annual rpt, discontinued, 2384–4

Alteration and repair spending for housing, by type, tenure, region, and other characteristics, quarterly rpt, 2382–7

American Housing Survey: inventory change from 1973, by reason, unit and household characteristics, and location, 1983, biennial rpt, 2485–14

American Housing Survey: unit and households characteristics, MSA fact sheet series, 2485–11

American Housing Survey: unit and households characteristics, unit and neighborhood quality, and journey to work by MSA location, for 11 MSAs, 1984 survey, supplement, 2485–8

American Housing Survey: unit and households detailed characteristics, and unit and neighborhood quality, MSA rpt series, 2485–6

American Housing Survey: unit and households detailed characteristics, and unit and neighborhood quality, 1987, biennial rpt, 2485–12; 2485–13

Assets of households, by type of holding and selected characteristics, 1988, Current Population Rpt, 2546–20.16

Census of Housing, 1990: inventory, occupancy, and costs, State fact sheet series, 2326–21

Census of Population and Housing, 1990: population and housing characteristics,

Index by Subjects and Names

households, and land area, by county, subdiv, and place, State rpt series, 2551–1

- Child rearing costs of married couple households, by expenditure type, child's age, income, and region, 1990 and projected to 2007, 1708–87
- Condominium completions and absorption rates, by size and price class, preliminary 1990, annual Current Housing Rpt, 2484–3
- Condominium completions by rent class and sales price, and market absorption rates, quarterly rpt, 2482–2
- Consumer Expenditure Survey, household income by source, and itemized spending, by selected characteristics and region, 1988-89, annual rpt, 6764–5
- Consumer Expenditure Survey, spending by category, and income, by selected household characteristics and location, 1990, annual press release, 6726–1.42
- Consumer Expenditure Survey, spending by category, selected household characteristics, and region, quarterly rpt, 6762–14
- Consumer spending, natl income and product accounts, *Survey of Current Business,* monthly rpt, 2702–1.25
- Cost of living and quality of life indicators for 14 MSAs, 1980s, GAO rpt, 26123–346
- CPI by component for US city average, and by region, population size, and for 27 metro areas, monthly rpt, 6762–2
- CPI changes for selected items, 1981-90, annual article, 6722–1.226
- CPI components relative importance, by selected MSA, region, population size, and for US city average, 1990, annual rpt, 6884–1
- Developing countries economic and social conditions from 1960s, and Intl Dev Cooperation Agency and AID activities and funding, FY90-92, annual rpt, 9904–4
- Developing countries housing and urban dev program of AID, financial statements, FY90, annual rpt, 9914–4
- Economic indicators and components, and Fed Reserve 4th District business and financial conditions, monthly chartbook, 9377–10
- Economic indicators and components, current data and annual trends, monthly rpt, 23842–1.4
- Energy prices and spending, by fuel type, end-use sector, and State, 1989, annual rpt, 3164–64
- Equity returns counted as income, and other income definitions effects on household income and poverty status, by recipient characteristics, 1990, annual Current Population Rpt, 2546–6.69
- FmHA activities, and loans and grants by program and State, FY90 and trends from FY70, annual rpt, 1184–17
- FmHA loans and borrower supervision activities in farm and housing programs, by type and State, monthly rpt, 1182–1
- Food stamp recipient household size, composition, income, and income and deductions allowed, summer 1988, annual rpt, 1364–8

Foreign countries living costs, State Dept indexes, housing allowances, and hardship differentials by country and major city, quarterly rpt, 7002–7

- Govt spending, coverage, and benefits for social welfare programs, late 1930s-89, annual rpt, 4744–3.1
- Govt spending for public welfare programs, by program type and level of govt, FY65-88, annual article, 4742–1.202
- Home mortgages FHA-insured, financial, property, and mortgagor characteristics, by metro area, 1990, annual rpt, 5144–24
- Home mortgages FHA-insured, financial, property, and mortgagor characteristics, by State, 1990, annual rpt, 5144–1
- Home mortgages FHA-insured, financial, property, and mortgagor characteristics, total and by State and outlying area, 1990, annual rpt, 5144–25
- Home mortgages FHA-insured, financial, property, and mortgagor characteristics, 1990, annual rpt, 5144–17; 5144–23
- Homelessness issues, population at risk, contributing factors, and Federal funding for services and prevention, with bibl, 1991 compilation of papers, 25928–9
- Japan financial instns and stock market conditions, and other economic indicators, with intl comparisons, 1980s-90, hearing, 21248–152
- Massachusetts housing prices economic impacts over business cycle expansion, 1984-87, article, 9373–1.216
- Men (never married) housing costs, by type and selected characteristics, 1987, article, 1702–1.208
- Mobile home fires, casualties, damage, and impacts of safety standards, with data on Michigan trailer parks, 1980s, hearing, 21248–145
- Mobile home placements and prices by State, and dealer inventories, by region, monthly rpt, 2382–1
- Natl income and product accounts and components, *Survey of Current Business,* monthly rpt, 2702–1.24
- New construction (public and private) put in place, value by type, monthly rpt, 2382–4
- New England States economic indicators, Fed Reserve 1st District, monthly rpt, 9373–2.6
- New England States, FHLB 1st District thrifts financial operations compared to banks, and housing industry indicators, bimonthly rpt with articles, 9302–4
- New housing construction and sales by region, permits by State and MSA, costs, and material prices, bimonthly rpt with articles, 2042–1
- New single and multifamily units, by structural and financial characteristics, inside-outside MSAs, and region, 1986-90, annual rpt, 2384–1
- New single-family houses sold and for sale, by price, stage of construction, months on market, and region, monthly rpt, 2382–3
- New single-family houses sold, prices and price index by region, quarterly rpt, 2382–8
- Older persons migration to southern coastal areas, household finances, services needs, and local economic impacts, for selected counties, 1990, 2068–38

Housing energy use

- Racial integration promotion through mortgage subsidy programs, effectiveness and impacts on housing prices, 1983-89, working paper, 9377–9.108
- Retirement housing centers tax-exempt bond use and other financing, defaults, and facility and resident characteristics, 1991 GAO rpt, 26119–328
- Rural areas housing loan programs of FmHA, and housing voucher demonstration program results, 1980s, hearing, 21248–143
- Savings instns failures, inventory of real estate assets available from Resolution Trust Corp, 1989, semiannual listing, 9722–2.1
- Savings instns failures, inventory of real estate assets available from Resolution Trust Corp, 1990, semiannual listing, 9722–2.2; 9722–2.3; 9722–2.5; 9722–2.6; 9722–2.7; 9722–2.8
- Savings instns failures, inventory of real estate assets available from Resolution Trust Corp, 1991, semiannual listing, 9722–2.11; 9722–2.12; 9722–2.13; 9722–2.14
- Savings rates in natl income and product accounts, under alternative estimates of imputed rent for housing and consumer goods, 1950s-90, article, 9373–1.218
- Soviet Union GNP by detailed income and outlay component, 1985, 2326–18.59
- *State and Metro Area Data Book,* 1991 data compilation, 2328–54
- *Statistical Abstract of US,* 1991 annual data compilation, 2324–1.26
- Vacant housing characteristics and costs, and occupancy and vacancy rates, by region and metro-nonmetro location, quarterly rpt, 2482–1
- Vacant housing characteristics, and occupancy and vacancy rates, by tenure and location, 1960s-90, annual rpt, 2484–1
- *see also* Federal aid to housing
- *see also* Housing sales
- *see also* Mortgages
- *see also* Property value
- *see also* Rent
- *see also* Rent supplements

Housing energy use

- American Housing Survey: inventory change from 1973, by reason, unit and household characteristics, and location, 1983, biennial rpt, 2485–14
- American Housing Survey: unit and households detailed characteristics, and unit and neighborhood quality, MSA rpt series, 2485–6
- American Housing Survey: unit and households detailed characteristics, and unit and neighborhood quality, 1987, biennial rpt, 2485–12
- Apartment completions by region and metro-nonmetro location, and absorption rate, by size and rent class, preliminary 1990, annual Current Housing Rpt, 2484–3
- Apartment market absorption rates, by whether utilities included in rent, 1989, annual Current Housing Rpt, 2484–2
- Attic insulation radiant barriers performance impacts of ventilation and dust, 1990 rpt, 3308–97

Housing energy use

Bonneville Power Admin energy conservation and resource planning activities, FY89-90, 3228–11

Bonneville Power Admin housing energy conservation program activities, cost effectiveness, and participation, series, 3226–1

Bonneville Power Admin mgmt of Fed Columbia River Power System, finances and sales, summary data, quarterly rpt, 3222–2

Building codes for energy efficiency, effect on house construction practices in BPA service areas, 1987, 3228–15

Business statistics, detailed data for major industries and economic indicators, *Survey of Current Business*, monthly rpt, 2702–1.13

Coal, coke, and breeze supply, demand, prices, trade, and stocks, by end-use sector and State, quarterly rpt with articles, 3162–37

Coal production, stocks, and shipments, by State of origin and destination, end-use sector, and mode of transport, quarterly rpt, 3162–8

Conservation measures impacts on energy consumption, by component and end-use sector, 1970s-88 and projected under alternative oil prices to 1995, 3308–93

Consumer Expenditure Survey, household income by source, and itemized spending, by selected characteristics and region, 1988-89, annual rpt, 6764–5

Consumer Expenditure Survey, spending by category, and income, by selected household characteristics and location, 1990, annual press release, 6726–1.42

CPI by component for US city average, and by region, population size, and for 27 metro areas, monthly rpt, 6762–2

CPI components relative importance, by selected MSA, region, population size, and for US city average, 1990, annual rpt, 6884–1

Developing countries energy use, and economic and environmental impacts, by fuel type, world area, and country, 1980s-90, 26358–232

Electric power billings for housing, and rankings, by State, as of Jan 1990, annual rpt, 1244–1.6

Electric power plants production and capacity by fuel type, prices, demand, and air pollution law impacts, by region, 1989-90 and projected to 2010, annual rpt, 3164–81

Electric power plants production, capacity, sales, and fuel stocks, use, and costs, by State, 1985-89, annual rpt, 3164–11

Electric power plants production, fuel use, stocks, and costs by fuel type, and sales, by State, monthly rpt with articles, 3162–35

Electric power sales and revenue, by end-use sector, consumption level, and utility, 1989, annual rpt, 3164–91

Electric utilities finances and operations, detailed data for publicly owned firms, 1989, annual rpt, 3164–24

Electric utilities privately owned, finances and operations, detailed data, 1989, annual rpt, 3164–23

Energy supply, demand, and prices, by fuel type and end-use sector, alternative projections 1989-2010, annual rpt, 3164–75

Energy supply, demand, and prices, by fuel type and end-use sector, projections and underlying assumptions, 1990-2010, annual rpt, 3164–90

Energy supply, demand, and prices, by fuel type and end-use sector, with foreign comparisons, 1990 and trends from 1949, annual rpt, 3164–74

Energy supply, demand, and prices, by fuel type, end-use sector, and country, detailed data, monthly rpt with articles, 3162–24

Energy supply, demand, and prices, forecasts by resource type, quarterly rpt, 3162–34

Energy use, by detailed fuel type, end-use sector, and State, 1960-89, State Energy Data System annual rpt, 3164–39

Energy use in transportation and other sectors, by fuel type, 1970s-89, annual rpt, 3304–5

Fuel oil and kerosene sales and deliveries, by end-use, PAD district, and State, 1989, annual rpt, 3164–94

Heating fuel use in housing, shares by type and region, 1989 and summary for 1950, fact sheet, 2326–17.34

Heating fuels production, imports, stocks, and prices, by selected PAD district and State, seasonal weekly rpt, 3162–45

Home mortgages FHA-insured, financial, property, and mortgagor characteristics, by metro area, 1990, annual rpt, 5144–24

Home mortgages FHA-insured, financial, property, and mortgagor characteristics, by State, 1990, annual rpt, 5144–1

Home mortgages FHA-insured, financial, property, and mortgagor characteristics, 1990, annual rpt, 5144–23

Housing units completed, single and multifamily units by structural and financial characteristics, inside-outside MSAs, and region, 1986-90, annual rpt, 2384–1

Housing units completed, single and multifamily units by structural characteristics, monthly rpt, quarterly tables, 2382–2.2

Lumber (veneer log) production, mill receipts, and trade, by species, with residue use, for North Central States, 1988, quadrennial rpt, 1208–220

Natl Energy Strategy plans for conservation and pollution reduction, impacts of technology and regulation proposals, projected 1990-2030, 3166–6.47

Natl Energy Strategy plans for conservation, impacts on energy use and pollution under alternative technology investment assumptions, projected 1990-2030, 3166–6.48

Natl income and product accounts and components, *Survey of Current Business*, monthly rpt, 2702–1.24

Natural and supplemental gas production, prices, trade, use, reserves, and pipeline company finances, by firm and State, monthly rpt with articles, 3162–4

Natural gas interstate pipeline company detailed financial and operating data, by firm, 1989, annual rpt, 3164–38

New England States electric power sales, Fed Reserve 1st District, monthly rpt, 9373–2.4

Oil and gas supply, demand, and prices, alternative projections 1989-2010, annual rpt, 3164–89

Index by Subjects and Names

Oil and refined products supply, demand, prices, and refinery capacity and stocks, by State, 1960-91, annual rpt, 3164–95

Oil products sales and purchases of refiners, processors, and distributors, by product, end-use sector, PAD district, and State, monthly rpt with articles, 3162–11

Pacific Northwest electric power capacity and use, by energy source, projected under alternative load and demand cases, 1991-2011, annual rpt, 3224–3

Pollution (air) contributing to global warming, emissions factors and control costs, by pollutant and source, 1990 rpt, 9198–124

Pollution (air) contributing to global warming, US and foreign emissions and control measures, 1980s and projected to 2020, 26358–233

Pollution (air) indoor levels and emissions rates, by pollutant type and source, 1990 handbook, 3326–1.2

Pollution (air) levels for 6 pollutants, by source, 1970-89 and trends from 1940, annual rpt, 9194–13

Prices and spending for fuel, by type, end-use sector, and State, 1989, annual rpt, 3164–64

Prices of energy for housing, by fuel and State, 1989 and forecast 1990-91, 3166–6.54

Public housing renovation costs and alternative funding methods, by project type and region, 1990 rpt, 5188–127

Solar collector and photovoltaic module shipments by end-use sector and State, and trade, 1989, annual rpt, 3164–62

State and Metro Area Data Book, 1991 data compilation, 2328–54

Statistical Abstract of US, 1991 annual data compilation, 2324–1.19

Tax (income) returns filed by type of filer, selected income items, quarterly rpt, 8302–2.1

Taxes on energy, economic and energy demand impacts of alternative taxation methods, projected 1991-2000, 3166–6.57

TVA electric power purchases and resales, with electricity use, average bills, and rates by customer class, by distributor, 1990, annual tables, 9804–14

TVA electric power purchases of municipal and cooperative distributors, and prices and use by distributor and consumer sector, monthly rpt, 9802–1

Wood, waste, and alcohol fuel use, by end-use sector and region, 1989, 3166–6.56

see also Low-income energy assistance

Housing insulation

see Insulation

Housing maintenance and repair

American Housing Survey: unit and households detailed characteristics, and unit and neighborhood quality, MSA rpt series, 2485–6

American Housing Survey: unit and households detailed characteristics, and unit and neighborhood quality, 1987, biennial rpt, 2485–12

Census of Construction Industries, 1987: finances and operations, by SIC 4-digit industry and State, final rpt series, 2373–1

Index by Subjects and Names

Construction put in place, permits, housing sales, costs, material prices, and employment, bimonthly rpt with articles, 2042–1

Consumer Expenditure Survey, household income by source, and itemized spending, by selected characteristics and region, 1988-89, annual rpt, 6764–5

CPI by component for US city average, and by region, population size, and for 27 metro areas, monthly rpt, 6762–2

CPI components relative importance, by selected MSA, region, population size, and for US city average, 1990, annual rpt, 6884–1

Expenditures for housing alterations and repair, by characteristics of property and region, annual rpt, discontinued, 2384–4

Expenditures for housing alterations and repair, by type, tenure, region, and other characteristics, quarterly rpt, 2382–7

Farm income, expenses, receipts by commodity, assets, liabilities, and ratios, 1990 and trends from 1945, annual rpt, 1544–16

FmHA activities, and loans and grants by program and State, FY90 and trends from FY70, annual rpt, 1184–17

Franchise business opportunities by firm and kind of business, and sources of aid and info, 1990 annual listing, 2104–7

Historic buildings rehabilitation tax incentives, projects, costs, ownership, and use, FY77-90, annual rpt, 5544–17

Home mortgages FHA-insured, financial, property, and mortgagor characteristics, by metro area, 1990, annual rpt, 5144–24

Home mortgages FHA-insured, financial, property, and mortgagor characteristics, by State, 1990, annual rpt, 5144–1

Home mortgages FHA-insured, financial, property, and mortgagor characteristics, 1990, annual rpt, 5144–17; 5144–23

HUD activities, and housing programs operations and funding, 1989, annual rpt, 5004–10

Indian Health Service facilities, funding, operations, and Indian health and other characteristics, 1950s-90, annual chartbook, 4084–1

Lead paint in privately owned housing, levels, exposure, and testing and abatement costs, 1990 rpt, 5188–128

Low income housing construction and repair loans of HUD to nonprofit organizations, project delays, and starts, 1980s, GAO rpt, 26113–506

Low income housing energy aid, funding sources, costs, and participation, by State, FY89, annual rpt, 4694–8

Lumber and pulp products supply and use, and timber resources, detailed data, 1950s-87 and alternative projections to 2040, 1208–24.20

Mortgage applications by disposition, and secondary loan market sales by purchaser type, by applicant and neighborhood characteristics, 1990, article, 9362–1.206

Mortgages FHA-insured for 1-family units, by loan type and mortgage characteristics, quarterly rpt, 5142–45

Price indexes (producer) for material inputs, by construction industry, monthly rpt, 6762–6

Housing supply and requirements

Price indexes for department store inventories, by class of item, monthly table, 6762–7

Public housing renovation costs and alternative funding methods, by project type and region, 1990 rpt, 5188–127

Rental housing rehabilitation funding and activities of HUD, by program and region, FY90, annual rpt, 5124–7

Service industries census, 1987: establishments, receipts by source, payroll, and employment, by SIC 2- to 4-digit kind of business, State, and MSA, 2393–4

Soviet Union GNP by detailed income and outlay component, 1985, 2326–18.59

Statistical Abstract of US, 1991 annual data compilation, 2324–1.26

see also Insulation

Housing rehabilitation

see Housing maintenance and repair

see Urban renewal

Housing sales

Condominium absorption rates, by sales class and size, 1989, annual Current Housing Rpt, 2484–2

Condominium completions and absorption rates, by size and price class, preliminary 1990, annual Current Housing Rpt, 2484–3

Economic indicators and components, current data and annual trends, monthly rpt, 23842–1.3

FmHA property acquired through foreclosure, 1-family homes, value, sales, and leases, by State, monthly rpt, 1182–7

Housing units (1-family) acquired by Fed Govt through foreclosure and savings instn failure, inventory by State, acquisition costs, and sales, for 4 agencies, 1986-90, GAO rpt, 26113–513

Indian (Navajo and Hopi) relocation program activities and caseloads, monthly rpt, 16002–1

Indian (Navajo and Hopi) relocation program activities and caseloads, 1975-90, 16008–5

Inventory of unsold new units, share of builders reporting declining, stable, and advancing trends, monthly press release, 5142–20

New and existing housing units sold, and average price, by region, bimonthly rpt, 2042–1.2

New England States, FHLB 1st District thrifts financial operations compared to banks, and housing industry indicators, bimonthly rpt with articles, 9302–4

New single and multifamily units, by structural and financial characteristics, inside-outside MSAs, and region, 1986-90, annual rpt, 2384–1

New single-family houses sold and for sale, by price, stage of construction, months on market, and region, monthly rpt, 2382–3

New single-family houses sold, prices and price index by region, quarterly rpt, 2382–8

New single-family housing units by selected structural characteristics, sales, and prices, 1970s-90, article, 1702–1.205

Southeastern States, FHLB 4th District, employment and housing and mortgage market indicators by State, quarterly rpt, 9302–36

Statistical Abstract of US, 1991 annual data compilation, 2324–1.26

Housing starts

see Housing construction

Housing supply and requirements

Alaska rural areas population characteristics, and energy resources dev effects, series, 5736–5

American Housing Survey: inventory change from 1973, by reason, unit and household characteristics, and location, 1983, biennial rpt, 2485–14

American Housing Survey: unit and households detailed characteristics, and unit and neighborhood quality, MSA rpt series, 2485–6

Apartment and condominium completions by rent class and sales price, and market absorption rates, quarterly rpt, 2482–2

Apartment market absorption rates and characteristics for nonsubsidized furnished and unfurnished units, 1989, annual Current Housing Rpt, 2484–2

Census Bur data coverage and availability, 1991 pamphlet, 2326–7.77

Census Bur rpts and data files, coverage and availability, 1991 annual listing, 2304–2

Census of Housing, 1990: inventory, occupancy, and costs, State fact sheet series, 2326–21

Census of Population and Housing, 1990: housing units occupied and vacant, persons in group quarters, and household size, by region, census div, and State, press release, 2328–71

Census of Population and Housing, 1990: voting age and total population by race, and housing units, by block, redistricting counts required under PL 94-171, State CD-ROM series, 2551–6

Census of Population and Housing, 1990: voting age and total population by race, and housing units, by county and city, redistricting counts required under PL 94-171, State summary rpt series, 2551–5

Census of Population, 1990: urban areas land area, housing units, and population, by State and compared to rural areas, press release, 2328–39

Current Housing Reports, unit and household characteristics, subject rpt series, 2486–1

Fed Govt property acquired through foreclosure and savings instn failure, 1-family homes inventory by State, acquisition costs, and sales, for 4 agencies, 1986-90, GAO rpt, 26113–513

Low income housing supply impacts of HUD programs to maintain supply and to deter insured mortgage prepayment, 1986-90 and projected to 2005, GAO rpt, 26131–84

New single-family houses sold and for sale, by price, stage of construction, months on market, and region, monthly rpt, 2382–3

North Central States, FHLB 7th District housing vacancy rates for single and multifamily units and mobile homes, by ZIP code, annual MSA rpt series, 9304–18

Public housing renovation costs and alternative funding methods, by project type and region, 1990 rpt, 5188–127

Statistical Abstract of US, 1991 annual data compilation, 2324–1.26

Housing supply and requirements

Supply, demand, and financing of housing, and construction industry operations, biennial rpt, discontinued, 5184–5

Texas economic and housing conditions, bank failures, and thrift and Federal regulators real estate holdings, 1980s-90, hearings, 21248–146

Vacant housing characteristics and costs, and occupancy and vacancy rates, by region and metro-nonmetro location, quarterly rpt, 2482–1

Vacant housing characteristics, and occupancy and vacancy rates, by tenure and location, 1960s-90, annual rpt, 2484–1

West Central States, FHLB 10th District housing vacancy rates for single and multifamily units and mobile homes, by ZIP code, annual MSA rpt series, 9304–22

Western States, FHLB 12th District housing vacancy rates for single and multifamily units and mobile homes, by ZIP code, annual MSA rpt series, 9304–21

see also Building permits

see also Housing condition and occupancy

see also Housing construction

see also Housing costs and financing

see also Housing sales

see also Urban renewal

see also Wrecking and demolition

Housing tenure

Affordability indicators for housing, by current tenure, 1988, fact sheet, 2326–17.31

Affordability indicators for housing, by household composition, income, and current tenure, 1988, 2486–1.11

Alteration and repair spending for housing, by type, tenure, region, and other characteristics, quarterly rpt, 2382–7

American Housing Survey: inventory change from 1973, by reason, unit and household characteristics, and location, 1983, biennial rpt, 2485–14

American Housing Survey: unit and households characteristics, MSA fact sheet series, 2485–11

American Housing Survey: unit and households characteristics, unit and neighborhood quality, and journey to work by MSA location, for 11 MSAs, 1984 survey, supplement, 2485–8

American Housing Survey: unit and households detailed characteristics, and unit and neighborhood quality, MSA rpt series, 2485–6

American Housing Survey: unit and households detailed characteristics, and unit and neighborhood quality, 1987, biennial rpt, 2485–12; 2485–13

Assets of households, by type of holding and selected characteristics, 1988, Current Population Rpt, 2546–20.16

Census of Housing, 1990: inventory, occupancy, and costs, State fact sheet series, 2326–21

Census of Population and Housing, 1990: population and housing characteristics, households, and land area, by county, subdiv, and place, State rpt series, 2551–1

Census of Population and Housing, 1990: population and housing selected characteristics, by region, press release, 2328–74

Consumer Expenditure Survey, household income by source, and itemized spending, by selected characteristics and region, 1988-89, annual rpt, 6764–5

Consumer Expenditure Survey, spending by category, and income, by selected household characteristics and location, 1990, annual press release, 6726–1.42

Consumer Income, socioeconomic characteristics of persons, families, and households, detailed cross-tabulations, Current Population Rpt series, 2546–6

Crime victimization, by victim characteristics, offense, and whether reported to police, 1973-88, 6066–3.45

Crime victimization of women, by relation to offender, circumstances, and victim characteristics, for rape and other violent offenses, 1973-87, 6068–243

Crime victimization rates, by victim and offender characteristics, circumstances, and offense, 1988 survey, annual rpt, 6066–3.42

Crime victimization rates, by victim and offender characteristics, circumstances, and offense, 1989 survey, annual rpt, 6066–3.44

Food spending, by item, household composition, income, age, race, and region, 1980-88, Consumer Expenditure Survey biennial rpt, 1544–30

Hispanic Americans social and economic characteristics, by detailed origin, 1991, Current Population Rpt, 2546–1.448; 2546–1.451

Households and family characteristics, by location, 1990, annual Current Population Rpt, 2546–1.447

Households by tenure and population size, by age group, State, and county, 1980 and 1985, 2546–3.169

Income and consumer spending of households, for selected population groups, quarterly journal, 1702–1

Living arrangements, family relationships, and marital status, by selected characteristics, 1990, annual Current Population Rpt, 2546–1.449

Ownership of homes, rates by location and age of householder, quarterly rpt, 2482–1

Ownership rates, changes by State, and for householders under age 35 by region, 1980s, fact sheet, 2326–17.28

Puerto Rico population and housing characteristics, 1990 Census of Population and Housing, press release, 2328–78

State and Metro Area Data Book, 1991 data compilation, 2328–54

Statistical Abstract of US, 1991 annual data compilation, 2324–1.26

Taxes, spending, and govt efficiency, public opinion by respondent characteristics, 1991 survey, annual rpt, 10044–2

Vacant housing characteristics and costs, and occupancy and vacancy rates, by region and metro-nonmetro location, quarterly rpt, 2482–1

Vacant housing characteristics, and occupancy and vacancy rates, by tenure and location, 1960s-90, annual rpt, 2484–1

Victimizations by region and victim characteristics, and rpts to police, by offense, 1973-90, annual rpt, 6066–25.35; 6066–25.41

Index by Subjects and Names

Virgin Islands population and housing characteristics, 1990 Census of Population and Housing, press release, 2328–81

Voting and registration, by socioeconomic and demographic characteristics, 1990 congressional election, biennial Current Population Rpt, 2546–1.454

see also Condominiums and cooperatives

see also Housing sales

see also Rent

Houston, Tex.

CPI by component for US city average, and by region, population size, and for 15 metro areas, monthly rpt, 6762–1

CPI by component for US city average, and by region, population size, and for 27 metro areas, monthly rpt, 6762–2

CPI by major component for 2 Texas MSAs, monthly rpt, 6962–2

Drug test results at arrest, by drug type, offense, and sex, for selected urban areas, quarterly rpt, 6062–3

Employment, earnings, hours, and CPI changes, for Houston metro area, 1970s-90, annual rpt, 6964–1

Housing starts and completions authorized by building permits in 40 MSAs, quarterly rpt, 2382–9

Housing vacancy and property value appreciation rates for 4 metro areas, 1991 GAO rpt, 26131–84

Oil prices by product, for 4 cities, seasonal weekly rpt, 3162–45

Wages by occupation, for office and plant workers, 1991 survey, periodic MSA rpt, 6785–12.3

see also under By City and By SMSA or MSA in the "Index by Categories"

Howe, Geoffrey R.

"Cohort Study of Fat Intake and Risk of Breast Cancer", 4472–1.204

Howe, Howard

"Political and Institutional Independence of U.S. Monetary Policy", 9385–8.106

Howell, Embry M.

"Comparison of Medicaid and Non-Medicaid Obstetrical Care in California", 4652–1.241

Howenstine, Ned G.

"Alternative Measures of the Rate of Return on Direct Investment", 2702–1.217

Hrubovcak, James

"Agriculture and Capital Gains Taxation", 1561–16.202

Hu, Patricia S.

"Light-Duty Vehicle Summary: First Six Months of Model Year 1991", 3302–4

"Transportation Energy Data Book: Edition 11", 3304–5

HUD

see Department of Housing and Urban Development

Hudson, Patrick L.

"Chironomidae of the Southeastern U.S.: A Checklist of Species and Notes on Biology, Distribution, and Habitat", 5506–13.3

Hudson River

Water supply and quality in streams and lakes, and groundwater levels in wells, by drainage basin, 1988, annual State rpt series, 5666–16

Water supply and quality in streams and lakes, and groundwater levels in wells, by drainage basin, 1989, annual State rpt series, 5666–12

Water supply and quality in streams and lakes, and groundwater levels in wells, by drainage basin, 1990, annual State rpt series, 5666–10

Water supply in northeastern US, precipitation and stream runoff by station, monthly rpt, 2182–3

Water supply in US and southern Canada, streamflow, surface and groundwater conditions, and reservoir levels, by location, monthly rpt, 5662–3

Huffman, G. C.
"Ground-Water Data for Michigan, 1988", 5666–28.2

Huffman, Gregory W.
"Tax Analysis in a Real Business Cycle Model: On Measuring Harberger Triangles and Okun Gaps", 9383–20.8

Hughes, Arthur L.
"Feasibility of Collecting Drug Abuse Data by Telephone", 4042–3.230

Hughes, John S.
"Procedure Codes: Potential Modifiers of Diagnosis-Related Groups", 4652–1.204

Hughes, Merritt R.
"Do Advance Deficiency Payments Affect Credit Markets?", 1541–1.204

Hukill, Craig
"Labor and the Supreme Court: Significant Issues of 1990-91", 6722–1.208

Human experimentation
Cell cultures with genetic abnormalities, availability and cultures shipped, 1990-91, biennial listing, 4474–23
NIH activities, funding by program and recipient type, staff, and clinic patients, by inst, FY90, annual rpt, 4434–3
Reproduction and population research, Fed Govt funding by project, FY89, annual listing, 4474–9

Human Genetic Mutant Cell Repository
Cell cultures with genetic abnormalities, availability and cultures shipped, 1990-91, biennial listing, 4474–23

Human immunodeficiency virus
see Acquired immune deficiency syndrome

Human Nutrition Information Service
Budget of US, obligations and authority by function, agency, and program, with summaries, analyses, and historical tables, FY92, annual rpt, 104–2
Food composition, detailed data on nutrients, calories, and waste, for raw, processed, and prepared foods, series, 1356–3
Food consumption, dietary composition, and nutrient intake, 1987/88 natl survey, preliminary rpt series, 1356–1

Human resources management
see Civil service system
see Employee development
see Employee performance and appraisal
see Employment services
see Personnel management

Human rights
see Civil rights

Humanities
see Arts and the humanities

Humpage, Owen F.
"Central-Bank Intervention: Recent Literature, Continuing Controversy", 9377–1.205

Humphrey, David B.
"Measurement and Efficiency Issues in Commercial Banking", 9366–6.265
"Scope Economies: Fixed Costs, Complementarity, and Functional Form", 9389–19.28

Hung, Juann H.
"Effectiveness of Sterilized U.S. Foreign Exchange Intervention: An Empirical Study Based on the Noise Trading Approach", 9385–8.114
"Noise Trading and the Effectiveness of Sterilized Foreign Exchange Intervention", 9385–8.107

Hungary
Agricultural exports of high-value commodities, indexes and sales by commodity, world area, and country, 1960s-86, 1528–323
Agricultural production, trade, and policies in foreign countries, summary data by country, 1989-90, annual factbook, 1924–12
Agricultural trade of US, by detailed commodity and country, 1989, annual rpt, 1524–8
Agricultural trade of US, by detailed commodity and country, 1990, semiannual rpt, 1522–4
Bearings (ball) from 14 countries, injury to US industry from foreign subsidized and less than fair value imports, investigation with background financial and operating data, 1991 rpt, 9886–19.74
Debt to foreign lenders by component, trade, balances, and other economic indicators, by Eastern Europe country, 1985-89, hearing, 21248–148
Drug abuse indicators, by world region and selected country, 1990 semiannual conf, 4492–5.1
Economic aid of US and other donor countries by type and recipient, and role in advancing economic interests, 1980s-90, 2048–152
Economic aid to Eastern Europe from US, by agency and country, FY90-92, GAO rpt, 26123–319
Economic and military aid and loans from US and intl agencies, by program and country, FY46-90, annual rpt, 9914–5
Economic conditions in USSR, Eastern Europe, OECD, and selected other countries, 1960s-90, annual rpt, 9114–4
Economic conditions, policy, and trade practices, by country, 1988-90, annual rpt, 21384–5
Economic, social, political, and geographic summary data, by country, 1991, annual factbook, 9114–2
Energy production, trade, use, and AID dev assistance, for 3 Eastern Europe countries, 1980s-91, 25318–81
Export licensing, monitoring, and enforcement activities, FY90, annual rpt, 2024–1
Exports and imports of US, by commodity and country, 1970-89, world area rpt, 9116–1.3
Exports and imports of US, by selected country, country group, and commodity group, 1990, annual rpt, 2044–37
Exports and imports of US, by transport mode, country, and SITC 1- to 3-digit commodity, 1990, annual rpt, 2424–12

Exports and imports of US with Communist countries, by detailed commodity and country, quarterly rpt with articles, 9882–2
Exports, imports, and balances of US with major trading partners, by product category, 1986-90, annual chartbook, 9884–21
Exports of US, detailed Schedule B commodities with countries of destination, 1990, annual rpt, 2424–10
Human rights conditions in 170 countries, and US economic and military aid, 1990, annual rpt, 21384–3
Market economy transition of Eastern Europe countries, economic conditions and energy balance, by country, 1985-90, 9118–13
Market economy transition of Eastern Europe countries, with trade agreements and bilateral US trade data by country, late 1980s-90, annual rpt, 444–2
Military aid of US, arms sales, and training programs costs and budget requests, by program, world region, and country, FY90-92, annual rpt, 7144–13
Nuclear power plant capacity and operating status, by plant and communist and regulated market country, as of Dec 1990, annual rpt, 3164–57.2
Older persons health condition and care research, data availability and collection methodology, for US and selected countries, 1988 conf, 4147–5.6
Poultry products exports of US, EC, and 3 leading countries, by world area, 1986-90, semiannual rpt, 1925–33.1
Steel imports of US under voluntary restraint agreement, by product, customs district, and country, with US industry operating data, quarterly rpt, 9882–13
UN voting record and share of votes in agreement with US, by issue, country, and world area, 1990, annual rpt, 7004–18
see also under By Foreign Country in the "Index by Categories"

Hunger
see Food assistance
see Food supply
see Nutrition and malnutrition

Hunter, Gillian
"Report to Congress on the Effect of the Full Funding Limit on Pension Benefit Security", 8008–152

Hunter, Linda C.
"Europe 1992: An Overview", 9379–1.201

Hunter, William B.
"Mental Health and Mental Illness", 4088–2
"Violence", 4088–2

Hunter, William C.
"Quasi-Fixed Inputs in the Estimation of Bank Scale Economies", 9371–10.54
"Some Evidence on the Impact of Quasi-Fixed Inputs on Bank Scale Economy Estimates", 9371–1.208
"Stochastic Dominance Approach to the Evaluation of Foreign Exchange Forecasts", 9371–10.63
"Supply Shocks and Household Demand for Motor Fuel", 9371–1.204

Hunterdon County, N.J.
Wages by occupation, and benefits for office and plant workers, 1990 survey, periodic MSA rpt, 6785–11.4

Hunterdon County, N.J.

see also under By SMSA or MSA in the "Index by Categories"

Hunting and fishing licenses

Birds (sandhill crane) hunting activity and permits, by State and county, 1989/90-1990/91, annual rpt, 5504–31

California sport and commercial fish and shellfish landings, permits issued, and harbor facilities, 1916-86, 5738–20

Duck hunting stamps philatelic and sales info, 1991/92, annual supplement, 5504–25

Duck stamps sold, by State and flyway, and permits by Canada Province, 1989-90, annual rpt, 5504–28

Holders of fishing and hunting licenses, by State, FY90, annual rpt, 5504–13

Issues of fishing and hunting licenses, and costs, by State, FY90, annual tables, 5504–16

State govt revenue by source, spending and debt by function, and holdings, FY90, annual rpt, 2466–2.6

Statistical Abstract of US, 1991 annual data compilation, 2324–1.7

Tax collections of State govts by detailed type of tax, and tax rates, by State, FY90, annual rpt, 2466–2.7

Hunting and trapping

Alabama hunter characteristics and expenditures, 1990 conf papers, annual rpt, 1204–38

Alaska rural areas population characteristics, and energy resources dev effects, series, 5736–5

Bears (grizzly) in Yellowstone Natl Park area, monitoring results, 1990, annual rpt, 5544–4

Birds (mourning dove) population, by hunting and nonhunting State, 1966-91, annual rpt, 5504–15

Birds (sandhill crane) hunting activity and permits, by State and county, 1989/90-1990/91, annual rpt, 5504–31

Birds (waterfowl) hunter harvest, age and sex ratios by species, State, and flyway, 1986-90, annual rpt, 5504–32

Birds (waterfowl) hunter harvest and unretrieved kills, and duck stamps sold, by species, State, and flyway, 1989-90, annual rpt, 5504–28

Birds (woodcock) population in US and Canada from 1968, and hunter harvest, by State, 1991, annual rpt, 5504–11

Coastal areas recreation facilities, by State, county, estuary, and level of govt, 1972-84, 2178–29

Coastal areas recreation facilities of Fed Govt and States, visitor and site characteristics, 1987-90 survey, regional rpt series, 2176–9

County Business Patterns, 1988: employment, establishments, and payroll, by SIC 2- to 4-digit industry and county, annual State rpt series, 2326–6

County Business Patterns, 1989: employment, establishments, and payroll, by SIC 2- to 4-digit industry and county, annual State rpt series, 2326–8

Fish and Wildlife Service restoration and hunter safety funding, by State, FY92, semiannual press release, 5502–1

Fish and Wildlife Service restoration programs finances by State, and excise tax collections, FY90, annual rpt, 5504–13

Fish and Wildlife Service restoration programs funding, land purchases, and project listing, by State, FY89, annual rpt, 5504–1

Forest Service activities and finances, by region and State, FY90, annual rpt, 1204–1.1

Forest Service mgmt of public lands and resources dev, environmental, economic, and social impacts of alternative programs, projected to 2040, 1208–24

Forests (natl) recreational use, by type of activity and State, 1990, annual rpt, 1204–17

Great Lakes area economic conditions and outlook, for US and Canada, 1970s-90, 9375–15

Marine mammals protection activities and funding, populations, and harvests, by species, 1989, annual rpt, 5504–12

Public lands acreage, grants, use, revenues, and allocations, by State, FY90, annual rpt, 5724–1.2

Public lands recreation facilities and use, and Land Mgmt Bur mgmt activities, funding, and plans, State rpt series, 5726–5

Research of State fish and wildlife agencies, federally funded wildlife projects and costs by species and State, 1990, annual listing, 5504–24

Tax (income) returns of sole proprietorships, income statement items, by industry group, 1989, annual article, 8302–2.214

Whales (bowhead) population in Arctic areas, impacts of subsistence whaling, shipping, noise, and other human activity, mid 1970s-80s, 5738–30

see also Fish and fishing industry

see also Fishing, sport

see also Hunting and fishing licenses

Huntington Beach, Calif.

see also under By City in the "Index by Categories"

Huntington, W.Va.

see also under By SMSA or MSA in the "Index by Categories"

Huntley, M. Stephen, Jr.

"Civilian Training in High-Altitude Flight Physiology", 7506–10.92

"Use and Design of Flightcrew Checklists and Manuals", 7506–10.86

Huntsville, Ala.

Wages by occupation, for office and plant workers, 1991 survey, periodic MSA rpt, 6785–12.2

see also under By City and By SMSA or MSA in the "Index by Categories"

Hurricanes

see Storms

Hutchins, Cecil C., Jr.

"Southern Pulpwood Production, 1989", 1204–23

Hutchinson, Fred, Cancer Research Center

"Population-Based Study of Hospice, Parts I-IV", 4658–53

Hutchison, Michael

"Central Bank Secrecy and Money Surprises: International Evidence", 9393–10.16

Hyberg, Bengt

"Sunflower Acreage Response to Increased Commodity Program Flexibility", 1561–3.201

Hyde, William F.

"Welfare Gains from Wood Preservatives Research", 1502–3.202

Hydrocarbons

see Petrochemicals

Hydroelectric power

Army Corps of Engineers water resources dev projects, characteristics, and costs, 1950s-89, biennial State rpt series, 3756–1

Army Corps of Engineers water resources dev projects, characteristics, and costs, 1950s-91, biennial State rpt series, 3756–2

Bonneville Power Admin mgmt of Fed Columbia River Power System, finances, operations, and sales by customer, FY90, annual rpt, 3224–1

Business statistics, detailed data for major industries and economic indicators, *Survey of Current Business,* monthly rpt, 2702–1.13

Certification applications filed with FERC, for small power production and cogeneration facilities, FY80-90, annual listing, 3084–13

Certification of hydroelectric projects, rate regulation, and other FERC activities, FY90, annual rpt, 3084–9

Colorado River Basin Federal reservoir and power operations and revenues, 1990-91, annual rpt, 5824–6

Consumption of energy, by detailed fuel type, end-use sector, and State, 1960-89, State Energy Data System annual rpt, 3164–39

Environmental Quality, status of problems, protection programs, research, and intl issues, 1991 annual rpt, 484–1

Foreign and US energy production and use, by energy type and country, 1980-89, annual rpt, 3164–50.1; 3164–50.5; 3164–50.8

Natl Energy Strategy plans for conservation and pollution reduction, impacts of technology and regulation proposals, projected 1990-2030, 3166–6.47

Natl Energy Strategy plans for renewable energy dev, supply projected under alternative cost and capacity use assumptions, 1990-2030, 3166–6.50

Pacific Northwest electric power capacity and use, by energy source, projected under alternative load and demand cases, 1991-2011, annual rpt, 3224–3

Pacific Northwest surplus energy from hydroelectric power, monthly 1929-78, 3224–3.2

Power plants (hydroelectric) licensed by FERC, characteristics and location, as of Oct 1991, annual listing, 3084–11

Power plants and capacity, by fuel used, owner, location, and operating status, 1990, and for units planned 1991-2000, annual listing, 3164–36

Power plants capital and production costs, operations, and fuel use, by fuel type, plant, utility, and location, 1989, annual rpt, 3164–9

Power plants production, fuel use, stocks, and costs by fuel type, and sales, by State, monthly rpt with articles, 3162–35

Production, plant capacity, and fuel use, by fuel type, census div, and State, 1985-89, annual rpt, 3164–11.1

Index by Subjects and Names

Ice conditions

Reclamation Bur irrigation activities, finances, and project impacts in western US, 1989, annual rpt, 5824–12

Rural Electrification Admin financed electric power plants, with location, capacity, and owner, as of Jan 1991, annual listing, 1244–6

Southwestern Fed Power System financial statements, sales by customer, and operations and costs by project, FY90, annual rpt, 3244–1

State and Metro Area Data Book, 1991 data compilation, 2328–54

Statistical Abstract of US, 1991 annual data compilation, 2324–1.19

Supply, demand, and prices, by fuel type and end-use sector, alternative projections 1989-2010, annual rpt, 3164–75

Supply, demand, and prices, by fuel type and end-use sector, projections and underlying assumptions, 1990-2010, annual rpt, 3164–90

Supply, demand, and prices, by fuel type and end-use sector, with foreign comparisons, 1990 and trends from 1949, annual rpt, 3164–74

Supply, demand, and prices, by fuel type, end-use sector, and country, detailed data, monthly rpt with articles, 3162–24

Supply, demand, and prices of energy, forecasts by resource type, quarterly rpt, 3162–34

Tennessee Valley river control activities, and hydroelectric power generation and capacity, 1989, annual rpt, 9804–7

TVA finances and operations by program and facility, FY90, annual rpt, 9804–32

Utilities finances and operations, detailed data for privately owned firms, 1989, annual rpt, 3164–23

Utilities finances and operations, detailed data for publicly owned firms, 1989, annual rpt, 3164–24

Water supply in US and southern Canada, streamflow, surface and groundwater conditions, and reservoir levels, by location, monthly rpt, 5662–3

Water use by end use, well withdrawals, and public supply deliveries, by county, State rpt series, 5666–24

Western Area Power Admin activities by plant, financial statements, and sales by customer, FY90, annual rpt, 3254–1

Hydrogen

see Gases

Hydrology

Alaska OCS environmental conditions and oil dev impacts, compilation of papers, series, 2176–1

California OCS oil and gas dev impacts on water quality, marine life, and sediments, by site, 1986-89, annual rpt, 5734–11

Coastal and estuarine environmental conditions, research results and methodology, series, 2176–7

Coastal and riparian areas environmental conditions, fish, wildlife, use, and mgmt, for individual ecosystems, series, 5506–9

Colorado River sand deposit characteristics, and density of campsites, 1920s-80s, 5668–122

DOE R&D projects and funding at natl labs, universities, and other instns, FY90, annual summary rpt, 3004–18.2

Estuary environmental conditions, and fish and shellfish catch by species and region, 1980s, 2178–27

Geological Survey activities and funding, FY90, annual rpt, 5664–8

Great Lakes Environmental Research Lab activities, FY90 annual rpt, 2144–26

Groundwater supply, quality, chemistry, and use, State and local area rpt series, 5666–28

Groundwater supply, quality, chemistry, other characteristics, and use, regional rpt series, 5666–25

Radioactive low-level waste repository site design, characteristics, and monitoring techniques, 1987 conf, 5668–116

Research on water resources, data collection and analysis activities of USGS Water Resources Div Districts, with project descriptions, series, 5666–26

Water quality, chemistry, hydrology, and other characteristics, local area studies, series, 5666–27

Water supply, hydrologic events, and end use, by State, 1988-89, annual rpt, 5664–12

Water supply in US and southern Canada, streamflow, surface and groundwater conditions, and reservoir levels, by location, monthly rpt, 5662–3

Wetlands acreage, resources, soil and water properties, and conservation efforts, by wetland type, State rpt series, 5506–11

see also Oceanography

see also Water area

see also Water pollution

see also Water power

see also Water resources development

see also Water supply and use

see also Watershed projects

Hydrothermal power

see Geothermal resources

Hyland, Stephanie L.

"Age-Related Reductions in Life Insurance Benefits", 6722–1.216

Hypertension

Blood pressure home monitoring by hypertensives, health condition and risk behavior compared to other hypertensives, local area study, 1991 article, 4042–3.207

Cases of acute and chronic conditions, disability, absenteeism, and health services use, by selected characteristics, 1987, CD-ROM, 4147–10.177

Deaths and rates, by cause and age, preliminary 1989-90, US Vital Statistics annual rpt, 4144–7

Deaths and rates, by cause, provisional data, monthly rpt, 4142–1.2

Deaths and rates, by detailed cause and demographic characteristics, 1988 and trends from 1900, US Vital Statistics annual rpt, 4144–2

Developing countries aged population and selected characteristics, 1980s and projected to 2020, country rpt series, 2326–19

Drug and diet effects on hypertension, and nonprescription diet pills and analgesics sales and adverse reactions, 1980s-90, hearing, 21728–77

Health condition and health care resources, use, and spending, 1950s-89, annual data compilation, 4144–11

Health maintenance organizations Medicare enrollees quality of care indicators compared to fee-for-service, demonstration projects results, mid 1980s, 4658–46

Indians and Alaska Natives chronic disease prevalence, for 8 conditions by age and sex, 1987, 4186–8.20

Kidney end-stage disease cases, treatment, outcomes, and characteristics of patients, organ donors, and facilities, late 1970s-88, annual rpt, 4474–37

Kidney end-stage disease treatment facilities, Medicare enrollment and reimbursement, survival, and patient characteristics, 1983-89, annual rpt, 4654–16

Minority group and women health condition, services use, payment sources, and health care labor force, by poverty status, 1940s-89, chartbook, 4118–56

Minority group health condition, services use, costs, and indicators of services need, 1950s-88, 4118–55

Natl Heart, Lung, and Blood Inst activities, and grants by recipient and location, FY90 and disease trends from 1940, annual rpt, 4474–15

Preventive disease and health improvement goals and recommended activities for 2000, with trends 1970s-80s, 4048–10

Women's hypertension risk, by age and race, aggregate 1976-80, article, 4042–3.231

see also under By Disease in the "Index by Categories"

Hysterectomy

see Sexual sterilization

Iams, Howard M.

"Childcare Effects on Social Security Benefits", 2626–10.138

"Predictors of Mortality Among Newly Retired Workers", 4742–1.206

IBRD

see International Bank for Reconstruction and Development

Ibuprofen

see Drugs

ICC

see Interstate Commerce Commission

Ice conditions

Alaska OCS environmental conditions and oil dev impacts, compilation of papers, series, 2176–1

Bering Sea and Alaska north coast ice conditions, monthly rpt, 2182–5

Global climate change environmental, infrastructure, and health impacts, with model results and background data, 1850s-2100, 9188–113

Weather trends and deviations, by world region, 1880s-1990, annual chartbook, 2184–9

Whales (bowhead) population in Arctic areas, behavioral differences by location, 1970s-80s, 5738–29

Whales (bowhead) population in Beaufort Sea, and fall aerial survey operations, 1979-90, annual rpt, 5734–10

Whales (bowhead and white) migration through Beaufort Sea, behavior impacts of oil drilling and aircraft noise, spring 1989, 5738–27

see also Glaciers

Ice, manufactured

Ice, manufactured

County Business Patterns, 1988: employment, establishments, and payroll, by SIC 2- to 4-digit industry and county, annual State rpt series, 2326–6

County Business Patterns, 1989: employment, establishments, and payroll, by SIC 2- to 4-digit industry and county, annual State rpt series, 2326–8

Manufacturing annual survey, 1989: finances and operations, by SIC 2- to 4-digit industry, series, 2506–15

Manufacturing census, 1987: finances and operations, by SIC 2- to 4-digit industry, State, and MSA, with trends from 1849, 2497–1

Manufacturing census, 1987: finances and operations, by type of organization and SIC 2- to 4-digit industry, subject rpt, 2497–5

Occupational injury and illness rates, by SIC 2- to 4-digit industry, 1988-89, annual rpt, 6844–7

Price indexes (producer), by stage of processing and detailed commodity, monthly rpt, 6762–6

Price indexes (producer), by stage of processing and detailed commodity, monthly 1990, annual rpt, 6764–2

Iceland

Agricultural exports of high-value commodities, indexes and sales by commodity, world area, and country, 1960s-86, 1528–323

Agricultural trade of US, by detailed commodity and country, 1989, annual rpt, 1524–8

Agricultural trade of US, by detailed commodity and country, 1990, semiannual rpt, 1522–4

AID loans repayment status and terms by program and country, and status of predecessor agency loans, quarterly rpt, 9912–3

Economic and military aid and loans from US and intl agencies, by program and country, FY46-90, annual rpt, 9914–5

Economic conditions, investment and export opportunities, and trade practices, 1991 country market research rpt, 2046–6.5

Economic, social, political, and geographic summary data, by country, 1991, annual factbook, 9114–2

Exports and imports of NATO members with PRC, by country, 1987-90, annual rpt, 7144–14

Exports and imports of OECD members, by country, 1989, annual rpt, 7144–10

Exports and imports of US, by transport mode, country, and SITC 1- to 3-digit commodity, 1990, annual rpt, 2424–12

Exports of US, detailed Schedule B commodities with countries of destination, 1990, annual rpt, 2424–10

GNP and GNP growth for OECD members, by country, 1980-90, annual rpt, 7144–8

Human rights conditions in 170 countries, and US economic and military aid, 1990, annual rpt, 21384–3

Oil production, trade, use, and stocks, by selected country and country group, monthly rpt, 3162–42

UN voting record and share of votes in agreement with US, by issue, country, and world area, 1990, annual rpt, 7004–18

Idaho

Banks (insured commercial and savings) deposits by instn, State, MSA, and county, as of June 1990, annual regional rpt, 9295–3.6

Bears (grizzly) in Yellowstone Natl Park area, monitoring results, 1990, annual rpt, 5544–4

Birds of prey, rodent, and vegetation distribution and characteristics, for Idaho Snake River area, research results, 1990, annual rpt, 5724–14

County Business Patterns, 1989: employment, establishments, and payroll, by SIC 2- to 4-digit industry and county, annual State rpt, 2326–8.14

DOD prime contract awards, by contractor, service branch, State, and city, FY90, annual rpt, 3544–22

Energy-efficiency building codes, effect on house construction practices in Bonneville Power Admin service areas, 1987, 3228–15

Fed Govt spending in States and local areas, by type, State, county, and city, FY90, annual rpt, 2464–3

Fed Govt spending in States, by type, program, agency, and State, FY90, annual rpt, 2464–2

Gemstone production in selected States, Mineral Industry Surveys, 1988-90, advance annual rpt, 5614–5.10

HHS financial aid, by program, recipient, State, and city, FY90, annual regional listing, 4004–3.10

Hospital deaths of Medicare patients, actual and expected rates by diagnosis, and hospital characteristics, by instn, FY87-89, annual regional rpt, 4654–14.10

Income (personal) per capita and by source, and earnings by industry div, by State, MSA, and county, 1984-89, annual regional rpt, 2704–2.5

Jail adult and juvenile population, employment, spending, instn conditions, and inmate programs, by county and facility, 1988, regional rpt series, 6068–144.5

Land Mgmt Bur activities and finances, and public land acreage and use, FY90, annual State rpt, 5724–11.4

Land Mgmt Bur activities and finances, and public land acreage and use, FY91, annual State rpt, 5724–11.2

Marriages, divorces, and rates, by characteristics of spouses, State, and county, 1987 and trends from 1920, US Vital Statistics annual rpt, 4144–4

Mineral industries census, 1987: finances and operations, by SIC 2- to 4-digit industry, State, and county, census div rpt, 2515–1.8

Mineral Industry Surveys, State reviews of production, 1990, preliminary annual rpt, 5614–6

Minerals (industrial) reserves, production, and use, and characteristics of individual deposits, 1991 State rpt, 5606–10.1

Minerals Yearbook, 1989, Vol 2: State review of production and sales by commodity, and business activity, annual rpt, 5604–16.13

Minerals Yearbook, 1989, Vol 2: State reviews of production, sales, and firms, by commodity, and business activity, annual rpt, 5604–34

Onion farm acreage, pesticide use, operators, and other characteristics, for 6 producer States, 1989, article, 1561–11.201

Physicians, by specialty, age, sex, and location of training and practice, 1989, State rpt, 4116–6.13

Population and housing census, 1990: population and housing characteristics, households, and land area, by county, subdiv, and place, State rpt, 2551–1.14

Population and housing census, 1990: voting age and total population by race, and housing units, by block, redistricting counts required under PL 94-171, State CD-ROM release, 2551–6.2

Population and housing census, 1990: voting age and total population by race, and housing units, by county and city, redistricting counts required under PL 94-171, State summary rpt, 2551–5.13

Radiation monitoring results of Idaho Natl Engineering Lab, for facilities and nearby areas, 1990, annual rpt, 3354–10

Soil and water conditions, land use, and conservation needs on non-Federal lands, 1982 and 1987, State rpt, 1266–5.1

Statistical Abstract of US, 1991 annual data compilation, 2324–1

Supplemental Security Income payments and beneficiaries, by type of eligibility, State, and county, Dec 1989, annual rpt, 4744–27.10

Timber in northwestern US and British Columbia, production, prices, trade, and employment, quarterly rpt, 1202–3

Timber insect and disease incidence and damage, and control activities, 1989, State rpt, 1206–49.1

Water (groundwater) supply, quality, chemistry, and use, 1982-85, local area rpt, 5666–28.11

Water resources dev projects of Army Corps of Engineers, characteristics, and costs, 1950s-89, biennial State rpt, 3756–1.13

Water supply and quality in streams and lakes, and groundwater levels in wells, by drainage basin, 1990, annual State rpt, 5666–10.11

Water supply, and snow survey results, monthly State rpt, 1266–2.4

Wildlife mgmt activities and funding, acreage by habitat type, and scientific staff, for Bur of Land Mgmt, 1990 State rpt, 5726–7.2

see also under By State in the "Index by Categories"

Idaho National Engineering Laboratory

"Environmental Monitoring for EG&G Idaho Facilities at the Idaho National Engineering Laboratory, Annual Report, 1990", 3354–10

see also Department of Energy National Laboratories

Identification papers

see Government forms and paperwork

Illegitimacy

see Births out of wedlock

Illinois

Banks (insured commercial and savings) deposits by instn, State, MSA, and county, as of June 1990, annual regional rpt, 9295–3.3

Banks (multinatl) US branches assets and liabilities, total and for 3 States, monthly rpt, quarterly data, 9362–1.4

Index by Subjects and Names

Immigration and emigration

Carbon dioxide in atmosphere, North Central States economic and agricultural impacts, model descriptions and results, 1980s and projected to 2030, 3006–11.15

Child welfare programs funding by source, and foster care program operations and client characteristics, for selected States, 1960s-95, 25368–169

Coal production and mines by county, prices, productivity, miners, and reserves, by mining method and State, 1989-90, annual rpt, 3164–25

County Business Patterns, 1989: employment, establishments, and payroll, by SIC 2- to 4-digit industry and county, annual State rpt, 2326–8.15

DOD prime contract awards, by contractor, service branch, State, and city, FY90, annual rpt, 3544–22

Economic conditions and outlook, for US and Canada Great Lakes area, 1970s-90, 9375–15

Fed Govt spending in States and local areas, by type, State, county, and city, FY90, annual rpt, 2464–3

Fed Govt spending in States, by type, program, agency, and State, FY90, annual rpt, 2464–2

Foster care placements, discharges, and returns to care, by selected characteristics of children, and length of stay factors, 1985-86, GAO rpt, 26121–432

HHS financial aid, by program, recipient, State, and city, FY90, annual regional listing, 4004–3.5

Hospital deaths of Medicare patients, actual and expected rates by diagnosis, and hospital characteristics, by instn, FY87-89, annual regional rpt, 4654–14.5

Housing vacancy rates for single and multifamily units and mobile homes in FHLB 7th District, by ZIP code, annual MSA rpt series, 9304–18

Income (personal) per capita and by source, and earnings by industry div, by State, MSA, and county, 1984-89, annual regional rpt, 2704–2.2

Jail adult and juvenile population, employment, spending, instn conditions, and inmate programs, by county and facility, 1988, regional rpt series, 6068–144.3

Lumber (veneer log) production, mill receipts, and trade, by species, with residue use, for North Central States, 1988, quadrennial rpt, 1208–220

Marriages, divorces, and rates, by characteristics of spouses, State, and county, 1987 and trends from 1920, US Vital Statistics annual rpt, 4144–4

Mineral Industry Surveys, State reviews of production, 1990, preliminary annual rpt, 5614–6

Minerals Yearbook, 1989, Vol 2: State review of production and sales by commodity, and business activity, annual rpt, 5604–16.14

Minerals Yearbook, 1989, Vol 2: State reviews of production, sales, and firms, by commodity, and business activity, annual rpt, 5604–34

Mortgage interest fixed and adjustable rates and fees offered by Illinois S&Ls, monthly rpt, 9302–6

Physicians, by specialty, age, sex, and location of training and practice, 1989, State rpt, 4116–6.14

Population and housing census, 1990: population and housing characteristics, households, and land area, by county, subdiv, and place, State rpt, 2551–1.15

Population and housing census, 1990: voting age and total population by race, and housing units, by block, redistricting counts required under PL 94-171, State CD-ROM release, 2551–6.1

Population and housing census, 1990: voting age and total population by race, and housing units, by county and city, redistricting counts required under PL 94-171, State summary rpt, 2551–5.14

Savings instns, FHLB 7th District and natl cost of funds indexes, and mortgage rates, monthly rpt, 9302–30

Statistical Abstract of US, 1991 annual data compilation, 2324–1

Supplemental Security Income payments and beneficiaries, by type of eligibility, State, and county, Dec 1989, annual rpt, 4744–27.5

Tornadoes in Plainfield, Ill, storm characteristics, deaths, and Natl Weather Service forecast accuracy, 1990, 2186–6.3

Water (groundwater) supply, quality, chemistry, and use, 1984-87, State rpt, 5666–28.5

Water resources dev projects of Army Corps of Engineers, characteristics, and costs, 1950s-89, biennial State rpt, 3756–1.14

Water supply and quality in streams and lakes, and groundwater levels in wells, by drainage basin, 1990, annual State rpt, 5666–10.12

see also Chicago, Ill.
see also Joliet, Ill.
see also Lake County, Ill.
see also Moline, Ill.
see also Peoria, Ill.
see also Plainfield, Ill.
see also Rock Island, Ill.
see also under By State in the "Index by Categories"

Illinois River

Water supply and quality in streams and lakes, and groundwater levels in wells, by drainage basin, 1988, annual State rpt series, 5666–16

Water supply and quality in streams and lakes, and groundwater levels in wells, by drainage basin, 1989, annual State rpt series, 5666–12

Water supply and quality in streams and lakes, and groundwater levels in wells, by drainage basin, 1990, annual State rpt series, 5666–10

Illiteracy

see Literacy and illiteracy

Illness

see Disabled and handicapped persons
see Diseases and disorders
see Hospitalization

ILO

see International Labor Organization

Imitation food products

see Synthetic food products

Immigration and emigration

Admissions to US of immigrants, by country of birth, FY81-90, annual rpt, 6264–4

Admissions to US of immigrants, by occupational group and country of birth, preliminary FY90, annual table, 6264–1

Applications for legal residence under Immigration Reform and Control Act, by selected characteristics, State, and country, periodic rpt, 6262–3

Applications processing, inspections, staffing, and funding, for INS, FY85-90, GAO rpt, 26119–317

Court civil and criminal caseloads for Federal district, appeals, and bankruptcy courts, by type of suit and offense, circuit, and district, 1990, annual rpt, 18204–11

Court civil and criminal caseloads for Federal district, appeals, and special courts, 1990, annual rpt, 18204–8

Court civil and criminal caseloads for Federal district courts, 1991, annual rpt, 18204–2.1

Crime, criminal justice admin and enforcement, and public opinion, data compilation, 1991 annual rpt, 6064–6

Criminal case processing in Federal district courts, and dispositions, by offense, district, and offender characteristics, 1986, annual rpt, 6064–29

Criminal case processing in Federal district courts, and dispositions, by offense, 1980-89, annual rpt, 6064–31

Criminal cases by type and disposition, and collections, for US attorneys, by Federal district, FY90, annual rpt, 6004–2.1; 6004–2.7

Criminal cases in Federal district courts, by offense, disposition, and district, 1980-90, last issue of annual rpt, 18204–1

Criminal defendants for Federal offenses pretrial processing, detention, and release, by defendant characteristics and district, 1988, hearing, 25528–114

Criminal sentences for Federal offenses, guidelines use and results by offense and district, and Sentencing Commission activities, 1990, annual rpt, 17664–1

Data on immigration admin, issues, and trends, series, 6266–1

Data on immigration enforcement, issues and trends, fact sheet series, 6266–2

Earnings of immigrants compared to native-born persons, relation to social and demographic characteristics, model description and results, 1970 and 1980, technical paper, 9385–8.100; 9385–8.101

Economic and labor force impacts of immigration, alien workers, amnesty programs, and employer sanctions, series, 6366–5

Education (bilingual) programs enrollment, funding, and services, by State, FY85-89, series, 4808–20

Education Dept programs funding, operations, and effectiveness, FY90, annual rpt, 4804–5

Education programs for immigrant children, Fed Govt and school districts funding, and student characteristics, 1980s, GAO rpt, 26121–418

Emigration of foreign-born from US, by world region and selected country of origin, 1975-79, fact sheet, 6266–2.5

Immigration and emigration

Exports and imports of Canada and US, impacts of immigration, with background data, 1960s-86, technical paper, 9379–12.64

Foreign countries human rights conditions in 170 countries, 1990, annual rpt, 21384–3

Illegal entry and smuggling of aliens, Federal sentencing guidelines by offense and circumstances, series, 17668–1

Population characteristics and fertility of foreign-born in US, by birthplace and compared to native born, 1980s, Current Population Rpt, 2546–2.162

Population size and characteristics, 1969-88, Current Population Rpt, biennial rpt, 2546–2.161

Research on population and reproduction, Federal funding by project, FY89, annual listing, 4474–9

Science and engineering employment and education, and R&D spending, for US and selected foreign countries, 1991 annual rpt, 9627–35.2

Soviet Union Jewish emigration, and share to Israel, 1968-90, hearings, 21168–49

State and Metro Area Data Book, 1991 data compilation, 2328–54

Statistical Abstract of US, 1991 annual data compilation, 2324–1.1; 2324–1.5

Visas of US issued and refused to immigrants and nonimmigrants, by class, issuing office, and nationality, FY89, annual rpt, 7184–1

see also Alien workers

see also Aliens

see also Deportation

see also Foreign medical graduates

see also Foreign students

see also Mexicans in the U.S.

see also Passports and visas

see also Refugees

Immigration and Naturalization Service

Admissions to US of aliens, by class of admission, port, country, and State of destination, quarterly rpt, discontinued, 6262–2

Admissions to US of immigrants, by country of birth, FY81-90, annual rpt, 6264–4

Admissions to US of immigrants, by occupational group and country of birth, preliminary FY90, annual table, 6264–1

Applications for legal residence under Immigration Reform and Control Act, by selected characteristics, State, and country, periodic rpt, 6262–3

Budget of US, obligations and authority by function, agency, and program, with summaries, analyses, and historical tables, FY92, annual rpt, 104–2

Data on immigration admin, issues, and trends, series, 6266–1

Data on immigration enforcement, issues and trends, fact sheet series, 6266–2

Illegal alien worker and Fair Labor Standards Act employer compliance, hiring impacts, and aliens overstaying visas by country and State, 1986-90, annual rpt, 6264–6

Illegal aliens overstaying visas, by class of admission, mode of arrival, age, country of origin, and State of sojourn, FY85-88, annual rpt, 6264–5

Jail inmates held for Federal authorities, by county and State, 1988, regional rpt series, 6068–144

Mgmt effectiveness of INS, applications processing, inspections, staffing, and funding, FY85-90, GAO rpt, 26119–317

Immigration Reform and Control Act

Admissions to US of aliens, by class of admission, impact of IRCA, FY84-89, 6266–1.1

Admissions to US of immigrants, by class of admission and for top 15 countries of birth, FY89-90, fact sheet, 6266–2.8

Applications for legal residence under IRCA, by selected characteristics, State, and country, periodic rpt, 6262–3

Economic and labor force impacts of immigration, alien workers, amnesty programs, and employer sanctions, series, 6366–5

Employer illegal alien worker and Fair Labor Standards Act compliance, hiring impacts, and aliens overstaying visas by country and State, 1986-90, annual rpt, 6264–6

Farm labor costs and trade of US, effects of immigration restrictions on selected industries, 1980s, 1598–276

Immunity disorders

Cancer deaths and rates, by body site, provisional data, monthly rpt, 4142–1.2

Deaths and rates, by detailed cause and demographic characteristics, 1988 and trends from 1900, US Vital Statistics annual rpt, 4144–2

HHS financial aid, by program, recipient, State, and city, FY90, annual regional listings, 4004–3

Natl Inst of Allergy and Infectious Diseases activities, grants by recipient and location, and disease cases, FY83-90, annual rpt, 4474–30

see also Acquired immune deficiency syndrome

see also Allergies

see also under By Disease in the "Index by Categories"

Immunity from prosecution

see Privileges and immunities

Immunology

see Vaccination and vaccines

Impacted areas

Education Dept programs funding, operations, and effectiveness, FY90, annual rpt, 4804–5

Expenditures of Fed Govt in States, by type, program, agency, and State, FY90, annual rpt, 2464–2

Forests (natl) revenue share paid to States, and acreage, by forest, region, county, and congressional district, FY90, annual rpt, 1204–33

Home mortgages FHA-insured for 1-family units, by loan type and mortgage characteristics, quarterly rpt, 5142–45

Land Mgmt Bur activities in Southwestern US, FY90, annual rpt, 5724–15

Public lands acreage and use, and Land Mgmt Bur activities and finances, annual State rpt series, 5724–11

Public lands, Fed Govt payments to local govts in lieu of property taxes, by State and county, FY91, annual rpt, 5724–9

Public lands, Fed Govt payments to local govts in lieu of property taxes, by State, FY91, annual press release, 5306–4.10

State govt payments to local govts in lieu of property taxes, by State, 1989, annual rpt, 10044–1

Index by Subjects and Names

Import restrictions

see Tariffs and foreign trade controls

Imports

see Agricultural exports and imports

see Coal exports and imports

see East-West trade

see Energy exports and imports

see Foreign trade

see Motor vehicle exports and imports

see Natural gas exports and imports

see Petroleum exports and imports

Impoundment

see Executive impoundment of appropriated funds

Imprisonment

see Correctional institutions

see Juvenile detention and correctional institutions

see Military prisons

see Prisoners

see Prisoners of war

Imrohoroglu, Ayse

"Seignorage as a Tax: A Quantitative Evaluation", 9383–20.2

Inciardi, James A.

"Crack-Cocaine in Miami", 4498–74

Income

see Business income and expenses, general

see Business income and expenses, specific industry

see Earnings, general

see Earnings, local and regional

see Farm income

see Income maintenance

see Income taxes

see National income and product accounts

see Personal and household income

see Poverty

see Professionals' fees

see Underground economy

see under By Income in the "Index by Categories"

Income maintenance

Assistance (financial and nonfinancial) of Fed Govt, 1991 base edition with supplements, annual listing, 104–5

Assistance programs under Ways and Means Committee jurisdiction, finances, operations, and participant characteristics, FY70s-90, annual rpt, 21784–11

Benefits, beneficiary characteristics, and trust funds of OASDHI, Medicaid, SSI, and related programs, selected years 1937-89, annual rpt, 4744–3

Birth outcomes and prenatal care use effects of Medicaid coverage, charges, and Medicaid payments, for California, 1983, article, 4652–1.241

Budget of US, CBO analysis and review of FY92 budget by function, annual rpt, 26304–2

Budget of US, CBO analysis of savings and revenues under alternative spending cuts and tax changes, projected FY92-97, 26306–3.118

Budget of US, House concurrent resolution, with spending and revenue targets, FY92 and projected to FY96, annual rpt, 21264–2

Budget of US, midsession review of FY92 budget, by function, annual rpt, 104–7

Budget of US, obligations and authority by function, agency, and program, with summaries, analyses, and historical tables, FY92, annual rpt, 104–2

Index by Subjects and Names

Income taxes

Budget of US, Senate concurrent resolution, with spending and revenue targets, FY92, annual rpt, 25254–1

Child and family health, education, and welfare condition, findings and recommendations, 1991 rpt, 15528–1

Employer tax credit for hiring from groups with high unemployment rates, participation by State, and effectiveness, FY88, GAO rpt, 26121–407

Expenditures of Fed Govt in States and local areas, by type, State, and county, FY90, annual rpt, 2464–3.1

Expenditures of Fed Govt in States, by type, program, agency, and State, FY90, annual rpt, 2464–2

Finances of govts, revenues by source and spending by function, natl income and product accounts, *Survey of Current Business,* monthly rpt, 2702–1.25

Govt census, 1987: employment, payroll, and average earnings, by function, level of govt, State, county, and population size, 2455–2

Govt finances, tax systems and revenue, and fiscal structure, by level of govt and State, 1991 with historical trends, annual rpt, 10044–1

HHS financial aid, by program, recipient, State, and city, FY90, annual regional listings, 4004–3

Income (household) and poverty status under alternative income definitions, by recipient characteristics, 1990, annual Current Population Rpt, 2546–6.69

Income (household, family, and personal), by source, detailed characteristics, and region, 1988-89, annual Current Population Rpt, 2546–6.68

Income (household, family, and personal), by source, detailed characteristics, and region, 1990, annual Current Population Rpt, 2546–6.70

Income (personal) per capita and by source, and earnings by industry div, by State, MSA, and county, 1984-89, annual regional rpts, 2704–2

Job Training Partnership Act funding and performance indicators in service delivery areas, by urban-rural location, 1987-88, 1598–266

Job Training Partnership Act participation by selected characteristics and State, and outcomes, by urban-rural location, 1987-88, 1598–267

Natl income and product accounts and components, *Survey of Current Business,* monthly rpt, 2702–1.24

Poverty status of population and families, by detailed characteristics, 1988-89, annual Current Population Rpt, 2546–6.67

Poverty status of population and families, by detailed characteristics, 1990, annual Current Population Rpt, 2546–6.71

Puerto Rico statehood referendum proposal, impacts on Federal tax revenue and aid outlays, corporations tax-favored status, and economic conditions, projected FY91-2000, hearing, 25368–168; 26306–3.112

Refugee resettlement programs and funding, arrivals by country of origin, and indicators of adjustment, by State, FY90, annual rpt, 4694–5

Research rpts and microdata files of SSA, 1991 biennial listing, 4744–12

Social Security Bulletin, OASDHI and other program operations and beneficiary characteristics, from 1940, monthly journal, 4742–1

State and Metro Area Data Book, 1991 data compilation, 2328–54

Statistical Abstract of US, 1991 annual data compilation, 2324–1.12

Survey of Current Business, detailed financial and business data, and economic indicators, monthly rpt, 2702–1.4

Survey of Income and Program Participation, data collection, methodology, and use, 1990 annual conf papers, 2624–1

Survey of Income and Program Participation, household composition, income, benefits, and labor force status, methodology, working paper series, 2626–10

Tax expenditures, Federal revenues forgone through income tax deductions and exclusions by type, FY92-96, annual rpt, 21784–10

see also Aid to Families with Dependent Children

see also Disability benefits and insurance

see also Food stamp programs

see also Low-income energy assistance

see also Maternity benefits

see also Medicaid

see also Medicare

see also Old-Age, Survivors, Disability, and Health Insurance

see also Public welfare programs

see also Rent supplements

see also Social security

see also State funding for social welfare

see also Supplemental Security Income

see also Unemployment insurance

see also Workers compensation

Income taxes

Admin and compliance issues, and taxpayer views, 1990 conf, 8304–25

Assets and debts of private sector, balance sheets by segment, 1945-90, semiannual rpt, 9365–4.1

Boycotts (intl) by OPEC and other countries, US firms and shareholders cooperation and tax benefits denied, 1986, annual rpt, 8004–13

Budget of US, authoritative financial statements with appropriations, outlays, and receipts, by category and agency, FY90, annual rpt, 8104–2.1

Budget of US, CBO analysis and review of FY92 budget by function, annual rpt, 26304–2

Budget of US, CBO analysis of revenue and spending alternatives and projections of economic indicators, FY92-96, annual rpt, 26304–3

Budget of US, CBO analysis of savings and revenues under alternative spending cuts and tax changes, projected FY92-97, 26306–3.118

Budget of US, midsession review of FY92 budget, by function, annual rpt, 104–7

Budget of US, obligations and authority by function, agency, and program, with summaries, analyses, and historical tables, FY92, annual rpt, 104–2

Budget of US, receipts by source, outlays by agency and program, and balances, monthly rpt, 8102–3

Child support overdue payments deducted from income tax refunds, by State, FY85-89, annual rpt, 4694–6

Collections, enforcement, and litigation activity of IRS, with data by type of tax, region, and State, FY90, annual rpt, 8304–3

Collections of taxes, by level of govt, type of tax, State, and selected counties, quarterly rpt, 2462–3

Competitiveness (intl) and taxation issues, with comparisons of US and foreign tax rates and revenue, 1988-91, press release, 8008–150

Consumer Expenditure Survey, household income by source, and itemized spending, by selected characteristics and region, 1988-89, annual rpt, 6764–5

Corporations and individual income taxes, monthly rpt, quarterly and annual data, 23842–1.6

Corporations income tax returns, income and tax items by asset size and detailed industry, 1987, annual rpt, 8304–4

Corporations income tax returns, income and tax items by asset size and detailed industry, 1988, annual rpt, 8304–21

Corporations income tax returns, summary data by asset size and industry div, 1987, annual article, 8302–2.204

Corporations income tax returns, summary data by asset size and industry div, 1988, annual article, 8302–2.215; 8302–2.217

Corporations income tax revenue, impacts of tax reform and other factors, 1990 hearing, 25368–173

Economic Report of the President for 1991, Joint Economic Committee critique and policy recommendations, annual rpt, 23844–2

Electric utilities finances and operations, detailed data for publicly owned firms, 1989, annual rpt, 3164–24

Electric utilities privately owned, finances and operations, detailed data, 1989, annual rpt, 3164–23

Energy producers finances and operations, by energy type for US firms domestic and foreign operations, 1989, annual rpt, 3164–44

Farm sector balance sheet, and marketing receipts by detailed commodity, by State, 1985-89, annual rpt, 1544–18

Fed Govt consolidated financial statements based on business accounting methods, FY89-90, annual rpt, 8104–5

Fed Govt finances, cash and debt transactions, daily tables, 8102–4

Fed Govt internal revenue and refunds, by type of tax, quarterly rpt, 8302–2.1

Fed Govt receipts by source and outlays by agency, *Treasury Bulletin,* quarterly rpt, 8002–4.1

Fed Govt tax provisions and receipts overview, by tax type, with background data, 1900s-91 and projected to 2000, 21788–197

Finances of govts, by level of govt, State, and for large cities and counties, annual rpt series, 2466–2

Finances of govts, tax systems and revenue, and fiscal structure, by level of govt and State, 1991 and historical trends, annual rpt, 10044–1

Income taxes

Flow-of-funds accounts, savings, investments, and credit statements, quarterly rpt, 9365–3.3

Foreign and US economic conditions and competitiveness issues, with data by country, 1960s-90, 21788–204

Foreign-controlled US corporations income tax returns, assets and income statement items by industry div and country, 1988, article, 8302–2.219

Foreign-owned corporate activity in US, income tax returns, assets, and income statement items, by industry div and selected country, 1986-87, article, 8302–2.205

Households income and poverty status under alternative income definitions, by recipient characteristics, 1990, annual Current Population Rpt, 2546–6.69

Individual income tax rates effects of indexing to adjust for inflation, under alternative tax codes, 1970-88, working paper, 9377–9.117

Individual income tax returns processing and taxpayer info activity, electronic filings, and refunds, periodic press release, 8302–6

Individual income tax returns, selected income and tax items by adjusted gross income and State, 1986-88, article, 8302–2.201

Individual income tax returns, selected income and tax items by income level, preliminary 1989, annual article, 8302–2.209

Individual income tax returns, taxable income, and tax generated, by tax rate and income level, 1987, annual article, 8302–2.211

Indochina refugees social and economic adjustment indicators, FY90, annual rpt, 4694–5

Inflation relation to individual income taxes and other economic indicators, model description and results, 1950s-89, working paper, 9377–9.110

Insurance (property and casualty) companies tax and income impacts of tax reform, with background financial data, 1970s-91, 8008–151

IRS correspondence regarding adjustments to taxpayer accounts, quality, and accuracy of returns processing, 1987-90, GAO rpt, 26119–329

Multinatl firms US affiliates, finances, and operations, by industry, world area of parent firm, and State, 1988-89, annual rpt, 2704–4

Multinatl US firms and foreign affiliates finances and operations, by industry and world area of parent firm, 1989 benchmark survey, preliminary annual rpt, 2704–5

Multinatl US firms foreign affiliates income tax returns, income statement items, by asset size, industry, and country, 1986, biennial article, 8302–2.212

Natl income and product accounts and components, *Survey of Current Business*, monthly rpt, 2702–1.24; 2702–1.25

Natural gas interstate pipeline company detailed financial and operating data, by firm, 1989, annual rpt, 3164–38

New England States economic indicators, Fed Reserve 1st District, monthly rpt, 9373–2.5

Nonprofit charitable organizations finances, and revenue and investments of top 10 instns, 1986-87, article, 8302–2.210

Nonprofit charitable organizations finances, 1988, table, 8302–2.220

North Central States, FHLB 6th District insured S&Ls financial condition and operations by State, quarterly rpt, 9302–23

OASDI benefit payments, trust fund finances, and economic and demographic assumptions, 1970-90 and alternative projections to 2000, actuarial rpt, 4706–1.105

Partnership income tax returns, income statement and balance sheet items by industry group, 1989, annual article, 8302–2.216; 8304–18

Public opinion on taxes, spending, and govt efficiency, by respondent characteristics, 1991 survey, annual rpt, 10044–2

Puerto Rico and other US possessions corporations income tax returns, income and tax items, and employment, by selected industry, 1987, article, 8302–2.213

Returns and supplemental documents filed, by type, FY90 and projected to FY99, semiannual rpt, 8302–4

Returns filed, by type, IRS service center, and whether full-paid, refund, and electronically filed, 1990 and projected to 1998, semiannual rpt, 8302–7

Returns filed, by type of filer, detailed preliminary and supplementary data, quarterly rpt with articles, 8302–2

Returns filed, by type of tax and IRS district, 1989 and projected 1990-97, annual rpt, 8304–24

Returns filed, by type of tax, region, and IRS service center, projected 1990-97 and trends from 1978, annual rpt, 8304–9

Returns preparation services negligent and fraudulent tax practices, IRS civil penalty cases and examiners views of program admin, 1989, GAO rpt, 26119–315

Returns processing and info distribution of IRS, effectiveness, 1988-90, GAO rpt, 26119–319

Returns processing, IRS workload forecasts, compliance, and enforcement, data compilation, 1991 annual rpt, 8304–8

Returns with IRS Service Center and taxpayer errors, by type of error, 1990-91, GAO rpt, 26119–346

Savings instns insured by Savings Assn Insurance Fund, finances by profitability group, district, and State, quarterly rpt, 8432–4

Sole proprietorship income tax returns, income statement items by industry group, 1989, annual article, 8302–2.214

Southeastern States, Fed Reserve 5th District insured commercial banks financial statements, by State, quarterly rpt, 9389–18

State and local govt competition in taxes, services, regulation, and dev incentives, 1970-89, 10048–79

State and Metro Area Data Book, 1991 data compilation, 2328–54

Statistical Abstract of US, 1991 annual data compilation, 2324–1.9; 2324–1.10; 2324–1.17

Index by Subjects and Names

Tax expenditures, Federal revenues forgone through income tax deductions and exclusions by type, FY92-96, annual rpt, 21784–10

Telephone and telegraph firms detailed finances and operations, 1989, annual rpt, 9284–6

Telephone firms borrowing under Rural Telephone Program, and financial and operating data, by State, 1990, annual rpt, 1244–2

Timber sales of Forest Service, expenses, and operations, by region, State, and natl forest, FY90, annual rpts, 1204–36

Transit systems finances and operations, by mode of transport, size of fleet, and for 468 systems, 1989, annual rpt, 7884–4

Truck and bus interstate carriers finances and operations, by district, 1989, annual rpt, 9486–6.3

see also Tax delinquency and evasion

see also Tax incentives and shelters

see also Tax protests and appeals

see also Windfall profit tax

see also Withholding tax

Incontinence

see Digestive diseases

see Urogenital diseases

Independence, Mo.

see also under By City in the "Index by Categories"

Independent agencies

see Federal independent agencies

Indexes

see Bibliographies

see CD-ROM catalogs and guides

see Computer data file guides

see Consumer Price Index

see Cost of living

see Directories

see Government publications lists

see Industrial production indexes

see Labor costs and cost indexes

see Producer Price Index

India

Agricultural exports of high-value commodities, indexes and sales by commodity, world area, and country, 1960s-86, 1528–323

Agricultural exports of US, for grains, oilseed products, hides, skins, and cotton, by country, weekly rpt, 1922–3

Agricultural exports of US, impacts of foreign agricultural and trade policy, with data by commodity and country, 1989, annual rpt, 1924–8

Agricultural production, prices, and trade, by country, 1960s-90, annual world area rpt, 1524–4.2

Agricultural production, trade, and policies in foreign countries, summary data by country, 1989-90, annual factbook, 1924–12

Agricultural trade of US, by detailed commodity and country, 1989, annual rpt, 1524–8

Agricultural trade of US, by detailed commodity and country, 1990, semiannual rpt, 1522–4

AID economic aid to developing countries, obligations and disbursements by country, quarterly rpt, 9912–4

AID loans repayment status and terms by program and country, and status of predecessor agency loans, quarterly rpt, 9912–3

Index by Subjects and Names

Drug (ibuprofen) imports from India, injury to US industry from foreign subsidized and less than fair value imports, investigation with background financial and operating data, 1991 rpt, 9886–19.77

Economic and military aid and loans from US and intl agencies, by program and country, FY46-90, annual rpt, 9914–5

Economic and social conditions of developing countries from 1960s, and Intl Dev Cooperation Agency and AID activities and funding, FY90-92, annual rpt, 9904–4

Economic conditions in USSR, Eastern Europe, OECD, and selected other countries, 1960s-90, annual rpt, 9114–4

Economic conditions, policy, and trade practices, by country, 1988-90, annual rpt, 21384–5

Economic, social, and agricultural data, US and other aid sources, and AID activity, 1985 country rpt, 9916–12.29

Economic, social, political, and geographic summary data, by country, 1991, annual factbook, 9114–2

Energy use in developing countries, and economic and environmental impacts, by fuel type, world area, and country, 1980s-90, 26358–232

Exports and imports of US, by commodity and country, 1970-89, world area rpt, 9116–1.7

Exports and imports of US, by Harmonized System 6-digit commodity and country, 1990, annual rpt, 2424–13

Exports and imports of US, by selected country, country group, and commodity group, 1990, annual rpt, 2044–37

Exports and imports of US, by transport mode, country, and SITC 1- to 3-digit commodity, 1990, annual rpt, 2424–12

Exports, imports, and balances of US with major trading partners, by product category, 1986-90, annual chartbook, 9884–21

Exports of US, detailed Schedule B commodities with countries of destination, 1990, annual rpt, 2424–10

Fish exports of India by commodity, and frozen shrimp exports by country and region, FY84-88, article, 2162–1.203

Grain production and needs, and related economic outlook, by world area and selected country, forecast 1990/91-1991/92, 1528–313

Human rights conditions in 170 countries, and US economic and military aid, 1990, annual rpt, 21384–3

Imports of goods, services, and investment from US, trade barriers, impacts, and US actions, by country, 1990, annual rpt, 444–2

Labor conditions, union coverage, and work accidents, 1991 annual country rpt, 6366–4.21

Military aid of US, arms sales, and training programs costs and budget requests, by program, world region, and country, FY90-92, annual rpt, 7144–13

Military weapons trade, production, and defense industry finances, with data by firm and country, 1980s-91, 26358–241

Multinatl US firms and foreign affiliates finances and operations, by industry and world area of parent firm, 1989 benchmark survey, preliminary annual rpt, 2704–5

Multinatl US firms foreign affiliates, income statement items by country and world area, 1986, biennial article, 8302–2.212

Nuclear power generation in US and 20 countries, monthly rpt, 3162–24.10

Nuclear power plant capacity, generation, and operating status, by plant and foreign and US location, 1990 and projected to 2030, annual rpt, 3164–57

Space programs activities, missions, launchings, payloads, and flight duration, for foreign and US programs, 1957-90, annual rpt, 21704–4

Spacecraft and satellite launches since 1957, quarterly listing, 9502–2

Steel wire rope from 4 countries, injury to US industry from foreign subsidized and less than fair value imports, investigation with background financial and operating data, 1991 rpt, 9886–19.79

Steel wire rope from 8 countries, injury to US industry from foreign subsidized and less than fair value imports, investigation with background financial and operating data, 1990 rpt, 9886–19.73

Timber in Pacific basin, sandalwood resources, habitat, harvest, exports, and uses, 1990 conf, 1208–366

UN voting record and share of votes in agreement with US, by issue, country, and world area, 1990, annual rpt, 7004–18

see also under By Foreign Country in the "Index by Categories"

Indian claims

Alaska submerged land grant holdings of Alaska Natives, exchange for upland acreage, impacts on conservation acreage and acquisition, 1989-90, 5728–38

Indian Health Service

Budget of US, obligations and authority by function, agency, and program, with summaries, analyses, and historical tables, FY92, annual rpt, 104–2

Disease and disorder cases among Indians and Alaska Natives, deaths, and health services use, by tribe, reservation, and IHS service area, late 1950s-86, 4088–2

Education funding of Fed Govt, and enrollment, degrees, and program grants and fellowships by State, for Indians, late 1960s-FY89, annual rpt, 14874–1

Employment of Indians and non-Indians, training, hires, and quits, for IHS by occupation, FY89, annual rpt, 4084–6

Facilities, funding, and operations of IHS, and Indian health and other characteristics, 1950s-90, annual chartbook, 4084–1

Facilities of IHS, use, and Indian health and other characteristics, by IHS region, 1980s-89, annual chartbook, 4084–7

Financial aid of HHS, by program, recipient, State, and city, FY90, annual regional listings, 4004–3

Health care access for Indians and Alaska Natives, indicators by selected characteristics, 1987, 4186–8.18

Health care coverage of Indians and Alaska Natives, by type, employment status, and other characteristics, 1987, 4186–8.17

Hospital admissions, length of stay, beds, and births, by IHS and tribal facility and service area, FY89-90, with trends from FY70, annual rpt, 4084–4

Indiana

Hospital capacity, use, and births, by area and IHS and tribal facility, quarterly rpt, 4082–1

Hospitalization in IHS, tribal, and contract facilities, by diagnosis, age, sex, and service area, FY89, annual rpt, 4084–5

Nursing staff of IHS, shortages, workload, and pay, by IHS service unit, mid 1980s-90, hearing, 25418–6

Outpatient services provided at IHS facilities, by reason for visit and age, FY88-89, annual rpt, 4084–2

Outpatient visits, by facility and IHS service area, FY89-90, annual rpt, 4084–8

Outpatient visits to IHS and tribal facilities, by type of provider, selected hospital, and service area, FY90, annual rpt, 4084–3

Research and evaluation programs of HHS, 1970-90, annual listing, 4004–30

Indian Ocean

Environmental summary data, and intl claims and disputes, 1991 annual factbook, 9114–2

Hurricanes and tropical storms in Pacific and Indian Oceans, paths and surveillance, 1990, annual rpt, 3804–8

Mariners Weather Log, quarterly journal, 2152–8

Temperature of sea surface by ocean and for US coastal areas, and Bering Sea ice conditions, monthly rpt, 2182–5

Tide height and time daily at coastal points, forecast 1992, annual rpt, 2174–2.5

Indiana

Banks (insured commercial and savings) deposits by instn, State, MSA, and county, as of June 1990, annual regional rpt, 9295–3.3

Coal production and mines by county, prices, productivity, miners, and reserves, by mining method and State, 1989-90, annual rpt, 3164–25

County Business Patterns, 1989: employment, establishments, and payroll, by SIC 2- to 4-digit industry and county, annual State rpt, 2326–8.16

DOD prime contract awards, by contractor, service branch, State, and city, FY90, annual rpt, 3544–22

Earthquakes in midwestern States, intensity, time, and seismograph locations, 1977-90, annual rpt, 9634–10

Economic conditions and outlook, for US and Canada Great Lakes area, 1970s-90, 9375–15

Fed Govt spending in States and local areas, by type, State, county, and city, FY90, annual rpt, 2464–3

Fed Govt spending in States, by type, program, agency, and State, FY90, annual rpt, 2464–2

HHS financial aid, by program, recipient, State, and city, FY90, annual regional listing, 4004–3.5

Hospital deaths of Medicare patients, actual and expected rates by diagnosis, and hospital characteristics, by instn, FY87-89, annual regional rpt, 4654–14.5

Income (personal) per capita and by source, and earnings by industry div, by State, MSA, and county, 1984-89, annual regional rpt, 2704–2.2

Jail adult and juvenile population, employment, spending, instn conditions, and inmate programs, by county and facility, 1988, regional rpt series, 6068–144.3

Indiana

Land subsidence above coal mines, State property insurance program income and expenses in 6 States, 1990, GAO rpt, 26113–530

Lumber (veneer log) production, mill receipts, and trade, by species, with residue use, for North Central States, 1988, quadrennial rpt, 1208–220

Marriages, divorces, and rates, by characteristics of spouses, State, and county, 1987 and trends from 1920, US Vital Statistics annual rpt, 4144–4

Mineral Industry Surveys, State reviews of production, 1990, preliminary annual rpt, 5614–6

Minerals Yearbook, 1989, Vol 2: State review of production and sales by commodity, and business activity, annual rpt, 5604–16.15

Minerals Yearbook, 1989, Vol 2: State reviews of production, sales, and firms, by commodity, and business activity, annual rpt, 5604–34

Physicians, by specialty, age, sex, and location of training and practice, 1989, State rpt, 4116–6.15

Population and housing census, 1990: population and housing characteristics, households, and land area, by county, subdiv, and place, State rpt, 2551–1.16

Population and housing census, 1990: voting age and total population by race, and housing units, by block, redistricting counts required under PL 94-171, State CD-ROM release, 2551–6.4

Population and housing census, 1990: voting age and total population by race, and housing units, by county and city, redistricting counts required under PL 94-171, State summary rpt, 2551–5.15

Savings and loan assns, FHLB 6th District insured members financial condition and operations by State, quarterly rpt, 9302–23

Savings instns, FHLB 6th District members financial condition and operations by State, monthly rpt, 9302–11

Statistical Abstract of US, 1991 annual data compilation, 2324–1

Supplemental Security Income payments and beneficiaries, by type of eligibility, State, and county, Dec 1989, annual rpt, 4744–27.5

Timber in Indiana, resources and removals, by species, forest characteristics, ownership, and county, 1985-86, 1208–368

Water quality, chemistry, hydrology, and other characteristics, 1989 local area study, 5666–27.8; 5666–27.15

Water quality, chemistry, hydrology, and other characteristics, 1990 local area study, 5666–27.19; 5666–27.20

Water supply and quality in streams and lakes, and groundwater levels in wells, by drainage basin, 1990, annual State rpt, 5666–10.13

see also Gary, Ind.
see also Hamilton County, Ind.
see also Indianapolis, Ind.
see also Johnson County, Ind.
see also Lake County, Ind.
see also Logansport, Ind.
see also Peru, Ind.

see also under By State in the "Index by Categories"

Indianapolis, Ind.

Drug test results at arrest, by drug type, offense, and sex, for selected urban areas, quarterly rpt, 6062–3

Housing and households characteristics, unit and neighborhood quality, and journey to work by MSA location, for 11 MSAs, 1984 survey, supplement, 2485–8

Housing and households detailed characteristics, and unit and neighborhood quality, by location, 1988 survey, MSA rpt, 2485–6.4

Wages by occupation, for office and plant workers, 1990 survey, periodic MSA rpt, 6785–11.2

see also under By City and By SMSA or MSA in the "Index by Categories"

Indians

Agriculture census, 1987: farms, farmland, production, finances, and operator characteristics, by county, final State rpt series, 2331–1

AIDS cases by risk group, race, sex, age, State, and MSA, and deaths, monthly rpt, 4202–9

Arrests and prisoners, by offense, offender characteristics, and location, data compilation, 1991 annual rpt, 6064–6.4; 6064–6.6

Arrests, by offense, offender characteristics, and location, 1990, annual rpt, 6224–2.2

Assistance (financial and nonfinancial) of Fed Govt, 1991 base edition with supplements, annual listing, 104–5

Births and rates, by characteristics of birth, infant, and parents, 1989 and trends from 1940, US Vital Statistics advance annual rpt, 4146–5.123

Budget of US, formula grant program obligations to State and local govts, by agency, program, and State, FY92, annual rpt, 104–30

Budget of US, Senate concurrent resolution, with spending and revenue targets, FY92, annual rpt, 25254–1

Bur of Indian Affairs funding under increased tribal authority, by program, tribe, and region, FY78-90, GAO rpt, 26113–508

Business mgmt and financial aid from Minority Business Dev Centers, and characteristics of businesses, by region and State, FY90, annual rpt, 2104–6

Cancer death rates of minorities, by body site, age, sex, and substate area, 1950s-80, atlas, 4478–78

Census of Population and Housing, 1990: population and housing characteristics, households, and land area, by county, subdiv, and place, State rpt series, 2551–1

Census of Population and Housing, 1990: voting age and total population by race, and housing units, by block, redistricting counts required under PL 94-171, State CD-ROM series, 2551–6

Census of Population and Housing, 1990: voting age and total population by race, and housing units, by county and city, redistricting counts required under PL 94-171, State summary rpt series, 2551–5

Census of Population, 1990: Indian and Alaska Native population on reservations and in other designated areas, by selected site, press release, 2328–76

Census of Population, 1990: metro area population by race, Hispanic origin, and MSA, press release, 2328–75

Census of Population, 1990: population by detailed Native American, Asian, and Pacific Islander group, race, region, and State, with data for 1980, press release, 2328–72

Census of Population, 1990: population by race and detailed Hipanic origin, region, and State, with data for 1980, press release, 2328–73

Census of Population, 1990: population by race, Hispanic origin, region, census div, and State, with data for 1980, fact sheet, 2326–20.2

Census of Population, 1990: post-enumeration survey results compared to census counts, by race, sex, city, county, and State, press release, 2328–69

Cherokee Indian Agency activities in North Carolina, FY91, annual rpt, 5704–4

Child accident deaths and death rates, by cause, age, sex, race, and State, 1980-85, 4108–54

Coal Surface Mining Reclamation and Enforcement Office activities and funding, by State and Indian tribe, FY90, annual rpt, 5644–1

Community Dev Block Grant activities and funding, by program, FY75-90, annual rpt, 5124–8

Criminal cases by type and disposition, and collections, for US attorneys, by Federal district, FY90, annual rpt, 6004–2.1; 6004–2.7

Deaths and rates, by detailed cause and demographic characteristics, 1988 and trends from 1900, US Vital Statistics annual rpt, 4144–2

Disease and disorder cases among Indians and Alaska Natives, deaths, and health services use, by tribe, reservation, and Indian Health Service area, late 1950s-86, 4088–2

Diseases (chronic) prevalence among Indians and Alaska Natives, for 8 conditions by age and sex, 1987, 4186–8.20

Drug abuse prevalence among minorities, related health effects and crime, treatment, and research status and needs, mid 1970s-90, 4498–72

Drug and alcohol abuse treatment facilities, services, use, funding, staff, and client characteristics, 1989, biennial rpt, 4494–10

Education (special) enrollment by age, staff, funding, and needs, by type of handicap and State, 1989/90, annual rpt, 4944–4

Education data compilation, 1991 annual rpt, 4824–2

Education Dept programs funding, operations, and effectiveness, FY90, annual rpt, 4804–5

Education funding by Federal agency, program, and recipient type, and instn spending, FY80-90, annual rpt, 4824–8

Education funding of Fed Govt, and enrollment, degrees, and program grants and fellowships by State, for Indians, late 1960s-FY89, annual rpt, 14874–1

Educational performance and conditions, characteristics, attitudes, activities, and plans, 1988 8th grade class, natl longitudinal survey, series, 4826–9

Index by Subjects and Names

Educational performance of elementary and secondary students, and factors affecting proficiency, by selected characteristics, 1990 natl assessments, subject rpt series, 4896–8

Educational service delivery and discipline, and discrimination indicators by State, 1988, biennial rpt, 4804–33

Electric power sales by customer, activities by plant, and financial statements of Western Area Power Admin, FY90, annual rpt, 3254–1

Energy aid for low income households, funding sources, costs, and participation, by State, FY89, annual rpt, 4694–8

EPA pollution control grant program activities, monthly rpt, 9182–8

Fed Equal Opportunity Recruitment Program activity, and employment by sex, race, pay grade, and occupational group, FY90, annual rpt, 9844–33

Fed Govt employment of minorities and women, and compliance with EEOC standards, by occupation and agency, FY88-92, GAO rpt, 26119–342

Fed Govt spending in States, by type, program, agency, and State, FY90, annual rpt, 2464–2

Fetal alcohol syndrome prevention program for Indians, evaluation, 1988-89 local area study, article, 4042–3.239

Fish Hatchery Natl System activities and deliveries, by species, hatchery, and jurisdiction of waters stocked, FY90, annual rpt, 5504–10

FmHA activities, and loans and grants by program and State, FY90 and trends from FY70, annual rpt, 1184–17

FmHA loans, by type, borrower characteristics, and State, quarterly rpt, 1182–8

FmHA loans, by type, borrower race, and State, quarterly rpt, 1182–5

Food aid program of USDA for women, infants, and children, participants and costs by State and Indian agency, FY88, annual tables, 1364–12

Food aid program of USDA for women, infants, and children, participants by race, State, and Indian agency, Apr 1990, annual rpt, 1364–16

Food aid program of USDA for women, infants, and children, participants, clinics, and costs, by State and Indian agency, monthly tables, 1362–16

Food aid programs of USDA, costs and participation by program, FY69-89, annual rpt, 1364–9

Head Start enrollment, funding, and staff, FY90, annual rpt, 4604–8

Head Start handicapped enrollment, by handicap, State, and for Indian and migrant programs, 1987/88, annual rpt, 4604–1

Health care access for Indians and Alaska Natives, indicators by selected characteristics, 1987, 4186–8.18

Health care coverage of Indians and Alaska Natives, by type, employment status, and other characteristics, 1987, 4186–8.17

Health care employment of Indians and non-Indians by Indian Health Service, training, hires, and quits, by occupation, FY89, annual rpt, 4084–6

Health care outpatient services provided at Indian Health Service facilities, by reason for visit and age, FY88-89, annual rpt, 4084–2

Health care outpatient visits to Indian Health Service and tribal facilities, by type of provider, selected hospital, and service area, FY90, annual rpt, 4084–3

Health care outpatient visits to Indian Health Service facilities, by facility and IHS service area, FY89-90, annual rpt, 4084–8

Health condition and other characteristics of Indians, and Indian Health Service facilities and use, by IHS region, 1980s-89, annual chartbook, 4084–7

Health condition and other characteristics of Indians, and Indian Health Service facilities, funding, and operations, 1950s-90, annual chartbook, 4084–1

Health condition improvement and disease prevention goals and recommended activities for 2000, with trends 1970s-80s, 4048–10

Health condition indicators and health occupations school enrollment, 1950s-89, annual data compilation, 4144–11

Health condition of minorities, services use, costs, and indicators of services need, 1950s-88, 4118–55

Health condition, services use, payment sources, and health care labor force, for minorities and women by poverty status, 1940s-89, chartbook, 4118–56

Health maintenance practices of Indians and Alaska Natives, exams by type, and smoking and overweight status, by selected characteristics, 1987, 4186–8.19

HHS financial aid, by program, recipient, State, and city, FY90, annual regional listings, 4004–3

Higher education degrees awarded, by level, field, race, and sex, 1988/89 with trends from 1978/79, biennial rpt, 4844–17

Hospital admissions, length of stay, beds, and births, by Indian Health Service and tribal facility and service area, FY89-90, with trends from FY70, annual rpt, 4084–4

Hospital capacity, use, and births, by area and Indian Health Service and tribal facility, quarterly rpt, 4082–1

Hospitalization in Indian Health Service, tribal, and contract facilities, by diagnosis, age, sex, and IHS service area, FY89, annual rpt, 4084–5

Housing programs of HUD, operations and funding, 1989, annual rpt, 5004–10

Infant death rates, and racial misclassification on death certificates, for Oklahoma Indians, 1975-88, article, 4042–3.209

Land acreage, by use, ownership, and State, 1987 and trends from 1910, 1588–48

Lands (public) acreage, grants, use, revenues, and allocations, by State, FY90, annual rpt, 5724–1.3

Minerals resources and availability on public lands, State rpt series, 5606–7

Nuclear engineering enrollment and degrees granted by instn and State, and grad placement, by student characteristics, 1990, annual rpt, 3004–5

Oil, gas, and minerals leasing, production, and revenue on Federal and Indian land, by State, 1980s and trends from 1920, 5738–21

Individual retirement arrangements

Oil, gas, and minerals production and revenue on Federal and Indian land, by State, 1990 and trends from 1920, annual rpt, 5734–2

Prisoners, characteristics, and movements, by State, 1989, annual rpt, 6064–26

Radiation exposure of population near Hanford, Wash, nuclear plant, with methodology, 1944-66, series, 3356–5

Radiation exposure of uranium miners and risk of death from cancer and lung diseases, for Indians and compared to whites and foreign countries, 1950s-84, hearing, 25548–101

Radiation protection and health physics enrollment and degrees granted by instn and State, and grad placement, by student characteristics, 1990, annual rpt, 3004–7

Relocation program for Navajo and Hopi, activities and caseloads, annual rpt, discontinued, 16004–1

Relocation program for Navajo and Hopi, activities and caseloads, monthly rpt, 16002–1

Relocation program for Navajo and Hopi, activities and caseloads, 1975-90, 16008–5

Science and engineering grad enrollment, by field, source of funds, and characteristics of student and instn, 1975-89, annual rpt, 9627–7

Science and engineering PhDs, by field, instn, employment prospects, sex, race, and other characteristics, 1960s-90, annual rpt, 9627–30

Science and engineering PhDs employment and other characteristics, by field and State, 1989, biennial rpt, 9627–18

State and local govt employment of minorities and women, by occupation, function, pay level, and State, 1990, annual rpt, 9244–6

State and Metro Area Data Book, 1991 data compilation, 2328–54

Statistical Abstract of US, 1991 annual data compilation, 2324–1

Student aid funding and participation, by Federal program, instn type and control, and State, various periods 1959-89, annual rpt, 4804–28

Timber mgmt programs of Bur of Indian Affairs, funding, acreage, harvest, and tribal investment, by tribe and location, FY77-89 and projected to FY96, hearing, 25418–4

Uranium reserves and industry operations, by region and State, various periods 1966-90, annual rpt, 3164–65.1

see also Alaska Natives

see also Indian claims

see also under By Race and Ethnic Group in the "Index by Categories"

Indigent defense

see Legal aid

Individual retirement arrangements

Banks (insured commercial) domestic and foreign office consolidated financial statements, monthly rpt, quarterly data, 9362–1.4

Banks (insured commercial and savings) finances, for foreign and domestic offices, by asset size, 1989, annual rpt, 9294–4.2

Coverage under pension plans by industry, vestment, and recipient income, by participant characteristics, 1987, Current Population Rpt, 2546–20.18

Individual retirement arrangements

Credit unions federally insured, finances by instn characteristics and State, as of June 1991, semiannual rpt, 9532–6

Credit unions federally insured, finances, 1989-90, annual rpt, 9534–1

Employee benefit plan coverage, by benefit type and worker characteristics, late 1970s-80s, 15496–1.11

Households assets, by type of holding and selected characteristics, 1988, Current Population Rpt, 2546–20.16

Households IRA holdings and relation to other assets, 1985, working paper, 2626–10.132

OASDI retired-worker benefits, effect of proposal to privatize excess trust funds into individual accounts, 1990 GAO rpt, 26121–397

Participation in IRAs, by selected characteristics, 1987, fact sheet, 2326–17.35

Savings and Investment Incentive Act issues, with IRA participation and other background data, 1980s, 25368–175

Southeastern States, Fed Reserve 5th District insured commercial banks financial statements, by State, quarterly rpt, 9389–18

Statistical Abstract of US, 1991 annual data compilation, 2324–1.12

Tax (income) returns filed by type of filer, selected income items, quarterly rpt, 8302–2.1

Tax (income) returns of individuals, selected income and tax items by income level, preliminary 1989, annual article, 8302–2.209

Tax (income) withholding and related documents filed, by type and IRS service center, 1990 and projected 1991-98, annual rpt, 8304–22

Tax expenditures, Federal revenues forgone through income tax deductions and exclusions by type, FY92-96, annual rpt, 21784–10

Indochina

see Cambodia

see Laos

see Southeast Asia

see Vietnam

Indonesia

Agricultural exports of high-value commodities, indexes and sales by commodity, world area, and country, 1960s-86, 1528–323

Agricultural exports of US, impacts of foreign agricultural and trade policy, with data by commodity and country, 1989, annual rpt, 1924–8

Agricultural production, prices, and trade, by country, 1960s-90, annual world area rpt, 1524–4.2

Agricultural production, trade, and policies in foreign countries, summary data by country, 1989-90, annual factbook, 1924–12

Agricultural trade of US, by detailed commodity and country, 1989, annual rpt, 1524–8

Agricultural trade of US, by detailed commodity and country, 1990, semiannual rpt, 1522–4

AID economic aid to developing countries, obligations and disbursements by country, quarterly rpt, 9912–4

AID loans repayment status and terms by program and country, and status of predecessor agency loans, quarterly rpt, 9912–3

Child and infant survival programs of AID, effectiveness with background data, 1970s-87, 9916–1.73

Economic and military aid and loans from US and intl agencies, by program and country, FY46-90, annual rpt, 9914–5

Economic and social conditions of developing countries from 1960s, and Intl Dev Cooperation Agency and AID activities and funding, FY90-92, annual rpt, 9904–4

Economic conditions in USSR, Eastern Europe, OECD, and selected other countries, 1960s-90, annual rpt, 9114–4

Economic conditions, income, production, prices, employment, and trade, 1991 periodic country rpt, 2046–4.31; 2046–4.62

Economic conditions, policy, and trade practices, by country, 1988-90, annual rpt, 21384–5

Economic, social, political, and geographic summary data, by country, 1991, annual factbook, 9114–2

Exports and imports of US, by commodity and country, 1970-89, world area rpt, 9116–1.7

Exports and imports of US, by Harmonized System 6-digit commodity and country, 1990, annual rpt, 2424–13

Exports and imports of US, by selected country, country group, and commodity group, 1990, annual rpt, 2044–37

Exports and imports of US, by transport mode, country, and SITC 1- to 3-digit commodity, 1990, annual rpt, 2424–12

Exports of US, detailed Schedule B commodities with countries of destination, 1990, annual rpt, 2424–10

Human rights conditions in 170 countries, and US economic and military aid, 1990, annual rpt, 21384–3

Imports of goods, services, and investment from US, trade barriers, impacts, and US actions, by country, 1990, annual rpt, 444–2

Labor conditions, union coverage, and work accidents, 1991 annual country rpt, 6366–4.48

Military aid of US, arms sales, and training programs costs and budget requests, by program, world region, and country, FY90-92, annual rpt, 7144–13

Multinatl US firms and foreign affiliates finances and operations, by industry and world area of parent firm, 1989 benchmark survey, preliminary annual rpt, 2704–5

Multinatl US firms foreign affiliates, income statement items by country and world area, 1986, biennial article, 8302–2.212

Natural gas and liquefied gas trade of US with 5 countries, by US firm, 1955-90, annual article, 3162–4.208

Oil production, and exports and prices for US, by major exporting country, detailed data, monthly rpt with articles, 3162–24

Oil production, trade, use, and stocks, by selected country and country group, monthly rpt, 3162–42

Index by Subjects and Names

Shrimp aquaculture harvest by Southeast Asia country, and Thailand revenues and costs, 1984-89, article, 2162–1.203

Spacecraft and satellite launches since 1957, quarterly listing, 9502–2

Tobacco and cigarette production and trade, for Indonesia, 1970-90, article, 1925–16.208

UN voting record and share of votes in agreement with US, by issue, country, and world area, 1990, annual rpt, 7004–18

see also under By Foreign Country in the "Index by Categories"

Industrial accidents and safety

see Hazardous substances

see Mine accidents and safety

see Occupational health and safety

see Railroad accidents and safety

see Transportation accidents and safety

Industrial and commercial energy use

Bonneville Power Admin energy conservation and resource planning activities, FY89-90, 3228–11

Bonneville Power Admin mgmt of Fed Columbia River Power System, finances and sales, summary data, quarterly rpt, 3222–2

Bonneville Power Admin mgmt of Fed Columbia River Power System, finances, operations, and sales by customer, FY90, annual rpt, 3224–1

Bonneville Power Admin sales, revenues, and rates, by customer and customer type, 1990, semiannual rpt, 3222–1

Building (commercial) energy use, costs, and conservation, by building characteristics, survey rpt series, 3166–8

Business statistics, detailed data for major industries and economic indicators, *Survey of Current Business*, monthly rpt, 2702–1.13; 2702–1.18

Coal, coke, and breeze supply, demand, prices, trade, and stocks, by end-use sector and State, quarterly rpt with articles, 3162–37

Coal production and mines by county, prices, productivity, miners, and reserves, by mining method and State, 1989-90, annual rpt, 3164–25

Coal production, prices, exports, and use by sector, with data by region, projected 1995-2010 and trends from 1970, annual rpt, 3164–68

Coal production, stocks, and shipments, by State of origin and destination, end-use sector, and mode of transport, quarterly rpt, 3162–8

Coal receipts, use, stocks, and delivered price to electric utilities, by State, weekly rpt, monthly data, 3162–1.2

Conservation measures impacts on energy consumption, by component and end-use sector, 1970s-88 and projected under alternative oil prices to 1995, 3308–93

Conservation of energy, State programs aid from Fed Govt, and energy savings, by State, 1989, annual rpt, 3304–1

Construction industries census, 1987: establishments, employment, receipts, and expenditures, by SIC 4-digit industry and State, final industry rpt series, 2373–1

Developing countries energy use, and economic and environmental impacts, by fuel type, world area, and country, 1980s-90, 26358–232

Index by Subjects and Names

Electric power plants production and capacity by fuel type, prices, demand, and air pollution law impacts, by region, 1989-90 and projected to 2010, annual rpt, 3164–81

Electric power plants production and capital costs, operations, and fuel use, by fuel type, plant, utility, and location, 1989, annual rpt, 3164–9

Electric power plants production, capacity, sales, and fuel stocks, use, and costs, by State, 1985-89, annual rpt, 3164–11

Electric power plants production, fuel use, stocks, and costs by fuel type, and sales, by State, monthly rpt with articles, 3162–35

Electric power sales and revenue, by end-use sector, consumption level, and utility, 1989, annual rpt, 3164–91

Electric power use indexes, by SIC 2- to 4-digit industry, monthly rpt, 9365–2.24

Electric power wholesale purchases of REA borrowers, by borrower, supplier, and State, 1940-89, annual rpt, 1244–5

Electric utilities finances and operations, detailed data for publicly owned firms, 1989, annual rpt, 3164–24

Electric utilities privately owned, finances and operations, detailed data, 1989, annual rpt, 3164–23

Energy supply, demand, and prices, by fuel type and end-use sector, alternative projections 1989-2010, annual rpt, 3164–75

Energy supply, demand, and prices, by fuel type and end-use sector, projections and underlying assumptions, 1990-2010, annual rpt, 3164–90

Energy supply, demand, and prices, by fuel type and end-use sector, with foreign comparisons, 1990 and trends from 1949, annual rpt, 3164–74

Energy supply, demand, and prices, by fuel type, end-use sector, and country, detailed data, monthly rpt with articles, 3162–24

Energy supply, demand, and prices, forecasts by resource type, quarterly rpt, 3162–34

Energy use, by detailed fuel type, end-use sector, and State, 1960-89, State Energy Data System annual rpt, 3164–39

Energy use in transportation and other sectors, by fuel type, 1970s-89, annual rpt, 3304–5

Enterprise Statistics, 1987: auxiliaries of multi-establishment firms, finances and operations by function, industry, and State, 2329–6

Environmental Quality, status of problems, protection programs, research, and intl issues, 1991 annual rpt, 484–1

Fuel oil and kerosene sales and deliveries, by end-use, PAD district, and State, 1989, annual rpt, 3164–94

Gasoline and other motor fuel use, by consuming sector and State, 1990, annual rpt, 7554–1.1

Health Care Financing Review, provider prices, price inputs and indexes, and labor, quarterly journal, 4652–1.1

Lumber (veneer log) production, mill receipts, and trade, by species, with residue use, for North Central States, 1988, quadrennial rpt, 1208–220

Industrial capacity and utilization

Manufacturing annual survey, 1989: establishments, employment, finances, inventories, and energy use, by SIC 2- to 4-digit industry, 2506–15.1

Manufacturing annual survey, 1989: finances and operations, by SIC 2- and 3-digit industry and State, 2506–15.3

Manufacturing census, 1987: finances and operations, by SIC 2- to 4-digit industry, State, and MSA, with trends from 1849, 2497–1

Manufacturing energy use and prices, 1988 survey, series, 3166–13

Mineral industries census, 1987: energy use and costs, by fuel type, SIC 2- to 4-digit industry, and State, subject rpt, 2517–2

Mineral industries census, 1987: finances and operations, by establishment characteristics, SIC 2- to 4-digit industry, and State, subject rpt, 2517–1

Mineral industries census, 1987: finances and operations, by SIC 2- to 4-digit industry, State, and county, census div rpt series, 2515–1

Natl Energy Strategy plans for conservation and pollution reduction, impacts of technology and regulation proposals, projected 1990-2030, 3166–6.47

Natl Energy Strategy plans for conservation, impacts on energy use and pollution under alternative technology investment assumptions, projected 1990-2030, 3166–6.48

Natural and supplemental gas production, prices, trade, use, reserves, and pipeline company finances, by firm and State, monthly rpt with articles, 3162–4

Natural gas interstate pipeline company detailed financial and operating data, by firm, 1989, annual rpt, 3164–38

Natural gas interstate pipeline company sales and contract deliveries, by firm and State, 1984-89, annual article, 3162–4.204

Natural gas use, by end-use sector and PAD district, seasonal weekly rpt, 3162–45

New England States electric power sales, Fed Reserve 1st District, monthly rpt, 9373–2.4

Oil and gas primary use prohibited for power and industrial plants, and gas use by State, 1977-90, annual rpt, 3334–1

Oil and gas supply, demand, and prices, alternative projections 1989-2010, annual rpt, 3164–89

Oil and refined products supply, demand, prices, and refinery capacity and stocks, by State, 1960-91, annual rpt, 3164–95

Oil products sales and purchases of refiners, processors, and distributors, by product, end-use sector, PAD district, and State, monthly rpt with articles, 3162–11

Oil refinery capacity, closings, and acquisitions by plant, and fuel used, by PAD district, 1973-89, annual rpt, 3164–2.1

Oil refinery operations and finances, with ownership changes, shutdowns, and reactivations, by firm, 1970s-90, 3168–119

Pacific Northwest electric power capacity and use, by energy source, projected under alternative load and demand cases, 1991-2011, annual rpt, 3224–3

Pollution (air) contributing to global warming, emissions factors and control costs, by pollutant and source, 1990 rpt, 9198–124

Pollution (air) contributing to global warming, US and foreign emissions and control measures, 1980s and projected to 2020, 26358–233

Pollution (air) levels for 6 pollutants, by source, 1970-89 and trends from 1940, annual rpt, 9194–13

Prices and spending for fuel, by type, end-use sector, and State, 1989, annual rpt, 3164–64

Retail trade census, 1987: depreciable assets, capital and operating expenses, sales, value added, and inventories, by SIC 2- to 4-digit kind of business, 2399–2

Service industries census, 1987: depreciable assets, capital and operating expenses, and receipts, by SIC 2- to 4-digit kind of business, 2393–2

Solar collector and photovoltaic module shipments by end-use sector and State, and trade, 1989, annual rpt, 3164–62

State and Metro Area Data Book, 1991 data compilation, 2328–54

Statistical Abstract of US, 1991 annual data compilation, 2324–1.19

TVA electric power purchases and resales, with electricity use, average bills, and rates by customer class, by distributor, 1990, annual tables, 9804–14

TVA electric power purchases of municipal and cooperative distributors, and prices and use by distributor and consumer sector, monthly rpt, 9802–1

TVA energy use by fuel type, and conservation costs and savings, FY90, annual rpt, 9804–26

Warehouse services finances, and inventory, by SIC 3- to 4-digit industry, 1988 survey, annual rpt, 2413–14

Wholesale trade census, 1987: depreciable assets, capital and operating expenses, sales, value added, and inventories, by SIC 2- to 3-digit kind of business, 2407–2

Wood, waste, and alcohol fuel use, by end-use sector and region, 1989, 3166–6.56

see also Agricultural energy use

see also Electric power and heat cogeneration

see also Transportation energy use

Industrial arts

Enrollment in single-sex and mixed classes, and schools offering courses, by course, 1988, biennial rpt, 4804–33

Higher education course completions, by detailed program, sex, race, and instn type, for 1972 high school class, as of 1984, 4888–4

Industrial capacity and utilization

Capacity use rates for manufacturers from 1948, and for mining and utilities, 1967-90, annual rpt, 204–1.3

Economic indicators and components, and Fed Reserve 4th District business and financial conditions, monthly chartbook, 9377–10

Economic indicators and components, current data and annual trends, monthly rpt, 23842–1.3

Industrial capacity and utilization

Economic indicators, monthly rpt, 9362–1.2

Electric power capacity and use in Pacific Northwest, by energy source, projected under alternative load and demand cases, 1991-2011, annual rpt, 3224–3

Electric power plants production and capacity by fuel type, prices, demand, and air pollution law impacts, by region, 1989-90 and projected to 2010, annual rpt, 3164–81

Electric power plants production and capital costs, operations, and fuel use, by fuel type, plant, utility, and location, 1989, annual rpt, 3164–9

Electric power plants production, capacity, sales, and fuel stocks, use, and costs, by State, 1985-89, annual rpt, 3164–11

Electric utilities privately owned, finances and operations, detailed data, 1989, annual rpt, 3164–23

Energy conservation measures impacts on consumption, by component and end-use sector, 1970s-88 and projected under alternative oil prices to 1995, 3308–93

Energy supply, demand, and prices, by fuel type and end-use sector, projections and underlying assumptions, 1990-2010, annual rpt, 3164–90

Energy supply, demand, and prices, by fuel type and end-use sector, with foreign comparisons, 1990 and trends from 1949, annual rpt, 3164–74

Exports, imports, balances, US consumption, and operations of industries affected, by industry, 1986-90, semiannual rpt, 9882–9

Fertilizer production capacity by firm, for US and Canada, 1986-91 and projected to 1997, triennial rpt, 9808–66

Gear production for selected uses under alternative production requirements, and industry finances and operations, late 1940s-89, 2028–1

Hydroelectric power generation and capacity, for TVA projects, 1989, annual rpt, 9804–7

Imports and tariff provisions effect on US industries and products, investigations with background financial and operating data, series, 9886–4

Imports injury to US industries from foreign subsidized products and sales at less than fair value, investigations with background financial and operating data, series, 9886–19

Imports injury to US industries from foreign subsidized products, investigations with background financial and operating data, series, 9886–15

Imports injury to US industries from sales at less than fair value, investigations with background financial and operating data, series, 9886–14

Imports under Generalized System of Preferences, status, and US tariffs, with trade by country and US economic impacts, for selected commodities, 1986-90, annual rpt, 9884–23

Lumber and pulp products supply and use, and timber resources, detailed data, 1950s-87 and alternative projections to 2040, 1208–24.20

Manufacturing capacity growth rate, by major industry group, 1950s-80s, technical paper, 9385–8.92

Natural gas production and wellhead capacity, by production area, 1980-89 and alternative forecasts 1990-91, biennial rpt, 3164–93

Natural gas underground storage facilities and capacities, and withdrawals and injections, by State and region, 1975/76-1990/91, annual article, 3162–4.203

Nuclear power plant capacity, generation, and capacity use, monthly rpt, 3162–24.8

Nuclear power plant capacity, generation, and operating status, by plant and foreign and US location, 1990 and projected to 2030, annual rpt, 3164–57

Nuclear power plant safety standards and research, design, licensing, construction, operation, and finances, with data by reactor, quarterly journal, 3352–4

Nuclear reactors operations, by commercial facility, 1990, annual rpt, 9634–12

Oil and refined products supply, demand, prices, and refinery capacity and stocks, by State, 1960-91, annual rpt, 3164–95

Oil refinery capacity and use, weekly rpt, 3162–32

Oil refinery capacity, closings, and acquisitions by plant, and fuel used, by PAD district, 1973-89, annual rpt, 3164–2.1

Oil refinery capacity use, 1988-89, annual rpt, 3164–44.3

Oil refinery crude received from Iraq, and capacity, by company, daily press release, 3162–44

Oil refinery operating and idle capacity, inputs by type, and oil quality, by PAD district, monthly rpt, 3162–6.2

Oil refinery operations and finances, with ownership changes, shutdowns, and reactivations, by firm, 1970s-90, 3168–119

OPEC oil production and capacity, by member, monthly rpt, 9112–2

Southwestern Fed Power System financial statements, sales by customer, and operations and costs by project, FY90, annual rpt, 3244–1

Statistical Abstract of US, 1991 annual data compilation, 2324–1.27

Steel imports of US under voluntary restraint agreement, by product, customs district, and country, with US industry operating data, quarterly rpt, 9882–13

Steel industry finances, operations, and modernization efforts, with data on major companies and foreign industry, 1968-91, last issue of annual rpt, 9884–24

Uranium mill capacity by plant, and production, by operating status, 1986-90, annual rpt, 3164–65.1

Industrial controls

see Instruments and measuring devices

see Quality control and testing

Industrial location

see Industrial siting

Industrial management

see Business management

see Consultants

see Executives and managers

see Industrial siting

see Labor-management relations, general

Index by Subjects and Names

Industrial plant closings

see Business failures and closings

Industrial plants and equipment

Arson incidents by whether structure occupied, property value, and arrest rate, by property type, 1990, annual rpt, 6224–2.1

Assets and debts of private sector, balance sheets by segment, 1945-90, semiannual rpt, 9365–4.1

Budget deficits under Reagan Admin, impact on capital stock, foreign debt, and other economic indicators, with background data, 1950s-88, article, 9393–8.201

Business statistics, detailed data for major industries and economic indicators, *Survey of Current Business,* monthly rpt, 2702–1.17

Capital stock measures, by type and industry, 1950s-80s, technical paper, 9385–8.92

Construction (industrial and commercial) contracts, *Survey of Current Business,* cyclical indicators, monthly rpt, 2702–1.1

Construction industries census, 1987: establishments, employment, receipts, and expenditures, by SIC 4-digit industry and State, final industry rpt series, 2373–1

Construction put in place, permits, housing sales, costs, material prices, and employment, bimonthly rpt with articles, 2042–1

Construction put in place, value of new public and private structures, by type, monthly rpt, 2382–4

County Business Patterns, 1988: employment, establishments, and payroll, by SIC 2- to 4-digit industry and county, annual State rpt series, 2326–6

County Business Patterns, 1989: employment, establishments, and payroll, by SIC 2- to 4-digit industry and county, annual State rpt series, 2326–8

DOD prime contract awards, by category, contractor type, and State, FY88-90, annual rpt, 3544–11

DOD prime contract awards, by detailed procurement category, FY87-90, annual rpt, 3544–18

Economic indicators and components, and Fed Reserve 4th District business and financial conditions, monthly chartbook, 9377–10

Employment, earnings, and hours, by SIC 1- to 4-digit industry, monthly and annual averages, selected years 1909-90, annual rpt, 6744–4

Energy producers finances and operations, by energy type for US firms domestic and foreign operations, 1989, annual rpt, 3164–44

Energy use and prices for manufacturing industries, 1988 survey, series, 3166–13

Engineering and architectural establishments, receipts by type of client and project, payroll, and employment, by State, 1987 Census of Service Industries, 2393–4.16

Enterprise Statistics, 1987: auxiliaries of multi-establishment firms, finances and operations by function, industry, and State, 2329–6

Enterprise Statistics, 1987: finances and operations for companies, by size, level of diversification, form of organization, and industry group, 2329–8

Index by Subjects and Names — Industrial production

Expenditures for plant and equipment, by major industry group, quarterly rpt, 2502–2

Exports and imports of US, by country and detailed commodity, monthly rpt, 2422–12

Exports and imports of US, by Harmonized System 6-digit commodity and country, 1990, annual rpt, 2424–13

Exports and imports of US, by selected country, country group, and commodity group, 1990, annual rpt, 2044–37

Exports and imports of US, by transport mode, country, and SITC 1- to 3-digit commodity, 1990, annual rpt, 2424–12

Exports of US, detailed Schedule B commodities with countries of destination, 1990, annual rpt, 2424–10

Fed Govt-owned real property inventory and costs, worldwide summary by purpose, agency, and location, 1989, annual rpt, 9454–5

Fishery employment, vessels, plants, and cooperatives, by State, 1989 and trends from 1970, annual rpt, 2164–1.10

Foreign direct investment in US, major transactions by type, industry, country, and US location, 1989, annual rpt, 2044–20

Gear production for selected uses under alternative production requirements, and industry finances and operations, late 1940s-89, 2028–1

Input-output structure of US economy, detailed interindustry transactions for 84 industries, and components of final demand, 1986, annual article, 2702–1.206

Input-output structure of US economy, detailed interindustry transactions for 85 industries, 1982 benchmark data, 2702–1.213

Labor productivity, indexes of output, hours, and employment by SIC 2- to 4-digit industry, 1967-89, annual rpt, 6824–1.3

Manufacturing annual survey, 1989: finances and operations, by SIC 2- to 4-digit industry, series, 2506–15

Manufacturing census, 1987: finances and operations, by SIC 2- to 4-digit industry, State, and MSA, with trends from 1849, 2497–1

Manufacturing census, 1987: finances and operations, by type of organization and SIC 2- to 4-digit industry, subject rpt, 2497–5

Manufacturing finances and operations, by SIC 2- to 4-digit industry, forecast 1991, annual rpt, 2044–28

Meat and poultry inspection activities and staff of Federal, State, and foreign govts, FY90, annual rpt, 1374–1

Meat plants inspected and certified for exporting to US, by country, 1990, annual listing, 1374–2

Meat production, livestock slaughter, and slaughter plants, by species and State, 1990, annual rpt, 1623–10

Mineral Industry Surveys, commodity reviews of production, trade, use, and industry operations, advance annual rpt series, 5614–5

Mines (underground coal) back injuries, by circumstances, victim characteristics, and treatment, mid 1980s, 5608–166

Mines occupational deaths, by circumstances and selected victim characteristics, semiannual rpt series, 6662–3

Multinatl firms US affiliates, finances, and operations, by industry, world area of parent firm, and State, 1988-89, annual rpt, 2704–4

Multinatl firms US affiliates, investment trends and impact on US economy, 1991 annual rpt, 2004–9

Natl income and product accounts and components, *Survey of Current Business,* monthly rpt, 2702–1.25

Natural gas interstate pipeline company detailed financial and operating data, by firm, 1989, annual rpt, 3164–38

Occupational deaths, by equipment type, circumstances, and OSHA standards violated, series, 6606–2

Occupational injuries, by circumstances, body site, equipment type, and industry, with safety measures, series, 6846–1

Occupational injury and illness rates, by SIC 2- to 4-digit industry, 1988-89, annual rpt, 6844–7

Occupational injury and illness rates, by SIC 2- to 4-digit industry, 1989, annual rpt, 6844–1

OECD trade, total and for 4 major countries, and US trade by country, by commodity, 1970-89, world area rpt series, 9116–1

Oil and gas primary use prohibited for power and industrial plants, and gas use by State, 1977-90, annual rpt, 3334–1

Oil and refined products supply, demand, prices, and refinery capacity and stocks, by State, 1960-91, annual rpt, 3164–95

Oil refinery capacity, closings, and acquisitions by plant, and fuel used, by PAD district, 1973-89, annual rpt, 3164–2.1

Price indexes (producer), by stage of processing and detailed commodity, monthly rpt, 6762–6

Price indexes (producer), by stage of processing and detailed commodity, monthly 1990, annual rpt, 6764–2

Production, shipments, trade, stocks, orders, use, and firms, by product, periodic Current Industrial Rpt series, 2506–12

Productivity of labor and capital, indexes and percent change, 1948-90, annual press release, 6824–2

Puerto Rico economic censuses, 1987: wholesale and retail trade and service industry finances and operations, by SIC 2- to 4-digit industry and municipio, 2591–1

Savings instns failures, inventory of real estate assets available from Resolution Trust Corp, 1990, semiannual listing, 9722–2.4

Savings instns failures, inventory of real estate assets available from Resolution Trust Corp, 1991, semiannual listing, 9722–2.10

Service industries census, 1987: establishments, receipts by source, payroll, and employment, by SIC 2- to 4-digit kind of business, State, and MSA, 2393–4

Shipbuilding and repair facilities, capacity, and employment, by shipyard, 1990, annual rpt, 7704–9

Solar collector and photovoltaic module shipments by end-use sector and State, and trade, 1989, annual rpt, 3164–62

Soviet Union GNP by detailed income and outlay component, 1985, 2326–18.59

Tax (income) returns of corporations, income and tax items by asset size and detailed industry, 1987, annual rpt, 8304–4

Tax (income) returns of corporations, income and tax items by asset size and detailed industry, 1988, annual rpt, 8304–21

Telephone and telegraph firms detailed finances and operations, 1989, annual rpt, 9284–6

Tennessee Valley industrial dev and employment, by SIC 2-digit industry, firm, and location, 1990, annual rpt, 9804–3

Water use by end use, well withdrawals, and public supply deliveries, by county, State rpt series, 5666–24

Wholesale trade census, 1987: establishments, sales by customer class, employment, inventories, and expenses, by SIC 2- to 4-digit kind of business, 2407–4

see also Business firms and establishments, number

see also Business machines and equipment

see also Capital investments, general

see also Capital investments, specific industry

see also Depreciation

see also Electric power plants and equipment

see also Foundries

see also Grain storage and facilities

see also Industrial capacity and utilization

see also Industrial robots

see also Industrial siting

see also Railroad equipment and vehicles

see also Warehouses

Industrial pollution

see Air pollution

see Environmental pollution and control

see Hazardous waste and disposal

see Lead poisoning and pollution

see Marine pollution

see Noise

see Water pollution

Industrial production

China economic indicators and reform issues, with background data, 1950s-90, compilation of papers, 23848–155

Communist and OECD countries economic conditions, 1989, annual rpt, 7144–11

Competitiveness (intl) of US industries, with selected foreign and US operating data by major firm and product, series, 2046–12

Economic and employment conditions, alternative BLS projections to 2005 and trends 1970s-90, biennial article, 6722–1.253

Economic indicators and components, and Fed Reserve 4th District business and financial conditions, monthly chartbook, 9377–10

Economic indicators and components, current data and annual trends, monthly rpt, 23842–1.3

Economic indicators compounded annual rates of change, 1971-90, annual rpt, 9391–9.2

Economic indicators, monthly rpt, 9362–1.2

Industrial production

Index by Subjects and Names

Foreign and US economic conditions and competitiveness issues, with data by country, 1960s-90, 21788–204

Foreign and US economic conditions, and trade devs and balances, with data by selected country and country group, monthly rpt, 9882–14

Foreign countries *Background Notes*, summary social, political, and economic data, series, 7006–2

Foreign countries economic and monetary trends, compounded annual rates of change for US and 10 major trading partners, quarterly rpt, 9391–7

Foreign countries economic conditions and implications for US, periodic country rpt series, 2046–4

Foreign countries economic indicators, and trade and investment flows, for selected countries and country groups, selected years 1946-90, annual rpt, 204–1.9

GDP and GNP as measures of production, factor income components, and receipts from and payments to foreigners, 1980s-91, article, 2702–1.215

GNP by industry, and constant dollar estimate revisions, data sources and reliability, 1977-88, article, 2702–1.201

GNP by industry group, 1986-89, article, 2702–1.208

Imports and tariff provisions effect on US industries and products, investigations with background financial and operating data, series, 9886–4

Imports injury to US industries from foreign subsidized products, investigations with background financial and operating data, series, 9886–15

Imports injury to US industries from sales at less than fair value, investigations with background financial and operating data, series, 9886–14

Industry finances and operations, by SIC 2- to 4-digit industry, forecast 1991, annual rpt, 2044–28

Input-output structure of US economy, detailed interindustry transactions for 84 industries, and components of final demand, 1986, annual article, 2702–1.206

Input-output structure of US economy, detailed interindustry transactions for 85 industries, 1982 benchmark data, 2702–1.213

Manufacturing annual survey, 1989: value of shipments, by SIC 4- to 5-digit product class, 2506–15.2

Manufacturing census, 1987: employment and shipments under Fed Govt contracts, by SIC 4-digit industry, 2497–7

Manufacturing census, 1987: finances and operations, by type of organization and SIC 2- to 4-digit industry, subject rpt, 2497–5

Manufacturing industries operations and performance, analytical rpt series, 2506–16

Manufacturing shipments and new and unfilled orders, 1947-90, annual rpt, 204–1.3

Manufacturing shipments, inventories, and orders, by SIC 2- to 3-digit industry, monthly Current Industrial Rpt, 2506–3.1

Middle Atlantic and East North Central census div shares of US manufacturing output, by industry and State, alternative estimates, 1963 and 1986, working paper, 9375–13.59

Middle Atlantic States manufacturing business outlook, monthly survey rpt, 9387–11

North Carolina environmental and socioeconomic conditions, and impacts of proposed OCS oil and gas exploration, 1970s-90 and projected to 2020, 5738–22

OECD intl trade position for US and 4 countries, and factors affecting US competition, periodic pamphlet, 2042–25

Overseas Business Reports: economic conditions, investment and export opportunities, and trade practices, country market research rpt series, 2046–6

PPI and components correlation with GNP and industrial production over business cycles, 1957-89, article, 9383–6.204

Rocky Mountain region employment and income, and economic dependence on shipments outside area, by industry and county group, 1980s, 1208–362

Soviet Union, Eastern Europe, OECD, and selected other countries economic conditions, 1960s-90, annual rpt, 9114–4

State and Metro Area Data Book, 1991 data compilation, 2328–54

Statistical Abstract of US, 1991 annual data compilation, 2324–1.27

Stock price and industrial production indexes, correlations among 4 industrial countries, 1966-90, technical paper, 9385–8.105

Survey of Current Business, detailed data for major industries and economic indicators, monthly rpt, 2702–1

Taiwan interest rate relation to money supply, industrial production, and US interest rate, late 1980s, working paper, 9371–10.56

see also Business inventories

see also Business orders

see also Gross Domestic Product

see also Industrial capacity and utilization

see also Industrial production indexes

see also Industrial purchasing

see also Labor productivity

see also Production costs

see also Productivity

see also Value added tax

see also under names of specific industries or industry groups

Industrial production indexes

DC production index, by component, 1987-91, article, 9389–1.203

Diffusion indexes of industrial production, monthly 1967-90, article, 9362–1.205

Economic indicators and components, current data and annual trends, monthly rpt, 23842–1.3

Economic indicators compounded annual rates of change, monthly rpt, 9391–3

Economic indicators, monthly rpt, 9362–1.2

Forecasts of industrial production growth and business cycle turning points, performance of diffusion indexes, 1960s-90, technical paper, 9366–6.277

Foreign and US economic conditions, for major industrial countries, biweekly rpt, 9112–1

Foreign and US industrial production indexes and CPI, for US and 6 OECD countries, current data and annual trends, monthly rpt, 23842–1.7

Foreign and US industrial production indexes, for 7 OECD countries, *Survey of Current Business*, monthly rpt, 2702–1.2

Foreign countries economic conditions and implications for US, periodic country rpt series, 2046–4

Manufacturing census, 1987: finances and operations, by SIC 2- to 4-digit industry, State, and MSA, with trends from 1849, 2497–1

Middle Atlantic States manufacturing output index, monthly rpt, 9387–12

Postal Service productivity, indexes of output and labor, capital, and other inputs, alternative model descriptions and results, 1960s-89, 9688–6

Production and capacity use indexes, by SIC 2- to 4-digit industry, monthly rpt, 9365–2.24

Production indexes for selected manufacturing groups, 1947-90, with trends for major industry divs from 1939, annual rpt, 204–1.3

Productivity of labor and capital, indexes and percent change, 1948-90, annual press release, 6824–2

Southeastern States, Fed Reserve 5th District, economic indicators by State, quarterly rpt, 9389–16

Soviet Union, Eastern Europe, OECD, and selected other countries economic conditions, 1960s-90, annual rpt, 9114–4.2

Statistical Abstract of US, 1991 annual data compilation, 2324–1.27

Survey of Current Business, detailed data for major industries and economic indicators, monthly rpt, 2702–1.4

Telecommunications industry intl competitiveness, with financial and operating data by product or service, firm, and country, 1990 rpt, 2008–30

Industrial purchasing

Manufacturing census, 1987: employment and shipments under Fed Govt contracts, by SIC 4-digit industry, 2497–7

Manufacturing census, 1987: finances and operations, by SIC 2- to 4-digit industry, State, and MSA, with trends from 1849, 2497–1

Manufacturing census, 1987: finances and operations, by type of organization and SIC 2- to 4-digit industry, subject rpt, 2497–5

Natl income and product accounts and components, *Survey of Current Business*, monthly rpt, 2702–1.25

Retail trade census, 1987: depreciable assets, capital and operating expenses, sales, value added, and inventories, by SIC 2- to 4-digit kind of business, 2399–2

Wholesale trade census, 1987: depreciable assets, capital and operating expenses, sales, value added, and inventories, by SIC 2- to 3-digit kind of business, 2407–2

Wholesale trade census, 1987: establishments, sales by customer class, employment, inventories, and expenses, by SIC 2- to 4-digit kind of business, 2407–4

Index by Subjects and Names

see also Business orders

Industrial relations

see Labor-management relations, general

see Work stoppages

Industrial revenue bonds

see Tax exempt securities

Industrial robots

Exports of US, detailed Schedule B commodities with countries of destination, 1990, annual rpt, 2424–10

Manufacturing finances and operations, by SIC 2- to 4-digit industry, forecast 1991, annual rpt, 2044–28

NSF R&D grant awards, by div and program, FY89, periodic rpt, 9626–7.3

Statistical Abstract of US, 1991 annual data compilation, 2324–1.27

Industrial siting

Farmland value, rent, taxes, foreign ownership, and transfers by probable use and lender type, with data by region and State, 1980-91, article, 1561–16.202

Financial instns location relation to ZIP code area income and minority population, by instn type for 5 cities, 1977-89, article, 9377–1.208

Landfills distance from wetlands and water habitats, for 11 States, 1990 rpt, 9188–115

Nuclear power plant safety standards and research, design, licensing, construction, operation, and finances, with data by reactor, quarterly journal, 3352–4

Radioactive waste and spent fuel generation, inventory, and disposal, 1960s-89 and projected to 2020, annual rpt, 3364–2

Tennessee Valley industrial dev and employment, by SIC 2-digit industry, firm, and location, 1990, annual rpt, 9804–3

Water quality, chemistry, hydrology, and other characteristics, local area studies, series, 5666–27

Industrial standards

Auto and light truck fuel economy performance by make, standards, and enforcement, 1978-91 model years, annual rpt, 7764–9

Computer systems purchase and use, and data recording, processing, and transfer, Fed Govt standards, series, 2216–2

Export and import product standards under GATT, Natl Inst of Standards and Technology info activities, and proposed standards by agency and country, 1990, annual rpt, 2214–6

Exports of goods, services, and investment, trade barriers, impacts, and US actions, by country, 1989, annual rpt, 444–2

Gold and silver fineness standards of US and EC, 1990 hearing, 25388–58

Mobile home fires, casualties, damage, and impacts of safety standards, with data on Michigan trailer parks, 1980s, hearing, 21248–145

Natl Inst of Standards and Technology rpts, 1990, annual listing, 2214–1

Nuclear power plant safety standards and research, design, licensing, construction, operation, and finances, with data by reactor, quarterly journal, 3352–4

Occupational exposure to hazardous substances and conditions, measurement, and proposed standards, series, 4246–1

Performance, weights, and measures standards dev, proposals, and policies, 1991 annual conf, 2214–7

see also Quality control and testing

see also Weights and measures

Industry

see Business and industry

see under By Industry in the "Index by Categories"

Industry conversion

see Conversion of industry

Industry wage surveys

Auto and auto parts manufacturing wages, employment, and benefits, by occupation, region, and selected labor market area, 1989 survey, 6787–6.252

Lumber industry workers and wages by occupation, annual State survey rpt series, 6787–7

Textile production workers and wages by occupation, and benefits, by location, 1990 survey, 6787–6.251

Wages, hours, and employment by occupation, and benefits, for selected locations, industry survey rpt series, 6787–6

see also Area wage surveys

INF treaty

see Intermediate-Range Nuclear Forces Treaty

Infant health

see Breast-feeding

see Infant mortality

see Obstetrics and gynecology

see Pediatrics

see Prenatal care

Infant mortality

Accident deaths of children, by cause, age, sex, race, and State, 1980-85, 4108–54

Deaths and rates, by cause, age, sex, race, and State, preliminary 1989-90 and trends from 1960, US Vital Statistics annual rpt, 4144–7

Deaths and rates, by detailed cause and demographic characteristics, 1988 and trends from 1900, US Vital Statistics annual rpt, 4144–2

Deaths of infants, by cause, region, and race, 1980-87, article, 4202–7.208

Deaths recorded in 121 cities, by age group and for infants, weekly rpt, 4202–1

Developing countries child health and welfare indicators, and economic conditions, 1950s-80s, hearing, 25388–57

Developing countries economic and social conditions from 1960s, and Intl Dev Cooperation Agency and AID activities and funding, FY90-92, annual rpt, 9904–4

Food aid program of USDA for women, infants, and children, health services need of participants, for Rhode Island, 1983-84, article, 4042–3.247

Foreign countries *Background Notes,* summary social, political, and economic data, series, 7006–2

Foreign countries economic, social, political, and geographic summary data, by country, 1991, annual factbook, 9114–2

Health condition and health care resources, use, and spending, 1950s-89, annual data compilation, 4144–11

Health condition and services use, for children, 1990 chartbook, 4108–49

Hispanic Americans deaths and rates, by cause, age, sex, and detailed origin, average 1979-81, 4147–20.18

Homeless teens pregnancy prevalence and outcomes, services availability, health condition, and drug abuse, 1989 conf, 4108–55

Indian and Alaska Native disease and disorder cases, deaths, and health services use, by tribe, reservation, and Indian Health Service area, late 1950s-86, 4088–2

Indian Health Service facilities and use, and Indian health and other characteristics, by IHS region, 1980s-89, annual chartbook, 4084–7

Indian Health Service facilities, funding, operations, and Indian health and other characteristics, 1950s-90, annual chartbook, 4084–1

Indian infant death rates, and racial misclassification on death certificates, for Oklahoma, 1975-88, article, 4042–3.209

Indonesia child and infant survival programs of AID, effectiveness with background data, 1970s-87, 9916–1.73

Medicaid coverage effects on prenatal care use and birth outcomes, charges, and Medicaid payments, for California, 1983, article, 4652–1.241

Minority group and women health condition, services use, payment sources, and health care labor force, by poverty status, 1940s-89, chartbook, 4118–56

Minority group health condition, services use, costs, and indicators of services need, 1950s-88, 4118–55

Palau admin, and social, economic, and govtl data, FY90, annual rpt, 7004–6

Population size and characteristics, 1969-88, Current Population Rpt, biennial rpt, 2546–2.161

Preventive disease and health improvement goals and recommended activities for 2000, with trends 1970s-80s, 4048–10

State and Metro Area Data Book, 1991 data compilation, 2328–54

Statistical Abstract of US, 1991 annual data compilation, 2324–1.2

Vital statistics provisional data, monthly rpt, 4142–1

see also Fetal deaths

Infective and parasitic diseases

Cases of acute and chronic conditions, disability, absenteeism, and health services use, by selected characteristics, 1987, CD-ROM, 4147–10.177

Deaths and rates, by cause and age, preliminary 1989-90, US Vital Statistics annual rpt, 4144–7

Deaths and rates, by cause, provisional data, monthly rpt, 4142–1.2

Deaths and rates, by detailed cause and demographic characteristics, 1988 and trends from 1900, US Vital Statistics annual rpt, 4144–2

Dientamoeba fragilis testing methods of State public health labs, 1985, article, 4042–3.225

Drug abuse indicators for selected metro areas, research results, data collection, and policy issues, 1991 semiannual conf, 4492–5

Foreign travel vaccination needs by country, and disease prevention recommendations, 1991 annual rpt, 4204–11

Health condition and health care resources, use, and spending, 1950s-89, annual data compilation, 4144–11

Infective and parasitic diseases

Helicobacter pylori infection relation to gastric cancer risk, 1982-89 study, article, 4472–1.236

Hepatitis B and C screening of blood donors, PHS guidelines, 1991 rpt, 4206–2.40

Hepatitis B virus transmission in health care settings, occupational exposure, prevention policies, and OSHA regulation, 1990 hearings, 21348–119

Hepatitis cases by infection source, age, sex, race, and State, and deaths, by strain, 1988 and trends from 1966, 4205–2

Hepatitis infection and other factors relation to hepatocellular cancer risk, 1984-90 local area study, article, 4472–1.237

HHS financial aid, by program, recipient, State, and city, FY90, annual regional listings, 4004–3

Hospital deaths of Medicare patients, actual and expected rates by diagnosis, with hospital characteristics, by instn, FY87-89, annual regional rpt series, 4654–14

Hospital discharges and length of stay, by diagnosis, patient and instn characteristics, procedure performed, and payment source, 1988, annual rpt, 4147–13.107

Hospital discharges and length of stay by region and diagnosis, and procedures performed, by age and sex, 1989, annual rpt, 4146–8.198

Hospital discharges by detailed diagnostic and procedure category, primary diagnosis, and length of stay, by age, sex, and region, 1988, annual rpt, 4147–13.105; 4147–13.108

Indian and Alaska Native disease and disorder cases, deaths, and health services use, by tribe, reservation, and Indian Health Service area, late 1950s-86, 4088–2

Indian Health Service, tribal, and contract facilities hospitalization, by diagnosis, age, sex, and service area, FY89, annual rpt, 4084–5

Infant death rate, by cause, region, and race, 1980-87, article, 4202–7.208

Malaria cases in US, for military personnel and US and foreign natls, and by country of infection, 1966-89, annual rpt, 4205–4

Malaria treatment with parenteral quinidine gluconate, CDC recommendations, 1991 rpt, 4206–2.40

Measles cases among New York State high school and college students, and vaccination and treatment costs, 1989, article, 4042–3.227

Minority group health condition, services use, costs, and indicators of services need, 1950s-88, 4118–55

Morbidity and Mortality Weekly Report, infectious notifiable disease cases and deaths, and other public health issues, periodic journal, 4202–7

Morbidity and Mortality Weekly Report, infectious notifiable disease cases by age, race, and State, and deaths, 1930s-90, annual rpt, 4204–1

Morbidity and Mortality Weekly Report, infectious notifiable disease cases by State, and public health issues, 4202–1

Morbidity and Mortality Weekly Report, special supplements, series, 4206–2

Natl Inst of Allergy and Infectious Diseases activities, grants by recipient and location, and disease cases, FY83-90, annual rpt, 4474–30

Neurological Disorders and Stroke Natl Inst activities, and disorder cases, FY90, annual rpt, 4474–25

Notifiable diseases reporting to health depts, physicians compliance, 1986-88 local area study, article, 4042–3.252

Polio history of population, 1987, CD-ROM, 4147–10.177

Preventive disease and health improvement goals and recommended activities for 2000, with trends 1970s-80s, 4048–10

State and Metro Area Data Book, 1991 data compilation, 2328–54

Waste (medical) generation, sources, health worker exposure and risk, and incineration emissions, 1980s, 4078–1

see also Acquired immune deficiency syndrome

see also Animal diseases and zoonoses

see also Food and waterborne diseases

see also Pneumonia and influenza

see also Rabies

see also Septicemia

see also Sexually transmitted diseases

see also Tuberculosis

see also Vaccination and vaccines

see also under By Disease in the "Index by Categories"

Infertility

see Fertility

see Sexual sterilization

see Urogenital diseases

Inflammable materials

Injuries from use of consumer products, by severity, victim age, and detailed product, 1990, annual rpt, 9164–6

Transport of hazardous material, accidents, casualties, and damage, by mode of transport, with DOT control activities, 1989, annual rpt, 7304–4

Inflation

Argentina and Brazil inflation rates and public debt burden, 1980s-91, technical paper, 9379–12.69

Argentina and Brazil inflation relation to money supply and public debt, model description and results, 1980s-90, technical paper, 9379–12.75

Assets and liabilities of US, and impacts of inflation, 1990 and trends from 1948, article, 9391–1.220

Brazil price variability among products and cities, relation to inflation, alternative model results for 1980s, working paper, 9379–14.14

Budget of US, CBO analysis of revenue and spending alternatives and projections of economic indicators, FY92-96, annual rpt, 26304–3

Business cycle variation and growth rates of GNP and components, inflation, and money supply, for 10 industrial countries, 1850s-1980s, working paper, 9383–20.15

Costs of inflation over long term, with background data on unemployment and GNP growth for high- and low-inflation countries, 1980s, article, 9385–1.207

CPI and Personal Consumption Expenditure Index inflation measures under alternative weighting systems, monthly rpt, periodic article, 6762–2

Developing countries economic and social conditions from 1960s, and Intl Dev Cooperation Agency and AID activities and funding, FY90-92, annual rpt, 9904–4

Developing countries inflation control programs using exchange rate policies, evaluation, 1980s-91, technical paper, 9366–7.256

Dollar exchange rate relation to interest rate differentials and inflation, for selected currencies and trade-weighted index, model description and results, 1974-90, technical paper, 9366–7.262

EC economic integration economic impacts, with background data by country, 1988-90, article, 9379–1.201

Economic indicators and relation to govt finances by level of govt, selected years 1929-90, annual rpt, 10044–1

Economic indicators compounded annual rates of change, monthly rpt, 9391–3

Economic indicators compounded annual rates of change, 1971-90, annual rpt, 9391–9.2

Economic indicators performance, and Fed Reserve monetary policy objectives, as of July 1991, semiannual rpt, 9362–4

Exports and export prices of US, impact of domestic and foreign price levels and other factors, 1970s-89, article, 9393–8.203

Fed Govt agencies civil fines imposed, and proposed inflation adjustments, FY87, hearing, 21408–124

Food price dispersion impacts of inflation, by city, model results, 1981-82, working paper, 6886–6.79

Forecasts of GNP and inflation, performance of alternative monetary aggregates, model description and results, 1948-87, working paper, 9371–10.53

Forecasts of inflation, performance of alternative models, impact of adjusting for prior announcement of forecast, 1970s-86, working paper, 9387–8.249

Forecasts of inflation, performance of expected long run inflation rate and other models for Japan and Germany, 1970s-89, technical paper, 9366–7.268

Forecasts of inflation, performance of interest rate spreads and yield curve, 1960s-88, technical paper, 9385–8.118

Forecasts of inflation, performance of money supply, unemployment, and other monetary and economic indicators, 1959-88, article, 9379–1.204

Foreign and US economic indicators, trade balances, and exchange rates, for selected OECD and Asian countries, 1991 semiannual rpt, 8002–14

Foreign countries economic and monetary trends, compounded annual rates of change and quarterly indicators for US and 7 major industrialized countries, quarterly rpt, 9391–7

Germany hyperinflation after WWI, money demand impact of relative prices of investment and consumer goods, model description and results, 1921-23, working paper, 9371–10.66

GNP and GNP deflator variability, alternative models assessment and results, 1869-1988, article, 9379–1.205

GNP implicit price deflators, monthly rpt, quarterly data, 23842–1.1

GNP implicit price deflators, total and major components, *Survey of Current Business*, monthly rpt, 2702–1.24

Index by Subjects and Names

Income tax rates for individuals, effects of indexing to adjust for inflation, under alternative tax codes, 1970-88, working paper, 9377–9.117

Interest rates over long run, relation to inflation and other economic indicators, model description and results for UK indexed bonds, 1982-88, technical paper, 9385–8.119

Monetary aggregates and aggregate indexes, relation to inflation, 1963-89, article, 9391–1.202

Monetary aggregates relation to inflation, 1950s-89, article, 9379–1.203

Mortgages (price level adjusted) impacts on housing affordability, 1991 article, 9373–1.204

Price indexes as inflation targets, actual and expected inflation rates based on alternative price indexes, 1950s-87, article, 9377–1.201

Statistical Abstract of US, 1991 annual data compilation, 2324–1.15

Stock returns relation to inflation, model description and results, 1950s-89, working paper, 9379–14.12

Survey of Current Business, detailed data for major industries and economic indicators, monthly rpt, 2702–1.5

Survey of Current Business, detailed financial and business data, and economic indicators, monthly rpt, 2702–1.4

Switzerland alternative monetary aggregates indexes relation to inflation and monetary base, 1970s-89, article, 9391–1.221

Tax (income) and other economic indicators relation to inflation, model description and results, 1950s-89, working paper, 9377–9.110

Turkey GNP, trade, investment, and inflation following currency devaluation, 1970s-90, technical paper, 9385–8.112

UK inflation and GNP forecasting performance of indexed bond prices and other factors, 1950s-91, article, 9385–1.214

Unemployment and Fed Reserve inflation forecast accuracy indicators, relation to inflation, 1960s-83, working paper, 9387–8.240

see also Consumer Price Index

see also Cost of living

see also Food prices

see also Interest rates

see also Monetary policy

see also Money supply

see also Price regulation

see also Prices

see also Producer Price Index

Influenza

see Pneumonia and influenza

Information access

see Freedom of information

see Government information

see Information sciences

see Information services

see Information storage and retrieval systems

Information sciences

Degrees awarded in higher education, by level, field, race, and sex, 1988/89 with trends from 1978/79, biennial rpt, 4844–17

Higher education course completions, by detailed program, sex, race, and instn type, for 1972 high school class, as of 1984, 4888–4

Natl Commission on Libraries and Info Science activities, FY90, annual rpt, 15634–1

NSF R&D grant awards, by div and program, periodic rpt series, 9626–7

Training in library science, grants for disadvantaged students, by instn and State, FY90, annual listing, 4874–1

see also CD-ROM technology and use

see also Computer sciences

Information services

County Business Patterns, 1988: employment, establishments, and payroll, by SIC 2- to 4-digit industry and county, annual State rpt series, 2326–6

County Business Patterns, 1989: employment, establishments, and payroll, by SIC 2- to 4-digit industry and county, annual State rpt series, 2326–8

Family planning and population activities of AID, grants by project and recipient, and contraceptive shipments, by country, FY90, annual rpt series, 9914–13

Finances and operations, by SIC 2- to 4-digit industry, forecast 1991, annual rpt, 2044–28

Service industries census, 1987: establishments, receipts by source, payroll, and employment, by SIC 2- to 4-digit kind of business, State, and MSA, 2393–4

Technology dev programs of govts, info sources and funding, 1990 rpt, 10048–81

Telecommunications industry intl competitiveness, with financial and operating data by product or service, firm, and country, 1990 rpt, 2008–30

Weather services activities and funding, by Federal agency, planned FY91-92, annual rpt, 2144–2

see also Government information

see also Information storage and retrieval systems

see also Libraries

see also Mass media

see also Research

Information storage and retrieval systems

Air Force fiscal mgmt system operations and techniques, quarterly rpt, 3602–1

Airline computer reservation system operations, travel agency revenues by firm, and frequent flyer awards by carrier, 1988, 7308–199.9

Criminal records checks of firearm purchasers, and firearms use in crime, with data by State, 1987-90, 26358–244

Criminal records repository characteristics, holdings, use, and reporting requirements, by State, 1989, 6068–241

Drug (prescription) mail service industry structure, finances, and operations, 1989 survey, 4658–60

Educational Resources Info Center (ERIC) activities, 1990-91, annual rpt, 4814–3

Environmental and natural resource data sources, and aerial survey R&D rpts, quarterly listing, 9502–7

Fed Govt computer and telecommunication systems acquisition plans and obligations, by agency, FY89-91, last issue of annual rpt, 104–20

Fed Govt computer and telecommunication systems acquisition plans and obligations, by agency, FY90-95, annual rpt, 104–33

Information storage and retrieval systems

Fed Govt computer systems and equipment, by type, make, and agency, 2nd half FY90, semiannual listing, 9452–9

Fed Govt computer systems with sensitive unclassified data, security plans by characteristics of info and system, and agency, 1989, 2218–85

Fed Govt data collection activities, and quality and privacy issues, 1990 conf, 106–4.14

Fed Govt standards for data recording, processing, and transfer, and for purchase and use of computer systems, series, 2216–2

Global climate change trends and contributing gases levels, Federal and intl data collection activities, mgmt, and inventory, 1990 rpt, 3028–4

Govt admin and tax records use in data collection, methodological and disclosure issues, 1988-89 annual conf papers, 8304–17

Health care services outcome research and practice guidelines dev activities and funding of Agency for Health Care Policy and Research, FY88-89, 4188–70

Health care treatments effectiveness info, feasibility of linking Federal and other databases, 1991 narrative rpt, 4188–73

Libraries technological aid, project descriptions and funding, FY89, annual listing, 4874–6

Library of Congress activities, acquisitions, services, and financial statements, FY90, annual rpt, 26404–1

Money laundering investigations of Fed Govt using IRS large cash transaction rpts, and rpts filed and penalties for nonfiling by region, 1989-91, GAO rpt, 26119–356

NIH Natl Library of Medicine activities, holdings, and grants, FY88-90, annual rpt, 4464–1

Public welfare computer records matching, Federal and State agencies compliance with recipient protection provisions before benefits reduction, 1990, GAO rpt, 26121–404

R&D facilities for biological and medical sciences, space and equipment adequacy, needs, and funding by source, by instn type, 1990, biennial rpt, 4434–17

Space science and related data sources, use by format and user type, FY90, annual rpt, 9504–11

Space science missions data archival storage of NASA, holdings, and missions not archived, 1950s-91, 26125–43

Survey of Income and Program Participation, data collection, methodology, and comparisons to other data bases, working paper series, 2626–10

Survey of Income and Program Participation, data collection, methodology, and use, 1990 annual conf papers, 2624–1

Tax (income) returns computer matching program to indentify underreported income, effectiveness, 1987, GAO rpt, 26119–325

see also CD-ROM catalogs and guides

see also CD-ROM releases

see also CD-ROM technology and use

see also Computer data file guides
see also Computer industry and products
see also Computer networks
see also Microforms
see also Statistical programs and activities

Infrastructure
see Public works

Inglewood, Calif.
see also under By City in the "Index by Categories"

Inhalation therapy
see Respiratory therapy

Inheritance tax
see Estate tax

Injuries
see Accidental deaths
see Accidents and accident prevention
see Agricultural accidents and safety
see Aviation accidents and safety
see Drowning
see Marine accidents and safety
see Mine accidents and safety
see Occupational health and safety
see Railroad accidents and safety
see Spinal cord injuries
see Traffic accidents and safety
see Transportation accidents and safety

Inland water transportation
Army Corps of Engineers water resources dev projects, characteristics, and costs, 1950s-89, biennial State rpt series, 3756–1
Army Corps of Engineers water resources dev projects, characteristics, and costs, 1950s-91, biennial State rpt series, 3756–2
Census of Transportation, 1987: finances and operations by size, ownership, and State, and revenues by MSA, by SIC 2- to 4-digit industry, 2579–1
Coal production, stocks, and shipments, by State of origin and destination, end-use sector, and mode of transport, quarterly rpt, 3162–8
Condition, mgmt, R&D, and funding, for transportation and environmental public works, 1986-91, 26358–235
County Business Patterns, 1988: employment, establishments, and payroll, by SIC 2- to 4-digit industry and county, annual State rpt series, 2326–6
County Business Patterns, 1989: employment, establishments, and payroll, by SIC 2- to 4-digit industry and county, annual State rpt series, 2326–8
Employment, earnings, and hours, by SIC 1- to 4-digit industry, monthly and annual averages, selected years 1909-90, annual rpt, 6744–4
Energy use by mode of transport, fuel supply, and demographic and economic factors of vehicle use, 1970s-89, annual rpt, 3304–5
Exports and imports (waterborne) of US, by type of service, customs district, port, and world area, monthly rpt, 2422–7
Fed Govt Inland Waterways Trust Fund financial condition, monthly rpt, 8102–9.8
Foreign countries economic, social, political, and geographic summary data, by country, 1991, annual factbook, 9114–2
Govt census, 1987: employment, payroll, and average earnings, by function, level of govt, State, county, and population size, 2455–2

Govt employment and payroll, by function, level of govt, and jurisdiction, 1990, annual rpt series, 2466–1
Govt finances, by level of govt, State, and for large cities and counties, annual rpt series, 2466–2
Grain shipments and rates for barge and rail loadings, periodic situation rpt with articles, 1561–4
Great Lakes area economic conditions and outlook, for US and Canada, 1970s-90, 9375–15
Military and personal property shipments, passenger traffic, and costs, by service branch and mode of transport, quarterly rpt, 3702–1
Mississippi River system freight traffic by commodity and waterway, 1988 and projected to 2000, article, 9391–16.202
Natl transportation system planning, use, condition, accidents, and needs, by mode of transport, 1940s-90 and projected to 2020, 7308–202
Occupational injury and illness rates, by SIC 2- to 4-digit industry, 1988-89, annual rpt, 6844–7
Occupational injury and illness rates, by SIC 2- to 4-digit industry, 1989, annual rpt, 6844–1
Price indexes (producer), by stage of processing and detailed commodity, monthly rpt, 6762–6
St Lawrence Seaway Dev Corp finances and activities, and Seaway cargo tonnage, 1989, annual rpt, 7744–1
St Lawrence Seaway ship, cargo, and passenger traffic, and toll revenue, 1990 and trends from 1959, annual rpt, 7744–2
Statistical Abstract of US, 1991 annual data compilation, 2324–1.22
TVA finances and operations by program and facility, FY90, annual rpt, 9804–32
see also Barges
see also Dredging

Inner cities
see Central cities

Inoculation
see Vaccination and vaccines

Inorganic chemicals
see Chemicals and chemical industry

Input-output analysis
Import restraint elimination impacts on US economy and selected service industries, 1970s-90, 9886–4.173
Import restraint elimination impacts on US economy by selected sector, model description and results, 1988, 9886–4.174
Input-output structure of US economy, detailed interindustry transactions for 84 industries, and components of final demand, 1986, annual article, 2702–1.206
Input-output structure of US economy, detailed interindustry transactions for 85 industries, 1982 benchmark data, 2702–1.213
Input-output tables construction of BEA, comparison to Census Bur source data, 1972 and 1977, working paper, 9375–13.53
Regional multipliers derived from input-output models, use in estimating economic impacts of spending changes, 1991 article, 9391–1.206

Rocky Mountain region employment and income, and economic dependence on shipments outside area, by industry and county group, 1980s, 1208–362

Insecticides
see Pesticides

Insects
see Animal diseases and zoonoses
see Honey and beekeeping
see Infective and parasitic diseases
see Pests and pest control

Inspection of industrial products
see Quality control and testing

Inspectors General reports
see Federal Inspectors General reports

Installment credit
see Consumer credit

Institute of Museum Services
see National Foundation on the Arts and the Humanities

Institute of Peace
see U.S. Institute of Peace

Instructional materials
see Educational materials

Instruments and measuring devices
Collective bargaining agreements expiring during year, and workers covered, by firm, union, industry group, and State, 1991, annual rpt, 6784–9
County Business Patterns, 1988: employment, establishments, and payroll, by SIC 2- to 4-digit industry and county, annual State rpt series, 2326–6
County Business Patterns, 1989: employment, establishments, and payroll, by SIC 2- to 4-digit industry and county, annual State rpt series, 2326–8
DOD prime contract awards, by detailed procurement category, FY87-90, annual rpt, 3544–18
Electronic communications systems and related products shipments, trade, use, and firms, 1990, annual Current Industrial Rpt, 2506–12.35
Employment, earnings, and hours, by SIC 1- to 4-digit industry, monthly and annual averages, selected years 1909-90, annual rpt, 6744–4
Employment in manufacturing, by detailed occupation and SIC 2-digit industry, 1989 survey, triennial rpt, 6748–52
Employment, unemployment, and labor force characteristics, by region and census div, 1990, annual rpt, 6744–7.1
Energy use and prices for manufacturing industries, 1988 survey, series, 3166–13
Enterprise Statistics, 1987: auxiliaries of multi-establishment firms, finances and operations by function, industry, and State, 2329–6
Enterprise Statistics, 1987: finances and operations for companies, by size, level of diversification, form of organization, and industry group, 2329–8
Exports and imports between US and outlying areas, by detailed commodity and mode of transport, 1990, annual rpt, 2424–11
Exports and imports of US, by country and detailed commodity, monthly rpt, 2422–12
Exports and imports of US, by Harmonized System 6-digit commodity and country, 1990, annual rpt, 2424–13

Index by Subjects and Names

Insurance and insurance industry

Exports and imports of US, by selected country, country group, and commodity group, 1990, annual rpt, 2044–37

Exports and imports of US, by transport mode, country, and SITC 1- to 3-digit commodity, 1990, annual rpt, 2424–12

Exports of US, detailed commodities by country, monthly CD-ROM, 2422–13

Exports of US, detailed Schedule B commodities with countries of destination, 1990, annual rpt, 2424–10

Glassware shipments, trade, use, and firms, by product, 1990, annual Current Industrial Rpt, 2506–9.3

Imports, exports, and employment impacts, by SIC 2- to 4-digit industry and commodity, quarterly rpt, 2322–2

Imports of US, detailed commodities by country, monthly CD-ROM, 2422–14

Imports of US given duty-free treatment for value of US material sent abroad, by commodity and country, 1989, annual rpt, 9884–14

Industrial control equipment shipments, trade, use, and firms, by product, 1990, annual Current Industrial Rpt, 2506–12.11

Injuries from use of consumer products, by severity, victim age, and detailed product, 1990, annual rpt, 9164–6

Input-output structure of US economy, detailed interindustry transactions for 84 industries, and components of final demand, 1986, annual article, 2702–1.206

Input-output structure of US economy, detailed interindustry transactions for 85 industries, 1982 benchmark data, 2702–1.213

Labor productivity, indexes of output, hours, and employment by SIC 2- to 4-digit industry, 1967-89, annual rpt, 6824–1.3

Manufacturing annual survey, 1989: finances and operations, by SIC 2- to 4-digit industry, series, 2506–15

Manufacturing census, 1987: employment and shipments under Fed Govt contracts, by SIC 4-digit industry, 2497–7

Manufacturing census, 1987: finances and operations, by SIC 2- to 4-digit industry, State, and MSA, with trends from 1849, 2497–1

Manufacturing census, 1987: finances and operations, by type of organization and SIC 2- to 4-digit industry, subject rpt, 2497–5

Manufacturing corporations financial statements, by selected SIC 2- to 3-digit industry, quarterly rpt, 2502–1

Manufacturing finances and operations, by SIC 2- to 4-digit industry, forecast 1991, annual rpt, 2044–28

Manufacturing industries operations and performance, analytical rpt series, 2506–16

Manufacturing production, shipments, inventories, orders, and pollution control costs, periodic Current Industrial Rpt series, 2506–3

Multinatl US firms and foreign affiliates finances and operations, by industry and world area of parent firm, 1989 benchmark, survey, preliminary annual rpt, 2704–5

Natural gas interstate pipeline company detailed financial and operating data, by firm, 1989, annual rpt, 3164 38

Occupational injury and illness rates, by SIC 2- to 4-digit industry, 1988-89, annual rpt, 6844–7

Occupational injury and illness rates, by SIC 2- to 4-digit industry, 1989, annual rpt, 6844–1

OECD trade, total and for 4 major countries, and US trade by country, by commodity, 1970-89, world area rpt series, 9116–1

Pollution (air) emissions factors, by detailed pollutant and source, data compilation, 1990 rpt, 9198–120

Pollution abatement capital and operating costs, by SIC 2-digit industry, 1989, advance annual Current Industrial Rpt, 2506–3.6

Price indexes (producer), by stage of processing and detailed commodity, monthly rpt, 6762–6

Price indexes (producer), by stage of processing and detailed commodity, monthly 1990, annual rpt, 6764–2

Puerto Rico and other US possessions corporations income tax returns, income and tax items, and employment, by selected industry, 1987, article, 8302–2.213

R&D funding, and scientists and engineers education and employment, for US and selected foreign countries, 1991 annual rpt, 9627–35.1

Shipments, trade, use, and firms, for instruments and related products by detailed type, 1989, annual Current Industrial Rpt, 2506–12.26

Standards dev, proposals, and policies, for weights, measures, and performance, 1991 annual conf, 2214–7

Tariff Schedule of US, classifications and rates of duty by detailed imported commodity, 1992 base edition, 9886–13

Tax (income) returns of corporations, income and tax items by asset size and detailed industry, 1987, annual rpt, 8304–4

Tax (income) returns of corporations, income and tax items by asset size and detailed industry, 1988, annual rpt, 8304–21

Tax (income) returns of corporations with foreign tax credit, income and tax items by industry group, 1986, biennial article, 8302–2.203

Tax (income) returns of multinatl US firms foreign affiliates, income statement items, by asset size and industry, 1986, biennial article, 8302–2.212

see also Aeronautical navigation

see also Medical supplies and equipment

see also Radar

see also Scientific equipment and apparatus

see also Watches and clocks

see also under By Commodity in the "Index by Categories"

see also under By Industry in the "Index by Categories"

Instruments, musical

see Musical instruments

Insulation

Bonneville Power Admin housing energy conservation program activities, cost effectiveness, and participation, series, 3226–1

Building codes for energy efficiency, effect on house construction practices in BPA service areas, 1987, 3228–15

Commercial buildings energy use, costs, and conservation, by building characteristics, survey rpt series, 3166–8

Exports and imports of US, by country and detailed commodity, monthly rpt, 2422–12

Exports and imports of US, by Harmonized System 6-digit commodity and country, 1990, annual rpt, 2424–13

Exports of US, detailed Schedule B commodities with countries of destination, 1990, annual rpt, 2424–10

Housing and households detailed characteristics, and unit and neighborhood quality, by location, 1989, biennial rpt, 2485–12

Housing and households detailed characteristics, and unit and neighborhood quality, MSA surveys, series, 2485–6

Housing attic insulation radiant barriers performance impacts of ventilation and dust, 1990 rpt, 3308–97

Injuries from use of consumer products, by severity, victim age, and detailed product, 1990, annual rpt, 9164–6

Manufacturing annual survey, 1989: finances and operations, by SIC 2- to 4-digit industry, series, 2506–15

Price indexes (producer), by stage of processing and detailed commodity, monthly rpt, 6762–6

Price indexes (producer) for building materials, by type, bimonthly rpt, 2042–1.5

Stockpiling of strategic material by Fed Govt, activity, and inventory by commodity, as of Mar 1991, semiannual rpt, 3542–22

Insulin

see Hormones

Insurance and insurance industry

Budget of US, obligations and authority by function, agency, and program, with summaries, analyses, and historical tables, FY92, annual rpt, 104–2

Classification codes concordance of Canada and US SICs, for 1- to 4-digit levels, 1991 rpt, 2628–31

Collective bargaining agreements expiring during year, and workers covered, by firm, union, industry group, and State, 1991, annual rpt, 6784–9

Consumer Expenditure Survey, spending by category, and income, by selected household characteristics and location, 1990, annual press release, 6726–1.42

County Business Patterns, 1988: employment, establishments, and payroll, by SIC 2- to 4-digit industry and county, annual State rpt series, 2326–6

County Business Patterns, 1989: employment, establishments, and payroll, by SIC 2- to 4-digit industry and county, annual State rpt series, 2326–8

Court civil and criminal caseloads for Federal district, appeals, and bankruptcy courts, by type of suit and offense, circuit, and district, 1990, annual rpt, 18204–11

Insurance and insurance industry

Court civil and criminal caseloads for Federal district, appeals, and special courts, 1990, annual rpt, 18204–8

Court civil and criminal caseloads for Federal district courts, 1991, annual rpt, 18204–2.1

Credit reporting and collection establishments, and receipts by source and class of client, by MSA, 1987 Census of Service Industries, 2393–4.4

Electric utilities privately owned, finances and operations, detailed data, 1989, annual rpt, 3164–23

Employment, earnings, and hours, by SIC 1- to 4-digit industry, monthly and annual averages, selected years 1909-90, annual rpt, 6744–4

Eximbank financial condition, with credit and insurance authorizations and loan activity by country, FY90, annual rpt, 9254–1

Exports and imports of services, direct and among multinatl firms affiliates, by industry and world area, 1986-90, article, 2702–1.223

Farm debt outstanding, by lender type, 1990, annual rpt, 1544–16.2

Farm finances, debts, assets, and receipts, and lenders financial condition, quarterly rpt with articles, 1541–1

Farm loans by purpose and source, quarterly rpt, 9365–3.10

Farm loans outstanding, by lender, and farm and nonfarm banks and assets held, 1990 conf papers, 9368–90

Farmland value, rent, taxes, foreign ownership, and transfers by probable use and lender type, with data by region and State, 1980-91, article, 1561–16.202

Fed Govt loans, loan guarantees, and insurance programs outstanding amounts, by agency and program, FY88-90, GAO rpt, 26111–65

Fed Govt spending in States, by type, program, agency, and State, FY90, annual rpt, 2464–2

Finances and operations, by SIC 2- to 4-digit industry, forecast 1991, annual rpt, 2044–28

Finances of financial instns by type and selected instn, and deposit insurance reform issues, 1970s-90, GAO rpt, 26119–320

Finances of insurance industry, underwriting activities, and investment plan mgmt, 1960s-90, 21248–159

Flow-of-funds accounts, savings, investments, and credit statements, quarterly rpt, 9365–3.3

Foreign countries insurance excise tax collections of IRS, quarterly rpt, 8302–2.1

Foreign direct investment in US, by industry group and world area, 1987-90, annual article, 2702–1.219

Foreign direct investment in US, by industry group of US affiliate and country of parent firm, 1980-86, 2708–41

Franchise business opportunities by firm and kind of business, and sources of aid and info, 1990 annual listing, 2104–7

Legal services establishments, lawyers by field, receipts by class of client, expenses, and employment, by MSA, 1987 Census of Service Industries, 2393–4.13

Mail volume to and from households, use, and views, by class, source, content, and household characteristics, 1987-88, annual rpt, 9864–10

Mortgage debt outstanding by purpose and holder type, 1978-89, annual rpt, 8434–3.3

Mortgage loan activity, by type of lender, loan, and mortgaged property, monthly press release, 5142–18

Mortgage loan activity, by type of lender, loan, and mortgaged property, quarterly press release, 5142–30

Mortgages FHA-insured, financial, property, and mortgagor characteristics, by metro area, 1990, annual rpt, 5144–24

Mortgages FHA-insured, financial, property, and mortgagor characteristics, by State, 1990, annual rpt, 5144–1

Mortgages FHA-insured, financial, property, and mortgagor characteristics, total and by State and outlying area, 1990, annual rpt, 5144–25

Mortgages FHA-insured, financial, property, and mortgagor characteristics, 1990, annual rpt, 5144–17; 5144–23

Mortgages insured by private companies, for 1-4 family units, monthly press release, 5142–38

Multinatl firms US affiliates, finances, and operations, by industry, world area of parent firm, and State, 1988-89, annual rpt, 2704–4

Multinatl US firms and foreign affiliates finances and operations, by industry and world area of parent firm, 1989 benchmark survey, preliminary annual rpt, 2704–5

Natural gas interstate pipeline company detailed financial and operating data, by firm, 1989, annual rpt, 3164–38

Occupational injury and illness rates, by SIC 2- to 4-digit industry, 1988-89, annual rpt, 6844–7

Occupational injury and illness rates, by SIC 2- to 4-digit industry, 1989, annual rpt, 6844–1

Pension Benefit Guaranty Corp activities and finances, FY90, annual rpt, 9674–1

Postal Service special services revenue and volume, quarterly rpt, 9862–1

SEC registration, firms required to file annual rpts, as of Sept 1990, annual listing, 9734–5

Statistical Abstract of US, 1991 annual data compilation, 2324–1.16

Student guaranteed loans, defaults, and collections, by type of loan, lender, and guarantee agency, with data by State and top lender, FY90, annual rpt, 4804–38

Tax (excise) collections of IRS, by source, quarterly rpt, 8302–1

Tax (income) returns filed by type of filer, selected income items, quarterly rpt, 8302–2.1

Tax (income) returns of corporations, income and tax items by asset size and detailed industry, 1987, annual rpt, 8304–4

Tax (income) returns of corporations, income and tax items by asset size and detailed industry, 1988, annual rpt, 8304–21

Tax (income) returns of corporations with foreign tax credit, income and tax items by industry group, 1986, biennial article, 8302–2.203

Index by Subjects and Names

Tax (income) returns of multinatl US firms foreign affiliates, income statement items, by asset size and industry, 1986, biennial article, 8302–2.212

Tax (income) returns of partnerships, income statement and balance sheet items, by industry group, 1989, annual article, 8302–2.216; 8304–18

Tax (income) returns of sole proprietorships, income statement items, by industry group, 1989, annual article, 8302–2.214

Tax collections of State govts by detailed type of tax, and tax rates, by State, FY90, annual rpt, 2466–2.7

Tax expenditures, Federal revenues forgone through income tax deductions and exclusions by type, FY92-96, annual rpt, 21784–10

Tax rates and revenue of State and local govts, by source and State, 1991 and historical trends, annual rpt, 10044–1

see also Agricultural insurance

see also Automobile insurance

see also Deposit insurance

see also Disability benefits and insurance

see also Employee benefits

see also Federal Deposit Insurance Corp.

see also Federal Savings and Loan Insurance Corp.

see also Health insurance

see also Life insurance

see also Medicare

see also Old-Age, Survivors, Disability, and Health Insurance

see also Property and casualty insurance

see also Servicepersons life insurance programs

see also Surety bonds

see also Unemployment insurance

see also Workers compensation

see also under By Industry in the "Index by Categories"

Integrated circuits

see Semiconductors

Integrated Postsecondary Education Data System

Data collection activities and programs of NCES, 1991, annual listing, 4824–7

Finances of higher education instns, revenue by source and spending by function, by State and instn control, FY80-88, annual rpt, 4844–6

Higher education enrollment, by student and instn characteristics, fall 1989, biennial rpt, 4844–2

Higher education enrollment, faculty, finances, and degrees, by instn level and control, and State, FY87, annual rpt, 4844–13

Intellectual property

see Copyright

see Patents

see Trademarks

Intelligence levels

Drug abuse residual neurological, behavioral, and cognitive effects, 1989 conf, 4498–69

Lead levels in environment, sources of emissions and exposure, and health effects, literature review, 1990 rpt, 9198–84

Military active duty and recruit social, economic, and parents characteristics, by service branch and State, FY89, annual rpt, 3544–41

Index by Subjects and Names

Military reserve forces personnel strengths and characteristics, by component, FY90, annual rpt, 3544–38

Military reserve forces personnel strengths and characteristics, by component, quarterly rpt, 3542–4

see also Educational tests
see also Literacy and illiteracy
see also Mental health and illness
see also Mental retardation

Intelligence services

see also Bureau of Intelligence and Research, State Department
see also Central Intelligence Agency
see also Defense Intelligence Agency
see also Defense Security Assistance Agency
see also Detective and protective services
see also Espionage
see also Military intelligence

Intelligence tests

see Intelligence levels

INTELSAT

see International Telecommunications Satellite Organization

Inter-American Development Bank

Loan activity by purpose and country, and funds by source, FY89, annual rpt, 15344–1.7

Loans and grants for economic and military aid from US and intl agencies, by program and country, FY46-90, annual rpt, 9914–5

Inter-American Foundation

Activities, grants by recipient, and fellowships of IAF, by country, FY90, annual rpt, 14424–1

Budget of US, authoritative financial statements with appropriations, outlays, and receipts, by category and agency, FY90, annual rpt, 8104–2.1

Budget of US, obligations and authority by function, agency, and program, with summaries, analyses, and historical tables, FY92, annual rpt, 104–2

Grants by program area, and fellowships by field and instn, by country, with IAF finances and staff, FY72-90, annual rpt, 14424–2

Interagency Task Force on Acid Precipitation

Research on acid rain, activities of Natl Acid Precipitation Assessment Program, 1990 annual rpt, 14354–1

Interdepartment Radio Advisory Committee

Radio frequency assignments for Federal use, by agency, 1st half 1990, semiannual rpt, 2802–1

Interest groups

see Lobbying and lobbying groups
see Nonprofit organizations and foundations
see Political action committees

Interest payments

Agricultural Stabilization and Conservation Service producer payments, by program and State, 1990, annual table, 1804–12

Agriculture census, 1987: farms, farmland, production, finances, and operator characteristics, by county, final State rpt series, 2331–1

AID loans repayment status and terms by program and country, and status of predecessor agency loans, quarterly rpt, 9912–3

Banks (insured commercial and savings) finances, for foreign and domestic offices, by asset size, 1989, annual rpt, 9294–4.2

Banks (insured commercial and savings) financial condition and performance, by asset size and region, quarterly rpt, 9292–1

Budget of US, authoritative financial statements with appropriations, outlays, and receipts, by category and agency, FY90, annual rpt, 8104–2.1

Budget of US, CBO analysis and review of FY92 budget by function, annual rpt, 26304–2

Budget of US, CBO analysis of revenue and spending alternatives and projections of economic indicators, FY92-96, annual rpt, 26304–3

Budget of US, compilation of background material on fiscal and tax policy, 1960s-96, 21788–203

Budget of US, House concurrent resolution, with spending and revenue targets, FY92 and projected to FY96, annual rpt, 21264–2

Budget of US, midsession review of FY92 budget, by function, annual rpt, 104–7

Budget of US, obligations and authority by function, agency, and program, with summaries, analyses, and historical tables, FY92, annual rpt, 104–2

Budget of US, receipts by source, outlays by agency and program, and balances, monthly rpt, 8102–3

Budget of US, Senate concurrent resolution, with spending and revenue targets, FY92, annual rpt, 25254–1

Consumer interest paid to business, and interest received as personal income, 1929-90, annual rpt, 204–1.1

Credit unions federally insured, finances by instn characteristics and State, as of June 1991, semiannual rpt, 9532–6

Credit unions federally insured, finances, 1989-90, annual rpt, 9534–1

Developing countries foreign debt, and IMF credit outstanding, by country, 1984-90, 9118–11

Eastern Europe foreign debt components, trade, balances, and other economic indicators, by country, 1985-89, hearing, 21248–148

Electric power distribution loans from REA, and borrower operating and financial data, by firm and State, 1990, annual rpt, 1244–1

Electric power plants production and capital costs, operations, and fuel use, by fuel type, plant, utility, and location, 1989, annual rpt, 3164–9

Electric utilities finances and operations, detailed data for public and privately owned firms, 1989, annual rpt, 3164–11.4

Electric utilities finances and operations, detailed data for publicly owned firms, 1989, annual rpt, 3164–24

Electric utilities privately owned, finances and operations, detailed data, 1989, annual rpt, 3164–23

Energy producers finances and operations, by energy type for US firms domestic and foreign operations, 1989, annual rpt, 3164–44.1

Farm income, expenses, receipts by commodity, assets, liabilities, and ratios, 1990 and trends from 1945, annual rpt, 1544–16

Farm production itemized costs, by farm sales size and region, 1990, annual rpt, 1614–3

Farm production itemized costs, receipts, and returns, by commodity and region, 1987-89, annual rpt, 1544–20

Farm sector balance sheet, and receipts by detailed commodity, by State, 1985-89, annual rpt, 1544–18

Fed Govt consolidated financial statements based on business accounting methods, FY89-90, annual rpt, 8104–5

Fed Govt finances, cash and debt transactions, daily tables, 8102–4

Fed Govt obligations object class analysis, by agency, Budget of US, FY92, annual rpt, 104–9

Fed Govt programs under Ways and Means Committee jurisdiction, finances, operations, and participant characteristics, FY70s-90, annual rpt, 21784–11

Fed Govt trust funds financial condition, by fund, periodic rpt series, 8102–9

Financial operations of Fed Govt, detailed data, *Treasury Bulletin*, quarterly rpt, 8002–4

FmHA activities, and loans and grants by program and State, FY90 and trends from FY70, annual rpt, 1184–17

Foreign govt and private obligors debt to US, by country and program, periodic rpt, 8002–6

Govt finances, by level of govt, State, and for large cities and counties, annual rpt series, 2466–2

Govt finances, tax systems and revenue, and fiscal structure, by level of govt and State, 1991 with historical trends, annual rpt, 10044–1

Govt revenues and spending by level of govt, natl income and product accounts, selected years 1929-92, annual rpt, 204–1.6

Income (household, family, and personal), by source, detailed characteristics, and region, 1988-89, annual Current Population Rpt, 2546–6.68

Income (household, family, and personal), by source, detailed characteristics, and region, 1990, annual Current Population Rpt, 2546–6.70

Income from US sources and tax withheld for foreign natls not residing in US, by country and tax treaty status, 1988, annual article, 8302–2.206

Massachusetts State govt spending and employment by program, revenues by source, debt, and public works financing, compared to other States, 1990 compilation of papers, 9373–4.27

Mortgages FHA-insured, financial, property, and mortgagor characteristics, by metro area, 1990, annual rpt, 5144–24

Mortgages FHA-insured, financial, property, and mortgagor characteristics, by State, 1990, annual rpt, 5144–1

Mortgages FHA-insured, financial, property, and mortgagor characteristics, 1990, annual rpt, 5144–23

Multinatl firms US affiliates, finances, and operations, by industry, world area of parent firm, and State, 1988-89, annual rpt, 2704–4

Natl income and product accounts and components, *Survey of Current Business*, monthly rpt, 2702–1.24

Interest payments

Natl income and product accounts benchmark revisions of GDP and natl income, various periods 1959-80, tables, 2702–1.227

Natural gas interstate pipeline company detailed financial and operating data, by firm, 1989, annual rpt, 3164–38

Nonprofit charitable organizations finances, by asset size and State, 1987, article, 8302–2.218

Nonprofit charitable organizations finances, by size of contributions received, 1987, article, 8302–2.218

Nursing home reimbursement by Medicaid, States payment ratesetting methods, limits, and allowances, 1988, article, 4652–1.253

OASDHI, Medicaid, SSI, and related programs benefits, beneficiary characteristics, and trust funds, selected years 1937-89, annual rpt, 4744–3

Older persons in rural areas, household income sources, and poverty status, 1983-84, 1598–268

Postal Service activities, finances, and mail volume and subsidies, FY90, annual rpt, 9864–5.3

Public debt, net interest paid by Fed Govt, monthly rpt, quarterly and annual data, 23842–1.6

Rural Electrification Program lending, by State, FY90, annual rpt, 1244–7

Rural Telephone Program loan activity, by State, FY90, annual tables, 1244–8

Savings and loan assns, FHLB 6th District insured members financial condition and operations by State, quarterly rpt, 9302–23

Savings banks insured by Bank Insurance Fund, financial condition and performance, by asset size and region, quarterly rpt, 9292–5

Savings instns, FHLB 6th District members financial condition and operations by State, monthly rpt, 9302–11

Savings instns insured by Savings Assn Insurance Fund, assets, liabilities, and deposit and loan activity, by conservatorship status, monthly rpt, 8432–1

Southeastern States, Fed Reserve 5th District insured commercial banks financial statements, by State, quarterly rpt, 9389–18

Survey of Current Business, detailed financial and business data, and economic indicators, monthly rpt, 2702–1.4

Tax (income) deduction for interest payments, impacts on savings rates, with indicators for US, Canada, and other OECD countries, 1990 article, 9377–1.202

Tax (income) returns filed by type of filer, selected income items, quarterly rpt, 8302–2.1

Tax (income) returns for foreign corporate activity in US, assets, and income statement items, by industry div and selected country, 1986-87, article, 8302–2.205

Tax (income) returns of corporations, income and tax items by asset size and detailed industry, 1987, annual rpt, 8304–4

Tax (income) returns of corporations, income and tax items by asset size and detailed industry, 1988, annual rpt, 8304–21

Tax (income) returns of corporations, summary data by asset size and industry div, 1988, annual article, 8302–2.217

Tax (income) returns of corporations with foreign tax credit, income, and tax items, by country and world region of credit, 1986, biennial article, 8302–2.207

Tax (income) returns of corporations with foreign tax credit, income and tax items by industry group, 1986, biennial article, 8302–2.203

Tax (income) returns of individuals, selected income and tax items, by adjusted gross income and State, 1986-88, article, 8302–2.201

Tax (income) returns of individuals, selected income and tax items by income level, preliminary 1989, annual article, 8302–2.209

Tax (income) returns of partnerships, income statement and balance sheet items, by industry group, 1989, annual article, 8302–2.216; 8304–18

Tax (income) returns of sole proprietorships, income statement items, by industry group, 1989, annual article, 8302–2.214

Tax (income) returns of US corporations under foreign control, assets and income statement items by industry div and country, 1988, article, 8302–2.219

Tax (income) withholding and related documents filed, by type and IRS service center, 1990 and projected 1991-98, annual rpt, 8304–22

Tax expenditures, Federal revenues forgone through income tax deductions and exclusions by type, FY92-96, annual rpt, 21784–10

Telephone and telegraph firms detailed finances and operations, 1989, annual rpt, 9284–6

Telephone firms borrowing under Rural Telephone Program, and financial and operating data, by State, 1990, annual rpt, 1244–2

Interest rates

Banks (insured commercial) assets, income, and financial ratios, by asset size and State, quarterly rpt, 13002–3

Banks Fed Reserve discount window borrowing, relation to interest rate spreads and banks financial performance indicators, 1980s-90, technical paper, 9385–8.111

Banks Fed Reserve discount window borrowing, relation to interest rate spreads and discount borrowing outstanding, by bank asset size, 1981-90, article, 9385–1.209

Banks Fed Reserve discount window borrowing, relation to interest rate spreads, 1980s-90, technical paper, 9385–8.110

Banks interest rates on loans and deposits, relation to market concentration indicators, 1985-90, technical paper, 9366–6.283

Banks market concentration indicators and Treasury security rates relation to bank deposit interest rates, 1980s, technical paper, 9366–6.261

Index by Subjects and Names

Banks profitability, balance sheet and income statement items, and financial ratios, by asset size, 1985-90, annual article, 9362–1.204

Bond (junk) holdings of Resolution Trust Corp, quarterly press release, 9722–4

Bond yields and interest rates on public and private securities, 1929-90, annual rpt, 204–1.5

Budget of US, CBO analysis of revenue and spending alternatives and projections of economic indicators, FY92-96, annual rpt, 26304–3

Business cycle recession forecasting performance of experimental indicators indexes and interest rate spreads, with data for 1940s-91, article, 9375–1.212

Business statistics, detailed data for major industries and economic indicators, *Survey of Current Business*, monthly rpt, 2702–1.9

Credit (installment) outstanding, and terms, by lender and credit type, monthly rpt, 9365–2.6

Credit unions federally insured, finances by instn characteristics and State, as of June 1991, semiannual rpt, 9532–6

Economic indicators and components, and Fed Reserve 4th District business and financial conditions, monthly chartbook, 9377–10

Economic indicators and components, current data and annual trends, monthly rpt, 23842–1.5

Economic indicators impacts of commercial paper-bank loan firm financing mix and selected interest rate spreads, model description and results, 1960s-89, technical paper, 9366–6.268

Economic indicators performance, and Fed Reserve monetary policy objectives, as of July 1991, semiannual rpt, 9362–4

Economic indicators relation to interest rates and financial market regulatory and structural changes, 1950s-80s, technical paper, 9385–8.73

Eurodollar and total market liabilities, US bank foreign branches market share, and Eurodollar deposit rates, quarterly rpt, 9391–7

Eurodollar deposit rates, interest arbitrage, and other short-term rates, current and 4-year trends, weekly chartbook, 9365–1.5

European Monetary System countries interest rate differentials with Germany, relation to fiscal policy, with model results for Italy, 1979-90, technical paper, 9366–7.259

Exchange rate relation to interest rate differentials and inflation, for selected currencies and trade-weighted index, model description and results, 1974-90, technical paper, 9366–7.262

Exchange rate relation to interest rate differentials for France and West Germany, model description and results, 1980s, technical paper, 9366–7.249

Eximbank financial condition, with credit and insurance authorizations and loan activity by country, FY90, annual rpt, 9254–1

Farm credit, terms, delinquency, agricultural bank failures, and credit conditions by Fed Reserve District, quarterly rpt, 9365–3.10

Index by Subjects and Names

Interest rates

Farm mortgage and other loans interest rates, by lender type, quarterly rpt with articles, 1541–1

Farm prices received for major products and paid for farm inputs and living items, by commodity and State, monthly rpt, 1629–1

Fed Financing Bank holdings and transactions, by borrower, monthly prcss release, 12802–1

Fed Govt consolidated financial statements based on business accounting methods, FY89-90, annual rpt, 8104–5

Fed Govt debt issued, redeemed, and outstanding, by series and source, and gifts to reduce debt, monthly rpt, 8242–2

Fed Govt financial operations, detailed data, *Treasury Bulletin*, quarterly rpt, 8002–4

Fed Reserve banks interest rates, Dec 1990, annual rpt, 9364–1.1

Fed Reserve monetary policy targets and interest rates relation to unexpected employment news, 1970s-91, article, 9389–1.205

Financial and business detailed statistics, *Fed Reserve Bulletin*, monthly rpt with articles, 9362–1

Financial and economic analysis of banking and nonbanking sectors, working paper series, 9381–10

Financial and monetary conditions, selected US summary data, weekly rpt, 9391–4

Financial instruments and home mortgages interest rates, monthly rpt, 9365–2.14

Food marketing cost indexes, by expense category, monthly rpt with articles, 1502–4

Forecasts of interest rates, performance of Treasury bill and other security yields at alternative maturities, 1950s-80s, article, 9389–1.201

Foreign and US economic conditions, and trade devs and balances, with data by selected country and country group, monthly rpt, 9882–14

Foreign countries central banks discount and short-term interest rates, monthly rpt, 9362–1.3

Foreign countries economic conditions and implications for US, periodic country rpt series, 2046–4

Foreign countries economic conditions, policy, and trade practices, by country, 1988-90, annual rpt, 21384–5

Futures trading in selected commodities and financial instruments and indexes, NYC, Chicago, and other markets activity, semimonthly rpt, 11922–5

GNP and components, impact of interest rates, alternative regression results, late 1950s-80s, technical paper, 9385–8.79

GNP relation to bank loan commitments, selected interest rates, and other factors, 1973-87, technical paper, 9385–8.75

Govt-sponsored enterprises financial condition and capital adequacy, with data by enterprise, 1970s-90 and projected to 1996, 26308–99

Housing affordability indicators, by household composition, income, and current tenure, 1988, 2486–1.11

Housing and households detailed characteristics, and unit and neighborhood quality, MSA surveys, series, 2485–6

Inflation and other economic indicators relation to long-run real interest rate, model description and results for UK indexed bonds, 1982-88, technical paper, 9385–8.119

Inflation forecasting performance of interest rate spreads and yield curve, 1960s-88, technical paper, 9385–8.118

Italy interest rates and spread relation to regional income and debt, and outside borrowing, model description and results, 1981-84, technical paper, 9366–7.248

Japan economic conditions, financial and intl policies, and trade devs, 1950s-80s and projected to 2050, compilation of papers, 23848–220

Japan interest rates relation to monetary policy and financial instn regulation, with background data and model results, 1960s-91, article, 9385–1.213; 9385–8.116

Monetary trends, Fed Reserve Bank of St Louis monthly rpt, 9391–2

Money supply impact on interest rate, alternative model results, 1950s-90, technical paper, 9366–7.257

Money supply relation to GNP and interest rates, alternative models description and results, 1953-88, article, 9391–1.210

Mortgage (home) terms on conventional loans closed, by lender type, with quarterly data for 32 MSAs, monthly rpt, 9442–2

Mortgage applications to FHA for new and existing units, refinancings, and housing starts, monthly rpt, 5142–44

Mortgage, bond, and construction loan interest rates, bimonthly rpt, 2042–1.5

Mortgage debt outstanding, and terms, for fixed- and adjustable-rate mortgages, 1950s-89, technical paper, 9366–6.263

Mortgage interest fixed and adjustable rates and fees offered by Illinois S&Ls, monthly rpt, 9302–6

Mortgage interest fixed and adjustable rates and fees offered by Wisconsin S&Ls, monthly rpt, 9302–7

Mortgages (price level adjusted) impacts on housing affordability, 1991 article, 9373–1.204

Mortgages FHA-insured, financial, property, and mortgagor characteristics, 1990, annual rpt, 5144–17

Mortgages FHA-insured for 1-family units, by loan type and mortgage characteristics, quarterly rpt, 5142–45

Mortgages FHA-insured, secondary market prices and yields, and interest rates on construction and conventional mortgage loans, by region, monthly press release, 5142–20

New England States economic indicators, Fed Reserve 1st District, monthly rpt, 9373–2.7

New England States, FHLB 1st District thrifts financial operations compared to banks, and housing industry indicators, bimonthly rpt with articles, 9302–4

North Central States farm credit conditions and economic devs, Fed Reserve 7th District, monthly rpt, 9375–10

North Central States farm credit conditions, earnings, and expenses, Fed Reserve 9th District, quarterly rpt, 9383–11

North Central States, FHLB 6th District and natl cost of funds indexes for savings instns, and mortgage and Treasury bill rates, monthly rpt, 9302–38

North Central States, FHLB 6th District savings instns financial condition and operations by State, monthly rpt, 9302–11

North Central States, FHLB 7th District and natl cost of funds indexes for savings instns, and mortgage rates, monthly rpt, 9302–30

OASDI benefit payments, trust fund finances, and economic and demographic assumptions, 1970-90 and alternative projections to 2000, actuarial rpt, 4706–1.105

OECD interest rates, for US and 3 countries, 1980-90, article, 6722–1.233

Prime rate changes by selected major banks, probability related to cost of funds and selected bank characteristics, 1990 working paper, 9387–8.235

Public debt burden on future generations forecast under alternative economic and fiscal policy assumptions, 1991 working paper, 9377–9.111

Savings and loan assns, FHLB 6th District insured members financial condition and operations by State, quarterly rpt, 9302–23

Savings instns finances and operations by district and State, mortgage loan activity and terms by MSA, and FHLB finances, 1989 and trends from 1900, annual rpt, 8434–3

Savings instns insured by Savings Assn Insurance Fund, assets, liabilities, and deposit and loan activity, by conservatorship status, monthly rpt, 8432–1

Savings instns interest rate differentials for short- and long-term assets and liabilities, risk analysis for solvent 4th FHLB District banks, 1984-88, working paper, 9371–10.65

Securities issues for corporations, terms, value, and yield relation to call provisions, 1970s-90, technical paper, 9366–6.269

Southwestern States farm credit conditions and real estate values, Fed Reserve 11th District, quarterly rpt, 9379–11

Statistical Abstract of US, 1991 annual data compilation, 2324–1.16

Stock price volatility relation to interest rates, oil and gold prices, and US money supply, for 10 countries, model description and results, 1970s-88, working paper, 9381–10.116

Student aid funding and participation, by Federal program, instn type and control, and State, various periods 1959-89, annual rpt, 4804–28

Student guaranteed loans, defaults, and collections, by type of loan, lender, and guarantee agency, with data by State and top lender, FY90, annual rpt, 4804–38

Survey of Current Business, detailed financial and business data, and economic indicators, monthly rpt, 2702–1.1

Swap contracts, by contract and counterparty type, and currency, late 1980s, article, 9371–1.205

Taiwan interest rate relation to money supply, industrial production, and US interest rate, late 1980s, working paper, 9371–10.56

Interest rates

Treasury bill offerings, auction results by Fed Reserve District, and terms, periodic press release series, 8002–7

Treasury bills, notes, and bonds market bid yields at constant maturities, *Treasury Bulletin*, quarterly rpt, 8002–4.8

Western States, FHLB 11th District and natl cost of funds indexes for savings instns, and mortgage and Treasury bill rates, monthly rpt, 9302–38

Intergovernmental relations

Assistance (financial and nonfinancial) of Fed Govt, 1991 base edition with supplements, annual listing, 104–5

Deaths of beneficiaries, erroneous benefit payments, and use of SSA and other sources of death info, by agency, 1990, GAO rpt, 26121–406

Fed Reserve political independence issues, with proposed restructuring legislation, 1970s-90, technical paper, 9385–8.106

Intergovernmental Perspective, quarterly journal, 10042–1

Public opinion on taxes, spending, and govt efficiency, by respondent characteristics, 1991 survey, annual rpt, 10044–2

see also Federal-local relations

see also Federal-State relations

see also Foreign relations

see also International cooperation in law enforcement

see also Interstate compacts

see also Interstate relations

see also Regional planning

see also State-local relations

Interindustry transactions

see Input-output analysis

Interior Department

see Department of Interior

Intermediate-Range Nuclear Forces Treaty

Inspections at US and USSR nuclear weapons sites under INF, and US costs and staffing, FY89-91, GAO rpt, 26123–364

Internal combustion engines

see Engines and motors

Internal Revenue Service

Activities of IRS, collection, enforcement, and litigation, with data by type of tax, region, and State, FY90, annual rpt, 8304–3

Admin and compliance issues, and taxpayer views, 1990 conf, 8304–25

Agents attrition, separations by reason, and hires, by region and district, FY87-90, GAO rpt, 26119–345

Asset Forfeiture Program of Justice Dept, seizures, finances, and disbursements, FY86-90, annual rpt, 6004–21

Audits of tax returns, rates by type of tax, FY64-89, hearing, 21408–125

Boycotts (intl) by OPEC and other countries, US taxpayers IRS filings, cooperation, and tax benefits denied, 1976-86, GAO rpt, 26119–349

Budget of US, obligations and authority by function, agency, and program, with summaries, analyses, and historical tables, FY92, annual rpt, 104–2

Computer matching program of IRS to indentify income underreported on tax returns, effectiveness, 1987, GAO rpt, 26119–325

Corporations income tax returns, income and tax items by asset size and detailed industry, 1987, annual rpt, 8304–4

Corporations income tax returns, income and tax items by asset size and detailed industry, 1988, annual rpt, 8304–21

Correspondence of IRS regarding adjustments to taxpayer accounts, quality, and accuracy of returns processing, 1987-90, GAO rpt, 26119–329

Data collection using tax and other govt admin records, methodological and disclosure issues, 1988-89 annual conf papers, 8304–17

Excise tax collections of IRS, by source, quarterly rpt, 8302–1

Money laundering enforcement activities of IRS, staff, and funding, abatement, 1985-90, GAO rpt, 26123–338

Partnership income tax returns, income statement and balance sheet items by industry group, 1989, annual rpt, 8304–18

Refunds of income tax applied by IRS to outstanding debts to Fed Govt, impacts on subsequent taxpayer compliance, 1984-87, GAO rpt, 26119–339

Returns and supplemental documents filed, by type, FY90 and projected to FY99, semiannual rpt, 8302–4

Returns filed, by type, IRS service center, and whether full-paid, refund, and electronically filed, 1990 and projected to 1998, semiannual rpt, 8302–7

Returns filed, by type of filer, detailed preliminary and supplementary data, quarterly rpt with articles, 8302–2

Returns filed, by type of tax and IRS district, 1989 and projected 1990-97, annual rpt, 8304–24

Returns filed, by type of tax, region, and IRS service center, projected 1990-97 and trends from 1978, annual rpt, 8304–9

Returns of high income individuals not filed, by selected characteristics, 1987, and assessments under alternative IRS enforcement programs, 1990, GAO rpt, 26119–322

Returns preparation services negligent and fraudulent tax practices, IRS civil penalty cases and examiners views of program admin, 1989, GAO rpt, 26119–315

Returns processing and info distribution of IRS, effectiveness, 1988-90, GAO rpt, 26119–319

Returns processing and taxpayer info activity, electronic filings, and refunds, for individual income tax, periodic press release, 8302–6

Returns processing, IRS workload forecasts, compliance, and enforcement, data compilation, 1991 annual rpt, 8304–8

Returns with IRS Service Center and taxpayer errors, by type of error, 1990-91, GAO rpt, 26119–346

Statistical programs of Fed Govt, index of spending for 4 agencies, 1976-88, hearing, 23848–218

Unpaid income tax accounts receivable of IRS by collection status, and IRS budget and staff, with data by district, 1980s-91, hearing, 21788–200

Withholding and related documents filed, by type and IRS service center, 1990 and projected 1991-98, annual rpt, 8304–22

Internal security

Embassy and other US diplomatic facilities security improvement construction projects costs and activities, 1986-90, GAO rpt, 26123–322

Info security nondisclosure agreements for Federal and contractor employees, prepublication reviews, and costs, 1988-90, GAO rpt, 26123–328

Info Security Oversight Office monitoring of Federal security measures and classification actions, FY90, annual rpt, 9454–21

Info security plans for Fed Govt computer systems with sensitive unclassified data, by characteristics of info and system, and agency, 1989, 2218–85

Labor laws enacted, by State, 1990, annual article, 6722–1.209

Labor productivity of Federal employees, indexes of output and labor costs by function, 1967-89, annual rpt, 6824–1.6

Military chemical and biological weapons research labs security measures, and govt and contractor staff, 1988-90, GAO rpt, 26123–356

Natl Archives and Records Admin activities, finances, holdings, and staff, FY90, annual rpt, 9514–2

Nuclear weapons facilities of DOE, contract security forces skill deficiencies, and costs compared to Federal security, late 1980s, GAO rpt, 26113–493

US attorneys civil and criminal cases by type and disposition, and collections, by Federal district, FY90, annual rpt, 6004–2.7

International agreements

see Executive agreements

see Trade agreements

see Treaties and conventions

International assistance

Africa (Sahel) grain production, use, imports, and stocks, by country, 1989/90, 9918–18

Africa economic and dev aid fund of AID, funding by project, 1980s-90, GAO rpt, 26123–333

Agricultural and economic conditions in developing countries, and agricultural exports of US, effects of US aid, 1989 conf papers, 1548–372

Agricultural technical aid of USDA, personnel and agreements by project, world area, and country, annual rpt, discontinued, 1954–2

AID and higher education instns collaboration on aid projects, and funding, by purpose and world region, 1960s-89, 26358–247

AID and Intl Dev Cooperation Agency activities and funding, FY90-92, with developing countries economic and social conditions from 1960s, annual rpt, 9904–4

AID dev funds obligated but unspent by country, and impacts of alternative allocation formulas, FY87-90, GAO rpt, 26123–327

AID dev project procurement under host country contracts, oversight issues with background data, 1991 GAO rpt, 26123–342

AID dev projects and socioeconomic impacts, evaluation rpt series, 9916–1

Index by Subjects and Names

International cooperation in conservation

AID dev projects, special study series, 9916–3

AID economic aid to developing countries, obligations and disbursements by country, quarterly rpt, 9912–4

AID loans repayment status and terms by program and country, and status of predecessor agency loans, quarterly rpt, 9912–3

Background Notes, foreign countries summary social, political, and economic data, series, 7006–2

Budget of US, balances of budget authority obligated and unobligated, by function and agency, FY90-92, annual rpt, 104–8

Budget of US, House concurrent resolution, with spending and revenue targets, FY92 and projected to FY96, annual rpt, 21264–2

Budget of US, obligations and authority by function, agency, and program, with summaries, analyses, and historical tables, FY92, annual rpt, 104–2

Budget of US, receipts by source, outlays by agency and program, and balances, monthly rpt, 8102–3

Budget of US, Senate concurrent resolution, with spending and revenue targets, FY92, annual rpt, 25254–1

China economic indicators and reform issues, with background data, 1950s-90, compilation of papers, 23848–155

Counterpart funds impacts on US aid programs effectiveness and developing countries economic and fiscal condition, literature review, 1991 rpt, 9918–21

Currency (foreign) accounts owned by US under AID admin and by foreign govts with joint AID control, status by program and country, quarterly rpt, 9912–1

Currency (foreign) holdings of US, transactions and balances by program and country, 1st half FY91, semiannual rpt, 8102–7

Debt to US of foreign govts and private obligors, by country and program, periodic rpt, 8002–6

Developing countries child health and welfare indicators, and economic conditions, 1950s-80s, hearing, 25388–57

Developing countries economic aid from US, bilateral and through intl dev banks, by program and world region, 1991 annual rpt, 9904–1

Developing countries economic aid from US, military spending and imports measures to determine aid eligibility, by country, 1986-87, annual rpt, 9914–1

Developing countries economic and military aid from US, USSR, PRC, and selected other countries, 1954-90, annual rpt, 9114–4.9

Developing countries economic, population, and agricultural data, US and other aid sources, and AID activity, country rpt series, 9916–12

Disabled persons in developing countries aid program activities and funding, for UN, AID, and Intl Labor Organization, late 1970s-90, GAO rpt, 26123–321

Disasters, casualties, damage, and aid by US and others, by country, FY90 and trends from FY64, annual rpt, 9914–12

Eastern Europe economic aid of US, by agency and country, FY90-92, GAO rpt, 26123–319

Eastern Europe transition to market economies, economic conditions, intl aid, and energy balance, by country, 1985-90, 9118–13

Economic aid of US and other donor countries by type and recipient, and role in advancing economic interests, 1980s-90, 2048–152

Economic conditions in foreign countries and implications for US, periodic country rpt series, 2046–4

Economic conditions, policy, and trade practices, by country, 1988-90, annual rpt, 21384–5

Economic, social, political, and geographic summary data, by country, 1991, annual factbook, 9114–2

Energy assistance to developing countries, and global warming reduction activities, for AID, 1980s-FY92, GAO rpt, 26123–352

Ethiopia agricultural conditions, grain production and use, and dev aid by major donor, 1960s-80s, hearing, 23848–216

Expenditures for intl organizations by US and other countries, by organization and program, FY90, annual rpt, 7004–9

Exports and imports of US, by Harmonized System 6-digit commodity and country, 1990, annual rpt, 2424–13

Exports of US, detailed Schedule B commodities with countries of destination, 1990, annual rpt, 2424–10

Family planning and population activities of AID, grants by project and recipient, and contraceptive shipments, by country, FY90, annual rpt series, 9914–13

Fed Govt contingent liabilities and claims paid on insured and guaranteed contracts with foreign obligors, by country and program, periodic rpt, 8002–12

Fed Govt economic and military aid, by program and country, selected years 1940-88, annual rpt, 15344–1.1

Financial instns (intl) funds by source and disbursements by purpose, by country, with US policy review, FY89, annual rpt, 15344–1

Food supply, needs, and aid for developing countries, status and alternative forecasts, world area rpt series, 1526–8

Housing and urban dev program of AID, financial statements, FY90, annual rpt, 9914–4

Human rights conditions in 170 countries, and US economic and military aid, 1990, annual rpt, 21384–3

Inter-American Foundation activities, grants by recipient, and fellowships, by country, FY90, annual rpt, 14424–1

Israel aid from US, 1984-89, hearing, 21388–58

Japan economic conditions, financial and intl policies, and trade devs, 1950s-80s and projected to 2050, compilation of papers, 23848–220

Latin America dev grants of Inter-American Foundation by program area, and fellowships by field and instn, by country, FY72-90, annual rpt, 14424–2

Loans and grants for economic and military aid from US and intl agencies, by program and country, FY46-90, annual rpt, 9914–5

Loans and loan guarantees of Fed Govt, outstanding amounts by agency and program, *Treasury Bulletin*, quarterly rpt, 8002–4.9

Middle East and East Africa economic and military aid from US and intl agencies, and US defense spending, FY80-90, GAO rpt, 26123–360

Military surplus property donations to intl and State relief programs, FY86-90, GAO rpt, 26123–316

NATO members and Japan economic aid to developing countries and Eastern Europe, 1980-89, annual rpt, 3544–28

Panama economic aid after US sanctions and military invasion, AID funding by program, as of 1991, GAO rpt, 26123–330

Peace Corps activities, funding by program, and volunteers, by country, FY92, annual rpt, 9654–1

Rice exports under Federal programs, periodic situation rpt, 1561–8

Statistical Abstract of US, 1991 annual data compilation, 2324–1.29; 2324–1.31

USIA English language program enrollment and staff, by country and world region, FY90, annual rpt, 9854–2

see also Export-Import Bank

see also Military assistance

see also Public Law 480

see also Refugees

see also War relief

International Atomic Energy Agency

Developing countries aid by intl agencies, Intl Dev Cooperation Agency oversight of US contributions, FY92, annual rpt, 9904–4.2

Expenditures for intl organizations by US and other countries, by organization and program, FY90, annual rpt, 7004–9

International Bank for Reconstruction and Development

Loan activity by purpose and country, and funds by source, FY89, annual rpt, 15344–1.4

Loans and grants for economic and military aid from US and intl agencies, by program and country, FY46-90, annual rpt, 9914–5

Middle East and East Africa economic and military aid from US and intl agencies, and US defense spending, FY80-90, GAO rpt, 26123–360

UN participation of US, and member and nonmember shares of UN budget by country, FY89-91, annual rpt, 7004–5

see also International Development Association

see also International Finance Corp.

International Boundary and Water Commission, U.S. and Mexico

Budget of US, obligations and authority by function, agency, and program, with summaries, analyses, and historical tables, FY92, annual rpt, 104–2

Hydroelectric power plants capacity and other characteristics, for western US, FY90, annual rpt, 3254–1

International cooperation in conservation

Developing countries economic and social conditions from 1960s, and Intl Dev Cooperation Agency and AID activities and funding, FY90-92, annual rpt, 9904–4

International cooperation in conservation

Endangered animals and plants US trade and permits, by species, purpose, disposition, and country, 1989, annual rpt, 5504–19

EPA pollution control grant program activities, monthly rpt, 9182–8

Expenditures for intl organizations by US and other countries, by organization and program, FY90, annual rpt, 7004–9

Global warming contributing air pollutants, US and foreign emissions and control measures, 1980s and projected to 2020, 26358–233

Marine mammals protection, Federal and intl regulatory and research activities, 1990, annual rpt, 14734–1

Treaties and agreements on environmental and wildlife conservation, provisions, status, and signatories, as of 1991, listing, 9886–4.169

Treaties and other bilateral and multilateral agreements of US in force, by country, as of Jan 1991, annual listing, 7004–1

Walrus population, habitat mgmt, and intl conservation needs, by world region, 1990 conf, 14738–9

see also International cooperation in environmental sciences

International cooperation in cultural activities

Arts Natl Endowment activities and grants, FY90, annual rpt, 9564–3

English language program of USIA, enrollment and staff, by country and world region, FY90, annual rpt, 9854–2

Environmental and wildlife conservation intl agreements provisions, status, and signatories, as of 1991, listing, 9886–4.169

Expenditures for intl organizations by US and other countries, by organization and program, FY90, annual rpt, 7004–9

Japan-US Friendship Commission educational and cultural exchange activities, grants, and trust fund status, FY89-90, biennial report, 14694–1

Treaties and other bilateral and multilateral agreements of US in force, by country, as of Jan 1991, annual listing, 7004–1

USIA library holdings, use, and staff, by country and city, FY90, annual rpt, 9854–4

see also Educational exchanges

see also Exchange of persons programs

International cooperation in environmental sciences

Developing countries economic and social conditions from 1960s, and Intl Dev Cooperation Agency and AID activities and funding, FY90-92, annual rpt, 9904–4

Exchange and training programs of Federal agencies, participants by world area, and funding, by program, FY89, annual rpt, 9854–8

Expenditures for intl organizations by US and other countries, by organization and program, FY90, annual rpt, 7004–9

Geological Survey activities and funding, FY90, annual rpt, 5664–8

Global climate change trends and contributing gases levels, Federal and intl data collection activities, mgmt, and inventory, 1990 rpt, 3028–4

Industrial pollutant concentrations and costs by process and waste prevention or treatment method, 1990 biennial conf, 9184–22

Oceanographic research and distribution activities of World Data Center A by country, and cruises by ship, 1989, annual rpt, 2144–15

Radiation and radionuclide concentrations, monitoring results of intl and foreign agencies, quarterly rpt, 9192–5

Radioactive strontium fallout, monitoring results for 65 sites worldwide, quarterly 1986 and trends from 1958, annual rpt, 3004–29

Treaties and other bilateral and multilateral agreements of US in force, by country, as of Jan 1991, annual listing, 7004–1

Weather services activities and funding, by Federal agency, planned FY91-92, annual rpt, 2144–2

see also International cooperation in conservation

International cooperation in law enforcement

Drug (illegal) production, eradication, and seizures, by substance, with US aid, by country, 1987-91, annual rpt, 7004–17

Drug abuse indicators for selected metro areas, research results, data collection, and policy issues, 1991 semiannual conf, 4492–5

Drug enforcement aid of US, by country, FY89, annual rpt, 21384–3

Expenditures for intl organizations by US and other countries, by organization and program, FY90, annual rpt, 7004–9

Terrorism incidents in US, related activity, and casualties, by attack type, target, group, and location, 1990, annual rpt, 6224–6

Treaties and other bilateral and multilateral agreements of US in force, by country, as of Jan 1991, annual listing, 7004–1

International cooperation in science and technology

Agricultural research grants of USDA, by program, subagency, and country, FY90, annual listing, 1954–3

Allergy and Infectious Diseases Natl Inst activities, grants by recipient and location, and disease cases, FY83-90, annual rpt, 4474–30

Assistance (financial and nonfinancial) of Fed Govt, 1991 base edition with supplements, annual listing, 104–5

Cancer Natl Inst activities, grants by recipient, and cancer deaths and cases, FY90 and trends, annual rpt, 4474–13

Dental Research Natl Inst research and training grants, by recipient, FY89, annual listing, 4474–19

Exchange and training programs of Federal agencies, participants by world area, and funding, by program, FY89, annual rpt, 9854–8

Expenditures for intl organizations by US and other countries, by organization and program, FY90, annual rpt, 7004–9

Hazardous material transport accidents, casualties, and damage, by mode of transport, with DOT control activities, 1989, annual rpt, 7304–4

Heart, Lung, and Blood Natl Inst activities, and grants by recipient and location, FY90 and disease trends from 1940, annual rpt, 4474–15

HHS financial aid, by program, recipient, State, and city, FY90, annual regional listings, 4004–3

Index by Subjects and Names

Industry (US) intl competitiveness, with selected foreign and US operating data by major firm and product, series, 2046–12

NASA R&D funding to higher education instns, by field, instn, and State, FY90, annual listing, 9504–7

NIH activities, funding by program and recipient type, staff, and clinic patients, by inst, FY90, annual rpt, 4434–3

NIH grants for R&D, training, construction, and medical libraries, by location and recipient, FY90, annual listings, 4434–7

NIH intl program activities and funding, by inst and country, FY90, annual rpt, 4474–6

NSF grants and contracts, by field, instn, and State, FY89, annual rpt, 9624–26

NSF R&D grant awards, by div and program, periodic rpt series, 9626–7

Nuclear engineering and science educational facilities, student aid, and degrees granted, by instn, 1990, 3008–126

R&D funding by Fed Govt, by field, performer type, agency, and State, FY89-91, annual rpt, 9627–20

Spacecraft launches and other activities of NASA and USSR, with flight data, 1957-90, annual rpt, 9504–6.1

Treaties and other bilateral and multilateral agreements of US in force, by country, as of Jan 1991, annual listing, 7004–1

see also European Space Agency

see also International cooperation in environmental sciences

see also Technology transfer

International corporations

see Foreign corporations

see Multinational corporations

International crime

see also Air piracy

see also International cooperation in law enforcement

see also Smuggling

see also Terrorism

International debts

see Foreign debts

International Development Association

Loan activity by purpose and country, and funds by source, FY89, annual rpt, 15344–1.5

Loans and grants for economic and military aid from US and intl agencies, by program and country, FY46-90, annual rpt, 9914–5

UN participation of US, and member and nonmember shares of UN budget by country, FY89-91, annual rpt, 7004–5

International Development Cooperation Agency

see U.S. International Development Cooperation Agency

International economic relations

see Balance of payments

see Foreign competition

see Foreign debts

see Foreign economic relations

see Foreign investments

see Foreign trade

see International finance

see Multinational corporations

International employees

Congressional Directory, members of 102nd Congress, other officials, elections, and districts, 1991-92, biennial rpt, 23874–1

Index by Subjects and Names

International organizations

UN employment, and US natls share of staff, by agency, as of Dec 1990, annual rpt, 7004–5

International finance

Banks (US) foreign lending at all US and foreign offices, by country group and country, quarterly rpt, 13002–1

Banks balance sheets, by Fed Reserve District, for major banks in NYC, and for US branches and agencies of foreign banks, weekly rpt, 9365–1.3

Capital intl market financial data by firm, and Intl Finance Corp finances, by country, 1990 hearing, 21248–149

Capital movements between US and foreign countries, *Treasury Bulletin*, quarterly rpt, 8002–4.11

Developing countries debt burden and related indicators, by country and for 9 US money-center banks, 1960s-89, article, 9292–4.201

Finance (intl) and financial policy, and external factors affecting US economy, technical paper series, 9366–7

Financial and economic analysis, technical paper series, 9385–8

Financial instns (intl) funds by source and disbursements by purpose, by country, with US policy review, FY89, annual rpt, 15344–1

Foreign and US intl transactions, debt, security holdings, interest and exchange rates, and US reserve assets, monthly rpt, 9362–1.3

Japan economic conditions, financial and intl policies, and trade devs, 1950s-80s and projected to 2050, compilation of papers, 23848–220

see also African Development Bank
see also African Development Fund
see also Asian Development Bank
see also Balance of payments
see also Eurocurrency
see also Export-Import Bank
see also Foreign debts
see also Foreign economic relations
see also Foreign exchange
see also Foreign investments
see also Inter-American Development Bank
see also International Bank for Reconstruction and Development
see also International Development Association
see also International Monetary Fund
see also International reserves
see also Multinational corporations
see also Organization for Economic Cooperation and Development
see also Overseas Private Investment Corp.
see also Special Drawing Rights

International Finance Corp.

Finances of IFC, and intl capital market financial data by firm, by country, 1990 hearing, 21248–149

Loan activity by purpose and country, FY89, annual rpt, 15344–1.6

Loans and grants for economic and military aid from US and intl agencies, by program and country, FY46-90, annual rpt, 9914–5

International Joint Commission, U.S. and Canada

Birds (bald eagle) Great Lakes population, breeding, and research status, 1990 conf, 14648–26

Great Lakes flood prevention activities of Army Corps of Engineers and Intl Joint Commission, monthly rpt and supplements, 3752–1

Great Lakes wastewater treatment by municipal and industrial facilities, releases, methods, effectiveness, pollutant limits, and enforcement, 1985-88, 14648–24

Pollution (air) emissions and levels in Detroit area, by pollutant, 1980-90, 14648–25

International labor

see Foreign labor conditions

International Labor Organization

Disabled persons in developing countries aid program activities and funding, for UN, AID, and Intl Labor Organization, late 1970s-90, GAO rpt, 26123–321

Expenditures for intl organizations by US and other countries, by organization and program, FY90, annual rpt, 7004–9

Respiratory diseases related to occupational hazards, epidemiology, diagnosis, and treatment, for selected industries and work settings, 1988 conf, 4248–90

International law

Intl organizations funding by US and other countries, by organization and program, FY90, annual rpt, 7004–9

UN voting record and share of votes in agreement with US, by issue, country, and world area, 1990, annual rpt, 7004–18

see also Citizenship
see also Diplomatic and consular service
see also Executive agreements
see also Expropriation of alien property
see also International cooperation in law enforcement
see also International military forces
see also International sanctions
see also Maritime law
see also Passports and visas
see also Territorial waters
see also Treaties and conventions

International military forces

US military aid, arms sales, and training programs costs and budget requests, by program, world region, and country, FY90-92, annual rpt, 7144–13

International Monetary Fund

Budget of US, authoritative financial statements with appropriations, outlays, and receipts, by category and agency, FY90, annual rpt, 8104–2.1

Developing countries foreign debt, and IMF credit outstanding, by country, 1984-90, 9118–11

Fed Govt receipts by source and outlays by agency, *Treasury Bulletin*, quarterly rpt, 8002–4.1

Investment (intl) position of US, by component, industry, world region, and country, 1989-90, annual article, 2702–1.212

Loan activity and voting power, by member country, FY89, annual rpt, 15344–1.3

Reserve assets of US by type, *Treasury Bulletin*, quarterly rpt, 8002–4.10

International Organization of Securities Commissions

Regulation of securities and commodity trading, activities and interagency coordination, FY91, annual rpt, 11924–4

International organizations

AID economic aid to developing countries, obligations and disbursements by country, quarterly rpt, 9912–4

AID loans repayment status and terms by program and country, and status of predecessor agency loans, quarterly rpt, 9912–3

Budget of US, obligations and authority by function, agency, and program, with summaries, analyses, and historical tables, FY92, annual rpt, 104–2

Congressional Directory, members of 102nd Congress, other officials, elections, and districts, 1991-92, biennial rpt, 23874–1

Developing countries aid by intl agencies, Intl Dev Cooperation Agency oversight of US contributions, FY92, annual rpt, 9904–4.2

Economic, social, political, and geographic summary data, by country, 1991, annual factbook, 9114–2

Expenditures for intl organizations by US and other countries, by organization and program, FY90, annual rpt, 7004–9

Financial instns (intl) funds by source and disbursements by purpose, by country, with US policy review, FY89, annual rpt, 15344–1

Iraq invasion of Kuwait, alien worker refugees fleeing from Iraq and Kuwait, intl aid by source, and costs to host and native countries, 1990-91, GAO rpt, 26123–326

Labor unions intl secretariats, membership and organization, 1988-91, 6366–4.53

Labor unions reporting to Labor Dept, parent bodies and locals by location, 1990 listing, 6468–17

Loans and grants for economic and military aid from US and intl agencies, by program and country, FY46-90, annual rpt, 9914–5

Loans of US banks to foreigners at all US and foreign offices, by country group and country, quarterly rpt, 13002–1

Military aid of US, arms sales, and training, by country, FY50-90, annual rpt, 3904–3

PL 480 exports by commodity, and recipients, by program, sponsor, and country, FY88 and cumulative from FY55, annual rpt, 1924–7

R&D funding by Fed Govt, by field, performer type, agency, and State, FY89-91, annual rpt, 9627–20

State Dept officers, ambassadors, and Chiefs of US overseas missions, by country and intl agency, 1778-1990, 7008–1

Treaties and other bilateral and multilateral agreements of US in force, by country, as of Jan 1991, annual listing, 7004–1

see also African Development Bank
see also African Development Fund
see also Asian Development Bank
see also Association of Southeast Asian Nations
see also Central Treaty Organization
see also Common markets and free trade areas
see also European Space Agency
see also Inter-American Development Bank
see also International Atomic Energy Agency
see also International Bank for Reconstruction and Development

International organizations

see also International Development Association
see also International employees
see also International Finance Corp.
see also International Labor Organization
see also International Monetary Fund
see also International Telecommunications Satellite Organization
see also North Atlantic Treaty Organization
see also Organization for Economic Cooperation and Development
see also Organization of American States
see also Red Cross
see also United Nations
see also Warsaw Pact

International relations

see Diplomatic and consular service
see Foreign economic relations
see Foreign relations
see International law
see International military forces
see International sanctions
see Military intervention
see Military invasion and occupation
see United Nations

International reserves

- Banks capital requirements for holding foreign currency assets, alternative measures of exchange rate risk, 1991 technical paper, 9366–7.254
- Developing countries counterpart funds impacts on US aid programs effectiveness and domestic economic and fiscal condition, literature review, 1991 rpt, 9918–21
- Economic conditions in foreign countries and implications for US, periodic country rpt series, 2046–4
- Economic indicators and components, current data and annual trends, monthly rpt, 23842–1.7
- Foreign and US intl transactions, debt, security holdings, interest and exchange rates, and US reserve assets, monthly rpt, 9362–1.3
- Imports/reserves ratio, and money supply growth rates, by selected country, 1950s-71, article, 9391–1.214
- Soviet Union, Eastern Europe, OECD, and selected other countries economic conditions, 1960s-90, annual rpt, 9114–4
- *Statistical Abstract of US,* 1991 annual data compilation, 2324–1.29; 2324–1.31

see also Special Drawing Rights

International sanctions

- Iraq invasion of Kuwait, oil embargo impacts on OPEC and US oil supply and industry, 1989-91, hearing, 21368–132
- Panama economic aid after US sanctions and military invasion, AID funding by program, as of 1991, GAO rpt, 26123–330
- UN voting record and share of votes in agreement with US, by issue, country, and world area, 1990, annual rpt, 7004–18

see also Boycotts

International Telecommunications Satellite Organization

- Launchings of satellites and other space objects since 1957, quarterly listing, 9502–2

International trade

see Balance of payments
see Foreign competition

see Foreign exchange
see Foreign investments
see Foreign trade
see Foreign trade promotion
see Maritime law
see Multinational corporations
see Ships and shipping
see Tariffs and foreign trade controls
see Trade agreements

International Trade Administration

- Auto trade of Canada and US, and production, sales, prices, and employment, selected years 1965-88, annual rpt, 2044–35
- Budget of US, obligations and authority by function, agency, and program, with summaries, analyses, and historical tables, FY92, annual rpt, 104–2
- *Business America,* foreign and domestic commerce, and US investment and trade opportunities, biweekly journal, 2042–24
- Caribbean Basin Initiative investment incentives, economic impacts, with finances and employment by country, 1984-90, 2048–141
- Competitiveness (intl) of US industries, with selected foreign and US operating data by major firm and product, series, 2046–12
- Construction put in place, permits, housing sales, costs, material prices, and employment, bimonthly rpt with articles, 2042–1
- Eastern Europe imports from US, and trade opportunities, periodic rpt, 2042–33
- Economic aid of US and other donor countries by type and recipient, and role in advancing economic interests, 1980s-90, 2048–152
- Electric current characteristics, by country and selected city, 1991 rpt, 2048–1
- Exports and imports of US, by selected country, country group, and commodity group, annual rpt, suspended, 2044–38
- Exports and imports of US, by selected country, country group, and commodity group, 1990, annual rpt, 2044–37
- Exports, imports, and balances of US by commodity group, world area, and country, and related employment, annual rpt, discontinued, 2044–26
- Exports, imports, and balances of US, by selected country, country group, and commodity group, preliminary data, monthly rpt, 2042–34
- Foreign countries economic conditions and implications for US, periodic country rpt series, 2046–4
- Foreign countries economic indicators, and trade and trade flows by commodity, by country, data compilation, monthly CD-ROM, 2002–6
- Franchise business opportunities by firm and kind of business, and sources of aid and info, annual rpt, issuing agency change, 2044–27
- Imports of textiles, total and from US, by commodity and country, 1987-89, 2048–155
- Industry finances and operations, by SIC 2- to 4-digit industry, forecast 1991, annual rpt, 2044–28
- Investment (foreign direct) in US, major transactions by type, industry, country, and US location, 1989, annual rpt, 2044–20

Index by Subjects and Names

- Japan manufacturing firms US affiliates, employment, and wages, by selected industry and State, 1980s, 2048–151
- Mexico imports from US, by industry and State, 1987-90, 2048–154
- North America free trade area proposal for Canada, US, and Mexico, outlook with trade data, 1990, 2048–153
- OECD intl trade position for US and 4 countries, and factors affecting US competition, periodic pamphlet, 2042–25
- *Overseas Business Reports:* economic conditions, investment and export opportunities, and trade practices, country market research rpt series, 2046–6
- Textile Agreement Category System import classification codes, correlation with TSUSA, 1992 annual rpt, 2044–31
- Textile imports, by country of origin, monthly rpt, 2042–27
- Textile imports, by product and country of origin, monthly rpt series, 2046–8; 2046–9

see also Foreign Trade Zones Board

International Trade Commission

see U.S. International Trade Commission

International transactions

see Balance of payments

Interstate agreements

see Interstate compacts

Interstate commerce

- Criminal cases by type and disposition, and collections, for US attorneys, by Federal district, FY90, annual rpt, 6004–2.1
- Criminal cases in Federal district courts, by offense, disposition, and district, 1980-90, last issue of annual rpt, 18204–1
- Criminal sentences for Federal offenses, guidelines by offense and circumstances, series, 17668–1
- Telecommunications domestic and intl rates, by type of service and area served, 1989, annual rpt, 9284–6.6

see also Antitrust law
see also Buses
see also Contraband
see also Freight
see also Inland water transportation
see also Pipelines
see also Railroads
see also Ships and shipping
see also Transportation and transportation equipment
see also Trucks and trucking industry

Interstate Commerce Commission

- Budget of US, authoritative financial statements with appropriations, outlays, and receipts, by category and agency, FY90, annual rpt, 8104–2.1
- Budget of US, obligations and authority by function, agency, and program, with summaries, analyses, and historical tables, FY92, annual rpt, 104–2
- Bus (Class I) passengers and selected revenue data, for individual large carriers, quarterly rpt, 9482–13
- Railroad employment by occupational group, for Class I line-haul railroads, monthly rpt, 9482–3
- Railroad employment, earnings, and hours, by occupation for Class I railroads, 1990, annual table, 9484–5
- Railroad revenue, income, freight, and rate of return, by Class I freight railroad and district, quarterly rpt, 9482–2

Index by Subjects and Names

Investments

Truck, bus, and rail carriers finances and operations, detailed data, 1989, annual rpt series, 9486–6

Truck transport of household goods, financial and operating data by firm, quarterly rpt, 9482–14

Truck transport of household goods, performance and disposition of damage claims, for selected carriers, 1990, annual rpt, 9484–11

Truck transport of property, financial and operating data by region and firm, quarterly rpt, 9482–5

Interstate Commission on the Potomac River Basin

Budget of US, authoritative financial statements with appropriations, outlays, and receipts, by category and agency, FY90, annual rpt, 8104–2.1

Interstate compacts

Radioactive low-level waste disposal activities of States and interstate compacts, with data by disposal facility and reactor, 1989, annual rpt, 3354–14

Interstate highways

see Federal aid to highways

see Highways, streets, and roads

Interstate relations

Child Support Enforcement Program finances and operations, by State, FY85-89, annual rpt, 4694–6

see also Interstate compacts

see also Regional planning

Inventions

Energy-related inventions recommended by Natl Inst of Standards and Technology for DOE support, awards, and evaluation status, 1990, annual listing, 2214–5

Energy-related inventions supported by DOE, sales, jobs created, and inventor financing, 1980-88, 3308–91

Fed Govt employee incentive awards, costs, and benefits, by award type and agency, FY89, annual rpt, 9844–20

NASA activities and funding, 1990, annual compilation of papers, 21704–1

see also Patents

see also Technological innovations

see also Technology transfer

Inventories

see Agricultural stocks

see Agricultural surpluses

see Business inventories

see Energy stocks and inventories

see Stockpiling

Inventory of Mental Health Organizations and General Hospital Mental Health Services

Mental health care facilities, staff, service, and patient characteristics, series, 4506–4

Investigations

see Congressional investigations

see Criminal investigations

see Government investigations

Investment banking

see Financial institutions

Investments

Airline finances, by carrier, carrier group, and for total certificated system, quarterly rpt, 7302–7

Assets and debts of private sector, balance sheets by segment, 1945-90, semiannual rpt, 9365–4.1

Banks (commercial) loans and investments, 1972-90, annual rpt, 204–1.5

Banks (natl) charters, mergers, liquidations, enforcement cases, and financial performance, with data by instn and State, quarterly rpt, 8402–3

Capital gains counted as income, and other income definitions effects on household income and poverty status, by recipient characteristics, 1990, annual Current Population Rpt, 2546–6.69

Capital gains preferential tax treatment impacts on agricultural finances and operations, 1991 article, 1561–16.202

County Business Patterns, 1988: employment, establishments, and payroll, by SIC 2- to 4-digit industry and county, annual State rpt series, 2326–6

County Business Patterns, 1989: employment, establishments, and payroll, by SIC 2- to 4-digit industry and county, annual State rpt series, 2326–8

Credit Union Natl Admin Central Liquidity Facility, financial statements, FY90, annual rpt, 9534–5

Credit unions federally insured, finances by instn characteristics and State, as of June 1991, semiannual rpt, 9532–6

Credit unions federally insured, finances, 1989-90, annual rpt, 9534–1

Economic indicators and components, and Fed Reserve 4th District business and financial conditions, monthly chartbook, 9377–10

Economic indicators and components, current data and annual trends, monthly rpt, 23842–1.5

Economic indicators compounded annual rates of change, 1971-90, annual rpt, 9391–9.2

Economic Report of the President for 1991, with economic trends from 1929, annual rpt, 204–1.1

Electric power distribution loans from REA, and borrower operating and financial data, by firm and State, 1990, annual rpt, 1244–1

Electric utilities finances and operations, detailed data for public and privately owned firms, 1989, annual rpt, 3164–11.4

Electric utilities finances and operations, detailed data for publicly owned firms, 1989, annual rpt, 3164–24

Electric utilities privately owned, finances and operations, detailed data, 1989, annual rpt, 3164–23

Energy producers finances and operations, by energy type for US firms domestic and foreign operations, 1989, annual rpt, 3164–44

Flow-of-funds accounts, savings, investments, and credit statements, quarterly rpt, 9365–3.3

Foreign and US economic conditions and competitiveness issues, with data by country, 1960s-90, 21788–204

Households assets, by type of holding and selected characteristics, 1988, Current Population Rpt, 2546–20.16

Housing units owned for recreation and investment, by selected unit characteristics, 1987, biennial rpt supplement, 2485–13

Income (household, family, and personal), by source, detailed characteristics, and region, 1988-89, annual Current Population Rpt, 2546–6.68

Income (household, family, and personal), by source, detailed characteristics, and region, 1990, annual Current Population Rpt, 2546–6.70

Income (personal) per capita and by source, and earnings by industry div, by State, MSA, and county, 1984-89, annual regional rpts, 2704–2

Income disparity between wealthiest and other families, and income sources, 1980s and trends from 1949, 23848–219

Input-output structure of US economy, detailed interindustry transactions for 84 industries, and components of final demand, 1986, annual article, 2702–1.206

Input-output structure of US economy, detailed interindustry transactions for 85 industries, 1982 benchmark data, 2702–1.213

Insurance industry finances, underwriting activities, and investment plan mgmt, 1960s-90, 21248–159

Monetary trends, Fed Reserve Bank of St Louis monthly rpt, 9391–2

Multinatl firms US affiliates, finances, and operations, by industry, world area of parent firm, and State, 1988-89, annual rpt, 2704–4

Multinatl firms US affiliates, investment trends and impact on US economy, 1991 annual rpt, 2004–9

Multinatl US firms and foreign affiliates finances and operations, by industry and world area of parent firm, 1989 benchmark survey, preliminary annual rpt, 2704–5

Natl income and product accounts and components, *Survey of Current Business*, monthly rpt, 2702–1.24

Natl income and product accounts benchmark revisions of GDP and natl income, various periods 1959-80, tables, 2702–1.227

Natural gas interstate pipeline company detailed financial and operating data, by firm, 1989, annual rpt, 3164–38

Nonprofit charitable organizations finances, and revenue and investments of top 10 instns, 1986-87, article, 8302–2.210

Nonprofit charitable organizations finances, by asset size and State, 1987, article, 8302–2.218

Nonprofit charitable organizations finances, 1988, table, 8302–2.220

North Central States business and economic conditions, Fed Reserve 9th District, quarterly journal, 9383–19

North Central States, FHLB 6th District insured S&Ls financial condition and operations by State, quarterly rpt, 9302–23

Older persons in rural areas, household income sources, and poverty status, 1983-84, 1598–268

Pension systems of State and local govts, finances, coverage, and benefits, by system, FY88, annual rpt, 2466–2.1

Pension systems of State and local govts, finances, coverage, and benefits, by system, FY89, annual rpt, 2466–2.8

Poverty status of population and families, by detailed characteristics, 1988-89, annual Current Population Rpt, 2546–6.67

Investments

Poverty status of population and families, by detailed characteristics, 1990, annual Current Population Rpt, 2546–6.71

Railroad (Class I) finances and operations, detailed data by firm, class of service, and district, 1989, annual rpt, 9486–6.1

Railroad retirement system funding and benefits findings and recommendations, with background industry data, 1960s-90 and projected to 2060, 9708–1

Return on investments under alternative valuation methods, for US business and for direct foreign investment in and of US, 1982-90, article, 2702–1.217

Savings and Investment Incentive Act issues, with IRA participation and other background data, 1980s, 25368–175

Service industries census, 1987: establishments, receipts by source, payroll, and employment, by SIC 2- to 4-digit kind of business, State, and MSA, 2393–4

Southeastern States, Fed Reserve 5th District insured commercial banks financial statements, by State, quarterly rpt, 9389–18

Statistical Abstract of US, 1991 annual data compilation, 2324–1.14

Survey of Current Business, detailed financial and business data, and economic indicators, monthly rpt, 2702–1.4

Tax (income) returns filed by type of filer, selected income items, quarterly rpt, 8302–2.1

Tax (income) returns for foreign corporate activity in US, assets, and income statement items, by industry div and selected country, 1986-87, article, 8302–2.205

Tax (income) returns of corporations, income and tax items by asset size and detailed industry, 1987, annual rpt, 8304–4

Tax (income) returns of corporations, income and tax items by asset size and detailed industry, 1988, annual rpt, 8304–21

Tax (income) returns of individuals, selected income and tax items, by adjusted gross income and State, 1986-88, article, 8302–2.201

Tax (income) returns of individuals, selected income and tax items by income level, preliminary 1989, annual article, 8302–2.209

Tax (income) returns of partnerships, income statement and balance sheet items, by industry group, 1989, annual article, 8302–2.216; 8304–18

Tax (income) returns of US corporations under foreign control, assets and income statement items by industry div and country, 1988, article, 8302–2.219

Tax (income) withholding and related documents filed, by type and IRS service center, 1990 and projected 1991-98, annual rpt, 8304–22

Tax reform and investment stimulation proposals, with background data, 1990 hearings, 25368–170

Taxation and intl competitiveness issues, with comparisons of US and foreign tax rates and revenue, 1988-91, press release, 8008–150

Telephone and telegraph firms detailed finances and operations, 1989, annual rpt, 9284–6

Telephone firms borrowing under Rural Telephone Program, and financial and operating data, by State, 1990, annual rpt, 1244–2

Turkey GNP, trade, investment, and inflation following currency devaluation, 1970s-90, technical paper, 9385–8.112

West Central States economic indicators, Fed Reserve 10th District, quarterly rpt, 9381–16.2

Western States, FHLB 11th District S&Ls, offices, and financial condition, 1991 annual listing, 9304–23

see also Capital investments, general

see also Capital investments, specific industry

see also Divestiture

see also Foreign investments

see also Futures trading

see also Government securities

see also Individual retirement arrangements

see also Joint ventures

see also Loans

see also Mortgages

see also Mutual funds

see also New York Stock Exchange

see also Options trading

see also Securities

see also Stock exchanges

see also Venture capital

Iowa

Banks (insured commercial and savings) deposits by instn, State, MSA, and county, as of June 1990, annual regional rpt, 9295–3.5

Coal production and mines by county, prices, productivity, miners, and reserves, by mining method and State, 1989-90, annual rpt, 3164–25

County Business Patterns, 1989: employment, establishments, and payroll, by SIC 2- to 4-digit industry and county, annual State rpt, 2326–8.17

DOD prime contract awards, by contractor, service branch, State, and city, FY90, annual rpt, 3544–22

Fed Govt spending in States and local areas, by type, State, county, and city, FY90, annual rpt, 2464–3

Fed Govt spending in States, by type, program, agency, and State, FY90, annual rpt, 2464–2

HHS financial aid, by program, recipient, State, and city, FY90, annual regional listing, 4004–3.7

Hospital deaths of Medicare patients, actual and expected rates by diagnosis, and hospital characteristics, by instn, FY87-89, annual regional rpt, 4654–14.7

Income (personal) per capita and by source, and earnings by industry div, by State, MSA, and county, 1984-89, annual regional rpt, 2704–2.3

Jail adult and juvenile population, employment, spending, instn conditions, and inmate programs, by county and facility, 1988, regional rpt series, 6068–144.3

Lumber (veneer log) production, mill receipts, and trade, by species, with residue use, for North Central States, 1988, quadrennial rpt, 1208–220

Index by Subjects and Names

Marriages, divorces, and rates, by characteristics of spouses, State, and county, 1987 and trends from 1920, US Vital Statistics annual rpt, 4144–4

Mineral Industry Surveys, State reviews of production, 1990, preliminary annual rpt, 5614–6

Minerals Yearbook, 1989, Vol 2: State review of production and sales by commodity, and business activity, annual rpt, 5604–16.16

Minerals Yearbook, 1989, Vol 2: State reviews of production, sales, and firms, by commodity, and business activity, annual rpt, 5604–34

Physicians, by specialty, age, sex, and location of training and practice, 1989, State rpt, 4116–6.16

Population and housing census, 1990: population and housing characteristics, households, and land area, by county, subdiv, and place, State rpt, 2551–1.17

Population and housing census, 1990: voting age and total population by race, and housing units, by block, redistricting counts required under PL 94-171, State CD-ROM release, 2551–6.9

Population and housing census, 1990: voting age and total population by race, and housing units, by county and city, redistricting counts required under PL 94-171, State summary rpt, 2551–5.16

Statistical Abstract of US, 1991 annual data compilation, 2324–1

Supplemental Security Income payments and beneficiaries, by type of eligibility, State, and county, Dec 1989, annual rpt, 4744–27.7

Water supply and quality in streams and lakes, and groundwater levels in wells, by drainage basin, 1990, annual State rpt, 5666–10.14

see also Cedar Falls, Iowa

see also Cedar Rapids, Iowa

see also Davenport, Iowa

see also Des Moines, Iowa

see also Waterloo, Iowa

see also under By State in the "Index by Categories"

Iowa City, Iowa

see also under By SMSA or MSA in the "Index by Categories"

Iran

Agricultural exports of high-value commodities, indexes and sales by commodity, world area, and country, 1960s-86, 1528–323

Agricultural production, prices, and trade, by country, 1960s-90, annual world area rpt, 1524–4.2

Agricultural trade of US, by detailed commodity and country, 1989, annual rpt, 1524–8

Agricultural trade of US, by detailed commodity and country, 1990, semiannual rpt, 1522–4

AID loans repayment status and terms by program and country, and status of predecessor agency loans, quarterly rpt, 9912–3

Economic and military aid and loans from US and intl agencies, by program and country, FY46-90, annual rpt, 9914–5

Economic conditions, policy, and trade practices, by country, 1988-90, annual rpt, 21384–5

Index by Subjects and Names

Economic, social, political, and geographic summary data, by country, 1991, annual factbook, 9114–2

Export controls and trade of US with Middle East countries, with dual-use commodity licenses and arms sales, 1980s-90, GAO rpt, 26123–339

Exports and imports of US, by commodity and country, 1970-89, world area rpt, 9116–1.1

Exports and imports of US, by selected country, country group, and commodity group, 1990, annual rpt, 2044–37

Exports and imports of US, by transport mode, country, and SITC 1- to 3-digit commodity, 1990, annual rpt, 2424–12

Exports of US, detailed Schedule B commodities with countries of destination, 1990, annual rpt, 2424–10

Human rights conditions in 170 countries, and US economic and military aid, 1990, annual rpt, 21384–3

Oil production, and exports and prices for US, by major exporting country, detailed data, monthly rpt with articles, 3162–24

Oil production, trade, use, and stocks, by selected country and country group, monthly rpt, 3162–42

Refugee resettlement programs and funding, arrivals by country of origin, and indicators of adjustment, by State, FY90, annual rpt, 4694–5

UN voting record and share of votes in agreement with US, by issue, country, and world area, 1990, annual rpt, 7004–18

see also under By Foreign Country in the "Index by Categories"

Iraq

Agricultural exports of high-value commodities, indexes and sales by commodity, world area, and country, 1960s-86, 1528–323

Agricultural exports of US, impacts of foreign agricultural and trade policy, with data by commodity and country, 1989, annual rpt, 1924–8

Agricultural imports of Iraq under CCC export credit guarantee programs, FY81-90, GAO rpt, 26123–314

Agricultural production, prices, and trade, by country, 1960s-90, annual world area rpt, 1524–4.2

Agricultural trade by commodity and country, prices, and world market devs, monthly rpt, 1922–12

Agricultural trade of US, by detailed commodity and country, 1989, annual rpt, 1524–8

Agricultural trade of US, by detailed commodity and country, 1990, semiannual rpt, 1522–4

CCC credit guarantee program sales to Iraq, FY81-90, with contingent liabilities projected to FY97, hearing, 21248–155

Economic and military aid and loans from US and intl agencies, by program and country, FY46-90, annual rpt, 9914–5

Economic conditions, policy, and trade practices, by country, 1988-90, annual rpt, 21384–5

Economic, social, political, and geographic summary data, by country, 1991, annual factbook, 9114–2

Export controls and trade of US with Middle East countries, with dual-use commodity licenses and arms sales, 1980s-90, GAO rpt, 26123–339

Exports and imports of US, by commodity and country, 1970-89, world area rpt, 9116–1.1

Exports and imports of US, by Harmonized System 6-digit commodity and country, 1990, annual rpt, 2424–13

Exports and imports of US, by selected country, country group, and commodity group, 1990, annual rpt, 2044–37

Exports and imports of US, by transport mode, country, and SITC 1- to 3-digit commodity, 1990, annual rpt, 2424–12

Exports of US, detailed Schedule B commodities with countries of destination, 1990, annual rpt, 2424–10

Human rights conditions in 170 countries, and US economic and military aid, 1990, annual rpt, 21384–3

Kuwait invasion by Iraq, alien worker refugees fleeing from Iraq and Kuwait, intl aid by source, and costs to host and native countries, 1990-91, GAO rpt, 26123–326

Kuwait invasion by Iraq, impacts on oil supply and prices, selected indicators, daily press release, 3162–44

Military weapons trade, production, and defense industry finances, with data by firm and country, 1980s-91, 26358–241

Oil production and exports to US, by major exporting country, detailed data, monthly rpt with articles, 3162–24

Oil production, trade, use, and stocks, by selected country and country group, monthly rpt, 3162–42

UN voting record and share of votes in agreement with US, by issue, country, and world area, 1990, annual rpt, 7004–18

see also under By Foreign Country in the "Index by Categories"

Iraq-Kuwait crisis

see Military intervention

see Military invasion and occupation

Ireland

Agricultural exports of high-value commodities, indexes and sales by commodity, world area, and country, 1960s-86, 1528–323

Agricultural production, prices, and trade, by country, 1970s-90, and forecast 1991, annual world region rpt, 1524–4.4

Agricultural production, trade, and policies in foreign countries, summary data by country, 1989-90, annual factbook, 1924–12

Agricultural trade of US, by detailed commodity and country, 1989, annual rpt, 1524–8

Agricultural trade of US, by detailed commodity and country, 1990, semiannual rpt, 1522–4

AID loans repayment status and terms by program and country, and status of predecessor agency loans, quarterly rpt, 9912–3

Economic and military aid and loans from US and intl agencies, by program and country, FY46-90, annual rpt, 9914–5

Economic and social conditions of developing countries from 1960s, and Intl Dev Cooperation Agency and AID activities and funding, FY90-92, annual rpt, 9904–4

Economic conditions, income, production, prices, employment, and trade, 1991 periodic country rpt, 2046–4.45

Iron and steel industry

Economic conditions, investment and export opportunities, and trade practices, 1991 country market research rpt, 2046–6.3

Economic conditions, policy, and trade practices, by country, 1988-90, annual rpt, 21384–5

Economic, social, political, and geographic summary data, by country, 1991, annual factbook, 9114–2

Exports and imports of OECD members, by country, 1989, annual rpt, 7144–10

Exports and imports of US, by Harmonized System 6-digit commodity and country, 1990, annual rpt, 2424–13

Exports and imports of US, by selected country, country group, and commodity group, 1990, annual rpt, 2044–37

Exports and imports of US, by transport mode, country, and SITC 1- to 3-digit commodity, 1990, annual rpt, 2424–12

Exports and imports of US with EC by country, and total agricultural trade, selected years 1958-90, annual rpt, 7144–7

Exports of US, detailed Schedule B commodities with countries of destination, 1990, annual rpt, 2424–10

GNP and GNP growth for OECD members, by country, 1980-90, annual rpt, 7144–8

Human rights conditions in 170 countries, and US economic and military aid, 1990, annual rpt, 21384–3

Labor conditions, union coverage, and work accidents, 1991 annual country rpt, 6366–4.39

Multinatl US firms and foreign affiliates finances and operations, by industry and world area of parent firm, 1989 benchmark survey, preliminary annual rpt, 2704–5

Multinatl US firms foreign affiliates, income statement items by country and world area, 1986, biennial article, 8302–2.212

Oil production, trade, use, and stocks, by selected country and country group, monthly rpt, 3162–42

Tax revenue, by level of govt and type of tax, for OECD countries, mid 1960s-89, annual rpt, 10044–1.2

UN voting record and share of votes in agreement with US, by issue, country, and world area, 1990, annual rpt, 7004–18

see also under By Foreign Country in the "Index by Categories"

Iron and steel industry

Building materials shipments and PPI, by type, bimonthly rpt, 2042–1.5; 2042–1.6

Business statistics, detailed data for major industries and economic indicators, *Survey of Current Business*, monthly rpt, 2702–1.17

County Business Patterns, 1988: employment, establishments, and payroll, by SIC 2- to 4-digit industry and county, annual State rpt series, 2326–6

County Business Patterns, 1989: employment, establishments, and payroll, by SIC 2- to 4-digit industry and county, annual State rpt series, 2326–8

Drums and pails (steel shipping) shipments, trade, use, and firms, quarterly Current Industrial Rpt, 2506–11.5

Employment, earnings, and hours, by SIC 1- to 4-digit industry, monthly and annual averages, selected years 1909-90, annual rpt, 6744–4

Iron and steel industry

Energy use and prices for manufacturing industries, 1988 survey, series, 3166–13

Enterprise Statistics, 1987: finances and operations for companies, by size, level of diversification, form of organization, and industry group, 2329–8

Exports and imports between US and outlying areas, by detailed commodity and mode of transport, 1990, annual rpt, 2424–11

Exports and imports of building materials, by commodity and country, 1989-90, article, 2042–1.204

Exports and imports of US, by country and detailed commodity, monthly rpt, 2422–12

Exports and imports of US, by Harmonized System 6-digit commodity and country, 1990, annual rpt, 2424–13

Exports and imports of US, by transport mode, country, and SITC 1- to 3-digit commodity, 1990, annual rpt, 2424–12

Exports and imports of US shipped through Canada, by detailed commodity, customs district, and country, 1989, annual rpt, 7704–11

Exports of US, detailed commodities by country, monthly CD-ROM, 2422–13

Exports of US, detailed Schedule B commodities with countries of destination, 1990, annual rpt, 2424–10

Finances, operations, and modernization efforts of steel industry, with data on major companies and foreign industry, 1968-91, last issue of annual rpt, 9884–24

Foreign countries economic, social, political, and geographic summary data, by country, 1991, annual factbook, 9114–2

Furniture (office) shipments by product, and metals used by type, 1990, annual Current Industrial Rpt, 2506–7.8

Great Lakes area economic conditions and outlook, for US and Canada, 1970s-90, 9375–15

Hwy construction material prices and indexes for Federal-aid system, by type of material and urban-rural location, quarterly rpt, 7552–7

Hwy construction material prices and indexes for Federal-aid system, by type of material, quarterly press release, 7552–16

Hwy construction material use by type, and spending, by State, various periods 1944-90, annual rpt, 7554–29

Imports injury to US industries from foreign subsidized products and sales at less than fair value, investigations with background financial and operating data, series, 9886–19

Imports injury to US industries from foreign subsidized products, investigations with background financial and operating data, series, 9886–15

Imports of steel sheet piling from Canada at less than fair value, injury to US industry, investigation with background financial and operating data, 1991 rpt, 9886–14.311

Imports of steel under voluntary restraint agreement, by product, customs district, and country, with US industry operating data, quarterly rpt, 9882–13

Imports of US, detailed commodities by country, monthly CD-ROM, 2422–14

Index by Subjects and Names

Imports of US given duty-free treatment for value of US material sent abroad, by commodity and country, 1989, annual rpt, 9884–14

Input-output structure of US economy, detailed interindustry transactions for 84 industries, and components of final demand, 1986, annual article, 2702–1.206

Input-output structure of US economy, detailed interindustry transactions for 85 industries, 1982 benchmark data, 2702–1.213

Manufacturing annual survey, 1989: finances and operations, by SIC 2- to 4-digit industry, series, 2506–15

Manufacturing census, 1987: finances and operations, by SIC 2- to 4-digit industry, State, and MSA, with trends from 1849, 2497–1

Manufacturing census, 1987: finances and operations, by type of organization and SIC 2- to 4-digit industry, subject rpt, 2497–5

Manufacturing corporations financial statements, by selected SIC 2- to 3-digit industry, quarterly rpt, 2502–1

Manufacturing finances and operations, by SIC 2- to 4-digit industry, forecast 1991, annual rpt, 2044–28

Military and personal property shipments, passenger traffic, and costs, by service branch and mode of transport, quarterly rpt, 3702–1

Mineral industries census, 1987: energy use and costs, by fuel type, SIC 2- to 4-digit industry, and State, subject rpt, 2517–2

Mineral industries census, 1987: finances and operations, by establishment characteristics, SIC 2- to 4-digit industry, and State, subject rpt, 2517–1

Mineral industries census, 1987: finances and operations, by SIC 2- to 4-digit industry, State, and county, census div rpt series, 2515–1

Mineral Industry Surveys, commodity review of production, trade, and use, 1990, advance annual rpt, 5614–5.7

Mineral Industry Surveys, commodity review of production, trade, stocks, and use, monthly rpt, 5612–1.11; 5612–1.12

Minerals Yearbook, 1988, Vol 3: foreign country reviews of production, trade, and policy, by commodity, annual rpt series, 5604–17

Minerals Yearbook, 1989, Vol 1: commodity reviews of production, reserves, supply, use, and trade, annual rpt series, 5604–15

Minerals Yearbook, 1989, Vol 2: State reviews of production and sales by commodity, and business activity, annual rpt series, 5604–16

Minerals Yearbook, 1989, Vol 2: State reviews of production, sales, and firms, by commodity, and business activity, annual rpt, 5604–34

Minerals Yearbook, 1990, Vol 1: commodity reviews of production, reserves, supply, use, and trade, annual rpt series, 5604–20

Mines (metal) and related operations occupational injuries and incidence, employment, and hours, 1989, annual rpt, 6664–3

Multinatl firms US affiliates, investment trends and impact on US economy, 1991 annual rpt, 2004–9

Multinatl US firms and foreign affiliates finances and operations, by industry and world area of parent firm, 1989 benchmark survey, preliminary annual rpt, 2704–5

North Central States business and economic conditions, Fed Reserve 9th District, quarterly journal, 9383–19

Occupational injury and illness rates, by SIC 2- to 4-digit industry, 1988-89, annual rpt, 6844–7

Occupational injury and illness rates, by SIC 2- to 4-digit industry, 1989, annual rpt, 6844–1

OECD trade, total and for 4 major countries, and US trade by country, by commodity, 1970-89, world area rpt series, 9116–1

Pollution (air) abatement equipment shipments by industry, and new and backlog orders, by product, 1990, annual Current Industrial Rpt, 2506–12.5

Pollution (air) contributing to global warming, emissions factors and control costs, by pollutant and source, 1990 rpt, 9198–124

Pollution (air) emissions factors, by detailed pollutant and source, data compilation, 1990 rpt, 9198–120

Price indexes (producer), by stage of processing and detailed commodity, monthly rpt, 6762–6

Price indexes (producer), by stage of processing and detailed commodity, monthly 1990, annual rpt, 6764–2

Production, prices, trade, and foreign and US industry devs, by commodity, bimonthly rpt with articles, 5602–4

Production, prices, trade, use, employment, tariffs, and stockpiles, by mineral, with foreign comparisons, 1986-90, annual rpt, 5604–18

Production, shipments, trade, stocks, and material used, for primary metals by product, periodic Current Industrial Rpt series, 2506–10

Productivity of labor and capital, and indexes of output, hours, and employment, 1967-89, annual rpt, 6824–1.2; 6824–1.3; 6824–1.5

Respiratory diseases related to occupational hazards, epidemiology, diagnosis, and treatment, for selected industries and work settings, 1988 conf, 4248–90

Rope (steel wire) from Canada at less than fair value, injury to US industry, investigation with background financial and operating data, 1991 rpt, 9886–14.323

Rope (steel wire) from 2 countries at less than fair value, injury to US industry, investigation with background financial and operating data, 1991 rpt, 9886–14.324

Rope (steel wire) from 4 countries, injury to US industry from foreign subsidized and less than fair value imports, investigation with background financial and operating data, 1991 rpt, 9886–19.79

Rope (steel wire) from 8 countries, injury to US industry from foreign subsidized and less than fair value imports, investigation with background financial and operating data, 1990 rpt, 9886–19.73

Soviet Union, Eastern Europe, OECD, and selected other countries minerals production, by commodity, 1960s-90, annual rpt, 9114–4.6

Statistical Abstract of US, 1991 annual data compilation, 2324–1.25; 2324–1.27

Tax (income) returns of corporations, income and tax items by asset size and detailed industry, 1987, annual rpt, 8304–4

Tax (income) returns of corporations, income and tax items by asset size and detailed industry, 1988, annual rpt, 8304–21

Technologically advanced structural materials devs, use, and R&D funding, for ceramics, metal alloys, polymers, and composites, 1960s-80s and projected to 2000, 5608–162

see also under By Commodity in the "Index by Categories"

Irrigation

Acreage of land, by use, ownership, and State, 1987 and trends from 1910, 1588–48

Acreage of non-Federal land by use, soil and water conditions, and conservation needs, 1987, State rpt series, 1266–5

Africa (sub-Saharan) agricultural conditions by country, with Ethiopia grain production and use, and dev aid by major donor, 1960s-80s, hearing, 23848–216

Agricultural Conservation Program participation and payments, by practice and State, FY90, annual rpt, 1804–7

Agricultural data compilation, 1990 and trends from 1920, annual rpt, 1004–14

Army Corps of Engineers water resources dev projects, characteristics, and costs, 1950s-89, biennial State rpt series, 3756–1

Army Corps of Engineers water resources dev projects, characteristics, and costs, 1950s-91, biennial State rpt series, 3756–2

California drought impacts, Central Valley reservoir storage and capacity, and Kern County crop production and irrigation, 1989-91, article, 1561–6.202

Census of Agriculture, 1987: farms, farmland, production, finances, and operator characteristics, by county, final State rpt series, 2331–1

Columbia River Power System projects, plant investment allocation schedule, FY90, annual rpt, 3224–1

Costs of production, itemized by farm sales size and region, 1990, annual rpt, 1614–3

Cotton farms fertilizer, pesticide and irrigation use, soil conservation practices, and water quality impacts, 1989, 1588–151

County Business Patterns, 1988: employment, establishments, and payroll, by SIC 2- to 4-digit industry and county, annual State rpt series, 2326–6

County Business Patterns, 1989: employment, establishments, and payroll, by SIC 2- to 4-digit industry and county, annual State rpt series, 2326–8

Developing countries agricultural supply, demand, and market for US exports, with socioeconomic conditions, country rpt series, 1526–6

Energy conservation and resource planning activities of Bonneville Power Admin, FY89-90, 3228–11

Environmental Quality, status of problems, protection programs, research, and intl issues, 1991 annual rpt, 484–1

Farm production inputs, finances, mgmt, and land value and transfers, periodic situation rpt with articles, 1561–16

Farm production itemized costs, receipts, and returns, by commodity and region, 1987-89, annual rpt, 1544–20

FmHA activities, and loans and grants by program and State, FY90 and trends from FY70, annual rpt, 1184–17

Global climate change environmental, infrastructure, and health impacts, with model results and background data, 1850s-2100, 9188–113

Groundwater supply, quality, chemistry, and use, State and local area rpt series, 5666–28

Groundwater supply, quality, chemistry, other characteristics, and use, regional rpt series, 5666–25

Horticultural specialties census, 1988: producers, finances, and operations, by crop and State, 1987 Census of Agriculture, 2337–1

Occupational injury and illness rates, by SIC 2- to 4-digit industry, 1988-89, annual rpt, 6844–7

Occupational injury and illness rates, by SIC 2- to 4-digit industry, 1989, annual rpt, 6844–1

Pollution (groundwater) from farm chemicals use and animal wastes, and reduction strategies, 1960s-90, 26358–231

Rental of farmland by assessment method, and rent receipts per acre and as share of land value by land type and State, 1960s-80s, 1548–377

State and Metro Area Data Book, 1991 data compilation, 2328–54

Statistical Abstract of US, 1991 annual data compilation, 2324–1.23

Water quality, chemistry, hydrology, and other characteristics, local area studies, series, 5666–27

Water supply in US and southern Canada, streamflow, surface and groundwater conditions, and reservoir levels, by location, monthly rpt, 5662–3

Water use by end use, well withdrawals, and public supply deliveries, by county, State rpt series, 5666–24

Water value estimates for sport fishing and irrigation, by river basin, 1991 article, 1502–7.203

Western Area Power Admin activities by plant, financial statements, and sales by customer, FY90, annual rpt, 3254–1

Western US irrigation projects of Reclamation Bur, acreage limits monitoring activities by region, 1988-90, annual rpt, 5824–13

Western US irrigation projects of Reclamation Bur, crop production and acreage by commodity, State, and project, 1989, annual rpt, 5824–12

Wetlands acreage, resources, soil and water properties, and conservation efforts, by wetland type, State rpt series, 5506–11

see also Watershed projects

IRS

see Internal Revenue Service

Irvine, Calif.

see also under By City in the "Index by Categories"

Irving, Tex.

see also under By City in the "Index by Categories"

Islands

see Coral reefs and islands

Israel

Agricultural exports of high-value commodities, indexes and sales by commodity, world area, and country, 1960s-86, 1528–323

Agricultural exports of US, impacts of foreign agricultural and trade policy, with data by commodity and country, 1989, annual rpt, 1924–8

Agricultural production, trade, and policies in foreign countries, summary data by country, 1989-90, annual factbook, 1924–12

Agricultural trade of US, by detailed commodity and country, 1989, annual rpt, 1524–8

Agricultural trade of US, by detailed commodity and country, 1990, semiannual rpt, 1522–4

AID economic aid to developing countries, obligations and disbursements by country, quarterly rpt, 9912–4

AID loans repayment status and terms by program and country, and status of predecessor agency loans, quarterly rpt, 9912–3

Background Notes, summary social, political, and economic data, 1991 rpt, 7006–2.23

Economic and military aid and loans from US and intl agencies, by program and country, FY46-90, annual rpt, 9914–5

Economic and social conditions of developing countries from 1960s, and Intl Dev Cooperation Agency and AID activities and funding, FY90-92, annual rpt, 9904–4

Economic conditions, income, production, prices, employment, and trade, 1991 periodic country rpt, 2046–4.74

Economic conditions, policy, and trade practices, by country, 1988-90, annual rpt, 21384–5

Economic, social, political, and geographic summary data, by country, 1991, annual factbook, 9114–2

Export controls and trade of US with Middle East countries, with dual-use commodity licenses and arms sales, 1980s-90, GAO rpt, 26123–339

Exports and imports of US, by Harmonized System 6-digit commodity and country, 1990, annual rpt, 2424–13

Exports and imports of US, by selected country, country group, and commodity group, 1990, annual rpt, 2044–37

Exports and imports of US, by transport mode, country, and SITC 1- to 3-digit commodity, 1990, annual rpt, 2424–12

Exports, imports, and balances of US with major trading partners, by product category, 1986-90, annual chartbook, 9884–21

Exports of US, detailed Schedule B commodities with countries of destination, 1990, annual rpt, 2424–10

Israel

Govt budgets, foreign debt, and economic indicators of Israel and Egypt, 1980s, hearing, 21388–58

Human rights conditions in 170 countries, and US economic and military aid, 1990, annual rpt, 21384–3

Imports of goods, services, and investment from US, trade barriers, impacts, and US actions, by country, 1990, annual rpt, 444–2

Investment (foreign direct) in US, by industry group of US affiliate and country of parent firm, 1980-86, 2708–41

Labor conditions, union coverage, and work accidents, 1990 annual country rpt, 6366–4.8

Military aid of US, arms sales, and training programs costs and budget requests, by program, world region, and country, FY90-92, annual rpt, 7144–13

Military weapons trade, production, and defense industry finances, with data by firm and country, 1980s-91, 26358–241

Multinatl US firms and foreign affiliates finances and operations, by industry and world area of parent firm, 1989 benchmark survey, preliminary annual rpt, 2704–5

Multinatl US firms foreign affiliates, income statement items by country and world area, 1986, biennial article, 8302–2.212

Soviet Union Jewish emigration, and share to Israel, 1968-90, hearings, 21168–49

Space programs activities, missions, launchings, payloads, and flight duration, for foreign and US programs, 1957-90, annual rpt, 21704–4

Spacecraft and satellite launches since 1957, quarterly listing, 9502–2

Steel wire rope from 8 countries, injury to US industry from foreign subsidized and less than fair value imports, investigation with background financial and operating data, 1990 rpt, 9886–19.73

Tobacco and cigarette production, use, and trade, for Israel, 1981-90, article, 1925–16.202

UN voting record and share of votes in agreement with US, by issue, country, and world area, 1990, annual rpt, 7004–18

see also under By Foreign Country in the "Index by Categories"

Israelevich, Philip R.

"Census Content of Bureau of Economic Analysis Input-Output Data", 9375–13.53

"Deregulation, Cost Economies and Allocative Efficiency of Large Commercial Banks", 9375–13.50

"Hog Butchers No Longer: 20 Years of Employment Change in Metropolitan Chicago", 9375–1.204

"Productive Efficiency in Banking", 9375–1.209

"Scale Elasticity and Efficiency for U.S. Banks", 9375–13.66

Italy

Agricultural exports of high-value commodities, indexes and sales by commodity, world area, and country, 1960s-86, 1528–323

Agricultural production, prices, and trade, by country, 1970s-90, and forecast 1991, annual world region rpt, 1524–4.4

Agricultural production, trade, and policies in foreign countries, summary data by country, 1989-90, annual factbook, 1924–12

Agricultural trade of US, by detailed commodity and country, 1989, annual rpt, 1524–8

Agricultural trade of US, by detailed commodity and country, 1990, semiannual rpt, 1522–4

AID economic aid to developing countries, obligations and disbursements by country, quarterly rpt, 9912–4

AID loans repayment status and terms by program and country, and status of predecessor agency loans, quarterly rpt, 9912–3

Background Notes, summary social, political, and economic data, 1990 rpt, 7006–2.2

Dollar exchange rates of selected foreign countries, weekly chartbook, 9365–1.5

Drug abuse indicators, by world region and selected country, 1990 semiannual conf, 4492–5.1

Economic aid of US and other donor countries by type and recipient, and role in advancing economic interests, 1980s-90, 2048–152

Economic and military aid and loans from US and intl agencies, by program and country, FY46-90, annual rpt, 9914–5

Economic and monetary trends, compounded annual rates of change and quarterly indicators for US and 7 major industrialized countries, quarterly rpt, 9391–7

Economic conditions, and oil supply and demand, for major industrial countries, biweekly rpt, 9112–1

Economic conditions, consumer and stock prices and production indexes, 6 OECD countries and US, *Business Conditions Digest*, monthly rpt, 2702–1.2

Economic conditions in USSR, Eastern Europe, OECD, and selected other countries, 1960s-90, annual rpt, 9114–4

Economic conditions, income, production, prices, employment, and trade, 1991 periodic country rpt, 2046–4.61

Economic conditions, policy, and trade practices, by country, 1988-90, annual rpt, 21384–5

Economic indicators, and dollar exchange rates, for selected OECD countries, 1991 semiannual rpt, 8002–14

Economic, social, political, and geographic summary data, by country, 1991, annual factbook, 9114–2

Energy prices, by fuel type and end use, for 10 countries, 1980-89 annual rpt, 3164–50.6

Energy production by type, and oil trade, and use, by country group and selected country, monthly rpt, 9112–2

European Monetary System countries interest rate differentials with Germany, relation to fiscal policy, with model results for Italy, 1979-90, technical paper, 9366–7.259

Exports and imports of NATO members with PRC, by country, 1987-90, annual rpt, 7144–14

Exports and imports of OECD members, by country, 1989, annual rpt, 7144–10

Index by Subjects and Names

Exports and imports of US by country, and trade shifts by commodity, 1990, semiannual rpt, 9882–9

Exports and imports of US, by Harmonized System 6-digit commodity and country, 1990, annual rpt, 2424–13

Exports and imports of US, by selected country, country group, and commodity group, 1990, annual rpt, 2044–37

Exports and imports of US, by transport mode, country, and SITC 1- to 3-digit commodity, 1990, annual rpt, 2424–12

Exports and imports of US with EC by country, and total agricultural trade, selected years 1958-90, annual rpt, 7144–7

Exports, imports, and balances of US with major trading partners, by product category, 1986-90, annual chartbook, 9884–21

Exports of US, detailed Schedule B commodities with countries of destination, 1990, annual rpt, 2424–10

Fish (squid) catch, trade, consumption, and cold storage holdings, by country and species, 1963-90, 2166–19.10

Fish trade between Italy and US, by commodity, 1981-88, article, 2162–1.201

GNP and GNP growth for OECD members, by country, 1980-90, annual rpt, 7144–8

Hazelnut production, supply, trade, and use, by country, 1989-92, article, 1925–34.246

Human rights conditions in 170 countries, and US economic and military aid, 1990, annual rpt, 21384–3

Imports of goods, services, and investment from US, trade barriers, impacts, and US actions, by country, 1990, annual rpt, 444–2

Interest rates and spread relation to regional income and debt, and outside borrowing, model description and results for Italy, 1981-84, technical paper, 9366–7.248

Intl transactions of US with 9 countries, 1986-88, *Survey of Current Business*, monthly rpt, annual table, 2702–1.26

Investment (foreign direct) in US, by industry group of US affiliate and country of parent firm, 1980-86, 2708–41

Multinatl US firms and foreign affiliates finances and operations, by industry and world area of parent firm, 1989 benchmark survey, preliminary annual rpt, 2704–5

Multinatl US firms foreign affiliates, income statement items by country and world area, 1986, biennial article, 8302–2.212

Nuclear power generation in US and 20 countries, monthly rpt, 3162–24.10

Nuclear power plant capacity, generation, and operating status, by plant and foreign and US location, 1990 and projected to 2030, annual rpt, 3164–57

Oil production, trade, use, and stocks, by selected country and country group, monthly rpt, 3162–42

Oil production, use, stocks, and exports to US, by country, detailed data, monthly rpt with articles, 3162–24

Paper (coated groundwood) from 9 countries at less than fair value, injury to US industry, investigation with background financial and operating data, 1991 rpt, 9886–14.306

Index by Subjects and Names

Science and engineering employment and education, and R&D spending, for US and selected foreign countries, 1991 annual rpt, 9627–35

Ships in world merchant fleet, tonnage, and new ship construction and deliveries, by vessel type and country, as of Jan 1990, annual rpt, 7704–3

Spacecraft and satellite launches since 1957, quarterly listing, 9502–2

Tax revenue, by level of govt and type of tax, for OECD countries, mid 1960s-89, annual rpt, 10044–1.2

Telecommunications industry intl competitiveness, with financial and operating data by product or service, firm, and country, 1990 rpt, 2008–30

Transportation energy use, fuel prices, vehicle registrations, and mileage, by selected country, 1970s-89, annual rpt, 3304–5.1

Travel to US, trade shows and other promotional activities, with magazine ad costs and circulation, for selected countries, 1991-92, annual rpt, 2904–11

UN voting record and share of votes in agreement with US, by issue, country, and world area, 1990, annual rpt, 7004–18

see also San Marino

see also Vatican City

see also under By Foreign Country in the "Index by Categories"

Iversen, Kirsten

"Dynamics of Hospital Services: Changing Patterns in the Services Provided by Hospitals from 1980 to 1987", 17206–2.22

"Medicaid Hospital Payment", 17206–1.11

Ivory Coast

Agricultural exports of high-value commodities, indexes and sales by commodity, world area, and country, 1960s-86, 1528–323

Agricultural production, prices, and trade, by country, 1960s-90, annual world area rpt, 1524–4.2

Agricultural production, trade, and policies in foreign countries, summary data by country, 1989-90, annual factbook, 1924–12

Agricultural trade of US, by detailed commodity and country, 1989, annual rpt, 1524–8

Agricultural trade of US, by detailed commodity and country, 1990, semiannual rpt, 1522–4

AID economic aid to developing countries, obligations and disbursements by country, quarterly rpt, 9912–4

AID loans repayment status and terms by program and country, and status of predecessor agency loans, quarterly rpt, 9912–3

Dairy imports, consumption, and market conditions, by sub-Saharan Africa country, 1961-88, 1528–321

Economic and military aid and loans from US and intl agencies, by program and country, FY46-90, annual rpt, 9914–5

Economic and social conditions of developing countries from 1960s, and Intl Dev Cooperation Agency and AID activities and funding, FY90-92, annual rpt, 9904–4

Economic conditions, income, production, prices, employment, and trade, 1990 periodic country rpt, 2046–4.1

Economic, social, political, and geographic summary data, by country, 1991, annual factbook, 9114–2

Exports and imports of US, by commodity and country, 1970-89, world area rpt, 9116–1.6

Exports and imports of US, by selected country, country group, and commodity group, 1990, annual rpt, 2044–37

Exports and imports of US, by transport mode, country, and SITC 1- to 3-digit commodity, 1990, annual rpt, 2424–12

Exports of US, detailed Schedule B commodities with countries of destination, 1990, annual rpt, 2424–10

Food supply, needs, and aid for developing countries, status and alternative forecasts, 1991 world area rpt, 1526–8.1

Human rights conditions in 170 countries, and US economic and military aid, 1990, annual rpt, 21384–3

Military aid of US, arms sales, and training programs costs and budget requests, by program, world region, and country, FY90-92, annual rpt, 7144–13

UN voting record and share of votes in agreement with US, by issue, country, and world area, 1990, annual rpt, 7004–18

see also under By Foreign Country in the "Index by Categories"

Iyasu, Solomon

"Surveillance of Postneonatal Mortality, U.S., 1980-87", 4202–7.208

Jackson, Mich.

see also under By SMSA or MSA in the "Index by Categories"

Jackson, Miss.

Wages by occupation, for office and plant workers, 1991 survey, periodic MSA rpt, 6785–12.1

see also under By City and By SMSA or MSA in the "Index by Categories"

Jackson, Tenn.

see also under By SMSA or MSA in the "Index by Categories"

Jacksonville, Fla.

Housing starts and completions authorized by building permits in 40 MSAs, quarterly rpt, 2382–9

Wages by occupation, for office and plant workers, 1990 survey, periodic MSA rpt, 6785–3.4

see also under By City and By SMSA or MSA in the "Index by Categories"

Jacksonville, N.C.

Wages by occupation, for office and plant workers, 1991 survey, periodic MSA rpt, 6785–3.9

see also under By SMSA or MSA in the "Index by Categories"

Jaditz, Ted

"Economic Markets and the Standard Industrial Classification", 6886–6.74

Jagger, Craig

"Farmer-Owned Reserve—Old Name, New Game: An Analysis of New Rules and 1990 Wheat Crop Entry", 1561–12.201

Jamaica

Jails

see Correctional institutions

Jain, Rita S.

"Trends in Employer-Provided Health Care Benefits", 6722–1.214

Jamaica

Agricultural exports of high-value commodities, indexes and sales by commodity, world area, and country, 1960s-86, 1528–323

Agricultural exports of US, impacts of foreign agricultural and trade policy, with data by commodity and country, 1989, annual rpt, 1924–8

Agricultural trade of US, by detailed commodity and country, 1989, annual rpt, 1524–8

Agricultural trade of US, by detailed commodity and country, 1990, semiannual rpt, 1522–4

AID economic aid to developing countries, obligations and disbursements by country, quarterly rpt, 9912–4

AID loans repayment status and terms by program and country, and status of predecessor agency loans, quarterly rpt, 9912–3

Economic and military aid and loans from US and intl agencies, by program and country, FY46-90, annual rpt, 9914–5

Economic and social conditions of developing countries from 1960s, and Intl Dev Cooperation Agency and AID activities and funding, FY90-92, annual rpt, 9904–4

Economic conditions, policy, and trade practices, by country, 1988-90, annual rpt, 21384–5

Economic, social, political, and geographic summary data, by country, 1991, annual factbook, 9114–2

Exports and imports of US, by commodity and country, 1970-89, world area rpt, 9116–1.5

Exports and imports of US, by Harmonized System 6-digit commodity and country, 1990, annual rpt, 2424–13

Exports and imports of US, by selected country, country group, and commodity group, 1990, annual rpt, 2044–37

Exports and imports of US, by transport mode, country, and SITC 1- to 3-digit commodity, 1990, annual rpt, 2424–12

Exports of US, detailed Schedule B commodities with countries of destination, 1990, annual rpt, 2424–10

Grain production and needs, and related economic outlook, by world area and selected country, forecast 1990/91-1991/92, 1528–313

Human rights conditions in 170 countries, and US economic and military aid, 1990, annual rpt, 21384–3

Investment (direct) incentives of Caribbean Basin Initiative, economic impacts, with finances and employment by country, 1984-90, 2048–141

Military aid of US, arms sales, and training programs costs and budget requests, by program, world region, and country, FY90-92, annual rpt, 7144–13

Multinatl US firms and foreign affiliates finances and operations, by industry and world area of parent firm, 1989 benchmark survey, preliminary annual rpt, 2704–5

Jamaica

Older population and selected characteristics, 1980s and projected to 2020, country rpt, 2326–19.6

Rum imports (duty-free) of US under Caribbean Basin Initiative, by country, 1989-90, annual rpt, 9884–15

UN voting record and share of votes in agreement with US, by issue, country, and world area, 1990, annual rpt, 7004–18

see also under By Foreign Country in the "Index by Categories"

James, Levy M.

"Temporal Trends in the Prevalence of Congenital Malformations at Birth Based on the Birth Defects Monitoring Program, U.S., 1979-87", 4202–7.203

James River

Ships in Natl Defense Reserve Fleet at James River, as of Jan 1991, semiannual listing, 7702–2

Jameson, Rosemary

"Domestic Natural Gas Reserves and Production Dedicated to Interstate Pipeline Companies, 1990", 3162–4.209

Jamestown, N.Y.

see also under By SMSA or MSA in the "Index by Categories"

Jamison, David

"1990 Promotional Activities Under Federal Milk Orders", 1317–4.204

Jamison, Ellen

"Scientists and Engineers in Canada and Sweden", 2326–18.63

"Scientists and Engineers in Industrialized Societies: An Update for France, West Germany, and the UK", 2326–18.62

"Scientists and Engineers in Malaysia, South Korea, and Taiwan", 2326–18.61

Janesville, Wis.

see also under By SMSA or MSA in the "Index by Categories"

Janitorial and maintenance services

County Business Patterns, 1988: employment, establishments, and payroll, by SIC 2- to 4-digit industry and county, annual State rpt series, 2326–6

County Business Patterns, 1989: employment, establishments, and payroll, by SIC 2- to 4-digit industry and county, annual State rpt series, 2326–8

Employee (temporary) supply establishments by occupation supplied, receipts by source, and payroll, by MSA, 1987 Census of Service Industries, 2393–4.8

Employment, earnings, and hours, by SIC 1- to 4-digit industry, monthly and annual averages, selected years 1909-90, annual rpt, 6744–4

Enterprise Statistics, 1987: finances and operations for companies, by size, level of diversification, form of organization, and industry group, 2329–8

Franchise business opportunities by firm and kind of business, and sources of aid and info, 1990 annual listing, 2104–7

Manufacturing employment, by detailed occupation and SIC 2-digit industry, 1989 survey, triennial rpt, 6748–52

Occupational injury and illness rates, by SIC 2- to 4-digit industry, 1988-89, annual rpt, 6844–7

Occupational injury and illness rates, by SIC 2- to 4-digit industry, 1989, annual rpt, 6844–1

Postal Service operating costs, itemized by class of mail, FY90, annual rpt, 9864–4

Receipts for services, by SIC 2- to 4-digit kind of business, 1990, annual rpt, 2413–8

Service industries census, 1987: depreciable assets, capital and operating expenses, and receipts, by SIC 2- to 4-digit kind of business, 2393–2

Service industries census, 1987: establishments, receipts by source, payroll, and employment, by SIC 2- to 4-digit kind of business, State, and MSA, 2393–4

see also Domestic workers and services

Jankowski, Louis W.

"Jail Inmates, 1990", 6066–25.38

"Probation and Parole 1989", 6066–25.34

Jansen, Anicca

"Rural Counties Lead Urban in Education Spending, but Is That Enough?", 1502–7.201

Japan

Agricultural exports of high-value commodities from developing countries to OECD, 1970s-87, 1528–316

Agricultural exports of high-value commodities, indexes and sales by commodity, world area, and country, 1960s-86, 1528–323

Agricultural exports of US, for grains, oilseed products, hides, skins, and cotton, by country, weekly rpt, 1922–3

Agricultural exports of US, impacts of foreign agricultural and trade policy, with data by commodity and country, 1989, annual rpt, 1924–8

Agricultural imports of Japan, total and from US, by commodity, 1989-90, article, 1925–34.215

Agricultural production, prices, and trade, by country, 1980s and forecast 1991, annual world region rpt, 1524–4.5

Agricultural production, trade, and policies in foreign countries, summary data by country, 1989-90, annual factbook, 1924–12

Agricultural trade by commodity and country, prices, and world market devs, monthly rpt, 1922–12

Agricultural trade of US, by detailed commodity and country, 1989, annual rpt, 1524–8

Agricultural trade of US, by detailed commodity and country, 1990, semiannual rpt, 1522–4

AID loans repayment status and terms by program and country, and status of predecessor agency loans, quarterly rpt, 9912–3

Auto industry finances and operations, trade by country, and prices of selected US and foreign models, monthly rpt, 9882–8

Autos (minivans) from Japan at less than fair value, injury to US industry, investigation with background financial and operating data, 1991 rpt, 9886–14.320

Background Notes, summary social, political, and economic data, 1990 rpt, 7006–2.12

Balance of payments by component, and foreign securities purchases by country, for Japan, 1980s-90, article, 9393–8.204

Balance of trade with US and other countries, for Japan, mid 1960s-88, article, 9391–1.209

Index by Subjects and Names

Banking intl competition and deposit insurance reform issues, with background data, 1990 hearings, 25248–122

Banking intl competition issues, with background data, 1980s, 21248–153

Banks capital costs, operating ratios, and intl market shares, for US and 5 OECD countries, 1980s-90, article, 9385–1.203

Banks financial performance, risk assessment, and regulation, 1990 annual conf papers, 9375–7

Banks in Japan, US affiliates loans by borrower type, late 1984-89, technical paper, 9385–8.97

Banks restrictions on business equity ownership, issues, with data for venture capital financing and comparisons to West Germany and Japan, 1970s-90, article, 9393–8.206

Beef imports under quota, from US, Australia, and New Zealand, 1977-90, semiannual rpt, 1925–33.2

Benzyl paraben from Japan at less than fair value, injury to US industry, investigation with background financial and operating data, 1991 rpt, 9886–14.303

Biotechnology commercial applications, industry finances and capitalization, patents, and govt support, for US, Japan, and EC, late 1970s-91, 26358–248

Businesses (foreign) activity in US, income tax returns, assets, and income statement items, by industry div and selected country, 1986-87, article, 8302–2.205

Capital cost indicators and contributing factors, for US and Japan, 1920s-90, article, 9385–1.202

Cement (portland) and clinker from Japan at less than fair value, injury to US industry, investigation with background financial and operating data, 1991 rpt, 9886–14.309

Computer displays (high-info content flat panel) from Japan at less than fair value, injury to US industry, investigation with background financial and operating data, 1991 rpt, 9886–14.328

Coral harvest of Japan by species, and imports by country, 1981-88, article, 2162–1.201

Corporations in Japan, finances of firms affiliated with integrated conglomerates and independent firms, 1976-89, article, 9375–1.203

Corporations in US under foreign control, income tax returns, assets and income statement items by industry div, country, and world area, 1988, article, 8302–2.219

Dollar exchange rate trade-weighted index of Fed Reserve Bank of Dallas, by world area, monthly rpt, 9379–13

Dollar exchange rates of yen and mark, impact of Fed Reserve policy interventions and other economic indicators, 1985-89, technical paper, 9385–8.114

Drug (methamphetamine) abuse, availability, health effects, and treatment, 1990 conf papers, 4498–75

Economic aid of US and other donor countries by type and recipient, and role in advancing economic interests, 1980s-90, 2048–152

Economic and military aid and loans from US and intl agencies, by program and country, FY46-90, annual rpt, 9914–5

Index by Subjects and Names

Japan

Economic and monetary trends, compounded annual rates of change and quarterly indicators for US and 7 major industrialized countries, quarterly rpt, 9391–7

Economic conditions, and oil supply and demand, for major industrial countries, biweekly rpt, 9112–1

Economic conditions, consumer and stock prices and production indexes, 6 OECD countries and US, *Business Conditions Digest*, monthly rpt, 2702–1.2

Economic conditions, financial and intl policies, and trade devs, for Japan, 1950s-80s and projected to 2050, compilation of papers, 23848–220

Economic conditions in Communist and OECD countries, 1989, annual rpt, 7144–11

Economic conditions in USSR, Eastern Europe, OECD, and selected other countries, 1960s-90, annual rpt, 9114–4

Economic conditions, policy, and trade practices, by country, 1988-90, annual rpt, 21384–5

Economic indicators, and dollar exchange rates, for selected OECD countries, 1991 semiannual rpt, 8002–14

Economic, social, political, and geographic summary data, by country, 1991, annual factbook, 9114–2

Education and cultural exchange activities of Japan-US Friendship Commission, grants, and trust fund status, FY89-90, biennial rpt, 14694–1

Energy conservation measures impacts on consumption, by component and end-use sector, 1970s-88 and projected under alternative oil prices to 1995, 3308–93

Energy prices, by fuel type and end use, for 10 countries, 1980-89 annual rpt, 3164–50.6

Energy production by type, and oil trade, and use, by country group and selected country, monthly rpt, 9112–2

Energy use and production, by fuel type, country, and country group, projected 1995-2010 and trends from 1970, annual rpt, 3164–84

Exports and imports between Japan and US, bilateral trade balances and indicators of surplus and deficit persistence for detailed commodity groups, 1962-88, technical paper, 9366–7.264

Exports and imports, intl position of US and 4 OECD countries, and factors affecting US competition, periodic pamphlet, 2042–25

Exports and imports of OECD members, by country, 1989, annual rpt, 7144–10

Exports and imports of OECD, total and for 4 major countries, and US trade by country, by commodity, 1970-89, world area rpt series, 9116–1

Exports and imports of US by country, and trade shifts by commodity, 1990, semiannual rpt, 9882–9

Exports and imports of US, by Harmonized System 6-digit commodity and country, 1990, annual rpt, 2424–13

Exports and imports of US, by selected country, country group, and commodity group, 1990, annual rpt, 2044–37

Exports and imports of US, by transport mode, country, and SITC 1- to 3-digit commodity, 1990, annual rpt, 2424–12

Exports and imports, trade agreements and relations, and USITC investigations, 1990, annual rpt, 9884–5

Exports, imports, and balances of US, by selected country, country group, and commodity group, preliminary data, monthly rpt, 2042–34

Exports, imports, and balances of US with major trading partners, by product category, 1986-90, annual chartbook, 9884–21

Exports of US, detailed Schedule B commodities with countries of destination, 1990, annual rpt, 2424–10

Film (polyethylene terephthalate) from 2 countries at less than fair value, injury to US industry, investigation with background financial and operating data, 1991 rpt, 9886–14.313

Financial instns and stock market conditions, and other economic indicators, for Japan with intl comparisons, 1980s-90, hearing, 21248–152

Financial instns with intl operations, assets by selected banking and securities instn, and financial performance indicators by selected country, late 1980s-90, article, 9385–1.206

Fish (squid) catch, trade, consumption, and cold storage holdings, by country and species, 1963-90, 2166–19.10

Fish (surimi) production and trade by country, and Japan import and catch quotas, 1975-89, article, 2162–1.202

Fish and shellfish aquaculture in US and Japan, mgmt, methods, and biological data for selected species, 1988 conf, annual rpt, 2164–15

Fish catch, prices, and trade of Japan, by selected species, and foreign fisheries aid by country, 1976-88, articles, 2162–1.201

Fish catch, prices, trade by country, cold storage holdings, and market devs, for Japan, semimonthly press release, 2162–7

Fish imports of Japan from Vietnam, by commodity, 1984-88, article, 2162–1.204

GNP and GNP growth for OECD members, by country, 1980-90, annual rpt, 7144–8

Health care cost control measures and insurance provisions, for Germany, France, and Japan, 1960s-91, GAO rpt, 26121–437

Human rights conditions in 170 countries, and US economic and military aid, 1990, annual rpt, 21384–3

Import restraint elimination impacts on US economy and selected service industries, 1970s-90, 9886–4.173

Imports of goods, services, and investment from US, trade barriers, impacts, and US actions, by country, 1990, annual rpt, 444–2

Imports of US given duty-free treatment for value of US material sent abroad, by commodity and country, 1989, annual rpt, 9884–14

Inflation forecasting performance of expected long run inflation rate and other models, for Japan and Germany, 1970s-89, technical paper, 9366–7.268

Interest and exchange rates, security yields, and stock indexes, for selected foreign countries, weekly chartbook, 9365–1.5

Interest rates relation to monetary policy and financial instn regulation in Japan,

with background data and model results, 1960s-91, article, 9385–1.213; 9385–8.116

Investment (foreign direct) in US, by industry group and world area, 1987-90, annual article, 2702–1.219

Investment (foreign direct) in US, by industry group of US affiliate and country of parent firm, 1980-86, 2708–41

Investment (foreign direct) in US, major transactions by type, industry, country, and US location, 1989, annual rpt, 2044–20

Investment (foreign direct) in US manufacturing, impacts on trade balances, with data by industry, 1980s-93, technical paper, 9385–8.91

Labor conditions, union coverage, and work accidents, 1991 annual country rpt, 6366–4.30

Labor costs and indexes, by selected country, 1990, semiannual rpt, 6822–3

Labor shortages, for Japan and 4 east Asia countries, 1991 rpt, 6366–4.17

Lenses (aspherical ophthalmoscopy) from Japan at less than fair value, injury to US industry, investigation with background financial and operating data, 1991 rpt, 9886–14.318

Manufacturing firms of Japan, US affiliates, employment, and wages, by selected industry and State, 1980s, 2048–151

Microwave ovens (commercial) from Japan at less than fair value, injury to US industry, investigation with background financial and operating data, 1991 rpt, 9886–14.322

Military spending and indicators of ability to support common defense, for NATO members and Japan, 1970s-89, annual rpt, 3544–28

Military weapons trade, production, and defense industry finances, with data by firm and country, 1980s-91, 26358–241

Money supply forecast accuracy impact of monetary target announcements, for US and Japan, 1978-88, working paper, 9393–10.16

Multinatl firms US affiliates, finances, and operations, by industry, world area of parent firm, and State, 1988-89, annual rpt, 2704–4

Multinatl firms US affiliates, investment trends and impact on US economy, 1991 annual rpt, 2004–9

Multinatl US firms and foreign affiliates finances and operations, by industry and world area of parent firm, 1989 benchmark survey, preliminary annual rpt, 2704–5

Multinatl US firms foreign affiliates, income statement items by country and world area, 1986, biennial article, 8302–2.212

Natural gas and liquefied gas trade of US with 5 countries, by US firm, 1955-90, annual article, 3162–4.208

Nuclear power generation in US and 20 countries, monthly rpt, 3162–24.10

Nuclear power plant capacity, generation, and operating status, by plant and foreign and US location, 1990 and projected to 2030, annual rpt, 3164–57

Oil production, trade, use, and stocks, by selected country and country group, monthly rpt, 3162–42

Japan

Oil supply, demand, and stock forecasts, by world area, quarterly rpt, 3162–34

Oil use and stocks for selected OECD countries, monthly rpt, 3162–24.10

Science and engineering employment and education, and R&D spending, for US and selected foreign countries, 1991 annual rpt, 9627–35

Securities firms equity capital costs and financial ratios, with data by firm, for US and Japan, 1980s-91, article, 9385–1.212

Semiconductors and related equipment import dependency of US firms, and sales from Japan firms delayed and denied, 1988-91, GAO rpt, 26123–361

Ships freight rates for lumber from Alaska and Puget Sound to Asian markets, by product and port, 1988, 1208–358

Ships in world merchant fleet, tonnage, and new ship construction and deliveries, by vessel type and country, as of Jan 1990, annual rpt, 7704–3

Space programs activities, missions, launchings, payloads, and flight duration, for foreign and US programs, 1957-90, annual rpt, 21704–4

Space programs involvement by private sector, govt contracts, costs, revenue, and R&D spending, 1970s-80s and projected to 2000, 26306–6.154

Spacecraft and satellite launches since 1957, quarterly listing, 9502–2

Steel imports of US under voluntary restraint agreement, by product, customs district, and country, with US industry operating data, quarterly rpt, 9882–13

Stock and bond returns for foreign and domestic instruments, relationship to selected economic indicators for US, UK, and Japan, 1970s-80s, article, 9385–1.211

Stock margin requirements impact on stock prices, volatility, and trading activity, 1951-88, technical paper, 9385–8.72

Tax revenue, by level of govt and type of tax, for OECD countries, mid 1960s-89, annual rpt, 10044–1.2

Telecommunications industry intl competitiveness, with financial and operating data by product or service, firm, and country, 1990 rpt, 2008–30

Tidal currents, daily time and velocity by station for North America and Asia coasts, forecast 1992, annual rpt, 2174–1.2

Timber in northwestern US and British Columbia, production, prices, trade, and employment, quarterly rpt, 1202–3

Timber products consumption, and imports by country, for Japan, 1960s-2010, 1208–365; 1208–367

Transportation energy use, fuel prices, vehicle registrations, and mileage, by selected country, 1970s-89, annual rpt, 3304–5.1

Travel to US, trade shows and other promotional activities, with magazine ad costs and circulation, for selected countries, 1991-92, annual rpt, 2904–11

UN voting record and share of votes in agreement with US, by issue, country, and world area, 1990, annual rpt, 7004–18

US military presence in Pacific basin, personnel, dependents, aircraft, ships, and costs, by service branch and location, 1990, GAO rpt, 26123–357

Wheat quality indicators, for US exports and foreign wheat production, 1960s-90, hearing, 25168–75

Word processors (personal) from Japan and Singapore at less than fair value, injury to US industry, investigation with background financial and operating data, 1990 rpt, 9886–14.302

Word processors from Japan at less than fair value, injury to US industry, investigation with background financial and operating data, 1991 rpt, 9886–14.325

see also under By Foreign Country in the "Index by Categories"

Japan-U.S. Friendship Commission

Budget of US, authoritative financial statements with appropriations, outlays, and receipts, by category and agency, FY90, annual rpt, 8104–2.1

Budget of US, obligations and authority by function, agency, and program, with summaries, analyses, and historical tables, FY92, annual rpt, 104–2

Education and cultural exchange activities, grants, and trust fund status, FY89-90, biennial rpt, 14694–1

Education funding by Federal agency, program, and recipient type, and instn spending, FY80-90, annual rpt, 4824–8

Japanese Americans

see Asian Americans

Jefferis, Richard H., Jr.

"Expectations and the Core Rate of Inflation", 9377–1.201

Jefferson County, Ala.

Housing and households characteristics, unit and neighborhood quality, and journey to work by MSA location, for 11 MSAs, 1984 survey, supplement, 2485–8

Jeffries, Steven J.

"Population Status and Condition of the Harbor Seal, *Phoca vitulina richardsi*, in the Waters of the State of Washington: 1975-80", 14738–7

Jencks, Stephen F.

"Accessibility and Effectiveness of Care Under Medicaid", 4652–1.210

Jenkins, Sarah

"Lender Profitability in the Student Loan Program", 4808–36

Jennings, Jerry T.

"Voting and Registration in the Election of November 1990", 2546–1.454

Jersey City, N.J.

see also under By City and By SMSA or MSA in the "Index by Categories"

Jervis, Lance

"1990 Promotional Activities Under Federal Milk Orders", 1317–4.204

Jet fuel

see Aviation fuels

Jewelry

County Business Patterns, 1988: employment, establishments, and payroll, by SIC 2- to 4-digit industry and county, annual State rpt series, 2326–6

County Business Patterns, 1989: employment, establishments, and payroll, by SIC 2- to 4-digit industry and county, annual State rpt series, 2326–8

CPI by component for US city average, and by region, population size, and for 27 metro areas, monthly rpt, 6762–2

Employment, earnings, and hours, by SIC 1- to 4-digit industry, monthly and annual averages, selected years 1909-90, annual rpt, 6744–4

Index by Subjects and Names

Endangered animals and plants US trade and permits, by species, purpose, disposition, and country, 1989, annual rpt, 5504–19

Exports and imports of jewelry, gold jewelry production and sales, and US and EC gold and silver fineness standards, by country, 1980s, hearing, 25388–58

Exports and imports of US, by Harmonized System 6-digit commodity and country, 1990, annual rpt, 2424–13

Exports and imports of US, by selected country, country group, and commodity group, 1990, annual rpt, 2044–37

Exports and imports of US, by transport mode, country, and SITC 1- to 3-digit commodity, 1990, annual rpt, 2424–12

Exports of US, detailed Schedule B commodities with countries of destination, 1990, annual rpt, 2424–10

Imports of US given duty-free treatment for value of US material sent abroad, by commodity and country, 1989, annual rpt, 9884–14

Injuries from use of consumer products, by severity, victim age, and detailed product, 1990, annual rpt, 9164–6

Manufacturing annual survey, 1989: finances and operations, by SIC 2- to 4-digit industry, series, 2506–15

Manufacturing census, 1987: finances and operations, by SIC 2- to 4-digit industry, State, and MSA, with trends from 1849, 2497–1

Manufacturing census, 1987: finances and operations, by type of organization and SIC 2- to 4-digit industry, subject rpt, 2497–5

Manufacturing finances and operations, by SIC 2- to 4-digit industry, forecast 1991, annual rpt, 2044–28

Occupational injury and illness rates, by SIC 2- to 4-digit industry, 1988-89, annual rpt, 6844–7

Occupational injury and illness rates, by SIC 2- to 4-digit industry, 1989, annual rpt, 6844–1

OECD trade, total and for 4 major countries, and US trade by country, by commodity, 1970-89, world area rpt series, 9116–1

Price indexes (producer), by stage of processing and detailed commodity, monthly rpt, 6762–6

Price indexes (producer), by stage of processing and detailed commodity, monthly 1990, annual rpt, 6764–2

Price indexes for department store inventories, by class of item, monthly table, 6762–7

Puerto Rico economic censuses, 1987: wholesale and retail trade and service industry finances and operations, by SIC 2- to 4-digit industry and municipio, 2591–1

Retail trade census, 1987: finances and employment, for establishments with and without payroll, by SIC 2- to 4-digit kind of business, State, and MSA, 2401–1

Retail trade sales and inventories, by kind of business, region, and selected State, MSA, and city, monthly rpt, 2413–3

Retail trade sales, inventories, purchases, gross margin, and accounts receivable, by SIC 2- to 4-digit kind of business and form of ownership, 1989, annual rpt, 2413–5

Index by Subjects and Names

Thefts, and value of property stolen and recovered, by property type, 1990, annual rpt, 6224–2.1

see also Gemstones

Jinkins, John E.

"Profile of Specialized Fruit and Vegetable Farms in 1989", 1541–1.209

"Small Farmers Weathered 1980's Financial Stress Better than Large Farmers", 1502–7.202

"Which Farmers Will Be Most Affected by Increasing Oil Prices?", 1541–1.203

Job Corps

Forest Service acreage, staff, finances, and mgmt activities in Pacific Northwest, with data by forest, 1970s-89, annual rpt, 1204–37

Forest Service activities and finances, by region and State, FY90, annual rpt, 1204–1.4

Fraud and abuse in DOL programs, audits and investigations, 2nd half FY91, semiannual rpt, 6302–2

Reclamation Bur activities and finances, FY90, annual rpt, 5824–1

Job creation

Disabled persons workshops finances, operations, and Federal procurement, FY80-90, annual rpt, 11714–1

Economic Dev Admin activities, and funding by program, recipient, State, and county, FY90 and cumulative from FY66, annual rpt, 2064–2

Employment conditions, alternative BLS projections to 2005 and trends 1970s-90, biennial article, 6722–1.253

Energy-related inventions supported by DOE, sales, jobs created, and inventor financing, 1980-88, 3308–91

Exports and export-related employment generated by Overseas Private Investment Corp projects, FY90, annual rpt, 9904–2

Forecasts of employment conditions, alternative BLS projections to 2005 and trends 1970s-90, biennial article, 6722–1.254

Manufacturing job creation, elimination, and reallocation rates, and relation to industry and establishment characteristics, 1970s-86, working paper, 9375–13.56

North Carolina environmental and socioeconomic conditions, and impacts of proposed OCS oil and gas exploration, 1970s-90 and projected to 2020, 5738–22

State and Metro Area Data Book, 1991 data compilation, 2328–54

Tax (income) returns filed by type of filer, selected income items, quarterly rpt, 8302–2.1

Tax credit for hiring from groups with high unemployment rates, participation by State, and effectiveness, FY88, GAO rpt, 26121–407

Tax expenditures, Federal revenues forgone through income tax deductions and exclusions by type, FY92-96, annual rpt, 21784–10

Tennessee Valley industrial dev and employment, by SIC 2-digit industry, firm, and location, 1990, annual rpt, 9804–3

Job discrimination

see Discrimination in employment

Job placement

see Employment services

Job tenure

Air traffic control and airway facilities supervisors task priorities, skills needed, and other characteristics, 1990 survey, technical rpt, 7506–10.84

Black American displaced workers, by demographic and current and former employment characteristics, and compared to whites, 1978-86, article, 6722–1.234

Earnings impact of educational attainment and work experience, model description and results for men, by census div, 1979-88, article, 9373–1.213

Education data compilation, 1991 annual rpt, 4824–2

Entry level employment, and share without previous experience in field, by detailed occupation, 1986, article, 6742–1.201

Fed Bur of Prisons correctional staff by selected characteristics, and inmates, by facility, data compilation, 1991 annual rpt, 6064–6.1

Fed Govt Senior Executive Service membership characteristics, entries, exits, and awards, FY79-90, annual rpt, 9844–36

IRS revenue agent attrition, separations by reason, and hires, by region and district, FY87-90, GAO rpt, 26119–345

Law enforcement officer assaults and deaths by circumstances, agency, victim and offender characteristics, and location, 1990, annual rpt, 6224–3

Military pay and benefits for active duty personnel, reserves, retirees, and survivors, 1940s-80s and projected to 2049, 21208–34

Military reserve forces personnel strengths and characteristics, by component, FY90, annual rpt, 3544–38

Military women personnel on active and reserve duty, by demographic and service characteristics and service branch, FY89, annual chartbook, 3544–26

Mines (underground coal) back injuries, by circumstances, victim characteristics, and treatment, mid 1980s, 5608–166

Mines occupational deaths, by circumstances and selected victim characteristics, semiannual rpt series, 6662–3

NASA staff characteristics and personnel actions, FY90, annual rpt, 9504–1

Pension benefits disparity between men and women in small business plans by selected participant and plan characteristics, impacts of 1986 Tax Reform Act, 1984-85, GAO rpt, 26121–412

Statistical Abstract of US, 1991 annual data compilation, 2324–1.13

Teacher employment, vacancies, and pay, by State, region, and school enrollment size, 1987/88, 4836–3.6

Teachers in higher education instns, personnel policies, pay, work conditions, and other characteristics, by instn type and control, 1987/88 survey, quadrennial rpt series, 4846–4

Teachers in private schools, selected characteristics by instn level, size, and orientation, various periods 1979-88, 4838–47

Truck accidents, by carrier financial and operating conditions and driver characteristics, 1980s, GAO rpt, 26131–82

Job vacancy

Vacation days paid, by length of service, 1988, 6722–1.204; 15496–1.11

see also Labor mobility

see also Labor turnover

Job training

see Apprenticeship

see Employee development

see Manpower training programs

see Vocational education and training

see Vocational rehabilitation

Job Training Partnership Act

Expenditures and performance indicators in JTPA service delivery areas, by urban-rural location, 1987-88, 1598–266

Expenditures of Fed Govt in States, by type, program, agency, and State, FY90, annual rpt, 2464–2

Fraud and abuse in DOL programs, audits and investigations, 2nd half FY91, semiannual rpt, 6302–2

Participation in JTPA by selected characteristics and State, and outcomes, by urban-rural location, 1987-88, 1598–267

Participation in JTPA, by selected characteristics, FY90, annual rpt, 6304–1

State and local govt JTPA admin, funding, effectiveness, and participants, GAO rpt series, 26106–8

Unemployed displaced and economically disadvantaged workers, training program operations and performance, series, 6406–10

Unemployed displaced workers and other hard-to-serve groups, factors contributing to unemployment, and training programs operations, series, 15496–1

Job vacancy

Help-wanted ads index and ratio to unemployment, *Survey of Current Business*, cyclical indicators, monthly rpt, 2702–1.1

Indian Health Service employment of Indians and non-Indians, training, hires, and quits, by occupation, FY89, annual rpt, 4084–6

Indian Health Service nursing staff, shortages, workload, and pay, by IHS service unit, mid 1980s-90, hearing, 25418–6

Judgeships vacant, by Federal district and appeals court, 1986-91, annual rpt, 18204–3

Labor force, wages, hours, and payroll costs, by major industry group and demographic characteristics, *Survey of Current Business*, monthly rpt, 2702–1.8

New England States economic indicators, Fed Reserve 1st District, monthly rpt, 9373–2.2

New England States, FHLB 1st District thrifts financial operations compared to banks, and housing industry indicators, bimonthly rpt with articles, 9302–4

North Central States business and economic conditions, Fed Reserve 9th District, quarterly journal, 9383–19

Statistical Abstract of US, 1991 annual data compilation, 2324–1.13

Teacher employment, vacancies, and pay, by State, region, and school enrollment size, 1987/88, 4836–3.6

VA health care staff and turnover, by occupation, physician specialty, and location, 1990, annual rpt, 8604–8

Job vacancy

see also Labor turnover

Jobs

see Employee performance and appraisal

see Employment and unemployment, general

see Employment and unemployment, local and regional

see Employment and unemployment, specific industry

see Job creation

see Job tenure

see Job vacancy

see Labor turnover

see Minority employment

see Occupations

see Part-time employment

see Temporary and seasonal employment

see Veterans employment

see Women's employment

see Youth employment

see under By Occupation in the "Index by Categories"

Johansson, Gunnar

"Propylene Glycol Ethers and Their Acetates. NEG and NIOSH Basis for an Occupational Health Standard", 4246–4.3

John, A.

"External Increasing Returns, Short-Lived Agents and Long-Lived Waste", 9389–19.27

Johns Hopkins Injury Prevention Center

"Childhood Injury: State-by-State Mortality Facts", 4108–54

Johnson, Ayah E.

"Prevalence of Chronic Diseases: A Summary of Data from the Survey of American Indians and Alaska Natives. National Medical Expenditure Survey", 4186–8.20

Johnson, Cheryl

"Sources of Revisions to the USDA Income Accounts", 1541–1.202

Johnson City, Tenn.

see also under By SMSA or MSA in the "Index by Categories"

Johnson, Clifford L.

"Hemoglobin and Selected Iron-Related Findings of Persons 1-74 Years of Age: U.S., 1971-74", 4147–16.5

Johnson County, Ind.

Housing and households characteristics, unit and neighborhood quality, and journey to work by MSA location, for 11 MSAs, 1984 survey, supplement, 2485–8

Housing and households detailed characteristics, and unit and neighborhood quality, by location, 1988 survey, MSA rpt, 2485–6.4

Johnson, Doyle C.

"California Water Crisis", 1561–6.202

"Floriculture and Environmental Horticulture Products: A Production and Marketing Statistical Review, 1960-88", 1568–293

"1990/91 Outlook for Floriculture Production and Greenhouse and Nursery Trade", 1004–16.1

Johnson, Eric S.

"Nested Case-Control Study of Lung Cancer in the Meat Industry", 4472–1.223

Johnson, Frank H.

"Early Estimates. Key Statistics for Public and Private Elementary and Secondary Education, School Year 1990-91", 4834–19

Johnson, Jim

"What Do Farmers Consider Important When Making Management Decisions?", 1541–1.206

Johnson, Joan M.

"Criminal Victimization in the U.S., 1973-88 Trends", 6066–3.45

"Criminal Victimization, 1989", 6066–25.35

Johnson, Marie-Louise T.

"Prevalence, Disability, and Health Care for Psoriasis Among Persons 1-74 Years: U.S.", 4147–16.5

Johnson, Murray L.

"Population Status and Condition of the Harbor Seal, *Phoca vitulina richardsi*, in the Waters of the State of Washington: 1975-80", 14738–7

Johnson, Ronald

"Bank Credit 'Crumble' ", 9385–1.208

Johnson, Terry R.

"Evaluation of the Impacts of the Washington Alternative Work Search Experiment", 6406–6.35

Johnson, Tony G.

"Forest Statistics for North Carolina, 1990", 1206–4.13

"Forest Statistics for the Mountains of North Carolina, 1990", 1206–4.15

Johnston, Lloyd D.

"Drug Use Among American High School Students, College Students and Young Adults, 1975-90", 4494–4

Johnston, Paul V.

"Influence of the Commodity Composition of Trade on Economic Growth", 1502–3.202

Johnstown, Pa.

see also under By SMSA or MSA in the "Index by Categories"

Joint committees

see Congressional joint committees

Joint Economic Committee

Africa (sub-Saharan) agricultural conditions by country, with Ethiopia grain production and use, and dev aid by major donor, 1960s-80s, hearing, 23848–216

China economic indicators and reform issues, with background data, 1950s-90, compilation of papers, 23848–155

Eastern Europe transition to market economies, economic conditions, intl aid, and energy balance, by country, 1985-90, 9118–13

Economic indicators and components, current data and annual trends, monthly rpt, 23842–1

Economic Report of the President for 1991, Joint Economic Committee critique and policy recommendations, annual rpt, 23844–2

Education funding of Fed Govt, Head Start and GI Bill costs, benefits, and participation, 1950s-90, hearing, 23848–217

Employment situation, earnings, hours, and other BLS economic indicators, transcripts of BLS Commissioner's monthly testimony, periodic rpt, 23846–4

Income disparity between wealthiest and other families, and income sources, 1980s and trends from 1949, 23848–219

Japan economic conditions, financial and intl policies, and trade devs, 1950s-80s and projected to 2050, compilation of papers, 23848–220

Pesticide and fertilizer use reduction, environmental and economic impacts by commodity and region, alternative forecasts 1989-94, hearing, 23848–222

Poverty threshold and rates under alternative threshold adjustment methodologies, 1980s-90, hearing, 23848–221

Soviet Union GNP by component and industry sector, and CIA estimation methods, 1950s-87, 23848–223

Statistical programs of Fed Govt, index of spending for 4 agencies, 1976-88, hearing, 23848–218

Joint Printing Committee

Congressional Directory, members of 102nd Congress, other officials, elections, and districts, 1991-92, biennial rpt, 23874–1

Joint Taxation Committee

Foreign and US economic conditions and competitiveness issues, with data by country, 1960s-90, 21788–204

Savings and Investment Incentive Act issues, with IRA participation and other background data, 1980s, 25368–175

Tax expenditures, Federal revenues forgone through income tax deductions and exclusions by type, FY92-96, annual rpt, 21784–10

Joint ventures

AID dev projects and socioeconomic impacts, evaluation rpt series, 9916–1

Auto and light truck fuel economy, sales, and market shares, by size and model for US and foreign makes, 1991 model year, semiannual rpt, 3302–4

Biotechnology commercial applications, industry finances and capitalization, patents, and govt support, for US, Japan, and EC, late 1970s-91, 26358–248

Energy resources of US, foreign direct investment by energy type and firm, and US affiliates, operations, as of 1989, annual rpt, 3164–80

Fish (surimi) production of Japan, by nationality of vessel landing fish, 1975-89, article, 2162–1.202

Fishing (ocean sport and commercial) catch and quotas for US and Canada, by species for North Atlantic Ocean, 1990, annual rpt, 2164–14

Foreign direct investment in US, major transactions by type, industry, country, and US location, 1989, annual rpt, 2044–20

Japan-US joint venture, affiliated firm assets, by industry, 1987, paper compilation, 23848–220

Steel industry finances, operations, and modernization efforts, with data on major companies and foreign industry, 1968-91, last issue of annual rpt, 9884–24

Uranium reserves and industry operations, by region and State, various periods 1966-90, annual rpt, 3164–65.1

Joliet, Ill.

Housing vacancy rates for single and multifamily units and mobile homes, by city and ZIP code, 1991, annual MSA rpt, 9304–18.5

Wages by occupation, for office and plant workers, 1990 survey, periodic MSA rpt, 6785–11.2

see also under By SMSA or MSA in the "Index by Categories"

Index by Subjects and Names

Jones, John

"Cash Rents for Farms, Cropland, and Pasture, 1960-89", 1548–377

"Returns to Cash Rented Farmland and Common Stock, 1940-90", 1561–16.202

Jones, Larry E.

"Reconsideration of the Problem of Social Cost: Free Riders and Monopolists", 9383–20.12

Jones, Sidney J.

"1991 Outlook for the U.S. Economy", 1004–16.1

Jonkers, Loretta

"Competitive Assessment of the U.S. Industrial Air Pollution Control Equipment Industry", 2046–12.45

Joplin, Mo.

see also under By SMSA or MSA in the "Index by Categories"

Jordan

- Agricultural exports of high-value commodities, indexes and sales by commodity, world area, and country, 1960s-86, 1528–323
- Agricultural exports of US, impacts of foreign agricultural and trade policy, with data by commodity and country, 1989, annual rpt, 1924–8
- Agricultural trade of US, by detailed commodity and country, 1989, annual rpt, 1524–8
- Agricultural trade of US, by detailed commodity and country, 1990, semiannual rpt, 1522–4
- AID economic aid to developing countries, obligations and disbursements by country, quarterly rpt, 9912–4
- AID loans repayment status and terms by program and country, and status of predecessor agency loans, quarterly rpt, 9912–3
- Economic and military aid and loans from US and intl agencies, by program and country, FY46-90, annual rpt, 9914–5
- Economic and social conditions of developing countries from 1960s, and Intl Dev Cooperation Agency and AID activities and funding, FY90-92, annual rpt, 9904–4
- Economic conditions, income, production, prices, employment, and trade, 1991 periodic country rpt, 2046–4.29
- Economic conditions, policy, and trade practices, by country, 1988-90, annual rpt, 21384–5
- Economic, social, political, and geographic summary data, by country, 1991, annual factbook, 9114–2
- Export controls and trade of US with Middle East countries, with dual-use commodity licenses and arms sales, 1980s-90, GAO rpt, 26123–339
- Exports and imports of US, by commodity and country, 1970-89, world area rpt, 9116–1.1
- Exports and imports of US, by selected country, country group, and commodity group, 1990, annual rpt, 2044–37
- Exports and imports of US, by transport mode, country, and SITC 1- to 3-digit commodity, 1990, annual rpt, 2424–12
- Exports of US, detailed Schedule B commodities with countries of destination, 1990, annual rpt, 2424–10

Human rights conditions in 170 countries, and US economic and military aid, 1990, annual rpt, 21384–3

Iraq invasion of Kuwait, alien worker refugees fleeing from Iraq and Kuwait, intl aid by source, and costs to host and native countries, 1990-91, GAO rpt, 26123–326

Military aid of US, arms sales, and training programs costs and budget requests, by program, world region, and country, FY90-92, annual rpt, 7144–13

UN voting record and share of votes in agreement with US, by issue, country, and world area, 1990, annual rpt, 7004–18

see also under By Foreign Country in the "Index by Categories"

Jorgensen, Cynthia M.

"Monitoring the Exposure of 'America Responds to AIDS' PSA Campaign", 4042–3.256

Journalism

- County Business Patterns, 1988: employment, establishments, and payroll, by SIC 2- to 4-digit industry and county, annual State rpt series, 2326–6
- County Business Patterns, 1989: employment, establishments, and payroll, by SIC 2- to 4-digit industry and county, annual State rpt series, 2326–8
- Education (postsecondary) course completions, by detailed program, sex, race, and instn type, for 1972 high school class, as of 1984, 4888–4
- Hospital deaths, analysis of newspaper coverage of HCFA data releases, Dec 1987, article, 4042–3.242
- Service industries census, 1987: establishments, receipts by source, payroll, and employment, by SIC 2- to 4-digit kind of business, State, and MSA, 2393–4

see also Freedom of the press

see also Government and the press

see also Newspapers

see also Periodicals

Joyce, Mary E.

"Petroleum: An Energy Profile", 3164–95

Judd, John P.

"Central Bank Secrecy and Money Surprises: International Evidence", 9393–10.16

Judges

- Assaults and deaths of law enforcement officers, by circumstances, agency, victim and offender characteristics, and location, 1990, annual rpt, 6224–3
- Criminal caseload, positions authorized, misconduct, terms, salaries, and selected other characteristics of judges, data compilation, 1991 annual rpt, 6064–6.1; 6064–6.5
- Drug testing of criminal defendants, demonstration program operations, offender characteristics, and judges views, 1987-90, 18208–11
- Federal district and appeals court caseloads, actions, procedure duration, judges, and jurors, by court, 1986-91, annual rpt, 18204–3
- Federal district and appeals court judgeships and visiting judge services, 1960s-90, annual rpt, 18204–8.10; 18204–8.14; 18204–8.30

Judgments, civil procedure

- Federal district and appeals court judgeships, 1991, annual rpt, 18204–2.1
- Federal district court personnel, by court, 1990, annual report, 17664–1
- Judicial Conf proceedings and findings, spring 1991, semiannual rpt, 18202–2
- Pension systems of State and local govts, finances, coverage, and benefits, by system, FY88, annual rpt, 2466–2.1
- Pension systems of State and local govts, finances, coverage, and benefits, by system, FY89, annual rpt, 2466–2.8
- Wiretaps authorized, costs, arrests, trials, and convictions, by offense and jurisdiction, 1990, annual rpt, 18204–7
- Workers compensation contested claims, caseload, and commissioners and hearing officers, by State, 1987-90, annual rpt, 6504–9

see also Judicial ethics

see also Judicial powers

see also Judicial reform

Judgments, civil procedure

- Coal Surface Mining Reclamation and Enforcement Office activities and funding, by State and Indian tribe, FY90, annual rpt, 5644–1
- Copyright infringement lawsuit damages and legal fee awards, by case, 1930s-87, hearing, 21528–82
- Customs Service activities, collections, entries processed by mode of transport, and seizures, FY86-90, annual rpt, 8144–1
- Employment (illegal) of minors, and penalties, FY89, annual rpt, 6504–2.1
- Fed Govt accounts receivable, delinquent debt cases and collections of Justice Dept and private law firms, pilot project results, FY90, annual rpt, 6004–20
- Fed Govt benefit programs overpayment recovery and judgment enforcement cases filed in Federal district courts, 1991, annual rpt, 18204–2.1; 18204–8.13
- Federal district, appeals, and bankruptcy courts, civil cases terminated by circuit and district, 1990, annual rpt, 18204–11
- Nuclear power plant operating, maintenance, and capital additions costs, relation to plant characteristics and regulation, 1974-89, 3168–108
- Nuclear Regulatory Commission activities, finances, and staff, with data for individual power plants, FY90, annual rpt, 9634–2
- Pension laws admin and enforcement under Employee Retirement Income Security Act (ERISA), 1990, annual rpt, 6684–1
- Tax collection, enforcement, and litigation activity of IRS, with data by type of tax, region, and State, FY90, annual rpt, 8304–3
- Tax Court of US caseloads and recoveries, FY90, annual tables, 18224–5
- Tax Court of US caseloads and tax due, by disposition, FY90, annual tables, 18224–3
- US attorneys case processing and collections, by case type and Federal district, FY90, annual rpt, 6004–2

see also Child support and alimony

see also Fines and settlements

Judicial Branch

Judicial Branch

see Administrative Office of the U.S. Courts
see Court of International Trade
see Court of Military Appeals
see Federal bankruptcy courts
see Federal courts of appeals
see Federal district courts
see Federal Judicial Center
see Supreme Court
see U.S. Court of Appeals for the Federal Circuit

Judicial Conference of the U.S.

Proceedings and findings of conf, spring 1991, semiannual rpt, 18202–2

Proceedings and findings of semiannual confs, 1990, annual rpt, 18204–8

Judicial ethics

Judges misconduct cases by disposition, and judicial conduct commissions staff and budgets, by State, data compilation, 1991 annual rpt, 6064–6.1; 6064–6.5

Judicial Conf proceedings and findings, spring 1991, semiannual rpt, 18202–2

Public opinion on crime and crime-related issues, by respondent characteristics, data compilation, 1991 annual rpt, 6064–6.2

Judicial powers

Judicial Conf proceedings and findings, spring 1991, semiannual rpt, 18202–2

Judicial reform

Appellate court pre-argument conferences impacts on case processing, disposition, and duration, for Federal 6th circuit, 1985-86, 18408–45

Judicial Conf proceedings and findings, spring 1991, semiannual rpt, 18202–2

Sentences for Federal crimes, guidelines use and results by offense and district, and Sentencing Commission activities, 1990, annual rpt, 17664–1

Sentences for Federal offenses, guidelines by offense and circumstances, series, 17668–1

Judkins, David R.

"National Survey of Family Growth: Design, Estimation, and Inference. Vital and Health Statistics Series 2", 4147–2.112

Junior colleges

Condition of Education, detail for higher education, 1960s-90, annual rpt, 4824–1.2

Course completions, by detailed program, sex, race, and instn type, for 1972 high school class, as of 1984, 4888–4

Degrees awarded in higher education, by level, field, race, and sex, 1988/89 with trends from 1978/79, biennial rpt, 4844–17

Digest of Education Statistics, 1991 annual data compilation, 4824–2

Enrollment and degrees awarded by sex, and instn finances, by instn level and control, 1990-91, annual rpt, 4844–14

Enrollment and degrees awarded in higher education, by sex, full- and part-time status, and instn level and control, fall 1990, annual rpt, 4844–16

Enrollment, by grade, instn type and control, and student characteristics, 1989 and trends from 1947, annual Current Population Rpt, 2546–1.453

Enrollment, faculty, finances, and degrees in higher education, by instn level and control, and State, FY87, annual rpt, 4844–13

Enrollment in higher education, by characteristics of instn, fall 1989, biennial rpt, 4844–2

Pell grants and applicants, by tuition, family and student income, instn type and control, and State, 1989/90, annual rpt, 4804–1

R&D and related funding of Fed Govt to higher education and nonprofit instns, by field, instn, agency, and State, FY89, annual rpt, 9627–17

Remedial education programs in higher education instns, and enrollment, courses, and faculty, by instn characteristics, 1989/90, 4826–1.30

Statistical Abstract of US, 1991 annual data compilation, 2324–1.4

Student aid and other sources of support, with student expenses and characteristics, by instn type and control, 1990 triennial study, series, 4846–5

Student aid, costs, and income factors affecting access to undergrad education, 1990 rpt, 26306–6.153

Student aid funding and participation, by Federal program, instn type and control, and State, various periods 1959-89, annual rpt, 4804–28

Teachers in higher education instns, personnel policies, pay, work conditions, and other characteristics, by instn type and control, 1987/88 survey, quadrennial rpt series, 4846–4

Teachers in higher education, salaries by faculty rank, sex, instn type and control, and State, 1989/90, annual rpt, 4844–8

Veterans education aid under GI Bill and other programs, and participation by period of service and State, FY89, annual rpt, 8604–9

Vocational education in postsecondary instns, States performance measurement activities and related legislation, 1989/90, 4808–33

Juries

DC appeals and superior courts civil and criminal caseloads, 1971-88, hearing, 21308–27

Employee paid leave days for jury duty, by occupational group, for small businesses, 1990, biennial rpt, 6784–20

Federal district and appeals court caseloads, actions, procedure duration, judges, and jurors, by court, 1986-91, annual rpt, 18204–3

Federal district court criminal caseloads, by offense, disposition, and district, 1980-90, last issue of annual rpt, 18204–1

Federal district court grand and petit juror use, by circuit and district, 1990, annual rpt, 18204–11

Federal district court grand and petit juror use, June 1985-90, annual rpt, 18204–8

Federal district court grand and petit juror use, June 1987-91, annual rpt, 18204–2.1

Fees paid, and jury use and service, by State and for Federal system, data compilation, 1991 annual rpt, 6064–6.1

Public opinion on crime and crime-related issues, by respondent characteristics, data compilation, 1991 annual rpt, 6064–6.2

US attorneys case processing and collections, by case type and Federal district, FY90, annual rpt, 6004–2

Jurisdiction

see Administration of justice
see Administrative law and procedure
see Courts
see Law

Just, Brian

"Wheat Cleaning Practices of U.S. Commercial Elevators", 1561–12.204

Justice Department

see Department of Justice

Jute

see Natural fibers

Juvenile courts and cases

Case processing, and juveniles detained, by age, sex, race, and offense, data compilation, 1991 annual rpt, 6064–6.5

Caseloads (criminal) in Federal district courts, by offense, disposition, and district, 1980-90, last issue of annual rpt, 18204–1

Caseloads of Federal district courts, 1990, annual rpt, 18204–8.18; 18204–11

Caseloads of Federal district courts, 1991, annual rpt, 18204–2.1

Cases (delinquency), by offense, referral source, disposition, age, sex, race, State, and county, 1988, annual rpt, 6064–12

Data on juvenile justice issues, young offenders and victims, series, 6066–27

Runaway cases in juvenile courts, by referral source, disposition, and sex, 1985-86, 6066–27.4

Statistical Abstract of US, 1991 annual data compilation, 2324–1.5

Status offender detentions in secure facilities, and States compliance with Federal policies to reduce detentions, 1983-89, GAO rpt, 26119–333

US attorneys civil and criminal cases by type and disposition, and collections, by Federal district, FY90, annual rpt, 6004–2.1

Juvenile delinquency

Arrest rates, by offense, sex, age, and race, 1965-89, annual rpt, 6224–7

Arrests, by offense, offender characteristics, and location, 1990, annual rpt, 6224–2.2

Children and youth social, economic, and demographic characteristics, 1950s-90, 4818–5

Counseling for youth, school based program client risk behaviors and outcomes, 1988/89 study, hearing, 25548–104

Data on crime, criminal justice admin and enforcement, and public opinion, data compilation, 1991 annual rpt, 6064–6

Data on juvenile justice issues, young offenders and victims, series, 6066–27

Drug abuse relation to violent and criminal behavior, with data on street gang activity and selected population groups, 1989 conf, 4498–70

Fed Govt funding for juvenile delinquency prevention, by program and agency, annual rpt, discontinued, 6064–11

Sentences for Federal offenses, guidelines by offense and circumstances, series, 17668–1

Women prisoners in State instns, by offense, drug use history, whether abused, and other characteristics, 1986, 6066–19.61

see also Juvenile courts and cases

see also Juvenile detention and correctional institutions

see also Missing persons and runaways

Juvenile detention and correctional institutions

Court caseloads for juvenile delinquency, by offense, referral source, disposition, age, sex, race, State, and county, 1988, annual rpt, 6064–12

Drug abuse history of jail population, by offense, conviction status, criminal and family history, and selected other characteristics, 1989, 6066–19.63

Facilities for juveniles, population, and costs, by facility and resident characteristics, region, and State, 1985-89, biennial rpt, 6064–5

Facilities, inmates, and expenses, by instn and resident characteristics and State, for public and private instns, 1987, biennial rpt, 6064–13

Jail adult and juvenile population, employment, spending, instn conditions, and inmate programs, by county and facility, 1988, regional rpt series, 6068–144

Jail juvenile population, by sex, 1983-89, annual rpt, 6064–26.1

Jail population, by criminal, correctional, drug use, and family history, and selected other characteristics, 1989, 6066–19.62

Jail population by sex, race, and for 25 jurisdictions, and instn conditions, 1988-90, annual rpt, 6066–25.38

Jail population, by sociodemographic characteristics, criminal and drug use history, whether convicted, offense, and sentencing, 1989, annual rpt, 6064–26.3

Prisoners and movements, by offense, location, and selected other characteristics, data compilation, 1991 annual rpt, 6064–6.6

Prisoners in Federal instns, by sex, prison, security level, contract facility type, and region, monthly rpt series, 6242–1

Privately operated prisons and jails, costs and characteristics of instns, by facility and State, 1990, GAO rpt, 26119–321

Property offenses cases of juvenile courts, by disposition and offender age, sex, and race, 1985-86, 6066–27.5

State and Metro Area Data Book, 1991 data compilation, 2328–54

Statistical Abstract of US, 1991 annual data compilation, 2324–1.5

Status offender detentions in secure facilities, and States compliance with Federal policies to reduce detentions, 1983-89, GAO rpt, 26119–333

Violent crime victimizations, circumstances, victim characteristics, arrest, recidivism, sentences, and prisoners, 1980s, 6068–148

Kahn, George A.

"Does More Money Mean More Bank Loans?", 9381–1.208

Kalamazoo, Mich.

see also under By SMSA or MSA in the "Index by Categories"

Kalton, Graham

"Seam Effect in Panel Surveys", 2626–10.119

Kamin, Steven B.

"Argentina's Experience with Parallel Exchange Markets: 1981-90", 9366–7.261

"Exchange Rate Rules in Support of Disinflation Programs in Developing Countries", 9366–7.256

Kampuchea

see Cambodia

Kane, Michael B.

"Minority Participation in Higher Education", 4808–29

Kane, Michael D.

"Cooperatives' Growth Slowed Due to Slump in Net Income", 1122–1.209

"Key Financial Measures for 1989 Indicate Improved Co-op Performance", 1122–1.201

"Revenues Grow, but Net Income Slumps for Nation's Largest Cooperatives", 1122–1.207

"Share of Top 100 Earnings Used To Strengthen Member Ownership", 1122–1.210

"Top 100 Cooperatives, 1989 Financial Profile", 1124–3

Kankakee, Ill.

see also under By SMSA or MSA in the "Index by Categories"

Kansas

Banks (insured commercial and savings) deposits by instn, State, MSA, and county, as of June 1990, annual regional rpt, 9295–3.5

Carbon dioxide in atmosphere, North Central States economic and agricultural impacts, model descriptions and results, 1980s and projected to 2030, 3006–11.15

Coal production and mines by county, prices, productivity, miners, and reserves, by mining method and State, 1989-90, annual rpt, 3164–25

County Business Patterns, 1989: employment, establishments, and payroll, by SIC 2- to 4-digit industry and county, annual State rpt, 2326–8.18

DOD prime contract awards, by contractor, service branch, State, and city, FY90, annual rpt, 3544–22

Fed Govt spending in States and local areas, by type, State, county, and city, FY90, annual rpt, 2464–3

Fed Govt spending in States, by type, program, agency, and State, FY90, annual rpt, 2464–2

Financial and economic devs, Fed Reserve 10th District, quarterly rpt, 9381–16

HHS financial aid, by program, recipient, State, and city, FY90, annual regional listing, 4004–3.7

Hospital deaths of Medicare patients, actual and expected rates by diagnosis, and hospital characteristics, by instn, FY87-89, annual regional rpt, 4654–14.7

Income (personal) per capita and by source, and earnings by industry div, by State, MSA, and county, 1984-89, annual regional rpt, 2704–2.3

Jail adult and juvenile population, employment, spending, instn conditions, and inmate programs, by county and facility, 1988, regional rpt series, 6068–144.3

Land Mgmt Bur activities in Southwestern US, FY90, annual rpt, 5724–15

Marriages, divorces, and rates, by characteristics of spouses, State, and county, 1987 and trends from 1920, US Vital Statistics annual rpt, 4144–4

Mineral Industry Surveys, State reviews of production, 1990, preliminary annual rpt, 5614–6

Minerals Yearbook, 1989, Vol 2: State review of production and sales by commodity, and business activity, annual rpt, 5604–16.17

Minerals Yearbook, 1989, Vol 2: State reviews of production, sales, and firms, by commodity, and business activity, annual rpt, 5604–34

Natural gas production and wellhead capacity, by production area, 1980-89 and alternative forecasts 1990-91, biennial rpt, 3164–93

Physicians, by specialty, age, sex, and location of training and practice, 1989, State rpt, 4116–6.17

Population and housing census, 1990: population and housing characteristics, households, and land area, by county, subdiv, and place, State rpt, 2551–1.18

Population and housing census, 1990: voting age and total population by race, and housing units, by block, redistricting counts required under PL 94-171, State CD-ROM release, 2551–6.9

Population and housing census, 1990: voting age and total population by race, and housing units, by county and city, redistricting counts required under PL 94-171, State summary rpt, 2551–5.17

Statistical Abstract of US, 1991 annual data compilation, 2324–1

Supplemental Security Income payments and beneficiaries, by type of eligibility, State, and county, Dec 1989, annual rpt, 4744–27.7

Water (groundwater) supply, quality, chemistry, and use, 1985-88, local area rpt, 5666–28.13

Water (groundwater) supply, quality, chemistry, and use, 1987-88, regional rpt, 5666–28.3

Water resources data collection and analysis activities of USGS Water Resources Div District, with project descriptions, 1989 rpt, 5666–26.10

Water resources dev projects of Army Corps of Engineers, characteristics, and costs, 1950s-89, biennial State rpt, 3756–1.17

Water supply and quality in streams and lakes, and groundwater levels in wells, by drainage basin, 1990, annual State rpt, 5666–10.15

see also Kansas City, Kans.

see also under By State in the "Index by Categories"

Kansas City, Kans.

CPI by component for US city average, and by region, population size, and for 27 metro areas, monthly rpt, 6762–2

Drug test results at arrest, by drug type, offense, and sex, for selected urban areas, quarterly rpt, 6062–3

Housing starts and completions authorized by building permits in 40 MSAs, quarterly rpt, 2382–9

Housing vacancy rates for single and multifamily units and mobile homes, by city and ZIP code, annual MSA rpt, 9304–22.1

Kansas City, Kans.

Wages by occupation, for office and plant workers, 1991 survey, periodic MSA rpt, 6785–12.7

see also under By City and By SMSA or MSA in the "Index by Categories"

Kansas City, Mo.

CPI by component for US city average, and by region, population size, and for 27 metro areas, monthly rpt, 6762–2

Drug test results at arrest, by drug type, offense, and sex, for selected urban areas, quarterly rpt, 6062–3

Housing starts and completions authorized by building permits in 40 MSAs, quarterly rpt, 2382–9

Housing vacancy rates for single and multifamily units and mobile homes, by city and ZIP code, annual MSA rpt, 9304–22.1

Wages by occupation, for office and plant workers, 1991 survey, periodic MSA rpt, 6785–12.7

see also under By City and By SMSA or MSA in the "Index by Categories"

Kaplan, Paul A.

"Salary and Wage Statistics, Full-Time Employment in Non-Postal Agencies, Mar. 31, 1991", 9842–1.205

Karon, John M.

"HIV Prevalence Estimates and AIDS Case Projections for the U.S.: Report Based upon a Workshop", 4206–2.34

Karrenbrock, Jeffrey D.

"Behavior of Retail Gasoline Prices: Symmetric or Not?", 9391–1.216

"District Forestry Industry: Growing to New Heights?", 9391–16.204

"Internationalization of the Beer Brewing Industry", 9391–1.201

"Mississippi River System and Barge Industry", 9391–16.202

"U.S. and District Agricultural Economies: The Expansion Continues", 9391–16.209

Kashyap, Anil K.

"Monetary Policy and Credit Conditions: Evidence from the Composition of External Finance", 9366–6.268

Kaske, Neal K.

"College Library Technology and Cooperation Grants Program, HEA Title II-D: Abstracts and Analysis of Funded Projects 1989", 4874–6

Kasman, Bruce

"Financial Liberalization and Monetary Control in Japan", 9385–1.213

"Financial Reform and Monetary Control in Japan", 9385–8.116

Kastner, William M.

"Water Level Changes in the High Plains Aquifer Underlying Parts of South Dakota, Wyoming, Nebraska, Colorado, Kansas, New Mexico, Oklahoma, and Texas: Predevelopment Through Nonirrigation Season 1987-88", 5666–28.3

Kauffman, Bruce W.

"Status and Trends in Gypsy Moth Defoliation Hazard in Tennessee", 1208–344

Kaufman, George G.

"Capital in Banking: Past, Present and Future", 9375–13.61

"Diminishing Role of Commercial Banking in the U.S. Economy", 9375–13.62

Kaufman, Phillip

"Dropout Rates in the U.S.: 1990", 4834–23

"Quality of the Responses of Eighth-Grade Students in NELS:88. National Education Longitudinal Study of 1988", 4826–9.11

Kaufman, Steven

"1988 Schools and Staffing Survey Sample Design and Estimation: Schools and Staffing Survey", 4836–3.4

Keegan, Charles E.

"Montana's Log Home Industry: Development and Current Status", 1208–370

Keel, Keith

"Occupational Employment in Manufacturing Industries", 6748–52

Keene, Roger E.

"Use and Cost of Short-Stay Hospital Inpatient Services Under Medicare, 1988", 4652–1.207

Kehoe, Patrick J.

"International Evidence on the Historical Properties of Business Cycles", 9383–20.15

"Reputation with Multiple Relationships: Reviving Reputation Models of Debt", 9383–20.7

Kehoe, Timothy J.

"More on Money as a Medium of Exchange", 9383–20.10

Kelleher, Jeanette

"Financial Market Evolution and the Interest Sensitivity of Output", 9385–8.79

Kellogg, Earl D.

"Effects of Agricultural Growth in Developing Countries on Agricultural Imports, Particularly from the U.S.: Policy Implications", 1548–372

Kelly, John F.

"Longleaf Pine Resource", 1208–355

Kelly, Richard T.

"Human Factors in Self-Monitoring of Blood Glucose: Final Report", 4068–71

Kelso, Wash.

Housing vacancy rates for single and multifamily units and mobile homes, by city and ZIP code, 1991, annual MSA rpt, 9304–21.1

Kempema, E. W.

"Field Observations on Slush Ice Generated During Freezeup in Arctic Coastal Waters", 2176–1.38

"Flume Studies and Field Observations of the Interaction of Frazil Ice and Anchor Ice with Sediment", 2176–1.38

Kemper, Peter

"Case Management Agency Systems of Administering Long-Term Care: Evidence from the Channeling Demonstration", 4186–7.8

"Lifetime Use of Nursing Home Care", 4186–7.9

Kennedy, Hugh I.

"Ground-Water Levels in Wyoming, 1980 Through September 1989", 5666–28.4

Kennedy, James E.

"Empirical Relationships Between the Total Industrial Production Index and Its Diffusion Indexes", 9366–6.277

Kennedy, John F., Center for the Performing Arts, D.C.

Financial statements of Center and Natl Symphony Orchestra, and capital and maintenance costs and needs, 1970s-90, hearing, 21648–62

Index by Subjects and Names

Kennedy, Richard D.

"Differences Between Oklahoma Indian Infant Mortality and Other Races", 4042–3.209

Kennedy, Stephen D.

"Recipient Housing in the Housing Voucher and Certificate Programs", 5186–14.4

Kennewick, Wash.

Radiation exposure of population near Hanford, Wash, nuclear plant, with methodology, 1944-66, series, 3356–5

Wages by occupation, for office and plant workers, 1991 survey, periodic MSA rpt, 6785–3.6

see also under By SMSA or MSA in the "Index by Categories"

Kenosha, Wis.

Housing vacancy rates for single and multifamily units and mobile homes, by city and ZIP code, 1990, annual MSA rpt, 9304–18.1

see also under By SMSA or MSA in the "Index by Categories"

Kentucky

Appalachian Regional Commission funding, by project and State, planned FY91, annual rpt, 9084–3

Banks (insured commercial and savings) deposits by instn, State, MSA, and county, as of June 1990, annual regional rpt, 9295–3.3

Coal production and mines by county, prices, productivity, miners, and reserves, by mining method and State, 1989-90, annual rpt, 3164–25

County Business Patterns, 1989: employment, establishments, and payroll, by SIC 2- to 4-digit industry and county, annual State rpt, 2326–8.19

DOD prime contract awards, by contractor, service branch, State, and city, FY90, annual rpt, 3544–22

Economic and banking conditions, for Fed Reserve 8th District, quarterly rpt with articles, 9391–16

Education system in Appalachia, improvement initiatives, and indicators of success, by State, 1960s-89, 9088–36

Employment and unemployment, for 8 southeastern States, 1989-90, annual rpt, 6944–2

Employment by industry div, earnings, and hours, for 8 southeastern States, quarterly press release, 6942–7

Fed Govt spending in States and local areas, by type, State, county, and city, FY90, annual rpt, 2464–3

Fed Govt spending in States, by type, program, agency, and State, FY90, annual rpt, 2464–2

HHS financial aid, by program, recipient, State, and city, FY90, annual regional listing, 4004–3.4

Hospital deaths of Medicare patients, actual and expected rates by diagnosis, and hospital characteristics, by instn, FY87-89, annual regional rpt, 4654–14.4

Housing census, 1990: inventory, occupancy, and costs, State fact sheet, 2326–21.19

Income (personal) per capita and by source, and earnings by industry div, by State, MSA, and county, 1984-89, annual regional rpt, 2704–2.4

Jail adult and juvenile population, employment, spending, instn conditions, and inmate programs, by county and facility, 1988, regional rpt series, 6068–144.4

Land subsidence above coal mines, State property insurance program income and expenses in 6 States, 1990, GAO rpt, 26113–530

Marriages, divorces, and rates, by characteristics of spouses, State, and county, 1987 and trends from 1920, US Vital Statistics annual rpt, 4144–4

Mineral Industry Surveys, State reviews of production, 1990, preliminary annual rpt, 5614–6

Minerals Yearbook, 1989, Vol 2: State review of production and sales by commodity, and business activity, annual rpt, 5604–16.18

Minerals Yearbook, 1989, Vol 2: State reviews of production, sales, and firms, by commodity, and business activity, annual rpt, 5604–34

Physicians, by specialty, age, sex, and location of training and practice, 1989, State rpt, 4116–6.18

Population and housing census, 1990: population and housing characteristics, households, and land area, by county, subdiv, and place, State rpt, 2551–1.19

Population and housing census, 1990: voting age and total population by race, and housing units, by block, redistricting counts required under PL 94-171, State CD-ROM release, 2551–6.7

Population and housing census, 1990: voting age and total population by race, and housing units, by county and city, redistricting counts required under PL 94-171, State summary rpt, 2551–5.18

Statistical Abstract of US, 1991 annual data compilation, 2324–1

Supplemental Security Income payments and beneficiaries, by type of eligibility, State, and county, Dec 1989, annual rpt, 4744–27.4

Textile mill employment, earnings, and hours, for 8 Southeastern States, quarterly press release, 6942–1

Timber resources and removals, by species, ownership class, and county, 1975 and 1988, State rpt, 1206–12.15

Water resources dev projects of Army Corps of Engineers, characteristics, and costs, 1950s-91, biennial State rpt, 3756–2.18

Water supply and quality in streams and lakes, and groundwater levels in wells, by drainage basin, 1990, annual State rpt, 5666–10.16

see also Fayette County, Ky.

see also Lexington, Ky.

see also Louisville, Ky.

see also under By State in the "Index by Categories"

Kenya

Agricultural exports of high-value commodities, indexes and sales by commodity, world area, and country, 1960s-86, 1528–323

Agricultural production, trade, and policies in foreign countries, summary data by country, 1989-90, annual factbook, 1924–12

Agricultural trade of US, by detailed commodity and country, 1989, annual rpt, 1524–8

Agricultural trade of US, by detailed commodity and country, 1990, semiannual rpt, 1522–4

AID economic aid to developing countries, obligations and disbursements by country, quarterly rpt, 9912–4

AID loans repayment status and terms by program and country, and status of predecessor agency loans, quarterly rpt, 9912–3

Dairy imports, consumption, and market conditions, by sub-Saharan Africa country, 1961-88, 1528–321

Economic and military aid and loans from US and intl agencies, by program and country, FY46-90, annual rpt, 9914–5

Economic and social conditions of developing countries from 1960s, and Intl Dev Cooperation Agency and AID activities and funding, FY90-92, annual rpt, 9904–4

Economic conditions, policy, and trade practices, by country, 1988-90, annual rpt, 21384–5

Economic, population, and agricultural data, US and other aid sources, and AID activity, 1990 country rpt, 9916–12.45

Economic, social, political, and geographic summary data, by country, 1991, annual factbook, 9114–2

Energy use in developing countries, and economic and environmental impacts, by fuel type, world area, and country, 1980s-90, 26358–232

Exports and imports of US, by commodity and country, 1970-89, world area rpt, 9116–1.6

Exports and imports of US, by transport mode, country, and SITC 1- to 3-digit commodity, 1990, annual rpt, 2424–12

Exports of US, detailed Schedule B commodities with countries of destination, 1990, annual rpt, 2424–10

Food supply, needs, and aid for developing countries, status and alternative forecasts, 1991 world area rpt, 1526–8.1

Human rights conditions in 170 countries, and US economic and military aid, 1990, annual rpt, 21384–3

Labor conditions, union coverage, and work accidents, 1991 annual country rpt, 6366–4.46

Military aid of US, arms sales, and training programs costs and budget requests, by program, world region, and country, FY90-92, annual rpt, 7144–13

Multinatl US firms foreign affiliates, income statement items by country and world area, 1986, biennial article, 8302–2.212

UN voting record and share of votes in agreement with US, by issue, country, and world area, 1990, annual rpt, 7004–18

see also under By Foreign Country in the "Index by Categories"

Kenyon, Daphne A.

"Interjurisdictional Tax and Policy Competition: Good or Bad for the Federal System?", 10048–79

Keogh plans

see Individual retirement arrangements

Keough, Kristin

"Current Funds Revenues and Expenditures of Institutions of Higher Education, FY80-88", 4844–6

Kern County, Calif.

Agricultural production value and share of State production, and irrigation, impacts of California drought, for Kern County, 1989, article, 1561–6.202

Kerns, Wilmer L.

"Private Social Welfare Expenditures, 1972-88", 4742–1.204

Kerosene

Consumption of energy, by detailed fuel type, end-use sector, and State, 1960-89, State Energy Data System annual rpt, 3164–39

Exports and imports of US, by country and detailed commodity, monthly rpt, 2422–12

Housing (low income) energy aid, funding sources, costs, and participation, by State, FY89, annual rpt, 4694–8

Housing and households detailed characteristics, and unit and neighborhood quality, MSA surveys, series, 2485–6

Housing energy prices, by fuel and State, 1989 and forecast 1990-91, 3166–6.54

Housing inventory change from 1973, by reason, unit and household characteristics, and location, 1983 survey, biennial rpt, 2485–14

Injuries from use of consumer products, by severity, victim age, and detailed product, 1990, annual rpt, 9164–6

Minerals Yearbook, 1988, Vol 3: foreign country reviews of production, trade, and policy, by commodity, annual rpt series, 5604–17

Pollution (air) indoor levels and emissions rates, by pollutant type and source, 1990 handbook, 3326–1.2

Price indexes (producer), by stage of processing and detailed commodity, monthly rpt, 6762–6

Price indexes (producer), by stage of processing and detailed commodity, monthly 1990, annual rpt, 6764–2

Prices and spending for fuel, by type, end-use sector, and State, 1989, annual rpt, 3164–64

Prices and volume of oil products sold and purchased by refiners, processors, and distributors, by product, end-use sector, PAD district, and State, monthly rpt with articles, 3162–11

Sales and deliveries of fuel oil and kerosene, by end-use, PAD district, and State, 1989, annual rpt, 3164–94

Supply, demand, and movement of crude oil, gas liquids, and refined products, by PAD district and State, 1990, annual rpt, 3164–2

Supply, demand, and prices, by fuel type and end-use sector, alternative projections 1989-2010, annual rpt, 3164–75

Supply, demand, and prices, by fuel type and end-use sector, with foreign comparisons, 1990 and trends from 1949, annual rpt, 3164–74.1

Supply, demand, and prices of crude oil and refined products, and refinery capacity and stocks, by State, 1960-91, annual rpt, 3164–95

Supply, demand, trade, stocks, and refining of oil and gas liquids, by detailed product, State, and PAD district, monthly rpt with articles, 3162–6

Ketchikan, Alaska

Ketchikan, Alaska
Seals (harbor) population at selected southern Alaska coastal sites, 1976-88, 14738–6

Kickbacks
see Corruption and bribery

Kidnapping
Aircraft hijackings, on-board explosions, and other crime, US and foreign incidents, 1985-89, annual rpt, 7504–31
Arrests, prosecutions, convictions, and sentencing, for felony offenders, by offender characteristics and offense, 1988, 6066–25.33; 6066–25.39
Court civil and criminal caseloads for Federal district, appeals, and bankruptcy courts, by type of suit and offense, circuit, and district, 1990, annual rpt, 18204–11
Court civil and criminal caseloads for Federal district, appeals, and special courts, 1990, annual rpt, 18204–8
Court civil and criminal caseloads for Federal district courts, 1991, annual rpt, 18204–2.1
Court criminal case processing in Federal courts by disposition, and prisoners, by offense and jurisdiction, data compilation, 1991 annual rpt, 6064–6.5; 6064–6.6
Court criminal case processing in Federal district courts, and dispositions, by offense, district, and offender characteristics, 1986, annual rpt, 6064–29
Court criminal case processing in Federal district courts, and dispositions, by offense, 1980-89, annual rpt, 6064–31
Court criminal cases in Federal district courts, by offense, disposition, and district, 1980-90, last issue of annual rpt, 18204–1
Jail population, by criminal, correctional, drug use, and family history, and selected other characteristics, 1989, 6066–19.62
Jail population, by sociodemographic characteristics, criminal and drug use history, whether convicted, offense, and sentencing, 1989, annual rpt, 6064–26.3
Prison and parole admissions and releases, sentence length, and time served, by offense and offender characteristics, 1985, annual rpt, 6064–33
Sentences for Federal crimes, guidelines use and results by offense and district, and Sentencing Commission activities, 1990, annual rpt, 17664–1
Sentences for Federal offenses, guidelines by offense and circumstances, series, 17668–1
Terrorism (intl) incidents, casualties, and attacks on US targets, by attack type and country, 1990, annual rpt, 7004–22
Terrorism (intl) incidents, casualties, and attacks on US targets, by attack type and world area, 1990, annual rpt, 7004–13
US attorneys civil and criminal cases by type and disposition, and collections, by Federal district, FY90, annual rpt, 6004–2.1
Wiretaps authorized, costs, arrests, trials, and convictions, by offense and jurisdiction, 1990, annual rpt, 18204–7
Women prisoners in State instns, by offense, drug use history, whether abused, and other characteristics, 1986, 6066–19.61

see *also* Hostages

Kidney diseases
see Urogenital diseases

Killeen, Tex.
Wages by occupation, and benefits for office and plant workers, 1991 survey, periodic MSA rpt., 6785–3.8
see *also* under By SMSA or MSA in the "Index by Categories"

Kim, In-Moo
"Role of Energy in Real Business Cycle Models", 9375–13.57

Kindergarten
see Preschool education

King, Ann O.
"U.S.-Canada Free Trade Agreement: Eliminating Barriers to Commerce", 5602–4.201

King, B. Frank
"Commercial Bank Profitability: Hampered Again by Large Banks' Loan Problems", 9371–1.211

King, Robert G.
"Stochastic Trends and Economic Fluctuations", 9375–13.55

Kingsport, Tenn.
see *also* under By SMSA or MSA in the "Index by Categories"

Kinsella, Kevin G.
"Aging Trends: Jamaica", 2326–19.6

Kinsman, Blair
"Who Put the Wind Speeds in Admiral Beaufort's Force Scale? Part 2—The New Scales", 2152–8.201

Kintzle, Jack
"Energy Production and Other Industrial Feed Grain Uses", 1004–16.1

Kirby, Ronald
"Premigrational Movements and Behavior of Young Mallards and Wood Ducks in North-Central Minnesota", 5506–13.1

Kiribati
Economic, social, political, and geographic summary data, by country, 1991, annual factbook, 9114–2
Exports and imports of US, by transport mode, country, and SITC 1- to 3-digit commodity, 1990, annual rpt, 2424–12
Human rights conditions in 170 countries, and US economic and military aid, 1990, annual rpt, 21384–3

Kirshstein, Rita J.
"Escalating Costs of Higher Education", 4808–25
"Trends in Institutional Costs", 4808–24

Kitchen utensils and appliances
see Household appliances and equipment
see Household supplies and utensils

Klamath Falls, Oreg.
Wages by occupation, for office and plant workers, 1991 survey, periodic MSA rpt, 6785–3.6

Klein, Michael W.
"Foreign Exchange Intervention as a Signal of Monetary Policy", 9373–1.209

Klepinger, Daniel H.
"Evaluation of the Impacts of the Washington Alternative Work Search Experiment", 6406–6.35

Kletzer, Lori G.
"Job Displacement, 1979-86: How Blacks Fared Relative to Whites", 6722–1.234

Knapp, David
"Study To Evaluate the Use of Mail Service Pharmacies", 4658–60

Knapp, Gunnar
"Economic and Demographic Systems Analysis: Nome, Alaska", 5736–5.13
"Economic and Demographic Systems Analysis: Unalaska and Cold Bay, Alaska", 5736–5.14

Knapp, Michael S.
"Study of Academic Instruction for Disadvantaged Students: What Is Taught, and How, to the Children of Poverty. Interim Report from a Two-Year Investigation", 4808–28

Knight, Richard R.
"Yellowstone Grizzly Bear Investigations, Annual Report of the Interagency Study Team, 1990", 5544–4

Knit fabrics
see Clothing and clothing industry
see Textile industry and fabrics

Knoke, G. S.
"Performance and Compatibility Analysis of Oil Weathering and Transport-Related Models for Use in the Environmental Assessment Process", 2176–1.36

Knoxville, Tenn.
see *also* under By City and By SMSA or MSA in the "Index by Categories"

Koch, Hugo
"Office Visits by Black Patients, National Ambulatory Medical Care Survey: U.S., 1975-76", 4147–16.5
"Office Visits to Cardiovascular Specialists, National Ambulatory Medical Care Survey: U.S., 1975-76", 4147–16.5
"Office Visits to Ophthalmologists: National Ambulatory Medical Care Survey, U.S., 1976", 4147–16.4
"Office Visits to Orthopedic Surgeons, National Ambulatory Medical Care Survey: U.S., 1975-76", 4147–16.4
"Office Visits to Otolaryngologists: National Ambulatory Medical Care Survey, U.S.: 1975-76", 4147–16.4
"Office Visits to Urologists: National Ambulatory Medical Care Survey, U.S., 1975-76", 4147–16.4

Koch, Peter
"Spiral Grain and Annual Ring Width in Natural Unthinned Stands of Lodgepole Pine in North America", 1208–380

Kochanek, Kenneth D.
"Induced Terminations of Pregnancy: Reporting States, 1988", 4146–5.120

Kochhar, Satya
"Development of Diagnostic Data in the 10-Percent Sample of Disabled SSI Recipients", 4742–1.214

Kogan, Deborah
"Improving the Quality of Training Under JTPA", 6406–10.1

Kokomo, Ind.
see *also* under By SMSA or MSA in the "Index by Categories"

Kokoski, Mary F.
"Comparing Prices Across Cities: A Hedonic Approach", 6886–6.73
"Differences in Food Prices Across U.S. Cities: Evidence from CPI Data", 6886–6.78
"New Research on Interarea Consumer Price Differences", 6722–1.236

Kole, Linda S.

"Usefulness of P* Measures for Japan and Germany", 9366–7.268

Kominski, Robert

"Computer Use in the U.S.: 1989", 2546–2.158

"Educational Attainment in the U.S.: March 1989 and 1988", 2546–1.452

"School Enrollment—Social and Economic Characteristics of Students: October 1989", 2546–1.453

"SIPP Event History Calendar: Aiding Respondents in the Dating of Longitudinal Processes", 2626–10.135

Koonin, Lisa M.

"Abortion Surveillance, U.S., 1988", 4202–7.207

"Maternal Mortality Surveillance, U.S., 1979-86", 4202–7.206

Koot, Ronald S.

"Measure of Federal Reserve Credibility", 9387–8.240

Kopcke, Richard W.

"Influence of Housing and Durables on Personal Saving", 9373–1.218

Kopstein, Andrea N.

"Drug Abuse Among Race/Ethnic Minorities", 4498–72

Korea, North

Agricultural exports of high-value commodities, indexes and sales by commodity, world area, and country, 1960s-86, 1528–323

Agricultural trade of US, by detailed commodity and country, 1990, semiannual rpt, 1522–4

Economic, social, political, and geographic summary data, by country, 1991, annual factbook, 9114–2

Exports and imports of US with Communist countries, by detailed commodity and country, quarterly rpt with articles, 9882–2

Human rights conditions in 170 countries, and US economic and military aid, 1990, annual rpt, 21384–3

see also under By Foreign Country in the "Index by Categories"

Korea, South

Agricultural exports of high-value commodities, indexes and sales by commodity, world area, and country, 1960s-86, 1528–323

Agricultural exports of US, impacts of foreign agricultural and trade policy, with data by commodity and country, 1989, annual rpt, 1924–8

Agricultural production, prices, and trade, by country, 1980s and forecast 1991, annual world region rpt, 1524–4.5

Agricultural production, trade, and policies in foreign countries, summary data by country, 1989-90, annual factbook, 1924–12

Agricultural subsidies of South Korea to producers and consumers, by commodity, 1987-89, article, 1522–3.205

Agricultural trade by commodity and country, prices, and world market devs, monthly rpt, 1922–12

Agricultural trade of US, by detailed commodity and country, 1989, annual rpt, 1524–8

Agricultural trade of US, by detailed commodity and country, 1990, semiannual rpt, 1522–4

AID loans repayment status and terms by program and country, and status of predecessor agency loans, quarterly rpt, 9912–3

Background Notes, summary social, political, and economic data, 1991 rpt, 7006–2.34

Bearings (ball) from 14 countries, injury to US industry from foreign subsidized and less than fair value imports, investigation with background financial and operating data, 1991 rpt, 9886–19.74

Drug (methamphetamine) abuse, availability, health effects, and treatment, 1990 conf papers, 4498–75

Economic and military aid and loans from US and intl agencies, by program and country, FY46-90, annual rpt, 9914–5

Economic conditions, and oil supply and demand, for major industrial countries, biweekly rpt, 9112–1

Economic conditions in USSR, Eastern Europe, OECD, and selected other countries, 1960s-90, annual rpt, 9114–4

Economic conditions, income, production, prices, employment, and trade, 1991 periodic country rpt, 2046–4.21

Economic conditions, policy, and trade practices, by country, 1988-90, annual rpt, 21384–5

Economic, social, political, and geographic summary data, by country, 1991, annual factbook, 9114–2

Export and import balances of US, and dollar exchange rates, with 5 Asian countries, 1991 semiannual rpt, 8002–14

Exports and imports of US, by commodity and country, 1970-89, world area rpt, 9116–1.7

Exports and imports of US by country, and trade shifts by commodity, 1990, semiannual rpt, 9882–9

Exports and imports of US, by Harmonized System 6-digit commodity and country, 1990, annual rpt, 2424–13

Exports and imports of US, by selected country, country group, and commodity group, 1990, annual rpt, 2044–37

Exports and imports of US, by transport mode, country, and SITC 1- to 3-digit commodity, 1990, annual rpt, 2424–12

Exports and imports, trade agreements and relations, and USITC investigations, 1990, annual rpt, 9884–5

Exports, imports, and balances of US with major trading partners, by product category, 1986-90, annual chartbook, 9884–21

Exports of US, detailed Schedule B commodities with countries of destination, 1990, annual rpt, 2424–10

Film (polyethylene terephthalate) from 2 countries at less than fair value, injury to US industry, investigation with background financial and operating data, 1991 rpt, 9886–14.313

Fish (surimi) production and trade by country, and Japan import and catch quotas, 1975-89, article, 2162–1.202

Human rights conditions in 170 countries, and US economic and military aid, 1990, annual rpt, 21384–3

Imports of goods, services, and investment from US, trade barriers, impacts, and US actions, by country, 1990, annual rpt, 444–2

Imports of US given duty-free treatment for value of US material sent abroad, by commodity and country, 1989, annual rpt, 9884–14

Labor conditions, union coverage, and work accidents, 1991 annual country rpt, 6366–4.28

Military aid of US, arms sales, and training programs costs and budget requests, by program, world region, and country, FY90-92, annual rpt, 7144–13

Multinatl US firms and foreign affiliates finances and operations, by industry and world area of parent firm, 1989 benchmark survey, preliminary annual rpt, 2704–5

Multinatl US firms foreign affiliates, income statement items by country and world area, 1986, biennial article, 8302–2.212

Mushroom (canned) trade, supply, and demand, for selected countries, 1980s-91, article, 1925–34.242

Nuclear power generation in US and 20 countries, monthly rpt, 3162–24.10

Nuclear power plant capacity, generation, and operating status, by plant and foreign and US location, 1990 and projected to 2030, annual rpt, 3164–57

Pipes and tubes (welded nonalloy steel) from 6 countries, injury to US industry from foreign subsidized and less than fair value imports, investigation with background financial and operating data, 1991 rpt, 9886–19.81

Science and engineering employment, by selected characteristics, for 3 countries, 1991 working paper, 2326–18.61

Ships freight rates for lumber from Alaska and Puget Sound to Asian markets, by product and port, 1988, 1208–358

Ships in world merchant fleet, tonnage, and new ship construction and deliveries, by vessel type and country, as of Jan 1990, annual rpt, 7704–3

Steel imports of US under voluntary restraint agreement, by product, customs district, and country, with US industry operating data, quarterly rpt, 9882–13

Telecommunications industry intl competitiveness, with financial and operating data by product or service, firm, and country, 1990 rpt, 2008–30

Timber in northwestern US and British Columbia, production, prices, trade, and employment, quarterly rpt, 1202–3

US military presence in Pacific basin, personnel, dependents, aircraft, ships, and costs, by service branch and location, 1990, GAO rpt, 26123–357

see also under By Foreign Country in the "Index by Categories"

Korean War

see Veterans benefits and pensions

see War

Korn, Steven

"Reaction of Interest Rates to the Employment Report: The Role of Policy Anticipations", 9389–1.205

Koslowe, Patricia A.

"Characteristics of Persons Served by Private Psychiatric Hospitals, U.S.: 1986", 4506–3.47

Kosrae

Kosrae
see Micronesia Federated States

Kossoff, Amy
"Analyses of DRG Classification and Assignment", 17206–2.18

Kott, Phillip S.
"What Does Performing Linear Regression on Sample Survey Data Mean?", 1502–3.202

Kraenzle, Charles A.
"California's $7.4 Billion Sales Leads States in Cooperative Business Volume", 1122–1.202
"Co-ops Report Extent of Business Transacted on Noncooperative Basis", 1122–1.203
"Co-ops' Share of Grains, Milk, Cotton Up in 1989", 1122–1.204

Kramer, Carol S.
"Food Marketing and New Product Development in Response to Health Concerns", 1004–16.1

Kramer, Deborah A.
"Lightweight Materials for New Cars: Driving Toward Better Mileage", 5602–4.202

Kramer, Natalie
"Employer-Sponsored Prescription Drug Benefits", 6722–1.215

Kraus, John F.
"Genecology of Longleaf Pine in Georgia and Florida", 1208–345

Krause, Kenneth R.
"Cattle Feeding, 1962-89: Location and Feedlot Size", 1568–300
"Changing Importance of Large Cattle Feedlots", 1561–7.203

Kraushaar, Jonathan M.
"Fiber Deployment Update, End of Year 1990", 9284–18

Kravetz, Alan
"Trends in the Problem Resolution Program", 8304–8.1

Kronenfeld, Jennie J.
"Medicaid Prospective Payment: Case-Mix Increase", 4652–1.206

Kronson, Marc E.
"Substance Abuse Coverage Provided by Employer Medical Plans", 6722–1.221

Kuester, Kathleen A.
"Market-Based Deposit Insurance Premiums: An Evaluation", 9366–6.264

Kumar, Krishna
"Assessment of the Impact of AID's Participant Training Programs in Nepal", 9916–3.62

Kumar, Vikram
"Effects of Devaluation with a Partial Wage Floor", 9371–10.58

Kupiec, Paul
"Noise Traders, Excess Volatility, and a Securities Transaction Tax", 9366–6.280
"Prudential Margin Policy in a Futures-Style Settlement System", 9366–6.278
"Stock Market Volatility in OECD Countries: Recent Trends, Consequences for the Real Economy, and Proposals for Reform", 9366–6.279

Kurtzweg, Laurie
"Measures of Soviet Gross National Product in 1982 Prices", 23848–223

Kutner, Mark A.
"Review of the National Workplace Literacy Program", 4808–37

Kutscher, Ronald E.
"New BLS Projections: Findings and Implications", 6722–1.250

Kuttner, Kenneth N.
"Using Noisy Indicators To Measure Potential Output", 9375–13.65

Kuwait
Agricultural exports of high-value commodities, indexes and sales by commodity, world area, and country, 1960s-86, 1528–323
Agricultural exports of US, impacts of foreign agricultural and trade policy, with data by commodity and country, 1989, annual rpt, 1924–8
Agricultural trade of US, by detailed commodity and country, 1989, annual rpt, 1524–8
Agricultural trade of US, by detailed commodity and country, 1990, semiannual rpt, 1522–4
Economic and military aid and loans from US and intl agencies, by program and country, FY46-90, annual rpt, 9914–5
Economic conditions, policy, and trade practices, by country, 1988-90, annual rpt, 21384–5
Economic, social, political, and geographic summary data, by country, 1991, annual factbook, 9114–2
Export controls and trade of US with Middle East countries, with dual-use commodity licenses and arms sales, 1980s-90, GAO rpt, 26123–339
Exports and imports of US, by commodity and country, 1970-89, world area rpt, 9116–1.1
Exports and imports of US, by Harmonized System 6-digit commodity and country, 1990, annual rpt, 2424–13
Exports and imports of US, by selected country, country group, and commodity group, 1990, annual rpt, 2044–37
Exports and imports of US, by transport mode, country, and SITC 1- to 3-digit commodity, 1990, annual rpt, 2424–12
Exports of US, detailed Schedule B commodities with countries of destination, 1990, annual rpt, 2424–10
Human rights conditions in 170 countries, and US economic and military aid, 1990, annual rpt, 21384–3
Iraq invasion of Kuwait, alien worker refugees fleeing from Iraq and Kuwait, intl aid by source, and costs to host and native countries, 1990-91, GAO rpt, 26123–326
Iraq invasion of Kuwait, impacts on oil supply and prices, selected indicators, daily press release, 3162–44
Iraq invasion of Kuwait, oil embargo impacts on OPEC and US oil supply and industry, 1989-91, hearing, 21368–132
Oil production and exports to US, by major exporting country, detailed data, monthly rpt with articles, 3162–24
Oil production, trade, use, and stocks, by selected country and country group, monthly rpt, 3162–42
Persian Gulf War damage in Kuwait, Army Corps of Engineers reconstruction contract awards by firm and purpose, 1st qtr 1991, article, 2042–1.203
UN voting record and share of votes in agreement with US, by issue, country, and world area, 1990, annual rpt, 7004–18

see also under By Foreign Country in the "Index by Categories"

Kyanite
see Nonmetallic minerals and mines

La Crosse, Wis.
Wages by occupation, and benefits for office and plant workers, 1991 survey, periodic labor market rpt, 6785–3.9
see also By SMSA or MSA in the "Index by Categories"

Labadie, Pamela
"Term Structure of Interest Rates over the Business Cycle", 9366–6.273

Labeling
Alcoholic and nonalcoholic beverages, youth ability to distinguish among brands, 1991 survey, 4006–10.2
Drug (chemotherapy) use for indications not listed on drug label, costs, and insurance reimbursement problems, 1990 physicians survey, GAO rpt, 26131–81
Exports of goods, services, and investment, trade barriers, impacts, and US actions, by country, 1989, annual rpt, 444–2
Hazardous substances and conditions occupational exposure, measurement, and proposed standards, series, 4246–1
Imports detained by FDA, by reason, product, shipper, brand, and country, monthly listing, 4062–2
Meat and poultry inspection activities and staff of Federal, State, and foreign govts, FY90, annual rpt, 1374–1
see also Trademarks

Labich, Carol J.
"New England Outlook", 9302–4.201

Labor
see terms listed under Employment and unemployment, general, Labor supply and demand, and Occupations

Labor Agreement Information Retrieval System
Collective bargaining agreements of Federal employees, coverage, unions, and location, by agency, for contracts expiring 1990-91, annual listing, 9847–1
Collective bargaining multi-unit agreements of Fed Govt, by agency and labor union, annual listing, discontinued, 9847–4

Labor costs and cost indexes
Costs and productivity of labor for private, nonfarm business, and manufacturing sectors, revised data, quarterly rpt, 6822–2
Costs and productivity of labor, indexes, preliminary data, quarterly rpt, 6822–1
Economic indicators compounded annual rates of change, monthly rpt, 9391–3
Economic indicators compounded annual rates of change, 1971-90, annual rpt, 9391–9.2
Economic indicators, prices, labor costs, and productivity, BLS econometric analyses and methodology, working paper series, 6886–6
Employer Cost Index by region, quarterly press release, 6942–8
Employment and Earnings, detailed data, monthly rpt, 6742–2.7
Employment Cost Index and percent change by occupational group, industry div, region, and metro-nonmetro area, quarterly press release, 6782–5

Index by Subjects and Names

Employment Cost Index changes for nonfarm workers, by occupation, industry div, region, and bargaining status, monthly rpt, 6782–1

Employment Cost Index, current data and annual trends, monthly rpt, 23842–1.2

Employment, earnings, and hours, by SIC 1- to 4-digit industry, monthly and annual averages, selected years 1909-90, annual rpt, 6744–4

Employment, earnings, and hours, monthly press release, 6742–5

Employment, earnings, hours, and productivity, by industry div, selected years 1929-90, annual rpt, 204–1.2

Farm employment, wages, and hours, by payment method, worker type, region, and State, 1910-90, 1618–21

Food marketing cost indexes, by expense category, monthly rpt with articles, 1502–4

Foreign and US industrial output, compensation, unit labor costs, and indexes, Monthly Labor Review, 6722–1.6

Foreign and US manufacturing labor costs and indexes, by selected country, 1990, semiannual rpt, 6822–3

Health Care Financing Review, provider prices, price inputs and indexes, and labor, quarterly journal, 4652–1.1

Health condition and health care resources, use, and spending, 1950s-89, annual data compilation, 4144–11

Hospital reimbursement by Medicare under prospective payment system, analyses of alternative payment plans, series, 17206–1

Hospital reimbursement by Medicare under prospective payment system, and effect on services, finances, and beneficiary payments, 1979-90, annual rpt, 17204–2

Hospital reimbursement by Medicare under prospective payment system, effect of adjusting wage index for occupational mix, 1990 rpt, 17206–2.17

Hospital reimbursement by Medicare under prospective payment system, methodology, inputs, and data by diagnostic group, 1991 annual rpt, 17204–1

Hourly costs, by component, industry sector, worker class, and firm size, 1990, annual rpt, 6744–22

Medicare Economic Index for physician reimbursement rebased to 1989, methodology and results, with projections to 1995, article, 4652–1.246

Medicare input price index rebased to 1987, methodology and results, 1991, article, 4652–1.231

Mineral industries census, 1987: finances and operations, by establishment characteristics, SIC 2- to 4-digit industry, and State, subject rpt, 2517–1

Monthly Labor Review, output, compensation, unit labor costs, and indexes, 6722–1.1; 6722–1.3; 6722–1.5

Physicians practice cost indexes and components, by State, MSA, and for rural areas, 1989 rpt, 4658–50

Postal Service productivity, indexes of output and labor, capital, and other inputs, alternative model descriptions and results, 1960s-89, 9688–6

Statistical Abstract of US, 1991 annual data compilation, 2324–1.13

Steel industry finances, operations, and modernization efforts, with data on major companies and foreign industry, 1968-91, last issue of annual rpt, 9884–24

Survey of Current Business, detailed data for major industries and economic indicators, monthly rpt, 2702–1

see also Employee benefits

see also Payroll

see also Social security tax

see also Unemployment insurance tax

see also Workers compensation

Labor Department

see Department of Labor

Labor force

see Employment and unemployment, general

see Employment and unemployment, local and regional

see Employment and unemployment, specific industry

see Foreign labor conditions

see Labor supply and demand

Labor law

Alien workers (unauthorized) and Fair Labor Standards Act employer compliance, hiring impacts, and aliens overstaying visas by country and State, 1986-90, annual rpt, 6264–6

Alien workers, amnesty programs, and employer sanctions impacts on US economy and labor force, series, 6366–5

Black lung benefits and claims by State, trust fund receipts by source, and disbursements, 1990, annual rpt, 6504–3

Child labor law violations and injuries by industry group, and employment of minors by selected characteristics, 1983-90, GAO rpt, 26121–426

Collective bargaining devs, 1990, annual narrative article, 6722–1.207

Court civil and criminal caseloads for Federal district, appeals, and bankruptcy courts, by type of suit and offense, circuit, and district, 1990, annual rpt, 18204–11

Court civil and criminal caseloads for Federal district, appeals, and special courts, 1990, annual rpt, 18204–8

Court civil and criminal caseloads for Federal district courts, 1991, annual rpt, 18204–2.1

Court criminal case processing in Federal district courts, and dispositions, by offense, district, and offender characteristics, 1986, annual rpt, 6064–29

Court criminal case processing in Federal district courts, and dispositions, by offense, 1980-89, annual rpt, 6064–31

Discrimination complaints of Federal employees, processing, and disposition, by complaint type and agency, FY89, annual rpt, 9244–11

DOD prime contract awards, by size and type of contract, service branch, competitive status, category, and labor standard, FY90, annual rpt, 3544–19

Equal employment laws compliance by Fed Govt contractors, FY90, 6508–36

Fair Labor Standards Act admin, with coverage under minimum wage and overtime provisions, and illegal employment of minors, by industry div, FY89, annual rpt, 6504–2.1

Labor-management relations, general

Fed Labor Relations Authority and Fed Services Impasses Panel activities, and cases by union, agency, and disposition, FY85-90, annual rpt, 13364–1

Industrial relations devs and collective bargaining agreements expiring during month, Monthly Labor Review, 6722–1

Mines safety and health enforcement, training, and funding, with casualties, by type of mine and State, FY89, annual rpt, 6664–6

Natl Labor Relations Board activities, cases, elections conducted, and litigation, FY89, annual rpt, 9584–1

Pension laws admin and enforcement under Employee Retirement Income Security Act (ERISA), 1990, annual rpt, 6684–1

States labor laws enacted, by State, 1989 annual article, 6722–1.209

Supreme Court docket labor-related cases, 1990-91, annual narrative article, 6722–1.208

Unemployment insurance laws of States, changes in coverage, benefits, tax rates, and penalties, by State, 1990, annual article, 6722–1.211

Unemployment insurance laws of States, comparison of provisions, 1991, base edition with semiannual revisions, 6402–2

Unemployment insurance programs of States, benefits, coverage, and tax provisions, as of Jan 1991, semiannual listing, 6402–7

US attorneys civil and criminal cases by type and disposition, and collections, by Federal district, FY90, annual rpt, 6004–2.1; 6004–2.7

Workers compensation laws of States and Fed Govt, 1991 semiannual rpt, 6502–1

Workers compensation laws of States, changes in coverage, benefits, and premium rates, by State, 1990, annual article, 6722–1.210

Workers compensation programs of States, admin, coverage, benefits, finances, processing, and staff, 1987-90, annual rpt, 6504–9

see also Minimum wage

Labor-management relations, general

Assistance (financial and nonfinancial) of Fed Govt, 1991 base edition with supplements, annual listing, 104–5

Collective bargaining agreement coverage of plant and office workers, by industry div and MSA, aggregate 1986-90, annual rpt, 6785–1.3

Collective bargaining agreements expiring during year, and workers covered, by firm, union, industry group, and State, 1991, annual rpt, 6784–9

Collective bargaining agreements expiring during year, and workers covered, by industry and level of govt, 1992, 6726–1.43

Collective bargaining contract expirations, and industrial relations devs, current statistics and articles, Monthly Labor Review, 6722–1

Collective bargaining contract expirations, wage increases, and coverage, by major industry group, 1991, annual article, 6722–1.206

Collective bargaining devs, 1990, annual narrative article, 6722–1.207

Labor-management relations, general

Collective bargaining wage and benefit changes, quarterly press release, 6782–2

Collective bargaining wage changes and coverage, by industry sector and whether contract includes escalator clause and lump sum payment, 1980-90, annual article, 6722–1.227

Developing countries labor standards impacts on social and economic dev, 1988 conf papers, 6368–9

Foreign countries labor conditions, union coverage, and work accidents, annual country rpt series, 6366–4

Genetic damage and trait monitoring and screening of employees, use, costs, benefits, and procedures, 1980s, 26358–230

Health condition screening and monitoring of employees, businesses practices and views, 1989 survey, 26358–250

Labor Dept programs fraud and abuse, audits and investigations activity, and racketeering cases by type and disposition, FY88-89, GAO rpt, 26111–74

Labor laws enacted, by State, 1990, annual article, 6722–1.209

Mediation and arbitration activities of Fed Mediation and Conciliation Service, and cases by issue, region, and State, FY84-89, annual rpt, 9344–1

Natl Labor Relations Board activities, cases, elections conducted, and litigation, FY89, annual rpt, 9584–1

Quality mgmt practices of corporations, effects on employee and customer relations, operations, and finances, 1988-89, GAO rpt, 26123–345

Representation elections conducted by NLRB, results, monthly rpt, 9582–2

Statistical Abstract of US, 1991 annual data compilation, 2324–1.13

Teachers in higher education instns, personnel policies, pay, work conditions, and other characteristics, by instn type and control, 1987/88 survey, quadrennial rpt series, 4846–4

Wage and benefit changes from collective bargaining and mgmt decisions, by industry div, monthly rpt, 6782–1

see also Absenteeism

see also Discrimination in employment

see also Employee benefits

see also Employee performance and appraisal

see also Escalator clauses

see also Labor-management relations in government

see also Labor unions

see also Pensions and pension funds

see also Personnel management

see also Work conditions

see also Work stoppages

Labor-management relations in government

Census of Govts, 1987: State and local labor-mgmt policies, agreements, and coverage and bargaining units, by function, level of govt, and State, 2455–3

Collective bargaining agreements expiring during year, and workers covered, by firm, union, industry group, and State, 1991, annual rpt, 6784–9

Collective bargaining agreements expiring during year, and workers covered, by industry and level of govt, 1992, 6726–1.43

Collective bargaining contract expirations, wage increases, and coverage, by major industry group, 1991, annual article, 6722–1.206

Collective bargaining multi-unit agreements of Fed Govt, by agency and labor union, annual listing, discontinued, 9847–4

Discrimination complaints of Federal employees, processing, and disposition, by complaint type and agency, FY89, annual rpt, 9244–11

Drug testing of Federal employees, results, and costs, by agency, FY87-92, GAO rpt, 26119–344

Fed Govt civilian employees demographic and employment characteristics, as of Sept 1990, annual article, 9842–1.201

Fed Govt collective bargaining agreements, coverage, unions, and location, by agency, for contracts expiring 1990-91, annual listing, 9847–1

Fed Govt labor unions recognized, coverage by agency and union, biennial rpt, discontinued, 9844–17

Fed Labor Relations Authority and Fed Services Impasses Panel activities, and cases by union, agency, and disposition, FY85-90, annual rpt, 13364–1

Mediation and arbitration activities of Fed Mediation and Conciliation Service, and cases by issue, region, and State, FY84-89, annual rpt, 9344–1

Merit system oversight and enforcement activities of OPM, series, 9496–2

Merit Systems Protection Board decisions on appeals of Fed Govt personnel actions, by agency and region, FY90, annual rpt, 9494–2

NASA staff characteristics and personnel actions, FY90, annual rpt, 9504–1

Natl Agricultural Statistics Service minority group staff, promotion, and discrimination complaints, 1988-90, GAO rpt, 26119–326

State and local govt collective bargaining, wage and benefit changes and coverage, 1st half 1991, semiannual press release, 6782–6

Statistical Abstract of US, 1991 annual data compilation, 2324–1.9

Wage and benefit changes from collective bargaining and mgmt decisions, by industry div, monthly rpt, 6782–1

see also Civil service system

Labor-Management Services Administration

see Office of Labor-Management Standards

Labor mobility

Black American displaced workers, by demographic and current and former employment characteristics, and compared to whites, 1978-86, article, 6722–1.234

Displaced workers losing job 1985-90, by demographic and former and current employment characteristics, as of Jan 1990, article, 6722–1.225

Fed Govt Senior Executive Service membership characteristics, entries, exits, and awards, FY79-90, annual rpt, 9844–36

Housing characteristics of recent movers for new and previous unit, and household characteristics, by location, 1989, biennial rpt, 2485–12

Housing characteristics of recent movers for new and previous unit, and household characteristics, MSA surveys, series, 2485–6

Housing location at birth and age 16, and residential preference in 5 years, by selected housing and household characteristics, 1985, biennial rpt supplement, 2485–13

Manufacturing job creation, elimination, and reallocation rates, and relation to industry and establishment characteristics, 1970s-86, working paper, 9375–13.56

Population size and characteristics, historical index to *Current Population Rpts,* 1991 listing, 2546–2.160

Teachers in higher education instns, employment and other characteristics, by instn type and control, 1987/88 survey, 4846–4.4

see also Job tenure

see also Labor turnover

see also Migrant workers

see also Migration

Labor productivity

Auto assembly plant productivity and relation to labor reserves, model description and results, 1990 working paper, 6886–6.72

China economic indicators and reform issues, with background data, 1950s-90, compilation of papers, 23848–155

Coal miners working daily, mines, and labor productivity, quarterly rpt, 3162–37.4

Coal mining productivity by mining method in US, Australia, and South Africa, 1980-89, annual rpt, 3164–77.1

Coal production and mines by county, prices, productivity, miners, and reserves, by mining method and State, 1989-90, annual rpt, 3164–25

Coal production per workhour, 1989 and trends from 1949, annual rpt, 3164–74.4

Competitiveness (intl) of US industries, with selected foreign and US operating data by major firm and product, series, 2046–12

Drug and alcohol abuse and mental illness direct and indirect costs, by type, 1970s-88, article, 4042–3.219

Eastern Europe foreign debt components, trade, balances, and other economic indicators, by country, 1985-89, hearing, 21248–148

Eastern Europe transition to market economies, economic conditions, intl aid, and energy balance, by country, 1985-90, 9118–13

Economic indicators and components, current data and annual trends, monthly rpt, 23842–1.2

Economic indicators compounded annual rates of change, 1971-90, annual rpt, 9391–9.2

Economic Report of the President for 1991, Joint Economic Committee critique and policy recommendations, annual rpt, 23844–2

Employment and unemployment current statistics, Monthly Labor Review, 6722–1.1

Farm and garden equipment industry productivity measures, 1958-88, article, 6722–1.232

Farm production inputs, output, and productivity, by commodity and region, 1947-89, annual rpt, 1544–17

Food prices (farm-retail), marketing cost components, and industry finances and productivity, 1960s-90, annual rpt, 1544–9.3

Index by Subjects and Names

Foreign and US industrial output, compensation, unit labor costs, and indexes, Monthly Labor Review, 6722–1.6

Foreign countries labor conditions, union coverage, and work accidents, annual country rpt series, 6366–4

Gear production for selected uses under alternative production requirements, and industry finances and operations, late 1940s-89, 2028–1

Hospital reimbursement by Medicare under prospective payment system, and effect on services, finances, and beneficiary payments, 1979-90, annual rpt, 17204–2

Hospital reimbursement by Medicare under prospective payment system, methodology, inputs, and data by diagnostic group, 1991 annual rpt, 17204–1

Imports injury to US industries from foreign subsidized products and sales at less than fair value, investigations with background financial and operating data, series, 9886–19

Manufacturing wages impacts of foreign competition and other factors, late 1950s-89, article, 9385–1.204

Mental illness and drug and alcohol abuse direct and indirect costs, by age and sex, 1985, 4048–35

Mines (coal) and related operations occupational injuries and incidence, employment, and hours, 1989, annual rpt, 6664–4

Output, compensation, labor and nonlabor unit costs, and indexes, Monthly Labor Review, 6722–1.5

Output per hour, and compensation and unit labor costs, percent change, monthly rpt, 6742–2.7

Output per hour, and compensation and unit labor costs, 1947-90, annual rpt, 204–1.1; 204–1.2

Productivity and costs of labor for private, nonfarm business, and manufacturing sectors, revised data, quarterly rpt, 6822–2

Productivity and costs of labor, indexes, preliminary data, quarterly rpt, 6822–1

Productivity of labor and capital, indexes and percent change, 1948-90, annual press release, 6824–2

Productivity of labor and for other inputs, indexes and changes for 2- to 4-digit industries and govt functions, 1984-89, annual article, 6722–1.228

Productivity of labor, indexes of output, hours, and employment by SIC 2- to 4-digit industry, 1967-89, annual rpt, 6824–1

State gross product impact of foreign labor productivity and dollar exchange rate, by industry sector and State, 1972-86, working paper, 9387–8.255

Statistical Abstract of US, 1991 annual data compilation, 2324–1.13

Steel industry finances, operations, and modernization efforts, with data on major companies and foreign industry, 1968-91, last issue of annual rpt, 9884–24

Telecommunications industry intl competitiveness, with financial and operating data by product or service, firm, and country, 1990 rpt, 2008–30

see also Employee performance and appraisal

see also Government efficiency

see also Industrial production indexes

see also Labor costs and cost indexes

see also Production costs

Labor supply and demand

Economic indicators and components, current data and annual trends, monthly rpt, 23842–1.2

Forecasts of employment conditions, alternative BLS projections to 2005 and trends 1970s-90, biennial article, 6722–1.252

Labor force, wages, hours, and payroll costs, by major industry group and demographic characteristics, *Survey of Current Business,* monthly rpt, 2702–1.8

Labor supply trends, with characteristics of working-age population not in labor force, part-time workers, and multiple-jobholders, late 1960s-90, article, 9362–1.203

Manufacturing job creation, elimination, and reallocation rates, and relation to industry and establishment characteristics, 1970s-86, working paper, 9375–13.56

Monthly Labor Review, current statistics and articles, 6722–1

New England States economic indicators, Fed Reserve 1st District, monthly rpt, 9373–2.2

Recruitment, hiring, compensation, and other employment practices of large firms, 1989 survey, GAO rpt, 26119–324

Rural areas economic conditions and dev, quarterly journal, 1502–8

State and Metro Area Data Book, 1991 data compilation, 2328–54

Statistical Abstract of US, 1991 annual data compilation, 2324–1.13

see also Absenteeism

see also Agricultural labor

see also Alien workers

see also Blue collar workers

see also Child labor

see also Clerical workers

see also Employee benefits

see also Employee development

see also Employment and unemployment, general

see also Employment and unemployment, local and regional

see also Employment and unemployment, specific industry

see also Federal employees

see also Forced labor

see also Foreign labor conditions

see also Health occupations

see also Hours of labor

see also Job tenure

see also Job vacancy

see also Labor law

see also Labor-management relations, general

see also Labor mobility

see also Labor productivity

see also Labor turnover

see also Labor unions

see also Manpower training programs

see also Merchant seamen

see also Migrant workers

see also Military personnel

see also Minority employment

see also Occupational health and safety

see also Occupational testing and certification

see also Occupations

see also Old-Age, Survivors, Disability, and Health Insurance

see also Part-time employment

see also Pensions and pension funds

see also Production workers

see also Professional and technical workers

see also Retirement

see also Sales workers

see also State and local employees

see also Temporary and seasonal employment

see also Underemployment

see also Unemployment insurance

see also Unpaid family workers

see also Vacations and holidays

see also Veterans employment

see also Women's employment

see also Youth employment

see also under names of specific occupations

Labor turnover

Black American displaced workers, by demographic and current and former employment characteristics, and compared to whites, 1978-86, article, 6722–1.234

Displaced and economically disadvantaged workers, training program performance and operations, series, 6406–10

Displaced workers and homemakers Pell grants recipients, by family income and grant level, 1989/90, annual rpt, 4804–1

Displaced workers and other hard-to-serve groups, factors contributing to unemployment, and training programs operations, series, 15496–1

Displaced workers losing job 1985-90, by demographic and former and current employment characteristics, as of Jan 1990, article, 6722–1.225

Displaced workers provisions under States unemployment insurance laws, 1991, base edition with semiannual revisions, 6402–2

Employment of DOT, by subagency, occupation, and selected personnel characteristics, FY90, annual rpt, 7304–18

Entry level employment, and share without previous experience in field, by detailed occupation, 1986, article, 6742–1.201

Fed Govt civilian employees accessions and separations, by citizenship status and agency for DC metro area and elsewhere, bimonthly rpt, 9842–1.3

Fed Govt employment of minorities, women, and disabled, by agency and occupation, FY89, annual rpt, 9244–10

Fed Govt personnel action appeals, decisions of Merit Systems Protection Board by agency and region, FY90, annual rpt, 9494–2

Fed Govt Senior Executive Service membership characteristics, entries, exits, and awards, FY79-90, annual rpt, 9844–36

HHS employment of Hispanics in Mountain region, hiring and promotion practices, 1980s, GAO rpt, 26121–393

Households composition, income, benefits, and labor force status, Survey of Income and Program Participation methodology, working paper series, 2626–10

Labor turnover

Imports, exports, and employment impacts, by SIC 2- to 4-digit industry and commodity, quarterly rpt, 2322–2

Indian Health Service employment of Indians and non-Indians, training, hires, and quits, by occupation, FY89, annual rpt, 4084–6

Indian Health Service nursing staff, shortages, workload, and pay, by IHS service unit, mid 1980s-90, hearing, 25418–6

IRS revenue agent attrition, separations by reason, and hires, by region and district, FY87-90, GAO rpt, 26119–345

Japan economic conditions, financial and intl policies, and trade devs, 1950s-80s and projected to 2050, compilation of papers, 23848–220

Labor force not at work, unemployed, and working less than 35 hours, by reason, sex, race, region, and State, 1990, annual rpt, 6744–7.1; 6744–7.2

Labor laws enacted, by State, 1990, annual article, 6722–1.209

Law enforcement spending and employment, by activity and level of govt, data compilation, 1991 annual rpt, 6064–6.1

Leave for illness, disability, and dependent care, coverage, provisions, terminations, costs, and methods of covering for absent worker, by firm size, 1988 survey, 9768–21

Manufacturing job creation, elimination, and reallocation rates, and relation to industry and establishment characteristics, 1970s-86, working paper, 9375–13.56

Military enlistments and reenlistment rates, by service branch, FY79-90, annual rpt, 3544–1.2

Military personnel on active duty, recruits, and reenlistment, by race, sex, and service branch, quarterly press release, 3542–7

Military recruits and reenlistment rates, by service branch, quarterly rpt, 3542–14.4

Military reserve forces attrition, by reason, personnel characteristics, reserve component, and State, FY88, GAO rpt, 26123–329

Military women personnel on active and reserve duty, by demographic and service characteristics and service branch, FY89, annual chartbook, 3544–26

NASA staff characteristics and personnel actions, FY90, annual rpt, 9504–1

Nuclear power plant occupational radiation exposure, by site, 1968-87, annual rpt, 9634–3

SSA staff reductions impacts on client services, 1980s, GAO rpt, 26121–415

State and local govt employment of minorities and women, by occupation, function, pay level, and State, 1990, annual rpt, 9244–6

State and Metro Area Data Book, 1991 data compilation, 2328–54

Teacher attrition, by selected school and teacher characteristics, 1987/88-1988/89, 4836–3.5

Teacher employment, vacancies, and pay, by State, region, and school enrollment size, 1987/88, 4836–3.6

Teachers leaving profession and subsequent employment, by urban-rural location and public-private control of school, 1986-87, annual rpt, 4824–1.1

Timber industry impacts of northern spotted owl conservation in Pacific Northwest, and local govts Federal payments and severance taxes, 1980s and projected to 2000, hearing, 21168–50

Timber industry impacts of northern spotted owl conservation in Pacific Northwest, and worker aid programs, 1980s and projected to 2000, hearing, 21728–76

Unemployment by reason, detailed data, monthly rpt, 6742–2

Unemployment by reason, monthly press release, 6742–5

Unemployment by reason, transcripts of BLS Commissioner's monthly testimony, periodic rpt, 23846–4

Unemployment, by reason, 1947-90, annual rpt, 204–1.2

Unemployment insurance job search services, impacts on UI claims activity and reemployment, and claimant characteristics, for Tacoma, Wash, 1986-87, 6406–6.35

VA health care staff and turnover, by occupation, physician specialty, and location, 1990, annual rpt, 8604–8

see also Job tenure

see also Job vacancy

Labor unions

Collective bargaining agreements expiring during year, and workers covered, by firm, union, industry group, and State, 1991, annual rpt, 6784–9

Construction and building materials trade and professional assns, and labor unions, 1991 listing, article, 2042–1.202

County Business Patterns, 1988: employment, establishments, and payroll, by SIC 2- to 4-digit industry and county, annual State rpt series, 2326–6

County Business Patterns, 1989: employment, establishments, and payroll, by SIC 2- to 4-digit industry and county, annual State rpt series, 2326–8

Coverage by unions of workers and earnings, by age, sex, race, occupational group, and industry div, 1989-90, press release, 6726–1.36

Criminal sentences for Federal offenses, guidelines by offense and circumstances, series, 17668–1

Elections for representation conducted by NLRB, results, monthly rpt, 9582–2

Employment and earnings by union affiliation, monthly rpt, periodic data, 6742–2

Employment Cost Index and percent change by occupational group, industry div, region, and metro-nonmetro area, quarterly press release, 6782–5

Employment Cost Index, by industry sector and union status, monthly rpt, 6782–1.1

Employment, earnings, and hours, by SIC 1- to 4-digit industry, monthly and annual averages, selected years 1909-90, annual rpt, 6744–4

Fed Govt collective bargaining agreements, coverage, unions, and location, by agency, for contracts expiring 1990-91, annual listing, 9847–1

Fed Govt collective bargaining multi-unit agreements, by agency and labor union, annual listing, discontinued, 9847–4

Fed Govt labor unions recognized, coverage by agency and union, biennial rpt, discontinued, 9844–17

Index by Subjects and Names

Fed Labor Relations Authority and Fed Services Impasses Panel activities, and cases by union, agency, and disposition, FY85-90, annual rpt, 13364–1

Foreign countries economic, social, political, and geographic summary data, by country, 1991, annual factbook, 9114–2

Foreign countries labor conditions, union coverage, and work accidents, annual country rpt series, 6366–4

Genetic damage and trait monitoring and screening of employees, use, costs, benefits, and procedures, 1980s, 26358–230

Japan economic conditions, financial and intl policies, and trade devs, 1950s-80s and projected to 2050, compilation of papers, 23848–220

Labor Dept programs fraud and abuse, audits and investigations activity, and racketeering cases by type and disposition, FY88-89, GAO rpt, 26111–74

Manufacturing employment by selected characteristics, wages, and import and export penetration rates, by SIC 2- to 4- digit industry, 1982-89, 6366–3.27

Manufacturing wages impacts of foreign competition and other factors, late 1950s-89, article, 9385–1.204

Multinatl firms US affiliates, finances, and operations, by industry, world area of parent firm, and State, 1988-89, annual rpt, 2704–4

Natl Labor Relations Board activities, cases, elections conducted, and litigation, FY89, annual rpt, 9584–1

Natl Labor Relations Board cases, backlog, and processing time, 1960s-89, GAO rpt, 26121–395

Pension coverage by industry, vestment, and recipient income, by participant characteristics, 1987, Current Population Rpt, 2546–20.18

Pension plans coverage, by union status, 1979 and 1983, 15496–1.11

Political action committees, by type, 1974-91, semiannual press release, 9276–1.86; 9276–1.91

Political action committees contributions by party and finances, by PAC type, 1989-90, press release, 9276–1.89

Railroad retirement system funding and benefits findings and recommendations, with background industry data, 1960s-90 and projected to 2060, 9708–1

Registrations of unions with Labor Dept, parent bodies and locals by location, 1990 listing, 6468–17

State and Metro Area Data Book, 1991 data compilation, 2328–54

Statistical Abstract of US, 1991 annual data compilation, 2324–1.13

Trade adjustment aid for workers, petitions by disposition, selected industry, union, and State, monthly rpt, 6402–13

Unemployment insurance job search services, impacts on UI claims activity and reemployment, and claimant characteristics, for Tacoma, Wash, 1986-87, 6406–6.35

Wage and benefit changes from collective bargaining and mgmt decisions, by industry div, monthly rpt, 6782–1

Work stoppages, workers involved, and days idle, 1990 and trends from 1947, annual press release, 6784–12

see also Industry wage surveys
see also Labor-management relations, general
see also Labor-management relations in government

Laboratories

Acid rain data quality and accuracy, for 2 natl field and lab data collection programs, 1989, annual rpt, 5664–17

Acid rain data quality and accuracy, for 2 natl field data collection programs, 1978-89, 5668–124

County Business Patterns, 1988: employment, establishments, and payroll, by SIC 2- to 4-digit industry and county, annual State rpt series, 2326–6

County Business Patterns, 1989: employment, establishments, and payroll, by SIC 2- to 4-digit industry and county, annual State rpt series, 2326–8

DOE R&D projects and funding at natl labs, universities, and other instns, periodic summary rpt series, 3004–18

Drug (illegal) lab seizures, by substance and location, 1989-90, annual rpt, 6284–3

Drug (illegal) production, eradication, and seizures, by substance, with US aid, by country, 1987-91, annual rpt, 7004–17

Employment, earnings, and hours, by SIC 1- to 4-digit industry, monthly and annual averages, selected years 1909-90, annual rpt, 6744–4

Energy use in commercial buildings, costs, and conservation, by building characteristics, survey rpt series, 3166–8

Health maintenance organizations and other prepaid managed care plans Medicaid enrollment and use, for 20 States, 1985-89, chartbook, 4108–29

HHS financial aid, by program, recipient, State, and city, FY90, annual regional listings, 4004–3

Higher education instn R&D equipment, acquisition and service costs, condition, and financing, by field and subfield, 1988-90, triennial survey series, 9627–27

Hospital services and facilities availability, by selected instn characteristics, 1980, 1983, and 1987, 17206–2.22

Hospitals, receipts by source, contract services, expenses, and employment, by facility type and State, 1987 Census of Service Industries, 2393–4.12

Indian Health Service facilities, funding, operations, and Indian health and other characteristics, 1950s-90, annual chartbook, 4084–1

Medicare and Medicaid beneficiaries and program operations, 1991, annual fact book, 4654–18

Medicare claims approved, charges, and reimbursements by type of service, from 1974, monthly rpt, quarterly data, 4742–1.11

Medicare facilities, by type and State, 1989, and by type, 1967-89, annual rpt, 4744–3.5

Medicare reimbursement of hospitals under prospective payment system, and effect on services, finances, and beneficiary payments, 1979-90, annual rpt, 17204–2

Military chemical and biological weapons research labs security measures, and govt and contractor staff, 1988-90, GAO rpt, 26123–356

NIH grants for R&D, training, construction, and medical libraries, by location and recipient, FY90, annual listings, 4434–7

Oceanographic research ships, fleet condition, funding, voyages, and modernization costs, for NOAA, 1980s-90 and projected to 2020, 2148–60

Paternity determination through genetic testing, labs, services, and costs, 1991 listing, 4698–4

Pollution (air) emissions factors, by detailed pollutant and source, data compilation, 1990 rpt, 9198–120

Profitability and cost indexes for independent clinical labs by customer type, and impacts of Medicare fee caps, 1988-89, GAO rpt, 26121–425

Puerto Rico economic censuses, 1987: wholesale and retail trade and service industry finances and operations, by SIC 2- to 4-digit industry and municipio, 2591–1

Puerto Rico economic censuses, 1987: wholesale, retail, and service industries finances and operations, by establishment characteristics and SIC 2- and 3-digit industry, subject rpts, 2591–2

Service industries census, 1987: depreciable assets, capital and operating expenses, and receipts, by SIC 2- to 4-digit kind of business, 2393–2

Service industries census, 1987: establishments, receipts by source, payroll, and employment, by SIC 2- to 4-digit kind of business, State, and MSA, 2393–4

Service industries receipts, by SIC 2- to 4-digit kind of business, 1990, annual rpt, 2413–8

Tax (income) returns of corporations, income and tax items by asset size and detailed industry, 1987, annual rpt, 8304–4

Tax (income) returns of corporations, income and tax items by asset size and detailed industry, 1988, annual rpt, 8304–21

Tax (income) returns of sole proprietorships, income statement items, by industry group, 1989, annual article, 8302–2.214

Veterinary Services Natl Labs activities, biologic drug products evaluation and disease testing, FY90, annual rpt, 1394–17

Waste (medical) generation, sources, health worker exposure and risk, and incineration emissions, 1980s, 4078–1

see also Clinical laboratory technicians
see also Department of Energy National Laboratories

Lacker, Jeffrey M.

"Money, Trade Credit and Asset Prices", 9389–19.29

Laderman, Elizabeth S.

"Interstate Banking and Competition: Evidence from the Behavior of Stock Returns", 9393–8.205

"Location, Branching, and Bank Portfolio Diversification: The Case of Agricultural Lending", 9393–8.202

Lafayette, Ind.

see under By SMSA or MSA in the "Index by Categories"

Lafayette, La.

see also under By SMSA or MSA in the "Index by Categories"

Lair, Tamra J.

"Mental Health and Functional Status of Residents of Nursing and Personal Care Homes. National Medical Expenditure Survey", 4186–8.11

LAIRS

see Labor Agreement Information Retrieval System

Laity, Jim

"Coca Economy in the Upper Huallaga", 9918–19

Lake Charles, La.

Wages by occupation, and benefits for office and plant workers, 1991 survey, periodic MSA rpt, 6785–3.6

see also under By SMSA or MSA in the "Index by Categories"

Lake County, Ill.

CPI by component for US city average, and by region, population size, and for 15 metro areas, monthly rpt, 6762–1

CPI by component for US city average, and by region, population size, and for 27 metro areas, monthly rpt, 6762–2

Housing starts and completions authorized by building permits in 40 MSAs, quarterly rpt, 2382–9

Housing vacancy rates for single and multifamily units and mobile homes, by city and ZIP code, 1990, annual MSA rpt, 9304–18.2

see also under By SMSA or MSA in the "Index by Categories"

Lake County, Ind.

CPI by component for US city average, and by region, population size, and for 15 metro areas, monthly rpt, 6762–1

CPI by component for US city average, and by region, population size, and for 27 metro areas, monthly rpt, 6762–2

Lake County, Ohio

Housing and households characteristics, unit and neighborhood quality, and journey to work by MSA location, for 11 MSAs, 1984 survey, supplement, 2485–8

Housing and households detailed characteristics, and unit and neighborhood quality, by location, 1988 survey, MSA rpt, 2485–6.3

Lakeland, Fla.

see also under By SMSA or MSA in the "Index by Categories"

Lakes and lakeshores

Acid rain and air pollution environmental impacts, and methods of neutralizing acidified water bodies, summary research rpt series, 5506–5

Army Corps of Engineers water resources dev projects, characteristics, and costs, 1950s-89, biennial State rpt series, 3756–1

Army Corps of Engineers water resources dev projects, characteristics, and costs, 1950s-91, biennial State rpt series, 3756–2

Environmental conditions, fish, wildlife, use, and mgmt, for individual coastal and riparian ecosystems, series, 5506–9

Environmental Quality, status of problems, protection programs, research, and intl issues, 1991 annual rpt, 484–1

Lakes and lakeshores

Fish and Wildlife Service restoration programs funding, land purchases, and project listing, by State, FY89, annual rpt, 5504–1

Fish Hatchery Natl System activities and deliveries, by species, hatchery, and jurisdiction of waters stocked, FY90, annual rpt, 5504–10

Fish kills in coastal areas related to pollution and natural causes, by land use, State, and county, 1980s, 2178–32

Fishery research of State fish and wildlife agencies, federally funded projects and costs by species and State, 1990, annual listing, 5504–23

Gazetteer of US places, mountains, bodies of water, and other political and physical features, 1990 rpt, 5668–117

Global climate change environmental, infrastructure, and health impacts, with model results and background data, 1850s-2100, 9188–113

Landfills distance from wetlands and water habitats, for 11 States, 1990 rpt, 9188–115

Natl park system visits and overnight stays, by park and State, monthly rpt, 5542–4

Natl parks and other land under Natl Park Service mgmt, acreage by site, ownership, and region, FY91, semiannual rpt, 5542–1

Northeastern US recreation areas use, mgmt, and tourism dev issues, 1990 conf, 1208–356

Pollution (water) fish kills, by pollution source, month, location, and State, 1977-87, last issue of annual rpt, 9204–3

Public lands acreage, grants, use, revenues, and allocations, by State, FY90, annual rpt, 5724–1.2

Water quality, chemistry, hydrology, and other characteristics, local area studies, series, 5666–27

Water supply and quality in streams and lakes, and groundwater levels in wells, by drainage basin, 1988, annual State rpt series, 5666–16

Water supply and quality in streams and lakes, and groundwater levels in wells, by drainage basin, 1989, annual State rpt series, 5666–12

Water supply and quality in streams and lakes, and groundwater levels in wells, by drainage basin, 1990, annual State rpt series, 5666–10

Water supply, hydrologic events, and end use, by State, 1988-89, annual rpt, 5664–12

Western US activities of Reclamation Bur, land and population served, and recreation areas, by location, 1989, annual rpt, 5824–12

Wetlands (riparian) acreage, and Bur of Land Mgmt activities, mgmt plans, and scientific staff, State rpt series, 5726–8

Wetlands acreage, resources, soil and water properties, and conservation efforts, by wetland type, State rpt series, 5506–11

Wildlife and plant research results, habitat study series, 5506–13

Wildlife mgmt activities and funding, acreage, staff, and plans of Bur of Land Mgmt, habitat study series, 5726–6

see also Dredging

see also Great Lakes

see also Reservoirs

see also Wetlands

Lakewood, Colo.

see also under By City in the "Index by Categories"

Lakin, K. Charlie

"Medicaid-Financed Residential Care for Persons with Mental Retardation", 4652–1.219

"Medicaid Services for Persons with Mental Retardation and Related Conditions", 4658–49

Lalich, Nina

"Guide for the Management, Analysis, and Interpretation of Occupational Mortality Data", 4248–89

Lamas, Enrique J.

"Measuring the Effect of Benefits and Taxes on Income and Poverty: 1990", 2546–6.69

Lamb

see Meat and meat products

Lambert, Susan C.

"Water Use in South Carolina, 1985", 5666–24.9

Lambou, Victor W.

"Proximity of Sanitary Landfills to Wetlands and Deepwater Habitats: An Evaluation and Comparison of 1,153 Sanitary Landfills in 11 States", 9188–115

Lamps, electric

see Lighting equipment

Lancaster, Pa.

see also under By SMSA or MSA in the "Index by Categories"

Land

see Arid zones

see Farms and farmland

see Forests and forestry

see Geography

see Homesteads

see Land area

see Land ownership and rights

see Land reform

see Land use

see Pasture and rangeland

see Property condemnation

see Public lands

see Real estate business

see Reclamation of land

see Soil pollution

see Soils and soil conservation

see Topography

Land area

Acreage of land, by use, ownership, and State, 1987 and trends from 1910, 1588–48

Acreage of non-Federal land by use, soil and water conditions, and conservation needs, 1987, State rpt series, 1266–5

Acreage of wetlands, water, and land, by State, 1780s and 1980s, 5508–107

Agricultural export-related employment, land, and capital inputs, by commodity and country of destination, and compared to imports, 1977-87, 1548–373

Alabama timber acreage and value, by species, forest type, ownership, and county, 1990, series, 1206–30

Arizona timber resources by species, forest and tree characteristics, ownership, and county, 1984-85, 1208–374

Census of Population and Housing, 1990: population and housing characteristics,

Index by Subjects and Names

households, and land area, by county, subdiv, and place, State rpt series, 2551–1

Census of Population and Housing, 1990: voting age and total population by race, and housing units, by block, redistricting counts required under PL 94-171, State CD-ROM series, 2551–6

Census of Population, 1990: top 39 MSAs and 40 cities population, with trends from 1900, fact sheet, 2326–20.3

Census of Population, 1990: urban areas land area, housing units, and population, by State and compared to rural areas, press release, 2328–39

Coal leasing activity on Federal land, acreage, production, and reserves, by coal region and State, FY90, annual rpt, 5724–10

Coastal areas recreation facilities of Fed Govt and States, visitor and site characteristics, 1987-90 survey, regional rpt series, 2176–9

Developing countries agricultural supply, demand, and market for US exports, with socioeconomic conditions, country rpt series, 1526–6

Estuary environmental conditions, and fish and shellfish catch by species and region, 1980s, 2178–27

Fed Govt-leased real property inventory and rental costs, worldwide summary by location and agency, 1989, annual rpt, 9454–10

Fed Govt-owned real property inventory and costs, worldwide summary by purpose, agency, and location, 1989, annual rpt, 9454–5

Fish and Wildlife Service restoration programs funding, land purchases, and project listing, by State, FY89, annual rpt, 5504–1

Foreign countries economic, social, political, and geographic summary data, by country, 1991, annual factbook, 9114–2

Foreign countries *Geographic Notes*, boundaries, claims, nomenclature, and other devs, periodic rpt, 7142–3

Forest fires and acres burned on Forest Service land, by cause, forest, and State, 1989, annual rpt, 1204–6

Forest Service acreage, staff, finances, and mgmt activities in Pacific Northwest, with data by forest, 1970s-89, annual rpt, 1204–37

Forest Service mgmt of public lands and resources dev, environmental, economic, and social impacts of alternative programs, projected to 2040, 1208–24

Forests (natl) and other lands under Forest Service mgmt, acreage by forest and location, 1990, annual rpt, 1204–2

Forests (natl) revenue share paid to States, and acreage, by forest, region, county, and congressional district, FY90, annual rpt, 1204–33

Global climate change environmental, infrastructure, and health impacts, with model results and background data, 1850s-2100, 9188–113

Indiana timber resources and removals, by species, forest characteristics, ownership, and county, 1985-86, 1208–368

Military base support costs by function, and personnel and acreage by installation, by service branch, FY91, annual rpt, 3504–11

Index by Subjects and Names

Montana timber outside natl forests, acreage, resources, and mortality, by species and ownership class, 1988-89, 1206–25

North Carolina timber acreage, resources, and removals, by species, ownership class, and county, 1989/90, series, 1206–4

Northeastern US timber resources and removals, by species, ownership, and county, State rpt series, 1206–12

Park natl system and other land under Natl Park Service mgmt, acreage by site, ownership, and region, FY91, semiannual rpt, 5542–1

Park natl system visits and overnight stays, by park and State, 1990, annual rpt, 5544–12

Public lands acreage, grants, use, revenues, and allocations, by State, FY90 and trends, annual rpt, 5724–1

Public lands minerals resources and availability, State rpt series, 5606–7

Public lands recreation facilities and use, and Land Mgmt Bur mgmt activities, funding, and plans, State rpt series, 5726–5

Real estate assets of failed thrifts, inventory of properties available from Resolution Trust Corp, semiannual listing series, 9722–2

Recreation (outdoor) coastal facilities, by State, county, estuary, and level of govt, 1972-84, 2178–29

Southeastern US longleaf pine mgmt and use, 1989 conf, 1208–355

State and Metro Area Data Book, 1991 data compilation, 2328–54

Statistical Abstract of US, 1991 annual data compilation, 2324–1; 2324–1.6

Timber acreage, by ownership, forest type, and State, 1950s-87 and projected to 2040, 1208–357

Timber and orchard damage from natural disaster, USDA restoration aid and program participation by practice and State, FY89-90, annual rpt, 1804–24

Timber and planting and dev, by State, FY90, annual rpt, 1204–7

Timber insect and disease incidence and damage, and control activities, State rpt series, 1206–49

Timber insect and disease incidence and damage, annual regional rpt series, 1206–11

Water resources data collection and analysis activities of USGS Water Resources Div Districts, with project descriptions, series, 5666–26

Western US activities of Reclamation Bur, land and population served, and recreation areas, by location, 1989, annual rpt, 5824–12

Wetlands (riparian) acreage, and Bur of Land Mgmt activities, mgmt plans, and scientific staff, State rpt series, 5726–8

Wetlands acreage, and agreements and payments to farmers under Water Bank Program, by State, 1972-91, annual rpt, 1804–21

Wetlands preservation under Water Bank Program, acreage, agreements, and payments, by State, monthly rpt, 1802–5

Wildlife and plant research results, habitat study series, 5506–13

Wildlife mgmt activities and funding, acreage by habitat type, and scientific staff, for Bur of Land Mgmt, State rpt series, 5726–7

Wildlife mgmt activities and funding, acreage, staff, and plans of Bur of Land Mgmt, habitat study series, 5726–6

Wildlife refuges and other land under Fish and Wildlife Service mgmt, acreage by site and State, as of Sept 1991, annual rpt, 5504–8

see also Farms and farmland

see also Land use

Land claims

see Indian claims

Land, Garland H.

"Changes in Characteristics of Women Who Smoke During Pregnancy: Missouri, 1978-88", 4042–3.203

Land ownership and rights

Acreage of land, by use, ownership, and State, 1987 and trends from 1910, 1588–48

Agriculture census, 1987: farms, farmland, production, finances, and operator characteristics, by county, final State rpt series, 2331–1

Alabama timber acreage and value, by species, forest type, ownership, and county, 1990, series, 1206–30

Alaska land area by ownership, and availability for mineral exploration and dev, 1984-86, 5608–152

Alaska submerged land grant holdings of Alaska Natives, exchange for upland acreage, impacts on conservation acreage and acquisition, 1989-90, 5728–38

Alaska timber production, trade, and Pacific basin market demand, 1960s-2010, 1208–365

Arizona timber resources by species, forest and tree characteristics, ownership, and county, 1984-85, 1208–374

Assets and debts of private sector, balance sheets by segment, 1945-90, semiannual rpt, 9365–4.1

Corn farms, finances, acreage, and production, by size, region, and State, 1987, 1568–304

Farm production inputs, finances, mgmt, and land value and transfers, periodic situation rpt with articles, 1561–16

Farmland in US owned by foreigners, holdings, acquisitions, and disposals by land use, owner type and country, and State, 1990, annual rpt, 1584–2

Farmland in US owned by foreigners, holdings, acreage, and value by land use, owner country, State, and county, 1990, annual rpt, 1584–3

Farms, farmland, and sales distribution, by sales size, various periods 1969-84, 1588–150

Foreign direct investment in US by country, and finances, employment, and acreage owned, by industry group of business acquired or established, 1984-90, annual article, 2702–1.210

Foreign direct investment in US commercial real estate, by State and country, 1980s, GAO rpt, 26123–350

Foreign direct investment in US, major transactions by type, industry, country, and US location, 1989, annual rpt, 2044–20

Forest Service mgmt of public lands and resources dev, environmental, economic, and social impacts of alternative programs, projected to 2040, 1208–24

Historic buildings rehabilitation tax incentives, projects, costs, ownership, and use, FY77-90, annual rpt, 5544–17

Indiana timber resources and removals, by species, forest characteristics, ownership, and county, 1985-86, 1208–368

Loan activity for mortgages, by type of lender, loan, and mortgaged property, quarterly press release, 5142–30

Minerals foreign and US supply under alternative market conditions, reserves, and background industry data, series, 5606–4

Montana timber outside natl forests, acreage, resources, and mortality, by species and ownership class, 1988-89, 1206–25

Multinatl firms US affiliates, finances, and operations, by industry, world area of parent firm, and State, 1988-89, annual rpt, 2704–4

New Hampshire and Vermont public opinion on natural resources use and mgmt, 1991 rpt, 1208–371

North Carolina timber acreage, resources, and removals, by species, ownership class, and county, 1989/90, series, 1206–4

Northeastern US forest wildlife habitat characteristics, by location, State rpt series, 1206–44

Northeastern US timber resources, and related manufacturing industries employment and finances, by State, 1977-87, 1208–375

Northeastern US timber resources and removals, by species, ownership, and county, State rpt series, 1206–12

Oklahoma timber resources, growth, and removals, by species, forest type, ownership, and county, 1986, regional rpt series, 1206–39

Oregon (western) timber resources, acreage by land use and ownership, 1961-86, 1208–353

Park natl system and other land under Natl Park Service mgmt, acreage by site, ownership, and region, FY91, semiannual rpt, 5542–1

Productivity of labor and capital, indexes and percent change, 1948-90, annual press release, 6824–2

Southeastern US longleaf pine mgmt and use, 1989 conf, 1208–355

Tax (income) returns filed by type of filer, selected income items, quarterly rpt, 8302–2.1

Timber acreage, by ownership, forest type, and State, 1950s-87 and projected to 2040, 1208–357

Timber insect and disease incidence and damage, and control activities, State rpt series, 1206–49

Timber insect and disease incidence and damage, annual regional rpt series, 1206–11

Uranium reserves and industry operations, by region and State, various periods 1966-90, annual rpt, 3164–65.1

Virginia timber resources, growth, and removals, by species, ownership, treatment, and county, 1990-91, series, 1206–6

Land ownership and rights

see also Government supplies and property
see also Homesteads
see also Housing tenure
see also Public lands
see also Real estate business
see also Vacant and abandoned property

Land reclamation
see Reclamation of land

Land reform
Eastern Europe agricultural production, trade, and land reform, with selected economic indicators, by country, 1960s-90, article, 1522–3.202

Land surveying
see Land area

Land tax
see Property tax

Land use
- Acreage of land, by use, ownership, and State, 1987 and trends from 1910, 1588–48
- Acreage of non-Federal land by use, soil and water conditions, and conservation needs, 1987, State rpt series, 1266–5
- Aerial survey R&D rpts, and sources of natural resource and environmental data, quarterly listing, 9502–7
- Aircraft noise abatement measures, and industry compliance costs, aggregate FY90-2000, GAO rpt, 26113–534
- Coastal areas environmental and socioeconomic conditions, and potential impact of oil and gas OCS leases, final statement series, 5736–1
- Developing countries agricultural supply, demand, and market for US exports, with socioeconomic conditions, country rpt series, 1526–6
- Developing countries economic, population, and agricultural data, US and other aid sources, and AID activity, country rpt series, 9916–12
- *Environmental Quality*, status of problems, protection programs, research, and intl issues, 1991 annual rpt, 484–1
- Estuary environmental conditions, and fish and shellfish catch by species and region, 1980s, 2178–27
- Fish kills in coastal areas related to pollution and natural causes, by land use, State, and county, 1980s, 2178–32
- Florida environmental, social, and economic conditions, and impacts of proposed OCS oil and gas leases in southern coastal areas, 1990 compilation of papers, 5738–19
- Foreign countries economic, social, political, and geographic summary data, by country, 1991, annual factbook, 9114–2
- Foreign ownership of US farmland, holdings, acquisitions, and disposals by land use, owner type and country, and State, 1990, annual rpt, 1584–2
- Foreign ownership of US farmland, holdings, acreage, and value by land use, owner country, State, and county, 1990, annual rpt, 1584–3
- Forest Service mgmt of public lands and resources dev, environmental, economic, and social impacts of alternative programs, projected to 2040, 1208–24
- New Hampshire and Vermont public opinion on natural resources use and mgmt, 1991 rpt, 1208–371

North Carolina environmental and socioeconomic conditions, and impacts of proposed OCS oil and gas exploration, 1970s-90 and projected to 2020, 5738–22

Pollution (water) fish kills, by pollution source, month, location, and State, 1977-87, last issue of annual rpt, 9204–3

Research (agricultural) funding and staffing for USDA, State agencies, and other instns, by topic, FY90, annual rpt, 1744–2

State and Metro Area Data Book, 1991 data compilation, 2328–54

Statistical Abstract of US, 1991 annual data compilation, 2324–1.6

Washington State marine sanctuaries proposal, environmental and economic impacts, with background data, 1984-89, 2178–30

Water (groundwater) supply, quality, chemistry, and use, State and local area rpt series, 5666–28

Water quality, chemistry, hydrology, and other characteristics, local area studies, series, 5666–27

see also City and town planning
see also Farms and farmland
see also Forests and forestry
see also Industrial siting
see also Land ownership and rights
see also Land reform
see also Mines and mineral resources
see also Pasture and rangeland
see also Property condemnation
see also Public lands
see also Reclamation of land
see also Regional planning
see also Zoning and zoning laws

Lande, James L.
"Telephone Rates Update", 9282–8

Landefeld, J. Steven
"Valuation of the U.S. Net International Investment Position", 2702–1.211

Landfills
- Air pollution emissions factors, by detailed pollutant and source, data compilation, 1990 rpt, 9198–120
- Methane recovered from landfills, use by region, 1989, 3166–6.56
- New York Bight pollution levels, sources, treatment costs, economic losses, and environmental and health effects, 1990 conf, 9208–131
- Water quality, chemistry, hydrology, and other characteristics, 1989 local area study, 5666–27.11
- Wetlands and water habitats distance from landfills, for 11 States, 1990 rpt, 9188–115

Landscape protection
see Environmental pollution and control
see Land use

Lang, William W.
"Housing Appraisals and Redlining", 9387–8.242

Langan, Patrick A.
"Race of Prisoners Admitted to State and Federal Institutions, 1926-86", 6068–245

Lange, W. Robert
"Followup Study of Possible HIV Seropositivity Among Abusers of Parenteral Drugs in 1971-72", 4042–3.237

Index by Subjects and Names

Langer, Judith A.
"Learning to Read in Our Nation's Schools. National Assessment of Educational Progress, 1988", 4896–7.2

Langley, Suchada V.
"Thailand: Emergence of a Sugar Superpower", 1561–14.201

Language arts
- Copyrights Register activities, registrations by material type, and fees, FY90 and trends from 1790, annual rpt, 26404–2
- DOD Dependents Schools basic skills and college entrance test scores, 1990-91, annual rpt, 3504–16
- Education data compilation, 1991 annual rpt, 4824–2
- Elementary and secondary students educational performance in math, science, reading, and writing, 1970s-90, 4898–32
- Fed Govt aid to higher education and nonprofit instns for R&D and related activities, by field, instn, agency, and State, FY89, annual rpt, 9627–17
- High school advanced placement for college credit, programs by selected characteristics and school control, 1984-86, 4838–46
- Higher education course completions, by detailed program, sex, race, and instn type, for 1972 high school class, as of 1984, 4888–4
- Higher education grad programs enrollment in science and engineering, by field, source of funds, and characteristics of student and instn, 1975-89, annual rpt, 9627–7
- Migrant workers children education programs enrollment, staff, and effectiveness, by State, 1980s, 4808–30
- Natl Education Goals progress indicators, by State, 1991, annual rpt, 15914–1
- Natl Endowment for Arts activities and grants, FY90, annual rpt, 9564–3
- USIA English language program enrollment and staff, by country and world region, FY90, annual rpt, 9854–2
- *see also* Area studies
- *see also* Writers and writing

Language use and ability
- Children with limited English proficiency, FY88-90, biennial rpt, 4804–14
- *Condition of Education*, detail for elementary and secondary education, 1920s-90 and projected to 2001, annual rpt, 4824–1.1
- *Digest of Education Statistics*, 1991 annual data compilation, 4824–2
- Eighth grade class of 1988: educational performance and conditions, characteristics, attitudes, activities, and plans, natl longitudinal survey, series, 4826–9
- Elementary and secondary students educational performance in math, science, reading, and writing, 1970s-90, 4898–32
- Higher education remedial programs, enrollment, courses, and faculty, by instn characteristics, 1989/90, 4826–1.30
- Hispanic Americans in counties bordering Mexico, by selected characteristics, 1980, Current Population Rpt, 2546–2.159
- Immigrant children education programs funding by Fed Govt and school districts, and student characteristics, 1980s, GAO rpt, 26121–418

Index by Subjects and Names

Latin America

Poverty area schools academic environment and teaching methods impacts on student performance, 1989/90 study, 4808–28

Refugee resettlement programs and funding, arrivals by country of origin, and indicators of adjustment, by State, FY90, annual rpt, 4694–5

Special education programs, enrollment by age, staff, funding, and needs, by type of handicap and State, 1989/90, annual rpt, 4944–4

Writing ability of elementary and secondary students, and factors affecting proficiency, by selected characteristics, 1988 natl assessments, subject rpt series, 4896–7.1

see also Bilingual education

see also Compensatory education

see also Foreign languages

see also Language arts

see also Learning disabilities

see also Literacy and illiteracy

see also Reading ability and habits

see also Speech pathology and audiology

see also Writers and writing

Langwell, Kathryn

"Rising Health Care Costs: Causes, Implications, and Strategies", 26306–6.155

"Trends in Health Expenditures by Medicare and the Nation", 26308–98

Lansing, Mich.

see also under By City and By SMSA or MSA in the "Index by Categories"

Lantz, Paula M.

"Mammography Screening and Increased Incidence of Breast Cancer in Wisconsin", 4472–1.229

Laos

Agricultural exports of high-value commodities, indexes and sales by commodity, world area, and country, 1960s-86, 1528–323

Agricultural trade of US, by detailed commodity and country, 1989, annual rpt, 1524–8

Agricultural trade of US, by detailed commodity and country, 1990, semiannual rpt, 1522–4

AID loans repayment status and terms by program and country, and status of predecessor agency loans, quarterly rpt, 9912–3

Background Notes, summary social, political, and economic data, 1991 rpt, 7006–2.26

Economic and military aid and loans from US and intl agencies, by program and country, FY46-90, annual rpt, 9914–5

Economic conditions, income, production, prices, employment, and trade, 1991 periodic country rpt, 2046–4.68

Economic, social, political, and geographic summary data, by country, 1991, annual factbook, 9114–2

Export licensing, monitoring, and enforcement activities, FY90, annual rpt, 2024–1

Exports and imports of US, by transport mode, country, and SITC 1- to 3-digit commodity, 1990, annual rpt, 2424–12

Exports and imports of US with Communist countries, by detailed commodity and country, quarterly rpt with articles, 9882–2

Human rights conditions in 170 countries, and US economic and military aid, 1990, annual rpt, 21384–3

Refugee resettlement programs and funding, arrivals by country of origin, and indicators of adjustment, by State, FY90, annual rpt, 4694–5

Refugees from Indochina, arrivals, and departures, by country of origin and resettlement, camp, and ethnicity, monthly rpt, 7002–4

UN voting record and share of votes in agreement with US, by issue, country, and world area, 1990, annual rpt, 7004–18

see also under By Foreign Country in the "Index by Categories"

Larceny

see Robbery and theft

Lard

see Oils, oilseeds, and fats

Laredo, Tex.

see also under By City and By SMSA or MSA in the "Index by Categories"

Larsen, Richard J.

"EML Surface Air Sampling Program, 1989 Data", 3004–31

"Worldwide Deposition of Strontium-90 Through 1986", 3004–29

Larson, Bruce

"Direct Approach for Estimating Nitrogen, Phosphorus, and Land Demands at the Regional Level", 1588–152

Las Cruces, N.Mex.

Wages by occupation, and benefits for office and plant workers, 1991 survey, periodic MSA rpt, 6785–3.5

see also under By SMSA or MSA in the "Index by Categories"

Las Vegas, Nev.

Air traffic, and passenger and freight enplanements, by airport, 1960s-90 and projected to 2010, hub area rpt, 7506–7.41

Housing starts and completions authorized by building permits in 40 MSAs, quarterly rpt, 2382–9

Wages by occupation, and benefits for office and plant workers, 1990 survey, periodic MSA rpt, 6785–3.1

see also under By City and By SMSA or MSA in the "Index by Categories"

Lasers

Exports and imports of US, by Harmonized System 6-digit commodity and country, 1990, annual rpt, 2424–13

Price indexes (producer), by stage of processing and detailed commodity, monthly rpt, 6762–6

Price indexes (producer), by stage of processing and detailed commodity, monthly 1990, annual rpt, 6764–2

Shipments, trade, use, and firms, for electronic communications systems and related products, 1990, annual Current Industrial Rpt, 2506–12.35

Lassuy, Dennis R.

"Pacific Herring. Species Profiles: Life Histories and Environmental Requirements of Coastal Fishes and Invertebrates (Pacific Northwest)", 5506–8.133

Latin America

Agricultural production, prices, and trade, by country, 1960s-90, annual world area rpt, 1524–4.2

Agricultural subsidies to producers and consumers in 6 Latin America countries, by selected commodity, 1982-87, 1528–324

AID dev funds obligated but unspent by country, and impacts of alternative allocation formulas, FY87-90, GAO rpt, 26123–327

AIDS virus infection prevalence in developing countries, by sex, selected city, urban-rural location, and country, 1991, semiannual rpt, 2322–4

Coal trade flows and reserves, by country, 1980-89 and projected to 2010, annual rpt, 3164–77

Cocaine production, eradication, and seizures, by Latin American country, 1988-90, 236–2.1

Construction contract awards and billings, by country of contractor and world area of award, 1989, annual article, 2042–1.201

Corporations in US under foreign control, income tax returns, assets and income statement items by industry div, country, and world area, 1988, article, 8302–2.219

Economic and social conditions of developing countries from 1960s, and Intl Dev Cooperation Agency and AID activities and funding, FY90-92, annual rpt, 9904–4

Energy production by type, and oil trade, and use, by country group and selected country, monthly rpt, 9112–2

Energy use and production, by fuel type, country, and country group, projected 1995-2010 and trends from 1970, annual rpt, 3164–84

Energy use and trade, by selected Latin America country, 1970s-80s and projected to 2000, 3408–1

Energy use in developing countries, and economic and environmental impacts, by fuel type, world area, and country, 1980s-90, 26358–232

English language program of USIA, enrollment and staff, by country and world region, FY90, annual rpt, 9854–2

Exchange and training programs of Federal agencies, participants by world area, and funding, by program, FY89, annual rpt, 9854–8

Export and investment promotion projects of AID in Latin America and Caribbean, effectiveness, 1974-89, 9916–3.63

Exports and imports (waterborne) of US, by type of service, commodity, country, route, and US port, 1988, annual rpt, 7704–2

Exports and imports (waterborne) of US, by type of service, customs district, port, and world area, monthly rpt, 2422–7

Exports and imports of US, by Harmonized System 6-digit commodity and country, 1990, annual rpt, 2424–13

Exports and imports of US, by selected country, country group, and commodity group, 1990, annual rpt, 2044–37

Exports and imports of US, by transport mode, country, and SITC 1- to 3-digit commodity, 1990, annual rpt, 2424–12

Exports, imports, and balances of US with major trading partners, by product category, 1986-90, annual chartbook, 9884–21

Family planning and population activities of AID, grants by project and recipient, and contraceptive shipments, by country, FY90, annual rpt series, 9914–13

Latin America

Immigrant and nonimmigrant visas of US issued and refused, by class, issuing office, and nationality, FY89, annual rpt, 7184–1

Immigrants admitted to US, by country of birth, FY81-90, annual rpt, 6264–4

Immigrants admitted to US, by occupational group and country of birth, preliminary FY90, annual table, 6264–1

Immigrants in US, population characteristics and fertility, by birthplace and compared to native born, 1980s, Current Population rpt, 2546–2.162

Immigration, alien workers, amnesty programs, and employer sanctions impacts on US economy and labor force, series, 6366–5

Inter-American Foundation activities, grants by recipient, and fellowships, by country, FY90, annual rpt, 14424–1

Inter-American Foundation dev grants by program area, and fellowships by field and instn, by country, FY72-90, annual rpt, 14424–2

Investment (foreign direct) in US, by industry group and world area, 1987-90, annual article, 2702–1.219

Investment (foreign direct) in US, by industry group of US affiliate and country of parent firm, 1980-86, 2708–41

Investment (foreign direct) of US, by industry group and world area, 1987-90, annual article, 2702–1.220

Loans of US banks to foreigners at all US and foreign offices, by country group and country, quarterly rpt, 13002–1

Military aid of US, arms sales, and training programs costs and budget requests, by program, world region, and country, FY90-92, annual rpt, 7144–13

Military spending and imports of developing countries, measures to determine eligibility for US economic aid, by country, 1986-87, annual rpt, 9914–1

Multinatl firms US affiliates, finances, and operations, by industry, world area of parent firm, and State, 1988-89, annual rpt, 2704–4

Multinatl US firms and foreign affiliates finances and operations, by industry and world area of parent firm, 1989 benchmark survey, preliminary annual rpt, 2704–5

Peace Corps activities, funding by program, and volunteers, by country, FY92, annual rpt, 9654–1

Refugee arrivals in US by world area and country of origin, and quotas, monthly rpt, 7002–4

Refugee arrivals in US by world area of origin and State of settlement, and Federal aid, FY90-91 and proposed FY92 allocations, annual rpt, 7004–16

Refugee resettlement programs and funding, arrivals by country of origin, and indicators of adjustment, by State, FY90, annual rpt, 4694–5

Terrorism (intl) incidents, casualties, and attacks on US targets, by attack type and world area, 1990, annual rpt, 7004–13

Tide height and time daily at coastal points, forecast 1992, annual rpt, 2174–2.2; 2174–2.3

Travel to and from US on US and foreign flag air carriers, by country, world area, and US port, monthly rpt, 7302–2

UN voting record and share of votes in agreement with US, by issue, country, and world area, 1990, annual rpt, 7004–18

US military and civilian personnel and dependents, by service branch, world area, and country, quarterly rpt, 3542–20

USIA library holdings, use, and staff, by country and city, FY90, annual rpt, 9854–4

Weather conditions and effect on agriculture, by US region, State, and city, and world area, weekly rpt, 2182–7

Weather events and anomalies, precipitation and temperature for US and foreign locations, weekly rpt, 2182–6

see also Anguilla
see also Antigua and Barbuda
see also Argentina
see also Aruba
see also Bahamas
see also Belize
see also Bermuda
see also Bolivia
see also Brazil
see also British Virgin Islands
see also Caribbean area
see also Cayman Islands
see also Central America
see also Chile
see also Colombia
see also Costa Rica
see also Cuba
see also Dominica
see also Dominican Republic
see also Ecuador
see also El Salvador
see also French Guiana
see also Grenada
see also Guatemala
see also Guyana
see also Haiti
see also Honduras
see also Inter-American Development Bank
see also Jamaica
see also Mexico
see also Netherlands Antilles
see also Nicaragua
see also Organization of American States
see also Panama
see also Paraguay
see also Peru
see also Puerto Rico
see also South America
see also St. Christopher and Nevis
see also St. Lucia
see also St. Vincent and The Grenadines
see also Suriname
see also Trinidad and Tobago
see also Uruguay
see also U.S. Virgin Islands
see also Venezuela
see also under By Foreign Country in the "Index by Categories"

Latinos

see Hispanic Americans
see Mexicans in the U.S.

Latta, Viola B.

"Medicare Short-Stay Hospital Services by Diagnosis-Related Groups", 4652–1.250

"Use and Cost of Short-Stay Hospital Inpatient Services Under Medicare, 1988", 4652–1.207

Index by Subjects and Names

Latvia

Human rights conditions in 170 countries, and US economic and military aid, 1990, annual rpt, 21384–3

Laundre, John W.

"Status, Distribution, and Management of Mountain Goats in the Greater Yellowstone Ecosystem", 5548–19

Laundry and cleaning services

County Business Patterns, 1988: employment, establishments, and payroll, by SIC 2- to 4-digit industry and county, annual State rpt series, 2326–6

County Business Patterns, 1989: employment, establishments, and payroll, by SIC 2- to 4-digit industry and county, annual State rpt series, 2326–8

CPI by component for US city average, and by region, population size, and for 27 metro areas, monthly rpt, 6762–2

Enterprise Statistics, 1987: finances and operations for companies, by size, level of diversification, form of organization, and industry group, 2329–8

Franchise business opportunities by firm and kind of business, and sources of aid and info, 1990 annual listing, 2104–7

Labor productivity, indexes of output, hours, and employment by SIC 2- to 4-digit industry, 1967-89, annual rpt, 6824–1.4

Occupational injury and illness rates, by SIC 2- to 4-digit industry, 1988-89, annual rpt, 6844–7

Occupational injury and illness rates, by SIC 2- to 4-digit industry, 1989, annual rpt, 6844–1

Pollution (air) emissions factors, by detailed pollutant and source, data compilation, 1990 rpt, 9198–120

Pollution (water) industrial releases in wastewater, levels, treatment, costs, and regulation, with background financial and operating data, 1989 industry rpt, 9206–4.10

Puerto Rico economic censuses, 1987: wholesale and retail trade and service industry finances and operations, by SIC 2- to 4-digit industry and municipio, 2591–1

Puerto Rico economic censuses, 1987: wholesale, retail, and service industries finances and operations, by establishment characteristics and SIC 2- and 3-digit industry, subject rpts, 2591–2

Receipts for services, by SIC 2- to 4-digit kind of business, 1990, annual rpt, 2413–8

Service industries census, 1987: depreciable assets, capital and operating expenses, and receipts, by SIC 2- to 4-digit kind of business, 2393–2

Service industries census, 1987: establishments, receipts by source, payroll, and employment, by SIC 2- to 4-digit kind of business, State, and MSA, 2393–4

Tax (income) returns of partnerships, income statement and balance sheet items, by industry group, 1989, annual article, 8302–2.216; 8304–18

Tax (income) returns of sole proprietorships, income statement items, by industry group, 1989, annual article, 8302–2.214

see also Janitorial and maintenance services

Index by Subjects and Names

Law

Foreign countries economic, social, political, and geographic summary data, by country, 1991, annual factbook, 9114–2

Smoking bans in public places, local ordinances provisions, as of 1989, 4478–196

see also Administration of justice

see also Administrative law and procedure

see also Alcoholic beverages control laws

see also Antitrust law

see also Building codes

see also Civil procedure

see also Commercial law

see also Constitutional law

see also Courts

see also Criminal procedure

see also Due process of law

see also Environmental regulation

see also Financial institutions regulation

see also Government-citizen lawsuits

see also International cooperation in law enforcement

see also International law

see also Labor law

see also Law enforcement

see also Lawyers and legal services

see also Legal aid

see also Legal education

see also Maritime law

see also Military law

see also State laws

see also Tax laws and courts

see also Traffic laws and courts

see also U.S. statutes

see also Zoning and zoning laws

Law enforcement

Data on crime, criminal justice admin and enforcement, and public opinion, data compilation, 1991 annual rpt, 6064–6

Drug and alcohol abuse and mental illness direct and indirect costs, by type and patient age and sex, 1985 with 1980 and 1988 comparisons, 4038–35

Education data compilation, 1991 annual rpt, 4824–2

Employment, payroll, and spending for criminal justice, by level of govt, State, and selected city and county, FY71-88, annual rpt, 6064–9

Employment, payroll, and spending for criminal justice, by level of govt, State, and selected city and county, 1984-86, biennial rpt, 6064–4

Forest Service acreage, staff, finances, and mgmt activities in Pacific Northwest, with data by forest, 1970s-89, annual rpt, 1204–37

Govt census, 1987: local govt employment by function, payroll, and average earnings, for individual counties, cities, and school and special districts, 2455–1

Govt spending measures using indicators of service costs and demand, with comparisons to fiscal capacity and actual outlays, by State, for State and local govts, 1986-87, 10048–77

Justice Natl Inst rpts, 1983-89, listing, 6068–240

Palau admin, and social, economic, and govtl data, FY90, annual rpt, 7004–6

Statistical Abstract of US, 1991 annual data compilation, 2324–1.5

see also Administration of justice

see also Administrative law and procedure

see also Arrest

see also Campus security

see also Correctional institutions

see also Courts

see also Crime and criminals

see also Criminal investigations

see also Criminal procedure

see also Electronic surveillance

see also Federal aid to law enforcement

see also Forensic sciences

see also International cooperation in law enforcement

see also Juvenile detention and correctional institutions

see also Organized crime

see also Police

see also Pretrial detention and release

see also Searches and seizures

see also State funding for public safety

see also Traffic laws and courts

Law of the sea

see Maritime law

Law schools

see Legal education

Lawn and garden equipment

County Business Patterns, 1988: employment, establishments, and payroll, by SIC 2- to 4-digit industry and county, annual State rpt series, 2326–6

County Business Patterns, 1989: employment, establishments, and payroll, by SIC 2- to 4-digit industry and county, annual State rpt series, 2326–8

CPI by component for US city average, and by region, population size, and for 27 metro areas, monthly rpt, 6762–2

Exports and imports of US, by Harmonized System 6-digit commodity and country, 1990, annual rpt, 2424–13

Exports of US, detailed Schedule B commodities with countries of destination, 1990, annual rpt, 2424–10

Franchise business opportunities by firm and kind of business, and sources of aid and info, 1990 annual listing, 2104–7

Injuries from use of consumer products, by severity, victim age, and detailed product, 1990, annual rpt, 9164–6

Injuries from use of consumer products, related deaths and costs, and recalls by brand, by product type, FY89, annual rpt, 9164–2

Labor productivity, indexes of output, hours, and employment by SIC 2- to 4-digit industry, 1967-89, annual rpt, 6824–1.3

Manufacturing annual survey, 1989: finances and operations, by SIC 2- to 4-digit industry, series, 2506–15

Manufacturing census, 1987: finances and operations, by SIC 2- to 4-digit industry, State, and MSA, with trends from 1849, 2497–1

Manufacturing census, 1987: finances and operations, by type of organization and SIC 2- to 4-digit industry, subject rpt, 2497–5

Manufacturing finances and operations, by SIC 2- to 4-digit industry, forecast 1991, annual rpt, 2044–28

Occupational injury and illness rates, by SIC 2- to 4-digit industry, 1988-89, annual rpt, 6844–7

Occupational injury and illness rates, by SIC 2- to 4-digit industry, 1989, annual rpt, 6844–1

Lawyers and legal services

Price indexes (producer), by stage of processing and detailed commodity, monthly rpt, 6762–6

Price indexes (producer), by stage of processing and detailed commodity, monthly 1990, annual rpt, 6764–2

Productivity measures for farm and garden equipment industry, 1958-88, article, 6722–1.232

Productivity of labor and capital, and indexes of output, hours, and employment, 1967-89, annual rpt, 6824–1.5

Puerto Rico economic censuses, 1987: wholesale and retail trade and service industry finances and operations, by SIC 2- to 4-digit industry and municipio, 2591–1

Shipments, trade, use, and firms, for farm and garden equipment by product, 1990, annual Current Industrial Rpt, 2506–12.1

Wholesale trade census, 1987: establishments, sales by customer class, employment, inventories, and expenses, by SIC 2- to 4-digit kind of business, 2407–4

Lawnmowers

see Lawn and garden equipment

Lawrence Berkeley Laboratory

see also Department of Energy National Laboratories

Lawrence, Kans.

see also under By SMSA or MSA in the "Index by Categories"

Lawrence Livermore National Laboratory

see also Department of Energy National Laboratories

Lawrence, Mass.

CPI by component for US city average, and by region, population size, and for 15 metro areas, monthly rpt, 6762–1

CPI by component for US city average, and by region, population size, and for 27 metro areas, monthly rpt, 6762–2

see also under By SMSA or MSA in the "Index by Categories"

Lawson, Ann M.

"Alternative Measures of the Rate of Return on Direct Investment", 2702–1.217

"Valuation of the U.S. Net International Investment Position", 2702–1.211

Lawton, Okla.

Wages by occupation, for office and plant workers, 1991 survey, periodic MSA rpt, 6785–3.5

see also under By SMSA or MSA in the "Index by Categories"

Lawyers and legal services

Aircraft accidents victims compensation, legal costs, and time to disposition, under intl agreements and US liability system, aggregate 1970-84, GAO rpt, 26113–501

Appellate court pre-argument conferences impacts on case processing, disposition, and duration, for Federal 6th circuit, 1985-86, 18408–45

Attorneys general of US and Canada, 1990 listing, 4208–34

Child abuse and neglect victims representation in legal proceedings, caseloads, State requirements, and compensation, by State and county, 1989, 4608–28

Copyright infringement lawsuit damages and legal fee awards, by case, 1930s-87, hearing, 21528–82

Lawyers and legal services

County Business Patterns, 1988: employment, establishments, and payroll, by SIC 2- to 4-digit industry and county, annual State rpt series, 2326–6

County Business Patterns, 1989: employment, establishments, and payroll, by SIC 2- to 4-digit industry and county, annual State rpt series, 2326–8

CPI by component for US city average, and by region, population size, and for 27 metro areas, monthly rpt, 6762–2

Defense lawyers subpoenas by Federal prosecutors, and public and private indigent defense lawyers pay by State, 1986-90, hearing, 21408–123

Employment and spending for law enforcement, by activity and level of govt, data compilation, 1991 annual rpt, 6064–6.1

Employment, earnings, and hours, by SIC 1- to 4-digit industry, monthly and annual averages, selected years 1909-90, annual rpt, 6744–4

Employment, payroll, and spending for criminal justice, by level of govt, State, and selected city and county, FY71-88, annual rpt, 6064–9

Enterprise Statistics, 1987: auxiliaries of multi-establishment firms, finances and operations by function, industry, and State, 2329–6

Enterprise Statistics, 1987: finances and operations for companies, by size, level of diversification, form of organization, and industry group, 2329–8

Exports and imports of services, direct and among multinatl firms affiliates, by industry and world area, 1986-90, article, 2702–1.223

Fed Govt accounts receivable, delinquent debt cases and collections of Justice Dept and private law firms, pilot project results, FY90, annual rpt, 6004–20

Federal judicial personnel, by position, June 1989-90, annual rpt, 18204–8.10

Federal judicial personnel, by position, 1990-91, annual rpt, 18204–2.1

Finances and operations, by SIC 2- to 4-digit industry, forecast 1991, annual rpt, 2044–28

Occupational injury and illness rates, by SIC 2- to 4-digit industry, 1988-89, annual rpt, 6844–7

Occupational injury and illness rates, by SIC 2- to 4-digit industry, 1989, annual rpt, 6844–1

Puerto Rico economic censuses, 1987: wholesale and retail trade and service industry finances and operations, by SIC 2- to 4-digit industry and municipio, 2591–1

Puerto Rico economic censuses, 1987: wholesale, retail, and service industries finances and operations, by establishment characteristics and SIC 2- and 3-digit industry, subject rpts, 2591–2

Receipts for services, by SIC 2- to 4-digit kind of business, 1990, annual rpt, 2413–8

Senate receipts, itemized expenses by payee, and balances, 1st half FY91, semiannual listing, 25922–1

Service industries census, 1987: depreciable assets, capital and operating expenses, and receipts, by SIC 2- to 4-digit kind of business, 2393–2

Service industries census, 1987: establishments, receipts by source, payroll, and employment, by SIC 2- to 4-digit kind of business, State, and MSA, 2393–4

State and Metro Area Data Book, 1991 data compilation, 2328–54

Statistical Abstract of US, 1991 annual data compilation, 2324–1.5

Tax (income) returns of corporations, income and tax items by asset size and detailed industry, 1987, annual rpt, 8304–4

Tax (income) returns of corporations, income and tax items by asset size and detailed industry, 1988, annual rpt, 8304–21

Tax (income) returns of partnerships, income statement and balance sheet items, by industry group, 1989, annual article, 8302–2.216; 8304–18

Tax (income) returns of sole proprietorships, income statement items, by industry group, 1989, annual article, 8302–2.214

Workers compensation contested claims cases represented by attorneys, by State, 1987-90, annual rpt, 6504–9

Workers compensation laws of States and Fed Govt, 1991 semiannual rpt, 6502–1

see also Judges

see also Legal aid

see also Legal arbitration and mediation

see also Legal education

see also Legal ethics

see also U.S. attorneys

see also under By Industry in the "Index by Categories"

Layoffs

see Labor turnover

Lazenby, Helen C.

"National Health Expenditures, 1989", 4652–1.221

Lead and lead industry

Business statistics, detailed data for major industries and economic indicators, *Survey of Current Business,* monthly rpt, 2702–1.17

Castings (nonferrous) shipments, by metal type, 1990, annual Current Industrial Rpt, 2506–10.5

Exports and imports between US and outlying areas, by detailed commodity and mode of transport, 1990, annual rpt, 2424–11

Exports and imports of US, by country and detailed commodity, monthly rpt, 2422–12

Exports and imports of US, by Harmonized System 6-digit commodity and country, 1990, annual rpt, 2424–13

Exports and imports of US, by transport mode, country, and SITC 1- to 3-digit commodity, 1990, annual rpt, 2424–12

Exports of US, detailed Schedule B commodities with countries of destination, 1990, annual rpt, 2424–10

Manufacturing annual survey, 1989: finances and operations, by SIC 2- to 4-digit industry, series, 2506–15

Manufacturing finances and operations, by SIC 2- to 4-digit industry, forecast 1991, annual rpt, 2044–28

Mineral Industry Surveys, commodity review of production, trade, stocks, and use, monthly rpt, 5612–1.13

Index by Subjects and Names

Mineral Industry Surveys, State reviews of production, 1990, preliminary annual rpt, 5614–6

Minerals Yearbook, 1988, Vol 3: foreign country reviews of production, trade, and policy, by commodity, annual rpt series, 5604–17

Minerals Yearbook, 1989, Vol 1: commodity review of production, reserves, supply, use, and trade, annual rpt, 5604–15.38

Minerals Yearbook, 1989, Vol 2: State reviews of production and sales by commodity, and business activity, annual rpt series, 5604–16

Minerals Yearbook, 1989, Vol 2: State reviews of production, sales, and firms, by commodity, and business activity, annual rpt, 5604–34

Mines (metal) and related operations occupational injuries and incidence, employment, and hours, 1989, annual rpt, 6664–3

Occupational injury and illness rates, by SIC 2- to 4-digit industry, 1988-89, annual rpt, 6844–7

Pollution (air) emissions factors, by detailed pollutant and source, data compilation, 1990 rpt, 9198–120

Price indexes (producer), by stage of processing and detailed commodity, monthly rpt, 6762–6

Price indexes (producer), by stage of processing and detailed commodity, monthly 1990, annual rpt, 6764–2

Production, prices, trade, and foreign and US industry devs, by commodity, bimonthly rpt with articles, 5602–4

Production, prices, trade, use, employment, tariffs, and stockpiles, by mineral, with foreign comparisons, 1986-90, annual rpt, 5604–18

Statistical Abstract of US, 1991 annual data compilation, 2324–1.25

Stockpiling of strategic material by Fed Govt, activity, and inventory by commodity, as of Mar 1991, semiannual rpt, 3542–22

Stockpiling of strategic material, inventories and needs, by commodity, as of Jan 1991, annual rpt, 3544–37

see also Lead poisoning and pollution

see also under By Commodity in the "Index by Categories"

Lead poisoning and pollution

Air pollution emissions factors, by detailed pollutant and source, data compilation, 1990 rpt, 9198–120

Air pollution levels for 6 pollutants, by source and selected MSA, 1980-89, annual rpt, 9194–1

Air pollution levels for 6 pollutants, by source, 1970-89 and trends from 1940, annual rpt, 9194–13

California OCS oil and gas dev impacts on water quality, marine life, and sediments, by site, 1986-89, annual rpt, 5734–11

Child lead poisoning cases and rates by race, and Hispanic origin, and screening tests conducted, for NYC, 1988, article, 4202–7.201

Coastal and estuarine pollutant concentrations in fish, shellfish, and environment, series, 2176–3

Deaths and rates, by detailed cause and demographic characteristics, 1988 and trends from 1900, US Vital Statistics annual rpt, 4144–2

Index by Subjects and Names

Environmental Quality, status of problems, protection programs, research, and intl issues, 1991 annual rpt, 484–1

Great Lakes wastewater treatment by municipal and industrial facilities, releases, methods, effectiveness, pollutant limits, and enforcement, 1985-88, 14648–24

Health condition and health care resources, use, and spending, 1950s-89, annual data compilation, 4144–11

Health effects of lead, sources of emissions and exposure, and levels in environment, literature review, 1990 rpt, 9198–84

Housing (public) renovation costs and alternative funding methods, by project type and region, 1990 rpt, 5188–127

Imports detained by FDA, by reason, product, shipper, brand, and country, monthly listing, 4062–2

Industrial wastewater pollution releases, levels, treatment, costs, and regulation, with background financial and operating data, industry rpt series, 9206–4

New York Bight pollution levels, sources, treatment costs, economic losses, and environmental and health effects, 1990 conf, 9208–131

Pacific Ocean coast pollutant concentrations in fish and sediments, by contaminant, fish species, and site, 1984-86, 2168–121

Paint (lead-based) in private housing, levels, exposure, and testing and abatement costs, 1990 rpt, 5188–128

Tax (excise) on hazardous waste generation and disposal, rates, and firms filing returns, by substance type, 1988, annual article, 8302–2.202

Water quality, chemistry, hydrology, and other characteristics, local area studies, series, 5666–27

Water supply and quality in streams and lakes, and groundwater levels in wells, by drainage basin, 1988, annual State rpt series, 5666–16

Water supply and quality in streams and lakes, and groundwater levels in wells, by drainage basin, 1989, annual State rpt series, 5666–12

Water supply and quality in streams and lakes, and groundwater levels in wells, by drainage basin, 1990, annual State rpt series, 5666–10

Leading indicators

see Economic indicators

Leahy, Michael P.

"Determining Foreign Exchange Risk and Bank Capital Requirements", 9366–7.254

"Usefulness of P* Measures for Japan and Germany", 9366–7.268

Learning disabilities

Child developmental, learning, and emotional problems, cases and share receiving special treatment and education, by selected characteristics, 1988, 4146–8.193

Digest of Education Statistics, 1991 annual data compilation, 4824–2

Family structure relation to child health, behavioral, emotional, and school problems, by selected characteristics, 1988, 4147–10.178

Population of learning disabled by sex and race, testing costs, and employment and training services, 1960s-90, 6406–10.4

State and Metro Area Data Book, 1991 data compilation, 2328–54

Leasing

see Mineral leases

see Motor vehicle rental

see Oil and gas leases

see Rental industries

Leather industry and products

Business statistics, detailed data for major industries and economic indicators, *Survey of Current Business*, monthly rpt, 2702–1.15

Collective bargaining agreements expiring during year, and workers covered, by firm, union, industry group, and State, 1991, annual rpt, 6784–9

County Business Patterns, 1988: employment, establishments, and payroll, by SIC 2- to 4-digit industry and county, annual State rpt series, 2326–6

County Business Patterns, 1989: employment, establishments, and payroll, by SIC 2- to 4-digit industry and county, annual State rpt series, 2326–8

Employment, earnings, and hours, by SIC 1- to 4-digit industry, monthly and annual averages, selected years 1909-90, annual rpt, 6744–4

Employment in manufacturing, by detailed occupation and SIC 2-digit industry, 1989 survey, triennial rpt, 6748–52

Employment related to agriculture, by industry, region, and metro-nonmetro location, 1987, 1598–271

Endangered animals and plants US trade and permits, by species, purpose, disposition, and country, 1989, annual rpt, 5504–19

Energy use and prices for manufacturing industries, 1988 survey, series, 3166–13

Enterprise Statistics, 1987: auxiliaries of multi-establishment firms, finances and operations by function, industry, and State, 2329–6

Enterprise Statistics, 1987: finances and operations for companies, by size, level of diversification, form of organization, and industry group, 2329–8

Exports and imports between US and outlying areas, by detailed commodity and mode of transport, 1990, annual rpt, 2424–11

Exports and imports of dairy, livestock, and poultry products, by commodity and country, FAS monthly circular, 1925–32

Exports and imports of US, by country and detailed commodity, monthly rpt, 2422–12

Exports and imports of US, by Harmonized System 6-digit commodity and country, 1990, annual rpt, 2424–13

Exports and imports of US, by transport mode, country, and SITC 1- to 3-digit commodity, 1990, annual rpt, 2424–12

Exports of US, detailed commodities by country, monthly CD-ROM, 2422–13

Exports of US, detailed Schedule B commodities with countries of destination, 1990, annual rpt, 2424–10

Imports, exports, and employment impacts, by SIC 2- to 4-digit industry and commodity, quarterly rpt, 2322–2

Imports of US, detailed commodities by country, monthly CD-ROM, 2422–14

Leather industry and products

Imports of US given duty-free treatment for value of US material sent abroad, by commodity and country, 1989, annual rpt, 9884–14

Input-output structure of US economy, detailed interindustry transactions for 84 industries, and components of final demand, 1986, annual article, 2702–1.206

Input-output structure of US economy, detailed interindustry transactions for 85 industries, 1982 benchmark data, 2702–1.213

Manufacturing annual survey, 1989: finances and operations, by SIC 2- to 4-digit industry, series, 2506–15

Manufacturing census, 1987: finances and operations, by SIC 2- to 4-digit industry, State, and MSA, with trends from 1849, 2497–1

Manufacturing census, 1987: finances and operations, by type of organization and SIC 2- to 4-digit industry, subject rpt, 2497–5

Manufacturing finances and operations, by SIC 2- to 4-digit industry, forecast 1991, annual rpt, 2044–28

Manufacturing industries operations and performance, analytical rpt series, 2506–16

Manufacturing production, shipments, inventories, orders, and pollution control costs, periodic Current Industrial Rpt series, 2506–3

Mexico imports from US, by industry and State, 1987-90, 2048–154

Occupational injury and illness rates, by SIC 2- to 4-digit industry, 1988-89, annual rpt, 6844–7

Occupational injury and illness rates, by SIC 2- to 4-digit industry, 1989, annual rpt, 6844–1

OECD trade, total and for 4 major countries, and US trade by country, by commodity, 1970-89, world area rpt series, 9116–1

Pollution abatement capital and operating costs, by SIC 2-digit industry, 1989, advance annual Current Industrial Rpt, 2506–3.6

Price indexes (producer), by stage of processing and detailed commodity, monthly rpt, 6762–6

Price indexes (producer), by stage of processing and detailed commodity, monthly 1990, annual rpt, 6764–2

Puerto Rico and other US possessions corporations income tax returns, income and tax items, and employment, by selected industry, 1987, article, 8302–2.213

Puerto Rico economic censuses, 1987: wholesale and retail trade and service industry finances and operations, by SIC 2- to 4-digit industry and municipio, 2591–1

Retail trade census, 1987: finances and employment, for establishments with and without payroll, by SIC 2- to 4-digit kind of business, State, and MSA, 2401–1

Tariff Schedule of US, classifications and rates of duty by detailed imported commodity, 1992 base edition, 9886–13

Tax (income) returns of corporations, income and tax items by asset size and detailed industry, 1987, annual rpt, 8304–4

Leather industry and products

Tax (income) returns of corporations, income and tax items by asset size and detailed industry, 1988, annual rpt, 8304–21

Tax (income) returns of corporations with foreign tax credit, income and tax items by industry group, 1986, biennial article, 8302–2.203

Tax (income) returns of sole proprietorships, income statement items, by industry group, 1989, annual article, 8302–2.214

see also Hides and skins

see also Shoes and shoe industry

see also under By Commodity in the "Index by Categories"

see also under By Industry in the "Index by Categories"

Lebanon

- Agricultural exports of high-value commodities, indexes and sales by commodity, world area, and country, 1960s-86, 1528–323
- Agricultural trade of US, by detailed commodity and country, 1989, annual rpt, 1524–8
- Agricultural trade of US, by detailed commodity and country, 1990, semiannual rpt, 1522–4
- AID economic aid to developing countries, obligations and disbursements by country, quarterly rpt, 9912–4
- AID loans repayment status and terms by program and country, and status of predecessor agency loans, quarterly rpt, 9912–3
- *Background Notes*, summary social, political, and economic data, 1990 rpt, 7006–2.18
- Economic and military aid and loans from US and intl agencies, by program and country, FY46-90, annual rpt, 9914–5
- Economic and social conditions of developing countries from 1960s, and Intl Dev Cooperation Agency and AID activities and funding, FY90-92, annual rpt, 9904–4
- Economic, social, political, and geographic summary data, by country, 1991, annual factbook, 9114–2
- Exports and imports of US, by selected country, country group, and commodity group, 1990, annual rpt, 2044–37
- Exports and imports of US, by transport mode, country, and SITC 1- to 3-digit commodity, 1990, annual rpt, 2424–12
- Exports of US, detailed Schedule B commodities with countries of destination, 1990, annual rpt, 2424–10
- Hostages held in Lebanon, and released, listing as of Jan 1991, annual rpt, 7004–13
- Hostages kidnapped in Lebanon, listing as of 1990, 7004–22
- Human rights conditions in 170 countries, and US economic and military aid, 1990, annual rpt, 21384–3
- Military aid of US, arms sales, and training programs costs and budget requests, by program, world region, and country, FY90-92, annual rpt, 7144–13
- UN voting record and share of votes in agreement with US, by issue, country, and world area, 1990, annual rpt, 7004–18

see also under By Foreign Country in the "Index by Categories"

Lebanon, Pa.

see also under By SMSA or MSA in the "Index by Categories"

LeBlanc, Michael

"Agriculture and Capital Gains Taxation", 1561–16.202

Lee, Chinkook

"Factor Intensity of U.S. Agricultural Trade", 1548–373

Lee, David

"Risk Aversion Through Nontraditional Export Promotion Programs in Central America", 1528–312

Lee, I-Min

"Physical Activity and Risk of Developing Colorectal Cancer Among College Alumni", 4472–1.222

Lee, Robert Y.

"International Financing Programs and U.S. International Economic Competitiveness", 2048–152

Lee, William

"Corporate Leverage and the Consequences of Macroeconomic Instability", 9385–8.78

Leendertse, J. J.

"Modeling the Alaskan Continental Shelf Waters", 2176–1.36

Leeper, Eric M.

"In Search of the Liquidity Effect", 9366–7.257

Leesville, La.

Wages by occupation, and benefits for office and plant workers, 1991 survey, periodic MSA rpt, 6785–3.6

Leeward and Windward Islands

see Caribbean area

Leeworthy, Vernon R.

- "Expenditure Profiles of Visitors to Southern California Coastal Areas. Public Area Recreation Visitors Survey", 2176–9.6
- "Socioeconomic Profile of Recreationists at Public Outdoor Recreation Sites in Coastal Areas: Volume 1. Public Area Recreation Visitors Survey", 2176–9.1
- "Socioeconomic Profile of Recreationists at Public Outdoor Recreation Sites in Coastal Areas: Volume 2. Public Area Recreation Visitors Survey", 2176–9.2
- "Socioeconomic Profile of Recreationists at Public Outdoor Recreation Sites in Coastal Areas: Volume 3. Public Area Recreation Visitors Survey", 2176–9.3
- "Socioeconomic Profile of Recreationists at Public Outdoor Recreation Sites in Coastal Areas: Volume 4. Public Area Recreation Visitors Survey", 2176–9.4
- "Socioeconomic Profile of Recreationists at Public Outdoor Recreation Sites in Coastal Areas: Volume 5. Public Area Recreation Visitors Survey", 2176–9.5
- "Socioeconomic Profile of Recreationists at Public Outdoor Recreation Sites in Coastal Areas: Volume 6. Public Area Recreation Visitors Survey", 2176–9.7

Lefebvre, Lynn W.

"Manatee Grazing Impacts on Seagrasses in Hobe Sound and Jupiter Sound in Southeast Florida During the Winter of 1988-89", 14738–12

Lefkowitz, Doris C.

"Mental Health and Functional Status of Residents of Nursing and Personal Care Homes. National Medical Expenditure Survey", 4186–8.11

Index by Subjects and Names

"Personal Health Practices: Findings from the Survey of American Indians and Alaska Natives. National Medical Expenditure Survey", 4186–8.19

Legal aid

- Assistance (financial and nonfinancial) of Fed Govt, 1991 base edition with supplements, annual listing, 104–5
- Assistance of Fed Govt, Equal Access to Justice Act petitions and decisions, June 1987-91, annual rpt, 18204–2.1
- Employment and spending for law enforcement, by activity and level of govt, data compilation, 1991 annual rpt, 6064–6.1
- Employment in Federal district courts, by court, 1990, annual report, 17664–1
- Employment, payroll, and spending for criminal justice, by level of govt, State, and selected city and county, FY71-88, annual rpt, 6064–9
- Employment, payroll, and spending for criminal justice, by level of govt, State, and selected city and county, 1984-86, biennial rpt, 6064–4
- Expenditures of Fed Govt in States, by type, program, agency, and State, FY90, annual rpt, 2464–2
- Judicial Conf proceedings and findings, spring 1991, semiannual rpt, 18202–2
- Older persons aid programs funding, and long term care ombudsman funding and visits by State, 1988-90, 25248–126
- Pay for public defenders and private indigent defense lawyers, by State, 1989-90, hearing, 21408–123
- Public defender workloads in Federal district courts, and Equal Access to Justice Act petitions and decisions, 1990, annual rpt, 18204–8.8; 18204–8.15; 18204–8.26
- Service industries census, 1987: establishments, receipts by source, payroll, and employment, by SIC 2- to 4-digit kind of business, State, and MSA, 2393–4

Legal arbitration and mediation

- Community Relations Service investigation and mediation of minority discrimination disputes, FY90, annual rpt, 6004–9
- Court-annexed arbitration for civil cases, pilot program evaluation, 1984-86, 18408–46
- Financial stress indicators for farms, operator quits, and loan problems and mediation, 1970s-90, 1598–272
- Futures trading oversight of CFTC and individual exchanges, foreign activity, and customer views, late 1980s, hearing, 25168–77
- Labor-mgmt mediation and arbitration activities of Fed Mediation and Conciliation Service, and cases by issue, region, and State, FY84-89, annual rpt, 9344–1
- Medical malpractice claims resolution through arbitration and litigation, Michigan program cases, awards, duration, and costs, late 1970s-80s, GAO rpt, 26121–394
- Older persons discrimination in Federal aid programs, Age Discrimination Act enforcement by agency, FY90, annual rpt, 4004–27

Index by Subjects and Names

Legal education

Course completions, by detailed program, sex, race, and instn type, for 1972 high school class, as of 1984, 4888–4

Degrees awarded in higher education, by level, field, race, and sex, 1988/89 with trends from 1978/79, biennial rpt, 4844–17

Digest of Education Statistics, 1991 annual data compilation, 4824–2

Education Dept programs funding, operations, and effectiveness, FY90, annual rpt, 4804–5

Student aid funding and participation, by Federal program, instn type and control, and State, various periods 1959-89, annual rpt, 4804–28

Legal ethics

Public opinion on crime and crime-related issues, by respondent characteristics, data compilation, 1991 annual rpt, 6064–6.2

see also Judicial ethics

Legal services

see Lawyers and legal services

see Legal aid

Legal Services Corp.

Budget of US, authoritative financial statements with appropriations, outlays, and receipts, by category and agency, FY90, annual rpt, 8104–2.1

Budget of US, obligations and authority by function, agency, and program, with summaries, analyses, and historical tables, FY92, annual rpt, 104–2

Expenditures of Fed Govt in States, by type, program, agency, and State, FY90, annual rpt, 2464–2

Legel, Ellen

"Corporation Income Tax Returns, Income Year 1987", 8302–2.204

Leger, Mireille L.

"Recipient Housing in the Housing Voucher and Certificate Programs", 5186–14.4

Legislative bodies

see Congress

see House of Representatives

see Senate

see State legislatures

Legumes

see Vegetables and vegetable products

Leisure

see Recreation

Lemieux, Catharine

"Deposit Growth, Nonperforming Assets, and Return on Assets, by County" Includes 3 charts. (p. 41-45), 9381–14.1

"Three Decades of Banking", 9381–14.1

Lemons

see Citrus fruits

Lentils

see Vegetables and vegetable products

Leominster, Mass.

see also under By SMSA or MSA in the "Index by Categories"

Leon, Joel

"Current and Projected Availability of Special Nursing Home Programs for Alzheimer's Disease Patients. National Medical Expenditure Survey", 4186–8.12

Leonard, Dorothy L.

"Quality of Shellfish Growing Waters on the West Coast of the U.S.", 2176–7.21

Leonard, Mary L.

"Pollution Abatement and Control Expenditures, 1987-89", 2702–1.229

Leptospirosis

see Animal diseases and zoonoses

Lesotho

Agricultural exports of high-value commodities, indexes and sales by commodity, world area, and country, 1960s-86, 1528–323

Agricultural trade of US, by detailed commodity and country, 1989, annual rpt, 1524–8

Agricultural trade of US, by detailed commodity and country, 1990, semiannual rpt, 1522–4

AID economic aid to developing countries, obligations and disbursements by country, quarterly rpt, 9912–4

Background Notes, summary social, political, and economic data, 1990 rpt, 7006–2.6

Dairy imports, consumption, and market conditions, by sub-Saharan Africa country, 1961-88, 1528–321

Economic and military aid and loans from US and intl agencies, by program and country, FY46-90, annual rpt, 9914–5

Economic and social conditions of developing countries from 1960s, and Intl Dev Cooperation Agency and AID activities and funding, FY90-92, annual rpt, 9904–4

Economic, population, and agricultural data, US and other aid sources, and AID activity, 1989 country rpt, 9916–12.32

Economic, social, political, and geographic summary data, by country, 1991, annual factbook, 9114–2

Exports and imports of US, by transport mode, country, and SITC 1- to 3-digit commodity, 1990, annual rpt, 2424–12

Exports of US, detailed Schedule B commodities with countries of destination, 1990, annual rpt, 2424–10

Human rights conditions in 170 countries, and US economic and military aid, 1990, annual rpt, 21384–3

Military aid of US, arms sales, and training programs costs and budget requests, by program, world region, and country, FY90-92, annual rpt, 7144–13

UN voting record and share of votes in agreement with US, by issue, country, and world area, 1990, annual rpt, 7004–18

see also under By Foreign Country in the "Index by Categories"

Lester, Gordon H.

"Child Support and Alimony: 1989", 2546–6.72

Letsch, Suzanne W.

"National Health Expenditures, 1989", 4652–1.221

Letter carriers

see Postal employees

Lettuce

see Vegetables and vegetable products

Leukemia

see Blood diseases and disorders

Leutz, Walter

"Financial Performance in the Social Health Maintenance Organization, 1985-88", 4652–1.202

Levedahl, J. William

"Role of Functional Form in Estimating the Effect of a Cash-Only Food Stamp Program", 1502–3.203

Levine, Richard M.

"Mineral Industries of the USSR, 1989", 5604–39

Levins, W. P.

"Cooling Season Energy Measurements of Dust and Ventilation Effects on Radiant Barriers", 3308–97

Levit, Katharine R.

"Burden of Health Care Costs: Business, Households, and Governments", 4652–1.230

"National Health Expenditures, 1990", 4652–1.252

LeVoir, James W.

"Lower Profits at Tenth District Banks", 9381–16.201

Lew, Judy F.

"Recommendations for Collection of Laboratory Specimens Associated with Outbreaks of Gastroenteritis", 4206–2.32

Lewin/ICF

"Health Care Financing System and the Uninsured", 4658–54

Lewis, A. D.

"Review of the South Pacific Tuna Baitfisheries: Small Pelagic Fisheries Associated with Coral Reefs", 2162–1.201

Lewis, Caroline

"Birth and Fertility Rates by Education: 1980-85. Vital and Health Statistics Series 21", 4147–21.49

Lewis, Margaret P.

"Controlled Foreign Corporations, 1986", 8302–2.212

Lewiston, Maine

see also under By SMSA or MSA in the "Index by Categories"

Lexington, Ky.

Wages by occupation, for office and plant workers, 1991 survey, periodic MSA rpt, 6785–3.10

see also under By City and By SMSA or MSA in the "Index by Categories"

Ley, Catherine

"Determinants of Genital Human Papillomavirus Infection in Young Women", 4472–1.215

LGL Ltd.

"Acoustic Effects of Oil Production Activities on Bowhead and White Whales Visible During Spring Migration Near Point Barrow Alaska—1989 Phase: Sound Propagation and Whale Responses to Playbacks of Continuous Drilling Noise from an Ice Platform, as Studied in Pack Ice Conditions", 5738–27

"Behavior of Bowhead Whales of the Davis Strait and Bering/Beaufort Stocks vs. Regional Differences in Human Activities", 5738–30

"Comparison of Behavior of Bowhead Whales of the Davis Strait and Bering/Beaufort Stocks", 5738–29

Li, Anlong

"Optimal Bank Portfolio Choice Under Fixed-Rate Deposit Insurance", 9377–9.120

Liability insurance

Liability insurance
see Property and casualty insurance

Liang, J. Nellie
"Changes in the Cost of Equity Capital for Bank Holding Companies and the Effects on Raising Capital", 9366–6.274
"Equity Underwriting Risk", 9366–6.260
"Inferring Market Power from Time-Series Data: The Case of the Banking Firm", 9366–6.261

Libel and slander
Court caseloads for Federal district courts, 1990, annual rpt, 18204–8.18
Court civil and criminal caseloads for Federal district, appeals, and bankruptcy courts, by type of suit and offense, circuit, and district, 1990, annual rpt, 18204–11
Court civil and criminal caseloads for Federal district courts, 1991, annual rpt, 18204–2.1

Liberia
Agricultural exports of high-value commodities, indexes and sales by commodity, world area, and country, 1960s-86, 1528–323
Agricultural trade of US, by detailed commodity and country, 1989, annual rpt, 1524–8
Agricultural trade of US, by detailed commodity and country, 1990, semiannual rpt, 1522–4
AID economic aid to developing countries, obligations and disbursements by country, quarterly rpt, 9912–4
AID loans repayment status and terms by program and country, and status of predecessor agency loans, quarterly rpt, 9912–3
Dairy imports, consumption, and market conditions, by sub-Saharan Africa country, 1961-88, 1528–321
Economic and military aid and loans from US and intl agencies, by program and country, FY46-90, annual rpt, 9914–5
Economic and social conditions of developing countries from 1960s, and Intl Dev Cooperation Agency and AID activities and funding, FY90-92, annual rpt, 9904–4
Economic, social, political, and geographic summary data, by country, 1991, annual factbook, 9114–2
Exports and imports of US, by transport mode, country, and SITC 1- to 3-digit commodity, 1990, annual rpt, 2424–12
Exports of US, detailed Schedule B commodities with countries of destination, 1990, annual rpt, 2424–10
Food supply, needs, and aid for developing countries, status and alternative forecasts, 1991 world area rpt, 1526–8.1
Human rights conditions in 170 countries, and US economic and military aid, 1990, annual rpt, 21384–3
Military aid of US, arms sales, and training programs costs and budget requests, by program, world region, and country, FY90-92, annual rpt, 7144–13
Multinatl US firms foreign affiliates, income statement items by country and world area, 1986, biennial article, 8302–2.212
Ships in world merchant fleet, tonnage, and new ship construction and deliveries, by vessel type and country, as of Jan 1990, annual rpt, 7704–3

UN voting record and share of votes in agreement with US, by issue, country, and world area, 1990, annual rpt, 7004–18
see also under By Foreign Country in the "Index by Categories"

Librarians
Blind and disabled persons library services, readership, circulation, staff, funding, and holdings, FY90, annual listing, 26404–3
Digest of Education Statistics, 1991 annual data compilation, 4824–2
Education Dept programs funding, operations, and effectiveness, FY90, annual rpt, 4804–5
Elementary and secondary public school systems enrollment, finances, staff, and high school grads, by State, FY88-89, annual rpt, 4834–6
Employment and payroll, by function and level of govt, 1990, annual rpt series, 2466–1
Fed Govt labor productivity, indexes of output and labor costs by function, FY67-89, annual rpt, 6824–1.6
Govt census, 1987: employment, payroll, and average earnings, by function, level of govt, State, county, and population size, 2455–2
Govt census, 1987: local govt employment by function, payroll, and average earnings, for individual counties, cities, and school and special districts, 2455–1
Higher education instn libraries, outlays, holdings, outlays, staff, and instn characteristics, 1969-88, 4468–4
Public libraries finances, staff, and operations, by State and population size, 1989, annual rpt, 4824–6
Training in library science, grants for disadvantaged students, by instn and State, FY90, annual listing, 4874–1
USIA library holdings, use, and staff, by country and city, FY90, annual rpt, 9854–4
VA Medicine and Surgery Dept trainees, by detailed program and city, FY90, annual rpt, 8704–4

Libraries
Audiovisual activities and spending of Fed Govt, by whether performed in-house and agency, FY90, annual rpt, 9514–1
Blind and disabled persons library services, readership, circulation, staff, funding, and holdings, FY90, annual listing, 26404–3
County Business Patterns, 1988: employment, establishments, and payroll, by SIC 2- to 4-digit industry and county, annual State rpt series, 2326–6
County Business Patterns, 1989: employment, establishments, and payroll, by SIC 2- to 4-digit industry and county, annual State rpt series, 2326–8
Data collection activities and programs of NCES, 1991, annual listing, 4824–7
Data on education, computer files from Office of Educational Research and Improvement, 1991 listing, 4868–10
Depository libraries for Federal publications, 1991 annual listing, 2214–1; 2304–2
Digest of Education Statistics, 1991 annual data compilation, 4824–2
Education Dept Research Library proposed services, educators and librarians views, 1990 survey, GAO rpt, 26121–414

Index by Subjects and Names

English as second language programs and services of public libraries, project descriptions and funding, by State, FY87, annual rpt, 4874–10
Govt finances, by level of govt, State, and for large cities and counties, annual rpt series, 2466–2
Higher education enrollment, faculty, finances, and degrees, by instn level and control, and State, FY87, annual rpt, 4844–13
Higher education instn libraries, outlays, holdings, outlays, staff, and instn characteristics, 1969-88, 4468–4
Higher education instn revenue by source and spending by function, by State and instn control, FY80-88, annual rpt, 4844–6
Higher education instn tuition costs relation to quality, indicators for private instns, regression results, 1985/86, 4888–3
Jails under court order to reduce overcrowding and to improve conditions, 1988, regional rpt series, 6068–144.1
Japan-US Friendship Commission educational and cultural exchange activities, grants, and trust fund status, FY89-90, biennial report, 14694–1
Library of Congress activities, acquisitions, services, and financial statements, FY90, annual rpt, 26404–1
Natl Archives and Records Admin activities, finances, holdings, and staff, FY90, annual rpt, 9514–2
Older persons migration to southern coastal areas, household finances, services needs, and local economic impacts, for selected counties, 1990, 2068–38
Presidential libraries holdings, use, and costs, by instn, FY90, annual rpt, 9514–2
Public libraries finances, staff, and operations, by State and population size, 1989, annual rpt, 4824–6
School and public libraries, selected data, 1991 edition, annual rpt, 4824–2.30
Service industries census, 1987: establishments, receipts by source, payroll, and employment, by SIC 2- to 4-digit kind of business, State, and MSA, 2393–4
Smoking bans in public places, local ordinances provisions, as of 1989, 4478–196
Statistical Abstract of US, 1991 annual data compilation, 2324–1.4
Urban resource libraries dev projects and funding, by city and State, FY84-88, listing, 4878–4
USIA library holdings, use, and staff, by country and city, FY90, annual rpt, 9854–4
see also Federal aid to libraries
see also Librarians
see also Medical libraries

Library of Congress
Activities, acquisitions, services, and financial statements of LC, FY90, annual rpt, 26404–1
Blind and disabled persons library services, readership, circulation, staff, funding, and holdings, FY90, annual listing, 26404–3
Budget of US, authoritative financial statements with appropriations, outlays, and receipts, by category and agency, FY90, annual rpt, 8104–2.1

Index by Subjects and Names

Budget of US, obligations and authority by function, agency, and program, with summaries, analyses, and historical tables, FY92, annual rpt, 104–2

Buildings and grounds under Capitol Architect supervision, itemized outlays by payee and function, 1st half FY91, semiannual rpt, 25922–2

Copyrights Register activities, registrations by material type, and fees, FY90 and trends from 1790, annual rpt, 26404–2

Education funding by Federal agency, program, and recipient type, and instn spending, FY80-90, annual rpt, 4824–8

Employment of LC by race, Hispanic origin, and sex, and affirmative action needs, 1989, hearing, 21428–9

Pollution (air) indoor levels in workplace, and health impacts, for LC Madison building, 1989 study, series, 4248–92

Publications and products of LC, 1990, annual listing, 26404–6

Publications and recordings of LC, 1991, biennial listing, 26404–5

R&D funding by Fed Govt, by field, performer type, agency, and State, FY89-91, annual rpt, 9627–20

see also Congressional Research Service *see also* Copyright Royalty Tribunal

Library sciences

see Information sciences

Libya

Agricultural trade of US, by detailed commodity and country, 1990, semiannual rpt, 1522–4

AID loans repayment status and terms by program and country, and status of predecessor agency loans, quarterly rpt, 9912–3

Debt of Communist countries to US and other Western banks, by country, 1980s, conf, 25388–56

Economic and military aid and loans from US and intl agencies, by program and country, FY46-90, annual rpt, 9914–5

Economic, social, political, and geographic summary data, by country, 1991, annual factbook, 9114–2

Export controls and trade of US with Middle East countries, with dual-use commodity licenses and arms sales, 1980s-90, GAO rpt, 26123–339

Exports and imports of US, by commodity and country, 1970-89, world area rpt, 9116–1.1

Exports and imports of US, by transport mode, country, and SITC 1- to 3-digit commodity, 1990, annual rpt, 2424–12

Human rights conditions in 170 countries, and US economic and military aid, 1990, annual rpt, 21384–3

Oil production and exports to US, by major exporting country, detailed data, monthly rpt with articles, 3162–24

Oil production, trade, use, and stocks, by selected country and country group, monthly rpt, 3162–42

UN voting record and share of votes in agreement with US, by issue, country, and world area, 1990, annual rpt, 7004–18

see also under By Foreign Country in the "Index by Categories"

Licenses and permits

Agriculture census, 1987: farms, farmland, production, finances, and operator characteristics, by county, final State rpt series, 2331–1

Aircraft registered with FAA, by type and characteristics of aircraft, make, carrier, State, and county, 1989, annual rpt, 7504–3

Alcohol, Tobacco, and Firearms Bur regulatory activities, staff, and funding, and tax revenues and rates, 1980s-91, GAO rpt, 26119–335

Animal protection, licensing, and inspection activities of USDA, and animals used in research, by State, FY89, annual rpt, 1394–10

Board and care homes regulation and rules enforcement by States, 1988, 4008–112

Boat registrations, by class, propulsion type, hull material, and State, 1990, annual rpt, 7404–1.1

Budget of US, authoritative financial statements with appropriations, outlays, and receipts, by category and agency, FY90, annual rpt, 8104–2.1

Coal leasing activity on Federal land, acreage, production, and reserves, by coal region and State, FY90, annual rpt, 5724–10

Coal Surface Mining Reclamation and Enforcement Office activities and funding, by State and Indian tribe, FY90, annual rpt, 5644–1

Credit unions federally insured, finances, 1989-90, annual rpt, 9534–1

Drug marketing application processing of FDA, by drug, purpose, and producer, 1990, annual rpt, 4064–14

Electric power and industrial plants exempt from oil and gas primary use prohibition, 1990, annual rpt, 3334–1

Electric power plants certification applications filed with FERC, for small production and cogeneration facilities, FY80-90, annual listing, 3084–13

Endangered animals and plants US trade and permits, by species, purpose, disposition, and country, 1989, annual rpt, 5504–19

Energy suppliers rate regulation, and hydroelectric project licensing, for FERC, FY90, annual rpt, 3084–9

Export licensing, monitoring, and enforcement activities, FY90, annual rpt, 2024–1

Exports and imports of services, direct and among multinatl firms affiliates, by industry and world area, 1986-90, article, 2702–1.223

Exports of goods, services, and investment, trade barriers, impacts, and US actions, by country, 1989, annual rpt, 444–2

Farm production itemized costs, by farm sales size and region, 1990, annual rpt, 1614–3

Fishing commercial operations permits, by vessel type, for North Atlantic Ocean, 1990, annual rpt, 2164–14

Forest Service activities and finances, by region and State, FY90, annual rpt, 1204–1.1

Govt finances, by level of govt, State, and for large cities and counties, annual rpt series, 2466–2

Licenses and permits

Govt finances, tax systems and revenue, and fiscal structure, by level of govt and State, 1991 with historical trends, annual rpt, 10044–1

Grazing of livestock on natl forest lands, by region and State, 1990, annual rpt, 1204–5

Hazardous material transport license applications by disposition, and certified test facilities by State and country, 1989, annual rpt, 7304–4

Hazardous waste treatment facility closures, by EPA review status and waste disposal method, 1991, GAO rpt, 26113–528

Historic buildings rehabilitation tax incentives, projects, costs, ownership, and use, FY77-90, annual rpt, 5544–17

Hospices operations, services, costs, and patient characteristics, for instns without Medicare certification, FY85-86, 4658–52

Hydroelectric power plants licensed by FERC, characteristics and location, as of Oct 1991, annual listing, 3084–11

Meat plants inspected and certified for exporting to US, by country, 1990, annual listing, 1374–2

Medicare supplemental private insurance loss ratio performance, sales abuse cases, and State enforcement, late 1980s, GAO rpt, 26121–410

Mentally retarded persons care facilities and residents by selected characteristics, and use of Medicaid services and waiver programs, by State, late 1970s-80s, 4658–49

Middle East export controls of US, with trade, dual-use commodity licenses, and arms sales, by country, 1980s-90, GAO rpt, 26123–339

Minimum wage exemption certificates and employment under Fair Labor Standards Act, FY88-89, annual rpt, 6504–2.1

Nuclear power plant operating licenses, and construction permits granted and pending, monthly rpt, 3162–24.8

Nuclear power plant safety standards and research, design, licensing, construction, operation, and finances, with data by reactor, quarterly journal, 3352–4

Nuclear reactors operations, by commercial facility, 1990, annual rpt, 9634–12

Nuclear Regulatory Commission activities, finances, and staff, with data for individual power plants, FY90, annual rpt, 9634–2

Nursing home Alzheimer's disease units, and beds, by facility characteristics, 1987, 4186–8.12

Nursing home residents with mental, behavioral, and functional disorders, by age, sex, and instn characteristics, 1987, 4186–8.11

Nursing home residents with mental disorders, by disorder type and resident and instn characteristics, 1985, 4147–13.106

Oil and gas OCS exploration and drilling activity on Federal leases, by ocean area and State, 1950s-90, annual rpt, 5734–3.3

Oil and gas OCS reserves, and leasing and dev activity, periodic regional rpt series, 5736–3

Licenses and permits

Park natl system visits and overnight stays, by park and State, 1990, annual rpt, 5544–12

Public lands acreage and use, and Land Mgmt Bur activities and finances, annual State rpt series, 5724–11

Public lands acreage, grants, use, revenues, and allocations, by State, FY90, annual rpt, 5724–1.2; 5724–1.3

Public lands recreation facilities and use, and Land Mgmt Bur mgmt activities, funding, and plans, State rpt series, 5726–5

SEC activities, securities industry finances, and exchange activity, selected years 1938-FY90, annual rpt, 9734–2

Small Business Investment Companies capital holdings, SBA obligation, and ownership, as of July 1991, semiannual listing, 9762–4

State and Metro Area Data Book, 1991 data compilation, 2328–54

Truck itemized costs per mile, finances, and operations, for agricultural carriers, 1990, annual rpt, 1311–15

Truck transport of fruit and vegetables, itemized costs per mile by item for fleets and owner-operator trucks, monthly table, 1272–1

TV channel allocation and license status, for commercial and noncommercial UHF and VHF stations by market, as of June 30, 1991, semiannual rpt, 9282–6

West Central States drilling permits, by State, quarterly rpt, 9381–16.2

see also Building permits

see also Drivers licenses

see also Hunting and fishing licenses

see also Motor vehicle registrations

see also Occupational testing and certification

see also Royalties

see also Water permits

Liebermann, Timothy D.

"Characteristics and Trends of Streamflow and Dissolved Solids in the Upper Colorado River Basin, Arizona, Colorado, New Mexico, Utah, and Wyoming", 5666–27.17

Liechtenstein

Agricultural trade of US, by detailed commodity and country, 1990, semiannual rpt, 1522–4

Economic, social, political, and geographic summary data, by country, 1991, annual factbook, 9114–2

Exports and imports of US, by transport mode, country, and SITC 1- to 3-digit commodity, 1990, annual rpt, 2424–12

Multinatl US firms foreign affiliates, income statement items by country and world area, 1986, biennial article, 8302–2.212

UN voting record and share of votes in agreement with US, by issue, country, and world area, 1990, annual rpt, 7004–18

Life expectancy

AIDS and AIDS virus infection patients service use and costs under Medicaid, 1991, article, 4652–1.215

Cancer cases, deaths, and survival rates, by sex, race, age, and body site, 1973-88, annual rpt, 4474–35

Deaths and years of potential life lost from selected chronic diseases, weekly rpt, annual table, 4202–1

Developing countries aged population and selected characteristics, 1980s and projected to 2020, country rpt series, 2326–19

Developing countries child health and welfare indicators, and economic conditions, 1950s-80s, hearing, 25388–57

Developing countries economic and social conditions from 1960s, and Intl Dev Cooperation Agency and AID activities and funding, FY90-92, annual rpt, 9904–4

Eastern Europe economic and political conditions, and impacts of geographic factors, by country, 1990 conf, 9118–18

Foreign countries *Background Notes*, summary social, political, and economic data, series, 7006–2

Foreign countries economic, social, political, and geographic summary data, by country, 1991, annual factbook, 9114–2

Health condition and health care resources, use, and spending, 1950s-89, annual data compilation, 4144–11

Health condition improvement and disease prevention goals and recommended activities for 2000, with trends 1970s-80s, 4048–10

Indian and Alaska Native disease and disorder cases, deaths, and health services use, by tribe, reservation, and Indian Health Service area, late 1950s-86, 4088–2

Indian Health Service facilities and use, and Indian health and other characteristics, by IHS region, 1980s-89, annual chartbook, 4084–7

Indian Health Service facilities, funding, operations, and Indian health and other characteristics, 1950s-90, annual chartbook, 4084–1

Life tables, 1988 and trends from 1900, US Vital Statistics annual rpt, 4144–2.6

Life tables, 1989, and life expectancy by race and sex, from 1950, US Vital Statistics annual rpt, 4144–7

Mental illness and drug and alcohol abuse direct and indirect costs, by age and sex, 1985, 4048–35

Minority group and women health condition, services use, payment sources, and health care labor force, by poverty status, 1940s-89, chartbook, 4118–56

Minority group health condition, services use, costs, and indicators of services need, 1950s-88, 4118–55

OASDI benefit payments, trust fund finances, and economic and demographic assumptions, 1970-90 and alternative projections to 2000, actuarial rpt, 4706–1.105

Population size and characteristics, 1969-88, Current Population Rpt, biennial rpt, 2546–2.161

Soviet Union, Eastern Europe, OECD, and selected other countries living standards and commodity production, 1960s-90, annual rpt, 9114–4.1

State and Metro Area Data Book, 1991 data compilation, 2328–54

Statistical Abstract of US, 1991 annual data compilation, 2324–1.2

Life insurance

Assets and debts of private sector, balance sheets by segment, 1945-90, semiannual rpt, 9365–4.1

Assets and liabilities of life insurance companies, monthly rpt, 9362–1.4

Consumer Expenditure Survey, household income by source, and itemized spending, by selected characteristics and region, 1988-89, annual rpt, 6764–5

Employer-provided life insurance plan benefits and age-related reductions, by employee characteristics, 1989, article, 6722–1.216

Expenditures, coverage, and benefits for social welfare programs, late 1930s-89, annual rpt, 4744–3.1

Fed Govt civilian employees demographic and employment characteristics, as of Sept 1990, annual article, 9842–1.201

Fed Govt civilian employees life insurance coverage, claims by age, and program finances, FY89 with trends from FY83, annual rpt, 9844–35.3

Fed Govt civilian employees work-years, pay rates, and benefits use and costs, by agency, FY89, annual rpt, 9844–31

Finances and operations, by SIC 2- to 4-digit industry, forecast 1991, annual rpt, 2044–28

Finances of life insurance companies, performance ratios, and problem holdings, by firm, 1989-90, hearing, 21368–133

Govt census, 1987: State and local govt employment, payroll, OASDHI coverage, and employee benefits costs, by level of govt and State, 2455–4

Health care (long-term) and nursing home financing using life insurance predeath benefits, payout terms, 1990, and coverage by beneficiary characteristics, 1984, 2626–10.128

Mortgage applications by disposition, and secondary loan market sales by purchaser type, by applicant and neighborhood characteristics, 1990, article, 9362–1.206

Occupational injury and illness rates, by SIC 2- to 4-digit industry, 1988-89, annual rpt, 6844–7

Occupational injury and illness rates, by SIC 2- to 4-digit industry, 1989, annual rpt, 6844–1

Small business employees benefit plan coverage and provisions, by plan type and occupational group, 1990, biennial rpt, 6784–20

Statistical Abstract of US, 1991 annual data compilation, 2324–1.16

Survivor benefits of employer-sponsored plans, coverage by plan type and payment method, 1989, article, 6722–1.230

Veterans and servicepersons life insurance, actuarial analyses of VA programs, 1990, annual rpt, 8604–1

Veterans and servicepersons life insurance of VA, finances and coverage by program and State, 1990, annual rpt, 8604–4

see also Area wage surveys

see also Old-Age, Survivors, Disability, and Health Insurance

see also Servicepersons life insurance programs

Index by Subjects and Names

Light
see also Fiber optics
see also Lasers
see also Lighting equipment

Light bulbs
see Household supplies and utensils

Lighthouses and lightships
Mariners Weather Log, quarterly journal, 2152–8

Lighting equipment
Bulb production, shipments, stocks, trade, and firms, by type, monthly and quarterly Current Industrial Rpts, 2506–12.13; 2506–12.33
Commercial buildings energy use, costs, and conservation, by building characteristics, survey rpt series, 3166–8
County Business Patterns, 1988: employment, establishments, and payroll, by SIC 2- to 4-digit industry and county, annual State rpt series, 2326–6
County Business Patterns, 1989: employment, establishments, and payroll, by SIC 2- to 4-digit industry and county, annual State rpt series, 2326–8
Exports and imports of US, by Harmonized System 6-digit commodity and country, 1990, annual rpt, 2424–13
Exports and imports of US, by transport mode, country, and SITC 1- to 3-digit commodity, 1990, annual rpt, 2424–12
Exports of US, detailed Schedule B commodities with countries of destination, 1990, annual rpt, 2424–10
Fluorescent light ballast shipments, trade, and firms, by ballast type, quarterly Current Industrial Rpt, 2506–12.14
Injuries from use of consumer products, by severity, victim age, and detailed product, 1990, annual rpt, 9164–6
Price indexes (producer), by stage of processing and detailed commodity, monthly rpt, 6762–6
Price indexes (producer), by stage of processing and detailed commodity, monthly 1990, annual rpt, 6764–2
Shipments, trade, firms, and use, for lighting fixtures by product, 1990, annual Current Industrial Rpt, 2506–12.19

Lillie-Blanton, Marsha
"Black-White Differences in Alcohol Use by Women: Baltimore Survey Findings", 4042–3.212

Lima, Ohio
Wages by occupation, and benefits for office and plant workers, 1991 survey, periodic labor market rpt, 6785–3.10
see also under By SMSA or MSA in the "Index by Categories"

Lime
see Fertilizers
see Nonmetallic minerals and mines

Lin, Biing-Hwan
"Substitutability of Crop Rotations for Agrichemicals: Preliminary Results", 1561–16.204

Lincoln, Nebr.
see also under By City and By SMSA or MSA in the "Index by Categories"

Lindsey, Phoebe A.
"Medicaid Home and Community-Based Waivers for Acquired Immunodeficiency Syndrome Patients", 4652–1.216

Linens
see Household supplies and utensils

Lino, Mark
"Expenditures on a Child by Husband-Wife Families: 1990", 1708–87
"Expenditures on a Child by Single-Parent Families", 1702–1.203
"Income and Expenditures of Families with a Baby", 1702–1.211

Linseed
see Oils, oilseeds, and fats

Lipman, Barbara J.
"State and Local Initiatives on Productivity, Technology, and Innovation: Enhancing a National Resource for International Competitiveness", 10048–81

Liquefied natural gas
see Natural gas liquids

Liquefied petroleum gas
Agriculture census, 1987: farms, farmland, production, finances, and operator characteristics, by county, final State rpt series, 2331–1
Business statistics, detailed data for major industries and economic indicators, *Survey of Current Business*, monthly rpt, 2702–1.18
California minerals production by commodity, shipments, and liquefied petroleum gas transport by mode, 1986-87, conf, 5668–119
Consumption of energy, by detailed fuel type, end-use sector, and State, 1960-89, State Energy Data System annual rpt, 3164–39
Eastern Europe energy production, trade, use, and AID dev assistance, for 3 countries, 1980s-91, 25318–81
Exports and imports of US, by country and detailed commodity, monthly rpt, 2422–12
Exports and imports of US, by Harmonized System 6-digit commodity and country, 1990, annual rpt, 2424–13
Exports and imports of US, by transport mode, country, and SITC 1- to 3-digit commodity, 1990, annual rpt, 2424–12
Exports of US, detailed Schedule B commodities with countries of destination, 1990, annual rpt, 2424–10
Farm prices received and paid, by commodity and State, 1990, annual rpt, 1629–5
Farm prices received for major products and paid for farm inputs and living items, by commodity and State, monthly rpt, 1629–1
Farm production inputs supply, demand, and prices, 1970s-90 and projected to 1995, article, 1561–16.201
Farm production inputs supply, demand, and prices, 1980s-91 and forecast 1992, article, 1561–16.204
Farm production itemized costs, by farm sales size and region, 1990, annual rpt, 1614–3
Foreign and US oil prices, by refined product and country, 1980-89, annual rpt, 3164–50.6
Futures trading in selected commodities and financial instruments and indexes, NYC, Chicago, and other markets activity, semimonthly rpt, 11922–5
Heating fuels production, imports, stocks, and prices, by selected PAD district and State, seasonal weekly rpt, 3162–45

Liquefied petroleum gas

Housing (low income) energy aid, funding sources, costs, and participation, by State, FY89, annual rpt, 4694–8
Housing and households detailed characteristics, and unit and neighborhood quality, by location, 1989, biennial rpt, 2485–12
Housing and households detailed characteristics, and unit and neighborhood quality, MSA surveys, series, 2485–6
Housing energy prices, by fuel and State, 1989 and forecast 1990-91, 3166–6.54
Housing inventory change from 1973, by reason, unit and household characteristics, and location, 1983 survey, biennial rpt, 2485–14
Manufacturing energy use and prices, 1988 survey, series, 3166–13
Minerals Yearbook, 1988, Vol 3: foreign country reviews of production, trade, and policy, by commodity, annual rpt series, 5604–17
Naval Petroleum and Oil Shale Reserves production and revenue by fuel type, sales by purchaser, and wells, by reserve, FY90, annual rpt, 3334–3
Price indexes (producer), by stage of processing and detailed commodity, monthly rpt, 6762–6
Prices and spending for fuel, by type, end-use sector, and State, 1989, annual rpt, 3164–64
Propane stocks in PAD Districts 1-3, daily press release, weekly data, 3162–44
Retail trade census, 1987: finances and employment, for establishments with and without payroll, by SIC 2- to 4-digit kind of business, State, and MSA, 2401–1
Statistical Abstract of US, 1991 annual data compilation, 2324–1.25
Supply, demand, and movement of crude oil, gas liquids, and refined products, by PAD district and State, 1990, annual rpt, 3164–2
Supply, demand, and prices, by fuel type and end-use sector, alternative projections 1989-2010, annual rpt, 3164–75
Supply, demand, and prices, by fuel type and end-use sector, projections and underlying assumptions, 1990-2010, annual rpt, 3164–90
Supply, demand, and prices, by fuel type and end-use sector, with foreign comparisons, 1990 and trends from 1949, annual rpt, 3164–74.1; 3164–74.2
Supply, demand, and prices, by fuel type, end-use sector, and country, detailed data, monthly rpt with articles, 3162–24
Supply, demand, and prices of crude oil and refined products, and refinery capacity and stocks, by State, 1960-91, annual rpt, 3164–95
Supply, demand, trade, stocks, and refining of oil and gas liquids, by detailed product, State, and PAD district, monthly rpt with articles, 3162–6
Tax provisions of States for motor fuel, auto registration fees, and disposition of receipts, by State, as of Jan 1991, biennial rpt, 7554–37
Tax rates for motor fuel, by fuel type and State, monthly rpt, 7552–1
Transportation energy use by mode, fuel supply, and demographic and economic factors of vehicle use, 1970s-89, annual rpt, 3304–5

Liquefied petroleum gas

Wholesale trade census, 1987: oil bulk stations, sales and storage capacity by product, inventories, expenses, employment, and modes of transport, 2407–4.2

Liquor and liquor industry

- Business statistics, detailed data for major industries and economic indicators, *Survey of Current Business*, monthly rpt, 2702–1.14
- County Business Patterns, 1988: employment, establishments, and payroll, by SIC 2- to 4-digit industry and county, annual State rpt series, 2326–6
- County Business Patterns, 1989: employment, establishments, and payroll, by SIC 2- to 4-digit industry and county, annual State rpt series, 2326–8
- CPI by component for US city average, and by region, population size, and for 27 metro areas, monthly rpt, 6762–2
- Employment, earnings, and hours, by SIC 1- to 4-digit industry, monthly and annual averages, selected years 1909-90, annual rpt, 6744–4
- Enterprise Statistics, 1987: finances and operations for companies, by size, level of diversification, form of organization, and industry group, 2329–8
- Exports and imports (agricultural) of US, by detailed commodity and country, 1990, semiannual rpt, 1522–4
- Exports and imports of US, by Harmonized System 6-digit commodity and country, 1990, annual rpt, 2424–13
- Exports and imports of US, by selected country, country group, and commodity group, 1990, annual rpt, 2044–37
- Exports and imports of US, by transport mode, country, and SITC 1- to 3-digit commodity, 1990, annual rpt, 2424–12
- Exports and imports of US shipped through Canada, by detailed commodity, customs district, and country, 1989, annual rpt, 7704–11
- Exports of US, detailed Schedule B commodities with countries of destination, 1990, annual rpt, 2424–10
- Govt (State) liquor store employment, payroll, and average earnings, by function, State, county, and population size, 1987 Census of Govts, 2455–2
- Govt finances, by level of govt, State, and for large cities and counties, annual rpt series, 2466–2
- Grain (feed) consumption, by end use, periodic situation rpt with articles, 1561–4
- Grain production, prices, trade, and export inspections by US port and country of destination, by grain type, weekly rpt, 1313–2
- Hotels and other lodging places, receipts, payroll, employment, and ownership, by State and MSA, 1987 Census of Service Industries, subject rpt, 2393–3.2
- Manufacturing annual survey, 1989: finances and operations, by SIC 2- to 4-digit industry, series, 2506–15
- Manufacturing census, 1987: finances and operations, by SIC 2- to 4-digit industry, State, and MSA, with trends from 1849, 2497–1
- Manufacturing census, 1987: finances and operations, by type of organization and SIC 2- to 4-digit industry, subject rpt, 2497–5

Manufacturing finances and operations, by SIC 2- to 4-digit industry, forecast 1991, annual rpt, 2044–28

- Molasses supply, use, wholesale prices by market, and imports by country, 1985-90, annual rpt, 1311–19
- Occupational injury and illness rates, by SIC 2- to 4-digit industry, 1988-89, annual rpt, 6844–7
- Occupational injury and illness rates, by SIC 2- to 4-digit industry, 1989, annual rpt, 6844–1
- Price indexes (producer), by stage of processing and detailed commodity, monthly rpt, 6762–6
- Price indexes (producer), by stage of processing and detailed commodity, monthly 1990, annual rpt, 6764–2
- Production of distilled spirits, stocks, materials used, and taxable and tax-free removals, by State, monthly rpt, 8486–1.3
- Puerto Rico economic censuses, 1987: wholesale and retail trade and service industry finances and operations, by SIC 2- to 4-digit industry and municipio, 2591–1
- Puerto Rico economic censuses, 1987: wholesale, retail, and service industries finances and operations, by establishment characteristics and SIC 2- and 3-digit industry, subject rpts, 2591–2
- Retail trade census, 1987: depreciable assets, capital and operating expenses, sales, value added, and inventories, by SIC 2- to 4-digit kind of business, 2399–2
- Retail trade census, 1987: finances and employment, for establishments with and without payroll, by SIC 2- to 4-digit kind of business, State, and MSA, 2401–1
- Retail trade sales and inventories, by kind of business, region, and selected State, MSA, and city, monthly rpt, 2413–3
- Retail trade sales, by kind of business, advance monthly rpt, 2413–2
- Retail trade sales, inventories, purchases, gross margin, and accounts receivable, by SIC 2- to 4-digit kind of business and form of ownership, 1989, annual rpt, 2413–5
- Rum production, trade by country, and use, 1989-90, annual rpt, 9884–15
- State govt liquor store employment and payroll, by State, 1990, annual rpt series, 2466–1.1
- State govt liquor store labor productivity and indexes of output, FY67-89, annual rpt, 6824–1.6
- *Statistical Abstract of US*, 1991 annual data compilation, 2324–1.27
- Tax (excise) collections of IRS, by source, quarterly rpt, 8302–2.1
- Tax (income) returns of corporations, income and tax items by asset size and detailed industry, 1987, annual rpt, 8304–4
- Tax (income) returns of corporations, income and tax items by asset size and detailed industry, 1988, annual rpt, 8304–21
- Tax collections of State govts by detailed type of tax, and tax rates, by State, FY90, annual rpt, 2466–2.7
- Tax rates and revenue of State and local govts, by source and State, 1991 and historical trends, annual rpt, 10044–1

Index by Subjects and Names

- Tax revenue, by level of govt, type of tax, State, and selected large county, quarterly rpt, 2462–3
- Tax revenues and rates, regulatory activities, staff, and funding of Bur of Alcohol, Tobacco, and Firearms, 1980s-91, GAO rpt, 26119–335
- Wholesale trade census, 1987: depreciable assets, capital and operating expenses, sales, value added, and inventories, by SIC 2- to 3-digit kind of business, 2407–2
- Wholesale trade census, 1987: establishments, sales by customer class, employment, inventories, and expenses, by SIC 2- to 4-digit kind of business, 2407–4
- Wholesale trade sales and inventories, by SIC 2- to 3-digit kind of business, monthly rpt, 2413–7
- Wholesale trade sales, inventories, purchases, and gross margins, by SIC 2- to 3-digit kind of business, 1990, annual rpt, 2413–13
- Youth alcohol use, knowledge, attitudes, and info sources, series, 4006–10
- *see also* Alcohol abuse and treatment
- *see also* Alcohol use
- *see also* Alcoholic beverages control laws
- *see also* Beer and breweries
- *see also* Wine and winemaking

Liquor laws

see Alcoholic beverages control laws

Lisella, Lynn W.

"National AIDS Hotline: HIV and AIDS Information Service Through a Toll-Free Telephone System", 4042–3.256

Liss, Susan

"1990 Nationwide Personal Transportation Study: Early Results", 7556–6.1

Lister, C. Kendall

"Forest Pest Conditions in the Rocky Mountain Region, 1990", 1206–11.3

Listerosis

see Animal diseases and zoonoses

Literacy and illiteracy

- Developing countries aged population and selected characteristics, 1980s and projected to 2020, country rpt series, 2326–19
- Developing countries economic and social conditions from 1960s, and Intl Dev Cooperation Agency and AID activities and funding, FY90-92, annual rpt, 9904–4
- Foreign countries economic, social, political, and geographic summary data, by country, 1991, annual factbook, 9114–2
- Natl Education Goals progress indicators, by State, 1991, annual rpt, 15914–1
- Student aid funding and participation, by Federal program, instn type and control, and State, various periods 1959-89, annual rpt, 4804–28
- Workplace literacy program of Education Dept, project descriptions and funding, FY90, annual listing, 4804–40
- Workplace literacy programs, demonstration projects funding and participant characteristics, FY88, 4808–37
- Young adults literacy and reading scores, by race and education, 1985, annual rpt, 4824–2.28
- *see also* Reading ability and habits

Index by Subjects and Names

Livestock and livestock industry

Literature
see Language arts

Lithium
see Metals and metal industries

Lithuania
Human rights conditions in 170 countries, and US economic and military aid, 1990, annual rpt, 21384–3

Litter
see Refuse and refuse disposal

Little, Jane S.
"Medicaid", 9373–4.27
"Medicaid (in Massachusetts)", 9373–1.203

Little Rock, Ark.
Economic and banking conditions, for Fed Reserve 8th District, quarterly rpt with articles, 9391–16
Wages by occupation, for office and plant workers, 1991 survey, periodic MSA rpt, 6785–12.7
see also under By City and By SMSA or MSA in the "Index by Categories"

Littman, Mark S.
"Poverty Areas and the 'Underclass': Untangling the Web", 6722–1.219
"Poverty in the U.S., 1988-89", 2546–6.67
"Poverty in the U.S.: 1990", 2546–6.71

Litz, Diane
"Multifactor Productivity in Farm and Garden Equipment", 6722–1.232

Liu, Lillian
"Social Security for State-Sector Workers in the PRC: The Reform Decade and Beyond", 4742–1.218

Liu, Shiao-Kung
"Modeling the Alaskan Continental Shelf Waters", 2176–1.36

Liver diseases
see Digestive diseases

Livestock and livestock industry
Africa (sub-Saharan) agricultural conditions by country, with Ethiopia grain production and use, and dev aid by major donor, 1960s-80s, hearing, 23848–216
Agricultural data compilation, 1990 and trends from 1920, annual rpt, 1004–14
Agricultural Stabilization and Conservation Service producer payments, by program and State, 1990, annual table, 1804–12
Agricultural Statistics, 1990, annual rpt, 1004–1
Agriculture census, 1987: farms, farmland, production, finances, and operator characteristics, by county, final State rpt series, 2331–1
Australia agricultural input and output indexes, and freight rates, 1950s-80s, 1528–311
Business statistics, detailed data for major industries and economic indicators, *Survey of Current Business,* monthly rpt, 2702–1.14
Cattle (dairy) slaughtered under Federal inspection, by region, 1990, annual rpt, 1317–1.6
Cattle and calves for beef and milk, by State, as of July 1991, semiannual press release, 1623–1
Cattle and calves on feed, inventory and marketings by State, monthly release, 1623–2
Cattle feedlots and fed cattle marketings, by feedlot capacity, 1980 and 1990, article, 1561–7.203

Cattle feedlots and marketing, by lot size and State, selected years 1955-89, 1568–300
Cattle sales by feedlot size, and production costs by type, 1972-88, article, 9381–1.201
Coastal and riparian areas environmental conditions, fish, wildlife, use, and mgmt, for individual ecosystems, series, 5506–9
Developing countries agricultural supply, demand, and market for US exports, with socioeconomic conditions, country rpt series, 1526–6
Economic Indicators of the Farm Sector, balance sheets, and receipts by detailed commodity, by State, 1985-89, annual rpt, 1544–18
Economic Indicators of the Farm Sector, income, expenses, receipts by commodity, assets, and liabilities, 1990 and trends from 1945, annual rpt, 1544–16
Employment on farms, wages, and hours, by payment method, worker type, region, and State, 1910-90, 1618–21
Exports (agricultural) of high-value commodities, indexes and sales value by commodity, world area, and country, 1960s-86, 1528–323
Exports (agricultural) of US, impacts of foreign agricultural and trade policy, with data by commodity and country, 1989, annual rpt, 1924–8
Exports and imports (agricultural) commodity and country, prices, and world market devs, monthly rpt, 1922–12
Exports and imports (agricultural) of US, by commodity and country, bimonthly rpt, 1522–1
Exports and imports (agricultural) of US, by detailed commodity and country, 1989, annual rpt, 1524–8
Exports and imports (agricultural) of US, by detailed commodity and country, 1990, semiannual rpt, 1522–4
Exports and imports between US and outlying areas, by detailed commodity and mode of transport, 1990, annual rpt, 2424–11
Exports and imports of dairy, livestock, and poultry products, by commodity and country, FAS monthly circular, 1925–32
Exports and imports of US, by country and detailed commodity, monthly rpt, 2422–12
Exports and imports of US, by Harmonized System 6-digit commodity and country, 1990, annual rpt, 2424–13
Exports and imports of US, by transport mode, country, and SITC 1- to 3-digit commodity, 1990, annual rpt, 2424–12
Exports of US, detailed commodities by country, monthly CD-ROM, 2422–13
Exports of US, detailed Schedule B commodities with countries of destination, 1990, annual rpt, 2424–10
Farm credit, terms, delinquency, agricultural bank failures, and credit conditions by Fed Reserve District, quarterly rpt, 9365–3.10
Farm financial and marketing conditions, forecast 1991, annual chartbook, 1504–8
Farm financial and marketing conditions, forecast 1991, annual conf, 1004–16
Foreign and US dairy production, trade, and use, by selected country, FAS semiannual circular series, 1925–33

Foreign countries agricultural production, prices, and trade, by country, 1980-90 and forecast 1991, annual world area rpt series, 1524–4
Foreign countries agricultural production, trade, and policies, summary data by country, 1989-90, annual factbook, 1924–12
Forest Service mgmt of public lands and resources dev, environmental, economic, and social impacts of alternative programs, projected to 2040, 1208–24
Futures and options trading volume, by commodity and exchange, FY90, annual rpt, 11924–2
Futures trading in selected commodities and financial instruments and indexes, NYC, Chicago, and other markets activity, semimonthly rpt, 11922–5
Hog farms financial condition, 1987, 1566–8.6
Hogs inventory, value, farrowings, and farms, by State, quarterly release, 1623–3
Horse and burro wild herd areas in western States, population, adoption, and mgmt costs, as of FY89, biennial rpt, 5724–8
Imports of US, detailed commodities by country, monthly CD-ROM, 2422–14
Input-output structure of US economy, detailed interindustry transactions for 84 industries, and components of final demand, 1986, annual article, 2702–1.206
Input-output structure of US economy, detailed interindustry transactions for 85 industries, 1982 benchmark data, 2702–1.213
Marketing data for livestock, meat, and wool, by species and market, weekly rpt, 1315–1
Natl forests livestock grazing, by region and State, 1990, annual rpt, 1204–5
Packers purchases and feeding, and livestock markets, dealers, and sales, by State, 1989, annual rpt, 1384–1
Pesticide and fertilizer use reduction, environmental and economic impacts by commodity and region, alternative forecasts 1989-94, hearing, 23848–222
Pollution (air) emissions factors, by detailed pollutant and source, data compilation, 1990 rpt, 9198–120
Pollution (groundwater) from farm chemicals use and animal wastes, and reduction strategies, 1960s-90, 26358–231
Pollution (water) impacts of livestock industry regional concentration, 1991 article, 1522–3.204
Price indexes (producer), by stage of processing and detailed commodity, monthly rpt, 6762–6
Price support program changes and other effects on farm income and production, for livestock and program and nonprogram crop producers, model results, 1988, 1548–375
Prices received and paid by farmers, by commodity and State, 1990, annual rpt, 1629–5
Prices received by farmers for major products, and paid for farm inputs and living items, by State, monthly rpt, 1629–1

Livestock and livestock industry

Production inputs, output, and productivity for farms, by commodity and region, 1947-89, annual rpt, 1544–17

Production itemized costs, by farm sales size and region, 1990, annual rpt, 1614–3

Production itemized costs, receipts, and returns, by commodity and region, 1987-89, annual rpt, 1544–20

Production, prices, receipts, and disposition for meat animals, by species and State, 1988-90, annual rpt, 1623–8

Production, prices, trade, and marketing, by commodity, current situation and forecast, monthly rpt with articles, 1502–4

Production, prices, trade, and stocks, monthly rpt, 1561–17

Production, prices, trade, stocks, and use, periodic situation rpt with articles, 1561–7

Public lands acreage and use, and Land Mgmt Bur activities and finances, annual State rpt series, 5724–11

Public lands acreage, grants, use, revenues, and allocations, by State, FY90, annual rpt, 5724–1.2

Sheep, lamb, and goat inventory, by State, 1989-91, annual press release, 1623–4

Sheep, lamb, and goat loss to predators and other causes, by region and State, 1990, 1618–20

Sheep slaughter, stock, and feeder lamb and ewe prices, weekly and biweekly rpt, 1315–2

Slaughter and meat production, by livestock type and State, monthly rpt, 1623–9

Slaughter of livestock, meat production, and slaughter plants, by species and State, 1990, annual rpt, 1623–10

Soviet Union agricultural reform issues, with background data for USSR and US, 1970s-90, article, 9381–1.210

Soviet Union GNP by component and industry sector, and CIA estimation methods, 1950s-87, 23848–223

State and Metro Area Data Book, 1991 data compilation, 2328–54

Statistical Abstract of US, 1991 annual data compilation, 2324–1.23

Tax (income) returns of partnerships, income statement and balance sheet items, by industry group, 1989, annual article, 8302–2.216; 8304–18

Thefts, and value of property stolen and recovered, by property type, 1990, annual rpt, 6224–2.1

Water use by end use, well withdrawals, and public supply deliveries, by county, State rpt series, 5666–24

Wholesale trade census, 1987: establishments, sales by customer class, employment, inventories, and expenses, by SIC 2- to 4-digit kind of business, 2407–4

see also Animal diseases and zoonoses

see also Dairy industry and products

see also Hides and skins

see also Meat and meat products

see also Pasture and rangeland

see also Poultry industry and products

see also Veterinary medicine

see also under By Commodity in the "Index by Categories"

see also under By Industry in the "Index by Categories"

Livezey, Janet

"U.S. Rice Imports and Domestic Use", 1561–8.206

Living arrangements

AFDC beneficiaries demographic and financial characteristics, by State, FY89, annual rpt, 4694–1

Census of Population and Housing, 1990: population and housing characteristics, households, and land area, by county, subdiv, and place, State rpt series, 2551–1

Census of Population and Housing, 1990: population and housing selected characteristics, by region, press release, 2328–74

Child welfare programs funding by source, and foster care program operations and client characteristics, for selected States, 1960s-95, 25368–169

Children (handicapped) enrollment by age, and special education programs staff, funding, and needs, by type of handicap and State, 1989/90, annual rpt, 4944–4

Children and youth social, economic, and demographic characteristics, 1950s-90, 4818–5

Cohabitation, marriage, marriage dissolution, and remarriage, for women, by age and race, 1988, 4146–8.196

Consumer Income, socioeconomic characteristics of persons, families, and households, detailed cross-tabulations, Current Population Rpt series, 2546–6

Disability, acute and chronic health conditions, absenteeism, and health services use, by selected characteristics, 1987, CD-ROM, 4147–10.177

Family economic impacts of departure, absence, and presence of parents, 1983-86, Current Population Rpt, 2546–20.17

Homeless and runaway youth programs, funding, activities, and participant characteristics, FY90, annual rpt, 4604–3

Hospices operations, services, costs, and patient characteristics, for instns without Medicare certification, FY85-86, 4658–52

Households composition, income, benefits, and labor force status, Survey of Income and Program Participation methodology, working paper series, 2626–10

Income (household) and poverty status under alternative income definitions, by recipient characteristics, 1990, annual Current Population Rpt, 2546–6.69

Injuries, by type, circumstances, and victim characteristics, and related activity limitations, 1985-87, 4147–10.176

Injuries, related impairments, and activity limitations, by circumstances and victim characteristics, 1985-87, 4147–10.179

Living arrangements, family relationships, and marital status, by selected characteristics, 1990, annual Current Population Rpt, 2546–1.449

Nursing home residents with mental disorders, by disorder type and resident and instn characteristics, 1985, 4147–13.106

Older persons living arrangements, by poverty status, 1989, annual rpt, 4744–3.1

Older persons with functional limitations, long-term care sources, and health and other characteristics, 1984-85, 4147–13.104

Index by Subjects and Names

Older women's household income by source, and expenses by type, by living arrangement and other characteristics, 1988, article, 1702–1.210

Population size and characteristics, historical index to *Current Population Rpts,* 1991 listing, 2546–2.160

Puerto Rico population and housing characteristics, 1990 Census of Population and Housing, press release, 2328–78

Statistical Abstract of US, 1991 annual data compilation, 2324–1.1

Supplemental Security Income and Medicaid eligibility and payment provisions, and beneficiaries living arrangements, by State, 1991, annual rpt, 4704–13

Supplemental Security Income recipients, by eligibility type and living arrangement, 1989, annual rpt, 4744–3.8

Supplemental Security Income recipients, by race and sex, monthly rpt, 4742–1.12

Veterans (homeless) domiciliary program of VA, participant characteristics and outcomes, 1990 annual rpt, 8604–10

Veterans (homeless) with mental illness, VA program services, costs, staff, client characteristics, and outcome, 1990, annual rpt, 8604–11

Virgin Islands population and housing characteristics, 1990 Census of Population and Housing, press release, 2328–81

Young adults living away from parents, living arrangements relation to selected characteristics, for US and 4 countries, 2546–2.157

see also Families and households

see also Foster home care

see also Group homes for the handicapped

see also Group quarters

see also Homeless population

see also Housing condition and occupancy

see also Retirement communities

see also Rooming and boarding houses

see also Transient housing

Living standard

see Cost of living

see Family budgets

see Personal and household income

see Quality of life

Livonia, Mich.

see also under By City in the "Index by Categories"

Loan delinquency and default

Acquisitions and mergers by type, with data for large transactions by payment method and firm, late 1960s-90, working paper, 9366–1.161

AID loans repayment status and terms by program and country, and status of predecessor agency loans, quarterly rpt, 9912–3

Banks (insured commercial) assets, income, and financial ratios, by asset size and State, quarterly rpt, 13002–3

Banks (insured commercial and savings) finances, for foreign and domestic offices, by asset size, 1989, annual rpt, 9294–4.2

Banks (insured commercial and savings) financial condition and performance, by asset size and region, quarterly rpt, 9292–1

Banks (natl) charters, mergers, liquidations, enforcement cases, and financial performance, with data by instn and State, quarterly rpt, 8402–3

Index by Subjects and Names

Loan delinquency and default

Banks and deposit insurance funds financial condition, potential losses, and regulatory issues, 1980s-90 and projected to 1995, 21248–147

Banks in Fed Reserve 8th District, financial performance indicators by asset size, 1987-90, annual article, 9391–16.208

Banks in Fed Reserve 9th District, finances and performance ratios, by State, quarterly journal, 9383–19

Banks in Fed Reserve 11th District, financial performance indicators by asset size and FDIC assistance receipt, 1987-90, article, 9379–1.206

Banks in northeast US, financial performance compared to rest of US, 1970s-90, article, 9373–1.220

Banks loan performance relation to loan commitments and selected financial ratios, 1975-86, working paper, 9377–9.105

Banks profitability, balance sheet and income statement items, and financial ratios, by asset size, 1985-90, annual article, 9362–1.204

Budget of US, obligations and authority by function, agency, and program, with summaries, analyses, and historical tables, FY92, annual rpt, 104–2

Credit reporting and collection establishments, and receipts by source and class of client, by MSA, 1987 Census of Service Industries, 2393–4.4

Credit unions (federally-insured) financial performance, by charter type and region, 1st half 1991, semiannual rpt, 9532–7

Credit unions federally insured, finances by instn characteristics and State, as of June 1991, semiannual rpt, 9532–6

Credit unions federally insured, finances, 1989-90, annual rpt, 9534–1

Credit unions mortage lending impacts on financial performance, for northeast States and total US, 1980s-90, article, 9536–1.6

DOD programs fraud and abuse, audits and investigations, 1st half FY91, semiannual rpt, 3542–18

Farm (small) loans, defaults, income, and financial condition, 1980-89, article, 1502–7.202

Farm Credit System and FmHA services to aid delinquent borrowers, activities, with background data, 1989 hearings, 25168–74

Farm Credit System financial condition, impacts of instn mergers, by district, 1982-89, 1548–381

Farm Credit System financial condition, quarterly rpt, 9262–2

Farm Credit System financial statements and loan activity by lender type, and borrower characteristics, 1990, annual rpt, 9264–2

Farm credit, terms, delinquency, agricultural bank failures, and credit conditions by Fed Reserve District, quarterly rpt, 9365–3.10

Farm finances, debts, assets, and receipts, and lenders financial condition, quarterly rpt with articles, 1541–1

Farm financial stress indicators, operator quits, and loan problems and mediation, 1970s-90, 1598–272

Fed Govt accounts receivable, delinquent debt cases and collections of Justice Dept and private law firms, pilot project results, FY90, annual rpt, 6004–20

Fed Govt consolidated financial statements based on business accounting methods, FY89-90, annual rpt, 8104–5

Fed Govt foreign loan and credit arrearages, by program and country, as of Dec 1988, annual rpt, 15344–1.1

Fed Home Loan Mortgage Corp activities and financial statements, 1990, annual rpt, 9414–1

FmHA activities, and loans and grants by program and State, FY90 and trends from FY70, annual rpt, 1184–17

FmHA farm and rural housing program loan appeals filed in 3 States, by disposition, 1988-90, GAO rpt, 26113–516

FmHA guaranteed and direct loan program costs under alternative assumptions, 1981-89, 1598–273

FmHA loan servicing eligibility, use, and effects on borrowers solvency, 1988-89, GAO rpt, 26113–497

FmHA loans and borrower supervision activities in farm and housing programs, by type and State, monthly rpt, 1182–1

FmHA property acquired through foreclosure, value, acreage, and sales, for farm and nonfarm property by State, monthly rpt, 1182–6

FmHA property acquired through foreclosure, value, and acreage under conservation easements by State, 1989-90, GAO rpt, 26113–514

FmHA property acquired through foreclosure, 1-family homes, value, sales, and leases, by State, monthly rpt, 1182–7

Foreign govt and private obligors debt to US, by country and program, periodic rpt, 8002–6

Govt-sponsored enterprises financial condition and capital adequacy, with data by enterprise, 1970s-90 and projected to 1996, 26308–99

Govt-sponsored enterprises financial condition, capital adequacy, and impacts on Federal borrowing, with data by enterprise, 1980s-90, last issue of annual rpt, 8004–15

GSA programs fraud and abuse, audits and investigations, 2nd half FY91, semiannual rpt, 9452–8

Home equity lines of credit share of all loans, and delinquency compared to other loans, by southeastern State, 1988-90, article, 9391–16.206

Housing units (1-family) acquired by Fed Govt through foreclosure and savings instn failure, inventory by State, acquisition costs, and sales, for 4 agencies, 1986-90, GAO rpt, 26113–513

Housing units repossessed under Federal programs, by agency, 1989, 8608–7

Interior Dept programs fraud and abuse, audits and investigations, 2nd half FY91, semiannual rpt, 5302–2

Labor Dept programs fraud and abuse, audits and investigations, 2nd half FY91, semiannual rpt, 6302–2

Mortgage foreclosure court caseloads for Federal district courts, 1990, annual rpt, 18204–8.13; 18204–8.18; 18204–11

Mortgage foreclosure court caseloads for Federal district courts, 1991, annual rpt, 18204–2.1

Mortgage foreclosures and HUD multifamily housing stock, by region, 1990, GAO rpt, 26131–84

Mortgage purchases, sales, and other activity of Fed Natl Mortgage Assn, 1988-89, annual rpt, 5184–9

Mortgages insured by private companies, for 1-4 family units, monthly press release, 5142–38

Natural gas interstate pipeline company detailed financial and operating data, by firm, 1989, annual rpt, 3164–38

New England States thrifts loan delinquency rates by loan type, time past due, thrift charter type, and State, 1990, annual article, 9302–4.202

North Central States, FHLB 6th District insured S&Ls financial condition and operations by State, quarterly rpt, 9302–23

North Central States, FHLB 6th District savings instns financial condition and operations by State, monthly rpt, 9302–11

Retirement housing centers tax-exempt bond use and other financing, defaults, and facility and resident characteristics, 1991 GAO rpt, 26119–328

Rural Electrification Program lending, by State, FY90, annual rpt, 1244–7

Rural Telephone Program loan activity, by State, FY90, annual tables, 1244–8

Savings banks insured by Bank Insurance Fund, financial condition and performance, by asset size and region, quarterly rpt, 9292–5

Savings instns failure resolution costs to FSLIC, relation to asset quality indicators and tax benefit grants, 1984-87, article, 9292–4.202

Savings instns failures, financial performance of instns under Resolution Trust Corp conservatorship, quarterly rpt, 9722–5

Savings instns finances and operations by district and State, mortgage loan activity and terms by MSA, and FHLB finances, 1989 and trends from 1900, annual rpt, 8434–3

Savings instns insured by Savings Assn Insurance Fund, assets, liabilities, and deposit and loan activity, by conservatorship status, monthly rpt, 8432–1

Small Business Admin surety bond guarantee program finances, and contracts by contractor race, obligee type, and region, FY87-89, GAO rpt, 26113–526

South Central States agricultural banks financial ratios, and farm receipts by commodity, 1980s-90, annual article, 9391–16.209

Southeastern States, Fed Reserve 5th District insured commercial banks financial statements, by State, quarterly rpt, 9389–18

Southeastern States, Fed Reserve 8th District banking and economic conditions, quarterly rpt with articles, 9391–16

Southeastern States, FHLB 4th District, employment and housing and mortgage market indicators by State, quarterly rpt, 9302–36

Statistical Abstract of US, 1991 annual data compilation, 2324–1.16

Student aid funding and participation, by Federal program, instn type and control, and State, various periods 1959-89, annual rpt, 4804–28

Loan delinquency and default

Student guaranteed loan default rate, causes, defaulter characteristics, and preventive recommendations, FY81-90, 4808–35

Student guaranteed loans, defaults, and collections, by type of loan, lender, and guarantee agency, with data by State and top lender, FY90, annual rpt, 4804–38

Student loans of Fed Govt in default, losses, and rates, by instn and State, as of June 1990, annual rpt, 4804–18

Tax (income) returns filed by type of filer, selected income items, quarterly rpt, 8302–2.1

Tax (income) returns of corporations, income and tax items by asset size and detailed industry, 1987, annual rpt, 8304–4

Tax (income) returns of corporations, income and tax items by asset size and detailed industry, 1988, annual rpt, 8304–21

Tax (income) returns of partnerships, income statement and balance sheet items, by industry group, 1989, annual article, 8302–2.216; 8304–18

US attorneys case processing and collections, by case type and Federal district, FY90, annual rpt, 6004–2

USDA programs fraud and abuse, audits and investigations, 1st half FY91, semiannual rpt, 1002–4

Loans

Banking activity, consumer credit, and interest rates, monthly rpt series, 9365–2

Banks (commercial) loans and investments, 1972-90, annual rpt, 204–1.5

Banks (insured commercial and savings) finances, for foreign and domestic offices, by asset size, 1989, annual rpt, 9294–4.2

Banks (insured commercial and savings) financial condition and performance, by asset size and region, quarterly rpt, 9292–1

Banks (natl) charters, mergers, liquidations, enforcement cases, and financial performance, with data by instn and State, quarterly rpt, 8402–3

Banks finances and operations, by metro-nonmetro location, 1987-89, annual rpt, 1544–29

Banks loan amounts outstanding, for commercial and Fed Reserve banks, monthly rpt, 9362–1.1

Banks loan performance relation to loan commitments and selected financial ratios, 1975-86, working paper, 9377–9.105

Banks loan terms, monthly rpt, quarterly data, 9362–1.4

Banks profitability, balance sheet and income statement items, and financial ratios, by asset size, 1985-90, annual article, 9362–1.204

Banks profitability indicators for student loans and other financial services, 1985-89, 4808–36

Economic indicators impacts of commercial paper-bank loan firm financing mix and selected interest rate spreads, model description and results, 1960s-89, technical paper, 9366–6.268

Fed Financing Bank holdings and transactions, by borrower, monthly press release, 12802–1

Fed Govt financial operations, detailed data, *Treasury Bulletin*, quarterly rpt, 8002–4

Fed Reserve banks finances and staff, 1990, annual rpt, 9364–1.1

Financial, banking, and mortgage market activity, weekly rpt series, 9365–1

GNP relation to bank loan commitments, selected interest rates, and other factors, 1973-87, technical paper, 9385–8.75

Govt-sponsored enterprises financial condition and capital adequacy, with data by enterprise, 1970s-90 and projected to 1996, 26308–99

Govt-sponsored enterprises financial condition and capital adequacy, with regulatory recommendations and data by enterprise, 1985-95, GAO rpt, 26119–296

Govt-sponsored enterprises financial condition, capital adequacy, and impacts on Federal borrowing, with data by enterprise, 1980s-90, last issue of annual rpt, 8004–15

Insurance industry finances, underwriting activities, and investment plan mgmt, 1960s-90, 21248–159

Japan bank affiliates in US, loans by borrower type, late 1984-89, technical paper, 9385–8.97

Monetary trends, Fed Reserve Bank of St Louis monthly rpt, 9391–2

Money supply impact on bank loans, 1970s-91, article, 9381–1.208

New England States economic indicators, Fed Reserve 1st District, monthly rpt, 9373–2.7

Nonprofit charitable organizations finances, by asset size and State, 1987, article, 8302–2.218

North Central States, FHLB 6th District insured S&Ls financial condition and operations by State, quarterly rpt, 9302–23

North Central States, FHLB 6th District insured savings instns financial condition and operations by State, monthly rpt, 9302–11

Savings banks insured by Bank Insurance Fund, financial condition and performance, by asset size and region, quarterly rpt, 9292–5

Savings instns finances and operations by district and State, mortgage loan activity and terms by MSA, and FHLB finances, 1989 and trends from 1900, annual rpt, 8434–3

Savings instns insured by Savings Assn Insurance Fund, assets, liabilities, and deposit and loan activity, by conservatorship status, monthly rpt, 8432–1

Securities credit issues of stockbrokers and other nonbank lenders, and brokers balance sheet, as of June 1990, annual rpt, 9365–5.1

Southeastern States, Fed Reserve 5th District, economic indicators by State, quarterly rpt, 9389–16

Southeastern States, Fed Reserve 5th District insured commercial banks financial statements, by State, quarterly rpt, 9389–18

Southeastern States, Fed Reserve 8th District banking and economic conditions, quarterly rpt with articles, 9391–16

Survey of Current Business, detailed financial and business data, and economic indicators, monthly rpt, 2702–1.1

Index by Subjects and Names

Tax (income) refunds applied by IRS to outstanding debts to Fed Govt, impacts on subsequent taxpayer compliance, 1984-87, GAO rpt, 26119–339

Tax (income) returns of corporations, income and tax items by asset size and detailed industry, 1987, annual rpt, 8304–4

West Central States economic indicators, Fed Reserve 10th District, quarterly rpt, 9381–16.2

Western States, FHLB 11th District S&Ls, offices, and financial condition, 1991 annual listing, 9304–23

see also Agricultural credit

see also Commercial credit

see also Consumer credit

see also Credit

see also Credit unions

see also Discrimination in credit

see also Export-Import Bank

see also Farm Credit System

see also Federal aid programs

see also Federal aid to arts and humanities

see also Federal aid to education

see also Federal aid to higher education

see also Federal aid to highways

see also Federal aid to housing

see also Federal aid to law enforcement

see also Federal aid to libraries

see also Federal aid to local areas

see also Federal aid to medical education

see also Federal aid to medicine

see also Federal aid to railroads

see also Federal aid to rural areas

see also Federal aid to States

see also Federal aid to transportation

see also Federal aid to vocational education

see also Federal funding for energy programs

see also Federal funding for research and development

see also Finance companies

see also Foreign debts

see also Government and business

see also Government assets and liabilities

see also Interest payments

see also Interest rates

see also International assistance

see also Loan delinquency and default

see also Military assistance

see also Mortgages

see also Public debt

see also Student aid

see also Veterans benefits and pensions

see also Veterans housing

Lobbying and lobbying groups

Tax (excise) collections of IRS, by source, quarterly rpt, 8302–1

see also Political action committees

Lobsters

see Shellfish

Local-Federal relations

see Federal-local relations

Local government

Alaska rural areas population characteristics, and energy resources dev effects, series, 5736–5

Construction put in place, value of new public and private structures, by type, monthly rpt, 2382–4

Criminal justice spending, employment, and payroll, by level of govt, State, and selected city and county, FY71-88, biennial rpt, 6064–9

Index by Subjects and Names

Criminal justice spending, employment, and payroll, by level of govt, State, and selected city and county, 1984-86, biennial rpt, 6064–4

Environmental protection programs costs to govts and households, by program type and city size, 1960s-88 and projected to 2000, 9188–114

Finances of govts, by level of govt, State, and for large cities and counties, annual rpt series, 2466–2

Finances of govts, tax systems and revenue, and fiscal structure, by level of govt and State, 1991 and historical trends, annual rpt, 10044–1

Finances of State and local govts, revenue by source and outlays by type, 1986-90, annual article, 2702–1.205

Flow-of-funds accounts, savings, investments, and credit statements, quarterly rpt, 9365–3.3

Hwy Statistics, detailed data by State, 1990, annual rpt, 7554–1

Job Training Partnership Act State and local admin, funding, effectiveness, and participants, GAO rpt series, 26106–8

Law enforcement spending and employment, by activity and level of govt, data compilation, 1991 annual rpt, 6064–6.1

Mental health care facilities, finances, caseload, staff, and characteristics of instn and patients, 1988, 4506–4.14

Public opinion on taxes, spending, and govt efficiency, by respondent characteristics, 1991 survey, annual rpt, 10044–2

Public works condition, mgmt, R&D, and funding, for transportation and environmental projects, 1986-91, 26358–235

Retirement systems of State and local govts, cash and security holdings and finances, quarterly rpt, 2462–2

Statistical Abstract of US, 1991 annual data compilation, 2324–1.9

see also Census of Governments

see also City and town planning

see also Federal aid to local areas

see also Federal-local relations

see also Fire departments

see also Municipal bonds

see also Police

see also School districts

see also Special districts

see also State and local employees

see also State and local employees pay

see also State and local taxes

see also State funding for local areas

see also State-local relations

see also Zoning and zoning laws

Location of industries

see Industrial siting

Locomotives

see Railroad equipment and vehicles

Lodging

see Hotels and motels

see Rooming and boarding houses

Log homes

see Prefabricated buildings

Logansport, Ind.

Wages by occupation, and benefits for office and plant workers, 1991 survey, periodic MSA rpt, 6785–3.7

Logistics

Army Reserve and National Guard wartime preparedness, for general support maintenance units, as of May 1990, GAO rpt, 26123–354

DOD budget, manpower needs, costs, and force readiness by service branch, FY92, annual rpt, 3504–1

DOD budget, R&D appropriations by item, service branch, and defense agency, FY90-93, annual rpt, 3544–33

Fed Govt labor productivity, indexes of output and labor costs by function, FY67-89, annual rpt, 6824–1.6

Military and personal property shipments, passenger traffic, and costs, by service branch and mode of transport, quarterly rpt, 3702–1

Persian Gulf War costs to US by category and service branch, and offsetting contributions by allied country, monthly rpt, 102–3

Persian Gulf War costs to US by category and service branch, and offsetting contributions by allied country, various periods FY90-91, annual rpt, 104–7

Reserve forces personnel and equipment strengths, and readiness, by reserve component, FY90, annual rpt, 3544–31

Soviet Union military weapons systems, presence, and force strengths, and compared to US, 1991 annual rpt, 3504–20

see also Military supplies and property

Lohoefener, Ren

"Association of Sea Turtles with Petroleum Platforms in the North-Central Gulf of Mexico", 5738–26

Lomax, Eugene

"Differences in Agricultural Research and Productivity Among 26 Countries", 1528–318

Lompoc, Calif.

Wages by occupation, for office and plant workers, 1991 survey, periodic MSA rpt, 6785–3.6

see also under By SMSA or MSA in the "Index by Categories"

London, Kathryn A.

"Cohabitation, Marriage, Marital Dissolution, and Remarriage: U.S., 1988", 4146–8.196

Long Beach, Calif.

Housing starts and completions authorized by building permits in 40 MSAs, quarterly rpt, 2382–9

Wages by occupation, for office and plant workers, 1990 survey, periodic MSA rpt, 6785–11.3

see also under By City and By SMSA or MSA in the "Index by Categories"

Long Island, N.Y.

CPI by component for US city average, and by region, population size, and for 15 metro areas, monthly rpt, 6762–1

CPI by component for US city average, and by region, population size, and for 27 metro areas, monthly rpt, 6762–2

Housing starts and completions authorized by building permits in 40 MSAs, quarterly rpt, 2382–9

Long, Sharon K.

"Children and Welfare: Patterns of Multiple Program Participation", 2626–10.133

Los Angeles, Calif.

"Wages and Employment Among the Working Poor: New Evidence from SIPP", 2626–10.122

"Welfare Participation and Welfare Recidivism: The Role of Family Events", 2626–10.126

Long, Stephen H.

"Effects of Being Uninsured on Health Care Service Use: Estimates from the Survey of Income and Program Participation", 2626–10.120

Longmont, Colo.

see also under By SMSA or MSA in the "Index by Categories"

Longshoremen

Accidents involving merchant ships, and casualties, by circumstances and characteristics of persons and vessels involved, 1988, annual rpt, 7404–11

Employment shipboard, shipyard, and longshore, FY89-90, annual rpt, 7704–14.3

Labor supply in 4 coastal regions, monthly rpt, 7702–1

Workers compensation laws of States and Fed Govt, 1991 semiannual rpt, 6502–1

Workers compensation programs under Federal admin, finances and operations, FY90, annual rpt, 6504–10

Longview, Tex.

see also under By SMSA or MSA in the "Index by Categories"

Longview, Wash.

Housing vacancy rates for single and multifamily units and mobile homes, by city and ZIP code, 1991, annual MSA rpt, 9304–21.1

Looker, Anne C.

"Comparing Serum Ferritin Values from Different Population Surveys. Vital and Health Statistics Series 2", 4147–2.111

Lorain, Ohio

CPI by component for US city average, and by region, population size, and for 15 metro areas, monthly rpt, 6762–1

CPI by component for US city average, and by region, population size, and for 27 metro areas, monthly rpt, 6762–2

see also under By SMSA or MSA in the "Index by Categories"

Lord, Ronald C.

"California's Sweetener Industries—Recent Developments and Prospects", 1561–14.206

"Canadian Sugar and HFCS Industries and U.S. Trade", 1561–14.203

"Procedures Used in Establishing 1991/92-Crop Loan Rates for Sugar and Minimum Support Prices for Sugarcane and Sugarbeets", 1561–14.207

Los Alamos Scientific Laboratory

see also Department of Energy National Laboratories

Los Angeles, Calif.

CPI by component for US city average, and by region, population size, and for 15 metro areas, monthly rpt, 6762–1

CPI by component for US city average, and by region, population size, and for 27 metro areas, monthly rpt, 6762–2

Drug abuse indicators for selected metro areas, research results, data collection, and policy issues, 1991 semiannual conf, 4492–5

Los Angeles, Calif.

Drug test results at arrest, by drug type, offense, and sex, for selected urban areas, quarterly rpt, 6062–3

Fruit and vegetable shipments, and arrivals in US and Canada cities, by mode of transport and State and country of origin, 1990, annual rpt, 1311–4.2

Housing starts and completions authorized by building permits in 40 MSAs, quarterly rpt, 2382–9

Housing vacancy and property value appreciation rates for 4 metro areas, 1991 GAO rpt, 26131–84

Oil prices by product, for 4 cities, seasonal weekly rpt, 3162–45

Wages by occupation, for office and plant workers, 1990 survey, periodic MSA rpt, 6785–11.3

see also under By City and By SMSA or MSA in the "Index by Categories"

Los Angeles County, Calif.

Foster care placements, discharges, and returns to care, by selected characteristics of children, and length of stay factors, 1985-86, GAO rpt, 26121–432

Medicaid coverage loss impacts on health services use, California transfer of selected Medicaid groups to county care, 1991 article, 4652–1.242

Lotteries

Govt finances, tax systems and revenue, and fiscal structure, by level of govt and State, 1991 with historical trends, annual rpt, 10044–1

Puerto Rico economic censuses, 1987: wholesale and retail trade and service industry finances and operations, by SIC 2- to 4-digit industry and municipio, 2591–1

State and Metro Area Data Book, 1991 data compilation, 2328–54

State govt revenue by source, spending and debt by function, and holdings, FY90, annual rpt, 2466–2.6

State govt tax collections by detailed type of tax, and tax rates, by State, FY90, annual rpt, 2466–2.7

Statistical Abstract of US, 1991 annual data compilation, 2324–1.9

Loudoun County, Va.

Fed Govt land acquisition and dev projects in DC metro area, characteristics and funding by agency and project, FY91-95, annual rpt, 15454–1

Louisiana

Banks (insured commercial and savings) deposits by instn, State, MSA, and county, as of June 1990, annual regional rpt, 9295–3.4

Black higher education instns finances, funding sources, enrollment, and student characteristics, with data for Louisiana instns, 1970s-90, hearing, 25258–24

Coal production and mines by county, prices, productivity, miners, and reserves, by mining method and State, 1989-90, annual rpt, 3164–25

County Business Patterns, 1989: employment, establishments, and payroll, by SIC 2- to 4-digit industry and county, annual State rpt, 2326–8.20

DOD prime contract awards, by contractor, service branch, State, and city, FY90, annual rpt, 3544–22

Economic indicators and oil rig growth forecasts for Louisiana, model description and results, 1991, article, 9379–1.202

Economic indicators by State and MSA, Fed Reserve 6th District, quarterly rpt, 9371–14

Employment by industry div, earnings, and hours, by southwestern State, monthly rpt, 6962–2

Estuary environmental and fishery conditions, research results and methodology, 1991 rpt, 2176–7.23

Fed Govt spending in States and local areas, by type, State, county, and city, FY90, annual rpt, 2464–3

Fed Govt spending in States, by type, program, agency, and State, FY90, annual rpt, 2464–2

Fish (catfish) raised on farms, inventory, stocks, and production, by major producer State, quarterly rpt, 1631–18

Fish and shellfish catch, wholesale receipts, prices, trade, and other market activities, weekly regional rpt, 2162–6.3

HHS financial aid, by program, recipient, State, and city, FY90, annual regional listing, 4004–3.6

Hospital deaths of Medicare patients, actual and expected rates by diagnosis, and hospital characteristics, by instn, FY87-89, annual regional rpt, 4654–14.6

Income (personal) per capita and by source, and earnings by industry div, by State, MSA, and county, 1984-89, annual regional rpt, 2704–2.4

Income per capita, impacts of industry mix and other factors, for 36 MSAs in Texas and Louisiana, 1969-88, article, 9379–1.209

Jail adult and juvenile population, employment, spending, instn conditions, and inmate programs, by county and facility, 1988, regional rpt series, 6068–144.4

Marriages, divorces, and rates, by characteristics of spouses, State, and county, 1987 and trends from 1920, US Vital Statistics annual rpt, 4144–4

Mineral Industry Surveys, State reviews of production, 1990, preliminary annual rpt, 5614–6

Minerals Yearbook, 1989, Vol 2: State review of production and sales by commodity, and business activity, annual rpt, 5604–16.19

Minerals Yearbook, 1989, Vol 2: State reviews of production, sales, and firms, by commodity, and business activity, annual rpt, 5604–34

Natural gas production and wellhead capacity, by production area, 1980-89 and alternative forecasts 1990-91, biennial rpt, 3164–93

Oil import traffic by US port and vessel type, marine oil pollution sources, and costs and operations of proposed offshore terminals, late 1980s, 5738–25

Physicians, by specialty, age, sex, and location of training and practice, 1989, State rpt, 4116–6.19

Population and housing census, 1990: population and housing characteristics, households, and land area, by county, subdiv, and place, State rpt, 2551–1.20

Population and housing census, 1990: voting age and total population by race, and housing units, by block, redistricting counts required under PL 94-171, State CD-ROM release, 2551–6.4

Population and housing census, 1990: voting age and total population by race, and housing units, by county and city, redistricting counts required under PL 94-171, State summary rpt, 2551–5.19

Rice market prices, inspections, sales, trade, supply, and use, for US and selected foreign markets, weekly rpt, 1313–8

Rice stocks on and off farms and total in all positions, periodic rpt, 1621–7

Statistical Abstract of US, 1991 annual data compilation, 2324–1

Supplemental Security Income payments and beneficiaries, by type of eligibility, State, and county, Dec 1989, annual rpt, 4744–27.6

Timber in Louisiana, prices for stumpage, sawtimber, and saw logs sold from private lands, by species, 1960-88, annual rpt, 1204–29

Water supply and quality in streams and lakes, and groundwater levels in wells, by drainage basin, 1990, annual State rpt, 5666–10.17

see also Alexandria, La.

see also Lake Charles, La.

see also Leesville, La.

see also New Orleans, La.

see also Shreveport, La.

see also under By State in the "Index by Categories"

Louisiana State University

Animals use in Army brain wound research, usefulness of LSU experiments, with results, 1980s, GAO rpt, 26121–396

Louisville, Ky.

Economic and banking conditions, for Fed Reserve 8th District, quarterly rpt with articles, 9391–16

see also under By City and By SMSA or MSA in the "Index by Categories"

Loungani, Prakash

"Role of Energy in Real Business Cycle Models", 9375–13.57

"Stock Market Dispersion and Business Cycles", 9375–1.201

"Structural Unemployment and Public Policy in Interwar Britain: A Review Essay", 9375–13.52

Loveland, Colo.

see also under By SMSA or MSA in the "Index by Categories"

Low-income energy assistance

Assistance for low income households, by type of aid from FY82, and by State, FY89, annual rpt, 4744–3.9

Assistance for low income households, funding sources, costs, and participation, by State, FY89, annual rpt, 4694–8

Fed Govt housing energy aid beneficiary households, by aid type, FY90, biennial article, 4742–1.217

State and Federal funding for low income housing energy aid, FY86-89, GAO rpt, 26121–401

States low income housing energy aid, program characteristics by State, FY90, annual rpt, 4694–9

Index by Subjects and Names

Utility allowances used in HUD public housing and rent assistance programs, coverage and adequacy, 1985-89, GAO rpt, 26113–512

Low-income housing

- American Housing Survey: unit and households detailed characteristics, and unit and neighborhood quality, MSA rpt series, 2485–6
- American Housing Survey: unit and households detailed characteristics, and unit and neighborhood quality, biennial rpt, 2485–12
- Community Dev Block Grant activities and funding, by program, FY75-90, annual rpt, 5124–8
- Construction and repair of low income housing, HUD loans nonprofit organizations, project delays, and starts, 1980s, GAO rpt, 26113–506
- Fed Govt financial and nonfinancial domestic aid, 1991 base edition with supplements, annual listing, 104–5
- Fed Govt spending in States, by type, program, agency, and State, FY90, annual rpt, 2464–2
- FmHA activities, and loans and grants by program and State, FY90 and trends from FY70, annual rpt, 1184–17
- FmHA loans and borrower supervision activities in farm and housing programs, by type and State, monthly rpt, 1182–1
- Homelessness issues, population at risk, contributing factors, and Federal funding for services and prevention, with bibl, 1991 compilation of papers, 25928–9
- Income (household) and poverty status under alternative income definitions, by recipient characteristics, 1990, annual Current Population Rpt, 2546–6.69
- Mortgages FHA-insured for 1-family units, by loan type and mortgage characteristics, quarterly rpt, 5142–45
- Poor households with high rent, and substandard units, worst case problems prevalence and households characteristics, 1970s-84, annual rpt, 5184–10
- Poverty status of population and families, by detailed characteristics, 1988-89, annual Current Population Rpt, 2546–6.67
- Poverty status of population and families, by detailed characteristics, 1990, annual Current Population Rpt, 2546–6.71
- Savings instns failures, inventory of real estate assets available from Resolution Trust Corp, 1989, semiannual listing, 9722–2.1
- Savings instns failures, inventory of real estate assets available from Resolution Trust Corp, 1990, semiannual listing, 9722–2.2; 9722–2.3
- Supply of low income housing, impacts of HUD programs to maintain supply and to deter insured mortgage prepayment, 1986-90 and projected to 2005, GAO rpt, 26131–84
- Tax credits for low income housing dev, and units constructed, by selected project and State, 1987-89, hearings, 25248–120
- Texas economic and housing conditions, bank failures, and thrift and Federal regulators real estate holdings, 1980s-90, hearings, 21248–146

see also Low-income energy assistance

see also Public housing
see also Rent supplements

Lowe, Jamison A.
"Fish Kills in Coastal Waters, 1980-89", 2178–32

Lowe, Jeffrey H.
"U.S. Direct Investment Abroad: 1989 Benchmark Survey Results", 2702–1.225

Lowell, Mass.
see also under By City and By SMSA or MSA in the "Index by Categories"

Lowenthal, Jim
"AID Economic Policy Reform Program in Senegal", 9916–1.75

Lown, Cara S.
"Indicator of Future Inflation Extracted from the Steepness of the Interest Rate Yield Curve Along Its Entire Length", 9385–8.118

LPG
see Liquefied petroleum gas

Lubbock, Tex.
see also under By City and By SMSA or MSA in the "Index by Categories"

Lucier, Gary
"U.S.-Mexican Vegetable Trade", 1561–11.202
"U.S. Potato Statistics, 1949-89", 1568–305

Luckett, Charles A.
"Payment of Household Debts", 9362–1.201

Luggage
see Leather industry and products

Lukasiewicz, John
"Occupational Employment Projections", 6722–1.254

Lumber industry and products

- Agriculture census, 1987: farms, farmland, production, finances, and operator characteristics, by county, final State rpt series, 2331–1
- Alaska timber production, trade, and Pacific basin market demand, 1960s-2010, 1208–365; 1208–367
- Birds (northern spotted owl) population and reproduction rate on lands open and closed to logging, estimation methodology, 1987, 1208–342
- Birds population impacts of timber harvest methods, by species, for Montana, 1989-90, 1208–372
- Business statistics, detailed data for major industries and economic indicators, *Survey of Current Business*, monthly rpt, 2702–1.16
- Collective bargaining agreements expiring during year, and workers covered, by firm, union, industry group, and State, 1991, annual rpt, 6784–9
- County Business Patterns, 1988: employment, establishments, and payroll, by SIC 2- to 4-digit industry and county, annual State rpt series, 2326–6
- County Business Patterns, 1989: employment, establishments, and payroll, by SIC 2- to 4-digit industry and county, annual State rpt series, 2326–8
- Disaster damage to timber and orchards, USDA restoration aid and program participation by practice and State, FY89-90, annual rpt, 1804–24
- DOD prime contract awards, by detailed procurement category, FY87-90, annual rpt, 3544–18

Employment, earnings, and hours, by SIC 1- to 4-digit industry, monthly and annual averages, selected years 1909-90, annual rpt, 6744–4

- Employment in manufacturing, by detailed occupation and SIC 2-digit industry, 1989 survey, triennial rpt, 6748–52
- Employment, unemployment, and labor force characteristics, by region and census div, 1990, annual rpt, 6744–7.1
- Energy use and prices for manufacturing industries, 1988 survey, series, 3166–13
- Enterprise Statistics, 1987: auxiliaries of multi-establishment firms, finances and operations by function, industry, and State, 2329–6
- Enterprise Statistics, 1987: finances and operations for companies, by size, level of diversification, form of organization, and industry group, 2329–8
- *Environmental Quality*, status of problems, protection programs, research, and intl issues, 1991 annual rpt, 484–1
- Exports (agricultural) of US, impacts of foreign agricultural and trade policy, with data by commodity and country, 1989, annual rpt, 1924–8
- Exports and imports (agricultural) commodity and country, prices, and world market devs, monthly rpt, 1922–12
- Exports and imports between US and outlying areas, by detailed commodity and mode of transport, 1990, annual rpt, 2424–11
- Exports and imports of building materials, by commodity and country, 1989-90, article, 2042–1.204
- Exports and imports of US, by country and detailed commodity, monthly rpt, 2422–12
- Exports and imports of US by country, and trade shifts by commodity, 1990, semiannual rpt, 9882–9
- Exports and imports of US, by Harmonized System 6-digit commodity and country, 1990, annual rpt, 2424–13
- Exports and imports of US, by selected country, country group, and commodity group, 1990, annual rpt, 2044–37
- Exports and imports of US, by transport mode, country, and SITC 1- to 3-digit commodity, 1990, annual rpt, 2424–12
- Exports and imports of US shipped through Canada, by detailed commodity, customs district, and country, 1989, annual rpt, 7704–11
- Exports, imports, and export promotion of US lumber and wood products by country, and trade balance, by commodity, FAS quarterly circular, 1925–36
- Exports of US, detailed commodities by country, monthly CD-ROM, 2422–13
- Exports of US, detailed Schedule B commodities with countries of destination, 1990, annual rpt, 2424–10
- Exports of US hardwood lumber to Europe and Asia, by species and country, 1981-89, 1208–373
- Farm financial and marketing conditions, forecast 1991, annual conf, 1004–16
- Farm income, expenses, receipts by commodity, assets, liabilities, and ratios, 1990 and trends from 1945, annual rpt, 1544–16

Lumber industry and products

Index by Subjects and Names

Florida industrial roundwood lumber production, by product and county, 1977-87, 1208–352

Forest Service acreage, staff, finances, and mgmt activities in Pacific Northwest, with data by forest, 1970s-89, annual rpt, 1204–37

Forest Service mgmt of public lands and resources dev, environmental, economic, and social impacts of alternative programs, projected to 2040, 1208–24

Futures and options trading volume, by commodity and exchange, FY90, annual rpt, 11924–2

Futures trading in selected commodities and financial instruments and indexes, NYC, Chicago, and other markets activity, semimonthly rpt, 11922–5

Great Lakes area economic conditions and outlook, for US and Canada, 1970s-90, 9375–15

Hwy construction material use by type, and spending, by State, various periods 1944-90, annual rpt, 7554–29

Imports, exports, and employment impacts, by SIC 2- to 4-digit industry and commodity, quarterly rpt, 2322–2

Imports of softwood lumber from Canada, injury to US industry from foreign subsidized products, investigation with background financial and operating data, 1991 rpt, 9886–15.78

Imports of US, detailed commodities by country, monthly CD-ROM, 2422–14

Imports of US given duty-free treatment for value of US material sent abroad, by commodity and country, 1989, annual rpt, 9884–14

Indian (Cherokee) Agency activities in North Carolina, FY91, annual rpt, 5704–4

Indian Affairs Bur timber mgmt programs funding, acreage, harvest, and tribal investment, by tribe and location, FY77-89 and projected to FY96, hearing, 25418–4

Indiana timber resources and removals, by species, forest characteristics, ownership, and county, 1985-86, 1208–368

Injuries from use of consumer products, by severity, victim age, and detailed product, 1990, annual rpt, 9164–6

Input-output structure of US economy, detailed interindustry transactions for 84 industries, and components of final demand, 1986, annual article, 2702–1.206

Input-output structure of US economy, detailed interindustry transactions for 85 industries, 1982 benchmark data, 2702–1.213

Labor productivity, indexes of output, hours, and employment by SIC 2- to 4-digit industry, 1967-89, annual rpt, 6824–1.3

Manufacturing annual survey, 1989: finances and operations, by SIC 2- to 4-digit industry, series, 2506–15

Manufacturing census, 1987: finances and operations, by SIC 2- to 4-digit industry, State, and MSA, with trends from 1849, 2497–1

Manufacturing census, 1987: finances and operations, by type of organization and SIC 2- to 4-digit industry, subject rpt, 2497–5

Manufacturing finances and operations, by SIC 2- to 4-digit industry, forecast 1991, annual rpt, 2044–28

Manufacturing industries operations and performance, analytical rpt series, 2506–16

Manufacturing production, shipments, inventories, orders, and pollution control costs, periodic Current Industrial Rpt series, 2506–3

Mexico imports from US, by industry and State, 1987-90, 2048–154

Montana log home manufacturers, sales, production, and timber use, 1960s-88, 1208–370

Multinatl US firms and foreign affiliates finances and operations, by industry and world area of parent firm, 1989 benchmark survey, preliminary annual rpt, 2704–5

Natl forests revenue, by source, forest, and State, FY90, annual rpt, 1204–34

Natl forests timber sales and harvests, by State, FY90, annual rpt, 1204–1

Natl forests timber sales of Forest Service, expenses, and operations, by region, State, and forest, FY90, annual rpts, 1204–36

New England timber acreage and resources, by State, 1982-85, pamphlet, 1208–363

New Hampshire and Vermont public opinion on natural resources use and mgmt, 1991 rpt, 1208–371

North Carolina timber acreage, resources, and removals, by species, ownership class, and county, 1989/90, series, 1206–4

North Central States timber harvest and industrial roundwood production, by product and county, State rpt series, 1206–10

North Central States veneer log production, mill receipts, and trade, by species, with residue use, 1988, quadrennial rpt, 1208–220

Northeastern US industrial roundwood production by product, State rpt series, 1206–15

Northeastern US pulpwood production by species and county, and shipments, by State, 1989, annual rpt, 1204–18

Northeastern US timber, change in value by species, with methodology, 1970s-85, 1208–348

Northeastern US timber resources, and related manufacturing industries employment and finances, by State, 1977-87, 1208–375

Northeastern US timber resources and removals, by species, ownership, and county, State rpt series, 1206–12

Northwestern US and British Columbia forest industry production, prices, trade, and employment, quarterly rpt, 1202–3

Occupational injury and illness rates, by SIC 2- to 4-digit industry, 1988-89, annual rpt, 6844–7

Occupational injury and illness rates, by SIC 2- to 4-digit industry, 1989, annual rpt, 6844–1

OECD trade, total and for 4 major countries, and US trade by country, by commodity, 1970-89, world area rpt series, 9116–1

Oklahoma timber resources, growth, and removals, by species, forest type, ownership, and county, 1986, regional rpt series, 1206–39

Oregon (western) timber resources, acreage by land use and ownership, 1961-86, 1208–353

Owl (northern spotted) conservation impacts on Pacific Northwest timber industry, and local govts Federal payments and severance taxes, 1980s and projected to 2000, hearing, 21168–50

Owl (northern spotted) conservation impacts on Pacific Northwest timber industry, and worker aid programs, 1980s and projected to 2000, hearing, 21728–76

Owl (northern spotted) conservation impacts on Pacific Northwest timber industry, 1980s and alternative projections to 2000, hearing, 21168–45

Owl (northern spotted) conservation impacts on Pacific Northwest timber sales of Forest Service, 1990 hearing, 21168–47

Pacific basin sandalwood resources, habitat, harvest, exports, and uses, 1990 conf, 1208–366

PL 480 long-term credit sales allocations, by commodity and country, periodic press release, 1922–7

Pollution (air) emissions factors, by detailed pollutant and source, data compilation, 1990 rpt, 9198–120

Pollution (air) emissions from burning of logging waste, 1982, 1208–343

Pollution abatement capital and operating costs, by SIC 2-digit industry, 1989, advance annual Current Industrial Rpt, 2506–3.6

Price indexes (producer), by stage of processing and detailed commodity, monthly rpt, 6762–6

Price indexes (producer), by stage of processing and detailed commodity, monthly 1990, annual rpt, 6764–2

Prices of lumber, timber value conversion standards for hardwood species, 1972 and 1984, 1208–361

Production, prices by region and State, trade by country, and use, for timber by species and product, 1960-88, annual rpt, 1204–29

Production, prices, employment, and trade, for hardwood lumber and products, quarterly rpt, 1202–4

Production, shipments, PPI, stocks, and trade of lumber products, by type, bimonthly rpt, 2042–1.5; 2042–1.6

Production, shipments, trade, stocks, and use of wood, paper, and related products, periodic Current Industrial Rpt series, 2506–7

Production, trade, and use of lumber and pulp products, and timber resources, detailed data, 1950s-87 and alternative projections to 2040, 1208–24.20

Public lands acreage and use, and Land Mgmt Bur activities and finances, annual State rpt series, 5724–11

Public lands acreage, grants, use, revenues, and allocations, by State, FY90, annual rpt, 5724–1.2

Puerto Rico economic censuses, 1987: wholesale and retail trade and service industry finances and operations, by SIC 2- to 4-digit industry and municipio, 2591–1

Puerto Rico economic censuses, 1987: wholesale, retail, and service industries finances and operations, by establishment characteristics and SIC 2- and 3-digit industry, subject rpts, 2591–2

Respiratory diseases related to occupational hazards, epidemiology, diagnosis, and treatment, for selected industries and work settings, 1988 conf, 4248–90

Ships freight rates for lumber from Alaska and Puget Sound to Asian markets, by product and port, 1988, 1208–358

South Carolina lumber and mill residue production, by product and species group, 1987-88, 1208–359

Southeastern US pine natural growth and plantation acreage, and lumber industries impacts of shift to plantation pine, 1989 conf papers, 1208–346

Southeastern US pulpwood and residue prices, spending, and transport shares by mode, 1988-89, annual rpt, 1204–22

Southeastern US timber resources, and industry employment and output, by State, 1980s, article, 9391–16.204

Southern US pulpwood production by county, and mill capacity by firm, by State, 1989, annual rpt, 1204–23

Southern US veneer log receipts, production, and shipments, by species and State, with residue use, 1988, 1208–43

Soviet Union, Eastern Europe, OECD, and selected other countries pollution and deforestation indicators, 1960s-90, annual rpt, 9114–4.10

Soviet Union GNP by component and industry sector, and CIA estimation methods, 1950s-87, 23848–223

Soviet Union GNP by detailed income and outlay component, 1985, 2326–18.59

State and Metro Area Data Book, 1991 data compilation, 2328–54

Statistical Abstract of US, 1991 annual data compilation, 2324–1.24

Taiwan imports of building materials, and share from US, by commodity, 1989-90, article, 2042–1.205

Tariff Schedule of US, classifications and rates of duty by detailed imported commodity, 1992 base edition, 9886–13

Tax (income) returns of corporations, income and tax items by asset size and detailed industry, 1987, annual rpt, 8304–4

Tax (income) returns of corporations, income and tax items by asset size and detailed industry, 1988, annual rpt, 8304–21

Tax (income) returns of corporations with foreign tax credit, income and tax items by industry group, 1986, biennial article, 8302–2.203

Tax (income) returns of partnerships, income statement and balance sheet items, by industry group, 1989, annual article, 8302–2.216; 8304–18

Tax (income) returns of sole proprietorships, income statement items, by industry group, 1989, annual article, 8302–2.214

Tax expenditures, Federal revenues forgone through income tax deductions and exclusions by type, FY92-96, annual rpt, 21784–10

Tennessee timber acreage at risk from gypsy moth infestation, by county, 1989, 1208–344

Virginia timber resources, growth, and removals, by species, ownership, treatment, and county, 1990-91, series, 1206–6

Wages and production workers by occupation, for logging and forestry industries, annual State survey rpt series, 6787–7

Wholesale trade census, 1987: establishments, sales by customer class, employment, inventories, and expenses, by SIC 2- to 4-digit kind of business, 2407–4

Wholesale trade sales and inventories, by SIC 2- to 3-digit kind of business, monthly rpt, 2413–7

Wood, waste, and alcohol fuel use, by end-use sector and region, 1989, 3166–6.56

see also Forests and forestry

see also Furniture and furnishings

see also Gum and wood chemicals

see also Paper and paper products

see also Wood fuel

see also under By Commodity in the "Index by Categories"

see also under By Industry in the "Index by Categories"

Lund, Adrian K.

"Motorcycle Helmet Use in Texas", 4042–3.251

Lundell, Mark R.

"Agricultural Privatization and Land Reform in Central Europe", 1522–3.202

Lundquist, John E.

"Forest Pest Conditions in the Rocky Mountain Region, 1990", 1206–11.3

Lundy, Janet

"Design of Health Plan Benefits for the Nonelderly", 23898–5

Lung diseases

see Black lung disease

see Pneumonia and influenza

see Respiratory diseases

see Tuberculosis

Luppold, William G.

"New Estimates of Hardwood Lumber Exports to Europe and Asia", 1208–373

Lussier, Frances M.

"Budgetary and Military Effects of a Treaty Limiting Conventional Forces in Europe", 26306–3.114

Luxembourg

Agricultural exports of high-value commodities, indexes and sales by commodity, world area, and country, 1960s-86, 1528–323

Agricultural production, prices, and trade, by country, 1970s-90, and forecast 1991, annual world region rpt, 1524–4.4

Agricultural production, trade, and policies in foreign countries, summary data by country, 1989-90, annual factbook, 1924–12

Agricultural trade of US, by detailed commodity and country, 1989, annual rpt, 1524–8

Agricultural trade of US, by detailed commodity and country, 1990, semiannual rpt, 1522–4

AID loans repayment status and terms by program and country, and status of predecessor agency loans, quarterly rpt, 9912–3

Economic and military aid and loans from US and intl agencies, by program and country, FY46-90, annual rpt, 9914–5

Economic conditions, income, production, prices, employment, and trade, 1991 periodic country rpt, 2046–4.72

Economic, social, political, and geographic summary data, by country, 1991, annual factbook, 9114–2

Exports and imports of NATO members with PRC, by country, 1987-90, annual rpt, 7144–14

Exports and imports of OECD members, by country, 1989, annual rpt, 7144–10

Exports and imports of US, by selected country, country group, and commodity group, 1990, annual rpt, 2044–37

Exports and imports of US, by transport mode, country, and SITC 1- to 3-digit commodity, 1990, annual rpt, 2424–12

Exports and imports of US with EC by country, and total agricultural trade, selected years 1958-90, annual rpt, 7144–7

Exports of US, detailed Schedule B commodities with countries of destination, 1990, annual rpt, 2424–10

GNP and GNP growth for OECD members, by country, 1980-90, annual rpt, 7144–8

Human rights conditions in 170 countries, and US economic and military aid, 1990, annual rpt, 21384–3

Intl transactions of US with 9 countries, 1986-88, *Survey of Current Business*, monthly rpt, annual table, 2702–1.26

Multinatl US firms and foreign affiliates finances and operations, by industry and world area of parent firm, 1989 benchmark survey, preliminary annual rpt, 2704–5

Multinatl US firms foreign affiliates, income statement items by country and world area, 1986, biennial article, 8302–2.212

Oil production, trade, use, and stocks, by selected country and country group, monthly rpt, 3162–42

Spacecraft and satellite launches since 1957, quarterly listing, 9502–2

Tax revenue, by level of govt and type of tax, for OECD countries, mid 1960s-89, annual rpt, 10044–1.2

UN voting record and share of votes in agreement with US, by issue, country, and world area, 1990, annual rpt, 7004–18

see also under By Foreign Country in the "Index by Categories"

Lymphoma

see Blood diseases and disorders

Lynch, Charles F.

"Cancer Registry Problems in Classifying Invasive Bladder Cancer", 4472–1.208

Lynchburg, Va.

see also under By SMSA or MSA in the "Index by Categories"

Maas, Kenneth M.

"Availability of Land for Mineral Exploration and Development in Northern Alaska, 1986", 5608–152.6

"Mineral Investigations in the Juneau Mining District, Alaska, 1984-88. Volume 3: Industrial Minerals", 5608–169.2

Mabbs-Zeno, Carl

"Progress for Developing Countries in the Uruguay Round", 1524–4.2

Macao

Agricultural exports of high-value commodities, indexes and sales by commodity, world area, and country, 1960s-86, 1528–323

Macao

Agricultural trade of US, by detailed commodity and country, 1989, annual rpt, 1524–8

Agricultural trade of US, by detailed commodity and country, 1990, semiannual rpt, 1522–4

Economic, social, political, and geographic summary data, by country, 1991, annual factbook, 9114–2

Exports and imports of US, by transport mode, country, and SITC 1- to 3-digit commodity, 1990, annual rpt, 2424–12

Exports of US, detailed Schedule B commodities with countries of destination, 1990, annual rpt, 2424–10

Human rights conditions in 170 countries, and US economic and military aid, 1990, annual rpt, 21384–3

MacAuley, Patrick H.

"Federal Construction-Related Expenditures, 1984-92", 2042–1.206

Machine-readable data file guides *see* CD-ROM catalogs and guides *see* Computer data file guides

Machine tools *see* Machines and machinery industry

Machines and machinery industry

- Accident deaths and rates, by cause, age, sex, race, and State, 1988, US Vital Statistics annual rpt, 4144–2
- Bearings (ball) from 14 countries, injury to US industry from foreign subsidized and less than fair value imports, investigation with background financial and operating data, 1991 rpt, 9886–19.74
- Business statistics, detailed data for major industries and economic indicators, *Survey of Current Business,* monthly rpt, 2702–1.17
- Capital expenditures for plant and equipment, by major industry group, quarterly rpt, 2502–2
- Collective bargaining agreements expiring during year, and workers covered, by firm, union, industry group, and State, 1991, annual rpt, 6784–9
- Communist countries trade with US, detailed commodity and country, quarterly rpt with articles, 9882–2
- Construction industries census, 1987: establishments, employment, receipts, and expenditures, by SIC 4-digit industry and State, final industry rpt series, 2373–1
- Construction machinery PPI, bimonthly rpt, 2042–1.5
- County Business Patterns, 1988: employment, establishments, and payroll, by SIC 2- to 4-digit industry and county, annual State rpt series, 2326–6
- County Business Patterns, 1989: employment, establishments, and payroll, by SIC 2- to 4-digit industry and county, annual State rpt series, 2326–8
- DOD prime contract awards, by detailed procurement category, FY87-90, annual rpt, 3544–18
- Employment, earnings, and hours, by SIC 1- to 4-digit industry, monthly and annual averages, selected years 1909-90, annual rpt, 6744–4
- Employment in manufacturing, by detailed occupation and SIC 2-digit industry, 1989 survey, triennial rpt, 6748–52
- Employment, unemployment, and labor force characteristics, by region and census div, 1990, annual rpt, 6744–7.1

Energy use and prices for manufacturing industries, 1988 survey, series, 3166–13

- Enterprise Statistics, 1987: auxiliaries of multi-establishment firms, finances and operations by function, industry, and State, 2329–6
- Export and import prices of machinery and transport equipment, impacts of dollar depreciation, 1985-90, article, 6722–1.233
- Exports and imports between US and outlying areas, by detailed commodity and mode of transport, 1990, annual rpt, 2424–11
- Exports and imports of US, by country and detailed commodity, monthly rpt, 2422–12
- Exports and imports of US by country, and trade shifts by commodity, 1990, semiannual rpt, 9882–9
- Exports and imports of US, by Harmonized System 6-digit commodity and country, 1990, annual rpt, 2424–13
- Exports and imports of US, by selected country, country group, and commodity group, 1990, annual rpt, 2044–37
- Exports and imports of US, by transport mode, country, and SITC 1- to 3-digit commodity, 1990, annual rpt, 2424–12
- Exports and imports of US shipped through Canada, by detailed commodity, customs district, and country, 1989, annual rpt, 7704–11
- Exports of agricultural products and nonelectrical machinery, *Survey of Current Business,* monthly rpt, 2702–1.2
- Exports of US, detailed commodities by country, monthly CD-ROM, 2422–13
- Exports of US, detailed Schedule B commodities with countries of destination, 1990, annual rpt, 2424–10
- Foreign direct investment in US, by industry group and world area, 1987-90, annual article, 2702–1.219
- Foreign direct investment in US, by industry group of US affiliate and country of parent firm, 1980-86, 2708–41
- Foreign direct investment of US, by industry group and world area, 1987-90, annual article, 2702–1.220
- Gear production for selected uses under alternative production requirements, and industry finances and operations, late 1940s-89, 2028–1
- Imports, exports, and employment impacts, by SIC 2- to 4-digit industry and commodity, quarterly rpt, 2322–2
- Imports of US, detailed commodities by country, monthly CD-ROM, 2422–14
- Imports of US given duty-free treatment for value of US material sent abroad, by commodity and country, 1989, annual rpt, 9884–14
- Injuries from use of consumer products, by severity, victim age, and detailed product, 1990, annual rpt, 9164–6
- Input-output structure of US economy, detailed interindustry transactions for 84 industries, and components of final demand, 1986, annual article, 2702–1.206
- Input-output structure of US economy, detailed interindustry transactions for 85 industries, 1982 benchmark data, 2702–1.213

Index by Subjects and Names

- Labor productivity, indexes of output, hours, and employment by SIC 2- to 4-digit industry, 1967-89, annual rpt, 6824–1.3
- Manufacturing annual survey, 1989: finances and operations, by SIC 2- to 4-digit industry, series, 2506–15
- Manufacturing census, 1987: employment and shipments under Fed Govt contracts, by SIC 4-digit industry, 2497–7
- Manufacturing census, 1987: finances and operations, by SIC 2- to 4-digit industry, State, and MSA, with trends from 1849, 2497–1
- Manufacturing census, 1987: finances and operations, by type of organization and SIC 2- to 4-digit industry, subject rpt, 2497–5
- Manufacturing corporations financial statements, by selected SIC 2- to 3-digit industry, quarterly rpt, 2502–1
- Manufacturing finances and operations, by SIC 2- to 4-digit industry, forecast 1991, annual rpt, 2044–28
- Manufacturing industries operations and performance, analytical rpt series, 2506–16
- Manufacturing production, shipments, inventories, orders, and pollution control costs, periodic Current Industrial Rpt series, 2506–3
- Mexico construction value and trade, and import duties on materials and equipment by type, 1991 article, 2042–1.207
- Mexico imports from US, by industry and State, 1987-90, 2048–154
- Middle East export controls of US, with trade, dual-use commodity licenses, and arms sales, by country, 1980s-90, GAO rpt, 26123–339
- Military and personal property shipments, passenger traffic, and costs, by service branch and mode of transport, quarterly rpt, 3702–1
- Military procurement of foreign-made machine tools, use of restriction waivers by service branch and country, FY86-89, GAO rpt, 26123–324
- Multinatl firms US affiliates, finances, and operations, by industry, world area of parent firm, and State, 1988-89, annual rpt, 2704–4
- Multinatl US firms and foreign affiliates finances and operations, by industry and world area of parent firm, 1989 benchmark survey, preliminary annual rpt, 2704–5
- Occupational deaths, by equipment type, circumstances, and OSHA standards violated, series, 6606–2
- Occupational injury and illness rates, by SIC 2- to 4-digit industry, 1988-89, annual rpt, 6844–7
- Occupational injury and illness rates, by SIC 2- to 4-digit industry, 1989, annual rpt, 6844–1
- OECD trade, total and for 4 major countries, and US trade by country, by commodity, 1970-89, world area rpt series, 9116–1
- Pollution (water) industrial releases in wastewater, levels, treatment, costs, and regulation, with background financial and operating data, 1989 industry rpt, 9206–4.13

Index by Subjects and Names

Maine

Pollution abatement capital and operating costs, by SIC 2-digit industry, 1989, advance annual Current Industrial Rpt, 2506–3.6

Price indexes (producer), by stage of processing and detailed commodity, monthly rpt, 6762–6

Price indexes (producer), by stage of processing and detailed commodity, monthly 1990, annual rpt, 6764–2

Production, shipments, trade, stocks, orders, use, and firms, by product, periodic Current Industrial Rpt series, 2506–12

Puerto Rico and other US possessions corporations income tax returns, income and tax items, and employment, by selected industry, 1987, article, 8302–2.213

Puerto Rico economic censuses, 1987: wholesale and retail trade and service industry finances and operations, by SIC 2- to 4-digit industry and municipio, 2591–1

Puerto Rico economic censuses, 1987: wholesale, retail, and service industries finances and operations, by establishment characteristics and SIC 2- and 3-digit industry, subject rpts, 2591–2

R&D funding, and scientists and engineers education and employment, for US and selected foreign countries, 1991 annual rpt, 9627–35.1

Rubber mechanical goods shipments, by product, 1990, annual Current Industrial Rpt, 2506–8.17

Soviet Union GNP by component and industry sector, and CIA estimation methods, 1950s-87, 23848–223

Soviet Union GNP by detailed income and outlay component, 1985, 2326–18.59

Tariff Schedule of US, classifications and rates of duty by detailed imported commodity, 1992 base edition, 9886–13

Tax (income) returns of corporations, income and tax items by asset size and detailed industry, 1987, annual rpt, 8304–4

Tax (income) returns of corporations, income and tax items by asset size and detailed industry, 1988, annual rpt, 8304–21

Tax (income) returns of corporations with foreign tax credit, income and tax items by industry group, 1986, biennial article, 8302–2.203

Tax (income) returns of multinatl US firms foreign affiliates, income statement items, by asset size and industry, 1986, biennial article, 8302–2.212

Tax (income) returns of partnerships, income statement and balance sheet items, by industry group, 1989, annual article, 8302–2.216; 8304–18

Tax (income) returns of sole proprietorships, income statement items, by industry group, 1989, annual article, 8302–2.214

Wholesale trade census, 1987: depreciable assets, capital and operating expenses, sales, value added, and inventories, by SIC 2- to 3-digit kind of business, 2407–2

Wholesale trade census, 1987: establishments, sales by customer class, employment, inventories, and expenses, by SIC 2- to 4-digit kind of business, 2407–4

Wholesale trade sales and inventories, by SIC 2- to 3-digit kind of business, monthly rpt, 2413–7

Wholesale trade sales, inventories, purchases, and gross margins, by SIC 2- to 3-digit kind of business, 1990, annual rpt, 2413–13

see also Agricultural machinery and equipment

see also Electric power plants and equipment

see also Electrical machinery and equipment

see also Engines and motors

see also Hardware

see also Industrial plants and equipment

see also Industrial robots

see also Lawn and garden equipment

see also Tools

see also Transportation and transportation equipment

see also Vending machines and stands

see also under By Commodity in the "Index by Categories"

see also under By Industry in the "Index by Categories"

MacKenzie, Clyde L., Jr.

"History of the Fisheries of Raritan Bay, New York and New Jersey", 2162–1.205

Mackie, Arthur B.

"World Oilseed and Products Trade, 1962-88", 1528–314

MacLean, Colin D.

"Changes in Area and Ownership of Timberland in Western Oregon: 1961-86", 1208–353

Macon, Ga.

Wages by occupation, for office and plant workers, 1990 survey, periodic MSA rpt, 6785–3.2

see also under By City and By SMSA or MSA in the "Index by Categories"

Madagascar

Agricultural exports of high-value commodities, indexes and sales by commodity, world area, and country, 1960s-86, 1528–323

Agricultural trade of US, by detailed commodity and country, 1989, annual rpt, 1524–8

Agricultural trade of US, by detailed commodity and country, 1990, semiannual rpt, 1522–4

AID economic aid to developing countries, obligations and disbursements by country, quarterly rpt, 9912–4

AID loans repayment status and terms by program and country, and status of predecessor agency loans, quarterly rpt, 9912–3

Dairy imports, consumption, and market conditions, by sub-Saharan Africa country, 1961-88, 1528–321

Economic and military aid and loans from US and intl agencies, by program and country, FY46-90, annual rpt, 9914–5

Economic and social conditions of developing countries from 1960s, and Intl Dev Cooperation Agency and AID activities and funding, FY90-92, annual rpt, 9904–4

Economic conditions, income, production, prices, employment, and trade, 1991 periodic country rpt, 2046–4.17

Economic, social, political, and geographic summary data, by country, 1991, annual factbook, 9114–2

Exports and imports of US, by transport mode, country, and SITC 1- to 3-digit commodity, 1990, annual rpt, 2424–12

Exports of US, detailed Schedule B commodities with countries of destination, 1990, annual rpt, 2424–10

Human rights conditions in 170 countries, and US economic and military aid, 1990, annual rpt, 21384–3

Military aid of US, arms sales, and training programs costs and budget requests, by program, world region, and country, FY90-92, annual rpt, 7144–13

UN voting record and share of votes in agreement with US, by issue, country, and world area, 1990, annual rpt, 7004–18

see also under By Foreign Country in the "Index by Categories"

Madell, Mary Lisa

"Agricultural Prospects Following German Unification", 1522–3.201

Madison, Wis.

see also under By City and By SMSA or MSA in the "Index by Categories"

Magazines

see Periodicals

Mager, Andreas, Jr.

"National Marine Fisheries Service Habitat Conservation Efforts in the Southeastern U.S. for 1988", 2162–1.202

Magistrates

see Judges

Magnesium

see Metals and metal industries

Mahidhara, Ramamohan

"Hog Butchers No Longer: 20 Years of Employment Change in Metropolitan Chicago", 9375–1.204

Mahler, Susan J.

"Environmental Excise Taxes, 1988", 8302–2.202

"Nonprofit Charitable Organizations, 1986 and 1987", 8302–2.218

Mahoney, Roberta

"Zambia Agricultural Sector Background", 9916–12.25

Mail

see Postal service

Mail order business

see Direct marketing

Mail, Patricia D.

"Substance Abuse", 4088–2

Maine

Acid rain effects on Maine streams water quality, acidity, and fish, 1986-87, 9208–130

Banks (insured commercial and savings) deposits by instn, State, MSA, and county, as of June 1990, annual regional rpt, 9295–3.1

County Business Patterns, 1989: employment, establishments, and payroll, by SIC 2- to 4-digit industry and county, annual State rpt, 2326–8.21

DOD prime contract awards, by contractor, service branch, State, and city, FY90, annual rpt, 3544–22

Economic indicators for New England States, Fed Reserve 1st District, monthly rpt, 9373–2

Fed Govt spending in States and local areas, by type, State, county, and city, FY90, annual rpt, 2464–3

Fed Govt spending in States, by type, program, agency, and State, FY90, annual rpt, 2464–2

Maine

Gemstone production in selected States, Mineral Industry Surveys, 1988-90, advance annual rpt, 5614–5.10

HHS financial aid, by program, recipient, State, and city, FY90, annual regional listing, 4004–3.1

Hospital deaths of Medicare patients, actual and expected rates by diagnosis, and hospital characteristics, by instn, FY87-89, annual regional rpt, 4654–14.1

Income (personal) per capita and by source, and earnings by industry div, by State, MSA, and county, 1984-89, annual regional rpt, 2704–2.2

Jail adult and juvenile population, employment, spending, instn conditions, and inmate programs, by county and facility, 1988, regional rpt series, 6068–144.2

Marriages, divorces, and rates, by characteristics of spouses, State, and county, 1987 and trends from 1920, US Vital Statistics annual rpt, 4144–4

Mineral Industry Surveys, State reviews of production, 1990, preliminary annual rpt, 5614–6

Minerals Yearbook, 1989, Vol 2: State review of production and sales by commodity, and business activity, annual rpt, 5604–16.20

Minerals Yearbook, 1989, Vol 2: State reviews of production, sales, and firms, by commodity, and business activity, annual rpt, 5604–34

Physicians, by specialty, age, sex, and location of training and practice, 1989, State rpt, 4116–6.20

Population and housing census, 1990: population and housing characteristics, households, and land area, by county, subdiv, and place, State rpt, 2551–1.21

Population and housing census, 1990: voting age and total population by race, and housing units, by block, redistricting counts required under PL 94-171, State CD-ROM release, 2551–6.2

Population and housing census, 1990: voting age and total population by race, and housing units, by county and city, redistricting counts required under PL 94-171, State summary rpt, 2551–5.20

Savings instns, FHLB 1st District members financial operations compared to banks, and related economic and housing indicators, bimonthly rpt with articles, 9302–4

Statistical Abstract of US, 1991 annual data compilation, 2324–1

Supplemental Security Income payments and beneficiaries, by type of eligibility, State, and county, Dec 1989, annual rpt, 4744–27.1

Wages by occupation, for office and plant workers, 1990 survey, periodic labor market rpt, 6785–3.4

Water supply and quality in streams and lakes, and groundwater levels in wells, by drainage basin, 1990, annual State rpt, 5666–10.18

Water supply in northeastern US, precipitation and stream runoff by station, monthly rpt, 2182–3

see also Portland, Maine

see also under By State in the "Index by Categories"

Maintenance services

see Janitorial and maintenance services

Majchrowicz, T. Alexander

"Employment Trends in Farm and Farm-Related Industries, 1975-87", 1598–271

Malagasy Republic

see Madagascar

Malaria

see Infective and parasitic diseases

Malawi

Agricultural exports of high-value commodities, indexes and sales by commodity, world area, and country, 1960s-86, 1528–323

Agricultural trade of US, by detailed commodity and country, 1989, annual rpt, 1524–8

Agricultural trade of US, by detailed commodity and country, 1990, semiannual rpt, 1522–4

AID economic aid to developing countries, obligations and disbursements by country, quarterly rpt, 9912–4

AID loans repayment status and terms by program and country, and status of predecessor agency loans, quarterly rpt, 9912–3

Dairy imports, consumption, and market conditions, by sub-Saharan Africa country, 1961-88, 1528–321

Economic and military aid and loans from US and intl agencies, by program and country, FY46-90, annual rpt, 9914–5

Economic and social conditions of developing countries from 1960s, and Intl Dev Cooperation Agency and AID activities and funding, FY90-92, annual rpt, 9904–4

Economic conditions, income, production, prices, employment, and trade, 1991 periodic country rpt, 2046–4.15

Economic, population, and agricultural data, US and other aid sources, and AID activity, 1989 country rpt, 9916–12.32; 9916–12.41

Economic, social, political, and geographic summary data, by country, 1991, annual factbook, 9114–2

Exports and imports of US, by transport mode, country, and SITC 1- to 3-digit commodity, 1990, annual rpt, 2424–12

Exports of US, detailed Schedule B commodities with countries of destination, 1990, annual rpt, 2424–10

Food supply, needs, and aid for developing countries, status and alternative forecasts, 1991 world area rpt, 1526–8.1

Human rights conditions in 170 countries, and US economic and military aid, 1990, annual rpt, 21384–3

Military aid of US, arms sales, and training programs costs and budget requests, by program, world region, and country, FY90-92, annual rpt, 7144–13

Tobacco auctioned and prices, for Malawi and Zimbabwe, 1989-90, article, 1925–16.205

UN voting record and share of votes in agreement with US, by issue, country, and world area, 1990, annual rpt, 7004–18

see also under By Foreign Country in the "Index by Categories"

Malaysia

Agricultural exports of high-value commodities, indexes and sales by commodity, world area, and country, 1960s-86, 1528–323

Agricultural exports of US, impacts of foreign agricultural and trade policy, with data by commodity and country, 1989, annual rpt, 1924–8

Agricultural production, prices, and trade, by country, 1960s-90, annual world area rpt, 1524–4.2

Agricultural production, trade, and policies in foreign countries, summary data by country, 1989-90, annual factbook, 1924–12

Agricultural trade of US, by detailed commodity and country, 1989, annual rpt, 1524–8

Agricultural trade of US, by detailed commodity and country, 1990, semiannual rpt, 1522–4

AID loans repayment status and terms by program and country, and status of predecessor agency loans, quarterly rpt, 9912–3

Economic and military aid and loans from US and intl agencies, by program and country, FY46-90, annual rpt, 9914–5

Economic conditions, policy, and trade practices, by country, 1988-90, annual rpt, 21384–5

Economic, social, political, and geographic summary data, by country, 1991, annual factbook, 9114–2

Exports and imports of US, by commodity and country, 1970-89, world area rpt, 9116–1.7

Exports and imports of US, by Harmonized System 6-digit commodity and country, 1990, annual rpt, 2424–13

Exports and imports of US, by selected country, country group, and commodity group, 1990, annual rpt, 2044–37

Exports and imports of US, by transport mode, country, and SITC 1- to 3-digit commodity, 1990, annual rpt, 2424–12

Exports of US, detailed Schedule B commodities with countries of destination, 1990, annual rpt, 2424–10

Human rights conditions in 170 countries, and US economic and military aid, 1990, annual rpt, 21384–3

Imports of goods, services, and investment from US, trade barriers, impacts, and US actions, by country, 1990, annual rpt, 444–2

Imports of US given duty-free treatment for value of US material sent abroad, by commodity and country, 1989, annual rpt, 9884–14

Military aid of US, arms sales, and training programs costs and budget requests, by program, world region, and country, FY90-92, annual rpt, 7144–13

Multinatl US firms and foreign affiliates finances and operations, by industry and world area of parent firm, 1989 benchmark survey, preliminary annual rpt, 2704–5

Multinatl US firms foreign affiliates, income statement items by country and world area, 1986, biennial article, 8302–2.212

Oil exports to US by OPEC and non-OPEC countries, monthly rpt, 3162–24.3

Rubber thread from Malaysia, injury to US industry from foreign subsidized and less than fair value imports, investigation with background financial and operating data, 1991 rpt, 9886–19.78

Science and engineering employment, by selected characteristics, for 3 countries, 1991 working paper, 2326–18.61

UN voting record and share of votes in agreement with US, by issue, country, and world area, 1990, annual rpt, 7004–18

see also under By Foreign Country in the "Index by Categories"

Maldives

Agricultural exports of high-value commodities, indexes and sales by commodity, world area, and country, 1960s-86, 1528–323

Economic and military aid and loans from US and intl agencies, by program and country, FY46-90, annual rpt, 9914–5

Economic, social, political, and geographic summary data, by country, 1991, annual factbook, 9114–2

Exports and imports of US, by transport mode, country, and SITC 1- to 3-digit commodity, 1990, annual rpt, 2424–12

Human rights conditions in 170 countries, and US economic and military aid, 1990, annual rpt, 21384–3

Military aid of US, arms sales, and training programs costs and budget requests, by program, world region, and country, FY90-92, annual rpt, 7144–13

UN voting record and share of votes in agreement with US, by issue, country, and world area, 1990, annual rpt, 7004–18

Mali

Agricultural exports of high-value commodities, indexes and sales by commodity, world area, and country, 1960s-86, 1528–323

Agricultural trade of US, by detailed commodity and country, 1989, annual rpt, 1524–8

Agricultural trade of US, by detailed commodity and country, 1990, semiannual rpt, 1522–4

AID economic aid to developing countries, obligations and disbursements by country, quarterly rpt, 9912–4

AID loans repayment status and terms by program and country, and status of predecessor agency loans, quarterly rpt, 9912–3

Dairy imports, consumption, and market conditions, by sub-Saharan Africa country, 1961-88, 1528–321

Economic and military aid and loans from US and intl agencies, by program and country, FY46-90, annual rpt, 9914–5

Economic and social conditions of developing countries from 1960s, and Intl Dev Cooperation Agency and AID activities and funding, FY90-92, annual rpt, 9904–4

Economic conditions, income, production, prices, employment, and trade, 1991 periodic country rpt, 2046–4.16

Economic, population, and agricultural data, US and other aid sources, and AID activity, 1988 country rpt, 9916–12.27

Economic, social, political, and geographic summary data, by country, 1991, annual factbook, 9114–2

Exports and imports of US, by transport mode, country, and SITC 1- to 3-digit commodity, 1990, annual rpt, 2424–12

Exports of US, detailed Schedule B commodities with countries of destination, 1990, annual rpt, 2424–10

Grain production, use, imports, and stocks, for Sahel region by country, 1989/90, 9918–18

Human rights conditions in 170 countries, and US economic and military aid, 1990, annual rpt, 21384–3

Military aid of US, arms sales, and training programs costs and budget requests, by program, world region, and country, FY90-92, annual rpt, 7144–13

UN voting record and share of votes in agreement with US, by issue, country, and world area, 1990, annual rpt, 7004–18

see also under By Foreign Country in the "Index by Categories"

Malnutrition

see Nutrition and malnutrition

Malpractice

see Medical malpractice

see Property and casualty insurance

Malt

see Beer and breweries

see Grains and grain products

Malta

Agricultural exports of high-value commodities, indexes and sales by commodity, world area, and country, 1960s-86, 1528–323

Agricultural trade of US, by detailed commodity and country, 1989, annual rpt, 1524–8

Agricultural trade of US, by detailed commodity and country, 1990, semiannual rpt, 1522–4

AID loans repayment status and terms by program and country, and status of predecessor agency loans, quarterly rpt, 9912–3

Economic and military aid and loans from US and intl agencies, by program and country, FY46-90, annual rpt, 9914–5

Economic, social, political, and geographic summary data, by country, 1991, annual factbook, 9114–2

Exports and imports of US, by transport mode, country, and SITC 1- to 3-digit commodity, 1990, annual rpt, 2424–12

Exports of US, detailed Schedule B commodities with countries of destination, 1990, annual rpt, 2424–10

Human rights conditions in 170 countries, and US economic and military aid, 1990, annual rpt, 21384–3

Military aid of US, arms sales, and training programs costs and budget requests, by program, world region, and country, FY90-92, annual rpt, 7144–13

UN voting record and share of votes in agreement with US, by issue, country, and world area, 1990, annual rpt, 7004–18

Mammography

see Medical examinations and tests

Management

see Business management

see Consultants

see Executives and managers

see Government efficiency

see Health facilities administration

see Labor-management relations, general

see Labor-management relations in government

see School administration and staff

Manatees

see Marine mammals

Manchester, N.H.

see also under By SMSA or MSA in the "Index by Categories"

Mandelbaum, Thomas B.

"Are District Services Jobs Bad Jobs?", 9391–16.205

"Consumer's Guide to Regional Economic Multipliers", 9391–1.206

"District Real Economy in 1990: Losing Its Fizz", 9391–16.207

"District Services: What They Are and Why They Have Grown", 9391–16.203

"Measuring State Exports: Is There a Better Way?", 9391–1.219

Manganese

see Metals and metal industries

Mangeno, J. J.

"Environmental Monitoring and Disposal of Radioactive Wastes from U.S. Naval Nuclear-Powered Ships and Their Support Facilities, 1990", 3804–11

"Occupational Radiation Exposure from U.S. Naval Nuclear Propulsion Plants and Their Support Facilities, 1990", 3804–10

Mangold, Robert D.

"Tree Planting in the U.S., 1990", 1204–7

Manned space flight

see Astronauts

Manpower

see Labor supply and demand

see under names of specific occupations

Manpower training programs

Assistance (financial and nonfinancial) of Fed Govt, 1991 base edition with supplements, annual listing, 104–5

Assistance programs under Ways and Means Committee jurisdiction, finances, operations, and participant characteristics, FY70s-90, annual rpt, 21784–11

Budget of US, CBO analysis and review of FY92 budget by function, annual rpt, 26304–2

Budget of US, formula grant program obligations to State and local govts, by agency, program, and State, FY92, annual rpt, 104–30

Budget of US, obligations and authority by function, agency, and program, with summaries, analyses, and historical tables, FY92, annual rpt, 104–2

Employment, earnings, and hours, by SIC 1- to 4-digit industry, monthly and annual averages, selected years 1909-90, annual rpt, 6744–4

Expenditures of Fed Govt in States, by type, program, agency, and State, FY90, annual rpt, 2464–2

Forest Service acreage, staff, finances, and mgmt activities in Pacific Northwest, with data by forest, 1970s-89, annual rpt, 1204–37

Job Training Partnership Act funding and performance indicators in service delivery areas, by urban-rural location, 1987-88, 1598–266

Job Training Partnership Act participants, by selected characteristics, FY90, annual rpt, 6304–1

Manpower training programs

Job Training Partnership Act participation by selected characteristics and State, and outcomes, by urban-rural location, 1987-88, 1598–267

Job Training Partnership Act State and local admin, funding, effectiveness, and participants, GAO rpt series, 26106–8

Labor Dept employment programs, training, and unemployment compensation, current devs and grants to States, press release series, 6406–2

Labor laws enacted, by State, 1990, annual article, 6722–1.209

Natl Commission for Employment Policy activities and rpts, 1990 annual rpt, 15494–1

Nepal economic dev projects manpower training program of AID, effectiveness, 1950s-80s, 9916–3.62

Steel industry finances, operations, and modernization efforts, with data on major companies and foreign industry, 1968-91, last issue of annual rpt, 9884–24

Timber industry impacts of northern spotted owl conservation in Pacific Northwest, and worker aid programs, 1980s and projected to 2000, hearing, 21728–76

Unemployed displaced and economically disadvantaged workers, training program operations and performance, series, 6406–10

Unemployed displaced workers and other hard-to-serve groups, factors contributing to unemployment, and training programs operations, series, 15496–1

Unemployment insurance reemployment and training services, and bonus for early reemployment, New Jersey demonstration project results, 1986-90, 6406–6.32

see also Apprenticeship

see also Employee development

see also Military training

see also Vocational education and training

see also Vocational rehabilitation

see also Work incentive programs

see also Youth Conservation Corps

Mansfield, Ohio

see also under By SMSA or MSA in the "Index by Categories"

Mansfield, Wendy

"College-Level Remedial Education in the Fall of 1989", 4826–1.30

"Teacher Survey on Safe, Disciplined, and Drug-Free Schools", 4826–1.31

Manton, Kenneth G.

"Functionally and Medically Defined Subgroups of Nursing Home Populations", 4652–1.205

Manufactured housing

see Mobile homes

Manufacturing

Acquisitions (leveraged buyout) in manufacturing, relation to industry size, concentration ratios, and financial indicators, 1988, technical paper, 9385–8.86

Agricultural crops (new and traditional) use in industry, replacement of imports and nonrenewable resources, R&D funding, and economic impacts, 1970s-90, 26358–239

Business statistics, detailed data for major industries and economic indicators, *Survey of Current Business,* monthly rpt, 2702–1

Capital expenditures for plant and equipment, by industry div, monthly rpt, quarterly data, 23842–1.1

Capital expenditures for plant and equipment, by major industry group, quarterly rpt, 2502–2

Capital expenditures relation to cash flow, working capital, and other factors, 1970s, working paper, 9375–13.49

Capital stock measures, by type and industry, 1950s-80s, technical paper, 9385–8.92

Census Bur rpts and data files, coverage and availability, 1991 annual listing, 2304–2

Chicago employment growth in service, manufacturing, and other industries, analysis of contributing factors, 1970s-87, article, 9375–1.204

Classification codes concordance of Canada and US SICs, for 1- to 4-digit levels, 1991 rpt, 2628–31

Coal receipts and prices at manufacturing plants, by SIC 2-digit industry, quarterly rpt, 3162–37.2

Collective bargaining agreements expiring during year, and workers covered, by firm, union, industry group, and State, 1991, annual rpt, 6784–9

Collective bargaining wage and benefit changes, quarterly press release, 6782–2

Collective bargaining wage changes and coverage, by industry sector and whether contract includes escalator clause and lump sum payment, 1980-90, annual article, 6722–1.227

Communist countries trade with US, by detailed commodity and country, quarterly rpt with articles, 9882–2

County Business Patterns, 1988: employment, establishments, and payroll, by SIC 2- to 4-digit industry and county, annual State rpt series, 2326–6

County Business Patterns, 1989: employment, establishments, and payroll, by SIC 2- to 4-digit industry and county, annual State rpt series, 2326–8

Developing countries labor standards impacts on social and economic dev, 1988 conf papers, 6368–9

Earnings and hours of work, weekly averages, monthly rpt, 23842–1.2

Earnings by industry div, and personal income per capita and by source, by State, MSA, and county, 1984-89, annual regional rpts, 2704–2

Economic indicators forecasts, performance of manufacturing activity index of Natl Assn of Purchasing Managers, various periods 1948-91, article, 9385–1.215; 9385–8.120

Employment and Earnings, detailed data, monthly rpt, 6742–2.5; 6742–2.6

Employment Cost Index and percent change by occupational group, industry div, region, and metro-nonmetro area, quarterly press release, 6782–5

Employment, earnings, and hours, by industry div and major manufacturing group, Monthly Labor Review, 6722–1.2

Employment, earnings, and hours, by SIC 1- to 4-digit industry, monthly and annual averages, selected years 1909-90, annual rpt, 6744–4

Employment, earnings, and hours, monthly press release, 6742–5

Index by Subjects and Names

Employment in manufacturing and nonagricultural industries, by MSA, 1989-90, annual press release, 6946–3.20

Employment in manufacturing, by detailed occupation and SIC 2-digit industry, 1989 survey, triennial rpt, 6748–52

Employment in manufacturing by selected characteristics, wages, and import and export penetration rates, by SIC 2- to 4-digit industry, 1982-89, 6366–3.27

Employment situation, earnings, hours, and other BLS economic indicators, transcripts of BLS Commissioner's monthly testimony, periodic rpt, 23846–4

Employment, unemployment, and labor force characteristics, by region, State, and selected metro area, 1990, annual rpt, 6744–7

Energy use and prices for manufacturing industries, 1988 survey, series, 3166–13

Energy use in commercial buildings, costs, and conservation, by building characteristics, survey rpt series, 3166–8

Enterprise Statistics, 1987: auxiliaries of multi-establishment firms, finances and operations by function, industry, and State, 2329–6

Enterprise Statistics, 1987: finances and operations for companies, by size, level of diversification, form of organization, and industry group, 2329–8

Export and import price indexes, by selected end-use category, monthly press release, 6762–15

Export and import price indexes for goods and services, and dollar exchange rate indexes, quarterly press release, 6762–13

Exports and imports between US and outlying areas, by detailed commodity and mode of transport, 1990, annual rpt, 2424–11

Exports and imports of finished goods and industrial supplies, with related indicators, by industry and country, mid 1970s-90, 9385–1.205; 9385–8.95

Exports and imports of US, by country and detailed commodity, monthly rpt, 2422–12

Exports and imports of US by country, and trade shifts by commodity, 1990, semiannual rpt, 9882–9

Exports and imports of US, by Harmonized System 6-digit commodity and country, 1990, annual rpt, 2424–13

Exports and imports of US, by selected country, country group, and commodity group, 1990, annual rpt, 2044–37

Exports and imports of US, by transport mode, country, and SITC 1- to 3-digit commodity, 1990, annual rpt, 2424–12

Exports, imports, and balances of US, by selected country, country group, and commodity group, preliminary data, monthly rpt, 2042–34

Exports, imports, and balances of US with major trading partners, by product category, 1986-90, annual chartbook, 9884–21

Exports, imports, and trade flows, by country and commodity, with background economic indicators, data compilation, monthly CD-ROM, 2002–6

Exports of manufactures, by State, alternative estimates, 1986-87, article, 9391–1.219

Index by Subjects and Names

Manufacturing

Exports of US, detailed commodities by country, monthly CD-ROM, 2422–13

Fed Govt labor productivity, indexes of output and labor costs by function, FY67-89, annual rpt, 6824–1.6

Finances and operations, by SIC 2- to 4-digit industry, forecast 1991, annual rpt, 2044–28

Financial statements for manufacturing, mining, and trade corporations, by selected SIC 2- to 3-digit industry, quarterly rpt, 2502–1

Foreign and US manufacturing labor costs and indexes, by selected country, 1990, semiannual rpt, 6822–3

Foreign countries economic conditions, policy, and trade practices, by country, 1988-90, annual rpt, 21384–5

Foreign countries economic, social, political, and geographic summary data, by country, 1991, annual factbook, 9114–2

Foreign direct investment impact on trade balance, with background data, late 1960s-90 and auto forecasts to 1993, article, 9385–1.210

Foreign direct investment in US, by industry group and world area, 1987-90, annual article, 2702–1.219

Foreign direct investment in US, by industry group of US affiliate and country of parent firm, 1980-86, 2708–41

Foreign direct investment in US, major transactions by type, industry, country, and US location, 1989, annual rpt, 2044–20

Foreign direct investment in US manufacturing, impacts on trade balances, with data by industry, 1980s-93, technical paper, 9385–8.91

Foreign direct investment of US, by industry group and world area, 1987-90, annual article, 2702–1.220

Great Lakes area economic conditions and outlook, for US and Canada, 1970s-90, 9375–15

Imports, exports, and employment impacts, by SIC 2- to 4-digit industry and commodity, quarterly rpt, 2322–2

Imports of US, detailed commodities by country, monthly CD-ROM, 2422–14

Income (personal) per capita disparity among States, with data by industrial base, 1979, 1989, and projected to 1995, 1548–379

Input-output structure of US economy, detailed interindustry transactions for 84 industries, and components of final demand, 1986, annual article, 2702–1.206

Input-output structure of US economy, detailed interindustry transactions for 85 industries, 1982 benchmark data, 2702–1.213

Inventories, sales, and inventory/sales ratios for manufacturing and trade, quarterly article, 2702–1.28

Investment spending of manufacturing industry groups, relation to concentration ratios and other factors, 1960s-82, technical paper, 9385–8.81

Investment spending relation to cash flow, by SIC 2-digit manufacturing industry, 1958-86, article, 9375–1.202

Investment spending relation to dollar exchange rate, by SIC 2-digit manufacturing industry, 1963-86, article, 9375–1.208

Japan financial instns and stock market conditions, and other economic indicators, with intl comparisons, 1980s-90, hearing, 21248–152

Japan manufacturing firms US affiliates, employment, and wages, by selected industry and State, 1980s, 2048–151

Job creation, elimination, and reallocation rates in manufacturing, and relation to industry and establishment characteristics, 1970s-86, working paper, 9375–13.56

Mexico imports from US, by industry and State, 1987-90, 2048–154

Middle Atlantic States manufacturing business outlook, monthly survey rpt, 9387–11

Middle Atlantic States manufacturing output index, monthly rpt, 9387–12

Multinatl firms US affiliates, finances, and operations, by industry, world area of parent firm, and State, 1988-89, annual rpt, 2704–4

Multinatl firms US affiliates, investment trends and impact on US economy, 1991 annual rpt, 2004–9

Multinatl US firms and foreign affiliates finances and operations, by industry and world area of parent firm, 1989 benchmark survey, preliminary annual rpt, 2704–5

Occupational injuries, illnesses, and workdays lost, by SIC 2-digit industry, 1989-90, annual press release, 6844–3

Occupational injury and illness rates, by SIC 2- to 4-digit industry, 1988-89, annual rpt, 6844–7

Occupational injury and illness rates, by SIC 2- to 4-digit industry, 1989, annual rpt, 6844–1

Operations and performance of manufacturing industries, analytical rpt series, 2506–16

Pollution (air) emissions factors, by detailed pollutant and source, data compilation, 1990 rpt, 9198–120

Price indexes (producer), by stage of processing and detailed commodity, monthly rpt, 6762–6

Price indexes (producer), by stage of processing and detailed commodity, monthly 1990, annual rpt, 6764–2

Producer Price Index, by major commodity group and subgroup, and processing stage, monthly press release, 6762–5

Production and capacity use indexes, by SIC 2- to 4-digit industry, monthly rpt, 9365–2.24

Production indexes, capital investment, and capacity use by industry div, and manufacturers and trade sales and inventories, 1947-90, annual rpt, 204–1.3

Production, shipments, inventories, and new orders, monthly rpt, 23842–1.3

Productivity and costs of labor for private, nonfarm business, and manufacturing sectors, revised data, quarterly rpt, 6822–2

Productivity and costs of labor, indexes, preliminary data, quarterly rpt, 6822–1

Productivity of labor and capital, indexes and percent change, 1948-90, annual press release, 6824–2

Puerto Rico and other US possessions corporations income tax returns, income and tax items, and employment, by selected industry, 1987, article, 8302–2.213

Science and engineering employment and education, and R&D spending, for US and selected foreign countries, 1991 annual rpt, 9627–35.2

SEC registration, firms required to file annual rpts, as of Sept 1990, annual listing, 9734–5

Shipments, inventories, orders, capacity use, and pollution control costs of manufacturers, periodic Current Industrial Rpt series, 2506–3

Southeastern States, Fed Reserve 5th District, economic indicators by State, quarterly rpt, 9389–16

Southeastern US services and manufacturing sectors, earnings and earnings distribution by State, 1989, article, 9391–16.205

Soviet Union GNP by component and industry sector, and CIA estimation methods, 1950s-87, 23848–223

Soviet Union GNP by detailed income and outlay component, 1985, 2326–18.59

State and Metro Area Data Book, 1991 data compilation, 2328–54

Statistical Abstract of US, 1991 annual data compilation, 2324–1.17; 2324–1.27

Tariff Schedule of US, classifications and rates of duty by detailed imported commodity, 1992 base edition, 9886–13

Tax (income) returns filed by type of filer, selected income items, quarterly rpt, 8302–2.1

Tax (income) returns for foreign corporate activity in US, assets, and income statement items, by industry div and selected country, 1986-87, article, 8302–2.205

Tax (income) returns of corporations, income and tax items by asset size and detailed industry, 1987, annual rpt, 8304–4

Tax (income) returns of corporations, income and tax items by asset size and detailed industry, 1988, annual rpt, 8304–21

Tax (income) returns of corporations with foreign tax credit, income and tax items by industry group, 1986, biennial article, 8302–2.203

Tax (income) returns of multinatl US firms foreign affiliates, income statement items, by asset size and industry, 1986, biennial article, 8302–2.212

Tax (income) returns of partnerships, income statement and balance sheet items, by industry group, 1989, annual article, 8302–2.216; 8304–18

Tax (income) returns of sole proprietorships, income statement items, by industry group, 1989, annual article, 8302–2.214

Tax (income) returns of US corporations under foreign control, assets and income statement items by industry div and country, 1988, article, 8302–2.219

Technology-intensive manufacturing methods use, by type and selected industry, 1988 survey, fact sheet, 2326–17.23

Trade zones (US) operations and movement of goods, by zone and commodity, FY88, annual rpt, 2044–30

Wage and benefit changes from collective bargaining and mgmt decisions, by industry div, monthly rpt, 6782–1

Manufacturing

Wages by occupation, and benefits for office and plant workers in selected MSAs, 1990, annual rpt, 6785–1

Wages by occupation, and benefits for office and plant workers, periodic MSA survey rpt series, 6785–11; 6785–12

Wages for 4 occupational groups, relative pay levels in 60 MSAs, 1990, annual rpt, 6785–8

Wages impacts of foreign competition in manufacturing industries, 1950s-89, article, 9385–1.204

Wages impacts of foreign competition, regression results, late 1950s-85, technical paper, 9385–8.89

see also Aerospace industry
see also Aircraft
see also Aluminum and aluminum industry
see also Annual Survey of Manufactures
see also Business machines and equipment
see also Cement and concrete
see also Census of Manufactures
see also Chemicals and chemical industry
see also Clay industry and products
see also Clothing and clothing industry
see also Copper and copper industry
see also Electrical machinery and equipment
see also Electronics industry and products
see also Food and food industry
see also Furniture and furnishings
see also Furs and fur industry
see also Glass and glass industry
see also Gum and wood chemicals
see also Household appliances and equipment
see also Ice, manufactured
see also Industrial capacity and utilization
see also Industrial plants and equipment
see also Industrial production
see also Instruments and measuring devices
see also Iron and steel industry
see also Leather industry and products
see also Lumber industry and products
see also Machines and machinery industry
see also Metals and metal industries
see also Motor vehicle industry
see also Musical instruments
see also Paints and varnishes
see also Paper and paper products
see also Petroleum and petroleum industry
see also Pharmaceutical industry
see also Plastics and plastics industry
see also Printing and publishing industry
see also Production workers
see also Rubber and rubber industry
see also Shipbuilding and repairing
see also Sporting goods
see also Stone products and quarries
see also Textile industry and fabrics
see also Tires and tire industry
see also Tobacco industry and products
see also Toys and games
see also Transportation and transportation equipment
see also Zinc and zinc industry
see also under By Commodity in the "Index by Categories"
see also under By Industry in the "Index by Categories"

Maps

Africa (Sahel) grain production, use, imports, and stocks, by country, 1989/90, 9918–18

Alaska land area by ownership, and availability for mineral exploration and dev, 1984-86, 5608–152

Alaska minerals resources and geologic characteristics, compilation of papers, 1989, annual rpt, 5664–15

Alaska minerals resources and production, by mineral and site, for Juneau region, 1987-88, 5608–169

Alaska minerals resources, production, oil and gas leases, reserves, and exploratory wells, with maps and bibl, 1989, annual rpt, 5664–11

Alaska OCS environmental conditions and oil dev impacts, compilation of papers, series, 2176–1

Alaska submerged land grant holdings of Alaska Natives, exchange for upland acreage, impacts on conservation acreage and acquisition, 1989-90, 5728–38

Birds (mourning dove) population, by hunting and nonhunting State, 1966-91, annual rpt, 5504–15

Birds (waterfowl) population, habitat conditions, and migratory flight forecasts, for Canada and US by region, 1991 and trends from 1955, annual rpt, 5504–27

Cancer death rates of minorities, by body site, age, sex, and substate area, 1950s-80, atlas, 4478–78

Census Bur rpts and data files, coverage and availability, 1991 annual listing, 2304–2

Census Bur rpts and data files, coverage, availability, and use, series, 2326–7

Census of Population and Housing, 1990: population and housing characteristics, households, and land area, by county, subdiv, and place, State rpt series, 2551–1

Census of Population, 1990: congressional redistricting data coverage and availability, guide, 2308–59

Coal production and mines by county, prices, productivity, miners, and reserves, by mining method and State, 1989-90, annual rpt, 3164–25

Coastal and estuarine pollutant concentrations in sediments, by contaminant and selected site, 1984-89, 2176–3.13

Coastal and riparian areas environmental conditions, fish, wildlife, use, and mgmt, for individual ecosystems, series, 5506–9

Coastal areas environmental and socioeconomic conditions, and potential impact of oil and gas OCS leases, final statement series, 5736–1

Congressional Directory, members of 102nd Congress, other officials, elections, and districts, 1991-92, biennial rpt, 23874–1

DC metro area land acquisition and dev projects of Fed Govt, characteristics and funding by agency and project, FY91-95, annual rpt, 15454–1

Developing countries economic, population, and agricultural data, US and other aid sources, and AID activity, country rpt series, 9916–12

Disasters and natl security incidents and mgmt, with data by major event and State, 1991 annual rpt, 9434–6

DOD contracts, payroll, and personnel, by service branch and location, with top 5 contractors and maps, by State and country, FY90, annual rpt, 3544–29

Earthquake intensity, time, location, damage, and seismic characteristics, for US and foreign earthquakes, 1985, annual rpt, 5664–13

Index by Subjects and Names

Environmental and natural resource data sources, and aerial survey R&D rpts, quarterly listing, 9502–7

Florida environmental, social, and economic conditions, and impacts of proposed OCS oil and gas leases in southern coastal areas, 1990 compilation of papers, 5738–19

Foreign countries agricultural production, trade, and policies, summary data by country, 1989-90, annual factbook, 1924–12

Foreign countries economic, social, political, and geographic summary data, by country, 1991, annual factbook, 9114–2

Foreign countries *Geographic Notes*, boundaries, claims, nomenclature, and other devs, periodic rpt, 7142–3

Forest fires and acres burned on Forest Service land, by cause, forest, and State, 1989, annual rpt, 1204–6

Geological Survey rpts and research journal articles, monthly listing, 5662–1

Geological Survey rpts, 1990, annual listing, 5664–4

Hurricanes and tropical storms in Pacific and Indian Oceans, paths and surveillance, 1990, annual rpt, 3804–8

Marine Fisheries Review, US and foreign fisheries resources, dev, mgmt, and research, quarterly journal, 2162–1

Mariners Weather Log, quarterly journal, 2152–8

Migrant workers and dependents by county, and health centers use and programs funding, by State, 1986-89, 4108–53

Minerals (strategic) supply and characteristics of individual deposits, by country, commodity rpt series, 5666–21

Minerals Mgmt Service OCS rpts, 1988, annual listing, 5734–5

Natural gas pipelines and owners, and fields, as of Sept 1989, map, 3088–21

North Carolina environmental and socioeconomic conditions, and impacts of proposed OCS oil and gas exploration, 1970s-90 and projected to 2020, 5738–22

Pacific Ocean coast pollutant concentrations in fish and sediments, by contaminant, fish species, and site, 1984-86, 2168–121

Pollution (air) levels for 6 pollutants, by source and selected MSA, 1980-89, annual rpt, 9194–1

Precipitation averages worldwide, estimates for map grid areas, 1850s-1989, 3006–11.14

Public lands minerals resources and availability, State rpt series, 5606–7

Soil surveys and maps for counties, 1899-1990, annual listing, 1264–11

Timber insect and disease incidence and damage, and control activities, State rpt series, 1206–49

Water (groundwater) supply, quality, chemistry, and use, State and local area rpt series, 5666–28

Water (groundwater) supply, quality, chemistry, other characteristics, and use, regional rpt series, 5666–25

Water quality, chemistry, hydrology, and other characteristics, local area studies, series, 5666–27

Water resources dev projects of Army Corps of Engineers, characteristics, and costs, 1950s-89, biennial State rpt series, 3756–1

Index by Subjects and Names

Water resources dev projects of Army Corps of Engineers, characteristics, and costs, 1950s-91, biennial State rpt series, 3756–2

Water supply, hydrologic events, and end use, by State, 1988-89, annual rpt, 5664–12

Water supply in US and southern Canada, streamflow, surface and groundwater conditions, and reservoir levels, by location, monthly rpt, 5662–3

Water supply in western US, and snow survey results, annual State rpt series, 1264–14

Water use by end use, well withdrawals, and public supply deliveries, by county, State rpt series, 5666–24

Weather conditions and effect on agriculture, by US region, State, and city, and world area, weekly rpt, 2182–7

Weather events and anomalies, precipitation and temperature for US and foreign locations, weekly rpt, 2182–6

Weather forecasts for US and Northern Hemisphere, precipitation and temperature by location, semimonthly rpt, 2182–1

Wetlands acreage, resources, soil and water properties, and conservation efforts, by wetland type, State rpt series, 5506–11

Wildlife and plant research results, habitat study series, 5506–13

Wildlife mgmt activities and funding, acreage, staff, and plans of Bur of Land Mgmt, habitat study series, 5726–6

see also Cartography

Margarine

see Oils, oilseeds, and fats

Mariana Islands

see Guam

see Northern Mariana Islands

Marietta, Ohio

see also under By SMSA or MSA in the "Index by Categories"

Marijuana

Abuse of cocaine and marijuana reported in household and telephone surveys, data accuracy, 1988, article, 4042–3.230

Abuse of drugs and alcohol, by selected characteristics, 1990 survey, biennial rpt, 4494–5

Abuse of drugs, emergency room admissions and deaths, by drug type and source, sex, race, age, and major metro area, 1990, annual rpt, 4494–8

Abuse of drugs, indicators for selected metro areas, research results, data collection, and policy issues, 1991 semiannual conf, 4492–5

Abuse of drugs, State treatment and prevention programs, funding, facilities, and patient characteristics, FY89, 4488–15

Abuse of drugs, treatment, biological and behavioral factors, and addiction potential of new drugs, research results, 1990 annual conf, 4494–11

Arrests, by offense, offender characteristics, and location, 1990, annual rpt, 6224–2.2

Arrests for drug- and nondrug-related offenses, urine test results by drug type, offense, and sex, for selected urban areas, quarterly rpt, 6062–3

Coast Guard drug, immigration, and fisheries enforcement activities, 2nd half FY91, semiannual rpt, 7402–4

Court civil and criminal caseloads for Federal district, appeals, and bankruptcy courts, by type of suit and offense, circuit, and district, 1990, annual rpt, 18204–11

Court civil and criminal caseloads for Federal district, appeals, and special courts, 1990, annual rpt, 18204–8

Court civil and criminal caseloads for Federal district courts, 1991, annual rpt, 18204–2.1

Court criminal cases in Federal district courts, by offense, disposition, and district, 1980-90, last issue of annual rpt, 18204–1

Cultivation of marijuana, DEA and local agencies eradication activities by State, and drug potency and prices, 1982-90, annual rpt, 6284–4

Customs Service activities, collections, entries processed by mode of transport, and seizures, FY86-90, annual rpt, 8144–1

Enforcement activities of drug control task forces by drug type and State, and organization, staff, and spending, 1988, 6068–244

Expenditures of users for illegal drugs, by user group and substance, 1988-90, 236–2.1

Fed Govt drug abuse and trafficking reduction programs activities, funding, staff, and Bush Admin budget request, by Federal agency and program area, FY90-92, 238–2

Fed Govt drug smuggling interdiction programs, budget, and seizures, FY87-90, GAO rpt, 26119–318

Foreign countries drug production, eradication, and seizures, by illegal substance, with US aid, by country, 1987-91, annual rpt, 7004–17

Health condition and health care resources, use, and spending, 1950s-89, annual data compilation, 4144–11

Jail population, by sociodemographic characteristics, criminal and drug use history, whether convicted, offense, and sentencing, 1989, annual rpt, 6064–26.3

Minority group drug abuse prevalence, related health effects and crime, treatment, and research status and needs, mid 1970s-90, 4498–72

Minority group health condition, services use, costs, and indicators of services need, 1950s-88, 4118–55

Neurological, cognitive, and behavioral residual effects of long-term drug abuse, 1989 conf, 4498–69

Organized Crime Drug Enforcement Task Forces regional investigation activities by agency and region, FY83-90, biennial rpt, 6004–17

Public lands marijuana cultivation, sinsemilla and other plants seized by State, FY89, annual rpt, 5724–13

Public opinion on crime and crime-related issues, by respondent characteristics, data compilation, 1991 annual rpt, 6064–6.2

Research on drug abuse and treatment, summaries of findings, resource materials, and grant listings, periodic rpt, 4492–4

Research on drug abuse, prevention, treatment, and health impacts, as of 1990, triennial rpt, 4498–68

Rural areas drug and alcohol abuse, related crime, and treatment, by substance and State, 1988-90, GAO rpt, 26131–79

Sentences for Federal offenses, guidelines by offense and circumstances, series, 17668–1

Supply of drugs in US by country of origin, abuse, prices, and seizures, by substance, 1990, annual rpt, 6284–2

Testing for drugs, urinalysis methods accuracy by drug type, 1991, 6066–26.6

Treatment services for drug and alcohol abuse, funding, staffing, and client load, characteristics, and outcomes, by setting, 1989 conf, 4498–73

Violent and criminal behavior relation to drug abuse, with data on street gang activity and selected population groups, 1989 conf, 4498–70

Youth drug, alcohol, and cigarette use and attitudes, by substance type and selected characteristics, 1975-90 surveys, annual rpt, 4494–4

Marine accidents and safety

Accidents involving ships and marine facilities, casualties, and circumstances, Coast Guard investigation results, periodic rpt, 9612–4

Boat registrations, and accidents, casualties, and damage by cause, by vessel characteristics and State, 1990, annual rpt, 7404–1

Coast Guard search and rescue missions, and lives and property lost and saved, by district and assisting unit, FY90, annual rpt, 7404–2

Deaths and rates, by detailed cause and demographic characteristics, 1988 and trends from 1900, US Vital Statistics annual rpt, 4144–2

Diving (underwater sport and occupational) deaths, by circumstances, diver characteristics, and location, 1970-89, annual rpt, 2144–5

Fed Govt spending in States, by type, program, agency, and State, FY90, annual rpt, 2464–2

Hazardous material transport accidents, casualties, and damage, by mode of transport, with DOT control activities, 1989, annual rpt, 7304–4

Injury and illness rates and causes, by SIC 2- to 4-digit industry, 1989, annual rpt, 6844–1

Injury and illness rates, by SIC 2- to 4-digit industry, 1988-89, annual rpt, 6844–7

Merchant ships accidents and casualties, by circumstances and characteristics of persons and vessels involved, 1988, annual rpt, 7404–11

Navy battleship *USS Iowa* explosion, safety and personnel mgmt issues, with technical analysis, FY89, GAO rpt, 26123–315

Recreational boats and engines recalls for safety-related defects, by make, periodic listing, 7402–5

Safety programs, and accidents, casualties, and damage, by mode of transport, 1989, annual rpt, 7304–19

Statistical Abstract of US, 1991 annual data compilation, 2324–1.22

Weather services activities and funding, by Federal agency, planned FY91-92, annual rpt, 2144–2

Marine accidents and safety

see also Drowning
see also Oil spills

Marine Corps

- Base support costs by function, and personnel and acreage by installation, by service branch, FY91, annual rpt, 3504–11
- Budget of DOD, procurement appropriations by item, service branch, and defense agency, FY90-93, annual rpt, 3544–32
- Budget of DOD, weapons acquisition costs by system and service branch, FY91-93, annual rpt, 3504–2
- Budget of US, obligations and authority by function, agency, and program, with summaries, analyses, and historical tables, FY92, annual rpt, 104–2
- Criminal case processing in military courts, and prisoners by facility, by service branch, data compilation, 1991 annual rpt, 6064–6.6
- Deaths by cause, age, race, and rank, and personnel captured and missing, by service branch, FY90, annual rpt, 3544–40
- Health care facilities of DOD in US and abroad, beds, admissions, outpatient visits, and births, by service branch, quarterly rpt, 3542–15
- Pacific basin US military personnel, dependents, aircraft, ships, and costs, by service branch and location, 1990, GAO rpt, 26123–357
- Personnel active duty and recruit social, economic, and parents characteristics, by service branch and State, FY89, annual rpt, 3544–41
- Personnel active duty strength, recruits, and reenlistment, by race, sex, and service branch, quarterly press release, 3542–7
- Personnel needs, costs, and force readiness, by service branch, FY92, annual rpt, 3504–1
- Personnel of DOD, and organization, budget, weapons, and property, by service branch, State, and country, 1991 annual summary rpt, 3504–13
- Personnel, procurement, equipment, and budget of Navy, planned FY91-93, annual fact sheet, 3804–16
- Personnel strengths, for active duty, civilians, and dependents, by service branch and US and foreign location, quarterly rpt, 3542–20
- Personnel strengths, for active duty, civilians, and reserves, by service branch, FY90 and trends, annual rpt, 3544–1
- Personnel strengths, for active duty, civilians, and reserves, by service branch, quarterly rpt, 3542–14
- Personnel strengths, for active duty enlisted and officers, by sex and race, 1970s-90, GAO rpt, 26123–325
- Personnel strengths in US and abroad, by service branch, world area, and country, quarterly press release, 3542–9
- Personnel strengths, summary by service branch, monthly press release, 3542–2
- Procurement of Navy, by contractor and location, FY90, annual rpt, 3804–13
- Shipments by DOD of military and personal property, passenger traffic, and costs, by service branch and mode of transport, quarterly rpt, 3702–1
- Training and education programs of DOD, funding, staff, students, and facilities, by service branch, FY92, annual rpt, 3504–5
- Women military personnel on active and reserve duty, by demographic and service characteristics and service branch, FY89, annual chartbook, 3544–26

see also Marine Reserve

Marine Mammal Commission

- Budget of US, authoritative financial statements with appropriations, outlays, and receipts, by category and agency, FY90, annual rpt, 8104–2.1
- Budget of US, obligations and authority by function, agency, and program, with summaries, analyses, and historical tables, FY92, annual rpt, 104–2
- Manatees (West Indian) population off Puerto Rico, and sightings by coastal region, 1976-89, 14738–11
- Manatees grazing effects on seagrass, by southeast Florida site, 1987-89, 14738–12
- Protection of marine mammals, Federal and intl regulatory and research activities, with bibl, 1990, annual rpt, 14734–1
- Research on marine mammals, Federal funding by topic, recipient, and agency, FY90, annual rpt, 14734–2
- Seals (harbor) population and physical characteristics at selected Washington State coastal sites, 1975-80, 14738–7
- Seals (harbor) population at selected southern Alaska coastal sites, 1976-88, 14738–6
- Strandings of marine mammals on land, physical characteristics and tests performed, for New England, 1970s, 14738–8
- Walrus population, habitat mgmt, and intl conservation needs, by world region, 1990 conf, 14738–9
- Whales (humpback) population and sightings off southeastern Alaska, 1979-86, 14738–10

Marine mammals

- Alaska OCS environmental conditions and oil dev impacts, compilation of papers, series, 2176–1
- Alaska rural areas population characteristics, and energy resources dev effects, series, 5736–5
- Coastal and riparian areas environmental conditions, fish, wildlife, use, and mgmt, for individual ecosystems, series, 5506–9
- Coastal areas environmental and socioeconomic conditions, and potential impact of oil and gas OCS leases, final statement series, 5736–1
- Endangered animals and plants conservation spending of Federal agencies and States, by species, FY90, annual rpt, 5504–33
- Endangered animals and plants population status and mgmt activity, by species, 1990, biennial rpt, 5504–35
- Foreign and US environmental and wildlife conservation agreements provisions, status, and signatories, as of 1991, listing, 9886–4.169
- Manatees (West Indian) population off Puerto Rico, and sightings by coastal region, 1976-89, 14738–11
- Manatees grazing effects on seagrass, by southeast Florida site, 1987-89, 14738–12
- Manatees killed in Florida and other US waters, by cause, 1978-90, annual rpt, 14734–1
- North Carolina environmental and socioeconomic conditions, and impacts of proposed OCS oil and gas exploration, 1970s-90 and projected to 2020, 5738–22
- Otters (sea) conservation measures taken after Exxon Valdez oil spill in Alaska, 1990 conf, 5508–110
- Otters (sea) population and behavior, for Pacific Ocean, 1914-90, 5508–109
- Otters (sea) population, and relocation project results, for California, 1982-89, annual rpt, 5504–12
- Otters (sea) population off California coast, 1982-90, annual rpt, 14734–1
- Pacific Ocean marine mammal and bird population density and distribution, by species and selected northeast location, literature and data base review, 1950s-88, 5738–28
- Porpoise kills by tuna fishery, and Federal and intl marine mammal protection activity, with bibl, 1990, annual rpt, 14734–1
- Protection of marine mammals, activities, funding, populations, and harvests, by species, 1989, annual rpt, 5504–12
- Protection of marine mammals, Federal and intl regulatory and research activities, with bibl, 1990, annual rpt, 14734–1
- Research on marine mammals, Federal funding by topic, recipient, and agency, FY90, annual rpt, 14734–2
- Seals (harbor) population and physical characteristics at selected Washington State coastal sites, 1975-80, 14738–7
- Seals (harbor) population at selected southern Alaska coastal sites, 1976-88, 14738–6
- Strandings of marine mammals on land, physical characteristics and tests performed, for New England, 1970s, 14738–8
- Strandings of marine mammals, research results, 1987 conf, 2168–127
- Walrus and polar bear harvest by Alaska Natives, by village, 1988/89, annual rpt, 5504–12
- Walrus population, habitat mgmt, and intl conservation needs, by world region, 1990 conf, 14738–9
- Washington State marine sanctuaries proposal, environmental and economic impacts, with background data, 1984-89, 2178–30
- Wetlands acreage, resources, soil and water properties, and conservation efforts, by wetland type, State rpt series, 5506–11
- Whales (bowhead) catch and quota for Eskimos, and other marine mammals harvest, 1970s-91, annual rpt, 14734–1
- Whales (bowhead) population in Arctic areas, behavioral differences by location, 1970s-80s, 5738–29
- Whales (bowhead) population in Arctic areas, impacts of subsistence whaling, shipping, noise, and other human activity, mid 1970s-80s, 5738–30
- Whales (bowhead) population in Beaufort Sea, and fall aerial survey operations, 1979-90, annual rpt, 5734–10
- Whales (bowhead and white) migration through Beaufort Sea, behavior impacts of oil drilling and aircraft noise, spring 1989, 5738–27

Index by Subjects and Names

Maritime Administration

Whales (humpback) population and sightings off southeastern Alaska, 1979-86, 14738–10

Marine pollution

Alaska OCS environmental conditions and oil dev impacts, compilation of papers, series, 2176–1

Beach closings due to contamination and medical waste, and bacterial levels, for New York and New Jersey, 1987-89, hearing, 21568–50

California OCS oil and gas dev impacts on water quality, marine life, and sediments, by site, 1986-89, annual rpt, 5734–11

Coastal and estuarine environmental conditions, research results and methodology, series, 2176–7

Coastal and estuarine pollutant concentrations in fish, shellfish, and environment, series, 2176–3

Coastal and riparian areas environmental conditions, fish, wildlife, use, and mgmt, for individual ecosystems, series, 5506–9

Coastal areas environmental and socioeconomic conditions, and potential impact of oil and gas OCS leases, final statement series, 5736–1

Environmental Quality, status of problems, protection programs, research, and intl issues, 1991 annual rpt, 484–1

Estuary environmental conditions, and fish and shellfish catch by species and region, 1980s, 2178–27

Fish (striped bass) stocks status on Atlantic coast, and sport and commercial catch by State, 1979-88, annual rpt, 5504–29

Fish and shellfish catch, life cycles, and environmental needs, for selected coastal species and regions, series, 5506–8

Fish kills from water pollution, by pollution source, month, location, and State, 1977-87, last issue of annual rpt, 9204–3

Fish kills in coastal areas related to pollution and natural causes, by land use, State, and county, 1980s, 2178–32

Florida environmental, social, and economic conditions, and impacts of proposed OCS oil and gas leases in southern coastal areas, 1990 compilation of papers, 5738–19

Health effects of selected pollutants on animals by species and on humans, and environmental levels, series, 5506–14

Marine mammals protection, Federal and intl regulatory and research activities, 1990, annual rpt, 14734–1

New York Bight fish population and disease, and pollutant levels, near sewage sludge dumpsite, 1986-90, last issue of annual rpt, 2164–19

New York Bight pollution levels, sources, treatment costs, economic losses, and environmental and health effects, 1990 conf, 9208–131

North Carolina environmental and socioeconomic conditions, and impacts of proposed OCS oil and gas exploration, 1970s-90 and projected to 2020, 5738–22

Oil and gas OCS production water discharges, for Pacific lands under Federal lease by drilling platform, 1960s-89, annual rpt, 5734–9

Pacific Ocean coast pollutant concentrations in fish and sediments, by contaminant, fish species, and site, 1984-86, 2168–121

Radioactive waste from Navy nuclear-powered vessels and support facilities, releases in harbors, and public exposure, 1970s-90, annual rpt, 3804–11

Research and distribution of oceanographic data, World Data Center A activities by country, and cruises by ship, 1989, annual rpt, 2144–15

Sewage sludge discharges and water properties at Atlantic Ocean deepwater dumpsite, 1990, annual rpt, 2164–20

Washington State marine sanctuaries proposal, environmental and economic impacts, with background data, 1984-89, 2178–30

Wetlands acreage, resources, soil and water properties, and conservation efforts, by wetland type, State rpt series, 5506–11

see also Oil spills

Marine Reserve

Persian Gulf War Navy and Marine Corps reserves mobilized, 1990-91, GAO rpt, 26123–351

Personnel and equipment strengths, and readiness, by reserve component, FY90, annual rpt, 3544–31

Personnel attrition in reserves, by reason, personnel characteristics, reserve component, and State, FY88, GAO rpt, 26123–329

Personnel strengths and characteristics, by reserve component, FY90, annual rpt, 3544–38

Personnel strengths and characteristics, by reserve component, quarterly rpt, 3542–4

Personnel strengths for reserve components, by selected characteristics, FY90, annual rpt, 3544–1.5

Women military personnel on active and reserve duty, by demographic and service characteristics and service branch, FY89, annual chartbook, 3544–26

Marine resources

Aerial survey R&D rpts, and sources of natural resource and environmental data, quarterly listing, 9502–7

Coastal areas environmental and socioeconomic conditions, and potential impact of oil and gas OCS leases, final statement series, 5736–1

Coral harvest of Japan by species, and imports by country, 1981-88, article, 2162–1.201

Florida environmental, social, and economic conditions, and impacts of proposed OCS oil and gas leases in southern coastal areas, 1990 compilation of papers, 5738–19

North Carolina environmental and socioeconomic conditions, and impacts of proposed OCS oil and gas exploration, 1970s-90 and projected to 2020, 5738–22

Pacific Marine Environmental Lab research activities and bibl, FY90, annual rpt, 2144–21

see also Coastal areas

see also Continental shelf

see also Coral reefs and islands

see also Fish and fishing industry

see also Marine mammals

see also Marine pollution

see also Marine resources conservation

see also Offshore mineral resources

see also Offshore oil and gas

see also Oil spills

see also Shellfish

see also Water resources development

Marine resources conservation

Coastal and estuarine environmental conditions, research results and methodology, series, 2176–7

Coastal and riparian areas environmental conditions, fish, wildlife, use, and mgmt, for individual ecosystems, series, 5506–9

Environmental Quality, status of problems, protection programs, research, and intl issues, 1991 annual rpt, 484–1

Fish and shellfish catch, life cycles, and environmental needs, for selected coastal species and regions, series, 5506–8

Fishery mgmt and R&D, Fed Govt grants by project and State, and rpts, 1990, annual listing, 2164–3

Marine Fisheries Review, US and foreign fisheries resources, dev, mgmt, and research, quarterly journal, 2162–1

Washington State marine sanctuaries proposal, environmental and economic impacts, with background data, 1984-89, 2178–30

Wetlands acreage, resources, soil and water properties, and conservation efforts, by wetland type, State rpt series, 5506–11

see also Marine mammals

see also Marine pollution

Marine safety

see Marine accidents and safety

Marital status

see Marriage and divorce

see Widows and widowers

see under By Marital Status in the "Index by Categories"

Maritime academies

see Service academies

Maritime Administration

Activities, finances, and subsidies of MarAd, and world merchant fleet operations, FY90, annual rpt, 7704–14

Budget of US, obligations and authority by function, agency, and program, with summaries, analyses, and historical tables, FY92, annual rpt, 104–2

Bulk carrier ships in world fleet, characteristics by country of registry, and for Great Lakes fleet by owner, annual listing, discontinued, 7704–13

Containers (intermodal) and equipment owned by shipping and leasing companies, inventory by type and size, 1990, annual rpt, 7704–10

Employment of DOT, by subagency, occupation, and selected personnel characteristics, FY90, annual rpt, 7304–18

Exports and imports (waterborne) of US, by type of service, commodity, country, route, and US port, 1988, annual rpt, 7704–2

Exports and imports of US shipped through Canada, by detailed commodity, customs district, and country, 1989, annual rpt, 7704–11

Foreign and US merchant ships, tonnage, and new ship construction and deliveries, by vessel type and country, as of Jan 1990, annual rpt, 7704–3

Foreign-flag ships owned by US firms and foreign affiliates, by type, owner, and country of registry and construction, as of Jan. 1991, semiannual rpt, 7702–3

Maritime Administration

Merchant ships in US fleet and Natl Defense Reserve Fleet, vessels, tonnage, and owner, as of Jan 1991, semiannual listing, 7702–2

Merchant ships in US fleet, operating subsidies, construction, and ship-related employment, monthly rpt, 7702–1

Shipbuilding and deliveries, by vessel type and country of construction and registry, annual rpt, discontinued, 7704–4

Shipbuilding and repair facilities, capacity, and employment, by shipyard, 1990, annual rpt, 7704–9

Tanker ships in world fleet, characteristics by country of registry, annual listing, discontinued, 7704–17

Maritime industry

see Inland water transportation

see Longshoremen

see Marine accidents and safety

see Merchant seamen

see Shipbuilding and operating subsidies

see Shipbuilding and repairing

see Ships and shipping

Maritime law

- Court civil and criminal caseloads for Federal district, appeals, and bankruptcy courts, by type of suit and offense, circuit, and district, 1990, annual rpt, 18204–11
- Court civil and criminal caseloads for Federal district, appeals, and special courts, 1990, annual rpt, 18204–8
- Court civil and criminal caseloads for Federal district courts, 1991, annual rpt, 18204–2.1
- Environmental and wildlife conservation intl agreements provisions, status, and signatories, as of 1991, listing, 9886–4.169
- Maritime Commission activities, case filings by type and disposition, and civil penalties by shipper, FY90, annual rpt, 9334–1
- Treaties and other bilateral and multilateral agreements of US in force, by country, as of Jan 1991, annual listing, 7004–1
- US attorneys civil and criminal cases by type and disposition, and collections, by Federal district, FY90, annual rpt, 6004–2.5

Market research

- Agricultural export market research and promotion activities of USDA, with background data, 1991 GAO rpt, 26113–504
- Agricultural exports of US, impacts of foreign agricultural and trade policy, with data by commodity and country, 1989, annual rpt, 1924–8
- Agricultural production, consumption, and policies for selected countries, and US export dev and promotion, monthly journal, 1922–2
- Agricultural supply, demand, and market for US exports, with socioeconomic conditions, country rpt series, 1526–6
- Agricultural trade by commodity and country, prices, and world market devs, monthly rpt, 1922–12
- Agricultural trade, outlook and current situation, quarterly rpt, 1542–4
- *Business America*, foreign and domestic commerce, and US investment and trade opportunities, biweekly journal, 2042–24
- Dairy exports market conditions, with background data by country, 1986-89, 1128–65

Eastern Europe transition to market economies, US trade prospects, with background data by country, 1980s, hearing, 25728–42

Exports, imports, and trade flows, by country and commodity, with background economic indicators, data compilation, monthly CD-ROM, 2002–6

Fish and shellfish foreign market conditions for US products, country rpt series, 2166–19

Materials (advanced structural) devs, use, and R&D funding, for ceramics, metal alloys, polymers, and composites, 1960s-80s and projected to 2000, 5608–162

Overseas Business Reports: economic conditions, investment and export opportunities, and trade practices, country market research rpt series, 2046–6

Travel to US, market research data available from US Travel and Tourism Admin, 1991, annual rpt, 2904–15

Travel to US, trade shows and other promotional activities, with magazine ad costs and circulation, for selected countries, 1991-92, annual rpt, 2904–11

see also Consumer surveys

Market shares

see Economic concentration and diversification

Marketing

- Airline deregulation in 1978, impacts on industry structure, competition, fares, finances, operations, and intl service, with data by carrier and airport, 1980s, series, 7308–199
- Education (postsecondary) course completions, by detailed program, sex, race, and instn type, for 1972 high school class, as of 1984, 4888–4
- Minority Business Dev Centers mgmt and financial aid, and characteristics of businesses, by region and State, FY90, annual rpt, 2104–6

see also Advertising

see also Agricultural marketing

see also Competition

see also Consumer credit

see also Consumer protection

see also Consumer surveys

see also Credit

see also Direct marketing

see also Economic concentration and diversification

see also Foreign trade promotion

see also Labeling

see also Market research

see also Packaging and containers

see also Price regulation

see also Prices

see also Retail trade

see also Sales promotion

see also Sales workers

see also Shopping centers

see also Wholesale trade

see also under names of specific commodities or commodity groups

Marketing quotas

see Agricultural production quotas and price supports

Marlor, Felice S.

"Alternative Hospital Market Area Definitions", 17206–2.20

"Nonmetro, Metro, and U.S. Bank-Operating Statistics, 1987-89", 1544–29

Marquez, Jaime

"Econometrics of Elasticities or the Elasticity of Econometrics: An Empirical Analysis of the Behavior of U.S. Imports", 9366–7.250

Marquis, Kent H.

"SIPP Record Check Results: Implications for Measurement Principles and Practice", 2626–10.129

Marriage and divorce

- AFDC beneficiaries demographic and financial characteristics, by State, FY89, annual rpt, 4694–1
- Alcohol abuse by family members and spouses, population exposure by selected characteristics, 1988, 4146–8.207
- Black Americans social and economic characteristics, for South and total US, 1989-90 and trends from 1969, Current Population Rpt, 2546–1.450
- Certificates of birth, death, marriage, and divorce, and fetal death and abortion rpts, 1989 natl standard revisions, 4147–4.27
- Child health, behavioral, emotional, and school problems relation to family structure, by selected characteristics, 1988, 4147–10.178
- Children and youth social, economic, and demographic characteristics, 1950s-90, 4818–5
- *Consumer Income*, socioeconomic characteristics of persons, families, and households, detailed cross-tabulations, Current Population Rpt series, 2546–6
- Deaths and rates, by cause, age, sex, marital status, and race, 1988, US Vital Statistics annual rpt, 4144–2.1
- Divorce property settlement, by type, whether child support and alimony received, and selected characteristics of woman, 1989, biennial Current Population Rpt, 2546–6.72
- Divorces by age of spouses and duration of marriage, and children involved, by State, 1988 and trends from 1940, US Vital Statistics advance annual rpt, 4146–5.121
- Educational attainment, by sociodemographic characteristics and location, 1989 and trends from 1940, biennial Current Population Rpt, 2546–1.452
- Family economic impacts of departure, absence, and presence of parents, 1983-86, Current Population Rpt, 2546–20.17
- Family economic impacts of departure, absence, and presence of parents, 1983-86, fact sheet, 2326–17.27
- Food spending, by item, household composition, income, age, race, and region, 1980-88, Consumer Expenditure Survey biennial rpt, 1544–30
- Foreign countries family composition, poverty status, labor conditions, and welfare indicators and needs, by country, 1960s-88, hearing, 23846–4.30
- Hispanic Americans social and economic characteristics, by detailed origin, 1991, Current Population Rpt, 2546–1.448; 2546–1.451
- Households and family characteristics, by location, 1990, annual Current Population Rpt, 2546–1.447

Index by Subjects and Names

Maryland

Households composition, income, benefits, and labor force status, Survey of Income and Program Participation methodology, working paper series, 2626–10

Housing characteristics of recent movers for new and previous unit, and household characteristics, by location, 1989, biennial rpt, 2485–12

Immigrant and nonimmigrant visas of US issued and refused, by class, issuing office, and nationality, FY89, annual rpt, 7184–1

Immigrants admitted to US, by class of admission and for top 15 countries of birth, FY89-90, fact sheet, 6266–2.4; 6266–2.8

Income (household) and poverty status under alternative income definitions, by recipient characteristics, 1990, annual Current Population Rpt, 2546–6.69

Infertility prevalence among women, by age and parity, with infertility services use, selected years 1965-88, 4146–8.194

Insurance (health) provided by employer, coverage offered to and chosen by families with 2 working spouses, 1977 and 1987, 4186–8.16

Living arrangements, family relationships, and marital status, by selected characteristics, 1990, annual Current Population Rpt, 2546–1.449

Marriage, marriage dissolution, remarriage, and cohabitation, for women, by age and race, 1988, 4146–8.196

Marriages and rates, by age, race, education, previous marital status, and State, 1988, US Vital Statistics advance annual rpt, 4146–5.122

Marriages, divorces, and rates, by characteristics of spouses, State, and county, 1987 and trends from 1920, US Vital Statistics annual rpt, 4144–4

Marriages, divorces, and rates, by State, preliminary 1989-90, US Vital Statistics annual rpt, 4144–7

Minority group and women health condition, services use, payment sources, and health care labor force, by poverty status, 1940s-89, chartbook, 4118–56

OASDI benefit payments, trust fund finances, and economic and demographic assumptions, 1970-90 and alternative projections to 2000, actuarial rpt, 4706–1.105

Population size and characteristics, historical index to *Current Population Rpts,* 1991 listing, 2546–2.160

Population size and characteristics, 1969-88, Current Population Rpt, biennial rpt, 2546–2.161

Railroad retirement benefits for divorced spouses, monthly rpt, 9702–2

Remarriage of divorced and widowed women, duration of singlehood, and redivorce, by age, 1985, Current Population Survey, 2546–2.157

Research on population and reproduction, Federal funding by project, FY89, annual listing, 4474–9

State and Metro Area Data Book, 1991 data compilation, 2328–54

Statistical Abstract of US, 1991 annual data compilation, 2324–1.1; 2324–1.2

Vital and Health Statistics series: reprints of monthly rpt supplements, 4147–24

Vital statistics provisional data, monthly rpt, 4142–1

see also Births out of wedlock

see also Child support and alimony

see also Families and households

see also Widows and widowers

see also under By Marital Status in the "Index by Categories"

Marshall Islands

Agricultural trade of US, by detailed commodity and country, 1989, annual rpt, 1524–8

Agricultural trade of US, by detailed commodity and country, 1990, semiannual rpt, 1522–4

Banks (insured commercial and savings) deposits by instn, State, MSA, and county, as of June 1990, annual regional rpt, 9295–3.6

Economic conditions, population characteristics, and Federal aid, for Pacific territories, 1989 hearing, 21448–44

Economic, social, political, and geographic summary data, by country, 1991, annual factbook, 9114–2

Exports and imports of US, by transport mode, country, and SITC 1- to 3-digit commodity, 1990, annual rpt, 2424–12

Exports of US, detailed Schedule B commodities with countries of destination, 1990, annual rpt, 2424–10

Human rights conditions in 170 countries, and US economic and military aid, 1990, annual rpt, 21384–3

Physicians, by specialty, age, sex, and location of training and practice, 1989, State rpt, 4116–6.53

Marshall, Tex.

see also under By SMSA or MSA in the "Index by Categories"

Marshals Service

see U.S. Marshals Service

Marshes

see Wetlands

Martin, George

"Price, Market Security Big Factors in Farmers' Selection of Milk Handler", 1122–1.206

Martin, Jack, and Co.

"Non-Certified Hospice Cost Analysis: Final Report", 4658–52

Martin, Jeffrey D.

"Description of the Physical Environment and Coal-Mining History of West-Central Indiana, with Emphasis on Six Small Watersheds", 5666–27.19

"Effects of Surface Coal Mining and Reclamation on the Geohydrology of Six Small Watersheds in West-Central Indiana", 5666–27.20

Martin, Michael

"Note on the Value of the Right Data", 1502–3.203

Martini, Alberto

"Wages and Employment Among the Working Poor: New Evidence from SIPP", 2626–10.122

Maryland

Appalachian Regional Commission funding, by project and State, planned FY91, annual rpt, 9084–3

Apple production, marketing, and prices, for Appalachia and compared to other States, 1988-91, annual rpt, 1311–13

Banks (insured commercial), Fed Reserve 5th District members financial statements, by State, quarterly rpt, 9389–18

Banks (insured commercial and savings) deposits by instn, State, MSA, and county, as of June 1990, annual regional rpt, 9295–3.2

Coal production and mines by county, prices, productivity, miners, and reserves, by mining method and State, 1989-90, annual rpt, 3164–25

County Business Patterns, 1989: employment, establishments, and payroll, by SIC 2- to 4-digit industry and county, annual State rpt, 2326–8.22

DOD prime contract awards, by contractor, service branch, State, and city, FY90, annual rpt, 3544–22

Economic indicators by State, Fed Reserve 5th District, quarterly rpt, 9389–16

Education system in Appalachia, improvement initiatives, and indicators of success, by State, 1960s-89, 9088–36

Employment and housing and mortgage market indicators by State, FHLB 4th District, quarterly rpt, 9302–36

Fed Govt spending in States and local areas, by type, State, county, and city, FY90, annual rpt, 2464–3

Fed Govt spending in States, by type, program, agency, and State, FY90, annual rpt, 2464–2

Forest wildlife habitat characteristics, by location, 1986, State rpt, 1206–44.5

HHS financial aid, by program, recipient, State, and city, FY90, annual regional listing, 4004–3.3

Hospital charges and length of stay for heart and lung patients with selected nonsurgical procedures, for Maryland, FY84, article, 4652–1.204

Hospital deaths of Medicare patients, actual and expected rates by diagnosis, and hospital characteristics, by instn, FY87-89, annual regional rpt, 4654–14.3

Hospital reimbursement by Medicare under prospective payment system, effect of including moveable equipment costs, with results for Maryland, FY89, 17206–2.24

Housing census, 1990: inventory, occupancy, and costs, State fact sheet, 2326–21.22

Income (personal) per capita and by source, and earnings by industry div, by State, MSA, and county, 1984-89, annual regional rpt, 2704–2.2

Jail adult and juvenile population, employment, spending, instn conditions, and inmate programs, by county and facility, 1988, regional rpt series, 6068–144.4

Marriages, divorces, and rates, by characteristics of spouses, State, and county, 1987 and trends from 1920, US Vital Statistics annual rpt, 4144–4

Mineral Industry Surveys, State reviews of production, 1990, preliminary annual rpt, 5614–6

Minerals Yearbook, 1989, Vol 2: State review of production and sales by commodity, and business activity, annual rpt, 5604–16.21

Minerals Yearbook, 1989, Vol 2: State reviews of production, sales, and firms, by commodity, and business activity, annual rpt, 5604–34

Maryland

Nursing home reimbursement by Medicaid, States payment ratesetting methods, analysis for 7 States, 1980s, article, 4652–1.255

Physicians, by specialty, age, sex, and location of training and practice, 1989, State rpt, 4116–6.21

Population and housing census, 1990: population and housing characteristics, households, and land area, by county, subdiv, and place, State rpt, 2551–1.22

Population and housing census, 1990: voting age and total population by race, and housing units, by block, redistricting counts required under PL 94-171, State CD-ROM release, 2551–6.6

Population and housing census, 1990: voting age and total population by race, and housing units, by county and city, redistricting counts required under PL 94-171, State summary rpt, 2551–5.21

Statistical Abstract of US, 1991 annual data compilation, 2324–1

Supplemental Security Income payments and beneficiaries, by type of eligibility, State, and county, Dec 1989, annual rpt, 4744–27.3

Timber biomass volume, by characteristics of tree and forest, and county, 1986, State rpt, 1206–43.3

Water quality, chemistry, hydrology, and other characteristics, 1990 local area study, 5666–27.22

Water resources dev projects of Army Corps of Engineers, characteristics, and costs, 1950s-89, biennial State rpt, 3756–1.21

Water supply and quality in streams and lakes, and groundwater levels in wells, by drainage basin, 1990, annual State rpt, 5666–10.19

Water use by end use, well withdrawals, and public supply deliveries, by county, 1986, State rpt, 5666–24.8

see also Baltimore, Md.

see also Montgomery County, Md.

see also Prince George's County, Md.

see also under By State in the "Index by Categories"

Masis, Kathleen B.

"Comprehensive Local Program for the Prevention of Fetal Alcohol Syndrome", 4042–3.239

Mass media

AIDS public knowledge and info sources, for blacks and Hispanics, 1987 local area survey, article, 4042–3.210

AIDS public knowledge, attitudes, info sources, and testing, for blacks, 1990 survey, 4146–8.208

AIDS public knowledge, attitudes, info sources, and testing, for Hispanics, 1990 survey, 4146–8.209

AIDS public knowledge, attitudes, info sources, and testing, 1990 survey, 4146–8.195; 4146–8.201; 4146–8.205

Alcohol use, knowledge, attitudes, and info sources of youth, series, 4006–10

Fed Govt audiovisual activities and spending, by whether performed in-house and agency, FY90, annual rpt, 9514–1

Statistical Abstract of US, 1991 annual data compilation, 2324–1.18

see also Advertising

see also Motion pictures

see also Newspapers

see also Periodicals

see also Public broadcasting

see also Radio

see also Television

Mass transit

see Airlines

see Buses

see National Railroad Passenger Corp.

see Railroads

see Subways

see Urban transportation

Massachusetts

Banks (insured commercial and savings) deposits by instn, State, MSA, and county, as of June 1990, annual regional rpt, 9295–3.1

Child injury rates, by presence of injury prevention education program for preschoolers, local area study, 1979-82, article, 4042–3.236

County Business Patterns, 1989: employment, establishments, and payroll, by SIC 2- to 4-digit industry and county, annual State rpt, 2326–8.23

Cranberry production, prices, use, and acreage, for selected States, 1989-90 and forecast 1991, annual rpt, 1621–18.4

DOD prime contract awards, by contractor, service branch, State, and city, FY90, annual rpt, 3544–22

Economic indicators for New England States, Fed Reserve 1st District, monthly rpt, 9373–2

Employment variability in New England relation to service and financial industries employment, with data by selected industry group and State, 1970s-89, article, 9373–1.212

Fed Govt spending in States and local areas, by type, State, county, and city, FY90, annual rpt, 2464–3

Fed Govt spending in States, by type, program, agency, and State, FY90, annual rpt, 2464–2

Health maintenance organizations and other prepaid managed care plans Medicaid enrollment and use, for 20 States, 1985-89, chartbook, 4108–29

HHS financial aid, by program, recipient, State, and city, FY90, annual regional listing, 4004–3.1

Hospital deaths of Medicare patients, actual and expected rates by diagnosis, and hospital characteristics, by instn, FY87-89, annual regional rpt, 4654–14.1

Housing prices economic impacts over business cycle expansion, for Massachusetts, 1984-87, article, 9373–1.216

Income (personal) per capita and by source, and earnings by industry div, by State, MSA, and county, 1984-89, annual regional rpt, 2704–2.2

Jail adult and juvenile population, employment, spending, instn conditions, and inmate programs, by county and facility, 1988, regional rpt series, 6068–144.2

Marriages, divorces, and rates, by characteristics of spouses, State, and county, 1987 and trends from 1920, US Vital Statistics annual rpt, 4144–4

Medicaid beneficiaries and payments by eligibility category, and savings from optional benefit elimination, for Massachusetts, FY89, article, 9373–1.203

Index by Subjects and Names

Mineral Industry Surveys, State reviews of production, 1990, preliminary annual rpt, 5614–6

Minerals Yearbook, 1989, Vol 2: State review of production and sales by commodity, and business activity, annual rpt, 5604–16.22

Minerals Yearbook, 1989, Vol 2: State reviews of production, sales, and firms, by commodity, and business activity, annual rpt, 5604–34

Physicians, by specialty, age, sex, and location of training and practice, 1989, State rpt, 4116–6.22

Population and housing census, 1990: population and housing characteristics, households, and land area, by county, subdiv, and place, State rpt, 2551–1.23

Population and housing census, 1990: voting age and total population by race, and housing units, by block, redistricting counts required under PL 94-171, State CD-ROM release, 2551–6.7

Population and housing census, 1990: voting age and total population by race, and housing units, by county and city, redistricting counts required under PL 94-171, State summary rpt, 2551–5.22

Public works funding in Massachusetts, financing sources, and employment, by function and authority, 1980s and projected to 2000, article, 9373–1.207

Savings instns, FHLB 1st District members financial operations compared to banks, and related economic and housing indicators, bimonthly rpt with articles, 9302–4

State govt employment and spending, by program, for Massachusetts, FY80-91, article, 9373–1.202

State govt spending and employment by program, revenues by source, debt, and public works financing, compared to other States, 1990 compilation of papers, 9373–4.27

Statistical Abstract of US, 1991 annual data compilation, 2324–1

Supplemental Security Income payments and beneficiaries, by type of eligibility, State, and county, Dec 1989, annual rpt, 4744–27.1

Tax (property) increase referenda and outcomes, and relation to community characteristics, FY81-91, article, 9373–1.208

Wages by occupation, for office and plant workers, 1991 survey, periodic labor market rpt, 6785–3.3

Water supply and quality in streams and lakes, and groundwater levels in wells, by drainage basin, 1989, annual State rpt, 5666–12.20

Water supply and quality in streams and lakes, and groundwater levels in wells, by drainage basin, 1990, annual State rpt, 5666–10.20

Water supply in northeastern US, precipitation and stream runoff by station, monthly rpt, 2182–3

Wetlands acreage, resources, soil and water properties, and conservation efforts, by wetland type, 1989 State rpt, 5506–11.6

Wetlands and riparian soil and plant characteristics, 1990 rpt, 5506–10.12

see also Attleboro, Mass.
see also Boston, Mass.
see also Gloucester, Mass.
see also Lawrence, Mass.
see also Middlesex County, Mass.
see also New Bedford, Mass.
see also Salem, Mass.
see also under By State in the "Index by Categories"

Mast, Richard F.

"Estimates of Undiscovered Recoverable Conventional Oil and Gas Resources Beneath Onshore Wilderness Lands in the U.S.", 3166–6.51

Masterson, Nancy

"U.S. Refining Industry", 3164–2.1

Mataloni, Raymond J., Jr.

"Capital Expenditures by Majority-Owned Foreign Affiliates of U.S. Companies, Latest Plans for 1991", 2702–1.207

"U.S. Direct Investment Abroad: 1989 Benchmark Survey Results", 2702–1.225

Maternity

- Abortions, by method, pregnancy history, and other characteristics of woman, 1988, US Vital Statistics annual rpt, 4146–5.120
- Africa (sub-Saharan) AIDS epidemic impacts on population size and components of change, model description and results, 1990-2015, working paper, 2326–18.57
- AIDS cases by race, sex, and risk category, and deaths and survivors, projected 1989-93, 4206–2.34
- Births, fertility rates, and childless women, by selected characteristics, 1990, annual Current Population Rpt, 2546–1.455
- Cancer (breast) precursor hormonal changes risk relation to selected reproductive factors, 1983-89 study, article, 4472–1.227
- Chlamydia infection among pregnant women, and pregnancy outcomes, 1986-88 local area study, article, 4042–3.240
- Deaths and rates, by cause and age, preliminary 1989-90, US Vital Statistics annual rpt, 4144–7
- Deaths and rates, by cause, provisional data, monthly rpt, 4142–1.2
- Deaths related to pregnancy, and rates, by detailed cause and demographic characteristics, 1988, US Vital Statistics annual rpt, 4144–2
- Deaths related to pregnancy, by race, 1940s-86, chartbook, 4118–56
- Deaths related to pregnancy, rates, and risk, by pregnancy outcome, cause, and maternal characteristics, 1979-86, article, 4202–7.206
- Diabetes cases among pregnant Indian and Alaska Native women, by Indian Health Service area, 1981-85, 4088–2
- Disability related to pregnancy, absenteeism, and health services use, by selected characteristics, 1987, CD-ROM, 4147–10.177
- Drug abuse and treatment, research on biological and behavioral factors and addiction potential of new drugs, 1990 annual conf, 4494–11
- Drug abuse during pregnancy, States reporting policies and status of treatment funding, 1990, article, 4042–3.220
- Drug abuse prevalence among minorities, related health effects and crime, treatment, and research status and needs, mid 1970s-90, 4498–72
- Drug, alcohol, and cigarette use and quit rates among young pregnant women, by marital status, aggregate 1984-88, annual rpt, 4494–4
- Ectopic pregnancies and related deaths, by race, age, and region, 1970-87, article, 4202–7.202
- Genital human papillomavirus risk relation to presence of other cervical cancer risk factors, local area study, 1991 article, 4472–1.215
- Health condition and health care resources, use, and spending, 1950s-89, annual data compilation, 4144–11
- Health condition improvement and disease prevention goals and recommended activities for 2000, with trends 1970s-80s, 4048–10
- Homeless persons alcohol abuse, by sex, age, race, and additional diagnoses, aggregate 1985-87, 4488–14
- Hospital discharges and length of stay, by diagnosis, patient and instn characteristics, procedure performed, and payment source, 1988, annual rpt, 4147–13.107
- Hospital discharges and length of stay by region and diagnosis, and procedures performed, by age and sex, 1989, annual rpt, 4146–8.198
- Hospital discharges by detailed diagnostic and procedure category, primary diagnosis, and length of stay, by age, sex, and region, 1988, annual rpt, 4147–13.105; 4147–13.108
- Indian and Alaska Native disease and disorder cases, deaths, and health services use, by tribe, reservation, and Indian Health Service area, late 1950s-86, 4088–2
- Indian Health Service facilities and use, and Indian health and other characteristics, by IHS region, 1980s-89, annual chartbook, 4084–7
- Indian Health Service facilities, funding, operations, and Indian health and other characteristics, 1950s-90, annual chartbook, 4084–1
- Lead levels in environment, sources of emissions and exposure, and health effects, literature review, 1990 rpt, 9198–84
- Minority group health condition, services use, costs, and indicators of services need, 1950s-88, 4118–55
- Poor women's pregnancies, by whether intended, outcome, contraceptives use, marital status, and race, 1985-86 local area study, article, 4042–3.241
- Rubella vaccination of children and women of childbearing age, and surveillance, CDC guidelines, 1990 rpt, 4206–2.33
- Smoking during pregnancy, by age, race, education, marital status, and birth order, 1970s-80s, article, 4042–3.203
- Smoking exposure of children before and after birth, by source and degree of exposure and family characteristics, 1988, 4146–8.204
- *Statistical Abstract of US,* 1991 annual data compilation, 2324–1.2

see also Birth defects
see also Births
see also Births out of wedlock
see also Birthweight
see also Breast-feeding
see also Family planning
see also Fertility
see also Fetal deaths
see also Infant mortality
see also Maternity benefits
see also Midwives
see also Obstetrics and gynecology
see also Prenatal care
see also Teenage pregnancy

Maternity benefits

- Assistance (financial and nonfinancial) of Fed Govt, 1991 base edition with supplements, annual listing, 104–5
- Employee benefit plan coverage, by benefit type and worker characteristics, late 1970s-80s, 15496–1.11
- Employee leave for illness, disability, and dependent care, coverage, provisions, terminations, costs, and methods of covering for absent worker, by firm size, 1988 survey, 9768–21
- Food aid program of USDA for women, infants, and children, health services need of participants, for Rhode Island, 1983-84, article, 4042–3.247
- Food aid program of USDA for women, infants, and children, participants and costs by State and Indian agency, FY88, annual tables, 1364–12
- Food aid program of USDA for women, infants, and children, participants by race, State, and Indian agency, Apr 1990, annual rpt, 1364–16
- Food aid program of USDA for women, infants, and children, participants, clinics, and costs, by State and Indian agency, monthly tables, 1362–16
- Food aid program of USDA for women, infants, and children, prenatal participation effect on Medicaid costs and birth outcomes, for 5 States, 1987-88, 1368–2
- Food aid programs of USDA, costs and participation by program, FY69-89, annual rpt, 1364–9
- Food stamp use at farmers markets, costs and participation, demonstration project results for 14 States, 1989, hearing, 21168–46
- Labor laws enacted, by State, 1990, annual article, 6722–1.209
- Medicaid coverage effects on prenatal care use and birth outcomes, charges, and Medicaid payments, for California, 1983, article, 4652–1.241
- Medicaid prenatal care eligibility and availability, by State, 1987-90, article, 4652–1.213
- Small business employees benefit plan coverage and provisions, by plan type and occupational group, 1990, biennial rpt, 6784–20
- State and local govt employees benefit plan coverage, by benefit type, 1990, press release, 6726–1.41
- Urban areas health depts programs for mothers and children, activities and budgets, 1990, listing, 4108–51

Mathematic models and modeling

Index by Subjects and Names

Mathematic models and modeling

AIDS epidemic impacts on population size and components of change, for sub-Saharan Africa, model description and results, 1990-2015, working paper, 2326–18.57

Alaska economic and demographic impacts of energy resources dev, model description and results for Nome, 1980s and projected to 2010, 5736–5.13

Alaska rural areas population characteristics, and energy resources dev effects, series, 5736–5

Beef packing and processing plant operating costs, model methodology and results, 1988, 1568–301

Carbon dioxide in atmosphere, North Central States economic and agricultural impacts, model descriptions and results, 1980s and projected to 2030, 3006–11.15

Criminal justice system workload impacts of budgetary changes, model description, 1991 GAO rpt, 26119–340

Energy Info Admin forecasting and data analysis models, 1991, annual listing, 3164–87

Energy supply, demand, distribution, and regulatory impacts, series, 3166–6

Farm operators age and off-farm employment, sales, and land value changes relationship to farm sales size, model description and results, 1974-78, 1548–374

Fertilizer and cropland demand impacts of proposed environmental regulation, model description and inputs, 1964-89, 1588–152

Forest mgmt effects on timber, wildlife, and water resources supply and use, model description and results, 1980s-2030, 1208–24.19

Global climate change environmental, infrastructure, and health impacts, with model results and background data, 1850s-2100, 9188–113

Medicaid services use and costs in alternative treatment settings, model description and results, FY87, article, 4652–1.211

Radiation exposure of population near Hanford, Wash, nuclear plant, with methodology, 1944-66, series, 3356–5

Timber survival rates in northeastern US, by species, model description and results, 1990 rpt, 1208–369

Unemployment insurance programs of States and Fed Govt, benefits adequacy, and work disincentives, series, 6406–6

Weather forecasts accuracy evaluations, for US, UK, and European systems, quarterly rpt, 2182–8

Wheat and corn stocks, demand impacts of storage subsidy programs, model description and results, 1972-87, 1548–378

Wheat summer feed and residual use, alternative models description and results, 1991 article, 1561–12.203

see also Economic and econometric models

Mathematica Policy Research, Inc.

"National Medicare Competition Evaluation: An Evaluation of the Quality of the Process of Care. Final Analysis Report", 4658–46

"New Jersey Unemployment Insurance Reemployment Demonstration Project Follow-Up Report", 6406–6.32

"Savings in Medicaid Costs for Newborns and Their Mothers from Prenatal Participation in the WIC Program", 1368–2

"Wages and Employment Among the Working Poor: New Evidence from SIPP", 2626–10.122

Mathematics

Bilingual education and English immersion programs activities, structure, and effectiveness, 1984-88 longitudinal study, 4808–27

Condition of Education, detail for elementary and secondary education, 1920s-90 and projected to 2001, annual rpt, 4824–1.1

Degrees (PhD) in science and engineering, by field, instn, employment prospects, sex, race, and other characteristics, 1960s-90, annual rpt, 9627–30

Degrees awarded in higher education, by level, field, race, and sex, 1988/89 with trends from 1978/79, biennial rpt, 4844–17

Degrees awarded in science and engineering, by field, level, and sex, 1966-89, 9627–33

DOD Dependents Schools basic skills and college entrance test scores, 1990-91, annual rpt, 3504–16

Education data compilation, 1991 annual rpt, 4824–2

Eighth grade class of 1988: educational performance and conditions, characteristics, attitudes, activities, and plans, natl longitudinal survey, series, 4826–9

Elementary and secondary students educational performance in math, science, reading, and writing, 1970s-90, 4898–32

Elementary and secondary students math performance and factors affecting proficiency, by selected characteristics, 1990 natl assessments, 4896–8.1

Elementary and secondary students math performance by State and selected characteristics, 1990 natl assessments, 4896–8.2

Employment and other characteristics of science and engineering PhDs, by field and State, 1989, biennial rpt, 9627–18

Employment, unemployment, and labor force characteristics, by region and census div, 1990, annual rpt, 6744–7.1

Fed Govt aid to higher education and nonprofit instns for R&D and related activities, by field, instn, agency, and State, FY89, annual rpt, 9627–17

Foreign and US funding for R&D, and scientists and engineering employment and education, 1991 annual rpt, 9627–35.1

Gifted minority students science and math education programs, participation and outcomes, 1981-88 study, 4808–34

High school advanced placement for college credit, programs by selected characteristics and school control, 1984-86, 4838–46

Higher education course completions, by detailed program, sex, race, and instn type, for 1972 high school class, as of 1984, 4888–4

Higher education grad programs enrollment in science and engineering, by field, source of funds, and characteristics of student and instn, 1975-89, annual rpt, 9627–7

Higher education remedial programs, enrollment, courses, and faculty, by instn characteristics, 1989/90, 4826–1.30

Migrant workers children education programs enrollment, staff, and effectiveness, by State, 1980s, 4808–30

NASA R&D funding to higher education instns, by field, instn, and State, FY90, annual listing, 9504–7

Natl Education Goals progress indicators, by State, 1991, annual rpt, 15914–1

NSF activities, finances, and funding by program, FY90, annual rpt, 9624–6

NSF grants for science, engineering, and math education, by recipient and level, FY89, biennial listing, 9624–27

Poverty area schools academic environment and teaching methods impacts on student performance, 1989/90 study, 4808–28

R&D funding by Fed Govt, by field, performer type, agency, and State, FY89-91, annual rpt, 9627–20

R&D funding by higher education instns and federally funded centers, by field, instn, and State, FY89, annual rpt, 9627–13

Teachers of science and math, professional dev project funding of Fed Govt, participation, operations, and effectiveness, 1985-90, 4808–31

see also Computer sciences

see also Mathematic models and modeling

see also Statisticians

Mathews, Kenneth H., Jr.

"Production Profile of Sorghum Producers: Government Program Participants vs Nonparticipants", 1541–1.210

Matsui, Tetsuo

"Biology and Potential Use of Pacific Grenadier, *Coryphaenoides acrolepis*, Off California", 2162–1.204

Matten, Marlene R.

"Nurses' Knowledge, Attitudes, and Beliefs Regarding Organ and Tissue Donation and Transplantation", 4042–3.214

Mattoon, Richard H.

"Balancing Act: Tax Structure in the Seventh District", 9375–1.211

Mattresses

see Furniture and furnishings

Maurer, Jeffrey D.

"Deaths of Hispanic Origin, 15 Reporting States, 1979-81. Vital and Health Statistics Series 20", 4147–20.18

Mauritania

Agricultural exports of high-value commodities, indexes and sales by commodity, world area, and country, 1960s-86, 1528–323

Agricultural trade of US, by detailed commodity and country, 1989, annual rpt, 1524–8

Agricultural trade of US, by detailed commodity and country, 1990, semiannual rpt, 1522–4

AID economic aid to developing countries, obligations and disbursements by country, quarterly rpt, 9912–4

Dairy imports, consumption, and market conditions, by sub-Saharan Africa country, 1961-88, 1528–321

Index by Subjects and Names

Economic and military aid and loans from US and intl agencies, by program and country, FY46-90, annual rpt, 9914–5

Economic and social conditions of developing countries from 1960s, and Intl Dev Cooperation Agency and AID activities and funding, FY90-92, annual rpt, 9904–4

Economic conditions, income, production, prices, employment, and trade, 1990 periodic country rpt, 2046–4.4

Economic, population, and agricultural data, US and other aid sources, and AID activity, 1989 country rpt, 9916–12.34

Economic, social, political, and geographic summary data, by country, 1991, annual factbook, 9114–2

Exports and imports of US, by transport mode, country, and SITC 1- to 3-digit commodity, 1990, annual rpt, 2424–12

Exports of US, detailed Schedule B commodities with countries of destination, 1990, annual rpt, 2424–10

Grain production, use, imports, and stocks, for Sahel region by country, 1989/90, 9918–18

Human rights conditions in 170 countries, and US economic and military aid, 1990, annual rpt, 21384–3

UN voting record and share of votes in agreement with US, by issue, country, and world area, 1990, annual rpt, 7004–18

see also under By Foreign Country in the "Index by Categories"

Mauritius

Agricultural exports of high-value commodities, indexes and sales by commodity, world area, and country, 1960s-86, 1528–323

Agricultural trade of US, by detailed commodity and country, 1989, annual rpt, 1524–8

Agricultural trade of US, by detailed commodity and country, 1990, semiannual rpt, 1522–4

AID economic aid to developing countries, obligations and disbursements by country, quarterly rpt, 9912–4

Dairy imports, consumption, and market conditions, by sub-Saharan Africa country, 1961-88, 1528–321

Economic and military aid and loans from US and intl agencies, by program and country, FY46-90, annual rpt, 9914–5

Economic and social conditions of developing countries from 1960s, and Intl Dev Cooperation Agency and AID activities and funding, FY90-92, annual rpt, 9904–4

Economic, social, political, and geographic summary data, by country, 1991, annual factbook, 9114–2

Exports and imports of US, by transport mode, country, and SITC 1- to 3-digit commodity, 1990, annual rpt, 2424–12

Exports of US, detailed Schedule B commodities with countries of destination, 1990, annual rpt, 2424–10

Human rights conditions in 170 countries, and US economic and military aid, 1990, annual rpt, 21384–3

Military aid of US, arms sales, and training programs costs and budget requests, by program, world region, and country, FY90-92, annual rpt, 7144–13

UN voting record and share of votes in agreement with US, by issue, country, and world area, 1990, annual rpt, 7004–18

see also under By Foreign Country in the "Index by Categories"

Max, Timothy A.

"Statistical Estimators for Monitoring Spotted Owls in Oregon and Washington in 1987", 1208–342

May, Daniel S.

"Surveillance of Major Causes of Hospitalization Among the Elderly, 1988", 4202–7.205

May, Dennis M.

"Midsouth Veneer Industry", 1208–43

"Status and Trends in Gypsy Moth Defoliation Hazard in Tennessee", 1208–344

May, Philip A.

"Comprehensive Local Program for the Prevention of Fetal Alcohol Syndrome", 4042–3.239

Mayaguez, P.R.

see also under By SMSA or MSA in the "Index by Categories"

Mayes, Fred, Jr.

"Annual Prospects for World Coal Trade, 1991", 3164–77

Mayfield, Max

"North Atlantic Hurricanes, 1990", 2152–8.202

McAllen, Tex.

see also under By SMSA or MSA in the "Index by Categories"

McAndrews, James J.

"Evolution of Shared ATM Networks", 9387–1.203

"Worker Debt with Bankruptcy", 9387–8.241

McArthur, Edith

"Family Disruption and Economic Hardship: The Short-Run Picture for Children", 2546–20.17

McArthur, Timmie S.

"Tax Amnesty, Improving Compliance?", 8304–8.1

McAuliffe, Paul

"World Wheat Outlook, 1990/91", 1004–16.1

McBride, Timothy

"Spells Without Health Insurance: Distributions of Durations and Their Link to Point-in-Time Estimates of the Uninsured", 2626–10.142

"Spells Without Health Insurance: What Affects Spell Duration and Who Are the Chronically Uninsured?", 2626–10.141

McCaskill, Von

"Fertilizer and Pesticide Use and the Environment", 1004–16.1

McCauley, Robert N.

"Bank Cost of Capital and International Competition", 9385–1.203

"British Invasion: Explaining the Strength of UK Acquisitions of U.S. Firms in the Late 1980's", 9385–8.82

"Cost of Capital for Securities Firms in the U.S. and Japan", 9385–1.212

"Policies Toward Corporate Leveraging", 9385–8.88

McClelland, Robert

"Effects of Government Transfer Payments on Charitable Contributions", 6886–6.76

McKay, Steven F.

McCormick, Ian

"Canola: Prospects for an Emerging Market", 1561–3.203

"Minor Oilseeds and the 1990 Farm Bill: Rules, Regulations, and Initial Impacts", 1561–3.202

"Sunflower Acreage Response to Increased Commodity Program Flexibility", 1561–3.201

McCoy, John L.

"Predictors of Mortality Among Newly Retired Workers", 4742–1.206

McDermott, Kevin

"Cotton in a World of Change", 1004–16.1

McDowell, Bruce D.

"Grant Reform Reconsidered", 10042–1.202

McDowell, Howard

"U.S. Milk Markets Under Alternative Federal Order Pricing Policies", 1568–294

McDowell, Lena

"Public Elementary and Secondary Schools and Agencies in the U.S. and Outlying Areas: School Year 1989-90. Final Tabulations", 4834–17

McFadden, Karen

"Comparison of Urinalysis Technologies for Drug Testing in Criminal Justice", 6066–26.6

McGregor, Elizabeth

"Entry Level Jobs: Defining Them and Counting Them", 6742–1.201

McGuire, Sumiye O.

"Foreign Direct Investment in the U.S., Review and Analysis of Current Developments", 2004–9

McGuire, Thomas E.

"Evaluation of Diagnosis-Related Group Severity and Complexity Refinement", 4652–1.245

McGurk, Michael

"Early Life History of Pacific Herring: 1989 Prince William Sound Herring Egg Incubation Experiment", 2176–1.37

"Early Life History of Pacific Herring: 1989 Prince William Sound Herring Larvae Survey", 2176–1.37

McHugh, Patrick

"SEAS III and Beyond", 2152–8.203

MCI Communications

Fiber optics and copper wire mileage and access lines, and fiber systems investment, by telecommunications firm, 1985-90, annual rpt, 9284–18

Finances and operations of local and long distance firms, subscribership, and charges, late 1970s-91, semiannual rpt, 9282–7

Intl telecommunications operations of US carriers, finances, rates, and traffic by service type, firm, and country, 1975-89, annual rpt, 9284–17

McIntire, Robert J.

"New Seasonal Adjustment Factors for Household Data Series", 6742–2.205

"Revision of Seasonally Adjusted Labor Force Series", 6742–2.201

McKay, Steven F.

"Short-Range Actuarial Projections of the Old-Age, Survivors, and Disability Insurance Program, 1991", 4706–1.105

McKinney Homeless Assistance Act

McKinney Homeless Assistance Act
Assistance for homeless of Fed Govt, program descriptions and funding, by agency and State, FY90, annual GAO rpt, 26104–21

Assistance for homeless persons, Federal housing and food programs funding and operations, FY89, hearing, 25408–111

Fed Govt funding for homelessness services and prevention, with bibl, 1991 compilation of papers, 25928–9

Fed Govt surplus property donated to homeless aid organizations by State, and compared to other recipients, FY87-90, GAO rpt, 26113–538

McLean, Craig
"Soviet-American Sail, 1990", 2152–8.202

McLean, Garnet
"Selection Criteria for Alcohol Detection Methods", 7506–10.91

McLemore, Thomas
"1977 Summary: National Ambulatory Medical Care Survey", 4147–16.5

McLeod, Darryl
"North American Free Trade and the Peso: The Case for a North American Currency Area", 9379–12.77

McLeroy, Kenneth R.
"Nationwide Evaluation of Medicaid Competition Demonstrations. Volume 5. Access and Satisfaction", 4658–45.5

McManus, Douglas A.
"Effects of Closure Policies on Bank Risk-Taking", 9366–6.272

McMillan, Alma
"Trends and Patterns in Place of Death for Medicare Enrollees", 4652–1.201

McMillen, Marilyn M.
"Diversity of Private Schools. Schools and Staffing Survey", 4836–3.7
"Private Schools in the U.S.: A Statistical Profile, with Comparisons to Public Schools", 4838–47

McNally, James W.
"AIDS-Related Knowledge and Behavior Among Women 15-44 Years of Age: U.S., 1988", 4146–8.200

McNees, Stephen K.
"How Fast Can We Grow?", 9373–1.201
"'Whither New England?'", 9373–1.211

McNulty, James E.
"Estimating the Minimum Risk Maturity Gap", 9371–10.65

McNutt, Barry
"Energy Conservation Trends: Understanding the Factors That Affect Conservation Gains in the U.S. Economy", 3308–93

McWilliams, William H.
"Forest Statistics for Southeast Alabama Counties, 1990", 1206–30.9
"Forest Statistics for Southwest-South Alabama Counties, 1990", 1206–30.8

Meade, Ellen E.
"Using External Sustainability To Forecast the Dollar", 9366–7.252

Meade, Norman F.
"Socioeconomic Profile of Recreationists at Public Outdoor Recreation Sites in Coastal Areas: Volume 1. Public Area Recreation Visitors Survey", 2176–9.1

Measles
see Infective and parasitic diseases

Index by Subjects and Names

Measures
see Industrial standards
see Instruments and measuring devices
see Weights and measures

Meat and meat products
Agricultural Statistics, 1990, annual rpt, 1004–1

Agriculture census, 1987: farms, farmland, production, finances, and operator characteristics, by county, final State rpt series, 2331–1

Beef (choice) price and price spread data series revisions, with methodology, 1970s-90, 1568–295

Beef packing and processing plant operating costs, model methodology and results, 1988, 1568–301

Business statistics, detailed data for major industries and economic indicators, *Survey of Current Business*, monthly rpt, 2702–1.14

Cancer (lung) risk of meat handlers, by job tenure and occupation, as of 1986, local area study, article, 4472–1.223

Cold storage food stocks by commodity and census div, and warehouse space use, by State, monthly rpt, 1631–5

Cold storage food stocks by commodity, and warehouse space use, by census div, 1990, annual rpt, 1631–11

Consumer Expenditure Survey, food spending by item, household composition, income, age, race, and region, 1980-88, biennial rpt, 1544–30

Consumer Expenditure Survey, household income by source, and itemized spending, by selected characteristics and region, 1988-89, annual rpt, 6764–5

Consumption of food, dietary composition, and nutrient intake, 1987/88 natl survey, preliminary rpt series, 1356–1

Consumption, supply, trade, prices, spending, and indexes, by food commodity, 1989, annual rpt, 1544–4

County Business Patterns, 1988: employment, establishments, and payroll, by SIC 2- to 4-digit industry and county, annual State rpt series, 2326–6

County Business Patterns, 1989: employment, establishments, and payroll, by SIC 2- to 4-digit industry and county, annual State rpt series, 2326–8

CPI by component for US city average, and by region, population size, and for 27 metro areas, monthly rpt, 6762–2

Employment, earnings, and hours, by SIC 1- to 4-digit industry, monthly and annual averages, selected years 1909-90, annual rpt, 6744–4

Enterprise Statistics, 1987: finances and operations for companies, by size, level of diversification, form of organization, and industry group, 2329–8

Exports and imports (agricultural) commodity and country, prices, and world market devs, monthly rpt, 1922–12

Exports and imports (agricultural) of US, by commodity and country, bimonthly rpt, 1522–1

Exports and imports (agricultural) of US, by detailed commodity and country, 1989, annual rpt, 1524–8

Exports and imports (agricultural) of US, by detailed commodity and country, 1990, semiannual rpt, 1522–4

Exports and imports between US and outlying areas, by detailed commodity and mode of transport, 1990, annual rpt, 2424–11

Exports and imports of dairy, livestock, and poultry products, by commodity and country, FAS monthly circular, 1925–32

Exports and imports of US, by country and detailed commodity, monthly rpt, 2422–12

Exports and imports of US, by Harmonized System 6-digit commodity and country, 1990, annual rpt, 2424–13

Exports and imports of US, by transport mode, country, and SITC 1- to 3-digit commodity, 1990, annual rpt, 2424–12

Exports of US, detailed Schedule B commodities with countries of destination, 1990, annual rpt, 2424–10

Foreign and US agricultural production, prices, trade, and use, periodic rpt with articles, 1522–3

Foreign and US dairy production, trade, and use, by selected country, FAS semiannual circular series, 1925–33

Foreign countries agricultural production, prices, and trade, by country, 1980-90 and forecast 1991, annual world area rpt series, 1524–4

Foreign countries agricultural production, trade, and policies, summary data by country, 1989-90, annual factbook, 1924–12

Futures and options trading volume, by commodity and exchange, FY90, annual rpt, 11924–2

Futures trading in selected commodities and financial instruments and indexes, NYC, Chicago, and other markets activity, semimonthly rpt, 11922–5

Imports of meat under Meat Import Act, by country of origin, FAS monthly rpt, dropped data, 1925–31

Inspection and certification of meat plants for export to US, by country, 1990, annual listing, 1374–2

Inspection of meat and poultry, Federal, State, and foreign govts activities and staff, FY90, annual rpt, 1374–1

Labor productivity, indexes of output, hours, and employment by SIC 2- to 4-digit industry, 1967-89, annual rpt, 6824–1.3

Lamb meat from Australia and New Zealand, US industry intl competitiveness, investigation with background financial and operating data and foreign comparisons, 1990 rpt, 9886–4.166

Manufacturing annual survey, 1989: finances and operations, by SIC 2- to 4-digit industry, series, 2506–15

Manufacturing census, 1987: finances and operations, by SIC 2- to 4-digit industry, State, and MSA, with trends from 1849, 2497–1

Manufacturing census, 1987: finances and operations, by type of organization and SIC 2- to 4-digit industry, subject rpt, 2497–5

Manufacturing finances and operations, by SIC 2- to 4-digit industry, forecast 1991, annual rpt, 2044–28

Marketing data for livestock, meat, and wool, by species and market, weekly rpt, 1315–1

Index by Subjects and Names

Medicaid

Nutrient, caloric, and waste composition, detailed data for raw, processed, and prepared foods, 1991 rpt, 1356–3.15

Occupational injury and illness rates, by SIC 2- to 4-digit industry, 1988-89, annual rpt, 6844–7

Occupational injury and illness rates, by SIC 2- to 4-digit industry, 1989, annual rpt, 6844–1

OECD trade, total and for 4 major countries, and US trade by country, by commodity, 1970-89, world area rpt series, 9116–1

Pork consumption revised estimation factors, with retail and boneless cuts consumption, 1950s-90, article, 1561–7.201

Pork from Canada, injury to US industry from foreign subsidized imports, investigation supplement, 1991 rpt, 9886–15.77

Price indexes (producer), by stage of processing and detailed commodity, monthly rpt, 6762–6

Price indexes (producer), by stage of processing and detailed commodity, monthly 1990, annual rpt, 6764–2

Prices (farm-retail) for food, marketing cost components, and industry finances and productivity, 1920s-90, annual rpt, 1544–9

Prices (producer and retail) of meat and fish, 1981-91, semiannual situation rpt, 1561–15.3

Production of meat and livestock slaughter, by livestock type and State, monthly rpt, 1623–9

Production of meat, by species and State, 1990, annual rpt, 1623–10

Production, prices, receipts, and disposition for meat animals, by species and State, 1988-90, annual rpt, 1623–8

Production, prices, trade, and marketing, by commodity, current situation and forecast, monthly rpt with articles, 1502–4

Production, prices, trade, and stocks, monthly rpt, 1561–17

Production, prices, trade, stocks, and use, periodic situation rpt with articles, 1561–7

Puerto Rico economic censuses, 1987: wholesale, retail, and service industries finances and operations, by establishment characteristics and SIC 2- and 3-digit industry, subject rpts, 2591–2

Retail trade census, 1987: finances and employment, for establishments with and without payroll, by SIC 2- to 4-digit kind of business, State, and MSA, 2401–1

Retail trade sales and inventories, by kind of business, region, and selected State, MSA, and city, monthly rpt, 2413–3

Retail trade sales, inventories, purchases, gross margin, and accounts receivable, by SIC 2- to 4-digit kind of business and form of ownership, 1989, annual rpt, 2413–5

Soviet Union agricultural trade, by commodity and country, 1955-90, 1528–322

Soviet Union GNP by component and industry sector, and CIA estimation methods, 1950s-87, 23848–223

Statistical Abstract of US, 1991 annual data compilation, 2324–1.23

Supply and demand indicators for livestock and dairy products, and for selected foreign and US crops, monthly rpt, 1522–5

Tax (income) returns of corporations, income and tax items by asset size and detailed industry, 1987, annual rpt, 8304–4

Tax (income) returns of corporations, income and tax items by asset size and detailed industry, 1988, annual rpt, 8304–21

Wholesale trade census, 1987: establishments, sales by customer class, employment, inventories, and expenses, by SIC 2- to 4-digit kind of business, 2407–4

see also Oils, oilseeds, and fats

see also Poultry industry and products

see also under By Commodity in the "Index by Categories"

Meat Import Act

Imports of meat under Act, by country of origin, FAS monthly rpt, dropped data, 1925–31

Mecklenburg County, N.C.

Water quality, chemistry, hydrology, and other characteristics, 1989 local area study, 5666–27.11

Meckstroth, Alicia

"Private Foundation Returns, 1986 and 1987", 8302–2.210

Medals

see Awards, medals, and prizes

see Military awards, decorations, and medals

Medford, Oreg.

Housing vacancy rates for single and multifamily units and mobile homes, by city and ZIP code, 1991, annual MSA rpt, 9304–21.4

Wages by occupation, for office and plant workers, 1991 survey, periodic MSA rpt, 6785–3.6

see also under By SMSA or MSA in the "Index by Categories"

Media

see Mass media

Mediation

see Legal arbitration and mediation

Medicaid

Accessibility of health care, persons with and without usual care source by selected characteristics, 1987, 4186–8.22

Adult day care centers revenue by source, and expenses by type, by agency type, FY86, article, 4652–1.234

AFDC families leaving program, transitional Medicaid benefits program operations and subsequent medical costs, for 2 States, 1980s, article, 4652–1.217

AIDS and AIDS virus infection patients service use and costs under Medicaid, 1991, article, 4652–1.215

AIDS patient home and community services under Medicaid waiver in 6 States, 1988-89, article, 4652–1.216

AIDS patient hospital use and charges, by hospital and patient characteristics, and payment source, 1986-87, 4186–6.15

Beneficiaries and program operations, for Medicare and Medicaid, 1991, annual fact book, 4654–18

Beneficiaries, eligibility, coverage, and program finances, for Medicare and Medicaid, various periods 1966-91, biennial rpt, 4654–1

Beneficiary service use and costs by service type and eligibility, for Medicaid, 1975-89, article, 4652–1.209

Benefits and beneficiaries, by eligibility and service type, FY89, biennial article, 4742–1.217

Benefits, beneficiary characteristics, and trust funds of OASDHI, Medicaid, SSI, and related programs, selected years 1937-89, annual rpt, 4744–3

Benefits, trust fund finances, and services use, for Medicare and Medicaid, 1966-89 and projected to 1995, 21148–61

Birth outcomes and prenatal care use effects of Medicaid coverage, charges, and Medicaid payments, for California, 1983, article, 4652–1.241

Budget of US, CBO analysis of revenue and spending alternatives and projections of economic indicators, FY92-96, annual rpt, 26304–3

Budget of US, CBO analysis of savings and revenues under alternative spending cuts and tax changes, projected FY92-97, 26306–3.118

Census of Population data use in Federal formula grant allocation, and effects of data errors on funding, with data by program and State, FY91, GAO rpt, 26119–361

Child preventive health care visits, exams, and immunizations under Medicaid, for California, 1981-84, article, 4652–1.214

Computer records matching of welfare data, Federal and State agencies compliance with recipient protection provisions before benefits reduction, 1990, GAO rpt, 26121–404

Costs and use of health care, methodology and findings of natl survey and Medicare and Medicaid records, 1980, series, 4146–12

Coverage (universal) under natl health insurance, alternative proposals and indicators of need, 1989, 4658–54

Coverage expansion for Medicaid and employer-provided insurance plans under alternative proposals, and uninsured population characteristics, 1991 rpt, 26306–6.157

Coverage loss impacts on health services use, California transfer of selected Medicaid groups to county care, 1991 article, 4652–1.242

Coverage under health insurance, by insurance type and selected characteristics, 1989, 4146–8.203

Coverage under health insurance by source, and services reimbursed by type, 1991 rpt, 26306–6.155

Demonstration projects for Medicaid, evaluation for 6 States, 1988 rpt, 4658–45

Disabled low income enrollees and eligibility provisions under Medicaid and Medicare, by State, 1975-89, article, 4652–1.218

Disabled Medicare enrollees supplementary health insurance coverage, by enrollee characteristics, 1984, article, 4652–1.243

Eligibility and payment provisions for SSI and Medicaid, by State, 1991, annual rpt, 4704–13

Eligibility expansion provisions, adoption by States, and impacts on Medicaid service use and costs, 1984-89, GAO rpt, 26121–429

Medicaid

Index by Subjects and Names

Emergency room visits by Medicaid patients relation to availability of other sources of care, for upstate New York, 1985-87, article, 4652–1.232

Expenditures for health care by businesses, households, and govts, 1965-89, article, 4652–1.230

Expenditures for health care, by service type, payment source, and sector, projected 1990-2000 and trends from 1965, article, 4652–1.251

Expenditures for health care, by service type, payment source, and sector, 1960s-90, annual article, 4652–1.221; 4652–1.252

Expenditures for health care by type and payment source, with background data and foreign comparisons, 1960s-80s and projected to 2000, 26308–98

Expenditures for Medicaid, Fed Govt funding shares under alternative formulas, by State, FY89, GAO rpt, 26121–420

Expenditures of Fed Govt in States, by type, program, agency, and State, FY90, annual rpt, 2464–2

Finances and operations of programs under Ways and Means Committee jurisdiction, FY70s-90, annual rpt, 21784–11

Finances of govts, tax systems and revenue, and fiscal structure, by level of govt and State, 1991 and historical trends, annual rpt, 10044–1

Food aid program of USDA for women, infants, and children, prenatal participation effect on Medicaid costs and birth outcomes, for 5 States, 1987-88, 1368–2

Fraud in State programs, funding for remediation by State, FY90, annual regional listings, 4004–3

Health care services use and costs under Medicaid, for alternative treatment settings, model description and results, FY87, article, 4652–1.211

Health condition and health care resources, use, and spending, 1950s-89, annual data compilation, 4144–11

Health maintenance organizations and other prepaid managed care plans Medicaid enrollment and use, for 20 States, 1985-89, chartbook, 4108–29

Health maintenance organizations Medicaid enrollees, payments, terminations, services use, and State oversight, for Chicago, Ill, late 1980s, GAO rpt, 26121–399

Hospices use by cancer patients, by service type, use of other facilities, patient and instn characteristics, and other indicators, local area study, 1980-85, 4658–53

Hospital closures and rates, with financial, operating, and market characteristics, by location, late 1980s, GAO rpt, 26121–392

Hospital discharges and length of stay, by diagnosis, patient and instn characteristics, procedure performed, and payment source, 1988, annual rpt, 4147–13.107

Hospital discharges, by Medicaid eligibility and instn characteristics, for 2 States, 1984, article, 4652–1.249

Hospital reimbursement by Medicaid, impacts of Federal and State provisions, with services use, costs, and profits, by State, 1980s, 17206–1.11

Hospital reimbursement by Medicaid under prospective payment system, effect on maternity case-mix for South Carolina, various periods 1985-87, article, 4652–1.206

Hospital reimbursement by Medicare under prospective payment system for discharge delays due to limited nursing home space, 1985, 4658–55

Hospital tax exempt status dependent on acceptance of charity, Medicare, and Medicaid cases, proposal and issues with background data, 1989, press release, 8008–149

Households composition, income, benefits, and labor force status, Survey of Income and Program Participation methodology, working paper series, 2626–10

Income (household) and poverty status under alternative income definitions, by recipient characteristics, 1990, annual Current Population Rpt, 2546–6.69

Kidney transplants, needs, costs, payment sources, and impact of immunosuppressive drugs on outcome, 1950s-87 and projected to 1995, 4658–59

Long-term care institutional and community services, spending and use by type and payment source, FY88, and Medicaid growth since FY75, 26306–6.156

Long-term health care costs for aged, under alternative private insurance policy types, 1989 hearing, 23898–8

Massachusetts Medicaid beneficiaries and payments by eligibility category, and savings from optional benefit elimination, FY89, article, 9373–1.203

Massachusetts State govt spending and employment by program, revenues by source, debt, and public works financing, compared to other States, 1990 compilation of papers, 9373–4.27

Mental health and substance abuse treatment services outlays by Medicaid, by service type, diagnosis, and eligibility, for 2 states, 1984, article, 4652–1.256

Mental health care facilities, finances, caseload, staff, and characteristics of instn and patients, 1988, 4506–4.14

Mental health care facilities for emotionally disturbed children, use, funding, and characteristics of patients, staff, and instn, 1988, 4506–3.44

Mental health care facilities outlays, by function, instn type, funding source, and State, 1988, 4506–3.45

Mental health care in private hospitals, patients characteristics, 1986, 4506–3.47

Mentally retarded Medicaid beneficiaries instnl and community care services under waiver, late 1970s-80s, article, 4652–1.219

Mentally retarded persons care facilities and residents by selected characteristics, and use of Medicaid services and waiver programs, by State, late 1970s-80s, 4658–49

Minority group and women health condition, services use, payment sources, and health care labor force, by poverty status, 1940s-89, chartbook, 4118–56

Minority group health condition, services use, costs, and indicators of services need, 1950s-88, 4118–55

Montana health care access indicators, 1989 hearing, 23898–6

Nursing home admissions of Medicare patients, factors affecting change, 1983-85, article, 4652–1.222

Nursing home and other long term care services under Medicare hospital use reduction demonstration, results for Rochester, NY, 1980s, 4658–43

Nursing home capital investment reimbursement by Medicaid under alternative methodologies, 30-year financial results, article, 4652–1.236

Nursing home reimbursement by Medicaid, resident classification using patient and care characteristics, New York State, 1990 article, 4652–1.205

Nursing home reimbursement by Medicaid, States payment ratesetting methods, analysis for 7 States, 1980s, article, 4652–1.255

Nursing home reimbursement by Medicaid, States payment ratesetting methods, limits, and allowances, 1988, article, 4652–1.253

Nursing home reimbursement by Medicaid under alternative methods, relation to hospital length of stay and discharge destination for Medicare patients, 1985, article, 4652–1.225

Nursing home reimbursement by Medicaid under prospective and retrospective payment systems, effects on payment rate, model results, 1979-86, article, 4652–1.224

Nursing home residents with mental disorders, by disorder type and resident and instn characteristics, 1985, 4147–13.106

Older persons poverty status by health and other characteristics, and Medicaid income and asset eligibility limits by State, 1984-90, 23898–5

Physicians fee schedule under Medicare Supplementary Medical Insurance, methodology with data by procedure and specialty, 1991, annual rpt, 17264–1

Poverty status of population and families, by detailed characteristics, 1988-89, annual Current Population Rpt, 2546–6.67

Poverty status of population and families, by detailed characteristics, 1990, annual Current Population Rpt, 2546–6.71

Pregnancy and child health Medicaid services availability indicators, literature review, 1980s, article, 4652–1.210

Prenatal care Medicaid eligibility and availability, by State, 1987-90, article, 4652–1.213

Prepaid Medicaid plans for physician services, characteristics of selected plans in 4 States, various periods 1983-89, article, 4652–1.228

Private health insurance detection and use in the New York State Medicaid program, various periods 1984-89, article, 4652–1.212

Research activities and grants of HCFA, by program, FY90, annual listing, 4654–10

State and Metro Area Data Book, 1991 data compilation, 2328–54

Statistical Abstract of US, 1991 annual data compilation, 2324–1.3

Transplant patients immunosuppressive drug coverage under Medicare and other insurance sources, costs, and procedures, 1991 rpt, 26358–246

Index by Subjects and Names

Medical costs

Veterans health care, patients, visits, costs, and operating beds, by VA and contract facility, and region, quarterly rpt, 8602–4

Medical assistance

Assistance (financial and nonfinancial) of Fed Govt, 1991 base edition with supplements, annual listing, 104–5

Cancer treatments using chemotherapy drugs for indications not listed on drug label, costs, and insurance reimbursement problems, 1990 physicians survey, GAO rpt, 26131–81

Child health insurance coverage, by source, family composition, income, and parent employment status, 1977 and 1987, 4186–8.14

Coverage (universal) for health care and long term care financing, background data, 1990 rpt, 23898–5

Coverage (universal) under natl health insurance, alternative proposals and indicators of need, 1989, 4658–54

Coverage under health insurance, by insurance type and selected characteristics, 1989, 4146–8.203

Developing countries economic and social conditions from 1960s, and Intl Dev Cooperation Agency and AID activities and funding, FY90-92, annual rpt, 9904–4

Expenditures, coverage, and benefits for social welfare programs, late 1930s-89, annual rpt, 4744–3.1

Expenditures for health care by businesses, households, and govts, 1965-89, article, 4652–1.230

Expenditures for health care, by service type, payment source, and sector, projected 1990-2000 and trends from 1965, article, 4652–1.251

Expenditures for health care, by service type, payment source, and sector, 1960s-90, annual article, 4652–1.221; 4652–1.252

Expenditures for health care, cost containment methods, and insurance coverage issues, with background data, 1991 rpt, 26306–6.155

Expenditures for public welfare by program, FY50s-88, annual article, 4742–1.209

Expenditures for public welfare programs, by program type and level of govt, FY65-88, annual article, 4742–1.202

Germany (West) health condition of children and aged, health care costs, and natl health insurance payroll tax rates, 1985-88, 23898–5

Health condition and health care resources, use, and spending, 1950s-89, annual data compilation, 4144–11

HHS financial aid, by program, recipient, State, and city, FY90, annual regional listings, 4004–3

Homeless persons aid programs of Fed Govt, program descriptions and funding, by agency and State, FY87-90, annual GAO rpt, 26104–21

Hospital discharges and length of stay, by diagnosis, patient and instn characteristics, procedure performed, and payment source, 1988, annual rpt, 4147–13.107

Prenatal care subsidy need under alternative poverty indicators, for 8 southern States, 1984-87, article, 4042–3.226

Public opinion on taxes, spending, and govt efficiency, by respondent characteristics, 1991 survey, annual rpt, 10044–2

Refugee resettlement programs and funding, arrivals by country of origin, and indicators of adjustment, by State, FY90, annual rpt, 4694–5

Research activities and grants of HCFA, by program, FY90, annual listing, 4654–10

South Dakota poverty relief and medical aid programs of counties, spending by type, MSA, and county, 1989, hearing, 25368–176

see also Maternity benefits

see also Medicaid

see also Medicare

see also State funding for health and hospitals

Medical centers

see Hospitals

see Military health facilities and services

see Veterans health facilities and services

Medical costs

AFDC families leaving program, transitional Medicaid benefits program operations and subsequent medical costs, for 2 States, 1980s, article, 4652–1.217

AIDS and AIDS virus infection patients service use and costs under Medicaid, 1991, article, 4652–1.215

Canada universal health care system operations and costs, and implications for US, 1987-91, GAO rpt, 26121–424

Cancer treatments using chemotherapy drugs for indications not listed on drug label, costs, and insurance reimbursement problems, 1990 physicians survey, GAO rpt, 26131–81

Child rearing costs of married couple households, by expenditure type, child's age, income, and region, 1990 and projected to 2007, 1708–87

Consumer Expenditure Survey, household income by source, and itemized spending, by selected characteristics and region, 1988-89, annual rpt, 6764–5

Consumer Expenditure Survey, spending by category, and income, by selected household characteristics and location, 1990, annual press release, 6726–1.42

Consumer Expenditure Survey, spending by category, selected household characteristics, and region, quarterly rpt, 6762–14

Consumer Product Safety Commission activities, recalls by brand, and casualties and medical costs, by product type, FY89, annual rpt, 9164–2

Consumer spending, natl income and product accounts, *Survey of Current Business,* monthly rpt, 2702–1.25

Cost of living and quality of life indicators for 14 MSAs, 1980s, GAO rpt, 26123–346

Costs and use of health care, methodology and findings of natl survey and Medicare and Medicaid records, 1980, series, 4146–12

CPI by component for US city average, and by region, population size, and for 27 metro areas, monthly rpt, 6762–2

CPI components relative importance, by selected MSA, region, population size, and for US city average, 1990, annual rpt, 6884–1

CPI health care component, since 1950, monthly rpt, 4742–1.8

Crime victimization rates, by victim and offender characteristics, circumstances, and offense, 1988 survey, annual rpt, 6066–3.42

Crime victimization rates, by victim and offender characteristics, circumstances, and offense, 1989 survey, annual rpt, 6066–3.44

Disease direct and indirect costs, by diagnosis, 1988, annual rpt, 4474–15

Drug (prescription) spending by aged, and manufacturer and retail price changes, by drug type, 1981-88, 4658–56

Drug and alcohol abuse and mental illness direct and indirect costs, by type, 1970s-88, article, 4042–3.219

Drug and alcohol abuse treatment facilities, services, use, funding, staff, and client characteristics, 1989, biennial rpt, 4494–10

Economic indicators and components, current data and annual trends, monthly rpt, 23842–1.4

Employer-provided health insurance and cost containment activities, North Central States employers views, 1991 survey, article, 9383–19.202

Expenditures (private) for social welfare, by category, 1970s-88, annual article, 4742–1.204

Expenditures, coverage, and benefits for social welfare programs, late 1930s-89, annual rpt, 4744–3.1

Expenditures for health care by businesses, households, and govts, 1965-89, article, 4652–1.230

Expenditures for health care, by service type, payment source, and sector, projected 1990-2000 and trends from 1965, article, 4652–1.251

Expenditures for health care, by service type, payment source, and sector, 1960s-90, annual article, 4652–1.221; 4652–1.252

Expenditures for health care by type and payment source, with background data and foreign comparisons, 1960s-80s and projected to 2000, 26308–98

Expenditures for health care, cost containment methods, and insurance coverage issues, with background data, 1991 rpt, 26306–6.155

Expenditures for health care per capita and as share of GNP, alternative projections 1990-2065, technical paper, 9366–6.284

Expenditures for public welfare by program, FY50s-88, annual article, 4742–1.209

Eye exams average fees and waiting time to appointment, for optometrists and ophthalmologists, by region, 1989, article, 4042–3.238

Family health care charges relation to family health and sociodemographic characteristics, regression results, 1980, 4146–12.27

Food stamp recipient household size, composition, income, and income and deductions allowed, summer 1988, annual rpt, 1364–8

Foreign countries health care cost control measures and insurance provisions, for Germany, France, and Japan, 1960s-91, GAO rpt, 26121–437

Medical costs

Germany (West) health care spending, by funding source and service type, and resource growth, 1970-89, article, 4652–1.238

Health Care Financing Review, quarterly journal, 4652–1

Health care provider prices, price inputs and indexes, and labor, quarterly journal, 4652–1.1

Health condition and health care resources, use, and spending, 1950s-89, annual data compilation, 4144–11

Heart and lung patients nonsurgical procedures hospital charges and length of stay, for Maryland, FY84, article, 4652–1.204

Hospices operations, services, costs, and patient characteristics, for instns without Medicare certification, FY85-86, 4658–52

Hospital cost control through revenue and reimbursement caps, demonstration project results with background data, 1980s, 4658–48

Hospital costs and use, data compilation project analyses, series, 4186–6

Hospital inpatient case-mix specialization level related to industry structure and market characteristics, 1980-85, 4188–71

Hospital prospective payment system use of diagnostic related groups reflecting case severity and complexity to reduce payment variation, model results, 1986, article, 4652–1.245

Hospital reimbursement by Medicare under prospective payment system, and effect on services, finances, and beneficiary payments, 1979-90, annual rpt, 17204–2

Hospital reimbursement by Medicare under prospective payment system, impacts on costs, industry structure and operations, and quality of care, series, 17206–2

Hospital reimbursement by Medicare under prospective payment system, impacts on instns and beneficiaries, 1988, annual rpt, 4654–13

Hospital reimbursement by Medicare under prospective payment system, methodology, inputs, and data by diagnostic group, 1991 annual rpt, 17204–1

Hospitalization costs relation to services timing, by selected patient and hospital characteristics, for Medicare discharges, 1987-88, 17208–2

Hospitals in rural areas, financial and operating performance impacts of Medicare prospective payment reimbursement system, 1980s-87, 4658–51

Inflation rate impacts of health care price changes, with CPI components relative weights, 1986 and 1990, article, 9381–1.212

Kidney end-stage disease treatment access and quality of care indicators, impacts of Medicare payment reductions, 1980s, 4658–44

Kidney transplants, needs, costs, payment sources, and impact of immunosuppressive drugs on outcome, 1950s-87 and projected to 1995, 4658–59

Labs (independent clinical) profitability and cost indexes by customer type, and impacts of Medicare fee caps, 1988-89, GAO rpt, 26121–425

Long-term care institutional and community services, spending and use by type and payment source, FY88, and Medicaid growth since FY75, 26306–6.156

Long-term health care costs for aged, under alternative private insurance policy types, 1989 hearing, 23898–8

Measles cases among New York State high school and college students, and vaccination and treatment costs, 1989, article, 4042–3.227

Medicare Cost Report reviews, revisions ratio to initially reported costs, by category, FY84, article, 4652–1.233

Medicare Economic Index for physician reimbursement rebased to 1989, methodology and results, with projections to 1995, article, 4652–1.246

Medicare input price index rebased to 1987, methodology and results, 1991, article, 4652–1.231

Mental health care facilities for emotionally disturbed children, use, funding, and characteristics of patients, staff, and instn, 1988, 4506–3.44

Mental health care facilities outlays, by function, instn type, funding source, and State, 1988, 4506–3.45

Mental health care facilities, staff, service, and patient characteristics, series, 4506–4

Mental illness and drug and alcohol abuse direct and indirect costs, by age and sex, 1985, 4048–35

Military dependents and retirees managed health care demonstration projects, enrollment, workload, and costs, 1988-90, 26306–3.117

Minority group health condition, services use, costs, and indicators of services need, 1950s-88, 4118–55

Montana health care access indicators, 1989 hearing, 23898–6

Natl income and product accounts and components, *Survey of Current Business*, monthly rpt, 2702–1.24

Neurological Disorders and Stroke Natl Inst activities, and disorder cases, FY90, annual rpt, 4474–25

Neurosciences research and public policy issues, series, 26356–9

Nursing home residents with mental disorders, by disorder type and resident and instn characteristics, 1985, 4147–13.106

Older persons long-term care needs and costs, late 1980s and projected 2018-60, GAO rpt, 26121–433

Older persons poverty status by health and other characteristics, and Medicaid income and asset eligibility limits by State, 1984-90, 23898–5

Paternity determination through genetic testing, labs, services, and costs, 1991 listing, 4698–4

Price indexes for health care services, by selected metro area and region, model results, 1988-89, working paper, 6886–6.73

Prison health care spending, by State and for Federal prisoners, data compilation, 1991 annual rpt, 6064–6.1

Research activities and grants of HCFA, by program, FY90, annual listing, 4654–10

Statistical Abstract of US, 1991 annual data compilation, 2324–1.3

Index by Subjects and Names

Tax (income) returns filed by type of filer, selected income items, quarterly rpt, 8302–2.1

Tax (income) returns of individuals, selected income and tax items by income level, preliminary 1989, annual article, 8302–2.209

Tax expenditures, Federal revenues forgone through income tax deductions and exclusions by type, FY92-96, annual rpt, 21784–10

Transplant patients immunosuppressive drug coverage under Medicare and other insurance sources, costs, and procedures, 1991 rpt, 26358–246

VA and non-VA facilities health services sharing contracts, by service type and region, FY90, annual rpt, 8704–5

VA hospitals admissions and discharges by diagnosis, facilities operating costs, and other VA activities, FY90, annual rpt, 8604–3.3

VA mental health care services use, spending, and staff and patient characteristics, by State and services type, 1983 and 1986, 4506–3.43

Veterans (homeless) with mental illness, VA program services, costs, staff, client characteristics, and outcome, 1990, annual rpt, 8604–11

Vital and Health Statistics series: health condition, medical costs, and use of facilities and services, 4147–10

Workers compensation regulation of physician fees and hospital rates, provisions by State, 1991 semiannual rpt, 6502–1

see also Health insurance
see also Medicaid
see also Medical assistance
see also Medicare

Medical education

Degrees awarded in higher education, by level, field, race, and sex, 1988/89 with trends from 1978/79, biennial rpt, 4844–17

Digest of Education Statistics, 1991 annual data compilation, 4824–2

Drug and alcohol abuse treatment services, funding, staffing, and client load, characteristics, and outcomes, by setting, 1989 conf, 4498–73

Enrollment and applicants for medical schools, 1950s-87, series, 4006–8

Enrollment in science and engineering grad programs, by field, source of funds, and characteristics of student and instn, 1975-89, annual rpt, 9627–7

Epidemiologists, education, specialties, and State govt employment, for southern US, 1989, article, 4042–3.253

Health condition and health care resources, use, and spending, 1950s-89, annual data compilation, 4144–11

Hepatitis B cases, exposure, and vaccination policies for students in nursing and lab technician training programs, 1989, article, 4042–3.244

Higher education course completions, by detailed program, sex, race, and instn type, for 1972 high school class, as of 1984, 4888–4

Higher education enrollment, faculty, finances, and degrees, by instn level and control, and State, FY87, annual rpt, 4844–13

Index by Subjects and Names

Medical examinations and tests

Hospital discharges, by Medicaid eligibility and instn characteristics, for 2 States, 1984, article, 4652–1.249

Hospital operations, and services spending by type and payment source, with background data and foreign comparisons, 1960s-80s and projected to 2000, 26308–98

Hospital reimbursement by Medicaid, impacts of Federal and State provisions, with services use, costs, and profits, by State, 1980s, 17206–1.11

Hospital reimbursement by Medicare under prospective payment system, and effect on services, finances, and beneficiary payments, 1979-90, annual rpt, 17204–2

Hospital reimbursement by Medicare under prospective payment system, diagnosis related group code assignment and effects on care and instn finances, 1984/85, series, 4006–7

Hospital reimbursement by Medicare under prospective payment system, impacts on costs, industry structure and operations, and quality of care, series, 17206–2

Hospital reimbursement by Medicare under prospective payment system, impacts on instns and beneficiaries, 1988, annual rpt, 4654–13

Hospital reimbursement by Medicare under prospective payment system, methodology, inputs, and data by location, 1991 annual rpt, 17204–1

Hospitalization costs relation to services timing, by selected patient and hospital characteristics, for Medicare discharges, 1987-88, 17208–2

Hospitals in rural areas, financial and operating performance impacts of Medicare prospective payment reimbursement system, 1980s-87, regulation, 4658–51

Military health care personnel, and accessions by training source, by occupation, specialty, and service branch, FY89, annual rpt, 3544–24

Military training and education programs funding, staff, students, and facilities, by service branch, FY92, annual rpt, 3504–5

Minority group and women health condition, services use, payment sources, and health care labor force, by poverty status, 1940s-89, chartbook, 4118–56

Nursing training programs faculty, by race, Hispanic origin, and degree level, 1988, hearing, 25418–6

Physicians, by specialty, age, sex, and location of training and practice, 1989, State rpt series, 4116–6

Physicians consultations requested by attending physician, Medicare reimbursement issues, with use by diagnosis, specialty, location, and other characteristics, 1986, 4658–47

Physicians licensing and disciplinary activities of State medical boards, investigative staff, and licensing fees, by State, 1985-90, 4008–83

R&D facilities for biological and medical sciences, space and equipment adequacy, needs, and funding by source, by instn type, 1990, biennial rpt, 4434–17

Radiation protection and health physics enrollment and degrees granted by instn and State, and female grads plans and employment, 1990, annual rpt, 3006–8.15

Radiation protection and health physics enrollment and degrees granted by instn and State, and grad placement, by student characteristics, 1990, annual rpt, 3004–7

VA Medicine and Surgery Dept trainees, by detailed program and city, FY90, annual rpt, 8704–4

VA mental health care services, staff, research, and training programs, 1991 biennial listing, 8704–2

VA mental health care services use, spending, and staff and patient characteristics, by State and services type, 1983 and 1986, 4506–3.43

see also Federal aid to medical education

see also Foreign medical graduates

see also Medical research

Medical equipment

see Medical supplies and equipment

Medical ethics

AIDS knowledge, attitudes, and transmission prevention practices of physicians and RNs, 1990-91, 4186–9.11

Drug (prescription) marketing practices, spending by selected firm, and physicians views, 1990 hearings, 25548–103

Organ and tissue transplants, hospital nurses knowledge, beliefs, and requests for family consent, 1988 survey, article, 4042–3.214

see also Human experimentation

see also Medical malpractice

Medical examinations and tests

Acute and chronic health conditions, disability, absenteeism, and health services use, by selected characteristics, 1987, CD-ROM, 4147–10.177

AIDS and hepatitis viruses transmission in health care settings, occupational exposure, prevention policies, and OSHA regulation, 1990 hearings, 21348–119

AIDS cases in prisons and jails, and testing and control policies, 1989 survey, 6066–28.1

AIDS deaths in jails, and testing policies, by county and facility, 1988, regional rpt series, 6068–144

AIDS knowledge, attitudes, and transmission prevention practices of physicians and RNs, 1990-91, 4186–9.11

AIDS public knowledge, attitudes, info sources, and testing, for blacks, 1990 survey, 4146–8.208

AIDS public knowledge, attitudes, info sources, and testing, for Hispanics, 1990 survey, 4146–8.209

AIDS public knowledge, attitudes, info sources, and testing, 1990 survey, 4146–8.195; 4146–8.201; 4146–8.205

AIDS virus antibody testing lab staff, by type of test, Aug 1991, article, 4042–3.256

AIDS virus antibody tests and counseling sessions by setting, and CDC funding and funds uncommitted by State, 1989-90, GAO rpt, 26121–428

AIDS virus infection and risk factor prevalence, natl survey methodology and pretest results, 1989, 4148–30

Alcohol abuse among veterans, screening results by age and race, for 5 VA medical centers, 1990, GAO rpt, 26121–416

Asian Americans heart disease screening program effectiveness, for persons of Southeast Asian origin, 1989 local area study, article, 4042–3.222

Aviation medicine research and test results, technical rpt series, 7506–10

Black children's mineral levels in hair, serum, and urine, for healthy and anemic children, local area study, 1991 article, 4042–3.248

Cancer (breast) risk relation to breast self-examination practice and other risk factors, 1982-88 local area study, article, 4472–1.202

Cholesterol levels of Navy personnel, by sex, 1989 study, article, 4042–3.215

Diabetics health-related behaviors, weight, and body mass, by level of exercise, 1991 article, 4042–3.246

Diabetics home monitoring of blood glucose, and factors affecting test accuracy, 1990 rpt, 4068–71

Dientamoeba fragilis testing methods of State public health labs, 1985, article, 4042–3.225

Drug abuse residual neurological, behavioral, and cognitive effects, 1989 conf, 4498–69

Eye exams average fees and waiting time to appointment, for optometrists and ophthalmologists, by region, 1989, article, 4042–3.238

Gastroenteritis outbreaks, specimen collection and diagnosis procedures, CDC guidelines, 1990 rpt, 4206–2.32

Genetic damage and trait monitoring and screening of employees, use, costs, benefits, and procedures, 1980s, 26358–230

Health condition and health care resources, use, and spending, 1950s-89, annual data compilation, 4144–11

Health maintenance organizations Medicare enrollees quality of care indicators compared to fee-for-service, demonstration projects results, mid 1980s, 4658–46

Health promotion program availability and participation, by type of program and sponsor, 1986-87 local area study, article, 4042–3.223

Hepatitis B and C screening of blood donors, PHS guidelines, 1991 rpt, 4206–2.40

Hospital discharges and length of stay, by diagnosis, patient and instn characteristics, procedure performed, and payment source, 1988, annual rpt, 4147–13.107

Hospital discharges and length of stay by region and diagnosis, and procedures performed, by age and sex, 1989, annual rpt, 4146–8.198

Hospital discharges by detailed diagnostic and procedure category, primary diagnosis, and length of stay, by age, sex, and region, 1988, annual rpt, 4147–13.105; 4147–13.108

Hospital services and facilities availability, by selected instn characteristics, 1980, 1983, and 1987, 17206–2.22

Hypertensive persons monitoring own blood pressure at home, health condition and risk behavior, local area study, 1991 article, 4042–3.207

Indian Health Service facilities, funding, operations, and Indian health and other characteristics, 1950s-90, annual chartbook, 4084–1

Medical examinations and tests

Indian Health Service outpatient services provided, by reason for visit and age, FY88-89, annual rpt, 4084–2

Indian Health Service, tribal, and contract facilities hospitalization, by diagnosis, age, sex, and service area, FY89, annual rpt, 4084–5

Indians and Alaska Natives preventive health practices, exams by type, and smoking and overweight status, by selected characteristics, 1987, 4186–8.19

Insurance (health) coverage and provisions of small business employee benefit plans, by plan type and occupational group, 1990, biennial rpt, 6784–20

Lead poisoning among children, cases and rates by race, and screening tests conducted, for NYC, 1988, article, 4202–7.201

Mammography screening costs, by setting, model results, 1989 rpt, 17266–1.1

Mammography use, and breast cancer rates attributable to increased detection, by age, 1980-88 study, article, 4472–1.229

Mammography use relation to perceived safety and effectiveness and health care characteristics, 1987 local area study, article, 4042–3.233

Medicaid child preventive health care visits, exams, and immunizations, for California, 1981-84, article, 4652–1.214

Medicare and Medicaid eligibility, participation, coverage, and program finances, various periods 1966-91, biennial rpt, 4654–1

Medicare reimbursement of hospitals under prospective payment system, and effect on services, finances, and beneficiary payments, 1979-90, annual rpt, 17204–2

Mines (underground coal) back injuries, by circumstances, victim characteristics, and treatment, mid 1980s, 5608–166

Minority group health condition, services use, costs, and indicators of services need, 1950s-88, 4118–55

Occupational exposure to hazardous substances and conditions, measurement, and proposed standards, series, 4246–1

Occupational health condition screening and monitoring, businesses practices and views, 1989 survey, 26358–250

Paternity determination through genetic testing, labs, services, and costs, 1991 listing, 4698–4

Pelvic inflammatory disease prevention, diagnosis, treatment, and surveillance, CDC guidelines, 1991 rpt, 4206–2.41

Physicians consultations requested by attending physician, Medicare reimbursement issues, with use by diagnosis, specialty, location, and other characteristics, 1986, 4658–47

Physicians visits, by patient and practice characteristics, diagnosis, and services provided, 1989, 4146–8.206

Preventive disease and health improvement goals and recommended activities for 2000, with trends 1970s-80s, 4048–10

Respiratory diseases related to occupational hazards, epidemiology, diagnosis, and treatment, for selected industries and work settings, 1988 conf, 4248–90

Teenagers physicians office visits, by reason and characteristics of physicians, patients, and visit, 1985, 4146–8.199

Tuberculosis cases and deaths, by patient characteristics, State, and city, 1989 and trends from 1953, annual rpt, 4204–10

Tuberculosis prevention and screening methods among aliens, CDC guidelines, 1990 rpt, 4206–2.36

Tuberculosis testing and treatment for persons with AIDS virus infection, CDC guidelines, 1991 rpt, 4206–2.41

Tuberculosis transmission in health care settings, prevention and screening methods, CDC guidelines, 1990 rpt, 4206–2.35

Veterans health care, patients, visits, costs, and operating beds, by VA and contract facility, and region, quarterly rpt, 8602–4

see also Autopsies

see also Drug and alcohol testing

see also X-rays

Medical facilities and services

see Health facilities and services

Medical instruments

see Medical supplies and equipment

Medical insurance

see Blue Cross-Blue Shield

see Health insurance

see Health maintenance organizations

see Medicaid

see Medicare

Medical libraries

Assistance (financial and nonfinancial) of Fed Govt, 1991 base edition with supplements, annual listing, 104–5

HHS financial aid, by program, recipient, State, and city, FY90, annual regional listings, 4004–3

NIH grants and contracts, quarterly listing, 4432–1

NIH grants for R&D, training, construction, and medical libraries, by location and recipient, FY90, annual listings, 4434–7

NIH Natl Library of Medicine activities, holdings, and grants, FY88-90, annual rpt, 4464–1

NIH Research Resources Center activities and funding, by program, FY90, annual rpt, 4434–12

VA Medicine and Surgery Dept trainees, by detailed program and city, FY90, annual rpt, 8704–4

Medical malpractice

Claims for medical malpractice, resolution through arbitration and litigation, Michigan program cases, awards, duration, and costs, late 1970s-80s, GAO rpt, 26121–394

Court caseloads for Federal district courts, 1990, annual rpt, 18204–8.13; 18204–8.18

Court civil and criminal caseloads for Federal district, appeals, and bankruptcy courts, by type of suit and offense, circuit, and district, 1990, annual rpt, 18204–11

Court civil and criminal caseloads for Federal district courts, 1991, annual rpt, 18204–2.1

Insurance (malpractice) and other components of physicians practice cost indexes, by State, MSA, and for rural areas, 1989 rpt, 4658–50

States medical boards licensing and discipline of health professionals, 1950s-87, series, 4006–8

States medical boards licensing and discipline of physicians, investigative staff, and licensing fees, by State, 1985-90, 4008–83

Index by Subjects and Names

Medical personnel

see Health occupations

Medical research

Alcohol abuse research, treatment programs, and patient characteristics and health effects, quarterly journal, 4482–1

Alcohol, Drug Abuse and Mental Health Admin research grants and awards, by recipient, FY90, annual listing, 4044–13

Allergy and Infectious Diseases Natl Inst activities, grants by recipient and location, and disease cases, FY83-90, annual rpt, 4474–30

Assistance (financial and nonfinancial) of Fed Govt, 1991 base edition with supplements, annual listing, 104–5

Aviation medicine research and test results, technical rpt series, 7506–10

Budget of US, obligations and authority by function, agency, and program, with summaries, analyses, and historical tables, FY92, annual rpt, 104–2

Cancer epidemiology and biochemistry research, semimonthly journal, 4472–1

Cancer Natl Inst activities, grants by recipient, and cancer deaths and cases, FY90 and trends, annual rpt, 4474–13

Cancer Natl Inst epidemiology and biometry activities, FY90, annual rpt, 4474–29

Dental Research Natl Inst research and training grants, by recipient, FY89, annual listing, 4474–19

Developing countries family planning and population activities of AID, grants by project and recipient, and contraceptive shipments, by country, FY90, annual rpt series, 9914–13

Diabetes research and care services programs and funding, by Federal agency and NIH inst, FY90, annual rpt, 4474–34

Drug abuse and treatment, research on biological and behavioral factors and addiction potential of new drugs, 1990 annual conf, 4494–11

Drug abuse and treatment research summaries, resource materials and grant listings, periodic rpt, 4492–4

Drug abuse prevalence among minorities, related health effects and crime, treatment, and research status and needs, mid 1970s-90, 4498–72

Drug abuse, prevention, treatment, and health research results, as of 1990, triennial rpt, 4498–68

Drug abuse psychotherapy and counseling outcomes, research results and methodology, 1990 conf, 4498–71

Employment and other characteristics of science and engineering PhDs, by field and State, 1989, biennial rpt, 9627–18

Expenditures (private) for social welfare, by category, 1970s-88, annual article, 4742–1.204

Expenditures for health care, by service type, payment source, and sector, projected 1990-2000 and trends from 1965, article, 4652–1.251

Expenditures for health care, by service type, payment source, and sector, 1960s-90, annual article, 4652–1.221; 4652–1.252

Expenditures for health care by type and payment source, with background data and foreign comparisons, 1960s-80s and projected to 2000, 26308–98

Index by Subjects and Names

Expenditures for public welfare by program, FY50s-88, annual article, 4742–1.209

Expenditures for R&D and related activities of higher education and nonprofit instns by Fed Govt, by field, instn, agency, and State, FY89, annual rpt, 9627–17

Expenditures for R&D by Fed Govt, by field, performer type, agency, and State, FY89-91, annual rpt, 9627–20

Expenditures for R&D by higher education instns and federally funded centers, by field, instn, and State, FY89, annual rpt, 9627–13

Foreign and US funding for R&D, and scientists and engineering employment and education, 1991 annual rpt, 9627–35.1

Health Care Policy and Research Agency grants, by recipient and location, FY90, 4186–9.10

Health care services outcome research and practice guidelines dev activities and funding of Agency for Health Care Policy and Research, FY88-89, 4188–70

Health condition and health care resources, use, and spending, 1950s-89, annual data compilation, 4144–11

Health condition and quality of life measurement, rpts and other info sources, quarterly listing, 4122–1

Heart, Lung, and Blood Natl Inst activities, and grants by recipient and location, FY90 and disease trends from 1940, annual rpt, 4474–15

HHS financial aid, by program, recipient, State, and city, FY90, annual regional listings, 4004–3

Kidney end-stage disease research of CDC and HCFA, project listing, 1990, annual rpt, 4654–16

Medicare coverage of new health care technologies, risks and benefit evaluations, series, 4186–10

Mental illness and drug and alcohol abuse direct and indirect costs, by age and sex, 1985, 4048–35

Military health care personnel, and accessions by training source, by occupation, specialty, and service branch, FY89, annual rpt, 3544–24

Neurological Disorders and Stroke Natl Inst activities, and disorder cases, FY90, annual rpt, 4474–25

Neurosciences research and public policy issues, series, 26356–9

NIH activities and funding, by inst, FY89-90, biennial rpt, 4434–16

NIH activities, funding by program and recipient type, staff, and clinic patients, by inst, FY90, annual rpt, 4434–3

NIH grants and contracts, by inst and type of recipient, FY81-90, annual rpt, 4434–9

NIH grants and contracts, quarterly listing, 4432–1

NIH grants for R&D, training, construction, and medical libraries, by location and recipient, FY90, annual listings, 4434–7

NIH intl program activities and funding, by inst and country, FY90, annual rpt, 4474–6

NIH Research Resources Center activities and funding, by program, FY90, annual rpt, 4434–12

NIH rpts, 1991 annual listing, 4434–2

Physicians, by specialty, age, sex, and location of training and practice, 1989, State rpt series, 4116–6

Pollutants health effects assessment, methodology and data needs, series, 9186–9

Pollutants health effects for animals by species and for humans, and environmental levels, for selected substances, series, 5506–14

Population, family, and sexual behavior research activities and funding, 1960s-89, 4478–194

Primary health care research, methodology and findings, 1991 annual conf, 4184–4

Primary health care research, provider role, Federal funding, and provision to minority groups, 1990 conf papers, 4188–69

R&D facilities for biological and medical sciences, space and equipment adequacy, needs, and funding by source, by instn type, 1990, biennial rpt, 4434–17

Reproduction and population research, Fed Govt funding by project, FY89, annual listing, 4474–9

Reproduction and population research, Natl Inst of Child Health and Human Dev funding and activities, 1990, annual rpt, 4474–33

Toxicology Natl Program research and testing activities, FY89 and planned FY90, annual rpt, 4044–16

VA health care facilities physicians, dentists, and nurses, by selected employment characteristics and VA district, quarterly rpt, 8602–6

VA health care staff and turnover, by occupation, physician specialty, and location, 1990, annual rpt, 8604–8

VA Medicine and Surgery Dept trainees, by detailed program and city, FY90, annual rpt, 8704–4

VA mental health care services, staff, research, and training programs, 1991 biennial listing, 8704–2

Waste (medical) generation, sources, health worker exposure and risk, and incineration emissions, 1980s, 4078–1

see also Animal experimentation

see also Epidemiology and epidemiologists

see also Human experimentation

Medical supplies and equipment

Airline emergency medical kit items use, occupation of person administering aid, and patient symptoms, 1986-87, technical rpt, 7506–10.82

Airline emergency medical kit items use, 1986-88, technical rpt, 7506–10.81

Cardiac electronic defibrillator device implants, risks and benefit evaluation for Medicare coverage, 1991 rpt, 4186–10.5

Cell cultures with genetic abnormalities, availability and cultures shipped, 1990-91, biennial listing, 4474–23

Consumer Expenditure Survey, household income by source, and itemized spending, by selected characteristics and region, 1988-89, annual rpt, 6764–5

County Business Patterns, 1988: employment, establishments, and payroll, by SIC 2- to 4-digit industry and county, annual State rpt series, 2326–6

County Business Patterns, 1989: employment, establishments, and payroll, by SIC 2- to 4-digit industry and county, annual State rpt series, 2326–8

CPI by component for US city average, and by region, population size, and for 27 metro areas, monthly rpt, 6762–2

Diabetics home monitoring of blood glucose, and factors affecting test accuracy, 1990 rpt, 4068–71

DOD prime contract awards, by category, contract and contractor type, and service branch, FY81-1st half FY91, semiannual rpt, 3542–1

DOD prime contract awards, by category, contractor type, and State, FY88-90, annual rpt, 3544–11

DOD prime contract awards, by detailed procurement category, FY87-90, annual rpt, 3544–18

Employment, earnings, and hours, by SIC 1- to 4-digit industry, monthly and annual averages, selected years 1909-90, annual rpt, 6744–4

Enterprise Statistics, 1987: finances and operations for companies, by size, level of diversification, form of organization, and industry group, 2329–8

Expenditures for health care, by service type, payment source, and sector, projected 1990-2000 and trends from 1965, article, 4652–1.251

Expenditures for health care, by service type, payment source, and sector, 1960s-90, annual article, 4652–1.221; 4652–1.252

Expenditures for health care, cost containment methods, and insurance coverage issues, with background data, 1991 rpt, 26306–6.155

Exports and imports of US, by country and detailed commodity, monthly rpt, 2422–12

Exports and imports of US, by Harmonized System 6-digit commodity and country, 1990, annual rpt, 2424–13

Exports and imports of US, by selected country, country group, and commodity group, 1990, annual rpt, 2044–37

Exports and imports of US, by transport mode, country, and SITC 1- to 3-digit commodity, 1990, annual rpt, 2424–12

Exports of US, detailed Schedule B commodities with countries of destination, 1990, annual rpt, 2424–10

Franchise business opportunities by firm and kind of business, and sources of aid and info, 1990 annual listing, 2104–7

Gene amplification thermal cyclers and subassemblies from UK at less than fair value, injury to US industry, investigation with background financial and operating data, 1990 rpt, 9886–14.301; 9886–14.327

Health Care Financing Review, provider prices, price inputs and indexes, and labor, quarterly journal, 4652–1.1

Hearing aid performance test results, by make and model, 1991 annual rpt, 8704–3

Higher education instn R&D equipment, acquisition and service costs, condition, and financing, by field and subfield, 1988-90, triennial survey series, 9627–27

Hospices operations, services, costs, and patient characteristics, for instns without Medicare certification, FY85-86, 4658–52

Medical supplies and equipment

Hospital post-discharge service use, by type, for Medicare pneumonia, stroke, and hip replacement cases, 1981-86, article, 4652–1.223

Hospital services and facilities availability, by selected instn characteristics, 1980, 1983, and 1987, 17206–2.22

Implants of medical devices, by type, reason, duration, and user characteristics, 1988, 4146–8.197

Imports detained by FDA, by reason, product, shipper, brand, and country, monthly listing, 4062–2

Imports of US given duty-free treatment for value of US material sent abroad, by commodity and country, 1989, annual rpt, 9884–14

Injuries from use of consumer products, by severity, victim age, and detailed product, 1990, annual rpt, 9164–6

Insulin infusion pumps for continuous therapy, risks and benefit evaluation for Medicare coverage, 1991 rpt, 4186–10.4

Lenses (aspherical ophthalmoscopy) from Japan at less than fair value, injury to US industry, investigation with background financial and operating data, 1991 rpt, 9886–14.318

Manufacturing annual survey, 1989: finances and operations, by SIC 2- to 4-digit industry, series, 2506–15

Manufacturing census, 1987: employment and shipments under Fed Govt contracts, by SIC 4-digit industry, 2497–7

Manufacturing census, 1987: finances and operations, by SIC 2- to 4-digit industry, State, and MSA, with trends from 1849, 2497–1

Manufacturing census, 1987: finances and operations, by type of organization and SIC 2- to 4-digit industry, subject rpt, 2497–5

Manufacturing finances and operations, by SIC 2- to 4-digit industry, forecast 1991, annual rpt, 2044–28

Medicare reimbursement for radiology services by location, and for home medical equipment under alternative proposals, 1990 hearing, 21368–131

Medicare reimbursement of hospitals under prospective payment system, effect of including moveable equipment costs, with results for Maryland, FY89, 17206–2.24

Needle intravenous use and other drug abuse, by selected characteristics, 1990 survey, biennial rpt, 4494–5

Occupational injury and illness rates, by SIC 2- to 4-digit industry, 1988-89, annual rpt, 6844–7

Occupational injury and illness rates, by SIC 2- to 4-digit industry, 1989, annual rpt, 6844–1

OECD trade, total and for 4 major countries, and US trade by country, by commodity, 1970-89, world area rpt series, 9116–1

Optical goods stores finances and employment, for establishments with and without payroll, by State and MSA, 1987 Census of Retail Trade, 2401–1

Physicians practice cost indexes and components, by State, MSA, and for rural areas, 1989 rpt, 4658–50

Price indexes (producer), by stage of processing and detailed commodity, monthly rpt, 6762–6

Price indexes (producer), by stage of processing and detailed commodity, monthly 1990, annual rpt, 6764–2

Puerto Rico economic censuses, 1987: wholesale and retail trade and service industry finances and operations, by SIC 2- to 4-digit industry and municipio, 2591–1

Radiation from electronic devices, incidents by type of device, and FDA control activities, 1990, annual rpt, 4064–13

Service industries census, 1987: establishments, receipts by source, payroll, and employment, by SIC 2- to 4-digit kind of business, State, and MSA, 2393–4

Shipments, trade, use, and firms, for electronic medical equipment, by product, 1990, annual Current Industrial Rpt, 2506–12.34

Tax (income) returns of corporations, income and tax items by asset size and detailed industry, 1987, annual rpt, 8304–4

Tax (income) returns of corporations, income and tax items by asset size and detailed industry, 1988, annual rpt, 8304–21

Waste (medical) generation, sources, health worker exposure and risk, and incineration emissions, 1980s, 4078–1

Waste (medical) marine pollution, related beach closings in New Jersey and New York, 1987-89, hearing, 21568–50

Wholesale trade census, 1987: establishments, sales by customer class, employment, inventories, and expenses, by SIC 2- to 4-digit kind of business, 2407–4

see also Biologic drug products
see also Drugs
see also Prosthetics and orthotics
see also Vaccination and vaccines
see also X-rays

Medical technicians

see Allied health personnel
see Clinical laboratory technicians
see Health occupations

Medical transplants

Drug (immunosuppressive) for transplant patients, coverage under Medicare and other insurance sources, costs, and procedures, 1991 rpt, 26358–246

Hospital deaths of Medicare patients, actual and expected rates by diagnosis, with hospital characteristics, by instn, FY87-89, annual regional rpt series, 4654–14

Insurance (health) coverage and provisions of small business employee benefit plans, by plan type and occupational group, 1990, biennial rpt, 6784–20

Kidney end-stage disease cases, treatment, outcomes, and characteristics of patients, organ donors, and facilities, late 1970s-88, annual rpt, 4474–37

Kidney end-stage disease program of Medicare, outlays, and enrollment by age and treatment type, 1982-87, article, 4652–1.208

Kidney end-stage disease treatment access and quality of care indicators, impacts of Medicare payment reductions, 1980s, 4658–44

Kidney end-stage disease treatment facilities, Medicare enrollment and reimbursement, survival, and patient characteristics, 1983-89, annual rpt, 4654–16

Index by Subjects and Names

Kidney transplants, needs, costs, payment sources, and impact of immunosuppressive drugs on outcome, 1950s-87 and projected to 1995, 4658–59

Nurses knowledge of organ and tissue transplants, beliefs, and requests for family consent, 1988 survey, article, 4042–3.214

Statistical Abstract of US, 1991 annual data compilation, 2324–1.3

VA health care facilities surgery-related deaths and complications, by procedure and instn, and compared to non-VA instns, FY84-89, last issue of biennial rpt, 8704–1

Medicare

Accessibility of health care, persons with and without usual care source by selected characteristics, 1987, 4186–8.22

Actuarial studies, Medicare and OASDI future cost estimates and past experience analyses, series, 4706–1

Administrative law judges actions to reduce Medicare Hospital Insurance appeals backlog, effectiveness for Chicago office, FY89, GAO rpt, 26121–398

Adult day care centers revenue by source, and expenses by type, by agency type, FY86, article, 4652–1.234

AIDS patient hospital use and charges, by hospital and patient characteristics, and payment source, 1986-87, 4186–6.15

Anesthesiologists reimbursement by Medicare, charges, and time billed, 1987, GAO rpt, 26121–417

Assistance (financial and nonfinancial) of Fed Govt, 1991 base edition with supplements, annual listing, 104–5

Assistance of Fed Govt, by type, program, agency, and State, FY90, annual rpt, 2464–2

Beneficiaries and program operations, for Medicare and Medicaid, 1991, annual fact book, 4654–18

Beneficiaries, eligibility, coverage, and program finances, for Medicare and Medicaid, various periods 1966-91, biennial rpt, 4654–1

Benefits, beneficiary characteristics, and trust funds of OASDHI, Medicaid, SSI, and related programs, selected years 1937-89, annual rpt, 4744–3

Benefits by county, FY90, annual regional listings, 4004–3

Benefits overpayment recovery and judgment enforcement cases filed in Federal district courts, 1990, annual rpt, 18204–8.13

Benefits, trust fund finances, and services use, for Medicare and Medicaid, 1966-89 and projected to 1995, 21148–61

Budget of US, CBO analysis and review of FY92 budget by function, annual rpt, 26304–2

Budget of US, CBO analysis of revenue and spending alternatives and projections of economic indicators, FY92-96, annual rpt, 26304–3

Budget of US, CBO analysis of savings and revenues under alternative spending cuts and tax changes, projected FY92-97, 26306–3.118

Budget of US, House concurrent resolution, with spending and revenue targets, FY92 and projected to FY96, annual rpt, 21264–2

Index by Subjects and Names

Medicare

Budget of US, midsession review of FY92 budget, by function, annual rpt, 104–7

Budget of US, obligations and authority by function, agency, and program, with summaries, analyses, and historical tables, FY92, annual rpt, 104–2

Budget of US, receipts by source, outlays by agency and program, and balances, monthly rpt, 8102–3

Claims approved, charges, and reimbursements by type of service, from 1974, monthly rpt, quarterly data, 4742–1.11

Copayment limits for Medicare beneficiaries, alternative proposals, 1991, 26306–6.159

Costs and use of health care, methodology and findings of natl survey and Medicare and Medicaid records, 1980, series, 4146–12

Coverage (universal) under natl health insurance, alternative proposals and indicators of need, 1989, 4658–54

Coverage of new health care technologies under Medicare, risks and benefit evaluations, series, 4186–10

Coverage under health insurance, by insurance type and selected characteristics, 1989, 4146–8.203

Coverage under health insurance by source, and services reimbursed by type, 1991 rpt, 26306–6.155

Disability Insurance beneficiaries costs to Medicare until age 64 under alternative coverage assumptions, model results, 1989, article, 4742–1.208

Disabled low income enrollees and eligibility provisions under Medicaid and Medicare, by State, 1975-89, article, 4652–1.218

Disabled Medicare enrollees supplementary health insurance coverage, by enrollee characteristics, 1984, article, 4652–1.243

Enrollment, and use by type of service, annual rpt, discontinued, 4657–5

Expenditures for health care by businesses, households, and govts, 1965-89, article, 4652–1.230

Expenditures for health care, by service type, payment source, and sector, projected 1990-2000 and trends from 1965, article, 4652–1.251

Expenditures for health care, by service type, payment source, and sector, 1960s-90, annual article, 4652–1.221; 4652–1.252

Expenditures for health care by type and payment source, with background data and foreign comparisons, 1960s-80s and projected to 2000, 26308–98

Expenditures for health care per capita and as share of GNP, alternative projections 1990-2065, technical paper, 9366–6.284

Fed Govt civilian retirees health insurance coverage, by plan, FY89, annual rpt, 9844–35.2

Finances and operations of programs under Ways and Means Committee jurisdiction, FY70s-90, annual rpt, 21784–11

Finances of Fed Govt, cash and debt transactions, daily tables, 8102–4

Georgia Medicare Supplementary Medical Insurance claims processing, 1989-90, hearing, 21728–75

Health Care Financing Review, quarterly journal, 4652–1

Health condition and health care resources, use, and spending, 1950s-89, annual data compilation, 4144–11

Health maintenance organizations, factors affecting participation in Medicare risk-based contract, model description and results, 1984-86, article, 4652–1.226

Health maintenance organizations financial performance and services use, demonstration project results, 1985-89, article, 4652–1.235

Health maintenance organizations Medicare enrollees quality of care indicators compared to fee-for-service, demonstration projects results, mid 1980s, 4658–46

Health maintenance organizations reimbursement by Medicare under alternative geographic adjustment factors, for selected counties, 1983-87, article, 4652–1.203

Home health care agencies finances impacts of Medicare payment limits under alternative determination methods, with data by service type, 1984-89, GAO rpt, 26121–400

Home health care equipment reimbursement by Medicare under alternative proposals, 1990 hearing, 21368–131

Home health care services Medicare claim filings under prior and concurrent authorization, demonstration project results, 1987, 4658–57

Home health care services Medicare use and costs, by agency and service type, patient characteristics, and State, 1988-89, article, 4652–1.229

Home health care visits approved by Medicare, planned and actual visits by service type, 1986, article, 4652–1.254

Hospices operations, services, costs, and patient characteristics, for instns without Medicare certification, FY85-86, 4658–52

Hospices use by cancer patients, by service type, use of other facilities, patient and instn characteristics, and other indicators, local area study, 1980-85, 4658–53

Hospital closures and rates, with financial, operating, and market characteristics, by location, late 1980s, GAO rpt, 26121–392

Hospital deaths of Medicare patients, actual and expected rates by diagnosis, with hospital characteristics, by instn, FY87-89, annual regional rpt series, 4654–14

Hospital discharges and length of stay, by diagnosis, patient and instn characteristics, procedure performed, and payment source, 1988, annual rpt, 4147–13.107

Hospital discharges and rates, for aged Medicare beneficiaries by diagnosis, age, sex, and race, 1988, article, 4202–7.205

Hospital discharges, length of stay, and costs, for Medicare by type of beneficiary and location, 1972-88, article, 4652–1.207

Hospital discharges of Medicare beneficiaries, length of stay, case weights, and payments, by diagnosis, selected years 1983-88, article, 4652–1.250

Hospital Insurance and Supplementary Insurance trust funds finances, early 1990s and projected to 2060s, annual article, 4742–1.211

Hospital Insurance trust fund finances, 1966-90 and alternative projections to 2065, annual rpt, 4654–11

Hospital length of stay and discharge destination for Medicare patients, relation to insurance status and Medicaid nursing home reimbursement method, 1985, article, 4652–1.225

Hospital Medicare Cost Report reviews, revisions ratio to initially reported costs, by category, FY84, article, 4652–1.233

Hospital post-discharge service use, by type, for Medicare pneumonia, stroke, and hip replacement cases, 1981-86, article, 4652–1.223

Hospital reimbursement by Medicare under prospective payment system, analyses of alternative payment plans, series, 17206–1

Hospital reimbursement by Medicare under prospective payment system, and effect on services, finances, and beneficiary payments, 1979-90, annual rpt, 17204–2

Hospital reimbursement by Medicare under prospective payment system, construction cost indexes evaluation, 1991 article, 4652–1.247

Hospital reimbursement by Medicare under prospective payment system, diagnosis related group code assignment and effects on care and instn finances, 1984/85, series, 4006–7

Hospital reimbursement by Medicare under prospective payment system, diagnostic group weight calibration alternatives, FY84, article, 4652–1.227

Hospital reimbursement by Medicare under prospective payment system for discharge delays due to limited nursing home space, 1985, 4658–55

Hospital reimbursement by Medicare under prospective payment system, impacts on costs, industry structure and operations, and quality of care, series, 17206–2

Hospital reimbursement by Medicare under prospective payment system, impacts on instns and beneficiaries, 1988, annual rpt, 4654–13

Hospital reimbursement by Medicare under prospective payment system, methodology, inputs, and data by diagnostic group, 1991 annual rpt, 17204–1

Hospital reimbursement by Medicare under prospective payment system, regulatory adjustments review and diagnostic group weight calibration, annual rpt, discontinued, 17204–3

Hospital tax exempt status dependent on acceptance of charity, Medicare, and Medicaid cases, proposal and issues with background data, 1989, press release, 8008–149

Hospitalization costs relation to services timing, by selected patient and hospital characteristics, for Medicare discharges, 1987-88, 17208–2

Hospitals in rural areas, financial and operating performance impacts of Medicare prospective payment reimbursement system, 1980s-87, 4658–51

Income (household) and poverty status under alternative income definitions, by recipient characteristics, 1990, annual Current Population Rpt, 2546–6.69

Medicare

Kidney dialysis patients anemia treatment with Epoetin alfa, dosages, costs, Medicare reimbursement, and facility income effects, 1989, 4008–113

Kidney end-stage disease cases, treatment, outcomes, and characteristics of patients, organ donors, and facilities, late 1970s-88, annual rpt, 4474–37

Kidney end-stage disease program of Medicare, outlays, and enrollment by age and treatment type, 1982-87, article, 4652–1.208

Kidney end-stage disease treatment access and quality of care indicators, impacts of Medicare payment reductions, 1980s, 4658–44

Kidney end-stage disease treatment facilities, Medicare enrollment and reimbursement, survival, and patient characteristics, 1983-89, annual rpt, 4654–16

Kidney transplants, needs, costs, payment sources, and impact of immunosuppressive drugs on outcome, 1950s-87 and projected to 1995, 4658–59

Labs (independent clinical) profitability and cost indexes by customer type, and impacts of Medicare fee caps, 1988-89, GAO rpt, 26121–425

Long-term care institutional and community services, spending and use by type and payment source, FY88, and Medicaid growth since FY75, 26306–6.156

Managed care program for Medicare beneficiaries, cost savings, 1991 article, 4652–1.244

Mental health care facilities, finances, caseload, staff, and characteristics of instn and patients, 1988, 4506–4.14

Mental health care facilities for emotionally disturbed children, use, funding, and characteristics of patients, staff, and instn, 1988, 4506–3.44

Mental health care facilities outlays, by function, instn type, funding source, and State, 1988, 4506–3.45

Mental health care in private hospitals, patients characteristics, 1986, 4506–3.47

Minority group and women health condition, services use, payment sources, and health care labor force, by poverty status, 1940s-89, chartbook, 4118–56

Minority group health condition, services use, costs, and indicators of services need, 1950s-88, 4118–55

Nursing home admissions of Medicare patients, factors affecting change, 1983-85, article, 4652–1.222

Nursing home and other long term care services under Medicare hospital use reduction demonstration, results for Rochester, NY, 1980s, 4658–43

Nursing home residents with mental disorders, by disorder type and resident and instn characteristics, 1985, 4147–13.106

Nursing home skilled care benefit use and costs by aged and disabled Medicare beneficiaries, 1967-88, article, 4652–1.239

Physicians consultations requested by attending physician, Medicare reimbursement issues, with use by diagnosis, specialty, location, and other characteristics, 1986, 4658–47

Physicians fee schedule under Medicare Supplementary Medical Insurance, analyses of costs and other issues, series, 17266–1

Physicians fee schedule under Medicare Supplementary Medical Insurance, methodology with data by procedure and specialty, 1991, annual rpt, 17264–1

Physicians payments, charges by specialty and treatment setting, and assignment rate by State, for Medicare, 1970s-88, article, 4652–1.240

Physicians practice cost indexes and components, by State, MSA, and for rural areas, 1989 rpt, 4658–50

Physicians reimbursement under Medicare Economic Index rebased to 1989, methodology and results, with projections to 1995, article, 4652–1.246

Poverty status of population and families, by detailed characteristics, 1988-89, annual Current Population Rpt, 2546–6.67

Poverty status of population and families, by detailed characteristics, 1990, annual Current Population Rpt, 2546–6.71

Preferred provider organizations marketing outlook under Medicare, with beneficiaries views on switching to Medicare-assignment physicians, 1989 survey, article, 4652–1.248

Price index for Medicare inputs rebased to 1987, methodology and results, 1991, article, 4652–1.231

Radiology services reimbursement by Medicare, by location, 1990 hearing, 21368–131

Research activities and grants of HCFA, by program, FY90, annual listing, 4654–10

Rural areas hospitals closures related to selected factors, 1980s, GAO rpt, 26121–409

State and Metro Area Data Book, 1991 data compilation, 2328–54

Statistical Abstract of US, 1991 annual data compilation, 2324–1.3

Supplemental private insurance for Medicare, loss ratio performance, sales abuse cases, and State enforcement, late 1980s, GAO rpt, 26121–410

Supplemental private insurance for Medicare, premiums, costs, claims, and benefit provisions, with data by firm, 1988-90, hearing, 21788–198

Supplementary Medical Insurance trust fund finances, various periods 1966-90 and projected to 2001, annual rpt, 4654–12

Tax expenditures, Federal revenues forgone through income tax deductions and exclusions by type, FY92-96, annual rpt, 21784–10

Transplant patients immunosuppressive drug coverage under Medicare and other insurance sources, costs, and procedures, 1991 rpt, 26358–246

Trust funds finances of Medicare, receipts, outlays, and assets since 1966, monthly rpt, 4742–1.2

Trust funds financial condition, for Hospital Insurance, monthly rpt, 8102–9.15

Trust funds financial condition, for Medicare, monthly rpt, 8102–9.3

see also Old-Age, Survivors, Disability, and Health Insurance

Index by Subjects and Names

Medicine

see also Anesthesiology
see also Aviation medicine
see also Biologic drug products
see also Chemotherapy
see also Chiropractic and naturopathy
see also Dentists and dentistry
see also Diseases and disorders
see also Drugs
see also Epidemiology and epidemiologists
see also Federal aid to medical education
see also Federal aid to medicine
see also Geriatrics
see also Health condition
see also Health education
see also Health facilities administration
see also Health facilities and services
see also Health insurance
see also Health maintenance organizations
see also Health occupations
see also Hospitals
see also Medicaid
see also Medical assistance
see also Medical costs
see also Medical education
see also Medical ethics
see also Medical examinations and tests
see also Medical libraries
see also Medical malpractice
see also Medical research
see also Medical supplies and equipment
see also Medical transplants
see also Medicare
see also Nurses and nursing
see also Nursing homes
see also Obstetrics and gynecology
see also Optometry
see also Orthopedics
see also Osteopathy
see also Pathology
see also Pediatrics
see also Pharmaceutical industry
see also Pharmacists and pharmacy
see also Physicians
see also Physiology
see also Podiatry
see also Prenatal care
see also Preventive medicine
see also Psychiatry
see also Public health
see also Regional medical programs
see also State funding for health and hospitals
see also Surgeons and surgery
see also Vaccination and vaccines
see also Veterinary medicine

Medin, Dean E.

"Small Mammals of a Beaver Pond Ecosystem and Adjacent Riparian Habitat in Idaho", 1208–377

Mediterranean Sea

Exports and imports (waterborne) of US, by type of service, commodity, country, route, and US port, 1988, annual rpt, 7704–2

Tide height and time daily at coastal points, forecast 1992, annual rpt, 2174–2.4

Meeks, Ronald L.

"Indian Health Service: FY90 Hospital Inpatient Workload Summary and Comparison with Previous Year", 4084–4

"Utilization of IHS and Tribal Direct and Contract General Hospitals, FY89 and U.S. Non-Federal Short-Stay Hospitals, CY88", 4084–5

Index by Subjects and Names

Meert, J.
"Geophysical Investigations of the Western Ohio-Indiana Region, Annual Report, October 1989-September 1990", 9634–10

Mehl, Georg M.
"U.S. Exports to Mexico: A State-by-State Overview, 1987-90", 2048–154

Mehra, Yash P.
"Error-Correction Model of U.S. M2 Demand", 9389–1.202

Meierhoefer, Barbara S.
"Court-Annexed Arbitration in Ten District Courts", 18408–46

Meiners, Mark R.
"Overview of Nursing Home Characteristics: Provisional Data from the 1977 National Nursing Home Survey", 4147–16.4

Meisenheimer, Joseph R., II
"U.S. Labor Market Weakened in 1990", 6722–1.212

Melancon, J. Michael
"Estimated Oil and Gas Reserves, Gulf of Mexico, Dec. 31, 1989", 5734–6

Melbourne, Fla.
Wages by occupation, for office and plant workers, 1991 survey, periodic MSA rpt, 6785–3.3
see also under By SMSA or MSA in the "Index by Categories"

Mellemgaard, Anders
"Increased Risk of Renal Cell Carcinoma Among Obese Women", 4472–1.230

Melnick, Glenn A.
"How Services and Costs Vary by Day of Stay for Medicare Hospital Stays", 17208–2

Melons
see Fruit and fruit products

Meltzer, Allan H.
"U.S. Policy in the Bretton Woods Era", 9391–1.214

Membership organizations
American Historical Assn financial statements, and membership by State, 1989, annual rpt, 29574–2
County Business Patterns, 1988: employment, establishments, and payroll, by SIC 2- to 4-digit industry and county, annual State rpt series, 2326–6
County Business Patterns, 1989: employment, establishments, and payroll, by SIC 2- to 4-digit industry and county, annual State rpt series, 2326–8
CPI by component for US city average, and by region, population size, and for 27 metro areas, monthly rpt, 6762–2
Golf and tennis participation, for northeastern US by facility type and location, 1979-87, conf, 1208–356
Hotels and other lodging places, receipts, payroll, employment, ownership, and rooms, by State and MSA, 1987 Census of Service Industries, subject rpt, 2393–3
Mail volume to and from households, use, and views, by class, source, content, and household characteristics, 1987-88, annual rpt, 9864–10
Puerto Rico economic censuses, 1987: wholesale and retail trade and service industry finances and operations, by SIC 2- to 4-digit industry and municipio, 2591–1
Service industries census, 1987: establishments, receipts by source, payroll, and employment, by SIC 2- to 4-digit kind of business, State, and MSA, 2393–4

Service industries receipts, by SIC 2- to 4-digit kind of business, 1990, annual rpt, 2413–8
see also Associations
see also Consumer cooperatives
see also Cooperatives
see also Credit unions
see also Labor unions
see also Rural cooperatives

Memorials
see Monuments and memorials

Memphis, Tenn.
Economic and banking conditions, for Fed Reserve 8th District, quarterly rpt with articles, 9391–16
Housing and households characteristics, unit and neighborhood quality, and journey to work by MSA location, for 11 MSAs, 1984 survey, supplement, 2485–8
Housing and households characteristics, 1988 survey, MSA fact sheet, 2485–11.7
Housing and households detailed characteristics, and unit and neighborhood quality, by location, 1988 survey, MSA rpt, 2485–6.1
see also under By City and By SMSA or MSA in the "Index by Categories"

Men
AIDS cases by risk group, race, sex, age, State, and MSA, and deaths, monthly rpt, 4202–9
Arrest rates, by offense, sex, age, and race, 1965-89, annual rpt, 6224–7
Black Americans social and economic characteristics, for South and total US, 1989-90 and trends from 1969, Current Population Rpt, 2546–1.450
Cancer (breast) risk for men relation to incidence among relatives, 1983-86, article, 4472–1.213
Cancer (non-Hodgkin's lymphoma) risk among men with AIDS virus infection, 1981-88 and projected to 1992, article, 4472–1.212
Cancer (prostate) prevalence, latent tissue presence at autopsy by race and age, 1973-77, article, 4472–1.221
Cancer (testicular) contralateral tumor risk for men with prior cancer history, 1960-84 study, article, 4472–1.225
Cancer (testicular) risk among Vietnam veterans, by service branch, 1976-81 local area study, article, 4472–1.228
Cancer cases, deaths, and survival rates, by sex, race, age, and body site, 1973-88, annual rpt, 4474–35
Crimes, arrests, and rates, by offense, offender characteristics, population size, and jurisdiction, 1990, annual rpt, 6224–2.1; 6224–2.2
Deaths and rates, by detailed cause and demographic characteristics, 1988 and trends from 1900, US Vital Statistics annual rpt, 4144–2
Divorces by age of spouses and duration of marriage, and children involved, by State, 1988 and trends from 1940, US Vital Statistics advance annual rpt, 4146–5.121
Drug, alcohol, and cigarette use, by selected characteristics, 1990 survey, biennial rpt, 4494–5
Earnings impact of educational attainment and work experience, model description and results for men, by census div, 1979-88, article, 9373–1.213

Health condition and health care resources, use, and spending, 1950s-89, annual data compilation, 4144–11
High school class of 1972: women's employment and educational experiences compared to men, natl longitudinal study, as of 1986, 4888–6
Hispanic Americans social and economic characteristics, by detailed origin, 1991, Current Population Rpt, 2546–1.448; 2546–1.451
Households composition, income, benefits, and labor force status, Survey of Income and Program Participation methodology, working paper series, 2626–10
Housing costs of never married men, by type and selected characteristics, 1987, article, 1702–1.208
Immigrants earnings compared to native-born, relation to social and demographic characteristics, model description and results, 1970 and 1980, technical paper, 9385–8.101
Jail adult and juvenile population, employment, spending, instn conditions, and inmate programs, by county and facility, 1988, regional rpt series, 6068–144
Marriages and rates, by age, race, education, previous marital status, and State, 1988, US Vital Statistics advance annual rpt, 4146–5.122
Marriages, divorces, and rates, by characteristics of spouses, State, and county, 1987 and trends from 1920, US Vital Statistics annual rpt, 4144–4
Military draft registrants by State, FY90, annual rpt, 9744–1
Nurses employed by VA, men RNs, licensed practical nurses, and nursing assistants, by grade, quarterly rpt, 8602–6
OASDHI, Medicaid, SSI, and related programs benefits, beneficiary characteristics, and trust funds, selected years 1937-89, annual rpt, 4744–3
Older men's labor force status by urban-rural location, and distribution of men by age and occupation, 1860s-1980, article, 9371–1.202
Poor black men's drug and condom use and sexual behavior, local area study, 1991 article, 4042–3.254
Prisoners, characteristics, and movements, by State, 1989, annual rpt, 6064–26
Statistical Abstract of US, 1991 annual data compilation, 2324–1
Voting and registration, by socioeconomic and demographic characteristics, 1990 congressional election, biennial Current Population Rpt, 2546–1.454
see also Families and households
see also under By Sex in the "Index by Categories"

Mendenhall, Vivian M.
"Monitoring of Populations and Productivity of Seabirds at St. George Island, Cape Peirce, and Bluff, Alaska, 1989", 5738–31

Meningitis
see Infective and parasitic diseases

Menke, Terri
"Rising Health Care Costs: Causes, Implications, and Strategies", 26306–6.155

Mental health and illness

Index by Subjects and Names

Mental health and illness

Aircraft noise policies, health impacts, and aircraft replacement schedules and costs, 1960s-90 and projected to 2006, hearing, 21648–64

Assistance (financial and nonfinancial) of Fed Govt, 1991 base edition with supplements, annual listing, 104–5

Cases of acute and chronic conditions, disability, absenteeism, and health services use, by selected characteristics, 1987, CD-ROM, 4147–10.177

Child developmental, learning, and emotional problems, cases and share receiving special treatment and education, by selected characteristics, 1988, 4146–8.193

Child health, behavioral, emotional, and school problems relation to family structure, by selected characteristics, 1988, 4147–10.178

Cocaine abuse, user characteristics, and related crime and violence, 1988 conf, 4498–74

Costs (direct and indirect) of drug and alcohol abuse and mental illness, by type, 1970s-88, article, 4042–3.219

Costs (direct and indirect) of mental illness and drug and alcohol abuse, by type and patient age and sex, 1985 with 1980 and 1988 comparisons, 4048–35

Court insanity caseloads for Federal district courts, 1990, annual rpt, 18204–8.13; 18204–11

Court insanity caseloads for Federal district courts, 1991, annual rpt, 18204–2.1

Deaths and rates, by detailed cause and demographic characteristics, 1988 and trends from 1900, US Vital Statistics annual rpt, 4144–2

Drug (steroid) use prevalence and health effects, 1989 conf papers, 4498–67

Drug abuse relation to violent and criminal behavior, with data on street gang activity and selected population groups, 1989 conf, 4498–70

Drug abuse residual neurological, behavioral, and cognitive effects, 1989 conf, 4498–69

Education (special) enrollment by age, staff, funding, and needs, by type of handicap and State, 1989/90, annual rpt, 4944–4

Head Start handicapped enrollment, by handicap, State, and for Indian and migrant programs, 1987/88, annual rpt, 4604–1

Health condition and health care resources, use, and spending, 1950s-89, annual data compilation, 4144–11

Health condition improvement and disease prevention goals and recommended activities for 2000, with trends 1970s-80s, 4048–10

HHS financial aid, by program, recipient, State, and city, FY90, annual regional listings, 4004–3

Homeless and runaway youth programs, funding, activities, and participant characteristics, FY90, annual rpt, 4604–3

Homeless persons alcohol abuse, by sex, age, race, and additional diagnoses, aggregate 1985-87, 4488–14

Hospital discharges and length of stay, by diagnosis, patient and instn characteristics, procedure performed, and payment source, 1988, annual rpt, 4147–13.107

Hospital discharges and length of stay by region and diagnosis, and procedures performed, by age and sex, 1989, annual rpt, 4146–8.198

Hospital discharges by detailed diagnostic and procedure category, primary diagnosis, and length of stay, by age, sex, and region, 1988, annual rpt, 4147–13.105; 4147–13.108

Indian and Alaska Native disease and disorder cases, deaths, and health services use, by tribe, reservation, and Indian Health Service area, late 1950s-86, 4088–2

Indian Health Service, tribal, and contract facilities hospitalization, by diagnosis, age, sex, and service area, FY89, annual rpt, 4084–5

Law enforcement officer assaults and deaths by circumstances, agency, victim and offender characteristics, and location, 1990, annual rpt, 6224–3

Minority group and women health condition, services use, payment sources, and health care labor force, by poverty status, 1940s-89, chartbook, 4118–56

Minority group health condition, services use, costs, and indicators of services need, 1950s-88, 4118–55

Nursing home residents with mental, behavioral, and functional disorders, by age, sex, and instn characteristics, 1987, 4186–8.11

Nursing home residents with mental disorders, by disorder type and resident and instn characteristics, 1985, 4147–13.106

Research grants and awards of ADAMHA, by recipient, FY90, annual listing, 4044–13

Veterans (homeless) domiciliary program of VA, participant characteristics and outcomes, 1990 annual rpt, 8604–10

Veterans (homeless) with mental illness, VA program services, costs, staff, client characteristics, and outcome, 1990, annual rpt, 8604–11

Vocational rehabilitation cases of State agencies by disposition and applicant characteristics, and closures by reason, FY84-88, annual rpt, 4944–6

Wilderness areas use, mental health and educational benefits, and leadership training programs effectiveness, 1990 conf papers, 1208–347

see also Alzheimer's disease
see also Intelligence levels
see also Mental health facilities and services
see also Mental retardation
see also Neurological disorders
see also Psychiatry
see also Psychology
see also Suicide

Mental health facilities and services

Alcohol, Drug Abuse and Mental Health Admin research grants and awards, by recipient, FY90, annual listing, 4044–13

Assistance (financial and nonfinancial) of Fed Govt, 1991 base edition with supplements, annual listing, 104–5

Child developmental, learning, and emotional problems, cases and share receiving special treatment and education, by selected characteristics, 1988, 4146–8.193

Costs (direct and indirect) of mental illness and drug and alcohol abuse, by type and patient age and sex, 1985 with 1980 and 1988 comparisons, 4048–35

Criminal sentences for Federal offenses, guidelines by offense and circumstances, series, 17668–1

Drug and alcohol abuse treatment services, funding, staffing, and client load, characteristics, and outcomes, by setting, 1989 conf, 4498–73

Employment, earnings, and hours, by SIC 1- to 4-digit industry, monthly and annual averages, selected years 1909-90, annual rpt, 6744–4

Facilities, patients, services, and staff characteristics, series, 4506–4

Facilities, patients, services, and staff characteristics, *Statistical Notes* series, 4506–3

Health condition and health care resources, use, and spending, 1950s-89, annual data compilation, 4144–11

HHS financial aid, by program, recipient, State, and city, FY90, annual regional listings, 4004–3

Homeless persons aid programs of Fed Govt, program descriptions and funding, by agency and State, FY87-90, annual GAO rpt, 26104–21

Hospital services and facilities availability, by selected instn characteristics, 1980, 1983, and 1987, 17206–2.22

Insurance (health) coverage and provisions of small business employee benefit plans, by plan type and occupational group, 1990, biennial rpt, 6784–20

Jail adult and juvenile population, employment, spending, instn conditions, and inmate programs, by county and facility, 1988, regional rpt series, 6068–144

Juvenile correctional and detention public and private instns, inmates, and expenses, by instn and resident characteristics and State, 1987, biennial rpt, 6064–13

Medicaid beneficiaries and payments, and Medicare facilities, mid-1960s-89, annual rpt, 4744–3.5; 4744–3.6

Medicaid reimbursement of hospitals under Federal and State provisions, with services use, costs, and profits, by State, 1980s, 17206–1.11

Medicaid spending for mental health and substance abuse treatment services, by service type, diagnosis, and eligibility, for 2 states, 1984, article, 4652–1.256

Medicare and Medicaid beneficiaries and program operations, 1991, annual fact book, 4654–18

Medicare and Medicaid eligibility, participation, coverage, and program finances, various periods 1966-91, biennial rpt, 4654–1

Medicare reimbursement of hospitals under prospective payment system, and effect on services, finances, and beneficiary payments, 1979-90, annual rpt, 17204–2

Mentally retarded persons care facilities and residents by selected characteristics, and use of Medicaid services and waiver programs, by State, late 1970s-80s, 4658–49

Minority group and women health condition, services use, payment sources, and health care labor force, by poverty status, 1940s-89, chartbook, 4118–56

Index by Subjects and Names

Minority group health condition, services use, costs, and indicators of services need, 1950s-88, 4118–55

NIH grants for R&D, training, construction, and medical libraries, by location and recipient, FY90, annual listings, 4434–7

Older persons health care services use, by service type, discharge destination, and prior care source, 1986, 4188–72

Patients and admissions of State and county mental hospitals, by age, diagnosis, and State, FY89, annual rpt, 4504–2

Service industries census, 1987: establishments, receipts by source, payroll, and employment, by SIC 2- to 4-digit kind of business, State, and MSA, 2393–4

State and Metro Area Data Book, 1991 data compilation, 2328–54

Statistical Abstract of US, 1991 annual data compilation, 2324–1.3

VA hospitals admissions and discharges by diagnosis, facilities operating costs, and other VA activities, FY90, annual rpt, 8604–3.3

VA mental health care services, staff, research, and training programs, 1991 biennial listing, 8704–2

Veterans (homeless) with mental illness, VA program services, costs, staff, client characteristics, and outcome, 1990, annual rpt, 8604–11

Veterans health care, patients, visits, costs, and operating beds, by VA and contract facility, and region, quarterly rpt, 8602–4 *see also* Psychiatry

Mental retardation

Child developmental, learning, and emotional problems, cases and share receiving special treatment and education, by selected characteristics, 1988, 4146–8.193

Child welfare programs funding by source, and foster care cases, problems, and program operations for selected States, 1970s-90, hearings, 21788–202

Children (emotionally disturbed) residential facilities, use, funding, and characteristics of patients, staff, and instn, 1988, 4506–3.44

Deaths and rates, by detailed cause and demographic characteristics, 1988 and trends from 1900, US Vital Statistics annual rpt, 4144–2

Education (special) enrollment by age, staff, funding, and needs, by type of handicap and State, 1989/90, annual rpt, 4944–4

Educational service delivery and discipline, and discrimination indicators by State, 1988, biennial rpt, 4804–33

Facilities for mental health care, outpatient programs, use, and client characteristics by instn type and State, 1988, 4506–3.40; 4506–3.46

Facilities for mentally retarded, and residents, by selected characteristics, with Medicaid services and waiver programs use, by State, late 1970s-80s, 4658–49

Head Start handicapped enrollment, by handicap, State, and for Indian and migrant programs, 1987/88, annual rpt, 4604–1

Hospitals for mental health care of States and counties, patients and admissions by age, diagnosis, and State, FY89, annual rpt, 4504–2

Long-term care institutional and community services, spending and use by type and payment source, FY88, and Medicaid growth since FY75, 26306–6.156

Medicaid mentally retarded beneficiaries instnl and community care services under waiver, late 1970s-80s, article, 4652–1.219

Medicare and Medicaid eligibility, participation, coverage, and program finances, various periods 1966-91, biennial rpt, 4654–1

Nursing home residents with mental disorders, by disorder type and resident and instn characteristics, 1985, 4147–13.106

State and Metro Area Data Book, 1991 data compilation, 2328–54

Statistical Abstract of US, 1991 annual data compilation, 2324–1.3

Vocational rehabilitation cases of State agencies by disposition and applicant characteristics, and closures by reason, FY84-88, annual rpt, 4944–6

Merced, Calif.

see also under By SMSA or MSA in the "Index by Categories"

Merchant marine

see Merchant seamen see Ships and shipping

Merchant seamen

Accidents involving merchant ships, and casualties, by circumstances and characteristics of persons and vessels involved, 1988, annual rpt, 7404–11

Accidents involving ships and marine facilities, casualties, and circumstances, Coast Guard investigation results, periodic rpt, 9612–4

Employment, by type and ownership of vessel and license status of sailor, monthly rpt, 7702–1

Employment shipboard, shipyard, and longshore, FY89-90, annual rpt, 7704–14.3

Fed Govt civilian employees work-years, pay rates, and benefits use and costs, by agency, FY89, annual rpt, 9844–31

Statistical Abstract of US, 1991 annual data compilation, 2324–1.22

Mercury

see Mercury pollution *see* Trace metals

Mercury pollution

Air pollution emissions factors, by detailed pollutant and source, data compilation, 1990 rpt, 9198–120

California OCS oil and gas dev impacts on water quality, marine life, and sediments, by site, 1986-89, annual rpt, 5734–11

Coastal and estuarine pollutant concentrations in fish, shellfish, and environment, series, 2176–3

Great Lakes wastewater treatment by municipal and industrial facilities, releases, methods, effectiveness, pollutant limits, and enforcement, 1985-88, 14648–24

Industrial wastewater pollution releases, levels, treatment, costs, and regulation, with background financial and operating data, industry rpt series, 9206–4

New York Bight pollution levels, sources, treatment costs, economic losses, and environmental and health effects, 1990 conf, 9208–131

Metabolic and endocrine diseases

Pacific Ocean coast pollutant concentrations in fish and sediments, by contaminant, fish species, and site, 1984-86, 2168–121

Seals (harbor) population and physical characteristics at selected Washington State coastal sites, 1975-80, 14738–7

Tax (excise) on hazardous waste generation and disposal, rates, and firms filing returns, by substance type, 1988, annual article, 8302–2.202

Water quality, chemistry, hydrology, and other characteristics, local area studies, series, 5666–27

Water supply and quality in streams and lakes, and groundwater levels in wells, by drainage basin, 1988, annual State rpt series, 5666–16

Water supply and quality in streams and lakes, and groundwater levels in wells, by drainage basin, 1989, annual State rpt series, 5666–12

Water supply and quality in streams and lakes, and groundwater levels in wells, by drainage basin, 1990, annual State rpt series, 5666–10

Mergers

see Business acquisitions and mergers

Meriden, Conn.

see also under By SMSA or MSA in the "Index by Categories"

Meridian, Miss.

Wages by occupation, for office and plant workers, 1991 survey, periodic MSA rpt, 6785–3.8

Merit Systems Protection Board

Appeals decisions on Fed Govt personnel actions, by agency and region, FY90, annual rpt, 9494–2

Budget of US, authoritative financial statements with appropriations, outlays, and receipts, by category and agency, FY90, annual rpt, 8104–2.1

Budget of US, obligations and authority by function, agency, and program, with summaries, analyses, and historical tables, FY92, annual rpt, 104–2

Personnel Mgmt Office merit system oversight and enforcement activities, series, 9496–2

Violations and prohibited political activity reported by Federal employees, cases by type, annual rpt, issuing agency change, 9494–3

Mesa, Ariz.

see also under By City in the "Index by Categories"

Mesquite, Tex.

see also under By City in the "Index by Categories"

Mester, Loretta J.

"Expense Preference and the Fed Revisited", 9387–8.245

"Who Changes the Prime Rate?", 9387–8.235

Metabolic and endocrine diseases

Cancer cases among persons treated for thyroid disorders with radionuclide iodine-131, for Sweden, 1950-85 study, article, 4472–1.218

Cancer cases, deaths, and survival rates, by sex, race, age, and body site, 1973-88, annual rpt, 4474–35

Cancer death rates of minorities, by body site, age, sex, and substate area, 1950s-80, atlas, 4478–78

Metabolic and endocrine diseases

Deaths and rates, by detailed cause and demographic characteristics, 1988 and trends from 1900, US Vital Statistics annual rpt, 4144–2

Health condition and health care resources, use, and spending, 1950s-89, annual data compilation, 4144–11

HHS financial aid, by program, recipient, State, and city, FY90, annual regional listings, 4004–3

Hospital discharges and length of stay, by diagnosis, patient and instn characteristics, procedure performed, and payment source, 1988, annual rpt, 4147–13.107

Hospital discharges and length of stay by region and diagnosis, and procedures performed, by age and sex, 1989, annual rpt, 4146–8.198

Hospital discharges by detailed diagnostic and procedure category, primary diagnosis, and length of stay, by age, sex, and region, 1988, annual rpt, 4147–13.105; 4147–13.108

Indian Health Service, tribal, and contract facilities hospitalization, by diagnosis, age, sex, and service area, FY89, annual rpt, 4084–5

see also Allergies

see also Diabetes

see also Immunity disorders

see also Nutrition and malnutrition

see also under By Disease in the "Index by Categories"

Metals and metal industries

Alaska minerals resources and production, by mineral and site, for Juneau region, 1987-88, 5608–169

Alaska minerals resources, production, oil and gas leases, reserves, and exploratory wells, with maps and bibl, 1989, annual rpt, 5664–11

Auto weight, by component material, 1975-90, article, 5602–4.202

Building materials production and PPI, by type, bimonthly rpt, 2042–1.5; 2042–1.6

Business statistics, detailed data for major industries and economic indicators, *Survey of Current Business,* monthly rpt, 2702–1.17

Capital expenditures for plant and equipment, by major industry group, quarterly rpt, 2502–2

Coin production and monetary metals use and holdings of US Mint, by metal type, FY90, annual rpt, 8204–1

Collective bargaining agreements expiring during year, and workers covered, by firm, union, industry group, and State, 1991, annual rpt, 6784–9

County Business Patterns, 1988: employment, establishments, and payroll, by SIC 2- to 4-digit industry and county, annual State rpt series, 2326–6

County Business Patterns, 1989: employment, establishments, and payroll, by SIC 2- to 4-digit industry and county, annual State rpt series, 2326–8

DOD prime contract awards, by detailed procurement category, FY87-90, annual rpt, 3544–18

Employment, earnings, and hours, by SIC 1- to 4-digit industry, monthly and annual averages, selected years 1909-90, annual rpt, 6744–4

Employment in manufacturing, by detailed occupation and SIC 2-digit industry, 1989 survey, triennial rpt, 6748–52

Employment, unemployment, and labor force characteristics, by region and census div, 1990, annual rpt, 6744–7.1

Energy use and prices for manufacturing industries, 1988 survey, series, 3166–13

Enterprise Statistics, 1987: auxiliaries of multi-establishment firms, finances and operations by function, industry, and State, 2329–6

Enterprise Statistics, 1987: finances and operations for companies, by size, level of diversification, form of organization, and industry group, 2329–8

Explosives and blasting agents use, by type, industry, and State, 1990, Mineral Industry Surveys, annual rpt, 5614–22

Exports and imports between US and outlying areas, by detailed commodity and mode of transport, 1990, annual rpt, 2424–11

Exports and imports of finished goods and industrial supplies, with related indicators, by industry and country, mid 1970s-90, 9385–1.205

Exports and imports of US, by country and detailed commodity, monthly rpt, 2422–12

Exports and imports of US by country, and trade shifts by commodity, 1990, semiannual rpt, 9882–9

Exports and imports of US, by Harmonized System 6-digit commodity and country, 1990, annual rpt, 2424–13

Exports and imports of US, by selected country, country group, and commodity group, 1990, annual rpt, 2044–37

Exports and imports of US, by transport mode, country, and SITC 1- to 3-digit commodity, 1990, annual rpt, 2424–12

Exports of US, detailed commodities by country, monthly CD-ROM, 2422–13

Exports of US, detailed Schedule B commodities with countries of destination, 1990, annual rpt, 2424–10

Foreign and US minerals supply under alternative market conditions, reserves, and background industry data, series, 5606–4

Foreign direct investment impact on trade balance, with background data, late 1960s-90 and auto forecasts to 1993, article, 9385–1.210

Foreign direct investment in US, by industry group and world area, 1987-90, annual article, 2702–1.219

Foreign direct investment in US, by industry group of US affiliate and country of parent firm, 1980-86, 2708–41

Foreign direct investment in US manufacturing, impacts on trade balances, with data by industry, 1980s-93, technical paper, 9385–8.91

Foreign direct investment of US, by industry group and world area, 1987-90, annual article, 2702–1.220

Futures and options trading volume, by commodity and exchange, FY90, annual rpt, 11924–2

Futures trading in selected commodities and financial instruments and indexes, NYC, Chicago, and other markets activity, semimonthly rpt, 11922–5

Imports, exports, and employment impacts, by SIC 2- to 4-digit industry and commodity, quarterly rpt, 2322–2

Imports of US, detailed commodities by country, monthly CD-ROM, 2422–14

Imports of US given duty-free treatment for value of US material sent abroad, by commodity and country, 1989, annual rpt, 9884–14

Input-output structure of US economy, detailed interindustry transactions for 84 industries, and components of final demand, 1986, annual article, 2702–1.206

Input-output structure of US economy, detailed interindustry transactions for 85 industries, 1982 benchmark data, 2702–1.213

Labor productivity, indexes of output, hours, and employment by SIC 2- to 4-digit industry, 1967-89, annual rpt, 6824–1.3

Machinery for metalworking, shipments, unfilled orders, trade, and use, quarterly Current Industrial Rpt, 2506–12.12

Magnesium from Canada and Norway, injury to US industry from foreign subsidized and less than fair value imports, investigation with background financial and operating data, 1991 rpt, 9886–19.80

Manufacturing annual survey, 1989: finances and operations, by SIC 2- to 4-digit industry, series, 2506–15

Manufacturing census, 1987: employment and shipments under Fed Govt contracts, by SIC 4-digit industry, 2497–7

Manufacturing census, 1987: finances and operations, by SIC 2- to 4-digit industry, State, and MSA, with trends from 1849, 2497–1

Manufacturing census, 1987: finances and operations, by type of organization and SIC 2- to 4-digit industry, subject rpt, 2497–5

Manufacturing corporations financial statements, by selected SIC 2- to 3-digit industry, quarterly rpt, 2502–1

Manufacturing finances and operations, by SIC 2- to 4-digit industry, forecast 1991, annual rpt, 2044–28

Manufacturing industries operations and performance, analytical rpt series, 2506–16

Manufacturing production, shipments, inventories, orders, and pollution control costs, periodic Current Industrial Rpt series, 2506–3

Mexico imports from US, by industry and State, 1987-90, 2048–154

Mineral industries census, 1987: energy use and costs, by fuel type, SIC 2- to 4-digit industry, and State, subject rpt, 2517–2

Mineral industries census, 1987: finances and operations, by establishment characteristics, SIC 2- to 4-digit industry, and State, subject rpt, 2517–1

Mineral industries census, 1987: finances and operations, by SIC 2- to 4-digit industry, State, and county, census div rpt series, 2515–1

Mineral Industry Surveys, commodity reviews of production, trade, stocks, and use, monthly rpt series, 5612–1

Mineral Industry Surveys, commodity reviews of production, trade, stocks, and use, quarterly rpt series, 5612–2

Index by Subjects and Names

Meteorology

Mineral Industry Surveys, commodity reviews of production, trade, use, and industry operations, advance annual rpt series, 5614–5

Mineral Industry Surveys, State reviews of production, 1990, preliminary annual rpt, 5614–6

Minerals Yearbook, 1988, Vol 3: foreign country reviews of production, trade, and policy, by commodity, annual rpt series, 5604–17

Minerals Yearbook, 1989, Vol 1: commodity reviews of production, reserves, supply, use, and trade, annual rpt series, 5604–15

Minerals Yearbook, 1989, Vol 2: State reviews of production and sales by commodity, and business activity, annual rpt series, 5604–16

Minerals Yearbook, 1989, Vol 2: State reviews of production, sales, and firms, by commodity, and business activity, annual rpt, 5604–34

Minerals Yearbook, 1990, Vol 1: commodity reviews of production, reserves, supply, use, and trade, annual rpt series, 5604–20

Multinatl firms US affiliates, finances, and operations, by industry, world area of parent firm, and State, 1988-89, annual rpt, 2704–4

Multinatl US firms and foreign affiliates rpt, finances and operations, by industry and world area of parent firm, 1989 benchmark survey, preliminary annual 2704–5

Occupational deaths in mining accidents, by circumstances and selected victim characteristics, semiannual rpt series, 6662–3

Occupational injuries and incidence, employment, and hours in metal mines and related operations, 1989, annual rpt, 6664–3

Occupational injuries by circumstances, employment, and hours, for mining industries by type of operation and State, quarterly rpt, 6662–1

Occupational injury and illness rates, by SIC 2- to 4-digit industry, 1988-89, annual rpt, 6844–7

Occupational injury and illness rates, by SIC 2- to 4-digit industry, 1989, annual rpt, 6844–1

OECD trade, total and for 4 major countries, and US trade by country, by commodity, 1970-89, world area rpt series, 9116–1

Pension plans funding status under 1987 accounting standards, for defined benefit plans, 1987-89, technical paper, 9366–6.259

Pollution (air) emissions factors, by detailed pollutant and source, data compilation, 1990 rpt, 9198–120

Price indexes (producer), by stage of processing and detailed commodity, monthly rpt, 6762–6

Price indexes (producer), by stage of processing and detailed commodity, monthly 1990, annual rpt, 6764–2

Production, prices, trade, use, employment, tariffs, and stockpiles, by mineral, with foreign comparisons, 1986-90, annual rpt, 5604–18

Production, shipments, trade, stocks, and material used, for primary metals by product, periodic Current Industrial Rpt series, 2506–10

Public lands minerals resources and availability, State rpt series, 5606–7

Puerto Rico and other US possessions corporations income tax returns, income and tax items, and employment, by selected industry, 1987, article, 8302–2.213

Respiratory diseases related to occupational hazards, epidemiology, diagnosis, and treatment, for selected industries and work settings, 1988 conf, 4248–90

Shipments, trade, and inventories of intermediate metal products, periodic Current Industrial Rpt series, 2506–11

Soviet Union, Eastern Europe, OECD, and selected other countries minerals production, by commodity, 1960s-90, annual rpt, 9114–4.6

Soviet Union GNP by component and industry sector, and CIA estimation methods, 1950s-87, 23848–223

Soviet Union GNP by detailed income and outlay component, 1985, 2326–18.59

Soviet Union minerals production and trade, by commodity, 1985-89 and projected to 2005, annual rpt, 5604–39

Statistical Abstract of US, 1991 annual data compilation, 2324–1.25; 2324–1.27

Stockpiling of strategic material, inventories and needs, by commodity, as of Jan 1991, annual rpt, 3544–37

Tariff Schedule of US, classifications and rates of duty by detailed imported commodity, 1992 base edition, 9886–13

Tax (income) returns of corporations, income and tax items by asset size and detailed industry, 1987, annual rpt, 8304–4

Tax (income) returns of corporations, income and tax items by asset size and detailed industry, 1988, annual rpt, 8304–21

Tax (income) returns of corporations with foreign tax credit, income and tax items by industry group, 1986, biennial article, 8302–2.203

Tax (income) returns of multinatl US firms foreign affiliates, income statement items, by asset size and industry, 1986, biennial article, 8302–2.212

Tax (income) returns of sole proprietorships, income statement items, by industry group, 1989, annual article, 8302–2.214

Technologically advanced structural materials devs and data needs, 1989 conf, 5608–167

Technologically advanced structural materials devs, use, and R&D funding, for ceramics, metal alloys, polymers, and composites, 1960s-80s and projected to 2000, 5608–162

Tungsten ore from PRC at less than fair value, injury to US industry, investigation with background financial and operating data, 1991 rpt, 9886–14.307; 9886–14.332

Wholesale trade census, 1987: establishments, sales by customer class, employment, inventories, and expenses, by SIC 2- to 4-digit kind of business, 2407–4

see also Abrasive materials
see also Aluminum and aluminum industry
see also Copper and copper industry
see also Foundries
see also Gold
see also Hardware
see also Iron and steel industry
see also Lead and lead industry
see also Lead poisoning and pollution
see also Mercury pollution
see also Offshore mineral resources
see also Scrap metals
see also Silver
see also Stockpiling
see also Strategic materials
see also Tin and tin industry
see also Trace metals
see also Uranium
see also Zinc and zinc industry
see also under By Commodity in the "Index by Categories"
see also under By Industry in the "Index by Categories"

Meteorological satellites

Fed Govt weather services activities and funding, by agency, planned FY91-92, annual rpt, 2144–2

Hurricanes and tropical storms in Pacific and Indian Oceans, paths and surveillance, 1990, annual rpt, 3804–8

Launchings and other activities of NASA and Soviet Union, with flight data, 1957-90, annual rpt, 9504–6.1

Meteorology

Agricultural research funding and staffing for USDA, State agencies, and other instns, by topic, FY90, annual rpt, 1744–2

Atlantic Oceanographic and Meteorological Lab research activities and bibl, FY90, annual rpt, 2144–19

Carbon dioxide in atmosphere, DOE R&D programs and funding at natl labs, universities, and other instns, FY91, annual summary rpt, 3004–18.1; 3004–18.7

Data sources and availability for space sciences and related topics, 1991 annual listing, 9504–10

Data sources for space sciences and related topics, use by format and user type, FY90, annual rpt, 9504–11

Fed Govt weather services activities and funding, by agency, planned FY91-92, annual rpt, 2144–2

Forecasts accuracy, evaluations for US, UK, and European systems, quarterly rpt, 2182–8

Forecasts of severe storms, Natl Weather Service forecast accuracy and storm characteristics, series, 2186–6

Great Lakes Environmental Research Lab activities, FY90 annual rpt, 2144–26

Natl Weather Service station locations and types of observations made, 1990 annual listing, 2184–5

Oceanographic research and distribution activities of World Data Center A by country, and cruises by ship, 1989, annual rpt, 2144–15

Pacific Marine Environmental Lab research activities and bibl, FY90, annual rpt, 2144–21

Storms (severe) natl lab research activities and bibl, FY90, annual rpt, 2144–20

Meteorology

see also Global climate change
see also Meteorological satellites
see also Stratosphere
see also Weather

Methadone treatment
see Drug abuse and treatment

Methamphetamines
see Drug abuse and treatment

Methane
see Natural gas and gas industry

Methanol
see Alcohol fuels

Methodology

Agricultural Economics Research, quarterly journal, 1502–3

Agricultural research funding and staffing for USDA, State agencies, and other instns, by topic, FY90, annual rpt, 1744–2

AIDS cases by race, sex, and risk category, and deaths and survivors, projected 1989-93, 4206–2.34

Air traffic and other aviation activity forecasts of FAA, 1991 annual conf, 7504–28

Alaska OCS environmental conditions and oil dev impacts, compilation of papers, series, 2176–1

Astronomical tables, time conversion factors, and listing of observatories worldwide, 1992, annual rpt, 3804–7

Aviation medicine research and test results, technical rpt series, 7506–10

Beef (choice) price and price spread data series revisions, with methodology, 1970s-90, 1568–295

Birds (northern spotted owl) population and reproduction rate on lands open and closed to logging, estimation methodology, 1987, 1208–342

Birds population surveys design and trend analysis methodology, 1988 conf, 5508–108

Carbon dioxide in atmosphere, measurement, methodology, and research results, series, 3006–11

Coastal and estuarine environmental conditions, research results and methodology, series, 2176–7

CPI rounding errors impact on rebased index, 1991 article, 9375–1.206

CPI use in escalator clauses of collective bargaining agreements and other contracts, with conversion factors for index rebasing, 1991 guide, 6888–34

Disaster aid of USDA for producers of crops ineligible for price supports by State, and methodology, 1988-89, GAO rpt, 26113–533

Employment, earnings, and hours benchmarks by SIC 2- to 4-digit industry, 1983-90, and revised seasonal adjustment factors by major industry group, 1991, semiannual article, 6742–2.204

Energy conservation (housing) program of Bonneville Power Admin, activities, cost effectiveness, and participation, series, 3226–1

Finance (intl) and financial policy, and external factors affecting US economy, technical paper series, 9366–7

Financial and economic analysis and forecasting methodology, technical paper series, 9366–6; 9377–9

Financial and economic analysis of banking and nonbanking sectors, working paper series, 9381–10

Food cost index alternative to CPI, by category, region, and household income, size, race, and food budget level, 1980-85, 1598–275

Foreign countries economic and social conditions, working paper series, 2326–18

GDP and GNP as measures of production, factor income components, and receipts from and payments to foreigners, 1980s-91, article, 2702–1.215

GNP by industry, and constant dollar estimate revisions, data sources and reliability, 1977-88, article, 2702–1.201

Govt admin and tax records use in data collection, methodological and disclosure issues, 1988-89 annual conf papers, 8304–17

Govt spending measures using indicators of service costs and demand, with comparisons to fiscal capacity and actual outlays, by State, for State and local govts, 1986-87, 10048–77

GPO pricing and marketing policies, findings and recommendations, 1990 rpt, 26208–3

Health condition and quality of life measurement, rpts and other info sources, quarterly listing, 4122–1

High school dropout rates, and subsequent completion, by student and school characteristics, alternative estimates, 1990, annual rpt, 4834–23

Hospital deaths of Medicare patients, actual and expected rates by diagnosis and MSA, and methodology, FY87-89, annual rpt, 4654–14.11

Hospital reimbursement by Medicare under prospective payment system, impacts on costs, industry structure and operations, and quality of care, series, 17206–2

Income (personal) and earnings estimates by State, data sources and reliability, 1980-87, article, 2702–1.202

Inflation measured by CPI and Personal Consumption Expenditure Index, under alternative weighting systems, monthly rpt, periodic article, 6762–2

Investment (intl) position of US under alternative valuation methods, 1982-89, article, 2702–1.211

Investments rate of return under alternative valuation methods, for US business and for direct foreign investment in and of US, 1982-90, article, 2702–1.217

Lead levels in environment, sources of emissions and exposure, and health effects, literature review, 1990 rpt, 9198–84

Manufacturing exports, by State, alternative estimates, 1986-87, article, 9391–1.219

Medicaid reimbursement of hospitals under Federal and State provisions, with services use, costs, and profits, by State, 1980s, 17206–1.11

Medicare reimbursement of hospitals under prospective payment system, analyses of alternative payment plans, series, 17206–1

Medicare reimbursement of hospitals under prospective payment system, methodology, inputs, and data by diagnostic group, 1991 annual rpt, 17204–1

Medicare Supplementary Medical Insurance physicians fee schedule, analyses of costs and other issues, series, 17266–1

Medicare Supplementary Medical Insurance physicians fee schedule, methodology with data by procedure and specialty, 1991, annual rpt, 17264–1

Natl income and product accounts benchmark revisions, definition and classification changes, 1929-87, article, 2702–1.221

Natl income and product accounts benchmark revisions, new, dropped, and revised tables, 1991 article, 2702–1.224

Natl income and product accounts benchmark revisions, selected years 1977-90, article, 2702–1.226

Pollutants health effects assessment, methodology and data needs, series, 9186–9

Population size, intercensal estimates and conformity with census results, alternative methodologies, 1981-89, 2324–10

Poverty rate under alternative measurement methods, and public opinion on definition, 1988-89, hearing, 21968–56

Poverty threshold and rates under alternative threshold adjustment methodologies, 1980s-90, hearing, 23848–221

Recreation (outdoor) mgmt, research methods, and public opinion, 1990 conf papers, annual rpt, 1204–38

Savings rates in natl income and product accounts, under alternative estimates of imputed rent for housing and consumer goods, 1950s-90, article, 9373–1.218

Smoking cessation program in 11 communities, methods and effectiveness, 1983-88, article, 4472–1.231

Social security programs and related issues, technical paper series, 4746–26

Soil mgmt and characteristics, for western mountain forest areas, 1990 conf, 1208–378

Soviet Union economic conditions, CIA GNP estimation methods assessment, 1989, GAO rpt, 26123–365

Soviet Union GNP by component and industry sector, and CIA estimation methods, 1950s-87, 23848–223

Soviet Union GNP by detailed income and outlay component, 1985, 2326–18.59

Statistical Abstract of US, 1991 annual data compilation, 2324–1

Supplemental Security Income disabled beneficiaries by diagnosis, research file dev methodology, 1991 article, 4742–1.214

Tax (income) returns processing, IRS workload forecasts, compliance, and enforcement, data compilation, 1991 annual rpt, 8304–8

Timber in northeastern US, change in value by species, with methodology, 1970s-85, 1208–348

Timber value conversion standards, for hardwood species conversion to lumber, 1972 and 1984, 1208–361

Unemployment insurance programs of States and Fed Govt, benefits adequacy, and work disincentives, series, 6406–6

Weather forecasts accuracy evaluations, for US, UK, and European systems, quarterly rpt, 2182–8

Index by Subjects and Names

Mexico

Wetlands acreage, resources, soil and water properties, and conservation efforts, by wetland type, State rpt series, 5506–11
see also Classifications
see also Demonstration and pilot projects
see also Economic and econometric models
see also Mathematic models and modeling
see also Seasonal adjustment factors
see also Statistical programs and activities
see also under names of individual surveys (listed under Surveys)

Metrica, Inc.

"Cyclical Effects of the Unemployment Insurance (UI) Program: Final Report", 6406–6.34

Metrication

see Weights and measures

Metropolitan areas

see Central cities
see Metropolitan Statistical Areas
see Suburbs
see Urban areas
see under By City, By SMSA or MSA, and By Urban-Rural and Metro-Nonmetro in the "Index by Categories"

Metropolitan Statistical Areas

Census Bur geographic levels of data coverage, maps, and reference products, 1991 pamphlet, 2326–7.79

Census of Population, 1990: metro area population by race, Hispanic origin, and MSA, press release, 2328–75

Census of Population, 1990: top 39 MSAs and 40 cities population, with trends from 1900, fact sheet, 2326–20.3

Consumer Income, socioeconomic characteristics of persons, families, and households, detailed cross-tabulations, Current Population Rpt series, 2546–6

Crimes, arrests by offender characteristics, and rates, by offense, and law enforcement employees, by population size and jurisdiction, 1990, annual rpt, 6224–2

Housing starts and completions authorized by building permits in 40 MSAs, quarterly rpt, 2382–9

Income (personal) per capita and by source, and earnings by industry div, by State, MSA, and county, 1984-89, annual regional rpts, 2704–2

Manufacturing census, 1987: finances and operations, by SIC 2- to 4-digit industry, State, and MSA, with trends from 1849, 2497–1.4

Population size, by MSA, as of Apr 1990, annual press release, 2324–8

State and Metro Area Data Book, 1991 data compilation, 2328–54

Statistical Abstract of US, 1991 annual data compilation, 2324–1

see also Area wage surveys
see also Central cities
see also State Economic Areas
see also under By SMSA or MSA in the "Index by Categories"

Metzger, Michael R.

"Petroleum Tariffs as a Source of Government Revenue", 9406–1.61

Mexican Americans

see Hispanic Americans
see Mexicans in the U.S.

Mexicans in the U.S.

Admissions to US of aliens on parole status, by world region, type of admission, and State, FY89, fact sheet, 6266–2.6

Deaths in US, by State of occurrence and birthplace abroad, 1988, US Vital Statistics annual rpt, 4144–2.1; 4144–2.2

Economic and labor force impacts of immigration, alien workers, amnesty programs, and employer sanctions, series, 6366–5

Educational enrollment, by grade, instn type and control, and student characteristics, 1989 and trends from 1947, annual Current Population Rpt, 2546–1.453

Emigration of foreign-born from US, by world region and selected country of origin, 1975-79, fact sheet, 6266–2.5

Illegal alien worker and Fair Labor Standards Act employer compliance, hiring impacts, and aliens overstaying visas by country and State, 1986-90, annual rpt, 6264–6

Illegal aliens applications for legal residence under Immigration Reform and Control Act, by selected characteristics, State, and country, periodic rpt, 6262–3

Illegal aliens overstaying visas, by class of admission, mode of arrival, age, country, and State, FY85-88, annual rpt, 6264–5

Immigrants admitted to US, by country of birth, FY81-90, annual rpt, 6264–4

Population characteristics and fertility of foreign-born in US, by birthplace and compared to native born, 1980s, Current Population Rpt, 2546–2.162

Mexico

Abortions in US, by place of woman's residence and State of occurrence, 1988, US Vital Statistics annual rpt, 4146–5.120

Agricultural exports of high-value commodities, indexes and sales by commodity, world area, and country, 1960s-86, 1528–323

Agricultural exports of US, impacts of foreign agricultural and trade policy, with data by commodity and country, 1989, annual rpt, 1924–8

Agricultural production, prices, and trade, by country, 1960s-90, annual world area rpt, 1524–4.2

Agricultural production, trade, and policies in foreign countries, summary data by country, 1989-90, annual factbook, 1924–12

Agricultural subsidies to producers and consumers in 6 Latin America countries, by selected commodity, 1982-87, 1528–324

Agricultural trade by commodity and country, prices, and world market devs, monthly rpt, 1922–12

Agricultural trade of US, by detailed commodity and country, 1989, annual rpt, 1524–8

Agricultural trade of US, by detailed commodity and country, 1990, semiannual rpt, 1522–4

Agricultural trade of US with Mexico, and import tariffs, by commodity, 1989-90, article, 1925–34.238

Agricultural trade of US with Mexico by commodity, and trade restrictions, 1980s, GAO rpt, 26123–335

Agricultural trade of US with Mexico, by commodity group, 1988-90, article, 1925–34.219

AID economic aid to developing countries, obligations and disbursements by country, quarterly rpt, 9912–4

AID loans repayment status and terms by program and country, and status of predecessor agency loans, quarterly rpt, 9912–3

Auto imports duties and origin preference eligibility rules under proposed North American Free Trade Agreement, 1978-91, 9886–4.178

Background Notes, summary social, political, and economic data, 1991 rpt, 7006–2.50

Banks in Mexico, deregulation impacts on finances, with data by bank, 1960s-90, technical paper, 9385–8.121

Bearings (ball) from 14 countries, injury to US industry from foreign subsidized and less than fair value imports, investigation with background financial and operating data, 1991 rpt, 9886–19.74

Construction value and trade, and import duties on materials and equipment by type, for Mexico, 1991 article, 2042–1.207

Corporations in US under foreign control, income tax returns, assets and income statement items by industry div, country, and world area, 1988, article, 8302–2.219

Dollar exchange rates of Mexico peso and Canada dollar, relation to domestic and US prices and nominal exchange rate, model description and results, 1991 technical paper, 9379–12.77

Drug abuse indicators, by world region and selected country, 1990 semiannual conf, 4492–5.1

Drug abuse indicators, for selected countries, 1991 semiannual conf, 4492–5.2

Earthquakes of San Andreas Fault system, location and seismic characteristics, by event, 1769-1989, 5668–123

Economic and military aid and loans from US and intl agencies, by program and country, FY46-90, annual rpt, 9914–5

Economic and monetary trends, compounded annual rates of change for US and 13 trading partners, quarterly rpt annual supplement, 9391–7

Economic conditions in USSR, Eastern Europe, OECD, and selected other countries, 1960s-90, annual rpt, 9114–4

Economic conditions, policy, and trade practices, by country, 1988-90, annual rpt, 21384–5

Economic, social, political, and geographic summary data, by country, 1991, annual factbook, 9114–2

Electric power trade of US with Canada by Province, and with Mexico, by US region, 1988, annual rpt, 3164–92.1

Export and import agreement of Mexico and US, proposal economic impacts, with background trade and investment data, 1985-90, 9886–4.168

Exports (duty-free) of Caribbean area to US, by commodity and country, with consumer and industry impacts, 1984-90, annual rpt, 9884–20

Exports and imports of US, by commodity and country, 1970-89, world area rpt, 9116–1.2

Mexico

Exports and imports of US by country, and trade shifts by commodity, 1990, semiannual rpt, 9882–9

Exports and imports of US, by Harmonized System 6-digit commodity and country, 1990, annual rpt, 2424–13

Exports and imports of US, by selected country, country group, and commodity group, 1990, annual rpt, 2044–37

Exports and imports of US, by transport mode, country, and SITC 1- to 3-digit commodity, 1990, annual rpt, 2424–12

Exports and imports of US, Canada, and Mexico, and outlook for North America free trade area proposal, 1990, 2048–153

Exports and imports, trade agreements and relations, and USITC investigations, 1990, annual rpt, 9884–5

Exports, imports, and balances of US, by selected country, country group, and commodity group, preliminary data, monthly rpt, 2042–34

Exports, imports, and balances of US with major trading partners, by product category, 1986-90, annual chartbook, 9884–21

Exports of US, detailed Schedule B commodities with countries of destination, 1990, annual rpt, 2424–10

Fish and shellfish products imported through California and Arizona ports of entry, by country, semiweekly rpt, 2162–6.4

Fruit and vegetable exports to US, by commodity, country, and port of entry, 1975-87, 1568–299

Fruit trade of US with Mexico, and US import duties, by commodity, 1970s-90, article, 1561–6.203

Govt debt of Mexico, relation to deficit, model description, 1991 technical paper, 9379–12.78

Human rights conditions in 170 countries, and US economic and military aid, 1990, annual rpt, 21384–3

Imports of goods, services, and investment from US, trade barriers, impacts, and US actions, by country, 1990, annual rpt, 444–2

Imports of Mexico from US, by industry and State, 1987-90, 2048–154

Imports of US given duty-free treatment for value of US material sent abroad, by commodity and country, 1989, annual rpt, 9884–14

Intl transactions of US with 9 countries, 1986-88, *Survey of Current Business*, monthly rpt, annual table, 2702–1.26

Labor conditions, union coverage, and work accidents, 1991 annual country rpt, 6366–4.19

Military aid of US, arms sales, and training programs costs and budget requests, by program, world region, and country, FY90-92, annual rpt, 7144–13

Multinatl US firms and foreign affiliates finances and operations, by industry and world area of parent firm, 1989 benchmark survey, preliminary annual rpt, 2704–5

Multinatl US firms foreign affiliates, income statement items by country and world area, 1986, biennial article, 8302–2.212

Natural gas and liquefied gas trade of US with 5 countries, by US firm, 1955-90, annual article, 3162–4.208

Natural gas imports of US by country, 1988 and projected to 2030, Natl Energy Strategy, 3166–6.52

Nuclear power generation in US and 20 countries, monthly rpt, 3162–24.10

Nuclear power plant capacity, generation, and operating status, by plant and foreign and US location, 1990 and projected to 2030, annual rpt, 3164–57

Oil production, and exports and prices for US, by major exporting country, detailed data, monthly rpt with articles, 3162–24

Oil production, trade, use, and stocks, by selected country and country group, monthly rpt, 3162–42

Oil supply, demand, and stock forecasts, by world area, quarterly rpt, 3162–34

Orange juice processing plants evaporating capacity, for Mexico by plant and location, 1991, article, 1925–34.214

Pipes and tubes (welded nonalloy steel) from 6 countries, injury to US industry from foreign subsidized and less than fair value imports, investigation with background financial and operating data, 1991 rpt, 9886–19.81

R&D funding by Fed Govt, by field, performer type, agency, and State, FY89-91, annual rpt, 9627–20

Radiation and radionuclide concentrations, monitoring results of intl and foreign agencies, quarterly rpt, 9192–5

Raisin and prune production, trade, use, and stocks for EC and other countries, Turkey price supports, and Mexico production costs, 1985-91, annual article, 1925–34.250

Spacecraft and satellite launches since 1957, quarterly listing, 9502–2

Steel imports of US under voluntary restraint agreement, by product, customs district, and country, with US industry operating data, quarterly rpt, 9882–13

Steel wire rope from 2 countries at less than fair value, injury to US industry, investigation with background financial and operating data, 1991 rpt, 9886–14.324

Steel wire rope from 8 countries, injury to US industry from foreign subsidized and less than fair value imports, investigation with background financial and operating data, 1990 rpt, 9886–19.73

Strawberry trade of US and Mexico, and Mexico and Chile supply and use, 1986-91, annual article, 1925–34.218

Sugar production, acreage, use, and trade with US, for Mexico, 1960s-91, article, 1561–14.204

Tax (income) returns of corporations with foreign tax credit, income, and tax items, by country and world region of credit, 1986, biennial article, 8302–2.207

Telecommunications domestic and intl rates, by type of service and area served, 1989, annual rpt, 9284–6.6

Telecommunications industry intl competitiveness, with financial and operating data by product or service, firm, and country, 1990 rpt, 2008–30

Trade agreements of US with Canada and Mexico, economic impacts, business leaders views in North Central States, 1991 survey, article, 9383–19.204

Index by Subjects and Names

Travel to and from US, by world area, forecast 1991-92, annual rpt, 2904–9

Travel to and from US on US and foreign flag air carriers, by world area, 1990, annual rpt, 2904–13

Travel to US, trade shows and other promotional activities, with magazine ad costs and circulation, for selected countries, 1991-92, annual rpt, 2904–11

UN voting record and share of votes in agreement with US, by issue, country, and world area, 1990, annual rpt, 7004–18

Vegetable trade of Mexico with US and US import duties by commodity, and fresh tomato arrivals in US and Canada cities, 1970s-90, article, 1561–11.202

Water supplied by US from Colorado River Basin, for Mexico, 1981-85, annual rpt, 5824–6

Weather stations of Natl Weather Service, locations and types of observations made, 1990 annual listing, 2184–5

see also Gulf of Mexico

see also Mexicans in the U.S.

see also under By Foreign Country in the "Index by Categories"

Meyer, Leslie A.

"Analyzing Domestic Mill Consumption of U.S. Upland Cotton", 1561–1.202

"Cotton Production Estimates: A Historical Review", 1561–1.208

"Economic Implications of Planting Flexibility Provisions for U.S. Upland Cotton Farms", 1561–1.205

Meyer, Robert M.

"Status of the State-Federal Bovine Tuberculosis Eradication Program, FY90", 1394–13.2

Miami, Fla.

Air traffic and passenger and freight enplanements, by airport, 1960s-89 and projected to 2010, hub area rpt, 7506–7.40

Cocaine abuse, user characteristics, and related crime and violence, 1988 conf, 4498–74

CPI by component for US city average, and by region, population size, and for 15 metro areas, monthly rpt, 6762–1

CPI by component for US city average, and by region, population size, and for 27 metro areas, monthly rpt, 6762–2

Drug abuse indicators for selected metro areas, research results, data collection, and policy issues, 1991 semiannual conf, 4492–5

Fruit and vegetable shipments, and arrivals in US and Canada cities, by mode of transport and State and country of origin, 1990, annual rpt, 1311–4.1

Housing starts and completions authorized by building permits in 40 MSAs, quarterly rpt, 2382–9

Wages by occupation, and benefits for office and plant workers, 1990 survey, periodic MSA rpt, 6785–11.3

see also under By City and By SMSA or MSA in the "Index by Categories"

Mica

see Nonmetallic minerals and mines

Michigan

Auto and auto parts manufacturing wages, employment, and benefits, by occupation, region, and selected labor market area, 1989 survey, 6787–6.252

Index by Subjects and Names

Microscopes

Banks (insured commercial and savings) deposits by instn, State, MSA, and county, as of June 1990, annual regional rpt, 9295–3.3

Bus connector service between rural areas and Greyhound intercity routes, finances and operations by system, 1987-90, 7888–79

Business and economic conditions, Fed Reserve 9th District, quarterly journal, 9383–19

Celery acreage planted and growing, by growing area, monthly rpt, 1621–14

County Business Patterns, 1989: employment, establishments, and payroll, by SIC 2- to 4-digit industry and county, annual State rpt, 2326–8.24

DOD prime contract awards, by contractor, service branch, State, and city, FY90, annual rpt, 3544–22

Earthquakes in midwestern States, intensity, time, and seismograph locations, 1977-90, annual rpt, 9634–10

Economic conditions and outlook, for US and Canada Great Lakes area, 1970s-90, 9375–15

Fed Govt spending in States and local areas, by type, State, county, and city, FY90, annual rpt, 2464–3

Fed Govt spending in States, by type, program, agency, and State, FY90, annual rpt, 2464–2

Fertilizer and pesticide use and application rates, by type, crop, and State, 1990, 1616–1.2

HHS financial aid, by program, recipient, State, and city, FY90, annual regional listing, 4004–3.5

Homeless persons social services spending and client characteristics, and youth programs cases, for Michigan, 1980s, hearing, 25418–5

Hospital deaths of Medicare patients, actual and expected rates by diagnosis, and hospital characteristics, by instn, FY87-89, annual regional rpt, 4654–14.5

Income (personal) per capita and by source, and earnings by industry div, by State, MSA, and county, 1984-89, annual regional rpt, 2704–2.2

Jail adult and juvenile population, employment, spending, instn conditions, and inmate programs, by county and facility, 1988, regional rpt series, 6068–144.3

Lumber (veneer log) production, mill receipts, and trade, by species, with residue use, for North Central States, 1988, quadrennial rpt, 1208–220

Marriages, divorces, and rates, by characteristics of spouses, State, and county, 1987 and trends from 1920, US Vital Statistics annual rpt, 4144–4

Medicaid hospital discharges, by eligibility and instn characteristics, for 2 States, 1984, article, 4652–1.249

Medical malpractice claims resolution through arbitration and litigation, Michigan program cases, awards, duration, and costs, late 1970s-80s, GAO rpt, 26121–394

Mental health and substance abuse treatment services outlays by Medicaid, by service type, diagnosis, and eligibility, for 2 states, 1984, article, 4652–1.256

Mineral Industry Surveys, State reviews of production, 1990, preliminary annual rpt, 5614–6

Minerals Yearbook, 1989, Vol 2: State review of production and sales by commodity, and business activity, annual rpt, 5604–16.23

Minerals Yearbook, 1989, Vol 2: State reviews of production, sales, and firms, by commodity, and business activity, annual rpt, 5604–34

Mobile home fires, casualties, damage, and impacts of safety standards, with data on Michigan trailer parks, 1980s, hearing, 21248–145

Onion farm acreage, pesticide use, operators, and other characteristics, for 6 producer States, 1989, article, 1561–11.201

Physicians, by specialty, age, sex, and location of training and practice, 1989, State rpt, 4116–6.23

Pollution (air) emissions and levels in Detroit area, by pollutant, 1980-90, 14648–25

Population and housing census, 1990: population and housing characteristics, households, and land area, by county, subdiv, and place, State rpt, 2551–1.24

Population and housing census, 1990: voting age and total population by race, and housing units, by block, redistricting counts required under PL 94-171, State CD-ROM release, 2551–6.3

Population and housing census, 1990: voting age and total population by race, and housing units, by county and city, redistricting counts required under PL 94-171, State summary rpt, 2551–5.23

Savings and loan assns, FHLB 6th District insured members financial condition and operations by State, quarterly rpt, 9302–23

Savings instns, FHLB 6th District members financial condition and operations by State, monthly rpt, 9302–11

Statistical Abstract of US, 1991 annual data compilation, 2324–1

Supplemental Security Income payments and beneficiaries, by type of eligibility, State, and county, Dec 1989, annual rpt, 4744–27.5

Timber harvest and industrial roundwood production, by product and county, 1988, State rpt, 1206–10.11

Water (groundwater) supply, quality, chemistry, and use, 1974-87, local area rpt, 5666–28.10

Water (groundwater) supply, quality, chemistry, and use, 1988, State rpt, 5666–28.2

Water supply and quality in streams and lakes, and groundwater levels in wells, by drainage basin, 1990, annual State rpt, 5666–10.21

see also Alpena, Mich.
see also Ann Arbor, Mich.
see also Battle Creek, Mich.
see also Detroit, Mich.
see also Standish, Mich.
see also Tawas City, Mich.
see also under By State in the "Index by Categories"

Microforms

Census Bur activities, rpts, and user services, monthly rpt, 2302–3

Census Bur rpts and data files, coverage and availability, 1991 annual listing, 2304–2

Census Bur rpts and data files, coverage, availability, and use, series, 2326–7

Census Bur rpts and data files, monthly listing, 2302–6

Education Dept rpts, quarterly listing, 4812–1

Educational Resources Info Center (ERIC) activities, 1990-91, annual rpt, 4814–3

Export and import statistics, Census Bur publications and data files, 1991 guide, 2428–11

Fed Govt standards for data recording, processing, and transfer, and for purchase and use of computer systems, series, 2216–2

Geological Survey rpts and research journal articles, monthly listing, 5662–1

Libraries of higher education instns, holdings, outlays, staff, and instn characteristics, 1969-88, 4468–4

Library of Congress activities, acquisitions, services, and financial statements, FY90, annual rpt, 26404–1

Library of Congress rpts and products, 1990, annual listing, 26404–6

Natl Archives and Records Admin activities, finances, holdings, and staff, FY90, annual rpt, 9514–2

Price indexes (producer), by stage of processing and detailed commodity, monthly rpt, 6762–6

Space science and related data sources and availability, 1991 annual listing, 9504–10

Space science and related data sources, use by format and user type, FY90, annual rpt, 9504–11

Micronesia Federated States

Agricultural trade of US, by detailed commodity and country, 1989, annual rpt, 1524–8

Agricultural trade of US, by detailed commodity and country, 1990, semiannual rpt, 1522–4

Banks (insured commercial and savings) deposits by instn, State, MSA, and county, as of June 1990, annual regional rpt, 9295–3.6

Economic conditions, population characteristics, and Federal aid, for Pacific territories, 1989 hearing, 21448–44

Economic, social, political, and geographic summary data, by country, 1991, annual factbook, 9114–2

Exports and imports of US, by transport mode, country, and SITC 1- to 3-digit commodity, 1990, annual rpt, 2424–12

Exports of US, detailed Schedule B commodities with countries of destination, 1990, annual rpt, 2424–10

Human rights conditions in 170 countries, and US economic and military aid, 1990, annual rpt, 21384–3

Physicians, by specialty, age, sex, and location of training and practice, 1989, State rpt, 4116–6.53

Microscopes

see Scientific equipment and apparatus

Midanik, Lorraine T.

Midanik, Lorraine T.
"Home Blood Pressure Monitoring for Mild Hypertensives", 4002–3.207

Middle Atlantic States
Economic conditions, Fed Reserve 3rd District, quarterly rpt, 9387–10
Economic indicators and cyclical devs and outlook, by Fed Reserve Bank District, periodic rpt, 9362–8
Financial and economic devs, Fed Reserve Bank of Philadelphia bimonthly journal, 9387–1
Financial and economic devs, Fed Reserve Bank of Richmond bimonthly journal, 9389–1
Fish and shellfish catch, by species and Middle Atlantic and Chesapeake State and port, 1988-89, article, 2162–1.204
Fish and shellfish catch, life cycles, and environmental needs, for selected coastal species and regions, series, 5506–8
Fishing (ocean sport) activities, and catch by species, by angler characteristics and State, 1987-89, annual coastal area rpt, 2166–17.1
Fishing (ocean sport and commercial) catch and quotas for US and Canada, by species for North Atlantic Ocean, 1990, annual rpt, 2164–14
HHS financial aid, by program, recipient, State, and city, FY90, annual regional listing, 4004–3.2; 4004–3.3
Income (personal) per capita and by source, and earnings by industry div, by State, MSA, and county, 1984-89, annual regional rpt, 2704–2.2
Lumber (pulpwood) production by species and county, and shipments, by northeastern State, 1989, annual rpt, 1204–18
Manufacturing business outlook, for Fed Reserve 3rd District, monthly survey rpt, 9387–11
Manufacturing output index for Middle Atlantic States, monthly rpt, 9387–12
Manufacturing output of Middle Atlantic and East North Central census divs relative to US, by industry and State, alternative estimates 1963 and 1986, working paper, 9375–13.59
Peanut production, prices, stocks, exports, use, inspection, and quality, by region and State, 1980-90, annual rpt, 1311–5
Statistical Abstract of US, 1991 annual data compilation, 2324–1
Tide height and tidal current velocity daily at Middle Atlantic coastal stations, forecast 1992, annual rpt, 2174–11
Tide height and time daily at coastal points, forecast 1992, annual rpt, 2174–2.3
Wetlands in coastal areas, acreage by wetland type, estuarine basin, and county, 1989, 2178–31
see also Appalachia
see also under By Census Division in the "Index by Categories"
see also under names of individual States

Middle East
Agricultural exports of high-value commodities, indexes and sales by commodity, world area, and country, 1960s-86, 1528–323
Agricultural production, prices, and trade, by country, 1960s-90, annual world area rpt, 1524–4.2

Agricultural trade of US, by commodity and country, bimonthly rpt, 1522–1
Agricultural trade of US, by detailed commodity and country, 1989, annual rpt, 1524–8
Agricultural trade of US, by detailed commodity and country, 1990, semiannual rpt, 1522–4
AID economic aid to developing countries, obligations and disbursements by country, quarterly rpt, 9912–4
AID housing and urban dev program financial statements, FY90, annual rpt, 9914–4
AID loans repayment status and terms by program and country, and status of predecessor agency loans, quarterly rpt, 9912–3
Child health and welfare indicators, and economic conditions, for developing countries, 1950s-80s, hearing, 25388–57
Construction contract awards and billings, by country of contractor and world area of award, 1989, annual article, 2042–1.201
Economic and military aid and loans from US and intl agencies, by program and country, FY46-90, annual rpt, 9914–5
Economic and military aid from US and intl agencies, and US defense spending, for Middle East and East Africa, FY80-90, GAO rpt, 26123–360
Economic and social conditions of developing countries from 1960s, and Intl Dev Cooperation Agency and AID activities and funding, FY90-92, annual rpt, 9904–4
Energy producers finances and operations, by energy type for US firms domestic and foreign operations, 1989, annual rpt, 3164–44.2
Energy production by type, and oil trade, and use, by country group and selected country, monthly rpt, 9112–2
Energy use and production, by fuel type, country, and country group, projected 1995-2010 and trends from 1970, annual rpt, 3164–84
Energy use in developing countries, and economic and environmental impacts, by fuel type, world area, and country, 1980s-90, 26358–232
English language program of USIA, enrollment and staff, by country and world region, FY90, annual rpt, 9854–2
Exchange and training programs of Federal agencies, participants by world area, and funding, by program, FY89, annual rpt, 9854–8
Export controls and trade of US with Middle East countries, with dual-use commodity licenses and arms sales, 1980s-90, GAO rpt, 26123–339
Exports and imports (waterborne) of US, by type of service, commodity, country, route, and US port, 1988, annual rpt, 7704–2
Exports and imports of OECD, total and for 4 major countries, and US trade by country, by commodity, 1970-89, world area rpt, 9116–1.1
Exports and imports of US, by Harmonized System 6-digit commodity and country, 1990, annual rpt, 2424–13

Exports and imports of US, by selected country, country group, and commodity group, 1990, annual rpt, 2044–37
Exports and imports of US, by transport mode, country, and SITC 1- to 3-digit commodity, 1990, annual rpt, 2424–12
Family planning and population activities of AID, grants by project and recipient, and contraceptive shipments, by country, FY90, annual rpt series, 9914–13
Grain production and needs, and related economic outlook, by world area and selected country, forecast 1990/91-1991/92, 1528–313
Imports of goods, services, and investment from US, trade barriers, impacts, and US actions, by country, 1990, annual rpt, 444–2
Investment (foreign direct) in US, by industry group and world area, 1987-90, annual article, 2702–1.219
Investment (foreign direct) in US, by industry group of US affiliate and country of parent firm, 1980-86, 2708–41
Investment (foreign direct) of US, by industry group and world area, 1987-90, annual article, 2702–1.220
Military aid of US, arms sales, and training, by country, FY50-90, annual rpt, 3904–3
Military aid of US, arms sales, and training programs costs and budget requests, by program, world region, and country, FY90-92, annual rpt, 7144–13
Military spending and imports of developing countries, measures to determine eligibility for US economic aid, by country, 1986-87, annual rpt, 9914–1
Multinatl firms US affiliates, finances, and operations, by industry, world area of parent firm, and State, 1988-89, annual rpt, 2704–4
Multinatl US firms and foreign affiliates finances and operations, by industry and world area of parent firm, 1989 benchmark survey, preliminary annual rpt, 2704–5
Oil and gas reserves and discoveries, by country and country group, quarterly rpt, 3162–43
Oil supply and price impacts of Iraq invasion of Kuwait, selected indicators, daily press release, 3162–44
Persian Gulf War costs to US by category and service branch, and offsetting contributions by allied country, monthly rpt, 102–3
Persian Gulf War costs to US by category and service branch, and offsetting contributions by allied country, various periods FY90-91, annual rpt, 104–7
Persian Gulf War Navy and Marine Corps reserves mobilized, 1990-91, GAO rpt, 26123–351
R&D funding by Fed Govt, by field, performer type, agency, and State, FY89-91, annual rpt, 9627–20
Refugee arrivals in US by world area and country of origin, and quotas, monthly rpt, 7002–4
Refugee arrivals in US by world area of origin and State of settlement, and Federal aid, FY90-91 and proposed FY92 allocations, annual rpt, 7004–16
Refugee resettlement programs and funding, arrivals by country of origin, and indicators of adjustment, by State, FY90, annual rpt, 4694–5

Index by Subjects and Names — Military aircraft

Tax (income) returns of corporations with foreign tax credit, income, and tax items, by country and world region of credit, 1986, biennial article, 8302–2.207

Terrorism (intl) incidents, casualties, and attacks on US targets, by attack type and country, 1990, annual rpt, 7004–22

Terrorism (intl) incidents, casualties, and attacks on US targets, by attack type and world area, 1990, annual rpt, 7004–13

Tide height and time daily at coastal points, forecast 1992, annual rpt, 2174–2.5

Travel to US, by characteristics of visit and traveler, country, port city, and State of destination, quarterly rpt, 2902–1

UN voting record and share of votes in agreement with US, by issue, country, and world area, 1990, annual rpt, 7004–18

US military and civilian personnel and dependents, by service branch, world area, and country, quarterly rpt, 3542–20

USIA library holdings, use, and staff, by country and city, FY90, annual rpt, 9854–4

Weather forecasts for US and Northern Hemisphere, precipitation and temperature by location, semimonthly rpt, 2182–1

see also Bahrain
see also Central Treaty Organization
see also Cyprus
see also Egypt
see also Iran
see also Iraq
see also Israel
see also Jordan
see also Kuwait
see also Lebanon
see also Mediterranean Sea
see also Oman
see also Organization of Petroleum Exporting Countries
see also Qatar
see also Saudi Arabia
see also Syria
see also Turkey
see also United Arab Emirates
see also Yemen
see also Yemen, North
see also Yemen, South
see also under By Foreign Country in the "Index by Categories"

Middlesex County, Mass.

Older persons abuse and neglect by circumstances and characteristics of abuser and victim, and States protective services budgets and staff, by location, 1980s, hearing, 21148–62

Middlesex County, N.J.

Wages by occupation, and benefits for office and plant workers, 1990 survey, periodic MSA rpt, 6785–11.4

see also under By SMSA or MSA in the "Index by Categories"

Middletown, Conn.

see also under By SMSA or MSA in the "Index by Categories"

Midland, Mich.

see also under By SMSA or MSA in the "Index by Categories"

Midland, Tex.

see also under By SMSA or MSA in the "Index by Categories"

Midway Islands

Economic, social, political, and geographic summary data, by country, 1991, annual factbook, 9114–2

Midwestern States

see North Central States
see under By Region in the "Index by Categories"

Midwives

Births and rates, by characteristics of birth, infant, and parents, 1989 and trends from 1940, US Vital Statistics advance annual rpt, 4146–5.123

Indian Health Service and tribal facility outpatient visits, by type of provider, selected hospital, and service area, FY90, annual rpt, 4084–3

Military health care personnel, and accessions by training source, by occupation, specialty, and service branch, FY89, annual rpt, 3544–24

Migrant workers

Assistance (financial and nonfinancial) of Fed Govt, 1991 base edition with supplements, annual listing, 104–5

Education Dept programs funding, operations, and effectiveness, FY90, annual rpt, 4804–5

Education programs for immigrant children, Fed Govt and school districts funding, and student characteristics, 1980s, GAO rpt, 26121–418

Education programs for migrant workers children, enrollment, staff, and effectiveness, by State, 1980s, 4808–30

Education programs for migrant workers children, enrollment, staff, finances, and outcomes, 1980s, 4808–22

Head Start enrollment, funding, and staff, FY90, annual rpt, 4604–8

Head Start handicapped enrollment, by handicap, State, and for Indian and migrant programs, 1987/88, annual rpt, 4604–1

HHS financial aid, by program, recipient, State, and city, FY90, annual regional listings, 4004–3

Population of migrant workers and health centers dependents by county, and health centers use and programs funding, by State, 1986-89, 4108–53

Migration

Consumer Income, socioeconomic characteristics of persons, families, and households, detailed cross-tabulations, Current Population Rpt series, 2546–6

Deaths in US, by State of occurrence and birth, and birthplace abroad, 1988, US Vital Statistics annual rpt, 4144–2.1

Fetal deaths and rates, by characteristics of mother and birth, 1988, US Vital Statistics annual rpt, 4144–2.3

Higher education enrollment of State and out-of-State residents, by State, fall 1988, annual rpt, 4824–2.17

Households composition, income, benefits, and labor force status, Survey of Income and Program Participation methodology, working paper series, 2626–10

Housing and households characteristics, MSA surveys, fact sheet series, 2485–11

Housing characteristics of recent movers for new and previous unit, and household characteristics, by location, 1989, biennial rpt, 2485–12

Housing characteristics of recent movers for new and previous unit, and household characteristics, MSA surveys, series, 2485–6

Housing inventory change from 1973, by reason, unit and household characteristics, and location, 1983 survey, biennial rpt, 2485–14

Housing location at birth and age 16, and residential preference in 5 years, by selected housing and household characteristics, 1985, biennial rpt supplement, 2485–13

Income (personal) and poverty status changes, by selected characteristics, 1987-88, Current Population Rpt, 2546–20.19

Income (personal) per capita disparity between metro and nonmetro areas, and causal factors, by State, 1979-88, 1548–380

Minority group and women health condition, services use, payment sources, and health care labor force, by poverty status, 1940s-89, chartbook, 4118–56

Older persons migration to southern coastal areas, household finances, services needs, and local economic impacts, for selected counties, 1990, 2068–38

Research on population and reproduction, Federal funding by project, FY89, annual listing, 4474–9

Research on population, family, and sexual behavior, activities and funding, 1960s-89, 4478–194

Science and engineering PhDs, by field, instn, employment prospects, sex, race, and other characteristics, 1960s-90, annual rpt, 9627–30

Statistical Abstract of US, 1991 annual data compilation, 2324–1.1

see also Alien workers
see also Immigration and emigration
see also Labor mobility
see also Mexicans in the U.S.
see also Migrant workers
see also Refugees
see also Relocation

Migratory Bird Conservation Commission

Wetlands wildlife and migratory bird habitat acquisition, funding by State, FY92, press release, 5306–4.8; 5306–4.11

Mikesell, James J.

"Nonmetro, Metro, and U.S. Bank-Operating Statistics, 1987-89", 1544–29

Milford, Conn.

see also under By SMSA or MSA in the "Index by Categories"

Milham, Nick

"Longrun Competitiveness of Australian Agriculture", 1528–311

Military academies

see Service academies

Military aircraft

Budget of DOD, organization, personnel, weapons, and property, by service branch, State, and country, 1991 annual summary rpt, 3504–13

Budget of DOD, procurement appropriations by item, service branch, and defense agency, FY90-93, annual rpt, 3544–32

Budget of DOD, programs, policies, and operations, FY90, annual rpt, 3544–2

Military aircraft

Budget of DOD, weapons acquisition costs by system and service branch, FY91-93, annual rpt, 3504–2

Coast Guard drug, immigration, and fisheries enforcement activities, 2nd half FY91, semiannual rpt, 7402–4

Coast Guard search and rescue missions, and lives and property lost and saved, by district and assisting unit, FY90, annual rpt, 7404–2

Customs Service activities, collections, entries processed by mode of transport, and seizures, FY86-90, annual rpt, 8144–1

Expenditures and obligations of DOD, by function and service branch, quarterly rpt, 3542–3

Exports and imports of US, by Harmonized System 6-digit commodity and country, 1990, annual rpt, 2424–13

Exports of US, detailed Schedule B commodities with countries of destination, 1990, annual rpt, 2424–10

Foreign and US military weapons trade, production, and defense industry finances, with data by firm and country, 1980s-91, 26358–241

Foreign countries military aid and arms sales of US, by weapon type, as of Sept 1990, annual rpt, 3904–3

Manufacturing annual survey, 1989: value of shipments, by SIC 4- to 5-digit product class, 2506–15.2

Manufacturing census, 1987: employment and shipments under Fed Govt contracts, by SIC 4-digit industry, 2497–7

Natl Guard activities, personnel, and facilities, FY90, annual rpt, 3504–22

NATO and Japan military spending and indicators of ability to support common defense, by country, 1970s-89, annual rpt, 3544–28

NATO and Warsaw Pact military forces reductions under proposed treaty, and US budget savings, 1990 rpt, 26306–3.114

Navy budget, personnel, procurement, and equipment, planned FY91-93, annual fact sheet, 3804–16

Pacific basin US military personnel, dependents, aircraft, ships, and costs, by service branch and location, 1990, GAO rpt, 26123–357

Price indexes (producer), by stage of processing and detailed commodity, monthly rpt, 6762–6

Price indexes (producer), by stage of processing and detailed commodity, monthly 1990, annual rpt, 6764–2

Procurement, DOD prime contract awards by category, contract and contractor type, and service branch, FY81-1st half FY91, semiannual rpt, 3542–1

Procurement, DOD prime contract awards by category, contractor type, and State, FY88-90, annual rpt, 3544–11

Procurement, DOD prime contract awards by detailed procurement category, FY87-90, annual rpt, 3544–18

Procurement, DOD prime contract awards by size and type of contract, service branch, competitive status, category, and labor standard, FY90, annual rpt, 3544–19

Reserve forces personnel and equipment strengths, and readiness, by reserve component, FY90, annual rpt, 3544–31

Sales, orders, backlog, and firms, by product for govt, military, and other customers, 1990, annual Current Industrial Rpt, 2506–12.22

Soviet Union military weapons systems, presence, and force strengths, and compared to US, 1991 annual rpt, 3504–20

Statistical Abstract of US, 1991 annual data compilation, 2324–1.11

Military airlift

Persian Gulf War costs to US by category and service branch, and offsetting contributions by allied country, monthly rpt, 102–3

Persian Gulf War costs to US by category and service branch, and offsetting contributions by allied country, various periods FY90-91, annual rpt, 104–7

Shipments by DOD of military and personal property, passenger traffic, and costs, by service branch and mode of transport, quarterly rpt, 3702–1

Military appropriations

see Defense budgets and appropriations

Military assistance

Army Dept activities, personnel, discipline, budget, and assistance, FY83 summary data, annual rpt, 3704–11

Budget of DOD, organization, personnel, weapons, and property, by service branch, State, and country, 1991 annual summary rpt, 3504–13

Budget of DOD, programs, policies, and operations, FY90, annual rpt, 3544–2

Budget of DOD, R&D appropriations by item, service branch, and defense agency, FY90-93, annual rpt, 3544–33

Currency (foreign) holdings of US, transactions and balances by program and country, 1st half FY91, semiannual rpt, 8102–7

Debt to US of foreign govts and private obligors, by country and program, periodic rpt, 8002–6

Developing countries economic and military aid from US, USSR, PRC, and selected other countries, 1954-90, annual rpt, 9114–4.9

Developing countries economic and social conditions from 1960s, and Intl Dev Cooperation Agency and AID activities and funding, FY90-92, annual rpt, 9904–4

Economic and military aid and loans from US and intl agencies, by program and country, FY46-90, annual rpt, 9914–5

Economic conditions in foreign countries and implications for US, periodic country rpt series, 2046–4

Economic indicators and components, current data and annual trends, monthly rpt, 23842–1.7

Expenditures for DOD base support by function, and personnel and acreage by installation, by service branch, FY91, annual rpt, 3504–11

Foreign countries military aid of US, arms sales, and training programs costs and budget requests, by program, world region, and country, FY90-92, annual rpt, 7144–13

Foreign countries military and economic aid of US, by program and country, selected years 1940-88, annual rpt, 15344–1.1

Human rights conditions in 170 countries, and US economic and military aid, 1990, annual rpt, 21384–3

Loans and loan guarantees of Fed Govt, outstanding amounts by agency and program, *Treasury Bulletin*, quarterly rpt, 8002–4.9

Middle East and East Africa economic and military aid from US and intl agencies, and US defense spending, FY80-90, GAO rpt, 26123–360

Persian Gulf War costs to US by category and service branch, and offsetting contributions by allied country, monthly rpt, 102–3

Persian Gulf War costs to US by category and service branch, and offsetting contributions by allied country, various periods FY90-91, annual rpt, 104–7

Statistical Abstract of US, 1991 annual data compilation, 2324–1.11; 2324–1.29

Treaties and other bilateral and multilateral agreements of US in force, by country, as of Jan 1991, annual listing, 7004–1

see also Arms trade

Military aviation

Air traffic control and airway facilities improvement activities under Aviation System Capital Investment Plan, 1981-90 and projected to 2005, annual rpt, 7504–12

Atlantic Ocean intl air traffic and passengers, by aviation type and route, alternative forecasts 1991-2010 and trends from 1980, annual rpt, 7504–44

Budget of DOD, manpower needs, costs, and force readiness by service branch, FY92, annual rpt, 3504–1

Civil aircraft joint use of military airfields, and effectiveness in reducing airport congestion, FY85-89, GAO rpt, 26113–524

Civil aircraft joint use of military airfields, passenger enplanements by State, 1989, annual rpt, 7504–48.2

Instrument flight rule aircraft handled, by user type, FAA traffic control center, and region, FY85-90 and projected to FY2005, annual rpt, 7504–15

Natl Guard activities, personnel, and facilities, FY90, annual rpt, 3504–22

Navy aircraft pilots hours flown, by pilot category, aircraft type, and flight purpose, late 1980s, GAO rpt, 26123–332

Navy personnel strengths, accessions, and attrition, detailed statistics, quarterly rpt, 3802–4

Traffic, aircraft, carriers, airports, and FAA activities, detailed data, 1980-89, annual rpt, 7504–1

Traffic, aircraft, pilots, airports, and fuel use, forecast FY91-2002 and trends from FY81, annual rpt, 7504–6

Traffic and passenger and freight enplanements, by airport, 1960s-90 and projected to 2010, hub area rpt series, 7506–7

Traffic and passenger enplanements, by airport, region, and State, projected FY91-2005 and trends from FY83, annual rpt, 7504–7

Traffic, capacity, and performance, by carrier and type of operation, monthly rpt, 7302–6

Index by Subjects and Names

Traffic levels at FAA air traffic control facilities, by airport and State, FY90, annual rpt, 7504–27

Training and education programs of DOD, funding, staff, students, and facilities, by service branch, FY92, annual rpt, 3504–5

see also Military aircraft

see also Military airlift

Military awards, decorations, and medals

Incentive awards to Federal employees, costs, and benefits, by award type and agency, FY89, annual rpt, 9844–20

Military bases, posts, and reservations

Acreage and costs of real property owned by Fed Govt, worldwide summary by location, agency, and use, 1989, annual rpt, 9454–5

Acreage of land, by use, ownership, and State, 1987 and trends from 1910, 1588–48

Airfields (military) joint use by civil aircraft, and effectiveness in reducing airport congestion, FY85-89, GAO rpt, 26113–524

Budget of DOD, base construction and family housing appropriations by facility, service branch, and location, FY90-93, annual rpt, 3544–39

Budget of DOD, organization, personnel, weapons, and property, by service branch, State, and country, 1991 annual summary rpt, 3504–13

Budget of DOD, programs, policies, and operations, FY90, annual rpt, 3544–2

Budget of US, obligations and authority by function, agency, and program, with summaries, analyses, and historical tables, FY92, annual rpt, 104–2

Closings of bases and military spending reductions, employment impacts by region and State, 1988-89 and projected FY91-95, article, 9371–1.206

Closings of bases, costs and savings for 71 Army and Navy bases, FY92-97, GAO rpt, 26123–341

Closings of bases in Europe, by service branch and location, FY91, GAO rpt, 26123-336

Construction put in place, by type of construction, bimonthly rpt, 2042–1.1

Construction put in place, value of new public and private structures, by type, monthly rpt, 2382–4

Construction, renovation, and land acquisition for bases, DOD budget requests by project, service branch, State, and country, FY92-93, annual rpt, 3544–15

Construction spending by Fed Govt, by program and type of structure, FY85-92, annual article, 2042–1.206

Expenditures for contracts and payroll, and personnel, by service branch and location, with top 5 contractors and maps, by State and country, FY90, annual rpt, 3544–29

Fish Hatchery Natl System activities and deliveries, by species, hatchery, and jurisdiction of waters stocked, FY90, annual rpt, 5504–10

Fishery products purchases of Defense Logistics Agency, by base of destination, weekly regional rpt, 2162–6.5

Hazardous waste site remedial action at military installations, activities and funding by site and State, FY90, annual rpt, 3544–36

Minerals resources and availability on public lands, State rpt series, 5606–7

Natl Guard activities, personnel, and facilities, FY90, annual rpt, 3504–22

Navy budget, personnel, procurement, and equipment, planned FY91-93, annual fact sheet, 3804–16

Pentagon personnel, 1945-90, annual rpt, 3544–1.1

Persian Gulf War Operation Desert Storm deployment, for top 50 US installations, as of Feb 1991, annual rpt supplement, 3504–13

Personnel (civilian and military) of DOD, by service branch, major installation, and State, as of Sept 1990, annual rpt, 3544–7

Radioactivity levels at former AEC and Manhattan Project research and storage sites and nearby areas, test results series, 3006–9

Reserve forces personnel and equipment strengths, and readiness, by reserve component, FY90, annual rpt, 3544–31

Support of bases, DOD outlays by function, and personnel and acreage by installation, by service branch, FY91, annual rpt, 3504–11

Terrorism (intl) incidents, casualties, and attacks on US targets, by attack type and country, 1990, annual rpt, 7004–22

Terrorism (intl) incidents, casualties, and attacks on US targets, by attack type and world area, 1990, annual rpt, 7004–13

Training and education programs of DOD, funding, staff, students, and facilities, by service branch, FY92, annual rpt, 3504–5

see also Military housing

see also Military post exchanges and commissaries

see also Military prisons

Military benefits and pensions

Benefits and beneficiaries of govt pension plans, by type of plan and eligibility, and level of govt, selected years 1954-88, annual article, 4742–1.212

Benefits and pay for active duty personnel, reserves, retirees, and survivors, 1940s-80s and projected to 2049, 21208–34

Budget of DOD, programs, policies, and operations, FY90, annual rpt, 3544–2

Budget of US, object class analysis of obligations, by agency, FY92, annual rpt, 104–9

Budget of US, obligations and authority by function, agency, and program, with summaries, analyses, and historical tables, FY92, annual rpt, 104–2

Deaths of beneficiaries, erroneous benefit payments, and use of SSA and other sources of death info, by agency, 1990, GAO rpt, 26121–406

Education aid under GI Bill and other programs, and participation by period of service and State, FY89, annual rpt, 8604–9

Expenditures and obligations of DOD, by function and service branch, quarterly rpt, 3542–3

Expenditures, coverage, and benefits for social welfare programs, late 1930s-89, annual rpt, 4744–3.1; 4744–3.3

Expenditures for contracts and payroll, and personnel, by service branch and location, with top 5 contractors and maps, by State and country, FY90, annual rpt, 3544–29

Military dependents

Expenditures of Fed Govt in States, by type, program, agency, and State, FY90, annual rpt, 2464–2

Income (household, family, and personal), by source, detailed characteristics, and region, 1988-89, annual Current Population Rpt, 2546–6.68

Income (household, family, and personal), by source, detailed characteristics, and region, 1990, annual Current Population Rpt, 2546–6.70

Pension annuitants, DOD retired military personnel, FY50-90, annual rpt, 3544–1.4

Pension coverage by industry, vestment, and recipient income, by participant characteristics, 1987, Current Population Rpt, 2546–20.18

Soviet Union GNP by detailed income and outlay component, 1985, 2326–18.59

Tax expenditures, Federal revenues forgone through income tax deductions and exclusions by type, FY92-96, annual rpt, 21784–10

see also Civilian Health and Medical Program of the Uniformed Services

see also Servicepersons life insurance programs

see also Veterans benefits and pensions

Military cemeteries and funerals

Acreage of land under Natl Park Service mgmt, by site, ownership, and region, FY91, semiannual rpt, 5542–1

Burials in natl cemeteries, and disposition of gravesites, by location, FY90, annual rpt, 8604–3.6

Military contracts and procurement

see Defense contracts and procurement

Military courts

see Court of Military Appeals

see Courts-martial and courts of inquiry

Military dependents

Benefits and pay for active duty personnel, reserves, retirees, and survivors, 1940s-80s and projected to 2049, 21208–34

Dependents of DOD military and civilian personnel, by service branch and location, FY90, annual rpt, 3544–1.4

Dependents of DOD military and civilian personnel, by service branch and US and foreign location, quarterly rpt, 3542–20

Food aid programs of USDA, costs and participation by program, FY69-89, annual rpt, 1364–9

Health care facilities of DOD in US and abroad, beds, admissions, outpatient visits, and births, by service branch, quarterly rpt, 3542–15

Pacific basin US military personnel, dependents, aircraft, ships, and costs, by service branch and location, 1990, GAO rpt, 26123–357

Persian Gulf War Operation Desert Shield and Desert Storm deployment and deaths by selected personnel characteristics, 1990-91, annual rpt supplement, 3544–41.2

Persian Gulf War Operation Desert Storm deployment by personnel characteristics, and offsetting contributions by allied countries, 1990-91, annual rpt supplement, 3504–13

Schools for DOD dependents, student basic skills and college entrance test scores, 1990-91, annual rpt, 3504–16

Military dependents

see also Civilian Health and Medical Program of the Uniformed Services

Military education

Course completions, by detailed program, sex, race, and instn type, for 1972 high school class, as of 1984, 4888–4

Degrees awarded in higher education, by level, field, race, and sex, 1988/89 with trends from 1978/79, biennial rpt, 4844–17

Expenditures, staff, students, and facilities for DOD training and education programs, by service branch, FY92, annual rpt, 3504–5

Health care personnel, and accessions by training source, by occupation, specialty, and service branch, FY89, annual rpt, 3544–24

Navy personnel strengths, accessions, and attrition, detailed statistics, quarterly rpt, 3802–4

see also Military training

see also Reserve Officers Training Corps

see also Service academies

Military expenditures

see Defense budgets and appropriations

see Defense contracts and procurement

see Defense expenditures

see Military assistance

Military funerals

see Military cemeteries and funerals

Military health facilities and services

Admissions, beds, outpatient visits, and births in DOD health facilities in US and abroad, by service branch, quarterly rpt, 3542–15

Coverage under health insurance, by insurance type and selected characteristics, 1989, 4146–8.203

Dependents and retirees managed health care demonstration projects, enrollment, workload, and costs, 1988-90, 26306–3.117

Employment, and accessions by training source, by occupation, specialty, and service branch, FY89, annual rpt, 3544–24

Expenditures for health care, by service type, payment source, and sector, 1960s-90, annual article, 4652–1.221; 4652–1.252

Pacific territories economic conditions, population characteristics, and Federal aid, 1989 hearing, 21448–44

Procurement, DOD prime contract awards by detailed procurement category, FY87-90, annual rpt, 3544–18

see also Civilian Health and Medical Program of the Uniformed Services

see also Veterans health facilities and services

Military housing

Army strategic capability, force strengths, budget, and mgmt, FY74-93, annual rpt, 3704–13

Benefits and pay for active duty personnel, reserves, retirees, and survivors, 1940s-80s and projected to 2049, 21208–34

Budget of DOD, base construction and family housing appropriations by facility, service branch, and location, FY90-93, annual rpt, 3544–39

Budget of US, obligations and authority by function, agency, and program, with summaries, analyses, and historical tables, FY92, annual rpt, 104–2

Construction, renovation, and land acquisition for bases, DOD budget requests by project, service branch, State, and country, FY92-93, annual rpt, 3544–15

Expenditures and obligations of DOD, by function and service branch, quarterly rpt, 3542–3

Mortgages FHA-insured for 1-family units, by loan type and mortgage characteristics, quarterly rpt, 5142–45

Navy command proposed decentralization and relocation from DC area, savings, and cost of living indicators for 14 MSAs, 1980s, GAO rpt, 26123–346

Military intelligence

Budget of DOD, manpower needs, costs, and force readiness by service branch, FY92, annual rpt, 3504–1

Budget of DOD, programs, policies, and operations, FY90, annual rpt, 3544–2

Budget of DOD, R&D appropriations by item, service branch, and defense agency, FY90-93, annual rpt, 3544–33

see also Defense Intelligence Agency

see also Defense Security Assistance Agency

Military intervention

Persian Gulf War allied contributions to Operation Desert Storm offsetting US costs, by country, as of Apr 1991, annual rpt, 3544–28

Persian Gulf War Army and Air Natl Guard units and personnel mobilized, FY90, annual rpt, 3504–22

Persian Gulf War budget impact, CBO analysis, FY92-96, annual rpt, 26304–3

Persian Gulf War costs to US, and weapons budget requests, CBO analysis and review of FY92 Federal budget, annual rpt, 26304–2

Persian Gulf War costs to US by category and service branch, and offsetting contributions by allied country, monthly rpt, 102–3

Persian Gulf War costs to US by category and service branch, and offsetting contributions by allied country, various periods FY90-91, annual rpt, 104–7

Persian Gulf War fuel demand of US military by source, alternative estimates, 1990-91, article, 3162–44

Persian Gulf War impacts on US economic conditions compared to previous oil shock periods, and Saudi Arabia oil production and prices, 1990-92, hearings, 21248–156

Persian Gulf War Navy and Marine Corps reserves mobilized, 1990-91, GAO rpt, 26123–351

Persian Gulf War Operation Desert Shield and Desert Storm deployment and deaths by selected personnel characteristics, 1990-91, annual rpt supplement, 3544–41.2

Persian Gulf War Operation Desert Storm deployment by personnel characteristics, and offsetting contributions by allied countries, 1990-91, annual rpt supplement, 3504–13

Persian Gulf War shipping operations of Military Sealift Command, FY90, annual rpt, 3804–14

Military invasion and occupation

Iraq invasion of Kuwait, alien worker refugees fleeing from Iraq and Kuwait, intl aid by source, and costs to host and native countries, 1990-91, GAO rpt, 26123–326

Iraq invasion of Kuwait, impacts on oil prices and industry profits, as of 4th qtr 1990, 3166–6.46

Iraq invasion of Kuwait, impacts on oil supply and prices, selected indicators, daily press release, 3162–44

Iraq invasion of Kuwait, oil embargo impacts on OPEC and US oil supply and industry, 1989-91, hearing, 21368–132

Kuwait reconstruction after Persian Gulf War, Army Corps of Engineers contract awards by firm and purpose, 1st qtr 1991, article, 2042–1.203

Panama economic aid after US sanctions and military invasion, AID funding by program, as of 1991, GAO rpt, 26123–330

Military law

Navy battleship *USS Iowa* explosion, safety and personnel mgmt issues, with technical analysis, FY89, GAO rpt, 26123–315

Navy personnel strengths, accessions, and attrition, detailed statistics, quarterly rpt, 3802–4

US attorneys civil and criminal cases by type and disposition, and collections, by Federal district, FY90, annual rpt, 6004–2.1

see also Court of Military Appeals

see also Courts-martial and courts of inquiry

Military occupation

see Military invasion and occupation

Military pay

Budget of DOD, programs, policies, and operations, FY90, annual rpt, 3544–2

Budget of US, object class analysis of obligations, by agency, FY92, annual rpt, 104–9

Budget of US, obligations and authority by function, agency, and program, with summaries, analyses, and historical tables, FY92, annual rpt, 104–2

Census of Govts, 1987: employment, payroll, and average earnings, by function, level of govt, State, county, and population size, 2455–2

Earnings by industry div, and personal income per capita and by source, by State, MSA, and county, 1984-89, annual regional rpts, 2704–2

Employment, earnings, and hours, by SIC 1- to 4-digit industry, monthly and annual averages, selected years 1909-90, annual rpt, 6744–4

Expenditures and obligations of DOD, by function and service branch, quarterly rpt, 3542–3

Income (household, family, and personal), by source, detailed characteristics, and region, 1988-89, annual Current Population Rpt, 2546–6.68

Income (household, family, and personal), by source, detailed characteristics, and region, 1990, annual Current Population Rpt, 2546–6.70

Natl Guard activities, personnel, and facilities, FY90, annual rpt, 3504–22

Natl income and product accounts and components, *Survey of Current Business,* monthly rpt, 2702–1.24

Navy budget, personnel, procurement, and equipment, planned FY91-93, annual fact sheet, 3804–16

Navy command proposed decentralization and relocation from DC area, savings, and cost of living indicators for 14 MSAs, 1980s, GAO rpt, 26123–346

Index by Subjects and Names

Military personnel

Pay and benefits for active duty personnel, reserves, retirees, and survivors, 1940s-80s and projected to 2049, 21208–34

Payroll and employment, by function, level of govt, and State, 1990, annual rpt, 2466–1.1

Payroll of Fed Govt, by State and county, FY90, annual rpt, 2464–3.1

Payroll of Fed Govt, spending for civilian, military, and postal workers by State, FY90, annual rpt, 2464–2

Payroll, personnel, and contracts spending, by service branch and location, with top 5 contractors and maps, by State and country, FY90, annual rpt, 3544–29

Persian Gulf War costs to US by category and service branch, and offsetting contributions by allied country, monthly rpt, 102–3

Persian Gulf War costs to US by category and service branch, and offsetting contributions by allied country, various periods FY90-91, annual rpt, 104–7

Personnel of DOD, and organization, budget, weapons, and property, by service branch, State, and country, 1991 annual summary rpt, 3504–13

Reserve forces personnel attrition, by reason, personnel characteristics, reserve component, and State, FY88, GAO rpt, 26123–329

Reserve forces personnel strengths and characteristics, by component, FY90, annual rpt, 3544–38

Reserve forces personnel strengths and characteristics, by component, quarterly rpt, 3542–4

Sealift Military Command shipping operations, finances, and personnel, FY90, annual rpt, 3804–14

Soviet Union GNP by detailed income and outlay component, 1985, 2326–18.59

State and Metro Area Data Book, 1991 data compilation, 2328–54

see also Military benefits and pensions

Military personnel

Air Force recruiting compliance with gender-neutral selection, with aptitude test results by sex, FY86-90, GAO rpt, 26123–359

Army Dept activities, personnel, discipline, budget, and assistance, FY83 summary data, annual rpt, 3704–11

Army strategic capability, force strengths, budget, and mgmt, FY74-93, annual rpt, 3704–13

Base support costs by function, and personnel and acreage by installation, by service branch, FY91, annual rpt, 3504–11

Black Americans social and economic characteristics, for South and total US, 1989-90 and trends from 1969, Current Population Rpt, 2546–1.450

Budget of DOD, manpower needs, costs, and force readiness by service branch, FY92, annual rpt, 3504–1

Budget of DOD, programs, policies, and operations, FY90, annual rpt, 3544–2

Cholesterol levels of Navy personnel, by sex, 1989 study, article, 4042–3.215

Coast Guard military and civilian employment, by grade, sex, race, and location, FY90, annual rpt, 7304–18

Coast Guard search and rescue missions, and lives and property lost and saved, by district and assisting unit, FY90, annual rpt, 7404–2

Criminal case processing in military courts, and prisoners by facility, by service branch, data compilation, 1991 annual rpt, 6064–6.5; 6064–6.6

Deaths by cause, age, race, and rank, and personnel captured and missing, by service branch, FY90, annual rpt, 3544–40

Deaths of military personnel by service branch and age group, and veterans death rates, 1966-90, annual rpt, 8654–1

Disability, acute and chronic health conditions, absenteeism, and health services use, by selected characteristics, 1987, CD-ROM, 4147–10.177

Economic indicators and components, current data and annual trends, monthly rpt, 23842–1.2

Employee paid leave days for military duty, by occupational group, for small businesses, 1990, biennial rpt, 6784–20

Employment and Earnings, detailed data, monthly rpt, 6742–2.4

Employment and payroll, by function, level of govt, and State, 1990, annual rpt, 2466–1.1

Employment, earnings, and hours, by SIC 1- to 4-digit industry, monthly and annual averages, selected years 1909-90, annual rpt, 6744–4

Employment, earnings, and hours, monthly press release, 6742–5

Employment, payroll, and average earnings, by function, level of govt, State, county, and population size, 1987 Census of Govts, 2455–2

Employment situation, earnings, hours, and other BLS economic indicators, transcripts of BLS Commissioner's monthly testimony, periodic rpt, 23846–4

Food recipient household size, composition, income, and income and deductions allowed, summer 1988, annual rpt, 1364–8

Foreign countries economic, social, political, and geographic summary data, by country, 1991, annual factbook, 9114–2

Foreign countries military aid of US, arms sales, and training programs costs and budget requests, by program, world region, and country, FY90-92, annual rpt, 7144–13

Health care facilities of DOD in US and abroad, beds, admissions, outpatient visits, and births, by service branch, quarterly rpt, 3542–15

Health care personnel, and accessions by training source, by occupation, specialty, and service branch, FY89, annual rpt, 3544–24

Income (household, family, and personal), by source, detailed characteristics, and region, 1988-89, annual Current Population Rpt, 2546–6.68

Income (household, family, and personal), by source, detailed characteristics, and region, 1990, annual Current Population Rpt, 2546–6.70

Labor force, wages, hours, and payroll costs, by major industry group and demographic characteristics, *Survey of Current Business*, monthly rpt, 2702–1.8

Malaria cases in US, for military personnel and US and foreign natls, and by country of infection, 1966-89, annual rpt, 4205–4

Minority group higher education enrollment, degrees, factors affecting participation, and earnings, 1960s-88, 4808–29

Natl Guard activities, personnel, and facilities, FY90, annual rpt, 3504–22

NATO and Japan military spending and indicators of ability to support common defense, by country, 1970s-89, annual rpt, 3544–28

NATO and Warsaw Pact military forces reductions under proposed treaty, and US budget savings, 1990 rpt, 26306–3.114

Navy battleship *USS Iowa* explosion, safety and personnel mgmt issues, with technical analysis, FY89, GAO rpt, 26123–315

Navy budget, personnel, procurement, and equipment, planned FY91-93, annual fact sheet, 3804–16

Navy command proposed decentralization and relocation from DC area, savings, and cost of living indicators for 14 MSAs, 1980s, GAO rpt, 26123–346

Navy drug and alcohol abuse education and treatment program activity, semiannual tables, discontinued, 3802–6

Navy flag officers, captains awaiting promotion, and billets, by pay grade and rank, as of Feb 1991, GAO rpt, 26123–340

Navy personnel radiation exposure on nuclear-powered vessels and at support facilities, and injury claims, 1950s-90, annual rpt, 3804–10

Navy personnel strengths, accessions, and attrition, detailed statistics, quarterly rpt, 3802–4

Nuclear weapons elimination under Intermediate-Range Nuclear Forces Treaty, US and USSR on site inspections, and US costs and staffing, FY89-91, GAO rpt, 26123–364

Officers assigned to multiservice organizations, designation of critical positions for qualified joint specialty officers, 1987-90 and projected to 1994, GAO rpt, 26123–317

Pacific basin US military personnel, dependants, aircraft, ships, and costs, by service branch and location, 1990, GAO rpt, 26123–357

Persian Gulf War Operation Desert Shield and Desert Storm deployment and deaths by selected personnel characteristics, 1990-91, annual rpt supplement, 3544–41.2

Persian Gulf War Operation Desert Storm deployment by personnel charactcristics, and offsetting contributions by allied countries, 1990-91, annual rpt supplement, 3504–13

Personnel (civilian) of DOD, by service branch and defense agency, with summary military employment data, quarterly rpt, 3542–16

Personnel (civilian and military) of DOD, by service branch, major installation, and State, as of Sept 1990, annual rpt, 3544–7

Personnel active duty and recruit social, economic, and parents characteristics, by service branch and State, FY89, annual rpt, 3544–41

Military personnel

Personnel active duty strength, recruits, and reenlistment, by race, sex, and service branch, quarterly press release, 3542–7

Personnel, contracts, and payroll spending, by service branch and location, with top 5 contractors and maps, by State and country, FY90, annual rpt, 3544–29

Personnel of DOD, and organization, budget, weapons, and property, by service branch, State, and country, 1991 annual summary rpt, 3504–13

Personnel strengths, for active duty, civilians, and dependents, by service branch and US and foreign location, quarterly rpt, 3542–20

Personnel strengths, for active duty, civilians, and reserves, by service branch, FY90 and trends, annual rpt, 3544–1

Personnel strengths, for active duty, civilians, and reserves, by service branch, quarterly rpt, 3542–14

Personnel strengths, for active duty enlisted and officers, by sex and race, 1970s-90, GAO rpt, 26123–325

Personnel strengths in US and abroad, by service branch, world area, and country, quarterly press release, 3542–9

Personnel strengths, summary by service branch, monthly press release, 3542–2

Physicians, by specialty, age, sex, and location of training and practice, 1989, State rpt series, 4116–6

Reserve forces personnel and equipment strengths, and readiness, by reserve component, FY90, annual rpt, 3544–31

Reserve forces personnel attrition, by reason, personnel characteristics, reserve component, and State, FY88, GAO rpt, 26123–329

Reserve forces personnel strengths and characteristics, by component, FY90, annual rpt, 3544–38

Reserve forces personnel strengths and characteristics, by component, quarterly rpt, 3542–4

ROTC programs enrollment, grads, staff, scholarships, and costs, by service branch, FY86-89, GAO rpt, 26123–337

Sealift Military Command shipping operations, finances, and personnel, FY90, annual rpt, 3804–14

Shift rotation health and safety effects, and US and foreign regulation, by selected industry and occupation, 1970s-89, 26356–9.3

Soviet Union GNP by component and industry sector, and CIA estimation methods, 1950s-87, 23848–223

Soviet Union military weapons systems, presence, and force strengths, and compared to US, 1991 annual rpt, 3504–20

State and Metro Area Data Book, 1991 data compilation, 2328–54

Statistical Abstract of US, 1991 annual data compilation, 2324–1.11

Terrorism (intl) incidents, casualties, and attacks on US targets, by attack type and country, 1990, annual rpt, 7004–22

Terrorism (intl) incidents, casualties, and attacks on US targets, by attack type and world area, 1990, annual rpt, 7004–13

Terrorism incidents in US, related activity, and casualties, by attack type, target, group, and location, 1990, annual rpt, 6224–6

Transport of personnel by DOD, and costs, by service branch and mode of transport, quarterly rpt, 3702–1

War participants, deaths, veterans living, and compensation and pension recipients, for each US war, 1775-1990, annual rpt, 8604–2

Women military personnel on active and reserve duty, by demographic and service characteristics and service branch, FY89, annual chartbook, 3544–26

see also Courts-martial and courts of inquiry

see also Military benefits and pensions

see also Military dependents

see also Military education

see also Military pay

see also Military training

see also Retired military personnel

see also Selective service

see also Veterans

see also Voluntary military service

Military policy

see Arms trade

see Defense budgets and appropriations

see Military assistance

see Military strategy

see National defense

Military post exchanges and commissaries

Financial statements of Army and Air Force Exchange Service, FY88-89, annual rpt, 3504–21

Labor productivity of Federal employees, indexes of output and labor costs by function, 1967-89, annual rpt, 6824–1.6

Milk home delivery, and sales by wholesale outlet type, by region, 1989 survey, biennial article, 1317–4.201

Navy small and disadvantaged business procurement office locations, and supply and service codes, 1990 biennial listing, 3804–5

Sales by commodity, and operations, by post exchange and location worldwide, FY89, annual rpt, 3504–10

Military prisons

Prisoners in Federal instns, by sex, prison, security level, contract facility type, and region, monthly rpt series, 6242–1

Prisoners in military prisons, and capacity, by service branch and facility, data compilation, 1991 annual rpt, 6064–6.6

Military research

see Defense research

Military reserves

see Armed services reserves

Military science

Budget of DOD, R&D appropriations by item, service branch, and defense agency, FY90-93, annual rpt, 3544–33

Soviet Union military weapons systems, presence, and force strengths, and compared to US, 1991 annual rpt, 3504–20

see also Arms control and disarmament

see also Civil defense

see also Defense research

see also Logistics

see also Military strategy

Military service

see Selective service

see Voluntary military service

Military service academies

see Service academies

Military strategy

Army strategic capability, force strengths, budget, and mgmt, FY74-93, annual rpt, 3704–13

Base support costs by function, and personnel and acreage by installation, by service branch, FY91, annual rpt, 3504–11

Budget of DOD, manpower needs, costs, and force readiness by service branch, FY92, annual rpt, 3504–1

Budget of DOD, programs, policies, and operations, FY90, annual rpt, 3544–2

Budget of DOD, R&D appropriations by item, service branch, and defense agency, FY90-93, annual rpt, 3544–33

Foreign countries military aid of US, arms sales, and training programs costs and budget requests, by program, world region, and country, FY90-92, annual rpt, 7144–13

Reserve forces personnel and equipment strengths, and readiness, by reserve component, FY90, annual rpt, 3544–31

Soviet Union military weapons systems, presence, and force strengths, and compared to US, 1991 annual rpt, 3504–20

Military supplies and property

Army equipment unserviceable inventories, and repair and replacement costs, late 1980s, GAO rpt, 26123–312

Autos and light trucks owned and leased by service branch, and costs and savings from GSA leases, FY89, GAO rpt, 26123–344

Budget of DOD, programs, policies, and operations, FY90, annual rpt, 3544–2

Budget of DOD, R&D appropriations by item, service branch, and defense agency, FY90-93, annual rpt, 3544–33

Budget of DOD, weapons acquisition costs by system and service branch, FY91-93, annual rpt, 3504–2

Capital stock, by type and level of govt, 1989, article, 9391–1.208

Computer systems and equipment of Fed Govt, by type, make, and agency, 2nd half FY90, semiannual listing, 9452–9

Defense Logistics Agency processing of supply requisitions, duration and efficiency, FY89, GAO rpt, 26123–331

Drug enforcement support activities of Natl Guard, spending and needs by State, FY89-91, GAO rpt, 26123–343

Expenditures and obligations of DOD, by function and service branch, quarterly rpt, 3542–3

Expenditures for DOD base support by function, and personnel and acreage by installation, by service branch, FY91, annual rpt, 3504–11

Exports and imports of US, by country and detailed commodity, monthly rpt, 2422–12

Foreign countries military aid and arms sales of US, by weapon type, as of Sept 1990, annual rpt, 3904–3

Foreign countries military aid of US, arms sales, and training programs costs and budget requests, by program, world region, and country, FY90-92, annual rpt, 7144–13

Inventory of DOD property, supplies, and equipment, by service branch, FY90, annual rpt, 3544–6

Index by Subjects and Names

Military weapons

Leasing of military equipment by equipment type and service branch and feasibility of lease refinancing, 1988, GAO rpt, 26111–75

Mexico imports from US, by industry and State, 1987-90, 2048–154

Navy budget, personnel, procurement, and equipment, planned FY91-93, annual fact sheet, 3804–16

Navy command proposed decentralization and relocation from DC area, savings, and cost of living indicators for 14 MSAs, 1980s, GAO rpt, 26123–346

Persian Gulf War costs to US by category and service branch, and offsetting contributions by allied country, monthly rpt, 102–3

Persian Gulf War costs to US by category and service branch, and offsetting contributions by allied country, various periods FY90-91, annual rpt, 104–7

Persian Gulf War fuel demand of US military by source, alternative estimates, 1990-91, article, 3162–44

Railroad equipment of DOD, inventory, defects, and repair and inspection needs, 1990, GAO rpt, 26113–535

Reserve forces personnel and equipment strengths, and readiness, by reserve component, FY90, annual rpt, 3544–31

Sealift Military Command shipping operations, finances, and personnel, FY90, annual rpt, 3804–14

Shipments by DOD of military and personal property, passenger traffic, and costs, by service branch and mode of transport, quarterly rpt, 3702–1

Soviet Union military weapons systems, presence, and force strengths, and compared to US, 1991 annual rpt, 3504–20

Surplus military property donations to intl and State relief programs, FY86-90, GAO rpt, 26123–316

see also Ammunition

see also Arms trade

see also Defense contracts and procurement

see also Logistics

see also Military assistance

see also Military bases, posts, and reservations

see also Military vehicles

see also Military weapons

Military training

Army Reserve and National Guard wartime preparedness, for general support maintenance units, as of May 1990, GAO rpt, 26123–354

Budget of DOD, manpower needs, costs, and force readiness by service branch, FY92, annual rpt, 3504–1

Budget of DOD, programs, policies, and operations, FY90, annual rpt, 3544–2

Budget of DOD, R&D appropriations by item, service branch, and defense agency, FY90-93, annual rpt, 3544–33

Computer simulations use in large military exercises, costs and effectiveness in Army Germany deployment exercise, 1969-90, GAO rpt, 26123–318

Exchange and training programs of Federal agencies, participants by world area, and funding, by program, FY89, annual rpt, 9854–8

Expenditures for DOD base support by function, and personnel and acreage by installation, by service branch, FY91, annual rpt, 3504–11

Expenditures, staff, students, and facilities for DOD training and education programs, by service branch, FY92, annual rpt, 3504–5

Foreign countries economic and military aid loans and grants from US and intl agencies, by program and country, FY46-90, annual rpt, 9914–5

Foreign countries human rights conditions in 170 countries, and US economic and military aid, 1990, annual rpt, 21384–3

Foreign countries military aid of US, arms sales, and training, by country, FY50-90, annual rpt, 3904–3

Foreign countries military aid of US, arms sales, and training programs costs and budget requests, by program, world region, and country, FY90-92, annual rpt, 7144–13

Health care personnel, and accessions by training source, by occupation, specialty, and service branch, FY89, annual rpt, 3544–24

Natl Guard activities, personnel, and facilities, FY90, annual rpt, 3504–22

Navy personnel strengths, accessions, and attrition, detailed statistics, quarterly rpt, 3802–4

Personnel of DOD, and organization, budget, weapons, and property, by service branch, State, and country, 1991 annual summary rpt, 3504–13

Procurement, DOD prime contract awards by detailed procurement category, FY87-90, annual rpt, 3544–18

Reserve forces personnel and equipment strengths, and readiness, by reserve component, FY90, annual rpt, 3544–31

see also Military education

see also Reserve Officers Training Corps

see also Service academies

Military tribunals

see Courts-martial and courts of inquiry

Military vehicles

Budget of DOD, procurement appropriations by item, service branch, and defense agency, FY90-93, annual rpt, 3544–32

Budget of DOD, programs, policies, and operations, FY90, annual rpt, 3544–2

Budget of DOD, weapons acquisition costs by system and service branch, FY91-93, annual rpt, 3504–2

Budget of US, object class analysis of obligations, by agency, FY92, annual rpt, 104–9

Coast Guard search and rescue missions, and lives and property lost and saved, by district and assisting unit, FY90, annual rpt, 7404–2

Energy use by mode of transport, fuel supply, and demographic and economic factors of vehicle use, 1970s-89, annual rpt, 3304–5

Exports and imports of US, by country and detailed commodity, monthly rpt, 2422–12

Exports and imports of US, by Harmonized System 6-digit commodity and country, 1990, annual rpt, 2424–13

Exports of US, detailed Schedule B commodities with countries of destination, 1990, annual rpt, 2424–10

Foreign and US military weapons trade, production, and defense industry finances, with data by firm and country, 1980s-91, 26358–241

Foreign countries military aid and arms sales of US, by weapon type, as of Sept 1990, annual rpt, 3904–3

Manufacturing annual survey, 1989: finances and operations, by SIC 2- to 4-digit industry, series, 2506–15

Manufacturing census, 1987: employment and shipments under Fed Govt contracts, by SIC 4-digit industry, 2497–7

Manufacturing census, 1987: finances and operations, by SIC 2- to 4-digit industry, State, and MSA, with trends from 1849, 2497–1

Manufacturing census, 1987: finances and operations, by type of organization and SIC 2- to 4-digit industry, subject rpt, 2497–5

NATO and Warsaw Pact military forces reductions under proposed treaty, and US budget savings, 1990 rpt, 26306–3.114

Occupational injury and illness rates, by SIC 2- to 4-digit industry, 1988-89, annual rpt, 6844–7

Procurement, DOD prime contract awards by category, contract and contractor type, and service branch, FY81-1st half FY91, semiannual rpt, 3542–1

Procurement, DOD prime contract awards by category, contractor type, and State, FY88-90, annual rpt, 3544–11

Procurement, DOD prime contract awards by detailed procurement category, FY87-90, annual rpt, 3544–18

Shipments by DOD of military and personal property, passenger traffic, and costs, by service branch and mode of transport, quarterly rpt, 3702–1

Soviet Union military weapons systems, presence, and force strengths, and compared to US, 1991 annual rpt, 3504–20

Military weapons

Army strategic capability, force strengths, budget, and mgmt, FY74-93, annual rpt, 3704–13

Budget of DOD, organization, personnel, weapons, and property, by service branch, State, and country, 1991 annual summary rpt, 3504–13

Budget of DOD, programs, policies, and operations, FY90, annual rpt, 3544–2

Budget of DOD, R&D appropriations by item, service branch, and defense agency, FY90-93, annual rpt, 3544–33

Foreign countries military aid of US, arms sales, and training programs costs and budget requests, by program, world region, and country, FY90-92, annual rpt, 7144–13

Japan weapons equipment levels, by system, planned 1986-91, annual rpt, 3544–28

Manufacturing census, 1987: employment and shipments under Fed Govt contracts, by SIC 4-digit industry, 2497–7

NATO and Warsaw Pact military forces reductions under proposed treaty, and US budget savings, 1990 rpt, 26306–3.114

Price indexes (producer), by stage of processing and detailed commodity, monthly 1990, annual rpt, 6764–2

Military weapons

Sealift Military Command shipping operations, finances, and personnel, FY90, annual rpt, 3804–14

Shipments by DOD of military and personal property, passenger traffic, and costs, by service branch and mode of transport, quarterly rpt, 3702–1

Soviet Union military weapons systems, presences, and force strengths, and compared to US, 1991 annual rpt, 3504–20

Space programs activities, missions, launchings, payloads, and flight duration, for foreign and US programs, 1957-90, annual rpt, 21704–4

see also Ammunition

see also Arms trade

see also Chemical and biological warfare agents

see also Defense contracts and procurement

see also Defense expenditures

see also Military aircraft

see also Military assistance

see also Military vehicles

see also Missiles and rockets

see also Naval vessels

see also Nuclear weapons

see also Torpedoes

Militia

see National Guard

Milk and milk products

see Dairy industry and products

Miller, Gary W.

"Behavior of Bowhead Whales of the Davis Strait and Bering/Beaufort Stocks vs. Regional Differences in Human Activities", 5738–30

Miller, Glenn H., Jr.

"Tax Increases in the Tenth District: Where Will the Money Come From?", 9381–1.204

"Tenth District Cities: Recent Growth and Prospects for the 1990s", 9381–1.209

Miller, Herbert

"Directory of Energy Information Administration Models, 1991", 3164–87

Miller, L. K.

"Water-Quality Data, San Joaquin Valley, Calif., April 1987 to September 1988. Regional Aquifer-System Analysis", 5666–25.9

Miller, Louisa F.

"Remarriage Among Women in the U.S.: 1985", 2546–2.157

Miller, Patrick E.

"Forest Statistics for Alabama Counties, 1990", 1206–30.10

Miller, Preston J.

"Playing By the Rules: A Proposal for Federal Budget Reform", 9383–2

Miller, Richard D.

"Another Look at the Medically Uninsured Using the 1987 Consumer Expenditure Survey", 6886–6.75

"Helium Resources of the U.S., 1989", 5604–44

Millionaires

see Wealth

Mills, Leonard O.

"Persistence and Convergence in Relative Regional Incomes", 9387–8.232

"Understanding National and Regional Housing Trends", 9387–1.205

Millville, N.J.

see also under By SMSA or MSA in the "Index by Categories"

Milwaukee, Wis.

CPI by component for US city average, and by region, population size, and for 27 metro areas, monthly rpt, 6762–2

Housing and households characteristics, unit and neighborhood quality, and journey to work by MSA location, for 11 MSAs, 1984 survey, supplement, 2485–8

Housing and households characteristics, 1988 survey, MSA fact sheet, 2485–11.8

Housing and households detailed characteristics, and unit and neighborhood quality, by location, 1988 survey, MSA rpt, 2485–6.2

Wages by occupation, and benefits for office and plant workers, 1991 survey, periodic MSA rpt, 6785–12.4

see also under By City and By SMSA or MSA in the "Index by Categories"

Mine accidents and safety

Back injuries in underground coal mines, by circumstances, victim characteristics, and treatment, mid 1980s, 5608–166

Coal mining and related operations occupational injuries and incidence, employment, and hours, 1989, annual rpt, 6664–4

Deaths and rates, by cause, age, sex, race, and State, 1988, US Vital Statistics annual rpt, 4144–2.5

Deaths in mining accidents, by circumstances and selected victim characteristics, semiannual rpt series, 6662–3

Fed Govt spending in States, by type, program, agency, and State, FY90, annual rpt, 2464–2

Injuries by circumstances, employment, and hours, for mining industries by type of operation and State, quarterly rpt, 6662–1

Injuries, illnesses, and workdays lost, by SIC 2-digit industry, 1989-90, annual press release, 6844–3

Injury and illness rates by SIC 2- to 4-digit industry, and deaths by cause and industry div, 1989, annual rpt, 6844–1

Injury and illness rates, by SIC 2- to 4-digit industry, 1988-89, annual rpt, 6844–7

Metal mines and related operations occupational injuries and incidence, employment, and hours, 1989, annual rpt, 6664–3

Nonmetallic minerals mines and related operations occupational injuries and incidence, employment, and hours, 1989, annual rpt, 6664–1

Radiation exposure of uranium miners and risk of death from cancer and lung diseases, for Indians and compared to whites and foreign countries, 1950s-84, hearing, 25548–101

Safety and health enforcement, training, and funding, with casualties, by type of mine and State, FY89, annual rpt, 6664–6

Sand and gravel mines and related operations occupational injuries and incidence, employment, and hours, 1989, annual rpt, 6664–2

Statistical Abstract of US, 1991 annual data compilation, 2324–1.25

Stone mines and related operations occupational injuries and incidence, employment, and hours, 1989, annual rpt, 6664–5

see also Black lung disease

Mine Safety and Health Administration

Budget of US, obligations and authority by function, agency, and program, with summaries, analyses, and historical tables, FY92, annual rpt, 104–2

Coal mining and related operations occupational injuries and incidence, employment, and hours, 1989, annual rpt, 6664–4

Deaths in mining accidents, by circumstances and selected victim characteristics, semiannual rpt series, 6662–3

Enforcement activities of MSHA, training, and funding, with casualties, by type of mine and State, FY89, annual rpt, 6664–6

Expenditures of Fed Govt in States, by type, program, agency, and State, FY90, annual rpt, 2464–2

Injuries by circumstances, employment, and hours, for mining industries by type of operation and State, quarterly rpt, 6662–1

Metal mines and related operations occupational injuries and incidence, employment, and hours, 1989, annual rpt, 6664–3

Nonmetallic minerals mines and related operations occupational injuries and incidence, employment, and hours, 1989, annual rpt, 6664–1

Respiratory diseases related to occupational hazards, epidemiology, diagnosis, and treatment, for selected industries and work settings, 1988 conf, 4248–90

Sand and gravel mines and related operations occupational injuries and incidence, employment, and hours, 1989, annual rpt, 6664–2

Stone mines and related operations occupational injuries and incidence, employment, and hours, 1989, annual rpt, 6664–5

Mineral Industry Surveys

Explosives and blasting agents use, by type, industry, and State, 1990, annual rpt, 5614–22

Phosphate rock production, prices, sales, trade, and use, 1991, annual rpt, 5614–20

Potash production, prices, trade, use, and sales, 1990 crop year, annual rpt, 5614–19

Production of minerals, 1990, annual preliminary rpt, 5614–6

Production, trade, stocks, and use of minerals, monthly commodity rpt series, 5612–1

Production, trade, stocks, and use of minerals, quarterly commodity rpt series, 5612–2

Production, trade, use, and industry operations, advance annual commodity rpt series, 5614–5

Mineral leases

Alaska land area by ownership, and availability for mineral exploration and dev, 1984-86, 5608–152

Coal and other fossil fuel production on Federal land, 1990 and trends from 1949, annual rpt, 3164–74.1

Coal leasing activity on Federal land, acreage, production, and reserves, by coal region and State, FY90, annual rpt, 5724–10

Expenditures of Fed Govt in States, by type, program, agency, and State, FY90, annual rpt, 2464–2

Fed Govt receipts by source and outlays by agency, *Treasury Bulletin*, quarterly rpt, 8002–4.1

Flow-of-funds accounts, savings, investments, and credit statements, quarterly rpt, 9365–3.3

Forest Service acreage, staff, finances, and mgmt activities in Pacific Northwest, with data by forest, 1970s-89, annual rpt, 1204–37

Forest Service activities and finances, by region and State, FY90, annual rpt, 1204–1.1

Forest Service mgmt of public lands and resources dev, environmental, economic, and social impacts of alternative programs, projected to 2040, 1208–24

Forests (natl) revenue, by source, forest, and State, FY90, annual rpt, 1204–34

Geothermal resources, power plant capacity and operating status, leases, and wells, by location, 1960s-94, 3308–87

Land Mgmt Bur activities and funding by State, FY89, annual rpt, 5724–13

Land Mgmt Bur activities in Southwestern US, FY90, annual rpt, 5724–15

Multinatl firms US affiliates, finances, and operations, by industry, world area of parent firm, and State, 1988-89, annual rpt, 2704–4

Offshore oil, gas, and minerals production, revenue, and leasing activity, for Federal OCS lands by ocean area and State, 1950s-90, annual rpt, 5734–3

Production and revenue from oil, gas, and minerals on Federal and Indian lands, by State, 1990 and trends from 1920, annual rpt, 5734–2

Production, revenue, and leasing activities on Federal and Indian oil, gas, and minerals lands, by State, 1980-89 and trends from 1920, 5738–21

Public lands acreage and use, and Land Mgmt Bur activities and finances, annual State rpt series, 5724–11

Public lands acreage, grants, use, revenues, and allocations, by State, FY90 and trends, annual rpt, 5724–1

Public lands minerals resources and availability, State rpt series, 5606–7

see also Oil and gas leases

Minerals Management Service

Alaska rural areas population characteristics, and energy resources dev effects, series, 5736–5

Arctic Ocean fish catch and habitat impacts of oil and gas dev, and assessment methods, 1988 conf, 5738–24

Atlantic OCS environmental conditions, and oil and gas dev impacts, series, discontinued, 5736–6

Birds (waterfowl) coastal population and breeding success, for murre and kittiwake in Bering Sea colonies, 1979-89, 5738–31

Budget of US, obligations and authority by function, agency, and program, with summaries, analyses, and historical tables, FY92, annual rpt, 104–2

California OCS oil and gas dev impacts on water quality, marine life, and sediments, by site, 1986-89, annual rpt, 5734–11

California sport and commercial fish and shellfish landings, permits issued, and harbor facilities, 1916-86, 5738–20

Expenditures of Fed Govt in States, by type, program, agency, and State, FY90, annual rpt, 2464–2

Florida environmental, social, and economic conditions, and impacts of proposed OCS oil and gas leases in southern coastal areas, 1990 compilation of papers, 5738–19

Geese pre-migration feeding behavior impacts of aircraft disturbance, for 3 species at Izembek Lagoon, Alaska, 1970s-88, 5738–23

Gulf of Mexico oil and gas reserves, production, and leasing status, by location, 1989, annual rpt, 5734–6

Marine mammals and birds population and distribution, by species and northeast Pacific Ocean location, literature and data base review, 1950s-88, 5738–28

North Carolina environmental and socioeconomic conditions, and impacts of proposed OCS oil and gas exploration, 1970s-90 and projected to 2020, 5738–22

Oil and gas OCS lease bidding under alternative leasing systems, activity, royalty rates, and production, by sale, lessee type, and ocean area, FY79-89, annual rpt, 5734–12

Oil and gas OCS leases environmental and socioeconomic impact and coastal area description, final statement series, 5736–1

Oil and gas OCS leases suspended for environmental reasons and repurchased by Fed Govt, costs of cancellation for 3 States, 1990, GAO rpt, 26113–509

Oil and gas OCS reserves, and leasing and dev activity, periodic regional rpt series, 5736–3

Oil and gas OCS reserves of Fed Govt, leasing and exploration activity, production, revenue, and costs, by ocean area, FY90, annual rpt, 5734–4

Oil, gas, and minerals leasing, production, and revenue on Federal and Indian land, by State, 1980s and trends from 1920, 5738–21

Oil, gas, and minerals production and revenue on Federal and Indian land, by State, 1990 and trends from 1920, annual rpt, 5734–2

Oil, gas, and minerals production, revenue, and leasing activity, for Federal OCS lands by ocean region and State, 1950s-90, annual rpt, 5734–3

Oil import traffic by US port and vessel type, marine oil pollution sources, and costs and operations of proposed offshore terminals, late 1980s, 5738–25

Pacific Ocean OCS oil and gas production, and wells, by drilling platform under Federal lease, 1960s-89, annual rpt, 5734–9

Pacific Ocean oil and gas production, reserves, and wells drilled by location, 1989, annual rpt, 5734–7

Publications of MMS on OCS research, 1988, annual listing, 5734–5

Turtles (sea) population near oil drilling rigs, and habitat characteristics, 1988-90, 5738–26

Whales (bowhead) population in Arctic areas, behavioral differences by location, 1970s-80s, 5738–29

Whales (bowhead) population in Arctic areas, impacts of subsistence whaling, shipping, noise, and other human activity, mid 1970s-80s, 5738–30

Whales (bowhead) population in Beaufort Sea, and fall aerial survey operations, 1979-90, annual rpt, 5734–10

Whales (bowhead and white) migration through Beaufort Sea, behavior impacts of oil drilling and aircraft noise, spring 1989, 5738–27

Mines and mineral resources

Aerial survey R&D rpts, and sources of natural resource and environmental data, quarterly listing, 9502–7

Alaska land area by ownership, and availability for mineral exploration and dev, 1984-86, 5608–152

Alaska minerals resources and geologic characteristics, compilation of papers, 1989, annual rpt, 5664–15

Alaska minerals resources and production, by mineral and site, for Juneau region, 1987-88, 5608–169

Alaska minerals resources, production, oil and gas leases, reserves, and exploratory wells, with maps and bibl, 1989, annual rpt, 5664–11

California minerals production by commodity, shipments, and liquefied petroleum gas transport by mode, 1986-87, conf, 5668–119

Capital expenditures for plant and equipment, by industry div, monthly rpt, quarterly data, 23842–1.1

Capital expenditures for plant and equipment, by major industry group, quarterly rpt, 2502–2

Census Bur rpts and data files, coverage and availability, 1991 annual listing, 2304–2

China minerals production and trade, by commodity, 1988-89, annual rpt, 5604–38

Classification codes concordance of Canada and US SICs, for 1- to 4-digit levels, 1991 rpt, 2628–31

Communist countries trade with US, by detailed commodity and country, quarterly rpt with articles, 9882–2

County Business Patterns, 1988: employment, establishments, and payroll, by SIC 2- to 4-digit industry and county, annual State rpt series, 2326–6

County Business Patterns, 1989: employment, establishments, and payroll, by SIC 2- to 4-digit industry and county, annual State rpt series, 2326–8

Earnings by industry div, and personal income per capita and by source, by State, MSA, and county, 1984-89, annual regional rpts, 2704–2

Employment and Earnings, detailed data, monthly rpt, 6742–2.5

Employment, earnings, and hours, by SIC 1- to 4-digit industry, monthly and annual averages, selected years 1909-90, annual rpt, 6744–4

Mines and mineral resources

Index by Subjects and Names

Employment, earnings, and hours, monthly press release, 6742–5

Employment situation, earnings, hours, and other BLS economic indicators, transcripts of BLS Commissioner's monthly testimony, periodic rpt, 23846–4

Employment, unemployment, and labor force characteristics, by region and census div, 1990, annual rpt, 6744–7.1

Energy use by mode of transport, fuel supply, and demographic and economic factors of vehicle use, 1970s-89, annual rpt, 3304–5

Enterprise Statistics, 1987: auxiliaries of multi-establishment firms, finances and operations by function, industry, and State, 2329–6

Enterprise Statistics, 1987: finances and operations for companies, by size, level of diversification, form of organization, and industry group, 2329–8

Explosives and blasting agents use, by type, industry, and State, 1990, Mineral Industry Surveys, annual rpt, 5614–22

Exports and imports between US and outlying areas, by detailed commodity and mode of transport, 1990, annual rpt, 2424–11

Exports and imports of US, by country and detailed commodity, monthly rpt, 2422–12

Exports and imports of US by country, and trade shifts by commodity, 1990, semiannual rpt, 9882–9

Exports and imports of US, by Harmonized System 6-digit commodity and country, 1990, annual rpt, 2424–13

Exports and imports of US, by transport mode, country, and SITC 1- to 3-digit commodity, 1990, annual rpt, 2424–12

Exports of US, detailed Schedule B commodities with countries of destination, 1990, annual rpt, 2424–10

Fed Govt financial and nonfinancial domestic aid, 1991 base edition with supplements, annual listing, 104–5

Finances and operations, by SIC 2- to 4-digit industry, forecast 1991, annual rpt, 2044–28

Financial statements for manufacturing, mining, and trade corporations, by selected SIC 2- to 3-digit industry, quarterly rpt, 2502–1

Foreign and US minerals supply under alternative market conditions, reserves, and background industry data, series, 5606–4

Foreign direct investment in US, by industry group and world area, 1987-90, annual article, 2702–1.219

Foreign direct investment in US, by industry group of US affiliate and country of parent firm, 1980-86, 2708–41

Foreign direct investment in US, major transactions by type, industry, country, and US location, 1989, annual rpt, 2044–20

Foreign direct investment of US, by industry group and world area, 1987-90, annual article, 2702–1.220

Forest Service mgmt of public lands and resources dev, environmental, economic, and social impacts of alternative programs, projected to 2040, 1208–24

Geological Survey activities and funding, FY90, annual rpt, 5664–8

Imports, exports, and employment impacts, by SIC 2- to 4-digit industry and commodity, quarterly rpt, 2322–2

Imports of US given duty-free treatment for value of US material sent abroad, by commodity and country, 1989, annual rpt, 9884–14

Machinery and equipment for mining, shipments, firms, and exports by product, 1990, annual Current Industrial Rpt, 2506–12.4

Manufacturing census, 1987: finances and operations, by SIC 2- to 4-digit industry, State, and MSA, with trends from 1849, 2497–1

Manufacturing census, 1987: finances and operations, by type of organization and SIC 2- to 4-digit industry, subject rpt, 2497–5

Mexico imports from US, by industry and State, 1987-90, 2048–154

Mineral Industry Surveys, commodity reviews of production, trade, stocks, and use, monthly rpt series, 5612–1

Mineral Industry Surveys, commodity reviews of production, trade, stocks, and use, quarterly rpt series, 5612–2

Mineral Industry Surveys, commodity reviews of production, trade, use, and industry operations, advance annual rpt series, 5614–5

Mineral Industry Surveys, State reviews of production, 1990, preliminary annual rpt, 5614–6

Minerals Yearbook, 1988, data collection and availability, annual rpt, 5604–48

Minerals Yearbook, 1988, Vol 3: foreign country reviews of production, trade, and policy, by commodity, annual rpt series, 5604–17

Minerals Yearbook, 1989, Vol 1: commodity reviews of production, reserves, supply, use, and trade, annual rpt series, 5604–15

Minerals Yearbook, 1989, Vol 2: State reviews of production and sales by commodity, and business activity, annual rpt series, 5604–16

Minerals Yearbook, 1989, Vol 2: State reviews of production, sales, and firms, by commodity, and business activity, annual rpt, 5604–34

Minerals Yearbook, 1990, Vol 1: commodity reviews of production, reserves, supply, use, and trade, annual rpt series, 5604–20

Multinatl firms US affiliates, finances, and operations, by industry, world area of parent firm, and State, 1988-89, annual rpt, 2704–4

Multinatl US firms and foreign affiliates finances and operations, by industry and world area of parent firm, 1989 benchmark survey, preliminary annual rpt, 2704–5

OECD trade, total and for 4 major countries, and US trade by country, by commodity, 1970-89, world area rpt series, 9116–1

Pollution (air) emissions factors, by detailed pollutant and source, data compilation, 1990 rpt, 9198–120

Price indexes (producer), by stage of processing and detailed commodity, monthly rpt, 6762–6

Price indexes (producer), by stage of processing and detailed commodity, monthly 1990, annual rpt, 6764–2

Producer Price Index, by major commodity group and subgroup, and processing stage, monthly press release, 6762–5

Production and capacity use indexes, by SIC 2- to 4-digit industry, monthly rpt, 9365–2.24

Production, prices, trade, and foreign and US industry devs, by commodity, bimonthly rpt with articles, 5602–4

Production, prices, trade, use, employment, tariffs, and stockpiles, by mineral, with foreign comparisons, 1986-90, annual rpt, 5604–18

Production, reserves, and use of industrial minerals, and characteristics of individual deposits, State rpt series, 5606–10

Public lands acreage and use, and Land Mgmt Bur activities and finances, annual State rpt series, 5724–11

Public lands minerals resources and availability, State rpt series, 5606–7

Publications and patents of Mines Bur, monthly listing, 5602–2

Publications and patents of Mines Bur, 1985-89, quinquennial listing, 5608–168

Puerto Rico economic censuses, 1987: wholesale and retail trade and service industry finances and operations, by SIC 2- to 4-digit industry and municipio, 2591–1

Puerto Rico economic censuses, 1987: wholesale, retail, and service industries finances and operations, by establishment characteristics and SIC 2- and 3-digit industry, subject rpts, 2591–2

Real estate assets of failed thrifts, inventory of properties available from Resolution Trust Corp, 1990, semiannual listing, 9722–2.9

Real estate assets of failed thrifts, inventory of properties available from Resolution Trust Corp, 1991, semiannual listing, 9722–2.15

Science and engineering employment and education, and R&D spending, for US and selected foreign countries, 1991 annual rpt, 9627–35.2

SEC registration, firms required to file annual rpts, as of Sept 1990, annual listing, 9734–5

Soviet Union, Eastern Europe, OECD, and selected other countries minerals production, by commodity, 1960s-90, annual rpt, 9114–4.6

Soviet Union minerals production and trade, by commodity, 1985-89 and projected to 2005, annual rpt, 5604–39

State and Metro Area Data Book, 1991 data compilation, 2328–54

Statistical Abstract of US, 1991 annual data compilation, 2324–1.15; 2324–1.25

Tariff Schedule of US, classifications and rates of duty by detailed imported commodity, 1992 base edition, 9886–13

Tax (income) returns filed by type of filer, selected income items, quarterly rpt, 8302–2.1

Tax (income) returns for foreign corporate activity in US, assets, and income

Index by Subjects and Names

Minnesota

statement items, by industry div and selected country, 1986-87, article, 8302–2.205

Tax (income) returns of corporations, income and tax items by asset size and detailed industry, 1987, annual rpt, 8304–4

Tax (income) returns of corporations, income and tax items by asset size and detailed industry, 1988, annual rpt, 8304–21

Tax (income) returns of corporations with foreign tax credit, income and tax items by industry group, 1986, biennial article, 8302–2.203

Tax (income) returns of multinatl US firms foreign affiliates, income statement items, by asset size and industry, 1986, biennial article, 8302–2.212

Tax (income) returns of partnerships, income statement and balance sheet items, by industry group, 1989, annual article, 8302–2.216; 8304–18

Tax (income) returns of sole proprietorships, income statement items, by industry group, 1989, annual article, 8302–2.214

Tax (income) returns of US corporations under foreign control, assets and income statement items by industry div and country, 1988, article, 8302–2.219

Tax expenditures, Federal revenues forgone through income tax deductions and exclusions by type, FY92-96, annual rpt, 21784–10

Wage and benefit changes from collective bargaining and mgmt decisions, by industry div, monthly rpt, 6782–1

Water (groundwater) supply, quality, chemistry, other characteristics, and use, regional rpt series, 5666–25

Water use by end use, well withdrawals, and public supply deliveries, by county, State rpt series, 5666–24

Wholesale trade census, 1987: depreciable assets, capital and operating expenses, sales, value added, and inventories, by SIC 2- to 3-digit kind of business, 2407–2

Wholesale trade sales and inventories, by SIC 2- to 3-digit kind of business, monthly rpt, 2413–7

Wholesale trade sales, inventories, purchases, and gross margins, by SIC 2- to 3-digit kind of business, 1990, annual rpt, 2413–13

see also Abrasive materials
see also Aluminum and aluminum industry
see also Cement and concrete
see also Census of Mineral Industries
see also Clay industry and products
see also Coal and coal mining
see also Copper and copper industry
see also Gases
see also Gemstones
see also Gold
see also Iron and steel industry
see also Lead and lead industry
see also Metals and metal industries
see also Mine accidents and safety
see also Mineral leases
see also Natural gas and gas industry
see also Nonmetallic minerals and mines
see also Offshore mineral resources
see also Offshore oil and gas

see also Oil shale
see also Petroleum and petroleum industry
see also Phosphate
see also Potash
see also Radioactive materials
see also Sand and gravel
see also Severance taxes
see also Silver
see also Stockpiling
see also Stone products and quarries
see also Strategic materials
see also Tar sands
see also Tin and tin industry
see also Uranium
see also Zinc and zinc industry
see also under By Commodity in the "Index by Categories"
see also under By Industry in the "Index by Categories"

Minimum income

see Income maintenance

Minimum wage

American Samoa employment, earnings, and minimum wage, by establishment and industry, 1989, biennial rpt, 6504–6

Employer illegal alien worker and Fair Labor Standards Act compliance, hiring impacts, and aliens overstaying visas by country and State, 1986-90, annual rpt, 6264–6

Fair Labor Standards Act admin, with coverage under minimum wage and overtime provisions, and illegal employment of minors, by industry div, FY89, annual rpt, 6504–2.1

Fair Labor Standards Act minimum wage rates, 1938-91, annual rpt, 4744–3.1

Foreign countries labor conditions, union coverage, and work accidents, annual country rpt series, 6366–4

Labor laws enacted, by State, 1990, annual article, 6722–1.209

Statistical Abstract of US, 1991 annual data compilation, 2324–1.13

Mining

see Mine accidents and safety
see Mines and mineral resources

Minneapolis, Minn.

Airline deregulation in 1978, and regional and major carriers agreements, impacts on service to small communities, late 1980s, 7308–199.10

CPI by component for US city average, and by region, population size, and for 27 metro areas, monthly rpt, 6762–2

Drug abuse indicators for selected metro areas, research results, data collection, and policy issues, 1991 semiannual conf, 4492–5

Housing starts and completions authorized by building permits in 40 MSAs, quarterly rpt, 2382–9

Wages by occupation, and benefits for office and plant workers, 1991 survey, periodic MSA rpt, 6785–12.2

see also under By City and By SMSA or MSA in the "Index by Categories"

Minnesota

Banks (insured commercial and savings) deposits by instn, State, MSA, and county, as of June 1990, annual regional rpt, 9295–3.5

Business and economic conditions, Fed Reserve 9th District, quarterly journal, 9383–19

County Business Patterns, 1989: employment, establishments, and payroll, by SIC 2- to 4-digit industry and county, annual State rpt, 2326–8.25

Dairy prices, by product and selected area, with related marketing data, 1990, annual rpt, 1317–1

DOD prime contract awards, by contractor, service branch, State, and city, FY90, annual rpt, 3544–22

Economic conditions and outlook, for US and Canada Great Lakes area, 1970s-90, 9375–15

Fed Govt spending in States and local areas, by type, State, county, and city, FY90, annual rpt, 2464–3

Fed Govt spending in States, by type, program, agency, and State, FY90, annual rpt, 2464–2

Food aid program of USDA for women, infants, and children, prenatal participation effect on Medicaid costs and birth outcomes, for 5 States, 1987-88, 1368–2

HHS financial aid, by program, recipient, State, and city, FY90, annual regional listing, 4004–3.5

Hospital deaths of Medicare patients, actual and expected rates by diagnosis, and hospital characteristics, by instn, FY87-89, annual regional rpt, 4654–14.5

Hwy funds pooled by States from FHwA funds for specific projects, demonstration project results, FY88-90, GAO rpt, 26113–471

Income (personal) per capita and by source, and earnings by industry div, by State, MSA, and county, 1984-89, annual regional rpt, 2704–2.3

Jail adult and juvenile population, employment, spending, instn conditions, and inmate programs, by county and facility, 1988, regional rpt series, 6068–144.3

Lumber (veneer log) production, mill receipts, and trade, by species, with residue use, for North Central States, 1988, quadrennial rpt, 1208–220

Marriages, divorces, and rates, by characteristics of spouses, State, and county, 1987 and trends from 1920, US Vital Statistics annual rpt, 4144–4

Medicaid demonstration projects evaluation, for 6 States, 1988 rpt, 4658–45

Mineral Industry Surveys, State reviews of production, 1990, preliminary annual rpt, 5614–6

Minerals Yearbook, 1989, Vol 2: State review of production and sales by commodity, and business activity, annual rpt, 5604–16.24

Minerals Yearbook, 1989, Vol 2: State reviews of production, sales, and firms, by commodity, and business activity, annual rpt, 5604–34

Physicians, by specialty, age, sex, and location of training and practice, 1989, State rpt, 4116–6.24

Population and housing census, 1990: population and housing characteristics, households, and land area, by county, subdiv, and place, State rpt, 2551–1.25

Population and housing census, 1990: voting age and total population by race, and housing units, by block, redistricting counts required under PL 94-171, State CD-ROM release, 2551–6.9

Minnesota

Population and housing census, 1990: voting age and total population by race, and housing units, by county and city, redistricting counts required under PL 94-171, State summary rpt, 2551–5.24

Statistical Abstract of US, 1991 annual data compilation, 2324–1

Supplemental Security Income payments and beneficiaries, by type of eligibility, State, and county, Dec 1989, annual rpt, 4744–27.5

Water (groundwater) supply, quality, chemistry, and use, 1983-84, local area rpt, 5666–28.9

Water supply and quality in streams and lakes, and groundwater levels in wells, by drainage basin, 1989, annual State rpt, 5666–12.22

Wetlands water pH and calcium concentration, by Minnesota peatland type, 1987, 5508–113

Wildlife and plant research results, 1989 habitat study, 5506–13.1

see also Minneapolis, Minn.

see also St. Paul, Minn.

see also under By State in the "Index by Categories"

Minor-Harper, Stephanie

"Women in Prison", 6066–19.61

Minority Business Development Agency

Budget of US, obligations and authority by function, agency, and program, with summaries, analyses, and historical tables, FY92, annual rpt, 104–2

Expenditures and mgmt of MBDA special projects, FY85-90, GAO rpt, 26113–517

Franchise business opportunities by firm and kind of business, and sources of aid and info, 1990 annual listing, 2104–7

Mgmt and financial aid from Minority Business Dev Centers, and characteristics of businesses, by region and State, FY90, annual rpt, 2104–6

Minority businesses

- Agriculture census, 1987: farms, farmland, production, finances, and operator characteristics, by county, final State rpt series, 2331–1
- Airway facilities and services contract awards of FAA to minority- and woman-owned businesses, FY85-89, annual rpt, 7504–37
- Community Dev Block Grant activities and funding, by program, FY75-90, annual rpt, 5124–8
- DOD contractor subcontract awards to small and disadvantaged business, by firm and service branch, quarterly rpt, 3542–17
- DOD prime contract awards, by category, contract and contractor type, and service branch, FY81-1st half FY91, semiannual rpt, 3542–1
- DOD prime contract awards in labor surplus areas, by service branch, State, and area, 1st half FY91, semiannual rpt, 3542–19
- DOE contracts and grants, by category, State, and for top contractors, FY90, annual rpt, 3004–21
- Fed Govt accounts receivable, delinquent debt cases and collections of Justice Dept and private law firms, pilot project results, FY90, annual rpt, 6004–20
- Fed Govt financial and nonfinancial domestic aid, 1991 base edition with supplements, annual listing, 104–5

Hwy construction minority contractor training, funding by region, FY91, annual release, 7554–40

Land Mgmt Bur activities and funding by State, FY89, annual rpt, 5724–13

Mgmt and financial aid from Minority Business Dev Centers, and characteristics of businesses, by region and State, FY90, annual rpt, 2104–6

NASA procurement contract awards, by type, contractor, State, and country, FY91 with trends from 1961, semiannual rpt, 9502–6

Navy procurement awards to small, disadvantaged, and women-owned businesses, FY90, annual rpt, 3804–13.3

Navy small and disadvantaged business procurement office locations, and supply and service codes, 1990 biennial listing, 3804–5

NIH activities, funding by program and recipient type, staff, and clinic patients, by inst, FY90, annual rpt, 4434–3

Small Business Admin surety bond guarantee program finances, and contracts by contractor race, obligee type, and region, FY87-89, GAO rpt, 26113–526

Small Business Investment Companies capital holdings, SBA obligation, and ownership, as of July 1991, semiannual listing, 9762–4

State and Metro Area Data Book, 1991 data compilation, 2328–54

Statistical Abstract of US, 1991 annual data compilation, 2324–1.17

Travel agencies contracts of GSA, by business size and recipient, FY88-90, GAO rpt, 26119–331

see also Women-owned businesses

Minority employment

- Black American displaced workers, by demographic and current and former employment characteristics, and compared to whites, 1978-86, article, 6722–1.234
- Black Americans social and economic characteristics, for South and total US, 1989-90 and trends from 1969, Current Population Rpt, 2546–1.450
- Black women's labor force status, employment by age and education, and women's and families earnings, 1980-90, fact sheet, 6564–1.2
- DOT activities by subagency, budget, and summary accident data, FY88, annual rpt, 7304–1
- Employment, unemployment, and labor force characteristics, by region, State, and selected metro area, 1990, annual rpt, 6744–7
- Fed Govt civilian employment of minorities, women, veterans, and disabled persons, as of Sept 1988 and 1990, biennial article, 9842–1.202
- Fed Govt employment of minorities, women, and disabled, by agency and occupation, FY89, annual rpt, 9244–10
- Forecasts of employment conditions, alternative BLS projections to 2005 and trends 1970s-90, biennial article, 6722–1.254
- Forest Service acreage, staff, finances, and mgmt activities in Pacific Northwest, with data by forest, 1970s-89, annual rpt, 1204–37

HHS employment of Hispanics in Mountain region, hiring and promotion practices, 1980s, GAO rpt, 26121–393

Hispanic Americans social and economic characteristics, by detailed origin, 1991, Current Population Rpt, 2546–1.448; 2546–1.451

Income (household) of minorities by source, and spending by type, by householder characteristics, 1987, article, 1702–1.206

Income (household, family, and personal), by source, detailed characteristics, and region, 1990, annual Current Population Rpt, 2546–6.70

Indian Health Service facilities and use, and Indian health and other characteristics, by IHS region, 1980s-89, annual chartbook, 4084–7

Indians and Alaska Natives health care access indicators, by selected characteristics, 1987, 4186–8.18

Indians and Alaska Natives health care coverage, by type, employment status, and other characteristics, 1987, 4186–8.17

IRS employment of minorities and women, compared to Fed Govt and total civilian labor force, FY90, annual rpt, 8304–3.3

Job Training Partnership Act occupational training services, disparities in delivery to women and minorities, 1989-90, 26106–8.14

Labor force status, by race, detailed Hispanic origin, and sex, quarterly rpt, 6742–18

Labor force status, experience, and unemployment duration, by race and sex, 1989-90, annual press release, 6726–1.39

Labor force, wages, hours, and payroll costs, by major industry group and demographic characteristics, *Survey of Current Business*, monthly rpt, 2702–1.8

Library of Congress employment by race, Hispanic origin, and sex, and affirmative action needs, 1989, hearing, 21428–9

Military active duty and recruit social, economic, and parents characteristics, by service branch and State, FY89, annual rpt, 3544–41

NASA minority and women employment, by installation, FY81-90, FY90, annual rpt, 9504–6.2

NASA staff characteristics and personnel actions, FY90, annual rpt, 9504–1

Natl Agricultural Statistics Service minority group staff, promotion, and discrimination complaints, 1988-90, GAO rpt, 26119–326

Poverty status of population and families, by detailed characteristics, 1990, annual Current Population Rpt, 2546–6.71

Science and engineering PhDs employment and other characteristics, by field and State, 1989, biennial rpt, 9627–18

SSA activities, and OASDHI admin, 1930s-90 and projected to 2064, annual data compilation, 4704–12

SSA minority, handicapped, and women employees, by pay grade, FY90, annual rpt, 4704–6

State and local govt employment of minorities and women, by occupation, function, pay level, and State, 1990, annual rpt, 9244–6

State and Metro Area Data Book, 1991 data compilation, 2328–54

Index by Subjects and Names

Missiles and rockets

State Dept and Foreign Service minority and women employment, and hiring goals, FY89-90, biennial rpt, 7004–21

Statistical Abstract of US, 1991 annual data compilation, 2324–1.13

Teachers in higher education instns, employment and other characteristics, by instn type and control, 1987/88 survey, 4846–4.4

Unemployed displaced and economically disadvantaged workers, training program operations and performance, series, 6406–10

Unemployment of groups with historically high rates, 1985-89, biennial rpt, 6504–2.2

see also Discrimination in employment
see also Minority businesses
see also Racial discrimination
see also Women's employment
see also under By Race and Ethnic Group in the "Index by Categories"

Minority Enterprise Small Business Investment Companies

see Small Business Investment Companies

Minority groups

- AFDC beneficiaries demographic and financial characteristics, by State, FY89, annual rpt, 4694–1
- Arrest rates, by offense, sex, age, and race, 1965-89, annual rpt, 6224–7
- Arts Natl Endowment activities and grants, FY90, annual rpt, 9564–3
- Cancer death rates of minorities, by body site, age, sex, and substate area, 1950s-80, atlas, 4478–78
- Census Bur minority group data coverage and availability, 1991 pamphlet, 2326–7.80
- Census of Population and Housing, 1990: data item selection, questionnaire dev, and testing, 2626–11.14
- Census of Population and Housing, 1990: population and housing characteristics, households, and land area, by county, subdiv, and place, State rpt series, 2551–1
- Census of Population and Housing, 1990: population and housing selected characteristics, by region, press release, 2328–74
- Census of Population and Housing, 1990: voting age and total population by race, and housing units, by block, redistricting counts required under PL 94-171, State CD-ROM series, 2551–6
- Census of Population and Housing, 1990: voting age and total population by race, and housing units, by county and city, redistricting counts required under PL 94-171, State summary rpt series, 2551–5
- Census of Population, 1990: metro area population by race, Hispanic origin, and MSA, press release, 2328–75
- Drug abuse prevalence among minorities, related health effects and crime, treatment, and research status and needs, mid 1970s-90, 4498–72
- Education data compilation, 1991 annual rpt, 4824–2
- Education data, elementary and secondary enrollment, staff, finances, operations, programs, and policies, 1987/88 biennial survey, series, 4836–3

Education Dept programs funding, operations, and effectiveness, FY90, annual rpt, 4804–5

Educational performance and conditions, characteristics, attitudes, activities, and plans, 1988 8th grade class, natl longitudinal survey, series, 4826–9

FmHA farm and rural housing program loan appeals filed in 3 States, by disposition, 1988-90, GAO rpt, 26113–516

Food aid program of USDA for women, infants, and children, participants by race, State, and Indian agency, Apr 1990, annual rpt, 1364–16

Foreign countries *Background Notes*, summary social, political, and economic data, series, 7006–2

Foreign countries economic, social, political, and geographic summary data, by country, 1991, annual factbook, 9114–2

Health care (primary) research, methodology and findings, 1991 annual conf, 4184–4

Health care (primary) research, provider role, Federal funding, and provision to minority groups, 1990 conf papers, 4188–69

Health condition of minorities, services use, costs, and indicators of services need, 1950s-88, 4118–55

Health condition, services use, payment sources, and health care labor force, for minorities and women by poverty status, 1940s-89, chartbook, 4118–56

Heart, Lung, and Blood Natl Inst activities, and grants by recipient and location, FY90 and disease trends from 1940, annual rpt, 4474–15

High school advanced placement for college credit, programs by selected characteristics and school control, 1984-86, 4838–46

Higher education degrees awarded, by level, field, race, and sex, 1988/89 with trends from 1978/79, biennial rpt, 4844–17

Higher education remedial programs, enrollment, courses, and faculty, by instn characteristics, 1989/90, 4826–1.30

Households composition, income, benefits, and labor force status, Survey of Income and Program Participation methodology, working paper series, 2626–10

Income (household) of minorities by source, and spending by type, by householder characteristics, 1987, article, 1702–1.206

Jewish population size, by State, 1989, data compilation, 2328–54

NIH Research Resources Center activities and funding, by program, FY90, annual rpt, 4434–12

Prisoner admissions by State and for Federal instns, by race, 1926-86, 6068–245

Science and engineering grad enrollment, by field, source of funds, and characteristics of student and instn, 1975-89, annual rpt, 9627–7

Statistical Abstract of US, 1991 annual data compilation, 2324–1

Student aid funding and participation, by Federal program, instn type and control, and State, various periods 1959-89, annual rpt, 4804–28

Violence among minority youth, prevention strategies, 1990 conf, 4042–3.218

see also Alaska Natives

see also Asian Americans
see also Black Americans
see also Black students
see also Civil rights
see also Ethnic studies
see also Hispanic Americans
see also Indians
see also Minority businesses
see also Minority employment
see also Pacific Islands Americans
see also Racial discrimination
see also under By Race and Ethnic Group in the "Index by Categories"

Mint

see Spices and herbs

Mint Bureau

see U.S. Mint

Miscarriage

see Fetal deaths

Mishawaka, Ind.

see also under By SMSA or MSA in the "Index by Categories"

Missiaen, Margaret

"Economic Performance and Policy Adjustment: The Experience of Zimbabwe", 1528–319

Missiles and rockets

- County Business Patterns, 1988: employment, establishments, and payroll, by SIC 2- to 4-digit industry and county, annual State rpt series, 2326–6
- County Business Patterns, 1989: employment, establishments, and payroll, by SIC 2- to 4-digit industry and county, annual State rpt series, 2326–8
- DOD budget, organization, personnel, weapons, and property, by service branch, State, and country, 1991 annual summary rpt, 3504–13
- DOD budget, procurement appropriations by item, service branch, and defense agency, FY90-93, annual rpt, 3544–32
- DOD budget, programs, and policies, FY90, annual rpt, 3544–2
- DOD budget, weapons acquisition costs by system and service branch, FY91-93, annual rpt, 3504–2
- DOD outlays and obligations, by function and service branch, quarterly rpt, 3542–3
- DOD prime contract awards, by category, contract and contractor type, and service branch, FY81-1st half FY91, semiannual rpt, 3542–1
- DOD prime contract awards, by category, contractor type, and State, FY88-90, annual rpt, 3544–11
- DOD prime contract awards, by detailed procurement category, FY87-90, annual rpt, 3544–18
- DOD prime contract awards, by size and type of contract, service branch, competitive status, category, and labor standard, FY90, annual rpt, 3544–19
- Exports of US, detailed Schedule B commodities with countries of destination, 1990, annual rpt, 2424–10
- Foreign and US military weapons trade, production, and defense industry finances, with data by firm and country, 1980s-91, 26358–241
- Foreign and US space program activities, missions, launchings, payloads, and flight duration, 1957-90, annual rpt, 21704–4
- Foreign countries military aid and arms sales of US, by weapon type, as of Sept 1990, annual rpt, 3904–3

Missiles and rockets

Manufacturing annual survey, 1989: value of shipments, by SIC 4- to 5-digit product class, 2506–15.2

Manufacturing census, 1987: employment and shipments under Fed Govt contracts, by SIC 4-digit industry, 2497–7

Manufacturing census, 1987: finances and operations, by SIC 2- to 4-digit industry, State, and MSA, with trends from 1849, 2497–1

Manufacturing finances and operations, by SIC 2- to 4-digit industry, forecast 1991, annual rpt, 2044–28

NATO and Japan military spending and indicators of ability to support common defense, by country, 1970s-89, annual rpt, 3544–28

Occupational injury and illness rates, by SIC 2- to 4-digit industry, 1989, annual rpt, 6844–1

Soviet Union military weapons systems, presence, and force strengths, and compared to US, 1991 annual rpt, 3504–20

Missing persons and runaways

Arrests, by offense, offender characteristics, and location, data compilation, 1991 annual rpt, 6064–6.4

Arrests, by offense, offender characteristics, and location, 1990, annual rpt, 6224–2.2

Detroit metro area runaway and other youth services programs cases, and school dropouts, 1980s, hearing, 25418–5

HHS financial aid, by program, recipient, State, and city, FY90, annual regional listings, 4004–3

Juvenile courts delinquency cases, by offense, referral source, disposition, age, sex, race, State, and county, 1988, annual rpt, 6064–12

Juvenile courts runaway cases, by referral source, disposition, and sex, 1985-86, 6066–27.4

Military deaths by cause, age, race, and rank, and personnel captured and missing, by service branch, FY90, annual rpt, 3544–40

Pregnancy prevalence among homeless teens, outcomes, services availability, health condition, and drug abuse, 1989 conf, 4108–55

Youth (homeless and runaway) programs, funding, activities, and participant characteristics, FY90, annual rpt, 4604–3

Youths entering runaway and homeless centers, by selected characteristics, data compilation, 1991 annual rpt, 6064–6.6

Mission, Tex.

see also under By SMSA or MSA in the "Index by Categories"

Missions and missionaries

Malaria cases in US, for military personnel and US and foreign natls, and by country of infection, 1966-89, annual rpt, 4205–4

Mississippi

Appalachian Regional Commission funding, by project and State, planned FY91, annual rpt, 9084–3

Banks (insured commercial and savings) deposits by instn, State, MSA, and county, as of June 1990, annual regional rpt, 9295–3.4

County Business Patterns, 1989: employment, establishments, and payroll, by SIC 2- to 4-digit industry and county, annual State rpt, 2326–8.26

DOD prime contract awards, by contractor, service branch, State, and city, FY90, annual rpt, 3544–22

Economic indicators by State and MSA, Fed Reserve 6th District, quarterly rpt, 9371–14

Education system in Appalachia, improvement initiatives, and indicators of success, by State, 1960s-89, 9088–36

Employment and unemployment, for 8 southeastern States, 1989-90, annual rpt, 6944–2

Employment by industry div, earnings, and hours, for 8 southeastern States, quarterly press release, 6942–7

Estuary environmental and fishery conditions, research results and methodology, 1991 rpt, 2176–7.23

Fed Govt spending in States and local areas, by type, State, county, and city, FY90, annual rpt, 2464–3

Fed Govt spending in States, by type, program, agency, and State, FY90, annual rpt, 2464–2

Fish (catfish) raised on farms, inventory, stocks, and production, by major producer State, quarterly rpt, 1631–18

Fish and shellfish catch, wholesale receipts, prices, trade, and other market activities, weekly regional rpt, 2162–6.3

FmHA farm and rural housing program loan appeals filed in 3 States, by disposition, 1988-90, GAO rpt, 26113–516

HHS financial aid, by program, recipient, State, and city, FY90, annual regional listing, 4004–3.4

Hospital deaths of Medicare patients, actual and expected rates by diagnosis, and hospital characteristics, by instn, FY87-89, annual regional rpt, 4654–14.4

Income (personal) per capita and by source, and earnings by industry div, by State, MSA, and county, 1984-89, annual regional rpt, 2704–2.4

Jail adult and juvenile population, employment, spending, instn conditions, and inmate programs, by county and facility, 1988, regional rpt series, 6068–144.4

Marriages, divorces, and rates, by characteristics of spouses, State, and county, 1987 and trends from 1920, US Vital Statistics annual rpt, 4144–4

Mineral Industry Surveys, State reviews of production, 1990, preliminary annual rpt, 5614–6

Minerals Yearbook, 1989, Vol 2: State review of production and sales by commodity, and business activity, annual rpt, 5604–16.25

Minerals Yearbook, 1989, Vol 2: State reviews of production, sales, and firms, by commodity, and business activity, annual rpt, 5604–34

Physicians, by specialty, age, sex, and location of training and practice, 1989, State rpt, 4116–6.25

Population and housing census, 1990: population and housing characteristics, households, and land area, by county, subdiv, and place, State rpt, 2551–1.26

Population and housing census, 1990: voting age and total population by race, and housing units, by block, redistricting counts required under PL 94-171, State CD-ROM release, 2551–6.4

Population and housing census, 1990: voting age and total population by race, and housing units, by county and city, redistricting counts required under PL 94-171, State summary rpt, 2551–5.25

Rice stocks on and off farms and total in all positions, periodic rpt, 1621–7

Statistical Abstract of US, 1991 annual data compilation, 2324–1

Supplemental Security Income payments and beneficiaries, by type of eligibility, State, and county, Dec 1989, annual rpt, 4744–27.4

Textile mill employment, earnings, and hours, for 8 Southeastern States, quarterly press release, 6942–1

Water supply and quality in streams and lakes, and groundwater levels in wells, by drainage basin, 1990, annual State rpt, 5666–10.23

see also De Soto County, Miss.

see also Jackson, Miss.

see also Meridian, Miss.

see also under By State in the "Index by Categories"

Mississippi River

Army Corps of Engineers water resources dev projects, characteristics, and costs, 1950s-89, biennial State rpt series, 3756–1

Army Corps of Engineers water resources dev projects, characteristics, and costs, 1950s-91, biennial State rpt series, 3756–2

Freight (waterborne) on Mississippi River system by commodity and waterway, 1988 with projections to 2000, article, 9391–16.202

Water supply and quality in streams and lakes, and groundwater levels in wells, by drainage basin, 1988, annual State rpt series, 5666–16

Water supply and quality in streams and lakes, and groundwater levels in wells, by drainage basin, 1989, annual State rpt series, 5666–12

Water supply and quality in streams and lakes, and groundwater levels in wells, by drainage basin, 1990, annual State rpt series, 5666–10

Water supply in US and southern Canada, streamflow, surface and groundwater conditions, and reservoir levels, by location, monthly rpt, 5662–3

Missouri

Banks (insured commercial and savings) deposits by instn, State, MSA, and county, as of June 1990, annual regional rpt, 9295–3.5

Carbon dioxide in atmosphere, North Central States economic and agricultural impacts, model descriptions and results, 1980s and projected to 2030, 3006–11.15

Coal production and mines by county, prices, productivity, miners, and reserves, by mining method and State, 1989-90, annual rpt, 3164–25

County Business Patterns, 1989: employment, establishments, and payroll, by SIC 2- to 4-digit industry and county, annual State rpt, 2326–8.27

DOD prime contract awards, by contractor, service branch, State, and city, FY90, annual rpt, 3544–22

Index by Subjects and Names

Mobile homes

Economic and banking conditions, for Fed Reserve 8th District, quarterly rpt with articles, 9391–16

Fed Govt spending in States and local areas, by type, State, county, and city, FY90, annual rpt, 2464–3

Fed Govt spending in States, by type, program, agency, and State, FY90, annual rpt, 2464–2

Fertilizer use in 2 States, by county, 1988-89, hearing, 25168–76

Financial and economic devs, Fed Reserve 10th District, quarterly rpt, 9381–16

HHS financial aid, by program, recipient, State, and city, FY90, annual regional listing, 4004–3.7

Hospital deaths of Medicare patients, actual and expected rates by diagnosis, and hospital characteristics, by instn, FY87-89, annual regional rpt, 4654–14.7

Income (personal) per capita and by source, and earnings by industry div, by State, MSA, and county, 1984-89, annual regional rpt, 2704–2.3

Jail adult and juvenile population, employment, spending, instn conditions, and inmate programs, by county and facility, 1988, regional rpt series, 6068–144.3

Lumber (veneer log) production, mill receipts, and trade, by species, with residue use, for North Central States, 1988, quadrennial rpt, 1208–220

Marriages, divorces, and rates, by characteristics of spouses, State, and county, 1987 and trends from 1920, US Vital Statistics annual rpt, 4144–4

Medicaid demonstration projects evaluation, for 6 States, 1988 rpt, 4658–45

Mineral Industry Surveys, State reviews of production, 1990, preliminary annual rpt, 5614–6

Minerals Yearbook, 1989, Vol 2: State review of production and sales by commodity, and business activity, annual rpt, 5604–16.26

Minerals Yearbook, 1989, Vol 2: State reviews of production, sales, and firms, by commodity, and business activity, annual rpt, 5604–34

Physicians, by specialty, age, sex, and location of training and practice, 1989, State rpt, 4116–6.26

Population and housing census, 1990: population and housing characteristics, households, and land area, by county, subdiv, and place, State rpt, 2551–1.27

Population and housing census, 1990: voting age and total population by race, and housing units, by block, redistricting counts required under PL 94-171, State CD-ROM release, 2551–6.8

Population and housing census, 1990: voting age and total population by race, and housing units, by county and city, redistricting counts required under PL 94-171, State summary rpt, 2551–5.26

Pregnant women smoking, by age, race, education, marital status, and birth order, 1970s-80s, article, 4042–3.203

Rice stocks on and off farms and total in all positions, periodic rpt, 1621–7

Statistical Abstract of US, 1991 annual data compilation, 2324–1

Supplemental Security Income payments and beneficiaries, by type of eligibility, State, and county, Dec 1989, annual rpt, 4744–27.7

Water supply and quality in streams and lakes, and groundwater levels in wells, by drainage basin, 1990, annual State rpt, 5666–10.24

Wildlife and plant research results, 1989 habitat study, 5506–13.2

see also Kansas City, Mo.

see also St. Louis, Mo.

see also under By State in the "Index by Categories"

Missouri River

Army Corps of Engineers water resources dev projects, characteristics, and costs, 1950s-89, biennial State rpt series, 3756–1

Army Corps of Engineers water resources dev projects, characteristics, and costs, 1950s-91, biennial State rpt series, 3756–2

Water supply and quality in streams and lakes, and groundwater levels in wells, by drainage basin, 1988, annual State rpt series, 5666–16

Water supply and quality in streams and lakes, and groundwater levels in wells, by drainage basin, 1989, annual State rpt series, 5666–12

Water supply and quality in streams and lakes, and groundwater levels in wells, by drainage basin, 1990, annual State rpt series, 5666–10

Water supply in US and southern Canada, streamflow, surface and groundwater conditions, and reservoir levels, by location, monthly rpt, 5662–3

Mittelstaedt, H. Fred

"Impact of Liabilities for Retiree Health Benefits on Share Prices", 9366–6.270

Miyasaka, Emiko

"Desk Reference Guide to U.S. Agricultural Trade", 1924–9

Mobil Oil Corp.

North Carolina environmental and socioeconomic conditions, and impacts of proposed OCS oil and gas exploration, 1970s-90 and projected to 2020, 5738–22

Mobile, Ala.

see also under By City and By SMSA or MSA in the "Index by Categories"

Mobile homes

American Housing Survey: inventory change from 1973, by reason, unit and household characteristics, and location, 1983, biennial rpt, 2485–14

American Housing Survey: unit and households characteristics, unit and neighborhood quality, and journey to work by MSA location, for 11 MSAs, 1984 survey, supplement, 2485–8

American Housing Survey: unit and households detailed characteristics, and unit and neighborhood quality, MSA rpt series, 2485–6

American Housing Survey: unit and households detailed characteristics, and unit and neighborhood quality, 1987, biennial rpt, 2485–12; 2485–13

County Business Patterns, 1988: employment, establishments, and payroll, by SIC 2- to 4-digit industry and county, annual State rpt series, 2326–6

County Business Patterns, 1989: employment, establishments, and payroll, by SIC 2- to 4-digit industry and county, annual State rpt series, 2326–8

Employment, earnings, and hours, by SIC 1- to 4-digit industry, monthly and annual averages, selected years 1909-90, annual rpt, 6744–4

Finance companies credit outstanding and leasing activities, by credit type, monthly rpt, 9365–2.7

Fires in mobile homes, casualties, damage, and impacts of safety standards, with data on Michigan trailer parks and resident characteristics, 1980s, hearing, 21248–145

Flow-of-funds accounts, savings, investments, and credit statements, quarterly rpt, 9365–3.3

Injuries from use of consumer products, by severity, victim age, and detailed product, 1990, annual rpt, 9164–6

Loans FHA-insured, financial, property, and mortgagor characteristics, by State, 1990, annual rpt, 5144–1

Loans FHA-insured, financial, property, and mortgagor characteristics, total and by State and outlying area, 1990, annual rpt, 5144–25

Loans FHA-insured, financial, property, and mortgagor characteristics, 1990, annual rpt, 5144–23

Loans for mobile homes, monthly rpt, 23842–1.5

Loans for mobile homes outstanding, *Survey of Current Business,* monthly rpt, 2702–1.9

Loans outstanding, and terms, by lender and credit type, monthly rpt, 9365–2.6

Manufacturing annual survey, 1989: finances and operations, by SIC 2- to 4-digit industry, series, 2506–15

Manufacturing census, 1987: finances and operations, by SIC 2- to 4-digit industry, State, and MSA, with trends from 1849, 2497–1

Manufacturing census, 1987: finances and operations, by type of organization and SIC 2- to 4-digit industry, subject rpt, 2497–5

New single and multifamily units, by structural and financial characteristics, inside-outside MSAs, and region, 1986-90, annual rpt, 2384–1

North Central States, FHLB 7th District housing vacancy rates for single and multifamily units and mobile homes, by ZIP code, annual MSA rpt series, 9304–18

Occupational injury and illness rates, by SIC 2- to 4-digit industry, 1988-89, annual rpt, 6844–7

Occupational injury and illness rates, by SIC 2- to 4-digit industry, 1989, annual rpt, 6844–1

Price indexes (producer), by stage of processing and detailed commodity, monthly rpt, 6762–6

Price indexes (producer), by stage of processing and detailed commodity, monthly 1990, annual rpt, 6764–2

Puerto Rico economic censuses, 1987: wholesale and retail trade and service industry finances and operations, by SIC 2- to 4-digit industry and municipio, 2591–1

Mobile homes

Retail trade census, 1987: finances and employment, for establishments with and without payroll, by SIC 2- to 4-digit kind of business, State, and MSA, 2401–1

Savings instns failures, inventory of real estate assets available from Resolution Trust Corp, 1989, semiannual listing, 9722–2.1

Savings instns failures, inventory of real estate assets available from Resolution Trust Corp, 1990, semiannual listing, 9722–2.2; 9722–2.3; 9722–2.8

Savings instns failures, inventory of real estate assets available from Resolution Trust Corp, 1991, semiannual listing, 9722–2.14

Shipments and PPI for mobile homes, bimonthly rpt, 2042–1.2; 2042–1.5

Shipments of mobile homes, by State, monthly rpt, quarterly table, 2382–5

Shipments of mobile homes, by State, 1988-90, annual rpt, 2384–2

Shipments of mobile homes, dealer inventories, and home characteristics, by region, and placements and prices by State, monthly rpt, 2382–1

Shipments of mobile homes, *Survey of Current Business*, monthly rpt, 2702–1.6

Statistical Abstract of US, 1991 annual data compilation, 2324–1.26

Vacant housing characteristics, and occupancy and vacancy rates, by tenure and location, 1960s-90, annual rpt, 2484–1

Virgin Islands population and housing characteristics, 1990 Census of Population and Housing, press release, 2328–81

West Central States, FHLB 10th District housing vacancy rates for single and multifamily units and mobile homes, by ZIP code, annual MSA rpt series, 9304–22

Western States, FHLB 12th District housing vacancy rates for single and multifamily units and mobile homes, by ZIP code, annual MSA rpt series, 9304–21

see also Recreational vehicles

Mobile radio

Manufacturing finances and operations, by SIC 2- to 4-digit industry, forecast 1991, annual rpt, 2044–28

Price indexes (producer), by stage of processing and detailed commodity, monthly rpt, 6762–6

Price indexes (producer), by stage of processing and detailed commodity, monthly 1990, annual rpt, 6764–2

Shipments, trade, use, and firms, for electronic communications systems and related products, 1990, annual Current Industrial Rpt, 2506–12.35

Telephone firms borrowing under Rural Telephone Program, and financial and operating data, by State, 1990, annual rpt, 1244–2

Telephone firms mobile operations and revenue, 1989, annual rpt, 9284–6.2

TV (UHF) channels reassigned for land mobile use, by market, as of June 30, 1991, semiannual rpt, 9282–6

Mobile telephones

see Mobile radio

Mobility

see Labor mobility

see Migration

see Mobility limitations

Mobility limitations

Cases of acute and chronic conditions, disability, absenteeism, and health services use, by selected characteristics, 1987, CD-ROM, 4147–10.177

Child health condition and services use, 1990 chartbook, 4108–49

Children (handicapped) enrollment by age, and special education programs staff, funding, and needs, by type of handicap and State, 1989/90, annual rpt, 4944–4

Disabled persons and related activity limitation days and health services use, by health status, disability type, and other characteristics, 1984-88, 4146–8.202

Educational service delivery and discipline, and discrimination indicators by State, 1988, biennial rpt, 4804–33

Functional limitations, persons needing aid with activities of daily living, by age and household income, 1986, fact sheet, 2326–17.22

Health condition and health care resources, use, and spending, 1950s-89, annual data compilation, 4144–11

Health condition improvement and disease prevention goals and recommended activities for 2000, with trends 1970s-80s, 4048–10

Hospices operations, services, costs, and patient characteristics, for instns without Medicare certification, FY85-86, 4658–52

Injuries, by type, circumstances, and victim characteristics, and related activity limitations, 1985-87, 4147–10.176

Injuries, related impairments, and activity limitations, by circumstances and victim characteristics, 1985-87, 4147–10.179

Kidney transplants, needs, costs, payment sources, and impact of immunosuppressive drugs on outcome, 1950s-87 and projected to 1995, 4658–59

Mentally retarded persons care facilities and residents by selected characteristics, and use of Medicaid services and waiver programs, by State, late 1970s-80s, 4658–49

Mines (underground coal) back injuries, by circumstances, victim characteristics, and treatment, mid 1980s, 5608–166

Minority group and women health condition, services use, payment sources, and health care labor force, by poverty status, 1940s-89, chartbook, 4118–56

Minority group health condition, services use, costs, and indicators of services need, 1950s-88, 4118–55

Nursing home reimbursement by Medicaid, resident classification using patient and care characteristics, New York State, 1990 article, 4652–1.205

Nursing home residents with mental, behavioral, and functional disorders, by age, sex, and instn characteristics, 1987, 4186–8.11

Nursing home residents with mental disorders, by disorder type and resident and instn characteristics, 1985, 4147–13.106

Index by Subjects and Names

Older persons health condition and care research, data availability and collection methodology, for US and selected countries, 1988 conf, 4147–5.6

Older persons with functional limitations, cognitive disorders and disruptive behavior by type and severity, 1984, 4186–7.10

Older persons with functional limitations, long-term care sources, and health and other characteristics, 1984-85, 4147–13.104

Statistical Abstract of US, 1991 annual data compilation, 2324–1.3

Transit systems grants of Urban Mass Transportation Admin, by city and State, FY90, annual rpt, 7884–10

Vocational rehabilitation cases of State agencies by disposition and applicant characteristics, and closures by reason, FY84-88, annual rpt, 4944–6

see also Architectural barriers to the handicapped

Mobs

see Riots and disorders

Models

see Demonstration and pilot projects

see Economic and econometric models

see Mathematic models and modeling

Modems

see Telecommunication

Modesto, Calif.

see also under By City and By SMSA or MSA in the "Index by Categories"

Moen, Jon R.

"Fewer Older Men in the U.S. Work Force: Technological, Behavioral, and Legislative Contributions to the Decline", 9371–1.202

Moffatt, Ronald E.

"Oceanographic Data Exchange, 1989", 2144–15

Moffitt, Robert

"Effect of the Medicaid Program on Welfare Participation and Labor Supply", 2626–10.139

Mofjeld, Harold O.

"Final Report on Residual Tidal Currents and Processing of Pressure and Current Records from the Eastern Bering Sea Shelf", 2176–1.36

Mohair

see Wool and wool trade

Mohamed, Ahmed H.

"Impact of Domestic Market Structure on Exchange Rate Pass-Through", 9387–8.234

Mohr, Michael F.

"Gross National Product by Industry, 1987-89", 2702–1.208

Moini, Saira

"Update on AIDS in Prisons and Jails", 6066–28.1

Molasses

see Sugar industry and products

see Syrups and sweeteners

Moline, Ill.

Housing vacancy rates for single and multifamily units and mobile homes, by city and ZIP code, 1990, annual MSA rpt, 9304–18.4

Wages by occupation, for office and plant workers, 1991 survey, periodic MSA rpt, 6785–12.1

Index by Subjects and Names

see also under By SMSA or MSA in the "Index by Categories"

Molybdenum

see Metals and metal industries

Monaco

Economic, social, political, and geographic summary data, by country, 1991, annual factbook, 9114–2

Exports and imports of US, by transport mode, country, and SITC 1- to 3-digit commodity, 1990, annual rpt, 2424–12

Monetary policy

- Banks Fed Reserve discount window borrowing, relation to interest rate spreads and discount borrowing outstanding, by bank asset size, 1981-90, article, 9385–1.209
- Dollar exchange rate and domestic monetary policy impacts of foreign exchange intervention, for US and Germany, 1985-87, article, 9373–1.209
- Economic indicators impacts of monetary policy effect on bank loan volume, model description and results, 1960s-89, technical paper, 9366–6.268
- Economic indicators relation to interest rates and financial market regulatory and structural changes, 1950s-80s, technical paper, 9385–8.73
- Economic policy and banking practices, technical paper series, 9366–1
- *Economic Report of the President* for 1991, Joint Economic Committee critique and policy recommendations, annual rpt, 23844–2
- *Economic Report of the President* for 1991, with economic trends from 1929, annual rpt, 204–1
- Farm prices impact of monetary policy, alternative model results, 1976-90, article, 9391–1.217
- Fed Open Market Committee member monetary policy votes, relation to regional employment conditions, 1965-85, article, 9373–1.205
- Fed Reserve Bank District presidents and Board governors monetary policy votes relative to inflation and GNP growth forecasts, 1965-85, article, 9373–1.214
- Fed Reserve Board and Reserve banks finances, staff, and review of monetary policy and economic devs, 1990, annual rpt, 9364–1
- Fed Reserve monetary policy objectives, and performance of major economic indicators, as of July 1991, semiannual rpt, 9362–4
- Fed Reserve political independence issues, with proposed restructuring legislation, 1970s-90, technical paper, 9385–8.106
- Fed Reserve System, Board of Governors, and district banks financial statements, performance, and fiscal services, 1990-91, annual rpt, 9364–10
- Financial and economic analysis of banking and nonbanking sectors, working paper series, 9381–10
- Financial and economic analysis, technical paper series, 9379–12; 9383–20; 9389–19; 9393–10
- Financial and economic devs, Fed Reserve Bank of Dallas bimonthly journal, 9379–1
- Financial and economic devs, Fed Reserve Bank of Minneapolis quarterly journal, 9383–6

Financial and economic devs, Fed Reserve Bank of New York quarterly journal, 9385–1

Financial and economic devs, Fed Reserve Bank of Philadelphia bimonthly journal, 9387–1

Financial and economic devs, Fed Reserve Bank of St Louis bimonthly journal, 9391–1

- Foreign countries economic and monetary trends, compounded annual rates of change and monetary targets for US and 10 major trading partners, quarterly rpt, 9391–7
- Interest rates and Fed Reserve monetary policy targets, relation to unexpected employment news, 1970s-91, article, 9389–1.205
- Japan economic conditions, financial and intl policies, and trade devs, 1950s-80s and projected to 2050, compilation of papers, 23848–220
- Japan interest rates relation to monetary policy and financial instn regulation, with background data and model results, 1960s-91, article, 9385–1.213; 9385–8.116
- Switzerland alternative monetary aggregates indexes relation to inflation and monetary base, 1970s-89, article, 9391–1.221
- *see also* Credit
- *see also* Fiscal policy
- *see also* Foreign exchange
- *see also* Inflation
- *see also* Money supply

Monetti, Matthew A.

"Worldwide Deposition of Strontium-90 Through 1986", 3004–29

Money laundering

see Underground economy

Money market funds

see Mutual funds

Money supply

- Argentina and Brazil inflation relation to money supply and public debt, model description and results, 1980s-90, technical paper, 9379–12.75
- Banks loans impact of money supply, 1970s-91, article, 9381–1.208
- Business cycle models incorporating money supply impact on economic indicators, assessment of alternative models, 1991 articles, 9383–6.202
- Business cycle variation and growth rates of GNP and components, inflation, and money supply, for 10 industrial countries, 1850s-1980s, working paper, 9383–20.15
- Business statistics, detailed data for major industries and economic indicators, *Survey of Current Business*, monthly rpt, 2702–1.9
- Credit card ownership impact on money supply components, model description and results, 1983, working paper, 9379–12.74
- Currency and coin outstanding and in circulation, by type and denomination, *Treasury Bulletin*, quarterly rpt, 8002–4.16
- Currency in circulation and removed, and Fed Reserve costs of new currency, 1989-91, annual rpt, 9364–10.2
- Developing countries counterpart funds impacts on US aid programs effectiveness and domestic economic and fiscal condition, literature review, 1991 rpt, 9918–21

Money supply

- Economic indicators and components, and Fed Reserve 4th District business and financial conditions, monthly chartbook, 9377–10
- Economic indicators and components, current data and annual trends, monthly rpt, 23842–1.5
- Economic indicators compounded annual rates of change, 1971-90, annual rpt, 9391–9.1
- Fed Reserve monetary policy objectives, and performance of major economic indicators, as of July 1991, semiannual rpt, 9362–4
- Financial and economic analysis and forecasting methodology, technical paper series, 9366–6
- Financial and economic analysis, technical paper series, 9383–20; 9385–8; 9393–10
- Financial and economic devs, Fed Reserve Bank of St Louis bimonthly journal, 9391–1
- Financial and monetary conditions, selected US summary data, weekly rpt, 9391–4
- Forecasts of GNP and money supply, performance of alternative monetary policy rules, 1991 technical paper, 9379–12.66
- Forecasts of money supply, impacts of monetary target announcements on accuracy, for US and Japan, 1978-88, working paper, 9393–10.16
- Forecasts of money supply, performance of alternative models, 1950s-90, article, 9389–1.202
- Foreign and US economic conditions, for major industrial countries, biweekly rpt, 9112–1
- Foreign and US reserves/imports ratio, and money supply growth rates, by selected country, selected years 1951-71, article, 9391–1.214
- Foreign countries economic and monetary trends, compounded annual rates of change and quarterly indicators for US and 7 major industrialized countries, quarterly rpt, 9391–7
- Foreign countries economic conditions and implications for US, periodic country rpt series, 2046–4
- Germany hyperinflation after WWI, money demand impact of relative prices of investment and consumer goods, model description and results, 1921-23, working paper, 9371–10.66
- GNP and inflation forecasting performance of alternative monetary aggregates, model description and results, 1948-87, working paper, 9371–10.53
- GNP and interest rates, relation to money supply, alternative models description and results, 1953-88, article, 9391–1.210
- GNP relation to money supply, alternative model results, 1960s-90, working paper, 9377–9.104
- Inflation forecasting performance of money supply, unemployment, and other monetary and economic indicators, 1959-88, article, 9379–1.204
- Inflation relation to alternative monetary aggregates and aggregate indexes, 1963-89, article, 9391–1.202
- Inflation relation to monetary aggregates, 1950s-89, article, 9379–1.203

Money supply

Interest rates relation to money supply, alternative model results, 1950s-90, technical paper, 9366–7.257

Japan economic conditions, financial and intl policies, and trade devs, 1950s-80s and projected to 2050, compilation of papers, 23848–220

Monetary aggregates and velocities, monthly rpt, discontinued, 9362–6

Monetary aggregates, money stock measures and components, monthly rpt, 9362–1.1

Monetary policy impact on multiplier relating money supply and components to monetary base, various periods 1970-90, article, 9391–1.218

Monetary trends, Fed Reserve Bank of St Louis monthly rpt, 9391–2

Money stock components, 1959-90, annual rpt, 204–1.5

Seignorage use for financing fiscal deficits in EC, with background data for EC, 1970s-88, working paper, 9387–8.238

Statistical Abstract of US, 1991 annual data compilation, 2324–1.16

Stock price volatility relation to interest rates, oil and gold prices, and US money supply, for 10 countries, model description and results, 1970s-88, working paper, 9381–10.116

Survey of Current Business, detailed financial and business data, and economic indicators, monthly rpt, 2702–1.1

Switzerland alternative monetary aggregates indexes relation to inflation and monetary base, 1970s-89, article, 9391–1.221

Taiwan interest rate relation to money supply, industrial production, and US interest rate, late 1980s, working paper, 9371–10.56

see also Black market currency

see also Coins and coinage

see also Counterfeiting and forgery

see also Credit

see also Eurocurrency

see also Flow-of-funds accounts

see also Foreign exchange

see also International reserves

see also Monetary policy

see also Special foreign currency programs

Mongolia

Agricultural exports of high-value commodities, indexes and sales by commodity, world area, and country, 1960s-86, 1528–323

Agricultural trade of US, by detailed commodity and country, 1990, semiannual rpt, 1522–4

Economic and social conditions of developing countries from 1960s, and Intl Dev Cooperation Agency and AID activities and funding, FY90-92, annual rpt, 9904–4

Economic, social, political, and geographic summary data, by country, 1991, annual factbook, 9114–2

Exports and imports of US, by transport mode, country, and SITC 1- to 3-digit commodity, 1990, annual rpt, 2424–12

Exports and imports of US with Communist countries, by detailed commodity and country, quarterly rpt with articles, 9882–2

Human rights conditions in 170 countries, and US economic and military aid, 1990, annual rpt, 21384–3

UN voting record and share of votes in agreement with US, by issue, country, and world area, 1990, annual rpt, 7004–18

see also under By Foreign Country in the "Index by Categories"

Monheit, Alan C.

"Insuring the Children: A Decade of Change. National Medical Expenditure Survey", 4186–8.14

Monitored Retrievable Storage Commission

Nuclear power plant spent fuel storage pending opening of permanent repository, safety and costs of alternative methods, projected 1991-2050, 14818–1

Monmouth County, N.J.

Wages by occupation, and benefits for office and plant workers, 1991 survey, periodic MSA rpt, 6785–12.3

see also under By SMSA or MSA in the "Index by Categories"

Mono County, Calif.

Water quality, chemistry, hydrology, and other characteristics, 1989 local area study, 5666–27.7

Monopolies and cartels

Boycotts (intl) by OPEC and other countries, US firms and shareholders cooperation and tax benefits denied, 1986, annual rpt, 8004–13

see also Antitrust law

see also Organization of Petroleum Exporting Countries

Monroe, La.

see also under By SMSA or MSA in the "Index by Categories"

Montagne, Michael

"Descriptive Epidemiology of International Cocaine Trafficking", 4498–74

Montana

Banks (insured commercial and savings) deposits by instn, State, MSA, and county, as of June 1990, annual regional rpt, 9295–3.6

Bears (grizzly) in Yellowstone Natl Park area, monitoring results, 1990, annual rpt, 5544–4

Birds (raptors) population, habitat, and reproductive success, for coal mining areas of Montana and Wyoming, 1970s-80s, technical rpt, 5506–12.1

Business and economic conditions, Fed Reserve 9th District, quarterly journal, 9383–19

Coal production and mines by county, prices, productivity, miners, and reserves, by mining method and State, 1989-90, annual rpt, 3164–25

County Business Patterns, 1989: employment, establishments, and payroll, by SIC 2- to 4-digit industry and county, annual State rpt, 2326–8.28

DOD prime contract awards, by contractor, service branch, State, and city, FY90, annual rpt, 3544–22

Energy-efficiency building codes, effect on house construction practices in Bonneville Power Admin service areas, 1987, 3228–15

Fed Govt spending in States and local areas, by type, State, county, and city, FY90, annual rpt, 2464–3

Fed Govt spending in States, by type, program, agency, and State, FY90, annual rpt, 2464–2

Gemstone production in selected States, Mineral Industry Surveys, 1988-90, advance annual rpt, 5614–5.10

Health care access indicators, for Montana, 1989 hearing, 23898–6

HHS financial aid, by program, recipient, State, and city, FY90, annual regional listing, 4004–3.8

Hospital deaths of Medicare patients, actual and expected rates by diagnosis, and hospital characteristics, by instn, FY87-89, annual regional rpt, 4654–14.8

Income (personal) per capita and by source, and earnings by industry div, by State, MSA, and county, 1984-89, annual regional rpt, 2704–2.5

Jail adult and juvenile population, employment, spending, instn conditions, and inmate programs, by county and facility, 1988, regional rpt series, 6068–144.5

Log home manufacturers in Montana, sales, production, and timber use, 1960s-88, 1208–370

Marriages, divorces, and rates, by characteristics of spouses, State, and county, 1987 and trends from 1920, US Vital Statistics annual rpt, 4144–4

Mineral industries census, 1987: finances and operations, by SIC 2- to 4-digit industry, State, and county, census div rpt, 2515–1.8

Mineral Industry Surveys, State reviews of production, 1990, preliminary annual rpt, 5614–6

Minerals Yearbook, 1989, Vol 2: State review of production and sales by commodity, and business activity, annual rpt, 5604–16.27

Minerals Yearbook, 1989, Vol 2: State reviews of production, sales, and firms, by commodity, and business activity, annual rpt, 5604–34

Physicians, by specialty, age, sex, and location of training and practice, 1989, State rpt, 4116–6.27

Population and housing census, 1990: population and housing characteristics, households, and land area, by county, subdiv, and place, State rpt, 2551–1.28

Population and housing census, 1990: voting age and total population by race, and housing units, by block, redistricting counts required under PL 94-171, State CD-ROM release, 2551–6.8

Population and housing census, 1990: voting age and total population by race, and housing units, by county and city, redistricting counts required under PL 94-171, State summary rpt, 2551–5.27

Recreation (outdoor) facilities on public land, use, and Land Mgmt Bur mgmt activities, funding, and plans, 1990 State rpt, 5726–5.5

Statistical Abstract of US, 1991 annual data compilation, 2324–1

Supplemental Security Income payments and beneficiaries, by type of eligibility, State, and county, Dec 1989, annual rpt, 4744–27.8

Timber in Montana, harvest methods impacts on bird population by species, 1989-90, 1208–372

Timber in Montana outside natl forests, acreage, resources, and mortality by species and ownership class, 1988-89, series, 1206–25

Index by Subjects and Names

Morocco

Timber in northwestern US and British Columbia, production, prices, trade, and employment, quarterly rpt, 1202–3

Timber insect and disease incidence and damage, and control activities, 1989, State rpt, 1206–49.2

Water quality, chemistry, hydrology, and other characteristics, 1989 local area study, 5666–27.16

Water resources data collection and analysis activities of USGS Water Resources Div District, with project descriptions, 1989 rpt, 5666–26.11

Water supply and quality in streams and lakes, and groundwater levels in wells, by drainage basin, 1990, annual State rpt, 5666–10.25

Wildlife mgmt activities and funding, acreage by habitat type, and scientific staff, for Bur of Land Mgmt, 1990 State rpt, 5726–7.4

see also under By State in the "Index by Categories"

Monterey, Calif.

see also under By SMSA or MSA in the "Index by Categories"

Montgomery, Ala.

see also under By City and By SMSA or MSA in the "Index by Categories"

Montgomery County, Md.

Fed Govt land acquisition and dev projects in DC metro area, characteristics and funding by agency and project, FY91-95, annual rpt, 15454–1

Montgomery, John D.

"Market Segmentation and 1992: Toward a Theory of Trade in Financial Services", 9366–7.248

Montgomery, Patricia A.

"Hispanic Population in the U.S.: March 1990", 2546–1.448

"Hispanic Population in the U.S.: March 1991", 2546–1.451

Montreal, Canada

Fruit and vegetable shipments, and arrivals in US and Canada cities, by mode of transport and State and country of origin, 1990, annual rpt, 1311–4.1

Monuments and memorials

Acreage and costs of real property owned by Fed Govt, worldwide summary by location, agency, and use, 1989, annual rpt, 9454–5

Acreage of land under Forest Service mgmt, by forest and location, 1990, annual rpt, 1204–2

Acreage of land under Natl Park Service mgmt, by site, ownership, and region, FY91, semiannual rpt, 5542–1

DC metro area land acquisition and dev projects of Fed Govt, characteristics and funding by agency and project, FY91-95, annual rpt, 15454–1

Visits and overnight stays in natl park system, by park and State, monthly rpt, 5542–4

Visits and overnight stays in natl park system, by park and State, 1990, annual rpt, 5544–12

Moon, Choon-Geol

"Effect of Rent Control on Housing Quality Change: A Longitudinal Analysis", 9387–8.246

Moonlighting

Labor force moonlighting, by reason, and characteristics of workers and primary and secondary jobs, 1991, press release, 6726–1.40

Labor supply trends, with characteristics of working-age population not in labor force, part-time workers, and multiple-jobholders, late 1960s-90, article, 9362–1.203

Statistical Abstract of US, 1991 annual data compilation, 2324–1.13

Moore, David

"Encouraging Private Investment in Space Activities", 26306–6.154

"Large Nondefense R&D Projects in the Budget: 1980-96", 26306–3.116

Moore, Jeffrey C.

"Proxy Reports: Results from a Record Check Study", 2626–10.140

"SIPP Record Check Results: Implications for Measurement Principles and Practice", 2626–10.129

Moore, Robert R.

"Asymmetric Information, Repeated Lending, and Capital Structure", 9379–14.13

"Relative Price Variability and Inflation: Inter and Intracity Evidence from Brazil in the 1980's", 9379–14.14

Moore, W. Henson

"Current Energy Situation and the National Energy Strategy", 1004–16.1

Moore, William

"Trends in U.S. Soft Drink Consumption—Demand Implications for Low-Calorie and Other Sweeteners", 1561–14.210

Moorhead, Minn.

see also under By SMSA or MSA in the "Index by Categories"

Morality

see Ethics and morality

Moran, Larry R.

"Motor Vehicles, Model Year 1991", 2702–1.228

Morbidity

see Diseases and disorders

Morehart, Mitchell J.

"Financial Characteristics of Dairy Farms, 1989", 1561–2.201

Moreno, Ramon

"Explaining the U.S. Export Boom", 9393–8.203

Moreno Valley, Calif.

see also under By City in the "Index by Categories"

Morgan, Donald P.

"Bank Credit Commitments", 9381–10.121

"New Evidence Firms Are Financially Constrained", 9381–1.211

Morgan, Frank B.

"Public Elementary and Secondary Schools and Agencies in the U.S. and Outlying Areas: School Year 1989-90. Final Tabulations", 4834–17

Morgan, Robert L.

"Classification of Instructional Programs (CIP)", 4828–29

"Comparison of State Methods for Collecting, Aggregating, and Reporting State Average Daily Attendance (ADA) Totals to the National Center for Education Statistics", 4838–48

Morocco

Agricultural exports of high-value commodities, indexes and sales by commodity, world area, and country, 1960s-86, 1528–323

Agricultural exports of US, impacts of foreign agricultural and trade policy, with data by commodity and country, 1989, annual rpt, 1924–8

Agricultural production, trade, and policies in foreign countries, summary data by country, 1989-90, annual factbook, 1924–12

Agricultural trade of US, by detailed commodity and country, 1989, annual rpt, 1524–8

Agricultural trade of US, by detailed commodity and country, 1990, semiannual rpt, 1522–4

AID economic aid to developing countries, obligations and disbursements by country, quarterly rpt, 9912–4

AID loans repayment status and terms by program and country, and status of predecessor agency loans, quarterly rpt, 9912–3

Almond production, trade, use, and stocks, for 6 countries and US, 1987-92, article, 1925–34.240

Economic and military aid and loans from US and intl agencies, by program and country, FY46-90, annual rpt, 9914–5

Economic and social conditions of developing countries from 1960s, and Intl Dev Cooperation Agency and AID activities and funding, FY90-92, annual rpt, 9904–4

Economic conditions, income, production, prices, employment, and trade, 1991 periodic country rpt, 2046–4.30

Economic conditions, policy, and trade practices, by country, 1988-90, annual rpt, 21384–5

Economic, social, political, and geographic summary data, by country, 1991, annual factbook, 9114–2

Exports and imports of US, by commodity and country, 1970-89, world area rpt, 9116–1.1

Exports and imports of US, by selected country, country group, and commodity group, 1990, annual rpt, 2044–37

Exports and imports of US, by transport mode, country, and SITC 1- to 3-digit commodity, 1990, annual rpt, 2424–12

Exports of US, detailed Schedule B commodities with countries of destination, 1990, annual rpt, 2424–10

Food supply, needs, and aid for developing countries, status and alternative forecasts, 1991 world area rpt, 1526–8.1

Human rights conditions in 170 countries, and US economic and military aid, 1990, annual rpt, 21384–3

Military aid of US, arms sales, and training programs costs and budget requests, by program, world region, and country, FY90-92, annual rpt, 7144–13

Multinatl US firms foreign affiliates, income statement items by country and world area, 1986, biennial article, 8302–2.212

Phosphate rock exports of Morocco by country of destination, Mineral Industry Surveys, monthly rpt, periodic table, 5612–1.30

Morocco

UN voting record and share of votes in agreement with US, by issue, country, and world area, 1990, annual rpt, 7004–18 *see also* under By Foreign Country in the "Index by Categories"

Morris, Charles S.

"Lower Profits at Tenth District Banks", 9381–16.201

Morris, Victor F.

"Bonner Bridge Storm", 2152–8.202

Morrison, Peter H.

"Fire History and Pattern in a Cascade Range Landscape", 1208–354

Morrissey, Elizabeth S.

"Work and Poverty in Metro and Nonmetro Areas", 1598–274

Mortality

see Accidental deaths
see Child mortality
see Deaths
see Fetal deaths
see Homicide
see Infant mortality
see Life expectancy
see Suicide
see Traffic accident fatalities
see Vital statistics

Mortgages

Affordability indicators for housing, by household composition, income, and current tenure, 1988, 2486–1.11

American Housing Survey: inventory change from 1973, by reason, unit and household characteristics, and location, 1983, biennial rpt, 2485–14

American Housing Survey: unit and households detailed characteristics, and unit and neighborhood quality, MSA rpt series, 2485–6

American Housing Survey: unit and households detailed characteristics, and unit and neighborhood quality, 1987, biennial rpt, 2485–12

Applications for mortgages by disposition, and secondary loan market sales by purchaser type, by applicant and neighborhood characteristics, 1990, article, 9362–1.206

Assets and debts of private sector, balance sheets by segment, 1945-90, semiannual rpt, 9365–4.1

Atlanta metro area secondary mortgage market underwriting guidelines, and indicators of discrimination, 1989, GAO rpt, 26113–500

Bank deposit insurance fund finances, potential losses, and real estate lenders financial ratios compared to other US and Texas banks, 1990 hearings, 25248–125

Banks (insured commercial and savings) finances, for foreign and domestic offices, by asset size, 1989, annual rpt, 9294–4.2

Banks profitability indicators for student loans and other financial services, 1985-89, 4808–36

Business statistics, detailed data for major industries and economic indicators, *Survey of Current Business,* monthly rpt, 2702–1.6; 2702–1.9

Consumer Expenditure Survey, household income by source, and itemized spending, by selected characteristics and region, 1988-89, annual rpt, 6764–5

County Business Patterns, 1988: employment, establishments, and payroll, by SIC 2- to 4-digit industry and county, annual State rpt series, 2326–6

County Business Patterns, 1989: employment, establishments, and payroll, by SIC 2- to 4-digit industry and county, annual State rpt series, 2326–8

Credit unions mortage lending impacts on financial performance, for northeast States and total US, 1980s-90, article, 9536–1.6

Debt outstanding, by type of property and holder, 1939-90, annual rpt, 204–1.5

Fed Govt property acquired through foreclosure and savings instn failure, 1-family homes inventory by State, acquisition costs, and sales, for 4 agencies, 1986-90, GAO rpt, 26113–513

Fed Govt spending in States, by type, program, agency, and State, FY90, annual rpt, 2464–2

Fed Home Loan Mortgage Corp activities and financial statements, 1990, annual rpt, 9414–1

Fed Home Loan Mortgage Corp financial condition and capital adequacy, 1989, annual rpt, 5184–8

Fed Housing Financing Board new home mortgage yields, monthly rpt, 23842–1.5

Fed Natl Mortgage Assn activities and finances, 1988-89, annual rpt, 5184–9

FHA-insured mortgages, financial, property, and mortgagor characteristics, by metro area, 1990, annual rpt, 5144–24

FHA-insured mortgages, financial, property, and mortgagor characteristics, by State, 1990, annual rpt, 5144–1

FHA-insured mortgages, financial, property, and mortgagor characteristics, total and by State and outlying area, 1990, annual rpt, 5144–25

FHA-insured mortgages, financial, property, and mortgagor characteristics, 1990, annual rpt, 5144–17; 5144–23

FHA-insured mortgages for 1-family units, by loan type and mortgage characteristics, quarterly rpt, 5142–45

FHA-insured mortgages secondary market prices and yields, and interest rates on construction and conventional mortgage loans, by region, monthly press release, 5142–20

FHA mortgage applications for new and existing units, refinancings, and housing starts, monthly rpt, 5142–44

Finance companies credit outstanding and leasing activities, by credit type, monthly rpt, 9365–2.7

Flow-of-funds accounts, savings, investments, and credit statements, quarterly rpt, 9365–3.3

FmHA property acquired through foreclosure, 1-family homes, value, sales, and leases, by State, monthly rpt, 1182–7

Foreclosure of mortgages, caseloads for Federal district courts, 1990, annual rpt, 18204–8.13; 18204–8.18; 18204–11

Foreclosure of mortgages, caseloads for Federal district courts, 1991, annual rpt, 18204–2.1

Futures and options trading volume, by commodity and exchange, FY90, annual rpt, 11924–2

Govt Natl Mortgage Assn finances, and mortgage-backed securities program, FY90, annual rpt, 5144–6

Govt-sponsored enterprises financial condition and capital adequacy, with data by enterprise, 1970s-90 and projected to 1996, 26308–99

Govt-sponsored enterprises financial condition and capital adequacy, with regulatory recommendations and data by enterprise, 1985-95, GAO rpt, 26119–296

Govt-sponsored enterprises financial condition, capital adequacy, and impacts on Federal borrowing, with data by enterprise, 1980s-90, last issue of annual rpt, 8004–15

Households debt, and payment behavior and difficulties, by selected characteristics, 1980s-90, article, 9362–1.201

Housing units (1-family) by selected structural characteristics, sales, and prices, 1970s-90, article, 1702–1.205

Housing units completed, single and multifamily units by structural and financial characteristics, inside-outside MSAs, and region, 1986-90, annual rpt, 2384–1

Illinois S&Ls, mortgage interest fixed and adjustable rates and fees offered, monthly rpt, 9302–6

Insurance (private) on mortgages for 1-4 family units, monthly press release, 5142–38

Interest rates for commercial paper, govt securities, other financial instruments, and home mortgages, monthly rpt, 9365–2.14

Interest rates on home mortgages, bimonthly rpt, 2042–1.5

Interest rates on new mortgages for previously occupied homes, monthly rpt, 9302–30; 9302–38

Loan activity for mortgages, by type of lender, loan, and mortgaged property, monthly press release, 5142–18

Loan activity for mortgages, by type of lender, loan, and mortgaged property, quarterly press release, 5142–30

Low income housing supply impacts of HUD programs to maintain supply and to deter insured mortgage prepayment, 1986-90 and projected to 2005, GAO rpt, 26131–84

New England States economic indicators, Fed Reserve 1st District, monthly rpt, 9373–2.7

New England States, FHLB 1st District thrifts financial operations compared to banks, and housing industry indicators, bimonthly rpt with articles, 9302–4

Nonprofit charitable organizations finances, and revenue and investments of top 10 instns, 1986-87, article, 8302–2.210

North Central States business and economic conditions, Fed Reserve 9th District, quarterly journal, 9383–19

North Central States, FHLB 6th District insured S&Ls financial condition and operations by State, quarterly rpt, 9302–23

North Central States, FHLB 6th District savings instns financial condition and operations by State, monthly rpt, 9302–11

Originations by financial instn type, and impacts of mortgage market regulatory and structural changes on residential investment, 1970s-80s, technical paper, 9385–8.74

Originations of mortgages, by State, 1978-89, annual press release, 5144–21

Index by Subjects and Names

Outstanding mortgage debt, and terms, for fixed- and adjustable-rate mortgages, 1950s-89, technical paper, 9366–6.263

Price level adjusted mortgages impacts on housing affordability, 1991 article, 9373–1.204

Racial integration promotion through mortgage subsidy programs, effectiveness and impacts on housing prices, 1983-89, working paper, 9377–9.108

Recreation and investment housing units owned, by selected characteristics, 1987, biennial rpt supplement, 2485–13

Savings instns failure resolution activity and finances of Resolution Trust Corp, with data by asset type, State, region, and instn, monthly rpt, 9722–3

Savings instns failures, financial performance of instns under Resolution Trust Corp conservatorship, quarterly rpt, 9722–5

Savings instns finances and operations by district and State, mortgage loan activity and terms by MSA, and FHLB finances, 1989 and trends from 1900, annual rpt, 8434–3

Savings instns insured by Savings Assn Insurance Fund, assets, liabilities, and deposit and loan activity, by conservatorship status, monthly rpt, 8432–1

Savings instns mortgage debt holdings and other assets, returns on assets, and impacts of qualified lender regulations, 1970s-89, GAO rpt, 26119–337

Securities backed by mortgages, Fannie Mae and Freddie Mac pool holdings, 1980-89, article, 9391–16.201

Securities backed by mortgages, investments by major financial instns, quarterly press release, discontinued, 5002–12

Southeastern States, Fed Reserve 5th District, economic indicators by State, quarterly rpt, 9389–16

Southeastern States, Fed Reserve 5th District insured commercial banks financial statements, by State, quarterly rpt, 9389–18

Southeastern States, Fed Reserve 8th District banking and economic conditions, quarterly rpt with articles, 9391–16

Southeastern States, FHLB 4th District, employment and housing and mortgage market indicators by State, quarterly rpt, 9302–36

State and local govt employees pension system cash and security holdings and finances, quarterly rpt, 2462–2

State and Metro Area Data Book, 1991 data compilation, 2328–54

Statistical Abstract of US, 1991 annual data compilation, 2324–1.16

Survey of Current Business, detailed financial and business data, and economic indicators, monthly rpt, 2702–1.1

Tax (income) returns filed by type of filer, selected income items, quarterly rpt, 8302–2.1

Tax (income) returns of corporations, income and tax items by asset size and detailed industry, 1987, annual rpt, 8304–4

Tax (income) returns of corporations, income and tax items by asset size and detailed industry, 1988, annual rpt, 8304–21

Tax (income) withholding and related documents filed, by type and IRS service center, 1990 and projected 1991-98, annual rpt, 8304–22

Tax expenditures, Federal revenues forgone through income tax deductions and exclusions by type, FY92-96, annual rpt, 21784–10

Terms on conventional mortgages closed, by lender type, with quarterly data for 32 MSAs, monthly rpt, 9442–2

Terms, yields, secondary market activity, and debt outstanding, monthly rpt, 9362–1.1

Western States, FHLB 11th District S&Ls, offices, and financial condition, 1991 annual listing, 9304–23

Wisconsin S&Ls, mortgage interest fixed and adjustable rates and fees offered, monthly rpt, 9302–7

see also Agricultural credit

see also Farm Credit System

see also Veterans housing

Morticians and mortuaries

see Cemeteries and funerals

Morton, John D.

"How Firm Size and Industry Affect Employee Benefits", 6722–1.204

Moser, James T.

"Evidence on the Impact of Futures Margin Specifications on the Performance of Futures and Cash Markets", 9375–13.51

Mosher, David

"START Treaty and Beyond", 26306–6.161

Mosher, William D.

"AIDS-Related Knowledge and Behavior Among Women 15-44 Years of Age: U.S., 1988", 4146–8.200

"Fecundity and Infertility in the U.S., 1965-88", 4146–8.194

Moss, Abigail J.

"Children's Exposure to Environmental Cigarette Smoke Before and After Birth: Health of Our Nation's Children", 4146–8.204

"Use of Selected Medical Device Implants in the U.S., 1988", 4146–8.197

Motels

see Hotels and motels

Mothers

see Births

see Breast-feeding

see Families and households

see Fertility

see Maternity

see Maternity benefits

see Parents

see Teenage pregnancy

see Women

Motion pictures

Copyrights Register activities, registrations by material type, and fees, FY90 and trends from 1790, annual rpt, 26404–2

County Business Patterns, 1988: employment, establishments, and payroll, by SIC 2- to 4-digit industry and county, annual State rpt series, 2326–6

County Business Patterns, 1989: employment, establishments, and payroll, by SIC 2- to 4-digit industry and county, annual State rpt series, 2326–8

Education (postsecondary) course completions, by detailed program, sex, race, and instn type, for 1972 high school class, as of 1984, 4888–4

Motion pictures

Employment, earnings, and hours, by SIC 1- to 4-digit industry, monthly and annual averages, selected years 1909-90, annual rpt, 6744–4

Enterprise Statistics, 1987: auxiliaries of multi-establishment firms, finances and operations by function, industry, and State, 2329–6

Enterprise Statistics, 1987: finances and operations for companies, by size, level of diversification, form of organization, and industry group, 2329–8

Exports and imports of US, by country and detailed commodity, monthly rpt, 2422–12

Exports and imports of US, by Harmonized System 6-digit commodity and country, 1990, annual rpt, 2424–13

Exports and imports of US, by transport mode, country, and SITC 1- to 3-digit commodity, 1990, annual rpt, 2424–12

Exports of US, detailed Schedule B commodities with countries of destination, 1990, annual rpt, 2424–10

Fed Govt audiovisual activities and spending, by whether performed in-house and agency, FY90, annual rpt, 9514–1

Finances and operations, by SIC 2- to 4-digit industry, forecast 1991, annual rpt, 2044–28

Libraries (public) finances, staff, and operations, by State and population size, 1989, annual rpt, 4824–6

Library of Congress activities, acquisitions, services, and financial statements, FY90, annual rpt, 26404–1

Military post exchange operations, and sales by commodity, by facility and location worldwide, FY89, annual rpt, 3504–10

Multinatl US firms and foreign affiliates finances and operations, by industry and world area of parent firm, 1989 benchmark survey, preliminary annual rpt, 2704–5

Natl Archives and Records Admin activities, finances, holdings, and staff, FY90, annual rpt, 9514–2

Natl Endowment for Arts activities and grants, FY90, annual rpt, 9564–3

Occupational injury and illness rates, by SIC 2- to 4-digit industry, 1988-89, annual rpt, 6844–7

Price indexes (producer), by stage of processing and detailed commodity, monthly rpt, 6762–6

Puerto Rico economic censuses, 1987: wholesale and retail trade and service industry finances and operations, by SIC 2- to 4-digit industry and municipio, 2591–1

Puerto Rico economic censuses, 1987: wholesale, retail, and service industries finances and operations, by establishment characteristics and SIC 2- and 3-digit industry, subject rpts, 2591–2

Receipts for services, by SIC 2- to 4-digit kind of business, 1990, annual rpt, 2413–8

Service industries census, 1987: depreciable assets, capital and operating expenses, and receipts, by SIC 2- to 4-digit kind of business, 2393–2

Service industries census, 1987: establishments, receipts by source, payroll, and employment, by SIC 2- to 4-digit kind of business, State, and MSA, 2393–4

Motion pictures

Tax (income) returns of corporations, income and tax items by asset size and detailed industry, 1987, annual rpt, 8304–4

Tax (income) returns of corporations, income and tax items by asset size and detailed industry, 1988, annual rpt, 8304–21

Tax (income) returns of sole proprietorships, income statement items, by industry group, 1989, annual article, 8302–2.214

USDA rpts, computer data files, and visual aids, 1991 annual listing, 1004–13

see also Video recordings and equipment

Motor Freight Transportation and Warehousing Survey

Finances and inventory of truck and warehouse services, by SIC 2- to 4-digit industry, 1989 survey, annual rpt, 2413–14

Motor fuels

Alcohol (methanol) fuel substitution for gasoline, economic, environmental, and health impacts, projected 2000-2010, article, 9379–1.208

Alcohol (methanol) use in autos, oil price and economic impacts, 1990 technical paper, 9379–12.62

Alternative motor fuels costs, emissions, health impacts, and characteristics, series, 9196–5

Construction industries census, 1987: establishments, employment, receipts, and expenditures, by SIC 4-digit industry and State, final industry rpt series, 2373–1

Consumer spending for motor fuel, relation to prices and household income, 1970s-89, article, 9371–1.204

Consumption of fuel by transport mode, fuel supply, and demographic and economic factors of vehicle use, 1970s-89, annual rpt, 3304–5

Consumption of motor fuel, by consuming sector and State, 1990, annual rpt, 7554–1.1

Foreign countries transportation energy use, fuel prices, vehicle registrations, and mileage, by selected country, 1970s-89, annual rpt, 3304–5.1

Imports of oil, traffic by US port and vessel type, marine oil pollution sources, and costs and operations of proposed offshore terminals, late 1980s, 5738–25

Minerals Yearbook, 1988, Vol 3: foreign country reviews of production, trade, and policy, by commodity, annual rpt series, 5604–17

Price indexes (producer), by stage of processing and detailed commodity, monthly rpt, 6762–6

Service industries census, 1987: establishments, receipts by source, payroll, and employment, by SIC 2- to 4-digit kind of business, State, and MSA, 2393–4.10

see also Aviation fuels

see also Diesel fuel

see also Fuel tax

see also Gasohol

see also Gasoline

see also Transportation energy use

Motor transportation

see Automobiles

see Buses

see Motor vehicle industry

see Motorcycles

see Taxicabs

see Traffic accidents and safety

see Trucks and trucking industry

Motor vehicle exhaust

Abatement spending by govts, business, and consumers, 1987-89, annual article, 2702–1.229

Alcohol (methanol) fuel substitution for gasoline, economic, environmental, and health impacts, projected 2000-2010, article, 9379–1.208

Alternative motor fuels costs, emissions, health impacts, and characteristics, series, 9196–5

Emissions levels for 6 pollutants, by source and selected MSA, 1980-89, annual rpt, 9194–1

Emissions levels for 6 pollutants, by source, 1970-89 and trends from 1940, annual rpt, 9194–13

Energy natl strategy plans for conservation, impacts on energy use and pollution under alternative technology investment assumptions, projected 1990-2030, 3166–6.48

Energy use by mode of transport, fuel supply, and demographic and economic factors of vehicle use, 1970s-89, annual rpt, 3304–5

Global warming contributing pollutants emissions factors and control costs, by pollutant and source, 1990 rpt, 9198–124

Natl transportation system planning, use, condition, accidents, and needs, by mode of transport, 1940s-90 and projected to 2020, 7308–202

Motor vehicle exports and imports

Canada and US auto trade, production, sales, prices, and employment, selected years 1965-88, annual rpt, 2044–35

Energy conservation measures impacts on consumption, by component and end-use sector, 1970s-88 and projected under alternative oil prices to 1995, 3308–93

Energy economy performance of autos and light trucks by make, standards, and enforcement, 1978-91 model years, annual rpt, 7764–9

Energy economy test results for US and foreign makes, 1992 model year, annual rpt, 3304–11

Energy use by mode of transport, fuel supply, and demographic and economic factors of vehicle use, 1970s-89, annual rpt, 3304–5

Exports and imports between US and outlying areas, by detailed commodity and mode of transport, 1990, annual rpt, 2424–11

Exports and imports by country, US industry finances and operations, and prices of selected US and foreign models, monthly rpt, 9882–8

Exports and imports of US, by country and detailed commodity, monthly rpt, 2422–12

Exports and imports of US, by Harmonized System 6-digit commodity and country, 1990, annual rpt, 2424–13

Exports and imports of US, by selected country, country group, and commodity group, 1990, annual rpt, 2044–37

Exports and imports of US, by transport mode, country, and SITC 1- to 3-digit commodity, 1990, annual rpt, 2424–12

Exports of US, detailed Schedule B commodities with countries of destination, 1990, annual rpt, 2424–10

Great Lakes area economic conditions and outlook, for US and Canada, 1970s-90, 9375–15

Imports, exports, and employment impacts, by SIC 2- to 4-digit industry and commodity, quarterly rpt, 2322–2

Imports of autos and parts, *Survey of Current Business,* monthly rpt, 2702–1.2

Imports of US given duty-free treatment for value of US material sent abroad, by commodity and country, 1989, annual rpt, 9884–14

Investment (foreign direct) impact on manufacturing trade balance, with background data, late 1960s-90 and auto forecasts to 1993, article, 9385–1.210

Market shares, sales, and fuel economy, by size and model for domestic and foreign makes, 1991 model year, semiannual rpt, 3302–4

Minivans from Japan at less than fair value, injury to US industry, investigation with background financial and operating data, 1991 rpt, 9886–14.320

North American Free Trade Agreement proposals, auto imports duties and origin preference eligibility rules, 1978-91, 9886–4.178

OECD intl trade position for US and 4 countries, and factors affecting US competition, periodic pamphlet, 2042–25

OECD trade, total and for 4 major countries, and US trade by country, by commodity, 1970-89, world area rpt series, 9116–1

Price indexes for exports and imports, by selected end-use category, monthly press release, 6762–15

Safety of domestic and foreign autos, crash test results by model, press release series, 7766–7

Sales and prices for domestic and import autos and trucks, and auto production and inventories, 1991 model year, annual article, 2702–1.228

Sales of domestic and imported cars, monthly rpt, quarterly data, 23842–1.1

Statistical Abstract of US, 1991 annual data compilation, 2324–1.21

Theft rates of new autos, by make and model, 1989 model year, annual rpt, 7764–21

Motor vehicle fleets

Depreciable assets class lives measurement, investment, and operations, for fleet and other business vehicle rental industries, 1991 rpt, 8006–5.5

DOE fleet, and fuel efficiency, by vehicle type, FY90, annual rpt, 3004–27

Energy economy, sales, and market shares, by size and model for domestic and foreign makes, 1991 model year, semiannual rpt, 3302–4

Energy use, size, and trip characteristics, for motor vehicle fleets by type, 1970s-89, annual rpt, 3304–5.3

Fed Govt obligations object class analysis, by agency, Budget of US, FY92, annual rpt, 104–9

Index by Subjects and Names

Motor vehicle industry

Manufacturing census, 1987: employment and shipments under Fed Govt contracts, by SIC 4-digit industry, 2497–7

Military autos and light trucks owned and leased by service branch, and costs and savings from GSA leases, FY89, GAO rpt, 26123–344

Postal Service operating costs, itemized by class of mail, FY90, annual rpt, 9864–4

Registrations by public and private ownership and vehicle type, and revenues, by State, 1990, annual rpt, 7554–1.2

Retail trade census, 1987: depreciable assets, capital and operating expenses, sales, value added, and inventories, by SIC 2- to 4-digit kind of business, 2399–2

Service industries census, 1987: depreciable assets, capital and operating expenses, and receipts, by SIC 2- to 4-digit kind of business, 2393–2

Truck and warehouse services finances and inventory, by SIC 2- to 4-digit industry, 1989 survey, annual rpt, 2413–14

Truck transport of fruit and vegetables, itemized costs per mile by item for fleets and owner-operator trucks, monthly table, 1272–1

TVA energy use by fuel type, and conservation costs and savings, FY90, annual rpt, 9804–26

Wholesale trade census, 1987: depreciable assets, capital and operating expenses, sales, value added, and inventories, by SIC 2- to 3-digit kind of business, 2407–2

Motor vehicle industry

Business statistics, detailed data for major industries and economic indicators, *Survey of Current Business,* monthly rpt, 2702–1.23

Capital expenditures for plant and equipment, by major industry group, quarterly rpt, 2502–2

Consumer spending forecasting performance of consumer sentiment index, 1950s-90, technical paper, 9366–6.282

County Business Patterns, 1988: employment, establishments, and payroll, by SIC 2- to 4-digit industry and county, annual State rpt series, 2326–6

County Business Patterns, 1989: employment, establishments, and payroll, by SIC 2- to 4-digit industry and county, annual State rpt series, 2326–8

EC auto sales shares, by firm, total and for France and West Germany, 1988, article, 9371–1.210

Economic indicators and components, and Fed Reserve 4th District business and financial conditions, monthly chartbook, 9377–10

Electric-powered autos, R&D activity and DOE funding shares, FY90, annual rpt, 3304–2

Employment, earnings, and hours, by SIC 1- to 4-digit industry, monthly and annual averages, selected years 1909-90, annual rpt, 6744–4

Employment, unemployment, and labor force characteristics, by region and census div, 1990, annual rpt, 6744–7.1

Enterprise Statistics, 1987: finances and operations for companies, by size, level of diversification, form of organization, and industry group, 2329–8

Finances and operations of US auto industry, trade by country, and prices of selected US and foreign models, monthly rpt, 9882–8

Foreign direct investment in US manufacturing, impacts on trade balances, with data by industry, 1980s-93, technical paper, 9385–8.91

Great Lakes area economic conditions and outlook, for US and Canada, 1970s-90, 9375–15

Input-output structure of US economy, detailed interindustry transactions for 84 industries, and components of final demand, 1986, annual article, 2702–1.206

Input-output structure of US economy, detailed interindustry transactions for 85 industries, 1982 benchmark data, 2702–1.213

Japan manufacturing firms US affiliates, employment, and wages, by selected industry and State, 1980s, 2048–151

Mail volume to and from households, use, and views, by class, source, content, and household characteristics, 1987-88, annual rpt, 9864–10

Manufacturing annual survey, 1989: finances and operations, by SIC 2- to 4-digit industry, series, 2506–15

Manufacturing census, 1987: employment and shipments under Fed Govt contracts, by SIC 4-digit industry, 2497–7

Manufacturing census, 1987: finances and operations, by SIC 2- to 4-digit industry, State, and MSA, with trends from 1849, 2497–1

Manufacturing census, 1987: finances and operations, by type of organization and SIC 2- to 4-digit industry, subject rpt, 2497–5

Manufacturing corporations financial statements, by selected SIC 2- to 3-digit industry, quarterly rpt, 2502–1

Manufacturing finances and operations, by SIC 2- to 4-digit industry, forecast 1991, annual rpt, 2044–28

Market shares, sales, and fuel economy, by size and model for domestic and foreign makes, 1991 model year, semiannual rpt, 3302–4

Multinatl firms US affiliates, investment trends and impact on US economy, 1991 annual rpt, 2004–9

Multinatl US firms and foreign affiliates finances and operations, by industry and world area of parent firm, 1989 benchmark survey, preliminary annual rpt, 2704–5

Occupational injury and illness rates, by SIC 2- to 4-digit industry, 1988-89, annual rpt, 6844–7

Occupational injury and illness rates, by SIC 2- to 4-digit industry, 1989, annual rpt, 6844–1

Pollution (air) emissions factors, by detailed pollutant and source, data compilation, 1990 rpt, 9198–120

Pollution (water) industrial releases in wastewater, levels, treatment, costs, and regulation, with background financial and operating data, 1989 industry rpt, 9206–4.13

Price indexes (producer), by stage of processing and detailed commodity, monthly rpt, 6762–6

Price indexes (producer), by stage of processing and detailed commodity, monthly 1990, annual rpt, 6764–2

Production and capacity use indexes, by SIC 2- to 4-digit industry, monthly rpt, 9365–2.24

Productivity in auto assembly plants and relation to labor reserves, model description and results, 1990 working paper, 6886–6.72

Productivity of labor and capital, and indexes of output, hours, and employment, 1967-89, annual rpt, 6824–1.3; 6824–1.5

Puerto Rico economic censuses, 1987: wholesale and retail trade and service industry finances and operations, by SIC 2- to 4-digit industry and municipio, 2591–1

Puerto Rico economic censuses, 1987: wholesale, retail, and service industries finances and operations, by establishment characteristics and SIC 2- and 3-digit industry, subject rpts, 2591–2

R&D funding, and scientists and engineers education and employment, for US and selected foreign countries, 1991 annual rpt, 9627–35.1

Recalls of motor vehicles and equipment with safety-related defects, by make, monthly listing, 7762–12

Recalls of motor vehicles and equipment with safety-related defects, by make, quarterly listing, 7762–2

Retail trade census, 1987: depreciable assets, capital and operating expenses, sales, value added, and inventories, by SIC 2- to 4-digit kind of business, 2399–2

Retail trade census, 1987: finances and employment, for establishments with and without payroll, by SIC 2- to 4-digit kind of business, State, and MSA, 2401–1

Soviet Union, Eastern Europe, OECD, and selected other countries consumer and producer goods and services production and sales, 1960s-90, annual rpt, 9114–4.7

Statistical Abstract of US, 1991 annual data compilation, 2324–1.21

Tax (income) returns of corporations, income and tax items by asset size and detailed industry, 1987, annual rpt, 8304–4

Tax (income) returns of corporations, income and tax items by asset size and detailed industry, 1988, annual rpt, 8304–21

Tax (income) returns of corporations with foreign tax credit, income and tax items by industry group, 1986, biennial article, 8302–2.203

Tax (income) returns of multinatl US firms foreign affiliates, income statement items, by asset size and industry, 1986, biennial article, 8302–2.212

Wages, employment, and benefits in auto and auto parts manufacturing, by occupation, region, and selected labor market area, 1989 survey, 6787–6.252

Wholesale trade census, 1987: depreciable assets, capital and operating expenses, sales, value added, and inventories, by SIC 2- to 3-digit kind of business, 2407–2

Wholesale trade census, 1987: establishments, sales by customer class,

Motor vehicle industry

employment, inventories, and expenses, by SIC 2- to 4-digit kind of business, 2407–4

Wholesale trade sales, inventories, purchases, and gross margins, by SIC 2- to 3-digit kind of business, 1990, annual rpt, 2413–13

see also Automobile repair and maintenance
see also Automobiles
see also Buses
see also Chrysler Corp.
see also Ford Motor Co.
see also General Motors Corp.
see also Motor vehicle exhaust
see also Motor vehicle exports and imports
see also Motor vehicle fleets
see also Motor vehicle parts and supplies
see also Motor vehicle registrations
see also Motor vehicle rental
see also Motor vehicle safety devices
see also Motorcycles
see also Recreational vehicles
see also Tires and tire industry
see also Trucks and trucking industry

Motor vehicle parts and supplies

Alternative motor fuels costs, emissions, health impacts, and characteristics, series, 9196–5

Bumper manufacturing, maintenance, and disposal costs, and percent of vehicles, by material, 1967-88, 5608–162.3

County Business Patterns, 1988: employment, establishments, and payroll, by SIC 2- to 4-digit industry and county, annual State rpt series, 2326–6

County Business Patterns, 1989: employment, establishments, and payroll, by SIC 2- to 4-digit industry and county, annual State rpt series, 2326–8

CPI by component for US city average, and by region, population size, and for 27 metro areas, monthly rpt, 6762–2

Exports and imports of US, by selected country, country group, and commodity group, 1990, annual rpt, 2044–37

Exports and imports of US shipped through Canada, by detailed commodity, customs district, and country, 1989, annual rpt, 7704–11

Exports of US, detailed Schedule B commodities with countries of destination, 1990, annual rpt, 2424–10

Franchise business opportunities by firm and kind of business, and sources of aid and info, 1990 annual listing, 2104–7

Gear production for selected uses under alternative production requirements, and industry finances and operations, late 1940s-89, 2028–1

Imports of autos, duties and origin preference eligibility rules under proposed North American Free Trade Agreement, 1978-91, 9886–4.178

Instruments and related products shipments, trade, use, and firms, by detailed type, 1989, annual Current Industrial Rpt, 2506–12.26

Japan manufacturing firms US affiliates, employment, and wages, by selected industry and State, 1980s, 2048–151

Labor productivity, indexes of output, hours, and employment by SIC 2- to 4-digit industry, 1967-89, annual rpt, 6824–1.3

Lug nuts (chrome-plated) from PRC and Taiwan at less than fair value, injury to

US industry, investigation with background financial and operating data, 1991 rpt, 9886–14.329

Manufacturing annual survey, 1989: finances and operations, by SIC 2- to 4-digit industry, series, 2506–15

Manufacturing census, 1987: finances and operations, by SIC 2- to 4-digit industry, State, and MSA, with trends from 1849, 2497–1

Manufacturing census, 1987: finances and operations, by type of organization and SIC 2- to 4-digit industry, subject rpt, 2497–5

Price indexes (producer), by stage of processing and detailed commodity, monthly rpt, 6762–6

Recalls of motor vehicles and equipment with safety-related defects, by make, monthly listing, 7762–12

Recalls of motor vehicles and equipment with safety-related defects, by make, quarterly listing, 7762–2

Retail trade census, 1987: finances and employment, for establishments with and without payroll, by SIC 2- to 4-digit kind of business, State, and MSA, 2401–1

Service industries census, 1987: establishments, receipts by source, payroll, and employment, by SIC 2- to 4-digit kind of business, State, and MSA, 2393–4.10

Tax (excise) on auto equipment of Fed Govt and States, 1990, annual rpt, 7554–1

Wages, employment, and benefits in auto and auto parts manufacturing, by occupation, region, and selected labor market area, 1989 survey, 6787–6.252

Wheels (steel disc) from Brazil at less than fair value, injury to US industry, investigation supplement, 1991 rpt, 9886–14.333

Wholesale trade sales, inventories, purchases, and gross margins, by SIC 2- to 3-digit kind of business, 1990, annual rpt, 2413–13

see also Batteries
see also Engines and motors
see also Mobile radio
see also Motor vehicle safety devices
see also Tires and tire industry

Motor vehicle registrations

Auto registrations, 1900-89, 3168–120

Business statistics, detailed data for major industries and economic indicators, *Survey of Current Business*, monthly rpt, 2702–1.23

Costs of operating autos and motorcycles by component, and Fed Govt mileage reimbursement rates, 1989, annual rpt, 9454–13

CPI by component for US city average, and by region, population size, and for 27 metro areas, monthly rpt, 6762–2

Energy use by mode of transport, fuel supply, and demographic and economic factors of vehicle use, 1970s-89, annual rpt, 3304–5

Fees for registration by vehicle type, motor fuel tax provisions, and disposition of tax receipts, by State, as of Jan 1991, biennial rpt, 7554–37

Foreign countries transportation energy use, fuel prices, vehicle registrations, and mileage, by selected country, 1970s-89, annual rpt, 3304–5.1

Govt finances, tax systems and revenue, and fiscal structure, by level of govt and State, 1991 with historical trends, annual rpt, 10044–1

Hwy receipts by source, and spending by function, by level of govt and State, 1990, annual rpt, 7554–1.3

Hwy Statistics, registrations by public and private ownership and vehicle type, and revenues, by State, 1990, annual rpt, 7554–1.2

Hwy Statistics, summary data by State, 1989-90, annual rpt, 7554–24

Registrations and fuel use, by vehicle type, 1960-90, annual rpt, 3164–74.1

Revenue, by level of govt, type of tax, State, and selected large county, quarterly rpt, 2462–3

Revenue of State govts by detailed source, and tax rates, by State, FY90, annual rpt, 2466–2.7

Soviet Union, Eastern Europe, OECD, and selected other countries living standards and commodity production, 1960s-90, annual rpt, 9114–4.1

State and Metro Area Data Book, 1991 data compilation, 2328–54

State govt revenue by source, spending and debt by function, and holdings, FY90, annual rpt, 2466–2.6

Statistical Abstract of US, 1991 annual data compilation, 2324–1.21

Truck interstate carriers finances and operations, by district, 1989, annual rpt, 9486–6.2

Motor vehicle rental

County Business Patterns, 1988: employment, establishments, and payroll, by SIC 2- to 4-digit industry and county, annual State rpt series, 2326–6

County Business Patterns, 1989: employment, establishments, and payroll, by SIC 2- to 4-digit industry and county, annual State rpt series, 2326–8

Depreciable assets class lives measurement, investment, and operations, for fleet and other business vehicle rental industries, 1991 rpt, 8006–5.5

Depreciable assets class lives measurement, investment, and operations, for light trucks fleet and other business use, 1991 rpt, 8006–5.6

Energy use, size, and trip characteristics, for motor vehicle fleets by type, 1970s-89, annual rpt, 3304–5.3

Enterprise Statistics, 1987: finances and operations for companies, by size, level of diversification, form of organization, and industry group, 2329–8

Finance companies credit outstanding and leasing activities, by credit type, monthly rpt, 9365–2.7

Franchise business opportunities by firm and kind of business, and sources of aid and info, 1990 annual listing, 2104–7

Military autos and light trucks owned and leased by service branch, and costs and savings from GSA leases, FY89, GAO rpt, 26123–344

Multinatl US firms and foreign affiliates finances and operations, by industry and world area of parent firm, 1989 benchmark survey, preliminary annual rpt, 2704–5

Index by Subjects and Names

Motorcycles

Price indexes (producer), by stage of processing and detailed commodity, monthly rpt, 6762–6

Puerto Rico economic censuses, 1987: wholesale and retail trade and service industry finances and operations, by SIC 2- to 4-digit industry and municipio, 2591–1

Puerto Rico economic censuses, 1987: wholesale, retail, and service industries finances and operations, by establishment characteristics and SIC 2- and 3-digit industry, subject rpts, 2591–2

Receipts for services, by SIC 2- to 4-digit kind of business, 1990, annual rpt, 2413–8

Service industries census, 1987: depreciable assets, capital and operating expenses, and receipts, by SIC 2- to 4-digit kind of business, 2393–2

Service industries census, 1987: establishments, receipts by source, payroll, and employment, by SIC 2- to 4-digit kind of business, State, and MSA, 2393–4

Transportation census, 1987: finances and operations by size, ownership, and State, and revenues by MSA, by SIC 2- to 4-digit industry, 2579–1

Travel from US, characteristics of visit and traveler, and country of destination, 1990 in-flight survey, annual rpt, 2904–14

Travel to US, by characteristics of visit and traveler, world area of origin, and US destination, 1990 survey, annual rpt, 2904–12

Truck and warehouse services finances and inventory, by SIC 2- to 4-digit industry, 1989 survey, annual rpt, 2413–14

Motor vehicle safety

see Motor vehicle safety devices

see Traffic accident fatalities

see Traffic accidents and safety

Motor vehicle safety devices

Accidents (fatal), circumstances, and characteristics of persons and vehicles involved, 1990, semiannual rpt, 7762–11

Child restraints use, related injuries by severity, 1990, annual rpt, 9164–6

Child safety seats recalls, by make, monthly listing, 7762–12

Costs of safety improvement measures, and accident and death reductions by type of accident and improvement, 1990 conf, 7558–110

Crash test results by domestic and foreign model, press release series, 7766–7

Diabetics health-related behaviors, weight, and body mass, by level of exercise, 1991 article, 4042–3.246

Exports and imports of US, by Harmonized System 6-digit commodity and country, 1990, annual rpt, 2424–13

Health condition improvement and disease prevention goals and recommended activities for 2000, with trends 1970s-80s, 4048–10

Motorcycle helmet mandatory use law in Texas, impacts on use, 1987-89 study, article, 4042–3.251

Motorcycle helmet use and mandatory use laws impacts on accident casualties and costs, literature review, 1956-89, GAO rpt, 26113–537

Natl Hwy Traffic Safety Admin activities and grants, and fatal traffic accident data, 1989, annual rpt, 7764–1

Quality changes in autos since last model year, factory and retail value, 1991 model year, annual press release, 6764–3

Recalls of motor vehicles and equipment with safety-related defects, by make, monthly listing, 7762–12

Recalls of motor vehicles and equipment with safety-related defects, by make, quarterly listing, 7762–2

Seat belt and motorcycle helmet use, and other detailed circumstances of fatal accidents, 1989, annual rpt, 7764–10

Seat belt use and alcohol involvement, for drivers killed and surviving fatal accidents, 1989, annual rpt, 7764–16

Seat belt use and lives saved, impacts of State mandatory use laws, 1983-90, annual fact sheet, 7766–15.2

Seat belt use, and other circumstances of accidents, 1989, annual rpt, 7764–18

Truck accidents, casualties, and damage, by circumstances and characteristics of persons and vehicles involved, 1988, annual rpt, 7554–9

Motor vehicle theft

Arrest rates, by offense, sex, age, and race, 1965-89, annual rpt, 6224–7

Arrests, prosecutions, convictions, and sentencing, for felony offenders, by offender characteristics and offense, 1988, 6066–25.33; 6066–25.39

Court civil and criminal caseloads for Federal district, appeals, and bankruptcy courts, by type of suit and offense, circuit, and district, 1990, annual rpt, 18204–11

Court civil and criminal caseloads for Federal district, appeals, and special courts, 1990, annual rpt, 18204–8

Court civil and criminal caseloads for Federal district courts, 1991, annual rpt, 18204–2.1

Court criminal case processing in Federal district courts, and dispositions, by offense, district, and offender characteristics, 1986, annual rpt, 6064–29

Court criminal case processing in Federal district courts, and dispositions, by offense, 1980-89, annual rpt, 6064–31

Court criminal cases in Federal district courts, by offense, disposition, and district, 1980-90, last issue of annual rpt, 18204–1

Crime, criminal justice admin and enforcement, and public opinion, data compilation, 1991 annual rpt, 6064–6

Crime Index by population size and region, and offenses by large city, Jan-June 1991, semiannual rpt, 6222–1

Crimes, arrests by offender characteristics, and rates, by offense, and law enforcement employees, by population size and jurisdiction, 1990, annual rpt, 6224–2

Drug abuse history of jail population, by offense, conviction status, criminal and family history, and selected other characteristics, 1989, 6066–19.63

Drug test results at arrest, by drug type, offense, and sex, for selected urban areas, quarterly rpt, 6062–3

Jail population, by criminal, correctional, drug use, and family history, and selected other characteristics, 1989, 6066–19.62

Jail population, by sociodemographic characteristics, criminal and drug use history, whether convicted, offense, and sentencing, 1989, annual rpt, 6064–26.3

Juvenile courts delinquency cases, by offense, referral source, disposition, age, sex, race, State, and county, 1988, annual rpt, 6064–12

Juvenile courts property offenses cases, by disposition and offender age, sex, and race, 1985-86, 6066–27.5

Pretrial processing, detention, and release, for Federal offenders, by defendant characteristics and district, 1988, hearing, 25528–114

Prison and parole admissions and releases, sentence length, and time served, by offense and offender characteristics, 1985, annual rpt, 6064–33

Sentences for Federal crimes, guidelines use and results by offense and district, and Sentencing Commission activities, 1990, annual rpt, 17664–1

Sentences for Federal offenses, guidelines by offense and circumstances, series, 17668–1

State and Metro Area Data Book, 1991 data compilation, 2328–54

Theft rates of new autos, by make and model, 1989 model year, annual rpt, 7764–21

US attorneys civil and criminal cases by type and disposition, and collections, by Federal district, FY90, annual rpt, 6004–2.1; 6004–2.7

Victimization rates, by victim and offender characteristics, circumstances, and offense, survey rpt series, 6066–3

Victimizations by region and victim characteristics, and rpts to police, by offense, 1973-90, annual rpt, 6066–25.35; 6066–25.41

Victimizations of households, by offense, household characteristics, and location, 1975-90, annual rpt, 6066–25.40

Women prisoners in State instns, by offense, drug use history, whether abused, and other characteristics, 1986, 6066–19.61

Motorcycles

Accident deaths and rates, by cause, age, sex, race, and State, 1988, US Vital Statistics annual rpt, 4144–2.5

Accidents (fatal), circumstances, and characteristics of persons and vehicles involved, 1990, semiannual rpt, 7762–11

Accidents (fatal), deaths, and rates, by circumstances, characteristics of persons and vehicles involved, and location, 1989, annual rpt, 7764–10

Accidents at hwy-railroad grade-crossings, detailed data by State and railroad, 1989, annual rpt, 7604–2

Accidents, casualties, circumstances, and characteristics of persons and vehicles involved, 1989, annual rpt, 7764–18

Child accident deaths and death rates, by cause, age, sex, race, and State, 1980-85, 4108–54

Costs of operating motorcycles by component, for 4 makes, and Fed Govt mileage reimbursement rates, 1989, annual rpt, 9454–13.3

Motorcycles

CPI by component for US city average, and by region, population size, and for 27 metro areas, monthly rpt, 6762–2

Drivers licenses issued and in force by age and sex, fees, and renewal, by license class and State, 1989, annual rpt, 7554–16

Energy economy, sales, and market shares, by size and model for domestic and foreign makes, 1991 model year, semiannual rpt, 3302–4

Energy use and vehicle registrations, by vehicle type, 1960-90, annual rpt, 3164–74.1

Energy use by mode of transport, fuel supply, and demographic and economic factors of vehicle use, 1970s-89, annual rpt, 3304–5

Exports and imports of US, by country and detailed commodity, monthly rpt, 2422–12

Exports and imports of US, by Harmonized System 6-digit commodity and country, 1990, annual rpt, 2424–13

Exports and imports of US, by transport mode, country, and SITC 1- to 3-digit commodity, 1990, annual rpt, 2424–12

Exports of US, detailed Schedule B commodities with countries of destination, 1990, annual rpt, 2424–10

Helmet mandatory use law in Texas, impacts on use, 1987-89 study, article, 4042–3.251

Helmet use and mandatory use laws impacts on accident casualties and costs, literature review, 1956-89, GAO rpt, 26113–537

Housing and households characteristics, unit and neighborhood quality, and journey to work by MSA location, for 11 MSAs, 1984 survey, supplement, 2485–8

Housing and households detailed characteristics, and unit and neighborhood quality, by location, 1985, biennial rpt supplement, 2485–13

Hwy Statistics, detailed data by State, 1990, annual rpt, 7554–1

Hwy Statistics, summary data by State, 1989-90, annual rpt, 7554–24

Manufacturing annual survey, 1989: finances and operations, by SIC 2- to 4-digit industry, series, 2506–15

Manufacturing finances and operations, by SIC 2- to 4-digit industry, forecast 1991, annual rpt, 2044–28

Natl transportation system planning, use, condition, accidents, and needs, by mode of transport, 1940s-90 and projected to 2020, 7308–202

OECD trade, total and for 4 major countries, and US trade by country, by commodity, 1970-89, world area rpt series, 9116–1

Price indexes (producer), by stage of processing and detailed commodity, monthly rpt, 6762–6

Price indexes (producer), by stage of processing and detailed commodity, monthly 1990, annual rpt, 6764–2

Recalls of motor vehicles and equipment with safety-related defects, by make, monthly listing, 7762–12

Recalls of motor vehicles and equipment with safety-related defects, by make, quarterly listing, 7762–2

Retail trade census, 1987: finances and employment, for establishments with and without payroll, by SIC 2- to 4-digit kind of business, State, and MSA, 2401–1

Safety programs, and accidents, casualties, and damage, by mode of transport, 1989, annual rpt, 7304–19

State and Metro Area Data Book, 1991 data compilation, 2328–54

Statistical Abstract of US, 1991 annual data compilation, 2324–1.21

Travel patterns, personal and household characteristics, and auto and public transport use, 1990 survey, series, 7556–6

Motors

see Engines and motors

Mountain-Plains States

see Western States

see under By Region in the "Index by Categories"

Movie industry

see Motion pictures

see Video recordings and equipment

Mozambique

Agricultural exports of high-value commodities, indexes and sales by commodity, world area, and country, 1960s-86, 1528–323

Agricultural trade of US, by detailed commodity and country, 1989, annual rpt, 1524–8

Agricultural trade of US, by detailed commodity and country, 1990, semiannual rpt, 1522–4

AID economic aid to developing countries, obligations and disbursements by country, quarterly rpt, 9912–4

Dairy imports, consumption, and market conditions, by sub-Saharan Africa country, 1961-88, 1528–321

Economic and military aid and loans from US and intl agencies, by program and country, FY46-90, annual rpt, 9914–5

Economic and social conditions of developing countries from 1960s, and Intl Dev Cooperation Agency and AID activities and funding, FY90-92, annual rpt, 9904–4

Economic conditions, income, production, prices, employment, and trade, 1991 periodic country rpt, 2046–4.63

Economic, population, and agricultural data, US and other aid sources, and AID activity, 1989 country rpt, 9916–12.32

Economic, population, and agricultural data, US and other aid sources, and AID activity, 1990 country rpt, 9916–12.44

Economic, social, political, and geographic summary data, by country, 1991, annual factbook, 9114–2

Exports and imports of US, by transport mode, country, and SITC 1- to 3-digit commodity, 1990, annual rpt, 2424–12

Exports of US, detailed Schedule B commodities with countries of destination, 1990, annual rpt, 2424–10

Food supply, needs, and aid for developing countries, status and alternative forecasts, 1991 world area rpt, 1526–8.1

Grain production and needs, and related economic outlook, by world area and selected country, forecast 1990/91-1991/92, 1528–313

Index by Subjects and Names

Human rights conditions in 170 countries, and US economic and military aid, 1990, annual rpt, 21384–3

Military aid of US, arms sales, and training programs costs and budget requests, by program, world region, and country, FY90-92, annual rpt, 7144–13

UN voting record and share of votes in agreement with US, by issue, country, and world area, 1990, annual rpt, 7004–18

see also under By Foreign Country in the "Index by Categories"

MSA

see Metropolitan Statistical Areas

see under By SMSA or MSA in the "Index by Categories"

Much, David H.

"Prevalence of Chlamydia trachomatis Infection in Pregnant Patients", 4042–3.240

Mueller, E. A., Inc.

"Indoor Air Quality Environmental Information Handbook: Combustion Sources, 1989 Update", 3326–1.2

Muench, R. D.

"Northeast Gulf of Alaska Program", 2176–1.36

Mullin, John J.

"Speculative Effects of Anticipated Trade Policy Under Dual Exchange Rates", 9385–8.104

Mullis, Ina V.

"State of Mathematics Achievement: NAEP's 1990 Assessment of the Nation and the Trial Assessment of the States. National Assessment of Educational Progress, 1990", 4896–8.1

Multilateral development banks

see African Development Bank

see Asian Development Bank

see Inter-American Development Bank

see International Bank for Reconstruction and Development

Multinational corporations

Bank deposit insurance system reform issues, with background industry financial data, 1970s-90, GAO rpt, 26119–320

Banks (insured commercial and savings) deposits by instn, State, MSA, and county, as of June 1990, annual regional rpt series, 9295–3

Banks (insured commercial and savings) finances, for foreign and domestic offices, by asset size, 1989, annual rpt, 9294–4.2

Banks (natl) charters, mergers, liquidations, enforcement cases, and financial performance, with data by instn and State, quarterly rpt, 8402–3

Banks (US) foreign branches assets and liabilities, by world region and country, quarterly rpt, 9365–3.7

Banks (US) foreign lending at all US and foreign offices, by country group and country, quarterly rpt, 13002–1

Banks balance sheets, by Fed Reserve District, for major banks in NYC, and for US branches and agencies of foreign banks, weekly rpt, 9365–1.3

Banks owned by foreigners, US subsidiaries, assets, and regulatory issues, with data by State and firm, 1989-90, hearing, 21248–155

Capital expenditures of multinatl US firms foreign affiliates, by major industry group, world area, and country, 1986-91, semiannual article, 2702–1.207; 2702–1.222

Index by Subjects and Names

Currency (foreign) positions of US firms and foreign branches or affiliates, *Treasury Bulletin*, quarterly rpt, 8002–4.12

Energy producers finances and operations, by energy type for US firms domestic and foreign operations, 1989, annual rpt, 3164–44

Energy resources of US, foreign direct investment by energy type and firm, and US affiliates operations, as of 1989, annual rpt, 3164–80

Finances and operations of foreign firms US affiliates, by industry div, country of parent firm, and State, 1988-89, annual article, 2702–1.214; 2702–1.218

Finances and operations of foreign firms US affiliates, by industry, world area of parent firm, and State, 1988-89, annual rpt, 2704–4

Finances and operations of foreign firms US affiliates, trends and impact on US economy, 1991 annual rpt, 2004–9

Finances and operations of multinatl US firms and foreign affiliates, by industry and world area of parent firm, 1989 benchmark survey, preliminary annual rpt, 2704–5

Finances and operations of multinatl US firms and foreign affiliates, by industry of parent firm and affiliate, world area, and selected country, 1989, annual article, 2702–1.225

Foreign direct investment in US, by industry group and world area, 1987-90, annual article, 2702–1.219

Foreign direct investment in US, by industry group of US affiliate and country of parent firm, 1980-86, 2708–41

Foreign direct investment in US, major transactions by type, industry, country, and US location, 1989, annual rpt, 2044–20

Foreign direct investment in US, new and established affiliates assets, and acquisitions, by industry div, 1980s, technical paper, 9366–7.255

Foreign direct investment of US, by industry group and world area, 1987-90, annual article, 2702–1.220

Great Lakes area economic conditions and outlook, for US and Canada, 1970s-90, 9375–15

Imports of US given duty-free treatment for value of US material sent abroad, by commodity and country, 1989, annual rpt, 9884–14

Investments rate of return under alternative valuation methods, for US business and for direct foreign investment in and of US, 1982-90, article, 2702–1.217

Japan manufacturing firms US affiliates, employment, and wages, by selected industry and State, 1980s, 2048–151

Service industries exports and imports of US, direct and among multinatl firms affiliates, by industry and world area, 1986-90, article, 2702–1.223

Ships under foreign flag owned by US firms and foreign affiliates, by type, owner, and country of registry and construction, as of Jan 1991, semiannual rpt, 7702–3

Statistical Abstract of US, 1991 annual data compilation, 2324–1.16; 2324–1.17

Tax (income) returns for foreign corporate activity in US, assets, and income

statement items, by industry div and selected country, 1986-87, article, 8302–2.205

Tax (income) returns of corporations with foreign tax credit, income, and tax items, by country and world region of credit, 1986, biennial article, 8302–2.207

Tax (income) returns of corporations with foreign tax credit, income and tax items by industry group, 1986, biennial article, 8302–2.203

Tax (income) returns of multinatl US firms foreign affiliates, income statement items, by asset size, industry, and country, 1986, biennial article, 8302–2.212

Tax (income) returns of US corporations under foreign control, assets and income statement items by industry div and country, 1988, article, 8302–2.219

Telecommunications industry intl competitiveness, with financial and operating data by product or service, firm, and country, 1990 rpt, 2008–30

UK firms acquisition of US firms, financing, sources, and rates of return, with data by firm, 1980s, technical paper, 9385–8.82

Muncie, Ind.

see also under By SMSA or MSA in the "Index by Categories"

Municipal bonds

Finances of govts, by level of govt, State, and for large cities and counties, annual rpt series, 2466–2

Finances of govts, tax systems and revenue, and fiscal structure, by level of govt and State, 1991 and historical trends, annual rpt, 10044–1

Futures and options trading volume, by commodity and exchange, FY90, annual rpt, 11924–2

Futures trading in selected commodities and financial instruments and indexes, NYC, Chicago, and other markets activity, semimonthly rpt, 11922–5

Hwy receipts by source, and spending by function, by level of govt and State, 1990, annual rpt, 7554–1.3

Interest rates for commercial paper, govt securities, other financial instruments, and home mortgages, monthly rpt, 9365–2.14

State and local govt employees pension system cash and security holdings and finances, quarterly rpt, 2462–2

Wastewater treatment facilities funding, by source, 1960s-88, 9188–114

Yields of municipal and Treasury bonds, relation to tax policies, 1970-89, article, 9373–1.215

Yields on corporate, Treasury, and municipal long-term bonds, *Treasury Bulletin*, quarterly rpt, 8002–4.8

Yields on govt and private issues, weekly rpt, 9391–4

Yields, *Survey of Current Business*, cyclical indicators, monthly rpt, 2702–1.1

Municipal employees

see State and local employees

Municipal government

see Census of Governments

see Local government

Municipal taxation

see State and local taxes

Musculoskeletal diseases

Municipal transportation

see Urban transportation

Munley, Vincent

"Structure of State Aid to Elementary and Secondary Education", 10048–78

Munnell, Alicia H.

"Financing Capital Expenditures in Massachusetts", 9373–1.207; 9373–4.27

"Massachusetts in the 1990s: The Role of State Government. Overview", 9373–1.202; 9373–4.27

Muraskin, Lana D.

"Education in Appalachia: Accomplishments and Prospects in a National Context", 9088–36

Murder

see Homicide

Murriner, Edward C.

"West Virginia Timber Products Output, 1987", 1206–15.9

Murtaugh, Christopher M.

"Lifetime Use of Nursing Home Care", 4186–7.9

Musculoskeletal diseases

Cancer cases, deaths, and survival rates, by sex, race, age, and body site, 1973-88, annual rpt, 4474–35

Cancer death rates of minorities, by body site, age, sex, and substate area, 1950s-80, atlas, 4478–78

Children (handicapped) enrollment by age, and special education programs staff, funding, and needs, by type of handicap and State, 1989/90, annual rpt, 4944–4

Deaths and rates, by detailed cause and demographic characteristics, 1988 and trends from 1900, US Vital Statistics annual rpt, 4144–2

Dental Research Natl Inst research and training grants, by recipient, FY89, annual listing, 4474–19

Disabled persons and related activity limitation days and health services use, by health status, disability type, and other characteristics, 1984-88, 4146–8.202

Fluoride exposure by source, and health risks and benefits, with research results, 1930s-89, 4048–36

Head Start handicapped enrollment, by handicap, State, and for Indian and migrant programs, 1987/88, annual rpt, 4604–1

Health condition and health care resources, use, and spending, 1950s-89, annual data compilation, 4144–11

HHS financial aid, by program, recipient, State, and city, FY90, annual regional listings, 4004–3

Hip fractures and repair procedures, actual and expected death rates for Medicare hospital providers, by instn, 1989, annual regional rpt series, 4654–14

Hip fractures physicians consultations requested by attending physician, and Medicare reimbursement issues, 1986, 4658–47

Hospital discharges and length of stay, by diagnosis, patient and instn characteristics, procedure performed, and payment source, 1988, annual rpt, 4147–13.107

Hospital discharges and length of stay by region and diagnosis, and procedures performed, by age and sex, 1989, annual rpt, 4146–8.198

Musculoskeletal diseases

Hospital discharges by detailed diagnostic and procedure category, primary diagnosis, and length of stay, by age, sex, and region, 1988, annual rpt, 4147–13.105; 4147–13.108

Indian and Alaska Native disease and disorder cases, deaths, and health services use, by tribe, reservation, and Indian Health Service area, late 1950s-86, 4088–2

Indian Health Service, tribal, and contract facilities hospitalization, by diagnosis, age, sex, and service area, FY89, annual rpt, 4084–5

Indians and Alaska Natives chronic disease prevalence, for 8 conditions by age and sex, 1987, 4186–8.20

Injuries, by type, circumstances, and victim characteristics, and related activity limitations, 1985-87, 4147–10.176

Mines (underground coal) back injuries, by circumstances, victim characteristics, and treatment, mid 1980s, 5608–166

Neurological Disorders and Stroke Natl Inst activities, and disorder cases, FY90, annual rpt, 4474–25

Vocational rehabilitation cases of State agencies by disposition and applicant characteristics, and closures by reason, FY84-88, annual rpt, 4944–6

see also under By Disease in the "Index by Categories"

Musell, R. Mark

"Changing the Classification of Federal White-Collar Jobs: Potential Management and Budgetary Impacts", 26306–3.119

Museums

Coastal areas recreation facilities of Fed Govt and States, visitor and site characteristics, 1987-90 survey, regional rpt series, 2176–9

County Business Patterns, 1988: employment, establishments, and payroll, by SIC 2- to 4-digit industry and county, annual State rpt series, 2326–6

County Business Patterns, 1989: employment, establishments, and payroll, by SIC 2- to 4-digit industry and county, annual State rpt series, 2326–8

DC metro area land acquisition and dev projects of Fed Govt, characteristics and funding by agency and project, FY91-95, annual rpt, 15454–1

Employment, earnings, and hours, by SIC 1- to 4-digit industry, monthly and annual averages, selected years 1909-90, annual rpt, 6744–4

Endangered animals and plants US trade and permits, by species, purpose, disposition, and country, 1989, annual rpt, 5504–19

Fed Govt spending in States, by type, program, agency, and State, FY90, annual rpt, 2464–2

Inst of Museum Services activities and finances, and grants by recipient, FY90, annual rpt, 9564–7

Mail volume to and from households, use, and views, by class, source, content, and household characteristics, 1987-88, annual rpt, 9864–10

Natl Archives and Records Admin activities, finances, holdings, and staff, FY90, annual rpt, 9514–2

Natl Endowment for Arts activities and grants, FY90, annual rpt, 9564–3

Natl Endowment for Humanities activities and grants, FY90, annual rpt, 9564–2

Occupational injury and illness rates, by SIC 2- to 4-digit industry, 1988-89, annual rpt, 6844–7

Occupational injury and illness rates, by SIC 2- to 4-digit industry, 1989, annual rpt, 6844–1

Service industries census, 1987: establishments, receipts by source, payroll, and employment, by SIC 2- to 4-digit kind of business, State, and MSA, 2393–4

Smoking bans in public places, local ordinances provisions, as of 1989, 4478–196

see also Botanical gardens

see also Zoological parks

Mushrooms

see Vegetables and vegetable products

Music

Copyrights Register activities, registrations by material type, and fees, FY90 and trends from 1790, annual rpt, 26404–2

Education (postsecondary) course completions, by detailed program, sex, race, and instn type, for 1972 high school class, as of 1984, 4888–4

Employment, earnings, and hours, by SIC 1- to 4-digit industry, monthly and annual averages, selected years 1909-90, annual rpt, 6744–4

Exports and imports of sheet music, by country, 1990, annual rpt, 2424–13

Exports and imports of US, by selected country, country group, and commodity group, 1990, annual rpt, 2044–37

Exports of sheet music, by country of destination, 1990, annual rpt, 2424–10

Industry finances and operations, by SIC 2- to 4-digit industry, forecast 1991, annual rpt, 2044–28

Library of Congress activities, acquisitions, services, and financial statements, FY90, annual rpt, 26404–1

Natl Endowment for Arts activities and grants, FY90, annual rpt, 9564–3

Puerto Rico economic censuses, 1987: wholesale and retail trade and service industry finances and operations, by SIC 2- to 4-digit industry and municipio, 2591–1

Retail trade census, 1987: finances and employment, for establishments with and without payroll, by SIC 2- to 4-digit kind of business, State, and MSA, 2401–1

Service industries census, 1987: establishments, receipts by source, payroll, and employment, by SIC 2- to 4-digit kind of business, State, and MSA, 2393–4

Musical instruments

County Business Patterns, 1988: employment, establishments, and payroll, by SIC 2- to 4-digit industry and county, annual State rpt series, 2326–6

County Business Patterns, 1989: employment, establishments, and payroll, by SIC 2- to 4-digit industry and county, annual State rpt series, 2326–8

Employment, earnings, and hours, by SIC 1- to 4-digit industry, monthly and annual averages, selected years 1909-90, annual rpt, 6744–4

Index by Subjects and Names

Exports and imports of US, by country and detailed commodity, monthly rpt, 2422–12

Exports and imports of US, by Harmonized System 6-digit commodity and country, 1990, annual rpt, 2424–13

Exports of US, detailed Schedule B commodities with countries of destination, 1990, annual rpt, 2424–10

Injuries from use of consumer products, by severity, victim age, and detailed product, 1990, annual rpt, 9164–6

Manufacturing annual survey, 1989: finances and operations, by SIC 2- to 4-digit industry, series, 2506–15

Manufacturing census, 1987: finances and operations, by SIC 2- to 4-digit industry, State, and MSA, with trends from 1849, 2497–1

Manufacturing census, 1987: finances and operations, by type of organization and SIC 2- to 4-digit industry, subject rpt, 2497–5

Manufacturing finances and operations, by SIC 2- to 4-digit industry, forecast 1991, annual rpt, 2044–28

Occupational injury and illness rates, by SIC 2- to 4-digit industry, 1988-89, annual rpt, 6844–7

Occupational injury and illness rates, by SIC 2- to 4-digit industry, 1989, annual rpt, 6844–1

OECD trade, total and for 4 major countries, and US trade by country, by commodity, 1970-89, world area rpt series, 9116–1

Price indexes (producer), by stage of processing and detailed commodity, monthly rpt, 6762–6

Price indexes (producer), by stage of processing and detailed commodity, monthly 1990, annual rpt, 6764–2

Puerto Rico economic censuses, 1987: wholesale and retail trade and service industry finances and operations, by SIC 2- to 4-digit industry and municipio, 2591–1

Retail trade census, 1987: finances and employment, for establishments with and without payroll, by SIC 2- to 4-digit kind of business, State, and MSA, 2401–1

Muskegon, Mich.

see also under By SMSA or MSA in the "Index by Categories"

Musselman, Bryan L.

"Electronic Filing: Who's Participating and Who Isn't", 8304–8.1

Mutchler, Jan E.

"Household and Nonhousehold Living Arrangements in Later Life: A Longitudinal Analysis of a Social Process", 2626–10.134

"Racial Differences in Health and Health Care Service Utilization: The Effect of Socioeconomic Status", 2626–10.127

Mutual funds

Asset allocation funds performance relative to stock index and Treasury bill rates, model description and alternative results, 1980s-90, technical paper, 9385–8.87

Assets and debts of private sector, balance sheets by segment, 1945-90, semiannual rpt, 9365–4.1

Credit unions federally insured, finances by instn characteristics and State, as of June 1991, semiannual rpt, 9532–6

Credit unions federally insured, finances, 1989-90, annual rpt, 9534–1

Finances and operations, by SIC 2- to 4-digit industry, forecast 1991, annual rpt, 2044–28

Financial and monetary conditions, selected US summary data, weekly rpt, 9391–4

Financial performance of mutual funds, impacts of selected mgmt decisions, model results, late 1970s-84, technical paper, 9385–8.80

Flow-of-funds accounts, savings, investments, and credit statements, quarterly rpt, 9365–3.3

Foreign and US economic conditions, for major industrial countries, biweekly rpt, 9112–1

Households assets, by type of holding and selected characteristics, 1988, Current Population Rpt, 2546–20.16

Mail volume to and from households, use, and views, by class, source, content, and household characteristics, 1987-88, annual rpt, 9864–10

Statistical Abstract of US, 1991 annual data compilation, 2324–1.16

Myanmar

UN voting record and share of votes in agreement with US, by issue, country, and world area, 1990, annual rpt, 7004–18

see also Burma

Mycoses

see Infective and parasitic diseases

Myers, Forest

"Three Decades of Banking", 9381–14.1

Myers, Jennifer G.

"Job Task—Competency Linkages for FAA First-Level Supervisors", 7506–10.84

"Two Studies on Participation in Decision-Making and Equity Among FAA Personnel", 7506–10.89

Myers, Patricia M.

"Minority Households: A Comparison of Selected Characteristics and Expenditures Contributing to Future Economic Well-Being", 1702–1.206

Myers, Peter C.

"Outlook for Farm Credit", 1004–16.1

Myers, Robert C.

"Biannual Water-Resources Review, White Sands Missile Range, New Mexico, 1986-87", 5666–28.7

Nacht, Michael

"Assessment of the Impact of AID's Participant Training Programs in Nepal", 9916–3.62

Nakagawara, Van B.

"Effect of Simulated Altitude on the Visual Fields of Glaucoma Patients and the Elderly", 7506–10.80

"Prevalence of Aphakia in the Civil Airman Population", 7506–10.93

Nakamura, Leonard I.

"Delegated Monitoring with Diseconomies of Scale", 9387–8.248

"Housing Appraisals and Redlining", 9387–8.242

"Optimal Acceptance Policies for Journals", 9387–8.254

"Reforming Deposit Insurance When Banks Conduct Loan Workouts and Runs Are Possible", 9387–8.239

"Worker Debt with Bankruptcy", 9387–8.241

Namibia

Agricultural trade of US, by detailed commodity and country, 1989, annual rpt, 1524–8

Agricultural trade of US, by detailed commodity and country, 1990, semiannual rpt, 1522–4

Background Notes, summary social, political, and economic data, 1991 rpt, 7006–2.31

Economic and military aid and loans from US and intl agencies, by program and country, FY46-90, annual rpt, 9914–5

Economic and social conditions of developing countries from 1960s, and Intl Dev Cooperation Agency and AID activities and funding, FY90-92, annual rpt, 9904–4

Economic, social, political, and geographic summary data, by country, 1991, annual factbook, 9114–2

Exports and imports of US, by transport mode, country, and SITC 1- to 3-digit commodity, 1990, annual rpt, 2424–12

Human rights conditions in 170 countries, and US economic and military aid, 1990, annual rpt, 21384–3

Military aid of US, arms sales, and training programs costs and budget requests, by program, world region, and country, FY90-92, annual rpt, 7144–13

UN voting record and share of votes in agreement with US, by issue, country, and world area, 1990, annual rpt, 7004–18

Napa, Calif.

see also under By SMSA or MSA in the "Index by Categories"

Naples, Fla.

see also under By SMSA or MSA in the "Index by Categories"

Narcotics

see Drug abuse and treatment

see Drug and narcotics offenses

see Drugs

NASA

see National Aeronautics and Space Administration

Nashua, N.H.

see also under By SMSA or MSA in the "Index by Categories"

Nashville, Tenn.

Transportation natl system planning, use, condition, accidents, and needs, by mode of transport, 1940s-90 and projected to 2020, 7308–202

see also under By City and By SMSA or MSA in the "Index by Categories"

Nassau County, N.Y.

see also under By SMSA or MSA in the "Index by Categories"

Nathan, Robert R., Associates, Inc.

"Development Impact of U.S. Program Food Assistance: Evidence from the AID Evaluation Literature", 9918–20

Nathenson, Manuel

"Chemistry of Lake Tahoe, California-Nevada, and Nearby Springs", 5666–27.6

National Academy of Public Administration

"Study of the Cost and Financing of a Commercially Developed Space Facility (CDSF)", 21708–129

National Aeronautics and Space Administration

National accounts

see National income and product accounts

National Adult Literacy Survey

Data collection activities and programs of NCES, 1991, annual listing, 4824–7

National Advisory Council on Child Nutrition

USDA child nutrition programs evaluation, biennial narrative rpt, discontinued, 14854–1

National Advisory Council on Educational Research and Improvement

Office of Educational Research and Improvement activities, FY90, annual narrative rpt, 4814–1

National Advisory Council on Indian Education

Activities of NACIE, with Indian education funding of Fed Govt, and enrollment, degrees, and program grants and fellowships by State, late 1960s-FY89, annual rpt, 14874–1

National Advisory Council on International Monetary and Financial Policies

Intl financial instns funds by source and disbursements by purpose, by country, with US policy review, FY89, annual rpt, 15344–1

National Aeronautics and Space Administration

Activities and budgets for aeronautics and space by Federal agency, and foreign programs, 1957-FY90, annual rpt, 9504–9

Activities and finances of NASA, and data on US and USSR space launches, 1957-90, annual rpt, 9504–6

Activities and funding of NASA, 1990, annual compilation of papers, 21704–1

Activities, missions, launchings, payloads, and flight duration, for foreign and US space programs, 1957-90, annual rpt, 21704–4

Advisory Committee on Future of US Space Program recommendations, 1990 rpt, 9508–38

Aerial survey R&D rpts, and sources of natural resource and environmental data, quarterly listing, 9502–7

Budget of US, authoritative financial statements with appropriations, outlays, and receipts, by category and agency, FY90, annual rpt, 8104–2.1

Budget of US, obligations and authority by function, agency, and program, with summaries, analyses, and historical tables, FY92, annual rpt, 104–2

Data archival storage of NASA space science missions, holdings, and missions not archived, 1950s-91, 26125–43

Data sources and availability for space sciences and related topics, 1991 annual listing, 9504–10

Data sources for space sciences and related topics, use by format and user type, FY90, annual rpt, 9504–11

Education funding by Federal agency, program, and recipient type, and instn spending, FY80-90, annual rpt, 4824–8

Employee characteristics and personnel actions, FY90, annual rpt, 9504–1

Expenditures of Fed Govt in States, by type, program, agency, and State, FY90, annual rpt, 2464–2

Fraud and abuse in NASA programs, audits and investigations, 2nd half FY91, semiannual rpt, 9502–9

National Aeronautics and Space Administration

Launch schedules and technical descriptions of NASA projects, press release series, 9506–2

Launchings of satellites and other space objects since 1957, quarterly listing, 9502–2

Manufacturing census, 1987: employment and shipments under Fed Govt contracts, by SIC 4-digit industry, 2497–7

Ozone in stratosphere, levels, depletion rates and climate impacts, and properties of chlorofluorocarbons and substitutes, 1990 rpt, 9508–37

Private sector involvement in space programs, commercial dev centers funding sources and flight requests, 1986-90, GAO rpt, 26123–353

Procurement contract awards of NASA, by type, contractor, State, and country, FY91 with trends from 1961, semiannual rpt, 9502–6

R&D and related funding of Fed Govt to higher education and nonprofit instns, by field, instn, agency, and State, FY89, annual rpt, 9627–17

R&D funding by Fed Govt, by field, performer type, agency, and State, FY89-91, annual rpt, 9627–20

R&D funding by NASA to higher education instns, by field, instn, and State, FY90, annual listing, 9504–7

Science and engineering staff retirement rates for NASA, projected 1991-95, GAO rpt, 26123–348

Space station commercial dev and operating costs and income under alternative financing options, projected 1989-2000, 21708–129

National Agricultural Statistics Service

Budget of US, obligations and authority by function, agency, and program, with summaries, analyses, and historical tables, FY92, annual rpt, 104–2

Minority group employment in NASS, promotion, and discrimination complaints, 1988-90, GAO rpt, 26119–326

see also Agricultural Statistics Board

National Ambulatory Medical Care Survey

Physicians visits, by patient and practice characteristics, diagnosis, and services provided, 1989, 4146–8.206

Teenagers physicians office visits, by reason and characteristics of physicians, patients, and visit, 1985, 4146–8.199

National Archives and Records Administration

Activities, finances, holdings, and staff of NARA, FY90, annual rpt, 9514–2

Audiovisual activities and spending of Fed Govt, by whether performed in-house and agency, FY90, annual rpt, 9514–1

Budget of US, authoritative financial statements with appropriations, outlays, and receipts, by category and agency, FY90, annual rpt, 8104–2.1

Budget of US, obligations and authority by function, agency, and program, with summaries, analyses, and historical tables, FY92, annual rpt, 104–2

Education funding by Federal agency, program, and recipient type, and instn spending, FY80-90, annual rpt, 4824–8

R&D funding by Fed Govt, by field, performer type, agency, and State, FY89-91, annual rpt, 9627–20

Index by Subjects and Names

National Assessment of Educational Progress

Data collection activities and programs of NCES, 1991, annual listing, 4824–7

Educational performance by subject and selected student characteristics, standard test results and credits, 1991 edition, annual rpt, 4824–2.12

Elementary and secondary students educational performance, and factors affecting proficiency, by selected characteristics, 1988 natl assessments, subject rpt series, 4896–7

Elementary and secondary students educational performance, and factors affecting proficiency, by selected characteristics, 1990 natl assessments, subject rpt series, 4896–8

Elementary and secondary students educational performance in math, science, reading, and writing, 1970s-90, 4898–32

National Association of Blue Shield Plans *see* Blue Cross-Blue Shield

National Association of State Alcohol and Drug Abuse Directors, Inc.

"State Resources and Services Related to Alcohol and Other Drug Abuse Problems, FY89: An Analysis of State Alcohol and Drug Abuse Profile Data", 4488–15

National Black Child Development Institute

"Parental Drug Abuse and African American Children in Foster Care: Issues and Study Findings", 4008–114

National Bureau of Standards *see* National Institute of Standards and Technology

National Cancer Institute

Activities and funding of NIH, by inst, FY89-90, biennial rpt, 4434–16

Activities of NCI epidemiology and biometry programs, FY90, annual rpt, 4474–29

Activities of NCI, grants by recipient, and cancer deaths and cases, FY90 and trends, annual rpt, 4474–13

Cases of cancer, deaths, and survival rates, by age, sex, race, and body site, 1973-88, annual rpt, 4474–35

Minority group cancer death rates, by body site, age, sex, and substate area, 1950s-80, atlas, 4478–78

Research on cancer epidemiology and biochemistry, semimonthly journal, 4472–1

Smoking and smokeless tobacco use, attitudes, and smoking intervention research spending and results, with bibl, 1960s-90, 4478–195

Smoking bans in public places, local ordinances provisions, as of 1989, 4478–196

National Capital Planning Commission

Budget of US, authoritative financial statements with appropriations, outlays, and receipts, by category and agency, FY90, annual rpt, 8104–2.1

Budget of US, obligations and authority by function, agency, and program, with summaries, analyses, and historical tables, FY92, annual rpt, 104–2

Land acquisition and dev projects of Fed Govt in DC metro area, characteristics and funding by agency and project, FY91-95, annual rpt, 15454–1

National Center for Appropriate Technology

"State Catalog of FY90 Low Income Home Energy Assistance Program Characteristics", 4694–9

National Center for Education Statistics *see* Office of Educational Research and Improvement

National Center for Health Services Research and Health Care Technology Assessment *see* Agency for Health Care Policy and Research

National Center for Health Statistics

AIDS virus infection and risk factor prevalence, natl survey methodology and pretest results, 1989, 4148–30

Deaths and rates, by detailed cause and demographic characteristics, 1988 and trends from 1900, US Vital Statistics annual rpt, 4144–2

Health care services use and costs, methodology and findings of natl survey and Medicare and Medicaid records, 1980, series, 4146–12

Health condition and health care resources, use, and spending, 1950s-89, annual data compilation, 4144–11

Health condition and quality of life measurement, rpts and other info sources, quarterly listing, 4122–1

Marriages, divorces, and rates, by characteristics of spouses, State, and county, 1987 and trends from 1920, US Vital Statistics annual rpt, 4144–4

Publications of NCHS, quarterly listing, 4122–2

Publications of NCHS, 1980-89, annual listing, 4124–1

Vital and Health Statistics Natl Committee activities, FY90, annual narrative rpt, 4164–1

Vital and Health Statistics series: advance data rpts, 4146–8

Vital and Health Statistics series: conf rpts, 4147–4

Vital and Health Statistics series: death rates for selected causes and population groups, 4147–20

Vital and Health Statistics series: foreign and US comparative data, 4147–5

Vital and Health Statistics series: health care facilities use and labor force, 4147–13

Vital and Health Statistics series: health condition, medical costs, and use of facilities and services, 4147–10

Vital and Health Statistics series: methodology, survey design, and data evaluation, 4147–2

Vital and Health Statistics series: natality, marriage, and divorce trends, 4147–21

Vital and Health Statistics series: program and data collection procedures, 4147–1

Vital and Health Statistics series: reprints of advance data rpts, 4147–16

Vital and Health Statistics series: reprints of monthly rpt supplements, 4147–24

Vital statistics, preliminary 1989-90 and trends from 1950, annual rpt, 4144–7

Vital statistics provisional data, monthly rpt, 4142–1

Vital statistics provisional data, supplements to monthly rpts, series, 4146–5

National Center for Human Genome Research

Activities and funding of NIH, by inst, FY89-90, biennial rpt, 4434–16

Index by Subjects and Names

National forests

National Center for Nursing Research
Activities and funding of NIH, by inst, FY89-90, biennial rpt, 4434–16

National Center for Research Resources, NIH
Activities and funding of NCRR, by program, FY90, annual rpt, 4434–12
Activities and funding of NIH, by inst, FY89-90, biennial rpt, 4434–16

National Commission for Employment Policy
Activities and rpts of NCEP, 1990 annual rpt, 15494–1
Unemployed displaced workers and other hard-to-serve groups, factors contributing to unemployment, and training programs operations, series, 15496–1

National Commission on Children
Health, education, and welfare condition of children and families, findings and recommendations, 1991 rpt, 15528–1

National Commission on Libraries and Information Science
Activities of NCLIS, FY90, annual rpt, 15634–1
Budget of US, authoritative financial statements with appropriations, outlays, and receipts, by category and agency, FY90, annual rpt, 8104–2.1
Budget of US, obligations and authority by function, agency, and program, with summaries, analyses, and historical tables, FY92, annual rpt, 104–2
Expenditures for education by Federal agency, program, and recipient type, and instn spending, FY80-90, annual rpt, 4824–8

National commissions
see Federal boards, committees, and commissions
see Federal independent agencies

National Committee on Vital and Health Statistics
Vital and Health Statistics series: conf rpts, 4147–4

National Credit Union Administration
Assets, members, and location of credit unions, 1991 annual listing, 9534–6
Budget of US, authoritative financial statements with appropriations, outlays, and receipts, by category and agency, FY90, annual rpt, 8104–2.1
Budget of US, obligations and authority by function, agency, and program, with summaries, analyses, and historical tables, FY92, annual rpt, 104–2
Economic outlook, with credit union financial performance and employment over business cycles, 1988-92, release, 9538–8
Finances of federally insured credit unions, by instn characteristics and State, as of June 1991, semiannual rpt, 9532–6
Finances, operations, and regulation of credit unions, series, 9536–1
Financial performance of federally-insured credit unions, by charter type and region, 1st half 1991, semiannual rpt, 9532–7
Financial statements of Central Liquidity Facility, FY90, annual rpt, 9534–5
Financial statements of NCUA and credit unions, 1989-90, annual rpt, 9534–1
Foreign and US credit unions, assets, and members, for 13 countries and 5 regional confederations, 1986 and 1989, release, 9538–9

Insurance fund of NCUA, losses and financial statements, with federally insured credit union finances, mergers, and closings, FY90, annual rpt, 9534–7

National Crime Survey
Victimization rates, by victim and offender characteristics, circumstances, and offense, survey rpt series, 6066–3

National debt
see Foreign debts
see Government assets and liabilities
see Public debt

National defense
Eastern Europe economic and political conditions, and impacts of geographic factors, by country, 1990 conf, 9118–18
Foreign countries economic, social, political, and geographic summary data, by country, 1991, annual factbook, 9114–2
Soviet Union military weapons systems, presence, and force strengths, and compared to US, 1991 annual rpt, 3504–20
Space programs activities, missions, launchings, payloads, and flight duration, for foreign and US programs, 1957-90, annual rpt, 21704–4
see also Armed services reserves
see also Arms control and disarmament
see also Arms trade
see also Chemical and biological warfare agents
see also Civil defense
see also Defense agencies
see also Defense budgets and appropriations
see also Defense contracts and procurement
see also Defense expenditures
see also Defense industries
see also Defense research
see also Department of Defense
see also Espionage
see also Internal security
see also Logistics
see also Military aircraft
see also Military airlift
see also Military assistance
see also Military aviation
see also Military awards, decorations, and medals
see also Military bases, posts, and reservations
see also Military benefits and pensions
see also Military education
see also Military health facilities and services
see also Military housing
see also Military intelligence
see also Military intervention
see also Military invasion and occupation
see also Military law
see also Military pay
see also Military personnel
see also Military post exchanges and commissaries
see also Military prisons
see also Military science
see also Military strategy
see also Military supplies and property
see also Military training
see also Military vehicles
see also Military weapons
see also National Guard
see also Naval vessels
see also Nuclear weapons

see also Service academies
see also Strategic Defense Initiative
see also Strategic materials
see also War

National Drug and Alcoholism Treatment Utilization Survey
Treatment facilities for drug and alcohol abuse, services, use, funding, staff, and client characteristics, 1989, biennial rpt, 4494–10

National Education Goals Panel
Natl Education Goals progress indicators, by State, 1991, annual rpt, 15914–1

National Education Longitudinal Survey
Eighth grade class of 1988: educational performance and conditions, characteristics, attitudes, activities, and plans, natl longitudinal survey, series, 4826–9

National Endowment for the Arts
see National Foundation on the Arts and the Humanities

National Endowment for the Humanities
see National Foundation on the Arts and the Humanities

National Environmental Policy Act
Environmental Quality, status of problems, protection programs, research, and intl issues, 1991 annual rpt, 484–1

National Environmental Satellite, Data, and Information Service
Foreign and US air pressure, temperature, and precipitation, by location, monthly 1971-80, decennial rpt series, 2156–4
Heating and cooling degree days weighted by population, by census div and State, with area-weighted temperature and precipitation, monthly rpt, 2152–13
Mariners Weather Log, quarterly journal, 2152–8
Storms and unusual weather phenomena characteristics, casualties, and property damage, by State, monthly listing, 2152–3
Weather data for stations in continental US and outlying areas, 1990 and historic trends, annual rpt, 2154–8
Weather data for surface and upper air, averages by foreign and US station, monthly rpt, 2152–4

National Eye Institute
Activities and funding of NIH, by inst, FY89-90, biennial rpt, 4434–16

National forests
Acreage and costs of real property owned by Fed Govt, worldwide summary by location, agency, and use, 1989, annual rpt, 9454–5
Acreage, grants, use, revenues, and allocations, for public lands by State, FY90 and trends, annual rpt, 5724–1
Acreage of land under Forest Service mgmt, by forest and location, 1990, annual rpt, 1204–2
Alabama timber acreage and value, by species, forest type, ownership, and county, 1990, series, 1206–30
Alaska timber production, trade, and Pacific basin market demand, 1960s-2010, 1208–365
Arizona timber resources by species, forest and tree characteristics, ownership, and county, 1984-85, 1208–374
Birds (northern spotted owl) population and reproduction rate on lands open and closed to logging, estimation methodology, 1987, 1208–342

National forests

Expenditures of Fed Govt in States, by type, program, agency, and State, FY90, annual rpt, 2464–2

Fires on Forest Service land and acres burned, by cause, forest, and State, 1989, annual rpt, 1204–6

Fish and wildlife activities funding, by source, FY88-90, GAO rpt, 26113–529

Forest Service activities and finances, by region and State, FY90, annual rpt, 1204–1

Grazing of livestock on natl forest lands, by region and State, 1990, annual rpt, 1204–5

Horse and burro wild herd areas in western States, population, adoption, and mgmt costs, as of FY89, biennial rpt, 5724–8

Indiana timber resources and removals, by species, forest characteristics, ownership, and county, 1985-86, 1208–368

Insect and disease incidence and damage in forests, and control activities, State rpt series, 1206–49

Insect and disease incidence and damage in forests, annual regional rpt series, 1206–11

Land Mgmt Bur activities and funding by State, FY89, annual rpt, 5724–13

Lumber production, prices by region and State, trade by country, and use, by species and product, 1960-88, annual rpt, 1204–29

Mgmt of public lands and resources dev, environmental, economic, and social impacts of alternative Forest Service programs, projected to 2040, 1208–24

Minerals resources and availability on public lands, State rpt series, 5606–7

North Carolina timber acreage, resources, and removals, by species, ownership class, and county, 1989/90, series, 1206–4

Northeastern US forest wildlife habitat characteristics, by location, State rpt series, 1206–44

Northeastern US timber resources and removals, by species, ownership, and county, State rpt series, 1206–12

Northwestern US and British Columbia forest industry production, prices, trade, and employment, quarterly rpt, 1202–3

Oklahoma timber resources, growth, and removals, by species, forest type, ownership, and county, 1986, regional rpt series, 1206–39

Oregon (western) timber resources, acreage by land use and ownership, 1961-86, 1208–353

Pacific Northwest acreage, staff, finances, and mgmt activities of Forest Service, with data by forest, 1970s-89, annual rpt, 1204–37

Planting and dev of forests, by State, FY90, annual rpt, 1204–7

Recreation programs of Forest Service, funding and cost sharing pledges, 1980s-91, GAO rpt, 26113–518

Recreation sites in natl forests, capacity, funding, and maintenance needs, 1980s-90, GAO rpt, 26113–502

Recreation use of natl forests, by type of activity and State, 1990, annual rpt, 1204–17

Revenue of natl forest land, by source, forest, and State, FY90, annual rpt, 1204–34

Revenue of natl forest land, share paid to States, and acreage, by forest, region, county, and congressional district, FY90, annual rpt, 1204–33

Rocky Mountain region employment and income, and economic dependence on shipments outside area, by industry and county group, 1980s, 1208–362

State and Metro Area Data Book, 1991 data compilation, 2328–54

Statistical Abstract of US, 1991 annual data compilation, 2324–1.7; 2324–1.24

Timber sales of Forest Service, expenses, and operations, by region, State, and natl forest, FY90, annual rpts, 1204–36

Timber sales of Forest Service, impacts of northern spotted owl conservation in Pacific Northwest, 1990 hearing, 21168–47

Virginia timber resources, growth, and removals, by species, ownership, treatment, and county, 1990-91, series, 1206–6

Visits and fees for Federal outdoor recreation facilities, by managing agency, FY88-90, annual rpt, 5544–14

see also Wilderness areas

National Forum on Education Statistics

Data collection and reporting improvement for Federal and State educational agencies, recommendations, 1991 rpt, 4828–39

National Foundation on the Arts and the Humanities

Arts Natl Endowment activities and grants, FY90, annual rpt, 9564–3

Budget of US, authoritative financial statements with appropriations, outlays, and receipts, by category and agency, FY90, annual rpt, 8104–2.1

Budget of US, obligations and authority by function, agency, and program, with summaries, analyses, and historical tables, FY92, annual rpt, 104–2

Education funding by Federal agency, program, and recipient type, and instn spending, FY80-90, annual rpt, 4824–8

Expenditures of Fed Govt in States, by type, program, agency, and State, FY90, annual rpt, 2464–2

Humanities Natl Endowment activities and grants, FY90, annual rpt, 9564–2

Museum Services Inst activities and finances, and grants by recipient, FY90, annual rpt, 9564–7

Performing arts commercial and nonprofit organizations, receipts by source, SIC 2- to 4-digit kind of business, and State, 1987 Census of Service Industries, 2393–4.11

National grasslands

Acreage and costs of real property owned by Fed Govt, worldwide summary by location, agency, and use, 1989, annual rpt, 9454–5

Acreage and use of public lands, and Land Mgmt Bur activities and finances, annual State rpt series, 5724–11

Acreage, grants, use, revenues, and allocations, for public lands by State, FY90 and trends, annual rpt, 5724–1

Acreage of land under Forest Service mgmt, by forest and location, 1990, annual rpt, 1204–2

Index by Subjects and Names

Expenditures of Fed Govt in States, by type, program, agency, and State, FY90, annual rpt, 2464–2

Grazing of livestock on natl forest lands, by region and State, 1990, annual rpt, 1204–5

Land Mgmt Bur activities and funding by State, FY89, annual rpt, 5724–13

Land Mgmt Bur activities in Southwestern US, FY90, annual rpt, 5724–15

Pacific Northwest acreage, staff, finances, and mgmt activities of Forest Service, with data by forest, 1970s-89, annual rpt, 1204–37

Rocky Mountain region employment and income, and economic dependence on shipments outside area, by industry and county group, 1980s, 1208–362

National Guard

Activities, personnel, and facilities of Army and Air Natl Guard, FY90, annual rpt, 3504–22

Activities, personnel, discipline, budget, and assistance, FY83 summary data, annual rpt, 3704–11

Drug enforcement support activities of Natl Guard, spending and needs by State, FY89-91, GAO rpt, 26123–343

Expenditures of Fed Govt in States, by type, program, agency, and State, FY90, annual rpt, 2464–2

Personnel active duty strength, recruits, and reenlistment, by race, sex, and service branch, quarterly press release, 3542–7

Personnel and equipment strengths, and readiness, by reserve component, FY90, annual rpt, 3544–31

Personnel attrition in reserves, by reason, personnel characteristics, reserve component, and State, FY88, GAO rpt, 26123–329

Personnel strengths and characteristics, by reserve component, FY90, annual rpt, 3544–38

Personnel strengths and characteristics, by reserve component, quarterly rpt, 3542–4

Personnel strengths for reserve components, by selected characteristics, FY90, annual rpt, 3544–1.5

Personnel strengths, force structure and training, for reserves of US and 5 European countries, as of 1990, GAO rpt, 26123–358

Statistical Abstract of US, 1991 annual data compilation, 2324–1.11

Training and education programs of DOD, funding, staff, students, and facilities, by service branch, FY92, annual rpt, 3504–5

Women military personnel on active and reserve duty, by demographic and service characteristics and service branch, FY89, annual chartbook, 3544–26

National Health and Nutrition Examination Survey

Methodology and sample characteristics for survey followup study, 1990 rpt, 4147–1.26

National Health Examination Survey

see National Health and Nutrition Examination Survey

National Health Interview Survey

Health condition, medical costs, and use of health facilities and services, Vital and Health Statistics series, 4147–10

Index by Subjects and Names

Vital and Health Statistics series: advance data rpts, 4146–8
Vital and Health Statistics series: reprints of advance data rpts, 4147–16

National Health Interview Survey on Child Health

Developmental, learning, and emotional problems in children, and share receiving special treatment and education, by selected characteristics, 1988, 4146–8.193

Insurance (health) coverage of children, and children with a regular source of care, by selected characteristics, 1988, 4146–8.192

National Health Survey

see Hispanic Health and Nutrition Examination Survey

see National Ambulatory Medical Care Survey

see National Health and Nutrition Examination Survey

see National Health Interview Survey

see National Health Interview Survey on Child Health

see National Hospital Discharge Survey

see National Medical Expenditure Survey

see National Natality Survey

see National Survey of Family Growth

National Heart, Lung, and Blood Institute

Activities and funding of NIH, by inst, FY89-90, biennial rpt, 4434–16

Activities of NHLBI, and grants by recipient and location, FY90 and disease trends from 1940, annual rpt, 4474–15

National Highway Traffic Safety Administration

Accidents (fatal), circumstances, and characteristics of persons and vehicles involved, 1990, semiannual rpt, 7762–11

Accidents (fatal), deaths, and rates, by circumstances, characteristics of persons and vehicles involved, and location, 1989, annual rpt, 7764–10

Accidents and safety data, annual fact sheet series, 7766–15

Accidents, casualties, circumstances, and characteristics of persons and vehicles involved, 1989, annual rpt, 7764–18

Accidents, injuries, and deaths, by circumstances and characteristics of persons and vehicles involved, annual rpt, discontinued, 7764–13

Activities of NHTSA, grants awarded, and fatal traffic accident data, 1989, annual rpt, 7764–1

Auto safety, crash test results by domestic and foreign model, press release series, 7766–7

Auto theft rates of new cars, by make and model, 1989 model year, annual rpt, 7764–21

Budget of US, obligations and authority by function, agency, and program, with summaries, analyses, and historical tables, FY92, annual rpt, 104–2

Bus (school) accidents, circumstances, victim characteristics, and vehicle type, 1989, annual rpt, 7764–22

Deaths in traffic accidents by region, and death rates for miles traveled, monthly rpt, 7762–7

Drunk drivers and others involved in fatal accidents, alcohol levels by circumstances and characteristics of persons and vehicles, 1989, annual rpt, 7764–16

National Institute for Occupational Safety and Health

Employment of DOT, by subagency, occupation, and selected personnel characteristics, FY90, annual rpt, 7304–18

Energy economy performance of autos and light trucks by make, standards, and enforcement, 1978-91 model years, annual rpt, 7764–9

Expenditures of Fed Govt in States, by type, program, agency, and State, FY90, annual rpt, 2464–2

Recalls of motor vehicles and equipment with safety-related defects, by make, monthly listing, 7762–12

Recalls of motor vehicles and equipment with safety-related defects, by make, quarterly listing, 7762–2

Safety improvement measures, costs, and accident and death reductions by type of accident and improvement, 1990 conf, 7558–110

Speed limit impacts on traffic accidents, with accident circumstances and speed averages, for States with 55 and 65 mph limit, 1986-89, annual rpt, 7764–15

Tire quality ratings, by type and brand, as of Sept 1991, annual rpt, 7764–17

Truck accidents, circumstances, severity, and characteristics of drivers and vehicles, 1989, annual rpt, 7764–20

National Hospital Discharge Survey

Discharges and length of stay, by diagnosis, patient and instn characteristics, procedure performed, and payment source, 1988, annual rpt, 4147–13.107

Discharges and length of stay by region and diagnosis, and procedures performed, by age and sex, 1989, annual rpt, 4146–8.198

Hospital discharges by detailed diagnostic and procedure category, primary diagnosis, and length of stay, by age, sex, and region, 1988, annual rpt, 4147–13.105; 4147–13.108

National Household Education Survey

Data collection activities and programs of NCES, 1991, annual listing, 4824–7

National Household Seroprevalence Survey

AIDS virus infection and risk factor prevalence, natl survey methodology and pretest results, 1989, 4148–30

National Household Survey on Drug Abuse

Abuse of drugs and alcohol, by selected characteristics, 1990 survey, biennial rpt, 4494–5

Cocaine and marijuana use reported in household and telephone surveys, data accuracy, 1988, article, 4042–3.230

National income and product accounts

Assets and liabilities of US, and impacts of inflation, 1990 and trends from 1948, article, 9391–1.220

Budget of US, CBO analysis of revenue and spending alternatives and projections of economic indicators, FY92-96, annual rpt, 26304–3

Budget of US, obligations and authority by function, agency, and program, with summaries, analyses, and historical tables, FY92, annual rpt, 104–2

Budget of US, receipts and outlays on natl income and product basis, FY92, annual article, 2702–1.204

Business statistics, detailed data for major industries and economic indicators, *Survey of Current Business,* monthly rpt, 2702–1

Consumer spending, natl income and product accounts, *Survey of Current Business,* monthly rpt, 2702–1.25

Exports, imports, and trade flows, by country and commodity, with background economic indicators, data compilation, monthly CD-ROM, 2002–6

Fed Govt nondefense, defense, and total spending, natl income accounts budget, compounded annual rates of change, 1971-90, annual rpt, 9391–9.2

Flow-of-funds accounts, savings, investments, and credit statements, quarterly rpt, 9365–3.3

Govt revenue by source and outlays by type, for State and local govts, 1986-90, annual article, 2702–1.205

Govt revenues and spending by level of govt, natl income and product accounts, selected years 1929-92, annual rpt, 204–1.6

Govt revenues by source, natl income and product accounts, *Survey of Current Business,* monthly rpt, 2702–1.25

Natl income and product accounts and components, *Survey of Current Business,* monthly rpt, 2702–1.24; 2702–1.25

Natl income and product accounts benchmark revisions, definition and classification changes, 1929-87, article, 2702–1.221

Natl income and product accounts benchmark revisions, new, dropped, and revised tables, 1991 article, 2702–1.224

Natl income and product accounts benchmark revisions of GDP and natl income, various periods 1959-80, tables, 2702–1.227

Natl income and product accounts benchmark revisions, selected years 1977-90, article, 2702–1.226

Savings rates in natl income and product accounts, under alternative estimates of imputed rent for housing and consumer goods, 1950s-90, article, 9373–1.218

Statistical Abstract of US, 1991 annual data compilation, 2324–1.14

Tax (income) returns filed by type of filer, selected income items, quarterly rpt, 8302–2.1

see also Gross Domestic Product

see also Gross National Product

National Institute for Occupational Safety and Health

Air pollution indoor levels in workplace, and health impacts, for Library of Congress Madison Building, 1989 study, series, 4248–92

Data on occupational deaths, States collection and processing, Natl Inst for Occupational Safety and Health guidelines, 1990 rpt, 4248–89

Hazardous substances and conditions occupational exposure and health effects, literature review, series, 4246–4

Hazardous substances and conditions occupational exposure, measurement, and proposed standards, series, 4246–1

Research and demonstration grants of NIOSH for occupational safety and health by State, and project listing, FY90, annual rpt, 4244–2

Respiratory diseases related to occupational hazards, epidemiology, diagnosis, and treatment, for selected industries and work settings, 1988 conf, 4248–90

Smoking involuntary exposure, health effects, and toxic substance levels of sidestream smoke, literature review, 1970s-90, 4248–91

Toxicology Natl Program research and testing activities, FY89 and planned FY90, annual rpt, 4044–16

National Institute of Allergy and Infectious Diseases

Activities and funding of NIH, by inst, FY89-90, biennial rpt, 4434–16

Activities of NIAID, grants by recipient and location, and disease cases, FY83-90, annual rpt, 4474–30

National Institute of Arthritis and Musculoskeletal and Skin Diseases

Activities and funding of NIH, by inst, FY89-90, biennial rpt, 4434–16

National Institute of Child Health and Human Development

Activities and funding of NIH, by inst, FY89-90, biennial rpt, 4434–16

Population, family, and sexual behavior research activities and funding, 1960s-89, 4478–194

Research contracts and grants of NICHD, annual listing, discontinued, 4474–36

Research on population and reproduction, Federal funding by project, FY89, annual listing, 4474–9

Research on population and reproduction, NICHD funding and activities, 1990, annual rpt, 4474–33

see also Center for Population Research

National Institute of Dental Research

Activities and funding of NIH, by inst, FY89-90, biennial rpt, 4434–16

Grants for research and training awarded by Inst, by recipient instn, FY89, annual listing, 4474–19

National Institute of Diabetes and Digestive and Kidney Diseases

Activities and funding of NIH, by inst, FY89-90, biennial rpt, 4434–16

Diabetes research and care services programs and funding, by Federal agency and NIH inst, FY90, annual rpt, 4474–34

Kidney end-stage disease cases, treatment, outcomes, and characteristics of patients, organ donors, and facilities, late 1970s-88, annual rpt, 4474–37

National Institute of Education

see also Office of Educational Research and Improvement

National Institute of Environmental Health Sciences

Activities and funding of NIH, by inst, FY89-90, biennial rpt, 4434–16

Toxicology Natl Program research and testing activities, FY89 and planned FY90, annual rpt, 4044–16

National Institute of General Medical Sciences

Activities and funding of NIH, by inst, FY89-90, biennial rpt, 4434–16

Cell cultures with genetic abnormalities, availability and cultures shipped, 1990-91, biennial listing, 4474–23

National Institute of Justice

AIDS cases and policies in criminal justice system, series, 6066–28

Crime and criminal justice research results, series, 6066–26

Drug abuse relation to violent and criminal behavior, with data on street gang activity and selected population groups, 1989 conf, 4498–70

Drug enforcement programs of State and local govts, FY90, annual rpt, 6064–32

Drug test results at arrest, by drug type, offense, and sex, for selected urban areas, quarterly rpt, 6062–3

Publications of NIJ, 1983-89, listing, 6068–240

National Institute of Mental Health

Facilities, patients, services, and staff characteristics, series, 4506–4

Facilities, patients, services, and staff characteristics, *Statistical Notes* series, 4506–3

States and counties mental health care hospitals, patients and admissions by age, diagnosis, and State, FY89, annual rpt, 4504–2

National Institute of Neurological Disorders and Stroke

Activities and funding of NIH, by inst, FY89-90, biennial rpt, 4434–16

Activities of NINDS, and disorder cases, FY90, annual rpt, 4474–25

National Institute of Standards and Technology

Budget of US, obligations and authority by function, agency, and program, with summaries, analyses, and historical tables, FY92, annual rpt, 104–2

Computer systems of Fed Govt with sensitive unclassified data, security plans by characteristics of info and system, and agency, 1989, 2218–85

Computer systems purchase and use, and data recording, processing, and transfer, Fed Govt standards, series, 2216–2

Energy-related inventions recommended by NIST for DOE support, awards, and evaluation status, 1990, annual listing, 2214–5

GATT Standards Code info activities of NIST, and proposed standards by agency and country, 1990, annual rpt, 2214–6

Publications of NIST, 1990, annual listing, 2214–1

Semiconductor and fiber optics industries quality control spending, effectiveness, and views, survey results, 1980s, 2218–84

Weights, measures, and performance standards dev, proposals, and policies, 1991 annual conf, 2214–7

National Institute on Aging

Activities and funding of NIH, by inst, FY89-90, biennial rpt, 4434–16

National Institute on Alcohol Abuse and Alcoholism

Abuse of alcohol, related injury and illness, series, 4486–1

Homeless persons alcohol abuse, by sex, age, race, and additional diagnoses, aggregate 1985-87, 4488–14

Research on alcoholism, treatment programs, and patient characteristics, quarterly journal, 4482–1

Treatment facilities for drug and alcohol abuse, services, use, funding, staff, and client characteristics, 1989, biennial rpt, 4494–10

National Institute on Deafness and Other Communication Disorders

Activities and funding of NIH, by inst, FY89-90, biennial rpt, 4434–16

National Institute on Drug Abuse

Abuse of drugs and alcohol, by selected characteristics, 1990 survey, biennial rpt, 4494–5

Abuse of drugs, emergency room admissions and deaths by drug type and major metro area, semiannual rpt, discontinued, 4492–3

Abuse of drugs, emergency room admissions and deaths, by drug type and source, sex, race, age, and major metro area, 1990, annual rpt, 4494–8

Abuse of drugs, indicators for selected metro areas, research results, data collection, and policy issues, 1991 semiannual conf, 4492–5

Cocaine abuse, user characteristics, and related crime and violence, 1988 conf, 4498–74

Drug (steroid) use prevalence and health effects, 1989 conf papers, 4498–67

Drug abuse, prevention, treatment, and health research results, as of 1990, triennial rpt, 4498–68

Drug abuse psychotherapy and counseling outcomes, research results and methodology, 1990 conf, 4498–71

Drug abuse residual neurological, behavioral, and cognitive effects, 1989 conf, 4498–69

Drug and alcohol abuse treatment services, funding, staffing, and client load, characteristics, and outcomes, by setting, 1989 conf, 4498–73

Methamphetamine abuse, availability, health effects, and treatment, 1990 conf papers, 4498–75

Minority group drug abuse prevalence, related health effects and crime, treatment, and research status and needs, mid 1970s-90, 4498–72

Research on drug abuse and treatment, biological and behavioral factors, and addiction potential of new drugs, 1990 annual conf, 4494–11

Research on drug abuse and treatment, summaries of findings, resource materials, and grant listings, periodic rpt, 4492–4

Treatment facilities for drug and alcohol abuse, services, use, funding, staff, and client characteristics, 1989, biennial rpt, 4494–10

Violent and criminal behavior relation to drug abuse, with data on street gang activity and selected population groups, 1989 conf, 4498–70

Youth drug, alcohol, and cigarette use and attitudes, by substance type and selected characteristics, 1975-90 surveys, annual rpt, 4494–4

National Institutes of Health

Activities and funding of NIH, by inst, FY89-90, biennial rpt, 4434–16

Activities of NIH, funding by program and recipient type, staff, and clinic patients, by inst, FY90, annual rpt, 4434–3

Budget of US, obligations and authority by function, agency, and program, with summaries, analyses, and historical tables, FY92, annual rpt, 104–2

Financial aid of HHS, by program, recipient, State, and city, FY90, annual regional listings, 4004–3

Grants and awards of NIH, quarterly listing, 4432–1

Grants and contracts of NIH, by inst and type of recipient, FY81-90, annual rpt, 4434–9

Grants of NIH for R&D, training, construction, and medical libraries, by location and recipient, FY90, annual listings, 4434–7

Intl programs of NIH, activities and funding by inst and country, FY90, annual rpt, 4474–6

Publications of NIH, 1991 annual listing, 4434–2

R&D facilities for biological and medical sciences, space and equipment adequacy, needs, and funding by source, by instn type, 1990, biennial rpt, 4434–17

Research and evaluation programs of HHS, 1970-90, annual listing, 4004–30

Toxicology Natl Program research and testing activities, FY89 and planned FY90, annual rpt, 4044–16

see also Division of Research Grants, NIH

see also Fogarty International Center for Advanced Study in the Health Sciences

see also National Cancer Institute

see also National Center for Nursing Research

see also National Center for Research Resources, NIH

see also National Eye Institute

see also National Heart, Lung, and Blood Institute

see also National Institute of Allergy and Infectious Diseases

see also National Institute of Arthritis and Musculoskeletal and Skin Diseases

see also National Institute of Child Health and Human Development

see also National Institute of Dental Research

see also National Institute of Diabetes and Digestive and Kidney Diseases

see also National Institute of Environmental Health Sciences

see also National Institute of General Medical Sciences

see also National Institute of Neurological Disorders and Stroke

see also National Institute on Aging

see also National Institute on Deafness and Other Communication Disorders

see also National Library of Medicine

National Labor Relations Board

Activities, cases, elections conducted, and litigation, FY89, annual rpt, 9584–1

Budget of US, authoritative financial statements with appropriations, outlays, and receipts, by category and agency, FY90, annual rpt, 8104–2.1

Budget of US, obligations and authority by function, agency, and program, with summaries, analyses, and historical tables, FY92, annual rpt, 104–2

Cases, backlog, and processing time, for NLRB, 1960s-89, GAO rpt, 26121–395

Representation elections conducted by NLRB, results, monthly rpt, 9582–2

National Library of Medicine

Activities and funding of NIH, by inst, FY89-90, biennial rpt, 4434–16

Activities, holdings, and grants of Library, FY88-90, annual rpt, 4464–1

Libraries of higher education instns, holdings, outlays, staff, and instn characteristics, 1969-88, 4468–4

National Long Term Care Survey

Cognitive impairment prevalence, accuracy of estimates derived from natl surveys, 1991 rpt, 4186–7.7

National Longitudinal Study of High School Seniors

Athletes in college, educational and employment performance compared to other students, for 1972 high school class, as of 1986, 4888–5

High school class of 1972: education, employment, and family characteristics, activities, and attitudes, natl longitudinal study, series, 4836–1

Women's employment and educational experiences compared to men, for high school class of 1972, natl longitudinal study, as of 1986, 4888–6

National Marine Fisheries Service

Activities, funding, and staff of Federal food safety and quality regulation agencies, 1980s, GAO rpt, 26113–503

Alaska fish catch in excess of domestic processor needs, and use of estimates for fishing rights allocation, 1984-90, GAO rpt, 26113–523

Aquaculture in US and Japan, mgmt, methods, and biological data for selected species, 1988 conf, annual rpt, 2164–15

Atlantic Ocean fish and shellfish distribution, bottom trawl survey results by species and location, periodic rpt series, 2164–18

Atlantic Ocean sport and commercial fishing catch and quotas for US and Canada, by species, 1990, annual rpt, 2164–14

Bass (striped) stocks status on Atlantic coast, and sport and commercial catch by State, 1972-89, annual rpt, 5504–29

Cold storage holdings of fish and shellfish, by product and species, preliminary data, monthly press release, 2162–2

Fish (groundfish) juvenile population distribution by species, for New England area, 1968-86, 2168–122

Fish and shellfish catch and stocks in northwest Atlantic, by species and location, 1887-1991 and forecast to 1993, semiannual conf, 2162–9

Fish and shellfish catch, wholesale receipts, prices, trade, and other market activities, weekly regional rpts, 2162–6

Fish catch, trade, use, and fishery operations, with selected foreign data, by species, 1980s-90, annual rpt, 2164–1

Fish meal and oil production and trade, quarterly tables, 2162–3

Fishing (ocean sport) activities, and catch by species, by angler characteristics and State, annual coastal area rpt series, 2166–17

Fishing (sport) from California commercial passenger boats with refrigeration equipment, anglers views, 1989 survey, 2168–125

Foreign countries market conditions for US fish and shellfish products, country rpt series, 2166–19

Japan fish catch, prices, trade by country, cold storage holdings, import quotas, and market devs, semimonthly press release, 2162–7

Larvae abundance, distribution, and growth, for fish at selected Western Hemisphere sites, 1989 conf papers, 2168–126

Marine Fisheries Review, US and foreign fisheries resources, dev, mgmt, and research, quarterly journal, 2162–1

Marine mammals strandings, research results, 1987 conf, 2168–127

New York Bight fish population and disease, and pollutant levels, near sewage sludge dumpsite, 1986-90, last issue of annual rpt, 2164–19

Pacific Ocean coast pollutant concentrations in fish and sediments, by contaminant, fish species, and site, 1984-86, 2168–121

Production of processed fish by location, and trade, by species and product, 1987-90, annual rpts, 2166–6

R&D and mgmt of fisheries, Fed Govt grants by project and State, and rpts, 1990, annual listing, 2164–3

Sewage sludge discharges and water properties at Atlantic Ocean deepwater dumpsite, 1990, annual rpt, 2164–20

Sharks and other fish tagged and recovered, by species, 1990, annual rpt, 2164–21

Sharks and rays population, physical characteristics, landings, and fishery mgmt, 1987 conf, 2168–124

Turtles (sea) population near oil drilling rigs, and habitat characteristics, 1988-90, 5738–26

National Mediation Board

Budget of US, authoritative financial statements with appropriations, outlays, and receipts, by category and agency, FY90, annual rpt, 8104–2.1

Budget of US, obligations and authority by function, agency, and program, with summaries, analyses, and historical tables, FY92, annual rpt, 104–2

National Medical Care Expenditure Survey

see also National Medical Expenditure Survey

National Medical Care Utilization and Expenditure Survey

Methodology and findings of natl survey and Medicare and Medicaid records, 1980, series, 4146–12

National Medical Expenditure Survey

Cognitive impairment prevalence, accuracy of estimates derived from natl surveys, 1991 rpt, 4186–7.7

Data accuracy and response rates for 2 organizations conducting NMES screenings, 1986, 4188–68

Data on health care use and costs, methodology and findings of natl survey, series, 4186–8

National monuments

see Monuments and memorials

National Narcotics Intelligence Consumers Committee

Supply of drugs in US by country of origin, abuse, prices, and seizures, by substance, 1990, annual rpt, 6284–2

National Natality Survey

Birth, marriage, and divorce trends, series, 4147–21

Smoking during pregnancy, by age, race, education, marital status, and birth order, 1970s-80s, article, 4042–3.203

National Ocean Service

National Ocean Service

Alaska OCS environmental conditions and oil dev impacts, compilation of papers, series, 2176–1

Charting and Geodetic Service activities and funding, by State, FY91-92, biennial rpt, 2174–10

Coastal and estuarine environmental conditions, research results and methodology, series, 2176–7

Great Lakes water levels, daily and monthly averages by site, 1990 and cumulative from 1900, annual rpt, 2174–3

Middle Atlantic States tide height and tidal current velocity daily at selected coastal stations, forecast 1992, annual rpt, 2174–11

Pollutant concentrations in coastal and estuarine fish, shellfish, and environment, series, 2176–3

Tidal currents, daily time and velocity by station for North America and Asia coasts, forecast 1992, annual rpts, 2174–1

Tide height and time daily at coastal points worldwide, forecast 1992, annual rpt series, 2174–2

National Oceanic and Atmospheric Administration

Atlantic Ocean currents, temperatures, and salinity, from Florida straits to northern Brazil, series, 2146–7

Atlantic Oceanographic and Meteorological Lab research activities and bibl, FY90, annual rpt, 2144–19

Budget of US, obligations and authority by function, agency, and program, with summaries, analyses, and historical tables, FY92, annual rpt, 104–2

Diving (underwater sport and occupational) deaths, by circumstances, diver characteristics, and location, 1970-89, annual rpt, 2144–5

Environmental Research Labs of NOAA, staff rpts, FY90, annual listing, 2144–25

Estuary environmental conditions, and fish and shellfish catch by species and region, 1980s, 2178–27

Expenditures of Fed Govt in States, by type, program, agency, and State, FY90, annual rpt, 2464–2

Fish (salmon and trout) wild and hatchery juvenile population and characteristics, for Pacific Northwest, 1981-85, 2168–123

Fish kills in coastal areas related to pollution and natural causes, by land use, State, and county, 1980s, 2178–32

Great Lakes Environmental Research Lab activities, FY90 annual rpt, 2144–26

Natl Severe Storms Lab research activities and bibl, FY90, annual rpt, 2144–20

Oceanographic research and distribution activities of World Data Center A by country, and cruises by ship, 1989, annual rpt, 2144–15

Pacific Marine Environmental Lab research activities and bibl, FY90, annual rpt, 2144–21

Pollutants contributing to climate change, atmospheric concentrations by monitoring site, 1989, annual rpt, 2144–28

Recreation (outdoor) coastal facilities and finances, by site and level of govt, State rpt series, discontinued, 2176–6

Recreation (outdoor) coastal facilities, by State, county, estuary, and level of govt, 1972-84, 2178–29

Recreation (outdoor) coastal facilities of Fed Govt and States, visitor and site characteristics, 1987-90 survey, regional rpt series, 2176–9

Shellfish recreational harvesters selected characteristics, location of harvest and residence, and spending, 1985 survey, 2178–28

Ships for oceanographic research, fleet condition, funding, voyages, and modernization costs, for NOAA, 1980s-90 and projected to 2020, 2148–60

Washington State marine sanctuaries proposal, environmental and economic impacts, with background data, 1984-89, 2178–30

Weather services activities and funding, by Federal agency, planned FY91-92, annual rpt, 2144–2

Wetlands in coastal areas, acreage by wetland type, estuarine basin, and county, 1989, 2178–31

see also National Environmental Satellite, Data, and Information Service

see also National Marine Fisheries Service

see also National Ocean Service

see also National Weather Service

National Park Service

Accidents, crimes, and hazardous waste sites in natl parks, and funding, 1971-91, GAO rpt, 26113–545

Acreage of land under NPS mgmt, by site, ownership, and region, FY91, semiannual rpt, 5542–1

Alaska submerged land grant holdings of Alaska Natives, exchange for upland acreage, impacts on conservation acreage and acquisition, 1989-90, 5728–38

Bears (grizzly) in Yellowstone Natl Park area, monitoring results, 1990, annual rpt, 5544–4

Budget of US, obligations and authority by function, agency, and program, with summaries, analyses, and historical tables, FY92, annual rpt, 104–2

Deaths of natl park system visitors, by cause, victim age, region, and park, 1980-90, annual rpt, 5544–6

Expenditures of Fed Govt in States, by type, program, agency, and State, FY90, annual rpt, 2464–2

Goats (mountain) population in Yellowstone and Grand Teton Natl Parks, and habitat mgmt options, 1970s-89, 5548–19

Historic buildings rehabilitation tax incentives, projects, costs, ownership, and use, FY77-90, annual rpt, 5544–17

Historic Preservation Fund grants, by State, FY92, annual table, 5544–9

Land and Water Conservation Fund allocations for outdoor recreation area dev, by State, FY91, annual table, 5544–15

Land and Water Conservation Fund grants, State matching funds, and balances, by State, FY90, annual rpt, 5544–18

Urban areas park and recreation facilities rehabilitation funding, by city and State, FY91, press release, 5306–4.7

Visits and fees for Federal outdoor recreation facilities, by managing agency, FY88-90, annual rpt, 5544–14

Index by Subjects and Names

Visits and overnight stays in natl park system, by park and State, monthly rpt, 5542–4

Visits and overnight stays in natl park system, by park and State, 1990, annual rpt, 5544–12

National parks

Accidents, crimes, and hazardous waste sites in natl parks, and funding, 1971-91, GAO rpt, 26113–545

Acreage and costs of real property owned by Fed Govt, worldwide summary by location, agency, and use, 1989, annual rpt, 9454–5

Acreage of land under Natl Park Service mgmt, by site, ownership, and region, FY91, semiannual rpt, 5542–1

Alaska land area by ownership, and availability for mineral exploration and dev, 1984-86, 5608–152

Badlands Natl Park juniper forest and mixed grass rangeland habitats, bird population and species diversity by season, 1991 rpt, 1208–364

Bears (grizzly) in Yellowstone Natl Park area, monitoring results, 1990, annual rpt, 5544–4

Coastal areas recreation facilities of Fed Govt and States, visitor and site characteristics, 1987-90 survey, regional rpt series, 2176–9

Crimes committed in natl parks, by offense, data compilation, 1991 annual rpt, 6064–6.3

Deaths of natl park system visitors, by cause, victim age, region, and park, 1980-90, annual rpt, 5544–6

Environmental Quality, status of problems, protection programs, research, and intl issues, 1991 annual rpt, 484–1

Global climate change environmental, infrastructure, and health impacts, with model results and background data, 1850s-2100, 9188–113

Goats (mountain) population in Yellowstone and Grand Teton Natl Parks, and habitat mgmt options, 1970s-89, 5548–19

Great Smoky Mountain region visitor activities and opinions, 1990 conf papers, annual rpt, 1204–38

Minerals resources and availability on public lands, State rpt series, 5606–7

Northeastern US recreation areas use, mgmt, and tourism dev issues, 1990 conf, 1208–356

State and Metro Area Data Book, 1991 data compilation, 2328–54

Statistical Abstract of US, 1991 annual data compilation, 2324–1.7

Visits and fees for Federal outdoor recreation facilities, by managing agency, FY88-90, annual rpt, 5544–14

Visits and overnight stays in natl park system, by park and State, monthly rpt, 5542–4

Visits and overnight stays in natl park system, by park and State, 1990, annual rpt, 5544–12

Visits in natl park system, *Survey of Current Business*, monthly rpt, 2702–1.11

Wetlands plant, soil, and water characteristics, for Big Meadows area in Rocky Mountain Natl Park, 1987-88, 5508–113

see also National forests
see also National trails
see also Wilderness areas
see also Wildlife refuges

National planning
see Economic policy
see Fiscal policy
see Monetary policy

National Postsecondary Student Aid Study
Assistance and other sources of support, with student expenses and characteristics, by instn type and control, 1990 triennial study, series, 4846–5
Data collection activities and programs of NCES, 1991, annual listing, 4824–7

National Railroad Passenger Corp.
Energy use by mode of transport, fuel supply, and demographic and economic factors of vehicle use, 1970s-89, annual rpt, 3304–5
Finances and ridership of Amtrak, FY78-88, annual rpt, 7304–1
Great Lakes area economic conditions and outlook, for US and Canada, 1970s-90, 9375–15
Operations and finances of Amtrak, FY90, annual rpt, 29524–1

National school lunch and breakfast programs
see School lunch and breakfast programs

National Science Foundation
Activities of NSF, finances, and funding by program, FY90, annual rpt, 9624–6
Budget of US, authoritative financial statements with appropriations, outlays, and receipts, by category and agency, FY90, annual rpt, 8104–2.1
Budget of US, obligations and authority by function, agency, and program, with summaries, analyses, and historical tables, FY92, annual rpt, 104–2
Degrees (PhD) in science and engineering, by field, instn, employment prospects, sex, race, and other characteristics, 1960s-90, annual rpt, 9627–30
Degrees awarded in science and engineering, by field, level, and sex, 1966-89, 9627–33
Education funding by Federal agency, program, and recipient type, and instn spending, FY80-90, annual rpt, 4824–8
Education in science and engineering, grad programs enrollment by field, source of funds, and characteristics of student and instn, 1975-89, annual rpt, 9627–7
Education in science, engineering, and math, NSF grants by recipient and level, FY89, biennial listing, 9624–27
Employment and other characteristics of science and engineering PhDs, by field and State, 1989, biennial rpt, 9627–18
Employment in science and engineering of NSF, and outside investigator research grant proposals and awards, 1980s-90, 9628–84
Employment of scientists and engineers, and related topics, fact sheet series, discontinued, 9626–2
Engineering research and education grants of NSF, FY90, annual listing, 9624–24
Expenditures of Fed Govt in States, by type, program, agency, and State, FY90, annual rpt, 2464–2
Fraud and abuse in NSF programs, audits and investigations, 2nd half FY91, semiannual rpt, 9622–1

Grants and contracts of NSF, by field, instn, and State, FY89, annual rpt, 9624–26
Higher education and nonprofit instns R&D and related activities funding by Fed Govt, by field, instn, agency, and State, FY89, annual rpt, 9627–17
Higher education instn and federally funded center R&D funding, by field, instn, and State, FY89, annual rpt, 9627–13
Higher education instn science and engineering research system status, R&D performance, and Federal support, 1950s-88, 9628–83
Intl exchange and training programs of Federal agencies, participants by world area, and funding, by program, FY89, annual rpt, 9854–8
Publications of NSF Science Resources Studies Div, 1988-91, listing, 9627–22
Publications of NSF, 1990 annual listing, 9624–16
R&D equipment of higher education instns, acquisition and service costs, condition, and financing, by field and subfield, 1988-90, triennial survey series, 9627–27
R&D funding, and scientists and engineers education and employment, for US and selected foreign countries, 1991 annual rpt, 9627–35
R&D funding by Fed Govt, by field, performer type, agency, and State, FY89-91, annual rpt, 9627–20
R&D grant awards of NSF, by div and program, periodic rpt series, 9626–7
Research grants to predominantly undergrad instns, by NSF div, and principal investigator sex and race, FY88, 9628–85
Women scientists and engineers seeking 1st Federal grant and reentering career, NSF support program proposal submissions, grant awards, and applicants views, FY85-89, 9628–82

National security
see Internal security
see National defense

National Security Council
Budget of US, authoritative financial statements with appropriations, outlays, and receipts, by category and agency, FY90, annual rpt, 8104–2.1
Budget of US, obligations and authority by function, agency, and program, with summaries, analyses, and historical tables, FY92, annual rpt, 104–2

National Severe Storms Lab
see National Oceanic and Atmospheric Administration

National stockpiles
see Stockpiling

National Survey of Family Growth
Infertility prevalence among women, by age and parity, with infertility services use, selected years 1965-88, 4146–8.194
Marriage, marriage dissolution, remarriage, and cohabitation, for women, by age and race, 1988, 4146–8.196
Methodology, sample design, and estimation procedures for 1988 survey, 1991 rpt, 4147–2.112

National Survey of Postsecondary Faculty
Data collection activities and programs of NCES, 1991, annual listing, 4824–7

National Technical Information Service
Computer data files of NTIS, 1991 annual listing, 2224–3
EPA rpts in NTIS collection, quarterly listing, 9182–5

National Telecommunications and Information Administration
Budget of US, obligations and authority by function, agency, and program, with summaries, analyses, and historical tables, FY92, annual rpt, 104–2
Expenditures of Fed Govt in States, by type, program, agency, and State, FY90, annual rpt, 2464–2
Publications of NTIA, FY90, annual listing, 2804–3
Radio frequency assignments for Federal use, by agency, 1st half 1990, semiannual rpt, 2802–1

National Toxicology Program
Research and testing activities under program, FY89 and planned FY90, annual rpt, 4044–16

National trails
Acreage of land under Natl Park Service mgmt, by site, ownership, and region, FY91, semiannual rpt, 5542–1
Forest Service recreation programs funding, and cost sharing pledges, 1980s-91, GAO rpt, 26113–518
Land Mgmt Bur recreation sites mgmt activities, plans, and use, State rpt series, 5726–5
Visits and overnight stays in natl park system, by park and State, 1990, annual rpt, 5544–12

National Transportation Safety Board
Aircraft (general aviation) accidents, by circumstances, characteristics of persons and aircraft involved, and type of flying, 1988, annual rpt, 9614–3
Aircraft accidents and circumstances, for US operations of domestic and foreign airlines and general aviation, periodic rpt, 9612–1
Aircraft accidents, casualties, and damage, for commercial operations by detailed circumstances, 1987, annual rpt, 9614–2
Aircraft accidents, deaths, and circumstances, by carrier and carrier type, preliminary 1990, annual press release, 9614–9
Budget of US, authoritative financial statements with appropriations, outlays, and receipts, by category and agency, FY90, annual rpt, 8104–2.1
Budget of US, obligations and authority by function, agency, and program, with summaries, analyses, and historical tables, FY92, annual rpt, 104–2
Deaths in transportation accidents, by mode, 1989-90, annual press release, 9614–6
Oil spill from tanker Exxon Valdez, safety issues, with oil lost and crew alcohol and drug test results, 1989, 9618–17
Ships and marine facilities accidents, casualties, and circumstances, Coast Guard investigation results, periodic rpt, 9612–4

National Trust for Historic Preservation
Grants to Natl Trust and to States, FY92, annual table, 5544–9

National Veterinary Services Laboratories

National Veterinary Services Laboratories Activities of NVSL, biologic drug product evaluation and disease testing, FY90, annual rpt, 1394–17

National Weather Service Forecasts accuracy, evaluations for US, UK, and European systems, quarterly rpt, 2182–8 Forecasts of precipitation and temperature for US and Northern Hemisphere, by location, semimonthly rpt, 2182–1 Forecasts of severe storms, Natl Weather Service forecast accuracy and storm characteristics, series, 2186–6 Hurricanes and tropical storms frequency, intensity, deaths, and damage, by State and selected city, 1886-1989, 2188–15 Northeastern US water supply, precipitation and stream runoff by station, monthly rpt, 2182–3 Ocean surface temperature by ocean and for US coastal areas, and Bering Sea ice conditions, monthly rpt, 2182–5 Precipitation and temperature for US and foreign locations, major events and anomalies, weekly rpt, 2182–6 Station locations and types of observations made, 1990 annual listing, 2184–5 Weather conditions and effect on agriculture, by US region, State, and city, and world area, weekly rpt, 2182–7 Weather trends and deviations, by world region, 1880s-1990, annual chartbook, 2184–9 Western US water supply, streamflow and reservoir storage forecasts by stream and station, Jan-May monthly rpt, 1262–1

National Wildlife Refuge System *see* Wildlife refuges

Nationality *see* Citizenship

Nationalization *see* Expropriation of alien property *see* Government ownership *see* Socialism

Nationwide Food Consumption Survey Food consumption, dietary composition, and nutrient intake, 1987/88 natl survey, preliminary rpt series, 1356–1

Nationwide Personal Transportation Study Households and personal travel patterns, characteristics, and auto and public transport use, 1990 survey, series, 7556–6 Travel patterns, personal and household characteristics, and auto use, 1990 survey, annual rpt, 7554–1.6

Native Americans *see* Alaska Natives *see* Indians

Nativity *see* Birthplace

NATO *see* North Atlantic Treaty Organization

Natural disasters *see* Avalanches *see* Disasters *see* Drought *see* Earthquakes *see* Floods *see* Forest fires *see* Storms *see* Volcanoes

Natural fibers County Business Patterns, 1988: employment, establishments, and payroll, by SIC 2- to 4-digit industry and county, annual State rpt series, 2326–6 County Business Patterns, 1989: employment, establishments, and payroll, by SIC 2- to 4-digit industry and county, annual State rpt series, 2326–8 Employment, earnings, and hours, by SIC 1- to 4-digit industry, monthly and annual averages, selected years 1909-90, annual rpt, 6744–4 Exports and imports (agricultural) of US, by commodity and country, bimonthly rpt, 1522–1 Exports and imports (agricultural) of US, by detailed commodity and country, 1989, annual rpt, 1524–8 Exports and imports (agricultural) of US, by detailed commodity and country, 1990, semiannual rpt, 1522–4 Exports and imports between US and outlying areas, by detailed commodity and mode of transport, 1990, annual rpt, 2424–11 Exports and imports of US, by country and detailed commodity, monthly rpt, 2422–12 Exports and imports of US, by Harmonized System 6-digit commodity and country, 1990, annual rpt, 2424–13 Exports and imports of US, by transport mode, country, and SITC 1- to 3-digit commodity, 1990, annual rpt, 2424–12 Exports of US, detailed Schedule B commodities with countries of destination, 1990, annual rpt, 2424–10 Foreign countries agricultural production, prices, and trade, by country, 1980-90 and forecast 1991, annual world area rpt series, 1524–4 Imports of textiles, by country of origin, monthly rpt, 2042–27 Imports of textiles, by product and country of origin, monthly rpt series, 2046–8; 2046–9 Imports of textiles under Multifiber Arrangement by product and country, and status of bilateral agreements, 1987-90, annual rpt, 9884–18 Manufacturing annual survey, 1989: finances and operations, by SIC 2- to 4-digit industry, series, 2506–15 OECD trade, total and for 4 major countries, and US trade by country, by commodity, 1970-89, world area rpt series, 9116–1 Price indexes (producer), by stage of processing and detailed commodity, monthly rpt, 6762–6 Price indexes (producer), by stage of processing and detailed commodity, monthly 1990, annual rpt, 6764–2 Production itemized costs, receipts, and returns, by commodity and region, 1987-89, annual rpt, 1544–20 Production, prices, trade, and use of natural fibers, periodic situation rpt with articles, 1561–1 Production, trade, sales, stocks, and material used, by product, region, and State, periodic Current Industrial Rpt series, 2506–5

Index by Subjects and Names

Statistical Abstract of US, 1991 annual data compilation, 2324–1.27 Stockpiling of strategic material by Fed Govt, activity, and inventory by commodity, as of Mar 1991, semiannual rpt, 3542–22 Stockpiling of strategic material, inventories and needs, by commodity, as of Jan 1991, annual rpt, 3544–37 *see also* Cotton *see also* Silk *see also* Wool and wool trade *see also* under By Commodity in the "Index by Categories"

Natural gas and gas industry Agriculture census, 1987: farms, farmland, production, finances, and operator characteristics, by county, final State rpt series, 2331–1 Auto alternative fuels costs, emissions, health impacts, and characteristics, 1990 rpt, 9196–5.2; 9196–5.3 Business statistics, detailed data for major industries and economic indicators, *Survey of Current Business,* monthly rpt, 2702–1.13 China economic indicators and reform issues, with background data, 1950s-90, compilation of papers, 23848–155 Commercial buildings energy use, costs, and conservation, by building characteristics, survey rpt series, 3166–8 Compressor stations and pipelines construction costs, 1984-87, annual rpt, 3084–3 Conservation measures impacts on energy consumption, by component and end-use sector, 1970s-88 and projected under alternative oil prices to 1995, 3308–93 Construction industries census, 1987: establishments, employment, receipts, and expenditures, by SIC 4-digit industry and State, final industry rpt series, 2373–1 Construction put in place (public and private), by type, bimonthly rpt, 2042–1.1 Construction put in place, value of new public and private structures, by type, monthly rpt, 2382–4 Consumer Expenditure Survey, household income by source, and itemized spending, by selected characteristics and region, 1988-89, annual rpt, 6764–5 Consumption of energy, by detailed fuel type, end-use sector, and State, 1960-89, State Energy Data System annual rpt, 3164–39 County Business Patterns, 1988: employment, establishments, and payroll, by SIC 2- to 4-digit industry and county, annual State rpt series, 2326–6 County Business Patterns, 1989: employment, establishments, and payroll, by SIC 2- to 4-digit industry and county, annual State rpt series, 2326–8 Developing countries energy use, and economic and environmental impacts, by fuel type, world area, and country, 1980s-90, 26358–232 Eastern Europe energy production, trade, use, and AID dev assistance, for 3 countries, 1980s-91, 25318–81 Electric power and industrial plants prohibited from oil and gas primary use, and gas use by State, 1977-90, annual rpt, 3334–1

Index by Subjects and Names

Electric power plants (steam) fuel receipts, costs, and quality, by fuel, plant, utility, and State, 1990, annual rpt, 3164–42

Electric power plants and capacity, by fuel used, owner, location, and operating status, 1990 and for units planned 1991-2000, annual listing, 3164–36

Electric power plants production and capacity by fuel type, prices, demand, and air pollution law impacts, by region, 1989-90 and projected to 2010, annual rpt, 3164–81

Electric power plants production and capital costs, operations, and fuel use, by fuel type, plant, utility, and location, 1989, annual rpt, 3164–9

Electric power plants production, capacity, sales, and fuel stocks, use, and costs, by State, 1985-89, annual rpt, 3164–11

Electric power plants production, fuel use, stocks, and costs by fuel type, and sales, by State, monthly rpt with articles, 3162–35

Employment, earnings, and hours, by SIC 1- to 4-digit industry, monthly and annual averages, selected years 1909-90, annual rpt, 6744–4

Environmental Quality, status of problems, protection programs, research, and intl issues, 1991 annual rpt, 484–1

Farm production itemized costs, by farm sales size and region, 1990, annual rpt, 1614–3

Fed Govt energy use and efficiency, by agency and fuel type, FY90, annual rpt, 3304–22

Finances and operations, by SIC 2- to 4-digit industry, forecast 1991, annual rpt, 2044–28

Finances and operations of energy producers, by energy type for US firms domestic and foreign operations, 1989, annual rpt, 3164–44

Foreign and US energy production, trade, use, and reserves, and oil and refined products supply and prices, by country, 1980-89, annual rpt, 3164–50

Foreign and US energy use and production, by fuel type, country, and country group, projected 1995-2010 and trends from 1970, annual rpt, 3164–84

Foreign and US natural gas production, by market economy country, monthly rpt, 9112–2

Foreign direct investment in US energy sources by type and firm, and US affiliates operations, as of 1989, annual rpt, 3164–80

Futures and options trading volume, by commodity and exchange, FY90, annual rpt, 11924–2

Futures trading in selected commodities and financial instruments and indexes, NYC, Chicago, and other markets activity, semimonthly rpt, 11922–5

Govt census, 1987: employment, payroll, and average earnings, by function, level of govt, State, county, and population size, 2455–2

Govt census, 1987: local govt employment by function, payroll, and average earnings, for individual counties, cities, and school and special districts, 2455–1

Govt employment and payroll, by function, level of govt, and jurisdiction, 1990, annual rpt series, 2466–1

Natural gas and gas industry

Heating fuels production, imports, stocks, and prices, by selected PAD district and State, seasonal weekly rpt, 3162–45

Helium and other components of natural gas, analyses of individual wells and pipelines, 1917-90, annual rpt, 5604–2

Housing (low income) energy aid, funding sources, costs, and participation, by State, FY89, annual rpt, 4694–8

Housing (rental) market absorption rates, by whether utilities included in rent, 1989, annual Current Housing Rpt, 2484–2

Housing and households detailed characteristics, and unit and neighborhood quality, by location, 1989, biennial rpt, 2485–12

Housing and households detailed characteristics, and unit and neighborhood quality, MSA surveys, series, 2485–6

Housing heating and air conditioning equipment shipments by type of fuel used, bimonthly rpt, 2042–1.6

Housing inventory change from 1973, by reason, unit and household characteristics, and location, 1983 survey, biennial rpt, 2485–14

Housing units (1-family) by selected structural characteristics, sales, and prices, 1970s-90, article, 1702–1.205

Housing units completed, single and multifamily units by structural and financial characteristics, inside-outside MSAs, and region, 1986-90, annual rpt, 2384–1

Labor productivity, indexes of output, hours, and employment by SIC 2- to 4-digit industry, 1967-89, annual rpt, 6824–1.4

Latin America energy use and trade, by selected country, 1970s-80s and projected to 2000, 3408–1

Manufacturing energy use and prices, 1988 survey, series, 3166–13

Methane production in coal fields, and proved reserves, by State, 1989-90, 3164–46.3

Methane production in coal fields by basin, and resources remaining, 1970s-89, article, 3162–4.201

Methane recovered from landfills, use by region, 1989, 3166–6.56

Mineral industries census, 1987: energy use and costs, by fuel type, SIC 2- to 4-digit industry, and State, subject rpt, 2517–2

Mineral industries census, 1987: finances and operations, by SIC 2- to 4-digit industry, State, and county, census div rpt series, 2515–1

Minerals Yearbook, 1988, Vol 3: foreign country reviews of production, trade, and policy, by commodity, annual rpt series, 5604–17

Natl Energy Strategy plans for conservation and pollution reduction, impacts of technology and regulation proposals, projected 1990-2030, 3166–6.47

Natl Energy Strategy plans for conservation and pollution reduction, impacts on electric power supply, costs, and emissions, projected under alternative assumptions, 1995-2030, 3166–6.49

Naval Petroleum and Oil Shale Reserves production and revenue by fuel type, sales by purchaser, and wells, by reserve, FY90, annual rpt, 3334–3

North Carolina environmental and socioeconomic conditions, and impacts of proposed OCS oil and gas exploration, 1970s-90 and projected to 2020, 5738–22

Occupational injury and illness rates, by SIC 2- to 4-digit industry, 1988-89, annual rpt, 6844–7

Occupational injury and illness rates, by SIC 2- to 4-digit industry, 1989, annual rpt, 6844–1

Pollution (air) contributing to global warming, emissions factors and control costs, by pollutant and source, 1990 rpt, 9198–124

Pollution (air) emissions factors, by detailed pollutant and source, data compilation, 1990 rpt, 9198–120

Pollution (air) indoor levels and emissions rates, by pollutant type and source, 1990 handbook, 3326–1.2

Pollution (air) levels for 6 pollutants, by source, 1970-89 and trends from 1940, annual rpt, 9194–13

Production and reserves of oil and gas, and coal production, by major country and world area, late 1930s-90, article, 9371–1.213

Production and reserves of oil, gas, and gas liquids, by State and substate area, 1990, annual rpt, 3164–46

Production and wellhead capacity for natural gas, by production area, 1980-89 and alternative forecasts 1990-91, biennial rpt, 3164–93

Production, deliverability, and flow capacity from large gas fields in selected States, projections and production trends, discontinued series, 3166–10

Production, dev, and distribution firms revenues and income, quarterly rpt, 3162–38

Production, prices, trade, use, reserves, pipeline finances, and wells classified, for natural and supplemental gas, by firm and State, monthly rpt with articles, 3162–4

Soviet Union, Eastern Europe, OECD, and selected other countries energy reserves, production, and use, and oil trade and revenue, 1960s-90, annual rpt, 9114–4.4

State and Metro Area Data Book, 1991 data compilation, 2328–54

Statistical Abstract of US, 1991 annual data compilation, 2324–1.19; 2324–1.25

Supply, demand, and distribution of energy, and regulatory impacts, series, 3166–6

Supply, demand, and prices, by fuel type and end-use sector, alternative projections 1989-2010, annual rpt, 3164–75

Supply, demand, and prices, by fuel type and end-use sector, projections and underlying assumptions, 1990-2010, annual rpt, 3164–90

Supply, demand, and prices, by fuel type and end-use sector, with foreign comparisons, 1990 and trends from 1949, annual rpt, 3164–74

Supply, demand, and prices, by fuel type, end-use sector, and country, detailed data, monthly rpt with articles, 3162–24

Supply, demand, and prices of energy, forecasts by resource type, quarterly rpt, 3162–34

Supply, demand, and prices of oil and gas, alternative projections 1989-2010, annual rpt, 3164–89

Natural gas and gas industry

Tax (income) returns of corporations, income and tax items by asset size and detailed industry, 1987, annual rpt, 8304–4

Tax (income) returns of corporations, income and tax items by asset size and detailed industry, 1988, annual rpt, 8304–21

Transportation energy use by mode, fuel supply, and demographic and economic factors of vehicle use, 1970s-89, annual rpt, 3304–5

Underground gas storage injections and withdrawals during heating season and offseason, and facility construction projects by company and location, 1970s-90, article, 3162–4.205

Utilities privately owned, detailed finances and operations by firm, 1989, annual rpt, 3164–23

see also Energy exploration and drilling
see also Liquefied petroleum gas
see also Natural gas exports and imports
see also Natural gas liquids
see also Natural gas prices
see also Natural gas reserves
see also Offshore oil and gas
see also Oil and gas leases
see also Pipelines
see also under By Commodity in the "Index by Categories"
see also under By Industry in the "Index by Categories"

Natural gas exports and imports

Eastern Europe and USSR natural gas trade, by country, monthly rpt, 9112–2

Exports and imports between US and outlying areas, by detailed commodity and mode of transport, 1990, annual rpt, 2424–11

Exports and imports of gas, by country of origin and destination, 1988, annual rpt, 3164–50.3

Exports and imports of US, by country and detailed commodity, monthly rpt, 2422–12

Exports and imports of US, by Harmonized System 6-digit commodity and country, 1990, annual rpt, 2424–13

Exports and imports of US, by transport mode, country, and SITC 1- to 3-digit commodity, 1990, annual rpt, 2424–12

Exports, imports, production, prices, use, reserves, and pipeline finances, for natural gas, by firm and State, monthly rpt with articles, 3162–4

Exports of US, detailed Schedule B commodities with countries of destination, 1990, annual rpt, 2424–10

Heating fuels production, imports, stocks, and prices, by selected PAD district and State, seasonal weekly rpt, 3162–45

Liquids (gas) supply, demand, and movement, by PAD district and State, 1990, annual rpt, 3164–2

Liquids (gas) supply, demand, trade, stocks, and refining, by detailed product and PAD district, monthly rpt with articles, 3162–6

Minerals Yearbook, 1988, Vol 3: foreign country reviews of production, trade, and policy, by commodity, annual rpt series, 5604–17

Natl Energy Strategy, natural gas imports of US by country, 1988 and projected to 2030, 3166–6.52

Index by Subjects and Names

Natl Energy Strategy plans for conservation and pollution reduction, impacts of technology and regulation proposals, projected 1990-2030, 3166–6.47

Supply, demand, and prices, by fuel type and end-use sector, alternative projections 1989-2010, annual rpt, 3164–75

Supply, demand, and prices, by fuel type and end-use sector, projections and underlying assumptions, 1990-2010, annual rpt, 3164–90

Supply, demand, and prices, by fuel type and end-use sector, with foreign comparisons, 1990 and trends from 1949, annual rpt, 3164–74

Supply, demand, and prices, by fuel type, end-use sector, and country, detailed data, monthly rpt with articles, 3162–24

Supply, demand, and prices of energy, forecasts by resource type, quarterly rpt, 3162–34

Supply, demand, and prices of oil and gas, alternative projections 1989-2010, annual rpt, 3164–89

Natural gas liquids

Exports and imports of natural gas and liquefied gas with 5 countries, and average price, by US firm, 1955-90, annual article, 3162–4.208

Exports and imports of US, by Harmonized System 6-digit commodity and country, 1990, annual rpt, 2424–13

Exports of US, detailed Schedule B commodities with countries of destination, 1990, annual rpt, 2424–10

Foreign and US natural gas plant liquids production, by country group and selected country, monthly rpt, 3162–42

Mineral industries census, 1987: finances and operations, by establishment characteristics, SIC 2- to 4-digit industry, and State, subject rpt, 2517–1

Mineral industries census, 1987: finances and operations, by SIC 2- to 4-digit industry, State, and county, census div rpt series, 2515–1

Minerals Yearbook, 1988, Vol 3: foreign country reviews of production, trade, and policy, by commodity, annual rpt series, 5604–17

Natl Energy Strategy, natural gas imports of US by country, 1988 and projected to 2030, 3166–6.52

Natl Energy Strategy, oil and gas reserves, 1988 and projected under alternative technology and policy assumptions to 2030, 3166–6.51

Natl Energy Strategy plans for conservation and pollution reduction, impacts of technology and regulation proposals, projected 1990-2030, 3166–6.47

Occupational injury and illness rates, by SIC 2- to 4-digit industry, 1989, annual rpt, 6844–1

Oil refinery operations and finances, with ownership changes, shutdowns, and reactivations, by firm, 1970s-90, 3168–119

Price indexes (producer), by stage of processing and detailed commodity, monthly rpt, 6762–6

Price indexes (producer), by stage of processing and detailed commodity, monthly 1990, annual rpt, 6764–2

Production and reserves of oil, gas, and gas liquids, by State and substate area, 1990, annual rpt, 3164–46

Statistical Abstract of US, 1991 annual data compilation, 2324–1.25

Supply, demand, and movement of crude oil, gas liquids, and refined products, by PAD district and State, 1990, annual rpt, 3164–2

Supply, demand, and prices, by fuel type and end-use sector, with foreign comparisons, 1990 and trends from 1949, annual rpt, 3164–74

Supply, demand, and prices of oil and gas, alternative projections 1989-2010, annual rpt, 3164–89

Supply, demand, trade, stocks, and refining of oil and gas liquids, by detailed product, State, and PAD district, monthly rpt with articles, 3162–6

Natural gas prices

Auto alternative fuels costs, emissions, health impacts, and characteristics, 1990 rpt, 9196–5.2; 9196–5.3

CPI by component for US city average, and by region, population size, and for 27 metro areas, monthly rpt, 6762–2

Electric power plants (steam) fuel receipts, costs, and quality, by fuel, plant, utility, and State, 1990, annual rpt, 3164–42

Electric power plants production, capacity, sales, and fuel stocks, use, and costs, by State, 1985-89, annual rpt, 3164–11

Electric power plants production, fuel use, stocks, and costs by fuel type, and sales, by State, monthly rpt with articles, 3162–35

Exports and imports of natural gas and liquefied gas with 5 countries, and average price, by US firm, 1955-90, annual article, 3162–4.208

Food marketing cost indexes, by expense category, monthly rpt with articles, 1502–4

Heating fuels production, imports, stocks, and prices, by selected PAD district and State, seasonal weekly rpt, 3162–45

Housing energy prices, by fuel and State, 1989 and forecast 1990-91, 3166–6.54

Natl Energy Strategy plans for conservation and pollution reduction, impacts of technology and regulation proposals, projected 1990-2030, 3166–6.47

Naval Petroleum and Oil Shale Reserves sales and contract prices, by purchaser and reserve, FY90, annual rpt, 3334–3

OECD energy prices, by fuel type and end use, for 10 countries, 1980-89 annual rpt, 3164–50.6

Prices and spending for fuel, by type, end-use sector, and State, 1989, annual rpt, 3164–64

Prices, production, trade, use, reserves, and pipeline company finances, for natural gas, by firm and State, monthly rpt with articles, 3162–4

Prices, supply, and demand, by fuel type and end-use sector, alternative projections 1989-2010, annual rpt, 3164–75

Prices, supply, and demand, by fuel type and end-use sector, projections and underlying assumptions, 1990-2010, annual rpt, 3164–90

Prices, supply, and demand, by fuel type and end-use sector, with foreign comparisons, 1990 and trends from 1949, annual rpt, 3164–74

Prices, supply, and demand of energy, forecasts by resource type, quarterly rpt, 3162–34

Prices, supply, and demand of oil and gas, alternative projections 1989-2010, annual rpt, 3164–89

Producer price indexes, by stage of processing and detailed commodity, monthly rpt, 6762–6

Producer price indexes, by stage of processing and detailed commodity, monthly 1990, annual rpt, 6764–2

Spot and futures prices of natural gas, daily press release, weekly data, 3162–44

Wholesale and wellhead prices to electric plants, and prices to residential customers, monthly rpt, 3162–24.9

Natural gas reserves

Alaska minerals resources, production, oil and gas leases, reserves, and exploratory wells, with maps and bibl, 1989, annual rpt, 5664–11

Field codes and locations, for oil and gas, 1990, annual listing, 3164–70

Field locations, for natural gas, as of Sept 1989, map, 3088–21

Foreign and US energy reserves, by type of fuel and country, as of Jan 1990, annual rpt, 3164–50.7

Foreign countries oil and gas reserves and discoveries, by country and country group, quarterly rpt, 3162–43

Gulf of Mexico oil and gas reserves, production, and leasing status, by location, 1989, annual rpt, 5734–6

Helium resources in storage and natural gas reserves, by State, 1950-89 and projected to 2020, biennial rpt, 5604–44

Methane production in coal fields by basin, and resources remaining, 1970s-89, article, 3162–4.201

Minerals Yearbook, 1988, Vol 3: foreign country reviews of production, trade, and policy, by commodity, annual rpt series, 5604–17

Natl Energy Strategy, oil and gas reserves, 1988 and projected under alternative technology and policy assumptions to 2030, 3166–6.51

Natl Energy Strategy plans for conservation and pollution reduction, impacts of technology and regulation proposals, projected 1990-2030, 3166–6.47

Offshore oil and gas reserves, and leasing and dev activity, periodic regional rpt series, 5736–3

Offshore oil and gas reserves of Fed Govt, production, leasing and exploration activity, revenue, and costs, by ocean area, FY90, annual rpt, 5734–4

Offshore oil and gas reserves on Federal leases, by ocean area, 1980-90, annual rpt, 5734–3.5

Pacific Ocean oil and gas production, reserves, and wells drilled by location, 1989, annual rpt, 5734–7

Pipeline interstate company gas reserves and production, 1963-90, annual article, 3162–4.209

Producers finances and operations, by energy type for US firms domestic and foreign operations, 1989, annual rpt, 3164–44.2

Public lands minerals resources and availability, State rpt series, 5606–7

Reserves and production of oil, gas, and gas liquids, by State and substate area, 1990, annual rpt, 3164–46

Reserves, production, prices, trade, use, reserves, and pipeline finances, for natural and supplemental gas, by firm and State, monthly rpt with articles, 3162–4

Resources of economically recoverable conventional oil and gas in US, by region and probability level, as of Dec 1986 and 1988, annual rpt, 3164–89

Soviet Union, Eastern Europe, OECD, and selected other countries energy reserves, production, and use, and oil trade and revenue, 1960s-90, annual rpt, 9114–4.4

State and Metro Area Data Book, 1991 data compilation, 2328–54

Supply, demand, and prices, by fuel type and end-use sector, projections and underlying assumptions, 1990-2010, annual rpt, 3164–90

Supply, demand, and prices, by fuel type and end-use sector, with foreign comparisons, 1990 and trends from 1949, annual rpt, 3164–74

Natural resources

Aerial survey R&D rpts, and sources of natural resource and environmental data, quarterly listing, 9502–7

Developing countries economic, population, and agricultural data, US and other aid sources, and AID activity, country rpt series, 9916–12

Foreign countries economic, social, political, and geographic summary data, by country, 1991, annual factbook, 9114–2

Overseas Business Reports: economic conditions, investment and export opportunities, and trade practices, country market research rpt series, 2046–6

see also Conservation of natural resources

see also Energy resources and consumption

see also Fish and fishing industry

see also Forests and forestry

see also Geothermal resources

see also Marine resources

see also Mines and mineral resources

see also Plants and vegetation

see also Reclamation of land

see also Severance taxes

see also State funding for natural resources and conservation

see also Strategic materials

see also Water area

see also Water power

see also Water resources development

see also Water supply and use

Naturalization

see Citizenship

Naturopathy

see Chiropractic and naturopathy

Nauru

Economic, social, political, and geographic summary data, by country, 1991, annual factbook, 9114–2

Exports and imports of US, by transport mode, country, and SITC 1- to 3-digit commodity, 1990, annual rpt, 2424–12

Human rights conditions in 170 countries, and US economic and military aid, 1990, annual rpt, 21384–3

Navajo and Hopi Indian Relocation Commission

Activities and caseloads, annual rpt, discontinued, 16004–1

Budget of US, obligations and authority by function, agency, and program, with summaries, analyses, and historical tables, FY92, annual rpt, 104–2

see also Office of Navajo and Hopi Indian Relocation

Naval Observatory

see U.S. Naval Observatory

Naval Oceanography Command

Hurricanes and tropical storms in Pacific and Indian Oceans, paths and surveillance, 1990, annual rpt, 3804–8

Naval Petroleum Reserves

Production and revenue by fuel type, sales by purchaser, and wells, by reserve, FY90, annual rpt, 3334–3

Naval stores

see Gum and wood chemicals

Naval vessels

Battleship *USS Iowa* explosion, safety and personnel mgmt issues, with technical analysis, FY89, GAO rpt, 26123–315

Budget of DOD, manpower needs, costs, and force readiness by service branch, FY92, annual rpt, 3504–1

Budget of DOD, organization, personnel, weapons, and property, by service branch, State, and country, 1991 annual summary rpt, 3504–13

Budget of DOD, procurement appropriations by item, service branch, and defense agency, FY90-93, annual rpt, 3544–32

Budget of DOD, programs, policies, and operations, FY90, annual rpt, 3544–2

Budget of DOD, weapons acquisition costs by system and service branch, FY91-93, annual rpt, 3504–2

Budget of Navy, personnel, procurement, and equipment, planned FY91-93, annual fact sheet, 3804–16

Coast Guard search and rescue missions, and lives and property lost and saved, by district and assisting unit, FY90, annual rpt, 7404–2

Customs Service activities, collections, entries processed by mode of transport, and seizures, FY86-90, annual rpt, 8144–1

Drug, immigration, and fisheries enforcement activities of Coast Guard, 2nd half FY91, semiannual rpt, 7402–4

Expenditures and obligations of DOD, by function and service branch, quarterly rpt, 3542–3

Foreign countries military aid and arms sales of US, by weapon type, as of Sept 1990, annual rpt, 3904–3

Foreign-flag ships subject to US control, by type and country of registry and construction, as of Jan. 1991, semiannual rpt, 7702–3

Homeport construction proposals of Navy, assignments and costs compared to existing ports, 1990s, GAO rpt, 26123–347

Manufacturing annual survey, 1989: finances and operations, by SIC 2- to 4-digit industry, series, 2506–15

Military Sealift Command shipping operations, finances, and personnel, FY90, annual rpt, 3804–14

Natl Defense Reserve Fleet inventory, by location, as of Jan 1991, semiannual listing, 7702–2

Naval vessels

Natl Defense Reserve Fleet inventory from FY45, and ships and tonnage by vessel type, with location, FY90, annual rpt, 7704-14.2; 7704-14.4

NATO and Japan military spending and indicators of ability to support common defense, by country, 1970s-89, annual rpt, 3544-28

Pacific basin US military personnel, dependents, aircraft, ships, and costs, by service branch and location, 1990, GAO rpt, 26123-357

Persian Gulf War costs to US by category and service branch, and offsetting contributions by allied country, monthly rpt, 102-3

Persian Gulf War costs to US by category and service branch, and offsetting contributions by allied country, various periods FY90-91, annual rpt, 104-7

Price indexes (producer), by stage of processing and detailed commodity, monthly 1990, annual rpt, 6764-2

Procurement, DOD prime contract awards by category, contract and contractor type, and service branch, FY81-1st half FY91, semiannual rpt, 3542-1

Procurement, DOD prime contract awards by category, contractor type, and State, FY88-90, annual rpt, 3544-11

Procurement, DOD prime contract awards by detailed procurement category, FY87-90, annual rpt, 3544-18

Procurement, DOD prime contract awards by size and type of contract, service branch, competitive status, category, and labor standard, FY90, annual rpt, 3544-19

Repair and modernization of Navy ships, programs costs and admin, FY87, GAO rpt, 26123-320

Soviet Union military weapons systems, presence, and force strengths, and compared to US, 1991 annual rpt, 3504-20

see also Nuclear-powered ships

see also Submarines

Navigation

Army Corps of Engineers water resources dev projects, characteristics, and costs, 1950s-89, biennial State rpt series, 3756-1

Army Corps of Engineers water resources dev projects, characteristics, and costs, 1950s-91, biennial State rpt series, 3756-2

Exports and imports of US, by Harmonized System 6-digit commodity and country, 1990, annual rpt, 2424-13

Exports of US, detailed Schedule B commodities with countries of destination, 1990, annual rpt, 2424-10

Fed Govt financial and nonfinancial domestic aid, 1991 base edition with supplements, annual listing, 104-5

Instruments and related products shipments, trade, use, and firms, by detailed type, 1989, annual Current Industrial Rpt, 2506-12.26

Manufacturing census, 1987: employment and shipments under Fed Govt contracts, by SIC 4-digit industry, 2497-7

Mariners Weather Log, quarterly journal, 2152-8

see also Aeronautical navigation

see also Lighthouses and lightships

see also Marine accidents and safety

see also Radar

Navy

Aircraft pilots hours flown, by pilot category, aircraft type, and flight purpose, for Navy, late 1980s, GAO rpt, 26123-332

Base closings, costs and savings for 71 Army and Navy bases, FY92-97, GAO rpt, 26123-341

Battleship *USS Iowa* explosion, safety and personnel mgmt issues, with technical analysis, FY89, GAO rpt, 26123-315

Criminal case processing in military courts, and prisoners by facility, by service branch, data compilation, 1991 annual rpt, 6064-6.6

Deaths by cause, age, race, and rank, and personnel captured and missing, by service branch, FY90, annual rpt, 3544-40

Drug and alcohol abuse education and treatment programs activity of Navy, semiannual tables, discontinued, 3802-6

Flag officers, captains awaiting promotion, and billets, for Navy by pay grade and rank, as of Feb 1991, GAO rpt, 26123-340

Health care facilities of DOD in US and abroad, beds, admissions, outpatient visits, and births, by service branch, quarterly rpt, 3542-15

Military Sealift Command shipping operations, finances, and personnel, FY90, annual rpt, 3804-14

Pacific basin US military personnel, dependents, aircraft, ships, and costs, by service branch and location, 1990, GAO rpt, 26123-357

Persian Gulf War costs to US by category and service branch, and offsetting contributions by allied country, monthly rpt, 102-3

Persian Gulf War costs to US by category and service branch, and offsetting contributions by allied country, various periods FY90-91, annual rpt, 104-7

Persian Gulf War Navy and Marine Corps reserves mobilized, 1990-91, GAO rpt, 26123-351

Personnel (civilian and military) of DOD, by service branch, major installation, and State, as of Sept 1990, annual rpt, 3544-7

Personnel active duty and recruit social, economic, and parents characteristics, by service branch and State, FY89, annual rpt, 3544-41

Personnel active duty strength, recruits, and reenlistment, by race, sex, and service branch, quarterly press release, 3542-7

Personnel, contracts, and payroll, by service branch and location, with top 5 contractors and maps, by State and country, FY90, annual rpt, 3544-29

Personnel needs, costs, and force readiness, by service branch, FY92, annual rpt, 3504-1

Personnel of DOD, and organization, budget, weapons, and property, by service branch, State, and country, 1991 annual summary rpt, 3504-13

Personnel, procurement, equipment, and budget of Navy, planned FY91-93, annual fact sheet, 3804-16

Personnel strengths, accessions, and attrition, detailed statistics for Navy and Naval Reserve, quarterly rpt, 3802-4

Personnel strengths, for active duty, civilians, and dependents, by service branch and US and foreign location, quarterly rpt, 3542-20

Personnel strengths, for active duty, civilians, and reserves, by service branch, FY90 and trends, annual rpt, 3544-1

Personnel strengths, for active duty, civilians, and reserves, by service branch, quarterly rpt, 3542-14

Personnel strengths, for active duty enlisted and officers, by sex and race, 1970s-90, GAO rpt, 26123-325

Personnel strengths in US and abroad, by service branch, world area, and country, quarterly press release, 3542-9

Personnel strengths, summary by service branch, monthly press release, 3542-2

Reserve forces personnel strengths and characteristics, by component, FY90, annual rpt, 3544-38

Reserve forces personnel strengths and characteristics, by component, quarterly rpt, 3542-4

ROTC programs enrollment, grads, staff, scholarships, and costs, by service branch, FY86-89, GAO rpt, 26123-337

Ship modernization program costs and admin, for Navy, FY87, GAO rpt, 26123-320

Training and education programs of DOD, funding, staff, students, and facilities, by service branch, FY92, annual rpt, 3504-5

Women military personnel on active and reserve duty, by demographic and service characteristics and service branch, FY89, annual chartbook, 3544-26

see also Department of Navy

see also Marine Corps

see also Naval Petroleum Reserves

see also Naval vessels

Neal, Edith G.

"Apparel Expenditures of Older Consumers", 1702-1.202

Near East

see Middle East

Nebraska

Banks (insured commercial and savings) deposits by instn, State, MSA, and county, as of June 1990, annual regional rpt, 9295-3.5

Carbon dioxide in atmosphere, North Central States economic and agricultural impacts, model descriptions and results, 1980s and projected to 2030, 3006-11.15

County Business Patterns, 1989: employment, establishments, and payroll, by SIC 2- to 4-digit industry and county, annual State rpt, 2326-8.29

DOD prime contract awards, by contractor, service branch, State, and city, FY90, annual rpt, 3544-22

Fed Govt spending in States and local areas, by type, State, county, and city, FY90, annual rpt, 2464-3

Fed Govt spending in States, by type, program, agency, and State, FY90, annual rpt, 2464-2

Index by Subjects and Names

Neoplasms

Financial and economic devs, Fed Reserve 10th District, quarterly rpt, 9381–16

HHS financial aid, by program, recipient, State, and city, FY90, annual regional listing, 4004–3.7

Hospital deaths of Medicare patients, actual and expected rates by diagnosis, and hospital characteristics, by instn, FY87-89, annual regional rpt, 4654–14.7

Income (personal) per capita and by source, and earnings by industry div, by State, MSA, and county, 1984-89, annual regional rpt, 2704–2.3

Jail adult and juvenile population, employment, spending, instn conditions, and inmate programs, by county and facility, 1988, regional rpt series, 6068–144.3

Marriages, divorces, and rates, by characteristics of spouses, State, and county, 1987 and trends from 1920, US Vital Statistics annual rpt, 4144–4

Mineral Industry Surveys, State reviews of production, 1990, preliminary annual rpt, 5614–6

Minerals Yearbook, 1989, Vol 2: State review of production and sales by commodity, and business activity, annual rpt, 5604–16.28

Minerals Yearbook, 1989, Vol 2: State reviews of production, sales, and firms, by commodity, and business activity, annual rpt, 5604–34

Physicians, by specialty, age, sex, and location of training and practice, 1989, State rpt, 4116–6.28

Population and housing census, 1990: population and housing characteristics, households, and land area, by county, subdiv, and place, State rpt, 2551–1.29

Population and housing census, 1990: voting age and total population by race, and housing units, by block, redistricting counts required under PL 94-171, State CD-ROM release, 2551–6.1

Population and housing census, 1990: voting age and total population by race, and housing units, by county and city, redistricting counts required under PL 94-171, State summary rpt, 2551–5.28

Statistical Abstract of US, 1991 annual data compilation, 2324–1

Supplemental Security Income payments and beneficiaries, by type of eligibility, State, and county, Dec 1989, annual rpt, 4744–27.7

Water (groundwater) supply, quality, chemistry, and use, 1987-88, regional rpt, 5666–28.3

Water supply and quality in streams and lakes, and groundwater levels in wells, by drainage basin, 1990, annual State rpt, 5666–10.26

see also Grand Island, Nebr.

see also Hastings, Nebr.

see also Omaha, Nebr.

see also under By State in the "Index by Categories"

Nederlof, Kees P.

"Ectopic Pregnancy Surveillance, U.S., 1970-87", 4202–7.202

Needleman, Jack

"Health Care Financing System and the Uninsured", 4658–54

Neenah, Wis.

see also under By SMSA or MSA in the "Index by Categories"

Neff, Evaline B.

"Library Programs: Library Services for Individuals with Limited English Proficiency, FY87", 4874–10

Neff, Liana

"Developing Countries' Trade with the European Community", 1524–4.2

Negotiable orders of withdrawal accounts

Banks (insured commercial) domestic and foreign office consolidated financial statements, monthly rpt, quarterly data, 9362–1.4

Banks (insured commercial and savings) finances, for foreign and domestic offices, by asset size, 1989, annual rpt, 9294–4.2

Debits, deposits, and deposit turnover, for commercial banks by type of account, monthly rpt, 9365–2.5

Savings instns insured by Savings Assn Insurance Fund, assets, liabilities, and deposit and loan activity, by conservatorship status, monthly rpt, 8432–1

Southeastern States, Fed Reserve 5th District insured commercial banks financial statements, by State, quarterly rpt, 9389–18

Negotiations

see Labor-management relations, general

see Labor-management relations in government

see Legal arbitration and mediation

see Strategic Arms Reduction Talks

see Treaties and conventions

Negroes

see Black Americans

Nehring, Richard F.

"Output and Input Subsidy Policy Options in Bangladesh", 1502–3.203

Neighborhood Reinvestment Corp.

Budget of US, authoritative financial statements with appropriations, outlays, and receipts, by category and agency, FY90, annual rpt, 8104–2.1

Budget of US, obligations and authority by function, agency, and program, with summaries, analyses, and historical tables, FY92, annual rpt, 104–2

Neighborhoods

Crime and crime-related issues, public opinion by respondent characteristics, data compilation, 1991 annual rpt, 6064–6.2

Financial instns location relation to ZIP code area income and minority population, by instn type for 5 cities, 1977-89, article, 9377–1.208

Mortgage applications by disposition, and secondary loan market sales by purchaser type, by applicant and neighborhood characteristics, 1990, article, 9362–1.206

Mortgage subsidy programs to promote neighborhood racial integration, effectiveness and impacts on housing prices, 1983-89, working paper, 9377–9.108

Quality of housing and neighborhoods, and rents paid under housing voucher and Section 8 certificate programs, 1985-87 survey, 5186–14.4

Quality of housing and neighborhoods, indicators and attitudes, by householder type and location, for 11 MSAs, 1984 survey, supplement, 2485–8

Quality of housing and neighborhoods, indicators and attitudes, by householder type and location, 1987, biennial rpt supplement, 2485–13

Quality of housing and neighborhoods, indicators and attitudes, by householder type and location, 1989, biennial rpt, 2485–12

Quality of housing and neighborhoods, indicators and attitudes, MSA surveys, series, 2485–6

see also Blocks, city

see also Census tracts

see also Community development

see also Wards, city

see also ZIP codes

Nelson, Charles T.

"Measuring the Effect of Benefits and Taxes on Income and Poverty: 1990", 2546–6.69

"Pensions: Worker Coverage and Retirement Benefits, 1987", 2546–20.18

Nelson, Cheryl

"Office Visits by Adolescents", 4146–8.199

Nelson, David M.

"Distribution and Abundance of Fishes and Invertebrates in Southeast Estuaries", 2176–7.25

Nelson, Douglas D.

"Textural and Mineralogic Analyses of Surficial Sediments Offshore of Myrtle Beach, S.C.", 5668–115

Nelson, Kenneth E.

"Beefpacking and Processing Plants: Computer-Assisted Cost Analysis", 1568–301

Nelson, Lyle

"Medigap Preferred Provider Organizations: Issues, Implications, and Early Experience", 4652–1.248

Nelson, Richard R.

"State Labor Legislation Enacted in 1990", 6722–1.209

Nelson, Scott H.

"Mental Health and Mental Illness", 4088–2

Nelson, William J., Jr.

"Workers' Compensation: Coverage, Benefits, and Costs, 1988", 4742–1.207

Neoplasms

Agent Orange exposure of Vietnam veterans, and other factors relation to dev of rare cancers, 1984-88, 4208–33

Alcohol (methanol) fuel substitution for gasoline, economic, environmental, and health impacts, projected 2000-2010, article, 9379–1.208

Asbestos in buildings, EPA aid for removal, occupational asbestos exposure cancer cases and deaths, and Catholic schools abatement costs, 1985-90, hearing, 25328–32

Auto alternative fuels costs, emissions, health impacts, and characteristics, series, 9196–5

Cases of cancer, deaths, and survival rates, by age, sex, race, and body site, 1973-88, annual rpt, 4474–35

Cases of cancer, knowledge, attitudes, and risk factors, 1987, CD-ROM, 4147–10.177

Chemotherapy drugs use for indications not listed on drug label, costs, and insurance reimbursement problems, 1990 physicians survey, GAO rpt, 26131–81

Neoplasms

Cuba and Cuban-born Americans cancer deaths, by body site, 1970s-83, article, 4042–3.205

Deaths and rates, by cause and age, preliminary 1989-90, US Vital Statistics annual rpt, 4144–7

Deaths and rates, by detailed cause and demographic characteristics, 1988 and trends from 1900, US Vital Statistics annual rpt, 4144–2

Deaths and rates for cancer, by body site, provisional data, monthly rpt, 4142–1.2

Fluoride exposure by source, and health risks and benefits, with research results, 1930s-89, 4048–36

Health condition and health care resources, use, and spending, 1950s-89, annual data compilation, 4144–11

Health maintenance organizations Medicare enrollees quality of care indicators compared to fee-for-service, demonstration projects results, mid 1980s, 4658–46

HHS financial aid, by program, recipient, State, and city, FY90, annual regional listings, 4004–3

Hospices operations, services, costs, and patient characteristics, for instns without Medicare certification, FY85-86, 4658–52

Hospices use by cancer patients, by service type, use of other facilities, patient and instn characteristics, and other indicators, local area study, 1980-85, 4658–53

Hospital charges and length of stay for heart and lung patients with selected nonsurgical procedures, for Maryland, FY84, article, 4652–1.204

Hospital discharges and length of stay, by diagnosis, patient and instn characteristics, procedure performed, and payment source, 1988, annual rpt, 4147–13.107

Hospital discharges and length of stay by region and diagnosis, and procedures performed, by age and sex, 1989, annual rpt, 4146–8.198

Hospital discharges by detailed diagnostic and procedure category, primary diagnosis, and length of stay, by age, sex, and region, 1988, annual rpt, 4147–13.105; 4147–13.108

Indian and Alaska Native disease and disorder cases, deaths, and health services use, by tribe, reservation, and Indian Health Service area, late 1950s-86, 4088–2

Indian Health Service facilities and use, and Indian health and other characteristics, by IHS region, 1980s-89, annual chartbook, 4084–7

Indian Health Service facilities, funding, operations, and Indian health and other characteristics, 1950s-90, annual chartbook, 4084–1

Indian Health Service, tribal, and contract facilities hospitalization, by diagnosis, age, sex, and service area, FY89, annual rpt, 4084–5

Indians and Alaska Natives chronic disease prevalence, for 8 conditions by age and sex, 1987, 4186–8.20

Minority group and women health condition, services use, payment sources, and health care labor force, by poverty status, 1940s-89, chartbook, 4118–56

Minority group cancer death rates, by body site, age, sex, and substate area, 1950s-80, atlas, 4478–78

Minority group health condition, services use, costs, and indicators of services need, 1950s-88, 4118–55

Natl Cancer Inst activities, grants by recipient, and cancer deaths and cases, FY90 and trends, annual rpt, 4474–13

Natl Cancer Inst epidemiology and biometry activities, FY90, annual rpt, 4474–29

Navy personnel radiation exposure on nuclear-powered vessels and at support facilities, and injury claims, 1950s-90, annual rpt, 3804–10

Older persons deaths in hospitals, nursing homes, and own home, by cause, age, marital status, and region, 1986, article, 4652–1.201

Preventive disease and health improvement goals and recommended activities for 2000, with trends 1970s-80s, 4048–10

Research on cancer epidemiology and biochemistry, semimonthly journal, 4472–1

Smoking involuntary exposure, health effects, and toxic substance levels of sidestream smoke, literature review, 1970s-90, 4248–91

State and Metro Area Data Book, 1991 data compilation, 2328–54

Statistical Abstract of US, 1991 annual data compilation, 2324–1.2

see also Carcinogens

see also under By Disease in the "Index by Categories"

Nepal

Agricultural exports of high-value commodities, indexes and sales by commodity, world area, and country, 1960s-86, 1528–323

Agricultural trade of US, by detailed commodity and country, 1989, annual rpt, 1524–8

Agricultural trade of US, by detailed commodity and country, 1990, semiannual rpt, 1522–4

AID economic aid to developing countries, obligations and disbursements by country, quarterly rpt, 9912–4

AID economic dev projects manpower training program for Nepal, effectiveness, 1950s-80s, 9916–3.62

AID loans repayment status and terms by program and country, and status of predecessor agency loans, quarterly rpt, 9912–3

Background Notes, summary social, political, and economic data, 1990 rpt, 7006–2.15

Economic and military aid and loans from US and intl agencies, by program and country, FY46-90, annual rpt, 9914–5

Economic and social conditions of developing countries from 1960s, and Intl Dev Cooperation Agency and AID activities and funding, FY90-92, annual rpt, 9904–4

Economic conditions, income, production, prices, employment, and trade, 1991 periodic country rpt, 2046–4.12

Economic, social, political, and geographic summary data, by country, 1991, annual factbook, 9114–2

Exports and imports of US, by transport mode, country, and SITC 1- to 3-digit commodity, 1990, annual rpt, 2424–12

Exports of US, detailed Schedule B commodities with countries of destination, 1990, annual rpt, 2424–10

Human rights conditions in 170 countries, and US economic and military aid, 1990, annual rpt, 21384–3

Military aid of US, arms sales, and training programs costs and budget requests, by program, world region, and country, FY90-92, annual rpt, 7144–13

UN voting record and share of votes in agreement with US, by issue, country, and world area, 1990, annual rpt, 7004–18

see also under By Foreign Country in the "Index by Categories"

Nepheline syenite

see Chemicals and chemical industry

Nervous system disorders

see Neurological disorders

Netherlands

Agricultural exports of high-value commodities, indexes and sales by commodity, world area, and country, 1960s-86, 1528–323

Agricultural production, prices, and trade, by country, 1970s-90, and forecast 1991, annual world region rpt, 1524–4.4

Agricultural production, trade, and policies in foreign countries, summary data by country, 1989-90, annual factbook, 1924–12

Agricultural trade of US, by detailed commodity and country, 1989, annual rpt, 1524–8

Agricultural trade of US, by detailed commodity and country, 1990, semiannual rpt, 1522–4

AID loans repayment status and terms by program and country, and status of predecessor agency loans, quarterly rpt, 9912–3

Background Notes, summary social, political, and economic data, 1991 rpt, 7006–2.25

Businesses (foreign) activity in US, income tax returns, assets, and income statement items, by industry div and selected country, 1986-87, article, 8302–2.205

Corporations in US under foreign control, income tax returns, assets and income statement items by industry div, country, and world area, 1988, article, 8302–2.219

Economic and military aid and loans from US and intl agencies, by program and country, FY46-90, annual rpt, 9914–5

Economic and monetary trends, compounded annual rates of change for US and 10 major trading partners, quarterly rpt, 9391–7

Economic conditions in USSR, Eastern Europe, OECD, and selected other countries, 1960s-90, annual rpt, 9114–4

Economic conditions, income, production, prices, employment, and trade, 1991 periodic country rpt, 2046–4.60

Economic conditions, policy, and trade practices, by country, 1988-90, annual rpt, 21384–5

Economic, social, political, and geographic summary data, by country, 1991, annual factbook, 9114–2

Energy prices, by fuel type and end use, for 10 countries, 1980-89 annual rpt, 3164–50.6

Exports and imports of NATO members with PRC, by country, 1987-90, annual rpt, 7144–14

Index by Subjects and Names

Neurological disorders

Exports and imports of OECD members, by country, 1989, annual rpt, 7144–10

Exports and imports of US, by Harmonized System 6-digit commodity and country, 1990, annual rpt, 2424–13

Exports and imports of US, by selected country, country group, and commodity group, 1990, annual rpt, 2044–37

Exports and imports of US, by transport mode, country, and SITC 1- to 3-digit commodity, 1990, annual rpt, 2424–12

Exports and imports of US with EC by country, and total agricultural trade, selected years 1958-90, annual rpt, 7144–7

Exports of US, detailed Schedule B commodities with countries of destination, 1990, annual rpt, 2424–10

Farmland in US owned by foreigners, holdings, acreage, and value by land use, owner country, State, and county, 1990, annual rpt, 1584–3

GNP and GNP growth for OECD members, by country, 1980-90, annual rpt, 7144–8

Human rights conditions in 170 countries, and US economic and military aid, 1990, annual rpt, 21384–3

Interest and exchange rates, security yields, and stock indexes, for selected foreign countries, weekly chartbook, 9365–1.5

Intl transactions of US with 9 countries, 1986-88, *Survey of Current Business*, monthly rpt, annual table, 2702–1.26

Investment (foreign direct) in US, by industry group of US affiliate and country of parent firm, 1980-86, 2708–41

Investment (foreign direct) in US, major transactions by type, industry, country, and US location, 1989, annual rpt, 2044–20

Labor conditions, union coverage, and work accidents, 1990 annual country rpt, 6366–4.2

Military reserve forces structure and training, for US and 5 European countries, as of 1990, GAO rpt, 26123–358

Multinatl firms US affiliates, finances, and operations, by industry, world area of parent firm, and State, 1988-89, annual rpt, 2704–4

Multinatl US firms and foreign affiliates finances and operations, by industry and world area of parent firm, 1989 benchmark survey, preliminary annual rpt, 2704–5

Multinatl US firms foreign affiliates, income statement items by country and world area, 1986, biennial article, 8302–2.212

Nuclear power generation in US and 20 countries, monthly rpt, 3162–24.10

Nuclear power plant capacity, generation, and operating status, by plant and foreign and US location, 1990 and projected to 2030, annual rpt, 3164–57

Oil exports to US by OPEC and non-OPEC countries, monthly rpt, 3162–24.3

Oil production, trade, use, and stocks, by selected country and country group, monthly rpt, 3162–42

Older persons health condition and care research, data availability and collection methodology, for US and selected countries, 1988 conf, 4147–5.6

Paper (coated groundwood) from 9 countries at less than fair value, injury to US

industry, investigation with background financial and operating data, 1991 rpt, 9886–14.306

Rayon yarn (high-tenacity filament) from 2 countries at less than fair value, injury to US industry, investigation with background financial and operating data, 1991 rpt, 9886–14.331

Spacecraft and satellite launches since 1957, quarterly listing, 9502–2

Tax revenue, by level of govt and type of tax, for OECD countries, mid 1960s-89, annual rpt, 10044–1.2

Travel to US, trade shows and other promotional activities, with magazine ad costs and circulation, for selected countries, 1991-92, annual rpt, 2904–11

UN voting record and share of votes in agreement with US, by issue, country, and world area, 1990, annual rpt, 7004–18

see also Netherlands Antilles

see also under By Foreign Country in the "Index by Categories"

Netherlands Antilles

Agricultural exports of US, impacts of foreign agricultural and trade policy, with data by commodity and country, 1989, annual rpt, 1924–8

Agricultural trade of US, by detailed commodity and country, 1989, annual rpt, 1524–8

Agricultural trade of US, by detailed commodity and country, 1990, semiannual rpt, 1522–4

Businesses (foreign) activity in US, income tax returns, assets, and income statement items, by industry div and selected country, 1986-87, article, 8302–2.205

Corporations in US under foreign control, income tax returns, assets and income statement items by industry div, country, and world area, 1988, article, 8302–2.219

Economic, social, political, and geographic summary data, by country, 1991, annual factbook, 9114–2

Exports and imports of US, by selected country, country group, and commodity group, 1990, annual rpt, 2044–37

Exports and imports of US, by transport mode, country, and SITC 1- to 3-digit commodity, 1990, annual rpt, 2424–12

Farmland in US owned by foreigners, holdings, acreage, and value by land use, owner country, State, and county, 1990, annual rpt, 1584–3

Investment (direct) incentives of Caribbean Basin Initiative, economic impacts, with finances and employment by country, 1984-90, 2048–141

Multinatl US firms and foreign affiliates finances and operations, by industry and world area of parent firm, 1989 benchmark survey, preliminary annual rpt, 2704–5

Multinatl US firms foreign affiliates, income statement items by country and world area, 1986, biennial article, 8302–2.212

Oil exports to US by OPEC and non-OPEC countries, monthly rpt, 3162–24.3

Networks

see Computer networks

see Information storage and retrieval systems

see Public broadcasting

see Radio

see Television

Neugut, Alfred I.

"Association of Asbestos Exposure with Colorectal Adenomatous Polyps and Cancer", 4472–1.238

"Obesity and Colorectal Adenomatous Polyps", 4472–1.206

Neunlist, Lindsay L.

"Market Cycles and Their Effect on Real Estate Lending by Credit Unions: Case Study of Region I", 9536–1.6

Neurological disorders

Cancer (brain and central nervous system) cases and rates, by whether confirmed by radiography alone, for Connecticut, 1960s-88, article, 4472–1.234

Cancer cases, deaths, and survival rates, by sex, race, age, and body site, 1973-88, annual rpt, 4474–35

Cancer death rates of minorities, by body site, age, sex, and substate area, 1950s-80, atlas, 4478–78

Cancer deaths and rates, by body site, provisional data, monthly rpt, 4142–1.2

Cases of acute and chronic conditions, disability, absenteeism, and health services use, by selected characteristics, 1987, CD-ROM, 4147–10.177

Cognitive impairment prevalence, accuracy of estimates derived from natl surveys, 1991 rpt, 4186–7.7

Deaths and rates, by detailed cause and demographic characteristics, 1988 and trends from 1900, US Vital Statistics annual rpt, 4144–2

Drug abuse residual neurological, behavioral, and cognitive effects, 1989 conf, 4498–69

HHS financial aid, by program, recipient, State, and city, FY90, annual regional listings, 4004–3

Hospital discharges and length of stay, by diagnosis, patient and instn characteristics, procedure performed, and payment source, 1988, annual rpt, 4147–13.107

Hospital discharges and length of stay by region and diagnosis, and procedures performed, by age and sex, 1989, annual rpt, 4146–8.198

Hospital discharges by detailed diagnostic and procedure category, primary diagnosis, and length of stay, by age, sex, and region, 1988, annual rpt, 4147–13.105; 4147–13.108

Hospitals for mental health care of States and counties, patients and admissions by age, diagnosis, and State, FY89, annual rpt, 4504–2

Hospitals for mental health care, private instns patients characteristics, 1986, 4506–3.47

Indian Health Service, tribal, and contract facilities hospitalization, by diagnosis, age, sex, and service area, FY89, annual rpt, 4084–5

Infectious notifiable disease cases, by age, race, and State, and deaths, 1930s-90, annual rpt, 4204–1

Lead levels in environment, sources of emissions and exposure, and health effects, literature review, 1990 rpt, 9198–84

Morbidity and Mortality Weekly Report, infectious notifiable disease cases by State, and public health issues, 4202–1

Neurological disorders

Natl Inst of Neurological Disorders and Stroke activities, and disorder cases, FY90, annual rpt, 4474–25

Nursing home residents with mental disorders, by disorder type and resident and instn characteristics, 1985, 4147–13.106

Older persons with functional limitations, cognitive disorders and disruptive behavior by type and severity, 1984, 4186–7.10

Research in neurosciences and public policy issues, series, 26356–9

VA mental health care services, staff, research, and training programs, 1991 biennial listing, 8704–2

Veterans disability and death compensation cases of VA, by entitlement type, period of service, sex, age, and State, FY89, annual rpt, 8604–7

Veterans health care, patients, visits, costs, and operating beds, by VA and contract facility, and region, quarterly rpt, 8602–4

see also Alzheimer's disease

see also Learning disabilities

see also Mental health and illness

see also Rabies

see also Spinal cord injuries

see also under By Disease in the "Index by Categories"

Nevada

- Air traffic, and passenger and freight enplanements, by airport, 1960s-90 and projected to 2010, hub area rpt, 7506–7.41
- Banks (insured commercial and savings) deposits by instn, State, MSA, and county, as of June 1990, annual regional rpt, 9295–3.6
- County Business Patterns, 1989: employment, establishments, and payroll, by SIC 2- to 4-digit industry and county, annual State rpt, 2326–8.30
- DOD prime contract awards, by contractor, service branch, State, and city, FY90, annual rpt, 3544–22
- Earthquakes of San Andreas Fault system, location and seismic characteristics, by event, 1769-1989, 5668–123
- Fed Govt spending in States and local areas, by type, State, county, and city, FY90, annual rpt, 2464–3
- Fed Govt spending in States, by type, program, agency, and State, FY90, annual rpt, 2464–2
- Gemstone production in selected States, Mineral Industry Surveys, 1988-90, advance annual rpt, 5614–5.10
- HHS financial aid, by program, recipient, State, and city, FY90, annual regional listing, 4004–3.9
- Hospital deaths of Medicare patients, actual and expected rates by diagnosis, and hospital characteristics, by instn, FY87-89, annual regional rpt, 4654–14.9
- Income (personal) per capita and by source, and earnings by industry div, by State, MSA, and county, 1984-89, annual regional rpt, 2704–2.5
- Jail adult and juvenile population, employment, spending, instn conditions, and inmate programs, by county and facility, 1988, regional rpt series, 6068–144.5

Marriages, divorces, and rates, by characteristics of spouses, State, and county, 1987 and trends from 1920, US Vital Statistics annual rpt, 4144–4

- Mineral industries census, 1987: finances and operations, by SIC 2- to 4-digit industry, State, and county, census div rpt, 2515–1.8
- Mineral Industry Surveys, State reviews of production, 1990, preliminary annual rpt, 5614–6
- Minerals resources and availability on public lands, 1985, State rpt, 5606–7.6
- *Minerals Yearbook, 1989*, Vol 2: State review of production and sales by commodity, and business activity, annual rpt, 5604–16.29
- *Minerals Yearbook, 1989*, Vol 2: State reviews of production, sales, and firms, by commodity, and business activity, annual rpt, 5604–34
- Physicians, by specialty, age, sex, and location of training and practice, 1989, State rpt, 4116–6.29
- Population and housing census, 1990: population and housing characteristics, households, and land area, by county, subdiv, and place, State rpt, 2551–1.30
- Population and housing census, 1990: voting age and total population by race, and housing units, by block, redistricting counts required under PL 94-171, State CD-ROM release, 2551–6.8
- Population and housing census, 1990: voting age and total population by race, and housing units, by county and city, redistricting counts required under PL 94-171, State summary rpt, 2551–5.29
- Radioactive low-level waste disposal activities of States and interstate compacts, with data by disposal facility and reactor, 1989, annual rpt, 3354–14
- *Statistical Abstract of US*, 1991 annual data compilation, 2324–1
- Supplemental Security Income payments and beneficiaries, by type of eligibility, State, and county, Dec 1989, annual rpt, 4744–27.9
- Truck accidents in Nevada, by cause, 1988, 25268–78
- Water (groundwater) supply, quality, chemistry, other characteristics, and use, 1991 regional rpt, 5666–25.13
- Water quality, chemistry, hydrology, and other characteristics, 1989 local area study, 5666–27.6
- Water quality, chemistry, hydrology, and other characteristics, 1990 local area study, 5666–27.12; 5666–27.14
- Water resources dev projects of Army Corps of Engineers, characteristics, and costs, 1950s-89, biennial State rpt, 3756–1.29
- Water supply and quality in streams and lakes, and groundwater levels in wells, by drainage basin, 1988, annual State rpt, 5666–16.27
- Water supply, and snow survey results, monthly State rpt, 1266–2.6
- Water supply, and snow survey results, 1990, annual State rpt, 1264–14.6
- Water supply in Nevada and eastern California, streamflow, precipitation, and reservoir storage, 1991 water year, annual rpt, 1264–8

see also Las Vegas, Nev.

see also Tonopah, Nev.

see also under By State in the "Index by Categories"

Nevel, Robert L., Jr.

"Timber Industries of Delaware, 1985", 1206–15.10

New Bedford, Mass.

Fish and shellfish catch, wholesale receipts, prices, trade, and other market activities, weekly regional rpt, 2162–6.5

see also under By SMSA or MSA in the "Index by Categories"

New Bern, N.C.

Wages by occupation, for office and plant workers, 1991 survey, periodic MSA rpt, 6785–3.9

New Britain, Conn.

see also under By SMSA or MSA in the "Index by Categories"

New Caledonia

- Economic, social, political, and geographic summary data, by country, 1991, annual factbook, 9114–2
- Exports and imports of US, by transport mode, country, and SITC 1- to 3-digit commodity, 1990, annual rpt, 2424–12

New England

see Northeast States

see under By Census Division in the "Index by Categories"

New England Aquarium

"Marine Mammal Strandings: The New England Aquarium Stranding Network", 14738–8

New Guinea

see Papua New Guinea

New Hampshire

- Banks (insured commercial and savings) deposits by instn, State, MSA, and county, as of June 1990, annual regional rpt, 9295–3.1
- County Business Patterns, 1989: employment, establishments, and payroll, by SIC 2- to 4-digit industry and county, annual State rpt, 2326–8.31
- DOD prime contract awards, by contractor, service branch, State, and city, FY90, annual rpt, 3544–22
- Economic indicators for New England States, Fed Reserve 1st District, monthly rpt, 9373–2
- Fed Govt spending in States and local areas, by type, State, county, and city, FY90, annual rpt, 2464–3
- Fed Govt spending in States, by type, program, agency, and State, FY90, annual rpt, 2464–2
- HHS financial aid, by program, recipient, State, and city, FY90, annual regional listing, 4004–3.1
- Hospital deaths of Medicare patients, actual and expected rates by diagnosis, and hospital characteristics, by instn, FY87-89, annual regional rpt, 4654–14.1
- Income (personal) per capita and by source, and earnings by industry div, by State, MSA, and county, 1984-89, annual regional rpt, 2704–2.2
- Jail adult and juvenile population, employment, spending, instn conditions, and inmate programs, by county and facility, 1988, regional rpt series, 6068–144.2

Index by Subjects and Names

New Mexico

Marriages, divorces, and rates, by characteristics of spouses, State, and county, 1987 and trends from 1920, US Vital Statistics annual rpt, 4144–4

Mineral Industry Surveys, State reviews of production, 1990, preliminary annual rpt, 5614–6

Minerals Yearbook, 1989, Vol 2: State review of production and sales by commodity, and business activity, annual rpt, 5604–16.30

Minerals Yearbook, 1989, Vol 2: State reviews of production, sales, and firms, by commodity, and business activity, annual rpt, 5604–34

Natural resources use and mgmt, New Hampshire and Vermont public opinion, 1991 rpt, 1208–371

Physicians, by specialty, age, sex, and location of training and practice, 1989, State rpt, 4116–6.30

Population and housing census, 1990: population and housing characteristics, households, and land area, by county, subdiv, and place, State rpt, 2551–1.31

Population and housing census, 1990: voting age and total population by race, and housing units, by block, redistricting counts required under PL 94-171, State CD-ROM release, 2551–6.3

Population and housing census, 1990: voting age and total population by race, and housing units, by county and city, redistricting counts required under PL 94-171, State summary rpt, 2551–5.30

Savings instns, FHLB 1st District members financial operations compared to banks, and related economic and housing indicators, bimonthly rpt with articles, 9302–4

Statistical Abstract of US, 1991 annual data compilation, 2324–1

Supplemental Security Income payments and beneficiaries, by type of eligibility, State, and county, Dec 1989, annual rpt, 4744–27.1

Water supply and quality in streams and lakes, and groundwater levels in wells, by drainage basin, 1990, annual State rpt, 5666–10.28

Water supply in northeastern US, precipitation and stream runoff by station, monthly rpt, 2182–3

see also under By State in the "Index by Categories"

New Haven, Conn.

see also under By City and By SMSA or MSA in the "Index by Categories"

New Hebrides

see Vanuatu

New Jersey

AIDS patient home and community services under Medicaid waiver in 6 States, 1988-89, article, 4652–1.216

Banks (insured commercial and savings) deposits by instn, State, MSA, and county, as of June 1990, annual regional rpt, 9295–3.1

County Business Patterns, 1989: employment, establishments, and payroll, by SIC 2- to 4-digit industry and county, annual State rpt, 2326–8.32

Cranberry production, prices, use, and acreage; for selected States, 1989-90 and forecast 1991, annual rpt, 1621–18.4

DOD prime contract awards, by contractor, service branch, State, and city, FY90, annual rpt, 3544–22

Employment growth and unemployment rates, Fed Reserve 3rd District, quarterly rpt, 9387–10

Estuary eutrophication and algal blooms, causes and environmental effects, 1991 conf, 2176–7.22

Fed Govt spending in States and local areas, by type, State, county, and city, FY90, annual rpt, 2464–3

Fed Govt spending in States, by type, program, agency, and State, FY90, annual rpt, 2464–2

HHS financial aid, by program, recipient, State, and city, FY90, annual regional listing, 4004–3.2

Hospital deaths of Medicare patients, actual and expected rates by diagnosis, and hospital characteristics, by instn, FY87-89, annual regional rpt, 4654–14.2

Housing census, 1990: inventory, occupancy, and costs, State fact sheet, 2326–21.32

Income (personal) per capita and by source, and earnings by industry div, by State, MSA, and county, 1984-89, annual regional rpt, 2704–2.2

Jail adult and juvenile population, employment, spending, instn conditions, and inmate programs, by county and facility, 1988, regional rpt series, 6068–144.2

Marriages, divorces, and rates, by characteristics of spouses, State, and county, 1987 and trends from 1920, US Vital Statistics annual rpt, 4144–4

Medicaid demonstration projects evaluation, for 6 States, 1988 rpt, 4658–45

Mineral Industry Surveys, State reviews of production, 1990, preliminary annual rpt, 5614–6

Minerals Yearbook, 1989, Vol 2: State review of production and sales by commodity, and business activity, annual rpt, 5604–16.31

Minerals Yearbook, 1989, Vol 2: State reviews of production, sales, and firms, by commodity, and business activity, annual rpt, 5604–34

Physicians, by specialty, age, sex, and location of training and practice, 1989, State rpt, 4116–6.31

Pollution (marine) bacterial levels, and beach closings due to contamination and medical waste, for New York and New Jersey, 1987-89, hearing, 21568–50

Pollution levels in New York Bight, sources, treatment costs, economic losses, and environmental and health effects, 1990 conf, 9208–131

Population and housing census, 1990: population and housing characteristics, households, and land area, by county, subdiv, and place, State rpt, 2551–1.32

Population and housing census, 1990: voting age and total population by race, and housing units, by block, redistricting counts required under PL 94-171, State CD-ROM release, 2551–6.10

Population and housing census, 1990: voting age and total population by race, and housing units, by county and city, redistricting counts required under PL 94-171, State summary rpt, 2551–5.31

Radioactivity levels at former AEC and Manhattan Project research and storage sites and nearby areas, 1985-86, 3006–9.13

Radioactivity levels at former AEC and Manhattan Project research and storage sites and nearby areas, 1987, 3006–9.10; 3006–9.11

Radioactivity levels at former AEC and Manhattan Project research and storage sites and nearby areas, 1988, 3006–9.9; 3006–9.12; 3006–9.14

Statistical Abstract of US, 1991 annual data compilation, 2324–1

Supplemental Security Income payments and beneficiaries, by type of eligibility, State, and county, Dec 1989, annual rpt, 4744–27.2

Timber resources and removals, by species, ownership class, and county, 1987, State rpt, 1206–12.14

Unemployment insurance reemployment and training services, and bonus for early reemployment, New Jersey demonstration project results, 1986-90, 6406–6.32

Water supply and quality in streams and lakes, and groundwater levels in wells, by drainage basin, 1990, annual State rpt, 5666–10.29

Wetlands acreage, resources, soil and water properties, and conservation efforts, by wetland type, 1987 State rpt, 5506–11.1

see also Bergen County, N.J.

see also Hunterdon County, N.J.

see also Middlesex County, N.J.

see also Monmouth County, N.J.

see also Newark, N.J.

see also Ocean County, N.J.

see also Passaic, N.J.

see also Somerset County, N.J.

see also Trenton, N.J.

see also under By State in the "Index by Categories"

New London, Conn.

see also under By SMSA or MSA in the "Index by Categories"

New Mexico

AIDS patient home and community services under Medicaid waiver in 6 States, 1988-89, article, 4652–1.216

Banks (insured commercial and savings) deposits by instn, State, MSA, and county, as of June 1990, annual regional rpt, 9295–3.6

Coal production and mines by county, prices, productivity, miners, and reserves, by mining method and State, 1989-90, annual rpt, 3164–25

County Business Patterns, 1989: employment, establishments, and payroll, by SIC 2- to 4-digit industry and county, annual State rpt, 2326–8.33

DOD prime contract awards, by contractor, service branch, State, and city, FY90, annual rpt, 3544–22

Employment by industry div, earnings, and hours, by southwestern State, monthly rpt, 6962–2

Fed Govt spending in States and local areas, by type, State, county, and city, FY90, annual rpt, 2464–3

Fed Govt spending in States, by type, program, agency, and State, FY90, annual rpt, 2464–2

New Mexico

Financial and economic devs, Fed Reserve 10th District, quarterly rpt, 9381–16

HHS financial aid, by program, recipient, State, and city, FY90, annual regional listing, 4004–3.6

Hispanic Americans in counties bordering Mexico, by selected characteristics, 1980, Current Population Rpt, 2546–2.159

Hospital deaths of Medicare patients, actual and expected rates by diagnosis, and hospital characteristics, by instn, FY87-89, annual regional rpt, 4654–14.6

Income (personal) per capita and by source, and earnings by industry div, by State, MSA, and county, 1984-89, annual regional rpt, 2704–2.5

Jail adult and juvenile population, employment, spending, instn conditions, and inmate programs, by county and facility, 1988, regional rpt series, 6068–144.5

Land Mgmt Bur activities in Southwestern US, FY90, annual rpt, 5724–15

Marriages, divorces, and rates, by characteristics of spouses, State, and county, 1987 and trends from 1920, US Vital Statistics annual rpt, 4144–4

Methane production in coal fields by basin, and resources remaining, 1970s-89, article, 3162–4.201

Mineral industries census, 1987: finances and operations, by SIC 2- to 4-digit industry, State, and county, census div rpt, 2515–1.8

Mineral Industry Surveys, State reviews of production, 1990, preliminary annual rpt, 5614–6

Minerals Yearbook, 1989, Vol 2 rpts: State review of production and sales by commodity, and business activity, annual rpt, 5604–16.32

Minerals Yearbook, 1989, Vol 2: State reviews of production, sales, and firms, by commodity, and business activity, annual rpt, 5604–34

Natural gas production and wellhead capacity, by production area, 1980-89 and alternative forecasts 1990-91, biennial rpt, 3164–93

Physicians, by specialty, age, sex, and location of training and practice, 1989, State rpt, 4116–6.32

Population and housing census, 1990: population and housing characteristics, households, and land area, by county, subdiv, and place, State rpt, 2551–1.33

Population and housing census, 1990: voting age and total population by race, and housing units, by block, redistricting counts required under PL 94-171, State CD-ROM release, 2551–6.7

Population and housing census, 1990: voting age and total population by race, and housing units, by county and city, redistricting counts required under PL 94-171, State summary rpt, 2551–5.32

Potash production, prices, trade, use, and sales, 1990 crop year, Mineral Industry Surveys, annual rpt, 5614–19

Statistical Abstract of US, 1991 annual data compilation, 2324–1

Supplemental Security Income payments and beneficiaries, by type of eligibility, State, and county, Dec 1989, annual rpt, 4744–27.6

Water (groundwater) supply, quality, chemistry, and use, 1986-87, local area rpt, 5666–28.7

Water (groundwater) supply, quality, chemistry, and use, 1987-88, regional rpt, 5666–28.3

Water (groundwater) supply, quality, chemistry, other characteristics, and use, 1991 regional rpt, 5666–25.13

Water quality, chemistry, hydrology, and other characteristics, 1989 local area study, 5666–27.17

Water supply and quality in streams and lakes, and groundwater levels in wells, by drainage basin, 1990, annual State rpt, 5666–10.30

Water supply, and snow survey results, monthly State rpt, 1266–2.11

Water supply, and snow survey results, 1990, annual State rpt, 1264–14.7

Wetlands (riparian) acreage, and Bur of Land Mgmt activities, mgmt plans, and scientific staff, 1990 State rpt, 5726–8.2

Wildlife mgmt activities and funding, acreage by habitat type, and scientific staff, for Bur of Land Mgmt, 1989 State rpt, 5726–7.1

see also Alamogordo, N.Mex.

see also Las Cruces, N.Mex.

see also under By State in the "Index by Categories"

New Orleans, La.

Drug abuse indicators for selected metro areas, research results, data collection, and policy issues, 1991 semiannual conf, 4492–5

Drug test results at arrest, by drug type, offense, and sex, for selected urban areas, quarterly rpt, 6062–3

Fish and shellfish catch, wholesale receipts, prices, trade, and other market activities, weekly regional rpt, 2162–6.3

Fruit and vegetable shipments, and arrivals in US and Canada cities, by mode of transport and State and country of origin, 1990, annual rpt, 1311–4.2

Housing starts and completions authorized by building permits in 40 MSAs, quarterly rpt, 2382–9

Wages by occupation, for office and plant workers, 1990 survey, periodic MSA rpt, 6785–11.2

see also under By City and By SMSA or MSA in the "Index by Categories"

New York Bight

Fish population and disease, and pollutant levels, near New York Bight sewage sludge dumpsite, 1986-90, last issue of annual rpt, 2164–19

Pollutant concentrations in coastal and estuarine sediments, by contaminant and selected site, 1984-89, 2176–3.13

Pollution levels in New York Bight, sources, treatment costs, economic losses, and environmental and health effects, 1990 conf, 9208–131

New York City

AIDS knowledge, attitudes, and transmission prevention practices of physicians and RNs, 1990-91, 4186–9.11

Airline market entry impacts of carrier control of airports, facility and aircraft availability, noise regulation, and other barriers, late 1980s and projected to 1997, 7308–199.8

Index by Subjects and Names

Banks (commercial) debits to demand deposits, and demand deposits and turnover, monthly rpt, 9365–2.5

Banks balance sheets, by Fed Reserve District, for major banks in NYC, and for US branches and agencies of foreign banks, weekly rpt, 9365–1.3

Census of Population and Housing, 1990: New York State and NYC data collection activities and status, hearing, 21628–90

Child welfare programs funding by source, and foster care cases, problems, and program operations for selected States, 1970s-90, hearings, 21788–202

CPI by component for US city average, and by region, population size, and for 15 metro areas, monthly rpt, 6762–1

CPI by component for US city average, and by region, population size, and for 27 metro areas, monthly rpt, 6762–2

Drug abuse indicators for selected metro areas, research results, data collection, and policy issues, 1991 semiannual conf, 4492–5

Drug abuse relation to violent and criminal behavior, with data on street gang activity and selected population groups, 1989 conf, 4498–70

Drug enforcement personnel, arrests, and seizures, for NYC, 1985-90, hearing, 25528–117

Drug test results at arrest, by drug type, offense, and sex, for selected urban areas, quarterly rpt, 6062–3

Firearm purchasers criminal records checks, and firearms use in crime, with data by State, 1987-90, 26358–244

Fish and shellfish catch, wholesale receipts, prices, trade, and other market activities, weekly regional rpt, 2162–6.3; 2162–6.5

Foster care placements, discharges, and returns to care, by selected characteristics of children, and length of stay factors, 1985-86, GAO rpt, 26121–432

Fruit and vegetable shipments, and arrivals in US and Canada cities, by mode of transport and State and country of origin, 1990, annual rpt, 1311–4.1

Fruit and vegetable wholesale prices in NYC by State, and shipments and arrivals by mode of transport, by commodity, weekly rpt, 1311–20

Fruit and vegetable wholesale prices in NYC, Chicago, and selected shipping points, by crop, 1990, annual rpt, 1311–8

Global climate change environmental, infrastructure, and health impacts, with model results and background data, 1850s-2100, 9188–113

Housing starts and completions authorized by building permits in 40 MSAs, quarterly rpt, 2382–9

Infectious notifiable disease cases and current outbreaks, by region and State, weekly rpt, 4202–1

Infectious notifiable disease cases, by age and State, and deaths, 1930s-90, annual rpt, 4204–1

Lead poisoning among children, cases and rates by race, and screening tests conducted, for NYC, 1988, article, 4202–7.201

Oil prices by product, for 4 cities, seasonal weekly rpt, 3162–45

Rent control impacts on rental housing condition, for NYC, late 1970s-87, working paper, 9387–8.246

Wages by occupation, for office and plant workers, 1991 survey, periodic MSA rpt, 6785–12.6

see also under By City and By SMSA or MSA in the "Index by Categories"

New York State

Appalachian Regional Commission funding, by project and State, planned FY91, annual rpt, 9084–3

Banks (insured commercial and savings) deposits by instn, State, MSA, and county, as of June 1990, annual regional rpt, 9295–3.1

Banks (multinatl) US branches assets and liabilities, total and for 3 States, monthly rpt, quarterly data, 9362–1.4

Celery acreage planted and growing, by growing area, monthly rpt, 1621–14

Child welfare programs funding by source, and foster care cases, problems, and program operations for selected States, 1970s-90, hearings, 21788–202

Child welfare programs funding by source, and foster care program operations and client characteristics, for selected States, 1960s-95, 25368–169

County Business Patterns, 1989: employment, establishments, and payroll, by SIC 2- to 4-digit industry and county, annual State rpt, 2326–8.34

Dairy prices, by product and selected area, with related marketing data, 1990, annual rpt, 1317–1

DOD prime contract awards, by contractor, service branch, State, and city, FY90, annual rpt, 3544–22

Economic conditions and outlook, for US and Canada Great Lakes area, 1970s-90, 9375–15

Education system in Appalachia, improvement initiatives, and indicators of success, by State, 1960s-89, 9088–36

Estuary eutrophication and algal blooms, causes and environmental effects, 1991 conf, 2176–7.22

Fed Govt spending in States and local areas, by type, State, county, and city, FY90, annual rpt, 2464–3

Fed Govt spending in States, by type, program, agency, and State, FY90, annual rpt, 2464–2

Foster care placements, discharges, and returns to care, by selected characteristics of children, and length of stay factors, 1985-86, GAO rpt, 26121–432

HHS financial aid, by program, recipient, State, and city, FY90, annual regional listing, 4004–3.2

Hospital deaths of Medicare patients, actual and expected rates by diagnosis, and hospital characteristics, by instn, FY87-89, annual regional rpt, 4654–14.2

Housing census, 1990: inventory, occupancy, and costs, State fact sheet, 2326–21.34

Hwy funds pooled by States from FHwA funds for specific projects, demonstration project results, FY88-90, GAO rpt, 26113–471

Income (personal) per capita and by source, and earnings by industry div, by State, MSA, and county, 1984-89, annual regional rpt, 2704–2.2

Jail adult and juvenile population, employment, spending, instn conditions, and inmate programs, by county and facility, 1988, regional rpt series, 6068–144.2

Marriages, divorces, and rates, by characteristics of spouses, State, and county, 1987 and trends from 1920, US Vital Statistics annual rpt, 4144–4

Measles cases among New York State high school and college students, and vaccination and treatment costs, 1989, article, 4042–3.227

Medicaid beneficiaries emergency room visits relation to availability of other sources of care, for upstate New York, 1985-87, article, 4652–1.232

Medicaid demonstration projects evaluation, for 6 States, 1988 rpt, 4658–45

Medicaid programs detection and use of private health insurance, for New York State, 1984-89, article, 4652–1.212

Mineral Industry Surveys, State reviews of production, 1990, preliminary annual rpt, 5614–6

Minerals Yearbook, 1989, Vol 2: State review of production and sales by commodity, and business activity, annual rpt, 5604–16.33

Minerals Yearbook, 1989, Vol 2: State reviews of production, sales, and firms, by commodity, and business activity, annual rpt, 5604–34

Nursing home reimbursement by Medicaid, resident classification using patient and care characteristics, New York State, 1990 article, 4652–1.205

Onion farm acreage, pesticide use, operators, and other characteristics, for 6 producer States, 1989, article, 1561–11.201

Physicians, by specialty, age, sex, and location of training and practice, 1989, State rpt, 4116–6.33

Pollution (marine) bacterial levels, and beach closings due to contamination and medical waste, for New York and New Jersey, 1987-89, hearing, 21568–50

Pollution levels in New York Bight, sources, treatment costs, economic losses, and environmental and health effects, 1990 conf, 9208–131

Population and housing census, 1990: population and housing characteristics, households, and land area, by county, subdiv, and place, State rpt, 2551–1.34

Population and housing census, 1990: voting age and total population by race, and housing units, by block, redistricting counts required under PL 94-171, State CD-ROM release, 2551–6.5

Population and housing census, 1990: voting age and total population by race, and housing units, by county and city, redistricting counts required under PL 94-171, State summary rpt, 2551–5.33

Statistical Abstract of US, 1991 annual data compilation, 2324–1

Supplemental Security Income payments and beneficiaries, by type of eligibility, State, and county, Dec 1989, annual rpt, 4744–27.2

Wages by occupation, and benefits for office and plant workers, 1991 survey, periodic labor market rpt, 6785–3.7

Water supply and quality in streams and lakes, and groundwater levels in wells, by drainage basin, 1990, annual State rpt, 5666–12.31

Water supply in northeastern US, precipitation and stream runoff by station, monthly rpt, 2182–3

see also Albany, N.Y.

see also Buffalo, N.Y.

see also Erie County, N.Y.

see also Long Island, N.Y.

see also New York Bight

see also New York City

see also Niagara Falls, N.Y.

see also Rochester, N.Y.

see also Schenectady, N.Y.

see also Troy, N.Y.

see also under By State in the "Index by Categories"

New York Stock Exchange

Price indexes of NYSE for common stock, by type, 1966-90 with trends from 1949, annual rpt, 204–1.7

Short selling of stocks, activity indicators, and regulatory issues, 1980s-89 and trends from 1940, hearings, 21408–122

Stockbrokers with NYSE membership, securities credit issues, as of June 1990, annual rpt, 9365–5.1

Trading volume on NYSE, monthly rpt, 9362–1.1

Trading volume, securities listed by type, and finances, by exchange, selected years 1938-89, annual rpt, 9734–2.1; 9734–2.2

New Zealand

Agricultural exports of high-value commodities, indexes and sales by commodity, world area, and country, 1960s-86, 1528–323

Agricultural exports of US, impacts of foreign agricultural and trade policy, with data by commodity and country, 1989, annual rpt, 1924–8

Agricultural production, prices, and trade, by country, 1980s and forecast 1991, annual world region rpt, 1524–4.5

Agricultural production, trade, and policies in foreign countries, summary data by country, 1989-90, annual factbook, 1924–12

Agricultural trade of US, by detailed commodity and country, 1989, annual rpt, 1524–8

Agricultural trade of US, by detailed commodity and country, 1990, semiannual rpt, 1522–4

Economic and military aid and loans from US and intl agencies, by program and country, FY46-90, annual rpt, 9914–5

Economic conditions in Communist and OECD countries, 1989, annual rpt, 7144–11

Economic conditions, income, production, prices, employment, and trade, 1991 periodic country rpt, 2046–4.25

Economic conditions, policy, and trade practices, by country, 1988-90, annual rpt, 21384–5

Economic, social, political, and geographic summary data, by country, 1991, annual factbook, 9114–2

Exports and imports of OECD members, by country, 1989, annual rpt, 7144–10

Exports and imports of US, by Harmonized System 6-digit commodity and country, 1990, annual rpt, 2424–13

New Zealand

Exports and imports of US, by selected country, country group, and commodity group, 1990, annual rpt, 2044–37

Exports and imports of US, by transport mode, country, and SITC 1- to 3-digit commodity, 1990, annual rpt, 2424–12

Exports of US, detailed Schedule B commodities with countries of destination, 1990, annual rpt, 2424–10

Fish (surimi) production and trade by country, and Japan import and catch quotas, 1975-89, article, 2162–1.202

GNP and GNP growth for OECD members, by country, 1980-90, annual rpt, 7144–8

Human rights conditions in 170 countries, and US economic and military aid, 1990, annual rpt, 21384–3

Imports of goods, services, and investment from US, trade barriers, impacts, and US actions, by country, 1990, annual rpt, 444–2

Kiwifruit from New Zealand at less than fair value, injury to US industry, investigation with background financial and operating data, 1991 rpt, 9886–14.316

Labor conditions, union coverage, and work accidents, 1991 annual country rpt, 6366–4.57

Lamb meat from Australia and New Zealand, US industry intl competitiveness, investigation with background financial and operating data and foreign comparisons, 1990 rpt, 9886–4.166

Multinatl US firms and foreign affiliates finances and operations, by industry and world area of parent firm, 1989 benchmark survey, preliminary annual rpt, 2704–5

Multinatl US firms foreign affiliates, income statement items by country and world area, 1986, biennial article, 8302–2.212

Oil production, trade, use, and stocks, by selected country and country group, monthly rpt, 3162–42

Oil supply, demand, and stock forecasts, by world area, quarterly rpt, 3162–34

R&D funding by Fed Govt, by field, performer type, agency, and State, FY89-91, annual rpt, 9627–20

Tax revenue, by level of govt and type of tax, for OECD countries, mid 1960s-89, annual rpt, 10044–1.2

UN voting record and share of votes in agreement with US, by issue, country, and world area, 1990, annual rpt, 7004–18

see also under By Foreign Country in the "Index by Categories"

Newark, N.J.

Drug abuse indicators for selected metro areas, research results, data collection, and policy issues, 1991 semiannual conf, 4492–5

Fruit and vegetable shipments, and arrivals in US and Canada cities, by mode of transport and State and country of origin, 1990, annual rpt, 1311–4.1

Wages by occupation, for office and plant workers, 1991 survey, periodic MSA rpt, 6785–12.3

see also under By City and By SMSA or MSA in the "Index by Categories"

Newcomb, Polly A.

"Breast Self-Examination in Relation to the Occurrence of Advanced Breast Cancer", 4472–1.202

Newcomer, Robert J.

"Social Health Maintenance Organizations' Service Use and Costs, 1985-89", 4652–1.235

Newport News, Va.

Housing and households characteristics, unit and neighborhood quality, and journey to work by MSA location, for 11 MSAs, 1984 survey, supplement, 2485–8

Housing and households characteristics, 1988 survey, MSA fact sheet, 2485–11.9

Housing starts and completions authorized by building permits in 40 MSAs, quarterly rpt, 2382–9

Wages by occupation, and benefits for office and plant workers, 1990 survey, periodic MSA rpt, 6785–3.1

Wages by occupation, for office and plant workers, 1991 survey, periodic MSA rpt, 6785–3.7

see also under By City and By SMSA or MSA in the "Index by Categories"

News reporting

see Freedom of the press
see Government and the press
see Journalism

Newspapers

Advertising in newspapers, spending by ad type, *Survey of Current Business*, monthly rpt, 2702–1.7

County Business Patterns, 1988: employment, establishments, and payroll, by SIC 2- to 4-digit industry and county, annual State rpt series, 2326–6

County Business Patterns, 1989: employment, establishments, and payroll, by SIC 2- to 4-digit industry and county, annual State rpt series, 2326–8

CPI by component for US city average, and by region, population size, and for 27 metro areas, monthly rpt, 6762–2

Employment, earnings, and hours, by SIC 1- to 4-digit industry, monthly and annual averages, selected years 1909-90, annual rpt, 6744–4

Exports and imports of US, by Harmonized System 6-digit commodity and country, 1990, annual rpt, 2424–13

Exports of US, detailed Schedule B commodities with countries of destination, 1990, annual rpt, 2424–10

Foreign travel to US, trade shows and other promotional activities, with magazine ad costs and circulation, for selected countries, 1991-92, annual rpt, 2904–11

Mail volume to and from households, use, and views, by class, source, content, and household characteristics, 1987-88, annual rpt, 9864–10

Manufacturing annual survey, 1989: finances and operations, by SIC 2- to 4-digit industry, series, 2506–15

Manufacturing census, 1987: finances and operations, by SIC 2- to 4-digit industry, State, and MSA, with trends from 1849, 2497–1

Manufacturing census, 1987: finances and operations, by type of organization and SIC 2- to 4-digit industry, subject rpt, 2497–5

Manufacturing finances and operations, by SIC 2- to 4-digit industry, forecast 1991, annual rpt, 2044–28

Occupational injury and illness rates, by SIC 2- to 4-digit industry, 1988-89, annual rpt, 6844–7

Index by Subjects and Names

Occupational injury and illness rates, by SIC 2- to 4-digit industry, 1989, annual rpt, 6844–1

Price indexes (producer), by stage of processing and detailed commodity, monthly rpt, 6762–6

Price indexes (producer), by stage of processing and detailed commodity, monthly 1990, annual rpt, 6764–2

Retail trade census, 1987: finances and employment, for establishments with and without payroll, by SIC 2- to 4-digit kind of business, State, and MSA, 2401–1

State and Metro Area Data Book, 1991 data compilation, 2328–54

Statistical Abstract of US, 1991 annual data compilation, 2324–1.18

Tax (income) returns of corporations, income and tax items by asset size and detailed industry, 1987, annual rpt, 8304–4

Tax (income) returns of corporations, income and tax items by asset size and detailed industry, 1988, annual rpt, 8304–21

see also Journalism

Newton, John L.

"Temperature and Salinity Structure of the Wintertime Bering Sea Marginal Ice Zone", 2176–1.38

Niagara Falls, N.Y.

CPI by component for US city average, and by region, population size, and for 27 metro areas, monthly rpt, 6762–2

Housing and households characteristics, unit and neighborhood quality, and journey to work by MSA location, for 11 MSAs, 1984 survey, supplement, 2485–8

see also under By SMSA or MSA in the "Index by Categories"

Nicaragua

Agricultural exports of high-value commodities, indexes and sales by commodity, world area, and country, 1960s-86, 1528–323

Agricultural trade of US, by detailed commodity and country, 1989, annual rpt, 1524–8

Agricultural trade of US, by detailed commodity and country, 1990, semiannual rpt, 1522–4

AID economic aid to developing countries, obligations and disbursements by country, quarterly rpt, 9912–4

AID loans repayment status and terms by program and country, and status of predecessor agency loans, quarterly rpt, 9912–3

Debt of Communist countries to US and other Western banks, by country, 1980s, conf, 25388–56

Economic and military aid and loans from US and intl agencies, by program and country, FY46-90, annual rpt, 9914–5

Economic and social conditions of developing countries from 1960s, and Intl Dev Cooperation Agency and AID activities and funding, FY90-92, annual rpt, 9904–4

Economic conditions, policy, and trade practices, by country, 1988-90, annual rpt, 21384–5

Economic, social, political, and geographic summary data, by country, 1991, annual factbook, 9114–2

Exports and imports of US, by commodity and country, 1970-89, world area rpt, 9116–1.2

Exports and imports of US, by selected country, country group, and commodity group, 1990, annual rpt, 2044–37

Exports and imports of US, by transport mode, country, and SITC 1- to 3-digit commodity, 1990, annual rpt, 2424–12

Exports of US, detailed Schedule B commodities with countries of destination, 1990, annual rpt, 2424–10

Human rights conditions in 170 countries, and US economic and military aid, 1990, annual rpt, 21384–3

Investment (direct) incentives of Caribbean Basin Initiative, economic impacts, with finances and employment by country, 1984-90, 2048–141

Military aid of US, arms sales, and training programs costs and budget requests, by program, world region, and country, FY90-92, annual rpt, 7144–13

UN voting record and share of votes in agreement with US, by issue, country, and world area, 1990, annual rpt, 7004–18

see also under By Foreign Country in the "Index by Categories"

Nichols, Bonnie L.

"Projections of Returns To Be Filed in FY91-98", 8302–2.208

Nichols, Vance E.

"Withdrawal and Distribution of Water by Public Water Supplies in Ohio in 1985", 5666–24.7

Nickel

see Metals and metal industries

Nicotine

see Smoking

Niemeier, Paul

"Chinese Shrimp Culture", 1524–4.3

Niendorff, William J.

"Oral Diseases", 4088–2

Niger

Agricultural exports of high-value commodities, indexes and sales by commodity, world area, and country, 1960s-86, 1528–323

Agricultural trade of US, by detailed commodity and country, 1989, annual rpt, 1524–8

Agricultural trade of US, by detailed commodity and country, 1990, semiannual rpt, 1522–4

AID economic aid to developing countries, obligations and disbursements by country, quarterly rpt, 9912–4

AID loans repayment status and terms by program and country, and status of predecessor agency loans, quarterly rpt, 9912–3

Dairy imports, consumption, and market conditions, by sub-Saharan Africa country, 1961-88, 1528–321

Economic and military aid and loans from US and intl agencies, by program and country, FY46-90, annual rpt, 9914–5

Economic and social conditions of developing countries from 1960s, and Intl Dev Cooperation Agency and AID activities and funding, FY90-92, annual rpt, 9904–4

Economic, social, political, and geographic summary data, by country, 1991, annual factbook, 9114–2

Exports and imports of US, by transport mode, country, and SITC 1- to 3-digit commodity, 1990, annual rpt, 2424–12

Grain production, use, imports, and stocks, for Sahel region by country, 1989/90, 9918–18

Human rights conditions in 170 countries, and US economic and military aid, 1990, annual rpt, 21384–3

Military aid of US, arms sales, and training programs costs and budget requests, by program, world region, and country, FY90-92, annual rpt, 7144–13

UN voting record and share of votes in agreement with US, by issue, country, and world area, 1990, annual rpt, 7004–18

see also under By Foreign Country in the "Index by Categories"

Nigeria

Agricultural exports of high-value commodities, indexes and sales by commodity, world area, and country, 1960s-86, 1528–323

Agricultural exports of US, impacts of foreign agricultural and trade policy, with data by commodity and country, 1989, annual rpt, 1924–8

Agricultural production, prices, and trade, by country, 1960s-90, annual world area rpt, 1524–4.2

Agricultural production, trade, and policies in foreign countries, summary data by country, 1989-90, annual factbook, 1924–12

Agricultural trade of US, by detailed commodity and country, 1989, annual rpt, 1524–8

Agricultural trade of US, by detailed commodity and country, 1990, semiannual rpt, 1522–4

AID economic aid to developing countries, obligations and disbursements by country, quarterly rpt, 9912–4

AID loans repayment status and terms by program and country, and status of predecessor agency loans, quarterly rpt, 9912–3

Background Notes, summary social, political, and economic data, 1991 rpt, 7006–2.32

Dairy imports, consumption, and market conditions, by sub-Saharan Africa country, 1961-88, 1528–321

Economic and military aid and loans from US and intl agencies, by program and country, FY46-90, annual rpt, 9914–5

Economic and social conditions of developing countries from 1960s, and Intl Dev Cooperation Agency and AID activities and funding, FY90-92, annual rpt, 9904–4

Economic conditions in USSR, Eastern Europe, OECD, and selected other countries, 1960s-90, annual rpt, 9114–4

Economic conditions, income, production, prices, employment, and trade, 1991 periodic country rpt, 2046–4.55

Economic conditions, policy, and trade practices, by country, 1988-90, annual rpt, 21384–5

Economic, social, political, and geographic summary data, by country, 1991, annual factbook, 9114–2

Exports and imports of US, by commodity and country, 1970-89, world area rpt, 9116–1.6

Exports and imports of US, by Harmonized System 6-digit commodity and country, 1990, annual rpt, 2424–13

Exports and imports of US, by selected country, country group, and commodity group, 1990, annual rpt, 2044–37

Exports and imports of US, by transport mode, country, and SITC 1- to 3-digit commodity, 1990, annual rpt, 2424–12

Exports of US, detailed Schedule B commodities with countries of destination, 1990, annual rpt, 2424–10

Food supply, needs, and aid for developing countries, status and alternative forecasts, 1991 world area rpt, 1526–8.1

Human rights conditions in 170 countries, and US economic and military aid, 1990, annual rpt, 21384–3

Imports of goods, services, and investment from US, trade barriers, impacts, and US actions, by country, 1990, annual rpt, 444–2

Labor conditions, union coverage, and work accidents, 1991 annual country rpt, 6366–4.54

Military aid of US, arms sales, and training programs costs and budget requests, by program, world region, and country, FY90-92, annual rpt, 7144–13

Multinatl US firms and foreign affiliates finances and operations, by industry and world area of parent firm, 1989 benchmark survey, preliminary annual rpt, 2704–5

Multinatl US firms foreign affiliates, income statement items by country and world area, 1986, biennial article, 8302–2.212

Oil production, and exports and prices for US, by major exporting country, detailed data, monthly rpt with articles, 3162–24

Oil production, trade, use, and stocks, by selected country and country group, monthly rpt, 3162–42

UN voting record and share of votes in agreement with US, by issue, country, and world area, 1990, annual rpt, 7004–18

see also under By Foreign Country in the "Index by Categories"

NIH

see National Institutes of Health

Nikishka, Alaska

Tide height and time daily at coastal points, forecast 1992, annual rpt, 2174–2.1

NIMH

see National Institute of Mental Health

Nimick, Ellen H.

"Juvenile Court Property Cases", 6066–27.5

Nitrocellulose

see Chemicals and chemical industry

Nitrogen

see Gases

Nitrogen oxides

see Air pollution

NOAA

see National Oceanic and Atmospheric Administration

Noble, Denis L.

"Guardians of the Eighth Sea", 2152–8.204

Noble, Gary R.

"Organizational Structure and Resources of CDC's HIV-AIDS Prevention Program", 4042–3.256

Noell, Jay

Noell, Jay
"Student Aid and the Cost of Postsecondary Education", 26306–6.153

Noise
Coastal areas environmental and socioeconomic conditions, and potential impact of oil and gas OCS leases, final statement series, 5736–1
Electric utilities privately owned, pollution abatement outlays by type of pollutant and equipment, and firm, 1989, annual rpt, 3164–23
Fed Govt financial and nonfinancial domestic aid, 1991 base edition with supplements, annual listing, 104–5
Health condition and health care resources, use, and spending, 1950s-89, annual data compilation, 4144–11
Neighborhood and housing quality, indicators and attitudes, by householder type and location, for 11 MSAs, 1984 survey, supplement, 2485–8
Neighborhood and housing quality, indicators and attitudes, by householder type and location, 1987, biennial rpt supplement, 2485–13
Neighborhood and housing quality, indicators and attitudes, by householder type and location, 1989, biennial rpt, 2485–12
Neighborhood and housing quality, indicators and attitudes, MSA surveys, series, 2485–6
Whales (bowhead) population in Arctic areas, impacts of subsistence whaling, shipping, noise, and other human activity, mid 1970s-80s, 5738–30
Whales (bowhead and white) migration through Beaufort Sea, behavior impacts of oil drilling and aircraft noise, spring 1989, 5738–27
see also Aircraft noise

Nolley, Jean W.
"Bulletin of Hardwood Market Statistics", 1202–4

Nomura, Abraham M.
"Prospective Study of Serum Cholesterol Levels and Large-Bowel Cancer", 4472–1.226

Non-ferrous metals industry
see Aluminum and aluminum industry
see Copper and copper industry
see Lead and lead industry
see Metals and metal industries
see Tin and tin industry
see Zinc and zinc industry

Non-Hodgkin's lymphoma
see Blood diseases and disorders

Nonappropriated funds
Budget of US, CBO analysis of revenue and spending alternatives and projections of economic indicators, FY92-96, annual rpt, 26304–3
Budget of US, obligations and authority by function, agency, and program, with summaries, analyses, and historical tables, FY92, annual rpt, 104–2

Nonmarket economies
see Centrally planned economies

Nonmetallic minerals and mines
Alaska minerals resources, production, oil and gas leases, reserves, and exploratory wells, with maps and bibl, 1989, annual rpt, 5664–11

County Business Patterns, 1988: employment, establishments, and payroll, by SIC 2- to 4-digit industry and county, annual State rpt series, 2326–6
County Business Patterns, 1989: employment, establishments, and payroll, by SIC 2- to 4-digit industry and county, annual State rpt series, 2326–8
Employment, earnings, and hours, by SIC 1- to 4-digit industry, monthly and annual averages, selected years 1909-90, annual rpt, 6744–4
Enterprise Statistics, 1987: auxiliaries of multi-establishment firms, finances and operations by function, industry, and State, 2329–6
Enterprise Statistics, 1987: finances and operations for companies, by size, level of diversification, form of organization, and industry group, 2329–8
Exports and imports between US and outlying areas, by detailed commodity and mode of transport, 1990, annual rpt, 2424–11
Exports and imports of US, by country and detailed commodity, monthly rpt, 2422–12
Exports and imports of US, by Harmonized System 6-digit commodity and country, 1990, annual rpt, 2424–13
Exports and imports of US, by transport mode, country, and SITC 1- to 3-digit commodity, 1990, annual rpt, 2424–12
Exports of US, detailed commodities by country, monthly CD-ROM, 2422–13
Exports of US, detailed Schedule B commodities with countries of destination, 1990, annual rpt, 2424–10
Foreign and US minerals supply under alternative market conditions, reserves, and background industry data, series, 5606–4
Imports, exports, and employment impacts, by SIC 2- to 4-digit industry and commodity, quarterly rpt, 2322–2
Imports of US, detailed commodities by country, monthly CD-ROM, 2422–14
Labor productivity, indexes of output, hours, and employment by SIC 2- to 4-digit industry, 1967-89, annual rpt, 6824–1.2
Manufacturing annual survey, 1989: finances and operations, by SIC 2- to 4-digit industry, series, 2506–15
Manufacturing census, 1987: finances and operations, by SIC 2- to 4-digit industry, State, and MSA, with trends from 1849, 2497–1
Manufacturing census, 1987: finances and operations, by type of organization and SIC 2- to 4-digit industry, subject rpt, 2497–5
Mineral industries census, 1987: energy use and costs, by fuel type, SIC 2- to 4-digit industry, and State, subject rpt, 2517–2
Mineral industries census, 1987: finances and operations, by establishment characteristics, SIC 2- to 4-digit industry, and State, subject rpt, 2517–1
Mineral industries census, 1987: finances and operations, by SIC 2- to 4-digit industry, State, and county, census div rpt series, 2515–1
Mineral Industry Surveys, commodity reviews of production, trade, stocks, and use, monthly rpt series, 5612–1

Index by Subjects and Names

Mineral Industry Surveys, commodity reviews of production, trade, stocks, and use, quarterly rpt series, 5612–2
Mineral Industry Surveys, commodity reviews of production, trade, use, and industry operations, advance annual rpt series, 5614–5
Mineral Industry Surveys, State reviews of production, 1990, preliminary annual rpt, 5614–6
Minerals Yearbook, 1988, Vol 3: foreign country reviews of production, trade, and policy, by commodity, annual rpt series, 5604–17
Minerals Yearbook, 1989, Vol 1: commodity reviews of production, reserves, supply, use, and trade, annual rpt series, 5604–15
Minerals Yearbook, 1989, Vol 2: State reviews of production and sales by commodity, and business activity, annual rpt series, 5604–16
Minerals Yearbook, 1989, Vol 2: State reviews of production, sales, and firms, by commodity, and business activity, annual rpt, 5604–34
Minerals Yearbook, 1990, Vol 1: commodity reviews of production, reserves, supply, use, and trade, annual rpt series, 5604–20
Multinatl US firms and foreign affiliates finances and operations, by industry and world area of parent firm, 1989 benchmark survey, preliminary annual rpt, 2704–5
Occupational deaths in mining accidents, by circumstances and selected victim characteristics, semiannual rpt series, 6662–3
Occupational injuries and incidence, employment, and hours in nonmetallic minerals mines and related operations, 1989, annual rpt, 6664–1
Occupational injury and illness rates, by SIC 2- to 4-digit industry, 1988-89, annual rpt, 6844–7
Occupational injury and illness rates, by SIC 2- to 4-digit industry, 1989, annual rpt, 6844–1
Occupational safety and health enforcement, training, and funding, with casualties, by type of mine and State, FY89, annual rpt, 6664–6
Price indexes (producer), by stage of processing and detailed commodity, monthly rpt, 6762–6
Price indexes (producer), by stage of processing and detailed commodity, monthly 1990, annual rpt, 6764–2
Production, prices, trade, use, employment, tariffs, and stockpiles, by mineral, with foreign comparisons, 1986-90, annual rpt, 5604–18
Production, reserves, and use of industrial minerals, and characteristics of individual deposits, State rpt series, 5606–10
Public lands minerals resources and availability, State rpt series, 5606–7
Publications and patents of Mines Bur, monthly listing, 5602–2
Publications and patents of Mines Bur, 1985-89, quinquennial listing, 5608–168
Respiratory diseases related to occupational hazards, epidemiology, diagnosis, and treatment, for selected industries and work settings, 1988 conf, 4248–90

Index by Subjects and Names

Salt production capacity, by firm and facility, 1990, annual listing, 5614–30

Selenium levels in Western States arid areas, and plant and animal exposure effects, 1990 conf, 5668–121

Silicon metal from Argentina at less than fair value, injury to US industry, investigation with background financial and operating data, 1991 rpt, 9886–14.330

Silicon metal from Brazil at less than fair value, injury to US industry, investigation with background financial and operating data, 1991 rpt, 9886–14.321

Silicon metal from PRC at less than fair value, injury to US industry, investigation with background financial and operating data, 1991 rpt, 9886–14.314

Soviet Union minerals production and trade, by commodity, 1985-89 and projected to 2005, annual rpt, 5604–39

Statistical Abstract of US, 1991 annual data compilation, 2324–1.25

Tax (income) returns of corporations, income and tax items by asset size and detailed industry, 1987, annual rpt, 8304–4

Tax (income) returns of corporations, income and tax items by asset size and detailed industry, 1988, annual rpt, 8304–21

Tax (income) returns of corporations with foreign tax credit, income and tax items by industry group, 1986, biennial article, 8302–2.203

Tax (income) returns of sole proprietorships, income statement items, by industry group, 1989, annual article, 8302–2.214

Technologically advanced structural materials devs, use, and R&D funding, for ceramics, metal alloys, polymers, and composites, 1960s-80s and projected to 2000, 5608–162

see also Asbestos contamination
see also Cement and concrete
see also Clay industry and products
see also Coal and coal mining
see also Fertilizers
see also Gases
see also Gemstones
see also Glass and glass industry
see also Natural gas and gas industry
see also Offshore mineral resources
see also Offshore oil and gas
see also Oil shale
see also Petroleum and petroleum industry
see also Phosphate
see also Potash
see also Pottery and porcelain products
see also Sand and gravel
see also Stockpiling
see also Stone products and quarries
see also Strategic materials
see also Tar sands
see also under By Commodity in the "Index by Categories"
see also under By Industry in the "Index by Categories"

Nonmetropolitan areas

see Rural areas
see under By Urban-Rural and Metro-Nonmetro in the "Index by Categories"

Nonprofit organizations and foundations

AID loans repayment status and terms by program and country, and status of predecessor agency loans, quarterly rpt, 9912–3

Alcohol, Drug Abuse and Mental Health Admin research grants and awards, by recipient, FY90, annual listing, 4044–13

Allergy and Infectious Diseases Natl Inst activities, grants by recipient and location, and disease cases, FY83-90, annual rpt, 4474–30

Arts Natl Endowment activities and grants, FY90, annual rpt, 9564–3

Assets and debts of private sector, balance sheets by segment, 1945-90, semiannual rpt, 9365–4.1

Blind and disabled persons reading materials from nonprofit agencies, FY90, annual listing, 26404–3

County Business Patterns, 1988: employment, establishments, and payroll, by SIC 2- to 4-digit industry and county, annual State rpt series, 2326–6

County Business Patterns, 1989: employment, establishments, and payroll, by SIC 2- to 4-digit industry and county, annual State rpt series, 2326–8

Dental Research Natl Inst research and training grants, by recipient, FY89, annual listing, 4474–19

Disabled persons workshops finances, operations, and Federal procurement, FY80-90, annual rpt, 11714–1

DOD prime contract awards, by category, contract and contractor type, and service branch, FY81-1st half FY91, semiannual rpt, 3542–1

DOD prime contract awards, by category, contractor type, and State, FY88-90, annual rpt, 3544–11

DOD prime contract awards for R&D, for top 500 contractors, FY90, annual listing, 3544–4

DOD prime contract awards for R&D to US and foreign nonprofit instns and govt agencies, by instn and location, FY90, annual listing, 3544–17

DOE contracts and grants, by category, State, and for top contractors, FY90, annual rpt, 3004–21

Energy conservation aid of Fed Govt to public and nonprofit private instns, by building type and State, 1990, annual rpt, 3304–15

Fed Govt financial and nonfinancial domestic aid, 1991 base edition with supplements, annual listing, 104–5

Fed Govt surplus personal property donations to govt and nonprofit agencies, with data by State, FY88-90, biennial rpt, 9454–22

Finances of nonprofit charitable organizations, and revenue and investments of top 10 instns, 1986-87, article, 8302–2.210

Finances of nonprofit charitable organizations, by asset size and State, 1987, article, 8302–2.218

Finances of nonprofit charitable organizations, 1988, table, 8302–2.220

Food aid program for children during summer vacation, nonprofit sponsors compliance with USDA regulations, 1989-90, GAO rpt, 26113–541

Foreign countries disasters, casualties, damage, and aid by US and others, FY90 and trends from FY64, annual rpt, 9914–12

Health care facilities for kidney end-stage disease treatment, by ownership, 1985-89, annual rpt, 4654–16.5

Health care R&D funding, by type of source and performer, 1981-90, annual rpt, 4434–3

Health promotion program availability and participation, by type of program and sponsor, 1986-87 local area study, article, 4042–3.223

HHS financial aid, by program, recipient, State, and city, FY90, annual regional listings, 4004–3

Homeless aid organizations donations of surplus Federal property by State, and compared to other recipients, FY87-80, GAO rpt, 26113–538

Homeless and runaway youth programs, funding, activities, and participant characteristics, FY90, annual rpt, 4604–3

Hospices use by cancer patients, by service type, use of other facilities, patient and instn characteristics, and other indicators, local area study, 1980-85, 4658–53

Hospital deaths of Medicare patients, actual and expected rates by diagnosis, with hospital characteristics, by instn, FY87-89, annual regional rpt series, 4654–14

Hospital reimbursement by Medicare under prospective payment system, impacts on instns and beneficiaries, 1988, annual rpt, 4654–13

Housing (low income) construction and repair loans of HUD to nonprofit organizations, project delays, and starts, 1980s, GAO rpt, 26113–506

Humanities Natl Endowment activities and grants, FY90, annual rpt, 9564–2

Mail operating costs of USPS, itemized by class of mail, FY90, annual rpt, 9864–4

Mail revenue and subsidy for revenue forgone, by class of mail, FY90, and volume from FY86, annual rpt, 9864–1

Mail revenue, costs, and volume, by class of mail, FY90, annual rpt, 9864–2

Mail volume, revenues, and subsidies for revenue forgone, by class of mail, FY90, annual rpt, 9864–5.2; 9864–5.3

Mail volume to and from households, use, and views, by class, source, content, and household characteristics, 1987-88, annual rpt, 9864–10

Medical and biological R&D facilities, space and equipment adequacy, needs, and funding by source, by instn type, 1990, biennial rpt, 4434–17

Mental health care facilities, staff, and patient characteristics, *Statistical Notes* series, 4506–3

NASA funding by program and type of performer, and contract awards by State, FY90, annual rpt, 9504–6.2

NASA procurement contract awards, by type, contractor, State, and country, FY91 with trends from 1961, semiannual rpt, 9502–6

Natl income and product accounts and components, *Survey of Current Business,* monthly rpt, 2702–1.24

Navy procurement, by contractor and location, FY90, annual rpt, 3804–13

Nonprofit organizations and foundations

NIH grants and contracts, by inst and type of recipient, FY81-90, annual rpt, 4434–9

NSF grants and contracts, by field, instn, and State, FY89, annual rpt, 9624–26

NSF R&D grant awards, by div and program, periodic rpt series, 9626–7

PL 480 exports by commodity, and recipients, by program, sponsor, and country, FY88 and cumulative from FY55, annual rpt, 1924–7

R&D and related funding of Fed Govt to higher education and nonprofit instns, by field, instn, agency, and State, FY89, annual rpt, 9627–17.1

R&D funding by Fed Govt, by field, performer type, agency, and State, FY89-91, annual rpt, 9627–20

Refugee arrivals and resettlement in US, by age, sex, sponsoring agency, State, and country, monthly rpt, 4692–2

Refugee resettlement programs and funding, arrivals by country of origin, and indicators of adjustment, by State, FY90, annual rpt, 4694–5

Science and engineering PhDs, by field, instn, employment prospects, sex, race, and other characteristics, 1960s-90, annual rpt, 9627–30

Science and engineering PhDs employment and other characteristics, by field and State, 1989, biennial rpt, 9627–18

Service industries census, 1987: establishments, receipts by source, payroll, and employment, by SIC 2- to 4-digit kind of business, State, and MSA, 2393–4

State and Metro Area Data Book, 1991 data compilation, 2328–54

Statistical Abstract of US, 1991 annual data compilation, 2324–1.12; 2324–1.28

Transit systems under private, public, and nonprofit ownership, funding, staff, and service and area characteristics, 1990 rpt, 7888–81

Unemployment insurance laws of States, comparison of provisions, 1991, base edition with semiannual revisions, 6402–2

see also Membership organizations

see also Political action committees

see also Religious organizations

Nordland, Willis J.

"Federal Employees' Compensation Act", 6722–1.241

Norfolk, Va.

Housing and households characteristics, unit and neighborhood quality, and journey to work by MSA location, for 11 MSAs, 1984 survey, supplement, 2485–8

Housing and households characteristics, 1988 survey, MSA fact sheet, 2485–11.9

Housing starts and completions authorized by building permits in 40 MSAs, quarterly rpt, 2382–9

Wages by occupation, and benefits for office and plant workers, 1990 survey, periodic MSA rpt, 6785–3.1

Wages by occupation, for office and plant workers, 1991 survey, periodic MSA rpt, 6785–3.7

see also under By City and By SMSA or MSA in the "Index by Categories"

Normal, Ill.

see also under By SMSA or MSA in the "Index by Categories"

North America

Agricultural exports of high-value commodities, indexes and sales by commodity, world area, and country, 1960s-86, 1528–323

Agricultural exports of US, for grains, oilseed products, hides, skins, and cotton, by country, weekly rpt, 1922–3

Agricultural trade of US, by commodity and country, bimonthly rpt, 1522–1

Agricultural trade of US, by detailed commodity and country, 1990, semiannual rpt, 1522–4

Air traffic and passengers, for intl routes over north Atlantic, by aviation type and route, alternative forecasts 1991-2010 and trends from 1980, annual rpt, 7504–44

Alien workers (unauthorized) and Fair Labor Standards Act employer compliance, hiring impacts, and aliens overstaying visas by country and State, 1986-90, annual rpt, 6264–6

Aliens (illegal) overstaying visas, by class of admission, mode of arrival, age, country, and State, FY85-88, annual rpt, 6264–5

Exports and imports (waterborne) of US, by type of service, customs district, port, and world area, monthly rpt, 2422–7

Exports, imports, and balances of US with major trading partners, by product category, 1986-90, annual chartbook, 9884–21

Fish larvae abundance, distribution, and growth, for selected Western Hemisphere sites, 1989 conf, 2168–126

Immigrant and nonimmigrant visas of US issued and refused, by class, issuing office, and nationality, FY89, annual rpt, 7184–1

Immigrants admitted to US, by country of birth, FY81-90, annual rpt, 6264–4

Immigrants admitted to US, by occupational group and country of birth, preliminary FY90, annual table, 6264–1

Immigrants in US, population characteristics and fertility, by birthplace and compared to native born, 1980s, Current Population rpt, 2546–2.162

Oil and gas reserves and discoveries, by country and country group, quarterly rpt, 3162–43

Oils, oilseeds, and meal imports, by commodity, world area of destination, and major producer, 1960s-88, 1528–314

Terrorism (intl) incidents, casualties, and attacks on US targets, by attack type and world area, 1990, annual rpt, 7004–13

Tidal currents, daily time and velocity by station for North America and Asia coasts, forecast 1992, annual rpts, 2174–1

Tide height and time daily at coastal points, forecast 1992, annual rpt, 2174–2.2; 2174–2.3

Travel to and from US on US and foreign flag air carriers, by country, world area, and US port, monthly rpt, 7302–2

US military and civilian personnel and dependents, by service branch, world area, and country, quarterly rpt, 3542–20

Weather, air pressure, temperature, and precipitation data for US and foreign locations, monthly 1971-80, decennial rpt, 2156–4.1

Index by Subjects and Names

Weather events and anomalies, precipitation and temperature for US and foreign locations, weekly rpt, 2182–6

Weather forecasts for US and Northern Hemisphere, precipitation and temperature by location, semimonthly rpt, 2182–1

see also Canada

see also Caribbean area

see also Greenland

see also Gulf of Mexico

see also Mexico

see also under By Foreign Country in the "Index by Categories"

North Atlantic Treaty Organization

Base construction, renovation, and land acquisition, DOD budget requests by project, service branch, State, and country, FY92-93, annual rpt, 3544–15

DOD budget, procurement appropriations by item, service branch, and defense agency, FY90-93, annual rpt, 3544–32

DOD civilian and military personnel and dependents, by service branch and US and foreign location, quarterly rpt, 3542–20

Economic conditions in Communist and OECD countries, 1989, annual rpt, 7144–11

Expenditures for intl organizations by US and other countries, by organization and program, FY90, annual rpt, 7004–9

Exports and imports of NATO members with PRC, by country, 1987-90, annual rpt, 7144–14

Exports and imports of OECD members, by country, 1989, annual rpt, 7144–10

GNP and GNP growth for OECD members, by country, 1980-90, annual rpt, 7144–8

Helsinki Final Act implementation by NATO and Warsaw Pact, Apr 1990-Mar 1991, last issue of semiannual rpt, 7002–1

Military forces reductions of NATO and Warsaw Pact under proposed treaty, and US budget savings, 1990 rpt, 26306–3.114

Military personnel of US abroad, by country, FY90, annual rpt, 3544–1.2

Military personnel of US abroad, by service branch, outlying area, and country, quarterly rpt, 3542–14.5

Military personnel of US abroad, by service branch, world area, and country, quarterly press release, 3542–9

Military spending and indicators of ability to support common defense, for NATO members and Japan, 1970s-89, annual rpt, 3544–28

Spacecraft and satellite launches since 1957, quarterly listing, 9502–2

UN voting record and share of votes in agreement with US, by issue, country, and world area, 1990, annual rpt, 7004–18

North Carolina

Appalachian Regional Commission funding, by project and State, planned FY91, annual rpt, 9084–3

Banks (insured commercial), Fed Reserve 5th District members financial statements, by State, quarterly rpt, 9389–18

Banks (insured commercial and savings) deposits by instn, State, MSA, and county, as of June 1990, annual regional rpt, 9295–3.2

County Business Patterns, 1989: employment, establishments, and payroll, by SIC 2- to 4-digit industry and county, annual State rpt, 2326–8.35

DOD prime contract awards, by contractor, service branch, State, and city, FY90, annual rpt, 3544–22

Economic indicators by State, Fed Reserve 5th District, quarterly rpt, 9389–16

Education system in Appalachia, improvement initiatives, and indicators of success, by State, 1960s-89, 9088–36

Employment and housing and mortgage market indicators by State, FHLB 4th District, quarterly rpt, 9302–36

Employment and unemployment, for 8 southeastern States, 1989-90, annual rpt, 6944–2

Employment by industry div, earnings, and hours, for 8 southeastern States, quarterly press release, 6942–7

Estuary environmental and fishery conditions, research results and methodology, 1991 rpt, 2176–7.25

Fed Govt spending in States and local areas, by type, State, county, and city, FY90, annual rpt, 2464–3

Fed Govt spending in States, by type, program, agency, and State, FY90, annual rpt, 2464–2

Fish and shellfish catch, wholesale receipts, prices, trade, and other market activities, weekly regional rpt, 2162–6.3

Food aid program of USDA for women, infants, and children, prenatal participation effect on Medicaid costs and birth outcomes, for 5 States, 1987-88, 1368–2

Gemstone production in selected States, Mineral Industry Surveys, 1988-90, advance annual rpt, 5614–5.10

HHS financial aid, by program, recipient, State, and city, FY90, annual regional listing, 4004–3.4

Hospital deaths of Medicare patients, actual and expected rates by diagnosis, and hospital characteristics, by instn, FY87-89, annual regional rpt, 4654–14.4

Hurricane Hugo relief funding and response by FEMA, 1989-90, GAO rpt, 26113–511

Hurricane Hugo storm characteristics, and Natl Weather Service forecast accuracy, 1989, 2186–6.1

Income (personal) per capita and by source, and earnings by industry div, by State, MSA, and county, 1984-89, annual regional rpt, 2704–2.4

Indian (Cherokee) Agency activities in North Carolina, FY91, annual rpt, 5704–4

Jail adult and juvenile population, employment, spending, instn conditions, and inmate programs, by county and facility, 1988, regional rpt series, 6068–144.4

Marriages, divorces, and rates, by characteristics of spouses, State, and county, 1987 and trends from 1920, US Vital Statistics annual rpt, 4144–4

Mineral Industry Surveys, State reviews of production, 1990, preliminary annual rpt, 5614–6

Minerals Yearbook, 1989, Vol 2: State review of production and sales by commodity, and business activity, annual rpt, 5604–16.34

Minerals Yearbook, 1989, Vol 2: State reviews of production, sales, and firms, by commodity, and business activity, annual rpt, 5604–34

Oil and gas OCS leases suspended for environmental reasons and repurchased by Fed Govt, costs of cancellation for 3 States, 1990, GAO rpt, 26113–509

Oil and gas proposed exploration off North Carolina, environmental and socioeconomic impacts, 1970s-90 and projected to 2020, 5738–22

Physicians, by specialty, age, sex, and location of training and practice, 1989, State rpt, 4116–6.34

Population and housing census, 1990: population and housing characteristics, households, and land area, by county, subdiv, and place, State rpt, 2551–1.35

Population and housing census, 1990: voting age and total population by race, and housing units, by block, redistricting counts required under PL 94-171, State CD-ROM release, 2551–6.6

Population and housing census, 1990: voting age and total population by race, and housing units, by county and city, redistricting counts required under PL 94-171, State summary rpt, 2551–5.34

Statistical Abstract of US, 1991 annual data compilation, 2324–1

Supplemental Security Income payments and beneficiaries, by type of eligibility, State, and county, Dec 1989, annual rpt, 4744–27.4

Textile mill employment, earnings, and hours, for 8 Southeastern States, quarterly press release, 6942–1

Textile production workers and wages by occupation, and benefits, by location, 1990 survey, 6787–6.251

Timber in North Carolina, acreage, resources, and removals by species, ownership class, and county, 1989/90, series, 1206–4

Water (groundwater) supply, quality, chemistry, and use, 1987, State rpt, 5666–28.1

Water supply and quality in streams and lakes, and groundwater levels in wells, by drainage basin, 1990, annual State rpt, 5666–10.32

see also Asheville, N.C.
see also Charlotte, N.C.
see also Durham, N.C.
see also Fayetteville, N.C.
see also Gastonia, N.C.
see also Jacksonville, N.C.
see also Mecklenburg County, N.C.
see also New Bern, N.C.
see also Raleigh, N.C.
see also under By State in the "Index by Categories"

North Central States

Banking industry structure, performance, and financial devs, for Fed Reserve 10th District, 1990, annual rpt, 9381–14

Birds (duck) breeding population, by species, State, and Canada Province, 1990-91 and trends from 1955, annual rpt, 5504–30

Business and economic conditions, Fed Reserve 9th District, quarterly journal, 9383–19

Carbon dioxide in atmosphere, North Central States economic and agricultural impacts, model descriptions and results, 1980s and projected to 2030, 3006–11.15

CPI by component for US city average, and by region, population size, and for 27 metro areas, monthly rpt, 6762–2

Dairy prices, by product and selected area, with related marketing data, 1990, annual rpt, 1317–1

Earthquakes in midwestern States, intensity, time, and seismograph locations, 1977-90, annual rpt, 9634–10

Economic conditions and outlook, for US and Canada Great Lakes area, 1970s-90, 9375–15

Economic indicators and cyclical devs and outlook, by Fed Reserve Bank District, periodic rpt, 9362–8

Farm credit conditions and economic devs, Fed Reserve 7th District, monthly rpt, 9375–10

Farm credit conditions, earnings, and expenses, Fed Reserve 9th District, quarterly rpt, 9383–11

Financial and economic analysis, and economic issues affecting North Central States, working paper series, 9375–13

Financial and economic devs, Fed Reserve Bank of Chicago bimonthly journal, 9375–1

Financial and economic devs, Fed Reserve Bank of Cleveland quarterly journal, 9377–1

Financial and economic devs, Fed Reserve Bank of Kansas City bimonthly journal, 9381–1

Financial and economic devs, Fed Reserve Bank of Minneapolis quarterly journal, 9383–6

Financial and economic devs, Fed Reserve Bank of St Louis bimonthly journal, 9391–1

Govt revenues and tax capacity for State and local govts, by source and western State, 1988, article, 9381–1.204

Head Start enrollment and operations, by North Central State, annual chartbook, discontinued, 4604–12

HHS financial aid, by program, recipient, State, and city, FY90, annual regional listing, 4004–3.5; 4004–3.7

Hogs inventory, value, farrowings, and farms, by State, quarterly release, 1623–3

Housing vacancy rates for single and multifamily units and mobile homes in FHLB 10th District, by ZIP code, annual MSA rpt series, 9304–22

Income (personal) per capita and by source, and earnings by industry div, by State, MSA, and county, 1984-89, annual regional rpt, 2704–2.2; 2704–2.3

Industry diversification, and employment and output relation to natl economic conditions, by industry and North Central State, 1950s-89, working paper, 9375–13.63

Lumber (industrial roundwood) production for North Central States, by product and county, State rpt series, 1206–10

Lumber (veneer log) production, mill receipts, and trade, by species, with residue use, for North Central States, 1988, quadrennial rpt, 1208–220

Manufacturing output of Middle Atlantic and East North Central census divs relative to US, by industry and State, alternative estimates 1963 and 1986, working paper, 9375–13.59

Population, income, and employment growth for Fed Reserve 10th District, by MSA, metro-nonmetro location, and State, 1970s-90s, article, 9381–1.209

North Central States

Savings and loan assns, FHLB 6th District insured members financial condition and operations by State, quarterly rpt, 9302–23

Savings and loan assns, FHLB 8th District members, locations, assets, and savings, 1991, annual listing, 9304–9

Savings instns, FHLB 6th and 11th District and natl cost of funds indexes, and mortgage and Treasury bill rates, monthly rpt, 9302–38

Savings instns, FHLB 6th District members financial condition and operations by State, monthly rpt, 9302–11

Savings instns, FHLB 7th District and natl cost of funds indexes, and mortgage rates, monthly rpt, 9302–30

Savings instns, FHLB 8th District members financial operations by State and SMSA, quarterly rpt, discontinued, 9302–9

Statistical Abstract of US, 1991 annual data compilation, 2324–1

Tax structure and revenue changes, for North Central States, 1980s, article, 9375–1.211

Water (groundwater) supply, quality, chemistry, other characteristics, and use, 1989 regional rpt, 5666–25.10

see also under By Region in the "Index by Categories"

see also under names of individual States

North Dakota

AIDS public knowledge, for North Dakota, 1987-89 surveys, article, 4042–3.211

Banks (insured commercial and savings) deposits by instn, State, MSA, and county, as of June 1990, annual regional rpt, 9295–3.5

Birds in Badlands Natl Park juniper forest and mixed grass rangeland habitats, population and species diversity by season, 1991 rpt, 1208–364

Business and economic conditions, Fed Reserve 9th District, quarterly journal, 9383–19

Coal production and mines by county, prices, productivity, miners, and reserves, by mining method and State, 1989-90, annual rpt, 3164–25

County Business Patterns, 1989: employment, establishments, and payroll, by SIC 2- to 4-digit industry and county, annual State rpt, 2326–8.36

DOD prime contract awards, by contractor, service branch, State, and city, FY90, annual rpt, 3544–22

Fed Govt spending in States and local areas, by type, State, county, and city, FY90, annual rpt, 2464–3

Fed Govt spending in States, by type, program, agency, and State, FY90, annual rpt, 2464–2

HHS financial aid, by program, recipient, State, and city, FY90, annual regional listing, 4004–3.8

Hospital deaths of Medicare patients, actual and expected rates by diagnosis, and hospital characteristics, by instn, FY87-89, annual regional rpt, 4654–14.8

Income (personal) per capita and by source, and earnings by industry div, by State, MSA, and county, 1984-89, annual regional rpt, 2704–2.3

Jail adult and juvenile population, employment, spending, instn conditions,

and inmate programs, by county and facility, 1988, regional rpt series, 6068–144.3

Marriages, divorces, and rates, by characteristics of spouses, State, and county, 1987 and trends from 1920, US Vital Statistics annual rpt, 4144–4

Mineral Industry Surveys, State reviews of production, 1990, preliminary annual rpt, 5614–6

Minerals Yearbook, 1989, Vol 2: State review of production and sales by commodity, and business activity, annual rpt, 5604–16.35

Minerals Yearbook, 1989, Vol 2: State reviews of production, sales, and firms, by commodity, and business activity, annual rpt, 5604–34

Physicians, by specialty, age, sex, and location of training and practice, 1989, State rpt, 4116–6.35

Population and housing census, 1990: population and housing characteristics, households, and land area, by county, subdiv, and place, State rpt, 2551–1.36

Population and housing census, 1990: voting age and total population by race, and housing units, by block, redistricting counts required under PL 94-171, State CD-ROM release, 2551–6.3

Population and housing census, 1990: voting age and total population by race, and housing units, by county and city, redistricting counts required under PL 94-171, State summary rpt, 2551–5.35

Recreation (outdoor) facilities on public land, use, and Land Mgmt Bur mgmt activities, funding, and plans, 1990 State rpt, 5726–5.5

Statistical Abstract of US, 1991 annual data compilation, 2324–1

Supplemental Security Income payments and beneficiaries, by type of eligibility, State, and county, Dec 1989, annual rpt, 4744–27.8

Wages by occupation, for office and plant workers, 1991 survey, periodic labor market rpt, 6785–3.9

Wildlife mgmt activities and funding, acreage by habitat type, and scientific staff, for Bur of Land Mgmt, 1990 State rpt, 5726–7.4

see also under By State in the "Index by Categories"

North Little Rock, Ark.

Wages by occupation, for office and plant workers, 1991 survey, periodic MSA rpt, 6785–12.7

North Sea

Oil supply, demand, and stock forecasts, by world area, quarterly rpt, 3162–34

Northeast States

Banks in northeast US, financial performance compared to rest of US, 1970s-90, article, 9373–1.220

CPI by component for US city average, and by region, population size, and for 27 metro areas, monthly rpt, 6762–2

Dairy prices, by product and selected area, with related marketing data, 1990, annual rpt, 1317–1

Economic and financial devs, Fed Reserve Bank of Boston quarterly journal, 9373–25

Index by Subjects and Names

Economic indicators and cyclical devs and outlook, by Fed Reserve Bank District, periodic rpt, 9362–8

Economic indicators for New England States, Fed Reserve 1st District, monthly rpt, 9373–2

Employment and personal income growth rates, and unemployment, by New England State, 1989-90 and projected to 1993, semiannual article, 9302–4.201; 9302–4.203

Employment growth rates for New England, and performance of alternative forecasts, 1950s-91, article, 9373–1.211

Employment over business cycles, by census div and State, 1988-92, release, 9538–8

Employment variability in New England relation to service and financial industries employment, with data by selected industry group and State, 1970s-89, article, 9373–1.212

Financial and economic devs, Fed Reserve Bank of Boston bimonthly journal, 9373–1

Fish (groundfish) juvenile population distribution by species, for New England area, 1968-86, 2168–122

Fish and shellfish catch, by species and New England State and port, 1988-89, article, 2162–1.204

Fish and shellfish catch, life cycles, and environmental needs, for selected coastal species and regions, series, 5506–8

Fish catch off Northeast States by species, 1988-89 and compared to record years, article, 2162–1.203

Fishing (ocean sport) activities, and catch by species, by angler characteristics and State, 1987-89, annual coastal area rpt, 2166–17.1

Fishing (ocean sport and commercial) catch and quotas for US and Canada, by species for North Atlantic Ocean, 1990, annual rpt, 2164–14

Forest wildlife habitat characteristics in northeastern US, by location, State rpt series, 1206–44

HHS financial aid, by program, recipient, State, and city, FY90, annual regional listing, 4004–3.1

Income (personal) per capita and by source, and earnings by industry div, by State, MSA, and county, 1984-89, annual regional rpt, 2704–2.2

Lumber (industrial roundwood) production in northeastern US, by product, State rpt series, 1206–15

Lumber (pulpwood) production by species and county, and shipments, by northeastern State, 1989, annual rpt, 1204–18

Marine mammals strandings on land, physical characteristics and tests performed, for New England, 1970s, 14738–8

Recreation (outdoor) coastal facilities of Fed Govt and States, visitor and site characteristics, 1987-90 survey, regional rpt, 2176–9.2; 2176–9.7

Recreation areas use in northeastern US, mgmt, and tourism dev issues, 1990 conf, 1208–356

Savings banks insured by Bank Insurance Fund, financial condition and performance, by asset size and region, quarterly rpt, 9292–1.2; 9292–5

Index by Subjects and Names

Savings instns, FHLB 1st District members financial operations compared to banks, and related economic and housing indicators, bimonthly rpt with articles, 9302–4

Statistical Abstract of US, 1991 annual data compilation, 2324–1

Textile production workers and wages by occupation, and benefits, by location, 1990 survey, 6787–6.251

Tide height and time daily at coastal points, forecast 1992, annual rpt, 2174–2.3

Timber in New England, acreage and resources by State, 1982-85, pamphlet, 1208–363

Timber in New England, growth and relationship to tree and site characteristics, 1900s-85, 1208–349

Timber in northeastern US, biomass volume by characteristics of tree and forest, and county, State rpt series, 1206–43

Timber in northeastern US, change in value by species, with methodology, 1970s-85, 1208–348

Timber in northeastern US, resources, and related manufacturing industries employment and finances, by State, 1977-87, 1208–375

Timber in northeastern US, resources and removals by species, ownership class, and county, State rpt series, 1206–12

Timber survival rates in northeastern US, by species, model description and results, 1990 rpt, 1208–369

Water supply in northeastern US, precipitation and stream runoff by station, monthly rpt, 2182–3

Wetlands in coastal areas, acreage by wetland type, estuarine basin, and county, 1989, 2178–31

see also Appalachia

see also under By Region in the "Index by Categories"

see also under names of individual States

Northern Economics

"Economic Impacts of the S.S. Glacier Bay Oil Spill. Alaska Social and Economic Study", 5736–5.15

Northern Mariana Islands

Agriculture census, 1987: farms, farmland, production, finances, and operator characteristics, by island and island group, 1990, final outlying area rpt, 2331–1.56

Banks (insured commercial and savings) deposits by instn, State, MSA, and county, as of June 1990, annual regional rpt, 9295–3.6

Economic, social, political, and geographic summary data, by country, 1991, annual factbook, 9114–2

Exports and imports between US and outlying areas, by detailed commodity and mode of transport, 1990, annual rpt, 2424–11

Fed Govt spending in States and local areas, by type, State, county, and city, FY90, annual rpt, 2464–3

Fed Govt spending in States, by type, program, agency, and State, FY90, annual rpt, 2464–2

HHS financial aid, by program, recipient, State, and city, FY90, annual regional listing, 4004–3.9

Physicians, by specialty, age, sex, and location of training and practice, 1989, State rpt, 4116–6.53

Statistical Abstract of US, 1991 annual data compilation, 2324–1.30

Supplemental Security Income payments and beneficiaries by State and for Northern Mariana Islands, monthly rpt, 4742–1.4

Supplemental Security Income payments and recipients by State and for Northern Mariana Islands, monthly rpt, 4742–1.12

see also under By Outlying Area in the "Index by Categories"

Northern spotted owl

see Birds and bird conservation

Norton, Arthur J.

"Remarriage Among Women in the U.S.: 1985", 2546–2.157

Norwalk, Conn.

see also under By SMSA or MSA in the "Index by Categories"

Norway

Agricultural exports of high-value commodities, indexes and sales by commodity, world area, and country, 1960s-86, 1528–323

Agricultural exports of US, impacts of foreign agricultural and trade policy, with data by commodity and country, 1989, annual rpt, 1924–8

Agricultural production, prices, and trade, by country, 1970s-90, and forecast 1991, annual world region rpt, 1524–4.4

Agricultural production, trade, and policies in foreign countries, summary data by country, 1989-90, annual factbook, 1924–12

Agricultural trade of US, by detailed commodity and country, 1989, annual rpt, 1524–8

Agricultural trade of US, by detailed commodity and country, 1990, semiannual rpt, 1522–4

AID loans repayment status and terms by program and country, and status of predecessor agency loans, quarterly rpt, 9912–3

Economic and military aid and loans from US and intl agencies, by program and country, FY46-90, annual rpt, 9914–5

Economic conditions, income, production, prices, employment, and trade, 1991 periodic country rpt, 2046–4.69

Economic conditions, policy, and trade practices, by country, 1988-90, annual rpt, 21384–5

Economic, social, political, and geographic summary data, by country, 1991, annual factbook, 9114–2

Exports and imports of NATO members with PRC, by country, 1987-90, annual rpt, 7144–14

Exports and imports of OECD members, by country, 1989, annual rpt, 7144–10

Exports and imports of US, by Harmonized System 6-digit commodity and country, 1990, annual rpt, 2424–13

Exports and imports of US, by selected country, country group, and commodity group, 1990, annual rpt, 2044–37

Exports and imports of US, by transport mode, country, and SITC 1- to 3-digit commodity, 1990, annual rpt, 2424–12

Exports of US, detailed Schedule B commodities with countries of destination, 1990, annual rpt, 2424–10

Nose and throat disorders

Fish (salmon) aquaculture production, farms, and exports, for Norway, 1971-88 with projections to 1990, article, 2162–1.204

Fish (salmon) from Norway, injury to US industry from foreign subsidized and less than fair value imports, investigation with background financial and operating data, 1991 rpt, 9886–19.75

GNP and GNP growth for OECD members, by country, 1980-90, annual rpt, 7144–8

Human rights conditions in 170 countries, and US economic and military aid, 1990, annual rpt, 21384–3

Imports of goods, services, and investment from US, trade barriers, impacts, and US actions, by country, 1990, annual rpt, 444–2

Magnesium from Canada and Norway, injury to US industry from foreign subsidized and less than fair value imports, investigation with background financial and operating data, 1991 rpt, 9886–19.80

Military reserve forces structure and training, for US and 5 European countries, as of 1990, GAO rpt, 26123–358

Multinatl US firms and foreign affiliates finances and operations, by industry and world area of parent firm, 1989 benchmark survey, preliminary annual rpt, 2704–5

Multinatl US firms foreign affiliates, income statement items by country and world area, 1986, biennial article, 8302–2.212

Oil exports to US by OPEC and non-OPEC countries, monthly rpt, 3162–24.3

Oil production, trade, use, and stocks, by selected country and country group, monthly rpt, 3162–42

Ships in world merchant fleet, tonnage, and new ship construction and deliveries, by vessel type and country, as of Jan 1990, annual rpt, 7704–3

Tax revenue, by level of govt and type of tax, for OECD countries, mid 1960s-89, annual rpt, 10044–1.2

UN voting record and share of votes in agreement with US, by issue, country, and world area, 1990, annual rpt, 7004–18

see also under By Foreign Country in the "Index by Categories"

Norwich, Conn.

see also under By SMSA or MSA in the "Index by Categories"

Nosal, Ed

"Note on Labor Contracts with Private Information and Household Production", 9383–20.1

Nose and throat disorders

Agent Orange exposure of Vietnam veterans, and other factors relation to dev of rare cancers, 1984-88, 4208–33

Cancer cases, deaths, and survival rates, by sex, race, age, and body site, 1973-88, annual rpt, 4474–35

Cancer death rates of minorities, by body site, age, sex, and substate area, 1950s-80, atlas, 4478–78

Cases of acute and chronic conditions, disability, absenteeism, and health services use, by selected characteristics, 1987, CD-ROM, 4147–10.177

Deaths and rates, by detailed cause and demographic characteristics, 1988 and trends from 1900, US Vital Statistics annual rpt, 4144–2

Notifiable diseases

Notifiable diseases
see Infective and parasitic diseases

Notions
see Clothing and clothing industry
see Household supplies and utensils

Novara, Albert N.
"Preliminary Estimates of Age and Sex Compositions of Ducks and Geese Harvested in the 1990 Hunting Season in Comparison with Prior Years", 5504–32
"Sandhill Crane Harvest and Hunter Activity in the Central Flyway During the 1990-91 Hunting Season", 5504–31

NOW accounts
see Negotiable orders of withdrawal accounts

NSF
see National Science Foundation

Nuclear accidents and safety
Chernobyl, USSR nuclear reactor accident, radionuclide releases and concentrations in food and water, by selected Soviet Republic, 1986-87 article, 4042–3.201
DOE and DOE-contractor sites radiation exposure, by facility type and contractor, 1987, annual rpt, 3324–1
Hanford, Wash nuclear plant, nearby population radiation exposure, with methodology, 1944-66, series, 3356–5
Incidents and mgmt of disasters and natl security threats, with data by major event and State, 1991 annual rpt, 9434–6
Inspection, regulatory, and licensing activities of NRC, budget and staff, by program, FY90-93, annual rpt, 9634–9
Inspection, regulatory, and licensing activities of NRC, with data for individual power plants, FY90, annual rpt, 9634–2
Operations of commercial reactors, by facility, 1990, annual rpt, 9634–12
Radiation and radionuclide concentrations in surface air at selected monitoring sites worldwide, and effects of nuclear tests and accidents, 1989, annual rpt, 3004–31
Radiation exposure of workers at nuclear power plants and related facilities, by site, 1968-87, annual rpt, 9634–3
Radiation protection and health physics enrollment and degrees granted by instn and State, and female grads plans and employment, 1990, annual rpt, 3006–8.15
Radiation protection and health physics enrollment and degrees granted by instn and State, and grad placement, by student characteristics, 1990, annual rpt, 3004–7
Safety standards and research, design, licensing, construction, operation, and finances, for nuclear power plants with data by reactor, quarterly journal, 3352–4
Shift rotation health and safety effects, and US and foreign regulation, by selected industry and occupation, 1970s-89, 26356–9.3

Nuclear explosives and explosions
Radiation and radionuclide concentrations in surface air at selected monitoring sites worldwide, and effects of nuclear tests and accidents, 1989, annual rpt, 3004–31
Strontium-90 fallout, monitoring results for 65 sites worldwide, quarterly 1986 and trends from 1958, annual rpt, 3004–29
see also Nuclear weapons

Nuclear fallout
see Nuclear explosives and explosions
see Radiation

Nuclear industries
see Nuclear power

Nuclear medicine and radiology
Cancer (brain and central nervous system) cases and rates, by whether confirmed by radiography alone, for Connecticut, 1960s-88, article, 4472–1.234
Cancer (childhood) survivors risk of miscarriage, stillbirth, and birth defects, by chemotherapy and radiotherapy exposure, study, 1991 article, 4472–1.233
Cancer cases among persons treated for thyroid disorders with radionuclide iodine-131, for Sweden, 1950-85 study, article, 4472–1.218
Education in nuclear engineering and science, facilities, student aid, and degrees granted, by instn, as of Sept 1990, 3008–126
Equipment shipments, trade, use, and firms, for electronic medical equipment by product, 1990, annual Current Industrial Rpt, 2506–12.34
Hospital discharges and length of stay, by diagnosis, patient and instn characteristics, procedure performed, and payment source, 1988, annual rpt, 4147–13.107
Hospital discharges by detailed diagnostic and procedure category, primary diagnosis, and length of stay, by age, sex, and region, 1988, annual rpt, 4147–13.105; 4147–13.108
Hospital services and facilities availability, by selected instn characteristics, 1980, 1983, and 1987, 17206–2.22
Labor supply of physicians, by specialty, age, sex, and location of training and practice, 1989, State rpt series, 4116–6
Manufacturing finances and operations, by SIC 2- to 4-digit industry, forecast 1991, annual rpt, 2044–28
Medicare reimbursement for radiology services by location, and for home medical equipment under alternative proposals, 1990 hearing, 21368–131
Medicare Supplementary Medical Insurance physicians fee schedule, methodology with data by procedure and specialty, 1991, annual rpt, 17264–1
Military health care personnel, and accessions by training source, by occupation, specialty, and service branch, FY89, annual rpt, 3544–24
Radiation exposure of workers at nuclear power plants and related facilities, by site, 1968-87, annual rpt, 9634–3
Radiation from electronic devices, incidents by type of device, and FDA control activities, 1990, annual rpt, 4064–13
Radiation protection and health physics enrollment and degrees granted by instn and State, and female grads plans and employment, 1990, annual rpt, 3006–8.15
Radiation protection and health physics enrollment and degrees granted by instn and State, and grad placement, by student characteristics, 1990, annual rpt, 3004–7
Respiratory diseases related to occupational hazards, epidemiology, diagnosis, and treatment, for selected industries and work settings, 1988 conf, 4248–90

Teenagers physicians office visits, by reason and characteristics of physicians, patients, and visit, 1985, 4146–8.199
VA health care facilities physicians, dentists, and nurses, by selected employment characteristics and VA district, quarterly rpt, 8602–6
VA health care staff and turnover, by occupation, physician specialty, and location, 1990, annual rpt, 8604–8
VA Medicine and Surgery Dept trainees, by detailed program and city, FY90, annual rpt, 8704–4
Waste (radioactive) generation, inventory, and disposal, 1960s-89 and projected to 2020, annual rpt, 3364–2
see also X-rays

Nuclear power
Construction industries census, 1987: establishments, employment, receipts, and expenditures, by SIC 4-digit industry and State, final industry rpt series, 2373–1
Consumption of energy, by detailed fuel type, end-use sector, and State, 1960-89, State Energy Data System annual rpt, 3164–39
Criminal cases by type and disposition, and collections, for US attorneys, by Federal district, FY90, annual rpt, 6004–2.1
Engineering (nuclear) and science educational facilities, student aid, and degrees granted, by instn, 1990, 3008–126
Engineering (nuclear) enrollment and degrees by instn and State, and women grads plans and employment, 1974-90, annual rpt, 3006–8.14
Engineering (nuclear) enrollment and degrees granted by instn and State, and grad placement, by student characteristics, 1990, annual rpt, 3004–5
Environmental Quality, status of problems, protection programs, research, and intl issues, 1991 annual rpt, 484–1
Exports and imports of US, by Harmonized System 6-digit commodity and country, 1990, annual rpt, 2424–13
Exports of US, detailed Schedule B commodities with countries of destination, 1990, annual rpt, 2424–10
Finances and operations of energy producers, by energy type for US firms domestic and foreign operations, 1989, annual rpt, 3164–44
Foreign and US energy production and use, by energy type and country, 1980-89, annual rpt, 3164–50.1; 3164–50.5; 3164–50.8
Foreign and US energy use and production, by fuel type, country, and country group, projected 1995-2010 and trends from 1970, annual rpt, 3164–84
Foreign and US nuclear power generation, by market economy country, monthly rpt, 9112–2
Foreign and US nuclear power plant capacity, generation, and construction and operating status, by plant and location, as of 1990 and projected to 2030, annual rpt, 3164–57
Natl Energy Strategy plans for conservation and pollution reduction, impacts of technology and regulation proposals, projected 1990-2030, 3166–6.47

Natl Energy Strategy plans for conservation and pollution reduction, impacts on electric power supply, costs, and emissions, projected under alternative assumptions, 1995-2030, 3166–6.49

Power plants and capacity, by fuel used, owner, location, and operating status, 1990, and for units planned 1991-2000, annual listing, 3164–36

Power plants capital and production costs, operations, and fuel use, by fuel type, plant, utility, and location, 1989, annual rpt, 3164–9

Power plants operating, maintenance, and capital additions costs, relation to plant characteristics and regulation, 1974-89, 3168–108

Power plants production and capacity by fuel type, prices, demand, and air pollution law impacts, by region, 1989-90 and projected to 2010, annual rpt, 3164–81

Power plants production, capacity, and fuel use, by fuel type, census div, and State, 1985-89, annual rpt, 3164–11.1

Power plants production, fuel use, stocks, and costs by fuel type, and sales, by State, monthly rpt with articles, 3162–35

Prices and spending for fuel, by type, end-use sector, and State, 1989, annual rpt, 3164–64

Reactors for domestic use and export by function and operating status, with owner, operating characteristics, and location, 1990, annual listing, 3354–15

Reactors operations, by commercial facility, 1990, annual rpt, 9634–12

Regulatory, inspection, and licensing activities of NRC, budget and staff, by program, FY90-93, annual rpt, 9634–9

Regulatory, inspection, and licensing activities of NRC, with data for individual power plants, FY90, annual rpt, 9634–2

Rural Electrification Admin financed electric power plants, with location, capacity, and owner, as of Jan 1991, annual listing, 1244–6

Soviet Union, Eastern Europe, OECD, and selected other countries energy reserves, production, and use, and oil trade and revenue, 1960s-90, annual rpt, 9114–4.4

State and Metro Area Data Book, 1991 data compilation, 2328–54

Statistical Abstract of US, 1991 annual data compilation, 2324–1.19

Supply, demand, and prices, by fuel type and end-use sector, alternative projections 1989-2010, annual rpt, 3164–75

Supply, demand, and prices, by fuel type and end-use sector, projections and underlying assumptions, 1990-2010, annual rpt, 3164–90

Supply, demand, and prices, by fuel type and end-use sector, with foreign comparisons, 1990 and trends from 1949, annual rpt, 3164–74

Supply, demand, and prices, by fuel type, end-use sector, and country, detailed data, monthly rpt with articles, 3162–24

Supply, demand, and prices of energy, forecasts by resource type, quarterly rpt, 3162–34

TVA finances and operations by program and facility, FY90, annual rpt, 9804–32

Utilities finances and operations, detailed data for privately owned firms, 1989, annual rpt, 3164–23

Utilities finances and operations, detailed data for publicly owned firms, 1989, annual rpt, 3164–24

see also Nuclear accidents and safety

see also Nuclear explosives and explosions

see also Nuclear-powered ships

see also Nuclear weapons

see also Radiation

see also Radioactive waste and disposal

see also Uranium

Nuclear-powered ships

Budget of DOD, programs, policies, and operations, FY90, annual rpt, 3544–2

Radiation exposure of Navy personnel on nuclear-powered vessels and at support facilities, and injury claims, 1950s-90, annual rpt, 3804–10

Radioactive waste from Navy nuclear-powered vessels and support facilities, releases in harbors, and public exposure, 1970s-90, annual rpt, 3804–11

Reactors for domestic use and export by function and operating status, with owner, operating characteristics, and location, 1990, annual listing, 3354–15

Soviet Union military weapons systems, presence, and force strengths, and compared to US, 1991 annual rpt, 3504–20

Nuclear radiation

see Radiation

Nuclear Regulatory Commission

Activities, finances, and staff of NRC, with data for individual power plants, FY90, annual rpt, 9634–2

Activities of NRC, budget, staff, and activities by program, FY90-93, annual rpt, 9634–9

Budget of US, authoritative financial statements with appropriations, outlays, and receipts, by category and agency, FY90, annual rpt, 8104–2.1

Budget of US, obligations and authority by function, agency, and program, with summaries, analyses, and historical tables, FY92, annual rpt, 104–2

Earthquakes in midwestern States, intensity, time, and seismograph locations, 1977-90, annual rpt, 9634–10

Education funding by Federal agency, program, and recipient type, and instn spending, FY80-90, annual rpt, 4824–8

Inspection and operations of commercial reactors, by facility, monthly rpt, periodicity change, 9632–1

Nuclear engineering enrollment and degrees granted by instn and State, and grad placement, by student characteristics, 1990, annual rpt, 3004–5

Occupational radiation exposure at nuclear power plants and related facilities, by site, 1968-87, annual rpt, 9634–3

Operations of commercial reactors, by facility, 1990, annual rpt, 9634–12

Penalties assessed by NRC, 1974-89, 3168–108

R&D and related funding of Fed Govt to higher education and nonprofit instns, by field, instn, agency, and State, FY89, annual rpt, 9627–17

R&D funding by Fed Govt, by field, performer type, agency, and State, FY89-91, annual rpt, 9627–20

Radiation protection and health physics enrollment and degrees granted by instn and State, and grad placement, by student characteristics, 1990, annual rpt, 3004–7

Radioactive waste from nuclear power plants, releases and waste composition by plant, 1988, annual rpt, 9634–1

Nuclear weapons

Budget of US, obligations and authority by function, agency, and program, with summaries, analyses, and historical tables, FY92, annual rpt, 104–2

DOD budget, programs, and policies, FY90, annual rpt, 3544–2

DOD prime contract awards, by detailed procurement category, FY87-90, annual rpt, 3544–18

DOE and nuclear weapons labs screening of contractors for foreign ownership, control, or influence, compliance by lab, FY88-90, GAO rpt, 26113–520

NATO and Japan military spending and indicators of ability to support common defense, by country, 1970s-89, annual rpt, 3544–28

Radiation exposure at DOE and DOE-contractor sites, by facility type and contractor, dose type, and worker age, sex, and occupation, 1988, annual rpt, 3324–1

Reactors for domestic use and export by function and operating status, with owner, operating characteristics, and location, 1990, annual listing, 3354–15

Security forces under contract at DOE nuclear weapons facilities, skill deficiencies, and costs compared to Federal security, late 1980s, GAO rpt, 26113–493

Soviet Union and US nuclear weapons systems, costs, and military forces survival after attack, projected under alternative arms control proposals, FY92-2006, 26306–6.161

Soviet Union military weapons systems, presence, and force strengths, and compared to US, 1991 annual rpt, 3504–20

Statistical Abstract of US, 1991 annual data compilation, 2324–1.11

UN voting record and share of votes in agreement with US, by issue, country, and world area, 1990, annual rpt, 7004–18

Waste (radioactive) at DOE nuclear weapons facilities, storage plans, and mgmt issues, 1988, 26358–236

Waste (radioactive) generation, inventory, and disposal, 1960s-89 and projected to 2020, annual rpt, 3364–2

Waste (radioactive and hazardous) at DOE facilities, disposal and remediation activities and funding, planned FY91-97, annual rpt, 3024–7

see also Intermediate-Range Nuclear Forces Treaty

see also Nuclear explosives and explosions

see also Strategic Arms Reduction Talks

Numismatics

see Coins and coinage

Nurseries

see Child day care

Nurseries and nursery products

see Flowers and nursery products

Nursery schools

Nursery schools
see Preschool education

Nurses and nursing

AIDS knowledge, attitudes, and transmission prevention practices of physicians and RNs, 1990-91, 4186–9.11

Drug and alcohol abuse treatment facilities, services, use, funding, staff, and client characteristics, 1989, biennial rpt, 4494–10

Earnings, annual average percent changes for selected occupational groups, selected MSAs, monthly rpt, 6782–1.1

Education in nursing, faculty by race, Hispanic origin, and degree level, 1988, hearing, 25418–6

Education in science and engineering, grad programs enrollment by field, source of funds, and characteristics of student and instn, 1975-89, annual rpt, 9627–7

Germany (West) health care spending, by funding source and service type, and resource growth, 1970-89, article, 4652–1.238

Health condition and health care resources, use, and spending, 1950s-89, annual data compilation, 4144–11

Hepatitis B cases, exposure, and vaccination policies for students in nursing and lab technician training programs, 1989, article, 4042–3.244

HHS financial aid, by program, recipient, State, and city, FY90, annual regional listings, 4004–3

Home health care agencies finances impacts of Medicare payment limits under alternative determination methods, with data by service type, 1984-89, GAO rpt, 26121–400

Home health care services Medicare use and costs, by agency and service type, patient characteristics, and State, 1988-89, article, 4652–1.229

Home health care visits approved by Medicare, planned and actual visits by service type, 1986, article, 4652–1.254

Hospices operations, services, costs, and patient characteristics, for instns without Medicare certification, FY85-86, 4658–52

Hospital deaths of Medicare patients, actual and expected rates by diagnosis, with hospital characteristics, by instn, FY87-89, annual regional rpt series, 4654–14

Hospital nursing staff registered nurses share, and earnings growth rate, various periods 1980-88, annual rpt, 4654–13

Indian Health Service and tribal facility outpatient visits, by type of provider, selected hospital, and service area, FY90, annual rpt, 4084–3

Indian Health Service facilities, funding, operations, and Indian health and other characteristics, 1950s-90, annual chartbook, 4084–1

Indian Health Service nursing staff, shortages, workload, and pay, by IHS service unit, mid 1980s-90, hearing, 25418–6

Medicare input price index rebased to 1987, methodology and results, 1991, article, 4652–1.231

Medicare reimbursement of hospitals under prospective payment system, and effect on services, finances, and beneficiary payments, 1979-90, annual rpt, 17204–2

Mental health care facilities, staff, and patient characteristics, *Statistical Notes* series, 4506–3

Military health care personnel, and accessions by training source, by occupation, specialty, and service branch, FY89, annual rpt, 3544–24

Military reserve medical personnel, by specialty and reserve component, FY90, annual rpt, 3544–31.1

Minority group and women health condition, services use, payment sources, and health care labor force, by poverty status, 1940s-89, chartbook, 4118–56

Navy personnel strengths, accessions, and attrition, detailed statistics, quarterly rpt, 3802–4

Nursing home reimbursement by Medicaid, resident classification using patient and care characteristics, New York State, 1990 article, 4652–1.205

Organ and tissue transplants, hospital nurses knowledge, beliefs, and requests for family consent, 1988 survey, article, 4042–3.214

Shift rotation health and safety effects, and US and foreign regulation, by selected industry and occupation, 1970s-89, 26356–9.3

State and Metro Area Data Book, 1991 data compilation, 2328–54

Statistical Abstract of US, 1991 annual data compilation, 2324–1.3

Tax (income) returns of sole proprietorships, income statement items, by industry group, 1989, annual article, 8302–2.214

VA health care facilities physicians, dentists, and nurses, by selected employment characteristics and VA district, quarterly rpt, 8602–6

VA health care professionals employment, by district and facility, quarterly rpt, 8602–4

VA health care staff and turnover, by occupation, physician specialty, and location, 1990, annual rpt, 8604–8

VA Medicine and Surgery Dept trainees, by detailed program and city, FY90, annual rpt, 8704–4

see also Midwives

Nursing homes

Adult day care centers revenue by source, and expenses by type, by agency type, FY86, article, 4652–1.234

Alzheimer's disease special units and beds in nursing homes, by facility characteristics, 1987, 4186–8.12

Construction put in place, private and public, by type and region, monthly rpt, annual tables, 2382–4

Costs of long-term health care for aged, under alternative private insurance policy types, 1989 hearing, 23898–8

County Business Patterns, 1988: employment, establishments, and payroll, by SIC 2- to 4-digit industry and county, annual State rpt series, 2326–6

County Business Patterns, 1989: employment, establishments, and payroll, by SIC 2- to 4-digit industry and county, annual State rpt series, 2326–8

Deaths of aged in hospitals, nursing homes, and own home, by cause, age, marital status, and region, 1986, article, 4652–1.201

Index by Subjects and Names

Employment, earnings, and hours, by SIC 1- to 4-digit industry, monthly and annual averages, selected years 1909-90, annual rpt, 6744–4

Energy use in commercial buildings, costs, and conservation, by building characteristics, survey rpt series, 3166–8

Enterprise Statistics, 1987: finances and operations for companies, by size, level of diversification, form of organization, and industry group, 2329–8

Expenditures for health care, by service type, payment source, and sector, projected 1990-2000 and trends from 1965, article, 4652–1.251

Expenditures for health care, by service type, payment source, and sector, 1960s-90, annual article, 4652–1.221; 4652–1.252

Expenditures for health care, cost containment methods, and insurance coverage issues, with background data, 1991 rpt, 26306–6.155

Govt finances, by level of govt, State, and for large cities and counties, annual rpt series, 2466–2

Health Care Financing Admin research activities and grants, by program, FY90, annual listing, 4654–10

Health Care Financing Review, provider prices, price inputs and indexes, and labor, quarterly journal, 4652–1.1

Health condition and health care resources, use, and spending, 1950s-89, annual data compilation, 4144–11

Health maintenance organizations financial performance and services use, demonstration project results, 1985-89, article, 4652–1.235

Hospices use by cancer patients, by service type, use of other facilities, patient and instn characteristics, and other indicators, local area study, 1980-85, 4658–53

Hospital post-discharge service use, by type, for Medicare pneumonia, stroke, and hip replacement cases, 1981-86, article, 4652–1.223

Hospital services and facilities availability, by selected instn characteristics, 1980, 1983, and 1987, 17206–2.22

Insurance (health) for long-term care, affordability and State regulation issues, 1986-90, hearing, 21368–130

Insurance (life) predeath benefits use to finance long-term care, payout terms, 1990, and coverage by beneficiary characteristics, 1984, 2626–10.128

Length of stay in nursing homes, effects of data adjustment to reflect short-term hospital stays, model results, 1987, 4186–8.15

Long-term care institutional and community services, spending and use by type and payment source, FY88, and Medicaid growth since FY75, 26306–6.156

Medicaid beneficiaries services use and costs, by service type and eligibility, 1975-89, article, 4652–1.209

Medicaid nursing home capital investment reimbursement under alternative methodologies, 30-year financial results, 1991 article, 4652–1.236

Medicaid reimbursement of nursing homes, resident classification using patient and care characteristics, New York State, 1990 article, 4652–1.205

Medicaid reimbursement of nursing homes, States payment ratesetting methods, analysis for 7 States, 1980s, article, 4652–1.255

Medicaid reimbursement of nursing homes, States payment ratesetting methods, limits, and allowances, 1988, article, 4652–1.253

Medicaid reimbursement of nursing homes under prospective and retrospective payment systems, effects on payment rate, model results, 1979-86, article, 4652–1.224

Medicare admissions to nursing homes, factors affecting change, 1983-85, article, 4652–1.222

Medicare and Medicaid beneficiaries and program operations, 1991, annual fact book, 4654–18

Medicare and Medicaid benefits, trust fund finances, and services use, 1966-89 and projected to 1995, 21148–61

Medicare and Medicaid eligibility, participation, coverage, and program finances, various periods 1966-91, biennial rpt, 4654–1

Medicare and Medicaid enrollees, benefits, reimbursements, and services use, mid-1960s-89, annual rpt, 4744–3.5; 4744–3.6

Medicare beneficiaries hospitalization length of stay and discharge destination related to insurance status and Medicaid nursing home reimbursement method, 1985, article, 4652–1.225

Medicare beneficiaries nursing home skilled care benefit use and costs, 1967-88, article, 4652–1.239

Medicare claims approved, charges, and reimbursements by type of service, from 1974, monthly rpt, quarterly data, 4742–1.11

Medicare hospital use reduction demonstration providing nursing home and other long term care services, results for Rochester, NY, 1980s, 4658–43

Medicare reimbursement of hospitals under prospective payment system, and effect on services, finances, and beneficiary payments, 1979-90, annual rpt, 17204–2

Medicare reimbursement of hospitals under prospective payment system for discharge delays due to limited nursing home space, 1985, 4658–55

Medicare reimbursement of hospitals under prospective payment system, impacts on instns and beneficiaries, 1988, annual rpt, 4654–13

Mental, behavioral, and functional disorders among nursing home residents, by age, sex, and instn characteristics, 1987, 4186–8.11

Mental illness among nursing home residents, by type of resident and instn characteristics, 1987, 4147–13.106

Mental illness and drug and alcohol abuse direct and indirect costs, by age and sex, 1985, 4048–35

Mentally retarded persons care facilities and residents by selected characteristics, and use of Medicaid services and waiver programs, by State, late 1970s-80s, 4658–49

Minority group health condition, services use, costs, and indicators of services need, 1950s-88, 4118–55

Montana health care access indicators, 1989 hearing, 23898–6

NIH grants for R&D, training, construction, and medical libraries, by location and recipient, FY90, annual listings, 4434–7

Occupational injury and illness rates, by SIC 2- to 4-digit industry, 1988-89, annual rpt, 6844–7

Occupational injury and illness rates, by SIC 2- to 4-digit industry, 1989, annual rpt, 6844–1

Older persons health care services use, by service type, discharge destination, and prior care source, 1986, 4188–72

Older persons long-term care needs and costs, late 1980s and projected 2018-60, GAO rpt, 26121–433

Older persons use of nursing homes, prevalence by length of stay and selected characteristics, 1986 and 1990, 4186–7.9

Older persons with functional limitations, long-term care sources, and health and other characteristics, 1984-85, 4147–13.104

Ombudsman programs for long term care facility residents, funding and visits by State, 1988-90, 25248–126

Pennsylvania aid to aged for prescription drugs, program enrollment, use, and costs, FY85-87, article, 4652–1.237

Receipts for services, by SIC 2- to 4-digit kind of business, 1990, annual rpt, 2413–8

Service industries census, 1987: establishments, receipts by source, payroll, and employment, by SIC 2- to 4-digit kind of business, State, and MSA, 2393–4

State and Metro Area Data Book, 1991 data compilation, 2328–54

Statistical Abstract of US, 1991 annual data compilation, 2324–1.3

Supplemental Security Income and Medicaid eligibility and payment provisions, and beneficiaries living arrangements, by State, 1991, annual rpt, 4704–13

Tax (income) returns of corporations, income and tax items by asset size and detailed industry, 1987, annual rpt, 8304–4

Tax (income) returns of corporations, income and tax items by asset size and detailed industry, 1988, annual rpt, 8304–21

Tax (income) returns of sole proprietorships, income statement items, by industry group, 1989, annual article, 8302–2.214

Veterans characteristics, and VA activities and programs, FY90, annual rpt, 8604–3

Veterans health care, patients, visits, costs, and operating beds, by VA and contract facility, and region, quarterly rpt, 8602–4

Vital and Health Statistics series: health care facilities use and labor force, 4147–13

Waste (medical) generation, sources, health worker exposure and risk, and incineration emissions, 1980s, 4078–1

Nutrition and malnutrition

Cases of acute and chronic conditions, disability, absenteeism, and health services use, by selected characteristics, 1987, CD-ROM, 4147–10.177

Deaths and rates, by cause, provisional data, monthly rpt, 4142–1.2

Deaths and rates, by detailed cause and demographic characteristics, 1988 and trends from 1900, US Vital Statistics annual rpt, 4144–2

Developing countries agricultural supply, demand, and market for US exports, with socioeconomic conditions, country rpt series, 1526–6

Developing countries economic and social conditions from 1960s, and Intl Dev Cooperation Agency and AID activities and funding, FY90-92, annual rpt, 9904–4

Developing countries food supply, needs, and aid, status and alternative forecasts, world area rpt series, 1526–8

Developing countries grains production and needs, and related economic outlook, by world area and selected country, forecast 1990/91-1991/92, 1528–313

Education natl goals progress indicators, by State, 1991, annual rpt, 15914–1

Farm financial and marketing conditions, forecast 1991, annual conf, 1004–16

Fed Govt financial and nonfinancial domestic aid, 1991 base edition with supplements, annual listing, 104–5

Foreign countries agricultural research grants of USDA, by program, subagency, and country, FY90, annual listing, 1954–3

Foreign countries disasters, casualties, damage, and aid by US and others, FY90 and trends from FY64, annual rpt, 9914–12

Health condition improvement and disease prevention goals and recommended activities for 2000, with trends 1970s-80s, 4048–10

HHS financial aid, by program, recipient, State, and city, FY90, annual regional listings, 4004–3

Minority group health condition, services use, costs, and indicators of services need, 1950s-88, 4118–55

NIH activities, funding by program and recipient type, staff, and clinic patients, by inst, FY90, annual rpt, 4434–3

Prenatal care nutritional and educational programs for women at risk of preterm delivery, and rate of anemia and low-weight births, 1985-86, article, 4042–3.235

Research and education grants, USDA competitive awards by program and recipient, FY90, annual listing, 1764–1

Statistical Abstract of US, 1991 annual data compilation, 2324–1.3

see also Breast-feeding

see also Dietitians and nutritionists

see also Food assistance

see also Food consumption

see also Food ingredients and additives

see also Food supply

see also Obesity

see also School lunch and breakfast programs

see also Vitamins and nutrients

see also under By Disease in the "Index by Categories"

Nuts

Agricultural Statistics, 1990, annual rpt, 1004–1

Agriculture census, 1987: farms, farmland, production, finances, and operator characteristics, by county, final State rpt series, 2331–1

Nuts

Almond production, trade, use, and stocks, for 6 countries and US, 1987-92, article, 1925–34.240

Cold storage food stocks by commodity and census div, and warehouse space use, by State, monthly rpt, 1631–5

Cold storage food stocks by commodity, and warehouse space use, by census div, 1990, annual rpt, 1631–11

Confectionery shipments, trade, use, and ingredients used, by product, 1990, annual Current Industrial Rpt, 2506–4.5

Consumer Expenditure Survey, food spending by item, household composition, income, age, race, and region, 1980-88, biennial rpt, 1544–30

Consumption of food, dietary composition, and nutrient intake, 1987/88 natl survey, preliminary rpt series, 1356–1

Consumption, supply, trade, prices, spending, and indexes, by food commodity, 1989, annual rpt, 1544–4

Exports (agricultural) of high-value commodities, indexes and sales value by commodity, world area, and country, 1960s-86, 1528–323

Exports (agricultural) of US, impacts of foreign agricultural and trade policy, with data by commodity and country, 1989, annual rpt, 1924–8

Exports and imports (agricultural) of US, by commodity and country, bimonthly rpt, 1522–1

Exports and imports (agricultural) of US, by detailed commodity and country, 1989, annual rpt, 1524–8

Exports and imports (agricultural) of US, by detailed commodity and country, 1990, semiannual rpt, 1522–4

Exports and imports between US and outlying areas, by detailed commodity and mode of transport, 1990, annual rpt, 2424–11

Exports and imports of US, by country and detailed commodity, monthly rpt, 2422–12

Exports and imports of US, by Harmonized System 6-digit commodity and country, 1990, annual rpt, 2424–13

Exports of US, detailed Schedule B commodities with countries of destination, 1990, annual rpt, 2424–10

Farm financial and marketing conditions, forecast 1991, annual chartbook, 1504–8

Farm income, expenses, receipts by commodity, assets, liabilities, and ratios, 1990 and trends from 1945, annual rpt, 1544–16

Farm sector balance sheet, and receipts by detailed commodity, by State, 1985-89, annual rpt, 1544–18

Foreign and US fresh and processed fruit, vegetable, and nut production and trade, FAS monthly circular with articles, 1925–34

Foreign countries agricultural production, trade, and policies, summary data by country, 1989-90, annual factbook, 1924–12

Hazelnut production, supply, trade, and use, by country, 1989-92, article, 1925–34.246

Hazelnut production, 1989-91, annual rpt, 1621–18.5

Irrigation projects of Reclamation Bur in western US, crop production and acreage by commodity, State, and project, 1989, annual rpt, 5824–12

Manufacturing annual survey, 1989: finances and operations, by SIC 2- to 4-digit industry, series, 2506–15

Manufacturing census, 1987: finances and operations, by type of organization and SIC 2- to 4-digit industry, subject rpt, 2497–5

Pecan wholesale prices at selected shipping points, 1990, annual rpt, 1311–8

Pistachio production and imports for selected countries, various periods 1980-89, article, 1925–34.205

Pistachio production, trade, stocks, and use, for 5 countries, 1988/89-1990/91, annual article, 1925–34.248

Pistachio production, 1989-91, annual rpt, 1621–18.6

Price indexes (producer), by stage of processing and detailed commodity, monthly rpt, 6762–6

Price indexes (producer), by stage of processing and detailed commodity, monthly 1990, annual rpt, 6764–2

Prices (wholesale) of fruit and vegetables in NYC by State, and shipments and arrivals by mode of transport, by commodity, weekly rpt, 1311–20

Prices received and paid by farmers, by commodity and State, 1990, annual rpt, 1629–5

Prices received by farmers for major products, and paid for farm inputs and living items, by State, monthly rpt, 1629–1

Production, farms, acreage, and related data, by selected crop and State, monthly rpt, 1621–1

Production, prices, and use of fruit and nuts, 1988-91, annual rpt series, 1621–18

Production, prices, trade, stocks, and use, by selected crop, periodic situation rpt with articles, 1561–6

Statistical Abstract of US, 1991 annual data compilation, 2324–1.23

Walnut production and use, 1989-91, annual rpt, 1621–18.8

Walnut production, trade, stocks, and use, for 6 countries, 1989/90-1991/92, annual article, 1925–34.247

see also Oils, oilseeds, and fats

see also Peanuts

see also under By Commodity in the "Index by Categories"

Nuts, metal

see Hardware

Nye, Lendell G.

"Some Personality Characteristics of Air Traffic Control Specialist Trainees: Interactions of Personality and Aptitude Test Scores with FAA Academy Success and Career Expectations", 7506–10.87

Oak Ridge Associated Universities

"University Programs and Facilities in Nuclear Science and Engineering, Seventh Edition", 3008–126

Oak Ridge National Laboratory

"Cooling Season Energy Measurements of Dust and Ventilation Effects on Radiant Barriers", 3308–97

Index by Subjects and Names

"Effects of Utility DSM Programs on Electricity Costs and Prices", 3308–99

"Electricity Savings Among Participants Three Years After Weatherization in Bonneville's 1986 Residential Weatherization Program", 3226–1.7

"Energy Efficiency Improvement Potential of Commercial Aircraft to 2010", 3028–6

"Energy-Related Inventions Program: Commercial Progress of Participants Through 1988", 3308–91

"Impact of Bonneville's Model Conservation Standards on the Energy Efficiency of New Home Construction", 3228–15

"Integrated Data Base for 1990: U.S. Spent Fuel and Radioactive Waste Inventories, Projections, and Characteristics", 3364–2

"Light-Duty Vehicle Summary: First Six Months of Model Year 1991", 3302–4

"Possible Effects of Electric-Utility DSM Programs, 1990-2010", 3308–98

"Results of the Preliminary Radiological Survey at the Former Diamond Magnesium Company Site, Luckey, Ohio (DML001)", 3006–9.8

"Results of the Radiological Survey at 6 Hancock Street, Lodi, N.J. (LJ033)", 3006–9.13

"Results of the Radiological Survey at 79 Avenue B, Lodi, N.J. (LJ091)", 3006–9.9

"Results of the Radiological Survey at 90 C Avenue, Lodi, N.J. (LJ079)", 3006–9.14

"Results of the Radiological Survey at 113 Avenue E, Lodi, N.J. (LJ081)", 3006–9.12

"Results of the Radiological Survey at 160 Essex Street, Lodi, N.J. (LJ072)", 3006–9.11

"Results of the Radiological Survey at 174 Essex Street, Lodi, N.J. (LJ073)", 3006–9.10

"Transportation Energy Data Book: Edition 11", 3304–5

see also Department of Energy National Laboratories

Oakland, Calif.

Cancer cases, by race, income, education, and area population density, for 3 metro areas, 1978-82, article, 4472–1.210

CPI by component for US city average, and by region, population size, and for 15 metro areas, monthly rpt, 6762–1

CPI by component for US city average, and by region, population size, and for 27 metro areas, monthly rpt, 6762–2

Fruit and vegetable shipments, and arrivals in US and Canada cities, by mode of transport and State and country of origin, 1990, annual rpt, 1311–4.2

Wages by occupation, and benefits for office and plant workers, 1991 survey, periodic MSA rpt, 6785–12.2

see also under By City and By SMSA or MSA in the "Index by Categories"

OAS

see Organization of American States

OASDHI

see Old-Age, Survivors, Disability, and Health Insurance

Oats

see Animal feed

see Grains and grain products

Index by Subjects and Names

Oberheu, Howard D.

"Applications Received in 1987 and Allowance Rates for Supplemental Security Income", 4742–1.213

Obesity

- Cancer (renal) risk relation to obesity, by age and sex, for Denmark, 1977-87, article, 4472–1.230
- Child health condition and services use, 1990 chartbook, 4108–49
- Colon polyps cases and risk, effects of body mass, 1986-88 local area study, article, 4472–1.206
- Deaths and rates, by detailed cause and demographic characteristics, 1988 and trends from 1900, US Vital Statistics annual rpt, 4144–2
- Diabetics health-related behaviors, weight, and body mass, by level of exercise, 1991 article, 4042–3.246
- Drug and diet effects on hypertension, and nonprescription diet pills and analgesics sales and adverse reactions, 1980s-90, hearing, 21728–77
- Health condition and health care resources, use, and spending, 1950s-89, annual data compilation, 4144–11
- Heart disease deaths and risk factors, for PRC, Finland, and US, 1980s, article, 4042–3.202
- Hypertensive persons monitoring own blood pressure at home, health condition and risk behavior, local area study, 1991 article, 4042–3.207
- Indians and Alaska Natives preventive health practices, exams by type, and smoking and overweight status, by selected characteristics, 1987, 4186–8.19
- Minority group and women health condition, services use, payment sources, and health care labor force, by poverty status, 1940s-89, chartbook, 4118–56
- Minority group health condition, services use, costs, and indicators of services need, 1950s-88, 4118–55
- Preventive disease and health improvement goals and recommended activities for 2000, with trends 1970s-80s, 4048–10

O'Brien, Catherine

"Subject Index to Current Population Reports", 2546–2.160

O'Brien, James M.

"Equity Underwriting Risk", 9366–6.260

"Market-Based Deposit Insurance Premiums: An Evaluation", 9366–6.264

O'Brien, Renee A.

- "Forest Statistics for Land Outside National Forests in Eastern Montana, 1989", 1206–25.8
- "Forest Statistics for Land Outside National Forests in Northwestern Montana, 1989", 1206–25.11
- "Forest Statistics for Land Outside National Forests in West-Central Montana, 1989", 1206–25.9

Obscenity and pornography

- Court criminal case processing in Federal district courts, and dispositions, by offense, district, and offender characteristics, 1986, annual rpt, 6064–29
- Court criminal case processing in Federal district courts, and dispositions, by offense, 1980-89, annual rpt, 6064–31

Postal Service inspection activities, 2nd half FY91, semiannual rpt, 9862–2

- Public opinion on crime and crime-related issues, by respondent characteristics, data compilation, 1991 annual rpt, 6064–6.2
- Sentences for Federal offenses, guidelines by offense and circumstances, series, 17668–1
- US attorneys civil and criminal cases by type and disposition, and collections, by Federal district, FY90, annual rpt, 6004–2.1

Obstetrics and gynecology

- Health condition and health care resources, use, and spending, 1950s-89, annual data compilation, 4144–11
- Hospital discharges and length of stay, by diagnosis, patient and instn characteristics, procedure performed, and payment source, 1988, annual rpt, 4147–13.107
- Hospital discharges and length of stay by region and diagnosis, and procedures performed, by age and sex, 1989, annual rpt, 4146–8.198
- Hospital discharges by detailed diagnostic and procedure category, primary diagnosis, and length of stay, by age, sex, and region, 1988, annual rpt, 4147–13.105; 4147–13.108
- Indian Health Service and tribal facility outpatient visits, by type of provider, selected hospital, and service area, FY90, annual rpt, 4084–3
- Indian Health Service outpatient services provided, by reason for visit and age, FY88-89, annual rpt, 4084–2
- Indian Health Service, tribal, and contract facilities hospitalization, by diagnosis, age, sex, and service area, FY89, annual rpt, 4084–5
- Labor supply of physicians, by specialty, age, sex, and location of training and practice, 1989, State rpt series, 4116–6
- Medicaid maternity and child health services availability indicators, literature review, 1980s, article, 4652–1.210
- Medicaid reimbursement of hospitals under prospective payment system, effect on maternity case-mix for South Carolina, various periods 1985-87, article, 4652–1.206
- Military health care personnel, and accessions by training source, by occupation, specialty, and service branch, FY89, annual rpt, 3544–24
- VA health care facilities physicians, dentists, and nurses, by selected employment characteristics and VA district, quarterly rpt, 8602–6
- VA health care staff and turnover, by occupation, physician specialty, and location, 1990, annual rpt, 8604–8
- Visits to physicians, by patient and practice characteristics, diagnosis, and services provided, 1989, 4146–8.206
- *see also* Maternity
- *see also* Prenatal care

Ocala, Fla.

see also under By SMSA or MSA in the "Index by Categories"

Occupational health and safety

- AIDS and hepatitis viruses transmission in health care settings, occupational exposure, prevention policies, and OSHA regulation, 1990 hearings, 21348–119

Occupational health and safety

- Aircraft (general aviation) accidents, by circumstances, characteristics of persons and aircraft involved, and type of flying, 1988, annual rpt, 9614–3
- Aircraft accidents and circumstances, for US operations of domestic and foreign airlines and general aviation, periodic rpt, 9612–1
- Asbestos in buildings, EPA aid for removal, occupational asbestos exposure cancer cases and deaths, and Catholic schools abatement costs, 1985-90, hearing, 25328–32
- Assistance (financial and nonfinancial) of Fed Govt, 1991 base edition with supplements, annual listing, 104–5
- Aviation medicine research and test results, technical rpt series, 7506–10
- Bus (school) accidents, circumstances, victim characteristics, and vehicle type, 1989, annual rpt, 7764–22
- Cancer (bladder) cases and risk among chemical plant workers, 1973-88, local area study, article, 4472–1.209
- Cancer (lung) death risk from occupational beryllium exposure, 1952-88, article, 4472–1.224
- Cancer (lung) risk of meat handlers, by job tenure and occupation, as of 1986, local area study, article, 4472–1.223
- Child accident deaths and injuries by cause, and victimization, rates by race, sex, and age, 1979-88, chartbook, 4108–56
- Child labor law violations and injuries by industry group, and employment of minors by selected characteristics, 1983-90, GAO rpt, 26121–426
- Construction industry occupational deaths, by cause, age, industry, and region, 1985-89, 6608–4
- Court civil and criminal caseloads for Federal district courts, 1991, annual rpt, 18204–2.1
- Criminal cases by type and disposition, and collections, for US attorneys, by Federal district, FY90, annual rpt, 6004–2.1
- Deaths and rates, by detailed cause and demographic characteristics, 1988 and trends from 1900, US Vital Statistics annual rpt, 4144–2
- Deaths related to work injuries, by equipment type, circumstances, and OSHA standards violated, series, 6606–2
- Deaths related to work injuries, data collection and processing by States, Natl Inst for Occupational Safety and Health guidelines, 1990 rpt, 4248–89
- Deaths related to work injuries, data collection from multiple sources, BLS pilot study results for 2 States, 1990, article, 6722–1.249
- Deaths related to work injuries, data collection methods of BLS and Texas, with Texas data by accident type and industry div, 1986, article, 6722–1.205
- Developing countries labor standards impacts on social and economic dev, 1988 conf papers, 6368–9
- Disability, acute and chronic health conditions, absenteeism, and health services use, by selected characteristics, 1987, CD-ROM, 4147–10.177
- Diving (underwater sport and occupational) deaths, by circumstances, diver characteristics, and location, 1970-89, annual rpt, 2144–5

Occupational health and safety

Fed Govt spending in States, by type, program, agency, and State, FY90, annual rpt, 2464–2

Foreign countries labor conditions, union coverage, and work accidents, annual country rpt series, 6366–4

Genetic damage and trait monitoring and screening of employees, use, costs, benefits, and procedures, 1980s, 26358–230

Hazardous substances and conditions occupational exposure and health effects, literature review, series, 4246–4

Hazardous substances and conditions occupational exposure, measurement, and proposed standards, series, 4246–1

Hazardous waste incinerators health and safety violations, by type of violation, 1991 rpt, 6608–5

Health condition and health care resources, use, and spending, 1950s-89, annual data compilation, 4144–11

Health condition screening and monitoring of employees, businesses practices and views, 1989 survey, 26358–250

HHS financial aid, by program, recipient, State, and city, FY90, annual regional listings, 4004–3

Injuries at workplace, by circumstances, body site, equipment type, and industry, with safety measures, series, 6846–1

Injuries, by type, circumstances, and victim characteristics, and related activity limitations, 1985-87, 4147–10.176

Injuries, illnesses, and workdays lost, by industry div and major manufacturing group, Monthly Labor Review, 6722–1.7

Injuries, illnesses, and workdays lost, by SIC 2-digit industry, 1989-90, annual press release, 6844–3

Injuries on job, relation to increases in workers compensation benefits, model description and results, 1991 working paper, 6886–6.80

Injuries, related impairments, and activity limitations, by circumstances and victim characteristics, 1985-87, 4147–10.179

Injury and illness rates by SIC 2- to 4-digit industry, and deaths by cause and industry div, 1989, annual rpt, 6844–1

Injury and illness rates, by SIC 2- to 4-digit industry, 1988-89, annual rpt, 6844–7

Labor laws enacted, by State, 1990, annual article, 6722–1.209

Law enforcement officer deaths by circumstances, agency, victim characteristics, and location, 1990, annual rpt, 6224–3

Medical waste generation, sources, health workers exposure and risk, and incineration emissions, 1980s, 4078–1

Navy personnel radiation exposure on nuclear-powered vessels and at support facilities, and injury claims, 1950s-90, annual rpt, 3804–10

Nuclear power plant occupational radiation exposure, by site, 1968-87, annual rpt, 9634–3

Nuclear radiation exposure at DOE and DOE-contractor sites, by facility type and contractor, 1987, annual rpt, 3324–1

Occupational Safety and Health admin standards, enforcement, and training activities, inspectors views, 1989-90, GAO rpt, 26121–391

Physicians, by specialty, age, sex, and location of training and practice, 1989, State rpt series, 4116–6

Pollution (air) indoor levels in workplace, and health impacts, for Library of Congress Madison building, 1989 study, series, 4248–92

Preventive disease and health improvement goals and recommended activities for 2000, with trends 1970s-80s, 4048–10

Radiation protection and health physics enrollment and degrees granted by instn and State, and female grads plans and employment, 1990, annual rpt, 3006–8.15

Radiation protection and health physics enrollment and degrees granted by instn and State, and grad placement, by student characteristics, 1990, annual rpt, 3004–7

Radioactive low-level waste repository site design, characteristics, and monitoring techniques, 1987 conf, 5668–116

Radioactive waste from nuclear power plants, storage pending opening of permanent repository, safety and costs of alternative methods, projected 1991-2050, 14818–1

Railroad accidents, casualties, and damage, by cause, railroad, and State, 1990, annual rpt, 7604–1

Railroad accidents, casualties, and damage, Fed Railroad Admin activities, and safety inspectors by State, 1989, annual rpt, 7604–12

Railroad-hwy grade-crossing accidents, detailed data by State and railroad, 1989, annual rpt, 7604–2

Railroad safety violation claims settled, by carrier, FY90, annual rpt, 7604–10

Research and demonstration grants of NIOSH for occupational safety and health by State, and project listing, FY90, annual rpt, 4244–2

Respiratory diseases related to occupational hazards, epidemiology, diagnosis, and treatment, for selected industries and work settings, 1988 conf, 4248–90

Restaurant and drinking place occupational injury and illness rates, and workdays lost by State, 1989, article, 6722–1.231

Shift rotation health and safety effects, and US and foreign regulation, by selected industry and occupation, 1970s-89, 26356–9.3

Ships accidents and casualties, by circumstances and characteristics of persons and vessels involved, 1988, annual rpt, 7404–11

Ships and marine facilities accidents, casualties, and circumstances, Coast Guard investigation results, periodic rpt, 9612–4

Smoking bans in public places, local ordinances provisions, as of 1989, 4478–196

Statistical Abstract of US, 1991 annual data compilation, 2324–1.13

Subway accidents, casualties, and damage, by circumstances and system, 1989, annual rpt, 7884–5

Transportation safety programs, and accidents, casualties, and damage, by mode of transport, 1989, annual rpt, 7304–19

Truck accidents, by carrier financial and operating conditions and driver characteristics, 1980s, GAO rpt, 26131–82

Truck accidents, casualties, and damage, by circumstances and characteristics of persons and vehicles involved, 1988, annual rpt, 7554–9

Truck accidents, circumstances, severity, and characteristics of drivers and vehicles, 1989, annual rpt, 7764–20

Youth illegally employed in hazardous work under Fair Labor Labor Standards Act, by occupation, FY89, annual rpt, 6504–2.1

see also Agricultural accidents and safety

see also Assaults on police

see also Black lung disease

see also Mine accidents and safety

see also Workers compensation

Occupational Safety and Health Administration

Activities of OSHA, standards, enforcement, and training, inspectors views, 1989-90, GAO rpt, 26121–391

AIDS and hepatitis viruses transmission in health care settings, occupational exposure, prevention policies, and OSHA regulation, 1990 hearings, 21348–119

Budget of US, obligations and authority by function, agency, and program, with summaries, analyses, and historical tables, FY92, annual rpt, 104–2

Construction industry occupational deaths, by cause, age, industry, and region, 1985-89, 6608–4

Deaths related to work injuries, by equipment type, circumstances, and OSHA standards violated, series, 6606–2

Expenditures of Fed Govt in States, by type, program, agency, and State, FY90, annual rpt, 2464–2

Hazardous waste incinerators health and safety violations, by type of violation, 1991 rpt, 6608–5

Respiratory diseases related to occupational hazards, epidemiology, diagnosis, and treatment, for selected industries and work settings, 1988 conf, 4248–90

Occupational Safety and Health Review Commission

Budget of US, obligations and authority by function, agency, and program, with summaries, analyses, and historical tables, FY92, annual rpt, 104–2

Occupational testing and certification

Air Force recruiting compliance with gender-neutral selection, with aptitude test results by sex, FY86-90, GAO rpt, 26123–359

Air traffic control qualification course similarity to controller tasks, 1990, annual rpt, 7506–10.83

Air traffic control screening impacts on field training performance, 1981-86, technical rpt, 7506–10.79

Aircraft pilot and nonpilot certificates held and issued, by type of certificate, region, State, and for women, 1989, annual rpt, 7504–1.7

Aircraft pilot and nonpilot certificates held, by type of certificate, age, sex, region, and State, 1990, annual rpt, 7504–2

Child day care providers health and safety training, by facility size, for California, 1987 survey, article, 4042–3.243

Index by Subjects and Names

Futures trading oversight of CFTC and individual exchanges, foreign activity, and customer views, late 1980s, hearing, 25168–77

Health care professionals licensing and disciplinary actions of State medical boards, 1950s-87, series, 4006–8

Mental health care services, staffing, research, and training programs in VA facilities, 1991 biennial listing, 8704–2

Navy battleship *USS Iowa* explosion, safety and personnel mgmt issues, with technical analysis, FY89, GAO rpt, 26123–315

Physicians and dentists with board certification, VA employment by specialty, quarterly rpt, 8602–6

Physicians, by specialty, age, sex, and location of training and practice, 1989, State rpt series, 4116–6

Physicians licensing and disciplinary activities of State medical boards, investigative staff, and licensing fees, by State, 1985-90, 4008–83

Physicians with board certification, and other characteristics of Medicare hospital providers, by instn, 1989, annual regional rpt series, 4654–14

Security forces under contract at DOE nuclear weapons facilities, skill deficiencies, and costs compared to Federal security, late 1980s, GAO rpt, 26113–493

Teacher employment, vacancies, and pay, by State, region, and school enrollment size, 1987/88, 4836–3.6

Teacher testing for State certification, listing of laws, 1991 annual data compilation, 4824–2.14

Teachers and other special education staff, training, degrees, and certification, by field and State, FY89, annual rpt, 4944–4

Teachers in private schools, selected characteristics by instn level, size, and orientation, various periods 1979-88, 4838–47

Occupational therapy

Home health care agencies finances impacts of Medicare payment limits under alternative determination methods, with data by service type, 1984-89, GAO rpt, 26121–400

Home health care visits approved by Medicare, planned and actual visits by service type, 1986, article, 4652–1.254

Hospices operations, services, costs, and patient characteristics, for instns without Medicare certification, FY85-86, 4658–52

Mental health care in private hospitals, patients characteristics, 1986, 4506–3.47

Military health care personnel, and accessions by training source, by occupation, specialty, and service branch, FY89, annual rpt, 3544–24

Special education programs, enrollment by age, staff, funding, and needs, by type of handicap and State, 1989/90, annual rpt, 4944–4

VA health care staff and turnover, by occupation, physician specialty, and location, 1990, annual rpt, 8604–8

see also Vocational rehabilitation

Occupational training

see Employee development

see Vocational education and training

Occupational wage surveys

see Area wage surveys

see Industry wage surveys

Occupations

Credit unions finances, by occupational membership category, as of June 1991, semiannual rpt, 9532–6

Criminal sentences for Federal offenses, guidelines by offense and circumstances, series, 17668–1

Dictionary of Occupational Titles, with classification codes, 1991 base edition and supplements, 6406–1

Employment conditions, alternative BLS projections to 2005 and trends 1970s-90, biennial article, 6722–1.254

Entry level employment, and share without previous experience in field, by detailed occupation, 1986, article, 6742–1.201

Immigrants admitted to US, by class of admission and for top 15 countries of birth, FY89-90, fact sheet, 6266–2.4; 6266–2.8

Manufacturing employment, by detailed occupation and SIC 2-digit industry, 1989 survey, triennial rpt, 6748–52

Occupational Outlook Quarterly, journal, 6742–1

Statistical Abstract of US, 1991 annual data compilation, 2324–1.13

Women's labor force status, earnings, and other characteristics, with comparisons to men, fact sheet series, 6564–1

see also Agricultural labor

see also Blue collar workers

see also Business management

see also Clergy

see also Clerical workers

see also Consultants

see also Domestic workers and services

see also Employee development

see also Engineers and engineering

see also Executives and managers

see also Health occupations

see also Job tenure —

see also Judges

see also Lawyers and legal services

see also Librarians

see also Military personnel

see also Occupational testing and certification

see also Pilots

see also Postal employees

see also Production workers

see also Professional and technical workers

see also Sales workers

see also Scientists and technicians

see also Service workers

see also Teachers

see also Vocational education and training

see also Vocational guidance

see also Writers and writing

see also under By Occupation in the "Index by Categories"

Ocean County, N.J.

Wages by occupation, and benefits for office and plant workers, 1991 survey, periodic MSA rpt, 6785–12.3

see also under By SMSA or MSA in the "Index by Categories"

Ocean liners

see Passenger ships

Ocean pollution

see Marine pollution

Ocean resources

see Marine resources

Oceania

Agricultural exports of US, for grains, oilseed products, hides, skins, and cotton, by country, weekly rpt, 1922–3

Agricultural trade of US, by commodity and country, bimonthly rpt, 1522–1

Agricultural trade of US, by detailed commodity and country, 1989, annual rpt, 1524–8

Agricultural trade of US, by detailed commodity and country, 1990, semiannual rpt, 1522–4

AIDS virus infection prevalence in developing countries, by sex, selected city, urban-rural location, and country, 1991, semiannual rpt, 2322–4

Alien workers (unauthorized) and Fair Labor Standards Act employer compliance, hiring impacts, and aliens overstaying visas by country and State, 1986-90, annual rpt, 6264–6

Aliens (illegal) overstaying visas, by class of admission, mode of arrival, age, country, and State, FY85-88, annual rpt, 6264–5

Corporations in US under foreign control, income tax returns, assets and income statement items by industry div, country, and world area, 1988, article, 8302–2.219

Developing countries economic, social, and agricultural data, US and other aid sources, and AID activity, 1988 world area rpt, 9916–12.28

Economic and military aid and loans from US and intl agencies, by program and country, FY46-90, annual rpt, 9914–5

Exports and imports (waterborne) of US, by type of service, commodity, country, route, and US port, 1988, annual rpt, 7704–2

Exports and imports (waterborne) of US, by type of service, customs district, port, and world area, monthly rpt, 2422–7

Fish (baitfish) catch distribution by species and South Pacific country or territory, 1965-85, article, 2162–1.201

Immigrant and nonimmigrant visas of US issued and refused, by class, issuing office, and nationality, FY89, annual rpt, 7184–1

Immigrants admitted to US, by country of birth, FY81-90, annual rpt, 6264–4

Immigrants admitted to US, by occupational group and country of birth, preliminary FY90, annual table, 6264–1

Multinatl US firms foreign affiliates, income statement items by country and world area, 1986, biennial article, 8302–2.212

Oil and gas reserves and discoveries, by country and country group, quarterly rpt, 3162–43

Oils, oilseeds, and meal imports, by commodity, world area of destination, and major producer, 1960s-88, 1528–314

Peace Corps activities, funding by program, and volunteers, by country, FY92, annual rpt, 9654–1

Tax (income) returns of corporations with foreign tax credit, income, and tax items, by country and world region of credit, 1986, biennial article, 8302–2.207

Oceania

Tide height and time daily at coastal points, forecast 1992, annual rpt, 2174–2.5

Timber in Pacific basin, sandalwood resources, habitat, harvest, exports, and uses, 1990 conf, 1208–366

Travel to and from US on US and foreign flag air carriers, by country, world area, and US port, monthly rpt, 7302–2

Travel to and from US on US and foreign flag air carriers, by world area, 1990, annual rpt, 2904–13

Travel to US, by characteristics of visit and traveler, country, port city, and State of destination, quarterly rpt, 2902–1

US military and civilian personnel and dependents, by service branch, world area, and country, quarterly rpt, 3542–20

Weather stations of Natl Weather Service, locations and types of observations made, 1990 annual listing, 2184–5

see also American Samoa
see also Australia
see also Cook Islands
see also Fiji
see also Guam
see also Kiribati
see also Marshall Islands
see also Micronesia Federated States
see also Nauru
see also New Caledonia
see also New Zealand
see also Northern Mariana Islands
see also Palau
see also Papua New Guinea
see also Solomon Islands
see also Tonga
see also Tuvalu
see also Vanuatu
see also Western Samoa
see also under By Foreign Country in the "Index by Categories"

Oceanography

Alaska minerals resources and geologic characteristics, compilation of papers, 1989, annual rpt, 5664–15

Alaska OCS environmental conditions and oil dev impacts, compilation of papers, series, 2176–1

Arctic Ocean fish catch and habitat impacts of oil and gas dev, and assessment methods, 1988 conf, 5738–24

Atlantic Ocean currents, temperatures, and salinity, from Florida straits to northern Brazil, series, 2146–7

Atlantic Oceanographic and Meteorological Lab research activities and bibl, FY90, annual rpt, 2144–19

Carbon dioxide in atmosphere, measurement, methodology, and research results, series, 3006–11

Employment and other characteristics of science and engineering PhDs, by field and State, 1989, biennial rpt, 9627–18

Fed Govt aid to higher education and nonprofit instns for R&D and related activities, by field, instn, agency, and State, FY89, annual rpt, 9627–17

Global climate change environmental, infrastructure, and health impacts, with model results and background data, 1850s-2100, 9188–113

Higher education grad programs enrollment in science and engineering, by field, source of funds, and characteristics of student and instn, 1975-89, annual rpt, 9627–7

NASA R&D funding to higher education instns, by field, instn, and State, FY90, annual listing, 9504–7

Pacific Marine Environmental Lab research activities and bibl, FY90, annual rpt, 2144–21

R&D funding by Fed Govt, by field, performer type, agency, and State, FY89-91, annual rpt, 9627–20

R&D funding by higher education instns and federally funded centers, by field, instn, and State, FY89, annual rpt, 9627–13

Research and distribution of oceanographic data, World Data Center A activities by country, and cruises by ship, 1989, annual rpt, 2144–15

Ships for oceanographic research, fleet condition, funding, voyages, and modernization costs, for NOAA, 1980s-90 and projected to 2020, 2148–60

Temperature of sea surface by ocean and for US coastal areas, and Bering Sea ice conditions, monthly rpt, 2182–5

Weather trends and deviations, by world region, 1880s-1990, annual chartbook, 2184–9

see also Ice conditions
see also Marine pollution
see also Marine resources
see also Marine resources conservation
see also Navigation
see also Tides and currents

Oceans and seas

see Arctic Ocean
see Atlantic Ocean
see Bering Sea
see Chukchi Sea
see Coastal areas
see Continental shelf
see Coral reefs and islands
see Gulf of Alaska
see Gulf of Mexico
see Indian Ocean
see Marine accidents and safety
see Marine pollution
see Marine resources
see Marine resources conservation
see Mediterranean Sea
see North Sea
see Oceanography
see Offshore mineral resources
see Offshore oil and gas
see Pacific Ocean
see Tides and currents
see Tsunamis

Oceanside, Calif.

see also under By City in the "Index by Categories"

O'Connell, Martin

"Late Expectations: Childbearing Patterns of American Women for the 1990's", 2546–2.162

O'Connor, Thomas P.

"Coastal Environmental Quality in the U.S., 1990: Chemical Contamination in Sediment and Tissues", 2176–3.12

Odessa, Tex.

see also under By SMSA or MSA in the "Index by Categories"

O'Driscoll, Gerald P., Jr.

"Learning from One Another: The U.S. and European Banking Experience", 9379–12.70

Index by Subjects and Names

OECD

see Organization for Economic Cooperation and Development

Office buildings

see Commercial buildings
see Public buildings

Office equipment

see Business machines and equipment
see Computer industry and products
see Office supplies

Office of Bilingual Education and Minority Language Affairs

Enrollment, funding, and services of bilingual education programs, by State, FY85-89, series, 4808–20

Office of Child Support Enforcement

see Family Support Administration

Office of Community Services

see Family Support Administration

Office of Education

see Department of Education

Office of Educational Research and Improvement

Activities of OERI, FY90, annual narrative rpt, 4814–1

Athletes in college, educational and employment performance compared to other students, for 1972 high school class, as of 1986, 4888–5

Budget of US, obligations and authority by function, agency, and program, with summaries, analyses, and historical tables, FY92, annual rpt, 104–2

Children and youth social, economic, and demographic characteristics, 1950s-90, 4818–5

Condition of Education, detail for elementary, secondary, and higher education, 1920s-90 and projected to 2001, annual rpt, 4824–1

Curricula classification codes and descriptions, by program area, 1990, rpt, 4828–29

Data collection and reporting improvement, and performance indicators dev, recommendations, 1991 rpt, 4828–40

Data collection and reporting improvement for Federal and State educational agencies, recommendations, 1991 rpt, 4828–39

Data on education, computer files from Office of Educational Research and Improvement, 1991 listing, 4868–10

Digest of Education Statistics, 1991 annual data compilation, 4824–2

Education data collection activities and programs of NCES, 1991, annual listing, 4824–7

Education data, selected trends and projections 1978-2001, pamphlet, 4828–27

Education data, 1960s-89, pamphlet, 4828–26

Educational Resources Info Center (ERIC) activities, 1990-91, annual rpt, 4814–3

Eighth grade class of 1988: educational performance and conditions, characteristics, attitudes, activities, and plans, natl longitudinal survey, series, 4826–9

Elementary and secondary education enrollment, staff, finances, operations, programs, and policies, 1987/88 biennial survey, series, 4836–3

Index by Subjects and Names

Elementary and secondary education enrollment, teachers, high school grads, and spending, by instn control and State, 1990/91, annual rpt, 4834–19

Elementary and secondary public school agencies, by enrollment size and location, fall 1989, annual listing, 4834–1

Elementary and secondary public school systems enrollment, finances, staff, and high school grads, by State, FY88-89, annual rpt, 4834–6

Elementary and secondary public schools and enrollment, by State, 1989/90, annual rpt, 4834–17

Elementary and secondary public schools, enrollment and other characteristics, for top 100 districts, 1988/89, annual rpt, 4834–22

Elementary and secondary public schools, enrollment, teachers, funding, and other characteristics, by region and State, 1988/89, annual rpt, 4834–20

Enrollment in public elementary and secondary schools, under alternative average daily attendance computation methods, by State, 1985-86, 4838–48

Fast Response Survey System, estimates for education data, series, 4826–1

Fed Govt education funding by agency, program, and recipient type, and instn spending, FY80-90, annual rpt, 4824–8

High school advanced placement for college credit, programs by selected characteristics and school control, 1984-86, 4838–46

High school class of 1972: education, employment, and family characteristics, activities, and attitudes, natl longitudinal study, series, 4836–1

High school dropout rates, and subsequent completion, by student and school characteristics, alternative estimates, 1990, annual rpt, 4834–23

Higher education course completions, by detailed program, sex, race, and instn type, for 1972 high school class, as of 1984, 4888–4

Higher education degrees awarded, by level, field, race, and sex, 1988/89 with trends from 1978/79, biennial rpt, 4844–17

Higher education enrollment and degrees awarded by sex, and instn finances, by instn level and control, 1990-91, annual rpt, 4844–14

Higher education enrollment and degrees awarded, by sex, full- and part-time status, and instn level and control, fall 1990, annual rpt, 4844–16

Higher education enrollment, by student and instn characteristics, fall 1989, biennial rpt, 4844–2

Higher education enrollment, faculty, finances, and degrees, by instn level and control, and State, FY87, annual rpt, 4844–13

Higher education instn revenue by source and spending by function, by State and instn control, FY80-88, annual rpt, 4844–6

Higher education instn student aid and other sources of support, with student expenses and characteristics, by instn type and control, 1990 triennial study, series, 4846–5

Higher education instn tuition costs relation to quality, indicators for private instns, regression results, 1985/86, 4888–3

Libraries (major urban resource centers) dev projects and funding, by city and State, FY84-88, listing, 4878–4

Libraries (public) English as second language programs and services, project descriptions and funding, by State, FY87, annual rpt, 4874–10

Libraries (public) finances, staff, and operations, by State and population size, 1989, annual rpt, 4824–6

Libraries technological aid, project descriptions and funding, FY89, annual listing, 4874–6

Library (research) of Education Dept, educators and librarians views of proposed services, 1990 survey, GAO rpt, 26121–414

Library science training grants for disadvantaged students, by instn and State, FY90, annual listing, 4874–1

Private elementary and secondary schools, enrollment, teachers, and high school grads, annual rpt, suspended, 4834–21

Private elementary and secondary schools, students, and staff characteristics, various periods 1979-88, 4838–47

Publications of Education Dept, quarterly listing, 4812–1

Publications of Natl Center for Education Statistics, periodic listing, 4822–1

Teachers in higher education instns, personnel policies, pay, work conditions, and other characteristics, by instn type and control, 1987/88 survey, quadrennial rpt series, 4846–4

Teachers in higher education, salaries by faculty rank, sex, instn type and control, and State, 1989/90, annual rpt, 4844–8

Women's employment and educational experiences compared to men, for high school class of 1972, natl longitudinal study, as of 1986, 4888–6

Office of Energy Research
see Department of Energy

Office of Family Assistance
see Family Support Administration

Office of Federal Statistical Policy and Standards
see Office of Management and Budget

Office of Government Ethics
Budget of US, obligations and authority by function, agency, and program, with summaries, analyses, and historical tables, FY92, annual rpt, 104–2

Office of Grants and Program Systems, USDA
Research and education grants, USDA competitive awards by program and recipient, FY90, annual listing, 1764–1

Office of Human Development Services
Budget of US, obligations and authority by function, agency, and program, with summaries, analyses, and historical tables, FY92, annual rpt, 104–2

Child abuse and neglect victims representation in legal proceedings, caseloads, State requirements, and compensation, by State and county, 1989, 4608–28

Expenditures of Fed Govt in States, by type, program, agency, and State, FY90, annual rpt, 2464–2

Office of Management and Budget

Financial aid of HHS, by program, recipient, State, and city, FY90, annual regional listings, 4004–3

Research and evaluation programs of HHS, 1970-90, annual listing, 4004–30

see also Administration for Children, Youth, and Families

see also Administration for Native Americans

see also Administration on Aging

see also Administration on Developmental Disabilities

Office of International Cooperation and Development, USDA

Budget of US, obligations and authority by function, agency, and program, with summaries, analyses, and historical tables, FY92, annual rpt, 104–2

Education and training programs of USDA, foreign participants by program, sponsor, and country, annual rpt, discontinued, 1954–1

Research grants of USDA, by program, subagency, and country, FY90, annual listing, 1954–3

Technical aid of USDA, personnel and agreements by project, world area, and country, annual rpt, discontinued, 1954–2

Office of Justice Programs

Activities and funding of OJP, FY90, annual rpt, 6064–18

Budget of US, obligations and authority by function, agency, and program, with summaries, analyses, and historical tables, FY92, annual rpt, 104–2

Expenditures of Fed Govt in States, by type, program, agency, and State, FY90, annual rpt, 2464–2

see also Bureau of Justice Assistance

see also Bureau of Justice Statistics

see also National Institute of Justice

see also Office of Juvenile Justice and Delinquency Prevention

Office of Juvenile Justice and Delinquency Prevention

Court caseloads for juvenile delinquency, by offense, referral source, disposition, age, sex, race, State, and county, 1988, annual rpt, 6064–12

Data on juvenile justice issues, young offenders and victims, series, 6066–27

Expenditures for juvenile delinquency prevention, by program and Federal agency, annual rpt, discontinued, 6064–11

Facilities for juveniles, population, and costs, by facility and resident characteristics, region, and State, 1985-89, biennial rpt, 6064–5

Status offender detentions in secure facilities, and States compliance with Federal policies to reduce detentions, 1983-89, GAO rpt, 26119–333

Office of Labor-Management Standards

Labor unions reporting to Labor Dept, parent bodies and locals by location, 1990 listing, 6468–17

Office of Management and Budget

Assistance (financial and nonfinancial) of Fed Govt, 1991 base edition with supplements, annual listing, 104–5

Budget of US, authoritative financial statements with appropriations, outlays, and receipts, by category and agency, FY90, annual rpt, 8104–2.1

Office of Management and Budget

Budget of US, authority rescissions and deferrals, monthly rpt, 102–2

Budget of US, balances of budget authority obligated and unobligated, by function and agency, FY90-92, annual rpt, 104–8

Budget of US, formula grant program obligations to State and local govts, by agency, program, and State, FY92, annual rpt, 104–30

Budget of US, historical data, selected years FY34-90 and projected to FY96, annual rpt, 104–22

Budget of US, midsession review of FY92 budget, by function, annual rpt, 104–7

Budget of US, object class analysis of obligations, by agency, FY92, annual rpt, 104–9

Budget of US, obligations and authority by function, agency, and program, with summaries, analyses, and historical tables, FY92, annual rpt, 104–2

Budget of US, receipts by source and outlays by agency, final statements compared to OMB forecasts, FY91, press release, 8008–153

Computer and telecommunication systems acquisition plans and obligations of Fed Govt, by agency, FY89-91, last issue of annual rpt, 104–20

Computer and telecommunication systems acquisition plans and obligations of Fed Govt, by agency, FY90-95, annual rpt, 104–33

Fraud and abuse in Fed Govt, audits and investigations by agency, FY90, annual rpt, 104–29

Info mgmt activities of Fed Govt, technology spending, and paperwork burden, by agency, planned FY91-92, annual rpt, 104–19

Persian Gulf War costs to US by category and service branch, and offsetting contributions by allied country, monthly rpt, 102–3

Regulatory programs of Fed Govt, evaluation, review process, and actions taken, by agency, 1980s-90, annual rpt, 104–28

Statistical programs of Fed Govt, funding by agency, FY90-92, annual rpt, 104–10

Statistical programs of Fed Govt, policies relating to technical operation, methodology, and use of data, working paper series, 106–4

Office of Minority Business Enterprise *see* Minority Business Development Agency

Office of National Drug Control Policy

Abuse and enforcement issues, series, 236–2

Abuse, treatment, and enforcement policy issues, series, 236–1

Budget of US, obligations and authority by function, agency, and program, with summaries, analyses, and historical tables, FY92, annual rpt, 104–2

Drug abuse and trafficking reduction programs activities, funding, staff, and Bush Admin budget request, by Federal agency and program area, FY90-92, 238–2

Drug abuse and trafficking reduction programs funding, and Bush Admin budget request, by Federal agency and program area, FY90-92, 238–1

Office of Navajo and Hopi Indian Relocation

Activities and caseloads of relocation program, monthly rpt, 16002–1

Activities and caseloads, 1975-90, 16008–5

see also Navajo and Hopi Indian Relocation Commission

Office of Personnel Management

Budget of US, authoritative financial statements with appropriations, outlays, and receipts, by category and agency, FY90, annual rpt, 8104–2.1

Budget of US, obligations and authority by function, agency, and program, with summaries, analyses, and historical tables, FY92, annual rpt, 104–2

Civil service retirement system actuarial valuation, FY79-90 and projected to FY2065, annual rpt, 9844–34

Collective bargaining agreements of Federal employees, coverage, unions, and location, by agency, for contracts expiring 1990-91, annual listing, 9847–1

Collective bargaining multi-unit agreements of Fed Govt, by agency and labor union, annual listing, discontinued, 9847–4

Employment (civilian) of Fed Govt, work-years, pay rates, and benefits use and costs, by agency, FY89, annual rpt, 9844–31

Employment and payroll (civilian) of Fed Govt, by agency in DC metro area, total US, and abroad, bimonthly rpt, 9842–1

Employment and payroll (civilian) of Fed Govt, by occupation, pay grade, sex, agency, and location, 1989, biennial rpt, 9844–4

Employment and payroll (civilian) of Fed Govt, by pay system, agency, and location, 1990, annual rpt, 9844–6

Employment of Fed Govt, by pay system, agency, and location, biennial rpt, discontinued, 9844–8

Equal Opportunity Recruitment Program activity, and Fed Govt employment by sex, race, pay grade, and occupational group, FY90, annual rpt, 9844–33

Incentive awards to Federal employees, costs, and benefits, by award type and agency, FY89, annual rpt, 9844–20

Insurance (health and life) programs of Fed Govt, coverage and finances, FY89 with trends from FY84, annual rpt, 9844–35

Labor unions recognized in Fed Govt, coverage by agency and union, biennial rpt, discontinued, 9844–17

Leave transfer to other employees, Federal pilot programs operations and costs by agency, FY89, 9848–40

Merit system oversight and enforcement activities of OPM, series, 9496–2

Senior Executive Service membership characteristics, entries, exits, and awards, FY79-90, annual rpt, 9844–36

Office of Policy Development

Budget of US, obligations and authority by function, agency, and program, with summaries, analyses, and historical tables, FY92, annual rpt, 104–2

Office of Policy, SSA

Publications and microdata files of SSA, 1991, biennial listing, 4744–12

see also Office of Research and Statistics, SSA

Index by Subjects and Names

Office of Refugee Resettlement *see* Family Support Administration

Office of Research and Statistics, SSA

OASDHI, Medicaid, SSI, and related programs benefits, beneficiary characteristics, and trust funds, selected years 1937-89, annual rpt, 4744–3

OASDI benefits and beneficiaries, by type of benefit, State, and county, as of Dec 1990, annual rpt, 4744–28

Social Security Bulletin, OASDHI and other program operations and beneficiary characteristics, from 1940, monthly journal, 4742–1

Social security programs and related issues, technical paper series, 4746–26

Supplemental Security Income payments and beneficiaries, by type of eligibility, State, and county, Dec 1989, annual rpt, 4744–27

Office of Science and Technology Policy

Budget of US, authoritative financial statements with appropriations, outlays, and receipts, by category and agency, FY90, annual rpt, 8104–2.1

Budget of US, obligations and authority by function, agency, and program, with summaries, analyses, and historical tables, FY92, annual rpt, 104–2

Office of Special Counsel

Violations and prohibited political activity reported by Federal employees, cases by type, FY90, annual rpt, 9894–1

Office of Special Education and Rehabilitative Services

Blind-operated vending facilities on Federal and non-Federal property, finances and operations by agency and State, FY90, annual rpt, 4944–2

Budget of US, obligations and authority by function, agency, and program, with summaries, analyses, and historical tables, FY92, annual rpt, 104–2

Disabled persons rehabilitation, Federal and State activities and funding, FY90, annual rpt, 4944–1

Enrollment by age, staff, funding, and needs of special education programs, by type of handicap and State, 1989/90, annual rpt, 4944–4

Vocational rehabilitation cases of State agencies by disposition and applicant characteristics, and closures by reason, FY84-88, annual rpt, 4944–6

Vocational rehabilitation cases of State agencies, by disposition and State, FY90 and trends from FY21, annual rpt, 4944–5

Vocational rehabilitation cases rejected by State agencies, by reason, applicant characteristics, and selected State, annual rpt, suspended, 4944–11

Office of Surface Mining Reclamation and Enforcement

Activities and funding of OSM, by State and Indian tribe, FY90, annual rpt, 5644–1

Budget of US, obligations and authority by function, agency, and program, with summaries, analyses, and historical tables, FY92, annual rpt, 104–2

Expenditures of Fed Govt in States, by type, program, agency, and State, FY90, annual rpt, 2464–2

Land subsidence above coal mines, State property insurance program income and expenses in 6 States, 1990, GAO rpt, 26113–530

Index by Subjects and Names

Office of Technology Assessment

Activities of OTA, and rpts, FY90, annual rpt, 26354–3

Agricultural crops (new and traditional) use in industry, replacement of imports and nonrenewable resources, R&D funding, and economic impacts, 1970s-90, 26358–239

Biotechnology commercial applications, industry finances and capitalization, patents, and govt support, for US, Japan, and EC, late 1970s-91, 26358–248

Budget of US, obligations and authority by function, agency, and program, with summaries, analyses, and historical tables, FY92, annual rpt, 104–2

Dairy industry biotechnology devs, and bST impacts on farm finances and Federal support programs, 1980s and projected to 1998, 26358–237

Developing countries aid projects collaboration of AID and US higher education instns, and funding, by purpose and world region, 1960s-89, 26358–247

Developing countries energy use, and economic and environmental impacts, by fuel type, world area, and country, 1980s-90, 26358–232

Energy production and demand impacts of alternative Federal policies and new technologies, 1970s-89 and projected to 2015, 26358–243

Energy spending, and conservation retrofit costs and savings, for Federal buildings, 1988-90, 26358–240

Firearm purchasers criminal records checks, and firearms use in crime, with data by State, 1987-90, 26358–244

Genetic damage and trait monitoring and screening of employees, use, costs, benefits, and procedures, 1980s, 26358–230

Global warming contributing air pollutants, US and foreign emissions and control measures, 1980s and projected to 2020, 26358–233

Health condition screening and monitoring of employees, businesses practices and views, 1989 survey, 26358–250

HHS research and evaluation programs, 1970-90, annual listing, 4004–30

Hwy and mass transit funding and regulation by Fed Govt and States, FY91 with projections to FY96, 26358–242

Military forces, research, and manufacturing base restructuring following relaxation of East-West tensions, with background data, FY87-93, 26358–245

Military weapons trade, production, and defense industry finances, with data by firm and country, 1980s-91, 26358–241

Neurosciences research and public policy issues, series, 26356–9

Pollution (groundwater) from farm chemicals use and animal wastes, and reduction strategies, 1960s-90, 26358–231

Public works condition, mgmt, R&D, and funding, for transportation and environmental projects, 1986-91, 26358–235

R&D funding and policy of Fed Govt, issues, 1950s-91, 26358–238

Radioactive waste at DOE nuclear weapons facilities, storage plans, and mgmt issues, 1988, 26358–236

Transplant patients immunosuppressive drug coverage under Medicare and other insurance sources, costs, and procedures, 1991 rpt, 26358–246

Youth health condition, risk factors, and preventive and treatment services use and availability, 1970s-89, 26358–234

Office of Territorial and International Affairs

Budget of US, obligations and authority by function, agency, and program, with summaries, analyses, and historical tables, FY92, annual rpt, 104–2

Expenditures of Fed Govt in States, by type, program, agency, and State, FY90, annual rpt, 2464–2

Office of the Comptroller of Currency

Activities of Comptroller, and natl banks charters, mergers, liquidations, and financial performance, with data by instn and State, quarterly rpt, 8402–3

Banks regulatory enforcement activities of Federal agencies, effectiveness, with data on capital-deficient banks, late 1980s-90, GAO rpt, 26119–334

Budget of US, obligations and authority by function, agency, and program, with summaries, analyses, and historical tables, FY92, annual rpt, 104–2

Office of the Secretary of Defense

Base construction, renovation, and land acquisition, DOD budget requests by project, service branch, State, and country, FY92-93, annual rpt, 3544–15

Budget of DOD, base construction and family housing appropriations by facility, service branch, and location, FY90-93, annual rpt, 3544–39

Budget of DOD, procurement appropriations by item, service branch, and defense agency, FY90-93, annual rpt, 3544–32

Budget of DOD, programs, policies, and operations, FY90, annual rpt, 3544–2

Budget of DOD, R&D appropriations by item, service branch, and defense agency, FY90-93, annual rpt, 3544–33

Deaths by cause, age, race, and rank, and personnel captured and missing, by service branch, FY90, annual rpt, 3544–40

Deaths by cause, age, race, and rank, and personnel captured and missing, by service branch, semiannual rpt, periodicity change, 3542–21

Expenditures and obligations of DOD, by function and service branch, quarterly rpt, 3542–3

Expenditures for contracts and payroll, and personnel, by service branch and location, with top 5 contractors and maps, by State and country, FY90, annual rpt, 3544–29

Fraud and abuse in DOD programs, audits and investigations, 1st half FY91, semiannual rpt, 3542–18

Hazardous waste site remedial action at military installations, activities and funding by site and State, FY90, annual rpt, 3544–36

Health care facilities of DOD in US and abroad, beds, admissions, outpatient visits, and births, by service branch, quarterly rpt, 3542–15

Health care personnel, and accessions by training source, by occupation, specialty, and service branch, FY89, annual rpt, 3544–24

Office of the Secretary of Defense

Military women personnel on active and reserve duty, by demographic and service characteristics and service branch, FY89, annual chartbook, 3544–26

NATO and Japan military spending and indicators of ability to support common defense, by country, 1970s-89, annual rpt, 3544–28

Personnel (civilian) of DOD, by service branch and defense agency, with summary military employment data, quarterly rpt, 3542–16

Personnel (civilian and military) of DOD, by service branch, major installation, and State, as of Sept 1990, annual rpt, 3544–7

Personnel active duty and recruit social, economic, and parents characteristics, by service branch and State, FY89, annual rpt, 3544–41

Personnel active duty strength, recruits, and reenlistment, by race, sex, and service branch, quarterly press release, 3542–7

Personnel strengths, for active duty, civilians, and dependents, by service branch and US and foreign location, quarterly rpt, 3542–20

Personnel strengths, for active duty, civilians, and reserves, by service branch, FY90 and trends, annual rpt, 3544–1

Personnel strengths, for active duty, civilians, and reserves, by service branch, quarterly rpt, 3542–14

Personnel strengths in US and abroad, by service branch, world area, and country, quarterly press release, 3542–9

Personnel strengths, summary by service branch, monthly press release, 3542–2

Procurement, DOD prime contract awards by category, contract and contractor type, and service branch, FY81-1st half FY91, semiannual rpt, 3542–1

Procurement, DOD prime contract awards by category, contractor type, and State, FY88-90, annual rpt, 3544–11

Procurement, DOD prime contract awards by contractor, service branch, State, and city, FY90, annual rpt, 3544–22

Procurement, DOD prime contract awards by detailed procurement category, FY87-90, annual rpt, 3544–18

Procurement, DOD prime contract awards by service branch and State, 1st half FY91, semiannual rpt, 3542–5

Procurement, DOD prime contract awards by size and type of contract, service branch, competitive status, category, and labor standard, FY90, annual rpt, 3544–19

Procurement, DOD prime contract awards for top 100 contractors, FY90, annual listing, 3544–5

Procurement, DOD prime contract awards in labor surplus areas, by service branch, State, and area, 1st half FY91, semiannual rpt, 3542–19

Procurement, subcontract awards by DOD contractors to small and disadvantaged business, by firm and service branch, quarterly rpt, 3542–17

Property, supply, and equipment inventory of DOD, by service branch, FY90, annual rpt, 3544–6

Publications of DOD Directorate for Info Operations and Rpts, annual rpt, periodicity change, 3544–16

Office of the Secretary of Defense

Publications of DOD Directorate for Info Operations and Rpts, 1989 listing, 3548–21

R&D prime contract awards of DOD, for top 500 contractors, FY90, annual listing, 3544–4

R&D prime contract awards of DOD to US and foreign nonprofit instns and govt agencies, by instn and location, FY90, annual listing, 3544–17

Reserve forces personnel and equipment strengths, and readiness, by reserve component, FY90, annual rpt, 3544–31

Reserve forces personnel strengths and characteristics, by component, FY90, annual rpt, 3544–38

Reserve forces personnel strengths and characteristics, by component, quarterly rpt, 3542–4

Strategic material stockpile inventories and needs, by commodity, as of Jan 1991, annual rpt, 3544–37

Strategic material stockpiling by Fed Govt, activity, and inventory by commodity, as of Mar 1991, semiannual rpt, 3542–22

Office of the Secretary of Energy

Aircraft fuel use and efficiency under alternative technological improvements and load factors, by model, projected 1995-2010, 3028–6

Budget of DOE, authority by program and subagency, FY91, annual rpt, 3024–5

Global climate change economic impacts, projected to 2100 with background data for 1980s, 3028–5

Global climate change trends and contributing gases levels, Federal and intl data collection activities, mgmt, and inventory, 1990 rpt, 3028–4

Radioactive and hazardous waste at DOE facilities, disposal and remediation activities and funding, planned FY91-97, annual rpt, 3024–7

Office of the Special Representative for Trade Negotiations

see Office of the U.S. Trade Representative

Office of the U.S. Trade Representative

Budget of US, authoritative financial statements with appropriations, outlays, and receipts, by category and agency, FY90, annual rpt, 8104–2.1

Budget of US, obligations and authority by function, agency, and program, with summaries, analyses, and historical tables, FY92, annual rpt, 104–2

Export and import agreements, negotiations, and related legislation, 1990, annual rpt, 444–1

Exports of goods, services, and investment, trade barriers, impacts, and US actions, by country, 1989, annual rpt, 444–2

Office of the Vice President

Budget of US, authoritative financial statements with appropriations, outlays, and receipts, by category and agency, FY90, annual rpt, 8104–2.1

Budget of US, obligations and authority by function, agency, and program, with summaries, analyses, and historical tables, FY92, annual rpt, 104–2

Congressional Directory, members of 102nd Congress, other officials, elections, and districts, 1991-92, biennial rpt, 23874–1

Office of Thrift Supervision

Budget of US, obligations and authority by function, agency, and program, with summaries, analyses, and historical tables, FY92, annual rpt, 104–2

Fraud and abuse in banks and thrifts, Federal criminal enforcement activities, case dispositions, and settlements, with data by district, 1982-90, hearing, 21248–142

Savings instns finances and operations by district and State, mortgage loan activity and terms by MSA, and FHLB finances, 1989 and trends from 1900, annual rpt, 8434–3

Savings instns insured by Savings Assn Insurance Fund, assets, liabilities, and deposit and loan activity, by conservatorship status, monthly rpt, 8432–1

Savings instns insured by Savings Assn Insurance Fund, finances by profitability group, district, and State, quarterly rpt, 8432–4

see also Federal Home Loan Bank Board

Office of Transportation, USDA

Truck transport of fruit and vegetables, itemized costs per mile by item for fleets and owner-operator trucks, monthly table, 1272–1

Office of Youth Development

see Office of Human Development Services

Office supplies

County Business Patterns, 1988: employment, establishments, and payroll, by SIC 2- to 4-digit industry and county, annual State rpt series, 2326–6

County Business Patterns, 1989: employment, establishments, and payroll, by SIC 2- to 4-digit industry and county, annual State rpt series, 2326–8

DOD prime contract awards, by detailed procurement category, FY87-90, annual rpt, 3544–18

Employment, earnings, and hours, by SIC 1- to 4-digit industry, monthly and annual averages, selected years 1909-90, annual rpt, 6744–4

Exports and imports between US and outlying areas, by detailed commodity and mode of transport, 1990, annual rpt, 2424–11

Exports and imports of US, by country and detailed commodity, monthly rpt, 2422–12

Exports and imports of US, by Harmonized System 6-digit commodity and country, 1990, annual rpt, 2424–13

Exports and imports of US, by transport mode, country, and SITC 1- to 3-digit commodity, 1990, annual rpt, 2424–12

Exports of US, detailed Schedule B commodities with countries of destination, 1990, annual rpt, 2424–10

House of Representatives salaries, expenses, and contingent fund disbursement, detailed listings, quarterly rpt, 21942–1

Injuries from use of consumer products, by severity, victim age, and detailed product, 1990, annual rpt, 9164–6

Manufacturing annual survey, 1989: finances and operations, by SIC 2- to 4-digit industry, series, 2506–15

Manufacturing census, 1987: finances and operations, by type of organization and SIC 2- to 4-digit industry, subject rpt, 2497–5

Index by Subjects and Names

Occupational injury and illness rates, by SIC 2- to 4-digit industry, 1988-89, annual rpt, 6844–7

Occupational injury and illness rates, by SIC 2- to 4-digit industry, 1989, annual rpt, 6844–1

Price indexes (producer), by stage of processing and detailed commodity, monthly rpt, 6762–6

Price indexes (producer), by stage of processing and detailed commodity, monthly 1990, annual rpt, 6764–2

Retail trade census, 1987: depreciable assets, capital and operating expenses, sales, value added, and inventories, by SIC 2- to 4-digit kind of business, 2399–2

Senate receipts, itemized expenses by payee, and balances, 1st half FY91, semiannual listing, 25922–1

Service industries census, 1987: depreciable assets, capital and operating expenses, and receipts, by SIC 2- to 4-digit kind of business, 2393–2

Wholesale trade census, 1987: depreciable assets, capital and operating expenses, sales, value added, and inventories, by SIC 2- to 3-digit kind of business, 2407–2

Office workers

see Clerical workers

Official publications

see Government documents

Officials

Criminal case processing in Federal courts, by offense, disposition, and jurisdiction, data compilation, 1991 annual rpt, 6064–6.5

Foreign countries economic, social, political, and geographic summary data, by country, 1991, annual factbook, 9114–2

Foreign govt Chiefs of State and Cabinet members, by country, bimonthly listing, 9112–4

Pension systems of State and local govts, finances, coverage, and benefits, by system, FY88, annual rpt, 2466–2.1

Pension systems of State and local govts, finances, coverage, and benefits, by system, FY89, annual rpt, 2466–2.8

State Dept officers, ambassadors, and Chiefs of US overseas missions, by country and intl agency, 1778-1990, 7008–1

Workers compensation programs of States, top officials, salaries, and hours, by State, as of 1990, annual rpt, 6504–9

see also Congressional employees

see also Executives and managers

see also Federal employees

see also Government employees

see also International employees

see also Presidential appointments

see also State and local employees

Offshore mineral resources

Leasing activity, production, and revenue, for oil, gas, and minerals on Federal OCS lands by ocean region and State, 1950s-90, annual rpt, 5734–3

Mineral industries census, 1987: finances and operations, by establishment characteristics, SIC 2- to 4-digit industry, and State, subject rpt, 2517–1

Production and revenue from oil, gas, and minerals on Federal and Indian lands, by State, 1990 and trends from 1920, annual rpt, 5734–2

Index by Subjects and Names

Ohio

Production, revenue, and leasing activities on Federal and Indian oil, gas, and minerals lands, by State, 1980-89 and trends from 1920, 5738–21

South Carolina, Myrtle Beach offshore mineral resources, 1989 rpt, 5668–115

see also Offshore oil and gas

Offshore oil and gas

Alaska North Slope oil production, and impacts of lifting export controls on US oil trade, West Coast prices, and shipping industry, 1988 and forecast 1995, GAO rpt, 26113–496

Alaska OCS environmental conditions and oil dev impacts, compilation of papers, series, 2176–1

Arctic Ocean fish catch and habitat impacts of oil and gas dev, and assessment methods, 1988 conf, 5738–24

Atlantic OCS environmental conditions, and oil and gas dev impacts, series, discontinued, 5736–6

California OCS oil and gas dev impacts on water quality, marine life, and sediments, by site, 1986-89, annual rpt, 5734–11

Coastal and riparian areas environmental conditions, fish, wildlife, use, and mgmt, for individual ecosystems, series, 5506–9

Drilling rigs construction financing guarantees of MarAd, FY90, annual rpt, 7704–14.1

Environmental and socioeconomic conditions, and potential impact of oil and gas OCS leases, final statement series, 5736–1

Field codes and locations, for oil and gas, 1990, annual listing, 3164–70

Florida environmental, social, and economic conditions, and impacts of proposed OCS oil and gas leases in southern coastal areas, 1990 compilation of papers, 5738–19

Gulf of Mexico oil and gas reserves, production, and leasing status, by location, 1989, annual rpt, 5734–6

Helicopters, use, and landing facilities, by craft type, region, and State, 1989, 7508–75

Lease bidding for OCS oil and gas under alternative leasing systems, activity, royalty rates, and production, by sale, lessee type, and ocean area, FY79-89, annual rpt, 5734–12

Lease revenue sharing payments for OCS oil and gas by State, 1991 annual press release, 5306–4.9

Leases for OCS oil and gas suspended for environmental reasons and repurchased by Fed Govt, costs of cancellation for 3 States, 1990, GAO rpt, 26113–509

Leasing activity, production, and revenue, for oil, gas, and minerals on Federal OCS lands by ocean region and State, 1950s-90, annual rpt, 5734–3

Mineral industries census, 1987: energy use and costs, by fuel type, SIC 2- to 4-digit industry, and State, subject rpt, 2517–2

Mineral industries census, 1987: finances and operations, by SIC 2- to 4-digit industry, State, and county, census div rpt series, 2515–1

Natural and supplemental gas production, prices, trade, use, reserves, and pipeline company finances, by firm and State, monthly rpt with articles, 3162–4

Natural gas production and wellhead capacity, by production area, 1980-89 and alternative forecasts 1990-91, biennial rpt, 3164–93

North Carolina environmental and socioeconomic conditions, and impacts of proposed OCS oil and gas exploration, 1970s-90 and projected to 2020, 5738–22

Pacific Ocean OCS oil and gas production, and wells, by drilling platform under Federal lease, 1960s-89, annual rpt, 5734–9

Pacific Ocean oil and gas production, reserves, and wells drilled by location, 1989, annual rpt, 5734–7

Pipeline and compressor station construction costs, 1984-87, annual rpt, 3084–3

Pollution (water) industrial releases in wastewater, levels, treatment, costs, and regulation, with background financial and operating data, 1989 industry rpt, 9206–4.12

Price indexes (producer), by stage of processing and detailed commodity, monthly 1990, annual rpt, 6764–2

Producers finances and operations, by energy type for US firms domestic and foreign operations, 1989, annual rpt, 3164–44.2

Production and reserves of oil, gas, and gas liquids, by State and substate area, 1990, annual rpt, 3164–46

Production and revenue from oil, gas, and minerals on Federal and Indian lands, by State, 1990 and trends from 1920, annual rpt, 5734–2

Production, leasing and exploration activity, revenue, and costs, for Fed Govt OCS oil and gas reserves, by ocean area, FY90, annual rpt, 5734–4

Production, revenue, and leasing activities on Federal and Indian oil, gas, and minerals lands, by State, 1980-89 and trends from 1920, 5738–21

Reserves of OCS oil and gas, and leasing and dev activity, periodic regional rpt series, 5736–3

Seismic exploration crews and activity, monthly rpt, 3162–24.5

Ships accidents and casualties, by circumstances and characteristics of persons and vessels involved, 1988, annual rpt, 7404–11

Statistical Abstract of US, 1991 annual data compilation, 2324–1.25

Supply, demand, and prices, by fuel type and end-use sector, with foreign comparisons, 1990 and trends from 1949, annual rpt, 3164–74.1; 3164–74.2

Supply, demand, and prices of crude oil and refined products, and refinery capacity and stocks, by State, 1960-91, annual rpt, 3164–95

Supply, demand, and prices of oil and gas, alternative projections 1989-2010, annual rpt, 3164–89

Turtles (sea) population near oil drilling rigs, and habitat characteristics, 1988-90, 5738–26

Water discharges from oil and gas OCS production, for Pacific lands under Federal lease by drilling platform, 1960s-89, annual rpt, 5734–9

Ogden, Utah

Housing starts and completions authorized by building permits in 40 MSAs, quarterly rpt, 2382–9

Wages by occupation, for office and plant workers, 1990 survey, periodic MSA rpt, 6785–11.2

see also under By SMSA or MSA in the "Index by Categories"

Oh, Soo-Nam

"Contracts, Constraints, and Consumption", 9383–20.13

O'Hanlon, Michael

"START Treaty and Beyond", 26306–6.161

Ohio

AIDS patient home and community services under Medicaid waiver in 6 States, 1988-89, article, 4652–1.216

Appalachian Regional Commission funding, by project and State, planned FY91, annual rpt, 9084–3

Banks (insured commercial and savings) deposits by instn, State, MSA, and county, as of June 1990, annual regional rpt, 9295–3.3

Coal production and mines by county, prices, productivity, miners, and reserves, by mining method and State, 1989-90, annual rpt, 3164–25

County Business Patterns, 1989: employment, establishments, and payroll, by SIC 2- to 4-digit industry and county, annual State rpt, 2326–8.37

DOD prime contract awards, by contractor, service branch, State, and city, FY90, annual rpt, 3544–22

Earthquakes in midwestern States, intensity, time, and seismograph locations, 1977-90, annual rpt, 9634–10

Economic conditions and outlook, for US and Canada Great Lakes area, 1970s-90, 9375–15

Economic indicators and components, and Fed Reserve 4th District business and financial conditions, monthly chartbook, 9377–10

Education system in Appalachia, improvement initiatives, and indicators of success, by State, 1960s-89, 9088–36

Fed Govt spending in States and local areas, by type, State, county, and city, FY90, annual rpt, 2464–3

Fed Govt spending in States, by type, program, agency, and State, FY90, annual rpt, 2464–2

Floods in Shadyside, Ohio, storm characteristics, deaths, and Natl Weather Service forecast accuracy for flash floods, 1990, 2186–6.2

HHS financial aid, by program, recipient, State, and city, FY90, annual regional listing, 4004–3.5

Hospital deaths of Medicare patients, actual and expected rates by diagnosis, and hospital characteristics, by instn, FY87-89, annual regional rpt, 4654–14.5

Income (personal) per capita and by source, and earnings by industry div, by State, MSA, and county, 1984-89, annual regional rpt, 2704–2.2

Jail adult and juvenile population, employment, spending, instn conditions, and inmate programs, by county and facility, 1988, regional rpt series, 6068–144.3

Ohio

Land subsidence above coal mines, State property insurance program income and expenses in 6 States, 1990, GAO rpt, 26113–530

Marriages, divorces, and rates, by characteristics of spouses, State, and county, 1987 and trends from 1920, US Vital Statistics annual rpt, 4144–4

Mineral Industry Surveys, State reviews of production, 1990, preliminary annual rpt, 5614–6

Minerals Yearbook, 1989, Vol 2: State review of production and sales by commodity, and business activity, annual rpt, 5604–16.36

Minerals Yearbook, 1989, Vol 2: State reviews of production, sales, and firms, by commodity, and business activity, annual rpt, 5604–34

Nursing home reimbursement by Medicaid, States payment ratesetting methods, analysis for 7 States, 1980s, article, 4652–1.255

Physicians, by specialty, age, sex, and location of training and practice, 1989, State rpt, 4116–6.36

Population and housing census, 1990: population and housing characteristics, households, and land area, by county, subdiv, and place, State rpt, 2551–1.37

Population and housing census, 1990: voting age and total population by race, and housing units, by block, redistricting counts required under PL 94-171, State CD-ROM release, 2551–6.6

Population and housing census, 1990: voting age and total population by race, and housing units, by county and city, redistricting counts required under PL 94-171, State summary rpt, 2551–5.36

Radioactivity levels at former AEC and Manhattan Project research and storage sites, 1988, 3006–9.8

Statistical Abstract of US, 1991 annual data compilation, 2324–1

Supplemental Security Income payments and beneficiaries, by type of eligibility, State, and county, Dec 1989, annual rpt, 4744–27.5

Water supply and quality in streams and lakes, and groundwater levels in wells, by drainage basin, 1990, annual State rpt, 5666–10.34

Water use by end use, well withdrawals, and public supply deliveries, by county, 1985, State rpt, 5666–24.7

see also Akron, Ohio
see also Chillicothe, Ohio
see also Cincinnati, Ohio
see also Cleveland, Ohio
see also Cuyahoga County, Ohio
see also Dayton, Ohio
see also Gallipolis, Ohio
see also Hamilton, Ohio
see also Lake County, Ohio
see also Lima, Ohio
see also Lorain, Ohio
see also Portsmouth, Ohio
see also Sandusky, Ohio
see also Shadyside, Ohio
see also Shaker Heights, Ohio
see also Springfield, Ohio
see also Toledo, Ohio
see also under By State in the "Index by Categories"

Ohio River

Army Corps of Engineers water resources dev projects, characteristics, and costs, 1950s-89, biennial State rpt series, 3756–1

Army Corps of Engineers water resources dev projects, characteristics, and costs, 1950s-91, biennial State rpt series, 3756–2

Water supply and quality in streams and lakes, and groundwater levels in wells, by drainage basin, 1988, annual State rpt series, 5666–16

Water supply and quality in streams and lakes, and groundwater levels in wells, by drainage basin, 1989, annual State rpt series, 5666–12

Water supply and quality in streams and lakes, and groundwater levels in wells, by drainage basin, 1990, annual State rpt series, 5666–10

Water supply in US and southern Canada, streamflow, surface and groundwater conditions, and reservoir levels, by location, monthly rpt, 5662–3

Ohsfeldt, Robert L.

"Medicaid Payment Rates for Nursing Homes, 1979-86", 4652–1.224

Oil

see Aviation fuels
see Diesel fuel
see Fuel oil
see Gasoline
see Kerosene
see Offshore oil and gas
see Oil and gas leases
see Oil depletion allowances
see Oil shale
see Oil spills
see Oils, oilseeds, and fats
see Petroleum and petroleum industry
see Petroleum exports and imports
see Petroleum prices
see Petroleum reserves
see Tar sands

Oil and gas leases

Alaska minerals resources, production, oil and gas leases, reserves, and exploratory wells, with maps and bibl, 1989, annual rpt, 5664–11

Alaska OCS environmental conditions and oil dev impacts, compilation of papers, series, 2176–1

Budget of US, obligations and authority by function, agency, and program, with summaries, analyses, and historical tables, FY92, annual rpt, 104–2

Coastal and riparian areas environmental conditions, fish, wildlife, use, and mgmt, for individual ecosystems, series, 5506–9

Environmental and socioeconomic conditions, and potential impact of oil and gas OCS leases, final statement series, 5736–1

Florida environmental, social, and economic conditions, and impacts of proposed OCS oil and gas leases in southern coastal areas, 1990 compilation of papers, 5738–19

Gulf of Mexico oil and gas reserves, production, and leasing status, by location, 1989, annual rpt, 5734–6

Land Mgmt Bur activities and funding by State, FY89, annual rpt, 5724–13

Land Mgmt Bur activities in Southwestern US, FY90, annual rpt, 5724–15

Naval Petroleum and Oil Shale Reserves production and revenue by fuel type, sales by purchaser, and wells, by reserve, FY90, annual rpt, 3334–3

North Carolina environmental and socioeconomic conditions, and impacts of proposed OCS oil and gas exploration, 1970s-90 and projected to 2020, 5738–22

Offshore oil and gas lease bidding under alternative leasing systems, activity, royalty rates, and production, by sale, lessee type, and ocean area, FY79-89, annual rpt, 5734–12

Offshore oil and gas leases, revenue sharing payments by State, 1991 annual press release, 5306–4.9

Offshore oil and gas leases suspended for environmental reasons and repurchased by Fed Govt, costs of cancellation for 3 States, 1990, GAO rpt, 26113–509

Offshore oil and gas reserves, and leasing and dev activity, periodic regional rpt series, 5736–3

Offshore oil and gas reserves of Fed Govt, production, leasing and exploration activity, revenue, and costs, by ocean area, FY90, annual rpt, 5734–4

Offshore oil, gas, and minerals production, revenue, and leasing activity, for Federal OCS lands by ocean area and State, 1950s-90, annual rpt, 5734–3

Pacific Ocean OCS oil and gas production, and wells, by drilling platform under Federal lease, 1960s-89, annual rpt, 5734–9

Production and revenue from oil, gas, and minerals on Federal and Indian lands, by State, 1990 and trends from 1920, annual rpt, 5734–2

Production, revenue, and leasing activities on Federal and Indian oil, gas, and minerals lands, by State, 1980-89 and trends from 1920, 5738–21

Public lands acreage and use, and Land Mgmt Bur activities and finances, annual State rpt series, 5724–11

Public lands acreage, grants, use, revenues, and allocations, by State, FY90, annual rpt, 5724–1.2

Oil depletion allowances

Producers finances and operations, by energy type for US firms domestic and foreign operations, 1989, annual rpt, 3164–44.1

Oil shale

Natl Energy Strategy plans for conservation and pollution reduction, impacts of technology and regulation proposals, projected 1990-2030, 3166–6.47

Naval Petroleum and Oil Shale Reserves production and revenue by fuel type, sales by purchaser, and wells, by reserve, FY90, annual rpt, 3334–3

Occupational injuries and incidence, employment, and hours in nonmetallic minerals mines and related operations, 1989, annual rpt, 6664–1

Pollution (air) contributing to global warming, emissions factors and control costs, by pollutant and source, 1990 rpt, 9198–124

Index by Subjects and Names

Oils, oilseeds, and fats

Oil spills

Alaska OCS environmental conditions and oil dev impacts, compilation of papers, series, 2176–1

Alaska oil spill from tanker Exxon Valdez, Federal cleanup and damage assessment costs, and reimbursement from Exxon, by agency, as of Sept 1990, GAO rpt, 26113–510

Alaska oil spill from tanker Exxon Valdez, impacts on marine mammals, and resulting legislation, 1990 annual rpt, 14734–1

Alaska oil spill from tanker Exxon Valdez, safety issues, with oil lost and crew alcohol and drug test results, 1989, 9618–17

Alaska oil spill from tanker Exxon Valdez, sea otter conservation measures, 1990 conf, 5508–110

Alaska oil spill from tanker Glacier Bay, cleanup costs and area economic benefits, with data by firm and agency, 1987, 5736–5.15

Bonneville Power Admin operations, maintenance, and environmental protection plans, FY90-99, 3228–14

Coastal and riparian areas environmental conditions, fish, wildlife, use, and mgmt, for individual ecosystems, series, 5506–9

Coastal areas environmental and socioeconomic conditions, and potential impact of oil and gas OCS leases, final statement series, 5736–1

Environmental Quality, status of problems, protection programs, research, and intl issues, 1991 annual rpt, 484–1

Fish kills from water pollution, by pollution source, month, location, and State, 1977-87, last issue of annual rpt, 9204–3

Fish kills in coastal areas related to pollution and natural causes, by land use, State, and county, 1980s, 2178–32

Florida environmental, social, and economic conditions, and impacts of proposed OCS oil and gas leases in southern coastal areas, 1990 compilation of papers, 5738–19

North Carolina environmental and socioeconomic conditions, and impacts of proposed OCS oil and gas exploration, 1970s-90 and projected to 2020, 5738–22

Spills, seepage, and well blowouts in waters under Federal lease, and tanker spills worldwide, selected years 1964-90, annual rpt, 5734–3.6

Statistical Abstract of US, 1991 annual data compilation, 2324–1.6

Terminals (offshore) for unloading oil tankers, impacts on marine oil pollution, 1990 rpt, 5738–25

Oil wells

see Energy exploration and drilling

Oils, essential

see Spices and herbs

Oils, oilseeds, and fats

Acreage planted and harvested, by crop and State, 1989-90 and planned as of June 1991, annual rpt, 1621–23

Acreage planted, by selected crop and State, 1982-90 and planned 1991, annual rpt, 1621–22

Agricultural Statistics, 1990, annual rpt, 1004–1

Agriculture census, 1987: farms, farmland, production, finances, and operator characteristics, by county, final State rpt series, 2331–1

Communist countries trade with US, by detailed commodity and country, quarterly rpt with articles, 9882–2

Confectionery shipments, trade, use, and ingredients used, by product, 1990, annual Current Industrial Rpt, 2506–4.5

Consumer Expenditure Survey, food spending by item, household composition, income, age, race, and region, 1980-88, biennial rpt, 1544–30

Consumer Expenditure Survey, household income by source, and itemized spending, by selected characteristics and region, 1988-89, annual rpt, 6764–5

Consumption of food, dietary composition, and nutrient intake, 1987/88 natl survey, preliminary rpt series, 1356–1

Consumption, supply, trade, prices, spending, and indexes, by food commodity, 1989, annual rpt, 1544–4

Cotton linters production, stocks, use, and prices, monthly rpt, 1309–10

Cottonseed prices and quality, by State, seasonal weekly rpt, 1309–14

Cottonseed quality factors, by State, 1990 crop, annual rpt, 1309–5

County Business Patterns, 1988: employment, establishments, and payroll, by SIC 2- to 4-digit industry and county, annual State rpt series, 2326–6

County Business Patterns, 1989: employment, establishments, and payroll, by SIC 2- to 4-digit industry and county, annual State rpt series, 2326–8

CPI by component for US city average, and by region, population size, and for 27 metro areas, monthly rpt, 6762–2

Employment, earnings, and hours, by SIC 1- to 4-digit industry, monthly and annual averages, selected years 1909-90, annual rpt, 6744–4

Exports (agricultural) of high-value commodities, indexes and sales value by commodity, world area, and country, 1960s-86, 1528–323

Exports (agricultural) of US, impacts of foreign agricultural and trade policy, with data by commodity and country, 1989, annual rpt, 1924–8

Exports and imports (agricultural) commodity and country, prices, and world market devs, monthly rpt, 1922–12

Exports and imports (agricultural) of US, by commodity and country, bimonthly rpt, 1522–1

Exports and imports (agricultural) of US, by detailed commodity and country, 1989, annual rpt, 1524–8

Exports and imports (agricultural) of US, by detailed commodity and country, 1990, semiannual rpt, 1522–4

Exports and imports between US and outlying areas, by detailed commodity and mode of transport, 1990, annual rpt, 2424–11

Exports and imports of dairy, livestock, and poultry products, by commodity and country, FAS monthly circular, 1925–32

Exports and imports of US, by country and detailed commodity, monthly rpt, 2422–12

Exports and imports of US, by Harmonized System 6-digit commodity and country, 1990, annual rpt, 2424–13

Exports and imports of US, by selected country, country group, and commodity group, 1990, annual rpt, 2044–37

Exports and imports of US, by transport mode, country, and SITC 1- to 3-digit commodity, 1990, annual rpt, 2424–12

Exports of grains, oilseed products, hides, skins, and cotton, by country, weekly rpt, 1922–3

Exports of US, detailed Schedule B commodities with countries of destination, 1990, annual rpt, 2424–10

Farm financial and marketing conditions, forecast 1991, annual chartbook, 1504–8

Farm financial and marketing conditions, forecast 1991, annual conf, 1004–16

Farm income, expenses, receipts by commodity, assets, liabilities, and ratios, 1990 and trends from 1945, annual rpt, 1544–16

Farm sector balance sheet, and receipts by detailed commodity, by State, 1985-89, annual rpt, 1544–18

Fish (processed) production by location, and trade, by species and product, 1987-90, annual rpts, 2166–6

Fish catch, prices, trade by country, cold storage holdings, and market devs, for Japan, semimonthly press release, 2162–7

Fish catch, trade, use, and fishery operations, with selected foreign data, by species, 1980s-90, annual rpt, 2164–1

Fish meal and oil production and trade, quarterly tables, 2162–3

Foreign and US agricultural production, acreage, and yield for selected crops, forecasts by selected world region and country, FAS monthly circular, 1925–28

Foreign and US agricultural production, prices, trade, and use, periodic rpt with articles, 1522–3

Foreign and US oils, oilseeds, and fats production and trade, FAS periodic circular series, 1925–1

Foreign countries agricultural production, prices, and trade, by country, 1980-90 and forecast 1991, annual world area rpt series, 1524–4

Foreign countries agricultural production, trade, and policies, summary data by country, 1989-90, annual factbook, 1924–12

Futures and options trading volume, by commodity and exchange, FY90, annual rpt, 11924–2

Imports of oils, oilseeds, and meal, by commodity, world area of destination, and major producer, 1960s-88, 1528–314

Industrial uses of new and traditional agricultural crops, replacement of imports and nonrenewable resources, R&D funding, and economic impacts, 1970s-90, 26358–239

Inspection of grain for export, test results by commodity and port region, 1988-90, annual rpt series, 1294–2

Low-fat and nonfat foods introduced, by product type, 1990, article, 1502–4.204

Manufacturing annual survey, 1989: finances and operations, by SIC 2- to 4-digit industry, series, 2506–15

Oils, oilseeds, and fats

Manufacturing census, 1987: finances and operations, by SIC 2- to 4-digit industry, State, and MSA, with trends from 1849, 2497–1

Manufacturing census, 1987: finances and operations, by type of organization and SIC 2- to 4-digit industry, subject rpt, 2497–5

Nutrient, caloric, and waste composition, detailed data for raw, processed, and prepared foods, 1991 rpt, 1356–3.15

Occupational injury and illness rates, by SIC 2- to 4-digit industry, 1988-89, annual rpt, 6844–7

Occupational injury and illness rates, by SIC 2- to 4-digit industry, 1989, annual rpt, 6844–1

OECD trade, total and for 4 major countries, and US trade by country, by commodity, 1970-89, world area rpt series, 9116–1

PL 480 long-term credit sales allocations, by commodity and country, periodic press release, 1922–7

Price indexes (producer), by stage of processing and detailed commodity, monthly rpt, 6762–6

Price indexes (producer), by stage of processing and detailed commodity, monthly 1990, annual rpt, 6764–2

Price support program provisions, for selected commodities, 1961-90, 1568–303

Price support programs for oilseeds, eligibility requirements, and market loan and repayment rates, 1990-92, article, 1561–3.202

Prices (farm-retail) for food, marketing cost components, and industry finances and productivity, 1920s-90, annual rpt, 1544–9

Prices received and paid by farmers, by commodity and State, 1990, annual rpt, 1629–5

Prices received by farmers and production value, by detailed crop and State, 1988-90, annual rpt, 1621–2

Prices received by farmers for major products, and paid for farm inputs and living items, by State, monthly rpt, 1629–1

Production, farms, acreage, and related data, by selected crop and State, monthly rpt, 1621–1

Production inputs, output, and productivity for farms, by commodity and region, 1947-89, annual rpt, 1544–17

Production of oil and fat, consumption by end use, and stocks, by type, quarterly Current Industrial Rpt, 2506–4.4

Production of oil, crushings, and stocks, by oilseed type and State, quarterly Current Industrial Rpt, 2506–4.3

Production, prices, trade, and export inspections by US port and country of destination, by grain type, weekly rpt, 1313–2

Production, prices, trade, and marketing, by commodity, current situation and forecast, monthly rpt with articles, 1502–4

Production, prices, trade, and use of oils and fats, periodic situation rpt with articles, 1561–3

Soviet Union agricultural trade, by commodity and country, 1955-90, 1528–322

Sunflower seed stocks by region and market city, and seed inspected for export, weekly rpt, 1313–4

Tallow and grease foreign and US production, trade, and use, by selected country, FAS semiannual circular series, 1925–33

see also Animal feed

see also Corn

see also Peanuts

see also Soybeans

see also under By Commodity in the "Index by Categories"

Oklahoma

Banks (insured commercial and savings) deposits by instn, State, MSA, and county, as of June 1990, annual regional rpt, 9295–3.4

Coal production and mines by county, prices, productivity, miners, and reserves, by mining method and State, 1989-90, annual rpt, 3164–25

County Business Patterns, 1989: employment, establishments, and payroll, by SIC 2- to 4-digit industry and county, annual State rpt, 2326–8.38

DOD prime contract awards, by contractor, service branch, State, and city, FY90, annual rpt, 3544–22

Employment by industry div, earnings, and hours, by southwestern State, monthly rpt, 6962–2

Fed Govt spending in States and local areas, by type, State, county, and city, FY90, annual rpt, 2464–3

Fed Govt spending in States, by type, program, agency, and State, FY90, annual rpt, 2464–2

Financial and economic devs, Fed Reserve 10th District, quarterly rpt, 9381–16

Floods on Arkansas, Red, and Trinity Rivers, storm characteristics, and Natl Weather Service forecast accuracy, 1990, 2186–6.4

HHS financial aid, by program, recipient, State, and city, FY90, annual regional listing, 4004–3.6

Hospital deaths of Medicare patients, actual and expected rates by diagnosis, and hospital characteristics, by instn, FY87-89, annual regional rpt, 4654–14.6

Income (personal) per capita and by source, and earnings by industry div, by State, MSA, and county, 1984-89, annual regional rpt, 2704–2.5

Indian infant death rates, and racial misclassification on death certificates, for Oklahoma, 1975-88, article, 4042–3.209

Jail adult and juvenile population, employment, spending, instn conditions, and inmate programs, by county and facility, 1988, regional rpt series, 6068–144.4

Land Mgmt Bur activities in Southwestern US, FY90, annual rpt, 5724–15

Marriages, divorces, and rates, by characteristics of spouses, State, and county, 1987 and trends from 1920, US Vital Statistics annual rpt, 4144–4

Mineral Industry Surveys, State reviews of production, 1990, preliminary annual rpt, 5614–6

Minerals Yearbook, 1989, Vol 2: State review of production and sales by commodity, and business activity, annual rpt, 5604–16.37

Index by Subjects and Names

Minerals Yearbook, 1989, Vol 2: State reviews of production, sales, and firms, by commodity, and business activity, annual rpt, 5604–34

Natural gas production and wellhead capacity, by production area, 1980-89 and alternative forecasts 1990-91, biennial rpt, 3164–93

Physicians, by specialty, age, sex, and location of training and practice, 1989, State rpt, 4116–6.37

Population and housing census, 1990: population and housing characteristics, households, and land area, by county, subdiv, and place, State rpt, 2551–1.38

Population and housing census, 1990: voting age and total population by race, and housing units, by block, redistricting counts required under PL 94-171, State CD-ROM release, 2551–6.1

Population and housing census, 1990: voting age and total population by race, and housing units, by county and city, redistricting counts required under PL 94-171, State summary rpt, 2551–5.37

Statistical Abstract of US, 1991 annual data compilation, 2324–1

Supplemental Security Income payments and beneficiaries, by type of eligibility, State, and county, Dec 1989, annual rpt, 4744–27.6

Timber in Oklahoma, resources, growth, and removals, by species, forest type, ownership, and county, 1986, regional rpt series, 1206–39

Water (groundwater) supply, quality, chemistry, and use, 1987-88, regional rpt, 5666–28.3

Water supply and quality in streams and lakes, and groundwater levels in wells, by drainage basin, 1989, annual State rpt, 5666–12.35

see also Altus, Okla.

see also Cleveland County, Okla.

see also Lawton, Okla.

see also Oklahoma City, Okla.

see also Oklahoma County, Okla.

see also Tulsa, Okla.

see also under By State in the "Index by Categories"

Oklahoma City, Okla.

Housing and households characteristics, unit and neighborhood quality, and journey to work by MSA location, for 11 MSAs, 1984 survey, supplement, 2485–8

Housing and households detailed characteristics, and unit and neighborhood quality, by location, 1988 survey, MSA rpt, 2485–6.6

Wages by occupation, for office and plant workers, 1991 survey, periodic MSA rpt, 6785–3.9

see also under By City and By SMSA or MSA in the "Index by Categories"

Oklahoma County, Okla.

Housing and households characteristics, unit and neighborhood quality, and journey to work by MSA location, for 11 MSAs, 1984 survey, supplement, 2485–8

Housing and households detailed characteristics, and unit and neighborhood quality, by location, 1988 survey, MSA rpt, 2485–6.6

Index by Subjects and Names

Old-Age, Survivors, Disability, and Health Insurance

Old age

see Aged and aging

Old age assistance

Assistance (financial and nonfinancial) of Fed Govt, 1991 base edition with supplements, annual listing, 104–5

Assistance for aged, funding by program, and long term care ombudsman funding and visits by State, 1988-90, 25248–126

Assistance programs under Ways and Means Committee jurisdiction, finances, operations, and participant characteristics, FY70s-90, annual rpt, 21784–11

Budget of US, formula grant program obligations to State and local govts, by agency, program, and State, FY92, annual rpt, 104–30

Energy aid for low income households, funding sources, costs, and participation, by State, FY89, annual rpt, 4694–8

Energy aid for low income households, program characteristics by State, FY90, annual rpt, 4694–9

Food aid programs of USDA, costs and participation by program, FY69-89, annual rpt, 1364–9

Food stamp eligibility and payment errors, by type, recipient characteristics, and State, FY89, annual rpt, 1364–15

Food stamp recipient household size, composition, income, and income and deductions allowed, summer 1988, annual rpt, 1364–8

Food stamp use at farmers markets, costs and participation, demonstration project results for 14 States, 1989, hearing, 21168–46

HHS financial aid, by program, recipient, State, and city, FY90, annual regional listings, 4004–3

Housing (public) renovation costs and alternative funding methods, by project type and region, 1990 rpt, 5188–127

Medicaid and SSI recipients, by eligibility type, from 1970s, and by State, 1989, annual rpt, 4744–3.8

Pennsylvania aid to aged for prescription drugs, program enrollment, use, and costs, FY85-87, article, 4652–1.237

Recreation (outdoor) facilities of Fed Govt, Golden Age Passports issued, FY88-90, annual rpt, 5544–14

see also Medicare

see also Old-Age, Survivors, Disability, and Health Insurance

see also Pensions and pension funds

see also Supplemental Security Income

Old-Age, Survivors, Disability, and Health Insurance

Actuarial studies, Medicare and OASDI future cost estimates and past experience analyses, series, 4706–1

Admin of OASDHI, and SSA activities, 1930s-90 and projected to 2064, annual data compilation, 4704–12

Assistance (financial and nonfinancial) of Fed Govt, 1991 base edition with supplements, annual listing, 104–5

Assistance of Fed Govt, by type, program, agency, and State, FY90, annual rpt, 2464–2

Benefits and beneficiaries of OASDI, by type of benefit, State, and county, as of Dec 1990, annual rpt, 4744–28

Benefits, beneficiary characteristics, and trust funds of OASDHI, Medicaid, SSI, and related programs, selected years 1937-89, annual rpt, 4744–3

Benefits by county, FY90, annual regional listings, 4004–3

Budget of US, balances of budget authority obligated and unobligated, by function and agency, FY90-92, annual rpt, 104–8

Budget of US, CBO analysis and review of FY92 budget by function, annual rpt, 26304–2

Budget of US, CBO analysis of revenue and spending alternatives and projections of economic indicators, FY92-96, annual rpt, 26304–3

Budget of US, CBO analysis of savings and revenues under alternative spending cuts and tax changes, projected FY92-97, 26306–3.118

Budget of US, House concurrent resolution, with spending and revenue targets, FY92 and projected to FY96, annual rpt, 21264–2

Budget of US, midsession review of FY92 budget, by function, annual rpt, 104–7

Budget of US, obligations and authority by function, agency, and program, with summaries, analyses, and historical tables, FY92, annual rpt, 104–2

Budget of US, receipts by source, outlays by agency and program, and balances, monthly rpt, 8102–3

Budget of US, Senate concurrent resolution, with spending and revenue targets, FY92, annual rpt, 25254–1

Court civil and criminal caseloads for Federal district, appeals, and bankruptcy courts, by type of suit and offense, circuit, and district, 1990, annual rpt, 18204–11

Court civil and criminal caseloads for Federal district, appeals, and special courts, 1990, annual rpt, 18204–8

Court civil and criminal caseloads for Federal district courts, 1991, annual rpt, 18204–2.1

Court criminal cases in Federal district courts, by offense, disposition, and district, 1980-90, last issue of annual rpt, 18204–1

Disability Insurance beneficiaries costs to Medicare until age 64 under alternative coverage assumptions, model results, 1989, article, 4742–1.208

Disability Insurance beneficiaries sociodemographic and medical characteristics, annual rpt, discontinued, 4704–14

Earnings replacement rates of pension plans and OASI benefits, by age, salary, years of participation, and occupational group, 1989, article, 6722–1.238

Expenditures of Fed Govt by type, and other finances, selected years 1952-89, annual rpt, 10044–1

Fed Govt civilian employees demographic and employment characteristics, as of Sept 1990, annual article, 9842–1.201

Finances and operations of programs under Ways and Means Committee jurisdiction, FY70s-90, annual rpt, 21784–11

Finances of govts, revenue by source, spending by function, debt, and assets, by level of govt, FY89, annual rpt, 2466–2.2

Finances of SSA programs, and litigation, FY90, annual rpt, 4704–6

Financial consolidated statements of Fed Govt based on business accounting methods, FY89-90, annual rpt, 8104–5

Food stamp recipient household size, composition, income, and income and deductions allowed, summer 1988, annual rpt, 1364–8

Govt census, 1987: State and local govt employment, payroll, OASDHI coverage, and employee benefits costs, by level of govt and State, 2455–4

Households composition, income, benefits, and labor force status, Survey of Income and Program Participation methodology, working paper series, 2626–10

Income (household) and poverty status under alternative income definitions, by recipient characteristics, 1990, annual Current Population Rpt, 2546–6.69

Income (household) by source, and itemized spending, by selected characteristics and region, 1988-89 Consumer Expenditure Survey, annual rpt, 6764–5

Income of retired pension recipients, by selected characteristics, 1986, Current Population Rpt, 2546–20.18

Medicaid and Medicare low income disabled enrollees and eligibility provisions, by State, 1975-89, article, 4652–1.218

Poverty status of population and families, by detailed characteristics, 1988-89, annual Current Population Rpt, 2546–6.67

Poverty status of population and families, by detailed characteristics, 1990, annual Current Population Rpt, 2546–6.71

Research on social security programs and related issues, technical paper series, 4746–26

Research rpts and microdata files of SSA, 1991 biennial listing, 4744–12

Retired-worker OASDI benefits, effect of proposal to privatize excess trust funds into individual accounts, 1990 GAO rpt, 26121–397

Rural areas aged household income sources, and poverty status, 1983-84, 1598–268

Social Security Bulletin, OASDHI and other program operations and beneficiary characteristics, from 1940, monthly journal, 4742–1

State and local govt employees covered under OASDHI, by system, FY88, annual rpt, 2466–2.1

State and local govt employees covered under OASDHI, by system, FY89, annual rpt, 2466–2.8

State and Metro Area Data Book, 1991 data compilation, 2328–54

Statistical Abstract of US, 1991 annual data compilation, 2324–1.12

Student aid Pell grants and applicants, by tuition, income level, instn type and control, and State, 1989/90, annual rpt, 4804–1

Supplemental Security Income beneficiaries income from OASI and other sources, and work history, 1988, article, 4742–1.216

Tax (income) returns of individuals, selected income and tax items by income level, preliminary 1989, annual article, 8302–2.209

Tax expenditures, Federal revenues forgone through income tax deductions and exclusions by type, FY92-96, annual rpt, 21784–10

Old-Age, Survivors, Disability, and Health Insurance

Trust funds finances for OASDI, 1937-FY90 and alternative projections to 2065, annual rpt, 4704–4

Trust funds financial condition, for Disability Insurance, monthly rpt, 8102–9.14

Trust funds financial condition, for OASI, monthly rpt, 8102–9.2

Trust funds of OASDHI, financial status forecasts, evaluation of demographic and economic assumptions, 1991 article, 9391–1.207

Trust funds of OASDI, finances, effects of inclusion in budget deficit figures, and social security tax reduction proposals, 1990 hearing, 25368–171

US attorneys civil cases, by type and disposition, FY90, annual rpt, 6004–2.5

see also Medicare

see also Social security tax

Old Dog Cross, Phyllis

"Violence", 4088–2

Older Americans Act

Assistance for aged, funding by program, and long term care ombudsman funding and visits by State, 1988-90, 25248–126

Oleomargarine

see Oils, oilseeds, and fats

Olive oil

see Oils, oilseeds, and fats

Olives

see Fruit and fruit products

Olsson, Hakan

"Her-2/neu and INT2 Proto-oncogene Amplification in Malignant Breast Tumors in Relation to Reproductive Factors and Exposure to Exogenous Hormones", 4472–1.227

Oltmann, Richard N.

"Rainfall and Runoff Quantity and Quality Characteristics of Four Urban Land-Use Catchments in Fresno, Calif., October 1981-April 1983", 5666–27.2

Olympia, Wash.

see also under By SMSA or MSA in the "Index by Categories"

Omaha, Nebr.

Drug test results at arrest, by drug type, offense, and sex, for selected urban areas, quarterly rpt, 6062–3

Housing vacancy rates for single and multifamily units and mobile homes, by city and ZIP code, 1991, annual MSA rpt, 9304–22.4

Wages by occupation, and benefits for office and plant workers, 1990 survey, periodic MSA rpt, 6785–11.2

see also under By City and By SMSA or MSA in the "Index by Categories"

Oman

Agricultural exports of high-value commodities, indexes and sales by commodity, world area, and country, 1960s-86, 1528–323

Agricultural trade of US, by detailed commodity and country, 1989, annual rpt, 1524–8

Agricultural trade of US, by detailed commodity and country, 1990, semiannual rpt, 1522–4

AID economic aid to developing countries, obligations and disbursements by country, quarterly rpt, 9912–4

AID loans repayment status and terms by program and country, and status of predecessor agency loans, quarterly rpt, 9912–3

Economic and military aid and loans from US and intl agencies, by program and country, FY46-90, annual rpt, 9914–5

Economic and social conditions of developing countries from 1960s, and Intl Dev Cooperation Agency and AID activities and funding, FY90-92, annual rpt, 9904–4

Economic conditions, income, production, prices, employment, and trade, 1991 periodic country rpt, 2046–4.39

Economic conditions, policy, and trade practices, by country, 1988-90, annual rpt, 21384–5

Economic, social, political, and geographic summary data, by country, 1991, annual factbook, 9114–2

Exports and imports of US, by commodity and country, 1970-89, world area rpt, 9116–1.1

Exports and imports of US, by selected country, country group, and commodity group, 1990, annual rpt, 2044–37

Exports and imports of US, by transport mode, country, and SITC 1- to 3-digit commodity, 1990, annual rpt, 2424–12

Exports of US, detailed Schedule B commodities with countries of destination, 1990, annual rpt, 2424–10

Human rights conditions in 170 countries, and US economic and military aid, 1990, annual rpt, 21384–3

Military aid of US, arms sales, and training programs costs and budget requests, by program, world region, and country, FY90-92, annual rpt, 7144–13

UN voting record and share of votes in agreement with US, by issue, country, and world area, 1990, annual rpt, 7004–18

see also under By Foreign Country in the "Index by Categories"

Omnibus Budget Reconciliation Act

Budget of US, CBO analysis of revenue and spending alternatives and projections of economic indicators, FY92-96, annual rpt, 26304–3

Pension plans (defined benefit) impacts of OBRA contribution deductibility limit, 1984-89, 8008–152

On-Site Inspection Agency

Nuclear weapons elimination under Intermediate-Range Nuclear Forces Treaty, US and USSR on site inspections, and US costs and staffing, FY89-91, GAO rpt, 26123–364

Onions

see Vegetables and vegetable products

Ontario, Calif.

see also under By City in the "Index by Categories"

Ontario Province, Canada

Economic conditions and outlook, for US and Canada Great Lakes area, 1970s-90, 9375–15

Great Lakes wastewater treatment by municipal and industrial facilities, releases, methods, effectiveness, pollutant limits, and enforcement, 1985-88, 14648–24

Health care universal system in Canada, operations and costs, and implications for US, 1987-91, GAO rpt, 26121–424

Pollution (air) emissions and levels in Detroit area, by pollutant, 1980-90, 14648–25

Index by Subjects and Names

OPEC

see Organization of Petroleum Exporting Countries

Open housing

see Discrimination in housing

Operating costs

see Business income and expenses, general

see Business income and expenses, specific industry

see Operating ratios

see Production costs

Operating ratios

Acquisitions (leveraged buyout) impacts on financial performance, for 4 transactions, 1980s-90, GAO rpt, 26119–355

Acquisitions (leveraged buyout) in manufacturing, relation to industry size, concentration ratios, and financial indicators, 1988, technical paper, 9385–8.86

Agricultural cooperatives finances, aggregate for top 100 assns by commodity group, 1989, annual rpt, 1124–3

Agricultural Outlook, production, prices, marketing, and trade, by commodity, forecast and current situation, monthly rpt with articles, 1502–4

Air traffic, capacity, and performance, by carrier and type of operation, monthly rpt, 7302–6

Air traffic, capacity, and performance for medium regionals, by carrier, quarterly rpt, 7302–8

Airline deregulation in 1978, impacts on industry structure, competition, fares, finances, operations, and intl service, with data by carrier and airport, 1980s, series, 7308–199

Airline finances, by carrier, carrier group, and for total certificated system, quarterly rpt, 7302–7

Airline financial and operating summary data, quarterly rpt, 7502–16

Airline operations and passenger, cargo, and mail traffic, by type of service, air carrier, State, and country, 1980-89, annual rpt, 7504–1.6

Assets and liabilities of US, and impacts of inflation, 1990 and trends from 1948, article, 9391–1.220

Bank deposit insurance fund finances, potential losses, and real estate lenders financial ratios compared to other US and Texas banks, 1990 hearings, 25248–125

Bank holding company equity capital costs and impact on ability to raise capital, 1960s-80s, technical paper, 9366–6.274

Bank holding company subsidiaries dealing in bank-ineligible securities, subsidiary and parent firm finances, 1989-91, GAO rpt, 26119–280

Banking and economic conditions, for Fed Reserve 8th District, quarterly rpt with articles, 9391–16

Banking industry structure and deposit insurance reform, findings and recommendations, with background data, 1989-90, 8008–147

Banking industry structure, performance, and financial devs, for Fed Reserve 10th District, 1990, annual rpt, 9381–14

Banking intl competition and deposit insurance reform issues, with background data, 1990 hearings, 25248–122; 25248–123

Index by Subjects and Names

Operating ratios

Banking intl competition issues, with background data, 1980s, 21248–153

Banks (agricultural) financial performance, before and after Farm Credit System mergers, by district, 1986-89, article, 1541–1.205

Banks (agricultural) financial ratios, for South Central States, 1980s-90, annual article, 9391–16.209

Banks (insured commercial) assets, income, and financial ratios, by asset size and State, quarterly rpt, 13002–3

Banks (insured commercial) financial ratios, by State, 1986-89, annual rpt, 9294–4

Banks (insured commercial and savings) financial condition and performance, by asset size and region, quarterly rpt, 9292–1

Banks (natl) charters, mergers, liquidations, enforcement cases, and financial performance, with data by instn and State, quarterly rpt, 8402–3

Banks acquisitions purchase price relation to target and acquiring banks earnings variability and other factors, 1980s, working paper, 9371–10.57

Banks and deposit insurance funds financial condition, potential losses, and regulatory issues, 1980s-90 and projected to 1995, 21248–147

Banks and thrifts in Texas, profitability and solvency indicators, and problem assets by type, 1980s, working paper, 9379–14.11

Banks, assets, and financial performance, by asset size, 1970s-90, article, 9383–6.203

Banks capital aid receipt relation to bank holding company affiliation and other factors, with data for Texas, 1985-88, article, 9391–1.205

Banks capital by component, and capital/asset ratios compared to other industry groups, 1900s-80s, working paper, 9375–13.61

Banks commercial loan growth, by bank financial and district employment characteristics, 1989-90, article, 9385–1.208

Banks failures declarations relation to selected regulatory activity indicators, 1960s-89, working paper, 9377–9.115

Banks failures forecasting performance of bank financial ratios and local market economic conditions, 1980s-89, article, 9377–1.203

Banks failures forecasting performance of measures using alternative capital/asset ratio requirements, 1982-89, working paper, 9377–9.109

Banks finances and operations, by metro-nonmetro location, 1987-89, annual rpt, 1544–29

Banks financial performance, for undercapitalized instns by State and inside-outside Texas, aggregate 1985-89, article, 9391–1.212

Banks financial performance in Fed Reserve 10th District, by urban-rural location and State, 1989-90, article, 9381–16.201

Banks financial performance relation to deposit insurance value and other financial and accounting measures, 1986-87, technical paper, 9366–6.264

Banks financial performance, risk assessment, and regulation, 1990 annual conf papers, 9375–7

Banks in Fed Reserve 3rd District, assets, income, and rates of return, by major instn, quarterly rpt, annual table, 9387–10

Banks in Fed Reserve 6th District, financial ratios by asset size and State, 1986-90, annual article, 9371–1.211

Banks in Fed Reserve 8th District, financial performance indicators by asset size, 1987-90, annual article, 9391–16.208

Banks in Fed Reserve 9th District, finances and performance ratios, by State, quarterly journal, 9383–19

Banks in Fed Reserve 11th District, financial performance indicators by asset size and FDIC assistance receipt, 1987-90, article, 9379–1.206

Banks in northeast US, financial performance compared to rest of US, 1970s-90, article, 9373–1.220

Banks loan performance relation to loan commitments and selected financial ratios, 1975-86, working paper, 9377–9.105

Banks profitability, balance sheet and income statement items, and financial ratios, by asset size, 1985-90, annual article, 9362–1.204

Banks profitability indicators for student loans and other financial services, 1985-89, 4808–36

Bus (Class I) passengers and selected revenue data, for individual large carriers, quarterly rpt, 9482–13

Business statistics, detailed data for major industries and economic indicators, *Survey of Current Business*, monthly rpt, 2702–1.4

Capital cost indicators and contributing factors, for US and Japan, 1920s-90, article, 9385–1.202

Construction industries census, 1987: establishments, employment, receipts, and expenditures, by SIC 4-digit industry and State, final industry rpt series, 2373–1

Corporations financial statements for manufacturing, mining, and trade, by selected SIC 2- to 3-digit industry, quarterly rpt, 2502–1

Corporations profits by industry div, profit tax liability, and dividends, monthly rpt, quarterly data, 23842–1.1

Corporations profits by industry div, stockholders equity, and costs per unit of output, 1929-90, annual rpt, 204–1.1; 204–1.7

Corporations profits, natl compounded annual rates of change, monthly rpt, 9391–3

Credit Union Natl Admin Central Liquidity Facility, financial statements, FY90, annual rpt, 9534–5

Credit unions (federally-insured) financial performance, by charter type and region, 1st half 1991, semiannual rpt, 9532–7

Credit unions federally insured, finances by instn characteristics and State, as of June 1991, semiannual rpt, 9532–6

Credit unions federally insured, finances, mergers, closings, and insurance fund losses and financial statements, FY90, annual rpt, 9534–7

Credit unions federally insured, finances, 1989-90, annual rpt, 9534–1

Credit unions in Fed Reserve 8th District, finances and members by State, 1984 and 1990, article, 9391–16.210

Credit unions mortage lending impacts on financial performance, for northeast States and total US, 1980s-90, article, 9536–1.6

Debt and business cycle sensitivity of major industry sectors, with intl comparisons, 1970s-88, technical paper, 9385–8.103

Debt impacts on financial performance during recessions, with data by industry group, 1970s-80s, technical paper, 9385–8.78

Debt/asset ratios impact on investment and employment, 1971-87, technical paper, 9385–8.77

Debt/equity ratio trends, issues and factors, 1990 compilation of papers, 9385–8.88

Electric power distribution loans from REA, and borrower operating and financial data, by firm and State, 1990, annual rpt, 1244–1

Electric utilities privately owned, finances and operations, detailed data, 1989, annual rpt, 3164–23

Energy producers finances and operations, by energy type for US firms domestic and foreign operations, 1989, annual rpt, 3164–44

Energy resources of US, foreign direct investment by energy type and firm, and US affiliates operations, as of 1989, annual rpt, 3164–80

Energy use in manufacturing, ratio to other operating characteristics by industry, 1988 survey, 3166–13.5

Enterprise Statistics, 1987: finances and operations for companies, by size, level of diversification, form of organization, and industry group, 2329–8

Farm Credit System financial condition, impacts of instn mergers, by district, 1982-89, 1548–381

Farm credit, terms, delinquency. agricultural bank failures, and credit conditions by Fed Reserve District, quarterly rpt, 9365–3.10

Farm finances, debts, assets, and receipts, and lenders financial condition, quarterly rpt with articles, 1541–1

Farm financial condition, by commodity, 1987, series, 1566–8

Farm income, expenses, receipts by commodity, assets, liabilities, and ratios, 1990 and trends from 1945, annual rpt, 1544–16

Farm sector balance sheet, and marketing receipts by detailed commodity, by State, 1985-89, annual rpt, 1544–18

Financial instns with intl operations, assets by selected banking and securities instn, and financial performance indicators by selected country, late 1980s-90, article, 9385–1.206

Food prices (farm-retail), marketing cost components, and industry finances and productivity, 1960s-90, annual rpt, 1544–9.3

Fruit and nut production, prices, trade, stocks, and use, by selected crop, periodic situation rpt with articles, 1561–6

Govt-sponsored enterprises capital adequacy and outstanding debt and mortgage pools, by enterprise, 1970s-89, article, 9391–16.201

Govt-sponsored enterprises financial condition and capital adequacy, with data by enterprise, 1970s-90 and projected to 1996, 26308–99

Operating ratios

Index by Subjects and Names

Govt-sponsored enterprises financial condition and capital adequacy, with regulatory recommendations and data by enterprise, 1985-95, GAO rpt, 26119–296

Govt-sponsored enterprises financial condition, capital adequacy, and impacts on Federal borrowing, with data by enterprise, 1980s-90, last issue of annual rpt, 8004–15

Grain cooperatives finances and operations, by grain handled and selected characteristics, 1983-85, series, 1128–44

Health care spending by type and payment source, with background data and foreign comparisons, 1960s-80s and projected to 2000, 26308–98

Health maintenance organizations financial performance and services use, demonstration project results, 1985-89, article, 4652–1.235

Home health care services Medicare use and costs, by agency and service type, patient characteristics, and State, 1988-89, article, 4652–1.229

Hospital closures and rates, with financial, operating, and market characteristics, by location, late 1980s, GAO rpt, 26121–392

Hospital investment spending relation to instn interest costs, cash flow, size, and chain membership, 1981-85, working paper, 9387–8.243

Hospital reimbursement by Medicaid, impacts of Federal and State provisions, with services use, costs, and profits, by State, 1980s, 17206–1.11

Hospital reimbursement by Medicare under prospective payment system, analyses of alternative payment plans, series, 17206–1

Hospital reimbursement by Medicare under prospective payment system, and effect on services, finances, and beneficiary payments, 1979-90, annual rpt, 17204–2

Hospital reimbursement by Medicare under prospective payment system, impacts on costs, industry structure and operations, and quality of care, series, 17206–2

Hospital reimbursement by Medicare under prospective payment system, impacts on instns and beneficiaries, 1988, annual rpt, 4654–13

Hospitals in rural areas, financial and operating performance impacts of Medicare prospective payment reimbursement system, 1980s-87, 4658–51

Imports and tariff provisions effect on US industries and products, investigations with background financial and operating data, series, 9886–4

Imports injury to US industries from foreign subsidized products and sales at less than fair value, investigations with background financial and operating data, series, 9886–19

Imports injury to US industries from foreign subsidized products, investigations with background financial and operating data, series, 9886–15

Imports injury to US industries from sales at less than fair value, investigations with background financial and operating data, series, 9886–14

Industry (US) intl competitiveness, with selected foreign and US operating data by major firm and product, series, 2046–12

Insurance (health) to supplement Medicare, premiums, costs, claims, and benefit provisions, with data by firm, 1988-90, hearing, 21788–198

Insurance (life) companies finances, performance ratios, and problem holdings, by firm, 1989-90, hearing, 21368–133

Intl Finance Corp finances, and intl capital market financial data by firm, by country, 1990 hearing, 21248–149

Japan corporations finances, for firms affiliated with integrated conglomerates and independent firms, 1976-89, article, 9375–1.203

Labs (independent clinical) profitability and cost indexes by customer type, and impacts of Medicare fee caps, 1988-89, GAO rpt, 26121–425

Manufacturing and trade inventories, sales, and inventory/sales ratios, quarterly article, 2702–1.28

Manufacturing capital investment spending, relation to cash flow, working capital, and other factors, 1970s, working paper, 9375–13.49

Manufacturing census, 1987: finances and operations, by SIC 2- to 4-digit industry, State, and MSA, with trends from 1849, 2497–1

Mexico banks deregulation impacts on finances, with data by bank, 1960s-90, technical paper, 9385–8.121

Minerals foreign and US supply under alternative market conditions, reserves, and background industry data, series, 5606–4

Natural gas interstate pipeline company detailed financial and operating data, by firm, 1989, annual rpt, 3164–38

Nursing home reimbursement by Medicaid, States payment ratesetting methods, analysis for 7 States, 1980s, article, 4652–1.255

Nursing home reimbursement by Medicaid, States payment ratesetting methods, limits, and allowances, 1988, article, 4652–1.253

OASDI benefit payments, trust fund finances, and economic and demographic assumptions, 1970-90 and alternative projections to 2000, actuarial rpt, 4706–1.105

Oil company production and imports by type, and financial data, 1977-89, annual rpt, 3164–74.1

Oil refinery operations and finances, with ownership changes, shutdowns, and reactivations, by firm, 1970s-90, 3168–119

Pension plans funding status under 1987 accounting standards, for defined benefit plans, 1987-89, technical paper, 9366–6.259

Puerto Rico economic censuses, 1987: wholesale and retail trade and service industry finances and operations, by SIC 2- to 4-digit industry and municipio, 2591–1

Puerto Rico economic censuses, 1987: wholesale, retail, and service industries finances and operations, by establishment characteristics and SIC 2- and 3-digit industry, subject rpts, 2591–2

Railroad retirement system funding and benefits findings and recommendations, with background industry data, 1960s-90 and projected to 2060, 9708–1

Railroad revenue, income, freight, and rate of return, by Class I freight railroad and district, quarterly rpt, 9482–2

Retail trade census, 1987: depreciable assets, capital and operating expenses, sales, value added, and inventories, by SIC 2- to 4-digit kind of business, 2399–2

Retail trade census, 1987: finances and employment, for establishments with and without payroll, by SIC 2- to 4-digit kind of business, State, and MSA, 2401–1

Retail trade inventory/sales ratios, by selected kind of business, monthly rpt, 2413–3.2

Retail trade sales, inventories, purchases, gross margin, and accounts receivable, by SIC 2- to 4-digit kind of business and form of ownership, 1989, annual rpt, 2413–5

Savings and loan assns, FHLB 6th District insured members financial condition and operations by State, quarterly rpt, 9302–23

Savings banks insured by Bank Insurance Fund, financial condition and performance, by asset size and region, quarterly rpt, 9292–5

Savings instns facing insolvency, financial performance by whether recovered, 1980s, working paper, 9377–9.121

Savings instns, FHLB 1st District members financial operations compared to banks, and related economic and housing indicators, bimonthly rpt with articles, 9302–4

Savings instns, FHLB 6th District members financial condition and operations by State, monthly rpt, 9302–11

Savings instns finances and operations by district and State, mortgage loan activity and terms by MSA, and FHLB finances, 1989 and trends from 1900, annual rpt, 8434–3

Savings instns insured by Savings Assn Insurance Fund, assets, liabilities, and deposit and loan activity, by conservatorship status, monthly rpt, 8432–1

Savings instns insured by Savings Assn Insurance Fund, finances by profitability group, district, and State, quarterly rpt, 8432–4

Savings instns interest rate differentials for short- and long-term assets and liabilities, risk analysis for solvent 4th FHLB District banks, 1984-88, working paper, 9371–10.65

Savings instns mortgage debt holdings and other assets, returns on assets, and impacts of qualified lender regulations, 1970s-89, GAO rpt, 26119–337

Securities firms equity capital costs and financial ratios, with data by firm, for US and Japan, 1980s-91, article, 9385–1.212

Securities industry finances, for broker-dealers and individual stock exchanges and clearing agencies, 1985-89, annual rpt, 9734–2.1

Service industries census, 1987: depreciable assets, capital and operating expenses, and receipts, by SIC 2- to 4-digit kind of business, 2393–2

Index by Subjects and Names

Small businesses investment spending, impacts of bank loan commitments, 1980-84, article, 9381–1.211

Space station commercial dev and operating costs and income under alternative financing options, projected 1989-2000, 21708–129

State gross product growth, impact of State bank credit conditions, 1980-86, article, 9377–1.206

Steel imports of US under voluntary restraint agreement, by product, customs district, and country, with US industry operating data, quarterly rpt, 9882–13

Steel industry finances, operations, and modernization efforts, with data on major companies and foreign industry, 1968-91, last issue of annual rpt, 9884–24

Stock (common) prices and earnings ratios, current data and annual trends, monthly rpt, 23842–1.5

Telecommunications finances, rates, and traffic for US carriers intl operations, by service type, firm, and country, 1975-89, annual rpt, 9284–17

Telephone and telegraph firms detailed finances and operations, 1989, annual rpt, 9284–6

Telephone firms borrowing under Rural Telephone Program, and financial and operating data, by State, 1990, annual rpt, 1244–2

Transit systems finances and operations, by mode of transport, size of fleet, and for 468 systems, 1989, annual rpt, 7884–4

Transportation census, 1987: finances and operations by size, ownership, and State, and revenues by MSA, by SIC 2- to 4-digit industry, 2579–1

Truck accidents, by carrier financial and operating conditions and driver characteristics, 1980s, GAO rpt, 26131–82

Truck itemized costs per mile, finances, and operations, for agricultural carriers, 1990, annual rpt, 1311–15

Truck transport of fruit and vegetables, itemized costs per mile by item for fleets and owner-operator trucks, monthly table, 1272–1

Truck transport of household goods, financial and operating data by firm, quarterly rpt, 9482–14

Truck transport of property, financial and operating data by region and firm, quarterly rpt, 9482–5

UK firms acquisition of US firms, financing, sources, and rates of return, with data by firm, 1980s, technical paper, 9385–8.82

Wholesale trade census, 1987: depreciable assets, capital and operating expenses, sales, value added, and inventories, by SIC 2- to 3-digit kind of business, 2407–2

Wholesale trade sales, inventories, purchases, and gross margins, by SIC 2- to 3-digit kind of business, 1990, annual rpt, 2413–13

see also Agricultural productivity

see also Industrial capacity and utilization

see also Labor productivity

see also Productivity

OPIC

see Overseas Private Investment Corp.

Opinion and attitude surveys

AIDS knowledge, attitudes, and transmission prevention practices of physicians and RNs, 1990-91, 4186–9.11

AIDS public knowledge and info sources, for blacks and Hispanics, 1987 local area survey, article, 4042–3.210

AIDS public knowledge, attitudes, and risk behaviors, for women, 1988 survey, 4146–8.200

AIDS public knowledge, attitudes, info sources, and testing, for blacks, 1990 survey, 4146–8.208

AIDS public knowledge, attitudes, info sources, and testing, for Hispanics, 1990 survey, 4146–8.209

AIDS public knowledge, attitudes, info sources, and testing, 1990 survey, 4146–8.195; 4146–8.201; 4146–8.205

AIDS public knowledge, for North Dakota, 1987-89 surveys, article, 4042–3.211

Carpool high occupancy vehicle lanes use, design, enforcement, and drivers views, for California, 1988-89, 7308–203

Children and youth social, economic, and demographic characteristics, 1950s-90, 4818–5

Crime and crime-related issues, public opinion by respondent characteristics, data compilation, 1991 annual rpt, 6064–6.2

Crime victimization of teens, by whether reported to police and reason for not reporting, 1985-88 surveys, 6066–3.43

Crime victimization rates, by offense and reasons for reporting and not reporting crime to police, 1988 survey, annual rpt, 6066–3.42

Crime victimization rates, by offense, whether reported to police, reasons for not reporting, and police response, 1989 survey, annual rpt, 6066–3.44

Data collection activities of Fed Govt, and quality and privacy issues, 1990 conf, 106–4.14

Drug (steroid) use prevalence and health effects, 1989 conf papers, 4498–67

Drug, alcohol, and cigarette use and attitudes of youth, by substance type and selected characteristics, 1975-90 surveys, annual rpt, 4494–4

Education data compilation, 1991 annual rpt, 4824–2

Education data, detail for elementary and secondary education, 1920s-90 and projected to 2001, annual rpt, 4824–1.1

Education in private elementary and secondary schools, students, and staff characteristics, various periods 1979-88, 4838–47

Educational performance and conditions, characteristics, attitudes, activities, and plans, 1988 8th grade class, natl longitudinal survey, series, 4826–9

Educational performance of elementary and secondary students, and factors affecting proficiency, by selected characteristics, 1988 natl assessments, subject rpt series, 4896–7

Educational performance of elementary and secondary students, and factors affecting proficiency, by selected characteristics, 1990 natl assessments, subject rpt series, 4896–8

Genetic damage and trait monitoring and screening of employees, use, costs, benefits, and procedures, 1980s, 26358–230

High school class of 1972: education, employment, and family characteristics, activities, and attitudes, natl longitudinal study, series, 4836–1

Homeless persons ratings of factors contributing to homelessness, aggregate 1985-87, 4488–14

Housing and neighborhood quality, indicators and attitudes, by householder type and location, for 11 MSAs, 1984 survey, supplement, 2485–8

Housing and neighborhood quality, indicators and attitudes, by householder type and location, 1987, biennial rpt supplement, 2485–13

Housing and neighborhood quality, indicators and attitudes, by householder type and location, 1989, biennial rpt, 2485–12

Housing and neighborhood quality, indicators and attitudes, MSA surveys, series, 2485–6

Kidney transplantation public knowledge and attitudes, 1987 survey, 4658–59

Natl service for youth, proposed program operations and youth attitudes, 1990 rpt, 26306–3.115

New Hampshire and Vermont public opinion on natural resources use and mgmt, 1991 rpt, 1208–371

Occupational Safety and Health admin standards, enforcement, and training activities, inspectors views, 1989-90, GAO rpt, 26121–391

Poverty rate under alternative measurement methods, and public opinion on definition, 1988-89, hearing, 21968–56

Recreation areas use in northeastern US, mgmt, and tourism dev issues, 1990 conf, 1208–356

Smoking initiation, influence of family, peers, and setting, 1988 local area survey, article, 4042–3.217

Tax (income) admin and compliance issues, and taxpayer views, 1990 conf, 8304–25

Tax (income) returns processing, IRS workload forecasts, compliance, and enforcement, data compilation, 1991 annual rpt, 8304–8

Taxes, spending, and govt efficiency, public opinion by respondent characteristics, 1991 survey, annual rpt, 10044–2

Teachers in higher education instns, personnel policies, pay, work conditions, and other characteristics, by instn type and control, 1987/88 survey, quadrennial rpt series, 4846–4

Teachers views on safety, discipline, and student drug use, for elementary and secondary schools, 1991 survey, 4826–1.31

Women's employment and educational experiences compared to men, for high school class of 1972, natl longitudinal study, as of 1986, 4888–6

Youth alcohol use, knowledge, attitudes, and info sources, series, 4006–10

see also Business outlook and attitude surveys

see also Consumer surveys

Opinion and attitude surveys

see also Foreign opinion of U.S.
see also Market research

Opium and opiates
see Drug abuse and treatment
see Drug and narcotics offenses
see Drugs

Optical instruments
see Instruments and measuring devices
see Scientific equipment and apparatus

Options
see Futures trading
see Options trading

Options trading
Banks (insured commercial and savings) finances, for foreign and domestic offices, by asset size, 1989, annual rpt, 9294–4.2
Short selling of stocks, activity indicators, and regulatory issues, 1980s-89 and trends from 1940, hearings, 21408–122
Swap contracts, by contract and counterparty type, and currency, late 1980s, article, 9371–1.205
Trading activity and system automation, with data by country, stock exchange, security type, and individual contract, 1980s-90, article, 9371–1.209
Trading activity by commodity and exchange, and Commodity Futures Trading Commission oversight, FY90, annual rpt, 11924–2
see also Futures trading

Optoelectronics
see Fiber optics

Optometric instruments
see Medical supplies and equipment

Optometry
County Business Patterns, 1988: employment, establishments, and payroll, by SIC 2- to 4-digit industry and county, annual State rpt series, 2326–6
County Business Patterns, 1989: employment, establishments, and payroll, by SIC 2- to 4-digit industry and county, annual State rpt series, 2326–8
CPI by component for US city average, and by region, population size, and for 27 metro areas, monthly rpt, 6762–2
Degrees awarded in higher education, by level, field, race, and sex, 1988/89 with trends from 1978/79, biennial rpt, 4844–17
Eye exams average fees and waiting time to appointment, for optometrists and ophthalmologists, by region, 1989, article, 4042–3.238
Franchise business opportunities by firm and kind of business, and sources of aid and info, 1990 annual listing, 2104–7
Health condition and health care resources, use, and spending, 1950s-89, annual data compilation, 4144–11
Indian Health Service and tribal facility outpatient visits, by type of provider, selected hospital, and service area, FY90, annual rpt, 4084–3
Insurance (health) coverage and provisions of small business employee benefit plans, by plan type and occupational group, 1990, biennial rpt, 6784–20
Labor supply of physicians, by specialty, age, sex, and location of training and practice, 1989, State rpt series, 4116–6
Lenses (aspherical ophthalmoscopy) from Japan at less than fair value, injury to US industry, investigation with background financial and operating data, 1991 rpt, 9886–14.318

Medicare Supplementary Medical Insurance physicians fee schedule, methodology with data by procedure and specialty, 1991, annual rpt, 17264–1
Military health care personnel, and accessions by training source, by occupation, specialty, and service branch, FY89, annual rpt, 3544–24
Minority group and women health condition, services use, payment sources, and health care labor force, by poverty status, 1940s-89, chartbook, 4118–56
Receipts for services, by SIC 2- to 4-digit kind of business, 1990, annual rpt, 2413–8
Service industries census, 1987: establishments, receipts by source, payroll, and employment, by SIC 2- to 4-digit kind of business, State, and MSA, 2393–4
Tax (income) returns of sole proprietorships, income statement items, by industry group, 1989, annual article, 8302–2.214
VA Medicine and Surgery Dept trainees, by detailed program and city, FY90, annual rpt, 8704–4
see also Vision

Orange, Calif.
see also under By City in the "Index by Categories"

Orange County, Calif.
Medicaid coverage loss impacts on health services use, California transfer of selected Medicaid groups to county care, 1991 article, 4652–1.242

Orange County, N.Y.
see also under By SMSA or MSA in the "Index by Categories"

Oranges
see Citrus fruits

Orchards
see Fruit and fruit products

Orders
see Business orders

Ordnance
see Ammunition
see Military supplies and property
see Military weapons

Oregon
Banks (insured commercial and savings) deposits by instn, State, MSA, and county, as of June 1990, annual regional rpt, 9295–3.6
Birds (northern spotted owl) population and reproduction rate on lands open and closed to logging, estimation methodology, 1987, 1208–342
Coastal areas pollutant concentrations in fish and sediments, by contaminant, fish species, and Pacific coast site, 1984-86, 2168–121
County Business Patterns, 1989: employment, establishments, and payroll, by SIC 2- to 4-digit industry and county, annual State rpt, 2326–8.39
Cranberry production, prices, use, and acreage, for selected States, 1989-90 and forecast 1991, annual rpt, 1621–18.4
DOD prime contract awards, by contractor, service branch, State, and city, FY90, annual rpt, 3544–22
Energy-efficiency building codes, effect on house construction practices in Bonneville Power Admin service areas, 1987, 3228–15

Index by Subjects and Names

Fed Govt spending in States and local areas, by type, State, county, and city, FY90, annual rpt, 2464–3
Fed Govt spending in States, by type, program, agency, and State, FY90, annual rpt, 2464–2
Fish (salmon and trout) wild and hatchery juvenile population and characteristics, for Pacific Northwest, 1981-85, 2168–123
Fish and shellfish catch, wholesale receipts, prices, trade, and other market activities, weekly regional rpt, 2162–6.5
Forest fires in Oregon Cascade Range area, historical frequency and severity, 1150-1985, 1208–354
Forest Service acreage, staff, finances, and mgmt activities in Pacific Northwest, with data by forest, 1970s-89, annual rpt, 1204–37
Foster care placements, discharges, and returns to care, by selected characteristics of children, and length of stay factors, 1985-86, GAO rpt, 26121–432
Gemstone production in selected States, Mineral Industry Surveys, 1988-90, advance annual rpt, 5614–5.10
Hazelnut production, 1989-91, annual rpt, 1621–18.5
HHS financial aid, by program, recipient, State, and city, FY90, annual regional listing, 4004–3.10
Hospital deaths of Medicare patients, actual and expected rates by diagnosis, and hospital characteristics, by instn, FY87-89, annual regional rpt, 4654–14.10
Income (personal) per capita and by source, and earnings by industry div, by State, MSA, and county, 1984-89, annual regional rpt, 2704–2.5
Jail adult and juvenile population, employment, spending, instn conditions, and inmate programs, by county and facility, 1988, regional rpt series, 6068–144.5
Land Mgmt Bur activities and finances, and public land acreage and use, FY90, annual State rpt, 5724–11.1
Land Mgmt Bur activities and funding by State, FY89, annual rpt, 5724–13
Marine mammals and birds population and distribution, by species and northeast Pacific Ocean location, literature and data base review, 1950s-88, 5738–28
Marriages, divorces, and rates, by characteristics of spouses, State, and county, 1987 and trends from 1920, US Vital Statistics annual rpt, 4144–4
Medicaid prepaid plans for physician services, characteristics of selected plans in 4 States, various periods 1983-89, article, 4652–1.228
Mineral Industry Surveys, State reviews of production, 1990, preliminary annual rpt, 5614–6
Minerals Yearbook, 1989, Vol 2: State review of production and sales by commodity, and business activity, annual rpt, 5604–16.38
Minerals Yearbook, 1989, Vol 2: State reviews of production, sales, and firms, by commodity, and business activity, annual rpt, 5604–34
Onion farm acreage, pesticide use, operators, and other characteristics, for 6 producer States, 1989, article, 1561–11.201

Index by Subjects and Names

Physicians, by specialty, age, sex, and location of training and practice, 1989, State rpt, 4116–6.38

Population and housing census, 1990: population and housing characteristics, households, and land area, by county, subdiv, and place, State rpt, 2551–1.39

Population and housing census, 1990: voting age and total population by race, and housing units, by block, redistricting counts required under PL 94-171, State CD-ROM release, 2551–6.1

Population and housing census, 1990: voting age and total population by race, and housing units, by county and city, redistricting counts required under PL 94-171, State summary rpt, 2551–5.38

Radiation exposure of population near Hanford, Wash, nuclear plant, with methodology, 1944-66, series, 3356–5

Recreation (outdoor) facilities on public land, use, and Land Mgmt Bur mgmt activities, funding, and plans, 1990 State rpt, 5726–5.3

Statistical Abstract of US, 1991 annual data compilation, 2324–1

Supplemental Security Income payments and beneficiaries, by type of eligibility, State, and county, Dec 1989, annual rpt, 4744–27.10

Timber in northwestern US and British Columbia, production, prices, trade, and employment, quarterly rpt, 1202–3

Timber in Oregon (western), acreage by land use and ownership, 1961-86, 1208–353

Timber in Oregon, acreage on railroad grant lands returned to Federal ownership, by county, FY90, annual rpt, 5724–1.1

Timber industry impacts of northern spotted owl conservation in Pacific Northwest, and local govts Federal payments and severance taxes, 1980s and projected to 2000, hearing, 21168–50

Timber industry impacts of northern spotted owl conservation in Pacific Northwest, and worker aid programs, 1980s and projected to 2000, hearing, 21728–76

Timber industry impacts of northern spotted owl conservation in Pacific Northwest, 1980s and alternative projections to 2000, hearings, 21168–45

Timber sales of Forest Service, impacts of northern spotted owl conservation in Pacific Northwest, 1990 hearing, 21168–47

Water (groundwater) supply, quality, chemistry, and use, 1982-85, local area rpt, 5666–28.11

Water quality, chemistry, hydrology, and other characteristics, 1991 local area study, 5666–27.21

Water resources dev projects of Army Corps of Engineers, characteristics, and costs, 1950s-89, biennial State rpt, 3756–1.38

Water supply and quality in streams and lakes, and groundwater levels in wells, by drainage basin, 1990, annual State rpt, 5666–10.36

Water supply, and snow survey results, monthly State rpt, 1266–2.7

Water supply, and snow survey results, 1990, annual State rpt, 1264–14.3

Water supply in Oregon, streamflow by station and reservoir storage, 1991, annual rpt, 1264–9

see also Eugene, Oreg.
see also Grants Pass, Oreg.
see also Klamath Falls, Oreg.
see also Medford, Oreg.
see also Pendleton, Oreg.
see also Portland, Oreg.
see also Roseburg, Oreg.
see also Springfield, Oreg.
see also under By State in the "Index by Categories"

Orem, Utah

see also under By SMSA or MSA in the "Index by Categories"

Organ transplants

see Medical transplants

Organization for Economic Cooperation and Development

Agricultural exports of high-value commodities from developing countries to OECD, 1970s-87, 1528–316

Bank deposit insurance programs of OECD members, operations by country, 1970s-80s, technical paper, 9385–8.93

Economic conditions, and oil supply and demand, for major industrial countries, biweekly rpt, 9112–1

Economic conditions in Communist and OECD countries, 1989, annual rpt, 7144–11

Economic conditions in USSR, Eastern Europe, OECD, and selected other countries, 1960s-90, annual rpt, 9114–4

Economic indicators, and dollar exchange rates, for selected OECD countries, 1991 semiannual rpt, 8002–14

Energy conservation measures impacts on consumption, by component and end-use sector, 1970s-88 and projected under alternative oil prices to 1995, 3308–93

Energy prices, by fuel type and end use, for 10 countries, 1980-89 annual rpt, 3164–50.6

Energy production by type, and oil trade, and use, by country group and selected country, monthly rpt, 9112–2

Energy use and production, by fuel type, country, and country group, projected 1995-2010 and trends from 1970, annual rpt, 3164–84

Expenditures for intl organizations by US and other countries, by organization and program, FY90, annual rpt, 7004–9

Exports and imports, intl position of US and 4 OECD countries, and factors affecting US competition, periodic pamphlet, 2042–25

Exports and imports of OECD members, by country, 1989, annual rpt, 7144–10

Exports and imports of OECD, total and for 4 major countries, and US trade by country, by commodity, 1970-89, world area rpt series, 9116–1

Global climate change economic impacts, projected to 2100 with background data for 1980s, 3028–5

GNP and GNP growth for OECD members, by country, 1980-90, annual rpt, 7144–8

Health care spending by type and payment source, with background data and foreign comparisons, 1960s-80s and projected to 2000, 26308–98

Industrial production, consumer price, and stock price indexes for 6 OECD countries and US, *Survey of Current Business*, monthly rpt, 2702–1.2

Organization of Petroleum Exporting Countries

Industrial production indexes and CPI, for US and 6 OECD countries, current data and annual trends, monthly rpt, 23842–1.7

Labor costs and indexes, by selected country, 1990, semiannual rpt, 6822–3

Nuclear power plant capacity, generation, and operating status, by plant and foreign and US location, 1990 and projected to 2030, annual rpt, 3164–57

Oil and refined products stocks of OECD, quarterly 1986-89, annual rpt, 3164–50.2

Oil production, trade, use, and stocks, by selected country and country group, monthly rpt, 3162–42

Oil stocks and use by OECD countries, selected years 1960-90, annual rpt, 3164–74.8

Oil supply, demand, and stock forecasts, by world area, quarterly rpt, 3162–34

Oil use and stocks for selected OECD countries, monthly rpt, 3162–24.10

Savings rates impacts of income tax deduction for interest payments, with indicators for US, Canada, and other OECD countries, 1990 article, 9377–1.202

Statistical Abstract of US, 1991 annual data compilation, 2324–1.31

Stock indexes in 15 OECD countries, returns volatility and inter-country correlations, 1960s-90, technical paper, 9366–6.279

Tax burden indicators for OECD, by type of tax and country, 1990 hearing, 25368–173

Tax revenue, by level of govt and type of tax, for OECD countries, mid 1960s-89, annual rpt, 10044–1.2

Organization of American States

Background Notes, OAS history, structure, and programs, 1991 rpt, 7006–2.53

Developing countries aid by intl agencies, Intl Dev Cooperation Agency oversight of US contributions, FY92, annual rpt, 9904–4.2

Expenditures for intl organizations by US and other countries, by organization and program, FY90, annual rpt, 7004–9

Organization of Petroleum Exporting Countries

Boycotts (intl) by OPEC and other countries, US firms and shareholders cooperation and tax benefits denied, 1986, annual rpt, 8004–13

Boycotts (intl) by OPEC and other countries, US taxpayers IRS filings, cooperation, and tax benefits denied, 1976-86, GAO rpt, 26119–349

Economic conditions in USSR, Eastern Europe, OECD, and selected other countries, 1960s-90, annual rpt, 9114–4

Energy use and production, by fuel type, country, and country group, projected 1995-2010 and trends from 1970, annual rpt, 3164–84

Exports and imports of OECD members, by country, 1989, annual rpt, 7144–10

Exports and imports of US by country, and trade shifts by commodity, 1990, semiannual rpt, 9882–9

Exports and imports of US, by world area, periodic pamphlet, 2042–25

Investment (direct) in US oil and other industries, by OPEC members, as of 1989, annual rpt, 3164–80

Organization of Petroleum Exporting Countries

Investment (foreign direct) in US, by industry group of US affiliate and country of parent firm, 1980-86, 2708–41

Iraq invasion of Kuwait, oil embargo impacts on OPEC and US oil supply and industry, 1989-91, hearing, 21368–132

Loans of US banks to foreigners at all US and foreign offices, by country group and country, quarterly rpt, 13002–1

Multinatl firms US affiliates, finances, and operations, by industry, world area of parent firm, and State, 1988-89, annual rpt, 2704–4

Multinatl US firms and foreign affiliates finances and operations, by industry and world area of parent firm, 1989 benchmark survey, preliminary annual rpt, 2704–5

Multinatl US firms foreign affiliates capital expenditures, by major industry group, world area, and country, 1986-91, semiannual article, 2702–1.207

Multinatl US firms foreign affiliates capital expenditures, by major industry group, world area, and country, 1987-91, semiannual article, 2702–1.222

Oil and gas reserves and discoveries, by country and country group, quarterly rpt, 3162–43

Oil crude, gas liquids, and refined products supply, demand, and movement, by PAD district and State, 1990, annual rpt, 3164–2

Oil import costs, by crude type and country or group of origin, monthly rpt, 3162–11

Oil prices of OPEC and non-OPEC countries, weekly rpt, 3162–32

Oil prices of OPEC, biweekly rpt, 9112–1

Oil production, and exports and prices for US, by major exporting country, detailed data, monthly rpt with articles, 3162–24

Oil production and exports to US, by OPEC member, 1960-90, annual rpt, 3164–74.2; 3164–74.8

Oil production, capacity, use, and exports by country, by OPEC member, monthly rpt, 9112–2

Oil production relation to prices and other factors for OPEC and non-OPEC countries, alternative model results, 1970s-80s, technical paper, 9379–12.68

Oil production, trade, use, and stocks, by selected country and country group, monthly rpt, 3162–42

Oil, refined products, and gas liquids supply, demand, trade, stocks, and refining, by detailed product, State, and PAD district, monthly rpt with articles, 3162–6

Rice production, trade, stocks, and use, by world region, country, and country group, 1966/67-1989/90, FAS circular, 1925–2.6

Tax (income) returns of corporations with foreign tax credit, income, and tax items, by country and world region of credit, 1986, biennial article, 8302–2.207

Organized crime

Court civil and criminal caseloads for Federal district, appeals, and bankruptcy courts, by type of suit and offense, circuit, and district, 1990, annual rpt, 18204–11

Court civil and criminal caseloads for Federal district, appeals, and special courts, 1990, annual rpt, 18204–8

Court civil and criminal caseloads for Federal district courts, 1991, annual rpt, 18204–2.1

Court criminal case processing in Federal district courts, and dispositions, by offense, district, and offender characteristics, 1986, annual rpt, 6064–29

Court criminal case processing in Federal district courts, and dispositions, by offense, 1980-89, annual rpt, 6064–31

Court criminal cases in Federal district courts, by offense, disposition, and district, 1980-90, last issue of annual rpt, 18204–1

Drug abuse relation to violent and criminal behavior, with data on street gang activity and selected population groups, 1989 conf, 4498–70

Drug enforcement regional task forces investigation of organized crime, activities by agency and region, FY83-90, biennial rpt, 6004–17

Drug-related money laundering operations, US and foreign govts enforcement activities, 1989, annual rpt, 7004–17

Labor Dept programs fraud and abuse, audits and investigations activity, and racketeering cases by type and disposition, FY88-89, GAO rpt, 26111–74

Labor Dept programs fraud and abuse, audits and investigations, 2nd half FY91, semiannual rpt, 6302–2

Sentences for Federal crimes, guidelines use and results by offense and district, and Sentencing Commission activities, 1990, annual rpt, 17664–1

Sentences for Federal offenses, guidelines by offense and circumstances, series, 17668–1

US attorneys civil and criminal cases by type and disposition, and collections, by Federal district, FY90, annual rpt, 6004–2.1; 6004–2.7

Wiretaps authorized, costs, arrests, trials, and convictions, by offense and jurisdiction, 1990, annual rpt, 18204–7

Organized Crime Drug Enforcement Task Forces

Activities of task forces by agency and region, FY83-90, biennial rpt, 6004–17

Organized labor

see Labor unions

Organochlorides

see Chemicals and chemical industry

see Pesticides

Oriental Americans

see Asian Americans

Orlando, Fla.

Housing starts and completions authorized by building permits in 40 MSAs, quarterly rpt, 2382–9

Wages by occupation, for office and plant workers, 1990 survey, periodic MSA rpt, 6785–11.2

Water quality, chemistry, hydrology, and other characteristics, 1989 local area study, 5666–27.3

see also under By City and By SMSA or MSA in the "Index by Categories"

Orr, James A.

"Foreign Direct Investment in U.S. Manufacturing: Effects on the Trade Balance", 9385–8.91

Index by Subjects and Names

"Trade Balance Effects of Foreign Direct Investment in U.S. Manufacturing", 9385–1.210

Orthopedic impairments

see Musculoskeletal diseases

Orthopedics

Labor supply of physicians, by specialty, age, sex, and location of training and practice, 1989, State rpt series, 4116–6

Medicare payments to physicians, charges by specialty and treatment setting, and assignment rate by State, 1970s-88, article, 4652–1.240

Military health care personnel, and accessions by training source, by occupation, specialty, and service branch, FY89, annual rpt, 3544–24

VA health care facilities physicians, dentists, and nurses, by selected employment characteristics and VA district, quarterly rpt, 8602–6

VA health care staff and turnover, by occupation, physician specialty, and location, 1990, annual rpt, 8604–8

Visits to physicians, by patient and practice characteristics, diagnosis, and services provided, 1989, 4146–8.206

see also Podiatry

see also Prosthetics and orthotics

Orthotics

see Prosthetics and orthotics

Oshkosh, Wis.

see also under By SMSA or MSA in the "Index by Categories"

Osteopathy

County Business Patterns, 1988: employment, establishments, and payroll, by SIC 2- to 4-digit industry and county, annual State rpt series, 2326–6

County Business Patterns, 1989: employment, establishments, and payroll, by SIC 2- to 4-digit industry and county, annual State rpt series, 2326–8

Degrees awarded in higher education, by level, field, race, and sex, 1988/89 with trends from 1978/79, biennial rpt, 4844–17

Health condition and health care resources, use, and spending, 1950s-89, annual data compilation, 4144–11

Minority group and women health condition, services use, payment sources, and health care labor force, by poverty status, 1940s-89, chartbook, 4118–56

Receipts for services, by SIC 2- to 4-digit kind of business, 1990, annual rpt, 2413–8

Service industries census, 1987: depreciable assets, capital and operating expenses, and receipts, by SIC 2- to 4-digit kind of business, 2393–2

Service industries census, 1987: establishments, receipts by source, payroll, and employment, by SIC 2- to 4-digit kind of business, State, and MSA, 2393–4

Tax (income) returns of sole proprietorships, income statement items, by industry group, 1989, annual article, 8302–2.214

Visits to physicians, by patient and practice characteristics, diagnosis, and services provided, 1989, 4146–8.206

Index by Subjects and Names

Ownership of enterprise

Osterberg, William P.
"Risk Premium in Forward Foreign Exchange Markets and G-3 Central Bank Intervention: Evidence of Daily Effects, 1985-90", 9377–9.118

Osterkamp, T. E.
"Subsea Permafrost: Probing, Thermal Regime, and Data Analyses, 1975-81", 2176–1.39

Osterlind, Anne
"Risk of Bilateral Testicular Germ Cell Cancer in Denmark: 1960-84", 4472–1.225

Ostroff, Stephen M.
"Surveillance of Escherichia coli O157 Isolation and Confirmation, U.S., 1988", 4202–7.204

Otitis
see Ear diseases and infections

Ott, David E.
"Survivor Income Benefits Provided by Employers", 6722–1.230

Otters
see Marine mammals

Outdoor recreation
see Recreation

Outer continental shelf
see Continental shelf

Outlying areas
see American Samoa
see Census of Outlying Areas
see Guam
see Midway Islands
see Northern Mariana Islands
see Puerto Rico
see Territories of the U.S.
see U.S. Virgin Islands
see Wake Island
see under By Outlying Area in the "Index by Categories"

Output of labor
see Labor productivity

Outward Bound Program
Wilderness areas use, mental health and educational benefits, and leadership training programs effectiveness, 1990 conf papers, 1208–347

Overland Park, Kans.
see also under By City in the "Index by Categories"

Overman, JoAnne R.
"GATT Standards Code Activities of the National Institute of Standards and Technology, 1990", 2214–6

Overpeck, Mary D.
"Children's Exposure to Environmental Cigarette Smoke Before and After Birth: Health of Our Nation's Children", 4146–8.204

Overseas Private Investment Corp.
Activities and finances of OPIC, with list of insured projects and firms, FY90, annual rpt, 9904–2
Budget of US, authoritative financial statements with appropriations, outlays, and receipts, by category and agency, FY90, annual rpt, 8104–2.1
Budget of US, obligations and authority by function, agency, and program, with summaries, analyses, and historical tables, FY92, annual rpt, 104–2
Debt to US of foreign govts and private obligors, by country and program, periodic rpt, 8002–6

Liabilities (contingent) and claims paid by Fed Govt on federally insured and guaranteed contracts with foreign obligors, by country and program, periodic rpt, 8002–12

Overtime
Employer illegal alien worker and Fair Labor Standards Act compliance, hiring impacts, and aliens overstaying visas by country and State, 1986-90, annual rpt, 6264–6
Employment and Earnings, detailed data, monthly rpt, 6742–2.6
Fair Labor Standards Act admin, with coverage under minimum wage and overtime provisions, and illegal employment of minors, by industry div, FY89, annual rpt, 6504–2.1
Fed Govt civilian employees work-years by schedule, overtime, holidays, and personnel cost components, FY89-90, annual article, 9842–1.204
Fed Govt civilian employees work-years, pay rates, and benefits use and costs, by agency, FY89, annual rpt, 9844–31
Labor force, wages, hours, and payroll costs, by major industry group and demographic characteristics, *Survey of Current Business*, monthly rpt, 2702–1.8
Manufacturing production and nonsupervisory workers average weekly hours, 1909-90, annual rpt, 6744–4
Mines (underground coal) back injuries, by circumstances, victim characteristics, and treatment, mid 1980s, 5608–166
Railroad employment, earnings, and hours, by occupation for Class I railroads, 1990, annual table, 9484–5
Rural areas labor force characteristics, with comparisons to urban areas, 1987, 1598–264
SSA activities, and OASDHI admin, 1930s-90 and projected to 2064, annual data compilation, 4704–12
Survey of Current Business, detailed financial and business data, and economic indicators, monthly rpt, 2702–1.1
see also Area wage surveys

Overweight
see Obesity

Owens, Raymond E.
"Survey Evidence of Tighter Credit Conditions: What Does It Mean?", 9389–19.30

Owensboro, Ky.
see also under By SMSA or MSA in the "Index by Categories"

Owings, Jeffrey
"Careers in Teaching: Following Members of the High School Class of 1972 In and Out of Teaching", 4836–1.13

Ownership of enterprise
Agriculture census, 1987: farms, farmland, production, finances, and operator characteristics, by county, final State rpt series, 2331–1
Agriculture census, 1987: horticultural specialties producers, finances, and operations, by crop and State, 1988 survey, 2337–1
AIDS patient hospital use and charges, by hospital and patient characteristics, and payment source, 1986-87, 4186–6.15
Enterprise Statistics, 1987: auxiliaries of multi-establishment firms, finances and operations by function, industry, and State, 2329–6

Enterprise Statistics, 1987: finances and operations for companies, by size, level of diversification, form of organization, and industry group, 2329–8
Farm operators reorganizations to remain under USDA crop subsidy payment limits, effectiveness of laws to prevent abuse, 1989, GAO rpt, 26113–546
Health Care Financing Review, provider prices, price inputs and indexes, and labor, quarterly journal, 4652–1.1
Home health care agencies finances impacts of Medicare payment limits under alternative determination methods, with data by service type, 1984-89, GAO rpt, 26121–400
Home health care services Medicare use and costs, by agency and service type, patient characteristics, and State, 1988-89, article, 4652–1.229
Hospital closures and rates, with financial, operating, and market characteristics, by location, late 1980s, GAO rpt, 26121–392
Hospital deaths of Medicare patients, actual and expected rates by diagnosis, with hospital characteristics, by instn, FY87-89, annual regional rpt series, 4654–14
Hospital operations, and services spending by type and payment source, with background data and foreign comparisons, 1960s-80s and projected to 2000, 26308–98
Hospital reimbursement by Medicaid, impacts of Federal and State provisions, with services use, costs, and profits, by State, 1980s, 17206–1.11
Hospital reimbursement by Medicare under prospective payment system, analyses of alternative payment plans, series, 17206–1
Hospital reimbursement by Medicare under prospective payment system, and effect on services, finances, and beneficiary payments, 1979-90, annual rpt, 17204–2
Hospital reimbursement by Medicare under prospective payment system, diagnosis related group code assignment and effects on care and instn finances, 1984/85, series, 4006–7
Hospital reimbursement by Medicare under prospective payment system, impacts on costs, industry structure and operations, and quality of care, series, 17206–2
Hospitals in rural areas, financial and operating performance impacts of Medicare prospective payment reimbursement system, 1980s-87, 4658–51
Hotels and other lodging places, receipts, payroll, employment, ownership, and rooms, by State and MSA, 1987 Census of Service Industries, subject rpt, 2393–3
Manufacturing census, 1987: finances and operations, by type of organization and SIC 2- to 4-digit industry, subject rpt, 2497–5
Mineral industries census, 1987: finances and operations, by establishment characteristics, SIC 2- to 4-digit industry, and State, subject rpt, 2517–1
Nursing home admissions of Medicare patients, factors affecting change, 1983-85, article, 4652–1.222

Ownership of enterprise

Nursing home Alzheimer's disease units, and beds, by facility characteristics, 1987, 4186–8.12

Nursing home reimbursement by Medicaid, States payment ratesetting methods, analysis for 7 States, 1980s, article, 4652–1.255

Nursing home residents with mental, behavioral, and functional disorders, by age, sex, and instn characteristics, 1987, 4186–8.11

Nursing home residents with mental disorders, by disorder type and resident and instn characteristics, 1985, 4147–13.106

Puerto Rico economic censuses, 1987: wholesale, retail, and service industries finances and operations, by size, form of organization, and SIC 2- and 3-digit industry, subject rpt, 2591–2.1

Retail trade census, 1987: depreciable assets, capital and operating expenses, sales, value added, and inventories, by SIC 2- to 4-digit kind of business, 2399–2

Securities purchases, sales, and holdings, by issuer and type and ownership of security, monthly listing, 9732–2

Service industries census, 1987: depreciable assets, capital and operating expenses, and receipts, by SIC 2- to 4-digit kind of business, 2393–2

Service industries census, 1987: establishments, receipts by source, payroll, and employment, by SIC 2- to 4-digit kind of business, State, and MSA, 2393–4

Ships under foreign flag owned by US firms and foreign affiliates, by type, owner, and country of registry and construction, as of Jan 1991, semiannual rpt, 7702–3

Small Business Investment Companies capital holdings, SBA obligation, and ownership, as of July 1991, semiannual listing, 9762–4

Tax (income) returns filed, by type of return and IRS district, 1989 and projected 1990-97, annual rpt, 8304–24

Tax (income) returns filed, by type of tax and IRS region and service center, projected 1990-97 and trends from 1978, annual rpt, 8304–9

Transportation census, 1987: finances and operations by size, ownership, and State, and revenues by MSA, by SIC 2- to 4-digit industry, 2579–1

Wholesale trade census, 1987: depreciable assets, capital and operating expenses, sales, value added, and inventories, by SIC 2- to 3-digit kind of business, 2407–2

see also Bank holding companies
see also Business acquisitions and mergers
see also Consumer cooperatives
see also Cooperatives
see also Corporations
see also Divestiture
see also Foreign corporations
see also Franchises
see also Government corporations and enterprises
see also Government ownership
see also Holding companies
see also Joint ventures
see also Minority businesses

Index by Subjects and Names

see also Monopolies and cartels
see also Multinational corporations
see also Partnerships
see also Proprietorships
see also Rural cooperatives
see also Securities
see also Self-employment
see also Women-owned businesses

Oxnard, Calif.
see also under By City and By SMSA or MSA in the "Index by Categories"

Oxygen
see Gases

Ozment, D'Ann M.
"Money Growth, Supply Shocks, and Inflation", 9379–1.204

Ozone
see Air pollution
see Stratosphere

Pacific Islands Americans

Agriculture census, 1987: farms, farmland, production, finances, and operator characteristics, by county, final State rpt series, 2331–1

Census of Population, 1990: population by detailed Native American, Asian, and Pacific Islander group, race, region, and State, with data for 1980, press release, 2328–72

Census of Population, 1990: population by race and detailed Hipanic origin, region, and State, with data for 1980, press release, 2328–73

Census of Population, 1990: population by race, Hispanic origin, region, census div, and State, with data for 1980, fact sheet, 2326–20.2

Deaths and rates, by detailed cause and demographic characteristics, 1988 and trends from 1900, US Vital Statistics annual rpt, 4144–2

Education data compilation, 1991 annual rpt, 4824–2

Health condition improvement and disease prevention goals and recommended activities for 2000, with trends 1970s-80s, 4048–10

Statistical Abstract of US, 1991 annual data compilation, 2324–1

Pacific Marine Environmental Laboratory
see National Oceanic and Atmospheric Administration

Pacific Northwest
see Western States

Pacific Northwest Laboratory
see also Department of Energy National Laboratories

Pacific Ocean

Environmental summary data, and intl claims and disputes, 1991 annual factbook, 9114–2

Estuary environmental and fishery conditions, research results and methodology, 1991 rpt, 2176–7.24

Estuary environmental conditions, and fish and shellfish catch by species and region, 1980s, 2178–27

Estuary waters approved and prohibited for shellfish harvest, and pollution sources, 1985, 2176–7.21

Exports and imports (waterborne) of US, by type of service, commodity, country, route, and US port, 1988, annual rpt, 7704–2

Fish and shellfish catch, life cycles, and environmental needs, for selected coastal species and regions, series, 5506–8

Fish and shellfish catch, wholesale receipts, prices, trade, and other market activities, semiweekly regional rpt, 2162–6.4

Fish catch, trade, use, and fishery operations, with selected foreign data, by species, 1980s-90, annual rpt, 2164–1

Hurricanes and tropical storms in north Pacific Ocean, characteristics, 1990, annual article, 2152–8.202

Hurricanes and tropical storms in Pacific and Indian Oceans, paths and surveillance, 1990, annual rpt, 3804–8

Japan fish catch, prices, trade by country, cold storage holdings, import quotas, and market devs, semimonthly press release, 2162–7

Marine Fisheries Review, US and foreign fisheries resources, dev, mgmt, and research, quarterly journal, 2162–1

Marine mammals and birds population and distribution, by species and northeast Pacific Ocean location, literature and data base review, 1950s-88, 5738–28

Mariners Weather Log, quarterly journal, 2152–8

Mineral industries census, 1987: finances and operations, by establishment characteristics, SIC 2- to 4-digit industry, and State, subject rpt, 2517–1

Oil and gas dev impacts on California OCS water quality, marine life, and sediments, by site, 1986-89, annual rpt, 5734–11

Oil and gas OCS production, and wells, for Pacific lands under Federal lease, by drilling platform, 1960s-89, annual rpt, 5734–9

Oil and gas OCS production, reserves, and wells drilled, for Pacific Ocean by location, 1989, annual rpt, 5734–7

Oil and gas OCS reserves, and leasing and dev activity, 1990 periodic regional rpt, 5736–3.1

Oil and gas OCS reserves of Fed Govt, leasing and exploration activity, production, revenue, and costs, by ocean area, FY90, annual rpt, 5734–4

Oil, gas, and minerals production, revenue, and leasing activity, for Federal OCS lands by ocean region and State, 1950s-90, annual rpt, 5734–3

Otters (sea) population and behavior, for Pacific Ocean, 1914-90, 5508–109

Pollutant concentrations in coastal and estuarine sediments, by contaminant and selected site, 1984-89, 2176–3.13

Pollutant concentrations in fish and sediments, by contaminant, fish species, and Pacific coast site, 1984-86, 2168–121

Recreation (outdoor) coastal facilities of California, visitor spending by purpose at 5 coastal sites, 1989, 2176–9.6

Recreation (outdoor) coastal facilities of Fed Govt and States, visitor and site characteristics, 1987-90 survey, regional rpt, 2176–9.5; 2176–9.7

Research activities of Pacific Marine Environmental Lab, and bibl, FY90, annual rpt, 2144–21

Seals (harbor) population and physical characteristics at selected Washington State coastal sites, 1975-80, 14738–7

Temperature of sea surface by ocean and for US coastal areas, and Bering Sea ice conditions, monthly rpt, 2182–5

Tidal currents, daily time and velocity by station for North America and Asia coasts, forecast 1992, annual rpt, 2174–1.2

Tide height and time daily at coastal points, forecast 1992, annual rpt, 2174–2.2; 2174–2.5

Walrus population, habitat mgmt, and intl conservation needs, by world region, 1990 conf, 14738–9

Washington State marine sanctuaries proposal, environmental and economic impacts, with background data, 1984-89, 2178–30

Wetlands in coastal areas, acreage by wetland type, estuarine basin, and county, 1989, 2178–31

Whales (humpback) population and sightings off southeastern Alaska, 1979-86, 14738–10

see also Bering Sea

see also Gulf of Alaska

see also Oceania

Pacific Science and Engineering

"Human Factors in Self-Monitoring of Blood Glucose: Final Report", 4068–71

Pacific States

see Western States

see under By Census Division in the "Index by Categories"

Packaging and containers

Beverage containers natl deposit law proposal, public views, with State deposit laws effectiveness, 1970s-89, GAO rpt, 26113–494

Business statistics, detailed data for major industries and economic indicators, *Survey of Current Business*, monthly rpt, 2702–1.19; 2702–1.21

Closures for containers, shipments, trade, use, and firms, quarterly Current Industrial Rpt, 2506–11.4

Costs of manufacture, maintenance, and disposal, by selected product and material, 1967-88, 5608–162.3

County Business Patterns, 1988: employment, establishments, and payroll, by SIC 2- to 4-digit industry and county, annual State rpt series, 2326–6

County Business Patterns, 1989: employment, establishments, and payroll, by SIC 2- to 4-digit industry and county, annual State rpt series, 2326–8

DOD prime contract awards, by detailed procurement category, FY87-90, annual rpt, 3544–18

Drums and pails (steel shipping) shipments, trade, use, and firms, quarterly Current Industrial Rpt, 2506–11.5

Employment, earnings, and hours, by SIC 1- to 4-digit industry, monthly and annual averages, selected years 1909-90, annual rpt, 6744–4

Exports and imports of US, by country and detailed commodity, monthly rpt, 2422–12

Exports and imports of US, by Harmonized System 6-digit commodity and country, 1990, annual rpt, 2424–13

Exports and imports of US, by transport mode, country, and SITC 1- to 3-digit commodity, 1990, annual rpt, 2424–12

Exports of US, detailed Schedule B commodities with countries of destination, 1990, annual rpt, 2424–10

Farm prices received for major products and paid for farm inputs and living items, by commodity and State, monthly rpt, 1629–1

Farm production itemized costs, by farm sales size and region, 1990, annual rpt, 1614–3

Food marketing cost indexes, by expense category, monthly rpt with articles, 1502–4

Food prices (farm-retail), marketing cost components, and industry finances and productivity, 1920s-90, annual rpt, 1544–9

Fruit and vegetable wholesale prices in NYC by State, and shipments and arrivals by mode of transport, by commodity, weekly rpt, 1311–20

Fruit and vegetable wholesale prices in NYC, Chicago, and selected shipping points, by crop, 1990, annual rpt, 1311–8

Glass container production, shipments, stocks, trade, and use, by type, monthly Current Industrial Report, 2506–9.4

Hazardous material transport cylinder test facilities, certifications by State and country, 1989, annual rpt, 7304–4

Injuries from use of consumer products, by severity, victim age, and detailed product, 1990, annual rpt, 9164–6

Injuries from use of consumer products, related deaths and costs, and recalls by brand, by product type, FY89, annual rpt, 9164–2

Input-output structure of US economy, detailed interindustry transactions for 84 industries, and components of final demand, 1986, annual article, 2702–1.206

Input-output structure of US economy, detailed interindustry transactions for 85 industries, 1982 benchmark data, 2702–1.213

Labor productivity, indexes of output, hours, and employment by SIC 2- to 4-digit industry, 1967-89, annual rpt, 6824–1.3

Manufacturing annual survey, 1989: finances and operations, by SIC 2- to 4-digit industry, series, 2506–15

Manufacturing census, 1987: finances and operations, by SIC 2- to 4-digit industry, State, and MSA, with trends from 1849, 2497–1

Manufacturing census, 1987: finances and operations, by type of organization and SIC 2- to 4-digit industry, subject rpt, 2497–5

Manufacturing finances and operations, by SIC 2- to 4-digit industry, forecast 1991, annual rpt, 2044–28

Milk order market sales, by container size and type, outlet type, and market area, 1989, biennial rpt, 1317–6

Milk sales, by type and size of container, milk product, and region, 1989 survey, biennial article, 1317–4.203

Occupational injury and illness rates, by SIC 2- to 4-digit industry, 1988-89, annual rpt, 6844–7

Occupational injury and illness rates, by SIC 2- to 4-digit industry, 1989, annual rpt, 6844–1

Paints and varnishes

Pollution (water) industrial releases in wastewater, levels, treatment, costs, and regulation, with background financial and operating data, 1989 industry rpt, 9206–4.8

Price indexes (producer), by stage of processing and detailed commodity, monthly rpt, 6762–6

Price indexes (producer), by stage of processing and detailed commodity, monthly 1990, annual rpt, 6764–2

Service industries census, 1987: establishments, receipts by source, payroll, and employment, by SIC 2- to 4-digit kind of business, State, and MSA, 2393–4

Tax (income) returns of corporations, income and tax items by asset size and detailed industry, 1987, annual rpt, 8304–4

Tax (income) returns of corporations, income and tax items by asset size and detailed industry, 1988, annual rpt, 8304–21

Transportation census, 1987: finances and operations by size, ownership, and State, and revenues by MSA, by SIC 2- to 4-digit industry, 2579–1

see also Containerization

see also Labeling

Packers and Stockyards Administration

Budget of US, obligations and authority by function, agency, and program, with summaries, analyses, and historical tables, FY92, annual rpt, 104–2

Livestock packers purchases and feeding, and livestock markets, dealers, and sales, by State, 1989, annual rpt, 1384–1

Paints and varnishes

Agricultural crops (new and traditional) use in industry, replacement of imports and nonrenewable resources, R&D funding, and economic impacts, 1970s-90, 26358–239

Business statistics, detailed data for major industries and economic indicators, *Survey of Current Business*, monthly rpt, 2702–1.12

County Business Patterns, 1988: employment, establishments, and payroll, by SIC 2- to 4-digit industry and county, annual State rpt series, 2326–6

County Business Patterns, 1989: employment, establishments, and payroll, by SIC 2- to 4-digit industry and county, annual State rpt series, 2326–8

Employment, earnings, and hours, by SIC 1- to 4-digit industry, monthly and annual averages, selected years 1909-90, annual rpt, 6744–4

Exports and imports between US and outlying areas, by detailed commodity and mode of transport, 1990, annual rpt, 2424–11

Exports and imports of US, by country and detailed commodity, monthly rpt, 2422–12

Exports and imports of US, by Harmonized System 6-digit commodity and country, 1990, annual rpt, 2424–13

Exports and imports of US, by transport mode, country, and SITC 1- to 3-digit commodity, 1990, annual rpt, 2424–12

Exports of US, detailed Schedule B commodities with countries of destination, 1990, annual rpt, 2424–10

Paints and varnishes

Housing alteration and repair spending, by property and job characteristics, and region, quarterly rpt, annual tables, 2382–7.2

Injuries from use of consumer products, by severity, victim age, and detailed product, 1990, annual rpt, 9164–6

Input-output structure of US economy, detailed interindustry transactions for 84 industries, and components of final demand, 1986, annual article, 2702–1.206

Input-output structure of US economy, detailed interindustry transactions for 85 industries, 1982 benchmark data, 2702–1.213

Labor productivity, indexes of output, hours, and employment by SIC 2- to 4-digit industry, 1967-89, annual rpt, 6824–1.3

Lead paint abatement and other public housing renovation costs and alternative funding methods, 1990 rpt, 5188–127

Lead paint in privately owned housing, levels, exposure, and testing and abatement costs, 1990 rpt, 5188–128

Manufacturing annual survey, 1989: finances and operations, by SIC 2- to 4-digit industry, series, 2506–15

Manufacturing census, 1987: finances and operations, by SIC 2- to 4-digit industry, State, and MSA, with trends from 1849, 2497–1

Manufacturing census, 1987: finances and operations, by type of organization and SIC 2- to 4-digit industry, subject rpt, 2497–5

Manufacturing finances and operations, by SIC 2- to 4-digit industry, forecast 1991, annual rpt, 2044–28

Occupational injury and illness rates, by SIC 2- to 4-digit industry, 1988-89, annual rpt, 6844–7

Occupational injury and illness rates, by SIC 2- to 4-digit industry, 1989, annual rpt, 6844–1

OECD trade, total and for 4 major countries, and US trade by country, by commodity, 1970-89, world area rpt series, 9116–1

Oil and fat production, consumption by end use, and stocks, by type, quarterly Current Industrial Rpt, 2506–4.4

Oils, oilseeds, and fats production, prices, trade, and use, periodic situation rpt with articles, 1561–3

Pollution (air) emissions factors, by detailed pollutant and source, data compilation, 1990 rpt, 9198–120

Pollution (water) industrial releases in wastewater, levels, treatment, costs, and regulation, with background financial and operating data, 1989 industry rpt, 9206–4.7

Price indexes (producer), by stage of processing and detailed commodity, monthly rpt, 6762–6

Price indexes (producer), by stage of processing and detailed commodity, monthly 1990, annual rpt, 6764–2

Production by State, shipments, trade, and use, by product for inorganic chemicals, 1990, annual Current Industrial Rpt, 2506–8.14

Production of synthetic organic chemicals, by detailed product, quarterly rpt, 9882–1

Propylene glycol ethers occupational exposure of factory and printing industry workers, health effects, literature review, 1991 rpt, 4246–4.3

Puerto Rico economic censuses, 1987: wholesale and retail trade and service industry finances and operations, by SIC 2- to 4-digit industry and municipio, 2591–1

Shipments and PPI for building materials, by type, bimonthly rpt, 2042–1.5; 2042–1.6

Shipments, trade, and use of paint and related products, quarterly Current Industrial Rpt, 2506–8.4

Shipments, trade, and use of paint and related products, 1990, annual Current Industrial Rpt, 2506–8.16

Tax (income) returns of corporations, income and tax items by asset size and detailed industry, 1987, annual rpt, 8304–4

Tax (income) returns of corporations, income and tax items by asset size and detailed industry, 1988, annual rpt, 8304–21

Wholesale trade census, 1987: establishments, sales by customer class, employment, inventories, and expenses, by SIC 2- to 4-digit kind of business, 2407–4

see also under By Commodity in the "Index by Categories"

Pakistan

Agricultural exports of high-value commodities, indexes and sales by commodity, world area, and country, 1960s-86, 1528–323

Agricultural exports of US, impacts of foreign agricultural and trade policy, with data by commodity and country, 1989, annual rpt, 1924–8

Agricultural production, prices, and trade, by country, 1960s-90, annual world area rpt, 1524–4.2

Agricultural production, trade, and policies in foreign countries, summary data by country, 1989-90, annual factbook, 1924–12

Agricultural trade of US, by detailed commodity and country, 1989, annual rpt, 1524–8

Agricultural trade of US, by detailed commodity and country, 1990, semiannual rpt, 1522–4

AID economic aid to developing countries, obligations and disbursements by country, quarterly rpt, 9912–4

AID loans repayment status and terms by program and country, and status of predecessor agency loans, quarterly rpt, 9912–3

Cotton production, trade, and use, for selected countries, FAS monthly circular, 1925–4.2

Economic and military aid and loans from US and intl agencies, by program and country, FY46-90, annual rpt, 9914–5

Economic and social conditions of developing countries from 1960s, and Intl Dev Cooperation Agency and AID activities and funding, FY90-92, annual rpt, 9904–4

Economic conditions in USSR, Eastern Europe, OECD, and selected other countries, 1960s-90, annual rpt, 9114–4

Index by Subjects and Names

Economic conditions, income, production, prices, employment, and trade, 1991 periodic country rpt, 2046–4.38

Economic conditions, policy, and trade practices, by country, 1988-90, annual rpt, 21384–5

Economic, social, political, and geographic summary data, by country, 1991, annual factbook, 9114–2

Exports and imports of US, by commodity and country, 1970-89, world area rpt, 9116–1.7

Exports and imports of US, by Harmonized System 6-digit commodity and country, 1990, annual rpt, 2424–13

Exports and imports of US, by selected country, country group, and commodity group, 1990, annual rpt, 2044–37

Exports and imports of US, by transport mode, country, and SITC 1- to 3-digit commodity, 1990, annual rpt, 2424–12

Exports of US, detailed Schedule B commodities with countries of destination, 1990, annual rpt, 2424–10

Human rights conditions in 170 countries, and US economic and military aid, 1990, annual rpt, 21384–3

Imports of goods, services, and investment from US, trade barriers, impacts, and US actions, by country, 1990, annual rpt, 444–2

Labor conditions, union coverage, and work accidents, 1991 annual country rpt, 6366–4.20

Military aid of US, arms sales, and training programs costs and budget requests, by program, world region, and country, FY90-92, annual rpt, 7144–13

Nuclear power generation in US and 20 countries, monthly rpt, 3162–24.10

Nuclear power plant capacity, generation, and operating status, by plant and foreign and US location, 1990 and projected to 2030, annual rpt, 3164–57

Spacecraft and satellite launches since 1957, quarterly listing, 9502–2

UN voting record and share of votes in agreement with US, by issue, country, and world area, 1990, annual rpt, 7004–18

see also under By Foreign Country in the "Index by Categories"

Palau

Agricultural trade of US, by detailed commodity and country, 1990, semiannual rpt, 1522–4

Banks (insured commercial and savings) deposits by instn, State, MSA, and county, as of June 1990, annual regional rpt, 9295–3.6

Economic conditions, population characteristics, and Federal aid, for Pacific territories, 1989 hearing, 21448–44

Economic, social, political, and geographic summary data, by country, 1991, annual factbook, 9114–2

Exports and imports of US, by transport mode, country, and SITC 1- to 3-digit commodity, 1990, annual rpt, 2424–12

Exports of US, detailed Schedule B commodities with countries of destination, 1990, annual rpt, 2424–10

Population social, economic, health, and govtl data, for Palau, FY90, annual rpt, 7004–6

Index by Subjects and Names

Palm Bay, Fla.
Wages by occupation, for office and plant workers, 1991 survey, periodic MSA rpt, 6785–3.3
see also under By SMSA or MSA in the "Index by Categories"

Palm oil
see Oils, oilseeds, and fats

Panama
Agricultural exports of high-value commodities, indexes and sales by commodity, world area, and country, 1960s-86, 1528–323
Agricultural exports of US, impacts of foreign agricultural and trade policy, with data by commodity and country, 1989, annual rpt, 1924–8
Agricultural trade of US, by detailed commodity and country, 1989, annual rpt, 1524–8
Agricultural trade of US, by detailed commodity and country, 1990, semiannual rpt, 1522–4
AID economic aid to developing countries, obligations and disbursements by country, quarterly rpt, 9912–4
AID loans repayment status and terms by program and country, and status of predecessor agency loans, quarterly rpt, 9912–3
Economic aid to Panama after US sanctions and military invasion, AID funding by program, as of 1991, GAO rpt, 26123–330
Economic and military aid and loans from US and intl agencies, by program and country, FY46-90, annual rpt, 9914–5
Economic and social conditions of developing countries from 1960s, and Intl Dev Cooperation Agency and AID activities and funding, FY90-92, annual rpt, 9904–4
Economic conditions, policy, and trade practices, by country, 1988-90, annual rpt, 21384–5
Economic, population, and agricultural data, US and other aid sources, and AID activity, 1986 country rpt, 9916–12.20
Economic, social, political, and geographic summary data, by country, 1991, annual factbook, 9114–2
Exports and imports of US, by commodity and country, 1970-89, world area rpt, 9116–1.2
Exports and imports of US, by selected country, country group, and commodity group, 1990, annual rpt, 2044–37
Exports and imports of US, by transport mode, country, and SITC 1- to 3-digit commodity, 1990, annual rpt, 2424–12
Exports of US, detailed Schedule B commodities with countries of destination, 1990, annual rpt, 2424–10
Human rights conditions in 170 countries, and US economic and military aid, 1990, annual rpt, 21384–3
Investment (direct) incentives of Caribbean Basin Initiative, economic impacts, with finances and employment by country, 1984-90, 2048–141
Investment (foreign direct) in US, by industry group of US affiliate and country of parent firm, 1980-86, 2708–41
Military aid of US, arms sales, and training programs costs and budget requests, by program, world region, and country, FY90-92, annual rpt, 7144–13

Multinatl US firms and foreign affiliates finances and operations, by industry and world area of parent firm, 1989 benchmark survey, preliminary annual rpt, 2704–5
Multinatl US firms foreign affiliates, income statement items by country and world area, 1986, biennial article, 8302–2.212
Ships in world merchant fleet, tonnage, and new ship construction and deliveries, by vessel type and country, as of Jan 1990, annual rpt, 7704–3
UN voting record and share of votes in agreement with US, by issue, country, and world area, 1990, annual rpt, 7004–18
see also Panama Canal
see also under By Foreign Country in the "Index by Categories"

Panama Canal
Traffic and tolls of Canal by commodity, and local public utilities and services, FY90, annual rpt, 9664–3

Panama Canal Commission
Activities and finances of Commission, with Canal traffic and local govt operations, FY90, annual rpt, 9664–3
Budget of US, authoritative financial statements with appropriations, outlays, and receipts, by category and agency, FY90, annual rpt, 8104–2.1
Budget of US, obligations and authority by function, agency, and program, with summaries, analyses, and historical tables, FY92, annual rpt, 104–2

Panama City, Fla.
see also under By SMSA or MSA in the "Index by Categories"

Papademetriou, Demetrios G.
"Employer Sanctions and U.S. Labor Markets: First Report", 6366–5.2
"Employer Sanctions and U.S. Labor Markets: Second Report", 6366–5.3

Paper and paper products
Agricultural crops (new and traditional) use in industry, replacement of imports and nonrenewable resources, R&D funding, and economic impacts, 1970s-90, 26358–239
Business statistics, detailed data for major industries and economic indicators, *Survey of Current Business*, monthly rpt, 2702–1.19
Capital expenditures for plant and equipment, by major industry group, quarterly rpt, 2502–2
Collective bargaining agreements expiring during year, and workers covered, by firm, union, industry group, and State, 1991, annual rpt, 6784–9
County Business Patterns, 1988: employment, establishments, and payroll, by SIC 2- to 4-digit industry and county, annual State rpt series, 2326–6
County Business Patterns, 1989: employment, establishments, and payroll, by SIC 2- to 4-digit industry and county, annual State rpt series, 2326–8
CPI by component for US city average, and by region, population size, and for 27 metro areas, monthly rpt, 6762–2
Employment, earnings, and hours, by SIC 1- to 4-digit industry, monthly and annual averages, selected years 1909-90, annual rpt, 6744–4

Employment in manufacturing, by detailed occupation and SIC 2-digit industry, 1989 survey, triennial rpt, 6748–52
Employment, unemployment, and labor force characteristics, by region and census div, 1990, annual rpt, 6744–7.1
Energy use and prices for manufacturing industries, 1988 survey, series, 3166–13
Enterprise Statistics, 1987: auxiliaries of multi-establishment firms, finances and operations by function, industry, and State, 2329–6
Enterprise Statistics, 1987: finances and operations for companies, by size, level of diversification, form of organization, and industry group, 2329–8
Exports and imports between US and outlying areas, by detailed commodity and mode of transport, 1990, annual rpt, 2424–11
Exports and imports of US, by country and detailed commodity, monthly rpt, 2422–12
Exports and imports of US, by Harmonized System 6-digit commodity and country, 1990, annual rpt, 2424–13
Exports and imports of US, by selected country, country group, and commodity group, 1990, annual rpt, 2044–37
Exports and imports of US, by transport mode, country, and SITC 1- to 3-digit commodity, 1990, annual rpt, 2424–12
Exports of US, detailed commodities by country, monthly CD-ROM, 2422–13
Exports of US, detailed Schedule B commodities with countries of destination, 1990, annual rpt, 2424–10
Imports, exports, and employment impacts, by SIC 2- to 4-digit industry and commodity, quarterly rpt, 2322–2
Imports of coated groundwood paper from 5 countries at less than fair value, injury to US industry, investigation with background financial and operating data, 1991 rpt, 9886–14.336
Imports of coated groundwood paper from 9 countries at less than fair value, injury to US industry, investigation with background financial and operating data, 1991 rpt, 9886–14.306
Imports of US, detailed commodities by country, monthly CD-ROM, 2422–14
Imports of US given duty-free treatment for value of US material sent abroad, by commodity and country, 1989, annual rpt, 9884–14
Injuries from use of consumer products, by severity, victim age, and detailed product, 1990, annual rpt, 9164–6
Input-output structure of US economy, detailed interindustry transactions for 84 industries, and components of final demand, 1986, annual article, 2702–1.206
Input-output structure of US economy, detailed interindustry transactions for 85 industries, 1982 benchmark data, 2702–1.213
Labor productivity, indexes of output, hours, and employment by SIC 2- to 4-digit industry, 1967-89, annual rpt, 6824–1.3
Manufacturing annual survey, 1989: finances and operations, by SIC 2- to 4-digit industry, series, 2506–15

Paper and paper products

Manufacturing census, 1987: finances and operations, by SIC 2- to 4-digit industry, State, and MSA, with trends from 1849, 2497–1

Manufacturing census, 1987: finances and operations, by type of organization and SIC 2- to 4-digit industry, subject rpt, 2497–5

Manufacturing corporations financial statements, by selected SIC 2- to 3-digit industry, quarterly rpt, 2502–1

Manufacturing finances and operations, by SIC 2- to 4-digit industry, forecast 1991, annual rpt, 2044–28

Manufacturing industries operations and performance, analytical rpt series, 2506–16

Manufacturing production, shipments, inventories, orders, and pollution control costs, periodic Current Industrial Rpt series, 2506–3

Mexico imports from US, by industry and State, 1987-90, 2048–154

Multinatl US firms and foreign affiliates finances and operations, by industry and world area of parent firm, 1989 benchmark survey, preliminary annual rpt, 2704–5

Northeastern US pulpwood production by species and county, and shipments, by State, 1989, annual rpt, 1204–18

Northeastern US timber resources, and related manufacturing industries employment and finances, by State, 1977-87, 1208–375

Occupational injury and illness rates, by SIC 2- to 4-digit industry, 1988-89, annual rpt, 6844–7

Occupational injury and illness rates, by SIC 2- to 4-digit industry, 1989, annual rpt, 6844–1

OECD trade, total and for 4 major countries, and US trade by country, by commodity, 1970-89, world area rpt series, 9116–1

Pollution (air) abatement equipment shipments by industry, and new and backlog orders, by product, 1990, annual Current Industrial Rpt, 2506–12.5

Pollution (air) emissions factors, by detailed pollutant and source, data compilation, 1990 rpt, 9198–120

Pollution (water) industrial releases in wastewater, levels, treatment, costs, and regulation, with background financial and operating data, 1989 industry rpt, 9206–4.1

Pollution abatement capital and operating costs, by SIC 2-digit industry, 1989, advance annual Current Industrial Rpt, 2506–3.6

Price indexes (producer), by stage of processing and detailed commodity, monthly rpt, 6762–6

Price indexes (producer), by stage of processing and detailed commodity, monthly 1990, annual rpt, 6764–2

Production, prices by region and State, trade by country, and use, for timber by species and product, 1960-88, annual rpt, 1204–29

Production, trade, and use of lumber and pulp products, and timber resources, detailed data, 1950s-87 and alternative projections to 2040, 1208–24.20

Puerto Rico and other US possessions corporations income tax returns, income and tax items, and employment, by selected industry, 1987, article, 8302–2.213

Puerto Rico economic censuses, 1987: wholesale and retail trade and service industry finances and operations, by SIC 2- to 4-digit industry and municipio, 2591–1

Puerto Rico economic censuses, 1987: wholesale, retail, and service industries finances and operations, by establishment characteristics and SIC 2- and 3-digit industry, subject rpts, 2591–2

Retail trade census, 1987: finances and employment, for establishments with and without payroll, by SIC 2- to 4-digit kind of business, State, and MSA, 2401–1

Southeastern US pine natural growth and plantation acreage, and lumber industries impacts of shift to plantation pine, 1989 conf papers, 1208–346

Southeastern US pulpwood and residue prices, spending, and transport shares by mode, 1988-89, annual rpt, 1204–22

Soviet Union, Eastern Europe, OECD, and selected other countries pollution and deforestation indicators, 1960s-90, annual rpt, 9114–4.10

Statistical Abstract of US, 1991 annual data compilation, 2324–1.24

Tariff Schedule of US, classifications and rates of duty by detailed imported commodity, 1992 base edition, 9886–13

Tax (income) returns of corporations, income and tax items by asset size and detailed industry, 1987, annual rpt, 8304–4

Tax (income) returns of corporations, income and tax items by asset size and detailed industry, 1988, annual rpt, 8304–21

Tax (income) returns of corporations with foreign tax credit, income and tax items by industry group, 1986, biennial article, 8302–2.203

Tax (income) returns of sole proprietorships, income statement items, by industry group, 1989, annual article, 8302–2.214

Wholesale trade census, 1987: depreciable assets, capital and operating expenses, sales, value added, and inventories, by SIC 2- to 3-digit kind of business, 2407–2

Wholesale trade census, 1987: establishments, sales by customer class, employment, inventories, and expenses, by SIC 2- to 4-digit kind of business, 2407–4

Wholesale trade sales and inventories, by SIC 2- to 3-digit kind of business, monthly rpt, 2413–7

Wholesale trade sales, inventories, purchases, and gross margins, by SIC 2- to 3-digit kind of business, 1990, annual rpt, 2413–13

Wood, waste, and alcohol fuel use, by end-use sector and region, 1989, 3166–6.56

see also under By Commodity in the "Index by Categories"

see also under By Industry in the "Index by Categories"

Index by Subjects and Names

Paper gold

see Special Drawing Rights

Paperwork

see Government forms and paperwork

Paperwork Reduction Act

Fed Govt info mgmt activities, technology spending, and paperwork burden, by agency, planned FY91-92, annual rpt, 104–19

Papua New Guinea

Agricultural exports of high-value commodities, indexes and sales by commodity, world area, and country, 1960s-86, 1528–323

Agricultural trade of US, by detailed commodity and country, 1989, annual rpt, 1524–8

Agricultural trade of US, by detailed commodity and country, 1990, semiannual rpt, 1522–4

Economic and military aid and loans from US and intl agencies, by program and country, FY46-90, annual rpt, 9914–5

Economic, social, and agricultural data, US and other aid sources, and AID activity, 1988 country rpt, 9916–12.28

Economic, social, political, and geographic summary data, by country, 1991, annual factbook, 9114–2

Exports and imports of US, by transport mode, country, and SITC 1- to 3-digit commodity, 1990, annual rpt, 2424–12

Exports of US, detailed Schedule B commodities with countries of destination, 1990, annual rpt, 2424–10

Human rights conditions in 170 countries, and US economic and military aid, 1990, annual rpt, 21384–3

Military aid of US, arms sales, and training programs costs and budget requests, by program, world region, and country, FY90-92, annual rpt, 7144–13

Timber in Pacific basin, sandalwood resources, habitat, harvest, exports, and uses, 1990 conf, 1208–366

UN voting record and share of votes in agreement with US, by issue, country, and world area, 1990, annual rpt, 7004–18

see also under By Foreign Country in the "Index by Categories"

Paraguay

Agricultural exports of high-value commodities, indexes and sales by commodity, world area, and country, 1960s-86, 1528–323

Agricultural production, trade, and policies in foreign countries, summary data by country, 1989-90, annual factbook, 1924–12

Agricultural trade of US, by detailed commodity and country, 1989, annual rpt, 1524–8

Agricultural trade of US, by detailed commodity and country, 1990, semiannual rpt, 1522–4

AID economic aid to developing countries, obligations and disbursements by country, quarterly rpt, 9912–4

AID loans repayment status and terms by program and country, and status of predecessor agency loans, quarterly rpt, 9912–3

Economic and military aid and loans from US and intl agencies, by program and country, FY46-90, annual rpt, 9914–5

Economic conditions, policy, and trade practices, by country, 1988-90, annual rpt, 21384–5

Economic, social, political, and geographic summary data, by country, 1991, annual factbook, 9114–2

Exports and imports of US, by selected country, country group, and commodity group, 1990, annual rpt, 2044–37

Exports and imports of US, by transport mode, country, and SITC 1- to 3-digit commodity, 1990, annual rpt, 2424–12

Exports of US, detailed Schedule B commodities with countries of destination, 1990, annual rpt, 2424–10

Human rights conditions in 170 countries, and US economic and military aid, 1990, annual rpt, 21384–3

Military aid of US, arms sales, and training programs costs and budget requests, by program, world region, and country, FY90-92, annual rpt, 7144–13

UN voting record and share of votes in agreement with US, by issue, country, and world area, 1990, annual rpt, 7004–18

see also under By Foreign Country in the "Index by Categories"

Paraplegia

see Spinal cord injuries

Paraprofessionals

Education (special) enrollment by age, staff, funding, and needs, by type of handicap and State, 1989/90, annual rpt, 4944–4

Education services for homeless adults, funding, participation, and staff, by State, 1989, annual rpt series, 4804–39

Legal services establishments, lawyers by field, receipts by class of client, expenses, and employment, by MSA, 1987 Census of Service Industries, 2393–4.13

State and local govt employment of minorities and women, by occupation, function, pay level, and State, 1990, annual rpt, 9244–6

see also Allied health personnel

Pardons

Criminal case processing in Federal courts, by offense, disposition, and jurisdiction, data compilation, 1991 annual rpt, 6064–6.5

Parente, Stephen L.

"Technology Adoption and Growth", 9383–20.6

Parents

Black Americans social and economic characteristics, for South and total US, 1989-90 and trends from 1969, Current Population Rpt, 2546–1.450

Consumer Income, socioeconomic characteristics of persons, families, and households, detailed cross-tabulations, Current Population Rpt series, 2546–6

Developmental, learning, and emotional problems in children, and share receiving special treatment and education, by selected characteristics, 1988, 4146–8.193

Divorces and children involved, by marriage duration, race and age of spouses, and State, 1987 and trends from 1950, US Vital Statistics annual rpt, 4144–4.2

Divorces by age of spouses and duration of marriage, and children involved, by State, 1988 and trends from 1940, US Vital Statistics advance annual rpt, 4146–5.121

Education data compilation, 1991 annual rpt, 4824–2

Educational performance and conditions, characteristics, attitudes, activities, and plans, 1988 8th grade class, natl longitudinal survey, series, 4826–9

Educational performance of elementary and secondary students, and factors affecting proficiency, by selected characteristics, 1988 natl assessments, subject rpt series, 4896–7

Educational performance of elementary and secondary students, and factors affecting proficiency, by selected characteristics, 1990 natl assessments, subject rpt series, 4896–8

Employee benefit plan coverage and provisions in small businesses, by plan type and occupational group, 1990, biennial rpt, 6784–20

Employee benefit plan coverage, by benefit type and worker characteristics, late 1970s-80s, 15496–1.11

Employee leave for illness, disability, and dependent care, coverage, provisions, terminations, costs, and methods of covering for absent worker, by firm size, 1988 survey, 9768–21

Family economic impacts of departure, absence, and presence of parents, 1983-86, Current Population Rpt, 2546–20.17

Family economic impacts of departure, absence, and presence of parents, 1983-86, fact sheet, 2326–17.27

Foster care placement of black children whose parents abuse drugs, by placement reason and outcome, and household and parent characteristics, 1986-90, 4008–114

Foster care placements, discharges, and returns to care, by selected characteristics of children, and length of stay factors, 1985-86, GAO rpt, 26121–432

Homeless and runaway youth programs, funding, activities, and participant characteristics, FY90, annual rpt, 4604–3

Households composition, income, benefits, and labor force status, Survey of Income and Program Participation methodology, working paper series, 2626–10

Immigrants admitted to US, by class of admission and for top 15 countries of birth, FY89-90, fact sheet, 6266–2.4; 6266–2.8

Insurance (health) coverage of children, and children with a regular source of care, by selected characteristics, 1988, 4146–8.192

Labor force status of family members and earnings, by family composition and race, quarterly press release, 6742–21

Labor force status of mothers, impacts of child care needs, and unemployed mothers characteristics, 1986, article, 6722–1.245

Living arrangements, family relationships, and marital status, by selected characteristics, 1990, annual Current Population Rpt, 2546–1.449

Military active duty and recruit social, economic, and parents characteristics, by service branch and State, FY89, annual rpt, 3544–41

Part-time employment by health insurance coverage and worker characteristics, and temporary and contract employment, 1979-89, GAO rpt, 26121–411

Paternity determination through genetic testing, labs, services, and costs, 1991 listing, 4698–4

Paternity establishment under Child Support Enforcement Program, FY85-89, annual rpt, 4694–6

Prisoner population of women in State instns, by offense, drug use history, whether abused, and other characteristics, with comparisons to men, 1986, 6066–19.61

Prisoners (women) in State instns, by number of children, whether abused, and other characteristics, data compilation, 1991 annual rpt, 6064–6.6

Private elementary and secondary schools, students, and staff characteristics, various periods 1979-88, 4838–47

Rural areas children in poverty by selected family characteristics, and compared to urban areas, 1987-88, 1598–270

Smoking exposure of children before and after birth, by source and degree of exposure and family characteristics, 1988, 4146–8.204

Veterans compensation and pension recipients, for each US war, 1775-1990, annual rpt, 8604–2

Veterans disability and death compensation and pension cases, by type of entitlement and period of service, monthly rpt, 8602–5

Veterans disability and death compensation cases of VA, by entitlement type, period of service, sex, age, and State, FY89, annual rpt, 8604–7

Women's employment and educational experiences compared to men, for high school class of 1972, natl longitudinal study, as of 1986, 4888–6

see also Adoption

see also Children

see also Families and households

see also Maternity

see also Maternity benefits

see also Single parents

see also Teenage pregnancy

Pari-mutuel wagering

State govt revenue by source, spending and debt by function, and holdings, FY90, annual rpt, 2466–2.6

State govt tax collections by detailed type of tax, and tax rates, by State, FY90, annual rpt, 2466–2.7

Statistical Abstract of US, 1991 annual data compilation, 2324–1.9

Tax rates and revenue of State and local govts, by source and State, 1991 and historical trends, annual rpt, 10044–1

see also Horse racing

Park, Sangkyun

"Bank Failure Contagion in Historical Perspective", 9385–8.99

"Triggering Mechanism of Economy-Wide Bank Runs", 9385–8.98

Parker, Robert P.

"Preview of the Comprehensive Revision of the National Income and Product Accounts: Definitional and Classificational Changes", 2702–1.221

"Preview of the Comprehensive Revision of the National Income and Product Accounts: New and Redesigned Tables", 2702–1.224

Parkersburg, W.Va.

see *also* under By SMSA or MSA in the "Index by Categories"

Parking facilities

Apartment completions by region and metro-nonmetro location, and absorption rate, by size and rent class, preliminary 1990, annual Current Housing Rpt, 2484–3

Apartment market absorption rates and characteristics for nonsubsidized furnished and unfurnished units, 1989, annual Current Housing Rpt, 2484–2

Construction industries census, 1987: establishments, employment, receipts, and expenditures, by SIC 4-digit industry and State, final industry rpt series, 2373–1

County Business Patterns, 1988: employment, establishments, and payroll, by SIC 2- to 4-digit industry and county, annual State rpt series, 2326–6

County Business Patterns, 1989: employment, establishments, and payroll, by SIC 2- to 4-digit industry and county, annual State rpt series, 2326–8

Crime victimization of women, by relation to offender, circumstances, and victim characteristics, for rape and other violent offenses, 1973-87, 6068–243

Crime victimization rates, by victim and offender characteristics, circumstances, and offense, 1988 survey, annual rpt, 6066–3.42

Crime victimization rates, by victim and offender characteristics, circumstances, and offense, 1989 survey, annual rpt, 6066–3.44

DC metro area land acquisition and dev projects of Fed Govt, characteristics and funding by agency and project, FY91-95, annual rpt, 15454–1

Govt revenue by source, spending by function, debt, and assets, by level of govt, FY89, annual rpt, 2466–2.2

Govt revenue by source, spending by function, debt, and assets, by level of govt, FY90, preliminary annual rpt, 2466–2.9

Home mortgages FHA-insured, financial, property, and mortgagor characteristics, by metro area, 1990, annual rpt, 5144–24

Home mortgages FHA-insured, financial, property, and mortgagor characteristics, by State, 1990, annual rpt, 5144–1

Home mortgages FHA-insured, financial, property, and mortgagor characteristics, total and by State and outlying area, 1990, annual rpt, 5144–25

Home mortgages FHA-insured, financial, property, and mortgagor characteristics, 1990, annual rpt, 5144–17; 5144–23

Housing and households characteristics, unit and neighborhood quality, and journey to work by MSA location, for 11 MSAs, 1984 survey, supplement, 2485–8

Housing and households detailed characteristics, and unit and neighborhood quality, by location, 1987, biennial rpt supplement, 2485–13

Housing and households detailed characteristics, and unit and neighborhood quality, by location, 1989, biennial rpt, 2485–12

Housing and households detailed characteristics, and unit and neighborhood quality, MSA surveys, series, 2485–6

Housing inventory change from 1973, by reason, unit and household characteristics, and location, 1983 survey, biennial rpt, 2485–14

Housing units completed, single and multifamily units by structural and financial characteristics, inside-outside MSAs, and region, 1986-90, annual rpt, 2384–1

Housing units completed, single and multifamily units by structural characteristics, monthly rpt, quarterly tables, 2382–2.2

Occupational injury and illness rates, by SIC 2- to 4-digit industry, 1988-89, annual rpt, 6844–7

Occupational injury and illness rates, by SIC 2- to 4-digit industry, 1989, annual rpt, 6844–1

Puerto Rico economic censuses, 1987: wholesale, retail, and service industries finances and operations, by establishment characteristics and SIC 2- and 3-digit industry, subject rpts, 2591–2

Recreation (outdoor) coastal facilities of Fed Govt and States, visitor and site characteristics, 1987-90 survey, regional rpt series, 2176–9

Service industries census, 1987: depreciable assets, capital and operating expenses, and receipts, by SIC 2- to 4-digit kind of business, 2393–2

Service industries census, 1987: establishments, receipts by source, payroll, and employment, by SIC 2- to 4-digit kind of business, State, and MSA, 2393–4

Service industries receipts, by SIC 2- to 4-digit kind of business, 1990, annual rpt, 2413–8

Tax (income) returns of partnerships, income statement and balance sheet items, by industry group, 1989, annual article, 8302–2.216; 8304–18

Tax (income) returns of sole proprietorships, income statement items, by industry group, 1989, annual article, 8302–2.214

Parks

Acreage of land, by use, ownership, and State, 1987 and trends from 1910, 1588–48

Acreage of land under Natl Park Service mgmt, by site, ownership, and region, FY91, semiannual rpt, 5542–1

Coastal areas recreation facilities, by State, county, estuary, and level of govt, 1972-84, 2178–29

Govt employment and payroll, by function, level of govt, and jurisdiction, 1990, annual rpt series, 2466–1

Service industries receipts, by SIC 2- to 4-digit kind of business, 1990, annual rpt, 2413–8

Statistical Abstract of US, 1991 annual data compilation, 2324–1.7

Urban areas park and recreation facilities rehabilitation funding, by city and State, FY91, press release, 5306–4.7

see *also* Amusement parks
see *also* National parks
see *also* State parks
see *also* Zoological parks

Parks, Wesley W.

"U.S. Trade in Tuna for Canning, 1987", 2162–1.202

Parlett, Ralph L., Jr.

"1991 Outlook for Food Prices", 1004–16.1

Parochial schools

see Private schools

Parole and probation

Admissions and releases from prison and parole, sentence length, and time served, by offense and offender characteristics, 1985, annual rpt, 6064–33

Caseloads (criminal) in Federal district courts, by offense, disposition, and district, 1980-90, last issue of annual rpt, 18204–1

Caseloads, decisions, and activities of US Parole Commission, FY87-90, annual rpt, 6004–3

Crime, criminal justice admin and enforcement, and public opinion, data compilation, 1991 annual rpt, 6064–6

Drug enforcement regional task forces investigation of organized crime, activities by agency and region, FY83-90, biennial rpt, 6004–17

Drug test results at arrest, by drug type, offense, and sex, for selected urban areas, quarterly rpt, 6062–3

Drug testing of criminal defendants, demonstration program operations, offender characteristics, and judges views, 1987-90, 18208–11

Employment, payroll, and spending for criminal justice, by level of govt, State, and selected city and county, FY71-88, annual rpt, 6064–9

Fed Probation System admissions, discharges, and caseloads, by type of supervision, 1990, annual rpt, 18204–8.5; 18204–8.19

Federal correctional instn parole and mandatory releases, and recidivism, by facility type and region, monthly rpt series, 6242–1

Federal criminal sentencing, guidelines use and results by offense and district, and Sentencing Commission activities, 1990, annual rpt, 17664–1

Federal district court criminal case processing and dispositions, by offense, district, and offender characteristics, 1986, annual rpt, 6064–29

Federal probation system admissions, discharges, and caseloads, by type of supervision, 1991, annual rpt, 18204–2.1

Felony arrests, prosecutions, convictions, and sentencing, by offender characteristics and offense, 1988, 6066–25.33; 6066–25.39

Jail population, by criminal, correctional, drug use, and family history, and selected other characteristics, 1989, 6066–19.62

Jail population, by sociodemographic characteristics, criminal and drug use history, whether convicted, offense, and sentencing, 1989, annual rpt, 6064–26.3

Judicial Conf proceedings and findings, spring 1991, semiannual rpt, 18202–2

Juvenile correctional and detention public and private instns, inmates, and expenses, by instn and resident characteristics and State, 1987, biennial rpt, 6064–13

Index by Subjects and Names

Part-time employment

Juvenile courts delinquency cases, by offense, referral source, disposition, age, sex, race, State, and county, 1988, annual rpt, 6064–12

Juvenile courts property offenses cases, by disposition and offender age, sex, and race, 1985-86, 6066–27.5

Juvenile facilities, population, and costs, by facility and resident characteristics, region, and State, 1985-89, biennial rpt, 6064–5

Parole and probation population, entries, and exits, by State, 1989, annual rpt, 6066–25.34

Prisoners, characteristics, and movements, by State, 1989, annual rpt, 6064–26

Sentences for Federal offenses, guidelines by offense and circumstances, series, 17668–1

State and Metro Area Data Book, 1991 data compilation, 2328–54

State court probation and split sentences for felony offenses, sentence lengths, case processing time, and felon characteristics, by offense, 1986, 6068–242

US attorneys civil and criminal cases by type and disposition, and collections, by Federal district, FY90, annual rpt, 6004–2.1

Parsonnet, Julie

"Helicobacter pylori Infection in Intestinal- and Diffuse-Type Gastric Adenocarcinomas", 4472–1.211

Part-time employment

AFDC beneficiaries demographic and financial characteristics, by State, FY89, annual rpt, 4694–1

Agriculture census, 1987: horticultural specialties producers, finances, and operations, by crop and State, 1988 survey, 2337–1

Child care benefits for employees, work schedule and leave policies coverage by firm size and industry group, 1987, 15496–1.11

Child support and alimony awards, and payment status, by selected characteristics of woman, 1989, biennial Current Population Rpt, 2546–6.72

Consumer Income, socioeconomic characteristics of persons, families, and households, detailed cross-tabulations, Current Population Rpt series, 2546–6

Credit unions federally insured, finances by instn characteristics and State, as of June 1991, semiannual rpt, 9532–6

DOD civilian employment, by service branch and defense agency, with summary military employment data, quarterly rpt, 3542–16

DOT employment, by subagency, occupation, and selected personnel characteristics, FY90, annual rpt, 7304–18

Drug, alcohol, and cigarette use, by selected characteristics, 1990 survey, biennial rpt, 4494–5

Drug and alcohol abuse treatment facilities, services, use, funding, staff, and client characteristics, 1989, biennial rpt, 4494–10

Economic indicators and components, current data and annual trends, monthly rpt, 23842–1.2

Education data compilation, 1991 annual rpt, 4824–2

Educational enrollment, by grade, instn type and control, and student characteristics, 1989 and trends from 1947, annual Current Population Rpt, 2546–1.453

Employment and Earnings, detailed data, monthly rpt, 6742–2

Employment, earnings, and hours, monthly press release, 6742–5

Employment part-time, by age, sex, industry div, and whether voluntary, 1969-89, article, 6722–1.218

Employment part-time by health insurance coverage and worker characteristics, and temporary and contract employment, 1979-89, GAO rpt, 26121–411

Employment situation, earnings, hours, and other BLS economic indicators, transcripts of BLS Commissioner's monthly testimony, periodic rpt, 23846–4

Employment, unemployment, and labor force characteristics, by region and State, 1990, annual rpt, 6744–7.1; 6744–7.2

Family economic impacts of departure, absence, and presence of parents, 1983-86, Current Population Rpt, 2546–20.17

Farming part-time, selected characteristics of operation, 1987, young readers pamphlet, 2346–1.4

Fed Govt civilian employees demographic and employment characteristics, as of Sept 1990, annual article, 9842–1.201

Fed Govt civilian employees work-years, pay rates, and benefits use and costs, by agency, FY89, annual rpt, 9844–31

Fed Govt civilian employment and payroll, by agency in DC metro area, total US, and abroad, bimonthly rpt, 9842–1

Fed Govt civilian employment, by work schedule, selected agency, State, and MSA, as of Dec 1990, biennial article, 9842–1.203

Fed Govt employee family-related and work schedule benefits, availability, admin, and personnel directors views, 1990 survey, 9496–2.7

Federal district court magistrate full- and part-time positions, 1990, annual rpt, 18204–8.10

Federal district court magistrate full- and part-time positions, 1991, annual rpt, 18204–2.1

Food stamp recipient household size, composition, income, and income and deductions allowed, summer 1988, annual rpt, 1364–8

Govt employment and payroll, by function, level of govt, and jurisdiction, 1990, annual rpt series, 2466–1

High school class of 1990: college enrollment, and labor force participation of grads and dropouts, by race and sex, press release, 6726–1.38

Hospital reimbursement by Medicare under prospective payment system, and effect on services, finances, and beneficiary payments, 1979-90, annual rpt, 17204–2

Households composition, income, benefits, and labor force status, Survey of Income and Program Participation methodology, working paper series, 2626–10

Income (household) and poverty status under alternative income definitions, by recipient characteristics, 1990, annual Current Population Rpt, 2546–6.69

Insurance (health) coverage by source, and services reimbursed by type, 1991 rpt, 26306–6.155

Insurance (health) coverage, uninsured persons by employment and other characteristics and State, 1988, GAO rpt, 26121–403

Insurance (health) provided by employer, coverage offered to and chosen by families with 2 working spouses, 1977 and 1987, 4186–8.16

Jail adult and juvenile population, employment, spending, instn conditions, and inmate programs, by county and facility, 1988, regional rpt series, 6068–144

Labor force status, experience, and unemployment duration, by race and sex, 1989-90, annual press release, 6726–1.39

Labor supply trends, with characteristics of working-age population not in labor force, part-time workers, and multiple-jobholders, late 1960s-90, article, 9362–1.203

Leave for illness, disability, and dependent care, coverage, provisions, terminations, costs, and methods of covering for absent worker, by firm size, 1988 survey, 9768–21

Manufacturing employment by selected characteristics, wages, and import and export penetration rates, by SIC 2- to 4- digit industry, 1982-89, 6366–3.27

Mental health care facilities staff, by discipline, full- and part-time status, and facility type, 1986, 4506–3.42

Military health care personnel, by full- and part-time status, occupation, and service branch, FY89, annual rpt, 3544–24.7

Monthly Labor Review, current statistics and articles, 6722–1

NASA staff characteristics and personnel actions, FY90, annual rpt, 9504–1

Poverty rate among workers in metro and nonmetro areas, relation to employment and other characteristics, 1987, 1598–274

Retired pension recipients income, by selected characteristics, 1986, Current Population Rpt, 2546–20.18

Rural areas labor force characteristics, with comparisons to urban areas, 1987, 1598–264

Small business employees benefit plan coverage and provisions, by plan type and occupational group, 1990, biennial rpt, 6784–20

State and local govt employment of minorities and women, by occupation, function, pay level, and State, 1990, annual rpt, 9244–6

Statistical Abstract of US, 1991 annual data compilation, 2324–1.13

Teachers in higher education instns, employment and other characteristics, by instn type and control, 1987/88 survey, 4846–4.4

Teachers in higher education instns, personnel policies, pay, work conditions, and other characteristics, by instn type and control, 1987/88 survey, quadrennial rpt series, 4846–4

Teachers in private schools, selected characteristics by instn level, size, and orientation, various periods 1979-88, 4838–47

Part-time employment

Unemployed displaced workers losing job 1985-90, by demographic and current and former employment characteristics, as of Jan 1990, article, 6722–1.225

Union coverage of workers and earnings, by age, sex, race, occupational group, and industry div, 1989-90, press release, 6726–1.36

VA employment characteristics and activities, FY90, annual rpt, 8604–3.8

VA health care facilities physicians, dentists, and nurses, by selected employment characteristics and VA district, quarterly rpt, 8602–6

VA health care professionals employment, by district and facility, quarterly rpt, 8602–4

VA mental health care services use, spending, and staff and patient characteristics, by State and services type, 1983 and 1986, 4506–3.43

VA physicians and dentists full- and part-time staff and vacancies, by specialty, 1990, annual rpt, 8604–8

Wages of full- and part-time workers, by selected characteristics, quarterly press release, 6742–20

see also Moonlighting

see also Temporary and seasonal employment

see also Underemployment

see also Worksharing

Particleboard

see Lumber industry and products

Particulates

see Air pollution

Partnerships

Agriculture census, 1987: farms, farmland, production, finances, and operator characteristics, by county, final State rpt series, 2331–1

Agriculture census, 1987: horticultural specialties producers, finances, and operations, by crop and State, 1988 survey, 2337–1

Boycotts (intl) by OPEC and other countries, US taxpayers IRS filings, cooperation, and tax benefits denied, 1976-86, GAO rpt, 26119–349

Enterprise Statistics, 1987: finances and operations for companies, by size, level of diversification, form of organization, and industry group, 2329–8

Farmland in US owned by foreigners, holdings, acquisitions, and disposals by land use, owner type and country, and State, 1990, annual rpt, 1584–2

Historic buildings rehabilitation tax incentives, projects, costs, ownership, and use, FY77-90, annual rpt, 5544–17

Hotels and other lodging places, receipts, payroll, employment, and ownership, by type and State, 1987 Census of Service Industries, subject rpt, 2393–3.1

Limited partnerships conversion to corporations, and impacts on share values, with data by firm, 1980s-91, hearing, 25248–124

Manufacturing census, 1987: finances and operations, by type of organization and SIC 2- to 4-digit industry, subject rpt, 2497–5

Mineral industries census, 1987: finances and operations, by establishment characteristics, SIC 2- to 4-digit industry, and State, subject rpt, 2517–1

Puerto Rico economic censuses, 1987: wholesale, retail, and service industries finances and operations, by size, form of organization, and SIC 2- and 3-digit industry, subject rpt, 2591–2.1

Retail trade census, 1987: finances and employment, for establishments with and without payroll, by SIC 2- to 4-digit kind of business, State, and MSA, 2401–1

Retail trade sales, inventories, purchases, gross margin, and accounts receivable, by SIC 2- to 4-digit kind of business and form of ownership, 1989, annual rpt, 2413–5

Service industries census, 1987: establishments, receipts by source, payroll, and employment, by SIC 2- to 4-digit kind of business, State, and MSA, 2393–4

Small Business Investment Companies capital holdings, SBA obligation, and ownership, as of July 1991, semiannual listing, 9762–4

Statistical Abstract of US, 1991 annual data compilation, 2324–1.17

Tax (income) collection, enforcement, and litigation activity of IRS, with data by type of tax, region, and State, FY90, annual rpt, 8304–3

Tax (income) returns and supplemental documents filed, by type, FY90 and projected to FY99, semiannual rpt, 8302–4

Tax (income) returns filed by type of filer, selected income items, quarterly rpt, 8302–2.1

Tax (income) returns filed, by type of return and IRS district, 1989 and projected 1990-97, annual rpt, 8304–24

Tax (income) returns filed, by type of tax and IRS region and service center, projected 1990-97 and trends from 1978, annual rpt, 8304–9

Tax (income) returns of corporations with foreign tax credit, income and tax items by industry group, 1986, biennial article, 8302–2.203

Tax (income) returns of partnerships, income statement and balance sheet items, by industry group, 1989, annual article, 8302–2.216; 8304–18

Tax (income) withholding and related documents filed, by type and IRS service center, 1990 and projected 1991-98, annual rpt, 8304–22

Tax returns and supplemental documents filed, by type, FY89 and projected to FY98, annual article, 8302–2.208

Transportation census, 1987: finances and operations by size, ownership, and State, and revenues by MSA, by SIC 2- to 4-digit industry, 2579–1

Women-owned businesses and sales, by industry div and ownership type, and data needs and availability, 1987, 9768–22

see also Joint ventures

Pasadena, Calif.

see also under By City in the "Index by Categories"

Pasadena, Tex.

see also under By City in the "Index by Categories"

Pascagoula, Miss.

see also under By SMSA or MSA in the "Index by Categories"

Pasco, Wash.

Wages by occupation, for office and plant workers, 1991 survey, periodic MSA rpt, 6785–3.6

see also under By SMSA or MSA in the "Index by Categories"

Pasek, Judith E.

"Forest Pest Conditions in the Rocky Mountain Region, 1989", 1206–11.1

Passaic, N.J.

Wages by occupation, for office and plant workers, 1990 survey, periodic MSA rpt, 6785–11.1

see also under By SMSA or MSA in the "Index by Categories"

Passenger ships

Accidents involving merchant ships, and casualties, by circumstances and characteristics of persons and vessels involved, 1988, annual rpt, 7404–11

Accidents involving ships and marine facilities, casualties, and circumstances, Coast Guard investigation results, periodic rpt, 9612–4

Aliens (illegal) overstaying visas, by class of admission, mode of arrival, age, country, and State, FY85-88, annual rpt, 6264–5

Census of Transportation, 1987: finances and operations by size, ownership, and State, and revenues by MSA, by SIC 2- to 4-digit industry, 2579–1

Construction and operating subsidies of MarAd by firm, and ship deliveries and fleet by country, by vessel type, FY90, annual rpt, 7704–14.1; 7704–14.2

Foreign-flag ships owned by US firms and foreign affiliates, by type, owner, and country of registry and construction, as of Jan. 1991, semiannual rpt, 7702–3

Foreign travel to US, by characteristics of visit and traveler, country, port city, and State of destination, monthly rpt, 2902–1

Sanitation inspection scores for passenger cruise ships, biweekly rpt, 4202–10

St Lawrence Seaway ship, cargo, and passenger traffic, and toll revenue, 1990 and trends from 1959, annual rpt, 7744–2

Passport Office

see Bureau of Consular Affairs, State Department

Passports and visas

Applications for passports handled by Federal district courts, by circuit and district, 1990, annual rpt, 18204–8.28

Criminal cases by type and disposition, and collections, for US attorneys, by Federal district, FY90, annual rpt, 6004–2.1

Criminal cases in Federal district courts, by offense, disposition, and district, 1980-90, last issue of annual rpt, 18204–1

Criminal sentences for Federal offenses, guidelines by offense and circumstances, series, 17668–1

Foreign travel to US, by characteristics of visit and traveler, country, port city, and State of destination, monthly rpt, 2902–1

Illegal alien worker and Fair Labor Standards Act employer compliance, hiring impacts, and aliens overstaying visas by country and State, 1986-90, annual rpt, 6264–6

Illegal aliens overstaying visas, by class of admission, mode of arrival, age, country, and State, FY85-88, annual rpt, 6264–5

Illegal aliens overstaying visas, by State of sojourn and world area of origin, 1985-88, fact sheet, 6266–2.1

Immigration Reform and Control Act impacts on visa application backlog, FY84-89, 6266–1.1

Passports issued, *Survey of Current Business*, monthly rpt, 2702–1.11

Visas of US issued and refused to immigrants and nonimmigrants, by class, issuing office, and nationality, FY89, annual rpt, 7184–1

Pasture and rangeland

Acreage of land, by use, ownership, and State, 1987 and trends from 1910, 1588–48

Acreage of non-Federal land by use, soil and water conditions, and conservation needs, 1987, State rpt series, 1266–5

Agricultural Statistics, 1990, annual rpt, 1004–1

Agriculture census, 1987: farms, farmland, production, finances, and operator characteristics, by county, final State rpt series, 2331–1

Birds in Badlands Natl Park juniper forest and mixed grass rangeland habitats, population and species diversity by season, 1991 rpt, 1208–364

Conservation program of USDA, participation and payments by practice and State, FY90, annual rpt, 1804–7

Corn farms, finances, acreage, and production, by size, region, and State, 1987, 1568–304

Economic Indicators of the Farm Sector, itemized production costs, receipts, and returns, by commodity and region, 1987-89, annual rpt, 1544–20

Environmental Quality, status of problems, protection programs, research, and intl issues, 1991 annual rpt, 484–1

Farm prices received for major products and paid for farm inputs and living items, by commodity and State, monthly rpt, 1629–1

Farm production itemized costs, by farm sales size and region, 1990, annual rpt, 1614–3

Farms, farmland, and sales distribution, by sales size, various periods 1969-84, 1588–150

FmHA activities, and loans and grants by program and State, FY90 and trends from FY70, annual rpt, 1184–17

Foreign ownership of US farmland, holdings, acquisitions, and disposals by land use, owner type and country, and State, 1990, annual rpt, 1584–2

Foreign ownership of US farmland, holdings, acreage, and value by land use, owner country, State, and county, 1990, annual rpt, 1584–3

Forest Service acreage, staff, finances, and mgmt activities in Pacific Northwest, with data by forest, 1970s-89, annual rpt, 1204–37

Irrigation projects of Reclamation Bur in western US, crop production and acreage by commodity, State, and project, 1989, annual rpt, 5824–12

Mgmt of public lands and resources dev, environmental, economic, and social impacts of alternative Forest Service programs, projected to 2040, 1208–24

Natl forests livestock grazing, by region and State, 1990, annual rpt, 1204–5

Natl forests revenue, by source, forest, and State, FY90, annual rpt, 1204–34

Public lands acreage, grants, use, revenues, and allocations, by State, FY90, annual rpt, 5724–1.2

Public lands grazing and receipts, by animal type and State, FY90, annual rpt, 1204–1.1

Rental of farmland by assessment method, and rent receipts per acre and as share of land value by land type and State, 1960s-80s, 1548–377

Rental of pasture, and cattle grazing rates, by region and State, 1986-90, article, 1561–16.202

Research and education grants, USDA competitive awards by program and recipient, FY90, annual listing, 1764–1

Shrublands in western US, ecology, biology, and cheatgrass invasion and related fire threat, 1989 conf papers, 1208–351

Southwestern States farm credit conditions and real estate values, Fed Reserve 11th District, quarterly rpt, 9379–11

State and Metro Area Data Book, 1991 data compilation, 2328–54

see also National grasslands

Patent and Trademark Office

Activities of PTO, applications, grants, fees, and litigation, FY71-90, annual rpt, 2244–1

Budget of US, obligations and authority by function, agency, and program, with summaries, analyses, and historical tables, FY92, annual rpt, 104–2

Fees for patent application, issuance, and protection, and PTO revenues, under alternative fee schedules, FY92-93, GAO rpt, 26113–543

Grants of patents to US and foreign applicants, by State and country, 1989-90, annual press release, 2244–2

Patents

Applications, grants, fees, and litigation, for patents and trademarks, FY71-90, annual rpt, 2244–1

Biotechnology commercial applications, industry finances and capitalization, patents, and govt support, for US, Japan, and EC, late 1970s-91, 26358–248

County Business Patterns, 1988: employment, establishments, and payroll, by SIC 2- to 4-digit industry and county, annual State rpt series, 2326–6

County Business Patterns, 1989: employment, establishments, and payroll, by SIC 2- to 4-digit industry and county, annual State rpt series, 2326–8

Court civil and criminal caseloads for Federal district, appeals, and bankruptcy courts, by type of suit and offense, circuit, and district, 1990, annual rpt, 18204–11

Court civil and criminal caseloads for Federal district, appeals, and special courts, 1990, annual rpt, 18204–8

Court civil and criminal caseloads for Federal district courts, 1991, annual rpt, 18204–2.1

Energy-related inventions supported by DOE, sales, jobs created, and inventor financing, 1980-88, 3308–91

Exports of goods, services, and investment, trade barriers, impacts, and US actions, by country, 1989, annual rpt, 444–2

Fed Govt employee incentive awards, costs, and benefits, by award type and agency, FY89, annual rpt, 9844–20

Fed Govt R&D labs technology transfer cooperative agreements, patents, royalties, and incentive payments to employees, by agency, FY89, GAO rpt, 26131–85

Foreign countries economic conditions, policy, and trade practices, by country, 1988-90, annual rpt, 21384–5

Grants of patents to US and foreign applicants, by country, 1970-89, annual rpt, 9627–35.3

Grants of patents to US and foreign applicants, by State and country, 1989-90, annual press release, 2244–2

Intl and domestic patent and copyright protection, products excluded, and countries and agreements involved, 1990 article, 9391–1.203

Land Mgmt Bur activities and finances, and public land acreage and use, annual State rpt series, 5724–11

Lands (public) acreage, grants, use, revenues, and allocations, by State, FY90, annual rpt, 5724–1.2

Mines Bur rpts and patents, monthly listing, 5602–2

Mines Bur rpts and patents, 1985-89, quinquennial listing, 5608–168

NASA activities and funding, 1990, annual compilation of papers, 21704–1

NIH activities, funding by program and recipient type, staff, and clinic patients, by inst, FY90, annual rpt, 4434–3

NSF grantees retaining patent rights and number transferred to NSF, FY90, annual rpt, 9624–6

Overseas Business Reports: economic conditions, investment and export opportunities, and trade practices, country market research rpt series, 2046–6

Patent and Trademark Office patent application, issuance, and protection fees and revenues under alternative fee schedules, FY92-93, GAO rpt, 26113–543

Science and engineering academic research system status, R&D performance, and Fed Govt support, 1950s-88 with trends and projections, 9628–83

State and Metro Area Data Book, 1991 data compilation, 2328–54

Statistical Abstract of US, 1991 annual data compilation, 2324–1.17

see also Trademarks

Paternity determination

see Medical examinations and tests

see Parents

Paterson, N.J.

see also under By City in the "Index by Categories"

Pathology

Aviation medicine research and test results, technical rpt series, 7506–10

Education in science and engineering, grad programs enrollment by field, source of funds, and characteristics of student and instn, 1975-89, annual rpt, 9627–7

Pathology

Labor supply of physicians, by specialty, age, sex, and location of training and practice, 1989, State rpt series, 4116–6

Medicare Supplementary Medical Insurance physicians fee schedule, methodology with data by procedure and specialty, 1991, annual rpt, 17264–1

Military health care personnel, and accessions by training source, by occupation, specialty, and service branch, FY89, annual rpt, 3544–24

Older persons health condition and care research, data availability and collection methodology, for US and selected countries, 1988 conf, 4147–5.6

Respiratory diseases related to occupational hazards, epidemiology, diagnosis, and treatment, for selected industries and work settings, 1988 conf, 4248–90

VA health care facilities physicians, dentists, and nurses, by selected employment characteristics and VA district, quarterly rpt, 8602–6

VA health care staff and turnover, by occupation, physician specialty, and location, 1990, annual rpt, 8604–8

see also Diseases and disorders

see also Medical examinations and tests

Pauls, B. Dianne

"Re-Assessment of the Relationship Between Real Exchange Rates and Real Interest Rates: 1974-90", 9366–7.262

Pavelko, Amy

"Corporation Income Tax Returns, 1988", 8302–2.217

Pawtucket, R.I.

Housing and households characteristics, 1988 survey, MSA fact sheet, 2485–11.10

Housing and households detailed characteristics, and unit and neighborhood quality, by location, 1988 survey, MSA rpt, 2485–6.7

Wages by occupation, for office and plant workers, 1991 survey, periodic MSA rpt, 6785–12.6

see also under By SMSA or MSA in the "Index by Categories"

Payment-in-kind program, USDA

see Agricultural production quotas and price supports

Payroll

Banks (Fed Reserve) and branch officers, staff, and salary, 1990, annual rpt, 9364–1.1

Construction industries census, 1987: establishments, employment, receipts, and expenditures, by SIC 4-digit industry and State, final industry rpt series, 2373–1

Costs (hourly) of labor, by component, industry sector, worker class, and firm size, 1990, annual rpt, 6744–22

County Business Patterns, 1988: employment, establishments, and payroll, by SIC 2- to 4-digit industry and county, annual State rpt series, 2326–6

County Business Patterns, 1989: employment, establishments, and payroll, by SIC 2- to 4-digit industry and county, annual State rpt series, 2326–8

Credit unions federally insured, finances by instn characteristics and State, as of June 1991, semiannual rpt, 9532–6

Disabled persons workshops finances, operations, and Federal procurement, FY80-90, annual rpt, 11714–1

Electric utilities privately owned, finances and operations, detailed data, 1989, annual rpt, 3164–23

Enterprise Statistics, 1987: auxiliaries of multi-establishment firms, finances and operations by function, industry, and State, 2329–6

Enterprise Statistics, 1987: finances and operations for companies, by size, level of diversification, form of organization, and industry group, 2329–8

Fed Reserve System, Board of Governors, and district banks financial statements, performance, and fiscal services, 1990-91, annual rpt, 9364–10

Health Care Financing Review, provider prices, price inputs and indexes, and labor, quarterly journal, 4652–1.1

Hotels and other lodging places, receipts, payroll, employment, ownership, and rooms, by State and MSA, 1987 Census of Service Industries, subject rpt, 2393–3

Lumber industry firms, employment, and payroll in northeast States, by industry, 1982-86, 1208–375

Manufacturing annual survey, 1989: establishments, employment, finances, inventories, and energy use, by SIC 2- to 4-digit industry, 2506–15.1

Manufacturing annual survey, 1989: finances and operations, by SIC 2- and 3-digit industry and State, 2506–15.3

Manufacturing census, 1987: finances and operations, by SIC 2- to 4-digit industry, State, and MSA, with trends from 1849, 2497–1

Manufacturing census, 1987: finances and operations, by type of organization and SIC 2- to 4-digit industry, subject rpt, 2497–5

Mental health care facilities outlays, by function, instn type, funding source, and State, 1988, 4506–3.45

Mineral industries census, 1987: finances and operations, by establishment characteristics, SIC 2- to 4-digit industry, and State, subject rpt, 2517–1

Mineral industries census, 1987: finances and operations, by SIC 2- to 4-digit industry, State, and county, census div rpt series, 2515–1

Multinatl firms US affiliates finances and operations, by industry div, country of parent firm, and State, 1988-89, annual article, 2702–1.214

Multinatl firms US affiliates, finances, and operations, by industry, world area of parent firm, and State, 1988-89, annual rpt, 2704–4

Multinatl US firms and foreign affiliates finances and operations, by industry and world area of parent firm, 1989 benchmark survey, preliminary annual rpt, 2704–5

Multinatl US firms and foreign affiliates finances and operations, by industry of parent firm and affiliate, world area, and selected country, 1989, annual article, 2702–1.225

Natural gas interstate pipeline company detailed financial and operating data, by firm, 1989, annual rpt, 3164–38

Nonprofit charitable organizations finances, and revenue and investments of top 10 instns, 1986-87, article, 8302–2.210

Index by Subjects and Names

Nonprofit charitable organizations finances, by size of contributions received, 1987, article, 8302–2.218

Oil bulk stations, sales and storage capacity by product, inventories, expenses, employment, and modes of transport, 1987 Census of Wholesale Trade, 2407–4.2

Puerto Rico economic censuses, 1987: wholesale and retail trade and service industry finances and operations, by SIC 2- to 4-digit industry and municipio, 2591–1

Puerto Rico economic censuses, 1987: wholesale, retail, and service industries finances and operations, by establishment characteristics and SIC 2- and 3-digit industry, subject rpts, 2591–2

Railroad (Class I) finances and operations, detailed data by firm, class of service, and district, 1989, annual rpt, 9486–6.1

Retail trade census, 1987: depreciable assets, capital and operating expenses, sales, value added, and inventories, by SIC 2- to 4-digit kind of business, 2399–2

Retail trade census, 1987: finances and employment, for establishments with and without payroll, by SIC 2- to 4-digit kind of business, State, and MSA, 2401–1

Service industries census, 1987: depreciable assets, capital and operating expenses, and receipts, by SIC 2- to 4-digit kind of business, 2393–2

Service industries census, 1987: establishments, receipts by source, payroll, and employment, by SIC 2- to 4-digit kind of business, State, and MSA, 2393–4

Southeastern States, Fed Reserve 5th District insured commercial banks financial statements, by State, quarterly rpt, 9389–18

State and Metro Area Data Book, 1991 data compilation, 2328–54

Statistical Abstract of US, 1991 annual data compilation, 2324–1.17

Steel imports of US under voluntary restraint agreement, by product, customs district, and country, with US industry operating data, quarterly rpt, 9882–13

Tax (income) returns filed by type of filer, selected income items, quarterly rpt, 8302–2.1

Tax (income) returns of partnerships, income statement and balance sheet items, by industry group, 1989, annual article, 8302–2.216; 8304–18

Tax (income) returns of sole proprietorships, income statement items, by industry group, 1989, annual article, 8302–2.214

Telephone and telegraph firms detailed finances and operations, 1989, annual rpt, 9284–6

Transportation census, 1987: finances and operations by size, ownership, and State, and revenues by MSA, by SIC 2- to 4-digit industry, 2579–1

Truck and bus interstate carriers finances and operations, by district, 1989, annual rpt, 9486–6.3

Truck and warehouse services finances and inventory, by SIC 2- to 4-digit industry, 1989 survey, annual rpt, 2413–14

Truck interstate carriers finances and operations, by district, 1989, annual rpt, 9486–6.2

Wholesale trade census, 1987: depreciable assets, capital and operating expenses, sales, value added, and inventories, by SIC 2- to 3-digit kind of business, 2407–2

Wholesale trade census, 1987: establishments, sales by customer class, employment, inventories, and expenses, by SIC 2- to 4-digit kind of business, 2407–4

see also Agricultural wages
see also Earnings, general
see also Earnings, specific industry
see also Educational employees pay
see also Federal pay
see also Government pay
see also Military pay
see also Social security tax
see also State and local employees pay
see also Unemployment insurance tax
see also Wage deductions

Payroll tax
see Social security tax
see Unemployment insurance tax

PCBs
see Carcinogens
see Hazardous substances
see Hazardous waste and disposal

Peace Corps

Activities of PC, funding by program, and volunteers, by country, FY92, annual rpt, 9654–1

Budget of US, authoritative financial statements with appropriations, outlays, and receipts, by category and agency, FY90, annual rpt, 8104–2.1

Budget of US, obligations and authority by function, agency, and program, with summaries, analyses, and historical tables, FY92, annual rpt, 104–2

Expenditures for economic and military aid, by program and country, FY46-90, annual rpt, 9914–5

Human rights conditions in 170 countries, and US economic and military aid, 1990, annual rpt, 21384–3

Palau admin, and social, economic, and govtl data, FY90, annual rpt, 7004–6

Participation by world area, and funding, for Fed Govt exchange and training programs, FY89, annual rpt, 9854–8

Peace Institute
see U.S. Institute of Peace

Peacekeeping forces
see International military forces

Peanuts

Acreage planted and harvested, by crop and State, 1989-90 and planned as of June 1991, annual rpt, 1621–23

Acreage planted, by selected crop and State, 1982-90 and planned 1991, annual rpt, 1621–22

Acreage under Agricultural Stabilization and Conservation Service programs, rankings by commodity and congressional district, 1989, biennial rpt, 1804–17

Agricultural Statistics, 1990, annual rpt, 1004–1

Agriculture census, 1987: farms, farmland, production, finances, and operator characteristics, by county, final State rpt series, 2331–1

CCC financial condition and major commodity program operations, FY62-87, annual chartbook, 1824–2

Cold storage food stocks by commodity, and warehouse space use, by census div, 1990, annual rpt, 1631–11

Confectionery shipments, trade, use, and ingredients used, by product, 1990, annual Current Industrial Rpt, 2506–4.5

Consumption, supply, trade, prices, spending, and indexes, by food commodity, 1989, annual rpt, 1544–4

Exports and imports (agricultural) of US, by detailed commodity and country, 1989, annual rpt, 1524–8

Exports and imports (agricultural) of US, by detailed commodity and country, 1990, semiannual rpt, 1522–4

Exports and imports between US and outlying areas, by detailed commodity and mode of transport, 1990, annual rpt, 2424–11

Exports and imports of US, by country and detailed commodity, monthly rpt, 2422–12

Exports and imports of US, by Harmonized System 6-digit commodity and country, 1990, annual rpt, 2424–13

Exports of US, detailed Schedule B commodities with countries of destination, 1990, annual rpt, 2424–10

Farm income, expenses, receipts by commodity, assets, liabilities, and ratios, 1990 and trends from 1945, annual rpt, 1544–16

Foreign and US oils, oilseeds, and fats production and trade, FAS periodic circular series, 1925–1

Imports of peanuts, injury to price-supported US industry, investigation with background financial and operating data, 1991 rpt, 9886–10.10

Price indexes (producer), by stage of processing and detailed commodity, monthly 1990, annual rpt, 6764–2

Price support program provisions, for selected commodities, 1961-90, 1568–303

Prices received and paid by farmers, by commodity and State, 1990, annual rpt, 1629–5

Prices received by farmers and production value, by detailed crop and State, 1988-90, annual rpt, 1621–2

Production and US exports by country, prices, and stocks, for peanuts, weekly rpt, 1311–1

Production, farms, acreage, and related data, by selected crop and State, monthly rpt, 1621–1

Production itemized costs, receipts, and returns, by commodity and region, 1987-89, annual rpt, 1544–20

Production, prices, stocks, exports, use, inspection, and quality, for peanuts, by region and State, 1980-90, annual rpt, 1311–5

Production, prices, trade, and use of oils and fats, periodic situation rpt with articles, 1561–3

Stocks, millings, and use, by peanut grade and type, monthly rpt, 1621–6

see also under By Commodity in the "Index by Categories"

Pearcy, William G.

"Distribution and Abundance of Juvenile Salmonids off Oregon and Washington, 1981-85", 2168–123

Pearrow, Joan

"Pumpkins: A Commodity Highlight", 1561–11.203

"U.S. Imports of Fruits and Vegetables Under Plant Quarantine Regulations, FY88", 1524–7

Peas
see Vegetables and vegetable products

Peat
see Fertilizers
see Nonmetallic minerals and mines

Pedestrians

Accident deaths and injuries of children by cause, and victimization, rates by race, sex, and age, 1979-88, chartbook, 4108–56

Accident deaths and rates, by cause, age, sex, race, and State, 1988, US Vital Statistics annual rpt, 4144–2

Accidents (fatal), circumstances, and characteristics of persons and vehicles involved, 1990, semiannual rpt, 7762–11

Accidents (fatal), deaths, and rates, by circumstances, characteristics of persons and vehicles involved, and location, 1989, annual rpt, 7764–10

Accidents and deaths of pedestrians and bicyclists involving autos, 1980-90, annual fact sheet, 7766–15.5

Accidents at hwy-railroad grade-crossings, detailed data by State and railroad, 1989, annual rpt, 7604–2

Accidents, casualties, circumstances, and characteristics of persons and vehicles involved, 1989, annual rpt, 7764–18

Bus (school) accidents, circumstances, victim characteristics, and vehicle type, 1989, annual rpt, 7764–22

Child accident deaths and death rates, by cause, age, sex, race, and State, 1980-85, 4108–54

Safety improvement measures, costs, and accident and death reductions by type of accident and improvement, 1990 conf, 7558–110

Safety programs, and accidents, casualties, and damage, by mode of transport, 1989, annual rpt, 7304–19

Travel patterns, personal and household characteristics, and auto and public transport use, 1990 survey, series, 7556–6

Pediatrics

Health condition and health care resources, use, and spending, 1950s-89, annual data compilation, 4144–11

Indian Health Service outpatient services provided, by reason for visit and age, FY88-89, annual rpt, 4084–2

Indian Health Service, tribal, and contract facilities hospitalization, by diagnosis, age, sex, and service area, FY89, annual rpt, 4084–5

Labor supply of physicians, by specialty, age, sex, and location of training and practice, 1989, State rpt series, 4116–6

Medicaid child preventive health care visits, exams, and immunizations, for California, 1981-84, article, 4652–1.214

Medicaid demonstration projects evaluation, for 6 States, 1988 rpt, 4658–45

Medicaid maternity and child health services availability indicators, literature review, 1980s, article, 4652–1.210

Pediatrics

Military health care personnel, and accessions by training source, by occupation, specialty, and service branch, FY89, annual rpt, 3544–24

Teenagers physicians office visits, by reason and characteristics of physicians, patients, and visit, 1985, 4146–8.199

Urban areas health depts programs for mothers and children, activities and budgets, 1990, listing, 4108–51

VA health care facilities physicians, dentists, and nurses, by selected employment characteristics and VA district, quarterly rpt, 8602–6

Visits to physicians, by patient and practice characteristics, diagnosis, and services provided, 1989, 4146–8.206

Peek, Joe

"Real, Affordable Mortgage", 9373–1.204

Pehrsson, Pamela R.

"Composition of Foods. Snacks and Sweets: Raw, Processed, Prepared", 1356–3.16

Pelavin Associates, Inc.

"Escalating Costs of Higher Education", 4808–25

"Minority Participation in Higher Education", 4808–29

"Review of the National Workplace Literacy Program", 4808–37

"Trends in Institutional Costs", 4808–24

Pelavin, Sol H.

"Minority Participation in Higher Education", 4808–29

Pell grants

see Student aid

Pelvic inflammatory disease

see Urogenital diseases

Penalties

see Fines and settlements

see Judgments, civil procedure

see Sentences, criminal procedure

Pendleton, Oreg.

Wages by occupation, for office and plant workers, 1991 survey, periodic MSA rpt, 6785–3.6

Pennsylvania

Appalachian Regional Commission funding, by project and State, planned FY91, annual rpt, 9084–3

Apple production, marketing, and prices, for Appalachia and compared to other States, 1988-91, annual rpt, 1311–13

Banks (insured commercial and savings) deposits by instn, State, MSA, and county, as of June 1990, annual regional rpt, 9295–3.1

Census of Population and Housing, 1990: Pennsylvania data collection activities and status, hearing, 21628–89

Census of Population and Housing, 1990: Pennsylvania preparations for count, hearing, 21628–87

Coal (Pennsylvania anthracite) production, use, and stocks, weekly rpt, 3162–1

Coal production and mines by county, prices, productivity, miners, and reserves, by mining method and State, 1989-90, annual rpt, 3164–25

County Business Patterns, 1989: employment, establishments, and payroll, by SIC 2- to 4-digit industry and county, annual State rpt, 2326–8.40

Dairy prices, by product and selected area, with related marketing data, 1990, annual rpt, 1317–1

DOD prime contract awards, by contractor, service branch, State, and city, FY90, annual rpt, 3544–22

Drug (prescription) aid program for aged in Pennsylvania, enrollment, use, and costs, FY85-87, article, 4652–1.237

Economic conditions and outlook, for US and Canada Great Lakes area, 1970s-90, 9375–15

Education system in Appalachia, improvement initiatives, and indicators of success, by State, 1960s-89, 9088–36

Employment growth and unemployment rates, Fed Reserve 3rd District, quarterly rpt, 9387–10

Fed Govt spending in States and local areas, by type, State, county, and city, FY90, annual rpt, 2464–3

Fed Govt spending in States, by type, program, agency, and State, FY90, annual rpt, 2464–2

HHS financial aid, by program, recipient, State, and city, FY90, annual regional listing, 4004–3.3

Hospital deaths of Medicare patients, actual and expected rates by diagnosis, and hospital characteristics, by instn, FY87-89, annual regional rpt, 4654–14.3

Housing census, 1990: inventory, occupancy, and costs, State fact sheet, 2326–21.40

Income (personal) per capita and by source, and earnings by industry div, by State, MSA, and county, 1984-89, annual regional rpt, 2704–2.2

Jail adult and juvenile population, employment, spending, instn conditions, and inmate programs, by county and facility, 1988, regional rpt series, 6068–144.2

Marriages, divorces, and rates, by characteristics of spouses, State, and county, 1987 and trends from 1920, US Vital Statistics annual rpt, 4144–4

Medicaid prepaid plans for physician services, characteristics of selected plans in 4 States, various periods 1983-89, article, 4652–1.228

Mineral Industry Surveys, State reviews of production, 1990, preliminary annual rpt, 5614–6

Minerals Yearbook, 1989, Vol 2: State review of production and sales by commodity, and business activity, annual rpt, 5604–16.39

Minerals Yearbook, 1989, Vol 2: State reviews of production, sales, and firms, by commodity, and business activity, annual rpt, 5604–34

Physicians, by specialty, age, sex, and location of training and practice, 1989, State rpt, 4116–6.39

Population and housing census, 1990: population and housing characteristics, households, and land area, by county, subdiv, and place, State rpt, 2551–1.40

Population and housing census, 1990: voting age and total population by race, and housing units, by block, redistricting counts required under PL 94-171, State CD-ROM release, 2551–6.9

Population and housing census, 1990: voting age and total population by race, and housing units, by county and city, redistricting counts required under PL 94-171, State summary rpt, 2551–5.39

Index by Subjects and Names

Statistical Abstract of US, 1991 annual data compilation, 2324–1

Supplemental Security Income payments and beneficiaries, by type of eligibility, State, and county, Dec 1989, annual rpt, 4744–27.3

Uranium tailings at inactive mills, remedial action activities by site, and funding, FY90, annual rpt, 3354–9

Water (groundwater) supply, quality, chemistry, and use, 1985-87, local area rpt, 5666–28.8

Water resources dev projects of Army Corps of Engineers, characteristics, and costs, 1950s-89, biennial State rpt, 3756–1.39

Water supply and quality in streams and lakes, and groundwater levels in wells, by drainage basin, 1989, annual State rpt, 5666–12.37

see also Allegheny County, Pa.

see also Philadelphia, Pa.

see also Pittsburgh, Pa.

see also Scranton, Pa.

see also Wilkes-Barre, Pa.

see also under By State in the "Index by Categories"

Pennsylvania Avenue Development Corp.

Budget of US, authoritative financial statements with appropriations, outlays, and receipts, by category and agency, FY90, annual rpt, 8104–2.1

Budget of US, obligations and authority by function, agency, and program, with summaries, analyses, and historical tables, FY92, annual rpt, 104–2

Pensacola, Fla.

see also under By SMSA or MSA in the "Index by Categories"

Pension and Welfare Benefits Administration

Employee Retirement Income Security Act (ERISA) admin and enforcement, 1990, annual rpt, 6684–1

Pension Benefit Guaranty Corp.

Activities and finances of PBGC, FY90, annual rpt, 9674–1

Budget of US, obligations and authority by function, agency, and program, with summaries, analyses, and historical tables, FY92, annual rpt, 104–2

Finances and operations of programs under Ways and Means Committee jurisdiction, FY70s-90, annual rpt, 21784–11

Pensions and pension funds

Acquisitions (leveraged buyout) affecting pensions, plans finances, participation, terminations, and replacements, 1982-87, GAO rpt, 26121–408

Assets and debts of private sector, balance sheets by segment, 1945-90, semiannual rpt, 9365–4.1

Consumer Expenditure Survey, spending by category, and income, by selected household characteristics and location, 1990, annual press release, 6726–1.42

Coverage and provisions of employee benefit plans, by plan type, firm size, and industry sector, 1988, article, 6722–1.204

Coverage under employee benefit plans, by benefit type and worker characteristics, late 1970s-80s, 15496–1.11

Coverage under pension plans by industry, and 401(k) and IRA participation, 1987, fact sheet, 2326–17.35

Coverage under pension plans by industry, vestment, and recipient income, by participant characteristics, 1987, Current Population Rpt, 2546–20.18

Index by Subjects and Names

Periodicals

Defined benefit pension plans impacts of Omnibus Budget Reconciliation Act contribution deductibility limit, 1984-89, 8008–152

Defined benefit plans funding status under 1987 accounting standards, 1987-89, technical paper, 9366–6.259

Earnings replacement rates of pension plans and OASI benefits, by age, salary, years of participation, and occupational group, 1989, article, 6722–1.238

Employee Retirement Income Security Act (ERISA) admin and enforcement, 1990, annual rpt, 6684–1

Expenditures (private) for social welfare, by category, 1970s-88, annual article, 4742–1.204

Expenditures, coverage, and benefits for social welfare programs, late 1930s-89, annual rpt, 4744–3.1; 4744–3.3

Flow-of-funds accounts, savings, investments, and credit statements, quarterly rpt, 9365–3.3

Households composition, income, benefits, and labor force status, Survey of Income and Program Participation methodology, working paper series, 2626–10

Income (household) by source, and itemized spending, by selected characteristics and region, 1988-89 Consumer Expenditure Survey, annual rpt, 6764–5

Income (household, family, and personal), by source, detailed characteristics, and region, 1988-89, annual Current Population Rpt, 2546–6.68

Income (household, family, and personal), by source, detailed characteristics, and region, 1990, annual Current Population Rpt, 2546–6.70

Insurance industry finances, underwriting activities, and investment plan mgmt, 1960s-90, 21248–159

Japan economic conditions, financial and intl policies, and trade devs, 1950s-80s and projected to 2050, compilation of papers, 23848–220

Labor hourly costs, by component, industry sector, worker class, and firm size, 1990, annual rpt, 6744–22

Mortgage loan activity, by type of lender, loan, and mortgaged property, monthly press release, 5142–18

Mortgage loan activity, by type of lender, loan, and mortgaged property, quarterly press release, 5142–30

Pension Benefit Guaranty Corp activities and finances, FY90, annual rpt, 9674–1

Poverty status of population and families, by detailed characteristics, 1988-89, annual Current Population Rpt, 2546–6.67

Poverty status of population and families, by detailed characteristics, 1990, annual Current Population Rpt, 2546–6.71

Railroad (Amtrak) finances and operations, FY90, annual rpt, 29524–1

Railroad employee benefits program finances and beneficiaries, FY90, annual rpt, 9704–1

Railroad retirement, survivors, unemployment, and health insurance programs, monthly rpt, 9702–2

Railroad retirement system funding and benefits findings and recommendations, with background industry data, 1960s-90 and projected to 2060, 9708–1

Rural areas aged household income sources, and poverty status, 1983-84, 1598–268

Small business employees benefit plan coverage and provisions, by plan type and occupational group, 1990, biennial rpt, 6784–20

Small businesses pension plan benefits disparity between men and women by selected participant and plan characteristics, impacts of 1986 Tax Reform Act, 1984-85, GAO rpt, 26121–412

Soviet Union GNP by detailed income and outlay component, 1985, 2326–18.59

State and local govt employees benefit plan coverage, by benefit type, 1990, press release, 6726–1.41

Statistical Abstract of US, 1991 annual data compilation, 2324–1.12

Survivor benefits of employer-sponsored plans, coverage by plan type and payment method, 1989, article, 6722–1.230

Tax (excise) collections of IRS, by source, quarterly rpt, 8302–1

Tax (income) returns filed by type of filer, selected income items, quarterly rpt, 8302–2.1

Tax (income) returns of individuals, selected income and tax items by income level, preliminary 1989, annual article, 8302–2.209

Tax (income) withholding and related documents filed, by type and IRS service center, 1990 and projected 1991-98, annual rpt, 8304–22

Tax deductions for pension plan contributions, effects of limits on savings rate, 1950s-90, article, 9373–1.219

Tax expenditures, Federal revenues forgone through income tax deductions and exclusions by type, FY92-96, annual rpt, 21784–10

Telephone and telegraph firms detailed finances and operations, 1989, annual rpt, 9284–6.2; 9284–6.3

see also Area wage surveys

see also Civil service pensions

see also Individual retirement arrangements

see also Military benefits and pensions

see also Old-Age, Survivors, Disability, and Health Insurance

see also Social security

see also Veterans benefits and pensions

People's Democratic Republic of Yemen

see Yemen, South

People's Republic of China

see China, Peoples Republic

Peoria, Ill.

Wages by occupation, and benefits for office and plant workers, 1991 survey, periodic labor market rpt, 6785–3.9

see also under By City and By SMSA or MSA in the "Index by Categories"

Pepper Commission

see U.S. Bipartisan Commission on Comprehensive Health Care

Per capita income

see Personal and household income

Perez, Agnes M.

"Size and Geographics of U.S. Turkey Growout Operations", 1561–7.202

Perez, Jacob

"Tracking Offenders, 1987", 6066–25.33

"Tracking Offenders, 1988", 6066–25.39

Perez-Stable, Eliseo J.

"Evaluation of 'Guia para Dejar de Fumar,' a Self-help Guide in Spanish To Quit Smoking", 4042–3.249

Performing arts

Copyrights Register activities, registrations by material type, and fees, FY90 and trends from 1790, annual rpt, 26404–2

County Business Patterns, 1988: employment, establishments, and payroll, by SIC 2- to 4-digit industry and county, annual State rpt series, 2326–6

County Business Patterns, 1989: employment, establishments, and payroll, by SIC 2- to 4-digit industry and county, annual State rpt series, 2326–8

Education (postsecondary) course completions, by detailed program, sex, race, and instn type, for 1972 high school class, as of 1984, 4888–4

Educational and employment performance of college athletes compared to other students, for 1972 high school class, as of 1986, 4888–5

Kennedy Center for Performing Arts and Natl Symphony Orchestra financial statements, and capital and maintenance costs and needs, 1970s-90, hearing, 21648–62

Natl Endowment for Arts activities and grants, FY90, annual rpt, 9564–3

Occupational injury and illness rates, by SIC 2- to 4-digit industry, 1988-89, annual rpt, 6844–7

Service industries census, 1987: establishments, receipts by source, payroll, and employment, by SIC 2- to 4-digit kind of business, State, and MSA, 2393–4

Service industries receipts, by SIC 2- to 4-digit kind of business, 1990, annual rpt, 2413–8

Statistical Abstract of US, 1991 annual data compilation, 2324–1.7

Tax (income) returns of sole proprietorships, income statement items, by industry group, 1989, annual article, 8302–2.214

see also Dance

see also Motion pictures

see also Theater

Periodicals

Copyrights Register activities, registrations by material type, and fees, FY90 and trends from 1790, annual rpt, 26404–2

County Business Patterns, 1988: employment, establishments, and payroll, by SIC 2- to 4-digit industry and county, annual State rpt series, 2326–6

County Business Patterns, 1989: employment, establishments, and payroll, by SIC 2- to 4-digit industry and county, annual State rpt series, 2326–8

Employment, earnings, and hours, by SIC 1- to 4-digit industry, monthly and annual averages, selected years 1909-90, annual rpt, 6744–4

Enterprise Statistics, 1987: finances and operations for companies, by size, level of diversification, form of organization, and industry group, 2329–8

Exports and imports of US, by country and detailed commodity, monthly rpt, 2422–12

Exports and imports of US, by Harmonized System 6-digit commodity and country, 1990, annual rpt, 2424–13

Periodicals

Exports of US, detailed Schedule B commodities with countries of destination, 1990, annual rpt, 2424–10

Libraries (public) finances, staff, and operations, by State and population size, 1989, annual rpt, 4824–6

Libraries for blind and handicapped, readership, circulation, staff, funding, and holdings, FY90, annual listing, 26404–3

Libraries of higher education instns, holdings, outlays, staff, and instn characteristics, 1969-88, 4468–4

Library of Congress activities, acquisitions, services, and financial statements, FY90, annual rpt, 26404–1

Mail revenue and subsidy for revenue forgone, by class of mail, FY90, and volume from FY86, annual rpt, 9864–1

Mail volume to and from households, use, and views, by class, source, content, and household characteristics, 1987-88, annual rpt, 9864–10

Manufacturing annual survey, 1989: finances and operations, by SIC 2- to 4-digit industry, series, 2506–15

Manufacturing census, 1987: finances and operations, by SIC 2- to 4-digit industry, State, and MSA, with trends from 1849, 2497–1

Manufacturing census, 1987: finances and operations, by type of organization and SIC 2- to 4-digit industry, subject rpt, 2497–5

Manufacturing finances and operations, by SIC 2- to 4-digit industry, forecast 1991, annual rpt, 2044–28

Occupational injury and illness rates, by SIC 2- to 4-digit industry, 1988-89, annual rpt, 6844–7

Occupational injury and illness rates, by SIC 2- to 4-digit industry, 1989, annual rpt, 6844–1

Price indexes (producer), by stage of processing and detailed commodity, monthly rpt, 6762–6

Price indexes (producer), by stage of processing and detailed commodity, monthly 1990, annual rpt, 6764–2

Senate receipts, itemized expenses by payee, and balances, 1st half FY91, semiannual listing, 25922–1

Statistical Abstract of US, 1991 annual data compilation, 2324–1.18

Tax (income) returns of corporations, income and tax items by asset size and detailed industry, 1987, annual rpt, 8304–4

Tax (income) returns of corporations, income and tax items by asset size and detailed industry, 1988, annual rpt, 8304–21

Travel to US, trade shows and other promotional activities, with magazine ad costs and circulation, for selected countries, 1991-92, annual rpt, 2904–11

USDA rpts, computer data files, and visual aids, 1991 annual listing, 1004–13

USIA library holdings, use, and staff, by country and city, FY90, annual rpt, 9854–4

see also Journalism

see also Newspapers

see also Research journals

Index by Subjects and Names

Peristiani, Stavros

"Disaggregate Analysis of Discount Window Borrowing", 9385–1.209

"Empirical Investigation of the Determinants of Discount Window Borrowing: A Disaggregate Analysis", 9385–8.110

"Margin Requirements, Speculative Trading and Stock Price Fluctuations: The Case of Japan", 9385–8.72

"Permanent and Transient Influences on the Reluctance To Borrow at the Discount Window", 9385–8.111

Perlite

see Nonmetallic minerals and mines

Permits

see Building permits

see Drivers licenses

see Hunting and fishing licenses

see Licenses and permits

see Occupational testing and certification

see Water permits

Perng, Shien S.

"Opinion Survey of Taxpayers Contacted by IRS Collection", 8304–8.1

"Survey of Payers and Payees with IRS-Identified Invalid TINs", 8304–8.1

Perquisites

see Employee benefits

see Employee bonuses and work incentives

Perry, Charles A.

"Source, Extent, and Degradation of Herbicides in a Shallow Aquifer Near Hesston, Kansas", 5666–28.13

Perry, Janet

"Profile of Specialized Fruit and Vegetable Farms in 1989", 1541–1.209

Persian Gulf

see Middle East

Persian Gulf War

see Military intervention

see Military invasion and occupation

Personal and household income

AFDC beneficiaries demographic and financial characteristics, by State, FY89, annual rpt, 4694–1

Alaska subsistence fishing role in local economies, with indicators for Yakutat, 1980s, 1208–350

Alien nonresidents income from US sources and tax withheld by country and US tax treaty status, 1988, annual article, 8302–2.206

Births, fertility rates, and childless women, by selected characteristics, 1990, annual Current Population Rpt, 2546–1.455

Black Americans social and economic characteristics, for South and total US, 1989-90 and trends from 1969, Current Population Rpt, 2546–1.450

Budget of US, compilation of background material on fiscal and tax policy, 1960s-96, 21788–203

Business statistics, detailed data for major industries and economic indicators, *Survey of Current Business*, monthly rpt, 2702–1

Children and youth social, economic, and demographic characteristics, 1950s-90, 4818–5

Coastal areas environmental and socioeconomic conditions, and potential impact of oil and gas OCS leases, final statement series, 5736–1

Consumer Expenditure Survey, household income by source, and itemized spending, by selected characteristics and region, 1988-89, annual rpt, 6764–5

Consumer Income, socioeconomic characteristics of persons, families, and households, detailed cross-tabulations, Current Population Rpt series, 2546–6

Consumer spending, ratio to lifetime income, by age and sex, 1991 working paper, 9377–9.116

Data on income from Survey of Income and Program Participation compared to Current Population Survey, 1984, technical paper, 4746–26.8

Developing countries aged population and selected characteristics, 1980s and projected to 2020, country rpt series, 2326–19

Developing countries aided by Peace Corps, quality of life indicators, FY92, annual rpt, 9654–1

Disparity between incomes of wealthiest and other families, and income sources, 1980s and trends from 1949, 23848–219

Eastern Europe transition to market economies, economic conditions, intl aid, and energy balance, by country, 1985-90, 9118–13

Economic indicators and components, and Fed Reserve 4th District business and financial conditions, monthly chartbook, 9377–10

Economic indicators and relation to govt finances by level of govt, selected years 1929-90, annual rpt, 10044–1

Economic indicators compounded annual rates of change, monthly rpt, 9391–3

Economic indicators compounded annual rates of change, 1971-90, annual rpt, 9391–9.2

Economic indicators, monthly rpt, 9362–1.2

Economic Report of the President for 1991, Joint Economic Committee critique and policy recommendations, annual rpt, 23844–2

Educational attainment, by sociodemographic characteristics and location, 1989 and trends from 1940, biennial Current Population Rpt, 2546–1.452

Educational attainment relation to income, by sex, 1987, fact sheet, 2326–17.25

Energy use by mode of transport, fuel supply, and demographic and economic factors of vehicle use, 1970s-89, annual rpt, 3304–5

Financial instns location relation to ZIP code area income and minority population, by instn type for 5 cities, 1977-89, article, 9377–1.208

Food spending, by item, household composition, income, age, race, and region, 1980-88, Consumer Expenditure Survey biennial rpt, 1544–30

Food stamp recipient household size, composition, income, and income and deductions allowed, summer 1988, annual rpt, 1364–8

Foreign countries family composition, poverty status, labor conditions, and welfare indicators and needs, by country, 1960s-88, hearing, 23846–4.30

Foster care placement of black children whose parents abuse drugs, by placement reason and outcome, and household and parent characteristics, 1986-90, 4008–114

Index by Subjects and Names

Personal and household income

Govt spending measures using indicators of service costs and demand, with comparisons to fiscal capacity and actual outlays, by State, for State and local govts, 1986-87, 10048–77

Hispanic Americans in counties bordering Mexico, by selected characteristics, 1980, Current Population Rpt, 2546–2.159

Hispanic Americans social and economic characteristics, by detailed origin, 1991, Current Population Rpt, 2546–1.448; 2546–1.451

Home mortgages FHA-insured, financial, property, and mortgagor characteristics, by metro area, 1990, annual rpt, 5144–24

Home mortgages FHA-insured, financial, property, and mortgagor characteristics, by State, 1990, annual rpt, 5144–1

Home mortgages FHA-insured, financial, property, and mortgagor characteristics, total and by State and outlying area, 1990, annual rpt, 5144–25

Home mortgages FHA-insured, financial, property, and mortgagor characteristics, 1990, annual rpt, 5144–23

Households and family characteristics, by location, 1990, annual Current Population Rpt, 2546–1.447

Households and housing characteristics, unit and neighborhood quality, and journey to work by MSA location, for 11 MSAs, 1984 survey, supplement, 2485–8

Households and housing detailed characteristics, and unit and neighborhood quality, by location, 1987, biennial rpt supplement, 2485–13

Households and housing detailed characteristics, and unit and neighborhood quality, by location, 1989, biennial rpt, 2485–12

Households and housing detailed characteristics, and unit and neighborhood quality, MSA surveys, series, 2485–6

Households income and poverty status under alternative income definitions, by recipient characteristics, 1990, annual Current Population Rpt, 2546–6.69

Households income indicators by composition, 1969-89, Current Population Rpt, biennial rpt, 2546–2.161

Housing affordability and family income relation to housing costs, 1989 survey, fact sheet, 2326–17.33

Housing affordability indicators, by household composition, income, and current tenure, 1988, 2486–1.11

Housing inventory change from 1973, by reason, unit and household characteristics, and location, 1983 survey, biennial rpt, 2485–14

Louisiana economic indicators and oil rig growth forecasts, model description and results, 1991, article, 9379–1.202

Lower middle-class household income by source and spending by type, for 2-parent and single mother families by selected characteristics, 1987, article, 1702–1.207

Married couple families income and expenses, and wife's employment status, before and after having children, 1987-89, article, 1702–1.211

Married couple families with one spouse working, and income by source and expenses by type, by selected characteristics, 1987, article, 1702–1.201

Minority group and women health condition, services use, payment sources, and health care labor force, by poverty status, 1940s-89, chartbook, 4118–56

Minority group household income by source, and spending by type, by householder characteristics, 1987, article, 1702–1.206

Mortgage applications by disposition, and secondary loan market sales by purchaser type, by applicant and neighborhood characteristics, 1990, article, 9362–1.206

Natl income and product accounts and components, *Survey of Current Business*, monthly rpt, 2702–1.24

Natl income and product accounts benchmark revisions of GDP and natl income, various periods 1959-80, tables, 2702–1.227

New England States economic indicators, Fed Reserve 1st District, monthly rpt, 9373–2.3

New England States, FHLB 1st District thrifts financial operations compared to banks, and housing industry indicators, bimonthly rpt with articles, 9302–4

North Central States business and economic conditions, Fed Reserve 9th District, quarterly journal, 9383–19

OASDI benefits share of personal income, by selected characteristics, 1986-88, annual rpt, 4744–3.1; 4744–3.3

Older persons household income by source, and spending by type, 1987, article, 1702–1.204

Older persons in rural areas, household income sources, and poverty status, 1983-84, 1598–268

Older women's household income by source, and expenses by type, by living arrangement and other characteristics, 1988, article, 1702–1.210

Parents departure, absence, and presence, family economic impacts, 1983-86, Current Population Rpt, 2546–20.17

Parents departure, absence, and presence, family economic impacts, 1983-86, fact sheet, 2326–17.27

Personal and per capita income, and earnings by industry group, by region and State, 1988-90, annual article, 2702–1.216

Personal income (per capita), by region compared to total US, alternative model results, 1929-87, working paper, 9387–8.232

Personal income (per capita) disparity among States, with data by industrial base, 1979, 1989, and projected to 1995, 1548–379

Personal income (per capita) disparity between metro and nonmetro areas, and causal factors, 1979-88, 1548–380

Personal income (per capita and total) by source, and earnings by industry div, by State, MSA, and county, 1984-89, annual regional rpts, 2704–2

Personal income (per capita and total), by State, MSA, county, and metro-nonmetro location, 1987-89, annual article, 2702–1.209

Personal income and earnings estimates by State, data sources and reliability, 1980-87, article, 2702–1.202

Personal income by source, disposition, and disposable income, 1929-90, annual rpt, 204–1.1

Personal income, by source, monthly rpt, 23842–1.1

Personal income totals, by region, census div, and State, quarterly article, 2702–1.27

Population size and characteristics, historical index to *Current Population Rpts*, 1991 listing, 2546–2.160

Poverty threshold and rates under alternative threshold adjustment methodologies, 1980s-90, hearing, 23848–221

Rent supplement programs evaluation, housing vouchers compared to Section 8 certificates, 1985-88, series, 5186–14

Retired pension recipients income, by selected characteristics, 1986, Current Population Rpt, 2546–20.18

Rocky Mountain region employment and income, and economic dependence on shipments outside area, by industry and county group, 1980s, 1208–362

Rural areas economic and social indicators used to determine Federal aid need, late 1960s-86, 1598–265

Rural areas economic conditions and dev, quarterly journal, 1502–8

Single mothers earnings, employment and welfare benefits, and poverty status, 1989, GAO rpt, 26121–413

South Central States employment by industry div, income, and other economic indicators, for 4 States, 1989-90 and forecast 1991-92, annual article, 9391–16.207

Southeastern States, Fed Reserve 5th District, economic indicators by State, quarterly rpt, 9389–16

Southeastern States, Fed Reserve 8th District banking and economic conditions, quarterly rpt with articles, 9391–16

Soviet Union GNP by component and industry sector, and CIA estimation methods, 1950s-87, 23848–223

Soviet Union GNP by detailed income and outlay component, 1985, 2326–18.59

State and Metro Area Data Book, 1991 data compilation, 2328–54

Statistical Abstract of US, 1991 annual data compilation, 2324–1.14

Student aid Pell grants and applicants, by tuition, income level, instn type and control, and State, 1989/90, annual rpt, 4804–1

Survey of Income and Program Participation, data collection, methodology, and use, 1990 annual conf papers, 2624–1

Survey of Income and Program Participation, household composition, income, benefits, and labor force status, methodology, working paper series, 2626–10

Survey of Income and Program Participation, household income and socioeconomic characteristics, special study series, 2546–20

Tax (income) returns filed by type of filer, selected income items, quarterly rpt, 8302–2.1

Tax (income) returns of individuals, selected income and tax items, by adjusted gross income and State, 1986-88, article, 8302–2.201

Personal and household income

Tax (income) returns of individuals, selected income and tax items by income level, preliminary 1989, annual article, 8302–2.209

Tax (income) returns of individuals, taxable income, and tax generated, by tax rate and income level, 1987, annual article, 8302–2.211

Texas and Louisiana per capita income, impacts of industry mix and other factors, for 36 MSAs, 1969-88, article, 9379–1.209

Travel from US, characteristics of visit and traveler, and country of destination, 1990 in-flight survey, annual rpt, 2904–14

Travel to US, by characteristics of visit and traveler, world area of origin, and US destination, 1990 survey, annual rpt, 2904–12

Vocational rehabilitation cases of State agencies by disposition and applicant characteristics, and closures by reason, FY84-88, annual rpt, 4944–6

West Central States economic indicators, Fed Reserve 10th District, quarterly rpt, 9381–16.2

West Central States population, income, and employment growth, by MSA, metro-nonmetro location, and State, for Fed Reserve 10th District, 1970s-90s, article, 9381–1.209

Women's labor force status, earnings, and other characteristics, with comparisons to men, fact sheet series, 6564–1

Youth employment impacts on family income, and expenses by type, with selected family characteristics, 1989, article, 1702–1.213

see also Child support and alimony
see also Earnings, general
see also Earnings, local and regional
see also Earnings, specific industry
see also Family budgets
see also under By Income in the "Index by Categories"

Personal assets

see Wealth

Personal care products

Consumer Expenditure Survey, household income by source, and itemized spending, by selected characteristics and region, 1988-89, annual rpt, 6764–5

Consumer Expenditure Survey, spending by category, and income, by selected household characteristics and location, 1990, annual press release, 6726–1.42

Consumer spending, natl income and product accounts, *Survey of Current Business,* monthly rpt, 2702–1.25

CPI by component for US city average, and by region, population size, and for 27 metro areas, monthly rpt, 6762–2

Electric housewares and fans shipments, trade, use, and firms, by product, 1990, annual Current Industrial Rpt, 2506–12.15

Exports and imports between US and outlying areas, by detailed commodity and mode of transport, 1990, annual rpt, 2424–11

Exports and imports of US, by Harmonized System 6-digit commodity and country, 1990, annual rpt, 2424–13

Exports of US, detailed Schedule B commodities with countries of destination, 1990, annual rpt, 2424–10

Injuries from use of consumer products, by severity, victim age, and detailed product, 1990, annual rpt, 9164–6

Manufacturing census, 1987: finances and operations, by type of organization and SIC 2- to 4-digit industry, subject rpt, 2497–5

Manufacturing finances and operations, by SIC 2- to 4-digit industry, forecast 1991, annual rpt, 2044–28

Price indexes (producer), by stage of processing and detailed commodity, monthly rpt, 6762–6

Price indexes (producer), by stage of processing and detailed commodity, monthly 1990, annual rpt, 6764–2

Price indexes for department store inventories, by class of item, monthly table, 6762–7

Toxicology Natl Program research and testing activities, FY89 and planned FY90, annual rpt, 4044–16

see also Contraceptives
see also Cosmetics and toiletries
see also Drugs
see also Vitamins and nutrients
see also under By Commodity in the "Index by Categories"

Personal computers

see Computer industry and products

Personal consumption

Child rearing costs of married couple households, by expenditure type, child's age, income, and region, 1990 and projected to 2007, 1708–87

Children and youth social, economic, and demographic characteristics, 1950s-90, 4818–5

Clothing expenditures, by type, 1982-90, article, 1702–1.209

Clothing expenses of aged, by selected characteristics, 1987, 1702–1.202

Economic and employment conditions, alternative BLS projections to 2005 and trends 1970s-90, biennial article, 6722–1.251

Economic indicators and components, and Fed Reserve 4th District business and financial conditions, monthly chartbook, 9377–10

Economic indicators and components, current data and annual trends, monthly rpt, 23842–1.1

Economic indicators compounded annual rates of change, monthly rpt, 9391–3

Economic indicators compounded annual rates of change, 1971-90, annual rpt, 9391–9.2

Expenditures by category, and income, by selected household characteristics and location, Consumer Expenditure Survey, 1990, annual press release, 6726–1.42

Expenditures by category, selected household characteristics, and region, Consumer Expenditure Survey, quarterly rpt, 6762–14

Expenditures by category, 1929-90, annual rpt, 204–1.1

Expenditures for selected categories, Consumer Expenditure Survey, 1991 semiannual pamphlet, 2322–3

Family Economics Review, consumer goods prices and supply, and home economics, quarterly journal, 1702–1

Index by Subjects and Names

Forecasts of consumer spending, performance of consumer sentiment index, 1950s-90, technical paper, 9366–6.282

Forecasts of durable goods spending, performance of consumer confidence levels as indicators, 1970s-91, article, 9381–1.206

Income over lifetime, ratio to personal consumption, by age and sex, 1991 working paper, 9377–9.116

Inflation measured by CPI and Personal Consumption Expenditure Index, under alternative weighting systems, monthly rpt, periodic article, 6762–2

Input-output structure of US economy, detailed interindustry transactions for 84 industries, and components of final demand, 1986, annual article, 2702–1.206

Input-output structure of US economy, detailed interindustry transactions for 85 industries, 1982 benchmark data, 2702–1.213

Interest rates impact on GNP and components, alternative regression results, late 1950s-80s, technical paper, 9385–8.79

Natl income and product accounts and components, *Survey of Current Business,* monthly rpt, 2702–1.24; 2702–1.25

Natl income and product accounts benchmark revisions of GDP and natl income, various periods 1959-80, tables, 2702–1.227

Pollution abatement spending by govts, business, and consumers, 1987-89, annual article, 2702–1.229

Poverty threshold and rates under alternative threshold adjustment methodologies, 1980s-90, hearing, 23848–221

Puerto Rico economic censuses, 1987: wholesale and retail trade sales by customer class, and employment, by SIC 2- and 3-digit kind of business, subject rpt, 2591–2.2

Retail trade sales per capita, 1989, annual rpt, 2413–5

Savings rates in natl income and product accounts, under alternative estimates of imputed rent for housing and consumer goods, 1950s-90, article, 9373–1.218

Soviet Union and US production and consumption of selected commodities, by commodity, 1960s-90, annual rpt, 9114–4.3

Soviet Union GNP by component and industry sector, and CIA estimation methods, 1950s-87, 23848–223

Soviet Union GNP by detailed income and outlay component, 1985, 2326–18.59

Statistical Abstract of US, 1991 annual data compilation, 2324–1.14

Survey of Current Business, detailed financial and business data, and economic indicators, monthly rpt, 2702–1.1; 2702–1.4

Travel from US, characteristics of visit and traveler, and country of destination, 1990 in-flight survey, annual rpt, 2904–14

Travel to US, by characteristics of visit and traveler, world area of origin, and US destination, 1990 survey, annual rpt, 2904–12

Index by Subjects and Names

UK personal consumption impacts of govt spending, alternative model results, 1950s-86, technical paper, 9385–8.83

Wholesale trade census, 1987: establishments, sales by customer class, employment, inventories, and expenses, by SIC 2- to 4-digit kind of business, 2407–4

see also Cost of living
see also Family budgets
see also Food consumption
see also Housing energy use
see also Wealth

Personal debt

Assets and liabilities of US, and impacts of inflation, 1990 and trends from 1948, article, 9391–1.220

Debt and assets of private sector, balance sheets by segment, 1945-90, semiannual rpt, 9365–4.1

Debt outstanding, by sector and type of debt and holder, monthly rpt, 9362–1.1

Economic indicators and components, and Fed Reserve 4th District business and financial conditions, monthly chartbook, 9377–10

Flow-of-funds accounts, savings, investments, and credit statements, quarterly rpt, 9365–3.3

Households composition, income, benefits, and labor force status, Survey of Income and Program Participation methodology, working paper series, 2626–10

Households debt, and payment behavior and difficulties, by selected characteristics, 1980s-90, article, 9362–1.201

Student loan debt burden of 1986 college grads, by selected student characteristics and instn control, 1987, 4808–26

see also Consumer credit
see also Credit bureaus and agencies
see also Loans
see also Mortgages

Personal income

see Personal and household income

Personal property

see Housing tenure
see Land ownership and rights
see Ownership of enterprise
see Personal debt
see Property
see Savings
see Wealth

Personick, Martin E.

"Profiles in Safety and Health: Eating and Drinking Places", 6722–1.231

Personnel management

Fed Govt employee family-related and work schedule benefits, availability, admin, and personnel directors views, 1990 survey, 9496–2.7

Leave for illness, disability, and dependent care, coverage, provisions, terminations, costs, and methods of covering for absent worker, by firm size, 1988 survey, 9768–21

Minority Business Dev Centers mgmt and financial aid, and characteristics of businesses, by region and State, FY90, annual rpt, 2104–6

Recruiting tactics, including targeting of nontraditional applicant groups, 1988, 15496–1.12

Recruitment, hiring, compensation, and other employment practices of large firms, 1989 survey, GAO rpt, 26119–324

see also Employee development
see also Employee performance and appraisal

Peru

Agricultural exports of high-value commodities, indexes and sales by commodity, world area, and country, 1960s-86, 1528–323

Agricultural exports of US, impacts of foreign agricultural and trade policy, with data by commodity and country, 1989, annual rpt, 1924–8

Agricultural production, trade, and policies in foreign countries, summary data by country, 1989-90, annual factbook, 1924–12

Agricultural supply, demand, and market for US exports, with socioeconomic conditions, 1989 country rpt, 1526–6.14

Agricultural trade of US, by detailed commodity and country, 1989, annual rpt, 1524–8

Agricultural trade of US, by detailed commodity and country, 1990, semiannual rpt, 1522–4

AID economic aid to developing countries, obligations and disbursements by country, quarterly rpt, 9912–4

AID loans repayment status and terms by program and country, and status of predecessor agency loans, quarterly rpt, 9912–3

Cocaine production, acreage, and economic impacts of crop eradication and conversion to legitimate agricultural use, 1960s-87, 9918–19

Cocaine production, eradication, and legal use, worldwide and for South America, 1970s-80s, conf, 4498–74

Economic and military aid and loans from US and intl agencies, by program and country, FY46-90, annual rpt, 9914–5

Economic and social conditions of developing countries from 1960s, and Intl Dev Cooperation Agency and AID activities and funding, FY90-92, annual rpt, 9904–4

Economic conditions, policy, and trade practices, by country, 1988-90, annual rpt, 21384–5

Economic, population, and agricultural data, US and other aid sources, and AID activity, 1988 country rpt, 9916–12.26

Economic, social, political, and geographic summary data, by country, 1991, annual factbook, 9114–2

Exports and imports of US, by commodity and country, 1970-89, world area rpt, 9116–1.4

Exports and imports of US, by Harmonized System 6-digit commodity and country, 1990, annual rpt, 2424–13

Exports and imports of US, by selected country, country group, and commodity group, 1990, annual rpt, 2044–37

Exports and imports of US, by transport mode, country, and SITC 1- to 3-digit commodity, 1990, annual rpt, 2424–12

Exports of US, detailed Schedule B commodities with countries of destination, 1990, annual rpt, 2424–10

Grain production and needs, and related economic outlook, by world area and selected country, forecast 1990/91-1991/92, 1528–313

Pesticides

Human rights conditions in 170 countries, and US economic and military aid, 1990, annual rpt, 21384–3

Labor conditions, union coverage, and work accidents, 1991 annual country rpt, 6366–4.45

Military aid of US, arms sales, and training programs costs and budget requests, by program, world region, and country, FY90-92, annual rpt, 7144–13

Multinatl US firms and foreign affiliates finances and operations, by industry and world area of parent firm, 1989 benchmark survey, preliminary annual rpt, 2704–5

Multinatl US firms foreign affiliates, income statement items by country and world area, 1986, biennial article, 8302–2.212

UN voting record and share of votes in agreement with US, by issue, country, and world area, 1990, annual rpt, 7004–18

see also under By Foreign Country in the "Index by Categories"

Peru, Ind.

Wages by occupation, and benefits for office and plant workers, 1991 survey, periodic MSA rpt, 6785–3.7

Pesticides

Agricultural cooperatives, finances, operations, activities, and membership, 1950s-88, commodity rpt, 1126–1.6

Agricultural Outlook, production, prices, marketing, and trade, by commodity, forecast and current situation, monthly rpt with articles, 1502–4

Agriculture census, 1987: farms, farmland, production, finances, and operator characteristics, by county, final State rpt series, 2331–1

Agriculture census, 1987: horticultural specialties producers, finances, and operations, by crop and State, 1988 survey, 2337–1

Air pollution indoor levels in workplace, and health impacts, for Library of Congress Madison Building, 1989 study, series, 4248–92

Assistance (financial and nonfinancial) of Fed Govt, 1991 base edition with supplements, annual listing, 104–5

Cancer (non-Hodgkin's lymphoma) cases in areas using phenoxy herbicides, local area study, 1985-88, article, 4472–1.207

Canine lymphoma risk relation to herbicide exposure and other factors, and implications for humans, 1984-88, article, 4472–1.220

Coastal and estuarine pollutant concentrations in fish, shellfish, and environment, series, 2176–3

Cotton farms fertilizer, pesticide and irrigation use, soil conservation practices, and water quality impacts, 1989, 1588–151

Criminal cases by type and disposition, and collections, for US attorneys, by Federal district, FY90, annual rpt, 6004–2.1

Dicofol levels in soil, and in wildlife by species, with toxicity indicators, 1950s-87, technical rpt, 5506–12.2

Employment, earnings, and hours, by SIC 1- to 4-digit industry, monthly and annual averages, selected years 1909-90, annual rpt, 6744–4

Pesticides

Environmental Quality, status of problems, protection programs, research, and intl issues, 1991 annual rpt, 484–1

EPA pollution control grant program activities, monthly rpt, 9182–8

Exports and imports (agricultural) of US, by commodity and country, bimonthly rpt, 1522–1

Exports and imports (agricultural) of US, by detailed commodity and country, 1989, annual rpt, 1524–8

Exports and imports (agricultural) of US, by detailed commodity and country, 1990, semiannual rpt, 1522–4

Exports and imports of US, by country and detailed commodity, monthly rpt, 2422–12

Exports and imports of US, by Harmonized System 6-digit commodity and country, 1990, annual rpt, 2424–13

Exports and imports of US, by transport mode, country, and SITC 1- to 3-digit commodity, 1990, annual rpt, 2424–12

Exports of US, detailed Schedule B commodities with countries of destination, 1990, annual rpt, 2424–10

Farm fertilizer and pesticide use, and application rates, by type, crop, and State, series, 1616–1

Farm finances and environmental benefits of alternative policies to Food Security Act conservation programs, projected 1991-2005, 1588–153

Farm income, expenses, receipts by commodity, assets, liabilities, and ratios, 1990 and trends from 1945, annual rpt, 1544–16

Farm pesticide and fertilizer use reduction, environmental and economic impacts by commodity and region, alternative forecasts 1989-94, hearing, 23848–222

Farm prices received for major products and paid for farm inputs and living items, by commodity and State, monthly rpt, 1629–1

Farm production inputs, finances, mgmt, and land value and transfers, periodic situation rpt with articles, 1561–16

Farm production itemized costs, by farm sales size and region, 1990, annual rpt, 1614–3

Farm production itemized costs, receipts, and returns, by commodity and region, 1987-89, annual rpt, 1544–20

Fish kills in coastal areas related to pollution and natural causes, by land use, State, and county, 1980s, 2178–32

Food pesticide levels, comparison of US and UN standards, 1988-90, GAO rpt, 26131–88

Forest Service pesticides use and acreage treated, by product and purpose, FY90, annual rpt, 1204–1.2

Health effects of selected pollutants on animals by species and on humans, and environmental levels, series, 5506–14

Imports detained by FDA, by reason, product, shipper, brand, and country, monthly listing, 4062–2

Injuries from use of consumer products, by severity, victim age, and detailed product, 1990, annual rpt, 9164–6

Labor productivity, indexes of output, hours, and employment by SIC 2- to 4-digit industry, 1967-89, annual rpt, 6824–1.3

Manufacturing annual survey, 1989: finances and operations, by SIC 2- to 4-digit industry, series, 2506–15

Manufacturing census, 1987: finances and operations, by SIC 2- to 4-digit industry, State, and MSA, with trends from 1849, 2497–1

Manufacturing finances and operations, by SIC 2- to 4-digit industry, forecast 1991, annual rpt, 2044–28

New York Bight fish population and disease, and pollutant levels, near sewage sludge dumpsite, 1986-90, last issue of annual rpt, 2164–19

OECD trade, total and for 4 major countries, and US trade by country, by commodity, 1970-89, world area rpt series, 9116–1

Onion farm acreage, pesticide use, operators, and other characteristics, for 6 producer States, 1989, article, 1561–11.201

Pacific Ocean coast pollutant concentrations in fish and sediments, by contaminant, fish species, and site, 1984-86, 2168–121

Pollution (air) emissions factors, by detailed pollutant and source, data compilation, 1990 rpt, 9198–120

Pollution (groundwater) from farm chemicals use and animal wastes, and reduction strategies, 1960s-90, 26358–231

Pollution (groundwater) from farm chemicals use, with background data and farmers views, 1970s-80s, hearing, 25168–76

Price indexes (producer), by stage of processing and detailed commodity, monthly rpt, 6762–6

Price indexes (producer), by stage of processing and detailed commodity, monthly 1990, annual rpt, 6764–2

Prices received and paid by farmers, by commodity and State, 1990, annual rpt, 1629–5

Production, trade, and additives, by pesticide type, with manufacturers listing, 1987-89, annual rpt, 1804–5

Regulation of pesticides, economic impacts of revised EPA standards, with data for tomatoes, 1984-88, conf papers, 1588–154

Statistical Abstract of US, 1991 annual data compilation, 2324–1.6; 2324–1.23

Timber insect and disease incidence and damage, and control activities, State rpt series, 1206–49

Timber insect and disease incidence and damage, annual regional rpt series, 1206–11

Toxicology Natl Program research and testing activities, FY89 and planned FY90, annual rpt, 4044–16

Vegetable crops consumer and producer costs, impacts of proposed EBDC pesticide ban, 1985-89, article, 1561–11.204

Vegetable integrated pest mgmt programs acreage, costs, savings, and funding sources and recipients, by State, 1980s, 1568–298

Water (groundwater) supply, quality, chemistry, and use, State and local area rpt series, 5666–28

Water (groundwater) supply, quality, chemistry, other characteristics, and use, 1991 regional rpt, 5666–25.12

Index by Subjects and Names

Water pollution fish kills, by pollution source, month, location, and State, 1977-87, last issue of annual rpt, 9204–3

Water pollution industrial releases in wastewater, levels, treatment, costs, and regulation, with background financial and operating data, 1989 industry rpt, 9206–4.2

Water quality, chemistry, hydrology, and other characteristics, local area studies, series, 5666–27

Water supply and quality in streams and lakes, and groundwater levels in wells, by drainage basin, 1988, annual State rpt series, 5666–16

Water supply and quality in streams and lakes, and groundwater levels in wells, by drainage basin, 1989, annual State rpt series, 5666–12

Water supply and quality in streams and lakes, and groundwater levels in wells, by drainage basin, 1990, annual State rpt series, 5666–10

see also Dioxins

Pests and pest control

Agricultural research and education grants, USDA competitive awards by program and recipient, FY90, annual listing, 1764–1

Agricultural research funding and staffing for USDA, State agencies, and other instns, by topic, FY90, annual rpt, 1744–2

Agricultural research grants of USDA, by program, subagency, and country, FY90, annual listing, 1954–3

Cheatgrass invasion and related fire threat in western US shrublands, 1989 conf papers, 1208–351

County Business Patterns, 1988: employment, establishments, and payroll, by SIC 2- to 4-digit industry and county, annual State rpt series, 2326–6

County Business Patterns, 1989: employment, establishments, and payroll, by SIC 2- to 4-digit industry and county, annual State rpt series, 2326–8

Foreign countries disasters, casualties, damage, and aid by US and others, FY90 and trends from FY64, annual rpt, 9914–12

Forest Service acreage, staff, finances, and mgmt activities in Pacific Northwest, with data by forest, 1970s-89, annual rpt, 1204–37

Forest Service mgmt of public lands and resources dev, environmental, economic, and social impacts of alternative programs, projected to 2040, 1208–24

Gypsy moth infestation in Tennessee, timber at risk, by county, 1989, 1208–344

Housing and neighborhood quality, indicators and attitudes, by householder type and location, for 11 MSAs, 1984 survey, supplement, 2485–8

Housing and neighborhood quality, indicators and attitudes, by householder type and location, 1987, biennial rpt supplement, 2485–13

Housing and neighborhood quality, indicators and attitudes, by householder type and location, 1989, biennial rpt, 2485–12

Housing and neighborhood quality, indicators and attitudes, MSA surveys, series, 2485–6

Index by Subjects and Names

Imports detained by FDA, by reason, product, shipper, brand, and country, monthly listing, 4062–2

Puerto Rico economic censuses, 1987: wholesale and retail trade and service industry finances and operations, by SIC 2- to 4-digit industry and municipio, 2591–1

Receipts for services, by SIC 2- to 4-digit kind of business, 1990, annual rpt, 2413–8

Service industries census, 1987: establishments, receipts by source, payroll, and employment, by SIC 2- to 4-digit kind of business, State, and MSA, 2393–4

Soil mgmt and characteristics, for western mountain forest areas, 1990 conf, 1208–378

Sugarcane clones yields, stability, and fungi resistance, 1990/91, annual rpt, 1704–2

Timber in Yellowstone Natl Park area, insect infestation and damage following 1988 forest fires, 1989-90, 1208–379

Timber insect and disease incidence and damage, and control activities, State rpt series, 1206–49

Timber insect and disease incidence and damage, annual regional rpt series, 1206–11

Vegetable integrated pest mgmt programs acreage, costs, savings, and funding sources and recipients, by State, 1980s, 1568–298

see also Pesticides

Pet food and supplies

County Business Patterns, 1989: employment, establishments, and payroll, by SIC 2- to 4-digit industry and county, annual State rpt series, 2326–8

CPI by component for US city average, and by region, population size, and for 27 metro areas, monthly rpt, 6762–2

Exports and imports (agricultural) of US, by detailed commodity and country, 1990, semiannual rpt, 1522–4

Exports and imports between US and outlying areas, by detailed commodity and mode of transport, 1990, annual rpt, 2424–11

Exports and imports of US, by Harmonized System 6-digit commodity and country, 1990, annual rpt, 2424–13

Exports of US, detailed Schedule B commodities with countries of destination, 1990, annual rpt, 2424–10

Injuries from use of consumer products, by severity, victim age, and detailed product, 1990, annual rpt, 9164–6

Price indexes (producer), by stage of processing and detailed commodity, monthly rpt, 6762–6

Price indexes (producer), by stage of processing and detailed commodity, monthly 1990, annual rpt, 6764–2

Petaluma, Calif.

see also under By SMSA or MSA in the "Index by Categories"

Peterkin, Betty B.

"Dietary Guidelines for Americans, 1990 Revision", 1004–16.1

Petersburg, Va.

Wages by occupation, for office and plant workers, 1991 survey, periodic MSA rpt, 6785–12.5

see also under By SMSA or MSA in the "Index by Categories"

Petersen, Bruce C.

"Cyclicality of Cash Flow and Investment in U.S. Manufacturing", 9375–1.202

"Investment Smoothing with Working Capital: New Evidence on the Impact of Financial Constraints", 9375–13.49

Peterson, R. Neal

"Single Equation Approach to Estimating Nonstationary Markov Matrices: The Case of U.S. Agriculture, 1974-78", 1548–374

Petrochemicals

Consumption of fossil fuel by end use, and trade, by type, 1990 and trends from 1949, annual rpt, 3164–74.1; 3164–74.2

County Business Patterns, 1988: employment, establishments, and payroll, by SIC 2- to 4-digit industry and county, annual State rpt series, 2326–6

County Business Patterns, 1989: employment, establishments, and payroll, by SIC 2- to 4-digit industry and county, annual State rpt series, 2326–8

Exports and imports between US and outlying areas, by detailed commodity and mode of transport, 1990, annual rpt, 2424–11

Exports and imports of US, by country and detailed commodity, monthly rpt, 2422–12

Exports and imports of US, by Harmonized System 6-digit commodity and country, 1990, annual rpt, 2424–13

Exports and imports of US, by transport mode, country, and SITC 1- to 3-digit commodity, 1990, annual rpt, 2424–12

Exports of US, detailed Schedule B commodities with countries of destination, 1990, annual rpt, 2424–10

Manufacturing annual survey, 1989: finances and operations, by SIC 2- to 4-digit industry, series, 2506–15

Manufacturing census, 1987: finances and operations, by SIC 2- to 4-digit industry, State, and MSA, with trends from 1849, 2497–1

Manufacturing finances and operations, by SIC 2- to 4-digit industry, forecast 1991, annual rpt, 2044–28

Occupational injury and illness rates, by SIC 2- to 4-digit industry, 1988-89, annual rpt, 6844–7

Occupational injury and illness rates, by SIC 2- to 4-digit industry, 1989, annual rpt, 6844–1

Pollution (air) emissions factors, by detailed pollutant and source, data compilation, 1990 rpt, 9198–120

Price indexes (producer), by stage of processing and detailed commodity, monthly rpt, 6762–6

Price indexes (producer), by stage of processing and detailed commodity, monthly 1990, annual rpt, 6764–2

Prices and spending for fuel, by type, end-use sector, and State, 1989, annual rpt, 3164–64

Production, dev, and distribution firms revenues and income, quarterly rpt, 3162–38

Production of synthetic organic chemicals, by detailed product, quarterly rpt, 9882–1

Petroleum and petroleum industry

Supply, demand, and movement of crude oil, gas liquids, and refined products, by PAD district and State, 1990, annual rpt, 3164–2

Supply, demand, and prices, by fuel type and end-use sector, alternative projections 1989-2010, annual rpt, 3164–75

Supply, demand, and prices of crude oil and refined products, and refinery capacity and stocks, by State, 1960-91, annual rpt, 3164–95

Supply, demand, trade, stocks, and refining of oil and gas liquids, by detailed product, State, and PAD district, monthly rpt with articles, 3162–6

Tax (excise) on hazardous waste generation and disposal, rates, and firms filing returns, by substance type, 1988, annual article, 8302–2.202

see also under By Commodity in the "Index by Categories"

Petroleum and petroleum industry

Agriculture census, 1987: farms, farmland, production, finances, and operator characteristics, by county, final State rpt series, 2331–1

Alaska North Slope oil production, and impacts of lifting export controls on US oil trade, West Coast prices, and shipping industry, 1988 and forecast 1995, GAO rpt, 26113–496

American Samoa employment, earnings, and minimum wage, by establishment and industry, 1989, biennial rpt, 6504–6

Business statistics, detailed data for major industries and economic indicators, *Survey of Current Business*, monthly rpt, 2702–1.18

Capital expenditures for plant and equipment, by major industry group, quarterly rpt, 2502–2

China economic indicators and reform issues, with background data, 1950s-90, compilation of papers, 23848–155

Collective bargaining agreements expiring during year, and workers covered, by firm, union, industry group, and State, 1991, annual rpt, 6784–9

Consumption of energy, by air pollutant source, fuel type, and State, annual rpt, discontinued, 9194–14

Consumption of energy, by detailed fuel type, end-use sector, and State, 1960-89, State Energy Data System annual rpt, 3164–39

County Business Patterns, 1988: employment, establishments, and payroll, by SIC 2- to 4-digit industry and county, annual State rpt series, 2326–6

County Business Patterns, 1989: employment, establishments, and payroll, by SIC 2- to 4-digit industry and county, annual State rpt series, 2326–8

Developing countries energy use, and economic and environmental impacts, by fuel type, world area, and country, 1980s-90, 26358–232

DOD prime contract awards, by category, contractor type, and State, FY88-90, annual rpt, 3544–11

DOD prime contract awards, by size and type of contract, service branch, competitive status, category, and labor standard, FY90, annual rpt, 3544–19

Petroleum and petroleum industry

Electric power and industrial plants prohibited from oil and gas primary use, and gas use by State, 1977-90, annual rpt, 3334–1

Electric power plants (steam) fuel receipts, costs, and quality, by fuel, plant, utility, and State, 1990, annual rpt, 3164–42

Electric power plants and capacity, by fuel used, owner, location, and operating status, 1990 and for units planned 1991-2000, annual listing, 3164–36

Electric power plants production and capacity by fuel type, prices, demand, and air pollution law impacts, by region, 1989-90 and projected to 2010, annual rpt, 3164–81

Electric power plants production and capital costs, operations, and fuel use, by fuel type, plant, utility, and location, 1989, annual rpt, 3164–9

Electric power plants production, capacity, sales, and fuel stocks, use, and costs, by State, 1985-89, annual rpt, 3164–11

Electric power plants production, fuel use, stocks, and costs by fuel type, and sales, by State, monthly rpt with articles, 3162–35

Employment, earnings, and hours, by SIC 1- to 4-digit industry, monthly and annual averages, selected years 1909-90, annual rpt, 6744–4

Employment in manufacturing, by detailed occupation and SIC 2-digit industry, 1989 survey, triennial rpt, 6748–52

Enterprise Statistics, 1987: finances and operations for companies, by size, level of diversification, form of organization, and industry group, 2329–8

Environmental Quality, status of problems, protection programs, research, and intl issues, 1991 annual rpt, 484–1

Farm income, expenses, receipts by commodity, assets, liabilities, and ratios, 1990 and trends from 1945, annual rpt, 1544–16

Farm production itemized costs, by farm sales size and region, 1990, annual rpt, 1614–3

Finances and operations, by SIC 2- to 4-digit industry, forecast 1991, annual rpt, 2044–28

Finances and operations of energy producers, by energy type for US firms domestic and foreign operations, 1989, annual rpt, 3164–44

Foreign and US economic conditions, for major industrial countries, biweekly rpt, 9112–1

Foreign and US energy production, trade, use, and reserves, and oil and refined products supply and prices, by country, 1980-89, annual rpt, 3164–50

Foreign and US energy use and production, by fuel type, country, and country group, projected 1995-2010 and trends from 1970, annual rpt, 3164–84

Foreign and US oil dependency, energy demand, and efficiency measures, for 6 OECD countries, 1970s-88, article, 9375–1.210

Foreign and US oil production, trade, and use, by country group and selected country, monthly rpt, 9112–2

Foreign and US oil production, trade, use, and stocks, by country group and selected country, monthly rpt, 3162–42

Foreign countries economic conditions, policy, and trade practices, by country, 1988-90, annual rpt, 21384–5

Foreign countries oil and gas reserves and discoveries, by country and country group, quarterly rpt, 3162–43

Foreign direct investment in US, by industry group and world area, 1987-90, annual article, 2702–1.219

Foreign direct investment in US, by industry group of US affiliate and country of parent firm, 1980-86, 2708–41

Foreign direct investment in US energy sources by type and firm, and US affiliates operations, as of 1989, annual rpt, 3164–80

Foreign direct investment of US, by industry group and world area, 1987-90, annual article, 2702–1.220

Futures market dev for energy, and crude oil contract activity, Aug 1990, article, 3162–11.201

Heating fuels production, imports, stocks, and prices, by selected PAD district and State, seasonal weekly rpt, 3162–45

Hwy construction material use by type, and spending, by State, various periods 1944-90, annual rpt, 7554–29

Injuries from use of consumer products, related deaths and costs, and recalls by brand, by product type, FY89, annual rpt, 9164–2

Input-output structure of US economy, detailed interindustry transactions for 84 industries, and components of final demand, 1986, annual article, 2702–1.206

Input-output structure of US economy, detailed interindustry transactions for 85 industries, 1982 benchmark data, 2702–1.213

Iraq invasion of Kuwait, impacts on oil prices and industry profits, as of 4th qtr 1990, 3166–6.46

Iraq invasion of Kuwait, impacts on oil supply and prices, selected indicators, daily press release, 3162–44

Iraq invasion of Kuwait, oil embargo impacts on OPEC and US oil supply and industry, 1989-91, hearing, 21368–132

Labor productivity, indexes of output, hours, and employment by SIC 2- to 4-digit industry, 1967-89, annual rpt, 6824–1.3

Manufacturing annual survey, 1989: finances and operations, by SIC 2- to 4-digit industry, series, 2506–15

Manufacturing census, 1987: employment and shipments under Fed Govt contracts, by SIC 4-digit industry, 2497–7

Manufacturing census, 1987: finances and operations, by SIC 2- to 4-digit industry, State, and MSA, with trends from 1849, 2497–1

Manufacturing census, 1987: finances and operations, by type of organization and SIC 2- to 4-digit industry, subject rpt, 2497–5

Manufacturing corporations financial statements, by selected SIC 2- to 3-digit industry, quarterly rpt, 2502–1

Manufacturing energy use and prices, 1988 survey, series, 3166–13

Manufacturing production, shipments, inventories, orders, and pollution control costs, periodic Current Industrial Rpt series, 2506–3

Index by Subjects and Names

Military and personal property shipments, passenger traffic, and costs, by service branch and mode of transport, quarterly rpt, 3702–1

Military Sealift Command shipping operations, finances, and personnel, FY90, annual rpt, 3804–14

Mineral industries census, 1987: energy use and costs, by fuel type, SIC 2- to 4-digit industry, and State, subject rpt, 2517–2

Mineral industries census, 1987: finances and operations, by SIC 2- to 4-digit industry, State, and county, census div rpt series, 2515–1

Minerals Yearbook, 1988, Vol 3: foreign country reviews of production, trade, and policy, by commodity, annual rpt series, 5604–17

Multinatl firms US affiliates, finances, and operations, by industry, world area of parent firm, and State, 1988-89, annual rpt, 2704–4

Multinatl US firms and foreign affiliates finances and operations, by industry and world area of parent firm, 1989 benchmark survey, preliminary annual rpt, 2704–5

Natl Energy Strategy plans for conservation and pollution reduction, impacts on electric power supply, costs, and emissions, projected under alternative assumptions, 1995-2030, 3166–6.49

North Carolina environmental and socioeconomic conditions, and impacts of proposed OCS oil and gas exploration, 1970s-90 and projected to 2020, 5738–22

Occupational injury and illness rates, by SIC 2- to 4-digit industry, 1988-89, annual rpt, 6844–7

Occupational injury and illness rates, by SIC 2- to 4-digit industry, 1989, annual rpt, 6844–1

Pollution (air) abatement equipment shipments by industry, and new and backlog orders, by product, 1990, annual Current Industrial Rpt, 2506–12.5

Pollution (air) contributing to global warming, emissions factors and control costs, by pollutant and source, 1990 rpt, 9198–124

Pollution (air) emissions factors, by detailed pollutant and source, data compilation, 1990 rpt, 9198–120

Pollution (water) industrial releases in wastewater, levels, treatment, costs, and regulation, with background financial and operating data, 1989 industry rpt, 9206–4.6

Pollution abatement capital and operating costs, by SIC 2-digit industry, 1989, advance annual Current Industrial Rpt, 2506–3.6

Production and reserves of oil and gas, and coal production, by major country and world area, late 1930s-90, article, 9371–1.213

Production and reserves of oil, gas, and gas liquids, by State and substate area, 1990, annual rpt, 3164–46

Production, dev, and distribution firms revenues and income, quarterly rpt, 3162–38

Production of oil relation to prices and other factors for OPEC and non-OPEC countries, alternative model results, 1970s-80s, technical paper, 9379–12.68

Index by Subjects and Names

Petroleum exports and imports

Puerto Rico and other US possessions corporations income tax returns, income and tax items, and employment, by selected industry, 1987, article, 8302–2.213

Puerto Rico economic censuses, 1987: wholesale and retail trade and service industry finances and operations, by SIC 2- to 4-digit industry and municipio, 2591–1

Puerto Rico economic censuses, 1987: wholesale, retail, and service industries finances and operations, by establishment characteristics and SIC 2- and 3-digit industry, subject rpts, 2591–2

Purchases and sales of oil products by refiners, processors, and distributors, by product, end-use sector, PAD district, and State, monthly rpt with articles, 3162–11

Refinery operations and finances, with ownership changes, shutdowns, and reactivations, by firm, 1970s-90, 3168–119

Soviet Union, Eastern Europe, OECD, and selected other countries energy reserves, production, and use, and oil trade and revenue, 1960s-90, annual rpt, 9114–4.4

Soviet Union oil production, exports, and investments, 1980s and projected to 1994, GAO rpt, 26123–349

State and Metro Area Data Book, 1991 data compilation, 2328–54

Statistical Abstract of US, 1991 annual data compilation, 2324–1.19; 2324–1.25

Supply and demand of oil and refined products, refinery capacity and use, and prices, weekly rpt, 3162–32

Supply, demand, and distribution of energy, and regulatory impacts, series, 3166–6

Supply, demand, and movement of crude oil, gas liquids, and refined products, by PAD district and State, 1990, annual rpt, 3164–2

Supply, demand, and prices, by fuel type and end-use sector, alternative projections 1989-2010, annual rpt, 3164–75

Supply, demand, and prices, by fuel type and end-use sector, projections and underlying assumptions, 1990-2010, annual rpt, 3164–90

Supply, demand, and prices, by fuel type and end-use sector, with foreign comparisons, 1990 and trends from 1949, annual rpt, 3164–74

Supply, demand, and prices, by fuel type, end-use sector, and country, detailed data, monthly rpt with articles, 3162–24

Supply, demand, and prices of crude oil and refined products, and refinery capacity and stocks, by State, 1960-91, annual rpt, 3164–95

Supply, demand, and prices of energy, forecasts by resource type, quarterly rpt, 3162–34

Supply, demand, and prices of oil and gas, alternative projections 1989-2010, annual rpt, 3164–89

Supply, demand, trade, stocks, and refining of oil and gas liquids, by detailed product, State, and PAD district, monthly rpt with articles, 3162–6

Tax (excise) on hazardous waste generation and disposal, rates, and firms filing returns, by substance type, 1988, annual article, 8302–2.202

Tax (income) returns of corporations, income and tax items by asset size and detailed industry, 1988, annual rpt, 8304–21

Tax (income) returns of corporations with foreign tax credit, income and tax items by industry group, 1986, biennial article, 8302–2.203

Tax (income) returns of multinatl US firms foreign affiliates, income statement items, by asset size and industry, 1986, biennial article, 8302–2.212

Underground storage of oil and other hazardous substances, systems and facilities subject to EPA regulation, as of 1988, article, 3162–6.203

Underground storage of oil, Federal trust fund for leaking tanks, financial condition, monthly rpt, 8102–9.11

Water (groundwater) supply, quality, chemistry, other characteristics, and use, regional rpt series, 5666–25

Wholesale trade census, 1987: depreciable assets, capital and operating expenses, sales, value added, and inventories, by SIC 2- to 3-digit kind of business, 2407–2

Wholesale trade census, 1987: finances and operations by SIC 2- to 4-digit kind of business, and oil bulk station operations by State, 2407–4

Wholesale trade sales and inventories, by SIC 2- to 3-digit kind of business, monthly rpt, 2413–7

Wholesale trade sales, inventories, purchases, and gross margins, by SIC 2- to 3-digit kind of business, 1990, annual rpt, 2413–13

see also Asphalt and tar
see also Aviation fuels
see also Diesel fuel
see also Energy exploration and drilling
see also Fuel oil
see also Gasoline
see also Gasoline service stations
see also Kerosene
see also Liquefied petroleum gas
see also Motor fuels
see also Natural gas and gas industry
see also Naval Petroleum Reserves
see also Offshore oil and gas
see also Oil and gas leases
see also Oil depletion allowances
see also Oil shale
see also Oil spills
see also Organization of Petroleum Exporting Countries
see also Petrochemicals
see also Petroleum exports and imports
see also Petroleum prices
see also Petroleum reserves
see also Petroleum stocks
see also Pipelines
see also Strategic Petroleum Reserve
see also Synthetic fuels
see also Tar sands
see also Windfall profit tax
see also under By Commodity in the "Index by Categories"
see also under By Industry in the "Index by Categories"

Petroleum exports and imports

Alaska North Slope oil production, and impacts of lifting export controls on US oil trade, West Coast prices, and shipping industry, 1988 and forecast 1995, GAO rpt, 26113–496

Business statistics, detailed data for major industries and economic indicators, *Survey of Current Business*, monthly rpt, 2702–1.18

Economic and employment conditions, alternative BLS projections to 2005 and trends 1970s-90, biennial article, 6722–1.251

Exports and imports between US and outlying areas, by detailed commodity and mode of transport, 1990, annual rpt, 2424–11

Exports and imports of US, by country and detailed commodity, monthly rpt, 2422–12

Exports and imports of US, by Harmonized System 6-digit commodity and country, 1990, annual rpt, 2424–13

Exports and imports of US, by selected country, country group, and commodity group, 1990, annual rpt, 2044–37

Exports and imports of US, by transport mode, country, and SITC 1- to 3-digit commodity, 1990, annual rpt, 2424–12

Exports, imports, production, and use, by country group and selected country, monthly rpt, 9112–2

Exports, imports, production, use, and stocks of oil, by country group and selected country, monthly rpt, 3162–42

Exports of US, detailed Schedule B commodities with countries of destination, 1990, annual rpt, 2424–10

Foreign and US oil production, trade, and stocks, by product and country, 1986-89, annual rpt, 3164–50.2

Gasohol trade, use, prices, efficiency, and specifications, by type, annual rpt, 3304–5.4

Heating fuels production, imports, stocks, and prices, by selected PAD district and State, seasonal weekly rpt, 3162–45

Imports, exports, and employment impacts, by SIC 2- to 4-digit industry and commodity, quarterly rpt, 2322–2

Imports of oil and refined products, *Survey of Current Business*, monthly rpt, 2702–1.2

Imports of oil, traffic by US port and vessel type, marine oil pollution sources, and costs and operations of proposed offshore terminals, late 1980s, 5738–25

Intl transactions summary, 1980s-90, annual article, 9362–1.202

Iraq invasion of Kuwait, impacts on oil supply and prices, selected indicators, daily press release, 3162–44

Iraq invasion of Kuwait, oil embargo impacts on OPEC and US oil supply and industry, 1989-91, hearing, 21368–132

Latin America energy use and trade, by selected country, 1970s-80s and projected to 2000, 3408–1

Mexico imports from US, by industry and State, 1987-90, 2048–154

Minerals Yearbook, 1988, Vol 3: foreign country reviews of production, trade, and policy, by commodity, annual rpt series, 5604–17

Natl Energy Strategy plans for conservation and pollution reduction, impacts of technology and regulation proposals, projected 1990-2030, 3166–6.47

OECD intl trade position for US and 4 countries, and factors affecting US competition, periodic pamphlet, 2042–25

Petroleum exports and imports

OECD trade, total and for 4 major countries, and US trade by country, by commodity, 1970-89, world area rpt series, 9116–1

Price indexes for exports and imports, by selected end-use category, monthly press release, 6762–15

Soviet Union, Eastern Europe, OECD, and selected other countries energy reserves, production, and use, and oil trade and revenue, 1960s-90, annual rpt, 9114–4.4

Soviet Union oil production, exports, and investments, 1980s and projected to 1994, GAO rpt, 26123–349

Statistical Abstract of US, 1991 annual data compilation, 2324–1.19

Strategic Petroleum Reserve oil deliveries, by country and State of origin, quarterly rpt, annual data, 3002–13

Supply and demand of oil and refined products, refinery capacity and use, and prices, weekly rpt, 3162–32

Supply, demand, and movement of crude oil, gas liquids, and refined products, by PAD district and State, 1990, annual rpt, 3164–2

Supply, demand, and prices, by fuel type and end-use sector, alternative projections 1989-2010, annual rpt, 3164–75

Supply, demand, and prices, by fuel type and end-use sector, with foreign comparisons, 1990 and trends from 1949, annual rpt, 3164–74

Supply, demand, and prices, by fuel type, end-use sector, and country, detailed data, monthly rpt with articles, 3162–24

Supply, demand, and prices of crude oil and refined products, and refinery capacity and stocks, by State, 1960-91, annual rpt, 3164–95

Supply, demand, and prices of energy, forecasts by resource type, quarterly rpt, 3162–34

Supply, demand, and prices of oil and gas, alternative projections 1989-2010, annual rpt, 3164–89

Supply, demand, trade, stocks, and refining of oil and gas liquids, by detailed product, State, and PAD district, monthly rpt with articles, 3162–6

Tariffs and excise taxes on oil imports, economic impacts, model description and results, 1991 paper, 9406–1.61

Taxes on energy, economic and energy demand impacts of alternative taxation methods, projected 1991-2000, 3166–6.57

Petroleum prices

Airline fuel prices for domestic and intl operations, quarterly rpt, 7502–16

Alaska minerals resources, production, oil and gas leases, reserves, and exploratory wells, with maps and bibl, 1989, annual rpt, 5664–11

Alaska North Slope oil production, and impacts of lifting export controls on US oil trade, West Coast prices, and shipping industry, 1988 and forecast 1995, GAO rpt, 26113–496

Alcohol (methanol) use in autos, oil price and economic impacts, 1990 technical paper, 9379–12.62

Business statistics, detailed data for major industries and economic indicators, *Survey of Current Business*, monthly rpt, 2702–1.18

Conservation measures impacts on energy consumption, by component and end-use sector, 1970s-88 and projected under alternative oil prices to 1995, 3308–93

CPI by component for US city average, and by region, population size, and for 27 metro areas, monthly rpt, 6762–2

Electric power plants (steam) fuel receipts, costs, and quality, by fuel, plant, utility, and State, 1990, annual rpt, 3164–42

Electric power plants production, capacity, sales, and fuel stocks, use, and costs, by State, 1985-89, annual rpt, 3164–11

Electric power plants production, fuel use, stocks, and costs by fuel type, and sales, by State, monthly rpt with articles, 3162–35

Farm diesel and other fuel costs, impacts of oil price increases, 1989, article, 1541–1.203

Farm prices received and paid, by commodity and State, 1990, annual rpt, 1629–5

Farm prices received for major products and paid for farm inputs and living items, by commodity and State, monthly rpt, 1629–1

Farm production inputs supply, demand, and prices, 1970s-90 and projected to 1995, article, 1561–16.201

Farm production inputs supply, demand, and prices, 1980s-91 and forecast 1992, article, 1561–16.204

Food marketing cost indexes, by expense category, monthly rpt with articles, 1502–4

Foreign and US energy use and production, by fuel type, country, and country group, projected 1995-2010 and trends from 1970, annual rpt, 3164–84

Foreign and US oil prices, by refined product and country, 1980-89, annual rpt, 3164–50.6

Foreign countries transportation energy use, fuel prices, vehicle registrations, and mileage, by selected country, 1970s-89, annual rpt, 3304–5.1

Gasoline retail price response to wholesale price changes, by grade, 1983-90, article, 9391–1.216

Gasoline supply, demand, prices, taxes, and auto registrations and mileage, 1900s-89, 3168–120

Heating fuels production, imports, stocks, and prices, by selected PAD district and State, seasonal weekly rpt, 3162–45

Housing energy prices, by fuel and State, 1989 and forecast 1990-91, 3166–6.54

Import and export price indexes, by selected end-use category, monthly press release, 6762–15

Iraq invasion of Kuwait, impacts on oil prices and industry profits, as of 4th qtr 1990, 3166–6.46

Iraq invasion of Kuwait, impacts on oil supply and prices, selected indicators, daily press release, 3162–44

Iraq invasion of Kuwait, oil embargo impacts on OPEC and US oil supply and industry, 1989-91, hearing, 21368–132

Natl Energy Strategy plans for conservation and pollution reduction, impacts of technology and regulation proposals, projected 1990-2030, 3166–6.47

Index by Subjects and Names

Naval Petroleum and Oil Shale Reserves sales and contract prices, by purchaser and reserve, FY90, annual rpt, 3334–3

OPEC and world crude oil prices, 1973-90, annual rpt, 9114–4.2

OPEC oil sales price, biweekly rpt, 9112–1

Overcharge settlements, use in low income energy assistance, by State, FY89, annual rpt, 4694–8

Persian Gulf War impacts on US economic conditions compared to previous oil shock periods, and Saudi Arabia oil production and prices, 1990-92, hearings, 21248–156

Prices and spending for fuel, by type, end-use sector, and State, 1989, annual rpt, 3164–64

Prices of imported and domestic oil and wholesale and retail fuels, and dealer margins, monthly rpt, 3162–24.9

Prices of oil and refined products, spot market, OPEC, non-OPEC, and refiners costs, weekly rpt, 3162–32

Prices, supply, and demand, by fuel type and end-use sector, alternative projections 1989-2010, annual rpt, 3164–75

Prices, supply, and demand, by fuel type and end-use sector, projections and underlying assumptions, 1990-2010, annual rpt, 3164–90

Prices, supply, and demand, by fuel type and end-use sector, with foreign comparisons, 1990 and trends from 1949, annual rpt, 3164–74

Prices, supply, and demand of energy, forecasts by resource type, quarterly rpt, 3162–34

Prices, supply, and demand of oil and gas, alternative projections 1989-2010, annual rpt, 3164–89

Producer price indexes, by stage of processing and detailed commodity, monthly rpt, 6762–6

Producer price indexes, by stage of processing and detailed commodity, monthly 1990, annual rpt, 6764–2

Refined product prices and sales volume, 1988-89, annual rpt, 3164–44.3

Refiners, processors, and distributors sales and purchases, by product, end-use sector, PAD district, and State, monthly rpt with articles, 3162–11

Refinery operations and finances, with ownership changes, shutdowns, and reactivations, by firm, 1970s-90, 3168–119

Statistical Abstract of US, 1991 annual data compilation, 2324–1.15

Stock price volatility relation to interest rates, oil and gold prices, and US money supply, for 10 countries, model description and results, 1970s-88, working paper, 9381–10.116

Supply, demand, and prices of crude oil and refined products, and refinery capacity and stocks, by State, 1960-91, annual rpt, 3164–95

Texas (west) crude oil prices, quarterly rpt, 9381–16.2

Transportation energy use by mode, fuel supply, and demographic and economic factors of vehicle use, 1970s-89, annual rpt, 3304–5.2

Index by Subjects and Names

Pharmaceutical industry

Petroleum reserves

Alaska minerals resources, production, oil and gas leases, reserves, and exploratory wells, with maps and bibl, 1989, annual rpt, 5664–11

Alaska socioeconomic impacts of OCS oil resources dev, 1980-89 and projected to 2020, 5736–5.11

Field codes and locations, for oil and gas, 1990, annual listing, 3164–70

Florida environmental, social, and economic conditions, and impacts of proposed OCS oil and gas leases in southern coastal areas, 1990 compilation of papers, 5738–19

Foreign and US energy reserves, by type of fuel and country, as of Jan 1990, annual rpt, 3164–50.7

Foreign countries oil and gas reserves and discoveries, by country and country group, quarterly rpt, 3162–43

Gulf of Mexico oil and gas reserves, production, and leasing status, by location, 1989, annual rpt, 5734–6

Minerals Yearbook, 1988, Vol 3: foreign country reviews of production, trade, and policy, by commodity, annual rpt series, 5604–17

Natl Energy Strategy, oil and gas reserves, 1988 and projected under alternative technology and policy assumptions to 2030, 3166–6.51

Natl Energy Strategy plans for conservation and pollution reduction, impacts of technology and regulation proposals, projected 1990-2030, 3166–6.47

Offshore oil and gas leases environmental and socioeconomic impact, and coastal area description, final statement series, 5736–1

Offshore oil and gas reserves, and leasing and dev activity, periodic regional rpt series, 5736–3

Offshore oil and gas reserves of Fed Govt, production, leasing and exploration activity, revenue, and costs, by ocean area, FY90, annual rpt, 5734–4

Offshore oil and gas reserves on Federal leases, by ocean area, 1980-90, annual rpt, 5734–3.5

Pacific Ocean oil and gas production, reserves, and wells drilled by location, 1989, annual rpt, 5734–7

Producers finances and operations, by energy type for US firms domestic and foreign operations, 1989, annual rpt, 3164–44.2

Public lands minerals resources and availability, State rpt series, 5606–7

Research on enhanced oil recovery under DOE contract, project summaries, funding, and bibl, quarterly rpt, 3002–14

Reserves and production of oil, gas, and gas liquids, by State and substate area, 1990, annual rpt, 3164–46

Resources of economically recoverable conventional oil and gas in US, by region and probability level, as of Dec 1986 and 1988, annual rpt, 3164–89

Soviet Union, Eastern Europe, OECD, and selected other countries energy reserves, production, and use, and oil trade and revenue, 1960s-90, annual rpt, 9114–4.4

State and Metro Area Data Book, 1991 data compilation, 2328–54

Supply, demand, and prices, by fuel type and end-use sector, projections and underlying assumptions, 1990-2010, annual rpt, 3164–90

Supply, demand, and prices, by fuel type and end-use sector, with foreign comparisons, 1990 and trends from 1949, annual rpt, 3164–74

Supply, demand, and prices of crude oil and refined products, and refinery capacity and stocks, by State, 1960-91, annual rpt, 3164–95

see also Natural gas reserves

see also Naval Petroleum Reserves

see also Strategic Petroleum Reserve

Petroleum stocks

Business statistics, detailed data for major industries and economic indicators, *Survey of Current Business*, monthly rpt, 2702–1.18

Electric power plants production, capacity, sales, and fuel stocks, use, and costs, by State, 1985-89, annual rpt, 3164–11

Electric power plants production, fuel use, stocks, and costs by fuel type, and sales, by State, monthly rpt with articles, 3162–35

Heating fuels production, imports, stocks, and prices, by selected PAD district and State, seasonal weekly rpt, 3162–45

Iraq invasion of Kuwait, impacts on oil supply and prices, selected indicators, daily press release, 3162–44

Manufacturing storage capacity for fuel oil and liquefied petroleum gas, by industry, 1988 survey, 3166–13.5

OECD oil crude and refined products stocks, quarterly 1986-89, annual rpt, 3164–50.2

OECD oil stocks, for US and 16 countries, monthly rpt, 9112–2

OECD oil stocks, monthly rpt, 3162–42

Refinery operations and finances, with ownership changes, shutdowns, and reactivations, by firm, 1970s-90, 3168–119

Supply and demand of oil and refined products, refinery capacity and use, and prices, weekly rpt, 3162–32

Supply, demand, and movement of crude oil, gas liquids, and refined products, by PAD district and State, 1990, annual rpt, 3164–2

Supply, demand, and prices, by fuel type and end-use sector, alternative projections 1989-2010, annual rpt, 3164–75

Supply, demand, and prices, by fuel type and end-use sector, with foreign comparisons, 1990 and trends from 1949, annual rpt, 3164–74.2

Supply, demand, and prices, by fuel type, end-use sector, and country, detailed data, monthly rpt with articles, 3162–24

Supply, demand, and prices of crude oil and refined products, and refinery capacity and stocks, by State, 1960-91, annual rpt, 3164–95

Supply, demand, and prices of energy, forecasts by resource type, quarterly rpt, 3162–34

Supply, demand, trade, stocks, and refining of oil and gas liquids, by detailed product, State, and PAD district, monthly rpt with articles, 3162–6

Wholesale trade census, 1987: oil bulk stations, sales and storage capacity by product, inventories, expenses, employment, and modes of transport, 2407–4.2

see also Naval Petroleum Reserves

see also Strategic Petroleum Reserve

Petroni, Rita

"Nonresponse Research for the Survey of Income and Program Participation", 2626–10.118

Pets

Franchise business opportunities by firm and kind of business, and sources of aid and info, 1990 annual listing, 2104–7

Retail trade census, 1987: finances and employment, for establishments with and without payroll, by SIC 2- to 4-digit kind of business, State, and MSA, 2401–1

Statistical Abstract of US, 1991 annual data compilation, 2324–1.7

see also Pet food and supplies

Pham-Thi, Hop

"Energy Profiles of Czechoslovakia, Hungary and Poland, and Their Emerging Free-Market Economies", 25318–81

Pharmaceutical industry

Competitiveness (intl) of US pharmaceutical industry, investigation with background financial and operating data and foreign comparisons, 1991 rpt, 9886–4.176

County Business Patterns, 1988: employment, establishments, and payroll, by SIC 2- to 4-digit industry and county, annual State rpt series, 2326–6

County Business Patterns, 1989: employment, establishments, and payroll, by SIC 2- to 4-digit industry and county, annual State rpt series, 2326–8

Employment, earnings, and hours, by SIC 1- to 4-digit industry, monthly and annual averages, selected years 1909-90, annual rpt, 6744–4

Enterprise Statistics, 1987: finances and operations for companies, by size, level of diversification, form of organization, and industry group, 2329–8

Finances and operations, by SIC 2- to 4-digit industry, forecast 1991, annual rpt, 2044–28

Input-output structure of US economy, detailed interindustry transactions for 84 industries, and components of final demand, 1986, annual article, 2702–1.206

Input-output structure of US economy, detailed interindustry transactions for 85 industries, 1982 benchmark data, 2702–1.213

Labor productivity, indexes of output, hours, and employment by SIC 2- to 4-digit industry, 1967-89, annual rpt, 6824–1.3

Manufacturing annual survey, 1989: finances and operations, by SIC 2- to 4-digit industry, series, 2506–15

Manufacturing census, 1987: finances and operations, by SIC 2- to 4-digit industry, State, and MSA, with trends from 1849, 2497–1

Manufacturing census, 1987: finances and operations, by type of organization and SIC 2- to 4-digit industry, subject rpt, 2497–5

Manufacturing corporations financial statements, by selected SIC 2- to 3-digit industry, quarterly rpt, 2502–1

Pharmaceutical industry

Marketing applications for drugs, FDA processing by drug, purpose, and producer, 1990, annual rpt, 4064–14

Marketing of prescription drugs, practices, spending by selected firm, and physicians views, 1990 hearings, 25548–103

Multinatl US firms and foreign affiliates finances and operations, by industry and world area of parent firm, 1989 benchmark survey, preliminary annual rpt, 2704–5

Occupational injury and illness rates, by SIC 2- to 4-digit industry, 1988-89, annual rpt, 6844–7

Occupational injury and illness rates, by SIC 2- to 4-digit industry, 1989, annual rpt, 6844–1

Pollution (air) emissions factors, by detailed pollutant and source, data compilation, 1990 rpt, 9198–120

Pollution (water) industrial releases in wastewater, levels, treatment, costs, and regulation, with background financial and operating data, 1989 industry rpt, 9206–4.4

Price indexes (producer), by stage of processing and detailed commodity, monthly rpt, 6762–6

Price indexes (producer), by stage of processing and detailed commodity, monthly 1990, annual rpt, 6764–2

Puerto Rico and other US possessions corporations income tax returns, income and tax items, and employment, by selected industry, 1987, article, 8302–2.213

Puerto Rico economic censuses, 1987: wholesale and retail trade and service industry finances and operations, by SIC 2- to 4-digit industry and municipio, 2591–1

Puerto Rico economic censuses, 1987: wholesale, retail, and service industries finances and operations, by establishment characteristics and SIC 2- and 3-digit industry, subject rpts, 2591–2

Tax (income) returns of corporations, income and tax items by asset size and detailed industry, 1987, annual rpt, 8304–4

Tax (income) returns of corporations, income and tax items by asset size and detailed industry, 1988, annual rpt, 8304–21

Wholesale trade census, 1987: depreciable assets, capital and operating expenses, sales, value added, and inventories, by SIC 2- to 3-digit kind of business, 2407–2

Wholesale trade census, 1987: establishments, sales by customer class, employment, inventories, and expenses, by SIC 2- to 4-digit kind of business, 2407–4

Wholesale trade sales and inventories, by SIC 2- to 3-digit kind of business, monthly rpt, 2413–7

Wholesale trade sales, inventories, purchases, and gross margins, by SIC 2- to 3-digit kind of business, 1990, annual rpt, 2413–13

see also Biologic drug products
see also Drugs
see also Drugstores

see also Pharmacists and pharmacy

Pharmacists and pharmacy

Advertising of prescription drugs direct to consumer, benefits and problems, review of studies published 1984-91, GAO rpt, 26131–86

Degrees awarded in higher education, by level, field, race, and sex, 1988/89 with trends from 1978/79, biennial rpt, 4844–17

Education in science and engineering, grad programs enrollment by field, source of funds, and characteristics of student and instn, 1975-89, annual rpt, 9627–7

Germany (West) health care spending, by funding source and service type, and resource growth, 1970-89, article, 4652–1.238

Health condition and health care resources, use, and spending, 1950s-89, annual data compilation, 4144–11

Hospitals, receipts by source, contract services, expenses, and employment, by facility type and State, 1987 Census of Service Industries, 2393–4.12

Indian Health Service and tribal facility outpatient visits, by type of provider, selected hospital, and service area, FY90, annual rpt, 4084–3

Mail service pharmacy industry structure, finances, and operations, 1989 survey, 4658–60

Military health care personnel, and accessions by training source, by occupation, specialty, and service branch, FY89, annual rpt, 3544–24

Minority group and women health condition, services use, payment sources, and health care labor force, by poverty status, 1940s-89, chartbook, 4118–56

Smoking bans in public places, local ordinances provisions, as of 1989, 4478–196

VA health care staff and turnover, by occupation, physician specialty, and location, 1990, annual rpt, 8604–8

VA Medicine and Surgery Dept trainees, by detailed program and city, FY90, annual rpt, 8704–4

VA pharmacies prescriptions issued and filled, FY89-90, annual rpt, 8604–3.4

see also Drugs
see also Drugstores

Phaup, Marvin

"Budgetary Treatment of Deposit Insurance: A Framework for Reform", 26308–100

Phelps, Robert B.

"Carbon Cycle Impacts of Future Forest Products Utilization and Recycling Trends", 1004–16.1

"Outlook for Timber Products", 1004–16.1

Philadelphia, Pa.

Commuting accessibility impact on auto ownership, employment location, and housing values, for Philadelphia metro area census tracts, 1980, working paper, 9387–8.231

CPI by component for US city average, and by region, population size, and for 15 metro areas, monthly rpt, 6762–1

CPI by component for US city average, and by region, population size, and for 27 metro areas, monthly rpt, 6762–2

Drug abuse indicators for selected metro areas, research results, data collection, and policy issues, 1991 semiannual conf, 4492–5

Index by Subjects and Names

Drug test results at arrest, by drug type, offense, and sex, for selected urban areas, quarterly rpt, 6062–3

Employment growth and unemployment rates, Fed Reserve 3rd District, quarterly rpt, 9387–10

Financial instns location relation to ZIP code area income and minority population, by instn type for 5 cities, 1977-89, article, 9377–1.208

Fruit and vegetable shipments, and arrivals in US and Canada cities, by mode of transport and State and country of origin, 1990, annual rpt, 1311–4.1

Housing value capitalization of property tax, model description and results for Philadelphia, 1982, working paper, 9387–8.252

Wages by occupation, for office and plant workers, 1990 survey, periodic MSA rpt, 6785–11.3

Water quality, chemistry, hydrology, and other characteristics, 1989 local area study, 5666–27.9

see also under By City and By SMSA or MSA in the "Index by Categories"

Philanthropy

see Gifts and private contributions
see Nonprofit organizations and foundations

Philippine Americans

see Pacific Islands Americans

Philippines

Agricultural exports of high-value commodities, indexes and sales by commodity, world area, and country, 1960s-86, 1528–323

Agricultural exports of US, impacts of foreign agricultural and trade policy, with data by commodity and country, 1989, annual rpt, 1924–8

Agricultural imports tariffs, by commodity, for Philippines, 1991-95, article, 1925–34.235

Agricultural production, prices, and trade, by country, 1960s-90, annual world area rpt, 1524–4.2

Agricultural production, trade, and policies in foreign countries, summary data by country, 1989-90, annual factbook, 1924–12

Agricultural trade of US, by detailed commodity and country, 1989, annual rpt, 1524–8

Agricultural trade of US, by detailed commodity and country, 1990, semiannual rpt, 1522–4

AID economic aid to developing countries, obligations and disbursements by country, quarterly rpt, 9912–4

AID loans repayment status and terms by program and country, and status of predecessor agency loans, quarterly rpt, 9912–3

Economic and military aid and loans from US and intl agencies, by program and country, FY46-90, annual rpt, 9914–5

Economic and social conditions of developing countries from 1960s, and Intl Dev Cooperation Agency and AID activities and funding, FY90-92, annual rpt, 9904–4

Economic conditions in USSR, Eastern Europe, OECD, and selected other countries, 1960s-90, annual rpt, 9114–4

Index by Subjects and Names

Economic conditions, income, production, prices, employment, and trade, 1991 periodic country rpt, 2046–4.20

Economic conditions, policy, and trade practices, by country, 1988-90, annual rpt, 21384–5

Economic, population, and agricultural data, US and other aid sources, and AID activity, 1990 country rpt, 9916–12.46

Economic, social, political, and geographic summary data, by country, 1991, annual factbook, 9114–2

Exports and imports of US, by commodity and country, 1970-89, world area rpt, 9116–1.7

Exports and imports of US, by Harmonized System 6-digit commodity and country, 1990, annual rpt, 2424–13

Exports and imports of US, by selected country, country group, and commodity group, 1990, annual rpt, 2044–37

Exports and imports of US, by transport mode, country, and SITC 1- to 3-digit commodity, 1990, annual rpt, 2424–12

Exports of US, detailed Schedule B commodities with countries of destination, 1990, annual rpt, 2424–10

Grain production and needs, and related economic outlook, by world area and selected country, forecast 1990/91-1991/92, 1528–313

Hostages kidnapped in Philippines, listing as of 1990, 7004–22

Human rights conditions in 170 countries, and US economic and military aid, 1990, annual rpt, 21384–3

Imports of goods, services, and investment from US, trade barriers, impacts, and US actions, by country, 1990, annual rpt, 444–2

Labor conditions, union coverage, and work accidents, 1991 annual country rpt, 6366–4.16

Military aid of US, arms sales, and training programs costs and budget requests, by program, world region, and country, FY90-92, annual rpt, 7144–13

Multinatl US firms and foreign affiliates finances and operations, by industry and world area of parent firm, 1989 benchmark survey, preliminary annual rpt, 2704–5

Multinatl US firms foreign affiliates, income statement items by country and world area, 1986, biennial article, 8302–2.212

Pineapple (canned fruit and juice) production and exports, by country, 1988-91, annual article, 1925–34.216

Pineapple (canned fruit and juice) production and exports, for 2 countries, forecast 1991, semiannual article, 1925–34.243

Ships in world merchant fleet, tonnage, and new ship construction and deliveries, by vessel type and country, as of Jan 1990, annual rpt, 7704–3

Shrimp aquaculture harvest by Southeast Asia country, and Thailand revenues and costs, 1984-89, article, 2162–1.203

Tidal currents, daily time and velocity by station for North America and Asia coasts, forecast 1992, annual rpt, 2174–1.2

Tobacco and cigarette production, use, and trade, for Philippines, 1980-90, article, 1925–16.203

UN voting record and share of votes in agreement with US, by issue, country, and world area, 1990, annual rpt, 7004–18

US military presence in Pacific basin, personnel, dependents, aircraft, ships, and costs, by service branch and location, 1990, GAO rpt, 26123–357

US veterans living abroad, disability and death compensation cases by entitlement type, period of service, sex, and age, FY89, annual rpt, 8604–7

US veterans living abroad, VA expenses by type and location, FY90, annual rpt, 8604–3.9

US veterans programs spending, by US and foreign location, FY90, annual rpt, 8604–6

see also under By Foreign Country in the "Index by Categories"

Philliber Research Associates

"Teen Outreach: The Fifth Year of National Replication", 25548–104

Philliber, Susan

"Teen Outreach: The Fifth Year of National Replication", 25548–104

Phillips, Keith R.

"Effect of the Growing Service Sector on Wages in Texas", 9379–1.210

Phillips Petroleum Co.

Leveraged buyouts impacts on financial performance, for 4 transactions, 1980s-90, GAO rpt, 26119–355

Phillips, Robert L.

- "Distribution and Abundance of Golden Eagles and Other Raptors in Campbell and Converse Counties, Wyoming", 5506–12.1
- "Nesting Ecology of Golden Eagles and Other Raptors in Southeastern Montana and Northern Wyoming", 5506–12.1

Phillips, Steven P.

"Quantity and Quality of Ground-Water Inflow to the San Joaquin River, California", 5666–28.14

Philosophy

see Arts and the humanities

Phoenix, Ariz.

Drug abuse indicators for selected metro areas, research results, data collection, and policy issues, 1991 semiannual conf, 4492–5

Drug test results at arrest, by drug type, offense, and sex, for selected urban areas, quarterly rpt, 6062–3

Housing starts and completions authorized by building permits in 40 MSAs, quarterly rpt, 2382–9

Wages by occupation, and benefits for office and plant workers, 1991 survey, periodic MSA rpt, 6785–12.4

see also under By City and By SMSA or MSA in the "Index by Categories"

Phonograph

see Home video and audio equipment

Phonograph records

see Recording industry

Phosphate

County Business Patterns, 1988: employment, establishments, and payroll, by SIC 2- to 4-digit industry and county, annual State rpt series, 2326–6

County Business Patterns, 1989: employment, establishments, and payroll, by SIC 2- to 4-digit industry and county, annual State rpt series, 2326–8

Photography and photographic equipment

Exports and imports (agricultural) of US, by detailed commodity and country, 1990, semiannual rpt, 1522–4

Fertilizer (inorganic) shipments, trade, use, and firms, by product and State, with stocks, 1990, annual Current Industrial Rpt, 2506–8.13

Fertilizer consumption, by type and region, 1947-89, annual rpt, 1544–17.2

Fertilizer production capacity by firm, for US and Canada, 1986-91 and projected to 1997, triennial rpt, 9808–66

Mineral industries census, 1987: energy use and costs, by fuel type, SIC 2- to 4-digit industry, and State, subject rpt, 2517–2

Mineral industries census, 1987: finances and operations, by establishment characteristics, SIC 2- to 4-digit industry, and State, subject rpt, 2517–1

Mineral industries census, 1987: finances and operations, by SIC 2- to 4-digit industry, State, and county, census div rpt series, 2515–1

Mineral Industry Surveys, commodity review of production, trade, stocks, and use, monthly rpt, 5612–1.30

Minerals Yearbook, 1988, Vol 3: foreign country reviews of production, trade, and policy, by commodity, annual rpt series, 5604–17

Minerals Yearbook, 1989, Vol 1: commodity review of production, reserves, supply, use, and trade, annual rpt, 5604–15.51

Minerals Yearbook, 1989, Vol 2: State reviews of production, sales, and firms, by commodity, and business activity, annual rpt, 5604–34

Minerals Yearbook, 1990, Vol 1: commodity review of production, reserves, supply, use, and trade, annual rpt, 5604–20.45

Mines (nonmetallic minerals) and related operations occupational injuries and incidence, employment, and hours, 1989, annual rpt, 6664–1

Pollution (air) emissions factors, by detailed pollutant and source, data compilation, 1990 rpt, 9198–120

Price indexes (producer), by stage of processing and detailed commodity, monthly 1990, annual rpt, 6764–2

Production of phosphate rock, prices, sales, trade, and use, 1991, Mineral Industry Surveys, annual rpt, 5614–20

Production, prices, trade, and foreign and US industry devs, by commodity, bimonthly rpt with articles, 5602–4

Production, prices, trade, use, employment, tariffs, and stockpiles, by mineral, with foreign comparisons, 1986-90, annual rpt, 5604–18

Statistical Abstract of US, 1991 annual data compilation, 2324–1.25

Phosphorus

see Nonmetallic minerals and mines

Photography and photographic equipment

Coastal areas recreation facilities of Fed Govt and States, visitor and site characteristics, 1987-90 survey, regional rpt series, 2176–9

County Business Patterns, 1988: employment, establishments, and payroll, by SIC 2- to 4-digit industry and county, annual State rpt series, 2326–6

County Business Patterns, 1989: employment, establishments, and payroll, by SIC 2- to 4-digit industry and county, annual State rpt series, 2326–8

Photography and photographic equipment

CPI by component for US city average, and by region, population size, and for 27 metro areas, monthly rpt, 6762–2

DOD prime contract awards, by category, contract and contractor type, and service branch, FY81-1st half FY91, semiannual rpt, 3542–1

DOD prime contract awards, by category, contractor type, and State, FY88-90, annual rpt, 3544–11

DOD prime contract awards, by detailed procurement category, FY87-90, annual rpt, 3544–18

Employment, earnings, and hours, by SIC 1- to 4-digit industry, monthly and annual averages, selected years 1909-90, annual rpt, 6744–4

Enterprise Statistics, 1987: finances and operations for companies, by size, level of diversification, form of organization, and industry group, 2329–8

Exports and imports of US, by country and detailed commodity, monthly rpt, 2422–12

Exports and imports of US, by Harmonized System 6-digit commodity and country, 1990, annual rpt, 2424–13

Exports and imports of US, by transport mode, country, and SITC 1- to 3-digit commodity, 1990, annual rpt, 2424–12

Exports of US, detailed Schedule B commodities with countries of destination, 1990, annual rpt, 2424–10

Imports of US given duty-free treatment for value of US material sent abroad, by commodity and country, 1989, annual rpt, 9884–14

Imports purchasing decisions of consumers, importance of brand name, authenticity, origin, and other factors, 1984 survey, hearing, 25528–115

Injuries from use of consumer products, by severity, victim age, and detailed product, 1990, annual rpt, 9164–6

Labor productivity, indexes of output, hours, and employment by SIC 2- to 4-digit industry, 1967-89, annual rpt, 6824–1.3

Library of Congress activities, acquisitions, services, and financial statements, FY90, annual rpt, 26404–1

Manufacturing annual survey, 1989: finances and operations, by SIC 2- to 4-digit industry, series, 2506–15

Manufacturing census, 1987: employment and shipments under Fed Govt contracts, by SIC 4-digit industry, 2497–7

Manufacturing census, 1987: finances and operations, by SIC 2- to 4-digit industry, State, and MSA, with trends from 1849, 2497–1

Manufacturing census, 1987: finances and operations, by type of organization and SIC 2- to 4-digit industry, subject rpt, 2497–5

Manufacturing finances and operations, by SIC 2- to 4-digit industry, forecast 1991, annual rpt, 2044–28

Natl Archives and Records Admin activities, finances, holdings, and staff, FY90, annual rpt, 9514–2

Occupational injury and illness rates, by SIC 2- to 4-digit industry, 1988-89, annual rpt, 6844–7

Occupational injury and illness rates, by SIC 2- to 4-digit industry, 1989, annual rpt, 6844–1

OECD trade, total and for 4 major countries, and US trade by country, by commodity, 1970-89, world area rpt series, 9116–1

Pollution (air) emissions factors, by detailed pollutant and source, data compilation, 1990 rpt, 9198–120

Price indexes (producer), by stage of processing and detailed commodity, monthly rpt, 6762–6

Price indexes (producer), by stage of processing and detailed commodity, monthly 1990, annual rpt, 6764–2

Puerto Rico economic censuses, 1987: wholesale and retail trade and service industry finances and operations, by SIC 2- to 4-digit industry and municipio, 2591–1

Puerto Rico economic censuses, 1987: wholesale, retail, and service industries finances and operations, by establishment characteristics and SIC 2- and 3-digit industry, subject rpts, 2591–2

Retail trade census, 1987: finances and employment, for establishments with and without payroll, by SIC 2- to 4-digit kind of business, State, and MSA, 2401–1

Senate receipts, itemized expenses by payee, and balances, 1st half FY91, semiannual listing, 25922–1

Service industries census, 1987: depreciable assets, capital and operating expenses, and receipts, by SIC 2- to 4-digit kind of business, 2393–2

Service industries census, 1987: establishments, receipts by source, payroll, and employment, by SIC 2- to 4-digit kind of business, State, and MSA, 2393–4

Service industries receipts, by SIC 2- to 4-digit kind of business, 1990, annual rpt, 2413–8

Space science and related data sources and availability, 1991 annual listing, 9504–10

Space science and related data sources, use by format and user type, FY90, annual rpt, 9504–11

Statistical Abstract of US, 1991 annual data compilation, 2324–1.7

Tax (income) returns of corporations, income and tax items by asset size and detailed industry, 1987, annual rpt, 8304–4

Tax (income) returns of corporations, income and tax items by asset size and detailed industry, 1988, annual rpt, 8304–21

Tax (income) returns of sole proprietorships, income statement items, by industry group, 1989, annual article, 8302–2.214

USDA rpts, computer data files, and visual aids, 1991 annual listing, 1004–13

Wholesale trade census, 1987: establishments, sales by customer class, employment, inventories, and expenses, by SIC 2- to 4-digit kind of business, 2407–4

PHS

see Public Health Service

Physical characteristics

see also Birthweight

see also Body measurements

see also Disabled and handicapped persons

see also Health condition

see also Obesity

Physical education and training

Enrollment in single-sex and mixed classes, and schools offering courses, by course, 1988, biennial rpt, 4804–33

Higher education course completions, by detailed program, sex, race, and instn type, for 1972 high school class, as of 1984, 4888–4

Special education programs, enrollment by age, staff, funding, and needs, by type of handicap and State, 1989/90, annual rpt, 4944–4

Physical exercise

Cancer (colorectal) risk relation to physical activity level, 1960s-88, article, 4472–1.222

Children and youth social, economic, and demographic characteristics, 1950s-90, 4818–5

Diabetics health-related behaviors, weight, and body mass, by level of exercise, 1991 article, 4042–3.246

Fed Govt financial and nonfinancial domestic aid, 1991 base edition with supplements, annual listing, 104–5

Franchise business opportunities by firm and kind of business, and sources of aid and info, 1990 annual listing, 2104–7

Health condition improvement and disease prevention goals and recommended activities for 2000, with trends 1970s-80s, 4048–10

Injuries from use of consumer products, by severity, victim age, and detailed product, 1990, annual rpt, 9164–6

Service industries census, 1987: establishments, receipts by source, payroll, and employment, by SIC 2- to 4-digit kind of business, State, and MSA, 2393–4

see also Physical education and training

see also Sports and athletics

Physical sciences

Degrees (PhD) in science and engineering, by field, instn, employment prospects, sex, race, and other characteristics, 1960s-90, annual rpt, 9627–30

Degrees awarded in higher education, by level, field, race, and sex, 1988/89 with trends from 1978/79, biennial rpt, 4844–17

Degrees awarded in science and engineering, by field, level, and sex, 1966-89, 9627–33

DOE R&D projects and funding at natl labs, universities, and other instns, periodic summary rpt series, 3004–18

Employment and other characteristics of science and engineering PhDs, by field and State, 1989, biennial rpt, 9627–18

Fed Govt aid to higher education and nonprofit instns for R&D and related activities, by field, instn, agency, and State, FY89, annual rpt, 9627–17

Foreign and US funding for R&D, and scientists and engineering employment and education, 1991 annual rpt, 9627–35.1

High school advanced placement for college credit, programs by selected characteristics and school control, 1984-86, 4838–46

Higher education course completions, by detailed program, sex, race, and instn type, for 1972 high school class, as of 1984, 4888–4

Index by Subjects and Names

Physicians

Higher education grad programs enrollment in science and engineering, by field, source of funds, and characteristics of student and instn, 1975-89, annual rpt, 9627–7

NASA R&D funding to higher education instns, by field, instn, and State, FY90, annual listing, 9504–7

NSF activities, finances, and funding by program, FY90, annual rpt, 9624–6

R&D equipment of higher education instns, acquisition and service costs, condition, and financing, by field and subfield, 1988-90, triennial survey series, 9627–27

R&D funding by Fed Govt, by field, performer type, agency, and State, FY89-91, annual rpt, 9627–20

R&D funding by higher education instns and federally funded centers, by field, instn, and State, FY89, annual rpt, 9627–13

see also Astronomy
see also Chemistry
see also Earth sciences
see also Environmental sciences
see also Geography
see also Mathematics
see also Oceanography
see also Physics

Physical therapy

Home health care agencies finances impacts of Medicare payment limits under alternative determination methods, with data by service type, 1984-89, GAO rpt, 26121–400

Home health care services Medicare use and costs, by agency and service type, patient characteristics, and State, 1988-89, article, 4652–1.229

Home health care visits approved by Medicare, planned and actual visits by service type, 1986, article, 4652–1.254

Hospices operations, services, costs, and patient characteristics, for instns without Medicare certification, FY85-86, 4658–52

Indian Health Service and tribal facility outpatient visits, by type of provider, selected hospital, and service area, FY90, annual rpt, 4084–3

Medicare and Medicaid beneficiaries and program operations, 1991, annual fact book, 4654–18

Military health care personnel, and accessions by training source, by occupation, specialty, and service branch, FY89, annual rpt, 3544–24

Physicians visits, by patient and practice characteristics, diagnosis, and services provided, 1989, 4146–8.206

Special education programs, enrollment by age, staff, funding, and needs, by type of handicap and State, 1989/90, annual rpt, 4944–4

VA health care staff and turnover, by occupation, physician specialty, and location, 1990, annual rpt, 8604–8

Physically handicapped

see Blind
see Deaf
see Disabled and handicapped persons

Physician Payment Review Commission

Medicare Supplementary Medical Insurance physicians fee schedule, analyses of costs and other issues, series, 17266–1

Medicare Supplementary Medical Insurance physicians fee schedule, methodology with data by procedure and specialty, 1991, annual rpt, 17264–1

Physicians

Accessibility of health care, persons with and without usual care source by selected characteristics, 1987, 4186–8.22

Acute and chronic health conditions, disability, absenteeism, and health services use, by selected characteristics, 1987, CD-ROM, 4147–10.177

AIDS and AIDS virus infection patients service use and costs under Medicaid, 1991, article, 4652–1.215

AIDS knowledge, attitudes, and transmission prevention practices of physicians and RNs, 1990-91, 4186–9.11

Allergy and Infectious Diseases Natl Inst activities, grants by recipient and location, and disease cases, FY83-90, annual rpt, 4474–30

Births and rates, by characteristics of birth, infant, and parents, 1989 and trends from 1940, US Vital Statistics advance annual rpt, 4146–5.123

Cancer treatments using chemotherapy drugs for indications not listed on drug label, costs, and insurance reimbursement problems, 1990 physicians survey, GAO rpt, 26131–81

Child health condition and services use, 1990 chartbook, 4108–49

Child health insurance coverage, and children with a regular source of care, by selected characteristics, 1988, 4146–8.192

Consultations requested by attending physician, Medicare reimbursement issues, with use by diagnosis, specialty, location, and other characteristics, 1986, 4658–47

Cost indexes for physicians practices, and components, by State, MSA, and for rural areas, 1989 rpt, 4658–50

County Business Patterns, 1988: employment, establishments, and payroll, by SIC 2- to 4-digit industry and county, annual State rpt series, 2326–6

County Business Patterns, 1989: employment, establishments, and payroll, by SIC 2- to 4-digit industry and county, annual State rpt series, 2326–8

CPI by component for US city average, and by region, population size, and for 27 metro areas, monthly rpt, 6762–2

Developing countries population/physician ratios, by country, 1960s-83, annual rpt, 9904–4

Disabled persons and related activity limitation days and health services use, by health status, disability type, and other characteristics, 1984-88, 4146–8.202

Drug (prescription) advertising direct to consumer, benefits and problems, review of studies published 1984-91, GAO rpt, 26131–86

Drug (prescription) marketing practices, spending by selected firm, and physicians views, 1990 hearings, 25548–103

Drug and alcohol abuse treatment facilities, services, use, funding, staff, and client characteristics, 1989, biennial rpt, 4494–10

Employment, earnings, and hours, by SIC 1- to 4-digit industry, monthly and annual averages, selected years 1909-90, annual rpt, 6744–4

Enterprise Statistics, 1987: finances and operations for companies, by size, level of diversification, form of organization, and industry group, 2329–8

Expenditures for health care, by service type, payment source, and sector, projected 1990-2000 and trends from 1965, article, 4652–1.251

Expenditures for health care, by service type, payment source, and sector, 1960s-90, annual article, 4652–1.221; 4652–1.252

Expenditures for health care by type and payment source, with background data and foreign comparisons, 1960s-80s and projected to 2000, 26308–98

Expenditures for health care, cost containment methods, and insurance coverage issues, with background data, 1991 rpt, 26306–6.155

Germany (West) health care spending, by funding source and service type, and resource growth, 1970-89, article, 4652–1.238

Health Care Financing Review, provider prices, price inputs and indexes, and labor, quarterly journal, 4652–1.1

Health condition and health care resources, use, and spending, 1950s-89, annual data compilation, 4144–11

Health maintenance organizations and other prepaid managed care plans Medicaid enrollment and use, for 20 States, 1985-89, chartbook, 4108–29

HHS financial aid, by program, recipient, State, and city, FY90, annual regional listings, 4004–3

Hospices operations, services, costs, and patient characteristics, for instns without Medicare certification, FY85-86, 4658–52

Hospices use by cancer patients, by service type, use of other facilities, patient and instn characteristics, and other indicators, local area study, 1980-85, 4658–53

Hospital deaths of Medicare patients, actual and expected rates by diagnosis, with hospital characteristics, by instn, FY87-89, annual regional rpt series, 4654–14

Hospital post-discharge service use, by type, for Medicare pneumonia, stroke, and hip replacement cases, 1981-86, article, 4652–1.223

Hospitals in rural areas, financial and operating performance impacts of Medicare prospective payment reimbursement system, 1980s-87, 4658–51

Indian and Alaska Native disease and disorder cases, deaths, and health services use, by tribe, reservation, and Indian Health Service area, late 1950s-86, 4088–2

Indian Health Service and tribal facility outpatient visits, by type of provider, selected hospital, and service area, FY90, annual rpt, 4084–3

Insurance (health) coverage and provisions of small business employee benefit plans, by plan type and occupational group, 1990, biennial rpt, 6784–20

Insurance (health) coverage status relation to physician services use and hospitalization, 1984, working paper, 2626–10.120

Physicians

Kidney end-stage disease treatment access and quality of care indicators, impacts of Medicare payment reductions, 1980s, 4658–44

Labor supply of physicians, by specialty, age, sex, and location of training and practice, 1989, State rpt series, 4116–6

Licensing and discipline of physicians by State medical boards, investigative staff, and licensing fees, by State, 1985-90, 4008–83

Medicaid beneficiaries emergency room visits relation to availability of other sources of care, for upstate New York, 1985-87, article, 4652–1.232

Medicaid beneficiaries services use and costs, by service type and eligibility, 1975-89, article, 4652–1.209

Medicaid demonstration projects evaluation, for 6 States, 1988 rpt, 4658–45

Medicaid prepaid plans for physician services, characteristics of selected plans in 4 States, various periods 1983-89, article, 4652–1.228

Medicaid services use and costs in alternative treatment settings, model description and results, FY87, article, 4652–1.211

Medicare and Medicaid beneficiaries and program operations, 1991, annual fact book, 4654–18

Medicare and Medicaid benefits, trust fund finances, and services use, 1966-89 and projected to 1995, 21148–61

Medicare and Medicaid eligibility, participation, coverage, and program finances, various periods 1966-91, biennial rpt, 4654–1

Medicare and Medicaid enrollees, benefits, reimbursements, and services use, mid-1960s-89, annual rpt, 4744–3.5; 4744–3.6

Medicare claims approved, charges, and reimbursements by type of service, from 1974, monthly rpt, quarterly data, 4742–1.11

Medicare Economic Index for physician reimbursement rebased to 1989, methodology and results, with projections to 1995, article, 4652–1.246

Medicare payments to physicians, charges by specialty and treatment setting, and assignment rate by State, 1970s-88, article, 4652–1.240

Medicare Supplementary Medical Insurance physicians fee schedule, analyses of costs and other issues, series, 17266–1

Medicare Supplementary Medical Insurance physicians fee schedule, methodology with data by procedure and specialty, 1991, annual rpt, 17264–1

Mental illness and drug and alcohol abuse direct and indirect costs, by age and sex, 1985, 4048–35

Military dependents and retirees managed health care demonstration projects, enrollment, workload, and costs, 1988-90, 26306–3.117

Military health care personnel, and accessions by training source, by occupation, specialty, and service branch, FY89, annual rpt, 3544–24

Military reserve medical personnel, by specialty and reserve component, FY90, annual rpt, 3544–31.1

Minority group and women health condition, services use, payment sources, and health care labor force, by poverty status, 1940s-89, chartbook, 4118–56

Minority group health condition, services use, costs, and indicators of services need, 1950s-88, 4118–55

Navy personnel strengths, accessions, and attrition, detailed statistics, quarterly rpt, 3802–4

Nursing home and other long term care services under Medicare hospital use reduction demonstration, results for Rochester, NY, 1980s, 4658–43

Older persons health care services use, by service type, discharge destination, and prior care source, 1986, 4188–72

Older persons with functional limitations, long-term care sources, and health and other characteristics, 1984-85, 4147–13.104

Preferred provider organizations marketing outlook under Medicare, with beneficiaries views on switching to Medicare-assignment physicians, 1989 survey, article, 4652–1.248

Primary health care research, methodology and findings, 1991 annual conf, 4184–4

Primary health care research, provider role, Federal funding, and provision to minority groups, 1990 conf papers, 4188–69

Receipts for services, by SIC 2- to 4-digit kind of business, 1990, annual rpt, 2413–8

Service industries census, 1987: depreciable assets, capital and operating expenses, and receipts, by SIC 2- to 4-digit kind of business, 2393–2

Service industries census, 1987: establishments, receipts by source, payroll, and employment, by SIC 2- to 4-digit kind of business, State, and MSA, 2393–4

Shift rotation health and safety effects, and US and foreign regulation, by selected industry and occupation, 1970s-89, 26356–9.3

State and Metro Area Data Book, 1991 data compilation, 2328–54

Statistical Abstract of US, 1991 annual data compilation, 2324–1.3

Tax (income) returns of corporations, income and tax items by asset size and detailed industry, 1987, annual rpt, 8304–4

Tax (income) returns of corporations, income and tax items by asset size and detailed industry, 1988, annual rpt, 8304–21

Tax (income) returns of partnerships, income statement and balance sheet items, by industry group, 1989, annual article, 8302–2.216; 8304–18

Tax (income) returns of sole proprietorships, income statement items, by industry group, 1989, annual article, 8302–2.214

Teenagers physicians office visits, by reason and characteristics of physicians, patients, and visit, 1985, 4146–8.199

VA health care facilities physicians, dentists, and nurses, by selected employment characteristics and VA district, quarterly rpt, 8602–6

VA health care professionals employment, by district and facility, quarterly rpt, 8602–4

VA health care staff and turnover, by occupation, physician specialty, and location, 1990, annual rpt, 8604–8

VA Medicine and Surgery Dept trainees, by detailed program and city, FY90, annual rpt, 8704–4

Visits to physicians, by patient and practice characteristics, diagnosis, and services provided, 1989, 4146–8.206

Visits to physicians by uninsured persons as percent of insured persons use, 1977-86 surveys, article, 4652–1.220

Waste (medical) generation, sources, health worker exposure and risk, and incineration emissions, 1980s, 4078–1

Workers compensation laws of States and Fed Govt, 1991 semiannual rpt, 6502–1

see also Anesthesiology

see also Coroners

see also Foreign medical graduates

see also Geriatrics

see also Medical education

see also Medical ethics

see also Medical malpractice

see also Nuclear medicine and radiology

see also Obstetrics and gynecology

see also Orthopedics

see also Osteopathy

see also Pathology

see also Pediatrics

see also Podiatry

see also Psychiatry

see also Surgeons and surgery

Physicians assistants

see Allied health personnel

Physics

Budget of US, obligations and authority by function, agency, and program, with summaries, analyses, and historical tables, FY92, annual rpt, 104–2

Degrees (PhD) in science and engineering, by field, instn, employment prospects, sex, race, and other characteristics, 1960s-90, annual rpt, 9627–30

Degrees awarded in science and engineering, by field, level, and sex, 1966-89, 9627–33

Employment and other characteristics of science and engineering PhDs, by field and State, 1989, biennial rpt, 9627–18

Fed Govt aid to higher education and nonprofit instns for R&D and related activities, by field, instn, agency, and State, FY89, annual rpt, 9627–17

Higher education course completions, by detailed program, sex, race, and instn type, for 1972 high school class, as of 1984, 4888–4

Higher education grad programs enrollment in science and engineering, by field, source of funds, and characteristics of student and instn, 1975-89, annual rpt, 9627–7

NASA R&D funding to higher education instns, by field, instn, and State, FY90, annual listing, 9504–7

R&D funding by Fed Govt, by field, performer type, agency, and State, FY89-91, annual rpt, 9627–20

R&D funding by higher education instns and federally funded centers, by field, instn, and State, FY89, annual rpt, 9627–13

Index by Subjects and Names

Physiology

Aviation medicine research and test results, technical rpt series, 7506–10

Education in science and engineering, grad programs enrollment by field, source of funds, and characteristics of student and instn, 1975-89, annual rpt, 9627–7

Lead levels in environment, sources of emissions and exposure, and health effects, literature review, 1990 rpt, 9198–84

Piccot, Stephen D.

"Emissions and Cost Estimates for Globally Significant Anthropogenic Combustion Sources of NOx, N2O, CH4, CO, and CO2", 9198–124

Pickering, Margaret H.

"Review of Corporate Restructuring Activity, 1980-90", 9366–1.161

Pickle, Linda W.

"Atlas of U.S. Cancer Mortality Among Nonwhites: 1950-80", 4478–78

Pierce, John P.

"Smoking Initiation in the U.S.: A Role for Worksite and College Smoking Bans", 4472–1.216

Pigments

see Chemicals and chemical industry *see* Paints and varnishes

Pigs

see Livestock and livestock industry

Pilot projects

see Demonstration and pilot projects

Pilots

- Accidents and circumstances, for US operations of domestic and foreign airlines and general aviation, periodic rpt, 9612–1
- Accidents by type of aviation, near collisions, air traffic control and pilot errors, and runway incursions, monthly rpt, 7502–15
- Accidents, casualties, and damage for air carriers, by detailed circumstances, 1987, annual rpt, 9614–2
- Accidents in general aviation, by circumstances, characteristics of persons and aircraft involved, and type of flying, 1988, annual rpt, 9614–3
- Air traffic, pilots, airports, and fuel use, forecast FY91-2002 and trends from FY81, annual rpt, 7504–6
- Certificates for pilots and nonpilots held and issued, by type of certificate, region, State, and for women, 1989, annual rpt, 7504–1.7
- Certificates for pilots and nonpilots held, by type of certificate, age, sex, region, and State, 1990, annual rpt, 7504–2
- Eye defect (aphakia) and artificial lens implants among pilots, by sex, 1982-85, technical rpt, 7506–10.93
- General aviation activity, by type of pilot certificate and age, 1990, triennial survey rpt, 7508–3
- General aviation pilots and aircraft, by FAA region and State, 1989, annual rpt, 7504–3.3
- Instrument-rated and total pilots in Natl Airspace System, 1990-2005, annual rpt, 7504–12
- Medical research and test results for aviation, technical rpt series, 7506–10
- Navy aircraft pilots hours flown, by pilot category, aircraft type, and flight purpose, late 1980s, GAO rpt, 26123–332

Veterans education aid under GI Bill and other programs, and participation by period of service and State, FY89, annual rpt, 8604–9

Pine Bluff, Ark.

see also under By SMSA or MSA in the "Index by Categories"

Pineapples

see Fruit and fruit products

Pipelines

- Accident deaths and rates, by cause, age, sex, race, and State, 1988, US Vital Statistics annual rpt, 4144–2
- Accidents of pipelines, casualties, safety enforcement activity, and Federal funding, by State, 1989, annual rpt, 7304–5
- Coal production, stocks, and shipments, by State of origin and destination, end-use sector, and mode of transport, quarterly rpt, 3162–8
- Construction costs for pipelines and compressor stations, 1984-87, annual rpt, 3084–3
- Construction industries census, 1987: establishments, employment, receipts, and expenditures, by SIC 4-digit industry and State, final industry rpt series, 2373–1
- Construction put in place and cost indexes, by type of construction, bimonthly rpt, 2042–1.1; 2042–1.5
- Construction put in place, value of new public and private structures, by type, monthly rpt, 2382–4
- County Business Patterns, 1988: employment, establishments, and payroll, by SIC 2- to 4-digit industry and county, annual State rpt series, 2326–6
- County Business Patterns, 1989: employment, establishments, and payroll, by SIC 2- to 4-digit industry and county, annual State rpt series, 2326–8
- DOT activities by subagency, budget, and summary accident data, FY88, annual rpt, 7304–1
- Employment, earnings, and hours, by SIC 1- to 4-digit industry, monthly and annual averages, selected years 1909-90, annual rpt, 6744–4
- Energy producers finances and operations, by energy type for US firms domestic and foreign operations, 1989, annual rpt, 3164–44.1
- Energy use by mode of transport, fuel supply, and demographic and economic factors of vehicle use, 1970s-89, annual rpt, 3304–5
- Exports and imports of US, by Harmonized System 6-digit commodity and country, 1990, annual rpt, 2424–13
- Exports of US, detailed Schedule B commodities with countries of destination, 1990, annual rpt, 2424–10
- Foreign countries economic, social, political, and geographic summary data, by country, 1991, annual factbook, 9114–2
- Labor productivity, indexes of output, hours, and employment by SIC 2- to 4-digit industry, 1967-89, annual rpt, 6824–1.4
- Military and personal property shipments, passenger traffic, and costs, by service branch and mode of transport, quarterly rpt, 3702–1
- Natl transportation system planning, use, condition, accidents, and needs, by mode of transport, 1940s-90 and projected to 2020, 7308–202

Pipelines

- Natural and supplemental gas production, prices, trade, use, reserves, and pipeline company finances, by firm and State, monthly rpt with articles, 3162–4
- Natural gas composition and helium levels, analyses of individual wells and pipelines, by selected State and county, 1917-90, annual rpt, 5604–2
- Natural gas interstate pipeline company detailed financial and operating data, by firm, 1989, annual rpt, 3164–38
- Natural gas interstate pipeline company sales and contract deliveries, by firm and State, 1984-89, annual article, 3162–4.204
- Natural gas interstate pipeline company sales and price trends, monthly rpt, 3162–24.4; 3162–24.9
- Natural gas pipelines and owners, and fields, as of Sept 1989, map, 3088–21
- North Carolina environmental and socioeconomic conditions, and impacts of proposed OCS oil and gas exploration, 1970s-90 and projected to 2020, 5738–22
- Occupational injury and illness rates, by SIC 2- to 4-digit industry, 1988-89, annual rpt, 6844–7
- Occupational injury and illness rates, by SIC 2- to 4-digit industry, 1989, annual rpt, 6844–1
- Offshore oil and gas leases environmental and socioeconomic impact, and coastal area description, final statement series, 5736–1
- Offshore oil and gas pipeline construction and landfalls on Federal leases in 2 ocean areas, by State, 1951-90, annual rpt, 5734–3.3
- Offshore oil and gas reserves, and leasing and dev activity, periodic regional rpt series, 5736–3
- Offshore oil and gas reserves of Fed Govt, production, leasing and exploration activity, revenue, and costs, by ocean area, FY90, annual rpt, 5734–4
- Oil and refined products stocks, and interdistrict shipments by mode of transport, monthly rpt, 3162–6.3
- Oil bulk stations, sales and storage capacity by product, inventories, expenses, employment, and modes of transport, 1987 Census of Wholesale Trade, 2407–4.2
- Oil crude, gas liquids, and refined products supply, demand, and movement, by PAD district and State, 1990, annual rpt, 3164–2
- Price indexes (producer), by stage of processing and detailed commodity, monthly rpt, 6762–6
- Price indexes (producer), by stage of processing and detailed commodity, monthly 1990, annual rpt, 6764–2
- Reclamation Bur irrigation activities, finances, and project impacts in western US, 1989, annual rpt, 5824–12
- Safety programs, and accidents, casualties, and damage, by mode of transport, 1989, annual rpt, 7304–19
- *Statistical Abstract of US,* 1991 annual data compilation, 2324–1.21
- Tax (income) returns of corporations, income and tax items by asset size and detailed industry, 1987, annual rpt, 8304–4

Pipelines

Tax (income) returns of corporations, income and tax items by asset size and detailed industry, 1988, annual rpt, 8304–21

Pistachios
see Nuts

Pistols
see Firearms

Pitcher, Charles B.
"Directory of National Trade Associations, Professional Societies, and Labor Unions of the Construction and Building Materials Industries", 2042–1.202

Pitcher, Kenneth W.
"Harbor Seal Trend Count Surveys in Southern Alaska, 1988", 14738–6

Pitts, Joyce M.
"Child Support Received by Teenaged Mothers: 1987", 4698–5

Pittsburgh, Pa.
- CPI by component for US city average, and by region, population size, and for 15 metro areas, monthly rpt, 6762–1
- CPI by component for US city average, and by region, population size, and for 27 metro areas, monthly rpt, 6762–2
- Fruit and vegetable shipments, and arrivals in US and Canada cities, by mode of transport and State and country of origin, 1990, annual rpt, 1311–4.1
- Wages by occupation, for office and plant workers, 1991 survey, periodic MSA rpt, 6785–12.2
- *see also* under By City and By SMSA or MSA in the "Index by Categories"

Pittsfield, Mass.
see also under By SMSA or MSA in the "Index by Categories"

Place of birth
see Birthplace

Plainfield, Ill.
Tornadoes in Plainfield, Ill, storm characteristics, deaths, and Natl Weather Service forecast accuracy, 1990, 2186–6.3

Planned parenthood
see Contraceptives
see Family planning

Planning
see City and town planning
see Conversion of industry
see Economic policy
see Health planning and evaluation
see Logistics
see Military strategy
see Regional planning

Plano, Tex.
see also under By City in the "Index by Categories"

Plants and equipment
see Business firms and establishments, number
see Capital investments, general
see Capital investments, specific industry
see Electric power plants and equipment
see Industrial plants and equipment
see Industrial robots

Plants and vegetation
- Acid rain and air pollution environmental impacts, and methods of neutralizing acidified water bodies, summary research rpt series, 5506–5
- Carbon dioxide in atmosphere, measurement, methodology, and research results, series, 3006–11

Coastal and riparian areas environmental conditions, fish, wildlife, use, and mgmt, for individual ecosystems, series, 5506–9

- Endangered animals and plants conservation spending of Federal agencies and States, by species, FY90, annual rpt, 5504–33
- Endangered animals and plants population status and mgmt activity, by species, 1990, biennial rpt, 5504–35
- Endangered animals and plants US trade and permits, by species, purpose, disposition, and country, 1989, annual rpt, 5504–19
- Exports and imports of US, by country and detailed commodity, monthly rpt, 2422–12
- Exports and imports of US, by transport mode, country, and SITC 1- to 3-digit commodity, 1990, annual rpt, 2424–12
- Goats (mountain) population in Yellowstone and Grand Teton Natl Parks, and habitat mgmt options, 1970s-89, 5548–19
- Idaho Snake River area birds of prey, rodent, and vegetation distribution and characteristics, research results, 1990, annual rpt, 5724–14
- Manatees grazing effects on seagrass, by southeast Florida site, 1987-89, 14738–12
- Research of State fish and wildlife agencies, federally funded fishery projects and costs by species and State, 1990, annual listing, 5504–23
- Research of State fish and wildlife agencies, federally funded wildlife projects and costs by species and State, 1990, annual listing, 5504–24
- Research on fish and wildlife population, habitat, and mgmt, technical rpt series, 5506–12
- Research on wildlife and plants, habitat study series, 5506–13
- Shrublands in western US, ecology, biology, and cheatgrass invasion and related fire threat, 1989 conf papers, 1208–351
- Water quality, chemistry, hydrology, and other characteristics, local area studies, series, 5666–27
- Wetlands acreage, resources, soil and water properties, and conservation efforts, by wetland type, State rpt series, 5506–11
- Wetlands and riparian soil and plant characteristics, series, 5506–10
- Wetlands plant, soil, and water characteristics, for Big Meadows area in Rocky Mountain Natl Park, 1987-88, 5508–113
- *see also* Botanical gardens
- *see also* Botany
- *see also* Farms and farmland
- *see also* Flowers and nursery products
- *see also* Forests and forestry
- *see also* Horticulture
- *see also* Pasture and rangeland

Plastics and plastics industry
- Agricultural crops (new and traditional) use in industry, replacement of imports and nonrenewable resources, R&D funding, and economic impacts, 1970s-90, 26358–239
- Auto weight, by component material, 1975-90, article, 5602–4.202
- Building materials production and PPI, by type, bimonthly rpt, 2042–1.5; 2042–1.6

Index by Subjects and Names

- Business statistics, detailed data for major industries and economic indicators, *Survey of Current Business*, monthly rpt, 2702–1.12
- County Business Patterns, 1988: employment, establishments, and payroll, by SIC 2- to 4-digit industry and county, annual State rpt series, 2326–6
- County Business Patterns, 1989: employment, establishments, and payroll, by SIC 2- to 4-digit industry and county, annual State rpt series, 2326–8
- Employment, earnings, and hours, by SIC 1- to 4-digit industry, monthly and annual averages, selected years 1909-90, annual rpt, 6744–4
- Employment in manufacturing, by detailed occupation and SIC 2-digit industry, 1989 survey, triennial rpt, 6748–52
- Energy use and prices for manufacturing industries, 1988 survey, series, 3166–13
- Enterprise Statistics, 1987: finances and operations for companies, by size, level of diversification, form of organization, and industry group, 2329–8
- Exports and imports between US and outlying areas, by detailed commodity and mode of transport, 1990, annual rpt, 2424–11
- Exports and imports of US, by country and detailed commodity, monthly rpt, 2422–12
- Exports and imports of US, by Harmonized System 6-digit commodity and country, 1990, annual rpt, 2424–13
- Exports and imports of US, by selected country, country group, and commodity group, 1990, annual rpt, 2044–37
- Exports and imports of US, by transport mode, country, and SITC 1- to 3-digit commodity, 1990, annual rpt, 2424–12
- Exports of US, detailed commodities by country, monthly CD-ROM, 2422–13
- Exports of US, detailed Schedule B commodities with countries of destination, 1990, annual rpt, 2424–10
- Film (polyethylene terephthalate) from 2 countries at less than fair value, injury to US industry, investigation with background financial and operating data, 1991 rpt, 9886–14.313
- Imports, exports, and employment impacts, by SIC 2- to 4-digit industry and commodity, quarterly rpt, 2322–2
- Imports of US, detailed commodities by country, monthly CD-ROM, 2422–14
- Injuries from use of consumer products, by severity, victim age, and detailed product, 1990, annual rpt, 9164–6
- Input-output structure of US economy, detailed interindustry transactions for 84 industries, and components of final demand, 1986, annual article, 2702–1.206
- Input-output structure of US economy, detailed interindustry transactions for 85 industries, 1982 benchmark data, 2702–1.213
- Labor productivity, indexes of output, hours, and employment by SIC 2- to 4-digit industry, 1967-89, annual rpt, 6824–1.3
- Manufacturing annual survey, 1989: finances and operations, by SIC 2- to 4-digit industry, series, 2506–15

Index by Subjects and Names

Manufacturing census, 1987: finances and operations, by SIC 2- to 4-digit industry, State, and MSA, with trends from 1849, 2497–1

Manufacturing census, 1987: finances and operations, by type of organization and SIC 2- to 4-digit industry, subject rpt, 2497–5

Manufacturing corporations financial statements, by selected SIC 2- to 3-digit industry, quarterly rpt, 2502–1

Manufacturing finances and operations, by SIC 2- to 4-digit industry, forecast 1991, annual rpt, 2044–28

Multinatl US firms and foreign affiliates finances and operations, by industry and world area of parent firm, 1989 benchmark survey, preliminary annual rpt, 2704–5

Occupational injury and illness rates, by SIC 2- to 4-digit industry, 1988-89, annual rpt, 6844–7

Occupational injury and illness rates, by SIC 2- to 4-digit industry, 1989, annual rpt, 6844–1

OECD trade, total and for 4 major countries, and US trade by country, by commodity, 1970-89, world area rpt series, 9116–1

Oil and fat production, consumption by end use, and stocks, by type, quarterly Current Industrial Rpt, 2506–4.4

Plumbing fixtures shipments, stocks, trade, use, and firms, by product, quarterly Current Industrial Rpt, 2506–11.2

Pollution (air) emissions factors, by detailed pollutant and source, data compilation, 1990 rpt, 9198–120

Price indexes (producer), by stage of processing and detailed commodity, monthly rpt, 6762–6

Price indexes (producer), by stage of processing and detailed commodity, monthly 1990, annual rpt, 6764–2

Production of synthetic organic chemicals, by detailed product, quarterly rpt, 9882–1

Shoe production, shipments, trade, and use, by product, 1990, annual Current Industrial Rpt, 2506–6.8

Tariff Schedule of US, classifications and rates of duty by detailed imported commodity, 1992 base edition, 9886–13

Tax (income) returns of corporations, income and tax items by asset size and detailed industry, 1987, annual rpt, 8304–4

Tax (income) returns of corporations, income and tax items by asset size and detailed industry, 1988, annual rpt, 8304–21

Technologically advanced structural materials devs, use, and R&D funding, for ceramics, metal alloys, polymers, and composites, 1960s-80s and projected to 2000, 5608–162

Wholesale trade census, 1987: establishments, sales by customer class, employment, inventories, and expenses, by SIC 2- to 4-digit kind of business, 2407–4

see also Petrochemicals

see also under By Commodity in the "Index by Categories"

Plumbing and heating

see also under By Industry in the "Index by Categories"

Platinum

see Metals and metal industries

Plumbing and heating

Business statistics, detailed data for major industries and economic indicators, *Survey of Current Business*, monthly rpt, 2702–1.17

Commercial buildings energy use, costs, and conservation, by building characteristics, survey rpt series, 3166–8

County Business Patterns, 1988: employment, establishments, and payroll, by SIC 2- to 4-digit industry and county, annual State rpt series, 2326–6

County Business Patterns, 1989: employment, establishments, and payroll, by SIC 2- to 4-digit industry and county, annual State rpt series, 2326–8

DOD prime contract awards, by detailed procurement category, FY87-90, annual rpt, 3544–18

Employment, earnings, and hours, by SIC 1- to 4-digit industry, monthly and annual averages, selected years 1909-90, annual rpt, 6744–4

Energy aid for low income households, funding sources, costs, and participation, by State, FY89, annual rpt, 4694–8

Energy aid for low income households, State and Federal funding, FY86-89, GAO rpt, 26121–401

Energy conservation measures impacts on consumption, by component and end-use sector, 1970s-88 and projected under alternative oil prices to 1995, 3308–93

Energy supply, demand, and prices, by fuel type and end-use sector, projections and underlying assumptions, 1990-2010, annual rpt, 3164–90

Energy supply, demand, and prices, by fuel type and end-use sector, with foreign comparisons, 1990 and trends from 1949, annual rpt, 3164–74

Exports and imports of building materials, by commodity and country, 1989-90, article, 2042–1.204

Exports and imports of US, by Harmonized System 6-digit commodity and country, 1990, annual rpt, 2424–13

Exports and imports of US, by selected country, country group, and commodity group, 1990, annual rpt, 2044–37

Exports of US, detailed Schedule B commodities with countries of destination, 1990, annual rpt, 2424–10

Furnace shipments, trade, use, and firms, 1990, annual Current Industrial Rpt, 2506–12.7

Heating fuel use in housing, shares by type and region, 1989 and summary for 1950, fact sheet, 2326–17.34

Home mortgages FHA-insured, financial, property, and mortgagor characteristics, by metro area, 1990, annual rpt, 5144–24

Home mortgages FHA-insured, financial, property, and mortgagor characteristics, by State, 1990, annual rpt, 5144–1

Home mortgages FHA-insured, financial, property, and mortgagor characteristics, total and by State and outlying area, 1990, annual rpt, 5144–25

Home mortgages FHA-insured, financial, property, and mortgagor characteristics, 1990, annual rpt, 5144–17; 5144–23

Housing (low income) energy aid, program characteristics by assistance type and State, FY90, annual rpt, 4694–9

Housing alteration and repair spending, by property and job characteristics, and region, quarterly rpt, annual tables, 2382–7.2

Housing and households characteristics, unit and neighborhood quality, and journey to work by MSA location, for 11 MSAs, 1984 survey, supplement, 2485–8

Housing and households detailed characteristics, and unit and neighborhood quality, by location, 1987, biennial rpt supplement, 2485–13

Housing and households detailed characteristics, and unit and neighborhood quality, by location, 1989, biennial rpt, 2485–12

Housing and households detailed characteristics, and unit and neighborhood quality, MSA surveys, series, 2485–6

Housing and neighborhood quality, and rents paid under voucher and Section 8 certificate programs, 1985-87 survey, 5186–14.4

Housing inventory change from 1973, by reason, unit and household characteristics, and location, 1983 survey, biennial rpt, 2485–14

Housing units (1-family) by selected structural characteristics, sales, and prices, 1970s-90, article, 1702–1.205

Housing units completed, single and multifamily units by structural and financial characteristics, inside-outside MSAs, and region, 1986-90, annual rpt, 2384–1

Housing units completed, single and multifamily units by structural characteristics, monthly rpt, quarterly tables, 2382–2.2

Indian Health Service funding for housing sanitary facilities, and needs, FY60-90, annual rpt, 4084–1

Injuries from use of consumer products, by severity, victim age, and detailed product, 1990, annual rpt, 9164–6

Labor productivity, indexes of output, hours, and employment by SIC 2- to 4-digit industry, 1967-89, annual rpt, 6824–1.3

Manufacturing annual survey, 1989: finances and operations, by SIC 2- to 4-digit industry, series, 2506–15

Manufacturing census, 1987: finances and operations, by SIC 2- to 4-digit industry, State, and MSA, with trends from 1849, 2497–1

Manufacturing census, 1987: finances and operations, by type of organization and SIC 2- to 4-digit industry, subject rpt, 2497–5

Manufacturing finances and operations, by SIC 2- to 4-digit industry, forecast 1991, annual rpt, 2044–28

Occupational injury and illness rates, by SIC 2- to 4-digit industry, 1988-89, annual rpt, 6844–7

Occupational injury and illness rates, by SIC 2- to 4-digit industry, 1989, annual rpt, 6844–1

Pacific Northwest housing energy conservation program of Bonneville Power Admin, activities, cost effectiveness, and participation, series, 3226–1

Plumbing and heating

Pipe manufacturing, maintenance, and disposal costs, and price elasticity, by material, 1967-88, 5608–162.3

Pipes and tubes (welded nonalloy steel) from 6 countries, injury to US industry from foreign subsidized and less than fair value imports, investigation with background financial and operating data, 1991 rpt, 9886–19.81

Pollution (air) contributing to global warming, emissions factors and control costs, by pollutant and source, 1990 rpt, 9198–124

Pollution (air) indoor levels and emissions rates, by pollutant type and source, 1990 handbook, 3326–1.2

Price indexes (producer), by stage of processing and detailed commodity, monthly rpt, 6762–6

Producer price indexes, by stage of processing and detailed commodity, monthly 1990, annual rpt, 6764–2

Production, shipments, and PPI for building materials, by type, bimonthly rpt, 2042–1.5; 2042–1.6

Puerto Rico economic censuses, 1987: wholesale and retail trade and service industry finances and operations, by SIC 2- to 4-digit industry and municipio, 2591–1

R&D facilities for biological and medical sciences, space and equipment adequacy, needs, and funding by source, by instn type, 1990, biennial rpt, 4434–17

Respiratory diseases related to occupational hazards, epidemiology, diagnosis, and treatment, for selected industries and work settings, 1988 conf, 4248–90

Shipments, trade, use, and firms, for appliances by product, 1990, annual Current Industrial Rpt, 2506–12.16

Solar collector and photovoltaic module shipments by end-use sector and State, and trade, 1989, annual rpt, 3164–62

Statistical Abstract of US, 1991 annual data compilation, 2324–1.26

Taiwan imports of building materials, and share from US, by commodity, 1989-90, article, 2042–1.205

Tax (income) returns of corporations, income and tax items by asset size and detailed industry, 1987, annual rpt, 8304–4

Tax (income) returns of corporations, income and tax items by asset size and detailed industry, 1988, annual rpt, 8304–21

TVA electric power purchases of municipal and cooperative distributors, and prices and use by distributor and consumer sector, monthly rpt, 9802–1

Wholesale trade census, 1987: establishments, sales by customer class, employment, inventories, and expenses, by SIC 2- to 4-digit kind of business, 2407–4

see also Air conditioning

see also Electric power and heat cogeneration

see also Household appliances and equipment

Plummer, Charles

"Pumpkins: A Commodity Highlight", 1561–11.203

Plums and prunes

see Fruit and fruit products

Plunkert, Patricia A.

"Lightweight Materials for New Cars: Driving Toward Better Mileage", 5602–4.202

Pluta, Mark J.

"Enrollment in Higher Education, Fall 1989", 4844–2

Plutonium

see Radioactive materials

Plywood

see Lumber industry and products

Pneumonia and influenza

AIDS child patients *pneumocystis carinii* pneumonia prevention and control, CDC guidelines, 1991 rpt, 4206–2.38

Cases of acute and chronic conditions, disability, absenteeism, and health services use, by selected characteristics, 1987, CD-ROM, 4147–10.177

Deaths and rates, by cause and age, preliminary 1989-90, US Vital Statistics annual rpt, 4144–7

Deaths and rates, by cause, provisional data, monthly rpt, 4142–1.2

Deaths and rates, by detailed cause and demographic characteristics, 1988 and trends from 1900, US Vital Statistics annual rpt, 4144–2

Deaths recorded in 121 cities, weekly rpt, 4202–1

Health condition and health care resources, use, and spending, 1950s-89, annual data compilation, 4144–11

Hospital charges and length of stay for heart and lung patients with selected nonsurgical procedures, for Maryland, FY84, article, 4652–1.204

Hospital deaths of Medicare patients, actual and expected rates by diagnosis, with hospital characteristics, by instn, FY87-89, annual regional rpt series, 4654–14

Hospital post-discharge service use, by type, for Medicare pneumonia, stroke, and hip replacement cases, 1981-86, article, 4652–1.223

Influenza vaccination schedules and dosage by age, outbreak control, and surveillance, CDC guidelines, 1991 rpt, 4206–2.42

Influenza vaccine for *Haemophilus influenza* type b, child dosages and schedules, CDC guidelines, 1991 rpt, 4206–2.37

Morbidity and Mortality Weekly Report, infectious notifiable disease cases by State, and public health issues, 4202–1

Physicians consultations requested by attending physician, Medicare reimbursement issues, with use by diagnosis, specialty, location, and other characteristics, 1986, 4658–47

State and Metro Area Data Book, 1991 data compilation, 2328–54

see also under By Disease in the "Index by Categories"

Podiatry

County Business Patterns, 1988: employment, establishments, and payroll, by SIC 2- to 4-digit industry and county, annual State rpt series, 2326–6

County Business Patterns, 1989: employment, establishments, and payroll, by SIC 2- to 4-digit industry and county, annual State rpt series, 2326–8

Index by Subjects and Names

Degrees awarded in higher education, by level, field, race, and sex, 1988/89 with trends from 1978/79, biennial rpt, 4844–17

Health condition and health care resources, use, and spending, 1950s-89, annual data compilation, 4144–11

HHS financial aid, by program, recipient, State, and city, FY90, annual regional listings, 4004–3

Indian Health Service and tribal facility outpatient visits, by type of provider, selected hospital, and service area, FY90, annual rpt, 4084–3

Licensing and discipline of podiatrists by State medical boards, with medical school enrollment and applications, 1970s-87, 4006–8.4

Medicare payments to physicians, charges by specialty and treatment setting, and assignment rate by State, 1970s-88, article, 4652–1.240

Medicare Supplementary Medical Insurance physicians fee schedule, methodology with data by procedure and specialty, 1991, annual rpt, 17264–1

Military health care personnel, and accessions by training source, by occupation, specialty, and service branch, FY89, annual rpt, 3544–24

Minority group and women health condition, services use, payment sources, and health care labor force, by poverty status, 1940s-89, chartbook, 4118–56

Service industries census, 1987: establishments, receipts by source, payroll, and employment, by SIC 2- to 4-digit kind of business, State, and MSA, 2393–4

VA Medicine and Surgery Dept trainees, by detailed program and city, FY90, annual rpt, 8704–4

Podolsky, Arthur

"Public Libraries in 50 States and the District of Columbia: 1989", 4824–6

Pohnpei

see Micronesia Federated States

Pointer, Terri

"Nationwide Evaluation of Medicaid Competition Demonstrations. Volume 6. Administrative Costs", 4658–45.6

Poisoning and drug reaction

Alcohol (methanol) fuel substitution for gasoline, economic, environmental, and health impacts, projected 2000-2010, article, 9379–1.208

Cases of injury, by type, circumstances, and victim characteristics, and related activity limitations, 1985-87, 4147–10.176

Child accident deaths and death rates, by cause, age, sex, race, and State, 1980-85, 4108–54

Child accident deaths and injuries by cause, and victimization, rates by race, sex, and age, 1979-88, chartbook, 4108–56

Cocaine abuse, user characteristics, and related crime and violence, 1988 conf, 4498–74

Cocaine-related emergency room admissions, by user and use characteristics, for major metro areas, 1987-89, article, 4042–3.204

Costs (direct and indirect) of mental illness and drug and alcohol abuse, by type and patient age and sex, 1985 with 1980 and 1988 comparisons, 4048–35

Index by Subjects and Names

Police

Cyclosporine use in kidney transplants, effectiveness and costs, with comparison to other immunosuppressive protocols, 1985-87 study, 1989 rpt, 4658–59

Deaths and rates, by detailed cause and demographic characteristics, 1988 and trends from 1900, US Vital Statistics annual rpt, 4144–2

Diet pills (nonprescription) and analgesics sales and adverse reactions, and diet and drug effects on hypertension, 1980s-90, hearing, 21728–77

Drug abuse emergency room admissions and deaths, by drug type and major metro area, semiannual rpt, discontinued, 4492–3

Drug abuse emergency room admissions and deaths, by drug type and source, sex, race, age, and major metro area, 1990, annual rpt, 4494–8

Drug abuse indicators for selected metro areas, research results, data collection, and policy issues, 1991 semiannual conf, 4492–5

Drug abuse prevalence among minorities, related health effects and crime, treatment, and research status and needs, mid 1970s-90, 4498–72

HHS financial aid, by program, recipient, State, and city, FY90, annual regional listings, 4004–3

Homicides, by circumstance, victim and offender relationship, and type of weapon, 1990, annual rpt, 6224–2.1

Infant death rate, by cause, region, and race, 1980-87, article, 4202–7.208

Injuries from use of consumer products, by severity, victim age, and detailed product, 1990, annual rpt, 9164–6

Methamphetamine abuse, availability, health effects, and treatment, 1990 conf papers, 4498–75

Minority group health condition, services use, costs, and indicators of services need, 1950s-88, 4118–55

Occupational illness rates, by cause and SIC 2- to 3-digit industry, 1989, annual rpt, 6844–1

Pollutants health effects for animals by species and for humans, and environmental levels, for selected substances, series, 5506–14

Research and testing activities under Natl Toxicology Program, FY89 and planned FY90, annual rpt, 4044–16

Vaccination for diphtheria, tetanus, and pertussis, CDC guidelines for schedules, dosages, and precautions, 1991 rpt, 4206–2.46

Vaccine adverse reactions, *Morbidity and Mortality Weekly Report*, 4202–1

see also Food and waterborne diseases

see also Lead poisoning and pollution

Poland

Agricultural exports of high-value commodities, indexes and sales by commodity, world area, and country, 1960s-86, 1528–323

Agricultural exports of US, impacts of foreign agricultural and trade policy, with data by commodity and country, 1989, annual rpt, 1924–8

Agricultural production, trade, and policies in foreign countries, summary data by country, 1989-90, annual factbook, 1924–12

Agricultural trade of US, by detailed commodity and country, 1989, annual rpt, 1524–8

Agricultural trade of US, by detailed commodity and country, 1990, semiannual rpt, 1522–4

AID economic aid to developing countries, obligations and disbursements by country, quarterly rpt, 9912–4

AID loans repayment status and terms by program and country, and status of predecessor agency loans, quarterly rpt, 9912–3

Background Notes, summary social, political, and economic data, 1991 rpt, 7006–2.37

Bearings (ball) from 14 countries, injury to US industry from foreign subsidized and less than fair value imports, investigation with background financial and operating data, 1991 rpt, 9886–19.74

Debt to foreign lenders by component, trade, balances, and other economic indicators, by Eastern Europe country, 1985-89, hearing, 21248–148

Economic aid of US and other donor countries by type and recipient, and role in advancing economic interests, 1980s-90, 2048–152

Economic aid to Eastern Europe from US, by agency and country, FY90-92, GAO rpt, 26123–319

Economic and military aid and loans from US and intl agencies, by program and country, FY46-90, annual rpt, 9914–5

Economic conditions in USSR, Eastern Europe, OECD, and selected other countries, 1960s-90, annual rpt, 9114–4

Economic conditions, policy, and trade practices, by country, 1988-90, annual rpt, 21384–5

Economic, social, political, and geographic summary data, by country, 1991, annual factbook, 9114–2

Energy production, trade, use, and AID dev assistance, for 3 Eastern Europe countries, 1980s-91, 25318–81

Export licensing, monitoring, and enforcement activities, FY90, annual rpt, 2024–1

Exports and imports of US, by commodity and country, 1970-89, world area rpt, 9116–1.3

Exports and imports of US, by selected country, country group, and commodity group, 1990, annual rpt, 2044–37

Exports and imports of US, by transport mode, country, and SITC 1- to 3-digit commodity, 1990, annual rpt, 2424–12

Exports and imports of US with Communist countries, by detailed commodity and country, quarterly rpt with articles, 9882–2

Exports, imports, and balances of US with major trading partners, by product category, 1986-90, annual chartbook, 9884–21

Exports of US, detailed Schedule B commodities with countries of destination, 1990, annual rpt, 2424–10

Human rights conditions in 170 countries, and US economic and military aid, 1990, annual rpt, 21384–3

Labor force status by education level, sex, and sector, college enrollment, and grads by field, for Poland, 1960s-88, article, 6722–1.203

Market economy transition of Eastern Europe countries, economic conditions and energy balance, by country, 1985-90, 9118–13

Market economy transition of Eastern Europe countries, with trade agreements and bilateral US trade data by country, late 1980s-90, annual rpt, 444–2

Military aid of US, arms sales, and training programs costs and budget requests, by program, world region, and country, FY90-92, annual rpt, 7144–13

Refugee resettlement programs and funding, arrivals by country of origin, and indicators of adjustment, by State, FY90, annual rpt, 4694–5

Steel imports of US under voluntary restraint agreement, by product, customs district, and country, with US industry operating data, quarterly rpt, 9882–13

UN voting record and share of votes in agreement with US, by issue, country, and world area, 1990, annual rpt, 7004–18

see also under By Foreign Country in the "Index by Categories"

Polder, Jacquelyn A.

"Recommendations for Preventing Transmission of Human Immunodeficiency Virus and Hepatitis B Virus to Patients During Exposure-Prone Invasive Procedures", 4206–2.44

Polednak, Anthony P.

"Time Trends in Incidence of Brain and Central Nervous System Cancers in Connecticut", 4472–1.234

Police

Auto fleet size, trip characteristics, and energy use, by fleet type, 1970s-89, annual rpt, 3304–5.3

Bombing incidents, casualties, and damage, by target, circumstances, and State, 1990, annual rpt, 6224–5

Crime, criminal justice admin and enforcement, and public opinion, data compilation, 1991 annual rpt, 6064–6

Crime victimization by region and victim characteristics, and rpts to police, by offense, 1973-90, annual rpt, 6066–25.35; 6066–25.41

Crime victimization, by victim characteristics, offense, and whether reported to police, 1973-88, 6066–3.45

Crime victimization rates, by offense and reasons for reporting and not reporting crime to police, 1988 survey, annual rpt, 6066–3.42

Crime victimization rates, by offense, whether reported to police, reasons for not reporting, and police response, 1989 survey, annual rpt, 6066–3.44

Drug and alcohol abuse and mental illness direct and indirect costs, by type and patient age and sex, 1985 with 1980 and 1988 comparisons, 4048–35

Employee benefit plan coverage in State and local govts, by benefit type, 1987, 6726–1.41

Employment and payroll, by function and level of govt, 1990, annual rpt series, 2466–1

Employment and payroll, by level of govt, State, and selected city and county, 1984-86, biennial rpt, 6064–4

Employment of State and local law enforcement personnel and officers, by

Police

sex, population size, census div, and jurisdiction, as of Oct 1990, annual rpt, 6224–2.3

Employment, payroll, and spending for criminal justice, by level of govt, State, and selected city and county, FY71-88, annual rpt, 6064–9

Finances of govts, by level of govt, State, and for large cities and counties, annual rpt series, 2466–2

Govt census, 1987: employment, payroll, and average earnings, by function, level of govt, State, county, and population size, 2455–2

Govt census, 1987: local govt employment by function, payroll, and average earnings, for individual counties, cities, and school and special districts, 2455–1

Govt census, 1987: State and local labor-mgmt policies, agreements, and coverage and bargaining units, by function, level of govt, and State, 2455–3

Govt finances, tax systems and revenue, and fiscal structure, by level of govt and State, 1991 with historical trends, annual rpt, 10044–1

Helicopters, use, and landing facilities, by craft type, region, and State, 1989, 7508–75

Housing and households detailed characteristics, and unit and neighborhood quality, by location, 1985, biennial rpt supplement, 2485–13

Juvenile courts delinquency cases, by offense, referral source, disposition, age, sex, race, State, and county, 1988, annual rpt, 6064–12

Minority group and women employment in State and local govt, by occupation, function, and pay level, 1990, annual rpt, 9244–6.4

New York City drug enforcement personnel, arrests, and seizures, 1985-90, hearing, 25528–117

Soviet Union GNP by component and industry sector, and CIA estimation methods, 1950s-87, 23848–223

Soviet Union GNP by detailed income and outlay component, 1985, 2326–18.59

Statistical Abstract of US, 1991 annual data compilation, 2324–1.5

Teenagers crime victimization, by whether reported to police and reason for not reporting, 1985-88 surveys, 6066–3.43

Women's crime victimization, by whether reported to police and reasons for reporting and not reporting, for rape and other violent offenses, 1973-87, 6068–243

see also Assaults on police
see also Detective and protective services
see also Federal aid to law enforcement
see also Law enforcement
see also State police

Policy Development and Research, HUD

American Housing Survey: unit and households characteristics, MSA fact sheet series, 2485–11

Budget of US, obligations and authority by function, agency, and program, with summaries, analyses, and historical tables, FY92, annual rpt, 104–2

Fed Home Loan Mortgage Corp financial condition and capital adequacy, 1989, annual rpt, 5184–8

Fed Natl Mortgage Assn activities and finances, 1988-89, annual rpt, 5184–9

Housing supply, demand, and financing, and construction industry operations, biennial rpt, discontinued, 5184–5

Lead paint in privately owned housing, levels, exposure, and testing and abatement costs, 1990 rpt, 5188–128

Poor households with high rent, and substandard units, worst case problems prevalence and households characteristics, 1970s-84, annual rpt, 5184–10

Public housing renovation costs and alternative funding methods, by project type and region, 1990 rpt, 5188–127

Rent control ordinances and effects on housing supply and affordability, by selected jursidiction, 1968-89, 5188–130

Rent supplement programs evaluation, housing vouchers compared to Section 8 certificates, 1985-88, series, 5186–14

Policy Research, Inc.

"Health Status of Minorities and Low Income Groups: Third Edition", 4118–55

Policy Studies Associates, Inc.

"Review of Programs Involving College Students as Tutors or Mentors in Grades K-12", 4808–23

"State Administration of the Amended Chapter 1 Program", 4808–32

Polio

see Infective and parasitic diseases

Polissar, Lincoln

"Population-Based Study of Hospice, Parts I-IV", 4658–53

Political action committees

Committees, by type, 1974-91, semiannual press release, 9276–1.86; 9276–1.91

Congressional election campaign receipts and spending, by candidate and State, 1989-Dec 1990, press release, 9276–1.87

Finances of PACs and contributions by party, by PAC type, 1989-90, press release, 9276–1.89

Financing of campaigns and Fed Election Commission activities, various periods 1975-90, annual rpt, 9274–1

Senatorial campaign contributions by source, party, and State, 1991, press release, 9276–1.93

Statistical Abstract of US, 1991 annual data compilation, 2324–1.8

Political broadcasting

Broadcasting operating budgets for US Govt overseas radio and TV services, FY88 and FY91, annual rpt, 17594–1

see also Radio Free Europe
see also Radio Liberty
see also Voice of America

Political campaign funds

see Campaign funds
see Political action committees

Political ethics

Govt employees political activities prohibited under Hatch Act, cases initiated, FY90, annual rpt, 9894–1

Public opinion on crime and crime-related issues, by respondent characteristics, data compilation, 1991 annual rpt, 6064–6.2

see also Conflict of interests
see also Corruption and bribery
see also Lobbying and lobbying groups

Index by Subjects and Names

Political parties

Campaign finances and Fed Election Commission activities, various periods 1975-90, annual rpt, 9274–1

Campaign finances, elections, procedures, and Fed Election Commission activities, press release series, 9276–1

County Business Patterns, 1988: employment, establishments, and payroll, by SIC 2- to 4-digit industry and county, annual State rpt series, 2326–6

County Business Patterns, 1989: employment, establishments, and payroll, by SIC 2- to 4-digit industry and county, annual State rpt series, 2326–8

Foreign countries *Background Notes*, summary social, political, and economic data, series, 7006–2

Foreign countries economic, social, political, and geographic summary data, by country, 1991, annual factbook, 9114–2

Foreign countries human rights conditions in 170 countries, 1990, annual rpt, 21384–3

Statistical Abstract of US, 1991 annual data compilation, 2324–1.8

Votes cast by party, candidate, and State, 1990 natl elections, biennial rpt, 9274–5

see also Communist parties
see also Democratic Party
see also Republican Party

Political rights

see Civil rights

Political science

Degrees awarded in higher education, by level, field, race, and sex, 1988/89 with trends from 1978/79, biennial rpt, 4844–17

Degrees awarded in science and engineering, by field, level, and sex, 1966-89, 9627–33

Education Dept programs funding, operations, and effectiveness, FY90, annual rpt, 4804–5

Fed Govt aid to higher education and nonprofit instns for R&D and related activities, by field, instn, agency, and State, FY89, annual rpt, 9627–17

Higher education course completions, by detailed program, sex, race, and instn type, for 1972 high school class, as of 1984, 4888–4

Higher education grad programs enrollment in science and engineering, by field, source of funds, and characteristics of student and instn, 1975-89, annual rpt, 9627–7

R&D funding by Fed Govt, by field, performer type, agency, and State, FY89-91, annual rpt, 9627–20

R&D funding by higher education instns and federally funded centers, by field, instn, and State, FY89, annual rpt, 9627–13

Polls

see Elections
see Opinion and attitude surveys

Pollution

see Acid rain
see Air pollution
see Asbestos contamination
see Dioxins
see Environmental pollution and control
see Environmental regulation
see Global climate change

Index by Subjects and Names

see Marine pollution
see Mercury pollution
see Motor vehicle exhaust
see Noise
see Radiation
see Radon
see Soil pollution
see Water pollution

Polychlorinated biphenyls
see Carcinogens
see Hazardous substances
see Hazardous waste and disposal

Polyester
see Synthetic fibers and fabrics

Pomona, Calif.
see also under By City in the "Index by Categories"

Pompano Beach, Fla.
Housing starts and completions authorized by building permits in 40 MSAs, quarterly rpt, 2382–9
see also under By SMSA or MSA in the "Index by Categories"

Ponce, P.R.
see also under By SMSA or MSA in the "Index by Categories"

Poor
see Homeless population
see Poverty

Pope, Gregory C.
"Measuring Geographic Variations in Hospitals' Capital Costs", 4652–1.247

Population census
see Census of Population
see Census of Population and Housing

Population characteristics
Agricultural research funding and staffing for USDA, State agencies, and other instns, by topic, FY90, annual rpt, 1744–2
Alaska rural areas population characteristics, and energy resources dev effects, series, 5736–5
Census Bur rpts and data files, coverage and availability, 1991 annual listing, 2304–2
Census of Population and Current Population Survey data coverage and availability, 1991 pamphlet, 2326–7.78
Census of Population and Housing, 1990: population and housing characteristics, households, and land area, by county, subdiv, and place, State rpt series, 2551–1
Census of Population and Housing, 1990: population and housing selected characteristics, by region, press release, 2328–74
Census of Population and Housing, 1990: population size and characteristics, summary results and trends, fact sheet series, 2326–20
Coastal areas environmental and socioeconomic conditions, and potential impact of oil and gas OCS leases, final statement series, 5736–1
Current Population Reports, demographic, social, and economic characteristics, series, 2546–1
Current Population Reports, demographic subjects, special study series, 2546–2
Current Population Reports, income and socioeconomic characteristics of persons, families, and households, detailed cross-tabulations, series, 2546–6

Data on population and housing, and policy issues, fact sheet series, 2326–17
Developing countries economic and social conditions from 1960s, and Intl Dev Cooperation Agency and AID activities and funding, FY90-92, annual rpt, 9904–4
Developing countries economic, population, and agricultural data, US and other aid sources, and AID activity, country rpt series, 9916–12
Developing countries population and economic data, and AID dev projects, special study series, 9916–3
Florida environmental, social, and economic conditions, and impacts of proposed OCS oil and gas leases in southern coastal areas, 1990 compilation of papers, 5738–19
Foreign countries *Background Notes*, summary social, political, and economic data, series, 7006–2
Foreign countries economic and social conditions, working paper series, 2326–18
Foreign countries economic, social, political, and geographic summary data, by country, 1991, annual factbook, 9114–2
Govt spending measures using indicators of service costs and demand, with comparisons to fiscal capacity and actual outlays, by State, for State and local govts, 1986-87, 10048–77
Hispanic Americans in counties bordering Mexico, by selected characteristics, 1980, Current Population Rpt, 2546–2.159
Military active duty and recruit social, economic, and parents characteristics, by service branch and State, FY89, annual rpt, 3544–41
North Carolina environmental and socioeconomic conditions, and impacts of proposed OCS oil and gas exploration, 1970s-90 and projected to 2020, 5738–22
Overseas Business Reports: economic conditions, investment and export opportunities, and trade practices, country market research rpt series, 2046–6
Palau admin, and social, economic, and govtl data, FY90, annual rpt, 7004–6
Puerto Rico population and housing characteristics, 1990 Census of Population and Housing, press release, 2328–78
Research on population and reproduction, Federal funding by project, FY89, annual listing, 4474–9
Research on population and reproduction, Natl Inst of Child Health and Human Dev funding and activities, 1990, annual rpt, 4474–33
Research on population, family, and sexual behavior, activities and funding, 1960s-89, 4478–194
State and Metro Area Data Book, 1991 data compilation, 2328–54
Survey of Income and Program Participation, household composition, income, benefits, and labor force status, methodology, working paper series, 2626–10
Virgin Islands population and housing characteristics, 1990 Census of Population and Housing, press release, 2328–81
see also Aged and aging

Population projections

see also Birthplace
see also Body measurements
see also Children
see also Disabled and handicapped persons
see also Earnings, general
see also Educational attainment
see also Educational enrollment
see also Employment and unemployment, general
see also Families and households
see also Farm population
see also Fertility
see also Health condition
see also Homeless population
see also Housing condition and occupancy
see also Intelligence levels
see also Labor supply and demand
see also Life expectancy
see also Living arrangements
see also Marriage and divorce
see also Men
see also Migration
see also Nutrition and malnutrition
see also Occupations
see also Personal and household income
see also Personal consumption
see also Population projections
see also Population size
see also Poverty
see also Quality of life
see also Vital statistics
see also Wealth
see also Women
see also Youth

Population projections
AIDS cases by race, sex, and risk category, and deaths and survivors, projected 1989-93, 4206–2.34
Current Population Reports, population estimates and projections, by region and State, series, 2546–3
Developing countries aged population and selected characteristics, 1980s and projected to 2020, country rpt series, 2326–19
Foreign countries economic and social conditions, working paper series, 2326–18
Foreign countries economic indicators, and trade and trade flows by commodity, by country, data compilation, monthly CD-ROM, 2002–6
Foreign countries youth population declines relative to other age groups, by selected country, 1985 and projected to 2010, 9118–17
Great Lakes area economic conditions and outlook, for US and Canada, 1970s-90, 9375–15
North Carolina environmental and socioeconomic conditions, and impacts of proposed OCS oil and gas exploration, 1970s-90 and projected to 2020, 5738–22
OASDHI future cost estimates, actuarial study series, 4706–1
Older persons long-term care needs and costs, late 1980s and projected 2018-60, GAO rpt, 26121–433
State and Metro Area Data Book, 1991 data compilation, 2328–54
Statistical Abstract of US, 1991 annual data compilation, 2324–1.1; 2324–1.2
West Central States population, income, and employment growth, by MSA, metro-nonmetro location, and State, for Fed Reserve 10th District, 1970s-90s, article, 9381–1.209

Population size

Population size

Appalachia population, by State and county, 1980 and 1990, annual rpt, 9084–1

Cancer cases, by race, income, education, and area population density, for 3 metro areas, 1978-82, article, 4472–1.210

Census of Govts, 1987: employment, payroll, and average earnings, by function, level of govt, State, county, and population size, 2455–2

Census of Population and Current Population Survey data coverage and availability, 1991 pamphlet, 2326–7.78

Census of Population and Housing, 1990: population and housing characteristics, households, and land area, by county, subdiv, and place, State rpt series, 2551–1

Census of Population and Housing, 1990: population and housing selected characteristics, by region, press release, 2328–74

Census of Population and Housing, 1990: population size and characteristics, summary results and trends, fact sheet series, 2326–20

Census of Population and Housing, 1990: voting age and total population by race, and housing units, by block, redistricting counts required under PL 94-171, State CD-ROM series, 2551–6

Census of Population and Housing, 1990: voting age and total population by race, and housing units, by county and city, redistricting counts required under PL 94-171, State summary rpt series, 2551–5

Census of Population, 1990: Guam population by district, press release, 2328–79

Census of Population, 1990: Hispanic population by detailed origin, region, and State, with data for 1980, press release, 2328–73

Census of Population, 1990: homeless shelter and on-street population, by State and for 200 cities, press release, 2328–70

Census of Population, 1990: metro area population by race, Hispanic origin, and MSA, press release, 2328–75

Census of Population, 1990: population by detailed Native American, Asian, and Pacific Islander group, race, region, and State, with data for 1980, press release, 2328–72

Census of Population, 1990: population by State and region, with Federal and military personnel abroad by State of residence and agency, press release, 2328–66

Census of Population, 1990: post-enumeration survey results compared to census counts, by race, sex, city, county, and State, press release, 2328–69

Census of Population, 1990: urban areas land area, housing units, and population, by State and compared to rural areas, press release, 2328–39

Census of Population, 1990: urban areas population, for 396 areas, press release, 2328–37

Census of Population, 1990: Virgin Islands population by location, press release, 2328–77

Child population from age 10 and from birth, by county, 1988, annual rpt, 6064–12

Children and youth social, economic, and demographic characteristics, 1950s-90, 4818–5

City population size for cities with population over 100,000, as of Apr 1990, biennial press release, 2324–7

Communist and OECD countries economic conditions, 1989, annual rpt, 7144–11

County population size for counties with population over 100,000, as of Apr 1990, press release, 2328–68

Crimes, arrests by offender characteristics, and rates, by offense, and law enforcement employees, by population size and jurisdiction, 1990, annual rpt, 6224–2

Current Population Reports, demographic, social, and economic characteristics, series, 2546–1

Current Population Reports, demographic subjects, special study series, 2546–2

Current Population Reports, historical index, 1991 listing, 2546–2.160

Current Population Reports, population estimates and projections, by region and State, series, 2546–3

Current Population Reports, population estimates for civilian, resident, and total population, monthly rpt, 2542–1

Data on population and housing, and policy issues, fact sheet series, 2326–17

Developing countries aged population and selected characteristics, 1980s and projected to 2020, country rpt series, 2326–19

Developing countries agricultural supply, demand, and market for US exports, with socioeconomic conditions, country rpt series, 1526–6

Developing countries aided by Peace Corps, quality of life indicators, FY92, annual rpt, 9654–1

Developing countries economic and social conditions from 1960s, and Intl Dev Cooperation Agency and AID activities and funding, FY90-92, annual rpt, 9904–4

Developing countries economic, population, and agricultural data, US and other aid sources, and AID activity, country rpt series, 9916–12

Developing countries grains production and needs, and related economic outlook, by world area and selected country, forecast 1990/91-1991/92, 1528–313

Developing countries population and economic data, and AID dev projects, special study series, 9916–3

Developing countries urban population size, by selected city and country, 1991 annual rpt, 9914–4

Eastern Europe economic and political conditions, and impacts of geographic factors, by country, 1990 conf, 9118–18

Economic indicators and relation to govt finances by level of govt, selected years 1929-90, annual rpt, 10044–1

Energy use by mode of transport, fuel supply, and demographic and economic factors of vehicle use, 1970s-89, annual rpt, 3304–5

Environmental Quality, status of problems, protection programs, research, and intl issues, 1991 annual rpt, 484–1

Estuary environmental conditions, and fish and shellfish catch by species and region, 1980s, 2178–27

Foreign countries agricultural production, trade, and policies, summary data by country, 1989-90, annual factbook, 1924–12

Foreign countries *Background Notes*, summary social, political, and economic data, series, 7006–2

Foreign countries economic and social conditions, working paper series, 2326–18

Foreign countries economic indicators, and trade and trade flows by commodity, by country, data compilation, monthly CD-ROM, 2002–6

Foreign countries economic, social, political, and geographic summary data, by country, 1991, annual factbook, 9114–2

Foreign countries *Geographic Notes*, boundaries, claims, nomenclature, and other devs, periodic rpt, 7142–3

Foreign countries youth population declines relative to other age groups, by selected country, 1985 and projected to 2010, 9118–17

GNP changes related to labor force composition and changes in participation, model description and results, 1940s-2000, article, 9373–1.201

Govt spending measures using indicators of service costs and demand, with comparisons to fiscal capacity and actual outlays, by State, for State and local govts, 1986-87, 10048–77

Great Lakes area economic conditions and outlook, for US and Canada, 1970s-90, 9375–15

Health condition and health care resources, use, and spending, 1950s-89, annual data compilation, 4144–11

Hispanic Americans in counties bordering Mexico, by selected characteristics, 1980, Current Population Rpt, 2546–2.159

Income (personal) per capita disparity between metro and nonmetro areas, and causal factors, by State, 1979-88, 1548–380

Indian and Alaska Native population on reservations and in other designated areas, by selected site, 1990 census, press release, 2328–76

Japan economic conditions, financial and intl policies, and trade devs, 1950s-80s and projected to 2050, compilation of papers, 23848–220

Libraries (public) finances, staff, and operations, by State and population size, 1989, annual rpt, 4824–6

Minority group and women health condition, services use, payment sources, and health care labor force, by poverty status, 1940s-89, chartbook, 4118–56

Minority group health condition, services use, costs, and indicators of services need, 1950s-88, 4118–55

MSA population size, by area, as of Apr 1990, annual press release, 2324–8

NATO and Japan military spending and indicators of ability to support common defense, by country, 1970s-89, annual rpt, 3544–28

OASDI benefit payments, trust fund finances, and economic and demographic assumptions, 1970-90 and alternative projections to 2000, actuarial rpt, 4706–1.105

Pacific territories economic conditions, population characteristics, and Federal aid, 1989 hearing, 21448–44

Palau admin, and social, economic, and govtl data, FY90, annual rpt, 7004–6

Population size, by age, selected years 1929-90, annual rpt, 204–1.2

Population size, July 1981-89 and compared to 1980 and 1990, annual press release, 2324–10

Puerto Rico population and housing characteristics, 1990 Census of Population and Housing, press release, 2328–78

Research on population and reproduction, Federal funding by project, FY89, annual listing, 4474–9

Research on population and reproduction, Natl Inst of Child Health and Human Dev funding and activities, 1990, annual rpt, 4474–33

Rural areas economic conditions and dev, quarterly journal, 1502–8

Soviet Union, Eastern Europe, OECD, and selected other countries economic conditions, 1960s-90, annual rpt, 9114–4.2

State and Metro Area Data Book, 1991 data compilation, 2328–54

Statistical Abstract of US, 1991 annual data compilation, 2324–1.1

Virgin Islands population and housing characteristics, 1990 Census of Population and Housing, press release, 2328–81

Vital statistics provisional data, monthly rpt, 4142–1

Voting age population, by State, 1992 general elections, press release, 9276–1.92

Voting age population, by State, 1992 primary elections, press release, 9276–1.90

see also Births

see also Deaths

see also Family planning

see also Farm population

see also Fertility

see also Immigration and emigration

see also Migration

see also Population projections

see also Vital statistics

Porcelain products

see Pottery and porcelain products

Porcella, Ronald L.

"Catalogue of U.S. Geological Survey Strong-Motion Records, 1988", 5664–14

Porell, Frank W.

"Medicare Risk Contracting: Determinants of Market Entry", 4652–1.226

Pork

see Meat and meat products

Pornography

see Obscenity and pornography

Porpoises

see Marine mammals

Port Arthur, Tex.

Wages by occupation, and benefits for office and plant workers, 1991 survey, periodic MSA rpt, 6785–3.6

see also under By SMSA or MSA in the "Index by Categories"

Port authorities

see Special districts

Porter, Donna V.

"Nutrition Labeling: Current Status and Comparison of Various Proposals", 1004–16.1

Porterville, Calif.

see also under By SMSA or MSA in the "Index by Categories"

Portland, Maine

Wages by occupation, for office and plant workers, 1990 survey, periodic MSA rpt, 6785–11.3

see also under By SMSA or MSA in the "Index by Categories"

Portland, Oreg.

CPI by component for US city average, and by region, population size, and for 27 metro areas, monthly rpt, 6762–2

Drug test results at arrest, by drug type, offense, and sex, for selected urban areas, quarterly rpt, 6062–3

see also under By City and By SMSA or MSA in the "Index by Categories"

Ports

see Harbors and ports

Portsmouth, N.H.

see also under By SMSA or MSA in the "Index by Categories"

Portsmouth, Ohio

Wages by occupation, and benefits for office and plant workers, 1991 survey, periodic MSA rpt, 6785–3.5

Portsmouth, Va.

see also under By City in the "Index by Categories"

Portugal

Agricultural exports of high-value commodities, indexes and sales by commodity, world area, and country, 1960s-86, 1528–323

Agricultural production, prices, and trade, by country, 1970s-90, and forecast 1991, annual world region rpt, 1524–4.4

Agricultural production, trade, and policies in foreign countries, summary data by country, 1989-90, annual factbook, 1924–12

Agricultural trade of US, by detailed commodity and country, 1989, annual rpt, 1524–8

Agricultural trade of US, by detailed commodity and country, 1990, semiannual rpt, 1522–4

AID economic aid to developing countries, obligations and disbursements by country, quarterly rpt, 9912–4

AID loans repayment status and terms by program and country, and status of predecessor agency loans, quarterly rpt, 9912–3

Background Notes, summary social, political, and economic data, 1990 rpt, 7006–2.41

Economic and military aid and loans from US and intl agencies, by program and country, FY46-90, annual rpt, 9914–5

Economic and social conditions of developing countries from 1960s, and Intl Dev Cooperation Agency and AID activities and funding, FY90-92, annual rpt, 9904–4

Economic conditions, income, production, prices, employment, and trade, 1991 periodic country rpt, 2046–4.52

Economic conditions, investment and export opportunities, and trade practices, 1991 country market research rpt, 2046–6.1

Economic conditions, policy, and trade practices, by country, 1988-90, annual rpt, 21384–5

Economic, social, political, and geographic summary data, by country, 1991, annual factbook, 9114–2

Exports and imports of NATO members with PRC, by country, 1987-90, annual rpt, 7144–14

Exports and imports of OECD members, by country, 1989, annual rpt, 7144–10

Exports and imports of US, by Harmonized System 6-digit commodity and country, 1990, annual rpt, 2424–13

Exports and imports of US, by selected country, country group, and commodity group, 1990, annual rpt, 2044–37

Exports and imports of US, by transport mode, country, and SITC 1- to 3-digit commodity, 1990, annual rpt, 2424–12

Exports and imports of US with EC by country, and total agricultural trade, selected years 1958-90, annual rpt, 7144–7

Exports of US, detailed Schedule B commodities with countries of destination, 1990, annual rpt, 2424–10

Fish (squid) catch, trade, consumption, and cold storage holdings, by country and species, 1963-90, 2166–19.10

GNP and GNP growth for OECD members, by country, 1980-90, annual rpt, 7144–8

Human rights conditions in 170 countries, and US economic and military aid, 1990, annual rpt, 21384–3

Imports of goods, services, and investment from US, trade barriers, impacts, and US actions, by country, 1990, annual rpt, 444–2

Labor conditions, union coverage, and work accidents, 1990 annual country rpt, 6366–4.6

Military aid of US, arms sales, and training programs costs and budget requests, by program, world region, and country, FY90-92, annual rpt, 7144–13

Multinatl US firms and foreign affiliates finances and operations, by industry and world area of parent firm, 1989 benchmark survey, preliminary annual rpt, 2704–5

Multinatl US firms foreign affiliates, income statement items by country and world area, 1986, biennial article, 8302–2.212

Oil production, trade, use, and stocks, by selected country and country group, monthly rpt, 3162–42

Steel imports of US under voluntary restraint agreement, by product, customs district, and country, with US industry operating data, quarterly rpt, 9882–13

Tax revenue, by level of govt and type of tax, for OECD countries, mid 1960s-89, annual rpt, 10044–1.2

UN voting record and share of votes in agreement with US, by issue, country, and world area, 1990, annual rpt, 7004–18

see also Macao

see also under By Foreign Country in the "Index by Categories"

Porvaznik, John

"Digestive System Diseases", 4088–2

Post exchanges

see Military post exchanges and commissaries

Postal employees

Assaults and deaths of law enforcement officers, by circumstances, agency, victim and offender characteristics, and location, 1990, annual rpt, 6224–3

Budget of US, object class analysis of obligations, by agency, FY92, annual rpt, 104–9

Census of Govts, 1987: employment, payroll, and average earnings, by function, level of govt, State, county, and population size, 2455–2

Employment (civilian) of Fed Govt, by work schedule, selected agency, State, and MSA, as of Dec 1990, biennial article, 9842–1.203

Employment (civilian) of Fed Govt, work-years, pay rates, and benefits use and costs, by agency, FY89, annual rpt, 9844–31

Employment and payroll, by function, level of govt, and State, 1990, annual rpt, 2466–1.1

Employment and related expenses of USPS, FY90, annual rpt, 9864–5.1; 9864–5.3

Employment, earnings, and hours, by SIC 1- to 4-digit industry, monthly and annual averages, selected years 1909-90, annual rpt, 6744–4

Inspection activities of USPS, FY90, annual rpt, 9864–9

Labor productivity of Federal employees, indexes of output and labor costs by function, 1967-89, annual rpt, 6824–1.6

Pay and benefit costs, by type, for USPS, FY89-90, annual article, 9842–1.204

Payroll and other operating costs of USPS, itemized by class of mail, FY90, annual rpt, 9864–4

Payroll of Fed Govt, spending for civilian, military, and postal workers by State, FY90, annual rpt, 2464–2

Postal Service activities, financial statements, and employment, FY86-90, annual rpt, 9864–1

Postal Service postage rates since 1775, and city and rural delivery routes, FY89, annual rpt, special supplement, 9864–6

Postal Service revenue, costs, and volume, by service type and class of mail, FY90, annual rpt, 9864–2

Productivity of USPS, indexes of output and labor, capital, and other inputs, alternative model descriptions and results, 1960s-89, 9688–6

Postal Rate Commission

Productivity of USPS, indexes of inputs and output, labor costs, and efficiency, and model descriptions and results, 1960s-89, 9688–6

Postal service

Air mail (foreign and US) carried by US scheduled service carriers, by carrier, monthly rpt, 7302–6

Air mail carried by US certificated carriers, by airport and carrier, 1990, annual rpt, 7504–35

Air mail, passenger, and cargo traffic, and airline operations, by type of service, air carrier, State, and country, 1980-89, annual rpt, 7504–1.6

Airline finances, by carrier, carrier group, and for total certificated system, quarterly rpt, 7302–7

Airline operations and passenger, cargo, and mail traffic, by type of service, air carrier, State, and country, 1980-89, annual rpt, 7504–1.4

Bombing incidents, casualties, and damage, by target, circumstances, and State, 1990, annual rpt, 6224–5

Budget of US, obligations and authority by function, agency, and program, with summaries, analyses, and historical tables, FY92, annual rpt, 104–2

Court civil and criminal caseloads for Federal district, appeals, and bankruptcy courts, by type of suit and offense, circuit, and district, 1990, annual rpt, 18204–11

Court civil and criminal caseloads for Federal district, appeals, and special courts, 1990, annual rpt, 18204–8

Court civil and criminal caseloads for Federal district courts, 1991, annual rpt, 18204–2.1

CPI by component for US city average, and by region, population size, and for 27 metro areas, monthly rpt, 6762–2

Criminal case processing in Federal courts by disposition, and prisoners, by offense and jurisdiction, data compilation, 1991 annual rpt, 6064–6.5; 6064–6.6

Criminal cases by type and disposition, and collections, for US attorneys, by Federal district, FY90, annual rpt, 6004–2.1; 6004–2.7

Criminal cases in Federal district courts, by offense, disposition, and district, 1980-90, last issue of annual rpt, 18204–1

Criminal sentences for Federal offenses, guidelines by offense and circumstances, series, 17668–1

Customer satisfaction with USPS, and on-time 1st class mail delivery, by region and city, 1991 survey, press release, 9868–1

Customs Service activities, collections, entries processed by mode of transport, and seizures, FY86-90, annual rpt, 8144–1

Expenditures of Fed Govt, by function, FY89, annual rpt, 2466–2.2

Exports and imports of philatelic material, by country, 1990, annual rpt, 2424–13

Exports of philatelic material, by country of destination, 1990, annual rpt, 2424–10

Express parcel shipments and revenues of private air and surface carriers, and impact of State regulation, 1976-89, 7308–201

Finances of Fed Govt, cash and debt transactions, daily tables, 8102–4

Foreign and US domestic postal rates, for 14 countries, 1990, annual rpt, 9864–5.1

Foreign govt and private obligors debt to US, by country and program, periodic rpt, 8002–6

Govt finances, tax systems and revenue, and fiscal structure, by level of govt and State, 1991 with historical trends, annual rpt, 10044–1

House of Representatives salaries, expenses, and contingent fund disbursement, detailed listings, quarterly rpt, 21942–1

Households incoming and outgoing mail volume, use, and views, by class, source, content, and household characteristics, 1987-88, annual rpt, 9864–10

Inspection activities of USPS, FY90, annual rpt, 9864–9

Inspection activities of USPS, 2nd half FY91, semiannual rpt, 9862–2

Mail postage rates of USPS since 1775, and city and rural delivery routes, FY89, annual rpt, special supplement, 9864–6

Parcel deliveries to and from households, carrier preferences, and content, for USPS and competitors, 1987-88, annual rpt, 9864–10

Price indexes (producer), by stage of processing and detailed commodity, monthly rpt, 6762–6

Productivity of USPS, indexes of output and labor, capital, and other inputs, alternative model descriptions and results, 1960s-89, 9688–6

Revenue and subsidy for revenue forgone, by class of mail, FY90, annual rpt, 9864–5

Revenue and volume by class of mail, and special service transactions, quarterly rpt, 9862–1

Revenue and volume, by class of mail and type of service, FY86-90, annual rpt, 9864–1

Revenue, costs, and volume, by class of mail, FY90, annual rpt, 9864–2

Senate receipts, itemized expenses by payee, and balances, 1st half FY91, semiannual listing, 25922–1

Statistical Abstract of US, 1991 annual data compilation, 2324–1.18

see also Postal employees

see also ZIP codes

see also under By Industry in the "Index by Categories"

Postsecondary Education Transcript Study

Higher education course completions, by detailed program, sex, race, and instn type, for 1972 high school class, as of 1984, 4888–4

Postsecondary Quick Information System

Data collection activities and programs of NCES, 1991, annual listing, 4824–7

Potash

Fertilizer consumption, by type and region, 1947-89, annual rpt, 1544–17.2

Fertilizer production capacity by firm, for US and Canada, 1986-91 and projected to 1997, triennial rpt, 9808–66

Mineral industries census, 1987: energy use and costs, by fuel type, SIC 2- to 4-digit industry, and State, subject rpt, 2517–2

Mineral industries census, 1987: finances and operations, by SIC 2- to 4-digit industry, State, and county, census div rpt series, 2515–1

Mineral Industry Surveys, commodity review of production, trade, and use, 1990, advance annual rpt, 5614–5.20

Minerals Yearbook, 1989, Vol 2: State reviews of production, sales, and firms, by commodity, and business activity, annual rpt, 5604–34

Mines (nonmetallic minerals) and related operations occupational injuries and incidence, employment, and hours, 1989, annual rpt, 6664–1

Price indexes (producer), by stage of processing and detailed commodity, monthly 1990, annual rpt, 6764–2

Production of potash, prices, trade, use, and sales, 1990 crop year, Mineral Industry Surveys, annual rpt, 5614–19

Index by Subjects and Names

Production, prices, trade, use, employment, tariffs, and stockpiles, by mineral, with foreign comparisons, 1986-90, annual rpt, 5604–18

Statistical Abstract of US, 1991 annual data compilation, 2324–1.25

Potatoes

see Vegetables and vegetable products

Poterba, James M.

"Comparing the Cost of Capital in the U.S. and Japan: A Survey of Methods", 9385–1.202

Potomac River

- Army Corps of Engineers water resources dev projects, characteristics, and costs, 1950s-89, biennial State rpt series, 3756–1
- Army Corps of Engineers water resources dev projects, characteristics, and costs, 1950s-91, biennial State rpt series, 3756–2

Fish (striped bass) stocks status on Atlantic coast, and sport and commercial catch by State, 1979-88, annual rpt, 5504–29

Water quality, chemistry, hydrology, and other characteristics, 1990 local area study, 5666–27.22

- Water supply and quality in streams and lakes, and groundwater levels in wells, by drainage basin, 1988, annual State rpt series, 5666–16
- Water supply and quality in streams and lakes, and groundwater levels in wells, by drainage basin, 1989, annual State rpt series, 5666–12
- Water supply and quality in streams and lakes, and groundwater levels in wells, by drainage basin, 1990, annual State rpt series, 5666–10

Water supply in US and southern Canada, streamflow, surface and groundwater conditions, and reservoir levels, by location, monthly rpt, 5662–3

Potter, D. E.

"Data Collection Organization Effects in the National Medical Expenditure Survey", 4188–68

Pottery and porcelain products

- County Business Patterns, 1988: employment, establishments, and payroll, by SIC 2- to 4-digit industry and county, annual State rpt series, 2326–6
- County Business Patterns, 1989: employment, establishments, and payroll, by SIC 2- to 4-digit industry and county, annual State rpt series, 2326–8
- Exports and imports of US, by country and detailed commodity, monthly rpt, 2422–12
- Exports and imports of US, by Harmonized System 6-digit commodity and country, 1990, annual rpt, 2424–13
- Exports and imports of US, by transport mode, country, and SITC 1- to 3-digit commodity, 1990, annual rpt, 2424–12
- Exports of US, detailed Schedule B commodities with countries of destination, 1990, annual rpt, 2424–10
- Injuries from use of consumer products, by severity, victim age, and detailed product, 1990, annual rpt, 9164–6
- Manufacturing census, 1987: finances and operations, by SIC 2- to 4-digit industry, State, and MSA, with trends from 1849, 2497–1

Manufacturing census, 1987: finances and operations, by type of organization and SIC 2- to 4-digit industry, subject rpt, 2497–5

Plumbing fixtures shipments, stocks, trade, use, and firms, by product, quarterly Current Industrial Rpt, 2506–11.2

- Price indexes (producer), by stage of processing and detailed commodity, monthly rpt, 6762–6
- Price indexes (producer), by stage of processing and detailed commodity, monthly 1990, annual rpt, 6764–2
- Technologically advanced structural materials devs, use, and K&D funding, for ceramics, metal alloys, polymers, and composites, 1960s-80s and projected to 2000, 5608–162

Poughkeepsie, N.Y.

see also under By SMSA or MSA in the "Index by Categories"

Poultry industry and products

Agricultural Statistics, 1990, annual rpt, 1004–1

- Agriculture census, 1987: farms, farmland, production, finances, and operator characteristics, by county, final State rpt series, 2331–1
- Business statistics, detailed data for major industries and economic indicators, *Survey of Current Business,* monthly rpt, 2702–1.14
- Cold storage food stocks by commodity and census div, and warehouse space use, by State, monthly rpt, 1631–5
- Cold storage food stocks by commodity, and warehouse space use, by census div, 1990, annual rpt, 1631–11
- Consumer Expenditure Survey, food spending by item, household composition, income, age, race, and region, 1980-88, biennial rpt, 1544–30
- Consumer Expenditure Survey, household income by source, and itemized spending, by selected characteristics and region, 1988-89, annual rpt, 6764–5
- Consumption of food, dietary composition, and nutrient intake, 1987/88 natl survey, preliminary rpt series, 1356–1
- Consumption, supply, trade, prices, spending, and indexes, by food commodity, 1989, annual rpt, 1544–4
- County Business Patterns, 1988: employment, establishments, and payroll, by SIC 2- to 4-digit industry and county, annual State rpt series, 2326–6
- County Business Patterns, 1989: employment, establishments, and payroll, by SIC 2- to 4-digit industry and county, annual State rpt series, 2326–8
- CPI by component for US city average, and by region, population size, and for 27 metro areas, monthly rpt, 6762–2
- Developing countries agricultural supply, demand, and market for US exports, with socioeconomic conditions, country rpt series, 1526–6
- Egg production and layer inventory, by State, 1989-90, annual rpt, 1625–7
- Egg production and trade, by country, 1986-91, article, 1561–7.204
- Egg production by type of product, and eggs broken under Federal inspection by region, monthly rpt, 1625–2

Poultry industry and products

- Eggs set and chicks placed in broiler hatcheries, by State, weekly rpt, 1625–11
- Employment, earnings, and hours, by SIC 1- to 4-digit industry, monthly and annual averages, selected years 1909-90, annual rpt, 6744–4
- Exports (agricultural) of high-value commodities, indexes and sales value by commodity, world area, and country, 1960s-86, 1528–323
- Exports (agricultural) of US, impacts of foreign agricultural and trade policy, with data by commodity and country, 1989, annual rpt, 1924–8
- Exports and imports (agricultural) commodity and country, prices, and world market devs, monthly rpt, 1922–12
- Exports and imports (agricultural) of US, by commodity and country, bimonthly rpt, 1522–1
- Exports and imports (agricultural) of US, by detailed commodity and country, 1989, annual rpt, 1524–8
- Exports and imports (agricultural) of US, by detailed commodity and country, 1990, semiannual rpt, 1522–4
- Exports and imports between US and outlying areas, by detailed commodity and mode of transport, 1990, annual rpt, 2424–11
- Exports and imports of dairy, livestock, and poultry products, by commodity and country, FAS monthly circular, 1925–32
- Exports and imports of US, by country and detailed commodity, monthly rpt, 2422–12
- Exports and imports of US, by Harmonized System 6-digit commodity and country, 1990, annual rpt, 2424–13
- Exports and imports of US, by transport mode, country, and SITC 1- to 3-digit commodity, 1990, annual rpt, 2424–12
- Exports of US, detailed Schedule B commodities with countries of destination, 1990, annual rpt, 2424–10
- Farm financial and marketing conditions, forecast 1991, annual chartbook, 1504–8
- Farm financial and marketing conditions, forecast 1991, annual conf, 1004–16
- Farm income, expenses, receipts by commodity, assets, liabilities, and ratios, 1990 and trends from 1945, annual rpt, 1544–16
- Farm sector balance sheet, and receipts by detailed commodity, by State, 1985-89, annual rpt, 1544–18
- Foreign and US dairy production, trade, and use, by selected country, FAS semiannual circular series, 1925–33
- Foreign countries agricultural production, prices, and trade, by country, 1980-90 and forecast 1991, annual world area rpt series, 1524–4
- Foreign countries agricultural production, trade, and policies, summary data by country, 1989-90, annual factbook, 1924–12
- Inspection of meat and poultry, Federal, State, and foreign govts activities and staff, FY90, annual rpt, 1374–1
- Inspection of poultry slaughter by Fed Govt, pounds certified, and condemnations by cause, by State, monthly rpt, 1625–3
- Labor productivity, indexes of output, hours, and employment by SIC 2- to 4-digit industry, 1967-89, annual rpt, 6824–1.3

Poultry industry and products

Manufacturing annual survey, 1989: finances and operations, by SIC 2- to 4-digit industry, series, 2506–15

Manufacturing census, 1987: finances and operations, by SIC 2- to 4-digit industry, State, and MSA, with trends from 1849, 2497–1

Manufacturing census, 1987: finances and operations, by type of organization and SIC 2- to 4-digit industry, subject rpt, 2497–5

Manufacturing finances and operations, by SIC 2- to 4-digit industry, forecast 1991, annual rpt, 2044–28

Natl Poultry Improvement Plan participating hatcheries and birds, by species and disease program, 1991, annual listing, 1394–15

Nutrient, caloric, and waste composition, detailed data for raw, processed, and prepared foods, 1991 rpt, 1356–3.15

Occupational injury and illness rates, by SIC 2- to 4-digit industry, 1988-89, annual rpt, 6844–7

Occupational injury and illness rates, by SIC 2- to 4-digit industry, 1989, annual rpt, 6844–1

Price indexes (producer), by stage of processing and detailed commodity, monthly rpt, 6762–6

Price indexes (producer), by stage of processing and detailed commodity, monthly 1990, annual rpt, 6764–2

Prices (farm-retail) for food, marketing cost components, and industry finances and productivity, 1920s-90, annual rpt, 1544–9

Prices (producer and retail) of meat and fish, 1981-91, semiannual situation rpt, 1561–15.3

Prices and marketing of poultry and eggs, by selected region, State, and city, monthly and weekly 1990, annual rpt, 1317–2

Prices received and paid by farmers, by commodity and State, 1990, annual rpt, 1629–5

Prices received by farmers for major products, and paid for farm inputs and living items, by State, monthly rpt, 1629–1

Production and inventories for chickens, eggs, and turkeys, monthly rpt, 1625–1

Production and prices for chickens, eggs, and turkeys, by State, 1989-90, annual rpt, 1625–5

Production inputs, output, and productivity for farms, by commodity and region, 1947-89, annual rpt, 1544–17

Production itemized costs, by farm sales size and region, 1990, annual rpt, 1614–3

Production of chicken and turkey hatcheries, by State, 1989-90, annual rpt, 1625–8

Production, prices, trade, and marketing, by commodity, current situation and forecast, monthly rpt with articles, 1502–4

Production, prices, trade, and stocks, monthly rpt, 1561–17

Production, prices, trade, stocks, and use, periodic situation rpt with articles, 1561–7

Soviet Union agricultural trade, by commodity and country, 1955-90, 1528–322

State and Metro Area Data Book, 1991 data compilation, 2328–54

Statistical Abstract of US, 1991 annual data compilation, 2324–1.23

Supply and demand indicators for livestock and dairy products, and for selected foreign and US crops, monthly rpt, 1522–5

Tax (income) returns of partnerships, income statement and balance sheet items, by industry group, 1989, annual article, 8302–2.216; 8304–18

Turkey hatcheries egg inventory and poult placements, by region, monthly rpt, 1625–10

Turkey production by State, and farms, by region, 1960s-90, article, 1561–7.202

Turkey production by State, and losses by region, 1989-90, and hatchery plans, 1991, annual rpt, 1625–6

Wholesale trade census, 1987: establishments, sales by customer class, employment, inventories, and expenses, by SIC 2- to 4-digit kind of business, 2407–4

see also under By Commodity in the "Index by Categories"

Poverty

Agricultural Conservation Program participation by low-income farmers, by State, FY90, annual rpt, 1804–7

AIDS public knowledge, attitudes, and risk behaviors, for women, 1988 survey, 4146–8.200

Appalachia education system, improvement initiatives, and indicators of success, by State, 1960s-89, 9088–36

Black Americans social and economic characteristics, for South and total US, 1989-90 and trends from 1969, Current Population Rpt, 2546–1.450

Black poor men's drug and condom use and sexual behavior, local area study, 1991 article, 4042–3.254

Budget of US, compilation of background material on fiscal and tax policy, 1960s-96, 21788–203

Budget of US, House Budget Committee analysis of Bush Admin proposals and economic assumptions, FY92, 21268–42

CCC dairy price support program foreign donations and domestic donations to poor, schools, Prisons Bur, and VA, monthly rpt, 1802–2

Child and family health, education, and welfare condition, findings and recommendations, 1991 rpt, 15528–1

Child care needs impacts on mothers labor force status, and unemployed mothers characteristics, 1986, article, 6722–1.245

Child health, behavioral, emotional, and school problems relation to family structure, by selected characteristics, 1988, 4147–10.178

Child health condition and services use, 1990 chartbook, 4108–49

Child support and alimony awards, and payment status, by selected characteristics of woman, 1989, biennial Current Population Rpt, 2546–6.72

Children and youth social, economic, and demographic characteristics, 1950s-90, 4818–5

Children in poverty by selected family characteristics, for rural areas compared to urban areas, 1987-88, 1598–270

Index by Subjects and Names

Condition of Education, detail for elementary and secondary education, 1920s-90 and projected to 2001, annual rpt, 4824–1.1

Consumer Income, socioeconomic characteristics of persons, families, and households, detailed cross-tabulations, Current Population Rpt series, 2546–6

Developing countries economic and social conditions from 1960s, and Intl Dev Cooperation Agency and AID activities and funding, FY90-92, annual rpt, 9904–4

Disability, acute and chronic health conditions, absenteeism, and health services use, by selected characteristics, 1987, CD-ROM, 4147–10.177

Economic Report of the President for 1991, Joint Economic Committee critique and policy recommendations, annual rpt, 23844–2

Education (compensatory) programs in high poverty school districts, Federal grant program activities, participation, and coordinators views, 1989/90, 4808–32

Education in poverty areas, schools academic environment and teaching methods impacts on student performance, 1989/90 study, 4808–28

Elementary and secondary students educational performance, and factors affecting proficiency, by selected characteristics, 1988 natl assessments, subject rpt series, 4896–7

Employment and unemployment in metro and nonmetro poverty and nonpoverty areas, monthly rpt, quarterly data, 6742–2.9

Energy aid for low income households, funding sources, costs, and participation, by State, FY89, annual rpt, 4694–8

Family and population poverty status, by race, 1970-89, annual rpt, 204–1.1

Family economic impacts of departure, absence, and presence of parents, 1983-86, Current Population Rpt, 2546–20.17

Fed Govt programs under Ways and Means Committee jurisdiction, finances, operations, and participant characteristics, FY70s-90, annual rpt, 21784–11

Financial instns location relation to ZIP code area income and minority population, by instn type for 5 cities, 1977-89, article, 9377–1.208

Food stamp recipient household size, composition, income, and income and deductions allowed, summer 1988, annual rpt, 1364–8

Foreign countries family composition, poverty status, labor conditions, and welfare indicators and needs, by country, 1960s-88, hearing, 23846–4.30

Foreign countries labor conditions, union coverage, and work accidents, annual country rpt series, 6366–4

Foster care placement of black children whose parents abuse drugs, by placement reason and outcome, and household and parent characteristics, 1986-90, 4008–114

Health care device implants, by type, reason, duration, and user characteristics, 1988, 4146–8.197

Health condition improvement and disease prevention goals and recommended activities for 2000, with trends 1970s-80s, 4048–10

Index by Subjects and Names

Prefabricated buildings

Health condition, services use, payment sources, and health care labor force, for minorities and women by poverty status, 1940s-89, chartbook, 4118–56

Hispanic Americans in counties bordering Mexico, by selected characteristics, 1980, Current Population Rpt, 2546–2.159

Hispanic Americans social and economic characteristics, by detailed origin, 1991, Current Population Rpt, 2546–1.448; 2546–1.451

Hospital operations, and services spending by type and payment source, with background data and foreign comparisons, 1960s-80s and projected to 2000, 26308–98

Hospital reimbursement by Medicaid, impacts of Federal and State provisions, with services use, costs, and profits, by State, 1980s, 17206–1.11

Hospital reimbursement by Medicare under prospective payment system, alternative complexity indexes for diagnosis related groups, with background data, FY86-88, annual rpt, 17206–2.21

Hospital tax exempt status dependent on acceptance of charity, Medicare, and Medicaid cases, proposal and issues with background data, 1989, press release, 8008–149

Households composition, income, benefits, and labor force status, Survey of Income and Program Participation methodology, working paper series, 2626–10

Housing and households characteristics, unit and neighborhood quality, and journey to work by MSA location, for 11 MSAs, 1984 survey, supplement, 2485–8

Housing and households detailed characteristics, and unit and neighborhood quality, by location, 1987, biennial rpt supplement, 2485–13

Housing and households detailed characteristics, and unit and neighborhood quality, by location, 1989, biennial rpt, 2485–12

Housing and households detailed characteristics, and unit and neighborhood quality, MSA surveys, series, 2485–6

Housing inventory change from 1973, by reason, unit and household characteristics, and location, 1983 survey, biennial rpt, 2485–14

Housing worst case problems prevalence and households characteristics, for poor households with high rent, and substandard units, 1970s-84, annual rpt, 5184–10

Immigrants in US, population characteristics and fertility, by birthplace and compared to native born, 1980s, Current Population rpt, 2546–2.162

Income (household) and poverty status under alternative income definitions, by recipient characteristics, 1990, annual Current Population Rpt, 2546–6.69

Income (personal) and poverty status changes, by selected characteristics, 1987-88, Current Population Rpt, 2546–20.19

Income guidelines for Federal poverty definition, by family size, 1991, biennial article, 4742–1.217

Indian Health Service facilities and use, and Indian health and other characteristics, by IHS region, 1980s-89, annual chartbook, 4084–7

Insurance (health) coverage, by insurance type and selected characteristics, 1989, 4146–8.203

Insurance (health) coverage, uninsured population under age 65 by selected characteristics, 1987, 4186–8.13

Insurance (health) natl coverage alternative proposals and indicators of need, 1989, 4658–54

Job Training Partnership Act funding and performance indicators in service delivery areas, by urban-rural location, 1987-88, 1598–266

Medicare and Medicaid eligibility, participation, coverage, and program finances, various periods 1966-91, biennial rpt, 4654–1

Minority group health condition, services use, costs, and indicators of services need, 1950s-88, 4118–55

Older persons in rural areas, household income sources, and poverty status, 1983-84, 1598–268

Older persons poverty status by health and other characteristics, and Medicaid income and asset eligibility limits by State, 1984-90, 23898–5

Older persons with functional limitations, long-term care sources, and health and other characteristics, 1984-85, 4147–13.104

Population and families in poverty, by detailed socioeconomic characteristics, 1988-89 annual Current Population Rpt, 2546–6.67

Population and families in poverty, by detailed socioeconomic characteristics, 1990 annual Current Population Rpt, 2546–6.71

Population in poverty under alternative measurement methods, and public opinion on poverty definition, 1988-89, hearing, 21968–56

Population poverty status, and poverty area definitions, by metro-nonmetro location, 1972-89, article, 6722–1.219

Population poverty status by age group and living arrangements, and family poverty threshold, late 1930s-91, annual rpt, 4744–3.1

Population poverty status, threshold and rates under alternative threshold adjustment methodologies, 1980s-90, hearing, 23848–221

Population size and characteristics, historical index to *Current Population Rpts,* 1991 listing, 2546–2.160

Population size and characteristics, 1969-88, Current Population Rpt, biennial rpt, 2546–2.161

Pregnancies of poor women, by whether intended, outcome, contraceptives use, marital status, and race, 1985-86 local area study, article, 4042–3.241

Prenatal care subsidy need under alternative poverty indicators, for 8 southern States, 1984-87, article, 4042–3.226

Rural and urban areas workers poverty rate relation to employment and other characteristics, 1987, 1598–274

Rural areas economic and social indicators used to determine Federal aid need, late 1960s-86, 1598–265

Rural areas economic conditions and dev, quarterly journal, 1502–8

Rural areas housing loan programs of FmHA, and housing voucher demonstration program results, 1980s, hearing, 21248–143

Single mothers earnings, employment and welfare benefits, and poverty status, 1989, GAO rpt, 26121–413

Smoking exposure of children before and after birth, by source and degree of exposure and family characteristics, 1988, 4146–8.204

State and Metro Area Data Book, 1991 data compilation, 2328–54

Statistical Abstract of US, 1991 annual data compilation, 2324–1.14

Student Community Service Program activities, and volunteer and client characteristics, 1987-89, 9028–14

Teenage mothers child support awards, payment status, health insurance inclusion, and govt aid for collection, by selected characteristics, 1987, 4698–5

Telephone local service charges and low-income subsidies, by region, company, and city, 1980s-90, semiannual rpt, 9282–8

Women's labor force status, earnings, and other characteristics, with comparisons to men, fact sheet series, 6564–1

see also Homeless population

see also under By Income in the "Index by Categories"

Powell, James A.

"Manatee Grazing Impacts on Seagrasses in Hobe Sound and Jupiter Sound in Southeast Florida During the Winter of 1988-89", 14738–12

Power plants

see Electric power plants and equipment

Power resources

see terms listed under Energy resources and consumption

Power tools

see Tools

Pozdena, Randall J.

"Interstate Banking and Competition: Evidence from the Behavior of Stock Returns", 9393–8.205

"Why Banks Need Commerce Powers", 9393–8.206

Pratt, William F.

"Fecundity and Infertility in the U.S., 1965-88", 4146–8.194

PRC

see China, Peoples Republic

Precious metals

see Gold

see Silver

Precious stones

see Gemstones

Precipitation

see Weather

Predictions

see Projections and forecasts

Prefabricated buildings

County Business Patterns, 1988: employment, establishments, and payroll, by SIC 2- to 4-digit industry and county, annual State rpt series, 2326–6

County Business Patterns, 1989: employment, establishments, and payroll, by SIC 2- to 4-digit industry and county, annual State rpt series, 2326–8

Employment, earnings, and hours, by SIC 1- to 4-digit industry, monthly and annual averages, selected years 1909-90, annual rpt, 6744–4

Prefabricated buildings

Exports and imports of US, by country and detailed commodity, monthly rpt, 2422–12

Exports and imports of US, by Harmonized System 6-digit commodity and country, 1990, annual rpt, 2424–13

Exports and imports of US, by transport mode, country, and SITC 1- to 3-digit commodity, 1990, annual rpt, 2424–12

Exports of US, detailed Schedule B commodities with countries of destination, 1990, annual rpt, 2424–10

Log home manufacturers in Montana, sales, production, and timber use, 1960s-88, 1208–370

Manufacturing annual survey, 1989: finances and operations, by SIC 2- to 4-digit industry, series, 2506–15

Manufacturing census, 1987: finances and operations, by SIC 2- to 4-digit industry, State, and MSA, with trends from 1849, 2497–1

Manufacturing census, 1987: finances and operations, by type of organization and SIC 2- to 4-digit industry, subject rpt, 2497–5

Manufacturing finances and operations, by SIC 2- to 4-digit industry, forecast 1991, annual rpt, 2044–28

Mortgages FHA-insured, financial, property, and mortgagor characteristics, by State, 1990, annual rpt, 5144–1

Occupational injury and illness rates, by SIC 2- to 4-digit industry, 1988-89, annual rpt, 6844–7

Occupational injury and illness rates, by SIC 2- to 4-digit industry, 1989, annual rpt, 6844–1

Price indexes (producer), by stage of processing and detailed commodity, monthly rpt, 6762–6

Price indexes (producer), by stage of processing and detailed commodity, monthly 1990, annual rpt, 6764–2

Price indexes (producer) for building materials, by type, bimonthly rpt, 2042–1.5

see also Mobile homes

Pregnancy

see Abortion

see Births out of wedlock

see Fetal deaths

see Maternity

see Obstetrics and gynecology

see Prenatal care

see Teenage pregnancy

Prenatal care

Assistance for prenatal care, need under alternative poverty indicators, for 8 southern States, 1984-87, article, 4042–3.226

Births and rates, by characteristics of birth, infant, and parents, 1989 and trends from 1940, US Vital Statistics advance annual rpt, 4146–5.123

Child health condition and services use, 1990 chartbook, 4108–49

Education natl goals progress indicators, by State, 1991, annual rpt, 15914–1

Food aid program of USDA for women, infants, and children, prenatal participation effect on Medicaid costs and birth outcomes, for 5 States, 1987-88, 1368–2

Health condition and health care resources, use, and spending, 1950s-89, annual data compilation, 4144–11

Health condition improvement and disease prevention goals and recommended activities for 2000, with trends 1970s-80s, 4048–10

Hispanic Americans low birthweight cases and inadequate prenatal care, 1980s, article, 4042–3.234

Medicaid coverage effects on prenatal care use and birth outcomes, charges, and Medicaid payments, for California, 1983, article, 4652–1.241

Medicaid prenatal care eligibility and availability, by State, 1987-90, article, 4652–1.213

Minority group and women health condition, services use, payment sources, and health care labor force, by poverty status, 1940s-89, chartbook, 4118–56

Minority group health condition, services use, costs, and indicators of services need, 1950s-88, 4118–55

Montana health care access indicators, 1989 hearing, 23898–6

Nutritional and educational prenatal care programs for women at risk of preterm delivery, and rate of anemia and low-weight births, 1985-86, article, 4042–3.235

Statistical Abstract of US, 1991 annual data compilation, 2324–1.2

Preschool education

Condition of Education, detail for elementary and secondary education, 1920s-90 and projected to 2001, annual rpt, 4824–1.1

Data on public elementary and secondary education, schools, enrollment, teachers, funding, and other characteristics, by region and State, 1988/89, annual rpt, 4834–20

Digest of Education Statistics, 1991 annual data compilation, 4824–2

Enrollment, by grade, instn type and control, and student characteristics, 1989 and trends from 1947, annual Current Population Rpt, 2546–1.453

Enrollment, finances, staff, and high school grads, for elementary and secondary public school systems by State, FY88-89, annual rpt, 4834–6

Handicapped children early education project descriptions, 1990/91, annual listing, 4944–10

Natl Education Goals progress indicators, by State, 1991, annual rpt, 15914–1

Special education programs, enrollment by age, staff, funding, and needs, by type of handicap and State, 1989/90, annual rpt, 4944–4

Statistical Abstract of US, 1991 annual data compilation, 2324–1.4

see also Head Start Project

Prescott, Edward C.

"Seignorage as a Tax: A Quantitative Evaluation", 9383–20.2

"Technology Adoption and Growth", 9383–20.6

Prescott, John H.

"Marine Mammal Strandings: The New England Aquarium Stranding Network", 14738–8

Prescription drugs

see Drugs

Presidency of the U.S.

Congressional Directory, members of 102nd Congress, other officials, elections, and districts, 1991-92, biennial rpt, 23874–1

Election (presidential) campaign receipts and expenditures, by type, and by candidate and party, 1992 primary elections, press release, 9276–1.95

Election (presidential) campaign spending limits for candidates, and voting age population, by State, 1992 primary elections, press release, 9276–1.90

Election campaign finances and FEC activities, various periods 1975-90, annual rpt, 9274–1

Libraries (presidential) holdings, use, and costs, by instn, FY90, annual rpt, 9514–2

Statistical Abstract of US, 1991 annual data compilation, 2324–1.8

Threats against President, criminal case processing and dispositions in Federal district court, 1980-89, annual rpt, 6064–31

Threats against President, criminal case processing and dispositions in Federal district court, 1986, annual rpt, 6064–29

see also Executive Office of the President

see also Presidential appointments

Presidential advisory bodies

see Federal boards, committees, and commissions

see under names of individual Presidential commissions (starting with Presidential or President's)

Presidential appointments

Judges appointed to district and appeals courts, by previous experience and other characteristics, data compilation, 1991 annual rpt, 6064–6.1

Senior Executive Service membership characteristics, entries, exits, and awards, FY79-90, annual rpt, 9844–36

State Dept officers, ambassadors, and Chiefs of US overseas missions, by country and intl agency, 1778-1990, 7008–1

Presidential commissions

see Federal boards, committees, and commissions

see under names of individual Presidential commissions (starting with Presidential or President's)

Presidential-congressional relations

see Congressional-executive relations

Presidential elections

see Elections

Presidential powers

see also Congressional-executive relations

see also Executive agreements

see also Executive impoundment of appropriated funds

see also Presidential appointments

Presidential Working Group on Financial Markets

Securities and commodity trading regulatory activities and interagency coordination, FY91, annual rpt, 11924–4

Press

see Freedom of the press

see Government and the press

see Journalism

see Newspapers

Index by Subjects and Names

Prices

Presser, Theresa S.

"Geologic Sources, Mobilization, and Transport of Selenium from the California Coast Ranges to the Western San Joaquin Valley: A Reconnaissance Study", 5666–27.10

Pressure groups

see Lobbying and lobbying groups

see Political action committees

Pretrial detention and release

- Criminal activity while on release, Federal sentencing guidelines by offense and circumstances, series, 17668–1
- Criminal case processing in Federal courts, by offense, disposition, and jurisdiction, data compilation, 1991 annual rpt, 6064–6.5
- Drug test results at arrest, by drug type, offense, and sex, for selected urban areas, quarterly rpt, 6062–3
- Drug testing of criminal defendants, demonstration program operations, offender characteristics, and judges views, 1987-90, 18208–11
- Federal criminal offenders processing, detention, and release, by defendant characteristics and district, 1988, hearing, 25528–114
- Federal district court criminal case processing and dispositions, by offense, district, and offender characteristics, 1986, annual rpt, 6064–29
- Federal district court pretrial interviews and reports, 1991, annual rpt, 18204–2.1
- Federal district court pretrial reports, detention, supervision, and bail violations, 1990, annual rpt, 18204–8.24
- Federal district court pretrial service cases, by type of bail rpt, circuit, and district, 1990, annual rpt, 18204–11
- Felony defendants pretrial release and rearrests, by offense type and selected characteristics, 1988, 6066–25.36
- Marshals Service activities, FY89, annual rpt, 6294–1
- US attorneys civil and criminal cases by type and disposition, and collections, by Federal district, FY90, annual rpt, 6004–2.1

see also Habeas corpus

Preventive medicine

- AIDS and hepatitis viruses transmission in health care settings, occupational exposure, prevention policies, and OSHA regulation, 1990 hearings, 21348–119
- AIDS knowledge, attitudes, and transmission prevention practices of physicians and RNs, 1990-91, 4186–9.11
- AIDS public knowledge, attitudes, and risk behaviors, for women, 1988 survey, 4146–8.200
- AIDS public knowledge, attitudes, info sources, and testing, for blacks, 1990 survey, 4146–8.208
- AIDS public knowledge, attitudes, info sources, and testing, for Hispanics, 1990 survey, 4146–8.209
- AIDS public knowledge, attitudes, info sources, and testing, 1990 survey, 4146–8.195; 4146–8.201; 4146–8.205
- AIDS public knowledge, for North Dakota, 1987-89 surveys, article, 4042–3.211
- Child abuse and neglect prevention funding by States, and funding sources, FY89, GAO rpt, 26121–423

Child and maternal health programs of major urban health depts, activities and budgets, 1990, listing, 4108–51

- Fetal alcohol syndrome prevention program for Indians, evaluation, 1988-89 local area study, article, 4042–3.239
- Health condition and health care resources, use, and spending, 1950s-89, annual data compilation, 4144–11
- Health condition improvement and disease prevention goals and recommended activities for 2000, with trends 1970s-80s, 4048–10
- Health promotion program availability and participation, by type of program and sponsor, 1986-87 local area study, article, 4042–3.223
- Heart disease risk assessment program activities and costs, for South Carolina, 1987-88 study, article, 4042–3.245
- HHS financial aid, by program, recipient, State, and city, FY90, annual regional listings, 4004–3
- Indian Health Service outpatient services provided, by reason for visit and age, FY88-89, annual rpt, 4084–2
- Indians and Alaska Natives preventive health practices, exams by type, and smoking and overweight status, by selected characteristics, 1987, 4186–8.19
- Medicaid child preventive health care visits, exams, and immunizations, for California, 1981-84, article, 4652–1.214
- Medicare coverage of new health care technologies, risks and benefit evaluations, series, 4186–10
- Military health care personnel, and accessions by training source, by occupation, specialty, and service branch, FY89, annual rpt, 3544–24
- Minority group health condition, services use, costs, and indicators of services need, 1950s-88, 4118–55
- *Morbidity and Mortality Weekly Report*, infectious notifiable disease cases by State, and public health issues, 4202–1
- NIH activities, funding by program and recipient type, staff, and clinic patients, by inst, FY90, annual rpt, 4434–3
- Older persons health condition and care research, data availability and collection methodology, for US and selected countries, 1988 conf, 4147–5.6
- Physicians, by specialty, age, sex, and location of training and practice, 1989, State rpt series, 4116–6
- *Public Health Reports*, bimonthly journal, 4042–3
- Research activities and grants of HCFA, by program, FY90, annual listing, 4654–10
- Research on primary health care, methodology and findings, 1991 annual conf, 4184–4
- Research on primary health care, provider role, Federal funding, and provision to minority groups, 1990 conf papers, 4188–69
- Senate receipts, itemized expenses by payee, and balances, 1st half FY91, semiannual listing, 25922–1
- Smoking prevention, control, and surveillance activities and funding of States, and tobacco farm receipts, by State, 1989-90, 4206–2.47

Youth health condition, risk factors, and preventive and treatment services use and availability, 1970s-89, 26358–234

see also Health maintenance organizations

see also Medical examinations and tests

see also Prenatal care

see also Vaccination and vaccines

Price indexes

see Consumer Price Index

see Producer Price Index

Price, Kurt F.

"Moveable Capital Cost Weights, Final Report", 17206–2.24

Price regulation

- Energy suppliers rate regulation, and hydroelectric project licensing, for FERC, FY90, annual rpt, 3084–9
- Telephone service subscribership, charges, and local and long distance firm finances and operations, late 1970s-91, semiannual rpt, 9282–7
- Trucking industry deregulation by States, potential economic and market impacts, with background data, mid 1970s-80s, 7308–200
- TV (cable) deregulation in 1986, impacts on prices and services, 1986-91, GAO rpt, 26113–431

see also Agricultural production quotas and price supports

see also Rent control

Price, Richard H.

"Outpatient Drug Abuse Treatment Services, 1988: Results of a National Survey", 4498–73

Price, Timothy L.

"Outlook for Oilseeds: Farmer Perspective", 1004–16.1

Prices

- Airline consumer complaints to DOT about service by US and foreign carrier, and for travel and cargo service, by reason, monthly rpt, 7302–11
- Airline deregulation in 1978, impacts on industry structure, competition, fares, finances, operations, and intl service, with data by carrier and airport, 1980s, series, 7308–199
- Brazil price variability among products and cities, relation to inflation, alternative model results for 1980s, working paper, 9379–14.14
- Business statistics, detailed data for major industries and economic indicators, *Survey of Current Business*, monthly rpt, 2702–1
- China GNP estimation methodology and results, 1978-89, with yuan-dollar prices by commodity, 1981, working paper, 2326–18.58
- Department store inventory price indexes, by class of item, monthly table, 6762–7
- Eastern Europe foreign debt components, trade, balances, and other economic indicators, by country, 1985-89, hearing, 21248–148
- Economic indicators, monthly rpt, 9362–1.2
- Export and import price indexes, by selected end-use category, monthly press release, 6762–15
- Export and import price indexes for goods and services, and dollar exchange rate indexes, quarterly press release, 6762–13
- Exports, imports, and trade flows, by country and commodity, with background economic indicators, data compilation, monthly CD-ROM, 2002–6

Prices

Foreign and US economic conditions, and trade devs and balances, with data by selected country and country group, monthly rpt, 9882–14

Foreign and US economic conditions, for major industrial countries, biweekly rpt, 9112–1

Foreign countries economic indicators, and trade and investment flows, for selected countries and country groups, selected years 1946-90, annual rpt, 204–1.9

GNP and industrial production correlation with selected price indexes over business cycles, 1957-89, article, 9383–6.204

Imports and tariff provisions effect on US industries and products, investigations with background financial and operating data, series, 9886–4

Imports injury to US industries from foreign subsidized products and sales at less than fair value, investigations with background financial and operating data, series, 9886–19

Imports injury to US industries from foreign subsidized products, investigations with background financial and operating data, series, 9886–15

Imports injury to US industries from sales at less than fair value, investigations with background financial and operating data, series, 9886–14

Intl investment position of US, by component, industry, world region, and country, 1989-90, annual article, 2702–1.212

Middle Atlantic States manufacturing business outlook, monthly survey rpt, 9387–11

Natl income and product accounts and components, *Survey of Current Business*, monthly rpt, 2702–1.24

Soviet Union, Eastern Europe, OECD, and selected other countries economic conditions, 1960s-90, annual rpt, 9114–4.2

Statistical Abstract of US, 1991 annual data compilation, 2324–1.15

Stock returns on initial public offerings, impact of underwriter price support, 1982-83, technical paper, 9385–8.113

Telecommunications domestic and intl rates, by type of service and area served, 1989, annual rpt, 9284–6.6

Telecommunications finances, rates, and traffic for US carriers intl operations, by service type, firm, and country, 1975-89, annual rpt, 9284–17

Telephone local service charges and low-income subsidies, by region, company, and city, 1980s-90, semiannual rpt, 9282–8

Telephone service subscribership, charges, and local and long distance firm finances and operations, late 1970s-91, semiannual rpt, 9282–7

see also Agricultural prices

see also Agricultural production quotas and price supports

see also Coal prices

see also Consumer Price Index

see also Electric power prices

see also Energy prices

see also Family budgets

see also Food prices

see also Housing costs and financing

see also Inflation

see also Medical costs

see also Natural gas prices

see also Petroleum prices

see also Price regulation

see also Producer Price Index

see also Professionals' fees

see also under names of specific commodities or commodity groups

Primary Metropolitan Statistical Areas

see Metropolitan Statistical Areas

Primont, Diane F.

"Comparing Prices Across Cities: A Hedonic Approach", 6886–6.73

"Differences in Food Prices Across U.S. Cities: Evidence from CPI Data", 6886–6.78

Prince George's County, Md.

Fed Govt land acquisition and dev projects in DC metro area, characteristics and funding by agency and project, FY91-95, annual rpt, 15454–1

Prince William County, Va.

Fed Govt land acquisition and dev projects in DC metro area, characteristics and funding by agency and project, FY91-95, annual rpt, 15454–1

Prince William Sound, Alaska

Oil spill from tanker Exxon Valdez, Federal cleanup and damage assessment costs, and reimbursement from Exxon, by agency, as of Sept 1990, GAO rpt, 26113–510

Oil spill from tanker Exxon Valdez, impacts on marine mammals, and resulting legislation, 1990 annual rpt, 14734–1

Oil spill from tanker Exxon Valdez, safety issues, with oil lost and crew alcohol and drug test results, 1989, 9618–17

Otters (sea) conservation measures taken after Exxon Valdez oil spill in Alaska, 1990 conf, 5508–110

Seals (harbor) population at selected southern Alaska coastal sites, 1976-88, 14738–6

Tide height and time daily at coastal points, forecast 1992, annual rpt, 2174–2.1

Printing and publishing industry

American Samoa employment, earnings, and minimum wage, by establishment and industry, 1989, biennial rpt, 6504–6

Collective bargaining agreements expiring during year, and workers covered, by firm, union, industry group, and State, 1991, annual rpt, 6784–9

Computer use at home, school, and work, by purpose and selected user characteristics, 1989, Current Population Rpt, 2546–2.158

Consumer Expenditure Survey, spending by category, and income, by selected household characteristics and location, 1990, annual press release, 6726–1.42

County Business Patterns, 1988: employment, establishments, and payroll, by SIC 2- to 4-digit industry and county, annual State rpt series, 2326–6

County Business Patterns, 1989: employment, establishments, and payroll, by SIC 2- to 4-digit industry and county, annual State rpt series, 2326–8

CPI by component for US city average, and by region, population size, and for 27 metro areas, monthly rpt, 6762–2

Index by Subjects and Names

DOD prime contract awards, by detailed procurement category, FY87-90, annual rpt, 3544–18

Duplicating services establishments, receipts by source, payroll, and employment, by State and MSA, 1987 Census of Service Industries, 2393–4

Employment, earnings, and hours, by SIC 1- to 4-digit industry, monthly and annual averages, selected years 1909-90, annual rpt, 6744–4

Employment in manufacturing, by detailed occupation and SIC 2-digit industry, 1989 survey, triennial rpt, 6748–52

Employment, unemployment, and labor force characteristics, by region and census div, 1990, annual rpt, 6744–7.1

Energy use and prices for manufacturing industries, 1988 survey, series, 3166–13

Enterprise Statistics, 1987: auxiliaries of multi-establishment firms, finances and operations by function, industry, and State, 2329–6

Enterprise Statistics, 1987: finances and operations for companies, by size, level of diversification, form of organization, and industry group, 2329–8

Exports and imports between US and outlying areas, by detailed commodity and mode of transport, 1990, annual rpt, 2424–11

Exports and imports of US, by country and detailed commodity, monthly rpt, 2422–12

Exports and imports of US, by Harmonized System 6-digit commodity and country, 1990, annual rpt, 2424–13

Exports and imports of US, by selected country, country group, and commodity group, 1990, annual rpt, 2044–37

Exports and imports of US, by transport mode, country, and SITC 1- to 3-digit commodity, 1990, annual rpt, 2424–12

Exports of US, detailed commodities by country, monthly CD-ROM, 2422–13

Exports of US, detailed Schedule B commodities with countries of destination, 1990, annual rpt, 2424–10

Fed Govt and contractor employees nondisclosure agreements for info security, prepublication reviews, and costs, 1988-90, GAO rpt, 26123–328

Fed Govt labor productivity, indexes of output and labor costs by function, FY67-89, annual rpt, 6824–1.6

Fed Govt obligations object class analysis, by agency, Budget of US, FY92, annual rpt, 104–9

Franchise business opportunities by firm and kind of business, and sources of aid and info, 1990 annual listing, 2104–7

GPO activities, finances, and production, FY90, annual rpt, 26204–1

Imports, exports, and employment impacts, by SIC 2- to 4-digit industry and commodity, quarterly rpt, 2322-2

Imports of US, detailed commodities by country, monthly CD-ROM, 2422–14

Input-output structure of US economy, detailed interindustry transactions for 84 industries, and components of final demand, 1986, annual article, 2702–1.206

Input-output structure of US economy, detailed interindustry transactions for 85 industries, 1982 benchmark data, 2702–1.213

Index by Subjects and Names — Prisoners

Mail volume to and from households, use, and views, by class, source, content, and household characteristics, 1987-88, annual rpt, 9864–10

Manufacturing annual survey, 1989: finances and operations, by SIC 2- to 4-digit industry, series, 2506–15

Manufacturing census, 1987: finances and operations, by SIC 2- to 4-digit industry, State, and MSA, with trends from 1849, 2497–1

Manufacturing census, 1987: finances and operations, by type of organization and SIC 2- to 4-digit industry, subject rpt, 2497–5

Manufacturing corporations financial statements, by selected SIC 2- to 3-digit industry, quarterly rpt, 2502–1

Manufacturing finances and operations, by SIC 2- to 4-digit industry, forecast 1991, annual rpt, 2044–28

Manufacturing industries operations and performance, analytical rpt series, 2506–16

Manufacturing production, shipments, inventories, orders, and pollution control costs, periodic Current Industrial Rpt series, 2506–3

Mexico imports from US, by industry and State, 1987-90, 2048–154

Multinatl US firms and foreign affiliates finances and operations, by industry and world area of parent firm, 1989 benchmark survey, preliminary annual rpt, 2704–5

Occupational injury and illness rates, by SIC 2- to 4-digit industry, 1988-89, annual rpt, 6844–7

Occupational injury and illness rates, by SIC 2- to 4-digit industry, 1989, annual rpt, 6844–1

Pollution abatement capital and operating costs, by SIC 2-digit industry, 1989, advance annual Current Industrial Rpt, 2506–3.6

Price indexes (producer), by stage of processing and detailed commodity, monthly rpt, 6762–6

Price indexes (producer), by stage of processing and detailed commodity, monthly 1990, annual rpt, 6764–2

Propylene glycol ethers occupational exposure of factory and printing industry workers, health effects, literature review, 1991 rpt, 4246–4.3

Puerto Rico and other US possessions corporations income tax returns, income and tax items, and employment, by selected industry, 1987, article, 8302–2.213

Puerto Rico economic censuses, 1987: wholesale and retail trade and service industry finances and operations, by SIC 2- to 4-digit industry and municipio, 2591–1

Statistical Abstract of US, 1991 annual data compilation, 2324–1.18

Tax (income) returns of corporations, income and tax items by asset size and detailed industry, 1987, annual rpt, 8304–4

Tax (income) returns of corporations, income and tax items by asset size and detailed industry, 1988, annual rpt, 8304–21

Tax (income) returns of corporations with foreign tax credit, income and tax items by industry group, 1986, biennial article, 8302–2.203

Tax (income) returns of partnerships, income statement and balance sheet items, by industry group, 1989, annual article, 8302–2.216; 8304–18

Tax (income) returns of sole proprietorships, income statement items, by industry group, 1989, annual article, 8302–2.214

Wholesale trade census, 1987: establishments, sales by customer class, employment, inventories, and expenses, by SIC 2- to 4-digit kind of business, 2407–4

see also Books and bookselling

see also Copyright

see also Microforms

see also Newspapers

see also Periodicals

see also Writers and writing

see also under By Commodity in the "Index by Categories"

see also under By Industry in the "Index by Categories"

Prison sentences

see Sentences, criminal procedure

Prison work programs

Fed Prison Industries finances and operations, FY90, annual rpt, 6244–3

Fed Prison Industries sales, by commodity and Federal agency, FY90, annual rpt, 6244–5

Federal correctional instn inmates, by sex, prison, security level, contract facility type, and region, monthly rpt series, 6242–1

Jail adult and juvenile population, employment, spending, instn conditions, and inmate programs, by county and facility, 1988, regional rpt series, 6068–144

Participants of work programs, by Federal instn, 1991, annual listing, 6244–4

Participants of work release programs, and provisions for using inmate labor for prison construction, by State, data compilation, 1991 annual rpt, 6064–6.1; 6064–6.6

Prisoners

Admissions and releases from prison and parole, sentence length, and time served, by offense and offender characteristics, 1985, annual rpt, 6064–33

Admissions by State and for Federal instns, by race, 1926-86, 6068–245

AIDS cases in prisons and jails, and testing and control policies, 1989 survey, 6066–28.1

Court criminal case processing in Federal district courts, and dispositions, by offense, 1980-89, annual rpt, 6064–31

Criminal activity in prison, Federal sentencing guidelines by offense and circumstances, series, 17668–1

Drug abuse history of jail population, by offense, conviction status, criminal and family history, and selected other characteristics, 1989, 6066–19.63

Drug abuse indicators for selected metro areas, research results, data collection, and policy issues, 1991 semiannual conf, 4492–5

Drug abuse prevalence among minorities, related health effects and crime, treatment, and research status and needs, mid 1970s-90, 4498–72

Drug and alcohol abuse and mental illness direct and indirect costs, by type and patient age and sex, 1985 with 1980 and 1988 comparisons, 4048–35

Drug and alcohol abuse in rural areas, related crime, and treatment, with comparisons to nonrural areas, by substance and State, 1988-90, GAO rpt, 26131–79

Executions since 1930, and prisoners under death sentence by prison control and prisoner characteristics, by State, 1973-90, annual rpt, 6066–25.42

Fed Bur of Prisons activities, and inmate and staff characteristics, 1990, annual rpt, 6244–2

Federal correctional instn inmates, by sex, prison, security level, contract facility type, and region, monthly rpt series, 6242–1

Foreign countries human rights conditions in 170 countries, 1990, annual rpt, 21384–3

Halfway house placements of Federal prisoners, duration, and employment, and house capacity, 1990-91, GAO rpt, 26119–347

Jail adult and juvenile population, employment, spending, instn conditions, and inmate programs, by county and facility, 1988, regional rpt series, 6068–144

Jail population, by criminal, correctional, drug use, and family history, and selected other characteristics, 1989, 6066–19.62

Jail population by sex, race, and for 25 jurisdictions, and instn conditions, 1988-90, annual rpt, 6066–25.38

Marshals Service activities, FY89, annual rpt, 6294–1

Petitions of prisoners, and dispositions in Federal district and appeals courts, by type, 1990, annual rpt, 18204–8; 18204–11

Petitions of prisoners, and dispositions in Federal district and appeals courts, by type, 1991, annual rpt, 18204–2.1

Population and movements of prisoners, by offense, location, and selected other characteristics, data compilation, 1991 annual rpt, 6064–6.6

Population of Federal and State instns by sex, admissions, and instn capacity and overcrowding, by State, 1980s-90, annual rpt, 6066–25.37

Population of Federal and State instns, by sex and State, June 1991, semiannual rpt, 6062–4

Population of prisoners, characteristics, and movements, by State, 1989, annual rpt, 6064–26

State and Metro Area Data Book, 1991 data compilation, 2328–54

Statistical Abstract of US, 1991 annual data compilation, 2324–1.5

US attorneys civil and criminal cases by type and disposition, and collections, by Federal district, FY90, annual rpt, 6004–2.1

Violent crime victimizations, circumstances, victim characteristics, arrest, recidivism, sentences, and prisoners, 1980s, 6068–148

Prisoners

Women prisoners in State instns, by offense, drug use history, whether abused, and other characteristics, 1986, 6066–19.61

see also Community-based correctional programs

see also Parole and probation

see also Prison work programs

see also Prisoners of war

Prisoners of war

Claims against foreign govts by US natls, by claim type and country, 1990, annual rpt, 6004–16

Military deaths by cause, age, race, and rank, and personnel captured and missing, by service branch, FY90, annual rpt, 3544–40

Veterans health care, patients, visits, costs, and operating beds, by VA and contract facility, and region, quarterly rpt, 8602–4

Vietnam Orderly Departure Program, former re-education camp prisoners arrivals in US and refugee camps, monthly rpt, 7002–4

Prisons

see Correctional institutions

see Juvenile detention and correctional institutions

see Military prisons

see Prison work programs

see Prisoners

see Sentences, criminal procedure

Pritchard, Robert S.

"Chukchi Sea Ice Motions, 1981-82", 2176–1.38

"Interpolation, Analysis, and Archival of Data on Sea Ice Trajectories and Ocean Currents Obtained from Satellite-Linked Instruments", 2176–1.38

Privacy

see Right of privacy

Private School Study

Data collection activities and programs of NCES, 1991, annual listing, 4824–7

Private schools

Asbestos in buildings, EPA aid for removal, occupational asbestos exposure cancer cases and deaths, and Catholic schools abatement costs, 1985-90, hearing, 25328–32

Condition of Education, detail for elementary, secondary, and higher education, 1920s-90 and projected to 2001, annual rpt, 4824–1

Digest of Education Statistics, 1991 annual data compilation, 4824–2

Education data, selected trends and projections 1978-2001, pamphlet, 4828–27

Eighth grade class of 1988: educational performance and conditions, characteristics, attitudes, activities, and plans, natl longitudinal survey, series, 4826–9

Elementary and secondary education enrollment, staff, finances, operations, programs, and policies, 1987/88 biennial survey, series, 4836–3

Elementary and secondary education enrollment, teachers, high school grads, and spending, by instn control and State, 1990/91, annual rpt, 4834–19

Elementary and secondary private schools, enrollment, teachers, and high school grads, by instn religious orientation, annual rpt, suspended, 4834–21

Elementary and secondary private schools, students, and staff characteristics, various periods 1979-88, 4838–47

Elementary and secondary students educational performance, and factors affecting proficiency, by selected characteristics, 1990 natl assessments, subject rpt series, 4896–8

Enrollment, by grade, instn type and control, and student characteristics, 1989 and trends from 1947, annual Current Population Rpt, 2546–1.453

Enrollment, staff, and spending, by instn level and control, and teacher salaries, 1980s-92, annual press release, 4804–19

High school advanced placement for college credit, programs by selected characteristics and school control, 1984-86, 4838–46

High school dropout rates, and subsequent completion, by student and school characteristics, alternative estimates, 1990, annual rpt, 4834–23

Higher education enrollment and degrees awarded by sex, and instn finances, by instn level and control, 1990-91, annual rpt, 4844–14

Higher education enrollment and degrees awarded, by sex, full- and part-time status, and instn level and control, fall 1990, annual rpt, 4844–16

Higher education enrollment, by student and instn characteristics, fall 1989, biennial rpt, 4844–2

Higher education enrollment, faculty, finances, and degrees, by instn level and control, and State, FY87, annual rpt, 4844–13

Higher education instn revenue by source and spending by function, by State and instn control, FY80-88, annual rpt, 4844–6

Higher education instn student aid and other sources of support, with student expenses and characteristics, by instn type and control, 1990 triennial study, series, 4846–5

Higher education instn tuition and other costs, govt aid, impacts on enrollment, and cost containment methods, 1970s-90 and projected to 2001, 4808–25

Higher education instn tuition relation to other instn financial indicators, by instn control, 1960s-88, 4808–24

Housing and households detailed characteristics, and unit and neighborhood quality, by location, 1987, biennial rpt supplement, 2485–13

Indian education funding of Fed Govt, and enrollment, degrees, and program grants and fellowships by State, late 1960s-FY89, annual rpt, 14874–1

Pell grants and applicants, by tuition, family and student income, instn type and control, and State, 1989/90, annual rpt, 4804–1

R&D facilities for biological and medical sciences, space and equipment adequacy, needs, and funding by source, by instn type, 1990, biennial rpt, 4434–17

R&D funding by higher education instns and federally funded centers, by field, instn, and State, FY89, annual rpt, 9627–13

Remedial education programs in higher education instns, and enrollment, courses, and faculty, by instn characteristics, 1989/90, 4826–1.30

Science and engineering grad enrollment, by field, source of funds, and characteristics of student and instn, 1975-89, annual rpt, 9627–7

State and Metro Area Data Book, 1991 data compilation, 2328–54

Statistical Abstract of US, 1991 annual data compilation, 2324–1.4

Student aid, costs, and income factors affecting access to undergrad education, 1990 rpt, 26306–6.153

Student aid funding and participation, by Federal program, instn type and control, and State, various periods 1959-89, annual rpt, 4804–28

Student loan debt burden of 1986 college grads, by selected student characteristics and instn control, 1987, 4808–26

Teachers in higher education instns, personnel policies, pay, work conditions, and other characteristics, by instn type and control, 1987/88 survey, quadrennial rpt series, 4846–4

Teachers in higher education, salaries by faculty rank, sex, instn type and control, and State, 1989/90, annual rpt, 4844–8

Privileges and immunities

Tax amnesty programs of States for delinquent taxpayers, participation, collections, and costs, by tax type and State, 1980s-90, hearing, 21408–125

Witnesses immunity requests by Federal prosecutors to US Attorney General, and witnesses involved, data compilation, 1991 annual rpt, 6064–6.5

Prizes

see Awards, medals, and prizes

Probation

see Parole and probation

Processed foods

see Food and food industry

see Food ingredients and additives

Procurement

see Business orders

see Defense contracts and procurement

see Government contracts and procurement

see Industrial purchasing

Producer Price Index

Agricultural Outlook, production, prices, marketing, and trade, by commodity, forecast and current situation, monthly rpt with articles, 1502–4

Building materials PPI, by type, bimonthly rpt, 2042–1.5

Business statistics, detailed data for major industries and economic indicators, *Survey of Current Business*, monthly rpt, 2702–1

Canada and US auto trade, production, sales, prices, and employment, selected years 1965-88, annual rpt, 2044–35

Dairy products PPI, monthly rpt, 1317–4.2

Economic indicators and components, and Fed Reserve 4th District business and financial conditions, monthly chartbook, 9377–10

Economic indicators and components, current data and annual trends, monthly rpt, 23842–1.4

Economic indicators compounded annual rates of change, monthly rpt, 9391–3

Index by Subjects and Names

Economic indicators compounded annual rates of change, 1971-90, annual rpt, 9391–9.2

Economic indicators, monthly rpt, 9362–1.2

Food consumption, supply, trade, prices, spending, and indexes, by commodity, 1989, annual rpt, 1544–4

Footwear production, employment, use, prices, and US trade by country, quarterly rpt, 9882–6

Foreign countries economic and monetary trends, compounded annual rates of change for US and 10 major trading partners, quarterly rpt, 9391–7

Foreign countries economic conditions and implications for US, periodic country rpt series, 2046–4

Import prices relation to dollar exchange rate for 32 industries, and impacts of domestic market concentration, 1990 working paper, 9387–8.234

Inflation actual and expected rates based on alternative price indexes, 1950s-87, article, 9377–1.201

Lumber (hardwood) production, prices, employment, and trade, quarterly rpt, 1202–4

Lumber and pulp products supply and use, and timber resources, detailed data, 1950s-87 and alternative projections to 2040, 1208–24.20

Lumber production, prices by region and State, trade by country, and use, by species and product, 1960-88, annual rpt, 1204–29

Meat and fish retail and producer prices, 1981-91, semiannual situation rpt, 1561–15.3

Monthly Labor Review, CPI and PPI current statistics, 6722–1.4

North Central States farm credit conditions and economic devs, Fed Reserve 7th District, monthly rpt, 9375–10

OECD intl trade position for US and 4 countries, and factors affecting US competition, periodic pamphlet, 2042–25

Physicians practice cost indexes and components, by State, MSA, and for rural areas, 1989 rpt, 4658–50

Price indexes (consumer and producer), by commodity group, selected years 1929-90, annual rpt, 204–1.4

Price indexes (producer), by major commodity group and subgroup, and processing stage, monthly press release, 6762–5

Price indexes (producer), by stage of processing and detailed commodity, monthly rpt, 6762–6

Price indexes (producer), by stage of processing and detailed commodity, monthly 1990, annual rpt, 6764–2

Statistical Abstract of US, 1991 annual data compilation, 2324–1.15

Telephone local service charges and low-income subsidies, by region, company, and city, 1980s-90, semiannual rpt, 9282–8

Product safety

Consumer Product Safety Commission activities, recalls by brand, and casualties and medical costs, by product type, FY89, annual rpt, 9164–2

Imports detained by FDA, by reason, product, shipper, brand, and country, monthly listing, 4062–2

Injuries from use of consumer products, by severity, victim age, and detailed product, 1990, annual rpt, 9164–6

Mobile home fires, casualties, damage, and impacts of safety standards, with data on Michigan trailer parks, 1980s, hearing, 21248–145

Radiation from electronic devices, incidents by type of device, and FDA control activities, 1990, annual rpt, 4064–13

Statistical Abstract of US, 1991 annual data compilation, 2324–1.3

Torts for product liability, caseloads for Federal district courts, 1990, annual rpt, 18204–8.13; 18204–11

Torts for product liability, caseloads for Federal district courts, 1991, annual rpt, 18204–2.1

see also Defective products

see also Food ingredients and additives

see also Food inspection

see also Hazardous substances

see also Inflammable materials

see also Motor vehicle safety devices

see also Poisoning and drug reaction

see also Quality control and testing

Production

see Agricultural production

see Industrial production

see Industrial production indexes

see Producer Price Index

see Production costs

see Productivity

see Value added tax

Production capacity and utilization

see Industrial capacity and utilization

Production costs

Auto quality changes since last model year, factory and retail value, 1991 model year, annual press release, 6764–3

Competitiveness (intl) of US industries, with selected foreign and US operating data by major firm and product, series, 2046–12

Food prices (farm-retail), marketing cost components, and industry finances and productivity, 1920s-90, annual rpt, 1544–9

Manufacturing annual survey, 1989: finances and operations, by SIC 2- and 3-digit industry and State, 2506–15.3

Manufacturing census, 1987: finances and operations, by SIC 2- to 4-digit industry, State, and MSA, with trends from 1849, 2497–1

Mineral industries census, 1987: finances and operations, by SIC 2- to 4-digit industry, State, and county, census div rpt series, 2515–1

Minerals foreign and US supply under alternative market conditions, reserves, and background industry data, series, 5606–4

Tax (income) returns of corporations, income and tax items by asset size and detailed industry, 1987, annual rpt, 8304–4

Tax (income) returns of corporations, income and tax items by asset size and detailed industry, 1988, annual rpt, 8304–21

see also Agricultural production costs

Production workers

see also Business income and expenses, general

see also Business income and expenses, specific industry

see also Capital investments, general

see also Capital investments, specific industry

see also Energy production costs

see also Labor costs and cost indexes

see also Payroll

see also Producer Price Index

Production Credit Associations

see Farm Credit System

Production workers

Construction industries census, 1987: establishments, employment, receipts, and expenditures, by SIC 4-digit industry and State, final industry rpt series, 2373–1

Dallas-Fort Worth-Arlington metro area employment, earnings, hours, and CPI changes, late 1970s-90, annual rpt, 6964–2

Earnings and hours, by industry div and major manufacturing group, Monthly Labor Review, 6722–1.2

Earnings, annual average percent changes for selected occupational groups, selected MSAs, monthly rpt, 6782–1.1

Education (postsecondary) course completions, by detailed program, sex, race, and instn type, for 1972 high school class, as of 1984, 4888–4

Employee benefit plan coverage and provisions in small businesses, by plan type and occupational group, 1990, biennial rpt, 6784–20

Employment and Earnings, detailed data, monthly rpt, 6742–2.6

Employment, earnings, and hours, monthly press release, 6742–5

Employment situation, earnings, hours, and other BLS economic indicators, transcripts of BLS Commissioner's monthly testimony, periodic rpt, 23846–4

Health maintenance organizations enrollment and availability for production and office workers, by industry div, selected metro area, and region, 1984-89, article, 6722–1.222

Houston metro area employment, earnings, hours, and CPI changes, 1970s-90, annual rpt, 6964–1

Imports injury to US industries from foreign subsidized products, investigations with background financial and operating data, series, 9886–15

Imports injury to US industries from sales at less than fair value, investigations with background financial and operating data, series, 9886–14

Industry finances and operations, by SIC 2- to 4-digit industry, forecast 1991, annual rpt, 2044–28

Manufacturing annual survey, 1989: establishments, employment, finances, inventories, and energy use, by SIC 2- to 4-digit industry, 2506–15.1

Manufacturing annual survey, 1989: finances and operations, by SIC 2- and 3-digit industry and State, 2506–15.3

Manufacturing census, 1987: finances and operations, by SIC 2- to 4-digit industry, State, and MSA, with trends from 1849, 2497–1

Production workers

Manufacturing census, 1987: finances and operations, by type of organization and SIC 2- to 4-digit industry, subject rpt, 2497–5

Manufacturing employment, by detailed occupation and SIC 2-digit industry, 1989 survey, triennial rpt, 6748–52

Manufacturing employment by selected characteristics, wages, and import and export penetration rates, by SIC 2- to 4-digit industry, 1982-89, 6366–3.27

Southeastern US manufacturing hours and earnings, for 8 States, quarterly press release, 6942–7

Southwestern US employment by industry div, earnings, and hours, by State, monthly rpt, 6962–2

State and Metro Area Data Book, 1991 data compilation, 2328–54

Statistical Abstract of US, 1991 annual data compilation, 2324–1.13

see also under By Occupation in the "Index by Categories"

Productivity

Banks output relation to costs, technological devs, deregulation, and other factors, alternative measures, 1980s, technical paper, 9366–6.265

Economic indicators compounded annual rates of change, monthly rpt, 9391–3

Economic indicators, prices, labor costs, and productivity, BLS econometric analyses and methodology, working paper series, 6886–6

Farm and garden equipment industry productivity measures, 1958-88, article, 6722–1.232

Foreign and US industrial output, compensation, unit labor costs, and indexes, Monthly Labor Review, 6722–1.6

Manufacturing returns to scale relation to external economies, model description and results, 1991 technical paper, 9366–6.267

Monthly Labor Review, output, compensation, labor and nonlabor unit costs, and indexes, 6722–1.5

OECD intl trade position for US and 4 countries, and factors affecting US competition, periodic pamphlet, 2042–25

Productivity of labor and capital, indexes and percent change, 1948-90, annual press release, 6824–2

Public capital stock effect on productivity, with model adjustments for energy prices and technological change, 1948-89, article, 9391–1.211

Soviet Union aggregate and industrial factor productivity annual growth rate, 1961-90, annual rpt, 9114–4.3

see also Agricultural productivity

see also Government efficiency

see also Industrial capacity and utilization

see also Industrial production indexes

see also Labor productivity

Professional and technical workers

Air traffic control and airway facilities staff, by employment and other characteristics, FY89, annual rpt, 7504–41

Aircraft mechanics certified by FAA, by age, sex, region, and State, 1990, annual rpt, 7504–2

Educational attainment, by sociodemographic characteristics and location, 1989 and trends from 1940, biennial Current Population Rpt, 2546–1.452

Employee benefit plan coverage and provisions in small businesses, by plan type and occupational group, 1990, biennial rpt, 6784–20

Employment, earnings, and hours, monthly press release, 6742–5

Employment situation, earnings, hours, and other BLS economic indicators, transcripts of BLS Commissioner's monthly testimony, periodic rpt, 23846–4

Employment, unemployment, and labor force characteristics, by region, State, and selected metro area, 1990, annual rpt, 6744–7

Fed Govt civilian employment and payroll, by occupation, pay grade, sex, agency, and location, 1989, biennial rpt, 9844–4

Immigrants admitted to US, by occupational group and country of birth, preliminary FY90, annual table, 6264–1

Income (household, family, and personal), by source, detailed characteristics, and region, 1988-89, annual Current Population Rpt, 2546–6.68

Income (household, family, and personal), by source, detailed characteristics, and region, 1990, annual Current Population Rpt, 2546–6.70

Manufacturing employment, by detailed occupation and SIC 2-digit industry, 1989 survey, triennial rpt, 6748–52

Recruitment, hiring, compensation, and other employment practices of large firms, 1989 survey, GAO rpt, 26119–324

State and local govt employment of minorities and women, by occupation, function, pay level, and State, 1990, annual rpt, 9244–6

Transit systems finances and operations, by mode of transport, size of fleet, and for 468 systems, 1989, annual rpt, 7884–4

see also Area wage surveys

see also Consultants

see also Engineers and engineering

see also Executives and managers

see also Health occupations

see also Industry wage surveys

see also Paraprofessionals

see also Scientists and technicians

see also under By Occupation in the "Index by Categories"

see also under names of specific professions

Professional associations

see Associations

Professionals' fees

Anesthesiologists reimbursement by Medicare, charges, and time billed, 1987, GAO rpt, 26121–417

Child abuse and neglect victims representation in legal proceedings, caseloads, State requirements, and compensation, by State and county, 1989, 4608–28

Health Care Financing Review, provider prices, price inputs and indexes, and labor, quarterly journal, 4652–1.1

Health care spending by type and payment source, with background data and foreign comparisons, 1960s-80s and projected to 2000, 26308–98

Medicare claims approved, charges, and reimbursements by type of service, from 1974, monthly rpt, quarterly data, 4742–1.11

Medicare Economic Index for physician reimbursement rebased to 1989, methodology and results, with projections to 1995, article, 4652–1.246

Physicians charges and reimbursement from Medicare, by enrollee characteristics and region, late 1960s-86, biennial rpt, 4654–1

Physicians consultations requested by attending physician, Medicare reimbursement issues, with use by diagnosis, specialty, location, and other characteristics, 1986, 4658–47

Physicians fee schedule under Medicare Supplementary Medical Insurance, analyses of costs and other issues, series, 17266–1

Physicians fee schedule under Medicare Supplementary Medical Insurance, methodology with data by procedure and specialty, 1991, annual rpt, 17264–1

Physicians payment issues, HCFA research activities and grants, FY90, annual listing, 4654–10

Physicians payments, charges by specialty and treatment setting, and assignment rate by State, for Medicare, 1970s-88, article, 4652–1.240

Physicians practice cost indexes and components, by State, MSA, and for rural areas, 1989 rpt, 4658–50

Service industries census, 1987: depreciable assets, capital and operating expenses, and receipts, by SIC 2- to 4-digit kind of business, 2393–2

Service industries census, 1987: establishments, receipts by source, payroll, and employment, by SIC 2- to 4-digit kind of business, State, and MSA, 2393–4

Service industries receipts, by SIC 2- to 4-digit kind of business, 1990, annual rpt, 2413–8

Profits

see Business income and expenses, general

see Business income and expenses, specific industry

see Farm income

see Operating ratios

Program Fraud Civil Remedies Act

Fraud cases of Federal agencies involving small dollar amounts, investigations, dispositions, losses, and collections, 1986-90, GAO rpt, 26111–76

Project listings

see Demonstration and pilot projects

see Directories

Projections and forecasts

Air traffic (passenger), and aircraft operations by type, by airport and State, projected FY91-2005 and trends from FY83, annual rpt, 7504–7

Air traffic and other aviation activity forecasts of FAA, 1991 annual conf, 7504–28

Air traffic, and passenger and freight enplanements, by airport, 1960s-90 and projected to 2010, hub area rpt series, 7506–7

Air traffic and passengers, for intl routes over north Atlantic, by aviation type and route, alternative forecasts 1991-2010 and trends from 1980, annual rpt, 7504–44

Air traffic control and airway facilities improvement activities under Aviation

Index by Subjects and Names

Projections and forecasts

System Capital Investment Plan, 1981-90 and projected to 2005, annual rpt, 7504–12

Air traffic, pilots, airports, and fuel use, forecast FY91-2002 and trends from FY81, annual rpt, 7504–6

Aircraft handled by instrument flight rule, by user type, FAA traffic control center, and region, FY85-90 and projected to FY2005, annual rpt, 7504–15

Aircraft noise abatement measures, and industry compliance costs, aggregate FY90-2000, GAO rpt, 26113–534

Airline market entry impacts of carrier control of airports, facility and aircraft availability, noise regulation, and other barriers, late 1980s and projected to 1997, 7308–199.8

Airport capacity improvement projects and funding, traffic, and delays, by major airport, 1987-90 and forecast to 1998, annual rpt, 7504–43

Airport finances, operations by carrier, and capacity improvement and dev funding, by airport, 1977-87 and projected to 2020, hearing, 21648–59

Airport improvement program of FAA, activities, funding, and airport operations, by location, projected 1990-99, biennial rpt, 7504–42

Alaska socioeconomic impacts of OCS oil resources dev, 1980-89 and projected to 2020, 5736–5.11

Bank deposit insurance fund finances, potential losses, and real estate lenders financial ratios compared to other US and Texas banks, 1990 hearings, 25248–125

Banks and deposit insurance funds financial condition, potential losses, and regulatory issues, 1980s-90 and projected to 1995, 21248–147

Banks failures forecasting performance of bank financial ratios and local market economic conditions, 1980s-89, article, 9377–1.203

Banks failures forecasting performance of measures using alternative capital/asset ratio requirements, 1982-89, working paper, 9377–9.109

Banks failures, survival probability model forecasting performance, 1986-90, article, 9377–1.204

Banks stock price changes relation to regulatory exam results, 1980s, article, 9373–1.210

Budget of US, CBO analysis and review of FY92 budget by function, annual rpt, 26304–2

Budget of US, CBO analysis of revenue and spending alternatives and projections of economic indicators, FY92-96, annual rpt, 26304–3

Budget of US, CBO analysis of savings and revenues under alternative spending cuts and tax changes, projected FY92-97, 26306–3.118

Budget of US, compilation of background material on fiscal and tax policy, 1960s-96, 21788–203

Budget of US, House concurrent resolution, with spending and revenue targets, FY92 and projected to FY96, annual rpt, 21264–2

Budget of US, midsession review of FY92 budget, by function, annual rpt, 104–7

Budget of US, obligations and authority by function, agency, and program, with summaries, analyses, and historical tables, FY92, annual rpt, 104–2

Budget of US, Senate concurrent resolution, with spending and revenue targets, FY92, annual rpt, 25254–1

Business cycle recession forecasting performance of experimental indicators indexes and interest rate spreads, with data for 1940s-91, article, 9375–1.212

Carbon dioxide in atmosphere, measurement, methodology, and research results, series, 3006–11

Carbon dioxide in atmosphere, North Central States economic and agricultural impacts, model descriptions and results, 1980s and projected to 2030, 3006–11.15

Coastal areas environmental and socioeconomic conditions, and potential impact of oil and gas OCS leases, final statement series, 5736–1

Construction put in place, housing starts, and Fed Govt investment outlays, projected 1991-95 and trends from 1980, annual article, 2042–1.201

Consumer spending forecasting performance of consumer sentiment index, 1950s-90, technical paper, 9366–6.282

Developing countries economic, population, and agricultural data, US and other aid sources, and AID activity, country rpt series, 9916–12

Dollar exchange rate forecasting performance, assessment of alternative forecasts for 5 currencies, 1985-91, working paper, 9371–10.63

Dollar exchange rate forecasting performance of central bank policy intervention indicators, with model results for 2 currencies, 1985-90, working paper, 9377–9.118

Economic and employment conditions, alternative BLS projections to 2005 and trends 1970s-90, biennial article, 6722–1.251; 6722–1.253

Economic and social conditions of foreign countries, working paper series, 2326–18

Economic indicators forecasts, performance of preliminary estimates, 1966-90, technical paper, 9385–8.94

Economic indicators forecasts, 1991-92 with trends from 1948, annual article, 9383–6.201

Economic Report of the President for 1991, with economic trends from 1929, annual rpt, 204–1

Employment conditions, alternative BLS projections to 2005 and trends 1970s-90, biennial article, 6722–1.252; 6722–1.254

Environmental protection programs costs to govts and households, by program type and city size, 1960s-88 and projected to 2000, 9188–114

Fed Govt agencies budget requests and program costs and characteristics, series, 26306–3

Fed Govt civil service retirement system actuarial valuation, FY79-90 and projected to FY2065, annual rpt, 9844–34

Fed Govt programs of congressional interest, objectives, feasibility, benefits, and costs, series, 26306–6

Fed Govt tax provisions and receipts overview, by tax type, with background data, 1900s-91 and projected to 2000, 21788–197

Financial and economic analysis and forecasting methodology, technical paper series, 9366–6

Forest Service mgmt of public lands and resources dev, environmental, economic, and social impacts of alternative programs, projected to 2040, 1208–24

Global climate change economic impacts, projected to 2100 with background data for 1980s, 3028–5

Global climate change environmental, infrastructure, and health impacts, with model results and background data, 1850s-2100, 9188–113

Global warming contributing air pollutants, US and foreign emissions and control measures, 1980s and projected to 2020, 26358–233

GNP and employment forecasting performance of alternative models, with results, 1958-88, article, 9371–1.201

GNP and inflation forecasting performance of alternative monetary aggregates, model description and results, 1948-87, working paper, 9371–10.53

GNP and money supply forecasting performance of alternative monetary policy rules, 1991 technical paper, 9379–12.66

GNP changes related to labor force composition and changes in participation, model description and results, 1940s-2000, article, 9373–1.201

Govt-sponsored enterprises financial condition and capital adequacy, with data by enterprise, 1970s-90 and projected to 1996, 26308–99

Great Lakes and connecting channels water levels, and forecasts, semimonthly rpt, 3752–2

Health care spending by type and payment source, with background data and foreign comparisons, 1960s-80s and projected to 2000, 26308–98

Health care spending per capita and as share of GNP, alternative projections 1990-2065, technical paper, 9366–6.284

Health condition and health care resources, use, and spending, 1950s-89, annual data compilation, 4144–11

Health condition improvement and disease prevention goals and recommended activities for 2000, with trends 1970s-80s, 4048–10

Helium resources in storage and natural gas reserves, by State, 1950-89 and projected to 2020, biennial rpt, 5604–44

Higher education instn tuition and other costs, govt aid, impacts on enrollment, and cost containment methods, 1970s-90 and projected to 2001, 4808–25

Housing starts forecasts by region, 1991-2000, with background data, 1973-87, article, 9387–1.205

Hwy and mass transit funding and regulation by Fed Govt and States, FY91 with projections to FY96, 26358–242

Income (personal) per capita disparity among States, with data by industrial base, 1979, 1989, and projected to 1995, 1548–379

Projections and forecasts

Industrial production growth and business cycle turning points, forecasting performance of diffusion indexes, 1960s-90, technical paper, 9366–6.277

Industry (US) intl competitiveness, with selected foreign and US operating data by major firm and product, series, 2046–12

Industry finances and operations, by SIC 2- to 4-digit industry, forecast 1991, annual rpt, 2044–28

Inflation and GNP forecasting performance of indexed bond prices, for UK, 1950s-91, article, 9385–1.214

Inflation forecasting performance of alternative models, impact of adjusting for prior announcement of forecast, 1970s-86, working paper, 9387–8.249

Inflation forecasting performance of expected long run inflation rate and other models, for Japan and Germany, 1970s-89, technical paper, 9366–7.268

Inflation forecasting performance of interest rate spreads and yield curve, 1960s-88, technical paper, 9385–8.118

Inflation relation to unemployment and Fed Reserve inflation forecast accuracy indicators, 1960s-83, working paper, 9387–8.240

Interest rates and Fed Reserve monetary policy targets, relation to unexpected employment news, 1970s-91, article, 9389–1.205

Interest rates forecasting performance of Treasury bill and other security yields at alternative maturities, 1950s-80s, article, 9389–1.201

Japan economic conditions, financial and intl policies, and trade devs, 1950s-80s and projected to 2050, compilation of papers, 23848–220

Labor force data of BLS, major statistical and analytical programs and rpts, as of Feb 1991, listing, 6728–35

Louisiana economic indicators and oil rig growth forecasts, model description and results, 1991, article, 9379–1.202

Manufacturing activity index of Natl Assn of Purchasing Managers, economic indicator forecasting performance, various periods 1948-91, article, 9385–1.215; 9385–8.120

Massachusetts State govt spending and employment by program, revenues by source, debt, and public works financing, compared to other States, 1990 compilation of papers, 9373–4.27

Materials (advanced structural) devs, use, and R&D funding, for ceramics, metal alloys, polymers, and composites, 1960s-80s and projected to 2000, 5608–162

Medicare Hospital Insurance and Supplementary Medical Insurance trust funds finances, early 1990s and projected to 2060s, annual article, 4742–1.211

Medicare Hospital Insurance trust fund finances, 1966-90 and alternative projections to 2065, annual rpt, 4654–11

Military pay and benefits for active duty personnel, reserves, retirees, and survivors, 1940s-80s and projected to 2049, 21208–34

Minerals foreign and US supply under alternative market conditions, reserves, and background industry data, series, 5606–4

Mississippi River system freight traffic by commodity and waterway, 1988 and projected to 2000, article, 9391–16.202

Monetary policy votes of Fed Open Market Committee members, relation to regional employment conditions, 1965-85, article, 9373–1.205

Money supply forecast accuracy impact of monetary target announcements, for US and Japan, 1978-88, working paper, 9393–10.16

Money supply forecasting performance of alternative models, 1950s-90, article, 9389–1.202

NASA activities and funding, 1990, annual compilation of papers, 21704–1

NASA science and engineering staff retirement rates, projected 1991-95, GAO rpt, 26123–348

New England employment growth rates by selected industry, projected 1990s with background data for 1980s, article, 9373–25.201

New England States employment growth rates, and performance of alternative forecasts, 1950s-91, article, 9373–1.211

North Carolina environmental and socioeconomic conditions, and impacts of proposed OCS oil and gas exploration, 1970s-90 and projected to 2020, 5738–22

North Central States business and economic conditions, Fed Reserve 9th District, quarterly journal, 9383–19

OASDHI admin, and SSA activities, 1930s-90 and projected to 2064, annual data compilation, 4704–12

OASDHI future cost estimates, actuarial study series, 4706–1

OASDHI trust funds financial status forecasts, evaluation of demographic and economic assumptions, 1991 article, 9391–1.207

OASDI actuarial balance and contingency fund ratio projections under technical advisory panel economic assumptions, with accuracy of past forecasts, 1990 article, 4742–1.201

OASDI trust funds finances, FY90 and projected to 2060s, annual article, 4742–1.210

OASDI trust funds finances, 1937-FY90 and alternative projections to 2065, annual rpt, 4704–4

Oceanographic research ships, fleet condition, funding, voyages, and modernization costs, for NOAA, 1980s-90 and projected to 2020, 2148–60

Ozone in stratosphere, levels, depletion rates and climate impacts, and properties of chlorofluorocarbons and substitutes, 1990 rpt, 9508–37

Public debt burden on future generations forecast under alternative economic and fiscal policy assumptions, 1991 working paper, 9377–9.111

Public debt burden on future generations forecast under alternative fiscal policies, and ratio of consumption to lifetime income, by sex and age, 1991 working paper, 9377–9.116

Puerto Rico statehood referendum proposal, impacts on Federal tax revenue and aid outlays, corporations tax-favored status, and economic conditions, projected FY91-2000, hearing, 25368–168; 26306–3.112

Index by Subjects and Names

Railroad retirement system actuarial evaluation, 1989 and projected to 2064, annual rpt, 9704–1

Railroad retirement system funding and benefits findings and recommendations, with background industry data, 1960s-90 and projected to 2060, 9708–1

Science and engineering academic research system status, R&D performance, and Fed Govt support, 1950s-88 with trends and projections, 9628–83

South Central States employment by industry div, income, and other economic indicators, for 4 States, 1989-90 and forecast 1991-92, annual article, 9391–16.207

Space programs involvement by private sector, govt contracts, costs, revenue, and R&D spending, 1970s-80s and projected to 2000, 26306–6.154

Space station commercial dev and operating costs and income under alternative financing options, projected 1989-2000, 21708–129

State and Metro Area Data Book, 1991 data compilation, 2328–54

Statistical Abstract of US, 1991 annual data compilation, 2324–1

Stockpiling of strategic material, inventories and needs, by commodity, as of Jan 1991, annual rpt, 3544–37

Tax (income) returns and supplemental documents filed, by type, FY90 and projected to FY99, semiannual rpt, 8302–4

Tax (income) returns filed, accuracy of projections by return type, various periods 1983-90, article, 8304–8.1

Tax (income) returns filed, by type, IRS service center, and whether full-paid, refund, and electronically filed, 1990 and projected to 1998, semiannual rpt, 8302–7

Tax (income) returns processing, IRS workload forecasts, compliance, and enforcement, data compilation, 1991 annual rpt, 8304–8

Tax (income) withholding and related documents filed, by type and IRS service center, 1990 and projected 1991-98, annual rpt, 8304–22

Tax expenditures, Federal revenues forgone through income tax deductions and exclusions by type, FY92-96, annual rpt, 21784–10

Tax returns and supplemental documents filed, by type, FY89 and projected to FY98, annual article, 8302–2.208

Tax returns filed, by type of tax and IRS district, 1989 and projected 1990-97, annual rpt, 8304–24

Tax returns filed, by type of tax and IRS region and service center, projected 1990-97 and trends from 1978, annual rpt, 8304–9

Textile, apparel, and shoe import restriction proposals economic impacts, projected 1991-2000, with imports by country, 1989-90, 26306–6.162

Tidal currents, daily time and velocity by station for North America and Asia coasts, forecast 1992, annual rpts, 2174–1

Tide height and tidal current velocity daily at Middle Atlantic coastal stations, forecast 1992, annual rpt, 2174–11

Tide height and time daily at coastal points worldwide, forecast 1992, annual rpt series, 2174–2

Transportation natl system use, condition, accidents, and needs, by mode of transport, 1940s-90 and projected to 2020, 7308–202

Unemployment insurance programs of States, finances, operations, tax provisions, and vulnerability to recessions, 1970s-90s, hearing, 21788–201

Wastewater treatment facilities in small communities, construction and repair needs to meet Clean Water Act standards, by State and region, 1988 and 2008, 1588–155

Water (groundwater) supply, quality, chemistry, other characteristics, and use, regional rpt series, 5666–25

Water quality, chemistry, hydrology, and other characteristics, local area studies, series, 5666–27

Water supply in western US, streamflow and reservoir storage forecasts by stream and station, Jan-May monthly rpt, 1262–1

Weather forecasts accuracy evaluations, for US, UK, and European systems, quarterly rpt, 2182–8

Weather forecasts for US and Northern Hemisphere, precipitation and temperature by location, semimonthly rpt, 2182–1

Weather forecasts of severe storms, Natl Weather Service forecast accuracy and storm characteristics, series, 2186–6

West Central States population, income, and employment growth, by MSA, metro-nonmetro location, and State, for Fed Reserve 10th District, 1970s-90s, article, 9381–1.209

Wetlands (riparian) acreage, and Bur of Land Mgmt activities, mgmt plans, and scientific staff, State rpt series, 5726–8

Wildlife mgmt activities and funding, acreage by habitat type, and scientific staff, for Bur of Land Mgmt, State rpt series, 5726–7

see also Agricultural forecasts

see also Energy projections

see also Population projections

Propaganda

see also Political broadcasting

Property

Divorce property settlement, by type, whether child support and alimony received, and selected characteristics of woman, 1989, biennial Current Population Rpt, 2546–6.72

see also Business assets and liabilities, general

see also Business assets and liabilities, specific industry

see also Capital investments, general

see also Capital investments, specific industry

see also Educational facilities

see also Farms and farmland

see also Government supplies and property

see also Housing condition and occupancy

see also Housing tenure

see also Land ownership and rights

see also Land use

see also Military bases, posts, and reservations

see also Military supplies and property

see also Mortgages

see also Property and casualty insurance

see also Property condemnation

see also Property damage and loss

see also Property tax

see also Property value

see also Public buildings

see also Public lands

see also Real estate business

see also Rent

see also Surplus government property

see also Vacant and abandoned property

see also Wealth

Property and casualty insurance

Aircraft operating costs by component for private planes, and Fed Govt mileage reimbursement rates, 1989, annual rpt, 9454–13.2

Budget of US, obligations and authority by function, agency, and program, with summaries, analyses, and historical tables, FY92, annual rpt, 104–2

County Business Patterns, 1988: employment, establishments, and payroll, by SIC 2- to 4-digit industry and county, annual State rpt series, 2326–6

County Business Patterns, 1989: employment, establishments, and payroll, by SIC 2- to 4-digit industry and county, annual State rpt series, 2326–8

Crime insurance policies under Federal program by State, and claims paid, data compilation, 1991 annual rpt, 6064–6.3

Earthquake preparedness costs and benefits, with data for California events and effects of 1989 Loma Prieta quake, 1980s, hearings, 21248–154

Finances and operations, by SIC 2- to 4-digit industry, forecast 1991, annual rpt, 2044–28

Financial performance of property and casualty insurance industry, State monitoring system effectiveness, and firms designated for increased attention, 1980s, GAO rpt, 26119–316

Flood insurance natl program participation, and flood losses, 1970-89, 5664–12

Foreign and US economic aid by type and recipient, and role in advancing economic interests, 1980s-90, 2048–152

Health Care Financing Review, provider prices, price inputs and indexes, and labor, quarterly journal, 4652–1.1

Home mortgages FHA-insured, financial, property, and mortgagor characteristics, by metro area, 1990, annual rpt, 5144–24

Home mortgages FHA-insured, financial, property, and mortgagor characteristics, by State, 1990, annual rpt, 5144–1

Home mortgages FHA-insured, financial, property, and mortgagor characteristics, 1990, annual rpt, 5144–17; 5144–23

Housing and households detailed characteristics, and unit and neighborhood quality, by location, 1989, biennial rpt, 2485–12

Housing and households detailed characteristics, and unit and neighborhood quality, MSA surveys, series, 2485–6

Land subsidence above coal mines, State property insurance program income and expenses in 6 States, 1990, GAO rpt, 26113–530

Marine and war-risk insurance approved for US and foreign vessels, FY90, annual rpt, 7704–14.4

Property damage and loss

Medical malpractice insurance and other components of physicians practice cost indexes, by State, MSA, and for rural areas, 1989 rpt, 4658–50

Medicare Economic Index for physician reimbursement rebased to 1989, methodology and results, with projections to 1995, article, 4652–1.246

Occupational injury and illness rates, by SIC 2- to 4-digit industry, 1988-89, annual rpt, 6844–7

Occupational injury and illness rates, by SIC 2- to 4-digit industry, 1989, annual rpt, 6844–1

Overseas Private Investment Corp finances and activities, with list of insured projects and firms, FY90, annual rpt, 9904–2

Reinsurance recoverables for large property and casualty insurance firms, 1988, hearing, 21368–133

Statistical Abstract of US, 1991 annual data compilation, 2324–1.16

Tax and income impacts of tax reform, with background financial data, for property and casualty insurance industry, 1970s-91, 8008–151

Transit systems finances and operations, by mode of transport, size of fleet, and for 468 systems, 1989, annual rpt, 7884–4

Truck and warehouse services finances and inventory, by SIC 2- to 4-digit industry, 1989 survey, annual rpt, 2413–14

Truck itemized costs per mile, finances, and operations, for agricultural carriers, 1990, annual rpt, 1311–15

Truck transport of fruit and vegetables, itemized costs per mile by item for fleets and owner-operator trucks, monthly table, 1272–1

see also Automobile insurance

Property condemnation

Court civil and criminal caseloads for Federal district, appeals, and bankruptcy courts, by type of suit and offense, circuit, and district, 1990, annual rpt, 18204–11

Court civil and criminal caseloads for Federal district, appeals, and special courts, 1990, annual rpt, 18204–8

Court civil and criminal caseloads for Federal district courts, 1991, annual rpt, 18204–2.1

Housing characteristics of recent movers for new and previous unit, and household characteristics, by location, 1989, biennial rpt, 2485–12

US attorneys land condemnation cases, by disposition and district, FY90, annual rpt, 6004–2.6

Property damage and loss

Aircraft (general aviation) accidents, by circumstances, characteristics of persons and aircraft involved, and type of flying, 1988, annual rpt, 9614–3

Aircraft accidents and circumstances, for US operations of domestic and foreign airlines and general aviation, periodic rpt, 9612–1

Aircraft accidents, casualties, and damage, for commercial operations by detailed circumstances, 1987, annual rpt, 9614–2

Arson incidents by whether structure occupied, property value, and arrest rate, by property type, 1990, annual rpt, 6224–2.1

Property damage and loss

Boat accidents, casualties, and damage, by cause, vessel characteristics, and State, 1990, annual rpt, 7404–1.1

Bombing incidents, casualties, and damage, by target, circumstances, and State, 1990, annual rpt, 6224–5

Coast Guard search and rescue missions, and lives and property lost and saved, by district and assisting unit, FY90, annual rpt, 7404–2

Court civil and criminal caseloads for Federal district, appeals, and special courts, 1990, annual rpt, 18204–8

Court civil and criminal caseloads for Federal district courts, 1991, annual rpt, 18204–2.1

Crime victimization rates, by victim and offender characteristics, circumstances, and offense, 1988 survey, annual rpt, 6066–3.42

Crime victimization rates, by victim and offender characteristics, circumstances, and offense, 1989 survey, annual rpt, 6066–3.44

Crimes, by characteristics of victim and offender, circumstances, and location, data compilation, 1991 annual rpt, 6064–6.3

Disasters and natl security incidents and mgmt, with data by major event and State, 1991 annual rpt, 9434–6

Earthquake intensity, time, location, damage, and seismic characteristics, for US and foreign earthquakes, 1985, annual rpt, 5664–13

Earthquake preparedness costs and benefits, with data for California events and effects of 1989 Loma Prieta quake, 1980s, hearings, 21248–154

Farm income, expenses, receipts by commodity, assets, liabilities, and ratios, 1990 and trends from 1945, annual rpt, 1544–16

Farmland damaged by natural disaster, Emergency Conservation Program funding by region and State, monthly rpt, 1802–13

Fish (trout) raised on farms, production, sales, prices, and losses, 1990-91, annual rpt, 1631–16

Flood insurance natl program participation, and flood losses, 1970-89, 5664–12

Foreign countries disasters, casualties, damage, and aid by US and others, FY90 and trends from FY64, annual rpt, 9914–12

Forest fires and acres burned on Forest Service land, by cause, forest, and State, 1989, annual rpt, 1204–6

Global climate change economic impacts, projected to 2100 with background data for 1980s, 3028–5

Hazardous material transport accidents, casualties, and damage, by mode of transport, with DOT control activities, 1989, annual rpt, 7304–4

Housing characteristics of recent movers for new and previous unit, and household characteristics, by location, 1989, biennial rpt, 2485–12

Housing inventory change from 1973, by reason, unit and household characteristics, and location, 1983 survey, biennial rpt, 2485–14

Hurricanes and tropical storms frequency, intensity, deaths, and damage, by State and selected city, 1886-1989, 2188–15

Military personnel personal property shipped worldwide, and loss and damage claims, quarterly rpt, 3702–1

Mobile home fires, casualties, damage, and impacts of safety standards, with data on Michigan trailer parks, 1980s, hearing, 21248–145

Panama Canal fires, and related property loss, FY89-90, annual rpt, 9664–3.2

Railroad accidents, casualties, and damage, by cause, railroad, and State, 1990, annual rpt, 7604–1

Railroad accidents, casualties, and damage, Fed Railroad Admin activities, and safety inspectors by State, 1989, annual rpt, 7604–12

Ships accidents and casualties, by circumstances and characteristics of persons and vessels involved, 1988, annual rpt, 7404–11

Ships and marine facilities accidents, casualties, and circumstances, Coast Guard investigation results, periodic rpt, 9612–4

Ships in world merchant fleet, tonnage, and new ship construction and deliveries, by vessel type and country, as of Jan 1990, annual rpt, 7704–3

Storms and unusual weather phenomena characteristics, casualties, and property damage, by State, monthly listing, 2152–3

Subway accidents, casualties, and damage, by circumstances and system, 1989, annual rpt, 7884–5

Tax (income) returns of individuals, selected income and tax items by income level, preliminary 1989, annual article, 8302–2.209

Tax expenditures, Federal revenues forgone through income tax deductions and exclusions by type, FY92-96, annual rpt, 21784–10

Thefts, and value of property stolen and recovered, by property type, 1990, annual rpt, 6224–2.1

Timber insect and disease incidence and damage, and control activities, State rpt series, 1206–49

Timber insect and disease incidence and damage, annual regional rpt series, 1206–11

Traffic accidents, casualties, circumstances, and characteristics of persons and vehicles involved, 1989, annual rpt, 7764–18

Transportation safety programs, and accidents, casualties, and damage, by mode of transport, 1989, annual rpt, 7304–19

Truck accidents, casualties, and damage, by circumstances and characteristics of persons and vehicles involved, 1988, annual rpt, 7554–9

Truck accidents, circumstances, severity, and characteristics of drivers and vehicles, 1989, annual rpt, 7764–20

Truck transport of household goods, performance and disposition of damage claims, for selected carriers, 1990, annual rpt, 9484–11

Weather forecasts of severe storms, Natl Weather Service forecast accuracy and storm characteristics, series, 2186–6

see also Robbery and theft

Index by Subjects and Names

see also Shoplifting

Property loss

see Property damage and loss

Property tax

Agriculture census, 1987: farms, farmland, production, finances, and operator characteristics, by county, final State rpt series, 2331–1

Airport finances, operations by carrier, and capacity improvement and dev funding, by airport, 1977-87 and projected to 2020, hearing, 21648–59

Collections of taxes, by level of govt, type of tax, State, and selected counties, quarterly rpt, 2462–3

Consumer Expenditure Survey, household income by source, and itemized spending, by selected characteristics and region, 1988-89, annual rpt, 6764–5

Farm prices received for major products and paid for farm inputs and living items, by commodity and State, monthly rpt, 1629–1

Farm production itemized costs, by farm sales size and region, 1990, annual rpt, 1614–3

Farmland value, rent, taxes, foreign ownership, and transfers by probable use and lender type, with data by region and State, 1980-91, article, 1561–16.202

Finances of govts, by level of govt, State, and for large cities and counties, annual rpt series, 2466–2

Finances of govts, tax systems and revenue, and fiscal structure, by level of govt and State, 1991 and historical trends, annual rpt, 10044–1

Home mortgages FHA-insured, financial, property, and mortgagor characteristics, by metro area, 1990, annual rpt, 5144–24

Home mortgages FHA-insured, financial, property, and mortgagor characteristics, by State, 1990, annual rpt, 5144–1

Home mortgages FHA-insured, financial, property, and mortgagor characteristics, 1990, annual rpt, 5144–17; 5144–23

Housing and households detailed characteristics, and unit and neighborhood quality, by location, 1989, biennial rpt, 2485–12

Housing and households detailed characteristics, and unit and neighborhood quality, MSA surveys, series, 2485–6

Housing inventory change from 1973, by reason, unit and household characteristics, and location, 1983 survey, biennial rpt, 2485–14

Housing value capitalization of property tax, model description and results for Philadelphia, 1982, working paper, 9387–8.252

Hwy receipts by source, and spending by function, by level of govt and State, 1990, annual rpt, 7554–1.3

Income tax deductions and exclusions, Federal tax expenditures by item, FY92-96, annual rpt, 21784–10

Massachusetts property tax increase referenda and outcomes, and relation to community characteristics, FY81-91, article, 9373–1.208

Massachusetts State govt spending and employment by program, revenues by source, debt, and public works financing, compared to other States, 1990 compilation of papers, 9373–4.27

Index by Subjects and Names

Property value

Natl income and product accounts and components, *Survey of Current Business*, monthly rpt, 2702–1.24; 2702–1.25

North Central States tax structure and revenue changes, 1980s, article, 9375–1.211

Public lands, Fed Govt payments to local govts in lieu of property taxes, by State and county, FY91, annual rpt, 5724–9

Public lands, Fed Govt payments to local govts in lieu of property taxes, by State, FY91, annual press release, 5306–4.10

Public opinion on taxes, spending, and govt efficiency, by respondent characteristics, 1991 survey, annual rpt, 10044–2

State govt tax collections by detailed type of tax, and tax rates, by State, FY90, annual rpt, 2466–2.7

Statistical Abstract of US, 1991 annual data compilation, 2324–1.9

Telephone and telegraph firms detailed finances and operations, 1989, annual rpt, 9284–6.2; 9284–6.3

Transit systems finances and operations, by mode of transport, size of fleet, and for 468 systems, 1989, annual rpt, 7884–4

Property value

AFDC beneficiaries demographic and financial characteristics, by State, FY89, annual rpt, 4694–1

Agriculture census, 1987: farms, farmland, production, finances, and operator characteristics, by county, final State rpt series, 2331–1

Airport finances, operations by carrier, and capacity improvement and dev funding, by airport, 1977-87 and projected to 2020, hearing, 21648–59

Assets and debts of private sector, balance sheets by segment, 1945-90, semiannual rpt, 9365–4.1

Banks (insured commercial and savings) finances, for foreign and domestic offices, by asset size, 1989, annual rpt, 9294–4.2

Census of Population and Housing, 1990: population and housing selected characteristics, by region, press release, 2328–74

Commuting accessibility impact on auto ownership, employment location, and housing values, for Philadelphia metro area census tracts, 1980, working paper, 9387–8.231

Construction put in place, value of new public and private structures, by type, monthly rpt, 2382–4

DOD property, supply, and equipment inventory, by service branch, FY90, annual rpt, 3544–6

Electric utilities privately owned, finances and operations, detailed data, 1989, annual rpt, 3164–23

Enterprise Statistics, 1987: auxiliaries of multi-establishment firms, finances and operations by function, industry, and State, 2329–6

Farm credit, terms, delinquency, agricultural bank failures, and credit conditions by Fed Reserve District, quarterly rpt, 9365–3.10

Farm housing for operators and hired labor, market and rental value, 1989, article, 1541–1.211

Farm income, expenses, receipts by commodity, assets, liabilities, and ratios, 1990 and trends from 1945, annual rpt, 1544–16

Farm operators age and off-farm employment, sales, and land value changes relationship to farm sales size, model description and results, 1974-78, 1548–374

Farm production inputs, finances, mgmt, and land value and transfers, periodic situation rpt with articles, 1561–16

Farmland in US owned by foreigners, holdings, acquisitions, and disposals by land use, owner type and country, and State, 1990, annual rpt, 1584–2

Farmland in US owned by foreigners, holdings, acreage, and value by land use, owner country, State, and county, 1990, annual rpt, 1584–3

Farmland rental by assessment method, and rent receipts per acre and as share of land value by land type and State, 1960s-80s, 1548–377

Fed Govt-owned real property inventory and costs, worldwide summary by purpose, agency, and location, 1989, annual rpt, 9454–5

Fish and Wildlife Service restoration programs funding, land purchases, and project listing, by State, FY89, annual rpt, 5504–1

FmHA property acquired through foreclosure, value, acreage, and sales, for farm and nonfarm property by State, monthly rpt, 1182–6

FmHA property acquired through foreclosure, value, and acreage under conservation easements by State, 1989-90, GAO rpt, 26113–514

FmHA property acquired through foreclosure, 1-family homes, value, sales, and leases, by State, monthly rpt, 1182–7

Foreign direct investment in US commercial real estate, by State and country, 1980s, GAO rpt, 26123–350

Foreign direct investment in US, major transactions by type, industry, country, and US location, 1989, annual rpt, 2044–20

Forest Service activities and finances, by region and State, FY90, annual rpt, 1204–1.1

Historic buildings rehabilitation tax incentives, projects, costs, ownership, and use, FY77-90, annual rpt, 5544–17

Home mortgages FHA-insured, financial, property, and mortgagor characteristics, by metro area, 1990, annual rpt, 5144–24

Home mortgages FHA-insured, financial, property, and mortgagor characteristics, by State, 1990, annual rpt, 5144–1

Home mortgages FHA-insured, financial, property, and mortgagor characteristics, total and by State and outlying area, 1990, annual rpt, 5144–25

Home mortgages FHA-insured, financial, property, and mortgagor characteristics, 1990, annual rpt, 5144–17; 5144–23

Households assets, by type of holding and selected characteristics, 1988, Current Population Rpt, 2546–20.16

Housing and households characteristics, unit and neighborhood quality, and journey to work by MSA location, for 11 MSAs, 1984 survey, supplement, 2485–8

Housing and households detailed characteristics, and unit and neighborhood quality, by location, 1987, biennial rpt supplement, 2485–13

Housing and households detailed characteristics, and unit and neighborhood quality, by location, 1989, biennial rpt, 2485–12

Housing and households detailed characteristics, and unit and neighborhood quality, MSA surveys, series, 2485–6

Housing and population census, 1990: population and housing characteristics, households, and land area, by county, subdiv, and place, State rpt series, 2551–1

Housing inventory change from 1973, by reason, unit and household characteristics, and location, 1983 survey, biennial rpt, 2485–14

Housing market and monthly rental values, by selected characteristics and region, 1988-89 Consumer Expenditure Survey, annual rpt, 6764–5

Housing units (1-family) by selected structural characteristics, sales, and prices, 1970s-90, article, 1702–1.205

Housing units (1-family) sold and for sale by price, stage of construction, months on market, and region, monthly rpt, 2382–3

Housing units completed, single and multifamily units by structural and financial characteristics, inside-outside MSAs, and region, 1986-90, annual rpt, 2384–1

Housing vacancy and occupancy rates, and vacant unit characteristics, by tenure and location, 1960s-90, annual rpt, 2484–1

Housing vacancy and property value appreciation rates for 4 metro areas, 1991 GAO rpt, 26131–84

Housing value capitalization of property tax, model description and results for Philadelphia, 1982, working paper, 9387–8.252

Natural gas interstate pipeline company detailed financial and operating data, by firm, 1989, annual rpt, 3164–38

North Central States farm credit conditions and farmland market values, Fed Reserve 9th District, quarterly rpt, 9383–11

Nursing home reimbursement by Medicaid, States payment ratesetting methods, limits, and allowances, 1988, article, 4652–1.253

Public lands acreage, grants, use, revenues, and allocations, by State, FY90 and trends, annual rpt, 5724–1

Puerto Rico population and housing characteristics, 1990 Census of Population and Housing, press release, 2328–78

Savings rates relationship to housing value and limits on tax deductible pension contributions, 1950s-90, article, 9373–1.219

Southeastern States, Fed Reserve 5th District, economic indicators by State, quarterly rpt, 9389–16

Southeastern States, Fed Reserve 6th District, economic indicators by State and MSA, quarterly rpt, 9371–14

Southwestern States farm credit conditions and real estate values, Fed Reserve 11th District, quarterly rpt, 9379–11

State and Metro Area Data Book, 1991 data compilation, 2328–54

Statistical Abstract of US, 1991 annual data compilation, 2324–1.26

Property value

Tax (income) returns of corporations, income and tax items by asset size and detailed industry, 1987, annual rpt, 8304–4

Tax (income) returns of corporations, income and tax items by asset size and detailed industry, 1988, annual rpt, 8304–21

Vacant housing characteristics and costs, and occupancy and vacancy rates, by region and metro-nonmetro location, quarterly rpt, 2482–1

Virgin Islands population and housing characteristics, 1990 Census of Population and Housing, press release, 2328–81

West Central States farm real estate values, farm loan trends, and regional farm price index, Fed Reserve 10th District, quarterly rpt, 9381–16.1

Wildlife refuges and other land under Fish and Wildlife Service mgmt, acreage by site and State, as of Sept 1991, annual rpt, 5504–8

Proprietorships

Agriculture census, 1987: farms, farmland, production, finances, and operator characteristics, by county, final State rpt series, 2331–1

Agriculture census, 1987: horticultural specialties producers, finances, and operations, by crop and State, 1988 survey, 2337–1

Enterprise Statistics, 1987: finances and operations for companies, by size, level of diversification, form of organization, and industry group, 2329–8

Hotels and other lodging places, receipts, payroll, employment, and ownership, by type and State, 1987 Census of Service Industries, subject rpt, 2393–3.1

Manufacturing census, 1987: finances and operations, by type of organization and SIC 2- to 4-digit industry, subject rpt, 2497–5

Mineral industries census, 1987: finances and operations, by establishment characteristics, SIC 2- to 4-digit industry, and State, subject rpt, 2517–1

Puerto Rico economic censuses, 1987: wholesale, retail, and service industries finances and operations, by size, form of organization, and SIC 2- and 3-digit industry, subject rpt, 2591–2.1

Retail trade census, 1987: finances and employment, for establishments with and without payroll, by SIC 2- to 4-digit kind of business, State, and MSA, 2401–1

Retail trade sales, inventories, purchases, gross margin, and accounts receivable, by SIC 2- to 4-digit kind of business and form of ownership, 1989, annual rpt, 2413–5

Service industries census, 1987: establishments, receipts by source, payroll, and employment, by SIC 2- to 4-digit kind of business, State, and MSA, 2393–4

Statistical Abstract of US, 1991 annual data compilation, 2324–1.17

Tax (income) returns filed by type of filer, selected income items, quarterly rpt, 8302–2.1

Tax (income) returns of sole proprietorships, income statement items, by industry group, 1989, annual article, 8302–2.214

Transportation census, 1987: finances and operations by size, ownership, and State, and revenues by MSA, by SIC 2- to 4-digit industry, 2579–1

Women-owned businesses and sales, by industry div and ownership type, and data needs and availability, 1987, 9768–22

Prospective Payment Assessment Commission

Hospital reimbursement by Medicare under prospective payment system, analyses of alternative payment plans, series, 17206–1

Hospital reimbursement by Medicare under prospective payment system, and effect on services, finances, and beneficiary payments, 1979-90, annual rpt, 17204–2

Hospital reimbursement by Medicare under prospective payment system, impacts on costs, industry structure and operations, and quality of care, series, 17206–2

Hospital reimbursement by Medicare under prospective payment system, methodology, inputs, and data by diagnostic group, 1991 annual rpt, 17204–1

Hospital reimbursement by Medicare under prospective payment system, regulatory adjustments review and diagnostic group weight calibration, annual rpt, discontinued, 17204–3

Hospitalization costs relation to services timing, by selected patient and hospital characteristics, for Medicare discharges, 1987-88, 17208–2

Prosthetics and orthotics

Exports and imports of US, by country and detailed commodity, monthly rpt, 2422–12

Exports and imports of US, by Harmonized System 6-digit commodity and country, 1990, annual rpt, 2424–13

Exports of US, detailed Schedule B commodities with countries of destination, 1990, annual rpt, 2424–10

Hip replacement cases post-discharge hospital services use by type, for Medicare patients, 1981-86, article, 4652–1.223

Implants of medical devices, by type, reason, duration, and user characteristics, 1988, 4146–8.197

Injuries from use of consumer products, by severity, victim age, and detailed product, 1990, annual rpt, 9164–6

Manufacturing census, 1987: employment and shipments under Fed Govt contracts, by SIC 4-digit industry, 2497–7

Medicare reimbursement for radiology services by location, and for home medical equipment under alternative proposals, 1990 hearing, 21368–131

Price indexes (producer), by stage of processing and detailed commodity, monthly rpt, 6762–6

Price indexes (producer), by stage of processing and detailed commodity, monthly 1990, annual rpt, 6764–2

Statistical Abstract of US, 1991 annual data compilation, 2324–1.3

VA health care facilities surgery-related deaths and complications, by procedure and instn, and compared to non-VA instns, FY84-89, last issue of biennial rpt, 8704–1

VA Medicine and Surgery Dept trainees, by detailed program and city, FY90, annual rpt, 8704–4

Prostitution

AIDS cases among drug abusers, by drug use, sexual behavior, and other characteristics, 1984-88 local area study, article, 4042–3.206

Arrests and prisoners, by offense, offender characteristics, and location, data compilation, 1991 annual rpt, 6064–6.4; 6064–6.6

Arrests, by offense, offender characteristics, and location, 1990, annual rpt, 6224–2.2

Cocaine abuse, user characteristics, and related crime and violence, 1988 conf, 4498–74

Drug abuse relation to violent and criminal behavior, with data on street gang activity and selected population groups, 1989 conf, 4498–70

Drug test results at arrest, by drug type, offense, and sex, for selected urban areas, quarterly rpt, 6062–3

Sentences for Federal offenses, guidelines by offense and circumstances, series, 17668–1

US attorneys civil and criminal cases by type and disposition, and collections, by Federal district, FY90, annual rpt, 6004–2.1

Protective services

see Campus security

see Detective and protective services

see Security devices

Providence, R.I.

Housing and households characteristics, unit and neighborhood quality, and journey to work by MSA location, for 11 MSAs, 1984 survey, supplement, 2485–8

Housing and households characteristics, 1988 survey, MSA fact sheet, 2485–11.10

Housing and households detailed characteristics, and unit and neighborhood quality, by location, 1988 survey, MSA rpt, 2485–6.7

see also under By City and By SMSA or MSA in the "Index by Categories"

Provo, Utah

see also under By SMSA or MSA in the "Index by Categories"

Psittacosis

see Animal diseases and zoonoses

Psychiatry

Drug abuse psychotherapy and counseling outcomes, research results and methodology, 1990 conf, 4498–71

Drug and alcohol abuse treatment services, funding, staffing, and client load, characteristics, and outcomes, by setting, 1989 conf, 4498–73

Labor supply of physicians, by specialty, age, sex, and location of training and practice, 1989, State rpt series, 4116–6

Mental health care facilities, staff, and patient characteristics, *Statistical Notes* series, 4506–3

Military health care personnel, and accessions by training source, by occupation, specialty, and service branch, FY89, annual rpt, 3544–24

Private hospitals for mental health care, patients characteristics, 1986, 4506–3.47

VA health care facilities physicians, dentists, and nurses, by selected employment characteristics and VA district, quarterly rpt, 8602–6

VA health care staff and turnover, by occupation, physician specialty, and location, 1990, annual rpt, 8604–8

VA Medicine and Surgery Dept trainees, by detailed program and city, FY90, annual rpt, 8704–4

VA mental health care services, staff, research, and training programs, 1991 biennial listing, 8704–2

Visits to physicians, by patient and practice characteristics, diagnosis, and services provided, 1989, 4146–8.206

Psychological disorders

see Mental health and illness

Psychology

- Aviation medicine research and test results, technical rpt series, 7506–10
- Degrees (PhD) in science and engineering, by field, instn, employment prospects, sex, race, and other characteristics, 1960s-90, annual rpt, 9627–30
- Degrees awarded in higher education, by level, field, race, and sex, 1988/89 with trends from 1978/79, biennial rpt, 4844–17
- Degrees awarded in science and engineering, by field, level, and sex, 1966-89, 9627–33
- Drug (methamphetamine) abuse, availability, health effects, and treatment, 1990 conf papers, 4498–75
- Drug abuse and treatment, research on biological and behavioral factors and addiction potential of new drugs, 1990 annual conf, 4494–11
- Education (special) enrollment by age, staff, funding, and needs, by type of handicap and State, 1989/90, annual rpt, 4944–4
- Employment and other characteristics of science and engineering PhDs, by field and State, 1989, biennial rpt, 9627–18
- Fed Govt aid to higher education and nonprofit instns for R&D and related activities, by field, instn, agency, and State, FY89, annual rpt, 9627–17
- Foreign and US funding for R&D, and scientists and engineering employment and education, 1991 annual rpt, 9627–35.1
- Higher education course completions, by detailed program, sex, race, and instn type, for 1972 high school class, as of 1984, 4888–4
- Higher education grad programs enrollment in science and engineering, by field, source of funds, and characteristics of student and instn, 1975-89, annual rpt, 9627–7
- Medicare reimbursement of hospitals under prospective payment system, and effect on services, finances, and beneficiary payments, 1979-90, annual rpt, 17204–2
- NASA R&D funding to higher education instns, by field, instn, and State, FY90, annual listing, 9504–7
- Population, family, and sexual behavior research activities and funding, 1960s-89, 4478–194
- R&D funding by Fed Govt, by field, performer type, agency, and State, FY89-91, annual rpt, 9627–20

R&D funding by higher education instns and federally funded centers, by field, instn, and State, FY89, annual rpt, 9627–13

Public administration

- Budget of US, CBO analysis and review of FY92 budget by function, annual rpt, 26304–2
- Budget of US, House concurrent resolution, with spending and revenue targets, FY92 and projected to FY96, annual rpt, 21264–2
- Budget of US, midsession review of FY92 budget, by function, annual rpt, 104–7
- Budget of US, obligations and authority by function, agency, and program, with summaries, analyses, and historical tables, FY92, annual rpt, 104–2
- Budget of US, receipts by source, outlays by agency and program, and balances, monthly rpt, 8102–3
- Budget of US, Senate concurrent resolution, with spending and revenue targets, FY92, annual rpt, 25254–1
- Census Bur rpts and data files, coverage and availability, 1991 annual listing, 2304–2
- Classification codes concordance of Canada and US SICs, for 1- to 4-digit levels, 1991 rpt, 2628–31
- Employment and payroll, by function and level of govt, 1990, annual rpt series, 2466–1
- Finances of govts, by level of govt, State, and for large cities and counties, annual rpt series, 2466–2
- Gambia cash transfers from AID linked to fiscal and govt reforms, effectiveness, 1987-89, 9916–1.74
- Govt census, 1987: employment, payroll, and average earnings, by function, level of govt, State, county, and population size, 2455–2
- Govt census, 1987: local govt employment by function, payroll, and average earnings, for individual counties, cities, and school and special districts, 2455–1
- Minority group and women employment in State and local govt, by occupation, function, pay level, and State, 1990, annual rpt, 9244–6
- Senegal cash transfers from AID linked to fiscal and govt reforms, effectiveness, 1980s, 9916–1.75
- Soviet Union GNP by component and industry sector, and CIA estimation methods, 1950s-87, 23848–223
- Soviet Union GNP by detailed income and outlay component, 1985, 2326–18.59
- Truman, Harry S, Scholarship Foundation finances, and awards by student characteristics, FY90, annual rpt, 14314–1

see also Administrative law and procedure

see also Civil service system

see also Federal boards, committees, and commissions

see also Federal employees

see also Federal executive departments

see also Federal independent agencies

see also Government and business

see also Government assets and liabilities

see also Government efficiency

see also Government employees

see also Government revenues

see also Government spending

see also Government supplies and property

see also Labor-management relations in government

see also Local government

see also Officials

see also Political science

see also Public services

see also School administration and staff

see also School boards

see also State and local employees

see also State government

see also under By Industry in the "Index by Categories"

Public assistance

see Public welfare programs

Public broadcasting

- Fed Govt spending in States, by type, program, agency, and State, FY90, annual rpt, 2464–2
- Natl Endowment for Arts activities and grants, FY90, annual rpt, 9564–3
- *Statistical Abstract of US*, 1991 annual data compilation, 2324–1.18
- TV channel allocation and license status, for commercial and noncommercial UHF and VHF stations by market, as of June 30, 1991, semiannual rpt, 9282–6

see also Educational broadcasting

Public buildings

- Accident deaths and rates, by cause, age, sex, race, and State, 1988, US Vital Statistics annual rpt, 4144–2.5
- Arson incidents by whether structure occupied, property value, and arrest rate, by property type, 1990, annual rpt, 6224–2.1
- Budget of US, authoritative financial statements with appropriations, outlays, and receipts, by category and agency, FY90, annual rpt, 8104–2.1
- Capitol Architect activities, funding, costs, and contracts, FY88, annual rpt, 25944–1
- Capitol Architect outlays for salaries, supplies, and services, itemized by payee and function, 1st half FY91, semiannual rpt, 25922–2
- Capitol buildings and grounds, historical summary and floor plans, 1991-92, *Congressional Directory*, biennial rpt, 23874–1
- Construction put in place, permits, housing sales, costs, material prices, and employment, bimonthly rpt with articles, 2042–1
- Construction put in place, value of new public and private structures, by type, monthly rpt, 2382–4
- Court buildings mgmt by GSA, spending, and rental income, 1980s-91, hearing, 21648–60
- Criminal cases by type and disposition, and collections, for US attorneys, by Federal district, FY90, annual rpt, 6004–2.1
- DC metro area land acquisition and dev projects of Fed Govt, characteristics and funding by agency and project, FY91-95, annual rpt, 15454–1
- Disabled persons access to election polling places, precincts by barrier type and State, 1990 natl elections, biennial rpt, 9274–6
- Disabled persons access to Federal and federally funded facilities, complaints by disposition, FY90, annual rpt, 17614–1

Public buildings

DOE energy use, costs, and conservation, by end use, fuel type, and field office, FY90, annual rpt, 3004–27

Energy conservation aid of Fed Govt to public and nonprofit private instns, by building type and State, 1990, annual rpt, 3304–15

Energy spending, and conservation retrofit costs and savings, for Federal buildings, 1988-90, 26358–240

Energy use and efficiency of Fed Govt, by agency and fuel type, FY90, annual rpt, 3304–22

Energy use in commercial buildings, costs, and conservation, by building characteristics, survey rpt series, 3166–8

Engineering and architectural establishments, receipts by type of client and project, payroll, and employment, by State, 1987 Census of Service Industries, 2393–4.16

FDA activities, funding, facilities, and staff, findings and recommendations, 1980s-91, 4008–115

Fed Govt labor productivity, indexes of output and labor costs by function, FY67-89, annual rpt, 6824–1.6

Fed Reserve banks finances and staff, 1990, annual rpt, 9364–1.1

Govt finances, by level of govt, State, and for large cities and counties, annual rpt series, 2466–2

GSA activities and finances, FY90, annual rpt, 9454–1

Homeless persons housing and food aid of Fed Govt, funding and operations, with data by State and county, FY89, hearing, 25408–111

Inventory and costs of real property owned by Fed Govt, worldwide summary by location, agency, and use, 1989, annual rpt, 9454–5

Inventory and rental costs of real property leased by Fed Govt, worldwide summary by location and agency, 1989, annual rpt, 9454–10

Kennedy Center for Performing Arts and Natl Symphony Orchestra financial statements, and capital and maintenance costs and needs, 1970s-90, hearing, 21648–62

Navy command proposed decentralization and relocation from DC area, savings, and cost of living indicators for 14 MSAs, 1980s, GAO rpt, 26123–346

Pollution (air) indoor levels in workplace, and health impacts, for Library of Congress Madison building, 1989 study, series, 4248–92

Postal Service activities, finances, and mail volume and subsidies, FY90, annual rpt, 9864–5.3

Postal Service operating costs, itemized by class of mail, FY90, annual rpt, 9864–4

Postal Service revenue, costs, and volume, by service type and class of mail, FY90, annual rpt, 9864–2

Smoking bans in public places, local ordinances provisions, as of 1989, 4478–196

SSA activities, and OASDHI admin, 1930s-90 and projected to 2064, annual data compilation, 4704–12

Statistical Abstract of US, 1991 annual data compilation, 2324–1.10

TVA energy use by fuel type, and conservation costs and savings, FY90, annual rpt, 9804–26

see also Educational facilities

Public contracts

see Defense contracts and procurement

see Government contracts and procurement

Public debt

Borrowing and debt issues, by level of govt, selected years 1929-90, annual rpt, 204–1.5; 204–1.6

Budget deficits impact on trade deficit, model description and results, 1960s-89, working paper, 9371–10.60

Budget deficits impact on trade deficit, model description and results, 1970s-89, article, 9371–1.207

Budget deficits under Reagan Admin, impact on capital stock, foreign debt, and other economic indicators, with background data, 1950s-88, article, 9393–8.201

Budget of US, authoritative financial statements with appropriations, outlays, and receipts, by agency, FY90, annual rpt, 8104–2

Budget of US, CBO analysis and review of FY92 budget by function, annual rpt, 26304–2

Budget of US, CBO analysis of revenue and spending alternatives and projections of economic indicators, FY92-96, annual rpt, 26304–3

Budget of US, compilation of background material on fiscal and tax policy, 1960s-96, 21788–203

Budget of US, House Budget Committee analysis of Bush Admin proposals and economic assumptions, FY92, 21268–42

Budget of US, House concurrent resolution, with spending and revenue targets, FY92 and projected to FY96, annual rpt, 21264–2

Budget of US, legislative process overview with summary projections and glossary, FY90-95, 21268–43

Budget of US, midsession review of FY92 budget, by function, annual rpt, 104–7

Budget of US, obligations and authority by function, agency, and program, with summaries, analyses, and historical tables, FY92, annual rpt, 104–2

Budget of US, receipts by source, outlays by agency and program, and balances, monthly rpt, 8102–3

Budget of US, Senate concurrent resolution, with spending and revenue targets, FY92, annual rpt, 25254–1

Business statistics, detailed data for major industries and economic indicators, *Survey of Current Business,* monthly rpt, 2702–1.9

Economic indicators and components, and Fed Reserve 4th District business and financial conditions, monthly chartbook, 9377–10

Environmental protection programs costs to govts and households, by program type and city size, 1960s-88 and projected to 2000, 9188–114

Fed Govt consolidated financial statements based on business accounting methods, FY89-90, annual rpt, 8104–5

Fed Govt debt, by type and holder, monthly rpt, 9362–1.1

Index by Subjects and Names

Fed Govt debt interest payments, monthly rpt, quarterly and annual data, 23842–1.6

Fed Govt debt issued, redeemed, and outstanding, by series and source, and gifts to reduce debt, monthly rpt, 8242–2

Fed Govt finances, cash and debt transactions, daily tables, 8102–4

Fed Govt financial operations, detailed data, *Treasury Bulletin,* quarterly rpt, 8002–4

Fed Govt financial transactions, *Survey of Current Business,* monthly rpt, 2702–1.9

Fed Govt programs under Ways and Means Committee jurisdiction, finances, operations, and participant characteristics, FY70s-90, annual rpt, 21784–11

Fed Govt receipts, expenditures, and debt, Fed Reserve Bank of St Louis monthly rpt, 9391–2; 9391–3

Finances of govts, by level of govt, State, and for large cities and counties, annual rpt series, 2466–2

Forecasts of public debt burden on future generations, under alternative economic and fiscal policy assumptions, 1991 working paper, 9377–9.111

Forecasts of public debt burden on future generations under alternative fiscal policies, by sex and age, 1991 working paper, 9377–9.116

Foreign countries economic conditions and implications for US, periodic country rpt series, 2046–4

Foreign countries economic conditions, policy, and trade practices, by country, 1988-90, annual rpt, 21384–5

Govt finances, tax systems and revenue, and fiscal structure, by level of govt and State, 1991 with historical trends, annual rpt, 10044–1

Massachusetts State govt spending and employment by program, revenues by source, debt, and public works financing, compared to other States, 1990 compilation of papers, 9373–4.27

NATO and Japan military spending and indicators of ability to support common defense, by country, 1970s-89, annual rpt, 3544–28

North Central States public debt by State, and govt spending changes by purpose, 1980s, article, 9375–1.207

Postal Service activities, finances, and mail volume and subsidies, FY90, annual rpt, 9864–5.3

Statistical Abstract of US, 1991 annual data compilation, 2324–1.9

see also Foreign debts

see also Government securities

see also Municipal bonds

see also U.S. savings bonds

Public defenders

see Legal aid

Public demonstrations

see also Right of assembly

see also Riots and disorders

Public documents

see Government documents

Public finance

see Budget of the U.S.

see Fiscal policy

see Government assets and liabilities

see Government revenues

see Government securities

see Government spending

Index by Subjects and Names — Public lands

see Monetary policy
see Public debt
see Taxation

Public health

Assistance (financial and nonfinancial) of Fed Govt, 1991 base edition with supplements, annual listing, 104–5

Budget of US, House concurrent resolution, with spending and revenue targets, FY92 and projected to FY96, annual rpt, 21264–2

Budget of US, Senate concurrent resolution, with spending and revenue targets, FY92, annual rpt, 25254–1

Child and maternal health programs of major urban health depts, activities and budgets, 1990, listing, 4108–51

Criminal cases by type and disposition, and collections, for US attorneys, by Federal district, FY90, annual rpt, 6004–2.1

Employment and payroll, by function and level of govt, 1990, annual rpt series, 2466–1

Expenditures for health care, by service type, payment source, and sector, projected 1990-2000 and trends from 1965, article, 4652–1.251

Expenditures for health care, by service type, payment source, and sector, 1960s-90, annual article, 4652–1.221; 4652–1.252

Expenditures for public welfare by program, FY50s-88, annual article, 4742–1.209

Expenditures for public welfare programs, by program type and level of govt, FY65-88, annual article, 4742–1.202

Expenditures of Fed Govt in States, by type, program, agency, and State, FY90, annual rpt, 2464–2

Govt finances, by level of govt, State, and for large cities and counties, annual rpt series, 2466–2

Govt spending measures using indicators of service costs and demand, with comparisons to fiscal capacity and actual outlays, by State, for State and local govts, 1986-87, 10048–77

Health condition improvement and disease prevention goals and recommended activities for 2000, with trends 1970s-80s, 4048–10

HHS financial aid, by program, recipient, State, and city, FY90, annual regional listings, 4004–3

Morbidity and Mortality Weekly Report, infectious notifiable disease cases and deaths, and other public health issues, periodic journal, 4202–7

Morbidity and Mortality Weekly Report, special supplements, series, 4206–2

NIH rpts, 1991 annual listing, 4434–2

Physicians, by specialty, age, sex, and location of training and practice, 1989, State rpt series, 4116–6

Public Health Reports, bimonthly journal, 4042–3

State and local govt employment of minorities and women, by occupation, function, and pay level, 1990, annual rpt, 9244–6.4

see also Accidents and accident prevention
see also Air pollution
see also Asbestos contamination
see also Birth defects
see also Carcinogens
see also Child abuse and neglect
see also Child welfare
see also Community health services
see also Diseases and disorders
see also Domestic violence
see also Environmental pollution and control
see also Epidemiology and epidemiologists
see also Food inspection
see also Hazardous substances
see also Health condition
see also Health education
see also Health facilities administration
see also Health facilities and services
see also Health insurance
see also Health maintenance organizations
see also Health occupations
see also Infant mortality
see also Lead poisoning and pollution
see also Medicaid
see also Medical assistance
see also Medical costs
see also Medical education
see also Medical research
see also Medical supplies and equipment
see also Medical transplants
see also Mental health facilities and services
see also Mercury pollution
see also Noise
see also Occupational health and safety
see also Pesticides
see also Pests and pest control
see also Poisoning and drug reaction
see also Preventive medicine
see also Radiation
see also Refuse and refuse disposal
see also Regional medical programs
see also Sewage and wastewater systems
see also Smoking
see also Soil pollution
see also State funding for health and hospitals
see also State funding for public safety
see also Vaccination and vaccines
see also Water supply and use

Public Health Service

Budget of US, obligations and authority by function, agency, and program, with summaries, analyses, and historical tables, FY92, annual rpt, 104–2

Fluoride exposure by source, and health risks and benefits, with research results, 1930s-89, 4048–36

Physicians, by specialty, age, sex, and location of training and practice, 1989, State rpt series, 4116–6

Preventive disease and health improvement goals and recommended activities for 2000, with trends 1970s-80s, 4048–10

Public Health Reports, bimonthly journal, 4042–3

Research and evaluation programs of HHS, 1970-90, annual listing, 4004–30

Toxicology Natl Program research and testing activities, FY89 and planned FY90, annual rpt, 4044–16

see also Agency for Health Care Policy and Research

see also Agency for Toxic Substances and Disease Registry

see also Alcohol, Drug Abuse and Mental Health Administration

see also Bureau of Health Professions

see also Centers for Disease Control

see also Food and Drug Administration

see also Health Resources and Services Administration

see also Indian Health Service

see also National Center for Health Statistics

see also National Institute for Occupational Safety and Health

see also National Institute of Mental Health

see also National Institute on Alcohol Abuse and Alcoholism

see also National Institute on Drug Abuse

see also National Institutes of Health

see also National Library of Medicine

Public housing

AFDC beneficiaries demographic and financial characteristics, by State, FY89, annual rpt, 4694–1

American Housing Survey: inventory change from 1973, by reason, unit and household characteristics, and location, 1983, biennial rpt, 2485–14

American Housing Survey: unit and households detailed characteristics, and unit and neighborhood quality, MSA rpt series, 2485–6

American Housing Survey: unit and households detailed characteristics, and unit and neighborhood quality, 1987, biennial rpt, 2485–12

Construction put in place, permits, housing sales, costs, material prices, and employment, bimonthly rpt with articles, 2042–1

Construction put in place, value of new public and private structures, by type, monthly rpt, 2382–4

Employment and payroll, by function and level of govt, 1990, annual rpt series, 2466–1

Expenditures for public welfare by program, FY50s-88, annual article, 4742–1.209

Expenditures of Fed Govt in States, by type, program, agency, and State, FY90, annual rpt, 2464–2

Govt finances, by level of govt, State, and for large cities and counties, annual rpt series, 2466–2

HUD activities, and housing programs operations and funding, 1989, annual rpt, 5004–10

Inventory and costs of real property owned by Fed Govt, worldwide summary by location, agency, and use, 1989, annual rpt, 9454–5

Living arrangements, family relationships, and marital status, by selected characteristics, 1990, annual Current Population Rpt, 2546–1.449

Renovation costs and alternative funding methods for public housing, by project type and region, 1990 rpt, 5188–127

Statistical Abstract of US, 1991 annual data compilation, 2324–1.26

Utility allowances used in HUD public housing and rent assistance programs, coverage and adequacy, 1985-89, GAO rpt, 26113–512

see also Low-income housing

Public lands

Acreage and costs of real property owned by Fed Govt, worldwide summary by location, agency, and use, 1989, annual rpt, 9454–5

Acreage and use of public lands, and Land Mgmt Bur activities and finances, annual State rpt series, 5724–11

Public lands

Acreage, grants, use, revenues, and allocations, for public lands by State, FY90 and trends, annual rpt, 5724–1

Acreage of land, by use, ownership, and State, 1987 and trends from 1910, 1588–48

Acreage of land under Natl Park Service mgmt, by site, ownership, and region, FY91, semiannual rpt, 5542–1

Agriculture census, 1987: farms, farmland, production, finances, and operator characteristics, by county, final State rpt series, 2331–1

Alaska land area by ownership, and availability for mineral exploration and dev, 1984-86, 5608–152

Alaska submerged land grant holdings of Alaska Natives, exchange for upland acreage, impacts on conservation acreage and acquisition, 1989-90, 5728–38

Arizona timber resources by species, forest and tree characteristics, ownership, and county, 1984-85, 1208–374

Coal Surface Mining Reclamation and Enforcement Office activities and funding, by State and Indian tribe, FY90, annual rpt, 5644–1

Concession operations on public lands, receipts, and fees, by Federal agency and for top 100 firms, 1989, GAO rpt, 26113–531

Criminal cases by type and disposition, and collections, for US attorneys, by Federal district, FY90, annual rpt, 6004–2.1

DC metro area land acquisition and dev projects of Fed Govt, characteristics and funding by agency and project, FY91-95, annual rpt, 15454–1

Environmental Quality, status of problems, protection programs, research, and intl issues, 1991 annual rpt, 484–1

Fish and Wildlife Service restoration programs funding, land purchases, and project listing, by State, FY89, annual rpt, 5504–1

Horse and burro wild herd areas in western States, population, adoption, and mgmt costs, as of FY89, biennial rpt, 5724–8

Indiana public lands, recreational areas by type, and timberland by ownership, 1985-88, 1208–368

Land Mgmt Bur activities and funding by State, FY89, annual rpt, 5724–13

Local govt receipts from Fed Govt in lieu of property taxes on public lands, by State and county, FY91, annual rpt, 5724–9

Local govt receipts from Fed Govt in lieu of property taxes on public lands, by State, FY91, annual press release, 5306–4.10

Mgmt of public lands and resources dev, environmental, economic, and social impacts of alternative Forest Service programs, projected to 2040, 1208–24

Minerals resources and availability on public lands, State rpt series, 5606–7

North Carolina timber acreage, resources, and removals, by species, ownership class, and county, 1989/90, series, 1206–4

Northeastern US forest wildlife habitat characteristics, by location, State rpt series, 1206–44

Northeastern US timber resources and removals, by species, ownership, and county, State rpt series, 1206–12

Northwestern US and British Columbia forest industry production, prices, trade, and employment, quarterly rpt, 1202–3

Oregon (western) timber resources, acreage by land use and ownership, 1961-86, 1208–353

Recreation (outdoor) coastal facilities and finances, by site and level of govt, State rpt series, discontinued, 2176–6

Recreation (outdoor) coastal facilities, by State, county, estuary, and level of govt, 1972-84, 2178–29

Recreation (outdoor) facilities on public land, use, and Land Mgmt Bur mgmt activities, funding, and plans, State rpt series, 5726–5

Sheep (desert bighorn) population and mgmt on public land, by State, 1989 rpt, 5728–36

Southwestern US activities of Land Mgmt Bur, FY90, annual rpt, 5724–15

State and Metro Area Data Book, 1991 data compilation, 2328–54

Statistical Abstract of US, 1991 annual data compilation, 2324–1.6; 2324–1.7; 2324–1.10

Timber acreage, by ownership, forest type, and State, 1950s-87 and projected to 2040, 1208–357

Uranium reserves and industry operations, by region and State, various periods 1966-90, annual rpt, 3164–65.1

Western US activities of Reclamation Bur, land and population served, and recreation areas, by location, 1989, annual rpt, 5824–12

Wetlands (riparian) acreage, and Bur of Land Mgmt activities, mgmt plans, and scientific staff, State rpt series, 5726–8

Wetlands acreage, resources, soil and water properties, and conservation efforts, by wetland type, State rpt series, 5506–11

Wildlife and plant research results, habitat study series, 5506–13

Wildlife mgmt activities and funding, acreage by habitat type, and scientific staff, for Bur of Land Mgmt, State rpt series, 5726–7

Wildlife mgmt activities and funding, acreage, staff, and plans of Bur of Land Mgmt, habitat study series, 5726–6

Wildlife mgmt on public lands, endangered species, and BLM activities and funding, FY80-90, 5728–37

see also Homesteads

see also Military bases, posts, and reservations

see also Mineral leases

see also National forests

see also National grasslands

see also National parks

see also National trails

see also Oil and gas leases

see also Parks

see also Public buildings

see also State forests

see also State parks

see also Wilderness areas

see also Wildlife refuges

Public Law 480

Agricultural Statistics, 1990, annual rpt, 1004–1

CCC dairy price support program foreign donations and domestic donations to poor, schools, Prisons Bur, and VA, monthly rpt, 1802–2

Index by Subjects and Names

Credit sales (long-term) allocations under PL 480, by commodity and country, periodic press release, 1922–7

Credit sales agreement terms, by commodity and country, FY89, annual rpt, 15344–1.11

Currency (foreign) accounts owned by US under AID admin and by foreign govts with joint AID control, status by program and country, quarterly rpt, 9912–1

Currency (foreign) holdings of US, transactions and balances by program and country, 1st half FY91, semiannual rpt, 8102–7

Developing countries agricultural supply, demand, and market for US exports, with socioeconomic conditions, country rpt series, 1526–6

Developing countries economic and social conditions from 1960s, and Intl Dev Cooperation Agency and AID activities and funding, FY90-92, annual rpt, 9904–4

Developing countries economic dev impacts of PL 480 food aid, literature review, 1979-88, 9918–20

Disasters, casualties, damage, and aid by US and others, by country, FY90 and trends from FY64, annual rpt, 9914–12

Exports (agricultural) under federally financed programs, FY60-90, annual rpt, 1924–9

Exports under PL 480 by commodity, and recipients, by program, sponsor, and country, FY88 and cumulative from FY55, annual rpt, 1924–7

Grain and feed trade, and export and support prices, for US and major producer countries, FAS monthly circular, 1925–2.4

Human rights conditions in 170 countries, and US economic and military aid, 1990, annual rpt, 21384–3

Loan repayment status and terms by program and country, AID and predecessor agencies, quarterly rpt, 9912–3

Oils, oilseeds, and fats foreign and US production and trade, FAS periodic circular series, 1925–1

Rice exports under Federal programs, periodic situation rpt, 1561–8

Title I and II aid, by country, FY46-90, annual rpt, 9914–5

Public libraries

see Federal aid to libraries

see Libraries

Public opinion

see Consumer surveys

see Opinion and attitude surveys

Public ownership

see Government ownership

Public relations

County Business Patterns, 1988: employment, establishments, and payroll, by SIC 2- to 4-digit industry and county, annual State rpt series, 2326–6

County Business Patterns, 1989: employment, establishments, and payroll, by SIC 2- to 4-digit industry and county, annual State rpt series, 2326–8

Finances and operations, by SIC 2- to 4-digit industry, forecast 1991, annual rpt, 2044–28

Puerto Rico economic censuses, 1987: wholesale and retail trade and service industry finances and operations, by SIC 2- to 4-digit industry and municipio, 2591–1

Service industries census, 1987: establishments, receipts by source, payroll, and employment, by SIC 2- to 4-digit kind of business, State, and MSA, 2393–4

see also Advertising

Public schools

see Elementary and secondary education

see Higher education

see terms listed under Education and beginning with School

Public service employment

Forest Service acreage, staff, finances, and mgmt activities in Pacific Northwest, with data by forest, 1970s-89, annual rpt, 1204–37

Nepal economic dev projects manpower training program of AID, effectiveness, 1950s-80s, 9916–3.62

Wagner-Peyser Act grants, by State, 1991-92, press release, 6406–2.31

see also Job Corps

Public services

Budget of US, authoritative financial statements with appropriations, outlays, and receipts, by category and agency, FY90, annual rpt, 8104–2.1

Community Dev Block Grant activities and funding, by program, FY75-90, annual rpt, 5124–8

Fed Govt labor productivity, indexes of output and labor costs by function, FY67-89, annual rpt, 6824–1.6

Labor productivity of govt employees, indexes of output and labor costs by function, FY67-89, annual rpt, 6824–1.6

Older persons migration to southern coastal areas, household finances, services needs, and local economic impacts, for selected counties, 1990, 2068–38

State and local govt spending measures using indicators of service costs and demand, with comparisons to fiscal capacity and actual outlays, by State, 1986-87, 10048–77

see also Community health services

see also Fire departments

see also Police

see also Public health

see also Public service employment

see also Public utilities

see also Public welfare programs

see also Public works

see also Sewage and wastewater systems

see also Social security

see also Social services

see also Special districts

see also User fees

see also Water supply and use

Public transportation

see Subways

see Urban transportation

Public utilities

Bombing incidents, casualties, and damage, by target, circumstances, and State, 1990, annual rpt, 6224–5

Capital expenditures for plant and equipment, by industry div, monthly rpt, quarterly data, 23842–1.1

Capital expenditures for plant and equipment, by major industry group, quarterly rpt, 2502–2

Classification codes concordance of Canada and US SICs, for 1- to 4-digit levels, 1991 rpt, 2628–31

Collective bargaining agreements expiring during year, and workers covered, by firm, union, industry group, and State, 1991, annual rpt, 6784–9

Construction put in place and cost indexes, by type of construction, bimonthly rpt, 2042–1.1; 2042–1.5

Construction put in place, value of new public and private structures, by type, monthly rpt, 2382–4

Consumer Expenditure Survey, household income by source, and itemized spending, by selected characteristics and region, 1988-89, annual rpt, 6764–5

Consumer Expenditure Survey, spending by category, and income, by selected household characteristics and location, 1990, annual press release, 6726–1.42

Consumer Expenditure Survey, spending by category, selected household characteristics, and region, quarterly rpt, 6762–14

County Business Patterns, 1988: employment, establishments, and payroll, by SIC 2- to 4-digit industry and county, annual State rpt series, 2326–6

County Business Patterns, 1989: employment, establishments, and payroll, by SIC 2- to 4-digit industry and county, annual State rpt series, 2326–8

CPI by component for US city average, and by region, population size, and for 27 metro areas, monthly rpt, 6762–2

CPI components relative importance, by selected MSA, region, population size, and for US city average, 1990, annual rpt, 6884–1

Earnings by industry div, and personal income per capita and by source, by State, MSA, and county, 1984-89, annual regional rpts, 2704–2

Employment and Earnings, detailed data, monthly rpt, 6742–2.5

Employment, earnings, and hours, by SIC 1- to 4-digit industry, monthly and annual averages, selected years 1909-90, annual rpt, 6744–4

Employment, earnings, and hours, monthly press release, 6742–5

Employment situation, earnings, hours, and other BLS economic indicators, transcripts of BLS Commissioner's monthly testimony, periodic rpt, 23846–4

Employment, unemployment, and labor force characteristics, by region, State, and selected metro area, 1990, annual rpt, 6744–7

Energy conservation programs of States, Federal aid and savings, by State, 1989, annual rpt, 3304–1

Exports and export-related employment, by SIC 3-digit industry and State, model results, 1987, annual rpt, 2506–16.1

Foreign direct investment in US, major transactions by type, industry, country, and US location, 1989, annual rpt, 2044–20

Govt census, 1987: employment, payroll, and average earnings, by function, level of govt, State, county, and population size, 2455–2

Govt census, 1987: local govt employment by function, payroll, and average earnings, for individual counties, cities, and school and special districts, 2455–1

Govt employment and payroll, by function, level of govt, and jurisdiction, 1990, annual rpt series, 2466–1

Govt finances, by level of govt, State, and for large cities and counties, annual rpt series, 2466–2

Home mortgages FHA-insured, financial, property, and mortgagor characteristics, 1990, annual rpt, 5144–17

Housing (low income) utility allowances used in HUD public housing and rent assistance programs, coverage and adequacy, 1985-89, GAO rpt, 26113–512

Input-output structure of US economy, detailed interindustry transactions for 84 industries, and components of final demand, 1986, annual article, 2702–1.206

Input-output structure of US economy, detailed interindustry transactions for 85 industries, 1982 benchmark data, 2702–1.213

Labor productivity, indexes of output, hours, and employment by SIC 2- to 4-digit industry, 1967-89, annual rpt, 6824–1.4

Mail volume to and from households, use, and views, by class, source, content, and household characteristics, 1987-88, annual rpt, 9864–10

Occupational injuries, illnesses, and workdays lost, by SIC 2-digit industry, 1989-90, annual press release, 6844–3

Occupational injury and illness rates, by SIC 2- to 4-digit industry, 1988-89, annual rpt, 6844–7

Occupational injury and illness rates, by SIC 2- to 4-digit industry, 1989, annual rpt, 6844–1

Pollution (water) fish kills, by pollution source, month, location, and State, 1977-87, last issue of annual rpt, 9204–3

Production and capacity use indexes, by SIC 2- to 4-digit industry, monthly rpt, 9365–2.24

SEC registration, firms required to file annual rpts, as of Sept 1990, annual listing, 9734–5

Soviet Union GNP by component and industry sector, and CIA estimation methods, 1950s-87, 23848–223

Soviet Union GNP by detailed income and outlay component, 1985, 2326–18.59

State and local govt employment of minorities and women, by occupation, function, and pay level, 1990, annual rpt, 9244–6.4

Stock (common) price indexes, current data and annual trends, monthly rpt, 23842–1.5

Tax (income) returns filed by type of filer, selected income items, quarterly rpt, 8302–2.1

Tax (income) returns for foreign corporate activity in US, assets, and income statement items, by industry div and selected country, 1986-87, article, 8302–2.205

Tax (income) returns of corporations, income and tax items by asset size and detailed industry, 1987, annual rpt, 8304–4

Public utilities

Tax (income) returns of corporations, income and tax items by asset size and detailed industry, 1988, annual rpt, 8304–21

Tax (income) returns of corporations with foreign tax credit, income and tax items by industry group, 1986, biennial article, 8302–2.203

Tax (income) returns of partnerships, income statement and balance sheet items, by industry group, 1989, annual article, 8302–2.216; 8304–18

Tax (income) returns of sole proprietorships, income statement items, by industry group, 1989, annual article, 8302–2.214

Tax (income) returns of US corporations under foreign control, assets and income statement items by industry div and country, 1988, article, 8302–2.219

Tax collections of State govts by detailed type of tax, and tax rates, by State, FY90, annual rpt, 2466–2.7

Tax rates and revenue of State and local govts, by source and State, 1991 and historical trends, annual rpt, 10044–1

Tax revenue, by level of govt, type of tax, State, and selected large county, quarterly rpt, 2462–3

Uranium marketing, contracts, prices, utility shipments, and trade, 1982-90 and projected to 2000, annual rpt, 3164–65.2

Wage and benefit changes from collective bargaining and mgmt decisions, by industry div, monthly rpt, 6782–1

Wages by occupation, and benefits for office and plant workers in selected MSAs, 1990, annual rpt, 6785–1

Wages by occupation, and benefits for office and plant workers, periodic MSA survey rpt series, 6785–11; 6785–12

see also Buses

see also Electric power

see also Electric power plants and equipment

see also Electric power prices

see also Railroads

see also Refuse and refuse disposal

see also Rural electrification

see also Sewage and wastewater systems

see also Subways

see also Telephones and telephone industry

see also Water supply and use

see also under By Industry in the "Index by Categories"

Public welfare programs

Assistance (financial and nonfinancial) of Fed Govt, 1991 base edition with supplements, annual listing, 104–5

Assistance programs under Ways and Means Committee jurisdiction, finances, operations, and participant characteristics, FY70s-90, annual rpt, 21784–11

Benefits, beneficiary characteristics, and trust funds of OASDHI, Medicaid, SSI, and related programs, selected years 1937-89, annual rpt, 4744–3

Budget of US, CBO analysis and review of FY92 budget by function, annual rpt, 26304–2

Budget of US, CBO analysis of revenue and spending alternatives and projections of economic indicators, FY92-96, annual rpt, 26304–3

Budget of US, CBO analysis of savings and revenues under alternative spending cuts and tax changes, projected FY92-97, 26306–3.118

Budget of US, formula grant program obligations to State and local govts, by agency, program, and State, FY92, annual rpt, 104–30

Budget of US, House concurrent resolution, with spending and revenue targets, FY92 and projected to FY96, annual rpt, 21264–2

Budget of US, obligations and authority by function, agency, and program, with summaries, analyses, and historical tables, FY92, annual rpt, 104–2

Budget of US, receipts by source, outlays by agency and program, and balances, monthly rpt, 8102–3

Charitable contributions impacts of public welfare payments, model description and results, 1990 working paper, 6886–6.76

Employment and payroll, by function and level of govt, 1990, annual rpt series, 2466–1

Expenditures for public welfare by program, FY50s-88, annual article, 4742–1.209

Expenditures for public welfare programs, by program type and level of govt, FY65-88, annual article, 4742–1.202

Finances of govts, by level of govt, State, and for large cities and counties, annual rpt series, 2466–2

Finances of govts, revenues by source and spending by function, natl income and product accounts, *Survey of Current Business,* monthly rpt, 2702–1.25

Finances of govts, tax systems and revenue, and fiscal structure, by level of govt and State, 1991 and historical trends, annual rpt, 10044–1

Foreign countries family composition, poverty status, labor conditions, and welfare indicators and needs, by country, 1960s-88, hearing, 23846–4.30

Fraud and abuse in HHS programs, audits and investigations, 1st half FY91, semiannual rpt, 4002–6

Govt census, 1987: employment, payroll, and average earnings, by function, level of govt, State, county, and population size, 2455–2

Govt census, 1987: local govt employment by function, payroll, and average earnings, for individual counties, cities, and school and special districts, 2455–1

Govt census, 1987: State and local labor-mgmt policies, agreements, and coverage and bargaining units, by function, level of govt, and State, 2455–3

Govt spending measures using indicators of service costs and demand, with comparisons to fiscal capacity and actual outlays, by State, for State and local govts, 1986-87, 10048–77

HHS financial aid, by program, recipient, State, and city, FY90, annual regional listings, 4004–3

Homelessness issues, population at risk, contributing factors, and Federal funding for services and prevention, with bibl, 1991 compilation of papers, 25928–9

Income (household) and poverty status under alternative income definitions, by recipient characteristics, 1990, annual Current Population Rpt, 2546–6.69

Income (household) by source, and itemized spending, by selected characteristics and region, 1988-89 Consumer Expenditure Survey, annual rpt, 6764–5

Index by Subjects and Names

Income (household, family, and personal), by source, detailed characteristics, and region, 1988-89, annual Current Population Rpt, 2546–6.68

Income (household, family, and personal), by source, detailed characteristics, and region, 1990, annual Current Population Rpt, 2546–6.70

Income (personal) and poverty status changes, by selected characteristics, 1987-88, Current Population Rpt, 2546–20.19

Indian (Cherokee) Agency activities in North Carolina, FY91, annual rpt, 5704–4

Indians and Alaska Natives health care coverage, by type, employment status, and other characteristics, 1987, 4186–8.17

Labor productivity of Federal employees, indexes of output and labor costs by function, 1967-89, annual rpt, 6824–1.6

Older persons discrimination in Federal aid programs, Age Discrimination Act enforcement by agency, FY90, annual rpt, 4004–27

Poverty status of population and families, by detailed characteristics, 1988-89, annual Current Population Rpt, 2546–6.67

Poverty status of population and families, by detailed characteristics, 1990, annual Current Population Rpt, 2546–6.71

Refugee arrivals in US by world area of origin and State of settlement, and Federal aid, FY90-91 and proposed FY92 allocations, annual rpt, 7004–16

Refugee resettlement programs and funding, arrivals by country of origin, and indicators of adjustment, by State, FY90, annual rpt, 4694–5

Research and evaluation programs of HHS, 1970-90, annual listing, 4004–30

South Dakota poverty relief and medical aid programs of counties, spending by type, MSA, and county, 1989, hearing, 25368–176

State and local govt employment of minorities and women, by occupation, function, and pay level, 1990, annual rpt, 9244–6.4

State and Metro Area Data Book, 1991 data compilation, 2328–54

Statistical Abstract of US, 1991 annual data compilation, 2324–1.12

Survey of Income and Program Participation, data collection, methodology, and use, 1990 annual conf papers, 2624–1

Survey of Income and Program Participation, household composition, income, benefits, and labor force status, methodology, working paper series, 2626–10

Veterans (homeless) domiciliary program of VA, participant characteristics and outcomes, 1990 annual rpt, 8604–10

Veterans (homeless) with mental illness, VA program services, costs, staff, client characteristics, and outcome, 1990, annual rpt, 8604–11

see also Aid to blind

see also Aid to disabled and handicapped persons

see also Aid to Families with Dependent Children

Index by Subjects and Names

Puerto Rico

see also Child day care
see also Child welfare
see also Disability benefits and insurance
see also Disaster relief
see also Food assistance
see also Food stamp programs
see also Foster home care
see also Homemaker services
see also Income maintenance
see also Legal aid
see also Low-income energy assistance
see also Medicaid
see also Medical assistance
see also Medicare
see also Old age assistance
see also Public service employment
see also Rent supplements
see also School lunch and breakfast programs
see also Social security
see also Social services
see also Social work
see also State funding for social welfare
see also Supplemental Security Income
see also Vocational rehabilitation
see also Work incentive programs

Public works

- Appalachian Regional Commission funding, by project and State, planned FY91, annual rpt, 9084–3
- Army Corps of Engineers activities, FY88, annual rpt, 3754–1
- Assistance (financial and nonfinancial) of Fed Govt, 1991 base edition with supplements, annual listing, 104–5
- Budget of US, authoritative financial statements with appropriations, outlays, and receipts, by category and agency, FY90, annual rpt, 8104–2.1
- Budget of US, House concurrent resolution, with spending and revenue targets, FY92 and projected to FY96, annual rpt, 21264–2
- Budget of US, obligations and authority by function, agency, and program, with summaries, analyses, and historical tables, FY92, annual rpt, 104–2
- Community Dev Block Grant activities and funding, by program, FY75-90, annual rpt, 5124–8
- Condition, mgmt, R&D, and funding, for transportation and environmental public works, 1986-91, 26358–235
- Construction industries census, 1987: establishments, employment, receipts, and expenditures, by SIC 4-digit industry and State, final industry rpt series, 2373–1
- Construction put in place, permits, housing sales, costs, material prices, and employment, bimonthly rpt with articles, 2042–1
- Economic Dev Admin activities, and funding by program, recipient, State, and county, FY90 and cumulative from FY66, annual rpt, 2064–2
- Economic effects of Federal spending for public works and human resources, 1991 CBO rpt, 26306–6.158
- Economic impacts of public capital stock and investment spending, with data by type of stock and region, 1950s-88, conf, 9373–3.34
- Environmental protection programs costs to govts and households, by program type and city size, 1960s-88 and projected to 2000, 9188–114

Fed Govt grants for public works, proposed replacement with credit subsidies, with background data by project type, FY88, 26306–3.113

- Fed Govt spending in States, by type, program, agency, and State, FY90, annual rpt, 2464–2
- Global climate change environmental, infrastructure, and health impacts, with model results and background data, 1850s-2100, 9188–113
- Investigations of GAO, 1989-91, listing, 26106–10.5
- Lands (public) acreage, grants, use, revenues, and allocations, by State, FY90, annual rpt, 5724–1.2
- Massachusetts public works funding, financing sources, and employment, by function and authority, 1980s and projected to 2000, article, 9373–1.207
- Massachusetts State govt spending and employment by program, revenues by source, debt, and public works financing, compared to other States, 1990 compilation of papers, 9373–4.27
- Neighborhood and housing quality, indicators and attitudes, by householder type and location, 1987, biennial rpt supplement, 2485–13
- Neighborhood and housing quality, indicators and attitudes, by householder type and location, 1989, biennial rpt, 2485–12
- Pacific territories economic conditions, population characteristics, and Federal aid, 1989 hearing, 21448–44
- Productivity related to public capital stock, effects on model of energy prices and technological change, 1950-89, article, 9391–1.211
- Reclamation Bur irrigation activities, finances, and project impacts in western US, 1989, annual rpt, 5824–12
- State gross product impacts of public works stock, by region, 1970s-86, article, 9373–1.217
- *Statistical Abstract of US,* 1991 annual data compilation, 2324–1.9
- Transportation natl system planning, use, condition, accidents, and needs, by mode of transport, 1940s-90 and projected to 2020, 7308–202
- Wastewater treatment facilities construction loan funds for local govts, Federal and State funding by State, 1990, GAO rpt, 26113–521
- *see also* Public buildings
- *see also* Public service employment
- *see also* Water resources development

Publications catalogs

see Bibliographies

see Government publications lists

Publishing industry

see Printing and publishing industry

Pueblo, Colo.

see also under By SMSA or MSA in the "Index by Categories"

Puente, Celso

"Simulation of Rainfall-Runoff Response in Mined and Unmined Watersheds in Coal Areas of West Virginia", 5666–27.1

Puerto Ricans

see Hispanic Americans

see Puerto Rico

Puerto Rico

- Aircraft (general aviation), flight hours, and equipment, by type, use, and model of aircraft, region, and State, 1990, annual rpt, 7504–29
- Banks (insured commercial and savings) deposits by instn, State, MSA, and county, as of June 1990, annual regional rpt, 9295–3.1
- Cement (portland) shipments to Puerto Rico, bimonthly rpt, 2042–1.6
- Census of Population and Housing, 1990: Puerto Rico population and housing characteristics, press release, 2328–78
- Census of Population, 1990: urban areas population, for 396 areas, press release, 2328–37
- Corporations operating in Puerto Rico and other US possessions, income tax return items, and employment, by selected industry, 1987, article, 8302–2.213
- County Business Patterns, 1989: employment, establishments, and payroll, by SIC 2- to 4-digit industry and county, annual State rpt, 2326–8.53
- Economic Censuses of Puerto Rico, 1987: wholesale and retail trade and service industry finances and operations, by SIC 2- to 4-digit industry and municipio, 2591–1
- Economic Censuses of Puerto Rico, 1987: wholesale, retail, and service industries finances and operations, by establishment characteristics and SIC 2- and 3-digit industry, subject rpts, 2591–2
- Economic, social, political, and geographic summary data, by country, 1991, annual factbook, 9114–2
- Exports and imports between US and outlying areas, by detailed commodity and mode of transport, 1990, annual rpt, 2424–11
- Fed Govt spending in States and local areas, by type, State, county, and city, FY90, annual rpt, 2464–3
- Fed Govt spending in States, by type, program, agency, and State, FY90, annual rpt, 2464–2
- Fish and shellfish catch, wholesale receipts, prices, trade, and other market activities, semiweekly regional rpt, 2162–6.4
- HHS financial aid, by program, recipient, State, and city, FY90, annual regional listing, 4004–3.2
- Hospital deaths of Medicare patients, actual and expected rates by diagnosis, and hospital characteristics, by instn, FY87-89, annual regional rpt, 4654–14.2
- Hurricane Hugo relief funding and response by FEMA, 1989-90, GAO rpt, 26113–511
- Hurricane Hugo storm characteristics, and Natl Weather Service forecast accuracy, 1989, 2186–6.1
- Manatees (West Indian) population off Puerto Rico, and sightings by coastal region, 1976-89, 14738–11
- Marriages, divorces, and rates, by characteristics of spouses and county, 1987 and trends from 1940, US Vital Statistics annual rpt, 4144–4.3
- Mineral Industry Surveys, State reviews of production, 1990, preliminary annual rpt, 5614–6

Puerto Rico

Minerals Yearbook, 1989, Vol 2: State review of production and sales by commodity, and business activity, annual rpt, 5604–16.40

Minerals Yearbook, 1989, Vol 2: State reviews of production, sales, and firms, by commodity, and business activity, annual rpt, 5604–34

Multinatl US firms foreign affiliates, income statement items by country and world area, 1986, biennial article, 8302–2.212

Oil exports to US by OPEC and non-OPEC countries, monthly rpt, 3162–24.3

Physicians, by specialty, age, sex, and location of training and practice, 1989, State rpt, 4116–6.40

Rum production, trade by country, and use, 1989-90, annual rpt, 9884–15

Statehood for Puerto Rico, referendum proposal impacts on Federal tax revenue and aid outlays, corporations tax-favored status, and economic conditions, projected FY91-2000, hearing, 25368–168; 26306–3.112

Statistical Abstract of US, 1991 annual data compilation, 2324–1; 2324–1.30

Sugar production, acreage, yield, stocks, deliveries, and price by State, and trade by country, 1950s-90, 1568–306

Sugarcane growers, acreage, yield, and cane sugar production, quarterly situation rpt with articles, 1561–14

Tax (excise) collections of IRS, by source, region, and State, quarterly rpt, annual table, 8302–1

Tax (income) returns of corporations with foreign tax credit, income, and tax items, by country and world region of credit, 1986, biennial article, 8302–2.207

Terrorism incidents in US, related activity, and casualties, by attack type, target, group, and location, 1990, annual rpt, 6224–6

Tobacco production, prices, stocks, taxes by State, and trade and production by country, 1990, annual rpt, 1319–1

VA programs spending, by US and foreign location, FY90, annual rpt, 8604–6

Water resources dev projects of Army Corps of Engineers, characteristics, and costs, 1950s-89, biennial State rpt, 3756–1.52

Water supply and quality in streams and lakes, and groundwater levels in wells, by drainage basin, 1990, annual State rpt, 5666–10.48

Weather conditions and effect on agriculture, by US region, State, and city, and world area, weekly rpt, 2182–7

see also under By Outlying Area in the "Index by Categories"

Puget Sound

Seals (harbor) population and physical characteristics at selected Washington State coastal sites, 1975-80, 14738–7

Ships freight rates for lumber from Alaska and Puget Sound to Asian markets, by product and port, 1988, 1208–358

Pulley, Lawrence B.

"Scope Economies: Fixed Costs, Complementarity, and Functional Form", 9389–19.28

Pulp

see Paper and paper products

Pulses

see Vegetables and vegetable products

Pumice

see Abrasive materials

Pumpkins

see Vegetables and vegetable products

Pumps and compressors

see Machines and machinery industry

Punishment

see Capital punishment

see Fines and settlements

see Judgments, civil procedure

see Sentences, criminal procedure

see Student discipline

Purchasing

see Industrial purchasing

Purchasing power

see Personal and household income

Putnam, Judith J.

"Food Consumption, Prices, and Expenditures, 1968-89", 1544–4

Pyrites

see Nonmetallic minerals and mines

Pyrophyllite

see Nonmetallic minerals and mines

Qatar

Agricultural trade of US, by detailed commodity and country, 1989, annual rpt, 1524–8

Agricultural trade of US, by detailed commodity and country, 1990, semiannual rpt, 1522–4

Economic conditions, income, production, prices, employment, and trade, 1991 periodic country rpt, 2046–4.36

Economic, social, political, and geographic summary data, by country, 1991, annual factbook, 9114–2

Exports and imports of US, by commodity and country, 1970-89, world area rpt, 9116–1.1

Exports and imports of US, by selected country, country group, and commodity group, 1990, annual rpt, 2044–37

Exports and imports of US, by transport mode, country, and SITC 1- to 3-digit commodity, 1990, annual rpt, 2424–12

Exports of US, detailed Schedule B commodities with countries of destination, 1990, annual rpt, 2424–10

Human rights conditions in 170 countries, and US economic and military aid, 1990, annual rpt, 21384–3

Oil production and exports to US, by major exporting country, detailed data, monthly rpt with articles, 3162–24

Oil production, trade, use, and stocks, by selected country and country group, monthly rpt, 3162–42

UN voting record and share of votes in agreement with US, by issue, country, and world area, 1990, annual rpt, 7004–18

Quality control and testing

Acid rain data quality and accuracy, for 2 natl field and lab data collection programs, 1989, annual rpt, 5664–17

Acid rain data quality and accuracy, for 2 natl field data collection programs, 1978-89, 5668–124

Corporations quality mgmt practices effects on employee and customer relations, operations, and finances, 1988-89, GAO rpt, 26123–345

Cotton acreage planted by State and county, and fiber quality, by variety, 1991, annual rpt, 1309–6

Cotton fiber and processing test results, by variety, region, State, and production area, 1990, annual rpt, 1309–16

Cotton fiber grade, staple, and mike, for upland and American pima cotton by State, monthly rpt, 1309–11

Cotton fiber grade, staple, mike, and other quality indicators, for upland cotton by classing office, weekly rpt, 1309–15

Cotton quality, by State, 1990, annual rpt, 1309–7

Cotton quality, supply, and carryover, 1989-90, annual rpt, 1309–8

Cottonseed prices and quality, by State, seasonal weekly rpt, 1309–14

Cottonseed quality factors, by State, 1990 crop, annual rpt, 1309–5

DOE labs testing of environmental samples from DOE facilities, quality control performance, late 1980s, 3006–5.21

Employment, earnings, and hours, by SIC 1- to 4-digit industry, monthly and annual averages, selected years 1909-90, annual rpt, 6744–4

Environmental samples from DOE facilities, DOE natl labs testing costs compared to commercial labs, FY87-89, 3006–5.23

Equipment for industrial control, shipments, trade, use, and firms, 1990, annual Current Industrial Rpt, 2506–12.11

Hearing aid performance test results, by make and model, 1991 annual rpt, 8704–3

Manufacturing employment, by detailed occupation and SIC 2-digit industry, 1989 survey, triennial rpt, 6748–52

Nuclear reactors for domestic use and export by function and operating status, with owner, operating characteristics, and location, 1990 annual listing, 3354–15

Semiconductor and fiber optics industries quality control spending, effectiveness, and views, survey results, 1980s, 2218–84

Service industries census, 1987: establishments, receipts by source, payroll, and employment, by SIC 2- to 4-digit kind of business, State, and MSA, 2393–4

Steel industry product quality and customer service improvements, producers and purchasers opinions, 1968-91, last issue of annual rpt, 9884–24

Tire quality ratings, by type and brand, as of Sept 1991, annual rpt, 7764–17

see also Food inspection

see also Government inspections

Quality of life

Data on health condition and quality of life measures, rpts and other info sources, quarterly listing, 4122–1

Eastern Europe energy production, trade, use, and AID dev assistance, for 3 countries, 1980s-91, 25318–81

Eastern Europe foreign debt components, trade, balances, and other economic indicators, by country, 1985-89, hearing, 21248–148

Households composition, income, benefits, and labor force status, Survey of Income and Program Participation methodology, working paper series, 2626–10

Housing and neighborhood quality, indicators and attitudes, MSA surveys, series, 2485–6

Kidney transplants, needs, costs, payment sources, and impact of immunosuppressive drugs on outcome, 1950s-87 and projected to 1995, 4658–59

Neighborhood and housing quality, indicators and attitudes, by householder type and location, for 11 MSAs, 1984 survey, supplement, 2485–8

Neighborhood and housing quality, indicators and attitudes, by householder type and location, 1987, biennial rpt supplement, 2485–13

Neighborhood and housing quality, indicators and attitudes, by householder type and location, 1989, biennial rpt, 2485–12

Quality of life and cost of living indicators for 14 MSAs, 1980s, GAO rpt, 26123–346

Soviet Union, Eastern Europe, OECD, and selected other countries living standards and commodity production, 1960s-90, annual rpt, 9114–4.1

Urban areas quality of life ratings, for 130 cites, 1979/80, article, 9387–1.202

see also Health condition

see also Housing condition and occupancy

see also Living arrangements

see also Poverty

see also Work conditions

Quarries and quarrying

see Sand and gravel

see Stone products and quarries

Quartz

see Nonmetallic minerals and mines

Quasi-official agencies

see American National Red Cross

see Government corporations and enterprises

see Legal Services Corp.

see National Railroad Passenger Corp.

see Smithsonian Institution

see U.S. Institute of Peace

Questionnaires

see Consumer surveys

see Opinion and attitude surveys

see Statistical programs and activities

see under names of individual surveys (listed under Surveys)

Quijano, Alicia M.

"Growth in Japanese Lending and Direct Investment in the U.S.: Are They Related?", 9385–8.97

Quinn, Carolyn

"Opinion Survey of Taxpayers Contacted by IRS Collection", 8304–8.1

Quintero, Hector

"Distribution of West Indian Manatees (Trichechus manatus) in Puerto Rico: 1988-89", 14738–11

Quits

see Labor turnover

Rabies

Cases of rabies in animals and humans by State, and deaths, 1930s-90, annual rpt, 4204–1

Deaths and rates, by detailed cause and demographic characteristics, 1988 and trends from 1900, US Vital Statistics annual rpt, 4144–2

Foreign countries rabies-free, and disease prevention recommendations, 1991 annual rpt, 4204–11

Morbidity and Mortality Weekly Report, infectious notifiable disease cases by State, and public health issues, 4202–1

Treatment for rabies exposure, and vaccination of veterinarians and others at risk, CDC guidelines, 1991 rpt, 4206–2.39

Race/ethnic groups

see Alaska Natives

see Asian Americans

see Black Americans

see Ethnic studies

see Hispanic Americans

see Indians

see Minority employment

see Minority groups

see Pacific Islands Americans

see Racial discrimination

see under By Race and Ethnic Group in the "Index by Categories"

Racial discrimination

Community Relations Service investigation and mediation of minority discrimination disputes, FY90, annual rpt, 6004–9

Education Dept enforcement activities to eliminate discrimination within schools, and adequacy, FY81-91, GAO rpt, 26121–427

Educational service delivery and discipline, and discrimination indicators by State, 1988, biennial rpt, 4804–33

Fed Equal Opportunity Recruitment Program activity, and employment by sex, race, pay grade, and occupational group, FY90, annual rpt, 9844–33

Fed Govt employment of minorities and women, and compliance with EEOC standards, by occupation and agency, FY88-92, GAO rpt, 26119–342

Fed Govt personnel action appeals, decisions of Merit Systems Protection Board by agency and region, FY90, annual rpt, 9494–2

Foreign countries human rights conditions in 170 countries, 1990, annual rpt, 21384–3

Labor laws enacted, by State, 1990, annual article, 6722–1.209

Library of Congress employment by race, Hispanic origin, and sex, and affirmative action needs, 1989, hearing, 21428–9

Natl Agricultural Statistics Service minority group staff, promotion, and discrimination complaints, 1988-90, GAO rpt, 26119–326

Racine, Wis.

see also under By SMSA or MSA in the "Index by Categories"

Racketeering

see Organized crime

Radar

Air traffic control operations of FAA, by service and aviation type, and facility, 1980-89, annual rpt, 7504–1.2

Air traffic levels at FAA-operated control facilities, including instrument operations, by airport and State, FY90, annual rpt, 7504–27

Aircraft (general aviation), flight hours, and equipment, by type, use, and model of aircraft, region, and State, 1990, annual rpt, 7504–29

DOD budget, weapons acquisition costs by system and service branch, FY91-93, annual rpt, 3504–2

Exports and imports of US, by Harmonized System 6-digit commodity and country, 1990, annual rpt, 2424–13

Exports of US, detailed Schedule B commodities with countries of destination, 1990, annual rpt, 2424–10

Hurricanes and tropical storms in Pacific and Indian Oceans, paths and surveillance, 1990, annual rpt, 3804–8

Instruments and related products shipments, trade, use, and firms, by detailed type, 1989, annual Current Industrial Rpt, 2506–12.26

Price indexes (producer), by stage of processing and detailed commodity, monthly 1990, annual rpt, 6764–2

Shipments, trade, use, and firms, for electronic communications systems and related products, 1990, annual Current Industrial Rpt, 2506–12.35

Soviet Union military weapons systems, presence, and force strengths, and compared to US, 1991 annual rpt, 3504–20

Radecki, Lawrence J.

"Survey of the Origins and Purposes of Deposit Protection Programs", 9385–8.93

Radecki, Stephen E.

"Racial and Ethnic Comparison of Family Formation and Contraceptive Practices Among Low-Income Women", 4042–3.241

Radian Corp.

"Emissions and Cost Estimates for Globally Significant Anthropogenic Combustion Sources of NO_x, N_2O, CH_4, CO, and CO_2", 9198–124

Radiation

Assistance (financial and nonfinancial) of Fed Govt, 1991 base edition with supplements, annual listing, 104–5

Atmosphere (surface) radiation levels at selected monitoring sites worldwide, and effects of nuclear tests and accidents, 1989, annual rpt, 3004–31

Atmosphere (surface) radiation levels, by selected site, 1989, annual rpt, 2144–28

Cancer (leukemia and other) death risk for uranium miners and others exposed to radiation, 1950s-84, hearing, 25548–101

Electronic devices radiation incidents by type of device, and FDA control activities, 1990, annual rpt, 4064–13

Environmental Quality, status of problems, protection programs, research, and intl issues, 1991 annual rpt, 484–1

Environmental radiation and radionuclide concentrations in air, water, and milk, monitoring results by State and site, quarterly rpt, 9192–5

Exposure to radiation at DOE and DOE-contractor sites, by facility type and contractor, 1988, annual rpt, 3324–1

Hanford, Wash nuclear plant, nearby population radiation exposure, with methodology, 1944-66, series, 3356–5

Health physics and radiation protection enrollment and degrees granted by instn and State, and female grads plans and employment, 1974-90, annual rpt, 3006–8.15

Radiation

Health physics and radiation protection enrollment and degrees granted by instn and State, and grad placement, by student characteristics, 1990, annual rpt, 3004–7

Idaho Natl Engineering Lab radiation monitoring results, for facilities and nearby areas, 1990, annual rpt, 3354–10

Industrial wastewater pollution releases, levels, treatment, costs, and regulation, with background financial and operating data, industry rpt series, 9206–4

Navy nuclear-powered vessels and support facilities radioactive waste, releases in harbors, and public exposure, 1970s-90, annual rpt, 3804–11

Navy personnel radiation exposure on nuclear-powered vessels and at support facilities, and injury claims, 1950s-90, annual rpt, 3804–10

Research and testing activities under Natl Toxicology Program, FY89 and planned FY90, annual rpt, 4044–16

Strontium-90 fallout, monitoring results for 65 sites worldwide, quarterly 1986 and trends from 1958, annual rpt, 3004–29

Water supply and quality in streams and lakes, and groundwater levels in wells, by drainage basin, 1988, annual State rpt series, 5666–16

Water supply and quality in streams and lakes, and groundwater levels in wells, by drainage basin, 1989, annual State rpt series, 5666–12

Water supply and quality in streams and lakes, and groundwater levels in wells, by drainage basin, 1990, annual State rpt series, 5666–10

see also Nuclear accidents and safety

see also Nuclear explosives and explosions

see also Nuclear medicine and radiology

see also Nuclear power

see also Nuclear weapons

see also Radioactive materials

see also Radioactive waste and disposal

see also Radon

see also Uranium

see also X-rays

Radiation Control for Health and Safety Act

FDA admin of Act, and radiation incidents involving electronic devices, 1990, annual rpt, 4064–13

Radio

AIDS info and education activities and funding of CDC, and donation of media ads, 1987-92, articles, 4042–3.256

Employment, earnings, and hours, by SIC 1- to 4-digit industry, monthly and annual averages, selected years 1909-90, annual rpt, 6744–4

Fed Govt radio frequency assignments, by agency, 1st half 1990, semiannual rpt, 2802–1

Foreign countries economic, social, political, and geographic summary data, by country, 1991, annual factbook, 9114–2

Political broadcasting operating budgets for US Govt overseas radio and TV services, FY88 and FY91, annual rpt, 17594–1

Price indexes (producer), by stage of processing and detailed commodity, monthly rpt, 6762–6

State and Metro Area Data Book, 1991 data compilation, 2328–54

Stations on the air, by class of operation, monthly press release, 9282–4

Statistical Abstract of US, 1991 annual data compilation, 2324–1.18

see also Home video and audio equipment

see also Mobile radio

Radio Free Europe

Broadcasting and financial data for Radio Free Europe and Radio Liberty, FY90, annual rpt, 10314–1

Radio Liberty

Broadcasting and financial data for Radio Free Europe and Radio Liberty, FY90, annual rpt, 10314–1

Radioactive materials

Criminal sentences for Federal offenses, guidelines by offense and circumstances, series, 17668–1

Environmental Quality, status of problems, protection programs, research, and intl issues, 1991 annual rpt, 484–1

Exports and imports of US, by country and detailed commodity, monthly rpt, 2422–12

Exports and imports of US, by transport mode, country, and SITC 1- to 3-digit commodity, 1990, annual rpt, 2424–12

Inventory discrepancies for nuclear materials at DOE and contractor facilities, 1989/90, annual rpt, 3344–2

Mineral industries census, 1987: finances and operations, by establishment characteristics, SIC 2- to 4-digit industry, and State, subject rpt, 2517–1

Nuclear Regulatory Commission activities, finances, and staff, with data for individual power plants, FY90, annual rpt, 9634–2

OECD trade, total and for 4 major countries, and US trade by country, by commodity, 1970-89, world area rpt series, 9116–1

Safety standards and research, design, licensing, construction, operation, and finances, for nuclear power plants with data by reactor, quarterly journal, 3352–4

see also Radiation

see also Radioactive waste and disposal

see also Radon

see also Uranium

Radioactive waste and disposal

Atomic Energy Commission and Manhattan Project former research and storage sites and nearby areas, radioactive concentrations, test results series, 3006–9

DOE facilities radioactive and hazardous waste disposal and remediation activities and funding, planned FY91-97, annual rpt, 3024–7

DOE nuclear weapons facilities radioactive waste, storage plans, and mgmt issues, 1988, 26358–236

Foreign and US environmental and wildlife conservation agreements provisions, status, and signatories, as of 1991, listing, 9886–4.169

Idaho Natl Engineering Lab radiation monitoring results, for facilities and nearby areas, 1990, annual rpt, 3354–10

Navy nuclear-powered vessels and support facilities radioactive waste, releases in harbors, and public exposure, 1970s-90, annual rpt, 3804–11

Nuclear power plant occupational radiation exposure, by site, 1968-87, annual rpt, 9634–3

Index by Subjects and Names

Nuclear Regulatory Commission activities, finances, and staff, with data for individual power plants, FY90, annual rpt, 9634–2

Nuclear Waste Fund finances, and DOE Civilian Radioactive Waste Mgmt Office activities, quarterly GAO rpt, 26102–4

Nuclear Waste Fund finances, and DOE Civilian Radioactive Waste Mgmt Office R&D costs, FY88-89, annual rpt, 3364–1

Nuclear Waste Fund finances, and DOE Civilian Radioactive Waste Mgmt Program costs, quarterly rpt, 3362–1

Regulatory, inspection, and licensing activities of NRC, budget and staff, by program, FY90-93, annual rpt, 9634–9

Repository sites for low-level radioactive waste, design, characteristics, and monitoring techniques, 1987 conf, 5668–116

Safety standards and research, design, licensing, construction, operation, and finances, for nuclear power plants with data by reactor, quarterly journal, 3352–4

Soviet Union, Eastern Europe, OECD, and selected other countries pollution and deforestation indicators, 1960s-90, annual rpt, 9114–4.10

Spent fuel and demand for uranium and enrichment services of nuclear power plants, for US and other country groups, projected 1991-2040, annual rpt, 3164–72

Spent fuel and radioactive waste generation, inventory, and disposal, 1960s-89 and projected to 2020, annual rpt, 3364–2

Spent fuel and radioactive waste, releases and waste composition by plant, 1988, annual rpt, 9634–1

Spent fuel from nuclear power plants and additional storage capacity needed, by reactor, projected 1990-2040, annual rpt, 3354–2

Spent fuel from nuclear power plants, discharges, storage capacity, and inventories, by reactor, 1968-89, 3166–6.55

Spent fuel from nuclear power plants, storage pending opening of permanent repository, safety and costs of alternative methods, projected 1991-2050, 14818–1

State and interstate compact low-level radioactive disposal activities, with data by disposal facility and reactor, 1989, annual rpt, 3354–14

Storage and transport needs, disposal site characteristics, and costs, for proposed radioactive waste mgmt plan, 1991 rpt, 3368–1

Uranium tailings at inactive mills, remedial action activities by site, and funding, FY90, annual rpt, 3354–9

Radiology

see Nuclear medicine and radiology

see X-rays

Radium

see Radioactive materials

Radke, Lawrence F.

"Airborne Monitoring and Smoke Characterization of Prescribed Fires on Forest Lands in Western Washington and Oregon: Final Report", 1208–343

Index by Subjects and Names

Radon

EPA pollution control grant program activities, monthly rpt, 9182–8

Indian uranium miners radiation exposure and death risk from lung cancer and other diseases, with comparisons to whites and other countries, 1950s-84, hearing, 25548–101

Indoor air radon levels in Pacific Northwest, with geological and soil characteristics, by township, 1989 rpt, 5668–114

Mines safety and health enforcement, training, and funding, with casualties, by type of mine and State, FY89, annual rpt, 6664–6

Rafuse, Robert W., Jr.

"Fiscal Disparities in Chicagoland", 10042–1.203

"Representative Expenditures: Addressing the Neglected Dimension of Fiscal Capacity", 10048–77

Railroad accidents and safety

Accidents, and mgmt of disasters and natl security threats, with data by major event and State, 1991 annual rpt, 9434–6

Accidents, casualties, and damage, by cause, railroad, and State, 1990, annual rpt, 7604–1

Accidents, casualties, and damage involving railroads, Fed Railroad Admin activities, and safety inspectors by State, 1989, annual rpt, 7604–12

Deaths and rates, by detailed cause and demographic characteristics, 1988 and trends from 1900, US Vital Statistics annual rpt, 4144–2

DOT activities by subagency, budget, and summary accident data, FY88, annual rpt, 7304–1

Hazardous material transport accidents, casualties, and damage, by mode of transport, with DOT control activities, 1989, annual rpt, 7304–4

Hwy-railroad grade-crossing accidents, detailed data by State and railroad, 1989, annual rpt, 7604–2

Hwy safety program funding by State, and accident and death reductions, FY90, annual rpt, 7554–26

Injury and illness rates, by SIC 2- to 4-digit industry, 1988-89, annual rpt, 6844–7

Injury and illness rates, by SIC 2- to 4-digit industry, 1989, annual rpt, 6844–1

Inspections by Fed Railroad Admin, safety defects and violations reported, by type, 1985-89, GAO rpt, 26113–515

Military rail equipment inventory, defects, and repair and inspection needs, 1990, GAO rpt, 26113–535

Safety programs, and accidents, casualties, and damage, by mode of transport, 1989, annual rpt, 7304–19

Safety violation claims settled, by rail carrier, FY90, annual rpt, 7604–10

Railroad equipment and vehicles

Amtrak finances and operations, FY90, annual rpt, 29524–1

Business statistics, detailed data for major industries and economic indicators, *Survey of Current Business*, monthly rpt, 2702–1.23

Condition, mgmt, R&D, and funding, for transportation and environmental public works, 1986-91, 26358–235

Construction put in place (public and private), by type, bimonthly rpt, 2042–1.1

Construction put in place, value of new public and private structures, by type, monthly rpt, 2382–4

County Business Patterns, 1988: employment, establishments, and payroll, by SIC 2- to 4-digit industry and county, annual State rpt series, 2326–6

County Business Patterns, 1989: employment, establishments, and payroll, by SIC 2- to 4-digit industry and county, annual State rpt series, 2326–8

DOD prime contract awards, by detailed procurement category, FY87-90, annual rpt, 3544–18

Employment, earnings, and hours, by SIC 1- to 4-digit industry, monthly and annual averages, selected years 1909-90, annual rpt, 6744–4

Exports and imports of US, by country and detailed commodity, monthly rpt, 2422–12

Exports and imports of US, by Harmonized System 6-digit commodity and country, 1990, annual rpt, 2424–13

Exports and imports of US, by transport mode, country, and SITC 1- to 3-digit commodity, 1990, annual rpt, 2424–12

Exports of US, detailed Schedule B commodities with countries of destination, 1990, annual rpt, 2424–10

Finances and operations of Class I railroads, detailed data by firm, class of service, and district, 1989, annual rpt, 9486–6.1

Fires on Forest Service land and acres burned, by cause, forest, and State, 1989, annual rpt, 1204–6

Fuel oil and kerosene sales and deliveries, by end-use, PAD district, and State, 1989, annual rpt, 3164–94

Imports of US given duty-free treatment for value of US material sent abroad, by commodity and country, 1989, annual rpt, 9884–14

Lumber and pulp products supply and use, and timber resources, detailed data, 1950s-87 and alternative projections to 2040, 1208–24.20

Manufacturing annual survey, 1989: finances and operations, by SIC 2- to 4-digit industry, series, 2506–15

Manufacturing census, 1987: finances and operations, by SIC 2- to 4-digit industry, State, and MSA, with trends from 1849, 2497–1

Manufacturing census, 1987: finances and operations, by type of organization and SIC 2- to 4-digit industry, subject rpt, 2497–5

Natl transportation system planning, use, condition, accidents, and needs, by mode of transport, 1940s-90 and projected to 2020, 7308–202

Occupational injury and illness rates, by SIC 2- to 4-digit industry, 1988-89, annual rpt, 6844–7

Occupational injury and illness rates, by SIC 2- to 4-digit industry, 1989, annual rpt, 6844–1

OECD trade, total and for 4 major countries, and US trade by country, by commodity, 1970-89, world area rpt series, 9116–1

Railroads

Pollution (air) levels for 6 pollutants, by source, 1970-89 and trends from 1940, annual rpt, 9194–13

Pollution (water) industrial releases in wastewater, levels, treatment, costs, and regulation, with background financial and operating data, 1989 industry rpt, 9206–4.13

Price indexes (producer), by stage of processing and detailed commodity, monthly rpt, 6762–6

Price indexes (producer), by stage of processing and detailed commodity, monthly 1990, annual rpt, 6764–2

Rental of railroad cars, establishments, revenue, employees, payroll, and ownership, by State, 1987 Census of Transportation, 2579–1

Urban Mass Transportation Admin grants for transit systems, by city and State, FY90, annual rpt, 7884–10

see also Railroad accidents and safety

Railroad Retirement Board

Budget of US, authoritative financial statements with appropriations, outlays, and receipts, by category and agency, FY90, annual rpt, 8104–2.1

Budget of US, obligations and authority by function, agency, and program, with summaries, analyses, and historical tables, FY92, annual rpt, 104–2

Deaths of beneficiaries, erroneous benefit payments, and use of SSA and other sources of death info, by agency, 1990, GAO rpt, 26121–406

Railroad employee benefits program finances and beneficiaries, FY90, annual rpt, 9704–1

Railroad retirement, survivors, unemployment, and health insurance programs, monthly rpt, 9702–2

Railroad retirement system funding and benefits findings and recommendations, with background industry data, 1960s-90 and projected to 2060, 9708–1

Railroads

Business statistics, detailed data for major industries and economic indicators, *Survey of Current Business*, monthly rpt, 2702–1.11

California minerals production by commodity, shipments, and liquefied petroleum gas transport by mode, 1986-87, conf, 5668–119

Capital expenditures for plant and equipment, by major industry group, quarterly rpt, 2502–2

Coal shipments to electric utilities under contract, and rates, by firm, transport mode, and region, 1979-87, 3168–121

Construction industries census, 1987: establishments, employment, receipts, and expenditures, by SIC 4-digit industry and State, final industry rpt series, 2373–1

Customs Service activities, collections, entries processed by mode of transport, and seizures, FY86-90, annual rpt, 8144–1

Developing countries energy use, and economic and environmental impacts, by fuel type, world area, and country, 1980s-90, 26358–232

Electric utilities privately owned, finances and operations, detailed data, 1989, annual rpt, 3164–23

Railroads

Employee benefit program finances and beneficiaries, FY89, annual rpt, 9704–1

Employee retirement, disability, and unemployment insurance programs, beneficiaries and collections, monthly rpt, 4742–1.1

Employee retirement, survivors, unemployment, and health insurance programs, monthly rpt, 9702–2

Employee retirement system funding and benefits findings and recommendations, with background industry data, 1960s-90 and projected to 2060, 9708–1

Employee retirement, unemployment, and disability benefits, and program finances, late 1930s-88, annual rpt, 4744–3

Employment by functional group, for Class I line-haul railroads, monthly rpt, 9482–3

Employment, earnings, and hours, by occupation for Class I railroads, 1990, annual table, 9484–5

Employment, earnings, and hours, by SIC 1- to 4-digit industry, monthly and annual averages, selected years 1909-90, annual rpt, 6744–4

Energy use by mode of transport, fuel supply, and demographic and economic factors of vehicle use, 1970s-89, annual rpt, 3304–5

Finances and operations, by SIC 2- to 4-digit industry, forecast 1991, annual rpt, 2044–28

Finances and operations of Class I railroads, detailed data by firm, class of service, and district, 1989, annual rpt, 9486–6.1

Finances and operations of transit systems, by mode of transport, size of fleet, and for 468 systems, 1989, annual rpt, 7884–4

Finances, costs, and needs of transit systems, by selected system, 1987-89, biennial rpt, 7884–8

Foreign countries economic, social, political, and geographic summary data, by country, 1991, annual factbook, 9114–2

Grain shipments and rates for barge and rail loadings, periodic situation rpt with articles, 1561–4

Labor productivity, indexes of output, hours, and employment by SIC 2- to 4-digit industry, 1967-89, annual rpt, 6824–1.4

Land acreage, by use, ownership, and State, 1987 and trends from 1910, 1588–48

Military and personal property shipments, passenger traffic, and costs, by service branch and mode of transport, quarterly rpt, 3702–1

Natl transportation system planning, use, condition, accidents, and needs, by mode of transport, 1940s-90 and projected to 2020, 7308–202

Oil bulk stations, sales and storage capacity by product, inventories, expenses, employment, and modes of transport, 1987 Census of Wholesale Trade, 2407–4.2

Pollution (air) contributing to global warming, emissions factors and control costs, by pollutant and source, 1990 rpt, 9198–124

Price indexes (producer), by stage of processing and detailed commodity, monthly rpt, 6762–6

Price indexes (producer), by stage of processing and detailed commodity, monthly 1990, annual rpt, 6764–2

Respiratory diseases related to occupational hazards, epidemiology, diagnosis, and treatment, for selected industries and work settings, 1988 conf, 4248–90

Revenue, income, freight, and rate of return, by Class I freight railroad and district, quarterly rpt, 9482–2

Statistical Abstract of US, 1991 annual data compilation, 2324–1.21

Tax (income) returns of corporations, income and tax items by asset size and detailed industry, 1987, annual rpt, 8304–4

Tax (income) returns of corporations, income and tax items by asset size and detailed industry, 1988, annual rpt, 8304–21

Travel from US, characteristics of visit and traveler, and country of destination, 1990 in-flight survey, annual rpt, 2904–14

Travel to US, by characteristics of visit and traveler, world area of origin, and US destination, 1990 survey, annual rpt, 2904–12

Unemployment insurance claims and covered unemployment by program, and extended benefit triggers, by State, weekly rpt, 6402–15

Unemployment insurance claims, by program, weekly press release, 6402–14

see also Consolidated Rail Corp.

see also Federal aid to railroads

see also Freight

see also National Railroad Passenger Corp.

see also Railroad accidents and safety

see also Railroad equipment and vehicles

see also Subways

see also Urban transportation

see also under By Industry in the "Index by Categories"

Rainfall

see Weather

Rainy River

see Souris-Red-Rainy Rivers

Raisins

see Fruit and fruit products

Raleigh, N.C.

Wages by occupation, for office and plant workers, 1991 survey, periodic MSA rpt, 6785–3.7

see also under By SMSA or MSA in the "Index by Categories"

Ramirez, J. David

"Final Report: Longitudinal Study of Structured English Immersion Strategy, Early-Exit and Late-Exit Transitional Bilingual Education Programs for Language-Minority Children", 4808–27

Rancho Cucamonga, Calif.

see also under By City in the "Index by Categories"

RAND Corp.

"Methodology for Measuring Case-Mix Change: How Much Change in the Case Mix Index Is DRG Creep?", 17206–2.23

Rand, Michael R.

"Crime and the Nation's Households, 1990", 6066–25.40

Randolph, William C.

"Report to Congress on the Effect of the Full Funding Limit on Pension Benefit Security", 8008–152

Raney, Terri

"Developing Countries' Trade with the European Community", 1524–4.2

Rantoul, Ill.

see also under By SMSA or MSA in the "Index by Categories"

Rape

Arrest rates, by offense, sex, age, and race, 1965-89, annual rpt, 6224–7

Arrests, prosecutions, convictions, and sentencing, for felony offenders, by offender characteristics and offense, 1988, 6066–25.33; 6066–25.39

Child accident deaths and injuries by cause, and victimization, rates by race, sex, and age, 1979-88, chartbook, 4108–56

Court criminal case processing in Federal district courts, and dispositions, by offense, district, and offender characteristics, 1986, annual rpt, 6064–29

Court criminal case processing in Federal district courts, and dispositions, by offense, 1980-89, annual rpt, 6064–31

Court criminal cases in Federal district courts, by offense, disposition, and district, 1980-90, last issue of annual rpt, 18204–1

Crime, criminal justice admin and enforcement, and public opinion, data compilation, 1991 annual rpt, 6064–6

Crime Index by population size and region, and offenses by large city, Jan-June 1991, semiannual rpt, 6222–1

Crimes, arrests by offender characteristics, and rates, by offense, and law enforcement employees, by population size and jurisdiction, 1990, annual rpt, 6224–2

Drug abuse history of jail population, by offense, conviction status, criminal and family history, and selected other characteristics, 1989, 6066–19.63

Executions of prisoners, by offense and race, 1930-89, annual rpt, 6064–26.6

Jail population, by criminal, correctional, drug use, and family history, and selected other characteristics, 1989, 6066–19.62

Jail population, by sociodemographic characteristics, criminal and drug use history, whether convicted, offense, and sentencing, 1989, annual rpt, 6064–26.3

Juvenile courts delinquency cases, by offense, referral source, disposition, age, sex, race, State, and county, 1988, annual rpt, 6064–12

Minority group health condition, services use, costs, and indicators of services need, 1950s-88, 4118–55

Preventive disease and health improvement goals and recommended activities for 2000, with trends 1970s-80s, 4048–10

Prison and parole admissions and releases, sentence length, and time served, by offense and offender characteristics, 1985, annual rpt, 6064–33

Probation and split sentences by State courts for felony offenses, sentence lengths, case processing time, and felon characteristics, by offense, 1986, 6068–242

Sentences for Federal offenses, guidelines by offense and circumstances, series, 17668–1

State and Metro Area Data Book, 1991 data compilation, 2328–54

Statistical Abstract of US, 1991 annual data compilation, 2324–1.5

Victimization rates, by victim and offender characteristics, circumstances, and offense, survey rpt series, 6066–3

Victimizations by region and victim characteristics, and rpts to police, by offense, 1973-90, annual rpt, 6066–25.35; 6066–25.41

Victimizations by violent crime, circumstances, victim characteristics, arrest, recidivism, sentences, and prisoners, 1980s, 6068–148

Victimizations of households, by offense, household characteristics, and location, 1975-90, annual rpt, 6066–25.40

Victimizations of women, by relation to offender, circumstances, and victim characteristics, for rape and other violent offenses, 1973-87, 6068–243

Victimizations reported, by State, 1989-90, 25528–116

Women prisoners in State instns, by offense, drug use history, whether abused, and other characteristics, 1986, 6066–19.61

Rapid City, S.Dak.

see also under By SMSA or MSA in the "Index by Categories"

Rapid transit

see Subways

see Urban transportation

Rare earths

see Nonmetallic minerals and mines

Raritan Bay

Fishing (commercial and sport) activity in Bay, 1885-1989, article, 2162–1.205

Ras al-Khaimah

see United Arab Emirates

Rasmussen, Wayne D.

"Farmers, Cooperatives, and USDA: A History of Agricultural Cooperative Service", 1128–66

Raw materials

see Stockpiling

see Strategic materials

see terms listed under Agricultural commodities

see terms listed under Commodities

see terms listed under Natural resources

Rawlings, Steve W.

"Household and Family Characteristics: March 1990 and 1989", 2546–1.447

Rayon

see Synthetic fibers and fabrics

RCA Global Communications

Finances and operations, detail for telegraph firms, 1989, annual rpt, 9284–6.3

Finances, rates, and traffic for US telecommunications carriers intl operations, by service type, firm, and country, 1975-89, annual rpt, 9284–17

REA

see Rural Electrification Administration

Reactors

see Electric power plants and equipment

see Nuclear power

Reading ability and habits

Bilingual education and English immersion programs activities, structure, and effectiveness, 1984-88 longitudinal study, 4808–27

Condition of Education, detail for elementary and secondary education, 1920s-90 and projected to 2001, annual rpt, 4824–1.1

Digest of Education Statistics, 1991 annual data compilation, 4824–2

DOD Dependents Schools basic skills and college entrance test scores, 1990-91, annual rpt, 3504–16

Eighth grade class of 1988: educational performance and conditions, characteristics, attitudes, activities, and plans, natl longitudinal survey, series, 4826–9

Elementary and secondary students educational performance, and factors affecting proficiency, by selected characteristics, 1988 natl assessments, subject rpt series, 4896–7

Elementary and secondary students educational performance in math, science, reading, and writing, 1970s-90, 4898–32

Higher education remedial programs, enrollment, courses, and faculty, by instn characteristics, 1989/90, 4826–1.30

Migrant workers children education programs enrollment, staff, and effectiveness, by State, 1980s, 4808–30

Natl Education Goals progress indicators, by State, 1991, annual rpt, 15914–1

Poverty area schools academic environment and teaching methods impacts on student performance, 1989/90 study, 4808–28

Statistical Abstract of US, 1991 annual data compilation, 2324–1.7

see also Literacy and illiteracy

Reading, Pa.

see also under By SMSA or MSA in the "Index by Categories"

Real estate

see Apartment houses

see Commercial buildings

see Condominiums and cooperatives

see Farms and farmland

see Government supplies and property

see Homesteads

see Housing condition and occupancy

see Housing construction

see Housing costs and financing

see Housing supply and requirements

see Housing tenure

see Industrial plants and equipment

see Land area

see Land ownership and rights

see Land reform

see Land use

see Military bases, posts, and reservations

see Mortgages

see Property

see Property value

see Public buildings

see Public lands

see Real estate business

see Reclamation of land

Real estate business

Classification codes concordance of Canada and US SICs, for 1- to 4-digit levels, 1991 rpt, 2628–31

Collective bargaining agreements expiring during year, and workers covered, by firm, union, industry group, and State, 1991, annual rpt, 6784–9

Construction industries census, 1987: establishments, employment, receipts, and expenditures, by SIC 4-digit industry and State, final industry rpt series, 2373–1

County Business Patterns, 1988: employment, establishments, and payroll, by SIC 2- to 4-digit industry and county, annual State rpt series, 2326–6

County Business Patterns, 1989: employment, establishments, and payroll, by SIC 2- to 4-digit industry and county, annual State rpt series, 2326–8

Employment, earnings, and hours, by SIC 1- to 4-digit industry, monthly and annual averages, selected years 1909-90, annual rpt, 6744–4

Employment, unemployment, and labor force characteristics, by region and census div, 1990, annual rpt, 6744–7.1

Flow-of-funds accounts, savings, investments, and credit statements, quarterly rpt, 9365–3.3

Foreign direct investment in US, by industry group and world area, 1987-90, annual article, 2702–1.219

Foreign direct investment in US, by industry group of US affiliate and country of parent firm, 1980-86, 2708–41

Foreign direct investment in US commercial real estate, by State and country, 1980s, GAO rpt, 26123–350

Foreign direct investment in US, major transactions by type, industry, country, and US location, 1989, annual rpt, 2044–20

Franchise business opportunities by firm and kind of business, and sources of aid and info, 1990 annual listing, 2104–7

Legal services establishments, lawyers by field, receipts by class of client, expenses, and employment, by MSA, 1987 Census of Service Industries, 2393–4.13

Mail volume to and from households, use, and views, by class, source, content, and household characteristics, 1987-88, annual rpt, 9864–10

Multinatl firms US affiliates, finances, and operations, by industry, world area of parent firm, and State, 1988-89, annual rpt, 2704–4

Multinatl US firms and foreign affiliates finances and operations, by industry and world area of parent firm, 1989 benchmark survey, preliminary annual rpt, 2704–5

New England States employment variability relation to service and financial industries employment, with data by selected industry group and State, 1970s-89, article, 9373–1.212

North Central States farm credit conditions, earnings, and expenses, Fed Reserve 9th District, quarterly rpt, 9383–11

Occupational injury and illness rates, by SIC 2- to 4-digit industry, 1988-89, annual rpt, 6844–7

Occupational injury and illness rates, by SIC 2- to 4-digit industry, 1989, annual rpt, 6844–1

Partnerships (limited) conversion to corporations, and impacts on share values, with data by firm, 1980s-91, hearing, 25248–124

Receipts for services, by SIC 2- to 4-digit kind of business, 1990, annual rpt, 2413–8

Savings instns failure resolution activity of Resolution Trust Corp, assets, deposits, and assets availability and sales, periodic press release, 9722–1

Savings instns failures, inventory of real estate assets available from Resolution Trust Corp, semiannual listing series, 9722–2

Real estate business

SEC registration, firms required to file annual rpts, as of Sept 1990, annual listing, 9734–5

Statistical Abstract of US, 1991 annual data compilation, 2324–1.16

Tax (income) returns of corporations, income and tax items by asset size and detailed industry, 1987, annual rpt, 8304–4

Tax (income) returns of corporations, income and tax items by asset size and detailed industry, 1988, annual rpt, 8304–21

Tax (income) returns of corporations with foreign tax credit, income and tax items by industry group, 1986, biennial article, 8302–2.203

Tax (income) returns of partnerships, income statement and balance sheet items, by industry group, 1989, annual article, 8302–2.216; 8304–18

Tax (income) returns of sole proprietorships, income statement items, by industry group, 1989, annual article, 8302–2.214

Texas economic and housing conditions, bank failures, and thrift and Federal regulators real estate holdings, 1980s-90, hearings, 21248–146

Wage and benefit changes from collective bargaining and mgmt decisions, by industry div, monthly rpt, 6782–1

see also Housing costs and financing

see also Housing sales

see also Property value

see also Rent

see also under By Industry in the "Index by Categories"

Reaves, Brian A.

"Pretrial Release of Felony Defendants, 1988", 6066–25.36

Recent College Graduates Survey

Data collection activities and programs of NCES, 1991, annual listing, 4824–7

Recession

see Business cycles

Rechnitzer, James R.

"Black Lung Benefits Act: Annual Report on Administration of the Act During 1990", 6504–3

Recidivism

Federal district court criminal case processing and dispositions, by offense, district, and offender characteristics, 1986, annual rpt, 6064–29

Jail population, by sociodemographic characteristics, criminal and drug use history, whether convicted, offense, and sentencing, 1989, annual rpt, 6064–26.3

Parole discharges, by whether parole revoked, sentence length, time served, offense, and offender characteristics, 1985, annual rpt, 6064–33

Pretrial processing, detention, and release, for Federal offenders, by defendant characteristics and district, 1988, hearing, 25528–114

Pretrial release of felony defendants and rearrests, by offense type and selected characteristics, 1988, 6066–25.36

Prisoners and movements, by offense, location, and selected other characteristics, data compilation, 1991 annual rpt, 6064–6.6

Sentences for Federal offenses, guidelines by offense and circumstances, series, 17668–1

Violent crime victimizations, circumstances, victim characteristics, arrest, recidivism, sentences, and prisoners, 1980s, 6068–148

Women prisoners in State instns, by offense, drug use history, whether abused, and other characteristics, 1986, 6066–19.61

Reclamation of land

Bur of Reclamation activities and finances, FY90, annual rpt, 5824–1

Coal Surface Mining Reclamation and Enforcement Office activities and funding, by State and Indian tribe, FY90, annual rpt, 5644–1

Fed Govt-owned real property inventory and costs, worldwide summary by purpose, agency, and location, 1989, annual rpt, 9454–5

Fed Govt spending in States, by type, program, agency, and State, FY90, annual rpt, 2464–2

Public lands acreage, grants, use, revenues, and allocations, by State, FY90 and trends, annual rpt, 5724–1

Tax expenditures, Federal revenues forgone through income tax deductions and exclusions by type, FY92-96, annual rpt, 21784–10

see also Irrigation

Reclamation Reform Act

Irrigation projects of Reclamation Bur, acreage limits monitoring activities by region, 1988-90, annual rpt, 5824–13

Recording industry

Copyrights Register activities, registrations by material type, and fees, FY90 and trends from 1790, annual rpt, 26404–2

County Business Patterns, 1988: employment, establishments, and payroll, by SIC 2- to 4-digit industry and county, annual State rpt series, 2326–6

County Business Patterns, 1989: employment, establishments, and payroll, by SIC 2- to 4-digit industry and county, annual State rpt series, 2326–8

Exports and imports of US, by country and detailed commodity, monthly rpt, 2422–12

Exports and imports of US, by Harmonized System 6-digit commodity and country, 1990, annual rpt, 2424–13

Exports of US, detailed Schedule B commodities with countries of destination, 1990, annual rpt, 2424–10

Fed Govt audiovisual activities and spending, by whether performed in-house and agency, FY90, annual rpt, 9514–1

Libraries (public) finances, staff, and operations, by State and population size, 1989, annual rpt, 4824–6

Libraries for blind and handicapped, readership, circulation, staff, funding, and holdings, FY90, annual listing, 26404–3

Library of Congress activities, acquisitions, services, and financial statements, FY90, annual rpt, 26404–1

Library of Congress rpts and recordings, 1991, biennial listing, 26404–5

Manufacturing annual survey, 1989: finances and operations, by SIC 2- to 4-digit industry, series, 2506–15

Manufacturing census, 1987: finances and operations, by SIC 2- to 4-digit industry, State, and MSA, with trends from 1849, 2497–1

Manufacturing census, 1987: finances and operations, by type of organization and SIC 2- to 4-digit industry, subject rpt, 2497–5

Natl Archives and Records Admin activities, finances, holdings, and staff, FY90, annual rpt, 9514–2

Occupational injury and illness rates, by SIC 2- to 4-digit industry, 1988-89, annual rpt, 6844–7

Occupational injury and illness rates, by SIC 2- to 4-digit industry, 1989, annual rpt, 6844–1

OECD trade, total and for 4 major countries, and US trade by country, by commodity, 1970-89, world area rpt series, 9116–1

Price indexes (producer), by stage of processing and detailed commodity, monthly rpt, 6762–6

Senate receipts, itemized expenses by payee, and balances, 1st half FY91, semiannual listing, 25922–1

Statistical Abstract of US, 1991 annual data compilation, 2324–1.7

see also Video recordings and equipment

Recordkeeping Practices Survey

Data coverage, methodology, businesses views, and applications for 1992 economic censuses, 1989 survey, 2328–67

Recreation

Accident deaths and rates, by cause, age, sex, race, and State, 1988, US Vital Statistics annual rpt, 4144–2.5

Aircraft (general aviation) accidents, by circumstances, characteristics of persons and aircraft involved, and type of flying, 1988, annual rpt, 9614–3

Aircraft accidents and circumstances, for US operations of domestic and foreign airlines and general aviation, periodic rpt, 9612–1

Aircraft pilot and nonpilot certificates held, by type of certificate, age, sex, region, and State, 1990, annual rpt, 7504–2

Army Corps of Engineers water resources dev projects, characteristics, and costs, 1950s-89, biennial State rpt series, 3756–1

Army Corps of Engineers water resources dev projects, characteristics, and costs, 1950s-91, biennial State rpt series, 3756–2

Bombing incidents, casualties, and damage, by target, circumstances, and State, 1990, annual rpt, 6224–5

Budget of US, obligations and authority by function, agency, and program, with summaries, analyses, and historical tables, FY92, annual rpt, 104–2

Children and youth social, economic, and demographic characteristics, 1950s-90, 4818–5

Coastal areas environmental and socioeconomic conditions, and potential impact of oil and gas OCS leases, final statement series, 5736–1

Coastal areas recreation facilities and finances, by site and level of govt, State rpt series, discontinued, 2176–6

Coastal areas recreation facilities, by State, county, estuary, and level of govt, 1972-84, 2178–29

Coastal areas recreation facilities of Fed Govt and States, visitor and site characteristics, 1987-90 survey, regional rpt series, 2176–9

Index by Subjects and Names

Recreation

Construction authorized by building permits, by type of construction, region, State, and MSA, bimonthly rpt, 2042–1.3

Construction industries census, 1987: establishments, employment, receipts, and expenditures, by SIC 4-digit industry and State, final industry rpt series, 2373–1

Construction put in place, private and public, by type and region, monthly rpt, annual tables, 2382–4

Consumer Expenditure Survey, household income by source, and itemized spending, by selected characteristics and region, 1988-89, annual rpt, 6764–5

Consumer Expenditure Survey, spending by category, and income, by selected household characteristics and location, 1990, annual press release, 6726–1.42

Consumer Expenditure Survey, spending by category, selected household characteristics, and region, quarterly rpt, 6762–14

Consumer spending, natl income and product accounts, *Survey of Current Business,* monthly rpt, 2702–1.25

County Business Patterns, 1988: employment, establishments, and payroll, by SIC 2- to 4-digit industry and county, annual State rpt series, 2326–6

County Business Patterns, 1989: employment, establishments, and payroll, by SIC 2- to 4-digit industry and county, annual State rpt series, 2326–8

CPI by component for US city average, and by region, population size, and for 27 metro areas, monthly rpt, 6762–2

CPI components relative importance, by selected MSA, region, population size, and for US city average, 1990, annual rpt, 6884–1

Education (postsecondary) course completions, by detailed program, sex, race, and instn type, for 1972 high school class, as of 1984, 4888–4

Employment, earnings, and hours, by SIC 1- to 4-digit industry, monthly and annual averages, selected years 1909-90, annual rpt, 6744–4

Enterprise Statistics, 1987: auxiliaries of multi-establishment firms, finances and operations by function, industry, and State, 2329–6

Enterprise Statistics, 1987: finances and operations for companies, by size, level of diversification, form of organization, and industry group, 2329–8

Farmland value, rent, taxes, foreign ownership, and transfers by probable use and lender type, with data by region and State, 1980-91, article, 1561–16.202

Fed Govt financial and nonfinancial domestic aid, 1991 base edition with supplements, annual listing, 104–5

Fed Govt outdoor recreation facilities fees and visits, by managing agency, FY88-90, annual rpt, 5544–14

Fed Govt spending in States, by type, program, agency, and State, FY90, annual rpt, 2464–2

Florida environmental, social, and economic conditions, and impacts of proposed OCS oil and gas leases in southern coastal areas, 1990 compilation of papers, 5738–19

FmHA activities, and loans and grants by program and State, FY90 and trends from FY70, annual rpt, 1184–17

FmHA loans, by type, borrower race, and State, quarterly rpt, 1182–5

Food and alcoholic beverage spending, by place of purchase, 1968-90, annual rpt, 1544–4.5

Forest Service acreage, staff, finances, and mgmt activities in Pacific Northwest, with data by forest, 1970s-89, annual rpt, 1204–37

Forest Service mgmt of public lands and resources dev, environmental, economic, and social impacts of alternative programs, projected to 2040, 1208–24

Forests (natl) revenue, by source, forest, and State, FY90, annual rpt, 1204–34

Franchise business opportunities by firm and kind of business, and sources of aid and info, 1990 annual listing, 2104–7

Govt census, 1987: employment, payroll, and average earnings, by function, level of govt, State, county, and population size, 2455–2

Govt census, 1987: local govt employment by function, payroll, and average earnings, for individual counties, cities, and school and special districts, 2455–1

Govt employment and payroll, by function, level of govt, and jurisdiction, 1990, annual rpt series, 2466–1

Govt finances, by level of govt, State, and for large cities and counties, annual rpt series, 2466–2

Housing units owned for recreation and investment, by selected unit characteristics, 1987, biennial rpt supplement, 2485–13

Indiana public lands, recreational areas by type, and timberland by ownership, 1985-88, 1208–368

Injuries, by type, circumstances, and victim characteristics, and related activity limitations, 1985-87, 4147–10.176

Injuries from use of consumer products, by severity, victim age, and detailed product, 1990, annual rpt, 9164–6

Injuries, related impairments, and activity limitations, by circumstances and victim characteristics, 1985-87, 4147–10.179

Input-output structure of US economy, detailed interindustry transactions for 84 industries, and components of final demand, 1986, annual article, 2702–1.206

Input-output structure of US economy, detailed interindustry transactions for 85 industries, 1982 benchmark data, 2702–1.213

Jails under court order to reduce overcrowding and to improve conditions, 1988, regional rpt series, 6068–144.1

Land and Water Conservation Fund allocations for outdoor recreation area dev, by State, FY91, annual table, 5544–15

Land and Water Conservation Fund grants, State matching funds, and balances, by State, FY90, annual rpt, 5544–18

Land Mgmt Bur activities and funding by State, FY89, annual rpt, 5724–13

Mail volume to and from households, use, and views, by class, source, content, and household characteristics, 1987-88, annual rpt, 9864–10

New Hampshire and Vermont public opinion on natural resources use and mgmt, 1991 rpt, 1208–371

North Carolina environmental and socioeconomic conditions, and impacts of proposed OCS oil and gas exploration, 1970s-90 and projected to 2020, 5738–22

Northeastern US recreation areas use, mgmt, and tourism dev issues, 1990 conf, 1208–356

Occupational injury and illness rates, by SIC 2- to 4-digit industry, 1988-89, annual rpt, 6844–7

Occupational injury and illness rates, by SIC 2- to 4-digit industry, 1989, annual rpt, 6844–1

Older persons migration to southern coastal areas, household finances, services needs, and local economic impacts, for selected counties, 1990, 2068–38

Outdoor recreation mgmt, research methods, and public opinion, 1990 conf papers, annual rpt, 1204–38

Public lands acreage and use, and Land Mgmt Bur activities and finances, annual State rpt series, 5724–11

Public lands acreage, grants, use, revenues, and allocations, by State, FY90, annual rpt, 5724–1.2

Public lands recreation facilities and use, and Land Mgmt Bur mgmt activities, funding, and plans, State rpt series, 5726–5

Puerto Rico economic censuses, 1987: wholesale and retail trade and service industry finances and operations, by SIC 2- to 4-digit industry and municipio, 2591–1

Puerto Rico economic censuses, 1987: wholesale, retail, and service industries finances and operations, by establishment characteristics and SIC 2- and 3-digit industry, subject rpts, 2591–2

Real estate assets of failed thrifts, inventory of properties available from Resolution Trust Corp, 1990, semiannual listing, 9722–2.4

Real estate assets of failed thrifts, inventory of properties available from Resolution Trust Corp, 1991, semiannual listing, 9722–2.10

Service industries census, 1987: depreciable assets, capital and operating expenses, and receipts, by SIC 2- to 4-digit kind of business, 2393–2

Service industries census, 1987: establishments, receipts by source, payroll, and employment, by SIC 2- to 4-digit kind of business, State, and MSA, 2393–4

Service industries receipts, by SIC 2- to 4-digit kind of business, 1990, annual rpt, 2413–8

Shellfish recreational harvesters selected characteristics, location of harvest and residence, and spending, 1985 survey, 2178–28

Soviet Union GNP by component and industry sector, and CIA estimation methods, 1950s-87, 23848–223

Soviet Union GNP by detailed income and outlay component, 1985, 2326–18.59

State and Metro Area Data Book, 1991 data compilation, 2328–54

Recreation

Statistical Abstract of US, 1991 annual data compilation, 2324–1.7

Tax (income) returns of corporations, income and tax items by asset size and detailed industry, 1987, annual rpt, 8304–4

Tax (income) returns of corporations, income and tax items by asset size and detailed industry, 1988, annual rpt, 8304–21

Tax (income) returns of corporations with foreign tax credit, income and tax items by industry group, 1986, biennial article, 8302–2.203

Tax (income) returns of partnerships, income statement and balance sheet items, by industry group, 1989, annual article, 8302–2.216; 8304–18

Tax (income) returns of sole proprietorships, income statement items, by industry group, 1989, annual article, 8302–2.214

Tax collections of State govts by detailed type of tax, and tax rates, by State, FY90, annual rpt, 2466–2.7

Travel patterns, personal and household characteristics, and auto and public transport use, 1990 survey, series, 7556–6

TVA finances and operations by program and facility, FY90, annual rpt, 9804–32

Urban areas park and recreation facilities rehabilitation funding, by city and State, FY91, press release, 5306–4.7

VA Medicine and Surgery Dept trainees, by detailed program and city, FY90, annual rpt, 8704–4

Western US activities of Reclamation Bur, land and population served, and recreation areas, by location, 1989, annual rpt, 5824–12

Wetlands acreage, resources, soil and water properties, and conservation efforts, by wetland type, State rpt series, 5506–11

Wildlife mgmt on public lands, endangered species, and BLM activities and funding, FY80-90, 5728–37

see also Amusement parks
see also Boats and boating
see also Camping
see also Fishing, sport
see also Horse racing
see also Hunting and trapping
see also Motion pictures
see also National forests
see also National parks
see also National trails
see also Parks
see also Recreational vehicles
see also Sporting goods
see also Sports and athletics
see also State forests
see also Swimming
see also Swimming pools
see also Travel and tourism
see also Wilderness areas
see also Winter sports
see also under By Industry in the "Index by Categories"

Recreational vehicles

Accidents (fatal), deaths, and rates, by circumstances, characteristics of persons and vehicles involved, and location, 1989, annual rpt, 7764–10

Accidents involving consumer products, injuries by severity, victim age, and detailed product, 1990, annual rpt, 9164–6

County Business Patterns, 1988: employment, establishments, and payroll, by SIC 2- to 4-digit industry and county, annual State rpt series, 2326–6

County Business Patterns, 1989: employment, establishments, and payroll, by SIC 2- to 4-digit industry and county, annual State rpt series, 2326–8

Employment, earnings, and hours, by SIC 1- to 4-digit industry, monthly and annual averages, selected years 1909-90, annual rpt, 6744–4

Energy use by mode of transport, fuel supply, and demographic and economic factors of vehicle use, 1970s-89, annual rpt, 3304–5

Exports and imports of US, by Harmonized System 6-digit commodity and country, 1990, annual rpt, 2424–13

Exports of US, detailed Schedule B commodities with countries of destination, 1990, annual rpt, 2424–10

Manufacturing annual survey, 1989: finances and operations, by SIC 2- to 4-digit industry, series, 2506–15

Manufacturing census, 1987: finances and operations, by SIC 2- to 4-digit industry, State, and MSA, with trends from 1849, 2497–1

Manufacturing census, 1987: finances and operations, by type of organization and SIC 2- to 4-digit industry, subject rpt, 2497–5

Natl park system visits and overnight stays, by park and State, monthly rpt, 5542–4

Natl park system visits and overnight stays, by park and State, 1990, annual rpt, 5544–12

Occupational injury and illness rates, by SIC 2- to 4-digit industry, 1988-89, annual rpt, 6844–7

Occupational injury and illness rates, by SIC 2- to 4-digit industry, 1989, annual rpt, 6844–1

OECD trade, total and for 4 major countries, and US trade by country, by commodity, 1970-89, world area rpt series, 9116–1

Parks and campsites for recreational vehicles, receipts, payroll, employment, and ownership, 1987 Census of Service Industries, subject rpt, 2393–3.1

Price indexes (producer), by stage of processing and detailed commodity, monthly rpt, 6762–6

Price indexes (producer), by stage of processing and detailed commodity, monthly 1990, annual rpt, 6764–2

Public lands recreation facilities and use, and Land Mgmt Bur mgmt activities, funding, and plans, State rpt series, 5726–5

Retail trade census, 1987: finances and employment, for establishments with and without payroll, by SIC 2- to 4-digit kind of business, State, and MSA, 2401–1

Statistical Abstract of US, 1991 annual data compilation, 2324–1.21

Recruiting

see Voluntary military service

Recycling of waste materials

County Business Patterns, 1988: employment, establishments, and payroll, by SIC 2- to 4-digit industry and county, annual State rpt series, 2326–6

Index by Subjects and Names

County Business Patterns, 1989: employment, establishments, and payroll, by SIC 2- to 4-digit industry and county, annual State rpt series, 2326–8

Electric power plants and capacity, by fuel used, owner, location, and operating status, 1990 and for units planned 1991-2000, annual listing, 3164–36

Electric power plants certification applications filed with FERC, for small production and cogeneration facilities, FY80-90, annual listing, 3084–13

Employment, earnings, and hours, by SIC 1- to 4-digit industry, monthly and annual averages, selected years 1909-90, annual rpt, 6744–4

Energy from waste materials, use by source and region, 1989, 3166–6.56

Energy natl strategy plans for conservation and pollution reduction, impacts of technology and regulation proposals, projected 1990-2030, 3166–6.47

Energy natl strategy plans for renewable energy dev, supply projected under alternative cost and capacity use assumptions, 1990-2030, 3166–6.50

Enterprise Statistics, 1987: auxiliaries of multi-establishment firms, finances and operations by function, industry, and State, 2329–6

Environmental Quality, status of problems, protection programs, research, and intl issues, 1991 annual rpt, 484–1

Exports and imports of US, by country and detailed commodity, monthly rpt, 2422–12

Exports and imports of US, by Harmonized System 6-digit commodity and country, 1990, annual rpt, 2424–13

Exports and imports of US, by transport mode, country, and SITC 1- to 3-digit commodity, 1990, annual rpt, 2424–12

Exports of US, detailed Schedule B commodities with countries of destination, 1990, annual rpt, 2424–10

Health condition improvement and disease prevention goals and recommended activities for 2000, with trends 1970s-80s, 4048–10

Industrial pollutant concentrations and costs by process and waste prevention or treatment method, 1990 biennial conf, 9184–22

Input-output structure of US economy, detailed interindustry transactions for 84 industries, and components of final demand, 1986, annual article, 2702–1.206

Input-output structure of US economy, detailed interindustry transactions for 85 industries, 1982 benchmark data, 2702–1.213

Lumber (industrial roundwood) production for Florida, by product and county, 1977-87, 1208–352

Lumber (industrial roundwood) production for North Central States, by product and county, State rpt series, 1206–10

Lumber (industrial roundwood) production in northeastern US, by product, State rpt series, 1206–15

Lumber (veneer) receipts, production, and shipments, by species and southern State, with residue use, 1988, 1208–43

Index by Subjects and Names

Refugees

Lumber (veneer log) production, mill receipts, and trade, by species, with residue use, for North Central States, 1988, quadrennial rpt, 1208–220

Lumber and mill residue production, by product and species group, for South Carolina, 1987-88, 1208–359

Lumber and pulp products supply and use, and timber resources, detailed data, 1950s-87 and alternative projections to 2040, 1208–24.20

Lumber production, prices by region and State, trade by country, and use, by species and product, 1960-88, annual rpt, 1204–29

Mexico imports from US, by industry and State, 1987-90, 2048–154

Minerals and metal recycling, by commodity, 1986-90, annual rpt, 5604–18

Minerals Yearbook, 1989, Vol 1: commodity reviews of production, reserves, supply, use, and trade, annual rpt series, 5604–15

Minerals Yearbook, 1990, Vol 1: commodity reviews of production, reserves, supply, use, and trade, annual rpt series, 5604–20

Paper (waste) use and inventories, *Survey of Current Business,* monthly rpt, 2702–1.19

Paper and board mill recovery and use of recyclable paper, 1960-88, annual rpt, 1204–29

Pollution (water) industrial releases in wastewater, levels, treatment, costs, and regulation, with background financial and operating data, 1989 industry rpt, 9206–4.6; 9206–4.9

Price indexes (producer), by stage of processing and detailed commodity, monthly rpt, 6762–6

Price indexes (producer), by stage of processing and detailed commodity, monthly 1990, annual rpt, 6764–2

Puerto Rico economic censuses, 1987: wholesale and retail trade and service industry finances and operations, by SIC 2- to 4-digit industry and municipio, 2591–1

Retail trade census, 1987: finances and employment, for establishments with and without payroll, by SIC 2- to 4-digit kind of business, State, and MSA, 2401–1

Statistical Abstract of US, 1991 annual data compilation, 2324–1.6; 2324–1.24

Wholesale trade census, 1987: establishments, sales by customer class, employment, inventories, and expenses, by SIC 2- to 4-digit kind of business, 2407–4

see also Biomass energy
see also Scrap metals

Red Cross

Iraq invasion of Kuwait, alien worker refugees fleeing from Iraq and Kuwait, intl aid by source, and costs to host and native countries, 1990-91, GAO rpt, 26123–326

Refugee aid funding of US by program, agency, and intl organization, and admissions to US, 1980s-90, GAO rpt, 26123–334

see also American National Red Cross

Red River

Floods on Arkansas, Red, and Trinity Rivers, storm characteristics, and Natl Weather Service forecast accuracy, 1990, 2186–6.4

Water supply and quality in streams and lakes, and groundwater levels in wells, by drainage basin, 1988, annual State rpt series, 5666–16

Water supply and quality in streams and lakes, and groundwater levels in wells, by drainage basin, 1989, annual State rpt series, 5666–12

Water supply and quality in streams and lakes, and groundwater levels in wells, by drainage basin, 1990, annual State rpt series, 5666–10

Water supply in US and southern Canada, streamflow, surface and groundwater conditions, and reservoir levels, by location, monthly rpt, 5662–3

Red River of the North

see Souris-Red-Rainy Rivers

Redding, Calif.

see also under By SMSA or MSA in the "Index by Categories"

Redick, Richard W.

- "Availability and Distribution of Psychiatric Beds, U.S. and Each State, 1986", 4506–3.41
- "Outpatient Care Programs of Mental Health Organizations, U.S., 1988", 4506–3.46
- "Specialty Mental Health Organizations, U.S., 1988. Mental Health Service System Reports, Series CN", 4506–4.14
- "Staffing of Mental Health Organizations, U.S., 1986", 4506–3.42

Redman, John M.

- "Metro/Nonmetro Funding Allocation Under Title II-A, Job Training Partnership Act", 1598–266
- "Metro/Nonmetro Program Performance Under Title II-A, Job Training Partnership Act", 1598–267
- "State-Level Examination of Metro/Nonmetro Per Capita Income Inequality, 1979-87", 1548–380

Redmiles, Lissa

"Corporate Foreign Tax Credit, 1986: An Industry Focus", 8302–2.203

Reeder, Richard J.

"Targeting Aid to Distressed Rural Areas: Indicators of Fiscal and Community Well-Being", 1598–265

Reeves, Andree E.

"State-Local Relations Organizations: The ACIR Counterparts", 10048–80

Refractories

see Clay industry and products

Refrigeration

see Air conditioning
see Cold storage and refrigeration
see Household appliances and equipment

Refugees

Admissions to US, FY89-90, fact sheet, 6266–2.4; 6266–2.8

Admissions to US of aliens, by class of admission, impact of Immigration Reform and Control Act, FY84-89, 6266–1.1

AID economic aid to developing countries, obligations and disbursements by country, quarterly rpt, 9912–4

Amerasian refugees admitted to US, FY89-90, fact sheet, 6266–2.4; 6266–2.8

Amerasian refugees arrivals in US, and resettlement programs and funding, FY90, annual rpt, 4694–5

Arrivals and resettlement in US, by age, sex, sponsoring agency, State, and country, monthly rpt, 4692–2

Arrivals in US by world area of origin and State of settlement, and Federal aid, FY90-91 and proposed FY92 allocations, annual rpt, 7004–16

Arrivals in US, by world area of origin, processing, and nationality, monthly rpt, 7002–4

Assistance (financial and nonfinancial) of Fed Govt, 1991 base edition with supplements, annual listing, 104–5

Assistance for refugees, funding of US by program, agency, and intl organization, and admissions to US, 1980s-90, GAO rpt, 26123–334

Assistance for refugees, impacts of reduced Federal funding on States, with data by selected State and California county, late 1980s, GAO rpt, 26121–402

Cambodia refugees in Thailand border camps by site, and UN aid by donor country, 1980s, GAO rpt, 26123–313

Cuba and Haiti refugees resettlement activities of Community Relations Service, FY90, annual rpt, 6004–9

Education (bilingual) enrollment, and Education Dept activities and funding by program, by State, FY88-90, biennial rpt, 4804–14

Education (bilingual) programs enrollment, funding, and services, by State, FY85-89, series, 4808–20

Education Dept programs funding, operations, and effectiveness, FY90, annual rpt, 4804–5

Education programs for immigrant children, Fed Govt and school districts funding, and student characteristics, 1980s, GAO rpt, 26121–418

Fed Govt spending in States, by type, program, agency, and State, FY90, annual rpt, 2464–2

Foreign countries disasters, casualties, damage, and aid by US and others, FY90 and trends from FY64, annual rpt, 9914–12

Foreign countries *Geographic Notes,* boundaries, claims, nomenclature, and other devs, periodic rpt, 7142–3

HHS financial aid, by program, recipient, State, and city, FY90, annual regional listings, 4004–3

Indochina refugees, arrivals, and departures, by country of origin and resettlement, camp, and ethnicity, monthly rpt, 7002–4

Indochina refugees, arrivals and resettlement in US, by State, monthly rpt, 4692–2

Iraq invasion of Kuwait, alien worker refugees fleeing from Iraq and Kuwait, intl aid by source, and costs to host and native countries, 1990-91, GAO rpt, 26123–326

Military surplus property donations to intl and State relief programs, FY86-90, GAO rpt, 26123–316

PL 480 exports by commodity, and recipients, by program, sponsor, and country, FY88 and cumulative from FY55, annual rpt, 1924–7

Refugees

Resettlement programs and funding, arrivals by country of origin, and indicators of adjustment, by State, FY90, annual rpt, 4694–5

UN voting record and share of votes in agreement with US, by issue, country, and world area, 1990, annual rpt, 7004–18

Refuse and refuse disposal

Air pollution levels for 6 pollutants, by source and selected MSA, 1980-89, annual rpt, 9194–1

Assistance (financial and nonfinancial) of Fed Govt, 1991 base edition with supplements, annual listing, 104–5

Containers (beverage) natl deposit law proposal, public views, with State deposit laws effectiveness, 1970s-89, GAO rpt, 26113–494

Costs of environmental protection programs to govts and households, by program type and city size, 1960s-88 and projected to 2000, 9188–114

Costs of manufacture, maintenance, and disposal, by selected product and material, 1967-88, 5608–162.3

County Business Patterns, 1988: employment, establishments, and payroll, by SIC 2- to 4-digit industry and county, annual State rpt series, 2326–6

County Business Patterns, 1989: employment, establishments, and payroll, by SIC 2- to 4-digit industry and county, annual State rpt series, 2326–8

CPI by component for US city average, and by region, population size, and for 27 metro areas, monthly rpt, 6762–2

DOD prime contract awards, by detailed procurement category, FY87-90, annual rpt, 3544–18

Electric utilities privately owned, pollution abatement outlays by type of pollutant and equipment, and firm, 1989, annual rpt, 3164–23

Employment, earnings, and hours, by SIC 1- to 4-digit industry, monthly and annual averages, selected years 1909-90, annual rpt, 6744–4

Environmental Quality, status of problems, protection programs, research, and intl issues, 1991 annual rpt, 484–1

Expenditures for pollution abatement by govts, business, and consumers, 1987-89, annual article, 2702–1.229

Fires on Forest Service land and acres burned, by cause, forest, and State, 1989, annual rpt, 1204–6

Govt census, 1987: employment, payroll, and average earnings, by function, level of govt, State, county, and population size, 2455–2

Govt census, 1987: local govt employment by function, payroll, and average earnings, for individual counties, cities, and school and special districts, 2455–1

Govt census, 1987: State and local labor-mgmt policies, agreements, and coverage and bargaining units, by function, level of govt, and State, 2455–3

Govt employment and payroll, by function, level of govt, and jurisdiction, 1990, annual rpt series, 2466–1

Govt finances, by level of govt, State, and for large cities and counties, annual rpt series, 2466–2

Housing and households detailed characteristics, and unit and neighborhood quality, MSA surveys, series, 2485–6

Incinerators air pollution abatement equipment shipments, by product, 1990, annual Current Industrial Rpt, 2506–12.5

Manufacturing pollution abatement capital and operating costs, by SIC 2-digit industry, 1989, advance annual Current Industrial Rpt, 2506–3.6

Neighborhood and housing quality, indicators and attitudes, by householder type and location, for 11 MSAs, 1984 survey, supplement, 2485–8

Neighborhood and housing quality, indicators and attitudes, by householder type and location, 1987, biennial rpt supplement, 2485–13

Neighborhood and housing quality, indicators and attitudes, by householder type and location, 1989, biennial rpt, 2485–12

Neighborhood and housing quality, indicators and attitudes, MSA surveys, series, 2485–6

New Hampshire and Vermont public opinion on natural resources use and mgmt, 1991 rpt, 1208–371

Occupational injury and illness rates, by SIC 2- to 4-digit industry, 1988-89, annual rpt, 6844–7

Occupational injury and illness rates, by SIC 2- to 4-digit industry, 1989, annual rpt, 6844–1

Pollution (air) emissions factors, by detailed pollutant and source, data compilation, 1990 rpt, 9198–120

Pollution (air) levels for 6 pollutants, by source, 1970-89 and trends from 1940, annual rpt, 9194–13

Soviet Union, Eastern Europe, OECD, and selected other countries pollution and deforestation indicators, 1960s-90, annual rpt, 9114–4.10

State and local govt employment of minorities and women, by occupation, function, and pay level, 1990, annual rpt, 9244–6.4

Statistical Abstract of US, 1991 annual data compilation, 2324–1.6

Timber wastes burning, air pollution emissions, 1982, 1208–343

Transportation census, 1987: finances and operations by size, ownership, and State, and revenues by MSA, by SIC 2- to 4-digit industry, 2579–1

see also Hazardous waste and disposal

see also Landfills

see also Radioactive waste and disposal

see also Recycling of waste materials

see also Sewage and wastewater systems

Regional Financial Associates, Inc.

"Lender Profitability in the Student Loan Program", 4808–36

Regional medical programs

HHS financial aid, by program, recipient, State, and city, FY90, annual regional listings, 4004–3

Kidney end-stage disease treatment facilities, Medicare enrollment and reimbursement, survival, and patient characteristics, 1983-89, annual rpt, 4654–16

VA and non-VA facilities health services sharing contracts, by service type and region, FY90, annual rpt, 8704–5

Regional planning

Appalachia local dev projects, and funding by source, by program and State, FY90, annual rpt, 9084–1

Appalachian Regional Commission funding, by project and State, planned FY91, annual rpt, 9084–3

Assistance (financial and nonfinancial) of Fed Govt, 1991 base edition with supplements, annual listing, 104–5

DC metro area land acquisition and dev projects of Fed Govt, characteristics and funding by agency and project, FY91-95, annual rpt, 15454–1

Fed Govt spending in States, by type, program, agency, and State, FY90, annual rpt, 2464–2

New Hampshire and Vermont public opinion on natural resources use and mgmt, 1991 rpt, 1208–371

Northeastern US recreation areas use, mgmt, and tourism dev issues, 1990 conf, 1208–356

see also Regional medical programs

Regions of the U.S.

see Appalachia

see Middle Atlantic States

see North Central States

see Northeast States

see Southeastern States

see Southwestern States

see Western States

see under By Region, By Census Division, and By State in the "Index by Categories"

see under names of individual States

Regions of the world

see Africa

see Antarctica

see Arctic Ocean

see Asia

see Atlantic Ocean

see Caribbean area

see Central America

see Eastern Europe

see Europe

see Gulf of Alaska

see Gulf of Mexico

see Indian Ocean

see Latin America

see Mediterranean Sea

see Middle East

see North America

see North Sea

see Oceania

see Pacific Ocean

see South America

see Southeast Asia

Regulatory commissions

see Administrative law and procedure

see under names of individual agencies (listed under Federal independent agencies)

Rehabilitation

see Drug abuse and treatment

see Housing maintenance and repair

see Rehabilitation of criminals

see Rehabilitation of the disabled

see Respiratory therapy

see Veterans rehabilitation

see Vocational rehabilitation

Rehabilitation of criminals

Drug abuse prevalence among minorities, related health effects and crime, treatment, and research status and needs, mid 1970s-90, 4498–72

Index by Subjects and Names

Drug and alcohol abuse treatment facilities, services, use, funding, staff, and client characteristics, 1989, biennial rpt, 4494–10

Drug treatment programs in jails, finances and operations, FY89-90, 21408–120

Employer tax credit for hiring from groups with high unemployment rates, participation by State, and effectiveness, FY88, GAO rpt, 26121–407

Sex offenders treatment programs for adults and juveniles, by program type and State, data compilation, 1991 annual rpt, 6064–6.1; 6064–6.6

Shock incarceration programs participation and operations, for 14 States, 1990, 6064–32

Shock incarceration programs provisions and participation, by State, data compilation, 1991 annual rpt, 6064–6.6

States vocational rehabilitation agency cases by disposition and applicant characteristics, and closures by reason, FY84-88, annual rpt, 4944–6

see also Community-based correctional programs

see also Pardons

see also Parole and probation

see also Prison work programs

see also Recidivism

Rehabilitation of the disabled

Fed Govt and State rehabilitation activities and funding, FY90, annual rpt, 4944–1

Fed Govt spending in States, by type, program, agency, and State, FY90, annual rpt, 2464–2

Hospital deaths of Medicare patients, actual and expected rates by diagnosis, with hospital characteristics, by instn, FY87-89, annual regional rpt series, 4654–14

Hospital discharges by detailed diagnostic and procedure category, primary diagnosis, and length of stay, by age, sex, and region, 1989, annual rpt, 4147–13.108

Hospital services and facilities availability, by selected instn characteristics, 1980, 1983, and 1987, 17206–2.22

Medicaid reimbursement of hospitals under Federal and State provisions, with services use, costs, and profits, by State, 1980s, 17206–1.11

Medicare and Medicaid beneficiaries and program operations, 1991, annual fact book, 4654–18

Medicare reimbursement of hospitals under prospective payment system, and effect on services, finances, and beneficiary payments, 1979-90, annual rpt, 17204–2

Older persons health care services use, by service type, discharge destination, and prior care source, 1986, 4188–72

Physicians, by specialty, age, sex, and location of training and practice, 1989, State rpt series, 4116–6

Workers compensation laws of States and Fed Govt, 1991 semiannual rpt, 6502–1

see also Group homes for the handicapped

see also Occupational therapy

see also Physical therapy

see also Respiratory therapy

see also Sheltered workshops

see also Special education

see also Speech pathology and audiology

see also Veterans rehabilitation

see also Vocational rehabilitation

Reidy, Ruth

"Is Battered Women's Help Seeking Connected to the Level of Their Abuse?", 4042–3.228

Reilly, Thomas W.

"Trends in Medicaid Payments and Utilization, 1975-89", 4652–1.209

Reimnitz, Erk

"Anchor Ice and Bottom-Freezing in High-Latitude Marine Sedimentary Environments: Observations from the Alaskan Beaufort Sea", 2176–1.38

"Field Observations on Slush Ice Generated During Freezeup in Arctic Coastal Waters", 2176–1.38

Reimund, Donn A.

"Changes in Farm Structure", 1004–16.1

Reinert, Kenneth A.

"Effects of Domestic Agricultural Policy Reform on Environmental Quality", 1502–3.203

Reinhardt, Uwe E.

"West Germany's Health Care and Health-Insurance System: Combining Universal Access with Cost Control", 23898–5

Reining, Robert C.

"Structural Change in U.S. Farmland", 1588–150

Reinsdorf, Marshall B.

"New Evidence on the Relation Between Inflation and Price Dispersion", 6886–6.79

Reis, Eric

"Consequences of the Nuclear Power Plant Accident at Chernobyl", 4042–3.201

Reisner, Elizabeth R.

"Review of Programs Involving College Students as Tutors or Mentors in Grades K-12", 4808–23

Relf, Paula D.

"Rising Demand for Horticultural Products", 1004–16.1

Relief

see Disaster relief

see Food assistance

see Income maintenance

see International assistance

see Public welfare programs

see Refugees

see State funding for social welfare

see War relief

Religion

Children and youth social, economic, and demographic characteristics, 1950s-90, 4818–5

Degrees awarded in higher education, by level, field, race, and sex, 1988/89 with trends from 1978/79, biennial rpt, 4844–17

Education (postsecondary) course completions, by detailed program, sex, race, and instn type, for 1972 high school class, as of 1984, 4888–4

Education data compilation, 1991 annual rpt, 4824–2

Foreign countries *Background Notes*, summary social, political, and economic data, series, 7006–2

Foreign countries economic, social, political, and geographic summary data, by country, 1991, annual factbook, 9114–2

Religious organizations

Jewish population size, by State, 1989, data compilation, 2328–54

Statistical Abstract of US, 1991 annual data compilation, 2324–1.1

see also Clergy

see also Missions and missionaries

see also Religious liberty

see also Religious organizations

Religious liberty

Foreign countries human rights conditions in 170 countries, 1990, annual rpt, 21384–3

Jewish emigration from USSR, and share to Israel, 1968-90, hearings, 21168–49

Religious organizations

Books (religious) exports of US by country, 1990, annual rpt, 2424–10

Construction industries census, 1987: establishments, employment, receipts, and expenditures, by SIC 4-digit industry and State, final industry rpt series, 2373–1

Construction put in place, and authorized by selected MSA, by type and region, bimonthly rpt, 2042–1.1; 2042–1.3

Construction put in place, value of new public and private structures, by type, monthly rpt, 2382–4

Consumer spending for cash contributions, by charity type and selected characteristics, 1988/89, article, 1702–1.214

County Business Patterns, 1988: employment, establishments, and payroll, by SIC 2- to 4-digit industry and county, annual State rpt series, 2326–6

County Business Patterns, 1989: employment, establishments, and payroll, by SIC 2- to 4-digit industry and county, annual State rpt series, 2326–8

Education data, detail for elementary and secondary education, 1920s-90 and projected to 2001, annual rpt, 4824–1.1

Finances of nonprofit charitable organizations, by asset size and State, 1987, article, 8302–2.218

Health promotion program availability and participation, by type of program and sponsor, 1986-87 local area study, article, 4042–3.223

Hospital deaths of Medicare patients, actual and expected rates by diagnosis, with hospital characteristics, by instn, FY87-89, annual regional rpt series, 4654–14

Mail volume to and from households, use, and views, by class, source, content, and household characteristics, 1987-88, annual rpt, 9864–10

Marriages performed in civil and religious ceremonies, by characteristics of spouses and State, 1987, US Vital Statistics annual rpt, 4144–4.1

Refugee resettlement programs and funding, arrivals by country of origin, and indicators of adjustment, by State, FY90, annual rpt, 4694–5

Schools (Catholic) asbestos inspection and abatement costs, by selected city, 1990 hearing, 25328–32

Schools (elementary and secondary), enrollment, teachers, high school grads, and spending, by instn control and State, 1990/91, annual rpt, 4834–19

Schools (private elementary and secondary), students, and staff characteristics, various periods 1979-88, 4838–47

Religious organizations

Schools attended by selected instn characteristics, eighth grade class of 1988, natl longitudinal survey, 1991 rpt, 4826–9.10

Schools, students, staff, finances, and facilities, data compilation, 1991 annual rpt, 4824–2

State and Metro Area Data Book, 1991 data compilation, 2328–54

Statistical Abstract of US, 1991 annual data compilation, 2324–1.1

Terrorism (intl) incidents, casualties, and attacks on US targets, by attack type and country, 1990, annual rpt, 7004–22

Terrorism incidents in US, related activity, and casualties, by attack type, target, group, and location, 1990, annual rpt, 6224–6

see also Clergy

see also Missions and missionaries

Relocation

Housing characteristics of recent movers for new and previous unit, and household characteristics, by location, 1989, biennial rpt, 2485–12

Housing characteristics of recent movers for new and previous unit, and household characteristics, MSA surveys, series, 2485–6

Housing location at birth and age 16, and residential preference in 5 years, by selected housing and household characteristics, 1985, biennial rpt supplement, 2485–13

Indian (Navajo and Hopi) relocation program activities and caseloads, annual rpt, discontinued, 16004–1

Indian (Navajo and Hopi) relocation program activities and caseloads, monthly rpt, 16002–1

Indian (Navajo and Hopi) relocation program activities and caseloads, 1975-90, 16008–5

Navy command proposed decentralization and relocation from DC area, savings, and cost of living indicators for 14 MSAs, 1980s, GAO rpt, 26123–346

Railroad accidents involving hazardous materials, damage, and persons evacuated, by cause, railroad, and State, 1990, annual rpt, 7604–1

see also Migration

Remedial education

Eighth grade class of 1988: educational performance and conditions, characteristics, attitudes, activities, and plans, natl longitudinal survey, series, 4826–9

Elementary and secondary education enrollment, staff, finances, operations, programs, and policies, 1987/88 biennial survey, series, 4836–3

Higher education remedial instruction and tutoring offerings, by instn type and control, 1980-91, annual rpt, 4824–2.21

Higher education remedial programs, enrollment, courses, and faculty, by instn characteristics, 1989/90, 4826–1.30

Homeless children educational projects, activities, and funding, FY90, annual rpt, 4804–35

Job Training Partnership Act classroom and on-the-job training services, program and participant characteristics, 1986-88, 6406–10.1

see also Compensatory education

see also Special education

Remington, Susan B.

"New England and New York's Timber Economy: A Review of the Statistics", 1208–375

Remolona, Eli M.

"Do International Reactions of Stock and Bond Markets Reflect Macroeconomic Fundamentals?", 9385–1.211

"Global Stock Markets and Links in Real Activity", 9385–8.105

"Understanding International Differences in Leverage Trends", 9385–8.88

Renewable energy resources

see Alcohol fuels

see Biomass energy

see Geothermal resources

see Hydroelectric power

see Solar energy

see Water power

see Wind energy

see Wood fuel

Renfrew, William

"Academic Research Equipment and Equipment Needs in Selected Science and Engineering Fields, 1989-90", 9627–27.2

Renn, Danny E.

"Streamflow and Stream Quality in the Coal-Mining Region, Patoka River Basin, Southwestern Indiana, 1983-85", 5666–27.8

Reno, Nev.

see also under By City and By SMSA or MSA in the "Index by Categories"

Rent

Agriculture census, 1987: farms, farmland, production, finances, and operator characteristics, by county, final State rpt series, 2331–1

American Housing Survey: inventory change from 1973, by reason, unit and household characteristics, and location, 1983, biennial rpt, 2485–14

American Housing Survey: unit and households detailed characteristics, and unit and neighborhood quality, MSA rpt series, 2485–6

American Housing Survey: unit and households detailed characteristics, and unit and neighborhood quality, 1987, biennial rpt, 2485–12

Apartment and condominium completions by rent class and sales price, and market absorption rates, quarterly rpt, 2482–2

Apartment completions by region and metro-nonmetro location, and absorption rate, by size and rent class, preliminary 1990, annual Current Housing Rpt, 2484–3

Apartment market absorption rates and characteristics for nonsubsidized furnished and unfurnished units, 1989, annual Current Housing Rpt, 2484–2

Budget of US, authoritative financial statements with appropriations, outlays, and receipts, by category and agency, FY90, annual rpt, 8104–2.1

Census of Housing, 1990: inventory, occupancy, and costs, State fact sheet series, 2326–21

Census of Population and Housing, 1990: population and housing characteristics, households, and land area, by county, subdiv, and place, State rpt series, 2551–1

Index by Subjects and Names

Census of Population and Housing, 1990: population and housing selected characteristics, by region, press release, 2328–74

Construction industries census, 1987: establishments, employment, receipts, and expenditures, by SIC 4-digit industry and State, final industry rpt series, 2373–1

Consumer Expenditure Survey, household income by source, and itemized spending, by selected characteristics and region, 1988-89, annual rpt, 6764–5

Court buildings mgmt by GSA, spending, and rental income, 1980s-91, hearing, 21648–60

CPI by component for US city average, and by region, population size, and for 27 metro areas, monthly rpt, 6762–2

CPI components relative importance, by selected MSA, region, population size, and for US city average, 1990, annual rpt, 6884–1

CPI for rent, bimonthly rpt, 2042–1.5

Electric utilities privately owned, finances and operations, detailed data, 1989, annual rpt, 3164–23

Enterprise Statistics, 1987: auxiliaries of multi-establishment firms, finances and operations by function, industry, and State, 2329–6

Farm housing for operators and hired labor, market and rental value, 1989, article, 1541–1.211

Farm income, expenses, receipts by commodity, assets, liabilities, and ratios, 1990 and trends from 1945, annual rpt, 1544–16

Farm production itemized costs, by farm sales size and region, 1990, annual rpt, 1614–3

Farm production itemized costs, receipts, and returns, by commodity and region, 1987-89, annual rpt, 1544–20

Farm sector balance sheet, and marketing receipts by detailed commodity, by State, 1985-89, annual rpt, 1544–18

Farmland rental by assessment method, and rent receipts per acre and as share of land value by land type and State, 1960s-80s, 1548–377

Farmland value, rent, taxes, foreign ownership, and transfers by probable use and lender type, with data by region and State, 1980-91, article, 1561–16.202

Fed Govt-leased real property inventory and rental costs, worldwide summary by location and agency, 1989, annual rpt, 9454–10

Fed Govt obligations object class analysis, by agency, Budget of US, FY92, annual rpt, 104–9

FmHA property acquired through foreclosure, 1-family homes, value, sales, and leases, by State, monthly rpt, 1182–7

House of Representatives salaries, expenses, and contingent fund disbursement, detailed listings, quarterly rpt, 21942–1

Housing value capitalization of property tax, model description and results for Philadelphia, 1982, working paper, 9387–8.252

Income (personal) per capita and by source, and earnings by industry div, by State, MSA, and county, 1984-89, annual regional rpts, 2704–2

Index by Subjects and Names

Rental industries

Manufacturing census, 1987: finances and operations, by SIC 2- to 4-digit industry, State, and MSA, with trends from 1849, 2497–1

Mineral industries census, 1987: finances and operations, by establishment characteristics, SIC 2- to 4-digit industry, and State, subject rpt, 2517–1

Mineral industries census, 1987: finances and operations, by SIC 2- to 4-digit industry, State, and county, census div rpt series, 2515–1

Natl income and product accounts and components, *Survey of Current Business*, monthly rpt, 2702–1.24

Natural gas interstate pipeline company detailed financial and operating data, by firm, 1989, annual rpt, 3164–38

Nonprofit charitable organizations finances, and revenue and investments of top 10 instns, 1986-87, article, 8302–2.210

Nonprofit charitable organizations finances, by asset size and State, 1987, article, 8302–2.218

Older persons in rural areas, household income sources, and poverty status, 1983-84, 1598–268

Physicians practice cost indexes and components, by State, MSA, and for rural areas, 1989 rpt, 4658–50

Poor households with high rent, and substandard units, worst case problems prevalence and households characteristics, 1970s-84, annual rpt, 5184–10

Puerto Rico population and housing characteristics, 1990 Census of Population and Housing, press release, 2328–78

Railroad (Class I) finances and operations, detailed data by firm, class of service, and district, 1989, annual rpt, 9486–6.1

Retail trade census, 1987: depreciable assets, capital and operating expenses, sales, value added, and inventories, by SIC 2- to 4-digit kind of business, 2399–2

Retirement housing centers tax-exempt bond use and other financing, defaults, and facility and resident characteristics, 1991 GAO rpt, 26119–328

Senate receipts, itemized expenses by payee, and balances, 1st half FY91, semiannual listing, 25922–1

Service industries census, 1987: depreciable assets, capital and operating expenses, and receipts, by SIC 2- to 4-digit kind of business, 2393–2

Soviet Union GNP by component and industry sector, and CIA estimation methods, 1950s-87, 23848–223

Soviet Union GNP by detailed income and outlay component, 1985, 2326–18.59

State and Metro Area Data Book, 1991 data compilation, 2328–54

Statistical Abstract of US, 1991 annual data compilation, 2324–1.26

Survey of Current Business, detailed financial and business data, and economic indicators, monthly rpt, 2702–1.4

Tax (income) returns filed by type of filer, selected income items, quarterly rpt, 8302–2.1

Tax (income) returns of corporations, income and tax items by asset size and detailed industry, 1987, annual rpt, 8304–4

Tax (income) returns of corporations, income and tax items by asset size and detailed industry, 1988, annual rpt, 8304–21

Tax (income) returns of partnerships, income statement and balance sheet items, by industry group, 1989, annual article, 8302–2.216; 8304–18

Tax (income) returns of sole proprietorships, income statement items, by industry group, 1989, annual article, 8302–2.214

Telephone and telegraph firms detailed finances and operations, 1989, annual rpt, 9284–6.2; 9284–6.3

Truck and warehouse services finances and inventory, by SIC 2- to 4-digit industry, 1989 survey, annual rpt, 2413–14

Vacant housing characteristics and costs, and occupancy and vacancy rates, by region and metro-nonmetro location, quarterly rpt, 2482–1

Vacant housing characteristics, and occupancy and vacancy rates, by tenure and location, 1960s-90, annual rpt, 2484–1

Virgin Islands population and housing characteristics, 1990 Census of Population and Housing, press release, 2328–81

Wholesale trade census, 1987: depreciable assets, capital and operating expenses, sales, value added, and inventories, by SIC 2- to 3-digit kind of business, 2407–2

see also Housing tenure

see also Motor vehicle rental

see also Rent control

see also Rent supplements

see also Rental industries

Rent control

American Housing Survey: unit and households detailed characteristics, and unit and neighborhood quality, MSA rpt series, 2485–6

American Housing Survey: unit and households detailed characteristics, and unit and neighborhood quality, 1987, biennial rpt, 2485–12

NYC rent control impacts on rental housing condition, late 1970s-87, working paper, 9387–8.246

Ordinances on rent control, and effects on housing supply and affordability, by selected jurisdiction, 1968-89, 5188–130

Rent supplements

American Housing Survey: inventory change from 1973, by reason, unit and household characteristics, and location, 1983, biennial rpt, 2485–14

American Housing Survey: unit and households detailed characteristics, and unit and neighborhood quality, MSA rpt series, 2485–6

American Housing Survey: unit and households detailed characteristics, and unit and neighborhood quality, 1987, biennial rpt, 2485–12

Expenditures of Fed Govt in States, by type, program, agency, and State, FY90, annual rpt, 2464–2

Housing vouchers compared to Section 8 certificates, rent supplement programs evaluation, 1985-88, series, 5186–14

HUD activities, and housing programs operations and funding, 1989, annual rpt, 5004–10

Rehabilitation of rental housing, HUD funding and activities by program and region, FY90, annual rpt, 5124–7

Retirement housing centers tax-exempt bond use and other financing, defaults, and facility and resident characteristics, 1991 GAO rpt, 26119–328

Rural areas housing loan programs of FmHA, and housing voucher demonstration program results, 1980s, hearing, 21248–143

Supply of low income housing, impacts of HUD programs to maintain supply and to deter insured mortgage prepayment, 1986-90 and projected to 2005, GAO rpt, 26131–84

Utility allowances used in HUD public housing and rent assistance programs, coverage and adequacy, 1985-89, GAO rpt, 26113–512

Rental industries

Agriculture census, 1987: farms, farmland, production, finances, and operator characteristics, by county, final State rpt series, 2331–1

Banks (insured commercial and savings) finances, for foreign and domestic offices, by asset size, 1989, annual rpt, 9294–4.2

Computer systems and equipment of Fed Govt, by type, make, and agency, 2nd half FY90, semiannual listing, 9452–9

Construction industries census, 1987: establishments, employment, receipts, and expenditures, by SIC 4-digit industry and State, final industry rpt series, 2373–1

Containers (intermodal) and equipment owned by shipping and leasing companies, inventory by type and size, 1990, annual rpt, 7704–10

County Business Patterns, 1988: employment, establishments, and payroll, by SIC 2- to 4-digit industry and county, annual State rpt series, 2326–6

County Business Patterns, 1989: employment, establishments, and payroll, by SIC 2- to 4-digit industry and county, annual State rpt series, 2326–8

DOD prime contract awards, by detailed procurement category, FY87-90, annual rpt, 3544–18

Employment, earnings, and hours, by SIC 1- to 4-digit industry, monthly and annual averages, selected years 1909-90, annual rpt, 6744–4

Enterprise Statistics, 1987: finances and operations for companies, by size, level of diversification, form of organization, and industry group, 2329–8

Finance companies credit outstanding and leasing activities, by credit type, monthly rpt, 9365–2.7

Finances and operations, by SIC 2- to 4-digit industry, forecast 1991, annual rpt, 2044–28

Franchise business opportunities by firm and kind of business, and sources of aid and info, 1990 annual listing, 2104–7

Military equipment leases by equipment type and service branch and feasibility of lease refinancing, 1988, GAO rpt, 26111–75

Multinatl US firms and foreign affiliates finances and operations, by industry and world area of parent firm, 1989 benchmark survey, preliminary annual rpt, 2704–5

Rental industries

Partnerships (limited) conversion to corporations, and impacts on share values, with data by firm, 1980s-91, hearing, 25248–124

Puerto Rico economic censuses, 1987: wholesale and retail trade and service industry finances and operations, by SIC 2- to 4-digit industry and municipio, 2591–1

Puerto Rico economic censuses, 1987: wholesale, retail, and service industries finances and operations, by establishment characteristics and SIC 2- and 3-digit industry, subject rpts, 2591–2

Receipts for services, by SIC 2- to 4-digit kind of business, 1990, annual rpt, 2413–8

Service industries census, 1987: depreciable assets, capital and operating expenses, and receipts, by SIC 2- to 4-digit kind of business, 2393–2

Service industries census, 1987: establishments, receipts by source, payroll, and employment, by SIC 2- to 4-digit kind of business, State, and MSA, 2393–4

Southeastern States, Fed Reserve 5th District insured commercial banks financial statements, by State, quarterly rpt, 9389–18

Tax (income) returns of corporations, income and tax items by asset size and detailed industry, 1988, annual rpt, 8304–21

Tax (income) returns of partnerships, income statement and balance sheet items, by industry group, 1989, annual article, 8302–2.216; 8304–18

Tax (income) returns of sole proprietorships, income statement items, by industry group, 1989, annual article, 8302–2.214

Truck and warehouse services finances and inventory, by SIC 2- to 4-digit industry, 1989 survey, annual rpt, 2413–14

Wholesale trade census, 1987: depreciable assets, capital and operating expenses, sales, value added, and inventories, by SIC 2- to 3-digit kind of business, 2407–2

see also Motor vehicle rental

Renter households

see Housing tenure

Reorganization of government

see Government reorganization

Repair industries

Agriculture census, 1987: farms, farmland, production, finances, and operator characteristics, by county, final State rpt series, 2331–1

Aircraft maintenance by independent repair stations, airlines use and costs, 1980s-90, GAO rpt, 26113–492

Aircraft maintenance requirements of FAA for aging craft, airlines compliance and repair facilities operations, 1989-91, GAO rpt, 26113–527

Aircraft operating costs by component for private planes, and Fed Govt mileage reimbursement rates, 1989, annual rpt, 9454–13.2

Bonneville Power Admin operations, maintenance, and environmental protection plans, FY90-99, 3228–14

Construction industries census, 1987: establishments, employment, receipts, and expenditures, by SIC 4-digit industry and State, final industry rpt series, 2373–1

County Business Patterns, 1988: employment, establishments, and payroll, by SIC 2- to 4-digit industry and county, annual State rpt series, 2326–6

County Business Patterns, 1989: employment, establishments, and payroll, by SIC 2- to 4-digit industry and county, annual State rpt series, 2326–8

CPI by component for US city average, and by region, population size, and for 27 metro areas, monthly rpt, 6762–2

DOD prime contract awards, by detailed procurement category, FY87-90, annual rpt, 3544–18

Education (postsecondary) course completions, by detailed program, sex, race, and instn type, for 1972 high school class, as of 1984, 4888–4

Employment, earnings, and hours, by SIC 1- to 4-digit industry, monthly and annual averages, selected years 1909-90, annual rpt, 6744–4

Employment, unemployment, and labor force characteristics, by region and census div, 1990, annual rpt, 6744–7.1

Enterprise Statistics, 1987: auxiliaries of multi-establishment firms, finances and operations by function, industry, and State, 2329–6

Enterprise Statistics, 1987: finances and operations for companies, by size, level of diversification, form of organization, and industry group, 2329–8

Farm production itemized costs, receipts, and returns, by commodity and region, 1987-89, annual rpt, 1544–20

Fed Govt labor productivity, indexes of output and labor costs by function, FY67-89, annual rpt, 6824–1.6

Manufacturing census, 1987: finances and operations, by SIC 2- to 4-digit industry, State, and MSA, with trends from 1849, 2497–1

Occupational injury and illness rates, by SIC 2- to 4-digit industry, 1988-89, annual rpt, 6844–7

Occupational injury and illness rates, by SIC 2- to 4-digit industry, 1989, annual rpt, 6844–1

Pollution (water) industrial releases in wastewater, levels, treatment, costs, and regulation, with background financial and operating data, 1989 industry rpt, 9206–4.13

Puerto Rico economic censuses, 1987: wholesale and retail trade and service industry finances and operations, by SIC 2- to 4-digit industry and municipio, 2591–1

Puerto Rico economic censuses, 1987: wholesale, retail, and service industries finances and operations, by establishment characteristics and SIC 2- and 3-digit industry, subject rpts, 2591–2

Receipts for services, by SIC 2- to 4-digit kind of business, 1990, annual rpt, 2413–8

Retail trade census, 1987: depreciable assets, capital and operating expenses, sales, value added, and inventories, by SIC 2- to 4-digit kind of business, 2399–2

Service industries census, 1987: depreciable assets, capital and operating expenses, and receipts, by SIC 2- to 4-digit kind of business, 2393–2

Index by Subjects and Names

Service industries census, 1987: establishments, receipts by source, payroll, and employment, by SIC 2- to 4-digit kind of business, State, and MSA, 2393–4

Soviet Union GNP by component and industry sector, and CIA estimation methods, 1950s-87, 23848–223

Soviet Union GNP by detailed income and outlay component, 1985, 2326–18.59

Tax (income) returns filed by type of filer, selected income items, quarterly rpt, 8302–2.1

Tax (income) returns of corporations, income and tax items by asset size and detailed industry, 1987, annual rpt, 8304–4

Tax (income) returns of corporations, income and tax items by asset size and detailed industry, 1988, annual rpt, 8304–21

Tax (income) returns of corporations with foreign tax credit, income and tax items by industry group, 1986, biennial article, 8302–2.203

Tax (income) returns of partnerships, income statement and balance sheet items, by industry group, 1989, annual article, 8302–2.216; 8304–18

Tax (income) returns of sole proprietorships, income statement items, by industry group, 1989, annual article, 8302–2.214

Transit systems finances and operations, by mode of transport, size of fleet, and for 468 systems, 1989, annual rpt, 7884–4

Wholesale trade census, 1987: depreciable assets, capital and operating expenses, sales, value added, and inventories, by SIC 2- to 3-digit kind of business, 2407–2

see also Automobile repair and maintenance

see also Housing maintenance and repair

see also Shipbuilding and repairing

see also under By Industry in the "Index by Categories"

Republic of China

see Taiwan

Republic of Korea

see Korea, South

Republic of Yemen

see Yemen

Republican Party

Campaign finances, elections, procedures, and Fed Election Commission activities, press release series, 9276–1

Congressional Directory, members of 102nd Congress, other officials, elections, and districts, 1991-92, biennial rpt, 23874–1

Election campaign funds raised and spent by party committees, by State and party, 1989-90, press release, 9276–1.88

State and Metro Area Data Book, 1991 data compilation, 2328–54

Statistical Abstract of US, 1991 annual data compilation, 2324–1.8

Votes cast by party, candidate, and State, 1990 natl elections, biennial rpt, 9274–5

Research

China economic indicators and reform issues, with background data, 1950s-90, compilation of papers, 23848–155

County Business Patterns, 1988: employment, establishments, and payroll, by SIC 2- to 4-digit industry and county, annual State rpt series, 2326–6

Index by Subjects and Names

County Business Patterns, 1989: employment, establishments, and payroll, by SIC 2- to 4-digit industry and county, annual State rpt series, 2326–8

Crime and criminal justice research results, series, 6066–26

Employment, earnings, and hours, by SIC 1- to 4-digit industry, monthly and annual averages, selected years 1909-90, annual rpt, 6744–4

Endangered animals and plants US trade and permits, by species, purpose, disposition, and country, 1989, annual rpt, 5504–19

Fulbright-Hays academic exchanges, grants by purpose, and foreign govt share of costs, by country, FY90, annual rpt, 10324–1

Higher education enrollment, faculty, finances, and degrees, by instn level and control, and State, FY87, annual rpt, 4844–13

Higher education instn revenue by source and spending by function, by State and instn control, FY80-88, annual rpt, 4844–6

Juvenile justice issues, data on young offenders and victims, series, 6066–27

Occupational exposure to hazardous substances and conditions, measurement, and proposed standards, series, 4246–1

Occupational injury and illness rates, by SIC 2- to 4-digit industry, 1988-89, annual rpt, 6844–7

Occupational injury and illness rates, by SIC 2- to 4-digit industry, 1989, annual rpt, 6844–1

Science and engineering PhDs employment and other characteristics, by field and State, 1989, biennial rpt, 9627–18

Tax (income) returns filed by type of filer, selected income items, quarterly rpt, 8302–2.1

Tax (income) returns of corporations, income and tax items by asset size and detailed industry, 1988, annual rpt, 8304–21

see also Agricultural sciences and research

see also Animal experimentation

see also Business outlook and attitude surveys

see also Consumer surveys

see also Defense research

see also Demonstration and pilot projects

see also Educational research

see also Energy research and development

see also Federal funding for research and development

see also Human experimentation

see also Market research

see also Medical research

see also Opinion and attitude surveys

see also Research and development

see also Research journals

see also Statistical programs and activities

see also under specific academic and scientific disciplines

Research and development

Aerial survey R&D rpts, and sources of natural resource and environmental data, quarterly listing, 9502–7

County Business Patterns, 1988: employment, establishments, and payroll, by SIC 2- to 4-digit industry and county, annual State rpt series, 2326–6

County Business Patterns, 1989: employment, establishments, and payroll, by SIC 2- to 4-digit industry and county, annual State rpt series, 2326–8

Employment in high technology industries by region and State, and earnings, by industry group, 1989, 6722–1.235

Enterprise Statistics, 1987: auxiliaries of multi-establishment firms, finances and operations by function, industry, and State, 2329–6

Enterprise Statistics, 1987: finances and operations for companies, by size, level of diversification, form of organization, and industry group, 2329–8

Gear production for selected uses under alternative production requirements, and industry finances and operations, late 1940s-89, 2028–1

Great Lakes area economic conditions and outlook, for US and Canada, 1970s-90, 9375–15

Higher education instn and federally funded center R&D funding, by field, instn, and State, FY89, annual rpt, 9627–13

Higher education instn R&D equipment, acquisition and service costs, condition, and financing, by field and subfield, 1988-90, triennial survey series, 9627–27

Higher education instn science and engineering research system status, R&D performance, and Federal support, 1950s-88, 9628–83

Hwy construction and design R&D, quarterly journal, 7552–3

Industry (US) intl competitiveness, with selected foreign and US operating data by major firm and product, series, 2046–12

Multinatl firms US affiliates, finances, and operations, by industry, world area of parent firm, and State, 1988-89, annual rpt, 2704–4

Multinatl firms US affiliates, investment trends and impact on US economy, 1991 annual rpt, 2004–9

Multinatl US firms and foreign affiliates finances and operations, by industry and world area of parent firm, 1989 benchmark survey, preliminary annual rpt, 2704–5

Multinatl US firms and foreign affiliates finances and operations, by industry of parent firm and affiliate, world area, and selected country, 1989, annual article, 2702–1.225

Pollution abatement spending by govts, business, and consumers, 1987-89, annual article, 2702–1.229

Puerto Rico economic censuses, 1987: wholesale and retail trade and service industry finances and operations, by SIC 2- to 4-digit industry and municipio, 2591–1

Puerto Rico economic censuses, 1987: wholesale, retail, and service industries finances and operations, by establishment characteristics and SIC 2- and 3-digit industry, subject rpts, 2591–2

Science and engineering PhDs employment and other characteristics, by field and State, 1989, biennial rpt, 9627–18

Service industries census, 1987: depreciable assets, capital and operating expenses, and receipts, by SIC 2- to 4-digit kind of business, 2393–2

Research journals

Service industries census, 1987: establishments, receipts by source, payroll, and employment, by SIC 2- to 4-digit kind of business, State, and MSA, 2393–4

Service industries receipts, by SIC 2- to 4-digit kind of business, 1990, annual rpt, 2413–8

Soviet Union GNP by component and industry sector, and CIA estimation methods, 1950s-87, 23848–223

Soviet Union GNP by detailed income and outlay component, 1985, 2326–18.59

Space station commercial dev and operating costs and income under alternative financing options, projected 1989-2000, 21708–129

State and Metro Area Data Book, 1991 data compilation, 2328–54

Statistical Abstract of US, 1991 annual data compilation, 2324–1.20

Steel industry finances, operations, and modernization efforts, with data on major companies and foreign industry, 1968-91, last issue of annual rpt, 9884–24

Tax (income) returns of corporations, income and tax items by asset size and detailed industry, 1987, annual rpt, 8304–4

Tax (income) returns of corporations with foreign tax credit, income and tax items by industry group, 1986, biennial article, 8302–2.203

Telecommunications industry intl competitiveness, with financial and operating data by product or service, firm, and country, 1990 rpt, 2008–30

see also Defense research

see also Demonstration and pilot projects

see also Energy research and development

see also Federal funding for research and development

see also Federally Funded R&D Centers

see also Inventions

see also Technological innovations

Research and Evaluation Associates, Inc.

"State-Level Measurement of Performance Outcomes in Postsecondary Vocational Education", 4808–33

Research journals

Acid rain and air pollution environmental impacts, bibl, 1989 listing, 5506–5.26

Alcohol abuse research, treatment programs, and patient characteristics and health effects, quarterly journal, 4482–1

Cancer epidemiology and biochemistry research, semimonthly journal, 4472–1

Drug abuse and treatment research summaries, and resource materials and grant listings, periodic rpt, 4492–4

Geological Survey rpts and research journal articles, monthly listing, 5662–1

Geological Survey rpts, 1990, annual listing, 5664–4

Health Care Financing Review, quarterly journal, 4652–1

Health condition and quality of life measurement, rpts and other info sources, quarterly listing, 4122–1

Morbidity and Mortality Weekly Report, infectious notifiable disease cases and deaths, and other public health issues, periodic journal, 4202–7

Morbidity and Mortality Weekly Report, infectious notifiable disease cases by State, and public health issues, 4202–1

Research journals

NIH Natl Library of Medicine activities, holdings, and grants, FY88-90, annual rpt, 4464–1

NOAA Environmental Research Labs rpts, FY90, annual listing, 2144–25

NSF rpts, 1990 annual listing, 9624–16

Public Health Reports, bimonthly journal, 4042–3

Science and engineering academic research system status, R&D performance, and Fed Govt support, 1950s-88 with trends and projections, 9628–83

Scientific journal articles and citations, by field for US sources, selected years 1973-86, annual rpt, 9627–35.3

Social Security Bulletin, OASDHI and other program operations and beneficiary characteristics, from 1940, monthly journal, 4742–1

Research Triangle Institute

"National Household Seroprevalence Survey: Feasibility Study Final Report", 4148–30

"Nationwide Evaluation of Medicaid Competition Demonstrations", 4658–45

Reserve components

see Armed services reserves

see Coast Guard Reserve

see Marine Reserve

see National Guard

Reserve Officers Training Corps

- Army Dept activities, personnel, discipline, budget, and assistance, FY83 summary data, annual rpt, 3704–11
- Enrollment, grads, staff, scholarships, and costs, for ROTC programs by service branch, FY86-89, GAO rpt, 26123–337
- Expenditures, staff, students, and facilities for DOD training and education programs, by service branch, FY92, annual rpt, 3504–5
- Health care personnel, and accessions by training source, by occupation, specialty, and service branch, FY89, annual rpt, 3544–24
- Personnel of DOD, and organization, budget, weapons, and property, by service branch, State, and country, 1991 annual summary rpt, 3504–13
- Reserve forces personnel strengths and characteristics, by component, FY90, annual rpt, 3544–38

Reservoirs

- Agricultural Conservation Program participation and payments, by practice and State, FY90, annual rpt, 1804–7
- Army Corps of Engineers water resources dev projects, characteristics, and costs, 1950s-89, biennial State rpt series, 3756–1
- Army Corps of Engineers water resources dev projects, characteristics, and costs, 1950s-91, biennial State rpt series, 3756–2
- California drought impacts, Central Valley reservoir storage and capacity, and Kern County crop production and irrigation, 1989-91, article, 1561–6.202
- Capacity and area, by reservoir and State, 1988, 5668–120
- Colorado River Basin Federal reservoir and power operations and revenues, 1990-91, annual rpt, 5824–6
- Colorado water supply, streamflow, precipitation, and reservoir storage, 1991 water year, annual rpt, 1264–13

Index by Subjects and Names

Fish Hatchery Natl System activities and deliveries, by species, hatchery, and jurisdiction of waters stocked, FY90, annual rpt, 5504–10

- Fishery research of State fish and wildlife agencies, federally funded projects and costs by species and State, 1990, annual listing, 5504–23
- Global climate change environmental, infrastructure, and health impacts, with model results and background data, 1850s-2100, 9188–113
- Nevada and eastern California water supply, streamflow, precipitation, and reservoir storage, 1991 water year, annual rpt, 1264–8
- Oregon water supply, streamflow by station and reservoir storage, 1991, annual rpt, 1264–9
- Public lands acreage, grants, use, revenues, and allocations, by State, FY90, annual rpt, 5724–1.2
- Reclamation Bur irrigation activities, finances, and project impacts in western US, 1989, annual rpt, 5824–12
- Tennessee Valley river control activities, and hydroelectric power generation and capacity, 1989, annual rpt, 9804–7
- TVA finances and operations by program and facility, FY90, annual rpt, 9804–32
- Water supply and quality in streams and lakes, and groundwater levels in wells, by drainage basin, 1988, annual State rpt series, 5666–16
- Water supply and quality in streams and lakes, and groundwater levels in wells, by drainage basin, 1989, annual State rpt series, 5666–12
- Water supply and quality in streams and lakes, and groundwater levels in wells, by drainage basin, 1990, annual State rpt series, 5666–10
- Water supply, hydrologic events, and end use, by State, 1988-89, annual rpt, 5664–12
- Water supply in US and southern Canada, streamflow, surface and groundwater conditions, and reservoir levels, by location, monthly rpt, 5662–3
- Western US water supply, and snow survey results, monthly State rpt series, 1266–2
- Western US water supply, storage by reservoir and State, and streamflow conditions, as of Oct 1991, annual rpt, 1264–4
- Western US water supply, streamflow and reservoir storage forecasts by stream and station, Jan-May monthly rpt, 1262–1
- Wetlands acreage, resources, soil and water properties, and conservation efforts, by wetland type, State rpt series, 5506–11
- Wildlife and plant research results, habitat study series, 5506–13
- Wildlife mgmt activities and funding, acreage, staff, and plans of Bur of Land Mgmt, habitat study series, 5726–6

Residential energy use

see Housing energy use

Resins

see Chemicals and chemical industry

see Gum and wood chemicals

see Plastics and plastics industry

Resolution Trust Corp.

- Activities and financial statements of RTC, with data on savings instn conservatorships by instn and State, 1989, annual rpt, 9724–1
- Banks and thrifts fraud and abuse, Federal agencies enforcement activities and staff, with data by instn and location, 1988-90, hearing, 21408–119
- Bond (junk) holdings of RTC, quarterly press release, 9722–4
- Budget of US, authoritative financial statements with appropriations, outlays, and receipts, by category and agency, FY90, annual rpt, 8104–2.1
- Budget of US, CBO analysis and review of FY92 budget by function, annual rpt, 26304–2
- Budget of US, CBO analysis of revenue and spending alternatives and projections of economic indicators, FY92-96, annual rpt, 26304–3
- Budget of US, midsession review of FY92 budget, by function, annual rpt, 104–7
- Budget of US, obligations and authority by function, agency, and program, with summaries, analyses, and historical tables, FY92, annual rpt, 104–2
- Fed Govt finances, cash and debt transactions, daily tables, 8102–4
- Fraud and abuse in RTC programs, audits and investigations, 2nd half FY91, semiannual rpt, 9722–6
- Obligation limits compliance by RTC, with balance sheet, quarterly GAO rpt, 26102–6
- Property acquired by Fed Govt through foreclosure and savings instn failure, 1-family homes inventory by State, acquisition costs, and sales, for 4 agencies, 1986-90, GAO rpt, 26113–513
- Real estate assets of failed thrifts, inventory of properties available from RTC, semiannual listing series, 9722–2
- Savings instns failure resolution activity and finances of RTC, with data by asset type, State, region, and instn, monthly rpt, 9722–3
- Savings instns failure resolution activity of RTC, assets, deposits, and assets availability and sales, periodic press release, 9722–1
- Savings instns failure resolution activity of RTC, with assets and retained senior executives compensation, by instn, 1988-90, hearing, 21248–144
- Savings instns failure resolution activity of RTC, with instns assets and senior executives compensation, 1990, hearing, 21248–157
- Savings instns failure resolution activity of RTC, 1991 semiannual hearing, 21242–1
- Savings instns failures, financial performance of instns under RTC conservatorship, quarterly rpt, 9722–5

Resolution Trust Corporation Task Force. House

- Savings instns failure resolution activity of Resolution Trust Corp, with assets and retained senior executives compensation, by instn, 1988-90, hearing, 21248–144
- Savings instns failure resolution activity of Resolution Trust Corp, with instns assets and senior executive compensation, 1990, hearing, 21248–157

Index by Subjects and Names

Resorts

see Hotels and motels

Respiratory diseases

- Asthma (chronic) among children, relation to family structure, by selected characteristics, 1988, 4147–10.178
- Cancer (lung) death risk from occupational beryllium exposure, 1952-88, article, 4472–1.224
- Cancer (lung) tumors with genetic mutations, by patient smoking history and other characteristics, 1980-89, article, 4472–1.217
- Cancer cases, deaths, and survival rates, by sex, race, age, and body site, 1973-88, annual rpt, 4474–35
- Cancer death rates of minorities, by body site, age, sex, and substate area, 1950s-80, atlas, 4478–78
- Cancer death risk relation to smoking by body site, and compared to other smoking-related diseases, by sex, 1960s-91, article, 4472–1.219
- Cancer deaths and rates, by body site, provisional data, monthly rpt, 4142–1.2
- Cases of acute and chronic conditions, disability, absenteeism, and health services use, by selected characteristics, 1987, CD-ROM, 4147–10.177
- Deaths and rates, by cause and age, preliminary 1989-90, US Vital Statistics annual rpt, 4144–7
- Deaths and rates, by cause, provisional data, monthly rpt, 4142–1.2
- Deaths and rates, by detailed cause and demographic characteristics, 1988 and trends from 1900, US Vital Statistics annual rpt, 4144–2
- Deaths from heart disease, stroke, and chronic obstructive lung disease, by country and sex, 1987, annual rpt, 4474–6
- Health condition and health care resources, use, and spending, 1950s-89, annual data compilation, 4144–11
- HHS financial aid, by program, recipient, State, and city, FY90, annual regional listings, 4004–3
- Hospital charges and length of stay for heart and lung patients with selected nonsurgical procedures, for Maryland, FY84, article, 4652–1.204
- Hospital deaths of Medicare patients, actual and expected rates by diagnosis, with hospital characteristics, by instn, FY87-89, annual regional rpt series, 4654–14
- Hospital discharges and length of stay, by diagnosis, patient and instn characteristics, procedure performed, and payment source, 1988, annual rpt, 4147–13.107
- Hospital discharges and length of stay by region and diagnosis, and procedures performed, by age and sex, 1989, annual rpt, 4146–8.198
- Hospital discharges by detailed diagnostic and procedure category, primary diagnosis, and length of stay, by age, sex, and region, 1988, annual rpt, 4147–13.105; 4147–13.108
- Indian and Alaska Native disease and disorder cases, deaths, and health services use, by tribe, reservation, and Indian Health Service area, late 1950s-86, 4088–2

Indian Health Service, tribal, and contract facilities hospitalization, by diagnosis, age, sex, and service area, FY89, annual rpt, 4084–5

- Indians and Alaska Natives chronic disease prevalence, for 8 conditions by age and sex, 1987, 4186–8.20
- Minority group health condition, services use, costs, and indicators of services need, 1950s-88, 4118–55
- Natl Heart, Lung, and Blood Inst activities, and grants by recipient and location, FY90 and disease trends from 1940, annual rpt, 4474–15
- Natl Inst of Allergy and Infectious Diseases activities, grants by recipient and location, and disease cases, FY83-90, annual rpt, 4474–30
- Occupational illness rates, by cause and SIC 2- to 3-digit industry, 1989, annual rpt, 6844–1
- Occupational respiratory diseases epidemiology, diagnosis, and treatment, for selected industries and work settings, 1988 conf, 4248–90
- Radiation exposure of uranium miners and risk of death from cancer and lung diseases, for Indians and compared to whites and foreign countries, 1950s-84, hearing, 25548–101
- *State and Metro Area Data Book*, 1991 data compilation, 2328–54
- Veterans disability and death compensation cases of VA, by entitlement type, period of service, sex, age, and State, FY89, annual rpt, 8604–7
- *see also* Black lung disease
- *see also* Nose and throat disorders
- *see also* Pneumonia and influenza
- *see also* Respiratory therapy
- *see also* Tuberculosis
- *see also* under By Disease in the "Index by Categories"

Respiratory therapy

- VA health care staff and turnover, by occupation, physician specialty, and location, 1990, annual rpt, 8604–8

Respite care

- Hospices operations, services, costs, and patient characteristics, for instns without Medicare certification, FY85-86, 4658–52

Rest homes

see Nursing homes

Restaurants and drinking places

- *Agricultural Statistics, 1990*, annual rpt, 1004–1
- Blind-operated vending facilities on Federal and non-Federal property, finances and operations by agency and State, FY90, annual rpt, 4944–2
- Business statistics, detailed data for major industries and economic indicators, *Survey of Current Business*, monthly rpt, 2702–1.11
- Census of Retail Trade, 1987: depreciable assets, capital and operating expenses, sales, value added, and inventories, by SIC 2- to 4-digit kind of business, 2399–2
- Census of Retail Trade, 1987: finances and employment, for establishments with and without payroll, by SIC 2- to 4-digit kind of business, State, and MSA, 2401–1

Restaurants and drinking places

- Collective bargaining agreements expiring during year, and workers covered, by firm, union, industry group, and State, 1991, annual rpt, 6784–9
- Consumer Expenditure Survey, food spending by item, household composition, income, age, race, and region, 1980-88, biennial rpt, 1544–30
- Consumer Expenditure Survey, household income by source, and itemized spending, by selected characteristics and region, 1988-89, annual rpt, 6764–5
- Consumer Expenditure Survey, spending by category, and income, by selected household characteristics and location, 1990, annual press release, 6726–1.42
- Consumer Expenditure Survey, spending by category, selected household characteristics, and region, quarterly rpt, 6762–14
- Consumer research, food marketing, legislation, and regulation devs, and consumption and price trends, quarterly journal, 1541–7
- County Business Patterns, 1988: employment, establishments, and payroll, by SIC 2- to 4-digit industry and county, annual State rpt series, 2326–6
- County Business Patterns, 1989: employment, establishments, and payroll, by SIC 2- to 4-digit industry and county, annual State rpt series, 2326–8
- CPI by component for US city average, and by region, population size, and for 27 metro areas, monthly rpt, 6762–2
- CPI components relative importance, by selected MSA, region, population size, and for US city average, 1990, annual rpt, 6884–1
- Crime victimization rates, by victim and offender characteristics, circumstances, and offense, 1988 survey, annual rpt, 6066–3.42
- Crime victimization rates, by victim and offender characteristics, circumstances, and offense, 1989 survey, annual rpt, 6066–3.44
- Employee (temporary) supply establishments by occupation supplied, receipts by source, and payroll, by MSA, 1987 Census of Service Industries, 2393–4.8
- Employment, earnings, and hours, by SIC 1- to 4-digit industry, monthly and annual averages, selected years 1909-90, annual rpt, 6744–4
- Energy use in commercial buildings, costs, and conservation, by building characteristics, survey rpt series, 3166–8
- Enterprise Statistics, 1987: auxiliaries of multi-establishment firms, finances and operations by function, industry, and State, 2329–6
- Enterprise Statistics, 1987: finances and operations for companies, by size, level of diversification, form of organization, and industry group, 2329–8
- Expenditures for food and alcoholic beverages by place of purchase, and CPI, 1968-90, annual rpt, 1544–4.5
- Fast food nutrient, caloric, and waste composition, 1991 rpt, 1356–3.15
- Finances and operations, by SIC 2- to 4-digit industry, forecast 1991, annual rpt, 2044–28

Restaurants and drinking places

Franchise business opportunities by firm and kind of business, and sources of aid and info, 1990 annual listing, 2104–7

Households food and beverage spending and per capita consumption, by food and beverage type, 1980s-90, article, 1702–1.212

Input-output structure of US economy, detailed interindustry transactions for 84 industries, and components of final demand, 1986, annual article, 2702–1.206

Input-output structure of US economy, detailed interindustry transactions for 85 industries, 1982 benchmark data, 2702–1.213

Insurance (health) provided by employers, small business and restaurant owners views, 1989 hearings, 23898–7

Labor productivity, indexes of output, hours, and employment by SIC 2- to 4-digit industry, 1967-89, annual rpt, 6824–1.4

Mail volume to and from households, use, and views, by class, source, content, and household characteristics, 1987-88, annual rpt, 9864–10

Microwave ovens (commercial) from Japan at less than fair value, injury to US industry, investigation with background financial and operating data, 1991 rpt, 9886–14.322

Occupational injury and illness rates, and workdays lost by State, for restaurants and drinking places, 1989, article, 6722–1.231

Occupational injury and illness rates, by SIC 2- to 4-digit industry, 1988-89, annual rpt, 6844–7

Occupational injury and illness rates, by SIC 2- to 4-digit industry, 1989, annual rpt, 6844–1

Older persons migration to southern coastal areas, household finances, services needs, and local economic impacts, for selected counties, 1990, 2068–38

Price indexes, alternative food cost index by category, region, and household income, size, race, and food budget level, 1980-85, 1598–275

Prices (farm-retail) for food, marketing cost components, and industry finances and productivity, 1920s-90, annual rpt, 1544–9

Puerto Rico economic censuses, 1987: wholesale and retail trade and service industry finances and operations, by SIC 2- to 4-digit industry and municipio, 2591–1

Puerto Rico economic censuses, 1987: wholesale, retail, and service industries finances and operations, by establishment characteristics and SIC 2- and 3-digit industry, subject rpts, 2591–2

Sales and inventories, by kind of retail business, region, and selected State, MSA, and city, monthly rpt, 2413–3

Sales, inventories, purchases, gross margin, and accounts receivable, by SIC 2- to 4-digit kind of business and form of ownership, 1989, annual rpt, 2413–5

Sales of retailers, by kind of business, advance monthly rpt, 2413–2

Savings instns failures, inventory of real estate assets available from Resolution Trust Corp, 1990, semiannual listing, 9722–2.4

Savings instns failures, inventory of real estate assets available from Resolution Trust Corp, 1991, semiannual listing, 9722–2.10

Smoking bans in public places, local ordinances provisions, as of 1989, 4478–196

State and Metro Area Data Book, 1991 data compilation, 2328–54

Tax (income) returns of corporations, income and tax items by asset size and detailed industry, 1987, annual rpt, 8304–4

Tax (income) returns of corporations, income and tax items by asset size and detailed industry, 1988, annual rpt, 8304–21

Tax (income) returns of corporations with foreign tax credit, income and tax items by industry group, 1986, biennial article, 8302–2.203

Tax (income) returns of partnerships, income statement and balance sheet items, by industry group, 1989, annual article, 8302–2.216; 8304–18

Tax (income) returns of sole proprietorships, income statement items, by industry group, 1989, annual article, 8302–2.214

Restitution

see Crime victim compensation

see Fines and settlements

Retail centers

see Shopping centers

Retail trade

Business statistics, detailed data for major industries and economic indicators, *Survey of Current Business*, monthly rpt, 2702–1.7

Census Bur rpts and data files, coverage and availability, 1991 annual listing, 2304–2

Classification codes concordance of Canada and US SICs, for 1- to 4-digit levels, 1991 rpt, 2628–31

Collective bargaining agreements expiring during year, and workers covered, by firm, union, industry group, and State, 1991, annual rpt, 6784–9

County Business Patterns, 1988: employment, establishments, and payroll, by SIC 2- to 4-digit industry and county, annual State rpt series, 2326–6

County Business Patterns, 1989: employment, establishments, and payroll, by SIC 2- to 4-digit industry and county, annual State rpt series, 2326–8

Credit (installment) outstanding, and terms, by lender and credit type, monthly rpt, 9365–2.6

Credit (installment) outstanding, by type of holder, *Survey of Current Business*, monthly rpt, 2702–1.9

Credit reporting and collection establishments, and receipts by source and class of client, by MSA, 1987 Census of Service Industries, 2393–4.4

Earnings by industry div, and personal income per capita and by source, by State, MSA, and county, 1984-89, annual regional rpts, 2704–2

Earnings, weekly averages, monthly rpt, 23842–1.2

Economic indicators and components, and Fed Reserve 4th District business and financial conditions, monthly chartbook, 9377–10

Economic indicators compounded annual rates of change, monthly rpt, 9391–3

Economic indicators compounded annual rates of change, 1971-90, annual rpt, 9391–9.2

Economic indicators, monthly rpt, 9362–1.2

Employment and Earnings, detailed data, monthly rpt, 6742–2.5

Employment, earnings, and hours, by SIC 1- to 4-digit industry, monthly and annual averages, selected years 1909-90, annual rpt, 6744–4

Employment, earnings, and hours, monthly press release, 6742–5

Employment situation, earnings, hours, and other BLS economic indicators, transcripts of BLS Commissioner's monthly testimony, periodic rpt, 23846–4

Employment, unemployment, and labor force characteristics, by region and census div, 1990, annual rpt, 6744–7.1

Enterprise Statistics, 1987: auxiliaries of multi-establishment firms, finances and operations by function, industry, and State, 2329–6

Enterprise Statistics, 1987: finances and operations for companies, by size, level of diversification, form of organization, and industry group, 2329–8

Finance companies credit outstanding and leasing activities, by credit type, monthly rpt, 9365–2.7

Finances and operations, by SIC 2- to 4-digit industry, forecast 1991, annual rpt, 2044–28

Financial statements for manufacturing, mining, and trade corporations, by selected SIC 2- to 3-digit industry, quarterly rpt, 2502–1

Foreign direct investment in US, by industry group and world area, 1987-90, annual article, 2702–1.219

Foreign direct investment in US, by industry group of US affiliate and country of parent firm, 1980-86, 2708–41

Foreign direct investment in US, major transactions by type, industry, country, and US location, 1989, annual rpt, 2044–20

Foreign direct investment of US, by industry group and world area, 1987-90, annual article, 2702–1.220

Franchise business opportunities by firm and kind of business, and sources of aid and info, 1990 annual listing, 2104–7

Labor productivity, indexes of output, hours, and employment by SIC 2- to 4-digit industry, 1967-89, annual rpt, 6824–1.4

Multinatl firms US affiliates, finances, and operations, by industry, world area of parent firm, and State, 1988-89, annual rpt, 2704–4

Multinatl US firms and foreign affiliates finances and operations, by industry and world area of parent firm, 1989 benchmark survey, preliminary annual rpt, 2704–5

New England States economic indicators, Fed Reserve 1st District, monthly rpt, 9373–2.3

New England States, FHLB 1st District thrifts financial operations compared to banks, and housing industry indicators, bimonthly rpt with articles, 9302–4

Index by Subjects and Names

Retirement

North Central States business and economic conditions, Fed Reserve 9th District, quarterly journal, 9383–19

Occupational injuries, illnesses, and workdays lost, by SIC 2-digit industry, 1989-90, annual press release, 6844–3

Occupational injury and illness rates, by SIC 2- to 4-digit industry, 1988-89, annual rpt, 6844–7

Occupational injury and illness rates, by SIC 2- to 4-digit industry, 1989, annual rpt, 6844–1

Older persons migration to southern coastal areas, household finances, services needs, and local economic impacts, for selected counties, 1990, 2068–38

Puerto Rico and other US possessions corporations income tax returns, income and tax items, and employment, by selected industry, 1987, article, 8302–2.213

Puerto Rico economic censuses, 1987: wholesale and retail trade and service industry finances and operations, by SIC 2- to 4-digit industry and municipio, 2591–1

Puerto Rico economic censuses, 1987: wholesale, retail, and service industries finances and operations, by establishment characteristics and SIC 2- and 3-digit industry, subject rpts, 2591–2

Sales and inventories, by kind of retail business, region, and selected State, MSA, and city, monthly rpt, 2413–3

Sales and inventories, monthly rpt, 23842–1.3

Sales, inventories, and inventory/sales ratios for manufacturing and trade, quarterly article, 2702–1.28

Sales, inventories, purchases, gross margin, and accounts receivable, by SIC 2- to 4-digit kind of business and form of ownership, 1989, annual rpt, 2413–5

Sales of retailers, by kind of business, advance monthly rpt, 2413–2

Sales of retailers, by kind of business, region, and selected MSA, 1989-91, fact sheet, 2326–17.29

SEC registration, firms required to file annual rpts, as of Sept 1990, annual listing, 9734–5

Smoking bans in public places, local ordinances provisions, as of 1989, 4478–196

State and Metro Area Data Book, 1991 data compilation, 2328–54

Statistical Abstract of US, 1991 annual data compilation, 2324–1.17; 2324–1.28

Tax (income) returns of corporations, income and tax items by asset size and detailed industry, 1987, annual rpt, 8304–4

Tax (income) returns of corporations, income and tax items by asset size and detailed industry, 1988, annual rpt, 8304–21

Tax (income) returns of corporations with foreign tax credit, income and tax items by industry group, 1986, biennial article, 8302–2.203

Tax (income) returns of multinatl US firms foreign affiliates, income statement items, by asset size and industry, 1986, biennial article, 8302–2.212

Tax (income) returns of partnerships, income statement and balance sheet items, by industry group, 1989, annual article, 8302–2.216; 8304–18

Tax (income) returns of sole proprietorships, income statement items, by industry group, 1989, annual article, 8302–2.214

Wage and benefit changes from collective bargaining and mgmt decisions, by industry div, monthly rpt, 6782–1

Wages by occupation, and benefits for office and plant workers, periodic MSA survey rpt series, 6785–11; 6785–12

see also Advertising

see also Census of Retail Trade

see also Consumer credit

see also Consumer protection

see also Credit cards

see also Department stores

see also Direct marketing

see also Drugstores

see also Food stores

see also Gasoline service stations

see also Labeling

see also Military post exchanges and commissaries

see also Packaging and containers

see also Restaurants and drinking places

see also Sales promotion

see also Sales workers

see also Shoplifting

see also Shopping centers

see also Vending machines and stands

see also Warehouses

see also Wholesale trade

see also under By Industry in the "Index by Categories"

see also under names of specific commodities or commodity groups

Retchin, Sheldon

"National Medicare Competition Evaluation: An Evaluation of the Quality of the Process of Care. Final Analysis Report", 4658–46

Retired military personnel

Annuitants, DOD retired military personnel, FY50-90, annual rpt, 3544–1.4

Benefits and pay for active duty personnel, reserves, retirees, and survivors, 1940s-80s and projected to 2049, 21208–34

Fed Govt civilian employees demographic and employment characteristics, as of Sept 1990, annual article, 9842–1.201

Health care facilities of DOD in US and abroad, beds, admissions, outpatient visits, and births, by service branch, quarterly rpt, 3542–15

Health care retired personnel, by specialty, FY89, annual rpt, 3544–24.8

Navy personnel strengths, accessions, and attrition, detailed statistics, quarterly rpt, 3802–4

Personnel of DOD, and organization, budget, weapons, and property, by service branch, State, and country, 1991 annual summary rpt, 3504–13

Reserve forces personnel and equipment strengths, and readiness, by reserve component, FY90, annual rpt, 3544–31

Reserve forces personnel attrition, by reason, personnel characteristics, reserve component, and State, FY88, GAO rpt, 26123–329

Reserve forces personnel strengths and characteristics, by component, FY90, annual rpt, 3544–38

Reserve forces personnel strengths and characteristics, by component, quarterly rpt, 3542–4

see also Civilian Health and Medical Program of the Uniformed Services

see also Military benefits and pensions

see also Veterans

Retired Senior Volunteer Program

Activities and funding of ACTION, by program, FY90, annual rpt, 9024–2

Retirement

Air traffic control and airway facilities staff, by employment and other characteristics, FY89, annual rpt, 7504–41

Deaths within 8 years of retirement, by health and other characteristics, 1982-88, article, 4742–1.206

Earnings replacement rates of pension plans and OASI benefits, by age, salary, years of participation, and occupational group, 1989, article, 6722–1.238

EC retirement age under statutory social security programs, by sex and country, 1989, article, 4742–1.205

Fed Govt civilian retirees health insurance coverage by plan, and program finances, FY89, annual rpt, 9844–35.2

Fed Govt personnel action appeals, decisions of Merit Systems Protection Board by agency and region, FY90, annual rpt, 9494–2

Health insurance coverage for small business employees after retirement, 1990, biennial rpt, 6784–20

Migration of aged to southern coastal areas, household finances, services needs, and local economic impacts, for selected counties, 1990, 2068–38

NASA science and engineering staff retirement rates, projected 1991-95, GAO rpt, 26123–348

NASA staff characteristics and personnel actions, FY90, annual rpt, 9504–1

OASDI benefit payments, trust fund finances, and economic and demographic assumptions, 1970-90 and alternative projections to 2000, actuarial rpt, 4706–1.105

Poverty status of population and families, by detailed characteristics, 1988-89, annual Current Population Rpt, 2546–6.67

Poverty status of population and families, by detailed characteristics, 1990, annual Current Population Rpt, 2546–6.71

Railroad retirement system funding and benefits findings and recommendations, with background industry data, 1960s-90 and projected to 2060, 9708–1

Teachers in higher education instns, employment and other characteristics, by instn type and control, 1987/88 survey, 4846–4.4

see also Civil service pensions

see also Employee benefits

see also Individual retirement arrangements

see also Old age assistance

see also Old-Age, Survivors, Disability, and Health Insurance

see also Pensions and pension funds

see also Retired military personnel

see also Retired Senior Volunteer Program

see also Retirement communities

Retirement communities

Retirement communities

Tax-exempt bond use and other financing of retirement housing centers, defaults, and facility and resident characteristics, 1991 GAO rpt, 26119–328

Reunion

Economic, social, political, and geographic summary data, by country, 1991, annual factbook, 9114–2

Revco D.S., Inc.

Leveraged buyouts impacts on financial performance, for 4 transactions, 1980s-90, GAO rpt, 26119–355

Revenue sharing

- Budget of US, CBO analysis of savings and revenues under alternative spending cuts and tax changes, projected FY92-97, 26306–3.118
- Budget of US, Senate concurrent resolution, with spending and revenue targets, FY92, annual rpt, 25254–1
- Education funding by Federal agency, program, and recipient type, and instn spending, FY80-90, annual rpt, 4824–8
- Expenditures of Fed Govt in States, by type, program, agency, and State, FY90, annual rpt, 2464–2
- Forest Service acreage, staff, finances, and mgmt activities in Pacific Northwest, with data by forest, 1970s-89, annual rpt, 1204–37
- Forests (natl) revenue share paid to States, and acreage, by forest, region, county, and congressional district, FY90, annual rpt, 1204–33
- Govt finances, by level of govt, State, and for large cities and counties, annual rpt series, 2466–2
- Govt finances, tax systems and revenue, and fiscal structure, by level of govt and State, 1991 with historical trends, annual rpt, 10044–1
- Hwy Trust Fund receipts by source, and apportionments, by State, 1990, annual rpt, 7554–1.3
- Oil and gas OCS leases, revenue sharing payments by State, 1991 annual press release, 5306–4.9

Revolvers

see Firearms

Rhenium

see Metals and metal industries

Rheumatism

see Musculoskeletal diseases

Rhoades, Everett R.

"Indian Burden of Illness and Future Health Interventions", 4088–2

Rhode Island

- Banks (insured commercial and savings) deposits by instn, State, MSA, and county, as of June 1990, annual regional rpt, 9295–3.1
- County Business Patterns, 1989: employment, establishments, and payroll, by SIC 2- to 4-digit industry and county, annual State rpt, 2326–8.41
- DOD prime contract awards, by contractor, service branch, State, and city, FY90, annual rpt, 3544–22
- Economic indicators for New England States, Fed Reserve 1st District, monthly rpt, 9373–2
- Fed Govt spending in States and local areas, by type, State, county, and city, FY90, annual rpt, 2464–3

Index by Subjects and Names

- Fed Govt spending in States, by type, program, agency, and State, FY90, annual rpt, 2464–2
- Food aid program of USDA for women, infants, and children, health services need of participants, for Rhode Island, 1983-84, article, 4042–3.247
- HHS financial aid, by program, recipient, State, and city, FY90, annual regional listing, 4004–3.1
- Hospital deaths of Medicare patients, actual and expected rates by diagnosis, and hospital characteristics, by instn, FY87-89, annual regional rpt, 4654–14.1
- Hwy funds pooled by States from FHwA funds for specific projects, demonstration project results, FY88-90, GAO rpt, 26113–471
- Income (personal) per capita and by source, and earnings by industry div, by State, MSA, and county, 1984-89, annual regional rpt, 2704–2.2
- Marriages, divorces, and rates, by characteristics of spouses, State, and county, 1987 and trends from 1920, US Vital Statistics annual rpt, 4144–4
- Mineral Industry Surveys, State reviews of production, 1990, preliminary annual rpt, 5614–6
- *Minerals Yearbook, 1989,* Vol 2: State review of production and sales by commodity, and business activity, annual rpt, 5604–16.41
- *Minerals Yearbook, 1989,* Vol 2: State reviews of production, sales, and firms, by commodity, and business activity, annual rpt, 5604–34
- Physicians, by specialty, age, sex, and location of training and practice, 1989, State rpt, 4116–6.41
- Population and housing census, 1990: population and housing characteristics, households, and land area, by county, subdiv, and place, State rpt, 2551–1.41
- Population and housing census, 1990: voting age and total population by race, and housing units, by block, redistricting counts required under PL 94-171, State CD-ROM release, 2551–6.6
- Population and housing census, 1990: voting age and total population by race, and housing units, by county and city, redistricting counts required under PL 94-171, State summary rpt, 2551–5.40
- Savings instns, FHLB 1st District members financial operations compared to banks, and related economic and housing indicators, bimonthly rpt with articles, 9302–4
- *Statistical Abstract of US,* 1991 annual data compilation, 2324–1
- Supplemental Security Income payments and beneficiaries, by type of eligibility, State, and county, Dec 1989, annual rpt, 4744–27.1
- Water supply and quality in streams and lakes, and groundwater levels in wells, by drainage basin, 1989, annual State rpt, 5666–12.20
- Water supply and quality in streams and lakes, and groundwater levels in wells, by drainage basin, 1990, annual State rpt, 5666–10.20
- Water supply in northeastern US, precipitation and stream runoff by station, monthly rpt, 2182–3

Wetlands acreage, resources, soil and water properties, and conservation efforts, by wetland type, 1989 State rpt, 5506–11.7

see also Cranston, R.I.

see also Pawtucket, R.I.

see also Providence, R.I.

see also Warwick, R.I.

see also Woonsocket, R.I.

see also under By State in the "Index by Categories"

Rhodesia

see Zimbabwe

Ribaudo, Marc

"Summary of State Water Quality Laws Affecting Agriculture", 1561–16.203

Rice

- Acreage planted and harvested, by crop and State, 1989-90 and planned as of June 1991, annual rpt, 1621–23
- Acreage planted, by selected crop and State, 1982-90 and planned 1991, annual rpt, 1621–22
- Acreage reduction program compliance, enrollment, and yield on planted acreage, by commodity and State, annual press release series, 1004–20
- Acreage under Agricultural Stabilization and Conservation Service programs, rankings by commodity and congressional district, 1989, biennial rpt, 1804–17
- Agricultural Stabilization and Conservation Service producer payments and certificate value, by program, monthly rpt, 1802–10
- Agricultural Stabilization and Conservation Service producer payments, by program and State, 1990, annual table, 1804–12
- Agricultural Stabilization and Conservation Service rice programs, 1979-91, annual fact sheet, 1806–4.6
- *Agricultural Statistics, 1990,* annual rpt, 1004–1
- Agriculture census, 1987: farms, farmland, production, finances, and operator characteristics, by county, final State rpt series, 2331–1
- Beer production, stocks, material used, tax-free removals, and taxable removals by State, monthly rpt, 8486–1.1
- Business statistics, detailed data for major industries and economic indicators, *Survey of Current Business,* monthly rpt, 2702–1.14
- CCC certificate exchange activity, by commodity, biweekly press release, 1802–16
- Consumer Expenditure Survey, food spending by item, household composition, income, age, race, and region, 1980-88, biennial rpt, 1544–30
- Consumption, supply, trade, prices, spending, and indexes, by food commodity, 1989, annual rpt, 1544–4
- Cooperatives, finances, operations, activities, and membership, 1950s-88, commodity rpt, 1126–1.5
- County Business Patterns, 1988: employment, establishments, and payroll, by SIC 2- to 4-digit industry and county, annual State rpt series, 2326–6
- County Business Patterns, 1989: employment, establishments, and payroll, by SIC 2- to 4-digit industry and county, annual State rpt series, 2326–8
- Export licensing, monitoring, and enforcement activities, FY90, annual rpt, 2024–1

Index by Subjects and Names

Exports (agricultural) of high-value commodities, indexes and sales value by commodity, world area, and country, 1960s-86, 1528–323

Exports and imports (agricultural) commodity and country, prices, and world market devs, monthly rpt, 1922–12

Exports and imports (agricultural) of US, by commodity and country, bimonthly rpt, 1522–1

Exports and imports (agricultural) of US, by detailed commodity and country, 1989, annual rpt, 1524–8

Exports and imports (agricultural) of US, by detailed commodity and country, 1990, semiannual rpt, 1522–4

Exports and imports between US and outlying areas, by detailed commodity and mode of transport, 1990, annual rpt, 2424–11

Exports and imports of US, by country and detailed commodity, monthly rpt, 2422–12

Exports and imports of US, by Harmonized System 6-digit commodity and country, 1990, annual rpt, 2424–13

Exports and imports of US, by transport mode, country, and SITC 1- to 3-digit commodity, 1990, annual rpt, 2424–12

Exports of grains, oilseed products, hides, skins, and cotton, by country, weekly rpt, 1922–3

Exports of US, detailed Schedule B commodities with countries of destination, 1990, annual rpt, 2424–10

Farm income, expenses, receipts by commodity, assets, liabilities, and ratios, 1990 and trends from 1945, annual rpt, 1544–16

Farm sector balance sheet, and receipts by detailed commodity, by State, 1985-89, annual rpt, 1544–18

Fertilizer and pesticide use and application rates, by type, crop, and State, 1990, 1616–1.1

Foreign and US agricultural production, acreage, and yield for selected crops, forecasts by selected world region and country, FAS monthly circular, 1925–28

Foreign and US agricultural supply and demand indicators, by selected crop, monthly rpt, 1522–5

Foreign and US grain production, prices, trade, stocks, and use, FAS periodic circular series, 1925–2

Foreign and US rice production, prices, trade, stocks, and use, periodic situation rpt, 1561–8

Foreign countries agricultural production, prices, and trade, by country, 1980-90 and forecast 1991, annual world area rpt series, 1524–4

Futures and options trading volume, by commodity and exchange, FY90, annual rpt, 11924–2

Futures trading in selected commodities and financial instruments and indexes, NYC, Chicago, and other markets activity, semimonthly rpt, 11922–5

Irrigation projects of Reclamation Bur in western US, crop production and acreage by commodity, State, and project, 1989, annual rpt, 5824–12

Labor productivity, indexes of output, hours, and employment by SIC 2- to 4-digit industry, 1967-89, annual rpt, 6824–1.3

Loan support programs of USDA for grains, activity and status by grain and State, monthly rpt, 1802–3

Manufacturing annual survey, 1989: finances and operations, by SIC 2- to 4-digit industry, series, 2506–15

Manufacturing census, 1987: finances and operations, by type of organization and SIC 2- to 4-digit industry, subject rpt, 2497–5

OECD trade, total and for 4 major countries, and US trade by country, by commodity, 1970-89, world area rpt series, 9116–1

PL 480 long-term credit sales allocations, by commodity and country, periodic press release, 1922–7

Price indexes (producer), by stage of processing and detailed commodity, monthly rpt, 6762–6

Price indexes (producer), by stage of processing and detailed commodity, monthly 1990, annual rpt, 6764–2

Price support and other CCC program outlays, with production and marketing outlook, by commodity, projected 1990-96, 26306–6.160

Price support program provisions, for selected commodities, 1961-90, 1568–302

Prices, market activities, inspections, sales, trade, supply, and use of rice, for US and selected foreign markets, weekly rpt, 1313–8

Prices received and paid by farmers, by commodity and State, 1990, annual rpt, 1629–5

Prices received by farmers and production value, by detailed crop and State, 1988-90, annual rpt, 1621–2

Prices received by farmers for major products, and paid for farm inputs and living items, by State, monthly rpt, 1629–1

Production, farms, acreage, and related data, by selected crop and State, monthly rpt, 1621–1

Production itemized costs, receipts, and returns, by commodity and region, 1987-89, annual rpt, 1544–20

Production, prices, trade, and marketing, by commodity, current situation and forecast, monthly rpt with articles, 1502–4

Soviet Union agricultural trade, by commodity and country, 1955-90, 1528–322

Soviet Union, Eastern Europe, OECD, and selected other countries agricultural production, by commodity, 1960s-90, annual rpt, 9114–4.5

Stocks of grain on and off farms, by crop, quarterly rpt, 1621–4

Stocks of rice on and off farms and total, periodic rpt, 1621–7

see also under By Commodity in the "Index by Categories"

Rice, Dorothy P.

"Economic Costs of Alcohol and Drug Abuse and Mental Illness: 1985", 4048–35

"Estimates of Economic Costs of Alcohol and Drug Abuse and Mental Illness, 1985 and 1988", 4042–3.219

Right of privacy

Richardson, Ralph M.

"Business Volume Sets $77 Billion Record, but Farmer Cooperative Income Declines", 1122–1.211

"Farmer Cooperative Statistics, 1989", 1124–1

Richardson, W. John

"Acoustic Effects of Oil Production Activities on Bowhead and White Whales Visible During Spring Migration Near Point Barrow Alaska—1989 Phase: Sound Propagation and Whale Responses to Playbacks of Continuous Drilling Noise from an Ice Platform, as Studied in Pack Ice Conditions", 5738–27

"Comparison of Behavior of Bowhead Whales of the Davis Strait and Bering/Beaufort Stocks", 5738–29

Richland, Wash.

Radiation exposure of population near Hanford, Wash, nuclear plant, with methodology, 1944-66, series, 3356–5

Wages by occupation, for office and plant workers, 1991 survey, periodic MSA rpt, 6785–3.6

see also under By SMSA or MSA in the "Index by Categories"

Richmond, Va.

Wages by occupation, for office and plant workers, 1991 survey, periodic MSA rpt, 6785–12.5

see also under By City and By SMSA or MSA in the "Index by Categories"

Riddick, Howard A.

"Report on the 1987-88 Nationwide Food Consumption Survey", 1004–16.1

Riedman, Marianne L.

"Sea Otter (Enhydra lutris): Behavior, Ecology, and Natural History", 5508–109

Ries, Peter

"Characteristics of Persons With and Without Health Care Coverage: U.S., 1989", 4146–8.203

"Disability and Health: Characteristics of Persons by Limitation of Activity and Assessed Health Status, U.S., 1984-88", 4146–8.202

"Sociodemographic and Health Characteristics of Persons by Private Health Insurance Coverage and Type of Plan: U.S., 1975", 4147–16.4

Rifles

see Firearms

Riggins, Phillip E.

"State-Local Relations Organizations: The ACIR Counterparts", 10048–80

Right of assembly

Foreign countries human rights conditions in 170 countries, 1990, annual rpt, 21384–3

Right of privacy

Census of Population data on individuals, public availability, for 1790-1990 censuses, pamphlet, 2326–7.81

Criminal sentences for Federal offenses, guidelines by offense and circumstances, series, 17668–1

Data collection using tax and other govt admin records, methodological and disclosure issues, 1988-89 annual conf papers, 8304–17

Foreign countries human rights conditions in 170 countries, 1990, annual rpt, 21384–3

Info security plans for Fed Govt computer systems with sensitive unclassified data, by characteristics of info and system, and agency, 1989, 2218–85

Right of privacy

Labor laws enacted, by State, 1990, annual article, 6722–1.209

Survey of Income and Program Participation, data collection, methodology, and use, 1990 annual conf papers, 2624–1

Surveys and other data collection activities of Fed Govt, and quality and privacy issues, 1990 conf, 106–4.14

see also Electronic surveillance

Right to counsel

see also Legal aid

Riley, Margaret

"Private Foundation Returns, 1986 and 1987", 8302–2.210

Ring, Emily

"Individual Income Tax Returns, Preliminary Data, 1989", 8302–2.209

Rio Grande River

- Water supply and quality in streams and lakes, and groundwater levels in wells, by drainage basin, 1988, annual State rpt series, 5666–16
- Water supply and quality in streams and lakes, and groundwater levels in wells, by drainage basin, 1989, annual State rpt series, 5666–12
- Water supply and quality in streams and lakes, and groundwater levels in wells, by drainage basin, 1990, annual State rpt series, 5666–10
- Water supply in US and southern Canada, streamflow, surface and groundwater conditions, and reservoir levels, by location, monthly rpt, 5662–3

Riots and disorders

- Foreign countries disasters, casualties, damage, and aid by US and others, FY90 and trends from FY64, annual rpt, 9914–12
- Mgmt of disasters and natl security threats, with data by major event and State, 1991 annual rpt, 9434–6
- Minority group discrimination disputes investigation and mediation activities of Community Relations Service, FY90, annual rpt, 6004–9
- Police response to disturbances, officers assaulted and killed, by circumstances, 1990, annual rpt, 6224–3
- Terrorism (intl) incidents, casualties, and attacks on US targets, by attack type and country, 1990, annual rpt, 7004–22
- US attorneys civil and criminal cases by type and disposition, and collections, by Federal district, FY90, annual rpt, 6004–2.1

Ritchken, Peter

"On Flexibility, Capital Structure, and Investment Decisions for the Insured Bank", 9377–9.119

Rivers and waterways

- Acid rain and air pollution environmental impacts, and methods of neutralizing acidified water bodies, summary research rpt series, 5506–5
- Acid rain effects on Maine streams water quality, acidity, and fish, 1986-87, 9208–130
- Army Corps of Engineers water resources dev projects, characteristics, and costs, 1950s-89, biennial State rpt series, 3756–1
- Army Corps of Engineers water resources dev projects, characteristics, and costs, 1950s-91, biennial State rpt series, 3756–2

Beaver pond area rodent and shrew population and diversity compared to riparian habitat, 1988-89 study, 1208–377

- Coast Guard search and rescue missions, and lives and property lost and saved, by district and assisting unit, FY90, annual rpt, 7404–2
- Colorado water supply, streamflow, precipitation, and reservoir storage, 1991 water year, annual rpt, 1264–13
- Environmental conditions, fish, wildlife, use, and mgmt, for individual coastal and riparian ecosystems, series, 5506–9
- *Environmental Quality*, status of problems, protection programs, research, and intl issues, 1991 annual rpt, 484–1
- Fish catch, trade, use, and fishery operations, with selected foreign data, by species, 1980s-90, annual rpt, 2164–1
- Fish Hatchery Natl System activities and deliveries, by species, hatchery, and jurisdiction of waters stocked, FY90, annual rpt, 5504–10
- Fish kills in coastal areas related to pollution and natural causes, by land use, State, and county, 1980s, 2178–32
- Fishery research of State fish and wildlife agencies, federally funded projects and costs by species and State, 1990, annual listing, 5504–23
- Gazetteer of US places, mountains, bodies of water, and other political and physical features, 1990 rpt, 5668–117
- Hydroelectric power plants licensed by FERC, characteristics and location, as of Oct 1991, annual listing, 3084–11
- Landfills distance from wetlands and water habitats, for 11 States, 1990 rpt, 9188–115
- Natl forests and other land under Forest Service mgmt, acreage by forest and location, 1990, annual rpt, 1204–2
- Natl park system visits and overnight stays, by park and State, monthly rpt, 5542–4
- Natl park system visits and overnight stays, by park and State, 1990, annual rpt, 5544–12
- Natl parks and other land under Natl Park Service mgmt, acreage by site, ownership, and region, FY91, semiannual rpt, 5542–1
- Natl transportation system planning, use, condition, accidents, and needs, by mode of transport, 1940s-90 and projected to 2020, 7308–202
- Nevada and eastern California water supply, streamflow, precipitation, and reservoir storage, 1991 water year, annual rpt, 1264–8
- Northeastern US water supply, precipitation and stream runoff by station, monthly rpt, 2182–3
- Oregon water supply, streamflow by station and reservoir storage, 1991, annual rpt, 1264–9
- Pollution (water) fish kills, by pollution source, month, location, and State, 1977-87, last issue of annual rpt, 9204–3
- Public lands acreage, grants, use, revenues, and allocations, by State, FY90, annual rpt, 5724–1.2
- Public lands recreation facilities and use, and Land Mgmt Bur mgmt activities, funding, and plans, State rpt series, 5726–5

Index by Subjects and Names

- Soil and plant characteristics in wetlands and riparian areas, series, 5506–10
- *Statistical Abstract of US*, 1991 annual data compilation, 2324–1.6
- Trout (brown) population, habitat quality, and streamflow, for Douglas Creek, Wyo, 1970s-89, 5508–112
- Washington State marine sanctuaries proposal, environmental and economic impacts, with background data, 1984-89, 2178–30
- Water quality, chemistry, hydrology, and other characteristics, local area studies, series, 5666–27
- Water supply and quality in streams and lakes, and groundwater levels in wells, by drainage basin, 1988, annual State rpt series, 5666–16
- Water supply and quality in streams and lakes, and groundwater levels in wells, by drainage basin, 1989, annual State rpt series, 5666–12
- Water supply and quality in streams and lakes, and groundwater levels in wells, by drainage basin, 1990, annual State rpt series, 5666–10
- Water supply, hydrologic events, and end use, by State, 1988-89, annual rpt, 5664–12
- Water supply in US and southern Canada, streamflow, surface and groundwater conditions, and reservoir levels, by location, monthly rpt, 5662–3
- Western US water supply, and snow survey results, monthly State rpt series, 1266–2
- Western US water supply, storage by reservoir and State, and streamflow conditions, as of Oct 1991, annual rpt, 1264–4
- Western US water supply, streamflow and reservoir storage forecasts by stream and station, Jan-May monthly rpt, 1262–1
- Wetlands (riparian) acreage, and Bur of Land Mgmt activities, mgmt plans, and scientific staff, State rpt series, 5726–8
- Wetlands acreage, resources, soil and water properties, and conservation efforts, by wetland type, State rpt series, 5506–11
- Wildlife and plant research results, habitat study series, 5506–13
- Wildlife mgmt activities and funding, acreage, staff, and plans of Bur of Land Mgmt, habitat study series, 5726–6

see also Arkansas River

see also Bridges and tunnels

see also Canals

see also Chesapeake Bay

see also Colorado River

see also Columbia River

see also Dams

see also Delaware River

see also Dredging

see also Estuaries

see also Floods

see also Great Lakes

see also Harbors and ports

see also Hudson River

see also Illinois River

see also James River

see also Lakes and lakeshores

see also Mississippi River

see also Missouri River

see also New York Bight

see also Ohio River

see also Potomac River
see also Puget Sound
see also Raritan Bay
see also Red River
see also Rio Grande River
see also San Francisco Bay
see also Snake River
see also Souris-Red-Rainy Rivers
see also St. Lawrence River
see also Susquehanna River
see also Tennessee River
see also Water resources development
see also Willamette River

Riverside, Calif.

CPI by component for US city average, and by region, population size, and for 15 metro areas, monthly rpt, 6762–1

CPI by component for US city average, and by region, population size, and for 27 metro areas, monthly rpt, 6762–2

Housing starts and completions authorized by building permits in 40 MSAs, quarterly rpt, 2382–9

Wages by occupation, for office and plant workers, 1991 survey, periodic MSA rpt, 6785–12.6

see also under By City and By SMSA or MSA in the "Index by Categories"

Rizzo, John A.

"Financing Constraints and Investment: New Evidence from the U.S. Hospital Industry", 9387–8.243

Roads

see Highways, streets, and roads

Roanoke, Va.

see also under By SMSA or MSA in the "Index by Categories"

Robbery and theft

Arrest rates, by offense, sex, age, and race, 1965-89, annual rpt, 6224–7

Arrests, prosecutions, convictions, and sentencing, for felony offenders, by offender characteristics and offense, 1988, 6066–25.33; 6066–25.39

Assaults and deaths of law enforcement officers, by circumstances, agency, victim and offender characteristics, and location, 1990, annual rpt, 6224–3

Cocaine abuse, user characteristics, and related crime and violence, 1988 conf, 4498–74

Court civil and criminal caseloads for Federal district, appeals, and bankruptcy courts, by type of suit and offense, circuit, and district, 1990, annual rpt, 18204–11

Court civil and criminal caseloads for Federal district, appeals, and special courts, 1990, annual rpt, 18204–8

Court civil and criminal caseloads for Federal district courts, 1991, annual rpt, 18204–2.1

Court criminal case processing in Federal district courts, and dispositions, by offense, district, and offender characteristics, 1986, annual rpt, 6064–29

Court criminal case processing in Federal district courts, and dispositions, by offense, 1980-89, annual rpt, 6064–31

Court criminal cases in Federal district courts, by offense, disposition, and district, 1980-90, last issue of annual rpt, 18204–1

Crime, criminal justice admin and enforcement, and public opinion, data compilation, 1991 annual rpt, 6064–6

Crime Index by population size and region, and offenses by large city, Jan-June 1991, semiannual rpt, 6222–1

Crimes, arrests by offender characteristics, and rates, by offense, and law enforcement employees, by population size and jurisdiction, 1990, annual rpt, 6224–2

Drug abuse history of jail population, by offense, conviction status, criminal and family history, and selected other characteristics, 1989, 6066–19.63

Drug abuse relation to violent and criminal behavior, with data on street gang activity and selected population groups, 1989 conf, 4498–70

Drug test results at arrest, by drug type, offense, and sex, for selected urban areas, quarterly rpt, 6062–3

Homicides, by circumstance, victim and offender relationship, and type of weapon, 1990, annual rpt, 6224–2.1

Jail population, by criminal, correctional, drug use, and family history, and selected other characteristics, 1989, 6066–19.62

Jail population, by sociodemographic characteristics, criminal and drug use history, whether convicted, offense, and sentencing, 1989, annual rpt, 6064–26.3

Juvenile courts delinquency cases, by offense, referral source, disposition, age, sex, race, State, and county, 1988, annual rpt, 6064–12

Juvenile courts property offenses cases, by disposition and offender age, sex, and race, 1985-86, 6066–27.5

Minority group health condition, services use, costs, and indicators of services need, 1950s-88, 4118–55

Postal Service inspection activities, 2nd half FY91, semiannual rpt, 9862–2

Pretrial processing, detention, and release, for Federal offenders, by defendant characteristics and district, 1988, hearing, 25528–114

Prison and parole admissions and releases, sentence length, and time served, by offense and offender characteristics, 1985, annual rpt, 6064–33

Probation and split sentences by State courts for felony offenses, sentence lengths, case processing time, and felon characteristics, by offense, 1986, 6068–242

Sentences for Federal crimes, guidelines use and results by offense and district, and Sentencing Commission activities, 1990, annual rpt, 17664–1

Sentences for Federal offenses, guidelines by offense and circumstances, series, 17668–1

State and Metro Area Data Book, 1991 data compilation, 2328–54

Statistical Abstract of US, 1991 annual data compilation, 2324–1.5

Teenagers crime victimization, by victim and offender characteristics, circumstances, and offense, 1985-88 surveys, 6066–3.43

US attorneys civil and criminal cases by type and disposition, and collections, by Federal district, FY90, annual rpt, 6004–2.1

Victimization rates, by victim and offender characteristics, circumstances, and offense, survey rpt series, 6066–3

Victimizations by region and victim characteristics, and rpts to police, by offense, 1973-90, annual rpt, 6066–25.35; 6066–25.41

Victimizations of households, by offense, household characteristics, and location, 1975-90, annual rpt, 6066–25.40

Violent crime victimizations, circumstances, victim characteristics, arrest, recidivism, sentences, and prisoners, 1980s, 6068–148

Wiretaps authorized, costs, arrests, trials, and convictions, by offense and jurisdiction, 1990, annual rpt, 18204–7

Women prisoners in State instns, by offense, drug use history, whether abused, and other characteristics, 1986, 6066–19.61

Women's rape and other violent crime victimization, by relation to offender, circumstances, and victim characteristics, 1973-87, 6068–243

see also Federal Inspectors General reports
see also Motor vehicle theft
see also Security devices
see also Shoplifting

Roberds, William

"Monetary Aggregates as Monetary Targets: A Statistical Investigation", 9371–10.53

Roberts, Donna

"Government Intervention in Latin American Agriculture, 1982-87", 1528–324

Roberts, William S.

"Availability of Land for Mineral Exploration and Development in Southeastern Alaska, 1984", 5608–152.5

Robertson, Frederick N.

"Geochemistry of Ground Water in Alluvial Basins of Arizona and Adjacent Parts of Nevada, New Mexico, and California. Regional Aquifer-System Analysis", 5666–25.13

Robinson, Kenneth J.

"Deposit Insurance Reform in the Post-FIRREA Environment: Lessons from the Texas Deposit Market", 9379–14.11

"Stock Returns and Inflation: Further Tests of the Role of the Central Bank", 9379–14.12

Robotics

see Automation
see Industrial robots

Rochester Area Hospitals Corp.

"Hospital Experimental Payments Program: 1980-87", 4658–48

Rochester, Minn.

see also under By SMSA or MSA in the "Index by Categories"

Rochester, N.H.

see also under By SMSA or MSA in the "Index by Categories"

Rochester, N.Y.

Hospital cost control through revenue and reimbursement caps, demonstration project results with background data, 1980s, 4658–48

Nursing home and other long term care services under Medicare hospital use reduction demonstration, results for Rochester, NY, 1980s, 4658–43

see also under By City and By SMSA or MSA in the "Index by Categories"

Rock, Donald A.

Rock, Donald A.

"Psychometric Report for the NELS:88 Base Year Test Battery. National Education Longitudinal Study of 1988", 4826–9.9

"Tested Achievement: Eighth Grade Class. National Education Longitudinal Study of 1988", 4826–9.8

Rock Hill, S.C.

Housing starts and completions authorized by building permits in 40 MSAs, quarterly rpt, 2382–9

Wages by occupation, and benefits for office and plant workers, 1991 survey, periodic MSA rpt, 6785–12.7

see also under By SMSA or MSA in the "Index by Categories"

Rock Island, Ill.

Housing vacancy rates for single and multifamily units and mobile homes, by city and ZIP code, 1990, annual MSA rpt, 9304–18.4

Wages by occupation, for office and plant workers, 1991 survey, periodic MSA rpt, 6785–12.1

see also under By SMSA or MSA in the "Index by Categories"

Rockets

see Missiles and rockets

Rockford, Ill.

see also under By City and By SMSA or MSA in the "Index by Categories"

Rocky Mountain National Park

Wetlands plant, soil, and water characteristics, for Big Meadows area in Rocky Mountain Natl Park, 1987-88, 5508–113

Rodano, Edith M.

"Technical Assistance and Safety Programs: FY90 Project Directory", 7884–1

Rodgers, Jack

"Effects of Being Uninsured on Health Care Service Use: Estimates from the Survey of Income and Program Participation", 2626–10.120

"Selected Options for Expanding Health Insurance Coverage", 26306–6.157

Rodrigues, Anthony P.

"Financial Liberalization and Monetary Control in Japan", 9385–1.213

"Financial Reform and Monetary Control in Japan", 9385–8.116

"Tests of Mean-Variance Efficiency of International Equity Markets", 9381–10.116

Rogers, Carolyn C.

"Economic Well-Being of Nonmetro Children", 1598–270

Rogowski, Jeannette R.

"Comparison of Alternative Weight Recalibration Methods for Diagnosis-Related Groups", 4652–1.227

Romania

Agricultural exports of high-value commodities, indexes and sales by commodity, world area, and country, 1960s-86, 1528–323

Agricultural exports of US, impacts of foreign agricultural and trade policy, with data by commodity and country, 1989, annual rpt, 1924–8

Agricultural production, trade, and policies in foreign countries, summary data by country, 1989-90, annual factbook, 1924–12

Agricultural trade of US, by detailed commodity and country, 1989, annual rpt, 1524–8

Agricultural trade of US, by detailed commodity and country, 1990, semiannual rpt, 1522–4

Debt to foreign lenders by component, trade, balances, and other economic indicators, by Eastern Europe country, 1985-89, hearing, 21248–148

Economic and military aid and loans from US and intl agencies, by program and country, FY46-90, annual rpt, 9914–5

Economic conditions in USSR, Eastern Europe, OECD, and selected other countries, 1960s-90, annual rpt, 9114–4

Economic conditions, policy, and trade practices, by country, 1988-90, annual rpt, 21384–5

Economic, social, political, and geographic summary data, by country, 1991, annual factbook, 9114–2

Export licensing, monitoring, and enforcement activities, FY90, annual rpt, 2024–1

Exports and imports of US, by commodity and country, 1970-89, world area rpt, 9116–1.3

Exports and imports of US, by selected country, country group, and commodity group, 1990, annual rpt, 2044–37

Exports and imports of US, by transport mode, country, and SITC 1- to 3-digit commodity, 1990, annual rpt, 2424–12

Exports and imports of US with Communist countries, by detailed commodity and country, quarterly rpt with articles, 9882–2

Exports of US, detailed Schedule B commodities with countries of destination, 1990, annual rpt, 2424–10

Human rights conditions in 170 countries, and US economic and military aid, 1990, annual rpt, 21384–3

Market economy transition of Eastern Europe countries, economic conditions and energy balance, by country, 1985-90, 9118–13

Market economy transition of Eastern Europe countries, with trade agreements and bilateral US trade data by country, late 1980s-90, annual rpt, 444–2

Nuclear power plant capacity and operating status, by plant and communist and regulated market country, as of Dec 1990, annual rpt, 3164–57.2

Pipes and tubes (welded nonalloy steel) from 6 countries, injury to US industry from foreign subsidized and less than fair value imports, investigation with background financial and operating data, 1991 rpt, 9886–19.81

Refugee resettlement programs and funding, arrivals by country of origin, and indicators of adjustment, by State, FY90, annual rpt, 4694–5

Steel imports of US under voluntary restraint agreement, by product, customs district, and country, with US industry operating data, quarterly rpt, 9882–13

UN voting record and share of votes in agreement with US, by issue, country, and world area, 1990, annual rpt, 7004–18

see also under By Foreign Country in the "Index by Categories"

Rome, N.Y.

see also under By SMSA or MSA in the "Index by Categories"

Romig, Candace L.

"Welfare Reform: How Well Is It Working?", 10042–1.201

Roningen, Vernon

"Overview of the Static World Policy Simulation (SWOPSIM) Modeling Framework", 1528–315

Roodman, Stephanie

"School Enrollment—Social and Economic Characteristics of Students: October 1989", 2546–1.453

Rooming and boarding houses

Board and care homes regulation and rules enforcement by States, 1988, 4008–112

Census of Service Industries, 1987: hotels and other lodging places, receipts, payroll, employment, ownership, and rooms, by State and MSA, subject rpt, 2393–3

County Business Patterns, 1988: employment, establishments, and payroll, by SIC 2- to 4-digit industry and county, annual State rpt series, 2326–6

County Business Patterns, 1989: employment, establishments, and payroll, by SIC 2- to 4-digit industry and county, annual State rpt series, 2326–8

Housing and households detailed characteristics, and unit and neighborhood quality, by location, 1989, biennial rpt, 2485–12

Service industries census, 1987: establishments, receipts by source, payroll, and employment, by SIC 2- to 4-digit kind of business, State, and MSA, 2393–4

Supplemental Security Income and Medicaid eligibility and payment provisions, and beneficiaries living arrangements, by State, 1991, annual rpt, 4704–13

Tax (income) returns of sole proprietorships, income statement items, by industry group, 1989, annual article, 8302–2.214

Roop, Joseph M.

"Energy Conservation Trends: Understanding the Factors That Affect Conservation Gains in the U.S. Economy", 3308–93

Rose, Andrew K.

"Expected and Predicted Realignments: The FF/DM Exchange Rate During the EMS", 9366–7.249

"How Pervasive Is the Product Cycle? The Empirical Dynamics of American and Japanese Trade Flows", 9366–7.264

Roseburg, Oreg.

Wages by occupation, for office and plant workers, 1991 survey, periodic MSA rpt, 6785–3.6

Rosen, Stacey

"Dairy Imports in Sub-Saharan Africa and the Welfare Implications of Import Policies", 1528–321

"Food Aid in the Post-Uruguay Round", 1524–4.2

Rosenbaum, Mary S.

"Supply Shocks and Household Demand for Motor Fuel", 9371–1.204

Rosenberg, Lynn

"Hypothesis: Nonsteroidal Anti-Inflammatory Drugs Reduce the Incidence of Large-Bowel Cancer", 4472–1.205

Index by Subjects and Names

Rubber and rubber industry

Rosenblatt, Karin A.
"Breast Cancer in Men: Aspects of Familial Aggregation", 4472–1.213

Rosengren, Eric S.
"Foreign Exchange Intervention as a Signal of Monetary Policy", 9373–1.209

Rosensweig, Jeffrey A.
"Fiscal Policy and Trade Adjustment: Are the Deficits Really Twins?", 9371–10.60
"Investigating U.S. Government and Trade Deficits", 9371–1.207

Rosenthal, Stuart S.
"Econometric Analysis of Borrowing Constraints and Household Debt", 9379–12.73

Rosine, John
"Update on the Farm Economy", 9362–1.207

Ross, Murray N.
"National Service: Issues and Options", 26306–3.115

Rossiter, Louis F.
"Nationwide Evaluation of Medicaid Competition Demonstrations. Volume 6. Administrative Costs", 4658–45.6
"Nationwide Evaluation of Medicaid Competition Demonstrations. Volume 7. Rate Setting", 4658–45.7
"Payment to Health Maintenance Organizations and the Geographic Factor", 4652–1.203

Rossman, Charles E.
"Agricultural Productivity and International Food Trade: A Cross-Section Approach", 1548–372

ROTC
see Reserve Officers Training Corps

Roth, Patrice T.
"Drug Abuse Among Race/Ethnic Minorities", 4498–72

Rothberg, Paul F.
"Reauthorization of the Motor Carrier Safety Assistance Program (MCSAP): Options Intended To Improve Highway Safety", 25268–78

Roush, Sandra W.
"Availability and Use of Hepatitis B Vaccine in Laboratory and Nursing Schools in the U.S.", 4042–3.244

Row, Clark
"Carbon Cycle Impacts of Future Forest Products Utilization and Recycling Trends", 1004–16.1

Rowland, Diane
"Fewer Resources, Greater Burdens: Medical Care Coverage for Low-Income Elderly People", 23898–5

Rowley, Thomas D.
"Rapid Rise in State Per Capita Income Inequality in the 1980's: Sources and Prospects", 1548–379
"State-Level Examination of Metro/Nonmetro Per Capita Income Inequality, 1979-87", 1548–380

Royalties
Budget of US, authoritative financial statements with appropriations, outlays, and receipts, by category and agency, FY90, annual rpt, 8104–2.1
Coal leasing activity on Federal land, acreage, production, and reserves, by coal region and State, FY90, annual rpt, 5724–10
Copyright royalty fees for cable and satellite TV and jukeboxes, and funds available for distribution, 1989-90, annual rpt, 26404–2

Energy-related inventions supported by DOE, sales, jobs created, and inventor financing, 1980-88, 3308–91
Exports and imports of services, direct and among multinatl firms affiliates, by industry and world area, 1986-90, article, 2702–1.223
Fed Govt R&D labs technology transfer cooperative agreements, patents, royalties, and incentive payments to employees, by agency, FY89, GAO rpt, 26131–85
Foreign countries royalty payments and receipts for US, 1960-88, annual rpt, 9627–35.4
Forest Service activities and finances, by region and State, FY90, annual rpt, 1204–1.1
Multinatl US firms and foreign affiliates finances and operations, by industry and world area of parent firm, 1989 benchmark survey, preliminary annual rpt, 2704–5
Natural gas interstate pipeline company detailed financial and operating data, by firm, 1989, annual rpt, 3164–38
Naval Petroleum and Oil Shale Reserves production and revenue by fuel type, sales by purchaser, and wells, by reserve, FY90, annual rpt, 3334–3
Offshore oil, gas, and minerals production, revenue, and leasing activity, for Federal OCS lands by ocean area and State, 1950s-90, annual rpt, 5734–3
Oil and gas OCS lease bidding under alternative leasing systems, activity, royalty rates, and production, by sale, lessee type, and ocean area, FY79-89, annual rpt, 5734–12
Oil, gas, and minerals production and revenue on Federal and Indian land, by State, 1990 and trends from 1920, annual rpt, 5734–2
Oil, gas, and minerals production, revenue, and leasing activity on Federal and Indian land, by State, 1980s and trends from 1920, 5738–21
Performing arts commercial and nonprofit organizations, receipts by source, SIC 2- to 4-digit kind of business, and State, 1987 Census of Service Industries, 2393–4.11
Public lands acreage and use, and Land Mgmt Bur activities and finances, annual State rpt series, 5724–11
Tax (income) returns filed by type of filer, selected income items, quarterly rpt, 8302–2.1
Tax (income) returns of corporations, income and tax items by asset size and detailed industry, 1987, annual rpt, 8304–4
Tax (income) returns of corporations, income and tax items by asset size and detailed industry, 1988, annual rpt, 8304–21
Tax (income) returns of partnerships, income statement and balance sheet items, by industry group, 1989, annual article, 8302–2.216; 8304–18

Rubber and rubber industry
Auto weight, by component material, 1975-90, article, 5602–4.202
Business statistics, detailed data for major industries and economic indicators, *Survey of Current Business*, monthly rpt, 2702–1.20

Capital expenditures for plant and equipment, by major industry group, quarterly rpt, 2502–2
Collective bargaining agreements expiring during year, and workers covered, by firm, union, industry group, and State, 1991, annual rpt, 6784–9
County Business Patterns, 1988: employment, establishments, and payroll, by SIC 2- to 4-digit industry and county, annual State rpt series, 2326–6
County Business Patterns, 1989: employment, establishments, and payroll, by SIC 2- to 4-digit industry and county, annual State rpt series, 2326–8
Employment, earnings, and hours, by SIC 1- to 4-digit industry, monthly and annual averages, selected years 1909-90, annual rpt, 6744–4
Employment in manufacturing, by detailed occupation and SIC 2-digit industry, 1989 survey, triennial rpt, 6748–52
Employment, unemployment, and labor force characteristics, by region and census div, 1990, annual rpt, 6744–7.1
Enterprise Statistics, 1987: finances and operations for companies, by size, level of diversification, form of organization, and industry group, 2329–8
Exports and imports (agricultural) of US, by commodity and country, bimonthly rpt, 1522–1
Exports and imports (agricultural) of US, by detailed commodity and country, 1989, annual rpt, 1524–8
Exports and imports (agricultural) of US, by detailed commodity and country, 1990, semiannual rpt, 1522–4
Exports and imports between US and outlying areas, by detailed commodity and mode of transport, 1990, annual rpt, 2424–11
Exports and imports of US, by country and detailed commodity, monthly rpt, 2422–12
Exports and imports of US, by Harmonized System 6-digit commodity and country, 1990, annual rpt, 2424–13
Exports and imports of US, by transport mode, country, and SITC 1- to 3-digit commodity, 1990, annual rpt, 2424–12
Exports of US, detailed commodities by country, monthly CD-ROM, 2422–13
Exports of US, detailed Schedule B commodities with countries of destination, 1990, annual rpt, 2424–10
Footwear production, employment, use, prices, and US trade by country, quarterly rpt, 9882–6
Foreign countries agricultural production, prices, and trade, by country, 1980-90 and forecast 1991, annual world area rpt series, 1524–4
Imports, exports, and employment impacts, by SIC 2- to 4-digit industry and commodity, quarterly rpt, 2322–2
Imports of US, detailed commodities by country, monthly CD-ROM, 2422–14
Input-output structure of US economy, detailed interindustry transactions for 84 industries, and components of final demand, 1986, annual article, 2702–1.206
Input-output structure of US economy, detailed interindustry transactions for 85 industries, 1982 benchmark data, 2702–1.213

Rubber and rubber industry

Labor productivity, indexes of output, hours, and employment by SIC 2- to 4-digit industry, 1967-89, annual rpt, 6824–1.3

Manufacturing annual survey, 1989: finances and operations, by SIC 2- to 4-digit industry, series, 2506–15

Manufacturing census, 1987: employment and shipments under Fed Govt contracts, by SIC 4-digit industry, 2497–7

Manufacturing census, 1987: finances and operations, by SIC 2- to 4-digit industry, State, and MSA, with trends from 1849, 2497–1

Manufacturing census, 1987: finances and operations, by type of organization and SIC 2- to 4-digit industry, subject rpt, 2497–5

Manufacturing corporations financial statements, by selected SIC 2- to 3-digit industry, quarterly rpt, 2502–1

Manufacturing finances and operations, by SIC 2- to 4-digit industry, forecast 1991, annual rpt, 2044–28

Manufacturing production, shipments, inventories, orders, and pollution control costs, periodic Current Industrial Rpt series, 2506–3

Multinatl US firms and foreign affiliates finances and operations, by industry and world area of parent firm, 1989 benchmark survey, preliminary annual rpt, 2704–5

Occupational injury and illness rates, by SIC 2- to 4-digit industry, 1988-89, annual rpt, 6844–7

Occupational injury and illness rates, by SIC 2- to 4-digit industry, 1989, annual rpt, 6844–1

OECD trade, total and for 4 major countries, and US trade by country, by commodity, 1970-89, world area rpt series, 9116–1

Pollution abatement capital and operating costs, by SIC 2-digit industry, 1989, advance annual Current Industrial Rpt, 2506–3.6

Price indexes (producer), by stage of processing and detailed commodity, monthly rpt, 6762–6

Price indexes (producer), by stage of processing and detailed commodity, monthly 1990, annual rpt, 6764–2

Puerto Rico and other US possessions corporations income tax returns, income and tax items, and employment, by selected industry, 1987, article, 8302–2.213

Shipments of rubber mechanical goods, by product, 1990, annual Current Industrial Rpt, 2506–8.17

Shoe production, shipments, trade, and use, by product, 1990, annual Current Industrial Rpt, 2506–6.8

Soviet Union, Eastern Europe, OECD, and selected other countries agricultural production, by commodity, 1960s-90, annual rpt, 9114–4.5

Soviet Union, Eastern Europe, OECD, and selected other countries consumer and producer goods and services production and sales, 1960s-90, annual rpt, 9114–4.7

Statistical Abstract of US, 1991 annual data compilation, 2324–1.27

Stockpiling of strategic material by Fed Govt, activity, and inventory by commodity, as of Mar 1991, semiannual rpt, 3542–22

Stockpiling of strategic material, inventories and needs, by commodity, as of Jan 1991, annual rpt, 3544–37

Tariff Schedule of US, classifications and rates of duty by detailed imported commodity, 1992 base edition, 9886–13

Tax (income) returns of corporations, income and tax items by asset size and detailed industry, 1987, annual rpt, 8304–4

Thread (rubber) from Malaysia, injury to US industry from foreign subsidized and less than fair value imports, investigation with background financial and operating data, 1991 rpt, 9886–19.78

see also Tires and tire industry

see also under By Commodity in the "Index by Categories"

see also under By Industry in the "Index by Categories"

Rubella

see Infective and parasitic diseases

Rubidium

see Metals and metal industries

Rubin, Jeffrey I.

"Health Insurance Coverage Among Disabled Medicare Enrollees", 4652–1.243

Rudd, Joel

"Survey of Newspaper Coverage of HCFA Hospital Mortality Data", 4042–3.242

Ruddy, Barbara C.

"Summary of Selected Characteristics of Large Reservoirs in the U.S. and Puerto Rico, 1988", 5668–120

Rudes, Blair A.

"Handbook of Effective Migrant Education Practices", 4808–22

Rugs

see Carpets and rugs

Ruhl, James F.

"Water Resources of the Fond du Lac Indian Reservation, East-Central Minnesota", 5666–28.9

Ruhsam, Cynthia M.

"Report of Water Masses Receiving Wastes from Ocean Dumping at the 106-Mile Dumpsite, Jan. 1-Dec. 31, 1990", 2164–20

Runaways

see Missing persons and runaways

Runkle, David E.

"Bad News from a Forecasting Model of the U.S. Economy", 9383–6.201

Runner, Diana

"Changes in Unemployment Insurance Legislation During 1990", 6722–1.211

Ruppel, Fred J.

"Grain Shipper/Railroad Contract Disclosure: An Experimental Analysis", 1502–3.201

Rural areas

AID dev projects, special study series, 9916–3

Airline deregulation in 1978, and regional and major carriers agreements, impacts on service to small communities, late 1980s, 7308–199.10

Alaska rural areas population characteristics, and energy resources dev effects, series, 5736–5

Banks finances and operations, by metro-nonmetro location, 1987-89, annual rpt, 1544–29

Births, fertility rates, and childless women, by selected characteristics, 1990, annual Current Population Rpt, 2546–1.455

Bus connector service between rural areas and Greyhound intercity routes, finances and operations by system, 1987-90, 7888–79

Children in poverty by selected family characteristics, for rural areas compared to urban areas, 1987-88, 1598–270

Crime Index by population size and region, and offenses by large city, Jan-June 1991, semiannual rpt, 6222–1

Crime victimization of households, by offense, household characteristics, and location, 1975-90, annual rpt, 6066–25.40

Crimes, arrests by offender characteristics, and rates, by offense, and law enforcement employees, by population size and jurisdiction, 1990, annual rpt, 6224–2

Drug and alcohol abuse in rural areas, related crime, and treatment, with comparisons to nonrural areas, by substance and State, 1988-90, GAO rpt, 26131–79

Economic and social conditions, dev, and problems in rural areas, periodic journal, 1502–7

Economic and social indicators used to determine Federal aid need for rural areas, late 1960s-86, 1598–265

Economic conditions and dev in rural areas, quarterly journal, 1502–8

Educational enrollment, by grade, instn type and control, and student characteristics, 1989 and trends from 1947, annual Current Population Rpt, 2546–1.453

Food spending, by item, household composition, income, age, race, and region, 1980-88, Consumer Expenditure Survey biennial rpt, 1544–30

Health care (primary) research, methodology and findings, 1991 annual conf, 4184–4

Hispanic Americans social and economic characteristics, by detailed origin, 1991, Current Population Rpt, 2546–1.448; 2546–1.451

Home mortgages FHA-insured, financial, property, and mortgagor characteristics, by metro area, 1990, annual rpt, 5144–24

Home mortgages FHA-insured, financial, property, and mortgagor characteristics, by State, 1990, annual rpt, 5144–1

Home mortgages FHA-insured, financial, property, and mortgagor characteristics, total and by State and outlying area, 1990, annual rpt, 5144–25

Home mortgages FHA-insured, financial, property, and mortgagor characteristics, 1990, annual rpt, 5144–23

Hospital closures and rates, with financial, operating, and market characteristics, by location, late 1980s, GAO rpt, 26121–392

Hospital operations, and services spending by type and payment source, with background data and foreign comparisons, 1960s-80s and projected to 2000, 26308–98

Hospital reimbursement by Medicare under prospective payment system, effect of adjusting wage index for occupational mix, 1990 rpt, 17206–2.17

Index by Subjects and Names

Rural cooperatives

Hospital reimbursement by Medicare under prospective payment system, rural area instns financial performance and impacts of PPS policy changes, FY84-89, 17206–1.12

Hospitals in rural areas, closures related to selected factors, 1980s, GAO rpt, 26121–409

Hospitals in rural areas, financial and operating performance impacts of Medicare prospective payment reimbursement system, 1980s-87, 4658–51

Hospitals in rural areas, HCFA grants for improving financial stability, by program area, recipient, and State, FY89, 4658–58

Households and family characteristics, by location, 1990, annual Current Population Rpt, 2546–1.447

Housing and households detailed characteristics, and unit and neighborhood quality, by location, 1987, biennial rpt supplement, 2485–13

Housing and households detailed characteristics, and unit and neighborhood quality, by location, 1989, biennial rpt, 2485–12

Housing inventory change from 1973, by reason, unit and household characteristics, and location, 1983 survey, biennial rpt, 2485–14

Housing loan programs of FmHA in rural areas, and housing voucher demonstration program results, 1980s, hearing, 21248–143

Housing vacancy and occupancy rates, and vacant unit characteristics and costs, by region and metro-nonmetro location, quarterly rpt, 2482–1

Hwy Statistics, detailed data by State, 1990, annual rpt, 7554–1

Hwy traffic volume on rural roads and city streets, monthly rpt, 7552–8

Income (household) and poverty status under alternative income definitions, by recipient characteristics, 1990, annual Current Population Rpt, 2546–6.69

Income (personal) per capita disparity between metro and nonmetro areas, and causal factors, by State, 1979-88, 1548–380

Job Training Partnership Act funding and performance indicators in service delivery areas, by urban-rural location, 1987-88, 1598–266

Job Training Partnership Act participation by selected characteristics and State, and outcomes, by urban-rural location, 1987-88, 1598–267

Labor force characteristics in rural areas, with comparisons to urban areas, 1987, 1598–264

Montana health care access indicators, 1989 hearing, 23898–6

Older persons in rural areas, household income sources, and poverty status, 1983-84, 1598–268

Physicians practice cost indexes and components, by State, MSA, and for rural areas, 1989 rpt, 4658–50

Poverty rate among workers in metro and nonmetro areas, relation to employment and other characteristics, 1987, 1598–274

Poverty status of population and families, by detailed characteristics, 1988-89, annual Current Population Rpt, 2546–6.67

Poverty status of population and families, by detailed characteristics, 1990, annual Current Population Rpt, 2546–6.71

Research (agricultural) funding and staffing for USDA, State agencies, and other instns, by topic, FY90, annual rpt, 1744–2

Retail trade census, 1987: finances and employment, for establishments with and without payroll, by SIC 2- to 4-digit kind of business, State, and MSA, 2401–1

South Dakota poverty relief and medical aid programs of counties, spending by type, MSA, and county, 1989, hearing, 25368–176

State and Metro Area Data Book, 1991 data compilation, 2328–54

Statistical Abstract of US, 1991 annual data compilation, 2324–1

Telephone firms borrowing under Rural Telephone Program, and financial and operating data, by State, 1990, annual rpt, 1244–2

Wastewater treatment facilities in small communities, construction and repair needs to meet Clean Water Act standards, by State and region, 1988 and 2008, 1588–155

see also Farm income

see also Farm population

see also Farms and farmland

see also Federal aid to rural areas

see also Migrant workers

see also Rural electrification

see also under Agriculture and terms beginning with Agricultural

see also under By Urban-Rural and Metro-Nonmetro in the "Index by Categories"

Rural cooperatives

Agricultural cooperatives finances, aggregate for top 100 assns by commodity group, 1989, annual rpt, 1124–3

Agricultural cooperatives, finances, and membership, by type of service, commodity, and State, 1989, annual rpt, 1124–1

Agricultural cooperatives finances, operations, activities, and current issues, monthly journal, 1122–1

Agricultural cooperatives, finances, operations, activities, and membership, commodity rpt series, 1126–1

Agricultural cooperatives investments and net worth, 1990, annual rpt, 1544–16.2

Agricultural cooperatives, membership, farms, and income, historical review, 1913-81, 1128–66

Agricultural research funding and staffing for USDA, State agencies, and other instns, by topic, FY90, annual rpt, 1744–2

Agricultural Statistics, 1990, annual rpt, 1004–1

Dairy cooperatives exemption from antitrust laws, impacts on industry structure and pricing, with background data, 1930s-80s, GAO rpt, 26113–499

Economic Indicators of the Farm Sector, income, expenses, receipts by commodity, assets, and liabilities, 1990 and trends from 1945, annual rpt, 1544–16

Electric cooperatives financed by REA, finances and operations, 1987-89, annual rpt, 3164–24.3

Electric power distribution loans from REA, and borrower operating and financial data, by firm and State, 1990, annual rpt, 1244–1

Electric power facilities loans of REA, by State, FY90, annual rpt, 1244–7

Electric power plants and capacity, by fuel used, owner, location, and operating status, 1990 and for units planned 1991-2000, annual listing, 3164–36

Electric power plants financed by REA, with location, capacity, and owner, as of Jan 1991, annual listing, 1244–6

Electric power purchases from TVA and resales, with use, average bills, and rates by customer class, by distributor, 1990, annual tables, 9804–14

Electric power purchases of municipal and cooperative distributors, and prices and use by distributor and consumer sector, for TVA, monthly rpt, 9802–1

Electric power sales and revenue, by end-use sector, consumption level, and utility, 1989, annual rpt, 3164–91

Electric power sales by customer, activities by plant, and financial statements of Western Area Power Admin, FY90, annual rpt, 3254–1

Electric power sales by customer, for Southwestern Fed Power System, FY90, annual rpt, 3244–1

Electric power sales by customer, plants, and capacity of Southeastern Power Admin, FY90, annual rpt, 3234–1

Electric power sales of Bonneville Power Admin, by customer, FY90, annual rpt, 3224–1

Electric power sales, revenue, and rates of Bonneville Power Admin, by customer and customer type, 1990, semiannual rpt, 3222–1

Electric power wholesale purchases of REA borrowers, by borrower, supplier, and State, 1940-89, annual rpt, 1244–5

Electric power wholesale trade, by utility, type of ownership, and region, 1988, biennial rpt, 3164–92

Farm sector balance sheet, and receipts by detailed commodity, by State, 1985-89, annual rpt, 1544–18

Grain cooperatives finances and operations, by grain handled and selected characteristics, 1983-85, series, 1128–44

Milk order and cooperative prices, by selected area, 1990, annual rpt, 1317–1.5

Pest control integrated mgmt programs for vegetables, acreage, costs, savings, and funding sources and recipients, by State, 1980s, 1568–298

Statistical Abstract of US, 1991 annual data compilation, 2324–1.17; 2324–1.23

Tax returns filed, by type of tax and IRS district, 1989 and projected 1990-97, annual rpt, 8304–24

Tax returns filed, by type of tax and IRS region and service center, projected 1990-97 and trends from 1978, annual rpt, 8304–9

Telephone firms borrowing under Rural Telephone Program, and financial and operating data, by State, 1990, annual rpt, 1244–2

Rural cooperatives

Telephone firms borrowing under Rural Telephone Program, loan activity by State, FY90, annual tables, 1244–8

Tobacco stocks held by grower cooperatives, by type, quarterly rpt, 1319–3

Rural electrification

Agricultural Statistics, 1990, annual rpt, 1004–1

Bonneville Power Admin mgmt of Fed Columbia River Power System, finances, operations, and sales by customer, FY90, annual rpt, 3224–1

Capacity and plants, by fuel used, owner, location, and operating status, 1990, and for units planned 1991-2000, annual listing, 3164–36

Cooperatives financed by REA, finances and operations, 1987-89, annual rpt, 3164–24.3

Cooperatives, membership, and revenue for Rural Electric Cooperatives, by State, 1989, annual rpt, 1124–1

Loans of REA, and borrower operating and financial data, by distribution firm and State, 1990, annual rpt, 1244–1

Loans of REA, by State, FY90, annual rpt, 1244–7

Plants financed by REA, with location, capacity, and owner, as of Jan 1991, annual listing, 1244–6

Purchases (wholesale) of REA borrowers, by borrower, supplier, and State, 1940-89, annual rpt, 1244–5

Sales and revenue, by end-use sector, consumption level, and utility, 1989, annual rpt, 3164–91

Southeastern Power Admin sales by customer, plants, capacity, and Southeastern Fed Power Program financial statements, FY90, annual rpt, 3234–1

Southwestern Fed Power System financial statements, sales by customer, and operations and costs by project, FY90, annual rpt, 3244–1

TVA electric power purchases and resales, with electricity use, average bills, and rates by customer class, by distributor, 1990, annual tables, 9804–14

Western Area Power Admin activities by plant, financial statements, and sales by customer, FY90, annual rpt, 3254–1

Wholesale trade of electric power, by utility, type of ownership, and region, 1988, biennial rpt, 3164–92

Rural Electrification Administration

Budget of US, obligations and authority by function, agency, and program, with summaries, analyses, and historical tables, FY92, annual rpt, 104–2

Cooperatives financed by REA, finances and operations, 1987-89, annual rpt, 3164–24.3

Loans of REA, and borrower operating and financial data, by distribution firm and State, 1990, annual rpt, 1244–1

Loans of REA, by State, FY90, annual rpt, 1244–7

Plants financed by REA, with location, capacity, and owner, as of Jan 1991, annual listing, 1244–6

Purchases (wholesale) of REA borrowers, by borrower, supplier, and State, 1940-89, annual rpt, 1244–5

see also Rural Telephone Bank

Rural Telephone Bank

Financial statements of Bank, FY89, annual rpt, 1244–4

Loans to telephone firms under Rural Telephone Program, activity by State, FY90, annual tables, 1244–8

Loans under Rural Telephone Program, and borrower operations and finances, by State, 1990, annual rpt, 1244–2

Ruser, John W.

"Workers' Compensation and the Distribution of Occupational Injuries", 6886–6.80

Rush, Mark

"Cointegration: How Short Is the Long Run?", 9381–10.119

Russell, Steven

"Inflationary Implications of Reducing Market Interest Rates via Alternative Monetary Policy Instruments", 9371–10.59

Russell, Susan H.

"Profiles of Faculty in Higher Education Institutions, 1988: 1988 National Survey of Postsecondary Faculty", 4846–4.4

Russia

see Soviet Union

Ruther, Martin

"Medicare and Medicaid Data Book, 1990", 4654–1

Rutledge, Gary L.

"Pollution Abatement and Control Expenditures, 1987-89", 2702–1.229

Ruud, Judith S.

"Underwriter Price Support and the IPO Underpricing Puzzle", 9385–8.113

Rwanda

Agricultural trade of US, by detailed commodity and country, 1989, annual rpt, 1524–8

Agricultural trade of US, by detailed commodity and country, 1990, semiannual rpt, 1522–4

AID economic aid to developing countries, obligations and disbursements by country, quarterly rpt, 9912–4

Dairy imports, consumption, and market conditions, by sub-Saharan Africa country, 1961-88, 1528–321

Economic and military aid and loans from US and intl agencies, by program and country, FY46-90, annual rpt, 9914–5

Economic and social conditions of developing countries from 1960s, and Intl Dev Cooperation Agency and AID activities and funding, FY90-92, annual rpt, 9904–4

Economic, population, and agricultural data, US and other aid sources, and AID activity, 1987 country rpt, 9916–12.23

Economic, social, political, and geographic summary data, by country, 1991, annual factbook, 9114–2

Exports and imports of US, by transport mode, country, and SITC 1- to 3-digit commodity, 1990, annual rpt, 2424–12

Exports of US, detailed Schedule B commodities with countries of destination, 1990, annual rpt, 2424–10

Human rights conditions in 170 countries, and US economic and military aid, 1990, annual rpt, 21384–3

Military aid of US, arms sales, and training programs costs and budget requests, by program, world region, and country, FY90-92, annual rpt, 7144–13

Minerals Yearbook, 1988, Vol 3: foreign country review of production, trade, and policy, by commodity, annual rpt, 5604–17.80

UN voting record and share of votes in agreement with US, by issue, country, and world area, 1990, annual rpt, 7004–18

see also under By Foreign Country in the "Index by Categories"

Ryan, Barry

"Assessment of Wastewater Treatment Facilities in Small Communities", 1588–155

Ryan, James

"Finance Outlook: Guarded Optimism", 1004–16.1

Ryan, Kevin C.

"Insect Infestation of Fire-Injured Trees in the Greater Yellowstone Area", 1208–379

Rybicki, Nancy

"Data on the Distribution and Abundance of Submersed Aquatic Vegetation in the Tidal Potomac River and Transition Zone of the Potomac Estuary, Maryland, Virginia, and the District of Columbia, 1988", 5666–27.22

Ryding, John

"Housing Finance and the Transmission Mechanism of Monetary Policy", 9385–8.74

"Rise in U.S. Corporate Leveraging in the 1980s", 9385–8.88

Rye

see Animal feed

see Grains and grain products

see Pasture and rangeland

Ryscavage, Paul

"Earnings Inequality Accelerates in the 1980's", 6722–1.201

Sabotage

Aircraft hijackings, on-board explosions, and other crime, US and foreign incidents, 1985-89, annual rpt, 7504–31

Sentences for Federal offenses, guidelines by offense and circumstances, series, 17668–1

Terrorism (intl) incidents, casualties, and attacks on US targets, by attack type and country, 1990, annual rpt, 7004–22

Terrorism (intl) incidents, casualties, and attacks on US targets, by attack type and world area, 1990, annual rpt, 7004–13

Terrorism incidents in US, related activity, and casualties, by attack type, target, group, and location, 1990, annual rpt, 6224–6

US attorneys civil and criminal cases by type and disposition, and collections, by Federal district, FY90, annual rpt, 6004–2.1

Sacramento, Calif.

Housing starts and completions authorized by building permits in 40 MSAs, quarterly rpt, 2382–9

Wages by occupation, and benefits for office and plant workers, 1991 survey, periodic MSA rpt, 6785–12.5

see also under By City and By SMSA or MSA in the "Index by Categories"

Index by Subjects and Names

Safety

see Accidents and accident prevention
see Aviation accidents and safety
see Marine accidents and safety
see Mine accidents and safety
see Motor vehicle safety devices
see Occupational health and safety
see Product safety
see Railroad accidents and safety
see State funding for public safety
see Traffic accident fatalities
see Traffic accidents and safety
see Transportation accidents and safety

Safeway Stores, Inc.

Leveraged buyouts impacts on financial performance, for 4 transactions, 1980s-90, GAO rpt, 26119–355

Saginaw, Mich.

see also under By SMSA or MSA in the "Index by Categories"

Sailors

see Merchant seamen
see Military personnel

Saint

see under terms beginning St.

Salaries

see Agricultural wages
see Earnings, general
see Earnings, local and regional
see Earnings, specific industry
see Educational employees pay
see Federal pay
see Government pay
see Minimum wage
see Payroll
see Professionals' fees
see State and local employees pay

Salassi, Michael E.

"Planting Flexibility Options for Mississippi River Delta Rice Farms", 1561–8.201
"Representative U.S. Corn Farms, 1987", 1568–304

Salem, Mass.

CPI by component for US city average, and by region, population size, and for 15 metro areas, monthly rpt, 6762–1
CPI by component for US city average, and by region, population size, and for 27 metro areas, monthly rpt, 6762–2
see also under By SMSA or MSA in the "Index by Categories"

Salem, Oreg.

see also under By City and By SMSA or MSA in the "Index by Categories"

Sales, business

see Business income and expenses, general
see Business income and expenses, specific industry
see Farm income

Sales promotion

- Airline computer reservation system operations, travel agency revenues by firm, and frequent flyer awards by carrier, 1988, 7308–199.9
- Drug (prescription) marketing practices, spending by selected firm, and physicians views, 1990 hearings, 25548–103
- Electric utilities finances and operations, detailed data for public and privately owned firms, 1989, annual rpt, 3164–11.4
- Electric utilities finances and operations, detailed data for publicly owned firms, 1989, annual rpt, 3164–24

Electric utilities privately owned, finances and operations, detailed data, 1989, annual rpt, 3164–23

- Milk order advertising and promotion finances, and producer participation, by region, 1990, annual article, 1317–4.204
- Natural gas interstate pipeline company detailed financial and operating data, by firm, 1989, annual rpt, 3164–38

see also Advertising
see also Direct marketing
see also Foreign trade promotion
see also Market research
see also Sales workers

Sales tax

- Auto, private airplane, and motorcycle operating costs by component, and Fed Govt mileage reimbursement rates, 1989, annual rpt, 9454–13
- Collections of taxes, by level of govt, type of tax, State, and selected counties, quarterly rpt, 2462–3
- Finances of govts, by level of govt, State, and for large cities and counties, annual rpt series, 2466–2
- Finances of govts, tax systems and revenue, and fiscal structure, by level of govt and State, 1991 and historical trends, annual rpt, 10044–1
- Hwy Trust Fund revenues, tax rates, and spending, FY87-91 with projections to FY95, GAO rpt, 26113–544
- Natl income and product accounts and components, *Survey of Current Business*, monthly rpt, 2702–1.24; 2702–1.25
- North Central States business and economic conditions, Fed Reserve 9th District, quarterly journal, 9383–19
- Public opinion on taxes, spending, and govt efficiency, by respondent characteristics, 1991 survey, annual rpt, 10044–2
- Retail trade sales tax as share of sales, by SIC 2- to 4-digit kind of business, 1989, annual rpt, 2413–5
- *State and Metro Area Data Book*, 1991 data compilation, 2328–54
- Transit systems finances and operations, by mode of transport, size of fleet, and for 468 systems, 1989, annual rpt, 7884–4
- West Central States economic indicators, Fed Reserve 10th District, quarterly rpt, 9381–16.2

see also Excise tax
see also Fuel tax
see also Value added tax

Sales workers

- Educational attainment, by sociodemographic characteristics and location, 1989 and trends from 1940, biennial Current Population Rpt, 2546–1.452
- Employment, earnings, and hours, monthly press release, 6742–5
- Employment, unemployment, and labor force characteristics, by region, State, and selected metro area, 1990, annual rpt, 6744–7
- Enterprise Statistics, 1987: auxiliaries of multi-establishment firms, finances and operations by function, industry, and State, 2329–6
- Immigrants admitted to US, by occupational group and country of birth, preliminary FY90, annual table, 6264–1

Income (household, family, and personal), by source, detailed characteristics, and region, 1988-89, annual Current Population Rpt, 2546–6.68

- Income (household, family, and personal), by source, detailed characteristics, and region, 1990, annual Current Population Rpt, 2546–6.70
- Manufacturing employment, by detailed occupation and SIC 2-digit industry, 1989 survey, triennial rpt, 6748–52
- Puerto Rico economic censuses, 1987: wholesale and retail trade sales by customer class, and employment, by SIC 2- and 3-digit kind of business, subject rpt, 2591–2.2
- Wholesale trade census, 1987: establishments, sales by customer class, employment, inventories, and expenses, by SIC 2- to 4-digit kind of business, 2407–4

see also under By Occupation in the "Index by Categories"

Salin, Victoria

"Rum: Annual Report (Covering 1989 and 1990) on Selected Economic Indicators", 9884–15

Salinas, Calif.

see also under By City and By SMSA or MSA in the "Index by Categories"

Salinity control

see Water pollution

Salmon

see Aquaculture
see Fish and fishing industry

Salmonella

see Food and waterborne diseases

Salomon, Matthew

"Potential Economic Impacts of Changes in Puerto Rico's Status Under S. 712", 26306–3.112

Salt Lake City, Utah

- Housing and households characteristics, unit and neighborhood quality, and journey to work by MSA location, for 11 MSAs, 1984 survey, supplement, 2485–8
- Housing and households characteristics, 1988 survey, MSA fact sheet, 2485–11.11
- Housing and households detailed characteristics, and unit and neighborhood quality, by location, 1988 survey, MSA rpt, 2485–6.5
- Housing starts and completions authorized by building permits in 40 MSAs, quarterly rpt, 2382–9
- Wages by occupation, for office and plant workers, 1990 survey, periodic MSA rpt, 6785–11.2

see also under By City and By SMSA or MSA in the "Index by Categories"

Salt Lake County, Utah

Housing and households detailed characteristics, and unit and neighborhood quality, by location, 1988 survey, MSA rpt, 2485–6.5

Saluter, Arlene F.

"Marital Status and Living Arrangements: March 1990", 2546–1.449

Salvage

see also Recycling of waste materials
see also Scrap metals

Index by Subjects and Names

Samoa

Samoa
see American Samoa
see Western Samoa

Samolyk, Katherine A.
"Regional Perspective on the Credit View", 9377–1.206

San Angelo, Tex.
see also under By SMSA or MSA in the "Index by Categories"

San Antonio, Tex.
Drug test results at arrest, by drug type, offense, and sex, for selected urban areas, quarterly rpt, 6062–3
Housing starts and completions authorized by building permits in 40 MSAs, quarterly rpt, 2382–9
see also under By City and By SMSA or MSA in the "Index by Categories"

San Bernardino, Calif.
Housing starts and completions authorized by building permits in 40 MSAs, quarterly rpt, 2382–9
Wages by occupation, for office and plant workers, 1991 survey, periodic MSA rpt, 6785–12.6
see also under By City and By SMSA or MSA in the "Index by Categories"

San Diego, Calif.
CPI by component for US city average, and by region, population size, and for 27 metro areas, monthly rpt, 6762–2
Drug abuse indicators for selected metro areas, research results, data collection, and policy issues, 1991 semiannual conf, 4492–5
Drug test results at arrest, by drug type, offense, and sex, for selected urban areas, quarterly rpt, 6062–3
Housing and households characteristics, 1987 survey, MSA fact sheet, 2485–11.1
Housing starts and completions authorized by building permits in 40 MSAs, quarterly rpt, 2382–9
Wages by occupation, for office and plant workers, 1990 survey, periodic MSA rpt, 6785–11.3
see also under By City and By SMSA or MSA in the "Index by Categories"

San Francisco Bay
Pollutant concentrations in coastal and estuarine sediments, by contaminant and selected site, 1984-89, 2176–3.13
Ships in Natl Defense Reserve Fleet at Suisun Bay, as of Jan 1991, semiannual listing, 7702–2

San Francisco, Calif.
AIDS knowledge, attitudes, and transmission prevention practices of physicians and RNs, 1990-91, 4186–9.11
Cancer (colorectal) risk related to intake of fat, fiber, and carbohydrates, for Sha Giao, PRC, and San Francisco Chinese, 1991 article, 4472–1.201
Cancer cases, by race, income, education, and area population density, for 3 metro areas, 1978-82, article, 4472–1.210
CPI by component for US city average, and by region, population size, and for 15 metro areas, monthly rpt, 6762–1
CPI by component for US city average, and by region, population size, and for 27 metro areas, monthly rpt, 6762–2
Drug abuse indicators for selected metro areas, research results, data collection, and policy issues, 1991 semiannual conf, 4492–5

Fruit and vegetable shipments, and arrivals in US and Canada cities, by mode of transport and State and country of origin, 1990, annual rpt, 1311–4.2
Pumpkin farms, production costs, shipments, and sales by State, prices, and imports by country, 1978-90, article, 1561–11.203
Wages by occupation, for office and plant workers, 1991 survey, periodic MSA rpt, 6785–12.2
see also under By City and By SMSA or MSA in the "Index by Categories"

San Jose, Calif.
CPI by component for US city average, and by region, population size, and for 15 metro areas, monthly rpt, 6762–1
CPI by component for US city average, and by region, population size, and for 27 metro areas, monthly rpt, 6762–2
Drug test results at arrest, by drug type, offense, and sex, for selected urban areas, quarterly rpt, 6062–3
Housing and households characteristics, unit and neighborhood quality, and journey to work by MSA location, for 11 MSAs, 1984 survey, supplement, 2485–8
Housing and households detailed characteristics, and unit and neighborhood quality, by location, 1988 survey, MSA rpt, 2485–6.8
Wages by occupation, for office and plant workers, 1991 survey, periodic MSA rpt, 6785–12.3
see also under By City and By SMSA or MSA in the "Index by Categories"

San Juan, P.R.
see also under By SMSA or MSA in the "Index by Categories"

San Marino
Economic, social, political, and geographic summary data, by country, 1991, annual factbook, 9114–2
Exports and imports of US, by transport mode, country, and SITC 1- to 3-digit commodity, 1990, annual rpt, 2424–12

Sana
see Yemen, North

Sanctions
see International sanctions

Sand and gravel
Alaska minerals resources and production, by mineral and site, for Juneau region, 1987-88, 5608–169
Colorado River sand deposit characteristics, and density of campsites, 1920s-80s, 5668–122
Exports and imports between US and outlying areas, by detailed commodity and mode of transport, 1990, annual rpt, 2424–11
Exports of US, detailed Schedule B commodities with countries of destination, 1990, annual rpt, 2424–10
Mineral Industry Surveys, commodity review of production, trade, stocks, and use, quarterly rpt, 5612–2.20
Minerals Yearbook, 1989, Vol 1: commodity review of production, reserves, supply, use, and trade, annual rpt, 5604–15.57
Minerals Yearbook, 1989, Vol 2: State reviews of production, sales, and firms, by commodity, and business activity, annual rpt, 5604–34
Occupational injuries and incidence, employment, and hours in sand and gravel mines and related operations, 1989, annual rpt, 6664–2

Occupational injuries by circumstances, employment, and hours, for mining industries by type of operation and State, quarterly rpt, 6662–1
Price indexes (producer), by stage of processing and detailed commodity, monthly rpt, 6762–6
Price indexes (producer), by stage of processing and detailed commodity, monthly 1990, annual rpt, 6764–2
Production, reserves, and use of industrial minerals, and characteristics of individual deposits, State rpt series, 5606–10
Statistical Abstract of US, 1991 annual data compilation, 2324–1.25

Sanderson, Colin G.
"EML Surface Air Sampling Program, 1989 Data", 3004–31

Sanderson, Fred
"Prospects for Japan's Livestock Sector", 1524–4.5

Sandia National Laboratories
see also Department of Energy National Laboratories

Sandretto, Carmen L.
"Trends in Resource Protection Policies in Agriculture", 1561–16.203

Sandusky, Ohio
Wages by occupation, and benefits for office and plant workers, 1991 survey, periodic MSA rpt, 6785–3.4

Sanford, Scott O.
"Forecasting 1990/91 U.S. Upland Cotton Exports Using Weekly Shipments: An Application of Seasonal Factors", 1561–1.204
"Outlook for Cotton", 1004–16.1

Sanitary districts
see Special districts

Sanitary engineering
see Plumbing and heating
see Refuse and refuse disposal
see Sewage and wastewater systems

Santa Ana, Calif.
Housing starts and completions authorized by building permits in 40 MSAs, quarterly rpt, 2382–9
Wages by occupation, for office and plant workers, 1990 survey, periodic MSA rpt, 6785–11.2
see also under By City and By SMSA or MSA in the "Index by Categories"

Santa Barbara, Calif.
Wages by occupation, for office and plant workers, 1991 survey, periodic MSA rpt, 6785–3.6
see also under By SMSA or MSA in the "Index by Categories"

Santa Clara County, Calif.
Housing and households characteristics, unit and neighborhood quality, and journey to work by MSA location, for 11 MSAs, 1984 survey, supplement, 2485–8
Housing and households detailed characteristics, and unit and neighborhood quality, by location, 1988 survey, MSA rpt, 2485–6.8

Santa Clarita, Calif.
see also under By City in the "Index by Categories"

Santa Cruz, Calif.
see also under By SMSA or MSA in the "Index by Categories"

Santa Fe, N.Mex.
see also under By SMSA or MSA in the "Index by Categories"

Santa Maria, Calif.
Wages by occupation, for office and plant workers, 1991 survey, periodic MSA rpt, 6785–3.6
see also under By SMSA or MSA in the "Index by Categories"

Santa Rosa, Calif.
see also under By City and By SMSA or MSA in the "Index by Categories"

Santomero, Anthony M.
"De Novo Banking in the Third District", 9387–1.201

Sao Tome and Principe
Agricultural trade of US, by detailed commodity and country, 1990, semiannual rpt, 1522–4
AID economic aid to developing countries, obligations and disbursements by country, quarterly rpt, 9912–4
Background Notes, summary social, political, and economic data, 1991 rpt, 7006–2.49
Economic and military aid and loans from US and intl agencies, by program and country, FY46-90, annual rpt, 9914–5
Economic and social conditions of developing countries from 1960s, and Intl Dev Cooperation Agency and AID activities and funding, FY90-92, annual rpt, 9904–4
Economic, social, political, and geographic summary data, by country, 1991, annual factbook, 9114–2
Exports and imports of US, by transport mode, country, and SITC 1- to 3-digit commodity, 1990, annual rpt, 2424–12
Human rights conditions in 170 countries, and US economic and military aid, 1990, annual rpt, 21384–3
Minerals Yearbook, 1988, Vol 3: foreign country review of production, trade, and policy, by commodity, annual rpt, 5604–17.80
UN voting record and share of votes in agreement with US, by issue, country, and world area, 1990, annual rpt, 7004–18

Sarasota, Fla.
see also under By SMSA or MSA in the "Index by Categories"

Satellites
Data sources and availability for space sciences and related topics, 1991 annual listing, 9504–10
Data sources for space sciences and related topics, use by format and user type, FY90, annual rpt, 9504–11
DOD budget, weapons acquisition costs by system and service branch, FY91-93, annual rpt, 3504–2
Environmental and natural resource data sources, and aerial survey R&D rpts, quarterly listing, 9502–7
Foreign and US space launchings and characteristics of craft and flight, 1957-90, annual rpt, 9504–9.1
Foreign and US space program activities, missions, launchings, payloads, and flight duration, 1957-90, annual rpt, 21704–4
Launchings and other activities of NASA and Soviet Union, with flight data, 1957-90, annual rpt, 9504–6.1
Launchings of satellites and other space objects since 1957, quarterly listing, 9502–2

NASA project launch schedules and technical descriptions, press release series, 9506–2
Oceanographic research ships, fleet condition, funding, voyages, and modernization costs, for NOAA, 1980s-90 and projected to 2020, 2148–60
Private sector involvement in space programs, govt contracts, costs, revenue, and R&D spending, 1970s-80s and projected to 2000, 26306–6.154
Wildlife tracking using satellites, costs and performance indicators by system type, species, and location, 1985-88, technical rpt, 5506–12.3
see also Communications satellites
see also Meteorological satellites

Saudi Arabia
Agricultural exports of high-value commodities, indexes and sales by commodity, world area, and country, 1960s-86, 1528–323
Agricultural exports of US, impacts of foreign agricultural and trade policy, with data by commodity and country, 1989, annual rpt, 1924–8
Agricultural production, prices, and trade, by country, 1960s-90, annual world area rpt, 1524–4.2
Agricultural production, trade, and policies in foreign countries, summary data by country, 1989-90, annual factbook, 1924–12
Agricultural trade of US, by detailed commodity and country, 1989, annual rpt, 1524–8
Agricultural trade of US, by detailed commodity and country, 1990, semiannual rpt, 1522–4
Economic and military aid and loans from US and intl agencies, by program and country, FY46-90, annual rpt, 9914–5
Economic conditions in USSR, Eastern Europe, OECD, and selected other countries, 1960s-90, annual rpt, 9114–4
Economic conditions, investment and export opportunities, and trade practices, 1991 country market research rpt, 2046–6.9
Economic conditions, policy, and trade practices, by country, 1988-90, annual rpt, 21384–5
Economic, social, political, and geographic summary data, by country, 1991, annual factbook, 9114–2
Export controls and trade of US with Middle East countries, with dual-use commodity licenses and arms sales, 1980s-90, GAO rpt, 26123–339
Exports and imports of US, by commodity and country, 1970-89, world area rpt, 9116–1.1
Exports and imports of US, by Harmonized System 6-digit commodity and country, 1990, annual rpt, 2424–13
Exports and imports of US, by selected country, country group, and commodity group, 1990, annual rpt, 2044–37
Exports and imports of US, by transport mode, country, and SITC 1- to 3-digit commodity, 1990, annual rpt, 2424–12
Exports, imports, and balances of US with major trading partners, by product category, 1986-90, annual chartbook, 9884–21

Exports of US, detailed Schedule B commodities with countries of destination, 1990, annual rpt, 2424–10
Human rights conditions in 170 countries, and US economic and military aid, 1990, annual rpt, 21384–3
Multinatl US firms and foreign affiliates finances and operations, by industry and world area of parent firm, 1989 benchmark survey, preliminary annual rpt, 2704–5
Multinatl US firms foreign affiliates, income statement items by country and world area, 1986, biennial article, 8302–2.212
Oil production, and exports and prices for US, by major exporting country, detailed data, monthly rpt with articles, 3162–24
Oil production, trade, use, and stocks, by selected country and country group, monthly rpt, 3162–42
Oil supply and price impacts of Iraq invasion of Kuwait, selected indicators, daily press release, 3162–44
Persian Gulf War impacts on US economic conditions compared to previous oil shock periods, and Saudi Arabia oil production and prices, 1990-92, hearings, 21248–156
Spacecraft and satellite launches since 1957, quarterly listing, 9502–2
UN voting record and share of votes in agreement with US, by issue, country, and world area, 1990, annual rpt, 7004–18
see also under By Foreign Country in the "Index by Categories"

Saunders, Anthony
"Who Changes the Prime Rate?", 9387–8.235

Saunders, Norman C.
"U.S. Economy into the 21st Century", 6722–1.251

Savage, Howard A.
"Who Can Afford To Buy a House?", 2486–1.11

Savannah, Ga.
see also under By City and By SMSA or MSA in the "Index by Categories"

Savings
Economic indicators and components, and Fed Reserve 4th District business and financial conditions, monthly chartbook, 9377–10
Economic indicators compounded annual rates of change, monthly rpt, 9391–3
Economic indicators compounded annual rates of change, 1971-90, annual rpt, 9391–9.1
Economic indicators, monthly rpt, 9362–1.2
Financial and monetary conditions, selected US summary data, weekly rpt, 9391–4
Flow-of-funds accounts, savings, investments, and credit statements, quarterly rpt, 9365–3.3
Foreign and US economic conditions and competitiveness issues, with data by country, 1960s-90, 21788–204
Foreign countries economic conditions and implications for US, periodic country rpt series, 2046–4
Foreign countries economic conditions, policy, and trade practices, by country, 1988-90, annual rpt, 21384–5
GNP and balance of payments impacts of savings rate, 1950s-89 and projected to 2009, article, 9385–1.201

Savings

Households assets, by type of holding and selected characteristics, 1988, Current Population Rpt, 2546–20.16

Monetary trends, Fed Reserve Bank of St Louis monthly rpt, 9391–2

Natl income and product accounts and components, *Survey of Current Business*, monthly rpt, 2702–1.24

Natl income and product accounts benchmark revisions of GDP and natl income, various periods 1959-80, tables, 2702–1.227

North Central States, FHLB 6th District savings instns financial condition and operations by State, monthly rpt, 9302–11

OECD personal savings rates for selected countries, 1960s-90, annual rpt, 9114–4.2

Personal, business, and govt gross saving and investment from 1929, and personal savings by type, 1946-90, annual rpt, 204–1.1

Personal, business, and govt savings, *Survey of Current Business*, monthly rpt, 2702–1.2

Personal savings rates, and household assets by type, 1970s-90, article, 1702–1.215

Personal savings rates in natl income and product accounts under alternative estimates of imputed rent for housing and consumer goods, 1950s-90, article, 9373–1.218

Personal savings rates relationship to housing value and limits on tax deductible pension contributions, 1950s-90, article, 9373–1.219

Savings and Investment Incentive Act issues, with IRA participation and other background data, 1980s, 25368–175

Southeastern States, Fed Reserve 5th District insured commercial banks financial statements, by State, quarterly rpt, 9389–18

Soviet Union GNP by detailed income and outlay component, 1985, 2326–18.59

Statistical Abstract of US, 1991 annual data compilation, 2324–1.14

Survey of Current Business, detailed financial and business data, and economic indicators, monthly rpt, 2702–1.4

Tax (income) deduction for interest payments, impacts on savings rates, with indicators for US, Canada, and other OECD countries, 1990 article, 9377–1.202

Tax reform and investment stimulation proposals, with background data, 1990 hearings, 25368–170

see also Bank deposits

see also Certificates of deposit

see also Credit unions

see also Individual retirement arrangements

see also Investments

see also Negotiable orders of withdrawal accounts

see also Savings institutions

Savings and Investment Incentive Act

Individual retirement arrangement participation and other impacts of Act, with background data, 1980s, 25368–175

Savings Association Insurance Fund

Finances of thrifts insured by SAIF, by profitability group, district, and State, quarterly rpt, 8432–4

New England States thrifts loan delinquency rates by loan type, time past due, thrift charter type, and State, 1990, annual article, 9302–4.202

Reform of banking system and deposit insurance, findings and recommendations, with background data, 1989-90, 8008–147

Savings bonds

see U.S. savings bonds

Savings institutions

Assets and liabilities of depository instns, monthly rpt, 9362–1.1

Assets, liabilities, and deposit and loan activity, for thrifts insured by Savings Assn Insurance Fund, by conservatorship status, monthly rpt, 8432–1

Banks financial performance, risk assessment, and regulation, 1990 annual conf papers, 9375–7

Bond (junk) holdings of Resolution Trust Corp, quarterly press release, 9722–4

County Business Patterns, 1988: employment, establishments, and payroll, by SIC 2- to 4-digit industry and county, annual State rpt series, 2326–6

County Business Patterns, 1989: employment, establishments, and payroll, by SIC 2- to 4-digit industry and county, annual State rpt series, 2326–8

Credit (installment) outstanding, and terms, by lender and credit type, monthly rpt, 9365–2.6

Deposits in insured commercial and savings banks, by instn, State, MSA, and county, as of June 1990, annual regional rpt series, 9295–3

Economic indicators and components, and Fed Reserve 4th District business and financial conditions, monthly chartbook, 9377–10

Employment, earnings, and hours, by SIC 1- to 4-digit industry, monthly and annual averages, selected years 1909-90, annual rpt, 6744–4

Failures of thrifts, financial performance of instns under Resolution Trust Corp conservatorship, quarterly rpt, 9722–5

Failures of thrifts, resolution activity and finances of Resolution Trust Corp, with data by asset type, State, region, and instn, monthly rpt, 9722–3

Failures of thrifts, resolution activity of Resolution Trust Corp, assets, deposits, and assets availability and sales, periodic press release, 9722–1

Failures of thrifts, resolution activity of Resolution Trust Corp, with assets and retained senior executives compensation, by instn, 1988-90, hearing, 21248–144

Failures of thrifts, resolution activity of Resolution Trust Corp, with instns assets and senior executives compensation, 1990, hearing, 21248–157

Failures of thrifts, resolution activity of Resolution Trust Corp, 1991 semiannual hearing, 21242–1

Failures of thrifts, resolution costs to FSLIC, relation to asset quality indicators and tax benefit grants, 1984-87, article, 9292–4.202

Finances and operations, by SIC 2- to 4-digit industry, forecast 1991, annual rpt, 2044–28

Index by Subjects and Names

Finances and operations of savings instns by district and State, mortgage loan activity and terms by MSA, and FHLB finances, 1989 and trends from 1900, annual rpt, 8434–3

Finances of banks and thrifts, by instn type, 1990, annual rpt, 13004–2

Finances of financial instns by type and selected instn, and deposit insurance reform issues, 1970s-90, GAO rpt, 26119–320

Finances of insured commercial and savings banks, by State, 1989, annual rpt, 9294–4

Finances of thrifts insured by Savings Assn Insurance Fund, by profitability group, district, and State, quarterly rpt, 8432–4

Financial condition and performance of insured commercial and savings banks, by asset size and region, quarterly rpt, 9292–1

Financial condition and performance of thrifts insured by Bank Insurance Fund, by asset size and region, quarterly rpt, 9292–5

Financial condition of savings instns, and devs, working paper series, 9379–14

Financial performance of thrifts facing insolvency, by whether recovered, 1980s, working paper, 9377–9.121

Flow-of-funds accounts, savings, investments, and credit statements, quarterly rpt, 9365–3.3

Fraud and abuse in banks and thrifts, Federal agencies enforcement activities and staff, with data by instn and location, 1988-90, hearing, 21408–119

Fraud and abuse in banks and thrifts, Federal criminal enforcement activities, case dispositions, and settlements, with data by district, 1982-90, hearing, 21248–142

Fraud and abuse in thrifts, Federal indictments and case dispositions, FY89-91, press release, 6008–33

Interest rate differentials for thrifts short- and long-term assets and liabilities, risk analysis for solvent 4th FHLB District banks, 1984-88, working paper, 9371–10.65

Mortgage debt holdings and other assets of thrifts, returns on assets, and impacts of qualified lender regulations, 1970s-89, GAO rpt, 26119–337

New England States, FHLB 1st District thrifts financial operations compared to banks, and housing industry indicators, bimonthly rpt with articles, 9302–4

North Central States, FHLB 6th District and natl cost of funds indexes for savings instns, and mortgage rates, monthly rpt, 9302–38

North Central States, FHLB 6th District insured S&Ls financial condition and operations by State, quarterly rpt, 9302–23

North Central States, FHLB 6th District savings instns financial condition and operations by State, monthly rpt, 9302–11

North Central States, FHLB 7th District and natl cost of funds indexes for savings instns, and mortgage rates, monthly rpt, 9302–30

North Central States, FHLB 8th District S&Ls, locations, assets, and savings, 1991, annual listing, 9304–9

Index by Subjects and Names

North Central States, FHLB 8th District thrifts financial operations by State and SMSA, quarterly rpt, discontinued, 9302–9

Occupational injury and illness rates, by SIC 2- to 4-digit industry, 1988-89, annual rpt, 6844–7

Occupational injury and illness rates, by SIC 2- to 4-digit industry, 1989, annual rpt, 6844–1

Real estate assets of failed thrifts, inventory of properties available from Resolution Trust Corp, semiannual listing series, 9722–2

Reform of banking system and deposit insurance, findings and recommendations, with background data, 1989-90, 8008–147

Resolution Trust Corp programs fraud and abuse, audits and investigations, 2nd half FY91, semiannual rpt, 9722–6

South Central States, FHLB 9th District thrifts finances and operations by State, quarterly rpt, discontinued, 9302–31

Southeastern States, Fed Reserve 5th District, economic indicators by State, quarterly rpt, 9389–16

Southeastern States thrifts, industry review, periodic journal, suspended, 9302–2

State and Metro Area Data Book, 1991 data compilation, 2328–54

Statistical Abstract of US, 1991 annual data compilation, 2324–1.16

Tax (income) returns of corporations, income and tax items by asset size and detailed industry, 1987, annual rpt, 8304–4

Tax (income) returns of corporations, income and tax items by asset size and detailed industry, 1988, annual rpt, 8304–21

Texas banks and thrifts profitability and solvency indicators, and problem assets by type, 1980s, working paper, 9379–14.11

Texas economic and housing conditions, bank failures, and thrift and Federal regulators real estate holdings, 1980s-90, hearings, 21248–146

West Central States economic indicators, Fed Reserve 10th District, quarterly rpt, 9381–16.2

West Central States, FHLB 10th District thrifts, locations, assets, and deposits, 1991, annual listing, 9304–17

Western States, FHLB 11th District and natl cost of funds indexes for savings instns, and mortgage rates, monthly rpt, 9302–38

Western States, FHLB 11th District S&Ls, offices, and financial condition, 1991 annual listing, 9304–23

see also Mortgages

see also under By Industry in the "Index by Categories"

SBA

see Small Business Administration

Scales and balances

see Instruments and measuring devices

see Scientific equipment and apparatus

Scarlett, Margaret I.

"Private Organization and Public Agency Partnership in Community Health Education", 4042–3.256

Scavone, Robert S.

"Current Efforts To Improve the Soviet Freight Transportation System", 1004–16.1

Schacht, Susan

"Fiscal Shock: How New England State Budgets Lost Their Balance", 9373–25.202

Schantz, Nancy B.

"Enrollment in Higher Education, Fall 1989", 4844–2

Schaub, John

"Outlook for Farm Inputs", 1004–16.1

Schenectady, N.Y.

Wages by occupation, and benefits for office and plant workers, 1990 survey, periodic MSA rpt, 6785–3.1; 6785–3.2

see also under By SMSA or MSA in the "Index by Categories"

Schening, M. R.

"Data on the Distribution and Abundance of Submersed Aquatic Vegetation in the Tidal Potomac River and Transition Zone of the Potomac Estuary, Maryland, Virginia, and the District of Columbia, 1988", 5666–27.22

Schilling, Robert F.

"Building Skills of Recovering Women Drug Users To Reduce Heterosexual AIDS Transmission", 4042–3.221

"Drug Use and Sexual Behavior of Indigent African American Men", 4042–3.254

Schlenker, Robert E.

"Comparison of Medicaid Nursing Home Payment Systems", 4652–1.255

Schlieter, Joyce

"Spiral Grain and Annual Ring Width in Natural Unthinned Stands of Lodgepole Pine in North America", 1208–380

Schmidt, John C.

"Aggradation and Degradation of Alluvial Sand Deposits, 1965-86, Colorado River, Grand Canyon National Park, Ariz.", 5668–122

Schneider, Markus

"Health Care Cost Containment in the Federal Republic of Germany", 4652–1.238

Schnorbus, Robert H.

"Midwest Economy: Quantifying Growth and Diversification in the 1980's", 9375–13.63

Schoenborn, Charlotte A.

"Developmental, Learning, and Emotional Problems: Health of Our Nation's Children, U.S., 1988", 4146–8.193

"Exposure to Alcoholism in the Family: U.S., 1988", 4146–8.207

Scholarships

see Student aid

Scholastic Aptitude Test

see Educational tests

Scholl, Russell B.

"International Investment Position of the U.S. in 1990", 2702–1.212

Schondelmeyer, Stephen

"Manufacturers' Prices and Pharmacists' Charges for Prescription Drugs Used by the Elderly", 4658–56

School administration and staff

Compensatory education programs in high poverty school districts, Federal grant program activities, participation, and coordinators views, 1989/90, 4808–32

School administration and staff

Condition of Education, detail for elementary, secondary, and higher education, 1920s-90 and projected to 2001, annual rpt, 4824–1

County Business Patterns, 1988: employment, establishments, and payroll, by SIC 2- to 4-digit industry and county, annual State rpt series, 2326–6

County Business Patterns, 1989: employment, establishments, and payroll, by SIC 2- to 4-digit industry and county, annual State rpt series, 2326–8

Digest of Education Statistics, 1991 annual data compilation, 4824–2

DOD Dependents Schools and Uniformed Services University of Health Sciences civilian and military personnel, quarterly rpt, 3542–14.1

Eighth grade class of 1988: characteristics of schools attended, natl longitudinal survey, 1991 rpt, 4826–9.10

Elementary and secondary education enrollment, staff, finances, operations, programs, and policies, 1987/88 biennial survey, series, 4836–3

Elementary and secondary public school systems enrollment, finances, staff, and high school grads, by State, FY88-89, annual rpt, 4834–6

Elementary and secondary public schools, enrollment, teachers, funding, and other characteristics, by region and State, 1988/89, annual rpt, 4834–20

Employment and payroll, by function and level of govt, 1990, annual rpt series, 2466–1

Employment and payroll of State and local govts, monthly rpt, 6742–4

Employment, earnings, and hours, by SIC 1- to 4-digit industry, monthly and annual averages, selected years 1909-90, annual rpt, 6744–4

Employment, enrollment, and spending, by instn level and control, and teachers salaries, 1980s-92, annual press release, 4804–19

Employment, unemployment, and labor force characteristics, by region and census div, 1990, annual rpt, 6744–7.1

Enterprise Statistics, 1987: auxiliaries of multi-establishment firms, finances and operations by function, industry, and State, 2329–6

Enterprise Statistics, 1987: finances and operations for companies, by size, level of diversification, form of organization, and industry group, 2329–8

Govt census, 1987: employment, payroll, and average earnings, by function, level of govt, State, county, and population size, 2455–2

Govt census, 1987: local govt employment by function, payroll, and average earnings, for individual counties, cities, and school and special districts, 2455–1

Govt census, 1987: State and local labor-mgmt policies, agreements, and coverage and bargaining units, by function, level of govt, and State, 2455–3

Head Start enrollment, funding, and staff, FY90, annual rpt, 4604–8

Higher education instn tuition and other costs, govt aid, impacts on enrollment, and cost containment methods, 1970s-90 and projected to 2001, 4808–25

School administration and staff

Higher education instn tuition relation to other instn financial indicators, by instn control, 1960s-88, 4808–24

Indian education funding of Fed Govt, and enrollment, degrees, and program grants and fellowships by State, late 1960s-FY89, annual rpt, 14874–1

Migrant workers children education programs enrollment, staff, and effectiveness, by State, 1980s, 4808–30

Migrant workers children education programs enrollment, staff, finances, and outcomes, 1980s, 4808–22

Nuclear engineering and science educational facilities, student aid, and degrees granted, by instn, 1990, 3008–126

Occupational injury and illness rates, by SIC 2- to 4-digit industry, 1988-89, annual rpt, 6844–7

Occupational injury and illness rates, by SIC 2- to 4-digit industry, 1989, annual rpt, 6844–1

Private elementary and secondary schools, students, and staff characteristics, various periods 1979-88, 4838–47

Science and engineering academic research system status, R&D performance, and Fed Govt support, 1950s-88 with trends and projections, 9628–83

Science and engineering grad enrollment, by field, source of funds, and characteristics of student and instn, 1975-89, annual rpt, 9627–7

Science and engineering PhDs, by field, instn, employment prospects, sex, race, and other characteristics, 1960s-90, annual rpt, 9627–30

Science and engineering PhDs employment and other characteristics, by field and State, 1989, biennial rpt, 9627–18

Special education programs, enrollment by age, staff, funding, and needs, by type of handicap and State, 1989/90, annual rpt, 4944–4

Statistical Abstract of US, 1991 annual data compilation, 2324–1.4

Tutoring and mentoring of disadvantaged elementary and secondary students by college students, program and participant characteristics, 1989, 4808–23

see also Campus security
see also Educational employees pay
see also Educational finance
see also School boards
see also School districts
see also Teachers

School boards

Elementary and secondary public school agencies, by enrollment size and location, fall 1989, annual listing, 4834–1

School buildings

see Educational facilities

School busing

Accidents (fatal), deaths, and rates, by circumstances, characteristics of persons and vehicles involved, and location, 1989, annual rpt, 7764–10

Accidents at hwy-railroad grade-crossings, detailed data by State and railroad, 1989, annual rpt, 7604–2

Accidents of school buses, circumstances, victim characteristics, and vehicle type, 1989, annual rpt, 7764–22

County Business Patterns, 1988: employment, establishments, and payroll, by SIC 2- to 4-digit industry and county, annual State rpt series, 2326–6

County Business Patterns, 1989: employment, establishments, and payroll, by SIC 2- to 4-digit industry and county, annual State rpt series, 2326–8

Digest of Education Statistics, 1991 annual data compilation, 4824–2

Drivers licenses issued and in force by age and sex, fees, and renewal, by license class and State, 1989, annual rpt, 7554–16

Employment, earnings, and hours, by SIC 1- to 4-digit industry, monthly and annual averages, selected years 1909-90, annual rpt, 6744–4

Energy use by mode of transport, fuel supply, and demographic and economic factors of vehicle use, 1970s-89, annual rpt, 3304–5

Occupational injury and illness rates, by SIC 2- to 4-digit industry, 1988-89, annual rpt, 6844–7

Occupational injury and illness rates, by SIC 2- to 4-digit industry, 1989, annual rpt, 6844–1

Travel patterns, personal and household characteristics, and auto and public transport use, 1990 survey, series, 7556–6

School desegregation

see Discrimination in education

School districts

Census of Govts, 1987: local govt employment by function, payroll, and average earnings, for individual counties, cities, and school and special districts, 2455–1

Census of Govts, 1987: school system total and instructional employment, payroll, and average earnings, by enrollment size and State, 2455–2

Census of Govts, 1987: State and local govt employment, payroll, OASDHI coverage, and employee benefits costs, by level of govt and State, 2455–4

Census of Govts, 1987: State and local labor-mgmt policies, agreements, and coverage and bargaining units, by function, level of govt, and State, 2455–3

Districts, schools, and enrollment, by State and for selected systems, 1991 annual data compilation, 4824–2.10

Elementary and secondary public school agencies, by enrollment size and location, fall 1989, annual listing, 4834–1

Elementary and secondary public schools and enrollment, by State, 1989/90, annual rpt, 4834–17

Elementary and secondary public schools, enrollment and other characteristics, for top 100 districts, 1988/89, annual rpt, 4834–22

Elementary and secondary public schools, enrollment, teachers, funding, and other characteristics, by region and State, 1988/89, annual rpt, 4834–20

Employment and payroll, by function, level of govt, and State, 1990, annual rpt, 2466–1.1

Finances of govts, by level of govt, State, and for large cities and counties, annual rpt series, 2466–2

Finances, tax systems and revenue, and fiscal structure, by level of govt and State, 1991 and historical trends, annual rpt, 10044–1

Index by Subjects and Names

Financing of public elementary and secondary education systems, issues and indicators of school districts fiscal independence, 1960s-80s, 10048–78

Immigrant children education programs funding by Fed Govt and school districts, and student characteristics, 1980s, GAO rpt, 26121–418

Poverty area school districts compensatory education programs, Federal grant program activities, participation, and coordinators views, 1989/90, 4808–32

R&D and related funding of Fed Govt to higher education and nonprofit instns, by field, instn, agency, and State, FY89, annual rpt, 9627–17

Smoking prevention, control, and surveillance activities and funding of States, and tobacco farm receipts, by State, 1989-90, 4206–2.47

Teacher employment, vacancies, and pay, by State, region, and school enrollment size, 1987/88, 4836–3.6

Texas school district quality indicators, model description and results by district and county, 1989, technical paper, 9379–12.67

see also School boards

School dropouts

Appalachia education system, improvement initiatives, and indicators of success, by State, 1960s-89, 9088–36

Bilingual education programs enrollment, funding, and services, by State, FY85-89, series, 4808–20

Children and youth social, economic, and demographic characteristics, 1950s-90, 4818–5

Condition of Education, detail for elementary and secondary education, 1920s-90 and projected to 2001, annual rpt, 4824–1.1

Counseling for youth, school based program client risk behaviors and outcomes, 1988/89 study, hearing, 25548–104

Detroit metro area runaway and other youth services programs cases, and school dropouts, 1980s, hearing, 25418–5

Digest of Education Statistics, 1991 annual data compilation, 4824–2

Drug (illegal) spending, by user group and substance, 1988-90, 236–2.1

Drug abuse prevalence among minorities, related health effects and crime, treatment, and research status and needs, mid 1970s-90, 4498–72

Eighth grade class of 1988: educational performance and conditions, characteristics, attitudes, activities, and plans, natl longitudinal survey, series, 4826–9

Health condition and services use, for children, 1990 chartbook, 4108–49

High school class of 1972: education, employment, and family characteristics, activities, and attitudes, natl longitudinal study, series, 4836–1

High school class of 1990: college enrollment, and labor force participation of grads and dropouts, by race and sex, press release, 6726–1.38

High school dropout rates, and subsequent completion, by student and school characteristics, alternative estimates, 1990, annual rpt, 4834–23

Index by Subjects and Names

Homeless and runaway youth programs, funding, activities, and participant characteristics, FY90, annual rpt, 4604–3

Income (household) and poverty status under alternative income definitions, by recipient characteristics, 1990, annual Current Population Rpt, 2546–6.69

Minority group and women health condition, services use, payment sources, and health care labor force, by poverty status, 1940s-89, chartbook, 4118–56

Minority group higher education enrollment, degrees, factors affecting participation, and earnings, 1960s-88, 4808–29

Natl Education Goals progress indicators, by State, 1991, annual rpt, 15914–1

Population educational enrollment status and attainment, by selected characteristics, 1989 and trends from 1947, annual Current Population Rpt, 2546–1.453

Rural areas economic and social indicators used to determine Federal aid need, late 1960s-86, 1598–265

Special education programs, enrollment by age, staff, funding, and needs, by type of handicap and State, 1989/90, annual rpt, 4944–4

Statistical Abstract of US, 1991 annual data compilation, 2324–1.4

Unemployed displaced and economically disadvantaged workers, training program operations and performance, series, 6406–10

see also Educational retention rates

School enrollment

see Educational enrollment

School finance

see Educational finance

see Tuition and fees

School lunch and breakfast programs

CCC dairy price support program foreign donations and domestic donations to poor, schools, Prisons Bur, and VA, monthly rpt, 1802–2

Consumer research, food marketing, legislation, and regulation devs, and consumption and price trends, quarterly journal, 1541–7

Criminal cases by type and disposition, and collections, for US attorneys, by Federal district, FY90, annual rpt, 6004–2.1

Elementary and secondary education enrollment, staff, finances, operations, programs, and policies, 1987/88 biennial survey, series, 4836–3

Elementary and secondary public schools, enrollment and other characteristics, for top 100 districts, 1988/89, annual rpt, 4834–22

Eligibility for free lunch, share of enrollment by State, 1989/90, annual rpt, 4834–17

Expenditures for education by Federal agency, program, and recipient type, and instn spending, FY80-90, annual rpt, 4824–8

Fed Govt financial and nonfinancial domestic aid, 1991 base edition with supplements, annual listing, 104–5

Income (household) and poverty status under alternative income definitions, by recipient characteristics, 1990, annual Current Population Rpt, 2546–6.69

Milk order market sales, by container size and type, outlet type, and market area, 1989, biennial rpt, 1317–6

Participation and costs of USDA food aid programs, by program, FY69-89, annual rpt, 1364–9

PL 480 exports by commodity, and recipients, by program, sponsor, and country, FY88 and cumulative from FY55, annual rpt, 1924–7

Poverty status of population and families, by detailed characteristics, 1988-89, annual Current Population Rpt, 2546–6.67

Poverty status of population and families, by detailed characteristics, 1990, annual Current Population Rpt, 2546–6.71

State and Metro Area Data Book, 1991 data compilation, 2328–54

Statistical Abstract of US, 1991 annual data compilation, 2324–1.12

USDA child nutrition programs funding, by program and State, FY89-90, annual rpt, 4824–2.27

Schools

see Educational facilities

see Private schools

see terms listed under Education and beginning with School

Schools and Staffing Survey

Data collection activities and programs of NCES, 1991, annual listing, 4824–7

Elementary and secondary education enrollment, staff, finances, operations, programs, and policies, 1987/88 biennial survey, series, 4836–3

Schrager, Lewis

"Demographic Characteristics, Drug Use, and Sexual Behavior of IV Drug Users with AIDS in Bronx, N.Y.", 4042–3.206

Schramm, Margaret M.

"Surveillance of Communicable Disease in Vermont: Who Reports?", 4042–3.208

Schreft, Stacey L.

"Money, Trade Credit and Asset Prices", 9389–19.29

"Survey Evidence of Tighter Credit Conditions: What Does It Mean?", 9389–19.30

"Welfare-Improving Credit Controls", 9389–19.26

Schruefer, Dan

"Socioeconomic Profile of Recreationists at Public Outdoor Recreation Sites in Coastal Areas: Volume 4. Public Area Recreation Visitors Survey", 2176–9.4

Schuchardt, Jane

"Comparison of Lower Middle Income Two-Parent and Single-Mother Families", 1702–1.207

Schumacher, James D.

"Final Report on Residual Tidal Currents and Processing of Pressure and Current Records from the Eastern Bering Sea Shelf", 2176–1.36

"Transport Processes in the North Aleutian Shelf", 2176–1.36

Schur, Claudia L.

"Choices of Health Insurance and the Two-Worker Household. National Medical Expenditure Survey", 4186–8.16

"Health Care Coverage: Findings from the Survey of American Indians and Alaska Natives. National Medical Expenditure Survey", 4186–8.17

Schwandt, John W.

"Idaho Forest Pest Conditions and Program Summary, 1989", 1206–49.1

Science and technology

Schwartz, Sara J.

"Food Grain Outlook", 1004–16.1

"World Rice Trade: Prospects and Issues for the Nineties", 1561–8.203

Schwarzbach, S. E.

"Reconnaissance Investigation of Water Quality, Bottom Sediment, and Biota Associated with Irrigation Drainage in the Klamath Basin, California and Oregon, 1988-89", 5666–27.21

Schwenk, Frankie N.

"Income and Expenditure Patterns of Consumer Units with Reference Person Age 70 to 79 and 80 or Older", 1702–1.204

"Women 65 Years or Older: A Comparison of Economic Well-Being by Living Arrangement", 1702–1.210

Schwenk, Nancy E.

"Food Trends", 1702–1.212

"Trends in Housing", 1702–1.205

Science and technology

China economic indicators and reform issues, with background data, 1950s-90, compilation of papers, 23848–155

Higher education instn science and engineering research system status, R&D performance, and Federal support, 1950s-88, 9628–83

Japan economic conditions, financial and intl policies, and trade devs, 1950s-80s and projected to 2050, compilation of papers, 23848–220

Natl Inst of Standards and Technology rpts, 1990, annual listing, 2214–1

NSF grants and contracts, by field, instn, and State, FY89, annual rpt, 9624–26

NSF R&D grant awards, by div and program, periodic rpt series, 9626–7

NSF rpts, 1990 annual listing, 9624–16

Soviet Union GNP by component and industry sector, and CIA estimation methods, 1950s-87, 23848–223

see also Agricultural sciences and research

see also Astronomy

see also Atmospheric sciences

see also Aviation sciences

see also Biological sciences

see also Biotechnology

see also Botany

see also CD-ROM technology and use

see also Chemistry

see also Computer sciences

see also Defense research

see also Department of Energy National Laboratories

see also Earth sciences

see also Educational research

see also Educational technology

see also Energy research and development

see also Engineers and engineering

see also Environmental sciences

see also Federal aid to medicine

see also Federal funding for energy programs

see also Federal funding for research and development

see also Federally Funded R&D Centers

see also Forensic sciences

see also Genetics

see also Information sciences

see also International cooperation in science and technology

see also Inventions

see also Mathematics

Science and technology

see also Medical research
see also Meteorology
see also Military science
see also Oceanography
see also Physical sciences
see also Physics
see also Physiology
see also Psychology
see also Research
see also Research and development
see also Scientific education
see also Scientific equipment and apparatus
see also Scientists and technicians
see also Social sciences
see also Space programs
see also Space sciences
see also Technological innovations
see also Technology transfer
see also Zoology

Scientific education

- Asia science and engineering employment, by selected characteristics, for 3 countries, 1991 working paper, 2326–18.61
- Assistance (financial and nonfinancial) of Fed Govt, 1991 base edition with supplements, annual listing, 104–5
- *Condition of Education*, detail for elementary and secondary education, 1920s-90 and projected to 2001, annual rpt, 4824–1.1
- Degrees (PhD) in science and engineering, by field, instn, employment prospects, sex, race, and other characteristics, 1960s-90, annual rpt, 9627–30
- Degrees awarded in higher education, by level, field, race, and sex, 1988/89 with trends from 1978/79, biennial rpt, 4844–17
- Degrees awarded in science and engineering, by field, level, and sex, 1966-89, 9627–33
- *Digest of Education Statistics*, 1991 annual data compilation, 4824–2
- DOD Dependents Schools basic skills and college entrance test scores, 1990-91, annual rpt, 3504–16
- Education Dept programs funding, operations, and effectiveness, FY90, annual rpt, 4804–5
- Eighth grade class of 1988: test scores and proficiency, by subject area and student characteristics, natl longitudinal survey, 1991 rpt, 4826–9.8
- Elementary and secondary students educational performance in math, science, reading, and writing, 1970s-90, 4898–32
- Enrollment in science and engineering grad programs, by field, source of funds, and characteristics of student and instn, 1975-89, annual rpt, 9627–7
- Facilities for R&D of higher education instns, equipment acquisition and service costs, condition, and financing, by field and subfield, 1988-90, triennial survey series, 9627–27
- Fed Govt aid to higher education and nonprofit instns for R&D and related activities, by field, instn, agency, and State, FY89, annual rpt, 9627–17
- Foreign and US economic conditions and competitiveness issues, with data by country, 1960s-90, 21788–204
- Foreign countries science and engineering employment, by professional characteristics, age, and sex, for selected countries, 1991 working paper, 2326–18.62; 2326–18.63
- Gifted minority students science and math education programs, participation and outcomes, 1981-88 study, 4808–34
- Higher education course completions, by detailed program, sex, race, and instn type, for 1972 high school class, as of 1984, 4888–4
- Higher education instn science and engineering research system status, R&D performance, and Federal support, 1950s-88, 9628–83
- Natl Education Goals progress indicators, by State, 1991, annual rpt, 15914–1
- NSF activities, finances, and funding by program, FY90, annual rpt, 9624–6
- NSF grants and contracts, by field, instn, and State, FY89, annual rpt, 9624–26
- NSF grants for science, engineering, and math education, by recipient and level, FY89, biennial listing, 9624–27
- NSF R&D grant awards, by div and program, periodic rpt series, 9626–7
- Nuclear engineering and science educational facilities, student aid, and degrees granted, by instn, 1990, 3008–126
- Nuclear engineering enrollment and degrees granted by instn and State, and grad placement, by student characteristics, 1990, annual rpt, 3004–5
- Radiation protection and health physics enrollment and degrees granted by instn and State, and female grads plans and employment, 1990, annual rpt, 3006–8.15
- Radiation protection and health physics enrollment and degrees granted by instn and State, and grad placement, by student characteristics, 1990, annual rpt, 3004–7
- Student aid funding and participation, by Federal program, instn type and control, and State, various periods 1959-89, annual rpt, 4804–28
- Student loan debt burden of 1986 college grads, by selected student characteristics and instn control, 1987, 4808–26
- Teachers in higher education instns, employment and other characteristics, by instn type and control, 1987/88 survey, 4846–4.4
- Teachers of science and math, professional dev project funding of Fed Govt, participation, operations, and effectiveness, 1985-90, 4808–31

Scientific equipment and apparatus

- Earthquakes in midwestern States, intensity, time, and seismograph locations, 1977-90, annual rpt, 9634–10
- Education in science, engineering, and math, NSF grants by recipient and level, FY89, biennial listing, 9624–27
- Enterprise Statistics, 1987: finances and operations for companies, by size, level of diversification, form of organization, and industry group, 2329–8
- Exports and imports of US, by country and detailed commodity, monthly rpt, 2422–12
- Exports and imports of US, by transport mode, country, and SITC 1- to 3-digit commodity, 1990, annual rpt, 2424–12
- Exports of US, detailed Schedule B commodities with countries of destination, 1990, annual rpt, 2424–10
- Glassware shipments, trade, use, and firms, by product, 1990, annual Current Industrial Rpt, 2506–9.3
- Higher education instn R&D equipment, acquisition and service costs, condition, and financing, by field and subfield, 1988-90, triennial survey series, 9627–27
- Imports of US given duty-free treatment for value of US material sent abroad, by commodity and country, 1989, annual rpt, 9884–14
- Manufacturing census, 1987: employment and shipments under Fed Govt contracts, by SIC 4-digit industry, 2497–7
- Manufacturing census, 1987: finances and operations, by type of organization and SIC 2- to 4-digit industry, subject rpt, 2497–5
- Manufacturing finances and operations, by SIC 2- to 4-digit industry, forecast 1991, annual rpt, 2044–28
- Mexico imports from US, by industry and State, 1987-90, 2048–154
- NSF R&D grant awards, by div and program, FY87-88, periodic rpt, 9626–7.4
- Oceanographic research ships, fleet condition, funding, voyages, and modernization costs, for NOAA, 1980s-90 and projected to 2020, 2148–60
- OECD trade, total and for 4 major countries, and US trade by country, by commodity, 1970-89, world area rpt series, 9116–1
- Price indexes (producer), by stage of processing and detailed commodity, monthly rpt, 6762–6
- Price indexes (producer), by stage of processing and detailed commodity, monthly 1990, annual rpt, 6764–2
- Shipments, trade, use, and firms, for instruments and related products by detailed type, 1989, annual Current Industrial Rpt, 2506–12.26
- Standards dev, proposals, and policies, for weights, measures, and performance, 1991 annual conf, 2214–7
- *see also* Medical supplies and equipment

Scientific ethics

see also Medical ethics

Scientific research

see Research

Scientists and technicians

- Agricultural research funding and staffing for USDA, State agencies, and other instns, by topic, FY90, annual rpt, 1744–2
- Asia science and engineering employment, by selected characteristics, for 3 countries, 1991 working paper, 2326–18.61
- China economic indicators and reform issues, with background data, 1950s-90, compilation of papers, 23848–155
- DOT employment, by subagency, occupation, and selected personnel characteristics, FY90, annual rpt, 7304–18
- Employment and education of scientists and engineers, and R&D spending, for US and selected foreign countries, 1991 annual rpt, 9627–35.2
- Employment and other characteristics of science and engineering PhDs, by field and State, 1989, biennial rpt, 9627–18
- Employment of scientists and engineers, and related topics, fact sheet series, discontinued, 9626–2

Index by Subjects and Names

Energy-related employment of science and engineering PhDs, by field and work activity, mid 1970s-80s, biennial rpt, 3006–8.17

Energy-related employment of scientists and engineers, by field and industry segment, projected 1990 and 1996, 3006–8.16

Engineering and architectural establishments, receipts by type of client and project, payroll, and employment, by State, 1987 Census of Service Industries, 2393–4.16

Foreign countries science and engineering employment, by professional characteristics, age, and sex, for selected countries, 1991 working paper, 2326–18.62; 2326–18.63

Manufacturing employment, by detailed occupation and SIC 2-digit industry, 1989 survey, triennial rpt, 6748–52

NASA science and engineering staff retirement rates, projected 1991-95, GAO rpt, 26123–348

NASA staff characteristics and personnel actions, FY90, annual rpt, 9504–1

NSF science and engineering staff, and outside investigator research grant proposals and awards, 1980s-90, 9628–84

Nuclear engineering enrollment and degrees granted by instn and State, and grad placement, by student characteristics, 1990, annual rpt, 3004–5

Radiation protection and health physics enrollment and degrees granted by instn and State, and grad placement, by student characteristics, 1990, annual rpt, 3004–7

Statistical Abstract of US, 1991 annual data compilation, 2324–1.20

Temporary help supply establishments by occupation supplied, receipts by source, and payroll, by MSA, 1987 Census of Service Industries, 2393–4.8

Women scientists and engineers seeking 1st Federal grant and reentering career, NSF support program proposal submissions, grant awards, and applicants views, FY85-89, 9628–82

see also Scientific education

see also Statisticians

see also under specific scientific disciplines (listed under Science and technology)

Scotland

see United Kingdom

Scott, Charles G.

"Aged SSI Recipients: Income, Work History, and Social Security Benefits", 4742–1.216

Scott, Charles T.

"Forest Statistics for New Jersey, 1987", 1206–12.14

Scott, E. L.

"Blue Marlin, *Makaira nigricans*, Movements in the Western North Atlantic Ocean: Results of a Cooperative Game Fish Tagging Program, 1954-88", 2162–1.203

Scott, Linda

"Developing Countries as a Source of U.S. Export Growth", 1524–4.2

Scottsdale, Ariz.

see also under By City in the "Index by Categories"

Scranton, Pa.

Wages by occupation, and benefits for office and plant workers, 1991 survey, periodic MSA rpt, 6785–12.6

see also under By SMSA or MSA in the "Index by Categories"

Scrap metals

Business statistics, detailed data for major industries and economic indicators, *Survey of Current Business*, monthly rpt, 2702–1.17

Exports and imports of US, by country and detailed commodity, monthly rpt, 2422–12

Exports and imports of US, by Harmonized System 6-digit commodity and country, 1990, annual rpt, 2424–13

Exports and imports of US, by transport mode, country, and SITC 1- to 3-digit commodity, 1990, annual rpt, 2424–12

Exports and imports of US shipped through Canada, by detailed commodity, customs district, and country, 1989, annual rpt, 7704–11

Exports of US, detailed Schedule B commodities with countries of destination, 1990, annual rpt, 2424–10

Labor productivity, indexes of output, hours, and employment by SIC 2- to 4-digit industry, 1967-89, annual rpt, 6824–1.4

Mineral Industry Surveys, commodity review of production, trade, stocks, and use, monthly rpt, 5612–1.11

Minerals Yearbook, 1989, Vol 1: commodity reviews of production, reserves, supply, use, and trade, annual rpt series, 5604–15

Minerals Yearbook, 1990, Vol 1: commodity reviews of production, reserves, supply, use, and trade, annual rpt series, 5604–20

Price indexes (producer), by stage of processing and detailed commodity, monthly rpt, 6762–6

Price indexes (producer), by stage of processing and detailed commodity, monthly 1990, annual rpt, 6764–2

Production, prices, trade, use, employment, tariffs, and stockpiles, by mineral, with foreign comparisons, 1986-90, annual rpt, 5604–18

Screws

see Hardware

Screwworms

see Animal diseases and zoonoses

Sea pollution

see Marine pollution

Sea turtles

see Endangered species

Seafood

see Fish and fishing industry

see Shellfish

Seals

see Marine mammals

Seamen

see Merchant seamen

Search Institute

"Private Schools in the U.S.: A Statistical Profile, with Comparisons to Public Schools", 4838–47

Searches and seizures

Airport security operations to prevent hijacking, screening results, enforcement actions, and hijacking attempts, 2nd half 1989, semiannual rpt, 7502–5

Searches and seizures

Coast Guard drug, immigration, and fisheries enforcement activities, 2nd half FY91, semiannual rpt, 7402–4

Counterfeiting and other Secret Service investigations and arrests by type, and dispositions, FY90 and trends from FY81, annual rpt, 8464–1

Customs Service activities, collections, entries processed by mode of transport, and seizures, FY86-90, annual rpt, 8144–1

Drug (illegal) and related property seizures by Federal agencies, by type, data compilation, 1991 annual rpt, 6064–6.4

Drug (illegal) lab seizures, by substance and location, 1989-90, annual rpt, 6284–3

Drug (illegal) production, eradication, and seizures, by substance, with US aid, by country, 1987-91, annual rpt, 7004–17

Drug abuse and trafficking reduction programs activities, funding, staff, and Bush Admin budget request, by Federal agency and program area, FY90-92, 238–2

Drug abuse indicators for selected metro areas, research results, data collection, and policy issues, 1991 semiannual conf, 4492–5

Drug control task forces enforcement activities by drug type and State, and organization, staff, and spending, 1988, 6068–244

Drug enforcement personnel, arrests, and seizures, for NYC, 1985-90, hearing, 25528–117

Drug enforcement regional task forces investigation of organized crime, activities by agency and region, FY83-90, biennial rpt, 6004–17

Drug-related property seizures, caseloads for Federal district courts, 1991, annual rpt, 18204–2.1

Drug smuggling interdiction programs, budget, and seizures of Fed govt, FY87-90, GAO rpt, 26119–318

Drug supply in US by country of origin, abuse, prices, and seizures, by substance, 1990, annual rpt, 6284–2

Endangered animals and plants US trade and permits, by species, purpose, disposition, and country, 1989, annual rpt, 5504–19

Foreign countries human rights conditions in 170 countries, 1990, annual rpt, 21384–3

Immigration and Naturalization Service drug and property seizures, FY89, fact sheet, 6266–2.3

Justice Dept and Customs Service asset forfeiture programs finances, and disbursements by State and judicial district, FY85-90, hearing, 25408–112

Justice Dept Asset Forfeiture Program seizures, finances, and disbursements, FY86-90, annual rpt, 6004–21

Marijuana crop eradication activities of DEA and local agencies, and weapons and assets seized, by State, 1982-90, annual rpt, 6284–4

Marshals Service activities, FY89, annual rpt, 6294–1

Warrants issued for search and arrest, caseloads of Federal district courts, by circuit and district, 1990, annual rpt, 18204–8.27

Searls, Anthony W.

Searls, Anthony W.

"Estimated Oil and Gas Reserves: Pacific Outer Continental Shelf (as of Dec. 31, 1989)", 5734–7

Seashores

- Army Corps of Engineers water resources dev projects, characteristics, and costs, 1950s-89, biennial State rpt series, 3756–1
- Army Corps of Engineers water resources dev projects, characteristics, and costs, 1950s-91, biennial State rpt series, 3756–2
- Coastal areas environmental and socioeconomic conditions, and potential impact of oil and gas OCS leases, final statement series, 5736–1
- Environmental conditions, fish, wildlife, use, and mgmt, for individual coastal and riparian ecosystems, series, 5506–9
- Global climate change environmental, infrastructure, and health impacts, with model results and background data, 1850s-2100, 9188–113
- Natl park system visits and overnight stays, by park and State, monthly rpt, 5542–4
- Natl park system visits and overnight stays, by park and State, 1990, annual rpt, 5544–12
- Natl parks and other land under Natl Park Service mgmt, acreage by site, ownership, and region, FY91, semiannual rpt, 5542–1
- Northeastern US recreation areas use, mgmt, and tourism dev issues, 1990 conf, 1208–356
- Pollution (marine) bacterial levels, and beach closings due to contamination and medical waste, for New York and New Jersey, 1987-89, hearing, 21568–50
- Recreation (outdoor) coastal facilities, by State, county, estuary, and level of govt, 1972-84, 2178–29
- Recreation (outdoor) coastal facilities of Fed Govt and States, visitor and site characteristics, 1987-90 survey, regional rpt series, 2176–9
- Wetlands acreage, resources, soil and water properties, and conservation efforts, by wetland type, State rpt series, 5506–11
- Wetlands in coastal areas, acreage by wetland type, estuarine basin, and county, 1989, 2178–31

Seaside, Calif.

see also under By SMSA or MSA in the "Index by Categories"

Seasonal adjustment factors

- Balance of payments, seasonal adjustment statistical discrepancy, monthly rpt, 23842–1.7
- Construction put in place, value of new public and private structures, by type, monthly rpt, 2382–4
- Employment, earnings, and hours benchmarks by SIC 2- to 4-digit industry, 1983-90, and revised seasonal adjustment factors by major industry group, 1991, semiannual article, 6742–2.204
- Employment, earnings, and hours, by SIC 1- to 4-digit industry, monthly and annual averages, selected years 1909-90, annual rpt, 6744–4
- Employment situation, earnings, hours, and other BLS economic indicators, transcripts of BLS Commissioner's monthly testimony, periodic rpt, 23846–4

Housing starts, by units per structure and metro-nonmetro location, and mobile home placements and prices, by region, monthly rpt, 2382–1

- Housing units (1-family) sold and for sale by price, stage of construction, months on market, and region, monthly rpt, 2382–3
- Housing units authorized, by region, State, selected MSA, and permit-issuing place, monthly rpt, 2382–5
- Labor force data series of BLS, seasonal adjustment factors, 1991, semiannual article, 6742–2.201; 6742–2.205
- Labor force, revised estimates based on 1990 seasonal adjustment factors, monthly 1986-90, annual tables, 6742–2.203
- Monetary aggregates and components weekly and monthly Fed Reserve seasonal adjustment factors, monthly rpt with articles, 9362–1
- Retail trade sales and inventories, by kind of business, region, and selected State, MSA, and city, monthly rpt, 2413–3
- Wholesale trade sales and inventories, by SIC 2- to 3-digit kind of business, monthly rpt, 2413–7

Seasonal and summer employment

see Temporary and seasonal employment

Seasonal variations

- Birds in Badlands Natl Park juniper forest and mixed grass rangeland habitats, population and species diversity by season, 1991 rpt, 1208–364
- Crimes committed, monthly 1985-89, annual rpt, 6224–2.1
- Energy supply, demand, and prices, forecasts by resource type, quarterly rpt, 3162–34
- Food spending, by item, household composition, income, age, race, and region, 1980-88, Consumer Expenditure Survey biennial rpt, 1544–30
- Global climate change environmental, infrastructure, and health impacts, with model results and background data, 1850s-2100, 9188–113
- Ozone in stratosphere, levels, depletion rates and climate impacts, and properties of chlorofluorocarbons and substitutes, 1990 rpt, 9508–37
- Radiation and radionuclide concentrations in surface air at selected monitoring sites worldwide, and effects of nuclear tests and accidents, 1989, annual rpt, 3004–31
- Traffic fatal accidents, deaths, and rates, by circumstances, characteristics of persons and vehicles involved, and location, 1989, annual rpt, 7764–10

see also Business cycles

see also Seasonal adjustment factors

Seat belts

see Motor vehicle safety devices

Seattle, Wash.

- CPI by component for US city average, and by region, population size, and for 27 metro areas, monthly rpt, 6762–2
- Drug abuse indicators for selected metro areas, research results, data collection, and policy issues, 1991 semiannual conf, 4492–5
- Fish and shellfish catch, wholesale receipts, prices, trade, and other market activities, weekly regional rpt, 2162–6.5
- Fruit and vegetable shipments, and arrivals in US and Canada cities, by mode of transport and State and country of origin, 1990, annual rpt, 1311–4.2

Index by Subjects and Names

- Housing and households characteristics, 1987 survey, MSA fact sheet, 2485–11.2
- Housing starts and completions authorized by building permits in 40 MSAs, quarterly rpt, 2382–9
- Housing vacancy rates for single and multifamily units and mobile homes, by city and ZIP code, 1991, annual MSA rpt, 9304–21.2
- Wages by occupation, for office and plant workers, 1990 survey, periodic MSA rpt, 6785–11.3

see also under By City and By SMSA or MSA in the "Index by Categories"

SEC

see Securities and Exchange Commission

Secondary education

see Elementary and secondary education

Secret Service

see U.S. Secret Service

Securities

- Airport finances, operations by carrier, and capacity improvement and dev funding, by airport, 1977-87 and projected to 2020, hearing, 21648–59
- Asset allocation funds performance relative to stock index and Treasury bill rates, model description and alternative results, 1980s-90, technical paper, 9385–8.87
- Assets and debts of private sector, balance sheets by segment, 1945-90, semiannual rpt, 9365–4.1
- Bank holding company subsidiaries dealing in bank-ineligible securities, subsidiary and parent firm finances, 1989-91, GAO rpt, 26119–280
- Banking industry structure and deposit insurance reform, findings and recommendations, with background data, 1989-90, 8008–147
- Banks (insured commercial and savings) finances, for foreign and domestic offices, by asset size, 1989, annual rpt, 9294–4.2
- Banks (natl) charters, mergers, liquidations, enforcement cases, and financial performance, with data by instn and State, quarterly rpt, 8402–3
- Banks and deposit insurance funds financial condition, potential losses, and regulatory issues, 1980s-90 and projected to 1995, 21248–147
- Banks stock price changes relation to regulatory exam results, 1980s, article, 9373–1.210
- Banks stock returns impact of interstate and intrastate banking regulation, 1960s-89, article, 9393–8.205
- Business statistics, detailed data for major industries and economic indicators, *Survey of Current Business*, monthly rpt, 2702–1.9
- Court civil and criminal caseloads for Federal district, appeals, and bankruptcy courts, by type of suit and offense, circuit, and district, 1990, annual rpt, 18204–11
- Court civil and criminal caseloads for Federal district, appeals, and special courts, 1990, annual rpt, 18204–8
- Court civil and criminal caseloads for Federal district courts, 1991, annual rpt, 18204–2.1
- Credit (securities) issues of stockbrokers and other nonbank lenders, and brokers balance sheet, as of June 1990, annual rpt, 9365–5.1

Index by Subjects and Names

Securities

Credit unions federally insured, finances by instn characteristics and State, as of June 1991, semiannual rpt, 9532–6

Criminal cases in Federal district courts, by offense, disposition, and district, 1980-90, last issue of annual rpt, 18204–1

Economic and monetary trends, compounded annual rates of change and quarterly indicators for US and 7 major industrialized countries, quarterly rpt, 9391–7

Electric utilities privately owned, finances and operations, detailed data, 1989, annual rpt, 3164–23

Flow-of-funds accounts, savings, investments, and credit statements, quarterly rpt, 9365–3.3

Foreign and US industrial stock indexes and long-term govt bond yields, for selected countries, weekly chartbook, 9365–1.5

Foreign and US stock price indexes, for 7 OECD countries, *Survey of Current Business*, monthly rpt, 2702–1.2

Foreign govt assets and liabilities, and transactions in securities, monthly rpt, 9362–1.3

Foreign transactions in long-term domestic and foreign securities, purchases and sales, by country, *Treasury Bulletin*, quarterly rpt, 8002–4.11

Fraud involving securities, US attorneys cases by disposition, FY90, annual rpt, 6004–2.1

Futures and options trading volume, by commodity and exchange, FY90, annual rpt, 11924–2

Futures trading in selected commodities and financial instruments and indexes, NYC, Chicago, and other markets activity, semimonthly rpt, 11922–5

Grain cooperatives finances and operations, by grain handled and selected characteristics, 1983-85, series, 1128–44

Households assets, by type of holding and selected characteristics, 1988, Current Population Rpt, 2546–20.16

Insider trading, Federal sentencing guidelines by offense and circumstances, series, 17668–1

Interest rates for commercial paper, govt securities, other financial instruments, and home mortgages, monthly rpt, 9365–2.14

Intl Finance Corp finances, and intl capital market financial data by firm, by country, 1990 hearing, 21248–149

Intl investment position of US, by component, industry, world region, and country, 1989-90, annual article, 2702–1.212

Intl transactions summary, 1980s-90, annual article, 9362–1.202

Intl transactions, *Survey of Current Business*, monthly rpt, quarterly tables, 2702–1.26

Investment banking firms stock performance relation to returns on underwritten stock issues, late 1970s-87, technical paper, 9366–6.260

Issues of corporate stock, terms, value, and yield relation to call provisions, 1970s-90, technical paper, 9366–6.269

Japan and US securities firms equity capital costs and financial ratios, with data by firm, 1980s-91, article, 9385–1.212

Japan economic conditions, financial and intl policies, and trade devs, 1950s-80s and projected to 2050, compilation of papers, 23848–220

Japan financial instns and stock market conditions, and other economic indicators, with intl comparisons, 1980s-90, hearing, 21248–152

Japan stock margin requirements impact on stock prices, volatility, and trading activity, 1951-88, technical paper, 9385–8.72

Leveraged buyouts impacts on financial performance, for 4 transactions, 1980s-90, GAO rpt, 26119–355

Low-grade junk bond holdings of RTC, quarterly press release, 9722–4

Margin requirements set by Fed Reserve Board, 1934-74, annual rpt, 9364–1.2

Medium-term notes outstanding, issuers, and borrowings size, by industry group, 1983-90, technical paper, 9366–6.276

Mortgage-backed securities and other financial services, banks profitability indicators, 1985-89, 4808–36

Mortgage-backed securities interest rates, 1984-88, technical paper, 9366–6.263

Mortgage-backed securities investment by major financial instns, quarterly press release, discontinued, 5002–12

Mortgage-backed securities program of Govt Natl Mortgage Assn, private issues, FY90, annual rpt, 5144–6

Mortgage-backed security conduits lending activity, by type of loan and mortgaged property, monthly press release, 5142–18

Mortgage-backed security conduits lending activity, by type of loan and mortgaged property, quarterly press release, 5142–30

Multinatl firms US affiliates, finances, and operations, by industry, world area of parent firm, and State, 1988-89, annual rpt, 2704–4

Multinatl firms US affiliates, investment trends and impact on US economy, 1991 annual rpt, 2004–9

Natural gas interstate pipeline company detailed financial and operating data, by firm, 1989, annual rpt, 3164–38

Nonprofit charitable organizations finances, and revenue and investments of top 10 instns, 1986-87, article, 8302–2.210

Nonprofit charitable organizations finances, by asset size and State, 1987, article, 8302–2.218

Nonprofit charitable organizations finances, 1988, table, 8302–2.220

OECD stock indexes for 15 countries, returns volatility and inter-country correlations, 1960s-90, technical paper, 9366–6.279

Partnerships (limited) conversion to corporations, and impacts on share values, with data by firm, 1980s-91, hearing, 25248–124

Pools of finance company credit upon which securities have been issued, by credit type, monthly rpt, 9365–2.7

Pools of installment credit upon which securities have been issued, by credit type, monthly rpt, 9365–2.6

Price dispersion index for common stock, impact on GNP, 1948-87, article, 9375–1.201

Price indexes of common stock, trading volume, margin credit, and new govt and corporate issues, monthly rpt, 9362–1.1

Price volatility relation to interest rates, oil and gold prices, and US money supply, for 10 countries, model description and results, 1970s-88, working paper, 9381–10.116

Prices and yields of common stock and bonds, current data and annual trends, monthly rpt, 23842–1.5

Prices of stock, and industrial production indexes, correlations among 4 OECD countries, 1960s-90, technical paper, 9385–8.105

Prices of stock, relation to price volatility and trading volume, mid 1940s-80s, technical paper, 9366–6.266

Prices of stocks relation to dividends, alternative model results, 1960s-90, working paper, 9377–9.104

Pricing efficiency of stock market, model description and results, late 1920s-90, article, 9373–1.206

Purchases, sales, and holdings, by issuer and type and ownership of security, monthly listing, 9732–2

Regulation of securities and commodity trading, activities and interagency coordination, FY91, annual rpt, 11924–4

Regulation of securities industry, self-regulatory organizations oversight by SEC, violations, and complaints, FY86-89, GAO rpt, 26119–336

Returns on foreign and domestic stocks and bonds, relationship to selected economic indicators for US, UK, and Japan, 1970s-80s, article, 9385–1.211

Returns on stock and bills, various periods 1802-1990, article, 9387–1.204

Returns on stock initial public offerings, impact of underwriter price support, 1982-83, technical paper, 9385–8.113

Returns on stock, relation to inflation, model description and results, 1950s-89, working paper, 9379–14.12

Savings instns failure resolution activity of Resolution Trust Corp, assets, deposits, and assets availability and sales, periodic press release, 9722–1

Savings instns finances and operations by district and State, mortgage loan activity and terms by MSA, and FHLB finances, 1989 and trends from 1900, annual rpt, 8434–3

Savings instns insured by Savings Assn Insurance Fund, assets, liabilities, and deposit and loan activity, by conservatorship status, monthly rpt, 8432–1

SEC activities, securities industry finances, and exchange activity, selected years 1938-FY90, annual rpt, 9734–2

SEC registration, firms required to file annual rpts, as of Sept 1990, annual listing, 9734–5

Short selling of stocks, activity indicators, and regulatory issues, 1980s-89 and trends from 1940, hearings, 21408–122

Small business capital formation sources and issues, 1990 annual conf, 9734–4

Southeastern States, Fed Reserve 5th District insured commercial banks financial statements, by State, quarterly rpt, 9389–18

Southeastern States, Fed Reserve 8th District banking and economic conditions, quarterly rpt with articles, 9391–16

Securities

State and local govt employees pension system cash and security holdings and finances, quarterly rpt, 2462–2

Statistical Abstract of US, 1991 annual data compilation, 2324–1.16

Tax (income) returns of corporations, income and tax items by asset size and detailed industry, 1987, annual rpt, 8304–4

Tax (income) returns of corporations, income and tax items by asset size and detailed industry, 1988, annual rpt, 8304–21

Telecommunications industry intl competitiveness, with financial and operating data by product or service, firm, and country, 1990 rpt, 2008–30

Telephone and telegraph firms detailed finances and operations, 1989, annual rpt, 9284–6

Trading activity and system automation, with data by country, stock exchange, security type, and individual contract, 1980s-90, article, 9371–1.209

UK inflation and GNP forecasting performance of indexed bond prices and other factors, 1950s-91, article, 9385–1.214

Yields, interest rates, prices, and offerings, by type of bond and issuing sector, selected years 1929-90, annual rpt, 204–1.5

Yields on corporate, Treasury, and municipal long-term bonds, *Treasury Bulletin,* quarterly rpt, 8002–4.8

Yields on govt and private issues, weekly rpt, 9391–4

see also American Stock Exchange

see also Foreign investments

see also Government securities

see also Municipal bonds

see also Mutual funds

see also New York Stock Exchange

see also Options trading

see also Stockbrokers

see also Tax exempt securities

see also U.S. savings bonds

Securities and Exchange Commission

Activities of SEC, securities industry finances, and exchange activity, selected years 1938-FY90, annual rpt, 9734–2

Budget of US, authoritative financial statements with appropriations, outlays, and receipts, by category and agency, FY90, annual rpt, 8104–2.1

Budget of US, obligations and authority by function, agency, and program, with summaries, analyses, and historical tables, FY92, annual rpt, 104–2

Corporations required to file annual rpts with SEC, as of Sept 1990, annual listing, 9734–5

Regulation of securities and commodity trading, activities and interagency coordination, FY91, annual rpt, 11924–4

Securities purchases, sales, and holdings, by issuer and type and ownership of security, monthly listing, 9732–2

Self-regulatory organizations oversight by SEC, violations, and complaints, FY86-89, GAO rpt, 26119–336

Small business capital formation sources and issues, 1990 annual conf, 9734–4

Securities exchange

see American Stock Exchange

see New York Stock Exchange

see Stock exchanges

Security clearance

see Internal security

Security devices

Exports and imports of US, by Harmonized System 6-digit commodity and country, 1990, annual rpt, 2424–13

Exports of US, detailed Schedule B commodities with countries of destination, 1990, annual rpt, 2424–10

Price indexes (producer), by stage of processing and detailed commodity, monthly rpt, 6762–6

Price indexes (producer), by stage of processing and detailed commodity, monthly 1990, annual rpt, 6764–2

Service industries census, 1987: establishments, receipts by source, payroll, and employment, by SIC 2- to 4-digit kind of business, State, and MSA, 2393–4

Shipments, trade, use, and firms, for electronic communications systems and related products, 1990, annual Current Industrial Rpt, 2506–12.35

Security services

see Campus security

see Detective and protective services

see Internal security

see Security devices

Sedatives

see Drug abuse and treatment

see Drugs

Sedition

see Subversive activities

Seeds

Agricultural Statistics, 1990, annual rpt, 1004–1

Agriculture census, 1987: farms, farmland, production, finances, and operator characteristics, by county, final State rpt series, 2331–1

Agriculture census, 1987: horticultural specialties producers, finances, and operations, by crop and State, 1988 survey, 2337–1

Cooperatives, finances, operations, activities, and membership, 1950s-88, commodity rpt, 1126–1.6

Exports and imports (agricultural) commodity and country, prices, and world market devs, monthly rpt, 1922–12

Exports and imports (agricultural) of US, by commodity and country, bimonthly rpt, 1522–1

Exports and imports (agricultural) of US, by detailed commodity and country, 1989, annual rpt, 1524–8

Exports and imports (agricultural) of US, by detailed commodity and country, 1990, semiannual rpt, 1522–4

Exports and imports of US, by country and detailed commodity, monthly rpt, 2422–12

Exports and imports of US, by Harmonized System 6-digit commodity and country, 1990, annual rpt, 2424–13

Exports of seeds, by type, world region, and country, FAS quarterly rpt, 1925–13

Exports of US, detailed Schedule B commodities with countries of destination, 1990, annual rpt, 2424–10

Index by Subjects and Names

Farm finances, receipts by commodity, other income, expenses, assets, liabilities, and ratios, 1990, annual rpt, 1544–16

Farm production inputs, finances, mgmt, and land value and transfers, periodic situation rpt with articles, 1561–16

Farm production itemized costs, by farm sales size and region, 1990, annual rpt, 1614–3

Farm production itemized costs, receipts, and returns, by commodity and region, 1987-89, annual rpt, 1544–20

Farm sector balance sheet, and marketing receipts by detailed commodity, by State, 1985-89, annual rpt, 1544–18

Feed production, acreage, stocks, use, trade, prices, and price supports, periodic situation rpt with articles, 1561–4

Flower and foliage plant production, marketing, and trade by country, by State, 1960s-88, 1568–293

Irrigation projects of Reclamation Bur in western US, crop production and acreage by commodity, State, and project, 1989, annual rpt, 5824–12

Pine (longleaf) planting performance relation to seed source and site, for Florida and Georgia, 1968-83, 1208–345

Potato production, prices, stocks, and use, by State, 1981-90, annual rpt, 1621–11

Prices received and paid by farmers, by commodity and State, 1990, annual rpt, 1629–5

Prices received by farmers for major products, and paid for farm inputs and living items, by State, monthly rpt, 1629–1

Production, farms, acreage, and related data, by selected crop and State, monthly rpt, 1621–1

see also Oils, oilseeds, and fats

Segregation

see Discrimination in education

see Discrimination in housing

see School busing

Seibert, Warren F.

"Research Library Trends II: 35 Libraries in the 1970's and Beyond", 4468–4

"Research Library Trends, 1951-80 and Beyond: An Update of Purdue's 'Past and Likely Future of 58 Research Libraries' ", 4468–4

Seignorage

see Coins and coinage

see Money supply

Seitchik, Adam

"Employer Strategies for a Changing Labor Force: A Primer on Innovative Programs and Policies", 15496–1.12

Seizures

see Searches and seizures

Seldon, Barry J.

"Welfare Gains from Wood Preservatives Research", 1502–3.202

Seldovia, Alaska

Tide height and time daily at coastal points, forecast 1992, annual rpt, 2174–2.1

Selective service

Registrants by State, FY90, annual rpt, 9744–1

see also Draft evasion and protest

see also Voluntary military service

Index by Subjects and Names

Selective Service System

Activities of SSS, and registrants by State, FY90, annual rpt, 9744–1

Budget of US, authoritative financial statements with appropriations, outlays, and receipts, by category and agency, FY90, annual rpt, 8104–2.1

Budget of US, obligations and authority by function, agency, and program, with summaries, analyses, and historical tables, FY92, annual rpt, 104–2

Selenium

see Nonmetallic minerals and mines

Self-employment

- AFDC beneficiaries demographic and financial characteristics, by State, FY89, annual rpt, 4694–1
- Child day care employment by occupation, and mothers in labor force, 1976-88 with day care employment projected to 2000, article, 6722–1.202
- *Employment and Earnings*, detailed data, monthly rpt, 6742–2
- Employment conditions, alternative BLS projections to 2005 and trends 1970s-90, biennial article, 6722–1.254
- Employment, earnings, and hours, monthly press release, 6742–5
- Employment of self-employed, by occupation, industry, sex, and race, 1983 and 1990, article, 6742–1.202
- Employment situation, earnings, hours, and other BLS economic indicators, transcripts of BLS Commissioner's monthly testimony, periodic rpt, 23846–4
- Employment under contract, 1985 and 1988, GAO rpt, 26121–411
- Farm employment, wages, and hours, by payment method, worker type, region, and State, 1910-90, 1618–21
- Farm labor, wages, hours, and perquisites, by State, monthly rpt, 1631–1
- Food stamp recipient household size, composition, income, and income and deductions allowed, summer 1988, annual rpt, 1364–8
- Immigrants earnings compared to native-born, relation to social and demographic characteristics, model description and results, 1970 and 1980, technical paper, 9385–8.101
- Income (household) by source, and itemized spending, by selected characteristics and region, 1988-89 Consumer Expenditure Survey, annual rpt, 6764–5
- Income (household, family, and personal), by source, detailed characteristics, and region, 1988-89, annual Current Population Rpt, 2546–6.68
- Income (household, family, and personal), by source, detailed characteristics, and region, 1990, annual Current Population Rpt, 2546–6.70
- Indians and Alaska Natives health care coverage, by type, employment status, and other characteristics, 1987, 4186–8.17
- Insurance (health) provided by employer, coverage offered to and chosen by families with 2 working spouses, 1977 and 1987, 4186–8.16
- Moonlighting employment, by reason, and characteristics of workers and primary and secondary jobs, 1991, press release, 6726–1.40

OASDHI admin, and SSA activities, 1930s-90 and projected to 2064, annual data compilation, 4704–12

OASDHI coverage of employment and earnings, late 1930s-89, annual rpt, 4744–3.1; 4744–3.2

OASDI and Hospital Insurance tax rates for self-employed, 1990-99 and projected to 2000, biennial article, 4742–1.217

OASDI benefit payments, trust fund finances, and economic and demographic assumptions, 1970-90 and alternative projections to 2000, actuarial rpt, 4706–1.105

Poverty status of population and families, by detailed characteristics, 1988-89, annual Current Population Rpt, 2546–6.67

Poverty status of population and families, by detailed characteristics, 1990, annual Current Population Rpt, 2546–6.71

Science and engineering PhDs, by field, instn, employment prospects, sex, race, and other characteristics, 1960s-90, annual rpt, 9627–30

Social security earnings records errors and rates, by employment type, late 1930s-87, GAO rpt, 26121–422

Statistical Abstract of US, 1991 annual data compilation, 2324–1.13

Tax expenditures, Federal revenues forgone through income tax deductions and exclusions by type, FY92-96, annual rpt, 21784–10

Tax rates and revenue of State and local govts, by source and State, 1991 and historical trends, annual rpt, 10044–1

Unemployed displaced workers losing job 1985-90, by demographic and current and former employment characteristics, as of Jan 1990, article, 6722–1.225

Unemployment insurance laws of States, comparison of provisions, 1991, base edition with semiannual revisions, 6402–2

Voting and registration, by socioeconomic and demographic characteristics, 1990 congressional election, biennial Current Population Rpt, 2546–1.454

Semiconductors

- Competitiveness (intl) of US semiconductor manufacturing and testing equipment industry, investigation with background financial and operating data and foreign comparisons, 1991 rpt, 9886–4.175
- County Business Patterns, 1988: employment, establishments, and payroll, by SIC 2- to 4-digit industry and county, annual State rpt series, 2326–6
- County Business Patterns, 1989: employment, establishments, and payroll, by SIC 2- to 4-digit industry and county, annual State rpt series, 2326–8
- Exports and imports between US and outlying areas, by detailed commodity and mode of transport, 1990, annual rpt, 2424–11
- Exports and imports of US, by Harmonized System 6-digit commodity and country, 1990, annual rpt, 2424–13
- Exports of US, detailed Schedule B commodities with countries of destination, 1990, annual rpt, 2424–10
- Import dependency of US firms for semiconductors and related equipment, and sales from Japan firms delayed and denied, 1988-91, GAO rpt, 26123–361

Senate Agriculture, Nutrition, and Forestry Committee

Price indexes (producer), by stage of processing and detailed commodity, monthly 1990, annual rpt, 6764–2

Quality control spending in semiconductor and fiber optics industries, effectiveness, and views, survey results, 1980s, 2218–84

Shipments, trade, use, and firms, for semiconductors, printed circuit boards, and other electronic components, 1990, annual Current Industrial Rpt, 2506–12.36

Senate

- Budget of US, authoritative financial statements with appropriations, outlays, and receipts, by category and agency, FY90, annual rpt, 8104–2.1
- Budget of US, obligations and authority by function, agency, and program, with summaries, analyses, and historical tables, FY92, annual rpt, 104–2
- Buildings and grounds under Capitol Architect supervision, itemized outlays by payee and function, 1st half FY91, semiannual rpt, 25922–2
- *Congressional Directory*, members of 102nd Congress, other officials, elections, and districts, 1991-92, biennial rpt, 23874–1
- Election (senatorial) political party spending limits for candidates, and voting age population, by State, 1992 general elections, press release, 9276–1.92
- Election campaign finances and FEC activities, various periods 1975-90, annual rpt, 9274–1
- Election campaign funds raised and spent by party committees, by State and party, 1989-90, press release, 9276–1.88
- Election campaign receipts and spending of congressional candidates, by candidate and State, 1989-Dec 1990, press release, 9276–1.87
- Election campaign receipts and spending of senatorial candidates, by party and State, 1991, press release, 9276–1.93
- Finances of Senate, receipts, itemized expenses by payee, and balances, 1st half FY91, semiannual listing, 25922–1
- *State and Metro Area Data Book*, 1991 data compilation, 2328–54
- *Statistical Abstract of US*, 1991 annual data compilation, 2324–1.8
- Votes cast by party, candidate, and State, 1990 natl elections, biennial rpt, 9274–5
- *see also* Senate Documents
- *see also* Senate Special Publications
- *see also* under names of individual committees (starting with Senate or Joint)
- *see also* under names of individual subcommittees (starting with Subcommittee)

Senate Aging Committee, Special

Assistance for aged, funding by program, and long term care ombudsman funding and visits by State, 1988-90, 25248–126

Senate Agriculture and Forestry Committee

see Senate Agriculture, Nutrition, and Forestry Committee

Senate Agriculture, Nutrition, and Forestry Committee

Farm Credit System and FmHA services to aid delinquent borrowers, activities, with background data, 1989 hearings, 25168–74

Senate Agriculture, Nutrition, and Forestry Committee

Futures trading oversight of CFTC and individual exchanges, foreign activity, and customer views, late 1980s, hearing, 25168–77

Pollution (groundwater) from farm chemicals use, with background data and farmers views, 1970s-80s, hearing, 25168–76

Wheat quality indicators, for US exports and foreign wheat production, 1960s-90, hearing, 25168–75

Senate Banking, Housing, and Urban Affairs Committee

Bank deposit insurance fund finances, potential losses, and real estate lenders financial ratios compared to other US and Texas banks, 1990 hearings, 25248–125

Banking intl competition and deposit insurance reform issues, with background data, 1990 hearings, 25248–122; 25248–123

Homeless persons social services spending and client characteristics, and youth programs cases, for Michigan, 1980s, hearing, 25418–5

Intl banking competition and deposit insurance reform issues, with background data, 1990 hearings, 25248–121

Low income housing dev tax credits, and units constructed, by selected project and State, 1987-89, hearings, 25248–120

Partnerships (limited) conversion to corporations, and impacts on share values, with data by firm, 1980s-91, hearing, 25248–124

Senate Budget Committee

Black higher education instns finances, funding sources, enrollment, and student characteristics, with data for Louisiana instns, 1970s-90, hearing, 25258–24

Budget of US, Senate concurrent resolution, with spending and revenue targets, FY92, annual rpt, 25254–1

Senate Commerce, Science and Transportation Committee

Truck and bus safety inspections, fines, and vehicles and drivers ordered out of service, by State, with program funding, FY89, 25268–78

Senate Documents

Capitol Architect outlays for salaries, supplies, and services, itemized by payee and function, 1st half FY91, semiannual rpt, 25922–2

Finances of Senate, receipts, itemized expenses by payee, and balances, 1st half FY91, semiannual listing, 25922–1

Homelessness issues, population at risk, contributing factors, and Federal funding for services and prevention, with bibl, 1991 compilation of papers, 25928–9

Senate Energy and Natural Resources Committee

Eastern Europe energy production, trade, use, and AID dev assistance, for 3 countries, 1980s-91, 25318–81

Senate Environment and Public Works Committee

Asbestos in buildings, EPA aid for removal, occupational asbestos exposure cancer cases and deaths, and Catholic schools abatement costs, 1985-90, hearing, 25328–32

Hwy Trust Fund finances, unobligated balances by State, and receipt losses from increased ethanol use, 1980s-90, hearing, 25328–31

Senate Finance Committee

Child welfare programs funding by source, and foster care program operations and client characteristics, for selected States, 1960s-95, 25368–169

China trade with US and through Hong Kong, and impacts of revoking most favored nation status, 1987-90, hearing, 25368–174

Foreign countries economic conditions, policy, and trade practices, by country, 1988-90, annual rpt, 21384–5

OASDI trust funds finances, effects of inclusion in budget deficit figures, and social security tax reduction proposals, 1990 hearing, 25368–171

Puerto Rico statehood referendum proposal, impacts on Federal tax revenue and aid outlays, corporations tax-favored status, and economic conditions, projected FY91-2000, hearing, 25368–168

Savings and Investment Incentive Act issues, with IRA participation and other background data, 1980s, 25368–175

South Dakota poverty relief and medical aid programs of counties, spending by type, MSA, and county, 1989, hearing, 25368–176

Tax (income) revenue from corporations, impacts of tax reform and other factors, 1990 hearing, 25368–173

Tax expenditures, Federal revenues forgone through income tax deductions and exclusions by type, FY92-96, annual rpt, 21784–10

Tax reform and investment stimulation proposals, with background data, 1990 hearings, 25368–170

Senate Foreign Relations Committee

Child health and welfare indicators, and economic conditions, for developing countries, 1950s-80s, hearing, 25388–57

Communist countries debt to US and other Western banks, by country, 1980s, conf, 25388–56

Economic conditions, policy, and trade practices, by country, 1988-90, annual rpt, 21384–5

Human rights conditions in 170 countries, and US economic and military aid, 1990, annual rpt, 21384–3

Jewelry trade of US, gold jewelry production and sales, and US and EC gold and silver fineness standards, by country, 1980s, hearing, 25388–58

Senate Governmental Affairs Committee

Census of Population, 1990: cities population and undercounts, and related Federal aid losses, 1990 mayoral survey, hearing, 25408–113

Homeless persons housing and food aid of Fed Govt, funding and operations, with data by State and county, FY89, hearing, 25408–111

Justice Dept and Customs Service asset forfeiture programs finances, and disbursements by State and judicial district, FY85-90, hearing, 25408–112

Senate Human Resources Committee

see Senate Labor and Human Resources Committee

Senate Indian Affairs Committee, Select

Indian Health Service nursing staff, shortages, workload, and pay, by IHS service unit, mid 1980s-90, hearing, 25418–6

Index by Subjects and Names

Timber mgmt programs of Bur of Indian Affairs, funding, acreage, harvest, and tribal investment, by tribe and location, FY77-89 and projected to FY96, hearing, 25418–4

Senate Judiciary Committee

Drug enforcement personnel, arrests, and seizures, for NYC, 1985-90, hearing, 25528–117

Imports purchasing decisions of consumers, importance of brand name, authenticity, origin, and other factors, 1984 survey, hearing, 25528–115

Pretrial processing, detention, and release, for Federal offenders, by defendant characteristics and district, 1988, hearing, 25528–114

Rapes reported, by State, 1989-90, 25528–116

Senate Labor and Human Resources Committee

Child abuse reports, and related deaths, by State, late 1980s, hearing, 25548–102

Drug (prescription) marketing practices, spending by selected firm, and physicians views, 1990 hearings, 25548–103

Radiation exposure of uranium miners and risk of death from cancer and lung diseases, for Indians and compared to whites and foreign countries, 1950s-84, hearing, 25548–101

Youth counseling program based at schools, client risk behaviors and outcomes, 1988/89 study, hearing, 25548–104

Senate Labor and Public Welfare Committee see Senate Labor and Human Resources Committee

Senate Small Business Committee

Dev centers for small business, mgmt and technical aid activities, funding, and client satisfaction and performance, 1980s, hearing, 25728–43

Eastern Europe transition to market economies, US trade prospects, with background data by country, 1980s, hearing, 25728–42

Senate Special Publications

Capitol Architect activities, funding, costs, and contracts, FY88, annual rpt, 25944–1

Sendak, Paul E.

"New England and New York's Timber Economy: A Review of the Statistics", 1208–375

Senegal

Agricultural exports of high-value commodities, indexes and sales by commodity, world area, and country, 1960s-86, 1528–323

Agricultural production, trade, and policies in foreign countries, summary data by country, 1989-90, annual factbook, 1924–12

Agricultural trade of US, by detailed commodity and country, 1989, annual rpt, 1524–8

Agricultural trade of US, by detailed commodity and country, 1990, semiannual rpt, 1522–4

AID cash transfers to Senegal linked to fiscal and govt reforms, effectiveness, 1980s, 9916–1.75

AID economic aid to developing countries, obligations and disbursements by country, quarterly rpt, 9912–4

Index by Subjects and Names

Service academies

AID loans repayment status and terms by program and country, and status of predecessor agency loans, quarterly rpt, 9912–3

Background Notes, summary social, political, and economic data, 1991 rpt, 7006–2.46

Dairy imports, consumption, and market conditions, by sub-Saharan Africa country, 1961-88, 1528–321

Economic and military aid and loans from US and intl agencies, by program and country, FY46-90, annual rpt, 9914–5

Economic and social conditions of developing countries from 1960s, and Intl Dev Cooperation Agency and AID activities and funding, FY90-92, annual rpt, 9904–4

Economic conditions, income, production, prices, employment, and trade, 1990 periodic country rpt, 2046–4.2

Economic conditions, policy, and trade practices, by country, 1988-90, annual rpt, 21384–5

Economic, population, and agricultural data, US and other aid sources, and AID activity, 1987 country rpt, 9916–12.22

Economic, social, political, and geographic summary data, by country, 1991, annual factbook, 9114–2

Exports and imports of US, by transport mode, country, and SITC 1- to 3-digit commodity, 1990, annual rpt, 2424–12

Exports of US, detailed Schedule B commodities with countries of destination, 1990, annual rpt, 2424–10

Food supply, needs, and aid for developing countries, status and alternative forecasts, 1991 world area rpt, 1526–8.1

Human rights conditions in 170 countries, and US economic and military aid, 1990, annual rpt, 21384–3

Military aid of US, arms sales, and training programs costs and budget requests, by program, world region, and country, FY90-92, annual rpt, 7144–13

UN voting record and share of votes in agreement with US, by issue, country, and world area, 1990, annual rpt, 7004–18

see also under By Foreign Country in the "Index by Categories"

Seninger, Stephen

"Wage Differentials and Job Changes", 2626–10.121

Senior citizens

see Aged and aging

Senior Companion Program

Activities and funding of ACTION, by program, FY90, annual rpt, 9024–2

Sentences, criminal procedure

Assaults and deaths of law enforcement officers, by circumstances, agency, victim and offender characteristics, and location, 1990, annual rpt, 6224–3

Banks and thrifts fraud and abuse, Federal agencies enforcement activities and staff, with data by instn and location, 1988-90, hearing, 21408–119

Counterfeiting and other Secret Service investigations and arrests by type, and dispositions, FY90 and trends from FY81, annual rpt, 8464–1

Crime, criminal justice admin and enforcement, and public opinion, data compilation, 1991 annual rpt, 6064–6

Criminal records repository characteristics, holdings, use, and reporting requirements, by State, 1989, 6068–241

Drug abuse history of jail population, by offense, conviction status, criminal and family history, and selected other characteristics, 1989, 6066–19.63

Drug abuse indicators for selected metro areas, research results, data collection, and policy issues, 1991 semiannual conf, 4492–5

Drug enforcement regional task forces investigation of organized crime, activities by agency and region, FY83-90, biennial rpt, 6004–17

Environmental legislation enforcement activities of EPA and State govts, FY90, annual rpt, 9184–21

Federal criminal sentencing, guidelines by offense and circumstances, series, 17668–1

Federal criminal sentencing, guidelines use and results by offense and district, and Sentencing Commission activities, 1990, annual rpt, 17664–1

Federal district court criminal case processing and dispositions, by offense, district, and offender characteristics, 1986, annual rpt, 6064–29

Federal district court criminal case processing and dispositions, by offense, 1980-89, annual rpt, 6064–31

Federal district court criminal caseloads, by offense, disposition, and district, 1980-90, last issue of annual rpt, 18204–1

Federal district court dispositions of criminal defendants, 1990, annual rpt, 18204–8.18

Felony arrests, prosecutions, convictions, and sentencing, by offender characteristics and offense, 1988, 6066–25.33; 6066–25.39

Jail population, by criminal, correctional, drug use, and family history, and selected other characteristics, 1989, 6066–19.62

Jail population, by sociodemographic characteristics, criminal and drug use history, whether convicted, offense, and sentencing, 1989, annual rpt, 6064–26.3

Juvenile facilities, population, and costs, by facility and resident characteristics, region, and State, 1985-89, biennial rpt, 6064–5

Older persons abuse and neglect by circumstances and characteristics of abuser and victim, and States protective services budgets and staff, by location, 1980s, hearing, 21148–62

Pretrial release of felony defendants and rearrests, by offense type and selected characteristics, 1988, 6066–25.36

Prison and parole admissions and releases, sentence length, and time served, by offense and offender characteristics, 1985, annual rpt, 6064–33

Prisoners in Federal and State instns, admissions and outcomes by sentence and inmate characteristics, by State, 1989, annual rpt, 6064–26.4

Prisoners in Federal and State instns by sex, admissions, and instn capacity and overcrowding, by State, 1980s-90, annual rpt, 6066–25.37

Savings instns fraud and abuse, Federal indictments and case dispositions, FY89-91, press release, 6008–33

State court probation and split sentences for felony offenses, sentence lengths, case processing time, and felon characteristics, by offense, 1986, 6068–242

Statistical Abstract of US, 1991 annual data compilation, 2324–1.5

Tax litigation and enforcement activity of IRS, FY90, annual rpt, 8304–3.1

US attorneys civil and criminal cases by type and disposition, and collections, by Federal district, FY90, annual rpt, 6004–2.1; 6004–2.2

VA programs fraud and abuse, audits and investigations, 2nd half FY90, semiannual rpt, 8602–1

Violent crime victimizations, circumstances, victim characteristics, arrest, recidivism, sentences, and prisoners, 1980s, 6068–148

Women prisoners in State instns, by offense, drug use history, whether abused, and other characteristics, 1986, 6066–19.61

see also Capital punishment

see also Crime victim compensation

see also Fines and settlements

see also Pardons

see also Parole and probation

Separation of powers

see also Congressional-executive relations

Septicemia

Deaths and rates, by cause and age, preliminary 1989-90, US Vital Statistics annual rpt, 4144–7

Deaths and rates, by cause, provisional data, monthly rpt, 4142–1.2

Deaths and rates, by detailed cause and demographic characteristics, 1988 and trends from 1900, US Vital Statistics annual rpt, 4144–2

Hospital deaths of Medicare patients, actual and expected rates by diagnosis, with hospital characteristics, by instn, FY87-89, annual regional rpt series, 4654–14

see also under By Disease in the "Index by Categories"

Servants

see Domestic workers and services

Service academies

Costs of service academies by type, staffing, and grad advancement in military, FY88-90, GAO rpt, 26123–355

Enrollment, staff, outlays, and facilities for DOD training and education programs, by service branch, FY92, annual rpt, 3504–5

Expenditures for education by Federal agency, program, and recipient type, and instn spending, FY80-90, annual rpt, 4824–8

Maritime academy students receiving Fed Govt aid, monthly rpt, 7702–1

Officer candidates, by service branch, quarterly rpt, 3542–14

Officer candidates, FY46-90, annual rpt, 3544–1.2

Personnel of DOD, and organization, budget, weapons, and property, by service branch, State, and country, 1991 annual summary rpt, 3504–13

Reserve forces personnel strengths and characteristics, by component, FY90, annual rpt, 3544–38

Ships on loan to maritime academies, vessels and tonnage, as of Jan 1991, semiannual listing, 7702–2

Service industries

Index by Subjects and Names

Service industries

Alien nonresidents income from US sources and tax withheld by country and US tax treaty status, 1988, annual article, 8302–2.206

Business statistics, detailed data for major industries and economic indicators, *Survey of Current Business*, monthly rpt, 2702–1

Capital expenditures for plant and equipment, by major industry group, quarterly rpt, 2502–2

Caribbean Basin Initiative investment incentives, economic impacts, with finances and employment by country, 1984-90, 2048–141

Census Bur rpts and data files, coverage and availability, 1991 annual listing, 2304–2

Chicago employment growth in service, manufacturing, and other industries, analysis of contributing factors, 1970s-87, article, 9375–1.204

Classification codes concordance of Canada and US SICs, for 1- to 4-digit levels, 1991 rpt, 2628–31

Collective bargaining agreements expiring during year, and workers covered, by firm, union, industry group, and State, 1991, annual rpt, 6784–9

Collective bargaining wage and benefit changes, quarterly press release, 6782–2

Collective bargaining wage changes and coverage, by industry sector and whether contract includes escalator clause and lump sum payment, 1980-90, annual article, 6722–1.227

Consumer spending forecasting performance of consumer sentiment index, 1950s-90, technical paper, 9366–6.282

Consumer spending, monthly rpt, quarterly data, 23842–1.1

County Business Patterns, 1988: employment, establishments, and payroll, by SIC 2- to 4-digit industry and county, annual State rpt series, 2326–6

County Business Patterns, 1989: employment, establishments, and payroll, by SIC 2- to 4-digit industry and county, annual State rpt series, 2326–8

DC production index, by component, 1987-91, article, 9389–1.203

DOD contracts, payroll, and personnel, by service branch and location, with top 5 contractors and maps, by State and country, FY90, annual rpt, 3544–29

DOD prime contract awards, by category, contract and contractor type, and service branch, FY81-1st half FY91, semiannual rpt, 3542–1

DOD prime contract awards, by category, contractor type, and State, FY88-90, annual rpt, 3544–11

DOD prime contract awards, by detailed procurement category, FY87-90, annual rpt, 3544–18

DOD prime contract awards, by size and type of contract, service branch, competitive status, category, and labor standard, FY90, annual rpt, 3544–19

Earnings by industry div, and personal income per capita and by source, by State, MSA, and county, 1984-89, annual regional rpts, 2704–2

Economic and employment conditions, alternative BLS projections to 2005 and trends 1970s-90, biennial article, 6722–1.253

Economic indicators and components, current data and annual trends, monthly rpt, 23842–1.7

Economic indicators compounded annual rates of change, monthly rpt, 9391–3

Employment and Earnings, detailed data, monthly rpt, 6742–2.5

Employment Cost Index and percent change by occupational group, industry div, region, and metro-nonmetro area, quarterly press release, 6782–5

Employment, earnings, and hours, by SIC 1- to 4-digit industry, monthly and annual averages, selected years 1909-90, annual rpt, 6744–4

Employment, earnings, and hours, monthly press release, 6742–5

Employment situation, earnings, hours, and other BLS economic indicators, transcripts of BLS Commissioner's monthly testimony, periodic rpt, 23846–4

Employment, unemployment, and labor force characteristics, by region, State, and selected metro area, 1990, annual rpt, 6744–7

Enterprise Statistics, 1987: auxiliaries of multi-establishment firms, finances and operations by function, industry, and State, 2329–6

Enterprise Statistics, 1987: finances and operations for companies, by size, level of diversification, form of organization, and industry group, 2329–8

Export and import price indexes for goods and services, and dollar exchange rate indexes, quarterly press release, 6762–13

Exports and export-related employment, by SIC 3-digit industry and State, model results, 1987, annual rpt, 2506–16.1

Exports and imports of services, direct and among multinatl firms affiliates, by industry and world area, 1986-90, article, 2702–1.223

Exports of goods, services, and investment, trade barriers, impacts, and US actions, by country, 1989, annual rpt, 444–2

Finances and operations, by SIC 2- to 4-digit industry, forecast 1991, annual rpt, 2044–28

Foreign direct investment in US, major transactions by type, industry, country, and US location, 1989, annual rpt, 2044–20

Foreign direct investment of US, by industry group and world area, 1987-90, annual article, 2702–1.220

Franchise business opportunities by firm and kind of business, and sources of aid and info, 1990 annual listing, 2104–7

Import restraint elimination impacts on US economy and selected service industries, 1970s-90, 9886–4.173

Income (personal) per capita disparity among States, with data by industrial base, 1979, 1989, and projected to 1995, 1548–379

Input-output structure of US economy, detailed interindustry transactions for 84 industries, and components of final demand, 1986, annual article, 2702–1.206

Input-output structure of US economy, detailed interindustry transactions for 85 industries, 1982 benchmark data, 2702–1.213

Intl transactions accounts statistical discrepancy assessment, with data for services component, and alternative regression results, 1970s-90, technical paper, 9366–7.258

Intl transactions summary, 1980s-90, annual article, 9362–1.202

Labor hourly costs, by component, industry sector, worker class, and firm size, 1990, annual rpt, 6744–22

Mail volume to and from households, use, and views, by class, source, content, and household characteristics, 1987-88, annual rpt, 9864–10

Military post exchange operations, and sales by commodity, by facility and location worldwide, FY89, annual rpt, 3504–10

Multinatl firms US affiliates, finances, and operations, by industry, world area of parent firm, and State, 1988-89, annual rpt, 2704–4

Multinatl US firms and foreign affiliates finances and operations, by industry and world area of parent firm, 1989 benchmark survey, preliminary annual rpt, 2704–5

New England States employment variability relation to service and financial industries employment, with data by selected industry group and State, 1970s-89, article, 9373–1.212

Occupational injuries, illnesses, and workdays lost, by SIC 2-digit industry, 1989-90, annual press release, 6844–3

Occupational injury and illness rates, by SIC 2- to 4-digit industry, 1988-89, annual rpt, 6844–7

Occupational injury and illness rates, by SIC 2- to 4-digit industry, 1989, annual rpt, 6844–1

Public lands concession operations, receipts, and fees, by Federal agency and for top 100 firms, 1989, GAO rpt, 26113–531

Puerto Rico and other US possessions corporations income tax returns, income and tax items, and employment, by selected industry, 1987, article, 8302–2.213

Puerto Rico economic censuses, 1987: wholesale and retail trade and service industry finances and operations, by SIC 2- to 4-digit industry and municipio, 2591–1

Puerto Rico economic censuses, 1987: wholesale, retail, and service industries finances and operations, by establishment characteristics and SIC 2- and 3-digit industry, subject rpts, 2591–2

Receipts for services, by SIC 2- to 4-digit kind of business, 1990, annual rpt, 2413–8

Science and engineering employment and education, and R&D spending, for US and selected foreign countries, 1991 annual rpt, 9627–35.2

SEC registration, firms required to file annual rpts, as of Sept 1990, annual listing, 9734–5

Senate receipts, itemized expenses by payee, and balances, 1st half FY91, semiannual listing, 25922–1

Southeastern US services and manufacturing sectors, earnings and earnings distribution by State, 1989, article, 9391–16.205

Index by Subjects and Names

Southeastern US services sector employment growth and share of output by industry, by State, various periods 1979-89, article, 9391–16.203

Soviet Union GNP by component and industry sector, and CIA estimation methods, 1950s-87, 23848–223

Soviet Union GNP by detailed income and outlay component, 1985, 2326–18.59

State and Metro Area Data Book, 1991 data compilation, 2328–54

Statistical Abstract of US, 1991 annual data compilation, 2324–1.28

Tax (income) returns filed by type of filer, selected income items, quarterly rpt, 8302–2.1

Tax (income) returns for foreign corporate activity in US, assets, and income statement items, by industry div and selected country, 1986-87, article, 8302–2.205

Tax (income) returns of corporations, income and tax items by asset size and detailed industry, 1987, annual rpt, 8304–4

Tax (income) returns of corporations, income and tax items by asset size and detailed industry, 1988, annual rpt, 8304–21

Tax (income) returns of corporations with foreign tax credit, income and tax items by industry group, 1986, biennial article, 8302–2.203

Tax (income) returns of multinatl US firms foreign affiliates, income statement items, by asset size and industry, 1986, biennial article, 8302–2.212

Tax (income) returns of partnerships, income statement and balance sheet items, by industry group, 1989, annual article, 8302–2.216; 8304–18

Tax (income) returns of sole proprietorships, income statement items, by industry group, 1989, annual article, 8302–2.214

Tax (income) returns of US corporations under foreign control, assets and income statement items by industry div and country, 1988, article, 8302–2.219

Texas services sector growth impact on wages, with data by industry and sector, late 1970s-89, article, 9379–1.210

Wage and benefit changes from collective bargaining and mgmt decisions, by industry div, monthly rpt, 6782–1

Wages by occupation, and benefits for office and plant workers, periodic MSA survey rpt series, 6785–11; 6785–12

see also Accounting and auditing
see also Adult day care
see also Advertising
see also Agricultural services
see also Associations
see also Automobile repair and maintenance
see also Barber and beauty shops
see also Census of Service Industries
see also Child day care
see also Consultants
see also Courier services
see also Credit bureaus and agencies
see also Detective and protective services
see also Direct marketing
see also Domestic workers and services
see also Gasoline service stations
see also Health facilities and services

see also Hotels and motels
see also Information services
see also Janitorial and maintenance services
see also Labor unions
see also Laundry and cleaning services
see also Lawyers and legal services
see also Legal aid
see also Membership organizations
see also Motion pictures
see also Motor vehicle rental
see also Museums
see also Nonprofit organizations and foundations
see also Public relations
see also Public services
see also Rental industries
see also Repair industries
see also Service workers
see also Travel agencies
see also under By Industry in the "Index by Categories"

Service stations
see Gasoline service stations

Service workers

Educational attainment, by sociodemographic characteristics and location, 1989 and trends from 1940, biennial Current Population Rpt, 2546–1.452

Employment, earnings, and hours, monthly press release, 6742–5

Employment situation, earnings, hours, and other BLS economic indicators, transcripts of BLS Commissioner's monthly testimony, periodic rpt, 23846–4

Employment, unemployment, and labor force characteristics, by region, State, and selected metro area, 1990, annual rpt, 6744–7

Immigrants admitted to US, by occupational group and country of birth, preliminary FY90, annual table, 6264–1

Income (household, family, and personal), by source, detailed characteristics, and region, 1988-89, annual Current Population Rpt, 2546–6.68

Income (household, family, and personal), by source, detailed characteristics, and region, 1990, annual Current Population Rpt, 2546–6.70

Manufacturing employment, by detailed occupation and SIC 2-digit industry, 1989 survey, triennial rpt, 6748–52

State and local govt employment of minorities and women, by occupation, function, pay level, and State, 1990, annual rpt, 9244–6

Temporary help supply establishments by occupation supplied, receipts by source, and payroll, by MSA, 1987 Census of Service Industries, 2393–4.8

see also Area wage surveys
see also Domestic workers and services
see also Health occupations
see also Industry wage surveys
see also Police
see also Service industries
see also under By Occupation in the "Index by Categories"

Servicepersons life insurance programs

Actuarial analyses of VA life insurance programs for veterans and servicepersons, 1990, annual rpt, 8604–1

Budget of US, obligations and authority by function, agency, and program, with summaries, analyses, and historical tables, FY92, annual rpt, 104–2

Sewage and wastewater systems

Expenditures for VA programs, by State, county, and congressional district, FY90, annual rpt, 8604–6

Finances and coverage of VA life insurance for veterans and servicepersons, by program and State, 1990, annual rpt, 8604–4

Finances and operations of VA insurance programs, FY90 and cumulative from 1965, annual rpt, 8604–3.7

Financial statements and death rates, for servicepersons and veterans group life insurance programs, as of June 1991, annual rpt, 8654–1

see also Veterans benefits and pensions

Sesame seed
see Oils, oilseeds, and fats

Set-aside programs

see Agricultural production quotas and price supports

see Defense contracts and procurement

see Small business

Seth, Rama

"Explaining LBOs and Acquisitions", 9385–8.86

"Growth in Japanese Lending and Direct Investment in the U.S.: Are They Related?", 9385–8.97

"Leverage and Cyclicality", 9385–8.88

"Patterns of Corporate Leverage in Selected Industrialized Countries", 9385–8.103

Setia, Parveen P.

"Characteristics of U.S. Rice Farms and Operators", 1561–8.205

Setmire, James G.

"Reconnaissance Investigation of Water Quality, Bottom Sediment, and Biota Associated with Irrigation Drainage in the Salton Sea Area, California, 1986-87", 5666–27.4

Settlements

see Fines and settlements

Severance taxes

Energy producers finances and operations, by energy type for US firms domestic and foreign operations, 1989, annual rpt, 3164–44

Finances of govts, tax systems and revenue, and fiscal structure, by level of govt and State, 1991 and historical trends, annual rpt, 10044–1

State govt revenue by source, spending and debt by function, and holdings, FY90, annual rpt, 2466–2.6

State govt tax collections by detailed type of tax, and tax rates, by State, FY90, annual rpt, 2466–2.7

Statistical Abstract of US, 1991 annual data compilation, 2324–1.9

Timber industry impacts of northern spotted owl conservation in Pacific Northwest, and local govts Federal payments and severance taxes, 1980s and projected to 2000, hearing, 21168–50

Sewage and wastewater systems

Air pollution emissions factors, by detailed pollutant and source, data compilation, 1990 rpt, 9198–120

Assistance (financial and nonfinancial) of Fed Govt, 1991 base edition with supplements, annual listing, 104–5

Atlantic Ocean deepwater sewage sludge dumpsite, discharges and water properties, 1990, annual rpt, 2164–20

Sewage and wastewater systems

Budget of US, formula grant program obligations to State and local govts, by agency, program, and State, FY92, annual rpt, 104–30

Building materials PPI, by construction industry, monthly rpt, 6762–6

Condition, mgmt, R&D, and funding, for transportation and environmental public works, 1986-91, 26358–235

Construction and repair needs for small community wastewater treatment facilities to meet Clean Water Act standards, by State and region, 1988 and 2008, 1588–155

Construction industries census, 1987: establishments, employment, receipts, and expenditures, by SIC 4-digit industry and State, final industry rpt series, 2373–1

Construction of wastewater treatment plants, local govt loan funds Federal and State funding by State, 1990, GAO rpt, 26113–521

Construction put in place (public and private), by type, bimonthly rpt, 2042–1.1

Construction put in place, value of new public and private structures, by type, monthly rpt, 2382–4

Construction spending by Fed Govt, by program and type of structure, FY85-92, annual article, 2042–1.206

Costs of environmental protection programs to govts and households, by program type and city size, 1960s-88 and projected to 2000, 9188–114

DOD prime contract awards, by detailed procurement category, FY87-90, annual rpt, 3544–18

Environmental Quality, status of problems, protection programs, research, and intl issues, 1991 annual rpt, 484–1

EPA grants to State and local govts for wastewater treatment facility construction, by project, monthly listing, 9202–3

EPA pollution control grant program activities, monthly rpt, 9182–8

Estuary environmental conditions, and fish and shellfish catch by species and region, 1980s, 2178–27

Expenditures for pollution abatement by govts, business, and consumers, 1987-89, annual article, 2702–1.229

Expenditures of Fed Govt in States, by type, program, agency, and State, FY90, annual rpt, 2464–2

Farm chemicals use and animal wastes sources of groundwater pollution, and reduction strategies, 1960s-90, 26358–231

Fed Govt grants for public works, proposed replacement with credit subsidies, with background data by project type, FY88, 26306–3.113

Fish kills from water pollution, by pollution source, month, location, and State, 1977-87, last issue of annual rpt, 9204–3

Fish kills in coastal areas related to pollution and natural causes, by land use, State, and county, 1980s, 2178–32

FmHA activities, and loans and grants by program and State, FY90 and trends from FY70, annual rpt, 1184–17

Govt census, 1987: employment, payroll, and average earnings, by function, level of govt, State, county, and population size, 2455–2

Govt employment and payroll, by function, level of govt, and jurisdiction, 1990, annual rpt series, 2466–1

Govt finances, by level of govt, State, and for large cities and counties, annual rpt series, 2466–2

Govt finances, tax systems and revenue, and fiscal structure, by level of govt and State, 1991 with historical trends, annual rpt, 10044–1

Great Lakes wastewater treatment by municipal and industrial facilities, releases, methods, effectiveness, pollutant limits, and enforcement, 1985-88, 14648–24

Groundwater supply, quality, chemistry, and use, State and local area rpt series, 5666–28

Groundwater supply, quality, chemistry, other characteristics, and use, regional rpt series, 5666–25

Housing and households characteristics, unit and neighborhood quality, and journey to work by MSA location, for 11 MSAs, 1984 survey, supplement, 2485–8

Housing and households detailed characteristics, and unit and neighborhood quality, by location, 1987, biennial rpt supplement, 2485–13

Housing and households detailed characteristics, and unit and neighborhood quality, by location, 1989, biennial rpt, 2485–12

Housing and households detailed characteristics, and unit and neighborhood quality, MSA surveys, series, 2485–6

Housing inventory change from 1973, by reason, unit and household characteristics, and location, 1983 survey, biennial rpt, 2485–14

Indian Health Service funding for housing sanitary facilities, and needs, FY60-90, annual rpt, 4084–1

Industrial wastewater pollution releases, levels, treatment, costs, and regulation, with background financial and operating data, industry rpt series, 9206–4

Manufacturing pollution abatement capital and operating costs, by SIC 2-digit industry, 1989, advance annual Current Industrial Rpt, 2506–3.6

New York Bight fish population and disease, and pollutant levels, near sewage sludge dumpsite, 1986-90, last issue of annual rpt, 2164–19

New York Bight pollution levels, sources, treatment costs, economic losses, and environmental and health effects, 1990 conf, 9208–131

Public opinion on taxes, spending, and govt efficiency, by respondent characteristics, 1991 survey, annual rpt, 10044–2

Ship (passenger) sanitary inspection scores, biweekly rpt, 4202–10

Washington State marine sanctuaries proposal, environmental and economic impacts, with background data, 1984-89, 2178–30

Water quality, chemistry, hydrology, and other characteristics, local area studies, series, 5666–27

Water use by end use, well withdrawals, and public supply deliveries, by county, State rpt series, 5666–24

Sex

see Homosexuality

see Men

see Sex crimes

see Sex discrimination

see Sex education

see Sexual behavior

see Sexual sterilization

see Sexually transmitted diseases

see Women

see under By Sex in the "Index by Categories"

Sex crimes

Arrest rates, by offense, sex, age, and race, 1965-89, annual rpt, 6224–7

Arrests, by offense, offender characteristics, and location, 1990, annual rpt, 6224–2.2

Court civil and criminal caseloads for Federal district, appeals, and bankruptcy courts, by type of suit and offense, circuit, and district, 1990, annual rpt, 18204–11

Court civil and criminal caseloads for Federal district, appeals, and special courts, 1990, annual rpt, 18204–8

Court civil and criminal caseloads for Federal district courts, 1991, annual rpt, 18204–2.1

Court criminal case processing in Federal district courts, and dispositions, by offense, district, and offender characteristics, 1986, annual rpt, 6064–29

Court criminal case processing in Federal district courts, and dispositions, by offense, 1980-89, annual rpt, 6064–31

Court criminal cases in Federal district courts, by offense, disposition, and district, 1980-90, last issue of annual rpt, 18204–1

Crime, criminal justice admin and enforcement, and public opinion, data compilation, 1991 annual rpt, 6064–6

Drug test results at arrest, by drug type, offense, and sex, for selected urban areas, quarterly rpt, 6062–3

Homicides, by circumstance, victim and offender relationship, and type of weapon, 1990, annual rpt, 6224–2.1

Juvenile correctional and detention public and private instns, inmates, and expenses, by instn and resident characteristics and State, 1987, biennial rpt, 6064–13

Labor laws enacted, by State, 1990, annual article, 6722–1.209

Pretrial processing, detention, and release, for Federal offenders, by defendant characteristics and district, 1988, hearing, 25528–114

Prison and parole admissions and releases, sentence length, and time served, by offense and offender characteristics, 1985, annual rpt, 6064–33

Sentences for Federal crimes, guidelines use and results by offense and district, and Sentencing Commission activities, 1990, annual rpt, 17664–1

Sentences for Federal offenses, guidelines by offense and circumstances, series, 17668–1

Treatment programs for adult and juvenile sex offenders, by program type and State, data compilation, 1991 annual rpt, 6064–6.1; 6064–6.6

US attorneys civil and criminal cases by type and disposition, and collections, by Federal district, FY90, annual rpt, 6004–2.1

see also Prostitution
see also Rape

Sex discrimination

Air Force recruiting compliance with gender-neutral selection, with aptitude test results by sex, FY86-90, GAO rpt, 26123–359

Educational service delivery and discipline, and discrimination indicators by State, 1988, biennial rpt, 4804–33

Fed Equal Opportunity Recruitment Program activity, and employment by sex, race, pay grade, and occupational group, FY90, annual rpt, 9844–33

Fed Govt employment of minorities and women, and compliance with EEOC standards, by occupation and agency, FY88-92, GAO rpt, 26119–342

Fed Govt personnel action appeals, decisions of Merit Systems Protection Board by agency and region, FY90, annual rpt, 9494–2

Foreign countries human rights conditions in 170 countries, 1990, annual rpt, 21384–3

Harassment (sexual) allegations in Fed Govt personnel action appeals, and decisions of Merit Systems Protection Board by agency and region, FY90, annual rpt, 9494–2

Labor laws enacted, by State, 1990, annual article, 6722–1.209

Sex education

Enrollment in sex education, by grade level and course content, 1986, annual rpt, 4824–2.13

Sexual behavior

Africa (sub-Saharan) AIDS epidemic impacts on population size and components of change, model description and results, 1990-2015, working paper, 2326–18.57

AIDS cases among drug abusers, by drug use, sexual behavior, and other characteristics, 1984-88 local area study, article, 4042–3.206

AIDS cases at VA health care centers by sex, race, risk factor, and facility, and AIDS prevention and treatment issues, quarterly rpt, 8702–1

AIDS cases by risk group, race, sex, age, State, and MSA, and deaths, monthly rpt, 4202–9

AIDS knowledge, attitudes, and risk behaviors of women in methadone maintenance programs, effects of life skills training, 1988 local area study, article, 4042–3.221

AIDS public knowledge, attitudes, and risk behaviors, for women, 1988 survey, 4146–8.200

AIDS virus infection and risk factor prevalence, natl survey methodology and pretest results, 1989, 4148–30

Child health condition and services use, 1990 chartbook, 4108–49

Cocaine abuse, user characteristics, and related crime and violence, 1988 conf, 4498–74

Deaths and rates, by detailed cause and demographic characteristics, 1988 and trends from 1900, US Vital Statistics annual rpt, 4144–2

Genital human papillomavirus risk relation to presence of other cervical cancer risk factors, local area study, 1991 article, 4472–1.215

Health condition improvement and disease prevention goals and recommended activities for 2000, with trends 1970s-80s, 4048–10

Poor black men's drug and condom use and sexual behavior, local area study, 1991 article, 4042–3.254

Research on population and reproduction, Federal funding by project, FY89, annual listing, 4474–9

Research on population, family, and sexual behavior, activities and funding, 1960s-89, 4478–194

see also Contraceptives
see also Family planning
see also Homosexuality
see also Obscenity and pornography
see also Sex crimes
see also Sexually transmitted diseases

Sexual harassment

see Sex discrimination

Sexual sterilization

Abortions, by method, patient characteristics, and State, 1972-88, article, 4202–7.207

Abortions, by method, pregnancy history, and other characteristics of woman, 1988, US Vital Statistics annual rpt, 4146–5.120

Developing countries family planning and population activities of AID, grants by project and recipient, and contraceptive shipments, by country, FY90, annual rpt series, 9914–13

Hospital discharges and length of stay, by diagnosis, patient and instn characteristics, procedure performed, and payment source, 1988, annual rpt, 4147–13.107

Hysterectomies performed by Medicare hospital providers, actual and expected death rates by instn, 1989, annual regional rpt series, 4654–14

Research on population and reproduction, Federal funding by project, FY89, annual listing, 4474–9

Women's infertility prevalence, by age and parity, with infertility services use, selected years 1965-88, 4146–8.194

Sexually transmitted diseases

AIDS virus infection and risk factor prevalence, natl survey methodology and pretest results, 1989, 4148–30

Cases of STD and control activity, by strain, State, and selected city, 1940s-90, 4205–42

Chlamydia infection among pregnant women, and pregnancy outcomes, 1986-88 local area study, article, 4042–3.240

Deaths and rates, by cause, provisional data, monthly rpt, 4142–1.2

Deaths and rates, by detailed cause and demographic characteristics, 1988 and trends from 1900, US Vital Statistics annual rpt, 4144–2

Developing countries family planning and population activities of AID, grants by project and recipient, and contraceptive shipments, by country, FY90, annual rpt series, 9914–13

Genital human papillomavirus risk relation to presence of other cervical cancer risk factors, local area study, 1991 article, 4472–1.215

Health condition and health care resources, use, and spending, 1950s-89, annual data compilation, 4144–11

HHS financial aid, by program, recipient, State, and city, FY90, annual regional listings, 4004–3

Homeless persons alcohol abuse, by sex, age, race, and additional diagnoses, aggregate 1985-87, 4488–14

Morbidity and Mortality Weekly Report, infectious notifiable disease cases by age, race, and State, and deaths, 1930s-90, annual rpt, 4204–1

Morbidity and Mortality Weekly Report, infectious notifiable disease cases by State, and public health issues, 4202–1

Natl Inst of Allergy and Infectious Diseases activities, grants by recipient and location, and disease cases, FY83-90, annual rpt, 4474–30

Pelvic inflammatory disease prevention, diagnosis, treatment, and surveillance, CDC guidelines, 1991 rpt, 4206–2.41

Preventive disease and health improvement goals and recommended activities for 2000, with trends 1970s-80s, 4048–10

Research on population, family, and sexual behavior, activities and funding, 1960s-89, 4478–194

State and Metro Area Data Book, 1991 data compilation, 2328–54

see also Acquired immune deficiency syndrome

see also under By Disease in the "Index by Categories"

Seychelles

Agricultural trade of US, by detailed commodity and country, 1989, annual rpt, 1524–8

Agricultural trade of US, by detailed commodity and country, 1990, semiannual rpt, 1522–4

AID economic aid to developing countries, obligations and disbursements by country, quarterly rpt, 9912–4

Economic and military aid and loans from US and intl agencies, by program and country, FY46-90, annual rpt, 9914–5

Economic and social conditions of developing countries from 1960s, and Intl Dev Cooperation Agency and AID activities and funding, FY90-92, annual rpt, 9904–4

Economic, social, political, and geographic summary data, by country, 1991, annual factbook, 9114–2

Exports and imports of US, by transport mode, country, and SITC 1- to 3-digit commodity, 1990, annual rpt, 2424–12

Fish catch and vessels off Seychelles by country, and exports to US, 1982-89, article, 2162–1.203

Human rights conditions in 170 countries, and US economic and military aid, 1990, annual rpt, 21384–3

Military aid of US, arms sales, and training programs costs and budget requests, by program, world region, and country, FY90-92, annual rpt, 7144–13

UN voting record and share of votes in agreement with US, by issue, country, and world area, 1990, annual rpt, 7004–18

Shack-Marquez, Janice

"Issues in Labor Supply", 9362–1.203

Shadyside, Ohio

Floods in Shadyside, Ohio, storm characteristics, deaths, and Natl Weather Service forecast accuracy for flash floods, 1990, 2186–6.2

Shaffer, Sherrill

Shaffer, Sherrill
"Conduct in a Banking Duopoly", 9387–8.251
"Efficient Two-Part Tariffs with Uncertainty and Interdependent Demand", 9387–8.253
"Forecast Announcements and Locally Persistent Bias", 9387–8.249
"Lerner Index, Welfare, and the Structure-Conduct-Performance Linkage", 9387–8.236
"Optimal Acceptance Policies for Journals", 9387–8.254
"Regulation and Endogenous Contestability", 9387–8.237
"Stable Cartels with a Cournot Fringe", 9387–8.233

Shai, Donna
"Cancer Mortality in Cuba and Among the Cuban-Born in the U.S.: 1979-81", 4042–3.205

Shaker Heights, Ohio
Mortgage subsidy programs to promote neighborhood racial integration, effectiveness and impacts on housing prices, 1983-89, working paper, 9377–9.108

Shale oil
see Oil shale

Shapiro, Lewis H.
"Mechanical Properties of Sea Ice and Sea Ice Deformation in the Nearshore Zone", 2176–1.38

Shapouri, Shahla
"Dairy Imports in Sub-Saharan Africa and the Welfare Implications of Import Policies", 1528–321
"Economic Performance and Policy Adjustment: The Experience of Zimbabwe", 1528–319

Sharjah
see United Arab Emirates

Sharks
see Fish and fishing industry

Sharon, Pa.
see also under By SMSA or MSA in the "Index by Categories"

Sharp, Steve C.
"Biannual Water-Resources Review, White Sands Missile Range, New Mexico, 1986-87", 5666–28.7

Sharpe, Steven A.
"Debt Maturity and the Back-to-the-Wall Theory of Corporate Finance", 9366–6.285

Sharples, Jerry
"Longrun Competitiveness of Australian Agriculture", 1528–311

Shaw, Robert M.
"U.S. Foreign Trade in Selected Building Products", 2042–1.204

Shea, Dennis G.
"Living Benefits: Closing the Gap for LTC Financing", 2626–10.128

Shea, Martina
"Transitions in Income and Poverty Status: 1987-88", 2546–20.19

Sheboygan County, Wis.
see also under By SMSA or MSA in the "Index by Categories"

Sheep
see Livestock and livestock industry

Shelburne, Robert C.
"Trade and Employment Effects of the Caribbean Basin Economic Recovery Act", 6364–2

Shelby County, Tenn.
Housing and households characteristics, unit and neighborhood quality, and journey to work by MSA location, for 11 MSAs, 1984 survey, supplement, 2485–8
Housing and households detailed characteristics, and unit and neighborhood quality, by location, 1988 survey, MSA rpt, 2485–6.1

Shell, Karl
"Indivisibilities, Lotteries, and Sunspot Equilibria", 9383–20.3

Shellfish
Alaska OCS environmental conditions and oil dev impacts, compilation of papers, series, 2176–1
Aquaculture in US and Japan, mgmt, methods, and biological data for selected species, 1988 conf, annual rpt, 2164–15
Atlantic Ocean fish and shellfish catch and stocks, by species and northwest location, 1887-1991 and forecast to 1993, semiannual conf, 2162–9
Atlantic Ocean fish and shellfish distribution, bottom trawl survey results by species and location, periodic rpt series, 2164–18
Atlantic Ocean sport and commercial fishing catch and quotas for US and Canada, by species, 1990, annual rpt, 2164–14
California sport and commercial fish and shellfish landings, permits issued, and harbor facilities, 1916-86, 5738–20
China shrimp production and exports, 1982-90, article, 1524–4.3
Coastal and estuarine environmental conditions, research results and methodology, series, 2176–7
Coastal and riparian areas environmental conditions, fish, wildlife, use, and mgmt, for individual ecosystems, series, 5506–9
Coastal areas fish and shellfish catch, life cycles, and environmental needs, for selected species and regions, series, 5506–8
Coastal areas recreation facilities of Fed Govt and States, visitor and site characteristics, 1987-90 survey, regional rpt series, 2176–9
Cold storage holdings of fish and shellfish, by product and species, preliminary data, monthly press release, 2162–2
Consumer Expenditure Survey, food spending by item, household composition, income, age, race, and region, 1980-88, biennial rpt, 1544–30
Consumption, supply, trade, prices, spending, and indexes, by food commodity, 1989, annual rpt, 1544–4
Endangered animals and plants conservation spending of Federal agencies and States, by species, FY90, annual rpt, 5504–33
Endangered animals and plants population status and mgmt activity, by species, 1990, biennial rpt, 5504–35
Environmental Quality, status of problems, protection programs, research, and intl issues, 1991 annual rpt, 484–1
Estuary environmental conditions, and fish and shellfish catch by species and region, 1980s, 2178–27

Index by Subjects and Names

Exports and imports (agricultural) of US, by detailed commodity and country, 1989, annual rpt, 1524–8
Exports and imports (agricultural) of US, by detailed commodity and country, 1990, semiannual rpt, 1522–4
Exports and imports of US, by country and detailed commodity, monthly rpt, 2422–12
Exports and imports of US, by Harmonized System 6-digit commodity and country, 1990, annual rpt, 2424–13
Exports and imports of US, by transport mode, country, and SITC 1- to 3-digit commodity, 1990, annual rpt, 2424–12
Exports of US, detailed Schedule B commodities with countries of destination, 1990, annual rpt, 2424–10
Foreign countries market conditions for US fish and shellfish products, country rpt series, 2166–19
Japan fish catch, prices, trade by country, cold storage holdings, import quotas, and market devs, semimonthly press release, 2162–7
Landings and trade of commercial fisheries, by species, 1980-90, semiannual rpt, 1561–15.1
Landings, trade, use, and fishery operations, with selected foreign data, by species, 1980s-90, annual rpt, 2164–1
Landings, wholesale receipts, prices, trade, and other market activities, by region, weekly regional rpts, 2162–6
Manufacturing annual survey, 1989: finances and operations, by SIC 2- to 4-digit industry, series, 2506–15
Marine Fisheries Review, US and foreign fisheries resources, dev, mgmt, and research, quarterly journal, 2162–1
New York Bight fish population and disease, and pollutant levels, near sewage sludge dumpsite, 1986-90, last issue of annual rpt, 2164–19
New York Bight pollution levels, sources, treatment costs, economic losses, and environmental and health effects, 1990 conf, 9208–131
Nutrient, caloric, and waste composition, detailed data for raw, processed, and prepared foods, 1991 rpt, 1356–3.15
Pacific Ocean estuary waters approved and prohibited for shellfish harvest, and pollution sources, 1985, 2176–7.21
Pollutant concentrations in coastal and estuarine fish, shellfish, and environment, series, 2176–3
Price indexes (producer), by stage of processing and detailed commodity, monthly rpt, 6762–6
Price indexes (producer), by stage of processing and detailed commodity, monthly 1990, annual rpt, 6764–2
Production of processed fish by location, and trade, by species and product, 1987-90, annual rpts, 2166–6
R&D and mgmt of fisheries, Fed Govt grants by project and State, and rpts, 1990, annual listing, 2164–3
Recreational shellfish harvesters selected characteristics, location of harvest and residence, and spending, 1985 survey, 2178–28
Statistical Abstract of US, 1991 annual data compilation, 2324–1.24

Index by Subjects and Names

Washington State marine sanctuaries proposal, environmental and economic impacts, with background data, 1984-89, 2178–30

Wetlands acreage, resources, soil and water properties, and conservation efforts, by wetland type, State rpt series, 5506–11

Sheltered workshops

Finances, operations, and Federal procurement from sheltered workshops, FY80-88, annual rpt, 11714–1

Shelton, L. R.

"Water-Quality Data, San Joaquin Valley, Calif., April 1987 to September 1988. Regional Aquifer-System Analysis", 5666–25.9

Shelton, Wash.

Wages by occupation, and benefits for office and plant workers, 1991 survey, periodic MSA rpt, 6785–3.4

Shephard, William T.

"Human Factors in Aviation Maintenance Phase 1: Progress Report", 7506–10.95

Sherman, Tex.

see also Under By SMSA or MSA in the "Index by Categories"

Shields, Dennis A.

"U.S.-Mexico Fruit Trade", 1561–6.203

Shigella

see Food and waterborne diseases

Shipbuilding and operating subsidies

Assistance (financial and nonfinancial) of Fed Govt, 1991 base edition with supplements, annual listing, 104–5

DOT activities by subagency, budget, and summary accident data, FY88, annual rpt, 7304–1

Freight (waterborne) sponsored by Fed Govt, total and US-flag share by agency and program, 1989, annual rpt, 7704–14.3

MarAd activities, finances, subsidies, and world merchant fleet operations, FY90, annual rpt, 7704–14

Merchant ships in US fleet, operating subsidies, construction, and ship-related employment, monthly rpt, 7702–1

Shipbuilding and repairing

American Samoa employment, earnings, and minimum wage, by establishment and industry, 1989, biennial rpt, 6504–6

Construction and delivery of new ships, by vessel type and country of construction and registry, annual rpt, discontinued, 7704–4

Costs of merchant ship construction and conversion by owner and builder, fleet size, and employment, monthly rpt, 7702–1

County Business Patterns, 1988: employment, establishments, and payroll, by SIC 2- to 4-digit industry and county, annual State rpt series, 2326–6

County Business Patterns, 1989: employment, establishments, and payroll, by SIC 2- to 4-digit industry and county, annual State rpt series, 2326–8

DOD budget, procurement appropriations by item, service branch, and defense agency, FY90-93, annual rpt, 3544–32

Employment, earnings, and hours, by SIC 1- to 4-digit industry, monthly and annual averages, selected years 1909-90, annual rpt, 6744–4

Employment shipboard, shipyard, and longshore, FY89-90, annual rpt, 7704–14.3

Enterprise Statistics, 1987: finances and operations for companies, by size, level of diversification, form of organization, and industry group, 2329–8

Exports and imports of US, by country and detailed commodity, monthly rpt, 2422–12

Exports and imports of US, by Harmonized System 6-digit commodity and country, 1990, annual rpt, 2424–13

Exports and imports of US, by transport mode, country, and SITC 1- to 3-digit commodity, 1990, annual rpt, 2424–12

Exports of US, detailed Schedule B commodities with countries of destination, 1990, annual rpt, 2424–10

Facilities for shipbuilding and repair, capacity, and employment, by shipyard, 1990, annual rpt, 7704–9

Foreign and US merchant ships, tonnage, and new ship construction and deliveries, by vessel type and country, as of Jan 1990, annual rpt, 7704–3

Foreign-flag ships owned by US firms and foreign affiliates, by type, owner, and country of registry and construction, as of Jan. 1991, semiannual rpt, 7702–3

Gear production for selected uses under alternative production requirements, and industry finances and operations, late 1940s-89, 2028–1

Manufacturing annual survey, 1989: finances and operations, by SIC 2- to 4-digit industry, series, 2506–15

Manufacturing census, 1987: employment and shipments under Fed Govt contracts, by SIC 4-digit industry, 2497–7

Manufacturing census, 1987: finances and operations, by SIC 2- to 4-digit industry, State, and MSA, with trends from 1849, 2497–1

Manufacturing census, 1987: finances and operations, by type of organization and SIC 2- to 4-digit industry, subject rpt, 2497–5

Manufacturing finances and operations, by SIC 2- to 4-digit industry, forecast 1991, annual rpt, 2044–28

Merchant ships in US fleet and Natl Defense Reserve Fleet, vessels, tonnage, and owner, as of Jan 1991, semiannual listing, 7702–2

Navy budget, personnel, procurement, and equipment, planned FY91-93, annual fact sheet, 3804–16

Navy nuclear-powered vessels and support facilities radioactive waste, releases in harbors, and public exposure, 1970s-90, annual rpt, 3804–11

Navy personnel radiation exposure on nuclear-powered vessels and at support facilities, and injury claims, 1950s-90, annual rpt, 3804–10

Navy ship modernization program costs and admin, FY87, GAO rpt, 26123–320

Occupational injury and illness rates, by SIC 2- to 4-digit industry, 1988-89, annual rpt, 6844–7

Occupational injury and illness rates, by SIC 2- to 4-digit industry, 1989, annual rpt, 6844–1

Ships and shipping

Oceanographic research ships, fleet condition, funding, voyages, and modernization costs, for NOAA, 1980s-90 and projected to 2020, 2148–60

OECD trade, total and for 4 major countries, and US trade by country, by commodity, 1970-89, world area rpt series, 9116–1

Pollution (water) industrial releases in wastewater, levels, treatment, costs, and regulation, with background financial and operating data, 1989 industry rpt, 9206–4.13

Price indexes (producer), by stage of processing and detailed commodity, monthly rpt, 6762–6

Price indexes (producer), by stage of processing and detailed commodity, monthly 1990, annual rpt, 6764–2

Respiratory diseases related to occupational hazards, epidemiology, diagnosis, and treatment, for selected industries and work settings, 1988 conf, 4248–90

Statistical Abstract of US, 1991 annual data compilation, 2324–1.22

Tax (income) returns of corporations, income and tax items by asset size and detailed industry, 1987, annual rpt, 8304–4

Tax (income) returns of corporations, income and tax items by asset size and detailed industry, 1988, annual rpt, 8304–21

see also Shipbuilding and operating subsidies

Shipments, industrial

see Industrial production

Ships and shipping

American Samoa employment, earnings, and minimum wage, by establishment and industry, 1989, biennial rpt, 6504–6

Bulk carrier ships in world fleet, characteristics by country of registry, annual listing, discontinued, 7704–13

Census of Transportation, 1987: finances and operations by size, ownership, and State, and revenues by MSA, by SIC 2- to 4-digit industry, 2579–1

Containers (intermodal) and equipment owned by shipping and leasing companies, inventory by type and size, 1990, annual rpt, 7704–10

County Business Patterns, 1988: employment, establishments, and payroll, by SIC 2- to 4-digit industry and county, annual State rpt series, 2326–6

County Business Patterns, 1989: employment, establishments, and payroll, by SIC 2- to 4-digit industry and county, annual State rpt series, 2326–8

Customs Service activities, collections, entries processed by mode of transport, and seizures, FY86-90, annual rpt, 8144–1

Employment, earnings, and hours, by SIC 1- to 4-digit industry, monthly and annual averages, selected years 1909-90, annual rpt, 6744–4

Energy use by mode of transport, fuel supply, and demographic and economic factors of vehicle use, 1970s-89, annual rpt, 3304–5

Enterprise Statistics, 1987: finances and operations for companies, by size, level of diversification, form of organization, and industry group, 2329–8

Ships and shipping

Exports and imports (waterborne) of US, by type of service, commodity, country, route, and US port, 1988, annual rpt, 7704–2

Exports and imports (waterborne) of US, by type of service, customs district, port, and world area, monthly rpt, 2422–7

Exports and imports between US and outlying areas, by detailed commodity and mode of transport, 1990, annual rpt, 2424–11

Exports of US, detailed commodities by country, monthly CD-ROM, 2422–13

Finances and operations, by SIC 2- to 4-digit industry, forecast 1991, annual rpt, 2044–28

Fishery employment, vessels, plants, and cooperatives, by State, 1989 and trends from 1970, annual rpt, 2164–1.10

Foreign and US merchant ships, tonnage, and new ship construction and deliveries, by vessel type and country, as of Jan 1990, annual rpt, 7704–3

Foreign and US merchant ships, tonnage, shipments, crews, and other operations, as of 1990, annual rpt, 7704–14

Foreign-flag ships owned by US firms and foreign affiliates, by type, owner, and country of registry and construction, as of Jan. 1991, semiannual rpt, 7702–3

Fuel oil and kerosene sales and deliveries, by end-use, PAD district, and State, 1989, annual rpt, 3164–94

Import restraint elimination impacts on US economy and selected service industries, 1970s-90, 9886–4.173

Imports of US, detailed commodities by country, monthly CD-ROM, 2422–14

Lumber and pulp products supply and use, and timber resources, detailed data, 1950s-87 and alternative projections to 2040, 1208–24.20

Maritime Commission activities, case filings by type and disposition, and civil penalties by shipper, FY90, annual rpt, 9334–1

Merchant ships in US fleet and Natl Defense Reserve Fleet, vessels, tonnage, and owner, as of Jan 1991, semiannual listing, 7702–2

Natl transportation system planning, use, condition, accidents, and needs, by mode of transport, 1940s-90 and projected to 2020, 7308–202

Oceanographic research and distribution activities of World Data Center A by country, and cruises by ship, 1989, annual rpt, 2144–15

Oceanographic research ships, fleet condition, funding, voyages, and modernization costs, for NOAA, 1980s-90 and projected to 2020, 2148–60

Oil production on Alaska North Slope, and impacts of lifting export controls on US oil trade, West Coast prices, and shipping industry, 1988 and forecast 1990-95, GAO rpt, 26113–496

Overseas Business Reports: economic conditions, investment and export opportunities, and trade practices, country market research rpt series, 2046–6

Panama Canal traffic and tolls, by commodity, flag of vessel, and trade route, FY90, annual rpt, 9664–3.1

Pollution (air) contributing to global warming, emissions factors and control costs, by pollutant and source, 1990 rpt, 9198–124

Pollution (air) levels for 6 pollutants, by source, 1970-89 and trends from 1940, annual rpt, 9194–13

Price indexes (producer), by stage of processing and detailed commodity, monthly rpt, 6762–6

Publications and data files of Census Bur on foreign trade, 1991 guide, 2428–11

St Lawrence Seaway Dev Corp finances and activities, and Seaway cargo tonnage, 1989, annual rpt, 7744–1

St Lawrence Seaway ship, cargo, and passenger traffic, and toll revenue, 1990 and trends from 1959, annual rpt, 7744–2

Statistical Abstract of US, 1991 annual data compilation, 2324–1.22

Tax (income) returns of corporations, income and tax items by asset size and detailed industry, 1987, annual rpt, 8304–4

Tax (income) returns of corporations, income and tax items by asset size and detailed industry, 1988, annual rpt, 8304–21

Tax (income) returns of sole proprietorships, income statement items, by industry group, 1989, annual article, 8302–2.214

Traffic of waterborne domestic and foreign freight, by US port and State, 1989, annual rpt, 3754–7

Weather rpts and gale and wave observations received from ships, quarterly journal, 2152–8

Whales (bowhead) population in Arctic areas, impacts of subsistence whaling, shipping, noise, and other human activity, mid 1970s-80s, 5738–30

see also Barges

see also Boats and boating

see also Freight

see also Harbors and ports

see also Inland water transportation

see also Longshoremen

see also Marine accidents and safety

see also Maritime law

see also Merchant seamen

see also Naval vessels

see also Navigation

see also Nuclear-powered ships

see also Oil spills

see also Passenger ships

see also Shipbuilding and operating subsidies

see also Shipbuilding and repairing

see also Tanker ships

see also under By Industry in the "Index by Categories"

Shock incarceration programs

see Rehabilitation of criminals

Shoes and shoe industry

Business statistics, detailed data for major industries and economic indicators, *Survey of Current Business*, monthly rpt, 2702–1.15

Consumer Expenditure Survey, household income by source, and itemized spending, by selected characteristics and region, 1988-89, annual rpt, 6764–5

County Business Patterns, 1988: employment, establishments, and payroll, by SIC 2- to 4-digit industry and county, annual State rpt series, 2326–6

County Business Patterns, 1989: employment, establishments, and payroll, by SIC 2- to 4-digit industry and county, annual State rpt series, 2326–8

Index by Subjects and Names

CPI by component for US city average, and by region, population size, and for 27 metro areas, monthly rpt, 6762–2

CPI components relative importance, by selected MSA, region, population size, and for US city average, 1990, annual rpt, 6884–1

Employment, earnings, and hours, by SIC 1- to 4-digit industry, monthly and annual averages, selected years 1909-90, annual rpt, 6744–4

Enterprise Statistics, 1987: finances and operations for companies, by size, level of diversification, form of organization, and industry group, 2329–8

Exports and imports between US and outlying areas, by detailed commodity and mode of transport, 1990, annual rpt, 2424–11

Exports and imports of US, by country and detailed commodity, monthly rpt, 2422–12

Exports and imports of US by country, and trade shifts by commodity, 1990, semiannual rpt, 9882–9

Exports and imports of US, by Harmonized System 6-digit commodity and country, 1990, annual rpt, 2424–13

Exports and imports of US, by selected country, country group, and commodity group, 1990, annual rpt, 2044–37

Exports and imports of US, by transport mode, country, and SITC 1- to 3-digit commodity, 1990, annual rpt, 2424–12

Exports of US, detailed Schedule B commodities with countries of destination, 1990, annual rpt, 2424–10

Franchise business opportunities by firm and kind of business, and sources of aid and info, 1990 annual listing, 2104–7

Import restrictions proposed for textiles, apparel, and shoes, economic impacts, projected 1991-2000, with imports by country, 1989-90, 26306–6.162

Imports of clothing, footwear, luggage, toys, games, and sporting goods from PRC and other countries, 1985-90, article, 9882–2.201

Imports of US given duty-free treatment for value of US material sent abroad, by commodity and country, 1989, annual rpt, 9884–14

Injuries from use of consumer products, by severity, victim age, and detailed product, 1990, annual rpt, 9164–6

Input-output structure of US economy, detailed interindustry transactions for 84 industries, and components of final demand, 1986, annual article, 2702–1.206

Input-output structure of US economy, detailed interindustry transactions for 85 industries, 1982 benchmark data, 2702–1.213

Manufacturing annual survey, 1989: finances and operations, by SIC 2- to 4-digit industry, series, 2506–15

Manufacturing census, 1987: finances and operations, by SIC 2- to 4-digit industry, State, and MSA, with trends from 1849, 2497–1

Manufacturing census, 1987: finances and operations, by type of organization and SIC 2- to 4-digit industry, subject rpt, 2497–5

Index by Subjects and Names

Manufacturing finances and operations, by SIC 2- to 4-digit industry, forecast 1991, annual rpt, 2044–28

Occupational injury and illness rates, by SIC 2- to 4-digit industry, 1988-89, annual rpt, 6844–7

Occupational injury and illness rates, by SIC 2- to 4-digit industry, 1989, annual rpt, 6844–1

OECD trade, total and for 4 major countries, and US trade by country, by commodity, 1970-89, world area rpt series, 9116–1

Price indexes (producer), by stage of processing and detailed commodity, monthly rpt, 6762–6

Price indexes (producer), by stage of processing and detailed commodity, monthly 1990, annual rpt, 6764–2

Price indexes for department store inventories, by class of item, monthly table, 6762–7

Production, employment, use, prices, and US trade by country, quarterly rpt, 9882–6

Production, shipments, trade, and use of shoes, by product, 1990, annual Current Industrial Rpt, 2506–6.8

Production, shipments, trade, and use of shoes, quarterly Current Industrial Rpt, 2506–6.7

Productivity of labor and capital, and indexes of output, hours, and employment, 1967-89, annual rpt, 6824–1.3; 6824–1.5

Puerto Rico economic censuses, 1987: wholesale and retail trade and service industry finances and operations, by SIC 2- to 4-digit industry and municipio, 2591–1

Retail trade census, 1987: depreciable assets, capital and operating expenses, sales, value added, and inventories, by SIC 2- to 4-digit kind of business, 2399–2

Retail trade census, 1987: finances and employment, for establishments with and without payroll, by SIC 2- to 4-digit kind of business, State, and MSA, 2401–1

Retail trade sales and inventories, by kind of business, region, and selected State, MSA, and city, monthly rpt, 2413–3

Retail trade sales, by kind of business, advance monthly rpt, 2413–2

Retail trade sales, inventories, purchases, gross margin, and accounts receivable, by SIC 2- to 4-digit kind of business and form of ownership, 1989, annual rpt, 2413–5

Service industries census, 1987: establishments, receipts by source, payroll, and employment, by SIC 2- to 4-digit kind of business, State, and MSA, 2393–4

Soviet Union GNP by detailed income and outlay component, 1985, 2326–18.59

Statistical Abstract of US, 1991 annual data compilation, 2324–1.27

Tax (income) returns of corporations, income and tax items by asset size and detailed industry, 1987, annual rpt, 8304–4

Tax (income) returns of corporations, income and tax items by asset size and detailed industry, 1988, annual rpt, 8304–21

Wholesale trade census, 1987: establishments, sales by customer class, employment, inventories, and expenses, by SIC 2- to 4-digit kind of business, 2407–4

see also under By Commodity in the "Index by Categories"

Shook, Jonathan E.

"Corporation Income Tax Returns, Income Year 1987", 8302–2.204

Shopland, Donald R.

"Smoking-Attributable Cancer Mortality in 1991: Is Lung Cancer Now the Leading Cause of Death Among Smokers in the U.S.?", 4472–1.219

Shoplifting

Juvenile courts delinquency cases, by offense, referral source, disposition, age, sex, race, State, and county, 1988, annual rpt, 6064–12

Juvenile courts property offenses cases, by disposition and offender age, sex, and race, 1985-86, 6066–27.5

Shopping centers

Mail volume to and from households, use, and views, by class, source, content, and household characteristics, 1987-88, annual rpt, 9864–10

State and Metro Area Data Book, 1991 data compilation, 2328–54

Statistical Abstract of US, 1991 annual data compilation, 2324–1.28

Short, Genie D.

"Deposit Insurance Reform in the Post-FIRREA Environment: Lessons from the Texas Deposit Market", 9379–14.11

Short, Kathleen S.

"Living Arrangements of Young Adults Living Independently: Evidence from the Luxembourg Income Study", 2546–2.157

"Pensions: Worker Coverage and Retirement Benefits, 1987", 2546–20.18

"Transitions in Income and Poverty Status: 1987-88", 2546–20.19

Short, Pamela F.

"Estimates of the Uninsured Population, 1987. National Medical Expenditure Survey", 4186–8.13

"Standardizing Nursing-Home Admission Dates for Short-Term Hospital Stays. National Medical Expenditure Survey", 4186–8.15

Short, Sara D.

"Financial Characteristics of Dairy Farms, 1989", 1561–2.201

"Outlook for Dairy", 1004–16.1

Shreveport, La.

Wages by occupation, for office and plant workers, 1990 survey, periodic MSA rpt, 6785–11.3

see also under By City and By SMSA or MSA in the "Index by Categories"

Shrimp

see Aquaculture

see Shellfish

Shrubs

see Plants and vegetation

Shulters, Michael V.

"Rainfall and Runoff Quantity and Quality Characteristics of Four Urban Land-Use Catchments in Fresno, Calif., October 1981-April 1983", 5666–27.2

Sierra Leone

Sibert, Anne

"Government Finance in a Common Currency Area", 9381–10.120

Sichel, Daniel E.

"Cyclical Patterns in the Variance of Economic Activity", 9366–6.275

Sickle-cell anemia

Deaths and rates, by detailed cause and demographic characteristics, 1988 and trends from 1900, US Vital Statistics annual rpt, 4144–2

Sickmund, Melissa

"Offenders in Juvenile Court, 1987", 6066–27.6

"Runaways in Juvenile Courts", 6066–27.4

Sickness

see Absenteeism

see Diseases and disorders

see Health condition

see Hospitalization

Sieg, Carolyn H.

"Rocky Mountain Juniper Woodlands: Year-Round Avian Habitat", 1208–364

Siegel, D. I.

"Geochemistry of the Cambrian-Ordovician Aquifer System in the Northern Midwest, U.S. Regional Aquifer-System Analysis", 5666–25.10

Siegfried, Clifford A.

"Crangonid Shrimp. Species Profiles: Life Histories and Environmental Requirements of Coastal Fishes and Invertebrates (Pacific Northwest)", 5506–8.132

Sierra Leone

Agricultural exports of high-value commodities, indexes and sales by commodity, world area, and country, 1960s-86, 1528–323

Agricultural production, trade, and policies in foreign countries, summary data by country, 1989-90, annual factbook, 1924–12

Agricultural trade of US, by detailed commodity and country, 1989, annual rpt, 1524–8

Agricultural trade of US, by detailed commodity and country, 1990, semiannual rpt, 1522–4

AID economic aid to developing countries, obligations and disbursements by country, quarterly rpt, 9912–4

Dairy imports, consumption, and market conditions, by sub-Saharan Africa country, 1961-88, 1528–321

Economic and military aid and loans from US and intl agencies, by program and country, FY46-90, annual rpt, 9914–5

Economic and social conditions of developing countries from 1960s, and Intl Dev Cooperation Agency and AID activities and funding, FY90-92, annual rpt, 9904–4

Economic conditions, income, production, prices, employment, and trade, 1991 periodic country rpt, 2046–4.50

Economic, social, political, and geographic summary data, by country, 1991, annual factbook, 9114–2

Exports and imports of US, by transport mode, country, and SITC 1- to 3-digit commodity, 1990, annual rpt, 2424–12

Exports of US, detailed Schedule B commodities with countries of destination, 1990, annual rpt, 2424–10

Sierra Leone

Human rights conditions in 170 countries, and US economic and military aid, 1990, annual rpt, 21384–3

Military aid of US, arms sales, and training programs costs and budget requests, by program, world region, and country, FY90-92, annual rpt, 7144–13

UN voting record and share of votes in agreement with US, by issue, country, and world area, 1990, annual rpt, 7004–18

see also under By Foreign Country in the "Index by Categories"

Sigler, Stella

"Analyses of Natural Gases, 1990", 5604–2

Silicon

see Nonmetallic minerals and mines

Silk

- Broadwoven gray goods production, by fabric type, quarterly Current Industrial Rpt, 2506–5.11
- Exports and imports (agricultural) of US, by detailed commodity and country, 1989, annual rpt, 1524–8
- Exports and imports (agricultural) of US, by detailed commodity and country, 1990, semiannual rpt, 1522–4
- Exports and imports of US, by country and detailed commodity, monthly rpt, 2422–12
- Exports and imports of US, by Harmonized System 6-digit commodity and country, 1990, annual rpt, 2424–13
- Exports and imports of US, by transport mode, country, and SITC 1- to 3-digit commodity, 1990, annual rpt, 2424–12
- Exports of US, detailed Schedule B commodities with countries of destination, 1990, annual rpt, 2424–10
- Imports of silk-blend textiles, by product and country of origin, monthly rpt, 2046–8.6
- Imports of textiles, by country of origin, monthly rpt, 2042–27
- Imports of textiles, by product and country of origin, monthly rpt series, 2046–8; 2046–9
- Manufacturing annual survey, 1989: finances and operations, by SIC 2- to 4-digit industry, series, 2506–15
- Production, prices, trade, and use of natural fibers, periodic situation rpt with articles, 1561–1

Silver

- Business statistics, detailed data for major industries and economic indicators, *Survey of Current Business*, monthly rpt, 2702–1.9
- Coin production and monetary metals use and holdings of US Mint, by metal type, FY90, annual rpt, 8204–1
- County Business Patterns, 1988: employment, establishments, and payroll, by SIC 2- to 4-digit industry and county, annual State rpt series, 2326–6
- County Business Patterns, 1989: employment, establishments, and payroll, by SIC 2- to 4-digit industry and county, annual State rpt series, 2326–8
- Exports and imports of US, by country and detailed commodity, monthly rpt, 2422–12
- Exports and imports of US, by Harmonized System 6-digit commodity and country, 1990, annual rpt, 2424–13

Index by Subjects and Names

- Exports and imports of US, by transport mode, country, and SITC 1- to 3-digit commodity, 1990, annual rpt, 2424–12
- Exports of US, detailed Schedule B commodities with countries of destination, 1990, annual rpt, 2424–10
- Fineness of gold and silver, US and EC standards, 1990 hearing, 25388–58
- Futures and options trading volume, by commodity and exchange, FY90, annual rpt, 11924–2
- Futures trading in selected commodities and financial instruments and indexes, NYC, Chicago, and other markets activity, semimonthly rpt, 11922–5
- Mineral industries census, 1987: energy use and costs, by fuel type, SIC 2- to 4-digit industry, and State, subject rpt, 2517–2
- Mineral industries census, 1987: finances and operations, by establishment characteristics, SIC 2- to 4-digit industry, and State, subject rpt, 2517–1
- Mineral Industry Surveys, commodity review of production, trade, stocks, and use, monthly rpt, 5612–1.10
- Mineral Industry Surveys, State reviews of production, 1990, preliminary annual rpt, 5614–6
- *Minerals Yearbook, 1988*, Vol 3: foreign country reviews of production, trade, and policy, by commodity, annual rpt series, 5604–17
- *Minerals Yearbook, 1989*, Vol 1: commodity review of production, reserves, supply, use, and trade, annual rpt, 5604–15.59
- *Minerals Yearbook, 1989*, Vol 2: State reviews of production and sales by commodity, and business activity, annual rpt series, 5604–16
- *Minerals Yearbook, 1989*, Vol 2: State reviews of production, sales, and firms, by commodity, and business activity, annual rpt, 5604–34
- Mines (metal) and related operations occupational injuries and incidence, employment, and hours, 1989, annual rpt, 6664–3
- Price indexes (producer), by stage of processing and detailed commodity, monthly rpt, 6762–6
- Price indexes (producer), by stage of processing and detailed commodity, monthly 1990, annual rpt, 6764–2
- Production, prices, trade, use, employment, tariffs, and stockpiles, by mineral, with foreign comparisons, 1986-90, annual rpt, 5604–18
- *Statistical Abstract of US*, 1991 annual data compilation, 2324–1.25
- Stockpiling of strategic material by Fed Govt, activity, and inventory by commodity, as of Mar 1991, semiannual rpt, 3542–22
- Stockpiling of strategic material, inventories and needs, by commodity, as of Jan 1991, annual rpt, 3544–37

Silverman, B. P.

"Applying Sociotechnical Work System Design Principles in the IRS", 8304–8.1

Silverman, Herbert A.

- "Medicare-Covered Skilled Nursing Facility Services, 1967-88", 4652–1.239
- "Use of Medicare-Covered Home Health Agency Services, 1988", 4652–1.229

Silverware

see Household supplies and utensils

Silvestri, George T.

- "Occupational Employment Projections", 6722–1.254
- "Who Are the Self-Employed? Employment Profiles and Recent Trends", 6742–1.202

Simi Valley, Calif.

see also under By City in the "Index by Categories"

Simmons, Michele

"U.S. Petroleum Trade 1990", 3162–6.202

Simone, Mark

- "Canada's GRIP Program: A Boon for Canada's Wheat Producers?", 1561–12.202
- "Canola's Growing Importance in North American and Developed East Asian Oilseed Markets", 1524–4.5

Simons, Katerina

"Do Capital Markets Predict Problems in Large Commercial Banks?", 9373–1.210

Singapore

- Agricultural exports of high-value commodities, indexes and sales by commodity, world area, and country, 1960s-86, 1528–323
- Agricultural exports of US, impacts of foreign agricultural and trade policy, with data by commodity and country, 1989, annual rpt, 1924–8
- Agricultural production, prices, and trade, by country, 1980s and forecast 1991, annual world region rpt, 1524–4.5
- Agricultural production, trade, and policies in foreign countries, summary data by country, 1989-90, annual factbook, 1924–12
- Agricultural trade of US, by detailed commodity and country, 1989, annual rpt, 1524–8
- Agricultural trade of US, by detailed commodity and country, 1990, semiannual rpt, 1522–4
- AID economic aid to developing countries, obligations and disbursements by country, quarterly rpt, 9912–4
- Apple import demand in 4 countries, 1960s-83, 1568–296
- Economic and military aid and loans from US and intl agencies, by program and country, FY46-90, annual rpt, 9914–5
- Economic conditions, policy, and trade practices, by country, 1988-90, annual rpt, 21384–5
- Economic, social, political, and geographic summary data, by country, 1991, annual factbook, 9114–2
- Export and import balances of US, and dollar exchange rates, with 5 Asian countries, 1991 semiannual rpt, 8002–14
- Exports and imports of US, by commodity and country, 1970-89, world area rpt, 9116–1.7
- Exports and imports of US by country, and trade shifts by commodity, 1990, semiannual rpt, 9882–9
- Exports and imports of US, by Harmonized System 6-digit commodity and country, 1990, annual rpt, 2424–13
- Exports and imports of US, by selected country, country group, and commodity group, 1990, annual rpt, 2044–37
- Exports and imports of US, by transport mode, country, and SITC 1- to 3-digit commodity, 1990, annual rpt, 2424–12

Index by Subjects and Names

Small business

Exports of US, detailed Schedule B commodities with countries of destination, 1990, annual rpt, 2424–10

Fruit (fresh) trade of Singapore, by country and kind of fruit, 1990 and trends from 1986, article, 1925–34.229

Human rights conditions in 170 countries, and US economic and military aid, 1990, annual rpt, 21384–3

Imports of goods, services, and investment from US, trade barriers, impacts, and US actions, by country, 1990, annual rpt, 444–2

Imports of US given duty-free treatment for value of US material sent abroad, by commodity and country, 1989, annual rpt, 9884–14

Labor conditions, union coverage, and work accidents, 1991 annual country rpt, 6366–4.27

Military aid of US, arms sales, and training programs costs and budget requests, by program, world region, and country, FY90-92, annual rpt, 7144–13

Multinatl US firms and foreign affiliates finances and operations, by industry and world area of parent firm, 1989 benchmark survey, preliminary annual rpt, 2704–5

Multinatl US firms foreign affiliates, income statement items by country and world area, 1986, biennial article, 8302–2.212

Oranges (fresh) exports of US, demand indicators for 4 countries, with production, trade, and use, 1960s-90, 1528–317

Ships in world merchant fleet, tonnage, and new ship construction and deliveries, by vessel type and country, as of Jan 1990, annual rpt, 7704–3

Tobacco and cigarette production, use, and trade, for Singapore, 1980-90, article, 1925–16.212

Typewriters (portable electric) from Singapore at less than fair value, injury to US industry, investigation with background financial and operating data, 1991 rpt, 9886–14.312

UN voting record and share of votes in agreement with US, by issue, country, and world area, 1990, annual rpt, 7004–18

Word processors (personal) from Japan and Singapore at less than fair value, injury to US industry, investigation with background financial and operating data, 1990 rpt, 9886–14.302

see also under By Foreign Country in the "Index by Categories"

Singh, Rajendra P.

"Handling Single Wave Nonresponse in a Panel Survey", 2626–10.117

Single parents

Black Americans social and economic characteristics, for South and total US, 1989-90 and trends from 1969, Current Population Rpt, 2546–1.450

Child care arrangements, costs, and impacts on mothers labor force status, by selected characteristics, 1983 and 1988, article, 6722–1.246

Child care needs impacts on mothers labor force status, and unemployed mothers characteristics, 1986, article, 6722–1.245

Child health, behavioral, emotional, and school problems relation to family structure, by selected characteristics, 1988, 4147–10.178

Child rearing costs for single parent families, by expense type and age of child, 1990, article, 1702–1.203

Earnings, employment and welfare benefits, and poverty status of single mothers, 1989, GAO rpt, 26121–413

Family economic impacts of departure, absence, and presence of parents, 1983-86, Current Population Rpt, 2546–20.17

Family economic impacts of departure, absence, and presence of parents, 1983-86, fact sheet, 2326–17.27

Foreign countries family composition, poverty status, labor conditions, and welfare indicators and needs, by country, 1960s-88, hearing, 23846–4.30

Foster care placement of black children whose parents abuse drugs, by placement reason and outcome, and household and parent characteristics, 1986-90, 4008–114

Households and family characteristics, by location, 1990, annual Current Population Rpt, 2546–1.447

Income (household) by source and spending by type, for lower middle-class 2-parent and single mother families by selected characteristics, 1987, article, 1702–1.207

Insurance (health) coverage of children, by source, family composition, income, and parent employment status, 1977 and 1987, 4186–8.14

Living arrangements, family relationships, and marital status, by selected characteristics, 1990, annual Current Population Rpt, 2546–1.449

Rural areas children in poverty by selected family characteristics, and compared to urban areas, 1987-88, 1598–270

Statistical Abstract of US, 1991 annual data compilation, 2324–1.1

Sinnock, Pomeroy

"First 3 Years of the National AIDS Clearinghouse", 4042–3.256

Sioux City, Iowa

see also under By SMSA or MSA in the "Index by Categories"

Sioux Falls, S.Dak.

see also under By City and By SMSA or MSA in the "Index by Categories"

Skiles, Marilyn E.

"Stabilization and Financial Sector Reform in Mexico", 9385–8.121

Skin diseases

Cancer (melanoma) precursor nevi genetic transmission risk, 1991 article, 4472–1.235

Cancer cases, deaths, and survival rates, by sex, race, age, and body site, 1973-88, annual rpt, 4474–35

Cancer death rates of minorities, by body site, age, sex, and substate area, 1950s-80, atlas, 4478–78

Cancer deaths and rates, by body site, provisional data, monthly rpt, 4142–1.2

Cases of acute and chronic conditions, disability, absenteeism, and health services use, by selected characteristics, 1987, CD-ROM, 4147–10.177

Deaths and rates, by detailed cause and demographic characteristics, 1988 and trends from 1900, US Vital Statistics annual rpt, 4144–2

Hospital discharges and length of stay, by diagnosis, patient and instn characteristics, procedure performed, and payment source, 1988, annual rpt, 4147–13.107

Hospital discharges and length of stay by region and diagnosis, and procedures performed, by age and sex, 1989, annual rpt, 4146–8.198

Hospital discharges by detailed diagnostic and procedure category, primary diagnosis, and length of stay, by age, sex, and region, 1988, annual rpt, 4147–13.105; 4147–13.108

Indian Health Service, tribal, and contract facilities hospitalization, by diagnosis, age, sex, and service area, FY89, annual rpt, 4084–5

Occupational illness rates, by cause and SIC 2- to 3-digit industry, 1989, annual rpt, 6844–1

see also under By Disease in the "Index by Categories"

Skinner, Robert

"Cotton Production Estimates: A Historical Review", 1561–1.208

"Economic Implications of Planting Flexibility Provisions for U.S. Upland Cotton Farms", 1561–1.205

Skully, David

"Food Aid in the Post-Uruguay Round", 1524–4.2

Skyjacking

see Air piracy

Slackman, Joel

"Managed Care in the Military: The Catchment Area Management Demonstrations", 26306–3.117

Slag

see Iron and steel industry

Slander

see Libel and slander

Slaughter, Eric A.

"Quality of Shellfish Growing Waters on the West Coast of the U.S.", 2176–7.21

Slave labor

see Forced labor

Slebos, Robert J.

"Relationship Between K-ras Oncogene Activation and Smoking in Adenocarcinoma of the Human Lung", 4472–1.217

Sleemi, Fehmida

"Collective Bargaining During 1991", 6722–1.206

Sluder, Earl R.

"Genecology of Longleaf Pine in Georgia and Florida", 1208–345

Sludge

see Sewage and wastewater systems

Slum clearance

see Urban renewal

Small business

Capital formation sources and issues for small business, 1990 annual conf, 9734–4

Dev centers for small business, mgmt and technical aid activities, funding, and client satisfaction and performance, 1980s, hearing, 25728–43

Developing countries economic and social conditions from 1960s, and Intl Dev Cooperation Agency and AID activities and funding, FY90-92, annual rpt, 9904–4

DOD contractor subcontract awards to small and disadvantaged business, by firm and service branch, quarterly rpt, 3542–17

DOD prime contract awards, by category, contract and contractor type, and service branch, FY81-1st half FY91, semiannual rpt, 3542–1

Small business

DOD prime contract awards for R&D, for top 500 contractors, FY90, annual listing, 3544–4

DOD prime contract awards in labor surplus areas, by service branch, State, and area, 1st half FY91, semiannual rpt, 3542–19

DOE contracts and grants, by category, State, and for top contractors, FY90, annual rpt, 3004–21

DOE R&D projects and funding at natl labs, universities, and other instns, periodic summary rpt series, 3004–18

Employee benefit plan coverage and provisions in small businesses, by plan type and occupational group, 1990, biennial rpt, 6784–20

Eximbank financial condition, with credit and insurance authorizations and loan activity by country, FY90, annual rpt, 9254–1

Fed Govt financial and nonfinancial domestic aid, 1991 base edition with supplements, annual listing, 104–5

Fed Govt spending in States, by type, program, agency, and State, FY90, annual rpt, 2464–2

Forests (natl) set-aside sales in Pacific Northwest region, quarterly rpt, 1202–3

HHS financial aid, by program, recipient, State, and city, FY90, annual regional listings, 4004–3

Insurance (health) provided by employers, small business and restaurant owners views, 1989 hearings, 23898–7 *

Investment spending of small businesses, impacts of bank loan commitments, 1980-84, article, 9381–1.211

Land Mgmt Bur activities and funding by State, FY89, annual rpt, 5724–13

NASA procurement contract awards, by type, contractor, State, and country, FY91 with trends from 1961, semiannual rpt, 9502–6

Navy procurement, by contractor and location, FY90, annual rpt, 3804–13

Navy small and disadvantaged business procurement office locations, and supply and service codes, 1990 biennial listing, 3804–5

NIH activities, funding by program and recipient type, staff, and clinic patients, by inst, FY90, annual rpt, 4434–3

NIH grants for R&D, by location and recipient, FY90, annual listing, 4434–7.1

Pension benefits disparity between men and women in small business plans by selected participant and plan characteristics, impacts of 1986 Tax Reform Act, 1984-85, GAO rpt, 26121–412

Research and education grants, USDA competitive awards by program and recipient, FY90, annual listing, 1764–1

State and Metro Area Data Book, 1991 data compilation, 2328–54

Statistical Abstract of US, 1991 annual data compilation, 2324–1.17

Surety bond guarantee program of SBA, finances, and contracts by contractor race, obligee type, and region, FY87-89, GAO rpt, 26113–526

Tax (income) returns filed by type of filer, selected income items, quarterly rpt, 8302–2.1

Tax (income) returns of corporations, income and tax items by asset size and detailed industry, 1987, annual rpt, 8304–4

Index by Subjects and Names

Tax collection activity of IRS, by type of tax, FY90, annual rpt, 8304–3.1

Travel agencies contracts of GSA, by business size and recipient, FY88-90, GAO rpt, 26119–331

Workers compensation laws of States and Fed Govt, 1991 semiannual rpt, 6502–1

see also Franchises

see also Small Business Investment Companies

see also Venture capital

Small Business Administration

Budget of US, authoritative financial statements with appropriations, outlays, and receipts, by category and agency, FY90, annual rpt, 8104–2.1

Budget of US, obligations and authority by function, agency, and program, with summaries, analyses, and historical tables, FY92, annual rpt, 104–2

Dev centers for small business, mgmt and technical aid activities, funding, and client satisfaction and performance, 1980s, hearing, 25728–43

Fraud and abuse in SBA programs, audits and investigations, 1st half FY91, semiannual rpt, 9762–5

Leave for illness, disability, and dependent care, coverage, provisions, terminations, costs, and methods of covering for absent worker, by firm size, 1988 survey, 9768–21

Mgmt and financial aid from Minority Business Dev Centers, and SBA financial assistance, by region, FY90, annual rpt, 2104–6

Small Business Investment Companies capital holdings, SBA obligation, and ownership, as of July 1991, semiannual listing, 9762–4

Surety bond guarantee program of SBA, finances, and contracts by contractor race, obligee type, and region, FY87-89, GAO rpt, 26113–526

Women-owned businesses and sales, by industry div and ownership type, and data needs and availability, 1987, 9768–22

Small Business Investment Companies

Capital holdings, SBA obligation, and ownership of SBICs, as of July 1991, semiannual listing, 9762–4

Fraud and abuse in SBA programs, audits and investigations, 1st half FY91, semiannual rpt, 9762–5

Tax (income) returns of corporations, income and tax items by asset size and detailed industry, 1987, annual rpt, 8304–4

Tax (income) returns of corporations, income and tax items by asset size and detailed industry, 1988, annual rpt, 8304–21

Smallwood, David M.

"Food Spending in American Households, 1980-88", 1544–30

Smith, Delores S.

"Home Mortgage Disclosure Act: Expanded Data on Residential Lending", 9362–1.206

Smith, Eric

"Why Is Automobile Insurance in Philadelphia So Damn Expensive?", 9383–20.9

Smith, G. W.

"Trends in Duck Breeding Populations, 1955-91", 5504–30

Smith, Jo Ann R.

"Science-Driven Solutions to Food Safety Dilemmas: A Progress Report", 1004–16.1

Smith, Kermit

"Musculoskeletal System Diseases", 4088–2

Smith, Marcia S.

"Space Activities of the U.S., Soviet Union and Other Launching Countries/Organizations, 1957-90", 21704–4

Smith, Richard J.

"Unintentional Injuries", 4088–2

Smith, Robert B.

"Regionally Averaged Diameter Growth in New England Forests", 1208–349

Smith, Tim R.

"Tenth District Economy: Avoiding a Recession?", 9381–1.202

Smith, W. Brad

"Michigan Timber Industry: An Assessment of Timber Product Output and Use, 1988", 1206–10.11

"Veneer Industry and Timber Use, North Central Region, 1988", 1208–220

"Wisconsin Timber Industry: An Assessment of Timber Product Output and Use, 1988", 1206–10.12

Smithsonian Institution

American Historical Assn financial statements, and membership by State, 1989, annual rpt, 29574–2

Budget of US, authoritative financial statements with appropriations, outlays, and receipts, by category and agency, FY90, annual rpt, 8104–2.1

Budget of US, obligations and authority by function, agency, and program, with summaries, analyses, and historical tables, FY92, annual rpt, 104–2

Education funding by Federal agency, program, and recipient type, and instn spending, FY80-90, annual rpt, 4824–8

R&D funding by Fed Govt, by field, performer type, agency, and State, FY89-91, annual rpt, 9627–20

see also Kennedy, John F., Center for the Performing Arts, D.C.

Smog

see Air pollution

Smoking

Agent Orange exposure of Vietnam veterans, and other factors relation to dev of rare cancers, 1984-88, 4208–33

Airline consumer complaints to DOT about service, by reason and US and foreign carrier, monthly rpt, 7302–11

Bans on smoking in public places, local ordinances provisions, as of 1989, 4478–196

Canada tobacco and cigarette production, trade, and use, 1985-91, article, 1925–16.201

Cancer (hepatocellular) risk relation to hepatitis infection, race, smoking, drinking, and oral contraceptives and estrogen use, 1984-90 local area study, article, 4472–1.237

Cancer (lung) tumors with genetic mutations, by patient smoking history and other characteristics, 1980-89, article, 4472–1.217

Index by Subjects and Names

Soap and detergent industry

Cancer cases, deaths, and survival rates, by sex, race, age, and body site, 1973-88, annual rpt, 4474–35

Cancer death risk relation to smoking by body site, and compared to other smoking-related diseases, by sex, 1960s-91, article, 4472–1.219

Cessation of smoking program in 11 communities, methods and effectiveness, 1983-88, article, 4472–1.231

Child exposure to cigarette smoke before and after birth, by source and degree of exposure and family characteristics, 1988, 4146–8.204

Child health condition and services use, 1990 chartbook, 4108–49

Consumption of cigarettes and cigars, *Survey of Current Business*, monthly rpt, 2702–1.14

Consumption of cigarettes and other tobacco products per capita, and total spending, 1984-89, annual rpt, 1319–1.4

Consumption of cigarettes and smokeless tobacco, by selected characteristics, 1990 survey, biennial rpt, 4494–5

Consumption of tobacco products, quarterly situation rpt with articles, 1561–10

Deaths and rates, by detailed cause and demographic characteristics, 1988 and trends from 1900, US Vital Statistics annual rpt, 4144–2

Diabetics health-related behaviors, weight, and body mass, by level of exercise, 1991 article, 4042–3.246

Exposure (involuntary) to cigarette smoke, health effects, and toxic substance levels of sidestream smoke, literature review, 1970s-90, 4248–91

Fires on Forest Service land and acres burned, by cause, forest, and State, 1989, annual rpt, 1204–6

Genital human papillomavirus risk relation to presence of other cervical cancer risk factors, local area study, 1991 article, 4472–1.215

Health condition and health care resources, use, and spending, 1950s-89, annual data compilation, 4144–11

Heart disease deaths and risk factors, for PRC, Finland, and US, 1980s, article, 4042–3.202

Hispanic Americans smoking quit rates, effects of Spanish language self-help guide, 1987-88 local area study, article, 4042–3.249

Hong Kong tobacco and cigarette production, trade, and use, 1980-91, article, 1925–16.210

Indians and Alaska Natives preventive health practices, exams by type, and smoking and overweight status, by selected characteristics, 1987, 4186–8.19

Indonesia tobacco and cigarette production and trade, 1970-90, article, 1925–16.208

Initiation of smoking by age 25, by sex and age, 1987, article, 4472–1.216

Initiation of smoking, influence of family, peers, and setting, 1988 local area survey, article, 4042–3.217

Injuries from use of consumer products, by severity, victim age, and detailed product, 1990, annual rpt, 9164–6

Israel tobacco and cigarette production, trade, and use, 1981-90, article, 1925–16.202

Labor laws enacted, by State, 1990, annual article, 6722–1.209

Minority group and women health condition, services use, payment sources, and health care labor force, by poverty status, 1940s-89, chartbook, 4118–56

Minority group drug abuse prevalence, related health effects and crime, treatment, and research status and needs, mid 1970s-90, 4498–72

Minority group health condition, services use, costs, and indicators of services need, 1950s-88, 4118–55

Nicotine, tar, and carbon monoxide content of cigarettes, by brand, 1989, 9408–53

Philippines tobacco and cigarette production, trade, and use, 1980-90, article, 1925–16.203

Pollution (air) indoor levels and emissions rates, by pollutant type and source, 1990 handbook, 3326–1.2

Pollution (air) indoor levels in workplace, and health impacts, for Library of Congress Madison building, 1989 study, series, 4248–92

Pregnant women smoking, by age, race, education, marital status, and birth order, 1970s-80s, article, 4042–3.203

Preventive disease and health improvement goals and recommended activities for 2000, with trends 1970s-80s, 4048–10

Research on drug abuse and treatment, biological and behavioral factors, and addiction potential of new drugs, 1990 annual conf, 4494–11

Research on drug abuse, prevention, treatment, and health impacts, as of 1990, triennial rpt, 4498–68

Research on smoking and smokeless tobacco use, spending, intervention project results, and smoking prevalence, with bibl, 1960s-90, 4478–195

Respiratory diseases related to occupational hazards, epidemiology, diagnosis, and treatment, for selected industries and work settings, 1988 conf, 4248–90

Singapore tobacco and cigarette production, trade, and use, 1980-90, article, 1925–16.212

States smoking prevention, control, and surveillance activities and funding, and tobacco farm receipts, by State, 1989-90, 4206–2.47

Statistical Abstract of US, 1991 annual data compilation, 2324–1.3

Youth drug, alcohol, and cigarette use and attitudes, by substance type and selected characteristics, 1975-90 surveys, annual rpt, 4494–4

see also Tobacco industry and products

SMSA

see Metropolitan Statistical Areas

see under By SMSA or MSA in the "Index by Categories"

Smuggling

Arms trade and share of GNP by country, and US customs seizures and defense industry employment, 1980s-90, article, 9373–1.221

Customs Service activities, collections, entries processed by mode of transport, and seizures, FY86-90, annual rpt, 8144–1

Drug enforcement regional task forces investigation of organized crime, activities by agency and region, FY83-90, biennial rpt, 6004–17

Drug smuggling interdiction programs, budget, and seizures of Fed govt, FY87-90, GAO rpt, 26119–318

Sentences for Federal offenses, guidelines by offense and circumstances, series, 17668–1

Snack foods

see Food and food industry

Snake River

Birds of prey, rodent, and vegetation distribution and characteristics, for Idaho Snake River area, research results, 1990, annual rpt, 5724–14

Water supply and quality in streams and lakes, and groundwater levels in wells, by drainage basin, 1988, annual State rpt series, 5666–16

Water supply and quality in streams and lakes, and groundwater levels in wells, by drainage basin, 1989, annual State rpt series, 5666–12

Water supply and quality in streams and lakes, and groundwater levels in wells, by drainage basin, 1990, annual State rpt series, 5666–10

Water supply in US and southern Canada, streamflow, surface and groundwater conditions, and reservoir levels, by location, monthly rpt, 5662–3

Snell, James

"Zambia Agricultural Sector Background", 9916–12.25

Snell, William M.

"Burley Quota Underutilization", 1004–16.1

Snyder, Elisabeth F.

"Activities of the Alaska District Water Resources Division, USGS, 1990", 5666–26.13

Snyder, Howard N.

"Juvenile Court Statistics, 1988", 6064–12

Snyder, Thomas D.

"Digest of Education Statistics, 1991", 4824–2

Soap and detergent industry

Agricultural crops (new and traditional) use in industry, replacement of imports and nonrenewable resources, R&D funding, and economic impacts, 1970s-90, 26358–239

County Business Patterns, 1988: employment, establishments, and payroll, by SIC 2- to 4-digit industry and county, annual State rpt series, 2326–6

County Business Patterns, 1989: employment, establishments, and payroll, by SIC 2- to 4-digit industry and county, annual State rpt series, 2326–8

CPI by component for US city average, and by region, population size, and for 27 metro areas, monthly rpt, 6762–2

Employment, earnings, and hours, by SIC 1- to 4-digit industry, monthly and annual averages, selected years 1909-90, annual rpt, 6744–4

Enterprise Statistics, 1987: finances and operations for companies, by size, level of diversification, form of organization, and industry group, 2329–8

Exports and imports between US and outlying areas, by detailed commodity and mode of transport, 1990, annual rpt, 2424–11

Exports and imports of US, by country and detailed commodity, monthly rpt, 2422–12

Soap and detergent industry

Exports and imports of US, by Harmonized System 6-digit commodity and country, 1990, annual rpt, 2424–13

Exports and imports of US, by transport mode, country, and SITC 1- to 3-digit commodity, 1990, annual rpt, 2424–12

Exports of US, detailed Schedule B commodities with countries of destination, 1990, annual rpt, 2424–10

Injuries from use of consumer products, by severity, victim age, and detailed product, 1990, annual rpt, 9164–6

Labor productivity, indexes of output, hours, and employment by SIC 2- to 4-digit industry, 1967-89, annual rpt, 6824–1.3

Manufacturing annual survey, 1989: finances and operations, by SIC 2- to 4-digit industry, series, 2506–15

Manufacturing census, 1987: finances and operations, by SIC 2- to 4-digit industry, State, and MSA, with trends from 1849, 2497–1

Manufacturing census, 1987: finances and operations, by type of organization and SIC 2- to 4-digit industry, subject rpt, 2497–5

Manufacturing finances and operations, by SIC 2- to 4-digit industry, forecast 1991, annual rpt, 2044–28

Multinatl US firms and foreign affiliates finances and operations, by industry and world area of parent firm, 1989 benchmark survey, preliminary annual rpt, 2704–5

Occupational injury and illness rates, by SIC 2- to 4-digit industry, 1988-89, annual rpt, 6844–7

Occupational injury and illness rates, by SIC 2- to 4-digit industry, 1989, annual rpt, 6844–1

Oil and fat production, consumption by end use, and stocks, by type, quarterly Current Industrial Rpt, 2506–4.4

Oils, oilseeds, and fats production, prices, trade, and use, periodic situation rpt with articles, 1561–3

Price indexes (producer), by stage of processing and detailed commodity, monthly rpt, 6762–6

Price indexes (producer), by stage of processing and detailed commodity, monthly 1990, annual rpt, 6764–2

Tax (income) returns of corporations, income and tax items by asset size and detailed industry, 1987, annual rpt, 8304–4

Tax (income) returns of corporations, income and tax items by asset size and detailed industry, 1988, annual rpt, 8304–21

Toxicology Natl Program research and testing activities, FY89 and planned FY90, annual rpt, 4044–16

see also under By Commodity in the "Index by Categories"

Soapstone

see Nonmetallic minerals and mines

Social indicators

see Quality of life

see under names of specific indicators (listed under Population characteristics)

Social sciences

Asia science and engineering employment, by selected characteristics, for 3 countries, 1991 working paper, 2326–18.61

Degrees (PhD) in science and engineering, by field, instn, employment prospects, sex, race, and other characteristics, 1960s-90, annual rpt, 9627–30

Degrees awarded in higher education, by level, field, race, and sex, 1988/89 with trends from 1978/79, biennial rpt, 4844–17

Degrees awarded in science and engineering, by field, level, and sex, 1966-89, 9627–33

DOD Dependents Schools basic skills and college entrance test scores, 1990-91, annual rpt, 3504–16

Education data compilation, 1991 annual rpt, 4824–2

Employment and other characteristics of science and engineering PhDs, by field and State, 1989, biennial rpt, 9627–18

Fed Govt aid to higher education and nonprofit instns for R&D and related activities, by field, instn, agency, and State, FY89, annual rpt, 9627–17

Foreign and US funding for R&D, and scientists and engineering employment and education, 1991 annual rpt, 9627–35.1

Foreign countries science and engineering employment, by professional characteristics, age, and sex, for selected countries, 1991 working paper, 2326–18.62; 2326–18.63

High school advanced placement for college credit, programs by selected characteristics and school control, 1984-86, 4838–46

Higher education course completions, by detailed program, sex, race, and instn type, for 1972 high school class, as of 1984, 4888–4

Higher education grad programs enrollment in science and engineering, by field, source of funds, and characteristics of student and instn, 1975-89, annual rpt, 9627–7

NASA R&D funding to higher education instns, by field, instn, and State, FY90, annual listing, 9504–7

R&D funding by Fed Govt, by field, performer type, agency, and State, FY89-91, annual rpt, 9627–20

R&D funding by higher education instns and federally funded centers, by field, instn, and State, FY89, annual rpt, 9627–13

Research on population and reproduction, Federal funding by project, FY89, annual listing, 4474–9

see also Anthropology

see also Economics

see also Geography

see also History

see also Political science

see also Psychology

see also Sociology

Social security

EC retirement age under statutory social security programs, by sex and country, 1989, article, 4742–1.205

Expenditures for public welfare programs, by program type and level of govt, FY65-88, annual article, 4742–1.202

Japan economic conditions, financial and intl policies, and trade devs, 1950s-80s and projected to 2050, compilation of papers, 23848–220

Numbers for social security, new issues, 1937-89, annual rpt, 4744–3.2

Research and evaluation programs of HHS, 1970-90, annual listing, 4004–30

Research on social security programs and related issues, technical paper series, 4746–26

Research rpts and microdata files of SSA, 1991 biennial listing, 4744–12

Soviet Union GNP by detailed income and outlay component, 1985, 2326–18.59

Statistical Abstract of US, 1991 annual data compilation, 2324–1.12

see also Aid to Families with Dependent Children

see also Health insurance

see also Health maintenance organizations

see also Income maintenance

see also Medicaid

see also Medicare

see also Old age assistance

see also Old-Age, Survivors, Disability, and Health Insurance

see also Public welfare programs

see also Social security tax

see also Supplemental Security Income

see also Unemployment insurance

see also Workers compensation

Social Security Administration

Activities, litigation, finances, and staff of SSA, FY90, annual rpt, 4704–6

Activities of SSA, and OASDHI admin, 1930s-90 and projected to 2064, annual data compilation, 4704–12

Actuarial studies, Medicare and OASDI future cost estimates and past experience analyses, series, 4706–1

Budget of US, obligations and authority by function, agency, and program, with summaries, analyses, and historical tables, FY92, annual rpt, 104–2

Deaths of beneficiaries, erroneous benefit payments, and use of SSA and other sources of death info, by agency, 1990, GAO rpt, 26121–406

Disability Insurance beneficiaries sociodemographic and medical characteristics, annual rpt, discontinued, 4704–14

Earnings records of SSA, errors and rates by employment type, late 1930s-87, GAO rpt, 26121–422

Employment reductions of SSA, impacts on client services, 1980s, GAO rpt, 26121–415

Financial aid of HHS, by program, recipient, State, and city, FY90, annual regional listings, 4004–3

Medicare Hospital Insurance appeals backlog reduction actions of SSA Chicago administrative law judges, effectiveness, FY89, GAO rpt, 26121–398

OASDI trust funds finances, 1937-FY90 and alternative projections to 2065, annual rpt, 4704–4

Public access to SSA by telephone, local line availability and effects of nationwide 800 number, by State, 1989 and 1991, GAO rpt, 26121–434

Research and evaluation programs of HHS, 1970-90, annual listing, 4004–30

Supplemental Security Income and Medicaid eligibility and payment provisions, and beneficiaries living arrangements, by State, 1991, annual rpt, 4704–13

Index by Subjects and Names

Social services

Tax (income) returns computer matching program to indentify underreported income, effectiveness, 1987, GAO rpt, 26119–325

Telephone info service of SSA, performance, 1989-90, hearing, 21788–199

see also Office of Policy, SSA

see also Office of Research and Statistics, SSA

Social security tax

- Admin of OASDHI, and SSA activities, 1930s-90 and projected to 2064, annual data compilation, 4704–12
- Budget of US, authoritative financial statements with appropriations, outlays, and receipts, by category and agency, FY90, annual rpt, 8104–2.1
- Budget of US, CBO analysis and review of FY92 budget by function, annual rpt, 26304–2
- Budget of US, CBO analysis of revenue and spending alternatives and projections of economic indicators, FY92-96, annual rpt, 26304–3
- Budget of US, CBO analysis of savings and revenues under alternative spending cuts and tax changes, projected FY92-97, 26306–3.118
- Budget of US, midsession review of FY92 budget, by function, annual rpt, 104–7
- Budget of US, obligations and authority by function, agency, and program, with summaries, analyses, and historical tables, FY92, annual rpt, 104–2
- Budget of US, receipts by source, outlays by agency and program, and balances, monthly rpt, 8102–3
- Collections, enforcement, and litigation activity of IRS, with data by type of tax, region, and State, FY90, annual rpt, 8304–3
- Collections of Fed Govt, by source, *Treasury Bulletin*, quarterly rpt, 8002–4.1
- Collections of tax and beneficiaries for social insurance programs, monthly rpt, 4742–1.1
- Earnings by industry div, and personal income per capita and by source, by State, MSA, and county, 1984-89, annual regional rpts, 2704–2
- Farm income, expenses, receipts by commodity, assets, liabilities, and ratios, 1990 and trends from 1945, annual rpt, 1544–16
- Fed Govt civilian employees work-years, pay rates, and benefits use and costs, by agency, FY89, annual rpt, 9844–31
- Fed Govt internal revenue and refunds, by type of tax, quarterly rpt, 8302–2.1
- Fed Govt tax provisions and receipts overview, by tax type, with background data, 1900s-91 and projected to 2000, 21788–197
- Fed Govt trust fund receipts, by source and fund, Budget of US, FY92, annual rpt, 104–9
- Finances and operations of programs under Ways and Means Committee jurisdiction, FY70s-90, annual rpt, 21784–11
- Finances of SSA programs, and litigation, FY90, annual rpt, 4704–6
- Financial consolidated statements of Fed Govt based on business accounting methods, FY89-90, annual rpt, 8104–5

Germany (West) health condition of children and aged, health care costs, and natl health insurance payroll tax rates, 1985-88, 23898–5

- Govt census, 1987: State and local govt employment, payroll, OASDHI coverage, and employee benefits costs, by level of govt and State, 2455–4
- Health care spending by businesses, households, and govts, 1965-89, article, 4652–1.230
- Income (household) and poverty status under alternative income definitions, by recipient characteristics, 1990, annual Current Population Rpt, 2546–6.69
- Labor hourly costs, by component, industry sector, worker class, and firm size, 1990, annual rpt, 6744–22
- Medicare Hospital Insurance trust fund finances, 1966-90 and alternative projections to 2065, annual rpt, 4654–11
- Natl income and product accounts and components, *Survey of Current Business*, monthly rpt, 2702–1.24
- OASDHI, Medicaid, SSI, and related programs benefits, beneficiary characteristics, and trust funds, selected years 1937-89, annual rpt, 4744–3
- OASDI benefit payments, trust fund finances, and economic and demographic assumptions, 1970-90 and alternative projections to 2000, actuarial rpt, 4706–1.105
- OASDI trust funds finances, FY90 and projected to 2060s, annual article, 4742–1.210
- OASDI trust funds finances, 1937-FY90 and alternative projections to 2065, annual rpt, 4704–4
- Railroad retirement system funding and benefits findings and recommendations, with background industry data, 1960s-90 and projected to 2060, 9708–1
- Rates for OASDI and Hospital Insurance tax for employers, employees, and self-employed, 1990-99 and projected to 2000, biennial article, 4742–1.217
- Reduction of social security tax, proposals with OASDI trust funds finances and effects of inclusion in budget deficit figures, 1990 hearing, 25368–171
- State and local govt tax rates and revenue, by source and State, 1991 and historical trends, annual rpt, 10044–1
- *Statistical Abstract of US*, 1991 annual data compilation, 2324–1.12
- *Survey of Current Business*, detailed financial and business data, and economic indicators, monthly rpt, 2702–1.4; 2702–1.25
- Telephone and telegraph firms detailed finances and operations, 1989, annual rpt, 9284–6.2; 9284–6.3
- Transit systems finances and operations, by mode of transport, size of fleet, and for 468 systems, 1989, annual rpt, 7884–4

Social services

- Assistance (financial and nonfinancial) of Fed Govt, 1991 base edition with supplements, annual listing, 104–5
- Assistance (formula grants) of Fed Govt, use of Census of Population data for allocation, and effects of data errors on funding, with data by program and State, FY91, GAO rpt, 26119–361

Budget of US, formula grant program obligations to State and local govts, by agency, program, and State, FY92, annual rpt, 104–30

- Budget of US, midsession review of FY92 budget, by function, annual rpt, 104–7
- Budget of US, obligations and authority by function, agency, and program, with summaries, analyses, and historical tables, FY92, annual rpt, 104–2
- Budget of US, receipts by source, outlays by agency and program, and balances, monthly rpt, 8102–3
- County Business Patterns, 1988: employment, establishments, and payroll, by SIC 2- to 4-digit industry and county, annual State rpt series, 2326–6
- County Business Patterns, 1989: employment, establishments, and payroll, by SIC 2- to 4-digit industry and county, annual State rpt series, 2326–8
- DOD prime contract awards, by detailed procurement category, FY87-90, annual rpt, 3544–18
- Drug and alcohol abuse treatment facilities, services, use, funding, staff, and client characteristics, 1989, biennial rpt, 4494–10
- Employment, earnings, and hours, by SIC 1- to 4-digit industry, monthly and annual averages, selected years 1909-90, annual rpt, 6744–4
- Enterprise Statistics, 1987: auxiliaries of multi-establishment firms, finances and operations by function, industry, and State, 2329–6
- Enterprise Statistics, 1987: finances and operations for companies, by size, level of diversification, form of organization, and industry group, 2329–8
- Expenditures (private) for social welfare, by category, 1970s-88, annual article, 4742–1.204
- Fed Govt programs under Ways and Means Committee jurisdiction, finances, operations, and participant characteristics, FY70s-90, annual rpt, 21784–11
- Fed Govt spending in States, by type, program, agency, and State, FY90, annual rpt, 2464–2
- Govt employment and payroll, by function, level of govt, and jurisdiction, 1990, annual rpt series, 2466–1
- HHS financial aid, by program, recipient, State, and city, FY90, annual regional listings, 4004–3
- Home health care agencies finances impacts of Medicare payment limits under alternative determination methods, with data by service type, 1984-89, GAO rpt, 26121–400
- Homeless and runaway youth programs, funding, activities, and participant characteristics, FY90, annual rpt, 4604–3
- Homeless teens pregnancy prevalence and outcomes, services availability, health condition, and drug abuse, 1989 conf, 4108–55
- Hospices operations, services, costs, and patient characteristics, for instns without Medicare certification, FY85-86, 4658–52
- Input-output structure of US economy, detailed interindustry transactions for 84 industries, and components of final demand, 1986, annual article, 2702–1.206

Social services

Input-output structure of US economy, detailed interindustry transactions for 85 industries, 1982 benchmark data, 2702–1.213

Occupational injury and illness rates, by SIC 2- to 4-digit industry, 1988-89, annual rpt, 6844–7

Occupational injury and illness rates, by SIC 2- to 4-digit industry, 1989, annual rpt, 6844–1

Older persons aid programs funding, and long term care ombudsman funding and visits by State, 1988-90, 25248–126

Refugee resettlement programs and funding, arrivals by country of origin, and indicators of adjustment, by State, FY90, annual rpt, 4694–5

Service industries census, 1987: depreciable assets, capital and operating expenses, and receipts, by SIC 2- to 4-digit kind of business, 2393–2

Service industries census, 1987: establishments, receipts by source, payroll, and employment, by SIC 2- to 4-digit kind of business, State, and MSA, 2393–4

Tax (income) returns of corporations, income and tax items by asset size and detailed industry, 1987, annual rpt, 8304–4

Tax (income) returns of corporations, income and tax items by asset size and detailed industry, 1988, annual rpt, 8304–21

Tax expenditures, Federal revenues forgone through income tax deductions and exclusions by type, FY92-96, annual rpt, 21784–10

see also Adult day care
see also Child day care
see also Child welfare
see also Community health services
see also Counselors and counseling
see also Disaster relief
see also Foster home care
see also Group homes for the handicapped
see also Home health services
see also Homemaker services
see also Legal aid
see also Respite care
see also School lunch and breakfast programs
see also Social work
see also Vocational rehabilitation
see also Work incentive programs
see also under By Industry in the "Index by Categories"

Social work

Child abuse and neglect victims representation in legal proceedings, caseloads, State requirements, and compensation, by State and county, 1989, 4608–28

Drug and alcohol abuse treatment facilities, services, use, funding, staff, and client characteristics, 1989, biennial rpt, 4494–10

Education (special) enrollment by age, staff, funding, and needs, by type of handicap and State, 1989/90, annual rpt, 4944–4

HHS financial aid, by program, recipient, State, and city, FY90, annual regional listings, 4004–3

Home health care visits approved by Medicare, planned and actual visits by service type, 1986, article, 4652–1.254

Medicare reimbursement of hospitals under prospective payment system, and effect on services, finances, and beneficiary payments, 1979-90, annual rpt, 17204–2

Mental health care facilities, staff, and patient characteristics, *Statistical Notes* series, 4506–3

Military health care personnel, and accessions by training source, by occupation, specialty, and service branch, FY89, annual rpt, 3544–24

VA health care staff and turnover, by occupation, physician specialty, and location, 1990, annual rpt, 8604–8

VA Medicine and Surgery Dept trainees, by detailed program and city, FY90, annual rpt, 8704–4

see also Counselors and counseling
see also Social services

Socialism

China economic conditions after 1988 austerity program, with background data, 1978-90, 9118–9

Poland labor force status by education level, sex, and sector, college enrollment, and grads by field, 1960s-88, article, 6722–1.203

Sociology

Degrees awarded in science and engineering, by field, level, and sex, 1966-89, 9627–33

Drug abuse relation to violent and criminal behavior, with data on street gang activity and selected population groups, 1989 conf, 4498–70

Employment and other characteristics of science and engineering PhDs, by field and State, 1989, biennial rpt, 9627–18

Fed Govt aid to higher education and nonprofit instns for R&D and related activities, by field, instn, agency, and State, FY89, annual rpt, 9627–17

Higher education course completions, by detailed program, sex, race, and instn type, for 1972 high school class, as of 1984, 4888–4

Higher education grad programs enrollment in science and engineering, by field, source of funds, and characteristics of student and instn, 1975-89, annual rpt, 9627–7

R&D funding by Fed Govt, by field, performer type, agency, and State, FY89-91, annual rpt, 9627–20

R&D funding by higher education instns and federally funded centers, by field, instn, and State, FY89, annual rpt, 9627–13

Soft drink industry and products

Consumer Expenditure Survey, food spending by item, household composition, income, age, race, and region, 1980-88, biennial rpt, 1544–30

Consumption of food, dietary composition, and nutrient intake, 1987/88 natl survey, preliminary rpt series, 1356–1

Consumption of soft drinks, and sweetener deliveries for soft drink use by type, late 1960s-90, article, 1561–14.210

Consumption per capita of selected beverages, 1970s-90, FAS annual circular, 1925–15.3

Consumption, supply, trade, prices, spending, and indexes, by food commodity, 1989, annual rpt, 1544–4

County Business Patterns, 1988: employment, establishments, and payroll, by SIC 2- to 4-digit industry and county, annual State rpt series, 2326–6

County Business Patterns, 1989: employment, establishments, and payroll, by SIC 2- to 4-digit industry and county, annual State rpt series, 2326–8

CPI by component for US city average, and by region, population size, and for 27 metro areas, monthly rpt, 6762–2

Employment, earnings, and hours, by SIC 1- to 4-digit industry, monthly and annual averages, selected years 1909-90, annual rpt, 6744–4

Enterprise Statistics, 1987: finances and operations for companies, by size, level of diversification, form of organization, and industry group, 2329–8

Exports and imports (agricultural) of US, by detailed commodity and country, 1990, semiannual rpt, 1522–4

Exports and imports of US, by Harmonized System 6-digit commodity and country, 1990, annual rpt, 2424–13

Exports of US, detailed Schedule B commodities with countries of destination, 1990, annual rpt, 2424–10

Labor productivity, indexes of output, hours, and employment by SIC 2- to 4-digit industry, 1967-89, annual rpt, 6824–1.3

Manufacturing annual survey, 1989: finances and operations, by SIC 2- to 4-digit industry, series, 2506–15

Manufacturing census, 1987: finances and operations, by SIC 2- to 4-digit industry, State, and MSA, with trends from 1849, 2497–1

Manufacturing census, 1987: finances and operations, by type of organization and SIC 2- to 4-digit industry, subject rpt, 2497–5

Manufacturing finances and operations, by SIC 2- to 4-digit industry, forecast 1991, annual rpt, 2044–28

Occupational injury and illness rates, by SIC 2- to 4-digit industry, 1988-89, annual rpt, 6844–7

Occupational injury and illness rates, by SIC 2- to 4-digit industry, 1989, annual rpt, 6844–1

Price indexes (producer), by stage of processing and detailed commodity, monthly rpt, 6762–6

Price indexes (producer), by stage of processing and detailed commodity, monthly 1990, annual rpt, 6764–2

Tax (income) returns of corporations, income and tax items by asset size and detailed industry, 1987, annual rpt, 8304–4

Tax (income) returns of corporations, income and tax items by asset size and detailed industry, 1988, annual rpt, 8304–21

Software

see Computer industry and products

Soil Conservation Service

Acreage of non-Federal land by use, soil and water conditions, and conservation needs, 1987, State rpt series, 1266–5

Activities of SCS, FY90, annual rpt, 1264–2

Budget of US, obligations and authority by function, agency, and program, with summaries, analyses, and historical tables, FY92, annual rpt, 104–2

Index by Subjects and Names — Solar energy

Colorado water supply, streamflow, precipitation, and reservoir storage, 1991 water year, annual rpt, 1264–13

County soil surveys and maps, 1899-1990, annual listing, 1264–11

Expenditures of Fed Govt in States, by type, program, agency, and State, FY90, annual rpt, 2464–2

Field offices, funding, and staff of USDA subagencies responsible for farm programs, FY89, GAO rpt, 26113–507

Nevada and eastern California water supply, streamflow, precipitation, and reservoir storage, 1991 water year, annual rpt, 1264–8

Oregon water supply, streamflow by station and reservoir storage, 1991, annual rpt, 1264–9

Western US water supply, and snow survey results, annual State rpt series, 1264–14

Western US water supply, and snow survey results, monthly State rpt series, 1266–2

Western US water supply, storage by reservoir and State, and streamflow conditions, as of Oct 1991, annual rpt, 1264–4

Western US water supply, streamflow and reservoir storage forecasts by stream and station, Jan-May monthly rpt, 1262–1

Soil pollution

- Acid rain and air pollution environmental impacts, and methods of neutralizing acidified water bodies, summary research rpt series, 5506–5
- Coastal and riparian areas environmental conditions, fish, wildlife, use, and mgmt, for individual ecosystems, series, 5506–9
- Hazardous waste site remedial action under Superfund, current and proposed sites descriptions and status, periodic listings, series, 9216–3
- Health effects of selected pollutants on animals by species and on humans, and environmental levels, series, 5506–14
- Idaho Natl Engineering Lab radiation monitoring results, for facilities and nearby areas, 1990, annual rpt, 3354–10
- Lead paint in privately owned housing, levels, exposure, and testing and abatement costs, 1990 rpt, 5188–128
- Pesticide (dicofol) levels in soil, crops, and wildlife by species, with toxicity indicators, 1950s-87, technical rpt, 5506–12.2
- Radioactive low-level waste repository site design, characteristics, and monitoring techniques, 1987 conf, 5668–116
- Radioactive waste and spent fuel generation, inventory, and disposal, 1960s-89 and projected to 2020, annual rpt, 3364–2
- Radioactive waste at DOE nuclear weapons facilities, storage plans, and mgmt issues, 1988, 26358–236
- Wetlands acreage, resources, soil and water properties, and conservation efforts, by wetland type, State rpt series, 5506–11

Soils and soil conservation

- Acreage covered under Soil Conservation Service activities, FY90, annual rpt, 1264–2
- Agricultural Stabilization and Conservation Service producer payments and certificate value, by program, monthly rpt, 1802–10
- *Agricultural Statistics, 1990*, annual rpt, 1004–1

Census of Agriculture, 1987: farms, farmland, production, finances, and operator characteristics, by county, final State rpt series, 2331–1

- Coastal and riparian areas environmental conditions, fish, wildlife, use, and mgmt, for individual ecosystems, series, 5506–9
- Conservation program of USDA, participation and payments by practice and State, FY90, annual rpt, 1804–7
- Conservation programs of USDA, benefits denied for noncompliance, and appeals disposition, by State, periodic rpt, discontinued, 1802–18
- Conservation programs under Food Security Act, farm finances and environmental benefits of alternative policies, projected 1991-2005, 1588–153
- Conservation Reserve Program acreage, plantings, and impacts on farm production, soil erosion, water quality, and wildlife habitat, 1991 conf, 1208–360
- Conservation Reserve Program control enrollment economic impacts, by crop for 10 local areas, 1986-89, article, 1502–4.203
- Cotton farms fertilizer, pesticide and irrigation use, soil conservation practices, and water quality impacts, 1989, 1588–151
- County Business Patterns, 1988: employment, establishments, and payroll, by SIC 2- to 4-digit industry and county, annual State rpt series, 2326–6
- County Business Patterns, 1989: employment, establishments, and payroll, by SIC 2- to 4-digit industry and county, annual State rpt series, 2326–8
- County soil surveys and maps, 1899-1990, annual listing, 1264–11
- Emergency Conservation Program for farmland damaged by natural disaster, aid and participation by State, FY90, annual rpt, 1804–22
- Emergency Conservation Program for farmland damaged by natural disaster, funding by region and State, monthly rpt, 1802–13
- *Environmental Quality*, status of problems, protection programs, research, and intl issues, 1991 annual rpt, 484–1
- Environmental regulation impacts on agricultural trade, with indicators of pollution and fertilizer use intensity by crop, 1991 article, 1522–3.203
- Erosion rates on croplands, 1987, State rpt series, 1266–5
- Expenditures of Fed Govt in States, by type, program, agency, and State, FY90, annual rpt, 2464–2
- Farm production inputs, finances, mgmt, and land value and transfers, periodic situation rpt with articles, 1561–16
- Fed Govt financial and nonfinancial domestic aid, 1991 base edition with supplements, annual listing, 104–5
- Fertilizer and cropland demand impacts of proposed environmental regulation, model description and inputs, 1964-89, 1588–152
- FmHA loans, by type, borrower characteristics, and State, quarterly rpt, 1182–8
- FmHA property acquired through foreclosure, value, and acreage under conservation easements by State, 1989-90, GAO rpt, 26113–514

Forest Service mgmt of public lands and resources dev, environmental, economic, and social impacts of alternative programs, projected to 2040, 1208–24

- Pacific Northwest county soil survey rpt abstracts, 1989 rpt, 5668–114
- Pesticide and fertilizer use reduction, environmental and economic impacts by commodity and region, alternative forecasts 1989-94, hearing, 23848–222
- Public lands acreage, grants, use, revenues, and allocations, by State, FY90, annual rpt, 5724–1.2
- Timber in western mountain areas, soil characteristics and mgmt, 1990 conf, 1208–378
- Water quality, chemistry, hydrology, and other characteristics, local area studies, series, 5666–27
- Wetlands acreage, resources, soil and water properties, and conservation efforts, by wetland type, State rpt series, 5506–11
- Wetlands and riparian soil and plant characteristics, series, 5506–10
- *Yearbook of Agriculture*, special topics, 1991 annual compilation of papers, 1004–18
- *see also* Flood control
- *see also* Reclamation of land
- *see also* Soil pollution

Solar energy

- Collector (solar) and photovoltaic module shipments, by type and end use, 1974-89, annual rpt, 3164–74.7
- Electric power plants and capacity, by fuel used, owner, location, and operating status, 1990 and for units planned 1991-2000, annual listing, 3164–36
- Electric power plants certification applications filed with FERC, for small production and cogeneration facilities, FY80-90, annual listing, 3084–13
- Equipment shipments by end-use sector and State, and trade, for collectors and photovoltaic modules, 1989, annual rpt, 3164–62
- Exports of US, detailed Schedule B commodities with countries of destination, 1990, annual rpt, 2424–10
- Housing and households detailed characteristics, and unit and neighborhood quality, by location, 1989, biennial rpt, 2485–12
- Housing and households detailed characteristics, and unit and neighborhood quality, MSA surveys, series, 2485–6
- Housing inventory change from 1973, by reason, unit and household characteristics, and location, 1983 survey, biennial rpt, 2485–14
- Natl Energy Strategy plans for conservation and pollution reduction, impacts of technology and regulation proposals, projected 1990-2030, 3166–6.47
- Natl Energy Strategy plans for renewable energy dev, supply projected under alternative cost and capacity use assumptions, 1990-2030, 3166–6.50
- Photovoltaic R&D sponsored by DOE, projects, funding, and rpts, FY90, annual listing, 3304–20
- *Statistical Abstract of US*, 1991 annual data compilation, 2324–1.19
- Supply, demand, and prices, by fuel type and end-use sector, alternative projections 1989-2010, annual rpt, 3164–75

Solar energy

Supply, demand, and prices, by fuel type and end-use sector, projections and underlying assumptions, 1990-2010, annual rpt, 3164–90

Solar Energy Research Institute

"Photovoltaic Energy Program Summary, FY90", 3304–20

see also Department of Energy National Laboratories

Soldiers

see Military personnel

Soldiers' and Airmen's Home

Budget of US, obligations and authority by function, agency, and program, with summaries, analyses, and historical tables, FY92, annual rpt, 104–2

Soldiers pay and allowances

see Military benefits and pensions

see Military pay

Sole proprietorships

see Proprietorships

Solid waste

see Landfills

see Recycling of waste materials

see Refuse and refuse disposal

see Sewage and wastewater systems

Solomon Islands

Agricultural exports of high-value commodities, indexes and sales by commodity, world area, and country, 1960s-86, 1528–323

Economic, social, and agricultural data, US and other aid sources, and AID activity, 1988 country rpt, 9916–12.28

Economic, social, political, and geographic summary data, by country, 1991, annual factbook, 9114–2

Exports and imports of US, by transport mode, country, and SITC 1- to 3-digit commodity, 1990, annual rpt, 2424–12

Human rights conditions in 170 countries, and US economic and military aid, 1990, annual rpt, 21384–3

Military aid of US, arms sales, and training programs costs and budget requests, by program, world region, and country, FY90-92, annual rpt, 7144–13

UN voting record and share of votes in agreement with US, by issue, country, and world area, 1990, annual rpt, 7004–18

Somalia

Agricultural exports of high-value commodities, indexes and sales by commodity, world area, and country, 1960s-86, 1528–323

Agricultural trade of US, by detailed commodity and country, 1989, annual rpt, 1524–8

Agricultural trade of US, by detailed commodity and country, 1990, semiannual rpt, 1522–4

AID economic aid to developing countries, obligations and disbursements by country, quarterly rpt, 9912–4

AID loans repayment status and terms by program and country, and status of predecessor agency loans, quarterly rpt, 9912–3

Dairy imports, consumption, and market conditions, by sub-Saharan Africa country, 1961-88, 1528–321

Economic and military aid and loans from US and intl agencies, by program and country, FY46-90, annual rpt, 9914–5

Economic and social conditions of developing countries from 1960s, and Intl Dev Cooperation Agency and AID activities and funding, FY90-92, annual rpt, 9904–4

Economic, social, and agricultural data, US and other aid sources, and AID activity, 1989 country rpt, 9916–12.36

Economic, social, political, and geographic summary data, by country, 1991, annual factbook, 9114–2

Exports and imports of US, by commodity and country, 1970-89, world area rpt, 9116–1.6

Exports and imports of US, by transport mode, country, and SITC 1- to 3-digit commodity, 1990, annual rpt, 2424–12

Exports of US, detailed Schedule B commodities with countries of destination, 1990, annual rpt, 2424–10

Food supply, needs, and aid for developing countries, status and alternative forecasts, 1991 world area rpt, 1526–8.1

Human rights conditions in 170 countries, and US economic and military aid, 1990, annual rpt, 21384–3

Military aid of US, arms sales, and training programs costs and budget requests, by program, world region, and country, FY90-92, annual rpt, 7144–13

UN voting record and share of votes in agreement with US, by issue, country, and world area, 1990, annual rpt, 7004–18

see also under By Foreign Country in the "Index by Categories"

Somerset County, N.J.

Wages by occupation, and benefits for office and plant workers, 1990 survey, periodic MSA rpt, 6785–11.4

see also under By SMSA or MSA in the "Index by Categories"

Sonnefeld, Sally T.

"Projections of National Health Expenditures Through the Year 2000", 4652–1.251

Sonu, Sunee C.

"World Squid Supply and Market Study", 2166–19.10

Sorenson, Stephen K.

"Reconnaissance Investigation of Water Quality, Bottom Sediment, and Biota Associated with Irrigation Drainage in the Klamath Basin, California and Oregon, 1988-89", 5666–27.21

Sorghum

see Animal feed

see Grains and grain products

Soroka, Mordachai

"Comparison of Examination Fees and Availability of Routine Vision Care by Optometrists and Ophthalmologists", 4042–3.238

Souris-Red-Rainy Rivers

Water supply and quality in streams and lakes, and groundwater levels in wells, by drainage basin, 1988, annual State rpt series, 5666–16

Water supply and quality in streams and lakes, and groundwater levels in wells, by drainage basin, 1989, annual State rpt series, 5666–12

Water supply and quality in streams and lakes, and groundwater levels in wells, by drainage basin, 1990, annual State rpt series, 5666–10

Water supply in US and southern Canada, streamflow, surface and groundwater conditions, and reservoir levels, by location, monthly rpt, 5662–3

South Africa

Agricultural exports of high-value commodities, indexes and sales by commodity, world area, and country, 1960s-86, 1528–323

Agricultural exports of US, impacts of foreign agricultural and trade policy, with data by commodity and country, 1989, annual rpt, 1924–8

Agricultural production, trade, and policies in foreign countries, summary data by country, 1989-90, annual factbook, 1924–12

Agricultural trade of US, by detailed commodity and country, 1989, annual rpt, 1524–8

Agricultural trade of US, by detailed commodity and country, 1990, semiannual rpt, 1522–4

AID economic aid to developing countries, obligations and disbursements by country, quarterly rpt, 9912–4

Economic and military aid and loans from US and intl agencies, by program and country, FY46-90, annual rpt, 9914–5

Economic and social conditions of developing countries from 1960s, and Intl Dev Cooperation Agency and AID activities and funding, FY90-92, annual rpt, 9904–4

Economic conditions, policy, and trade practices, by country, 1988-90, annual rpt, 21384–5

Economic, population, and agricultural data, US and other aid sources, and AID activity, 1989 country rpt, 9916–12.32

Economic, social, political, and geographic summary data, by country, 1991, annual factbook, 9114–2

Exports and imports of US, by commodity and country, 1970-89, world area rpt, 9116–1.6

Exports and imports of US, by Harmonized System 6-digit commodity and country, 1990, annual rpt, 2424–13

Exports and imports of US, by selected country, country group, and commodity group, 1990, annual rpt, 2044–37

Exports and imports of US, by transport mode, country, and SITC 1- to 3-digit commodity, 1990, annual rpt, 2424–12

Exports of US, detailed Schedule B commodities with countries of destination, 1990, annual rpt, 2424–10

Human rights conditions in 170 countries, and US economic and military aid, 1990, annual rpt, 21384–3

Intl transactions of US with 9 countries, 1986-88, *Survey of Current Business*, monthly rpt, annual table, 2702–1.26

Labor conditions, union coverage, and work accidents, 1991 annual country rpt, 6366–4.43

Multinatl US firms and foreign affiliates finances and operations, by industry and world area of parent firm, 1989 benchmark survey, preliminary annual rpt, 2704–5

Multinatl US firms foreign affiliates, income statement items by country and world area, 1986, biennial article, 8302–2.212

Index by Subjects and Names — South Carolina

Nuclear power generation in US and 20 countries, monthly rpt, 3162–24.10

Nuclear power plant capacity, generation, and operating status, by plant and foreign and US location, 1990 and projected to 2030, annual rpt, 3164–57

Steel imports of US under voluntary restraint agreement, by product, customs district, and country, with US industry operating data, quarterly rpt, 9882–13

UN voting record and share of votes in agreement with US, by issue, country, and world area, 1990, annual rpt, 7004–18

see also under By Foreign Country in the "Index by Categories"

South America

Agricultural exports of high-value commodities, indexes and sales by commodity, world area, and country, 1960s-86, 1528–323

Agricultural exports of US, for grains, oilseed products, hides, skins, and cotton, by country, weekly rpt, 1922–3

Agricultural trade of US, by commodity and country, bimonthly rpt, 1522–1

Agricultural trade of US, by detailed commodity and country, 1989, annual rpt, 1524–8

Agricultural trade of US, by detailed commodity and country, 1990, semiannual rpt, 1522–4

AID economic aid to developing countries, obligations and disbursements by country, quarterly rpt, 9912–4

AID housing and urban dev program financial statements, FY90, annual rpt, 9914–4

AID loans repayment status and terms by program and country, and status of predecessor agency loans, quarterly rpt, 9912–3

Alien workers (unauthorized) and Fair Labor Standards Act employer compliance, hiring impacts, and aliens overstaying visas by country and State, 1986-90, annual rpt, 6264–6

Aliens (illegal) overstaying visas, by class of admission, mode of arrival, age, country, and State, FY85-88, annual rpt, 6264–5

Coastal currents, temperatures, and salinity, for Atlantic Ocean from Florida straits to northern Brazil, series, 2146–7

Corporations in US under foreign control, income tax returns, assets and income statement items by industry div, country, and world area, 1988, article, 8302–2.219

Deforestation, and OECD imports of tropical wood, by country, 1980s, annual rpt, 9114–4.10

Economic and military aid and loans from US and intl agencies, by program and country, FY46-90, annual rpt, 9914–5

Economic and social conditions of developing countries from 1960s, and Intl Dev Cooperation Agency and AID activities and funding, FY90-92, annual rpt, 9904–4

Exports (duty-free) of Caribbean area to US, by commodity and country, with consumer and industry impacts, 1984-90, annual rpt, 9884–20

Exports and imports (waterborne) of US, by type of service, commodity, country, route, and US port, 1988, annual rpt, 7704–2

Exports and imports of OECD, total and for 4 major countries, and US trade by country, by commodity, 1970-89, world area rpt, 9116–1.4

Fish larvae abundance, distribution, and growth, for selected Western Hemisphere sites, 1989 conf, 2168–126

Grain production and needs, and related economic outlook, by world area and selected country, forecast 1990/91-1991/92, 1528–313

Immigrants admitted to US, by country of birth, FY81-90, annual rpt, 6264–4

Immigrants admitted to US, by occupational group and country of birth, preliminary FY90, annual table, 6264–1

Inter-American Foundation activities, grants by recipient, and fellowships, by country, FY90, annual rpt, 14424–1

Inter-American Foundation dev grants by program area, and fellowships by field and instn, by country, FY72-90, annual rpt, 14424–2

Investment (foreign direct) of US, by industry group and world area, 1987-90, annual article, 2702–1.220

Loans of US banks to foreigners at all US and foreign offices, by country group and country, quarterly rpt, 13002–1

Military aid of US, arms sales, and training, by country, FY50-90, annual rpt, 3904–3

Military aid of US, arms sales, and training programs costs and budget requests, by program, world region, and country, FY90-92, annual rpt, 7144–13

Multinatl US firms and foreign affiliates finances and operations, by industry and world area of parent firm, 1989 benchmark survey, preliminary annual rpt, 2704–5

Multinatl US firms foreign affiliates, income statement items by country and world area, 1986, biennial article, 8302–2.212

Oil and gas reserves and discoveries, by country and country group, quarterly rpt, 3162–43

Oils, oilseeds, and meal imports, by commodity, world area of destination, and major producer, 1960s-88, 1528–314

Peace Corps activities, funding by program, and volunteers, by country, FY92, annual rpt, 9654–1

R&D funding by Fed Govt, by field, performer type, agency, and State, FY89-91, annual rpt, 9627–20

Tax (income) returns of corporations with foreign tax credit, income, and tax items, by country and world region of credit, 1986, biennial article, 8302–2.207

Terrorism (intl) incidents, casualties, and attacks on US targets, by attack type and country, 1990, annual rpt, 7004–22

Travel to and from US on US and foreign flag air carriers, by world area, 1990, annual rpt, 2904–13

Travel to US, by characteristics of visit and traveler, country, port city, and State of destination, quarterly rpt, 2902–1

Travel to US, trade shows and other promotional activities, with magazine ad costs and circulation, for selected countries, 1991-92, annual rpt, 2904–11

Weather stations of Natl Weather Service, locations and types of observations made, 1990 annual listing, 2184–5

see also Argentina
see also Bolivia
see also Brazil
see also Chile
see also Colombia
see also Ecuador
see also French Guiana
see also Guyana
see also Inter-American Development Bank
see also Organization of American States
see also Paraguay
see also Peru
see also Suriname
see also Uruguay
see also Venezuela
see also under By Foreign Country in the "Index by Categories"

South Bend, Ind.

see also under By City and By SMSA or MSA in the "Index by Categories"

South Carolina

AIDS patient home and community services under Medicaid waiver in 6 States, 1988-89, article, 4652–1.216

Appalachian Regional Commission funding, by project and State, planned FY91, annual rpt, 9084–3

Banks (insured commercial), Fed Reserve 5th District members financial statements, by State, quarterly rpt, 9389–18

Banks (insured commercial and savings) deposits by instn, State, MSA, and county, as of June 1990, annual regional rpt, 9295–3.2

County Business Patterns, 1989: employment, establishments, and payroll, by SIC 2- to 4-digit industry and county, annual State rpt, 2326–8.42

DOD prime contract awards, by contractor, service branch, State, and city, FY90, annual rpt, 3544–22

Economic indicators by State, Fed Reserve 5th District, quarterly rpt, 9389–16

Education system in Appalachia, improvement initiatives, and indicators of success, by State, 1960s-89, 9088–36

Employment and housing and mortgage market indicators by State, FHLB 4th District, quarterly rpt, 9302–36

Employment and unemployment, for 8 southeastern States, 1989-90, annual rpt, 6944–2

Employment by industry div, earnings, and hours, for 8 southeastern States, quarterly press release, 6942–7

Estuary environmental and fishery conditions, research results and methodology, 1991 rpt, 2176–7.25

Fed Govt spending in States and local areas, by type, State, county, and city, FY90, annual rpt, 2464–3

Fed Govt spending in States, by type, program, agency, and State, FY90, annual rpt, 2464–2

Food aid program of USDA for women, infants, and children, prenatal participation effect on Medicaid costs and birth outcomes, for 5 States, 1987-88, 1368–2

Foster care placements, discharges, and returns to care, by selected characteristics of children, and length of stay factors, 1985-86, GAO rpt, 26121–432

Heart disease risk assessment program activities and costs, for South Carolina, 1987-88 study, article, 4042–3.245

South Carolina

HHS financial aid, by program, recipient, State, and city, FY90, annual regional listing, 4004–3.4

Hospital deaths of Medicare patients, actual and expected rates by diagnosis, and hospital characteristics, by instn, FY87-89, annual regional rpt, 4654–14.4

Hurricane Hugo relief funding and response by FEMA, 1989-90, GAO rpt, 26113–511

Hurricane Hugo storm characteristics, and Natl Weather Service forecast accuracy, 1989, 2186–6.1

Income (personal) per capita and by source, and earnings by industry div, by State, MSA, and county, 1984-89, annual regional rpt, 2704–2.4

Jail adult and juvenile population, employment, spending, instn conditions, and inmate programs, by county and facility, 1988, regional rpt series, 6068–144.4

Marriages, divorces, and rates, by characteristics of spouses, State, and county, 1987 and trends from 1920, US Vital Statistics annual rpt, 4144–4

Medicaid reimbursement of hospitals under prospective payment system, effect on maternity case-mix for South Carolina, various periods 1985-87, article, 4652–1.206

Mineral Industry Surveys, State reviews of production, 1990, preliminary annual rpt, 5614–6

Minerals resources in sediment off Myrtle Beach, SC, coast, 1989 rpt, 5668–115

Minerals Yearbook, 1989, Vol 2: State review of production and sales by commodity, and business activity, annual rpt, 5604–16.42

Minerals Yearbook, 1989, Vol 2: State reviews of production, sales, and firms, by commodity, and business activity, annual rpt, 5604–34

Peaches production, marketing, and prices in 3 southeastern States and Appalachia, 1990, annual rpt, 1311–12

Physicians, by specialty, age, sex, and location of training and practice, 1989, State rpt, 4116–6.42

Population and housing census, 1990: population and housing characteristics, households, and land area, by county, subdiv, and place, State rpt, 2551–1.42

Population and housing census, 1990: voting age and total population by race, and housing units, by block, redistricting counts required under PL 94-171, State CD-ROM release, 2551–6.2

Population and housing census, 1990: voting age and total population by race, and housing units, by county and city, redistricting counts required under PL 94-171, State summary rpt, 2551–5.41

Radioactive low-level waste disposal activities of States and interstate compacts, with data by disposal facility and reactor, 1989, annual rpt, 3354–14

Statistical Abstract of US, 1991 annual data compilation, 2324–1

Supplemental Security Income payments and beneficiaries, by type of eligibility, State, and county, Dec 1989, annual rpt, 4744–27.4

Textile mill employment, earnings, and hours, for 8 Southeastern States, quarterly press release, 6942–1

Textile production workers and wages by occupation, and benefits, by location, 1990 survey, 6787–6.251

Timber in South Carolina, lumber and mill residue production by product and species group, 1987-88, 1208–359

Water supply and quality in streams and lakes, and groundwater levels in wells, by drainage basin, 1990, annual State rpt, 5666–10.38

Water use by end use, well withdrawals, and public supply deliveries, by county, 1985, State rpt, 5666–24.9

see also Aiken County, S.C.

see also Charleston, S.C.

see also Columbia, S.C.

see also Rock Hill, S.C.

see also under By State in the "Index by Categories"

South Dakota

Banks (insured commercial and savings) deposits by instn, State, MSA, and county, as of June 1990, annual regional rpt, 9295–3.5

Business and economic conditions, Fed Reserve 9th District, quarterly journal, 9383–19

County Business Patterns, 1989: employment, establishments, and payroll, by SIC 2- to 4-digit industry and county, annual State rpt, 2326–8.43

DOD prime contract awards, by contractor, service branch, State, and city, FY90, annual rpt, 3544–22

Fed Govt spending in States and local areas, by type, State, county, and city, FY90, annual rpt, 2464–3

Fed Govt spending in States, by type, program, agency, and State, FY90, annual rpt, 2464–2

HHS financial aid, by program, recipient, State, and city, FY90, annual regional listing, 4004–3.8

Hospital deaths of Medicare patients, actual and expected rates by diagnosis, and hospital characteristics, by instn, FY87-89, annual regional rpt, 4654–14.8

Income (personal) per capita and by source, and earnings by industry div, by State, MSA, and county, 1984-89, annual regional rpt, 2704–2.3

Jail adult and juvenile population, employment, spending, instn conditions, and inmate programs, by county and facility, 1988, regional rpt series, 6068–144.3

Marriages, divorces, and rates, by characteristics of spouses, State, and county, 1987 and trends from 1920, US Vital Statistics annual rpt, 4144–4

Mineral Industry Surveys, State reviews of production, 1990, preliminary annual rpt, 5614–6

Minerals Yearbook, 1989, Vol 2: State review of production and sales by commodity, and business activity, annual rpt, 5604–16.43

Minerals Yearbook, 1989, Vol 2: State reviews of production, sales, and firms, by commodity, and business activity, annual rpt, 5604–34

Index by Subjects and Names

Physicians, by specialty, age, sex, and location of training and practice, 1989, State rpt, 4116–6.43

Population and housing census, 1990: population and housing characteristics, households, and land area, by county, subdiv, and place, State rpt, 2551–1.43

Population and housing census, 1990: voting age and total population by race, and housing units, by block, redistricting counts required under PL 94-171, State CD-ROM release, 2551–6.4

Population and housing census, 1990: voting age and total population by race, and housing units, by county and city, redistricting counts required under PL 94-171, State summary rpt, 2551–5.42

Poverty relief and medical aid programs of South Dakota counties, spending by type, MSA, and county, 1989, hearing, 25368–176

Recreation (outdoor) facilities on public land, use, and Land Mgmt Bur mgmt activities, funding, and plans, 1990 State rpt, 5726–5.5

Statistical Abstract of US, 1991 annual data compilation, 2324–1

Supplemental Security Income payments and beneficiaries, by type of eligibility, State, and county, Dec 1989, annual rpt, 4744–27.8

Wages by occupation, for office and plant workers, 1991 survey, periodic labor market rpt, 6785–3.7

Water (groundwater) supply, quality, chemistry, and use, 1987-88, regional rpt, 5666–28.3

Water quality, chemistry, hydrology, and other characteristics, 1989 local area study, 5666–27.13

Water supply and quality in streams and lakes, and groundwater levels in wells, by drainage basin, 1990, annual State rpt, 5666–10.39

Wildlife mgmt activities and funding, acreage by habitat type, and scientific staff, for Bur of Land Mgmt, 1990 State rpt, 5726–7.4

see also under By State in the "Index by Categories"

South West Africa

see Namibia

Southeast Asia

Agricultural exports of high-value commodities, indexes and sales by commodity, world area, and country, 1960s-86, 1528–323

Agricultural trade of US, by detailed commodity and country, 1989, annual rpt, 1524–8

Agricultural trade of US, by detailed commodity and country, 1990, semiannual rpt, 1522–4

AID economic aid to developing countries, obligations and disbursements by country, quarterly rpt, 9912–4

Economic and military aid and loans from US and intl agencies, by program and country, FY46-90, annual rpt, 9914–5

Economic and social conditions of developing countries from 1960s, and Intl Dev Cooperation Agency and AID activities and funding, FY90-92, annual rpt, 9904–4

Index by Subjects and Names

Southeastern States

Exports and imports (waterborne) of US, by type of service, commodity, country, route, and US port, 1988, annual rpt, 7704–2

Exports and imports of US, by Harmonized System 6-digit commodity and country, 1990, annual rpt, 2424–13

Exports and imports of US, by selected country, country group, and commodity group, 1990, annual rpt, 2044–37

Exports and imports of US, by transport mode, country, and SITC 1- to 3-digit commodity, 1990, annual rpt, 2424–12

Grain production and needs, and related economic outlook, by world area and selected country, forecast 1990/91-1991/92, 1528–313

Military aid of US, arms sales, and training, by country, FY50-90, annual rpt, 3904–3

Oil and gas reserves and discoveries, by country and country group, quarterly rpt, 3162–43

Oils, oilseeds, and meal imports, by commodity, world area of destination, and major producer, 1960s-88, 1528–314

Refugee arrivals and resettlement in US, by age, sex, sponsoring agency, State, and country, monthly rpt, 4692–2

Refugee arrivals in US by world area of origin and State of settlement, and Federal aid, FY90-91 and proposed FY92 allocations, annual rpt, 7004–16

Refugee resettlement programs and funding, arrivals by country of origin, and indicators of adjustment, by State, FY90, annual rpt, 4694–5

Refugees from Indochina, arrivals, and departures, by country of origin and resettlement, camp, and ethnicity, monthly rpt, 7002–4

Tax (income) returns of corporations with foreign tax credit, income, and tax items, by country and world region of credit, 1986, biennial article, 8302–2.207

Tide height and time daily at coastal points, forecast 1992, annual rpt, 2174–2.5

Weather conditions and effect on agriculture, by US region, State, and city, and world area, weekly rpt, 2182–7

see also Association of Southeast Asian Nations

see also Brunei

see also Burma

see also Cambodia

see also Christmas Island

see also Indonesia

see also Laos

see also Malaysia

see also Myanmar

see also Philippines

see also Singapore

see also Thailand

see also Vietnam

see also under By Foreign Country in the "Index by Categories"

Southeastern Power Administration

Electric power wholesale purchases of REA borrowers, by borrower, supplier, and State, 1940-89, annual rpt, 1244–5

Finances and operations of Federal power admins and electric utilities, 1989, annual rpt, 3164–24.2

Sales by customer, plants, and capacity of SEPA, and Southeastern Fed Power Program financial statements, FY90, annual rpt, 3234–1

Southeastern States

Banks (insured commercial), Fed Reserve 5th District members financial statements, by State, quarterly rpt, 9389–18

Banks in southeastern States, mergers and acquisitions, assets and major institutions involved, by State, 1984-89, article, 9371–1.203

Black Americans social and economic characteristics, for South and total US, 1989-90 and trends from 1969, Current Population Rpt, 2546–1.450

Coastal areas environmental conditions, fish, wildlife, use, and mgmt, 1990 rpt, 5506–9.42

CPI by component for US city average, and by region, population size, and for 27 metro areas, monthly rpt, 6762–2

Dairy prices, by product and selected area, with related marketing data, 1990, annual rpt, 1317–1

Economic and banking conditions, for Fed Reserve 8th District, quarterly rpt with articles, 9391–16

Economic indicators and cyclical devs and outlook, by Fed Reserve Bank District, periodic rpt, 9362–8

Economic indicators by State and MSA, Fed Reserve 6th District, quarterly rpt, 9371–14

Economic indicators by State, Fed Reserve 5th District, quarterly rpt, 9389–16

Electric power sales by customer, plants, and capacity of Southeastern Power Admin, FY90, annual rpt, 3234–1

Employment and housing and mortgage market indicators by State, FHLB 4th District, quarterly rpt, 9302–36

Employment by industry div, earnings, and hours, for 8 southeastern States, quarterly press release, 6942–7

Employment by industry div, unemployment, and CPI, for 8 southeastern States, 1989-90, annual rpt, 6944–2

Employment conditions in southeastern States, suspended series, 6946–1

Employment conditions in southeastern States, with comparisons to other regions, press release series, 6946–3

Epidemiologists, education, specialties, and State govt employment, for southern US, 1989, article, 4042–3.253

Financial and banking devs in southeastern States, working paper series, 9371–10

Financial and economic devs, Fed Reserve Bank of Atlanta bimonthly journal, 9371–1

Financial and economic devs, Fed Reserve Bank of Richmond bimonthly journal, 9389–1

Financial and economic devs, Fed Reserve Bank of St Louis bimonthly journal, 9391–1

Fish and shellfish catch, life cycles, and environmental needs, for selected coastal species and regions, series, 5506–8

Fishing (ocean sport) activities, and catch by species, by angler characteristics and State, 1987-89, annual coastal area rpt, 2166–17.1

Global climate change environmental, infrastructure, and health impacts, with model results and background data, 1850s-2100, 9188–113

HHS financial aid, by program, recipient, State, and city, FY90, annual regional listing, 4004–3.3; 4004–3.4

Hogs inventory, value, farrowings, and farms, by State, quarterly release, 1623–3

Home equity lines of credit share of all loans, and delinquency compared to other loans, by southeastern State, 1988-90, article, 9391–16.206

Income (personal) per capita and by source, and earnings by industry div, by State, MSA, and county, 1984-89, annual regional rpt, 2704–2.4

Lumber (pulpwood) production by county, and mill capacity by firm, by southern State, 1989, annual rpt, 1204–23

Lumber (pulpwood and residue) prices, spending, and transport shares by mode, for southeast US, 1988-89, annual rpt, 1204–22

Lumber (veneer) receipts, production, and shipments, by species and southern State, with residue use, 1988, 1208–43

Natural gas production and wellhead capacity, by production area, 1980-89 and alternative forecasts 1990-91, biennial rpt, 3164–93

Older persons migration to southern coastal areas, household finances, services needs, and local economic impacts, for selected counties, 1990, 2068–38

Peaches production, marketing, and prices in 3 southeastern States and Appalachia, 1990, annual rpt, 1311–12

Peanut production, prices, stocks, exports, use, inspection, and quality, by region and State, 1980-90, annual rpt, 1311–5

Prenatal care subsidy need under alternative poverty indicators, for 8 southern States, 1984-87, article, 4042–3.226

Recreation (outdoor) coastal facilities of Fed Govt and States, visitor and site characteristics, 1987-90 survey, regional rpt, 2176–9.1; 2176–9.3; 2176–9.4; 2176–9.7

Savings instns, FHLB 9th District members finances and operations by State, quarterly rpt, discontinued, 9302–31

Savings instns in southeastern States, industry review, periodic journal, suspended, 9302–2

Services and manufacturing sectors earnings and earnings distribution by southeastern State, 1989, article, 9391–16.205

Services sector employment growth and share of output by industry, by southeastern State, various periods 1979-89, article, 9391–16.203

Statistical Abstract of US, 1991 annual data compilation, 2324–1

Textile mill employment, earnings, and hours, for 8 Southeastern States, quarterly press release, 6942–1

Textile mill employment in southern US, 1951-90, annual rpt, 6944–1

Tide height and time daily at coastal points, forecast 1992, annual rpt, 2174–2.3

Timber in southeastern US, longleaf pine mgmt and use, 1989 conf, 1208–355

Timber in southeastern US, pine natural growth and plantation acreage, and lumber industries impacts of shift to plantation pine, 1989 conf papers, 1208–346

Southeastern States

Timber in southeastern US, resources and industry employment and output, by State, 1980s, article, 9391–16.204

Wetlands acreage conserved and disturbed in southeastern US, by habitat and disturbance type and State, 1988, article, 2162–1.202

Wetlands in coastal areas, acreage by wetland type, estuarine basin, and county, 1989, 2178–31

Wildlife and plant research results, 1990 habitat study, 5506–13.3

see also Appalachia

see also under By Region in the "Index by Categories"

see also under names of individual States

Southwestern Power Administration

Electric power wholesale purchases of REA borrowers, by borrower, supplier, and State, 1940-89, annual rpt, 1244–5

Finances and operations of Federal power admins and electric utilities, 1989, annual rpt, 3164–24.2

Financial statements, sales by customer, and operations and costs by project, for Southwestern Fed Power System, FY90, annual rpt, 3244–1

Southwestern States

Economic indicators and cyclical devs and outlook, by Fed Reserve Bank District, periodic rpt, 9362–8

Electric power sales by customer, activities by plant, and financial statements of Western Area Power Admin, FY90, annual rpt, 3254–1

Employment by industry div, earnings, and hours, by southwestern State, monthly rpt, 6962–2

Farm credit conditions and real estate values, Fed Reserve 11th District, quarterly rpt, 9379–11

Financial and economic devs, Fed Reserve Bank of Dallas bimonthly journal, 9379–1

Fish and shellfish catch, life cycles, and environmental needs, for selected coastal species and regions, series, 5506–8

HHS financial aid, by program, recipient, State, and city, FY90, annual regional listing, 4004–3.6

Hispanic Americans in counties bordering Mexico, by selected characteristics, 1980, Current Population Rpt, 2546–2.159

Income (personal) per capita and by source, and earnings by industry div, by State, MSA, and county, 1984-89, annual regional rpt, 2704–2.5

Land Mgmt Bur activities in Southwestern US, FY90, annual rpt, 5724–15

Peanut production, prices, stocks, exports, use, inspection, and quality, by region and State, 1980-90, annual rpt, 1311–5

Savings instns, FHLB 9th District members finances and operations by State, quarterly rpt, discontinued, 9302–31

Statistical Abstract of US, 1991 annual data compilation, 2324–1

see also under By Region in the "Index by Categories"

see also under names of individual States

Soviet Union

Agricultural conditions and factors affecting US grain exports and CCC credit guarantees, for USSR, 1990 hearings, 21168–49

Agricultural exports of high-value commodities, indexes and sales by commodity, world area, and country, 1960s-86, 1528–323

Agricultural exports of US, for grains, oilseed products, hides, skins, and cotton, by country, weekly rpt, 1922–3

Agricultural exports of US, impacts of foreign agricultural and trade policy, with data by commodity and country, 1989, annual rpt, 1924–8

Agricultural production, prices, and trade, for USSR, 1960s-90 and forecast 1991, annual rpt, 1524–4.1

Agricultural production, trade, and policies in foreign countries, summary data by country, 1989-90, annual factbook, 1924–12

Agricultural reform issues for USSR, with background data on USSR and US, 1970s-90, article, 9381–1.210

Agricultural subsidies of USSR to producers and consumers, 1986, 1528–320

Agricultural trade by commodity and country, prices, and world market devs, monthly rpt, 1922–12

Agricultural trade of US, by detailed commodity and country, 1989, annual rpt, 1524–8

Agricultural trade of US, by detailed commodity and country, 1990, semiannual rpt, 1522–4

Agricultural trade of USSR, by commodity and country, 1955-90, 1528–322

Cocoa bean imports of USSR, by country, 1986-89, semiannual rpt, 1925–9.1

Cotton production, trade, and use, for selected countries, FAS monthly circular, 1925–4.2

Debt of Communist countries to US and other Western banks, by country, 1980s, conf, 25388–56

Drug abuse indicators, for selected countries, 1991 semiannual conf, 4492–5.2

Economic and military aid and loans from US and intl agencies, by program and country, FY46-90, annual rpt, 9914–5

Economic and social conditions of developing countries from 1960s, and Intl Dev Cooperation Agency and AID activities and funding, FY90-92, annual rpt, 9904–4

Economic conditions in Communist and OECD countries, 1989, annual rpt, 7144–11

Economic conditions in USSR, CIA estimation methods assessment, 1989, GAO rpt, 26123–365

Economic conditions in USSR, Eastern Europe, OECD, and selected other countries, 1960s-90, annual rpt, 9114–4

Economic conditions in USSR under General Secretary Gorbachev, 1990 and trends from 1975, annual rpt, 9114–6

Economic conditions, policy, and trade practices, by country, 1988-90, annual rpt, 21384–5

Economic, social, political, and geographic summary data, by country, 1991, annual factbook, 9114–2

Energy use and production, by fuel type, country, and country group, projected 1995-2010 and trends from 1970, annual rpt, 3164–84

Export licensing, monitoring, and enforcement activities, FY90, annual rpt, 2024–1

Exports and imports of OECD members, by country, 1989, annual rpt, 7144–10

Exports and imports of US, by commodity and country, 1970-89, world area rpt, 9116–1.3

Exports and imports of US, by Harmonized System 6-digit commodity and country, 1990, annual rpt, 2424–13

Exports and imports of US, by selected country, country group, and commodity group, 1990, annual rpt, 2044–37

Exports and imports of US, by transport mode, country, and SITC 1- to 3-digit commodity, 1990, annual rpt, 2424–12

Exports and imports of US with Communist countries, by detailed commodity and country, quarterly rpt with articles, 9882–2

Exports, imports, and balances of US with major trading partners, by product category, 1986-90, annual chartbook, 9884–21

Exports of US, detailed Schedule B commodities with countries of destination, 1990, annual rpt, 2424–10

GNP of USSR by component and industry sector, and CIA estimation methods, 1950s-87, 23848–223

GNP of USSR by detailed income and outlay component, 1985, 2326–18.59

Grain production, supply, trade, and use, by country and world region, forecasts and trends, FAS monthly circular, 1925–2.1

Helsinki Final Act implementation by NATO and Warsaw Pact, Apr 1990-Mar 1991, last issue of semiannual rpt, 7002–1

Human rights conditions in 170 countries, and US economic and military aid, 1990, annual rpt, 21384–3

Immigrants in US, population characteristics and fertility, by birthplace and compared to native born, 1980s, Current Population rpt, 2546–2.162

Jewish emigration from USSR, and share to Israel, 1968-90, hearings, 21168–49

Market economy transition of Eastern Europe countries, US trade prospects, with background data by country, 1980s, hearing, 25728–42

Market economy transition of USSR, with trade agreements and bilateral US trade data by country, late 1980s-90, annual rpt, 444–2

Military aid of US, arms sales, and training, by country, FY50-90, annual rpt, 3904–3

Military reserve forces structure and training, for US and 5 European countries, as of 1990, GAO rpt, 26123–358

Military weapons systems, presence, and force strengths of USSR, and compared to US, 1991 annual rpt, 3504–20

Minerals production and trade of USSR, by commodity, 1988-89, annual rpt, 5604–39

Nuclear power plant capacity and operating status, by plant and communist and regulated market country, as of Dec 1990, annual rpt, 3164–57.2

Nuclear reactor accident in Chernobyl, radionuclide releases and concentrations in food and water, by selected Soviet Republic, 1986-87 article, 4042–3.201

Index by Subjects and Names

Soybeans

Nuclear weapons elimination under Intermediate-Range Nuclear Forces Treaty, US and USSR on site inspections, and US costs and staffing, FY89-91, GAO rpt, 26123–364

Nuclear weapons systems of US and USSR, costs, and military forces survival after attack, projected under alternative arms control proposals, FY92-2006, 26306–6.161

Oil and gas production by region, use, and trade by country, monthly rpt, 9112–2

Oil production and exports to US, by major exporting country, detailed data, monthly rpt with articles, 3162–24

Oil production of USSR, exports, and investments, 1980s and projected to 1994, GAO rpt, 26123–349

Oil production, trade, use, and stocks, by selected country and country group, monthly rpt, 3162–42

Oil supply, demand, and stock forecasts, by world area, quarterly rpt, 3162–34

Radio Free Europe and Radio Liberty broadcast and financial data, FY90, annual rpt, 10314–1

Refugee arrivals in US by world area and country of origin, and quotas, monthly rpt, 7002–4

Refugee arrivals in US by world area of origin and State of settlement, and Federal aid, FY90-91 and proposed FY92 allocations, annual rpt, 7004–16

Refugee resettlement programs and funding, arrivals by country of origin, and indicators of adjustment, by State, FY90, annual rpt, 4694–5

Ships in world merchant fleet, tonnage, and new ship construction and deliveries, by vessel type and country, as of Jan 1990, annual rpt, 7704–3

Space launchings and characteristics of craft and flight, by country, 1957-90, annual rpt, 9504–9.1

Space programs activities, missions, launchings, payloads, and flight duration, for foreign and US programs, 1957-90, annual rpt, 21704–4

Space programs involvement by private sector, govt contracts, costs, revenue, and R&D spending, 1970s-80s and projected to 2000, 26306–6.154

Spacecraft and satellite launches since 1957, quarterly listing, 9502–2

Spacecraft launches and other activities of NASA and USSR, with flight data, 1957-90, annual rpt, 9504–6.1

UN voting record and share of votes in agreement with US, by issue, country, and world area, 1990, annual rpt, 7004–18

Weather conditions and effect on agriculture, by US region, State, and city, and world area, weekly rpt, 2182–7

Wheat quality indicators, for US exports and foreign wheat production, 1960s-90, hearing, 25168–75

see also Under By Foreign Country in the "Index by Categories"

Soybeans

Acreage planted and harvested, by crop and State, 1989-90 and planned as of June 1991, annual rpt, 1621–23

Acreage planted, by selected crop and State, 1982-90 and planned 1991, annual rpt, 1621–22

Acreage under Agricultural Stabilization and Conservation Service programs, rankings by commodity and congressional district, 1989, biennial rpt, 1804–17

Agricultural data compilation, 1990 and trends from 1920, annual rpt, 1004–14

Agricultural Statistics, 1990, annual rpt, 1004–1

Agriculture census, 1987: farms, farmland, production, finances, and operator characteristics, by county, final State rpt series, 2331–1

Andean countries cocaine and alternative crop production and impacts on US agricultural exports, with data for Bolivia, 1980s-91, GAO rpt, 26123–366

Beer production, stocks, material used, tax-free removals, and taxable removals by State, monthly rpt, 8486–1.1

CCC certificate exchange activity, by commodity, biweekly press release, 1802–16

CCC financial condition and major commodity program operations, FY62-87, annual chartbook, 1824–2

Cooperatives finances and operations, by grain handled and selected characteristics, 1983-85, series, 1128–44

Cooperatives, finances, operations, activities, and membership, 1950s-88, commodity rpt, 1126–1.5

County Business Patterns, 1988: employment, establishments, and payroll, by SIC 2- to 4-digit industry and county, annual State rpt series, 2326–6

County Business Patterns, 1989: employment, establishments, and payroll, by SIC 2- to 4-digit industry and county, annual State rpt series, 2326–8

Export demand for US corn, wheat, and soybeans, by selected country, 1960s-83, 1568–297

Exports and imports (agricultural) commodity and country, prices, and world market devs, monthly rpt, 1922–12

Exports and imports (agricultural) of US, by commodity and country, bimonthly rpt, 1522–1

Exports and imports (agricultural) of US, by detailed commodity and country, 1989, annual rpt, 1524–8

Exports and imports (agricultural) of US, by detailed commodity and country, 1990, semiannual rpt, 1522–4

Exports and imports between US and outlying areas, by detailed commodity and mode of transport, 1990, annual rpt, 2424–11

Exports and imports of US, by country and detailed commodity, monthly rpt, 2422–12

Exports and imports of US, by Harmonized System 6-digit commodity and country, 1990, annual rpt, 2424–13

Exports of grains, oilseed products, hides, skins, and cotton, by country, weekly rpt, 1922–3

Exports of US, detailed Schedule B commodities with countries of destination, 1990, annual rpt, 2424–10

Farm financial condition, 1987, commodity rpt, 1566–8.7

Farm income, expenses, receipts by commodity, assets, liabilities, and ratios, 1990 and trends from 1945, annual rpt, 1544–16

Farm sector balance sheet, and receipts by detailed commodity, by State, 1985-89, annual rpt, 1544–18

Fertilizer and pesticide use and application rates, by type, crop, and State, 1990, 1616–1.1

Foreign and US agricultural production, acreage, and yield for selected crops, forecasts by selected world region and country, FAS monthly circular, 1925–28

Foreign and US agricultural production, prices, trade, and use, periodic rpt with articles, 1522–3

Foreign and US agricultural supply and demand indicators, by selected crop, monthly rpt, 1522–5

Foreign and US oils, oilseeds, and fats production and trade, FAS periodic circular series, 1925–1

Foreign countries agricultural production, prices, and trade, by country, 1980-90 and forecast 1991, annual world area rpt series, 1524–4

Futures and options trading volume, by commodity and exchange, FY90, annual rpt, 11924–2

Futures contracts, stocks in deliverable position by type, weekly table, 11922–4.3

Futures trading in selected commodities and financial instruments and indexes, NYC, Chicago, and other markets activity, semimonthly rpt, 11922–5

Imports of oils, oilseeds, and meal, by commodity, world area of destination, and major producer, 1960s-88, 1528–314

Inspection of grain for domestic use and export, and foreign buyers complaints, FY90, annual rpt, 1294–1

Inspection of grain for export, test results by commodity and port region, 1988-90, annual rpt series, 1294–2

Irrigation projects of Reclamation Bur in western US, crop production and acreage by commodity, State, and project, 1989, annual rpt, 5824–12

Loan support programs of USDA for grains, activity and status by grain and State, monthly rpt, 1802–3

Manufacturing census, 1987: finances and operations, by SIC 2- to 4-digit industry, State, and MSA, with trends from 1849, 2497–1

Manufacturing census, 1987: finances and operations, by type of organization and SIC 2- to 4-digit industry, subject rpt, 2497–5

OECD trade, total and for 4 major countries, and US trade by country, by commodity, 1970-89, world area rpt series, 9116–1

Pesticide and fertilizer use reduction, environmental and economic impacts by commodity and region, alternative forecasts 1989-94, hearing, 23848–222

Price indexes (producer), by stage of processing and detailed commodity, monthly rpt, 6762–6

Price indexes (producer), by stage of processing and detailed commodity, monthly 1990, annual rpt, 6764–2

Price support and other CCC program outlays, with production and marketing outlook, by commodity, projected 1990-96, 26306–6.160

Soybeans

Price support program provisions, for selected commodities, 1961-90, 1568–303

Prices received and paid by farmers, by commodity and State, 1990, annual rpt, 1629–5

Prices received by farmers and production value, by detailed crop and State, 1988-90, annual rpt, 1621–2

Prices received by farmers for major products, and paid for farm inputs and living items, by State, monthly rpt, 1629–1

Production costs for corn, wheat, and soybeans in current and constant dollars, 1975-79, article, 1541–1.208

Production, farms, acreage, and related data, by selected crop and State, monthly rpt, 1621–1

Production itemized costs, receipts, and returns, by commodity and region, 1987-89, annual rpt, 1544–20

Production of oil and fat, consumption by end use, and stocks, by type, quarterly Current Industrial Rpt, 2506–4.4

Production of oil, crushings, and stocks, by oilseed type and State, quarterly Current Industrial Rpt, 2506–4.3

Production, prices, trade, and export inspections by US port and country of destination, by grain type, weekly rpt, 1313–2

Production, prices, trade, and marketing, by commodity, current situation and forecast, monthly rpt with articles, 1502–4

Production, prices, trade, and use of oils and fats, periodic situation rpt with articles, 1561–3

Rail loadings of grain and soybeans, periodic situation rpt with articles, 1561–4

Research and education grants, USDA competitive awards by program and recipient, FY90, annual listing, 1764–1

Soviet Union agricultural trade, by commodity and country, 1955-90, 1528–322

Soviet Union, Eastern Europe, OECD, and selected other countries agricultural production, by commodity, 1960s-90, annual rpt, 9114–4.5

State and Metro Area Data Book, 1991 data compilation, 2328–54

Statistical Abstract of US, 1991 annual data compilation, 2324–1.23

Stocks of grain by region and market city, and grain inspected for export, by type, weekly rpt, 1313–4

Stocks of grain on and off farms, by crop, quarterly rpt, 1621–4

see also under By Commodity in the "Index by Categories"

Space program accidents and safety

Foreign and US space program activities, missions, launchings, payloads, and flight duration, 1957-90, annual rpt, 21704–4

Space programs

Advisory Committee on Future of US Space Program recommendations, 1990 rpt, 9508–38

Budget of US, CBO analysis and review of FY92 budget by function, annual rpt, 26304–2

Budget of US, CBO analysis of savings and revenues under alternative spending cuts and tax changes, projected FY92-97, 26306–3.118

Budget of US, obligations and authority by function, agency, and program, with summaries, analyses, and historical tables, FY92, annual rpt, 104–2

China economic indicators and reform issues, with background data, 1950s-90, compilation of papers, 23848–155

Data sources and availability for space sciences and related topics, 1991 annual listing, 9504–10

DOD budget, programs, and policies, FY90, annual rpt, 3544–2

DOD budget, weapons acquisition costs by system and service branch, FY91-93, annual rpt, 3504–2

Employment and payroll, by function, level of govt, and State, 1990, annual rpt, 2466–1.1

Environmental and natural resource data sources, and aerial survey R&D rpts, quarterly listing, 9502–7

Expenditures of Fed Govt, by function, FY89, annual rpt, 2466–2.2

Expenditures of Fed Govt by type, and other finances, selected years 1952-89, annual rpt, 10044–1

Expenditures of Fed Govt in States, by type, program, agency, and State, FY90, annual rpt, 2464–2

Fed Govt aeronautics and space activities and budgets, by agency, and foreign programs, 1957-FY90, annual rpt, 9504–9

Finances and operations, by SIC 2- to 4-digit industry, forecast 1991, annual rpt, 2044–28

Foreign and US funding for R&D, and scientists and engineering employment and education, 1991 annual rpt, 9627–35.1

Foreign and US space program activities, missions, launchings, payloads, and flight duration, 1957-90, annual rpt, 21704–4

Fraud and abuse in NASA programs, audits and investigations, 2nd half FY91, semiannual rpt, 9502–9

NASA activities and finances, and data on US and USSR space launches, 1957-90, annual rpt, 9504–6

NASA activities and funding, 1990, annual compilation of papers, 21704–1

NASA project launch schedules and technical descriptions, press release series, 9506–2

Nuclear reactors for domestic use and export by function and operating status, with owner, operating characteristics, and location, 1990 annual listing, 3354–15

Private sector involvement in space programs, commercial dev centers funding sources and flight requests, 1986-90, GAO rpt, 26123–353

Private sector involvement in space programs, govt contracts, costs, revenue, and R&D spending, 1970s-80s and projected to 2000, 26306–6.154

Procurement contract awards of NASA, by type, contractor, State, and country, FY91 with trends from 1961, semiannual rpt, 9502–6

Soviet Union military weapons systems, presence, and force strengths, and compared to US, 1991 annual rpt, 3504–20

Index by Subjects and Names

Space station commercial dev and operating costs and income under alternative financing options, projected 1989-2000, 21708–129

Statistical Abstract of US, 1991 annual data compilation, 2324–1.20

see also Communications satellites

see also Meteorological satellites

see also Satellites

see also Space program accidents and safety

see also Space sciences

see also Spacecraft

see also Strategic Defense Initiative

Space sciences

Aerial survey R&D rpts, and sources of natural resource and environmental data, quarterly listing, 9502–7

Data archival storage of NASA space science missions, holdings, and missions not archived, 1950s-91, 26125–43

Data sources and availability for space sciences and related topics, 1991 annual listing, 9504–10

Data sources for space sciences and related topics, use by format and user type, FY90, annual rpt, 9504–11

NASA activities and finances, and data on US and USSR space launches, 1957-90, annual rpt, 9504–6

NASA project launch schedules and technical descriptions, press release series, 9506–2

NASA R&D funding to higher education instns, by field, instn, and State, FY90, annual listing, 9504–7

Private sector involvement in space programs, govt contracts, costs, revenue, and R&D spending, 1970s-80s and projected to 2000, 26306–6.154

Procurement contract awards of NASA, by type, contractor, State, and country, FY91 with trends from 1961, semiannual rpt, 9502–6

R&D funding by Fed Govt, by field, performer type, agency, and State, FY89-91, annual rpt, 9627–20

R&D funding by higher education instns and federally funded centers, by field, instn, and State, FY89, annual rpt, 9627–13

Spacecraft

County Business Patterns, 1988: employment, establishments, and payroll, by SIC 2- to 4-digit industry and county, annual State rpt series, 2326–6

County Business Patterns, 1989: employment, establishments, and payroll, by SIC 2- to 4-digit industry and county, annual State rpt series, 2326–8

Data sources and availability for space sciences and related topics, 1991 annual listing, 9504–10

DOD budget, weapons acquisition costs by system and service branch, FY91-93, annual rpt, 3504–2

DOD prime contract awards, by detailed procurement category, FY87-90, annual rpt, 3544–18

Exports and imports of US, by country and detailed commodity, monthly rpt, 2422–12

Foreign and US space launchings and characteristics of craft and flight, 1957-90, annual rpt, 9504–9.1

Index by Subjects and Names

Special districts

Foreign and US space program activities, missions, launchings, payloads, and flight duration, 1957-90, annual rpt, 21704–4

Launch schedules and technical descriptions of NASA projects, press release series, 9506–2

Launchings by US and USSR, 1957-90, annual rpt, 9504–6

Launchings of satellites and other space objects since 1957, quarterly listing, 9502–2

Manufacturing annual survey, 1989: value of shipments, by SIC 4- to 5-digit product class, 2506–15.2

Manufacturing census, 1987: employment and shipments under Fed Govt contracts, by SIC 4-digit industry, 2497–7

Manufacturing census, 1987: finances and operations, by SIC 2- to 4-digit industry, State, and MSA, with trends from 1849, 2497–1

Manufacturing census, 1987: finances and operations, by type of organization and SIC 2- to 4-digit industry, subject rpt, 2497–5

Manufacturing finances and operations, by SIC 2- to 4-digit industry, forecast 1991, annual rpt, 2044–28

Occupational injury and illness rates, by SIC 2- to 4-digit industry, 1989, annual rpt, 6844–1

Private sector involvement in space programs, govt contracts, costs, revenue, and R&D spending, 1970s-80s and projected to 2000, 26306–6.154

Space station commercial dev and operating costs and income under alternative financing options, projected 1989-2000, 21708–129

see also Communications satellites

see also Meteorological satellites

see also Satellites

see also Space program accidents and safety

Spain

Agricultural exports of high-value commodities, indexes and sales by commodity, world area, and country, 1960s-86, 1528–323

Agricultural production, prices, and trade, by country, 1970s-90, and forecast 1991, annual world region rpt, 1524–4.4

Agricultural production, trade, and policies in foreign countries, summary data by country, 1989-90, annual factbook, 1924–12

Agricultural trade of US, by detailed commodity and country, 1989, annual rpt, 1524–8

Agricultural trade of US, by detailed commodity and country, 1990, semiannual rpt, 1522–4

AID loans repayment status and terms by program and country, and status of predecessor agency loans, quarterly rpt, 9912–3

Background Notes, summary social, political, and economic data, 1991 rpt, 7006–2.30

Bearings (ball) from 14 countries, injury to US industry from foreign subsidized and less than fair value imports, investigation with background financial and operating data, 1991 rpt, 9886–19.74

Drug abuse indicators, by world region and selected country, 1990 semiannual conf, 4492–5.1

Economic and military aid and loans from US and intl agencies, by program and country, FY46-90, annual rpt, 9914–5

Economic and monetary trends, compounded annual rates of change for US and 13 trading partners, quarterly rpt annual supplement, 9391–7

Economic conditions in USSR, Eastern Europe, OECD, and selected other countries, 1960s-90, annual rpt, 9114–4

Economic conditions, investment and export opportunities, and trade practices, 1991 country market research rpt, 2046–6.8

Economic conditions, policy, and trade practices, by country, 1988-90, annual rpt, 21384–5

Economic, social, political, and geographic summary data, by country, 1991, annual factbook, 9114–2

Exports and imports of NATO members with PRC, by country, 1987-90, annual rpt, 7144–14

Exports and imports of OECD members, by country, 1989, annual rpt, 7144–10

Exports and imports of US, by Harmonized System 6-digit commodity and country, 1990, annual rpt, 2424–13

Exports and imports of US, by selected country, country group, and commodity group, 1990, annual rpt, 2044–37

Exports and imports of US, by transport mode, country, and SITC 1- to 3-digit commodity, 1990, annual rpt, 2424–12

Exports and imports of US with EC by country, and total agricultural trade, selected years 1958-90, annual rpt, 7144–7

Exports of US, detailed Schedule B commodities with countries of destination, 1990, annual rpt, 2424–10

Fish (squid) catch of Spain, and trade by country, by species, 1980-88, article, 2162–1.203

Fish (squid) catch, trade, consumption, and cold storage holdings, by country and species, 1963-90, 2166–19.10

GNP and GNP growth for OECD members, by country, 1980-90, annual rpt, 7144–8

Hazelnut production, supply, trade, and use, by country, 1989-92, article, 1925–34.246

Human rights conditions in 170 countries, and US economic and military aid, 1990, annual rpt, 21384–3

Imports of goods, services, and investment from US, trade barriers, impacts, and US actions, by country, 1990, annual rpt, 444–2

Labor conditions, union coverage, and work accidents, 1991 annual country rpt, 6366–4.15

Military aid of US, arms sales, and training programs costs and budget requests, by program, world region, and country, FY90-92, annual rpt, 7144–13

Multinatl US firms and foreign affiliates finances and operations, by industry and world area of parent firm, 1989 benchmark survey, preliminary annual rpt, 2704–5

Multinatl US firms foreign affiliates, income statement items by country and world area, 1986, biennial article, 8302–2.212

Nuclear power generation in US and 20 countries, monthly rpt, 3162–24.10

Nuclear power plant capacity, generation, and operating status, by plant and foreign and US location, 1990 and projected to 2030, annual rpt, 3164–57

Oil exports to US by OPEC and non-OPEC countries, monthly rpt, 3162–24.3

Oil production, trade, use, and stocks, by selected country and country group, monthly rpt, 3162–42

Spacecraft and satellite launches since 1957, quarterly listing, 9502–2

Steel imports of US under voluntary restraint agreement, by product, customs district, and country, with US industry operating data, quarterly rpt, 9882–13

Tax revenue, by level of govt and type of tax, for OECD countries, mid 1960s-89, annual rpt, 10044–1.2

Telecommunications industry intl competitiveness, with financial and operating data by product or service, firm, and country, 1990 rpt, 2008–30

UN voting record and share of votes in agreement with US, by issue, country, and world area, 1990, annual rpt, 7004–18

see also under By Foreign Country in the "Index by Categories"

Spanish heritage Americans

see Hispanic Americans

Spanish Sahara

see Western Sahara

Sparks, Amy L.

"Apple Import Demand: Four Markets for U.S. Fresh Apples", 1568–296

"Orange Import Demand: Four Markets for U.S. Fresh Oranges", 1528–317

Sparta, Wis.

Wages by occupation, and benefits for office and plant workers, 1991 survey, periodic labor market rpt, 6785–3.9

Spartanburg, S.C.

see also under By SMSA or MSA in the "Index by Categories"

Spatz, Karen J.

"Exporting: An Avenue for Dairy Cooperatives", 1128–65

Special districts

Census of Govts, 1987: employment, payroll, and average earnings, by function, level of govt, State, county, and population size, 2455–2

Census of Govts, 1987: local govt employment by function, payroll, and average earnings, for individual counties, cities, and school and special districts, 2455–1

Census of Govts, 1987: State and local govt employment, payroll, OASDHI coverage, and employee benefits costs, by level of govt and State, 2455–4

Census of Govts, 1987: State and local labor-mgmt policies, agreements, and coverage and bargaining units, by function, level of govt, and State, 2455–3

Electric power wholesale purchases of REA borrowers, by borrower, supplier, and State, 1940-89, annual rpt, 1244–5

Employment and payroll, by function, level of govt, and State, 1990, annual rpt, 2466–1.1

Finances of govts, by level of govt, State, and for large cities and counties, annual rpt series, 2466–2

Finances, tax systems and revenue, and fiscal structure, by level of govt and State, 1991 and historical trends, annual rpt, 10044–1

Special districts

Minority group and women employment in State and local govt, by occupation, function, pay grade, and level of govt, 1990, annual rpt, 9244–6.3

see also School districts

Special Drawing Rights

Assets and debts of private sector, balance sheets by segment, 1945-90, semiannual rpt, 9365–4.1

Budget of US, authoritative financial statements with appropriations, outlays, and receipts, by category and agency, FY90, annual rpt, 8104–2.1

Economic indicators and components, current data and annual trends, monthly rpt, 23842–1.7

Fed Govt receipts by source and outlays by agency, *Treasury Bulletin*, quarterly rpt, 8002–4.1

Fed Reserve banks finances and staff, 1990, annual rpt, 9364–1.1

Flow-of-funds accounts, savings, investments, and credit statements, quarterly rpt, 9365–3.3

Investment (intl) position of US, by component, industry, world region, and country, 1989-90, annual article, 2702–1.212

Reserve assets of US by type, *Treasury Bulletin*, quarterly rpt, 8002–4.10

Reserve assets of US, monthly rpt, 9362–1.3

Special education

Assistance (financial and nonfinancial) of Fed Govt, 1991 base edition with supplements, annual listing, 104–5

Condition of Education, detail for elementary and secondary education, 1920s-90 and projected to 2001, annual rpt, 4824–1.1

Developmental, learning, and emotional problems in children, and share receiving special treatment and education, by selected characteristics, 1988, 4146–8.193

Digest of Education Statistics, 1991 annual data compilation, 4824–2

Discrimination in education, indicators for service delivery and discipline, by State, 1988, biennial rpt, 4804–33

Discrimination within schools, Education Dept enforcement activities and adequacy, FY81-91, GAO rpt, 26121–427

Early childhood education for handicapped children, project descriptions, 1990/91, annual listing, 4944–10

Education Dept programs funding, operations, and effectiveness, FY90, annual rpt, 4804–5

Elementary and secondary education enrollment, staff, finances, operations, programs, and policies, 1987/88 biennial survey, series, 4836–3

Elementary and secondary public schools, enrollment, teachers, funding, and other characteristics, by region and State, 1988/89, annual rpt, 4834–20

Enrollment by age, staff, funding, and needs of special education programs, by type of handicap and State, 1989/90, annual rpt, 4944–4

Enrollment in public elementary and secondary schools, and facilities, by State, 1989/90, annual rpt, 4834–17

Expenditures of Fed Govt in States, by type, program, agency, and State, FY90, annual rpt, 2464–2

Gifted minority students science and math education programs, participation and outcomes, 1981-88 study, 4808–34

Head Start enrollment, funding, and staff, FY90, annual rpt, 4604–8

Head Start handicapped enrollment, by handicap, State, and for Indian and migrant programs, 1987/88, annual rpt, 4604–1

Homeless children educational projects, activities, and funding, FY90, annual rpt, 4804–35

Mental health care in private hospitals, patients characteristics, 1986, 4506–3.47

State and Metro Area Data Book, 1991 data compilation, 2328–54

Statistical Abstract of US, 1991 annual data compilation, 2324–1.4

see also Compensatory education

see also Remedial education

Special foreign currency programs

AID and Intl Dev Cooperation Agency activities and funding, FY90-92, with developing countries economic and social conditions from 1960s, annual rpt, 9904–4

Budget of US, obligations and authority by function, agency, and program, with summaries, analyses, and historical tables, FY92, annual rpt, 104–2

Currency (foreign) accounts owned by US under AID admin and by foreign govts with joint AID control, status by program and country, quarterly rpt, 9912–1

Currency (foreign) holdings of US, transactions and balances by program and country, 1st half FY91, semiannual rpt, 8102–7

DOD outlays and obligations, by function and service branch, quarterly rpt, 3542–3

NIH intl program activities and funding, by inst and country, FY90, annual rpt, 4474–6

PL 480 foreign currency status, by use, agency, and country, as of FY88, annual rpt, 1924–7

R&D funding by Fed Govt, by field, performer type, agency, and State, FY89-91, annual rpt, 9627–20

Special observances

see Vacations and holidays

Special Study Panel on Education Indicators

Data collection and reporting improvement, and performance indicators dev, recommendations, 1991 rpt, 4828–40

Spector, William D.

"Cognitive Impairment and Disruptive Behaviors Among Community-Based Elderly Persons: Implications for Targeting Long-Term Care", 4186–7.10

"Measuring Cognitive Impairment with Large Data Sets", 4186–7.7

Speech pathology and audiology

Child health, behavioral, emotional, and school problems relation to family structure, by selected characteristics, 1988, 4147–10.178

Education in science and engineering, grad programs enrollment by field, source of funds, and characteristics of student and instn, 1975-89, annual rpt, 9627–7

Index by Subjects and Names

Educational service delivery and discipline, and discrimination indicators by State, 1988, biennial rpt, 4804–33

Head Start handicapped enrollment, by handicap, State, and for Indian and migrant programs, 1987/88, annual rpt, 4604–1

Home health care agencies finances impacts of Medicare payment limits under alternative determination methods, with data by service type, 1984-89, GAO rpt, 26121–400

Home health care visits approved by Medicare, planned and actual visits by service type, 1986, article, 4652–1.254

Hospices operations, services, costs, and patient characteristics, for instns without Medicare certification, FY85-86, 4658–52

Military health care personnel, and accessions by training source, by occupation, specialty, and service branch, FY89, annual rpt, 3544–24

Special education programs, enrollment by age, staff, funding, and needs, by type of handicap and State, 1989/90, annual rpt, 4944–4

State and Metro Area Data Book, 1991 data compilation, 2328–54

VA health care staff and turnover, by occupation, physician specialty, and location, 1990, annual rpt, 8604–8

VA Medicine and Surgery Dept trainees, by detailed program and city, FY90, annual rpt, 8704–4

see also Ear diseases and infections

Speed limit

see Traffic laws and courts

Spence, Sandy

"National Commuter Transportation Survey, People and Programs", 7888–81

Spencer, John S., Jr.

"Indiana's Timber Resource, 1986: An Analysis", 1208–368

Spendable earnings

see Earnings, general

see Personal and household income

Spices and herbs

Agricultural Statistics, 1990, annual rpt, 1004–1

Agriculture census, 1987: farms, farmland, production, finances, and operator characteristics, by county, final State rpt series, 2331–1

Consumer Expenditure Survey, food spending by item, household composition, income, age, race, and region, 1980-88, biennial rpt, 1544–30

Consumption, supply, trade, prices, spending, and indexes, by food commodity, 1989, annual rpt, 1544–4

CPI by component for US city average, and by region, population size, and for 27 metro areas, monthly rpt, 6762–2

Exports and imports (agricultural) of US, by commodity and country, bimonthly rpt, 1522–1

Exports and imports (agricultural) of US, by detailed commodity and country, 1989, annual rpt, 1524–8

Exports and imports (agricultural) of US, by detailed commodity and country, 1990, semiannual rpt, 1522–4

Exports and imports of US, by country and detailed commodity, monthly rpt, 2422–12

Index by Subjects and Names

Exports and imports of US, by Harmonized System 6-digit commodity and country, 1990, annual rpt, 2424–13

Exports and imports of US, by transport mode, country, and SITC 1- to 3-digit commodity, 1990, annual rpt, 2424–12

Exports of essential oils, by type and country, FAS monthly circular with articles, 1925–34

Exports of US, detailed Schedule B commodities with countries of destination, 1990, annual rpt, 2424–10

Farm income, expenses, receipts by commodity, assets, liabilities, and ratios, 1990 and trends from 1945, annual rpt, 1544–16

Foreign and US tea and herbal production, prices, and trade, FAS annual circular series, 1925–15

Foreign countries agricultural production, prices, and trade, by country, 1980-90 and forecast 1991, annual world area rpt series, 1524–4

Imports of fruits and vegetables under quarantine, by crop, country, and port of entry, FY88 annual rpt, 1524–7

Irrigation projects of Reclamation Bur in western US, crop production and acreage by commodity, State, and project, 1989, annual rpt, 5824–12

Mint oil prices received by farmers and production value, by State, 1988-90, annual rpt, 1621–2

Mint oil production, yield, and farm prices by State, and NYC spot prices, various periods 1988-91, FAS annual circular, 1925–15.2

Nutrient, caloric, and waste composition, detailed data for raw, processed, and prepared foods, 1991 rpt, 1356–3.15

Price indexes (producer), by stage of processing and detailed commodity, monthly rpt, 6762–6

Price indexes (producer), by stage of processing and detailed commodity, monthly 1990, annual rpt, 6764–2

Prices (wholesale) of fruit and vegetables in NYC by State, and shipments and arrivals by mode of transport, by commodity, weekly rpt, 1311–20

Statistical Abstract of US, 1991 annual data compilation, 2324–1.23

Spies

see Espionage

Spinal cord injuries

Cases of injury, related impairments, and activity limitations, by circumstances and victim characteristics, 1985-87, 4147–10.179

Deaths and rates, by detailed cause and demographic characteristics, 1988 and trends from 1900, US Vital Statistics annual rpt, 4144–2

VA mental health care services, staff, research, and training programs, 1991 biennial listing, 8704–2

Veterans health care, patients, visits, costs, and operating beds, by VA and contract facility, and region, quarterly rpt, 8602–4

Spokane, Wash.

Wages by occupation, and benefits for office and plant workers, 1991 survey, periodic labor market rpt, 6785–3.10

see also under By City and By SMSA or MSA in the "Index by Categories"

Sporting goods

Accident deaths and injuries of children by cause, and victimization, rates by race, sex, and age, 1979-88, chartbook, 4108–56

County Business Patterns, 1988: employment, establishments, and payroll, by SIC 2- to 4-digit industry and county, annual State rpt series, 2326–6

County Business Patterns, 1989: employment, establishments, and payroll, by SIC 2- to 4-digit industry and county, annual State rpt series, 2326–8

CPI by component for US city average, and by region, population size, and for 27 metro areas, monthly rpt, 6762–2

DOD prime contract awards, by detailed procurement category, FY87-90, annual rpt, 3544–18

Employment, earnings, and hours, by SIC 1- to 4-digit industry, monthly and annual averages, selected years 1909-90, annual rpt, 6744–4

Exports and imports of US, by country and detailed commodity, monthly rpt, 2422–12

Exports and imports of US, by Harmonized System 6-digit commodity and country, 1990, annual rpt, 2424–13

Exports of US, detailed Schedule B commodities with countries of destination, 1990, annual rpt, 2424–10

Imports of clothing, footwear, luggage, toys, games, and sporting goods from PRC and other countries, 1985-90, article, 9882–2.201

Imports of US given duty-free treatment for value of US material sent abroad, by commodity and country, 1989, annual rpt, 9884–14

Injuries from use of consumer products, by severity, victim age, and detailed product, 1990, annual rpt, 9164–6

Injuries from use of consumer products, related deaths and costs, and recalls by brand, by product type, FY89, annual rpt, 9164–2

Manufacturing annual survey, 1989: finances and operations, by SIC 2- to 4-digit industry, series, 2506–15

Manufacturing census, 1987: finances and operations, by SIC 2- to 4-digit industry, State, and MSA, with trends from 1849, 2497–1

Manufacturing census, 1987: finances and operations, by type of organization and SIC 2- to 4-digit industry, subject rpt, 2497–5

Manufacturing finances and operations, by SIC 2- to 4-digit industry, forecast 1991, annual rpt, 2044–28

Occupational injury and illness rates, by SIC 2- to 4-digit industry, 1988-89, annual rpt, 6844–7

Occupational injury and illness rates, by SIC 2- to 4-digit industry, 1989, annual rpt, 6844–1

Price indexes (producer), by stage of processing and detailed commodity, monthly rpt, 6762–6

Price indexes (producer), by stage of processing and detailed commodity, monthly 1990, annual rpt, 6764–2

Puerto Rico economic censuses, 1987: wholesale and retail trade and service

Sports and athletics

industry finances and operations, by SIC 2- to 4-digit industry and municipio, 2591–1

Retail trade census, 1987: finances and employment, for establishments with and without payroll, by SIC 2- to 4-digit kind of business, State, and MSA, 2401–1

Retail trade sales and inventories, by kind of business, region, and selected State, MSA, and city, monthly rpt, 2413–3

Retail trade sales, inventories, purchases, gross margin, and accounts receivable, by SIC 2- to 4-digit kind of business and form of ownership, 1989, annual rpt, 2413–5

Statistical Abstract of US, 1991 annual data compilation, 2324–1.7

Tax (excise) collections of IRS, by source, quarterly rpt, 8302–1; 8302–2.1

Tax (excise) on hunting and fishing equipment, revenue of Fish and Wildlife Service restoration programs, FY90, annual rpt, 5504–13

Tax (income) returns of sole proprietorships, income statement items, by industry group, 1989, annual article, 8302–2.214

Wholesale trade census, 1987: establishments, sales by customer class, employment, inventories, and expenses, by SIC 2- to 4-digit kind of business, 2407–4

Wholesale trade sales, inventories, purchases, and gross margins, by SIC 2- to 3-digit kind of business, 1990, annual rpt, 2413–13

see also Bicycles

see also Boats and boating

see also Recreational vehicles

Sports and athletics

Accident deaths and injuries of children by cause, and victimization, rates by race, sex, and age, 1979-88, chartbook, 4108–56

Accident deaths and rates, by cause, age, sex, race, and State, 1988, US Vital Statistics annual rpt, 4144–2

Bowling centers occupational injury and illness rates, 1989, annual rpt, 6844–1

Coastal areas recreation facilities of Fed Govt and States, visitor and site characteristics, 1987-90 survey, regional rpt series, 2176–9

County Business Patterns, 1988: employment, establishments, and payroll, by SIC 2- to 4-digit industry and county, annual State rpt series, 2326–6

County Business Patterns, 1989: employment, establishments, and payroll, by SIC 2- to 4-digit industry and county, annual State rpt series, 2326–8

CPI by component for US city average, and by region, population size, and for 27 metro areas, monthly rpt, 6762–2

Drug (steroid) use prevalence and health effects, 1989 conf papers, 4498–67

Educational and employment performance of college athletes compared to other students, for 1972 high school class, as of 1986, 4888–5

Injuries from use of consumer products, by severity, victim age, and detailed product, 1990, annual rpt, 9164–6

Occupational injury and illness rates, by SIC 2- to 4-digit industry, 1988-89, annual rpt, 6844–7

Sports and athletics

Puerto Rico economic censuses, 1987: wholesale and retail trade and service industry finances and operations, by SIC 2- to 4-digit industry and municipio, 2591–1

Puerto Rico economic censuses, 1987: wholesale, retail, and service industries finances and operations, by establishment characteristics and SIC 2- and 3-digit industry, subject rpts, 2591–2

Service industries census, 1987: establishments, receipts by source, payroll, and employment, by SIC 2- to 4-digit kind of business, State, and MSA, 2393–4

Service industries receipts, by SIC 2- to 4-digit kind of business, 1990, annual rpt, 2413–8

Statistical Abstract of US, 1991 annual data compilation, 2324–1.7

Tax (income) returns of sole proprietorships, income statement items, by industry group, 1989, annual article, 8302–2.214

Tennis and golf participation, for northeastern US by facility type and location, 1979-87, conf, 1208–356

see also Baseball

see also Basketball

see also Bicycles

see also Boats and boating

see also Fishing, sport

see also Football

see also Golf

see also Horse racing

see also Physical exercise

see also Sporting goods

see also Swimming

see also Swimming pools

see also Winter sports

Springdale, Ark.

see also under By SMSA or MSA in the "Index by Categories"

Springfield, Ill.

see also under By City and By SMSA or MSA in the "Index by Categories"

Springfield, Mass.

see also under By City and By SMSA or MSA in the "Index by Categories"

Springfield, Mo.

see also under By City and By SMSA or MSA in the "Index by Categories"

Springfield, Ohio

Wages by occupation, and benefits for office and plant workers, 1990 survey, periodic MSA rpt, 6785–3.3

see also under By SMSA or MSA in the "Index by Categories"

Springfield, Oreg.

Wages by occupation, for office and plant workers, 1991 survey, periodic MSA rpt, 6785–3.6

see also under By SMSA or MSA in the "Index by Categories"

SRI International

"Improving the Quality of Training Under JTPA", 6406–10.1

Sri Lanka

Agricultural exports of high-value commodities, indexes and sales by commodity, world area, and country, 1960s-86, 1528–323

Agricultural exports of US, impacts of foreign agricultural and trade policy, with data by commodity and country, 1989, annual rpt, 1924–8

Agricultural trade of US, by detailed commodity and country, 1989, annual rpt, 1524–8

Agricultural trade of US, by detailed commodity and country, 1990, semiannual rpt, 1522–4

AID economic aid to developing countries, obligations and disbursements by country, quarterly rpt, 9912–4

AID loans repayment status and terms by program and country, and status of predecessor agency loans, quarterly rpt, 9912–3

Economic and military aid and loans from US and intl agencies, by program and country, FY46-90, annual rpt, 9914–5

Economic and social conditions of developing countries from 1960s, and Intl Dev Cooperation Agency and AID activities and funding, FY90-92, annual rpt, 9904–4

Economic conditions, income, production, prices, employment, and trade, 1991 periodic country rpt, 2046–4.11

Economic, social, political, and geographic summary data, by country, 1991, annual factbook, 9114–2

Exports and imports of US, by selected country, country group, and commodity group, 1990, annual rpt, 2044–37

Exports and imports of US, by transport mode, country, and SITC 1- to 3-digit commodity, 1990, annual rpt, 2424–12

Exports of US, detailed Schedule B commodities with countries of destination, 1990, annual rpt, 2424–10

Human rights conditions in 170 countries, and US economic and military aid, 1990, annual rpt, 21384–3

Labor conditions, union coverage, and work accidents, 1991 annual country rpt, 6366–4.52

Military aid of US, arms sales, and training programs costs and budget requests, by program, world region, and country, FY90-92, annual rpt, 7144–13

UN voting record and share of votes in agreement with US, by issue, country, and world area, 1990, annual rpt, 7004–18

see also under By Foreign Country in the "Index by Categories"

Sronce, Philip W.

"Outlook for Feed Grains", 1004–16.1

St. Christopher and Nevis

Agricultural trade of US, by detailed commodity and country, 1990, semiannual rpt, 1522–4

Economic, social, political, and geographic summary data, by country, 1991, annual factbook, 9114–2

Exports and imports of US, by transport mode, country, and SITC 1- to 3-digit commodity, 1990, annual rpt, 2424–12

Human rights conditions in 170 countries, and US economic and military aid, 1990, annual rpt, 21384–3

Investment (direct) incentives of Caribbean Basin Initiative, economic impacts, with finances and employment by country, 1984-90, 2048–141

Labor conditions, union coverage, and work accidents, 1991 annual regional rpt, 6366–4.56

Military aid of US, arms sales, and training programs costs and budget requests, by program, world region, and country, FY90-92, annual rpt, 7144–13

UN voting record and share of votes in agreement with US, by issue, country, and world area, 1990, annual rpt, 7004–18

St. Clair, Thomas

"Desk Reference Guide to U.S. Agricultural Trade", 1924–9

St. Cloud, Minn.

see also under By SMSA or MSA in the "Index by Categories"

St. Joseph, Mo.

see also under By SMSA or MSA in the "Index by Categories"

St. Kitts-Nevis

see St. Christopher and Nevis

St. Lawrence River

Traffic on Seaway for ships, cargo, and passengers, and toll revenue, 1990 and trends from 1959, annual rpt, 7744–2

Water levels of Great Lakes and connecting channels, and forecasts, semimonthly rpt, 3752–2

Water supply and quality in streams and lakes, and groundwater levels in wells, by drainage basin, 1988, annual State rpt series, 5666–16

Water supply and quality in streams and lakes, and groundwater levels in wells, by drainage basin, 1989, annual State rpt series, 5666–12

Water supply and quality in streams and lakes, and groundwater levels in wells, by drainage basin, 1990, annual State rpt series, 5666–10

Water supply in northeastern US, precipitation and stream runoff by station, monthly rpt, 2182–3

Water supply in US and southern Canada, streamflow, surface and groundwater conditions, and reservoir levels, by location, monthly rpt, 5662–3

St. Lawrence Seaway Development Corp.

Activities and finances of Corp, 1989, annual rpt, 7744–1

Budget of US, obligations and authority by function, agency, and program, with summaries, analyses, and historical tables, FY92, annual rpt, 104–2

Employment of DOT, by subagency, occupation, and selected personnel characteristics, FY90, annual rpt, 7304–18

Traffic on Seaway for ships, cargo, and passengers, and toll revenue, 1990 and trends from 1959, annual rpt, 7744–2

St. Louis, Mo.

Airline deregulation in 1978, and regional and major carriers agreements, impacts on service to small communities, late 1980s, 7308–199.10

CPI by component for US city average, and by region, population size, and for 15 metro areas, monthly rpt, 6762–1

CPI by component for US city average, and by region, population size, and for 27 metro areas, monthly rpt, 6762–2

Drug abuse indicators for selected metro areas, research results, data collection, and policy issues, 1991 semiannual conf, 4492–5

Drug test results at arrest, by drug type, offense, and sex, for selected urban areas, quarterly rpt, 6062–3

Economic and banking conditions, for Fed Reserve 8th District, quarterly rpt with articles, 9391–16

Index by Subjects and Names

Fruit and vegetable shipments, and arrivals in US and Canada cities, by mode of transport and State and country of origin, 1990, annual rpt, 1311–4.2

Housing and households characteristics, 1987 survey, MSA fact sheet, 2485–11.3

Housing starts and completions authorized by building permits in 40 MSAs, quarterly rpt, 2382–9

Housing vacancy rates for single and multifamily units and mobile homes, by city and ZIP code, 1991, annual MSA rpt, 9304–18.3

Wages by occupation, for office and plant workers, 1991 survey, periodic MSA rpt, 6785–12.3

see also under By City and By SMSA or MSA in the "Index by Categories"

St. Lucia

Agricultural trade of US, by detailed commodity and country, 1990, semiannual rpt, 1522–4

Economic, social, political, and geographic summary data, by country, 1991, annual factbook, 9114–2

Exports and imports of US, by transport mode, country, and SITC 1- to 3-digit commodity, 1990, annual rpt, 2424–12

Human rights conditions in 170 countries, and US economic and military aid, 1990, annual rpt, 21384–3

Investment (direct) incentives of Caribbean Basin Initiative, economic impacts, with finances and employment by country, 1984-90, 2048–141

Labor conditions, union coverage, and work accidents, 1991 annual regional rpt, 6366–4.56

Military aid of US, arms sales, and training programs costs and budget requests, by program, world region, and country, FY90-92, annual rpt, 7144–13

UN voting record and share of votes in agreement with US, by issue, country, and world area, 1990, annual rpt, 7004–18

St. Paul, Minn.

Airline deregulation in 1978, and regional and major carriers agreements, impacts on service to small communities, late 1980s, 7308–199.10

CPI by component for US city average, and by region, population size, and for 27 metro areas, monthly rpt, 6762–2

Drug abuse indicators for selected metro areas, research results, data collection, and policy issues, 1991 semiannual conf, 4492–5

Housing starts and completions authorized by building permits in 40 MSAs, quarterly rpt, 2382–9

Wages by occupation, and benefits for office and plant workers, 1991 survey, periodic MSA rpt, 6785–12.2

see also under By City and By SMSA or MSA in the "Index by Categories"

St. Petersburg, Fla.

Housing starts and completions authorized by building permits in 40 MSAs, quarterly rpt, 2382–9

see also under By City and By SMSA or MSA in the "Index by Categories"

St. Vincent and The Grenadines

Agricultural trade of US, by detailed commodity and country, 1990, semiannual rpt, 1522–4

Economic, social, political, and geographic summary data, by country, 1991, annual factbook, 9114–2

Exports and imports of US, by transport mode, country, and SITC 1- to 3-digit commodity, 1990, annual rpt, 2424–12

Human rights conditions in 170 countries, and US economic and military aid, 1990, annual rpt, 21384–3

Investment (direct) incentives of Caribbean Basin Initiative, economic impacts, with finances and employment by country, 1984-90, 2048–141

Labor conditions, union coverage, and work accidents, 1991 annual regional rpt, 6366–4.56

Military aid of US, arms sales, and training programs costs and budget requests, by program, world region, and country, FY90-92, annual rpt, 7144–13

UN voting record and share of votes in agreement with US, by issue, country, and world area, 1990, annual rpt, 7004–18

Staines, Verdon S.

"Policy Choices for Long-Term Care", 26306–6.156

Stam, Jerome M.

"Farm Financial Stress, Farm Exits, and Public Sector Assistance to the Farm Sector in the 1980's", 1598–272

Stamford, Conn.

see also under By City and By SMSA or MSA in the "Index by Categories"

Standard Consolidated Areas

see Metropolitan Statistical Areas

Standard Industrial Classification

Canada and US industrial classification codes concordance, for SIC 1- to 4-digit levels, 1991 rpt, 2628–31

Market structure delineation using SIC codes, correspondence with price groupings, 1990 working paper, 6886–6.74

Standard Metropolitan Statistical Areas

see Metropolitan Statistical Areas

see under By SMSA or MSA in the "Index by Categories"

see under Urban-Rural and Metro-Nonmetro in the "Index by Categories"

Standard of living

see Cost of living

see Family budgets

see Personal and household income

see Quality of life

Standards

see Industrial standards

see Quality control and testing

see Weights and measures

Standish, Mich.

Wages by occupation, and benefits for office and plant workers, 1991 survey, periodic MSA rpt, 6785–3.8

Stanecki, Karen

"Demographic Impact of an AIDS Epidemic on an African Country: Application of the iwgAIDS Model", 2326–18.57

Stanford Research Institute

see SRI International

Stark, John A.

"Industry Perspective", 1004–16.1

START

see Strategic Arms Reduction Talks

State and local employees

State aid programs

see Aid to Families with Dependent Children

see Medicaid

see Medical assistance

see State funding for economic development

see State funding for education

see State funding for health and hospitals

see State funding for higher education

see State funding for local areas

see State funding for public safety

see State funding for social welfare

see State government spending

see Supplemental Security Income

see Unemployment insurance

see Workers compensation

State and local employees

Census of Govts, 1987: employment, payroll, and average earnings, by function, level of govt, State, county, and population size, 2455–2

Census of Govts, 1987: local govt employment by function, payroll, and average earnings, for individual counties, cities, and school and special districts, 2455–1

Census of Govts, 1987: State and local govt employment, payroll, OASDHI coverage, and employee benefits costs, by level of govt and State, 2455–4

Child Support Enforcement Program finances and operations, by State, FY85-89, annual rpt, 4694–6

Criminal justice spending, employment, and payroll, by level of govt, State, and selected city and county, FY71-88, biennial rpt, 6064–9

Criminal justice spending, employment, and payroll, by level of govt, State, and selected city and county, 1984-86, biennial rpt, 6064–4

DC govt workers compensation under Fed Govt admin, program finances and operations, FY90, annual rpt, 6504–10

Drug control task forces enforcement activities by drug type and State, and organization, staff, and spending, 1988, 6068–244

Employment and payroll, by function and level of govt, 1990, annual rpt series, 2466–1

Employment and payroll, by level of govt and State, 1991 and historical trends, annual rpt, 10044–1

Employment and payroll of State and local govts, monthly rpt, 6742–4

Employment Cost Index and percent change by occupational group, industry div, region, and metro-nonmetro area, quarterly press release, 6782–5

Employment, earnings, and hours, by SIC 1- to 4-digit industry, monthly and annual averages, selected years 1909-90, annual rpt, 6744–4

Employment services local offices operations, State and Federal oversight, staff, and costs, 1983-91, GAO rpt, 26121–430

Employment situation, earnings, hours, and other BLS economic indicators, transcripts of BLS Commissioner's monthly testimony, periodic rpt, 23846–4

Epidemiologists, education, specialties, and State govt employment, for southern US, 1989, article, 4042–3.253

State and local employees

Health Care Financing Review, provider prices, price inputs and indexes, and labor, quarterly journal, 4652–1.1

Jail adult and juvenile population, employment, spending, instn conditions, and inmate programs, by county and facility, 1988, regional rpt series, 6068–144

Job Training Partnership Act State and local staff turnover, qualifications, training, and selected characteristics, 1987-90, 6406–10.2

Juvenile correctional and detention public and private instns, inmates, and expenses, by instn and resident characteristics and State, 1987, biennial rpt, 6064–13

Labor productivity of State and local employees, indexes of output by function, FY64-89, annual rpt, 6824–1.6

Law enforcement spending and employment, by activity and level of govt, data compilation, 1991 annual rpt, 6064–6.1

Libraries (public) finances, staff, and operations, by State and population size, 1989, annual rpt, 4824–6

Massachusetts public works funding, financing sources, and employment, by function and authority, 1980s and projected to 2000, article, 9373–1.207

Massachusetts State govt employment and spending, by program, FY80-91, article, 9373–1.202

Massachusetts State govt spending and employment by program, revenues by source, debt, and public works financing, compared to other States, 1990 compilation of papers, 9373–4.27

Meat and poultry inspection activities and staff of Federal, State, and foreign govts, FY90, annual rpt, 1374–1

Minority group and women employment in State and local govt, by occupation, function, pay level, and State, 1990, annual rpt, 9244–6

Railroad accidents, casualties, and damage, Fed Railroad Admin activities, and safety inspectors by State, 1989, annual rpt, 7604–12

Recreation (outdoor) coastal facilities of Fed Govt and States, visitor and site characteristics, 1987-90 survey, regional rpt series, 2176–9

Science and engineering PhDs employment and other characteristics, by field and State, 1989, biennial rpt, 9627–18

Southwestern US employment by industry div, earnings, and hours, by State, monthly rpt, 6962–2

State and Metro Area Book, 1991 data compilation, 2328–54

State-local relations advisory organizations activities, staff, and funding, 1990, 10048–80

Statistical Abstract of US, 1991 annual data compilation, 2324–1.9

Transit systems finances and operations, by mode of transport, size of fleet, and for 468 systems, 1989, annual rpt, 7884–4

Unemployment insurance coverage of establishments, employment, and wages, by SIC 4-digit industry and State, 1990, annual rpt, 6744–16

see also Civil service pensions

see also Civil service system

see also Fire departments

see also Labor-management relations in government

see also Officials

see also Police

see also State and local employees pay

see also State police

see also Teachers

State and local employees pay

American Samoa employment, earnings, and minimum wage, by establishment and industry, 1989, biennial rpt, 6504–6

Benefit plan coverage of State and local employees, by benefit type, 1987, 6726–1.41

Census of Govts, 1987: employment, payroll, and average earnings, by function, level of govt, State, county, and population size, 2455–2

Census of Govts, 1987: local govt employment by function, payroll, and average earnings, for individual counties, cities, and school and special districts, 2455–1

Census of Govts, 1987: State and local govt employment, payroll, OASDHI coverage, and employee benefits costs, by level of govt and State, 2455–4

Collective bargaining wage and benefit changes and coverage, monthly rpt, 6782–1

Collective bargaining wage and benefit changes and coverage, 1st half 1991, semiannual press release, 6782–6

Criminal justice spending, employment, and payroll, by level of govt, State, and selected city and county, FY71-88, biennial rpt, 6064–9

Criminal justice spending, employment, and payroll, by level of govt, State, and selected city and county, 1984-86, biennial rpt, 6064–4

Earnings by industry div, and personal income per capita and by source, by State, MSA, and county, 1984-89, annual regional rpts, 2704–2

Employment and payroll, by function and level of govt, 1990, annual rpt series, 2466–1

Employment, earnings, and hours, by SIC 1- to 4-digit industry, monthly and annual averages, selected years 1909-90, annual rpt, 6744–4

Finances of govts, by level of govt, State, and for large cities and counties, annual rpt series, 2466–2

Income (household, family, and personal), by source, detailed characteristics, and region, 1988-89, annual Current Population Rpt, 2546–6.68

Income (household, family, and personal), by source, detailed characteristics, and region, 1990, annual Current Population Rpt, 2546–6.70

Jail adult and juvenile population, employment, spending, instn conditions, and inmate programs, by county and facility, 1988, regional rpt series, 6068–144

Job Training Partnership Act State and local staff turnover, qualifications, training, and selected characteristics, 1987-90, 6406–10.2

Law enforcement spending and employment, by activity and level of govt, data compilation, 1991 annual rpt, 6064–6.1

Index by Subjects and Names

Lawyers for indigent defense, pay for public defenders and private practitioners by State, 1989-90, hearing, 21408–123

Libraries (public) finances, staff, and operations, by State and population size, 1989, annual rpt, 4824–6

Massachusetts State govt spending and employment by program, revenues by source, debt, and public works financing, compared to other States, 1990 compilation of papers, 9373–4.27

Minority group and women employment in State and local govt, by occupation, function, pay level, and State, 1990, annual rpt, 9244–6

Natl income and product accounts and components, *Survey of Current Business*, monthly rpt, 2702–1.24

Payroll and employment, by level of govt and State, 1991 and historical trends, annual rpt, 10044–1

Payroll and employment of State and local govts, monthly rpt, 6742–4

Public opinion on taxes, spending, and govt efficiency, by respondent characteristics, 1991 survey, annual rpt, 10044–2

Science and engineering PhDs employment and other characteristics, by field and State, 1989, biennial rpt, 9627–18

State and Metro Area Data Book, 1991 data compilation, 2328–54

Statistical Abstract of US, 1991 annual data compilation, 2324–1.9

Transit systems finances and operations, by mode of transport, size of fleet, and for 468 systems, 1989, annual rpt, 7884–4

Unemployment insurance coverage of establishments, employment, and wages, by SIC 4-digit industry and State, 1990, annual rpt, 6744–16

Workers compensation programs of States, top officials, salaries, and hours, by State, as of 1990, annual rpt, 6504–9

see also Civil service pensions

see also Educational employees pay

State and local taxes

Alaska socioeconomic impacts of OCS oil resources dev, 1980-89 and projected to 2020, 5736–5.11

Amnesty programs of States for delinquent taxpayers, participation, collections, and costs, by tax type and State, 1980s-90, hearing, 21408–125

Chicago metro area local govts fiscal capacity, 1987, article, 10042–1.203

Collections of taxes, by level of govt, type of tax, State, and selected counties, quarterly rpt, 2462–3

Competition among State and local govts in taxes, services, regulation, and dev incentives, 1970-89, 10048–79

Consumer Expenditure Survey, household income by source, and itemized spending, by selected characteristics and region, 1988-89, annual rpt, 6764–5

Cost of living and quality of life indicators for 14 MSAs, 1980s, GAO rpt, 26123–346

Energy producers finances and operations, by energy type for US firms domestic and foreign operations, 1989, annual rpt, 3164–44

Expenditures of State and local govts, measures using indicators of service costs and demand, with comparisons to fiscal capacity and actual outlays, by State, 1986-87, 10048–77

Index by Subjects and Names

Finances of govts, by level of govt, State, and for large cities and counties, annual rpt series, 2466–2

Finances of govts, revenue and spending by level of govt, natl income and product accounts, selected years 1929-92, annual rpt, 204–1.6

Finances of govts, tax systems and revenue, and fiscal structure, by level of govt and State, 1991 and historical trends, annual rpt, 10044–1

Gasoline and other motor fuel tax provisions, auto registration fees, and disposition of receipts, by State, as of Jan 1991, biennial rpt, 7554–37

Hwy receipts by source, and spending by function, by level of govt and State, 1990, annual rpt, 7554–1.3

Income (household) and poverty status under alternative income definitions, by recipient characteristics, 1990, annual Current Population Rpt, 2546–6.69

Income tax deductions and exclusions, Federal tax expenditures by item, FY92-96, annual rpt, 21784–10

Income tax returns of individuals, selected income and tax items by income level, preliminary 1989, annual article, 8302–2.209

Massachusetts State govt spending and employment by program, revenues by source, debt, and public works financing, compared to other States, 1990 compilation of papers, 9373–4.27

Natl income and product accounts and components, *Survey of Current Business*, monthly rpt, 2702–1.24; 2702–1.25

New England States economic indicators, Fed Reserve 1st District, monthly rpt, 9373–2.5

North Central States tax structure and revenue changes, 1980s, article, 9375–1.211

Public opinion on taxes, spending, and govt efficiency, by respondent characteristics, 1991 survey, annual rpt, 10044–2

Rural areas economic and social indicators used to determine Federal aid need, late 1960s-86, 1598–265

State and Metro Area Data Book, 1991 data compilation, 2328–54

Statistical Abstract of US, 1991 annual data compilation, 2324–1.9

Telephone and telegraph firms detailed finances and operations, 1989, annual rpt, 9284–6.2

Transit systems finances and operations, by mode of transport, size of fleet, and for 468 systems, 1989, annual rpt, 7884–4

Unemployment insurance programs of States, finances, operations, tax provisions, and vulnerability to recessions, 1970s-90s, hearing, 21788–201

Western US State and local govt revenues and tax capacity, by source and State, 1988, article, 9381–1.204

see also Excise tax

see also Fuel tax

see also Property tax

see also Revenue sharing

see also Sales tax

see also Severance taxes

State College, Pa.

see also under By SMSA or MSA in the "Index by Categories"

State courts

Expenditures and employment for law enforcement, by activity and level of govt, data compilation, 1991 annual rpt, 6064–6.1

Felony court filings, dispositions, and sentence lengths, by sentence type, and offense and offender characteristics, data compilation, 1991 annual rpt, 6064–6.5

Probation and split sentences by State courts for felony offenses, sentence lengths, case processing time, and felon characteristics, by offense, 1986, 6068–242

US attorneys work hours, by type of court and Federal district, FY90, annual rpt, 6004–2.6

Wiretaps authorized, costs, arrests, trials, and convictions, by offense and jurisdiction, 1990, annual rpt, 18204–7

State Department

see Department of State

State Economic Areas

Cancer death rates of minorities, by body site, age, sex, and substate area, 1950s-80, atlas, 4478–78

State forests

Mgmt of public lands and resources dev, environmental, economic, and social impacts of alternative Forest Service programs, projected to 2040, 1208–24

North Carolina timber acreage, resources, and removals, by species, ownership class, and county, 1989/90, series, 1206–4

Oklahoma timber resources, growth, and removals, by species, forest type, ownership, and county, 1986, regional rpt series, 1206–39

Planting and dev of forests, by State, FY90, annual rpt, 1204–7

Virginia timber resources, growth, and removals, by species, ownership, treatment, and county, 1990-91, series, 1206–6

State funding for economic development

Appalachia local dev projects, and funding by source, by program and State, FY90, annual rpt, 9084–1

Competition among State and local govts in taxes, services, regulation, and dev incentives, 1970-89, 10048–79

Construction put in place, value of new public and private structures, by type, monthly rpt, 2382–4

Finances of govts, by level of govt, State, and for large cities and counties, annual rpt series, 2466–2

Finances of govts, tax systems and revenue, and fiscal structure, by level of govt and State, 1991 and historical trends, annual rpt, 10044–1

Public works capital stock and investment spending economic impacts, with data by type of stock and region, 1950s-88, conf, 9373–3.34

State and Metro Area Data Book, 1991 data compilation, 2328–54

Technology dev programs of govts, info sources and funding, 1990 rpt, 10048–81

State funding for education

Bilingual education programs enrollment, funding, and services, by State, FY85-89, series, 4808–20

State funding for health and hospitals

Digest of Education Statistics, 1991 annual data compilation, 4824–2

Elementary and secondary public school systems enrollment, finances, staff, and high school grads, by State, FY88-89, annual rpt, 4834–6

Elementary and secondary public schools, enrollment, teachers, funding, and other characteristics, by region and State, 1988/89, annual rpt, 4834–20

Enrollment in public elementary and secondary schools, under alternative average daily attendance computation methods, by State, 1985-86, 4838–48

Finances of govts, by level of govt, State, and for large cities and counties, annual rpt series, 2466–2

Finances of govts, tax systems and revenue, and fiscal structure, by level of govt and State, 1991 and historical trends, annual rpt, 10044–1

Financing of public elementary and secondary education systems, issues and indicators of school districts fiscal independence, 1960s-80s, 10048–78

Govt census, 1987: employment, payroll, and average earnings, by function, level of govt, State, county, and population size, 2455–2

Homeless adults educational services, funding, participation, and staff, by State, 1989, annual rpt series, 4804–39

Libraries (public) English as second language programs and services, project descriptions and funding, by State, FY87, annual rpt, 4874–10

Libraries (public) finances, staff, and operations, by State and population size, 1989, annual rpt, 4824–6

Massachusetts State govt spending and employment by program, revenues by source, debt, and public works financing, compared to other States, 1990 compilation of papers, 9373–4.27

Smoking prevention, control, and surveillance activities and funding of States, and tobacco farm receipts, by State, 1989-90, 4206–2.47

Special education programs, enrollment by age, staff, funding, and needs, by type of handicap and State, 1989/90, annual rpt, 4944–4

State and Metro Area Data Book, 1991 data compilation, 2328–54

see also State funding for higher education

State funding for health and hospitals

Diarrhea bacteria *Escherichia coli* testing by State labs, and isolates confirmed, 1988, 4202–7.204

Drug abuse during pregnancy, States reporting policies and status of treatment funding, 1990, article, 4042–3.220

Drug and alcohol abuse treatment and prevention programs of States, funding, facilities, and patient characteristics, FY89, 4488–15

Drug and alcohol abuse treatment facilities, services, use, funding, staff, and client characteristics, 1989, biennial rpt, 4494–10

Drug and alcohol abuse treatment services, funding, staffing, and client load, characteristics, and outcomes, by setting, 1989 conf, 4498–73

State funding for health and hospitals

Employment and payroll, by function, level of govt, and State, 1990, annual rpt, 2466–1.1

Expenditures for health care by businesses, households, and govts, 1965-89, article, 4652–1.230

Expenditures for health care, by service type, payment source, and sector, projected 1990-2000 and trends from 1965, article, 4652–1.251

Expenditures for health care, by service type, payment source, and sector, 1960s-90, annual article, 4652–1.221; 4652–1.252

Finances of govts, by level of govt, State, and for large cities and counties, annual rpt series, 2466–2

Finances of govts, tax systems and revenue, and fiscal structure, by level of govt and State, 1991 and historical trends, annual rpt, 10044–1

Govt census, 1987: employment, payroll, and average earnings, by function, level of govt, State, county, and population size, 2455–2

Health condition and health care resources, use, and spending, 1950s-89, annual data compilation, 4144–11

Hospital operations, and services spending by type and payment source, with background data and foreign comparisons, 1960s-80s and projected to 2000, 26308–98

Insurance (health) for long-term care, affordability and State regulation issues, 1986-90, hearing, 21368–130

Mental health care facilities, finances, caseload, staff, and characteristics of instn and patients, 1988, 4506–4.14

Mental health care facilities, staff, and patient characteristics, *Statistical Notes* series, 4506–3

Mental illness and drug and alcohol abuse direct and indirect costs, by age and sex, 1985, 4048–35

Mentally retarded persons care facilities and residents by selected characteristics, and use of Medicaid services and waiver programs, by State, late 1970s-80s, 4658–49

Occupational deaths data collection and processing by States, Natl Inst for Occupational Safety and Health guidelines, 1990 rpt, 4248–89

Pennsylvania aid to aged for prescription drugs, program enrollment, use, and costs, FY85-87, article, 4652–1.237

R&D facilities for biological and medical sciences, space and equipment adequacy, needs, and funding by source, by instn type, 1990, biennial rpt, 4434–17

State and Metro Area Data Book, 1991 data compilation, 2328–54

Veterans health care, patients, visits, costs, and operating beds, by VA and contract facility, and region, quarterly rpt, 8602–4

see also Medicaid

State funding for higher education

Agricultural research funding and staffing for USDA, State agencies, and other instns, by topic, FY90, annual rpt, 1744–2

Assistance for higher education instns and students, tuition and other costs, impacts on enrollment, and cost containment methods, 1970s-90 and projected to 2001, 4808–25

Finances of govts, by level of govt, State, and for large cities and counties, annual rpt series, 2466–2

Finances of govts, tax systems and revenue, and fiscal structure, by level of govt and State, 1991 and historical trends, annual rpt, 10044–1

Finances of higher education instns, revenue by source and spending by function, by State and instn control, FY80-88, annual rpt, 4844–6

Govt census, 1987: employment, payroll, and average earnings, by function, level of govt, State, county, and population size, 2455–2

Higher education instn tuition relation to other instn financial indicators, by instn control, 1960s-88, 4808–24

Medical and biological R&D facilities, space and equipment adequacy, needs, and funding by source, by instn type, 1990, biennial rpt, 4434–17

R&D equipment of higher education instns, acquisition and service costs, condition, and financing, by field and subfield, 1988-90, triennial survey series, 9627–27

R&D funding by higher education instns and federally funded centers, by field, instn, and State, FY89, annual rpt, 9627–13

Student aid and other sources of support, with student expenses and characteristics, by instn type and control, 1990 triennial study, series, 4846–5

Student aid, costs, and income factors affecting access to undergrad education, 1990 rpt, 26306–6.153

Student aid funding and participation, by Federal program, instn type and control, and State, various periods 1959-89, annual rpt, 4804–28

Student guaranteed loans, defaults, and collections, by type of loan, lender, and guarantee agency, with data by State and top lender, FY90, annual rpt, 4804–38

Vocational education in postsecondary instns, States performance measurement activities and related legislation, 1989/90, 4808–33

State funding for local areas

Alaska subsistence fishing role in local economies, with indicators for Yakutat, 1980s, 1208–350

Appalachia local dev projects, and funding by source, by program and State, FY90, annual rpt, 9084–1

Community Dev Block Grant activities and funding, by program, FY75-90, annual rpt, 5124–8

Finances of govts, by level of govt, State, and for large cities and counties, annual rpt series, 2466–2

Finances of govts, tax systems and revenue, and fiscal structure, by level of govt and State, 1991 and historical trends, annual rpt, 10044–1

Hwy receipts by source, and spending by function, by level of govt and State, 1990, annual rpt, 7554–1.3

Hwy Statistics, summary data by State, 1989-90, annual rpt, 7554–24

Land and Water Conservation Fund grants, State matching funds, and balances, by State, FY90, annual rpt, 5544–18

Index by Subjects and Names

Massachusetts State govt spending and employment by program, revenues by source, debt, and public works financing, compared to other States, 1990 compilation of papers, 9373–4.27

Refugee aid funding of Fed Govt and States, impacts of reductions, with data by selected State and California county, late 1980s, GAO rpt, 26121–402

State and Metro Area Data Book, 1991 data compilation, 2328–54

Statistical Abstract of US, 1991 annual data compilation, 2324–1.9

Transit systems finances and operations, by mode of transport, size of fleet, and for 468 systems, 1989, annual rpt, 7884–4

Wastewater treatment facilities construction loan funds for local govts, Federal and State funding by State, 1990, GAO rpt, 26113–521

State funding for natural resources and conservation

Coal Surface Mining Reclamation and Enforcement Office activities and funding, by State and Indian tribe, FY90, annual rpt, 5644–1

Costs of environmental protection programs to govts and households, by program type and city size, 1960s-88 and projected to 2000, 9188–114

Employment and payroll, by function, level of govt, and State, 1990, annual rpt, 2466–1.1

Endangered animals and plants conservation spending of Federal agencies and States, by species, FY90, annual rpt, 5504–33

Enforcement of environmental legislation by EPA and State govts, activities, FY90, annual rpt, 9184–21

Finances of govts, by level of govt, State, and for large cities and counties, annual rpt series, 2466–2

Fish kills in coastal areas related to pollution and natural causes, by land use, State, and county, 1980s, 2178–32

Fishery mgmt and R&D, Fed Govt grants by project and State, and rpts, 1990, annual listing, 2164–3

Land and Water Conservation Fund grants, State matching funds, and balances, by State, FY90, annual rpt, 5544–18

Radioactive low-level waste disposal activities of States and interstate compacts, with data by disposal facility and reactor, 1989, annual rpt, 3354–14

Uranium tailings at inactive mills, remedial action activities by site, and funding, FY90, annual rpt, 3354–9

Wastewater treatment facilities construction loan funds for local govts, Federal and State funding by State, 1990, GAO rpt, 26113–521

Water pollution areas and sources identification activities of EPA and State, 1991, GAO rpt, 26113–536

State funding for public safety

Criminal justice spending, employment, and payroll, by level of govt, State, and selected city and county, FY71-88, biennial rpt, 6064–9

Criminal justice spending, employment, and payroll, by level of govt, State, and selected city and county, 1984-86, biennial rpt, 6064–4

Index by Subjects and Names

State government

Employment and payroll, by function, level of govt, and State, 1990, annual rpt, 2466–1.1

Finances of govts, by level of govt, State, and for large cities and counties, annual rpt series, 2466–2

Finances of govts, tax systems and revenue, and fiscal structure, by level of govt and State, 1991 and historical trends, annual rpt, 10044–1

Govt census, 1987: employment, payroll, and average earnings, by function, level of govt, State, county, and population size, 2455–2

Juvenile correctional and detention public and private instns, inmates, and expenses, by instn and resident characteristics and State, 1987, biennial rpt, 6064–13

Law enforcement spending and employment, by activity and level of govt, data compilation, 1991 annual rpt, 6064–6.1

Older persons abuse and neglect by circumstances and characteristics of abuser and victim, and States protective services budgets and staff, by location, 1980s, hearing, 21148–62

Pipeline accidents, casualties, safety enforcement activity, and Federal funding, by State, 1989, annual rpt, 7304–5

Prison construction and operating costs, capacity, and inmates, for Federal and State facilities, 1985-89, GAO rpt, 26119–341

State and Metro Area Data Book, 1991 data compilation, 2328–54

see also State police

State funding for social welfare

Adult day care centers revenue by source, and expenses by type, by agency type, FY86, article, 4652–1.234

AFDC Job Opportunities and Basic Skills Training Program Federal and State funding by State, and administrators views, 1989-91, GAO rpt, 26121–435

Beneficiaries families and children, and total and average payments, by public assistance program and State, since 1940, monthly rpt, 4742–1.5

Child abuse and neglect prevention funding by States, and funding sources, FY89, GAO rpt, 26121–423

Child abuse and neglect victims representation in legal proceedings, caseloads, State requirements, and compensation, by State and county, 1989, 4608–28

Child welfare programs funding by source, and foster care cases, problems, and program operations for selected States, 1970s-90, hearings, 21788–202

Child welfare programs funding by source, and foster care program operations and client characteristics, for selected States, 1960s-95, 25368–169

Computer records matching of welfare data, Federal and State agencies compliance with recipient protection provisions before benefits reduction, 1990, GAO rpt, 26121–404

Employment and payroll, by function, level of govt, and State, 1990, annual rpt, 2466–1.1

Energy aid for low income households, State and Federal funding, FY86-89, GAO rpt, 26121–401

Finances of govts, by level of govt, State, and for large cities and counties, annual rpt series, 2466–2

Finances of govts, tax systems and revenue, and fiscal structure, by level of govt and State, 1991 and historical trends, annual rpt, 10044–1

Govt census, 1987: employment, payroll, and average earnings, by function, level of govt, State, county, and population size, 2455–2

Job Training Partnership Act State and local admin, funding, effectiveness, and participants, GAO rpt series, 26106–8

Massachusetts State govt spending and employment by program, revenues by source, debt, and public works financing, compared to other States, 1990 compilation of papers, 9373–4.27

Refugee aid funding of Fed Govt and States, impacts of reductions, with data by selected State and California county, late 1980s, GAO rpt, 26121–402

Refugee resettlement programs and funding, arrivals by country of origin, and indicators of adjustment, by State, FY90, annual rpt, 4694–5

State and local govt competition in taxes, services, regulation, and dev incentives, 1970-89, 10048–79

State and Metro Area Data Book, 1991 data compilation, 2328–54

Timber industry impacts of northern spotted owl conservation in Pacific Northwest, and worker aid programs, 1980s and projected to 2000, hearing, 21728–76

Vocational rehabilitation cases of State agencies by disposition and applicant characteristics, and closures by reason, FY84-88, annual rpt, 4944–6

Vocational rehabilitation cases of State agencies, by disposition and State, FY90 and trends from FY21, annual rpt, 4944–5

Vocational rehabilitation cases rejected by State agencies, by reason, applicant characteristics, and selected State, annual rpt, suspended, 4944–11

Vocational rehabilitation programs of Fed Govt and States, activities and funding, FY90, annual rpt, 4944–1

Vocational rehabilitation programs of States, service provision based on severity of client disability, evaluation, FY88, GAO rpt, 26121–438

see also Aid to Families with Dependent Children

see also Medicaid

see also Supplemental Security Income

see also Unemployment insurance

see also Workers compensation

State funding for transportation

Employment and payroll, by function, level of govt, and State, 1990, annual rpt, 2466–1.1

Expenditures and regulation for surface transportation by Fed Govt and States, FY91 with projections to FY96, 26358–242

Finances of govts, by level of govt, State, and for large cities and counties, annual rpt series, 2466–2

Finances of govts, tax systems and revenue, and fiscal structure, by level of govt and State, 1991 and historical trends, annual rpt, 10044–1

Hwy Statistics, detailed data by State, 1990, annual rpt, 7554–1

Hwy Statistics, summary data by State, 1989-90, annual rpt, 7554–24

Massachusetts State govt spending and employment by program, revenues by source, debt, and public works financing, compared to other States, 1990 compilation of papers, 9373–4.27

Natl transportation system planning, use, condition, accidents, and needs, by mode of transport, 1940s-90 and projected to 2020, 7308–202

State and Metro Area Data Book, 1991 data compilation, 2328–54

Toll facilities, mileage, and operating status, by type of system, as of Jan 1990, biennial listing, 7554–39

Transit systems finances and operations, by mode of transport, size of fleet, and for 468 systems, 1989, annual rpt, 7884–4

Transit systems finances, costs, and needs, by selected system, 1987-89, biennial rpt, 7884–8

Trucking industry deregulation by States, potential economic and market impacts, with background data, mid 1970s-80s, 7308–200

State government

Finances of govts, by level of govt, State, and for large cities and counties, annual rpt series, 2466–2

Finances of govts, tax systems and revenue, and fiscal structure, by level of govt and State, 1991 and historical trends, annual rpt, 10044–1

Finances of State and local govts, revenue by source and outlays by type, 1986-90, annual article, 2702–1.205

Governors of States and territories, terms and salaries, 1991-92, *Congressional Directory*, biennial rpt, 23874–1

Public opinion on taxes, spending, and govt efficiency, by respondent characteristics, 1991 survey, annual rpt, 10044–2

State and Metro Area Data Book, 1991 data compilation, 2328–54

Statistical Abstract of US, 1991 annual data compilation, 2324–1.8; 2324–1.9

see also Census of Governments

see also Federal aid to States

see also Federal-State relations

see also Interstate compacts

see also Interstate relations

see also State and local employees

see also State and local employees pay

see also State and local taxes

see also State courts

see also State forests

see also State funding for economic development

see also State funding for education

see also State funding for health and hospitals

see also State funding for higher education

see also State funding for local areas

see also State funding for natural resources and conservation

see also State funding for public safety

see also State funding for social welfare

see also State funding for transportation

see also State government spending

see also State laws

see also State legislatures

State government

see also State-local relations
see also State parks
see also State police
see also under By State in the "Index by Categories"
see also under names of individual States

State government spending

Finances of govts, by level of govt, State, and for large cities and counties, annual rpt series, 2466–2

Finances of govts, tax systems and revenue, and fiscal structure, by level of govt and State, 1991 and historical trends, annual rpt, 10044–1

Finances of State and local govts, revenue by source and outlays by type, 1986-90, annual article, 2702–1.205

Flow-of-funds accounts, savings, investments, and credit statements, quarterly rpt, 9365–3.3

Hwy taxes provisions, fees, and disposition of receipts, by State, as of Jan 1991, biennial rpt, 7554–37

Massachusetts State govt employment and spending, by program, FY80-91, article, 9373–1.202

Massachusetts State govt spending and employment by program, revenues by source, debt, and public works financing, compared to other States, 1990 compilation of papers, 9373–4.27

New England States govt revenue and spending issues, with data by State, 1970s-80s, article, 9373–25.202

Palau admin, and social, economic, and govtl data, FY90, annual rpt, 7004–6

Pest control integrated mgmt programs for vegetables, acreage, costs, savings, and funding sources and recipients, by State, 1980s, 1568–298

Public opinion on taxes, spending, and govt efficiency, by respondent characteristics, 1991 survey, annual rpt, 10044–2

State and Metro Area Data Book, 1991 data compilation, 2328–54

State-local relations advisory organizations activities, staff, and funding, 1990, 10048–80

see also Aid to Families with Dependent Children
see also Medicaid
see also Medical assistance
see also State funding for economic development
see also State funding for education
see also State funding for health and hospitals
see also State funding for higher education
see also State funding for local areas
see also State funding for natural resources and conservation
see also State funding for public safety
see also State funding for social welfare
see also State funding for transportation
see also Supplemental Security Income
see also Unemployment insurance
see also Workers compensation

State Hospital Data Project

Costs and use of hospitals, data compilation project analyses, series, 4186–6

State laws

Black lung benefits and claims by State, trust fund receipts by source, and disbursements, 1990, annual rpt, 6504–3

Board and care homes regulation and rules enforcement by States, 1988, 4008–112

Capital offenses, execution methods, and minimum age for execution, provisions of States, 1990, annual rpt, 6066–25.42

Capital punishment sentencing provisions of States, 1989, annual rpt, 6064–26.6

Child abuse and neglect victims representation in legal proceedings, caseloads, State requirements, and compensation, by State and county, 1989, 4608–28

Criminal law statutes of States, and public opinion, data compilation, 1991 annual rpt, 6064–6.1; 6064–6.2

Criminal records repository characteristics, holdings, use, and reporting requirements, by State, 1989, 6068–241

Death investigation systems of US and Canada, jurisdictions, medical officers qualifications, types of deaths covered, and related statutes, 1990 listing, 4208–34

Drug abuse during pregnancy, States reporting policies and status of treatment funding, 1990, article, 4042–3.220

Finances of govts, tax systems and revenue, and fiscal structure, by level of govt and State, 1991 and historical trends, annual rpt, 10044–1

Labor laws enacted, by State, 1990, annual article, 6722–1.209

Older persons abuse, State agency reporting and investigation procedures, 1989 survey, article, 4042–3.213

Physicians licensing and disciplinary activities of State medical boards, investigative staff, and licensing fees, by State, 1985-90, 4008–83

Smoking prevention, control, and surveillance activities and funding of States, and tobacco farm receipts, by State, 1989-90, 4206–2.47

Supplemental Security Income and Medicaid eligibility and payment provisions, and beneficiaries living arrangements, by State, 1991, annual rpt, 4704–13

Trucking industry deregulation by States, potential economic and market impacts, with background data, mid 1970s-80s, 7308–200

Unemployment insurance laws of States, changes in coverage, benefits, tax rates, and penalties, by State, 1990, annual article, 6722–1.211

Unemployment insurance laws of States, comparison of provisions, 1991, base edition with semiannual revisions, 6402–2

Unemployment insurance programs of States, benefits, coverage, and tax provisions, as of Jan 1991, semiannual listing, 6402–7

Water (bottled) quality standards of FDA, EPA, and States, with use in 12 States, 1990, GAO rpt, 26113–519

Workers compensation laws of States and Fed Govt, 1991 semiannual rpt, 6502–1

Workers compensation laws of States, changes in coverage, benefits, and premium rates, by State, 1990, annual article, 6722–1.210

Workers compensation programs of States, admin, coverage, benefits, finances, processing, and staff, 1987-90, annual rpt, 6504–9

see also Alcoholic beverages control laws
see also Financial institutions regulation
see also Traffic laws and courts

State legislatures

Census of Population and Housing, 1990: voting age and total population by race, and housing units, by block, redistricting counts required under PL 94-171, State CD-ROM series, 2551–6

Census of Population and Housing, 1990: voting age and total population by race, and housing units, by county and city, redistricting counts required under PL 94-171, State summary rpt series, 2551–5

State and Metro Area Data Book, 1991 data compilation, 2328–54

Statistical Abstract of US, 1991 annual data compilation, 2324–1.8

State-local relations

Advisory organizations for State-local relations, activities, staff, and funding, 1990, 10048–80

Competition among State and local govts in taxes, services, regulation, and dev incentives, 1970-89, 10048–79

see also State funding for local areas

State parks

Alaska land area by ownership, and availability for mineral exploration and dev, 1984-86, 5608–152

Coastal areas recreation facilities of Fed Govt and States, visitor and site characteristics, 1987-90 survey, regional rpt series, 2176–9

Northeastern US recreation areas use, mgmt, and tourism dev issues, 1990 conf, 1208–356

State and Metro Area Data Book, 1991 data compilation, 2328–54

Statistical Abstract of US, 1991 annual data compilation, 2324–1.7

Visits and fees for State parks and recreation areas, FY88-90, annual rpt, 5544–14

see also State forests

State police

Assaults and deaths of law enforcement officers, by circumstances, agency, victim and offender characteristics, and location, 1990, annual rpt, 6224–3

Carpool and bus high occupancy vehicle lanes use, design, and enforcement, for US and Canada, 1989, 7888–80

Carpool high occupancy vehicle lanes use, design, enforcement, and drivers views, for California, 1988-89, 7308–203

Employment and payroll, by level of govt, State, and selected city and county, 1984-86, biennial rpt, 6064–4

Employment and spending for law enforcement, by activity and level of govt, data compilation, 1991 annual rpt, 6064–6.1

Employment of State and local law enforcement personnel and officers, by sex, population size, census div, and jurisdiction, as of Oct 1990, annual rpt, 6224–2.3

Employment, payroll, and spending for criminal justice, by level of govt, State, and selected city and county, FY71-88, annual rpt, 6064–9

Govt census, 1987: employment, payroll, and average earnings, by function, level of govt, State, county, and population size, 2455–2

Index by Subjects and Names

State prisons
see Correctional institutions
see Prisoners

State taxation
see State and local taxes

States
see terms beginning with State
see under By State in the "Index by Categories"
see under names of individual States

States' rights
see Federal-State relations

Statistical programs and activities
Agricultural data collection, Economic Research Service activities, funding, and staff, by branch, planned FY91, annual rpt, 1504–6
BLS major economic indicators, methodology, and time series revisions, transcripts of BLS Commissioner's monthly testimony, periodic rpt, 23846–4
Cancer Natl Inst epidemiology and biometry activities, FY90, annual rpt, 4474–29
Census Bur activities, rpts, and user services, monthly rpt, 2302–3
Census Bur data collection and publication operations, US Code Title 13 text, 1991 rpt, 21628–94
Census Bur rpts and data files, coverage and availability, 1991 annual listing, 2304–2
Census Bur rpts and data files, coverage, availability, and use, series, 2326–7
Computer systems purchase and use, and data recording, processing, and transfer, Fed Govt standards, series, 2216–2
CPI components relative importance, by selected MSA, region, population size, and for US city average, 1990, annual rpt, 6884–1
Crime and criminal justice data collection activities of Bur of Justice Statistics and States, annual rpt, discontinued, 6064–21
Crime and criminal justice data collection programs and rpts, 1989, annual listing, 6064–25
Crime and criminal justice research results, series, 6066–26
Crime, criminal justice admin and enforcement, and public opinion, data compilation, 1991 annual rpt, 6064–6
Data collection, methodology, and related issues, 1991 annual conf, 2624–2
Developing countries family planning and population activities of AID, grants by project and recipient, and contraceptive shipments, by country, FY90, annual rpt series, 9914–13
DOE data collection forms and related rpts, 1990, annual listing, 3164–86
Drug abuse indicators for selected metro areas, research results, data collection, and policy issues, 1991 semiannual conf, 4492–5
Drug abuse psychotherapy and counseling outcomes, research results and methodology, 1990 conf, 4498–71
Education data collection activities and programs of NCES, 1991, annual listing, 4824–7
Education data collection and reporting improvement, and performance indicators dev, recommendations, 1991 rpt, 4828–40
Education data collection and reporting improvement for Federal and State agencies, recommendations, 1991 rpt, 4828–39

Education data, estimates from Fast Response Survey System, series, 4826–1
Educational enrollment in public elementary and secondary schools, under alternative average daily attendance computation methods, by State, 1985-86, 4838–48
EIA data collection and analysis activities, 1987-90, annual narrative rpt, 26104–14
Employment Cost Index methodology, occupational definitions, and coverage, quarterly press release, 6782–5
Energy Info Admin activities, 1990, annual rpt, 3164–29
Energy Info Admin and alternative estimates of energy supply, demand, prices, and trade, with methodology, series, 3166–12
Export and import statistics, Census Bur publications and data files, 1991 guide, 2428–11
Exports and imports data series methodology, use, and sources, 1991 article, 9389–1.206
Farm income data sources and adjustment factors of USDA, with income by source, 1983-89, article, 1541–1.202
Fed Govt financial and nonfinancial domestic aid, 1991 base edition with supplements, annual listing, 104–5
Fed Govt policies relating to statistical programs technical operation, methodology, and use of data, working paper series, 106–4
Fed Govt statistical programs, funding by agency, FY90-92, annual rpt, 104–10
Fed Govt statistical programs, index of spending for 4 agencies, 1976-88, hearing, 23848–218
Fed Reserve System statistical series additions and revisions, monthly rpt with articles, 9362–1
Fishery mgmt and R&D, Fed Govt grants by project and State, and rpts, 1990, annual listing, 2164–3
Geological Survey Water Resources Div history, series, 5668–118
Global climate change trends and contributing gases levels, Federal and intl data collection activities, mgmt, and inventory, 1990 rpt, 3028–4
Govt admin and tax records use in data collection, methodological and disclosure issues, 1988-89 annual conf papers, 8304–17
Health care (primary) research, methodology and findings, 1991 annual conf, 4184–4
Health Care Financing Admin research activities and grants, by program, FY90, annual listing, 4654–10
HHS financial aid, by program, recipient, State, and city, FY90, annual regional listings, 4004–3
HHS research and evaluation programs, 1970-90, annual listing, 4004–30
Intl transactions accounts statistical discrepancy assessment, with data for services component, and alternative regression results, 1970s-90, technical paper, 9366–7.258
Labor force data of BLS, major statistical and analytical programs and rpts, as of Feb 1991, listing, 6728–35
Minerals Yearbook, 1988, data collection and availability, annual rpt, 5604–48

Natl Hwy Traffic Safety Admin activities and grants, and fatal traffic accident data, 1989, annual rpt, 7764–1
Occupational deaths data collection and processing by States, Natl Inst for Occupational Safety and Health guidelines, 1990 rpt, 4248–89
Occupational deaths data collection from multiple sources, BLS pilot study results for 2 States, 1990, article, 6722–1.249
Occupational injury death data collection methods of BLS and Texas, with Texas data by accident type and industry div, 1986, article, 6722–1.205
Older persons health condition and care research, data availability and collection methodology, for US and selected countries, 1988 conf, 4147–5.6
Population and reproduction research, Fed Govt funding by project, FY89, annual listing, 4474–9
Vital and Health Statistics series and other NCHS rpts, 1990, annual listing, 4124–1
Vital and Health Statistics series: methodology, survey design, and data evaluation, 4147–2
Vital and Health Statistics series: program and data collection procedures, 4147–1
Vital statistics reporting, natl standards revisions for birth, death, marriage, and divorce certificates, and for fetal death and abortion rpts, 1989, 4147–4.27
Women-owned businesses and sales, by industry div and ownership type, and data needs and availability, 1987, 9768–22
see also Business outlook and attitude surveys
see also Classifications
see also Computer data file guides
see also Consumer surveys
see also Economic and econometric models
see also Mathematic models and modeling
see also Methodology
see also Opinion and attitude surveys
see also Seasonal adjustment factors
see also Statisticians
see also under names of individual surveys (listed under Surveys)

Statisticians
Employment and other characteristics of science and engineering PhDs, by field and State, 1989, biennial rpt, 9627–18
Natl Agricultural Statistics Service minority group staff, promotion, and discrimination complaints, 1988-90, GAO rpt, 26119–326

Steblez, Walter G.
"Mineral Industries of the USSR, 1989", 5604–39

Steel industry
see Iron and steel industry

Steele, Christine E.
"Dec. 31, 1990, Federal Civilian Employment by State, Metropolitan Area, Overseas, Citizenship, Major Agency, Pay System Category, and Work Schedule", 9842–1.203
"Profile of the 'Typical' Federal Civilian Employee, Sept. 30, 1990", 9842–1.201

Steenland, Kyle
"Lung Cancer Incidence Among Patients with Beryllium Disease: A Cohort Mortality Study", 4472–1.224

Stehn, Robert A.

Stehn, Robert A.
"Response of Brant and Other Geese to Aircraft Disturbances at Izembek Lagoon, Alaska", 5738–23

Steindel, Charles
"Decline in U.S. Saving and Its Implications for Economic Growth", 9385–1.201
"Recent Trends in Capital Formation", 9385–8.92

Steinkampf, William C.
"Water-Quality Characteristics of the Columbia Plateau Regional Aquifer System in Parts of Washington, Oregon, and Idaho", 5666–28.11

Steinmeier, Thomas L.
"Pension Portability and Labor Mobility: Evidence from the Survey of Income and Program Participation", 2626–10.123

Stekler, Lois E.
"Adequacy of U.S. Direct Investment Data", 9366–7.255
"Statistical Discrepancy in the U.S. International Transactions Accounts: Sources and Suggested Remedies", 9366–7.258
"U.S. International Transactions in 1990", 9362–1.202

Stephan, James J.
"Jail Inmates, 1990", 6066–25.38

Sterilization
see Sexual sterilization

Sterling Heights, Mich.
see also under By City in the "Index by Categories"

Steroids
see Hormones

Steubenville, Ohio
see also under By SMSA or MSA in the "Index by Categories"

Stevedores
see Longshoremen

Stevens, E. J.
"Is There Any Rationale for Reserve Requirements?", 9377–1.207

Stevens, Guy V.
"Adequacy of U.S. Direct Investment Data", 9366–7.255

Stimulants
see Drug abuse and treatment
see Drugs

Stinson, Frederick S.
"Alcohol Consumption in a 1986 Sample of Deaths", 4482–1.201

Stobbe, Terrence J.
"Back Injuries in Underground Coal Mining", 5608–166

Stock exchanges
County Business Patterns, 1988: employment, establishments, and payroll, by SIC 2- to 4-digit industry and county, annual State rpt series, 2326–6
County Business Patterns, 1989: employment, establishments, and payroll, by SIC 2- to 4-digit industry and county, annual State rpt series, 2326–8
Employment, earnings, and hours, by SIC 1- to 4-digit industry, monthly and annual averages, selected years 1909-90, annual rpt, 6744–4
Futures trading oversight of CFTC and individual exchanges, foreign activity, and customer views, late 1980s, hearing, 25168–77
Intl securities markets computer use and risk mgmt methods, 1991 GAO rpt, 26125–44

Regulation of securities industry, self-regulatory organizations oversight by SEC, violations, and complaints, FY86-89, GAO rpt, 26119–336
Statistical Abstract of US, 1991 annual data compilation, 2324–1.16
Tax (income) returns of corporations, income and tax items by asset size and detailed industry, 1988, annual rpt, 8304–21
Trading activity and system automation, with data by country, stock exchange, security type, and individual contract, 1980s-90, article, 9371–1.209
Trading volume, securities listed by type, and finances, by exchange, selected years 1938-89, annual rpt, 9734–2.1; 9734–2.2
see also American Stock Exchange
see also New York Stock Exchange
see also Securities

Stock, James H.
"Simple Estimator of Cointegrating Vectors in Higher Order Integrated Systems", 9375–13.54

Stock market
see American Stock Exchange
see New York Stock Exchange
see Securities
see Stock exchanges
see Stockbrokers

Stockbauer, Joseph W.
"Changes in Characteristics of Women Who Smoke During Pregnancy: Missouri, 1978-88", 4042–3.203

Stockbrokers
Bank holding company subsidiaries dealing in bank-ineligible securities, subsidiary and parent firm finances, 1989-91, GAO rpt, 26119–280
County Business Patterns, 1988: employment, establishments, and payroll, by SIC 2- to 4-digit industry and county, annual State rpt series, 2326–6
County Business Patterns, 1989: employment, establishments, and payroll, by SIC 2- to 4-digit industry and county, annual State rpt series, 2326–8
Credit (securities) issues of stockbrokers and other nonbank lenders, and brokers balance sheet, as of June 1990, annual rpt, 9365–5.1
Employment, earnings, and hours, by SIC 1- to 4-digit industry, monthly and annual averages, selected years 1909-90, annual rpt, 6744–4
Finances of financial instns by type and selected instn, and deposit insurance reform issues, 1970s-90, GAO rpt, 26119–320
Finances of stockbrokers, 1985-89, annual rpt, 9734–2.1
Flow-of-funds accounts, savings, investments, and credit statements, quarterly rpt, 9365–3.3
Futures trading oversight of CFTC and individual exchanges, foreign activity, and customer views, late 1980s, hearing, 25168–77
Intl banking and securities instns assets by selected firm, and financial performance indicators by selected country, late 1980s-90, article, 9385–1.206
Intl banking competition and deposit insurance reform issues, with background data, 1990 hearings, 25248–122

Index by Subjects and Names

Mail volume to and from households, use, and views, by class, source, content, and household characteristics, 1987-88, annual rpt, 9864–10
Occupational injury and illness rates, by SIC 2- to 4-digit industry, 1988-89, annual rpt, 6844–7
Occupational injury and illness rates, by SIC 2- to 4-digit industry, 1989, annual rpt, 6844–1
Regulation of securities industry, self-regulatory organizations oversight by SEC, violations, and complaints, FY86-89, GAO rpt, 26119–336
Securities purchases, sales, and holdings, by issuer and type and ownership of security, monthly listing, 9732–2
Tax (income) returns of corporations, income and tax items by asset size and detailed industry, 1987, annual rpt, 8304–4
Tax (income) returns of corporations, income and tax items by asset size and detailed industry, 1988, annual rpt, 8304–21
Tax (income) returns of corporations with foreign tax credit, income and tax items by industry group, 1986, biennial article, 8302–2.203
Tax (income) returns of partnerships, income statement and balance sheet items, by industry group, 1989, annual article, 8302–2.216; 8304–18
Tax (income) returns of sole proprietorships, income statement items, by industry group, 1989, annual article, 8302–2.214
Tax (income) withholding and related documents filed, by type and IRS service center, 1990 and projected 1991-98, annual rpt, 8304–22

Stockman, Alan C.
"Tastes and Technology in a Two-Country Model of the Business Cycle: Explaining International Co-Movements", 9377–9.113

Stockpiling
GSA activities and finances, FY90, annual rpt, 9454–1
Materials (advanced structural) devs, use, and R&D funding, for ceramics, metal alloys, polymers, and composites, 1960s-80s and projected to 2000, 5608–162
Mineral Industry Surveys, commodity reviews of production, trade, stocks, and use, monthly rpt series, 5612–1
Mineral Industry Surveys, commodity reviews of production, trade, use, and industry operations, advance annual rpt series, 5614–5
Minerals production, prices, trade, use, employment, tariffs, and stockpiles, by mineral, with foreign comparisons, 1986-90, annual rpt, 5604–18
Strategic material stockpile inventories and needs, by commodity, as of Jan 1991, annual rpt, 3544–37
Strategic material stockpile inventories, costs, and goals, by commodity, semiannual rpt, discontinued, 3902–3
Strategic material stockpiling by Fed Govt, activity, and inventory by commodity, as of Mar 1991, semiannual rpt, 3542–22
Strategic material stockpiling by Fed Govt, activity, and inventory by commodity, semiannual rpt, discontinued, 3902–2

Index by Subjects and Names

see also Naval Petroleum Reserves
see also Strategic Petroleum Reserve

Stocks

see Agricultural stocks
see Business inventories
see Coal stocks
see Energy stocks and inventories
see Options trading
see Petroleum stocks
see Securities
see Stock exchanges
see Stockbrokers
see Stockpiling

Stockton, Calif.

Wages by occupation, for office and plant workers, 1991 survey, periodic MSA rpt, 6785–3.6

see also under By City and By SMSA or MSA in the "Index by Categories"

Stone, Michael P.

"Maintaining a Trained and Ready Total Force for the 1990s and Beyond. A Statement on the Posture of the U.S. Army, FY92-93", 3704–13

Stone products and quarries

Alaska minerals resources and production, by mineral and site, for Juneau region, 1987-88, 5608–169

Business statistics, detailed data for major industries and economic indicators, *Survey of Current Business*, monthly rpt, 2702–1.21

Capital expenditures for plant and equipment, by major industry group, quarterly rpt, 2502–2

Collective bargaining agreements expiring during year, and workers covered, by firm, union, industry group, and State, 1991, annual rpt, 6784–9

County Business Patterns, 1988: employment, establishments, and payroll, by SIC 2- to 4-digit industry and county, annual State rpt series, 2326–6

County Business Patterns, 1989: employment, establishments, and payroll, by SIC 2- to 4-digit industry and county, annual State rpt series, 2326–8

Employment, earnings, and hours, by SIC 1- to 4-digit industry, monthly and annual averages, selected years 1909-90, annual rpt, 6744–4

Employment in manufacturing, by detailed occupation and SIC 2-digit industry, 1989 survey, triennial rpt, 6748–52

Employment, unemployment, and labor force characteristics, by region and census div, 1990, annual rpt, 6744–7.1

Energy use and prices for manufacturing industries, 1988 survey, series, 3166–13

Enterprise Statistics, 1987: auxiliaries of multi-establishment firms, finances and operations by function, industry, and State, 2329–6

Enterprise Statistics, 1987: finances and operations for companies, by size, level of diversification, form of organization, and industry group, 2329–8

Exports and imports between US and outlying areas, by detailed commodity and mode of transport, 1990, annual rpt, 2424–11

Exports and imports of building materials, by commodity and country, 1989-90, article, 2042–1.204

Stone products and quarries

Exports and imports of US, by country and detailed commodity, monthly rpt, 2422–12

Exports and imports of US, by Harmonized System 6-digit commodity and country, 1990, annual rpt, 2424–13

Exports and imports of US, by transport mode, country, and SITC 1- to 3-digit commodity, 1990, annual rpt, 2424–12

Exports and imports of US shipped through Canada, by detailed commodity, customs district, and country, 1989, annual rpt, 7704–11

Exports of US, detailed commodities by country, monthly CD-ROM, 2422–13

Exports of US, detailed Schedule B commodities with countries of destination, 1990, annual rpt, 2424–10

Hwy construction material use by type, and spending, by State, various periods 1944-90, annual rpt, 7554–29

Imports, exports, and employment impacts, by SIC 2- to 4-digit industry and commodity, quarterly rpt, 2322–2

Imports of US, detailed commodities by country, monthly CD-ROM, 2422–14

Indian (Cherokee) Agency activities in North Carolina, FY91, annual rpt, 5704–4

Input-output structure of US economy, detailed interindustry transactions for 84 industries, and components of final demand, 1986, annual article, 2702–1.206

Input-output structure of US economy, detailed interindustry transactions for 85 industries, 1982 benchmark data, 2702–1.213

Labor productivity, indexes of output, hours, and employment by SIC 2- to 4-digit industry, 1967-89, annual rpt, 6824–1.2

Manufacturing annual survey, 1989: finances and operations, by SIC 2- to 4-digit industry, series, 2506–15

Manufacturing census, 1987: finances and operations, by SIC 2- to 4-digit industry, State, and MSA, with trends from 1849, 2497–1

Manufacturing census, 1987: finances and operations, by type of organization and SIC 2- to 4-digit industry, subject rpt, 2497–5

Manufacturing industries operations and performance, analytical rpt series, 2506–16

Manufacturing production, shipments, inventories, orders, and pollution control costs, periodic Current Industrial Rpt series, 2506–3

Mexico imports from US, by industry and State, 1987-90, 2048–154

Mineral industries census, 1987: energy use and costs, by fuel type, SIC 2- to 4-digit industry, and State, subject rpt, 2517–2

Mineral industries census, 1987: finances and operations, by establishment characteristics, SIC 2- to 4-digit industry, and State, subject rpt, 2517–1

Mineral industries census, 1987: finances and operations, by SIC 2- to 4-digit industry, State, and county, census div rpt series, 2515–1

Mineral Industry Surveys, commodity review of production, trade, stocks, and use, quarterly rpt, 5612–2.20

Mineral Industry Surveys, commodity reviews of production, trade, use, and industry operations, advance annual rpt series, 5614–5

Mineral Industry Surveys, State reviews of production, 1990, preliminary annual rpt, 5614–6

Minerals Yearbook, 1988, Vol 3: foreign country reviews of production, trade, and policy, by commodity, annual rpt series, 5604–17

Minerals Yearbook, 1989, Vol 1: commodity review of production, reserves, supply, use, and trade, annual rpt, 5604–15.1; 5604–15.61

Minerals Yearbook, 1989, Vol 2: State reviews of production and sales by commodity, and business activity, annual rpt series, 5604–16

Minerals Yearbook, 1989, Vol 2: State reviews of production, sales, and firms, by commodity, and business activity, annual rpt, 5604–34

Multinatl US firms and foreign affiliates finances and operations, by industry and world area of parent firm, 1989 benchmark survey, preliminary annual rpt, 2704–5

Occupational injuries and incidence, employment, and hours in stone mines and related operations, 1989, annual rpt, 6664–5

Occupational injuries by circumstances, employment, and hours, for mining industries by type of operation and State, quarterly rpt, 6662–1

Occupational injury and illness rates, by SIC 2- to 4-digit industry, 1988-89, annual rpt, 6844–7

Occupational injury and illness rates, by SIC 2- to 4-digit industry, 1989, annual rpt, 6844–1

Pollution abatement capital and operating costs, by SIC 2-digit industry, 1989, advance annual Current Industrial Rpt, 2506–3.6

Price indexes (producer) and sales of building materials, by type, bimonthly rpt, 2042–1.5; 2042–1.6

Price indexes (producer), by stage of processing and detailed commodity, monthly rpt, 6762–6

Price indexes (producer), by stage of processing and detailed commodity, monthly 1990, annual rpt, 6764–2

Production, prices, trade, use, employment, tariffs, and stockpiles, by mineral, with foreign comparisons, 1986-90, annual rpt, 5604–18

Production, reserves, and use of industrial minerals, and characteristics of individual deposits, State rpt series, 5606–10

Statistical Abstract of US, 1991 annual data compilation, 2324–1.25

Taiwan imports of building materials, and share from US, by commodity, 1989-90, article, 2042–1.205

Tariff Schedule of US, classifications and rates of duty by detailed imported commodity, 1992 base edition, 9886–13

Tax (income) returns of corporations, income and tax items by asset size and detailed industry, 1987, annual rpt, 8304–4

Stone products and quarries

Tax (income) returns of corporations, income and tax items by asset size and detailed industry, 1988, annual rpt, 8304–21

Tax (income) returns of corporations with foreign tax credit, income and tax items by industry group, 1986, biennial article, 8302–2.203

Tax (income) returns of sole proprietorships, income statement items, by industry group, 1989, annual article, 8302–2.214

see also Abrasive materials

see also Cement and concrete

see also Oil shale

see also Phosphate

see also Potash

see also Sand and gravel

see also under By Commodity in the "Index by Categories"

see also under By Industry in the "Index by Categories"

Storage

see Agricultural stocks

see Cold storage and refrigeration

see Grain storage and facilities

see Packaging and containers

see Stockpiling

see Warehouses

Storms

- Aircraft (general aviation) accidents, by circumstances, characteristics of persons and aircraft involved, and type of flying, 1988, annual rpt, 9614–3
- Deaths and rates, by detailed cause and demographic characteristics, 1988 and trends from 1900, US Vital Statistics annual rpt, 4144–2
- Farm water supply, crop moisture, and drought indexes, weekly rpt, seasonal data, 2182–7
- Farmland damaged by natural disaster, Emergency Conservation Program aid and participation by State, FY90, annual rpt, 1804–22
- Fish kills in coastal areas related to pollution and natural causes, by land use, State, and county, 1980s, 2178–32
- Forecasts of severe storms, Natl Weather Service forecast accuracy and storm characteristics, series, 2186–6
- Foreign countries disasters, casualties, damage, and aid by US and others, FY90 and trends from FY64, annual rpt, 9914–12
- Hurricane Hugo relief funding and response by FEMA, 1989-90, GAO rpt, 26113–511
- Hurricanes and tropical storms frequency, intensity, deaths, and damage, by State and selected city, 1886-1989, 2188–15
- Hurricanes and tropical storms in Pacific and Indian Oceans, paths and surveillance, 1990, annual rpt, 3804–8
- Incidents and mgmt of disasters and natl security threats, with data by major event and State, 1991 annual rpt, 9434–6
- Lightning and other causes of fires on Forest Service land, by forest and State, 1989, annual rpt, 1204–6
- *Mariners Weather Log*, quarterly journal, 2152–8
- Precipitation and temperature for US and foreign locations, major events and anomalies, weekly rpt, 2182–6

Research activities of Natl Severe Storms Lab, and bibl, FY90, annual rpt, 2144–20

Statistical Abstract of US, 1991 annual data compilation, 2324–1.6

Water supply, hydrologic events, and end use, by State, 1988-89, annual rpt, 5664–12

Weather phenomena and storm characteristics, casualties, and property damage, by State, monthly listing, 2152–3

Weather trends and deviations, by world region, 1880s-1990, annual chartbook, 2184–9

see also Floods

Stotsky, Janet G.

"Effect of Rent Control on Housing Quality Change: A Longitudinal Analysis", 9387–8.246

Strahan, Genevieve

"Mental Illness in Nursing Homes: U.S., 1985. Vital and Health Statistics Series 13", 4147–13.106

Strategic Arms Reduction Talks

Nuclear weapons systems of US and USSR, costs, and military forces survival after attack, projected under alternative arms control proposals, FY92-2006, 26306–6.161

Strategic Defense Initiative

Nuclear weapons systems of US and USSR, costs, and military forces survival after attack, projected under alternative arms control proposals, FY92-2006, 26306–6.161

Strategic materials

- Mineral Industry Surveys, commodity reviews of production, trade, stocks, and use, monthly rpt series, 5612–1
- Mineral Industry Surveys, commodity reviews of production, trade, use, and industry operations, advance annual rpt series, 5614–5
- Minerals (strategic) supply and characteristics of individual deposits, by country, commodity rpt series, 5666–21
- Nuclear material inventory discrepancies at DOE and contractor facilities, 1989/90, annual rpt, 3344–2
- Prices of sensitive materials, and indexes, *Survey of Current Business*, cyclical indicators, monthly rpt, 2702–1.1
- *Statistical Abstract of US*, 1991 annual data compilation, 2324–1.25
- *see also* Naval Petroleum Reserves
- *see also* Stockpiling
- *see also* Strategic Petroleum Reserve
- *see also* Uranium

Strategic Petroleum Reserve

Capacity, inventory, fill rate, and finances of SPR, quarterly rpt, 3002–13

Crude oil imports, domestic deliveries, and stocks, 1977-90, annual rpt, 3164–74.2

Energy supply, demand, and prices, forecasts by resource type, quarterly rpt, 3162–34

Military Sealift Command shipping operations, finances, and personnel, FY90, annual rpt, 3804–14

Oil imports and withdrawals from stocks, monthly rpt, 3162–24.3

Statistical Abstract of US, 1991 annual data compilation, 2324–1.19

Supply and demand of oil and refined products, refinery capacity and use, and prices, weekly rpt, 3162–32

Index by Subjects and Names

Supply, demand, and movement of crude oil, gas liquids, and refined products, by PAD district and State, 1990, annual rpt, 3164–2

Supply, demand, and prices, by fuel type and end-use sector, alternative projections 1989-2010, annual rpt, 3164–75

Stratosphere

- Global warming contributing air pollutants, US and foreign emissions and control measures, 1980s and projected to 2020, 26358–233
- Ozone and pollutant levels in stratosphere, 1990 rpt, 9188–113
- Ozone depletion in stratosphere, USDA competitive research grants by recipient, FY90, annual rpt, 1764–1
- Ozone in stratosphere, levels, depletion rates and climate impacts, and properties of chlorofluorocarbons and substitutes, 1990 rpt, 9508–37
- Pollutants contributing to climate change, atmospheric concentrations by monitoring site, 1989, annual rpt, 2144–28

Strauss, William A.

"Cyclicality of Cash Flow and Investment in U.S. Manufacturing", 9375–1.202

Straw, J. Ashley

"American Woodcock Harvest and Breeding Population Status, 1991", 5504–11

Strawberries

see Fruit and fruit products

Streams

see Rivers and waterways

Streetcars

see Urban transportation

Streets

see Highways, streets, and roads

Stress

see Mental health and illness

Strickland, Roger

"Sources of Revisions to the USDA Income Accounts", 1541–1.202

"1990 State-level Income and Balance Sheet Estimates", 1541–1.212

Strikes and lockouts

see Work stoppages

Stringer, William J.

"Remote Sensing Data Acquisition, Analysis, and Archival", 2176–1.38

Stringfield, Whitney J.

"Water Use in South Carolina, 1985", 5666–24.9

Stroke

see Cerebrovascular diseases

Strontium

see Radioactive materials

Stuart, Bruce

"Patterns of Outpatient Prescription Drug Use Among Pennsylvania Elderly", 4652–1.237

Stuart, Mary

"Ambulatory Practice Variation in Maryland: Implications for Medicaid Cost Management", 4652–1.211

Stuart, Michael J.

"Fruit and Vegetable Industry Perspective", 1004–16.1

Student aid

Alcohol, Drug Abuse and Mental Health Admin research grants and awards, by recipient, FY90, annual listing, 4044–13

Allergy and Infectious Diseases Natl Inst activities, grants by recipient and location, and disease cases, FY83-90, annual rpt, 4474–30

Index by Subjects and Names

Arts Natl Endowment activities and grants, FY90, annual rpt, 9564–3

Assistance (financial and nonfinancial) of Fed Govt, 1991 base edition with supplements, annual listing, 104–5

Assistance and other sources of support, with student expenses and characteristics, by instn type and control, 1990 triennial study, series, 4846–5

Assistance of Fed Govt, by type, program, agency, and State, FY90, annual rpt, 2464–2

Benefits overpayment recovery and judgment enforcement cases filed in Federal district courts, 1990, annual rpt, 18204–8.13

Benefits overpayment recovery and judgment enforcement cases filed in Federal district courts, 1991, annual rpt, 18204–2.1

Black higher education instns finances, funding sources, enrollment, and student characteristics, with data for Louisiana instns, 1970s-90, hearing, 25258–24

Dental Research Natl Inst research and training grants, by recipient, FY89, annual listing, 4474–19

Education Dept financial aid programs, 1991 annual listing, 4804–3

Education Dept programs funding, operations, and effectiveness, FY90, annual rpt, 4804–5

Expenditures and participation, by Federal student aid program, instn type and control, and State, various periods 1959-89, annual rpt, 4804–28

Expenditures for education by Federal agency, program, and recipient type, and instn spending, FY80-90, annual rpt, 4824–8

Expenditures for student aid supplemental grants, loans, and work-study awards, Federal shares by instn and State, 1991/92, annual listing, 4804–17

Flow-of-funds accounts, savings, investments, and credit statements, quarterly rpt, 9365–3.3

Fraud and abuse in Education Dept programs, audits and investigations, 2nd half FY91, semiannual rpt, 4802–1

Fulbright-Hays academic exchanges, grants by purpose, and foreign govt share of costs, by country, FY90, annual rpt, 10324–1

Guaranteed student loan activity, by program, guarantee agency, and State, quarterly rpt, 4802–2

Guaranteed student loan default rate, causes, defaulter characteristics, and preventive recommendations, FY81-90, 4808–35

Guaranteed student loans, defaults, and collections, by type of loan, lender, and guarantee agency, with data by State and top lender, FY90, annual rpt, 4804–38

Heart, Lung, and Blood Natl Inst activities, and grants by recipient and location, FY90 and disease trends from 1940, annual rpt, 4474–15

HHS financial aid, by program, recipient, State, and city, FY90, annual regional listings, 4004–3

Higher education enrollment, faculty, finances, and degrees, by instn level and control, and State, FY87, annual rpt, 4844–13

Higher education instn revenue by source and spending by function, by State and instn control, FY80-88, annual rpt, 4844–6

Higher education instn tuition and other costs, govt aid, impacts on enrollment, and cost containment methods, 1970s-90 and projected to 2001, 4808–25

Higher education instn tuition, fees, and student aid awards, by State, 1950s-91, annual rpt, 4824–2.22

Higher education instn tuition relation to other instn financial indicators, by instn control, 1960s-88, 4808–24

Humanities Natl Endowment activities and grants, FY90, annual rpt, 9564–2

Income (household, family, and personal), by source, detailed characteristics, and region, 1988-89, annual Current Population Rpt, 2546–6.68

Income (household, family, and personal), by source, detailed characteristics, and region, 1990, annual Current Population Rpt, 2546–6.70

Indian education funding of Fed Govt, and enrollment, degrees, and program grants and fellowships by State, late 1960s-FY89, annual rpt, 14874–1

Indian Health Service employment of Indians and non-Indians, training, hires, and quits, by occupation, FY89, annual rpt, 4084–6

Inter-American Foundation activities, grants by recipient, and fellowships, by country, FY90, annual rpt, 14424–1

Japan-US Friendship Commission educational and cultural exchange activities, grants, and trust fund status, FY89-90, biennial report, 14694–1

Latin America dev grants of Inter-American Foundation by program area, and fellowships by field and instn, by country, FY72-90, annual rpt, 14424–2

Library science training grants for disadvantaged students, by instn and State, FY90, annual listing, 4874–1

Loans and loan guarantees of Fed Govt, outstanding amounts by agency and program, *Treasury Bulletin*, quarterly rpt, 8002–4.9

Loans for students and other financial services, banks profitability indicators, 1985-89, 4808–36

Loans of Fed Govt to students, defaults, losses, and rates, by instn and State, as of June 1990, annual rpt, 4804–18

Loans to 1986 college grads, debt burden by selected student characteristics and instn control, 1987, 4808–26

Maritime academy students receiving Fed Govt aid, monthly rpt, 7702–1

Military health care personnel, and accessions by training source, by occupation, specialty, and service branch, FY89, annual rpt, 3544–24

Military training and education programs funding, staff, students, and facilities, by service branch, FY92, annual rpt, 3504–5

Natl service for youth, proposed program operations and youth attitudes, 1990 rpt, 26306–3.115

NIH activities, funding by program and recipient type, staff, and clinic patients, by inst, FY90, annual rpt, 4434–3

Student discipline

NIH grants and contracts, quarterly listing, 4432–1

NIH grants for R&D, training, construction, and medical libraries, by location and recipient, FY90, annual listings, 4434–7

NIH Research Resources Center activities and funding, by program, FY90, annual rpt, 4434–12

NSF grants and contracts, by field, instn, and State, FY89, annual rpt, 9624–26

Pell grants and applicants, by tuition, family and student income, instn type and control, and State, 1989/90, annual rpt, 4804–1

Reproduction and population research, Natl Inst of Child Health and Human Dev funding and activities, 1990, annual rpt, 4474–33

ROTC programs enrollment, grads, staff, scholarships, and costs, by service branch, FY86-89, GAO rpt, 26123–337

Science and engineering grad enrollment, by field, source of funds, and characteristics of student and instn, 1975-89, annual rpt, 9627–7

Science, engineering, and math education grants of NSF, by recipient and level, FY89, biennial listing, 9624–27

Science fellowship and traineeship funding of Fed Govt, by field, instn, agency, and State, FY89, annual rpt, 9627–17

Statistical Abstract of US, 1991 annual data compilation, 2324–1.4

Tax (income) refunds applied by IRS to outstanding debts to Fed Govt, impacts on subsequent taxpayer compliance, 1984-87, GAO rpt, 26119–339

Truman, Harry S, Scholarship Foundation finances, and awards by student characteristics, FY90, annual rpt, 14314–1

Truman, Harry S, Scholarship Fund receipts by source, transfers, and investment holdings and transactions, monthly rpt, 14312–1

Undergrad student aid, costs, and income factors affecting access to education, 1990 rpt, 26306–6.153

US attorneys civil and criminal cases by type and disposition, and collections, by Federal district, FY90, annual rpt, 6004–2.1; 6004–2.5

see also School lunch and breakfast programs

see also Veterans education

see also Work-study programs

Student Community Service Program

Activities and funding of ACTION, by program, FY90, annual rpt, 9024–2

Activities of SCSP, and volunteer and client characteristics, 1987-89, 9028–14

Student discipline

Children and youth social, economic, and demographic characteristics, 1950s-90, 4818–5

Condition of Education, detail for elementary and secondary education, 1920s-90 and projected to 2001, annual rpt, 4824–1.1

Counseling for youth, school based program client risk behaviors and outcomes, 1988/89 study, hearing, 25548–104

Digest of Education Statistics, 1991 annual data compilation, 4824–2

Student discipline

Discrimination in education, indicators for service delivery and discipline, by State, 1988, biennial rpt, 4804–33

Discrimination within schools, Education Dept enforcement activities and adequacy, FY81-91, GAO rpt, 26121–427

Family structure relation to child health, behavioral, emotional, and school problems, by selected characteristics, 1988, 4147–10.178

High school dropout rates, and subsequent completion, by student and school characteristics, alternative estimates, 1990, annual rpt, 4834–23

Natl Education Goals progress indicators, by State, 1991, annual rpt, 15914–1

Poverty area schools academic environment and teaching methods impacts on student performance, 1989/90 study, 4808–28

Private elementary and secondary schools, students, and staff characteristics, various periods 1979-88, 4838–47

Teachers views on safety, discipline, and student drug use, for elementary and secondary schools, 1991 survey, 4826–1.31

Student employment

see Work-study programs

see Youth employment

Student Loan Marketing Association

Budget of US, financial statements of federally sponsored enterprises, FY92, annual rpt, 104–2.5

Financial condition and capital adequacy of govt-sponsored enterprises, with data by enterprise, 1970s-90 and projected to 1996, 26308–99

Financial condition and capital adequacy of govt-sponsored enterprises, with impacts on Federal borrowing and data by enterprise, 1980s-90, last issue of annual rpt, 8004–15

Financial condition and capital adequacy of govt-sponsored enterprises, with regulatory recommendations and data by enterprise, 1985-95, GAO rpt, 26119–296

Guaranteed student loans, defaults, and collections, by type of loan, lender, and guarantee agency, with data by State and top lender, FY90, annual rpt, 4804–38

Student loans

see Student aid

Students

Aircraft (general aviation) accidents, by circumstances, characteristics of persons and aircraft involved, and type of flying, 1988, annual rpt, 9614–3

Aircraft pilot and nonpilot certificates held, by type of certificate, age, sex, region, and State, 1990, annual rpt, 7504–2

Athletes in college, educational and employment performance compared to other students, for 1972 high school class, as of 1986, 4888–5

Children and youth social, economic, and demographic characteristics, 1950s-90, 4818–5

Computer use at home, school, and work, by family income, 1989, fact sheet, 2326–17.30

Computer use at home, school, and work, by purpose and selected user characteristics, 1989, Current Population Rpt, 2546–2.158

Condition of Education, detail for elementary, secondary, and higher education, 1920s-90 and projected to 2001, annual rpt, 4824–1

Crime and crime-related issues, public opinion by respondent characteristics, data compilation, 1991 annual rpt, 6064–6.2

Crime victimization of teens, by victim and offender characteristics, circumstances, and offense, 1985-88 surveys, 6066–3.43

Digest of Education Statistics, 1991 annual data compilation, 4824–2

Discrimination in education, indicators for service delivery and discipline, by State, 1988, biennial rpt, 4804–33

Drug (illegal) spending, by user group and substance, 1988-90, 236–2.1

Drug, alcohol, and cigarette use and attitudes of youth, by substance type and selected characteristics, 1975-90 surveys, annual rpt, 4494–4

Eighth grade class of 1988: educational performance and conditions, characteristics, attitudes, activities, and plans, natl longitudinal survey, series, 4826–9

Elementary and secondary education enrollment, staff, finances, operations, programs, and policies, 1987/88 biennial survey, series, 4836–3

Elementary and secondary students educational performance, and factors affecting proficiency, by selected characteristics, 1988 natl assessments, subject rpt series, 4896–7

Elementary and secondary students educational performance, and factors affecting proficiency, by selected characteristics, 1990 natl assessments, subject rpt series, 4896–8

Food spending, by item, household composition, income, age, race, and region, 1980-88, Consumer Expenditure Survey biennial rpt, 1544–30

Food stamp recipient household size, composition, income, and income and deductions allowed, summer 1988, annual rpt, 1364–8

High school class of 1972: education, employment, and family characteristics, activities, and attitudes, natl longitudinal study, series, 4836–1

Higher education instn student aid and other sources of support, with student expenses and characteristics, by instn type and control, 1990 triennial study, series, 4846–5

Measles cases among New York State high school and college students, and vaccination and treatment costs, 1989, article, 4042–3.227

Natl Education Goals progress indicators, by State, 1991, annual rpt, 15914–1

OASDI beneficiaries and benefits, selected characteristics with data by State, late 1930s-89, annual rpt, 4744–3.3; 4744–3.4

Performance in school, indicators of problems and relation to family structure, by selected characteristics, 1988, 4147–10.178

Poverty status of population and families, by detailed characteristics, 1988-89, annual Current Population Rpt, 2546–6.67

Poverty status of population and families, by detailed characteristics, 1990, annual Current Population Rpt, 2546–6.71

Private elementary and secondary schools, students, and staff characteristics, various periods 1979-88, 4838–47

Remedial education programs in higher education instns, and enrollment, courses, and faculty, by instn characteristics, 1989/90, 4826–1.30

Tutoring and mentoring of disadvantaged elementary and secondary students by college students, program and participant characteristics, 1989, 4808–23

Women's employment and educational experiences compared to men, for high school class of 1972, natl longitudinal study, as of 1986, 4888–6

see also Black students

see also Educational attainment

see also Educational enrollment

see also Educational retention rates

see also Educational tests

see also Foreign students

see also Learning disabilities

see also School dropouts

see also Student aid

see also Student Community Service Program

see also Student discipline

see also Tuition and fees

Sturrock, John

"Potential Economic Impacts of Changes in Puerto Rico's Status Under S. 712", 26306–3.112

Stutzman, Thomas M.

"Job Task—Competency Linkages for FAA First-Level Supervisors", 7506–10.84

Suarez, Nydia R.

"U.S. Markets for Caribbean Basin Fruits and Vegetables: Selected Characteristics for 17 Fresh and Frozen Imports, 1975-87", 1568–299

Subcommittee on Agricultural Credit. Senate

Delinquent borrowers aid services of Farm Credit System and FmHA, activities, with background data, 1989 hearings, 25168–74

Subcommittee on Agricultural Research and General Legislation. Senate

Wheat quality indicators, for US exports and foreign wheat production, 1960s-90, hearing, 25168–75

Subcommittee on Aviation. House

Airport capacity expansion and improvement funding sources, alternative methods, late 1980s and projected to 2000, hearing, 21648–63

Airport finances, operations by carrier, and capacity improvement and dev funding, by airport, 1977-87 and projected to 2020, hearing, 21648–59

Child fare proposal impacts on family airline travel and industry revenue, with costs and accidents compared to auto travel, 1990 hearing, 21648–61

Noise policies, aircraft replacement schedules and costs, and health impacts, 1960s-90 and projected to 2006, hearing, 21648–64

Subcommittee on Census and Population. House

Census of Population and Housing, 1990: Budget of US constraints impacts on census operations, hearing, 21628–88

Index by Subjects and Names

Census of Population and Housing, 1990: data accuracy and quality issues, hearing, 21628–91

Census of Population and Housing, 1990: data collection progress, hearing, 21628–86

Census of Population and Housing, 1990: local govt review of preliminary results, issues, hearing, 21628–93

Census of Population and Housing, 1990: New York State and NYC data collection activities and status, hearing, 21628–90

Census of Population and Housing, 1990: Pennsylvania data collection activities and status, hearing, 21628–89

Census of Population and Housing, 1990: Pennsylvania preparations for count, hearing, 21628–87

Census of Population and Housing, 1990: Texas data collection activities and status, hearing, 21628–92

Census of Population, 1990: data coverage evaluation and improvement activities, and post-census sample use, hearing, 21628–96

Census of Population, 1990: data coverage evaluation and improvement activities, and revised counts for 1970-90 censuses, hearing, 21628–95

Subcommittee on Children, Family, Drugs and Alcoholism. Senate

Child abuse reports, and related deaths, by State, late 1980s, hearing, 25548–102

Subcommittee on Commerce, Consumer, and Monetary Affairs. House

Banks and thrifts fraud and abuse, Federal agencies enforcement activities and staff, with data by instn and location, 1988-90, hearing, 21408–119

Stock short selling activity indicators, and regulatory issues, 1980s-89 and trends from 1940, hearings, 21408–122

Tax amnesty programs of States for delinquent taxpayers, participation, collections, and costs, by tax type and State, 1980s-90, hearing, 21408–125

Subcommittee on Conservation and Forestry. Senate

Pollution (groundwater) from farm chemicals use, with background data and farmers views, 1970s-80s, hearing, 25168–76

Subcommittee on Constitution. Senate

Pretrial processing, detention, and release, for Federal offenders, by defendant characteristics and district, 1988, hearing, 25528–114

Subcommittee on Courts, Intellectual Property, and Administration of Justice. House

Copyright infringement damage award and video screening issues, 1990 hearing, 21528–82

Subcommittee on Crime. House

Drug (opium) legal production and US imports by country, and analgesics opium content, 1980s, hearing, 21528–81

Subcommittee on Domestic Marketing, Consumer Relations, and Nutrition. House

Food stamp use at farmers markets, costs and participation, demonstration project results for 14 States, 1989, hearing, 21168–46

Subcommittee on Legislation and National Security. House

Subcommittee on Education and Health. Joint

Education funding of Fed Govt, Head Start and GI Bill costs, benefits, and participation, 1950s-90, hearing, 23848–217

Subcommittee on Energy and Power. House

Iraq invasion of Kuwait, oil embargo impacts on OPEC and US oil supply and industry, 1989-91, hearing, 21368–132

Subcommittee on Environment, Energy, and Natural Resources. House

Forest Service mgmt activities, budget, priorities, and employee reward criteria, supervisor and staff views, 1989 survey, 1989, hearing, 21408–121

Subcommittee on Europe and Middle East. House

Israel and Egypt govt budgets, foreign debt, and economic indicators, 1980s, hearing, 21388–58

Subcommittee on Exports, Tax Policy, and Special Problems. House

Medicare claims processing issues in Georgia, with data on beneficiary satisfaction, payments, and subcontractor review activity and savings, 1989-90, hearing, 21728–75

Subcommittee on Financial Institutions Supervision, Regulation and Insurance. House

Banks and deposit insurance funds financial condition, potential losses, and regulatory issues, 1980s-90 and projected to 1995, 21248–147

Intl banking competition issues, with background data, 1980s, 21248–153

Japan financial instns and stock market conditions, and other economic indicators, with intl comparisons, 1980s-90, hearing, 21248–152

Savings instns failure resolution activity of Resolution Trust Corp, with assets and retained senior executives compensation, by instn, 1988-90, hearing, 21248–144

Savings instns failure resolution activity of Resolution Trust Corp, with instns assets and senior executive compensation, 1990, hearing, 21248–157

Subcommittee on Fisheries and Wildlife Conservation and Environment. House

Timber sales of Forest Service, impacts of northern spotted owl conservation in Pacific Northwest, 1990 hearing, 21168–47

Subcommittee on Forests, Family Farms, and Energy. House

Timber industry impacts of northern spotted owl conservation in Pacific Northwest, and local govts Federal payments and severance taxes, 1980s and projected to 2000, hearing, 21168–50

Timber industry impacts of northern spotted owl conservation in Pacific Northwest, 1980s and alternative projections to 2000, hearings, 21168–45

Timber sales of Forest Service, impacts of northern spotted owl conservation in Pacific Northwest, 1990 hearing, 21168–47

Subcommittee on Government Information, Justice, and Agriculture. House

Jail drug treatment programs finances and operations, FY89-90, 21408–120

Lawyers for defense, subpeonas by Federal prosecutors, and public and private indigent defense lawyers pay by State, 1986-90, hearing, 21408–123

Subcommittee on Health and Environment. House

Medicare reimbursement for radiology services by location, and for home medical equipment under alternative proposals, 1990 hearing, 21368–131

Subcommittee on Health and Long-Term Care. House

Older persons abuse and neglect by circumstances and characteristics of abuser and victim, and States protective services budgets and staff, by location, 1980s, hearing, 21148–62

Subcommittee on Health and Safety. House

AIDS and hepatitis viruses transmission in health care settings, occupational exposure, prevention policies, and OSHA regulation, 1990 hearings, 21348–119

Subcommittee on Health. House

Medicare supplemental private insurance premiums, costs, claims, and benefit provisions, with data by firm, 1988-90, hearing, 21788–198

Subcommittee on Housing and Community Development. House

Mobile home fires, casualties, damage, and impacts of safety standards, with data on Michigan trailer parks, 1980s, hearing, 21248–145

Rural areas housing loan programs of FmHA, and housing voucher demonstration program results, 1980s, hearing, 21248–143

Subcommittee on HUD/Mod Rehab Investigation. Senate

Low income housing dev tax credits, and units constructed, by selected project and State, 1987-89, hearings, 25248–120

Subcommittee on Human Resources. House

Child welfare programs funding by source, and foster care cases, problems, and program operations for selected States, 1970s-90, hearings, 21788–202

Unemployment insurance programs of States, finances, operations, tax provisions, and vulnerability to recessions, 1970s-90s, hearing, 21788–201

Subcommittee on Insular and International Affairs. House

Pacific territories economic conditions, population characteristics, and Federal aid, 1989 hearing, 21448–44

Subcommittee on International Development, Finance, Trade, and Monetary Policy. House

Eastern Europe foreign debt components, trade, balances, and other economic indicators, by country, 1985-89, hearing, 21248–148

Intl Finance Corp finances, and intl capital market financial data by firm, by country, 1990 hearing, 21248–149

Subcommittee on Judiciary and Education. House

DC appeals and superior courts civil and criminal caseloads, 1971-88, hearing, 21308–27

Subcommittee on Legislation and National Security. House

Fines (civil) imposed by Federal agencies, and proposed inflation adjustments, FY87, hearing, 21408–124

Subcommittee on Libraries and Memorials. House

Subcommittee on Libraries and Memorials. House
Library of Congress employment by race, Hispanic origin, and sex, and affirmative action needs, 1989, hearing, 21428–9

Subcommittee on National Parks and Public Lands. House
Timber sales of Forest Service, impacts of northern spotted owl conservation in Pacific Northwest, 1990 hearing, 21168–47

Subcommittee on Oceanography and Great Lakes. House
Pollution (marine) bacterial levels, and beach closings due to contamination and medical waste, for New York and New Jersey, 1987-89, hearing, 21568–50

Subcommittee on Oversight and Investigations, Energy and Commerce. House
Insurance (health) for long-term care, affordability and State regulation issues, 1986-90, hearing, 21368–130
Insurance company failures issues and contributing factors, with background data, 1988-90, hearing, 21368–133
Iraq invasion of Kuwait, oil embargo impacts on OPEC and US oil supply and industry, 1989-91, hearing, 21368–132

Subcommittee on Oversight. House
Tax (income) unpaid accounts receivable of IRS by collection status, and IRS budget and staff, with data by district, 1980s-91, hearing, 21788–200

Subcommittee on Patents, Copyrights, and Trademarks. Senate
Imports purchasing decisions of consumers, importance of brand name, authenticity, origin, and other factors, 1984 survey, hearing, 25528–115

Subcommittee on Policy Research and Insurance. House
Earthquake preparedness costs and benefits, with data for California events and effects of 1989 Loma Prieta quake, 1980s, hearings, 21248–154
Insurance industry finances, underwriting activities, and investment plan mgmt, 1960s-90, 21248–159

Subcommittee on Public Buildings and Grounds. House
Court buildings mgmt by GSA, spending, and rental income, 1980s-91, hearing, 21648–60
Kennedy Center for Performing Arts and Natl Symphony Orchestra financial statements, and capital and maintenance costs and needs, 1970s-90, hearing, 21648–62

Subcommittee on Regulation, Business Opportunities, and Energy. House
Drug and diet effects on hypertension, and nonprescription diet pills and analgesics sales and adverse reactions, 1980s-90, hearing, 21728–77
Timber industry impacts of northern spotted owl conservation in Pacific Northwest, and worker aid programs, 1980s and projected to 2000, hearing, 21728–76

Subcommittee on Securities. Senate
Partnerships (limited) conversion to corporations, and impacts on share values, with data by firm, 1980s-91, hearing, 25248–124

Subcommittee on Social Security. House
SSA telephone info service performance, 1989-90, hearing, 21788–199

Subcommittee on Space. House
NASA activities and funding, 1990, annual compilation of papers, 21704–1

Subcommittee on Space Science and Applications. House
Space station commercial dev and operating costs and income under alternative financing options, projected 1989-2000, 21708–129

Subcommittee on Technology and National Security. Joint
Eastern Europe transition to market economies, economic conditions, intl aid, and energy balance, by country, 1985-90, 9118–13

Subcommittee on Toxic Substances, Environmental Oversight, Research and Development. Senate
Asbestos in buildings, EPA aid for removal, occupational asbestos exposure cancer cases and deaths, and Catholic schools abatement costs, 1985-90, hearing, 25328–32

Subcommittee on Water Resources, Transportation, and Infrastructure. Senate
Hwy Trust Fund finances, unobligated balances by State, and receipt losses from increased ethanol use, 1980s-90, hearing, 25328–31

Subcommittee on Wheat, Soybeans, and Feed Grains. House
Grain price support and loan programs operations of USDA, with farmers views on Federal programs, by region and State, 1990 hearings, 21168–43
Soviet Union agricultural conditions and factors affecting US grain exports and CCC credit guarantees, 1990 hearings, 21168–49

Submarines
DOD budget, weapons acquisition costs by system and service branch, FY91-93, annual rpt, 3504–2
Radiation exposure of Navy personnel on nuclear-powered vessels and at support facilities, and injury claims, 1950s-90, annual rpt, 3804–10
Radioactive waste from Navy nuclear-powered vessels and support facilities, releases in harbors, and public exposure, 1970s-90, annual rpt, 3804–11
Soviet Union military weapons systems, presence, and force strengths, and compared to US, 1991 annual rpt, 3504–20
Statistical Abstract of US, 1991 annual data compilation, 2324–1.11

Submerged lands
see also Continental shelf
see also Offshore oil and gas

Subsidies
Budget of US, obligations and authority by function, agency, and program, with summaries, analyses, and historical tables, FY92, annual rpt, 104–2
Egypt govt domestic subsidies by type, FY87-89, hearing, 21388–58
Finances of govts, revenues by source and spending by function, natl income and product accounts, *Survey of Current Business,* monthly rpt, 2702–1.25

Index by Subjects and Names

Minerals depletion allowance of foreign countries and US, by nonfuel mineral, 1986-90, annual rpt, 5604–18
Natl income and product accounts and components, *Survey of Current Business,* monthly rpt, 2702–1.24
Postal Service activities, finances, and mail volume and subsidies, FY90, annual rpt, 9864–5.3
Postal Service operating costs, itemized by class of mail, FY90, annual rpt, 9864–4
Postal Service subsidy for revenue forgone, by class of mail, FY90, annual rpt, 9864–1
Telephone local service charges and low-income subsidies, by region, company, and city, 1980s-90, semiannual rpt, 9282–8
see also Agricultural production quotas and price supports
see also Agricultural subsidies
see also Federal aid programs
see also Federal aid to arts and humanities
see also Federal aid to education
see also Federal aid to higher education
see also Federal aid to highways
see also Federal aid to housing
see also Federal aid to law enforcement
see also Federal aid to libraries
see also Federal aid to local areas
see also Federal aid to medical education
see also Federal aid to medicine
see also Federal aid to railroads
see also Federal aid to rural areas
see also Federal aid to States
see also Federal aid to transportation
see also Federal aid to vocational education
see also Federal funding for energy programs
see also Federal funding for research and development
see also Rent supplements
see also Shipbuilding and operating subsidies
see also State funding for economic development
see also State funding for education
see also State funding for health and hospitals
see also State funding for higher education
see also State funding for local areas
see also State funding for natural resources and conservation
see also State funding for public safety
see also State funding for social welfare
see also State funding for transportation
see also State government spending
see also Tax expenditures
see also Tax incentives and shelters
see also Trade adjustment assistance

Substance abuse
see Alcohol abuse and treatment
see Cocaine
see Drug abuse and treatment
see Drug and alcohol testing
see Marijuana
see Smoking

Suburbs
Births, fertility rates, and childless women, by selected characteristics, 1990, annual Current Population Rpt, 2546–1.455
Census of Population, 1990: top 39 MSAs and 40 cities population, with trends from 1900, fact sheet, 2326–20.3
Crime Index by population size and region, and offenses by large city, Jan-June 1991, semiannual rpt, 6222–1

Index by Subjects and Names

Crime victimization of households, by offense, household characteristics, and location, 1975-90, annual rpt, 6066–25.40

Crimes, arrests by offender characteristics, and rates, by offense, and law enforcement employees, by population size and jurisdiction, 1990, annual rpt, 6224–2

Educational enrollment, by grade, instn type and control, and student characteristics, 1989 and trends from 1947, annual Current Population Rpt, 2546–1.453

Employment and unemployment in metro and nonmetro areas, monthly rpt, quarterly data, 6742–2.9

Home mortgages FHA-insured, financial, property, and mortgagor characteristics, by metro area, 1990, annual rpt, 5144–24

Home mortgages FHA-insured, financial, property, and mortgagor characteristics, by State, 1990, annual rpt, 5144–1

Home mortgages FHA-insured, financial, property, and mortgagor characteristics, total and by State and outlying area, 1990, annual rpt, 5144–25

Home mortgages FHA-insured, financial, property, and mortgagor characteristics, 1990, annual rpt, 5144–23

Households and family characteristics, by location, 1990, annual Current Population Rpt, 2546–1.447

Housing and households characteristics, MSA surveys, fact sheet series, 2485–11

Housing and households detailed characteristics, and unit and neighborhood quality, by location, 1987, biennial rpt supplement, 2485–13

Housing and households detailed characteristics, and unit and neighborhood quality, by location, 1989, biennial rpt, 2485–12

Housing and households detailed characteristics, and unit and neighborhood quality, MSA surveys, series, 2485–6

Housing inventory change from 1973, by reason, unit and household characteristics, and location, 1983 survey, biennial rpt, 2485–14

Housing vacancy and occupancy rates, and vacant unit characteristics and costs, by region and metro-nonmetro location, quarterly rpt, 2482–1

Income (household) and poverty status under alternative income definitions, by recipient characteristics, 1990, annual Current Population Rpt, 2546–6.69

Retail trade census, 1987: finances and employment, for establishments with and without payroll, by SIC 2- to 4-digit kind of business, State, and MSA, 2401–1

State and Metro Area Data Book, 1991 data compilation, 2328–54

see also Neighborhoods

see also Urban renewal

see also under By Urban-Rural and Metro-Nonmetro in the "Index by Categories"

Subversive activities

Foreign countries human rights conditions in 170 countries, 1990, annual rpt, 21384–3

Sentences for Federal offenses, guidelines by offense and circumstances, series, 17668–1

US attorneys civil and criminal cases by type and disposition, and collections, by Federal district, FY90, annual rpt, 6004–2.1; 6004–2.7

see also Espionage

see also Internal security

see also Sabotage

see also Terrorism

Subways

Accidents, casualties, and damage, by circumstances and system, 1989, annual rpt, 7884–5

Construction industries census, 1987: establishments, employment, receipts, and expenditures, by SIC 4-digit industry and State, final industry rpt series, 2373–1

Energy use by mode of transport, fuel supply, and demographic and economic factors of vehicle use, 1970s-89, annual rpt, 3304–5

Finances and operations of transit systems, by mode of transport, size of fleet, and for 468 systems, 1989, annual rpt, 7884–4

Finances, costs, and needs of transit systems, by selected system, 1987-89, biennial rpt, 7884–8

Manufacturing annual survey, 1989: finances and operations, by SIC 2- to 4-digit industry, series, 2506–15

Natl transportation system planning, use, condition, accidents, and needs, by mode of transport, 1940s-90 and projected to 2020, 7308–202

Safety programs, and accidents, casualties, and damage, by mode of transport, 1989, annual rpt, 7304–19

Urban Mass Transportation Admin grants for transit systems, by city and State, FY90, annual rpt, 7884–10

Sudan

Agricultural exports of high-value commodities, indexes and sales by commodity, world area, and country, 1960s-86, 1528–323

Agricultural trade of US, by detailed commodity and country, 1989, annual rpt, 1524–8

Agricultural trade of US, by detailed commodity and country, 1990, semiannual rpt, 1522–4

AID economic aid to developing countries, obligations and disbursements by country, quarterly rpt, 9912–4

AID loans repayment status and terms by program and country, and status of predecessor agency loans, quarterly rpt, 9912–3

Background Notes, summary social, political, and economic data, 1991 rpt, 7006–2.27

Dairy imports, consumption, and market conditions, by sub-Saharan Africa country, 1961-88, 1528–321

Economic and military aid and loans from US and intl agencies, by program and country, FY46-90, annual rpt, 9914–5

Economic and social conditions of developing countries from 1960s, and Intl Dev Cooperation Agency and AID activities and funding, FY90-92, annual rpt, 9904–4

Economic conditions, income, production, prices, employment, and trade, 1991 periodic country rpt, 2046–4.70

Economic, social, political, and geographic summary data, by country, 1991, annual factbook, 9114–2

Sugar industry and products

Exports and imports of US, by transport mode, country, and SITC 1- to 3-digit commodity, 1990, annual rpt, 2424–12

Exports of US, detailed Schedule B commodities with countries of destination, 1990, annual rpt, 2424–10

Food supply, needs, and aid for developing countries, status and alternative forecasts, 1991 world area rpt, 1526–8.1

Grain production and needs, and related economic outlook, by world area and selected country, forecast 1990/91-1991/92, 1528–313

Grain production, use, imports, and stocks, for Sahel region by country, 1989/90, 9918–18

Human rights conditions in 170 countries, and US economic and military aid, 1990, annual rpt, 21384–3

Military aid of US, arms sales, and training programs costs and budget requests, by program, world region, and country, FY90-92, annual rpt, 7144–13

UN voting record and share of votes in agreement with US, by issue, country, and world area, 1990, annual rpt, 7004–18

see also under By Foreign Country in the "Index by Categories"

Suffolk County, N.Y.

see also under By SMSA or MSA in the "Index by Categories"

Sugar industry and products

Acreage planted and harvested, by crop and State, 1989-90 and planned as of June 1991, annual rpt, 1621–23

Acreage planted, by selected crop and State, 1982-90 and planned 1991, annual rpt, 1621–22

Acreage under Agricultural Stabilization and Conservation Service programs, rankings by commodity and congressional district, 1989, biennial rpt, 1804–17

Agricultural Stabilization and Conservation Service sugar programs, 1990, annual fact sheet, 1806–4.4

Agricultural Statistics, 1990, annual rpt, 1004–1

Agriculture census, 1987: farms, farmland, production, finances, and operator characteristics, by county, final State rpt series, 2331–1

Alcoholic beverages production, stocks, materials used, and taxable and tax-free removals, for beer and distilled spirits by State, monthly rpt, 8486–1.1; 8486–1.3

Business statistics, detailed data for major industries and economic indicators, *Survey of Current Business*, monthly rpt, 2702–1.14

Cloned sugarcane yields, stability, and fungi resistance, 1990/91, annual rpt, 1704–2

Consumer Expenditure Survey, food spending by item, household composition, income, age, race, and region, 1980-88, biennial rpt, 1544–30

Consumer Expenditure Survey, household income by source, and itemized spending, by selected characteristics and region, 1988-89, annual rpt, 6764–5

Consumption of food, dietary composition, and nutrient intake, 1987/88 natl survey, preliminary rpt series, 1356–1

Consumption, supply, trade, prices, spending, and indexes, by food commodity, 1989, annual rpt, 1544–4

Sugar industry and products

County Business Patterns, 1988: employment, establishments, and payroll, by SIC 2- to 4-digit industry and county, annual State rpt series, 2326–6

County Business Patterns, 1989: employment, establishments, and payroll, by SIC 2- to 4-digit industry and county, annual State rpt series, 2326–8

CPI by component for US city average, and by region, population size, and for 27 metro areas, monthly rpt, 6762–2

Employment, earnings, and hours, by SIC 1- to 4-digit industry, monthly and annual averages, selected years 1909-90, annual rpt, 6744–4

Enterprise Statistics, 1987: finances and operations for companies, by size, level of diversification, form of organization, and industry group, 2329–8

Exports (agricultural) of high-value commodities, indexes and sales value by commodity, world area, and country, 1960s-86, 1528–323

Exports and imports (agricultural) commodity and country, prices, and world market devs, monthly rpt, 1922–12

Exports and imports (agricultural) of US, by commodity and country, bimonthly rpt, 1522–1

Exports and imports (agricultural) of US, by detailed commodity and country, 1989, annual rpt, 1524–8

Exports and imports (agricultural) of US, by detailed commodity and country, 1990, semiannual rpt, 1522–4

Exports and imports between US and outlying areas, by detailed commodity and mode of transport, 1990, annual rpt, 2424–11

Exports and imports of US, by country and detailed commodity, monthly rpt, 2422–12

Exports and imports of US, by Harmonized System 6-digit commodity and country, 1990, annual rpt, 2424–13

Exports and imports of US, by transport mode, country, and SITC 1- to 3-digit commodity, 1990, annual rpt, 2424–12

Exports and imports of US shipped through Canada, by detailed commodity, customs district, and country, 1989, annual rpt, 7704–11

Exports of US, detailed Schedule B commodities with countries of destination, 1990, annual rpt, 2424–10

Farm financial and marketing conditions, forecast 1991, annual chartbook, 1504–8

Farm financial and marketing conditions, forecast 1991, annual conf, 1004–16

Farm income, expenses, receipts by commodity, assets, liabilities, and ratios, 1990 and trends from 1945, annual rpt, 1544–16

Farm sector balance sheet, and receipts by detailed commodity, by State, 1985-89, annual rpt, 1544–18

Foreign and US production, prices, trade, and use, FAS periodic circular series, 1925–14

Foreign countries agricultural production, prices, and trade, by country, 1980-90 and forecast 1991, annual world area rpt series, 1524–4

Foreign countries agricultural production, trade, and policies, summary data by country, 1989-90, annual factbook, 1924–12

Futures and options trading volume, by commodity and exchange, FY90, annual rpt, 11924–2

Futures trading in selected commodities and financial instruments and indexes, NYC, Chicago, and other markets activity, semimonthly rpt, 11922–5

Imports of sugar and sugar-containing products under quota, by country, periodic rpt, 1922–9

Irrigation projects of Reclamation Bur in western US, crop production and acreage by commodity, State, and project, 1989, annual rpt, 5824–12

Labor productivity, indexes of output, hours, and employment by SIC 2- to 4-digit industry, 1967-89, annual rpt, 6824–1.3

Manufacturing annual survey, 1989: finances and operations, by SIC 2- to 4-digit industry, series, 2506–15

Manufacturing census, 1987: finances and operations, by SIC 2- to 4-digit industry, State, and MSA, with trends from 1849, 2497–1

Manufacturing census, 1987: finances and operations, by type of organization and SIC 2- to 4-digit industry, subject rpt, 2497–5

Molasses supply, use, wholesale prices by market, and imports by country, 1985-90, annual rpt, 1311–19

Nutrient, caloric, and waste composition, detailed data for raw, processed, and prepared snacks and sweets, 1991 rpt, 1356–3.16

Occupational injury and illness rates, by SIC 2- to 4-digit industry, 1988-89, annual rpt, 6844–7

Occupational injury and illness rates, by SIC 2- to 4-digit industry, 1989, annual rpt, 6844–1

OECD trade, total and for 4 major countries, and US trade by country, by commodity, 1970-89, world area rpt series, 9116–1

Price indexes (producer), by stage of processing and detailed commodity, monthly rpt, 6762–6

Price indexes (producer), by stage of processing and detailed commodity, monthly 1990, annual rpt, 6764–2

Price support program provisions, for selected commodities, 1961-90, 1568–303

Prices (farm-retail) for food, marketing cost components, and industry finances and productivity, 1920s-90, annual rpt, 1544–9

Prices received and paid by farmers, by commodity and State, 1990, annual rpt, 1629–5

Prices received by farmers and production value, by detailed crop and State, 1988-90, annual rpt, 1621–2

Production, acreage, yield, stocks, deliveries, and price, by State, and trade by country, 1950s-90, 1568–306

Production, farms, acreage, and related data, by selected crop and State, monthly rpt, 1621–1

Production inputs, output, and productivity for farms, by commodity and region, 1947-89, annual rpt, 1544–17

Production itemized costs, receipts, and returns, by commodity and region, 1987-89, annual rpt, 1544–20

Production, prices, trade, and marketing, by commodity, current situation and forecast, monthly rpt with articles, 1502–4

Production, prices, trade, supply, and use, quarterly situation rpt with articles, 1561–14

Production, trade, and use of sugar, quarterly rpt, 1621–28

Soviet Union agricultural trade, by commodity and country, 1955-90, 1528–322

Soviet Union, Eastern Europe, OECD, and selected other countries agricultural production, by commodity, 1960s-90, annual rpt, 9114–4.5

Statistical Abstract of US, 1991 annual data compilation, 2324–1.23

Tax (income) returns of corporations, income and tax items by asset size and detailed industry, 1987, annual rpt, 8304–4

Tax (income) returns of corporations, income and tax items by asset size and detailed industry, 1988, annual rpt, 8304–21

see also Candy and confectionery products

see also Syrups and sweeteners

see also under By Commodity in the "Index by Categories"

Suicide

Child accident deaths and death rates, by cause, age, sex, race, and State, 1980-85, 4108–54

Child accident deaths and injuries by cause, and victimization, rates by race, sex, and age, 1979-88, chartbook, 4108–56

Cocaine abuse, user characteristics, and related crime and violence, 1988 conf, 4498–74

Cocaine-related emergency room admissions, by user and use characteristics, for major metro areas, 1987-89, article, 4042–3.204

Deaths and rates, by cause and age, preliminary 1989-90, US Vital Statistics annual rpt, 4144–7

Deaths and rates, by cause, provisional data, monthly rpt, 4142–1.2

Deaths and rates, by detailed cause and demographic characteristics, 1988 and trends from 1900, US Vital Statistics annual rpt, 4144–2

Deaths by cause, age, race, and sex, 1950s-89, annual rpt, 4144–11

Drug abuse emergency room admissions and deaths, by drug type and source, sex, race, age, and major metro area, 1990, annual rpt, 4494–8

Firearms-related deaths and death rates, by motive, age, sex, and race, for persons aged 1-34, 1979-88, 4146–5.119

Health condition improvement and disease prevention goals and recommended activities for 2000, with trends 1970s-80s, 4048–10

Indian Health Service facilities and use, and Indian health and other characteristics, by IHS region, 1980s-89, annual chartbook, 4084–7

Indian Health Service facilities, funding, operations, and Indian health and other characteristics, 1950s-90, annual chartbook, 4084–1

Military deaths by cause, age, race, and rank, and personnel captured and missing, by service branch, FY90, annual rpt, 3544–40

Minority group health condition, services use, costs, and indicators of services need, 1950s-88, 4118–55

Pacific territories economic conditions, population characteristics, and Federal aid, 1989 hearing, 21448–44

Prisoners and movements, by offense, location, and selected other characteristics, data compilation, 1991 annual rpt, 6064–6.6

Prisoners in Federal and State instns, deaths by cause, sex, and State, 1989, annual rpt, 6064–26.4

Prisoners in jails, deaths by cause, by county and facility, 1988, regional rpt series, 6068–144

Prisoners in jails, deaths by cause, 1989-90, annual rpt, 6066–25.38

State and Metro Area Data Book, 1991 data compilation, 2328–54

Statistical Abstract of US, 1991 annual data compilation, 2324–1.2

Sulfur

see Nonmetallic minerals and mines

Sulfur oxides

see Acid rain

see Air pollution

Sulfuric acid

see Chemicals and chemical industry

Sullivan, David F.

"State and Local Government Fiscal Position in 1990", 2702–1.205

Sullivan, Gene D.

"Prospects for Energy Supplies", 9371–1.213

"Structural Change for Farm Lenders in the 1980s", 9368–90

Summer employment

see Temporary and seasonal employment

Summerson, John H.

"Association Between Exercise and Other Preventive Health Behaviors Among Diabetics", 4042–3.246

Sunflowers and sunflower seeds

see Oils, oilseeds, and fats

Sunnyvale, Calif.

Housing and households characteristics, unit and neighborhood quality, and journey to work by MSA location, for 11 MSAs, 1984 survey, supplement, 2485–8

Housing and households detailed characteristics, and unit and neighborhood quality, by location, 1988 survey, MSA rpt, 2485–6.8

see *also* under By City in the "Index by Categories"

Sunshine, Jonathan H.

"Determinants of Total Family Charges for Health Care: U.S., 1980", 4146–12.27

"Expenditures and Sources of Funds for Mental Health Organizations: U.S. and Each State, 1988", 4506–3.45

"Mental Health Services of the Veterans Administration, U.S., 1986", 4506–3.43

"Psychiatric Outpatient Care Services in Mental Health Organizations, U.S., 1986", 4506–3.40

"Residential Treatment Centers and Other Organized Mental Health Care for Children and Youth: U.S., 1988", 4506–3.44

Sunspots

see Astronomy

Superfund

see Hazardous waste and disposal

Supermarkets

see Food stores

Supervisors

see Business management

see Executives and managers

Supplemental Security Income

Admin of OASDHI, and SSA activities, 1930s-90 and projected to 2064, annual data compilation, 4704–12

AFDC beneficiaries demographic and financial characteristics, by State, FY89, annual rpt, 4694–1

Beneficiaries by diagnosis, research file dev methodology, 1991 article, 4742–1.214

Beneficiaries of SSI, income from OASI and other sources, and work history, 1988, article, 4742–1.216

Benefits and beneficiaries of SSI, by type of eligibility, State, and county, Dec 1989, annual rpt, 4744–27

Benefits award rate by applicant characteristics and eligibility class, for SSI, 1987, article, 4742–1.213

Benefits, beneficiaries, and recipient characteristics, with data by State, 1970s-89, annual rpt, 4744–3.8

Benefits by county, FY90, annual regional listings, 4004–3

Budget of US, obligations and authority by function, agency, and program, with summaries, analyses, and historical tables, FY92, annual rpt, 104–2

Court caseloads for SSI claims in Federal district courts, 1990, annual rpt, 18204–8.13; 18204–11

Court caseloads for SSI claims in Federal district courts, 1991, annual rpt, 18204–2.1

Eligibility and payment provisions for SSI and Medicaid, and beneficiaries living arrangements, by State, 1991, annual rpt, 4704–13

Expenditures, coverage, and benefits for social welfare programs, late 1930s-89, annual rpt, 4744–3.1

Expenditures of Fed Govt in States, by type, program, agency, and State, FY90, annual rpt, 2464–2

Finances and operations of programs under Ways and Means Committee jurisdiction, FY70s-90, annual rpt, 21784–11

Finances of Fed Govt, cash and debt transactions, daily tables, 8102–4

Finances of SSA programs, and litigation, FY90, annual rpt, 4704–6

Food stamp recipient household size, composition, income, and income and deductions allowed, summer 1988, annual rpt, 1364–8

Food stamp substitution with cash aid for aged and handicapped persons, pilot project results by area, as of July 1990, semiannual rpt, 1362–6

Households composition, income, benefits, and labor force status, Survey of Income and Program Participation methodology, working paper series, 2626–10

Households, family, and personal income, by source, detailed characteristics, and region, 1988-89, annual Current Population Rpt, 2546–6.68

Households, family, and personal income, by source, detailed characteristics, and region, 1990, annual Current Population Rpt, 2546–6.70

Households income and poverty status under alternative income definitions, by recipient characteristics, 1990, annual Current Population Rpt, 2546–6.69

Medicaid and Medicare low income disabled enrollees and eligibility provisions, by State, 1975-89, article, 4652–1.218

Medicaid beneficiaries services use and costs, by service type and eligibility, 1975-89, article, 4652–1.209

Medicaid hospital discharges, by eligibility and instn characteristics, for 2 States, 1984, article, 4652–1.249

Older persons in rural areas, household income sources, and poverty status, 1983-84, 1598–268

Social Security Bulletin, OASDHI and other program operations and beneficiary characteristics, from 1940, monthly journal, 4742–1

State and Metro Area Data Book, 1991 data compilation, 2328–54

Statistical Abstract of US, 1991 annual data compilation, 2324–1.12

Vocational rehabilitation cases of State agencies by disposition and applicant characteristics, and closures by reason, FY84-88, annual rpt, 4944–6

Vocational rehabilitation cases of State agencies, by social, employment, and disability characteristics, FY90, annual rpt, 4944–1

Supplementary Educational Opportunity Grant

see Student aid

Supplementary wage benefits

see Employee benefits

Supreme Court

Budget of US, authoritative financial statements with appropriations, outlays, and receipts, by category and agency, FY90, annual rpt, 8104–2.1

Budget of US, obligations and authority by function, agency, and program, with summaries, analyses, and historical tables, FY92, annual rpt, 104–2

Buildings and grounds under Capitol Architect supervision, itemized outlays by payee and function, 1st half FY91, semiannual rpt, 25922–2

Caseloads, dispositions, and backlog, for Supreme Court, Oct 1985-89, annual rpt, 18204–8.16

Crime, criminal justice admin and enforcement, and public opinion, data compilation, 1991 annual rpt, 6064–6

Criminal case processing in Federal courts, by offense, disposition, and jurisdiction, data compilation, 1991 annual rpt, 6064–6.5

Labor-related cases on Supreme Court docket, 1990-91, annual narrative article, 6722–1.208

Public opinion on crime and crime-related issues, by respondent characteristics, data compilation, 1991 annual rpt, 6064–6.2

Statistical Abstract of US, 1991 annual data compilation, 2324–1.5

Tax litigation, prosecutions, and interpretive law decisions, FY90, annual rpt, 8304–3.3

Writs of certiorari for review by Supreme Court on writs filed in Federal courts of appeals, petitions and disposition, 1990, annual rpt, 18204–8.17

Surety bonds

Surety bonds

Small Business Admin surety bond guarantee program finances, and contracts by contractor race, obligee type, and region, FY87-89, GAO rpt, 26113–526

Surgeons and surgery

- AIDS virus transmission from health care workers to patients during invasive procedures, CDC prevention guidelines, 1991 rpt, 4206–2.44
- Anesthesiologists reimbursement by Medicare, charges, and time billed, 1987, GAO rpt, 26121–417
- Deaths of Medicare patients, actual and expected rates by diagnosis, with hospital characteristics, by instn, FY87-89, annual regional rpt series, 4654–14
- Deaths related to surgery, and rates, by cause, age, sex, race, and State, 1988, US Vital Statistics annual rpt, 4144–2
- *Health Care Financing Review*, provider prices, price inputs and indexes, and labor, quarterly journal, 4652–1.1
- Health condition and health care resources, use, and spending, 1950s-89, annual data compilation, 4144–11
- Hepatitis cases by infection source, age, sex, race, and State, and deaths, by strain, 1988 and trends from 1966, 4205–2
- Hospital discharges and length of stay, by diagnosis, patient and instn characteristics, procedure performed, and payment source, 1988, annual rpt, 4147–13.107
- Hospital discharges and length of stay by region and diagnosis, and procedures performed, by age and sex, 1989, annual rpt, 4146–8.198
- Hospital discharges by detailed diagnostic and procedure category, primary diagnosis, and length of stay, by age, sex, and region, 1988, annual rpt, 4147–13.105; 4147–13.108
- Hospital services and facilities availability, by selected instn characteristics, 1980, 1983, and 1987, 17206–2.22
- Hospitalization costs relation to services timing, by selected patient and hospital characteristics, for Medicare discharges, 1987-88, 17208–2
- Insurance (health) coverage and provisions of small business employee benefit plans, by plan type and occupational group, 1990, biennial rpt, 6784–20
- Labor supply of physicians, by specialty, age, sex, and location of training and practice, 1989, State rpt series, 4116–6
- Medicare and Medicaid beneficiaries and program operations, 1991, annual fact book, 4654–18
- Medicare-certified ambulatory surgery centers, by region, selected years 1983-89, annual rpt, 4654–13
- Medicare claims approved, charges, and reimbursements by type of service, from 1974, monthly rpt, quarterly data, 4742–1.11
- Medicare coverage of new health care technologies, risks and benefit evaluations, series, 4186–10
- Medicare payments to physicians, charges by specialty and treatment setting, and assignment rate by State, 1970s-88, article, 4652–1.240
- Medicare reimbursement of hospitals under prospective payment system, and effect on services, finances, and beneficiary payments, 1979-90, annual rpt, 17204–2
- Medicare Supplementary Medical Insurance physicians fee schedule, analyses of costs and other issues, series, 17266–1
- Medicare Supplementary Medical Insurance physicians fee schedule, methodology with data by procedure and specialty, 1991, annual rpt, 17264–1
- Military health care personnel, and accessions by training source, by occupation, specialty, and service branch, FY89, annual rpt, 3544–24
- Minority group and women health condition, services use, payment sources, and health care labor force, by poverty status, 1940s-89, chartbook, 4118–56
- Minority group health condition, services use, costs, and indicators of services need, 1950s-88, 4118–55
- *State and Metro Area Data Book*, 1991 data compilation, 2328–54
- VA health care facilities physicians, dentists, and nurses, by selected employment characteristics and VA district, quarterly rpt, 8602–6
- VA health care facilities surgery-related deaths and complications, by procedure and instn, and compared to non-VA instns, FY84-89, last issue of biennial rpt, 8704–1
- VA health care staff and turnover, by occupation, physician specialty, and location, 1990, annual rpt, 8604–8
- VA hospitals admissions and discharges by diagnosis, facilities operating costs, and other VA activities, FY90, annual rpt, 8604–3.3
- VA Medicine and Surgery Dept trainees, by detailed program and city, FY90, annual rpt, 8704–4
- VA mental health care services, staff, research, and training programs, 1991 biennial listing, 8704–2
- Veterans health care, patients, visits, costs, and operating beds, by VA and contract facility, and region, quarterly rpt, 8602–4
- Visits to physicians, by patient and practice characteristics, diagnosis, and services provided, 1989, 4146–8.206

see also Medical transplants

Suriname

- Agricultural exports of high-value commodities, indexes and sales by commodity, world area, and country, 1960s-86, 1528–323
- Agricultural trade of US, by detailed commodity and country, 1989, annual rpt, 1524–8
- Agricultural trade of US, by detailed commodity and country, 1990, semiannual rpt, 1522–4
- AID economic aid to developing countries, obligations and disbursements by country, quarterly rpt, 9912–4
- AID loans repayment status and terms by program and country, and status of predecessor agency loans, quarterly rpt, 9912–3
- *Background Notes*, summary social, political, and economic data, 1991 rpt, 7006–2.54
- Economic and military aid and loans from US and intl agencies, by program and country, FY46-90, annual rpt, 9914–5
- Economic, social, political, and geographic summary data, by country, 1991, annual factbook, 9114–2

Index by Subjects and Names

- Exports and imports of US, by transport mode, country, and SITC 1- to 3-digit commodity, 1990, annual rpt, 2424–12
- Exports of US, detailed Schedule B commodities with countries of destination, 1990, annual rpt, 2424–10
- Human rights conditions in 170 countries, and US economic and military aid, 1990, annual rpt, 21384–3
- UN voting record and share of votes in agreement with US, by issue, country, and world area, 1990, annual rpt, 7004–18

Surplus government property

- Assistance (financial and nonfinancial) of Fed Govt, 1991 base edition with supplements, annual listing, 104–5
- Budget of US, authoritative financial statements with appropriations, outlays, and receipts, by category and agency, FY90, annual rpt, 8104–2.1
- Developing countries economic and social conditions from 1960s, and Intl Dev Cooperation Agency and AID activities and funding, FY90-92, annual rpt, 9904–4
- DOD property, supply, and equipment inventory, by service branch, FY90, annual rpt, 3544–6
- Donations of surplus Federal personal property to govt and nonprofit agencies, with data by State, FY88-90, biennial rpt, 9454–22
- Foreign countries military aid of US, arms sales, and training, by country, FY50-90, annual rpt, 3904–3
- Homeless aid organizations donations of surplus Federal property by State, and compared to other recipients, FY87-80, GAO rpt, 26113–538
- Homeless persons housing and food aid of Fed Govt, funding and operations, with data by State and county, FY89, hearing, 25408–111
- Military surplus property donations to intl and State relief programs, FY86-90, GAO rpt, 26123–316

Surveillance

see Electronic surveillance
see Espionage

Survey of Income and Program Participation

- Data collection, methodology, and comparisons to other data bases, working paper series, 2626–10
- Data collection, methodology, and use, 1990 annual conf papers, 2624–1
- *Household Economic Studies*, series, 2546–20
- Income data from SIPP compared to Current Population Survey, 1984, technical paper, 4746–26.8
- Population and housing data, and policy issues, fact sheet series, 2326–17

Surveys

- *see* Aerial surveys
- *see* American Housing Survey
- *see* Annual Survey of Manufactures
- *see* Area wage surveys
- *see* Business outlook and attitude surveys
- *see* Census of Agriculture
- *see* Census of Construction Industries
- *see* Census of Governments
- *see* Census of Housing
- *see* Census of Manufactures
- *see* Census of Mineral Industries

Index by Subjects and Names

Sweden

see Census of Outlying Areas
see Census of Population
see Census of Population and Housing
see Census of Retail Trade
see Census of Service Industries
see Census of Transportation
see Census of Wholesale Trade
see Consumer Expenditure Survey
see Consumer surveys
see Continuous Work History Sample
see Current Employment Survey
see Current Population Survey
see Economic censuses
see Enterprise Statistics Program
see Farm Costs and Returns Survey
see Fast Response Survey System
see General Aviation Pilot and Aircraft Activity Survey
see High School and Beyond Survey
see High School Transcript Study
see Hispanic Health and Nutrition Examination Survey
see Hospital Cost and Clinical Research Project
see Hospital Cost and Utilization Project
see Industry wage surveys
see Integrated Postsecondary Education Data System
see Inventory of Mental Health Organizations and General Hospital Mental Health Services
see Methodology
see Mineral Industry Surveys
see Motor Freight Transportation and Warehousing Survey
see National Adult Literacy Survey
see National Ambulatory Medical Care Survey
see National Assessment of Educational Progress
see National Crime Survey
see National Drug and Alcoholism Treatment Utilization Survey
see National Education Longitudinal Survey
see National Health and Nutrition Examination Survey
see National Health Interview Survey
see National Health Interview Survey on Child Health
see National Hospital Discharge Survey
see National Household Education Survey
see National Household Seroprevalence Survey
see National Household Survey on Drug Abuse
see National Long Term Care Survey
see National Longitudinal Study of High School Seniors
see National Medical Care Utilization and Expenditure Survey
see National Medical Expenditure Survey
see National Natality Survey
see National Postsecondary Student Aid Study
see National Survey of Family Growth
see National Survey of Postsecondary Faculty
see Nationwide Food Consumption Survey
see Nationwide Personal Transportation Study
see Opinion and attitude surveys
see Postsecondary Education Transcript Study
see Postsecondary Quick Information System

see Private School Study
see Recent College Graduates Survey
see Recordkeeping Practices Survey
see Schools and Staffing Survey
see State Hospital Data Project
see Statistical programs and activities
see Survey of Income and Program Participation

Survivors

see Old-Age, Survivors, Disability, and Health Insurance
see Widows and widowers

Susquehanna River

Water supply and quality in streams and lakes, and groundwater levels in wells, by drainage basin, 1988, annual State rpt series, 5666–16

Water supply and quality in streams and lakes, and groundwater levels in wells, by drainage basin, 1989, annual State rpt series, 5666–12

Water supply and quality in streams and lakes, and groundwater levels in wells, by drainage basin, 1990, annual State rpt series, 5666–10

Water supply in US and southern Canada, streamflow, surface and groundwater conditions, and reservoir levels, by location, monthly rpt, 5662–3

Susquehanna River Basin Commission

Budget of US, authoritative financial statements with appropriations, outlays, and receipts, by category and agency, FY90, annual rpt, 8104–2.1

Budget of US, obligations and authority by function, agency, and program, with summaries, analyses, and historical tables, FY92, annual rpt, 104–2

Sutphin, David M.

"International Strategic Minerals Inventory Summary Report: Tin", 5666–21.10

Suwaki, Hiroshi

"Methamphetamine Abuse in Japan", 4498–75

Svensson, Lars E.

"Expected and Predicted Realignments: The FF/DM Exchange Rate During the EMS", 9366–7.249

Swamps

see Wetlands

Swamy, P. A.

"Some Problems with Identification in Parametric Models", 9366–6.258

Swanson, Frederick J.

"Fire History and Pattern in a Cascade Range Landscape", 1208–354

Swartz, Katherine

"Spells Without Health Insurance: Distributions of Durations and Their Link to Point-in-Time Estimates of the Uninsured", 2626–10.142

"Spells Without Health Insurance: What Affects Spell Duration and Who Are the Chronically Uninsured?", 2626–10.141

Swaziland

Agricultural exports of high-value commodities, indexes and sales by commodity, world area, and country, 1960s-86, 1528–323

Agricultural trade of US, by detailed commodity and country, 1989, annual rpt, 1524–8

Agricultural trade of US, by detailed commodity and country, 1990, semiannual rpt, 1522–4

AID economic aid to developing countries, obligations and disbursements by country, quarterly rpt, 9912–4

AID loans repayment status and terms by program and country, and status of predecessor agency loans, quarterly rpt, 9912–3

Background Notes, summary social, political, and economic data, 1990 rpt, 7006–2.43

Economic and military aid and loans from US and intl agencies, by program and country, FY46-90, annual rpt, 9914–5

Economic and social conditions of developing countries from 1960s, and Intl Dev Cooperation Agency and AID activities and funding, FY90-92, annual rpt, 9904–4

Economic conditions, income, production, prices, employment, and trade, 1991 periodic country rpt, 2046–4.58

Economic, population, and agricultural data, US and other aid sources, and AID activity, 1989 country rpt, 9916–12.32; 9916–12.39

Economic, social, political, and geographic summary data, by country, 1991, annual factbook, 9114–2

Exports and imports of US, by transport mode, country, and SITC 1- to 3-digit commodity, 1990, annual rpt, 2424–12

Exports of US, detailed Schedule B commodities with countries of destination, 1990, annual rpt, 2424–10

Human rights conditions in 170 countries, and US economic and military aid, 1990, annual rpt, 21384–3

Military aid of US, arms sales, and training programs costs and budget requests, by program, world region, and country, FY90-92, annual rpt, 7144–13

UN voting record and share of votes in agreement with US, by issue, country, and world area, 1990, annual rpt, 7004–18

Sweden

Agricultural exports of high-value commodities, indexes and sales by commodity, world area, and country, 1960s-86, 1528–323

Agricultural exports of US, impacts of foreign agricultural and trade policy, with data by commodity and country, 1989, annual rpt, 1924–8

Agricultural production, prices, and trade, by country, 1970s-90, and forecast 1991, annual world region rpt, 1524–4.4

Agricultural production, trade, and policies in foreign countries, summary data by country, 1989-90, annual factbook, 1924–12

Agricultural trade of US, by detailed commodity and country, 1989, annual rpt, 1524–8

Agricultural trade of US, by detailed commodity and country, 1990, semiannual rpt, 1522–4

AID loans repayment status and terms by program and country, and status of predecessor agency loans, quarterly rpt, 9912–3

Cancer cases among persons treated for thyroid disorders with radionuclide iodine-131, for Sweden, 1950-85 study, article, 4472–1.218

Corporations in US under foreign control, income tax returns, assets and income statement items by industry div, country, and world area, 1988, article, 8302–2.219

Sweden

Economic and military aid and loans from US and intl agencies, by program and country, FY46-90, annual rpt, 9914–5

Economic and monetary trends, compounded annual rates of change for US and 10 major trading partners, quarterly rpt, 9391–7

Economic conditions in USSR, Eastern Europe, OECD, and selected other countries, 1960s-90, annual rpt, 9114–4

Economic conditions, income, production, prices, employment, and trade, 1991 periodic country rpt, 2046–4.47

Economic conditions, policy, and trade practices, by country, 1988-90, annual rpt, 21384–5

Economic, social, political, and geographic summary data, by country, 1991, annual factbook, 9114–2

Energy prices, by fuel type and end use, for 10 countries, 1980-89 annual rpt, 3164–50.6

Exports and imports of OECD members, by country, 1989, annual rpt, 7144–10

Exports and imports of US, by Harmonized System 6-digit commodity and country, 1990, annual rpt, 2424–13

Exports and imports of US, by selected country, country group, and commodity group, 1990, annual rpt, 2044–37

Exports and imports of US, by transport mode, country, and SITC 1- to 3-digit commodity, 1990, annual rpt, 2424–12

Exports of US, detailed Schedule B commodities with countries of destination, 1990, annual rpt, 2424–10

GNP and GNP growth for OECD members, by country, 1980-90, annual rpt, 7144–8

Human rights conditions in 170 countries, and US economic and military aid, 1990, annual rpt, 21384–3

Imports of goods, services, and investment from US, trade barriers, impacts, and US actions, by country, 1990, annual rpt, 444–2

Imports of US given duty-free treatment for value of US material sent abroad, by commodity and country, 1989, annual rpt, 9884–14

Investment (foreign direct) in US, by industry group of US affiliate and country of parent firm, 1980-86, 2708–41

Labor conditions, union coverage, and work accidents, 1990 annual country rpt, 6366–4.1

Multinatl US firms and foreign affiliates finances and operations, by industry and world area of parent firm, 1989 benchmark survey, preliminary annual rpt, 2704–5

Multinatl US firms foreign affiliates, income statement items by country and world area, 1986, biennial article, 8302–2.212

Nuclear power generation in US and 20 countries, monthly rpt, 3162–24.10

Nuclear power plant capacity, generation, and operating status, by plant and foreign and US location, 1990 and projected to 2030, annual rpt, 3164–57

Oil production, trade, use, and stocks, by selected country and country group, monthly rpt, 3162–42

Paper (coated groundwood) from 9 countries at less than fair value, injury to US industry, investigation with background financial and operating data, 1991 rpt, 9886–14.306

Science and engineering employment and education, and R&D spending, for US and selected foreign countries, 1991 annual rpt, 9627–35

Science and engineering employment, by professional characteristics, age, and sex, for selected countries, 1991 working paper, 2326–18.63

Spacecraft and satellite launches since 1957, quarterly listing, 9502–2

Tax revenue, by level of govt and type of tax, for OECD countries, mid 1960s-89, annual rpt, 10044–1.2

Telecommunications industry intl competitiveness, with financial and operating data by product or service, firm, and country, 1990 rpt, 2008–30

Transportation energy use, fuel prices, vehicle registrations, and mileage, by selected country, 1970s-89, annual rpt, 3304–5.1

UN voting record and share of votes in agreement with US, by issue, country, and world area, 1990, annual rpt, 7004–18

see also By Foreign Country in the "Index by Categories"

Sweeteners

see Honey and beekeeping

see Sugar industry and products

see Syrups and sweeteners

Swimming

Coastal areas recreation facilities of Fed Govt and States, visitor and site characteristics, 1987-90 survey, regional rpt series, 2176–9

Forest Service activities and finances, by region and State, FY90, annual rpt, 1204–1.1

Injuries from use of consumer products, by severity, victim age, and detailed product, 1990, annual rpt, 9164–6

Shigellosis risk from swimming in park pond, 1989 local area study, article, 4042–3.224

see also Drowning

see also Swimming pools

Swimming pools

Apartment completions by region and metro-nonmetro location, and absorption rate, by size and rent class, preliminary 1990, annual Current Housing Rpt, 2484–3

Apartment market absorption rates and characteristics for nonsubsidized furnished and unfurnished units, 1989, annual Current Housing Rpt, 2484–2

Coastal areas recreation facilities of Fed Govt and States, visitor and site characteristics, 1987-90 survey, regional rpt series, 2176–9

Construction industries census, 1987: establishments, employment, receipts, and expenditures, by SIC 4-digit industry and State, final industry rpt series, 2373–1

Franchise business opportunities by firm and kind of business, and sources of aid and info, 1990 annual listing, 2104–7

Injuries from use of consumer products, by severity, victim age, and detailed product, 1990, annual rpt, 9164–6

Solar collector and photovoltaic module shipments by end-use sector and State, and trade, 1989, annual rpt, 3164–62

Swine

see Livestock and livestock industry

Switzer, Josephine C.

"Catalogue of U.S. Geological Survey Strong-Motion Records, 1988", 5664–14

Switzerland

Agricultural exports of high-value commodities, indexes and sales by commodity, world area, and country, 1960s-86, 1528–323

Agricultural exports of US, impacts of foreign agricultural and trade policy, with data by commodity and country, 1989, annual rpt, 1924–8

Agricultural production, prices, and trade, by country, 1970s-90, and forecast 1991, annual world region rpt, 1524–4.4

Agricultural production, trade, and policies in foreign countries, summary data by country, 1989-90, annual factbook, 1924–12

Agricultural trade of US, by detailed commodity and country, 1989, annual rpt, 1524–8

Agricultural trade of US, by detailed commodity and country, 1990, semiannual rpt, 1522–4

Banks capital costs, operating ratios, and intl market shares, for US and 5 OECD countries, 1980s-90, article, 9385–1.203

Businesses (foreign) activity in US, income tax returns, assets, and income statement items, by industry div and selected country, 1986-87, article, 8302–2.205

Corporations in US under foreign control, income tax returns, assets and income statement items by industry div, country, and world area, 1988, article, 8302–2.219

Economic and military aid and loans from US and intl agencies, by program and country, FY46-90, annual rpt, 9914–5

Economic and monetary trends, compounded annual rates of change and quarterly indicators for US and 7 major industrialized countries, quarterly rpt, 9391–7

Economic conditions in USSR, Eastern Europe, OECD, and selected other countries, 1960s-90, annual rpt, 9114–4

Economic conditions, income, production, prices, employment, and trade, 1991 periodic country rpt, 2046–4.33; 2046–4.65

Economic conditions, policy, and trade practices, by country, 1988-90, annual rpt, 21384–5

Economic, social, political, and geographic summary data, by country, 1991, annual factbook, 9114–2

Exports and imports of OECD members, by country, 1989, annual rpt, 7144–10

Exports and imports of US, by Harmonized System 6-digit commodity and country, 1990, annual rpt, 2424–13

Exports and imports of US, by selected country, country group, and commodity group, 1990, annual rpt, 2044–37

Exports and imports of US, by transport mode, country, and SITC 1- to 3-digit commodity, 1990, annual rpt, 2424–12

Exports, imports, and balances of US with major trading partners, by product category, 1986-90, annual chartbook, 9884–21

Index by Subjects and Names

Exports of US, detailed Schedule B commodities with countries of destination, 1990, annual rpt, 2424–10

GNP and GNP growth for OECD members, by country, 1980-90, annual rpt, 7144–8

Human rights conditions in 170 countries, and US economic and military aid, 1990, annual rpt, 21384–3

Imports of goods, services, and investment from US, trade barriers, impacts, and US actions, by country, 1990, annual rpt, 444–2

Imports of US given duty-free treatment for value of US material sent abroad, by commodity and country, 1989, annual rpt, 9884–14

Interest and exchange rates, security yields, and stock indexes, for selected foreign countries, weekly chartbook, 9365–1.5

Investment (foreign direct) in US, by industry group of US affiliate and country of parent firm, 1980-86, 2708–41

Investment (foreign direct) in US, major transactions by type, industry, country, and US location, 1989, annual rpt, 2044–20

Labor conditions, union coverage, and work accidents, 1991 annual country rpt, 6366–4.36

Monetary aggregates alternative indexes relation to inflation and monetary base, for Switzerland, 1970s-89, article, 9391–1.221

Multinatl firms US affiliates, finances, and operations, by industry, world area of parent firm, and State, 1988-89, annual rpt, 2704–4

Multinatl US firms and foreign affiliates finances and operations, by industry and world area of parent firm, 1989 benchmark survey, preliminary annual rpt, 2704–5

Multinatl US firms foreign affiliates, income statement items by country and world area, 1986, biennial article, 8302–2.212

Nuclear power generation in US and 20 countries, monthly rpt, 3162–24.10

Nuclear power plant capacity, generation, and operating status, by plant and foreign and US location, 1990 and projected to 2030, annual rpt, 3164–57

Oil production, trade, use, and stocks, by selected country and country group, monthly rpt, 3162–42

Tax revenue, by level of govt and type of tax, for OECD countries, mid 1960s-89, annual rpt, 10044–1.2

see also under By Foreign Country in the "Index by Categories"

Symposiums

see Conferences

Synthetic fibers and fabrics

Business statistics, detailed data for major industries and economic indicators, *Survey of Current Business*, monthly rpt, 2702–1.22

Clothing and shoe production, shipments, trade, and use, by product, periodic Current Industrial Rpt series, 2506–6

County Business Patterns, 1988: employment, establishments, and payroll, by SIC 2- to 4-digit industry and county, annual State rpt series, 2326–6

County Business Patterns, 1989: employment, establishments, and payroll, by SIC 2- to 4-digit industry and county, annual State rpt series, 2326–8

Employment, earnings, and hours, by SIC 1- to 4-digit industry, monthly and annual averages, selected years 1909-90, annual rpt, 6744–4

Exports and imports of US, by country and detailed commodity, monthly rpt, 2422–12

Exports and imports of US, by Harmonized System 6-digit commodity and country, 1990, annual rpt, 2424–13

Exports and imports of US, by transport mode, country, and SITC 1- to 3-digit commodity, 1990, annual rpt, 2424–12

Exports of US, detailed Schedule B commodities with countries of destination, 1990, annual rpt, 2424–10

Imports of textiles, by country of origin, monthly rpt, 2042–27

Imports of textiles, by product and country of origin, monthly rpt series, 2046–8; 2046–9

Imports of textiles under Multifiber Arrangement by product and country, and status of bilateral agreements, 1987-90, annual rpt, 9884–18

Labor productivity, indexes of output, hours, and employment by SIC 2- to 4-digit industry, 1967-89, annual rpt, 6824–1.3

Manufacturing annual survey, 1989: finances and operations, by SIC 2- to 4-digit industry, series, 2506–15

Manufacturing census, 1987: finances and operations, by SIC 2- to 4-digit industry, State, and MSA, with trends from 1849, 2497–1

Manufacturing census, 1987: finances and operations, by type of organization and SIC 2- to 4-digit industry, subject rpt, 2497–5

Manufacturing finances and operations, by SIC 2- to 4-digit industry, forecast 1991, annual rpt, 2044–28

Occupational injury and illness rates, by SIC 2- to 4-digit industry, 1988-89, annual rpt, 6844–7

Occupational injury and illness rates, by SIC 2- to 4-digit industry, 1989, annual rpt, 6844–1

Price indexes (producer), by stage of processing and detailed commodity, monthly rpt, 6762–6

Price indexes (producer), by stage of processing and detailed commodity, monthly 1990, annual rpt, 6764–2

Production, prices, trade, and use of cotton, wool, and synthetic fibers, periodic situation rpt with articles, 1561–1

Production, trade, sales, stocks, and material used, by product, region, and State, periodic Current Industrial Rpt series, 2506–5

Rayon yarn (high-tenacity filament) from 2 countries at less than fair value, injury to US industry, investigation with background financial and operating data, 1991 rpt, 9886–14.331

Soviet Union, Eastern Europe, OECD, and selected other countries consumer and producer goods and services production and sales, 1960s-90, annual rpt, 9114–4.7

Statistical Abstract of US, 1991 annual data compilation, 2324–1.27

Synthetic food products

Nutrient, caloric, and waste composition of food, detailed data for raw, processed, and prepared foods, series, 1356–3

Synthetic fuels

Electric power plants and capacity, by fuel used, owner, location, and operating status, 1990 and for units planned 1991-2000, annual listing, 3164–36

Natl Energy Strategy, coal liquids production under alternative oil price and technology assumptions, projected 2000-2030, 3166–6.53

Natl Energy Strategy plans for conservation and pollution reduction, impacts of technology and regulation proposals, projected 1990-2030, 3166–6.47

Synthetic products

see Chemicals and chemical industry

see Plastics and plastics industry

see Synthetic fibers and fabrics

see Synthetic food products

see Synthetic fuels

Syphilis

see Sexually transmitted diseases

Syracuse, N.Y.

see also under By City and By SMSA or MSA in the "Index by Categories"

Syria

Agricultural exports of high-value commodities, indexes and sales by commodity, world area, and country, 1960s-86, 1528–323

Agricultural trade of US, by detailed commodity and country, 1989, annual rpt, 1524–8

Agricultural trade of US, by detailed commodity and country, 1990, semiannual rpt, 1522–4

AID economic aid to developing countries, obligations and disbursements by country, quarterly rpt, 9912–4

AID loans repayment status and terms by program and country, and status of predecessor agency loans, quarterly rpt, 9912–3

Economic and military aid and loans from US and intl agencies, by program and country, FY46-90, annual rpt, 9914–5

Economic conditions, income, production, prices, employment, and trade, 1991 periodic country rpt, 2046–4.28

Economic conditions, policy, and trade practices, by country, 1988-90, annual rpt, 21384–5

Economic, social, political, and geographic summary data, by country, 1991, annual factbook, 9114–2

Export controls and trade of US with Middle East countries, with dual-use commodity licenses and arms sales, 1980s-90, GAO rpt, 26123–339

Exports and imports of US, by commodity and country, 1970-89, world area rpt, 9116–1.1

Exports and imports of US, by selected country, country group, and commodity group, 1990, annual rpt, 2044–37

Exports and imports of US, by transport mode, country, and SITC 1- to 3-digit commodity, 1990, annual rpt, 2424–12

Exports of US, detailed Schedule B commodities with countries of destination, 1990, annual rpt, 2424–10

Syria

Human rights conditions in 170 countries, and US economic and military aid, 1990, annual rpt, 21384–3

UN voting record and share of votes in agreement with US, by issue, country, and world area, 1990, annual rpt, 7004–18

see also under By Foreign Country in the "Index by Categories"

Syrups and sweeteners

Agricultural Statistics, 1990, annual rpt, 1004–1

Confectionery shipments, trade, use, and ingredients used, by product, 1990, annual Current Industrial Rpt, 2506–4.5

Consumer Expenditure Survey, food spending by item, household composition, income, age, race, and region, 1980-88, biennial rpt, 1544–30

Consumption and trade by commodity, quarterly situation rpt with articles, 1561–14

Consumption, supply, trade, prices, spending, and indexes, by food commodity, 1989, annual rpt, 1544–4

County Business Patterns, 1988: employment, establishments, and payroll, by SIC 2- to 4-digit industry and county, annual State rpt series, 2326–6

County Business Patterns, 1989: employment, establishments, and payroll, by SIC 2- to 4-digit industry and county, annual State rpt series, 2326–8

Exports and imports (agricultural) of US, by commodity and country, bimonthly rpt, 1522–1

Exports and imports (agricultural) of US, by detailed commodity and country, 1989, annual rpt, 1524–8

Exports and imports (agricultural) of US, by detailed commodity and country, 1990, semiannual rpt, 1522–4

Exports and imports of US, by country and detailed commodity, monthly rpt, 2422–12

Exports and imports of US, by Harmonized System 6-digit commodity and country, 1990, annual rpt, 2424–13

Exports of US, detailed Schedule B commodities with countries of destination, 1990, annual rpt, 2424–10

Farm financial and marketing conditions, forecast 1991, annual conf, 1004–16

Farm income, expenses, receipts by commodity, assets, liabilities, and ratios, 1990 and trends from 1945, annual rpt, 1544–16

Futures and options trading volume, by commodity and exchange, FY90, annual rpt, 11924–2

Manufacturing annual survey, 1989: finances and operations, by SIC 2- to 4-digit industry, series, 2506–15

Manufacturing census, 1987: finances and operations, by SIC 2- to 4-digit industry, State, and MSA, with trends from 1849, 2497–1

Manufacturing census, 1987: finances and operations, by type of organization and SIC 2- to 4-digit industry, subject rpt, 2497–5

Molasses (feed) wholesale prices by market area, and trade, weekly rpt, 1311–16

Molasses supply, use, wholesale prices by market, and imports by country, 1985-90, annual rpt, 1311–19

Nutrient, caloric, and waste composition, detailed data for raw, processed, and prepared snacks and sweets, 1991 rpt, 1356–3.16

Occupational injury and illness rates, by SIC 2- to 4-digit industry, 1988-89, annual rpt, 6844–7

Occupational injury and illness rates, by SIC 2- to 4-digit industry, 1989, annual rpt, 6844–1

Price indexes (producer), by stage of processing and detailed commodity, monthly rpt, 6762–6

Price indexes (producer), by stage of processing and detailed commodity, monthly 1990, annual rpt, 6764–2

see also Honey and beekeeping

see also Sugar industry and products

Systan Inc.

"HOV Lane Violation Study", 7308–203

SysteMetrics/McGraw-Hill, Inc.

"Alternative Hospital Market Area Definitions", 17206–2.20

"Within DRG Case Complexity: Change Update and Distributional Differences", 17206–2.21

Szilagyi, John A.

"Whatever Happened to Child Care in 1989?", 8304–8.1

Tabellini, Guido

"Optimality of Nominal Contracts", 9379–12.76

Tableware

see Household supplies and utensils

Tacoma, Wash.

CPI by component for US city average, and by region, population size, and for 27 metro areas, monthly rpt, 6762–2

Fruit and vegetable shipments, and arrivals in US and Canada cities, by mode of transport and State and country of origin, 1990, annual rpt, 1311–4.2

Housing and households characteristics, 1987 survey, MSA fact sheet, 2485–11.2

Housing starts and completions authorized by building permits in 40 MSAs, quarterly rpt, 2382–9

Unemployment insurance job search services, impacts on UI claims activity and reemployment, and claimant characteristics, for Tacoma, Wash, 1986-87, 6406–6.35

Wages by occupation, for office and plant workers, 1991 survey, periodic MSA rpt, 6785–3.5

see also under By City and By SMSA or MSA in the "Index by Categories"

Taha, Fawzi A.

"Wool Prices Liberalized in International Markets", 1561–1.207

Taiwan

Agricultural exports of high-value commodities, indexes and sales by commodity, world area, and country, 1960s-86, 1528–323

Agricultural exports of US, impacts of foreign agricultural and trade policy, with data by commodity and country, 1989, annual rpt, 1924–8

Agricultural production, prices, and trade, by country, 1980s and forecast 1991, annual world region rpt, 1524–4.5

Index by Subjects and Names

Agricultural production, trade, and policies in foreign countries, summary data by country, 1989-90, annual factbook, 1924–12

Agricultural trade by commodity and country, prices, and world market devs, monthly rpt, 1922–12

Agricultural trade of US, by detailed commodity and country, 1989, annual rpt, 1524–8

Agricultural trade of US, by detailed commodity and country, 1990, semiannual rpt, 1522–4

AID loans repayment status and terms by program and country, and status of predecessor agency loans, quarterly rpt, 9912–3

Background Notes, summary social, political, and economic data, 1991 rpt, 7006–2.51

Bearings (ball) from 14 countries, injury to US industry from foreign subsidized and less than fair value imports, investigation with background financial and operating data, 1991 rpt, 9886–19.74

Building materials imports, and share from US, by commodity, 1989-90, article, 2042–1.205

Economic and military aid and loans from US and intl agencies, by program and country, FY46-90, annual rpt, 9914–5

Economic conditions, and oil supply and demand, for major industrial countries, biweekly rpt, 9112–1

Economic conditions in USSR, Eastern Europe, OECD, and selected other countries, 1960s-90, annual rpt, 9114–4

Economic conditions, income, production, prices, employment, and trade, 1990 periodic country rpt, 2046–4.8

Economic conditions, policy, and trade practices, by country, 1988-90, annual rpt, 21384–5

Economic, social, political, and geographic summary data, by country, 1991, annual factbook, 9114–2

Energy use in developing countries, and economic and environmental impacts, by fuel type, world area, and country, 1980s-90, 26358–232

Export and import balances of US, and dollar exchange rates, with 5 Asian countries, 1991 semiannual rpt, 8002–14

Exports and imports of US, by commodity and country, 1970-89, world area rpt, 9116–1.7

Exports and imports of US by country, and trade shifts by commodity, 1990, semiannual rpt, 9882–9

Exports and imports of US, by Harmonized System 6-digit commodity and country, 1990, annual rpt, 2424–13

Exports and imports of US, by selected country, country group, and commodity group, 1990, annual rpt, 2044–37

Exports and imports of US, by transport mode, country, and SITC 1- to 3-digit commodity, 1990, annual rpt, 2424–12

Exports and imports, trade agreements and relations, and USITC investigations, 1990, annual rpt, 9884–5

Exports, imports, and balances of US with major trading partners, by product category, 1986-90, annual chartbook, 9884–21

Exports of US, detailed Schedule B commodities with countries of destination, 1990, annual rpt, 2424–10

Human rights conditions in 170 countries, and US economic and military aid, 1990, annual rpt, 21384–3

Imports of goods, services, and investment from US, trade barriers, impacts, and US actions, by country, 1990, annual rpt, 444–2

Imports of US given duty-free treatment for value of US material sent abroad, by commodity and country, 1989, annual rpt, 9884–14

Interest rates relation to money supply, industrial production, and US interest rate, for Taiwan, late 1980s, working paper, 9371–10.56

Labor conditions, union coverage, and work accidents, 1990 annual country rpt, 6366–4.7

Labor force educational attainment index relation to GDP growth, for Taiwan, 1960s-86, working paper, 9371–10.55

Lug nuts (chrome-plated) from PRC and Taiwan at less than fair value, injury to US industry, investigation with background financial and operating data, 1991 rpt, 9886–14.329

Multinatl US firms and foreign affiliates finances and operations, by industry and world area of parent firm, 1989 benchmark survey, preliminary annual rpt, 2704–5

Multinatl US firms foreign affiliates, income statement items by country and world area, 1986, biennial article, 8302–2.212

Mushroom (canned) trade, supply, and demand, for selected countries, 1980s-91, article, 1925–34.242

Nuclear power generation in US and 20 countries, monthly rpt, 3162–24.10

Nuclear power plant capacity, generation, and operating status, by plant and foreign and US location, 1990 and projected to 2030, annual rpt, 3164–57

Pipes and tubes (welded nonalloy steel) from 6 countries, injury to US industry from foreign subsidized and less than fair value imports, investigation with background financial and operating data, 1991 rpt, 9886–19.81

Science and engineering employment, by selected characteristics, for 3 countries, 1991 working paper, 2326–18.61

Ships freight rates for lumber from Alaska and Puget Sound to Asian markets, by product and port, 1988, 1208–358

Steel wire rope from 4 countries, injury to US industry from foreign subsidized and less than fair value imports, investigation with background financial and operating data, 1991 rpt, 9886–19.79

Steel wire rope from 8 countries, injury to US industry from foreign subsidized and less than fair value imports, investigation with background financial and operating data, 1990 rpt, 9886–19.73

Timber in northwestern US and British Columbia, production, prices, trade, and employment, quarterly rpt, 1202–3

Talc

see Nonmetallic minerals and mines

Tallahassee, Fla.

see also under By City and By SMSA or MSA in the "Index by Categories"

Talley, Nicholas J.

"Gastric Adenocarcinoma and *Helicobacter pylori* Infection", 4472–1.236

Tallman, Ellis W.

"Fiscal Policy and Trade Adjustment: Are the Deficits Really Twins?", 9371–10.60

"Human Capital and Endogenous Growth: Evidence from Taiwan", 9371–10.55

"Investigating U.S. Government and Trade Deficits", 9371–1.207

"Money Demand and Relative Prices in the German Hyperinflation", 9371–10.66

Tallow and grease

see Oils, oilseeds, and fats

Tampa, Fla.

Housing starts and completions authorized by building permits in 40 MSAs, quarterly rpt, 2382–9

see also under By City and By SMSA or MSA in the "Index by Categories"

Tanker ships

Accidents involving merchant ships, and casualties, by circumstances and characteristics of persons and vessels involved, 1988, annual rpt, 7404–11

Accidents involving ships and marine facilities, casualties, and circumstances, Coast Guard investigation results, periodic rpt, 9612–4

Construction and operating subsidies of MarAd by firm, and ship deliveries and fleet by country, by vessel type, FY90, annual rpt, 7704–14.1; 7704–14.2

Construction and repair facilities, capacity, and employment, by shipyard, 1990, annual rpt, 7704–9

Exports and imports (waterborne) of US, by type of service, commodity, country, route, and US port, 1988, annual rpt, 7704–2

Exports and imports (waterborne) of US, by type of service, customs district, port, and world area, monthly rpt, 2422–7

Foreign and US merchant ships, tonnage, and new ship construction and deliveries, by vessel type and country, as of Jan 1990, annual rpt, 7704–3

Foreign and US tanker fleet, characteristics by country of registry, annual listing, discontinued, 7704–17

Foreign-flag ships owned by US firms and foreign affiliates, by type, owner, and country of registry and construction, as of Jan. 1991, semiannual rpt, 7702–3

Merchant ships in US fleet and Natl Defense Reserve Fleet, vessels, tonnage, and owner, as of Jan 1991, semiannual listing, 7702–2

Merchant ships in US fleet, operating subsidies, construction, and ship-related employment, monthly rpt, 7702–1

Military Sealift Command shipping operations, finances, and personnel, FY90, annual rpt, 3804–14

Natl transportation system planning, use, condition, accidents, and needs, by mode of transport, 1940s-90 and projected to 2020, 7308–202

Oil and refined products stocks, and interdistrict shipments by mode of transport, monthly rpt, 3162–6.3

Oil bulk stations, sales and storage capacity by product, inventories, expenses, employment, and modes of transport, 1987 Census of Wholesale Trade, 2407–4.2

Oil import traffic by US port and vessel type, marine oil pollution sources, and costs and operations of proposed offshore terminals, late 1980s, 5738–25

Oil refinery crude received, by mode of transport and PAD district, 1990, annual rpt, 3164–2.1

Oil spills from tankers worldwide, selected years 1964-90, annual rpt, 5734–3.6

Oil tanker inbound freight price indexes, quarterly press release, 6762–13

Publications and data files of Census Bur on foreign trade, 1991 guide, 2428–11

St Lawrence Seaway ship, cargo, and passenger traffic, and toll revenue, 1990 and trends from 1959, annual rpt, 7744–2

Tanks

see Military vehicles

Tannenwald, Robert

"Cyclical Swing or Secular Slide? Why Have New England's Banks Been Losing Money?", 9373–1.220

Tanning industry

see Hides and skins

see Leather industry and products

Tansey, John B.

"Changes in Florida's Industrial Roundwood Products Output, 1977-87", 1208–352

"Changes in South Carolina's Industrial Timber Products Output, 1988", 1208–359

Tanzania

Agricultural exports of high-value commodities, indexes and sales by commodity, world area, and country, 1960s-86, 1528–323

Agricultural production, trade, and policies in foreign countries, summary data by country, 1989-90, annual factbook, 1924–12

Agricultural trade of US, by detailed commodity and country, 1989, annual rpt, 1524–8

Agricultural trade of US, by detailed commodity and country, 1990, semiannual rpt, 1522–4

AID economic aid to developing countries, obligations and disbursements by country, quarterly rpt, 9912–4

AID loans repayment status and terms by program and country, and status of predecessor agency loans, quarterly rpt, 9912–3

Dairy imports, consumption, and market conditions, by sub-Saharan Africa country, 1961-88, 1528–321

Economic and military aid and loans from US and intl agencies, by program and country, FY46-90, annual rpt, 9914–5

Economic and social conditions of developing countries from 1960s, and Intl Dev Cooperation Agency and AID activities and funding, FY90-92, annual rpt, 9904–4

Economic conditions, income, production, prices, employment, and trade, 1990 periodic country rpt, 2046–4.6

Economic, population, and agricultural data, US and other aid sources, and AID activity, 1989 country rpt, 9916–12.32

Tanzania

Economic, social, political, and geographic summary data, by country, 1991, annual factbook, 9114–2

Exports and imports of US, by commodity and country, 1970-89, world area rpt, 9116–1.6

Exports and imports of US, by transport mode, country, and SITC 1- to 3-digit commodity, 1990, annual rpt, 2424–12

Exports of US, detailed Schedule B commodities with countries of destination, 1990, annual rpt, 2424–10

Food supply, needs, and aid for developing countries, status and alternative forecasts, 1991 world area rpt, 1526–8.1

Human rights conditions in 170 countries, and US economic and military aid, 1990, annual rpt, 21384–3

Military aid of US, arms sales, and training programs costs and budget requests, by program, world region, and country, FY90-92, annual rpt, 7144–13

UN voting record and share of votes in agreement with US, by issue, country, and world area, 1990, annual rpt, 7004–18

see also under By Foreign Country in the "Index by Categories"

Tape recordings and taping equipment

see Home video and audio equipment

see Recording industry

Tar

see Asphalt and tar

see Gum and wood chemicals

see Tar sands

Tar sands

Natl Energy Strategy, coal liquids production under alternative oil price and technology assumptions, projected 2000-2030, 3166–6.53

Natl Energy Strategy plans for conservation and pollution reduction, impacts of technology and regulation proposals, projected 1990-2030, 3166–6.47

Taren, Douglas L.

"Association of Prenatal Nutrition and Educational Services with Low Birth Weight Rates in a Florida Program", 4042–3.235

Tariff Commission

see U.S. International Trade Commission

Tariffs and foreign trade controls

Agricultural exports of US, impacts of foreign agricultural and trade policy, with data by commodity and country, 1989, annual rpt, 1924–8

Alaska North Slope oil production, and impacts of lifting export controls on US oil trade, West Coast prices, and shipping industry, 1988 and forecast 1995, GAO rpt, 26113–496

Auto imports duties and origin preference eligibility rules under proposed North American Free Trade Agreement, 1978-91, 9886–4.178

Auto trade of Canada and US, and production, sales, prices, and employment, selected years 1965-88, annual rpt, 2044–35

Bean (dried) prices by State, market activity, and foreign and US production, use, stocks, and trade, weekly rpt, 1311–17

Budget of US, authoritative financial statements with appropriations, outlays, and receipts, by category and agency, FY90, annual rpt, 8104–2.1

Budget of US, CBO analysis of revenue and spending alternatives and projections of economic indicators, FY92-96, annual rpt, 26304–3

Budget of US, midsession review of FY92 budget, by function, annual rpt, 104–7

Budget of US, obligations and authority by function, agency, and program, with summaries, analyses, and historical tables, FY92, annual rpt, 104–2

Budget of US, receipts by source, outlays by agency and program, and balances, monthly rpt, 8102–3

Bulgaria trade with US, US tariffs, and impacts of US granting most favored nation status, 1987-90, GAO rpt, 26123–323

Business America, foreign and domestic commerce, and US investment and trade opportunities, biweekly journal, 2042–24

Canada tariffs for storing and cleaning wheat, 1990 hearings, 25168–75

Caribbean area duty-free exports to US, and imports from US, by country, and impact on US employment, by commodity, 1990, annual rpt, 6364–2

Caribbean area duty-free exports to US, by commodity and country, with consumer and industry impacts, 1984-90, annual rpt, 9884–20

China trade policy changes, Jan 1988-Jan 1991, 9118–9

China trade with US and through Hong Kong, and impacts of revoking most favored nation status, 1987-90, hearing, 25368–174

Coffee production, trade and quotas, and use, by country, with US and intl prices, FAS periodic circular, 1925–5

Cotton, wool, and synthetic fiber production, prices, trade, and use, periodic situation rpt with articles, 1561–1

Criminal sentences for Federal offenses, guidelines by offense and circumstances, series, 17668–1

Customs collections, for top 15 ports, quarterly rpt, discontinued, 8142–1

Customs Service activities, and collections total and for selected ports, bimonthly journal, 8142–2

Customs Service activities, collections, entries processed by mode of transport, and seizures, FY86-90, annual rpt, 8144–1

Dairy imports under quota by commodity, by country of origin, FAS monthly rpt, 1925–31

Developing countries agricultural supply, demand, and market for US exports, with socioeconomic conditions, country rpt series, 1526–6

EC economic integration economic impacts, with background data by country, 1988-90, article, 9379–1.201

Employment and industry impacts of trade, series, 6366–3

Endangered animals and plants US trade and permits, by species, purpose, disposition, and country, 1989, annual rpt, 5504–19

Energy producers finances and operations, by energy type for US firms domestic and foreign operations, 1989, annual rpt, 3164–44.1

Export and import agreements, negotiations, and related legislation, 1990, annual rpt, 444–1

Export licensing, monitoring, and enforcement activities, FY90, annual rpt, 2024–1

Exports and imports, trade agreements and relations, and USITC investigations, 1990, annual rpt, 9884–5

Exports, imports, and trade flows, by country and commodity, with background economic indicators, data compilation, monthly CD-ROM, 2002–6

Exports of goods, services, and investment, trade barriers, impacts, and US actions, by country, 1989, annual rpt, 444–2

Fed Govt consolidated financial statements based on business accounting methods, FY89-90, annual rpt, 8104–5

Fed Govt receipts by source and outlays by agency, *Treasury Bulletin*, quarterly rpt, 8002–4.1

Fed Govt tax revenues, by type of tax, quarterly rpt, 2462–3

Fish (surimi) production and trade by country, and Japan import and catch quotas, 1975-89, article, 2162–1.202

Fish and shellfish foreign market conditions for US products, country rpt series, 2166–19

Fish import duties collected, 1980s-90, annual rpt, 2164–1.6

Foreign countries agricultural production, prices, and trade, by country, 1980-90 and forecast 1991, annual world area rpt series, 1524–4

Foreign countries economic conditions, policy, and trade practices, by country, 1988-90, annual rpt, 21384–5

Fruit trade of US with Mexico, and US import duties, by commodity, 1970s-90, article, 1561–6.203

GATT Standards Code info activities of Natl Inst of Standards and Technology, and proposed standards by agency and country, 1990, annual rpt, 2214–6

GATT Uruguay Round negotiations economic and trade impacts for US, with background data and foreign comparisons, 1970s-90, technical paper, 9385–8.115

Generalized System of Preferences status, and US tariffs, with trade by country and US economic impacts, for selected commodities, 1985-89, annual rpt, 9884–23

Imports and tariff provisions effect on US industries and products, investigations with background financial and operating data, series, 9886–4

Imports injury to US industries from foreign subsidized products and sales at less than fair value, investigations with background financial and operating data, series, 9886–19

Imports injury to US industries from foreign subsidized products, investigations with background financial and operating data, series, 9886–15

Imports injury to US industries from sales at less than fair value, investigations with background financial and operating data, series, 9886–14

Imports injury to US industries, trade-remedy law petitions brought, by provision, 1979-90, article, 9391–1.215

Index by Subjects and Names

Tax delinquency and evasion

Imports injury to US industries, USITC rpts, 1983-90, annual listing, 9884–12

Imports of US given duty-free treatment for value of US material sent abroad, by commodity and country, 1989, annual rpt, 9884–14

Japan economic conditions, financial and intl policies, and trade devs, 1950s-80s and projected to 2050, compilation of papers, 23848–220

Japan fish catch, prices, trade by country, cold storage holdings, import quotas, and market devs, semimonthly press release, 2162–7

Lumber and wood products exports, imports, and export promotion of US by country, and trade balance, by commodity, FAS quarterly circular, 1925–36

Machine tool procurement by DOD of foreign-made tools, use of restriction waivers by service branch and country, FY86-89, GAO rpt, 26123–324

Maritime Commission activities, case filings by type and disposition, and civil penalties by shipper, FY90, annual rpt, 9334–1

Meat plants inspected and certified for exporting to US, by country, 1990, annual listing, 1374–2

Mexico agricultural trade with US, and import tariffs, by commodity, 1989-90, article, 1925–34.238

Mexico agricultural trade with US by commodity, and trade restrictions, 1980s, GAO rpt, 26123–335

Mexico construction value and trade, and import duties on materials and equipment by type, 1991 article, 2042–1.207

Mexico-US trade agreement proposal, economic impacts with background trade and investment data, 1985-90, 9886–4.168

Mexico vegetable trade with US and US import duties by commodity, and fresh tomato arrivals in US and Canada cities, 1970s-90, article, 1561–11.202

Middle East export controls of US, with trade, dual-use commodity licenses, and arms sales, by country, 1980s-90, GAO rpt, 26123–339

Mineral Industry Surveys, commodity reviews of production, trade, use, and industry operations, advance annual rpt series, 5614–5

Minerals production, prices, trade, use, employment, tariffs, and stockpiles, by mineral, with foreign comparisons, 1986-90, annual rpt, 5604–18

Natl income and product accounts and components, *Survey of Current Business*, monthly rpt, 2702–1.24

Oil import tariff and excise tax economic impacts, model description and results, 1991 paper, 9406–1.61

Overseas Business Reports: economic conditions, investment and export opportunities, and trade practices, country market research rpt series, 2046–6

Philippines agricultural imports tariffs, by commodity, 1991-95, article, 1925–34.235

Pumpkin farms, production costs, shipments, and sales by State, prices, and imports by country, 1978-90, article, 1561–11.203

Rum imports (duty-free) of US under Caribbean Basin Initiative, by country, 1989-90, annual rpt, 9884–15

Senegal cash transfers from AID linked to fiscal and govt reforms, effectiveness, 1980s, 9916–1.75

Sugar and honey foreign and US production, prices, trade, and use, FAS periodic circular series, 1925–14

Sugar and sugar product imports of US under quota, by country, periodic rpt, 1922–9

Sugar production, acreage, use, and trade with US, for Canada, 1950s-98, article, 1561–14.203

Tariff Schedule of US, classifications and rates of duty for detailed imported commodities, and codes for ports and foreign countries, 1992 base edition, 9886–13

Textile, apparel, and shoe import restriction proposals economic impacts, projected 1991-2000, with imports by country, 1989-90, 26306–6.162

Tobacco tariff and tax rates, and antismoking restrictions, by country, as of Jan 1991, article, 1925–16.207

US attorneys civil and criminal cases by type and disposition, and collections, by Federal district, FY90, annual rpt, 6004–2.1

USITC activities, investigations, and rpts, FY90, annual rpt, 9884–1

see also Common markets and free trade areas

see also Dumping

see also International sanctions

Tarone, Robert E.

"Service in Vietnam and Risk of Testicular Cancer", 4472–1.228

Task Force on the International Competitiveness of U.S. Financial Institutions. House

Banking intl competition issues, with background data, 1980s, 21248–153

Japan financial instns and stock market conditions, and other economic indicators, with intl comparisons, 1980s-90, hearing, 21248–152

Task Force To Strengthen Public Health in the U.S.

Findings and recommendations, 1991 narrative rpt, 4042–3.255

Tatom, John A.

"Public Capital and Private Sector Performance", 9391–1.211

"Should Government Spending on Capital Goods Be Raised?", 9391–1.208

Tawas City, Mich.

Wages by occupation, and benefits for office and plant workers, 1991 survey, periodic MSA rpt, 6785–3.8

Tax appeals

see Tax protests and appeals

Tax Court of the U.S.

Budget of US, authoritative financial statements with appropriations, outlays, and receipts, by category and agency, FY90, annual rpt, 8104–2.1

Budget of US, obligations and authority by function, agency, and program, with summaries, analyses, and historical tables, FY92, annual rpt, 104–2

Caseloads of Court and recoveries, FY90, annual tables, 18224–5

Caseloads of US Tax Court, and tax due, by disposition, FY90, annual tables, 18224–3

IRS enforcement and litigation activity, with data by type of tax, FY90, annual rpt, 8304–3.3

Tax courts

see Tax Court of the U.S.

see Tax laws and courts

Tax credits

see Tax expenditures

see Tax incentives and shelters

Tax delinquency and evasion

Amnesty programs of States for delinquent taxpayers, participation, collections, and costs, by tax type and State, 1980s-90, hearing, 21408–125

Computer matching program of IRS to indentify income underreported on tax returns, effectiveness, 1987, GAO rpt, 26119–325

Court criminal case processing in Federal district courts, and dispositions, by offense, district, and offender characteristics, 1986, annual rpt, 6064–29

Court criminal case processing in Federal district courts, and dispositions, by offense, 1980-89, annual rpt, 6064–31

Court criminal cases in Federal district courts, by offense, disposition, and district, 1980-90, last issue of annual rpt, 18204–1

Debt delinquent on Federal accounts, cases and collections of Justice Dept and private law firms, pilot project results, FY90, annual rpt, 6004–20

Drug enforcement regional task forces investigation of organized crime, activities by agency and region, FY83-90, biennial rpt, 6004–17

Fed Govt tax provisions and receipts overview, by tax type, with background data, 1900s-91 and projected to 2000, 21788–197

High-income individuals income tax returns not filed, by selected characteristics, 1987, and assessments under alternative IRS enforcement programs, 1990, GAO rpt, 26119–322

Income tax admin and compliance issues, and taxpayer views, 1990 conf, 8304–25

Income tax returns processing, IRS workload forecasts, compliance, and enforcement, data compilation, 1991 annual rpt, 8304–8

Income tax unpaid accounts receivable of IRS by collection status, and IRS budget and staff, with data by district, 1980s-91, hearing, 21788–200

IRS collections, enforcement, and litigation activity, with data by type of tax, region, and State, FY90, annual rpt, 8304–3

Preparation services negligent and fraudulent tax practices, IRS civil penalty cases and examiners views of program admin, 1989, GAO rpt, 26119–315

Pretrial processing, detention, and release, for Federal offenders, by defendant characteristics and district, 1988, hearing, 25528–114

Refunds of income tax applied by IRS to outstanding debts to Fed Govt, impacts on subsequent taxpayer compliance, 1984-87, GAO rpt, 26119–339

Tax delinquency and evasion

Sentences for Federal crimes, guidelines use and results by offense and district, and Sentencing Commission activities, 1990, annual rpt, 17664–1

Sentences for Federal offenses, guidelines by offense and circumstances, series, 17668–1

Taxpayer opinions about quality of IRS income tax return audits and delinquent tax collection activity, 1989, article, 8304–8.1

Tax exempt organizations

Finances of nonprofit charitable organizations, by asset size and State, 1987, article, 8302–2.218

Hospital tax exempt status dependent on acceptance of charity, Medicare, and Medicaid cases, proposal and issues with background data, 1989, press release, 8008–149

Hotels and other lodging places, revenue, payroll, employment, and merchandise sales, for tax exempt firms by State, 1987 Census of Service Industries, subject rpt, 2393–3.4

IRS collections, by excise tax source, quarterly rpt, 8302–1

IRS collections, enforcement, and litigation activity, with data by type of tax, region, and State, FY90, annual rpt, 8304–3

IRS tax returns and supplemental documents filed, by type, FY89 and projected to FY98, annual article, 8302–2.208

IRS tax returns and supplemental documents filed, by type, FY90 and projected to FY99, semiannual rpt, 8302–4

IRS tax returns filed by type of filer, quarterly rpt, 8302–2.1

IRS tax returns filed, by type of tax and IRS district, 1989 and projected 1990-97, annual rpt, 8304–24

IRS tax returns filed, by type of tax and IRS region and service center, projected 1990-97 and trends from 1978, annual rpt, 8304–9

Service industries census, 1987: establishments, receipts by source, payroll, and employment, by SIC 2- to 4-digit kind of business, State, and MSA, 2393–4

Service industries receipts, by SIC 2- to 4-digit kind of business, 1990, annual rpt, 2413–8

State and Metro Area Data Book, 1991 data compilation, 2328–54

Tax exempt securities

Assets and debts of private sector, balance sheets by segment, 1945-90, semiannual rpt, 9365–4.1

Budget of US, CBO analysis of savings and revenues under alternative spending cuts and tax changes, projected FY92-97, 26306–3.118

Fed Govt tax provisions and receipts overview, by tax type, with background data, 1900s-91 and projected to 2000, 21788–197

Finances of govts, tax systems and revenue, and fiscal structure, by level of govt and State, 1991 and historical trends, annual rpt, 10044–1

Flow-of-funds accounts, savings, investments, and credit statements, quarterly rpt, 9365–3.3

Ownership of govt securities, dealer transactions and financing sources, and new State and local issues, monthly rpt, 9362–1.1

R&D facilities for biological and medical sciences, space and equipment adequacy, needs, and funding by source, by instn type, 1990, biennial rpt, 4434–17

Retirement housing centers tax-exempt bond use and other financing, defaults, and facility and resident characteristics, 1991 GAO rpt, 26119–328

State and local govt competition in taxes, services, regulation, and dev incentives, 1970-89, 10048–79

see also Municipal bonds

Tax expenditures

Budget of US, CBO analysis of revenue and spending alternatives and projections of economic indicators, FY92-96, annual rpt, 26304–3

Budget of US, House concurrent resolution, with spending and revenue targets, FY92 and projected to FY96, annual rpt, 21264–2

Budget of US, obligations and authority by function, agency, and program, with summaries, analyses, and historical tables, FY92, annual rpt, 104–2

Budget of US, Senate concurrent resolution, with spending and revenue targets, FY92, annual rpt, 25254–1

Education funding by Federal agency, program, and recipient type, and instn spending, FY80-90, annual rpt, 4824–8

Fed Govt consolidated financial statements based on business accounting methods, FY89-90, annual rpt, 8104–5

Fed Govt programs under Ways and Means Committee jurisdiction, finances, operations, and participant characteristics, FY70s-90, annual rpt, 21784–11

Fed Govt tax provisions and receipts overview, by tax type, with background data, 1900s-91 and projected to 2000, 21788–197

Income tax deductions and exclusions, Federal tax expenditures by item, FY92-96, annual rpt, 21784–10

Puerto Rico and other US possessions corporations income tax returns, income and tax items, and employment, by selected industry, 1987, article, 8302–2.213

State and local govt competition in taxes, services, regulation, and dev incentives, 1970-89, 10048–79

Statistical Abstract of US, 1991 annual data compilation, 2324–1.10

Tax incentives and shelters

Boycotts (intl) by OPEC and other countries, US firms and shareholders cooperation and tax benefits denied, 1986, annual rpt, 8004–13

Boycotts (intl) by OPEC and other countries, US taxpayers IRS filings, cooperation, and tax benefits denied, 1976-86, GAO rpt, 26119–349

Budget of US, CBO analysis and review of FY92 budget by function, annual rpt, 26304–2

Budget of US, CBO analysis of savings and revenues under alternative spending cuts and tax changes, projected FY92-97, 26306–3.118

Capital gains preferential tax treatment impacts on agricultural finances and operations, 1991 article, 1561–16.202

Caribbean area duty-free exports to US, by commodity and country, with consumer and industry impacts, 1984-90, annual rpt, 9884–20

Child and family health, education, and welfare condition, findings and recommendations, 1991 rpt, 15528–1

Corporations income tax returns, income and tax items by asset size and detailed industry, 1987, annual rpt, 8304–4

Corporations income tax returns, income and tax items by asset size and detailed industry, 1988, annual rpt, 8304–21

Corporations income tax returns, summary data by asset size and industry div, 1987, annual article, 8302–2.204

Corporations income tax returns, summary data by asset size and industry div, 1988, annual article, 8302–2.215; 8302–2.217

Electric utilities privately owned, finances and operations, detailed data, 1989, annual rpt, 3164–23

Employer tax credit for hiring from groups with high unemployment rates, participation by State, and effectiveness, FY88, GAO rpt, 26121–407

Energy producers finances and operations, by energy type for US firms domestic and foreign operations, 1989, annual rpt, 3164–44.1

Fed Govt programs under Ways and Means Committee jurisdiction, finances, operations, and participant characteristics, FY70s-90, annual rpt, 21784–11

Fed Govt tax provisions and receipts overview, by tax type, with background data, 1900s-91 and projected to 2000, 21788–197

Foreign-controlled US corporations income tax returns, assets and income statement items by industry div and country, 1988, article, 8302–2.219

Foreign countries tax credits on corporate income tax returns, income, and tax items, by country and world region of credit, 1986, biennial article, 8302–2.207

Foreign countries tax credits on corporate income tax returns, with income and tax items by industry group, 1986, biennial article, 8302–2.203

Foreign-owned corporate activity in US, income tax returns, assets, and income statement items, by industry div and selected country, 1986-87, article, 8302–2.205

Historic buildings rehabilitation tax incentives, projects, costs, ownership, and use, FY77-90, annual rpt, 5544–17

Housing (low income) dev tax credits, and units constructed, by selected project and State, 1987-89, hearings, 25248–120

Income tax admin and compliance issues, and taxpayer views, 1990 conf, 8304–25

Individual income tax returns, selected income and tax items by adjusted gross income and State, 1986-88, article, 8302–2.201

Individual income tax returns, selected income and tax items by income level, preliminary 1989, annual article, 8302–2.209

Insurance (property and casualty) companies tax and income impacts of tax reform, with background financial data, 1970s-91, 8008–151

Japan and US capital costs and contributing factors, 1920s-90, article, 9385–1.202

Litigation, enforcement, and collection activity of IRS, with data by type of tax, region, and State, FY90, annual rpt, 8304–3

Multinatl US firms foreign affiliates, income statement items by asset size, industry, and country, 1986, biennial article, 8302–2.212

Natural gas interstate pipeline company detailed financial and operating data, by firm, 1989, annual rpt, 3164–38

Pension plans (defined benefit) impacts of Omnibus Budget Reconciliation Act contribution deductibility limit, 1984-89, 8008–152

Pension plans contributions tax deductions, effects of limits on savings rate, 1950s-90, article, 9373–1.219

Puerto Rico and other US possessions corporations income tax returns, income and tax items, and employment, by selected industry, 1987, article, 8302–2.213

Puerto Rico statehood referendum proposal, impacts on Federal tax revenue and aid outlays, corporations tax-favored status, and economic conditions, projected FY91-2000, hearing, 25368–168; 26306–3.112

Returns filed, by type of filer, detailed preliminary and supplementary data, quarterly rpt with articles, 8302–2

Savings and Investment Incentive Act issues, with IRA participation and other background data, 1980s, 25368–175

Savings instns failure resolution costs to FSLIC, relation to asset quality indicators and tax benefit grants, 1984-87, article, 9292–4.202

Savings rates impacts of income tax deduction for interest payments, with indicators for US, Canada, and other OECD countries, 1990 article, 9377–1.202

State and local govt competition in taxes, services, regulation, and dev incentives, 1970-89, 10048–79

State and local govt tax rates and revenue, by source and State, 1991 and historical trends, annual rpt, 10044–1

Statistical Abstract of US, 1991 annual data compilation, 2324–1.17

see also Individual retirement arrangements

see also Oil depletion allowances

see also Tax exempt organizations

see also Tax exempt securities

see also Tax expenditures

Tax laws and courts

Boycotts (intl) by OPEC and other countries, US firms and shareholders cooperation and tax benefits denied, 1986, annual rpt, 8004–13

Boycotts (intl) by OPEC and other countries, US taxpayers IRS filings, cooperation, and tax benefits denied, 1976-86, GAO rpt, 26119–349

Court caseloads and recoveries, for US Tax Court, FY90, annual tables, 18224–5

Court caseloads for US Tax Court, and tax due, by disposition, FY90, annual tables, 18224–3

Court civil and criminal caseloads for Federal district, appeals, and bankruptcy courts, by type of suit and offense, circuit, and district, 1990, annual rpt, 18204–11

Court civil and criminal caseloads for Federal district, appeals, and special courts, 1990, annual rpt, 18204–8

Court civil and criminal caseloads for Federal district courts, 1991, annual rpt, 18204–2.1

Court criminal case processing in Federal courts by disposition, and prisoners, by offense and jurisdiction, data compilation, 1991 annual rpt, 6064–6.5; 6064–6.6

Court criminal cases in Federal district courts, by offense, disposition, and district, 1980-90, last issue of annual rpt, 18204–1

Depreciable assets class lives measurement, investment, and industry operations, industry rpt series, 8006–5

Fed Govt tax provisions and receipts overview, by tax type, with background data, 1900s-91 and projected to 2000, 21788–197

Income tax returns processing, IRS workload forecasts, compliance, and enforcement, data compilation, 1991 annual rpt, 8304–8

IRS collections, enforcement, and litigation activity, with data by type of tax, region, and State, FY90, annual rpt, 8304–3

Legal services establishments, lawyers by field, receipts by class of client, expenses, and employment, by MSA, 1987 Census of Service Industries, 2393–4.13

Money laundering investigations of Fed Govt using IRS large cash transaction rpts, and rpts filed and penalties for nonfiling by region, 1989-91, GAO rpt, 26119–356

Sentences for Federal offenses, guidelines by offense and circumstances, series, 17668–1

Unemployment insurance programs of States, benefits, coverage, and tax provisions, as of Jan 1991, semiannual listing, 6402–7

US attorneys civil and criminal cases by type and disposition, and collections, by Federal district, FY90, annual rpt, 6004–2.1; 6004–2.5

see also Tax delinquency and evasion

see also Tax protests and appeals

see also Tax reform

Tax loopholes

see Tax incentives and shelters

Tax protests and appeals

Court civil and criminal caseloads for Federal district, appeals, and bankruptcy courts, by type of suit and offense, circuit, and district, 1990, annual rpt, 18204–11

Court civil and criminal caseloads for Federal district, appeals, and special courts, 1990, annual rpt, 18204–8

Court civil and criminal caseloads for Federal district courts, 1991, annual rpt, 18204–2.1

IRS collections, enforcement, and litigation activity, with data by type of tax, region, and State, FY90, annual rpt, 8304–3

Tax reform

Budget of US, CBO analysis of savings and revenues under alternative spending cuts and tax changes, projected FY92-97, 26306–3.118

Budget of US, House Budget Committee analysis of Bush Admin proposals and economic assumptions, FY92, 21268–42

Corporations income tax revenue, impacts of tax reform and other factors, 1990 hearing, 25368–173

Income tax admin and compliance issues, and taxpayer views, 1990 conf, 8304–25

Insurance (property and casualty) companies tax and income impacts of tax reform, with background financial data, 1970s-91, 8008–151

Investment stimulation and tax reform proposals, with background data, 1990 hearings, 25368–170

Pension benefits disparity between men and women in small business plans by selected participant and plan characteristics, impacts of 1986 Tax Reform Act, 1984-85, GAO rpt, 26121–412

Pension plans (defined benefit) impacts of Omnibus Budget Reconciliation Act contribution deductibility limit, 1984-89, 8008–152

Returns and supplemental documents filed, by type, FY89 and projected to FY98, annual article, 8302–2.208

Savings rates impacts of income tax deduction for interest payments, with indicators for US, Canada, and other OECD countries, 1990 article, 9377–1.202

Tax sharing

see Revenue sharing

Taxation

Agricultural Statistics, 1990, annual rpt, 1004–1

Banking intl competition and deposit insurance reform issues, with background data, 1990 hearings, 25248–123

Budget of US, authoritative financial statements with appropriations, outlays, and receipts, by agency, FY90, annual rpt, 8104–2

Budget of US, CBO analysis and review of FY92 budget by function, annual rpt, 26304–2

Budget of US, CBO analysis of revenue and spending alternatives and projections of economic indicators, FY92-96, annual rpt, 26304–3

Budget of US, CBO analysis of savings and revenues under alternative spending cuts and tax changes, projected FY92-97, 26306–3.118

Budget of US, House concurrent resolution, with spending and revenue targets, FY92 and projected to FY96, annual rpt, 21264–2

Budget of US, midsession review of FY92 budget, by function, annual rpt, 104–7

Budget of US, obligations and authority by function, agency, and program, with summaries, analyses, and historical tables, FY92, annual rpt, 104–2

Budget of US, receipts by source, outlays by agency and program, and balances, monthly rpt, 8102–3

Budget of US, Senate concurrent resolution, with spending and revenue targets, FY92, annual rpt, 25254–1

Taxation

Competitiveness (intl) and taxation issues, with comparisons of US and foreign tax rates and revenue, 1988-91, press release, 8008–150

Corporations income tax returns, income and tax items by asset size and detailed industry, 1987, annual rpt, 8304–4

Corporations income tax returns, income and tax items by asset size and detailed industry, 1988, annual rpt, 8304–21

Electric power plants production and capital costs, operations, and fuel use, by fuel type, plant, utility, and location, 1989, annual rpt, 3164–9

Farm income, expenses, receipts by commodity, assets, liabilities, and ratios, 1990 and trends from 1945, annual rpt, 1544–16

Fed Govt consolidated financial statements based on business accounting methods, FY89-90, annual rpt, 8104–5

Fed Govt finances, cash and debt transactions, daily tables, 8102–4

Fed Govt internal revenue and refunds, by type of tax, quarterly rpt, 8302–2.1

Fed Govt receipts by source and outlays by agency, *Treasury Bulletin*, quarterly rpt, 8002–4.1

Fed Govt tax provisions and receipts overview, by tax type, with background data, 1900s-91 and projected to 2000, 21788–197

Fed Govt tax receipts, monthly rpt, quarterly and annual data, 23842–1.6

Finances of govts, tax systems and revenue, and fiscal structure, by level of govt and State, 1991 and historical trends, annual rpt, 10044–1

Flow-of-funds accounts, savings, investments, and credit statements, quarterly rpt, 9365–3.3

Households composition, income, benefits, and labor force status, Survey of Income and Program Participation methodology, working paper series, 2626–10

IRS collections, enforcement, and litigation activity, with data by type of tax, region, and State, FY90, annual rpt, 8304–3

Multinatl firms US affiliates, finances, and operations, by industry, world area of parent firm, and State, 1988-89, annual rpt, 2704–4

Multinatl US firms and foreign affiliates finances and operations, by industry and world area of parent firm, 1989 benchmark survey, preliminary annual rpt, 2704–5

Natl income and product accounts and components, *Survey of Current Business*, monthly rpt, 2702–1.24

Natural gas interstate pipeline company detailed financial and operating data, by firm, 1989, annual rpt, 3164–38

Nonprofit charitable organizations finances, and revenue and investments of top 10 instns, 1986-87, article, 8302–2.210

Nonprofit charitable organizations finances, 1988, table, 8302–2.220

Public debt burden on future generations forecast under alternative economic and fiscal policy assumptions, 1991 working paper, 9377–9.111

Public debt burden on future generations forecast under alternative fiscal policies, and ratio of consumption to lifetime income, by sex and age, 1991 working paper, 9377–9.116

Public opinion on taxes, spending, and govt efficiency, by respondent characteristics, 1991 survey, annual rpt, 10044–2

Puerto Rico statehood referendum proposal, impacts on Federal tax revenue and aid outlays, corporations tax-favored status, and economic conditions, projected FY91-2000, hearing, 25368–168

Retail trade census, 1987: depreciable assets, capital and operating expenses, sales, value added, and inventories, by SIC 2- to 4-digit kind of business, 2399–2

Securities yields, for municipal and Treasury bonds, relation to tax policies, 1970-89, article, 9373–1.215

Service industries census, 1987: depreciable assets, capital and operating expenses, and receipts, by SIC 2- to 4-digit kind of business, 2393–2

Soviet Union GNP by detailed income and outlay component, 1985, 2326–18.59

Statistical Abstract of US, 1991 annual data compilation, 2324–1.10

Telephone and telegraph firms detailed finances and operations, 1989, annual rpt, 9284–6

Telephone firms borrowing under Rural Telephone Program, and financial and operating data, by State, 1990, annual rpt, 1244–2

Truck and warehouse services finances and inventory, by SIC 2- to 4-digit industry, 1989 survey, annual rpt, 2413–14

Truck interstate carriers finances and operations, by district, 1989, annual rpt, 9486–6.2

Wholesale trade census, 1987: depreciable assets, capital and operating expenses, sales, value added, and inventories, by SIC 2- to 3-digit kind of business, 2407–2

see also Estate tax
see also Excise tax
see also Fuel tax
see also Gift tax
see also Income taxes
see also Licenses and permits
see also Oil depletion allowances
see also Property tax
see also Revenue sharing
see also Sales tax
see also Severance taxes
see also Social security tax
see also State and local taxes
see also Tariffs and foreign trade controls
see also Tax delinquency and evasion
see also Tax exempt organizations
see also Tax exempt securities
see also Tax expenditures
see also Tax incentives and shelters
see also Tax laws and courts
see also Tax protests and appeals
see also Tax reform
see also Unemployment insurance tax
see also Value added tax
see also Windfall profit tax
see also Withholding tax

Taxicabs

Auto fleet size, trip characteristics, and energy use, by fleet type, 1970s-89, annual rpt, 3304–5.3

County Business Patterns, 1988: employment, establishments, and payroll, by SIC 2- to 4-digit industry and county, annual State rpt series, 2326–6

Index by Subjects and Names

County Business Patterns, 1989: employment, establishments, and payroll, by SIC 2- to 4-digit industry and county, annual State rpt series, 2326–8

Drivers licenses issued and in force by age and sex, fees, and renewal, by license class and State, 1989, annual rpt, 7554–16

Employment, earnings, and hours, by SIC 1- to 4-digit industry, monthly and annual averages, selected years 1909-90, annual rpt, 6744–4

Housing and households characteristics, unit and neighborhood quality, and journey to work by MSA location, for 11 MSAs, 1984 survey, supplement, 2485–8

Housing and households detailed characteristics, and unit and neighborhood quality, by location, 1985, biennial rpt supplement, 2485–13

Occupational injury and illness rates, by SIC 2- to 4-digit industry, 1988-89, annual rpt, 6844–7

Occupational injury and illness rates, by SIC 2- to 4-digit industry, 1989, annual rpt, 6844–1

Tax (income) returns of sole proprietorships, income statement items, by industry group, 1989, annual article, 8302–2.214

Travel from US, characteristics of visit and traveler, and country of destination, 1990 in-flight survey, annual rpt, 2904–14

Travel to US, by characteristics of visit and traveler, world area of origin, and US destination, 1990 survey, annual rpt, 2904–12

Taylor, Amy K.

"Choices of Health Insurance and the Two-Worker Household. National Medical Expenditure Survey", 4186–8.16

"Prevalence of Chronic Diseases: A Summary of Data from the Survey of American Indians and Alaska Natives. National Medical Expenditure Survey", 4186–8.20

Taylor, Harold H.

"Fertilizer Application Timing", 1561–16.204

"Statistical Analysis of Fertilizer Application Rate Differences Between 1989 and 1990", 1561–16.201

Taylor, Jeffrey R.

"Dollar GNP Estimates for China", 2326–18.58

Taylor, Lori L.

"Government Budgets and Property Values", 9379–1.207

"Variations in Texas School Quality", 9379–12.67

Tea

Agricultural Statistics, 1990, annual rpt, 1004–1

Business statistics, detailed data for major industries and economic indicators, *Survey of Current Business*, monthly rpt, 2702–1.14

Consumer Expenditure Survey, food spending by item, household composition, income, age, race, and region, 1980-88, biennial rpt, 1544–30

Consumption of food, dietary composition, and nutrient intake, 1987/88 natl survey, preliminary rpt series, 1356–1

Consumption, supply, trade, prices, spending, and indexes, by food commodity, 1989, annual rpt, 1544–4

Index by Subjects and Names

Teachers

Exports and imports (agricultural) of US, by commodity and country, bimonthly rpt, 1522–1

Exports and imports (agricultural) of US, by detailed commodity and country, 1989, annual rpt, 1524–8

Exports and imports (agricultural) of US, by detailed commodity and country, 1990, semiannual rpt, 1522–4

Exports and imports of US, by country and detailed commodity, monthly rpt, 2422–12

Exports and imports of US, by Harmonized System 6-digit commodity and country, 1990, annual rpt, 2424–13

Exports and imports of US, by transport mode, country, and SITC 1- to 3-digit commodity, 1990, annual rpt, 2424–12

Exports of US, detailed Schedule B commodities with countries of destination, 1990, annual rpt, 2424–10

Foreign and US tea and herbal production, prices, and trade, FAS annual circular series, 1925–15

Foreign countries agricultural production, prices, and trade, by country, 1980-90 and forecast 1991, annual world area rpt series, 1524–4

Foreign countries agricultural production, trade, and policies, summary data by country, 1989-90, annual factbook, 1924–12

Manufacturing annual survey, 1989: finances and operations, by SIC 2- to 4-digit industry, series, 2506–15

Price indexes (producer), by stage of processing and detailed commodity, monthly rpt, 6762–6

Price indexes (producer), by stage of processing and detailed commodity, monthly 1990, annual rpt, 6764–2

Teacher education

Assistance (financial and nonfinancial) of Fed Govt, 1991 base edition with supplements, annual listing, 104–5

Bilingual education enrollment, and Education Dept activities and funding by program, by State, FY88-90, biennial rpt, 4804–14

Bilingual education programs enrollment, funding, and services, by State, FY85-89, series, 4808–20

Course completions, by detailed program, sex, race, and instn type, for 1972 high school class, as of 1984, 4888–4

Degrees awarded in higher education, by level, field, race, and sex, 1988/89 with trends from 1978/79, biennial rpt, 4844–17

Digest of Education Statistics, 1991 annual data compilation, 4824–2

Education Dept programs funding, operations, and effectiveness, FY90, annual rpt, 4804–5

Elementary and secondary students educational performance, and factors affecting proficiency, by selected characteristics, 1988 natl assessments, subject rpt series, 4896–7

Elementary and secondary students educational performance, and factors affecting proficiency, by selected characteristics, 1990 natl assessments, subject rpt series, 4896–8

Fulbright-Hays academic exchanges, grants by purpose, and foreign govt share of costs, by country, FY90, annual rpt, 10324–1

High school class of 1972: teaching employment experience by selected characteristics, natl longitudinal study, 1976-86, 4836–1.13

Higher education faculty employment and other characteristics, by instn type and control, 1987/88 survey, 4846–4.4

Private elementary and secondary schools, students, and staff characteristics, various periods 1979-88, 4838–47

Science and math teacher dev project funding of Fed Govt, participation, operations, and effectiveness, 1985-90, 4808–31

Science, engineering, and math education grants of NSF, by recipient and level, FY89, biennial listing, 9624–27

Special education staff, training, degrees, and certification, by field and State, FY89, annual rpt, 4944–4

Student aid funding and participation, by Federal program, instn type and control, and State, various periods 1959-89, annual rpt, 4804–28

Student loan debt burden of 1986 college grads, by selected student characteristics and instn control, 1987, 4808–26

USIA English language program enrollment and staff, by country and world region, FY90, annual rpt, 9854–2

Teachers

Appalachia education system, improvement initiatives, and indicators of success, by State, 1960s-89, 9088–36

Bilingual education and English immersion programs activities, structure, and effectiveness, 1984-88 longitudinal study, 4808–27

Condition of Education, detail for elementary, secondary, and higher education, 1920s-90 and projected to 2001, annual rpt, 4824–1

Data on education, selected trends and projections 1978-2001, pamphlet, 4828–27

Data on education, 1960s-89, pamphlet, 4828–26

Digest of Education Statistics, 1991 annual data compilation, 4824–2

Elementary and secondary education enrollment, staff, finances, operations, programs, and policies, 1987/88 biennial survey, series, 4836–3

Elementary and secondary education enrollment, teachers, high school grads, and spending, by instn control and State, 1990/91, annual rpt, 4834–19

Elementary and secondary public school systems enrollment, finances, staff, and high school grads, by State, FY88-89, annual rpt, 4834–6

Elementary and secondary public schools, enrollment and other characteristics, for top 100 districts, 1988/89, annual rpt, 4834–22

Elementary and secondary public schools, enrollment, teachers, funding, and other characteristics, by region and State, 1988/89, annual rpt, 4834–20

Elementary and secondary students educational performance, and factors

affecting proficiency, by selected characteristics, 1988 natl assessments, subject rpt series, 4896–7

Elementary and secondary students educational performance, and factors affecting proficiency, by selected characteristics, 1990 natl assessments, subject rpt series, 4896–8

Employment and payroll, by function and level of govt, 1990, annual rpt series, 2466–1

Employment, enrollment, and spending, by instn level and control, and teachers salaries, 1980s-92, annual press release, 4804–19

Employment, unemployment, and labor force characteristics, by region and census div, 1990, annual rpt, 6744–7.1

Flight and ground inspector certificates held and issued, by region, State, and for women, 1989, annual rpt, 7504–1.7

Flight and ground instructors certified by FAA, by age, sex, region, and State, 1990, annual rpt, 7504–2

Fulbright-Hays academic exchanges, grants by purpose, and foreign govt share of costs, by country, FY90, annual rpt, 10324–1

Govt census, 1987: employment, payroll, and average earnings, by function, level of govt, State, county, and population size, 2455–2

Govt census, 1987: State and local labor-mgmt policies, agreements, and coverage and bargaining units, by function, level of govt, and State, 2455–3

High school class of 1972: teaching employment experience by selected characteristics, natl longitudinal study, 1976-86, 4836–1.13

Higher education enrollment, faculty, finances, and degrees, by instn level and control, and State, FY87, annual rpt, 4844–13

Higher education faculty, personnel policies, pay, work conditions, and other characteristics, by instn type and control, 1987/88 survey, quadrennial rpt series, 4846–4

Higher education faculty salaries, by instn type and State, by rank and sex, 1989/90, annual rpt, 4844–8

Higher education instn tuition costs relation to quality, indicators for private instns, regression results, 1985/86, 4888–3

Higher education instn tuition relation to other instn financial indicators, by instn control, 1960s-88, 4808–24

Homeless adults educational services, funding, participation, and staff, by State, 1989, annual rpt series, 4804–39

Indian education funding of Fed Govt, and enrollment, degrees, and program grants and fellowships by State, late 1960s-FY89, annual rpt, 14874–1

Military training and education programs funding, staff, students, and facilities, by service branch, FY92, annual rpt, 3504–5

Natl Education Goals progress indicators, by State, 1991, annual rpt, 15914–1

Opinions of teachers on safety, discipline, and student drug use, for elementary and secondary schools, 1991 survey, 4826–1.31

Teachers

Physicians, by specialty, age, sex, and location of training and practice, 1989, State rpt series, 4116–6

Poverty area schools academic environment and teaching methods impacts on student performance, 1989/90 study, 4808–28

Private elementary and secondary schools, students, and staff characteristics, various periods 1979-88, 4838–47

Remedial education programs in higher education instns, and enrollment, courses, and faculty, by instn characteristics, 1989/90, 4826–1.30

Science and engineering PhDs employment and other characteristics, by field and State, 1989, biennial rpt, 9627–18

Special education programs, enrollment by age, staff, funding, and needs, by type of handicap and State, 1989/90, annual rpt, 4944–4

State and Metro Area Data Book, 1991 data compilation, 2328–54

Statistical Abstract of US, 1991 annual data compilation, 2324–1.4

USIA English language program enrollment and staff, by country and world region, FY90, annual rpt, 9854–2

see also Educational employees pay

see also Teacher education

Teaching aids and devices

see Educational materials

see Educational technology

Technical assistance

see International assistance

see Military assistance

Technical education

see Vocational education and training

Technicians

see Clinical laboratory technicians

see Scientists and technicians

Technological innovations

- Aircraft fuel use and efficiency under alternative technological improvements and load factors, by model, projected 1995-2010, 3028–6
- Auto (electric-powered) R&D activity and DOE funding shares, FY90, annual rpt, 3304–2
- Auto alternative fuels costs, emissions, health impacts, and characteristics, series, 9196–5
- Banks output relation to costs, technological devs, deregulation, and other factors, alternative measures, 1980s, technical paper, 9366–6.265
- Economic indicators, prices, labor costs, and productivity, BLS econometric analyses and methodology, working paper series, 6886–6
- Employment in high technology industries by region and State, and earnings, by industry group, 1989, 6722–1.235
- Energy conservation measures impacts on consumption, by component and end-use sector, 1970s-88 and projected under alternative oil prices to 1995, 3308–93
- Engineering research and education grants of NSF, FY90, annual listing, 9624–24
- *Environmental Quality*, status of problems, protection programs, research, and intl issues, 1991 annual rpt, 484–1
- Global warming contributing air pollutants, US and foreign emissions and control measures, 1980s and projected to 2020, 26358–233

Manufacturing high technology use, by type and selected industry, 1988 survey, fact sheet, 2326–17.23

Materials (advanced structural) devs and data needs, 1989 conf, 5608–167

Materials (advanced structural) devs, use, and R&D funding, for ceramics, metal alloys, polymers, and composites, 1960s-80s and projected to 2000, 5608–162

NSF R&D grant awards, by div and program, periodic rpt series, 9626–7

Statistical Abstract of US, 1991 annual data compilation, 2324–1.27

see also Automation

see also Energy research and development

see also Fiber optics

see also Industrial robots

see also Inventions

see also Lasers

see also Patents

see also Research

see also Research and development

see also Technology transfer

Technology

see Inventions

see Research

see Research and development

see Science and technology

see Technological innovations

see Technology transfer

Technology transfer

- AID economic aid to developing countries, obligations and disbursements by country, quarterly rpt, 9912–4
- Developing countries economic and social conditions from 1960s, and Intl Dev Cooperation Agency and AID activities and funding, FY90-92, annual rpt, 9904–4
- Export licensing, monitoring, and enforcement activities, FY90, annual rpt, 2024–1
- Fed Govt R&D labs technology transfer cooperative agreements, patents, royalties, and incentive payments to employees, by agency, FY89, GAO rpt, 26131–85
- Govt technology dev programs, info sources and funding, 1990 rpt, 10048–81
- Japan economic conditions, financial and intl policies, and trade devs, 1950s-80s and projected to 2050, compilation of papers, 23848–220
- NASA activities and funding, 1990, annual compilation of papers, 21704–1
- Nuclear weapons labs and DOE screening of contractors for foreign ownership, control, or influence, compliance by lab, FY88-90, GAO rpt, 26113–520

Teck, Richard M.

"Individual-Tree Probability of Survival Model for the Northeastern U.S.", 1208–369

Teenage pregnancy

- Abortions, by method, patient characteristics, and State, 1972-88, article, 4202–7.207
- Abortions, by method, pregnancy history, and other characteristics of woman, 1988, US Vital Statistics annual rpt, 4146–5.120
- Births and rates, by characteristics of birth, infant, and parents, 1989 and trends from 1940, US Vital Statistics advance annual rpt, 4146–5.123

Index by Subjects and Names

- Child health condition and services use, 1990 chartbook, 4108–49
- Child support awards to teen mothers, payment status, health insurance inclusion, and govt aid for collection, by selected characteristics, 1987, 4698–5
- Counseling for youth, school based program client risk behaviors and outcomes, 1988/89 study, hearing, 25548–104
- Deaths related to pregnancy, and rates, by detailed cause and demographic characteristics, 1988, US Vital Statistics annual rpt, 4144–2
- Fetal deaths and rates, by characteristics of mother and birth, 1988, US Vital Statistics annual rpt, 4144–2.3
- Food aid program of USDA for women, infants, and children, prenatal participation effect on Medicaid costs and birth outcomes, for 5 States, 1987-88, 1368–2
- Foreign countries motor vehicle accidental death rate for young men, and teen pregnancy rate, by selected country, 1980s, fact sheet, 2326–17.24
- Health condition improvement and disease prevention goals and recommended activities for 2000, with trends 1970s-80s, 4048–10
- HHS financial aid, by program, recipient, State, and city, FY90, annual regional listings, 4004–3
- Homeless teens pregnancy prevalence and outcomes, services availability, health condition, and drug abuse, 1989 conf, 4108–55
- Medicaid coverage effects on prenatal care use and birth outcomes, charges, and Medicaid payments, for California, 1983, article, 4652–1.241
- Research on population and reproduction, Federal funding by project, FY89, annual listing, 4474–9
- *State and Metro Area Data Book*, 1991 data compilation, 2328–54
- *Statistical Abstract of US*, 1991 annual data compilation, 2324–1.2
- Youth and children social, economic, and demographic characteristics, 1950s-90, 4818–5

Teenagers

see Elementary and secondary education

see Juvenile delinquency

see School dropouts

see Teenage pregnancy

see Youth

see Youth employment

Teigen, Lloyd D.

"Weather and Soybean Yield: A Regional Analysis", 1561–3.204

"Weather, Climate and Variability of U.S. Corn Yield", 1561–4.203

Telecommunication

- Air traffic control and airway facilities improvement activities under Aviation System Capital Investment Plan, 1981-90 and projected to 2005, annual rpt, 7504–12
- Competitiveness (intl) of US communications technology and equipment industries, investigation with background financial and operating data and foreign comparisons, 1991 rpt, 9886–4.177

Index by Subjects and Names

Telephones and telephone industry

Competitiveness (intl) of US telecommunications industry, with financial and operating data by product or service, firm, and country, 1990 rpt, 2008–30

Computer use at home, school, and work, by purpose and selected user characteristics, 1989, Current Population Rpt, 2546–2.158

Construction industries census, 1987: establishments, employment, receipts, and expenditures, by SIC 4-digit industry and State, final industry rpt series, 2373–1

Construction put in place, value of new public and private structures, by type, monthly rpt, 2382–4

County Business Patterns, 1988: employment, establishments, and payroll, by SIC 2- to 4-digit industry and county, annual State rpt series, 2326–6

County Business Patterns, 1989: employment, establishments, and payroll, by SIC 2- to 4-digit industry and county, annual State rpt series, 2326–8

DOD budget, programs, and policies, FY90, annual rpt, 3544–2

Eastern Europe economic and political conditions, and impacts of geographic factors, by country, 1990 conf, 9118–18

Enterprise Statistics, 1987: auxiliaries of multi-establishment firms, finances and operations by function, industry, and State, 2329–6

Equipment shipments, trade, use, and firms, for electronic communications systems and related products, 1990, annual Current Industrial Rpt, 2506–12.35

Exports and imports of services, direct and among multinatl firms affiliates, by industry and world area, 1986-90, article, 2702–1.223

Exports and imports of US, by country and detailed commodity, monthly rpt, 2422–12

Exports and imports of US, by Harmonized System 6-digit commodity and country, 1990, annual rpt, 2424–13

Exports and imports of US, by selected country, country group, and commodity group, 1990, annual rpt, 2044–37

Exports and imports of US, by transport mode, country, and SITC 1- to 3-digit commodity, 1990, annual rpt, 2424–12

Exports of US, detailed Schedule B commodities with countries of destination, 1990, annual rpt, 2424–10

Fed Govt computer and telecommunication systems acquisition plans and obligations, by agency, FY89-91, last issue of annual rpt, 104–20

Fed Govt computer and telecommunication systems acquisition plans and obligations, by agency, FY90-95, annual rpt, 104–33

Fed Govt labor productivity, indexes of output and labor costs by function, FY67-89, annual rpt, 6824–1.6

Fiber optics and copper wire mileage and access lines, and fiber systems investment, by telecommunications firm, 1985-90, annual rpt, 9284–18

Finances and operations, by SIC 2- to 4-digit industry, forecast 1991, annual rpt, 2044–28

Foreign countries economic, social, political, and geographic summary data, by country, 1991, annual factbook, 9114–2

GSA activities and finances, FY90, annual rpt, 9454–1

Intl telecommunications operations of US carriers, finances, rates, and traffic by service type, firm, and country, 1975-89, annual rpt, 9284–17

Manufacturing census, 1987: employment and shipments under Fed Govt contracts, by SIC 4-digit industry, 2497–7

Mineral industries census, 1987: finances and operations, by SIC 2- to 4-digit industry, State, and county, census div rpt series, 2515–1

Modem shipments, trade, use, and firms, 1990, annual Current Industrial Rpt, 2506–12.35

Natl Telecommunications and Info Admin rpts, FY90, annual listing, 2804–3

OECD trade, total and for 4 major countries, and US trade by country, by commodity, 1970-89, world area rpt series, 9116–1

Price indexes (producer), by stage of processing and detailed commodity, monthly rpt, 6762–6

Price indexes (producer), by stage of processing and detailed commodity, monthly 1990, annual rpt, 6764–2

Rates for domestic and intl service, by type of service and area served, various dates 1989, annual rpt, 9284–6.6

Retail trade census, 1987: depreciable assets, capital and operating expenses, sales, value added, and inventories, by SIC 2- to 4-digit kind of business, 2399–2

Service industries census, 1987: depreciable assets, capital and operating expenses, and receipts, by SIC 2- to 4-digit kind of business, 2393–2

Soviet Union, Eastern Europe, OECD, and selected other countries consumer and producer goods and services production and sales, 1960s-90, annual rpt, 9114–4.7

Tax rates and revenue of State and local govts, by source and State, 1991 and historical trends, annual rpt, 10044–1

Wholesale trade census, 1987: depreciable assets, capital and operating expenses, sales, value added, and inventories, by SIC 2- to 3-digit kind of business, 2407–2

Wire and cable (insulated) shipments, trade, use, and firms, by product, 1990, annual Current Industrial Rpt, 2506–10.8

see also Communications satellites

see also Educational broadcasting

see also Mobile radio

see also Public broadcasting

see also Radio

see also Telegraph

see also Telephones and telephone industry

see also Television

Telegraph

Competitiveness (intl) of US telecommunications industry, with financial and operating data by product or service, firm, and country, 1990 rpt, 2008–30

County Business Patterns, 1988: employment, establishments, and payroll, by SIC 2- to 4-digit industry and county, annual State rpt series, 2326–6

County Business Patterns, 1989: employment, establishments, and payroll, by SIC 2- to 4-digit industry and county, annual State rpt series, 2326–8

Exports and imports of US, by Harmonized System 6-digit commodity and country, 1990, annual rpt, 2424–13

Exports of US, detailed Schedule B commodities with countries of destination, 1990, annual rpt, 2424–10

Finances and operations, detail for telegraph firms, 1989, annual rpt, 9284–6

Intl telecommunications operations of US carriers, finances, rates, and traffic by service type, firm, and country, 1975-89, annual rpt, 9284–17

Manufacturing annual survey, 1989: finances and operations, by SIC 2- to 4-digit industry, series, 2506–15

Rates for domestic and intl service, by type of service and area served, various dates 1989, annual rpt, 9284–6.6

Shipments, trade, use, and firms, for electronic communications systems and related products, 1990, annual Current Industrial Rpt, 2506–12.35

Statistical Abstract of US, 1991 annual data compilation, 2324–1.18

Telephones and telephone industry

Agricultural Statistics, 1990, annual rpt, 1004–1

Bill payment transactions of households, by method, 1987-88, annual rpt, 9864–10

Competitiveness (intl) of US telecommunications industry, with financial and operating data by product or service, firm, and country, 1990 rpt, 2008–30

Construction put in place and cost indexes, by type of construction, bimonthly rpt, 2042–1.1

Consumer Expenditure Survey, household income by source, and itemized spending, by selected characteristics and region, 1988-89, annual rpt, 6764–5

County Business Patterns, 1988: employment, establishments, and payroll, by SIC 2- to 4-digit industry and county, annual State rpt series, 2326–6

County Business Patterns, 1989: employment, establishments, and payroll, by SIC 2- to 4-digit industry and county, annual State rpt series, 2326–8

CPI by component for US city average, and by region, population size, and for 27 metro areas, monthly rpt, 6762–2

Criminal cases by type and disposition, and collections, for US attorneys, by Federal district, FY90, annual rpt, 6004–2.1

Employment, earnings, and hours, by SIC 1- to 4-digit industry, monthly and annual averages, selected years 1909-90, annual rpt, 6744–4

Exports and imports of US, by country and detailed commodity, monthly rpt, 2422–12

Exports and imports of US, by Harmonized System 6-digit commodity and country, 1990, annual rpt, 2424–13

Exports of US, detailed Schedule B commodities with countries of destination, 1990, annual rpt, 2424–10

Farm average monthly local and total telephone bill, monthly rpt, annual table, 1629–1

Fiber optics and copper wire mileage and access lines, and fiber systems investment, by telecommunications firm, 1985-90, annual rpt, 9284–18

Telephones and telephone industry

Finances and operations, by SIC 2- to 4-digit industry, forecast 1991, annual rpt, 2044–28

Finances and operations, detail for telephone firms, 1989, annual rpt, 9284–6

Finances and operations of local and long distance firms, subscribership, and charges, late 1970s-91, semiannual rpt, 9282–7

Foreign countries economic, social, political, and geographic summary data, by country, 1991, annual factbook, 9114–2

Hispanic Americans social and economic characteristics, by detailed origin, 1991, Current Population Rpt, 2546–1.448; 2546–1.451

Hotels and other lodging places, receipts, payroll, employment, and ownership, by State and MSA, 1987 Census of Service Industries, subject rpt, 2393–3.2

House of Representatives salaries, expenses, and contingent fund disbursement, detailed listings, quarterly rpt, 21942–1

Households and housing detailed characteristics, and unit and neighborhood quality, by location, 1987, biennial rpt supplement, 2485–13

Households telephone service subscribership, by selected characteristics and State, periodic rpt, suspended, 9282–9

Households with telephones, MSA surveys, series, 2485–6

Housing and households characteristics, unit and neighborhood quality, and journey to work by MSA location, for 11 MSAs, 1984 survey, supplement, 2485–8

Housing inventory change from 1973, by reason, unit and household characteristics, and location, 1983 survey, biennial rpt, 2485–14

Indian Health Service facilities and use, and Indian health and other characteristics, by IHS region, 1980s-89, annual chartbook, 4084–7

Injuries from use of consumer products, by severity, victim age, and detailed product, 1990, annual rpt, 9164–6

Intl telecommunications operations of US carriers, finances, rates, and traffic by service type, firm, and country, 1975-89, annual rpt, 9284–17

Labor productivity, indexes of output, hours, and employment by SIC 2- to 4-digit industry, 1967-89, annual rpt, 6824–1.4

Local telephone rates and low-income subsidies, by region, company, and city, 1980s-90, semiannual rpt, 9282–8

Long-distance telephone service rates, by company, city, and time of day, 1950s-89, annual rpt, 9284–6.7

Mail volume to and from households, use, and views, by class, source, content, and household characteristics, 1987-88, annual rpt, 9864–10

Manufacturing annual survey, 1989: finances and operations, by SIC 2- to 4-digit industry, series, 2506–15

Occupational injury and illness rates, by SIC 2- to 4-digit industry, 1988-89, annual rpt, 6844–7

Occupational injury and illness rates, by SIC 2- to 4-digit industry, 1989, annual rpt, 6844–1

Palau admin, and social, economic, and govtl data, FY90, annual rpt, 7004–6

Price indexes (producer), by stage of processing and detailed commodity, monthly rpt, 6762–6

Price indexes (producer), by stage of processing and detailed commodity, monthly 1990, annual rpt, 6764–2

Rates for domestic and intl service, by type of service and area served, various dates 1989, annual rpt, 9284–6.6

Rural Telephone Bank financial statements, FY89, annual rpt, 1244–4

Rural Telephone Cooperatives, membership, and revenue, by State, 1989, annual rpt, 1124–1

Rural Telephone Program loan activity, by State, FY90, annual tables, 1244–8

Rural Telephone Program loans, and borrower operations and finances, by State, 1990, annual rpt, 1244–2

Service industries census, 1987: establishments, receipts by source, payroll, and employment, by SIC 2- to 4-digit kind of business, State, and MSA, 2393–4

Shipments, trade, use, and firms, for electronic communications systems and related products, 1990, annual Current Industrial Rpt, 2506–12.35

SSA public access by telephone, local line availability and effects of nationwide 800 number, by State, 1989 and 1991, GAO rpt, 26121–434

SSA telephone info service performance, 1989-90, hearing, 21788–199

Statistical Abstract of US, 1991 annual data compilation, 2324–1.18

Surveys and other data collection activities of Fed Govt, and quality and privacy issues, 1990 conf, 106–4.14

Tax (excise) collections of IRS, by source, quarterly rpt, 8302–1; 8302–2.1

Tax (income) aid telephone service activity of IRS, FY90, annual rpt, 8304–3

Tax (income) returns of individuals, IRS processing and taxpayer info activity, electronic filings, and refunds, periodic press release, 8302–6

see also Mobile radio

Television

AIDS info and education activities and funding of CDC, and donation of media ads, 1987-92, articles, 4042–3.256

Children and youth social, economic, and demographic characteristics, 1950s-90, 4818–5

China economic indicators and reform issues, with background data, 1950s-90, compilation of papers, 23848–155

Education data compilation, 1991 annual rpt, 4824–2

Educational performance and conditions, characteristics, attitudes, activities, and plans, 1988 8th grade class, natl longitudinal survey, series, 4826–9

Educational performance of elementary and secondary students, and factors affecting proficiency, by selected characteristics, 1988 natl assessments, subject rpt series, 4896–7

Educational performance of elementary and secondary students, and factors affecting proficiency, by selected characteristics, 1990 natl assessments, subject rpt series, 4896–8

Index by Subjects and Names

Employment, earnings, and hours, by SIC 1- to 4-digit industry, monthly and annual averages, selected years 1909-90, annual rpt, 6744–4

Foreign countries economic, social, political, and geographic summary data, by country, 1991, annual factbook, 9114–2

Licensing status and allocation of commercial and noncommercial UHF and VHF TV channels, by market, as of June 30, 1991, semiannual rpt, 9282–6

Palau admin, and social, economic, and govtl data, FY90, annual rpt, 7004–6

Political broadcasting operating budgets for US Govt overseas radio and TV services, FY88 and FY91, annual rpt, 17594–1

State and Metro Area Data Book, 1991 data compilation, 2328–54

Stations on the air, by class of operation, monthly press release, 9282–4

Statistical Abstract of US, 1991 annual data compilation, 2324–1.18

see also Cable television

see also Home video and audio equipment

see also Video recordings and equipment

Tellurium

see Metals and metal industries

Tempe, Ariz.

see also under By City in the "Index by Categories"

Temperature

see Global climate change

see Weather

Tempest, Bruce

"Respiratory Diseases", 4088–2

Temple, Tex.

Wages by occupation, and benefits for office and plant workers, 1991 survey, periodic MSA rpt,, 6785–3.8

see also under By SMSA or MSA in the "Index by Categories"

Temporary and seasonal employment

Agriculture census, 1987: farms, farmland, production, finances, and operator characteristics, by county, final State rpt series, 2331–1

Air traffic control and airway facilities staff, by employment and other characteristics, FY89, annual rpt, 7504–41

Capitol Architect outlays for salaries, supplies, and services, itemized by payee and function, 1st half FY91, semiannual rpt, 25922–2

Census Bur temporary hires for 1990 census, impact on natl employment trends, 1990, article, 6742–2.202

DOD civilian employment, by service branch and defense agency, with summary military employment data, quarterly rpt, 3542–16

DOT employment, by subagency, occupation, and selected personnel characteristics, FY90, annual rpt, 7304–18

Farm labor, wages, hours, and perquisites, by State, monthly rpt, 1631–1

Fed Govt agencies appointments of consultants and experts for temporary employment, and rule violations, 1986-89, GAO rpt, 26119–354

Fed Govt civilian employees work-years, pay rates, and benefits use and costs, by agency, FY89, annual rpt, 9844–31

Fed Govt civilian employment and payroll, by agency in DC metro area, total US, and abroad, bimonthly rpt, 9842–1

Index by Subjects and Names

Help supply agencies depreciable assets, capital and operating expenses, and receipts, 1987 Census of Service Industries, 2393–2

Help supply agencies finances and operations, by size, level of diversification, and form of organization, 1987 Enterprise Statistics survey, 2329–8

Help supply agencies receipts, 1990, annual rpt, 2413–8

Income (household, family, and personal), by source, detailed characteristics, and region, 1988-89, annual Current Population Rpt, 2546–6.68

Income (household, family, and personal), by source, detailed characteristics, and region, 1990, annual Current Population Rpt, 2546–6.70

NASA staff characteristics and personnel actions, FY90, annual rpt, 9504–1

Postal Service activities, financial statements, and employment, FY86-90, annual rpt, 9864–1

Radiation exposure of workers at nuclear power plants and related facilities, by site, 1968-87, annual rpt, 9634–3

Teachers in higher education instns, personnel policies, pay, work conditions, and other characteristics, by instn type and control, 1987/88 survey, quadrennial rpt series, 4846–4

Unemployment insurance laws of States, comparison of provisions, 1991, base edition with semiannual revisions, 6402–2

VA health care staff and turnover, by occupation, physician specialty, and location, 1990, annual rpt, 8604–8

Wages, hours, and employment by occupation, and benefits, for selected locations, industry survey rpt series, 6787–6

Youth labor force status by age, Apr and July 1991 and change from 1990, annual press release, 6744–13

Youth labor force status, by sex, race, and industry div, summer 1987-91, annual press release, 6744–14

see also Migrant workers

see also Part-time employment

Tennessee

Appalachian Regional Commission funding, by project and State, planned FY91, annual rpt, 9084–3

Banks (insured commercial and savings) deposits by instn, State, MSA, and county, as of June 1990, annual regional rpt, 9295–3.4

Coal production and mines by county, prices, productivity, miners, and reserves, by mining method and State, 1989-90, annual rpt, 3164–25

County Business Patterns, 1989: employment, establishments, and payroll, by SIC 2- to 4-digit industry and county, annual State rpt, 2326–8.44

DOD prime contract awards, by contractor, service branch, State, and city, FY90, annual rpt, 3544–22

Economic and banking conditions, for Fed Reserve 8th District, quarterly rpt with articles, 9391–16

Economic indicators by State and MSA, Fed Reserve 6th District, quarterly rpt, 9371–14

Education system in Appalachia, improvement initiatives, and indicators of success, by State, 1960s-89, 9088–36

Employment and unemployment, for 8 southeastern States, 1989-90, annual rpt, 6944–2

Employment by industry div, earnings, and hours, for 8 southeastern States, quarterly press release, 6942–7

Fed Govt spending in States and local areas, by type, State, county, and city, FY90, annual rpt, 2464–3

Fed Govt spending in States, by type, program, agency, and State, FY90, annual rpt, 2464–2

Food aid program of USDA for women, infants, and children, enrollment of children at high risk of poor nutrition, for Tennessee, 1982-84, article, 4042–3.216

Gemstone production in selected States, Mineral Industry Surveys, 1988-90, advance annual rpt, 5614–5.10

HHS financial aid, by program, recipient, State, and city, FY90, annual regional listing, 4004–3.4

Hospital deaths of Medicare patients, actual and expected rates by diagnosis, and hospital characteristics, by instn, FY87-89, annual regional rpt, 4654–14.4

Income (personal) per capita and by source, and earnings by industry div, by State, MSA, and county, 1984-89, annual regional rpt, 2704–2.4

Jail adult and juvenile population, employment, spending, instn conditions, and inmate programs, by county and facility, 1988, regional rpt series, 6068–144.4

Marriages, divorces, and rates, by characteristics of spouses, State, and county, 1987 and trends from 1920, US Vital Statistics annual rpt, 4144–4

Mineral Industry Surveys, State reviews of production, 1990, preliminary annual rpt, 5614–6

Minerals Yearbook, 1989, Vol 2: State review of production and sales by commodity, and business activity, annual rpt, 5604–16.44

Minerals Yearbook, 1989, Vol 2: State reviews of production, sales, and firms, by commodity, and business activity, annual rpt, 5604–34

Physicians, by specialty, age, sex, and location of training and practice, 1989, State rpt, 4116–6.44

Population and housing census, 1990: population and housing characteristics, households, and land area, by county, subdiv, and place, State rpt, 2551–1.44

Population and housing census, 1990: voting age and total population by race, and housing units, by block, redistricting counts required under PL 94-171, State CD-ROM release, 2551–6.7

Population and housing census, 1990: voting age and total population by race, and housing units, by county and city, redistricting counts required under PL 94-171, State summary rpt, 2551–5.43

Statistical Abstract of US, 1991 annual data compilation, 2324–1

Supplemental Security Income payments and beneficiaries, by type of eligibility, State, and county, Dec 1989, annual rpt, 4744–27.4

Tennessee Valley Authority

Textile mill employment, earnings, and hours, for 8 Southeastern States, quarterly press release, 6942–1

Timber in Tennessee, acreage at risk from gypsy moth infestation, by county, 1989, 1208–344

Water supply and quality in streams and lakes, and groundwater levels in wells, by drainage basin, 1989, annual State rpt, 5666–12.40

Water supply and quality in streams and lakes, and groundwater levels in wells, by drainage basin, 1990, annual State rpt, 5666–10.40

see also Chattanooga, Tenn.

see also Clarksville, Tenn.

see also Memphis, Tenn.

see also Nashville, Tenn.

see also Shelby County, Tenn.

see also Tennessee River

see also Tennessee Valley

see also under By State in the "Index by Categories"

Tennessee River

Army Corps of Engineers water resources dev projects, characteristics, and costs, 1950s-89, biennial State rpt series, 3756–1

Army Corps of Engineers water resources dev projects, characteristics, and costs, 1950s-91, biennial State rpt series, 3756–2

TVA river control activities, and hydroelectric power generation and capacity, 1989, annual rpt, 9804–7

Water supply and quality in streams and lakes, and groundwater levels in wells, by drainage basin, 1988, annual State rpt series, 5666–16

Water supply and quality in streams and lakes, and groundwater levels in wells, by drainage basin, 1989, annual State rpt series, 5666–12

Water supply and quality in streams and lakes, and groundwater levels in wells, by drainage basin, 1990, annual State rpt series, 5666–10

see also Tennessee Valley

Tennessee Valley

Electric power distributors of TVA, finances and operations by firm, annual rpt, discontinued, 9804–19

Industrial dev and employment, for Tennessee Valley by SIC 2-digit industry, firm, and location, 1990, annual rpt, 9804–3

River control activities of TVA, and hydroelectric power generation and capacity, 1989, annual rpt, 9804–7

TVA finances and operations by program and facility, FY90, annual rpt, 9804–32

Tennessee Valley Authority

Budget of US, authoritative financial statements with appropriations, outlays, and receipts, by category and agency, FY90, annual rpt, 8104–2.1

Budget of US, obligations and authority by function, agency, and program, with summaries, analyses, and historical tables, FY92, annual rpt, 104–2

Electric power distributors of TVA, finances and operations by firm, annual rpt, discontinued, 9804–19

Electric power purchases from TVA and resales, with use, average bills, and rates by customer class, by distributor, 1990, annual tables, 9804–14

Tennessee Valley Authority

Electric power purchases of municipal and cooperative distributors, and prices and use by distributor and consumer sector, for TVA, monthly rpt, 9802–1

Electric power wholesale purchases of REA borrowers, by borrower, supplier, and State, 1940-89, annual rpt, 1244–5

Employment (civilian) of Fed Govt, work-years, pay rates, and benefits use and costs, by agency, FY89, annual rpt, 9844–31

Energy use of TVA by fuel type, and conservation costs and savings, FY90, annual rpt, 9804–26

Expenditures of Fed Govt in States, by type, program, agency, and State, FY90, annual rpt, 2464–2

Fed Govt finances, cash and debt transactions, daily tables, 8102–4

Fertilizer production capacity by firm, for US and Canada, 1986-91 and projected to 1997, triennial rpt, 9808–66

Fertilizer use and costs by type, and acreage harvested, by State, 1970s-90, biennial rpt, 9804–5

Fertilizer use, by type and State, 1989-90, annual rpt, 9804–30

Finances and operations by program and facility, FY90, annual rpt, 9804–32

Finances and operations of Federal power admins and electric utilities, 1989, annual rpt, 3164–24.2

Finances and power sales, FY90, annual rpt, 9804–1

Industrial dev and employment, for Tennessee Valley by SIC 2-digit industry, firm, and location, 1990, annual rpt, 9804–3

R&D funding by Fed Govt, by field, performer type, agency, and State, FY89-91, annual rpt, 9627–20

Recreation (outdoor) facilities of Fed Govt, fees and visits by managing agency, FY88-90, annual rpt, 5544–14

River control activities of TVA, and hydroelectric power generation and capacity, 1989, annual rpt, 9804–7

Tenure

see Housing tenure

see Job tenure

Terre Haut, Ind.

see also under By SMSA or MSA in the "Index by Categories"

Territorial waters

Foreign countries economic, social, political, and geographic summary data, by country, 1991, annual factbook, 9114–2

Foreign countries *Geographic Notes*, boundaries, claims, nomenclature, and other devs, periodic rpt, 7142–3

Foreign countries maritime claims and boundary agreements, series, 7006–8

see also Continental shelf

Territories of the U.S.

Aircraft (general aviation), flight hours, and equipment, by type, use, and model of aircraft, region, and State, 1990, annual rpt, 7504–29

Assistance (financial and nonfinancial) of Fed Govt, 1991 base edition with supplements, annual listing, 104–5

Budget of US, formula grant program obligations to State and local govts, by agency, program, and State, FY92, annual rpt, 104–30

Community Dev Block Grant activities and funding, by program, FY75-90, annual rpt, 5124–8

Corporations in US under foreign control, income tax returns, assets and income statement items by industry div, country, and world area, 1988, article, 8302–2.219

Corporations operating in Puerto Rico and other US possessions, income tax return items, and employment, by selected industry, 1987, article, 8302–2.213

Death investigation systems of US and Canada, jurisdictions, medical officers qualifications, types of deaths covered, and related statutes, 1990 listing, 4208–34

DOD budget, organization, personnel, weapons, and property, by service branch, State, and country, 1991 annual summary rpt, 3504–13

DOD civilian and military personnel and dependents, by service branch and US and foreign location, quarterly rpt, 3542–20

Economic and military aid and loans from US and intl agencies, by program and country, FY46-90, annual rpt, 9914–5

Exports of US, detailed Schedule B commodities with countries of destination, 1990, annual rpt, 2424–10

Fed Govt civilian employees accessions and separations, by agency for DC metro area and elsewhere, bimonthly rpt, 9842–1.3

Fed Govt civilian employment and payroll, by pay system and location, 1990, annual rpt, 9844–6.1

Fed Govt-leased real property inventory and rental costs, worldwide summary by location and agency, 1989, annual rpt, 9454–10

Fed Govt-owned real property inventory and costs, worldwide summary by purpose, agency, and location, 1989, annual rpt, 9454–5

Fed Govt spending in States and local areas, by type, State, county, and city, FY90, annual rpt, 2464–3

Food stamp recipient household size, composition, income, and income and deductions allowed, summer 1988, annual rpt, 1364–8

Governors of States and territories, terms and salaries, 1991-92, *Congressional Directory*, biennial rpt, 23874–1

HHS financial aid, by program, recipient, State, and city, FY90, annual regional listing, 4004–3.2; 4004–3.9

Interior Dept programs fraud and abuse, audits and investigations, 2nd half FY91, semiannual rpt, 5302–2

Military base support costs by function, and personnel and acreage by installation, by service branch, FY91, annual rpt, 3504–11

Military presence of US in Pacific basin, personnel, dependents, aircraft, ships, and costs, by service branch and location, 1990, GAO rpt, 26123–357

Minerals Yearbook, 1989, Vol 2: State reviews of production, sales, and firms, by commodity, and business activity, annual rpt, 5604–34

Multinatl US firms foreign affiliates, income statement items by country and world area, 1986, biennial article, 8302–2.212

Index by Subjects and Names

Pacific territories admin, and Palau social, economic, and govtl data, FY90, annual rpt, 7004–6

R&D funding by Fed Govt, by field, performer type, agency, and State, FY89-91, annual rpt, 9627–20

R&D funding by higher education instns and federally funded centers, by field, instn, and State, FY89, annual rpt, 9627–13

Refugee resettlement programs and funding, arrivals by country of origin, and indicators of adjustment, by State, FY90, annual rpt, 4694–5

Science and engineering grad enrollment, by field, source of funds, and characteristics of student and instn, 1975-89, annual rpt, 9627–7

Statistical Abstract of US, 1991 annual data compilation, 2324–1.30

Tax (income) returns of corporations with foreign tax credit, income, and tax items, by country and world region of credit, 1986, biennial article, 8302–2.207

TV channel allocation and license status, for commercial and noncommercial UHF and VHF stations by market, as of June 30, 1991, semiannual rpt, 9282–6

VA expenses, by type and location, FY90, annual rpt, 8604–3.9

Weather data for stations in continental US and outlying areas, 1990 and historic trends, annual rpt, 2154–8

see also American Samoa

see also Guam

see also Midway Islands

see also Northern Mariana Islands

see also Puerto Rico

see also U.S. Virgin Islands

see also Wake Island

see also under By Outlying Area in the "Index by Categories"

Terrorism

Incidents of terrorism in US, related activity, and casualties, by attack type, target, group, and location, 1990, annual rpt, 6224–6

Intl terrorism incidents, casualties, and attacks on US targets, by attack type and country, 1990, annual rpt, 7004–22

Intl terrorism incidents, casualties, and attacks on US targets, by attack type and world area, 1968-90, annual rpt, 7004–13

Intl terrorism incidents involving US targets, by type of attack, and casualties, by target type, data compilation, 1991 annual rpt, 6064–6.3

Mgmt of disasters and natl security threats, with data by major event and State, 1991 annual rpt, 9434–6

see also Air piracy

see also Assassination

see also Hostages

see also Sabotage

Tesar, Linda L.

"Tastes and Technology in a Two-Country Model of the Business Cycle: Explaining International Co-Movements", 9377–9.113

Testa, William A.

"Calibrating Manufacturing Decline in the Midwest: Value Added, Gross State Product, and All Points Between", 9375–13.59

Index by Subjects and Names

Texas

Tests
see Drug and alcohol testing
see Educational tests
see Medical examinations and tests
see Occupational testing and certification
see Quality control and testing

Tetanus
see Infective and parasitic diseases

Texarkana, Ark.
see also under By SMSA or MSA in the "Index by Categories"

Texarkana, Tex.
see also under By SMSA or MSA in the "Index by Categories"

Texas

Bank deposit insurance fund finances, potential losses, and real estate lenders financial ratios compared to other US and Texas banks, 1990 hearings, 25248–125

Banks (insured commercial and savings) deposits by instn, State, MSA, and county, as of June 1990, annual regional rpt, 9295–3.4

Banks capital aid receipt relation to bank holding company affiliation and other factors, with data for Texas, 1985-88, article, 9391–1.205

Banks financial performance, for undercapitalized instns by State and inside-outside Texas, aggregate 1985-89, article, 9391–1.212

Banks in Texas, failures relation to portfolio risk indicators and year of establishment, 1980s, working paper, 9379–14.10

Census of Population and Housing, 1990: Texas data collection activities and status, hearing, 21628–92

Child welfare programs funding by source, and foster care program operations and client characteristics, for selected States, 1960s-95, 25368–169

Coal production and mines by county, prices, productivity, miners, and reserves, by mining method and State, 1989-90, annual rpt, 3164–25

County Business Patterns, 1989: employment, establishments, and payroll, by SIC 2- to 4-digit industry and county, annual State rpt, 2326–8.45

Dairy prices, by product and selected area, with related marketing data, 1990, annual rpt, 1317–1

DOD prime contract awards, by contractor, service branch, State, and city, FY90, annual rpt, 3544–22

Drug abuse indicators for selected metro areas, research results, data collection, and policy issues, 1991 semiannual conf, 4492–5

Economic and housing conditions in Texas, bank failures, and thrift and Federal regulators real estate holdings, 1980s-90, hearings, 21248–146

Employment by industry div, earnings, and hours, by southwestern State, with CPI by major component for 2 Texas MSAs, monthly rpt, 6962–2

Farm Credit System and FmHA services to aid delinquent borrowers, activities, with background data, 1989 hearings, 25168–74

Fed Govt spending in States and local areas, by type, State, county, and city, FY90, annual rpt, 2464–3

Fed Govt spending in States, by type, program, agency, and State, FY90, annual rpt, 2464–2

Fertilizer and pesticide use and application rates, by type, crop, and State, 1990, 1616–1.2

Fish and shellfish catch, wholesale receipts, prices, trade, and other market activities, weekly regional rpt, 2162–6.3

Floods on Arkansas, Red, and Trinity Rivers, storm characteristics, and Natl Weather Service forecast accuracy, 1990, 2186–6.4

FmHA farm and rural housing program loan appeals filed in 3 States, by disposition, 1988-90, GAO rpt, 26113–516

Food aid program of USDA for women, infants, and children, prenatal participation effect on Medicaid costs and birth outcomes, for 5 States, 1987-88, 1368–2

Foster care placements, discharges, and returns to care, by selected characteristics of children, and length of stay factors, 1985-86, GAO rpt, 26121–432

Goat inventory in Texas, 1989-91, annual press release, 1623–4

HHS financial aid, by program, recipient, State, and city, FY90, annual regional listing, 4004–3.6

Hispanic Americans in counties bordering Mexico, by selected characteristics, 1980, Current Population Rpt, 2546–2.159

Hospital deaths of Medicare patients, actual and expected rates by diagnosis, and hospital characteristics, by instn, FY87-89, annual regional rpt, 4654–14.6

Housing census, 1990: inventory, occupancy, and costs, State fact sheet, 2326–21.45

Hwy funds pooled by States from FHwA funds for specific projects, demonstration project results, FY88-90, GAO rpt, 26113–471

Income (personal) per capita and by source, and earnings by industry div, by State, MSA, and county, 1984-89, annual regional rpt, 2704–2.5

Income per capita, impacts of industry mix and other factors, for 36 MSAs in Texas and Louisiana, 1969-88, article, 9379–1.209

Jail adult and juvenile population, employment, spending, instn conditions, and inmate programs, by county and facility, 1988, regional rpt series, 6068–144.4

Land Mgmt Bur activities in Southwestern US, FY90, annual rpt, 5724–15

Marriages, divorces, and rates, by characteristics of spouses, State, and county, 1987 and trends from 1920, US Vital Statistics annual rpt, 4144–4

Mineral Industry Surveys, State reviews of production, 1990, preliminary annual rpt, 5614–6

Minerals Yearbook, 1989, Vol 2: State review of production and sales by commodity, and business activity, annual rpt, 5604–16.45

Minerals Yearbook, 1989, Vol 2: State reviews of production, sales, and firms, by commodity, and business activity, annual rpt, 5604–34

Motorcycle helmet mandatory use law in Texas, impacts on use, 1987-89 study, article, 4042–3.251

Natural gas production and wellhead capacity, by production area, 1980-89 and alternative forecasts 1990-91, biennial rpt, 3164–93

Nursing home reimbursement by Medicaid, States payment ratesetting methods, analysis for 7 States, 1980s, article, 4652–1.255

Occupational deaths data collection from multiple sources, BLS pilot study results for 2 States, 1990, article, 6722–1.249

Occupational injury death data collection methods of BLS and Texas, with Texas data by accident type and industry div, 1986, article, 6722–1.205

Oranges (fresh) exports of US, demand indicators for 4 countries, with production, trade, and use, 1960s-90, 1528–317

Physicians, by specialty, age, sex, and location of training and practice, 1989, State rpt, 4116–6.45

Population and housing census, 1990: population and housing characteristics, households, and land area, by county, subdiv, and place, State rpt, 2551–1.45

Population and housing census, 1990: voting age and total population by race, and housing units, by block, redistricting counts required under PL 94-171, State CD-ROM release, 2551–6.8

Population and housing census, 1990: voting age and total population by race, and housing units, by county and city, redistricting counts required under PL 94-171, State summary rpt, 2551–5.44

Rice market activities, prices, inspections, sales, trade, supply, and use, for US and selected foreign markets, weekly rpt, 1313–8

Rice stocks on and off farms and total in all positions, periodic rpt, 1621–7

Savings instns failures, inventory of real estate assets available from Resolution Trust Corp, 1990, semiannual listing, 9722–2.6

Savings instns failures, inventory of real estate assets available from Resolution Trust Corp, 1991, semiannual listing, 9722–2.12

Savings instns financial condition and devs, working paper series, 9379–14

School districts in Texas, educational quality indicators, model description and results by district and county, 1989, technical paper, 9379–12.67

Services sector growth in Texas, impact on wages, with data by industry and sector, late 1970s-89, article, 9379–1.210

Statistical Abstract of US, 1991 annual data compilation, 2324–1

Supplemental Security Income payments and beneficiaries, by type of eligibility, State, and county, Dec 1989, annual rpt, 4744–27.6

Wages by occupation, for office and plant workers, 1991 survey, periodic labor market rpt, 6785–3.10

Water (groundwater) supply, quality, chemistry, and use, 1987-88, regional rpt, 5666–28.3

see also Arlington, Tex.
see also Beaumont, Tex.
see also Brazoria, Tex.

Texas

see also Dallas County, Tex.
see also Dallas, Tex.
see also El Paso, Tex.
see also Fort Worth, Tex.
see also Galveston, Tex.
see also Houston, Tex.
see also Killeen, Tex.
see also Port Arthur, Tex.
see also San Antonio, Tex.
see also Temple, Tex.
see also Waco, Tex.
see also Wichita Falls, Tex.
see also under By State in the "Index by Categories"

Texas City, Tex.
see also under By SMSA or MSA in the "Index by Categories"

Texas Transportation Institute
"Description of High-Occupancy Vehicle Facilities in North America", 7888–80

Textbooks
see Educational materials

Textile industry and fabrics

Business statistics, detailed data for major industries and economic indicators, *Survey of Current Business,* monthly rpt, 2702–1.22

Capital expenditures for plant and equipment, by major industry group, quarterly rpt, 2502–2

Caribbean Basin Initiative investment incentives, economic impacts, with finances and employment by country, 1984-90, 2048–141

Collective bargaining agreements expiring during year, and workers covered, by firm, union, industry group, and State, 1991, annual rpt, 6784–9

County Business Patterns, 1988: employment, establishments, and payroll, by SIC 2- to 4-digit industry and county, annual State rpt series, 2326–6

County Business Patterns, 1989: employment, establishments, and payroll, by SIC 2- to 4-digit industry and county, annual State rpt series, 2326–8

Employment, earnings, and hours, by SIC 1- to 4-digit industry, monthly and annual averages, selected years 1909-90, annual rpt, 6744–4

Employment in manufacturing, by detailed occupation and SIC 2-digit industry, 1989 survey, triennial rpt, 6748–52

Employment related to agriculture, by industry, region, and metro-nonmetro location, 1987, 1598–271

Employment, unemployment, and labor force characteristics, by region and census div, 1990, annual rpt, 6744–7.1

Energy use and prices for manufacturing industries, 1988 survey, series, 3166–13

Enterprise Statistics, 1987: auxiliaries of multi-establishment firms, finances and operations by function, industry, and State, 2329–6

Enterprise Statistics, 1987: finances and operations for companies, by size, level of diversification, form of organization, and industry group, 2329–8

Exports and imports between US and outlying areas, by detailed commodity and mode of transport, 1990, annual rpt, 2424–11

Exports and imports of US, by country and detailed commodity, monthly rpt, 2422–12

Exports and imports of US by country, and trade shifts by commodity, 1990, semiannual rpt, 9882–9

Exports and imports of US, by Harmonized System 6-digit commodity and country, 1990, annual rpt, 2424–13

Exports and imports of US, by transport mode, country, and SITC 1- to 3-digit commodity, 1990, annual rpt, 2424–12

Exports of US, detailed commodities by country, monthly CD-ROM, 2422–13

Exports of US, detailed Schedule B commodities with countries of destination, 1990, annual rpt, 2424–10

Import classification codes under Textile Agreement Category System, correlation with TSUSA, 1992 annual rpt, 2044–31

Import restrictions proposed for textiles, apparel, and shoes, economic impacts, projected 1991-2000, with imports by country, 1989-90, 26306–6.162

Imports, exports, and employment impacts, by SIC 2- to 4-digit industry and commodity, quarterly rpt, 2322–2

Imports of textiles, by country of origin, monthly rpt, 2042–27

Imports of textiles, by product and country of origin, monthly rpt series, 2046–8; 2046–9

Imports of textiles, total and from US, by commodity and country, 1987-89, 2048–155

Imports of textiles under Multifiber Arrangement by product and country, and status of bilateral agreements, 1987-90, annual rpt, 9884–18

Imports of US, detailed commodities by country, monthly CD-ROM, 2422–14

Imports of US given duty-free treatment for value of US material sent abroad, by commodity and country, 1989, annual rpt, 9884–14

Input-output structure of US economy, detailed interindustry transactions for 84 industries, and components of final demand, 1986, annual article, 2702–1.206

Input-output structure of US economy, detailed interindustry transactions for 85 industries, 1982 benchmark data, 2702–1.213

Labor productivity, indexes of output, hours, and employment by SIC 2- to 4-digit industry, 1967-89, annual rpt, 6824–1.3

Manufacturing annual survey, 1989: finances and operations, by SIC 2- to 4-digit industry, series, 2506–15

Manufacturing census, 1987: finances and operations, by SIC 2- to 4-digit industry, State, and MSA, with trends from 1849, 2497–1

Manufacturing census, 1987: finances and operations, by type of organization and SIC 2- to 4-digit industry, subject rpt, 2497–5

Manufacturing corporations financial statements, by selected SIC 2- to 3-digit industry, quarterly rpt, 2502–1

Manufacturing finances and operations, by SIC 2- to 4-digit industry, forecast 1991, annual rpt, 2044–28

Manufacturing industries operations and performance, analytical rpt series, 2506–16

Manufacturing production, shipments, inventories, orders, and pollution control costs, periodic Current Industrial Rpt series, 2506–3

Mexico imports from US, by industry and State, 1987-90, 2048–154

Multinatl US firms and foreign affiliates finances and operations, by industry and world area of parent firm, 1989 benchmark survey, preliminary annual rpt, 2704–5

Occupational injury and illness rates, by SIC 2- to 4-digit industry, 1988-89, annual rpt, 6844–7

Occupational injury and illness rates, by SIC 2- to 4-digit industry, 1989, annual rpt, 6844–1

OECD trade, total and for 4 major countries, and US trade by country, by commodity, 1970-89, world area rpt series, 9116–1

Pollution abatement capital and operating costs, by SIC 2-digit industry, 1989, advance annual Current Industrial Rpt, 2506–3.6

Price indexes (producer), by stage of processing and detailed commodity, monthly rpt, 6762–6

Price indexes (producer), by stage of processing and detailed commodity, monthly 1990, annual rpt, 6764–2

Price indexes for department store inventories, by class of item, monthly table, 6762–7

Production, prices, trade, and use of cotton, wool, and synthetic fibers, periodic situation rpt with articles, 1561–1

Production, trade, sales, stocks, and material used, by product, region, and State, periodic Current Industrial Rpt series, 2506–5

Puerto Rico and other US possessions corporations income tax returns, income and tax items, and employment, by selected industry, 1987, article, 8302–2.213

Puerto Rico economic censuses, 1987: wholesale, retail, and service industries finances and operations, by establishment characteristics and SIC 2- and 3-digit industry, subject rpts, 2591–2

Research (agricultural) funding and staffing for USDA, State agencies, and other instns, by topic, FY90, annual rpt, 1744–2

Respiratory diseases related to occupational hazards, epidemiology, diagnosis, and treatment, for selected industries and work settings, 1988 conf, 4248–90

Retail trade census, 1987: finances and employment, for establishments with and without payroll, by SIC 2- to 4-digit kind of business, State, and MSA, 2401–1

Southeastern US textile mill employment, earnings, and hours, for 8 States, quarterly press release, 6942–1

Southern US textile mill employment, 1951-90, annual rpt, 6944–1

Statistical Abstract of US, 1991 annual data compilation, 2324–1.27

Tariff Schedule of US, classifications and rates of duty by detailed imported commodity, 1992 base edition, 9886–13

Tax (income) returns of corporations, income and tax items by asset size and detailed industry, 1987, annual rpt, 8304–4

Tax (income) returns of corporations, income and tax items by asset size and detailed industry, 1988, annual rpt, 8304–21

Tax (income) returns of corporations with foreign tax credit, income and tax items by industry group, 1986, biennial article, 8302–2.203

Tax (income) returns of sole proprietorships, income statement items, by industry group, 1989, annual article, 8302–2.214

Towels (shop) from Bangladesh at less than fair value, injury to US industry, investigation with background financial and operating data, 1991 rpt, 9886–14.310

Wages and production workers by occupation, and benefits, by location, 1990 survey, 6787–6.251

Wholesale trade census, 1987: establishments, sales by customer class, employment, inventories, and expenses, by SIC 2- to 4-digit kind of business, 2407–4

Wholesale trade sales, inventories, purchases, and gross margins, by SIC 2- to 3-digit kind of business, 1990, annual rpt, 2413–13

see also Carpets and rugs

see also Clothing and clothing industry

see also Cotton

see also Natural fibers

see also Silk

see also Synthetic fibers and fabrics

see also Wool and wool trade

see also under By Commodity in the "Index by Categories"

see also under By Industry in the "Index by Categories"

Thailand

Agricultural exports of high-value commodities, indexes and sales by commodity, world area, and country, 1960s-86, 1528–323

Agricultural exports of US, impacts of foreign agricultural and trade policy, with data by commodity and country, 1989, annual rpt, 1924–8

Agricultural production, prices, and trade, by country, 1960s-90, annual world area rpt, 1524–4.2

Agricultural production, trade, and policies in foreign countries, summary data by country, 1989-90, annual factbook, 1924–12

Agricultural trade of US, by detailed commodity and country, 1989, annual rpt, 1524–8

Agricultural trade of US, by detailed commodity and country, 1990, semiannual rpt, 1522–4

AID economic aid to developing countries, obligations and disbursements by country, quarterly rpt, 9912–4

AID loans repayment status and terms by program and country, and status of predecessor agency loans, quarterly rpt, 9912–3

Cambodia refugees in Thailand border camps by site, and UN aid by donor country, 1980s, GAO rpt, 26123–313

Drug abuse indicators, by world region and selected country, 1990 semiannual conf, 4492–5.1

Economic and military aid and loans from US and intl agencies, by program and country, FY46-90, annual rpt, 9914–5

Economic and social conditions of developing countries from 1960s, and Intl Dev Cooperation Agency and AID activities and funding, FY90-92, annual rpt, 9904–4

Economic conditions in USSR, Eastern Europe, OECD, and selected other countries, 1960s-90, annual rpt, 9114–4

Economic conditions, income, production, prices, employment, and trade, 1991 periodic country rpt, 2046–4.19; 2046–4.54

Economic conditions, policy, and trade practices, by country, 1988-90, annual rpt, 21384–5

Economic, social, political, and geographic summary data, by country, 1991, annual factbook, 9114–2

Exports and imports of US, by commodity and country, 1970-89, world area rpt, 9116–1.7

Exports and imports of US, by Harmonized System 6-digit commodity and country, 1990, annual rpt, 2424–13

Exports and imports of US, by selected country, country group, and commodity group, 1990, annual rpt, 2044–37

Exports and imports of US, by transport mode, country, and SITC 1- to 3-digit commodity, 1990, annual rpt, 2424–12

Exports of US, detailed Schedule B commodities with countries of destination, 1990, annual rpt, 2424–10

Fish (surimi) production and trade by country, and Japan import and catch quotas, 1975-89, article, 2162–1.202

Human rights conditions in 170 countries, and US economic and military aid, 1990, annual rpt, 21384–3

Imports of goods, services, and investment from US, trade barriers, impacts, and US actions, by country, 1990, annual rpt, 444–2

Labor conditions, union coverage, and work accidents, 1991 annual country rpt, 6366–4.50

Military aid of US, arms sales, and training programs costs and budget requests, by program, world region, and country, FY90-92, annual rpt, 7144–13

Multinatl US firms and foreign affiliates finances and operations, by industry and world area of parent firm, 1989 benchmark survey, preliminary annual rpt, 2704–5

Multinatl US firms foreign affiliates, income statement items by country and world area, 1986, biennial article, 8302–2.212

Pineapple (canned fruit and juice) production and exports, for 2 countries, forecast 1991, semiannual article, 1925–34.243

Pipe fittings (carbon steel) from 2 countries at less than fair value, injury to US industry, investigation with background financial and operating data, 1991 rpt, 9886–14.319

Poultry products exports of US, EC, and 3 leading countries, by world area, 1986-90, semiannual rpt, 1925–33.1

Rice market activities, prices, inspections, sales, trade, supply, and use, for US and selected foreign markets, weekly rpt, 1313–8

Shrimp aquaculture harvest by Southeast Asia country, and Thailand revenues and costs, 1984-89, article, 2162–1.203

Steel wire rope from 4 countries, injury to US industry from foreign subsidized and less than fair value imports, investigation with background financial and operating data, 1991 rpt, 9886–19.79

Steel wire rope from 8 countries, injury to US industry from foreign subsidized and less than fair value imports, investigation with background financial and operating data, 1990 rpt, 9886–19.73

Sugar exports by country, prices, acreage, production, and use, for Thailand, 1970s-91, article, 1561–14.201

UN voting record and share of votes in agreement with US, by issue, country, and world area, 1990, annual rpt, 7004–18

see also under By Foreign Country in the "Index by Categories"

Thallium

see Metals and metal industries

Thamke, Joanna N.

"Water Resources Activities of the USGS in Montana, Oct. 1987-Sept. 1989", 5666–26.11

Theater

County Business Patterns, 1988: employment, establishments, and payroll, by SIC 2- to 4-digit industry and county, annual State rpt series, 2326–6

County Business Patterns, 1989: employment, establishments, and payroll, by SIC 2- to 4-digit industry and county, annual State rpt series, 2326–8

Natl Endowment for Arts activities and grants, FY90, annual rpt, 9564–3

Service industries census, 1987: establishments, receipts by source, payroll, and employment, by SIC 2- to 4-digit kind of business, State, and MSA, 2393–4

Smoking bans in public places, local ordinances provisions, as of 1989, 4478–196

Theft

see Motor vehicle theft

see Robbery and theft

see Shoplifting

Theology

see Religion

Therapy

see Chemotherapy

see Occupational therapy

see Physical therapy

see Rehabilitation of the disabled

see Respiratory therapy

see Speech pathology and audiology

Thermal power

see Electric power and heat cogeneration

see Geothermal resources

Thibodaux, La.

see also under By SMSA or MSA in the "Index by Categories"

Third World countries

see Developing countries

Thomas, Anderia D.

"BLS Establishment Estimates Revised to March 1990 Benchmarks", 6742–2.204

Thomas, Charles P.

"Using External Sustainability To Forecast the Dollar", 9366–7.252

Thomas, D. R.

Thomas, D. R.
"Chukchi Sea Ice Motions, 1981-82", 2176–1.38

Thomas, Eric A.
"Rising Cost of Medical Care and Its Effect on Inflation", 9381–1.212

Thomas, James
"Chemical Trade Prospers in the 1980's", 6722–1.229

Thomas, Jesse G.
"Consumer Prices Rise Sharply in 1990", 6722–1.226

Thomas, Joseph
"Manufacturers' Prices and Pharmacists' Charges for Prescription Drugs Used by the Elderly", 4658–56

Thomas, R. Edward
"New Estimates of Hardwood Lumber Exports to Europe and Asia", 1208–373

Thomas, Robert L.
"ERIC Annual Report, 1991", 4814–3

Thompson, Andrew
"Bank Holding Company Performance", 9381–14.1

Thompson, Michael T.
"Forest Statistics for the Coastal Plain of Virginia, 1991", 1206–6.13

Thomson, James B.
"Insider's View of the Political Economy of the Too Big To Fail Doctrine", 9377–9.107
"Predicting Bank Failures in the 1980s", 9377–1.203

Thorium
see Radioactive materials

Thornton, Daniel L.
"Multiplier Approach to the Money Supply Process: A Precautionary Note", 9391–1.218

Thorsteinson, Lyman K.
"Arctic Fish Habitat Use Investigations: Nearshore Studies in the Alaskan Beaufort Sea, Summer 1988", 2176–1.37

Thousand Oaks, Calif.
see also under By City in the "Index by Categories"

Thrift institutions
see Credit unions
see Savings institutions

Throat disorders
see Nose and throat disorders

Throop, Adrian W.
"Fiscal Policy in the Reagan Years: A Burden on Future Generations?", 9393–8.201

Tibbals, C. H.
"Hydrology of the Floridan Aquifer System in East-Central Florida. Regional Aquifer-System Analysis", 5666–25.8

Tichler, J.
"Radioactive Materials Released from Nuclear Power Plants, Annual Report, 1988", 9634–1

Ticks
see Animal diseases and zoonoses

Tidal waves
see Tsunamis

Tides and currents
Alaska OCS environmental conditions and oil dev impacts, compilation of papers, series, 2176–1
Atlantic Ocean currents, temperatures, and salinity, from Florida straits to northern Brazil, series, 2146–7

California OCS oil and gas dev impacts on water quality, marine life, and sediments, by site, 1986-89, annual rpt, 5734–11
Coastal and estuarine environmental conditions, research results and methodology, series, 2176–7
Coastal currents, for US by ocean region, monthly rpt, 2182–5
Coastal tidal currents, daily time and velocity by station for North America and Asia, forecast 1992, annual rpts, 2174–1
Coastal tide height and time daily at points worldwide, forecast 1992, annual rpt series, 2174–2
Great Lakes water levels, daily and monthly averages by site, 1990 and cumulative from 1900, annual rpt, 2174–3
Mariners Weather Log, quarterly journal, 2152–8
Middle Atlantic States tide height and tidal current velocity daily at selected coastal stations, forecast 1992, annual rpt, 2174–11
North Carolina environmental and socioeconomic conditions, and impacts of proposed OCS oil and gas exploration, 1970s-90 and projected to 2020, 5738–22
Wetlands acreage, resources, soil and water properties, and conservation efforts, by wetland type, State rpt series, 5506–11

Tilly, Chris
"Reasons for the Continuing Growth of Part-Time Employment", 6722–1.218

Timber
see Forests and forestry
see Lumber industry and products
see Wood fuel

Time
see Chronologies
see Seasonal adjustment factors
see Seasonal variations
see Time of day

Time deposits
see Bank deposits
see Certificates of deposit

Time of day
Air traffic and other general aviation activity, 1990, triennial survey rpt, 7508–3
Air traffic, and passenger and freight enplanements, by airport, 1960s-90 and projected to 2010, hub area rpt series, 7506–7
Aircraft (general aviation) accidents, by circumstances, characteristics of persons and aircraft involved, and type of flying, 1988, annual rpt, 9614–3
Aircraft (general aviation) flight hours, by weather and light conditions, aircraft type and model, and region, 1990, annual rpt, 7504–29.2
Aircraft accidents and circumstances, for US operations of domestic and foreign airlines and general aviation, periodic rpt, 9612–1
Aircraft accidents, casualties, and damage, for commercial operations by detailed circumstances, 1987, annual rpt, 9614–2
Aircraft noise abatement measures, and industry compliance costs, aggregate FY90-2000, GAO rpt, 26113–534
Airline consumer complaints by reason, passengers denied boarding, and late flights, by reporting carrier and airport, monthly rpt, 7302–11

Assaults and deaths of law enforcement officers, by circumstances, agency, victim and offender characteristics, and location, 1990, annual rpt, 6224–3
Boat accidents, casualties, and damage, by cause, vessel and operator characteristics, and State, 1990, annual rpt, 7404–1.2
Bombing incidents, casualties, and damage, by target, circumstances, and State, 1990, annual rpt, 6224–5
Bus (school) accidents, circumstances, victim characteristics, and vehicle type, 1989, annual rpt, 7764–22
Carpool high occupancy vehicle lanes use, design, enforcement, and drivers views, for California, 1988-89, 7308–203
Crime victimization rates, by victim and offender characteristics, circumstances, and offense, 1988 survey, annual rpt, 6066–3.42
Crime victimization rates, by victim and offender characteristics, circumstances, and offense, 1989 survey, annual rpt, 6066–3.44
Crimes, by characteristics of victim and offender, circumstances, and location, data compilation, 1991 annual rpt, 6064–6.3
Earthquake intensity, time, location, damage, and seismic characteristics, for US and foreign earthquakes, 1985, annual rpt, 5664–13
Mines occupational deaths, by circumstances and selected victim characteristics, semiannual rpt series, 6662–3
Occupational injuries, by circumstances, body site, equipment type, and industry, with safety measures, series, 6846–1
Railroad-hwy grade-crossing accidents, detailed data by State and railroad, 1989, annual rpt, 7604–2
Ships and marine facilities accidents, casualties, and circumstances, Coast Guard investigation results, periodic rpt, 9612–4
Star position tables, planet coordinates, time conversion factors, and listing of observatories worldwide, 1992, annual rpt, 3804–7
Sunrise and sunset mean time every 5th day, by degree of latitude worldwide, forecast 1992, annual rpt series, 2174–2
Telephone rates for intl calls, and domestic long-distance rates by company, by time and area served, 1950s- 89, annual rpt, 9284–6.6; 9284–6.7
Tidal currents, daily time and velocity by station for North America and Asia coasts, forecast 1992, annual rpts, 2174–1
Tide height and tidal current velocity daily at Middle Atlantic coastal stations, forecast 1992, annual rpt, 2174–11
Tide height and time daily at coastal points worldwide, forecast 1992, annual rpt series, 2174–2
Traffic accidents, casualties, circumstances, and characteristics of persons and vehicles involved, 1989, annual rpt, 7764–18
Traffic fatal accidents, alcohol levels of drivers and others, by circumstances and characteristics of persons and vehicles, 1989, annual rpt, 7764–16
Traffic fatal accidents, circumstances, and characteristics of persons and vehicles involved, 1990, semiannual rpt, 7762–11

Index by Subjects and Names

Traffic fatal accidents, deaths, and rates, by circumstances, characteristics of persons and vehicles involved, and location, 1989, annual rpt, 7764–10

Truck accidents, casualties, and damage, by circumstances and characteristics of persons and vehicles involved, 1988, annual rpt, 7554–9

Timme, Stephen G.

"Quasi-Fixed Inputs in the Estimation of Bank Scale Economies", 9371–10.54

"Some Evidence on the Impact of Quasi-Fixed Inputs on Bank Scale Economy Estimates", 9371–1.208

"Stochastic Dominance Approach to the Evaluation of Foreign Exchange Forecasts", 9371–10.63

Timmerman, Tina

"AIDS Awareness in North Dakota: A Knowledge and Attitude Study of the General Population", 4042–3.211

Tin and tin industry

Business statistics, detailed data for major industries and economic indicators, *Survey of Current Business,* monthly rpt, 2702–1.17

Exports and imports between US and outlying areas, by detailed commodity and mode of transport, 1990, annual rpt, 2424–11

Exports and imports of US, by country and detailed commodity, monthly rpt, 2422–12

Exports and imports of US, by Harmonized System 6-digit commodity and country, 1990, annual rpt, 2424–13

Exports and imports of US, by transport mode, country, and SITC 1- to 3-digit commodity, 1990, annual rpt, 2424–12

Exports of US, detailed Schedule B commodities with countries of destination, 1990, annual rpt, 2424–10

Foreign and US strategic minerals supply and characteristics of individual deposits, by country, 1990 commodity rpt, 5666–21.10

Mineral Industry Surveys, commodity review of production, trade, stocks, and use, monthly rpt, 5612–1.24

Minerals Yearbook, 1988, Vol 3: foreign country reviews of production, trade, and policy, by commodity, annual rpt series, 5604–17

Minerals Yearbook, 1989, Vol 1: commodity review of production, reserves, supply, use, and trade, annual rpt, 5604–15.65

Minerals Yearbook, 1989, Vol 2: State reviews of production and sales by commodity, and business activity, annual rpt series, 5604–16

Minerals Yearbook, 1989, Vol 2: State reviews of production, sales, and firms, by commodity, and business activity, annual rpt, 5604–34

Mines (metal) and related operations occupational injuries and incidence, employment, and hours, 1989, annual rpt, 6664–3

OECD trade, total and for 4 major countries, and US trade by country, by commodity, 1970-89, world area rpt series, 9116–1

Price indexes (producer), by stage of processing and detailed commodity, monthly 1990, annual rpt, 6764–2

Production, prices, trade, use, employment, tariffs, and stockpiles, by mineral, with foreign comparisons, 1986-90, annual rpt, 5604–18

Statistical Abstract of US, 1991 annual data compilation, 2324–1.25

Stockpiling of strategic material by Fed Govt, activity, and inventory by commodity, as of Mar 1991, semiannual rpt, 3542–22

Stockpiling of strategic material, inventories and needs, by commodity, as of Jan 1991, annual rpt, 3544–37

see also under By Commodity in the "Index by Categories"

Tiner, Ralph W., Jr.

"National Wetlands Inventory. Preliminary Report of Vermont's Wetland Acreage", 5506–11.3

"National Wetlands Inventory. Preliminary Report on Connecticut's Wetland Acreage", 5506–11.4

"National Wetlands Inventory. Preliminary Report on Massachusetts' Wetland Acreage", 5506–11.6

"National Wetlands Inventory. Wetlands of Delaware", 5506–11.2

"National Wetlands Inventory. Wetlands of New Jersey", 5506–11.1

"National Wetlands Inventory. Wetlands of Rhode Island", 5506–11.7

"Soil-Vegetation Correlations in the Connecticut River Floodplain of Western Massachusetts", 5506–10.12

Tinsley, LaVerne C.

"State Workers' Compensation: Legislation Enacted in 1990", 6722–1.210

Tippett, Katherine

"Report on the Diet and Health Knowledge Survey", 1004–16.1

Tires and tire industry

Auto, private airplane, and motorcycle operating costs by component, and Fed Govt mileage reimbursement rates, 1989, annual rpt, 9454–13

Business statistics, detailed data for major industries and economic indicators, *Survey of Current Business,* monthly rpt, 2702–1.20

Canada and US auto trade, production, sales, prices, and employment, selected years 1965-88, annual rpt, 2044–35

County Business Patterns, 1988: employment, establishments, and payroll, by SIC 2- to 4-digit industry and county, annual State rpt series, 2326–6

County Business Patterns, 1989: employment, establishments, and payroll, by SIC 2- to 4-digit industry and county, annual State rpt series, 2326–8

CPI by component for US city average, and by region, population size, and for 27 metro areas, monthly rpt, 6762–2

DOD prime contract awards, by detailed procurement category, FY87-90, annual rpt, 3544–18

Employment, earnings, and hours, by SIC 1- to 4-digit industry, monthly and annual averages, selected years 1909-90, annual rpt, 6744–4

Exports and imports between US and outlying areas, by detailed commodity and mode of transport, 1990, annual rpt, 2424–11

Tires and tire industry

Exports and imports of US, by country and detailed commodity, monthly rpt, 2422–12

Exports and imports of US, by Harmonized System 6-digit commodity and country, 1990, annual rpt, 2424–13

Exports and imports of US, by selected country, country group, and commodity group, 1990, annual rpt, 2044–37

Exports and imports of US, by transport mode, country, and SITC 1- to 3-digit commodity, 1990, annual rpt, 2424–12

Exports of US, detailed Schedule B commodities with countries of destination, 1990, annual rpt, 2424–10

Farm prices received and paid, by commodity and State, 1990, annual rpt, 1629–5

Imports purchasing decisions of consumers, importance of brand name, authenticity, origin, and other factors, 1984 survey, hearing, 25528–115

Manufacturing annual survey, 1989: finances and operations, by SIC 2- to 4-digit industry, series, 2506–15

Manufacturing census, 1987: employment and shipments under Fed Govt contracts, by SIC 4-digit industry, 2497–7

Manufacturing census, 1987: finances and operations, by SIC 2- to 4-digit industry, State, and MSA, with trends from 1849, 2497–1

Manufacturing census, 1987: finances and operations, by type of organization and SIC 2- to 4-digit industry, subject rpt, 2497–5

Occupational injury and illness rates, by SIC 2- to 4-digit industry, 1988-89, annual rpt, 6844–7

Occupational injury and illness rates, by SIC 2- to 4-digit industry, 1989, annual rpt, 6844–1

Price indexes (producer), by stage of processing and detailed commodity, monthly rpt, 6762–6

Price indexes (producer), by stage of processing and detailed commodity, monthly 1990, annual rpt, 6764–2

Productivity of labor and capital, and indexes of output, hours, and employment, 1967-89, annual rpt, 6824–1.3; 6824–1.5

Quality ratings for tires, by type and brand, as of Sept 1991, annual rpt, 7764–17

Recalls of motor vehicles and equipment with safety-related defects, by make, monthly listing, 7762–12

Recalls of motor vehicles and equipment with safety-related defects, by make, quarterly listing, 7762–2

Service industries census, 1987: establishments, receipts by source, payroll, and employment, by SIC 2- to 4-digit kind of business, State, and MSA, 2393–4.10

Soviet Union, Eastern Europe, OECD, and selected other countries consumer and producer goods and services production and sales, 1960s-90, annual rpt, 9114–4.7

Tax (excise) collections of IRS, by source, quarterly rpt, 8302–1; 8302–2.1

Tire cord fabrics production, quarterly Current Industrial Rpt, 2506–5.11

Truck itemized costs per mile, finances, and operations, for agricultural carriers, 1990, annual rpt, 1311–15

Tires and tire industry

Truck transport of fruit and vegetables, itemized costs per mile by item for fleets and owner-operator trucks, monthly table, 1272–1

Wholesale trade census, 1987: establishments, sales by customer class, employment, inventories, and expenses, by SIC 2- to 4-digit kind of business, 2407–4

see also under By Commodity in the "Index by Categories"

Titanium

see Metals and metal industries

Titusville, Fla.

Wages by occupation, for office and plant workers, 1991 survey, periodic MSA rpt, 6785–3.3

see also under By SMSA or MSA in the "Index by Categories"

Tobacco industry and products

Acreage planted and harvested, by crop and State, 1989-90 and planned as of June 1991, annual rpt, 1621–23

Acreage planted, by selected crop and State, 1982-90 and planned 1991, annual rpt, 1621–22

Acreage under Agricultural Stabilization and Conservation Service programs, rankings by commodity and congressional district, 1989, biennial rpt, 1804–17

Advertising of tobacco in food and drug stores, prevalence and characteristics, 1987 local area study, article, 4042–3.250

Agricultural Stabilization and Conservation Service tobacco programs, 1960-91, annual fact sheet, 1806–4.2; 1806–4.3

Agricultural Stabilization and Conservation Service tobacco programs, 1987-91, annual fact sheet, 1806–4.7

Agricultural Statistics, 1990, annual rpt, 1004–1

Agriculture census, 1987: farms, farmland, production, finances, and operator characteristics, by county, final State rpt series, 2331–1

Business statistics, detailed data for major industries and economic indicators, *Survey of Current Business,* monthly rpt, 2702–1.14

CCC financial condition and major commodity program operations, FY62-87, annual chartbook, 1824–2

Collective bargaining agreements expiring during year, and workers covered, by firm, union, industry group, and State, 1991, annual rpt, 6784–9

Consumer Expenditure Survey, household income by source, and itemized spending, by selected characteristics and region, 1988-89, annual rpt, 6764–5

Consumer Expenditure Survey, spending by category, and income, by selected household characteristics and location, 1990, annual press release, 6726–1.42

County Business Patterns, 1988: employment, establishments, and payroll, by SIC 2- to 4-digit industry and county, annual State rpt series, 2326–6

County Business Patterns, 1989: employment, establishments, and payroll, by SIC 2- to 4-digit industry and county, annual State rpt series, 2326–8

CPI by component for US city average, and by region, population size, and for 27 metro areas, monthly rpt, 6762–2

Employment, earnings, and hours, by SIC 1- to 4-digit industry, monthly and annual averages, selected years 1909-90, annual rpt, 6744–4

Employment in manufacturing, by detailed occupation and SIC 2-digit industry, 1989 survey, triennial rpt, 6748–52

Employment related to agriculture, by industry, region, and metro-nonmetro location, 1987, 1598–271

Energy use and prices for manufacturing industries, 1988 survey, series, 3166–13

Enterprise Statistics, 1987: auxiliaries of multi-establishment firms, finances and operations by function, industry, and State, 2329–6

Enterprise Statistics, 1987: finances and operations for companies, by size, level of diversification, form of organization, and industry group, 2329–8

Exports (agricultural) of high-value commodities, indexes and sales value by commodity, world area, and country, 1960s-86, 1528–323

Exports (agricultural) of US, impacts of foreign agricultural and trade policy, with data by commodity and country, 1989, annual rpt, 1924–8

Exports and imports (agricultural) commodity and country, prices, and world market devs, monthly rpt, 1922–12

Exports and imports (agricultural) of US, by commodity and country, bimonthly rpt, 1522–1

Exports and imports (agricultural) of US, by detailed commodity and country, 1989, annual rpt, 1524–8

Exports and imports (agricultural) of US, by detailed commodity and country, 1990, semiannual rpt, 1522–4

Exports and imports between US and outlying areas, by detailed commodity and mode of transport, 1990, annual rpt, 2424–11

Exports and imports of US, by country and detailed commodity, monthly rpt, 2422–12

Exports and imports of US, by Harmonized System 6-digit commodity and country, 1990, annual rpt, 2424–13

Exports and imports of US, by selected country, country group, and commodity group, 1990, annual rpt, 2044–37

Exports and imports of US, by transport mode, country, and SITC 1- to 3-digit commodity, 1990, annual rpt, 2424–12

Exports of US, detailed commodities by country, monthly CD-ROM, 2422–13

Exports of US, detailed Schedule B commodities with countries of destination, 1990, annual rpt, 2424–10

Farm financial and marketing conditions, forecast 1991, annual chartbook, 1504–8

Farm financial and marketing conditions, forecast 1991, annual conf, 1004–16

Farm income, expenses, receipts by commodity, assets, liabilities, and ratios, 1990 and trends from 1945, annual rpt, 1544–16

Farm sector balance sheet, and receipts by detailed commodity, by State, 1985-89, annual rpt, 1544–18

Foreign and US tobacco production, prices, and trade, FAS monthly circular with articles, 1925–16

Index by Subjects and Names

Foreign countries agricultural production, prices, and trade, by country, 1980-90 and forecast 1991, annual world area rpt series, 1524–4

Foreign countries agricultural production, trade, and policies, summary data by country, 1989-90, annual factbook, 1924–12

Illegal commerce in cigarettes, Federal sentencing guidelines by offense and circumstances, series, 17668–1

Illegal commerce in cigarettes, US attorneys cases by disposition, FY90, annual rpt, 6004–2.1

Imports, exports, and employment impacts, by SIC 2- to 4-digit industry and commodity, quarterly rpt, 2322–2

Imports of US, detailed commodities by country, monthly CD-ROM, 2422–14

Input-output structure of US economy, detailed interindustry transactions for 84 industries, and components of final demand, 1986, annual article, 2702–1.206

Input-output structure of US economy, detailed interindustry transactions for 85 industries, 1982 benchmark data, 2702–1.213

Labor productivity, indexes of output, hours, and employment by SIC 2- to 4-digit industry, 1967-89, annual rpt, 6824–1.3

Manufacturing annual survey, 1989: finances and operations, by SIC 2- to 4-digit industry, series, 2506–15

Manufacturing census, 1987: finances and operations, by SIC 2- to 4-digit industry, State, and MSA, with trends from 1849, 2497–1

Manufacturing census, 1987: finances and operations, by type of organization and SIC 2- to 4-digit industry, subject rpt, 2497–5

Manufacturing corporations financial statements, by selected SIC 2- to 3-digit industry, quarterly rpt, 2502–1

Manufacturing production, shipments, inventories, orders, and pollution control costs, periodic Current Industrial Rpt series, 2506–3

Marketing activity, prices, and sales, by grade and type of tobacco, market, and State, 1989-90, annual rpt series, 1319–5

Mexico imports from US, by industry and State, 1987-90, 2048–154

Multinatl US firms and foreign affiliates finances and operations, by industry and world area of parent firm, 1989 benchmark survey, preliminary annual rpt, 2704–5

Nicotine, tar, and carbon monoxide content of cigarettes, by brand, 1989, 9408–53

Occupational injury and illness rates, by SIC 2- to 4-digit industry, 1988-89, annual rpt, 6844–7

Occupational injury and illness rates, by SIC 2- to 4-digit industry, 1989, annual rpt, 6844–1

OECD trade, total and for 4 major countries, and US trade by country, by commodity, 1970-89, world area rpt series, 9116–1

Pollution abatement capital and operating costs, by SIC 2-digit industry, 1989, advance annual Current Industrial Rpt, 2506–3.6

Index by Subjects and Names

Price indexes (producer), by stage of processing and detailed commodity, monthly rpt, 6762–6

Price indexes (producer), by stage of processing and detailed commodity, monthly 1990, annual rpt, 6764–2

Price support program provisions, for selected commodities, 1961-90, 1568–303

Prices received and paid by farmers, by commodity and State, 1990, annual rpt, 1629–5

Prices received by farmers and production value, by detailed crop and State, 1988-90, annual rpt, 1621–2

Prices received by farmers for major products, and paid for farm inputs and living items, by State, monthly rpt, 1629–1

Production, farms, acreage, and related data, by selected crop and State, monthly rpt, 1621–1

Production inputs, output, and productivity for farms, by commodity and region, 1947-89, annual rpt, 1544–17

Production, marketing, use, price supports, and trade, for tobacco, quarterly situation rpt with articles, 1561–10

Production, prices, stocks, and taxes by State, and trade and production by country, 1990, annual rpt, 1319–1

Production, prices, trade, and marketing, by commodity, current situation and forecast, monthly rpt with articles, 1502–4

Production, trade, and removals of tobacco products, by type, monthly rpt, 8486–1.4

Puerto Rico economic censuses, 1987: wholesale and retail trade and service industry finances and operations, by SIC 2- to 4-digit industry and municipio, 2591–1

Regulatory activities, staff, and funding of Bur of Alcohol, Tobacco, and Firearms, and tax revenues and rates, 1980s-91, GAO rpt, 26119–335

Retail trade census, 1987: finances and employment, for establishments with and without payroll, by SIC 2- to 4-digit kind of business, State, and MSA, 2401–1

Smokeless tobacco use and smoking research, spending, intervention project results, and smoking prevalence, with bibl, 1960s-90, 4478–195

Smokeless tobacco use, by selected characteristics, 1990 survey, biennial rpt, 4494–5

Statistical Abstract of US, 1991 annual data compilation, 2324–1.23; 2324–1.27

Stocks, production, sales, and import inspections by country, for tobacco leaf by product, quarterly rpt, 1319–3

Tax (excise) collections of IRS, by source, quarterly rpt, 8302–2.1

Tax (income) returns of corporations, income and tax items by asset size and detailed industry, 1987, annual rpt, 8304–4

Tax (income) returns of corporations, income and tax items by asset size and detailed industry, 1988, annual rpt, 8304–21

Tax (income) returns of corporations with foreign tax credit, income and tax items by industry group, 1986, biennial article, 8302–2.203

Tax collections of State govts by detailed type of tax, and tax rates, by State, FY90, annual rpt, 2466–2.7

Tax rates and revenue of State and local govts, by source and State, 1991 and historical trends, annual rpt, 10044–1

Tax revenue, by level of govt, type of tax, State, and selected large county, quarterly rpt, 2462–3

Toxicology Natl Program research and testing activities, FY89 and planned FY90, annual rpt, 4044–16

Wholesale trade census, 1987: establishments, sales by customer class, employment, inventories, and expenses, by SIC 2- to 4-digit kind of business, 2407–4

Zimbabwe agricultural conditions impacts of economic policies, 1980s, 1528–319

see also Smoking

see also under By Commodity in the "Index by Categories"

see also under By Industry in the "Index by Categories"

Tobalske, Bret W.

"Bird Populations in Logged and Unlogged Western Larch/Douglas-fir Forest in Northwestern Montana", 1208–372

Tobey, James A.

"Agricultural Trade Implications of Environmental Management", 1522–3.203

"Effects of Domestic Agricultural Policy Reform on Environmental Quality", 1502–3.203

Tobin, James

"Natural Gas Transportation Services: An Update", 3162–4.204

"Overview of Recent Developments in the Underground Storage Market", 3162–4.205

"Recent Trends and Regional Variability in Underground Storage Activities", 3162–4.203

Todd, Mary E.

"Pacific Outer Continental Shelf Region: Production Record by Platform, 1989", 5734–9

Todd, Walker F.

"Insider's View of the Political Economy of the Too Big To Fail Doctrine", 9377–9.107

Togo

Agricultural exports of high-value commodities, indexes and sales by commodity, world area, and country, 1960s-86, 1528–323

Agricultural trade of US, by detailed commodity and country, 1989, annual rpt, 1524–8

Agricultural trade of US, by detailed commodity and country, 1990, semiannual rpt, 1522–4

AID economic aid to developing countries, obligations and disbursements by country, quarterly rpt, 9912–4

Dairy imports, consumption, and market conditions, by sub-Saharan Africa country, 1961-88, 1528–321

Economic and military aid and loans from US and intl agencies, by program and country, FY46-90, annual rpt, 9914–5

Economic and social conditions of developing countries from 1960s, and Intl Dev Cooperation Agency and AID activities and funding, FY90-92, annual rpt, 9904–4

Tonga

Economic conditions, income, production, prices, employment, and trade, 1990 periodic country rpt, 2046–4.3

Economic, social, political, and geographic summary data, by country, 1991, annual factbook, 9114–2

Exports and imports of US, by transport mode, country, and SITC 1- to 3-digit commodity, 1990, annual rpt, 2424–12

Exports of US, detailed Schedule B commodities with countries of destination, 1990, annual rpt, 2424–10

Human rights conditions in 170 countries, and US economic and military aid, 1990, annual rpt, 21384–3

Military aid of US, arms sales, and training programs costs and budget requests, by program, world region, and country, FY90-92, annual rpt, 7144–13

UN voting record and share of votes in agreement with US, by issue, country, and world area, 1990, annual rpt, 7004–18

see also under By Foreign Country in the "Index by Categories"

Toiletries

see Cosmetics and toiletries

Toledo, Ohio

Auto and auto parts manufacturing wages, employment, and benefits, by occupation, region, and selected labor market area, 1989 survey, 6787–6.252

Wages by occupation, for office and plant workers, 1990 survey, periodic MSA rpt, 6785–11.4

see also under By City and By SMSA or MSA in the "Index by Categories"

Tolls

Facilities (toll), mileage, and operating status, by type of system, as of Jan 1990, biennial listing, 7554–39

Hwy funding, costs, and completion status of Federal-aid system, by State, as of June 1991, semiannual rpt, 7552–5

Hwy receipts by source, and spending by function, by level of govt and State, 1990, annual rpt, 7554–1.3

Panama Canal Commission finances and activities, with Canal traffic and local govt operations, FY90, annual rpt, 9664–3

St Lawrence Seaway ship, cargo, and passenger traffic, and toll revenue, 1990 and trends from 1959, annual rpt, 7744–2

State govt revenue by source, spending and debt by function, and holdings, FY90, annual rpt, 2466–2.6

Tolson, George C.

"Revision of the U.S. Standard Certificates and Reports, 1989. Vital and Health Statistics Series 4", 4147–4.27

Tomatoes

see Vegetables and vegetable products

Tonga

Economic, social, and agricultural data, US and other aid sources, and AID activity, 1988 country rpt, 9916–12.28

Economic, social, political, and geographic summary data, by country, 1991, annual factbook, 9114–2

Exports and imports of US, by transport mode, country, and SITC 1- to 3-digit commodity, 1990, annual rpt, 2424–12

Human rights conditions in 170 countries, and US economic and military aid, 1990, annual rpt, 21384–3

Tonga

Military aid of US, arms sales, and training programs costs and budget requests, by program, world region, and country, FY90-92, annual rpt, 7144–13

Tonopah, Nev.

Wages by occupation, and benefits for office and plant workers, 1990 survey, periodic MSA rpt, 6785–3.1

Tool and die industry

see Machines and machinery industry

Tools

- China exports of tools at less than fair value, injury to US industry, investigation with background financial and operating data, 1991 rpt, 9886–14.304
- County Business Patterns, 1988: employment, establishments, and payroll, by SIC 2- to 4-digit industry and county, annual State rpt series, 2326–6
- County Business Patterns, 1989: employment, establishments, and payroll, by SIC 2- to 4-digit industry and county, annual State rpt series, 2326–8
- DOD prime contract awards, by detailed procurement category, FY87-90, annual rpt, 3544–18
- Employment, earnings, and hours, by SIC 1- to 4-digit industry, monthly and annual averages, selected years 1909-90, annual rpt, 6744–4
- Exports and imports between US and outlying areas, by detailed commodity and mode of transport, 1990, annual rpt, 2424–11
- Exports and imports of US, by country and detailed commodity, monthly rpt, 2422–12
- Exports and imports of US, by Harmonized System 6-digit commodity and country, 1990, annual rpt, 2424–13
- Exports and imports of US, by transport mode, country, and SITC 1- to 3-digit commodity, 1990, annual rpt, 2424–12
- Exports of US, detailed Schedule B commodities with countries of destination, 1990, annual rpt, 2424–10
- Franchise business opportunities by firm and kind of business, and sources of aid and info, 1990 annual listing, 2104–7
- Imports of US given duty-free treatment for value of US material sent abroad, by commodity and country, 1989, annual rpt, 9884–14
- Injuries from use of consumer products, by severity, victim age, and detailed product, 1990, annual rpt, 9164–6
- Injuries from use of consumer products, related deaths and costs, and recalls by brand, by product type, FY89, annual rpt, 9164–2
- Labor productivity, indexes of output, hours, and employment by SIC 2- to 4-digit industry, 1967-89, annual rpt, 6824–1.3
- Manufacturing annual survey, 1989: finances and operations, by SIC 2- to 4-digit industry, series, 2506–15
- Manufacturing census, 1987: employment and shipments under Fed Govt contracts, by SIC 4-digit industry, 2497–7
- Manufacturing census, 1987: finances and operations, by SIC 2- to 4-digit industry, State, and MSA, with trends from 1849, 2497–1
- Manufacturing census, 1987: finances and operations, by type of organization and SIC 2- to 4-digit industry, subject rpt, 2497–5
- Manufacturing finances and operations, by SIC 2- to 4-digit industry, forecast 1991, annual rpt, 2044–28
- Occupational injury and illness rates, by SIC 2- to 4-digit industry, 1988-89, annual rpt, 6844–7
- Occupational injury and illness rates, by SIC 2- to 4-digit industry, 1989, annual rpt, 6844–1
- OECD trade, total and for 4 major countries, and US trade by country, by commodity, 1970-89, world area rpt series, 9116–1
- Price indexes (producer), by stage of processing and detailed commodity, monthly rpt, 6762–6
- Price indexes (producer), by stage of processing and detailed commodity, monthly 1990, annual rpt, 6764–2
- *Statistical Abstract of US,* 1991 annual data compilation, 2324–1.27
- *see also* Agricultural machinery and equipment
- *see also* Hardware
- *see also* Household supplies and utensils
- *see also* Lawn and garden equipment
- *see also* Machines and machinery industry
- *see also* under By Commodity in the "Index by Categories"

Tootell, Geoffrey M.

- "Are District Presidents More Conservative than Board Governors?", 9373–1.214
- "Regional Economic Conditions and the FOMC Votes of District Presidents", 9373–1.205
- " 'Whither New England?' ", 9373–1.211

Toothpaste

see Cosmetics and toiletries

Topeka, Kans.

see also under By City and By SMSA or MSA in the "Index by Categories"

Topography

- Elevations, highest and lowest points for regions and States, 1991 data compilation, 2328–54
- Foreign countries *Background Notes,* summary social, political, and economic data, series, 7006–2
- Foreign countries economic, social, political, and geographic summary data, by country, 1991, annual factbook, 9114–2
- Gazetteer of US places, mountains, bodies of water, and other political and physical features, 1990 rpt, 5668–117
- Natl Ocean Service Charting and Geodetic Service activities and funding, by State, FY91-92, biennial rpt, 2174–10
- *Statistical Abstract of US,* 1991 annual data compilation, 2324–1.6
- Water quality, chemistry, hydrology, and other characteristics, local area studies, series, 5666–27
- *see also* Arid zones
- *see also* Cartography
- *see also* Coastal areas
- *see also* Lakes and lakeshores
- *see also* Land area
- *see also* Rivers and waterways
- *see also* Seashores
- *see also* Water area

Tornadoes

see Storms

Toronto, Canada

- Drug abuse indicators, for selected countries, 1991 semiannual conf, 4492–5.2
- Fruit and vegetable shipments, and arrivals in US and Canada cities, by mode of transport and State and country of origin, 1990, annual rpt, 1311–4.1

Torpedoes

DOD budget, weapons acquisition costs by system and service branch, FY91-93, annual rpt, 3504–2

Torrance, Calif.

see also under By City in the "Index by Categories"

Torts

- Court civil and criminal caseloads for Federal district, appeals, and bankruptcy courts, by type of suit and offense, circuit, and district, 1990, annual rpt, 18204–11
- Court civil and criminal caseloads for Federal district, appeals, and special courts, 1990, annual rpt, 18204–8
- Court civil and criminal caseloads for Federal district courts, 1991, annual rpt, 18204–2.1
- Legal services establishments, lawyers by field, receipts by class of client, expenses, and employment, by MSA, 1987 Census of Service Industries, 2393–4.13
- Medical malpractice claims resolution through arbitration and litigation, Michigan program cases, awards, duration, and costs, late 1970s-80s, GAO rpt, 26121–394
- US attorneys civil cases, by type and disposition, FY90, annual rpt, 6004–2.5

Toscano, Guy

"Further Test of a Census Approach to Compiling Data on Fatal Work Injuries", 6722–1.249

Tourist travel

see Travel and tourism

Towels

see Household supplies and utensils

Town planning

see City and town planning

Towns

- *see* Central cities
- *see* Cities
- *see* Rural areas
- *see* Suburbs
- *see* Urban areas

Townsend, Terry P.

"Cotton Price Stability and the Outlook for 1991/92", 1004–16.1

Toxic substances

- *see* Dioxins
- *see* Hazardous substances
- *see* Hazardous waste and disposal
- *see* Pesticides
- *see* Poisoning and drug reaction

Toys and games

- Accident deaths and injuries of children by cause, and victimization, rates by race, sex, and age, 1979-88, chartbook, 4108–56
- Computer use at home, school, and work, by purpose and selected user characteristics, 1989, Current Population Rpt, 2546–2.158
- Consumer Expenditure Survey, household income by source, and itemized spending, by selected characteristics and region, 1988-89, annual rpt, 6764–5

Index by Subjects and Names

Trade adjustment assistance

County Business Patterns, 1988: employment, establishments, and payroll, by SIC 2- to 4-digit industry and county, annual State rpt series, 2326–6

County Business Patterns, 1989: employment, establishments, and payroll, by SIC 2- to 4-digit industry and county, annual State rpt series, 2326–8

CPI by component for US city average, and by region, population size, and for 27 metro areas, monthly rpt, 6762–2

Electronic communications systems and related products shipments, trade, use, and firms, 1990, annual Current Industrial Rpt, 2506–12.35

Employment, earnings, and hours, by SIC 1- to 4-digit industry, monthly and annual averages, selected years 1909-90, annual rpt, 6744–4

Exports and imports between US and outlying areas, by detailed commodity and mode of transport, 1990, annual rpt, 2424–11

Exports and imports of US, by country and detailed commodity, monthly rpt, 2422–12

Exports and imports of US, by Harmonized System 6-digit commodity and country, 1990, annual rpt, 2424–13

Exports and imports of US, by selected country, country group, and commodity group, 1990, annual rpt, 2044–37

Exports of US, detailed Schedule B commodities with countries of destination, 1990, annual rpt, 2424–10

Imports of clothing, footwear, luggage, toys, games, and sporting goods from PRC and other countries, 1985-90, article, 9882–2.201

Imports of US given duty-free treatment for value of US material sent abroad, by commodity and country, 1989, annual rpt, 9884–14

Injuries from use of consumer products, by severity, victim age, and detailed product, 1990, annual rpt, 9164–6

Injuries from use of consumer products, related deaths and costs, and recalls by brand, by product type, FY89, annual rpt, 9164–2

Manufacturing annual survey, 1989: finances and operations, by SIC 2- to 4-digit industry, series, 2506–15

Manufacturing census, 1987: finances and operations, by SIC 2- to 4-digit industry, State, and MSA, with trends from 1849, 2497–1

Manufacturing census, 1987: finances and operations, by type of organization and SIC 2- to 4-digit industry, subject rpt, 2497–5

Manufacturing finances and operations, by SIC 2- to 4-digit industry, forecast 1991, annual rpt, 2044–28

Occupational injury and illness rates, by SIC 2- to 4-digit industry, 1988-89, annual rpt, 6844–7

Occupational injury and illness rates, by SIC 2- to 4-digit industry, 1989, annual rpt, 6844–1

OECD trade, total and for 4 major countries, and US trade by country, by commodity, 1970-89, world area rpt series, 9116–1

Price indexes (producer), by stage of processing and detailed commodity, monthly rpt, 6762–6

Price indexes (producer), by stage of processing and detailed commodity, monthly 1990, annual rpt, 6764–2

Puerto Rico economic censuses, 1987: wholesale and retail trade and service industry finances and operations, by SIC 2- to 4-digit industry and municipio, 2591–1

Retail trade census, 1987: finances and employment, for establishments with and without payroll, by SIC 2- to 4-digit kind of business, State, and MSA, 2401–1

Wholesale trade census, 1987: establishments, sales by customer class, employment, inventories, and expenses, by SIC 2- to 4-digit kind of business, 2407–4

see also Sporting goods

see also under By Commodity in the "Index by Categories"

Trace metals

Acid rain and air pollution environmental impacts, and methods of neutralizing acidified water bodies, summary research rpt series, 5506–5

Acid rain effects on Maine streams water quality, acidity, and fish, 1986-87, 9208–130

Air pollution emissions factors, by detailed pollutant and source, data compilation, 1990 rpt, 9198–120

Alaska OCS environmental conditions and oil dev impacts, compilation of papers, series, 2176–1

California OCS oil and gas dev impacts on water quality, marine life, and sediments, by site, 1986-89, annual rpt, 5734–11

Coastal and estuarine pollutant concentrations in fish, shellfish, and environment, series, 2176–3

Detroit metro area air pollution emissions and levels, by pollutant, 1980-90, 14648–25

Environmental Quality, status of problems, protection programs, research, and intl issues, 1991 annual rpt, 484–1

Farm chemicals use and animal wastes sources of groundwater pollution, and reduction strategies, 1960s-90, 26358–231

Florida environmental, social, and economic conditions, and impacts of proposed OCS oil and gas leases in southern coastal areas, 1990 compilation of papers, 5738–19

Great Lakes wastewater treatment by municipal and industrial facilities, releases, methods, effectiveness, pollutant limits, and enforcement, 1985-88, 14648–24

Health effects of selected pollutants on animals by species and on humans, and environmental levels, series, 5506–14

Industrial wastewater pollution releases, levels, treatment, costs, and regulation, with background financial and operating data, industry rpt series, 9206–4

New York Bight pollution levels, sources, treatment costs, economic losses, and environmental and health effects, 1990 conf, 9208–131

North Carolina environmental and socioeconomic conditions, and impacts of proposed OCS oil and gas exploration, 1970s-90 and projected to 2020, 5738–22

Pacific Ocean coast pollutant concentrations in fish and sediments, by contaminant, fish species, and site, 1984-86, 2168–121

Toxicology Natl Program research and testing activities, FY89 and planned FY90, annual rpt, 4044–16

Water (groundwater) supply, quality, chemistry, and use, State and local area rpt series, 5666–28

Water quality, chemistry, hydrology, and other characteristics, local area studies, series, 5666–27

Water supply and quality in streams and lakes, and groundwater levels in wells, by drainage basin, 1988, annual State rpt series, 5666–16

Water supply and quality in streams and lakes, and groundwater levels in wells, by drainage basin, 1989, annual State rpt series, 5666–12

Water supply and quality in streams and lakes, and groundwater levels in wells, by drainage basin, 1990, annual State rpt series, 5666–10

see also Lead poisoning and pollution

see also Mercury pollution

Tractors

see Agricultural machinery and equipment

Trade

see Agricultural exports and imports

see Arms trade

see Balance of payments

see Coal exports and imports

see Common markets and free trade areas

see Contraband

see Customs administration

see East-West trade

see Energy exports and imports

see Foreign competition

see Foreign trade

see Foreign trade promotion

see International assistance

see Interstate commerce

see Marketing

see Military assistance

see Motor vehicle exports and imports

see Natural gas exports and imports

see Petroleum exports and imports

see Retail trade

see Smuggling

see Tariffs and foreign trade controls

see Trade adjustment assistance

see Trade agreements

see Wholesale trade

Trade adjustment assistance

Assistance programs under Ways and Means Committee jurisdiction, finances, operations, and participant characteristics, FY70s-90, annual rpt, 21784–11

Budget of US, CBO analysis of savings and revenues under alternative spending cuts and tax changes, projected FY92-97, 26306–3.118

Eligibility of workers, petitions by disposition, selected industry, union, and State, monthly rpt, 6402–13

Fed Govt financial and nonfinancial domestic aid, 1991 base edition with supplements, annual listing, 104–5

Manufacturing employment by selected characteristics, wages, and import and export penetration rates, by SIC 2- to 4- digit industry, 1982-89, 6366–3.27

Unemployment insurance laws of States, comparison of provisions, 1991, base edition with semiannual revisions, 6402–2

Trade agreements

Trade agreements

- Auto imports duties and origin preference eligibility rules under proposed North American Free Trade Agreement, 1978-91, 9886–4.178
- Bilateral and multilateral treaties and other agreements in force, by country, as of Jan 1991, annual listing, 7004–1
- Bulgaria trade with US, US tariffs, and impacts of US granting most favored nation status, 1987-90, GAO rpt, 26123–323
- Canada and Mexico trade agreements with US, economic impacts, North Central States business leaders views, 1991 survey, article, 9383–19.204
- Caribbean Basin Initiative duty-free exports to US which are ineligible under Generalized System of Preferences, by commodity, 1989, 9886–4.171
- Caribbean Basin Initiative investment incentives, economic impacts, with finances and employment by country, 1984-90, 2048–141
- China trade with US and through Hong Kong, and impacts of revoking most favored nation status, 1987-90, hearing, 25368–174
- Economic conditions, and trade devs and balances, with data by selected country and country group, monthly rpt, 9882–14
- Employment and industry impacts of trade, series, 6366–3
- Environmental and wildlife conservation intl agreements provisions, status, and signatories, as of 1991, listing, 9886–4.169
- Export and import agreements, negotiations, and related legislation, 1990, annual rpt, 444–1
- Exports and imports, trade agreements and relations, and USITC investigations, 1990, annual rpt, 9884–5
- GATT Standards Code info activities of Natl Inst of Standards and Technology, and proposed standards by agency and country, 1990, annual rpt, 2214–6
- GATT Uruguay Round negotiations economic and trade impacts for US, with background data and foreign comparisons, 1970s-90, technical paper, 9385–8.115
- Mexico-US trade agreement proposal, economic impacts with background trade and investment data, 1985-90, 9886–4.168
- *Overseas Business Reports*: economic conditions, investment and export opportunities, and trade practices, country market research rpt series, 2046–6
- Soviet Union and Eastern Europe market economy transition, with US trade agreements and trade data by country, late 1980s-90, annual rpt, 444–2
- Steel imports of US under voluntary restraint agreement, by product, customs district, and country, with US industry operating data, quarterly rpt, 9882–13
- Textile Agreement Category System import classification codes, correlation with TSUSA, 1992 annual rpt, 2044–31
- Textile, apparel, and shoe import restriction proposals economic impacts, projected 1991-2000, with imports by country, 1989-90, 26306–6.162
- Textile imports under Multifiber Arrangement by product and country, and status of bilateral agreements, 1987-90, annual rpt, 9884–18
- USITC activities, investigations, and rpts, FY90, annual rpt, 9884–1
- *see also* Common markets and free trade areas
- *see also* Tariffs and foreign trade controls

Trade balances

- *see* Balance of payments
- *see* Foreign trade

Trade fairs

- *see* Exhibitions and trade fairs

Trade investigations

- *see* Government investigations

Trade promotion

- *see* Foreign trade promotion

Trade regulation

- *see* Antitrust law
- *see* Consumer protection
- *see* Copyright
- *see* Government and business
- *see* Licenses and permits
- *see* Patents
- *see* Price regulation
- *see* Tariffs and foreign trade controls
- *see* Trade adjustment assistance
- *see* Trademarks

Trade unions

- *see* Labor unions

Trademarks

- Applications, grants, fees, and litigation, for patents and trademarks, FY71-90, annual rpt, 2244–1
- Court civil and criminal caseloads for Federal district, appeals, and bankruptcy courts, by type of suit and offense, circuit, and district, 1990, annual rpt, 18204–11
- Court civil and criminal caseloads for Federal district, appeals, and special courts, 1990, annual rpt, 18204–8
- Court civil and criminal caseloads for Federal district courts, 1991, annual rpt, 18204–2.1
- Criminal sentences for Federal offenses, guidelines by offense and circumstances, series, 17668–1
- Imports purchasing decisions of consumers, importance of brand name, authenticity, origin, and other factors, 1984 survey, hearing, 25528–115
- *Statistical Abstract of US*, 1991 annual data compilation, 2324–1.17

Traffic accident fatalities

- Accidents (fatal), circumstances, and characteristics of persons and vehicles involved, 1990, semiannual rpt, 7762–11
- Accidents (fatal), deaths, and rates, by circumstances, characteristics of persons and vehicles involved, and location, 1989, annual rpt, 7764–10
- Accidents, casualties, circumstances, and characteristics of persons and vehicles involved, 1989, annual rpt, 7764–18
- Auto weight impacts on fatal traffic accident rates, with data for young drivers, 1976-78 and 1986-88, GAO rpt, 26131–89
- Bus (school) accidents, circumstances, victim characteristics, and vehicle type, 1989, annual rpt, 7764–22
- Child accident deaths and death rates, by cause, age, sex, race, and State, 1980-85, 4108–54
- Child accident deaths and injuries by cause, and victimization, rates by race, sex, and age, 1979-88, chartbook, 4108–56
- Deaths and rates, by cause and age, preliminary 1989-90, US Vital Statistics annual rpt, 4144–7
- Deaths and rates, by cause, provisional data, monthly rpt, 4142–1.2
- Deaths and rates, by detailed cause and demographic characteristics, 1988 and trends from 1900, US Vital Statistics annual rpt, 4144–2
- Deaths by cause, age, race, and sex, 1950s-89, annual rpt, 4144–11
- Deaths in traffic accidents by circumstances and State, drunk drivers involved in fatal accidents, and impacts of minimum age drinking laws, 1982-89, annual fact sheet, 7766–15.1; 7766–15.4
- Deaths in traffic accidents by region, and death rates for miles traveled, monthly rpt, 7762–7
- Deaths in traffic accidents by type of vehicle involved, and Natl Hwy Traffic Safety Admin activities, 1979-89, annual rpt, 7764–1
- Drunk drivers and others involved in fatal accidents, alcohol levels by circumstances and characteristics of persons and vehicles, 1989, annual rpt, 7764–16
- Drunk driving accidents, deaths, and injuries, by alcohol level, data compilation, 1991 annual rpt, 6064–6.3
- Foreign countries motor vehicle accidental death rate for young men, and teen pregnancy rate, by selected country, 1980s, fact sheet, 2326–17.24
- Indian Health Service facilities and use, and Indian health and other characteristics, by IHS region, 1980s-89, annual chartbook, 4084–7
- Indian Health Service facilities, funding, operations, and Indian health and other characteristics, 1950s-90, annual chartbook, 4084–1
- Infant death rate, by cause, region, and race, 1980-87, article, 4202–7.208
- Law enforcement officer assaults and deaths by circumstances, agency, victim and offender characteristics, and location, 1990, annual rpt, 6224–3
- Minority group health condition, services use, costs, and indicators of services need, 1950s-88, 4118–55
- Motorcycle helmet use and mandatory use laws impacts on accident casualties and costs, literature review, 1956-89, GAO rpt, 26113–537
- Occupational deaths, by cause and industry div, 1989, annual rpt, 6844–1
- Park natl system visitor deaths, by cause, victim age, region, and park, 1980-90, annual rpt, 5544–6
- Pedestrian and bicyclist accidents and deaths involving autos, 1980-90, annual fact sheet, 7766–15.5
- Railroad-hwy grade-crossing accidents, detailed data by State and railroad, 1989, annual rpt, 7604–2
- Safety improvement measures, costs, and accident and death reductions by type of accident and improvement, 1990 conf, 7558–110
- Safety program funding by State, and accident and death reductions, FY90, annual rpt, 7554–26

Index by Subjects and Names

Traffic laws and courts

Seat belt use and lives saved, impacts of State mandatory use laws, 1983-90, annual fact sheet, 7766–15.2

Speed limit impacts on traffic accidents, with accident circumstances and speed averages, for States with 55 and 65 mph limit, 1986-89, annual rpt, 7764–15

State and Metro Area Data Book, 1991 data compilation, 2328–54

Statistical Abstract of US, 1991 annual data compilation, 2324–1.21

Truck accidents, casualties, and damage, by circumstances and characteristics of persons and vehicles involved, 1988, annual rpt, 7554–9

Truck accidents, circumstances, severity, and characteristics of drivers and vehicles, 1989, annual rpt, 7764–20

Traffic accidents and safety

Accidents and safety data, annual fact sheet series, 7766–15

Accidents, casualties, circumstances, and characteristics of persons and vehicles involved, 1989, annual rpt, 7764–18

Accidents, injuries, and deaths, by circumstances and characteristics of persons and vehicles involved, annual rpt, discontinued, 7764–13

Budget of US, formula grant program obligations to State and local govts, by agency, program, and State, FY92, annual rpt, 104–30

Bus (school) accidents, circumstances, victim characteristics, and vehicle type, 1989, annual rpt, 7764–22

Child accident deaths and injuries by cause, and victimization, rates by race, sex, and age, 1979-88, chartbook, 4108–56

Child fare proposal impacts on family airline travel and industry revenue, with costs and accidents compared to auto travel, 1990 hearing, 21648–61

Disability, acute and chronic health conditions, absenteeism, and health services use, by selected characteristics, 1987, CD-ROM, 4147–10.177

DOT activities by subagency, budget, and summary accident data, FY88, annual rpt, 7304–1

Drug and alcohol abuse and mental illness direct and indirect costs, by type and patient age and sex, 1985 with 1980 and 1988 comparisons, 4048–35

Fed Govt and State surface transportation funding and regulation, FY91 with projections to FY96, 26358–242

Fed Govt spending in States, by type, program, agency, and State, FY90, annual rpt, 2464–2

Hazardous material transport accidents, casualties, and damage, by mode of transport, with DOT control activities, 1989, annual rpt, 7304–4

Hwy Statistics, detailed data by State, 1990, annual rpt, 7554–1

Injuries, by type, circumstances, and victim characteristics, and related activity limitations, 1985-87, 4147–10.176

Injuries, related impairments, and activity limitations, by circumstances and victim characteristics, 1985-87, 4147–10.179

Railroad-hwy grade-crossing accidents and casualties, and Fed Railroad Admin activities, 1989, annual rpt, 7604–12

Railroad-hwy grade-crossing accidents, casualties, and damage, by cause, railroad, and State, 1990, annual rpt, 7604–1

Railroad-hwy grade-crossing accidents, detailed data by State and railroad, 1989, annual rpt, 7604–2

Safety improvement measures, costs, and accident and death reductions by type of accident and improvement, 1990 conf, 7558–110

Safety of domestic and foreign autos, crash test results by model, press release series, 7766–7

Safety program funding by State, and accident and death reductions, FY90, annual rpt, 7554–26

Safety programs, and accidents, casualties, and damage, by mode of transport, 1989, annual rpt, 7304–19

Speed limit impacts on traffic accidents, with accident circumstances and speed averages, for States with 55 and 65 mph limit, 1986-89, annual rpt, 7764–15

State and Metro Area Data Book, 1991 data compilation, 2328–54

Statistical Abstract of US, 1991 annual data compilation, 2324–1.21

Truck accidents, by carrier financial and operating conditions and driver characteristics, 1980s, GAO rpt, 26131–82

Truck accidents, casualties, and damage, by circumstances and characteristics of persons and vehicles involved, 1988, annual rpt, 7554–9

Truck accidents, circumstances, severity, and characteristics of drivers and vehicles, 1989, annual rpt, 7764–20

Truck and bus safety inspections, fines, and vehicles and drivers ordered out of service, by State, with program funding, FY89, 25268–78

Truck safety inspections of FHwA conducted FY87-88, compliance review status as of 1990, GAO rpt, 26113–505

see also Driving while intoxicated

see also Motor vehicle safety devices

see also Pedestrians

see also Traffic accident fatalities

see also Traffic engineering

see also Traffic laws and courts

Traffic engineering

Appalachia hwy system and access roads funding and completion status, by State, quarterly tables, 9082–1

Carpool and bus high occupancy vehicle lanes use, design, and enforcement, for US and Canada, 1989, 7888–80

Carpool high occupancy vehicle lanes use, design, enforcement, and drivers views, for California, 1988-89, 7308–203

Engineering and architectural establishments, receipts by type of client and project, payroll, and employment, by State, 1987 Census of Service Industries, 2393–4.16

Hwy construction and design R&D, quarterly journal, 7552–3

Hwy safety program funding by State, and accident and death reductions, FY90, annual rpt, 7554–26

Intersection traffic controls involvement in accidents, 1989, annual rpt, 7764–18

Intersection traffic controls involvement in fatal accidents, 1989, annual rpt, 7764–10

Railroad-hwy grade-crossing accidents, detailed data by State and railroad, 1989, annual rpt, 7604–2

Safety improvement measures, costs, and accident and death reductions by type of accident and improvement, 1990 conf, 7558–110

Safety research and funding of DOT, project listing, FY89, annual rpt, 7764–1

Traffic laws and courts

Carpool and bus high occupancy vehicle lanes use, design, and enforcement, for US and Canada, 1989, 7888–80

Carpool high occupancy vehicle lanes use, design, enforcement, and drivers views, for California, 1988-89, 7308–203

Court civil and criminal caseloads for Federal district, appeals, and bankruptcy courts, by type of suit and offense, circuit, and district, 1990, annual rpt, 18204–11

Court civil and criminal caseloads for Federal district, appeals, and special courts, 1990, annual rpt, 18204–8

Court civil and criminal caseloads for Federal district courts, 1991, annual rpt, 18204–2.1

Court criminal case processing in Federal district courts, and dispositions, by offense, district, and offender characteristics, 1986, annual rpt, 6064–29

Court criminal case processing in Federal district courts, and dispositions, by offense, 1980-89, annual rpt, 6064–31

Court criminal cases in Federal district courts, by offense, disposition, and district, 1980-90, last issue of annual rpt, 18204–1

Crime, criminal justice admin and enforcement, and public opinion, data compilation, 1991 annual rpt, 6064–6

Drug test results at arrest, by drug type, offense, and sex, for selected urban areas, quarterly rpt, 6062–3

Hwy Statistics, detailed data by State, 1990, annual rpt, 7554–1

Motorcycle helmet use and mandatory use laws impacts on accident casualties and costs, literature review, 1956-89, GAO rpt, 26113–537

Natl Hwy Traffic Safety Admin activities and grants, and fatal traffic accident data, 1989, annual rpt, 7764–1

Seat belt use and lives saved, impacts of State mandatory use laws, 1983-90, annual fact sheet, 7766–15.2

Speed averages and vehicles exceeding 55 mph, by State, FY90, annual rpt, 7554–1.4

Speed averages and vehicles exceeding 55 mph, by State, quarterly rpt, 7552–14

Speed limit impacts on traffic accidents, with accident circumstances and speed averages, for States with 55 and 65 mph limit, 1986-89, annual rpt, 7764–15

Speed limit posted and alcohol involvement, for fatal accidents, 1989, annual rpt, 7764–16

Speed limit posted and other circumstances of accidents, 1989, annual rpt, 7764–18

Speed limit posted and other circumstances of fatal accidents, 1990, semiannual rpt, 7762–11

Speed limit posted for places where fatal accidents occurred, selected years 1979-89, annual rpt, 7304–19

Traffic laws and courts

Speed limit posted, previous violations and license revocation of drivers involved, and other detailed circumstances of fatal accidents, 1989, annual rpt, 7764–10

Truck accidents, circumstances, severity, and characteristics of drivers and vehicles, 1989, annual rpt, 7764–20

see also Driving while intoxicated

Traffic violations

see Traffic accidents and safety

see Traffic laws and courts

Trails

see National trails

Training

see Apprenticeship

see Employee development

see Manpower training programs

see Military training

see Sheltered workshops

see Vocational education and training

Tranquilizers

see Drug abuse and treatment

see Drugs

Transfer payments

see terms listed under Income maintenance

Transient housing

- Census of Population, 1990: homeless shelter and on-street population, by State and for 200 cities, press release, 2328–70
- Census of Service Industries, 1987: hotels and other lodging places, receipts, payroll, employment, ownership, and rooms, by State and MSA, subject rpt, 2393–3
- County Business Patterns, 1988: employment, establishments, and payroll, by SIC 2- to 4-digit industry and county, annual State rpt series, 2326–6
- County Business Patterns, 1989: employment, establishments, and payroll, by SIC 2- to 4-digit industry and county, annual State rpt series, 2326–8
- Homeless children educational projects, activities, and funding, FY90, annual rpt, 4804–35
- Homeless persons aid programs of Fed Govt, program descriptions and funding, by agency and State, FY87-90, annual GAO rpt, 26104–21
- Homeless persons housing and food aid of Fed Govt, funding and operations, with data by State and county, FY89, hearing, 25408–111
- Homelessness issues, population at risk, contributing factors, and Federal funding for services and prevention, with bibl, 1991 compilation of papers, 25928–9

see also Group homes for the handicapped

see also Hotels and motels

Transit districts

see Special districts

Transportation accidents and safety

- Accidents, and mgmt of disasters and natl security threats, with data by major event and State, 1991 annual rpt, 9434–6
- Deaths and rates, by detailed cause and demographic characteristics, 1988 and trends from 1900, US Vital Statistics annual rpt, 4144–2
- Deaths in transportation accidents, by mode, 1989-90, annual press release, 9614–6
- DOT activities by subagency, budget, and summary accident data, FY88, annual rpt, 7304–1
- Fed Govt financial and nonfinancial domestic aid, 1991 base edition with supplements, annual listing, 104–5
- Injuries from use of consumer products, by severity, victim age, and detailed product, 1990, annual rpt, 9164–6
- Injuries, illnesses, and workdays lost, by SIC 2-digit industry, 1989-90, annual press release, 6844–3
- Injury and illness rates by SIC 2- to 4-digit industry, and deaths by cause and industry div, 1989, annual rpt, 6844–1
- Injury and illness rates, by SIC 2- to 4-digit industry, 1988-89, annual rpt, 6844–7
- Investigations of GAO, 1989-91, listing, 26106–10.5
- Natl transportation system planning, use, condition, accidents, and needs, by mode of transport, 1940s-90 and projected to 2020, 7308–202
- Pipeline accidents, casualties, safety enforcement activity, and Federal funding, by State, 1989, annual rpt, 7304–5
- Safety programs, and accidents, casualties, and damage, by mode of transport, 1989, annual rpt, 7304–19
- Shift rotation health and safety effects, and US and foreign regulation, by selected industry and occupation, 1970s-89, 26356–9.3
- *Statistical Abstract of US*, 1991 annual data compilation, 2324–1.21
- Subway accidents, casualties, and damage, by circumstances and system, 1989, annual rpt, 7884–5
- Transit systems finances and operations, by mode of transport, size of fleet, and for 468 systems, 1989, annual rpt, 7884–4
- Urban Mass Transportation Admin R&D projects and funding, FY90, annual listing, 7884–1

see also Aviation accidents and safety

see also Hazardous substances transport

see also Marine accidents and safety

see also Motor vehicle safety devices

see also Railroad accidents and safety

see also Traffic accident fatalities

see also Traffic accidents and safety

see also Traffic engineering

Transportation and transportation equipment

- Business statistics, detailed data for major industries and economic indicators, *Survey of Current Business*, monthly rpt, 2702–1.23
- Capital expenditures for plant and equipment, by industry div, monthly rpt, quarterly data, 23842–1.1
- Capital expenditures for plant and equipment, by major industry group, quarterly rpt, 2502–2
- Census Bur rpts and data files, coverage and availability, 1991 annual listing, 2304–2
- China economic indicators and reform issues, with background data, 1950s-90, compilation of papers, 23848–155
- Classification codes concordance of Canada and US SICs, for 1- to 4-digit levels, 1991 rpt, 2628–31
- Collective bargaining agreements expiring during year, and workers covered, by firm, union, industry group, and State, 1991, annual rpt, 6784–9
- Consumer Expenditure Survey, spending by category, and income, by selected household characteristics and location, 1990, annual press release, 6726–1.42
- Consumer Expenditure Survey, spending by category, selected household characteristics, and region, quarterly rpt, 6762–14
- County Business Patterns, 1988: employment, establishments, and payroll, by SIC 2- to 4-digit industry and county, annual State rpt series, 2326–6
- County Business Patterns, 1989: employment, establishments, and payroll, by SIC 2- to 4-digit industry and county, annual State rpt series, 2326–8
- CPI components relative importance, by selected MSA, region, population size, and for US city average, 1990, annual rpt, 6884–1
- Developing countries economic, population, and agricultural data, US and other aid sources, and AID activity, country rpt series, 9916–12
- DOD prime contract awards, by detailed procurement category, FY87-90, annual rpt, 3544–18
- Eastern Europe economic and political conditions, and impacts of geographic factors, by country, 1990 conf, 9118–18
- Education (postsecondary) course completions, by detailed program, sex, race, and instn type, for 1972 high school class, as of 1984, 4888–4
- Employment, earnings, and hours, by SIC 1- to 4-digit industry, monthly and annual averages, selected years 1909-90, annual rpt, 6744–4
- Employment in manufacturing, by detailed occupation and SIC 2-digit industry, 1989 survey, triennial rpt, 6748–52
- Employment, unemployment, and labor force characteristics, by region and census div, 1990, annual rpt, 6744–7.1
- Energy use and prices for manufacturing industries, 1988 survey, series, 3166–13
- Engineering and architectural establishments, receipts by type of client and project, payroll, and employment, by State, 1987 Census of Service Industries, 2393–4.16
- Enterprise Statistics, 1987: auxiliaries of multi-establishment firms, finances and operations by function, industry, and State, 2329–6
- Enterprise Statistics, 1987: finances and operations for companies, by size, level of diversification, form of organization, and industry group, 2329–8
- *Environmental Quality*, status of problems, protection programs, research, and intl issues, 1991 annual rpt, 484–1
- Export and import prices of machinery and transport equipment, impacts of dollar depreciation, 1985-90, article, 6722–1.233
- Exports and imports between US and outlying areas, by detailed commodity and mode of transport, 1990, annual rpt, 2424–11
- Exports and imports of US, by Harmonized System 6-digit commodity and country, 1990, annual rpt, 2424–13
- Exports and imports of US, by selected country, country group, and commodity group, 1990, annual rpt, 2044–37
- Exports and imports of US shipped through Canada, by detailed commodity, customs district, and country, 1989, annual rpt, 7704–11
- Exports of US, detailed commodities by country, monthly CD-ROM, 2422–13

Index by Subjects and Names

Transportation and transportation equipment

Exports of US, detailed Schedule B commodities with countries of destination, 1990, annual rpt, 2424–10

Finances and operations of Class I rail and motor carriers, detailed data, 1989, annual rpt series, 9486–6

Finances and operations of transit systems, by mode of transport, size of fleet, and for 468 systems, 1989, annual rpt, 7884–4

Foreign countries economic, social, political, and geographic summary data, by country, 1991, annual factbook, 9114–2

Foreign direct investment in US, major transactions by type, industry, country, and US location, 1989, annual rpt, 2044–20

Foreign direct investment of US, by industry group and world area, 1987-90, annual article, 2702–1.220

Imports, exports, and employment impacts, by SIC 2- to 4-digit industry and commodity, quarterly rpt, 2322–2

Imports of US, detailed commodities by country, monthly CD-ROM, 2422–14

Imports of US given duty-free treatment for value of US material sent abroad, by commodity and country, 1989, annual rpt, 9884–14

Industry finances and operations, by SIC 2- to 4-digit industry, forecast 1991, annual rpt, 2044–28

Input-output structure of US economy, detailed interindustry transactions for 84 industries, and components of final demand, 1986, annual article, 2702–1.206

Input-output structure of US economy, detailed interindustry transactions for 85 industries, 1982 benchmark data, 2702–1.213

Investigations of GAO, 1989-91, listing, 26106–10.5

Land acreage, by use, ownership, and State, 1987 and trends from 1910, 1588–48

Manufacturing annual survey, 1989: finances and operations, by SIC 2- to 4-digit industry, series, 2506–15

Manufacturing census, 1987: employment and shipments under Fed Govt contracts, by SIC 4-digit industry, 2497–7

Manufacturing census, 1987: finances and operations, by SIC 2- to 4-digit industry, State, and MSA, with trends from 1849, 2497–1

Manufacturing census, 1987: finances and operations, by type of organization and SIC 2- to 4-digit industry, subject rpt, 2497–5

Manufacturing corporations financial statements, by selected SIC 2- to 3-digit industry, quarterly rpt, 2502–1

Manufacturing industries operations and performance, analytical rpt series, 2506–16

Manufacturing production, shipments, inventories, orders, and pollution control costs, periodic Current Industrial Rpt series, 2506–3

Mexico imports from US, by industry and State, 1987-90, 2048–154

Multinatl US firms and foreign affiliates finances and operations, by industry and world area of parent firm, 1989 benchmark survey, preliminary annual rpt, 2704–5

Natl income and product accounts and components, *Survey of Current Business*, monthly rpt, 2702–1.24

Natl transportation system planning, use, condition, accidents, and needs, by mode of transport, 1940s-90 and projected to 2020, 7308–202

Occupational injury and illness rates, by SIC 2- to 4-digit industry, 1988-89, annual rpt, 6844–7

Occupational injury and illness rates, by SIC 2- to 4-digit industry, 1989, annual rpt, 6844–1

OECD trade, total and for 4 major countries, and US trade by country, by commodity, 1970-89, world area rpt series, 9116–1

Pollution (water) fish kills, by pollution source, month, location, and State, 1977-87, last issue of annual rpt, 9204–3

Pollution (water) industrial releases in wastewater, levels, treatment, costs, and regulation, with background financial and operating data, 1989 industry rpt, 9206–4.11

Pollution abatement capital and operating costs, by SIC 2-digit industry, 1989, advance annual Current Industrial Rpt, 2506–3.6

Price indexes (producer), by stage of processing and detailed commodity, monthly rpt, 6762–6

Price indexes (producer), by stage of processing and detailed commodity, monthly 1990, annual rpt, 6764–2

Publications and data files of Census Bur on foreign trade, 1991 guide, 2428–11

Puerto Rico and other US possessions corporations income tax returns, income and tax items, and employment, by selected industry, 1987, article, 8302–2.213

Puerto Rico economic censuses, 1987: wholesale and retail trade and service industry finances and operations, by SIC 2- to 4-digit industry and municipio, 2591–1

SEC registration, firms required to file annual rpts, as of Sept 1990, annual listing, 9734–5

Soviet Union GNP by component and industry sector, and CIA estimation methods, 1950s-87, 23848–223

Soviet Union GNP by detailed income and outlay component, 1985, 2326–18.59

Statistical Abstract of US, 1991 annual data compilation, 2324–1.21; 2324–1.22

Stock (common) price indexes, current data and annual trends, monthly rpt, 23842–1.5

Tariff Schedule of US, classifications and rates of duty by detailed imported commodity, 1992 base edition, 9886–13

Tax (income) returns of corporations, income and tax items by asset size and detailed industry, 1987, annual rpt, 8304–4

Tax (income) returns of corporations, income and tax items by asset size and detailed industry, 1988, annual rpt, 8304–21

Tax (income) returns of corporations with foreign tax credit, income and tax items by industry group, 1986, biennial article, 8302–2.203

Tax (income) returns of multinatl US firms foreign affiliates, income statement items, by asset size and industry, 1986, biennial article, 8302–2.212

Tax (income) returns of partnerships, income statement and balance sheet items, by industry group, 1989, annual article, 8302–2.216; 8304–18

Tax (income) returns of sole proprietorships, income statement items, by industry group, 1989, annual article, 8302–2.214

Wage and benefit changes from collective bargaining and mgmt decisions, by industry div, monthly rpt, 6782–1

Wholesale trade census, 1987: establishments, sales by customer class, employment, inventories, and expenses, by SIC 2- to 4-digit kind of business, 2407–4

see also Air travel

see also Aircraft

see also Airlines

see also Automobile repair and maintenance

see also Automobiles

see also Aviation accidents and safety

see also Bicycles

see also Boats and boating

see also Bridges and tunnels

see also Buses

see also Canals

see also Census of Transportation

see also Civil aviation

see also Commuting

see also Courier services

see also Drivers licenses

see also Federal aid to transportation

see also Ferries

see also Freight

see also Gasoline

see also General aviation

see also Harbors and ports

see also Hazardous substances transport

see also Helicopters

see also Highways, streets, and roads

see also Inland water transportation

see also Marine accidents and safety

see also Military vehicles

see also Motor fuels

see also Motor vehicle exhaust

see also Motor vehicle exports and imports

see also Motor vehicle fleets

see also Motor vehicle industry

see also Motor vehicle parts and supplies

see also Motor vehicle registrations

see also Motor vehicle rental

see also Motor vehicle safety devices

see also Motor vehicle theft

see also Motorcycles

see also Parking facilities

see also Passenger ships

see also Pipelines

see also Railroad accidents and safety

see also Railroad equipment and vehicles

see also Railroads

see also Recreational vehicles

see also Rivers and waterways

see also School busing

see also Shipbuilding and repairing

see also Ships and shipping

see also State funding for transportation

see also Subways

see also Tanker ships

see also Taxicabs

see also Traffic accident fatalities

Transportation and transportation equipment

Index by Subjects and Names

see also Traffic accidents and safety
see also Transportation accidents and safety
see also Transportation energy use
see also Travel agencies
see also Travel and tourism
see also Trucks and trucking industry
see also Urban transportation
see also under By Commodity in the "Index by Categories"
see also under By Industry in the "Index by Categories"

Transportation census
see Census of Transportation

Transportation Department
see Department of Transportation

Transportation energy use
- Alternative motor fuels costs, emissions, health impacts, and characteristics, series, 9196–5
- Auto and light truck fuel economy performance by make, standards, and enforcement, 1978-91 model years, annual rpt, 7764–9
- Auto and light truck fuel economy, sales, and market shares, by size and model for US and foreign makes, 1991 model year, semiannual rpt, 3302–4
- Auto fuel consumption, miles traveled, and mileage, 1967-88, 3168–120
- Auto fuel economy test results for US and foreign makes, 1992 model year, annual rpt, 3304–11
- Auto, private airplane, and motorcycle operating costs by component, and Fed Govt mileage reimbursement rates, 1989, annual rpt, 9454–13
- Business statistics, detailed data for major industries and economic indicators, *Survey of Current Business*, monthly rpt, 2702–1.13
- Conservation measures impacts on energy consumption, by component and end-use sector, 1970s-88 and projected under alternative oil prices to 1995, 3308–93
- Conservation of energy, State programs aid from Fed Govt, and energy savings, by State, 1989, annual rpt, 3304–1
- Consumer Expenditure Survey, household income by source, and itemized spending, by selected characteristics and region, 1988-89, annual rpt, 6764–5
- Consumer Expenditure Survey, spending by category, and income, by selected household characteristics and location, 1990, annual press release, 6726–1.42
- Consumer Expenditure Survey, spending by category, selected household characteristics, and region, quarterly rpt, 6762–14
- CPI by component for US city average, and by region, population size, and for 27 metro areas, monthly rpt, 6762–2
- CPI components relative importance, by selected MSA, region, population size, and for US city average, 1990, annual rpt, 6884–1
- Developing countries energy use, and economic and environmental impacts, by fuel type, world area, and country, 1980s-90, 26358–232
- DOE energy use, costs, and conservation, by end use, fuel type, and field office, FY90, annual rpt, 3004–27
- Electric utilities privately owned, finances and operations, detailed data, 1989, annual rpt, 3164–23

Energy supply, demand, and prices, by fuel type and end-use sector, alternative projections 1989-2010, annual rpt, 3164–75

Energy supply, demand, and prices, by fuel type and end-use sector, projections and underlying assumptions, 1990-2010, annual rpt, 3164–90

Energy supply, demand, and prices, by fuel type and end-use sector, with foreign comparisons, 1990 and trends from 1949, annual rpt, 3164–74

Energy supply, demand, and prices, by fuel type, end-use sector, and country, detailed data, monthly rpt with articles, 3162–24

Energy use, by detailed fuel type, end-use sector, and State, 1960-89, State Energy Data System annual rpt, 3164–39

Energy use by mode of transport, fuel supply, and demographic and economic factors of vehicle use, 1970s-89, annual rpt, 3304–5

Fed Govt energy use and efficiency, by agency and fuel type, FY90, annual rpt, 3304–22

Foreign and US oil dependency, energy demand, and efficiency measures, for 6 OECD countries, 1970s-88, article, 9375–1.210

Foreign countries transportation energy use, fuel prices, vehicle registrations, and mileage, by selected country, 1970s-89, annual rpt, 3304–5.1

Fuel oil and kerosene sales and deliveries, by end-use, PAD district, and State, 1989, annual rpt, 3164–94

Gasohol use, by region, 1989, 3166–6.56

Gasoline and other motor fuel use, by consuming sector and State, 1990, annual rpt, 7554–1.1

Hwy Statistics, summary data by State, 1989-90, annual rpt, 7554–24

Natl Energy Strategy plans for conservation and pollution reduction, impacts of technology and regulation proposals, projected 1990-2030, 3166–6.47

Natl Energy Strategy plans for conservation, impacts on energy use and pollution under alternative technology investment assumptions, projected 1990-2030, 3166–6.48

Natl transportation system planning, use, condition, accidents, and needs, by mode of transport, 1940s-90 and projected to 2020, 7308–202

Oil and gas supply, demand, and prices, alternative projections 1989-2010, annual rpt, 3164–89

Oil and refined products supply, demand, prices, and refinery capacity and stocks, by State, 1960-91, annual rpt, 3164–95

Pollution (air) contributing to global warming, US and foreign emissions and control measures, 1980s and projected to 2020, 26358–233

Prices and spending for fuel, by type, end-use sector, and State, 1989, annual rpt, 3164–64

R&D projects on automotive engines and powertrains, DOE contracts and funding by recipient, FY90, annual rpt, 3304–17

Railroad retirement system funding and benefits findings and recommendations, with background industry data, 1960s-90 and projected to 2060, 9708–1

State and Metro Area Data Book, 1991 data compilation, 2328–54

Statistical Abstract of US, 1991 annual data compilation, 2324–1.21

Taxes on energy, economic and energy demand impacts of alternative taxation methods, projected 1991-2000, 3166–6.57

Transit systems finances and operations, by mode of transport, size of fleet, and for 468 systems, 1989, annual rpt, 7884–4

Truck and warehouse services finances and inventory, by SIC 2- to 4-digit industry, 1989 survey, annual rpt, 2413–14

Truck itemized costs per mile, finances, and operations, for agricultural carriers, 1990, annual rpt, 1311–15

Truck transport of fruit and vegetables, itemized costs per mile by item for fleets and owner-operator trucks, monthly table, 1272–1

TVA energy use by fuel type, and conservation costs and savings, FY90, annual rpt, 9804–26
see also Aviation fuels
see also Motor vehicle exhaust

Transports
see Military aircraft
see Military vehicles
see Naval vessels

Trapido, Paul
"Government Intervention in Latin American Agriculture, 1982-87", 1528–324

Trapmann, William
- "Analysis of Long-Term Contracts for Imports of Canadian Natural Gas", 3162–4.206
- "Domestic Oil and Gas Recoverable Resource Base: Supporting Analysis for the National Energy Strategy", 3166–6.51
- "Outlook for Natural Gas Imports: Supporting Analysis for the National Energy Strategy", 3166–6.52

Trapping
see Hunting and trapping

Traub, Larry G.
"Value-Weighted Quantity Indices of Exports for High-Value Processed Agricultural Products", 1528–323

Travel agencies
- Airline computer reservation system operations, travel agency revenues by firm, and frequent flyer awards by carrier, 1988, 7308–199.9
- Census of Transportation, 1987: finances and operations by size, ownership, and State, and revenues by MSA, by SIC 2- to 4-digit industry, 2579–1
- County Business Patterns, 1988: employment, establishments, and payroll, by SIC 2- to 4-digit industry and county, annual State rpt series, 2326–6
- County Business Patterns, 1989: employment, establishments, and payroll, by SIC 2- to 4-digit industry and county, annual State rpt series, 2326–8
- Enterprise Statistics, 1987: finances and operations for companies, by size, level of diversification, form of organization, and industry group, 2329–8
- Foreign travel from US, characteristics of visit and traveler, and world area of destination, 1990 in-flight survey, annual rpt, 2904–14

Index by Subjects and Names

Treaties and conventions

Foreign travel to US, by characteristics of visit and traveler, world area of origin, and US destination, 1990 survey, annual rpt, 2904–12

Franchise business opportunities by firm and kind of business, and sources of aid and info, 1990 annual listing, 2104–7

GSA contracts to travel agencies, by business size and recipient, FY88-90, GAO rpt, 26119–331

Price indexes (producer), by stage of processing and detailed commodity, monthly rpt, 6762–6

Receipts for services, by SIC 2- to 4-digit kind of business, 1990, annual rpt, 2413–8

Statistical Abstract of US, 1991 annual data compilation, 2324–1.21

Travel and tourism

Alaska socioeconomic impacts of OCS oil resources dev, 1980-89 and projected to 2020, 5736–5.11

Aliens (illegal) overstaying visas, by class of admission, mode of arrival, age, country, and State, FY85-88, annual rpt, 6264–5

American Samoa employment, earnings, and minimum wage, by establishment and industry, 1989, biennial rpt, 6504–6

Arrivals and departures of US and foreign natls, *Survey of Current Business*, monthly rpt, 2702–1.11

Auto use, travel patterns, and personal and household characteristics, 1990 survey, annual rpt, 7554–1.6

Bus (Class I) passengers and selected revenue data, for individual large carriers, quarterly rpt, 9482–13

Caribbean Basin Initiative investment incentives, economic impacts, with finances and employment by country, 1984-90, 2048–141

Child rearing costs of married couple households, by expenditure type, child's age, income, and region, 1990 and projected to 2007, 1708–87

Coastal areas recreation facilities of Fed Govt and States, visitor and site characteristics, 1987-90 survey, regional rpt series, 2176–9

Colorado tourism visits, by site, trip purpose, and State of origin, 1985-87, 5726–5.1

Consumer Expenditure Survey, spending for selected categories, 1991 semiannual pamphlet, 2322–3

Consumer spending, natl income and product accounts, *Survey of Current Business*, monthly rpt, 2702–1.25

Exports and imports of services, direct and among multinatl firms affiliates, by industry and world area, 1986-90, article, 2702–1.223

Fed Govt employee travel expenses, operating costs for private autos, airplanes, and motorcycles, and reimbursement rates for business use, 1989, annual rpt, 9454–13

Fed Govt labor productivity, indexes of output and labor costs by function, FY67-89, annual rpt, 6824–1.6

Fed Govt obligations object class analysis, by agency, Budget of US, FY92, annual rpt, 104–9

Finances and operations, by SIC 2- to 4-digit industry, forecast 1991, annual rpt, 2044–28

Florida environmental, social, and economic conditions, and impacts of proposed OCS oil and gas leases in southern coastal areas, 1990 compilation of papers, 5738–19

Foreign countries *Background Notes*, summary social, political, and economic data, travel notes, series, 7006–2

Foreign countries economic conditions and implications for US, periodic country rpt series, 2046–4

Foreign countries human rights conditions in 170 countries, 1990, annual rpt, 21384–3

Foreign travel balance of US, current and annual trends, monthly rpt, 23842–1.7

Foreign travel from US, characteristics of visit and traveler, and world area of destination, 1990 in-flight survey, annual rpt, 2904–14

Foreign travel to and from US, by world area, forecast 1991-92, annual rpt, 2904–9

Foreign travel to US, by characteristics of visit and traveler, country, port city, and State of destination, monthly rpt, 2902–1

Foreign travel to US, by characteristics of visit and traveler, world area of origin, and US destination, 1990 survey, annual rpt, 2904–12

Foreign travel to US, market research data available from US Travel and Tourism Admin, 1991, annual rpt, 2904–15

Foreign travel to US, trade shows and other promotional activities, with magazine ad costs and circulation, for selected countries, 1991-92, annual rpt, 2904–11

Forest Service activities and finances, by region and State, FY90, annual rpt, 1204–1.1

Great Lakes area economic conditions and outlook, for US and Canada, 1970s-90, 9375–15

Hepatitis cases by infection source, age, sex, race, and State, and deaths, by strain, 1988 and trends from 1966, 4205–2

House of Representatives salaries, expenses, and contingent fund disbursement, detailed listings, quarterly rpt, 21942–1

Households and personal travel patterns, characteristics, and auto and public transport use, 1990 survey, series, 7556–6

Hwy Statistics, summary data by State, 1989-90, annual rpt, 7554–24

Hwy traffic volume on rural roads and city streets, monthly rpt, 7552–8

Malaria cases in US, for military personnel and US and foreign natls, and by country of infection, 1966-89, annual rpt, 4205–4

Natl transportation system planning, use, condition, accidents, and needs, by mode of transport, 1940s-90 and projected to 2020, 7308–202

Navy command proposed decentralization and relocation from DC area, savings, and cost of living indicators for 14 MSAs, 1980s, GAO rpt, 26123–346

Northeastern US recreation areas use, mgmt, and tourism dev issues, 1990 conf, 1208–356

Overseas Business Reports: economic conditions, investment and export opportunities, and trade practices, country market research rpt series, 2046–6

Palau admin, and social, economic, and govtl data, FY90, annual rpt, 7004–6

Price indexes (producer), by stage of processing and detailed commodity, monthly rpt, 6762–6

Puerto Rico economic censuses, 1987: wholesale and retail trade and service industry finances and operations, by SIC 2- to 4-digit industry and municipio, 2591–1

Puerto Rico economic censuses, 1987: wholesale, retail, and service industries finances and operations, by establishment characteristics and SIC 2- and 3-digit industry, subject rpts, 2591–2

Railroad (Amtrak) finances and operations, FY90, annual rpt, 29524–1

Senate receipts, itemized expenses by payee, and balances, 1st half FY91, semiannual listing, 25922–1

State and Metro Area Data Book, 1991 data compilation, 2328–54

Statistical Abstract of US, 1991 annual data compilation, 2324–1.7; 2324–1.21

Tax (income) returns of sole proprietorships, income statement items, by industry group, 1989, annual article, 8302–2.214

Vaccination needs for intl travel by country, and disease prevention recommendations, 1991 annual rpt, 4204–11

see also Air travel

see also Commuting

see also Passenger ships

see also Passports and visas

see also Transportation accidents and safety

see also Travel agencies

Travel and Tourism Administration

see U.S. Travel and Tourism Administration

Treacy, Stephen D.

"Aerial Surveys of Endangered Whales in the Beaufort Sea, Fall 1990", 5734–10

Treason

see Subversive activities

Treasury Department

see Department of Treasury

Treaties and conventions

Aircraft accidents victims compensation, legal costs, and time to disposition, under intl agreements and US liability system, aggregate 1970-84, GAO rpt, 26113–501

Bilateral and multilateral treaties and other agreements in force, by country, as of Jan 1991, annual listing, 7004–1

Copyright intl relations of US, by country, 1990, annual listing, 26404–2

Environmental and wildlife conservation intl agreements provisions, status, and signatories, as of 1991, listing, 9886–4.169

Foreign countries economic, social, political, and geographic summary data, by country, 1991, annual factbook, 9114–2

Geographic Notes, foreign countries boundaries, claims, nomenclature, and other devs, periodic rpt, 7142–3

Helsinki Final Act implementation by NATO and Warsaw Pact, Apr 1990-Mar 1991, last issue of semiannual rpt, 7002–1

Human rights conditions in 170 countries, and US economic and military aid, 1990, annual rpt, 21384–3

Maritime claims and boundary agreements of coastal countries, series, 7006–8

Treaties and conventions

OASDI beneficiaries abroad, benefits, and eligibility based on intl agreement, by program type and country, 1989, annual rpt, 4744–3.3

Patent and copyright intl and domestic protection, products excluded, and countries and agreements involved, 1990 article, 9391–1.203

Tax withheld and income from US sources for foreign natls not residing in US, by country and tax treaty status, 1988, annual article, 8302–2.206

see also Executive agreements

see also Intermediate-Range Nuclear Forces Treaty

see also Strategic Arms Reduction Talks

see also Trade agreements

see also Treaty on Conventional Armed Forces in Europe

Treaty on Conventional Armed Forces in Europe

NATO and Warsaw Pact military forces reductions under proposed treaty, and US budget savings, 1990 rpt, 26306–3.114

Trees

see Forests and forestry

Trent, Linda K.

"Prevalence of Elevated Serum Cholesterol in Personnel of the U.S. Navy", 4042–3.215

Trenton, N.J.

CPI by component for US city average, and by region, population size, and for 15 metro areas, monthly rpt, 6762–1

CPI by component for US city average, and by region, population size, and for 27 metro areas, monthly rpt, 6762–2

Wages by occupation, for office and plant workers, 1990 survey, periodic MSA rpt, 6785–11.3

see also By SMSA or MSA in the "Index by Categories"

Treubert, Patrice

"Corporation Income Tax Returns, 1988", 8302–2.217

Trials

Criminal case processing in Federal courts, by offense, disposition, and jurisdiction, data compilation, 1991 annual rpt, 6064–6.5

DC appeals and superior courts civil and criminal caseloads, 1971-88, hearing, 21308–27

Drug and alcohol abuse and mental illness direct and indirect costs, by type and patient age and sex, 1985 with 1980 and 1988 comparisons, 4048–35

Federal district and appeals court caseloads, actions, procedure duration, judges, and jurors, by court, 1986-91, annual rpt, 18204–3

Federal district court civil and criminal trials, and time to trial and case disposition, 1990, annual rpt, 18204–8.13; 18204–8.18

Federal district court criminal caseloads, by offense, disposition, and district, 1980-90, last issue of annual rpt, 18204–1

Tax litigation, prosecutions, and interpretive law decisions, FY90, annual rpt, 8304–3.3

US attorneys case processing and collections, by case type and Federal district, FY90, annual rpt, 6004–2

Wiretaps authorized, costs, arrests, trials, and convictions, by offense and jurisdiction, 1990, annual rpt, 18204–7

see also Courts-martial and courts of inquiry

see also Juries

Trichinosis

see Food and waterborne diseases

Trinidad and Tobago

Agricultural exports of high-value commodities, indexes and sales by commodity, world area, and country, 1960s-86, 1528–323

Agricultural exports of US, impacts of foreign agricultural and trade policy, with data by commodity and country, 1989, annual rpt, 1924–8

Agricultural trade of US, by detailed commodity and country, 1989, annual rpt, 1524–8

Agricultural trade of US, by detailed commodity and country, 1990, semiannual rpt, 1522–4

AID economic aid to developing countries, obligations and disbursements by country, quarterly rpt, 9912–4

Economic and military aid and loans from US and intl agencies, by program and country, FY46-90, annual rpt, 9914–5

Economic conditions, policy, and trade practices, by country, 1988-90, annual rpt, 21384–5

Economic, social, political, and geographic summary data, by country, 1991, annual factbook, 9114–2

Exports and imports of US, by commodity and country, 1970-89, world area rpt, 9116–1.5

Exports and imports of US, by Harmonized System 6-digit commodity and country, 1990, annual rpt, 2424–13

Exports and imports of US, by selected country, country group, and commodity group, 1990, annual rpt, 2044–37

Exports and imports of US, by transport mode, country, and SITC 1- to 3-digit commodity, 1990, annual rpt, 2424–12

Exports of US, detailed Schedule B commodities with countries of destination, 1990, annual rpt, 2424–10

Human rights conditions in 170 countries, and US economic and military aid, 1990, annual rpt, 21384–3

Investment (direct) incentives of Caribbean Basin Initiative, economic impacts, with finances and employment by country, 1984-90, 2048–141

Labor conditions, union coverage, and work accidents, 1991 annual country rpt, 6366–4.31

Military aid of US, arms sales, and training programs costs and budget requests, by program, world region, and country, FY90-92, annual rpt, 7144–13

Multinatl US firms and foreign affiliates finances and operations, by industry and world area of parent firm, 1989 benchmark survey, preliminary annual rpt, 2704–5

Oil exports to US by OPEC and non-OPEC countries, monthly rpt, 3162–24.3

Steel imports of US under voluntary restraint agreement, by product, customs district, and country, with US industry operating data, quarterly rpt, 9882–13

UN voting record and share of votes in agreement with US, by issue, country, and world area, 1990, annual rpt, 7004–18

see also under By Foreign Country in the "Index by Categories"

Tropical storms

see Storms

Trout

see Aquaculture

see Fish and fishing industry

Troy, N.Y.

Wages by occupation, and benefits for office and plant workers, 1990 survey, periodic MSA rpt, 6785–3.1; 6785–3.2

see also under By SMSA or MSA in the "Index by Categories"

TRT Telecommunications Corp.

Finances and operations, detail for telegraph firms, 1989, annual rpt, 9284–6.3

Finances, rates, and traffic for US telecommunications carriers intl operations, by service type, firm, and country, 1975-89, annual rpt, 9284–17

Trucks and trucking industry

Accidents (fatal), circumstances, and characteristics of persons and vehicles involved, 1990, semiannual rpt, 7762–11

Accidents (fatal), deaths, and rates, by circumstances, characteristics of persons and vehicles involved, and location, 1989, annual rpt, 7764–10

Accidents at hwy-railroad grade-crossings, detailed data by State and railroad, 1989, annual rpt, 7604–2

Accidents, casualties, and damage, by circumstances and characteristics of persons and trucks involved, 1988, annual rpt, 7554–9

Accidents, casualties, circumstances, and characteristics of persons and vehicles involved, 1989, annual rpt, 7764–18

Accidents impacts of speed limits, with accident circumstances and speed averages, for States with 55 and 65 mph limit, 1986-89, annual rpt, 7764–15

Accidents of trucks, by carrier financial and operating conditions and driver characteristics, 1980s, GAO rpt, 26131–82

Accidents of trucks, circumstances, severity, and characteristics of drivers and vehicles, 1989, annual rpt, 7764–20

Agriculture census, 1987: farms, farmland, production, finances, and operator characteristics, by county, final State rpt series, 2331–1

Business statistics, detailed data for major industries and economic indicators, *Survey of Current Business*, monthly rpt, 2702–1.11; 2702–1.23

California minerals production by commodity, shipments, and liquefied petroleum gas transport by mode, 1986-87, conf, 5668–119

Canada and US auto trade, production, sales, prices, and employment, selected years 1965-88, annual rpt, 2044–35

Census of Transportation, 1987: finances and operations by size, ownership, and State, and revenues by MSA, by SIC 2- to 4-digit industry, 2579–1

Coal shipments to electric utilities under contract, and rates, by firm, transport mode, and region, 1979-87, 3168–121

Index by Subjects and Names

Trucks and trucking industry

Collective bargaining agreements expiring during year, and workers covered, by firm, union, industry group, and State, 1991, annual rpt, 6784–9

Costs itemized per mile, finances, and operations, for agricultural carriers, 1990, annual rpt, 1311–15

Costs itemized per mile for transport of fruit and vegetables, by fleets and owner-operator trucks, monthly table, 1272–1

County Business Patterns, 1988: employment, establishments, and payroll, by SIC 2- to 4-digit industry and county, annual State rpt series, 2326–6

County Business Patterns, 1989: employment, establishments, and payroll, by SIC 2- to 4-digit industry and county, annual State rpt series, 2326–8

CPI by component for US city average, and by region, population size, and for 27 metro areas, monthly rpt, 6762–2

Customs Service activities, collections, entries processed by mode of transport, and seizures, FY86-90, annual rpt, 8144–1

Depreciable assets class lives measurement, investment, and operations, for light trucks fleet and other business use, 1991 rpt, 8006–5.6

Deregulation of trucking industry by States, potential economic and market impacts, with background data, mid 1970s-80s, 7308–200

Drivers licenses issued and in force by age and sex, fees, and renewal, by license class and State, 1989, annual rpt, 7554–16

Employee (temporary) supply establishments by occupation supplied, receipts by source, and payroll, by MSA, 1987 Census of Service Industries, 2393–4.8

Employment, earnings, and hours, by SIC 1- to 4-digit industry, monthly and annual averages, selected years 1909-90, annual rpt, 6744–4

Energy conservation measures impacts on consumption, by component and end-use sector, 1970s-88 and projected under alternative oil prices to 1995, 3308–93

Energy economy performance of autos and light trucks by make, standards, and enforcement, 1978-91 model years, annual rpt, 7764–9

Energy economy, sales, and market shares, by size and model for domestic and foreign makes, 1991 model year, semiannual rpt, 3302–4

Energy use and vehicle registrations, by vehicle type, 1960-90, annual rpt, 3164–74.1

Energy use by mode of transport, fuel supply, and demographic and economic factors of vehicle use, 1970s-89, annual rpt, 3304–5

Engine and powertrain R&D projects, DOE contracts and funding by recipient, FY90, annual rpt, 3304–17

Enterprise Statistics, 1987: finances and operations for companies, by size, level of diversification, form of organization, and industry group, 2329–8

Exports and imports by country, US industry finances and operations, and prices of selected US and foreign models, monthly rpt, 9882–8

Exports and imports of US, by country and detailed commodity, monthly rpt, 2422–12

Exports and imports of US, by Harmonized System 6-digit commodity and country, 1990, annual rpt, 2424–13

Exports and imports of US, by transport mode, country, and SITC 1- to 3-digit commodity, 1990, annual rpt, 2424–12

Exports of US, detailed Schedule B commodities with countries of destination, 1990, annual rpt, 2424–10

Farm income, expenses, receipts by commodity, assets, liabilities, and ratios, 1990 and trends from 1945, annual rpt, 1544–16

Farm production itemized costs, by farm sales size and region, 1990, annual rpt, 1614–3

Finances and inventory of truck and warehouse services, by SIC 2- to 4-digit industry, 1989 survey, annual rpt, 2413–14

Finances and operations, by SIC 2- to 4-digit industry, forecast 1991, annual rpt, 2044–28

Finances and operations of carriers of property, by region and firm, quarterly rpt, 9482–5

Finances and operations of interstate carriers, by district, 1989, annual rpt, 9486–6.2; 9486–6.3

Household goods carriers financial and operating data by firm, quarterly rpt, 9482–14

Household goods carriers performance and disposition of damage claims, for selected carriers, 1990, annual rpt, 9484–11

Households with autos and trucks available, by location, 1989, biennial rpt, 2485–12

Households with autos and trucks available, MSA surveys, series, 2485–6

Hwy Statistics, detailed data by State, 1990, annual rpt, 7554–1

Hwy Statistics, summary data by State, 1989-90, annual rpt, 7554–24

Labor productivity, indexes of output, hours, and employment by SIC 2- to 4-digit industry, 1967-89, annual rpt, 6824–1.4

Mail (express parcel) shipments and revenues of private air and surface carriers, and impact of State regulation, 1976-89, 7308–201

Manufacturing annual survey, 1989: finances and operations, by SIC 2- to 4-digit industry, series, 2506–15

Manufacturing census, 1987: employment and shipments under Fed Govt contracts, by SIC 4-digit industry, 2497–7

Manufacturing census, 1987: finances and operations, by SIC 2- to 4-digit industry, State, and MSA, with trends from 1849, 2497–1

Manufacturing employment, by detailed occupation and SIC 2-digit industry, 1989 survey, triennial rpt, 6748–52

Natl income and product accounts and components, *Survey of Current Business*, monthly rpt, 2702–1.24

Natl transportation system planning, use, condition, accidents, and needs, by mode of transport, 1940s-90 and projected to 2020, 7308–202

Natural gas (compressed) use in trucks, costs, emissions, health impacts, and fuel characteristics, 1990 rpt, 9196–5.3

Occupational injury and illness rates, by SIC 2- to 4-digit industry, 1988-89, annual rpt, 6844–7

Occupational injury and illness rates, by SIC 2- to 4-digit industry, 1989, annual rpt, 6844–1

OECD trade, total and for 4 major countries, and US trade by country, by commodity, 1970-89, world area rpt series, 9116–1

Oil bulk stations, sales and storage capacity by product, inventories, expenses, employment, and modes of transport, 1987 Census of Wholesale Trade, 2407–4.2

Price indexes (producer), by stage of processing and detailed commodity, monthly rpt, 6762–6

Price indexes (producer), by stage of processing and detailed commodity, monthly 1990, annual rpt, 6764–2

Prices received and paid by farmers, by commodity and State, 1990, annual rpt, 1629–5

Recalls of motor vehicles and equipment with safety-related defects, by make, monthly listing, 7762–12

Rental of autos and trucks, industry receipts, 1990, annual rpt, 2413–8

Safety inspections of trucks and buses, fines, and vehicles and drivers ordered out of service, by State, with program funding, FY89, 25268–78

Safety inspections of trucks conducted FY87-88, FHwA compliance review status as of 1990, GAO rpt, 26113–505

Safety of domestic and foreign autos, crash test results by model, press release series, 7766–7

Safety programs, and accidents, casualties, and damage, by mode of transport, 1989, annual rpt, 7304–19

Sales and prices for domestic and import autos and trucks, and auto production and inventories, 1991 model year, annual article, 2702–1.228

State and Metro Area Data Book, 1991 data compilation, 2328–54

Statistical Abstract of US, 1991 annual data compilation, 2324–1.21

Tax (excise) collections of IRS, by source, quarterly rpt, 8302–1

Tax (excise) returns filed, by type of return and IRS district, 1989 and projected 1990-97, annual rpt, 8304–24

Tax (excise) returns filed, by type of tax and IRS region and service center, projected 1990-97 and trends from 1978, annual rpt, 8304–9

Tax (income) returns of corporations, income and tax items by asset size and detailed industry, 1987, annual rpt, 8304–4

Tax (income) returns of corporations, income and tax items by asset size and detailed industry, 1988, annual rpt, 8304–21

Tax (income) returns of partnerships, income statement and balance sheet items, by industry group, 1989, annual article, 8302–2.216; 8304–18

Tax (income) returns of sole proprietorships, income statement items, by industry group, 1989, annual article, 8302–2.214

Trucks and trucking industry

Tax provisions of States for motor fuel, auto registration fees, and disposition of receipts, by State, as of Jan 1991, biennial rpt, 7554–37

Trailer shipments, exports, and firms, by trailer type, monthly Current Industrial Rpt, 2506–12.25

Weight and size limits, by truck and roadway type and State, 1991, 26358–242

Wholesale trade census, 1987: establishments, sales by customer class, employment, inventories, and expenses, by SIC 2- to 4-digit kind of business, 2407–4

see also Freight

see also under By Industry in the "Index by Categories"

Truk

see Micronesia Federated States

Truman, Harry S., Scholarship Foundation

Awards by student characteristics, and Foundation finances, FY90, annual rpt, 14314–1

Budget of US, authoritative financial statements with appropriations, outlays, and receipts, by category and agency, FY90, annual rpt, 8104–2.1

Budget of US, obligations and authority by function, agency, and program, with summaries, analyses, and historical tables, FY92, annual rpt, 104–2

Expenditures for education by Federal agency, program, and recipient type, and instn spending, FY80-90, annual rpt, 4824–8

Trust fund receipts by source, transfers, and investment holdings and transactions, monthly rpt, 14312–1

Trust funds

American Historical Assn financial statements, and membership by State, 1989, annual rpt, 29574–2

Assets and debts of private sector, balance sheets by segment, 1945-90, semiannual rpt, 9365–4.1

Boycotts (intl) by OPEC and other countries, US taxpayers IRS filings, cooperation, and tax benefits denied, 1976-86, GAO rpt, 26119–349

County Business Patterns, 1988: employment, establishments, and payroll, by SIC 2- to 4-digit industry and county, annual State rpt series, 2326–6

County Business Patterns, 1989: employment, establishments, and payroll, by SIC 2- to 4-digit industry and county, annual State rpt series, 2326–8

Farmland in US owned by foreigners, holdings, acquisitions, and disposals by land use, owner type and country, and State, 1990, annual rpt, 1584–2

Higher education instn endowment funds, for top 100 instns, FY87, annual rpt, 4824–2.25

Higher education instn revenue by source and spending by function, by State and instn control, FY80-88, annual rpt, 4844–6

Mortgage loan activity, by type of lender, loan, and mortgaged property, monthly press release, 5142–18

Mortgage loan activity, by type of lender, loan, and mortgaged property, quarterly press release, 5142–30

Tax returns filed, by type of tax and IRS district, 1989 and projected 1990-97, annual rpt, 8304–24

Tax returns filed, by type of tax and IRS region and service center, projected 1990-97 and trends from 1978, annual rpt, 8304–9

see also Government trust funds

see also Pensions and pension funds

see also Unemployment trust funds

Trust Territory of the Pacific Islands

see Marshall Islands

see Micronesia Federated States

see Northern Mariana Islands

see Palau

see Territories of the U.S.

Trzcinski, Eileen

"Leave Policies in Small Business: Findings from the U.S. Small Business Administration Employee Leave Survey", 9768–21

Tsunamis

Incidents and mgmt of disasters and natl security threats, with data by major event and State, 1991 annual rpt, 9434–6

Tuan, Francis C.

"U.S.-China Agricultural Trade over Two Decades", 1524–4.3

Tuberculosis

AIDS virus infection, TB testing and treatment, CDC guidelines, 1991 rpt, 4206–2.41

Aliens TB prevention and screening methods, CDC guidelines, 1990 rpt, 4206–2.36

Cases of acute and chronic conditions, disability, absenteeism, and health services use, by selected characteristics, 1987, CD-ROM, 4147–10.177

Cases of TB and deaths, by patient characteristics, State, and city, 1989 and trends from 1953, annual rpt, 4204–10

Cattle TB cases and cooperative Federal-State eradication activities, by State, FY89-90, annual rpt, 1394–13

Deaths and rates, by cause, provisional data, monthly rpt, 4142–1.2

Deaths and rates, by detailed cause and demographic characteristics, 1988 and trends from 1900, US Vital Statistics annual rpt, 4144–2

Health care settings transmission of TB, prevention and screening methods, CDC guidelines, 1990 rpt, 4206–2.35

Health condition and health care resources, use, and spending, 1950s-89, annual data compilation, 4144–11

HHS financial aid, by program, recipient, State, and city, FY90, annual regional listings, 4004–3

Homeless persons alcohol abuse, by sex, age, race, and additional diagnoses, aggregate 1985-87, 4488–14

Indian Health Service facilities and use, and Indian health and other characteristics, by IHS region, 1980s-89, annual chartbook, 4084–7

Indian Health Service facilities, funding, operations, and Indian health and other characteristics, 1950s-90, annual chartbook, 4084–1

Morbidity and Mortality Weekly Report, infectious notifiable disease cases by age, race, and State, and deaths, 1930s-90, annual rpt, 4204–1

Morbidity and Mortality Weekly Report, infectious notifiable disease cases by State, and public health issues, 4202–1

Radiation exposure of uranium miners and risk of death from cancer and lung diseases, for Indians and compared to whites and foreign countries, 1950s-84, hearing, 25548–101

see also under By Disease in the "Index by Categories"

Tucson, Ariz.

Housing starts and completions authorized by building permits in 40 MSAs, quarterly rpt, 2382–9

see also under By City and By SMSA or MSA in the "Index by Categories"

Tuition and fees

Child rearing costs of married couple households, by expenditure type, child's age, income, and region, 1990 and projected to 2007, 1708–87

Condition of Education, detail for higher education, 1960s-90, annual rpt, 4824–1.2

CPI by component for US city average, and by region, population size, and for 27 metro areas, monthly rpt, 6762–2

Digest of Education Statistics, 1991 annual data compilation, 4824–2

Higher education enrollment, faculty, finances, and degrees, by instn level and control, and State, FY87, annual rpt, 4844–13

Higher education instn revenue by source and spending by function, by State and instn control, FY80-88, annual rpt, 4844–6

Higher education instn student aid and other sources of support, with student expenses and characteristics, by instn type and control, 1990 triennial study, series, 4846–5

Higher education instn tuition and other costs, govt aid, impacts on enrollment, and cost containment methods, 1970s-90 and projected to 2001, 4808–25

Higher education instn tuition costs relation to quality, indicators for private instns, regression results, 1985/86, 4888–3

Higher education instn tuition relation to other instn financial indicators, by instn control, 1960s-88, 4808–24

Private elementary and secondary schools, students, and staff characteristics, various periods 1979-88, 4838–47

Statistical Abstract of US, 1991 annual data compilation, 2324–1.4

Undergrad student aid, costs, and income factors affecting access to education, 1990 rpt, 26306–6.153

Undergrad tuition and other costs, by instn control, 1959/60-1989/90, 4818–5

see also Student aid

Tulare, Calif.

see also under By SMSA or MSA in the "Index by Categories"

Tulsa, Marilyn

"Indian Health Service: FY90 Outpatient Visit Workload Summary and Comparison with Previous Year", 4084–8

"Outpatient Visits by Primary Health Provider, Indian Health Service and Tribally Operated Facilities, FY90", 4084–3

"Summary of Leading Causes for Outpatient Visits, Indian Health Service Direct and Contract Facilities, FY89", 4084–2

Tulsa, Okla.

Housing vacancy rates for single and multifamily units and mobile homes, by city and ZIP code, 1991, annual MSA rpt, 9304–22.3

Wages by occupation, and benefits for office and plant workers, 1991 survey, periodic MSA rpt, 6785–3.7

see also under By City and By SMSA or MSA in the "Index by Categories"

Tung nuts and oil

see Oils, oilseeds, and fats

Tungsten

see Metals and metal industries

Tunisia

Agricultural exports of high-value commodities, indexes and sales by commodity, world area, and country, 1960s-86, 1528–323

Agricultural exports of US, impacts of foreign agricultural and trade policy, with data by commodity and country, 1989, annual rpt, 1924–8

Agricultural production, trade, and policies in foreign countries, summary data by country, 1989-90, annual factbook, 1924–12

Agricultural trade of US, by detailed commodity and country, 1989, annual rpt, 1524–8

Agricultural trade of US, by detailed commodity and country, 1990, semiannual rpt, 1522–4

AID economic aid to developing countries, obligations and disbursements by country, quarterly rpt, 9912–4

AID loans repayment status and terms by program and country, and status of predecessor agency loans, quarterly rpt, 9912–3

Background Notes, summary social, political, and economic data, 1990 rpt, 7006–2.11

Economic and military aid and loans from US and intl agencies, by program and country, FY46-90, annual rpt, 9914–5

Economic and social conditions of developing countries from 1960s, and Intl Dev Cooperation Agency and AID activities and funding, FY90-92, annual rpt, 9904–4

Economic conditions, income, production, prices, employment, and trade, 1991 periodic country rpt, 2046–4.27; 2046–4.76

Economic conditions, policy, and trade practices, by country, 1988-90, annual rpt, 21384–5

Economic, social, political, and geographic summary data, by country, 1991, annual factbook, 9114–2

Exports and imports of US, by commodity and country, 1970-89, world area rpt, 9116–1.1

Exports and imports of US, by selected country, country group, and commodity group, 1990, annual rpt, 2044–37

Exports and imports of US, by transport mode, country, and SITC 1- to 3-digit commodity, 1990, annual rpt, 2424–12

Exports of US, detailed Schedule B commodities with countries of destination, 1990, annual rpt, 2424–10

Food supply, needs, and aid for developing countries, status and alternative forecasts, 1991 world area rpt, 1526–8.1

Human rights conditions in 170 countries, and US economic and military aid, 1990, annual rpt, 21384–3

Military aid of US, arms sales, and training programs costs and budget requests, by program, world region, and country, FY90-92, annual rpt, 7144–13

UN voting record and share of votes in agreement with US, by issue, country, and world area, 1990, annual rpt, 7004–18

see also under By Foreign Country in the "Index by Categories"

Tunnels

see Bridges and tunnels

Turkey

Agricultural exports of high-value commodities, indexes and sales by commodity, world area, and country, 1960s-86, 1528–323

Agricultural exports of US, impacts of foreign agricultural and trade policy, with data by commodity and country, 1989, annual rpt, 1924–8

Agricultural production, prices, and trade, by country, 1960s-90, annual world area rpt, 1524–4.2

Agricultural production, trade, and policies in foreign countries, summary data by country, 1989-90, annual factbook, 1924–12

Agricultural trade of US, by detailed commodity and country, 1989, annual rpt, 1524–8

Agricultural trade of US, by detailed commodity and country, 1990, semiannual rpt, 1522–4

AID economic aid to developing countries, obligations and disbursements by country, quarterly rpt, 9912–4

AID loans repayment status and terms by program and country, and status of predecessor agency loans, quarterly rpt, 9912–3

Almond production, trade, use, and stocks, for 6 countries and US, 1987-92, article, 1925–34.240

Background Notes, summary social, political, and economic data, 1991 rpt, 7006–2.22

Bearings (ball) from 14 countries, injury to US industry from foreign subsidized and less than fair value imports, investigation with background financial and operating data, 1991 rpt, 9886–19.74

Currency devaluation in Turkey and effects on GNP, trade, investment, and inflation, 1970s-90, technical paper, 9385–8.112

Economic and military aid and loans from US and intl agencies, by program and country, FY46-90, annual rpt, 9914–5

Economic and social conditions of developing countries from 1960s, and Intl Dev Cooperation Agency and AID activities and funding, FY90-92, annual rpt, 9904–4

Economic conditions, income, production, prices, employment, and trade, 1991 periodic country rpt, 2046–4.24

Economic conditions, policy, and trade practices, by country, 1988-90, annual rpt, 21384–5

Economic, social, political, and geographic summary data, by country, 1991, annual factbook, 9114–2

Exports and imports of NATO members with PRC, by country, 1987-90, annual rpt, 7144–14

Exports and imports of OECD members, by country, 1989, annual rpt, 7144–10

Exports and imports of US, by Harmonized System 6-digit commodity and country, 1990, annual rpt, 2424–13

Exports and imports of US, by selected country, country group, and commodity group, 1990, annual rpt, 2044–37

Exports and imports of US, by transport mode, country, and SITC 1- to 3-digit commodity, 1990, annual rpt, 2424–12

Exports of US, detailed Schedule B commodities with countries of destination, 1990, annual rpt, 2424–10

GNP and GNP growth for OECD members, by country, 1980-90, annual rpt, 7144–8

Hazelnut production, supply, trade, and use, by country, 1989-92, article, 1925–34.246

Human rights conditions in 170 countries, and US economic and military aid, 1990, annual rpt, 21384–3

Imports of goods, services, and investment from US, trade barriers, impacts, and US actions, by country, 1990, annual rpt, 444–2

Labor conditions, union coverage, and work accidents, 1991 annual country rpt, 6366–4.51

Military aid of US, arms sales, and training programs costs and budget requests, by program, world region, and country, FY90-92, annual rpt, 7144–13

Multinatl US firms and foreign affiliates finances and operations, by industry and world area of parent firm, 1989 benchmark survey, preliminary annual rpt, 2704–5

Multinatl US firms foreign affiliates, income statement items by country and world area, 1986, biennial article, 8302–2.212

Oil production, trade, use, and stocks, by selected country and country group, monthly rpt, 3162–42

Raisin and prune production, trade, use, and stocks for EC and other countries, Turkey price supports, and Mexico production costs, 1985-91, annual article, 1925–34.250

Tax revenue, by level of govt and type of tax, for OECD countries, mid 1960s-89, annual rpt, 10044–1.2

UN voting record and share of votes in agreement with US, by issue, country, and world area, 1990, annual rpt, 7004–18

see also under By Foreign Country in the "Index by Categories"

Turkeys

see Poultry industry and products

Turnbull, Brenda J.

"State Administration of the Amended Chapter 1 Program", 4808–32

Turnbull, Katherine F.

"Description of High-Occupancy Vehicle Facilities in North America", 7888–80

Turner, Barbara J.

"AIDS in U.S. Hospitals, 1986-87: A National Perspective", 4186–6.15

Turner, John W.

"Civilian Training in High-Altitude Flight Physiology", 7506–10.92

Turner, John W.

"Use and Design of Flightcrew Checklists and Manuals", 7506–10.86

Turnover of labor

see Job tenure

see Labor turnover

Turpentine

see Gum and wood chemicals

Tuscaloosa, Ala.

see also under By SMSA or MSA in the "Index by Categories"

Tuvalu

Economic, social, and agricultural data, US and other aid sources, and AID activity, 1988 country rpt, 9916–12.28

Economic, social, political, and geographic summary data, by country, 1991, annual factbook, 9114–2

Exports and imports of US, by transport mode, country, and SITC 1- to 3-digit commodity, 1990, annual rpt, 2424–12

TVA

see Tennessee Valley Authority

Tyler, Tex.

see also under By SMSA or MSA in the "Index by Categories"

Typewriters

see Business machines and equipment

Uctum, Merih

"Critical Evaluation of Exchange Rate Policy in Turkey", 9385–8.112

"Foreign Interest Rate Disturbance, Financial Flows and Physical Capital Accumulation in a Small Open Economy", 9385–8.102

Uganda

Agricultural exports of high-value commodities, indexes and sales by commodity, world area, and country, 1960s-86, 1528–323

Agricultural trade of US, by detailed commodity and country, 1989, annual rpt, 1524–8

Agricultural trade of US, by detailed commodity and country, 1990, semiannual rpt, 1522–4

AID economic aid to developing countries, obligations and disbursements by country, quarterly rpt, 9912–4

AID loans repayment status and terms by program and country, and status of predecessor agency loans, quarterly rpt, 9912–3

Background Notes, summary social, political, and economic data, 1991 rpt, 7006–2.28

Dairy imports, consumption, and market conditions, by sub-Saharan Africa country, 1961-88, 1528–321

Economic and military aid and loans from US and intl agencies, by program and country, FY46-90, annual rpt, 9914–5

Economic and social conditions of developing countries from 1960s, and Intl Dev Cooperation Agency and AID activities and funding, FY90-92, annual rpt, 9904–4

Economic conditions, income, production, prices, employment, and trade, 1990 periodic country rpt, 2046–4.9

Economic conditions, income, production, prices, employment, and trade, 1991 periodic country rpt, 2046–4.49

Economic, social, political, and geographic summary data, by country, 1991, annual factbook, 9114–2

Exports and imports of US, by transport mode, country, and SITC 1- to 3-digit commodity, 1990, annual rpt, 2424–12

Exports of US, detailed Schedule B commodities with countries of destination, 1990, annual rpt, 2424–10

Human rights conditions in 170 countries, and US economic and military aid, 1990, annual rpt, 21384–3

Military aid of US, arms sales, and training programs costs and budget requests, by program, world region, and country, FY90-92, annual rpt, 7144–13

UN voting record and share of votes in agreement with US, by issue, country, and world area, 1990, annual rpt, 7004–18

see also under By Foreign Country in the "Index by Categories"

Ulcers

see Digestive diseases

Ulrich, Alice H.

"U.S. Timber Production, Trade, Consumption, and Price Statistics, 1960-88", 1204–29

Umm al-Qaiwain

see United Arab Emirates

Unconventional warfare

see Chemical and biological warfare agents

Underdeveloped countries

see Developing countries

Underemployment

Employment, earnings, and hours, monthly press release, 6742–5

Foreign countries labor conditions, union coverage, and work accidents, annual country rpt series, 6366–4

Part-time employment, by age, sex, industry div, and whether voluntary, 1969-89, article, 6722–1.218

Part-time employment by health insurance coverage and worker characteristics, and temporary and contract employment, 1979-89, GAO rpt, 26121–411

Rural areas labor force characteristics, with comparisons to urban areas, 1987, 1598–264

Science and engineering PhDs employment and other characteristics, by field and State, 1989, biennial rpt, 9627–18

Youth labor force status, by sex, race, and industry div, summer 1987-91, annual press release, 6744–14

Underground economy

Drug enforcement regional task forces investigation of organized crime, activities by agency and region, FY83-90, biennial rpt, 6004–17

Money laundering and related activity, Federal sentencing guidelines by offense and circumstances, series, 17668–1

Money laundering enforcement activities of IRS, staff, and funding, abatement, 1985-90, GAO rpt, 26123–338

Money laundering investigation network of Treasury Dept, funding, and staff detailed from other agencies, 1990-91, GAO rpt, 26119–330

Money laundering investigations of Fed Govt using IRS large cash transaction rpts, and rpts filed and penalties for nonfiling by region, 1989-91, GAO rpt, 26119–356

Money laundering operations related to drug traffic, US and foreign govts enforcement activities, 1989, annual rpt, 7004–17

see also Black market currency

Underground movements

see also Terrorism

Underwood, Carol

"Personal Health Practices: Findings from the Survey of American Indians and Alaska Natives. National Medical Expenditure Survey", 4186–8.19

Unemployment

see Employment and unemployment, general

see Employment and unemployment, local and regional

see Employment and unemployment, specific industry

see Labor turnover

see Public welfare programs

see Underemployment

see Unemployment insurance

see Unemployment insurance tax

see Work incentive programs

Unemployment insurance

AFDC beneficiaries demographic and financial characteristics, by State, FY89, annual rpt, 4694–1

Beneficiaries, taxes collected, and State program operations by State, since 1940, monthly rpt, 4742–1.1; 4742–1.7

Benefits adequacy, State and Federal programs, and work disincentives, series, 6406–6

Benefits and benefit duration under UI, by State, 1991, biennial article, 4742–1.217

Benefits, claims, coverage, and exhaustions for UI, 1955-90, annual rpt, 204–1.2

Benefits, coverage, and tax provisions under State UI programs, as of Jan 1991, semiannual listing, 6402–7

Benefits, coverage, tax rates, and penalties, changes under State UI programs, 1990, annual article, 6722–1.211

Black American displaced workers, by demographic and current and former employment characteristics, and compared to whites, 1978-86, article, 6722–1.234

Budget of US, midsession review of FY92 budget, by function, annual rpt, 104–7

Budget of US, obligations and authority by function, agency, and program, with summaries, analyses, and historical tables, FY92, annual rpt, 104–2

Business cycle and economic indicators impacts of UI programs, regression results, 1950s-89, 6406–6.34

Census of Govts, 1987: State and local govt employment, payroll, OASDHI coverage, and employee benefits costs, by level of govt and State, 2455–4

Child support overdue payments deducted from UI benefits, by State, FY85-89, annual rpt, 4694–6

Claims (initial) under State programs, *Survey of Current Business*, cyclical indicators, monthly rpt, 2702–1.1

Claims for UI and covered unemployment by program, and extended benefit triggers, by State, weekly rpt, 6402–15

Claims for UI, by program, weekly press release, 6402–14

Coverage, benefits, tax rates, and other changes in State UI law provisions, 1991, base edition with semiannual revisions, 6402–2

Coverage of employment, establishments, and wages under UI, by SIC 4-digit industry and State, 1990, annual rpt, 6744–16

Index by Subjects and Names

Coverage of wages under UI, by industry div, State, and MSA, 1989-90, annual press releases, 6784–17

Economic indicators and components, current data and annual trends, monthly rpt, 23842–1.2

Employment and hours worked, impacts of alternative UI policies, with data for selected countries, 1970s, article, 9383–6.205

Expenditures (private) for social welfare, by category, 1970s-88, annual article, 4742–1.204

Expenditures, coverage, and benefits for social welfare programs, late 1930s-89, annual rpt, 4744–3.1; 4744–3.7

Expenditures for public welfare by program, FY50s-88, annual article, 4742–1.209

Expenditures of Fed Govt in States, by type, program, agency, and State, FY90, annual rpt, 2464–2

Finances and operations of programs under Ways and Means Committee jurisdiction, FY70s-90, annual rpt, 21784–11

Finances of Fed Govt, cash and debt transactions, daily tables, 8102–4

Finances of govts, revenue by source, spending by function, debt, and assets, by level of govt, FY89, annual rpt, 2466–2.2

Finances, operations, tax provisions, and vulnerability to recessions, for State UI programs, 1970s-90s, hearing, 21788–201

Food stamp recipient household size, composition, income, and income and deductions allowed, summer 1988, annual rpt, 1364–8

Govt revenue by source, spending by function, debt, and assets, by level of govt, FY90, preliminary annual rpt, 2466–2.9

Households composition, income, benefits, and labor force status, Survey of Income and Program Participation methodology, working paper series, 2626–10

Income (household, family, and personal), by source, detailed characteristics, and region, 1988-89, annual Current Population Rpt, 2546–6.68

Income (household, family, and personal), by source, detailed characteristics, and region, 1990, annual Current Population Rpt, 2546–6.70

Income tax returns of individuals, selected income and tax items by adjusted gross income and State, 1986-88, article, 8302–2.201

Income tax returns of individuals, selected income and tax items by income level, preliminary 1989, annual article, 8302–2.209

Job Training Partnership Act programs evaluation using UI wage records, 1986-87, 15496–1.13

Labor Dept activities and funding, by program and State, FY90, annual rpt, 6304–1

Labor Dept employment programs, training, and unemployment compensation, current devs and grants to States, press release series, 6406–2

Labor force, wages, hours, and payroll costs, by major industry group and demographic characteristics, *Survey of Current Business*, monthly rpt, 2702–1.8

North Central States business and economic conditions, Fed Reserve 9th District, quarterly journal, 9383–19

Railroad employee benefits program finances and beneficiaries, FY90, annual rpt, 9704–1

Railroad retirement, survivors, unemployment, and health insurance programs, monthly rpt, 9702–2

Railroad retirement system funding and benefits findings and recommendations, with background industry data, 1960s-90 and projected to 2060, 9708–1

Southeastern US wages covered under UI, by industry div, State, and metro area, 1989-90, annual press release, 6946–3.22

State and Metro Area Data Book, 1991 data compilation, 2328–54

State govt labor productivity, indexes of output by function, FY64-89, annual rpt, 6824–1.6

State govt revenue by source, spending and debt by function, and holdings, FY90, annual rpt, 2466–2.6

States UI programs quality appraisal results, FY90, annual rpt, 6404–16

Statistical Abstract of US, 1991 annual data compilation, 2324–1.12; 2324–1.13

see also Unemployment insurance tax

see also Unemployment trust funds

Unemployment insurance tax

Budget of US, authoritative financial statements with appropriations, outlays, and receipts, by category and agency, FY90, annual rpt, 8104–2.1

Budget of US, CBO analysis of savings and revenues under alternative spending cuts and tax changes, projected FY92-97, 26306–3.118

Budget of US, obligations and authority by function, agency, and program, with summaries, analyses, and historical tables, FY92, annual rpt, 104–2

Budget of US, receipts by source, outlays by agency and program, and balances, monthly rpt, 8102–3

Collections, enforcement, and litigation activity of IRS, with data by type of tax, region, and State, FY90, annual rpt, 8304–3

Collections of tax and beneficiaries for social insurance programs, monthly rpt, 4742–1.1

Costs (hourly) of labor, by component, industry sector, worker class, and firm size, 1990, annual rpt, 6744–22

Fed Govt receipts by source and outlays by agency, *Treasury Bulletin*, quarterly rpt, 8002–4.1

Fed Govt tax provisions and receipts overview, by tax type, with background data, 1900s-91 and projected to 2000, 21788–197

Fed Govt trust fund receipts, by source and fund, Budget of US, FY92, annual rpt, 104–9

Finances and operations of programs under Ways and Means Committee jurisdiction, FY70s-90, annual rpt, 21784–11

Finances of Fed Govt, cash and debt transactions, daily tables, 8102–4

Railroad retirement, survivors, unemployment, and health insurance programs, monthly rpt, 9702–2

Returns and supplemental documents filed, by type, FY90 and projected to FY99, semiannual rpt, 8302–4

Returns filed, accuracy of projections by return type, various periods 1983-90, article, 8304–8.1

State govt revenue by source, spending and debt by function, and holdings, FY90, annual rpt, 2466–2.6

States UI benefits, coverage, and tax provisions, as of Jan 1991, semiannual listing, 6402–7

States UI laws, changes in coverage, benefits, tax rates, and penalties, by State, 1990, annual article, 6722–1.211

States UI laws, comparison of provisions, 1991, base edition with semiannual revisions, 6402–2

States UI programs finances, operations, tax provisions, and vulnerability to recessions, 1970s-90s, hearing, 21788–201

Transit systems finances and operations, by mode of transport, size of fleet, and for 468 systems, 1989, annual rpt, 7884–4

Unemployment trust funds

Finances and operations of programs under Ways and Means Committee jurisdiction, FY70s-90, annual rpt, 21784–11

Financial condition of Federal UI trust funds, by State, monthly rpt, 8102–9.16

Financial condition of Federal UI trust funds, quarterly rpt, 8102–9.1

State govt revenue by source, spending and debt by function, and holdings, FY90, annual rpt, 2466–2.6

States UI programs finances, operations, tax provisions, and vulnerability to recessions, 1970s-90s, hearing, 21788–201

UNICOR

see Federal Prison Industries

Unions

see Labor unions

United Arab Emirates

Agricultural exports of high-value commodities, indexes and sales by commodity, world area, and country, 1960s-86, 1528–323

Agricultural exports of US, impacts of foreign agricultural and trade policy, with data by commodity and country, 1989, annual rpt, 1924–8

Agricultural production, trade, and policies in foreign countries, summary data by country, 1989-90, annual factbook, 1924–12

Agricultural trade of US, by detailed commodity and country, 1989, annual rpt, 1524–8

Agricultural trade of US, by detailed commodity and country, 1990, semiannual rpt, 1522–4

Background Notes, summary social, political, and economic data, 1991 rpt, 7006–2.47

Economic conditions, income, production, prices, employment, and trade, 1991 periodic country rpt, 2046–4.35

Economic conditions, policy, and trade practices, by country, 1988-90, annual rpt, 21384–5

Economic, social, political, and geographic summary data, by country, 1991, annual factbook, 9114–2

Exports and imports of US, by commodity and country, 1970-89, world area rpt, 9116–1.1

United Arab Emirates

Index by Subjects and Names

Exports and imports of US, by Harmonized System 6-digit commodity and country, 1990, annual rpt, 2424–13

Exports and imports of US, by selected country, country group, and commodity group, 1990, annual rpt, 2044–37

Exports and imports of US, by transport mode, country, and SITC 1- to 3-digit commodity, 1990, annual rpt, 2424–12

Exports of US, detailed Schedule B commodities with countries of destination, 1990, annual rpt, 2424–10

Human rights conditions in 170 countries, and US economic and military aid, 1990, annual rpt, 21384–3

Multinatl US firms and foreign affiliates finances and operations, by industry and world area of parent firm, 1989 benchmark survey, preliminary annual rpt, 2704–5

Oil production and exports to US, by major exporting country, detailed data, monthly rpt with articles, 3162–24

Oil production, trade, use, and stocks, by selected country and country group, monthly rpt, 3162–42

UN voting record and share of votes in agreement with US, by issue, country, and world area, 1990, annual rpt, 7004–18

see also under By Foreign Country in the "Index by Categories"

United Arab Republic

see Egypt

United Kingdom

Acquisitions of US firms by UK firms, financing, sources, and rates of return, with data by firm, 1980s, technical paper, 9385–8.82

Agricultural exports of high-value commodities, indexes and sales by commodity, world area, and country, 1960s-86, 1528–323

Agricultural production, prices, and trade, by country, 1970s-90, and forecast 1991, annual world region rpt, 1524–4.4

Agricultural production, trade, and policies in foreign countries, summary data by country, 1989-90, annual factbook, 1924–12

Agricultural trade of US, by detailed commodity and country, 1989, annual rpt, 1524–8

Agricultural trade of US, by detailed commodity and country, 1990, semiannual rpt, 1522–4

AID loans repayment status and terms by program and country, and status of predecessor agency loans, quarterly rpt, 9912–3

Apple import demand in 4 countries, 1960s-83, 1568–296

Background Notes, summary social, political, and economic data, 1990 rpt, 7006–2.3

Banks capital costs, operating ratios, and intl market shares, for US and 5 OECD countries, 1980s-90, article, 9385–1.203

Businesses (foreign) activity in US, income tax returns, assets, and income statement items, by industry div and selected country, 1986-87, article, 8302–2.205

Corporations in US under foreign control, income tax returns, assets and income statement items by industry div, country, and world area, 1988, article, 8302–2.219

Economic aid of US and other donor countries by type and recipient, and role in advancing economic interests, 1980s-90, 2048–152

Economic and military aid and loans from US and intl agencies, by program and country, FY46-90, annual rpt, 9914–5

Economic and monetary trends, compounded annual rates of change and quarterly indicators for US and 7 major industrialized countries, quarterly rpt, 9391–7

Economic conditions, and oil supply and demand, for major industrial countries, biweekly rpt, 9112–1

Economic conditions, consumer and stock prices and production indexes, 6 OECD countries and US, *Business Conditions Digest*, monthly rpt, 2702–1.2

Economic conditions in USSR, Eastern Europe, OECD, and selected other countries, 1960s-90, annual rpt, 9114–4

Economic conditions, income, production, prices, employment, and trade, 1991 periodic country rpt, 2046–4.43

Economic conditions, policy, and trade practices, by country, 1988-90, annual rpt, 21384–5

Economic indicators, and dollar exchange rates, for selected OECD countries, 1991 semiannual rpt, 8002–14

Economic, social, political, and geographic summary data, by country, 1991, annual factbook, 9114–2

Energy prices, by fuel type and end use, for 10 countries, 1980-89 annual rpt, 3164–50.6

Energy production by type, and oil trade, and use, by country group and selected country, monthly rpt, 9112–2

Exports and imports, intl position of US and 4 OECD countries, and factors affecting US competition, periodic pamphlet, 2042–25

Exports and imports of NATO members with PRC, by country, 1987-90, annual rpt, 7144–14

Exports and imports of OECD members, by country, 1989, annual rpt, 7144–10

Exports and imports of OECD, total and for 4 major countries, and US trade by country, by commodity, 1970-89, world area rpt series, 9116–1

Exports and imports of US by country, and trade shifts by commodity, 1990, semiannual rpt, 9882–9

Exports and imports of US, by Harmonized System 6-digit commodity and country, 1990, annual rpt, 2424–13

Exports and imports of US, by selected country, country group, and commodity group, 1990, annual rpt, 2044–37

Exports and imports of US, by transport mode, country, and SITC 1- to 3-digit commodity, 1990, annual rpt, 2424–12

Exports and imports of US with EC by country, and total agricultural trade, selected years 1958-90, annual rpt, 7144–7

Exports, imports, and balances of US with major trading partners, by product category, 1986-90, annual chartbook, 9884–21

Exports of US, detailed Schedule B commodities with countries of destination, 1990, annual rpt, 2424–10

Farmland in US owned by foreigners, holdings, acreage, and value by land use, owner country, State, and county, 1990, annual rpt, 1584–3

Gene amplification thermal cyclers and subassemblies from UK at less than fair value, injury to US industry, investigation with background financial and operating data, 1990 rpt, 9886–14.301; 9886–14.327

GNP and GNP growth for OECD members, by country, 1980-90, annual rpt, 7144–8

Govt spending impacts on personal consumption, for UK, alternative model results, 1950s-86, technical paper, 9385–8.83

Human rights conditions in 170 countries, and US economic and military aid, 1990, annual rpt, 21384–3

Imports of goods, services, and investment from US, trade barriers, impacts, and US actions, by country, 1990, annual rpt, 444–2

Imports of US given duty-free treatment for value of US material sent abroad, by commodity and country, 1989, annual rpt, 9884–14

Inflation and GNP forecasting performance of indexed bond prices, for UK, 1950s-91, article, 9385–1.214

Interest and exchange rates, security yields, and stock indexes, for selected foreign countries, weekly chartbook, 9365–1.5

Interest rates over long run, relation to inflation and other economic indicators, model description and results for UK indexed bonds, 1982-88, technical paper, 9385–8.119

Investment (foreign direct) in US, by industry group of US affiliate and country of parent firm, 1980-86, 2708–41

Investment (foreign direct) in US, major transactions by type, industry, country, and US location, 1989, annual rpt, 2044–20

Labor conditions, union coverage, and work accidents, 1991 annual country rpt, 6366–4.12

Military reserve forces structure and training, for US and 5 European countries, as of 1990, GAO rpt, 26123–358

Multinatl firms US affiliates, finances, and operations, by industry, world area of parent firm, and State, 1988-89, annual rpt, 2704–4

Multinatl firms US affiliates, investment trends and impact on US economy, 1991 annual rpt, 2004–9

Multinatl US firms and foreign affiliates finances and operations, by industry and world area of parent firm, 1989 benchmark survey, preliminary annual rpt, 2704–5

Multinatl US firms foreign affiliates, income statement items by country and world area, 1986, biennial article, 8302–2.212

Nuclear power generation in US and 20 countries, monthly rpt, 3162–24.10

Nuclear power plant capacity, generation, and operating status, by plant and foreign and US location, 1990 and projected to 2030, annual rpt, 3164–57

Oil production, trade, use, and stocks, by selected country and country group, monthly rpt, 3162–42

Index by Subjects and Names

Uranium

Oil production, use, stocks, and exports and prices for US, by country, detailed data, monthly rpt with articles, 3162–24

Paper (coated groundwood) from 5 countries at less than fair value, injury to US industry, investigation with background financial and operating data, 1991 rpt, 9886–14.336

Paper (coated groundwood) from 9 countries at less than fair value, injury to US industry, investigation with background financial and operating data, 1991 rpt, 9886–14.306

Science and engineering employment and education, and R&D spending, for US and selected foreign countries, 1991 annual rpt, 9627–35

Science and engineering employment, by professional characteristics, age, and sex, for selected countries, 1991 working paper, 2326–18.62

Ships in world merchant fleet, tonnage, and new ship construction and deliveries, by vessel type and country, as of Jan 1990, annual rpt, 7704–3

Sodium sulfur compounds from 4 countries at less than fair value, injury to US industry, investigation with background financial and operating data, 1991 rpt, 9886–14.305

Space programs activities, missions, launchings, payloads, and flight duration, for foreign and US programs, 1957-90, annual rpt, 21704–4

Spacecraft and satellite launches since 1957, quarterly listing, 9502–2

Stock and bond returns for foreign and domestic instruments, relationship to selected economic indicators for US, UK, and Japan, 1970s-80s, article, 9385–1.211

Tax revenue, by level of govt and type of tax, for OECD countries, mid 1960s-89, annual rpt, 10044–1.2

Tea imports of UK, and London auction prices, 1975-91, FAS annual circular, 1925–15.3

Telecommunications industry intl competitiveness, with financial and operating data by product or service, firm, and country, 1990 rpt, 2008–30

Transportation energy use, fuel prices, vehicle registrations, and mileage, by selected country, 1970s-89, annual rpt, 3304–5.1

Travel to US, trade shows and other promotional activities, with magazine ad costs and circulation, for selected countries, 1991-92, annual rpt, 2904–11

UN voting record and share of votes in agreement with US, by issue, country, and world area, 1990, annual rpt, 7004–18

Unemployment in UK, impacts of monetary policy, industry structure, and unemployment benefits, 1920-38, working paper, 9375–13.52

Weather forecasts accuracy evaluations, for US, UK, and European systems, quarterly rpt, 2182–8

see also Gibraltar

see also under By Foreign Country in the "Index by Categories"

United Nations

Cambodia refugees in Thailand border camps by site, and UN aid by donor country, 1980s, GAO rpt, 26123–313

Developing countries aid by intl agencies, Intl Dev Cooperation Agency oversight of US contributions, FY92, annual rpt, 9904–4.2

Disabled persons in developing countries aid program activities and funding, for UN, AID, and Intl Labor Organization, late 1970s-90, GAO rpt, 26123–321

Expenditures for intl organizations by US and other countries, by organization and program, FY90, annual rpt, 7004–9

Iraq invasion of Kuwait, alien worker refugees fleeing from Iraq and Kuwait, intl aid by source, and costs to host and native countries, 1990-91, GAO rpt, 26123–326

Loans and grants for economic and military aid from US and intl agencies, by program and country, FY46-90, annual rpt, 9914–5

Peace Corps activities, funding by program, and volunteers, by country, FY92, annual rpt, 9654–1

Persian Gulf War events and UN Security Council resolutions, listing, 1990-91, annual rpt supplement, 3504–13

Pesticide levels in food, comparison of US and UN standards, 1988-90, GAO rpt, 26131–88

PL 480 exports by commodity, and recipients, by program, sponsor, and country, FY88 and cumulative from FY55, annual rpt, 1924–7

Refugee aid funding of US by program, agency, and intl organization, and admissions to US, 1980s-90, GAO rpt, 26123–334

US participation in UN, and member and nonmember shares of UN budget by country, FY89-91, annual rpt, 7004–5

Voting record in UN and share of votes in agreement with US, by issue, country, and world area, 1990, annual rpt, 7004–18

see also International Atomic Energy Agency

see also International Bank for Reconstruction and Development

see also International Development Association

see also International Finance Corp.

see also International Labor Organization

see also International Monetary Fund

Universities

see Higher education

Unmanned space programs

see Communications satellites

see Meteorological satellites

see Satellites

see Space programs

Unpaid family workers

Employment and Earnings, detailed data, monthly rpt, 6742–2

Employment, earnings, and hours, monthly press release, 6742–5

Employment situation, earnings, hours, and other BLS economic indicators, transcripts of BLS Commissioner's monthly testimony, periodic rpt, 23846–4

Farm employment, wages, and hours, by payment method, worker type, region, and State, 1910-90, 1618–21

Farm labor, wages, hours, and perquisites, by State, monthly rpt, 1631–1

Mental illness and drug and alcohol abuse direct and indirect costs, by age and sex, 1985, 4048–35

Moonlighting employment, by reason, and characteristics of workers and primary and secondary jobs, 1991, press release, 6726–1.40

Puerto Rico economic censuses, 1987: wholesale, retail, and service industries finances and operations, by size, form of organization, and SIC 2- and 3-digit industry, subject rpt, 2591–2.1

Unemployment insurance laws of States, comparison of provisions, 1991, base edition with semiannual revisions, 6402–2

Unreported income

see Tax delinquency and evasion

see Underground economy

Upper Volta

see Burkina Faso

Uranium

County Business Patterns, 1988: employment, establishments, and payroll, by SIC 2- to 4-digit industry and county, annual State rpt series, 2326–6

County Business Patterns, 1989: employment, establishments, and payroll, by SIC 2- to 4-digit industry and county, annual State rpt series, 2326–8

Demand for uranium and enrichment services, and nuclear power plant spent fuel, for US and other country groups, projected 1991-2040, annual rpt, 3164–72

Enrichment facilities of DOE, financial statements, FY89-90, annual rpt, 3354–7

Environmental Quality, status of problems, protection programs, research, and intl issues, 1991 annual rpt, 484–1

Exports and imports of US, by country and detailed commodity, monthly rpt, 2422–12

Exports and imports of US, by Harmonized System 6-digit commodity and country, 1990, annual rpt, 2424–13

Exports and imports of US, by transport mode, country, and SITC 1- to 3-digit commodity, 1990, annual rpt, 2424–12

Exports of US, detailed Schedule B commodities with countries of destination, 1990, annual rpt, 2424–10

Foreign direct investment in US energy sources by type and firm, and US affiliates operations, as of 1989, annual rpt, 3164–80

Inventory discrepancies for nuclear materials at DOE and contractor facilities, 1989/90, annual rpt, 3344–2

Mills (inactive) uranium tailings, remedial action activities by site, and funding, FY90, annual rpt, 3354–9

Minerals Yearbook, 1988, Vol 3: foreign country reviews of production, trade, and policy, by commodity, annual rpt series, 5604–17

Minerals Yearbook, 1989, Vol 2: State reviews of production and sales by commodity, and business activity, annual rpt series, 5604–16

Mines (metal) and related operations occupational injuries and incidence, employment, and hours, 1989, annual rpt, 6664–3

Mines safety and health enforcement, training, and funding, with casualties, by type of mine and State, FY89, annual rpt, 6664–6

Uranium

OECD trade, total and for 4 major countries, and US trade by country, by commodity, 1970-89, world area rpt series, 9116–1

Pollution (air) emissions factors, by detailed pollutant and source, data compilation, 1990 rpt, 9198–120

Power plants capital and production costs, operations, and fuel use, by fuel type, plant, utility, and location, 1989, annual rpt, 3164–9

Price indexes (producer), by stage of processing and detailed commodity, monthly 1990, rpt, 6764–2

Public lands acreage, grants, use, revenues, and allocations, by State, FY90, annual rpt, 5724–1.2

Radiation exposure at DOE and DOE-contractor sites, by facility type and contractor, dose type, and worker age, sex, and occupation, 1988, annual rpt, 3324–1

Radiation exposure of uranium miners and risk of death from cancer and lung diseases, for Indians and compared to whites and foreign countries, 1950s-84, hearing, 25548–101

Radioactive waste and spent fuel generation, inventory, and disposal, 1960s-89 and projected to 2020, annual rpt, 3364–2

Reserves, by recovery cost category, as of Dec 1989, annual rpt, 3164–74.1

Statistical Abstract of US, 1991 annual data compilation, 2324–1.25

Supply and industry operations for uranium, various periods 1947-90 and projected to 2000, annual rpt, 3164–65

Supply, demand, and prices, by fuel type and end-use sector, with foreign comparisons, 1990 and trends from 1949, annual rpt, 3164–74

Urban areas

AID housing and urban dev program financial statements, FY90, annual rpt, 9914–4

Aircraft noise policies, health impacts, and aircraft replacement schedules and costs, 1960s-90 and projected to 2006, hearing, 21648–64

Births, fertility rates, and childless women, by selected characteristics, 1990, annual Current Population Rpt, 2546–1.455

Census of Population, 1990: urban areas land area, housing units, and population, by State and compared to rural areas, press release, 2328–39

Census of Population, 1990: urban areas population, for 396 areas, press release, 2328–37

Child and maternal health programs of major urban health depts, activities and budgets, 1990, listing, 4108–51

China urbanization, bibl, 1991 working paper, 2326–18.60

CPI by component for US city average, and by region, population size, and for 15 metro areas, monthly rpt, 6762–1

CPI by component for US city average, and by region, population size, and for 27 metro areas, monthly rpt, 6762–2

Crime Index by population size and region, and offenses by large city, Jan-June 1991, semiannual rpt, 6222–1

Crime victimization of households, by offense, household characteristics, and location, 1975-90, annual rpt, 6066–25.40

Crimes, arrests by offender characteristics, and rates, by offense, and law enforcement employees, by population size and jurisdiction, 1990, annual rpt, 6224–2

Educational enrollment, by grade, instn type and control, and student characteristics, 1989 and trends from 1947, annual Current Population Rpt, 2546–1.453

Environmental Quality, status of problems, protection programs, research, and intl issues, 1991 annual rpt, 484–1

Food spending, by item, household composition, income, age, race, and region, 1980-88, Consumer Expenditure Survey biennial rpt, 1544–30

Hispanic Americans social and economic characteristics, by detailed origin, 1991, Current Population Rpt, 2546–1.448; 2546–1.451

Home mortgages FHA-insured, financial, property, and mortgagor characteristics, by metro area, 1990, annual rpt, 5144–24

Home mortgages FHA-insured, financial, property, and mortgagor characteristics, by State, 1990, annual rpt, 5144–1

Home mortgages FHA-insured, financial, property, and mortgagor characteristics, total and by State and outlying area, 1990, annual rpt, 5144–25

Home mortgages FHA-insured, financial, property, and mortgagor characteristics, 1990, annual rpt, 5144–23

Hospitals in rural areas, financial and operating performance impacts of Medicare prospective payment reimbursement system, 1980s-87, 4658–51

Households and family characteristics, by location, 1990, annual Current Population Rpt, 2546–1.447

Housing and households characteristics, unit and neighborhood quality, and journey to work by MSA location, for 11 MSAs, 1984 survey, supplement, 2485–8

Housing and households detailed characteristics, and unit and neighborhood quality, by location, 1987, biennial rpt supplement, 2485–13

Housing and households detailed characteristics, and unit and neighborhood quality, by location, 1989, biennial rpt, 2485–12

Housing inventory change from 1973, by reason, unit and household characteristics, and location, 1983 survey, biennial rpt, 2485–14

Housing vacancy and occupancy rates, and vacant unit characteristics and costs, by region and metro-nonmetro location, quarterly rpt, 2482–1

Hwy Statistics, detailed data by State, 1990, annual rpt, 7554–1

Income (personal) per capita disparity between metro and nonmetro areas, and causal factors, by State, 1979-88, 1548–380

Land acreage, by use, ownership, and State, 1987 and trends from 1910, 1588–48

Libraries (major urban resource centers) dev projects and funding, by city and State, FY84-88, listing, 4878–4

Poverty status of population and families, by detailed characteristics, 1988-89, annual Current Population Rpt, 2546–6.67

Poverty status of population and families, by detailed characteristics, 1990, annual Current Population Rpt, 2546–6.71

Recreation (outdoor) facilities and parks in urban areas, rehabilitation funding by city and State, FY91, press release, 5306–4.7

Retail trade census, 1987: finances and employment, for establishments with and without payroll, by SIC 2- to 4-digit kind of business, State, and MSA, 2401–1

State and Metro Area Data Book, 1991 data compilation, 2328–54

Statistical Abstract of US, 1991 annual data compilation, 2324–1

Unemployment, by State and metro area, monthly press release, 6742–12

Wages by occupation, for office and plant workers in metro areas, by industry div and region, Aug 1990, annual rpt, 6785–9

Water quality, chemistry, hydrology, and other characteristics, local area studies, series, 5666–27

see also Central cities

see also Cities

see also City and town planning

see also Community development

see also Local government

see also Metropolitan Statistical Areas

see also Neighborhoods

see also Relocation

see also Suburbs

see also Urban renewal

see also Urban transportation

see also Zoning and zoning laws

see also under By City, By SMSA or MSA, and By Urban-Rural and Metro-Nonmetro in the "Index by Categories"

Urban Development Action Grants

Activities, funding, and jobs and taxes generated under UDAG, discontinued, 5124–5

Expenditures of Fed Govt in States, by type, program, agency, and State, FY90, annual rpt, 2464–2

Urban Institute

"Children and Welfare: Patterns of Multiple Program Participation", 2626–10.133

"Decline in Unemployment Insurance Claims Activity in the 1980s", 6406–6.33

"Geographic Medicare Economic Index: Alternative Approaches", 4658–50

"Spells Without Health Insurance: Distributions of Durations and Their Link to Point-in-Time Estimates of the Uninsured", 2626–10.142

"Spells Without Health Insurance: What Affects Spell Duration and Who Are the Chronically Uninsured?", 2626–10.141

"Welfare Participation and Welfare Recidivism: The Role of Family Events", 2626–10.126

Urban Mass Transportation Administration

Budget of US, obligations and authority by function, agency, and program, with summaries, analyses, and historical tables, FY92, annual rpt, 104–2

Bus connector service between rural areas and Greyhound intercity routes, finances and operations by system, 1987-90, 7888–79

Carpool and bus high occupancy vehicle lanes use, design, and enforcement, for US and Canada, 1989, 7888–80

Index by Subjects and Names

Urogenital diseases

Employment of DOT, by subagency, occupation, and selected personnel characteristics, FY90, annual rpt, 7304–18

Expenditures of Fed Govt in States, by type, program, agency, and State, FY90, annual rpt, 2464–2

Grants of UMTA for transit systems, by city and State, FY90, annual rpt, 7884–10

Grants of UMTA to higher education instns for research and training, by project, FY90, annual listing, 7884–7

R&D projects and funding of UMTA, FY90, annual listing, 7884–1

Subway accidents, casualties, and damage, by circumstances and system, 1989, annual rpt, 7884–5

Transit systems finances and operations, by mode of transport, size of fleet, and for 468 systems, 1989, annual rpt, 7884–4

Transit systems finances, costs, and needs, by selected system, 1987-89, biennial rpt, 7884–8

Transit systems under private, public, and nonprofit ownership, funding, staff, and service and area characteristics, 1990 rpt, 7888–81

Urban planning

see City and town planning

Urban renewal

Govt finances, by level of govt, State, and for large cities and counties, annual rpt series, 2466–2

see also Community Development Block Grants

see also Relocation

see also Urban Development Action Grants

Urban transportation

Budget of US, formula grant program obligations to State and local govts, by agency, program, and State, FY92, annual rpt, 104–30

Budget of US, obligations and authority by function, agency, and program, with summaries, analyses, and historical tables, FY92, annual rpt, 104–2

Business statistics, detailed data for major industries and economic indicators, *Survey of Current Business*, monthly rpt, 2702–1.11

Collective bargaining agreements expiring during year, and workers covered, by firm, union, industry group, and State, 1991, annual rpt, 6784–9

Condition, mgmt, R&D, and funding, for transportation and environmental public works, 1986-91, 26358–235

Construction industries census, 1987: establishments, employment, receipts, and expenditures, by SIC 4-digit industry and State, final industry rpt series, 2373–1

Consumer Expenditure Survey, household income by source, and itemized spending, by selected characteristics and region, 1988-89, annual rpt, 6764–5

Consumer Expenditure Survey, spending by category, and income, by selected household characteristics and location, 1990, annual press release, 6726–1.42

County Business Patterns, 1988: employment, establishments, and payroll, by SIC 2- to 4-digit industry and county, annual State rpt series, 2326–6

County Business Patterns, 1989: employment, establishments, and payroll, by SIC 2- to 4-digit industry and county, annual State rpt series, 2326–8

CPI by component for US city average, and by region, population size, and for 27 metro areas, monthly rpt, 6762–2

Crime victimization of women, by relation to offender, circumstances, and victim characteristics, for rape and other violent offenses, 1973-87, 6068–243

Crime victimization rates, by victim and offender characteristics, circumstances, and offense, 1988 survey, annual rpt, 6066–3.42

Crime victimization rates, by victim and offender characteristics, circumstances, and offense, 1989 survey, annual rpt, 6066–3.44

Employment, earnings, and hours, by SIC 1- to 4-digit industry, monthly and annual averages, selected years 1909-90, annual rpt, 6744–4

Energy use by mode of transport, fuel supply, and demographic and economic factors of vehicle use, 1970s-89, annual rpt, 3304–5

Fed Govt and State surface transportation funding and regulation, FY91 with projections to FY96, 26358–242

Fed Govt financial and nonfinancial domestic aid, 1991 base edition with supplements, annual listing, 104–5

Fed Govt spending in States, by type, program, agency, and State, FY90, annual rpt, 2464–2

Finances and operations of interstate carriers, 1989, annual rpt, 9486–6.3

Finances and operations of transit systems, by mode of transport, size of fleet, and for 468 systems, 1989, annual rpt, 7884–4

Finances, costs, and needs of transit systems, by selected system, 1987-89, biennial rpt, 7884–8

Govt census, 1987: employment, payroll, and average earnings, by function, level of govt, State, county, and population size, 2455–2

Govt census, 1987: local govt employment by function, payroll, and average earnings, for individual counties, cities, and school and special districts, 2455–1

Govt employment and payroll, by function, level of govt, and jurisdiction, 1990, annual rpt series, 2466–1

Housing and households characteristics, unit and neighborhood quality, and journey to work by MSA location, for 11 MSAs, 1984 survey, supplement, 2485–8

Housing and households detailed characteristics, and unit and neighborhood quality, by location, 1987, biennial rpt supplement, 2485–13

Hwy Trust Fund revenues, tax rates, and spending, FY87-91 with projections to FY95, GAO rpt, 26113–544

Natl transportation system planning, use, condition, accidents, and needs, by mode of transport, 1940s-90 and projected to 2020, 7308–202

Occupational injury and illness rates, by SIC 2- to 4-digit industry, 1988-89, annual rpt, 6844–7

Occupational injury and illness rates, by SIC 2- to 4-digit industry, 1989, annual rpt, 6844–1

R&D projects and funding of Urban Mass Transportation Admin, FY90, annual listing, 7884–1

Research and training grants of UMTA to higher education instns, by project, FY90, annual listing, 7884–7

Smoking bans in public places, local ordinances provisions, as of 1989, 4478–196

Tax (income) returns of corporations, income and tax items by asset size and detailed industry, 1987, annual rpt, 8304–4

Tax (income) returns of corporations, income and tax items by asset size and detailed industry, 1988, annual rpt, 8304–21

Tax (income) returns of sole proprietorships, income statement items, by industry group, 1989, annual article, 8302–2.214

Traffic volume on rural roads and city streets, monthly rpt, 7552–8

Travel patterns, personal and household characteristics, and auto and public transport use, 1990 survey, series, 7556–6

Urban Mass Transportation Admin grants for transit systems, by city and State, FY90, annual rpt, 7884–10

see also Buses

see also Commuting

see also Subways

see also Taxicabs

see also Traffic engineering

see also under By Industry in the "Index by Categories"

Urbana, Ill.

see also under By SMSA or MSA in the "Index by Categories"

Urogenital diseases

Cancer (bladder) cases and risk among chemical plant workers, 1973-88, local area study, article, 4472–1.209

Cancer (bladder) cases reported as invasive and noninvasive, accuracy, and 1- to 5-year survival rates, local area study, 1979-87, article, 4472–1.208

Cancer (breast) rates attributable to increased detection through mammography use, by age, 1980-88 study, article, 4472–1.229

Cancer (breast) risk for men relation to incidence among relatives, 1983-86, article, 4472–1.213

Cancer (breast) risk relation to breast self-examination practice and other risk factors, 1982-88 local area study, article, 4472–1.202

Cancer (breast) risk relation to dietary fat and nutrient intake, for Canada, 1982-87, article, 4472–1.204

Cancer (cervical) risk relation to blood selenium levels, local area study, 1991 article, 4472–1.203

Cancer (prostate) prevalence, latent tissue presence at autopsy by race and age, 1973-77, article, 4472–1.221

Cancer (renal) risk relation to obesity, by age and sex, for Denmark, 1977-87, article, 4472–1.230

Cancer (testicular) contralateral tumor risk for men with prior cancer history, 1960-84 study, article, 4472–1.225

Cancer (testicular) risk among Vietnam veterans, by service branch, 1976-81 local area study, article, 4472–1.228

Cancer cases, deaths, and survival rates, by sex, race, age, and body site, 1973-88, annual rpt, 4474–35

Urogenital diseases

Cancer death rates of minorities, by body site, age, sex, and substate area, 1950s-80, atlas, 4478–78

Cancer death risk relation to smoking by body site, and compared to other smoking-related diseases, by sex, 1960s-91, article, 4472–1.219

Cancer death, survival, and incidence rates, by type and body site, 1974 and 1986, article, 4472–1.232

Cancer deaths and rates, by body site, provisional data, monthly rpt, 4142–1.2

Cases of acute and chronic conditions, disability, absenteeism, and health services use, by selected characteristics, 1987, CD-ROM, 4147–10.177

Deaths and rates, by cause and age, preliminary 1989-90, US Vital Statistics annual rpt, 4144–7

Deaths and rates, by cause, provisional data, monthly rpt, 4142–1.2

Deaths and rates, by detailed cause and demographic characteristics, 1988 and trends from 1900, US Vital Statistics annual rpt, 4144–2

Enuresis (chronic) among children, relation to family structure, by selected characteristics, 1988, 4147–10.178

Genital human papillomavirus risk relation to presence of other cervical cancer risk factors, local area study, 1991 article, 4472–1.215

Health condition and health care resources, use, and spending, 1950s-89, annual data compilation, 4144–11

HHS financial aid, by program, recipient, State, and city, FY90, annual regional listings, 4004–3

Hospital deaths of Medicare patients, actual and expected rates by diagnosis, with hospital characteristics, by instn, FY87-89, annual regional rpt series, 4654–14

Hospital discharges and length of stay, by diagnosis, patient and instn characteristics, procedure performed, and payment source, 1988, annual rpt, 4147–13.107

Hospital discharges and length of stay by region and diagnosis, and procedures performed, by age and sex, 1989, annual rpt, 4146–8.198

Hospital discharges by detailed diagnostic and procedure category, primary diagnosis, and length of stay, by age, sex, and region, 1988, annual rpt, 4147–13.105; 4147–13.108

Incontinence among nursing home residents, by age and sex, 1987, 4186–8.11

Incontinence among nursing home residents with mental disorders, by resident and instn characteristics, 1985, 4147–13.106

Indian and Alaska Native disease and disorder cases, deaths, and health services use, by tribe, reservation, and Indian Health Service area, late 1950s-86, 4088–2

Indian Health Service, tribal, and contract facilities hospitalization, by diagnosis, age, sex, and service area, FY89, annual rpt, 4084–5

Infertility prevalence among women, by age and parity, with infertility services use, selected years 1965-88, 4146–8.194

Kidney dialysis facilities, receipts by source, payroll, and employment, by State and MSA, 1987 Census of Service Industries, 2393–4

Kidney dialysis patients anemia treatment with Epoetin alfa, dosages, costs, Medicare reimbursement, and facility income effects, 1989, 4008–113

Kidney end-stage disease cases among diabetics, deaths, and hospitalization, by age, sex, race, State, and region, 1980-86, annual rpt, 4205–41

Kidney end-stage disease cases, treatment, outcomes, and characteristics of patients, organ donors, and facilities, late 1970s-88, annual rpt, 4474–37

Kidney end-stage disease patients and Medicare reimbursements, 1974-86, biennial rpt, 4654–1

Kidney end-stage disease program of Medicare, enrollees hospitalization, days of care, and length of stay, 1981-87, annual rpt, 4654–13

Kidney end-stage disease program of Medicare, enrollment and program operations, 1991, annual fact book, 4654–18

Kidney end-stage disease program of Medicare, enrollment by age, sex, race, and region, and facilities, 1975-89, annual rpt, 4744–3.5

Kidney end-stage disease program of Medicare, outlays, and enrollment by age and treatment type, 1982-87, article, 4652–1.208

Kidney end-stage disease treatment access and quality of care indicators, impacts of Medicare payment reductions, 1980s, 4658–44

Kidney end-stage disease treatment facilities, Medicare enrollment and reimbursement, survival, and patient characteristics, 1983-89, annual rpt, 4654–16

Kidney transplants, needs, costs, payment sources, and impact of immunosuppressive drugs on outcome, 1950s-87 and projected to 1995, 4658–59

Minority group health condition, services use, costs, and indicators of services need, 1950s-88, 4118–55

Pelvic inflammatory disease prevention, diagnosis, treatment, and surveillance, CDC guidelines, 1991 rpt, 4206–2.41

Pollutants reproductive health and fetal dev effects, with production, trade, and Federal regulatory activities by selected substance, 1980s-90, GAO rpt, 26131–90

Research on population and reproduction, Federal funding by project, FY89, annual listing, 4474–9

Transplant patients immunosuppressive drug coverage under Medicare and other insurance sources, costs, and procedures, 1991 rpt, 26358–246

see also Sexually transmitted diseases

see also under By Disease in the "Index by Categories"

Uruguay

Agricultural exports of high-value commodities, indexes and sales by commodity, world area, and country, 1960s-86, 1528–323

Agricultural trade of US, by detailed commodity and country, 1989, annual rpt, 1524–8

Agricultural trade of US, by detailed commodity and country, 1990, semiannual rpt, 1522–4

Index by Subjects and Names

AID economic aid to developing countries, obligations and disbursements by country, quarterly rpt, 9912–4

AID loans repayment status and terms by program and country, and status of predecessor agency loans, quarterly rpt, 9912–3

Background Notes, summary social, political, and economic data, 1990 rpt, 7006–2.10

Economic and military aid and loans from US and intl agencies, by program and country, FY46-90, annual rpt, 9914–5

Economic and social conditions of developing countries from 1960s, and Intl Dev Cooperation Agency and AID activities and funding, FY90-92, annual rpt, 9904–4

Economic conditions, policy, and trade practices, by country, 1988-90, annual rpt, 21384–5

Economic, social, political, and geographic summary data, by country, 1991, annual factbook, 9114–2

Exports and imports of US, by commodity and country, 1970-89, world area rpt, 9116–1.4

Exports and imports of US, by selected country, country group, and commodity group, 1990, annual rpt, 2044–37

Exports and imports of US, by transport mode, country, and SITC 1- to 3-digit commodity, 1990, annual rpt, 2424–12

Exports of US, detailed Schedule B commodities with countries of destination, 1990, annual rpt, 2424–10

Human rights conditions in 170 countries, and US economic and military aid, 1990, annual rpt, 21384–3

Labor conditions, union coverage, and work accidents, 1991 annual country rpt, 6366–4.22

Military aid of US, arms sales, and training programs costs and budget requests, by program, world region, and country, FY90-92, annual rpt, 7144–13

Multinatl US firms foreign affiliates, income statement items by country and world area, 1986, biennial article, 8302–2.212

UN voting record and share of votes in agreement with US, by issue, country, and world area, 1990, annual rpt, 7004–18

see also under By Foreign Country in the "Index by Categories"

U.S. Advisory Commission on Public Diplomacy

USIA activities, finances, and info services, FY91, annual rpt, 17594–1

U.S. Architectural and Transportation Barriers Compliance Board

Budget of US, authoritative financial statements with appropriations, outlays, and receipts, by category and agency, FY90, annual rpt, 8104–2.1

Budget of US, obligations and authority by function, agency, and program, with summaries, analyses, and historical tables, FY92, annual rpt, 104–2

Building access for disabled to Federal and federally funded facilities, complaints by disposition, FY90, annual rpt, 17614–1

U.S. Arms Control and Disarmament Agency

Budget of US, authoritative financial statements with appropriations, outlays, and receipts, by category and agency, FY90, annual rpt, 8104–2.1

Index by Subjects and Names

Budget of US, obligations and authority by function, agency, and program, with summaries, analyses, and historical tables, FY92, annual rpt, 104–2

Education funding by Federal agency, program, and recipient type, and instn spending, FY80-90, annual rpt, 4824–8

R&D funding by Fed Govt, by field, performer type, agency, and State, FY89-91, annual rpt, 9627–20

U.S. Army Corps of Engineers see Army Corps of Engineers

U.S. attorneys

Banks and thrifts fraud and abuse, Federal agencies enforcement activities and staff, with data by instn and location, 1988-90, hearing, 21408–119

Case processing and collections of US attorneys, by case type and Federal district, FY90, annual rpt, 6004–2

Court criminal case processing in Federal district courts, and dispositions, by offense, district, and offender characteristics, 1986, annual rpt, 6064–29

Court criminal case processing in Federal district courts, and dispositions, by offense, 1980-89, annual rpt, 6064–31

Criminal case processing in Federal courts, by offense, disposition, and jurisdiction, data compilation, 1991 annual rpt, 6064–6.5

Debt delinquent on Federal accounts, cases and collections of Justice Dept and private law firms, pilot project results, FY90, annual rpt, 6004–20

Federal district court personnel, by court, 1990, annual report, 17664–1

Staffing disparities among US attorneys district offices, and caseload by litigation type, FY87-90, GAO rpt, 26119–323

U.S. Bipartisan Commission on Comprehensive Health Care

Costs of long-term health care for aged, under alternative private insurance policy types, 1989 hearing, 23898–8

Insurance (health) provided by employers, small business and restaurant owners views, 1989 hearings, 23898–7

Montana health care access indicators, 1989 hearing, 23898–6

Universal coverage for health care and long term care financing, background data, 1990 rpt, 23898–5

U.S. Border Patrol

Aliens (illegal) apprehensions and officer hours, for Border Patrol by location, 1980s, fact sheet, 6266–2.2

U.S. Budget see Budget of the U.S.

U.S. Claims Court

Cases, judgments, and appeals, 1990, annual rpt, 18204–8.23

Tax litigation, prosecutions, and interpretive law decisions, FY90, annual rpt, 8304–3.3

U.S. Coast Guard see Coast Guard

U.S. Commission on Civil Rights see Commission on Civil Rights

U.S. Court of Appeals for the Federal Circuit

Budget of US, obligations and authority by function, agency, and program, with summaries, analyses, and historical tables, FY92, annual rpt, 104–2

Cases filed and terminated, by source of appeal, 1990, annual rpt, 18204–8.22

Cases filed and terminated, by source of appeal, 1991, annual rpt, 18204–2.1

Intl Trade Court decisions appealed to Appeals Court, and dispositions, FY90-91, annual rpt, 18224–2

U.S. Court of International Trade see Court of International Trade

U.S. Customs Service

Activities, collections, entries processed by mode of transport, and seizures, FY86-90, annual rpt, 8144–1

Activities of Customs Service, and collections total and for selected ports, bimonthly journal, 8142–2

Asset forfeiture programs of Justice Dept and Customs Service, finances, and disbursements by State and judicial district, FY85-90, hearing, 25408–112

Budget of US, obligations and authority by function, agency, and program, with summaries, analyses, and historical tables, FY92, annual rpt, 104–2

Customs collections, for top 15 ports, quarterly rpt, discontinued, 8142–1

Drug enforcement training of US for foreign govts, enrollment in US and host countries by program, 1989-90, annual rpt, 7004–17

U.S. Employment Service see Employment and Training Administration

U.S. Fish and Wildlife Service see Fish and Wildlife Service

U.S. Geological Survey see Geological Survey

U.S. Holocaust Memorial Council

Budget of US, authoritative financial statements with appropriations, outlays, and receipts, by category and agency, FY90, annual rpt, 8104–2.1

Budget of US, obligations and authority by function, agency, and program, with summaries, analyses, and historical tables, FY92, annual rpt, 104–2

U.S. Information Agency

Activities, finances, and info services of USIA, FY91, annual rpt, 17594–1

Budget of US, authoritative financial statements with appropriations, outlays, and receipts, by category and agency, FY90, annual rpt, 8104–2.1

Budget of US, obligations and authority by function, agency, and program, with summaries, analyses, and historical tables, FY92, annual rpt, 104–2

Education funding by Federal agency, program, and recipient type, and instn spending, FY80-90, annual rpt, 4824–8

English language program of USIA, enrollment and staff, by country and world region, FY90, annual rpt, 9854–2

Exchange and training programs of Federal agencies, participants by world area, and funding, by program, FY89, annual rpt, 9854–8

Fulbright-Hays academic exchanges, grants by purpose, and foreign govt share of costs, by country, FY90, annual rpt, 10324–1

Libraries of USIA, holdings, use, and staff by country and city, FY90, annual rpt, 9854–4

U.S. International Trade Commission

R&D funding by Fed Govt, by field, performer type, agency, and State, FY89-91, annual rpt, 9627–20

see also Voice of America

U.S. Institute of Peace

Education funding by Federal agency, program, and recipient type, and instn spending, FY80-90, annual rpt, 4824–8

U.S. International Development Cooperation Agency

Activities and funding of IDCA and AID, FY90-92, and developing countries economic and social conditions from 1960s, annual rpt, 9904–4

Developing countries economic aid from US, bilateral and through intl dev banks, by program and world region, 1991 annual rpt, 9904–1

see also Agency for International Development

see also Overseas Private Investment Corp.

U.S. International Trade Commission

Activities, investigations, and rpts of USITC, FY90, annual rpt, 9884–1

Auto industry finances and operations, trade by country, and prices of selected US and foreign models, monthly rpt, 9882–8

Budget of US, authoritative financial statements with appropriations, outlays, and receipts, by category and agency, FY90, annual rpt, 8104–2.1

Budget of US, obligations and authority by function, agency, and program, with summaries, analyses, and historical tables, FY92, annual rpt, 104–2

Caribbean area duty-free exports to US, by commodity and country, with consumer and industry impacts, 1984-90, annual rpt, 9884–20

Chemicals (synthetic organic) production, by detailed product, quarterly rpt, 9882–1

Communist countries trade with US, by detailed commodity and country, quarterly rpt with articles, 9882–2

Exports and imports of US by country, and trade shifts by commodity, 1990, semiannual rpt, 9882–9

Exports and imports, trade agreements and relations, and USITC investigations, 1990, annual rpt, 9884–5

Exports, imports, and balances of US with major trading partners, by product category, 1986-90, annual chartbook, 9884–21

Footwear production, employment, use, prices, and US trade by country, quarterly rpt, 9882–6

Foreign and US economic conditions, and trade devs and balances, with data by selected country and country group, monthly rpt, 9882–14

Generalized System of Preferences status, and US tariffs, with trade by country and US economic impacts, for selected commodities, 1985-89, annual rpt, 9884–23

Imports and tariff provisions effect on US industries and products, investigations with background financial and operating data, series, 9886–4

Imports injury to price-supported US agricultural industry, investigations with background financial and operating data, series, 9886–10

U.S. International Trade Commission

Imports injury to US industries from foreign subsidized products and sales at less than fair value, investigations with background financial and operating data, series, 9886–19

Imports injury to US industries from foreign subsidized products, investigations with background financial and operating data, series, 9886–15

Imports injury to US industries from sales at less than fair value, investigations with background financial and operating data, series, 9886–14

Imports of US given duty-free treatment for value of US material sent abroad, by commodity and country, 1989, annual rpt, 9884–14

Publications of USITC, 1983-90, annual listing, 9884–12

R&D funding by Fed Govt, by field, performer type, agency, and State, FY89-91, annual rpt, 9627–20

Rum production, trade by country, and use, 1989-90, annual rpt, 9884–15

Steel imports of US under voluntary restraint agreement, by product, customs district, and country, with US industry operating data, quarterly rpt, 9882–13

Steel industry finances, operations, and modernization efforts, with data on major companies and foreign industry, 1968-91, last issue of annual rpt, 9884–24

Tariff Schedule of US, classifications and rates of duty by detailed imported commodity, 1992 base edition, 9886–13

Textile imports under Multifiber Arrangement by product and country, and status of bilateral agreements, 1987-90, annual rpt, 9884–18

U.S.-Liberia Radio Corp.

Finances and operations, detail for telegraph firms, 1989, annual rpt, 9284–6.3

Finances, rates, and traffic for US telecommunications carriers intl operations, by service type, firm, and country, 1975-89, annual rpt, 9284–17

U.S. Marshals Service

Activities of USMS, FY89, annual rpt, 6294–1

Jail inmates held for Federal authorities, by county and State, 1988, regional rpt series, 6068–144

U.S. Mint

Activities, finances, coin and medals production and holdings, and gold and silver transactions, by facility, FY90, annual rpt, 8204–1

Budget of US, obligations and authority by function, agency, and program, with summaries, analyses, and historical tables, FY92, annual rpt, 104–2

Coin production of US Mint, for US by denomination and mint, and for foreign countries, monthly table, 8202–1

U.S. Naval Observatory

Star position tables, planet coordinates, time conversion factors, and listing of observatories worldwide, 1992, annual rpt, 3804–7

U.S. Nuclear Regulatory Commission *see* Nuclear Regulatory Commission

U.S. Parole Commission

Activities of Commission, and parole decisions and caseloads, FY87-90, annual rpt, 6004–3

Budget of US, obligations and authority by function, agency, and program, with summaries, analyses, and historical tables, FY92, annual rpt, 104–2

Parole granted, and hearing examiner caseload by disposition, by region, data compilation, 1991 annual rpt, 6064–6.1; 6064–6.6

U.S. Postal Rate Commission *see* Postal Rate Commission

U.S. Postal Service

Activities of USPS, finances, and employment, FY86-90, annual rpt, 9864–1

Activities of USPS, finances, and mail volume and subsidies, FY90, annual rpt, 9864–5

Asset Forfeiture Program of Justice Dept, seizures, finances, and disbursements, FY86-90, annual rpt, 6004–21

Budget of US, authoritative financial statements with appropriations, outlays, and receipts, by category and agency, FY90, annual rpt, 8104–2.1

Budget of US, CBO analysis of revenue and spending alternatives and projections of economic indicators, FY92-96, annual rpt, 26304–3

Budget of US, obligations and authority by function, agency, and program, with summaries, analyses, and historical tables, FY92, annual rpt, 104–2

Budget of US, Senate concurrent resolution, with spending and revenue targets, FY92, annual rpt, 25254–1

Costs of operations itemized by class of mail, FY90, annual rpt, 9864–4

Customer satisfaction with USPS, and on-time 1st class mail delivery, by region and city, 1991 survey, press release, 9868–1

Expenditures of Fed Govt in States, by type, program, agency, and State, FY90, annual rpt, 2464–2

Households incoming and outgoing mail volume, use, and views, by class, source, content, and household characteristics, 1987-88, annual rpt, 9864–10

Inspection activities of USPS, FY90, annual rpt, 9864–9

Inspection activities of USPS, 2nd half FY91, semiannual rpt, 9862–2

Mail postage rates of USPS since 1775, and city and rural delivery routes, FY89, annual rpt, special supplement, 9864–6

Marketing and Customer Service Group of USPS, expenses by type, FY87-90, GAO rpt, 26119–338

Productivity of USPS, indexes of output and labor, capital, and other inputs, alternative model descriptions and results, 1960s-89, 9688–6

Property (real) of Fed Govt, leased inventory and rental costs, worldwide summary by location and agency, 1989, annual rpt, 9454–10

Revenue and volume by class of mail, and special service transactions, quarterly rpt, 9862–1

Revenue, costs, and volume, by class of mail, FY90, annual rpt, 9864–2

Statistical Abstract of US, 1991 annual data compilation, 2324–1.18

see also Postal employees

Index by Subjects and Names

see also Postal service

U.S. savings bonds

Assets and debts of private sector, balance sheets by segment, 1945-90, semiannual rpt, 9365–4.1

Farm income, expenses, receipts by commodity, assets, liabilities, and ratios, 1990 and trends from 1945, annual rpt, 1544–16

Farm sector balance sheet, and marketing receipts by detailed commodity, by State, 1985-89, annual rpt, 1544–18

Households and personal purchases and holdings of govt securities, terms, and purchase methods, 1980s-90, 8008–148

Households assets, by type of holding and selected characteristics, 1988, Current Population Rpt, 2546–20.16

Issues, redemptions, and bonds outstanding, by series, monthly table, 8242–1

Issues, redemptions, and bonds outstanding, monthly rpt, 8242–2

Sales and redemptions, *Treasury Bulletin,* quarterly rpt, 8002–4.6

Sales, redemptions, exchanges, and bonds outstanding, for series EE and HH, monthly rpt, 8442–1

Statistical Abstract of US, 1991 annual data compilation, 2324–1.10

U.S. Savings Bonds Division

Savings bonds sold, redeemed, exchanged, and outstanding, for series EE and HH, monthly rpt, 8442–1

U.S. Secret Service

Budget of US, obligations and authority by function, agency, and program, with summaries, analyses, and historical tables, FY92, annual rpt, 104–2

Counterfeiting and other Secret Service investigations and arrests by type, and dispositions, FY90 and trends from FY81, annual rpt, 8464–1

U.S. Sentencing Commission

Activities of USSC, and sentencing guidelines use and results for Federal offenses by offense type and district, 1990, annual rpt, 17664–1

Budget of US, obligations and authority by function, agency, and program, with summaries, analyses, and historical tables, FY92, annual rpt, 104–2

Guidelines for sentencing, by Federal offense and circumstances, series, 17668–1

U.S. Soldiers Home *see* Soldier's and Airmen's Home

US Sprint

Fiber optics and copper wire mileage and access lines, and fiber systems investment, by telecommunications firm, 1985-90, annual rpt, 9284–18

Finances and operations of local and long distance firms, subscribership, and charges, late 1970s-91, semiannual rpt, 9282–7

Intl telecommunications operations of US carriers, finances, rates, and traffic by service type, firm, and country, 1975-89, annual rpt, 9284–17

U.S. statutes

Assistance (financial and nonfinancial) of Fed Govt, authorizing legislation, 1991 base edition with supplements, annual listing, 104–5

Index by Subjects and Names

User fees

Budget of US, debt subject to statutory limits, and legislative history, FY40-90 and projected to FY96, annual rpt, 104–2.9

Budget of US, debt subject to statutory limits, daily tables, 8102–4

Budget of US, statutory debt limit and debt subject to limit, monthly rpt, 8242–2

Census Bur data collection and publication operations, US Code Title 13 text, 1991 rpt, 21628–94

Court civil and criminal caseloads for Federal district, appeals, and bankruptcy courts, by type of suit and offense, circuit, and district, 1990, annual rpt, 18204–11

Court civil and criminal caseloads for Federal district, appeals, and special courts, 1990, annual rpt, 18204–8

Court civil and criminal caseloads for Federal district courts, 1991, annual rpt, 18204–2.1

Court criminal cases in Federal district courts, by offense, disposition, and district, 1980-90, last issue of annual rpt, 18204–1

Criminal case processing in Federal courts, by offense, disposition, and jurisdiction, data compilation, 1991 annual rpt, 6064–6.5

Fed Govt civilian pay legislation, 1945-90, annual rpt, 9844–6.7

Foreign govt claims of US natls, by claim type and country, 1990, annual rpt, 6004–16

Imports injury to US industries, USITC activities, investigations, and rpts, FY90, annual rpt, 9884–1

Medicaid eligibility expansion provisions, adoption by States, and impacts on service use and costs, 1984-89, GAO rpt, 26121–429

Oil spill from tanker Exxon Valdez, impacts on marine mammals, and resulting legislation, 1990 annual rpt, 14734–1

Public lands minerals resources and availability, State rpt series, 5606–7

Sentences for Federal offenses, guidelines by offense and circumstances, series, 17668–1

Tariff Schedule of US, classifications and rates of duty by detailed imported commodity, 1992 base edition, 9886–13

U.S. Tax Court

see Tax Court of the U.S.

U.S. territories

see American Samoa

see Guam

see Puerto Rico

see Territories of the U.S.

see U.S. Virgin Islands

see under By Outlying Area in the "Index by Categories"

U.S. Travel and Tourism Administration

Air travel from US, characteristics of visit and traveler, and world area of destination, 1990 in-flight survey, annual rpt, 2904–14

Air travel to and from US on US and foreign flag carriers, by world area, 1990, annual rpt, 2904–13

Budget of US, obligations and authority by function, agency, and program, with summaries, analyses, and historical tables, FY92, annual rpt, 104–2

Foreign travel to and from US, by world area, forecast 1991-92, annual rpt, 2904–9

Foreign travel to US, by characteristics of visit and traveler, country, port city, and State of destination, monthly rpt, 2902–1

Foreign travel to US, by characteristics of visit and traveler, world area of origin, and US destination, 1990 survey, annual rpt, 2904–12

Market dev for foreign travel to US, trade shows and other promotional activities, with magazine ad costs and circulation, for selected countries, 1991-92, annual rpt, 2904–11

Market research data available from US Travel and Tourism Admin, 1991, annual rpt, 2904–15

U.S. Travel Service

see U.S. Travel and Tourism Administration

U.S. Virgin Islands

Banks (insured commercial and savings) deposits by instn, State, MSA, and county, as of June 1990, annual regional rpt, 9295–3.1

Census of Population and Housing, 1990: Virgin Islands population and housing characteristics, press release, 2328–81

Census of Population, 1990: Virgin Islands population by location, press release, 2328–77

Economic, social, political, and geographic summary data, by country, 1991, annual factbook, 9114–2

Exports and imports between US and outlying areas, by detailed commodity and mode of transport, 1990, annual rpt, 2424–11

Fed Govt spending in States and local areas, by type, State, county, and city, FY90, annual rpt, 2464–3

Fed Govt spending in States, by type, program, agency, and State, FY90, annual rpt, 2464–2

HHS financial aid, by program, recipient, State, and city, FY90, annual regional listing, 4004–3.2

Hospital deaths of Medicare patients, actual and expected rates by diagnosis, and hospital characteristics, by instn, FY87-89, annual regional rpt, 4654–14.2

Hurricane Hugo relief funding and response by FEMA, 1989-90, GAO rpt, 26113–511

Hurricane Hugo storm characteristics, and Natl Weather Service forecast accuracy, 1989, 2186–6.1

Marriages, divorces, and rates, by characteristics of spouses and county, 1987 and trends from 1940, US Vital Statistics annual rpt, 4144–4.3

Minerals Yearbook, 1989, Vol 2: State reviews of production, sales, and firms, by commodity, and business activity, annual rpt, 5604–34

Multinatl US firms foreign affiliates, income statement items by country and world area, 1986, biennial article, 8302–2.212

Oil exports to US by OPEC and non-OPEC countries, monthly rpt, 3162–24.3

Physicians, by specialty, age, sex, and location of training and practice, 1989, State rpt, 4116–6.54

Population and housing census, 1990: population and housing characteristics, households, and land area, by county, subdiv, and place, State rpt, 2551–1.55

Rum production, trade by country, and use, 1989-90, annual rpt, 9884–15

Statistical Abstract of US, 1991 annual data compilation, 2324–1.30

Wages by occupation, for office and plant workers, 1990 survey, periodic labor market rpt, 6785–3.2

Water resources dev projects of Army Corps of Engineers, characteristics, and costs, 1950s-89, biennial State rpt, 3756–1.52

Water supply and quality in streams and lakes, and groundwater levels in wells, by drainage basin, 1990, annual State rpt, 5666–10.48

see also Charlotte Amalie, V.I.

see also Christiansted, V.I.

see also Frederiksted, V.I.

see also under By Outlying Area in the "Index by Categories"

USDA

see Department of Agriculture

User fees

Budget of US, authoritative financial statements with appropriations, outlays, and receipts, by category and agency, FY90, annual rpt, 8104–2.1

Budget of US, CBO analysis of savings and revenues under alternative spending cuts and tax changes, projected FY92-97, 26306–3.118

Budget of US, House Budget Committee analysis of Bush Admin proposals and economic assumptions, FY92, 21268–42

Budget of US, House concurrent resolution, with spending and revenue targets, FY92 and projected to FY96, annual rpt, 21264–2

Budget of US, object class analysis of obligations, by agency, FY92, annual rpt, 104–9

Budget of US, obligations and authority by function, agency, and program, with summaries, analyses, and historical tables, FY92, annual rpt, 104–2

Copyrights Register activities, registrations by material type, and fees, FY90 and trends from 1790, annual rpt, 26404–2

Customs Service activities, collections, entries processed by mode of transport, and seizures, FY86-90, annual rpt, 8144–1

Environmental protection programs costs to govts and households, by program type and city size, 1960s-88 and projected to 2000, 9188–114

Fed Govt trust fund receipts, by source and fund, Budget of US, FY92, annual rpt, 104–9

Fed Reserve System, Board of Governors, and district banks financial statements, performance, and fiscal services, 1990-91, annual rpt, 9364–10

Forest Service acreage, staff, finances, and mgmt activities in Pacific Northwest, with data by forest, 1970s-89, annual rpt, 1204–37

Forest Service activities and finances, by region and State, FY90, annual rpt, 1204–1.1

Forests (natl) revenue, by source, forest, and State, FY90, annual rpt, 1204–34

Govt finances, by level of govt, State, and for large cities and counties, annual rpt series, 2466–2

User fees

Govt finances, tax systems and revenue, and fiscal structure, by level of govt and State, 1991 with historical trends, annual rpt, 10044–1

Grain inspected for domestic use and export, foreign buyers complaints, and handling facilities explosions, FY90, annual rpt, 1294–1

HHS Freedom of Info Act requests, disposition, costs, and fees, 1990, annual rpt, 4004–21

Hwy Trust Fund revenues, tax rates, and spending, FY87-91 with projections to FY95, GAO rpt, 26113–544

Land Mgmt Bur activities and finances, and public land acreage and use, annual State rpt series, 5724–11

Lands (public) acreage, grants, use, revenues, and allocations, by State, FY90, annual rpt, 5724–1.2; 5724–1.3

Minority Business Dev Centers mgmt and financial aid, and characteristics of businesses, by region and State, FY90, annual rpt, 2104–6

Nuclear Waste Fund finances, and DOE Civilian Radioactive Waste Mgmt Office activities, quarterly GAO rpt, 26102–4

Nuclear Waste Fund finances, and DOE Civilian Radioactive Waste Mgmt Office R&D costs, FY88-89, annual rpt, 3364–1

Nuclear Waste Fund finances, and DOE Civilian Radioactive Waste Mgmt Program costs, quarterly rpt, 3362–1

Patent and Trademark Office fee income, by source, FY87-90, annual rpt, 2244–1.1

Patent and Trademark Office patent application, issuance, and protection fees and revenues under alternative fee schedules, FY92-93, GAO rpt, 26113–543

Postal Service activities, finances, and mail volume and subsidies, FY90, annual rpt, 9864–5.3

Public lands concession operations, receipts, and fees, by Federal agency and for top 100 firms, 1989, GAO rpt, 26113–531

Public works condition, mgmt, R&D, and funding, for transportation and environmental projects, 1986-91, 26358–235

Recreation (outdoor) coastal facilities of Fed Govt and States, visitor and site characteristics, 1987-90 survey, regional rpt series, 2176–9

Recreation (outdoor) facilities of Fed Govt, fees and visits by managing agency, FY88-90, annual rpt, 5544–14

Transit systems finances and operations, by mode of transport, size of fleet, and for 468 systems, 1989, annual rpt, 7884–4

Transportation natl system planning, use, condition, accidents, and needs, by mode of transport, 1940s-90 and projected to 2020, 7308–202

Western US State and local govt revenues and tax capacity, by source and State, 1988, article, 9381–1.204

see also Royalties

see also Tolls

USIA

see U.S. Information Agency

USMC

see Marine Corps

USSR

see Soviet Union

Utah

Banks (insured commercial and savings) deposits by instn, State, MSA, and county, as of June 1990, annual regional rpt, 9295–3.6

Coal production and mines by county, prices, productivity, miners, and reserves, by mining method and State, 1989-90, annual rpt, 3164–25

County Business Patterns, 1989: employment, establishments, and payroll, by SIC 2- to 4-digit industry and county, annual State rpt, 2326–8.46

DOD prime contract awards, by contractor, service branch, State, and city, FY90, annual rpt, 3544–22

Fed Govt spending in States and local areas, by type, State, county, and city, FY90, annual rpt, 2464–3

Fed Govt spending in States, by type, program, agency, and State, FY90, annual rpt, 2464–2

Gemstone production in selected States, Mineral Industry Surveys, 1988-90, advance annual rpt, 5614–5.10

Health maintenance organizations and other prepaid managed care plans Medicaid enrollment and use, for 20 States, 1985-89, chartbook, 4108–29

HHS financial aid, by program, recipient, State, and city, FY90, annual regional listing, 4004–3.8

Hospital deaths of Medicare patients, actual and expected rates by diagnosis, and hospital characteristics, by instn, FY87-89, annual regional rpt, 4654–14.8

Income (personal) per capita and by source, and earnings by industry div, by State, MSA, and county, 1984-89, annual regional rpt, 2704–2.5

Jail adult and juvenile population, employment, spending, instn conditions, and inmate programs, by county and facility, 1988, regional rpt series, 6068–144.5

Land Mgmt Bur activities and finances, and public land acreage and use, FY90, annual State rpt, 5724–11.3

Marriages, divorces, and rates, by characteristics of spouses, State, and county, 1987 and trends from 1920, US Vital Statistics annual rpt, 4144–4

Mineral industries census, 1987: finances and operations, by SIC 2- to 4-digit industry, State, and county, census div rpt, 2515–1.8

Mineral Industry Surveys, State reviews of production, 1990, preliminary annual rpt, 5614–6

Minerals Yearbook, 1989, Vol 2: State review of production and sales by commodity, and business activity, annual rpt, 5604–16.46

Minerals Yearbook, 1989, Vol 2: State reviews of production, sales, and firms, by commodity, and business activity, annual rpt, 5604–34

Nursing home reimbursement by Medicaid, States payment ratesetting methods, analysis for 7 States, 1980s, article, 4652–1.255

Physicians, by specialty, age, sex, and location of training and practice, 1989, State rpt, 4116–6.46

Index by Subjects and Names

Population and housing census, 1990: population and housing characteristics, households, and land area, by county, subdiv, and place, State rpt, 2551–1.46

Population and housing census, 1990: voting age and total population by race, and housing units, by block, redistricting counts required under PL 94-171, State CD-ROM release, 2551–6.7

Population and housing census, 1990: voting age and total population by race, and housing units, by county and city, redistricting counts required under PL 94-171, State summary rpt, 2551–5.45

Recreation (outdoor) facilities on public land, use, and Land Mgmt Bur mgmt activities, funding, and plans, 1990 State rpt, 5726–5.4

Statistical Abstract of US, 1991 annual data compilation, 2324–1

Supplemental Security Income payments and beneficiaries, by type of eligibility, State, and county, Dec 1989, annual rpt, 4744–27.8

Water quality, chemistry, hydrology, and other characteristics, 1989 local area study, 5666–27.17

Water resources data collection and analysis activities of USGS Water Resources Div District, with project descriptions, 1990 rpt, 5666–26.15

Water salinity control program for Colorado River, participation and payments, FY87-90, annual rpt, 1804–23

Water supply and quality in streams and lakes, and groundwater levels in wells, by drainage basin, 1990, annual State rpt, 5666–10.42

Water supply, and snow survey results, monthly State rpt, 1266–2.8

Water supply, and snow survey results, 1990, annual State rpt, 1264–14.2

see also Davis County, Utah

see also Ogden, Utah

see also Salt Lake City, Utah

see also Salt Lake County, Utah

see also under By State in the "Index by Categories"

Utica, N.Y.

see also under By SMSA or MSA in the "Index by Categories"

Utilities

see Public utilities

VA

see Department of Veterans Affairs

see Veterans Administration

Vacant and abandoned property

Airport abandonments, by State, 1989, annual rpt, 7504–1.3

Arson incidents by whether structure occupied, property value, and arrest rate, by property type, 1990, annual rpt, 6224–2.1

Atomic Energy Commission and Manhattan Project former research and storage sites and nearby areas, radioactive concentrations, test results series, 3006–9

Coal Surface Mining Reclamation and Enforcement Office activities and funding, by State and Indian tribe, FY90, annual rpt, 5644–1

Commercial buildings energy use, costs, and conservation, by building characteristics, survey rpt series, 3166–8

Index by Subjects and Names

Fed Govt-owned real property inventory and costs, worldwide summary by purpose, agency, and location, 1989, annual rpt, 9454–5

Neighborhood and housing quality, indicators and attitudes, by householder type and location, 1989, biennial rpt, 2485–12

Neighborhood and housing quality, indicators and attitudes, MSA surveys, series, 2485–6

Neighborhoods with abandoned and boarded up buildings, and other characteristics of housing inventory by status in 1973 amd 1983, survey, biennial rpt, 2485–14

Office buildings vacancy rates, by selected city, 1980-90, 21248–147

Uranium tailings at inactive mills, remedial action activities by site, and funding, FY90, annual rpt, 3354–9

see also Housing condition and occupancy

Vacations and holidays

Employee benefit plan coverage and provisions, by plan type, firm size, and industry sector, 1988, article, 6722–1.204

Employee benefit plan coverage and provisions in small businesses, by plan type and occupational group, 1990, biennial rpt, 6784–20

Employee benefit plan coverage, by benefit type and worker characteristics, late 1970s-80s, 15496–1.11

Employee leave for illness, disability, and dependent care, coverage, provisions, terminations, costs, and methods of covering for absent worker, by firm size, 1988 survey, 9768–21

Fed Govt civilian employees work-years by schedule, overtime, holidays, and personnel cost components, FY89-90, annual article, 9842–1.204

Fed Govt civilian employees work-years, pay rates, and benefits use and costs, by agency, FY89, annual rpt, 9844–31

Fed Govt shutdown over Columbus Day holiday, employees affected, costs, and savings, Oct 1990, GAO rpt, 26119–311

Food aid program for children during summer vacation, nonprofit sponsors compliance with USDA regulations, 1989-90, GAO rpt, 26113–541

Foreign countries economic, social, political, and geographic summary data, by country, 1991, annual factbook, 9114–2

Foreign countries holidays observed by businesses, by country, biweekly rpt, annual listing, 2042–24

Labor force not at work, unemployed, and working less than 35 hours, by reason, sex, race, region, and State, 1990, annual rpt, 6744–7.1; 6744–7.2

Labor hourly costs, by component, industry sector, worker class, and firm size, 1990, annual rpt, 6744–22

Mail volume to and from households, use, and views, by class, source, content, and household characteristics, 1987-88, annual rpt, 9864–10

Overseas Business Reports: economic conditions, investment and export opportunities, and trade practices, country market research rpt series, 2046–6

State and local govt employees benefit plan coverage, by benefit type, 1990, press release, 6726–1.41

Transit systems finances and operations, by mode of transport, size of fleet, and for 468 systems, 1989, annual rpt, 7884–4

Travel from US, characteristics of visit and traveler, and country of destination, 1990 in-flight survey, annual rpt, 2904–14

Travel patterns, personal and household characteristics, and auto and public transport use, 1990 survey, series, 7556–6

Travel to US, by characteristics of visit and traveler, world area of origin, and US destination, 1990 survey, annual rpt, 2904–12

see also Area wage surveys

see also Industry wage surveys

Vaccination and vaccines

Child health condition and services use, 1990 chartbook, 4108–49

Developing countries economic and social conditions from 1960s, and Intl Dev Cooperation Agency and AID activities and funding, FY90-92, annual rpt, 9904–4.1

Diphtheria, tetanus, and pertussis vaccination schedules, dosages, and precautions, CDC recommendations, 1991 rpt, 4206–2.46

Exports and imports of US, by Harmonized System 6-digit commodity and country, 1990, annual rpt, 2424–13

Exports of US, detailed Schedule B commodities with countries of destination, 1990, annual rpt, 2424–10

Foreign travel vaccination needs by country, and disease prevention recommendations, 1991 annual rpt, 4204–11

Health condition and health care resources, use, and spending, 1950s-89, annual data compilation, 4144–11

Health condition improvement and disease prevention goals and recommended activities for 2000, with trends 1970s-80s, 4048–10

Hepatitis B cases, exposure, and vaccination policies for students in nursing and lab technician training programs, 1989, article, 4042–3.244

HHS financial aid, by program, recipient, State, and city, FY90, annual regional listings, 4004–3

Indian and Alaska Native disease and disorder cases, deaths, and health services use, by tribe, reservation, and Indian Health Service area, late 1950s-86, 4088–2

Influenza vaccination schedules and dosage by age, outbreak control, and surveillance, CDC guidelines, 1991 rpt, 4206–2.42

Influenza vaccine for *Haemophilus influenza* type b, child dosages and schedules, CDC guidelines, 1991 rpt, 4206–2.37

Insurance (health) coverage and provisions of small business employee benefit plans, by plan type and occupational group, 1990, biennial rpt, 6784–20

Manufacturing annual survey, 1989: value of shipments, by SIC 4- to 5-digit product class, 2506–15.2

Measles cases among New York State high school and college students, and vaccination and treatment costs, 1989, article, 4042–3.227

Medicaid child preventive health care visits, exams, and immunizations, for California, 1981-84, article, 4652–1.214

Minority group and women health condition, services use, payment sources, and health care labor force, by poverty status, 1940s-89, chartbook, 4118–56

Minority group health condition, services use, costs, and indicators of services need, 1950s-88, 4118–55

Morbidity and Mortality Weekly Report, infectious notifiable disease cases by State, and public health issues, 4202–1

Natl Inst of Allergy and Infectious Diseases activities, grants by recipient and location, and disease cases, FY83-90, annual rpt, 4474–30

Price indexes (producer), by stage of processing and detailed commodity, monthly rpt, 6762–6

Price indexes (producer), by stage of processing and detailed commodity, monthly 1990, annual rpt, 6764–2

Rabies post-exposure treatment, and vaccination of veterinarians and others at risk, CDC guidelines, 1991 rpt, 4206–2.39

Rubella vaccination of children and women of childbearing age, and surveillance, CDC guidelines, 1990 rpt, 4206–2.33

Statistical Abstract of US, 1991 annual data compilation, 2324–1.3

Tax (excise) collections of IRS, by source, quarterly rpt, 8302–1

Vail, Del

"Fisheries Habitat Management on Public Lands: A Strategy for the Future", 5726–6.3

Valdez, Alaska

Tide height and time daily at coastal points, forecast 1992, annual rpt, 2174–2.1

Weather data for Valdez, Alaska, 1988, 9618–17

Valdez, Charles D.

"FAA Altitude Chamber Training Flight Profile: A Survey of Altitude Reactions, 1965-89", 7506–10.78

Vallejo, Calif.

see also under By City and By SMSA or MSA in the "Index by Categories"

Value added tax

Competitiveness (intl) and taxation issues, with comparisons of US and foreign tax rates and revenue, 1988-91, press release, 8008–150

EC economic integration issues, with economic indicators and trade by country, 1985-89, article, 9371–1.210

Energy taxes economic and energy demand impacts, for alternative taxation methods, projected 1991-2000, 3166–6.57

Foreign and US economic conditions and competitiveness issues, with data by country, 1960s-90, 21788–204

OECD tax burden indicators, by type of tax and country, 1990 hearing, 25368–173

Van der Veen, Jan H.

"AID Economic Policy Reform Program in The Gambia", 9916–1.74

Van Haverbeke, David F.

"Twenty-two Year Results of a Scots Pine (*Pinus sylvestris* L.) Provenance Test in North Dakota", 1208–383

Van Meir, Larry

"Outlook for Feed Grains", 1004–16.1

Van Walleghem, Joe

Van Walleghem, Joe
"Banking Structure Laws: Current Status and Recommendations for Change", 9381–14.1

Vanadium
see Metals and metal industries

Vancouver, Canada
Fruit and vegetable shipments, and arrivals in US and Canada cities, by mode of transport and State and country of origin, 1990, annual rpt, 1311–4.2

Vancouver, Wash.
CPI by component for US city average, and by region, population size, and for 27 metro areas, monthly rpt, 6762–2
see also under By SMSA or MSA in the "Index by Categories"

Vandalism
Arrests, by offense, offender characteristics, and location, data compilation, 1991 annual rpt, 6064–6.4
Arrests, by offense, offender characteristics, and location, 1990, annual rpt, 6224–2.2
Drug and alcohol abuse and mental illness direct and indirect costs, by type and patient age and sex, 1985 with 1980 and 1988 comparisons, 4048–35
Juvenile courts delinquency cases, by offense, referral source, disposition, age, sex, race, State, and county, 1988, annual rpt, 6064–12
Juvenile courts property offenses cases, by disposition and offender age, sex, and race, 1985-86, 6066–27.5
Neighborhood and housing quality, indicators and attitudes, by householder type and location, 1989, biennial rpt, 2485–12
Railroad accidents, casualties, and damage, by cause, railroad, and State, 1990, annual rpt, 7604–1
Railroad accidents, casualties, and damage, Fed Railroad Admin activities, and safety inspectors by State, 1989, annual rpt, 7604–12
Sentences for Federal offenses, guidelines by offense and circumstances, series, 17668–1

Vanuatu
Background Notes, summary social, political, and economic data, 1990 rpt, 7006–2.44
Economic, social, and agricultural data, US and other aid sources, and AID activity, 1988 country rpt, 9916–12.28
Economic, social, political, and geographic summary data, by country, 1991, annual factbook, 9114–2
Exports and imports of US, by transport mode, country, and SITC 1- to 3-digit commodity, 1990, annual rpt, 2424–12
Human rights conditions in 170 countries, and US economic and military aid, 1990, annual rpt, 21384–3
Military aid of US, arms sales, and training programs costs and budget requests, by program, world region, and country, FY90-92, annual rpt, 7144–13
Timber in Pacific basin, sandalwood resources, habitat, harvest, exports, and uses, 1990 conf, 1208–366
UN voting record and share of votes in agreement with US, by issue, country, and world area, 1990, annual rpt, 7004–18

Varanasi, Usha
"National Benthic Surveillance Project, Pacific Coast: Part I, Summary and Overview of the Results for Cycles I to III (1984-86)", 2168–121.1
"National Benthic Surveillance Project, Pacific Coast: Part II, Technical Presentation of the Results for Cycles I to III (1984-86)", 2168–121.2

Varnishes
see Paints and varnishes

Vartiainen, Erkki
"Mortality, Cardiovascular Risk Factors, and Diet in China, Finland, and the U.S.", 4042–3.202

Vasectomy
see Sexual sterilization

VAT
see Value added tax

Vatican City
Economic, social, political, and geographic summary data, by country, 1991, annual factbook, 9114–2
Exports and imports of US, by transport mode, country, and SITC 1- to 3-digit commodity, 1990, annual rpt, 2424–12

Vaughan, Denton R.
"Reflections on the Income Estimates from the Initial Panel of the Survey of Income and Program Participation (SIPP)", 4746–26.8

Vegetable oils
see Oils, oilseeds, and fats

Vegetables and vegetable products
Acreage planted and harvested, by crop and State, 1989-90 and planned as of June 1991, annual rpt, 1621–23
Acreage planted, by selected crop and State, 1982-90 and planned 1991, annual rpt, 1621–22
Acreage under Agricultural Stabilization and Conservation Service programs, rankings by commodity and congressional district, 1989, biennial rpt, 1804–17
Agricultural Statistics, 1990, annual rpt, 1004–1
Agriculture census, 1987: farms, farmland, production, finances, and operator characteristics, by county, final State rpt series, 2331–1
Agriculture census, 1987: horticultural specialties producers, finances, and operations, by crop and State, 1988 survey, 2337–1
Bean (dried) prices by State, market activity, and foreign and US production, use, stocks, and trade, weekly rpt, 1311–17
Bean (dried) production and prices by State, exports and foreign production by country, and USDA food aid purchases, by bean type, 1984-90, annual rpt, 1311–18
Bean, pea, and lentil (dried) trade, by country, 1979/80-1990/91, 1925–2.5
Celery acreage planted and growing, by growing area, monthly rpt, 1621–14
Central America agricultural export promotion of nontraditional crops, impacts on income export stability, late 1970s-80s, 1528–312
Cold storage food stocks by commodity and census div, and warehouse space use, by State, monthly rpt, 1631–5
Cold storage food stocks by commodity, and warehouse space use, by census div, 1990, annual rpt, 1631–11

Index by Subjects and Names

Consumer Expenditure Survey, food spending by item, household composition, income, age, race, and region, 1980-88, biennial rpt, 1544–30
Consumer Expenditure Survey, household income by source, and itemized spending, by selected characteristics and region, 1988-89, annual rpt, 6764–5
Consumption of food, dietary composition, and nutrient intake, 1987/88 natl survey, preliminary rpt series, 1356–1
Consumption, supply, trade, prices, spending, and indexes, by food commodity, 1989, annual rpt, 1544–4
CPI by component for US city average, and by region, population size, and for 27 metro areas, monthly rpt, 6762–2
Employment, earnings, and hours, by SIC 1- to 4-digit industry, monthly and annual averages, selected years 1909-90, annual rpt, 6744–4
Exports (agricultural) of high-value commodities, indexes and sales value by commodity, world area, and country, 1960s-86, 1528–323
Exports and imports (agricultural) of US, by commodity and country, bimonthly rpt, 1522–1
Exports and imports (agricultural) of US, by detailed commodity and country, 1989, annual rpt, 1524–8
Exports and imports (agricultural) of US, by detailed commodity and country, 1990, semiannual rpt, 1522–4
Exports and imports between US and outlying areas, by detailed commodity and mode of transport, 1990, annual rpt, 2424–11
Exports and imports of US, by country and detailed commodity, monthly rpt, 2422–12
Exports and imports of US, by Harmonized System 6-digit commodity and country, 1990, annual rpt, 2424–13
Exports and imports of US, by transport mode, country, and SITC 1- to 3-digit commodity, 1990, annual rpt, 2424–12
Exports and imports of US shipped through Canada, by detailed commodity, customs district, and country, 1989, annual rpt, 7704–11
Exports of US, detailed Schedule B commodities with countries of destination, 1990, annual rpt, 2424–10
Farm financial and marketing conditions, forecast 1991, annual chartbook, 1504–8
Farm financial and marketing conditions, forecast 1991, annual conf, 1004–16
Farm financial condition, for fruit and vegetable operations, 1989, article, 1541–1.209
Farm income, expenses, receipts by commodity, assets, liabilities, and ratios, 1990 and trends from 1945, annual rpt, 1544–16
Farm sector balance sheet, and receipts by detailed commodity, by State, 1985-89, annual rpt, 1544–18
Fertilizer and pesticide use and application rates, by type, crop, and State, series, 1616–1
Foreign and US fresh and processed fruit, vegetable, and nut production and trade, FAS monthly circular with articles, 1925–34

Index by Subjects and Names

Vending machines and stands

Foreign countries agricultural production, prices, and trade, by country, 1980-90 and forecast 1991, annual world area rpt series, 1524–4

Foreign countries agricultural production, trade, and policies, summary data by country, 1989-90, annual factbook, 1924–12

Immigration restrictions effects on US agricultural labor costs and trade competitiveness, 1980s, 1598–276

Imports of fruits and vegetables under quarantine, by crop, country, and port of entry, FY88 annual rpt, 1524–7

Imports of US given duty-free treatment for value of US material sent abroad, by commodity and country, 1989, annual rpt, 9884–14

Irrigation projects of Reclamation Bur in western US, crop production and acreage by commodity, State, and project, 1989, annual rpt, 5824–12

Labor productivity, indexes of output, hours, and employment by SIC 2- to 4-digit industry, 1967-89, annual rpt, 6824–1.3

Manufacturing annual survey, 1989: finances and operations, by SIC 2- to 4-digit industry, series, 2506–15

Manufacturing finances and operations, by SIC 2- to 4-digit industry, forecast 1991, annual rpt, 2044–28

Mexico vegetable trade with US and US import duties by commodity, and fresh tomato arrivals in US and Canada cities, 1970s-90, article, 1561–11.202

Mushroom (canned) trade, supply, and demand, for selected countries, 1980s-91, article, 1925–34.242

Mushroom production, sales, and prices, by State, 1966/67-1990/91 and planned 1991/92, annual rpt, 1631–9

Nutrient, caloric, and waste composition, detailed data for raw, processed, and prepared foods, 1991 rpt, 1356–3.15

Occupational injury and illness rates, by SIC 2- to 4-digit industry, 1988-89, annual rpt, 6844–7

Occupational injury and illness rates, by SIC 2- to 4-digit industry, 1989, annual rpt, 6844–1

OECD trade, total and for 4 major countries, and US trade by country, by commodity, 1970-89, world area rpt series, 9116–1

Onion farm acreage, pesticide use, operators, and other characteristics, for 6 producer States, 1989, article, 1561–11.201

Pest control integrated mgmt programs for vegetables, acreage, costs, savings, and funding sources and recipients, by State, 1980s, 1568–298

Pesticide (EBDC) use on vegetable crops, consumer and producer cost impacts of proposed ban, 1985-89, article, 1561–11.204

Potato production, acreage, disposition, prices, and trade, by State and country, 1949-90, 1568–305

Potato production, prices, stocks, and use, by State, 1981-90, annual rpt, 1621–11

Potato production, stocks, processing, yields, and harvest losses, by State, periodic rpt, 1621–10

Price indexes (producer), by stage of processing and detailed commodity, monthly rpt, 6762–6

Price indexes (producer), by stage of processing and detailed commodity, monthly 1990, annual rpt, 6764–2

Prices (farm-retail) for food, marketing cost components, and industry finances and productivity, 1920s-90, annual rpt, 1544–9

Prices (wholesale) for fresh fruit and vegetables in NYC, Chicago, and selected shipping points, by crop, 1990, annual rpt, 1311–8

Prices (wholesale) of fruit and vegetables in NYC by State, and shipments and arrivals by mode of transport, by commodity, weekly rpt, 1311–20

Prices received and paid by farmers, by commodity and State, 1990, annual rpt, 1629–5

Prices received by farmers and production value, by detailed crop and State, 1988-90, annual rpt, 1621–2

Prices received by farmers for major products, and paid for farm inputs and living items, by State, monthly rpt, 1629–1

Production, acreage, and yield, current and forecast for selected fresh and processing vegetables by State, periodic rpt, 1621–12

Production, farms, acreage, and related data, by selected crop and State, monthly rpt, 1621–1

Production inputs, output, and productivity for farms, by commodity and region, 1947-89, annual rpt, 1544–17

Production of fruit and vegetables, imports by country, use, exports, and prices, by commodity, 1975-87, 1568–299

Production, prices, trade, and marketing, by commodity, current situation and forecast, monthly rpt with articles, 1502–4

Production, prices, trade, stocks, and use, for selected fresh and processing crops, periodic situation rpt with articles, 1561–11

Production, value, and acreage, for selected fresh and processing vegetables by State, 1988-90, annual rpts, 1621–25

Puerto Rico economic censuses, 1987: wholesale, retail, and service industries finances and operations, by establishment characteristics and SIC 2- and 3-digit industry, subject rpts, 2591–2

Pumpkin farms, production costs, shipments, and sales by State, prices, and imports by country, 1978-90, article, 1561–11.203

Radionuclide releases and concentrations in water, milk, and other food products after Chernobyl, USSR, reactor accident, for selected Republics, 1986-87, 4042–3.201

Seed exports, by type, world region, and country, FAS quarterly rpt, 1925–13

Shipments by mode of transport, arrivals, and imports, for fruit and vegetables by commodity and State and country of origin, weekly rpt, 1311–3

Shipments of fruit and vegetables, and arrivals in US and Canada cities, by mode of transport and State and country of origin, 1990, annual rpt series, 1311–4

Statistical Abstract of US, 1991 annual data compilation, 2324–1.23

Tax (income) returns of corporations, income and tax items by asset size and detailed industry, 1988, annual rpt, 8304–21

Tax (income) returns of partnerships, income statement and balance sheet items, by industry group, 1989, annual article, 8302–2.216; 8304–18

Tomato (paste and canned) imports of US, and Chile paste exports, by country, 1986-90, article, 1925–34.211

Tomato (paste, canned, and sauce) imports of US, and Mediterranean basin supply and use, by country, 1988-92, article, 1925–34.227

Tomato (processing) production, and paste and canned tomato supply, trade, and use, by selected country, 1987-91, article, 1925–34.202

Tomato crop fungicide use, and ban impacts on production and price, 1984-88, conf papers, 1588–154

Truck rates for fruit and vegetables weekly by growing area and market, and shipments monthly by State and country of origin, 1990, annual rpt, 1311–15

see also Fruit and fruit products

see also under By Commodity in the "Index by Categories"

Vegetation

see Plants and vegetation

Vending machines and stands

Blind-operated vending facilities on Federal and non-Federal property, finances and operations by agency and State, FY90, annual rpt, 4944–2

Census of Retail Trade, 1987: finances and employment, for establishments with and without payroll, by SIC 2- to 4-digit kind of business, State, and MSA, 2401–1

County Business Patterns, 1988: employment, establishments, and payroll, by SIC 2- to 4-digit industry and county, annual State rpt series, 2326–6

County Business Patterns, 1989: employment, establishments, and payroll, by SIC 2- to 4-digit industry and county, annual State rpt series, 2326–8

Electronic communications systems and related products shipments, trade, use, and firms, 1990, annual Current Industrial Rpt, 2506–12.35

Employment, earnings, and hours, by SIC 1- to 4-digit industry, monthly and annual averages, selected years 1909-90, annual rpt, 6744–4

Exports and imports of US, by Harmonized System 6-digit commodity and country, 1990, annual rpt, 2424–13

Exports of US, detailed Schedule B commodities with countries of destination, 1990, annual rpt, 2424–10

Franchise business opportunities by firm and kind of business, and sources of aid and info, 1990 annual listing, 2104–7

Injuries from use of consumer products, by severity, victim age, and detailed product, 1990, annual rpt, 9164–6

Jukebox copyright royalty fees, and funds available for distribution, 1989-90, annual rpt, 26404–2

Manufacturing annual survey, 1989: finances and operations, by SIC 2- to 4-digit industry, series, 2506–15

Manufacturing census, 1987: finances and operations, by SIC 2- to 4-digit industry, State, and MSA, with trends from 1849, 2497–1

Vending machines and stands

Manufacturing census, 1987: finances and operations, by type of organization and SIC 2- to 4-digit industry, subject rpt, 2497–5

Military post exchange operations, and sales by commodity, by facility and location worldwide, FY89, annual rpt, 3504–10

Occupational injury and illness rates, by SIC 2- to 4-digit industry, 1988-89, annual rpt, 6844–7

Occupational injury and illness rates, by SIC 2- to 4-digit industry, 1989, annual rpt, 6844–1

Price indexes (producer), by stage of processing and detailed commodity, monthly rpt, 6762–6

Price indexes (producer), by stage of processing and detailed commodity, monthly 1990, annual rpt, 6764–2

Puerto Rico economic censuses, 1987: wholesale and retail trade and service industry finances and operations, by SIC 2- to 4-digit industry and municipio, 2591–1

Service industries census, 1987: establishments, receipts by source, payroll, and employment, by SIC 2- to 4-digit kind of business, State, and MSA, 2393–4

Service industries receipts, by SIC 2- to 4-digit kind of business, 1990, annual rpt, 2413–8

Shipments of vending machines by product, trade, and use, 1990, Current Industrial Rpt, 2506–12.10

Thefts, and value of property stolen and recovered, by property type, 1990, annual rpt, 6224–2.1

Veneman, Peter L.

"Soil-Vegetation Correlations in the Connecticut River Floodplain of Western Massachusetts", 5506–10.12

Venereal diseases

see Sexually transmitted diseases

Venezuela

- Agricultural exports of high-value commodities, indexes and sales by commodity, world area, and country, 1960s-86, 1528–323
- Agricultural exports of US, impacts of foreign agricultural and trade policy, with data by commodity and country, 1989, annual rpt, 1924–8
- Agricultural production, prices, and trade, by country, 1960s-90, annual world area rpt, 1524–4.2
- Agricultural production, trade, and policies in foreign countries, summary data by country, 1989-90, annual factbook, 1924–12
- Agricultural subsidies to producers and consumers in 6 Latin America countries, by selected commodity, 1982-87, 1528–324
- Agricultural trade by commodity and country, prices, and world market devs, monthly rpt, 1922–12
- Agricultural trade of US, by detailed commodity and country, 1989, annual rpt, 1524–8
- Agricultural trade of US, by detailed commodity and country, 1990, semiannual rpt, 1522–4
- AID economic aid to developing countries, obligations and disbursements by country, quarterly rpt, 9912–4

AID loans repayment status and terms by program and country, and status of predecessor agency loans, quarterly rpt, 9912–3

Background Notes, summary social, political, and economic data, 1990 rpt, 7006–2.9

Cement (gray portland) and clinker from Venezuela, injury to US industry from foreign subsidized and less than fair value imports, investigation with background financial and operating data, 1991 rpt, 9886–19.76

Economic and military aid and loans from US and intl agencies, by program and country, FY46-90, annual rpt, 9914–5

Economic conditions in USSR, Eastern Europe, OECD, and selected other countries, 1960s-90, annual rpt, 9114–4

Economic conditions, policy, and trade practices, by country, 1988-90, annual rpt, 21384–5

Economic, social, political, and geographic summary data, by country, 1991, annual factbook, 9114–2

Exports and imports of US, by commodity and country, 1970-89, world area rpt, 9116–1.4

Exports and imports of US, by Harmonized System 6-digit commodity and country, 1990, annual rpt, 2424–13

Exports and imports of US, by selected country, country group, and commodity group, 1990, annual rpt, 2044–37

Exports and imports of US, by transport mode, country, and SITC 1- to 3-digit commodity, 1990, annual rpt, 2424–12

Exports, imports, and balances of US with major trading partners, by product category, 1986-90, annual chartbook, 9884–21

Exports of US, detailed Schedule B commodities with countries of destination, 1990, annual rpt, 2424–10

Human rights conditions in 170 countries, and US economic and military aid, 1990, annual rpt, 21384–3

Imports of goods, services, and investment from US, trade barriers, impacts, and US actions, by country, 1990, annual rpt, 444–2

Intl transactions of US with 9 countries, 1986-88, *Survey of Current Business*, monthly rpt, annual table, 2702–1.26

Labor conditions, union coverage, and work accidents, 1991 annual country rpt, 6366–4.26

Military aid of US, arms sales, and training programs costs and budget requests, by program, world region, and country, FY90-92, annual rpt, 7144–13

Multinatl US firms and foreign affiliates finances and operations, by industry and world area of parent firm, 1989 benchmark survey, preliminary annual rpt, 2704–5

Multinatl US firms foreign affiliates, income statement items by country and world area, 1986, biennial article, 8302–2.212

Oil production, and exports and prices for US, by major exporting country, detailed data, monthly rpt with articles, 3162–24

Oil production, trade, use, and stocks, by selected country and country group, monthly rpt, 3162–42

Index by Subjects and Names

Pipes and tubes (welded nonalloy steel) from 6 countries, injury to US industry from foreign subsidized and less than fair value imports, investigation with background financial and operating data, 1991 rpt, 9886–19.81

Steel imports of US under voluntary restraint agreement, by product, customs district, and country, with US industry operating data, quarterly rpt, 9882–13

UN voting record and share of votes in agreement with US, by issue, country, and world area, 1990, annual rpt, 7004–18

see also under By Foreign Country in the "Index by Categories"

Venti, Steven F.

"Aging and the Income Value of Housing Wealth", 2626–10.125

"Saving Effect of Tax-Deferred Retirement Accounts: Evidence from the SIPP", 2626–10.132

Ventura, Calif.

see also under By SMSA or MSA in the "Index by Categories"

Ventura, Stephanie

"Birth and Fertility Rates by Education: 1980-85. Vital and Health Statistics Series 21", 4147–21.49

Venture capital

- Banks restrictions on business equity ownership, issues, with data for venture capital financing and comparisons to West Germany and Japan, 1970s-90, article, 9393–8.206
- Biotechnology commercial applications, industry finances and capitalization, patents, and govt support, for US, Japan, and EC, late 1970s-91, 26358–248

see also Small Business Investment Companies

Vermiculite

see Nonmetallic minerals and mines

Vermont

- Banks (insured commercial and savings) deposits by instn, State, MSA, and county, as of June 1990, annual regional rpt, 9295–3.1
- County Business Patterns, 1989: employment, establishments, and payroll, by SIC 2- to 4-digit industry and county, annual State rpt, 2326–8.47
- Disease (infectious notifiable) cases reported to Vermont health dept by source, and reasons for nonreporting, 1986-87, article, 4042–3.208
- DOD prime contract awards, by contractor, service branch, State, and city, FY90, annual rpt, 3544–22
- Economic indicators for New England States, Fed Reserve 1st District, monthly rpt, 9373–2
- Fed Govt spending in States and local areas, by type, State, county, and city, FY90, annual rpt, 2464–3
- Fed Govt spending in States, by type, program, agency, and State, FY90, annual rpt, 2464–2
- HHS financial aid, by program, recipient, State, and city, FY90, annual regional listing, 4004–3.1
- Hospital deaths of Medicare patients, actual and expected rates by diagnosis, and hospital characteristics, by instn, FY87-89, annual regional rpt, 4654–14.1

Index by Subjects and Names

Housing census, 1990: inventory, occupancy, and costs, State fact sheet, 2326–21.47

Income (personal) per capita and by source, and earnings by industry div, by State, MSA, and county, 1984-89, annual regional rpt, 2704–2.2

Marriages, divorces, and rates, by characteristics of spouses, State, and county, 1987 and trends from 1920, US Vital Statistics annual rpt, 4144–4

Mineral Industry Surveys, State reviews of production, 1990, preliminary annual rpt, 5614–6

Minerals Yearbook, 1989, Vol 2: State review of production and sales by commodity, and business activity, annual rpt, 5604–16.47

Minerals Yearbook, 1989, Vol 2: State reviews of production, sales, and firms, by commodity, and business activity, annual rpt, 5604–34

Natural resources use and mgmt, New Hampshire and Vermont public opinion, 1991 rpt, 1208–371

Physicians, by specialty, age, sex, and location of training and practice, 1989, State rpt, 4116–6.47

Population and housing census, 1990: population and housing characteristics, households, and land area, by county, subdiv, and place, State rpt, 2551–1.47

Population and housing census, 1990: voting age and total population by race, and housing units, by block, redistricting counts required under PL 94-171, State CD-ROM release, 2551–6.10

Population and housing census, 1990: voting age and total population by race, and housing units, by county and city, redistricting counts required under PL 94-171, State summary rpt, 2551–5.46

Savings instns, FHLB 1st District members financial operations compared to banks, and related economic and housing indicators, bimonthly rpt with articles, 9302–4

Statistical Abstract of US, 1991 annual data compilation, 2324–1

Supplemental Security Income payments and beneficiaries, by type of eligibility, State, and county, Dec 1989, annual rpt, 4744–27.1

Water resources dev projects of Army Corps of Engineers, characteristics, and costs, 1950s-89, biennial State rpt, 3756–1.46

Water supply and quality in streams and lakes, and groundwater levels in wells, by drainage basin, 1990, annual State rpt, 5666–10.28

Water supply in northeastern US, precipitation and stream runoff by station, monthly rpt, 2182–3

Wetlands acreage, resources, soil and water properties, and conservation efforts, by wetland type, 1987 State rpt, 5506–11.3

see also under By State in the "Index by Categories"

Veterans

Agent Orange exposure of Vietnam veterans, and other factors relation to dev of rare cancers, 1984-88, 4208–33

Alcohol abuse among veterans, screening results by age and race, for 5 VA medical centers, 1990, GAO rpt, 26121–416

Veterans benefits and pensions

Cancer (testicular) risk among Vietnam veterans, by service branch, 1976-81 local area study, article, 4472–1.228

Deaths of military personnel by service branch and age group, and veterans death rates, 1966-90, annual rpt, 8654–1

Disability, acute and chronic health conditions, absenteeism, and health services use, by selected characteristics, 1987, CD-ROM, 4147–10.177

Homeless veterans domiciliary program of VA, participant characteristics and outcomes, 1990 annual rpt, 8604–10

Homeless veterans with mental illness, VA program services, costs, staff, client characteristics, and outcome, 1990, annual rpt, 8604–11

Jail population, by criminal, correctional, drug use, and family history, and selected other characteristics, 1989, 6066–19.62

Jail population, by sociodemographic characteristics, criminal and drug use history, whether convicted, offense, and sentencing, 1989, annual rpt, 6064–26.3

Population and characteristics of veterans, and VA activities and programs, FY90, annual rpt, 8604–3

Population of veterans, by period of service, age, and State, as of Mar 1991, annual rpt, 8604–12

Prisoners and movements, by offense, location, and selected other characteristics, data compilation, 1991 annual rpt, 6064–6.6

State and Metro Area Data Book, 1991 data compilation, 2328–54

Statistical Abstract of US, 1991 annual data compilation, 2324–1.11

War participants, deaths, veterans living, and compensation and pension recipients, for each US war, 1775-1990, annual rpt, 8604–2

Women veterans, by age, period of service, and State, annual tables, discontinued, 9924–25

see also Retired military personnel

see also Servicepersons life insurance programs

see also Veterans benefits and pensions

see also Veterans education

see also Veterans employment

see also Veterans health facilities and services

see also Veterans housing

see also Veterans rehabilitation

Veterans Administration

Expenditures of Fed Govt in States, by type, program, agency, and State, FY90, annual rpt, 2464–2

Health care facilities of VA, patient and employee biostatistical data, discontinued series, 9926–1

Women veterans, by age, period of service, and State, annual tables, discontinued, 9924–25

see also Department of Veterans Affairs

Veterans Benefits Administration

Budget of US, obligations and authority by function, agency, and program, with summaries, analyses, and historical tables, FY92, annual rpt, 104–2

Insurance (life) for veterans and servicepersons, financial statements of programs and death rates, as of June 1991, annual rpt, 8654–1

Veterans benefits and pensions

Assistance (financial and nonfinancial) of Fed Govt, 1991 base edition with supplements, annual listing, 104–5

Beneficiaries and taxes collected for social insurance programs since 1940, monthly rpt, 4742–1.1

Benefits overpayment recovery and judgment enforcement cases filed in Federal district courts, 1990, annual rpt, 18204–8.13

Benefits overpayment recovery and judgment enforcement cases filed in Federal district courts, 1991, annual rpt, 18204–2.1

Budget of US, CBO analysis and review of FY92 budget by function, annual rpt, 26304–2

Budget of US, formula grant program obligations to State and local govts, by agency, program, and State, FY92, annual rpt, 104–30

Budget of US, House concurrent resolution, with spending and revenue targets, FY92 and projected to FY96, annual rpt, 21264–2

Budget of US, midsession review of FY92 budget, by function, annual rpt, 104–7

Budget of US, obligations and authority by function, agency, and program, with summaries, analyses, and historical tables, FY92, annual rpt, 104–2

Budget of US, receipts by source, outlays by agency and program, and balances, monthly rpt, 8102–3

Budget of US, Senate concurrent resolution, with spending and revenue targets, FY92, annual rpt, 25254–1

Compensation and pension cases of VA, by type of entitlement and period of service, monthly rpt, 8602–5

Criminal cases in Federal district courts, by offense, disposition, and district, 1980-90, last issue of annual rpt, 18204–1

Disability and death compensation cases of VA, by entitlement type, period of service, sex, age, and State, FY89, annual rpt, 8604–7

Expenditures, coverage, and benefits for social welfare programs, late 1930s-89, annual rpt, 4744–3.1; 4744–3.3; 4744–3.7

Expenditures for public welfare by program, FY50s-88, annual article, 4742–1.209

Expenditures for public welfare programs, by program type and level of govt, FY65-88, annual article, 4742–1.202

Expenditures for VA programs, by State, county, and congressional district, FY90, annual rpt, 8604–6

Expenditures of Fed Govt in States, by type, program, agency, and State, FY90, annual rpt, 2464–2

Fed Govt programs under Ways and Means Committee jurisdiction, finances, operations, and participant characteristics, FY70s-90, annual rpt, 21784–11

Fraud and abuse in VA programs, audits and investigations, 2nd half FY91, semiannual rpt, 8602–1

Govt revenue by source, spending by function, debt, and assets, by level of govt, FY89, annual rpt, 2466–2.2

Govt revenue by source, spending by function, debt, and assets, by level of govt, FY90, preliminary annual rpt, 2466–2.9

Veterans benefits and pensions

Homeless persons aid programs of Fed Govt, program descriptions and funding, by agency and State, FY87-90, annual GAO rpt, 26104–21

Homeless veterans with mental illness, VA program services, costs, staff, client characteristics, and outcome, 1990, annual rpt, 8604–11

Households composition, income, benefits, and labor force status, Survey of Income and Program Participation methodology, working paper series, 2626–10

Income (household, family, and personal), by source, detailed characteristics, and region, 1988-89, annual Current Population Rpt, 2546–6.68

Income (household, family, and personal), by source, detailed characteristics, and region, 1990, annual Current Population Rpt, 2546–6.70

Insurance (life) for veterans and servicepersons, actuarial analyses of VA programs, 1990, annual rpt, 8604–1

Insurance (life) for veterans and servicepersons, finances and coverage by program and State, 1990, annual rpt, 8604–4

Insurance (life) for veterans and servicepersons, financial statements of programs and death rates, as of June 1991, annual rpt, 8654–1

Lands (public) acreage and grants, by State, FY90 and trends, annual rpt, 5724–1.1

Loans and loan guarantees of Fed Govt, outstanding amounts by agency and program, *Treasury Bulletin*, quarterly rpt, 8002–4.9

Rural areas aged household income sources, and poverty status, 1983-84, 1598–268

Statistical Abstract of US, 1991 annual data compilation, 2324–1.11

Tax expenditures, Federal revenues forgone through income tax deductions and exclusions by type, FY92-96, annual rpt, 21784–10

Unemployment insurance laws of States, comparison of provisions, 1991, base edition with semiannual revisions, 6402–2

US attorneys civil and criminal cases by type and disposition, and collections, by Federal district, FY90, annual rpt, 6004–2.1; 6004–2.5

VA activities and programs, and veterans characteristics, FY90, annual rpt, 8604–3

VA activities and programs, monthly rpt, discontinued, 8602–3

War participants, deaths, veterans living, and compensation and pension recipients, for each US war, 1775-1990, annual rpt, 8604–2

see also Military benefits and pensions
see also Servicepersons life insurance programs
see also Veterans education
see also Veterans health facilities and services
see also Veterans housing

Veterans education

Assistance and other sources of support, with student expenses and characteristics, by instn type and control, 1990 triennial study, series, 4846–5

Assistance under GI Bill and other programs, and participation by period of service and State, FY89, annual rpt, 8604–9

Budget of US, obligations and authority by function, agency, and program, with summaries, analyses, and historical tables, FY92, annual rpt, 104–2

Costs, benefits, and participation for Head Start and GI Bill education programs, 1950s-90, hearing, 23848–217

Education Dept programs funding, operations, and effectiveness, FY90, annual rpt, 4804–5

Pell grants and applicants, by tuition, family and student income, instn type and control, and State, 1989/90, annual rpt, 4804–1

Reserves education benefits under GI Bill, eligible personnel and applications by component, 1990, annual rpt, 3544–31.1

Statistical Abstract of US, 1991 annual data compilation, 2324–1.11

Student aid funding and participation, by Federal program, instn type and control, and State, various periods 1959-89, annual rpt, 4804–28

Training benefits and participation, and other VA activities, FY90, annual rpt, 8604–3.7

Veterans employment

DOT employment, by subagency, occupation, and selected personnel characteristics, FY90, annual rpt, 7304–18

Fed Govt civilian employees demographic and employment characteristics, as of Sept 1990, annual article, 9842–1.201

Fed Govt civilian employment of minorities, women, veterans, and disabled persons, as of Sept 1988 and 1990, biennial article, 9842–1.202

Homeless veterans domiciliary program of VA, participant characteristics and outcomes, 1990 annual rpt, 8604–10

Homeless veterans with mental illness, VA program services, costs, staff, client characteristics, and outcome, 1990, annual rpt, 8604–11

Tax credit for hiring from groups with high unemployment rates, participation by State, and effectiveness, FY88, GAO rpt, 26121–407

Training on job under GI Bill and other programs, participation by State, and costs, FY89, annual rpt, 8604–9

Unemployment insurance claims and covered unemployment by program, and extended benefit triggers, by State, weekly rpt, 6402–15

Unemployment insurance claims, by program, weekly press release, 6402–14

Unemployment of groups with historically high rates, 1985-89, biennial rpt, 6504–2.2

VA employment characteristics and activities, FY90, annual rpt, 8604–3.8

Vietnam veterans employment status, by age and race, monthly rpt, 6742–2

Vietnam veterans employment status, by age, monthly press release, 6742–5

Vietnam veterans employment status, transcripts of BLS Commissioner's monthly testimony, periodic rpt, 23846–4

Veterans health facilities and services

AIDS cases at VA health care centers by sex, race, risk factor, and facility, and AIDS prevention and treatment issues, quarterly rpt, 8702–1

Alcohol abuse among veterans, screening results by age and race, for 5 VA medical centers, 1990, GAO rpt, 26121–416

Assistance (financial and nonfinancial) of Fed Govt, 1991 base edition with supplements, annual listing, 104–5

Budget of US, obligations and authority by function, agency, and program, with summaries, analyses, and historical tables, FY92, annual rpt, 104–2

Contracts for sharing health services among VA and non-VA facilities, by service type and region, FY90, annual rpt, 8704–5

Coverage under health insurance by source, and services reimbursed by type, 1991 rpt, 26306–6.155

Employment of VA health facilities, and turnover, by occupation and location, 1990, annual rpt, 8604–8

Expenditures for health care, by service type, payment source, and sector, 1960s-90, annual article, 4652–1.221; 4652–1.252

Expenditures for health care by type and payment source, with background data and foreign comparisons, 1960s-80s and projected to 2000, 26308–98

Expenditures for public welfare by program, FY50s-88, annual article, 4742–1.209

Expenditures for VA programs, by State, county, and congressional district, FY90, annual rpt, 8604–6

Fraud and abuse in VA programs, audits and investigations, 2nd half FY91, semiannual rpt, 8602–1

Health condition and health care resources, use, and spending, 1950s-89, annual data compilation, 4144–11

Homeless veterans domiciliary program of VA, participant characteristics and outcomes, 1990 annual rpt, 8604–10

Homeless veterans with mental illness, VA program services, costs, staff, client characteristics, and outcome, 1990, annual rpt, 8604–11

Kidney dialysis centers of VA, patients and contract fees by service type, 1988-89, annual rpt, 4654–16.2

Medicine and Surgery Dept of VA, trainees by detailed program and city, FY90, annual rpt, 8704–4

Mental health care facilities, finances, caseload, staff, and characteristics of instn and patients, 1988, 4506–4.14

Mental health care facilities, staff, and patient characteristics, *Statistical Notes* series, 4506–3

Mental health care services, staffing, research, and training programs in VA facilities, 1991 biennial listing, 8704–2

Older persons health care services use, by service type, discharge destination, and prior care source, 1986, 4188–72

Patients and employees in VA medical facilities, biostatistical data, discontinued series, 9926–1

Patients, visits, costs, and operating beds, by VA and contract facility, and region, quarterly rpt, 8602–4

Statistical Abstract of US, 1991 annual data compilation, 2324–1.11

Surgery-related deaths and complications, by procedure and VA facility, and compared to non-VA instns, FY84-89, last issue of biennial rpt, 8704–1

Index by Subjects and Names

VA activities and programs, and veterans characteristics, FY90, annual rpt, 8604–3
VA activities and programs, monthly rpt, discontinued, 8602–3
see also Military health facilities and services
see also Veterans benefits and pensions
see also Veterans rehabilitation

Veterans Health Services and Research Administration

AIDS cases at VA health care centers by sex, race, risk factor, and facility, and AIDS prevention and treatment issues, quarterly rpt, 8702–1
Budget of US, obligations and authority by function, agency, and program, with summaries, analyses, and historical tables, FY92, annual rpt, 104–2
Contracts for sharing health services among VA and non-VA facilities, by service type and region, FY90, annual rpt, 8704–5
Health care staff and salary of VHSRA, by pay system and occupational group, 1990, annual rpt, 9844–6.3
Hearing aid performance test results, by make and model, 1991 annual rpt, 8704–3
Medicine and Surgery Dept of VA, trainees by detailed program and city, FY90, annual rpt, 8704–4
Mental health care services, staffing, research, and training programs in VA facilities, 1991 biennial listing, 8704–2
Surgery-related deaths and complications, by procedure and VA facility, and compared to non-VA instns, FY84-89, last issue of biennial rpt, 8704–1

Veterans hospitals
see Veterans health facilities and services

Veterans housing
American Housing Survey: unit and households detailed characteristics, and unit and neighborhood quality, MSA rpt series, 2485–6
American Housing Survey: unit and households detailed characteristics, and unit and neighborhood quality, 1987, biennial rpt, 2485–12
Atlanta metro area secondary mortgage market underwriting guidelines, and indicators of discrimination, 1989, GAO rpt, 26113–500
Budget of US, obligations and authority by function, agency, and program, with summaries, analyses, and historical tables, FY92, annual rpt, 104–2
Costs, terms, and user characteristics for VA housing programs, 1985-89, 8608–7
Expenditures for VA programs, by State, county, and congressional district, FY90, annual rpt, 8604–6
Expenditures of Fed Govt in States, by type, program, agency, and State, FY90, annual rpt, 2464–2
Loan guarantee operations of VA, quarterly rpt, discontinued, 8602–2
Mortgage loan activity, by type of lender, loan, and mortgaged property, quarterly press release, 5142–30
Mortgage loans guaranteed by VA, and other activities, FY90, annual rpt, 8604–3.7
Mortgages FHA-insured for 1-family units, by loan type and mortgage characteristics, quarterly rpt, 5142–45

New single and multifamily units, by structural and financial characteristics, inside-outside MSAs, and region, 1986-90, annual rpt, 2384–1
New single-family houses sold and sales price by type of financing, monthly rpt, quarterly tables, 2382–3.2
Statistical Abstract of US, 1991 annual data compilation, 2324–1.11

Veterans loans
see Veterans benefits and pensions
see Veterans housing

Veterans pensions
see Veterans benefits and pensions

Veterans rehabilitation
Education aid under GI Bill and other programs, and participation by period of service and State, FY89, annual rpt, 8604–9
Expenditures for VA programs, by State, county, and congressional district, FY90, annual rpt, 8604–6
Homeless veterans domiciliary program of VA, participant characteristics and outcomes, 1990 annual rpt, 8604–10
Medicine and Surgery Dept of VA, trainees by detailed program and city, FY90, annual rpt, 8704–4
Mental health care services, staffing, research, and training programs in VA facilities, 1991 biennial listing, 8704–2
Patients, visits, costs, and operating beds, by VA and contract facility, and region, quarterly rpt, 8602–4
States vocational rehabilitation agency cases by disposition and applicant characteristics, and closures by reason, FY84-88, annual rpt, 4944–6
VA activities and programs, and veterans characteristics, FY90, annual rpt, 8604–3
VA health care facilities physicians, dentists, and nurses, by selected employment characteristics and VA district, quarterly rpt, 8602–6

Veterinary medicine
Canine lymphoma risk relation to herbicide exposure and other factors, and implications for humans, 1984-88, article, 4472–1.220
Cattle tuberculosis cases and cooperative Federal-State eradication activities, by State, FY89-90, annual rpt, 1394–13
County Business Patterns, 1988: employment, establishments, and payroll, by SIC 2- to 4-digit industry and county, annual State rpt series, 2326–6
County Business Patterns, 1989: employment, establishments, and payroll, by SIC 2- to 4-digit industry and county, annual State rpt series, 2326–8
Dairy Herd Improvement Program cooperatives and cows tested, by State, 1989, annual rpt, 1124–1
Degrees awarded in higher education, by level, field, race, and sex, 1988/89 with trends from 1978/79, biennial rpt, 4844–17
Drug (veterinary) PPI, monthly rpt, 6762–6
Drug (veterinary) PPI, monthly 1990, annual rpt, 6764–2
Drug shipments, trade, and use, by product, 1990, annual Current Industrial Rpt, 2506–8.5
Education in science and engineering, grad programs enrollment by field, source of funds, and characteristics of student and instn, 1975-89, annual rpt, 9627–7

Video recordings and equipment

Farm production itemized costs, by farm sales size and region, 1990, annual rpt, 1614–3
Farm production itemized costs, receipts, and returns, by commodity and region, 1987-89, annual rpt, 1544–20
Foreign countries agricultural research grants of USDA, by program, subagency, and country, FY90, annual listing, 1954–3
Health condition and health care resources, use, and spending, 1950s-89, annual data compilation, 4144–11
Injuries from use of consumer products, by severity, victim age, and detailed product, 1990, annual rpt, 9164–6
Lab animals protection, licensing, and inspection activities of USDA, by State, FY89, annual rpt, 1394–10
Military health care personnel, and accessions by training source, by occupation, specialty, and service branch, FY89, annual rpt, 3544–24
Minority group and women health condition, services use, payment sources, and health care labor force, by poverty status, 1940s-89, chartbook, 4118–56
Natl Veterinary Services Labs activities, biologic drug products evaluation and disease testing, FY90, annual rpt, 1394–17
Rabies post-exposure treatment, and vaccination of veterinarians and others at risk, CDC guidelines, 1991 rpt, 4206–2.39
Research (agricultural) funding and staffing for USDA, State agencies, and other instns, by topic, FY90, annual rpt, 1744–2
Research and education grants, USDA competitive awards by program and recipient, FY90, annual listing, 1764–1
Tax (income) returns of sole proprietorships, income statement items, by industry group, 1989, annual article, 8302–2.214
Waste (medical) generation, sources, health worker exposure and risk, and incineration emissions, 1980s, 4078–1
see also Animal diseases and zoonoses

Vetterick, Paul
"Anadromous Fish Habitat Management on Public Lands: A Strategy for the Future", 5726–6.1

Veum, Jonathan R.
"Child Care: Arrangements and Costs", 6722–1.246

Vice Presidency of the U.S.
see Office of the Vice President

Victoria, Tex.
see also under By SMSA or MSA in the "Index by Categories"

Video recordings and equipment
Consumer Expenditure Survey, spending for selected categories, 1991 semiannual pamphlet, 2322–3
Copyright infringement and copying issues for prerecorded training videos, businesses views, 1987 survey, hearing, 21528–82
Fed Govt audiovisual activities and spending, by whether performed in-house and agency, FY90, annual rpt, 9514–1
Libraries (public) finances, staff, and operations, by State and population size, 1989, annual rpt, 4824–6

Video recordings and equipment

Library of Congress rpts and recordings, 1991, biennial listing, 26404–5
Natl Archives and Records Admin activities, finances, holdings, and staff, FY90, annual rpt, 9514–2
Price indexes (producer), by stage of processing and detailed commodity, monthly rpt, 6762–6
Price indexes (producer), by stage of processing and detailed commodity, monthly 1990, annual rpt, 6764–2
Puerto Rico economic censuses, 1987: wholesale and retail trade and service industry finances and operations, by SIC 2- to 4-digit industry and municipio, 2591–1
Puerto Rico economic censuses, 1987: wholesale, retail, and service industries finances and operations, by establishment characteristics and SIC 2- and 3-digit industry, subject rpts, 2591–2
Service industries census, 1987: establishments, receipts by source, payroll, and employment, by SIC 2- to 4-digit kind of business, State, and MSA, 2393–4
Shipments, trade, use, and firms, for consumer electronics by product, 1990, annual Current Industrial Rpt, 2506–12.20
Shipments, trade, use, and firms, for electronic communications systems and related products, 1990, annual Current Industrial Rpt, 2506–12.35
Space science and related data sources and availability, 1991 annual listing, 9504–10
Statistical Abstract of US, 1991 annual data compilation, 2324–1.7
USDA rpts, computer data files, and visual aids, 1991 annual listing, 1004–13

Vietnam

- Agricultural exports of high-value commodities, indexes and sales by commodity, world area, and country, 1960s-86, 1528–323
- Agricultural trade of US, by detailed commodity and country, 1989, annual rpt, 1524–8
- Agricultural trade of US, by detailed commodity and country, 1990, semiannual rpt, 1522–4
- AID loans repayment status and terms by program and country, and status of predecessor agency loans, quarterly rpt, 9912–3
- Amerasian refugees admitted to US, FY89-90, fact sheet, 6266–2.4; 6266–2.8
- Amerasian refugees arrivals in US, and resettlement programs and funding, FY90, annual rpt, 4694–5
- Debt of Communist countries to US and other Western banks, by country, 1980s, conf, 25388–56
- Economic and military aid and loans from US and intl agencies, by program and country, FY46-90, annual rpt, 9914–5
- Economic, social, political, and geographic summary data, by country, 1991, annual factbook, 9114–2
- Exports and imports of US, by transport mode, country, and SITC 1- to 3-digit commodity, 1990, annual rpt, 2424–12
- Exports and imports of US with Communist countries, by detailed commodity and country, quarterly rpt with articles, 9882–2

Fish imports of Japan from Vietnam, by commodity, 1984-88, article, 2162–1.204
Human rights conditions in 170 countries, and US economic and military aid, 1990, annual rpt, 21384–3
Refugee arrivals in US by world area of origin and State of settlement, and Federal aid, FY90-91 and proposed FY92 allocations, annual rpt, 7004–16
Refugee resettlement programs and funding, arrivals by country of origin, and indicators of adjustment, by State, FY90, annual rpt, 4694–5
Refugees from Indochina, arrivals, and departures, by country of origin and resettlement, camp, and ethnicity, monthly rpt, 7002–4
UN voting record and share of votes in agreement with US, by issue, country, and world area, 1990, annual rpt, 7004–18
see also under By Foreign Country in the "Index by Categories"

Vietnam War
see Veterans benefits and pensions
see War

Vigdorchik, Michael

"Geographic Based Information Management System for Permafrost Prediction in the Beaufort and Chukchi Seas. Part I: Submarine Permafrost on the Alaskan Shelf", 2176–1.39

Vilches, Ramon

"Changes in the Structure of Wages: A Regional Comparison", 9373–1.213

Villella, Rita F.

"Acid Rain Publications by the U.S. Fish and Wildlife Service, 1979-89", 5506–5.26

Villet, Ruxton H.

"Diversification of the Agricultural Product Portfolio Through Biotechnology", 1004–16.1

Vineis, Paolo

"Incidence Rates of Lymphomas and Soft-Tissue Sarcomas and Environmental Measurements of Phenoxy Herbicides", 4472–1.207

Vineland, N.J.
see also under By SMSA or MSA in the "Index by Categories"

Vinyl chloride
see Chemicals and chemical industry

Vinyl materials
see Plastics and plastics industry
see Synthetic fibers and fabrics

Violence

- Cocaine abuse, user characteristics, and related crime and violence, 1988 conf, 4498–74
- Crimes, by characteristics of victim and offender, circumstances, and location, data compilation, 1991 annual rpt, 6064–6.3
- Drug abuse relation to violent and criminal behavior, with data on street gang activity and selected population groups, 1989 conf, 4498–70
- Indian and Alaska Native disease and disorder cases, deaths, and health services use, by tribe, reservation, and Indian Health Service area, late 1950s-86, 4088–2
- Minority group health condition, services use, costs, and indicators of services need, 1950s-88, 4118–55

Older persons abuse and neglect by circumstances and characteristics of abuser and victim, and States protective services budgets and staff, by location, 1980s, hearing, 21148–62
Preventive disease and health improvement goals and recommended activities for 2000, with trends 1970s-80s, 4048–10
Youth violence among minorities, prevention strategies, 1990 conf, 4042–3.218
see also Assassination
see also Assault
see also Assaults on police
see also Child abuse and neglect
see also Crime and criminals
see also Domestic violence
see also Homicide
see also Rape
see also Riots and disorders
see also Terrorism
see also Vandalism
see also War
see also War casualties

Virgin Islands
see British Virgin Islands
see U.S. Virgin Islands

Virginia

- Appalachian Regional Commission funding, by project and State, planned FY91, annual rpt, 9084–3
- Apple production, marketing, and prices, for Appalachia and compared to other States, 1988-91, annual rpt, 1311–13
- Banks (insured commercial), Fed Reserve 5th District members financial statements, by State, quarterly rpt, 9389–18
- Banks (insured commercial and savings) deposits by instn, State, MSA, and county, as of June 1990, annual regional rpt, 9295–3.2
- Child welfare programs funding by source, and foster care cases, problems, and program operations for selected States, 1970s-90, hearings, 21788–202
- Coal production and mines by county, prices, productivity, miners, and reserves, by mining method and State, 1989-90, annual rpt, 3164–25
- County Business Patterns, 1989: employment, establishments, and payroll, by SIC 2- to 4-digit industry and county, annual State rpt, 2326–8.48
- DOD prime contract awards, by contractor, service branch, State, and city, FY90, annual rpt, 3544–22
- Economic indicators by State, Fed Reserve 5th District, quarterly rpt, 9389–16
- Education system in Appalachia, improvement initiatives, and indicators of success, by State, 1960s-89, 9088–36
- Employment and housing and mortgage market indicators by State, FHLB 4th District, quarterly rpt, 9302–36
- Fed Govt spending in States and local areas, by type, State, county, and city, FY90, annual rpt, 2464–3
- Fed Govt spending in States, by type, program, agency, and State, FY90, annual rpt, 2464–2
- HHS financial aid, by program, recipient, State, and city, FY90, annual regional listing, 4004–3.3
- Hospital deaths of Medicare patients, actual and expected rates by diagnosis, and hospital characteristics, by instn, FY87-89, annual regional rpt, 4654–14.3

Index by Subjects and Names

Vitamins and nutrients

Housing census, 1990: inventory, occupancy, and costs, State fact sheet, 2326–21.48
Income (personal) per capita and by source, and earnings by industry div, by State, MSA, and county, 1984-89, annual regional rpt, 2704–2.4
Jail adult and juvenile population, employment, spending, instn conditions, and inmate programs, by county and facility, 1988, regional rpt series, 6068–144.4
Marriages, divorces, and rates, by characteristics of spouses, State, and county, 1987 and trends from 1920, US Vital Statistics annual rpt, 4144–4
Mineral Industry Surveys, State reviews of production, 1990, preliminary annual rpt, 5614–6
Minerals Yearbook, 1989, Vol 2: State review of production and sales by commodity, and business activity, annual rpt, 5604–16.48
Minerals Yearbook, 1989, Vol 2: State reviews of production, sales, and firms, by commodity, and business activity, annual rpt, 5604–34
Physicians, by specialty, age, sex, and location of training and practice, 1989, State rpt, 4116–6.48
Population and housing census, 1990: population and housing characteristics, households, and land area, by county, subdiv, and place, State rpt, 2551–1.48
Population and housing census, 1990: voting age and total population by race, and housing units, by block, redistricting counts required under PL 94-171, State CD-ROM release, 2551–6.10
Population and housing census, 1990: voting age and total population by race, and housing units, by county and city, redistricting counts required under PL 94-171, State summary rpt, 2551–5.47
Statistical Abstract of US, 1991 annual data compilation, 2324–1
Supplemental Security Income payments and beneficiaries, by type of eligibility, State, and county, Dec 1989, annual rpt, 4744–27.3
Textile production workers and wages by occupation, and benefits, by location, 1990 survey, 6787–6.251
Timber in Virginia, resources, growth, and removals, by species, ownership, treatment, and county, 1990-91, series, 1206–6
Water quality, chemistry, hydrology, and other characteristics, 1990 local area study, 5666–27.22
see also Alexandria, Va.
see also Arlington, Va.
see also Fairfax County, Va.
see also Loudoun County, Va.
see also Newport News, Va.
see also Norfolk, Va.
see also Petersburg, Va.
see also Prince William County, Va.
see also Richmond, Va.
see also Virginia Beach, Va.
see also under By State in the "Index by Categories"

Virginia Beach, Va.
Housing and households characteristics, unit and neighborhood quality, and journey to work by MSA location, for 11 MSAs, 1984 survey, supplement, 2485–8

Housing and households characteristics, 1988 survey, MSA fact sheet, 2485–11.9
Housing starts and completions authorized by building permits in 40 MSAs, quarterly rpt, 2382–9
Wages by occupation, and benefits for office and plant workers, 1990 survey, periodic MSA rpt, 6785–3.1
Wages by occupation, for office and plant workers, 1991 survey, periodic MSA rpt, 6785–3.7
see also under By City and By SMSA or MSA in the "Index by Categories"

Visalia, Calif.
see also under By SMSA or MSA in the "Index by Categories"

Visher, Christy
"Comparison of Urinalysis Technologies for Drug Testing in Criminal Justice", 6066–26.6

Vision
Eye exams average fees and waiting time to appointment, for optometrists and ophthalmologists, by region, 1989, article, 4042–3.238
see also Blind
see also Eye diseases and defects
see also Optometry

Vissage, John S.
"Forest Statistics for Alabama Counties, 1990", 1206–30.10
"Midsouth Veneer Industry", 1208–43

VISTA
Activities and funding of ACTION, by program, FY90, annual rpt, 9024–2

Vital statistics
Certificates of birth, death, marriage, and divorce, and fetal death and abortion rpts, 1989 natl standard revisions, 4147–4.27
Developing countries population and economic data, and AID dev projects, special study series, 9916–3
Foreign countries economic and social conditions, working paper series, 2326–18
Health condition and health care resources, use, and spending, 1950s-89, annual data compilation, 4144–11
Minority group health condition, services use, costs, and indicators of services need, 1950s-88, 4118–55
Natl Vital and Health Statistics Committee activities, FY90, annual narrative rpt, 4164–1
Palau admin, and social, economic, and govtl data, FY90, annual rpt, 7004–6
Registrars of vital statistics, US and Canada records offices, 1990 listing, 4208–34
State and Metro Area Data Book, 1991 data compilation, 2328–54
Statistical Abstract of US, 1991 annual data compilation, 2324–1.2
Survey programs and data collection procedures, Vital and Health Statistics series, 4147–1
Vital and Health Statistics series: advance data rpts, 4146–8
Vital and Health Statistics series and other NCHS rpts, 1990, annual listing, 4124–1
Vital and Health Statistics series: foreign and US comparative data, 4147–5
Vital and Health Statistics series: methodology, survey design, and data evaluation, 4147–2

Vital and Health Statistics series: natality, marriage, and divorce trends, 4147–21
Vital and Health Statistics series: reprints of advance data rpts, 4147–16
Vital and Health Statistics series: reprints of monthly rpt supplements, 4147–24
Vital statistics, preliminary 1989-90 and trends from 1950, annual rpt, 4144–7
Vital statistics provisional data, monthly rpt, 4142–1
Vital statistics provisional data, supplements to monthly rpts, series, 4146–5
see also Births
see also Child mortality
see also Deaths
see also Fertility
see also Infant mortality
see also Life expectancy
see also Marriage and divorce

Vitamins and nutrients
Black children's mineral levels in hair, serum, and urine, for healthy and anemic children, local area study, 1991 article, 4042–3.248
Cancer (breast) risk relation to dietary fat and nutrient intake, for Canada, 1982-87, article, 4472–1.204
Cancer (cervical) risk relation to blood selenium levels, local area study, 1991 article, 4472–1.203
Consumer research, food marketing, legislation, and regulation devs, and consumption and price trends, quarterly journal, 1541–7
Consumption of food, dietary composition, and nutrient intake, 1987/88 natl survey, preliminary rpt series, 1356–1
Exports and imports of US, by country and detailed commodity, monthly rpt, 2422–12
Exports and imports of US, by Harmonized System 6-digit commodity and country, 1990, annual rpt, 2424–13
Exports of US, detailed Schedule B commodities with countries of destination, 1990, annual rpt, 2424–10
Fluoride exposure by source, and health risks and benefits, with research results, 1930s-89, 4048–36
Food composition, detailed data on nutrients, calories, and waste, for raw, processed, and prepared foods, series, 1356–3
Heart disease deaths and risk factors, for PRC, Finland, and US, 1980s, article, 4042–3.202
Manufacturing annual survey, 1989: value of shipments, by SIC 4- to 5-digit product class, 2506–15.2
Minority group health condition, services use, costs, and indicators of services need, 1950s-88, 4118–55
Prenatal care nutritional and educational programs for women at risk of preterm delivery, and rate of anemia and low-weight births, 1985-86, article, 4042–3.235
Prescriptions for drugs, by drug type and brand, and for new drugs, 1989, annual rpt, 4064–12
Price indexes (producer), by stage of processing and detailed commodity, monthly rpt, 6762–6
Price indexes (producer), by stage of processing and detailed commodity, monthly 1990, annual rpt, 6764–2

Vitamins and nutrients

Shipments, trade, and use of drugs, by product, 1990, annual Current Industrial Rpt, 2506–8.5

Statistical Abstract of US, 1991 annual data compilation, 2324–1.3

see also Cholesterol

Vocational education and training

- Appalachia education system, improvement initiatives, and indicators of success, by State, 1960s-89, 9088–36
- County Business Patterns, 1988: employment, establishments, and payroll, by SIC 2- to 4-digit industry and county, annual State rpt series, 2326–6
- County Business Patterns, 1989: employment, establishments, and payroll, by SIC 2- to 4-digit industry and county, annual State rpt series, 2326–8
- Data collection activities and programs of NCES, 1991, annual listing, 4824–7
- *Digest of Education Statistics*, 1991 annual data compilation, 4824–2
- Elementary and secondary education enrollment, staff, finances, operations, programs, and policies, 1987/88 biennial survey, series, 4836–3
- Elementary and secondary public schools, enrollment, teachers, funding, and other characteristics, by region and State, 1988/89, annual rpt, 4834–20
- Employment programs, training, and unemployment compensation, current devs and grants to States, press release series, 6406–2
- Enrollment, by grade, instn type and control, and student characteristics, 1989 and trends from 1947, annual Current Population Rpt, 2546–1.453
- Enrollment in public elementary and secondary schools, and facilities, by State, 1989/90, annual rpt, 4834–17
- Foreign countries labor conditions, union coverage, and work accidents, annual country rpt series, 6366–4
- Higher education course completions, by detailed program, sex, race, and instn type, for 1972 high school class, as of 1984, 4888–4
- Higher education vocational training performance measurement by States, activities and related legislation, 1989/90, 4808–33
- Homeless adults educational services, funding, participation, and staff, by State, 1989, annual rpt series, 4804–39
- Homeless persons aid programs of Fed Govt, program descriptions and funding, by agency and State, FY87-90, annual GAO rpt, 26104–21
- Indian education funding of Fed Govt, and enrollment, degrees, and program grants and fellowships by State, late 1960s-FY89, annual rpt, 14874–1
- Juvenile correctional and detention public and private instns, inmates, and expenses, by instn and resident characteristics and State, 1987, biennial rpt, 6064–13
- Labor laws enacted, by State, 1990, annual article, 6722–1.209
- Minority group higher education enrollment, degrees, factors affecting participation, and earnings, 1960s-88, 4808–29
- Occupational injury and illness rates, by SIC 2- to 4-digit industry, 1988-89, annual rpt, 6844–7

Occupational injury and illness rates, by SIC 2- to 4-digit industry, 1989, annual rpt, 6844–1

- Participants characteristics, effectiveness, and benefits of vocational training and education programs, 1980s, GAO rpt, 26121–431
- Private elementary and secondary schools, students, and staff characteristics, various periods 1979-88, 4838–47
- Service industries census, 1987: depreciable assets, capital and operating expenses, and receipts, by SIC 2- to 4-digit kind of business, 2393–2
- Service industries census, 1987: establishments, receipts by source, payroll, and employment, by SIC 2- to 4-digit kind of business, State, and MSA, 2393–4
- Veterans education aid under GI Bill and other programs, and participation by period of service and State, FY89, annual rpt, 8604–9
- Veterans education benefits and job training, and other VA activities, FY90, annual rpt, 8604–3.7

see also Adult education

see also Apprenticeship

see also Employee development

see also Federal aid to vocational education

see also Industrial arts

see also Manpower training programs

see also Sheltered workshops

see also Vocational guidance

see also Vocational rehabilitation

Vocational guidance

Occupational Outlook Quarterly, journal, 6742–1

Vocational rehabilitation

- Blind-operated vending facilities on Federal and non-Federal property, finances and operations by agency and State, FY90, annual rpt, 4944–2
- Education (special) enrollment by age, staff, funding, and needs, by type of handicap and State, 1989/90, annual rpt, 4944–4
- Education Dept programs funding, operations, and effectiveness, FY90, annual rpt, 4804–5
- Employer tax credit for hiring from groups with high unemployment rates, participation by State, and effectiveness, FY88, GAO rpt, 26121–407
- Expenditures for public welfare by program, FY50s-88, annual article, 4742–1.209
- Fed Govt and State rehabilitation activities and funding, FY90, annual rpt, 4944–1
- Govt spending, coverage, and benefits for social welfare programs, late 1930s-89, annual rpt, 4744–3.1
- Minimum wage exemption certificates and employment under Fair Labor Standards Act, FY88-89, annual rpt, 6504–2.1
- OASDI benefit payments, trust fund finances, and economic and demographic assumptions, 1970-90 and alternative projections to 2000, actuarial rpt, 4706–1.105
- *State and Metro Area Data Book*, 1991 data compilation, 2328–54
- States vocational rehabilitation agency cases and disposition, by State, FY90 and trends from FY21, annual rpt, 4944–5
- States vocational rehabilitation agency cases by disposition and applicant characteristics, and closures by reason, FY84-88, annual rpt, 4944–6

Index by Subjects and Names

- States vocational rehabilitation agency cases rejected, by reason, applicant characteristics, and selected State, annual report, suspended, 4944–11
- States vocational rehabilitation programs, service provision based on severity of client disability, evaluation, FY88, GAO rpt, 26121–438
- *Statistical Abstract of US*, 1991 annual data compilation, 2324–1.12
- Workers compensation laws of States and Fed Govt, 1991 semiannual rpt, 6502–1

see also Sheltered workshops

see also Veterans rehabilitation

Vocke, Gary

"Impact of Environmental Safeguards on the Livestock Sector", 1522–3.204

Voelker, David C.

"Quality of Water from Public-Supply Wells in Principal Aquifers of Illinois, 1984-87", 5666–28.5

Voice of America

Broadcasting operating budgets for US Govt overseas radio and TV services, FY88 and FY91, annual rpt, 17594–1

Voith, Richard

- "Property Taxes, Homeownership Capitalization Rates, and Housing Consumption", 9387–8.252
- "Transportation, Sorting, and House Values in the Philadelphia Metropolitan Area", 9387–8.231

Volcanoes

- Alaska minerals resources and geologic characteristics, compilation of papers, 1989, annual rpt, 5664–15
- Alaska OCS environmental conditions and oil dev impacts, compilation of papers, series, 2176–1
- Foreign countries disasters, casualties, damage, and aid by US and others, FY90 and trends from FY64, annual rpt, 9914–12
- Gazetteer of US places, mountains, bodies of water, and other political and physical features, 1990 rpt, 5668–117
- Incidents and mgmt of disasters and natl security threats, with data by major event and State, 1991 annual rpt, 9434–6

Vollrath, Thomas L.

- "Are Most-Favored-Nation Exclusions in the Interests of Developing Countries?", 1524–4.2
- "Developing Countries as a Source of U.S. Export Growth", 1524–4.2
- "Influence of the Commodity Composition of Trade on Economic Growth", 1502–3.202

Voluntary military service

- Budget of DOD, manpower needs, costs, and force readiness by service branch, FY92, annual rpt, 3504–1
- Enlistments and reenlistment rates, by service branch, FY79-90, annual rpt, 3544–1.2
- Enlistments and reenlistment rates, by service branch, quarterly rpt, 3542–14.4
- Enlistments and reenlistments, by race, sex, and service branch, quarterly press release, 3542–7
- Natl Guard activities, personnel, and facilities, FY90, annual rpt, 3504–22
- Navy budget, personnel, procurement, and equipment, planned FY91-93, annual fact sheet, 3804–16

Index by Subjects and Names

Wall coverings

Personnel active duty and recruit social, economic, and parents characteristics, by service branch and State, FY89, annual rpt, 3544–41

Personnel of DOD, and organization, budget, weapons, and property, by service branch, State, and country, 1991 annual summary rpt, 3504–13

Reserve forces personnel strengths and characteristics, by component, FY90, annual rpt, 3544–38

Reserve forces personnel strengths and characteristics, by component, quarterly rpt, 3542–4

Statistical Abstract of US, 1991 annual data compilation, 2324–1.11

Women military personnel on active and reserve duty, by demographic and service characteristics and service branch, FY89, annual chartbook, 3544–26

Youth natl service program proposal, operations and youth attitudes, 1990 rpt, 26306–3.115

see also Selective service

Volunteers

- ACTION activities and funding, by program, FY90, annual rpt, 9024–2
- Child abuse and neglect victims representation in legal proceedings, caseloads, State requirements, and compensation, by State and county, 1989, 4608–28
- Children and youth social, economic, and demographic characteristics, 1950s-90, 4818–5
- Drug and alcohol abuse treatment facilities, services, use, funding, staff, and client characteristics, 1989, biennial rpt, 4494–10
- Education data compilation, 1991 annual rpt, 4824–2
- Education services for homeless adults, funding, participation, and staff, by State, 1989, annual rpt series, 4804–39
- Forest Service acreage, staff, finances, and mgmt activities in Pacific Northwest, with data by forest, 1970s-89, annual rpt, 1204–37
- Forest Service activities and finances, by region and State, FY90, annual rpt, 1204–1.4
- Head Start enrollment, funding, and staff, FY90, annual rpt, 4604–8
- High school and college grads employment status and income, 1991 edition, annual rpt, 4824–2.28
- Hospices operations, services, costs, and patient characteristics, for instns without Medicare certification, FY85-86, 4658–52
- Hours and weeks served, type of organization, whether otherwise employed, and other characteristics of volunteers, 1989, article, 6722–1.213
- Juvenile correctional and detention public and private instns, inmates, and expenses, by instn and resident characteristics and State, 1987, biennial rpt, 6064–13
- Land Mgmt Bur activities in Southwestern US, FY90, annual rpt, 5724–15
- Older persons migration to southern coastal areas, household finances, services needs, and local economic impacts, for selected counties, 1990, 2068–38

Peace Corps activities, funding by program, and volunteers, by country, FY92, annual rpt, 9654–1

Schools (private elementary and secondary), students, and staff characteristics, various periods 1979-88, 4838–47

Statistical Abstract of US, 1991 annual data compilation, 2324–1.12

Tutoring and mentoring of disadvantaged elementary and secondary students by college students, program and participant characteristics, 1989, 4808–23

Women's employment and educational experiences compared to men, for high school class of 1972, natl longitudinal study, as of 1986, 4888–6

Youth natl service program proposal, operations and youth attitudes, 1990 rpt, 26306–3.115

see also Foster Grandparent Program

see also Retired Senior Volunteer Program

see also Senior Companion Program

see also Student Community Service Program

see also VISTA

see also Voluntary military service

Volunteers in Service to America *see* VISTA

Von Korff, Michael

"Is Battered Women's Help Seeking Connected to the Level of Their Abuse?", 4042–3.228

Voshell, Laura

"Two Notes on Relating the Risk of Disclosure for Microdata and Geographic Area Size", 2626–10.137

Voting

see Elections

Vroman, Wayne

"Decline in Unemployment Insurance Claims Activity in the 1980s", 6406–6.33

Vroomen, Harry

"Direct Approach for Estimating Nitrogen, Phosphorus, and Land Demands at the Regional Level", 1588–152

Vuono, Carl E.

"Maintaining a Trained and Ready Total Force for the 1990s and Beyond. A Statement on the Posture of the U.S. Army, FY92-93", 3704–13

Wabnick, Richard

"Debt Burden Facing College Graduates", 4808–26

Waco, Tex.

Wages by occupation, and benefits for office and plant workers, 1991 survey, periodic MSA rpt, 6785–3.8

see also under By City and By SMSA or MSA in the "Index by Categories"

Wage controls

see also Minimum wage

Wage deductions

- Child support overdue payments deducted from wages, by State, FY85-89, annual rpt, 4694–6
- Securities (govt) purchases and holdings of individuals and households, terms, and purchase methods, 1980s-90, 8008–148
- *see also* Employee benefits
- *see also* Social security tax
- *see also* Unemployment insurance tax
- *see also* Withholding tax

Wage garnishment

see Wage deductions

Wage surveys

see also Area wage surveys

see also Industry wage surveys

Wages and salaries

- *see* Agricultural wages
- *see* Earnings, general
- *see* Earnings, local and regional
- *see* Earnings, specific industry
- *see* Educational employees pay
- *see* Federal pay
- *see* Government pay
- *see* Labor costs and cost indexes
- *see* Minimum wage
- *see* Payroll
- *see* Professionals' fees
- *see* State and local employees pay

Wagner, Joachim

"More on the International Similarity of Interindustry Wage Differentials: Evidence from the Federal Republic of Germany and the U.S.", 9366–6.281

Wagner-Peyser Act

- Employment services local offices operations, State and Federal oversight, staff, and costs, 1983-91, GAO rpt, 26121–430
- Grants under Wagner-Peyser Act, by State, 1991-92, press release, 6406–2.31

Wailes, Eric J.

"U.S. Rice Imports and Domestic Use", 1561–8.206

Wake Island

- Economic, social, political, and geographic summary data, by country, 1991, annual factbook, 9114–2
- HHS financial aid, by program, recipient, State, and city, FY90, annual regional listing, 4004–3.9

Wakefield, Joseph C.

"Federal Fiscal Programs", 2702–1.204

Wales

see United Kingdom

Walker, Clarice

"Parental Drug Abuse and African American Children in Foster Care: Issues and Study Findings", 4008–114

Walker County, Ala.

Housing and households characteristics, unit and neighborhood quality, and journey to work by MSA location, for 11 MSAs, 1984 survey, supplement, 2485–8

Walker, Retia S.

"Income and Expenditure Patterns of Consumer Units with Reference Person Age 70 to 79 and 80 or Older", 1702–1.204

Wall coverings

- Exports and imports between US and outlying areas, by detailed commodity and mode of transport, 1990, annual rpt, 2424–11
- Exports and imports of US, by country and detailed commodity, monthly rpt, 2422–12
- Exports of US, detailed Schedule B commodities with countries of destination, 1990, annual rpt, 2424–10
- Price indexes (producer), by stage of processing and detailed commodity, monthly rpt, 6762–6
- Price indexes (producer), by stage of processing and detailed commodity, monthly 1990, annual rpt, 6764–2

Wall, Larry D.

Wall, Larry D.
"Southeastern Interstate Banking and Consolidation: 1984-89", 9371–1.203

Walla Walla, Wash.
Wages by occupation, for office and plant workers, 1991 survey, periodic MSA rpt, 6785–3.6

Wallace, George B.
"State Credit Subsidy Programs for Agricultural Producers", 1541–1.201

Wallack, Stanley S.
"Medicare Risk Contracting: Determinants of Market Entry", 4652–1.226

Waller, Anna E.
"Childhood Injury: State-by-State Mortality Facts", 4108–54

Waller, Robert R.
"National AIDS Hotline: HIV and AIDS Information Service Through a Toll-Free Telephone System", 4042–3.256

Walnuts
see Nuts

Walraven, Nicholas
"Update on the Farm Economy", 9362–1.207

Walruses
see Marine mammals

Walter, Martha
"Silent Killer—Hypothermia", 2152–8.204

Wang, Ping
"Human Capital and Endogenous Growth: Evidence from Taiwan", 9371–10.55
"Money Demand and Relative Prices in the German Hyperinflation", 9371–10.66

War
Claims against foreign govts by US natls, by claim type and country, 1990, annual rpt, 6004–16
Foreign countries disasters, casualties, damage, and aid by US and others, FY90 and trends from FY64, annual rpt, 9914–12
Participants and casualties in principal US wars, by service branch, 1775-1973, annual rpt, 3544–1.2
Participants and casualties in principal US wars, 1775-1973, annual summary rpt, 3504–13
Participants, deaths, veterans living, and compensation and pension recipients, for each US war, 1775-1990, annual rpt, 8604–2
see also Arms control and disarmament
see also Chemical and biological warfare agents
see also Civil defense
see also Military intervention
see also Military invasion and occupation
see also Military science
see also Military strategy
see also National defense
see also Prisoners of war
see also Veterans
see also Veterans benefits and pensions
see also War casualties
see also War relief

War casualties
Casualties and participants in principal US wars, by service branch, 1775-1973, annual rpt, 3544–1.2
Casualties and participants in principal US wars, 1775-1973, annual summary rpt, 3504–13
Deaths and rates, by detailed cause and demographic characteristics, 1988 and trends from 1900, US Vital Statistics annual rpt, 4144–2

Deaths by cause, age, race, and rank, and personnel captured and missing, by service branch, FY90, annual rpt, 3544–40
Deaths, participants, veterans living, and compensation and pension recipients, for each US war, 1775-1990, annual rpt, 8604–2
Foreign countries disasters, casualties, damage, and aid by US and others, FY90 and trends from FY64, annual rpt, 9914–12
Persian Gulf War Operation Desert Shield and Desert Storm deployment and deaths by selected personnel characteristics, 1990-91, annual rpt supplement, 3544–41.2

War prisoners
see Prisoners of war

War relief
Foreign countries disasters, casualties, damage, and aid by US and others, FY90 and trends from FY64, annual rpt, 9914–12
Iraq invasion of Kuwait, alien worker refugees fleeing from Iraq and Kuwait, intl aid by source, and costs to host and native countries, 1990-91, GAO rpt, 26123–326
Panama economic aid after US sanctions and military invasion, AID funding by program, as of 1991, GAO rpt, 26123–330
World War I debt to US of foreign govts, by country and program, periodic rpt, 8002–6

Ward, David H.
"Response of Brant and Other Geese to Aircraft Disturbances at Izembek Lagoon, Alaska", 5738–23

Ward, Elizabeth
"Excess Number of Bladder Cancers in Workers Exposed to Ortho-Toluidine and Aniline", 4472–1.209
"Lung Cancer Incidence Among Patients with Beryllium Disease: A Cohort Mortality Study", 4472–1.224

Wards, city
Census of Population and Housing, 1990: voting age and total population by race, and housing units, by block, redistricting counts required under PL 94-171, State CD-ROM series, 2551–6

Warehouses
Agricultural Stabilization and Conservation Service producer payments, by program and State, 1990, annual table, 1804–12
Arson incidents by whether structure occupied, property value, and arrest rate, by property type, 1990, annual rpt, 6224–2.1
Census of Transportation, 1987: finances and operations by size, ownership, and State, and revenues by MSA, by SIC 2- to 4-digit industry, 2579–1
Construction industries census, 1987: establishments, employment, receipts, and expenditures, by SIC 4-digit industry and State, final industry rpt series, 2373–1
Construction put in place, private and public, by type and region, monthly rpt, annual tables, 2382–4
Cotton ginning activity and charges, by State, 1990/91, annual rpt, 1564–3

County Business Patterns, 1988: employment, establishments, and payroll, by SIC 2- to 4-digit industry and county, annual State rpt series, 2326–6
County Business Patterns, 1989: employment, establishments, and payroll, by SIC 2- to 4-digit industry and county, annual State rpt series, 2326–8
Customs Service activities, collections, entries processed by mode of transport, and seizures, FY86-90, annual rpt, 8144–1
Employment, earnings, and hours, by SIC 1- to 4-digit industry, monthly and annual averages, selected years 1909-90, annual rpt, 6744–4
Employment related to agriculture, by industry, region, and metro-nonmetro location, 1987, 1598–271
Energy use in commercial buildings, costs, and conservation, by building characteristics, survey rpt series, 3166–8
Enterprise Statistics, 1987: auxiliaries of multi-establishment firms, finances and operations by function, industry, and State, 2329–6
Enterprise Statistics, 1987: finances and operations for companies, by size, level of diversification, form of organization, and industry group, 2329–8
Finances of warehouse services, by SIC 2- to 4-digit industry, 1989 survey, annual rpt, 2413–14
Foreign trade zones (US) operations and movement of goods, by zone and commodity, FY88, annual rpt, 2044–30
Occupational injury and illness rates, by SIC 2- to 4-digit industry, 1988-89, annual rpt, 6844–7
Occupational injury and illness rates, by SIC 2- to 4-digit industry, 1989, annual rpt, 6844–1
Oil and fat production, consumption by end use, and stocks, by type, quarterly Current Industrial Rpt, 2506–4.4
Puerto Rico economic censuses, 1987: warehouse storage space, and establishment sales, by wholesale kind of business, subject rpt, 2591–2.2
Savings instns failures, inventory of real estate assets available from Resolution Trust Corp, 1990, semiannual listing, 9722–2.4
Savings instns failures, inventory of real estate assets available from Resolution Trust Corp, 1991, semiannual listing, 9722–2.10
Statistical Abstract of US, 1991 annual data compilation, 2324–1.21
Tax (income) returns of partnerships, income statement and balance sheet items, by industry group, 1989, annual article, 8302–2.216; 8304–18
Tax (income) returns of sole proprietorships, income statement items, by industry group, 1989, annual article, 8302–2.214
Tobacco marketing activity, prices, and sales, by grade, type, market, and State, 1989-90, annual rpt series, 1319–5
see also Cold storage and refrigeration
see also Grain storage and facilities
see also under By Industry in the "Index by Categories"

Index by Subjects and Names

Washington State

Waring, George H.

"Survey of Federally-Funded Marine Mammal Research and Studies, FY74-90", 14734–2

Warner Robins, Ga.

Wages by occupation, for office and plant workers, 1990 survey, periodic MSA rpt, 6785–3.2

see also under By SMSA or MSA in the "Index by Categories"

Warnick, Rodney B.

"Market Share Analysis of Selected Recreation Activities in the Northeastern U.S.: 1979-87", 1208–356

Warren, Debra D.

"Production, Prices, Employment, and Trade in Northwest Forest Industries", 1202–3

Warren, Hugh

"Catfish Industry Perspective", 1004–16.1

Warren, Mich.

see also under By City in the "Index by Categories"

Warren, Ohio

see also under By SMSA or MSA in the "Index by Categories"

Warren, Robert

"Annual Estimates of Nonimmigrant Overstays in the U.S.: 1985-88", 6264–5

Warsaw Pact

Helsinki Final Act implementation by NATO and Warsaw Pact, Apr 1990-Mar 1991, last issue of semiannual rpt, 7002–1

Military forces reductions of NATO and Warsaw Pact under proposed treaty, and US budget savings, 1990 rpt, 26306–3.114

Warshawsky, Mark J.

"Financial Accounting for Pensions: Measures of Funding Status", 9366–6.259

"Impact of Liabilities for Retiree Health Benefits on Share Prices", 9366–6.270

"Projections of Health Care Expenditures as a Share of GNP: Actuarial and Economic Approaches", 9366–6.284

Warships

see Naval vessels

Warwick, R.I.

Housing and households characteristics, unit and neighborhood quality, and journey to work by MSA location, for 11 MSAs, 1984 survey, supplement, 2485–8

Housing and households characteristics, 1988 survey, MSA fact sheet, 2485–11.10

Housing and households detailed characteristics, and unit and neighborhood quality, by location, 1988 survey, MSA rpt, 2485–6.7

Wash, Darrel P.

"Child Day Care Services: An Industry at a Crossroads", 6722–1.202

Washington

see D.C.

see Washington State

Washington Metropolitan Area Transit Authority

Budget of US, authoritative financial statements with appropriations, outlays, and receipts, by category and agency, FY90, annual rpt, 8104–2.1

Budget of US, obligations and authority by function, agency, and program, with summaries, analyses, and historical tables, FY92, annual rpt, 104–2

Washington National Airport

Airline control issues and availability of facilities and aircraft, impacts on market entry and flight delays, 1985-89 with projections to 1997, 7308–199.8

Washington State

Banks (insured commercial and savings) deposits by instn, State, MSA, and county, as of June 1990, annual regional rpt, 9295–3.6

Birds (northern spotted owl) population and reproduction rate on lands open and closed to logging, estimation methodology, 1987, 1208–342

Coal production and mines by county, prices, productivity, miners, and reserves, by mining method and State, 1989-90, annual rpt, 3164–25

Coastal and offshore marine sanctuaries proposal for Washington, environmental and economic impacts, with background data, 1984-89, 2178–30

Coastal areas pollutant concentrations in fish and sediments, by contaminant, fish species, and Pacific coast site, 1984-86, 2168–121

County Business Patterns, 1989: employment, establishments, and payroll, by SIC 2- to 4-digit industry and county, annual State rpt, 2326–8.49

Cranberry production, prices, use, and acreage, for selected States, 1989-90 and forecast 1991, annual rpt, 1621–18.4

DOD prime contract awards, by contractor, service branch, State, and city, FY90, annual rpt, 3544–22

Energy-efficiency building codes, effect on house construction practices in Bonneville Power Admin service areas, 1987, 3228–15

Fed Govt spending in States and local areas, by type, State, county, and city, FY90, annual rpt, 2464–3

Fed Govt spending in States, by type, program, agency, and State, FY90, annual rpt, 2464–2

Fish (salmon and trout) wild and hatchery juvenile population and characteristics, for Pacific Northwest, 1981-85, 2168–123

Fish and shellfish catch, wholesale receipts, prices, trade, and other market activities, weekly regional rpt, 2162–6.5

Forest Service acreage, staff, finances, and mgmt activities in Pacific Northwest, with data by forest, 1970s-89, annual rpt, 1204–37

Hazelnut production, 1989-91, annual rpt, 1621–18.5

HHS financial aid, by program, recipient, State, and city, FY90, annual regional listing, 4004–3.10

Hospices use by cancer patients, by service type, use of other facilities, patient and instn characteristics, and other indicators, local area study, 1980-85, 4658–53

Hospital deaths of Medicare patients, actual and expected rates by diagnosis, and hospital characteristics, by instn, FY87-89, annual regional rpt, 4654–14.10

Income (personal) per capita and by source, and earnings by industry div, by State, MSA, and county, 1984-89, annual regional rpt, 2704–2.5

Jail adult and juvenile population, employment, spending, instn conditions,

and inmate programs, by county and facility, 1988, regional rpt series, 6068–144.5

Land Mgmt Bur activities and finances, and public land acreage and use, FY90, annual State rpt, 5724–11.1

Lumber industry workers and wages by occupation, 1990 survey, annual State rpt, 6787–7.1

Marine mammals and birds population and distribution, by species and northeast Pacific Ocean location, literature and data base review, 1950s-88, 5738–28

Marriages, divorces, and rates, by characteristics of spouses, State, and county, 1987 and trends from 1920, US Vital Statistics annual rpt, 4144–4

Medicaid prepaid plans for physician services, characteristics of selected plans in 4 States, various periods 1983-89, article, 4652–1.228

Mineral Industry Surveys, State reviews of production, 1990, preliminary annual rpt, 5614–6

Minerals Yearbook, 1989, Vol 2: State review of production and sales by commodity, and business activity, annual rpt, 5604–16.49

Minerals Yearbook, 1989, Vol 2: State reviews of production, sales, and firms, by commodity, and business activity, annual rpt, 5604–34

Physicians, by specialty, age, sex, and location of training and practice, 1989, State rpt, 4116–6.49

Population and housing census, 1990: population and housing characteristics, households, and land area, by county, subdiv, and place, State rpt, 2551–1.49

Population and housing census, 1990: voting age and total population by race, and housing units, by block, redistricting counts required under PL 94-171, State CD-ROM release, 2551–6.2

Population and housing census, 1990: voting age and total population by race, and housing units, by county and city, redistricting counts required under PL 94-171, State summary rpt, 2551–5.48

Radiation exposure of population near Hanford, Wash, nuclear plant, with methodology, 1944-66, series, 3356–5

Radioactive low-level waste disposal activities of States and interstate compacts, with data by disposal facility and reactor, 1989, annual rpt, 3354–14

Recreation (outdoor) facilities on public land, use, and Land Mgmt Bur mgmt activities, funding, and plans, 1990 State rpt, 5726–5.3

Seals (harbor) population and physical characteristics at selected Washington State coastal sites, 1975-80, 14738–7

Soil and water conditions, land use, and conservation needs on non-Federal lands, 1982 and 1987, State rpt, 1266–5.2

Statistical Abstract of US, 1991 annual data compilation, 2324–1

Supplemental Security Income payments and beneficiaries, by type of eligibility, State, and county, Dec 1989, annual rpt, 4744–27.10

Timber in northwestern US and British Columbia, production, prices, trade, and employment, quarterly rpt, 1202–3

Washington State

Timber industry impacts of northern spotted owl conservation in Pacific Northwest, and local govts Federal payments and severance taxes, 1980s and projected to 2000, hearing, 21168–50

Timber industry impacts of northern spotted owl conservation in Pacific Northwest, and worker aid programs, 1980s and projected to 2000, hearing, 21728–76

Timber industry impacts of northern spotted owl conservation in Pacific Northwest, 1980s and alternative projections to 2000, hearings, 21168–45

Timber sales of Forest Service, impacts of northern spotted owl conservation in Pacific Northwest, 1990 hearing, 21168–47

Water (groundwater) supply, quality, chemistry, and use, 1982-85, local area rpt, 5666–28.11

Water supply and quality in streams and lakes, and groundwater levels in wells, by drainage basin, 1990, annual State rpt, 5666–10.44

Water supply, and snow survey results, monthly State rpt, 1266–2.9

Water supply, and snow survey results, 1990, annual State rpt, 1264–14.1

see also Bellingham, Wash.

see also Bremerton, Wash.

see also Everett, Wash.

see also Kelso, Wash.

see also Kennewick, Wash.

see also Longview, Wash.

see also Pasco, Wash.

see also Richland, Wash.

see also Seattle, Wash.

see also Shelton, Wash.

see also Spokane, Wash.

see also Tacoma, Wash.

see also Vancouver, Wash.

see also Walla Walla, Wash.

see also Yakima, Wash.

see also under By State in the "Index by Categories"

Waste management

see Hazardous waste and disposal

see Landfills

see Radioactive waste and disposal

see Recycling of waste materials

see Refuse and refuse disposal

see Sewage and wastewater systems

Wastewater treatment

see Sewage and wastewater systems

Watches and clocks

County Business Patterns, 1988: employment, establishments, and payroll, by SIC 2- to 4-digit industry and county, annual State rpt series, 2326–6

County Business Patterns, 1989: employment, establishments, and payroll, by SIC 2- to 4-digit industry and county, annual State rpt series, 2326–8

CPI by component for US city average, and by region, population size, and for 27 metro areas, monthly rpt, 6762–2

Employment, earnings, and hours, by SIC 1- to 4-digit industry, monthly and annual averages, selected years 1909-90, annual rpt, 6744–4

Exports and imports of US, by country and detailed commodity, monthly rpt, 2422–12

Exports and imports of US, by Harmonized System 6-digit commodity and country, 1990, annual rpt, 2424–13

Exports and imports of US, by transport mode, country, and SITC 1- to 3-digit commodity, 1990, annual rpt, 2424–12

Exports of US, detailed Schedule B commodities with countries of destination, 1990, annual rpt, 2424–10

Imports purchasing decisions of consumers, importance of brand name, authenticity, origin, and other factors, 1984 survey, hearing, 25528–115

Injuries from use of consumer products, by severity, victim age, and detailed product, 1990, annual rpt, 9164–6

Manufacturing census, 1987: employment and shipments under Fed Govt contracts, by SIC 4-digit industry, 2497–7

Manufacturing census, 1987: finances and operations, by SIC 2- to 4-digit industry, State, and MSA, with trends from 1849, 2497–1

Manufacturing census, 1987: finances and operations, by type of organization and SIC 2- to 4-digit industry, subject rpt, 2497–5

Occupational injury and illness rates, by SIC 2- to 4-digit industry, 1989, annual rpt, 6844–1

OECD trade, total and for 4 major countries, and US trade by country, by commodity, 1970-89, world area rpt series, 9116–1

Price indexes (producer), by stage of processing and detailed commodity, monthly rpt, 6762–6

Price indexes (producer), by stage of processing and detailed commodity, monthly 1990, annual rpt, 6764–2

Water area

Acreage of non-Federal land by use, soil and water conditions, and conservation needs, 1987, State rpt series, 1266–5

Acreage of wetlands, water, and land, by State, 1780s and 1980s, 5508–107

Army Corps of Engineers water resources dev projects, characteristics, and costs, 1950s-89, biennial State rpt series, 3756–1

Army Corps of Engineers water resources dev projects, characteristics, and costs, 1950s-91, biennial State rpt series, 3756–2

Census of Population and Housing, 1990: voting age and total population by race, and housing units, by block, redistricting counts required under PL 94-171, State CD-ROM series, 2551–6

Coastal and estuarine environmental conditions, research results and methodology, series, 2176–7

Coastal and riparian areas environmental conditions, fish, wildlife, use, and mgmt, for individual ecosystems, series, 5506–9

Coastal areas recreation facilities of Fed Govt and States, visitor and site characteristics, 1987-90 survey, regional rpt series, 2176–9

Estuary environmental conditions, and fish and shellfish catch by species and region, 1980s, 2178–27

Foreign countries economic, social, political, and geographic summary data, by country, 1991, annual factbook, 9114–2

Forest Service mgmt of public lands and resources dev, environmental, economic, and social impacts of alternative programs, projected to 2040, 1208–24

Index by Subjects and Names

Great Lakes area economic conditions and outlook, for US and Canada, 1970s-90, 9375–15

Park natl system and other land under Natl Park Service mgmt, acreage by site, ownership, and region, FY91, semiannual rpt, 5542–1

Public lands acreage and use, and Land Mgmt Bur activities and finances, annual State rpt series, 5724–11

Public lands acreage, grants, use, revenues, and allocations, by State, FY90 and trends, annual rpt, 5724–1

Recreation (outdoor) coastal facilities, by State, county, estuary, and level of govt, 1972-84, 2178–29

Reservoirs capacity and area, by reservoir and State, 1988, 5668–120

State and Metro Area Data Book, 1991 data compilation, 2328–54

Statistical Abstract of US, 1991 annual data compilation, 2324–1.6

Tennessee Valley river control activities, and hydroelectric power generation and capacity, 1989, annual rpt, 9804–7

Water quality, chemistry, hydrology, and other characteristics, local area studies, series, 5666–27

Water supply and quality in streams and lakes, and groundwater levels in wells, by drainage basin, 1988, annual State rpt series, 5666–16

Water supply and quality in streams and lakes, and groundwater levels in wells, by drainage basin, 1989, annual State rpt series, 5666–12

Water supply and quality in streams and lakes, and groundwater levels in wells, by drainage basin, 1990, annual State rpt series, 5666–10

Wetlands (riparian) acreage, and Bur of Land Mgmt activities, mgmt plans, and scientific staff, State rpt series, 5726–8

Wetlands acreage, resources, soil and water properties, and conservation efforts, by wetland type, State rpt series, 5506–11

see also Water supply and use

Water fluoridation

Exposure to fluoride by source, and health risks and benefits, findings and recommendations, 1991 rpt, 4206–2.43

Exposure to fluoride by source, and health risks and benefits, with research results, 1930s-89, 4048–36

Health condition improvement and disease prevention goals and recommended activities for 2000, with trends 1970s-80s, 4048–10

Water permits

Coastal and riparian areas environmental conditions, fish, wildlife, use, and mgmt, for individual ecosystems, series, 5506–9

Coastal areas environmental and socioeconomic conditions, and potential impact of oil and gas OCS leases, final statement series, 5736–1

Water pollution

Abatement spending by govts, business, and consumers, 1987-89, annual article, 2702–1.229

Abatement spending, capital and operating costs by SIC 2-digit industry, 1989, advance annual Current Industrial Rpt, 2506–3.6

Index by Subjects and Names

Water resources development

Acid rain and air pollution environmental impacts, and methods of neutralizing acidified water bodies, summary research rpt series, 5506–5

Acid rain effects on Maine streams water quality, acidity, and fish, 1986-87, 9208–130

Agricultural Conservation Program participation and payments, by practice and State, FY90, annual rpt, 1804–7

Agricultural Stabilization and Conservation Service producer payments and certificate value, by program, monthly rpt, 1802–10

Agricultural Stabilization and Conservation Service producer payments, by program and State, 1990, annual table, 1804–12

Agricultural trade impacts of environmental regulation, with indicators of pollution and fertilizer use intensity by crop, 1991 article, 1522–3.203

Army Corps of Engineers water resources dev projects, characteristics, and costs, 1950s-89, biennial State rpt series, 3756–1

Army Corps of Engineers water resources dev projects, characteristics, and costs, 1950s-91, biennial State rpt series, 3756–2

Assistance (financial and nonfinancial) of Fed Govt, 1991 base edition with supplements, annual listing, 104–5

Coastal and estuarine environmental conditions, research results and methodology, series, 2176–7

Coastal and riparian areas environmental conditions, fish, wildlife, use, and mgmt, for individual ecosystems, series, 5506–9

Conservation Reserve Program acreage, plantings, and impacts on farm production, soil erosion, water quality, and wildlife habitat, 1991 conf, 1208–360

Costs of environmental protection programs to govts and households, by program type and city size, 1960s-88 and projected to 2000, 9188–114

Cotton farms fertilizer, pesticide and irrigation use, soil conservation practices, and water quality impacts, 1989, 1588–151

Electric utilities privately owned, pollution abatement outlays by type of pollutant and equipment, and firm, 1989, annual rpt, 3164–23

Environmental Quality, status of problems, protection programs, research, and intl issues, 1991 annual rpt, 484–1

EPA and State govt identification of polluted water locations and sources, activities, 1991, GAO rpt, 26113–536

EPA pollution control grant program activities, monthly rpt, 9182–8

Farm chemicals use and animal wastes sources of groundwater pollution, and reduction strategies, 1960s-90, 26358–231

Farm chemicals use sources of groundwater pollution, with background data and farmers views, 1970s-80s, hearing, 25168–76

Farm finances and environmental benefits of alternative policies to Food Security Act conservation programs, projected 1991-2005, 1588–153

Fish kills from water pollution, by pollution source, month, location, and State, 1977-87, last issue of annual rpt, 9204–3

Fish kills in coastal areas related to pollution and natural causes, by land use, State, and county, 1980s, 2178–32

Fishery research of State fish and wildlife agencies, federally funded projects and costs by species and State, 1990, annual listing, 5504–23

Foreign and US environmental and wildlife conservation agreements provisions, status, and signatories, as of 1991, listing, 9886–4.169

Great Lakes Environmental Research Lab activities, FY90 annual rpt, 2144–26

Great Lakes wastewater treatment by municipal and industrial facilities, releases, methods, effectiveness, pollutant limits, and enforcement, 1985-88, 14648–24

Groundwater supply, quality, chemistry, and use, State and local area rpt series, 5666–28

Groundwater supply, quality, chemistry, other characteristics, and use, regional rpt series, 5666–25

Hazardous waste site remedial action under Superfund, current and proposed sites descriptions and status, periodic listings, series, 9216–3

Health effects of selected pollutants on animals by species and on humans, and environmental levels, series, 5506–14

Idaho Natl Engineering Lab radiation monitoring results, for facilities and nearby areas, 1990, annual rpt, 3354–10

Industrial wastewater pollution releases, levels, treatment, costs, and regulation, with background financial and operating data, industry rpt series, 9206–4

Livestock industry regional concentration impacts on water pollution, 1991 article, 1522–3.204

Pesticide levels in drinking water, by selected State, 1989 hearing, 25168–76

Quality and supply of water in streams and lakes, and groundwater levels in wells, by drainage basin, 1988, annual State rpt series, 5666–16

Quality and supply of water in streams and lakes, and groundwater levels in wells, by drainage basin, 1989, annual State rpt series, 5666–12

Quality and supply of water in streams and lakes, and groundwater levels in wells, by drainage basin, 1990, annual State rpt series, 5666–10

Quality, chemistry, hydrology, and other characteristics of water, local area studies, series, 5666–27

Radiation and radionuclide concentrations in air, water, and milk, monitoring results by State and site, quarterly rpt, 9192–5

Radiation exposure of population near Hanford, Wash, nuclear plant, with methodology, 1944-66, series, 3356–5

Radioactive low-level waste repository site design, characteristics, and monitoring techniques, 1987 conf, 5668–116

Radioactive waste and spent fuel generation, inventory, and disposal, 1960s-89 and projected to 2020, annual rpt, 3364–2

Radioactive waste from nuclear power plants, releases and waste composition by plant, 1988, annual rpt, 9634–1

Radionuclide releases and concentrations in water, milk, and other food products after Chernobyl, USSR, reactor accident, for selected Republics, 1986-87, 4042–3.201

Research on water resources, data collection and analysis activities of USGS Water Resources Div Districts, with project descriptions, series, 5666–26

Rivers dissolved solids and water temperatures, for 6 rivers by monitoring site, monthly rpt, 5662–3

Rural Clean Water Program funding for control of pollution from farming, by region and State, monthly rpt, 1802–14

Salinity control program for Colorado River, participation and payments, FY87-90, annual rpt, 1804–23

Statistical Abstract of US, 1991 annual data compilation, 2324–1.6

Wetlands acreage, resources, soil and water properties, and conservation efforts, by wetland type, State rpt series, 5506–11

Yearbook of Agriculture, special topics, 1991 annual compilation of papers, 1004–18

see also Eutrophication

see also Food and waterborne diseases

see also Marine pollution

see also Oil spills

Water power

Shipments and firms for fluid power products, by type, 1990, annual Current Industrial Rpt, 2506–12.31

see also Dams

see also Hydroelectric power

Water Resources Council

Budget of US, authoritative financial statements with appropriations, outlays, and receipts, by category and agency, FY90, annual rpt, 8104–2.1

Water resources development

Agricultural Conservation Program participation and payments, by practice and State, FY90, annual rpt, 1804–7

Agricultural Stabilization and Conservation Service producer payments and certificate value, by program, monthly rpt, 1802–10

Agricultural Stabilization and Conservation Service producer payments, by program and State, 1990, annual table, 1804–12

Army Corps of Engineers activities, FY88, annual rpt, 3754–1

Army Corps of Engineers water resources dev projects, characteristics, and costs, 1950s-89, biennial State rpt series, 3756–1

Army Corps of Engineers water resources dev projects, characteristics, and costs, 1950s-91, biennial State rpt series, 3756–2

Budget of US, obligations and authority by function, agency, and program, with summaries, analyses, and historical tables, FY92, annual rpt, 104–2

Construction industries census, 1987: establishments, employment, receipts, and expenditures, by SIC 4-digit industry and State, final industry rpt series, 2373–1

Construction put in place (public and private), by type, bimonthly rpt, 2042–1.1

Construction put in place, value of new public and private structures, by type, monthly rpt, 2382–4

Electric utilities privately owned, finances and operations, detailed data, 1989, annual rpt, 3164–23

FmHA activities, and loans and grants by program and State, FY90 and trends from FY70, annual rpt, 1184–17

Water resources development

Forest Service acreage, staff, finances, and mgmt activities in Pacific Northwest, with data by forest, 1970s-89, annual rpt, 1204–37

Forest Service activities and finances, by region and State, FY90, annual rpt, 1204–1

Forest Service mgmt of public lands and resources dev, environmental, economic, and social impacts of alternative programs, projected to 2040, 1208–24

Groundwater supply, quality, chemistry, other characteristics, and use, regional rpt series, 5666–25

Public lands acreage and use, and Land Mgmt Bur activities and finances, annual State rpt series, 5724–11

Reclamation Bur activities and finances, FY90, annual rpt, 5824–1

Research on water resources, data collection and analysis activities of USGS Water Resources Div Districts, with project descriptions, series, 5666–26

Soil Conservation Service activities, FY90, annual rpt, 1264–2

Water Bank program agreements, payments to farmers, and wetlands acreage, by State, monthly rpt, 1802–5

Water Bank Program agreements, payments to farmers, and wetlands acreage, by State, 1972-91, annual rpt, 1804–21

Water quality, chemistry, hydrology, and other characteristics, local area studies, series, 5666–27

Wetlands acreage, resources, soil and water properties, and conservation efforts, by wetland type, State rpt series, 5506–11

see also Aquaculture

see also Canals

see also Dredging

see also Flood control

see also Hydroelectric power

see also Inland water transportation

see also Irrigation

see also Marine resources

see also Water power

see also Water supply and use

see also Watershed projects

Water supply and use

Aerial survey R&D rpts, and sources of natural resource and environmental data, quarterly listing, 9502–7

Agricultural Stabilization and Conservation Service producer payments and certificate value, by program, monthly rpt, 1802–10

Agriculture census, 1987: farms, farmland, production, finances, and operator characteristics, by island and island group, 1990, final outlying area rpt, 2331–1.55; 2331–1.56

Army Corps of Engineers water resources dev projects, characteristics, and costs, 1950s-89, biennial State rpt series, 3756–1

Army Corps of Engineers water resources dev projects, characteristics, and costs, 1950s-91, biennial State rpt series, 3756–2

Assistance (financial and nonfinancial) of Fed Govt, 1991 base edition with supplements, annual listing, 104–5

Bottled water quality standards of FDA, EPA, and States, with use in 12 States, 1990, GAO rpt, 26113–519

Budget of US, formula grant program obligations to State and local govts, by agency, program, and State, FY92, annual rpt, 104–30

Carbon dioxide in atmosphere, North Central States economic and agricultural impacts, model descriptions and results, 1980s and projected to 2030, 3006–11.15

Catfish raised on farms, operations, water use, and acreage, by State, 1989-91, semiannual situation rpt, 1561–15.2

Colorado River Basin Federal reservoir and power operations and revenues, 1990-91, annual rpt, 5824–6

Colorado water supply, streamflow, precipitation, and reservoir storage, 1991 water year, annual rpt, 1264–13

Consumption of water by end use, well withdrawals, and public supply deliveries, by county, State rpt series, 5666–24

County Business Patterns, 1988: employment, establishments, and payroll, by SIC 2- to 4-digit industry and county, annual State rpt series, 2326–6

County Business Patterns, 1989: employment, establishments, and payroll, by SIC 2- to 4-digit industry and county, annual State rpt series, 2326–8

Criminal sentences for Federal offenses, guidelines by offense and circumstances, series, 17668–1

DC metro area land acquisition and dev projects of Fed Govt, characteristics, funding, and impacts, by agency and project, FY91-95, annual rpt, 15454–1

Developing countries economic and social conditions from 1960s, and Intl Dev Cooperation Agency and AID activities and funding, FY90-92, annual rpt, 9904–4

Engineering and architectural establishments, receipts by type of client and project, payroll, and employment, by State, 1987 Census of Service Industries, 2393–4.16

Environmental Quality, status of problems, protection programs, research, and intl issues, 1991 annual rpt, 484–1

EPA pollution control grant program activities, monthly rpt, 9182–8

Farm production itemized costs, by farm sales size and region, 1990, annual rpt, 1614–3

Forest Service mgmt of public lands and resources dev, environmental, economic, and social impacts of alternative programs, projected to 2040, 1208–24

Franchise business opportunities by firm and kind of business, and sources of aid and info, 1990 annual listing, 2104–7

Geological Survey Water Resources Div history, series, 5668–118

Global climate change environmental, infrastructure, and health impacts, with model results and background data, 1850s-2100, 9188–113

Govt census, 1987: employment, payroll, and average earnings, by function, level of govt, State, county, and population size, 2455–2

Govt census, 1987: local govt employment by function, payroll, and average earnings, for individual counties, cities, and school and special districts, 2455–1

Index by Subjects and Names

Govt employment and payroll, by function, level of govt, and jurisdiction, 1990, annual rpt series, 2466–1

Govt finances, by level of govt, State, and for large cities and counties, annual rpt series, 2466–2

Great Lakes water levels, daily and monthly averages by site, 1990 and cumulative from 1900, annual rpt, 2174–3

Groundwater supply, quality, chemistry, and use, State and local area rpt series, 5666–28

Groundwater supply, quality, chemistry, other characteristics, and use, regional rpt series, 5666–25

Housing and households detailed characteristics, and unit and neighborhood quality, by location, 1987, biennial rpt supplement, 2485–13

Housing and households detailed characteristics, and unit and neighborhood quality, by location, 1989, biennial rpt, 2485–12

Housing and households detailed characteristics, and unit and neighborhood quality, MSA surveys, series, 2485–6

Housing inventory change from 1973, by reason, unit and household characteristics, and location, 1983 survey, biennial rpt, 2485–14

Nevada and eastern California water supply, streamflow, precipitation, and reservoir storage, 1991 water year, annual rpt, 1264–8

Northeastern US water supply, precipitation and stream runoff by station, monthly rpt, 2182–3

Occupational injury and illness rates, by SIC 2- to 4-digit industry, 1988-89, annual rpt, 6844–7

Occupational injury and illness rates, by SIC 2- to 4-digit industry, 1989, annual rpt, 6844–1

Oregon water supply, streamflow by station and reservoir storage, 1991, annual rpt, 1264–9

Panama Canal water supply and use, FY89-90, annual rpt, 9664–3.2

Public works condition, mgmt, R&D, and funding, for transportation and environmental projects, 1986-91, 26358–235

Research (agricultural) funding and staffing for USDA, State agencies, and other instns, by topic, FY90, annual rpt, 1744–2

Research on water resources, data collection and analysis activities of USGS Water Resources Div Districts, with project descriptions, series, 5666–26

Saline water withdrawal and use, for coastal areas, State rpt series, 5666–24

Ship (passenger) sanitary inspection scores, biweekly rpt, 4202–10

State and Metro Area Data Book, 1991 data compilation, 2328–54

Statistical Abstract of US, 1991 annual data compilation, 2324–1.6

Streamflow conditions in US and Puerto Rico, weekly rpt, monthly data, 2182–7

Supply and quality of water in streams and lakes, and groundwater levels in wells, by drainage basin, 1988, annual State rpt series, 5666–16

Index by Subjects and Names

Weapons

Supply and quality of water in streams and lakes, and groundwater levels in wells, by drainage basin, 1989, annual State rpt series, 5666–12

Supply and quality of water in streams and lakes, and groundwater levels in wells, by drainage basin, 1990, annual State rpt series, 5666–10

Supply of water, hydrologic events, and end use, by State, 1988-89, annual rpt, 5664–12

Supply of water in US and southern Canada, streamflow, surface and groundwater conditions, and reservoir levels, by location, monthly rpt, 5662–3

Tax (income) returns of corporations, income and tax items by asset size and detailed industry, 1988, annual rpt, 8304–21

Western US water supply, and snow survey results, annual State rpt series, 1264–14

Western US water supply, and snow survey results, monthly State rpt series, 1266–2

Western US water supply, storage by reservoir and State, and streamflow conditions, as of Oct 1991, annual rpt, 1264–4

Western US water supply, streamflow and reservoir storage forecasts by stream and station, Jan-May monthly rpt, 1262–1

see also Dams

see also Food and waterborne diseases

see also Hydroelectric power

see also Irrigation

see also Reservoirs

see also Water area

see also Water fluoridation

see also Water permits

see also Water pollution

see also Water power

see also Water resources development

see also Watershed projects

see also Weather

see also Wetlands

Waterloo, Iowa

Wages by occupation, and benefits for office and plant workers, 1991 survey, periodic MSA rpt, 6785–3.7

see also under By SMSA or MSA in the "Index by Categories"

Watershed projects

Acreage, grants, use, revenues, and allocations, for public lands by State, FY90, annual rpt, 5724–1.2

Agricultural Conservation Program participation and payments, by practice and State, FY90, annual rpt, 1804–7

Army Corps of Engineers water resources dev projects, characteristics, and costs, 1950s-89, biennial State rpt series, 3756–1

Army Corps of Engineers water resources dev projects, characteristics, and costs, 1950s-91, biennial State rpt series, 3756–2

Forest Service activities and finances, by region and State, FY90, annual rpt, 1204–1

Reclamation Bur irrigation activities, finances, and project impacts in western US, 1989, annual rpt, 5824–12

Soil Conservation Service activities, FY90, annual rpt, 1264–2

Waterways

see Canals

see Harbors and ports

see Inland water transportation

see Lakes and lakeshores

see Rivers and waterways

Watson, Mark W.

"Measures of Fit for Calibrated Models", 9375–13.60

"Simple Estimator of Cointegrating Vectors in Higher Order Integrated Systems", 9375–13.54

"Using Econometric Models To Predict Recessions", 9375–1.212

Waukesha County, Wis.

Housing and households characteristics, unit and neighborhood quality, and journey to work by MSA location, for 11 MSAs, 1984 survey, supplement, 2485–8

Housing and households detailed characteristics, and unit and neighborhood quality, by location, 1988 survey, MSA rpt, 2485–6.2

Wausau, Wis.

see also under By SMSA or MSA in the "Index by Categories"

Way, Peter O.

"Demographic Impact of an AIDS Epidemic on an African Country: Application of the iwgAIDS Model", 2326–18.57

Wealth

Assets and debts of private sector, balance sheets by segment, 1945-90, semiannual rpt, 9365–4.1

Assets and liabilities of US, and impacts of inflation, 1990 and trends from 1948, article, 9391–1.220

Households assets, by type of holding and selected characteristics, 1988, Current Population Rpt, 2546–20.16

Households composition, income, benefits, and labor force status, Survey of Income and Program Participation methodology, working paper series, 2626–10

Households debt holdings impact of credit constraints and other factors, model description and results, 1980-83, technical paper, 9379–12.73

Households net worth, by householder age, race, and income, 1988, fact sheet, 2326–17.26

Income disparity between wealthiest and other families, and income sources, 1980s and trends from 1949, 23848–219

State and Metro Area Data Book, 1991 data compilation, 2328–54

Statistical Abstract of US, 1991 annual data compilation, 2324–1.14

Student aid Pell grants and applicants, by tuition, income level, instn type and control, and State, 1989/90, annual rpt, 4804–1

Tax (income) returns of high income individuals not filed, by selected characteristics, 1987, and assessments under alternative IRS enforcement programs, 1990, GAO rpt, 26119–322

see also Business assets and liabilities, general

see also Business assets and liabilities, specific industry

see also Gross National Product

see also Investments

see also Money supply

see also National income and product accounts

see also Personal and household income

see also Personal debt

see also Poverty

see also Property

see also Savings

Weapons

Arrest rates, by offense, sex, age, and race, 1965-89, annual rpt, 6224–7

Arrests, by offense, offender characteristics, and location, 1990, annual rpt, 6224–2.2

Arrests, prosecutions, convictions, and sentencing, for felony offenders, by offender characteristics and offense, 1988, 6066–25.33; 6066–25.39

Court civil and criminal caseloads for Federal district, appeals, and bankruptcy courts, by type of suit and offense, circuit, and district, 1990, annual rpt, 18204–11

Court civil and criminal caseloads for Federal district, appeals, and special courts, 1990, annual rpt, 18204–8

Court civil and criminal caseloads for Federal district courts, 1991, annual rpt, 18204–2.1

Crime victimization of women, by relation to offender, circumstances, and victim characteristics, for rape and other violent offenses, 1973-87, 6068–243

Crime victimization rates, by victim and offender characteristics, circumstances, and offense, 1988 survey, annual rpt, 6066–3.42

Crime victimization rates, by victim and offender characteristics, circumstances, and offense, 1989 survey, annual rpt, 6066–3.44

Crimes, arrests, and rates, by offense, offender characteristics, population size, and jurisdiction, 1990, annual rpt, 6224–2.1; 6224–2.2

Criminal case processing in Federal district courts, and dispositions, by offense, district, and offender characteristics, 1986, annual rpt, 6064–29

Criminal case processing in Federal district courts, and dispositions, by offense, 1980-89, annual rpt, 6064–31

Criminal cases in Federal district courts, by offense, disposition, and district, 1980-90, last issue of annual rpt, 18204–1

Criminal sentences for Federal offenses, guidelines by offense and circumstances, series, 17668–1

Deaths and rates, by detailed cause and demographic characteristics, 1988 and trends from 1900, US Vital Statistics annual rpt, 4144–2

Drug test results at arrest, by drug type, offense, and sex, for selected urban areas, quarterly rpt, 6062–3

Exports and imports of US, by selected country, country group, and commodity group, 1990, annual rpt, 2044–37

Input-output structure of US economy, detailed interindustry transactions for 84 industries, and components of final demand, 1986, annual article, 2702–1.206

Input-output structure of US economy, detailed interindustry transactions for 85 industries, 1982 benchmark data, 2702–1.213

Weapons

Jail population, by criminal, correctional, drug use, and family history, and selected other characteristics, 1989, 6066–19.62

Jail population, by sociodemographic characteristics, criminal and drug use history, whether convicted, offense, and sentencing, 1989, annual rpt, 6064–26.3

Juvenile courts delinquency cases, by offense, referral source, disposition, age, sex, race, State, and county, 1988, annual rpt, 6064–12

Law enforcement officer assaults and deaths by circumstances, agency, victim and offender characteristics, and location, 1990, annual rpt, 6224–3

Marijuana crop eradication activities of DEA and local agencies, and weapons and assets seized, by State, 1982-90, annual rpt, 6284–4

Prison and parole admissions and releases, sentence length, and time served, by offense and offender characteristics, 1985, annual rpt, 6064–33

Teenagers crime victimization, by victim and offender characteristics, circumstances, and offense, 1985-88 surveys, 6066–3.43

Wiretaps authorized, costs, arrests, trials, and convictions, by offense and jurisdiction, 1990, annual rpt, 18204–7

Women prisoners in State instns, by offense, drug use history, whether abused, and other characteristics, 1986, 6066–19.61

see also Ammunition
see also Arms trade
see also Bombs
see also Chemical and biological warfare agents
see also Firearms
see also Military assistance
see also Military weapons
see also Missiles and rockets
see also Nuclear weapons
see also Torpedoes

Weather

Aircraft (general aviation) accidents, by circumstances, characteristics of persons and aircraft involved, and type of flying, 1988, annual rpt, 9614–3

Aircraft (general aviation) flight hours, by weather and light conditions, aircraft type and model, and region, 1990, annual rpt, 7504–29.2

Aircraft (general aviation) weather info services use, 1990, triennial survey rpt, 7508–3

Aircraft accidents and circumstances, for US operations of domestic and foreign airlines and general aviation, periodic rpt, 9612–1

Aircraft accidents, casualties, and damage, for commercial operations by detailed circumstances, 1987, annual rpt, 9614–2

Alaska OCS environmental conditions and oil dev impacts, compilation of papers, series, 2176–1

Alaska weather data, for Valdez station, 1988, 9618–17

Boat accidents, casualties, and damage, by cause, vessel and operator characteristics, and State, 1990, annual rpt, 7404–1.2

Coastal areas environmental and socioeconomic conditions, and potential impact of oil and gas OCS leases, final statement series, 5736–1

Index by Subjects and Names

Coastal currents driven by wind, velocity and direction by station for North America, forecast 1992, annual rpts, 2174–1

Colorado water supply, streamflow, precipitation, and reservoir storage, 1991 water year, annual rpt, 1264–13

Corn yield related to summer temperature and rainfall, 1991 article, 1561–4.203

Deaths and rates, by detailed cause and demographic characteristics, 1988 and trends from 1900, US Vital Statistics annual rpt, 4144–2

Deaths, injuries, and damage from weather phenomena, and storm characteristics, by State, monthly listing, 2152–3

Deaths of natl park system visitors, by cause, victim age, region, and park, 1980-90, annual rpt, 5544–6

Diving (underwater sport and occupational) deaths, by circumstances, diver characteristics, and location, 1970-89, annual rpt, 2144–5

Energy supply, demand, and price forecasts, economic and weather assumptions, quarterly rpt, 3162–34

Foreign and US air pressure, temperature, and precipitation, by location, monthly 1971-80, decennial rpt series, 2156–4

Foreign countries agricultural production, trade, and policies, summary data by country, 1989-90, annual factbook, 1924–12

Foreign countries *Background Notes*, summary social, political, and economic data, series, 7006–2

Foreign countries economic, social, political, and geographic summary data, by country, 1991, annual factbook, 9114–2

Groundwater supply, quality, chemistry, and use, State and local area rpt series, 5666–28

Groundwater supply, quality, chemistry, other characteristics, and use, regional rpt series, 5666–25

Heating and cooling degree days, by census div, monthly and cumulative for season, monthly rpt, 3162–24.1

Heating and cooling degree days, distribution for commercial buildings by building type, survey rpt series, 3166–8

Heating and cooling degree days, for 45 cities and total US, cumulative for season, weekly rpt, 3162–32.2; 3162–45.2

Heating and cooling degree days weighted by population, by census div and State, with area-weighted temperature and precipitation, monthly rpt, 2152–13

Labor force not at work, unemployed, and working less than 35 hours, by reason, sex, race, region, and State, 1990, annual rpt, 6744–7.1; 6744–7.2

Mariners Weather Log, quarterly journal, 2152–8

Natl Weather Service station locations and types of observations made, 1990 annual listing, 2184–5

Nevada and eastern California water supply, streamflow, precipitation, and reservoir storage, 1991 water year, annual rpt, 1264–8

Northeastern US water supply, precipitation and stream runoff by station, monthly rpt, 2182–3

Pacific Northwest housing energy conservation program of Bonneville Power Admin, activities, cost effectiveness, and participation, series, 3226–1

Precipitation, and groundwater and surface water supply and conditions, monthly rpt, 5662–3

Precipitation and temperature, and effect on agriculture, by US region, State, and city, and world area, weekly rpt, 2182–7

Precipitation and temperature for US and foreign locations, major events and anomalies, weekly rpt, 2182–6

Precipitation and temperature forecasts for US and Northern Hemisphere, by location, semimonthly rpt, 2182–1

Precipitation averages worldwide, estimates for map grid areas, 1850s-1989, 3006–11.14

Railroad accidents, casualties, and damage, by cause, railroad, and State, 1990, annual rpt, 7604–1

Railroad-hwy grade-crossing accidents, detailed data by State and railroad, 1989, annual rpt, 7604–2

Ships accidents and casualties, by circumstances and characteristics of persons and vessels involved, 1988, annual rpt, 7404–11

Ships and marine facilities accidents, casualties, and circumstances, Coast Guard investigation results, periodic rpt, 9612–4

Soil mgmt and characteristics, for western mountain forest areas, 1990 conf, 1208–378

Statistical Abstract of US, 1991 annual data compilation, 2324–1.6

Timber in New England, growth and relationship to tree and site characteristics, 1900s-85, 1208–349

Traffic accidents, casualties, circumstances, and characteristics of persons and vehicles involved, 1989, annual rpt, 7764–18

Traffic fatal accidents, deaths, and rates, by circumstances, characteristics of persons and vehicles involved, and location, 1989, annual rpt, 7764–10

Truck accidents, casualties, and damage, by circumstances and characteristics of persons and vehicles involved, 1988, annual rpt, 7554–9

Truck accidents, circumstances, severity, and characteristics of drivers and vehicles, 1989, annual rpt, 7764–20

Water quality, chemistry, hydrology, and other characteristics, local area studies, series, 5666–27

Water supply, hydrologic events, and end use, by State, 1988-89, annual rpt, 5664–12

Weather data for stations in continental US and outlying areas, 1990 and historic trends, annual rpt, 2154–8

Weather data for surface and upper air, averages by foreign and US station, monthly rpt, 2152–4

Weather trends and deviations, by world region, 1880s-1990, annual chartbook, 2184–9

Western US water supply, and snow survey results, annual State rpt series, 1264–14

Western US water supply, and snow survey results, monthly State rpt series, 1266–2

Index by Subjects and Names

Western US water supply, streamflow and reservoir storage forecasts by stream and station, Jan-May monthly rpt, 1262–1

Wetlands acreage, resources, soil and water properties, and conservation efforts, by wetland type, State rpt series, 5506–11

see also Drought

see also Floods

see also Glaciers

see also Global climate change

see also Ice conditions

see also Meteorological satellites

see also Meteorology

see also Storms

see also Wind energy

Weather Bureau

see National Environmental Satellite, Data, and Information Service

see National Weather Service

Weather satellites

see Meteorological satellites

Webb, Alan J.

"Farmland Values and Japanese Agriculture", 1524–4.5

Webb, Shwu-Eng H.

"China's Agricultural Commodity Policies in the 1980's", 1524–4.3

Weber, Bruce R.

"Grain Programs in the 1990 Farm Bill", 1004–16.1

Webre, Philip

"Large Nondefense R&D Projects in the Budget: 1980-96", 26306–3.116

Wei, Shang-Jin

"Anticipations of Foreign Exchange Volatility and Bid-Ask Spreads", 9366–7.263

Weight

see Body measurements

see Obesity

Weights and measures

- Auto and light truck fuel economy, sales, and market shares, by size and model for US and foreign makes, 1991 model year, semiannual rpt, 3302–4
- Auto weight, by component material, 1975-90, article, 5602–4.202
- Auto weight impacts on fatal traffic accident rates, with data for young drivers, 1976-78 and 1986-88, GAO rpt, 26131–89
- Natl Inst of Standards and Technology rpts, 1990, annual listing, 2214–1
- Standards dev, proposals, and policies, for weights, measures, and performance, 1991 annual conf, 2214–7
- *Statistical Abstract of US,* 1991 annual data compilation, 2324–1
- *see also* Industrial standards

Weirton, W.Va.

see also under By SMSA or MSA in the "Index by Categories"

Weis, Kathleen A.

"Nationwide Evaluation of Medicaid Competition Demonstrations. Volume 4. Quality of Care Study", 4658–45.4

Weisbrod, Rita R.

"Current Status of Health Promotion Activities in Four Midwest Cities", 4042–3.223

Weiss, David D.

"Calibrating Manufacturing Decline in the Midwest: Value Added, Gross State Product, and All Points Between", 9375–13.59

West Virginia

"Midwest Economy: Quantifying Growth and Diversification in the 1980's", 9375–13.63

Weitz, Stevenson

"Comprehensive and Workable Plan for the Abatement of Lead-Based Paint in Privately Owned Housing", 5188–128

Welch, John H.

- "Hyperinflation, and Internal Debt Repudiation in Argentina and Brazil: From Expectations Management to the 'Bonex' and 'Collor' Plans", 9379–12.69
- "North American Free Trade and the Peso: The Case for a North American Currency Area", 9379–12.77
- "Public Debts and Deficits in Mexico: A Comment", 9379–12.78
- "Rational Inflation and Real Internal Debt Bubbles in Argentina and Brazil?", 9379–12.75

Welch, W. Pete

- "Geographic Medicare Economic Index: Alternative Approaches", 4658–50
- "Giving Physicians Incentives To Contain Costs Under Medicaid", 4652–1.228

Welfare

see Aid to Families with Dependent Children

see Public welfare programs

see Social security

see State funding for social welfare

Welniak, Edward J., Jr.

- "Money Income of Households, Families, and Persons in the U.S.: 1988-89", 2546–6.68
- "Money Income of Households, Families, and Persons in the U.S.: 1990", 2546–6.70

Welty, Thomas K.

"Cardiovascular Disease", 4088–2

"End-Stage Renal Disease", 4088–2

"Infectious Diseases", 4088–2

Wenner, Mark

"Current and Potential Agricultural Trade Between Eastern and Central Europe and Developing Countries", 1524–4.2

West Indies

see Caribbean area

West Palm Beach, Fla.

Housing starts and completions authorized by building permits in 40 MSAs, quarterly rpt, 2382–9

see also under By SMSA or MSA in the "Index by Categories"

West Virginia

- Appalachian Regional Commission funding, by project and State, planned FY91, annual rpt, 9084–3
- Apple production, marketing, and prices, for Appalachia and compared to other States, 1988-91, annual rpt, 1311–13
- Banks (insured commercial), Fed Reserve 5th District members financial statements, by State, quarterly rpt, 9389–18
- Banks (insured commercial and savings) deposits by instn, State, MSA, and county, as of June 1990, annual regional rpt, 9295–3.2
- Coal production and mines by county, prices, productivity, miners, and reserves, by mining method and State, 1989-90, annual rpt, 3164–25
- County Business Patterns, 1989: employment, establishments, and payroll, by SIC 2- to 4-digit industry and county, annual State rpt, 2326–8.50

DOD prime contract awards, by contractor, service branch, State, and city, FY90, annual rpt, 3544–22

- Economic indicators by State, Fed Reserve 5th District, quarterly rpt, 9389–16
- Education system in Appalachia, improvement initiatives, and indicators of success, by State, 1960s-89, 9088–36
- Fed Govt spending in States and local areas, by type, State, county, and city, FY90, annual rpt, 2464–3
- Fed Govt spending in States, by type, program, agency, and State, FY90, annual rpt, 2464–2
- HHS financial aid, by program, recipient, State, and city, FY90, annual regional listing, 4004–3.3
- Hospital deaths of Medicare patients, actual and expected rates by diagnosis, and hospital characteristics, by instn, FY87-89, annual regional rpt, 4654–14.3
- Income (personal) per capita and by source, and earnings by industry div, by State, MSA, and county, 1984-89, annual regional rpt, 2704–2.4
- Jail adult and juvenile population, employment, spending, instn conditions, and inmate programs, by county and facility, 1988, regional rpt series, 6068–144.4
- Land subsidence above coal mines, State property insurance program income and expenses in 6 States, 1990, GAO rpt, 26113–530
- Marriages, divorces, and rates, by characteristics of spouses, State, and county, 1987 and trends from 1920, US Vital Statistics annual rpt, 4144–4
- Mineral Industry Surveys, State reviews of production, 1990, preliminary annual rpt, 5614–6
- *Minerals Yearbook, 1989,* Vol 2: State reviews of production, sales, and firms, by commodity, and business activity, annual rpt, 5604–34
- Nursing home reimbursement by Medicaid, States payment ratesetting methods, analysis for 7 States, 1980s, article, 4652–1.255
- Physicians, by specialty, age, sex, and location of training and practice, 1989, State rpt, 4116–6.50
- Population and housing census, 1990: population and housing characteristics, households, and land area, by county, subdiv, and place, State rpt, 2551–1.50
- Population and housing census, 1990: voting age and total population by race, and housing units, by block, redistricting counts required under PL 94-171, State CD-ROM release, 2551–6.2
- Population and housing census, 1990: voting age and total population by race, and housing units, by county and city, redistricting counts required under PL 94-171, State summary rpt, 2551–5.49
- *Statistical Abstract of US,* 1991 annual data compilation, 2324–1
- Supplemental Security Income payments and beneficiaries, by type of eligibility, State, and county, Dec 1989, annual rpt, 4744–27.3
- Timber and pulpwood production, by product, 1960s-87, State rpt, 1206–15.9

West Virginia

Timber resources and removals, by species, ownership class, and county, 1975 and 1989, State rpt, 1206–12.13

Water quality, chemistry, hydrology, and other characteristics, 1989 local area study, 5666–27.1

Water resources data collection and analysis activities of USGS Water Resources Div District, with project descriptions, 1990 rpt, 5666–26.12

Water supply and quality in streams and lakes, and groundwater levels in wells, by drainage basin, 1990, annual State rpt, 5666–10.45

see also By State in the "Index by Categories"

Westat, Inc.

"National Survey of Academic Research Instruments and Instrumentation Needs", 9627–27

"Preliminary Estimates on Student Financial Aid Recipients, 1989-90", 4846–5.1

Westcott, Paul

"Summer Quarter Feed and Residual Use of Wheat", 1561–12.203

"Trends in Costs of Production of Corn, Wheat, and Soybeans, 1975-89", 1541–1.208

Westerfield, Paul W.

"Ground-Water Levels in Arkansas, Spring 1990", 5666–28.12

"Ground-Water Levels in the Alluvial Aquifer in Eastern Arkansas, 1987", 5666–28.6

Western Area Power Administration

Activities of WAPA by plant, financial statements, and sales by customer, FY90, annual rpt, 3254–1

Electric power wholesale purchases of REA borrowers, by borrower, supplier, and State, 1940-89, annual rpt, 1244–5

Finances and operations of Federal power admins and electric utilities, 1989, annual rpt, 3164–24.2

Western Sahara

Agricultural trade of US, by detailed commodity and country, 1990, semiannual rpt, 1522–4

Economic, social, political, and geographic summary data, by country, 1991, annual factbook, 9114–2

Exports and imports of US, by transport mode, country, and SITC 1- to 3-digit commodity, 1990, annual rpt, 2424–12

Human rights conditions in 170 countries, and US economic and military aid, 1990, annual rpt, 21384–3

Western Samoa

Agricultural trade of US, by detailed commodity and country, 1989, annual rpt, 1524–8

Agricultural trade of US, by detailed commodity and country, 1990, semiannual rpt, 1522–4

Economic and military aid and loans from US and intl agencies, by program and country, FY46-90, annual rpt, 9914–5

Economic, social, and agricultural data, US and other aid sources, and AID activity, 1988 country rpt, 9916–12.28

Economic, social, political, and geographic summary data, by country, 1991, annual factbook, 9114–2

Exports and imports of US, by transport mode, country, and SITC 1- to 3-digit commodity, 1990, annual rpt, 2424–12

Exports of US, detailed Schedule B commodities with countries of destination, 1990, annual rpt, 2424–10

Human rights conditions in 170 countries, and US economic and military aid, 1990, annual rpt, 21384–3

UN voting record and share of votes in agreement with US, by issue, country, and world area, 1990, annual rpt, 7004–18

Western States

Banking industry structure, performance, and financial devs, for Fed Reserve 10th District, 1990, annual rpt, 9381–14

Birds (duck) breeding population, by species, State, and Canada Province, 1990-91 and trends from 1955, annual rpt, 5504–30

Bonneville Power Admin mgmt of Fed Columbia River Power System, finances and sales, summary data, quarterly rpt, 3222–2

Bonneville Power Admin mgmt of Fed Columbia River Power System, finances, operations, and sales by customer, FY90, annual rpt, 3224–1

Bonneville Power Admin sales, revenues, and rates, by customer and customer type, 1990, semiannual rpt, 3222–1

Coal production and mines by county, prices, productivity, miners, and reserves, by mining method and State, 1989-90, annual rpt, 3164–25

Coastal areas pollutant concentrations in fish and sediments, by contaminant, fish species, and Pacific coast site, 1984-86, 2168–121

CPI by component for US city average, and by region, population size, and for 27 metro areas, monthly rpt, 6762–2

Dairy prices, by product and selected area, with related marketing data, 1990, annual rpt, 1317–1

Economic indicators and cyclical devs and outlook, by Fed Reserve Bank District, periodic rpt, 9362–8

Electric power capacity and use in Pacific Northwest, by energy source, projected under alternative load and demand cases, 1991-2011, annual rpt, 3224–3

Electric power sales by customer, activities by plant, and financial statements of Western Area Power Admin, FY90, annual rpt, 3254–1

Employment and income in Rocky Mountain region, and economic dependence on shipments outside area, by industry and county group, 1980s, 1208–362

Energy conservation (housing) program of Bonneville Power Admin, activities, cost effectiveness, and participation, series, 3226–1

Energy conservation and resource planning activities of Bonneville Power Admin, FY89-90, 3228–11

Estuary environmental and fishery conditions, research results and methodology, 1991 rpt, 2176–7.24

Financial and economic devs, Fed Reserve Bank of Kansas City bimonthly journal, 9381–1

Financial and economic devs, Fed Reserve Bank of San Francisco quarterly journal, 9393–8

Financial and economic devs, Fed Reserve 10th District, quarterly rpt, 9381–16

Index by Subjects and Names

Fish and shellfish catch, life cycles, and environmental needs, for selected coastal species and regions, series, 5506–8

Fishing (sport) warmwater resources mgmt in western US, 1991 conf, 1208–381

Forest Service acreage, staff, finances, and mgmt activities in Pacific Northwest, with data by forest, 1970s-89, annual rpt, 1204–37

Govt revenues and tax capacity for State and local govts, by source and western States, 1988, article, 9381–1.204

HHS financial aid, by program, recipient, State, and city, FY90, annual regional listing, 4004–3.8; 4004–3.9; 4004–3.10

Horse and burro wild herd areas in western States, population, adoption, and mgmt costs, as of FY89, biennial rpt, 5724–8

Housing vacancy rates for single and multifamily units and mobile homes in FHLB 10th District, by ZIP code, annual MSA rpt series, 9304–22

Housing vacancy rates for single and multifamily units and mobile homes in FHLB 12th District, by ZIP code, annual MSA rpt series, 9304–21

Income (personal) per capita and by source, and earnings by industry div, by State, MSA, and county, 1984-89, annual regional rpt, 2704–2.5

Irrigation projects of Reclamation Bur, acreage limits monitoring activities by region, 1988-90, annual rpt, 5824–13

Mineral industries census, 1987: finances and operations, by SIC 2- to 4-digit industry, State, and county, census div rpt, 2515–1.8

Minerals resources and availability on public lands, State rpt series, 5606–7

Natural gas production and wellhead capacity, by production area, 1980-89 and alternative forecasts 1990-91, biennial rpt, 3164–93

Oil production on Alaska North Slope, and impacts of lifting export controls on US oil trade, West Coast prices, and shipping industry, 1988 and forecast 1995, GAO rpt, 26113–496

Population, income, and employment growth for Fed Reserve 10th District, by MSA, metro-nonmetro location, and State, 1970s-90s, article, 9381–1.209

Radon indoor air pollution levels in Pacific Northwest, with geological and soil characteristics, by township, 1989 rpt, 5668–114

Reclamation Bur activities and finances, FY90, annual rpt, 5824–1

Recreation (outdoor) coastal facilities of Fed Govt and States, visitor and site characteristics, 1987-90 survey, regional rpt, 2176–9.5; 2176–9.7

Recreation (outdoor) facilities on public land, use, and Land Mgmt Bur mgmt activities, funding, and plans, State rpt series, 5726–5

Savings and loan assns, FHLB 11th District members, offices, and financial condition, 1991 annual listing, 9304–23

Savings instns, FHLB 6th and 11th District and natl cost of funds indexes, and mortgage and Treasury bill rates, monthly rpt, 9302–38

Savings instns, FHLB 10th District members, locations, assets, and deposits, 1991, annual listing, 9304–17

Index by Subjects and Names — Wheat

Selenium levels in Western States arid areas, and plant and animal exposure effects, 1990 conf, 5668–121

Shrublands in western US, ecology, biology, and cheatgrass invasion and related fire threat, 1989 conf papers, 1208–351

Statistical Abstract of US, 1991 annual data compilation, 2324–1

Tidal currents, daily time and velocity by station for North America and Asia coasts, forecast 1992, annual rpt, 2174–1.2

Tide height and time daily at coastal points, forecast 1992, annual rpt, 2174–2.2

Timber in northwestern US and British Columbia, production, prices, trade, and employment, quarterly rpt, 1202–3

Timber in western mountain areas, soil characteristics and mgmt, 1990 conf, 1208–378

Timber in western US and Canada, lodgepole pine spiral grain defect incidence and severity, 1991 rpt, 1208–380

Timber insect and disease incidence and damage, 1989, annual regional rpt, 1206–11.1

Timber insect and disease incidence and damage, 1990, annual regional rpt, 1206–11.2; 1206–11.3

Uranium tailings at inactive mills, remedial action activities by site, and funding, FY90, annual rpt, 3354–9

Water supply in western US, and snow survey results, annual State rpt series, 1264–14

Water supply in western US, and snow survey results, monthly State rpt series, 1266–2

Water supply in western US, storage by reservoir and State, and streamflow conditions, as of Oct 1991, annual rpt, 1264–4

Water supply in western US, streamflow and reservoir storage forecasts by stream and station, Jan-May monthly rpt, 1262–1

Wetlands (riparian) acreage, and Bur of Land Mgmt activities, mgmt plans, and scientific staff, State rpt series, 5726–8

Wetlands in coastal areas, acreage by wetland type, estuarine basin, and county, 1989, 2178–31

see also under By Region in the "Index by Categories"

see also under names of individual States

Western Union Telegraph Co.

Finances and operations, detail for telegraph firms, 1989, annual rpt, 9284–6.3

Intl telecommunications operations of US carriers, finances, rates, and traffic by service type, firm, and country, 1975-89, annual rpt, 9284–17

Wetlands

Acreage of coastal wetlands, by type, estuarine basin, and county, 1989, 2178–31

Acreage of non-Federal land by use, soil and water conditions, and conservation needs, 1987, State rpt series, 1266–5

Acreage of wetlands, water, and land, by State, 1780s and 1980s, 5508–107

Acreage, resources, soil and water properties, and conservation efforts, by wetland type, State rpt series, 5506–11

Agricultural Stabilization and Conservation Service producer payments and certificate value, by program, monthly rpt, 1802–10

Alaska OCS environmental conditions and oil dev impacts, compilation of papers, series, 2176–1

Birds (waterfowl) population, habitat conditions, and migratory flight forecasts, for Canada and US by region, 1991 and trends from 1955, annual rpt, 5504–27

Birds (whooping crane) migration roosting sites and population by wetland type, 1990 rpt, 5508–111

Colorado Rocky Mountain Natl Park, Big Meadows wetlands plant, soil, and water characteristics, 1987-88, 5508–113

Conservation programs of USDA, benefits denied for noncompliance, and appeals disposition, by State, periodic rpt, discontinued, 1802–18

Environmental and socioeconomic conditions, and potential impact of oil and gas OCS leases, final statement series, 5736–1

Environmental conditions, fish, wildlife, use, and mgmt, for individual coastal and riparian ecosystems, series, 5506–9

Environmental conditions of coastal areas and estuaries, research results and methodology, series, 2176–7

Environmental Quality, status of problems, protection programs, research, and intl issues, 1991 annual rpt, 484–1

Estuary environmental conditions, and fish and shellfish catch by species and region, 1980s, 2178–27

Farm finances and environmental benefits of alternative policies to Food Security Act conservation programs, projected 1991-2005, 1588–153

Florida environmental, social, and economic conditions, and impacts of proposed OCS oil and gas leases in southern coastal areas, 1990 compilation of papers, 5738–19

Geese pre-migration feeding behavior impacts of aircraft disturbance, for 3 species at Izembek Lagoon, Alaska, 1970s-88, 5738–23

Global climate change environmental, infrastructure, and health impacts, with model results and background data, 1850s-2100, 9188–113

Land Mgmt Bur mgmt of riparian wetlands, activities, mgmt plans, and scientific staff, with acreage, State rpt series, 5726–8

Landfills distance from wetlands and water habitats, for 11 States, 1990 rpt, 9188–115

Migratory Bird Conservation Commission wetlands habitat acquisition, funding by State, FY92, press release, 5306–4.8; 5306–4.11

New York Bight pollution levels, sources, treatment costs, economic losses, and environmental and health effects, 1990 conf, 9208–131

North Carolina environmental and socioeconomic conditions, and impacts of proposed OCS oil and gas exploration, 1970s-90 and projected to 2020, 5738–22

Public lands acreage, grants, use, revenues, and allocations, by State, FY90, annual rpt, 5724–1.2

Soil and plant characteristics in wetlands and riparian areas, series, 5506–10

Southeastern US wetlands acreage conserved and disturbed, by habitat and disturbance type and State, 1988, article, 2162–1.202

Water Bank program agreements, payments to farmers, and wetlands acreage, by State, monthly rpt, 1802–5

Water Bank Program agreements, payments to farmers, and wetlands acreage, by State, 1972-91, annual rpt, 1804–21

Wildlife and plant research results, habitat study series, 5506–13

Wildlife mgmt activities and funding, acreage, staff, and plans of Bur of Land Mgmt, habitat study series, 5726–6

Wildlife research of State fish and wildlife agencies, federally funded projects and costs by species and State, 1990, annual listing, 5504–24

Wetterau, John M.

"Fluid Milk Sales by Method of Distribution", 1317–4.201

"Fluid Milk Sales by Size and Type of Container", 1317–4.203

Whalen, Gary

"Proportional Hazards Model of Bank Failure: An Examination of Its Usefulness as an Early Warning Tool", 9377–1.204

Whales

see Marine mammals

Wharton, Eric H.

"Timber Industries of Delaware, 1985", 1206–15.10

Wheat

Acreage of wheat and rye seeded, by State, 1989-91, annual rpt, 1621–30

Acreage planted and harvested, by crop and State, 1989-90 and planned as of June 1991, annual rpt, 1621–23

Acreage planted, by selected crop and State, 1982-90 and planned 1991, annual rpt, 1621–22

Acreage reduction program compliance, enrollment, and yield on planted acreage, by commodity and State, annual press release series, 1004–20

Acreage under Agricultural Stabilization and Conservation Service programs, rankings by commodity and congressional district, 1989, biennial rpt, 1804–17

Agricultural data compilation, 1990 and trends from 1920, annual rpt, 1004–14

Agricultural Stabilization and Conservation Service producer payments and certificate value, by program, monthly rpt, 1802–10

Agricultural Stabilization and Conservation Service producer payments, by program and State, 1990, annual table, 1804–12

Agricultural Stabilization and Conservation Service wheat programs, 1960-91, annual fact sheet, 1806–4.11

Agricultural Statistics, 1990, annual rpt, 1004–1

Agriculture census, 1987: farms, farmland, production, finances, and operator characteristics, by county, final State rpt series, 2331–1

Alcoholic beverages production, stocks, materials used, and taxable and tax-free removals, for beer and distilled spirits by State, monthly rpt, 8486–1.1; 8486–1.3

Business statistics, detailed data for major industries and economic indicators, *Survey of Current Business*, monthly rpt, 2702–1.14

Wheat

Index by Subjects and Names

Canada wheat producer subsidy costs and returns, 1990-92, article, 1561–12.202

CCC certificate exchange activity, by commodity, biweekly press release, 1802–16

CCC financial condition and major commodity program operations, FY62-87, annual chartbook, 1824–2

Consumption, supply, trade, prices, spending, and indexes, by food commodity, 1989, annual rpt, 1544–4

Cooperatives finances and operations, by grain handled and selected characteristics, 1983-85, series, 1128–44

Deficiency program payments freeze in 1985 for wheat, impacts on participation, production, costs, exports, and returns, model results, 1990 rpt, 1548–376

Durum wheat acreage, production, prices, stocks, use, and US and Canada exports by country, quarterly rpt, discontinued, 1313–6

Export demand for US corn, wheat, and soybeans, by selected country, 1960s-83, 1568–297

Export licensing, monitoring, and enforcement activities, FY90, annual rpt, 2024–1

Exports (agricultural) of high-value commodities, indexes and sales value by commodity, world area, and country, 1960s-86, 1528–323

Exports and imports (agricultural) commodity and country, prices, and world market devs, monthly rpt, 1922–12

Exports and imports (agricultural) of US, by commodity and country, bimonthly rpt, 1522–1

Exports and imports (agricultural) of US, by detailed commodity and country, 1989, annual rpt, 1524–8

Exports and imports (agricultural) of US, by detailed commodity and country, 1990, semiannual rpt, 1522–4

Exports and imports between US and outlying areas, by detailed commodity and mode of transport, 1990, annual rpt, 2424–11

Exports and imports of US, by country and detailed commodity, monthly rpt, 2422–12

Exports and imports of US, by Harmonized System 6-digit commodity and country, 1990, annual rpt, 2424–13

Exports and imports of US, by selected country, country group, and commodity group, 1990, annual rpt, 2044–37

Exports and imports of US, by transport mode, country, and SITC 1- to 3-digit commodity, 1990, annual rpt, 2424–12

Exports of grains, oilseed products, hides, skins, and cotton, by country, weekly rpt, 1922–3

Exports of US, detailed Schedule B commodities with countries of destination, 1990, annual rpt, 2424–10

Exports of US wheat, and wheat produced in other countries, quality indicators, 1960s-90, hearing, 25168–75

Farm financial and marketing conditions, forecast 1991, annual chartbook, 1504–8

Farm income, expenses, receipts by commodity, assets, liabilities, and ratios, 1990 and trends from 1945, annual rpt, 1544–16

Farm sector balance sheet, and receipts by detailed commodity, by State, 1985-89, annual rpt, 1544–18

Fertilizer and pesticide use and application rates, by type, crop, and State, 1990, 1616–1.1

Flour milling production by State, stocks, daily capacity, and exports by country, monthly Current Industrial Rpt, 2506–4.1

Foreign and US agricultural production, acreage, and yield for selected crops, forecasts by selected world region and country, FAS monthly circular, 1925–28

Foreign and US agricultural production, prices, trade, and use, periodic rpt with articles, 1522–3

Foreign and US agricultural supply and demand indicators, by selected crop, monthly rpt, 1522–5

Foreign and US grain production, prices, trade, stocks, and use, FAS periodic circular series, 1925–2

Foreign and US wheat production, prices, trade, stocks, and use, quarterly situation rpt with articles, 1561–12

Foreign countries agricultural production, prices, and trade, by country, 1980-90 and forecast 1991, annual world area rpt series, 1524–4

Futures and options trading volume, by commodity and exchange, FY90, annual rpt, 11924–2

Futures contracts, stocks in deliverable position by type, weekly tables, 11922–4

Futures trading in selected commodities and financial instruments and indexes, NYC, Chicago, and other markets activity, semimonthly rpt, 11922–5

Inspection of grain for domestic use and export, and foreign buyers complaints, FY90, annual rpt, 1294–1

Inspection of grain for export, test results by commodity and port region, 1988-90, annual rpt series, 1294–2

Irrigation projects of Reclamation Bur in western US, crop production and acreage by commodity, State, and project, 1989, annual rpt, 5824–12

Loan support programs of USDA for grains, activity and status by grain and State, monthly rpt, 1802–3

Manufacturing annual survey, 1989: finances and operations, by SIC 2- to 4-digit industry, series, 2506–15

OECD trade, total and for 4 major countries, and US trade by country, by commodity, 1970-89, world area rpt series, 9116–1

Pesticide and fertilizer use reduction, environmental and economic impacts by commodity and region, alternative forecasts 1989-94, hearing, 23848–222

PL 480 long-term credit sales allocations, by commodity and country, periodic press release, 1922–7

Price indexes (producer), by stage of processing and detailed commodity, monthly rpt, 6762–6

Price indexes (producer), by stage of processing and detailed commodity, monthly 1990, annual rpt, 6764–2

Price support and other CCC program outlays, with production and marketing outlook, by commodity, projected 1990-96, 26306–6.160

Prices received and paid by farmers, by commodity and State, 1990, annual rpt, 1629–5

Prices received by farmers and production value, by detailed crop and State, 1988-90, annual rpt, 1621–2

Prices received by farmers for major products, and paid for farm inputs and living items, by State, monthly rpt, 1629–1

Production and trade, by country, 1989-92, article, 1502–4.202

Production costs for corn, wheat, and soybeans in current and constant dollars, 1975-79, article, 1541–1.208

Production, farms, acreage, and related data, by selected crop and State, monthly rpt, 1621–1

Production itemized costs, receipts, and returns, by commodity and region, 1987-89, annual rpt, 1544–20

Production, prices, trade, and export inspections by US port and country of destination, by grain type, weekly rpt, 1313–2

Production, prices, trade, and marketing, by commodity, current situation and forecast, monthly rpt with articles, 1502–4

Soviet Union agricultural trade, by commodity and country, 1955-90, 1528–322

Soviet Union, Eastern Europe, OECD, and selected other countries agricultural production, by commodity, 1960s-90, annual rpt, 9114–4.5

State and Metro Area Data Book, 1991 data compilation, 2328–54

Statistical Abstract of US, 1991 annual data compilation, 2324–1.23

Stocks and prices of wheat estimated under alternative reserve storage assumptions, 1990-91, article, 1561–12.201

Stocks of grain by region and market city, and grain inspected for export, by type, weekly rpt, 1313–4

Stocks of grain on and off farms, by crop, quarterly rpt, 1621–4

Stocks of wheat and corn, demand impacts of storage subsidy programs, model description and results, 1972-87, 1548–378

Zimbabwe agricultural conditions impacts of economic policies, 1980s, 1528–319

see also under By Commodity in the "Index by Categories"

Wheelchairs

see Prosthetics and orthotics

Wheeler, Frances C.

"Evaluating South Carolina's Community Cardiovascular Disease Prevention Project", 4042–3.245

Wheeler, Judith C.

"Water Withdrawal and Use in Maryland, 1986", 5666–24.8

Wheeling, W.Va.

see also under By SMSA or MSA in the "Index by Categories"

Whichard, Obie G.

"U.S. International Sales and Purchases of Services: U.S. Cross-Border Transactions, 1987-90, and Sales by Affiliates, 1988-89", 2702–1.223

Index by Subjects and Names

Wholesale trade

Whipple, James W.
"Wisconsin Timber Industry: An Assessment of Timber Product Output and Use, 1988", 1206–10.12

Whitaker, Catherine J.
"Teenage Victims", 6066–3.43

White, A. Patricia
"Globex Trading System", 9366–6.271

White, Betsy B.
"U.S. Financial System: A Status Report and a Structural Perspective", 9385–8.84

White collar crime
see Fraud

White collar workers
see Area wage surveys
see Business management
see Clerical workers
see Executives and managers
see Industry wage surveys
see Paraprofessionals
see Professional and technical workers

White, Dennis L.
"Electricity Savings Among Participants Three Years After Weatherization in Bonneville's 1986 Residential Weatherization Program", 3226–1.7

White House
Acreage of land under Natl Park Service mgmt, by site, ownership, and region, FY91, semiannual rpt, 5542–1
Press members admitted to congressional and White House galleries, *Congressional Directory*, 1991-92, biennial rpt, 23874–1
Visits in natl park system, by park and State, monthly rpt, 5542–4
Visits in natl park system, by park and State, 1990, annual rpt, 5544–12
see also Executive Office of the President

White, T. Fred, Jr.
"Choice Beef Prices and Price Spreads Series: Methodology and Revisions", 1568–295

Whited, C. R.
"Ground-Water Data for Michigan, 1988", 5666–28.2

Whitehead, David D.
"Impact of Private-Sector Defense Cuts on Regions of the U.S.", 9371–1.206

Whiteman, Charles H.
"Monetary Aggregates as Monetary Targets: A Statistical Investigation", 9371–10.53

Whitesell, William C.
"Credit Cards and Money Demand: A Cross-Sectional Study", 9379–12.74

Whittemore, Alice S.
"Low-Grade, Latent Prostate Cancer Volume: Predictor of Clinical Cancer Incidence?", 4472–1.221

Whitton, Carolyn L.
"Background on Egypt's Cotton Sector", 1561–1.201

Wholesale Price Index
see Producer Price Index

Wholesale trade
Business statistics, detailed data for major industries and economic indicators, *Survey of Current Business*, monthly rpt, 2702–1.7
Census Bur rpts and data files, coverage and availability, 1991 annual listing, 2304–2
Classification codes concordance of Canada and US SICs, for 1- to 4-digit levels, 1991 rpt, 2628–31
Collective bargaining agreements expiring during year, and workers covered, by firm, union, industry group, and State, 1991, annual rpt, 6784–9

County Business Patterns, 1988: employment, establishments, and payroll, by SIC 2- to 4-digit industry and county, annual State rpt series, 2326–6
County Business Patterns, 1989: employment, establishments, and payroll, by SIC 2- to 4-digit industry and county, annual State rpt series, 2326–8
Earnings by industry div, and personal income per capita and by source, by State, MSA, and county, 1984-89, annual regional rpts, 2704–2
Employment and Earnings, detailed data, monthly rpt, 6742–2.5
Employment, earnings, and hours, by SIC 1- to 4-digit industry, monthly and annual averages, selected years 1909-90, annual rpt, 6744–4
Employment, earnings, and hours, monthly press release, 6742–5
Employment situation, earnings, hours, and other BLS economic indicators, transcripts of BLS Commissioner's monthly testimony, periodic rpt, 23846–4
Employment, unemployment, and labor force characteristics, by region and census div, 1990, annual rpt, 6744–7.1
Enterprise Statistics, 1987: auxiliaries of multi-establishment firms, finances and operations by function, industry, and State, 2329–6
Enterprise Statistics, 1987: finances and operations for companies, by size, level of diversification, form of organization, and industry group, 2329–8
Finance companies credit outstanding and leasing activities, by credit type, monthly rpt, 9365–2.7
Financial statements for manufacturing, mining, and trade corporations, by selected SIC 2- to 3-digit industry, quarterly rpt, 2502–1
Foreign countries economic conditions, policy, and trade practices, by country, 1988-90, annual rpt, 21384–5
Foreign direct investment in US, by industry group and world area, 1987-90, annual article, 2702–1.219
Foreign direct investment in US, by industry group of US affiliate and country of parent firm, 1980-86, 2708–41
Foreign direct investment in US, major transactions by type, industry, country, and US location, 1989, annual rpt, 2044–20
Foreign direct investment of US, by industry group and world area, 1987-90, annual article, 2702–1.220
Franchise business opportunities by firm and kind of business, and sources of aid and info, 1990 annual listing, 2104–7
Inventories, sales, and inventory/sales ratios for manufacturing and trade, quarterly article, 2702–1.28
Multinatl firms US affiliates, finances, and operations, by industry, world area of parent firm, and State, 1988-89, annual rpt, 2704–4
Multinatl US firms and foreign affiliates finances and operations, by industry and world area of parent firm, 1989 benchmark survey, preliminary annual rpt, 2704–5
Occupational injuries, illnesses, and workdays lost, by SIC 2-digit industry, 1989-90, annual press release, 6844–3

Occupational injury and illness rates, by SIC 2- to 4-digit industry, 1988-89, annual rpt, 6844–7
Occupational injury and illness rates, by SIC 2- to 4-digit industry, 1989, annual rpt, 6844–1
Puerto Rico and other US possessions corporations income tax returns, income and tax items, and employment, by selected industry, 1987, article, 8302–2.213
Puerto Rico economic censuses, 1987: wholesale and retail trade and service industry finances and operations, by SIC 2- to 4-digit industry and municipio, 2591–1
Puerto Rico economic censuses, 1987: wholesale, retail, and service industries finances and operations, by establishment characteristics and SIC 2- and 3-digit industry, subject rpts, 2591–2
Sales and inventories, by SIC 2- to 3-digit kind of business, monthly rpt, 2413–7
Sales and inventories, monthly rpt, 23842–1.3
Sales, inventories, purchases, and gross margins, by SIC 2- to 3-digit kind of business, 1990, annual rpt, 2413–13
SEC registration, firms required to file annual rpts, as of Sept 1990, annual listing, 9734–5
State and Metro Area Data Book, 1991 data compilation, 2328–54
Statistical Abstract of US, 1991 annual data compilation, 2324–1.17; 2324–1.28
Tax (income) returns of corporations, income and tax items by asset size and detailed industry, 1987, annual rpt, 8304–4
Tax (income) returns of corporations, income and tax items by asset size and detailed industry, 1988, annual rpt, 8304–21
Tax (income) returns of corporations with foreign tax credit, income and tax items by industry group, 1986, biennial article, 8302–2.203
Tax (income) returns of multinatl US firms foreign affiliates, income statement items, by asset size and industry, 1986, biennial article, 8302–2.212
Tax (income) returns of partnerships, income statement and balance sheet items, by industry group, 1989, annual article, 8302–2.216; 8304–18
Tax (income) returns of sole proprietorships, income statement items, by industry group, 1989, annual article, 8302–2.214
Wage and benefit changes from collective bargaining and mgmt decisions, by industry div, monthly rpt, 6782–1
Wages by occupation, and benefits for office and plant workers, periodic MSA survey rpt series, 6785–11; 6785–12
see also Agricultural marketing
see also Census of Wholesale Trade
see also Industrial purchasing
see also Retail trade
see also Warehouses
see also under By Industry in the "Index by Categories"
see also under names of specific commodities or commodity groups

Whooping cranes

Whooping cranes
see Birds and bird conservation

Wiatrowski, William J.
"New Survey Data on Pension Benefits", 6722–1.238

Wichita Falls, Tex.
Wages by occupation, for office and plant workers, 1991 survey, periodic MSA rpt, 6785–3.5
see also under By SMSA or MSA in the "Index by Categories"

Wichita, Kans.
see also under By City and By SMSA or MSA in the "Index by Categories"

Widmann, Richard H.
"Pulpwood Production in the Northeast, 1989", 1204–18
"West Virginia Timber Products Output, 1987", 1206–15.9

Widows and widowers
- Black Americans social and economic characteristics, for South and total US, 1989-90 and trends from 1969, Current Population Rpt, 2546–1.450
- Black lung benefits and beneficiaries by recipient type, from 1970, and by State, 1989, annual rpt, 4744–3.7
- *Consumer Income*, socioeconomic characteristics of persons, families, and households, detailed cross-tabulations, Current Population Rpt series, 2546–6
- Deaths and rates, by cause, age, sex, marital status, and race, 1988, US Vital Statistics annual rpt, 4144–2.1
- Earnings replacement rates of pension plans and OASI benefits, by age, salary, years of participation, and occupational group, 1989, article, 6722–1.238
- Educational attainment, by sociodemographic characteristics and location, 1989 and trends from 1940, biennial Current Population Rpt, 2546–1.452
- Hispanic Americans social and economic characteristics, by detailed origin, 1991, Current Population Rpt, 2546–1.448; 2546–1.451
- Households and family characteristics, by location, 1990, annual Current Population Rpt, 2546–1.447
- Living arrangements, family relationships, and marital status, by selected characteristics, 1990, annual Current Population Rpt, 2546–1.449
- Marriage, marriage dissolution, remarriage, and cohabitation, for women, by age and race, 1988, 4146–8.196
- Marriages and rates, by age, race, education, previous marital status, and State, 1988, US Vital Statistics advance annual rpt, 4146–5.122
- Marriages, by prior marital status and other characteristics of spouses, and State, 1987, US Vital Statistics annual rpt, 4144–4.1
- Military pay and benefits for active duty personnel, reserves, retirees, and survivors, 1940s-80s and projected to 2049, 21208–34
- OASDI benefit payments, trust fund finances, and economic and demographic assumptions, 1970-90 and alternative projections to 2000, actuarial rpt, 4706–1.105
- Railroad employee benefits program finances and beneficiaries, FY90, annual rpt, 9704–1

Railroad retirement, survivors, unemployment, and health insurance programs, monthly rpt, 9702–2

- Remarriage of divorced and widowed women, duration of singlehood, and redivorce, by age, 1985, Current Population Survey, 2546–2.157
- *Statistical Abstract of US*, 1991 annual data compilation, 2324–1.1; 2324–1.2
- Veterans compensation and pension recipients, for each US war, 1775-1990, annual rpt, 8604–2
- Veterans disability and death compensation and pension cases, by type of entitlement and period of service, monthly rpt, 8602–5
- Veterans disability and death compensation cases of VA, by entitlement type, period of service, sex, age, and State, FY89, annual rpt, 8604–7
- Workers compensation laws of States and Fed Govt, 1991 semiannual rpt, 6502–1
- *see also* Old-Age, Survivors, Disability, and Health Insurance
- *see also* under By Marital Status in the "Index by Categories"

Wiegert, Richard G.
"Tidal Salt Marshes of the Southeast Atlantic Coast: A Community Profile", 5506–9.42

Wigley, Susan E.
"Distribution of Sexually Immature Components of 10 Northwest Atlantic Groundfish Species Based on Northeast Fisheries Center Bottom Trawl Surveys, 1968-86", 2168–122

Wilburn, Anne M.
- "Current Velocity and Hydrographic Observations in the Southwestern North Atlantic Ocean: Subtropical Atlantic Climate Studies (STACS), 1989", 2146–7.7
- "Shipboard Acoustic Doppler Current Profiler Data Collected During the Subtropical Atlantic Climate Studies (STACS) Project (1983-86)", 2146–7.8

Wilcox-Gok, Virginia
"Health Insurance Coverage Among Disabled Medicare Enrollees", 4652–1.243

Wilcox, James A.
"Real, Affordable Mortgage", 9373–1.204

Wilderness areas
- Acreage and use of public lands, and Land Mgmt Bur activities and finances, annual State rpt series, 5724–11
- Acreage, grants, use, revenues, and allocations, for public lands by State, FY90, annual rpt, 5724–1.2
- Acreage of land, by use, ownership, and State, 1987 and trends from 1910, 1588–48
- Acreage of land under Forest Service mgmt, by forest and location, 1990, annual rpt, 1204–2
- Acreage of land under Natl Park Service mgmt, by site, ownership, and region, FY91, semiannual rpt, 5542–1
- Acreage of refuges and other land under Fish and Wildlife Service mgmt, by site and State, as of Sept 1991, annual rpt, 5504–8
- *Environmental Quality*, status of problems, protection programs, research, and intl issues, 1991 annual rpt, 484–1

Forest Service activities and finances, by region and State, FY90, annual rpt, 1204–1.1

- Forest Service mgmt of public lands and resources dev, environmental, economic, and social impacts of alternative programs, projected to 2040, 1208–24
- Forests (natl) recreational use, by type of activity and State, 1990, annual rpt, 1204–17
- Mental health and educational benefits of wilderness areas use, and leadership training programs effectiveness, 1990 conf papers, 1208–347
- Minerals resources and availability on public lands, State rpt series, 5606–7
- Oil and gas reserves, 1988 and projected under alternative technology and policy assumptions to 2030, Natl Energy Strategy, 3166–6.51
- Pacific Northwest acreage, staff, finances, and mgmt activities of Forest Service, with data by forest, 1970s-89, annual rpt, 1204–37
- Recreation programs of Forest Service, funding and cost sharing pledges, 1980s-91, GAO rpt, 26113–518
- Visits and overnight stays in natl park system, by park and State, monthly rpt, 5542–4
- Visits and overnight stays in natl park system, by park and State, 1990, annual rpt, 5544–12

Wildlife and wildlife conservation
- Acid rain and air pollution environmental impacts, and methods of neutralizing acidified water bodies, summary research rpt series, 5506–5
- Agricultural Conservation Program participation and payments, by practice and State, FY90, annual rpt, 1804–7
- Assistance (financial and nonfinancial) of Fed Govt, 1991 base edition with supplements, annual listing, 104–5
- Bears (grizzly) in Yellowstone Natl Park area, monitoring results, 1990, annual rpt, 5544–4
- Beaver pond area rodent and shrew population and diversity compared to riparian habitat, 1988-89 study, 1208–377
- Coastal and riparian areas environmental conditions, fish, wildlife, use, and mgmt, for individual ecosystems, series, 5506–9
- Coastal areas environmental and socioeconomic conditions, and potential impact of oil and gas OCS leases, final statement series, 5736–1
- Coastal areas recreation facilities of Fed Govt and States, visitor and site characteristics, 1987-90 survey, regional rpt series, 2176–9
- Colorado River Salinity Control Program participation and payments, FY87-90, annual rpt, 1804–23
- Criminal sentences for Federal offenses, guidelines by offense and circumstances, series, 17668–1
- Enforcement of wildlife protection laws, FWS activities, funding, costs, and staff, late 1970s-90, GAO rpt, 26113–525
- *Environmental Quality*, status of problems, protection programs, research, and intl issues, 1991 annual rpt, 484–1

Index by Subjects and Names

Williamson, Steve

Farm acreage enrolled in Conservation Reserve Program, plantings, and impacts on production, soil erosion, water quality, and wildlife habitat, 1991 conf, 1208–360

Fed Govt spending in States, by type, program, agency, and State, FY90, annual rpt, 2464–2

Fish and Wildlife Service conservation and habitat mgmt activities, and endangered species by group, FY90, biennial rpt, 5504–20

Florida environmental, social, and economic conditions, and impacts of proposed OCS oil and gas leases in southern coastal areas, 1990 compilation of papers, 5738–19

Foreign and US environmental and wildlife conservation agreements provisions, status, and signatories, as of 1991, listing, 9886–4.169

Forest Service acreage, staff, finances, and mgmt activities in Pacific Northwest, with data by forest, 1970s-89, annual rpt, 1204–37

Forest Service activities and finances, by region and State, FY90, annual rpt, 1204–1

Forest Service mgmt of public lands and resources dev, environmental, economic, and social impacts of alternative programs, projected to 2040, 1208–24

Forests (natl) recreational use, by type of activity and State, 1990, annual rpt, 1204–17

Global climate change environmental, infrastructure, and health impacts, with model results and background data, 1850s-2100, 9188–113

Goats (mountain) population in Yellowstone and Grand Teton Natl Parks, and habitat mgmt options, 1970s-89, 5548–19

Horse and burro wild herd areas in southwestern States, adoptions by State, 1990, annual rpt, 5724–15

Horse and burro wild herd areas in western States, population, adoption, and mgmt costs, as of FY89, biennial rpt, 5724–8

Horse and burro wild herd population, and Bur of Land Mgmt removals and disposition, by county, annual State rpt series, 5724–11

Horse and burro wild herd population and grazing on natl forest lands, by region and State, 1990, annual rpt, 1204–5

Idaho Snake River area birds of prey, rodent, and vegetation distribution and characteristics, research results, 1990, annual rpt, 5724–14

Land Mgmt Bur activities and funding by State, FY89, annual rpt, 5724–13

Land Mgmt Bur activities in Southwestern US, FY90, annual rpt, 5724–15

Land Mgmt Bur wildlife mgmt activities and funding, acreage by habitat type, and scientific staff, State rpt series, 5726–7

Land Mgmt Bur wildlife mgmt activities and funding, acreage, staff, and plans, habitat study series, 5726–6

Land under Fish and Wildlife Service mgmt, acreage by site and State, as of Sept 1991, annual rpt, 5504–8

Natl forests fish and wildlife activities funding, by source, FY88-90, GAO rpt, 26113–529

Northeastern US forest wildlife habitat characteristics, by location, State rpt series, 1206–44

Northeastern US recreation areas use, mgmt, and tourism dev issues, 1990 conf, 1208–356

Pollutants health effects for animals by species and for humans, and environmental levels, for selected substances, series, 5506–14

Public lands acreage and use, and Land Mgmt Bur activities and finances, annual State rpt series, 5724–11

Public lands acreage, grants, use, revenues, and allocations, by State, FY90, annual rpt, 5724–1.2

Public lands wildlife mgmt, endangered species, and BLM activities and funding, FY80-90, 5728–37

Research (agricultural) funding and staffing for USDA, State agencies, and other instns, by topic, FY90, annual rpt, 1744–2

Research of State fish and wildlife agencies, federally funded wildlife projects and costs by species and State, 1990, annual listing, 5504–24

Research on fish and wildlife population, habitat, and mgmt, technical rpt series, 5506–12

Research on wildlife and plants, habitat study series, 5506–13

Restoration and hunter safety funding of Fish and Wildlife Service, by State, FY92, semiannual press release, 5502–1

Restoration programs of Fish and Wildlife Service, finances by State, and excise tax collections, FY90, annual rpt, 5504–13

Restoration programs of Fish and Wildlife Service, funding, land purchases, and project listing, by State, FY89, annual rpt, 5504–1

Sheep, lamb, and goat loss to predators and other causes, by region and State, 1990, 1618–20

Wetlands acreage, resources, soil and water properties, and conservation efforts, by wetland type, State rpt series, 5506–11

see also Birds and bird conservation

see also Endangered species

see also Fish and fishing industry

see also Fishing, sport

see also Hunting and fishing licenses

see also Hunting and trapping

see also Marine mammals

see also Marine resources conservation

see also Wildlife refuges

see also Zoological parks

Wildlife refuges

Acreage and costs of real property owned by Fed Govt, worldwide summary by location, agency, and use, 1989, annual rpt, 9454–5

Acreage of land, by use, ownership, and State, 1987 and trends from 1910, 1588–48

Acreage of land under Forest Service mgmt, by forest and location, 1990, annual rpt, 1204–2

Acreage of land under Natl Park Service mgmt, by site, ownership, and region, FY91, semiannual rpt, 5542–1

Acreage of refuges and other land under Fish and Wildlife Service mgmt, by site and State, as of Sept 1991, annual rpt, 5504–8

Army Corps of Engineers water resources dev projects, characteristics, and costs, 1950s-89, biennial State rpt series, 3756–1

Army Corps of Engineers water resources dev projects, characteristics, and costs, 1950s-91, biennial State rpt series, 3756–2

Restoration programs of Fish and Wildlife Service, funding, land purchases, and project listing, by State, FY89, annual rpt, 5504–1

Visits and overnight stays in natl park system, by park and State, 1990, annual rpt, 5544–12

Washington State marine sanctuaries proposal, environmental and economic impacts, with background data, 1984-89, 2178–30

Wetlands acreage, resources, soil and water properties, and conservation efforts, by wetland type, State rpt series, 5506–11

Wetlands wildlife and migratory bird habitat acquisition, funding by State, FY92, press release, 5306–4.8; 5306–4.11

Wildman, Mark R.

"Chinese Shrimp Culture", 1524–4.3

Wilhelm, James A.

"1989 Examination Customer Satisfaction Survey", 8304–8.1

Wilhelmsen, Roger N.

"Environmental Monitoring for EG&G Idaho Facilities at the Idaho National Engineering Laboratory, Annual Report, 1990", 3354–10

Wilkes-Barre, Pa.

Wages by occupation, and benefits for office and plant workers, 1991 survey, periodic MSA rpt, 6785–12.6

see also under By SMSA or MSA in the "Index by Categories"

Willamette River

Water supply and quality in streams and lakes, and groundwater levels in wells, by drainage basin, 1988, annual State rpt series, 5666–16

Water supply and quality in streams and lakes, and groundwater levels in wells, by drainage basin, 1989, annual State rpt series, 5666–12

Water supply and quality in streams and lakes, and groundwater levels in wells, by drainage basin, 1990, annual State rpt series, 5666–10

Water supply in US and southern Canada, streamflow, surface and groundwater conditions, and reservoir levels, by location, monthly rpt, 5662–3

Willard, David G.

"Cobalt Availability: A Minerals Availability Appraisal", 5606–4.29

Williams, Deborah

"Adjusting a Wage Index for Geographic Differences in Occupational Mix", 17206–2.17

Williams, Linda S.

"Highway Vehicle MPG and Market Shares Report: Model Year 1990", 3302–4

Williams, Terry

"Soviet Agriculture System", 1004–16.1

Williamson, Steve

"Barter and Monetary Exchange Under Private Information", 9383–20.11

Williamsport, Pa.

Williamsport, Pa.
see also under By SMSA or MSA in the "Index by Categories"

Willis, Winnie O.
"Requiring Formal Training in Preventive Health Practices for Child Day Care Providers", 4042–3.243

Willoughby, Timothy C.
"External Quality-Assurance Results for the National Atmospheric Deposition Program and the National Trends Network During 1989", 5664–17

Wills, Darryl S.
"Factor Intensity of U.S. Agricultural Trade", 1548–373

Wilmington, Del.
CPI by component for US city average, and by region, population size, and for 15 metro areas, monthly rpt, 6762–1
CPI by component for US city average, and by region, population size, and for 27 metro areas, monthly rpt, 6762–2
see also under By SMSA or MSA in the "Index by Categories"

Wilmington, N.C.
see also under By SMSA or MSA in the "Index by Categories"

Wilson, C. Robert
"Energy-Related Inventions Program: Commercial Progress of Participants Through 1988", 3308–91

Wilson, Doug
"Shipboard Acoustic Doppler Current Profiler Data Collected During the Subtropical Atlantic Climate Studies (STACS) Project (1983-86)", 2146–7.8

Wilson, Richard
"We Fought Cape Horn . . . and the Horn Won", 2152–8.201

Wilson, Todd L.
"Consumer Price Rise Slows in First Half of 1991", 6722–1.247

Wind
see Meteorology
see Storms
see Weather
see Wind energy

Wind energy
Certification applications filed with FERC, for small power production and cogeneration facilities, FY80-90, annual listing, 3084–13
Electric power plants and capacity, by fuel used, owner, location, and operating status, 1990 and for units planned 1991-2000, annual listing, 3164–36
Natl Energy Strategy plans for conservation and pollution reduction, impacts of technology and regulation proposals, projected 1990-2030, 3166–6.47
Natl Energy Strategy plans for renewable energy dev, supply projected under alternative cost and capacity use assumptions, 1990-2030, 3166–6.50
Supply, demand, and prices, by fuel type and end-use sector, alternative projections 1989-2010, annual rpt, 3164–75
Supply, demand, and prices, by fuel type and end-use sector, projections and underlying assumptions, 1990-2010, annual rpt, 3164–90

Windau, Janice
"Further Test of a Census Approach to Compiling Data on Fatal Work Injuries", 6722–1.249

"Testing a Census Approach to Compiling Data on Fatal Work Injuries", 6722–1.205

Windfall profit tax
Collections of excise tax, by source, quarterly rpt, 8302–1
Collections, refunds, and taxes due IRS, by State and region, FY86, annual rpt, 8304–3
Producers finances and operations, by energy type for US firms domestic and foreign operations, 1989, annual rpt, 3164–44
Tax (excise) collections of IRS, by source, quarterly rpt, 8302–2.1

Windheim, Barry
"Individual Income Tax Returns Data by State, 1986-88", 8302–2.201

Windmuller, John P.
"International Trade Secretariats: The Industrial Trade Union Internationals", 6366–4.53

Wine and winemaking
Business statistics, detailed data for major industries and economic indicators, *Survey of Current Business*, monthly rpt, 2702–1.14
Consumer Expenditure Survey, food spending by item, household composition, income, age, race, and region, 1980-88, biennial rpt, 1544–30
Consumption of food, dietary composition, and nutrient intake, 1987/88 natl survey, preliminary rpt series, 1356–1
Consumption, supply, trade, prices, spending, and indexes, by food commodity, 1989, annual rpt, 1544–4
County Business Patterns, 1988: employment, establishments, and payroll, by SIC 2- to 4-digit industry and county, annual State rpt series, 2326–6
County Business Patterns, 1989: employment, establishments, and payroll, by SIC 2- to 4-digit industry and county, annual State rpt series, 2326–8
CPI by component for US city average, and by region, population size, and for 27 metro areas, monthly rpt, 6762–2
Employment, earnings, and hours, by SIC 1- to 4-digit industry, monthly and annual averages, selected years 1909-90, annual rpt, 6744–4
Exports (agricultural) of US, impacts of foreign agricultural and trade policy, with data by commodity and country, 1989, annual rpt, 1924–8
Exports and imports (agricultural) of US, by commodity and country, bimonthly rpt, 1522–1
Exports and imports (agricultural) of US, by detailed commodity and country, 1989, annual rpt, 1524–8
Exports and imports (agricultural) of US, by detailed commodity and country, 1990, semiannual rpt, 1522–4
Exports and imports of US, by country and detailed commodity, monthly rpt, 2422–12
Exports and imports of US, by Harmonized System 6-digit commodity and country, 1990, annual rpt, 2424–13
Exports of US, detailed Schedule B commodities with countries of destination, 1990, annual rpt, 2424–10

Index by Subjects and Names

Foreign and US fresh and processed fruit, vegetable, and nut production and trade, FAS monthly circular with articles, 1925–34
Fruit (noncitrus) and nut production, prices, and use, by crop and State, 1988-90, annual rpt, 1621–18.1
Inventory and supply of wine, by type of wine, source, and selected State, periodic situation rpt with articles, 1561–6
Manufacturing annual survey, 1989: finances and operations, by SIC 2- to 4-digit industry, series, 2506–15
Manufacturing census, 1987: finances and operations, by SIC 2- to 4-digit industry, State, and MSA, with trends from 1849, 2497–1
Manufacturing census, 1987: finances and operations, by type of organization and SIC 2- to 4-digit industry, subject rpt, 2497–5
Occupational injury and illness rates, by SIC 2- to 4-digit industry, 1988-89, annual rpt, 6844–7
Occupational injury and illness rates, by SIC 2- to 4-digit industry, 1989, annual rpt, 6844–1
Pollution (air) emissions factors, by detailed pollutant and source, data compilation, 1990 rpt, 9198–120
Price indexes (producer), by stage of processing and detailed commodity, monthly rpt, 6762–6
Price indexes (producer), by stage of processing and detailed commodity, monthly 1990, annual rpt, 6764–2
Production, prices, and use of noncitrus fruit and nuts, by crop and State, 1988-90, annual rpt, 1621–18.3
Production, stocks, and taxable and tax-free removals, for wine by State, monthly rpt, 8486–1.2
Tax rates and revenue of State and local govts, by source and State, 1991 and historical trends, annual rpt, 10044–1
Wholesale trade census, 1987: establishments, sales by customer class, employment, inventories, and expenses, by SIC 2- to 4-digit kind of business, 2407–4
Youth alcohol use, knowledge, attitudes, and info sources, series, 4006–10

Wineholt, David A.
"Grain Cooperatives", 1126–1.5

Winnipeg, Canada
Fruit and vegetable shipments, and arrivals in US and Canada cities, by mode of transport and State and country of origin, 1990, annual rpt, 1311–4.2

Winston-Salem, N.C.
see also under By City and By SMSA or MSA in the "Index by Categories"

Winter Haven, Fla.
see also under By SMSA or MSA in the "Index by Categories"

Winter sports
Forest Service activities and finances, by region and State, FY90, annual rpt, 1204–1.1
Forests (natl) recreational use, by type of activity and State, 1990, annual rpt, 1204–17
Injuries from use of consumer products, by severity, victim age, and detailed product, 1990, annual rpt, 9164–6

Index by Subjects and Names

Public lands acreage, grants, use, revenues, and allocations, by State, FY90, annual rpt, 5724–1.2

Public lands recreation facilities and use, and Land Mgmt Bur mgmt activities, funding, and plans, State rpt series, 5726–5

Wiretapping

see Electronic surveillance

Wiring, electrical

see Electrical machinery and equipment

see Electronics industry and products

Wisconsin

- Banks (insured commercial and savings) deposits by instn, State, MSA, and county, as of June 1990, annual regional rpt, 9295–3.3
- Business and economic conditions, Fed Reserve 9th District, quarterly journal, 9383–19
- Cancer (breast) rates attributable to increased detection through mammography use, by age, 1980-88 study, article, 4472–1.229
- County Business Patterns, 1989: employment, establishments, and payroll, by SIC 2- to 4-digit industry and county, annual State rpt, 2326–8.51
- Cranberry production, prices, use, and acreage, for selected States, 1989-90 and forecast 1991, annual rpt, 1621–18.4
- Dairy prices, by product and selected area, with related marketing data, 1990, annual rpt, 1317–1
- DOD prime contract awards, by contractor, service branch, State, and city, FY90, annual rpt, 3544–22
- Economic conditions and outlook, for US and Canada Great Lakes area, 1970s-90, 9375–15
- Fed Govt spending in States and local areas, by type, State, county, and city, FY90, annual rpt, 2464–3
- Fed Govt spending in States, by type, program, agency, and State, FY90, annual rpt, 2464–2
- HHS financial aid, by program, recipient, State, and city, FY90, annual regional listing, 4004–3.5
- Hospital deaths of Medicare patients, actual and expected rates by diagnosis, and hospital characteristics, by instn, FY87-89, annual regional rpt, 4654–14.5
- Housing vacancy rates for single and multifamily units and mobile homes in FHLB 7th District, by ZIP code, annual MSA rpt series, 9304–18
- Income (personal) per capita and by source, and earnings by industry div, by State, MSA, and county, 1984-89, annual regional rpt, 2704–2.2
- Jail adult and juvenile population, employment, spending, instn conditions, and inmate programs, by county and facility, 1988, regional rpt series, 6068–144.3
- Lumber (veneer log) production, mill receipts, and trade, by species, with residue use, for North Central States, 1988, quadrennial rpt, 1208–220
- Marriages, divorces, and rates, by characteristics of spouses, State, and county, 1987 and trends from 1920, US Vital Statistics annual rpt, 4144–4

Mineral Industry Surveys, State reviews of production, 1990, preliminary annual rpt, 5614–6

- *Minerals Yearbook, 1989,* Vol 2: State reviews of production, sales, and firms, by commodity, and business activity, annual rpt, 5604–34
- Mortgage interest fixed and adjustable rates and fees offered by Wisconsin S&Ls, monthly rpt, 9302–7
- Physicians, by specialty, age, sex, and location of training and practice, 1989, State rpt, 4116–6.51
- Population and housing census, 1990: population and housing characteristics, households, and land area, by county, subdiv, and place, State rpt, 2551–1.51
- Population and housing census, 1990: voting age and total population by race, and housing units, by block, redistricting counts required under PL 94-171, State CD-ROM release, 2551–6.3
- Population and housing census, 1990: voting age and total population by race, and housing units, by county and city, redistricting counts required under PL 94-171, State summary rpt, 2551–5.50
- Savings instns, FHLB 7th District and natl cost of funds indexes, and mortgage rates, monthly rpt, 9302–30
- *Statistical Abstract of US,* 1991 annual data compilation, 2324–1
- Supplemental Security Income payments and beneficiaries, by type of eligibility, State, and county, Dec 1989, annual rpt, 4744–27.5
- Timber harvest and industrial roundwood production, by product and county, 1988, State rpt, 1206–10.12
- Timber in Wisconsin, prices for sawlogs by species and grade, 1960-88, annual rpt, 1204–29

see also Kenosha, Wis.

see also La Crosse, Wis.

see also Milwaukee, Wis.

see also Sparta, Wis.

see also Waukesha County, Wis.

see also under By State in the "Index by Categories"

Wisdom, Harold W.

"Transportation Costs for Forest Products from the Puget Sound Area and Alaska to Pacific Rim Markets", 1208–358

Wise, David A.

"Aging and the Income Value of Housing Wealth", 2626–10.125

"Saving Effect of Tax-Deferred Retirement Accounts: Evidence from the SIPP", 2626–10.132

Withholding tax

- Admin and compliance issues, and taxpayer views, 1990 conf, 8304–25
- Alien nonresidents income from US sources and tax withheld by country and US tax treaty status, 1988, annual article, 8302–2.206
- Budget of US, authoritative financial statements with appropriations, outlays, and receipts, by category and agency, FY90, annual rpt, 8104–2.1
- Foreign countries tax credits on corporate income tax returns, income, and tax items, by country and world region of credit, 1986, biennial article, 8302–2.207

Woernle, Charles H.

- Foreign countries tax credits on corporate income tax returns, with income and tax items by industry group, 1986, biennial article, 8302–2.203
- Returns and supplemental documents filed, by type, FY89 and projected to FY98, annual article, 8302–2.208
- Returns and supplemental documents filed, by type, FY90 and projected to FY99, semiannual rpt, 8302–4
- Returns filed, by type of tax and IRS district, 1989 and projected 1990-97, annual rpt, 8304–24
- Returns filed, by type of tax, region, and IRS service center, projected 1990-97 and trends from 1978, annual rpt, 8304–9
- Returns processing, IRS workload forecasts, compliance, and enforcement, data compilation, 1991 annual rpt, 8304–8
- Statements of income tax withholding and related documents filed, by type and IRS service center, 1990 and projected 1991-98, annual rpt, 8304–22

see also Social security tax

Witnesses

- Criminal sentences for Federal offenses, guidelines by offense and circumstances, series, 17668–1
- Immunity requests by Federal prosecutors to US Attorney General, and witnesses involved, data compilation, 1991 annual rpt, 6064–6.5
- Marshals Service activities, FY89, annual rpt, 6294–1
- Paternity determination through genetic testing, labs expert witness availability and costs, 1991 listing, 4698–4

Witt, L. Alan

- "Cross-Level Inferences of Job Satisfaction in the Prediction of Intent To Leave", 7506–10.94
- "Exchange Ideology as a Moderator of the Procedural Justice-Satisfaction Relationship", 7506–10.90
- "Two Studies on Participation in Decision-Making and Equity Among FAA Personnel", 7506–10.89

Witte, James C.

- "Discrete Time Models of Entry into Marriage Based on Retrospective Marital Histories of Young Adults in the U.S. and the Federal Republic of Germany", 2626–10.143
- "Entry into Marriage and the Transition to Adulthood Among Recent Birth Cohorts of Young Adults in the U.S. and the Federal Republic of Germany", 2626–10.131

Witucki, Larry A.

"U.S. Broiler Exports to the USSR: Temporary Phenomena or Emerging Trend?", 1561–7.205

Witzell, W. N.

"Blue Marlin, *Makaira nigricans,* Movements in the Western North Atlantic Ocean: Results of a Cooperative Game Fish Tagging Program, 1954-88", 2162–1.203

Woernle, Charles H.

"Staff Patterns of Epidemiologists in the Health Departments of 12 Southern States", 4042–3.253

Wolf, Holger C.

Index by Subjects and Names

Wolf, Holger C.
"Procyclical Prices: A Demi-Myth?", 9383–6.204

Wolfe, Barbara
"Effect of the Medicaid Program on Welfare Participation and Labor Supply", 2626–10.139

Wolff, S. W.
"Brown Trout Population and Habitat Changes Associated with Increased Minimum Low Flows in Douglas Creek, Wyo.", 5508–112

Women
- Abuse of women by partners, interval between incident and seeking help, by type of abuse, 1987 local area study, article, 4042–3.228
- AIDS cases by risk group, race, sex, age, State, and MSA, and deaths, monthly rpt, 4202–9
- AIDS knowledge, attitudes, and risk behaviors of women in methadone maintenance programs, effects of life skills training, 1988 local area study, article, 4042–3.221
- AIDS public knowledge, attitudes, and risk behaviors, for women, 1988 survey, 4146–8.200
- Alcohol use and abuse by women related to race, employment status, and other characteristics, 1981 local area study, article, 4042–3.212
- Arrest rates, by offense, sex, age, and race, 1965-89, annual rpt, 6224–7
- Black Americans social and economic characteristics, for South and total US, 1989-90 and trends from 1969, Current Population Rpt, 2546–1.450
- Cancer (breast) precursor hormonal changes risk relation to selected reproductive factors, 1983-89 study, article, 4472–1.227
- Cancer (breast) rates attributable to increased detection through mammography use, by age, 1980-88 study, article, 4472–1.229
- Cancer (breast) risk relation to breast self-examination practice and other risk factors, 1982-88 local area study, article, 4472–1.202
- Cancer (breast) risk relation to dietary fat and nutrient intake, for Canada, 1982-87, article, 4472–1.204
- Cancer (cervical) risk relation to blood selenium levels, local area study, 1991 article, 4472–1.203
- Cancer cases, deaths, and survival rates, by sex, race, age, and body site, 1973-88, annual rpt, 4474–35
- Census of Population and Housing, 1990: population and housing characteristics, households, and land area, by county, subdiv, and place, State rpt series, 2551–1
- Child support and alimony awards, and payment status, by selected characteristics of woman, 1989, biennial Current Population Rpt, 2546–6.72
- Child support awards, receipt, and reasons for nonsupport, 1989-90, fact sheet, 2326–17.37
- Childless women, by selected characteristics, 1990, annual Current Population Rpt, 2546–1.455
- Crime, criminal justice admin and enforcement, and public opinion, data compilation, 1991 annual rpt, 6064–6
- Crime victimization of women, by relation to offender, circumstances, and victim characteristics, for rape and other violent offenses, 1973-87, 6068–243
- Crimes, arrests, and rates, by offense, offender characteristics, population size, and jurisdiction, 1990, annual rpt, 6224–2.1; 6224–2.2
- Deaths and rates, by detailed cause and demographic characteristics, 1988 and trends from 1900, US Vital Statistics annual rpt, 4144–2
- Developing countries economic, population, and agricultural data, US and other aid sources, and AID activity, country rpt series, 9916–12
- Divorces by age of spouses and duration of marriage, and children involved, by State, 1988 and trends from 1940, US Vital Statistics advance annual rpt, 4146–5.121
- Drug, alcohol, and cigarette use, by selected characteristics, 1990 survey, biennial rpt, 4494–5
- Drug and alcohol abuse treatment facilities, services, use, funding, staff, and client characteristics, 1989, biennial rpt, 4494–10
- Education Dept programs funding, operations, and effectiveness, FY90, annual rpt, 4804–5
- Genital human papillomavirus risk relation to presence of other cervical cancer risk factors, local area study, 1991 article, 4472–1.215
- Health condition and health care resources, use, and spending, 1950s-89, annual data compilation, 4144–11
- Health condition, services use, payment sources, and health care labor force, for minorities and women by poverty status, 1940s-89, chartbook, 4118–56
- High school class of 1972: women's employment and educational experiences compared to men, natl longitudinal study, as of 1986, 4888–6
- Higher education degrees awarded, by level, field, race, and sex, 1988/89 with trends from 1978/79, biennial rpt, 4844–17
- Hispanic Americans social and economic characteristics, by detailed origin, 1991, Current Population Rpt, 2546–1.448; 2546–1.451
- Homeless adults educational services, funding, participation, and staff, by State, 1989, annual rpt series, 4804–39
- Households composition, income, benefits, and labor force status, Survey of Income and Program Participation methodology, working paper series, 2626–10
- Hypertension risk for women, by age and race, aggregate 1976-80, article, 4042–3.231
- Income (household) and poverty status under alternative income definitions, by recipient characteristics, 1990, annual Current Population Rpt, 2546–6.69
- Jail adult and juvenile population, employment, spending, instn conditions, and inmate programs, by county and facility, 1988, regional rpt series, 6068–144
- Mammography screening costs, by setting, model results, 1989 rpt, 17266–1.1
- Marriage, marriage dissolution, remarriage, and cohabitation, for women, by age and race, 1988, 4146–8.196
- Marriages and rates, by age, race, education, previous marital status, and State, 1988, US Vital Statistics advance annual rpt, 4146–5.122
- Marriages, divorces, and rates, by characteristics of spouses, State, and county, 1987 and trends from 1920, US Vital Statistics annual rpt, 4144–4
- Nuclear engineering enrollment and degrees granted by instn and State, and grad placement, by student characteristics, 1990, annual rpt, 3004–5
- OASDHI, Medicaid, SSI, and related programs benefits, beneficiary characteristics, and trust funds, selected years 1937-89, annual rpt, 4744–3
- Older women's household income by source, and expenses by type, by living arrangement and other characteristics, 1988, article, 1702–1.210
- Pelvic inflammatory disease prevention, diagnosis, treatment, and surveillance, CDC guidelines, 1991 rpt, 4206–2.41
- Prisoner population of women in State instns, by offense, drug use history, whether abused, and other characteristics, with comparisons to men, 1986, 6066–19.61
- Prisoners, characteristics, and movements, by State, 1989, annual rpt, 6064–26
- Prisoners under death sentence by prison control and prisoner characteristics, and executions from 1930, by State, 1973-90, annual rpt, 6066–25.42
- Radiation exposure at DOE and DOE-contractor sites, for women employees and visitors of child-bearing age, by age and facility type, 1988, annual rpt, 3324–1.1
- Radiation protection and health physics enrollment and degrees granted by instn and State, and grad placement, by student characteristics, 1990, annual rpt, 3004–7
- Science and engineering grad enrollment, by field, source of funds, and characteristics of student and instn, 1975-89, annual rpt, 9627–7
- *State and Metro Area Data Book*, 1991 data compilation, 2328–54
- *Statistical Abstract of US*, 1991 annual data compilation, 2324–1
- Veteran women, by age, period of service, and State, annual tables, discontinued, 9924–25
- Veterans disability and death compensation cases of VA, by entitlement type, period of service, sex, age, and State, FY89, annual rpt, 8604–7
- Veterans population, by period of service and age, as of Mar 1991, annual rpt, 8604–12
- Voting and registration, by socioeconomic and demographic characteristics, 1990 congressional election, biennial Current Population Rpt, 2546–1.454
- *see also* Families and households
- *see also* Fertility
- *see also* Maternity
- *see also* Maternity benefits

Index by Subjects and Names

see also Prenatal care
see also Sex discrimination
see also Teenage pregnancy
see also Women-owned businesses
see also Women's employment
see also under By Sex in the "Index by Categories"

Women-owned businesses

Agriculture census, 1987: farms, farmland, production, finances, and operator characteristics, by county, final State rpt series, 2331–1

Airway facilities and services contract awards of FAA to minority- and woman-owned businesses, FY85-89, annual rpt, 7504–37

DOE contracts and grants, by category, State, and for top contractors, FY90, annual rpt, 3004–21

Firms and sales, by industry div and ownership type, and data needs and availability, 1987, 9768–22

FmHA loans, by type, borrower characteristics, and State, quarterly rpt, 1182–8

Land Mgmt Bur activities and funding by State, FY89, annual rpt, 5724–13

Mgmt and financial aid from Minority Business Dev Centers, and characteristics of businesses, by region and State, FY90, annual rpt, 2104–6

NASA procurement contract awards, by type, contractor, State, and country, FY91 with trends from 1961, semiannual rpt, 9502–6

Navy procurement awards to small, disadvantaged, and women-owned businesses, FY90, annual rpt, 3804–13.3

State and Metro Area Data Book, 1991 data compilation, 2328–54

Statistical Abstract of US, 1991 annual data compilation, 2324–1.17

Travel agencies contracts of GSA, by business size and recipient, FY88-90, GAO rpt, 26119–331

Women's Bureau

Labor force status, earnings, and other characteristics of women, with comparisons to men, fact sheet series, 6564–1

Women's employment

AFDC beneficiaries demographic and financial characteristics, by State, FY89, annual rpt, 4694–1

Air Force recruiting compliance with gender-neutral selection, with aptitude test results by sex, FY86-90, GAO rpt, 26123–359

Aircraft pilot and nonpilot certificates held and issued, by type of certificate, region, State, and for women, 1989, annual rpt, 7504–1.7

Aircraft pilot and nonpilot certificates held, by type of certificate, age, sex, region, and State, 1990, annual rpt, 7504–2

Alcohol use and abuse by women related to race, employment status, and other characteristics, 1981 local area study, article, 4042–3.212

Birth expectations, childbearing delay, and childlessness among women born late 1930s-72, by age, education, and marital and employment status, late 1970s-90, Current Population Rpt, 2546–2.162

Births, fertility rates, and childless women, by selected characteristics, 1990, annual Current Population Rpt, 2546–1.455

Black Americans social and economic characteristics, for South and total US, 1989-90 and trends from 1969, Current Population Rpt, 2546–1.450

Child care arrangements, costs, and impacts on mothers labor force status, by selected characteristics, 1983 and 1988, article, 6722–1.246

Child care needs impacts on mothers labor force status, and unemployed mothers characteristics, 1986, article, 6722–1.245

Child care-related interruption of women's employment, and impacts on social security benefits, 1990 working paper, 2626–10.138

Child health, behavioral, emotional, and school problems relation to family structure, by selected characteristics, 1988, 4147–10.178

Child support and alimony awards, and payment status, by selected characteristics of woman, 1989, biennial Current Population Rpt, 2546–6.72

Children and youth social, economic, and demographic characteristics, 1950s-90, 4818–5

Computer use at home, school, and work, by purpose and selected user characteristics, 1989, Current Population Rpt, 2546–2.158

Crime victimization of women, by relation to offender, circumstances, and victim characteristics, for rape and other violent offenses, 1973-87, 6068–243

Dallas-Fort Worth-Arlington metro area employment, earnings, hours, and CPI changes, late 1970s-90, annual rpt, 6964–2

DOT activities by subagency, budget, and summary accident data, FY88, annual rpt, 7304–1

DOT employment, by subagency, occupation, and selected personnel characteristics, FY90, annual rpt, 7304–18

Educational attainment, by sociodemographic characteristics and location, 1989 and trends from 1940, biennial Current Population Rpt, 2546–1.452

Educational enrollment, by grade, instn type and control, and student characteristics, 1989 and trends from 1947, annual Current Population Rpt, 2546–1.453

Employment and Earnings, detailed data, monthly rpt, 6742–2.5

Employment, earnings, and hours, by SIC 1- to 4-digit industry, monthly and annual averages, selected years 1909-90, annual rpt, 6744–4

Employment situation, earnings, hours, and other BLS economic indicators, transcripts of BLS Commissioner's monthly testimony, periodic rpt, 23846–4

Employment, unemployment, and labor force characteristics, by region, State, and selected metro area, 1990, annual rpt, 6744–7

Family economic impacts of departure, absence, and presence of parents, 1983-86, Current Population Rpt, 2546–20.17

Women's employment

Fed Equal Opportunity Recruitment Program activity, and employment by sex, race, pay grade, and occupational group, FY90, annual rpt, 9844–33

Fed Govt civilian employment and payroll, by occupation, pay grade, sex, agency, and location, 1989, biennial rpt, 9844–4

Fed Govt civilian employment of minorities, women, veterans, and disabled persons, as of Sept 1988 and 1990, biennial article, 9842–1.202

Fed Govt employment of minorities and women, and compliance with EEOC standards, by occupation and agency, FY88-92, GAO rpt, 26119–342

Fed Govt employment of minorities, women, and disabled, by agency and occupation, FY89, annual rpt, 9244–10

Forecasts of employment conditions, alternative BLS projections to 2005 and trends 1970s-90, biennial article, 6722–1.254

Foreign countries family composition, poverty status, labor conditions, and welfare indicators and needs, by country, 1960s-88, hearing, 23846–4.30

Forest Service acreage, staff, finances, and mgmt activities in Pacific Northwest, with data by forest, 1970s-89, annual rpt, 1204–37

Great Lakes area economic conditions and outlook, for US and Canada, 1970s-90, 9375–15

High school class of 1972: women's employment and educational experiences compared to men, natl longitudinal study, as of 1986, 4888–6

Hispanic Americans social and economic characteristics, by detailed origin, 1991, Current Population Rpt, 2546–1.448; 2546–1.451

Households and family characteristics, by location, 1990, annual Current Population Rpt, 2546–1.447

Houston metro area employment, earnings, hours, and CPI changes, 1970s-90, annual rpt, 6964–1

Income (household) and poverty status under alternative income definitions, by recipient characteristics, 1990, annual Current Population Rpt, 2546–6.69

Income (household) by source and expenses by type, for married couple families with one spouse working, by selected characteristics, 1987, article, 1702–1.201

Income (household, family, and personal), by source, detailed characteristics, and region, 1988-89, annual Current Population Rpt, 2546–6.68

Income (household, family, and personal), by source, detailed characteristics, and region, 1990, annual Current Population Rpt, 2546–6.70

Income of young single mothers relative to poverty under earnings and other sources of support assumptions, 1989, GAO rpt, 26121–413

Japan economic conditions, financial and intl policies, and trade devs, 1950s-80s and projected to 2050, compilation of papers, 23848–220

Job Training Partnership Act occupational training services, disparities in delivery to women and minorities, 1989-90, 26106–8.14

Women's employment

Labor force status by race and sex, selected years 1929-90, annual rpt, 204–1.2

Labor force status, by worker characteristics and industry group, 1982-90, semiannual article, 6722–1.212

Labor force status, earnings, and other characteristics of women, with comparisons to men, fact sheet series, 6564–1

Labor force status, experience, and unemployment duration, by race and sex, 1989-90, annual press release, 6726–1.39

Labor force status of family members and earnings, by family composition and race, quarterly press release, 6742–21

Labor force status of women, by age, race, and family status, quarterly rpt, 6742–17

Labor force, wages, hours, and payroll costs, by major industry group and demographic characteristics, *Survey of Current Business*, monthly rpt, 2702–1.8

Married couple families income and expenses, and wife's employment status, before and after having children, 1987-89, article, 1702–1.211

Military active duty and recruit social, economic, and parents characteristics, by service branch and State, FY89, annual rpt, 3544–41

Military officers, enlisted, and reserve personnel, by sex and service branch, FY90 and trends from 1945, annual rpt, 3544–1.2; 3544–1.5

Military personnel on active duty, recruits, and reenlistment, by race, sex, and service branch, quarterly press release, 3542–7

Military personnel strengths, for active duty enlisted and officers, by sex and race, 1970s-90, GAO rpt, 26123–325

Military reserve officer and enlisted personnel, by component, FY90, annual rpt, 3544–31.1

Military women personnel on active and reserve duty, by demographic and service characteristics and service branch, FY89, annual chartbook, 3544–26

Military women personnel on active duty, by rank, grade, and service branch, quarterly rpt, 3542–14.3

Mothers in labor force, and child day care employment, 1976-88, article, 6722–1.202

NASA minority and women employment, by installation, FY81-90, FY90, annual rpt, 9504–6.2

Navy personnel strengths, accessions, and attrition, detailed statistics, quarterly rpt, 3802–4

Nuclear engineering enrollment and degrees by instn and State, and women grads plans and employment, 1990, annual rpt, 3006–8.14

Pension coverage by industry, vestment, and recipient income, by participant characteristics, 1987, Current Population Rpt, 2546–20.18

Physicians, by specialty, age, sex, and location of training and practice, 1989, State rpt series, 4116–6

Population size and characteristics, 1969-88, Current Population Rpt, biennial rpt, 2546–2.161

Postal Service employment and related expenses, FY90, annual rpt, 9864–5.1

Poverty status of population and families, by detailed characteristics, 1988-89, annual Current Population Rpt, 2546–6.67

Poverty status of population and families, by detailed characteristics, 1990, annual Current Population Rpt, 2546–6.71

Prisoner population of women in State instns, by offense, drug use history, whether abused, and other characteristics, with comparisons to men, 1986, 6066–19.61

Radiation protection and health physics enrollment and degrees granted by instn and State, and female grads plans and employment, 1990, annual rpt, 3006–8.15

Science and engineering employment and education, and R&D spending, for US and selected foreign countries, 1991 annual rpt, 9627–35.2

Science and engineering PhDs employment and other characteristics, by field and State, 1989, biennial rpt, 9627–18

Science and engineering PhDs energy-realted employment, by field and work activity, mid 1970s-80s, biennial rpt, 3006–8.17

Science and engineering support program of NSF for women seeking 1st Federal grant and reentering career, proposals submitted, grant awards, and applicants views, FY85-89, 9628–82

Self-employment, by occupation, industry, sex, and race, 1983 and 1990, article, 6742–1.202

SSA minority, handicapped, and women employees, by pay grade, FY90, annual rpt, 4704–6

State and local govt employment of minorities and women, by occupation, function, pay level, and State, 1990, annual rpt, 9244–6

State and Metro Area Data Book, 1991 data compilation, 2328–54

State Dept and Foreign Service minority and women employment, and hiring goals, FY89-90, biennial rpt, 7004–21

Statistical Abstract of US, 1991 annual data compilation, 2324–1.13

Taxes, spending, and govt efficiency, public opinion by respondent characteristics, 1991 survey, annual rpt, 10044–2

Teachers in higher education instns, employment and other characteristics, by instn type and control, 1987/88 survey, 4846–4.4

Teachers in private schools, selected characteristics by instn level, size, and orientation, various periods 1979-88, 4838–47

Unemployed displaced and economically disadvantaged workers, training program operations and performance, series, 6406–10

Unemployment of groups with historically high rates, 1985-89, biennial rpt, 6504–2.2

Unemployment rates, current data and annual trends, monthly rpt, 23842–1.2

VA employment characteristics and activities, FY90, annual rpt, 8604–3.8

VA health care facilities physicians, dentists, and nurses, by selected employment characteristics and VA district, quarterly rpt, 8602–6

Index by Subjects and Names

Voting and registration, by socioeconomic and demographic characteristics, 1990 congressional election, biennial Current Population Rpt, 2546–1.454

see also Women-owned businesses

see also under By Sex in the "Index by Categories"

Woo, Danette

"Summary of State Water Quality Laws Affecting Agriculture", 1561–16.203

Wood

see Lumber industry and products

see Wood fuel

Wood fuel

Commercial buildings energy use, costs, and conservation, by building characteristics, survey rpt series, 3166–8

Consumption of energy, impacts of conservation measures by component and end-use sector, 1970s-88 and projected under alternative oil prices to 1995, 3308–93

Consumption of wood, waste, and alcohol fuels, by end-use sector and region, 1989, 3166–6.56

Consumption of wood, waste, and alcohol fuels, by region, and characteristics of wood-burning households, 1980-88, annual rpt, 3164–74.7

Developing countries energy use, and economic and environmental impacts, by fuel type, world area, and country, 1980s-90, 26358–232

Electric power plants and capacity, by fuel used, owner, location, and operating status, 1990 and for units planned 1991-2000, annual listing, 3164–36

Exports and imports of US, by country and detailed commodity, monthly rpt, 2422–12

Exports and imports of US, by Harmonized System 6-digit commodity and country, 1990, annual rpt, 2424–13

Exports and imports of US, by transport mode, country, and SITC 1- to 3-digit commodity, 1990, annual rpt, 2424–12

Exports of US, detailed Schedule B commodities with countries of destination, 1990, annual rpt, 2424–10

Florida industrial roundwood lumber production, by product and county, 1977-87, 1208–352

Forest Service acreage, staff, finances, and mgmt activities in Pacific Northwest, with data by forest, 1970s-89, annual rpt, 1204–37

Housing and households detailed characteristics, and unit and neighborhood quality, by location, 1989, biennial rpt, 2485–12

Housing and households detailed characteristics, and unit and neighborhood quality, MSA surveys, series, 2485–6

Housing inventory change from 1973, by reason, unit and household characteristics, and location, 1983 survey, biennial rpt, 2485–14

Natl Energy Strategy plans for conservation and pollution reduction, impacts of technology and regulation proposals, projected 1990-2030, 3166–6.47

Natl Energy Strategy plans for renewable energy dev, supply projected under alternative cost and capacity use assumptions, 1990-2030, 3166–6.50

North Central States timber harvest and industrial roundwood production, by product and county, State rpt series, 1206–10

North Central States veneer log residue use, 1988, quadrennial rpt, 1208–220

Northeastern US industrial roundwood production by product, State rpt series, 1206–15

Pacific Northwest housing energy conservation program of Bonneville Power Admin, activities, cost effectiveness, and participation, series, 3226–1

Pollution (air) contributing to global warming, emissions factors and control costs, by pollutant and source, 1990 rpt, 9198–124

Pollution (air) emissions factors, by detailed pollutant and source, data compilation, 1990 rpt, 9198–120

Pollution (air) indoor levels and emissions rates, by pollutant type and source, 1990 handbook, 3326–1.2

Pollution (air) levels for 6 pollutants, by source, 1970-89 and trends from 1940, annual rpt, 9194–13

Production, prices by region and State, trade by country, and use, for timber by species and product, 1960-88, annual rpt, 1204–29

Production, trade, and use of lumber and pulp products, and timber resources, detailed data, 1950s-87 and alternative projections to 2040, 1208–24.20

South Carolina lumber and mill residue production, by product and species group, 1987-88, 1208–359

Statistical Abstract of US, 1991 annual data compilation, 2324–1.19

Wood, Grayson B.

"Report of Water Masses Receiving Wastes from Ocean Dumping at the 106-Mile Dumpsite, Jan. 1-Dec. 31, 1990", 2164–20

Woods, Diana R.

"'America Responds to AIDS': Its Content, Development Process, and Outcome", 4042–3.256

Wool and wool trade

Acreage under Agricultural Stabilization and Conservation Service programs, rankings by commodity and congressional district, 1989, biennial rpt, 1804–17

Agricultural Stabilization and Conservation Service mohair programs, 1955-91, annual fact sheet, 1806–4.13

Agricultural Stabilization and Conservation Service producer payments and certificate value, by program, monthly rpt, 1802–10

Agricultural Stabilization and Conservation Service producer payments, by program and State, 1990, annual table, 1804–12

Agricultural Stabilization and Conservation Service wool programs, 1955-91, annual fact sheet, 1806–4.14

Agricultural Statistics, 1990, annual rpt, 1004–1

Agriculture census, 1987: farms, farmland, production, finances, and operator characteristics, by county, final State rpt series, 2331–1

Business statistics, detailed data for major industries and economic indicators, *Survey of Current Business,* monthly rpt, 2702–1.22

CCC financial condition and major commodity program operations, FY62-87, annual chartbook, 1824–2

Clothing and shoe production, shipments, trade, and use, by product, periodic Current Industrial Rpt series, 2506–6

County Business Patterns, 1988: employment, establishments, and payroll, by SIC 2- to 4-digit industry and county, annual State rpt series, 2326–6

County Business Patterns, 1989: employment, establishments, and payroll, by SIC 2- to 4-digit industry and county, annual State rpt series, 2326–8

Employment, earnings, and hours, by SIC 1- to 4-digit industry, monthly and annual averages, selected years 1909-90, annual rpt, 6744–4

Exports and imports (agricultural) of US, by commodity and country, bimonthly rpt, 1522–1

Exports and imports (agricultural) of US, by detailed commodity and country, 1989, annual rpt, 1524–8

Exports and imports (agricultural) of US, by detailed commodity and country, 1990, semiannual rpt, 1522–4

Exports and imports of dairy, livestock, and poultry products, by commodity and country, FAS monthly circular, 1925–32

Exports and imports of US, by country and detailed commodity, monthly rpt, 2422–12

Exports and imports of US, by Harmonized System 6-digit commodity and country, 1990, annual rpt, 2424–13

Exports and imports of US, by transport mode, country, and SITC 1- to 3-digit commodity, 1990, annual rpt, 2424–12

Exports of US, detailed Schedule B commodities with countries of destination, 1990, annual rpt, 2424–10

Farm financial and marketing conditions, forecast 1991, annual chartbook, 1504–8

Farm sector balance sheet, and receipts by detailed commodity, by State, 1985-89, annual rpt, 1544–18

Farm sector finances, and Fed Govt payments, 1990 and trends from 1945, annual rpt, 1544–16

Foreign countries agricultural production, prices, and trade, by country, 1980-90 and forecast 1991, annual world area rpt series, 1524–4

Imports of textiles, by country of origin, monthly rpt, 2042–27

Imports of textiles, by product and country of origin, monthly rpt series, 2046–8; 2046–9

Imports of textiles under Multifiber Arrangement by product and country, and status of bilateral agreements, 1987-90, annual rpt, 9884–18

Manufacturing annual survey, 1989: finances and operations, by SIC 2- to 4-digit industry, series, 2506–15

Manufacturing census, 1987: finances and operations, by SIC 2- to 4-digit industry, State, and MSA, with trends from 1849, 2497–1

Manufacturing census, 1987: finances and operations, by type of organization and SIC 2- to 4-digit industry, subject rpt, 2497–5

Marketing data for livestock, meat, and wool, by species and market, weekly rpt, 1315–1

Occupational injury and illness rates, by SIC 2- to 4-digit industry, 1988-89, annual rpt, 6844–7

Occupational injury and illness rates, by SIC 2- to 4-digit industry, 1989, annual rpt, 6844–1

Price indexes (producer), by stage of processing and detailed commodity, monthly rpt, 6762–6

Price indexes (producer), by stage of processing and detailed commodity, monthly 1990, annual rpt, 6764–2

Price support program provisions, for selected commodities, 1961-90, 1568–303

Prices received and paid by farmers, by commodity and State, 1990, annual rpt, 1629–5

Prices received by farmers for major products, and paid for farm inputs and living items, by State, monthly rpt, 1629–1

Prices, sales, trade, and stocks of wool, and sheep inventory, weekly and biweekly rpt, 1315–2

Production and prices of wool and mohair, by State, 1989-90, annual press release, 1623–6

Production itemized costs, receipts, and returns, by commodity and region, 1987-89, annual rpt, 1544–20

Production, prices, trade, and marketing, by commodity, current situation and forecast, monthly rpt with articles, 1502–4

Production, prices, trade, and use of wool, mohair, and other fibers, periodic situation rpt with articles, 1561–1

Production, trade, sales, stocks, and material used, by product, region, and State, periodic Current Industrial Rpt series, 2506–5

Woonsocket, R.I.

Wages by occupation, for office and plant workers, 1991 survey, periodic MSA rpt, 6785–12.6

see also under By SMSA or MSA in the "Index by Categories"

Wootton, Barbara

"Changes in Hospital Staffing Patterns", 6722–1.217

Worcester, Mass.

see also under By City and By SMSA or MSA in the "Index by Categories"

Word processing

see Computer industry and products

see Computer use

Work conditions

Education data compilation, 1991 annual rpt, 4824–2

Teachers in higher education instns, personnel policies, pay, work conditions, and other characteristics, by instn type and control, 1987/88 survey, quadrennial rpt series, 4846–4

see also Agricultural accidents and safety

see also Employee performance and appraisal

see also Job tenure

see also Labor-management relations, general

see also Labor-management relations in government

Work conditions

see also Mine accidents and safety
see also Occupational health and safety

Work incentive programs

- AFDC beneficiaries demographic and financial characteristics, by State, FY89, annual rpt, 4694–1
- AFDC Job Opportunities and Basic Skills Training Program Federal and State funding by State, and administrators views, 1989-91, GAO rpt, 26121–435
- AFDC work incentive program appropriations, by State, FY90-91, article, 10042–1.201
- Assistance (financial and nonfinancial) of Fed Govt, 1991 base edition with supplements, annual listing, 104–5
- Expenditures of Fed Govt in States, by type, program, agency, and State, FY90, annual rpt, 2464–2
- HHS financial aid, by program, recipient, State, and city, FY90, annual regional listings, 4004–3
- Tax (income) returns filed by type of filer, selected income items, quarterly rpt, 8302–2.1
- Unemployed displaced and economically disadvantaged workers, training program operations and performance, series, 6406–10
- Unemployment insurance laws of States, comparison of provisions, 1991, base edition with semiannual revisions, 6402–2

Work stoppages

- Developing countries labor standards impacts on social and economic dev, 1988 conf papers, 6368–9
- Food stamp recipient household size, composition, income, and income and deductions allowed, summer 1988, annual rpt, 1364–8
- Foreign countries labor conditions, union coverage, and work accidents, annual country rpt series, 6366–4
- Incidents of stoppages, workers involved, and days idle, 1990 and trends from 1947, annual press release, 6784–12
- Labor force, wages, hours, and payroll costs, by major industry group and demographic characteristics, *Survey of Current Business*, monthly rpt, 2702–1.8
- Los Alamos Natl Lab contract security strike, reasons and temporary replacement workers skill deficiencies, 1989, GAO rpt, 26113–493
- Mediation and arbitration activities of Fed Mediation and Conciliation Service, and cases by issue, region, and State, FY84-89, annual rpt, 9344–1
- *Monthly Labor Review*, work stoppages involving 1,000 workers or more, workers involved, and days idle, 6722–1.3
- Replacement worker hires and mgmt threats to hire during strikes, and workers affected, 1985 and 1989, GAO rpt, 26121–405
- *Statistical Abstract of US*, 1991 annual data compilation, 2324–1.13
- Wage and benefit changes from collective bargaining and mgmt decisions, by industry div, monthly rpt, 6782–1

Work-study programs

Assistance and other sources of support, with student expenses and characteristics, by instn type and control, 1990 triennial study, series, 4846–5

Education Dept programs funding, operations, and effectiveness, FY90, annual rpt, 4804–5

- Fed Govt education funding by agency, program, and recipient type, and instn spending, FY80-90, annual rpt, 4824–8
- Fed Govt share of student aid supplemental grants, loans, and work-study awards, by instn and State, 1991/92, annual listing, 4804–17
- Minimum wage exemption certificates and employment under Fair Labor Standards Act, FY88-89, annual rpt, 6504–2.1
- Science and engineering grad enrollment, by field, source of funds, and characteristics of student and instn, 1975-89, annual rpt, 9627–7
- Special education programs, enrollment by age, staff, funding, and needs, by type of handicap and State, 1989/90, annual rpt, 4944–4
- Student aid funding and participation, by Federal program, instn type and control, and State, various periods 1959-89, annual rpt, 4804–28
- Undergrad student aid, costs, and income factors affecting access to education, 1990 rpt, 26306–6.153
- Unemployment insurance laws of States, comparison of provisions, 1991, base edition with semiannual revisions, 6402–2

Work training

- *see* Employee development
- *see* Manpower training programs
- *see* Vocational education and training

Worker adjustment assistance

see Trade adjustment assistance

Worker incentives

see Employee bonuses and work incentives

Workers

- *see* Agricultural labor
- *see* Alien workers
- *see* Blue collar workers
- *see* Clerical workers
- *see* Employment and unemployment, general
- *see* Employment and unemployment, local and regional
- *see* Employment and unemployment, specific industry
- *see* Government employees
- *see* Job tenure
- *see* Labor supply and demand
- *see* Migrant workers
- *see* Minority employment
- *see* Occupational testing and certification
- *see* Production workers
- *see* Professional and technical workers
- *see* Sales workers
- *see* Service workers
- *see* Unpaid family workers
- *see* Women's employment
- *see* Work conditions
- *see* Youth employment

Workers compensation

- Beneficiaries and taxes collected for social insurance programs since 1940, monthly rpt, 4742–1.1
- Benefits and benefit duration under workers compensation, by State, 1990, biennial article, 4742–1.217
- Benefits and coverage under workers compensation, by type of program and insurer, and State, 1987-88, annual article, 4742–1.207

Index by Subjects and Names

- Black lung benefits and claims by State, trust fund receipts by source, and disbursements, 1990, annual rpt, 6504–3
- Black lung benefits by county, FY90, annual regional listings, 4004–3
- Black lung benefits to miners, widows, and dependents, with data by State reported quarterly, monthly rpt, 4742–1.6; 4742–1.13
- Black lung trust funds financial condition, monthly rpt, 8102–9.10
- Costs (hourly) of labor, by component, industry sector, worker class, and firm size, 1990, annual rpt, 6744–22
- Deaths of beneficiaries, erroneous benefit payments, and use of SSA and other sources of death info, by agency, 1990, GAO rpt, 26121–406
- Expenditures (private) for social welfare, by category, 1970s-88, annual article, 4742–1.204
- Expenditures, coverage, and benefits for social welfare programs, late 1930s-89, annual rpt, 4744–3.1; 4744–3.7
- Expenditures for health care by businesses, households, and govts, 1965-89, article, 4652–1.230
- Expenditures for health care, by service type, payment source, and sector, 1960s-90, annual article, 4652–1.221; 4652–1.252
- Expenditures for public welfare by program, FY50s-88, annual article, 4742–1.209
- Expenditures of Fed Govt in States, by type, program, agency, and State, FY90, annual rpt, 2464–2
- Fed Govt civilian employees work-years, pay rates, and benefits use and costs, by agency, FY89, annual rpt, 9844–31
- Fed Govt workers compensation program coverage, injuries, and costs, 1940-45, article, 6722–1.241
- Fed Govt workers compensation program finances and operations, FY90, annual rpt, 6504–10
- Fed Govt workers compensation program staff and budget ratios, and compared to 6 State systems, 1984-88, article, 6722–1.242
- Food stamp recipient household size, composition, income, and income and deductions allowed, summer 1988, annual rpt, 1364–8
- Hospital discharges and length of stay, by diagnosis, patient and instn characteristics, procedure performed, and payment source, 1988, annual rpt, 4147–13.107
- Income (household, family, and personal), by source, detailed characteristics, and region, 1988-89, annual Current Population Rpt, 2546–6.68
- Income (household, family, and personal), by source, detailed characteristics, and region, 1990, annual Current Population Rpt, 2546–6.70
- Injuries on job, relation to increases in workers compensation benefits, model description and results, 1991 working paper, 6886–6.80
- Postal Service employment and related expenses, FY90, annual rpt, 9864–5.1; 9864–5.3
- *State and Metro Area Data Book*, 1991 data compilation, 2328–54

Index by Subjects and Names

Wyoming

State govt revenue by source, spending and debt by function, and holdings, FY90, annual rpt, 2466–2.6

States workers compensation laws, and Fed Govt provisions, 1991 semiannual rpt, 6502–1

States workers compensation laws, changes in coverage, benefits, and premium rates, by State, 1990, annual article, 6722–1.210

States workers compensation programs, admin, coverage, benefits, finances, processing, and staff, 1987-90, annual rpt, 6504–9

Statistical Abstract of US, 1991 annual data compilation, 2324–1.12

Tax expenditures, Federal revenues forgone through income tax deductions and exclusions by type, FY92-96, annual rpt, 21784–10

Transit systems finances and operations, by mode of transport, size of fleet, and for 468 systems, 1989, annual rpt, 7884–4

Vocational rehabilitation cases of State agencies by disposition and applicant characteristics, and closures by reason, FY84-88, annual rpt, 4944–6

Working women

see Women-owned businesses

see Women's employment

Worksharing

Child care benefits for employees, work schedule and leave policies coverage by firm size and industry group, 1987, 15496–1.11

Unemployment insurance laws of States, comparison of provisions, 1991, base edition with semiannual revisions, 6402–2

Workshops

see Conferences

see Sheltered workshops

World Bank

see International Bank for Reconstruction and Development

see International Development Association

World Meteorological Organization

Weather data for surface and upper air, averages by foreign and US station, monthly rpt, 2152–4

World Wars

see Veterans benefits and pensions

see War

Worthington, Paula R.

"Investment and Market Power", 9375–13.58

"Investment and Market Power: Evidence from the U.S. Manufacturing Sector", 9385–8.81

"Investment, GNP, and Real Exchange Rates", 9375–1.208

Wrecking and demolition

County Business Patterns, 1988: employment, establishments, and payroll, by SIC 2- to 4-digit industry and county, annual State rpt series, 2326–6

County Business Patterns, 1989: employment, establishments, and payroll, by SIC 2- to 4-digit industry and county, annual State rpt series, 2326–8

Wright, George E.

"Alternative Hospital Market Area Definitions", 17206–2.20

"Medicaid Support of Alcohol, Drug Abuse, and Mental Health Services", 4652–1.256

Wright, James D.

"Correlates and Consequences of Alcohol Abuse in the National 'Health Care for the Homeless' Client Population", 4488–14

Wright, Randall

"Barter and Monetary Exchange Under Private Information", 9383–20.11

"Discussion of Cooley and Hansen's 'Welfare Costs of Moderate Inflations' ", 9383–20.4

"Indivisibilities, Lotteries, and Sunspot Equilibria", 9383–20.3

"Labor Market Implications of Unemployment Insurance and Short-Time Compensation", 9383–6.205

"Why Is Automobile Insurance in Philadelphia So Damn Expensive?", 9383–20.9

Writers and writing

Teachers in higher education instns, employment and other characteristics, by instn type and control, 1987/88 survey, 4846–4.4

see also Journalism

Writing ability

see Language use and ability

Wynne, Mark A.

"Government Purchases and Real Wages", 9379–12.65

Wyoming

Banks (insured commercial and savings) deposits by instn, State, MSA, and county, as of June 1990, annual regional rpt, 9295–3.6

Bears (grizzly) in Yellowstone Natl Park area, monitoring results, 1990, annual rpt, 5544–4

Birds (raptors) population, habitat, and reproductive success, for coal mining areas of Montana and Wyoming, 1970s-80s, technical rpt, 5506–12.1

Coal production and mines by county, prices, productivity, miners, and reserves, by mining method and State, 1989-90, annual rpt, 3164–25

County Business Patterns, 1989: employment, establishments, and payroll, by SIC 2- to 4-digit industry and county, annual State rpt, 2326–8.52

DOD prime contract awards, by contractor, service branch, State, and city, FY90, annual rpt, 3544–22

Fed Govt spending in States and local areas, by type, State, county, and city, FY90, annual rpt, 2464–3

Fed Govt spending in States, by type, program, agency, and State, FY90, annual rpt, 2464–2

Financial and economic devs, Fed Reserve 10th District, quarterly rpt, 9381–16

Fish (brown trout) population, habitat quality, and streamflow, for Douglas Creek, Wyo, 1970s-89, 5508–112

HHS financial aid, by program, recipient, State, and city, FY90, annual regional listing, 4004–3.8

Hospital deaths of Medicare patients, actual and expected rates by diagnosis, and hospital characteristics, by instn, FY87-89, annual regional rpt, 4654–14.8

Income (personal) per capita and by source, and earnings by industry div, by State, MSA, and county, 1984-89, annual regional rpt, 2704–2.5

Jail adult and juvenile population, employment, spending, instn conditions, and inmate programs, by county and facility, 1988, regional rpt series, 6068–144.5

Land Mgmt Bur activities and finances, and public land acreage and use, FY89, annual State rpt, 5724–11.5

Land Mgmt Bur activities and finances, and public land acreage and use, FY90, annual State rpt, 5724–11.6

Land subsidence above coal mines, State property insurance program income and expenses in 6 States, 1990, GAO rpt, 26113–530

Marriages, divorces, and rates, by characteristics of spouses, State, and county, 1987 and trends from 1920, US Vital Statistics annual rpt, 4144–4

Mineral industries census, 1987: finances and operations, by SIC 2- to 4-digit industry, State, and county, census div rpt, 2515–1.8

Mineral Industry Surveys, State reviews of production, 1990, preliminary annual rpt, 5614–6

Minerals Yearbook, 1989, Vol 2: State reviews of production, sales, and firms, by commodity, and business activity, annual rpt, 5604–34

Physicians, by specialty, age, sex, and location of training and practice, 1989, State rpt, 4116–6.52

Population and housing census, 1990: population and housing characteristics, households, and land area, by county, subdiv, and place, State rpt, 2551–1.52

Population and housing census, 1990: voting age and total population by race, and housing units, by block, redistricting counts required under PL 94-171, State CD-ROM release, 2551–6.4

Population and housing census, 1990: voting age and total population by race, and housing units, by county and city, redistricting counts required under PL 94-171, State summary rpt, 2551–5.51

Statistical Abstract of US, 1991 annual data compilation, 2324–1

Supplemental Security Income payments and beneficiaries, by type of eligibility, State, and county, Dec 1989, annual rpt, 4744–27.8

Timber in Yellowstone Natl Park area, insect infestation and damage following 1988 forest fires, 1989-90, 1208–379

Water (groundwater) supply, quality, chemistry, and use, 1980-89, State rpt, 5666–28.4

Water (groundwater) supply, quality, chemistry, and use, 1987-88, regional rpt, 5666–28.3

Water quality, chemistry, hydrology, and other characteristics, 1989 local area study, 5666–27.17

Water salinity control program for Colorado River, participation and payments, FY87-90, annual rpt, 1804–23

Water supply, and snow survey results, monthly State rpt, 1266–2.10

Water supply, and snow survey results, 1990, annual State rpt, 1264–14.5

see also under By State in the "Index by Categories"

X-rays

X-rays

County Business Patterns, 1988: employment, establishments, and payroll, by SIC 2- to 4-digit industry and county, annual State rpt series, 2326–6

County Business Patterns, 1989: employment, establishments, and payroll, by SIC 2- to 4-digit industry and county, annual State rpt series, 2326–8

Equipment shipments, trade, use, and firms, for electronic medical equipment by product, 1990, annual Current Industrial Rpt, 2506–12.34

Exports and imports of US, by country and detailed commodity, monthly rpt, 2422–12

Exports and imports of US, by Harmonized System 6-digit commodity and country, 1990, annual rpt, 2424–13

Exports of US, detailed Schedule B commodities with countries of destination, 1990, annual rpt, 2424–10

Health maintenance organizations and other prepaid managed care plans Medicaid enrollment and use, for 20 States, 1985-89, chartbook, 4108–29

Manufacturing census, 1987: employment and shipments under Fed Govt contracts, by SIC 4-digit industry, 2497–7

Manufacturing finances and operations, by SIC 2- to 4-digit industry, forecast 1991, annual rpt, 2044–28

Medicare and Medicaid beneficiaries and program operations, 1991, annual fact book, 4654–18

Occupational injury and illness rates, by SIC 2- to 4-digit industry, 1988-89, annual rpt, 6844–7

Occupational injury and illness rates, by SIC 2- to 4-digit industry, 1989, annual rpt, 6844–1

Physicians visits, by patient and practice characteristics, diagnosis, and services provided, 1989, 4146–8.206

Price indexes (producer), by stage of processing and detailed commodity, monthly rpt, 6762–6

Price indexes (producer), by stage of processing and detailed commodity, monthly 1990, annual rpt, 6764–2

Radiation from electronic devices, incidents by type of device, and FDA control activities, 1990, annual rpt, 4064–13

Respiratory diseases related to occupational hazards, epidemiology, diagnosis, and treatment, for selected industries and work settings, 1988 conf, 4248–90

Xylene

see Chemicals and chemical industry

Yager, Francis P.

"Changes in Financial Profile of Cooperatives Handling Grain: First-Handlers with $5 Million or More in Sales, 1983 and 1985", 1128–44.4

Yakima, Wash.

Wages by occupation, for office and plant workers, 1991 survey, periodic MSA rpt, 6785–3.6

see also under By SMSA or MSA in the "Index by Categories"

Yakutat, Alaska

Fishing for subsistence, role in Alaska communities economies, with indicators for Yakutat, 1980s, 1208–350

Yap

see Micronesia Federated States

Yarn

see Textile industry and fabrics *see* Wool and wool trade

Yeats, Kevin J.

"Return to Profitability: The Performance of Eleventh District Commercial Banks", 9379–1.206

Yeatts, Dale E.

"Financing Geriatric Programs in Community Health Centers", 4042–3.229

Yeh, Sze-Ya

"Prevalence of Chlamydia trachomatis Infection in Pregnant Patients", 4042–3.240

Yellowstone National Park

Bears (grizzly) in Yellowstone Natl Park area, monitoring results, 1990, annual rpt, 5544–4

Goats (mountain) population in Yellowstone and Grand Teton Natl Parks, and habitat mgmt options, 1970s-89, 5548–19

Timber in Yellowstone Natl Park area, insect infestation and damage following 1988 forest fires, 1989-90, 1208–379

Yemen

AID economic aid to developing countries, obligations and disbursements by country, quarterly rpt, 9912–4

AID loans repayment status and terms by program and country, and status of predecessor agency loans, quarterly rpt, 9912–3

Economic and social conditions of developing countries from 1960s, and Intl Dev Cooperation Agency and AID activities and funding, FY90-92, annual rpt, 9904–4

Economic, social, political, and geographic summary data, by country, 1991, annual factbook, 9114–2

Exports and imports of US, by selected country, country group, and commodity group, 1990, annual rpt, 2044–37

Human rights conditions in 170 countries, and US economic and military aid, 1990, annual rpt, 21384–3

UN voting record and share of votes in agreement with US, by issue, country, and world area, 1990, annual rpt, 7004–18

see also Yemen, North

see also Yemen, South

see also under By Foreign Country in the "Index by Categories"

Yemen Arab Republic

see Yemen, North

Yemen, North

Agricultural exports of high-value commodities, indexes and sales by commodity, world area, and country, 1960s-86, 1528–323

Agricultural trade of US, by detailed commodity and country, 1989, annual rpt, 1524–8

Agricultural trade of US, by detailed commodity and country, 1990, semiannual rpt, 1522–4

Economic and military aid and loans from US and intl agencies, by program and country, FY46-90, annual rpt, 9914–5

Exports and imports of US, by transport mode, country, and SITC 1- to 3-digit commodity, 1990, annual rpt, 2424–12

Exports of US, detailed Schedule B commodities with countries of destination, 1990, annual rpt, 2424–10

Yemen, South

Agricultural exports of high-value commodities, indexes and sales by commodity, world area, and country, 1960s-86, 1528–323

Agricultural trade of US, by detailed commodity and country, 1989, annual rpt, 1524–8

Agricultural trade of US, by detailed commodity and country, 1990, semiannual rpt, 1522–4

Economic and military aid and loans from US and intl agencies, by program and country, FY46-90, annual rpt, 9914–5

Export controls and trade of US with Middle East countries, with dual-use commodity licenses and arms sales, 1980s-90, GAO rpt, 26123–339

Exports and imports of US, by transport mode, country, and SITC 1- to 3-digit commodity, 1990, annual rpt, 2424–12

Exports of US, detailed Schedule B commodities with countries of destination, 1990, annual rpt, 2424–10

Yeung, K. S.

"Comparisons of Diet and Biochemical Characteristics of Stool and Urine Between Chinese Populations with Low and High Colorectal Cancer Rates", 4472–1.201

Yip, Chong K.

"On the Sustainability of International Coordination", 9371–10.61

Yip, Ray

"Using Linked Program and Birth Records To Evaluate Coverage and Targeting in Tennessee's WIC Program", 4042–3.216

Yonkers, N.Y.

see also under By City in the "Index by Categories"

York, Pa.

see also under By SMSA or MSA in the "Index by Categories"

Yoshimoto, Stacey S.

"Application of the Leslie Model to Commercial Catch and Effort of the Slipper Lobster, *Scyllarides squammosus*, Fishery in the Northwestern Hawaiian Islands", 2162–1.203

Young, Douglas L.

"Comment on the Role of Professional Journals in Facilitating Data Access", 1502–3.203

Young, Paula C.

"Benchmark Input-Output Accounts for the U.S. Economy, 1982", 2702–1.213

Youngstown, Ohio

see also under By SMSA or MSA in the "Index by Categories"

Youth

Alcohol use, knowledge, attitudes, and info sources of youth, series, 4006–10

Assistance (financial and nonfinancial) of Fed Govt, 1991 base edition with supplements, annual listing, 104–5

Budget of US, House Budget Committee analysis of Bush Admin proposals and economic assumptions, FY92, 21268–42

Index by Subjects and Names

Youth employment

Cancer cases, deaths, and survival rates, by sex, race, age, and body site, 1973-88, annual rpt, 4474–35

Census of Population and Housing, 1990: population and housing selected characteristics, by region, press release, 2328–74

Crime and crime-related issues, public opinion by respondent characteristics, data compilation, 1991 annual rpt, 6064–6.2

Crime victimization of teens, by victim and offender characteristics, circumstances, and offense, 1985-88 surveys, 6066–3.43

Deaths and rates, by detailed cause and demographic characteristics, 1988 and trends from 1900, US Vital Statistics annual rpt, 4144–2

Detroit metro area runaway and other youth services programs cases, and school dropouts, 1980s, hearing, 25418–5

Drug (steroid) use prevalence and health effects, 1989 conf papers, 4498–67

Drug abuse prevalence among minorities, related health effects and crime, treatment, and research status and needs, mid 1970s-90, 4498–72

Drug, alcohol, and cigarette use and attitudes of youth, by substance type and selected characteristics, 1975-90 surveys, annual rpt, 4494–4

Drug, alcohol, and cigarette use, by selected characteristics, 1990 survey, biennial rpt, 4494–5

Drug and alcohol abuse treatment facilities, services, use, funding, staff, and client characteristics, 1989, biennial rpt, 4494–10

Firearms-related deaths and death rates, by motive, age, sex, and race, for persons aged 1-34, 1979-88, 4146–5.119

Foreign countries youth population declines relative to other age groups, by selected country, 1985 and projected to 2010, 9118–17

Health, behavioral, emotional, and school problems of children relation to family structure, by selected characteristics, 1988, 4147–10.178

Health condition and health care resources, use, and spending, 1950s-89, annual data compilation, 4144–11

Health condition and services use, for children, 1990 chartbook, 4108–49

Health condition improvement and disease prevention goals and recommended activities for 2000, with trends 1970s-80s, 4048–10

Health condition of youths, risk factors, and preventive and treatment services use and availability, 1970s-89, 26358–234

Heart rate in children relationship to elevated blood pressure and mothers heart rate, 1971-73, article, 4042–3.232

HHS financial aid, by program, recipient, State, and city, FY90, annual regional listings, 4004–3

Homeless and runaway youth center arrivals, by selected characteristics, data compilation, 1991 annual rpt, 6064–6.6

Homeless and runaway youth programs, funding, activities, and participant characteristics, FY90, annual rpt, 4604–3

Insurance (health) coverage, uninsured population under age 65 by selected characteristics, 1987, 4186–8.13

Living arrangements, family relationships, and marital status, by selected characteristics, 1990, annual Current Population Rpt, 2546–1.449

Living arrangements relation to selected characteristics, for young adults living away from parents in US and 4 countries, 2546–2.157

Natl service for youth, proposed program operations and youth attitudes, 1990 rpt, 26306–3.115

Physicians office visits of teenagers, by reason and characteristics of physicians, patients, and visit, 1985, 4146–8.199

Population of children and youth, social, economic, and demographic characteristics, 1950s-90, 4818–5

Population of 16 and 18 year olds, for US and selected foreign countries, 1966-94, annual rpt, 9627–35.2

Sexual behavior, population, and family research activities and funding, 1960s-89, 4478–194

Smoking initiation by age 25, by sex and age, 1987, article, 4472–1.216

State and Metro Area Data Book, 1991 data compilation, 2328–54

Statistical Abstract of US, 1991 annual data compilation, 2324–1

Traffic fatal accident rates impacts of auto weight, with data for young drivers, 1976-78 and 1986-88, GAO rpt, 26131–89

Violence among minority youth, prevention strategies, 1990 conf, 4042–3.218

Voting and registration, by socioeconomic and demographic characteristics, 1990 congressional election, biennial Current Population Rpt, 2546–1.454

see also Child mortality

see also Children

see also Elementary and secondary education

see also Foster home care

see also Higher education

see also Juvenile courts and cases

see also Juvenile delinquency

see also Juvenile detention and correctional institutions

see also School dropouts

see also Students

see also Teenage pregnancy

see also Youth employment

see also under By Age in the "Index by Categories"

Youth Conservation Corps

Forest Service acreage, staff, finances, and mgmt activities in Pacific Northwest, with data by forest, 1970s-89, annual rpt, 1204–37

Forest Service activities and finances, by region and State, FY90, annual rpt, 1204–1.4

Youth employment

AFDC Job Opportunities and Basic Skills Training Program Federal and State funding by State, and administrators views, 1989-91, GAO rpt, 26121–435

Budget of US, formula grant program obligations to State and local govts, by agency, program, and State, FY92, annual rpt, 104–30

Children and youth social, economic, and demographic characteristics, 1950s-90, 4818–5

Condition of Education, detail for elementary and secondary education, 1920s-90 and projected to 2001, annual rpt, 4824–1.1

Dallas-Fort Worth-Arlington metro area employment, earnings, hours, and CPI changes, late 1970s-90, annual rpt, 6964–2

Educational enrollment, by grade, instn type and control, and student characteristics, 1989 and trends from 1947, annual Current Population Rpt, 2546–1.453

Educational performance and conditions, characteristics, attitudes, activities, and plans, 1988 8th grade class, natl longitudinal survey, series, 4826–9

Employment of youth by selected characteristics, with child labor law violations and injuries, 1983-90, GAO rpt, 26121–426

Employment situation, earnings, hours, and other BLS economic indicators, transcripts of BLS Commissioner's monthly testimony, periodic rpt, 23846–4

Employment, unemployment, and labor force characteristics, by region, State, and selected metro area, 1990, annual rpt, 6744–7

High school and college grads and dropouts employment status and income, 1991 edition, annual rpt, 4824–2.28

Houston metro area employment, earnings, hours, and CPI changes, 1970s-90, annual rpt, 6964–1

Income (family) and expenses by type, impacts of youth employment, with selected family characteristics, 1989, article, 1702–1.213

Job Training Partnership Act funding and performance indicators in service delivery areas, by urban-rural location, 1987-88, 1598–266

Job Training Partnership Act participation by selected characteristics and State, and outcomes, by urban-rural location, 1987-88, 1598–267

Labor force status by race and sex, employment by industry div, and unemployment duration and reason, selected years 1929-90, annual rpt, 204–1.2

Labor force status by sex, and employment by class and industry div, for youth by race, summer 1987-91, annual press release, 6744–14

Labor force status by sex and for teens, *Survey of Current Business*, monthly rpt, 2702–1.2

Labor force status, by worker characteristics and industry group, 1982-90, semiannual article, 6722–1.212

Labor force status of youth, by age, Apr and July 1991 and change from 1990, annual press release, 6744–13

Labor force status of youth, by school enrollment, educational attainment, sex, and race, monthly rpt, 6742–2.1

Natl service for youth, proposed program operations and youth attitudes, 1990 rpt, 26306–3.115

Statistical Abstract of US, 1991 annual data compilation, 2324–1.13

Tax credit for hiring from groups with high unemployment rates, participation by State, and effectiveness, FY88, GAO rpt, 26121–407

Youth employment

Unemployed displaced and economically disadvantaged workers, training program operations and performance, series, 6406–10

Unemployment of groups with historically high rates, 1985-89, biennial rpt, 6504–2.2

see also Apprenticeship

see also Child labor

Yu, Mimi C.

"Nonviral Risk Factors for Hepatocellular Carcinoma in a Low-Risk Population, the Non-Asians of Los Angeles County, California", 4472–1.237

Yuan, Florence L.

"Selected Bibliography on Urbanization in China", 2326–18.60

Yuba City, Calif.

see also under By SMSA or MSA in the "Index by Categories"

Yucel, Mine K.

"Methanol as an Alternative Fuel", 9379–12.62

"Methanol as an Alternative Fuel: Economic and Health Effects", 9379–1.208

"What Motivates Oil Producers?: Testing Alternative Hypotheses", 9379–12.68

Yudkowsky, Beth K.

"Preventive Health Care for Medicaid Children", 4652–1.214

Yue, Piyu

"Divisia Monetary Services Indexes for Switzerland: Are They Useful for Monetary Targeting?", 9391–1.221

Yuengert, Andrew M.

"Estimating Immigrant Assimilation Rates with Synthetic Panel Data", 9385–8.100

"Self-Employment and the Earnings of Male Immigrants in the U.S.", 9385–8.101

Yugoslavia

- Agricultural exports of high-value commodities, indexes and sales by commodity, world area, and country, 1960s-86, 1528–323
- Agricultural exports of US, impacts of foreign agricultural and trade policy, with data by commodity and country, 1989, annual rpt, 1924–8
- Agricultural production, trade, and policies in foreign countries, summary data by country, 1989-90, annual factbook, 1924–12
- Agricultural trade of US, by detailed commodity and country, 1989, annual rpt, 1524–8
- Agricultural trade of US, by detailed commodity and country, 1990, semiannual rpt, 1522–4
- AID loans repayment status and terms by program and country, and status of predecessor agency loans, quarterly rpt, 9912–3
- Bearings (ball) from 14 countries, injury to US industry from foreign subsidized and less than fair value imports, investigation with background financial and operating data, 1991 rpt, 9886–19.74
- Cherry juice and concentrate from 2 countries at less than fair value, injury to US industry, investigation with background financial and operating data, 1991 rpt, 9886–14.308
- Debt to foreign lenders by component, trade, balances, and other economic indicators, by Eastern Europe country, 1985-89, hearing, 21248–148

Economic and military aid and loans from US and intl agencies, by program and country, FY46-90, annual rpt, 9914–5

Economic conditions in Communist and OECD countries, 1989, annual rpt, 7144–11

Economic conditions in USSR, Eastern Europe, OECD, and selected other countries, 1960s-90, annual rpt, 9114–4

Economic conditions, policy, and trade practices, by country, 1988-90, annual rpt, 21384–5

Economic, social, political, and geographic summary data, by country, 1991, annual factbook, 9114–2

Exports and imports of US, by commodity and country, 1970-89, world area rpt, 9116–1.3

Exports and imports of US, by Harmonized System 6-digit commodity and country, 1990, annual rpt, 2424–13

Exports and imports of US, by selected country, country group, and commodity group, 1990, annual rpt, 2044–37

Exports and imports of US, by transport mode, country, and SITC 1- to 3-digit commodity, 1990, annual rpt, 2424–12

Exports, imports, and balances of US with major trading partners, by product category, 1986-90, annual chartbook, 9884–21

Exports of US, detailed Schedule B commodities with countries of destination, 1990, annual rpt, 2424–10

Human rights conditions in 170 countries, and US economic and military aid, 1990, annual rpt, 21384–3

Imports of goods, services, and investment from US, trade barriers, impacts, and US actions, by country, 1990, annual rpt, 444–2

Labor conditions, union coverage, and work accidents, 1991 annual country rpt, 6366–4.34

Market economy transition of Eastern Europe countries, economic conditions and energy balance, by country, 1985-90, 9118–13

Military aid of US, arms sales, and training programs costs and budget requests, by program, world region, and country, FY90-92, annual rpt, 7144–13

Nuclear power plant capacity, generation, and operating status, by plant and foreign and US location, 1990 and projected to 2030, annual rpt, 3164–57

Steel imports of US under voluntary restraint agreement, by product, customs district, and country, with US industry operating data, quarterly rpt, 9882–13

UN voting record and share of votes in agreement with US, by issue, country, and world area, 1990, annual rpt, 7004–18

see also under By Foreign Country in the "Index by Categories"

Yuma County, Ariz.

see also under By SMSA or MSA in the "Index by Categories"

Zadrozny, Peter A.

"Forecasting U.S. GNP at Monthly Intervals with an Estimated Bivariate Time Series Model", 9371–1.201

Index by Subjects and Names

Zaire

- Agricultural exports of high-value commodities, indexes and sales by commodity, world area, and country, 1960s-86, 1528–323
- Agricultural trade of US, by detailed commodity and country, 1989, annual rpt, 1524–8
- Agricultural trade of US, by detailed commodity and country, 1990, semiannual rpt, 1522–4
- AID economic aid to developing countries, obligations and disbursements by country, quarterly rpt, 9912–4
- AID loans repayment status and terms by program and country, and status of predecessor agency loans, quarterly rpt, 9912–3
- Dairy imports, consumption, and market conditions, by sub-Saharan Africa country, 1961-88, 1528–321
- Economic and military aid and loans from US and intl agencies, by program and country, FY46-90, annual rpt, 9914–5
- Economic and social conditions of developing countries from 1960s, and Intl Dev Cooperation Agency and AID activities and funding, FY90-92, annual rpt, 9904–4
- Economic conditions, income, production, prices, employment, and trade, 1991 periodic country rpt, 2046–4.41
- Economic conditions, investment and export opportunities, and trade practices, 1991 country market research rpt, 2046–6.4
- Economic conditions, policy, and trade practices, by country, 1988-90, annual rpt, 21384–5
- Economic, social, political, and geographic summary data, by country, 1991, annual factbook, 9114–2
- Exports and imports of US, by commodity and country, 1970-89, world area rpt, 9116–1.6
- Exports and imports of US, by selected country, country group, and commodity group, 1990, annual rpt, 2044–37
- Exports and imports of US, by transport mode, country, and SITC 1- to 3-digit commodity, 1990, annual rpt, 2424–12
- Exports of US, detailed Schedule B commodities with countries of destination, 1990, annual rpt, 2424–10
- Human rights conditions in 170 countries, and US economic and military aid, 1990, annual rpt, 21384–3
- Labor conditions, union coverage, and work accidents, 1991 annual country rpt, 6366–4.24
- Military aid of US, arms sales, and training programs costs and budget requests, by program, world region, and country, FY90-92, annual rpt, 7144–13
- *Minerals Yearbook, 1988,* Vol 3: foreign country review of production, trade, and policy, by commodity, annual rpt, 5604–17.80
- Multinatl US firms foreign affiliates, income statement items by country and world area, 1986, biennial article, 8302–2.212
- UN voting record and share of votes in agreement with US, by issue, country, and world area, 1990, annual rpt, 7004–18

see also under By Foreign Country in the "Index by Categories"

Index by Subjects and Names

Zambia

Agricultural exports of high-value commodities, indexes and sales by commodity, world area, and country, 1960s-86, 1528–323

Agricultural trade of US, by detailed commodity and country, 1989, annual rpt, 1524–8

Agricultural trade of US, by detailed commodity and country, 1990, semiannual rpt, 1522–4

AID economic aid to developing countries, obligations and disbursements by country, quarterly rpt, 9912–4

AID loans repayment status and terms by program and country, and status of predecessor agency loans, quarterly rpt, 9912–3

Background Notes, summary social, political, and economic data, 1991 rpt, 7006–2.33

Dairy imports, consumption, and market conditions, by sub-Saharan Africa country, 1961-88, 1528–321

Economic and military aid and loans from US and intl agencies, by program and country, FY46-90, annual rpt, 9914–5

Economic and social conditions of developing countries from 1960s, and Intl Dev Cooperation Agency and AID activities and funding, FY90-92, annual rpt, 9904–4

Economic conditions, income, production, prices, employment, and trade, 1991 periodic country rpt, 2046–4.56

Economic, population, and agricultural data, US and other aid sources, and AID activity, 1987 country rpt, 9916–12.25

Economic, population, and agricultural data, US and other aid sources, and AID activity, 1989 country rpt, 9916–12.32

Economic, social, political, and geographic summary data, by country, 1991, annual factbook, 9114–2

Exports and imports of US, by commodity and country, 1970-89, world area rpt, 9116–1.6

Exports and imports of US, by transport mode, country, and SITC 1- to 3-digit commodity, 1990, annual rpt, 2424–12

Exports of US, detailed Schedule B commodities with countries of destination, 1990, annual rpt, 2424–10

Food supply, needs, and aid for developing countries, status and alternative forecasts, 1991 world area rpt, 1526–8.1

Human rights conditions in 170 countries, and US economic and military aid, 1990, annual rpt, 21384–3

UN voting record and share of votes in agreement with US, by issue, country, and world area, 1990, annual rpt, 7004–18

see also under By Foreign Country in the "Index by Categories"

Zeimetz, Kathryn A.

"USSR Agricultural Trade", 1528–322

Zeitzer, Ilene R.

"Role of Assistive Technology in Promoting Return to Work for People with Disabilities: The U.S. and Swedish Systems", 4742–1.215

Zelman, William M.

"Financial Aspects of Adult Day Care: National Survey Results", 4652–1.234

Zempel, Alan

"Partnership Returns, 1989", 8302–2.216

Zill, Nicholas

"Developmental, Learning, and Emotional Problems: Health of Our Nation's Children, U.S., 1988", 4146–8.193

Zimbabwe

Agricultural conditions in Zimbabwe, impacts of economic policies, 1980s, 1528–319

Agricultural exports of high-value commodities, indexes and sales by commodity, world area, and country, 1960s-86, 1528–323

Agricultural production, trade, and policies in foreign countries, summary data by country, 1989-90, annual factbook, 1924–12

Agricultural trade of US, by detailed commodity and country, 1989, annual rpt, 1524–8

Agricultural trade of US, by detailed commodity and country, 1990, semiannual rpt, 1522–4

AID economic aid to developing countries, obligations and disbursements by country, quarterly rpt, 9912–4

AID loans repayment status and terms by program and country, and status of predecessor agency loans, quarterly rpt, 9912–3

Dairy imports, consumption, and market conditions, by sub-Saharan Africa country, 1961-88, 1528–321

Economic and military aid and loans from US and intl agencies, by program and country, FY46-90, annual rpt, 9914–5

Economic and social conditions of developing countries from 1960s, and Intl Dev Cooperation Agency and AID activities and funding, FY90-92, annual rpt, 9904–4

Economic conditions, income, production, prices, employment, and trade, 1991 periodic country rpt, 2046–4.40

Economic, population, and agricultural data, US and other aid sources, and AID activity, 1989 country rpt, 9916–12.32

Economic, social, political, and geographic summary data, by country, 1991, annual factbook, 9114–2

Exports and imports of US, by commodity and country, 1970-89, world area rpt, 9116–1.6

Exports and imports of US, by transport mode, country, and SITC 1- to 3-digit commodity, 1990, annual rpt, 2424–12

Exports of US, detailed Schedule B commodities with countries of destination, 1990, annual rpt, 2424–10

Food supply, needs, and aid for developing countries, status and alternative forecasts, 1991 world area rpt, 1526–8.1

Human rights conditions in 170 countries, and US economic and military aid, 1990, annual rpt, 21384–3

Labor conditions, union coverage, and work accidents, 1990 annual country rpt, 6366–4.9

Labor conditions, union coverage, and work accidents, 1991 annual country rpt, 6366–4.41

Military aid of US, arms sales, and training programs costs and budget requests, by program, world region, and country, FY90-92, annual rpt, 7144–13

Multinatl US firms foreign affiliates, income statement items by country and world area, 1986, biennial article, 8302–2.212

Tobacco auctioned and prices, for Malawi and Zimbabwe, 1989-90, article, 1925–16.205

UN voting record and share of votes in agreement with US, by issue, country, and world area, 1990, annual rpt, 7004–18

see also under By Foreign Country in the "Index by Categories"

Zimmer, Steven A.

"Bank Cost of Capital and International Competition", 9385–1.203

"Cost of Capital for Securities Firms in the U.S. and Japan", 9385–1.212

"Event Risk Premia and Bond Market Incentives for Corporate Leverage", 9385–8.88

Zinc and zinc industry

Business statistics, detailed data for major industries and economic indicators, *Survey of Current Business*, monthly rpt, 2702–1.17

Castings (nonferrous) shipments, by metal type, 1990, annual Current Industrial Rpt, 2506–10.5

Coin production and monetary metals use and holdings of US Mint, by metal type, FY90, annual rpt, 8204–1

Exports and imports between US and outlying areas, by detailed commodity and mode of transport, 1990, annual rpt, 2424–11

Exports and imports of US, by country and detailed commodity, monthly rpt, 2422–12

Exports and imports of US, by Harmonized System 6-digit commodity and country, 1990, annual rpt, 2424–13

Exports and imports of US, by transport mode, country, and SITC 1- to 3-digit commodity, 1990, annual rpt, 2424–12

Exports of US, detailed Schedule B commodities with countries of destination, 1990, annual rpt, 2424–10

Manufacturing annual survey, 1989: finances and operations, by SIC 2- to 4-digit industry, series, 2506–15

Manufacturing finances and operations, by SIC 2- to 4-digit industry, forecast 1991, annual rpt, 2044–28

Mineral Industry Surveys, commodity review of production, trade, stocks, and use, monthly rpt, 5612–1.27

Mineral Industry Surveys, State reviews of production, 1990, preliminary annual rpt, 5614–6

Minerals Yearbook, 1988, Vol 3: foreign country reviews of production, trade, and policy, by commodity, annual rpt series, 5604–17

Minerals Yearbook, 1989, Vol 1: commodity review of production, reserves, supply, use, and trade, annual rpt, 5604–15.70

Minerals Yearbook, 1989, Vol 2: State reviews of production and sales by commodity, and business activity, annual rpt series, 5604–16

Minerals Yearbook, 1989, Vol 2: State reviews of production, sales, and firms, by commodity, and business activity, annual rpt, 5604–34

Mines (metal) and related operations occupational injuries and incidence, employment, and hours, 1989, annual rpt, 6664–3

Zinc and zinc industry

Occupational injury and illness rates, by SIC 2- to 4-digit industry, 1988-89, annual rpt, 6844–7

OECD trade, total and for 4 major countries, and US trade by country, by commodity, 1970-89, world area rpt series, 9116–1

Pollution (air) emissions factors, by detailed pollutant and source, data compilation, 1990 rpt, 9198–120

Price indexes (producer), by stage of processing and detailed commodity, monthly rpt, 6762–6

Price indexes (producer), by stage of processing and detailed commodity, monthly 1990, annual rpt, 6764–2

Production, prices, trade, and foreign and US industry devs, by commodity, bimonthly rpt with articles, 5602–4

Production, prices, trade, use, employment, tariffs, and stockpiles, by mineral, with foreign comparisons, 1986-90, annual rpt, 5604–18

Statistical Abstract of US, 1991 annual data compilation, 2324–1.25

Stockpiling of strategic material by Fed Govt, activity, and inventory by commodity, as of Mar 1991, semiannual rpt, 3542–22

Stockpiling of strategic material, inventories and needs, by commodity, as of Jan 1991, annual rpt, 3544–37

see also under By Commodity in the "Index by Categories"

ZIP codes

Financial instns location relation to ZIP code area income and minority population, by instn type for 5 cities, 1977-89, article, 9377–1.208

Mail volume to and from households, use, and views, by class, source, content, and household characteristics, 1987-88, annual rpt, 9864–10

North Central States, FHLB 7th District housing vacancy rates for single and multifamily units and mobile homes, by ZIP code, annual MSA rpt series, 9304–18

West Central States, FHLB 10th District housing vacancy rates for single and multifamily units and mobile homes, by ZIP code, annual MSA rpt series, 9304–22

Western States, FHLB 12th District housing vacancy rates for single and multifamily units and mobile homes, by ZIP code, annual MSA rpt series, 9304–21

Zirconium

see Metals and metal industries

Zoning and zoning laws

Real estate assets of failed thrifts, inventory of properties available from Resolution Trust Corp, 1990, semiannual listing, 9722–2.9

Real estate assets of failed thrifts, inventory of properties available from Resolution Trust Corp, 1991, semiannual listing, 9722–2.15

see also Building permits

Zoological parks

County Business Patterns, 1988: employment, establishments, and payroll, by SIC 2- to 4-digit industry and county, annual State rpt series, 2326–6

County Business Patterns, 1989: employment, establishments, and payroll, by SIC 2- to 4-digit industry and county, annual State rpt series, 2326–8

Endangered animals and plants US trade and permits, by species, purpose, disposition, and country, 1989, annual rpt, 5504–19

Fish (shark and ray) population, physical characteristics, landings, and fishery mgmt, 1987 conf, 2168–124

Licensing and inspection of facilities, and other animal protection activities of USDA, with animals used in research, by State, FY89, annual rpt, 1394–10

Service industries census, 1987: establishments, receipts by source, payroll, and employment, by SIC 2- to 4-digit kind of business, State, and MSA, 2393–4

Zoology

Education in science and engineering, grad programs enrollment by field, source of funds, and characteristics of student and instn, 1975-89, annual rpt, 9627–7

Land Mgmt Bur wildlife mgmt activities and funding, acreage by habitat type, and scientific staff, State rpt series, 5726–7

Land Mgmt Bur wildlife mgmt activities and funding, acreage, staff, and plans, habitat study series, 5726–6

Marine mammals research, Federal funding by topic, recipient, and agency, FY90, annual rpt, 14734–2

Reproduction and population research, Fed Govt funding by project, FY89, annual listing, 4474–9

Research on wildlife and plants, habitat study series, 5506–13

see also Animals

see also Birds and bird conservation

see also Wildlife and wildlife conservation

see also Zoological parks

Zuckerman, Stephen

"Hospital Cost Variations Under PPS", 17206–2.26

Index by Categories

Index by Categories

Geographic Breakdowns		Economic Breakdowns		Demographic Breakdowns	
By Census Division	841	By Commodity	881	By Age	900
By City	842	By Federal Agency	885	By Disease	905
By County	846	By Income	887	By Educational Attainment	906
By Foreign Country	847	By Individual Company		By Marital Status	908
By Outlying Area	854	or Institution	888	By Race and	
By Region	857	By Industry	894	Ethnic Group	909
By SMSA or MSA	864	By Occupation	898	By Sex	914
By State	865				
By Urban-Rural and					
Metro-Nonmetro	879				

INTRODUCTION

The Index by Categories contains references to all publications, tables, and groups of tables that contain breakdowns of statistical data by any or several of the following 21 standard categories:

GEOGRAPHIC BREAKDOWNS

By Census Division	By Outlying Area
By City	By Region
By County	By SMSA or MSA
By Foreign Country	By State
	By Urban-Rural

ECONOMIC BREAKDOWNS

By Commodity	By Individual
By Federal Agency	Company
By Income	or Institution
By Industry	By Occupation

DEMOGRAPHIC BREAKDOWNS

By Age	By Marital Status
By Disease	By Race and Ethnic
By Educational	Group
Attainment	By Sex

SUBJECT SUBHEADINGS

Within each of the categories listed above, references have been grouped according to the subject matter of the publication or the statistical content being indexed. Nineteen subheadings have been used for this purpose; they are listed below. The kinds of material referenced under each subheading are noted, as well as cross-references to other, related subheadings.

Agriculture and Food — Covers all agricultural data, including commercial fishing and the fertilizer industry; agricultural credit of all kinds; agricultural land; farm population and labor; and all data on food except retail prices.

See also Natural Resources, Environment, and Pollution, for forestry data, additional conservation data
Prices and Cost of Living, for retail food prices

Banking, Finance, and Insurance — Covers all data on financial institutions and their activities; all banking and insurance data; consumer credit; bankruptcy; securities markets; and money supply, interest rates, and other financial indicators.

See also Other specific subheadings, for Federal insurance programs
Agriculture and Food, for agricultural credit
Government and Defense, for Government debt and securities
Health and Vital Statistics, for health insurance data
Housing and Construction, for mortgage data
Industry and Commerce, for general economic indicators

Communications and Transportation — Covers all data on industries in these sectors, including their finances, employment, occupational safety, and rates and regulation; highway data; Postal Service; all travel and tourism data, including accidents; and propaganda.

See also Energy Resources and Demand, for pipeline data
Industry and Commerce, for equipment and parts manufacturing and trade.

Education — Covers all data on education in general, including schools, faculty, students, graduates, and finances.

See also Government and Defense, for military academies
Health and Vital Statistics, for medical and dental schools and all data on health manpower training
Labor and Employment, for employment training programs, such as CETA and WIN, and for apprenticeships
Science and Technology, for education exclusively in science and engineering
Veterans Affairs, for GI Bill and other veterans' education

Energy Resources and Demand — Covers supply, consumption, and conservation of all types of energy. Includes exploration, extraction, R&D, transportation, distribution, and waste disposal of all energy forms; all data on energy industries; and energy use and costs.

See also Health and Vital Statistics, for accidents and occupational health in energy industries, including mines
Natural Resources, Environment, and Pollution, for additional data exclusively on energy reserves, and for pollution and radioactivity from energy resources
Prices and Cost of Living, for consumer utility bills

Geography and Climate — Covers all data on weather, climate, oceanography, and storms and other natural disasters.

See also Natural Resources, Environment, and Pollution, for data on water supply and land use

Government and Defense — Covers all data on government in general, including activities, finances, programs, and personnel; all data on defense activities and foreign affairs; taxes; coinage; passports; and elections and voting.

See also Other specific subheadings for data on government aid, employment, or regulation in specific areas
Health and Vital Statistics, for military medicine

Health and Vital Statistics—Covers all data on health condition, disease, and disability; occupational health and safety in general; medical care, costs, and insurance; medical facilities; health personnel and their education; and vital statistics.

See also Communications and Transportation, for all transportation accidents, including occupational accidents and health
Labor and Employment, for vocational rehabilitation and other training programs for disabled persons
Public Welfare and Social Security, for data on Medicare, Medicaid, and social security recipients
Veterans Affairs, for data on veterans' health and VA medical facilities

Housing and Construction — Covers all data on housing condition, finance, and occupancy; all data on the construction industry; all mortgages; urban renewal and community development; and government aid for housing or communities.

See also Communications and Transportation, for construction of highways and bridges
Natural Resources, Environment, and Pollution, for construction of dams, sewer plants, etc.

Industry and Commerce — Covers all data on industry in general, including production, finances, payrolls, and profits; productivity; trade and marketing; foreign trade, tariffs, and balance of payments; and economic indicators in general.

See also Other more specific subheadings for data on specific industry sectors Government and Defense, for corporate income tax data

Labor and Employment — Covers all data on the labor force and employment in general, including characteristics, earnings, hours, working conditions, and employee benefits; unemployment; labor unions; and employment training programs, such as CETA and WIN.

See also Other more specific subheadings for employment and employees in specific disciplines, such as health or science, or in specific industry sectors, such as agriculture or transportation Industry and Commerce, for general industry data including employment and payrolls

Law Enforcement — Covers all data on crime and the characteristics of criminals; and all data on the criminal justice system, including police, lawyers, courts, prisons, and sentences.

See also Other specific subheadings for civil proceedings and government regulation in specific areas

Natural Resources, Environment, and Pollution— Covers all data on natural resource supply and conservation, including energy reserves, forests, public lands, and wildlife; land use; water supply, dams, and flood control; environmental quality; all types of pollutants; wastes in general, including sewage disposal; oil spills; and radioactivity in the environment.

See also Agriculture and Food, for conservation specifically related to agriculture
Energy Resources and Demand, for additional data on energy reserves, disposal of wastes from energy production, and nuclear power
Health and Vital Statistics, for occupational hazards and for the health effects of pollutants

Population—Covers all data on population size; characteristics of the population in general; demographic groups such as youth, women, or blacks; and migration.

See also Other specific subheadings for data on special population groups such

as farmers, veterans, or mortgagors Health and Vital Statistics, for data on births and deaths

Prices and Cost of Living—Covers prices in general, both wholesale and retail; price indexes; consumer costs; and inflation.

See also Education, for tuition costs
Health and Vital Statistics, for medical costs
Industry and Commerce or other more specific subheadings, for data on production costs, farm value, etc.

Public Welfare and Social Security—Covers everything related to the social security program, including Medicare and disability insurance; everything related to welfare, public assistance, and medical assistance (Medicaid); food stamps and school lunch programs; and social services.

See also Health and Vital Statistics, for data on workers compensation and disabled persons in general
Labor and Employment, for unemployment insurance

Recreation and Leisure—Covers all data on recreation activities and recreation industries. Includes sport fishing, hunting, parks, museums, and the arts; and tourists promotion.

See also Communications and Transportation, for data on travel
Education, for libraries

Science and Technology—Covers activities, private and government funding, employment, and education, exclusively in scientific fields; all data on space programs; and inventions and patents.

See also Agriculture and Food, for agricultural sciences
Energy Resources and Demand, for R&D in energy fields
Geography and Climate, for meteorology, oceanography, etc.

Veterans Affairs—Covers everything that relates exclusively to veterans, including education, health, VA hospitals, housing and VA home loans, employment and employment programs, pensions, and disability payments.

See also Government and Defense, for data on the armed services

---

USING THE INDEX

In using the Category Index, you must keep in mind that the amount of detail provided in the various tabular breakdowns may vary considerably.

Breakdowns "By sex" or "By urban-rural" are, by definition, complete. Breakdowns "By census division," "By region," or "By State" are generally complete unless specific limitations are noted.

Breakdowns "By race and ethnic group" generally show white and nonwhite or white, black, and other. When substantial data on race/ethnic breakdowns are included, they are indexed specifically in the Index of Subjects and Names (i.e. Black Americans, Asian Americans, Indians, Hispanic Americans) as well as under the category "By race."

The greatest variation in the detail of category breakdowns occurs in such categories as "By county," "By foreign country," "By industry," "By commodity," and "By occupation." For these categories, we try, whenever possible, to indicate the degree of detail in the notations of content listed under the category terms and in the abstract of the publication.

For further information about using the Category Index, see the User Guide.

For use in conjunction with the Category Index, we have printed several standard classification systems that are frequently used in Federal statistical publications (see p. 1023). These classifications include regions of the U.S., SMSAs, Standard Industrial Classification, and Standard International Trade Classification.

Index by Categories

GEOGRAPHIC BREAKDOWNS

BY CENSUS DIVISION

Agriculture and Food

Cold storage food stocks by commodity and census div, and warehouse space use, by State, monthly rpt, 1631–5

Cold storage food stocks by commodity, and warehouse space use, by census div, 1990, annual rpt, 1631–11

Fertilizer (inorganic) shipments, trade, use, and firms, by product and State, with stocks, 1990, annual Current Industrial Rpt, 2506–8.13

Fertilizer use, by type and State, 1989-90, annual rpt, 9804–30

Banking, Finance, and Insurance

Banks financial performance, for undercapitalized instns by State and inside-outside Texas, aggregate 1985-89, article, 9391–1.212

Communications and Transportation

Travel from US, characteristics of visit and traveler, and country of destination, 1990 in-flight survey, annual rpt, 2904–14

Travel to US, by characteristics of visit and traveler, world area of origin, and US destination, 1990 survey, annual rpt, 2904–12

Education

Educational attainment, by sociodemographic characteristics and location, 1989 and trends from 1940, biennial Current Population Rpt, 2546–1.452

Elementary and secondary public schools, enrollment, teachers, funding, and other characteristics, by region and State, 1988/89, annual rpt, 4834–20

Energy Resources and Demand

Building (commercial) energy use, costs, and conservation, by building characteristics, survey rpt series, 3166–8

Coal, coke, and breeze supply, demand, prices, trade, and stocks, by end-use sector and State, quarterly rpt with articles, 3162–37

Coal production, stocks, and shipments, by State of origin and destination, end-use sector, and mode of transport, quarterly rpt, 3162–8

Coal stocks at electric utilities, by census div and State, weekly rpt, monthly data, 3162–1.2

Electric power plants (steam) fuel receipts, costs, and quality, by fuel, plant, utility, and State, 1990, annual rpt, 3164–42

Electric power plants and capacity, by fuel used, owner, location, and operating status, 1990 and for units planned 1991-2000, annual listing, 3164–36

Electric power plants certification applications filed with FERC, for small production and cogeneration facilities, FY80-90, annual listing, 3084–13

Electric power plants natural gas use, by State, 1977 and 1989, annual rpt, 3334–1

Electric power plants production, capacity, sales, and fuel stocks, use, and costs, by State, 1985-89, annual rpt, 3164–11

Electric power plants production, fuel use, stocks, and costs by fuel type, and sales, by State, monthly rpt with articles, 3162–35

Electric power sales and revenue, by end-use sector, consumption level, and utility, 1989, annual rpt, 3164–91

Natural gas interstate pipeline company sales and contract deliveries, by firm and State, 1984-89, annual article, 3162–4.204

Geography and Climate

Heating and cooling degree days, by census div, monthly and cumulative for season, monthly rpt, 3162–24.1

Heating and cooling degree days weighted by population, by census div and State, with area-weighted temperature and precipitation, monthly rpt, 2152–13

Government and Defense

DOD prime contract awards, by category, contractor type, and State, FY88-90, annual rpt, 3544–11

Military active duty and recruit social, economic, and parents characteristics, by service branch and State, FY89, annual rpt, 3544–41

Military spending reductions and base closings employment impacts, by region and State, 1988-89 and projected FY91-95, article, 9371–1.206

State and Metro Area Data Book, 1991 data compilation, 2328–54

Voting and registration, by socioeconomic and demographic characteristics, 1990 congressional election, biennial Current Population Rpt, 2546–1.454

Health and Vital Statistics

Births and rates, by characteristics of birth, infant, and parents, 1989 and trends from 1940, US Vital Statistics advance annual rpt, 4146–5.123

Births and rates by mother's age, and fertility rates, by mother's education, child's race, census div, and State, 1980 and 1985, 4147–21.49

Deaths and rates, by detailed cause and demographic characteristics, 1988 and trends from 1900, US Vital Statistics annual rpt, 4144–2

Divorces by age of spouses and duration of marriage, and children involved, by State, 1988 and trends from 1940, US Vital Statistics advance annual rpt, 4146–5.121

Health condition and health care resources, use, and spending, 1950s-89, annual data compilation, 4144–11

Home health care services Medicare use and costs, by agency and service type, patient characteristics, and State, 1988-89, article, 4652–1.229

Hospital closures and rates, with financial, operating, and market characteristics, by location, late 1980s, GAO rpt, 26121–392

Hospitals in rural areas, financial and operating performance impacts of Medicare prospective payment reimbursement system, 1980s-87, 4658–51

Infectious notifiable disease cases, by age, race, and State, and deaths, 1930s-90, annual rpt, 4204–1

Marriages and rates, by age, race, education, previous marital status, and State, 1988, US Vital Statistics advance annual rpt, 4146–5.122

Marriages, divorces, and rates, by characteristics of spouses, State, and county, 1987 and trends from 1920, US Vital Statistics annual rpt, 4144–4

Physicians, by specialty, age, sex, and location of training and practice, 1989, State rpt series, 4116–6

Radiation protection and health physics enrollment and degrees granted by instn and State, and grad placement, by student characteristics, 1990, annual rpt, 3004–7

Smoking and smokeless tobacco use, attitudes, and smoking intervention research spending and results, with bibl, 1960s-90, 4478–195

Tuberculosis cases and deaths, by patient characteristics, State, and city, 1989 and trends from 1953, annual rpt, 4204–10

Vital statistics provisional data, monthly rpt, 4142–1

Housing and Construction

Cement (portland) shipments to census divs, bimonthly rpt, 2042–1.6

Census of Population and Housing, 1990: housing units occupied and vacant, persons in group quarters, and household size, by region, census div, and State, press release, 2328–71

Clay (construction) production and shipments by region and State, trade, and use, by product, quarterly Current Industrial Rpt, 2506–9.2

Construction put in place, value of new public and private structures, by type, monthly rpt, 2382–4

Mobile home placements by structural characteristics, and price, by census div and State, monthly rpt, annual tables, 2382–1

New housing units authorized, by region, State, selected MSA, and permit-issuing place, monthly rpt, 2382–5

New housing units authorized, by State, MSA, and permit-issuing place, 1990, annual rpt, 2384–2

Public works capital stock and investment spending economic impacts, with data by type of stock and region, 1950s-88, conf, 9373–3.34

Industry and Commerce

Mineral industries census, 1987: finances and operations, by SIC 2- to 4-digit industry, State, and county, census div rpt series, 2515–1

Retail trade sales and inventories, by kind of business, region, and selected State, MSA, and city, monthly rpt, 2413–3

BY CENSUS DIVISION

State and Metro Area Data Book, 1991 data compilation, 2328–54

Statistical Abstract of US, 1991 annual data compilation, 2324–1

Labor and Employment

Earnings impact of educational attainment and work experience, model description and results for men, by census div, 1979-88, article, 9373–1.213

Employment over business cycles, by census div and State, 1988-92, release, 9538–8

Employment, unemployment, and labor force characteristics, by region and census div, 1990, annual rpt, 6744–7.1

Labor force status, by worker characteristics and industry group, 1982-90, semiannual article, 6722–1.212

Labor Relations Natl Board activities, cases, elections conducted, and litigation, FY89, annual rpt, 9584–1

Manufacturing job creation, elimination, and reallocation rates, and relation to industry and establishment characteristics, 1970s-86, working paper, 9375–13.56

Unemployment, employment, and labor force, by region and State, 1989-90, press release, 6726–1.37

Law Enforcement

Assaults and deaths of law enforcement officers, by circumstances, agency, victim and offender characteristics, and location, 1990, annual rpt, 6224–3

Crimes and rates by offense, and law enforcement employment, by population size and jurisdiction, 1990, annual rpt, 6224–2.1; 6224–2.3

Police employment and expenditures, by population size, metro status, and location, data compilation, 1991 annual rpt, 6064–6.1

Natural Resources, Environment, and Pollution

Electric utilities privately owned, air pollution emissions and abatement equipment by fuel type and State, 1985-89, annual rpt, 3164–11.5

Population

Census of Population, 1990: population by race, Hispanic origin, region, census div, and State, with data for 1980, fact sheet, 2326–20.2

Census of Population, 1990: population size, by State, census div, and region, and congressional seats apportioned by State, 1990 and trends from 1790, fact sheet, 2326–20.1

Census of Population, 1990: urban areas land area, housing units, and population, by State and compared to rural areas, press release, 2328–39

Income (household, family, and personal), by source, detailed characteristics, and region, 1988-89, annual Current Population Rpt, 2546–6.68

Income (household, family, and personal), by source, detailed characteristics, and region, 1990, annual Current Population Rpt, 2546–6.70

Income (personal) totals, by region, census div, and State, quarterly article, 2702–1.27

Population estimates and projections, by region and State, Current Population Rpt series, 2546–3

Population size, July 1981-89 and compared to 1980 and 1990, annual press release, 2324–10

Index by Categories

State and Metro Area Data Book, 1991 data compilation, 2328–54

Statistical Abstract of US, 1991 annual data compilation, 2324–1

Public Welfare and Social Security

Medicare and Medicaid eligibility, participation, coverage, and program finances, various periods 1966-91, biennial rpt, 4654–1

Medicare beneficiaries hospital discharges, length of stay, and costs, by type of beneficiary and location, 1972-88, article, 4652–1.207

Medicare Cost Report reviews, revisions ratio to initially reported costs, by category, FY84, article, 4652–1.233

Medicare reimbursement of hospitals under prospective payment system, alternative complexity indexes for diagnosis related groups, with background data, FY86-88, annual rpt, 17206–2.21

Medicare reimbursement of hospitals under prospective payment system, and effect on services, finances, and beneficiary payments, 1979-90, annual rpt, 17204–2

OASDHI, Medicaid, SSI, and related programs benefits, beneficiary characteristics, and trust funds, selected years 1937-89, annual rpt, 4744–3

Recreation and Leisure

Coastal areas recreation facilities of Fed Govt and States, out-of-State visitors by location of residence, 1987-90 survey, regional rpt series, 2176–9

Shellfish recreational harvesters selected characteristics, location of harvest and residence, and spending, 1985 survey, 2178–28

Science and Technology

Education in science and engineering, grad programs enrollment by field, source of funds, and characteristics of student and instn, 1975-89, annual rpt, 9627–7

Employment and other characteristics of science and engineering PhDs, by field and State, 1989, biennial rpt, 9627–18

Nuclear engineering enrollment and degrees granted by instn and State, and grad placement, by student characteristics, 1990, annual rpt, 3004–5

R&D and related funding of Fed Govt to higher education and nonprofit instns, by field, instn, agency, and State, FY89, annual rpt, 9627–17

R&D funding by Fed Govt, by field, performer type, agency, and State, FY89-91, annual rpt, 9627–20

R&D funding by higher education instns and federally funded centers, by field, instn, and State, FY89, annual rpt, 9627–13

BY CITY

Agriculture and Food

Cotton prices in 8 spot markets, futures prices at NYC exchange, farm prices, and CCC loan stocks, monthly rpt, 1309–1

Exports and imports (agricultural) of US, by commodity, country, and US port, 1950s-91, annual rpt, 1924–9

Fish (squid) exports of US by port, species, and country, 1963-90, 2166–19.10

Fish and shellfish catch, wholesale receipts, prices, trade, and other market activities, weekly regional rpts, 2162–6

Fish catch, by species, use, region, State, and major port, 1980s-90, annual rpt, 2164–1.1

Fruit and vegetable exports to US, by commodity, country, and port of entry, 1975-87, 1568–299

Fruit and vegetable imports under quarantine, by crop, country, and port of entry, FY88, annual rpt, 1524–7

Fruit and vegetable shipments, and arrivals in US and Canada cities, by mode of transport and State and country of origin, 1990, annual rpt series, 1311–4

Grain stocks by region and market city, and grain inspected for export, by type, weekly rpt, 1313–4

Molasses (feed) wholesale prices by market area, and trade, weekly rpt, 1311–16

Molasses supply, use, wholesale prices by market, and imports by country, 1985-90, annual rpt, 1311–19

Potato shipments, and arrivals by US city of origin, 1980-90, 1568–305

Salt production capacity, by firm and facility, 1990, annual listing, 5614–30

Tobacco marketing activity, prices, and sales, by grade, type, market, and State, 1989-90, annual rpt series, 1319–5

Tomato arrivals in US and Canada cities from Mexico, 1970s-90, article, 1561–11.202

Banking, Finance, and Insurance

Fed Financing Bank holdings and transactions, by borrower, monthly press release, 12802–1

Fraud and abuse in banks and thrifts, Federal agencies enforcement activities and staff, with data by instn and location, 1988-90, hearing, 21408–119

Savings instns failures, inventory of real estate assets available from Resolution Trust Corp, semiannual listing series, 9722–2

Texas economic and housing conditions, bank failures, and thrift and Federal regulators real estate holdings, 1980s-90, hearings, 21248–146

West Central States, FHLB 10th District thrifts, locations, assets, and deposits, 1991, annual listing, 9304–17

Communications and Transportation

Air traffic (passenger), and aircraft operations by type, by airport and State, projected FY91-2005 and trends from FY83, annual rpt, 7504–7

Air traffic (passenger and cargo), and departures by aircraft type, by carrier and airport, 1990, annual rpt, 7504–35

Air traffic (passenger and cargo), carrier enplanement shares, and FAA airport improvement program grants, by airport and State, 1989, annual rpt, 7504–48

Air traffic, and passenger and freight enplanements, by airport, 1960s-90 and projected to 2010, hub area rpt series, 7506–7

Air traffic, carriers, craft, airports, and FAA activities, detailed data, 1980-89, annual rpt, 7504–1

Air traffic control staffing levels, by job level and selected facility, FY88-90, GAO rpt, 26113–522

Air traffic levels at FAA-operated control facilities, by airport and State, FY90, annual rpt, 7504–27

Index by Categories

BY CITY

Aircraft accidents and circumstances, for US operations of domestic and foreign airlines and general aviation, periodic rpt, 9612–1

Aircraft handled by instrument flight rule, by user type, FAA traffic control center, and region, FY85-90 and projected to FY2005, annual rpt, 7504–15

Airline consumer complaints by reason, passengers denied boarding, and late flights, by reporting carrier and airport, monthly rpt, 7302–11

Airline deregulation in 1978, impacts on industry structure, competition, fares, finances, operations, and intl service, with data by carrier and airport, 1980s, series, 7308–199

Airport capacity expansion and improvement funding sources, alternative methods, late 1980s and projected to 2000, hearing, 21648–63

Airport capacity improvement projects and funding, traffic, and delays, by major airport, 1987-90 and forecast to 1998, annual rpt, 7504–43

Airport finances, operations by carrier, and capacity improvement and dev funding, by airport, 1977-87 and projected to 2020, hearing, 21648–59

Airport improvement program of FAA, activities and grants by State and airport, FY90, annual rpt, 7504–38

Airport improvement program of FAA, activities, funding, and airport operations, by location, projected 1990-99, biennial rpt, 7504–42

Airport planning and dev project grants of FAA, by airport and location, quarterly press release, 7502–14

Coast Guard search and rescue missions, and lives and property lost and saved, by district and assisting unit, FY90, annual rpt, 7404–2

Hwy and road miles and traffic volume, by city, 1990, annual rpt, 7554–1.4

Hwy toll facilities of State and local govts, receipts and disbursements by facility, 1989-90, annual rpt, 7554–1.3

Postal Service customer satisfaction, and on-time 1st class mail delivery, by region and city, 1991 survey, press release, 9868–1

Shipborne commerce (domestic and foreign) of US, freight by port and State, 1989, annual rpt, 3754–7

Shipborne trade of US, by type of service, commodity, country, route, and US port, 1988, annual rpt, 7704–2

Shipborne trade of US, by type of service, customs district, port, and world area, monthly rpt, 2422–7

Ships freight rates for lumber from Alaska and Puget Sound to Asian markets, by product and port, 1988, 1208–358

St Lawrence Seaway ship, cargo, and passenger traffic, and toll revenue, 1990 and trends from 1959, annual rpt, 7744–2

Telephone local service charges and low-income subsidies, by region, company, and city, 1980s-90, semiannual rpt, 9282–8

Telephone rates for long-distance telephone service, by company, city, and time of day, 1950s-89, annual rpt, 9284–6.7

Toll facilities, mileage, and operating status, by type of system, as of Jan 1990, biennial listing, 7554–39

Transit systems finances and operations, by mode of transport, size of fleet, and for 468 systems, 1989, annual rpt, 7884–4

Transit systems finances, costs, and needs, by selected system, 1987-89, biennial rpt, 7884–8

Transit systems grants of Urban Mass Transportation Admin, by city and State, FY90, annual rpt, 7884–10

Transportation natl system planning, use, condition, accidents, and needs, by mode of transport, 1940s-90 and projected to 2020, 7308–202

Travel to and from US on US and foreign flag air carriers, by country, world area, and US port, monthly rpt, 7302–2

Travel to US, by characteristics of visit and traveler, country, port city, and State of destination, quarterly rpt, 2902–1

Travel to US, by characteristics of visit and traveler, world area of origin, and US destination, 1990 survey, annual rpt, 2904–12

Truck rates for fresh vegetables, by crop, growing area, and market, periodic situation rpt with articles, 1561–11

Truck rates for fruit and vegetables, by growing area and market, weekly 1990, annual rpt, 1311–15

TV channel allocation and license status, for commercial and noncommercial UHF and VHF stations by market, as of June 30, 1991, semiannual rpt, 9282–6

Education

Elementary and secondary public schools, enrollment and other characteristics, for top 100 districts, 1988/89, annual rpt, 4834–22

Libraries (major urban resource centers) dev projects and funding, by city and State, FY84-88, listing, 4878–4

USIA library holdings, use, and staff, by country and city, FY90, annual rpt, 9854–4

Energy Resources and Demand

Bonneville Power Admin mgmt of Fed Columbia River Power System, finances, operations, and sales by customer, FY90, annual rpt, 3224–1

Bonneville Power Admin sales, revenues, and rates, by customer and customer type, 1990, semiannual rpt, 3222–1

Electric power and industrial plants exempt from oil and gas primary use prohibition, 1990, annual rpt, 3334–1

Electric power sales and revenue, by end-use sector, consumption level, and utility, 1989, annual rpt, 3164–91

Foreign countries electric current characteristics, by country and selected city, 1991 rpt, 2048–1

Nuclear reactors for domestic use and export by function and operating status, with owner, operating characteristics, and location, 1990 annual listing, 3354–15

Oil import traffic by US port and vessel type, marine oil pollution sources, and costs and operations of proposed offshore terminals, late 1980s, 5738–25

Southeastern Power Admin sales by customer, plants, capacity, and Southeastern Fed Power Program financial statements, FY90, annual rpt, 3234–1

Southwestern Fed Power System financial statements, sales by customer, and operations and costs by project, FY90, annual rpt, 3244–1

TVA electric power purchases and resales, with electricity use, average bills, and rates by customer class, by distributor, 1990, annual tables, 9804–14

TVA electric power purchases of municipal and cooperative distributors, and prices and use by distributor and consumer sector, monthly rpt, 9802–1

Western Area Power Admin activities by plant, financial statements, and sales by customer, FY90, annual rpt, 3254–1

Geography and Climate

Earthquake intensity, time, location, damage, and seismic characteristics, for US and foreign earthquakes, 1985, annual rpt, 5664–13

Earthquakes and other ground motion, intensity by station, 1988, annual rpt, 5664–14

Great Lakes water levels, daily and monthly averages by site, 1990 and cumulative from 1900, annual rpt, 2174–3

Heating and cooling degree days, for 45 cities and total US, cumulative for season, weekly rpt, 3162–32.2

Heating degree days for 45 cities and total US, cumulative for season, weekly rpt, 3162–45.2

Hurricanes and tropical storms frequency, intensity, deaths, and damage, by State and selected city, 1886-1989, 2188–15

Statistical Abstract of US, 1991 annual data compilation, 2324–1.6

Tidal currents, daily time and velocity by station for North America and Asia coasts, forecast 1992, annual rpts, 2174–1

Tide height and tidal current velocity daily at Middle Atlantic coastal stations, forecast 1992, annual rpt, 2174–11

Tide height and time daily at coastal points worldwide, forecast 1992, annual rpt series, 2174–2

Weather, air pressure, temperature, and precipitation data for US and foreign locations, monthly 1971-80, decennial rpt series, 2156–4

Weather conditions and effect on agriculture, by US region, State, and city, and world area, weekly rpt, 2182–7

Weather data for stations in continental US and outlying areas, 1990 and historic trends, annual rpt, 2154–8

Weather data for surface and upper air, averages by foreign and US station, monthly rpt, 2152–4

Weather events and anomalies, precipitation and temperature for US and foreign locations, weekly rpt, 2182–6

Weather forecasts for US and Northern Hemisphere, precipitation and temperature by location, semimonthly rpt, 2182–1

Government and Defense

Aliens admitted to US, by class of admission and selected port and country, FY89-90, fact sheet, 6266–2.7

Census of Govts, 1987: local govt employment by function, payroll, and average earnings, for individual counties, cities, and school and special districts, 2455–1

Customs collections, by district and port, FY90, annual rpt, 8104–2.1

Customs Service activities, and collections total and for selected ports, bimonthly journal, 8142–2

BY CITY

Index by Categories

DOD contracts, payroll, and personnel, by service branch and location, with top 5 contractors and maps, by State and country, FY90, annual rpt, 3544–29

DOD prime contract awards, by contractor, service branch, State, and city, FY90, annual rpt, 3544–22

DOD prime contract awards for R&D to US and foreign nonprofit instns and govt agencies, by instn and location, FY90, annual listing, 3544–17

DOD prime contract awards in labor surplus areas, by service branch, and area, 1st half FY91, semiannual rpt, 3542–19

Employment and payroll of city govts, by function, for 295 largest cities, 1990, annual rpt, 2466–1.2

Fed Govt spending in States and local areas, by type, State, county, and city, FY90, annual rpt, 2464–3.2

Finances of govts, by level of govt, State, and for large cities and counties, annual rpt series, 2466–2

Finances, tax systems and revenue, and fiscal structure, by level of govt and State, 1991 and historical trends, annual rpt, 10044–1

Immigrant and nonimmigrant visas of US issued and refused, by class, issuing office, and nationality, FY89, annual rpt, 7184–1

Military base support costs by function, and personnel and acreage by installation, by service branch, FY91, annual rpt, 3504–11

Natl Guard emergency response and strengths, by incident and location, FY90, annual rpt, 3504–22

Navy nuclear-powered vessels and support facilities radioactive waste, releases in harbors, and public exposure, 1970s-90, annual rpt, 3804–11

Navy procurement, by contractor and location, FY90, annual rpt, 3804–13

Property (real) of Fed Govt, leased inventory and rental costs, worldwide summary by location and agency, 1989, annual rpt, 9454–10

State and Metro Area Data Book, 1991 data compilation, 2328–54

Health and Vital Statistics

AIDS virus infection prevalence in developing countries, by sex, selected city, urban-rural location, and country, 1991, semiannual rpt, 2322–4

Alcohol, Drug Abuse and Mental Health Admin research grants and awards, by recipient, FY90, annual listing, 4044–13

Asbestos in buildings, EPA aid for removal, occupational asbestos exposure cancer cases and deaths, and Catholic schools abatement costs, 1985-90, hearing, 25328–32

Child and maternal health programs of major urban health depts, activities and budgets, 1990, listing, 4108–51

Cocaine abuse, user characteristics, and related crime and violence, 1988 conf, 4498–74

Deaths recorded in 121 cities, weekly rpt, 4202–1

Drug (methamphetamine) abuse, availability, health effects, and treatment, 1990 conf papers, 4498–75

Drug abuse indicators for selected metro areas, research results, data collection, and policy issues, 1991 semiannual conf, 4492–5

Firearm accident deaths and injuries by selected city, and effects of gun design modifications, 1988-89, GAO rpt, 26131–80

Fluoride exposure by source, and health risks and benefits, with research results, 1930s-89, 4048–36

HHS financial aid, by program, recipient, State, and city, FY90, annual regional listings, 4004–3

Motorcycle helmet mandatory use law in Texas, impacts on use, 1987-89 study, article, 4042–3.251

NIH grants for R&D, training, construction, and medical libraries, by location and recipient, FY90, annual listings, 4434–7

Sexually transmitted disease cases and control activity, by strain, State, and selected city, 1940s-90, 4205–42

Smoking cessation program in 11 communities, methods and effectiveness, 1983-88, article, 4472–1.231

Tuberculosis cases and deaths, by patient characteristics, State, and city, 1989 and trends from 1953, annual rpt, 4204–10

Housing and Construction

American Housing Survey: unit and households detailed characteristics, and unit and neighborhood quality, MSA rpt series, 2485–6

Census of Population and Housing, 1990: population and housing characteristics, households, and land area, by county, subdiv, and place, State rpt series, 2551–1

Census of Population and Housing, 1990: voting age and total population by race, and housing units, by block, redistricting counts required under PL 94-171, State CD-ROM series, 2551–6

Census of Population and Housing, 1990: voting age and total population by race, and housing units, by county and city, redistricting counts required under PL 94-171, State summary rpt series, 2551–5

Community Dev Block Grant allocation, by State, county, and city, FY84-91, 5128–17

Indian (Navajo and Hopi) relocation program activities and caseloads, 1975-90, 16008–5

New housing units authorized, by region, State, selected MSA, and permit-issuing place, monthly rpt, 2382–5

New housing units authorized, by State, MSA, and permit-issuing place, 1990, annual rpt, 2384–2

North Central States, FHLB 7th District housing vacancy rates for single and multifamily units and mobile homes, by ZIP code, annual MSA rpt series, 9304–18

Office buildings vacancy rates, by selected city, 1980-90, 21248–147

Public works condition, mgmt, R&D, and funding, for transportation and environmental projects, 1986-91, 26358–235

Rent control ordinances and effects on housing supply and affordability, by selected jurisdiction, 1968-89, 5188–130

Rent supplement programs evaluation, housing vouchers compared to Section 8 certificates, 1985-88, series, 5186–14

Southeastern States community dev grants from HUD, by purpose and location, quarterly rpt, 9389–16

West Central States, FHLB 10th District housing vacancy rates for single and multifamily units and mobile homes, by ZIP code, annual MSA rpt series, 9304–22

Western States, FHLB 12th District housing vacancy rates for single and multifamily units and mobile homes, by ZIP code, annual MSA rpt series, 9304–21

Industry and Commerce

Exports of US, detailed commodities by country, monthly CD-ROM, 2422–13

Foreign trade zones (US) operations and movement of goods, by zone and commodity, FY88, annual rpt, 2044–30

Imports of US, detailed commodities by country, monthly CD-ROM, 2422–14

Puerto Rico economic censuses, 1987: wholesale and retail trade and service industry finances and operations, by SIC 2- to 4-digit industry and municipio, 2591–1

Retail trade sales and inventories, by kind of business, region, and selected State, MSA, and city, monthly rpt, 2413–3

State and Metro Area Data Book, 1991 data compilation, 2328–54

Tennessee Valley industrial dev and employment, by SIC 2-digit industry, firm, and location, 1990, annual rpt, 9804–3

Labor and Employment

Alien workers (unauthorized) and Fair Labor Standards Act employer compliance, hiring impacts, and aliens overstaying visas by country and State, 1986-90, annual rpt, 6264–6

Employment and Earnings, detailed data, monthly rpt, 6742–2.8

Employment, unemployment, and labor force characteristics, by selected metro area and large city, 1990, annual rpt, 6744–7.3

Unemployment, employment, and labor force, by State, MSA, and city, monthly rpt, 6742–22

Law Enforcement

Aircraft hijackings, on-board explosions, and other crime, US and foreign incidents, 1985-89, annual rpt, 7504–31

Arrests, by offense, offender characteristics, and location, data compilation, 1991 annual rpt, 6064–6.4

Assaults and deaths of law enforcement officers, by circumstances, agency, victim and offender characteristics, and location, 1990, annual rpt, 6224–3

Crime Index by population size and region, and offenses by large city, Jan-June 1991, semiannual rpt, 6222–1

Crimes and rates by offense, and law enforcement employment, by population size and jurisdiction, 1990, annual rpt, 6224–2.1; 6224–2.3

Crimes, by characteristics of victim and offender, circumstances, and location, data compilation, 1991 annual rpt, 6064–6.3

Criminal justice spending, employment, and payroll, by level of govt, State, and selected city and county, FY71-88, biennial rpt, 6064–9

Criminal justice spending, employment, and payroll, by level of govt, State, and selected city and county, 1984-86, biennial rpt, 6064–4

Drug (illegal) lab seizures, by substance and location, 1989-90, annual rpt, 6284–3

Drug test results at arrest, by drug type, offense, and sex, for selected urban areas, quarterly rpt, 6062–3

Jail population by sex, race, and for 25 jurisdictions, and instn conditions, 1988-90, annual rpt, 6066–25.38

Index by Categories

BY CITY

Police employment and expenditures, by population size, metro status, and location, data compilation, 1991 annual rpt, 6064–6.1

Terrorism incidents in US, related activity, and casualties, by attack type, target, group, and location, 1990, annual rpt, 6224–6

Natural Resources, Environment, and Pollution

Alaska submerged land grant holdings of Alaska Natives, exchange for upland acreage, impacts on conservation acreage and acquisition, 1989-90, 5728–38

Coastal and estuarine pollutant concentrations in sediments, by contaminant and selected site, 1984-89, 2176–3.13

Global climate change environmental, infrastructure, and health impacts, with model results and background data, 1850s-2100, 9188–113

Hazardous waste site remedial action under Superfund, current and proposed sites descriptions and status, periodic listings, series, 9216–3

Hazardous waste site remedial action under Superfund, current and proposed sites priority ranking and status by location, series, 9216–5

Hazardous waste site remedial action under Superfund, EPA records of decision by site, FY89, annual rpt, 9214–5

Military installations hazardous waste site remedial action, activities and funding by site and State, FY90, annual rpt, 3544–36

Minerals (industrial) reserves, production, and use, and characteristics of individual deposits, State rpt series, 5606–10

Minerals resources and availability on public lands, State rpt series, 5606–7

Pacific Ocean coast pollutant concentrations in fish and sediments, by contaminant, fish species, and site, 1984-86, 2168–121

Radiation and radionuclide concentrations in air, water, and milk, monitoring results by State and site, quarterly rpt, 9192–5

Radiation and radionuclide concentrations in surface air at selected monitoring sites worldwide, and effects of nuclear tests and accidents, 1989, annual rpt, 3004–31

Radioactive strontium fallout, monitoring results for 65 sites worldwide, quarterly 1986 and trends from 1958, annual rpt, 3004–29

Radioactive waste from Navy nuclear-powered vessels and support facilities, releases in harbors, and public exposure, 1970s-90, annual rpt, 3804–11

Radon indoor air pollution levels in Pacific Northwest, with geological and soil characteristics, by township, 1989 rpt, 5668–114

Tennessee Valley river control activities, and hydroelectric power generation and capacity, 1989, annual rpt, 9804–7

Timber sales of Forest Service, expenses, and operations, by region, State, and natl forest, FY90, annual rpts, 1204–36

Uranium tailings at inactive mills, remedial action activities by site, and funding, FY90, annual rpt, 3354–9

Wastewater treatment facilities construction grants of EPA to State and local govts, by project, monthly listing, 9202–3

Water quality, chemistry, hydrology, and other characteristics, local area studies, series, 5666–27

Water resources dev projects of Army Corps of Engineers, characteristics, and costs, 1950s-89, biennial State rpt series, 3756–1

Water resources dev projects of Army Corps of Engineers, characteristics, and costs, 1950s-91, biennial State rpt series, 3756–2

Water supply and quality in streams and lakes, and groundwater levels in wells, by drainage basin, 1988, annual State rpt series, 5666–16

Water supply and quality in streams and lakes, and groundwater levels in wells, by drainage basin, 1989, annual State rpt series, 5666–12

Water supply and quality in streams and lakes, and groundwater levels in wells, by drainage basin, 1990, annual State rpt series, 5666–10

Water supply in northeastern US, precipitation and stream runoff by station, monthly rpt, 2182–3

Water supply in US and southern Canada, streamflow, surface and groundwater conditions, and reservoir levels, by location, monthly rpt, 5662–3

Water supply in western US, streamflow and reservoir storage forecasts by stream and station, Jan-May monthly rpt, 1262–1

Population

Alaska rural areas population characteristics, and energy resources dev effects, series, 5736–5

Census of Population and Housing, 1990: population and housing characteristics, households, and land area, by county, subdiv, and place, State rpt series, 2551–1

Census of Population and Housing, 1990: voting age and total population by race, and housing units, by block, redistricting counts required under PL 94-171, State CD-ROM series, 2551–6

Census of Population and Housing, 1990: voting age and total population by race, and housing units, by county and city, redistricting counts required under PL 94-171, State summary rpt series, 2551–5

Census of Population, 1990: cities population and undercounts, and related Federal aid losses, 1990 mayoral survey, hearing, 25408–113

Census of Population, 1990: homeless shelter and on-street population, by State and for 200 cities, press release, 2328–70

Census of Population, 1990: post-enumeration survey results compared to census counts, by race, sex, city, county, and State, press release, 2328–69

Census of Population, 1990: top 39 MSAs and 40 cities population, with trends from 1900, fact sheet, 2326–20.3

Census of Population, 1990: urban areas population, for 396 areas, press release, 2328–37

Population size of cities with population over 100,000, as of Apr 1990, biennial press release, 2324–7

Refugees from Indochina, arrivals, and departures, by country of origin and resettlement, camp, and ethnicity, monthly rpt, 7002–4

State and Metro Area Data Book, 1991 data compilation, 2328–54

Statistical Abstract of US, 1991 annual data compilation, 2324–1.14

Prices and Cost of Living

Auto insurance cost differentials among cities, premiums and cost factors for selected cities, mid 1980s, working paper, 9383–20.9

Brazil price variability among products and cities, relation to inflation, alternative model results for 1980s, working paper, 9379–14.14

Cotton prices at selected spot markets, NYC futures prices, and CCC loan rates, 1990/91 and trends from 1943, annual rpt, 1309–2

Dairy prices, by product and selected area, with related marketing data, 1990, annual rpt, 1317–1

Food price indexes, by city, model results, 1988-89, article, 6722–1.236

Foreign countries living costs, State Dept indexes, housing allowances, and hardship differentials by country and major city, quarterly rpt, 7002–7

Inflation impacts on food price dispersion, by city, model results, 1981-82, working paper, 6886–6.79

Milk farm, processor, and retail prices in 29 cities, 1980s-91, GAO rpt, 26113–540

Milk order and cooperative prices, by selected area, 1990, annual rpt, 1317–1.5

Poultry and egg prices and marketing, by selected region, State, and city, monthly and weekly 1990, annual rpt, 1317–2

Quality of life ratings, for 130 cites, 1979/80, article, 9387–1.202

Public Welfare and Social Security

Food aid programs purchases, by commodity, firm, and shipping point or destination, weekly rpt, 1302–3

HHS financial aid, by program, recipient, State, and city, FY90, annual regional listings, 4004–3

SSA activities, and OASDHI admin, 1930s-90 and projected to 2064, annual data compilation, 4704–12

Recreation and Leisure

Coastal areas recreation facilities of Fed Govt and States, visitor and site characteristics, 1987-90 survey, regional rpt series, 2176–9

Park natl system and other land under Natl Park Service mgmt, acreage by site, ownership, and region, FY91, semiannual rpt, 5542–1

Park natl system visitor deaths, by cause, victim age, region, and park, 1980-90, annual rpt, 5544–6

Public lands recreation facilities and use, and Land Mgmt Bur mgmt activities, funding, and plans, State rpt series, 5726–5

Urban areas park and recreation facilities rehabilitation funding, by city and State, FY91, press release, 5306–4.7

Veterans Affairs

Health care for veterans, patients, visits, costs, and operating beds, by VA and contract facility, and region, quarterly rpt, 8602–4

Health care professionals of VA, by selected employment characteristics and VA district and duty station, quarterly rpt, 8602–6

Homeless veterans domiciliary program of VA, participant characteristics and outcomes, 1990 annual rpt, 8604–10

BY CITY

Homeless veterans with mental illness, VA program services, costs, staff, client characteristics, and outcome, 1990, annual rpt, 8604–11

Medicine and Surgery Dept of VA, trainees by detailed program and city, FY90, annual rpt, 8704–4

BY COUNTY

Agriculture and Food

- Census of Agriculture, 1987: farms, farmland, production, finances, and operator characteristics, by county, final State rpt series, 2331–1
- Cotton acreage planted by State and county, and fiber quality, by variety, 1991, annual rpt, 1309–6
- Cotton ginnings and production, by State and county, 1990, annual rpt, 2344–1
- Cotton ginnings, by State and county, seasonal biweekly rpt, 1631–19
- Cotton ginnings, by State and county, seasonal monthly rpt, 2342–2
- Farmland in US owned by foreigners, holdings, acreage, and value by land use, owner country, State, and county, 1990, annual rpt, 1584–3
- Migrant workers and dependents by county, and health centers use and programs funding, by State, 1986-89, 4108–53

Banking, Finance, and Insurance

Banks (insured commercial and savings) deposits by instn, State, MSA, and county, as of June 1990, annual regional rpt series, 9295–3

Communications and Transportation

Aircraft registered with FAA, by type and characteristics of aircraft, make, carrier, State, and county, 1989, annual rpt, 7504–3

Education

Texas school district quality indicators, model description and results by district and county, 1989, technical paper, 9379–12.67

Energy Resources and Demand

- Bonneville Power Admin mgmt of Fed Columbia River Power System, finances, operations, and sales by customer, FY90, annual rpt, 3224–1
- Coal production and mines by county, prices, productivity, miners, and reserves, by mining method and State, 1989-90, annual rpt, 3164–25
- Coal receipts cost and quality, by electric utility, plant, State, and county, 1990, annual rpt, 3164–42
- Oil bulk station and terminal sales and storage capacity, by product and county, 1987 Census of Wholesale Trade, 2407–4.2

Government and Defense

- Census of Govts, 1987: employment, payroll, and average earnings, by function, level of govt, State, county, and population size, 2455–2
- Census of Govts, 1987: local govt employment by function, payroll, and average earnings, for individual counties, cities, and school and special districts, 2455–1
- DC metro area land acquisition and dev projects of Fed Govt, characteristics and funding by agency and project, FY91-95, annual rpt, 15454–1

DOD prime contract awards in labor surplus areas, by service branch, State, and area, 1st half FY91, semiannual rpt, 3542–19

- Employment and payroll of county govts, by function and population size, for 398 largest counties, 1990, annual rpt, 2466–1.3
- Fed Govt spending in States and local areas, by type, State, county, and city, FY90, annual rpt, 2464–3
- Finances of govts, by level of govt, State, and for large cities and counties, annual rpt series, 2466–2
- Finances, tax systems and revenue, and fiscal structure, by level of govt and State, 1991 and historical trends, annual rpt, 10044–1
- Public lands, Fed Govt payments to local govts in lieu of property taxes, by State and county, FY91, annual rpt, 5724–9
- *State and Metro Area Data Book,* 1991 data compilation, 2328–54
- Tax revenue, by level of govt, type of tax, State, and selected large county, quarterly rpt, 2462–3

Health and Vital Statistics

- Deaths and infant deaths, by cause, age, sex, race, and location, 1988, US Vital Statistics annual rpt, 4144–2.1; 4144–2.2
- HHS financial aid, by program, recipient, State, and city, FY90, annual regional listings, 4004–3
- Marriages, divorces, and rates, by characteristics of spouses, State, and county, 1987 and trends from 1920, US Vital Statistics annual rpt, 4144–4
- Physicians, by specialty, age, sex, and location of training and practice, 1989, State rpt series, 4116–6
- Radiation exposure of population near Hanford, Wash, nuclear plant, with methodology, 1944-66, series, 3356–5

Housing and Construction

- Census of Population and Housing, 1990: population and housing characteristics, households, and land area, by county, subdiv, and place, State rpt series, 2551–1
- Census of Population and Housing, 1990: voting age and total population by race, and housing units, by block, redistricting counts required under PL 94-171, State CD-ROM series, 2551–6
- Census of Population and Housing, 1990: voting age and total population by race, and housing units, by county and city, redistricting counts required under PL 94-171, State summary rpt series, 2551–5
- Community Dev Block Grant allocation, by State, county, and city, FY84-91, 5128–17
- Economic Dev Admin activities, and funding by program, recipient, State, and county, FY90 and cumulative from FY66, annual rpt, 2064–2
- Homeless persons housing and food aid of Fed Govt, funding and operations, with data by State and county, FY89, hearing, 25408–111
- New housing units authorized, by region, State, selected MSA, and permit-issuing place, monthly rpt, 2382–5
- New housing units authorized, by State, MSA, and permit-issuing place, 1990, annual rpt, 2384–2
- North Central States, FHLB 7th District housing vacancy rates for single and multifamily units and mobile homes, by ZIP code, annual MSA rpt series, 9304–18

West Central States, FHLB 10th District housing vacancy rates for single and multifamily units and mobile homes, by ZIP code, annual MSA rpt series, 9304–22

Western States, FHLB 12th District housing vacancy rates for single and multifamily units and mobile homes, by ZIP code, annual MSA rpt series, 9304–21

Industry and Commerce

- County Business Patterns, 1988: employment, establishments, and payroll, by SIC 2- to 4-digit industry and county, annual State rpt series, 2326–6
- County Business Patterns, 1989: employment, establishments, and payroll, by SIC 2- to 4-digit industry and county, annual State rpt series, 2326–8
- Lumber (industrial roundwood) production for Florida, by product and county, 1977-87, 1208–352
- Lumber (industrial roundwood) production for North Central States, by product and county, State rpt series, 1206–10
- Lumber (pulpwood) production by county, and mill capacity by firm, by southern State, 1989, annual rpt, 1204–23
- Lumber (pulpwood) production by species and county, and shipments, by northeastern State, 1989, annual rpt, 1204–18
- Mineral industries census, 1987: finances and operations, by SIC 2- to 4-digit industry, State, and county, census div rpt series, 2515–1
- *Minerals Yearbook, 1989,* Vol 2: State reviews of production and sales by commodity, and business activity, annual rpt series, 5604–16
- *Minerals Yearbook, 1989,* Vol 2: State reviews of production, sales, and firms, by commodity, and business activity, annual rpt, 5604–34
- Rocky Mountain region employment and income, and economic dependence on shipments outside area, by industry and county group, 1980s, 1208–362
- *State and Metro Area Data Book,* 1991 data compilation, 2328–54
- Tennessee Valley industrial dev and employment, by SIC 2-digit industry, firm, and location, 1990, annual rpt, 9804–3

Labor and Employment

Unemployment, employment, and labor force, by State, MSA, and city, monthly rpt, 6742–22

Law Enforcement

- Child abuse and neglect victims representation in legal proceedings, caseloads, State requirements, and compensation, by State and county, 1989, 4608–28
- Crimes and rates by offense, and law enforcement employment, by population size and jurisdiction, 1990, annual rpt, 6224–2.1; 6224–2.3
- Criminal justice spending, employment, and payroll, by level of govt, State, and selected city and county, FY71-88, biennial rpt, 6064–9
- Criminal justice spending, employment, and payroll, by level of govt, State, and selected city and county, 1984-86, biennial rpt, 6064–4
- Jail adult and juvenile population, employment, spending, instn conditions, and inmate programs, by county and facility, 1988, regional rpt series, 6068–144

Index by Categories

Jail population by sex, race, and for 25 jurisdictions, and instn conditions, 1988-90, annual rpt, 6066–25.38

Juvenile courts delinquency cases, by offense, referral source, disposition, age, sex, race, State, and county, 1988, annual rpt, 6064–12

Wiretaps authorized, costs, arrests, trials, and convictions, by offense and jurisdiction, 1990, annual rpt, 18204–7

Natural Resources, Environment, and Pollution

Birds (sandhill crane) hunting activity and permits, by State and county, 1989/90-1990/91, annual rpt, 5504–31

Fish kills in coastal areas related to pollution and natural causes, by land use, State, and county, 1980s, 2178–32

Forest wildlife habitat characteristics in northeastern US, by location, State rpt series, 1206–44

Forests (natl) and other lands under Forest Service mgmt, acreage by forest and location, 1990, annual rpt, 1204–2

Forests (natl) revenue share paid to States, and acreage, by forest, region, county, and congressional district, FY90, annual rpt, 1204–33

Helium and other components of natural gas, analyses of individual wells and pipelines, 1917-90, annual rpt, 5604–2

Oregon railroad grant lands, forest acreage returned to Federal ownership by county, FY90, annual rpt, 5724–1.1

Public lands acreage and use, and Land Mgmt Bur activities and finances, annual State rpt series, 5724–11

Soil survey rpt abstracts, for Pacific Northwest counties, 1989 rpt, 5668–114

Timber in Alabama, acreage and volume by species, forest type, ownership, and county, 1990, series, 1206–30

Timber in Arizona, resources by species, forest and tree characteristics, ownership, and county, 1984-85, 1208–374

Timber in Indiana, resources and removals, by species, forest characteristics, ownership, and county, 1985-86, 1208–368

Timber in Montana outside natl forests, acreage, resources, and mortality by species and ownership class, 1988-89, series, 1206–25

Timber in North Carolina, acreage, resources, and removals by species, ownership class, and county, 1989/90, series, 1206–4

Timber in northeastern US, biomass volume by characteristics of tree and forest, and county, State rpt series, 1206–43

Timber in northeastern US, resources and removals by species, ownership class, and county, State rpt series, 1206–12

Timber in Oklahoma, resources, growth, and removals, by species, forest type, ownership, and county, 1986, regional rpt series, 1206–39

Timber in Tennessee, acreage at risk from gypsy moth infestation, by county, 1989, 1208–344

Timber in Virginia, resources, growth, and removals, by species, ownership, treatment, and county, 1990-91, series, 1206–6

Timber insect and disease incidence and damage, and control activities, State rpt series, 1206–49

Wastewater treatment facilities construction grants of EPA to State and local govts, by project, monthly listing, 9202–3

Water (groundwater) supply, quality, chemistry, and use, State and local area rpt series, 5666–28

Water supply, hydrologic events, and end use, by State, 1988-89, annual rpt, 5664–12

Water use by end use, well withdrawals, and public supply deliveries, by county, State rpt series, 5666–24

Wetlands in coastal areas, acreage by wetland type, estuarine basin, and county, 1989, 2178–31

Population

Appalachia population, by State and county, 1980 and 1990, annual rpt, 9084–1

Census of Population and Housing, 1990: population and housing characteristics, households, and land area, by county, subdiv, and place, State rpt series, 2551–1

Census of Population and Housing, 1990: voting age and total population by race, and housing units, by block, redistricting counts required under PL 94-171, State CD-ROM series, 2551–6

Census of Population and Housing, 1990: voting age and total population by race, and housing units, by county and city, redistricting counts required under PL 94-171, State summary rpt series, 2551–5

Census of Population, 1990: post-enumeration survey results compared to census counts, by race, sex, city, county, and State, press release, 2328–69

Child population from age 10 and from birth, by county, 1988, annual rpt, 6064–12

Households by tenure and population size, by age group, State, and county, 1980 and 1985, 2546–3.169

Income (personal) per capita and by source, and earnings by industry div, by State, MSA, and county, 1984-89, annual regional rpts, 2704–2

Income (personal) per capita and total, by State, MSA, county, and metro-nonmetro location, 1987-89, annual article, 2702–1.209

Income (personal) per capita disparity between metro and nonmetro areas, and causal factors, by State, 1979-88, 1548–380

Population size of counties with population over 100,000, as of Apr 1990, press release, 2328–68

State and Metro Area Data Book, 1991 data compilation, 2328–54

Public Welfare and Social Security

Food stamp issues and participation, by State and county, as of July 1990, semiannual rpt, 1362–6

HHS financial aid, by program, recipient, State, and city, FY90, annual regional listings, 4004–3

OASDI benefits and beneficiaries, by type of benefit, State, and county, as of Dec 1990, annual rpt, 4744–28

Refugee aid funding of Fed Govt and States, impacts of reductions, with data by selected State and California county, late 1980s, GAO rpt, 26121–402

South Dakota poverty relief and medical aid programs of counties, spending by type, MSA, and county, 1989, hearing, 25368–176

BY FOREIGN COUNTRY

Supplemental Security Income payments and beneficiaries, by type of eligibility, State, and county, Dec 1989, annual rpt, 4744–27

Recreation and Leisure

Coastal areas recreation facilities, by State, county, estuary, and level of govt, 1972-84, 2178–29

Veterans Affairs

VA programs spending, by State, county, and congressional district, FY90, annual rpt, 8604–6

BY FOREIGN COUNTRY

Agriculture and Food

Africa (Sahel) grain production, use, imports, and stocks, by country, 1989/90, 9918–18

Africa (sub-Saharan) agricultural conditions by country, with Ethiopia grain production and use, and dev aid by major donor, 1960s-80s, hearing, 23848–216

Africa (sub-Saharan) dairy imports, consumption, and market conditions, by country, 1961-88, 1528–321

Agricultural Statistics, 1990, annual rpt, 1004–1

Apple import demand in 4 countries, 1960s-83, 1568–296

Bean (dried) prices by State, market activity, and foreign and US production, use, stocks, and trade, weekly rpt, 1311–17

Bean (dried) production and prices by State, exports and foreign production by country, and USDA food aid purchases, by bean type, 1984-90, annual rpt, 1311–18

Beer trade compared to domestic consumption and production, for 26 countries, mid 1970s-87, article, 9391–1.201

Central America agricultural export promotion of nontraditional crops, impacts on income export stability, late 1970s-80s, 1528–312

Cocoa and cocoa products foreign and US production, prices, and trade, 1980s-92, FAS semiannual circular, 1925–9

Coffee production, trade and quotas, and use, by country, with US and intl prices, FAS periodic circular, 1925–5

Corn, wheat, and soybeans export demand, by selected country, 1960s-83, 1568–297

Cotton (raw) imports of US, shipping costs and supply, by country and world region, 1986-91, article, 1561–1.206

Cotton production and trade for US and selected countries, FAS periodic circular series, 1925–4

Cotton, wool, and synthetic fiber production, prices, trade, and use, periodic situation rpt with articles, 1561–1

Dairy exports market conditions, with background data by country, 1986-89, 1128–65

Dairy imports and quotas, by commodity and country of origin, FAS monthly rpt, 1925–31

Dairy production, trade, use, and prices, for US and selected countries, forecast 1992 and trends from 1987, FAS semiannual circular, 1925–10

Developing countries agricultural exports of high-value commodities to OECD, 1970s-87, 1528–316

BY FOREIGN COUNTRY

Index by Categories

Developing countries agricultural supply, demand, and market for US exports, with socioeconomic conditions, country rpt series, 1526–6

Developing countries economic, population, and agricultural data, US and other aid sources, and AID activity, country rpt series, 9916–12

Developing countries food supply, needs, and aid, status and alternative forecasts, world area rpt series, 1526–8

Developing countries grains production and needs, and related economic outlook, by world area and selected country, forecast 1990/91-1991/92, 1528–313

Drug (opium) legal production and US imports by country, and analgesics opium content, 1980s, hearing, 21528–81

Eastern Europe agricultural production, trade, and land reform, with selected economic indicators, by country, 1960s-90, article, 1522–3.202

Egg production and trade, by country, 1986-91, article, 1561–7.204

Exports (agricultural) of high-value commodities, indexes and sales value by commodity, world area, and country, 1960s-86, 1528–323

Exports (agricultural) of US, impacts of foreign agricultural and trade policy, with data by commodity and country, 1989, annual rpt, 1924–8

Exports (agricultural) related employment, land, and capital inputs, by commodity and country of destination, and compared to imports, 1977-87, 1548–373

Exports and imports (agricultural) commodity and country, prices, and world market devs, monthly rpt, 1922–12

Exports and imports (agricultural) of US, by commodity and country, bimonthly rpt, 1522–1

Exports and imports (agricultural) of US, by commodity, country, and US port, 1950s-91, annual rpt, 1924–9

Exports and imports (agricultural) of US, by detailed commodity and country, 1989, annual rpt, 1524–8

Exports and imports (agricultural) of US, by detailed commodity and country, 1990, semiannual rpt, 1522–4

Exports and imports (agricultural) of US, outlook and current situation, quarterly rpt, 1542–4

Exports of grains, oilseed products, hides, skins, and cotton, by country, weekly rpt, 1922–3

Farmland (US) owned by foreigners, by owner country and State, as of Dec 1990, article, 1561–16.202

Farmland in US owned by foreigners, holdings, acquisitions, and disposals by land use, owner type and country, and State, 1990, annual rpt, 1584–2

Farmland in US owned by foreigners, holdings, acreage, and value by land use, owner country, State, and county, 1990, annual rpt, 1584–3

Fish (baitfish) catch distribution by species and South Pacific country or territory, 1965-85, article, 2162–1.201

Fish (shark and ray) population, physical characteristics, landings, and fishery mgmt, 1987 conf, 2168–124

Fish and shellfish catch and stocks in northwest Atlantic, by species and location, 1887-1991 and forecast to 1993, semiannual conf, 2162–9

Fish and shellfish foreign market conditions for US products, country rpt series, 2166–19

Fish catch by world region, processing, and US trade, 1982-89, semiannual rpt, 1561–15.1

Fish catch, trade, use, and fishery operations, with selected foreign data, by species, 1980s-90, annual rpt, 2164–1

Fish meal and oil production and trade, quarterly tables, 2162–3

Flour milling production by State, stocks, daily capacity, and exports by country, monthly Current Industrial Rpt, 2506–4.1

Flower and foliage plant production, marketing, and trade by country, by State, 1960s-88, 1568–293

Flower and foliage plant production, trade, farms, acreage, and sales, for US by crop, with spending by country, 1987-90, article, 1502–4.201

Fruit and nut trade, by selected crop and country, periodic situation rpt with articles, 1561–6

Fruit and vegetable exports to US, by commodity, country, and port of entry, 1975-87, 1568–299

Fruit and vegetable imports under quarantine, by crop, country, and port of entry, FY88, annual rpt, 1524–7

Fruit and vegetable shipments, and arrivals in US and Canada cities, by mode of transport and State and country of origin, 1990, annual rpt series, 1311–4

Fruit and vegetable shipments by mode of transport, arrivals, and imports, by commodity and State and country of origin, weekly rpt, 1311–3

Fruit and vegetable shipments by truck, monthly by State and country of origin, and rates weekly by growing area and market, 1990, annual rpt, 1311–15

Fruit, vegetable, and nut (fresh and processed) foreign and US production and trade, FAS monthly circular with articles, 1925–34

Grain foreign and US production, prices, trade, stocks, and use, FAS periodic circular series, 1925–2

Grain inspected for domestic use and export, foreign buyers complaints, and handling facilities explosions, FY90, annual rpt, 1294–1

Grain production, prices, trade, and export inspections by US port and country of destination, by grain type, weekly rpt, 1313–2

Honey production, prices, trade, stocks, marketing, and CCC honey loan and distribution activities, monthly rpt, 1311–2

Hops production, stocks, use, and US trade by country, monthly rpt, 1313–7

Imports injury to price-supported US agricultural industry, investigations with background financial and operating data, series, 9886–10

Japan fish catch, prices, trade by country, cold storage holdings, import quotas, and market devs, semimonthly press release, 2162–7

Livestock, meat, poultry, and egg production, prices, trade, and stocks, monthly rpt, 1561–17

Livestock, poultry, and dairy trade, by commodity and country, FAS monthly circular, 1925–32

Livestock, poultry, and products foreign and US production, trade, and use, by selected country, FAS semiannual circular series, 1925–33

Meat and poultry inspection activities and staff of Federal, State, and foreign govts, FY90, annual rpt, 1374–1

Meat imports under Meat Import Act, by country of origin, FAS monthly circular, 1925–31

Meat plants inspected and certified for exporting to US, by country, 1990, annual listing, 1374–2

Molasses (feed) wholesale prices by market area, and trade, weekly rpt, 1311–16

Molasses supply, use, wholesale prices by market, and imports by country, 1985-90, annual rpt, 1311–19

Oils, oilseeds, and fats foreign and US production and trade, FAS periodic circular series, 1925–1

Oils, oilseeds, and meal imports, by commodity, world area of destination, and major producer, 1960s-88, 1528–314

Oranges (fresh) exports of US, demand indicators for 4 countries, with production, trade, and use, 1960s-90, 1528–317

Peanut and peanut oil exports of US, and foreign production, by country, 1985-91 and forecast 1992, annual rpt, 1311–5.2

Peanut production and US exports by country, prices, and stocks, weekly rpt, 1311–1

PL 480 and CCC export credit sales agreement terms, by commodity and country, FY89, annual rpt, 15344–1.11

PL 480 exports by commodity, and recipients, by program, sponsor, and country, FY88 and cumulative from FY55, annual rpt, 1924–7

PL 480 food aid impacts on developing countries economic dev, literature review, 1979-88, 9918–20

PL 480 long-term credit sales allocations, by commodity and country, periodic press release, 1922–7

Potato production, acreage, disposition, prices, and trade, by State and country, 1949-90, 1568–305

Production, acreage, and yield for selected crops, forecasts by selected world region and country, FAS monthly circular, 1925–28

Production, consumption, and policies for selected countries, and US export dev and promotion, monthly journal, 1922–2

Production, prices, and trade of agricultural commodities, by country, 1980-90 and forecast 1991, annual world area rpt series, 1524–4

Production, prices, trade, and use, for foreign and US agriculture, periodic rpt with articles, 1522–3

Production, trade, and policies in foreign countries, summary data by country, 1989-90, annual factbook, 1924–12

Research (agricultural) investment impacts on productivity, indicators for developed and developing countries, late 1960s-80, 1528–318

Index by Categories

BY FOREIGN COUNTRY

Research (agricultural) of US, staffing by topic, performing organization, and for 6 countries, FY90, annual rpt, 1744–2.2

Research grants of USDA, by program, subagency, and country, FY90, annual listing, 1954–3

Rice foreign and US production, prices, trade, stocks, and use, periodic situation rpt, 1561–8

Rice market activities, prices, inspections, sales, trade, supply, and use, for US and selected foreign markets, weekly rpt, 1313–8

Rum imports (duty-free) of US under Caribbean Basin Initiative, by country, 1989-90, annual rpt, 9884–15

Salmon landings by species, and trade of US by country, 1980-89, article, 1561–15.201

Seed exports, by type, world region, and country, FAS quarterly rpt, 1925–13

Soviet Union agricultural trade, by commodity and country, 1955-90, 1528–322

Spice, essential oil, and tea foreign and US production, prices, and trade, FAS annual circular series, 1925–15

Sugar and honey foreign and US production, prices, trade, and use, FAS periodic circular series, 1925–14

Sugar and sugar product imports of US under quota, by country, periodic rpt, 1922–9

Sugar and sweeteners production, prices, trade, supply, and use, quarterly situation rpt with articles, 1561–14

Sugar production, acreage, yield, stocks, deliveries, and price by State, and trade by country, 1950s-90, 1568–306

Sugar production, trade, and use, quarterly rpt, 1621–28

Supply and demand indicators for selected foreign and US crops, monthly rpt, 1522–5

Tobacco and products foreign and US industry review, FAS monthly circular articles, 1925–16

Tobacco leaf stocks, production, sales, and import inspections by country, by product, quarterly rpt, 1319–3

Tobacco production and US trade, by country, 1985-90, annual rpt, 1319–1

Tobacco production, marketing, use, price supports, and trade, quarterly situation rpt with articles, 1561–10

Wheat and rye foreign and US production, prices, trade, stocks, and use, quarterly situation rpt with articles, 1561–12

Wheat production and trade, by country, 1989-92, article, 1502–4.202

Wheat quality indicators, for US exports and foreign wheat production, 1960s-90, hearing, 25168–75

Wool (virgin) use and imports, by country and world area, 1980-89, article, 1561–1.207

Banking, Finance, and Insurance

Bank deposit insurance programs of OECD members, operations by country, 1970s-80s, technical paper, 9385–8.93

Bank deposits in foreign banks, for 7 heavily indebted developing countries, 1982-89, technical paper, 9385–8.109

Banking industry structure and deposit insurance reform, findings and recommendations, with background data, 1989-90, 8008–147

Banking intl competition and deposit insurance reform issues, with background data, 1990 hearings, 25248–121; 25248–122; 25248–123

Banks (foreign-owned) assets in US, relation to foreign and domestic economic and financial indicators, by instn type, 1970s-89, technical paper, 9385–8.108

Banks (US) foreign branches assets and liabilities, by world region and country, quarterly rpt, 9365–3.7

Capital intl market financial data by firm, and Intl Finance Corp finances, by country, 1990 hearing, 21248–149

Capital movements between US and foreign countries, *Treasury Bulletin*, quarterly rpt, 8002–4.11

Communist countries debt to US and other Western banks, by country, 1980s, conf, 25388–56

Credit unions, assets, and members, for US, 12 countries, and 5 regional confederations, 1986 and 1989, release, 9538–9

Debt and business cycle sensitivity of major industry sectors, with intl comparisons, 1970s-88, technical paper, 9385–8.103

Debt to US of foreign govts and private obligors, by country and program, periodic rpt, 8002–6

Developing countries debt burden and related indicators, by country and for 9 US money-center banks, 1960s-89, article, 9292–4.201

Developing countries inflation control programs using exchange rate policies, evaluation, 1980s-91, technical paper, 9366–7.256

Dollar exchange rates of 35 countries, and interest rates and security yields for US and selected foreign countries, weekly chartbook, 9365–1.5

Dollar exchange rates offered by US disbursing offices, by country, quarterly rpt, 8102–6

Eastern Europe foreign debt components, trade, balances, and other economic indicators, by country, 1985-89, hearing, 21248–148

European Currency Unit weights, and dollar and ECU exchange rates for each currency, 1991 article, 9371–1.212

Eximbank financial condition, with credit and insurance authorizations and loan activity by country, FY90, annual rpt, 9254–1

Fed Financing Bank holdings and transactions, by borrower, monthly press release, 12802–1

Finance (intl) statistics, monthly rpt, 9362–1.3

Financial instns (intl) funds by source and disbursements by purpose, by country, with US policy review, FY89, annual rpt, 15344–1

Financial instns with intl operations, assets by selected banking and securities instn, and financial performance indicators by selected country, late 1980s-90, article, 9385–1.206

Investment (foreign direct) impact on manufacturing trade balance, with background data, late 1960s-90 and auto forecasts to 1993, article, 9385–1.210

Japan balance of payments by component, and foreign securities purchases by country, 1980s-90, article, 9393–8.204

Loans and grants for economic and military aid from US and intl agencies, by program and country, FY46-90, annual rpt, 9914–5

Loans of US banks to foreigners at all US and foreign offices, by country group and country, quarterly rpt, 13002–1

Overseas Private Investment Corp finances and activities, with list of insured projects and firms, FY90, annual rpt, 9904–2

Reserves/imports ratio, and money supply growth rates, by selected country, selected years 1951-71, article, 9391–1.214

Savings rates impacts of income tax deduction for interest payments, with indicators for US, Canada, and other OECD countries, 1990 article, 9377–1.202

Securities trading activity and automation, with data by country, exchange, security type, and individual contract, 1980s-90, article, 9371–1.209

Seignorage use for financing fiscal deficits in EC, with background data for EC, 1970s-88, working paper, 9387–8.238

Stock indexes in 15 OECD countries, returns volatility and inter-country correlations, 1960s-90, technical paper, 9366–6.279

Stock price and industrial production indexes, correlations among 4 industrial countries, 1966-90, technical paper, 9385–8.105

Stock price volatility relation to interest rates, oil and gold prices, and US money supply, for 10 countries, model description and results, 1970s-88, working paper, 9381–10.116

Communications and Transportation

Aircraft registered with FAA, by type and characteristics of aircraft, and country, 1989, annual rpt, 7504–3

Airline operations and passenger, cargo, and mail traffic, by type of service, air carrier, State, and country, 1980-89, annual rpt, 7504–1.4

Hazardous material transport cylinder test facilities, certifications by State and country, 1989, annual rpt, 7304–4

Mail (domestic) postal rates, for 14 countries, 1990, annual rpt, 9864–5.1

Panama Canal traffic and tolls, by commodity, flag of vessel, and trade route, FY90, annual rpt, 9664–3.1

Shipborne trade of US, by type of service, commodity, country, route, and US port, 1988, annual rpt, 7704–2

Ships in world merchant fleet, tonnage, and new ship construction and deliveries, by vessel type and country, as of Jan 1990, annual rpt, 7704–3

Ships in world merchant fleet, US transfers to foreign firms, and deliveries, by vessel type and country, FY90, annual rpt, 7704–14.1; 7704–14.2

Ships under foreign flag owned by US firms and foreign affiliates, by type, owner, and country of registry and construction, as of Jan 1991, semiannual rpt, 7702–3

St Lawrence Seaway ship, cargo, and passenger traffic, and toll revenue, 1990 and trends from 1959, annual rpt, 7744–2

Telecommunications finances, rates, and traffic for US carriers intl operations, by service type, firm, and country, 1975-89, annual rpt, 9284–17

Telecommunications industry intl competitiveness, with financial and operating data by product or service, firm, and country, 1990 rpt, 2008–30

BY FOREIGN COUNTRY

Index by Categories

Telephone and telegraph intl operations, revenue, and rates, by world area and country, various dates 1989-90, annual rpt, 9284–6

Travel from US, characteristics of visit and traveler, and country of destination, 1990 in-flight survey, annual rpt, 2904–14

Travel to and from US, by world area, forecast 1991-92, annual rpt, 2904–9

Travel to and from US on US and foreign flag air carriers, by country, world area, and US port, monthly rpt, 7302–2

Travel to US, by characteristics of visit and traveler, country, port city, and State of destination, quarterly rpt, 2902–1

Travel to US, market research data available from US Travel and Tourism Admin, 1991, annual rpt, 2904–15

Travel to US, trade shows and other promotional activities, with magazine ad costs and circulation, for selected countries, 1991-92, annual rpt, 2904–11

Education

Condition of Education, detail for elementary, secondary, and higher education, 1920s-90 and projected to 2001, annual rpt, 4824–1

Education data for foreign countries, and students enrolled in US higher education instns, 1991 edition, annual rpt, 4824–2.29

English language program of USIA, enrollment and staff, by country and world region, FY90, annual rpt, 9854–2

Exchange and training programs of Federal agencies, participants by world area, and funding, by program, FY89, annual rpt, 9854–8

Fulbright-Hays academic exchanges, grants by purpose, and foreign govt share of costs, by country, FY90, annual rpt, 10324–1

USIA library holdings, use, and staff, by country and city, FY90, annual rpt, 9854–4

Energy Resources and Demand

AID energy assistance to developing countries, and global warming reduction activities, 1980s-FY92, GAO rpt, 26123–352

Coal imports of US electric utilities, by utility and country of origin, 1986-90, annual rpt, 3164–42

Coal trade and average price, by country of destination and origin and customs district, weekly rpt, monthly data, 3162–1.2

Coal trade and average price, by world region, country, and customs district, quarterly rpt with articles, 3162–37

Coal trade flows and reserves, by country, 1980-89 and projected to 2010, annual rpt, 3164–77

Developing countries energy use, and economic and environmental impacts, by fuel type, world area, and country, 1980s-90, 26358–232

Electric current characteristics, by country and selected city, 1991 rpt, 2048–1

Electric power generation and losses in transmission, share by country, 1990 rpt, 9198–124

Electric power generation by fuel type, and fuel switching from oil to coal capability, by country, 1973-89, article, 3162–37.201

Energy production by type, and oil trade, and use, by country group and selected country, monthly rpt, 9112–2

Energy production, trade, use, and reserves, and oil and refined products supply and prices, by country, 1980-89, annual rpt, 3164–50

Energy supply, demand, and prices, by fuel type and end-use sector, with foreign comparisons, 1990 and trends from 1949, annual rpt, 3164–74

Energy supply, demand, and prices, by fuel type, end-use sector, and country, detailed data, monthly rpt with articles, 3162–24

Energy use and production, by fuel type, country, and country group, projected 1995-2010 and trends from 1970, annual rpt, 3164–84

Latin America energy use and trade, by selected country, 1970s-80s and projected to 2000, 3408–1

Natural gas imports of US by country, 1988 and projected to 2030, Natl Energy Strategy, 3166–6.52

Nuclear power generation in US and 20 countries, monthly rpt, 3162–24.10

Nuclear power plant capacity, generation, and operating status, by plant and foreign and US location, 1990 and projected to 2030, annual rpt, 3164–57

Nuclear power plant spent fuel and demand for uranium and enrichment services, for US and other country groups, projected 1991-2040, annual rpt, 3164–72

Nuclear reactors for domestic use and export by function and operating status, with owner, operating characteristics, and location, 1990 annual listing, 3354–15

Oil and gas production and reserves, and coal production, by major country and world area, late 1930s-90, article, 9371–1.213

Oil and gas reserves and discoveries, by country and country group, quarterly rpt, 3162–43

Oil and refined products supply, demand, prices, and refinery capacity and stocks, by State, 1960-91, annual rpt, 3164–95

Oil crude, gas liquids, and refined products supply, demand, and movement, by PAD district and State, 1990, annual rpt, 3164–2

Oil dependency, energy demand, and efficiency measures, for 6 OECD countries, 1970s-88, article, 9375–1.210

Oil import costs, by crude type and country or group of origin, monthly rpt, 3162–11

Oil prices of OPEC and non-OPEC countries, weekly rpt, 3162–32

Oil production relation to prices and other factors for OPEC and non-OPEC countries, alternative model results, 1970s-80s, technical paper, 9379–12.68

Oil production, trade, use, and stocks, by selected country and country group, monthly rpt, 3162–42

Oil production, use, stocks, and exports and prices for US, by country, detailed data, monthly rpt with articles, 3162–24

Oil, refined products, and gas liquids supply, demand, trade, stocks, and refining, by detailed product, State, and PAD district, monthly rpt with articles, 3162–6

Oil supply and industry of OPEC and US, impacts of oil embargo imposed after Iraq invasion of Kuwait, 1989-91, hearing, 21368–132

Oil supply and price impacts of Iraq invasion of Kuwait, selected indicators, daily press release, 3162–44

Soviet Union, Eastern Europe, OECD, and selected other countries energy reserves, production, and use, and oil trade and revenue, 1960s-90, annual rpt, 9114–4.4

Strategic Petroleum Reserve oil deliveries, by country and State of origin, quarterly rpt, annual data, 3002–13

Transportation energy use, fuel prices, vehicle registrations, and mileage, by selected country, 1970s-89, annual rpt, 3304–5.1

Geography and Climate

Aerial survey R&D rpts, and sources of natural resource and environmental data, quarterly listing, 9502–7

Borders (maritime) agreements and claims of coastal countries, series, 7006–8

Disasters, casualties, damage, and aid by US and others, by country, FY90 and trends from FY64, annual rpt, 9914–12

Geographic Notes, foreign countries boundaries, claims, nomenclature, and other devs, periodic rpt, 7142–3

Oceanographic research and distribution activities of World Data Center A by country, and cruises by ship, 1989, annual rpt, 2144–15

Tide height and time daily at coastal points worldwide, forecast 1992, annual rpt series, 2174–2

Weather, air pressure, temperature, and precipitation data for US and foreign locations, monthly 1971-80, decennial rpt series, 2156–4

Weather conditions and effect on agriculture, by US region, State, and city, and world area, weekly rpt, 2182–7

Weather data for surface and upper air, averages by foreign and US station, monthly rpt, 2152–4

Weather events and anomalies, precipitation and temperature for US and foreign locations, weekly rpt, 2182–6

Government and Defense

AID dev funds obligated but unspent by country, and impacts of alternative allocation formulas, FY87-90, GAO rpt, 26123–327

AID dev projects and socioeconomic impacts, evaluation rpt series, 9916–1

AID dev projects, special study series, 9916–3

AID economic aid to developing countries, obligations and disbursements by country, quarterly rpt, 9912–4

AID loans repayment status and terms by program and country, and status of predecessor agency loans, quarterly rpt, 9912–3

Aliens (illegal) legal residence applications under Immigration Reform and Control Act, by selected characteristics, State, and country, periodic rpt, 6262–3

Aliens admitted to US, by class of admission and selected port and country, FY89-90, fact sheet, 6266–2.7

Arms trade and share of GNP by country, and US customs seizures and defense industry employment, 1980s-90, article, 9373–1.221

Background Notes, foreign countries summary social, political, and economic data, series, 7006–2

Boycotts (intl) by OPEC and other countries, US taxpayers IRS filings, cooperation, and tax benefits denied, 1976-86, GAO rpt, 26119–349

Index by Categories

BY FOREIGN COUNTRY

Chiefs of State and Cabinet members, by country, bimonthly listing, 9112–4

Claims against foreign govts by US natls, by claim type and country, 1990, annual rpt, 6004–16

Coin production of US Mint, for US by denomination and mint, and for foreign countries, monthly table, 8202–1

Currency (foreign) accounts owned by US under AID admin and by foreign govts with joint AID control, status by program and country, quarterly rpt, 9912–1

Currency (foreign) holdings of US, transactions and balances by program and country, 1st half FY91, semiannual rpt, 8102–7

Currency (foreign) purchases of US with dollars, by country, 1st half FY91, semiannual rpt, 8102–5

Developing countries counterpart funds impacts on US aid programs effectiveness and domestic economic and fiscal condition, literature review, 1991 rpt, 9918–21

Developing countries economic and social conditions from 1960s, and Intl Dev Cooperation Agency and AID activities and funding, FY90-92, annual rpt, 9904–4

Developing countries economic, population, and agricultural data, US and other aid sources, and AID activity, country rpt series, 9916–12

Eastern Europe economic aid of US, by agency and country, FY90-92, GAO rpt, 26123–319

Economic aid of US and other donor countries by type and recipient, and role in advancing economic interests, 1980s-90, 2048–152

Economic and military aid and loans from US and intl agencies, by program and country, FY46-90, annual rpt, 9914–5

Economic and military aid of US, by program and country, and arrearages, selected years 1940-88, annual rpt, 15344–1.1

Economic, social, political, and geographic summary data, by country, 1991, annual factbook, 9114–2

Human rights conditions in 170 countries, and US economic and military aid, 1990, annual rpt, 21384–3

Immigrants admitted to US, by country of birth, FY81-90, annual rpt, 6264–4

Intl organizations funding by US and other countries, by organization and program, FY90, annual rpt, 7004–9

Latin America dev grants of Inter-American Foundation by program area, and fellowships by field and instn, by country, FY72-90, annual rpt, 14424–2

Latin America dev grants of Inter-American Foundation by recipient, and fellowships, by country, FY90, annual rpt, 14424–1

Military aid of US, arms sales, and training, by country, FY50-90, annual rpt, 3904–3

Military aid of US, arms sales, and training programs costs and budget requests, by program, world region, and country, FY90-92, annual rpt, 7144–13

Military spending and imports of developing countries, measures to determine eligibility for US economic aid, by country, 1986-87, annual rpt, 9914–1

Military weapons trade, production, and defense industry finances, with data by firm and country, 1980s-91, 26358–241

NATO and Japan military spending and indicators of ability to support common defense, by country, 1970s-89, annual rpt, 3544–28

NATO and Warsaw Pact military forces reductions under proposed treaty, and US budget savings, 1990 rpt, 26306–3.114

Peace Corps activities, funding by program, and volunteers, by country, FY92, annual rpt, 9654–1

Persian Gulf War costs to US by category and service branch, and offsetting contributions by allied country, monthly rpt, 102–3

Persian Gulf War costs to US by category and service branch, and offsetting contributions by allied country, various periods FY90-91, annual rpt, 104–7

Soviet Union, China, OECD, and selected other countries economic and military aid, by recipient, 1960s-90, annual rpt, 9114–4.9

Tax (income) returns for foreign corporate activity in US, assets, and income statement items, by industry div and selected country, 1986-87, article, 8302–2.205

Tax (income) returns of corporations with foreign tax credit, income, and tax items, by country and world region of credit, 1986, biennial article, 8302–2.207

Tax (income) returns of US corporations under foreign control, assets and income statement items by industry div and country, 1988, article, 8302–2.219

Tax withheld and income from US sources for foreign natls not residing in US, by country and tax treaty status, 1988, annual article, 8302–2.206

Taxation and intl competitiveness issues, with comparisons of US and foreign tax rates and revenue, 1988-91, press release, 8008–150

UN participation of US, and member and nonmember shares of UN budget by country, FY89-91, annual rpt, 7004–5

UN voting record and share of votes in agreement with US, by issue, country, and world area, 1990, annual rpt, 7004–18

US diplomatic facilities security improvement construction projects costs and activities, 1986-90, GAO rpt, 26123–322

US govt contingent liabilities and claims paid on federally insured and guaranteed contracts with foreign obligors, by country and program, periodic rpt, 8002–12

US govt-leased real property inventory and rental costs, worldwide summary by location and agency, 1989, annual rpt, 9454–10

US govt-owned real property inventory and costs, worldwide summary by location, agency, and use, 1989, annual rpt, 9454–5

US military and civilian personnel and dependents, by service branch and location, FY90, annual rpt, 3544–1

US military and civilian personnel and dependents, by service branch, world area, and country, quarterly rpt, 3542–20

US military base and family housing construction, DOD appropriations by facility, service branch, and location, FY90-93, annual rpt, 3544–39

US military base closings in Europe, by service branch and location, FY91, GAO rpt, 26123–336

US military base construction, renovation, and land acquisition, budget requests by project, service branch, State, and country, FY92-93, annual rpt, 3544–15

US military base support costs by function, and personnel and acreage by installation, by service branch, FY91, annual rpt, 3504–11

US military contracts, payroll, and personnel, by service branch and location, with top 5 contractors and maps, by State and country, FY90, annual rpt, 3544–29

US military deaths, by service branch and country, FY90, annual rpt, 3544–40

US military employment of civilians, by country, quarterly rpt, 3542–16

US military pay and benefits for active duty personnel, reserves, retirees, and survivors, 1940s-80s and projected to 2049, 21208–34

US military personnel abroad, by service branch, outlying area, and country, quarterly rpt, 3542–14.5

US military personnel abroad, by service branch, world area, and country, quarterly press release, 3542–9

US military post exchange operations, and sales by commodity, by facility and location worldwide, FY89, annual rpt, 3504–10

US military presence abroad, by service branch and country, 1991 annual summary rpt, 3504–13

US military prime contract awards for R&D, for top 500 contractors, FY90, annual listing, 3544–4

US military prime contract awards for R&D to US and foreign nonprofit instns and govt agencies, by instn and location, FY90, annual listing, 3544–17

US military procurement of foreign-made machine tools, use of restriction waivers by service branch and country, FY86-89, GAO rpt, 26123–324

Visas of US issued and refused to immigrants and nonimmigrants, by class, issuing office, and nationality, FY89, annual rpt, 7184–1

Health and Vital Statistics

AIDS virus infection prevalence in developing countries, by sex, selected city, urban-rural location, and country, 1991, semiannual rpt, 2322–4

Allergy and Infectious Diseases Natl Inst activities, grants by recipient and location, and disease cases, FY83-90, annual rpt, 4474–30

Cancer Natl Inst activities, grants by recipient, and cancer deaths and cases, FY90 and trends, annual rpt, 4474–13

Dental Research Natl Inst research and training grants, by recipient, FY89, annual listing, 4474–19

Developing countries economic and social conditions from 1960s, and Intl Dev Cooperation Agency and AID activities and funding, FY90-92, annual rpt, 9904–4

Diving (underwater sport and occupational) deaths, by circumstances, diver characteristics, and location, 1970-89, annual rpt, 2144–5

Family planning and population activities of AID, grants by project and recipient, and contraceptive shipments, by country, FY90, annual rpt series, 9914–13

BY FOREIGN COUNTRY

Index by Categories

Health care spending by type and payment source, with background data and foreign comparisons, 1960s-80s and projected to 2000, 26308–98

Health condition and health care resources, use, and spending, 1950s-89, annual data compilation, 4144–11

Health, welfare, and research aid from HHS, by program, recipient, and country, FY90, annual listing, 4004–3.10

Heart disease, stroke, and chronic obstructive lung disease deaths, by country and sex, 1987, annual rpt, 4474–6

Heart, Lung, and Blood Natl Inst activities, and grants by recipient and location, FY90 and disease trends from 1940, annual rpt, 4474–15

Kidney end-stage disease cases, new patients by country, 1983-88, annual rpt, 4654–16.1

Malaria cases in US, for military personnel and US and foreign natls, and by country of infection, 1966-89, annual rpt, 4205–4

NIH grants for R&D, training, construction, and medical libraries, by location and recipient, FY90, annual listings, 4434–7

NIH intl program activities and funding, by inst and country, FY90, annual rpt, 4474–6

Occupational health and safety effects of shift rotation, and US and foreign regulation, by selected industry and occupation, 1970s-89, 26356–9.3

Radiation exposure of uranium miners and risk of death from cancer and lung diseases, for Indians and compared to whites and foreign countries, 1950s-84, hearing, 25548–101

Tuberculosis cases in the US, by country of origin, 1989, annual rpt, 4204–10

Vaccination needs for intl travel by country, and disease prevention recommendations, 1991 annual rpt, 4204–11

Housing and Construction

Building materials trade, by commodity and country, 1989-90, article, 2042–1.204

Construction contract awards and billings, by country of contractor and world area of award, 1989, annual article, 2042–1.201

Industry and Commerce

Auto industry finances and operations, trade by country, and prices of selected US and foreign models, monthly rpt, 9882–8

Auto trade of Canada and US, by country, 1986-88, annual rpt, 2044–35

Boycotts (intl) by OPEC and other countries, US firms and shareholders cooperation and tax benefits denied, 1986, annual rpt, 8004–13

Business America, foreign and domestic commerce, and US investment and trade opportunities, biweekly journal, 2042–24

Business cycle transmission among 7 OECD countries, model description and results, 1960s-88, working paper, 9377–9.113

Business cycle variation and growth rates of GNP and components, inflation, and money supply, for 10 industrial countries, 1850s-1980s, working paper, 9383–20.15

Caribbean area duty-free exports to US, and imports from US, by country, and impact on US employment, by commodity, 1990, annual rpt, 6364–2

Caribbean area duty-free exports to US, by commodity and country, with consumer and industry impacts, 1984-90, annual rpt, 9884–20

Caribbean Basin Initiative investment incentives, economic impacts, with finances and employment by country, 1984-90, 2048–141

Communist and OECD countries economic conditions, 1989, annual rpt, 7144–11

Communist countries trade with US, by detailed commodity and country, quarterly rpt with articles, 9882–2

Competitiveness (intl) of US industries, with selected foreign and US operating data by major firm and product, series, 2046–12

Developing countries economic, population, and agricultural data, US and other aid sources, and AID activity, country rpt series, 9916–12

Eastern Europe economic and political conditions, and impacts of geographic factors, by country, 1990 conf, 9118–18

Eastern Europe foreign debt components, trade, balances, and other economic indicators, by country, 1985-89, hearing, 21248–148

Eastern Europe imports from US, and trade opportunities, periodic rpt, 2042–33

Eastern Europe transition to market economies, economic conditions, intl aid, and energy balance, by country, 1985-90, 9118–13

Eastern Europe transition to market economies, US trade prospects, with background data by country, 1980s, hearing, 25728–42

EC economic integration economic impacts, with background data by country, 1988-90, article, 9379–1.201

EC economic integration impacts on domestic economic conditions and US trade, 1985-90, 9886–4.170

EC economic integration issues, with economic indicators and trade by country, 1985-89, article, 9371–1.210

EC trade with US by country, and total agricultural trade, selected years 1958-90, annual rpt, 7144–7

Economic and monetary trends, compounded annual rates of change and quarterly indicators for US and 7 major industrialized countries, quarterly rpt, 9391–7

Economic and social conditions of foreign countries, working paper series, 2326–18

Economic conditions, and oil supply and demand, for major industrial countries, biweekly rpt, 9112–1

Economic conditions, and trade devs and balances, with data by selected country and country group, monthly rpt, 9882–14

Economic conditions, consumer and stock prices and production indexes, 6 OECD countries and US, *Business Conditions Digest*, monthly rpt, 2702–1.2

Economic conditions in foreign countries and implications for US, periodic country rpt series, 2046–4

Economic conditions in foreign countries and US, and competitiveness issues, 1960s-90, 21788–204

Economic conditions, policy, and trade practices, by country, 1988-90, annual rpt, 21384–5

Economic indicators, trade balances, and exchange rates, for selected OECD and Asian countries, 1991 semiannual rpt, 8002–14

Economic, social, political, and geographic summary data, by country, 1991, annual factbook, 9114–2

Export and import product standards under GATT, Natl Inst of Standards and Technology info activities, and proposed standards by agency and country, 1990, annual rpt, 2214–6

Export licensing, monitoring, and enforcement activities, FY90, annual rpt, 2024–1

Exports and imports of finished goods and industrial supplies, with related indicators, by industry and country, mid 1970s-90, 9385–1.205; 9385–8.95

Exports and imports of US, by country and detailed commodity, monthly rpt, 2422–12

Exports and imports of US by country, and trade shifts by commodity, 1990, semiannual rpt, 9882–9

Exports and imports of US, by Harmonized System 6-digit commodity and country, 1990, annual rpt, 2424–13

Exports and imports of US, by selected country, country group, and commodity group, 1990, annual rpt, 2044–37

Exports and imports of US, by transport mode, country, and SITC 1- to 3-digit commodity, 1990, annual rpt, 2424–12

Exports and imports of US, by world area, country, and commodity, *Survey of Current Business*, monthly rpt, 2702–1.10

Exports and imports of US shipped through Canada, by detailed commodity, customs district, and country, 1989, annual rpt, 7704–11

Exports and imports, trade agreements and relations, and USITC investigations, 1990, annual rpt, 9884–5

Exports, imports, and balances of US, by selected country, country group, and commodity group, preliminary data, monthly rpt, 2042–34

Exports, imports, and balances of US with major trading partners, by product category, 1986-90, annual chartbook, 9884–21

Exports, imports, and trade flows, by country and commodity, with background economic indicators, data compilation, monthly CD-ROM, 2002–6

Exports of US, detailed commodities by country, monthly CD-ROM, 2422–13

Exports of US, detailed Schedule B commodities with countries of destination, 1990, annual rpt, 2424–10

Flows of trade and investment, and economic indicators, for selected countries and country groups, selected years 1946-90, annual rpt, 204–1.9

Footwear production, employment, use, prices, and US trade by country, quarterly rpt, 9882–6

Imports and tariff provisions effect on US industries and products, investigations with background financial and operating data, series, 9886–4

Imports detained by FDA, by reason, product, shipper, brand, and country, monthly listing, 4062–2

Imports injury to US industries from foreign subsidized products and sales at less than fair value, investigations with background financial and operating data, series, 9886–19

Index by Categories

BY FOREIGN COUNTRY

Imports injury to US industries from foreign subsidized products, investigations with background financial and operating data, series, 9886–15

Imports injury to US industries from sales at less than fair value, investigations with background financial and operating data, series, 9886–14

Imports of goods, services, and investment from US, trade barriers, impacts, and US actions, by country, 1990, annual rpt, 444–2

Imports of US, detailed commodities by country, monthly CD-ROM, 2422–14

Imports of US given duty-free treatment for value of US material sent abroad, by commodity and country, 1989, annual rpt, 9884–14

Imports under Generalized System of Preferences, status, and US tariffs, with trade by country and US economic impacts, for selected commodities, 1986-90, annual rpt, 9884–23

Investment (direct) in US by country, and finances, employment, and acreage owned, by industry group of business acquired or established, 1984-90, annual article, 2702–1.210

Investment (foreign direct) in US, by industry group and world area, 1987-90, annual article, 2702–1.219

Investment (foreign direct) in US, by industry group of US affiliate and country of parent firm, 1980-86, 2708–41

Investment (foreign direct) in US commercial real estate, by State and investor country, 1980s, GAO rpt, 26123–350

Investment (foreign direct) in US, major transactions by type, industry, country, and US location, 1989, annual rpt, 2044–20

Investment (foreign direct) of US, by industry group and world area, 1987-90, annual article, 2702–1.220

Investment (intl) position of US, by component, industry, world region, and country, 1989-90, annual article, 2702–1.212

Japan economic conditions, financial and intl policies, and trade devs, 1950s-80s and projected to 2050, compilation of papers, 23848–220

Jewelry trade of US, gold jewelry production and sales, and US and EC gold and silver fineness standards, by country, 1980s, hearing, 25388–58

Latin America and Caribbean AID export and investment promotion projects effectiveness, 1974-89, 9916–3.63

Lumber (hardwood) exports of US to Europe and Asia, by species and country, 1981-89, 1208–373

Lumber (hardwood) production, prices, employment, and trade, quarterly rpt, 1202–4

Lumber and pulp products supply and use, and timber resources, detailed data, 1950s-87 and alternative projections to 2040, 1208–24.20

Lumber and wood products exports, imports, and export promotion of US by country, and trade balance, by commodity, FAS quarterly circular, 1925–36

Lumber exports from northwestern US ports, by selected country, quarterly rpt, 1202–3

Lumber production, prices by region and State, trade by country, and use, by species and product, 1960-88, annual rpt, 1204–29

Middle East export controls of US, with trade, dual-use commodity licenses, and arms sales, by country, 1980s-90, GAO rpt, 26123–339

Mineral Industry Surveys, commodity reviews of production, trade, stocks, and use, monthly rpt series, 5612–1

Mineral Industry Surveys, commodity reviews of production, trade, stocks, and use, quarterly rpt series, 5612–2

Mineral Industry Surveys, commodity reviews of production, trade, use, and industry operations, advance annual rpt series, 5614–5

Minerals (strategic) supply and characteristics of individual deposits, by country, commodity rpt series, 5666–21

Minerals foreign and US supply under alternative market conditions, reserves, and background industry data, series, 5606–4

Minerals production, prices, trade, use, employment, tariffs, and stockpiles, by mineral, with foreign comparisons, 1986-90, annual rpt, 5604–18

Minerals Yearbook, 1988, Vol 3: foreign country reviews of production, trade, and policy, by commodity, annual rpt series, 5604–17

Minerals Yearbook, 1989, Vol 1: commodity reviews of production, reserves, supply, use, and trade, annual rpt series, 5604–15

Minerals Yearbook, 1990, Vol 1: commodity reviews of production, reserves, supply, use, and trade, annual rpt series, 5604–20

Multinatl firms US affiliates finances and operations, by industry div, country of parent firm, and State, 1988-89, annual article, 2702–1.214; 2702–1.218

Multinatl firms US affiliates, finances, and operations, by industry, world area of parent firm, and State, 1988-89, annual rpt, 2704–4

Multinatl firms US affiliates, investment trends and impact on US economy, 1991 annual rpt, 2004–9

Multinatl US firms and foreign affiliates finances and operations, by industry and world area of parent firm, 1989 benchmark survey, preliminary annual rpt, 2704–5

Multinatl US firms and foreign affiliates finances and operations, by industry of parent firm and affiliate, world area, and selected country, 1989, annual article, 2702–1.225

Multinatl US firms foreign affiliates capital expenditures, by major industry group, world area, and country, 1986-91, semiannual article, 2702–1.207

Multinatl US firms foreign affiliates capital expenditures, by major industry group, world area, and country, 1987-91, semiannual article, 2702–1.222

Multinatl US firms foreign affiliates, income statement items by country and world area, 1986, biennial article, 8302–2.212

NATO members trade with PRC, by country, 1987-90, annual rpt, 7144–14

OECD intl trade position for US and 4 countries, and factors affecting US competition, periodic pamphlet, 2042–25

OECD members GNP and GNP growth, by country, 1980-90, annual rpt, 7144–8

OECD trade, by country, 1989, annual rpt, 7144–10

OECD trade, total and for 4 major countries, and US trade by country, by commodity, 1970-89, world area rpt series, 9116–1

Overseas Business Reports: economic conditions, investment and export opportunities, and trade practices, country market research rpt series, 2046–6

Production indexes and CPI, for US and 6 OECD countries, current data and annual trends, monthly rpt, 23842–1.7

Service industries exports and imports of US, direct and among multinatl firms affiliates, by industry and world area, 1986-90, article, 2702–1.223

Soviet Union, Eastern Europe, OECD, and selected other countries economic conditions, 1960s-90, annual rpt, 9114–4

Statistical Abstract of US, 1991 annual data compilation, 2324–1

Steel imports of US under voluntary restraint agreement, by product, customs district, and country, with US industry operating data, quarterly rpt, 9882–13

Steel industry finances, operations, and modernization efforts, with data on major companies and foreign industry, 1968-91, last issue of annual rpt, 9884–24

Textile, apparel, and shoe import restriction proposals economic impacts, projected 1991-2000, with imports by country, 1989-90, 26306–6.162

Textile imports, by country of origin, monthly rpt, 2042–27

Textile imports, by product and country of origin, monthly rpt series, 2046–8; 2046–9

Textile imports, total and from US, by commodity and country, 1987-89, 2048–155

Textile imports under Multifiber Arrangement by product and country, and status of bilateral agreements, 1987-90, annual rpt, 9884–18

Labor and Employment

Developing countries labor standards impacts on social and economic dev, 1988 conf papers, 6368–9

Employment, unemployment, and productivity indexes, for US and selected OECD countries, Monthly Labor Review, 6722–1.6

Immigrants admitted to US, by occupational group and country of birth, preliminary FY90, annual table, 6264–1

Immigration, alien workers, amnesty programs, and employer sanctions impacts on US economy and labor force, series, 6366–5

Labor conditions, union coverage, and work accidents in foreign countries, annual country rpt series, 6366–4

Manufacturing labor costs and indexes, by selected country, 1990, semiannual rpt, 6822–3

Unemployment insurance alternative policies impacts on employment and hours worked, with data for selected countries, 1970s, article, 9383–6.205

Law Enforcement

Aircraft hijackings, on-board explosions, and other crime, US and foreign incidents, 1985-89, annual rpt, 7504–31

Alien workers (unauthorized) and Fair Labor Standards Act employer compliance, hiring

BY FOREIGN COUNTRY

impacts, and aliens overstaying visas by country and State, 1986-90, annual rpt, 6264–6

- Aliens (illegal) enforcement activity of Coast Guard, by nationality, 2nd half FY91, semiannual rpt, 7402–4
- Aliens (illegal) overstaying visas, by class of admission, mode of arrival, age, country, and State, FY85-88, annual rpt, 6264–5
- Aliens (illegal) overstaying visas, by State of sojourn and world area of origin, 1985-88, fact sheet, 6266–2.1
- Cocaine production, eradication, and seizures, by Latin American country, 1988-90, 236–2.1
- Drug (illegal) production, eradication, and seizures, by substance, with US aid, by country, 1987-91, annual rpt, 7004–17
- Drug supply in US by country of origin, abuse, prices, and seizures, by substance, 1990, annual rpt, 6284–2
- Terrorism (intl) incidents, casualties, and attacks on US targets, by attack type and world area, 1990, annual rpt, 7004–13

Natural Resources, Environment, and Pollution

- Acid rain and air pollution environmental impacts, and methods of neutralizing acidified water bodies, summary research rpt series, 5506–5
- Endangered animals and plants US trade and permits, by species, purpose, disposition, and country, 1989, annual rpt, 5504–19
- Fish trace metal levels, standards by country, 1983, 9208–131
- Global climate change economic impacts, projected to 2100 with background data for 1980s, 3028–5
- Global warming contributing air pollutants, US and foreign emissions and control measures, 1980s and projected to 2020, 26358–233
- Radiation and radionuclide concentrations in surface air at selected monitoring sites worldwide, and effects of nuclear tests and accidents, 1989, annual rpt, 3004–31
- Soviet Union, Eastern Europe, OECD, and selected other countries pollution and deforestation indicators, 1960s-90, annual rpt, 9114–4.10
- Timber in Pacific basin, sandalwood resources, habitat, harvest, exports, and uses, 1990 conf, 1208–366

Population

- Developing countries aged population and selected characteristics, 1980s and projected to 2020, country rpt series, 2326–19
- Developing countries economic and social conditions from 1960s, and Intl Dev Cooperation Agency and AID activities and funding, FY90-92, annual rpt, 9904–4
- Developing countries economic, population, and agricultural data, US and other aid sources, and AID activity, country rpt series, 9916–12
- Developing countries urban population size, by selected city and country, 1991 annual rpt, 9914–4
- Economic, social, political, and geographic summary data, by country, 1991, annual factbook, 9114–2
- Emigration of foreign-born from US, by world region and selected country of origin, 1975-79, fact sheet, 6266–2.5

Family composition, poverty status, labor conditions, and welfare indicators and needs, by country, 1960s-88, hearing, 23846–4.30

- Immigrants admitted to US, by class of admission and for top 15 countries of birth, FY89-90, fact sheet, 6266–2.4; 6266–2.8
- Immigrants in US, population characteristics and fertility, by birthplace and compared to native born, 1980s, Current Population rpt, 2546–2.162
- Population social and economic conditions in foreign countries, working paper series, 2326–18
- Refugee arrivals and resettlement in US, by age, sex, sponsoring agency, State, and country, monthly rpt, 4692–2
- Refugee arrivals in US by world area and country of origin, and quotas, monthly rpt, 7002–4
- Refugee resettlement programs and funding, arrivals by country of origin, and indicators of adjustment, by State, FY90, annual rpt, 4694–5
- *Statistical Abstract of US*, 1991 annual data compilation, 2324–1
- Youth population declines relative to other age groups, by selected country, 1985 and projected to 2010, 9118–17

Prices and Cost of Living

- Food prices in selected world capitals, monthly rpt, semiannual data, 1922–12
- Imports of US, demand elasticities, assessment of alternative models, 1991 technical paper, 9366–7.250
- Living costs abroad, State Dept indexes, housing allowances, and hardship differentials by country and major city, quarterly rpt, 7002–7

Public Welfare and Social Security

- Developing countries child health and welfare indicators, and economic conditions, 1950s-80s, hearing, 25388–57
- Disabled persons in developing countries aid program activities and funding, for UN, AID, and Intl Labor Organization, late 1970s-90, GAO rpt, 26123–321
- Refugees fleeing from Iraq and Kuwait during Iraqi invasion, intl aid by source, and costs to host and native countries, 1990-91, GAO rpt, 26123–326
- Refugees from Cambodia in Thailand border camps by site, and UN aid by donor country, 1980s, GAO rpt, 26123–313
- US OASDI beneficiaries abroad, benefits, and eligibility based on intl agreement, by program type and country, 1989, annual rpt, 4744–3.3
- US social security programs admin and activities, 1930s-90 and projected to 2064, annual data compilation, 4704–12
- Welfare, health, and research aid from HHS, by program, recipient, and country, FY90, annual listing, 4004–3.10

Science and Technology

- Biotechnology commercial applications, industry finances and capitalization, patents, and govt support, for US, Japan, and EC, late 1970s-91, 26358–248
- Degrees (PhD) in science and engineering, by field, instn, employment prospects, sex, race, and other characteristics, 1960s-90, annual rpt, 9627–30
- NASA procurement contract awards, by type, contractor, State, and country, FY91 with trends from 1961, semiannual rpt, 9502–6

Index by Categories

- Patent and trademark (US) applications filed and granted, by country, FY87-90, annual rpt, 2244–1.2; 2244–1.3
- Patents (US) granted to US and foreign applicants, by State and country, 1989-90, annual press release, 2244–2
- R&D funding, and scientists and engineers education and employment, for US and selected foreign countries, 1991 annual rpt, 9627–35
- R&D funding by Fed Govt, by field, performer type, agency, and State, FY89-91, annual rpt, 9627–20
- Space launchings and characteristics of craft and flight, by country, 1957-90, annual rpt, 9504–9.1
- Space programs activities, missions, launchings, payloads, and flight duration, for foreign and US programs, 1957-90, annual rpt, 21704–4
- Spacecraft and satellite launches since 1957, quarterly listing, 9502–2

BY OUTLYING AREA

Agriculture and Food

- Agricultural Stabilization and Conservation Service producer payments, by program and State, 1990, annual table, 1804–12
- *Agricultural Statistics, 1990*, annual rpt, 1004–1
- Animal protection, licensing, and inspection activities of USDA, and animals used in research, by State, FY89, annual rpt, 1394–10
- Cattle tuberculosis cases and cooperative Federal-State eradication activities, by State, FY89-90, annual rpt, 1394–13
- Census of Agriculture, 1987: farms, farmland, production, finances, and operator characteristics, by county, final State rpt series, 2331–1
- Conservation program of USDA, funding by practice, region and State, monthly rpt, 1802–15
- Conservation program of USDA, participation and payments by practice and State, FY90, annual rpt, 1804–7
- Fish (processed) production by location, and trade, by species and product, 1987-90, annual rpts, 2166–6
- Fishery employment, vessels, plants, and cooperatives, by State, 1989 and trends from 1970, annual rpt, 2164–1.10
- Fishery mgmt and R&D, Fed Govt grants by project and State, and rpts, 1990, annual listing, 2164–3
- FmHA loans and borrower supervision activities in farm and housing programs, by type and State, monthly rpt, 1182–1
- FmHA loans, by type, borrower characteristics, and State, quarterly rpt, 1182–8
- FmHA loans, by type, borrower race, and State, quarterly rpt, 1182–5
- FmHA property acquired through foreclosure, value, acreage, and sales, for farm and nonfarm property by State, monthly rpt, 1182–6
- Food aid programs of USDA, costs and participation by program, FY69-89, annual rpt, 1364–9
- Fruit and vegetable imports under quarantine, by crop, country, and port of entry, FY88, annual rpt, 1524–7

Index by Categories

BY OUTLYING AREA

Meat and poultry inspection activities and staff of Federal, State, and foreign govts, FY90, annual rpt, 1374–1

Research (agricultural) funding and staffing for USDA, State agencies, and other instns, by topic, FY90, annual rpt, 1744–2

Tobacco production, prices, stocks, taxes by State, and trade and production by country, 1990, annual rpt, 1319–1

Banking, Finance, and Insurance

Banks (insured commercial) assets, income, and financial ratios, by asset size and State, quarterly rpt, 13002–3

Banks (insured commercial and savings) deposits by instn, State, MSA, and county, as of June 1990, annual regional rpt series, 9295–3

Banks (insured commercial and savings) finances, and changes in status, by State, 1989, annual rpt, 9294–4.1

Credit unions federally insured, finances by instn characteristics and State, as of June 1991, semiannual rpt, 9532–6

Credit unions federally insured, finances, 1989-90, annual rpt, 9534–1

Savings instns finances and operations by district and State, mortgage loan activity and terms by MSA, and FHLB finances, 1989 and trends from 1965, annual rpt, 8434–3.2

Savings instns insured by Savings Assn Insurance Fund, finances by profitability group, district, and State, quarterly rpt, 8432–4

Communications and Transportation

Air traffic (passenger), and aircraft operations by type, by airport and State, projected FY91-2005 and trends from FY83, annual rpt, 7504–7

Air traffic (passenger and cargo), and departures by aircraft type, by carrier and airport, 1990, annual rpt, 7504–35

Air traffic (passenger and cargo), carrier enplanement shares, and FAA airport improvement program grants, by airport and State, 1989, annual rpt, 7504–48

Air traffic levels at FAA-operated control facilities, by airport and State, FY90, annual rpt, 7504–27

Aircraft registered with FAA, by type and characteristics of aircraft, make, carrier, State, and county, 1989, annual rpt, 7504–3

Airport improvement program of FAA, activities and grants by State and airport, FY90, annual rpt, 7504–38

Airport improvement program of FAA, activities, funding, and airport operations, by location, projected 1990-99, biennial rpt, 7504–42

Airport planning and dev project grants of FAA, by airport and location, quarterly press release, 7502–14

FAA activities and finances, and staff by region, FY89-90, annual rpt, 7504–10

Fed Hwy Admin traffic safety grants, by program and State, FY89, annual rpt, 7764–1.1

Hazardous material transport cylinder test facilities, certifications by State and country, 1989, annual rpt, 7304–4

Hwy Statistics, detailed data by outlying area, 1990, annual rpt, 7554–1.5

Hwy Trust Fund status and net revenues, FY57-89, annual rpt, 7554–24

Shipborne trade of US, by type of service, commodity, country, route, and US port, 1988, annual rpt, 7704–2

Telephone firms borrowing under Rural Telephone Program, and financial and operating data, by State, 1990, annual rpt, 1244–2

Telephone firms borrowing under Rural Telephone Program, loan activity by State, FY90, annual tables, 1244–8

Telephone lines in residences and businesses, carriage equipment miles, and calls placed, by State, 1989, annual rpt, 9284–6.2

Urban Mass Transportation Admin grants for transit systems, by city and State, FY90, annual rpt, 7884–10

Education

American Historical Assn financial statements, and membership by State, 1989, annual rpt, 29574–2

Bilingual education enrollment, and Education Dept activities and funding by program, by State, FY88-90, biennial rpt, 4804–14

Bilingual education programs enrollment, funding, and services, by State, FY85-89, series, 4808–20

Digest of Education Statistics, 1991 annual data compilation, 4824–2

Elementary and secondary education enrollment, teachers, high school grads, and spending, by instn control and State, 1990/91, annual rpt, 4834–19

Elementary and secondary public school agencies, by enrollment size and location, fall 1989, annual listing, 4834–1

Elementary and secondary public school systems enrollment, finances, staff, and high school grads, by State, FY88-89, annual rpt, 4834–6

Elementary and secondary public schools and enrollment, by State, 1989/90, annual rpt, 4834–17

Head Start enrollment, funding, and staff, FY90, annual rpt, 4604–8

Head Start handicapped enrollment, by handicap, State, and for Indian and migrant programs, 1987/88, annual rpt, 4604–1

Higher education enrollment, by student and instn characteristics, fall 1989, biennial rpt, 4844–2

Homeless children educational projects, activities, and funding, FY90, annual rpt, 4804–35

Libraries (public) English as second language programs and services, project descriptions and funding, by State, FY87, annual rpt, 4874–10

Libraries for blind and handicapped, readership, circulation, staff, funding, and holdings, FY90, annual listing, 26404–3

Math ability of elementary and secondary students, and factors affecting proficiency, by selected characteristics, 1990 natl assessments, 4896–8.1

Natl Education Goals progress indicators, by State, 1991, annual rpt, 15914–1

Special education programs, enrollment by age, staff, funding, and needs, by type of handicap and State, 1989/90, annual rpt, 4944–4

Student aid funding and participation, by Federal program, instn type and control, and State, various periods 1959-89, annual rpt, 4804–28

Student guaranteed loans, defaults, and collections, by type of loan, lender, and guarantee agency, with data by State and top lender, FY90, annual rpt, 4804–38

Student loans of Fed Govt in default, losses, and rates, by instn and State, as of June 1990, annual rpt, 4804–18

Student supplemental grants, loans, and work-study awards, Federal share by instn and State, 1991/92, annual listing, 4804–17

Energy Resources and Demand

Conservation aid of Fed Govt to public and nonprofit private instns, by building type and State, 1990, annual rpt, 3304–15

Conservation of energy, State programs aid from Fed Govt, and energy savings, by State, 1989, annual rpt, 3304–1

Housing (low income) energy aid, funding sources, costs, and participation, by State, FY89, annual rpt, 4694–8

Oil crude, gas liquids, and refined products supply, demand, and movement, by PAD district and State, 1990, annual rpt, 3164–2

Rural Electrification Program lending, by State, FY90, annual rpt, 1244–7

Geography and Climate

Natl Ocean Service Charting and Geodetic Service activities and funding, by State, FY91-92, biennial rpt, 2174–10

Storms and unusual weather phenomena characteristics, casualties, and property damage, by State, monthly listing, 2152–3

Government and Defense

Budget of US, formula grant program obligations to State and local govts, by agency, program, and State, FY92, annual rpt, 104–30

Congressional Directory, members of 102nd Congress, other officials, elections, and districts, 1991-92, biennial rpt, 23874–1

DOD appropriations for base construction and family housing, by facility, service branch, and location, FY90-93, annual rpt, 3544–39

DOD budget requests for base construction, renovation, and land acquisition, by project, service branch, State, and country, FY92-93, annual rpt, 3544–15

DOD civilian and military personnel and dependents, by service branch and location, FY90, annual rpt, 3544–1

DOD civilian and military personnel and dependents, by service branch and US and foreign location, quarterly rpt, 3542–20

DOD contracts, payroll, and personnel, by service branch and location, with top 5 contractors and maps, by State and country, FY90, annual rpt, 3544–29

DOT employment, by subagency, occupation, and selected personnel characteristics, FY90, annual rpt, 7304–18

Fed Govt spending in States and local areas, by type, State, county, and city, FY90, annual rpt, 2464–3

Fed Govt spending in States, by type, program, agency, and State, FY90, annual rpt, 2464–2

Local govt receipts from Fed Govt in lieu of property taxes on public lands, by State and county, FY91, annual rpt, 5724–9

Local govt receipts from Fed Govt in lieu of property taxes on public lands, by State, FY91, annual press release, 5306–4.10

BY OUTLYING AREA

Index by Categories

Military base support costs by function, and personnel and acreage by installation, by service branch, FY91, annual rpt, 3504–11

Military deaths, by service branch and location, FY90, annual rpt, 3544–40

Military draft registrants by State, FY90, annual rpt, 9744–1

Military personnel of US abroad, by service branch, outlying area, and country, quarterly rpt, 3542–14.5

Military personnel of US abroad, by service branch, world area, and country, quarterly press release, 3542–9

Military reserve forces personnel strengths and characteristics, by component, FY90, annual rpt, 3544–38

Military reserve forces personnel strengths and characteristics, by component, quarterly rpt, 3542–4

Property (real) of Fed Govt, inventory and costs, worldwide summary by location, agency, and use, 1989, annual rpt, 9454–5

Votes cast by party, candidate, and State, 1990 natl elections, biennial rpt, 9274–5

Health and Vital Statistics

Abortions, by place of woman's residence and State of occurrence, 1988, US Vital Statistics annual rpt, 4146–5.120

AIDS cases by risk group, race, sex, age, State, and MSA, and deaths, monthly rpt, 4202–9

AIDS virus antibody tests and counseling sessions by setting, and CDC funding and funds uncommitted by State, 1989-90, GAO rpt, 26121–428

Deaths in US, by State of occurrence and birthplace abroad, 1988, US Vital Statistics annual rpt, 4144–2.1

Disabled persons rehabilitation, Federal and State activities and funding, FY90, annual rpt, 4944–1

Diving (underwater sport and occupational) deaths, by circumstances, diver characteristics, and location, 1970-89, annual rpt, 2144–5

Drug and alcohol abuse treatment and prevention programs of States, funding, facilities, and patient characteristics, FY89, 4488–15

Hepatitis cases by infection source, age, sex, race, and State, and deaths, by strain, 1988 and trends from 1966, 4205–2

HHS financial aid, by program, recipient, State, and city, FY90, annual regional listing, 4004–3.2; 4004–3.9

Infectious notifiable disease cases and current outbreaks, by region and State, weekly rpt, 4202–1

Infectious notifiable disease cases, by age, race, and State, and deaths, 1930s-90, annual rpt, 4204–1

Kidney end-stage disease treatment facilities, Medicare enrollment and reimbursement, survival, and patient characteristics, 1983-89, annual rpt, 4654–16

Marriages, divorces, and rates, by characteristics of spouses and county, 1987 and trends from 1940, US Vital Statistics annual rpt, 4144–4.3

Mines and mills injuries by circumstances, employment, and hours, by type of operation and State, quarterly rpt, 6662–1

NIH activities, funding by program and recipient type, staff, and clinic patients, by inst, FY90, annual rpt, 4434–3

NIH grants for R&D, training, construction, and medical libraries, by location and recipient, FY90, annual listings, 4434–7

Physicians, by specialty, age, sex, and location of training and practice, 1989, State rpt series, 4116–6

Sexually transmitted disease cases and control activity, by strain, State, and selected city, 1940s-90, 4205–42

Tuberculosis cases and deaths, by patient characteristics, State, and city, 1989 and trends from 1953, annual rpt, 4204–10

Workers compensation benefits and benefit duration, by State, 1990, biennial article, 4742–1.217

Workers compensation laws of States and Fed Govt, 1991 semiannual rpt, 6502–1

Housing and Construction

Economic Dev Admin activities, and funding by program, recipient, State, and county, FY90 and cumulative from FY66, annual rpt, 2064–2

FmHA property acquired through foreclosure, 1-family homes, value, sales, and leases, by State, monthly rpt, 1182–7

Mortgage originations, by State, 1978-89, annual press release, 5144–21

Mortgages FHA-insured, financial, property, and mortgagor characteristics, by State, 1990, annual rpt, 5144–1

Mortgages FHA-insured, financial, property, and mortgagor characteristics, total and by State and outlying area, 1990, annual rpt, 5144–25

New housing units authorized, by State, MSA, and permit-issuing place, 1990, annual rpt, 2384–2

Industry and Commerce

Exports and imports between US and outlying areas, by detailed commodity and mode of transport, 1990, annual rpt, 2424–11

Mineral Industry Surveys, commodity reviews of production, trade, stocks, and use, monthly rpt series, 5612–1

Mineral Industry Surveys, commodity reviews of production, trade, stocks, and use, quarterly rpt series, 5612–2

Minerals Yearbook, 1989, Vol 2: State reviews of production and sales by commodity, and business activity, annual rpt series, 5604–16

Minerals Yearbook, 1989, Vol 2: State reviews of production, sales, and firms, by commodity, and business activity, annual rpt, 5604–34

Statistical Abstract of US, 1991 annual data compilation, 2324–1.30

Vending facilities run by blind on Federal and non-Federal property, finances and operations by agency and State, FY90, annual rpt, 4944–2

Labor and Employment

Employment and Earnings, detailed data, monthly rpt, 6742–2.5; 6742–2.6

Employment and unemployment, by age, sex, race, marital and family status, industry div, and State, Monthly Labor Review, 6722–1.2

Employment programs, training, and unemployment compensation, current devs and grants to States, press release series, 6406–2

Labor-mgmt mediation and arbitration activities of Fed Mediation and

Conciliation Service, and cases by issue, region, and State, FY84-89, annual rpt, 9344–1

Labor Relations Natl Board activities, cases, elections conducted, and litigation, FY89, annual rpt, 9584–1

Unemployment insurance benefits and benefit duration, by State, 1991, biennial article, 4742–1.217

Unemployment insurance laws of States, comparison of provisions, 1991, base edition with semiannual revisions, 6402–2

Unemployment insurance programs of States, benefits, coverage, and tax provisions, as of Jan 1991, semiannual listing, 6402–7

Unemployment insurance programs of States, quality appraisal results, FY90, annual rpt, 6404–16

Unemployment insurance trust funds financial condition, by State, monthly rpt, 8102–9.16

Vocational rehabilitation cases of State agencies, by disposition and State, FY90 and trends from FY21, annual rpt, 4944–5

Vocational rehabilitation programs of Fed Govt and States, activities and funding, FY90, annual rpt, 4944–1

Law Enforcement

Aliens (illegal) overstaying visas, by class of admission, mode of arrival, age, country, and State, FY85-88, annual rpt, 6264–5

Assaults and deaths of law enforcement officers, by circumstances, agency, victim and offender characteristics, and location, 1990, annual rpt, 6224–3

Court caseloads, actions, procedure duration, judges, and jurors, by Federal district and appeals court, 1986-91, annual rpt, 18204–3

Court civil and criminal caseloads for Federal district, appeals, and bankruptcy courts, by type of suit and offense, circuit, and district, 1990, annual rpt, 18204–11

Court civil and criminal caseloads for Federal district, appeals, and special courts, 1990, annual rpt, 18204–8

Court civil and criminal caseloads for Federal district, appeals, and special courts, 1991, annual rpt, 18204–2

Office of Justice Programs activities and funding, FY90, annual rpt, 6064–18

Sentences for Federal crimes, guidelines use and results by offense and district, and Sentencing Commission activities, 1990, annual rpt, 17664–1

US attorneys case processing and collections, by case type and Federal district, FY90, annual rpt, 6004–2

Natural Resources, Environment, and Pollution

Endangered animals and plants population status and mgmt activity, by species, 1990, biennial rpt, 5504–35

EPA pollution control grant program activities, monthly rpt, 9182–8

Fish and Wildlife Service restoration and hunter safety funding, by State, FY92, semiannual press release, 5502–1

Fish and Wildlife Service restoration programs finances by State, and excise tax collections, FY90, annual rpt, 5504–13

Fish and Wildlife Service restoration programs funding, land purchases, and project listing, by State, FY89, annual rpt, 5504–1

Index by Categories

BY REGION

Fishery research of State fish and wildlife agencies, federally funded projects and costs by species and State, 1990, annual listing, 5504–23

Forests (natl) and other lands under Forest Service mgmt, acreage by forest and location, 1990, annual rpt, 1204–2

Hazardous waste site remedial action under Superfund, current and proposed sites descriptions and status, periodic listings, series, 9216–3

Hazardous waste site remedial action under Superfund, current and proposed sites priority ranking and status by location, series, 9216–5

Land Mgmt Bur allocations of public land revenues, by State and outlying area, FY90, annual rpt, 5724–1.3

Military installations hazardous waste site remedial action, activities and funding by site and State, FY90, annual rpt, 3544–36

Timber and planting and dev, by State, FY90, annual rpt, 1204–7

Water pollution areas and sources identification activities of EPA and State, 1991, GAO rpt, 26113–536

Water pollution fish kills, by pollution source, month, location, and State, 1977-87, last issue of annual rpt, 9204–3

Water resources dev projects of Army Corps of Engineers, characteristics, and costs, 1950s-89, biennial State rpt series, 3756–1

Water resources dev projects of Army Corps of Engineers, characteristics, and costs, 1950s-91, biennial State rpt series, 3756–2

Water supply and quality in streams and lakes, and groundwater levels in wells, by drainage basin, 1988, annual State rpt series, 5666–16

Water supply and quality in streams and lakes, and groundwater levels in wells, by drainage basin, 1989, annual State rpt series, 5666–12

Water supply and quality in streams and lakes, and groundwater levels in wells, by drainage basin, 1990, annual State rpt series, 5666–10

Water supply, hydrologic events, and end use, by State, 1988-89, annual rpt, 5664–12

Wildlife refuges and other land under Fish and Wildlife Service mgmt, acreage by site and State, as of Sept 1991, annual rpt, 5504–8

Wildlife research of State fish and wildlife agencies, federally funded projects and costs by species and State, 1990, annual listing, 5504–24

Population

Refugee arrivals and resettlement in US, by age, sex, sponsoring agency, State, and country, monthly rpt, 4692–2

Refugee arrivals in US by world area of origin and State of settlement, and Federal aid, FY90-91 and proposed FY92 allocations, annual rpt, 7004–16

Statistical Abstract of US, 1991 annual data compilation, 2324–1.30

Public Welfare and Social Security

Child Support Enforcement Program finances and operations, by State, FY85-89, annual rpt, 4694–6

Fed Govt spending in States, by type, program, agency, and State, FY90, annual rpt, 2464–2

Food aid program of USDA for women, infants, and children, participants and costs by State and Indian agency, FY88, annual tables, 1364–12

Food aid program of USDA for women, infants, and children, participants by race, State, and Indian agency, Apr 1990, annual rpt, 1364–16

Food aid program of USDA for women, infants, and children, participants, clinics, and costs, by State and Indian agency, monthly tables, 1362–16

Food stamp eligibility and payment errors, by type, recipient characteristics, and State, FY89, annual rpt, 1364–15

Food stamp issues and participation, by State and county, as of July 1990, semiannual rpt, 1362–6

HHS financial aid, by program, recipient, State, and city, FY90, annual regional listing, 4004–3.2; 4004–3.9

Homeless persons aid programs of Fed Govt, program descriptions and funding, by agency and State, FY87-90, annual GAO rpt, 26104–21

Medicare and Medicaid eligibility, participation, coverage, and program finances, various periods 1966-91, biennial rpt, 4654–1

OASDHI, Medicaid, SSI, and related programs benefits, beneficiary characteristics, and trust funds, selected years 1937-89, annual rpt, 4744–3

OASDI benefits and beneficiaries, by type of benefit, State, and county, as of Dec 1990, annual rpt, 4744–28

Social Security Bulletin, OASDHI and other program operations and beneficiary characteristics, from 1940, monthly journal, 4742–1

Recreation and Leisure

Boat registrations, and accidents, casualties, and damage by cause, by vessel characteristics and State, 1990, annual rpt, 7404–1

Historic Preservation Fund grants, by State, FY92, annual table, 5544–9

Land and Water Conservation Fund allocations for outdoor recreation area dev, by State, FY91, annual table, 5544–15

Land and Water Conservation Fund grants, State matching funds, and balances, by State, FY90, annual rpt, 5544–18

Park natl system visits and overnight stays, by park and State, 1990, annual rpt, 5544–12

Science and Technology

NSF grants and contracts, by field, instn, and State, FY89, annual rpt, 9624–26

Patents (US) granted to US and foreign applicants, by State and country, 1989-90, annual press release, 2244–2

Patents granted to US residents, by State, FY87-90, annual rpt, 2244–1.2

R&D and related funding of Fed Govt to higher education and nonprofit instns, by field, instn, agency, and State, FY89, annual rpt, 9627–17

BY REGION

Agriculture and Food

Acreage of cropland, total, idle, and grazed, by region and State, 1987 and trends from 1910, 1588–48

Conservation program of USDA, funding by practice, region and State, monthly rpt, 1802–15

Cooperatives loans, assets, net worth, and assns, for FCS by district, 1989, annual rpt, 1124–1

Corn farms, finances, acreage, and production, by size, region, and State, 1987, 1568–304

Cotton (upland) acreage estimated under alternative program planting assumptions, by region, 1988-91, article, 1561–1.205

Cotton farms fertilizer, pesticide and irrigation use, soil conservation practices, and water quality impacts, 1989, 1588–151

Cotton fiber and processing test results, by variety, region, State, and production area, 1990, annual rpt, 1309–16

Cotton linters production, stocks, use, and prices, monthly rpt, 1309–10

Cotton, wool, and synthetic fiber production, prices, trade, and use, periodic situation rpt with articles, 1561–1

Cottonseed prices and quality, by State, seasonal weekly rpt, 1309–14

Dairy farms financial statement, by size and region, 1985-89, annual article, 1561–2.201

Economic Indicators of the Farm Sector, itemized production costs, receipts, and returns, by commodity and region, 1987-89, annual rpt, 1544–20

Economic Indicators of the Farm Sector, production inputs, output, and productivity, by commodity and region, 1947-89, annual rpt, 1544–17

Egg production and layer inventory, by State, 1989-90, annual rpt, 1625–7

Egg production by type of product, and eggs broken under Federal inspection by region, monthly rpt, 1625–2

Emergency Conservation Program for farmland damaged by natural disaster, funding by region and State, monthly rpt, 1802–13

Employment on farms, wages, and hours, by payment method, worker type, region, and State, 1910-90, 1618–21

Employment on farms, wages, hours, and perquisites, by State, monthly rpt, 1631–1

Employment related to agriculture, by industry, region, and metro-nonmetro location, 1987, 1598–271

Farm Credit System financial statements and loan activity by lender type, and borrower characteristics, 1990, annual rpt, 9264–2

Farms and acreage, by sales size, region, and State, 1989-91, annual rpt, 1614–4

Fertilizer and pesticide use and application rates, by type, crop, and State, series, 1616–1

Fertilizer use and costs by type, and acreage harvested, by State, 1970s-90, biennial rpt, 9804–5

Fertilizer use, and effects on agricultural productivity, for selected US regions and PRC, 1989 hearing, 25168–76

Finances of farms, debts, assets, and receipts, and lenders financial condition, quarterly rpt with articles, 1541–1

Financial stress indicators for farms, operator quits, and loan problems and mediation, 1970s-90, 1598–272

Fish (processed) production by location, and trade, by species and product, 1987-90, annual rpts, 2166–6

BY REGION

Index by Categories

Fish and shellfish catch, wholesale receipts, prices, trade, and other market activities, weekly regional rpts, 2162–6

Fish catch, trade, use, and fishery operations, with selected foreign data, by species, 1980s-90, annual rpt, 2164–1

Fish Hatchery Natl System activities and deliveries, by species, hatchery, and jurisdiction of waters stocked, FY90, annual rpt, 5504–10

Food spending, by item, household composition, income, age, race, and region, 1980-88, Consumer Expenditure Survey biennial rpt, 1544–30

Fruit and vegetable shipments, and arrivals in US and Canada cities, by mode of transport and State and country of origin, 1990, annual rpt series, 1311–4

Grain price support and loan programs operations of USDA, with farmers views on Federal programs, by region and State, 1990 hearings, 21168–43

Grain production, prices, trade, and export inspections by US port and country of destination, by grain type, weekly rpt, 1313–2

Grain stocks by region and market city, and grain inspected for export, by type, weekly rpt, 1313–4

Honey production, prices, trade, stocks, marketing, and CCC honey loan and distribution activities, monthly rpt, 1311–2

Irrigation projects of Reclamation Bur, acreage limits monitoring activities by region, 1988-90, annual rpt, 5824–13

Irrigation projects of Reclamation Bur in western US, crop production and acreage by commodity, State, and project, 1989, annual rpt, 5824–12

Livestock grazing on natl forest lands, by region and State, 1990, annual rpt, 1204–5

Livestock packers purchases and feeding, and livestock markets, dealers, and sales, by State, 1989, annual rpt, 1384–1

Livestock slaughter, meat production, and slaughter plants, by species and State, 1990, annual rpt, 1623–10

Livestock slaughter under Fed Govt inspection, by livestock type and region, monthly rpt, 1623–9

Milk home delivery, and sales by wholesale outlet type, by region, 1989 survey, biennial article, 1317–4.201

Milk order market policy alternatives impacts on supply, interregional marketings, and pricing, by region, 1988, 1568–294

Milk order market prices and detailed operations, by State and market area, 1989-90, annual rpt, 1317–3

Milk order market prices and detailed operations, monthly rpt with articles, 1317–4

Milk order market sales, by container size and type, outlet type, and market area, 1989, biennial rpt, 1317–6

Molasses (feed) wholesale prices by market area, and trade, weekly rpt, 1311–16

Molasses supply, use, wholesale prices by market, and imports by country, 1985-90, annual rpt, 1311–19

Mushroom production, sales, and prices, by State, 1966/67-1990/91 and planned 1991/92, annual rpt, 1631–9

Oils, oilseeds, and fats production, prices, trade, and use, periodic situation rpt with articles, 1561–3

Peanut production and US exports by country, prices, and stocks, weekly rpt, 1311–1

Peanut production, prices, stocks, exports, use, inspection, and quality, by region and State, 1980-90, annual rpt, 1311–5

Pesticide (EBDC) use on vegetable crops, consumer and producer cost impacts of proposed ban, 1985-89, article, 1561–11.204

Pesticide and fertilizer use reduction, environmental and economic impacts by commodity and region, alternative forecasts 1989-94, hearing, 23848–222

Potato chip plants and potatoes processed, by region, 1989-90, annual rpt, 1621–11

Potato production, acreage, disposition, prices, and trade, by State and country, 1949-90, 1568–305

Poultry (chicken and turkey) hatchery production, 1989-90, annual rpt, 1625–8

Poultry (chicken, egg, and turkey) production and inventories, monthly rpt, 1625–1

Prices received and paid by farmers, by commodity and State, 1990, annual rpt, 1629–5

Prices received by farmers for major products, and paid for farm inputs and living items, by State, monthly rpt, 1629–1

Production inputs, finances, mgmt, and land value and transfers, periodic situation rpt with articles, 1561–16

Production itemized costs, by farm sales size and region, 1990, annual rpt, 1614–3

Research (agricultural) funding and staffing for USDA, State agencies, and other instns, by topic, FY90, annual rpt, 1744–2

Sheep, lamb, and goat loss to predators and other causes, by region and State, 1990, 1618–20

Sugar and sweeteners production, prices, trade, supply, and use, quarterly situation rpt with articles, 1561–14

Sugar production, acreage, yield, stocks, deliveries, and price by State, and trade by country, 1950s-90, 1568–306

Turkey hatcheries egg inventory and poult placements, by region, monthly rpt, 1625–10

Turkey production by State, and farms, by region, 1960s-90, article, 1561–7.202

Turkey production by State, and losses by region, 1989-90, and hatchery plans, 1991, annual rpt, 1625–6

Vegetable production, prices, trade, stocks, and use, for selected fresh and processing crops, periodic situation rpt with articles, 1561–11

Banking, Finance, and Insurance

Banks (insured commercial and savings) deposits by instn, State, MSA, and county, as of June 1990, annual regional rpt series, 9295–3

Banks (insured commercial and savings) financial condition and performance, by asset size and region, quarterly rpt, 9292–1

Banks (natl) charters, mergers, liquidations, enforcement cases, and financial performance, with data by instn and State, quarterly rpt, 8402–3

Banks balance sheets, by Fed Reserve District, for major banks in NYC, and for US branches and agencies of foreign banks, weekly rpt, 9365–1.3

Banks commercial loan growth, by bank financial and district employment characteristics, 1989-90, article, 9385–1.208

Banks finances and operations, by metro-nonmetro location, 1987-89, annual rpt, 1544–29

Banks regulatory enforcement activities of Federal agencies, effectiveness, with data on capital-deficient banks, late 1980s-90, GAO rpt, 26119–334

Credit unions (federally-insured) financial performance, by charter type and region, 1st half 1991, semiannual rpt, 9532–7

Credit unions federally insured, finances by instn characteristics and State, as of June 1991, semiannual rpt, 9532–6

Fed Home Loan Banks financial statements, monthly tables, 9442–1

Fed Home Loan Banks financial statements, 1988-90, annual rpt, 9444–1

Fed Reserve banks finances and staff, 1990, annual rpt, 9364–1.1

Fed Reserve banks financial statements and performance, by district, 1990-91, annual rpt, 9364–10.3

Govt-sponsored enterprises financial condition and capital adequacy, with data by enterprise, 1970s-90 and projected to 1996, 26308–99

Households assets, by type of holding and selected characteristics, 1988, Current Population Rpt, 2546–20.16

Money laundering investigations of Fed Govt using IRS large cash transaction rpts, and rpts filed and penalties for nonfiling by region, 1989-91, GAO rpt, 26119–356

Savings instns failure resolution activity and finances of Resolution Trust Corp, with data by asset type, State, region, and instn, monthly rpt, 9722–3

Savings instns finances and operations by district and State, mortgage loan activity and terms by MSA, and FHLB finances, 1989 and trends from 1965, annual rpt, 8434–3.2

Savings instns insured by Savings Assn Insurance Fund, finances by profitability group, district, and State, quarterly rpt, 8432–4

Communications and Transportation

Air taxi and commuter airlines operating certificates, FAA revocations for safety violations, 1987-91, GAO rpt, 26113–547

Air traffic (passenger), and aircraft operations by type, by airport and State, projected FY91-2005 and trends from FY83, annual rpt, 7504–7

Air traffic (passenger and cargo), carrier enplanement shares, and FAA airport improvement program grants, by airport and State, 1989, annual rpt, 7504–48

Air traffic and other general aviation activity, 1990, triennial survey rpt, 7508–3

Air traffic, carriers, craft, airports, and FAA activities, detailed data, 1980-89, annual rpt, 7504–1

Air traffic control and airway facilities staff, by employment and other characteristics, FY89, annual rpt, 7504–41

Air traffic control and airway facilities supervisors task priorities, skills needed, and other characteristics, 1990 survey, technical rpt, 7506–10.84

Index by Categories

BY REGION

Air traffic levels at FAA-operated control facilities, by airport and State, FY90, annual rpt, 7504–27

Air traffic, pilots, airports, and fuel use, forecast FY91-2002 and trends from FY81, annual rpt, 7504–6

Aircraft (general aviation), flight hours, and equipment, by type, use, and model of aircraft, region, and State, 1990, annual rpt, 7504–29

Aircraft handled by instrument flight rule, by user type, FAA traffic control center, and region, FY85-90 and projected to FY2005, annual rpt, 7504–15

Aircraft pilot and nonpilot certificates held, by type of certificate, age, sex, region, and State, 1990, annual rpt, 7504–2

Aircraft registered with FAA, by type and characteristics of aircraft, make, carrier, State, and county, 1989, annual rpt, 7504–3

Coast Guard search and rescue missions, and lives and property lost and saved, by district and assisting unit, FY90, annual rpt, 7404–2

FAA activities and finances, and staff by region, FY89-90, annual rpt, 7504–10

Helicopters, use, and landing facilities, by craft type, region, and State, 1989, 7508–75

Hwy construction material prices and indexes for Federal-aid system, by type of material and urban-rural location, quarterly rpt, 7552–7

Hwy construction minority contractor training, funding by region, FY91, annual release, 7554–40

Hwy traffic volume on rural roads and city streets, monthly rpt, 7552–8

Longshore employment in 4 coastal regions, monthly rpt, 7702–1

Mail volume to and from households, use, and views, by class, source, content, and household characteristics, 1987-88, annual rpt, 9864–10

Postal Service customer satisfaction, and on-time 1st class mail delivery, by region and city, 1991 survey, press release, 9868–1

Railroad (Class I) finances and operations, detailed data by firm, class of service, and district, 1989, annual rpt, 9486–6.1

Railroad revenue, income, freight, and rate of return, by Class I freight railroad and district, quarterly rpt, 9482–2

Shipborne trade of US, by type of service, commodity, country, route, and US port, 1988, annual rpt, 7704–2

Shipborne trade of US, by type of service, customs district, port, and world area, monthly rpt, 2422–7

Shipbuilding and repair facilities, capacity, and employment, by shipyard, 1990, annual rpt, 7704–9

Telephone firms borrowing under Rural Telephone Program, and financial and operating data, by State, 1990, annual rpt, 1244–2

Traffic accidents deaths by region, and death rates for miles traveled, monthly rpt, 7762–7

Traffic fatal accidents, circumstances, and characteristics of persons and vehicles involved, 1990, semiannual rpt, 7762–11

Travel to US, by characteristics of visit and traveler, world area of origin, and US destination, 1990 survey, annual rpt, 2904–12

Travel to US, market research data available from US Travel and Tourism Admin, 1991, annual rpt, 2904–15

Truck and bus interstate carriers finances and operations, by district, 1989, annual rpt, 9486–6.3

Truck interstate carriers finances and operations, by district, 1989, annual rpt, 9486–6.2

Truck rates for fruit and vegetables, by growing area and market, weekly 1990, annual rpt, 1311–15

Truck transport of property, financial and operating data by region and firm, quarterly rpt, 9482–5

Education

American Historical Assn financial statements, and membership by State, 1989, annual rpt, 29574–2

Bilingual education programs enrollment, funding, and services, by State, FY85-89, series, 4808–20

Educational attainment, by sociodemographic characteristics and location, 1989 and trends from 1940, biennial Current Population Rpt, 2546–1.452

Eighth grade class of 1988: educational performance and conditions, characteristics, attitudes, activities, and plans, natl longitudinal survey, series, 4826–9

Elementary and secondary education enrollment, staff, finances, operations, programs, and policies, 1987/88 biennial survey, series, 4836–3

Elementary and secondary public schools, enrollment, teachers, funding, and other characteristics, by region and State, 1988/89, annual rpt, 4834–20

Elementary and secondary students educational performance, and factors affecting proficiency, by selected characteristics, 1988 natl assessments, subject rpt series, 4896–7

Elementary and secondary students educational performance, and factors affecting proficiency, by selected characteristics, 1990 natl assessments, subject rpt series, 4896–8

Elementary and secondary students educational performance in math, science, reading, and writing, 1970s-90, 4898–32

Enrollment, by grade, instn type and control, and student characteristics, 1989 and trends from 1947, annual Current Population Rpt, 2546–1.453

High school advanced placement for college credit, programs by selected characteristics and school control, 1984-86, 4838–46

High school class of 1972: education, employment, and family characteristics, activities, and attitudes, natl longitudinal study, series, 4836–1

High school dropout rates, and subsequent completion, by student and school characteristics, alternative estimates, 1990, annual rpt, 4834–23

Natl Archives and Records Admin activities, finances, holdings, and staff, FY90, annual rpt, 9514–2

Private elementary and secondary schools, students, and staff characteristics, various periods 1979-88, 4838–47

Remedial education programs in higher education instns, and enrollment, courses, and faculty, by instn characteristics, 1989/90, 4826–1.30

Energy Resources and Demand

Coal leasing activity on Federal land, acreage, production, and reserves, by coal region and State, FY90, annual rpt, 5724–10

Coal production and mines by county, prices, productivity, miners, and reserves, by mining method and State, 1989-90, annual rpt, 3164–25

Coal production by State and region, trade, use, and stocks, weekly rpt, 3162–1

Coal production, prices, exports, and use by sector, with data by region, projected 1995-2010 and trends from 1970, annual rpt, 3164–68

Coal production, stocks, and shipments, by State of origin and destination, end-use sector, and mode of transport, quarterly rpt, 3162–8

Coal shipments to electric utilities under contract, and rates, by firm, transport mode, and region, 1979-87, 3168–121

Coal trade and average price, by world region, country, and customs district, quarterly rpt with articles, 3162–37

Electric power plants and capacity, by fuel used, owner, location, and operating status, 1990 and for units planned 1991-2000, annual listing, 3164–36

Electric power plants production and capacity by fuel type, prices, demand, and air pollution law impacts, by region, 1989-90 and projected to 2010, annual rpt, 3164–81

Electric power plants production, by North American Electric Reliability Council region, monthly rpt, 3162–35

Electric power plants production, capacity, sales, and fuel stocks, use, and costs, by State, 1985-89, annual rpt, 3164–11

Electric power wholesale trade, by type of ownership and North American Electric Reliability Council region, 1989, article, 3162–24.201; 3162–35.201

Electric power wholesale trade, by utility, type of ownership, and region, 1988, biennial rpt, 3164–92

Energy production, dev, and distribution firms revenues and income, quarterly rpt, 3162–38

Energy supply, demand, and prices, by fuel type and end-use sector, projections and underlying assumptions, 1990-2010, annual rpt, 3164–90

Energy supply, demand, and prices, by fuel type and end-use sector, with foreign comparisons, 1990 and trends from 1949, annual rpt, 3164–74

Fuel oil and kerosene sales and deliveries, by end-use, PAD district, and State, 1989, annual rpt, 3164–94

Heating fuels production, imports, stocks, and prices, by selected PAD district and State, seasonal weekly rpt, 3162–45

Housing (low income) energy aid, funding sources, costs, and participation, by State, FY89, annual rpt, 4694–8

Manufacturing energy use and prices, 1988 survey, series, 3166–13

Natl Energy Strategy plans for conservation and pollution reduction, impacts on electric power supply, costs, and emissions, projected under alternative assumptions, 1995-2030, 3166–6.49

BY REGION

Natural gas imports of US from Canada under long-term contracts by region, with contract provisions, 1986-90, article, 3162–4.206

Natural gas underground storage facilities and capacities, and withdrawals and injections, by State and region, 1975/76-1990/91, annual article, 3162–4.203

Nuclear power plant capacity, generation, and operating status, by plant and foreign and US location, 1990 and projected to 2030, annual rpt, 3164–57

Offshore oil and gas reserves, and leasing and dev activity, periodic regional rpt series, 5736–3

Offshore oil, gas, and minerals production, revenue, and leasing activity, for Federal OCS lands by ocean area and State, 1950s-90, annual rpt, 5734–3

Oil and gas economically recoverable conventional resources, by region and probability level, as of Dec 1986, annual rpt, 3164–89

Oil and gas OCS lease bidding under alternative leasing systems, activity, royalty rates, and production, by sale, lessee type, and ocean area, FY79-89, annual rpt, 5734–12

Oil and gas supply, demand, and prices, alternative projections 1989-2010, annual rpt, 3164–89

Oil crude, gas liquids, and refined products supply, demand, and movement, by PAD district and State, 1990, annual rpt, 3164–2

Oil import traffic by US port and vessel type, marine oil pollution sources, and costs and operations of proposed offshore terminals, late 1980s, 5738–25

Oil products sales and purchases of refiners, processors, and distributors, by product, end-use sector, PAD district, and State, monthly rpt with articles, 3162–11

Oil, refined products, and gas liquids supply, demand, trade, stocks, and refining, by detailed product, State, and PAD district, monthly rpt with articles, 3162–6

Oil refinery operations and finances, with ownership changes, shutdowns, and reactivations, by firm, 1970s-90, 3168–119

Pipeline and compressor station construction costs, 1984-87, annual rpt, 3084–3

Rural Electrification Admin loans, and borrower operating and financial data, by distribution firm and State, 1990, annual rpt, 1244–1

Uranium reserves and industry operations, by region and State, various periods 1966-90, annual rpt, 3164–65.1

Wood, waste, and alcohol fuel use, by end-use sector and region, 1989, 3166–6.56

Geography and Climate

Earthquake intensity, time, location, damage, and seismic characteristics, for US and foreign earthquakes, 1985, annual rpt, 5664–13

Oceanographic research ships, fleet condition, funding, voyages, and modernization costs, for NOAA, 1980s-90 and projected to 2020, 2148–60

Weather events and anomalies, precipitation and temperature for US and foreign locations, weekly rpt, 2182–6

Index by Categories

Government and Defense

City govt revenue and spending declines, share of cities by region, late 1980s, article, 9375–1.207

Collective bargaining agreements of Federal employees, coverage, unions, and location, by agency, for contracts expiring 1990-91, annual listing, 9847–1

Customs collections and entries processed, by district, FY86-90, annual rpt, 8144–1

Customs collections, by district and port, FY90, annual rpt, 8104–2.1

Fed Govt personnel action appeals, decisions of Merit Systems Protection Board by agency and region, FY90, annual rpt, 9494–2

Finances of govts, tax systems and revenue, and fiscal structure, by level of govt and State, 1991 and historical trends, annual rpt, 10044–1

IRS revenue agent attrition, separations by reason, and hires, by region and district, FY87-90, GAO rpt, 26119–345

Military active duty and recruit social, economic, and parents characteristics, by service branch and State, FY89, annual rpt, 3544–41

Military post exchange operations, and sales by commodity, by facility and location worldwide, FY89, annual rpt, 3504–10

Military spending reductions and base closings employment impacts, by region and State, 1988-89 and projected FY91-95, article, 9371–1.206

State and Metro Area Data Book, 1991 data compilation, 2328–54

Tax (excise) collections of IRS, by source, region, and State, quarterly rpt, annual table, 8302–1

Tax (income) returns filed, by type, IRS service center, and whether full-paid, refund, and electronically filed, 1990 and projected to 1998, semiannual rpt, 8302–7

Tax (income) returns processing, IRS workload forecasts, compliance, and enforcement, data compilation, 1991 annual rpt, 8304–8

Tax (income) withholding and related documents filed, by type and IRS service center, 1990 and projected 1991-98, annual rpt, 8304–22

Tax collection, enforcement, and litigation activity of IRS, with data by type of tax, region, and State, FY90, annual rpt, 8304–3

Tax returns filed, by type of tax and IRS district, 1989 and projected 1990-97, annual rpt, 8304–24

Tax returns filed, by type of tax and IRS region and service center, projected 1990-97 and trends from 1978, annual rpt, 8304–9

Taxes, spending, and govt efficiency, public opinion by respondent characteristics, 1991 survey, annual rpt, 10044–2

Treasury bill offerings, auction results by Fed Reserve District, and terms, periodic press release series, 8002–7

Voting and registration, by socioeconomic and demographic characteristics, 1990 congressional election, biennial Current Population Rpt, 2546–1.454

Health and Vital Statistics

Acute and chronic health conditions, disability, absenteeism, and health services use, by selected characteristics, 1987, CD-ROM, 4147–10.177

AIDS patient hospital use and charges, by hospital and patient characteristics, and payment source, 1986-87, 4186–6.15

Births, fertility rates, and childless women, by selected characteristics, 1990, annual Current Population Rpt, 2546–1.455

Cocaine abuse, user characteristics, and related crime and violence, 1988 conf, 4498–74

Construction industry occupational deaths, by cause, age, industry, and region, 1985-89, 6608–4

Deaths and rates, by region and State, preliminary 1989-90 and trends from 1960, US Vital Statistics annual rpt, 4144–7

Deaths within 8 years of retirement, by health and other characteristics, 1982-88, article, 4742–1.206

Diabetes and complications cases, deaths, and hospitalization, by age, sex, race, State, and region, 1980-86, annual rpt, 4205–41

Disabled persons and related activity limitation days and health services use, by health status, disability type, and other characteristics, 1984-88, 4146–8.202

Disabled persons rehabilitation, Federal and State activities and funding, FY90, annual rpt, 4944–1

Divorces by age of spouses and duration of marriage, and children involved, by State, 1988 and trends from 1940, US Vital Statistics advance annual rpt, 4146–5.121

Drug, alcohol, and cigarette use and attitudes of youth, by substance type and selected characteristics, 1975-90 surveys, annual rpt, 4494–4

Drug, alcohol, and cigarette use, by selected characteristics, 1990 survey, biennial rpt, 4494–5

Ectopic pregnancies and related deaths, by race, age, and region, 1970-87, article, 4202–7.202

Health care services use and costs, methodology and findings of natl survey, series, 4186–8

Health condition and health care resources, use, and spending, 1950s-89, annual data compilation, 4144–11

Health maintenance organizations enrollment and availability for production and office workers, by industry div, selected metro area, and region, 1984-89, article, 6722–1.222

HHS financial aid, by program, recipient, State, and city, FY90, annual regional listings, 4004–3

Home health care services Medicare use and costs, by agency and service type, patient characteristics, and State, 1988-89, article, 4652–1.229

Hospices operations, services, costs, and patient characteristics, for instns without Medicare certification, FY85-86, 4658–52

Hospital closures and rates, with financial, operating, and market characteristics, by location, late 1980s, GAO rpt, 26121–392

Hospital discharges and length of stay, by diagnosis, patient and instn characteristics, procedure performed, and payment source, 1988, annual rpt, 4147–13.107

Index by Categories

BY REGION

Hospital discharges by detailed diagnostic and procedure category, primary diagnosis, and length of stay, by age, sex, and region, 1988, annual rpt, 4147–13.105

Hospital discharges by detailed diagnostic and procedure category, primary diagnosis, and length of stay, by age, sex, and region, 1989, annual rpt, 4147–13.108

Hospitalization costs relation to services timing, by selected patient and hospital characteristics, for Medicare discharges, 1987-88, 17208–2

Hospitals in rural areas, HCFA grants for improving financial stability, by program area, recipient, and State, FY89, 4658–58

Implants of medical devices, by type, reason, duration, and user characteristics, 1988, 4146–8.197

Indian and Alaska Native disease and disorder cases, deaths, and health services use, by tribe, reservation, and Indian Health Service area, late 1950s-86, 4088–2

Indian Health Service and tribal facility outpatient visits, by type of provider, selected hospital, and service area, FY90, annual rpt, 4084–3

Indian Health Service and tribal hospital admissions, length of stay, beds, and births, by facility and service area, FY70-89, annual rpt, 4084–4

Indian Health Service and tribal hospital capacity, use, and births, by area and facility, quarterly rpt, 4082–1

Indian Health Service facilities and use, and Indian health and other characteristics, by IHS region, 1980s-89, annual chartbook, 4084–7

Indian Health Service nursing staff, shortages, workload, and pay, by IHS service unit, mid 1980s-90, hearing, 25418–6

Indian Health Service outpatient visits, by facility and IHS service area, FY89-90, annual rpt, 4084–8

Indian Health Service, tribal, and contract facilities hospitalization, by diagnosis, age, sex, and service area, FY89, annual rpt, 4084–5

Infant death rate, by cause, region, and race, 1980-87, article, 4202–7.208

Infectious notifiable disease cases and current outbreaks, by region and State, weekly rpt, 4202–1

Infectious notifiable disease cases, by age, race, and State, and deaths, 1930s-90, annual rpt, 4204–1

Injuries, by type, circumstances, and victim characteristics, and related activity limitations, 1985-87, 4147–10.176

Injuries, related impairments, and activity limitations, by circumstances and victim characteristics, 1985-87, 4147–10.179

Insurance (health) coverage, by insurance type and selected characteristics, 1989, 4146–8.203

Marriages and rates, by age, race, education, previous marital status, and State, 1988, US Vital Statistics advance annual rpt, 4146–5.122

Marriages, divorces, and rates, by characteristics of spouses, State, and county, 1987 and trends from 1920, US Vital Statistics annual rpt, 4144–4

Minority group and women health condition, services use, payment sources, and health care labor force, by poverty status, 1940s-89, chartbook, 4118–56

NIH grants for R&D, training, construction, and medical libraries, by location and recipient, FY90, annual listings, 4434–7

Nursing home residents with mental disorders, by disorder type and resident and instn characteristics, 1985, 4147–13.106

Occupational safety and health research and demonstration grants by State, and project listing, FY90, annual rpt, 4244–2

Older persons deaths in hospitals, nursing homes, and own home, by cause, age, marital status, and region, 1986, article, 4652–1.201

Physicians consultations requested by attending physician, Medicare reimbursement issues, with use by diagnosis, specialty, location, and other characteristics, 1986, 4658–47

Price indexes for health care services, by selected metro area and region, model results, 1988-89, working paper, 6886–6.73

Radiation exposure at DOE and DOE-contractor sites, by facility type and contractor, dose type, and worker age, sex, and occupation, 1988, annual rpt, 3324–1

Sexually transmitted disease cases and control activity, by strain, State, and selected city, 1940s-90, 4205–42

Tuberculosis cases and deaths, by patient characteristics, State, and city, 1989 and trends from 1953, annual rpt, 4204–10

Housing and Construction

Affordability indicators for housing, by household composition, income, and current tenure, 1988, 2486–1.11

Alteration and repair spending for housing, by type, tenure, region, and other characteristics, quarterly rpt, 2382–7

American Housing Survey: unit and households detailed characteristics, and unit and neighborhood quality, 1987, biennial rpt, 2485–12

American Housing Survey: unit and households detailed characteristics, and unit and neighborhood quality, 1987, biennial rpt supplement, 2485–13

Apartment and condominium completions by rent class and sales price, and market absorption rates, quarterly rpt, 2482–2

Apartment completions by region and metro-nonmetro location, and absorption rate, by size and rent class, preliminary 1990, annual Current Housing Rpt, 2484–3

Apartment market absorption rates and characteristics for nonsubsidized furnished and unfurnished units, 1989, annual Current Housing Rpt, 2484–2

Census of Population and Housing, 1990: housing units occupied and vacant, persons in group quarters, and household size, by region, census div, and State, press release, 2328–71

Clay (construction) production and shipments by region and State, trade, and use, by product, quarterly Current Industrial Rpt, 2506–9.2

Construction put in place, permits, housing sales, costs, material prices, and employment, bimonthly rpt with articles, 2042–1

Construction put in place, value of new public and private structures, by type, monthly rpt, 2382–4

Historic buildings rehabilitation tax incentives, projects, costs, ownership, and use, FY77-90, annual rpt, 5544–17

Homeownership rates, changes by State, and for householders under age 35 by region, 1980s, fact sheet, 2326–17.28

HUD multifamily housing stock and mortgage foreclosures, by region, 1990, GAO rpt, 26131–84

Low income housing construction and repair loans of HUD to nonprofit organizations, project delays, and starts, 1980s, GAO rpt, 26113–506

Mortgages FHA-insured, secondary market prices and yields, and interest rates on construction and conventional mortgage loans, by region, monthly press release, 5142–20

New housing starts, by units per structure and metro-nonmetro location, and mobile home placements and prices, by region, monthly rpt, 2382–1

New housing starts, forecasts by region, 1991-2000, with background data, 1973-87, article, 9387–1.205

New housing units authorized, by region, State, selected MSA, and permit-issuing place, monthly rpt, 2382–5

New housing units authorized, by State, MSA, and permit-issuing place, 1990, annual rpt, 2384–2

New housing units completed and under construction, by units per structure, region, and inside-outside MSAs, monthly rpt, 2382–2

New single and multifamily units, by structural and financial characteristics, inside-outside MSAs, and region, 1986-90, annual rpt, 2384–1

New single-family houses sold and for sale, by price, stage of construction, months on market, and region, monthly rpt, 2382–3

Poor households with high rent, and substandard units, worst case problems prevalence and households characteristics, 1970s-84, annual rpt, 5184–10

Public housing renovation costs and alternative funding methods, by project type and region, 1990 rpt, 5188–127

Public works capital stock and investment spending economic impacts, with data by type of stock and region, 1950s-88, conf, 9373–3.34

Public works stock impacts on State gross product, by region, 1970s-86, article, 9373–1.217

Rental housing rehabilitation funding and activities of HUD, by program and region, FY90, annual rpt, 5124–7

Retirement housing centers tax-exempt bond use and other financing, defaults, and facility and resident characteristics, 1991 GAO rpt, 26119–328

Vacant housing characteristics and costs, and occupancy and vacancy rates, by region and metro-nonmetro location, quarterly rpt, 2482–1

Vacant housing characteristics, and occupancy and vacancy rates, by tenure and location, 1960s-90, annual rpt, 2484–1

Industry and Commerce

Exports and imports of US shipped through Canada, by detailed commodity, customs district, and country, 1989, annual rpt, 7704–11

BY REGION

Index by Categories

Gross product for regions, by industry div, 1986, article, 9373–1.211

Imports detained by FDA, by reason, product, shipper, brand, and country, monthly listing, 4062–2

Lumber and pulp products supply and use, and timber resources, detailed data, 1950s-87 and alternative projections to 2040, 1208–24.20

Lumber production, prices by region and State, trade by country, and use, by species and product, 1960-88, annual rpt, 1204–29

Lumber production, prices, trade, and employment, for northwestern US and British Columbia, quarterly rpt, 1202–3

Minority Business Dev Centers mgmt and financial aid, and characteristics of businesses, by region and State, FY90, annual rpt, 2104–6

Multinatl firms US affiliates, investment trends and impact on US economy, 1991 annual rpt, 2004–9

Phosphate rock production, prices, sales, trade, and use, 1991, Mineral Industry Surveys, annual rpt, 5614–20

Puerto Rico economic censuses, 1987: wholesale and retail trade and service industry finances and operations, by SIC 2- to 4-digit industry and municipio, 2591–1

Retail trade sales and inventories, by kind of business, region, and selected State, MSA, and city, monthly rpt, 2413–3

Rural areas economic and social indicators used to determine Federal aid need, late 1960s-86, 1598–265

Small Business Admin surety bond guarantee program finances, and contracts by contractor race, obligee type, and region, FY87-89, GAO rpt, 26113–526

State and Metro Area Data Book, 1991 data compilation, 2328–54

Statistical Abstract of US, 1991 annual data compilation, 2324–1

Steel imports of US under voluntary restraint agreement, by product, customs district, and country, with US industry operating data, quarterly rpt, 9882–13

Textile mill production, trade, sales, stocks, and material used, by product, region, and State, periodic Current Industrial Rpt series, 2506–5

Vending facilities run by blind on Federal and non-Federal property, finances and operations by agency and State, FY90, annual rpt, 4944–2

Labor and Employment

Auto and auto parts manufacturing wages, employment, and benefits, by occupation, region, and selected labor market area, 1989 survey, 6787–6.252

Employer Cost Index by region, quarterly press release, 6942–8

Employment Cost Index and percent change by occupational group, industry div, region, and metro-nonmetro area, quarterly press release, 6782–5

Employment Cost Index changes for nonfarm workers, by occupation, industry div, region, and bargaining status, monthly rpt, 6782–1

Employment cost indexes, by occupation, industry div, and region, Monthly Labor Review, 6722–1.3

Employment, unemployment, and labor force characteristics, by region and census div, 1990, annual rpt, 6744–7.1

Fair Labor Standards Act admin, with coverage under minimum wage and overtime provisions, and illegal employment of minors, by industry div, FY89, annual rpt, 6504–2.1

Fed Govt contractor compliance with equal employment laws, FY90, 6508–36

Job Training Partnership Act funding and performance indicators in service delivery areas, by urban-rural location, 1987-88, 1598–266

Labor Dept activities and funding, by program and State, FY90, annual rpt, 6304–1

Labor force status, by worker characteristics and industry group, 1982-90, semiannual article, 6722–1.212

Labor-mgmt mediation and arbitration activities of Fed Mediation and Conciliation Service, and cases by issue, region, and State, FY84-89, annual rpt, 9344–1

Labor Relations Natl Board activities, cases, elections conducted, and litigation, FY89, annual rpt, 9584–1

Rural areas economic conditions and dev, quarterly journal, 1502–8

Technology-intensive employment by region and State, and earnings, by industry group, 1989, article, 6722–1.235

Textile production workers and wages by occupation, and benefits, by location, 1990 survey, 6787–6.251

Unemployment, employment, and labor force, by region and State, 1989-90, press release, 6726–1.37

Unemployment insurance claims and receipt, by reason and duration of unemployment, age, sex, and region, 1989-90, 6406–6.33

Vocational rehabilitation cases of State agencies, by disposition and State, FY90 and trends from FY21, annual rpt, 4944–5

Wages by occupation, for office and plant workers in metro areas, by industry div and region, Aug 1990, annual rpt, 6785–9

Wages, hours, and employment by occupation, and benefits, for selected locations, industry survey rpt series, 6787–6

Law Enforcement

Aliens (illegal) apprehensions and officer hours, for Border Patrol by location, 1980s, fact sheet, 6266–2.2

Assaults and deaths of law enforcement officers, by circumstances, agency, victim and offender characteristics, and location, 1990, annual rpt, 6224–3

Bombing incidents, casualties, and damage, by target, circumstances, and State, 1990, annual rpt, 6224–5

Court caseloads, actions, procedure duration, judges, and jurors, by Federal district and appeals court, 1986-91, annual rpt, 18204–3

Court civil and criminal caseloads for Federal district, appeals, and bankruptcy courts, by type of suit and offense, circuit, and district, 1990, annual rpt, 18204–11

Court civil and criminal caseloads for Federal district, appeals, and special courts, 1990, annual rpt, 18204–8

Court civil and criminal caseloads for Federal district, appeals, and special courts, 1991, annual rpt, 18204–2

Crime, criminal justice admin and enforcement, and public opinion, data compilation, 1991 annual rpt, 6064–6

Crime Index by population size and region, and offenses by large city, Jan-June 1991, semiannual rpt, 6222–1

Crimes, arrests by offender characteristics, and rates, by offense, and law enforcement employees, by population size and jurisdiction, 1990, annual rpt, 6224–2

Drug (illegal) lab seizures, by substance and location, 1989-90, annual rpt, 6284–3

Drug enforcement regional task forces investigation of organized crime, activities by agency and region, FY83-90, biennial rpt, 6004–17

Jail adult and juvenile population, employment, spending, instn conditions, and inmate programs, by county and facility, 1988, regional rpt series, 6068–144

Juvenile correctional and detention public and private instns, inmates, and expenses, by instn and resident characteristics and State, 1987, biennial rpt, 6064–13

Juvenile facilities, population, and costs, by facility and resident characteristics, region, and State, 1985-89, biennial rpt, 6064–5

Parole and probation population, entries, and exits, by State, 1989, annual rpt, 6066–25.34

Parole decisions, caseloads, and activities of US Parole Commission, FY87-90, annual rpt, 6004–3

Prison construction and operating costs, capacity, and inmates, for Federal and State facilities, 1985-89, GAO rpt, 26119–341

Prisoners, characteristics, and movements, by State, 1989, annual rpt, 6064–26

Prisoners in Federal and State instns, by sex and State, June 1991, semiannual rpt, 6062–4

Prisoners in Federal instns, by sex, prison, security level, contract facility type, and region, monthly rpt series, 6242–1

Rapes reported, by State, 1989-90, 25528–116

Sentences for Federal crimes, guidelines use and results by offense and district, and Sentencing Commission activities, 1990, annual rpt, 17664–1

Terrorism incidents in US, related activity, and casualties, by attack type, target, group, and location, 1990, annual rpt, 6224–6

Victimization rates, by victim and offender characteristics, circumstances, and offense, 1988 survey, annual rpt, 6066–3.42

Victimization rates, by victim and offender characteristics, circumstances, and offense, 1989 survey, annual rpt, 6066–3.44

Victimizations by region and victim characteristics, and rpts to police, by offense, 1973-90, annual rpt, 6066–25.35; 6066–25.41

Victimizations of households, by offense, household characteristics, and location, 1975-90, annual rpt, 6066–25.40

Violent crime victimizations, circumstances, victim characteristics, arrest, recidivism, sentences, and prisoners, 1980s, 6068–148

Index by Categories

Natural Resources, Environment, and Pollution

Air pollutant sulfur dioxide emissions, electric power generation and prices, and coal supply and demand, impacts of Clean Air Act, 1980s and projected to 2010, annual rpt, 3164–81

Army Corps of Engineers activities, FY88, annual rpt, 3754–1

Birds (bald eagle) Great Lakes population, breeding, and research status, 1990 conf, 14648–26

Birds (mourning dove) population, by hunting and nonhunting State, 1966-91, annual rpt, 5504–15

Birds (waterfowl) hunter harvest, age and sex ratios by species, State, and flyway, 1986-90, annual rpt, 5504–32

Birds (waterfowl) hunter harvest and unretrieved kills, and duck stamps sold, by species, State, Canada Province, and flyway, 1989-90, annual rpt, 5504–28

Birds (waterfowl) population, habitat conditions, and migratory flight forecasts, for Canada and US by region, 1991 and trends from 1955, annual rpt, 5504–27

Birds (woodcock) population in US and Canada from 1968, and hunter harvest, by State, 1991, annual rpt, 5504–11

Coastal and riparian areas environmental conditions, fish, wildlife, use, and mgmt, for individual ecosystems, series, 5506–9

Environmental Quality, status of problems, protection programs, research, and intl issues, 1991 annual rpt, 484–1

EPA pollution control grant program activities, monthly rpt, 9182–8

Estuary environmental conditions, and fish and shellfish catch by species and region, 1980s, 2178–27

Fish and Wildlife Service restoration programs finances by State, and excise tax collections, FY90, annual rpt, 5504–13

Fish kills in coastal areas related to pollution and natural causes, by land use, State, and county, 1980s, 2178–32

Forest fires and acres burned on Forest Service land, by cause, forest, and State, 1989, annual rpt, 1204–6

Forest Service activities and finances, by region and State, FY90, annual rpt, 1204–1

Forest Service mgmt of public lands and resources dev, environmental, economic, and social impacts of alternative programs, projected to 2040, 1208–24

Forests (natl) and other lands under Forest Service mgmt, acreage by forest and location, 1990, annual rpt, 1204–2

Forests (natl) revenue, by source, forest, and State, FY90, annual rpt, 1204–34

Forests (natl) revenue share paid to States, and acreage, by forest, region, county, and congressional district, FY90, annual rpt, 1204–33

Global climate change environmental, infrastructure, and health impacts, with model results and background data, 1850s-2100, 9188–113

Hazardous waste site remedial action under Superfund, current and proposed sites priority ranking and status by location, series, 9216–5

Helium resources in storage and natural gas reserves, by State, 1950-89 and projected to 2020, biennial rpt, 5604–44

Land acreage, by use, ownership, and State, 1987 and trends from 1910, 1588–48

Radioactive low-level waste disposal activities of States and interstate compacts, with data by disposal facility and reactor, 1989, annual rpt, 3354–14

Timber acreage, by ownership, forest type, and State, 1950s-87 and projected to 2040, 1208–357

Timber improvement program for private land, Fed Govt cost-sharing funds by region and State, monthly rpt, 1802–11

Timber insect and disease incidence and damage, annual regional rpt series, 1206–11

Timber mgmt programs of Bur of Indian Affairs, funding, acreage, harvest, and tribal investment, by tribe and location, FY77-89 and projected to FY96, hearing, 25418–4

Timber sales of Forest Service, expenses, and operations, by region and natl forest, FY90, annual rpt, 1204–36.2

Wastewater industrial releases pollution levels, treatment, costs, and regulation, with background financial and operating data, industry rpt series, 9206–4

Wastewater treatment facilities in small communities, construction and repair needs to meet Clean Water Act standards, by State and region, 1988 and 2008, 1588–155

Water (groundwater) supply, quality, chemistry, other characteristics, and use, regional rpt series, 5666–25

Water pollution fish kills, by pollution source, month, location, and State, 1977-87, last issue of annual rpt, 9204–3

Water pollution from farming, funding for control under Rural Clean Water Program by region and State, monthly rpt, 1802–14

Population

Census of Population and Housing, 1990: population and housing selected characteristics, by region, press release, 2328–74

Census of Population, 1990: Hispanic population by detailed origin, region, and State, with data for 1980, press release, 2328–73

Census of Population, 1990: population by detailed Native American, Asian, and Pacific Islander group, race, region, and State, with data for 1980, press release, 2328–72

Census of Population, 1990: population by race, Hispanic origin, region, census div, and State, with data for 1980, fact sheet, 2326–20.2

Census of Population, 1990: population size, by State, census div, and region, and congressional seats apportioned by State, 1990 and trends from 1790, fact sheet, 2326–20.1

Census of Population, 1990: top 39 MSAs and 40 cities population, with trends from 1900, fact sheet, 2326–20.3

Census of Population, 1990: urban areas land area, housing units, and population, by State and compared to rural areas, press release, 2328–39

Consumer Income, socioeconomic characteristics of persons, families, and households, detailed cross-tabulations, Current Population Rpt series, 2546–6

BY REGION

Households and family characteristics, by location, 1990, annual Current Population Rpt, 2546–1.447

Immigrants in US, population characteristics and fertility, by birthplace and compared to native born, 1980s, Current Population rpt, 2546–2.162

Income (household) and poverty status under alternative income definitions, by recipient characteristics, 1990, annual Current Population Rpt, 2546–6.69

Income (personal) and poverty status changes, by selected characteristics, 1987-88, Current Population Rpt, 2546–20.19

Income (personal) per capita and by source, and earnings by industry div, by State, MSA, and county, 1984-89, annual regional rpts, 2704–2

Income (personal) per capita and total, and earnings by industry group, by region and State, 1988-90, annual article, 2702–1.216

Income (personal) per capita, by region compared to total US, alternative model results, 1929-87, working paper, 9387–8.232

Income (personal) totals, by region, census div, and State, quarterly article, 2702–1.27

Income and consumer spending of households, for selected population groups, quarterly journal, 1702–1

Living arrangements, family relationships, and marital status, by selected characteristics, 1990, annual Current Population Rpt, 2546–1.449

Population estimates and projections, by region and State, Current Population Rpt series, 2546–3

Population size, July 1981-89 and compared to 1980 and 1990, annual press release, 2324–10

Poverty status of population and families, by detailed characteristics, 1988-89, annual Current Population Rpt, 2546–6.67

Poverty status of population and families, by detailed characteristics, 1990, annual Current Population Rpt, 2546–6.71

State and Metro Area Data Book, 1991 data compilation, 2328–54

Statistical Abstract of US, 1991 annual data compilation, 2324–1

Prices and Cost of Living

Child rearing costs of married couple households, by expenditure type, child's age, income, and region, 1990 and projected to 2007, 1708–87

Consumer Expenditure Survey, household income by source, and itemized spending, by selected characteristics and region, 1988-89, annual rpt, 6764–5

Consumer Expenditure Survey, spending by category, and income, by selected household characteristics and location, 1990, annual press release, 6726–1.42

Consumer Expenditure Survey, spending by category, selected household characteristics, and region, quarterly rpt, 6762–14

CPI by component for US city average, and by region, population size, and for 15 metro areas, monthly rpt, 6762–1

CPI by component for US city average, and by region, population size, and for 27 metro areas, monthly rpt, 6762–2

BY REGION

Index by Categories

CPI components relative importance, by selected MSA, region, population size, and for US city average, 1990, annual rpt, 6884–1

CPI current statistics, Monthly Labor Review, 6722–1.4

Dairy prices, by product and selected area, with related marketing data, 1990, annual rpt, 1317–1

Farm prices received and paid, by commodity and State, 1990, annual rpt, 1629–5

Food cost index alternative to CPI, by category, region, and household income, size, race, and food budget level, 1980-85, 1598–275

Food price indexes, by selected metro area and region, model results, 1988-89, working paper, 6886–6.78

Housing units (1-family) sold, price indexes by region, monthly rpt, quarterly tables, 2382–3.2

Housing units (1-family) sold, prices and price index by region, quarterly rpt, 2382–8

Milk order market prices and detailed operations, by State and market area, 1989-90, annual rpt, 1317–3

Milk order market prices and detailed operations, monthly rpt with articles, 1317–4

Poultry and egg prices and marketing, by selected region, State, and city, monthly and weekly 1990, annual rpt, 1317–2

Producer price indexes, by stage of processing and detailed commodity, monthly 1990, annual rpt, 6764–2

Public Welfare and Social Security

Food aid program of USDA for women, infants, and children, participants and costs by State and Indian agency, FY88, annual tables, 1364–12

Food aid program of USDA for women, infants, and children, participants by race, State, and Indian agency, Apr 1990, annual rpt, 1364–16

Food aid program of USDA for women, infants, and children, participants, clinics, and costs, by State and Indian agency, monthly tables, 1362–16

Food stamp issues and participation, by State and county, as of July 1990, semiannual rpt, 1362–6

HHS financial aid, by program, recipient, State, and city, FY90, annual regional listings, 4004–3

Homeless and runaway youth programs, funding, activities, and participant characteristics, FY90, annual rpt, 4604–3

Medicare and Medicaid beneficiaries and program operations, 1991, annual fact book, 4654–18

Medicare and Medicaid eligibility, participation, coverage, and program finances, various periods 1966-91, biennial rpt, 4654–1

Medicare beneficiaries hospital discharges, length of stay, and costs, by type of beneficiary and location, 1972-88, article, 4652–1.207

Medicare reimbursement of hospitals under prospective payment system, effect of adjusting wage index for occupational mix, 1990 rpt, 17206–2.17

Supplemental Security Income benefit award rate by applicant characteristics and eligibility class, 1987, article, 4742–1.213

Surplus personal property of Fed Govt donated to govt and nonprofit agencies, with data by State, FY88-90, biennial rpt, 9454–22

Recreation and Leisure

Coastal areas recreation facilities, by State, county, estuary, and level of govt, 1972-84, 2178–29

Coastal areas recreation facilities of Fed Govt and States, visitor and site characteristics, 1987-90 survey, regional rpt series, 2176–9

Fishing (ocean sport) activities, and catch by species, by angler characteristics and State, annual coastal area rpt series, 2166–17

Fishing (ocean sport) catch, by species, mode of fishing, and coastal region, 1990, annual rpt, 2164–1.2

Park natl system and other land under Natl Park Service mgmt, acreage by site, ownership, and region, FY91, semiannual rpt, 5542–1.4

Park natl system and other land under Natl Park Service mgmt, acreage by site, ownership, and region, 1990, semiannual rpt, 5542–1.2

Park natl system visitor deaths, by cause, victim age, region, and park, 1980-90, annual rpt, 5544–6

Park natl system visits and overnight stays, by park and State, monthly rpt, 5542–4

Park natl system visits and overnight stays, by park and State, 1990, annual rpt, 5544–12

Shellfish recreational harvesters selected characteristics, location of harvest and residence, and spending, 1985 survey, 2178–28

Science and Technology

Computer use at home, school, and work, by purpose and selected user characteristics, 1989, Current Population Rpt, 2546–2.158

Technology dev programs of govts, info sources and funding, 1990 rpt, 10048–81

Veterans Affairs

Health care for veterans, patients, visits, costs, and operating beds, by VA and contract facility, and region, quarterly rpt, 8602–4

Health care professionals of VA, by selected employment characteristics and VA district and duty station, quarterly rpt, 8602–6

Health care services sharing contracts among VA and non-VA facilities, by service type and region, FY90, annual rpt, 8704–5

Health care staff of VA, and turnover, by occupation and location, 1990, annual rpt, 8604–8

BY SMSA OR MSA

Banking, Finance, and Insurance

Banks (insured commercial and savings) deposits by instn, State, MSA, and county, as of June 1990, annual regional rpt, 9295–3.7

New England States, FHLB 1st District thrifts financial operations and housing industry indicators, monthly rpt with articles, 9302–4

Communications and Transportation

Transportation census, 1987: finances and operations by size, ownership, and State, and revenues by MSA, by SIC 2- to 4-digit industry, 2579–1

Education

Educational attainment, by sociodemographic characteristics and location, 1989 and trends from 1940, biennial Current Population Rpt, 2546–1.452

Government and Defense

Employment (civilian) of Fed Govt, by work schedule, selected agency, State, and MSA, as of Dec 1990, biennial article, 9842–1.203

Employment and payroll (civilian) of Fed Govt, by pay system and location, 1990, annual rpt, 9844–6.6

State and Metro Area Data Book, 1991 data compilation, 2328–54

Health and Vital Statistics

AIDS cases by risk group, race, sex, age, State, and MSA, and deaths, monthly rpt, 4202–9

Deaths and infant deaths, by cause, age, sex, race, and location, 1988, US Vital Statistics annual rpt, 4144–2.1; 4144–2.2

Drug abuse emergency room admissions and deaths, by drug type and source, sex, race, age, and major metro area, 1990, annual rpt, 4494–8

Drug abuse indicators for selected metro areas, research results, data collection, and policy issues, 1991 semiannual conf, 4492–5

Health maintenance organizations enrollment and availability for production and office workers, by industry div, selected metro area, and region, 1984-89, article, 6722–1.222

Hospital deaths of Medicare patients, actual and expected rates by diagnosis and MSA, and methodology, FY87-89, annual rpt, 4654–14.11

Marriages, divorces, and rates, by characteristics of spouses, State, and county, 1987 and trends from 1920, US Vital Statistics annual rpt, 4144–4

Physicians practice cost indexes and components, by State, MSA, and for rural areas, 1989 rpt, 4658–50

Price indexes for health care services, by selected metro area and region, model results, 1988-89, working paper, 6886–6.73

Housing and Construction

American Housing Survey: unit and households characteristics, MSA fact sheet series, 2485–11

American Housing Survey: unit and households detailed characteristics, and unit and neighborhood quality, MSA rpt series, 2485–6

Construction authorized by building permits, by type of construction, region, State, and MSA, bimonthly rpt, 2042–1.3

Hotels and other lodging places, receipts, payroll, employment, ownership, and rooms, by State and MSA, 1987 Census of Service Industries, subject rpt, 2393–3

Mortgage (home) terms on conventional loans closed, by lender type, with quarterly data for 32 MSAs, monthly rpt, 9442–2

Mortgages FHA-insured, financial, property, and mortgagor characteristics, by metro area, 1990, annual rpt, 5144–24

New housing starts and completions authorized by building permits in 40 MSAs, quarterly rpt, 2382–9

New housing units authorized, by region, State, selected MSA, and permit-issuing place, monthly rpt, 2382–5

Index by Categories

BY STATE

New housing units authorized, by State, MSA, and permit-issuing place, 1990, annual rpt, 2384–2

North Central States, FHLB 7th District housing vacancy rates for single and multifamily units and mobile homes, by ZIP code, annual MSA rpt series, 9304–18

Vacant housing characteristics, and occupancy and vacancy rates, by tenure and location, 1960s-90, annual rpt, 2484–1

West Central States, FHLB 10th District housing vacancy rates for single and multifamily units and mobile homes, by ZIP code, annual MSA rpt series, 9304–22

Western States, FHLB 12th District housing vacancy rates for single and multifamily units and mobile homes, by ZIP code, annual MSA rpt series, 9304–21

Industry and Commerce

Manufacturing census, 1987: finances and operations, by SIC 2- to 4-digit industry, State, and MSA, with trends from 1849, 2497–1.4

New England States economic indicators, Fed Reserve 1st District, monthly rpt, 9373–2

Retail trade census, 1987: finances and employment, for establishments with and without payroll, by SIC 2- to 4-digit kind of business, State, and MSA, 2401–1

Retail trade sales and inventories, by kind of business, region, and selected State, MSA, and city, monthly rpt, 2413–3

Service industries census, 1987: establishments, receipts by source, payroll, and employment, by SIC 2- to 4-digit kind of business, State, and MSA, 2393–4

Southeastern States, Fed Reserve 6th District, economic indicators by State and MSA, quarterly rpt, 9371–14

State and Metro Area Data Book, 1991 data compilation, 2328–54

Statistical Abstract of US, 1991 annual data compilation, 2324–1

Labor and Employment

Earnings, annual average percent changes for selected occupational groups, selected MSAs, monthly rpt, 6782–1.1

Employment and Earnings, detailed data, monthly rpt, 6742–2.5; 6742–2.6; 6742–2.8

Employment in manufacturing and nonagricultural industries, by MSA, 1989-90, annual press release, 6946–3.20

Employment, unemployment, and labor force characteristics, by selected metro area and large city, 1990, annual rpt, 6744–7.3

New England States economic indicators, Fed Reserve 1st District, monthly rpt, 9373–2.2

North Central States business and economic conditions, Fed Reserve 9th District, quarterly journal, 9383–19

Pay comparability of Fed Govt with private industry, by occupation for 22 MSAs, 1989, GAO rpt, 26119–332

Southeastern US employment, by selected MSA, 1989-90, annual rpt, 6944–2

Southeastern US wages covered under unemployment insurance, by industry div, State, and metro area, 1989-90, annual press release, 6946–3.22

Southeastern US wages of office and plant workers, for 27 MSAs, 1990, press release, 6946–3.21

Textile production workers and wages by occupation, and benefits, by location, 1990 survey, 6787–6.251

Unemployment, by State and metro area, monthly press release, 6742–12

Unemployment, employment, and labor force, by State, MSA, and city, monthly rpt, 6742–22

Wages by occupation, and benefits for office and plant workers in selected MSAs, 1990, annual rpt, 6785–1

Wages by occupation, and benefits for office and plant workers, periodic MSA survey rpt series, 6785–3; 6785–11; 6785–12

Wages by occupation, for office and plant workers in selected MSAs, 1991 surveys, annual rpt, 6785–5

Wages by occupation, for office and plant workers in selected MSAs, 1991 surveys, annual summary rpts, 6785–6

Wages for 4 occupational groups, relative pay levels in 60 MSAs, 1990, annual rpt, 6785–8

Wages for 4 occupational groups, relative pay levels in 75 labor market areas, 1990, annual rpt, 6785–13

Wages, hours, and employment by occupation, and benefits, for selected locations, industry survey rpt series, 6787–6

Wages of workers covered by unemployment insurance, by MSA, 1989-90, annual press release, 6784–17.2

Natural Resources, Environment, and Pollution

Air pollution levels for 6 pollutants, by source and selected MSA, 1980-89, annual rpt, 9194–1

Population

Census of Population, 1990: metro area population by race, Hispanic origin, and MSA, press release, 2328–75

Census of Population, 1990: top 39 MSAs and 40 cities population, with trends from 1900, fact sheet, 2326–20.3

Income (personal) per capita and by source, and earnings by industry div, by State, MSA, and county, 1984-89, annual regional rpts, 2704–2

Income (personal) per capita and total, by State, MSA, county, and metro-nonmetro location, 1987-89, annual article, 2702–1.209

Population size, by MSA, as of Apr 1990, annual press release, 2324–8

State and Metro Area Data Book, 1991 data compilation, 2328–54

Statistical Abstract of US, 1991 annual data compilation, 2324–1

Texas and Louisiana per capita income, impacts of industry mix and other factors, for 36 MSAs, 1969-88, article, 9379–1.209

West Central States population, income, and employment growth, by MSA, metro-nonmetro location, and State, for Fed Reserve 10th District, 1970s-90s, article, 9381–1.209

Prices and Cost of Living

Consumer Expenditure Survey, household income by source, and itemized spending, by selected characteristics and region, 1988-89, annual rpt, 6764–5

Cost of living and quality of life indicators for 14 MSAs, 1980s, GAO rpt, 26123–346

CPI by component for US city average, and by region, population size, and for 15 metro areas, monthly rpt, 6762–1

CPI by component for US city average, and by region, population size, and for 27 metro areas, monthly rpt, 6762–2

CPI components relative importance, by selected MSA, region, population size, and for US city average, 1990, annual rpt, 6884–1

CPI current statistics, Monthly Labor Review, 6722–1.4

Food price indexes, by selected metro area and region, model results, 1988-89, working paper, 6886–6.78

Poultry and egg prices and marketing, by selected region, State, and city, monthly and weekly 1990, annual rpt, 1317–2

Public Welfare and Social Security

Medicare reimbursement for radiology services by location, and for home medical equipment under alternative proposals, 1990 hearing, 21368–131

South Dakota poverty relief and medical aid programs of counties, spending by type, MSA, and county, 1989, hearing, 25368–176

BY STATE

Agriculture and Food

Acreage of cropland, total, idle, and grazed, by region and State, 1987 and trends from 1910, 1588–48

Acreage planted and harvested, by crop and State, 1989-90 and planned as of June 1991, annual rpt, 1621–23

Acreage planted, by selected crop and State, 1982-90 and planned 1991, annual rpt, 1621–22

Acreage reduction program compliance, enrollment, and yield on planted acreage, by commodity and State, annual press release series, 1004–20

Acreage under Agricultural Stabilization and Conservation Service programs, rankings by commodity and congressional district, 1989, biennial rpt, 1804–17

Agricultural data compilation, 1990 and trends from 1920, annual rpt, 1004–14

Agricultural Stabilization and Conservation Service producer payments, by program and State, 1990, annual table, 1804–12

Agricultural Statistics, 1990, annual rpt, 1004–1

Alcoholic beverages and tobacco production, removals, stocks, and material used, by State, monthly rpt series, 8486–1

Animal protection, licensing, and inspection activities of USDA, and animals used in research, by State, FY89, annual rpt, 1394–10

Apple production, marketing, and prices, for Appalachia and compared to other States, 1988-91, annual rpt, 1311–13

Bean (dried) prices by State, market activity, and foreign and US production, use, stocks, and trade, weekly rpt, 1311–17

Bean (dried) production and prices by State, exports and foreign production by country, and USDA food aid purchases, by bean type, 1984-90, annual rpt, 1311–18

Carbon dioxide in atmosphere, North Central States economic and agricultural impacts, model descriptions and results, 1980s and projected to 2030, 3006–11.15

BY STATE

Index by Categories

Catfish raised on farms, operations, water use, and acreage, by State, 1989-91, semiannual situation rpt, 1561–15.2

Cattle and calves for beef and milk, by State, as of July 1991, semiannual press release, 1623–1

Cattle and calves on feed, inventory and marketings by State, monthly release, 1623–2

Cattle feedlots and marketing, by lot size and State, selected years 1955-89, 1568–300

Cattle tuberculosis cases and cooperative Federal-State eradication activities, by State, FY89-90, annual rpt, 1394–13

Census of Agriculture, 1987: farms, farmland, production, finances, and operator characteristics, by county, final State rpt series, 2331–1

Census of Agriculture, 1987: horticultural specialties producers, finances, and operations, by crop and State, 1988 survey, 2337–1

Cherry production, by State, 1989-91, annual rpt, 1621–18.2

Citrus production, prices, and use, by commodity and State, 1988/89-1990/91, annual rpt, 1621–18.7

Cold storage food stocks by commodity and census div, and warehouse space use, by State, monthly rpt, 1631–5

Cold storage food stocks by commodity, and warehouse space use, by census div, 1990, annual rpt, 1631–11

Conservation program of USDA, funding by practice, region and State, monthly rpt, 1802–15

Conservation program of USDA, participation and payments by practice and State, FY90, annual rpt, 1804–7

Cooperatives, finances, and membership, by type of service, commodity, and State, 1989, annual rpt, 1124–1

Cooperatives, memberships and sales, by State, 1989, article, 1122–1.202

Corn farms, finances, acreage, and production, by size, region, and State, 1987, 1568–304

Cotton acreage planted by State and county, and fiber quality, by variety, 1991, annual rpt, 1309–6

Cotton farms fertilizer, pesticide and irrigation use, soil conservation practices, and water quality impacts, 1989, 1588–151

Cotton fiber and processing test results, by variety, region, State, and production area, 1990, annual rpt, 1309–16

Cotton fiber grade, staple, and mike, for upland and American pima cotton by State, monthly rpt, 1309–11

Cotton fiber grade, staple, mike, and other quality indicators, for upland cotton by classing office, weekly rpt, 1309–15

Cotton ginning activity and charges, by State, 1990/91, annual rpt, 1564–3

Cotton ginnings and production, by State and county, 1990, annual rpt, 2344–1

Cotton ginnings, by State and county, seasonal biweekly rpt, 1631–19

Cotton ginnings, by State and county, seasonal monthly rpt, 2342–2

Cotton ginnings, by State, seasonal semimonthly rpt, 2342–1

Cotton quality, by State, 1990, annual rpt, 1309–7

Cotton, wool, and synthetic fiber production, prices, trade, and use, periodic situation rpt with articles, 1561–1

Cottonseed prices and quality, by State, seasonal weekly rpt, 1309–14

Cottonseed quality factors, by State, 1990 crop, annual rpt, 1309–5

Cranberry production, prices, use, and acreage, for selected States, 1989-90 and forecast 1991, annual rpt, 1621–18.4

Dairy cattle, milk production, and grain and other concentrates fed, by State, monthly rpt, 1627–1

Dairy production by commodity, and plants, by State, 1990, annual rpt, 1627–5

Dairy production by State, stocks, prices, and CCC price support activities, by product type, monthly rpt, 1627–3

Dairy production, prices, trade, and use, periodic situation rpt with articles, 1561–2

Disaster aid of USDA for producers of crops ineligible for price supports by State, and methodology, 1988-89, GAO rpt, 26113–533

Economic Indicators of the Farm Sector, balance sheets, and receipts by detailed commodity, by State, 1985-89, annual rpt, 1544–18

Egg production and layer inventory, by State, 1989-90, annual rpt, 1625–7

Emergency Conservation Program for farmland damaged by natural disaster, funding by region and State, monthly rpt, 1802–13

Employment on farms, wages, and hours, by payment method, worker type, region, and State, 1910-90, 1618–21

Employment on farms, wages, hours, and perquisites, by State, monthly rpt, 1631–1

Exports and imports (agricultural) of US, by commodity, country, and US port, 1950s-91, annual rpt, 1924–9

Farmland damaged by natural disaster, Emergency Conservation Program aid and participation by State, FY90, annual rpt, 1804–22

Farmland in US owned by foreigners, holdings, acquisitions, and disposals by land use, owner type and country, and State, 1990, annual rpt, 1584–2

Farmland in US owned by foreigners, holdings, acreage, and value by land use, owner country, State, and county, 1990, annual rpt, 1584–3

Farmland rental by assessment method, and rent receipts per acre and as share of land value by land type and State, 1960s-80s, 1548–377

Farms and acreage, by sales size, region, and State, 1989-91, annual rpt, 1614–4

Farms, production, acreage, and related data, by selected crop and State, monthly rpt, 1621–1

Fertilizer (inorganic) shipments, trade, use, and firms, by product and State, with stocks, 1990, annual Current Industrial Rpt, 2506–8.13

Fertilizer and pesticide use and application rates, by type, crop, and State, series, 1616–1

Fertilizer use and costs by type, and acreage harvested, by State, 1970s-90, biennial rpt, 9804–5

Fertilizer use, by type and State, 1989-90, annual rpt, 9804–30

Finances of farms, income, expenses, assets by type, and debt by lender, by State, 1990, article, 1541–1.212

Financial stress indicators for farms, operator quits, and loan problems and mediation, 1970s-90, 1598–272

Fish (catfish) raised on farms, inventory, stocks, and production, by major producer State, quarterly rpt, 1631–18

Fish (processed) production by location, and trade, by species and product, 1987-90, annual rpts, 2166–6

Fish (squid) catch, trade, consumption, and cold storage holdings, by country and species, 1963-90, 2166–19.10

Fish (trout) raised on farms, production, sales, prices, and losses, 1990-91, annual rpt, 1631–16

Fish catch, by species, use, region, State, and major port, 1980s-90, annual rpt, 2164–1.1

Fish hatcheries and farms, production, costs, prices, and sales, for catfish and trout, 1970s-91, semiannual situation rpt, 1561–15

Fish Hatchery Natl System activities and deliveries, by species, hatchery, and jurisdiction of waters stocked, FY90, annual rpt, 5504–10

Fishery employment, vessels, plants, and cooperatives, by State, 1989 and trends from 1970, annual rpt, 2164–1.10

Fishery mgmt and R&D, Fed Govt grants by project and State, and rpts, 1990, annual listing, 2164–3

Flour milling production by State, stocks, daily capacity, and exports by country, monthly Current Industrial Rpt, 2506–4.1

Flower and foliage plant production, marketing, and trade by country, by State, 1960s-88, 1568–293

Flower and foliage plant production, sales, prices, and growers, by crop and State, 1989-90 and planting planned 1991, annual rpt, 1631–8

FmHA activities, and loans and grants by program and State, FY90 and trends from FY70, annual rpt, 1184–17

FmHA loans and borrower supervision activities in farm and housing programs, by type and State, monthly rpt, 1182–1

FmHA loans, by type, borrower characteristics, and State, quarterly rpt, 1182–8

FmHA loans, by type, borrower race, and State, quarterly rpt, 1182–5

FmHA property acquired through foreclosure, value, acreage, and sales, for farm and nonfarm property by State, monthly rpt, 1182–6

FmHA property acquired through foreclosure, value, and acreage under conservation easements by State, 1989-90, GAO rpt, 26113–514

Food (processed) production and stocks by State, shipments, exports, ingredients, and use, periodic Current Industrial Rpt series, 2506–4

Food aid programs of USDA, costs and participation by program, FY69-89, annual rpt, 1364–9

Fruit (noncitrus) and nut production, prices, and use, by crop and State, 1988-90, annual rpt, 1621–18.1; 1621–18.3

Fruit and nut production, prices, trade, stocks, and use, by selected crop, periodic situation rpt with articles, 1561–6

Index by Categories

BY STATE

Fruit and vegetable production, imports by country, use, exports, and prices, by commodity, 1975-87, 1568–299

Fruit and vegetable shipments, and arrivals in US and Canada cities, by mode of transport and State and country of origin, 1990, annual rpt series, 1311–4

Fruit and vegetable shipments by mode of transport, arrivals, and imports, by commodity and State and country of origin, weekly rpt, 1311–3

Fruit and vegetable shipments by truck, monthly by State and country of origin, and rates weekly by growing area and market, 1990, annual rpt, 1311–15

Fruit and vegetable wholesale prices in NYC by State, and shipments and arrivals by mode of transport, by commodity, weekly rpt, 1311–20

Grain price support and loan programs operations of USDA, with farmers views on Federal programs, by region and State, 1990 hearings, 21168–43

Grain stocks on and off farms, by crop, quarterly rpt, 1621–4

Grain storage facility and equipment loans to farmers under CCC program, by State, FY68-91, annual table, 1804–14

Grain support loan programs of USDA, activity and status by grain and State, monthly rpt, 1802–3

Hay (alfalfa and prairie) prices, for selected areas, weekly rpt, 1313–5

Hogs inventory, value, farrowings, and farms, by State, quarterly release, 1623–3

Honey production, prices, stocks, and bee colonies, by State, 1989-90, annual rpt, 1631–6

Honey production, prices, trade, stocks, marketing, and CCC honey loan and distribution activities, monthly rpt, 1311–2

Irrigation projects of Reclamation Bur in western US, crop production and acreage by commodity, State, and project, 1989, annual rpt, 5824–12

Livestock grazing on natl forest lands, by region and State, 1990, annual rpt, 1204–5

Livestock inspected by Fed Govt, by type, weekly rpt, 1315–1

Livestock packers purchases and feeding, and livestock markets, dealers, and sales, by State, 1989, annual rpt, 1384–1

Livestock slaughter and meat production, by livestock type and State, monthly rpt, 1623–9

Livestock slaughter, meat production, and slaughter plants, by species and State, 1990, annual rpt, 1623–10

Meat and poultry inspection activities and staff of Federal, State, and foreign govts, FY90, annual rpt, 1374–1

Meat animal production, prices, receipts, and disposition, by species and State, 1988-90, annual rpt, 1623–8

Migrant workers and dependents by county, and health centers use and programs funding, by State, 1986-89, 4108–53

Milk order market prices and detailed operations, by State and market area, 1989-90, annual rpt, 1317–3

Milk order market sales, by container size and type, outlet type, and market area, 1989, biennial rpt, 1317–6

Milk production, use, and receipts, and milk cow inventory, by State, 1988-90, annual rpt, 1627–4

Mink and pelt production, prices, and farms, selected years 1969-91, annual rpt, 1631–7

Mint oil production, yield, and farm prices by State, and NYC spot prices, various periods 1988-91, FAS annual circular, 1925–15.2

Mushroom production, sales, and prices, by State, 1966/67-1990/91 and planned 1991/92, annual rpt, 1631–9

Operators entries and exits, by State, late 1970s-87, 1598–269

Peaches production, marketing, and prices in 3 southeastern States and Appalachia, 1990, annual rpt, 1311–12

Peanut production and US exports by country, prices, and stocks, weekly rpt, 1311–1

Peanut production, prices, stocks, exports, use, inspection, and quality, by region and State, 1980-90, annual rpt, 1311–5

Pest control integrated mgmt programs for vegetables, acreage, costs, savings, and funding sources and recipients, by State, 1980s, 1568–298

Potato production, acreage, disposition, prices, and trade, by State and country, 1949-90, 1568–305

Potato production, prices, stocks, and use, by State, 1981-90, annual rpt, 1621–11

Potato production, stocks, processing, yields, and harvest losses, by State, periodic rpt, 1621–10

Poultry (broiler) hatcheries eggs set and chicks placed, by State, weekly rpt, 1625–11

Poultry (chicken and turkey) hatchery production, 1989-90, annual rpt, 1625–8

Poultry (chicken, egg, and turkey) production and inventories, monthly rpt, 1625–1

Poultry (chicken, egg, and turkey) production and prices, by State, 1989-90, annual rpt, 1625–5

Poultry slaughtered under Fed Govt inspection, pounds certified, and condemnations by cause, by State, monthly rpt, 1625–3

Prices received and paid by farmers, by commodity and State, 1990, annual rpt, 1629–5

Prices received by farmers and production value, by detailed crop and State, 1988-90, annual rpt, 1621–2

Prices received by farmers for major products, and paid for farm inputs and living items, by State, monthly rpt, 1629–1

Production inputs, finances, mgmt, and land value and transfers, periodic situation rpt with articles, 1561–16

Pumpkin farms, production costs, shipments, and sales by State, prices, and imports by country, 1978-90, article, 1561–11.203

Research (agricultural) funding and staffing for USDA, State agencies, and other instns, by topic, FY90, annual rpt, 1744–2

Restaurant and drinking place occupational injury and illness rates, and workdays lost by State, 1989, article, 6722–1.231

Rice foreign and US production, prices, trade, stocks, and use, periodic situation rpt, 1561–8

Rice market activities, prices, inspections, sales, trade, supply, and use, for US and selected foreign markets, weekly rpt, 1313–8

Sheep, lamb, and goat inventory, by State, 1989-91, annual press release, 1623–4

Sheep, lamb, and goat loss to predators and other causes, by region and State, 1990, 1618–20

Small farms loans, defaults, income, and financial condition, 1980-89, article, 1502–7.202

South Central States agricultural banks financial ratios, and farm receipts by commodity, 1980s-90, annual article, 9391–16.209

Storage facility and equipment loans to farmers under CCC grain program, by State, monthly table, 1802–9

Sugar and sweeteners production, prices, trade, supply, and use, quarterly situation rpt with articles, 1561–14

Sugar production, acreage, yield, stocks, deliveries, and price by State, and trade by country, 1950s-90, 1568–306

Sugar production, trade, and use, quarterly rpt, 1621–28

Timber and orchard damage from natural disaster, USDA restoration aid and program participation by practice and State, FY89-90, annual rpt, 1804–24

Tobacco marketing activity, prices, and sales, by grade, type, market, and State, 1989-90, annual rpt series, 1319–5

Tobacco production, marketing, use, price supports, and trade, quarterly situation rpt with articles, 1561–10

Tobacco production, prices, stocks, taxes by State, and trade and production by country, 1990, annual rpt, 1319–1

Turkey production by State, and farms, by region, 1960s-90, article, 1561–7.202

Turkey production by State, and losses by region, 1989-90, and hatchery plans, 1991, annual rpt, 1625–6

USDA subagencies responsible for farm programs, field offices, funding, and staff, FY89, GAO rpt, 26113–507

Vegetable production, acreage, and yield, current and forecast for selected fresh and processing crops by State, periodic rpt, 1621–12

Vegetable production, prices, trade, stocks, and use, for selected fresh and processing crops, periodic situation rpt with articles, 1561–11

Vegetable production, value, and acreage, for selected fresh and processing crops by State, 1988-90, annual rpts, 1621–25

Wheat and rye acreage seeded, by State, 1989-91, annual rpt, 1621–30

Wheat and rye foreign and US production, prices, trade, stocks, and use, quarterly situation rpt with articles, 1561–12

Wool and mohair production and prices, by State, 1989-90, annual press release, 1623–6

Banking, Finance, and Insurance

Acquisitions and mergers of banks in Southeastern States, assets and major institutions involved, by State, 1984-89, article, 9371–1.203

Banks (insured commercial) assets, income, and financial ratios, by asset size and State, quarterly rpt, 13002–3

Banks (insured commercial) financial ratios, by State, 1986-89, annual rpt, 9294–4

Banks (insured commercial and savings) deposits by instn, State, MSA, and county, as of June 1990, annual regional rpt series, 9295–3

BY STATE

Banks (insured commercial and savings) finances, and changes in status, by State, 1989, annual rpt, 9294–4.1

Banks (insured commercial and savings) finances, by State, 1989, annual rpt, 9294–4

Banks (natl) charters, mergers, liquidations, enforcement cases, and financial performance, with data by instn and State, quarterly rpt, 8402–3

Banks and deposit insurance funds financial condition, potential losses, and regulatory issues, 1980s-90 and projected to 1995, 21248–147

Banks financial performance, for undercapitalized instns by State and inside-outside Texas, aggregate 1985-89, article, 9391–1.212

Credit unions federally insured, finances by instn characteristics and State, as of June 1991, semiannual rpt, 9532–6

Credit unions federally insured, finances, 1989-90, annual rpt, 9534–1

Credit unions in Fed Reserve 8th District, finances and members by State, 1984 and 1990, article, 9391–16.210

Foreign-owned banks US subsidiaries, assets, and regulatory issues, with data by State and firm, 1989-90, hearing, 21248–155

Fraud and abuse in banks and thrifts, Federal agencies enforcement activities and staff, with data by instn and location, 1988-90, hearing, 21408–119

Futures industry registered traders, by type and State, FY90, annual rpt, 11924–2

New England States economic indicators, Fed Reserve 1st District, monthly rpt, 9373–2

New England States, FHLB 1st District thrifts financial operations compared to banks, and housing industry indicators, bimonthly rpt with articles, 9302–4

New England States thrifts loan delinquency rates by loan type, time past due, thrift charter type, and State, 1990, annual article, 9302–4.202

North Central States business and economic conditions, Fed Reserve 9th District, quarterly journal, 9383–19

Partnerships (limited) conversion to corporations, and impacts on share values, with data by firm, 1980s-91, hearing, 25248–124

Savings instns failure resolution activity and finances of Resolution Trust Corp, with data by asset type, State, region, and instn, monthly rpt, 9722–3

Savings instns failure resolution activity of Resolution Trust Corp, with data by State and instn, and RTC financial statements, 1989, annual rpt, 9724–1

Savings instns failures, inventory of real estate assets available from Resolution Trust Corp, semiannual listing series, 9722–2

Savings instns finances and operations by district and State, mortgage loan activity and terms by MSA, and FHLB finances, 1989 and trends from 1965, annual rpt, 8434–3.2

Savings instns insured by Savings Assn Insurance Fund, finances by profitability group, district, and State, quarterly rpt, 8432–4

Southeastern States, Fed Reserve 5th District insured commercial banks financial statements, by State, quarterly rpt, 9389–18

Southeastern States, Fed Reserve 6th District banks financial ratios, by asset size and State, 1986-90, annual article, 9371–1.211

West Central States, Fed Reserve 10th District banking industry structure, performance, and financial devs, 1990, annual rpt, 9381–14

West Central States, FHLB 10th District thrifts, locations, assets, and deposits, 1991, annual listing, 9304–17

Communications and Transportation

Air traffic (passenger), and aircraft operations by type, by airport and State, projected FY91-2005 and trends from FY83, annual rpt, 7504–7

Air traffic (passenger and cargo), and departures by aircraft type, by carrier and airport, 1990, annual rpt, 7504–35

Air traffic (passenger and cargo), carrier enplanement shares, and FAA airport improvement program grants, by airport and State, 1989, annual rpt, 7504–48

Air traffic, carriers, craft, airports, and FAA activities, detailed data, 1980-89, annual rpt, 7504–1

Air traffic levels at FAA-operated control facilities, by airport and State, FY90, annual rpt, 7504–27

Aircraft (general aviation), flight hours, and equipment, by type, use, and model of aircraft, region, and State, 1990, annual rpt, 7504–29

Aircraft accidents and circumstances, for US operations of domestic and foreign airlines and general aviation, periodic rpt, 9612–1

Aircraft accidents, by State, 1988, annual rpt, 9614–3

Aircraft near collisions, by State, monthly rpt, annual data, 7502–15

Aircraft pilot and nonpilot certificates held, by type of certificate, age, sex, region, and State, 1990, annual rpt, 7504–2

Aircraft registered with FAA, by type and characteristics of aircraft, make, carrier, State, and county, 1989, annual rpt, 7504–3

Airport improvement program of FAA, activities and grants by State and airport, FY90, annual rpt, 7504–38

Airport improvement program of FAA, activities, funding, and airport operations, by location, projected 1990-99, biennial rpt, 7504–42

Airport planning and dev project grants of FAA, by airport and location, quarterly press release, 7502–14

Appalachia hwy system and access roads funding and completion status, by State, quarterly tables, 9082–1

Bus (school) accidents, circumstances, victim characteristics, and vehicle type, 1989, annual rpt, 7764–22

Bus connector service between rural areas and Greyhound intercity routes, finances and operations by system, 1987-90, 7888–79

Drivers licenses issued and in force by age and sex, fees, and renewal, by license class and State, 1989, annual rpt, 7554–16

FAA activities and finances, and staff by region, FY89-90, annual rpt, 7504–10

Index by Categories

Fed Hwy Admin traffic safety grants, by program and State, FY89, annual rpt, 7764–1.1

Hazardous material transport accidents, casualties, and damage, by mode of transport, with DOT control activities, 1989, annual rpt, 7304–4

Helicopters, use, and landing facilities, by craft type, region, and State, 1989, 7508–75

Hwy and mass transit funding and regulation by Fed Govt and States, FY91 with projections to FY96, 26358–242

Hwy construction bids and contracts for Federal-aid hwys, by State, 1st half 1991, semiannual rpt, 7552–12

Hwy construction material prices and indexes for Federal-aid system, by type of material and urban-rural location, quarterly rpt, 7552–7

Hwy construction material use by type, and spending, by State, various periods 1944-90, annual rpt, 7554–29

Hwy funding, costs, and completion status of Federal-aid system, by State, as of June 1991, semiannual rpt, 7552–5

Hwy safety program funding by State, and accident and death reductions, FY90, annual rpt, 7554–26

Hwy speed averages and vehicles exceeding 55 mph, by State, quarterly rpt, 7552–14

Hwy Statistics, detailed data by State, 1990, annual rpt, 7554–1

Hwy Statistics, summary data by State, 1989-90, annual rpt, 7554–24

Hwy traffic volume on rural roads and city streets, monthly rpt, 7552–8

Hwy Trust Fund finances, unobligated balances by State, and receipt losses from increased ethanol use, 1980s-90, hearing, 25328–31

Mail (express parcel) shipments and revenues of private air and surface carriers, and impact of State regulation, 1976-89, 7308–201

Pipeline accidents, casualties, safety enforcement activity, and Federal funding, by State, 1989, annual rpt, 7304–5

Railroad accidents, casualties, and damage, by cause, railroad, and State, 1990, annual rpt, 7604–1

Railroad accidents, casualties, and damage, Fed Railroad Admin activities, and safety inspectors by State, 1989, annual rpt, 7604–12

Railroad-hwy grade-crossing accidents, detailed data by State and railroad, 1989, annual rpt, 7604–2

Safety belt usage rates, by State, 1989, annual rpt, 7764–1

Shipborne commerce (domestic and foreign) of US, freight by port and State, 1989, annual rpt, 3754–7

Telephone firms borrowing under Rural Telephone Program, and financial and operating data, by State, 1990, annual rpt, 1244–2

Telephone firms borrowing under Rural Telephone Program, loan activity by State, FY90, annual tables, 1244–8

Telephone lines in residences and businesses, carriage equipment miles, and calls placed, by State, 1989, annual rpt, 9284–6.2

Telephone service subscribership, charges, and local and long distance firm finances and operations, late 1970s-91, semiannual rpt, 9282–7

Index by Categories

BY STATE

Traffic accidents impacts of speed limits, with accident circumstances and speed averages, for States with 55 and 65 mph limit, 1986-89, annual rpt, 7764–15

Traffic deaths by circumstances and State, drunk drivers involved in fatal accidents, and impacts of minimum age drinking laws, 1982-89, annual fact sheet, 7766–15.1

Traffic deaths by circumstances and State, drunk drivers involved in fatal accidents, and impacts of minimum age drinking laws, 1982-90, annual fact sheet, 7766–15.4

Traffic fatal accidents, circumstances, and characteristics of persons and vehicles involved, 1990, semiannual rpt, 7762–11

Traffic fatal accidents, deaths, and rates, by circumstances, characteristics of persons and vehicles involved, and location, 1989, annual rpt, 7764–10

Transportation census, 1987: finances and operations by size, ownership, and State, and revenues by MSA, by SIC 2- to 4-digit industry, 2579–1

Travel to US, by characteristics of visit and traveler, country, port city, and State of destination, quarterly rpt, 2902–1

Travel to US, by characteristics of visit and traveler, world area of origin, and US destination, 1990 survey, annual rpt, 2904–12

Travel to US, market research data available from US Travel and Tourism Admin, 1991, annual rpt, 2904–15

Truck accidents, casualties, and damage, by circumstances and characteristics of persons and vehicles involved, 1988, annual rpt, 7554–9

Truck and bus safety inspections, fines, and vehicles and drivers ordered out of service, by State, with program funding, FY89, 25268–78

Trucking industry deregulation by States, potential economic and market impacts, with background data, mid 1970s-80s, 7308–200

Urban Mass Transportation Admin grants for transit systems, by city and State, FY90, annual rpt, 7884–10

Education

American Historical Assn financial statements, and membership by State, 1989, annual rpt, 29574–2

Appalachia education system, improvement initiatives, and indicators of success, by State, 1960s-89, 9088–36

Bilingual education enrollment, and Education Dept activities and funding by program, by State, FY88-90, biennial rpt, 4804–14

Bilingual education programs enrollment, funding, and services, by State, FY85-89, series, 4808–20

Digest of Education Statistics, 1991 annual data compilation, 4824–2

Discrimination in education, indicators for service delivery and discipline, by State, 1988, biennial rpt, 4804–33

Educational attainment, by sociodemographic characteristics and location, 1989 and trends from 1940, biennial Current Population Rpt, 2546–1.452

Elementary and secondary education enrollment, staff, finances, operations, programs, and policies, 1987/88 biennial survey, series, 4836–3

Elementary and secondary education enrollment, teachers, high school grads, and spending, by instn control and State, 1990/91, annual rpt, 4834–19

Elementary and secondary public school agencies, by enrollment size and location, fall 1989, annual listing, 4834–1

Elementary and secondary public school systems enrollment, finances, staff, and high school grads, by State, FY88-89, annual rpt, 4834–6

Elementary and secondary public schools and enrollment, by State, 1989/90, annual rpt, 4834–17

Elementary and secondary public schools, enrollment, teachers, funding, and other characteristics, by region and State, 1988/89, annual rpt, 4834–20

Enrollment in public elementary and secondary schools, by State, 1980s-92, annual press release, 4804–19

Enrollment in public elementary and secondary schools, under alternative average daily attendance computation methods, by State, 1985-86, 4838–48

Financing of public elementary and secondary education systems, issues and indicators of school districts fiscal independence, 1960s-80s, 10048–78

Head Start enrollment, funding, and staff, FY90, annual rpt, 4604–8

Head Start handicapped enrollment, by handicap, State, and for Indian and migrant programs, 1987/88, annual rpt, 4604–1

Higher education enrollment, by student and instn characteristics, fall 1989, biennial rpt, 4844–2

Higher education enrollment, faculty, finances, and degrees, by instn level and control, and State, FY87, annual rpt, 4844–13

Higher education instn revenue by source and spending by function, by State and instn control, FY80-88, annual rpt, 4844–6

Historical Publications and Records Natl Commission grants, by State, FY90, annual rpt, 9514–2

Homeless adults educational services, funding, participation, and staff, by State, 1989, annual rpt series, 4804–39

Homeless children educational projects, activities, and funding, FY90, annual rpt, 4804–35

Humanities Natl Endowment activities and grants, FY90, annual rpt, 9564–2

Indian education funding of Fed Govt, and enrollment, degrees, and program grants and fellowships by State, late 1960s-FY89, annual rpt, 14874–1

Libraries (major urban resource centers) dev projects and funding, by city and State, FY84-88, listing, 4878–4

Libraries (public) English as second language programs and services, project descriptions and funding, by State, FY87, annual rpt, 4874–10

Libraries (public) finances, staff, and operations, by State and population size, 1989, annual rpt, 4824–6

Libraries for blind and handicapped, readership, circulation, staff, funding, and holdings, FY90, annual listing, 26404–3

Libraries technological aid, project descriptions and funding, FY89, annual listing, 4874–6

Library science training grants for disadvantaged students, by instn and State, FY90, annual listing, 4874–1

Math ability of elementary and secondary students, and factors affecting proficiency, by selected characteristics, 1990 natl assessments, 4896–8.1

Math ability of elementary and secondary students, by State and selected characteristics, 1990 natl assessments, 4896–8.2

Migrant workers children education programs enrollment, staff, and effectiveness, by State, 1980s, 4808–30

Natl Education Goals progress indicators, by State, 1991, annual rpt, 15914–1

Rural areas education spending per student, by State, 1920s-87, article, 1502–7.201

Special education programs, enrollment by age, staff, funding, and needs, by type of handicap and State, 1989/90, annual rpt, 4944–4

Student aid funding and participation, by Federal program, instn type and control, and State, various periods 1959-89, annual rpt, 4804–28

Student aid Pell grants and applicants, by tuition, income level, instn type and control, and State, 1989/90, annual rpt, 4804–1

Student guaranteed loan activity, by program, guarantee agency, and State, quarterly rpt, 4802–2

Student guaranteed loans, defaults, and collections, by type of loan, lender, and guarantee agency, with data by State and top lender, FY90, annual rpt, 4804–38

Student loans of Fed Govt in default, losses, and rates, by instn and State, as of June 1990, annual rpt, 4804–18

Student supplemental grants, loans, and work-study awards, Federal share by instn and State, 1991/92, annual listing, 4804–17

Teachers in higher education, salaries by faculty rank, sex, instn type and control, and State, 1989/90, annual rpt, 4844–8

Energy Resources and Demand

Coal, coke, and breeze supply, demand, prices, trade, and stocks, by end-use sector and State, quarterly rpt with articles, 3162–37

Coal leasing activity on Federal land, acreage, production, and reserves, by coal region and State, FY90, annual rpt, 5724–10

Coal production and mines by county, prices, productivity, miners, and reserves, by mining method and State, 1989-90, annual rpt, 3164–25

Coal production by State and region, trade, use, and stocks, weekly rpt, 3162–1

Coal production, labor hours, and production value, by State, EIA and alternative estimates, with methodology, 1983-88, 3166–12.6

Coal production, stocks, and shipments, by State of origin and destination, end-use sector, and mode of transport, quarterly rpt, 3162–8

Coal reserves, by type, region, and State, as of Jan 1990, annual rpt, 3164–74.1

Conservation aid of Fed Govt to public and nonprofit private instns, by building type and State, 1990, annual rpt, 3304–15

BY STATE

Conservation of energy, State programs aid from Fed Govt, and energy savings, by State, 1989, annual rpt, 3304–1

Consumption of energy, by detailed fuel type, end-use sector, and State, 1960-89, State Energy Data System annual rpt, 3164–39

DOE contracts and grants, by category, State, and for top contractors, FY90, annual rpt, 3004–21

Electric power plants (steam) fuel receipts, costs, and quality, by fuel, plant, utility, and State, 1990, annual rpt, 3164–42

Electric power plants and capacity, by fuel used, owner, location, and operating status, 1990 and for units planned 1991-2000, annual listing, 3164–36

Electric power plants certification applications filed with FERC, for small production and cogeneration facilities, FY80-90, annual listing, 3084–13

Electric power plants natural gas use, by State, 1977 and 1989, annual rpt, 3334–1

Electric power plants production, capacity, sales, and fuel stocks, use, and costs, by State, 1985-89, annual rpt, 3164–11

Electric power plants production, fuel use, stocks, and costs by fuel type, and sales, by State, monthly rpt with articles, 3162–35

Electric power sales and revenue, by end-use sector, consumption level, and utility, 1989, annual rpt, 3164–91

Electric power wholesale purchases of REA borrowers, by borrower, supplier, and State, 1940-89, annual rpt, 1244–5

Electric power wholesale trade, by utility, type of ownership, and region, 1988, biennial rpt, 3164–92

Electric utilities privately owned, finances and operations, detailed data, 1989, annual rpt, 3164–23

Fed Govt and Indian land oil, gas, and minerals production and revenue, by State, 1990 and trends from 1920, annual rpt, 5734–2

Fed Govt and Indian land oil, gas, and minerals production, revenue, and leasing, by State, 1980s and trends from 1920, 5738–21

Fuel oil and kerosene sales and deliveries, by end-use, PAD district, and State, 1989, annual rpt, 3164–94

Gasohol and ethanol tax subsidies, by State, as of Aug 1990, 3166–6.56

Gasohol sales, and tax rates on all motor fuels, by State, 1983-90, annual rpt, 3304–9

Gasohol use, by State, 1980-87, annual rpt, 3304–5.2

Gasoline and other motor fuel use and tax rates, by State, monthly rpt, 7552–1

Geothermal resources, power plant capacity and operating status, leases, and wells, by location, 1960s-94, 3308–87

Heating fuels production, imports, stocks, and prices, by selected PAD district and State, seasonal weekly rpt, 3162–45

Housing (low income) energy aid, funding sources, costs, and participation, by State, FY89, annual rpt, 4694–8

Housing (low income) energy aid, program characteristics by assistance type and State, FY90, annual rpt, 4694–9

Housing (low income) energy aid, State and Federal funding, FY86-89, GAO rpt, 26121–401

Inventions recommended by Natl Inst of Standards and Technology for DOE support, awards, and evaluation status, 1990, annual listing, 2214–5

Mineral industries census, 1987: energy use and costs, by fuel type, SIC 2- to 4-digit industry, and State, subject rpt, 2517–2

Natural and supplemental gas production, prices, trade, use, reserves, and pipeline company finances, by firm and State, monthly rpt with articles, 3162–4

Natural gas interstate pipeline company sales and contract deliveries, by firm and State, 1984-89, annual article, 3162–4.204

Natural gas production and wellhead capacity, by production area, 1980-89 and alternative forecasts 1990-91, biennial rpt, 3164–93

Nuclear power plant capacity, generation, and operating status, by plant and foreign and US location, 1990 and projected to 2030, annual rpt, 3164–57

Nuclear reactors for domestic use and export by function and operating status, with owner, operating characteristics, and location, 1990 annual listing, 3354–15

Offshore oil and gas leases, revenue sharing payments by State, 1991 annual press release, 5306–4.9

Offshore oil, gas, and minerals production, revenue, and leasing activity, for Federal OCS lands by ocean area and State, 1950s-90, annual rpt, 5734–3

Oil and refined products supply, demand, prices, and refinery capacity and stocks, by State, 1960-91, annual rpt, 3164–95

Oil bulk stations, sales and storage capacity by product, inventories, expenses, employment, and modes of transport, 1987 Census of Wholesale Trade, 2407–4.2

Oil crude, gas liquids, and refined products supply, demand, and movement, by PAD district and State, 1990, annual rpt, 3164–2

Oil, gas, and gas liquids reserves and production, by State and substate area, 1990, annual rpt, 3164–46

Oil products sales and purchases of refiners, processors, and distributors, by product, end-use sector, PAD district, and State, monthly rpt with articles, 3162–11

Oil, refined products, and gas liquids supply, demand, trade, stocks, and refining, by detailed product, State, and PAD district, monthly rpt with articles, 3162–6

Rural Electrification Admin loans, and borrower operating and financial data, by distribution firm and State, 1990, annual rpt, 1244–1

Rural Electrification Program lending, by State, FY90, annual rpt, 1244–7

Solar collector and photovoltaic module shipments by end-use sector and State, and trade, 1989, annual rpt, 3164–62

Southeastern Power Admin sales by customer, plants, capacity, and Southeastern Fed Power Program financial statements, FY90, annual rpt, 3234–1

Uranium reserves and industry operations, by region and State, various periods 1966-90, annual rpt, 3164–65.1

Western Area Power Admin activities by plant, financial statements, and sales by customer, FY90, annual rpt, 3254–1

Index by Categories

Geography and Climate

Earthquake intensity, time, location, damage, and seismic characteristics, for US and foreign earthquakes, 1985, annual rpt, 5664–13

Gazetteer of US places, mountains, bodies of water, and other political and physical features, 1990 rpt, 5668–117

Heating and cooling degree days weighted by population, by census div and State, with area-weighted temperature and precipitation, monthly rpt, 2152–13

Hurricanes and tropical storms frequency, intensity, deaths, and damage, by State and selected city, 1886-1989, 2188–15

Natl Ocean Service Charting and Geodetic Service activities and funding, by State, FY91-92, biennial rpt, 2174–10

Storms and unusual weather phenomena characteristics, casualties, and property damage, by State, monthly listing, 2152–3

Weather conditions and effect on agriculture, by US region, State, and city, and world area, weekly rpt, 2182–7

Government and Defense

Aliens (illegal) legal residence applications under Immigration Reform and Control Act, by selected characteristics, State, and country, periodic rpt, 6262–3

Aliens admitted to US on parole status, by world region, type of admission, and State, FY89, fact sheet, 6266–2.6

Appalachia local dev projects, and funding by source, by program and State, FY90, annual rpt, 9084–1

Assistance (formula grants) of Fed Govt, use of Census of Population data for allocation, and effects of data errors on funding, with data by program and State, FY91, GAO rpt, 26119–361

Budget of US, formula grant program obligations to State and local govts, by agency, program, and State, FY92, annual rpt, 104–30

Census of Govts, 1987: employment, payroll, and average earnings, by function, level of govt, State, county, and population size, 2455–2

Census of Govts, 1987: State and local govt employment, payroll, OASDHI coverage, and employee benefits costs, by level of govt and State, 2455–4

Census of Govts, 1987: State and local labor-mgmt policies, agreements, and coverage and bargaining units, by function, level of govt, and State, 2455–3

Collective bargaining agreements of Federal employees, coverage, unions, and location, by agency, for contracts expiring 1990-91, annual listing, 9847–1

Congressional apportionment and official population counts, by State, 1990 Census of Population, 2328–22

Congressional Directory, members of 102nd Congress, other officials, elections, and districts, 1991-92, biennial rpt, 23874–1

DOD appropriations for base construction and family housing, by facility, service branch, and location, FY90-93, annual rpt, 3544–39

DOD budget, organization, personnel, weapons, and property, by service branch, State, and country, 1991 annual summary rpt, 3504–13

Index by Categories

BY STATE

DOD budget requests for base construction, renovation, and land acquisition, by project, service branch, State, and country, FY92-93, annual rpt, 3544–15

DOD civilian and military personnel, by service branch and State, FY90, annual rpt, 3544–1.1

DOD contracts, payroll, and personnel, by service branch and location, with top 5 contractors and maps, by State and country, FY90, annual rpt, 3544–29

DOD prime contract awards, by category, contractor type, and State, FY88-90, annual rpt, 3544–11

DOD prime contract awards, by contractor, service branch, State, and city, FY90, annual rpt, 3544–22

DOD prime contract awards, by service branch and State, 1st half FY91, semiannual rpt, 3542–5

DOD prime contract awards in labor surplus areas, by service branch, State, and area, 1st half FY91, semiannual rpt, 3542–19

DOT employment, by subagency, occupation, and selected personnel characteristics, FY90, annual rpt, 7304–18

Election (presidential) campaign spending limits for candidates, and voting age population, by State, 1992 primary elections, press release, 9276–1.90

Election (senatorial) political party spending limits for candidates, and voting age population, by State, 1992 general elections, press release, 9276–1.92

Election campaign funds raised and spent by party committees, by State and party, 1989-90, press release, 9276–1.88

Election campaign receipts and spending of congressional candidates, by candidate and State, 1989-Dec 1990, press release, 9276–1.87

Election campaign receipts and spending of senatorial candidates, by party and State, 1991, press release, 9276–1.93

Election polling places accessibility to aged and disabled, precincts by barrier type and State, 1990 natl elections, biennial rpt, 9274–6

Employment (civilian) of Fed Govt, by work schedule, selected agency, State, and MSA, as of Dec 1990, biennial article, 9842–1.203

Employment and payroll (civilian) of Fed Govt, by pay system and location, 1990, annual rpt, 9844–6.6

Employment and payroll, by function, level of govt, and State, 1990, annual rpt, 2466–1.1

Fed Govt contract awards per capita, by State, 1980s-91, fact sheet, 2326–17.36

Fed Govt revenues by source and State, *Treasury Bulletin*, quarterly rpt, annual data, 8002–4.1

Fed Govt spending in States and local areas, by type, State, county, and city, FY90, annual rpt, 2464–3

Fed Govt spending in States, by type, program, agency, and State, FY90, annual rpt, 2464–2

Fed Govt tax provisions and receipts overview, by tax type, with background data, 1900s-91 and projected to 2000, 21788–197

Finances of govts, by level of govt, State, and for large cities and counties, annual rpt series, 2466–2

Finances, tax systems and revenue, and fiscal structure, by level of govt and State, 1991 and historical trends, annual rpt, 10044–1

Gasoline and other motor fuel tax provisions, auto registration fees, and disposition of receipts, by State, as of Jan 1991, biennial rpt, 7554–37

Gasoline and other motor fuel tax rates, by State, 1980-89, annual table, 7554–32

Insurance (health) coverage of Federal civilian employees, by plan, FY89, annual rpt, 9844–35.1

Local govt receipts from Fed Govt in lieu of property taxes on public lands, by State and county, FY91, annual rpt, 5724–9

Local govt receipts from Fed Govt in lieu of property taxes on public lands, by State, FY91, annual press release, 5306–4.10

Military active duty and recruit social, economic, and parents characteristics, by service branch and State, FY89, annual rpt, 3544–41

Military and civilian personnel, by service branch, major installation, and State, as of Sept 1990, annual rpt, 3544–7

Military base support costs by function, and personnel and acreage by installation, by service branch, FY91, annual rpt, 3504–11

Military deaths, by service branch and home State, FY90, annual rpt, 3544–40

Military draft registrants by State, FY90, annual rpt, 9744–1

Military pay and benefits for active duty personnel, reserves, retirees, and survivors, 1940s-80s and projected to 2049, 21208–34

Military reserve forces attrition, by reason, personnel characteristics, reserve component, and State, FY88, GAO rpt, 26123–329

Military reserve forces personnel strengths and characteristics, by component, FY90, annual rpt, 3544–38

Military reserve forces personnel strengths and characteristics, by component, quarterly rpt, 3542–4

Military spending reductions and base closings employment impacts, by region and State, 1988-89 and projected FY91-95, article, 9371–1.206

Minority group and women employment in State and local govt, by occupation, pay level, and State, 1990, annual rpt, 9244–6.5

Natl Guard activities, personnel, and facilities, FY90, annual rpt, 3504–22

Navy personnel strengths, accessions, and attrition, detailed statistics, quarterly rpt, 3802–4

New England States govt revenue and spending issues, with data by State, 1970s-80s, article, 9373–25.202

North Central States tax structure and revenue changes, 1980s, article, 9375–1.211

Payroll (civilian) of Fed Govt, by pay system and location, as of Mar 1991, annual article, 9842–1.205

Property (real) of Fed Govt, inventory and costs, worldwide summary by location, agency, and use, 1989, annual rpt, 9454–5

Property (real) of Fed Govt, leased inventory and rental costs, worldwide summary by location and agency, 1989, annual rpt, 9454–10

Senior Executive Service membership characteristics, entries, exits, and awards, FY79-90, annual rpt, 9844–36

State and local govt competition in taxes, services, regulation, and dev incentives, 1970-89, 10048–79

State and local govt spending measures using indicators of service costs and demand, with comparisons to fiscal capacity and actual outlays, by State, 1986-87, 10048–77

State and Metro Area Data Book, 1991 data compilation, 2328–54

Tax (excise) collections of IRS, by source, region, and State, quarterly rpt, annual table, 8302–1

Tax (income) returns filed by type of filer, selected income items, quarterly rpt, 8302–2.1

Tax (income) returns of individuals, selected income and tax items, by adjusted gross income and State, 1986-88, article, 8302–2.201

Tax amnesty programs of States for delinquent taxpayers, participation, collections, and costs, by tax type and State, 1980s-90, hearing, 21408–125

Tax collection, enforcement, and litigation activity of IRS, with data by type of tax, region, and State, FY90, annual rpt, 8304–3

Tax collections of IRS, by type of tax, State, and substate area, FY90, annual rpt, 8104–2.1

Tax collections of State govts by detailed type of tax, and tax rates, by State, FY90, annual rpt, 2466–2.7

Tax revenue, by level of govt, type of tax, State, and selected large county, quarterly rpt, 2462–3

Votes cast by party, candidate, and State, 1990 natl elections, biennial rpt, 9274–5

Voting and registration, by socioeconomic and demographic characteristics, 1990 congressional election, biennial Current Population Rpt, 2546–1.454

Western US State and local govt revenues and tax capacity, by source and State, 1988, article, 9381–1.204

Health and Vital Statistics

Abortions, by method, patient characteristics, and State, 1972-88, article, 4202–7.207

Abortions, by place of woman's residence and State of occurrence, 1988, US Vital Statistics annual rpt, 4146–5.120

AIDS cases by risk group, race, sex, age, State, and MSA, and deaths, monthly rpt, 4202–9

AIDS virus antibody tests and counseling sessions by setting, and CDC funding and funds uncommitted by State, 1989-90, GAO rpt, 26121–428

Alcohol, Drug Abuse and Mental Health Admin research grants and awards, by recipient, FY90, annual listing, 4044–13

Allergy and Infectious Diseases Natl Inst activities, grants by recipient and location, and disease cases, FY83-90, annual rpt, 4474–30

Asbestos in buildings, EPA aid for removal, occupational asbestos exposure cancer cases and deaths, and Catholic schools abatement costs, 1985-90, hearing, 25328–32

BY STATE

Index by Categories

Births and rates, by characteristics of birth, infant, and parents, 1989 and trends from 1940, US Vital Statistics advance annual rpt, 4146–5.123

Births and rates by mother's age, and fertility rates, by mother's education, child's race, census div, and State, 1980 and 1985, 4147–21.49

Black lung benefits and claims by State, trust fund receipts by source, and disbursements, 1990, annual rpt, 6504–3

Board and care homes regulation and rules enforcement by States, 1988, 4008–112

Cancer cases, deaths, and survival rates, by sex, race, age, and body site, 1973-88, annual rpt, 4474–35

Child accident deaths and death rates, by cause, age, sex, race, and State, 1980-85, 4108–54

Deaths and rates, by detailed cause and demographic characteristics, 1988 and trends from 1900, US Vital Statistics annual rpt, 4144–2

Dental Research Natl Inst research and training grants, by recipient, FY89, annual listing, 4474–19

Diabetes and complications cases, deaths, and hospitalization, by age, sex, race, State, and region, 1980-86, annual rpt, 4205–41

Diarrhea bacteria *Escherichia coli* testing by State labs, and isolates confirmed, 1988, 4202–7.204

Disabled persons rehabilitation, Federal and State activities and funding, FY90, annual rpt, 4944–1

Diving (underwater sport and occupational) deaths, by circumstances, diver characteristics, and location, 1970-89, annual rpt, 2144–5

Divorces by age of spouses and duration of marriage, and children involved, by State, 1988 and trends from 1940, US Vital Statistics advance annual rpt, 4146–5.121

Drug abuse prevalence among minorities, related health effects and crime, treatment, and research status and needs, mid 1970s-90, 4498–72

Drug and alcohol abuse treatment and prevention programs of States, funding, facilities, and patient characteristics, FY89, 4488–15

Drug and alcohol abuse treatment facilities, services, use, funding, staff, and client characteristics, 1989, biennial rpt, 4494–10

Drug and alcohol abuse treatment services, funding, staffing, and client load, characteristics, and outcomes, by setting, 1989 conf, 4498–73

Epidemiologists, education, specialties, and State govt employment, for southern US, 1989, article, 4042–3.253

Health condition and health care resources, use, and spending, 1950s-89, annual data compilation, 4144–11

Health maintenance organizations and other prepaid managed care plans Medicaid enrollment and use, for 20 States, 1985-89, chartbook, 4108–29

Heart, Lung, and Blood Natl Inst activities, and grants by recipient and location, FY90 and disease trends from 1940, annual rpt, 4474–15

Hepatitis cases by infection source, age, sex, race, and State, and deaths, by strain, 1988 and trends from 1966, 4205–2

HHS financial aid, by program, recipient, State, and city, FY90, annual regional listings, 4004–3

Hispanic Americans infant deaths, for 21 States, average 1979-81, 4147–20.18

Home health care services Medicare use and costs, by agency and service type, patient characteristics, and State, 1988-89, article, 4652–1.229

Hospitals in rural areas, closures related to selected factors, 1980s, GAO rpt, 26121–409

Hospitals in rural areas, HCFA grants for improving financial stability, by program area, recipient, and State, FY89, 4658–58

Infectious notifiable disease cases and current outbreaks, by region and State, weekly rpt, 4202–1

Infectious notifiable disease cases, by age, race, and State, and deaths, 1930s-90, annual rpt, 4204–1

Insurance (health) coverage, uninsured persons by employment and other characteristics and State, 1988, GAO rpt, 26121–403

Kidney end-stage disease cases, treatment, outcomes, and characteristics of patients, organ donors, and facilities, late 1970s-88, annual rpt, 4474–37

Kidney end-stage disease treatment facilities, Medicare enrollment and reimbursement, survival, and patient characteristics, 1983-89, annual rpt, 4654–16

Malaria cases in US, for military personnel and US and foreign natls, and by country of infection, 1966-89, annual rpt, 4205–4

Marriages and rates, by age, race, education, previous marital status, and State, 1988, US Vital Statistics advance annual rpt, 4146–5.122

Marriages, divorces, and rates, by characteristics of spouses, State, and county, 1987 and trends from 1920, US Vital Statistics annual rpt, 4144–4

Mental health care facilities, beds, and bed/population ratios, by instn type and State, 1986, 4506–3.41

Mental health care facilities, finances, caseload, staff, and characteristics of instn and patients, 1988, 4506–4.14

Mental health care facilities for emotionally disturbed children, use, funding, and characteristics of patients, staff, and instn, 1988, 4506–3.44

Mental health care facilities of States and counties, patients and admissions by age, diagnosis, and State, FY89, annual rpt, 4504–2

Mental health care facilities outlays, by function, instn type, funding source, and State, 1988, 4506–3.45

Mental health care facilities outpatient care programs, use, and client characteristics, by instn type and State, 1988, 4506–3.40; 4506–3.46

Mentally retarded persons care facilities and residents by selected characteristics, and use of Medicaid services and waiver programs, by State, late 1970s-80s, 4658–49

Mines (coal) and related operations occupational injuries and incidence, employment, and hours, 1989, annual rpt, 6664–4

Mines (metal) and related operations occupational injuries and incidence, employment, and hours, 1989, annual rpt, 6664–3

Mines (nonmetallic minerals) and related operations occupational injuries and incidence, employment, and hours, 1989, annual rpt, 6664–1

Mines (sand and gravel) and related operations occupational injuries and incidence, employment, and hours, 1989, annual rpt, 6664–2

Mines (stone) and related operations occupational injuries and incidence, employment, and hours, 1989, annual rpt, 6664–5

Mines and mills injuries by circumstances, employment, and hours, by type of operation and State, quarterly rpt, 6662–1

Mines safety and health enforcement, training, and funding, with casualties, by type of mine and State, FY89, annual rpt, 6664–6

NIH activities, funding by program and recipient type, staff, and clinic patients, by inst, FY90, annual rpt, 4434–3

NIH grants and contracts, for top 15 States, FY81-90, annual rpt, 4434–9

NIH grants for R&D, training, construction, and medical libraries, by location and recipient, FY90, annual listings, 4434–7

Occupational safety and health research and demonstration grants by State, and project listing, FY90, annual rpt, 4244–2

Physicians, by specialty, age, sex, and location of training and practice, 1989, State rpt series, 4116–6

Physicians consultations requested by attending physician, Medicare reimbursement issues, with use by diagnosis, specialty, location, and other characteristics, 1986, 4658–47

Physicians licensing and disciplinary activities of State medical boards, investigative staff, and licensing fees, by State, 1985-90, 4008–83

Physicians payments, charges by specialty and treatment setting, and assignment rate by State, for Medicare, 1970s-88, article, 4652–1.240

Physicians practice cost indexes and components, by State, MSA, and for rural areas, 1989 rpt, 4658–50

Radiation protection and health physics enrollment and degrees granted by instn and State, and grad placement, by student characteristics, 1990, annual rpt, 3004–7

Sexually transmitted disease cases and control activity, by strain, State, and selected city, 1940s-90, 4205–42

Smoking and smokeless tobacco use, attitudes, and smoking intervention research spending and results, with bibl, 1960s-90, 4478–195

Smoking bans in public places, local ordinances provisions, as of 1989, 4478–196

Smoking prevention, control, and surveillance activities and funding of States, and tobacco farm receipts, by State, 1989-90, 4206–2.47

Tuberculosis cases and deaths, by patient characteristics, State, and city, 1989 and trends from 1953, annual rpt, 4204–10

Index by Categories

BY STATE

Vital statistics, preliminary 1989-90 and trends from 1950, annual rpt, 4144–7

Vital statistics provisional data, monthly rpt, 4142–1

Water (bottled) quality standards of FDA, EPA, and States, with use in 12 States, 1990, GAO rpt, 26113–519

Workers compensation benefits and benefit duration, by State, 1990, biennial article, 4742–1.217

Workers compensation coverage and benefits, by type of program and insurer, and State, 1987-88, annual article, 4742–1.207

Workers compensation laws of States and Fed Govt, 1991 semiannual rpt, 6502–1

Workers compensation laws of States, changes in coverage, benefits, and premium rates, by State, 1990, annual article, 6722–1.210

Workers compensation programs of States, admin, coverage, benefits, finances, processing, and staff, 1987-90, annual rpt, 6504–9

Housing and Construction

Census of Construction Industries, 1987: finances and operations, by SIC 4-digit industry and State, final rpt series, 2373–1

Census of Housing, 1990: inventory, occupancy, and costs, State fact sheet series, 2326–21

Census of Population and Housing, 1990: housing units occupied and vacant, persons in group quarters, and household size, by region, census div, and State, press release, 2328–71

Census of Population and Housing, 1990: population and housing characteristics, households, and land area, by county, subdiv, and place, State rpt series, 2551–1

Census of Population and Housing, 1990: voting age and total population by race, and housing units, by block, redistricting counts required under PL 94-171, State CD-ROM series, 2551–6

Census of Population and Housing, 1990: voting age and total population by race, and housing units, by county and city, redistricting counts required under PL 94-171, State summary rpt series, 2551–5

Clay (construction) production and shipments by region and State, trade, and use, by product, quarterly Current Industrial Rpt, 2506–9.2

Community Dev Block Grant allocation, by State, county, and city, FY84-91, 5128–17

Construction authorized by building permits, by type of construction, region, State, and MSA, bimonthly rpt, 2042–1.3

Economic Dev Admin activities, and funding by program, recipient, State, and county, FY90 and cumulative from FY66, annual rpt, 2064–2

Fed Govt property acquired through foreclosure and savings instn failure, 1-family homes inventory by State, acquisition costs, and sales, for 4 agencies, 1986-90, GAO rpt, 26113–513

FmHA property acquired through foreclosure, 1-family homes, value, sales, and leases, by State, monthly rpt, 1182–7

Homeless aid organizations donations of surplus Federal property by State, and compared to other recipients, FY87-80, GAO rpt, 26113–538

Homeless persons housing and food aid of Fed Govt, funding and operations, with data by State and county, FY89, hearing, 25408–111

Homeownership rates, changes by State, and for householders under age 35 by region, 1980s, fact sheet, 2326–17.28

Hotels and other lodging places, receipts, payroll, employment, ownership, and rooms, by State and MSA, 1987 Census of Service Industries, subject rpt, 2393–3

Low income housing dev tax credits, and units constructed, by selected project and State, 1987-89, hearings, 25248–120

Low income housing supply impacts of HUD programs to maintain supply and to deter insured mortgage prepayment, 1986-90 and projected to 2005, GAO rpt, 26131–84

Mobile home placements by structural characteristics, and price, by census div and State, monthly rpt, annual tables, 2382–1

Mobile home shipments from manufacturers, by State, monthly rpt, quarterly table, 2382–5

Mortgage originations, by State, 1978-89, annual press release, 5144–21

Mortgages FHA-insured, financial, property, and mortgagor characteristics, by State, 1990, annual rpt, 5144–1

Mortgages FHA-insured, financial, property, and mortgagor characteristics, total and by State and outlying area, 1990, annual rpt, 5144–25

New England States economic indicators, Fed Reserve 1st District, monthly rpt, 9373–2.6

New housing units authorized, by region, State, selected MSA, and permit-issuing place, monthly rpt, 2382–5

New housing units authorized, by State, MSA, and permit-issuing place, 1990, annual rpt, 2384–2

Rural areas housing loan programs of FmHA, and housing voucher demonstration program results, 1980s, hearing, 21248–143

Southeastern States, FHLB 4th District, employment and housing and mortgage market indicators by State, quarterly rpt, 9302–36

Vacant housing characteristics, and occupancy and vacancy rates, by tenure and location, 1960s-90, annual rpt, 2484–1

Industry and Commerce

Appalachian Regional Commission funding, by project and State, planned FY91, annual rpt, 9084–3

Chemicals (inorganic) production by State, shipments, trade, and use, by product, 1990, annual Current Industrial Rpt, 2506–8.14

County Business Patterns, 1988: employment, establishments, and payroll, by SIC 2- to 4-digit industry and county, annual State rpt series, 2326–6

County Business Patterns, 1989: employment, establishments, and payroll, by SIC 2- to 4-digit industry and county, annual State rpt series, 2326–8

Enterprise Statistics, 1987: auxiliaries of multi-establishment firms, finances and operations by function, industry, and State, 2329–6

Enterprise Statistics, 1987: finances and operations for companies, by size, level of diversification, form of organization, and industry group, 2329–8

Explosives and blasting agents use, by type, industry, and State, 1990, Mineral Industry Surveys, annual rpt, 5614–22

Exports of States by industry and country, data compilation, monthly CD-ROM, 2002–6

Foreign direct investment in US commercial real estate, by State and country, 1980s, GAO rpt, 26123–350

Foreign direct investment in US, major transactions by type, industry, country, and US location, 1989, annual rpt, 2044–20

Foreign trade zones (US) operations and movement of goods, by zone and commodity, FY88, annual rpt, 2044–30

Great Lakes area economic conditions and outlook, for US and Canada, 1970s-90, 9375–15

Gross State product impact of foreign labor productivity and dollar exchange rate, by industry sector and State, 1972-86, working paper, 9387–8.255

Japan manufacturing firms US affiliates, employment, and wages, by selected industry and State, 1980s, 2048–151

Lumber (industrial roundwood) production for North Central States, by product and county, State rpt series, 1206–10

Lumber (industrial roundwood) production in northeastern US, by product, State rpt series, 1206–15

Lumber (pulpwood) production by county, and mill capacity by firm, by southern State, 1989, annual rpt, 1204–23

Lumber (pulpwood) production by species and county, and shipments, by northeastern State, 1989, annual rpt, 1204–18

Lumber (pulpwood and residue) prices, spending, and transport shares by mode, for southeast US, 1988-89, annual rpt, 1204–22

Lumber (veneer) receipts, production, and shipments, by species and southern State, with residue use, 1988, 1208–43

Lumber (veneer log) production, mill receipts, and trade, by species, with residue use, for North Central States, 1988, quadrennial rpt, 1208–220

Lumber production by State, trade and use, by species, with mill stocks, 1990, annual Current Industrial Rpt, 2506–7.4

Lumber production, prices by region and State, trade by country, and use, by species and product, 1960-88, annual rpt, 1204–29

Lumber production, prices, trade, and employment, for northwestern US and British Columbia, quarterly rpt, 1202–3

Manufacturing annual survey, 1989: finances and operations, by SIC 2- and 3-digit industry and State, 2506–15.3

Manufacturing census, 1987: finances and operations, by SIC 2- to 4-digit industry, State, and MSA, with trends from 1849, 2497–1

Manufacturing exports, by State, alternative estimates, 1986-87, article, 9391–1.219

Manufacturing industries operations and performance, analytical rpt series, 2506–16

Manufacturing output of Middle Atlantic and East North Central census divs relative to US, by industry and State, alternative estimates 1963 and 1986, working paper, 9375–13.59

BY STATE

Index by Categories

Mexico imports from US, by industry and State, 1987-90, 2048–154

Mineral industries census, 1987: finances and operations, by establishment characteristics, SIC 2- to 4-digit industry, and State, subject rpt, 2517–1

Mineral industries census, 1987: finances and operations, by SIC 2- to 4-digit industry, State, and county, census div rpt series, 2515–1

Mineral Industry Surveys, commodity reviews of production, trade, stocks, and use, monthly rpt series, 5612–1

Mineral Industry Surveys, commodity reviews of production, trade, stocks, and use, quarterly rpt series, 5612–2

Mineral Industry Surveys, commodity reviews of production, trade, use, and industry operations, advance annual rpt series, 5614–5

Mineral Industry Surveys, State reviews of production, 1990, preliminary annual rpt, 5614–6

Minerals Yearbook, 1989, Vol 1: commodity reviews of production, reserves, supply, use, and trade, annual rpt series, 5604–15

Minerals Yearbook, 1989, Vol 2: State reviews of production and sales by commodity, and business activity, annual rpt series, 5604–16

Minerals Yearbook, 1989, Vol 2: State reviews of production, sales, and firms, by commodity, and business activity, annual rpt, 5604–34

Minerals Yearbook, 1990, Vol 1: commodity reviews of production, reserves, supply, use, and trade, annual rpt series, 5604–20

Minority Business Dev Centers mgmt and financial aid, and characteristics of businesses, by region and State, FY90, annual rpt, 2104–6

Multinatl firms US affiliates, finances, and operations, by industry, world area of parent firm, and State, 1988-89, annual rpt, 2704–4

Multinatl firms US affiliates, investment trends and impact on US economy, 1991 annual rpt, 2004–9

New England States economic indicators, Fed Reserve 1st District, monthly rpt, 9373–2

North Central States business and economic conditions, Fed Reserve 9th District, quarterly journal, 9383–19

North Central States industry diversification, and employment and output relation to natl economic conditions, by industry and State, 1950s-89, working paper, 9375–13.63

Retail trade census, 1987: finances and employment, for establishments with and without payroll, by SIC 2- to 4-digit kind of business, State, and MSA, 2401–1

Retail trade sales and inventories, by kind of business, region, and selected State, MSA, and city, monthly rpt, 2413–3

Service industries census, 1987: establishments, receipts by source, payroll, and employment, by SIC 2- to 4-digit kind of business, State, and MSA, 2393–4

Shoe production, shipments, trade, and use, by product, 1990, annual Current Industrial Rpt, 2506–6.8

Small business dev centers mgmt and technical aid activities, funding, and client satisfaction and performance, 1980s, hearing, 25728–43

Small Business Investment Companies capital holdings, SBA obligation, and ownership, as of July 1991, semiannual listing, 9762–4

Southeastern States, Fed Reserve 5th District, economic indicators by State, quarterly rpt, 9389–16

Southeastern States, Fed Reserve 6th District, economic indicators by State and MSA, quarterly rpt, 9371–14

Southeastern States, Fed Reserve 8th District banking and economic conditions, quarterly rpt with articles, 9391–16

State and Metro Area Data Book, 1991 data compilation, 2328–54

Statistical Abstract of US, 1991 annual data compilation, 2324–1

Textile mill production, trade, sales, stocks, and material used, by product, region, and State, periodic Current Industrial Rpt series, 2506–5

Vending facilities run by blind on Federal and non-Federal property, finances and operations by agency and State, FY90, annual rpt, 4944–2

West Central States economic indicators, Fed Reserve 10th District, quarterly rpt, 9381–16.2

Labor and Employment

Collective bargaining agreements expiring during year, and workers covered, by firm, union, industry group, and State, 1991, annual rpt, 6784–9

Employment and Earnings, detailed data, monthly rpt, 6742–2.5; 6742–2.6; 6742–2.8

Employment and unemployment, by age, sex, race, marital and family status, industry div, and State, Monthly Labor Review, 6722–1.2

Employment and unemployment, for 11 large States, monthly press release, 6742–5

Employment by industry and State, impacts of decline in employers voluntary reporting on Continuous Work History Sample, 1970s-86, article, 4742–1.203

Employment over business cycles, by census div and State, 1988-92, release, 9538–8

Employment programs, training, and unemployment compensation, current devs and grants to States, press release series, 6406–2

Employment, unemployment, and labor force characteristics, by State, 1990, annual rpt, 6744–7.2

Exports and export-related employment, by SIC 3-digit industry and State, model results, 1987, annual rpt, 2506–16.1

Fair Labor Standards Act admin, with coverage under minimum wage and overtime provisions, and illegal employment of minors, by industry div, FY89, annual rpt, 6504–2.1

Job Training Partnership Act participation by selected characteristics and State, and outcomes, by urban-rural location, 1987-88, 1598–267

Labor Dept activities and funding, by program and State, FY90, annual rpt, 6304–1

Labor-mgmt mediation and arbitration activities of Fed Mediation and Conciliation Service, and cases by issue, region, and State, FY84-89, annual rpt, 9344–1

Labor Relations Natl Board activities, cases, elections conducted, and litigation, FY89, annual rpt, 9584–1

Middle Atlantic States economic conditions, Fed Reserve 3rd District, quarterly rpt, 9387–10

New England States economic indicators, Fed Reserve 1st District, monthly rpt, 9373–2.2

New England States employment and personal income growth rates, and unemployment, by State, 1989-90 and projected to 1993, semiannual article, 9302–4.201; 9302–4.203

New England States employment variability relation to service and financial industries employment, with data by selected industry group and State, 1970s-89, article, 9373–1.212

Southeastern States, FHLB 4th District, employment and housing and mortgage market indicators by State, quarterly rpt, 9302–36

Southeastern US employment and unemployment, for 8 States, 1989-90, annual rpt, 6944–2

Southeastern US employment by industry div, earnings, and hours, for 8 States, quarterly press release, 6942–7

Southeastern US employment conditions, with comparisons to other regions, press release series, 6946–3

Southeastern US textile mill employment, earnings, and hours, for 8 States, quarterly press release, 6942–1

Southwestern US employment by industry div, earnings, and hours, by State, monthly rpt, 6962–2

Tax credit for hiring from groups with high unemployment rates, participation by State, and effectiveness, FY88, GAO rpt, 26121–407

Technology-intensive employment by region and State, and earnings, by industry group, 1989, article, 6722–1.235

Textile production workers and wages by occupation, and benefits, by location, 1990 survey, 6787–6.251

Trade adjustment aid for workers, petitions by disposition, selected industry, union, and State, monthly rpt, 6402–13

Unemployment, by State and metro area, monthly press release, 6742–12

Unemployment, employment, and labor force, by region and State, 1989-90, press release, 6726–1.37

Unemployment, employment, and labor force, by State, MSA, and city, monthly rpt, 6742–22

Unemployment insurance benefits and benefit duration, by State, 1991, biennial article, 4742–1.217

Unemployment insurance claims and covered unemployment by program, and extended benefit triggers, by State, weekly rpt, 6402–15

Unemployment insurance claims, by program, weekly press release, 6402–14

Unemployment insurance coverage of establishments, employment, and wages, by SIC 4-digit industry and State, 1990, annual rpt, 6744–16

Unemployment insurance laws of States, comparison of provisions, 1991, base edition with semiannual revisions, 6402–2

Unemployment insurance programs of States and Fed Govt, benefits adequacy, and work disincentives, series, 6406–6

Index by Categories

BY STATE

Unemployment insurance programs of States, benefits, coverage, and tax provisions, as of Jan 1991, semiannual listing, 6402–7

Unemployment insurance programs of States, finances, operations, tax provisions, and vulnerability to recessions, 1970s-90s, hearing, 21788–201

Unemployment insurance programs of States, quality appraisal results, FY90, annual rpt, 6404–16

Unemployment insurance trust funds financial condition, by State, monthly rpt, 8102–9.16

Unions reporting to Labor Dept, parent bodies and locals by location, 1990 listing, 6468–17

Vocational rehabilitation cases of State agencies, by disposition and State, FY90 and trends from FY21, annual rpt, 4944–5

Vocational rehabilitation programs of Fed Govt and States, activities and funding, FY90, annual rpt, 4944–1

Wages of workers covered by unemployment insurance, by State and industry div, 1989-90, annual press release, 6784–17.1

Law Enforcement

Alien workers (unauthorized) and Fair Labor Standards Act employer compliance, hiring impacts, and aliens overstaying visas by country and State, 1986-90, annual rpt, 6264–6

Aliens (illegal) overstaying visas, by class of admission, mode of arrival, age, country, and State, FY85-88, annual rpt, 6264–5

Aliens (illegal) overstaying visas, by State of sojourn and world area of origin, 1985-88, fact sheet, 6266–2.1

Assaults and deaths of law enforcement officers, by circumstances, agency, victim and offender characteristics, and location, 1990, annual rpt, 6224–3

Asset forfeiture programs of Justice Dept and Customs Service, finances, and disbursements by State and judicial district, FY85-90, hearing, 25408–112

Banks and thrifts fraud and abuse, Federal criminal enforcement activities, case dispositions, and settlements, with data by district, 1982-90, hearing, 21248–142

Bombing incidents, casualties, and damage, by target, circumstances, and State, 1990, annual rpt, 6224–5

Child abuse and neglect victims representation in legal proceedings, caseloads, State requirements, and compensation, by State and county, 1989, 4608–28

Child abuse reports, and related deaths, by State, late 1980s, hearing, 25548–102

Court-annexed arbitration for civil cases, pilot program evaluation, 1984-86, 18408–46

Court caseloads, actions, procedure duration, judges, and jurors, by Federal district and appeals court, 1986-91, annual rpt, 18204–3

Court civil and criminal caseloads for Federal district, appeals, and bankruptcy courts, by type of suit and offense, circuit, and district, 1990, annual rpt, 18204–11

Court civil and criminal caseloads for Federal district, appeals, and special courts, 1990, annual rpt, 18204–8

Court civil and criminal caseloads for Federal district, appeals, and special courts, 1991, annual rpt, 18204–2

Court criminal cases in Federal district courts, by offense, disposition, and district, 1980-90, last issue of annual rpt, 18204–1

Crime, criminal justice admin and enforcement, and public opinion, data compilation, 1991 annual rpt, 6064–6

Crimes, arrests by offender characteristics, and rates, by offense, and law enforcement employees, by population size and jurisdiction, 1990, annual rpt, 6224–2

Criminal case processing in Federal district courts, and dispositions, by offense, district, and offender characteristics, 1986, annual rpt, 6064–29

Criminal justice spending, employment, and payroll, by level of govt, State, and selected city and county, FY71-88, biennial rpt, 6064–9

Criminal justice spending, employment, and payroll, by level of govt, State, and selected city and county, 1984-86, biennial rpt, 6064–4

Drug abuse and trafficking reduction grant programs and funding, by Federal agency and State, FY90-92, 236–1.5

Drug abuse treatment, prevention, and enforcement grants to States, by Federal agency and State, FY87-91, 236–1.4

Drug and alcohol abuse in rural areas, related crime, and treatment, with comparisons to nonrural areas, by substance and State, 1988-90, GAO rpt, 26131–79

Drug control task forces enforcement activities by drug type and State, and organization, staff, and spending, 1988, 6068–244

Drug enforcement support activities of Natl Guard, spending and needs by State, FY89-91, GAO rpt, 26123–343

Executions since 1930, and prisoners under death sentence by prison control and prisoner characteristics, by State, 1973-90, annual rpt, 6066–25.42

Firearm purchasers criminal records checks, and firearms use in crime, with data by State, 1987-90, 26358–244

Jail adult and juvenile population, employment, spending, instn conditions, and inmate programs, by county and facility, 1988, regional rpt series, 6068–144

Juvenile correctional and detention public and private instns, inmates, and expenses, by instn and resident characteristics and State, 1987, biennial rpt, 6064–13

Juvenile courts delinquency cases, by offense, referral source, disposition, age, sex, race, State, and county, 1988, annual rpt, 6064–12

Juvenile facilities, population, and costs, by facility and resident characteristics, region, and State, 1985-89, biennial rpt, 6064–5

Juvenile status offender detentions in secure facilities, and States compliance with Federal policies to reduce detentions, 1983-89, GAO rpt, 26119–333

Lawyers for defense, subpeonas by Federal prosecutors, and public and private indigent defense lawyers pay by State, 1986-90, hearing, 21408–123

Marijuana crop eradication activities of DEA and local agencies by State, and drug potency and prices, 1982-90, annual rpt, 6284–4

Office of Justice Programs activities and funding, FY90, annual rpt, 6064–18

Older persons abuse and neglect by circumstances and characteristics of abuser and victim, and States protective services budgets and staff, by location, 1980s, hearing, 21148–62

Parole and probation population, entries, and exits, by State, 1989, annual rpt, 6066–25.34

Pretrial processing, detention, and release, for Federal offenders, by defendant characteristics and district, 1988, hearing, 25528–114

Prisoner admissions by State and for Federal instns, by race, 1926-86, 6068–245

Prisoners, characteristics, and movements, by State, 1989, annual rpt, 6064–26

Prisoners in Federal and State instns by sex, admissions, and instn capacity and overcrowding, by State, 1980s-90, annual rpt, 6066–25.37

Prisoners in Federal and State instns, by sex and State, June 1991, semiannual rpt, 6062–4

Prisoners rehabilitation shock incarceration programs participation and operations, for 14 States, 1990, 6064–32

Prisons and jails operated under private contract, costs and characteristics of instns, by facility and State, 1990, GAO rpt, 26119–321

Rapes reported, by State, 1989-90, 25528–116

Records (criminal) repository characteristics, holdings, use, and reporting requirements, by State, 1989, 6068–241

Sentences for Federal crimes, guidelines use and results by offense and district, and Sentencing Commission activities, 1990, annual rpt, 17664–1

US attorneys case processing and collections, by case type and Federal district, FY90, annual rpt, 6004–2

US attorneys staffing disparities among district offices, and caseload by litigation type, FY87-90, GAO rpt, 26119–323

Victims of crime, compensation and support service applications by disposition, and grant funding by State, 1986-91, GAO rpt, 26119–348

Wiretaps authorized, costs, arrests, trials, and convictions, by offense and jurisdiction, 1990, annual rpt, 18204–7

Natural Resources, Environment, and Pollution

Birds (bald eagle) Great Lakes population, breeding, and research status, 1990 conf, 14648–26

Birds (duck) breeding population, by species, State, and Canada Province, 1990-91 and trends from 1955, annual rpt, 5504–30

Birds (mourning dove) population, by hunting and nonhunting State, 1966-91, annual rpt, 5504–15

Birds (sandhill crane) hunting activity and permits, by State and county, 1989/90-1990/91, annual rpt, 5504–31

Birds (waterfowl) hunter harvest, age and sex ratios by species, State, and flyway, 1986-90, annual rpt, 5504–32

Birds (waterfowl) hunter harvest and unretrieved kills, and duck stamps sold, by species, State, Canada Province, and flyway, 1989-90, annual rpt, 5504–28

BY STATE — Index by Categories

Birds (waterfowl) population, habitat conditions, and migratory flight forecasts, for Canada and US by region, 1991 and trends from 1955, annual rpt, 5504–27

Birds (woodcock) population in US and Canada from 1968, and hunter harvest, by State, 1991, annual rpt, 5504–11

Carbon dioxide in atmosphere, North Central States economic and agricultural impacts, model descriptions and results, 1980s and projected to 2030, 3006–11.15

Coal Surface Mining Reclamation and Enforcement Office activities and funding, by State and Indian tribe, FY90, annual rpt, 5644–1

Coastal and riparian areas environmental conditions, fish, wildlife, use, and mgmt, for individual ecosystems, series, 5506–9

Containers (beverage) natl deposit law proposal, public views, with State deposit laws effectiveness, 1970s-89, GAO rpt, 26113–494

Electric utilities privately owned, air pollution emissions and abatement equipment by fuel type and State, 1985-89, annual rpt, 3164–11.5

Endangered animals and plants population status and mgmt activity, by species, 1990, biennial rpt, 5504–35

Environmental Quality, status of problems, protection programs, research, and intl issues, 1991 annual rpt, 484–1

EPA pollution control grant program activities, monthly rpt, 9182–8

Fish (striped bass) stocks status on Atlantic coast, and sport and commercial catch by State, 1979-88, annual rpt, 5504–29

Fish and Wildlife Service restoration and hunter safety funding, by State, FY92, semiannual press release, 5502–1

Fish and Wildlife Service restoration programs finances by State, and excise tax collections, FY90, annual rpt, 5504–13

Fish and Wildlife Service restoration programs funding, land purchases, and project listing, by State, FY89, annual rpt, 5504–1

Fish kills in coastal areas related to pollution and natural causes, by land use, State, and county, 1980s, 2178–32

Fishery research of State fish and wildlife agencies, federally funded projects and costs by species and State, 1990, annual listing, 5504–23

Forest fires and acres burned on Forest Service land, by cause, forest, and State, 1989, annual rpt, 1204–6

Forest Service activities and finances, by region and State, FY90, annual rpt, 1204–1

Forest Service mgmt of public lands and resources dev, environmental, economic, and social impacts of alternative programs, projected to 2040, 1208–24

Forest wildlife habitat characteristics in northeastern US, by location, State rpt series, 1206–44

Forests (natl) and other lands under Forest Service mgmt, acreage by forest and location, 1990, annual rpt, 1204–2

Forests (natl) revenue, by source, forest, and State, FY90, annual rpt, 1204–34

Forests (natl) revenue share paid to States, and acreage, by forest, region, county, and congressional district, FY90, annual rpt, 1204–33

Global climate change environmental, infrastructure, and health impacts, with model results and background data, 1850s-2100, 9188–113

Great Lakes wastewater treatment by municipal and industrial facilities, releases, methods, effectiveness, pollutant limits, and enforcement, 1985-88, 14648–24

Hazardous substances industrial releases, accuracy of EPA reporting, and nonreporting facilities by State and industry, 1987-90, GAO rpt, 26113–532

Hazardous waste site remedial action under Superfund, current and proposed sites descriptions and status, periodic listings, series, 9216–3

Hazardous waste site remedial action under Superfund, current and proposed sites priority ranking and status by location, series, 9216–5

Helium and other components of natural gas, analyses of individual wells and pipelines, 1917-90, annual rpt, 5604–2

Helium resources in storage and natural gas reserves, by State, 1950-89 and projected to 2020, biennial rpt, 5604–44

Horse and burro wild herd areas in western States, population, adoption, and mgmt costs, as of FY89, biennial rpt, 5724–8

Land acreage, by use, ownership, and State, 1987 and trends from 1910, 1588–48

Land acreage by use, soil and water conditions, and conservation needs, for non-Federal holdings, 1987, State rpt series, 1266–5

Land Mgmt Bur activities and funding by State, FY89, annual rpt, 5724–13

Land Mgmt Bur activities in Southwestern US, FY90, annual rpt, 5724–15

Land subsidence above coal mines, State property insurance program income and expenses in 6 States, 1990, GAO rpt, 26113–530

Landfills distance from wetlands and water habitats, for 11 States, 1990 rpt, 9188–115

Marine mammals research, Federal funding by topic, recipient, and agency, FY90, annual rpt, 14734–2

Military installations hazardous waste site remedial action, activities and funding by site and State, FY90, annual rpt, 3544–36

Minerals (industrial) reserves, production, and use, and characteristics of individual deposits, State rpt series, 5606–10

Minerals production and revenue on Federal and Indian land, by State, 1980s and trends from 1920, 5738–21

Minerals production and revenue on Federal and Indian land, by State, 1990 and trends from 1920, annual rpt, 5734–2

Minerals resources and availability on public lands, State rpt series, 5606–7

Public lands acreage and use, and Land Mgmt Bur activities and finances, annual State rpt series, 5724–11

Public lands acreage, grants, use, revenues, and allocations, by State, FY90 and trends, annual rpt, 5724–1

Radiation and radionuclide concentrations in air, water, and milk, monitoring results by State and site, quarterly rpt, 9192–5

Radioactive low-level waste disposal activities of States and interstate compacts, with data by disposal facility and reactor, 1989, annual rpt, 3354–14

Radioactive spent fuel discharges, storage capacity, and inventories, by reactor, 1968-89, 3166–6.55

Radioactive waste and spent fuel generation, inventory, and disposal, 1960s-89 and projected to 2020, annual rpt, 3364–2

Reservoirs capacity and area, by reservoir and State, 1988, 5668–120

Sheep (desert bighorn) population and mgmt on public land, by State, 1989 rpt, 5728–36

Timber acreage, by ownership, forest type, and State, 1950s-87 and projected to 2040, 1208–357

Timber and orchard damage from natural disaster, USDA restoration aid and program participation by practice and State, FY89-90, annual rpt, 1804–24

Timber and planting and dev, by State, FY90, annual rpt, 1204–7

Timber improvement program for private land, Fed Govt cost-sharing funds by region and State, monthly rpt, 1802–11

Timber improvement program for private land, participation and payments by State, FY90, annual rpt, 1804–20

Timber in New England, acreage and resources by State, 1982-85, pamphlet, 1208–363

Timber in New England, growth and relationship to tree and site characteristics, 1900s-85, 1208–349

Timber in northeastern US, biomass volume by characteristics of tree and forest, and county, State rpt series, 1206–43

Timber in northeastern US, resources, and related manufacturing industries employment and finances, by State, 1977-87, 1208–375

Timber in northeastern US, resources and removals by species, ownership class, and county, State rpt series, 1206–12

Timber in southeastern US, longleaf pine mgmt and use, 1989 conf, 1208–355

Timber insect and disease incidence and damage, and control activities, State rpt series, 1206–49

Timber insect and disease incidence and damage, annual regional rpt series, 1206–11

Timber sales of Forest Service, expenses, and operations, by State and natl forest, FY90, annual rpt, 1204–36.3

Wastewater industrial releases pollution levels, treatment, costs, and regulation, with background financial and operating data, industry rpt series, 9206–4

Wastewater treatment facilities construction grants of EPA to State and local govts, by project, monthly listing, 9202–3

Wastewater treatment facilities construction loan funds for local govts, Federal and State funding by State, 1990, GAO rpt, 26113–521

Wastewater treatment facilities in small communities, construction and repair needs to meet Clean Water Act standards, by State and region, 1988 and 2008, 1588–155

Water (groundwater) supply, quality, chemistry, and use, State and local area rpt series, 5666–28

Water pollution areas and sources identification activities of EPA and State, 1991, GAO rpt, 26113–536

Index by Categories

BY STATE

Water pollution fish kills, by pollution source, month, location, and State, 1977-87, last issue of annual rpt, 9204–3

Water pollution from farming, funding for control under Rural Clean Water Program by region and State, monthly rpt, 1802–14

Water quality, chemistry, hydrology, and other characteristics, local area studies, series, 5666–27

Water resources data collection and analysis activities of USGS Water Resources Div Districts, with project descriptions, series, 5666–26

Water resources dev projects of Army Corps of Engineers, characteristics, and costs, 1950s-89, biennial State rpt series, 3756–1

Water resources dev projects of Army Corps of Engineers, characteristics, and costs, 1950s-91, biennial State rpt series, 3756–2

Water supply and quality in streams and lakes, and groundwater levels in wells, by drainage basin, 1988, annual State rpt series, 5666–16

Water supply and quality in streams and lakes, and groundwater levels in wells, by drainage basin, 1989, annual State rpt series, 5666–12

Water supply and quality in streams and lakes, and groundwater levels in wells, by drainage basin, 1990, annual State rpt series, 5666–10

Water supply, hydrologic events, and end use, by State, 1988-89, annual rpt, 5664–12

Water supply in western US, and snow survey results, annual State rpt series, 1264–14

Water supply in western US, and snow survey results, monthly State rpt series, 1266–2

Water supply in western US, storage by reservoir and State, and streamflow conditions, as of Oct 1991, annual rpt, 1264–4

Water use by end use, well withdrawals, and public supply deliveries, by county, State rpt series, 5666–24

Water use from Colorado River Basin Project, by State and for Mexico, 1981-85, annual rpt, 5824–6

Wetlands (riparian) acreage, and Bur of Land Mgmt activities, mgmt plans, and scientific staff, State rpt series, 5726–8

Wetlands acreage, and agreements and payments to farmers under Water Bank Program, by State, 1972-91, annual rpt, 1804–21

Wetlands acreage, resources, soil and water properties, and conservation efforts, by wetland type, State rpt series, 5506–11

Wetlands in coastal areas, acreage by wetland type, estuarine basin, and county, 1989, 2178–31

Wetlands preservation under Water Bank Program, acreage, agreements, and payments, by State, monthly rpt, 1802–5

Wetlands, water, and land acreage, by State, 1780s and 1980s, 5508–107

Wetlands wildlife and migratory bird habitat acquisition, funding by State, FY92, press release, 5306–4.8; 5306–4.11

Wildlife and plant research results, habitat study series, 5506–13

Wildlife mgmt activities and funding, acreage by habitat type, and scientific staff, for Bur of Land Mgmt, State rpt series, 5726–7

Wildlife mgmt activities and funding, acreage, staff, and plans of Bur of Land Mgmt, habitat study series, 5726–6

Wildlife mgmt on public lands, endangered species, and BLM activities and funding, FY80-90, 5728–37

Wildlife refuges and other land under Fish and Wildlife Service mgmt, acreage by site and State, as of Sept 1991, annual rpt, 5504–8

Wildlife research of State fish and wildlife agencies, federally funded projects and costs by species and State, 1990, annual listing, 5504–24

Population

Census of Population and Housing, 1990: population and housing characteristics, households, and land area, by county, subdiv, and place, State rpt series, 2551–1

Census of Population and Housing, 1990: population counts for congressional districts and change from 1980, by State, press release, 2328–32

Census of Population and Housing, 1990: voting age and total population by race, and housing units, by block, redistricting counts required under PL 94-171, State CD-ROM series, 2551–6

Census of Population and Housing, 1990: voting age and total population by race, and housing units, by county and city, redistricting counts required under PL 94-171, State summary rpt series, 2551–5

Census of Population, 1990: Hispanic population by detailed origin, region, and State, with data for 1980, press release, 2328–73

Census of Population, 1990: population by detailed Native American, Asian, and Pacific Islander group, race, region, and State, with data for 1980, press release, 2328–72

Census of Population, 1990: population by race, Hispanic origin, region, census div, and State, with data for 1980, fact sheet, 2326–20.2

Census of Population, 1990: population by State and region, with Federal and military personnel abroad by State of residence and agency, press release, 2328–66

Census of Population, 1990: population size, by State, census div, and region, and congressional seats apportioned by State, 1990 and trends from 1790, fact sheet, 2326–20.1

Census of Population, 1990: post-enumeration survey results compared to census counts, by race, sex, city, county, and State, press release, 2328–69

Census of Population, 1990: urban areas land area, housing units, and population, by State and compared to rural areas, press release, 2328–39

Households by tenure and population size, by age group, State, and county, 1980 and 1985, 2546–3.169

Income (household), by source, detailed characteristics, region, and State, 1990, annual Current Population Rpt, 2546–6.70

Income (personal) and earnings estimates by State, data sources and reliability, 1980-87, article, 2702–1.202

Income (personal) per capita and by source, and earnings by industry div, by State, MSA, and county, 1984-89, annual regional rpts, 2704–2

Income (personal) per capita and total, and earnings by industry group, by region and State, 1988-90, annual article, 2702–1.216

Income (personal) per capita and total, by State, MSA, county, and metro-nonmetro location, 1987-89, annual article, 2702–1.209

Income (personal) per capita disparity among States, with data by industrial base, 1979, 1989, and projected to 1995, 1548–379

Income (personal) per capita disparity between metro and nonmetro areas, and causal factors, by State, 1979-88, 1548–380

Income (personal) totals, by region, census div, and State, quarterly article, 2702–1.27

Population estimates and projections, by region and State, Current Population Rpt series, 2546–3

Population size, July 1981-89 and compared to 1980 and 1990, annual press release, 2324–10

Poverty status of population and families, by detailed characteristics, 1990, annual Current Population Rpt, 2546–6.71

Refugee arrivals and resettlement in US, by age, sex, sponsoring agency, State, and country, monthly rpt, 4692–2

Refugee arrivals in US by world area of origin and State of settlement, and Federal aid, FY90-91 and proposed FY92 allocations, annual rpt, 7004–16

State and Metro Area Data Book, 1991 data compilation, 2328–54

Statistical Abstract of US, 1991 annual data compilation, 2324–1

West Central States population, income, and employment growth, by MSA, metro-nonmetro location, and State, for Fed Reserve 10th District, 1970s-90s, article, 9381–1.209

Prices and Cost of Living

Dairy prices, by product and selected area, with related marketing data, 1990, annual rpt, 1317–1

Electric power billings for housing, and rankings, by State, as of Jan 1990, annual rpt, 1244–1.6

Energy prices and spending, by fuel type, end-use sector, and State, 1989, annual rpt, 3164–64

Energy prices for housing, by fuel and State, 1989 and forecast 1990-91, 3166–6.54

Farm prices received and paid, by commodity and State, 1990, annual rpt, 1629–5

Farm prices received and production value, by detailed crop and State, 1988-90, annual rpt, 1621–2

Fruit and vegetable wholesale prices in NYC by State, and shipments and arrivals by mode of transport, by commodity, weekly rpt, 1311–20

Fruit and vegetable wholesale prices in NYC, Chicago, and selected shipping points, by crop, 1990, annual rpt, 1311–8

Heating oil retail prices, by State, and wholesale prices and dealer margins, monthly rpt, 3162–24.9

Milk order market prices and detailed operations, by State and market area, 1989-90, annual rpt, 1317–3

Oil and refined products supply, demand, reserves, trade, and prices, and refinery capacity, by State, 1960-91, annual rpt, 3164–95

BY STATE

Poultry and egg prices and marketing, by selected region, State, and city, monthly and weekly 1990, annual rpt, 1317–2

Public Welfare and Social Security

- AFDC beneficiaries demographic and financial characteristics, by State, FY89, annual rpt, 4694–1
- AFDC Job Opportunities and Basic Skills Training Program Federal and State funding by State, and administrators views, 1989-91, GAO rpt, 26121–435
- AFDC work incentive program appropriations, by State, FY90-91, article, 10042–1.201
- AIDS patient home and community services under Medicaid waiver in 6 States, 1988-89, article, 4652–1.216
- Child Support Enforcement Program finances and operations, by State, FY85-89, annual rpt, 4694–6
- Child welfare programs funding by source, and foster care program operations and client characteristics, for selected States, 1960s-95, 25368–169
- Computer records matching of welfare data, Federal and State agencies compliance with recipient protection provisions before benefits reduction, 1990, GAO rpt, 26121–404
- Fed Govt programs under Ways and Means Committee jurisdiction, finances, operations, and participant characteristics, FY70s-90, annual rpt, 21784–11
- Fed Govt spending in States, by type, program, agency, and State, FY90, annual rpt, 2464–2
- Food aid program for children during summer vacation, nonprofit sponsors compliance with USDA regulations, 1989-90, GAO rpt, 26113–541
- Food aid program of USDA for women, infants, and children, participants and costs by State and Indian agency, FY88, annual tables, 1364–12
- Food aid program of USDA for women, infants, and children, participants by race, State, and Indian agency, Apr 1990, annual rpt, 1364–16
- Food aid program of USDA for women, infants, and children, participants, clinics, and costs, by State and Indian agency, monthly tables, 1362–16
- Food stamp eligibility and payment errors, by type, recipient characteristics, and State, FY89, annual rpt, 1364–15
- Food stamp issues and participation, by State and county, as of July 1990, semiannual rpt, 1362–6
- Food stamp use at farmers markets, costs and participation, demonstration project results for 14 States, 1989, hearing, 21168–46
- HHS financial aid, by program, recipient, State, and city, FY90, annual regional listings, 4004–3
- Homeless persons aid programs of Fed Govt, program descriptions and funding, by agency and State, FY87-90, annual GAO rpt, 26104–21
- Homelessness issues, population at risk, contributing factors, and Federal funding for services and prevention, with bibl, 1991 compilation of papers, 25928–9
- Medicaid and Medicare low income disabled enrollees and eligibility provisions, by State, 1975-89, article, 4652–1.218
- Medicaid funding shares of Fed Govt under alternative formulas, by State, FY89, GAO rpt, 26121–420
- Medicaid income and asset eligibility limits for aged, by marital status and State, 1989, 23898–5
- Medicaid prenatal care eligibility and availability, by State, 1987-90, article, 4652–1.213
- Medicaid reimbursement of hospitals under Federal and State provisions, with services use, costs, and profits, by State, 1980s, 17206–1.11
- Medicaid reimbursement of nursing homes, States payment ratesetting methods, limits, and allowances, 1988, article, 4652–1.253
- Medicare and Medicaid eligibility, participation, coverage, and program finances, various periods 1966-91, biennial rpt, 4654–1
- Medicare and Medicaid outlays per enrollee, for aged and disabled beneficiaries by State, 1990, annual Current Population Rpt, 2546–6.69
- Medicare beneficiaries hospital discharges, length of stay, and costs, by type of beneficiary and location, 1972-88, article, 4652–1.207
- Medicare reimbursement of hospitals under prospective payment system for discharge delays due to limited nursing home space, 1985, 4658–55
- Medicare Supplementary Medical Insurance physicians fee schedule, analyses of costs and other issues, series, 17266–1
- Medicare Supplementary Medical Insurance physicians fee schedule, methodology with data by procedure and specialty, 1991, annual rpt, 17264–1
- Nonprofit charitable organizations finances, by asset size and State, 1987, article, 8302–2.218
- OASDHI, Medicaid, SSI, and related programs benefits, beneficiary characteristics, and trust funds, selected years 1937-89, annual rpt, 4744–3
- OASDI benefits and beneficiaries, by type of benefit, State, and county, as of Dec 1990, annual rpt, 4744–28
- Older persons aid programs funding, and long term care ombudsman funding and visits by State, 1988-90, 25248–126
- Paternity determination through genetic testing, labs, services, and costs, 1991 listing, 4698–4
- Refugee aid funding of Fed Govt and States, impacts of reductions, with data by selected State and California county, late 1980s, GAO rpt, 26121–402
- Refugee resettlement programs and funding, arrivals by country of origin, and indicators of adjustment, by State, FY90, annual rpt, 4694–5
- *Social Security Bulletin*, OASDHI and other program operations and beneficiary characteristics, from 1940, monthly journal, 4742–1
- Supplemental Security Income and Medicaid eligibility and payment provisions, and beneficiaries living arrangements, by State, 1991, annual rpt, 4704–13
- Supplemental Security Income payments and beneficiaries, by type of eligibility, State, and county, Dec 1989, annual rpt, 4744–27

Surplus personal property of Fed Govt donated to govt and nonprofit agencies, with data by State, FY88-90, biennial rpt, 9454–22

Recreation and Leisure

- Boat registrations, and accidents, casualties, and damage by cause, by vessel characteristics and State, 1990, annual rpt, 7404–1
- Coastal areas recreation facilities, by State, county, estuary, and level of govt, 1972-84, 2178–29
- Fishing (ocean sport) activities, and catch by species, by angler characteristics and State, annual coastal area rpt series, 2166–17
- Fishing and hunting licenses issued, and costs, by State, FY90, annual tables, 5504–16
- Forests (natl) recreational use, by type of activity and State, 1990, annual rpt, 1204–17
- Historic Preservation Fund grants, by State, FY92, annual table, 5544–9
- Land and Water Conservation Fund allocations for outdoor recreation area dev, by State, FY91, annual table, 5544–15
- Land and Water Conservation Fund grants, State matching funds, and balances, by State, FY90, annual rpt, 5544–18
- Park natl system visits and overnight stays, by park and State, 1990, annual rpt, 5544–12
- Public lands recreation facilities and use, and Land Mgmt Bur mgmt activities, funding, and plans, State rpt series, 5726–5
- Shellfish recreational harvesters selected characteristics, location of harvest and residence, and spending, 1985 survey, 2178–28
- Urban areas park and recreation facilities rehabilitation funding, by city and State, FY91, press release, 5306–4.7

Science and Technology

- Animal protection, licensing, and inspection activities of USDA, and animals used in research, by State, FY89, annual rpt, 1394–10
- Degrees (PhD) in science and engineering, by field, instn, employment prospects, sex, race, and other characteristics, 1960s-90, annual rpt, 9627–30
- Education in science and engineering, grad programs enrollment by field, source of funds, and characteristics of student and instn, 1975-89, annual rpt, 9627–7
- Employment and other characteristics of science and engineering PhDs, by field and State, 1989, biennial rpt, 9627–18
- Higher education instn science and engineering research system status, R&D performance, and Federal support, 1950s-88, 9628–83
- NASA funding by program and type of performer, and contract awards by State, FY90, annual rpt, 9504–6.2
- NASA procurement contract awards, by type, contractor, State, and country, FY91 with trends from 1961, semiannual rpt, 9502–6
- NASA R&D funding to higher education instns, by field, instn, and State, FY90, annual listing, 9504–7
- NSF grants and contracts, by field, instn, and State, FY89, annual rpt, 9624–26
- Nuclear engineering enrollment and degrees by instn and State, and women grads plans and employment, 1990, annual rpt, 3006–8.14

Index by Categories

Nuclear engineering enrollment and degrees granted by instn and State, and grad placement, by student characteristics, 1990, annual rpt, 3004–5

Patents (US) granted to US and foreign applicants, by State and country, 1989-90, annual press release, 2244–2

Patents granted to US residents, by State, FY87-90, annual rpt, 2244–1.2

R&D and related funding of Fed Govt to higher education and nonprofit instns, by field, instn, agency, and State, FY89, annual rpt, 9627–17

R&D funding by Fed Govt, by field, performer type, agency, and State, FY89-91, annual rpt, 9627–20

R&D funding by higher education instns and federally funded centers, by field, instn, and State, FY89, annual rpt, 9627–13

Radiation protection and health physics enrollment and degrees granted by instn and State, and female grads plans and employment, 1990, annual rpt, 3006–8.15

Technology dev programs of govts, info sources and funding, 1990 rpt, 10048–81

Veterans Affairs

Disability and death compensation cases of VA, by entitlement type, period of service, sex, age, and State, FY89, annual rpt, 8604–7

Education aid under GI Bill and other programs, and participation by period of service and State, FY89, annual rpt, 8604–9

Insurance (life) for veterans and servicepersons, finances and coverage by program and State, 1990, annual rpt, 8604–4

Mental health care services of VA, use, spending, and staff and patient characteristics, by State and services type, 1983 and 1986, 4506–3.43

Population and characteristics of veterans, and VA hospital and other activities, by State, FY90, annual rpt, 8604–3

Population of veterans, by period of service, age, and State, as of Mar 1991, annual rpt, 8604–12

VA programs spending, by State, county, and congressional district, FY90, annual rpt, 8604–6

BY URBAN-RURAL AND METRO-NONMETRO

Agriculture and Food

Banks agricultural loans share of all loans, impact of State branching laws, bank urban-rural location, and other factors, 1981-86, article, 9393–8.202

Employment related to agriculture, by industry, region, and metro-nonmetro location, 1987, 1598–271

Banking, Finance, and Insurance

Banks finances and operations, by metro-nonmetro location, 1987-89, annual rpt, 1544–29

Banks financial performance in Fed Reserve 10th District, by urban-rural location and State, 1989-90, article, 9381–16.201

Communications and Transportation

Hwy construction material prices and indexes for Federal-aid system, by type of material and urban-rural location, quarterly rpt, 7552–7

BY URBAN-RURAL AND METRO-NONMETRO

Hwy speed averages and vehicles exceeding 55 mph, by State, quarterly rpt, 7552–14

Hwy Statistics, detailed data by State, 1990, annual rpt, 7554–1

Hwy Statistics, summary data by State, 1989-90, annual rpt, 7554–24

Mail volume to and from households, use, and views, by class, source, content, and household characteristics, 1987-88, annual rpt, 9864–10

Railroad-hwy grade-crossing accidents, detailed data by State and railroad, 1989, annual rpt, 7604–2

Telephone local service charges and low-income subsidies, by region, company, and city, 1980s-90, semiannual rpt, 9282–8

Toll facilities, mileage, and operating status, by type of system, as of Jan 1990, biennial listing, 7554–39

Traffic accidents, casualties, circumstances, and characteristics of persons and vehicles involved, 1989, annual rpt, 7764–18

Traffic accidents impacts of speed limits, with accident circumstances and speed averages, for States with 55 and 65 mph limit, 1986-89, annual rpt, 7764–15

Traffic fatal accidents, alcohol levels of drivers and others, by circumstances and characteristics of persons and vehicles, 1989, annual rpt, 7764–16

Traffic fatal accidents, circumstances, and characteristics of persons and vehicles involved, 1990, semiannual rpt, 7762–11

Traffic fatal accidents, deaths, and rates, by circumstances, characteristics of persons and vehicles involved, and location, 1989, annual rpt, 7764–10

Transportation natl system planning, use, condition, accidents, and needs, by mode of transport, 1940s-90 and projected to 2020, 7308–202

Truck accidents, circumstances, severity, and characteristics of drivers and vehicles, 1989, annual rpt, 7764–20

Education

Appalachia education system, improvement initiatives, and indicators of success, by State, 1960s-89, 9088–36

Digest of Education Statistics, 1991 annual data compilation, 4824–2

Educational attainment, by sociodemographic characteristics and location, 1989 and trends from 1940, biennial Current Population Rpt, 2546–1.452

Eighth grade class of 1988: educational performance and conditions, characteristics, attitudes, activities, and plans, natl longitudinal survey, series, 4826–9

Elementary and secondary education enrollment, staff, finances, operations, programs, and policies, 1987/88 biennial survey, series, 4836–3

Elementary and secondary public school agencies, by enrollment size and location, fall 1989, annual listing, 4834–1

Elementary and secondary public schools, enrollment, teachers, funding, and other characteristics, by region and State, 1988/89, annual rpt, 4834–20

Elementary and secondary students educational performance, and factors affecting proficiency, by selected characteristics, 1988 natl assessments, subject rpt series, 4896–7

Elementary and secondary students educational performance, and factors affecting proficiency, by selected characteristics, 1990 natl assessments, subject rpt series, 4896–8

Enrollment, by grade, instn type and control, and student characteristics, 1989 and trends from 1947, annual Current Population Rpt, 2546–1.453

High school dropout rates, and subsequent completion, by student and school characteristics, alternative estimates, 1990, annual rpt, 4834–23

Private elementary and secondary schools, students, and staff characteristics, various periods 1979-88, 4838–47

Teachers leaving profession and subsequent employment, by urban-rural location and public-private control of school, 1986-87, annual rpt, 4824–1.1

Energy Resources and Demand

Building (commercial) energy use, costs, and conservation, by building characteristics, survey rpt series, 3166–8

Government and Defense

Census of Govts, 1987: employment, payroll, and average earnings, by function, level of govt, State, county, and population size, 2455–2

Property (real) of Fed Govt, inventory and costs, worldwide summary by location, agency, and use, 1989, annual rpt, 9454–5

Property (real) of Fed Govt, leased inventory and rental costs, worldwide summary by location and agency, 1989, annual rpt, 9454–10

State and Metro Area Data Book, 1991 data compilation, 2328–54

Taxes, spending, and govt efficiency, public opinion by respondent characteristics, 1991 survey, annual rpt, 10044–2

Voting and registration, by socioeconomic and demographic characteristics, 1990 congressional election, biennial Current Population Rpt, 2546–1.454

Health and Vital Statistics

Abortions, by method, pregnancy history, and other characteristics of woman, 1988, US Vital Statistics annual rpt, 4146–5.120

Accessibility of health care, persons with and without usual care source by selected characteristics, 1987, 4186–8.22

Acute and chronic health conditions, disability, absenteeism, and health services use, by selected characteristics, 1987, CD-ROM, 4147–10.177

AIDS virus infection prevalence in developing countries, by sex, selected city, urban-rural location, and country, 1991, semiannual rpt, 2322–4

Birth outcomes and prenatal care use effects of Medicaid coverage, charges, and Medicaid payments, for California, 1983, article, 4652–1.241

Births, fertility rates, and childless women, by selected characteristics, 1990, annual Current Population Rpt, 2546–1.455

Child developmental, learning, and emotional problems, cases and share receiving special treatment and education, by selected characteristics, 1988, 4146–8.193

Deaths within 8 years of retirement, by health and other characteristics, 1982-88, article, 4742–1.206

BY URBAN-RURAL AND METRO-NONMETRO

Disabled persons and related activity limitation days and health services use, by health status, disability type, and other characteristics, 1984-88, 4146–8.202

Drug abuse prevalence among minorities, related health effects and crime, treatment, and research status and needs, mid 1970s-90, 4498–72

Drug, alcohol, and cigarette use and attitudes of youth, by substance type and selected characteristics, 1975-90 surveys, annual rpt, 4494–4

Drug, alcohol, and cigarette use, by selected characteristics, 1990 survey, biennial rpt, 4494–5

Food aid program of USDA for women, infants, and children, prenatal participation effect on Medicaid costs and birth outcomes, for 5 States, 1987-88, 1368–2

Health condition and health care resources, use, and spending, 1950s-89, annual data compilation, 4144–11

Home health care agencies finances impacts of Medicare payment limits under alternative determination methods, with data by service type, 1984-89, GAO rpt, 26121–400

Hospices use by cancer patients, by service type, use of other facilities, patient and instn characteristics, and other indicators, local area study, 1980-85, 4658–53

Hospital closures and rates, with financial, operating, and market characteristics, by location, late 1980s, GAO rpt, 26121–392

Hospital operations, and services spending by type and payment source, with background data and foreign comparisons, 1960s-80s and projected to 2000, 26308–98

Hospitals in rural areas, financial and operating performance impacts of Medicare prospective payment reimbursement system, 1980s-87, 4658–51

Implants of medical devices, by type, reason, duration, and user characteristics, 1988, 4146–8.197

Injuries, by type, circumstances, and victim characteristics, and related activity limitations, 1985-87, 4147–10.176

Injuries, related impairments, and activity limitations, by circumstances and victim characteristics, 1985-87, 4147–10.179

Insurance (health) coverage, by insurance type and selected characteristics, 1989, 4146–8.203

Insurance (health) coverage of children, and children with a regular source of care, by selected characteristics, 1988, 4146–8.192

Lead paint in privately owned housing, levels, exposure, and testing and abatement costs, 1990 rpt, 5188–128

Minority group and women health condition, services use, payment sources, and health care labor force, by poverty status, 1940s-89, chartbook, 4118–56

Nursing home Alzheimer's disease units, and beds, by facility characteristics, 1987, 4186–8.12

Nursing home residents with mental disorders, by disorder type and resident and instn characteristics, 1985, 4147–13.106

Physicians, by specialty, age, sex, and location of training and practice, 1989, State rpt series, 4116–6

Smoking exposure of children before and after birth, by source and degree of exposure and family characteristics, 1988, 4146–8.204

Housing and Construction

American Housing Survey: inventory change from 1973, by reason, unit and household characteristics, and location, 1983, biennial rpt, 2485–14

American Housing Survey: unit and households detailed characteristics, and unit and neighborhood quality, 1987, biennial rpt, 2485–12

American Housing Survey: unit and households detailed characteristics, and unit and neighborhood quality, 1987, biennial rpt supplement, 2485–13

Apartment and condominium completions by rent class and sales price, and market absorption rates, quarterly rpt, 2482–2

Apartment completions by region and metro-nonmetro location, and absorption rate, by size and rent class, preliminary 1990, annual Current Housing Rpt, 2484–3

Apartment market absorption rates and characteristics for nonsubsidized furnished and unfurnished units, 1989, annual Current Housing Rpt, 2484–2

Census of Population and Housing, 1990: voting age and total population by race, and housing units, by block, redistricting counts required under PL 94-171, State CD-ROM series, 2551–6

Community Dev Block Grant allocation, by State, county, and city, FY84-91, 5128–17

Mortgages FHA-insured, financial, property, and mortgagor characteristics, by metro area, 1990, annual rpt, 5144–24

Mortgages FHA-insured, financial, property, and mortgagor characteristics, by State, 1990, annual rpt, 5144–1

Mortgages FHA-insured, financial, property, and mortgagor characteristics, total and by State and outlying area, 1990, annual rpt, 5144–25

Mortgages FHA-insured, financial, property, and mortgagor characteristics, 1990, annual rpt, 5144–17; 5144–23

New housing starts and completions, by location inside-outside SMSAs, bimonthly rpt, 2042–1.2

New housing starts, by units per structure and metro-nonmetro location, and mobile home placements and prices, by region, monthly rpt, 2382–1

New housing units completed and under construction, by units per structure, region, and inside-outside MSAs, monthly rpt, 2382–2

New single and multifamily units, by structural and financial characteristics, inside-outside MSAs, and region, 1986-90, annual rpt, 2384–1

Poor households with high rent, and substandard units, worst case problems prevalence and households characteristics, 1970s-84, annual rpt, 5184–10

Vacant housing characteristics and costs, and occupancy and vacancy rates, by region and metro-nonmetro location, quarterly rpt, 2482–1

Vacant housing characteristics, and occupancy and vacancy rates, by tenure and location, 1960s-90, annual rpt, 2484–1

Index by Categories

Industry and Commerce

Retail trade census, 1987: finances and employment, for establishments with and without payroll, by SIC 2- to 4-digit kind of business, State, and MSA, 2401–1

State and Metro Area Data Book, 1991 data compilation, 2328–54

Labor and Employment

Employment and unemployment in metro and nonmetro areas, monthly rpt, quarterly data, 6742–2.9

Employment Cost Index and percent change by occupational group, industry div, region, and metro-nonmetro area, quarterly press release, 6782–5

Employment Cost Index changes for nonfarm workers, by occupation, industry div, region, and bargaining status, monthly rpt, 6782–1

Job Training Partnership Act funding and performance indicators in service delivery areas, by urban-rural location, 1987-88, 1598–266

Job Training Partnership Act participation by selected characteristics and State, and outcomes, by urban-rural location, 1987-88, 1598–267

Labor force characteristics in rural areas, with comparisons to urban areas, 1987, 1598–264

Older men's labor force status by urban-rural location, and distribution of men by age and occupation, 1860s-1980, article, 9371–1.202

Poverty rate among workers in metro and nonmetro areas, relation to employment and other characteristics, 1987, 1598–274

Wages, hours, and employment by occupation, and benefits, for selected locations, industry survey rpt series, 6787–6

Law Enforcement

Arrests, by offense, offender characteristics, and location, data compilation, 1991 annual rpt, 6064–6.4

Assaults and deaths of law enforcement officers, by circumstances, agency, victim and offender characteristics, and location, 1990, annual rpt, 6224–3

Crime, criminal justice admin and enforcement, and public opinion, data compilation, 1991 annual rpt, 6064–6

Crime Index by population size and region, and offenses by large city, Jan-June 1991, semiannual rpt, 6222–1

Crimes, arrests by offender characteristics, and rates, by offense, and law enforcement employees, by population size and jurisdiction, 1990, annual rpt, 6224–2

Juvenile correctional and detention public and private instns, inmates, and expenses, by instn and resident characteristics and State, 1987, biennial rpt, 6064–13

Teenagers crime victimization, by victim and offender characteristics, circumstances, and offense, 1985-88 surveys, 6066–3.43

Victimization rates, by victim and offender characteristics, circumstances, and offense, 1988 survey, annual rpt, 6066–3.42

Victimization rates, by victim and offender characteristics, circumstances, and offense, 1989 survey, annual rpt, 6066–3.44

Victimizations by region and victim characteristics, and rpts to police, by offense, 1973-90, annual rpt, 6066–25.35; 6066–25.41

Index by Categories

BY COMMODITY

Victimizations, by victim characteristics, offense, and whether reported to police, 1973-88, 6066–3.45

Victimizations of households, by offense, household characteristics, and location, 1975-90, annual rpt, 6066–25.40

Women's rape and other violent crime victimization, by relation to offender, circumstances, and victim characteristics, 1973-87, 6068–243

Natural Resources, Environment, and Pollution

Wetlands acreage, resources, soil and water properties, and conservation efforts, by wetland type, State rpt series, 5506–11

Population

Black Americans social and economic characteristics, for South and total US, 1989-90 and trends from 1969, Current Population Rpt, 2546–1.450

Census of Population and Housing, 1990: voting age and total population by race, and housing units, by block, redistricting counts required under PL 94-171, State CD-ROM series, 2551–6

Census of Population, 1990: urban areas land area, housing units, and population, by State and compared to rural areas, press release, 2328–39

Children in poverty by selected family characteristics, for rural areas compared to urban areas, 1987-88, 1598–270

Consumer Income, socioeconomic characteristics of persons, families, and households, detailed cross-tabulations, Current Population Rpt series, 2546–6

Hispanic Americans social and economic characteristics, by detailed origin, 1991, Current Population Rpt, 2546–1.448; 2546–1.451

Households and family characteristics, by location, 1990, annual Current Population Rpt, 2546–1.447

Immigrants in US, population characteristics and fertility, by birthplace and compared to native born, 1980s, Current Population rpt, 2546–2.162

Income (household) and poverty status under alternative income definitions, by recipient characteristics, 1990, annual Current Population Rpt, 2546–6.69

Income (personal) and poverty status changes, by selected characteristics, 1987-88, Current Population Rpt, 2546–20.19

Income (personal) per capita and by source, and earnings by industry div, by State, MSA, and county, 1984-89, annual regional rpts, 2704–2

Income (personal) per capita and total, by State, MSA, county, and metro-nonmetro location, 1987-89, annual article, 2702–1.209

Income (personal) per capita disparity between metro and nonmetro areas, and causal factors, by State, 1979-88, 1548–380

Income and consumer spending of households, for selected population groups, quarterly journal, 1702–1

Living arrangements, family relationships, and marital status, by selected characteristics, 1990, annual Current Population Rpt, 2546–1.449

Poverty area definitions, and population, by metro-nonmetro location, 1972-89, article, 6722–1.219

Poverty status of population and families, by detailed characteristics, 1988-89, annual Current Population Rpt, 2546–6.67

Poverty status of population and families, by detailed characteristics, 1990, annual Current Population Rpt, 2546–6.71

State and Metro Area Data Book, 1991 data compilation, 2328–54

Statistical Abstract of US, 1991 annual data compilation, 2324–1

West Central States population, income, and employment growth, by MSA, metro-nonmetro location, and State, for Fed Reserve 10th District, 1970s-90s, article, 9381–1.209

Prices and Cost of Living

Child rearing costs, by expense type and urban-rural location, 1981 and 1989, 4818–5

Consumer Expenditure Survey, household income by source, and itemized spending, by selected characteristics and region, 1988-89, annual rpt, 6764–5

Consumer Expenditure Survey, spending by category, and income, by selected household characteristics and location, 1990, annual press release, 6726–1.42

Public Welfare and Social Security

Medicaid hospital discharges, by eligibility and instn characteristics, for 2 States, 1984, article, 4652–1.249

Medicaid reimbursement of hospitals under Federal and State provisions, with services use, costs, and profits, by State, 1980s, 17206–1.11

Medicare beneficiaries hospital discharges, length of stay, and costs, by type of beneficiary and location, 1972-88, article, 4652–1.207

Medicare Cost Report reviews, revisions ratio to initially reported costs, by category, FY84, article, 4652–1.233

Medicare reimbursement of hospitals under prospective payment system, analyses of alternative payment plans, series, 17206–1

Medicare reimbursement of hospitals under prospective payment system, and effect on services, finances, and beneficiary payments, 1979-90, annual rpt, 17204–2

Medicare reimbursement of hospitals under prospective payment system, diagnosis related group code assignment and effects on care and instn finances, 1984/85, series, 4006–7

Medicare reimbursement of hospitals under prospective payment system, impacts on costs, industry structure and operations, and quality of care, series, 17206–2

Medicare reimbursement of hospitals under prospective payment system, impacts on instns and beneficiaries, 1988, annual rpt, 4654–13

Medicare reimbursement of hospitals under prospective payment system, methodology, inputs, and data by diagnostic group, 1991 annual rpt, 17204–1

Medicare Supplementary Medical Insurance physicians fee schedule, analyses of costs and other issues, series, 17266–1

Medicare Supplementary Medical Insurance physicians fee schedule, methodology with data by procedure and specialty, 1991, annual rpt, 17264–1

Student Community Service Program activities, and volunteer and client characteristics, 1987-89, 9028–14

Recreation and Leisure

Park natl system visits and overnight stays, by park and State, monthly rpt, 5542–4

ECONOMIC BREAKDOWNS

BY COMMODITY

Agriculture and Food

Acreage harvested, by crop, selected years 1962-89, 1588–48

Acreage planted and harvested, by crop and State, 1989-90 and planned as of June 1991, annual rpt, 1621–23

Acreage planted, by selected crop and State, 1982-90 and planned 1991, annual rpt, 1621–22

Acreage reduction program compliance, enrollment, and yield on planted acreage, by commodity and State, annual press release series, 1004–20

Acreage under Agricultural Stabilization and Conservation Service programs, rankings by commodity and congressional district, 1989, biennial rpt, 1804–17

Agricultural data compilation, 1990 and trends from 1920, annual rpt, 1004–14

Agricultural Outlook, production, prices, marketing, and trade, by commodity, forecast and current situation, monthly rpt with articles, 1502–4

Agricultural Stabilization and Conservation Service programs, annual commodity fact sheet series, 1806–4

Agricultural Statistics, 1990, annual rpt, 1004–1

Alien workers legal residence applications, by crop and country of origin, periodic rpt, 6262–3

Australia agricultural input and output indexes, and freight rates, 1950s-80s, 1528–311

Business statistics, detailed data for major industries and economic indicators, *Survey of Current Business*, monthly rpt, 2702–1.14

Carbon dioxide in atmosphere, North Central States economic and agricultural impacts, model descriptions and results, 1980s and projected to 2030, 3006–11.15

CCC certificate exchange activity, by commodity, biweekly press release, 1802–16

CCC commodities for sale, and prices, monthly press release, 1802–4

CCC financial condition and major commodity program operations, FY62-87, annual chartbook, 1824–2

CCC loan activities by commodity, and agency operating results, monthly press release, 1802–7

Census of Agriculture, 1987: farms, farmland, production, finances, and operator characteristics, by county, final State rpt series, 2331–1

Cold storage food stocks by commodity and census div, and warehouse space use, by State, monthly rpt, 1631–5

BY COMMODITY

Index by Categories

Cold storage food stocks by commodity, and warehouse space use, by census div, 1990, annual rpt, 1631–11

Conservation programs under Food Security Act, farm finances and environmental benefits of alternative policies, projected 1991-2005, 1588–153

Cooperatives finances, aggregate for top 100 assns by commodity group, 1989, annual rpt, 1124–3

Cooperatives, finances, and membership, by type of service, commodity, and State, 1989, annual rpt, 1124–1

Cooperatives finances, operations, activities, and current issues, monthly journal, 1122–1

Developing countries agricultural exports of high-value commodities to OECD, 1970s-87, 1528–316

Developing countries agricultural supply, demand, and market for US exports, with socioeconomic conditions, country rpt series, 1526–6

Developing countries food supply, needs, and aid, status and alternative forecasts, world area rpt series, 1526–8

Disaster aid of USDA for producers of crops ineligible for price supports by State, and methodology, 1988-89, GAO rpt, 26113–533

Eastern Europe agricultural production, trade, and land reform, with selected economic indicators, by country, 1960s-90, article, 1522–3.202

Economic Indicators of the Farm Sector, balance sheets, and receipts by detailed commodity, by State, 1985-89, annual rpt, 1544–18

Economic Indicators of the Farm Sector, income, expenses, receipts by commodity, assets, and liabilities, 1990 and trends from 1945, annual rpt, 1544–16

Economic Indicators of the Farm Sector, itemized production costs, receipts, and returns, by commodity and region, 1987-89, annual rpt, 1544–20

Economic Indicators of the Farm Sector, production inputs, output, and productivity, by commodity and region, 1947-89, annual rpt, 1544–17

Environmental regulation impacts on agricultural trade, with indicators of pollution and fertilizer use intensity by crop, 1991 article, 1522–3.203

Exports (agricultural) of high-value commodities, indexes and sales value by commodity, world area, and country, 1960s-86, 1528–323

Exports (agricultural) of US, impacts of foreign agricultural and trade policy, with data by commodity and country, 1989, annual rpt, 1924–8

Exports (agricultural) related employment, land, and capital inputs, by commodity and country of destination, and compared to imports, 1977-87, 1548–373

Exports and imports (agricultural) commodity and country, prices, and world market devs, monthly rpt, 1922–12

Exports and imports (agricultural) of US, by commodity and country, bimonthly rpt, 1522–1

Exports and imports (agricultural) of US, by commodity, country, and US port, 1950s-91, annual rpt, 1924–9

Exports and imports (agricultural) of US, by detailed commodity and country, 1989, annual rpt, 1524–8

Exports and imports (agricultural) of US, by detailed commodity and country, 1990, semiannual rpt, 1522–4

Exports and imports (agricultural) of US, outlook and current situation, quarterly rpt, 1542–4

Exports of grains, oilseed products, hides, skins, and cotton, by country, weekly rpt, 1922–3

Farms, production, acreage, and related data, by selected crop and State, monthly rpt, 1621–1

Fertilizer and pesticide use and application rates, by type, crop, and State, series, 1616–1

Fertilizer use, and effects on agricultural productivity, for selected US regions and PRC, 1989 hearing, 25168–76

Finances and operations of farm sector, 1970s-91, article, 9362–1.207

Finances of farms, debts, assets, and receipts, and lenders financial condition, quarterly rpt with articles, 1541–1

Financial and marketing conditions of farms, forecast 1991, annual chartbook, 1504–8

Financial condition of farm sector, and prices, supply, and demand by commodity, 1988-90 and forecast 1991, annual article, 9381–1.203

Financial stress indicators for farms, operator quits, and loan problems and mediation, 1970s-90, 1598–272

Food (processed) production and stocks by State, shipments, exports, ingredients, and use, periodic Current Industrial Rpt series, 2506–4

Food composition, detailed data on nutrients, calories, and waste, for raw, processed, and prepared foods, series, 1356–3

Food consumer research, marketing, legislation, and regulation devs, and consumption and price trends, quarterly journal, 1541–7

Food consumption, dietary composition, and nutrient intake, 1987/88 natl survey, preliminary rpt series, 1356–1

Food consumption, supply, trade, prices, spending, and indexes, by commodity, 1989, annual rpt, 1544–4

Food industry vertically integrated markets, and farm products produced under contract, 1960s-90, article, 9381–1.205

Food spending, by item, household composition, income, age, race, and region, 1980-88, Consumer Expenditure Survey biennial rpt, 1544–30

Foreign and US agricultural production, acreage, and yield for selected crops, forecasts by selected world region and country, FAS monthly circular, 1925–28

Foreign and US agricultural production, prices, trade, and use, periodic rpt with articles, 1522–3

Foreign and US agricultural supply and demand indicators, by selected crop, monthly rpt, 1522–5

Foreign and US fresh and processed fruit, vegetable, and nut production and trade, FAS monthly circular with articles, 1925–34

Foreign countries agricultural production, consumption, and policies, and US export dev and promotion, monthly journal, 1922–2

Foreign countries agricultural production, prices, and trade, by country, 1980-90 and forecast 1991, annual world area rpt series, 1524–4

Foreign countries agricultural production, trade, and policies, summary data by country, 1989-90, annual factbook, 1924–12

Fruit and nut production, prices, and use, 1988-91, annual rpt series, 1621–18

Fruit and nut production, prices, trade, stocks, and use, by selected crop, periodic situation rpt with articles, 1561–6

Fruit and vegetable shipments, and arrivals in US and Canada cities, by mode of transport and State and country of origin, 1990, annual rpt series, 1311–4

Fruit and vegetable shipments by mode of transport, arrivals, and imports, by commodity and State and country of origin, weekly rpt, 1311–3

Fruit and vegetable wholesale prices in NYC by State, and shipments and arrivals by mode of transport, by commodity, weekly rpt, 1311–20

Households food and beverage spending and per capita consumption, by food and beverage type, 1980s-90, article, 1702–1.212

Immigration restrictions effects on US agricultural labor costs and trade competitiveness, 1980s, 1598–276

Imports injury to price-supported US agricultural industry, investigations with background financial and operating data, series, 9886–10

Industrial uses of new and traditional agricultural crops, replacement of imports and nonrenewable resources, R&D funding, and economic impacts, 1970s-90, 26358–239

Iraq agricultural imports under CCC export credit guarantee programs, FY81-90, GAO rpt, 26123–314

Irrigation projects of Reclamation Bur in western US, crop production and acreage by commodity, State, and project, 1989, annual rpt, 5824–12

Japan economic conditions, financial and intl policies, and trade devs, 1950s-80s and projected to 2050, compilation of papers, 23848–220

Korea (South) agricultural subsidies to producers and consumers, by commodity, 1987-89, article, 1522–3.205

Latin America agricultural subsidies to producers and consumers, by selected commodity for 6 countries, 1982-87, 1528–324

Livestock, poultry, and dairy trade, by commodity and country, FAS monthly circular, 1925–32

Livestock, poultry, and products foreign and US production, trade, and use, by selected country, FAS semiannual circular series, 1925–33

Low-fat and nonfat foods introduced, by product type, 1990, article, 1502–4.204

Mexico agricultural trade with US by commodity, and trade restrictions, 1980s, GAO rpt, 26123–335

Mexico vegetable trade with US and US import duties by commodity, and fresh tomato arrivals in US and Canada cities, 1970s-90, article, 1561–11.202

Index by Categories

BY COMMODITY

Pesticide and fertilizer use reduction, environmental and economic impacts by commodity and region, alternative forecasts 1989-94, hearing, 23848–222

PL 480 and CCC export credit sales agreement terms, by commodity and country, FY89, annual rpt, 15344–1.11

PL 480 exports by commodity, and recipients, by program, sponsor, and country, FY88 and cumulative from FY55, annual rpt, 1924–7

PL 480 long-term credit sales allocations, by commodity and country, periodic press release, 1922–7

Price support and other CCC program outlays, with production and marketing outlook, by commodity, projected 1990-96, 26306–6.160

Prices received and paid by farmers, by commodity and State, 1990, annual rpt, 1629–5

Prices received by farmers and production value, by detailed crop and State, 1988-90, annual rpt, 1621–2

Prices received by farmers for major products, and paid for farm inputs and living items, by State, monthly rpt, 1629–1

Production inputs, finances, mgmt, and land value and transfers, periodic situation rpt with articles, 1561–16

Research (agricultural) funding and staffing for USDA, State agencies, and other instns, by topic, FY90, annual rpt, 1744–2

South Central States agricultural banks financial ratios, and farm receipts by commodity, 1980s-90, annual article, 9391–16.209

Soviet Union agricultural conditions and factors affecting US grain exports and CCC credit guarantees, 1990 hearings, 21168–49

Soviet Union agricultural reform issues, with background data for USSR and US, 1970s-90, article, 9381–1.210

Soviet Union agricultural subsidies to producers and consumers, by selected commodity, 1986, 1528–320

Soviet Union agricultural trade, by commodity and country, 1955-90, 1528–322

Soviet Union, Eastern Europe, OECD, and selected other countries agricultural production, by commodity, 1960s-90, annual rpt, 9114–4.5

Subsidy rates of Fed Govt under 1985 and 1990 farm bills, by selected program and commodity, 1990 rpt, 1008–54

Vegetable production, acreage, and yield, current and forecast for selected fresh and processing crops by State, periodic rpt, 1621–12

Vegetable production, prices, trade, stocks, and use, for selected fresh and processing crops, periodic situation rpt with articles, 1561–11

Vegetable production, value, and acreage, for selected fresh and processing crops by State, 1988-90, annual rpts, 1621–25

Weather conditions and effect on agriculture, by US region, State, and city, and world area, weekly rpt, 2182–7

Banking, Finance, and Insurance

Futures and options trading volume, by commodity and exchange, FY90, annual rpt, 11924–2

Futures trading in selected commodities and financial instruments and indexes, NYC, Chicago, and other markets activity, semimonthly rpt, 11922–5

Futures trading oversight of CFTC and individual exchanges, foreign activity, and customer views, late 1980s, hearing, 25168–77

Communications and Transportation

Freight and distance hauled, by commodity and mode of transport, selected years 1970-89, annual rpt, 3304–5.5

Mississippi River system freight traffic by commodity and waterway, 1988 and projected to 2000, article, 9391–16.202

Panama Canal traffic and tolls, by commodity, flag of vessel, and trade route, FY90, annual rpt, 9664–3.1

Railroad retirement system funding and benefits findings and recommendations, with background industry data, 1960s-90 and projected to 2060, 9708–1

Shipborne trade of US, by type of service, commodity, country, route, and US port, 1988, annual rpt, 7704–2

St Lawrence Seaway ship, cargo, and passenger traffic, and toll revenue, 1990 and trends from 1959, annual rpt, 7744–2

Truck freight revenue, by commodity, 1989 survey, annual rpt, 2413–14

Truck rates for fruit and vegetables, by growing area and market, weekly 1990, annual rpt, 1311–15

Trucking industry deregulation by States, potential economic and market impacts, with background data, mid 1970s-80s, 7308–200

Government and Defense

DOD prime contract awards, by detailed procurement category, FY87-90, annual rpt, 3544–18

Military and personal property shipments, passenger traffic, and costs, by service branch and mode of transport, quarterly rpt, 3702–1

Military post exchange operations, and sales by commodity, by facility and location worldwide, FY89, annual rpt, 3504–10

Prison Industries (Federal) sales, by commodity and Federal agency, FY90, annual rpt, 6244–5

Strategic material stockpile inventories and needs, by commodity, as of Jan 1991, annual rpt, 3544–37

Strategic material stockpiling by Fed Govt, activity, and inventory by commodity, as of Mar 1991, semiannual rpt, 3542–22

Tax (excise) collections of IRS, by source, quarterly rpt, 8302–1

Health and Vital Statistics

Injuries from use of consumer products, by severity, victim age, and detailed product, 1990, annual rpt, 9164–6

Injuries from use of consumer products, related deaths and costs, and recalls by brand, by product type, FY89, annual rpt, 9164–2

Housing and Construction

Building materials production, shipments, and PPI, by type, bimonthly rpt, 2042–1.5; 2042–1.6

Building materials trade, by commodity and country, 1989-90, article, 2042–1.204

Industry and Commerce

Bulgaria trade with US, US tariffs, and impacts of US granting most favored nation status, 1987-90, GAO rpt, 26123–323

Business statistics, detailed data for major industries and economic indicators, *Survey of Current Business*, monthly rpt, 2702–1

Canada and US minerals trade, by commodity, 1987-89, article, 5602–4.201

Caribbean area duty-free exports to US, and imports from US, by country, and impact on US employment, by commodity, 1990, annual rpt, 6364–2

Caribbean area duty-free exports to US, by commodity and country, with consumer and industry impacts, 1984-90, annual rpt, 9884–20

Caribbean Basin Initiative duty-free exports to US which are ineligible under Generalized System of Preferences, by commodity, 1989, 9886–4.171

Caribbean Basin Initiative investment incentives, economic impacts, with finances and employment by country, 1984-90, 2048–141

Chemicals export and import price indexes, by commodity, 1985-90, article, 6722–1.229

China GNP estimation methodology and results, 1978-89, with yuan-dollar prices by commodity, 1981, working paper, 2326–18.58

China minerals production and trade, by commodity, 1988-89, annual rpt, 5604–38

China trade with US and through Hong Kong, and impacts of revoking most favored nation status, 1987-90, hearing, 25368–174

Communist countries trade with US, by detailed commodity and country, quarterly rpt with articles, 9882–2

Competitiveness (intl) of US industries, with selected foreign and US operating data by major firm and product, series, 2046–12

Eastern Europe imports from US, and trade opportunities, periodic rpt, 2042–33

Export and import balances of US, by major commodity group, monthly rpt, 9882–14

Export licensing, monitoring, and enforcement activities, FY90, annual rpt, 2024–1

Exports and imports between US and outlying areas, by detailed commodity and mode of transport, 1990, annual rpt, 2424–11

Exports and imports of US, by country and detailed commodity, monthly rpt, 2422–12

Exports and imports of US by country, and trade shifts by commodity, 1990, semiannual rpt, 9882–9

Exports and imports of US, by Harmonized System 6-digit commodity and country, 1990, annual rpt, 2424–13

Exports and imports of US, by selected country, country group, and commodity group, 1990, annual rpt, 2044–37

Exports and imports of US, by transport mode, country, and SITC 1- to 3-digit commodity, 1990, annual rpt, 2424–12

Exports and imports of US shipped through Canada, by detailed commodity, customs district, and country, 1989, annual rpt, 7704–11

Exports and imports, trade agreements and relations, and USITC investigations, 1990, annual rpt, 9884–5

BY COMMODITY

Index by Categories

Exports, imports, and balances of US, by selected country, country group, and commodity group, preliminary data, monthly rpt, 2042–34

Exports, imports, and trade flows, by country and commodity, with background economic indicators, data compilation, monthly CD-ROM, 2002–6

Exports of US, detailed commodities by country, monthly CD-ROM, 2422–13

Exports of US, detailed Schedule B commodities with countries of destination, 1990, annual rpt, 2424–10

Foreign countries economic conditions and implications for US, periodic country rpt series, 2046–4

Foreign trade zones (US) operations and movement of goods, by zone and commodity, FY88, annual rpt, 2044–30

Imports and tariff provisions effect on US industries and products, investigations with background financial and operating data, series, 9886–4

Imports detained by FDA, by reason, product, shipper, brand, and country, monthly listing, 4062–2

Imports, exports, and employment impacts, by SIC 2- to 4-digit industry and commodity, quarterly rpt, 2322–2

Imports injury to US industries from foreign subsidized products, investigations with background financial and operating data, series, 9886–15

Imports injury to US industries from sales at less than fair value, investigations with background financial and operating data, series, 9886–14

Imports of US, detailed commodities by country, monthly CD-ROM, 2422–14

Imports of US given duty-free treatment for value of US material sent abroad, by commodity and country, 1989, annual rpt, 9884–14

Imports under Generalized System of Preferences, status, and US tariffs, with trade by country and US economic impacts, for selected commodities, 1986-90, annual rpt, 9884–23

Input-output structure of US economy, detailed interindustry transactions for 84 industries, and components of final demand, 1986, annual article, 2702–1.206

Input-output structure of US economy, detailed interindustry transactions for 85 industries, 1982 benchmark data, 2702–1.213

Japan and US bilateral trade balances, indicators of surplus and deficit persistence for detailed commodity groups, 1962-88, technical paper, 9366–7.264

Japan balance of trade with US and other countries, mid 1960s-88, article, 9391–1.209

Machinery and transport equipment export and import prices, impacts of dollar depreciation, 1985-90, article, 6722–1.233

Manufacturing annual survey, 1989: value of shipments, by SIC 4- to 5-digit product class, 2506–15.2

Mexico imports from US, by industry and State, 1987-90, 2048–154

Mineral Industry Surveys, commodity reviews of production, trade, stocks, and use, monthly rpt series, 5612–1

Mineral Industry Surveys, commodity reviews of production, trade, stocks, and use, quarterly rpt series, 5612–2

Mineral Industry Surveys, commodity reviews of production, trade, use, and industry operations, advance annual rpt series, 5614–5

Mineral Industry Surveys, State reviews of production, 1990, preliminary annual rpt, 5614–6

Minerals foreign and US supply under alternative market conditions, reserves, and background industry data, series, 5606–4

Minerals production, prices, trade, use, employment, tariffs, and stockpiles, by mineral, with foreign comparisons, 1986-90, annual rpt, 5604–18

Minerals resources and production of Juneau, Alaska region, by mineral and site, 1987-88, 5608–169

Minerals resources of Alaska, production, oil and gas leases, reserves, and exploratory wells, with maps and bibl, 1989, annual rpt, 5664–11

Minerals Yearbook, 1988, Vol 3: foreign country reviews of production, trade, and policy, by commodity, annual rpt series, 5604–17

Minerals Yearbook, 1989, Vol 1: commodity reviews of production, reserves, supply, use, and trade, annual rpt series, 5604–15

Minerals Yearbook, 1989, Vol 2: State reviews of production and sales by commodity, and business activity, annual rpt series, 5604–16

Minerals Yearbook, 1989, Vol 2: State reviews of production, sales, and firms, by commodity, and business activity, annual rpt, 5604–34

Minerals Yearbook, 1990, Vol 1: commodity reviews of production, reserves, supply, use, and trade, annual rpt series, 5604–20

Multinatl US firms and foreign affiliates finances and operations, by industry and world area of parent firm, 1989 benchmark survey, preliminary annual rpt, 2704–5

OECD trade, total and for 4 major countries, and US trade by country, by commodity, 1970-89, world area rpt series, 9116–1

Overseas Business Reports: economic conditions, investment and export opportunities, and trade practices, country market research rpt series, 2046–6

Soviet Union and US production and consumption of selected commodities, by commodity, 1960s-90, annual rpt, 9114–4.3

Soviet Union, Eastern Europe, OECD, and selected other countries industrial production and trade, by commodity, 1960s-90, annual rpt, 9114–4

Soviet Union minerals production and trade, by commodity, 1985-89 and projected to 2005, annual rpt, 5604–39

Textile imports, total and from US, by commodity and country, 1987-89, 2048–155

Wholesale trade sales and inventories, by SIC 2- to 3-digit kind of business, monthly rpt, 2413–7

Natural Resources, Environment, and Pollution

Endangered animals and plants US trade and permits, by species, purpose, disposition, and country, 1989, annual rpt, 5504–19

Prices and Cost of Living

Brazil price variability among products and cities, relation to inflation, alternative model results for 1980s, working paper, 9379–14.14

CPI by component for US city average, and by region, population size, and for 15 metro areas, monthly rpt, 6762–1

CPI by component for US city average, and by region, population size, and for 27 metro areas, monthly rpt, 6762–2

CPI changes for selected items, 1981-90, annual article, 6722–1.226

CPI components relative importance, by selected MSA, region, population size, and for US city average, 1990, annual rpt, 6884–1

CPI current statistics, Monthly Labor Review, 6722–1.4

Department store inventory price indexes, by class of item, monthly table, 6762–7

Export and import price indexes, by selected end-use category, monthly press release, 6762–15

Export and import price indexes for goods and services, and dollar exchange rate indexes, quarterly press release, 6762–13

Farm prices received and paid, by commodity and State, 1990, annual rpt, 1629–5

Farm prices received and production value, by detailed crop and State, 1988-90, annual rpt, 1621–2

Farm prices received for major products and paid for farm inputs and living items, by commodity and State, monthly rpt, 1629–1

Food consumer research, marketing, legislation, and regulation devs, and consumption and price trends, quarterly journal, 1541–7

Food cost index alternative to CPI, by category, region, and household income, size, race, and food budget level, 1980-85, 1598–275

Food prices (farm-retail), marketing cost components, and industry finances and productivity, 1920s-90, annual rpt, 1544–9

Foreign and US economic conditions, for major industrial countries, biweekly rpt, 9112–1

Fruit and vegetable wholesale prices in NYC by State, and shipments and arrivals by mode of transport, by commodity, weekly rpt, 1311–20

Fruit and vegetable wholesale prices in NYC, Chicago, and selected shipping points, by crop, 1990, annual rpt, 1311–8

North Central States farm credit conditions and economic devs, Fed Reserve 7th District, monthly rpt, 9375–10

Price indexes (consumer and producer), by commodity group, selected years 1929-90, annual rpt, 204–1.4

Producer Price Index, by major commodity group and subgroup, and processing stage, monthly press release, 6762–5

Producer price indexes, by stage of processing and detailed commodity, monthly rpt, 6762–6

Producer price indexes, by stage of processing and detailed commodity, monthly 1990, annual rpt, 6764–2

Statistical Abstract of US, 1991 annual data compilation, 2324–1.15

Index by Categories

Survey of Current Business, detailed data for major industries and economic indicators, monthly rpt, 2702–1.5

Texas, Dallas-Ft Worth and Houston MSAs, CPI by major component, monthly rpt, 6962–2

Public Welfare and Social Security

Food aid programs purchases, by commodity, firm, and shipping point or destination, weekly rpt, 1302–3

BY FEDERAL AGENCY

Agriculture and Food

Food safety and quality regulation activities, funding, and staff, by Federal agency, 1980s, GAO rpt, 26113–503

PL 480 exports by commodity, and recipients, by program, sponsor, and country, FY88 and cumulative from FY55, annual rpt, 1924–7

Banking, Finance, and Insurance

Debt delinquent on Federal accounts, cases and collections of Justice Dept and private law firms, pilot project results, FY90, annual rpt, 6004–20

Fed Financing Bank holdings and transactions, by borrower, monthly press release, 12802–1

Money laundering investigations of Fed Govt using IRS large cash transaction rpts, and rpts filed and penalties for nonfiling by region, 1989-91, GAO rpt, 26119–356

Communications and Transportation

Audiovisual activities and spending of Fed Govt, by whether performed in-house and agency, FY90, annual rpt, 9514–1

Hwy and mass transit funding and regulation by Fed Govt and States, FY91 with projections to FY96, 26358–242

Hwy funding provisions, by Federal agency and program, as of Jan 1991, biennial rpt, 7554–37

Radio frequency assignments for Federal use, by agency, 1st half 1990, semiannual rpt, 2802–1

Shipborne cargo sponsored by Fed Govt, total and US-flag share by agency and program, 1989, annual rpt, 7704–14.3

Education

Exchange and training programs of Federal agencies, participants by world area, and funding, by program, FY89, annual rpt, 9854–8

Expenditures for education by Federal agency, program, and recipient type, and instn spending, FY80-90, annual rpt, 4824–8

Expenditures for education, by Federal agency, program, and State, FY80-90, annual rpt, 4824–2.27

Energy Resources and Demand

Bonneville Power Admin mgmt of Fed Columbia River Power System, finances, operations, and sales by customer, FY90, annual rpt, 3224–1

Electric power admins and utlities of Fed Govt, finances and operations, 1989, annual rpt, 3164–24.2

Energy use and efficiency of Fed Govt, by agency and fuel type, FY90, annual rpt, 3304–22

Energy use of Fed Govt, by agency and fuel type, FY77-90, annual rpt, 3164–74.1

Geography and Climate

Weather services activities and funding, by Federal agency, planned FY91-92, annual rpt, 2144–2

Government and Defense

Advisory committees of Fed Govt, and members, staff, meetings, and costs by agency, FY90, annual rpt, 9454–18

Assistance (financial) of Fed Govt to State and local govts, by program, budget function, and agency, FY90, GAO rpt, 26121–421

Assistance (financial and nonfinancial) of Fed Govt, 1991 base edition with supplements, annual listing, 104–5

Budget of US, authoritative financial statements with appropriations, outlays, and receipts, by agency, FY90, annual rpt, 8104–2

Budget of US, authority rescissions and deferrals, monthly rpt, 102–2

Budget of US, balances of budget authority obligated and unobligated, by function and agency, FY90-92, annual rpt, 104–8

Budget of US, House Budget Committee analysis of Bush Admin proposals and economic assumptions, FY92, 21268–42

Budget of US, object class analysis of obligations, by agency, FY92, annual rpt, 104–9

Budget of US, obligations and authority by function, agency, and program, with summaries, analyses, and historical tables, FY92, annual rpt, 104–2

Budget of US, receipts by source and outlays by agency, final statements compared to OMB forecasts, FY91, press release, 8008–153

Budget of US, receipts by source, outlays by agency and program, and balances, monthly rpt, 8102–3

Collective bargaining agreements of Federal employees, coverage, unions, and location, by agency, for contracts expiring 1990-91, annual listing, 9847–1

Consultants and experts appointed for temporary employment in Federal agencies, and rule violations, 1986-89, GAO rpt, 26119–354

Consulting services contracts of Fed Govt, obligations by agency, FY87-89, GAO rpt, 26119–343

Currency (foreign) holdings of US, transactions and balances by program and country, 1st half FY91, semiannual rpt, 8102–7

DC metro area land acquisition and dev projects of Fed Govt, characteristics and funding by agency and project, FY91-95, annual rpt, 15454–1

Eastern Europe economic aid of US, by agency and country, FY90-92, GAO rpt, 26123–319

Employee appeals of personnel actions, decisions of Merit Systems Protection Board by agency and region, FY90, annual rpt, 9494–2

Employee incentive awards, costs, and benefits, by award type and agency, FY89, annual rpt, 9844–20

Employee leave transfer to other employees, Federal pilot programs operations and costs by agency, FY89, 9848–40

Employment (civilian) of Fed Govt, work-years, pay rates, and benefits use and costs, by agency, FY89, annual rpt, 9844–31

BY FEDERAL AGENCY

Employment and payroll (civilian) of Fed Govt, by agency in DC metro area, total US, and abroad, bimonthly rpt, 9842–1

Employment and payroll (civilian) of Fed Govt, by occupation, pay grade, sex, agency, and location, 1989, biennial rpt, 9844–4

Employment and payroll (civilian) of Fed Govt, by pay system, agency, and location, 1990, annual rpt, 9844–6.1; 9844–6.2

Employment discrimination complaints, processing, and disposition, by complaint type and Federal agency, FY89, annual rpt, 9244–11

Expenditures of Fed Govt in States, by type, program, agency, and State, FY90, annual rpt, 2464–2

Finances of Fed Govt, cash and debt transactions, daily tables, 8102–4

Financial consolidated statements of Fed Govt based on business accounting methods, FY89-90, annual rpt, 8104–5

Financial operations of Fed Govt, detailed data, *Treasury Bulletin*, quarterly rpt, 8002–4

Fines (civil) imposed by Federal agencies, and proposed inflation adjustments, FY87, hearing, 21408–124

Fraud cases of Federal agencies involving small dollar amounts, investigations, dispositions, losses, and collections, 1986-90, GAO rpt, 26111–76

Info security nondisclosure agreements for Federal and contractor employees, prepublication reviews, and costs, 1988-90, GAO rpt, 26123–328

Info Security Oversight Office monitoring of Federal security measures and classification actions, FY90, annual rpt, 9454–21

Inspectors General audits and investigations of fraud and abuse, by agency, FY90, annual rpt, 104–29

Investigations of Federal agency and program operations, summaries of findings, 1981-90, annual GAO rpt, 26104–5

Labor Relations Fed Authority and Fed Service Impasses Panel activities, and cases by union, agency, and disposition, FY85-90, annual rpt, 13364–1

Loans, loan guarantees, and insurance programs of Fed Govt, outstanding amounts by agency and program, FY88-90, GAO rpt, 26111–65

Minority group, women, and disabled employment of Fed Govt, by agency and occupation, FY89, annual rpt, 9244–10

Prison Industries (Federal) sales, by commodity and Federal agency, FY90, annual rpt, 6244–5

Property (real) of Fed Govt, inventory and costs, worldwide summary by location, agency, and use, 1989, annual rpt, 9454–5

Property (real) of Fed Govt, leased inventory and rental costs, worldwide summary by location and agency, 1989, annual rpt, 9454–10

Property (real) spending, by selected agency, FY84-89, hearing, 21648–60

Regulatory programs of Fed Govt, evaluation, review process, and actions taken, by agency, 1980s-90, annual rpt, 104–28

Senior Executive Service membership characteristics, entries, exits, and awards, FY79-90, annual rpt, 9844–36

BY FEDERAL AGENCY

Shutdown of Fed Govt over Columbus Day holiday, employees affected, costs, and savings, Oct 1990, GAO rpt, 26119–311

Statistical programs of Fed Govt, funding by agency, FY90-92, annual rpt, 104–10

Trust funds of Fed Govt, financial condition, periodic rpt series, 8102–9

Health and Vital Statistics

Diabetes research and care services programs and funding, by Federal agency and NIH inst, FY90, annual rpt, 4474–34

Disabled persons rehabilitation, Federal and State activities and funding, FY90, annual rpt, 4944–1

Health condition and health care resources, use, and spending, 1950s-89, annual data compilation, 4144–11

Neurosciences research and public policy issues, series, 26356–9

Pollutants reproductive health and fetal dev effects, with production, trade, and Federal regulatory activities by selected substance, 1980s-90, GAO rpt, 26131–90

R&D in medicine, funding by type of source and performer, 1981-90, annual rpt, 4434–3

Reproduction and population research, Fed Govt funding by project, FY89, annual listing, 4474–9

Industry and Commerce

Export and import product standards under GATT, Natl Inst of Standards and Technology info activities, and proposed standards by agency and country, 1990, annual rpt, 2214–6

Manufacturing census, 1987: employment and shipments under Fed Govt contracts, by SIC 4-digit industry, 2497–7

Vending facilities run by blind on Federal and non-Federal property, finances and operations by agency and State, FY90, annual rpt, 4944–2

Law Enforcement

Assaults and deaths of law enforcement officers, by circumstances, agency, victim and offender characteristics, and location, 1990, annual rpt, 6224–3

Assaults on law enforcement officers and offenders involved, by agency, data compilation, 1991 annual rpt, 6064–6.3

Drug abuse and trafficking reduction grant programs and funding, by Federal agency and State, FY90-92, 236–1.5

Drug abuse and trafficking reduction programs activities, funding, staff, and Bush Admin budget request, by Federal agency and program area, FY90-92, 238–2

Drug abuse and trafficking reduction programs funding, and Bush Admin budget request, by Federal agency and program area, FY90-92, 238–1

Drug abuse treatment, prevention, and enforcement grants to States, by Federal agency and State, FY87-91, 236–1.4

Drug enforcement regional task forces investigation of organized crime, activities by agency and region, FY83-90, biennial rpt, 6004–17

Drug testing of Federal employees, results, and costs, by agency, FY87-92, GAO rpt, 26119–344

US attorneys civil cases and amounts involved, and criminal cases declined, by agency, FY90, annual rpt, 6004–2.5; 6004–2.7

Natural Resources, Environment, and Pollution

Alaska land area by ownership, and availability for mineral exploration and dev, 1984-86, 5608–152

Endangered animals and plants conservation spending of Federal agencies and States, by species, FY90, annual rpt, 5504–33

Environmental Quality, status of problems, protection programs, research, and intl issues, 1991 annual rpt, 484–1

Geological Survey reimbursable program funds from other Federal agencies, by program and agency, FY87-90, annual rpt, 5664–8

Lands (public) disposition and withdrawals from inventory, by agency and State, FY90, annual rpt, 5724–1.2

Marine mammals research, Federal funding by topic, recipient, and agency, FY90, annual rpt, 14734–2

Minerals resources and availability on public lands, State rpt series, 5606–7

Oil spill from tanker Exxon Valdez, Federal cleanup and damage assessment costs, and reimbursement from Exxon, by agency, as of Sept 1990, GAO rpt, 26113–510

Population

Census of Population, 1990: population by State and region, with Federal and military personnel abroad by State of residence and agency, press release, 2328–66

Public Welfare and Social Security

Beneficiaries deaths, erroneous benefit payments, and use of SSA and other sources of death info, by agency, 1990, GAO rpt, 26121–406

Expenditures of Fed Govt in States, by type, program, agency, and State, FY90, annual rpt, 2464–2

Homeless persons aid programs of Fed Govt, program descriptions and funding, by agency and State, FY87-90, annual GAO rpt, 26104–21

Homelessness issues, population at risk, contributing factors, and Federal funding for services and prevention, with bibl, 1991 compilation of papers, 25928–9

Older persons discrimination in Federal aid programs, Age Discrimination Act enforcement by agency, FY90, annual rpt, 4004–27

Refugee aid funding of US by program, agency, and intl organization, and admissions to US, 1980s-90, GAO rpt, 26123–334

Recreation and Leisure

Coastal areas recreation facilities, by State, county, estuary, and level of govt, 1972-84, 2178–29

Concession operations on public lands, receipts, and fees, by Federal agency and for top 100 firms, 1989, GAO rpt, 26113–531

Visits and fees for Federal outdoor recreation facilities, by managing agency, FY88-90, annual rpt, 5544–14

Science and Technology

Biotechnology commercial applications, industry finances and capitalization, patents, and govt support, for US, Japan, and EC, late 1970s-91, 26358–248

Computer and telecommunication systems acquisition plans and obligations of Fed Govt, by agency, FY89-91, last issue of annual rpt, 104–20

Index by Categories

Computer and telecommunication systems acquisition plans and obligations of Fed Govt, by agency, FY90-95, annual rpt, 104–33

Computer mainframe and related equipment procurement and compatibility, for Federal agencies, FY86-89, GAO rpt series, 26125–41

Computer systems and equipment of Fed Govt, by type, make, and agency, 2nd half FY90, semiannual listing, 9452–9

Computer systems of Fed Govt with sensitive unclassified data, security plans by characteristics of info and system, and agency, 1989, 2218–85

DOD prime contract awards for R&D to US and foreign nonprofit instns and govt agencies, by instn and location, FY90, annual listing, 3544–17

Education in science and engineering, grad programs enrollment by field, source of funds, and characteristics of student and instn, 1975-89, annual rpt, 9627–7

Higher education instn science and engineering research system status, R&D performance, and Federal support, 1950s-88, 9628–83

Info mgmt activities of Fed Govt, technology spending, and paperwork burden, by agency, planned FY91-92, annual rpt, 104–19

Labs of Fed Govt, technology transfer cooperative agreements, patents, royalties, and incentive payments to employees, by agency, FY89, GAO rpt, 26131–85

Materials (advanced structural) devs, use, and R&D funding, for ceramics, metal alloys, polymers, and composites, 1960s-80s and projected to 2000, 5608–162

Patents granted to Federal agencies, FY81-90, annual rpt, 2244–1.2

R&D and related funding of Fed Govt to higher education and nonprofit instns, by field, instn, agency, and State, FY89, annual rpt, 9627–17

R&D equipment of higher education instns, acquisition and service costs, condition, and financing, by field and subfield, 1988-90, triennial survey series, 9627–27

R&D funding by Fed Govt, by field, performer type, agency, and State, FY89-91, annual rpt, 9627–20

R&D prime contract awards of DOD, for top 500 contractors, FY90, annual listing, 3544–4

R&D spending for large nondefense projects, by field, budget function, and Federal agency, FY80-91 and projected to FY96, 26306–3.116

Space and aeronautics activities and budgets, by Federal agency, FY59-91, annual rpt, 9504–9.2

Space programs procurement contract awards of NASA and other agencies, by type, contractor, State, and country, FY91 with trends from 1961, semiannual rpt, 9502–6

Spacecraft launches and other activities of NASA and USSR, with flight data, 1957-90, annual rpt, 9504–6.1

Index by Categories

BY INCOME

Agriculture and Food

Food spending, by item, household composition, income, age, race, and region, 1980-88, Consumer Expenditure Survey biennial rpt, 1544–30

Production itemized costs, by farm sales size and region, 1990, annual rpt, 1614–3

Banking, Finance, and Insurance

Households assets, by type of holding and selected characteristics, 1988, Current Population Rpt, 2546–20.16

Communications and Transportation

Mail volume to and from households, use, and views, by class, source, content, and household characteristics, 1987-88, annual rpt, 9864–10

Telephone local service charges and low-income subsidies, by region, company, and city, 1980s-90, semiannual rpt, 9282–8

Travel patterns, personal and household characteristics, and auto and public transport use, 1990 survey, series, 7556–6

Travel patterns, personal and household characteristics, and auto use, 1990 survey, annual rpt, 7554–1.6

Truck accidents, by carrier financial and operating conditions and driver characteristics, 1980s, GAO rpt, 26131–82

Education

American Historical Assn financial statements, and membership by State, 1989, annual rpt, 29574–2

Eighth grade class of 1988: educational performance and conditions, characteristics, attitudes, activities, and plans, natl longitudinal survey, series, 4826–9

Enrollment, by grade, instn type and control, and student characteristics, 1989 and trends from 1947, annual Current Population Rpt, 2546–1.453

Higher education instn student aid and other sources of support, with student expenses and characteristics, by instn type and control, 1990 triennial study, series, 4846–5

Higher education instn tuition and other costs, govt aid, impacts on enrollment, and cost containment methods, 1970s-90 and projected to 2001, 4808–25

Private elementary and secondary schools, students, and staff characteristics, various periods 1979-88, 4838–47

Student aid, costs, and income factors affecting access to undergrad education, 1990 rpt, 26306–6.153

Student aid Pell grants and applicants, by tuition, income level, instn type and control, and State, 1989/90, annual rpt, 4804–1

Energy Resources and Demand

Housing (low income) energy aid, funding sources, costs, and participation, by State, FY89, annual rpt, 4694–8

Government and Defense

Securities (govt) purchases and holdings of individuals and households, terms, and purchase methods, 1980s-90, 8008–148

Tax (income) returns filed by type of filer, selected income items, quarterly rpt, 8302–2.1

Tax (income) returns filed, by whether filed electronically, taxpayer characteristics, and reason for not filing electronically, 1990, article, 8304–8.1

Tax (income) returns of high income individuals not filed, by selected characteristics, 1987, and assessments under alternative IRS enforcement programs, 1990, GAO rpt, 26119–322

Tax (income) returns of individuals, selected income and tax items, by adjusted gross income and State, 1986-88, article, 8302–2.201

Tax (income) returns of individuals, selected income and tax items by income level, preliminary 1989, annual article, 8302–2.209

Tax (income) returns of individuals, taxable income, and tax generated, by tax rate and income level, 1987, annual article, 8302–2.211

Tax rates and revenue of State and local govts, by source and State, 1991 and historical trends, annual rpt, 10044–1

Tax returns filed, by type of tax and IRS region and service center, projected 1990-97 and trends from 1978, annual rpt, 8304–9

Taxes, spending, and govt efficiency, public opinion by respondent characteristics, 1991 survey, annual rpt, 10044–2

Voting and registration, by socioeconomic and demographic characteristics, 1990 congressional election, biennial Current Population Rpt, 2546–1.454

Health and Vital Statistics

Acute and chronic health conditions, disability, absenteeism, and health services use, by selected characteristics, 1987, CD-ROM, 4147–10.177

Alcohol abuse by family members and spouses, population exposure by selected characteristics, 1988, 4146–8.207

Births, fertility rates, and childless women, by selected characteristics, 1990, annual Current Population Rpt, 2546–1.455

Cancer cases, by race, income, education, and area population density, for 3 metro areas, 1978-82, article, 4472–1.210

Child developmental, learning, and emotional problems, cases and share receiving special treatment and education, by selected characteristics, 1988, 4146–8.193

Child health, behavioral, emotional, and school problems relation to family structure, by selected characteristics, 1988, 4147–10.178

Disability (functional), persons needing aid with activities of daily living, by age and household income, 1986, fact sheet, 2326–17.22

Disabled persons and related activity limitation days and health services use, by health status, disability type, and other characteristics, 1984-88, 4146–8.202

Drug, alcohol, and cigarette use, by selected characteristics, and for DC, 1990 survey, biennial rpt, 4494–5.3

Health condition and health care resources, use, and spending, 1950s-89, annual data compilation, 4144–11

Hospices use by cancer patients, by service type, use of other facilities, patient and instn characteristics, and other indicators, local area study, 1980-85, 4658–53

Implants of medical devices, by type, reason, duration, and user characteristics, 1988, 4146–8.197

Injuries, by type, circumstances, and victim characteristics, and related activity limitations, 1985-87, 4147–10.176

Injuries, related impairments, and activity limitations, by circumstances and victim characteristics, 1985-87, 4147–10.179

Insurance (health) coverage of children, and children with a regular source of care, by selected characteristics, 1988, 4146–8.192

Insurance (health) coverage of children, by source, family composition, income, and parent employment status, 1977 and 1987, 4186–8.14

Insurance (health) coverage, uninsured persons by employment and other characteristics and State, 1988, GAO rpt, 26121–403

Insurance (health) coverage, uninsured population under age 65 by selected characteristics, 1987, 4186–8.13

Insurance (health) natl coverage alternative proposals and indicators of need, 1989, 4658–54

Insurance (life) predeath benefits use to finance long-term care, payout terms, 1990, and coverage by beneficiary characteristics, 1984, 2626–10.128

Minority group and women health condition, services use, payment sources, and health care labor force, by poverty status, 1940s-89, chartbook, 4118–56

Minority group health condition, services use, costs, and indicators of services need, 1950s-88, 4118–55

Smoking exposure of children before and after birth, by source and degree of exposure and family characteristics, 1988, 4146–8.204

Housing and Construction

Affordability indicators for housing, by household composition, income, and current tenure, 1988, 2486–1.11

American Housing Survey: inventory change from 1973, by reason, unit and household characteristics, and location, 1983, biennial rpt, 2485–14

American Housing Survey: unit and households characteristics, unit and neighborhood quality, and journey to work by MSA location, for 11 MSAs, 1984 survey, supplement, 2485–8

American Housing Survey: unit and households detailed characteristics, and unit and neighborhood quality, MSA rpt series, 2485–6

American Housing Survey: unit and households detailed characteristics, and unit and neighborhood quality, 1987, biennial rpt, 2485–12

American Housing Survey: unit and households detailed characteristics, and unit and neighborhood quality, 1987, biennial rpt supplement, 2485–13

Housing value capitalization of property tax, model description and results for Philadelphia, 1982, working paper, 9387–8.252

Mortgage applications by disposition, and secondary loan market sales by purchaser type, by applicant and neighborhood characteristics, 1990, article, 9362–1.206

Mortgages FHA-insured, financial, property, and mortgagor characteristics, by metro area, 1990, annual rpt, 5144–24

BY INCOME

Mortgages FHA-insured, financial, property, and mortgagor characteristics, by State, 1990, annual rpt, 5144–1

Mortgages FHA-insured, financial, property, and mortgagor characteristics, 1990, annual rpt, 5144–17; 5144–23

Retirement housing centers tax-exempt bond use and other financing, defaults, and facility and resident characteristics, 1991 GAO rpt, 26119–328

Labor and Employment

Insurance (life) benefits and age-related reductions of employee plans, by employee characteristics, 1989, article, 6722–1.216

Part-time employment by health insurance coverage and worker characteristics, and temporary and contract employment, 1979-89, GAO rpt, 26121–411

Vocational rehabilitation cases of State agencies by disposition and applicant characteristics, and closures by reason, FY84-88, annual rpt, 4944–6

Youth employment by selected characteristics, with child labor law violations and injuries, 1983-90, GAO rpt, 26121–426

Law Enforcement

Crimes, by characteristics of victim and offender, circumstances, and location, data compilation, 1991 annual rpt, 6064–6.3

Criminal case processing in Federal district courts, and dispositions, by offense, district, and offender characteristics, 1986, annual rpt, 6064–29

Jail population, by criminal, correctional, drug use, and family history, and selected other characteristics, 1989, 6066–19.62

Jail population drug abuse history, by offense, conviction status, criminal and family history, and selected other characteristics, 1989, 6066–19.63

Prisoners and movements, by offense, location, and selected other characteristics, data compilation, 1991 annual rpt, 6064–6.6

Public opinion on crime and crime-related issues, by respondent characteristics, data compilation, 1991 annual rpt, 6064–6.2

Victimization rates, by victim and offender characteristics, circumstances, and offense, 1988 survey, annual rpt, 6066–3.42

Victimization rates, by victim and offender characteristics, circumstances, and offense, 1989 survey, annual rpt, 6066–3.44

Victimizations by region and victim characteristics, and rpts to police, by offense, 1973-90, annual rpt, 6066–25.35; 6066–25.41

Victimizations of households, by offense, household characteristics, and location, 1975-90, annual rpt, 6066–25.40

Women's rape and other violent crime victimization, by relation to offender, circumstances, and victim characteristics, 1973-87, 6068–243

Population

Black Americans social and economic characteristics, for South and total US, 1989-90 and trends from 1969, Current Population Rpt, 2546–1.450

Consumer Income, socioeconomic characteristics of persons, families, and households, detailed cross-tabulations, Current Population Rpt series, 2546–6

Index by Categories

Disparity between incomes of wealthiest and other families, and income sources, 1980s and trends from 1949, 23848–219

Hispanic Americans social and economic characteristics, by detailed origin, 1991, Current Population Rpt, 2546–1.448; 2546–1.451

Households and family characteristics, by location, 1990, annual Current Population Rpt, 2546–1.447

Households income and consumer spending, for selected population groups, quarterly journal, 1702–1

Households income and poverty status under alternative income definitions, by recipient characteristics, 1990, annual Current Population Rpt, 2546–6.69

Immigrants in US, population characteristics and fertility, by birthplace and compared to native born, 1980s, Current Population rpt, 2546–2.162

Indian Health Service facilities and use, and Indian health and other characteristics, by IHS region, 1980s-89, annual chartbook, 4084–7

Living arrangements, family relationships, and marital status, by selected characteristics, 1990, annual Current Population Rpt, 2546–1.449

Poverty status of population and families, by detailed characteristics, 1988-89, annual Current Population Rpt, 2546–6.67

Poverty status of population and families, by detailed characteristics, 1990, annual Current Population Rpt, 2546–6.71

Prices and Cost of Living

Child rearing costs of married couple households, by expenditure type, child's age, income, and region, 1990 and projected to 2007, 1708–87

Consumer Expenditure Survey, household income by source, and itemized spending, by selected characteristics and region, 1988-89, annual rpt, 6764–5

Consumer Expenditure Survey, spending by category, and income, by selected household characteristics and location, 1990, annual press release, 6726–1.42

Consumer Expenditure Survey, spending by category, selected household characteristics, and region, quarterly rpt, 6762–14

Foreign countries living costs, State Dept indexes, housing allowances, and hardship differentials by country and major city, quarterly rpt, 7002–7

Public Welfare and Social Security

Child care arrangements, costs, and impacts on mothers labor force status, by selected characteristics, 1983 and 1988, article, 6722–1.246

Child support and alimony awards, and payment status, by selected characteristics of woman, 1989, biennial Current Population Rpt, 2546–6.72

Earnings replacement rates of pension plans and OASI benefits, by age, salary, years of participation, and occupational group, 1989, article, 6722–1.238

Food stamp eligibility and payment errors, by type, recipient characteristics, and State, FY89, annual rpt, 1364–15

Food stamp recipient household size, composition, income, and income and deductions allowed, summer 1988, annual rpt, 1364–8

Medicare disabled enrollees supplementary health insurance coverage, by enrollee characteristics, 1984, article, 4652–1.243

OASDHI, Medicaid, SSI, and related programs benefits, beneficiary characteristics, and trust funds, selected years 1937-89, annual rpt, 4744–3

Student Community Service Program activities, and volunteer and client characteristics, 1987-89, 9028–14

Recreation and Leisure

Coastal areas recreation facilities of Fed Govt and States, visitor and site characteristics, 1987-90 survey, regional rpt series, 2176–9

Shellfish recreational harvesters selected characteristics, location of harvest and residence, and spending, 1985 survey, 2178–28

Science and Technology

Computer use at home, school, and work, by family income, 1989, fact sheet, 2326–17.30

Computer use at home, school, and work, by purpose and selected user characteristics, 1989, Current Population Rpt, 2546–2.158

Veterans Affairs

Homeless veterans domiciliary program of VA, participant characteristics and outcomes, 1990 annual rpt, 8604–10

Homeless veterans with mental illness, VA program services, costs, staff, client characteristics, and outcome, 1990, annual rpt, 8604–11

Housing programs of VA, costs, terms, and user characteristics, 1985-89, 8608–7

BY INDIVIDUAL COMPANY OR INSTITUTION

Agriculture and Food

Beer brewing intl licensing agreements, by major firm, 1987, article, 9391–1.201

Cooperatives, finances, operations, activities, and membership, commodity rpt series, 1126–1

Cooperatives sales, for 14 coops on *Fortune* 500 list, 1990, article, 1122–1.205

Fertilizer production capacity by firm, for US and Canada, 1986-91 and projected to 1997, triennial rpt, 9808–66

Fish Hatchery Natl System activities and deliveries, by species, hatchery, and jurisdiction of waters stocked, FY90, annual rpt, 5504–10

Food retailers after-tax profits, aggregate and for 16 supermarket chains, 1990, annual rpt, 1544–9.3

Foreign countries agricultural research grants of USDA, by program, subagency, and country, FY90, annual listing, 1954–3

Grain handling facility explosions and casualties, by firm, FY90, annual rpt, 1294–1

Livestock, meat, and wool, market news summary data by animal type and market, weekly rpt, 1315–1

Meat plants inspected and certified for exporting to US, by country, 1990, annual listing, 1374–2

PL 480 exports by commodity, and recipients, by program, sponsor, and country, FY88 and cumulative from FY55, annual rpt, 1924–7

Poultry Natl Improvement Plan participating hatcheries and birds, by species and disease program, 1991, annual listing, 1394–15

Index by Categories

BY INDIVIDUAL COMPANY OR INSTITUTION

Research (agricultural) funding and staffing for USDA, State agencies, and other instns, by topic, FY90, annual rpt, 1744–2

Research and education grants, USDA competitive awards by program and recipient, FY90, annual listing, 1764–1

Salt production capacity, by firm and facility, 1990, annual listing, 5614–30

Snack foods and sweets nutrient, caloric, and waste composition, detailed data for raw, processed, and prepared products by brand, 1991 rpt, 1356–3.16

Banking, Finance, and Insurance

- Acquisitions and mergers by type, with data for large transactions by payment method and firm, late 1960s-90, working paper, 9366–1.161
- Acquisitions and mergers of banks in Southeastern States, assets and major institutions involved, by State, 1984-89, article, 9371–1.203
- Bank deposit insurance system reform issues, with background industry financial data, 1970s-90, GAO rpt, 26119–320
- Banking intl competition and deposit insurance reform issues, with background data, 1990 hearings, 25248–121; 25248–122
- Bankruptcy filings with SEC participation, by firm, FY90, annual rpt, 9734–2.4
- Banks (insured commercial and savings) deposits by instn, State, MSA, and county, as of June 1990, annual regional rpt series, 9295–3
- Banks (natl) charters, mergers, liquidations, enforcement cases, and financial performance, with data by instn and State, quarterly rpt, 8402–3
- Banks and deposit insurance funds financial condition, potential losses, and regulatory issues, 1980s-90 and projected to 1995, 21248–147
- Banks failures, assets and losses to FDIC, for State-chartered Fed Reserve members by instn, 1984-90, hearing, 21242–1
- Banks failures, interbank exposure risk indicators by bank size, 1980s-90, working paper, 9377–9.107
- Banks failures involving assets over $90 million, listing by instn, 1973-89, working paper, 9377–9.115
- Banks financial performance, risk assessment, and regulation, 1990 annual conf papers, 9375–7
- Banks in Fed Reserve 3rd District, assets, income, and rates of return, by major instn, quarterly rpt, annual table, 9387–10
- Banks in Fed Reserve 3rd District established since 1985, assets by firm, as of Jan 1990, article, 9387–1.201
- Banks market value calculation method to expose undercapitalization, with model results and background data for selected failed banks, 1960s-89, working paper, 9377–9.112
- Banks mergers and consolidations approved by Fed Reserve Board of Governors, 1990, annual rpt, 9364–1.2
- Banks mergers approved, and assets and offices involved, by instn, 1989, annual rpt, 9294–5
- Bond (junk) holdings of Resolution Trust Corp, quarterly press release, 9722–4
- Credit unions assets, members, and location, 1991 annual listing, 9534–6

Credit unions federally insured, finances by instn characteristics and State, as of June 1991, semiannual rpt, 9532–6

- Credit unions federally insured, finances, mergers, closings, and insurance fund losses and financial statements, FY90, annual rpt, 9534–7
- Credit unions federally insured, finances, 1989-90, annual rpt, 9534–1
- Eximbank financial condition, with credit and insurance authorizations and loan activity by country, FY90, annual rpt, 9254–1
- Fed Financing Bank holdings and transactions, by borrower, monthly press release, 12802–1
- Fed Home Loan Banks financial statements, 1988-90, annual rpt, 9444–1
- Foreign-owned banks US subsidiaries, assets, and regulatory issues, with data by State and firm, 1989-90, hearing, 21248–155
- Fraud and abuse in banks and thrifts, Federal agencies enforcement activities and staff, with data by instn and location, 1988-90, hearing, 21408–119
- Futures and options trading volume, by commodity and exchange, FY90, annual rpt, 11924–2
- Insurance (life) companies finances, performance ratios, and problem holdings, by firm, 1989-90, hearing, 21368–133
- Insurance (property and casualty) industry recoverable reinsurance, by firm, 1988, hearing, 21368–133
- Intl banking and securities instns assets by selected firm, and financial performance indicators by selected country, late 1980s-90, article, 9385–1.206
- Intl financial instns funds by source and disbursements by purpose, by country, with US policy review, FY89, annual rpt, 15344–1
- Investment banking firms stock performance relation to returns on underwritten stock issues, late 1970s-87, technical paper, 9366–6.260
- Japan financial instns and stock market conditions, and other economic indicators, with intl comparisons, 1980s-90, hearing, 21248–152
- Mexico banks deregulation impacts on finances, with data by bank, 1960s-90, technical paper, 9385–8.121
- North Central States, FHLB 8th District S&Ls, locations, assets, and savings, 1991, annual listing, 9304–9
- Overseas Private Investment Corp finances and activities, with list of insured projects and firms, FY90, annual rpt, 9904–2
- Partnerships (limited) conversion to corporations, and impacts on share values, with data by firm, 1980s-91, hearing, 25248–124
- Savings instns failure resolution activity and finances of Resolution Trust Corp, with data by asset type, State, region, and instn, monthly rpt, 9722–3
- Savings instns failure resolution activity of Resolution Trust Corp, assets, deposits, and assets availability and sales, periodic press release, 9722–1
- Savings instns failure resolution activity of Resolution Trust Corp, with assets and retained senior executives compensation, by instn, 1988-90, hearing, 21248–144

Savings instns failure resolution activity of Resolution Trust Corp, with data by State and instn, and RTC financial statements, 1989, annual rpt, 9724–1

- Savings instns failure resolution activity of Resolution Trust Corp, with instns assets and senior executive compensation, 1990, hearing, 21248–157
- Savings instns failures, inventory of real estate assets available from Resolution Trust Corp, semiannual listing series, 9722–2
- Securities firms equity capital costs and financial ratios, with data by firm, for US and Japan, 1980s-91, article, 9385–1.212
- Securities purchases, sales, and holdings, by issuer and type and ownership of security, monthly listing, 9732–2
- Securities trading activity and automation, with data by country, exchange, security type, and individual contract, 1980s-90, article, 9371–1.209
- Stock exchange trading volume, securities listed by type, and finances, by exchange, selected years 1938-89, annual rpt, 9734–2.1; 9734–2.2
- Stock short selling activity indicators, and regulatory issues, 1980s-89 and trends from 1940, hearings, 21408–122
- Texas economic and housing conditions, bank failures, and thrift and Federal regulators real estate holdings, 1980s-90, hearings, 21248–146
- UK firms acquisition of US firms, financing sources, and rates of return, with data by firm, 1980s, technical paper, 9385–8.82
- West Central States, Fed Reserve 10th District banking industry structure, performance, and financial devs, 1990, annual rpt, 9381–14
- West Central States, FHLB 10th District thrifts, locations, assets, and deposits, 1991, annual listing, 9304–17
- Western States, FHLB 11th District S&Ls, offices, and financial condition, 1991 annual listing, 9304–23

Communications and Transportation

- Air traffic (passenger), and aircraft operations by type, by airport and State, projected FY91-2005 and trends from FY83, annual rpt, 7504–7
- Air traffic (passenger and cargo), and departures by aircraft type, by carrier and airport, 1990, annual rpt, 7504–35
- Air traffic (passenger and cargo), carrier enplanement shares, and FAA airport improvement program grants, by airport and State, 1989, annual rpt, 7504–48
- Air traffic, and passenger and freight enplanements, by airport, 1960s-90 and projected to 2010, hub area rpt series, 7506–7
- Air traffic, capacity, and performance, by carrier and type of operation, monthly rpt, 7302–6
- Air traffic, capacity, and performance for medium regionals, by carrier, quarterly rpt, 7302–8
- Air traffic, carriers, craft, airports, and FAA activities, detailed data, 1980-89, annual rpt, 7504–1
- Air traffic levels at FAA-operated control facilities, by airport and State, FY90, annual rpt, 7504–27

BY INDIVIDUAL COMPANY OR INSTITUTION

Index by Categories

Air traffic, pilots, airports, and fuel use, forecast FY91-2002 and trends from FY81, annual rpt, 7504–6

Aircraft (general aviation), flight hours, and equipment, by type, use, and model of aircraft, region, and State, 1990, annual rpt, 7504–29

Aircraft accidents and circumstances, for US operations of domestic and foreign airlines and general aviation, periodic rpt, 9612–1

Aircraft accidents, deaths, and circumstances, by carrier and carrier type, preliminary 1990, annual press release, 9614–9

Aircraft maintenance requirements of FAA for aging craft, airlines compliance and repair facilities operations, 1989-91, GAO rpt, 26113–527

Aircraft registered with FAA, by type and characteristics of aircraft, make, carrier, State, and county, 1989, annual rpt, 7504–3

Airline consumer complaints by reason, passengers denied boarding, and late flights, by reporting carrier and airport, monthly rpt, 7302–11

Airline consumer complaints, passengers denied boarding, and late flights, by carrier, 1985-91, GAO rpt, 26113–542

Airline deregulation in 1978, impacts on industry structure, competition, fares, finances, operations, and intl service, with data by carrier and airport, 1980s, series, 7308–199

Airline finances, by carrier, carrier group, and for total certificated system, quarterly rpt, 7302–7

Airline financial and operating summary data, quarterly rpt, 7502–16

Airline flight and engine hours, and shutdown rates, by aircraft and engine model, and air carrier, monthly rpt, 7502–13

Airport improvement program of FAA, activities and grants by State and airport, FY90, annual rpt, 7504–38

Airport planning and dev project grants of FAA, by airport and location, quarterly press release, 7502–14

Auto and auto equipment recalls for safety-related defects, by make, monthly listing, 7762–12

Auto engine and power train R&D projects, DOE contracts and funding by recipient, FY90, annual rpt, 3304–17

Auto safety, crash test results by domestic and foreign model, press release series, 7766–7

Boats (recreational) and engines recalls for safety-related defects, by make, periodic listing, 7402–5

Bus (Class I) passengers and selected revenue data, for individual large carriers, quarterly rpt, 9482–13

Bus connector service between rural areas and Greyhound intercity routes, finances and operations by system, 1987-90, 7888–79

Bus finances and operations, by carrier, 1989, annual rpt, 9486–6.3

Coast Guard search and rescue missions, and lives and property lost and saved, by district and assisting unit, FY90, annual rpt, 7404–2

Containers (intermodal) and equipment owned by shipping and leasing companies, inventory by type and size, 1990, annual rpt, 7704–10

Hazardous materials transport violations and DOT penalties assessed, by company, 1989, annual rpt, 7304–4

Helicopters, use, and landing facilities, by craft type, region, and State, 1989, 7508–75

Hwy construction bids and contracts for Federal-aid hwys, by State, 1st half 1991, semiannual rpt, 7552–12

Magazine ad costs and circulation, for travel magazines in selected countries, 1991-92, annual rpt, 2904–11

Maritime Commission activities, case filings by type and disposition, and civil penalties by shipper, FY90, annual rpt, 9334–1

Motorcycle operating costs by component, for 4 makes, and Fed Govt mileage reimbursement rates, 1989, annual rpt, 9454–13.3

Parcel deliveries to and from households, carrier preferences, and content, for USPS and competitors, 1987-88, annual rpt, 9864–10

Railroad (Class I) finances and operations, detailed data by firm, class of service, and district, 1989, annual rpt, 9486–6.1

Railroad accidents, casualties, and damage, by cause, railroad, and State, 1990, annual rpt, 7604–1

Railroad-hwy grade-crossing accidents, detailed data by State and railroad, 1989, annual rpt, 7604–2

Railroad retirement system funding and benefits findings and recommendations, with background industry data, 1960s-90 and projected to 2060, 9708–1

Railroad revenue, income, freight, and rate of return, by Class I freight railroad and district, quarterly rpt, 9482–2

Railroad safety violation claims settled, by carrier, FY90, annual rpt, 7604–10

Shipbuilding and conversion costs for merchant ships by owner and builder, fleet size, and employment, monthly rpt, 7702–1

Shipbuilding and operating subsidies of MarAd, by vessel type and firm, FY90, annual rpt, 7704–14.1; 7704–14.2

Shipbuilding and repair facilities, capacity, and employment, by shipyard, 1990, annual rpt, 7704–9

Ships and marine facilities accidents, casualties, and circumstances, Coast Guard investigation results, periodic rpt, 9612–4

Ships in US merchant fleet and Natl Defense Reserve Fleet, vessels, tonnage, and owner, as of Jan 1991, semiannual listing, 7702–2

Ships under foreign flag owned by US firms and foreign affiliates, by type, owner, and country of registry and construction, as of Jan 1991, semiannual rpt, 7702–3

Ships weather rpts, and gale and wave observations, quarterly journal, 2152–8

Subway accidents, casualties, and damage, by circumstances and system, 1989, annual rpt, 7884–5

Telecommunications fiber optics and copper wire mileage and access lines, and fiber systems investment, by firm, 1985-90, annual rpt, 9284–18

Telecommunications finances, rates, and traffic for US carriers intl operations, by service type, firm, and country, 1975-89, annual rpt, 9284–17

Telecommunications industry intl competitiveness, with financial and operating data by product or service, firm, and country, 1990 rpt, 2008–30

Telephone and telegraph firms detailed finances and operations, 1989, annual rpt, 9284–6

Telephone firms borrowing under Rural Telephone Program, and financial and operating data, by State, 1990, annual rpt, 1244–2

Telephone service subscribership, charges, and local and long distance firm finances and operations, late 1970s-91, semiannual rpt, 9282–7

Transit systems finances and operations, by mode of transport, size of fleet, and for 468 systems, 1989, annual rpt, 7884–4

Travel agencies contracts of GSA, by business size and recipient, FY88-90, GAO rpt, 26119–331

Truck transport of household goods, financial and operating data by firm, quarterly rpt, 9482–14

Truck transport of household goods, performance and disposition of damage claims, for selected carriers, 1990, annual rpt, 9484–11

Truck transport of property, financial and operating data by region and firm, quarterly rpt, 9482–5

Urban Mass Transportation Admin research and training grants to higher education instns, by project, FY90, annual listing, 7884–7

Education

Assns for education and library professionals, staff and membership, by assn, 1991 GAO rpt, 26121–414

Black higher education instns finances, funding sources, enrollment, and student characteristics, with data for Louisiana instns, 1970s-90, hearing, 25258–24

Catholic school enrollment in top 20 dioceses, 1987/88, 4838–47

Digest of Education Statistics, 1991 annual data compilation, 4824–2

Elementary and secondary public school agencies, by enrollment size and location, fall 1989, annual listing, 4834–1

Higher education admissions applicants from in- and out-of-State, for 8 public instns, 1970s-88, 4808–24

Higher education instn endowment funds, for top 100 instns, FY87, annual rpt, 4824–2.25

Humanities Natl Endowment activities and grants, FY90, annual rpt, 9564–2

Japan-US Friendship Commission educational and cultural exchange activities, grants, and trust fund status, FY89-90, biennial report, 14694–1

Libraries for blind and handicapped, readership, circulation, staff, funding, and holdings, FY90, annual listing, 26404–3

Libraries selected characteristics, for largest public and higher education facilities, 1991 edition, annual rpt, 4824–2.30

Libraries technological aid, project descriptions and funding, FY89, annual listing, 4874–6

Library science training grants for disadvantaged students, by instn and State, FY90, annual listing, 4874–1

Index by Categories

BY INDIVIDUAL COMPANY OR INSTITUTION

Literacy programs in workplaces, demonstration projects funding and participant characteristics, FY88, 4808–37

Literacy programs in workplaces, Education Dept funding and project descriptions, FY90, annual listing, 4804–40

Student guaranteed loan activity, by program, guarantee agency, and State, quarterly rpt, 4802–2

Student guaranteed loans, defaults, and collections, by type of loan, lender, and guarantee agency, with data by State and top lender, FY90, annual rpt, 4804–38

Student loans of Fed Govt in default, losses, and rates, by instn and State, as of June 1990, annual rpt, 4804–18

Student supplemental grants, loans, and work-study awards, Federal share by instn and State, 1991/92, annual listing, 4804–17

Energy Resources and Demand

Alaska minerals resources, production, oil and gas leases, reserves, and exploratory wells, with maps and bibl, 1989, annual rpt, 5664–11

Auto and light truck fuel economy performance by make, standards, and enforcement, 1978-91 model years, annual rpt, 7764–9

Auto fuel economy test results for US and foreign makes, 1992 model year, annual rpt, 3304–11

Bonneville Power Admin mgmt of Fed Columbia River Power System, finances, operations, and sales by customer, FY90, annual rpt, 3224–1

Bonneville Power Admin sales, revenues, and rates, by customer and customer type, 1990, semiannual rpt, 3222–1

Coal imports and prices, total and for individual power plants, by country and State of origin, quarterly rpt, 3162–37.5

Coal leasing activity on Federal land, acreage, production, and reserves, by coal region and State, FY90, annual rpt, 5724–10

Coal production by top 20 companies, total and from new mines, 1989, annual rpt, 3164–25

Coal production, stocks, and shipments, by State of origin and destination, end-use sector, and mode of transport, quarterly rpt, 3162–8

Coal shipments to electric utilities under contract, and rates, by firm, transport mode, and region, 1979-87, 3168–121

Conservation aid of Fed Govt to public and nonprofit private instns, by building type and State, 1990, annual rpt, 3304–15

DOE contracts and grants, by category, State, and for top contractors, FY90, annual rpt, 3004–21

Electric power and industrial plants prohibited from oil and gas primary use, and gas use by State, 1977-90, annual rpt, 3334–1

Electric power plants (steam) fuel receipts, costs, and quality, by fuel, plant, utility, and State, 1990, annual rpt, 3164–42

Electric power plants and capacity, by fuel used, owner, location, and operating status, 1990 and for units planned 1991-2000, annual listing, 3164–36

Electric power plants certification applications filed with FERC, for small production and cogeneration facilities, FY80-90, annual listing, 3084–13

Electric power plants production and capital costs, operations, and fuel use, by fuel type, plant, utility, and location, 1989, annual rpt, 3164–9

Electric power plants, production and fuel use and costs, by utility and plant, monthly rpt, 3162–35

Electric power sales and revenue, by end-use sector, consumption level, and utility, 1989, annual rpt, 3164–91

Electric power wholesale purchases of REA borrowers, by borrower, supplier, and State, 1940-89, annual rpt, 1244–5

Electric power wholesale trade, by utility, type of ownership, and region, 1988, biennial rpt, 3164–92

Electric utilities privately owned, finances and operations, detailed data, 1989, annual rpt, 3164–23

Electric utilities publicly owned, finances and operations, 1989, annual rpt, 3164–24.1

Electric utilities purchase contracts with nonutility generators, competitive bidding use, 1980s-90, GAO rpt, 26113–498

Foreign countries oil and gas reserves and discoveries, by country and country group, quarterly rpt, 3162–43

Foreign direct investment in US energy sources by type and firm, and US affiliates operations, as of 1989, annual rpt, 3164–80

Geothermal resources, power plant capacity and operating status, leases, and wells, by location, 1960s-94, 3308–87

Helium and other components of natural gas, analyses of individual wells and pipelines, 1917-90, annual rpt, 5604–2

Hydroelectric power plants licensed by FERC, characteristics and location, as of Oct 1991, annual listing, 3084–11

Hydrogen energy R&D activity and funding of DOE, and project listing, FY90, annual rpt, 3304–18

Inventions recommended by Natl Inst of Standards and Technology for DOE support, awards, and evaluation status, 1990, annual listing, 2214–5

Natural and supplemental gas production, prices, trade, use, reserves, and pipeline company finances, by firm and State, monthly rpt with articles, 3162–4

Natural gas and liquefied gas trade of US with 5 countries, by US firm, 1955-90, annual article, 3162–4.208

Natural gas interstate pipeline company detailed financial and operating data, by firm, 1989, annual rpt, 3164–38

Natural gas interstate pipeline company sales and contract deliveries, by firm and State, 1984-89, annual article, 3162–4.204

Natural gas take-or-pay contracts, settlement costs under FERC Order 500 by interstate pipeline firm, as of Oct 1990, article, 3162–4.202

Naval Petroleum and Oil Shale Reserves sales and contract prices, by purchaser and reserve, FY90, annual rpt, 3334–3

Nuclear material inventory discrepancies at DOE and contractor facilities, 1989/90, annual rpt, 3344–2

Nuclear power plant capacity, generation, and operating status, by plant and foreign and US location, 1990 and projected to 2030, annual rpt, 3164–57

Nuclear power plant fuel processing and waste facilities capacity, owner, and foreign and US location, projected 1991-2040, annual rpt, 3164–72

Nuclear power plant operating, maintenance, and capital additions costs, relation to plant characteristics and regulation, 1974-89, 3168–108

Nuclear power plant safety standards and research, design, licensing, construction, operation, and finances, with data by reactor, quarterly journal, 3352 4

Nuclear power plant spent fuel discharges and additional storage capacity needed, by reactor, projected 1990-2040, annual rpt, 3354–2

Nuclear reactors for domestic use and export by function and operating status, with owner, operating characteristics, and location, 1990 annual listing, 3354–15

Nuclear reactors operations, by commercial facility, 1990, annual rpt, 9634–12

Nuclear Regulatory Commission activities, finances, and staff, with data for individual power plants, FY90, annual rpt, 9634–2

Offshore oil and gas production by operator, for Federal leases in 2 ocean areas, 1990, annual rpt, 5734–3.4

Offshore oil and gas reserves, and leasing and dev activity, periodic regional rpt series, 5736–3

Oil (crude) and products imports, for top 10 US firms, 1990, article, 3162–6.202

Oil enhanced recovery research contracts of DOE, project summaries, funding, and bibl, quarterly rpt, 3002–14

Oil refinery capacity, closings, and acquisitions by plant, and fuel used, by PAD district, 1973-89, annual rpt, 3164–2.1

Oil refinery crude received from Iraq, and capacity, by company, daily press release, 3162–44

Oil refinery operations and finances, with ownership changes, shutdowns, and reactivations, by firm, 1970s-90, 3168–119

Oil supply and industry of OPEC and US, impacts of oil embargo imposed after Iraq invasion of Kuwait, 1989-91, hearing, 21368–132

Pacific Northwest electric power capacity and use, by energy source, projected under alternative load and demand cases, 1991-2011, annual rpt, 3224–3

Pacific Northwest energy conservation and resource planning activities of Bonneville Power Admin, FY89-90, 3228–11

Pipeline and compressor station construction costs, 1984-87, annual rpt, 3084–3

R&D projects and funding of DOE at natl labs, universities, and other instns, periodic summary rpt series, 3004–18

Rural Electrification Admin financed electric power plants, with location, capacity, and owner, as of Jan 1991, annual listing, 1244–6

Rural Electrification Admin loans, and borrower operating and financial data, by distribution firm and State, 1990, annual rpt, 1244–1

Solar photovoltaic R&D sponsored by DOE, projects, funding, and rpts, FY90, annual listing, 3304–20

Southeastern Power Admin sales by customer, plants, capacity, and Southeastern Fed Power Program financial statements, FY90, annual rpt, 3234–1

BY INDIVIDUAL COMPANY OR INSTITUTION

Index by Categories

Southwestern Fed Power System financial statements, sales by customer, and operations and costs by project, FY90, annual rpt, 3244–1

Tennessee Valley river control activities, and hydroelectric power generation and capacity, 1989, annual rpt, 9804–7

TVA electric power purchases and resales, with electricity use, average bills, and rates by customer class, by distributor, 1990, annual tables, 9804–14

TVA electric power purchases of municipal and cooperative distributors, and prices and use by distributor and consumer sector, monthly rpt, 9802–1

Uranium mill capacity by plant, and production, by operating status, 1986-90, annual rpt, 3164–65.1

Western Area Power Admin activities by plant, financial statements, and sales by customer, FY90, annual rpt, 3254–1

Geography and Climate

Disasters, casualties, damage, and aid by US and others, by country, FY90 and trends from FY64, annual rpt, 9914–12

Oceanographic research and distribution activities of World Data Center A by country, and cruises by ship, 1989, annual rpt, 2144–15

Government and Defense

AID loans repayment status and terms by program and country, and status of predecessor agency loans, quarterly rpt, 9912–3

Capitol Architect outlays for salaries, supplies, and services, itemized by payee and function, 1st half FY91, semiannual rpt, 25922–2

Collective bargaining agreements of Federal employees, coverage, unions, and location, by agency, for contracts expiring 1990-91, annual listing, 9847–1

DC metro area land acquisition and dev projects of Fed Govt, characteristics and funding by agency and project, FY91-95, annual rpt, 15454–1

Developing countries economic and social conditions from 1960s, and Intl Dev Cooperation Agency and AID activities and funding, FY90-92, annual rpt, 9904–4

DOD appropriations for base construction and family housing, by facility, service branch, and location, FY90-93, annual rpt, 3544–39

DOD budget requests for base construction, renovation, and land acquisition, by project, service branch, State, and country, FY92-93, annual rpt, 3544–15

DOD budget, weapons acquisition costs by prime contractor and system, FY91-93, annual rpt, 3504–2

DOD contractor subcontract awards to small and disadvantaged business, by firm and service branch, quarterly rpt, 3542–17

DOD contracts, payroll, and personnel, by service branch and location, with top 5 contractors and maps, by State and country, FY90, annual rpt, 3544–29

DOD prime contract awards, by contractor, service branch, State, and city, FY90, annual rpt, 3544–22

DOD prime contract awards for R&D, for top 500 contractors, FY90, annual listing, 3544–4

DOD prime contract awards for R&D to US and foreign nonprofit instns and govt agencies, by instn and location, FY90, annual listing, 3544–17

DOD prime contract awards, for top 100 contractors, FY90, annual rpt, 3504–13; 3544–5

House of Representatives salaries, expenses, and contingent fund disbursement, detailed listings, quarterly rpt, 21942–1

Insurance (health) coverage of Federal civilian employees, by plan, FY89, annual rpt, 9844–35.1

Inter-American Foundation activities, grants by recipient, and fellowships, by country, FY90, annual rpt, 14424–1

Intl organizations funding by US and other countries, by organization and program, FY90, annual rpt, 7004–9

Japan military components sales to US firms, for top 10 Japanese firms, FY89, compilation of papers, 23848–220

Latin America dev grants of Inter-American Foundation by program area, and fellowships by field and instn, by country, FY72-90, annual rpt, 14424–2

Military and civilian personnel, by service branch, major installation, and State, as of Sept 1990, annual rpt, 3544–7

Military base support costs by function, and personnel and acreage by installation, by service branch, FY91, annual rpt, 3504–11

Military industrial base restructuring following relaxation of East-West tensions, with top US and foreign DOD contract awards, FY87-93, 26358–245

Military post exchange operations, and sales by commodity, by facility and location worldwide, FY89, annual rpt, 3504–10

Military prisons population and capacity, by service branch and facility, data compilation, 1991 annual rpt, 6064–6.6

Military training and education programs funding, staff, students, and facilities, by service branch, FY92, annual rpt, 3504–5

Military weapons trade, production, and defense industry finances, with data by firm and country, 1980s-91, 26358–241

NASA funding by program and type of performer, and contract awards by State, FY90, annual rpt, 9504–6.2

Navy procurement, by contractor and location, FY90, annual rpt, 3804–13

Navy procurement, by contractor, FY90, annual rpt, 3804–13.4

Political action committees contributions by party and finances, by PAC type, 1989-90, press release, 9276–1.89

Presidential libraries holdings, use, and costs, by instn, FY90, annual rpt, 9514–2

Senate receipts, itemized expenses by payee, and balances, 1st half FY91, semiannual listing, 25922–1

Health and Vital Statistics

Alcohol, Drug Abuse and Mental Health Admin research grants and awards, by recipient, FY90, annual listing, 4044–13

Allergy and Infectious Diseases Natl Inst activities, grants by recipient and location, and disease cases, FY83-90, annual rpt, 4474–30

Cancer Natl Inst activities, grants by recipient, and cancer deaths and cases, FY90 and trends, annual rpt, 4474–13

Cigarette smoke tar, nicotine, and carbon monoxide content, by brand, 1989, 9408–53

Dental Research Natl Inst research and training grants, by recipient, FY89, annual listing, 4474–19

Drug marketing application processing of FDA, by drug, purpose, and producer, 1990, annual rpt, 4064–14

Drug prescriptions, by drug type and brand, and for new drugs, 1989, annual rpt, 4064–12

Family planning and population activities of AID, grants by project and recipient, and contraceptive shipments, by country, FY90, annual rpt series, 9914–13

Health Care Financing Admin research activities and grants, by program, FY90, annual listing, 4654–10

Health Care Policy and Research Agency grants, by recipient and location, FY90, 4186–9.10

Hearing aid performance test results, by make and model, 1991 annual rpt, 8704–3

Heart, Lung, and Blood Natl Inst activities, and grants by recipient and location, FY90 and disease trends from 1940, annual rpt, 4474–15

HHS financial aid, by program, recipient, State, and city, FY90, annual regional listings, 4004–3

HHS research and evaluation programs, 1970-90, annual listing, 4004–30

Hospital deaths of Medicare patients, actual and expected rates by diagnosis, with hospital characteristics, by instn, FY87-89, annual regional rpt series, 4654–14

Hospitals in rural areas, HCFA grants for improving financial stability, by program area, recipient, and State, FY89, 4658–58

Indian Health Service and tribal facility outpatient visits, by type of provider, selected hospital, and service area, FY90, annual rpt, 4084–3

Indian Health Service and tribal hospital admissions, length of stay, beds, and births, by facility and service area, FY70-89, annual rpt, 4084–4

Indian Health Service and tribal hospital capacity, use, and births, by area and facility, quarterly rpt, 4082–1

Indian Health Service outpatient visits, by facility and IHS service area, FY89-90, annual rpt, 4084–8

Insurance (life) predeath benefits use to finance long-term care, payout terms, 1990, and coverage by beneficiary characteristics, 1984, 2626–10.128

Kidney dialysis patients anemia treatment with Epoetin alfa, dosages, costs, Medicare reimbursement, and facility income effects, 1989, 4008–113

Kidney end-stage disease research of CDC and HCFA, project listing, 1990, annual rpt, 4654–16

Labs (independent clinical) profitability and cost indexes by customer type, and impacts of Medicare fee caps, 1988-89, GAO rpt, 26121–425

Migrant workers children education programs enrollment, staff, finances, and outcomes, 1980s, 4808–22

NIH grants and contracts, quarterly listing, 4432–1

Index by Categories

NIH grants and contracts to top recipients, FY89, annual rpt, 4434–9

NIH grants for R&D, training, construction, and medical libraries, by location and recipient, FY90, annual listings, 4434–7

Occupational safety and health research and demonstration grants by State, and project listing, FY90, annual rpt, 4244–2

Physicians, by specialty, State of practice, and school of graduation, 1989, State rpt series, 4116–6

Radiation exposure at DOE and DOE-contractor sites, by facility type and contractor, dose type, and worker age, sex, and occupation, 1988, annual rpt, 3324–1

Radiation exposure of workers at nuclear power plants and related facilities, by site, 1968-87, annual rpt, 9634–3

Radiation protection and health physics enrollment and degrees granted by instn and State, and grad placement, by student characteristics, 1990, annual rpt, 3004–7

Reproduction and population research, Fed Govt funding by project, FY89, annual listing, 4474–9

Housing and Construction

Economic Dev Admin activities, and funding by program, recipient, State, and county, FY90 and cumulative from FY66, annual rpt, 2064–2

Kuwait reconstruction after Persian Gulf War, Army Corps of Engineers contract awards by firm and purpose, 1st qtr 1991, article, 2042–1.203

Low income housing dev tax credits, and units constructed, by selected project and State, 1987-89, hearings, 25248–120

Industry and Commerce

Auto and auto equipment recalls for safety-related defects, by make, quarterly listing, 7762–2

Auto and light truck fuel economy, sales, and market shares, by size and model for US and foreign makes, 1991 model year, semiannual rpt, 3302–4

Auto industry in US, Japan firms investment, production capacity, and sales, as of 1990, technical paper, 9385–8.91

Auto industry sales, profits, and loss, by US make, monthly rpt, annual data, 9882–8

Competitiveness (intl) of US industries, with selected foreign and US operating data by major firm and product, series, 2046–12

Exporters (US) antiboycott law violations and fines by firm, and invitations to boycott by country, FY90, annual rpt, 2024–1

Foreign direct investment in US, major transactions by type, industry, country, and US location, 1989, annual rpt, 2044–20

Franchise business opportunities by firm and kind of business, and sources of aid and info, 1990 annual listing, 2104–7

Imports detained by FDA, by reason, product, shipper, brand, and country, monthly listing, 4062–2

Japan corporations finances, for firms affiliated with integrated conglomerates and independent firms, 1976-89, article, 9375–1.203

Lumber (pulpwood) production by county, and mill capacity by firm, by southern State, 1989, annual rpt, 1204–23

Minerals foreign and US supply under alternative market conditions, reserves, and background industry data, series, 5606–4

Minerals Yearbook, 1989, Vol 1: commodity reviews of production, reserves, supply, use, and trade, annual rpt series, 5604–15

Minerals Yearbook, 1989, Vol 2: State reviews of production, sales, and firms, by commodity, and business activity, annual rpt, 5604–34

Minerals Yearbook, 1990, Vol 1: commodity reviews of production, reserves, supply, use, and trade, annual rpt series, 5604–20

Small Business Investment Companies capital holdings, SBA obligation, and ownership, as of July 1991, semiannual listing, 9762–4

Steel industry finances, operations, and modernization efforts, with data on major companies and foreign industry, 1968-91, last issue of annual rpt, 9884–24

Tennessee Valley industrial dev and employment, by SIC 2-digit industry, firm, and location, 1990, annual rpt, 9804–3

Labor and Employment

Alaska rural areas population characteristics, and energy resources dev effects, series, 5736–5

American Samoa employment, earnings, and minimum wage, by establishment and industry, 1989, biennial rpt, 6504–6

Collective bargaining agreements expiring during year, and workers covered, by firm, union, industry group, and State, 1991, annual rpt, 6784–9

Fed Labor Relations Authority and Fed Services Impasses Panel activities, and cases by union, agency, and disposition, FY85-90, annual rpt, 13364–1

Trade adjustment aid for workers, petitions by disposition, selected industry, union, and State, monthly rpt, 6402–13

Union representation elections conducted by NLRB, results, monthly rpt, 9582–2

Unions reporting to Labor Dept, parent bodies and locals by location, 1990 listing, 6468–17

Wage and benefit changes from collective bargaining and mgmt decisions, by industry div, monthly rpt, 6782–1

Work stoppages, workers involved, and days idle, 1990 and trends from 1947, annual press release, 6784–12

Law Enforcement

Aircraft hijackings, on-board explosions, and other crime, US and foreign incidents, 1985-89, annual rpt, 7504–31

Auto theft rates of new cars, by make and model, 1989 model year, annual rpt, 7764–21

Higher education instn law enforcement personnel, and crimes by offense, by instn, 1990, annual rpt, 6224–2.1; 6224–2.3

Jail adult and juvenile population, employment, spending, instn conditions, and inmate programs, by county and facility, 1988, regional rpt series, 6068–144

Prisoners from Federal instns, halfway house placements, duration, and employment, and house capacity, 1990-91, GAO rpt, 26119–347

Prisoners in Federal instns, by sex, prison, security level, contract facility type, and region, monthly rpt series, 6242–1

Prisons and jails operated under private contract, costs and characteristics of instns, by facility and State, 1990, GAO rpt, 26119–321

BY INDIVIDUAL COMPANY OR INSTITUTION

Prisons Bur admin offices and correctional instns, facility characteristics, 1991, annual listing, 6244–4

Prisons Bur correctional staff by selected characteristics, and inmates, by facility, data compilation, 1991 annual rpt, 6064–6.1

Terrorism (intl) organizations, activities and strengths, listing, 1990, annual rpt, 7004–13

Terrorism incidents in US, related activity, and casualties, by attack type, target, group, and location, 1990, annual rpt, 6224–6

Trials (civil and criminal) of 20 days or more terminated in Federal district courts, case and trial characteristics, 1990, annual rpt, 18204–8.18

Natural Resources, Environment, and Pollution

EPA R&D programs and funding, FY90, annual listing, 9184–18

Hazardous waste site remedial action under Superfund, current and proposed sites descriptions and status, periodic listings, series, 9216–3

Hazardous waste site remedial action under Superfund, current and proposed sites priority ranking and status by location, series, 9216–5

Marine mammals research, Federal funding by topic, recipient, and agency, FY90, annual rpt, 14734–2

Nuclear power plant spent fuel discharges, storage capacity, and inventories, by reactor, 1968-89, 3166–6.55

Nuclear Waste Fund program costs, by contractor, quarterly GAO rpt, supplemental data, 26102–4

Radioactive low-level waste disposal activities of States and interstate compacts, with data by disposal facility and reactor, 1989, annual rpt, 3354–14

Radioactive waste and spent fuel generation, inventory, and disposal, 1960s-89 and projected to 2020, annual rpt, 3364–2

Radioactive waste at DOE nuclear weapons facilities, storage plans, and mgmt issues, 1988, 26358–236

Radioactive waste from nuclear power plants, releases and waste composition by plant, 1988, annual rpt, 9634–1

Radioactivity levels at former AEC and Manhattan Project research and storage sites and nearby areas, test results series, 3006–9

Reservoirs capacity and area, by reservoir and State, 1988, 5668–120

Wastewater industrial releases pollution levels, treatment, costs, and regulation, with background financial and operating data, industry rpt series, 9206–4

Population

Census of Population, 1990: Indian and Alaska Native population on reservations and in other designated areas, by selected site, press release, 2328–76

Prices and Cost of Living

Auto industry finances and operations, trade by country, and prices of selected US and foreign models, monthly rpt, 9882–8

Public Welfare and Social Security

Food aid programs purchases, by commodity, firm, and shipping point or destination, weekly rpt, 1302–3

BY INDIVIDUAL COMPANY OR INSTITUTION

Homelessness issues, population at risk, contributing factors, and Federal funding for services and prevention, with bibl, 1991 compilation of papers, 25928–9

Medicaid HMO enrollees, payments, terminations, services use, and State oversight, for Chicago, Ill, late 1980s, GAO rpt, 26121–399

Medicaid prepaid plans for physician services, characteristics of selected plans in 4 States, various periods 1983-89, article, 4652–1.228

Medicare supplemental private insurance premiums, costs, claims, and benefit provisions, with data by firm, 1988-90, hearing, 21788–198

Nonprofit charitable organizations finances, and revenue and investments of top 10 instns, 1986-87, article, 8302–2.210

Nonprofit charitable organizations revenue and assets, for top organizations, 1987, article, 8302–2.218

Refugee arrivals and resettlement in US, by age, sex, sponsoring agency, State, and country, monthly rpt, 4692–2

Refugee resettlement programs and funding, arrivals by country of origin, and indicators of adjustment, by State, FY90, annual rpt, 4694–5

Recreation and Leisure

Arts Natl Endowment activities and grants, FY90, annual rpt, 9564–3

Concession operations on public lands, receipts, and fees, by Federal agency and for top 100 firms, 1989, GAO rpt, 26113–531

Museum Services Inst activities and finances, and grants by recipient, FY90, annual rpt, 9564–7

Science and Technology

Astronomical tables, time conversion factors, and listing of observatories worldwide, 1992, annual rpt, 3804–7

Biotechnology commercial applications, industry finances and capitalization, patents, and govt support, for US, Japan, and EC, late 1970s-91, 26358–248

Computer mainframe and related equipment procurement and compatibility, for Federal agencies, FY86-89, GAO rpt series, 26125–41

Computer systems and equipment of Fed Govt, by type, make, and agency, 2nd half FY90, semiannual listing, 9452–9

Degrees (PhD) in science and engineering, by field, instn, employment prospects, sex, race, and other characteristics, 1960s-90, annual rpt, 9627–30

Education in science and engineering, grad programs enrollment by field, source of funds, and characteristics of student and instn, 1975-89, annual rpt, 9627–7

Education in science, engineering, and math, NSF grants by recipient and level, FY89, biennial listing, 9624–27

Engineering research and education grants of NSF, FY90, annual listing, 9624–24

Higher education instn science and engineering research system status, R&D performance, and Federal support, 1950s-88, 9628–83

Military computer systems engineering and technical support contract costs, late 1980s, GAO rpt, 26125–45

NASA procurement contract awards, by type, contractor, State, and country, FY91 with trends from 1961, semiannual rpt, 9502–6

NASA R&D funding to higher education instns, by field, instn, and State, FY90, annual listing, 9504–7

NSF grants and contracts, by field, instn, and State, FY89, annual rpt, 9624–26

Nuclear engineering and science educational facilities, student aid, and degrees granted, by instn, 1990, 3008–126

Nuclear engineering enrollment and degrees by instn and State, and women grads plans and employment, 1990, annual rpt, 3006–8.14

Nuclear engineering enrollment and degrees granted by instn and State, and grad placement, by student characteristics, 1990, annual rpt, 3004–5

R&D and related funding of Fed Govt to higher education and nonprofit instns, by field, instn, agency, and State, FY89, annual rpt, 9627–17

R&D funding by Fed Govt, by field, performer type, agency, and State, FY89-91, annual rpt, 9627–20

R&D funding by higher education instns and federally funded centers, by field, instn, and State, FY89, annual rpt, 9627–13

Radiation protection and health physics enrollment and degrees granted by instn and State, and female grads plans and employment, 1990, annual rpt, 3006–8.15

Space programs involvement by private sector, govt contracts, costs, revenue, and R&D spending, 1970s-80s and projected to 2000, 26306–6.154

Spacecraft launches and other activities of NASA and USSR, with flight data, 1957-90, annual rpt, 9504–6.1

Veterans Affairs

AIDS cases at VA health care centers by sex, race, risk factor, and facility, and AIDS prevention and treatment issues, quarterly rpt, 8702–1

Health care for veterans, patients, visits, costs, and operating beds, by VA and contract facility, and region, quarterly rpt, 8602–4

Health care staff of VA, and turnover, by occupation and location, 1990, annual rpt, 8604–8

Hospital and nursing home use, beds, daily census, and construction projects, by VA facility, FY90, annual rpt, 8604–3

Medicine and Surgery Dept of VA, trainees by detailed program and city, FY90, annual rpt, 8704–4

Mental health care services, staffing, research, and training programs in VA facilities, 1991 biennial listing, 8704–2

Surgery-related deaths and complications, by procedure and VA facility, and compared to non-VA instns, FY84-89, last issue of biennial rpt, 8704–1

BY INDUSTRY

Agriculture and Food

Employment related to agriculture, by industry, region, and metro-nonmetro location, 1987, 1598–271

Index by Categories

Banking, Finance, and Insurance

Capital gains preferential tax treatment impacts on agricultural finances and operations, 1991 article, 1561–16.202

Debt and business cycle sensitivity of major industry sectors, with intl comparisons, 1970s-88, technical paper, 9385–8.103

Foreign direct investment impact on trade balance, with background data, late 1960s-90 and auto forecasts to 1993, article, 9385–1.210

Securities (medium-term) outstanding, issuers, and borrowings size, by industry group, 1983-90, technical paper, 9366–6.276

Communications and Transportation

Mail volume to and from households, use, and views, by class, source, content, and household characteristics, 1987-88, annual rpt, 9864–10

Energy Resources and Demand

Coal receipts and prices at manufacturing plants, by SIC 2-digit industry, quarterly rpt, 3162–37.2

Electric power use indexes, by SIC 2- to 4-digit industry, monthly rpt, 9365–2.24

Manufacturing energy use and prices, 1988 survey, series, 3166–13

Manufacturing sector energy efficiency, by industry, 1980-85, annual rpt, 3164–74.1

Natl Energy Strategy plans for conservation, impacts on energy use and pollution under alternative technology investment assumptions, projected 1990-2030, 3166–6.48

Government and Defense

Boycotts (intl) by OPEC and other countries, US taxpayers IRS filings, cooperation, and tax benefits denied, 1976-86, GAO rpt, 26119–349

Manufacturing census, 1987: employment and shipments under Fed Govt contracts, by SIC 4-digit industry, 2497–7

Puerto Rico and other US possessions corporations income tax returns, income and tax items, and employment, by selected industry, 1987, article, 8302–2.213

Tax (income) returns filed by type of filer, selected income items, quarterly rpt, 8302–2.1

Tax (income) returns for foreign corporate activity in US, assets, and income statement items, by industry div and selected country, 1986-87, article, 8302–2.205

Tax (income) returns of corporations, income and tax items by asset size and detailed industry, 1987, annual rpt, 8304–4

Tax (income) returns of corporations, income and tax items by asset size and detailed industry, 1988, annual rpt, 8304–21

Tax (income) returns of corporations, summary data by asset size and industry div, 1987, annual article, 8302–2.204

Tax (income) returns of corporations, summary data by asset size and industry div, 1988, annual article, 8302–2.215; 8302–2.217

Tax (income) returns of corporations with foreign tax credit, income and tax items by industry group, 1986, biennial article, 8302–2.203

Tax (income) returns of partnerships, income statement and balance sheet items, by industry group, 1989, annual article, 8302–2.216; 8304–18

Index by Categories

BY INDUSTRY

Tax (income) returns of sole proprietorships, income statement items, by industry group, 1989, annual article, 8302–2.214

Tax (income) returns of US corporations under foreign control, assets and income statement items by industry div and country, 1988, article, 8302–2.219

Tax (sales) collections of retailers as share of sales, by SIC 2- to 4-digit kind of business, 1989, annual rpt, 2413–5

Health and Vital Statistics

Acute and chronic health conditions, disability, absenteeism, and health services use, by selected characteristics, 1987, CD-ROM, 4147–10.177

Deaths related to work injuries, by equipment type, circumstances, and OSHA standards violated, series, 6606–2

Drug and alcohol use in workplace, and drinkers reporting adverse effects, for young adults by selected characteristics, 1984, article, 6722–1.237

Health care spending by businesses, households, and govts, 1965-89, article, 4652–1.230

Health maintenance organizations enrollment and availability for production and office workers, by industry div, selected metro area, and region, 1984-89, article, 6722–1.222

Injuries at workplace, by circumstances, body site, equipment type, and industry, with safety measures, series, 6846–1

Injuries, illnesses, and workdays lost, by industry div and major manufacturing group, Monthly Labor Review, 6722–1.7

Injuries, illnesses, and workdays lost, by SIC 2-digit industry, 1989-90, annual press release, 6844–3

Injury and illness rates by SIC 2- to 4-digit industry, and deaths by cause and industry div, 1989, annual rpt, 6844–1

Injury and illness rates, by SIC 2- to 4-digit industry, 1988-89, annual rpt, 6844–7

Insurance (health) coverage, uninsured persons by employment and other characteristics and State, 1988, GAO rpt, 26121–403

Insurance (health) natl coverage alternative proposals and indicators of need, 1989, 4658–54

Respiratory diseases related to occupational hazards, epidemiology, diagnosis, and treatment, for selected industries and work settings, 1988 conf, 4248–90

Shift rotation health and safety effects, and US and foreign regulation, by selected industry and occupation, 1970s-89, 26356–9.3

Industry and Commerce

Business statistics, detailed data for major industries and economic indicators, *Survey of Current Business*, monthly rpt, 2702–1

Capital expenditures for plant and equipment, by industry div, bimonthly rpt, 2042–1.4

Capital expenditures for plant and equipment, by major industry group, quarterly rpt, 2502–2

Capital stock measures, by type and industry, 1950s-80s, technical paper, 9385–8.92

Corporations debt impacts on financial performance during recessions, with data by industry group, 1970s-80s, technical paper, 9385–8.78

Corporations financial statements for manufacturing, mining, and trade, by selected SIC 2- to 3-digit industry, quarterly rpt, 2502–1

Corporations profits, by industry div, selected years 1929-90, annual rpt, 204–1.7

County Business Patterns, 1988: employment, establishments, and payroll, by SIC 2- to 4-digit industry and county, annual State rpt series, 2326–6

County Business Patterns, 1989: employment, establishments, and payroll, by SIC 2- to 4-digit industry and county, annual State rpt series, 2326–8

DC production index, by component, 1987-91, article, 9389–1.203

Depreciable assets class lives measurement, investment, and industry operations, industry rpt series, 8006–5

Economic and employment conditions, alternative BLS projections to 2005 and trends 1970s-90, biennial article, 6722–1.253

Enterprise Statistics, 1987: auxiliaries of multi-establishment firms, finances and operations by function, industry, and State, 2329–6

Enterprise Statistics, 1987: finances and operations for companies, by size, level of diversification, form of organization, and industry group, 2329–8

Explosives and blasting agents use, by type, industry, and State, 1990, Mineral Industry Surveys, annual rpt, 5614–22

Exports and imports of finished goods and industrial supplies, with related indicators, by industry and country, mid 1970s-90, 9385–1.205; 9385–8.95

Exports, imports, balances, US consumption, and operations of industries affected, by industry, 1986-90, semiannual rpt, 9882–9

Finances and operations, by SIC 2- to 4-digit industry, forecast 1991, annual rpt, 2044–28

Foreign direct investment in US, by industry group and world area, 1987-90, annual article, 2702–1.219

Foreign direct investment in US, by industry group of US affiliate and country of parent firm, 1980-86, 2708–41

Foreign direct investment in US, major transactions by type, industry, country, and US location, 1989, annual rpt, 2044–20

Foreign direct investment in US manufacturing, impacts on trade balances, with data by industry, 1980s-93, technical paper, 9385–8.91

Foreign direct investment in US, new and established affiliates assets, and acquisitions, by industry div, 1980s, technical paper, 9366–7.255

Foreign direct investment of US, by industry group and world area, 1987-90, annual article, 2702–1.220

Foreign direct investment of US, in oil, selected manufacturing industries, and wholesale trade, by country, 1988-90, annual rpt, 21384–5

GNP by industry, and constant dollar estimate revisions, data sources and reliability, 1977-88, article, 2702–1.201

GNP by industry div, 1947-88, annual rpt, 204–1.1

GNP by industry group, 1986-89, article, 2702–1.208

Great Lakes area economic conditions and outlook, for US and Canada, 1970s-90, 9375–15

Gross product for regions, by industry div, 1986, article, 9373–1.211

Import restraint elimination impacts on US economy and selected service industries, 1970s-90, 9886–4.173

Imports and tariff provisions effect on US industries and products, investigations with background financial and operating data, series, 9886–4

Imports injury to US industries from foreign subsidized products, investigations with background financial and operating data, series, 9886–15

Imports injury to US industries from sales at less than fair value, investigations with background financial and operating data, series, 9886–14

Input-output structure of US economy, detailed interindustry transactions for 84 industries, and components of final demand, 1986, annual article, 2702–1.206

Input-output structure of US economy, detailed interindustry transactions for 85 industries, 1982 benchmark data, 2702–1.213

Investment (foreign direct) in US by country, and finances, employment, and acreage owned, by industry group of business acquired or established, 1984-90, annual article, 2702–1.210

Investment (intl) position of US, by component, industry, world region, and country, 1989-90, annual article, 2702–1.212

Investment spending relation to cash flow, by SIC 2-digit manufacturing industry, 1958-86, article, 9375–1.202

Japan economic conditions, financial and intl policies, and trade devs, 1950s-80s and projected to 2050, compilation of papers, 23848–220

Japan manufacturing firms US affiliates, employment, and wages, by selected industry and State, 1980s, 2048–151

Manufacturing annual survey, 1989: finances and operations, by SIC 2- to 4-digit industry, series, 2506–15

Manufacturing census, 1987: finances and operations, by SIC 2- to 4-digit industry, State, and MSA, with trends from 1849, 2497–1

Manufacturing census, 1987: finances and operations, by type of organization and SIC 2- to 4-digit industry, subject rpt, 2497–5

Manufacturing industries operations and performance, analytical rpt series, 2506–16

Manufacturing output of Middle Atlantic and East North Central census divs relative to US, by industry and State, alternative estimates 1963 and 1986, working paper, 9375–13.59

Manufacturing production and selected measures of capacity use, for 16 industry groups, monthly rpt, 23842–1.3

Manufacturing production, shipments, inventories, orders, and pollution control costs, periodic Current Industrial Rpt series, 2506–3

Mexico-US trade agreement proposal, economic impacts with background trade and investment data, 1985-90, 9886–4.168

BY INDUSTRY

Index by Categories

Middle Atlantic States manufacturing output index, monthly rpt, 9387–12

Mineral industries census, 1987: finances and operations, by establishment characteristics, SIC 2- to 4-digit industry, and State, subject rpt, 2517–1

Minority Business Dev Centers mgmt and financial aid, and characteristics of businesses, by region and State, FY90, annual rpt, 2104–6

Multinatl firms US affiliates finances and operations, by industry div, country of parent firm, and State, 1988-89, annual article, 2702–1.214; 2702–1.218

Multinatl firms US affiliates, finances, and operations, by industry, world area of parent firm, and State, 1988-89, annual rpt, 2704–4

Multinatl firms US affiliates, investment trends and impact on US economy, 1991 annual rpt, 2004–9

Multinatl US firms and foreign affiliates finances and operations, by industry and world area of parent firm, 1989 benchmark survey, preliminary annual rpt, 2704–5

Multinatl US firms and foreign affiliates finances and operations, by industry of parent firm and affiliate, world area, and selected country, 1989, annual article, 2702–1.225

Multinatl US firms foreign affiliates capital expenditures, by major industry group, world area, and country, 1986-91, semiannual article, 2702–1.207

Multinatl US firms foreign affiliates capital expenditures, by major industry group, world area, and country, 1987-91, semiannual article, 2702–1.222

North Central States industry diversification, and employment and output relation to natl economic conditions, by industry and State, 1950s-89, working paper, 9375–13.63

OPEC members direct investment in US, by industry div, as of 1989, annual rpt, 3164–80

Overseas Business Reports: economic conditions, investment and export opportunities, and trade practices, country market research rpt series, 2046–6

Production and capacity use indexes, by SIC 2- to 4-digit industry, monthly rpt, 9365–2.24

Production indexes, capital investment, and capacity use by industry div, and manufacturers and trade sales and inventories, 1947-90, annual rpt, 204–1.3

Puerto Rico economic censuses, 1987: wholesale and retail trade and service industry finances and operations, by SIC 2- to 4-digit industry and municipio, 2591–1

Puerto Rico economic censuses, 1987: wholesale, retail, and service industries finances and operations, by establishment characteristics and SIC 2- and 3-digit industry, subject rpts, 2591–2

Retail trade census, 1987: depreciable assets, capital and operating expenses, sales, value added, and inventories, by SIC 2- to 4-digit kind of business, 2399–2

Retail trade census, 1987: finances and employment, for establishments with and without payroll, by SIC 2- to 4-digit kind of business, State, and MSA, 2401–1

Retail trade sales and inventories, by kind of business, region, and selected State, MSA, and city, monthly rpt, 2413–3

Retail trade sales, by kind of business, advance monthly rpt, 2413–2

Retail trade sales, inventories, purchases, gross margin, and accounts receivable, by SIC 2- to 4-digit kind of business and form of ownership, 1989, annual rpt, 2413–5

Rocky Mountain region employment and income, and economic dependence on shipments outside area, by industry and county group, 1980s, 1208–362

Service industries census, 1987: depreciable assets, capital and operating expenses, and receipts, by SIC 2- to 4-digit kind of business, 2393–2

Service industries census, 1987: establishments, receipts by source, payroll, and employment, by SIC 2- to 4-digit kind of business, State, and MSA, 2393–4

Service industries exports and imports of US, direct and among multinatl firms affiliates, by industry and world area, 1986-90, article, 2702–1.223

Service industries receipts, by SIC 2- to 4-digit kind of business, 1990, annual rpt, 2413–8

Southeastern US services sector employment growth and share of output by industry, by State, various periods 1979-89, article, 9391–16.203

Soviet Union GNP by component and industry sector, and CIA estimation methods, 1950s-87, 23848–223

Soviet Union GNP by detailed income and outlay component, 1985, 2326–18.59

Soviet Union industrial production annual growth rate, by major industry, 1960s-90, annual rpt, 9114–4.3

State and Metro Area Data Book, 1991 data compilation, 2328–54

State gross product impact of foreign labor productivity and dollar exchange rate, by industry sector and State, 1972-86, working paper, 9387–8.255

Statistical Abstract of US, 1991 annual data compilation, 2324–1

Tax (income) returns of multinatl US firms foreign affiliates, income statement items, by asset size and industry, 1986, biennial article, 8302–2.212

Tennessee Valley industrial dev and employment, by SIC 2-digit industry, firm, and location, 1990, annual rpt, 9804–3

Wholesale trade census, 1987: depreciable assets, capital and operating expenses, sales, value added, and inventories, by SIC 2- to 3-digit kind of business, 2407–2

Wholesale trade census, 1987: establishments, sales by customer class, employment, inventories, and expenses, by SIC 2- to 4-digit kind of business, 2407–4

Wholesale trade sales, inventories, purchases, and gross margins, by SIC 2- to 3-digit kind of business, 1990, annual rpt, 2413–13

Women-owned businesses and sales, by industry div and ownership type, and data needs and availability, 1987, 9768–22

Labor and Employment

Alaska rural areas population characteristics, and energy resources dev effects, series, 5736–5

Alien workers (unauthorized) and Fair Labor Standards Act employer compliance, hiring impacts, and aliens overstaying visas by country and State, 1986-90, annual rpt, 6264–6

American Samoa employment, earnings, and minimum wage, by establishment and industry, 1989, biennial rpt, 6504–6

Black American displaced workers, by demographic and current and former employment characteristics, and compared to whites, 1978-86, article, 6722–1.234

Child labor law violations and injuries by industry group, and employment of minors by selected characteristics, 1983-90, GAO rpt, 26121–426

Collective bargaining agreements expiring during year, and workers covered, by firm, union, industry group, and State, 1991, annual rpt, 6784–9

Collective bargaining agreements expiring during year, and workers covered, by industry and level of govt, 1992, 6726–1.43

Collective bargaining contract expirations, wage increases, and coverage, by major industry group, 1991, annual article, 6722–1.206

Dallas-Fort Worth-Arlington metro area employment, earnings, hours, and CPI changes, late 1970s-90, annual rpt, 6964–2

Developing countries labor standards impacts on social and economic dev, 1988 conf papers, 6368–9

Displaced workers losing job 1985-90, by demographic and former and current employment characteristics, as of Jan 1990, article, 6722–1.225

Earnings by industry div, and personal income per capita and by source, by State, MSA, and county, 1984-89, annual regional rpts, 2704–2

Earnings by industry group, region, and State, 1988-90, annual article, 2702–1.216

Earnings distribution by sex, race, industry div, and occupation, 1960-89, article, 6722–1.201

Economic and employment conditions, alternative BLS projections to 2005 and trends 1970s-90, biennial article, 6722–1.253

Employee benefit plan coverage, by benefit type and worker characteristics, late 1970s-80s, 15496–1.11

Employee leave for illness, disability, and dependent care, coverage, provisions, terminations, costs, and methods of covering for absent worker, by firm size, 1988 survey, 9768–21

Employment and Earnings, detailed data, monthly rpt, 6742–2

Employment and unemployment, by age, sex, race, marital and family status, industry div, and State, Monthly Labor Review, 6722–1.2

Employment by industry and State, impacts of decline in employers voluntary reporting on Continuous Work History Sample, 1970s-86, article, 4742–1.203

Employment by industry div and State, monthly press release, 6742–12

Employment Cost Index and percent change by occupational group, industry div, region, and metro-nonmetro area, quarterly press release, 6782–5

Index by Categories

BY INDUSTRY

Employment Cost Index changes for nonfarm workers, by occupation, industry div, region, and bargaining status, monthly rpt, 6782–1

Employment cost indexes, by occupation, industry div, and region, Monthly Labor Review, 6722–1.3

Employment, earnings, and hours, by SIC 1- to 4-digit industry, monthly and annual averages, selected years 1909-90, annual rpt, 6744–4

Employment, earnings, and hours, monthly press release, 6742–5

Employment, earnings, hours, and productivity, by industry div, selected years 1929-90, annual rpt, 204–1.2

Employment situation, earnings, hours, and other BLS economic indicators, transcripts of BLS Commissioner's monthly testimony, periodic rpt, 23846–4

Employment, unemployment, and labor force characteristics, by region, State, and selected metro area, 1990, annual rpt, 6744–7

Exports and export-related employment, by SIC 3-digit industry and State, model results, 1987, annual rpt, 2506–16.1

Fair Labor Standards Act admin, with coverage under minimum wage and overtime provisions, and illegal employment of minors, by industry div, FY89, annual rpt, 6504–2.1

Foreign countries labor conditions, union coverage, and work accidents, annual country rpt series, 6366–4

Houston metro area employment, earnings, hours, and CPI changes, 1970s-90, annual rpt, 6964–1

Immigration, alien workers, amnesty programs, and employer sanctions impacts on US economy and labor force, series, 6366–5

Imports (duty-free) from Caribbean area, impact on US employment by industry, 1990, annual rpt, 6364–2

Imports, exports, and employment impacts, by SIC 2- to 4-digit industry and commodity, quarterly rpt, 2322–2

Labor force status, by worker characteristics and industry group, 1982-90, semiannual article, 6722–1.212

Labor force, wages, hours, and payroll costs, by major industry group and demographic characteristics, *Survey of Current Business*, monthly rpt, 2702–1.8

Labor Relations Natl Board activities, cases, elections conducted, and litigation, FY89, annual rpt, 9584–1

Manufacturing employment, by detailed occupation and SIC 2-digit industry, 1989 survey, triennial rpt, 6748–52

Manufacturing employment by selected characteristics, wages, and import and export penetration rates, by SIC 2- to 4- digit industry, 1982-89, 6366–3.27

Manufacturing job creation, elimination, and reallocation rates, and relation to industry and establishment characteristics, 1970s-86, working paper, 9375–13.56

Moonlighting employment, by reason, and characteristics of workers and primary and secondary jobs, 1991, press release, 6726–1.40

New England employment growth rates by selected industry, projected 1990s with background data for 1980s, article, 9373–25.201

New England States economic indicators, Fed Reserve 1st District, monthly rpt, 9373–2.2

New England States employment variability relation to service and financial industries employment, with data by selected industry group and State, 1970s-89, article, 9373–1.212

North Central States business and economic conditions, Fed Reserve 9th District, quarterly journal, 9383–19

Part-time employment, by age, sex, industry div, and whether voluntary, 1969-89, article, 6722–1.218

Part-time employment by health insurance coverage and worker characteristics, and temporary and contract employment, 1979-89, GAO rpt, 26121–411

Pension benefits disparity between men and women in small business plans by selected participant and plan characteristics, impacts of 1986 Tax Reform Act, 1984-85, GAO rpt, 26121–412

Pension coverage by industry, and 401(k) and IRA participation, 1987, fact sheet, 2326–17.35

Pension coverage by industry, vestment, and recipient income, by participant characteristics, 1987, Current Population Rpt, 2546–20.18

Productivity of labor and for other inputs, indexes and changes for 2- to 4-digit industries and govt functions, 1984-89, annual article, 6722–1.228

Productivity of labor, indexes by selected SIC 2- to 4-digit industry, Monthly Labor Review, 6722–1.5

Productivity of labor, indexes of output, hours, and employment by SIC 2- to 4-digit industry, 1967-89, annual rpt, 6824–1

Rural areas economic conditions and dev, quarterly journal, 1502–8

Self-employment, by occupation, industry, sex, and race, 1983 and 1990, article, 6742–1.202

South Central States employment by industry div, income, and other economic indicators, for 4 States, 1989-90 and forecast 1991-92, annual article, 9391–16.207

Southeastern States, Fed Reserve 8th District banking and economic conditions, quarterly rpt with articles, 9391–16

Southeastern US employment, by industry div, 1989-90, annual rpt, 6944–2

Southeastern US wages covered under unemployment insurance, by industry div, State, and metro area, 1989-90, annual press release, 6946–3.22

Southwestern US employment by major industry div, earnings, and hours, by State, monthly rpt, 6962–2

State and Metro Area Data Book, 1991 data compilation, 2328–54

Technology-intensive employment by region and State, and earnings, by industry group, 1989, article, 6722–1.235

Texas services sector growth impact on wages, with data by industry and sector, late 1970s-89, article, 9379–1.210

Trade adjustment aid for workers, petitions by disposition, selected industry, union, and State, monthly rpt, 6402–13

Unemployment insurance coverage of establishments, employment, and wages, by SIC 4-digit industry and State, 1990, annual rpt, 6744–16

Union coverage of workers and earnings, by age, sex, race, occupational group, and industry div, 1989-90, press release, 6726–1.36

Wage and benefit changes from collective bargaining and mgmt decisions, by industry div, monthly rpt, 6782–1

Wage differentials among industries, by industry and country, and correlation of differentials between countries, for US and West Germany, 1979-87, technical paper, 9366–6.281

Wages by occupation, for office and plant workers in metro areas, by industry div and region, Aug 1990, annual rpt, 6785–9

Wages, hourly and weekly averages by industry div, monthly press release, 6742–3

Wages, hours, and employment by occupation, and benefits, for selected locations, industry survey rpt series, 6787–6

Wages of workers covered by unemployment insurance, by State and industry div, 1989-90, annual press release, 6784–17.1

West Central States economic indicators, Fed Reserve 10th District, quarterly rpt, 9381–16.2

Western US employment growth by industry div and manufacturing group, Fed Reserve 10th District, 1989-90, annual article, 9381–1.202

Youth labor force status, by sex, race, and industry div, summer 1987-91, annual press release, 6744–14

Natural Resources, Environment, and Pollution

Air pollution abatement equipment shipments by industry, and new and backlog orders, by product, 1990, annual Current Industrial Rpt, 2506–12.5

Air pollution emissions factors, by detailed pollutant and source, data compilation, 1990 rpt, 9198–120

Air pollution levels for 6 pollutants, by source, 1970-89 and trends from 1940, annual rpt, 9194–13

Environmental Quality, status of problems, protection programs, research, and intl issues, 1991 annual rpt, 484–1

Fish kills in coastal areas related to pollution and natural causes, by land use, State, and county, 1980s, 2178–32

Global warming contributing air pollutants, US and foreign emissions and control measures, 1980s and projected to 2020, 26358–233

Hazardous substances industrial releases, accuracy of EPA reporting, and nonreporting facilities by State and industry, 1987-90, GAO rpt, 26113–532

Pollution abatement capital and operating costs, by SIC 2-digit industry, 1989, advance annual Current Industrial Rpt, 2506–3.6

Wastewater industrial releases pollution levels, treatment, costs, and regulation, with background financial and operating data, industry rpt series, 9206–4

Water pollution fish kills, by pollution source, month, location, and State, 1977-87, last issue of annual rpt, 9204–3

BY INDUSTRY

Water supply, hydrologic events, and end use, by State, 1988-89, annual rpt, 5664–12

Population

Income (household, family, and personal), by source, detailed characteristics, and region, 1988-89, annual Current Population Rpt, 2546–6.68

Income (household, family, and personal), by source, detailed characteristics, and region, 1990, annual Current Population Rpt, 2546–6.70

Prices and Cost of Living

Import prices relation to dollar exchange rate for 32 industries, and impacts of domestic market concentration, 1990 working paper, 9387–8.234

Producer Price Index, by major commodity group and subgroup, and processing stage, monthly press release, 6762–5

Producer Price Index current statistics, Monthly Labor Review, 6722–1.4

Producer price indexes, by stage of processing and detailed commodity, monthly rpt, 6762–6

Producer price indexes, by stage of processing and detailed commodity, monthly 1990, annual rpt, 6764–2

Public Welfare and Social Security

OASDI disabled worker beneficiaries, by diagnostic group and industry div, 1988, annual rpt, 4744–3.4

Science and Technology

Asia science and engineering employment, by selected characteristics, for 3 countries, 1991 working paper, 2326–18.61

Computer use at home, school, and work, by purpose and selected user characteristics, 1989, Current Population Rpt, 2546–2.158

Foreign countries science and engineering employment, by professional characteristics, age, and sex, for selected countries, 1991 working paper, 2326–18.62; 2326–18.63

Materials (advanced structural) devs, use, and R&D funding, for ceramics, metal alloys, polymers, and composites, 1960s-80s and projected to 2000, 5608–162

R&D funding, and scientists and engineers education and employment, for US and selected foreign countries, 1991 annual rpt, 9627–35

BY OCCUPATION

Banking, Finance, and Insurance

Credit unions finances, by occupational membership category, as of June 1991, semiannual rpt, 9532–6

Communications and Transportation

Air traffic control and airway facilities staff, by employment and other characteristics, FY89, annual rpt, 7504–41

Railroad accidents, casualties, and damage, by cause, railroad, and State, 1990, annual rpt, 7604–1

Railroad employment by occupational group, for Class I line-haul railroads, monthly rpt, 9482–3

Railroad employment, earnings, and hours, by occupation for Class I railroads, 1990, annual table, 9484–5

Education

Athletes in college, educational and employment performance compared to other students, for 1972 high school class, as of 1986, 4888–5

Educational attainment, by sociodemographic characteristics and location, 1989 and trends from 1940, biennial Current Population Rpt, 2546–1.452

Indian education funding of Fed Govt, and enrollment, degrees, and program grants and fellowships by State, late 1960s-FY89, annual rpt, 14874–1

Special education programs, enrollment by age, staff, funding, and needs, by type of handicap and State, 1989/90, annual rpt, 4944–4

Student loan debt burden of 1986 college grads, by selected student characteristics and instn control, 1987, 4808–26

Women's employment and educational experiences compared to men, for high school class of 1972, natl longitudinal study, as of 1986, 4888–6

Government and Defense

DOT employment, by subagency, occupation, and selected personnel characteristics, FY90, annual rpt, 7304–18

Employment (civilian) of Fed Govt, by demographic and employment characteristics, as of Sept 1990, annual article, 9842–1.201

Employment and payroll (civilian) of Fed Govt, by occupation, pay grade, sex, agency, and location, 1989, biennial rpt, 9844–4

Employment of minorities, women, and disabled in Fed Govt, by agency and occupation, FY89, annual rpt, 9244–10

Equal Opportunity Recruitment Program activity, and Fed Govt employment by sex, race, pay grade, and occupational group, FY90, annual rpt, 9844–33

Military active duty and recruit social, economic, and parents characteristics, by service branch and State, FY89, annual rpt, 3544–41

Military reserve forces attrition, by reason, personnel characteristics, reserve component, and State, FY88, GAO rpt, 26123–329

Military reserve forces personnel strengths and characteristics, by component, FY90, annual rpt, 3544–38

Military reserve forces personnel strengths and characteristics, by component, quarterly rpt, 3542–4

Military women personnel on active and reserve duty, by demographic and service characteristics and service branch, FY89, annual chartbook, 3544–26

Minority group and women employment by Fed Govt, and compliance with EEOC standards, by occupation and agency, FY88-92, GAO rpt, 26119–342

Minority group and women employment in State and local govt, by occupation, function, pay level, and State, 1990, annual rpt, 9244–6

Navy personnel strengths, accessions, and attrition, detailed statistics, quarterly rpt, 3802–4

Senior Executive Service membership characteristics, entries, exits, and awards, FY79-90, annual rpt, 9844–36

Index by Categories

Taxes, spending, and govt efficiency, public opinion by respondent characteristics, 1991 survey, annual rpt, 10044–2

Voting and registration, by socioeconomic and demographic characteristics, 1990 congressional election, biennial Current Population Rpt, 2546–1.454

Health and Vital Statistics

Births, fertility rates, and childless women, by selected characteristics, 1990, annual Current Population Rpt, 2546–1.455

Deaths related to work injuries, by equipment type, circumstances, and OSHA standards violated, series, 6606–2

Deaths within 8 years of retirement, by health and other characteristics, 1982-88, article, 4742–1.206

Disabled persons rehabilitation, Federal and State activities and funding, FY90, annual rpt, 4944–1

Drug and alcohol use in workplace, and drinkers reporting adverse effects, for young adults by selected characteristics, 1984, article, 6722–1.237

Hospices use by cancer patients, by service type, use of other facilities, patient and instn characteristics, and other indicators, local area study, 1980-85, 4658–53

Hospital employment, by detailed occupation, 1989, article, 6722–1.217

Indian Health Service employment of Indians and non-Indians, training, hires, and quits, by occupation, FY89, annual rpt, 4084–6

Injuries at workplace, by circumstances, body site, equipment type, and industry, with safety measures, series, 6846–1

Military health care personnel, and accessions by training source, by occupation, specialty, and service branch, FY89, annual rpt, 3544–24

Mines (coal) and related operations occupational injuries and incidence, employment, and hours, 1989, annual rpt, 6664–4

Mines (metal) and related operations occupational injuries and incidence, employment, and hours, 1989, annual rpt, 6664–3

Mines (nonmetallic minerals) and related operations occupational injuries and incidence, employment, and hours, 1989, annual rpt, 6664–1

Mines (sand and gravel) and related operations occupational injuries and incidence, employment, and hours, 1989, annual rpt, 6664–2

Mines (stone) and related operations occupational injuries and incidence, employment, and hours, 1989, annual rpt, 6664–5

Mines (underground coal) back injuries, by circumstances, victim characteristics, and treatment, mid 1980s, 5608–166

Mines occupational deaths, by circumstances and selected victim characteristics, semiannual rpt series, 6662–3

Mines safety and health enforcement, training, and funding, with casualties, by type of mine and State, FY89, annual rpt, 6664–6

Radiation exposure at DOE and DOE-contractor sites, by facility type and contractor, dose type, and worker age, sex, and occupation, 1988, annual rpt, 3324–1

Index by Categories

BY OCCUPATION

Respiratory diseases related to occupational hazards, epidemiology, diagnosis, and treatment, for selected industries and work settings, 1988 conf, 4248–90

Shift rotation health and safety effects, and US and foreign regulation, by selected industry and occupation, 1970s-89, 26356–9.3

Waste (medical) generation, sources, health worker exposure and risk, and incineration emissions, 1980s, 4078–1

Labor and Employment

Alaska rural areas population characteristics, and energy resources dev effects, series, 5736–5

Aliens (illegal) legal residence applications under Immigration Reform and Control Act, by selected characteristics, State, and country, periodic rpt, 6262–3

Black American displaced workers, by demographic and current and former employment characteristics, and compared to whites, 1978-86, article, 6722–1.234

Dallas-Fort Worth-Arlington metro area employment, earnings, hours, and CPI changes, late 1970s-90, annual rpt, 6964–2

Displaced workers losing job 1985-90, by demographic and former and current employment characteristics, as of Jan 1990, article, 6722–1.225

Earnings, annual average percent changes for selected occupational groups, selected MSAs, monthly rpt, 6782–1.1

Earnings distribution by sex, race, industry div, and occupation, 1960-89, article, 6722–1.201

Employee benefit plan coverage and provisions, by plan type, firm size, and industry sector, 1988, article, 6722–1.204

Employee benefit plan coverage, by benefit type and worker characteristics, late 1970s-80s, 15496–1.11

Employment and Earnings, detailed data, monthly rpt, 6742–2

Employment conditions, alternative BLS projections to 2005 and trends 1970s-90, biennial article, 6722–1.254

Employment Cost Index and percent change by occupational group, industry div, region, and metro-nonmetro area, quarterly press release, 6782–5

Employment Cost Index changes for nonfarm workers, by occupation, industry div, region, and bargaining status, monthly rpt, 6782–1

Employment cost indexes, by occupation, industry div, and region, Monthly Labor Review, 6722–1.3

Employment, unemployment, and labor force characteristics, by region, State, and selected metro area, 1990, annual rpt, 6744–7

Entry level employment, and share without previous experience in field, by detailed occupation, 1986, article, 6742–1.201

Foreign countries labor conditions, union coverage, and work accidents, annual country rpt series, 6366–4

High school and college grads employment status and income, 1991 edition, annual rpt, 4824–2.28

Hispanic Americans social and economic characteristics, by detailed origin, 1991, Current Population Rpt, 2546–1.448; 2546–1.451

Houston metro area employment, earnings, hours, and CPI changes, 1970s-90, annual rpt, 6964–1

Immigrants admitted to US, by occupational group and country of birth, preliminary FY90, annual table, 6264–1

Labor force status, by worker characteristics and industry group, 1982-90, semiannual article, 6722–1.212

Labor force, wages, hours, and payroll costs, by major industry group and demographic characteristics, *Survey of Current Business*, monthly rpt, 2702–1.8

Lumber industry workers and wages by occupation, annual State survey rpt series, 6787–7

Manufacturing employment, by detailed occupation and SIC 2-digit industry, 1989 survey, triennial rpt, 6748–52

Moonlighting employment, by reason, and characteristics of workers and primary and secondary jobs, 1991, press release, 6726–1.40

Older men's labor force status by urban-rural location, and distribution of men by age and occupation, 1860s-1980, article, 9371–1.202

Pay comparability of Fed Govt with private industry, by occupation for 22 MSAs, 1989, GAO rpt, 26119–332

Poverty rate among workers in metro and nonmetro areas, relation to employment and other characteristics, 1987, 1598–274

Recruitment, hiring, compensation, and other employment practices of large firms, 1989 survey, GAO rpt, 26119–324

Self-employment, by occupation, industry, sex, and race, 1983 and 1990, article, 6742–1.202

Small business employees benefit plan coverage and provisions, by plan type and occupational group, 1990, biennial rpt, 6784–20

Southeastern US wages of office and plant workers, for 27 MSAs, 1990, press release, 6946–3.21

State and Metro Area Data Book, 1991 data compilation, 2328–54

Statistical Abstract of US, 1991 annual data compilation, 2324–1.13

Temporary help supply establishments by occupation supplied, receipts by source, and payroll, by MSA, 1987 Census of Service Industries, 2393–4.8

Unemployment insurance job search services, impacts on UI claims activity and reemployment, and claimant characteristics, for Tacoma, Wash, 1986-87, 6406–6.35

Unemployment major indicators, by occupational group, monthly press release, 6742–5

Unemployment major indicators, transcripts of BLS Commissioner's monthly testimony, periodic rpt, 23846–4

Union coverage of workers and earnings, by age, sex, race, occupational group, and industry div, 1989-90, press release, 6726–1.36

Vocational rehabilitation cases of State agencies by disposition and applicant characteristics, and closures by reason, FY84-88, annual rpt, 4944–6

Wages by occupation, and benefits for office and plant workers in selected MSAs, 1990, annual rpt, 6785–1

Wages by occupation, and benefits for office and plant workers, periodic MSA survey rpt series, 6785–3; 6785–11; 6785–12

Wages by occupation, for office and plant workers in metro areas, by industry div and region, Aug 1990, annual rpt, 6785–9

Wages by occupation, for office and plant workers in selected MSAs, 1991 surveys, annual rpt, 6785–5

Wages by occupation, for office and plant workers in selected MSAs, 1991 surveys, annual summary rpts, 6785–6

Wages, hours, and employment by occupation, and benefits, for selected locations, industry survey rpt series, 6787–6

Wages of full- and part-time workers, by selected characteristics, quarterly press release, 6742–20

Women's employment in skilled manual occupations, and apprenticeships, 1978-89, 6564–1.1

Law Enforcement

Crimes, by characteristics of victim and offender, circumstances, and location, data compilation, 1991 annual rpt, 6064–6.3

Public opinion on crime and crime-related issues, by respondent characteristics, data compilation, 1991 annual rpt, 6064–6.2

Population

Black Americans social and economic characteristics, for South and total US, 1989-90 and trends from 1969, Current Population Rpt, 2546–1.450

Consumer Income, socioeconomic characteristics of persons, families, and households, detailed cross-tabulations, Current Population Rpt series, 2546–6

Developing countries aged population and selected characteristics, 1980s and projected to 2020, country rpt series, 2326–19

Hispanic Americans in counties bordering Mexico, by selected characteristics, 1980, Current Population Rpt, 2546–2.159

Immigrants in US, population characteristics and fertility, by birthplace and compared to native born, 1980s, Current Population rpt, 2546–2.162

Income (household) by source and expenses by type, for married couple families with one spouse working, by selected characteristics, 1987, article, 1702–1.201

Prices and Cost of Living

Consumer Expenditure Survey, household income by source, and itemized spending, by selected characteristics and region, 1988-89, annual rpt, 6764–5

Consumer Expenditure Survey, spending by category, and income, by selected household characteristics and location, 1990, annual press release, 6726–1.42

Public Welfare and Social Security

Child day care employment by occupation, and mothers in labor force, 1976-88 with day care employment projected to 2000, article, 6722–1.202

Disability Insurance beneficiaries costs to Medicare until age 64 under alternative coverage assumptions, model results, 1989, article, 4742–1.208

Earnings replacement rates of pension plans and OASI benefits, by age, salary, years of participation, and occupational group, 1989, article, 6722–1.238

BY OCCUPATION

Science and Technology

Asia science and engineering employment, by selected characteristics, for 3 countries, 1991 working paper, 2326–18.61

Computer use at home, school, and work, by purpose and selected user characteristics, 1989, Current Population Rpt, 2546–2.158

Employment and education of scientists and engineers, and R&D spending, for US and selected foreign countries, 1991 annual rpt, 9627–35.2

Employment and other characteristics of science and engineering PhDs, by field and State, 1989, biennial rpt, 9627–18

Foreign countries science and engineering employment, by professional characteristics, age, and sex, for selected countries, 1991 working paper, 2326–18.62; 2326–18.63

NASA staff characteristics and personnel actions, FY90, annual rpt, 9504–1

Veterans Affairs

Health care staff of VA, and turnover, by occupation and location, 1990, annual rpt, 8604–8

Medicine and Surgery Dept of VA, trainees by detailed program and city, FY90, annual rpt, 8704–4

DEMOGRAPHIC BREAKDOWNS

BY AGE

Agriculture and Food

Census of Agriculture, 1987: farms, farmland, production, finances, and operator characteristics, by county, final State rpt series, 2331–1

Food consumption, dietary composition, and nutrient intake, 1987/88 natl survey, preliminary rpt series, 1356–1

Food spending, by item, household composition, income, age, race, and region, 1980-88, Consumer Expenditure Survey biennial rpt, 1544–30

Operators entries and exits, by State, late 1970s-87, 1598–269

Banking, Finance, and Insurance

Households assets, by type of holding and selected characteristics, 1988, Current Population Rpt, 2546–20.16

Communications and Transportation

Air traffic control and airway facilities staff, by employment and other characteristics, FY89, annual rpt, 7504–41

Air traffic control and airway facilities supervisors task priorities, skills needed, and other characteristics, 1990 survey, technical rpt, 7506–10.84

Aircraft accidents and circumstances, for US operations of domestic and foreign airlines and general aviation, periodic rpt, 9612–1

Aircraft accidents, pilots involved by age, 1988, annual rpt, 9614–3

Aircraft pilot and nonpilot certificates held, by type of certificate, age, sex, region, and State, 1990, annual rpt, 7504–2

Aircraft pilots in general aviation, by type of certificate and age, 1990, triennial survey rpt, 7508–3

Bus (school) accidents, circumstances, victim characteristics, and vehicle type, 1989, annual rpt, 7764–22

Drivers licenses in force, by age, sex, and State, 1989-90, annual rpt, 7554–24

Drivers licenses in force by license type, sex, and age, and revenues, by State, 1990, annual rpt, 7554–1.2

Drivers licenses issued and in force by age and sex, fees, and renewal, by license class and State, 1989, annual rpt, 7554–16

Mail volume to and from households, use, and views, by class, source, content, and household characteristics, 1987-88, annual rpt, 9864–10

Traffic accidents, casualties, circumstances, and characteristics of persons and vehicles involved, 1989, annual rpt, 7764–18

Traffic fatal accidents, alcohol levels of drivers and others, by circumstances and characteristics of persons and vehicles, 1989, annual rpt, 7764–16

Traffic fatal accidents, circumstances, and characteristics of persons and vehicles involved, 1990, semiannual rpt, 7762–11

Traffic fatal accidents, deaths, and rates, by circumstances, characteristics of persons and vehicles involved, and location, 1989, annual rpt, 7764–10

Travel from US, characteristics of visit and traveler, and country of destination, 1990 in-flight survey, annual rpt, 2904–14

Travel patterns, personal and household characteristics, and auto and public transport use, 1990 survey, series, 7556–6

Travel patterns, personal and household characteristics, and auto use, 1990 survey, annual rpt, 7554–1.6

Travel to US, by characteristics of visit and traveler, country, port city, and State of destination, quarterly rpt, 2902–1

Travel to US, by characteristics of visit and traveler, world area of origin, and US destination, 1990 survey, annual rpt, 2904–12

Truck accidents, by carrier financial and operating conditions and driver characteristics, 1980s, GAO rpt, 26131–82

Truck accidents, casualties, and damage, by circumstances and characteristics of persons and vehicles involved, 1988, annual rpt, 7554–9

Truck accidents, circumstances, severity, and characteristics of drivers and vehicles, 1989, annual rpt, 7764–20

Education

Condition of Education, detail for elementary, secondary, and higher education, 1920s-90 and projected to 2001, annual rpt, 4824–1

Digest of Education Statistics, 1991 annual data compilation, 4824–2

Educational attainment, by sociodemographic characteristics and location, 1989 and trends from 1940, biennial Current Population Rpt, 2546–1.452

Educational enrollment rates, 1960s-89, pamphlet, 4828–26

Elementary and secondary education enrollment, staff, finances, operations, programs, and policies, 1987/88 biennial survey, series, 4836–3

Elementary and secondary public schools, enrollment and other characteristics, for top 100 districts, 1988/89, annual rpt, 4834–22

Elementary and secondary students educational performance, and factors

Index by Categories

affecting proficiency, by selected characteristics, 1988 natl assessments, subject rpt series, 4896–7

Elementary and secondary students educational performance in math, science, reading, and writing, 1970s-90, 4898–32

Enrollment, by grade, instn type and control, and student characteristics, 1989 and trends from 1947, annual Current Population Rpt, 2546–1.453

High school dropout rates, and subsequent completion, by student and school characteristics, alternative estimates, 1990, annual rpt, 4834–23

Higher education instn student aid and other sources of support, with student expenses and characteristics, by instn type and control, 1990 triennial study, series, 4846–5

Homeless adults educational services, funding, participation, and staff, by State, 1989, annual rpt series, 4804–39

Literacy programs in workplaces, demonstration projects funding and participant characteristics, FY88, 4808–37

Special education programs, enrollment by age, staff, funding, and needs, by type of handicap and State, 1989/90, annual rpt, 4944–4

Student aid Pell grants and applicants, by tuition, income level, instn type and control, and State, 1989/90, annual rpt, 4804–1

Teachers in higher education instns, employment and other characteristics, by instn type and control, 1987/88 survey, 4846–4.4

Teachers in private schools, selected characteristics by instn level, size, and orientation, various periods 1979-88, 4838–47

Government and Defense

Aliens (illegal) legal residence applications under Immigration Reform and Control Act, by selected characteristics, State, and country, periodic rpt, 6262–3

Insurance (life) coverage, and claims by age, for Federal civilian employees, FY89 with trends from FY84, annual rpt, 9844–35.3

Military active duty and recruit social, economic, and parents characteristics, by service branch and State, FY89, annual rpt, 3544–41

Military deaths by cause, age, race, and rank, and personnel captured and missing, by service branch, FY90, annual rpt, 3544–40

Military personnel, by selected characteristics, 1991 annual summary rpt, 3504–13

Military personnel deaths by service branch and age group, and veterans death rates, 1966-90, annual rpt, 8654–1

Military personnel on active duty, by age, 1963-90, annual rpt, 3544–1.2

Military reserve forces personnel strengths and characteristics, by component, FY90, annual rpt, 3544–38

Military reserve forces personnel strengths and characteristics, by component, quarterly rpt, 3542–4

Navy personnel strengths, accessions, and attrition, detailed statistics, quarterly rpt, 3802–4

Public debt burden on future generations forecast under alternative economic and fiscal policy assumptions, 1991 working paper, 9377–9.111

Index by Categories

BY AGE

Public debt burden on future generations forecast under alternative fiscal policies, and ratio of consumption to lifetime income, by sex and age, 1991 working paper, 9377–9.116

Senior Executive Service membership characteristics, entries, exits, and awards, FY79-90, annual rpt, 9844–36

Tax (income) returns filed, by whether filed electronically, taxpayer characteristics, and reason for not filing electronically, 1990, article, 8304–8.1

Tax (income) returns of high income individuals not filed, by selected characteristics, 1987, and assessments under alternative IRS enforcement programs, 1990, GAO rpt, 26119–322

Taxes, spending, and govt efficiency, public opinion by respondent characteristics, 1991 survey, annual rpt, 10044–2

Voting and registration, by socioeconomic and demographic characteristics, 1990 congressional election, biennial Current Population Rpt, 2546–1.454

Health and Vital Statistics

Abortions, by method, patient characteristics, and State, 1972-88, article, 4202–7.207

Abortions, by method, pregnancy history, and other characteristics of woman, 1988, US Vital Statistics annual rpt, 4146–5.120

Acute and chronic health conditions, disability, absenteeism, and health services use, by selected characteristics, 1987, CD-ROM, 4147–10.177

AIDS cases by risk group, race, sex, age, State, and MSA, and deaths, monthly rpt, 4202–9

AIDS public knowledge, attitudes, and risk behaviors, for women, 1988 survey, 4146–8.200

AIDS public knowledge, attitudes, info sources, and testing, for blacks, 1990 survey, 4146–8.208

AIDS public knowledge, attitudes, info sources, and testing, for Hispanics, 1990 survey, 4146–8.209

AIDS public knowledge, attitudes, info sources, and testing, 1990 survey, 4146–8.195; 4146–8.201; 4146–8.205

AIDS virus infection and risk factor prevalence, natl survey methodology and pretest results, 1989, 4148–30

Alcohol abuse by family members and spouses, population exposure by selected characteristics, 1988, 4146–8.207

Alcohol users by consumption level, and abstainers, deaths by cause, age, and sex, 1986-87, article, 4482–1.201

Birth expectations, childbearing delay, and childlessness among women born late 1930s-72, by age, education, and marital and employment status, late 1970s-90, Current Population Rpt, 2546–2.162

Birth outcomes and prenatal care use effects of Medicaid coverage, charges, and Medicaid payments, for California, 1983, article, 4652–1.241

Births and rates, by characteristics of birth, infant, and parents, 1989 and trends from 1940, US Vital Statistics advance annual rpt, 4146–5.123

Births, fertility rates, and childless women, by selected characteristics, 1990, annual Current Population Rpt, 2546–1.455

Cancer cases by body site and population characteristics, research results, semimonthly journal, 4472–1

Cancer cases, deaths, and survival rates, by sex, race, age, and body site, 1973-88, annual rpt, 4474–35

Cancer death rates of minorities, by body site, age, sex, and substate area, 1950s-80, atlas, 4478–78

Cancer deaths by age, and cases, by sex, 1985 and 1990, annual rpt, 4474–13

Child accident deaths and death rates, by cause, age, sex, race, and State, 1980-85, 4108–54

Child accident deaths and injuries by cause, and victimization, rates by race, sex, and age, 1979-88, chartbook, 4108–56

Child developmental, learning, and emotional problems, cases and share receiving special treatment and education, by selected characteristics, 1988, 4146–8.193

Child health, behavioral, emotional, and school problems relation to family structure, by selected characteristics, 1988, 4147–10.178

Cirrhosis of liver deaths, by age, sex, race, and whether alcohol involved, 1987 and trends from 1910, 4486–1.10

Construction industry occupational deaths, by cause, age, industry, and region, 1985-89, 6608–4

Deaths and rates, by cause, age, sex, race, and State, preliminary 1989-90 and trends from 1960, US Vital Statistics annual rpt, 4144–7

Deaths and rates, by detailed cause and demographic characteristics, 1988 and trends from 1900, US Vital Statistics annual rpt, 4144–2

Deaths and rates, provisional data, monthly rpt, 4142–1.2

Deaths recorded in 121 cities, by age group and for infants, weekly rpt, 4202–1

Deaths within 8 years of retirement, by health and other characteristics, 1982-88, article, 4742–1.206

Diabetes and complications cases, deaths, and hospitalization, by age, sex, race, State, and region, 1980-86, annual rpt, 4205–41

Disability (functional), persons needing aid with activities of daily living, by age and household income, 1986, fact sheet, 2326–17.22

Disabled persons and related activity limitation days and health services use, by health status, disability type, and other characteristics, 1984-88, 4146–8.202

Disabled persons rehabilitation, Federal and State activities and funding, FY90, annual rpt, 4944–1

Diving (underwater sport and occupational) deaths, by circumstances, diver characteristics, and location, 1970-89, annual rpt, 2144–5

Divorces by age of spouses and duration of marriage, and children involved, by State, 1988 and trends from 1940, US Vital Statistics advance annual rpt, 4146–5.121

Drug abuse emergency room admissions and deaths, by drug type and source, sex, race, age, and major metro area, 1990, annual rpt, 4494–8

Drug abuse indicators for selected metro areas, research results, data collection, and policy issues, 1991 semiannual conf, 4492–5

Drug abuse prevalence among minorities, related health effects and crime, treatment, and research status and needs, mid 1970s-90, 4498–72

Drug, alcohol, and cigarette use, by selected characteristics, 1990 survey, biennial rpt, 4494–5

Drug and alcohol abuse treatment and prevention programs of States, funding, facilities, and patient characteristics, FY89, 4488–15

Drug and alcohol abuse treatment facilities, services, use, funding, staff, and client characteristics, 1989, biennial rpt, 4494–10

Drug and alcohol abuse treatment services, funding, staffing, and client load, characteristics, and outcomes, by setting, 1989 conf, 4498–73

Ectopic pregnancies and related deaths, by race, age, and region, 1970-87, article, 4202–7.202

Expenditures for health care, by service type, payment source, and sector, 1960s-90, annual article, 4652–1.221

Firearms-related deaths and death rates, by motive, age, sex, and race, for persons aged 1-34, 1979-88, 4146–5.119

Food aid program of USDA for women, infants, and children, prenatal participation effect on Medicaid costs and birth outcomes, for 5 States, 1987-88, 1368–2

Health care services use and costs, methodology and findings of natl survey, series, 4186–8

Health condition and health care resources, use, and spending, 1950s-89, annual data compilation, 4144–11

Hepatitis cases by infection source, age, sex, race, and State, and deaths, by strain, 1988 and trends from 1966, 4205–2

Hispanic Americans deaths and rates, by cause, age, sex, and detailed origin, average 1979-81, 4147–20.18

Home health care services Medicare use and costs, by agency and service type, patient characteristics, and State, 1988-89, article, 4652–1.229

Homeless persons alcohol abuse, by sex, age, race, and additional diagnoses, aggregate 1985-87, 4488–14

Hospices operations, services, costs, and patient characteristics, for instns without Medicare certification, FY85-86, 4658–52

Hospices use by cancer patients, by service type, use of other facilities, patient and instn characteristics, and other indicators, local area study, 1980-85, 4658–53

Hospital discharges and length of stay, by diagnosis, patient and instn characteristics, procedure performed, and payment source, 1988, annual rpt, 4147–13.107

Hospital discharges and length of stay by region and diagnosis, and procedures performed, by age and sex, 1989, annual rpt, 4146–8.198

Hospital discharges and rates, for aged Medicare beneficiaries by diagnosis, age, sex, and race, 1988, article, 4202–7.205

Hospital discharges by detailed diagnostic and procedure category, primary diagnosis, and length of stay, by age, sex, and region, 1988, annual rpt, 4147–13.105

Hospital discharges by detailed diagnostic and procedure category, primary diagnosis, and length of stay, by age, sex, and region, 1989, annual rpt, 4147–13.108

BY AGE

Index by Categories

Hypertension risk for women, by age and race, aggregate 1976-80, article, 4042–3.231

Implants of medical devices, by type, reason, duration, and user characteristics, 1988, 4146–8.197

Indian Health Service facilities, funding, operations, and Indian health and other characteristics, 1950s-90, annual chartbook, 4084–1

Indian Health Service outpatient services provided, by reason for visit and age, FY88-89, annual rpt, 4084–2

Indian Health Service, tribal, and contract facilities hospitalization, by diagnosis, age, sex, and service area, FY89, annual rpt, 4084–5

Infectious notifiable disease cases, by age, race, and State, and deaths, 1930s-90, annual rpt, 4204–1

Infertility prevalence among women, by age and parity, with infertility services use, selected years 1965-88, 4146–8.194

Injuries, by type, circumstances, and victim characteristics, and related activity limitations, 1985-87, 4147–10.176

Injuries from use of consumer products, by severity, victim age, and detailed product, 1990, annual rpt, 9164–6

Injuries from use of consumer products, related deaths and costs, and recalls by brand, by product type, FY89, annual rpt, 9164–2

Injuries, related impairments, and activity limitations, by circumstances and victim characteristics, 1985-87, 4147–10.179

Insurance (health) coverage, by insurance type and selected characteristics, 1989, 4146–8.203

Insurance (health) coverage of children, and children with a regular source of care, by selected characteristics, 1988, 4146–8.192

Insurance (health) coverage, uninsured persons by employment and other characteristics and State, 1988, GAO rpt, 26121–403

Insurance (health) natl coverage alternative proposals and indicators of need, 1989, 4658–54

Kidney end-stage disease cases, treatment, outcomes, and characteristics of patients, organ donors, and facilities, late 1970s-88, annual rpt, 4474–37

Kidney end-stage disease program of Medicare, outlays, and enrollment by age and treatment type, 1982-87, article, 4652–1.208

Kidney end-stage disease treatment facilities, Medicare enrollment and reimbursement, survival, and patient characteristics, 1983-89, annual rpt, 4654–16

Kidney transplants, needs, costs, payment sources, and impact of immunosuppressive drugs on outcome, 1950s-87 and projected to 1995, 4658–59

Life tables, 1988 and trends from 1900, US Vital Statistics annual rpt, 4144–2.6

Marriage, marriage dissolution, remarriage, and cohabitation, for women, by age and race, 1988, 4146–8.196

Marriages and rates, by age, race, education, previous marital status, and State, 1988, US Vital Statistics advance annual rpt, 4146–5.122

Marriages, divorces, and rates, by characteristics of spouses, State, and county, 1987 and trends from 1920, US Vital Statistics annual rpt, 4144–4

Mental health care facilities for emotionally disturbed children, use, funding, and characteristics of patients, staff, and instn, 1988, 4506–3.44

Mental health care facilities of States and counties, patients and admissions by age, diagnosis, and State, FY89, annual rpt, 4504–2

Mental health care facilities outpatient care programs, use, and client characteristics, by instn type and State, 1988, 4506–3.40; 4506–3.46

Mental health care in private hospitals, patients characteristics, 1986, 4506–3.47

Mental illness and drug and alcohol abuse direct and indirect costs, by age and sex, 1985, 4048–35

Mentally retarded persons care facilities and residents by selected characteristics, and use of Medicaid services and waiver programs, by State, late 1970s-80s, 4658–49

Mines (underground coal) back injuries, by circumstances, victim characteristics, and treatment, mid 1980s, 5608–166

Mines occupational deaths, by circumstances and selected victim characteristics, semiannual rpt series, 6662–3

Minority group and women health condition, services use, payment sources, and health care labor force, by poverty status, 1940s-89, chartbook, 4118–56

Minority group health condition, services use, costs, and indicators of services need, 1950s-88, 4118–55

Nursing home residents with mental, behavioral, and functional disorders, by age, sex, and instn characteristics, 1987, 4186–8.11

Nursing home residents with mental disorders, by disorder type and resident and instn characteristics, 1985, 4147–13.106

Nursing home use prevalence among aged, by length of stay and selected characteristics, 1986 and 1990, 4186–7.9

Occupational injuries, by circumstances, body site, equipment type, and industry, with safety measures, series, 6846–1

Older persons deaths in hospitals, nursing homes, and own home, by cause, age, marital status, and region, 1986, article, 4652–1.201

Older persons with functional limitations, long-term care sources, and health and other characteristics, 1984-85, 4147–13.104

Physicians, by specialty, age, sex, and location of training and practice, 1989, State rpt series, 4116–6

Physicians visits, by patient and practice characteristics, diagnosis, and services provided, 1989, 4146–8.206

Pregnancy-related deaths, rates, and risk, by pregnancy outcome, cause, and maternal characteristics, 1979-86, article, 4202–7.206

Radiation exposure at DOE and DOE-contractor sites, by facility type and contractor, dose type, and worker age, sex, and occupation, 1988, annual rpt, 3324–1

Sexually transmitted disease cases, by strain, age, and sex, 1981-90, annual rpt, 4205–42

Smoking and smokeless tobacco use, attitudes, and smoking intervention research spending and results, with bibl, 1960s-90, 4478–195

Tuberculosis cases and deaths, by patient characteristics, State, and city, 1989 and trends from 1953, annual rpt, 4204–10

Housing and Construction

Affordability indicators for housing, by household composition, income, and current tenure, 1988, 2486–1.11

American Housing Survey: inventory change from 1973, by reason, unit and household characteristics, and location, 1983, biennial rpt, 2485–14

American Housing Survey: unit and households characteristics, unit and neighborhood quality, and journey to work by MSA location, for 11 MSAs, 1984 survey, supplement, 2485–8

American Housing Survey: unit and households detailed characteristics, and unit and neighborhood quality, MSA rpt series, 2485–6

American Housing Survey: unit and households detailed characteristics, and unit and neighborhood quality, 1987, biennial rpt, 2485–12

American Housing Survey: unit and households detailed characteristics, and unit and neighborhood quality, 1987, biennial rpt supplement, 2485–13

Homeownership rates, by household type, householder age and sex, and location, 1960s-90, annual rpt, 2484–1.3

Homeownership rates, by location and age of householder, quarterly rpt, 2482–1

Mortgages FHA-insured, financial, property, and mortgagor characteristics, by metro area, 1990, annual rpt, 5144–24

Mortgages FHA-insured, financial, property, and mortgagor characteristics, by State, 1990, annual rpt, 5144–1

Mortgages FHA-insured, financial, property, and mortgagor characteristics, 1990, annual rpt, 5144–17; 5144–23

Labor and Employment

Black women's labor force status, employment by age and education, and women's and families earnings, 1980-90, fact sheet, 6564–1.2

Displaced workers losing job 1985-90, by demographic and former and current employment characteristics, as of Jan 1990, article, 6722–1.225

Employee benefit plan coverage, by benefit type and worker characteristics, late 1970s-80s, 15496–1.11

Employment and Earnings, detailed data, monthly rpt, 6742–2

Employment and unemployment, by age, sex, race, marital and family status, industry div, and State, Monthly Labor Review, 6722–1.2

Employment conditions, alternative BLS projections to 2005 and trends 1970s-90, biennial article, 6722–1.252

Employment, earnings, and hours, monthly press release, 6742–5

Employment situation, earnings, hours, and other BLS economic indicators, transcripts of BLS Commissioner's monthly testimony, periodic rpt, 23846–4

Index by Categories

BY AGE

Insurance (life) benefits and age-related reductions of employee plans, by employee characteristics, 1989, article, 6722–1.216

Job Training Partnership Act participants, by selected characteristics, FY90, annual rpt, 6304–1

Labor force status, by worker characteristics and industry group, 1982-90, semiannual article, 6722–1.212

Labor supply trends, with characteristics of working-age population not in labor force, part-time workers, and multiple-jobholders, late 1960s-90, article, 9362–1.203

Manufacturing employment by selected characteristics, wages, and import and export penetration rates, by SIC 2- to 4-digit industry, 1982-89, 6366–3.27

Men (older) labor force status by urban-rural location, and distribution of men by age and occupation, 1860s-1980, article, 9371–1.202

Moonlighting employment, by reason, and characteristics of workers and primary and secondary jobs, 1991, press release, 6726–1.40

Part-time employment, by age, sex, industry div, and whether voluntary, 1969-89, article, 6722–1.218

Pension coverage by industry, vestment, and recipient income, by participant characteristics, 1987, Current Population Rpt, 2546–20.18

Pension coverage in private sector, age and length of service requirements by occupational group, 1990, biennial rpt, 6784–20

Poverty rate among workers in metro and nonmetro areas, relation to employment and other characteristics, 1987, 1598–274

Rural areas labor force characteristics, with comparisons to urban areas, 1987, 1598–264

Tax credit for hiring from groups with high unemployment rates, participation by State, and effectiveness, FY88, GAO rpt, 26121–407

Unemployment insurance claims and receipt, by reason and duration of unemployment, age, sex, and region, 1989-90, 6406–6.33

Unemployment insurance job search services, impacts on UI claims activity and reemployment, and claimant characteristics, for Tacoma, Wash, 1986-87, 6406–6.35

Unemployment of groups with historically high rates, 1985-89, biennial rpt, 6504–2.2

Unemployment rates, current data and annual trends, monthly rpt, 23842–1.2

Union coverage of workers and earnings, by age, sex, race, occupational group, and industry div, 1989-90, press release, 6726–1.36

Vocational rehabilitation cases of State agencies by disposition and applicant characteristics, and closures by reason, FY84-88, annual rpt, 4944–6

Volunteer workers by organization type, time served, whether otherwise employed, and other characteristics, 1989, article, 6722–1.213

Wages of full- and part-time workers, by selected characteristics, quarterly press release, 6742–20

Women's labor force status, by age, race, and family status, quarterly rpt, 6742–17

Law Enforcement

Aliens (illegal) overstaying visas, by class of admission, mode of arrival, age, country, and State, FY85-88, annual rpt, 6264–5

Arrests, prosecutions, convictions, and sentencing, for felony offenders, by offender characteristics and offense, 1988, 6066–25.33; 6066–25.39

Assaults and deaths of law enforcement officers, by circumstances, agency, victim and offender characteristics, and location, 1990, annual rpt, 6224–3

Crime, criminal justice admin and enforcement, and public opinion, data compilation, 1991 annual rpt, 6064–6

Crimes, arrests, and rates, by offense, offender characteristics, population size, and jurisdiction, 1990, annual rpt, 6224–2.1; 6224–2.2

Criminal case processing in Federal district courts, and dispositions, by offense, district, and offender characteristics, 1986, annual rpt, 6064–29

Drug test results at arrest, by drug type, offense, and sex, for selected urban areas, quarterly rpt, 6062–3

Drug testing of criminal defendants, demonstration program operations, offender characteristics, and judges views, 1987-90, 18208–11

Jail population, by criminal, correctional, drug use, and family history, and selected other characteristics, 1989, 6066–19.62

Jail population, by sociodemographic characteristics, criminal and drug use history, whether convicted, offense, and sentencing, 1989, annual rpt, 6064–26.3

Jail population drug abuse history, by offense, conviction status, criminal and family history, and selected other characteristics, 1989, 6066–19.63

Juvenile correctional and detention public and private instns, inmates, and expenses, by instn and resident characteristics and State, 1987, biennial rpt, 6064–13

Juvenile courts delinquency cases, by offense, referral source, disposition, age, sex, race, State, and county, 1988, annual rpt, 6064–12

Juvenile courts property offenses cases, by disposition and offender age, sex, and race, 1985-86, 6066–27.5

Juvenile facilities, population, and costs, by facility and resident characteristics, region, and State, 1985-89, biennial rpt, 6064–5

Older persons abuse and neglect by circumstances and characteristics of abuser and victim, and States protective services budgets and staff, by location, 1980s, hearing, 21148–62

Pretrial processing, detention, and release, for Federal offenders, by defendant characteristics and district, 1988, hearing, 25528–114

Pretrial release of felony defendants and rearrests, by offense type and selected characteristics, 1988, 6066–25.36

Prison and parole admissions and releases, sentence length, and time served, by offense and offender characteristics, 1985, annual rpt, 6064–33

Prisoners under death sentence, and executions from 1930, by offense, prisoner characteristics, and State, 1989, annual rpt, 6064–26.6

Prisoners under death sentence by prison control and prisoner characteristics, and executions from 1930, by State, 1973-90, annual rpt, 6066–25.42

Probation and split sentences by State courts for felony offenses, sentence lengths, case processing time, and felon characteristics, by offense, 1986, 6068–242

Sentences for Federal crimes, guidelines use and results by offense and district, and Sentencing Commission activities, 1990, annual rpt, 17664–1

Teenagers crime victimization, by victim and offender characteristics, circumstances, and offense, 1985-88 surveys, 6066–3.43

Victimization rates, by victim and offender characteristics, circumstances, and offense, 1988 survey, annual rpt, 6066–3.42

Victimization rates, by victim and offender characteristics, circumstances, and offense, 1989 survey, annual rpt, 6066–3.44

Victimizations by region and victim characteristics, and rpts to police, by offense, 1973-90, annual rpt, 6066–25.35; 6066–25.41

Victimizations, by victim characteristics, offense, and whether reported to police, 1973-88, 6066–3.45

Violent crime victimizations, circumstances, victim characteristics, arrest, recidivism, sentences, and prisoners, 1980s, 6068–148

Women prisoners in State instns, by offense, drug use history, whether abused, and other characteristics, 1986, 6066–19.61

Women's rape and other violent crime victimization, by relation to offender, circumstances, and victim characteristics, 1973-87, 6068–243

Population

Alaska rural areas population characteristics, and energy resources dev effects, series, 5736–5

Black Americans social and economic characteristics, for South and total US, 1989-90 and trends from 1969, Current Population Rpt, 2546–1.450

Census of Population and Housing, 1990: population and housing characteristics, households, and land area, by county, subdiv, and place, State rpt series, 2551–1

Census of Population and Housing, 1990: population and housing selected characteristics, by region, press release, 2328–74

Children and youth social, economic, and demographic characteristics, 1950s-90, 4818–5

Consumer Income, socioeconomic characteristics of persons, families, and households, detailed cross-tabulations, Current Population Rpt series, 2546–6

Foreign countries youth population declines relative to other age groups, by selected country, 1985 and projected to 2010, 9118–17

Hispanic Americans in counties bordering Mexico, by selected characteristics, 1980, Current Population Rpt, 2546–2.159

Hispanic Americans social and economic characteristics, by detailed origin, 1991, Current Population Rpt, 2546–1.448; 2546–1.451

Households and family characteristics, by location, 1990, annual Current Population Rpt, 2546–1.447

BY AGE

Index by Categories

Immigrants in US, population characteristics and fertility, by birthplace and compared to native born, 1980s, Current Population rpt, 2546–2.162

Income (household) and poverty status under alternative income definitions, by recipient characteristics, 1990, annual Current Population Rpt, 2546–6.69

Income (personal) and poverty status changes, by selected characteristics, 1987-88, Current Population Rpt, 2546–20.19

Income and consumer spending of households, for selected population groups, quarterly journal, 1702–1

Living arrangements, family relationships, and marital status, by selected characteristics, 1990, annual Current Population Rpt, 2546–1.449

Population size and characteristics, 1969-88, Current Population Rpt, biennial rpt, 2546–2.161

Population size, by age, selected years 1929-90, annual rpt, 204–1.2

Poverty status of population and families, by detailed characteristics, 1988-89, annual Current Population Rpt, 2546–6.67

Poverty status of population and families, by detailed characteristics, 1990, annual Current Population Rpt, 2546–6.71

Poverty threshold and rates under alternative threshold adjustment methodologies, 1980s-90, hearing, 23848–221

Puerto Rico population and housing characteristics, 1990 Census of Population and Housing, press release, 2328–78

Refugee arrivals and resettlement in US, by age, sex, sponsoring agency, State, and country, monthly rpt, 4692–2

Remarriage of divorced and widowed women, duration of singlehood, and redivorce, by age, 1985, Current Population Survey, 2546–2.157

Retired pension recipients income, by selected characteristics, 1986, Current Population Rpt, 2546–20.18

Rural areas children in poverty by selected family characteristics, and compared to urban areas, 1987-88, 1598–270

State and Metro Area Data Book, 1991 data compilation, 2328–54

Statistical Abstract of US, 1991 annual data compilation, 2324–1

Virgin Islands population and housing characteristics, 1990 Census of Population and Housing, press release, 2328–81

Prices and Cost of Living

Child rearing costs of married couple households, by expenditure type, child's age, income, and region, 1990 and projected to 2007, 1708–87

Consumer Expenditure Survey, household income by source, and itemized spending, by selected characteristics and region, 1988-89, annual rpt, 6764–5

Consumer Expenditure Survey, spending by category, and income, by selected household characteristics and location, 1990, annual press release, 6726–1.42

Consumer Expenditure Survey, spending by category, selected household characteristics, and region, quarterly rpt, 6762–14

Public Welfare and Social Security

AFDC beneficiaries demographic and financial characteristics, by State, FY89, annual rpt, 4694–1

Child support and alimony awards, and payment status, by selected characteristics of woman, 1989, biennial Current Population Rpt, 2546–6.72

Child welfare programs funding by source, and foster care program operations and client characteristics, for selected States, 1960s-95, 25368–169

Disability Insurance beneficiaries costs to Medicare until age 64 under alternative coverage assumptions, model results, 1989, article, 4742–1.208

Earnings replacement rates of pension plans and OASI benefits, by age, salary, years of participation, and occupational group, 1989, article, 6722–1.238

Food stamp recipient household size, composition, income, and income and deductions allowed, summer 1988, annual rpt, 1364–8

Foster care placements, discharges, and returns to care, by selected characteristics of children, and length of stay factors, 1985-86, GAO rpt, 26121–432

Homeless and runaway youth programs, funding, activities, and participant characteristics, FY90, annual rpt, 4604–3

Medicaid services use and costs in alternative treatment settings, model description and results, FY87, article, 4652–1.211

Medicare and Medicaid beneficiaries and program operations, 1991, annual fact book, 4654–18

Medicare and Medicaid eligibility, participation, coverage, and program finances, various periods 1966-91, biennial rpt, 4654–1

Medicare disabled enrollees supplementary health insurance coverage, by enrollee characteristics, 1984, article, 4652–1.243

Medicare reimbursement of hospitals under prospective payment system, impacts on instns and beneficiaries, 1988, annual rpt, 4654–13

OASDHI admin, and SSA activities, 1930s-90 and projected to 2064, annual data compilation, 4704–12

OASDHI, Medicaid, SSI, and related programs benefits, beneficiary characteristics, and trust funds, selected years 1937-89, annual rpt, 4744–3

OASDI benefit payments, trust fund finances, and economic and demographic assumptions, 1970-90 and alternative projections to 2000, actuarial rpt, 4706–1.105

Student Community Service Program activities, and volunteer and client characteristics, 1987-89, 9028–14

Supplemental Security Income beneficiaries income from OASI and other sources, and work history, 1988, article, 4742–1.216

Supplemental Security Income benefit award rate by applicant characteristics and eligibility class, 1987, article, 4742–1.213

Teenage mothers child support awards, payment status, health insurance inclusion, and govt aid for collection, by selected characteristics, 1987, 4698–5

Recreation and Leisure

Boat accidents, casualties, and damage, by cause, vessel and operator characteristics, and State, 1990, annual rpt, 7404–1.2

Coastal areas recreation facilities of Fed Govt and States, visitor and site characteristics, 1987-90 survey, regional rpt series, 2176–9

Fishing (ocean sport) activities, and catch by species, by angler characteristics and State, annual coastal area rpt series, 2166–17

Park natl system visitor deaths, by cause, victim age, region, and park, 1980-90, annual rpt, 5544–6

Shellfish recreational harvesters selected characteristics, location of harvest and residence, and spending, 1985 survey, 2178–28

Science and Technology

Asia science and engineering employment, by selected characteristics, for 3 countries, 1991 working paper, 2326–18.61

Computer use at home, school, and work, by purpose and selected user characteristics, 1989, Current Population Rpt, 2546–2.158

Employment and education of scientists and engineers, and R&D spending, for US and selected foreign countries, 1991 annual rpt, 9627–35.2

Employment and other characteristics of science and engineering PhDs, by field and State, 1989, biennial rpt, 9627–18

Foreign countries science and engineering employment, by professional characteristics, age, and sex, for selected countries, 1991 working paper, 2326–18.62; 2326–18.63

NASA staff characteristics and personnel actions, FY90, annual rpt, 9504–1

Veterans Affairs

Agent Orange exposure of Vietnam veterans, and other factors relation to dev of rare cancers, 1984-88, 4208–33

Alcohol abuse among veterans, screening results by age and race, for 5 VA medical centers, 1990, GAO rpt, 26121–416

Disability and death compensation cases of VA, by entitlement type, period of service, sex, age, and State, FY89, annual rpt, 8604–7

Health care professionals of VA, by selected employment characteristics and VA district, quarterly rpt, 8602–6

Homeless veterans domiciliary program of VA, participant characteristics and outcomes, 1990 annual rpt, 8604–10

Homeless veterans with mental illness, VA program services, costs, staff, client characteristics, and outcome, 1990, annual rpt, 8604–11

Housing programs of VA, costs, terms, and user characteristics, 1985-89, 8608–7

Insurance (life) for veterans and servicepersons, actuarial analyses of VA programs, 1990, annual rpt, 8604–1

Mental health care services of VA, use, spending, and staff and patient characteristics, by State and services type, 1983 and 1986, 4506–3.43

Population and characteristics of veterans, and VA hospital and other activities, by State, FY90, annual rpt, 8604–3

Population of veterans, by period of service, age, and State, as of Mar 1991, annual rpt, 8604–12

Index by Categories

BY DISEASE

Communications and Transportation

Railroad accidents, casualties, and damage, by cause, railroad, and State, 1990, annual rpt, 7604–1

Education

Head Start handicapped enrollment, by handicap, State, and for Indian and migrant programs, 1987/88, annual rpt, 4604–1

Special education programs, enrollment by age, staff, funding, and needs, by type of handicap and State, 1989/90, annual rpt, 4944–4

Government and Defense

Employment of disabled in Fed Govt, by disability and agency, FY89, annual rpt, 9244–10.2

Health and Vital Statistics

Acute and chronic health conditions, disability, absenteeism, and health services use, by selected characteristics, 1987, CD-ROM, 4147–10.177

Alcohol users by consumption level, and abstainers, deaths by cause, age, and sex, 1986-87, article, 4482–1.201

Cancer death rates of minorities, by body site, age, sex, and substate area, 1950s-80, atlas, 4478–78

Children and youth social, economic, and demographic characteristics, 1950s-90, 4818–5

Costs (direct and indirect) of disease, by diagnosis, 1988, annual rpt, 4474–15

Deaths and rates, by cause and age, preliminary 1989-90, US Vital Statistics annual rpt, 4144–7

Deaths and rates, by detailed cause and demographic characteristics, 1988 and trends from 1900, US Vital Statistics annual rpt, 4144–2

Deaths and rates, provisional data, monthly rpt, 4142–1.2

Deaths from 10 leading causes, 1989, annual rpt, 4474–15

Disabled persons and related activity limitation days and health services use, by health status, disability type, and other characteristics, 1984-88, 4146–8.202

Disabled persons rehabilitation, Federal and State activities and funding, FY90, annual rpt, 4944–1

Drug prescriptions, by drug type and brand, and for new drugs, 1989, annual rpt, 4064–12

Foreign travel vaccination needs by country, and disease prevention recommendations, 1991 annual rpt, 4204–11

Genetic damage and trait monitoring and screening of employees, use, costs, benefits, and procedures, 1980s, 26358–230

Health condition and health care resources, use, and spending, 1950s-89, annual data compilation, 4144–11

Hispanic Americans deaths and rates, by cause, age, sex, and detailed origin, average 1979-81, 4147–20.18

Homeless persons alcohol abuse, by sex, age, race, and additional diagnoses, aggregate 1985-87, 4488–14

Hospices operations, services, costs, and patient characteristics, for instns without Medicare certification, FY85-86, 4658–52

Hospital deaths of Medicare patients, actual and expected rates by diagnosis, with hospital characteristics, by instn, FY87-89, annual regional rpt series, 4654–14

Hospital discharges and length of stay, by diagnosis, patient and instn characteristics, procedure performed, and payment source, 1988, annual rpt, 4147–13.107

Hospital discharges and length of stay by region and diagnosis, and procedures performed, by age and sex, 1989, annual rpt, 4146–8.198

Hospital discharges by detailed diagnostic and procedure category, primary diagnosis, and length of stay, by age, sex, and region, 1988, annual rpt, 4147–13.105

Hospital discharges by detailed diagnostic and procedure category, primary diagnosis, and length of stay, by age, sex, and region, 1989, annual rpt, 4147–13.108

Hospital discharges of Medicare beneficiaries, length of stay, case weights, and payments, by diagnosis, selected years 1983-88, article, 4652–1.250

Hospitalization costs relation to services timing, by selected patient and hospital characteristics, for Medicare discharges, 1987-88, 17208–2

Indian and Alaska Native disease and disorder cases, deaths, and health services use, by tribe, reservation, and Indian Health Service area, late 1950s-86, 4088–2

Indian Health Service facilities and use, and Indian health and other characteristics, by IHS region, 1980s-89, annual chartbook, 4084–7

Indian Health Service facilities, funding, operations, and Indian health and other characteristics, 1950s-90, annual chartbook, 4084–1

Indian Health Service outpatient services provided, by reason for visit and age, FY88-89, annual rpt, 4084–2

Indian Health Service, tribal, and contract facilities hospitalization, by diagnosis, age, sex, and service area, FY89, annual rpt, 4084–5

Indians and Alaska Natives health care access indicators, by selected characteristics, 1987, 4186–8.18

Infectious notifiable disease cases and current outbreaks, by region and State, weekly rpt, 4202–1

Injuries, by type, circumstances, and victim characteristics, and related activity limitations, 1985-87, 4147–10.176

Injuries, related impairments, and activity limitations, by circumstances and victim characteristics, 1985-87, 4147–10.179

Kidney end-stage disease treatment facilities, Medicare enrollment and reimbursement, survival, and patient characteristics, 1983-89, annual rpt, 4654–16

Mental health care facilities of States and counties, patients and admissions by age, diagnosis, and State, FY89, annual rpt, 4504–2

Mental health care in private hospitals, patients characteristics, 1986, 4506–3.47

Mentally retarded persons care facilities and residents by selected characteristics, and use of Medicaid services and waiver programs, by State, late 1970s-80s, 4658–49

Mines (nonmetallic minerals) and related operations occupational injuries and incidence, employment, and hours, 1989, annual rpt, 6664–1

Minority group and women health condition, services use, payment sources, and health care labor force, by poverty status, 1940s-89, chartbook, 4118–56

Minority group health condition, services use, costs, and indicators of services need, 1950s-88, 4118–55

Morbidity and Mortality Weekly Report, infectious notifiable disease cases and deaths, and other public health issues, periodic journal, 4202–7

Morbidity and Mortality Weekly Report, infectious notifiable disease cases by age, race, and State, and deaths, 1930s-90, annual rpt, 4204–1

Occupational health condition screening and monitoring, businesses practices and views, 1989 survey, 26358–250

Occupational injury and illness rates by SIC 2- to 4-digit industry, and deaths by cause and industry div, 1989, annual rpt, 6844–1

Older persons deaths in hospitals, nursing homes, and own home, by cause, age, marital status, and region, 1986, article, 4652–1.201

Older persons with functional limitations, long-term care sources, and health and other characteristics, 1984-85, 4147–13.104

Physicians consultations requested by attending physician, Medicare reimbursement issues, with use by diagnosis, specialty, location, and other characteristics, 1986, 4658–47

Physicians visits, by patient and practice characteristics, diagnosis, and services provided, 1989, 4146–8.206

Pregnancy-related deaths, rates, and risk, by pregnancy outcome, cause, and maternal characteristics, 1979-86, article, 4202–7.206

Preventive disease and health improvement goals and recommended activities for 2000, with trends 1970s-80s, 4048–10

State and Metro Area Data Book, 1991 data compilation, 2328–54

Statistical Abstract of US, 1991 annual data compilation, 2324–1.2; 2324–1.3

Teenagers physicians office visits, by reason and characteristics of physicians, patients, and visit, 1985, 4146–8.199

Labor and Employment

Vocational rehabilitation cases of State agencies by disposition and applicant characteristics, and closures by reason, FY84-88, annual rpt, 4944–6

Public Welfare and Social Security

Disability Insurance beneficiaries costs to Medicare until age 64 under alternative coverage assumptions, model results, 1989, article, 4742–1.208

Medicare reimbursement of hospitals under prospective payment system, diagnosis related group code assignment and effects on care and instn finances, 1984/85, series, 4006–7

Medicare reimbursement of hospitals under prospective payment system for discharge delays due to limited nursing home space, 1985, 4658–55

Medicare reimbursement of hospitals under prospective payment system, impacts on instns and beneficiaries, 1988, annual rpt, 4654–13

BY DISEASE

Medicare reimbursement of hospitals under prospective payment system, methodology, inputs, and data by diagnostic group, 1991 annual rpt, 17204–1

OASDHI, Medicaid, SSI, and related programs benefits, beneficiary characteristics, and trust funds, selected years 1937-89, annual rpt, 4744–3

Veterans Affairs

Hospitals of VA, patients discharged by diagnosis, compensation and pension status, and other characteristics, FY90, annual rpt, 8604–3.3

Surgery-related deaths and complications, by procedure and VA facility, and compared to non-VA instns, FY84-89, last issue of biennial rpt, 8704–1

BY EDUCATIONAL ATTAINMENT

Banking, Finance, and Insurance

Households assets, by type of holding and selected characteristics, 1988, Current Population Rpt, 2546–20.16

Communications and Transportation

Air traffic control and airway facilities staff, by employment and other characteristics, FY89, annual rpt, 7504–41

Mail volume to and from households, use, and views, by class, source, content, and household characteristics, 1987-88, annual rpt, 9864–10

Education

Condition of Education, detail for elementary, secondary, and higher education, 1920s-90 and projected to 2001, annual rpt, 4824–1

Degrees awarded in higher education, by level, field, race, and sex, 1988/89 with trends from 1978/79, biennial rpt, 4844–17

Digest of Education Statistics, 1991 annual data compilation, 4824–2

Eighth grade class of 1988: test scores and proficiency, by subject area and student characteristics, natl longitudinal survey, 1991 rpt, 4826–9.8

Elementary and secondary education enrollment, staff, finances, operations, programs, and policies, 1987/88 biennial survey, series, 4836–3

Enrollment, by grade, instn type and control, and student characteristics, 1989 and trends from 1947, annual Current Population Rpt, 2546–1.453

High school class of 1972: education, employment, and family characteristics, activities, and attitudes, natl longitudinal study, series, 4836–1

High school class of 1990: college enrollment, and labor force participation of grads and dropouts, by race and sex, press release, 6726–1.38

Population educational attainment, by sociodemographic characteristics and location, 1989 and trends from 1940, biennial Current Population Rpt, 2546–1.452

Private elementary and secondary schools, students, and staff characteristics, various periods 1979-88, 4838–47

Government and Defense

Military active duty and recruit social, economic, and parents characteristics, by service branch and State, FY89, annual rpt, 3544–41

Index by Categories

Military personnel, by selected characteristics, 1991 annual summary rpt, 3504–13

Military personnel on active duty, and reserves, by education, FY90, annual rpt, 3544–1.2; 3544–1.5

Military reserve forces personnel strengths and characteristics, by component, FY90, annual rpt, 3544–38

Military reserve forces personnel strengths and characteristics, by component, quarterly rpt, 3542–4

Military women personnel on active and reserve duty, by demographic and service characteristics and service branch, FY89, annual chartbook, 3544–26

Navy personnel strengths, accessions, and attrition, detailed statistics, quarterly rpt, 3802–4

Senior Executive Service membership characteristics, entries, exits, and awards, FY79-90, annual rpt, 9844–36

Tax (income) returns filed, by whether filed electronically, taxpayer characteristics, and reason for not filing electronically, 1990, article, 8304–8.1

Taxes, spending, and govt efficiency, public opinion by respondent characteristics, 1991 survey, annual rpt, 10044–2

Voting and registration, by socioeconomic and demographic characteristics, 1990 congressional election, biennial Current Population Rpt, 2546–1.454

Health and Vital Statistics

Abortions, by method, pregnancy history, and other characteristics of woman, 1988, US Vital Statistics annual rpt, 4146–5.120

Acute and chronic health conditions, disability, absenteeism, and health services use, by selected characteristics, 1987, CD-ROM, 4147–10.177

AIDS public knowledge, attitudes, info sources, and testing, for blacks, 1990 survey, 4146–8.208

AIDS public knowledge, attitudes, info sources, and testing, for Hispanics, 1990 survey, 4146–8.209

AIDS public knowledge, attitudes, info sources, and testing, 1990 survey, 4146–8.195; 4146–8.201; 4146–8.205

Alcohol abuse by family members and spouses, population exposure by selected characteristics, 1988, 4146–8.207

Birth expectations, childbearing delay, and childlessness among women born late 1930s-72, by age, education, and marital and employment status, late 1970s-90, Current Population Rpt, 2546–2.162

Births and rates, by characteristics of birth, infant, and parents, 1989 and trends from 1940, US Vital Statistics advance annual rpt, 4146–5.123

Births and rates by mother's age, and fertility rates, by mother's education, child's race, census div, and State, 1980 and 1985, 4147–21.49

Births, fertility rates, and childless women, by selected characteristics, 1990, annual Current Population Rpt, 2546–1.455

Cancer cases, by race, income, education, and area population density, for 3 metro areas, 1978-82, article, 4472–1.210

Child developmental, learning, and emotional problems, cases and share receiving special treatment and education, by selected characteristics, 1988, 4146–8.193

Child health, behavioral, emotional, and school problems relation to family structure, by selected characteristics, 1988, 4147–10.178

Deaths within 8 years of retirement, by health and other characteristics, 1982-88, article, 4742–1.206

Disabled persons rehabilitation, Federal and State activities and funding, FY90, annual rpt, 4944–1

Drug abuse indicators for selected metro areas, research results, data collection, and policy issues, 1991 semiannual conf, 4492–5

Drug, alcohol, and cigarette use, by selected characteristics, 1990 survey, biennial rpt, 4494–5

Food aid program of USDA for women, infants, and children, prenatal participation effect on Medicaid costs and birth outcomes, for 5 States, 1987-88, 1368–2

Hospices use by cancer patients, by service type, use of other facilities, patient and instn characteristics, and other indicators, local area study, 1980-85, 4658–53

Implants of medical devices, by type, reason, duration, and user characteristics, 1988, 4146–8.197

Injuries, by type, circumstances, and victim characteristics, and related activity limitations, 1985-87, 4147–10.176

Injuries, related impairments, and activity limitations, by circumstances and victim characteristics, 1985-87, 4147–10.179

Insurance (health) coverage, by insurance type and selected characteristics, 1989, 4146–8.203

Marriages and rates, by age, race, education, previous marital status, and State, 1988, US Vital Statistics advance annual rpt, 4146–5.122

Marriages, divorces, and rates, by characteristics of spouses, State, and county, 1987 and trends from 1920, US Vital Statistics annual rpt, 4144–4

Minority group and women health condition, services use, payment sources, and health care labor force, by poverty status, 1940s-89, chartbook, 4118–56

Minority group health condition, services use, costs, and indicators of services need, 1950s-88, 4118–55

Nursing home use prevalence among aged, by length of stay and selected characteristics, 1986 and 1990, 4186–7.9

Smoking exposure of children before and after birth, by source and degree of exposure and family characteristics, 1988, 4146–8.204

Housing and Construction

American Housing Survey: inventory change from 1973, by reason, unit and household characteristics, and location, 1983, biennial rpt, 2485–14

American Housing Survey: unit and households detailed characteristics, and unit and neighborhood quality, MSA rpt series, 2485–6

American Housing Survey: unit and households detailed characteristics, and unit and neighborhood quality, 1987, biennial rpt, 2485–12

Index by Categories

BY EDUCATIONAL ATTAINMENT

Labor and Employment

Black American displaced workers, by demographic and current and former employment characteristics, and compared to whites, 1978-86, article, 6722–1.234

Black women's labor force status, employment by age and education, and women's and families earnings, 1980-90, fact sheet, 6564–1.2

Employment conditions, alternative BLS projections to 2005 and trends 1970s-90, biennial article, 6722–1.254

Job Training Partnership Act participants, by selected characteristics, FY90, annual rpt, 6304–1

Manufacturing employment by selected characteristics, wages, and import and export penetration rates, by SIC 2- to 4-digit industry, 1982-89, 6366–3.27

Poland labor force status by education level, sex, and sector, college enrollment, and grads by field, 1960s-88, article, 6722–1.203

Poverty rate among workers in metro and nonmetro areas, relation to employment and other characteristics, 1987, 1598–274

Rural areas labor force characteristics, with comparisons to urban areas, 1987, 1598–264

Unemployment insurance job search services, impacts on UI claims activity and reemployment, and claimant characteristics, for Tacoma, Wash, 1986-87, 6406–6.35

Vocational rehabilitation cases of State agencies by disposition and applicant characteristics, and closures by reason, FY84-88, annual rpt, 4944–6

Volunteer workers by organization type, time served, whether otherwise employed, and other characteristics, 1989, article, 6722–1.213

Law Enforcement

Crime, criminal justice admin and enforcement, and public opinion, data compilation, 1991 annual rpt, 6064–6

Crimes, by characteristics of victim and offender, circumstances, and location, data compilation, 1991 annual rpt, 6064–6.3

Criminal case processing in Federal district courts, and dispositions, by offense, district, and offender characteristics, 1986, annual rpt, 6064–29

Drug testing of criminal defendants, demonstration program operations, offender characteristics, and judges views, 1987-90, 18208–11

Jail population, by criminal, correctional, drug use, and family history, and selected other characteristics, 1989, 6066–19.62

Jail population, by sociodemographic characteristics, criminal and drug use history, whether convicted, offense, and sentencing, 1989, annual rpt, 6064–26.3

Jail population drug abuse history, by offense, conviction status, criminal and family history, and selected other characteristics, 1989, 6066–19.63

Pretrial processing, detention, and release, for Federal offenders, by defendant characteristics and district, 1988, hearing, 25528–114

Prison and parole admissions and releases, sentence length, and time served, by offense and offender characteristics, 1985, annual rpt, 6064–33

Prisoners and movements, by offense, location, and selected other characteristics, data compilation, 1991 annual rpt, 6064–6.6

Prisoners under death sentence, and executions from 1930, by offense, prisoner characteristics, and State, 1989, annual rpt, 6064–26.6

Prisoners under death sentence by prison control and prisoner characteristics, and executions from 1930, by State, 1973-90, annual rpt, 6066–25.42

Public opinion on crime and crime-related issues, by respondent characteristics, data compilation, 1991 annual rpt, 6064–6.2

Victimization rates, by victim and offender characteristics, circumstances, and offense, 1988 survey, annual rpt, 6066–3.42

Victimization rates, by victim and offender characteristics, circumstances, and offense, 1989 survey, annual rpt, 6066–3.44

Women prisoners in State instns, by offense, drug use history, whether abused, and other characteristics, 1986, 6066–19.61

Population

Black Americans social and economic characteristics, for South and total US, 1989-90 and trends from 1969, Current Population Rpt, 2546–1.450

Children and youth social, economic, and demographic characteristics, 1950s-90, 4818–5

Consumer Income, socioeconomic characteristics of persons, families, and households, detailed cross-tabulations, Current Population Rpt series, 2546–6

Hispanic Americans in counties bordering Mexico, by selected characteristics, 1980, Current Population Rpt, 2546–2.159

Hispanic Americans social and economic characteristics, by detailed origin, 1991, Current Population Rpt, 2546–1.448; 2546–1.451

Households and family characteristics, by location, 1990, annual Current Population Rpt, 2546–1.447

Immigrants in US, population characteristics and fertility, by birthplace and compared to native born, 1980s, Current Population rpt, 2546–2.162

Income (household) and poverty status under alternative income definitions, by recipient characteristics, 1990, annual Current Population Rpt, 2546–6.69

Income (personal) and poverty status changes, by selected characteristics, 1987-88, Current Population Rpt, 2546–20.19

Income and consumer spending of households, for selected population groups, quarterly journal, 1702–1

Indian Health Service facilities and use, and Indian health and other characteristics, by IHS region, 1980s-89, annual chartbook, 4084–7

Indian Health Service facilities, funding, operations, and Indian health and other characteristics, 1950s-90, annual chartbook, 4084–1

Living arrangements, family relationships, and marital status, by selected characteristics, 1990, annual Current Population Rpt, 2546–1.449

Population size and characteristics, 1969-88, Current Population Rpt, biennial rpt, 2546–2.161

Poverty status of population and families, by detailed characteristics, 1988-89, annual Current Population Rpt, 2546–6.67

Poverty status of population and families, by detailed characteristics, 1990, annual Current Population Rpt, 2546–6.71

Retired pension recipients income, by selected characteristics, 1986, Current Population Rpt, 2546–20.18

State and Metro Area Data Book, 1991 data compilation, 2328–54

Statistical Abstract of US, 1991 annual data compilation, 2324–1

Prices and Cost of Living

Consumer Expenditure Survey, household income by source, and itemized spending, by selected characteristics and region, 1988-89, annual rpt, 6764–5

Public Welfare and Social Security

Child care needs impacts on mothers labor force status, and unemployed mothers characteristics, 1986, article, 6722–1.245

Child support and alimony awards, and payment status, by selected characteristics of woman, 1989, biennial Current Population Rpt, 2546–6.72

Disability Insurance beneficiaries costs to Medicare until age 64 under alternative coverage assumptions, model results, 1989, article, 4742–1.208

Foster care placements, discharges, and returns to care, by selected characteristics of children, and length of stay factors, 1985-86, GAO rpt, 26121–432

Homeless and runaway youth programs, funding, activities, and participant characteristics, FY90, annual rpt, 4604–3

Medicare disabled enrollees supplementary health insurance coverage, by enrollee characteristics, 1984, article, 4652–1.243

Student Community Service Program activities, and volunteer and client characteristics, 1987-89, 9028–14

Teenage mothers child support awards, payment status, health insurance inclusion, and govt aid for collection, by selected characteristics, 1987, 4698–5

Recreation and Leisure

Coastal areas recreation facilities of Fed Govt and States, visitor and site characteristics, 1987-90 survey, regional rpt series, 2176–9

Shellfish recreational harvesters selected characteristics, location of harvest and residence, and spending, 1985 survey, 2178–28

Science and Technology

Computer use at home, school, and work, by purpose and selected user characteristics, 1989, Current Population Rpt, 2546–2.158

Employment and education of scientists and engineers, and R&D spending, for US and selected foreign countries, 1991 annual rpt, 9627–35.2

NASA staff characteristics and personnel actions, FY90, annual rpt, 9504–1

Nuclear engineering enrollment and degrees by instn and State, and women grads plans and employment, 1990, annual rpt, 3006–8.14

Radiation protection and health physics enrollment and degrees granted by instn and State, and female grads plans and employment, 1990, annual rpt, 3006–8.15

BY EDUCATIONAL ATTAINMENT

Veterans Affairs

Agent Orange exposure of Vietnam veterans, and other factors relation to dev of rare cancers, 1984-88, 4208–33

Homeless veterans domiciliary program of VA, participant characteristics and outcomes, 1990 annual rpt, 8604–10

Housing programs of VA, costs, terms, and user characteristics, 1985-89, 8608–7

BY MARITAL STATUS

Agriculture and Food

FmHA loans, by type, borrower characteristics, and State, quarterly rpt, 1182–8

Food spending, by item, household composition, income, age, race, and region, 1980-88, Consumer Expenditure Survey biennial rpt, 1544–30

Banking, Finance, and Insurance

Households assets, by type of holding and selected characteristics, 1988, Current Population Rpt, 2546–20.16

Education

Educational attainment, by sociodemographic characteristics and location, 1989 and trends from 1940, biennial Current Population Rpt, 2546–1.452

Elementary and secondary education enrollment, staff, finances, operations, programs, and policies, 1987/88 biennial survey, series, 4836–3

Enrollment, by grade, instn type and control, and student characteristics, 1989 and trends from 1947, annual Current Population Rpt, 2546–1.453

High school class of 1972: education, employment, and family characteristics, activities, and attitudes, natl longitudinal study, series, 4836–1

Higher education instn student aid and other sources of support, with student expenses and characteristics, by instn type and control, 1990 triennial study, series, 4846–5

Student loan debt burden of 1986 college grads, by selected student characteristics and instn control, 1987, 4808–26

Teachers in public schools, demographic and employment characteristics, 1991 annual data compilation, 4824–2.9

Government and Defense

Aliens (illegal) legal residence applications under Immigration Reform and Control Act, by selected characteristics, State, and country, periodic rpt, 6262–3

Military active duty and recruit social, economic, and parents characteristics, by service branch and State, FY89, annual rpt, 3544–41

Military women personnel on active and reserve duty, by demographic and service characteristics and service branch, FY89, annual chartbook, 3544–26

Tax (income) returns of high income individuals not filed, by selected characteristics, 1987, and assessments under alternative IRS enforcement programs, 1990, GAO rpt, 26119–322

Tax (income) returns of individuals, taxable income, and tax generated, by tax rate and income level, 1987, annual article, 8302–2.211

Tax rates and revenue of State and local govts, by source and State, 1991 and historical trends, annual rpt, 10044–1

Taxes, spending, and govt efficiency, public opinion by respondent characteristics, 1991 survey, annual rpt, 10044–2

Health and Vital Statistics

Abortions, by method, patient characteristics, and State, 1972-88, article, 4202–7.207

Abortions, by method, pregnancy history, and other characteristics of woman, 1988, US Vital Statistics annual rpt, 4146–5.120

AIDS public knowledge, attitudes, and risk behaviors, for women, 1988 survey, 4146–8.200

AIDS virus infection and risk factor prevalence, natl survey methodology and pretest results, 1989, 4148–30

Alcohol abuse by family members and spouses, population exposure by selected characteristics, 1988, 4146–8.207

Birth expectations, childbearing delay, and childlessness among women born late 1930s-72, by age, education, and marital and employment status, late 1970s-90, Current Population Rpt, 2546–2.162

Births, fertility rates, and childless women, by selected characteristics, 1990, annual Current Population Rpt, 2546–1.455

Deaths and rates, by cause, age, sex, marital status, and race, 1988, US Vital Statistics annual rpt, 4144–2.1

Deaths within 8 years of retirement, by health and other characteristics, 1982-88, article, 4742–1.206

Drug abuse indicators for selected metro areas, research results, data collection, and policy issues, 1991 semiannual conf, 4492–5

Drug, alcohol, and cigarette use and quit rates among young pregnant women, by marital status, aggregate 1984-88, annual rpt, 4494–4

Fetal deaths and rates, by characteristics of mother and birth, 1988, US Vital Statistics annual rpt, 4144–2.3

Food aid program of USDA for women, infants, and children, prenatal participation effect on Medicaid costs and birth outcomes, for 5 States, 1987-88, 1368–2

Genital human papillomavirus risk relation to presence of other cervical cancer risk factors, local area study, 1991 article, 4472–1.215

Health care services use and costs, methodology and findings of natl survey, series, 4186–8

Hospices operations, services, costs, and patient characteristics, for instns without Medicare certification, FY85-86, 4658–52

Hospices use by cancer patients, by service type, use of other facilities, patient and instn characteristics, and other indicators, local area study, 1980-85, 4658–53

Injuries, related impairments, and activity limitations, by circumstances and victim characteristics, 1985-87, 4147–10.179

Insurance (health) coverage, uninsured persons by employment and other characteristics and State, 1988, GAO rpt, 26121–403

Marriages and rates, by age, race, education, previous marital status, and State, 1988, US Vital Statistics advance annual rpt, 4146–5.122

Marriages, divorces, and rates, by characteristics of spouses, State, and county, 1987 and trends from 1920, US Vital Statistics annual rpt, 4144–4

Minority group health condition, services use, costs, and indicators of services need, 1950s-88, 4118–55

Nursing home residents with mental disorders, by disorder type and resident and instn characteristics, 1985, 4147–13.106

Nursing home use prevalence among aged, by length of stay and selected characteristics, 1986 and 1990, 4186–7.9

Older persons deaths in hospitals, nursing homes, and own home, by cause, age, marital status, and region, 1986, article, 4652–1.201

Older persons with functional limitations, long-term care sources, and health and other characteristics, 1984-85, 4147–13.104

Housing and Construction

American Housing Survey: unit and households characteristics, unit and neighborhood quality, and journey to work by MSA location, for 11 MSAs, 1984 survey, supplement, 2485–8

American Housing Survey: unit and households detailed characteristics, and unit and neighborhood quality, MSA rpt series, 2485–6

American Housing Survey: unit and households detailed characteristics, and unit and neighborhood quality, 1987, biennial rpt, 2485–12

American Housing Survey: unit and households detailed characteristics, and unit and neighborhood quality, 1987, biennial rpt supplement, 2485–13

Mortgages FHA-insured, financial, property, and mortgagor characteristics, by metro area, 1990, annual rpt, 5144–24

Mortgages FHA-insured, financial, property, and mortgagor characteristics, by State, 1990, annual rpt, 5144–1

Mortgages FHA-insured, financial, property, and mortgagor characteristics, total and by State and outlying area, 1990, annual rpt, 5144–25

Mortgages FHA-insured, financial, property, and mortgagor characteristics, 1990, annual rpt, 5144–17; 5144–23

Labor and Employment

Black American displaced workers, by demographic and current and former employment characteristics, and compared to whites, 1978-86, article, 6722–1.234

Employment and Earnings, detailed data, monthly rpt, 6742–2.2; 6742–2.3; 6742–2.4

Employment and unemployment, by age, sex, race, marital and family status, industry div, and State, Monthly Labor Review, 6722–1.2

Employment, unemployment, and labor force characteristics, by region, State, and selected metro area, 1990, annual rpt, 6744–7

Labor force status of family members and earnings, by family composition and race, quarterly press release, 6742–21

Labor force, wages, hours, and payroll costs, by major industry group and demographic characteristics, *Survey of Current Business*, monthly rpt, 2702–1.8

Index by Categories

Moonlighting employment, by reason, and characteristics of workers and primary and secondary jobs, 1991, press release, 6726–1.40

Vocational rehabilitation cases of State agencies by disposition and applicant characteristics, and closures by reason, FY84-88, annual rpt, 4944–6

Volunteer workers by organization type, time served, whether otherwise employed, and other characteristics, 1989, article, 6722–1.213

Women's labor force status, by age, race, and family status, quarterly rpt, 6742–17

Law Enforcement

Criminal case processing in Federal district courts, and dispositions, by offense, district, and offender characteristics, 1986, annual rpt, 6064–29

Jail population, by criminal, correctional, drug use, and family history, and selected other characteristics, 1989, 6066–19.62

Jail population, by sociodemographic characteristics, criminal and drug use history, whether convicted, offense, and sentencing, 1989, annual rpt, 6064–26.3

Pretrial processing, detention, and release, for Federal offenders, by defendant characteristics and district, 1988, hearing, 25528–114

Prisoners and movements, by offense, location, and selected other characteristics, data compilation, 1991 annual rpt, 6064–6.6

Prisoners under death sentence, and executions from 1930, by offense, prisoner characteristics, and State, 1989, annual rpt, 6064–26.6

Prisoners under death sentence by prison control and prisoner characteristics, and executions from 1930, by State, 1973-90, annual rpt, 6066–25.42

Victimization rates, by victim and offender characteristics, circumstances, and offense, 1988 survey, annual rpt, 6066–3.42

Victimization rates, by victim and offender characteristics, circumstances, and offense, 1989 survey, annual rpt, 6066–3.44

Women prisoners in State instns, by offense, drug use history, whether abused, and other characteristics, 1986, 6066–19.61

Women's rape and other violent crime victimization, by relation to offender, circumstances, and victim characteristics, 1973-87, 6068–243

Population

Black Americans social and economic characteristics, for South and total US, 1989-90 and trends from 1969, Current Population Rpt, 2546–1.450

Consumer Income, socioeconomic characteristics of persons, families, and households, detailed cross-tabulations, Current Population Rpt series, 2546–6

Families with children by householder marital status, and birth rates for all and unmarried women, 1950s-90, 4818–5

Hispanic Americans in counties bordering Mexico, by selected characteristics, 1980, Current Population Rpt, 2546–2.159

Hispanic Americans social and economic characteristics, by detailed origin, 1991, Current Population Rpt, 2546–1.448; 2546–1.451

BY RACE AND ETHNIC GROUP

Immigrants in US, population characteristics and fertility, by birthplace and compared to native born, 1980s, Current Population rpt, 2546–2.162

Income (personal) and poverty status changes, by selected characteristics, 1987-88, Current Population Rpt, 2546–20.19

Income and consumer spending of households, for selected population groups, quarterly journal, 1702–1

Population size and characteristics, 1969-88, Current Population Rpt, biennial rpt, 2546–2.161

Poverty status of population and families, by detailed characteristics, 1988-89, annual Current Population Rpt, 2546–6.67

Poverty status of population and families, by detailed characteristics, 1990, annual Current Population Rpt, 2546–6.71

Statistical Abstract of US, 1991 annual data compilation, 2324–1

Public Welfare and Social Security

Child care arrangements, costs, and impacts on mothers labor force status, by selected characteristics, 1983 and 1988, article, 6722–1.246

Child care needs impacts on mothers labor force status, and unemployed mothers characteristics, 1986, article, 6722–1.245

Child support and alimony awards, and payment status, by selected characteristics of woman, 1989, biennial Current Population Rpt, 2546–6.72

Food stamp eligibility and payment errors, by type, recipient characteristics, and State, FY89, annual rpt, 1364–15

Medicare disabled enrollees supplementary health insurance coverage, by enrollee characteristics, 1984, article, 4652–1.243

OASDHI, Medicaid, SSI, and related programs benefits, beneficiary characteristics, and trust funds, selected years 1937-89, annual rpt, 4744–3

OASDI benefit payments, trust fund finances, and economic and demographic assumptions, 1970-90 and alternative projections to 2000, actuarial rpt, 4706–1.105

Supplemental Security Income beneficiaries income from OASI and other sources, and work history, 1988, article, 4742–1.216

Supplemental Security Income benefit award rate by applicant characteristics and eligibility class, 1987, article, 4742–1.213

Teenage mothers child support awards, payment status, health insurance inclusion, and govt aid for collection, by selected characteristics, 1987, 4698–5

Science and Technology

Computer use at home, school, and work, by purpose and selected user characteristics, 1989, Current Population Rpt, 2546–2.158

Veterans Affairs

Agent Orange exposure of Vietnam veterans, and other factors relation to dev of rare cancers, 1984-88, 4208–33

Homeless veterans domiciliary program of VA, participant characteristics and outcomes, 1990 annual rpt, 8604–10

Hospitals of VA, patients discharged by diagnosis, compensation and pension status, and other characteristics, FY90, annual rpt, 8604–3.3

Housing programs of VA, costs, terms, and user characteristics, 1985-89, 8608–7

BY RACE AND ETHNIC GROUP

Agriculture and Food

Census of Agriculture, 1987: farms, farmland, production, finances, and operator characteristics, by county, final State rpt series, 2331–1

FmHA loans, by type, borrower characteristics, and State, quarterly rpt, 1182–8

FmHA loans, by type, borrower race, and State, quarterly rpt, 1182–5

Food spending, by item, household composition, income, age, race, and region, 1980-88, Consumer Expenditure Survey biennial rpt, 1544–30

Banking, Finance, and Insurance

Households assets, by type of holding and selected characteristics, 1988, Current Population Rpt, 2546–20.16

Communications and Transportation

Air traffic control and airway facilities staff, by employment and other characteristics, FY89, annual rpt, 7504–41

Air traffic control and airway facilities supervisors task priorities, skills needed, and other characteristics, 1990 survey, technical rpt, 7506–10.84

Postal Service employment and related expenses, FY90, annual rpt, 9864–5.1

Education

Athletes in college, educational and employment performance compared to other students, for 1972 high school class, as of 1986, 4888–5

Condition of Education, detail for elementary, secondary, and higher education, 1920s-90 and projected to 2001, annual rpt, 4824–1

Degrees awarded in higher education, by level, field, race, and sex, 1988/89 with trends from 1978/79, biennial rpt, 4844–17

Digest of Education Statistics, 1991 annual data compilation, 4824–2

Discrimination in education, indicators for service delivery and discipline, by State, 1988, biennial rpt, 4804–33

DOD Dependents Schools basic skills and college entrance test scores, 1990-91, annual rpt, 3504–16

Educational attainment, by sociodemographic characteristics and location, 1989 and trends from 1940, biennial Current Population Rpt, 2546–1.452

Eighth grade class of 1988: educational performance and conditions, characteristics, attitudes, activities, and plans, natl longitudinal survey, series, 4826–9

Elementary and secondary education enrollment, staff, finances, operations, programs, and policies, 1987/88 biennial survey, series, 4836–3

Elementary and secondary public schools, enrollment and other characteristics, for top 100 districts, 1988/89, annual rpt, 4834–22

Elementary and secondary students educational performance, and factors affecting proficiency, by selected characteristics, 1988 natl assessments, subject rpt series, 4896–7

BY RACE AND ETHNIC GROUP

Elementary and secondary students educational performance, and factors affecting proficiency, by selected characteristics, 1990 natl assessments, subject rpt series, 4896–8

Elementary and secondary students educational performance in math, science, reading, and writing, 1970s-90, 4898–32

Enrollment, by grade, instn type and control, and student characteristics, 1989 and trends from 1947, annual Current Population Rpt, 2546–1.453

Enrollment in public elementary and secondary schools, minorities share by group and State, 1989/90, annual rpt, 4834–17

Head Start enrollment, funding, and staff, FY90, annual rpt, 4604–8

High school class of 1972: education, employment, and family characteristics, activities, and attitudes, natl longitudinal study, series, 4836–1

High school class of 1990: college enrollment, and labor force participation of grads and dropouts, by race and sex, press release, 6726–1.38

High school dropout rates, and subsequent completion, by student and school characteristics, alternative estimates, 1990, annual rpt, 4834–23

Higher education course completions, by detailed program, sex, race, and instn type, for 1972 high school class, as of 1984, 4888–4

Higher education enrollment of minorities, degrees, factors affecting participation, and earnings, by race, 1960s-88, 4808–29

Higher education instn student aid and other sources of support, with student expenses and characteristics, by instn type and control, 1990 triennial study, series, 4846–5

Homeless adults educational services, funding, participation, and staff, by State, 1989, annual rpt series, 4804–39

Immigrant children education programs funding by Fed Govt and school districts, and student characteristics, 1980s, GAO rpt, 26121–418

Library of Congress employment by race, Hispanic origin, and sex, and affirmative action needs, 1989, hearing, 21428–9

Literacy programs in workplaces, demonstration projects funding and participant characteristics, FY88, 4808–37

Migrant workers children education programs enrollment, staff, and effectiveness, by State, 1980s, 4808–30

Private elementary and secondary schools, students, and staff characteristics, various periods 1979-88, 4838–47

Teachers in higher education instns, employment and other characteristics, by instn type and control, 1987/88 survey, 4846–4.4

Truman, Harry S, Scholarship Foundation finances, and awards by student characteristics, FY90, annual rpt, 14314–1

Women's employment and educational experiences compared to men, for high school class of 1972, natl longitudinal study, as of 1986, 4888–6

Government and Defense

Army Dept activities, personnel, discipline, budget, and assistance, FY83 summary data, annual rpt, 3704–11

DOT employment, by subagency, occupation, and selected personnel characteristics, FY90, annual rpt, 7304–18

Employment (civilian) of Fed Govt, by demographic and employment characteristics, as of Sept 1990, annual article, 9842–1.201

Employment of minorities and women by Fed Govt, and compliance with EEOC standards, by occupation and agency, FY88-92, GAO rpt, 26119–342

Employment of minorities, women, and disabled in Fed Govt, by agency and occupation, FY89, annual rpt, 9244–10

Equal Opportunity Recruitment Program activity, and Fed Govt employment by sex, race, pay grade, and occupational group, FY90, annual rpt, 9844–33

IRS employment of minorities and women, compared to Fed Govt and total civilian labor force, FY90, annual rpt, 8304–3.3

Military active duty and recruit social, economic, and parents characteristics, by service branch and State, FY89, annual rpt, 3544–41

Military deaths by cause, age, race, and rank, and personnel captured and missing, by service branch, FY90, annual rpt, 3544–40

Military personnel, by selected characteristics, 1991 annual summary rpt, 3504–13

Military personnel on active duty, recruits, and reenlistment, by race, sex, and service branch, quarterly press release, 3542–7

Military personnel strengths, for active duty enlisted and officers, by sex and race, 1970s-90, GAO rpt, 26123–325

Military reserve forces personnel strengths and characteristics, by component, FY90, annual rpt, 3544–38

Military reserve forces personnel strengths and characteristics, by component, quarterly rpt, 3542–4

Military reserve forces personnel strengths, by selected characteristics and reserve component, FY90, annual rpt, 3544–1.5

Military women personnel on active and reserve duty, by demographic and service characteristics and service branch, FY89, annual chartbook, 3544–26

Senior Executive Service membership characteristics, entries, exits, and awards, FY79-90, annual rpt, 9844–36

State and local govt employment of minorities and women, by occupation, function, pay level, and State, 1990, annual rpt, 9244–6

State Dept and Foreign Service minority and women employment, and hiring goals, FY89-90, biennial rpt, 7004–21

Taxes, spending, and govt efficiency, public opinion by respondent characteristics, 1991 survey, annual rpt, 10044–2

Voting and registration, by socioeconomic and demographic characteristics, 1990 congressional election, biennial Current Population Rpt, 2546–1.454

Health and Vital Statistics

Abortions, by method, patient characteristics, and State, 1972-88, article, 4202–7.207

Index by Categories

Abortions, by method, pregnancy history, and other characteristics of woman, 1988, US Vital Statistics annual rpt, 4146–5.120

Acute and chronic health conditions, disability, absenteeism, and health services use, by selected characteristics, 1987, CD-ROM, 4147–10.177

AIDS cases by race, sex, and risk category, and deaths and survivors, projected 1989-93, 4206–2.34

AIDS cases by risk group, race, sex, age, State, and MSA, and deaths, monthly rpt, 4202–9

AIDS patient hospital use and charges, by hospital and patient characteristics, and payment source, 1986-87, 4186–6.15

AIDS public knowledge and info sources, for blacks and Hispanics, 1987 local area survey, article, 4042–3.210

AIDS public knowledge, attitudes, and risk behaviors, for women, 1988 survey, 4146–8.200

AIDS public knowledge, attitudes, info sources, and testing, for blacks, 1990 survey, 4146–8.208

AIDS public knowledge, attitudes, info sources, and testing, 1990 survey, 4146–8.195; 4146–8.201; 4146–8.205

AIDS virus infection and risk factor prevalence, natl survey methodology and pretest results, 1989, 4148–30

Alcohol abuse by family members and spouses, population exposure by selected characteristics, 1988, 4146–8.207

Alcohol use and abuse by women related to race, employment status, and other characteristics, 1981 local area study, article, 4042–3.212

Birth outcomes and prenatal care use effects of Medicaid coverage, charges, and Medicaid payments, for California, 1983, article, 4652–1.241

Births and rates, by characteristics of birth, infant, and parents, 1989 and trends from 1940, US Vital Statistics advance annual rpt, 4146–5.123

Births and rates by mother's age, and fertility rates, by mother's education, child's race, census div, and State, 1980 and 1985, 4147–21.49

Births, fertility rates, and childless women, by selected characteristics, 1990, annual Current Population Rpt, 2546–1.455

Cancer cases by body site and population characteristics, research results, semimonthly journal, 4472–1

Cancer cases, deaths, and survival rates, by sex, race, age, and body site, 1973-88, annual rpt, 4474–35

Cancer death rates of minorities, by body site, age, sex, and substate area, 1950s-80, atlas, 4478–78

Child accident deaths and death rates, by cause, age, sex, race, and State, 1980-85, 4108–54

Child accident deaths and injuries by cause, and victimization, rates by race, sex, and age, 1979-88, chartbook, 4108–56

Child developmental, learning, and emotional problems, cases and share receiving special treatment and education, by selected characteristics, 1988, 4146–8.193

Child health, behavioral, emotional, and school problems relation to family structure, by selected characteristics, 1988, 4147–10.178

Index by Categories

BY RACE AND ETHNIC GROUP

Child health condition and services use, 1990 chartbook, 4108–49

Cirrhosis of liver deaths, by age, sex, race, and whether alcohol involved, 1987 and trends from 1910, 4486–1.10

Cocaine abuse, user characteristics, and related crime and violence, 1988 conf, 4498–74

Deaths and rates by age, and life expectancy, by sex and race, preliminary 1989-90 and trends from 1950, US Vital Statistics annual rpt, 4144–7

Deaths and rates, by detailed cause and demographic characteristics, 1988 and trends from 1900, US Vital Statistics annual rpt, 4144–2

Deaths and rates, provisional data, monthly rpt, 4142–1.2

Deaths within 8 years of retirement, by health and other characteristics, 1982-88, article, 4742–1.206

Diabetes and complications cases, deaths, and hospitalization, by age, sex, race, State, and region, 1980-86, annual rpt, 4205–41

Disabled persons and related activity limitation days and health services use, by health status, disability type, and other characteristics, 1984-88, 4146–8.202

Disabled persons rehabilitation, Federal and State activities and funding, FY90, annual rpt, 4944–1

Drug abuse emergency room admissions and deaths, by drug type and source, sex, race, age, and major metro area, 1990, annual rpt, 4494–8

Drug abuse indicators for selected metro areas, research results, data collection, and policy issues, 1991 semiannual conf, 4492–5

Drug abuse prevalence among minorities, related health effects and crime, treatment, and research status and needs, mid 1970s-90, 4498–72

Drug, alcohol, and cigarette use and attitudes of youth, by substance type and selected characteristics, 1975-90 surveys, annual rpt, 4494–4

Drug, alcohol, and cigarette use, by selected characteristics, 1990 survey, biennial rpt, 4494–5

Drug and alcohol abuse treatment and prevention programs of States, funding, facilities, and patient characteristics, FY89, 4488–15

Drug and alcohol abuse treatment facilities, services, use, funding, staff, and client characteristics, 1989, biennial rpt, 4494–10

Drug and alcohol abuse treatment services, funding, staffing, and client load, characteristics, and outcomes, by setting, 1989 conf, 4498–73

Drug and alcohol use in workplace, and drinkers reporting adverse effects, for young adults by selected characteristics, 1984, article, 6722–1.237

Ectopic pregnancies and related deaths, by race, age, and region, 1970-87, article, 4202–7.202

Firearms-related deaths and death rates, by motive, age, sex, and race, for persons aged 1-34, 1979-88, 4146–5.119

Food aid program of USDA for women, infants, and children, prenatal participation effect on Medicaid costs and birth outcomes, for 5 States, 1987-88, 1368–2

Health care services use and costs, methodology and findings of natl survey, series, 4186–8

Health condition and health care resources, use, and spending, 1950s-89, annual data compilation, 4144–11

Health condition of minorities, services use, costs, and indicators of services need, 1950s-88, 4118–55

Health condition, services use, payment sources, and health care labor force, for minorities and women by poverty status, 1940s-89, chartbook, 4118–56

Hepatitis cases by infection source, age, sex, race, and State, and deaths, by strain, 1988 and trends from 1966, 4205–2

Homeless persons alcohol abuse, by sex, age, race, and additional diagnoses, aggregate 1985-87, 4488–14

Hospices operations, services, costs, and patient characteristics, for instns without Medicare certification, FY85-86, 4658–52

Hospices use by cancer patients, by service type, use of other facilities, patient and instn characteristics, and other indicators, local area study, 1980-85, 4658–53

Hospital discharges and length of stay, by diagnosis, patient and instn characteristics, procedure performed, and payment source, 1988, annual rpt, 4147–13.107

Hospital discharges and rates, for aged Medicare beneficiaries by diagnosis, age, sex, and race, 1988, article, 4202–7.205

Implants of medical devices, by type, reason, duration, and user characteristics, 1988, 4146–8.197

Infant death rate, by cause, region, and race, 1980-87, article, 4202–7.208

Infectious notifiable disease cases, by age, race, and State, and deaths, 1930s-90, annual rpt, 4204–1

Injuries, by type, circumstances, and victim characteristics, and related activity limitations, 1985-87, 4147–10.176

Injuries, related impairments, and activity limitations, by circumstances and victim characteristics, 1985-87, 4147–10.179

Insurance (health) coverage, by insurance type and selected characteristics, 1989, 4146–8.203

Insurance (health) coverage of children, and children with a regular source of care, by selected characteristics, 1988, 4146–8.192

Insurance (health) coverage, uninsured persons by employment and other characteristics and State, 1988, GAO rpt, 26121–403

Insurance (health) natl coverage alternative proposals and indicators of need, 1989, 4658–54

Kidney end-stage disease cases, treatment, outcomes, and characteristics of patients, organ donors, and facilities, late 1970s-88, annual rpt, 4474–37

Kidney end-stage disease treatment facilities, Medicare enrollment and reimbursement, survival, and patient characteristics, 1983-89, annual rpt, 4654–16

Lead paint in privately owned housing, levels, exposure, and testing and abatement costs, 1990 rpt, 5188–128

Lead poisoning among children, cases and rates by race, and screening tests conducted, for NYC, 1988, article, 4202–7.201

Life tables, 1988 and trends from 1900, US Vital Statistics annual rpt, 4144–2.6

Marriage, marriage dissolution, remarriage, and cohabitation, for women, by age and race, 1988, 4146–8.196

Marriages and rates, by age, race, education, previous marital status, and State, 1988, US Vital Statistics advance annual rpt, 4146–5.122

Marriages, divorces, and rates, by characteristics of spouses, State, and county, 1987 and trends from 1920, US Vital Statistics annual rpt, 4144–4

Mental health care facilities for emotionally disturbed children, use, funding, and characteristics of patients, staff, and instn, 1988, 4506–3.44

Mental health care facilities outpatient care programs, use, and client characteristics, by instn type and State, 1988, 4506–3.40; 4506–3.46

Mental health care in private hospitals, patients characteristics, 1986, 4506–3.47

Nursing home use prevalence among aged, by length of stay and selected characteristics, 1986 and 1990, 4186–7.9

Nursing training programs faculty, by race, Hispanic origin, and degree level, 1988, hearing, 25418–6

Older persons with functional limitations, long-term care sources, and health and other characteristics, 1984-85, 4147–13.104

Physicians visits, by patient and practice characteristics, diagnosis, and services provided, 1989, 4146–8.206

Pregnancies of poor women, by whether intended, outcome, contraceptives use, marital status, and race, 1985-86 local area study, article, 4042–3.241

Pregnancy-related deaths, rates, and risk, by pregnancy outcome, cause, and maternal characteristics, 1979-86, article, 4202–7.206

Radiation protection and health physics enrollment and degrees granted by instn and State, and grad placement, by student characteristics, 1990, annual rpt, 3004–7

Smoking and smokeless tobacco use, attitudes, and smoking intervention research spending and results, with bibl, 1960s-90, 4478–195

Smoking exposure of children before and after birth, by source and degree of exposure and family characteristics, 1988, 4146–8.204

Teenagers physicians office visits, by reason and characteristics of physicians, patients, and visit, 1985, 4146–8.199

Tuberculosis cases and deaths, by patient characteristics, State, and city, 1989 and trends from 1953, annual rpt, 4204–10

Housing and Construction

Affordability indicators for housing, by household composition, income, and current tenure, 1988, 2486–1.11

American Housing Survey: inventory change from 1973, by reason, unit and household characteristics, and location, 1983, biennial rpt, 2485–14

American Housing Survey: unit and households characteristics, MSA fact sheet series, 2485–11

American Housing Survey: unit and households characteristics, unit and

BY RACE AND ETHNIC GROUP

neighborhood quality, and journey to work by MSA location, for 11 MSAs, 1984 survey, supplement, 2485–8

- American Housing Survey: unit and households detailed characteristics, and unit and neighborhood quality, MSA rpt series, 2485–6
- American Housing Survey: unit and households detailed characteristics, and unit and neighborhood quality, 1987, biennial rpt, 2485–12
- American Housing Survey: unit and households detailed characteristics, and unit and neighborhood quality, 1987, biennial rpt supplement, 2485–13
- Atlanta metro area secondary mortgage market underwriting guidelines, and indicators of discrimination, 1989, GAO rpt, 26113–500
- Census of Housing, 1990: inventory, occupancy, and costs, State fact sheet series, 2326–21
- Census of Population and Housing, 1990: population and housing selected characteristics, by region, press release, 2328–74
- Mortgage applications by disposition, and secondary loan market sales by purchaser type, by applicant and neighborhood characteristics, 1990, article, 9362–1.206
- Mortgages FHA-insured, financial, property, and mortgagor characteristics, by metro area, 1990, annual rpt, 5144–24
- Mortgages FHA-insured, financial, property, and mortgagor characteristics, by State, 1990, annual rpt, 5144–1
- Mortgages FHA-insured, financial, property, and mortgagor characteristics, total and by State and outlying area, 1990, annual rpt, 5144–25
- Mortgages FHA-insured, financial, property, and mortgagor characteristics, 1990, annual rpt, 5144–17; 5144–23
- Retirement housing centers tax-exempt bond use and other financing, defaults, and facility and resident characteristics, 1991 GAO rpt, 26119–328

Industry and Commerce

- Business mgmt and financial aid from Minority Business Dev Centers, and characteristics of businesses, by region and State, FY90, annual rpt, 2104–6
- Small Business Admin surety bond guarantee program finances, and contracts by contractor race, obligee type, and region, FY87-89, GAO rpt, 26113–526

Labor and Employment

- Black American displaced workers, by demographic and current and former employment characteristics, and compared to whites, 1978-86, article, 6722–1.234
- Dallas-Fort Worth-Arlington metro area employment, earnings, hours, and CPI changes, late 1970s-90, annual rpt, 6964–2
- Displaced workers losing job 1985-90, by demographic and former and current employment characteristics, as of Jan 1990, article, 6722–1.225
- Earnings distribution by sex, race, industry div, and occupation, 1960-89, article, 6722–1.201
- *Employment and Earnings*, detailed data, monthly rpt, 6742–2
- Employment and unemployment, by age, sex, race, marital and family status, industry div, and State, Monthly Labor Review, 6722–1.2

Employment conditions, alternative BLS projections to 2005 and trends 1970s-90, biennial article, 6722–1.252; 6722–1.254

- Employment, earnings, and hours, monthly press release, 6742–5
- Employment situation, earnings, hours, and other BLS economic indicators, transcripts of BLS Commissioner's monthly testimony, periodic rpt, 23846–4
- Employment, unemployment, and labor force characteristics, by region, State, and selected metro area, 1990, annual rpt, 6744–7
- Family members labor force status and earnings, by family composition and race, quarterly press release, 6742–21
- Houston metro area employment, earnings, hours, and CPI changes, 1970s-90, annual rpt, 6964–1
- Job Training Partnership Act occupational training services, disparities in delivery to women and minorities, 1989-90, 26106–8.14
- Job Training Partnership Act participants, by selected characteristics, FY90, annual rpt, 6304–1
- Labor force status by race and sex, employment by industry div, and unemployment duration and reason, selected years 1929-90, annual rpt, 204–1.2
- Labor force status, by race, detailed Hispanic origin, and sex, quarterly rpt, 6742–18
- Labor force status, by worker characteristics and industry group, 1982-90, semiannual article, 6722–1.212
- Labor force status, experience, and unemployment duration, by race and sex, 1989-90, annual press release, 6726–1.39
- Labor force, wages, hours, and payroll costs, by major industry group and demographic characteristics, *Survey of Current Business*, monthly rpt, 2702–1.8
- Minimum wage provisions of Fair Labor Standards Act, coverage of nonsupervisory workers by race and sex, FY89, annual rpt, 6504–2.1
- Moonlighting employment, by reason, and characteristics of workers and primary and secondary jobs, 1991, press release, 6726–1.40
- Poverty rate among workers in metro and nonmetro areas, relation to employment and other characteristics, 1987, 1598–274
- Rural areas labor force characteristics, with comparisons to urban areas, 1987, 1598–264
- Self-employment, by occupation, industry, sex, and race, 1983 and 1990, article, 6742–1.202
- Unemployment insurance job search services, impacts on UI claims activity and reemployment, and claimant characteristics, for Tacoma, Wash, 1986-87, 6406–6.35
- Unemployment of groups with historically high rates, 1985-89, biennial rpt, 6504–2.2
- Unemployment rates, current data and annual trends, monthly rpt, 23842–1.2
- Union coverage of workers and earnings, by age, sex, race, occupational group, and industry div, 1989-90, press release, 6726–1.36
- Vocational rehabilitation cases of State agencies by disposition and applicant characteristics, and closures by reason, FY84-88, annual rpt, 4944–6

Index by Categories

- Volunteer workers by organization type, time served, whether otherwise employed, and other characteristics, 1989, article, 6722–1.213
- Wages of full- and part-time workers, by selected characteristics, quarterly press release, 6742–20
- Women's labor force status, by age, race, and family status, quarterly rpt, 6742–17
- Women's labor force status, earnings, and other characteristics, with comparisons to men, fact sheet series, 6564–1
- Youth employment by selected characteristics, with child labor law violations and injuries, 1983-90, GAO rpt, 26121–426
- Youth labor force status, by sex, race, and industry div, summer 1987-91, annual press release, 6744–14

Law Enforcement

- Arrest rates, by offense, sex, age, and race, 1965-89, annual rpt, 6224–7
- Arrests, prosecutions, convictions, and sentencing, for felony offenders, by offender characteristics and offense, 1988, 6066–25.33; 6066–25.39
- Assaults and deaths of law enforcement officers, by circumstances, agency, victim and offender characteristics, and location, 1990, annual rpt, 6224–3
- Crime, criminal justice admin and enforcement, and public opinion, data compilation, 1991 annual rpt, 6064–6
- Crimes, arrests, and rates, by offense, offender characteristics, population size, and jurisdiction, 1990, annual rpt, 6224–2.1; 6224–2.2
- Criminal case processing in Federal district courts, and dispositions, by offense, district, and offender characteristics, 1986, annual rpt, 6064–29
- Drug test results at arrest, by drug type, offense, and sex, for selected urban areas, quarterly rpt, 6062–3
- Jail adult and juvenile population, employment, spending, instn conditions, and inmate programs, by county and facility, 1988, regional rpt series, 6068–144
- Jail population, by criminal, correctional, drug use, and family history, and selected other characteristics, 1989, 6066–19.62
- Jail population by sex, race, and for 25 jurisdictions, and instn conditions, 1988-90, annual rpt, 6066–25.38
- Jail population drug abuse history, by offense, conviction status, criminal and family history, and selected other characteristics, 1989, 6066–19.63
- Juvenile correctional and detention public and private instns, inmates, and expenses, by instn and resident characteristics and State, 1987, biennial rpt, 6064–13
- Juvenile courts delinquency cases, by offense, referral source, disposition, age, sex, race, State, and county, 1988, annual rpt, 6064–12
- Juvenile courts property offenses cases, by disposition and offender age, sex, and race, 1985-86, 6066–27.5
- Juvenile facilities, population, and costs, by facility and resident characteristics, region, and State, 1985-89, biennial rpt, 6064–5
- Pretrial processing, detention, and release, for Federal offenders, by defendant characteristics and district, 1988, hearing, 25528–114

Index by Categories

BY RACE AND ETHNIC GROUP

Prison and parole admissions and releases, sentence length, and time served, by offense and offender characteristics, 1985, annual rpt, 6064–33

Prisoner admissions by State and for Federal instns, by race, 1926-86, 6068–245

Prisoners, characteristics, and movements, by State, 1989, annual rpt, 6064–26

Prisoners under death sentence by prison control and prisoner characteristics, and executions from 1930, by State, 1973-90, annual rpt, 6066–25.42

Probation and split sentences by State courts for felony offenses, sentence lengths, case processing time, and felon characteristics, by offense, 1986, 6068–242

Sentences for Federal crimes, guidelines use and results by offense and district, and Sentencing Commission activities, 1990, annual rpt, 17664–1

Teenagers crime victimization, by victim and offender characteristics, circumstances, and offense, 1985-88 surveys, 6066–3.43

Victimization rates, by victim and offender characteristics, circumstances, and offense, 1988 survey, annual rpt, 6066–3.42

Victimization rates, by victim and offender characteristics, circumstances, and offense, 1989 survey, annual rpt, 6066–3.44

Victimizations by region and victim characteristics, and rpts to police, by offense, 1973-90, annual rpt, 6066–25.35; 6066–25.41

Victimizations, by victim characteristics, offense, and whether reported to police, 1973-88, 6066–3.45

Victimizations of households, by offense, household characteristics, and location, 1975-90, annual rpt, 6066–25.40

Violent crime victimizations, circumstances, victim characteristics, arrest, recidivism, sentences, and prisoners, 1980s, 6068–148

Women prisoners in State instns, by offense, drug use history, whether abused, and other characteristics, 1986, 6066–19.61

Women's rape and other violent crime victimization, by relation to offender, circumstances, and victim characteristics, 1973-87, 6068–243

Population

Black Americans social and economic characteristics, for South and total US, 1989-90 and trends from 1969, Current Population Rpt, 2546–1.450

Census of Population and Housing, 1990: population and housing characteristics, households, and land area, by county, subdiv, and place, State rpt series, 2551–1

Census of Population and Housing, 1990: population and housing selected characteristics, by region, press release, 2328–74

Census of Population and Housing, 1990: voting age and total population by race, and housing units, by block, redistricting counts required under PL 94-171, State CD-ROM series, 2551–6

Census of Population and Housing, 1990: voting age and total population by race, and housing units, by county and city, redistricting counts required under PL 94-171, State summary rpt series, 2551–5

Census of Population, 1990: metro area population by race, Hispanic origin, and MSA, press release, 2328–75

Census of Population, 1990: population by detailed Native American, Asian, and Pacific Islander group, race, region, and State, with data for 1980, press release, 2328–72

Census of Population, 1990: population by race and detailed Hipanic origin, region, and State, with data for 1980, press release, 2328–73

Census of Population, 1990: population by race, Hispanic origin, region, census div, and State, with data for 1980, fact sheet, 2326–20.2

Census of Population, 1990: post-enumeration survey results compared to census counts, by race, sex, city, county, and State, press release, 2328–69

Census of Population, 1990: post-enumeration survey use for adjusting census counts, with estimates of undercount by race, 1950-80, GAO rpt, 26119–327

Children and youth social, economic, and demographic characteristics, 1950s-90, 4818–5

Consumer Income, socioeconomic characteristics of persons, families, and households, detailed cross-tabulations, Current Population Rpt series, 2546–6

Households and family characteristics, by location, 1990, annual Current Population Rpt, 2546–1.447

Immigrants in US, population characteristics and fertility, by birthplace and compared to native born, 1980s, Current Population rpt, 2546–2.162

Income (household) and poverty status under alternative income definitions, by recipient characteristics, 1990, annual Current Population Rpt, 2546–6.69

Income (personal) and poverty status changes, by selected characteristics, 1987-88, Current Population Rpt, 2546–20.19

Income (personal) by sex, and poverty status of families and persons, by race, 1970-89, annual rpt, 204–1.1

Income and consumer spending of households, for selected population groups, quarterly journal, 1702–1

Living arrangements, family relationships, and marital status, by selected characteristics, 1990, annual Current Population Rpt, 2546–1.449

Parents departure, absence, and presence, family economic impacts, 1983-86, Current Population Rpt, 2546–20.17

Poverty status of population and families, by detailed characteristics, 1988-89, annual Current Population Rpt, 2546–6.67

Poverty status of population and families, by detailed characteristics, 1990, annual Current Population Rpt, 2546–6.71

Rural areas children in poverty by selected family characteristics, and compared to urban areas, 1987-88, 1598–270

State and Metro Area Data Book, 1991 data compilation, 2328–54

Statistical Abstract of US, 1991 annual data compilation, 2324–1

Prices and Cost of Living

Consumer Expenditure Survey, household income by source, and itemized spending, by selected characteristics and region, 1988-89, annual rpt, 6764–5

Consumer Expenditure Survey, spending by category, and income, by selected household characteristics and location, 1990, annual press release, 6726–1.42

Food cost index alternative to CPI, by category, region, and household income, size, race, and food budget level, 1980-85, 1598–275

Public Welfare and Social Security

AFDC beneficiaries demographic and financial characteristics, by State, FY89, annual rpt, 4694–1

AIDS patient home and community services under Medicaid waiver in 6 States, 1988-89, article, 4652–1.216

Child care needs impacts on mothers labor force status, and unemployed mothers characteristics, 1986, article, 6722–1.245

Child support and alimony awards, and payment status, by selected characteristics of woman, 1989, biennial Current Population Rpt, 2546–6.72

Child welfare programs funding by source, and foster care program operations and client characteristics, for selected States, 1960s-95, 25368–169

Disability Insurance beneficiaries costs to Medicare until age 64 under alternative coverage assumptions, model results, 1989, article, 4742–1.208

Food aid program of USDA for women, infants, and children, participants by race, State, and Indian agency, Apr 1990, annual rpt, 1364–16

Food stamp recipient household size, composition, income, and income and deductions allowed, summer 1988, annual rpt, 1364–8

Foster care placements, discharges, and returns to care, by selected characteristics of children, and length of stay factors, 1985-86, GAO rpt, 26121–432

Homeless and runaway youth programs, funding, activities, and participant characteristics, FY90, annual rpt, 4604–3

Medicaid services use and costs in alternative treatment settings, model description and results, FY87, article, 4652–1.211

Medicare and Medicaid beneficiaries and program operations, 1991, annual fact book, 4654–18

Medicare and Medicaid eligibility, participation, coverage, and program finances, various periods 1966-91, biennial rpt, 4654–1

Medicare reimbursement of hospitals under prospective payment system, impacts on instns and beneficiaries, 1988, annual rpt, 4654–13

OASDHI admin, and SSA activities, 1930s-90 and projected to 2064, annual data compilation, 4704–12

OASDHI, Medicaid, SSI, and related programs benefits, beneficiary characteristics, and trust funds, selected years 1937-89, annual rpt, 4744–3

Supplemental Security Income benefit award rate by applicant characteristics and eligibility class, 1987, article, 4742–1.213

Supplemental Security Income recipients, by race and sex, monthly rpt, 4742–1.12

Teenage mothers child support awards, payment status, health insurance inclusion, and govt aid for collection, by selected characteristics, 1987, 4698–5

BY RACE AND ETHNIC GROUP

Youth natl service program proposal, operations and youth attitudes, 1990 rpt, 26306–3.115

Recreation and Leisure

Coastal areas recreation facilities of Fed Govt and States, visitor and site characteristics, 1987-90 survey, regional rpt series, 2176–9

Shellfish recreational harvesters selected characteristics, location of harvest and residence, and spending, 1985 survey, 2178–28

Science and Technology

Computer use at home, school, and work, by purpose and selected user characteristics, 1989, Current Population Rpt, 2546–2.158

Degrees (PhD) in science and engineering, by field, instn, employment prospects, sex, race, and other characteristics, 1960s-90, annual rpt, 9627–30

Education in science and engineering, grad programs enrollment by field, source of funds, and characteristics of student and instn, 1975-89, annual rpt, 9627–7

Employment and other characteristics of science and engineering PhDs, by field and State, 1989, biennial rpt, 9627–18

Higher education instn science and engineering research system status, R&D performance, and Federal support, 1950s-88, 9628–83

NASA staff characteristics and personnel actions, FY90, annual rpt, 9504–1

NSF research grants to predominantly undergrad instns, by NSF div, and principal investigator sex and race, FY88, 9628–85

Nuclear engineering enrollment and degrees granted by instn and State, and grad placement, by student characteristics, 1990, annual rpt, 3004–5

Veterans Affairs

Agent Orange exposure of Vietnam veterans, and other factors relation to dev of rare cancers, 1984-88, 4208–33

AIDS cases at VA health care centers by sex, race, risk factor, and facility, and AIDS prevention and treatment issues, quarterly rpt, 8702–1

Alcohol abuse among veterans, screening results by age and race, for 5 VA medical centers, 1990, GAO rpt, 26121–416

Homeless veterans domiciliary program of VA, participant characteristics and outcomes, 1990 annual rpt, 8604–10

Homeless veterans with mental illness, VA program services, costs, staff, client characteristics, and outcome, 1990, annual rpt, 8604–11

Housing programs of VA, costs, terms, and user characteristics, 1985-89, 8608–7

Mental health care services of VA, use, spending, and staff and patient characteristics, by State and services type, 1983 and 1986, 4506–3.43

VA employment characteristics and activities, FY90, annual rpt, 8604–3.8

BY SEX

Agriculture and Food

Census of Agriculture, 1987: farms, farmland, production, finances, and operator characteristics, by county, final State rpt series, 2331–1

FmHA loans, by type, borrower characteristics, and State, quarterly rpt, 1182–8

Food consumption, dietary composition, and nutrient intake, 1987/88 natl survey, preliminary rpt series, 1356–1

Food spending, by item, household composition, income, age, race, and region, 1980-88, Consumer Expenditure Survey biennial rpt, 1544–30

Banking, Finance, and Insurance

Households assets, by type of holding and selected characteristics, 1988, Current Population Rpt, 2546–20.16

Communications and Transportation

Air traffic control and airway facilities staff, by employment and other characteristics, FY89, annual rpt, 7504–41

Air traffic control and airway facilities supervisors task priorities, skills needed, and other characteristics, 1990 survey, technical rpt, 7506–10.84

Aircraft pilot and nonpilot certificates held, by type of certificate, age, sex, region, and State, 1990, annual rpt, 7504–2

Drivers licenses in force, by age, sex, and State, 1989-90, annual rpt, 7554–24

Drivers licenses in force by license type, sex, and age, and revenues, by State, 1990, annual rpt, 7554–1.2

Drivers licenses issued and in force by age and sex, fees, and renewal, by license class and State, 1989, annual rpt, 7554–16

Traffic accidents, casualties, circumstances, and characteristics of persons and vehicles involved, 1989, annual rpt, 7764–18

Traffic fatal accidents, alcohol levels of drivers and others, by circumstances and characteristics of persons and vehicles, 1989, annual rpt, 7764–16

Traffic fatal accidents, circumstances, and characteristics of persons and vehicles involved, 1990, semiannual rpt, 7762–11

Traffic fatal accidents, deaths, and rates, by circumstances, characteristics of persons and vehicles involved, and location, 1989, annual rpt, 7764–10

Travel from US, characteristics of visit and traveler, and country of destination, 1990 in-flight survey, annual rpt, 2904–14

Travel patterns, personal and household characteristics, and auto and public transport use, 1990 survey, series, 7556–6

Travel patterns, personal and household characteristics, and auto use, 1990 survey, annual rpt, 7554–1.6

Travel to US, by characteristics of visit and traveler, world area of origin, and US destination, 1990 survey, annual rpt, 2904–12

Truck accidents, circumstances, severity, and characteristics of drivers and vehicles, 1989, annual rpt, 7764–20

Education

American Historical Assn financial statements, and membership by State, 1989, annual rpt, 29574–2

Athletes in college, educational and employment performance compared to other students, for 1972 high school class, as of 1986, 4888–5

Condition of Education, detail for elementary, secondary, and higher education, 1920s-90 and projected to 2001, annual rpt, 4824–1

Index by Categories

Degrees awarded in higher education, by level, field, race, and sex, 1988/89 with trends from 1978/79, biennial rpt, 4844–17

Digest of Education Statistics, 1991 annual data compilation, 4824–2

Discrimination in education, indicators for service delivery and discipline, by State, 1988, biennial rpt, 4804–33

DOD Dependents Schools basic skills and college entrance test scores, 1990-91, annual rpt, 3504–16

Educational attainment, by sociodemographic characteristics and location, 1989 and trends from 1940, biennial Current Population Rpt, 2546–1.452

Eighth grade class of 1988: educational performance and conditions, characteristics, attitudes, activities, and plans, natl longitudinal survey, series, 4826–9

Elementary and secondary education enrollment, staff, finances, operations, programs, and policies, 1987/88 biennial survey, series, 4836–3

Elementary and secondary students educational performance, and factors affecting proficiency, by selected characteristics, 1988 natl assessments, subject rpt series, 4896–7

Elementary and secondary students educational performance, and factors affecting proficiency, by selected characteristics, 1990 natl assessments, subject rpt series, 4896–8

Elementary and secondary students educational performance in math, science, reading, and writing, 1970s-90, 4898–32

Enrollment, by grade, instn type and control, and student characteristics, 1989 and trends from 1947, annual Current Population Rpt, 2546–1.453

High school class of 1972: education, employment, and family characteristics, activities, and attitudes, natl longitudinal study, series, 4836–1

High school class of 1972: women's employment and educational experiences compared to men, natl longitudinal study, as of 1986, 4888–6

High school class of 1990: college enrollment, and labor force participation of grads and dropouts, by race and sex, press release, 6726–1.38

High school dropout rates, and subsequent completion, by student and school characteristics, alternative estimates, 1990, annual rpt, 4834–23

Higher education course completions, by detailed program, sex, race, and instn type, for 1972 high school class, as of 1984, 4888–4

Higher education enrollment and degrees awarded by sex, and instn finances, by instn level and control, 1990-91, annual rpt, 4844–14

Higher education enrollment and degrees awarded, by sex, full- and part-time status, and instn level and control, fall 1990, annual rpt, 4844–16

Higher education enrollment, by student and instn characteristics, fall 1989, biennial rpt, 4844–2

Higher education instn student aid and other sources of support, with student expenses and characteristics, by instn type and control, 1990 triennial study, series, 4846–5

Index by Categories

BY SEX

Higher education instn tuition and other costs, govt aid, impacts on enrollment, and cost containment methods, 1970s-90 and projected to 2001, 4808–25

Indian education funding of Fed Govt, and enrollment, degrees, and program grants and fellowships by State, late 1960s-FY89, annual rpt, 14874–1

Library of Congress employment by race, Hispanic origin, and sex, and affirmative action needs, 1989, hearing, 21428–9

Literacy programs in workplaces, demonstration projects funding and participant characteristics, FY88, 4808–37

Migrant workers children education programs enrollment, staff, and effectiveness, by State, 1980s, 4808–30

Minority group higher education enrollment, degrees, factors affecting participation, and earnings, 1960s-88, 4808–29

Student loan debt burden of 1986 college grads, by selected student characteristics and instn control, 1987, 4808–26

Teachers in higher education instns, employment and other characteristics, by instn type and control, 1987/88 survey, 4846–4.4

Teachers in higher education, salaries by faculty rank, sex, instn type and control, and State, 1989/90, annual rpt, 4844–8

Teachers in private schools, selected characteristics by instn level, size, and orientation, various periods 1979-88, 4838–47

Truman, Harry S, Scholarship Foundation finances, and awards by student characteristics, FY90, annual rpt, 14314–1

Government and Defense

Air Force recruiting compliance with gender-neutral selection, with aptitude test results by sex, FY86-90, GAO rpt, 26123–359

Aliens (illegal) legal residence applications under Immigration Reform and Control Act, by selected characteristics, State, and country, periodic rpt, 6262–3

Army Dept activities, personnel, discipline, budget, and assistance, FY83 summary data, annual rpt, 3704–11

DOT employment, by subagency, occupation, and selected personnel characteristics, FY90, annual rpt, 7304–18

Employment (civilian) of Fed Govt, by demographic and employment characteristics, as of Sept 1990, annual article, 9842–1.201

Employment (civilian) of Fed Govt, minorities, women, veterans, and disabled persons, as of Sept 1988 and 1990, biennial article, 9842–1.202

Employment and payroll (civilian) of Fed Govt, by occupation, pay grade, sex, agency, and location, 1989, biennial rpt, 9844–4

Employment of minorities, women, and disabled in Fed Govt, by agency and occupation, FY89, annual rpt, 9244–10

Equal Opportunity Recruitment Program activity, and Fed Govt employment by sex, race, pay grade, and occupational group, FY90, annual rpt, 9844–33

Military active duty and recruit social, economic, and parents characteristics, by service branch and State, FY89, annual rpt, 3544–41

Military personnel, by selected characteristics, 1991 annual summary rpt, 3504–13

Military personnel on active duty, recruits, and reenlistment, by race, sex, and service branch, quarterly press release, 3542–7

Military personnel strengths, for active duty enlisted and officers, by sex and race, 1970s-90, GAO rpt, 26123–325

Military reserve forces personnel strengths and characteristics, by component, FY90, annual rpt, 3544–38

Military reserve forces personnel strengths and characteristics, by component, quarterly rpt, 3542–4

Military reserve forces personnel strengths, by selected characteristics and reserve component, FY90, annual rpt, 3544–1.5

Navy personnel strengths, accessions, and attrition, detailed statistics, quarterly rpt, 3802–4

Public debt burden on future generations forecast under alternative economic and fiscal policy assumptions, 1991 working paper, 9377–9.111

Public debt burden on future generations forecast under alternative fiscal policies, and ratio of consumption to lifetime income, by sex and age, 1991 working paper, 9377–9.116

Senior Executive Service membership characteristics, entries, exits, and awards, FY79-90, annual rpt, 9844–36

State and local govt employment of minorities and women, by occupation, function, pay level, and State, 1990, annual rpt, 9244–6

State Dept and Foreign Service minority and women employment, and hiring goals, FY89-90, biennial rpt, 7004–21

Taxes, spending, and govt efficiency, public opinion by respondent characteristics, 1991 survey, annual rpt, 10044–2

Voting and registration, by socioeconomic and demographic characteristics, 1990 congressional election, biennial Current Population Rpt, 2546–1.454

Health and Vital Statistics

Acute and chronic health conditions, disability, absenteeism, and health services use, by selected characteristics, 1987, CD-ROM, 4147–10.177

AIDS cases by race, sex, and risk category, and deaths and survivors, projected 1989-93, 4206–2.34

AIDS cases by risk group, race, sex, age, State, and MSA, and deaths, monthly rpt, 4202–9

AIDS patient hospital use and charges, by hospital and patient characteristics, and payment source, 1986-87, 4186–6.15

AIDS public knowledge, attitudes, info sources, and testing, for blacks, 1990 survey, 4146–8.208

AIDS public knowledge, attitudes, info sources, and testing, for Hispanics, 1990 survey, 4146–8.209

AIDS public knowledge, attitudes, info sources, and testing, 1990 survey, 4146–8.195; 4146–8.201; 4146–8.205

AIDS virus infection and risk factor prevalence, natl survey methodology and pretest results, 1989, 4148–30

AIDS virus infection prevalence in developing countries, by sex, selected city, urban-rural location, and country, 1991, semiannual rpt, 2322–4

Alcohol abuse by family members and spouses, population exposure by selected characteristics, 1988, 4146–8.207

Alcohol users by consumption level, and abstainers, deaths by cause, age, and sex, 1986-87, article, 4482–1.201

Asbestos in buildings, EPA aid for removal, occupational asbestos exposure cancer cases and deaths, and Catholic schools abatement costs, 1985-90, hearing, 25328–32

Births and rates, by characteristics of birth, infant, and parents, 1989 and trends from 1940, US Vital Statistics advance annual rpt, 4146–5.123

Cancer (childhood) survivors risk of miscarriage, stillbirth, and birth defects, by chemotherapy and radiotherapy exposure, study, 1991 article, 4472–1.233

Cancer cases by body site and population characteristics, research results, semimonthly journal, 4472–1

Cancer cases, deaths, and survival rates, by sex, race, age, and body site, 1973-88, annual rpt, 4474–35

Cancer death rates of minorities, by body site, age, sex, and substate area, 1950s-80, atlas, 4478–78

Cancer deaths by age, and cases, by sex, 1985 and 1990, annual rpt, 4474–13

Child accident deaths and death rates, by cause, age, sex, race, and State, 1980-85, 4108–54

Child accident deaths and injuries by cause, and victimization, rates by race, sex, and age, 1979-88, chartbook, 4108–56

Child developmental, learning, and emotional problems, cases and share receiving special treatment and education, by selected characteristics, 1988, 4146–8.193

Child health, behavioral, emotional, and school problems relation to family structure, by selected characteristics, 1988, 4147–10.178

Child health condition and services use, 1990 chartbook, 4108–49

Cirrhosis of liver deaths, by age, sex, race, and whether alcohol involved, 1987 and trends from 1910, 4486–1.10

Cocaine abuse, user characteristics, and related crime and violence, 1988 conf, 4498–74

Deaths and rates by age, and life expectancy, by sex and race, preliminary 1989-90 and trends from 1950, US Vital Statistics annual rpt, 4144–7

Deaths and rates, by detailed cause and demographic characteristics, 1988 and trends from 1900, US Vital Statistics annual rpt, 4144–2

Deaths and rates, provisional data, monthly rpt, 4142–1.2

Deaths within 8 years of retirement, by health and other characteristics, 1982-88, article, 4742–1.206

Diabetes and complications cases, deaths, and hospitalization, by age, sex, race, State, and region, 1980-86, annual rpt, 4205–41

Disabled persons and related activity limitation days and health services use, by health status, disability type, and other characteristics, 1984-88, 4146–8.202

Disabled persons rehabilitation, Federal and State activities and funding, FY90, annual rpt, 4944–1

BY SEX

Index by Categories

Diving (underwater sport and occupational) deaths, by circumstances, diver characteristics, and location, 1970-89, annual rpt, 2144–5

Drug abuse emergency room admissions and deaths, by drug type and source, sex, race, age, and major metro area, 1990, annual rpt, 4494–8

Drug abuse indicators for selected metro areas, research results, data collection, and policy issues, 1991 semiannual conf, 4492–5

Drug abuse prevalence among minorities, related health effects and crime, treatment, and research status and needs, mid 1970s-90, 4498–72

Drug, alcohol, and cigarette use and attitudes of youth, by substance type and selected characteristics, 1975-90 surveys, annual rpt, 4494–4

Drug, alcohol, and cigarette use, by selected characteristics, 1990 survey, biennial rpt, 4494–5

Drug and alcohol abuse treatment and prevention programs of States, funding, facilities, and patient characteristics, FY89, 4488–15

Drug and alcohol abuse treatment facilities, services, use, funding, staff, and client characteristics, 1989, biennial rpt, 4494–10

Drug and alcohol abuse treatment services, funding, staffing, and client load, characteristics, and outcomes, by setting, 1989 conf, 4498–73

Drug and alcohol use in workplace, and drinkers reporting adverse effects, for young adults by selected characteristics, 1984, article, 6722–1.237

Drug prescriptions, by drug type and brand, and for new drugs, 1989, annual rpt, 4064–12

Firearms-related deaths and death rates, by motive, age, sex, and race, for persons aged 1-34, 1979-88, 4146–5.119

Fluoride exposure by source, and health risks and benefits, with research results, 1930s-89, 4048–36

Health care services use and costs, methodology and findings of natl survey, series, 4186–8

Health condition and health care resources, use, and spending, 1950s-89, annual data compilation, 4144–11

Heart disease death rates for US and 31 other countries by sex, 1987, annual rpt, 4474–15

Heart disease, stroke, and chronic obstructive lung disease deaths, by country and sex, 1987, annual rpt, 4474–6

Hepatitis cases by infection source, age, sex, race, and State, and deaths, by strain, 1988 and trends from 1966, 4205–2

Hispanic Americans deaths and rates, by cause, age, sex, and detailed origin, average 1979-81, 4147–20.18

Home health care services Medicare use and costs, by agency and service type, patient characteristics, and State, 1988-89, article, 4652–1.229

Homeless persons alcohol abuse, by sex, age, race, and additional diagnoses, aggregate 1985-87, 4488–14

Hospices operations, services, costs, and patient characteristics, for instns without Medicare certification, FY85-86, 4658–52

Hospices use by cancer patients, by service type, use of other facilities, patient and instn characteristics, and other indicators, local area study, 1980-85, 4658–53

Hospital discharges and length of stay, by diagnosis, patient and instn characteristics, procedure performed, and payment source, 1988, annual rpt, 4147–13.107

Hospital discharges and length of stay by region and diagnosis, and procedures performed, by age and sex, 1989, annual rpt, 4146–8.198

Hospital discharges and rates, for aged Medicare beneficiaries by diagnosis, age, sex, and race, 1988, article, 4202–7.205

Hospital discharges by detailed diagnostic and procedure category, primary diagnosis, and length of stay, by age, sex, and region, 1988, annual rpt, 4147–13.105

Hospital discharges by detailed diagnostic and procedure category, primary diagnosis, and length of stay, by age, sex, and region, 1989, annual rpt, 4147–13.108

Implants of medical devices, by type, reason, duration, and user characteristics, 1988, 4146–8.197

Indian Health Service facilities and use, and Indian health and other characteristics, by IHS region, 1980s-89, annual chartbook, 4084–7

Indian Health Service facilities, funding, operations, and Indian health and other characteristics, 1950s-90, annual chartbook, 4084–1

Indian Health Service outpatient services provided, by reason for visit and age, FY88-89, annual rpt, 4084–2

Indian Health Service, tribal, and contract facilities hospitalization, by diagnosis, age, sex, and service area, FY89, annual rpt, 4084–5

Infant death rate, by cause, region, and race, 1980-87, article, 4202–7.208

Injuries, by type, circumstances, and victim characteristics, and related activity limitations, 1985-87, 4147–10.176

Injuries, related impairments, and activity limitations, by circumstances and victim characteristics, 1985-87, 4147–10.179

Insurance (health) coverage, by insurance type and selected characteristics, 1989, 4146–8.203

Insurance (health) coverage of children, and children with a regular source of care, by selected characteristics, 1988, 4146–8.192

Insurance (health) coverage, uninsured persons by employment and other characteristics and State, 1988, GAO rpt, 26121–403

Insurance (health) natl coverage alternative proposals and indicators of need, 1989, 4658–54

Kidney end-stage disease cases, treatment, outcomes, and characteristics of patients, organ donors, and facilities, late 1970s-88, annual rpt, 4474–37

Kidney end-stage disease treatment facilities, Medicare enrollment and reimbursement, survival, and patient characteristics, 1983-89, annual rpt, 4654–16

Life tables, 1988 and trends from 1900, US Vital Statistics annual rpt, 4144–2.6

Marriages and rates, by age, race, education, previous marital status, and State, 1988, US Vital Statistics advance annual rpt, 4146–5.122

Marriages, divorces, and rates, by characteristics of spouses, State, and county, 1987 and trends from 1920, US Vital Statistics annual rpt, 4144–4

Mental health care facilities for emotionally disturbed children, use, funding, and characteristics of patients, staff, and instn, 1988, 4506–3.44

Mental health care facilities outpatient care programs, use, and client characteristics, by instn type and State, 1988, 4506–3.40; 4506–3.46

Mental health care in private hospitals, patients characteristics, 1986, 4506–3.47

Mental illness and drug and alcohol abuse direct and indirect costs, by age and sex, 1985, 4048–35

Minority group and women health condition, services use, payment sources, and health care labor force, by poverty status, 1940s-89, chartbook, 4118–56

Minority group health condition, services use, costs, and indicators of services need, 1950s-88, 4118–55

Nursing home residents with mental, behavioral, and functional disorders, by age, sex, and instn characteristics, 1987, 4186–8.11

Nursing home residents with mental disorders, by disorder type and resident and instn characteristics, 1985, 4147–13.106

Nursing home use prevalence among aged, by length of stay and selected characteristics, 1986 and 1990, 4186–7.9

Occupational injuries, by circumstances, body site, equipment type, and industry, with safety measures, series, 6846–1

Older persons with functional limitations, long-term care sources, and health and other characteristics, 1984-85, 4147–13.104

Physicians, by specialty, age, sex, and location of training and practice, 1989, State rpt series, 4116–6

Physicians visits, by patient and practice characteristics, diagnosis, and services provided, 1989, 4146–8.206

Radiation exposure at DOE and DOE-contractor sites, by facility type and contractor, dose type, and worker age, sex, and occupation, 1988, annual rpt, 3324–1

Radiation protection and health physics enrollment and degrees granted by instn and State, and grad placement, by student characteristics, 1990, annual rpt, 3004–7

Sexually transmitted disease cases, by strain, age, and sex, 1981-90, annual rpt, 4205–42

Smoking and smokeless tobacco use, attitudes, and smoking intervention research spending and results, with bibl, 1960s-90, 4478–195

Teenagers physicians office visits, by reason and characteristics of physicians, patients, and visit, 1985, 4146–8.199

Tuberculosis cases and deaths, by patient characteristics, State, and city, 1989 and trends from 1953, annual rpt, 4204–10

Housing and Construction

Affordability indicators for housing, by household composition, income, and current tenure, 1988, 2486–1.11

American Housing Survey: inventory change from 1973, by reason, unit and household characteristics, and location, 1983, biennial rpt, 2485–14

Index by Categories

BY SEX

American Housing Survey: unit and households characteristics, unit and neighborhood quality, and journey to work by MSA location, for 11 MSAs, 1984 survey, supplement, 2485–8

American Housing Survey: unit and households detailed characteristics, and unit and neighborhood quality, 1987, biennial rpt, 2485–12

American Housing Survey: unit and households detailed characteristics, and unit and neighborhood quality, 1987, biennial rpt supplement, 2485–13

Homeownership rates, by household type, householder age and sex, and location, 1960s-90, annual rpt, 2484–1.3

Mortgage applications by disposition, and secondary loan market sales by purchaser type, by applicant and neighborhood characteristics, 1990, article, 9362–1.206

Mortgages FHA-insured, financial, property, and mortgagor characteristics, by metro area, 1990, annual rpt, 5144–24

Mortgages FHA-insured, financial, property, and mortgagor characteristics, by State, 1990, annual rpt, 5144–1

Mortgages FHA-insured, financial, property, and mortgagor characteristics, total and by State and outlying area, 1990, annual rpt, 5144–25

Mortgages FHA-insured, financial, property, and mortgagor characteristics, 1990, annual rpt, 5144–17; 5144–23

Labor and Employment

Black American displaced workers, by demographic and current and former employment characteristics, and compared to whites, 1978-86, article, 6722–1.234

Dallas-Fort Worth-Arlington metro area employment, earnings, hours, and CPI changes, late 1970s-90, annual rpt, 6964–2

Displaced workers losing job 1985-90, by demographic and former and current employment characteristics, as of Jan 1990, article, 6722–1.225

Earnings distribution by sex, race, industry div, and occupation, 1960-89, article, 6722–1.201

Employee benefit plan coverage, by benefit type and worker characteristics, late 1970s-80s, 15496–1.11

Employment and Earnings, detailed data, monthly rpt, 6742–2

Employment and unemployment, by age, sex, race, marital and family status, industry div, and State, Monthly Labor Review, 6722–1.2

Employment conditions, alternative BLS projections to 2005 and trends 1970s-90, biennial article, 6722–1.252; 6722–1.254

Employment, earnings, and hours, monthly press release, 6742–5

Employment situation, earnings, hours, and other BLS economic indicators, transcripts of BLS Commissioner's monthly testimony, periodic rpt, 23846–4

Employment, unemployment, and labor force characteristics, by region, State, and selected metro area, 1990, annual rpt, 6744–7

Family members labor force status and earnings, by family composition and race, quarterly press release, 6742–21

Foreign countries labor conditions, union coverage, and work accidents, annual country rpt series, 6366–4

Houston metro area employment, earnings, hours, and CPI changes, 1970s-90, annual rpt, 6964–1

Job Training Partnership Act occupational training services, disparities in delivery to women and minorities, 1989-90, 26106–8.14

Job Training Partnership Act participants, by selected characteristics, FY90, annual rpt, 6304–1

Labor force status by race and sex, employment by industry div, and unemployment duration and reason, selected years 1929-90, annual rpt, 204–1.2

Labor force status by sex and for teens, *Survey of Current Business*, monthly rpt, 2702–1.2

Labor force status, by worker characteristics and industry group, 1982-90, semiannual article, 6722–1.212

Labor force status, earnings, and other characteristics of women, with comparisons to men, fact sheet series, 6564–1

Labor force status, experience, and unemployment duration, by race and sex, 1989-90, annual press release, 6726–1.39

Labor force, wages, hours, and payroll costs, by major industry group and demographic characteristics, *Survey of Current Business*, monthly rpt, 2702–1.8

Labor supply trends, with characteristics of working-age population not in labor force, part-time workers, and multiple-jobholders, late 1960s-90, article, 9362–1.203

Manufacturing employment by selected characteristics, wages, and import and export penetration rates, by SIC 2- to 4-digit industry, 1982-89, 6366–3.27

Minimum wage provisions of Fair Labor Standards Act, coverage of nonsupervisory workers by race and sex, FY89, annual rpt, 6504–2.1

Minority group labor force status, by race, detailed Hispanic origin, and sex, quarterly rpt, 6742–18

Moonlighting employment, by reason, and characteristics of workers and primary and secondary jobs, 1991, press release, 6726–1.40

Part-time employment, by age, sex, industry div, and whether voluntary, 1969-89, article, 6722–1.218

Pension benefits disparity between men and women in small business plans by selected participant and plan characteristics, impacts of 1986 Tax Reform Act, 1984-85, GAO rpt, 26121–412

Pension coverage by industry, vestment, and recipient income, by participant characteristics, 1987, Current Population Rpt, 2546–20.18

Poland labor force status by education level, sex, and sector, college enrollment, and grads by field, 1960s-88, article, 6722–1.203

Rural areas labor force characteristics, with comparisons to urban areas, 1987, 1598–264

Unemployment insurance claims and receipt, by reason and duration of unemployment, age, sex, and region, 1989-90, 6406–6.33

Unemployment insurance job search services, impacts on UI claims activity and reemployment, and claimant characteristics, for Tacoma, Wash, 1986-87, 6406–6.35

Unemployment of groups with historically high rates, 1985-89, biennial rpt, 6504–2.2

Unemployment rates, current data and annual trends, monthly rpt, 23842–1.2

Union coverage of workers and earnings, by age, sex, race, occupational group, and industry div, 1989-90, press release, 6726–1.36

Vocational rehabilitation cases of State agencies by disposition and applicant characteristics, and closures by reason, FY84-88, annual rpt, 4944–6

Volunteer workers by organization type, time served, whether otherwise employed, and other characteristics, 1989, article, 6722–1.213

Wages by occupation, and benefits for office and plant workers, periodic MSA survey rpt series, 6785–11; 6785–12

Wages, hours, and employment by occupation, and benefits, for selected locations, industry survey rpt series, 6787–6

Wages of full- and part-time workers, by selected characteristics, quarterly press release, 6742–20

Youth labor force status, by sex, race, and industry div, summer 1987-91, annual press release, 6744–14

Law Enforcement

Aircraft hijackings, on-board explosions, and other crime, US and foreign incidents, 1985-89, annual rpt, 7504–31

Arrest rates, by offense, sex, age, and race, 1965-89, annual rpt, 6224–7

Arrests, prosecutions, convictions, and sentencing, for felony offenders, by offender characteristics and offense, 1988, 6066–25.33; 6066–25.39

Assaults and deaths of law enforcement officers, by circumstances, agency, victim and offender characteristics, and location, 1990, annual rpt, 6224–3

Crime, criminal justice admin and enforcement, and public opinion, data compilation, 1991 annual rpt, 6064–6

Crime victimization of women, by relation to offender, circumstances, and victim characteristics, for rape and other violent offenses, with comparisons to men, 1973-87, 6068–243

Crimes, arrests, and rates, by offense, offender characteristics, population size, and jurisdiction, 1990, annual rpt, 6224–2.1; 6224–2.2

Criminal case processing in Federal district courts, and dispositions, by offense, district, and offender characteristics, 1986, annual rpt, 6064–29

Drug test results at arrest, by drug type, offense, and sex, for selected urban areas, quarterly rpt, 6062–3

Drug testing of criminal defendants, demonstration program operations, offender characteristics, and judges views, 1987-90, 18208–11

Employment of State and local law enforcement personnel and officers, by sex, population size, census div, and jurisdiction, as of Oct 1990, annual rpt, 6224–2.3

Jail adult and juvenile population, employment, spending, instn conditions, and inmate programs, by county and facility, 1988, regional rpt series, 6068–144

BY SEX

Index by Categories

Jail population, by criminal, correctional, drug use, and family history, and selected other characteristics, 1989, 6066–19.62

Jail population by sex, race, and for 25 jurisdictions, and instn conditions, 1988-90, annual rpt, 6066–25.38

Jail population drug abuse history, by offense, conviction status, criminal and family history, and selected other characteristics, 1989, 6066–19.63

Juvenile correctional and detention public and private instns, inmates, and expenses, by instn and resident characteristics and State, 1987, biennial rpt, 6064–13

Juvenile courts delinquency cases, by offense, referral source, disposition, age, sex, race, State, and county, 1988, annual rpt, 6064–12

Juvenile courts property offenses cases, by disposition and offender age, sex, and race, 1985-86, 6066–27.5

Juvenile facilities, population, and costs, by facility and resident characteristics, region, and State, 1985-89, biennial rpt, 6064–5

Older persons abuse and neglect by circumstances and characteristics of abuser and victim, and States protective services budgets and staff, by location, 1980s, hearing, 21148–62

Pretrial processing, detention, and release, for Federal offenders, by defendant characteristics and district, 1988, hearing, 25528–114

Pretrial release of felony defendants and rearrests, by offense type and selected characteristics, 1988, 6066–25.36

Prison and parole admissions and releases, sentence length, and time served, by offense and offender characteristics, 1985, annual rpt, 6064–33

Prisoner population of women in State instns, by offense, drug use history, whether abused, and other characteristics, with comparisons to men, 1986, 6066–19.61

Prisoners, characteristics, and movements, by State, 1989, annual rpt, 6064–26

Prisoners from Federal instns, halfway house placements, duration, and employment, and house capacity, 1990-91, GAO rpt, 26119–347

Prisoners in Federal and State instns by sex, admissions, and instn capacity and overcrowding, by State, 1980s-90, annual rpt, 6066–25.37

Prisoners in Federal and State instns, by sex and State, June 1991, semiannual rpt, 6062–4

Prisoners in Federal instns, by sex, prison, security level, contract facility type, and region, monthly rpt series, 6242–1

Prisoners under death sentence by prison control and prisoner characteristics, and executions from 1930, by State, 1973-90, annual rpt, 6066–25.42

Prisons and jails operated under private contract, costs and characteristics of instns, by facility and State, 1990, GAO rpt, 26119–321

Probation and split sentences by State courts for felony offenses, sentence lengths, case processing time, and felon characteristics, by offense, 1986, 6068–242

Runaway cases in juvenile courts, by referral source, disposition, and sex, 1985-86, 6066–27.4

Sentences for Federal crimes, guidelines use and results by offense and district, and Sentencing Commission activities, 1990, annual rpt, 17664–1

Teenagers crime victimization, by victim and offender characteristics, circumstances, and offense, 1985-88 surveys, 6066–3.43

Victimization rates, by victim and offender characteristics, circumstances, and offense, 1988 survey, annual rpt, 6066–3.42

Victimization rates, by victim and offender characteristics, circumstances, and offense, 1989 survey, annual rpt, 6066–3.44

Victimizations by region and victim characteristics, and rpts to police, by offense, 1973-90, annual rpt, 6066–25.35; 6066–25.41

Victimizations, by victim characteristics, offense, and whether reported to police, 1973-88, 6066–3.45

Violent crime victimizations, circumstances, victim characteristics, arrest, recidivism, sentences, and prisoners, 1980s, 6068–148

Population

Alaska rural areas population characteristics, and energy resources dev effects, series, 5736–5

Black Americans social and economic characteristics, for South and total US, 1989-90 and trends from 1969, Current Population Rpt, 2546–1.450

Census of Population and Housing, 1990: population and housing characteristics, households, and land area, by county, subdiv, and place, State rpt series, 2551–1

Census of Population and Housing, 1990: population and housing selected characteristics, by region, press release, 2328–74

Census of Population, 1990: post-enumeration survey results compared to census counts, by race, sex, city, county, and State, press release, 2328–69

Children and youth social, economic, and demographic characteristics, 1950s-90, 4818–5

Consumer Income, socioeconomic characteristics of persons, families, and households, detailed cross-tabulations, Current Population Rpt series, 2546–6

Developing countries aged population and selected characteristics, 1980s and projected to 2020, country rpt series, 2326–19

Hispanic Americans in counties bordering Mexico, by selected characteristics, 1980, Current Population Rpt, 2546–2.159

Hispanic Americans social and economic characteristics, by detailed origin, 1991, Current Population Rpt, 2546–1.448; 2546–1.451

Households and family characteristics, by location, 1990, annual Current Population Rpt, 2546–1.447

Immigrants in US, population characteristics and fertility, by birthplace and compared to native born, 1980s, Current Population rpt, 2546–2.162

Income (household) and poverty status under alternative income definitions, by recipient characteristics, 1990, annual Current Population Rpt, 2546–6.69

Income (personal) and poverty status changes, by selected characteristics, 1987-88, Current Population Rpt, 2546–20.19

Income (personal), by sex and race, 1970-89, annual rpt, 204–1.1

Income and consumer spending of households, for selected population groups, quarterly journal, 1702–1

Living arrangements, family relationships, and marital status, by selected characteristics, 1990, annual Current Population Rpt, 2546–1.449

Population size and characteristics, 1969-88, Current Population Rpt, biennial rpt, 2546–2.161

Poverty status of population and families, by detailed characteristics, 1988-89, annual Current Population Rpt, 2546–6.67

Poverty status of population and families, by detailed characteristics, 1990, annual Current Population Rpt, 2546–6.71

Puerto Rico population and housing characteristics, 1990 Census of Population and Housing, press release, 2328–78

Refugee arrivals and resettlement in US, by age, sex, sponsoring agency, State, and country, monthly rpt, 4692–2

Retired pension recipients income, by selected characteristics, 1986, Current Population Rpt, 2546–20.18

State and Metro Area Data Book, 1991 data compilation, 2328–54

Statistical Abstract of US, 1991 annual data compilation, 2324–1

Virgin Islands population and housing characteristics, 1990 Census of Population and Housing, press release, 2328–81

Prices and Cost of Living

Consumer Expenditure Survey, household income by source, and itemized spending, by selected characteristics and region, 1988-89, annual rpt, 6764–5

Public Welfare and Social Security

AFDC beneficiaries demographic and financial characteristics, by State, FY89, annual rpt, 4694–1

Disability Insurance beneficiaries costs to Medicare until age 64 under alternative coverage assumptions, model results, 1989, article, 4742–1.208

Food stamp recipient household size, composition, income, and income and deductions allowed, summer 1988, annual rpt, 1364–8

Foster care placements, discharges, and returns to care, by selected characteristics of children, and length of stay factors, 1985-86, GAO rpt, 26121–432

Homeless and runaway youth programs, funding, activities, and participant characteristics, FY90, annual rpt, 4604–3

Medicaid services use and costs in alternative treatment settings, model description and results, FY87, article, 4652–1.211

Medicare and Medicaid beneficiaries and program operations, 1991, annual fact book, 4654–18

Medicare and Medicaid eligibility, participation, coverage, and program finances, various periods 1966-91, biennial rpt, 4654–1

Medicare disabled enrollees supplementary health insurance coverage, by enrollee characteristics, 1984, article, 4652–1.243

Medicare reimbursement of hospitals under prospective payment system, impacts on instns and beneficiaries, 1988, annual rpt, 4654–13

Index by Categories

BY SEX

OASDHI admin, and SSA activities, 1930s-90 and projected to 2064, annual data compilation, 4704–12

OASDHI, Medicaid, SSI, and related programs benefits, beneficiary characteristics, and trust funds, selected years 1937-89, annual rpt, 4744–3

OASDI benefit payments, trust fund finances, and economic and demographic assumptions, 1970-90 and alternative projections to 2000, actuarial rpt, 4706–1.105

OASDI benefits and beneficiaries, by type of benefit, State, and county, as of Dec 1990, annual rpt, 4744–28

OASDI benefits and beneficiaries, for aged by sex and State, monthly rpt, 4742–1.10

Supplemental Security Income beneficiaries income from OASI and other sources, and work history, 1988, article, 4742–1.216

Supplemental Security Income benefit award rate by applicant characteristics and eligibility class, 1987, article, 4742–1.213

Supplemental Security Income recipients, by race and sex, monthly rpt, 4742–1.12

Youth natl service program proposal, operations and youth attitudes, 1990 rpt, 26306–3.115

Recreation and Leisure

Coastal areas recreation facilities of Fed Govt and States, visitor and site characteristics, 1987-90 survey, regional rpt series, 2176–9

Fishing (ocean sport) activities, and catch by species, by angler characteristics and State, annual coastal area rpt series, 2166–17

Shellfish recreational harvesters selected characteristics, location of harvest and residence, and spending, 1985 survey, 2178–28

Science and Technology

Asia science and engineering employment, by selected characteristics, for 3 countries, 1991 working paper, 2326–18.61

Computer use at home, school, and work, by purpose and selected user characteristics, 1989, Current Population Rpt, 2546–2.158

Degrees (PhD) in science and engineering, by field, instn, employment prospects, sex, race, and other characteristics, 1960s-90, annual rpt, 9627–30

Degrees awarded in science and engineering, by field, level, and sex, 1966-89, 9627–33

Education in science and engineering, grad programs enrollment by field, source of funds, and characteristics of student and instn, 1975-89, annual rpt, 9627–7

Employment and education of scientists and engineers, and R&D spending, for US and selected foreign countries, 1991 annual rpt, 9627–35.2

Employment and other characteristics of science and engineering PhDs, by field and State, 1989, biennial rpt, 9627–18

Foreign countries science and engineering employment, by professional characteristics, age, and sex, for selected countries, 1991 working paper, 2326–18.62; 2326–18.63

Higher education instn science and engineering research system status, R&D performance, and Federal support, 1950s-88, 9628–83

NASA staff characteristics and personnel actions, FY90, annual rpt, 9504–1

NSF research grants to predominantly undergrad instns, by NSF div, and principal investigator sex and race, FY88, 9628–85

Nuclear engineering enrollment and degrees granted by instn and State, and grad placement, by student characteristics, 1990, annual rpt, 3004–5

Veterans Affairs

AIDS cases at VA health care centers by sex, race, risk factor, and facility, and AIDS prevention and treatment issues, quarterly rpt, 8702–1

Disability and death compensation cases of VA, by entitlement type, period of service, sex, age, and State, FY89, annual rpt, 8604–7

Homeless veterans domiciliary program of VA, participant characteristics and outcomes, 1990 annual rpt, 8604–10

Homeless veterans with mental illness, VA program services, costs, staff, client characteristics, and outcome, 1990, annual rpt, 8604–11

Hospitals of VA, patients discharged by diagnosis, compensation and pension status, and other characteristics, FY90, annual rpt, 8604–3.3

Housing programs of VA, costs, terms, and user characteristics, 1985-89, 8608–7

Mental health care services of VA, use, spending, and staff and patient characteristics, by State and services type, 1983 and 1986, 4506–3.43

VA employment characteristics and activities, FY90, annual rpt, 8604–3.8

Index by Titles

Index by Titles

Titles are listed alphabetically in natural word order, as they appear in the Abstracts Section. Titles beginning with numbers (e.g. "1990 Census . . . ") appear at the end of the Index. Where appropriate, alternate word-orders of titles have also been provided.

In addition to publication titles, individual report titles within a publication series are indexed, as are the titles of all periodical articles receiving individual abstracts.

AAFES Annual Report, 1988, 3504–21
AAFES Annual Report, 1989, 3504–21
AAFES Facts for Vendors, 1990, 3504–10
Abortion Surveillance, U.S., 1988, 4202–7.207
Abrasive Materials: Minerals Yearbook, Volume 1, 1989, 5604–15.3
Abuse and Mismanagement of HUD, Volume II, 25248–120
Academic Research Equipment and Equipment Needs in Selected Science and Engineering Fields, 1989-90, 9627–27.2
Academic Research Equipment and Equipment Needs in the Physical Sciences, 1989, 9627–27.3
Academic Research Equipment in Computer Science, Central Computer Facilities and Engineering, 1989, 9627–27.1
Academic Science/Engineering: Graduate Enrollment and Support, Fall 1989, 9627–7
Academic Science/Engineering R&D Expenditures, FY89, 9627–13
Academic Science/Engineering R&D Funds, 9627–13
Access: Catalogs and Technical Publications, 26404–6
Access: CDS, 26404–6
ACCESS: Medicare Program: Reducing Hospital Use Among Medicare Beneficiaries, 4658–43
Access to Health Care: Findings from the Survey of American Indians and Alaska Natives. National Medical Expenditure Survey, 4186–8.18
Access to Hospital Care for California and Michigan Medicaid Recipients, 4652–1.249
Access to Medicaid and Medicare by the Low-Income Disabled, 4652–1.218
Accessibility and Effectiveness of Care Under Medicaid, 4652–1.210
Accident/Incident Bulletin, 1990, No. 159, 7604–1
Accidental Shootings: Many Deaths and Injuries Caused by Firearms Could Be Prevented, 26131–80
Accidents, Fatalities and Rates: Air Carriers and General Aviation, 9614–9
Accidents of Motor Carriers of Property, 1988, 7554–9
Achievements, 1990, 9844–20
Acid Rain Publications by the U.S. Fish and Wildlife Service, 1979-89, 5506–5.26
Acidic Deposition: State of Science and Technology. Summary Report of the U.S. National Acid Precipitation Assessment Program, 14354–1

ACIR: The Year in Review, 32nd Annual Report, 10044–3
Acoustic Effects of Oil Production Activities on Bowhead and White Whales Visible During Spring Migration Near Point Barrow Alaska—1989 Phase: Sound Propagation and Whale Responses to Playbacks of Continuous Drilling Noise from an Ice Platform, as Studied in Pack Ice Conditions, 5738–27
ACP Monthly Progress Report, By State and Area for Period Ending (Date), 1802–15
Acreage, 1621–23
Acreage Reduction Program Enrollment, 1004–20
ACTION Annual Report, FY90, 9024–2
Action Needed To Improve Case-Processing Time at Headquarters. National Labor Relations Board, 26121–395
Actions Needed To Improve Its Usefulness. Education's Library, 26121–414
Active Compensation, Pension and Retirement Cases by Period of Service, 8602–5
Active Corporation Income Tax Returns, July 1988-June 1989. Source Book, Statistics of Income, 8304–21
Active Foreign Agricultural Research Grants, 1990, 1954–3
Activities of EPA Assistance Programs and Interagency-Intergovernmental Agreements, 9182–8
Activities of the Alaska District Water Resources Division, USGS, 1990, 5666–26.13
Activities of the Oil Implementation Task Force and Contracts for Field Projects and Supporting Research on Enhanced Oil Recovery, 3002–14
Actuarial Analysis of 1990 Operations for Life Insurance Programs Administered by the Department of Veterans Affairs, 8604–1
Actuarial Status of the HI and SMI Trust Funds, 4742–1.211
Actuarial Status of the OASI and DI Trust Funds, 4742–1.210
Actuarial Studies, 4706–1
Addendum (October 1991) to Division of Science Resources Studies Publications List: 1978-88 (NSF 88-335), 9627–22
Addendum to 1985 National Survey of Fishing, Hunting, and Wildlife-Associated Recreation: Recreational Shellfishing in the U.S., 2178–28
Additional FAA Oversight Needed of Aging Aircraft Repairs. Aircraft Maintenance, 26113–527
Additional 1990 Census Population, Housing Information Released for the Virgin Islands by Census Bureau, 2328–81
Additions and Resident Patients at End of Year: State and County Mental Hospitals, by Age and Diagnosis, by State, U.S., 1989, 4504–2
Adequacy of U.S. Direct Investment Data, 9366–7.255
Adjusted Census Data Would Redistribute Small Percentage of Funds to States. Formula Programs, 26119–361

Adjusting a Wage Index for Geographic Differences in Occupational Mix, 17206–2.17
Adjustments to the Medicare Prospective Payment System: Report to the Congress, 17204–3
Administration of the Marine Mammal Protection Act of 1972, Annual Report, Jan. 1-Dec. 31, 1989, 5504–12
Administration of the Radiation Control for Health and Safety Act of 1968, Public Law 90-602, 1990 Annual Report, 4064–13
Administration of the Wild Free-Roaming Horse and Burro Act: 8th Report to Congress, 1990, 5724–8
Administration's Budget Proposal for the SBA for FY91, Part 3, 25728–43
Administrative Office of the U.S. Courts, Annual Report of the Director, 1990, 18204–8
Administrative Office of the U.S. Courts, Report of the Director, 18204–16
Administrative Office of the U.S. Courts, 1991 Annual Report of the Director, 18204–2.2
Administratively Necessary Days, 4658–55
Adolescent Health, 26358–234
Adolescent Health. Volume I: Summary and Policy Options, 26358–234.1
ADP Procurement: Contracting and Market Share Information, 26125–41
Adult Learning and Literacy: Education for Homeless Adults, 4804–39
Adults' Accounts of Onset of Regular Smoking: Influences of School, Work, and Other Settings, 4042–3.217
Advance Data from Vital and Health Statistics of the National Center for Health Statistics, 4146–8
Advance Monthly Retail Sales, Current Business Reports, 2413–2
Advance Report of Final Divorce Statistics, 1987, 4147–24.4
Advance Report of Final Divorce Statistics, 1988, 4146–5.121
Advance Report of Final Marriage Statistics, 1987, 4147–24.4
Advance Report of Final Marriage Statistics, 1988, 4146–5.122
Advance Report of Final Mortality Statistics, 1987, 4147–24.4
Advance Report of Final Natality Statistics, 1987, 4147–24.4
Advance Report of Final Natality Statistics, 1989, 4146–5.123
Advanced Energy Projects, FY91 Research Summaries, 3004–18.6
Advanced Manufacturing Technology. Statistical Brief, 2326–17.23
Advanced Materials: Outlook and Information Requirements. Proceedings of a Bureau of Mines Conference, Nov. 7-8, 1989, Arlington, VA, 5608–167
Advanced Placement Programs in Public and Private Schools: Characteristics of Schools and Program Offerings, 1984-86, 4838–46
Advertising, Marketing and Promotional Practices of the Pharmaceutical Industry, 25548–103

Adviser, BLM: New Mexico,...

Index by Titles

Adviser, BLM: New Mexico, Oklahoma, Texas and Kansas, 1990, 5724–15

Aerial Surveys of Endangered Whales in the Beaufort Sea, Fall 1989, 5734–10

Aerial Surveys of Endangered Whales in the Beaufort Sea, Fall 1990, 5734–10

Aeronautics and Space Report of the President, 1988 Activities, 9504–9

Aeronautics and Space Report of the President, 1989-90 Activities, 9504–9

Aerospace Industry (Orders, Sales, and Backlog), 1990, Current Industrial Report, 2506–12.22

AFDC Recipient Characteristics Study, 1989, 4694–1

Affirmative Action Multi-Year Plan (MYP), 7004–21

Affirmative Employment Statistics for Executive Branch (Non-Postal) Agencies, as of Sept. 30, 1990, 9842–1.202

African Food Needs Assessment: Situation and Outlook Report, 1526–8.1

Aged SSI Recipients: Income, Work History, and Social Security Benefits, 4742–1.216

Agencies Need Death Information from Social Security To Avoid Erroneous Payments. Federal Benefit Payments, 26121–406

Age-Related Reductions in Life Insurance Benefits, 6722–1.216

Age-Specific Arrest Rates and Race-Specific Arrest Rates for Selected Offenses, 1965-89, 6224–7

AgExporter, 1922–2

Aggradation and Degradation of Alluvial Sand Deposits, 1965-86, Colorado River, Grand Canyon National Park, Ariz., 5668–122

Aggregate Reserves of Depository Institutions and Monetary Base, 9365–1

Aggregate Summaries of Annual Surveys of Securities Credit Extension, as of June 30, 1990, 9365–5.1

Aggregates, Directory of Principal Producers in the U.S. in 1990: Mineral Industry Surveys Annual Advance Summary Supplement, 5614–5.4

Aging and the Income Value of Housing Wealth, 2626–10.125

Aging Trends, 2326–19

Agricultural Chartbook, 1504–3

Agricultural Chemical Usage, 1616–1

Agricultural Commodities as Industrial Raw Materials, 26358–239

Agricultural Conservation Program (ACP) Monthly Progress Report, By State and Area for Period Ending (Date), 1802–15

Agricultural Conservation Program, FY90 Statistical Summary, 1804–7

Agricultural Credit Conditions Survey: Federal Reserve Bank of Minneapolis, 9383–11

Agricultural Finance Databook, 9365–3.10

Agricultural Income and Finance Situation and Outlook Report, 1541–1

Agricultural Interest Rates and Inflationary Expectations: A Regional Analysis, 1502–3.201

Agricultural Land Values and Markets Situation and Outlook Report. Agricultural Resources, 1561–16.202

Agricultural Letter, Federal Reserve Bank of Chicago, 9375–10

Agricultural Outlook, 1502–4

Agricultural Outlook Conference Proceedings, 1004–16

Agricultural Prices, Monthly Report, 1629–1

Agricultural Prices, 1990 Summary, 1629–5

Agricultural Privatization and Land Reform in Central Europe, 1522–3.202

Agricultural Productivity and International Food Trade: A Cross-Section Approach, 1548–372

Agricultural Prospects Following German Unification, 1522–3.201

Agricultural Resources Situation and Outlook Report, 1561–16

Agricultural Stabilization and Conservation Service Commodity Fact Sheets, 1806–4

Agricultural Stabilization and Conservation Service Payments to Producers by State and Program During 1990, 1804–12

Agricultural Statistics Board Catalog, 1991 Releases, 1614–1

Agricultural Statistics, 1990, 1004–1

Agricultural Trade Highlights, 1922–12

Agricultural Trade Implications of Environmental Management, 1522–3.203

Agricultural Trade Outlook, 1004–16.1

Agricultural Work Force: A Statistical Profile, 1594–2

Agriculture and Capital Gains Taxation, 1561–16.202

Agriculture and the Environment: 1991 Yearbook of Agriculture, 1004–18

Agriculture and Trade Reports, Situation and Outlook Series, 1524–4

Agriculture in a North American Free Trade Agreement, 1524–4.2

Agriculture in a World of Change: USDA Annual Outlook Conference, 1004–16

Agriculture Payments: Effectiveness of Efforts To Reduce Farm Payments Has Been Limited, 26113–546

AHCPR Grant Awards, FY90, 4186–9.10

AHCPR Health Technology Assessment Reports, 1990, 4186–10

AHCPR Program Notes, 4186–9

AID Can Improve Its Management and Oversight of Host Country Contracts. Foreign Assistance, 26123–342

AID, Congressional Presentation, FY92, 9904–4

AID, Congressional Presentation, FY92. Main Volume, 9904–4.1

AID, Congressional Presentation, FY92. Statistical Annex, 9904–4.5

AID Economic Policy Reform Program in Senegal, 9916–1.75

AID Economic Policy Reform Program in The Gambia, 9916–1.74

AID Energy Assistance and Global Warming. Foreign Assistance, 26123–352

AID Evaluation Special Studies, 9916–3

AID Impact Evaluation Reports, 9916–1

AID, Summary Tables, FY92, 9904–4.4

Aid to Panama: Status of Emergency Assistance To Revitalize the Economy, 26123–330

AIDS Awareness in North Dakota: A Knowledge and Attitude Study of the General Population, 4042–3.211

AIDS Gram, 8702–1

AIDS in U.S. Hospitals, 1986-87: A National Perspective, 4186–6.15

AIDS Knowledge and Attitudes of Black Americans: U.S., 1990. Provisional Data from the National Health Interview Survey, 4146–8.208

AIDS Knowledge and Attitudes of Hispanic Americans: U.S., 1990. Provisional Data from the National Health Interview Survey, 4146–8.209

AIDS Knowledge and Attitudes for April-June 1990. Provisional Data from the National Health Interview Survey, 4146–8.195

AIDS Knowledge and Attitudes for July-September 1990. Provisional Data from the National Health Interview Survey, 4146–8.201

AIDS Knowledge and Attitudes for October-December 1990. Provisional Data from the National Health Interview Survey, 4146–8.205

AIDS Knowledge in Low-Income and Minority Populations, 4042–3.210

AIDS Patient Registry, 8702–1

AIDS Weekly Surveillance Report, 4202–9

AIDS-Prevention Programs: High-Risk Groups Still Prove Hard To Reach, 26121–428

AIDS-Related Knowledge and Behavior Among Women 15-44 Years of Age: U.S., 1988, 4146–8.200

Air Carrier Aircraft Utilization and Propulsion Reliability Report, 7502–13

Air Carrier Financial Statistics Quarterly, 7302–7

Air Carrier Industry Scheduled Service Traffic Statistics Quarterly, 7302–8

Air Carrier Passenger Enplanements, All Cargo Landings and Apportionments, 1989, 7504–48

Air Carrier Traffic Statistics Monthly, 7302–6

Air Force and Army Processes for Selected Bases To Close in Europe. Overseas Basing, 26123–336

Air Force Comptroller, 3602–1

Air Force Revises Job Availability but Entry Screening Needs Review. Women in the Military, 26123–359

Air Pollution and Acid Rain Reports, 5506–5

Air Quality Criteria for Lead, 9198–84

Air Travel Consumer Report: Flight Delays, Mishandled Baggage, Oversales, and Consumer Complaints, 7302–11

Air Travel: Passengers Could Be Better Informed of Their Rights, 26113–542

Airborne Monitoring and Smoke Characterization of Prescribed Fires on Forest Lands in Western Washington and Oregon: Final Report, 1208–343

Aircraft Accident Reports: Brief Format, U.S. Civil and Foreign Aviation, 9612–1

Aircraft Maintenance: Additional FAA Oversight Needed of Aging Aircraft Repairs, 26113–527

Aircraft Maintenance: Potential Shortage in National Aircraft Repair Capacity, 26113–492

Airport Activity Statistics of Certificated Route Air Carriers, 1990, 7504–35

Airport and Airway Trust Fund, 8102–9.5

Airport Capacity: Civilian Use of Military Airfields Has Added Little to System Capacity, 26113–524

Airport Capacity Enhancement Plan, 7504–43

Airport Grant Allocations, 7502–14

Airport Improvement Program, 9th Annual Report of Accomplishments, FY90, 7504–38

Alaska Coastal Wetlands Survey, 5506–11.5

Alaska Cooperative Snow Survey Data of Federal-State-Private Cooperative Snow Surveys, Water Year 1990, 1264–14.4

Alaska OCS Oil and Gas Lease Sale 124, Beaufort Sea Planning Area. Final Environmental Impact Statement, 5736–1.22

Index by Titles

Alaska Riparian Area Management Strategy, 5726–8.3

Alaska Statewide and Regional Economic and Demographic Systems: Effects of OCS Exploration and Development, 1990, 5736–5.11

Alaska Submerged Lands Act Report Analysis of Inholdings, Acquisition Priorities and Recommendations to Reduce Impacts on Conservation System Units in Alaska, 5728–38

Alaska's Mineral Resources, 1990 Annual Report, 5664–11

Alcohol Consumption in a 1986 Sample of Deaths, 4482–1.201

Alcohol, Drug Abuse, and Mental Health Research Grant Awards, FY90, 4044–13

Alcohol Epidemiologic Data System Surveillance Reports, 4486–1

Alcohol Health and Research World, 4482–1

Alcohol Involvement in Fatal Traffic Crashes, 1989, 7764–16

Alcoholism Screening Procedures Should Be Improved. VA Health Care, 26121–416

Algebra of Price Stability, 9379–12.79

Alternative Agriculture: Perspectives of the National Academy of Sciences and the Council for Agricultural Sciences and Technology, 23848–222

Alternative Allocations of Water in Rural Areas, 1502–7.203

Alternative Garden Crops for the 21st Century, 1004–16.1

Alternative Hospital Market Area Definitions, 17206–2.20

Alternative Measures of Money as Indicators of Inflation: A Survey and Some New Evidence, 9391–1.202

Alternative Measures of the Rate of Return on Direct Investment, 2702–1.217

Alternatives for Improving the Distribution of Funds. Medicaid, 26121–420

Aluminum Industry: Mineral Industry Surveys, 5612–1.1

Aluminum Ingot and Mill Products, Current Industrial Report, 2506–10.9

Ambulatory Practice Variation in Maryland: Implications for Medicaid Cost Management, 4652–1.211

"America Responds to AIDS": Its Content, Development Process, and Outcome, 4042–3.256

American Historical Association, Annual Report, 1989, 29574–2

American Housing Brief. Housing Profiles, 2485–11

American Housing Survey for Selected Metropolitan Areas: 1984, Supplement, 2485–8

American Housing Survey for the Cleveland Metropolitan Area in 1988, 2485–6.3

American Housing Survey for the Indianapolis Metropolitan Area in 1988, 2485–6.4

American Housing Survey for the Memphis Metropolitan Area in 1988, 2485–6.1

American Housing Survey for the Milwaukee Metropolitan Area in 1988, 2485–6.2

American Housing Survey for the Oklahoma City Metropolitan Area in 1988, 2485–6.6

American Housing Survey for the Providence-Pawtucket-Warwick, Metropolitan Area in 1988, 2485–6.7

American Housing Survey for the Salt Lake City Metropolitan Area in 1988, 2485–6.5

American Housing Survey for the San Jose Metropolitan Area in 1988, 2485–6.8

American Housing Survey for the U.S. in 1985, Supplement, 2485–13

American Housing Survey for the U.S. in 1987, Supplement, 2485–13

American Housing Survey for the U.S. in 1989, 2485–12

American Housing Survey: Metropolitan Areas, 2485–6

American Red Cross Annual Report, 1989-90, 29254–1

American Woodcock Harvest and Breeding Population Status, 1991, 5504–11

Americans in Agriculture: 1990 Yearbook of Agriculture, 1004–18

America's Agriculture, 2346–1

America's Agriculture: Part-Time Farmers, 2346–1.4

America's Wars, 8604–2

AMS Food Purchases: Weekly Summary, 1302–3

Anabolic Steroid Abuse, 4498–67

Anadromous Fish Habitat Management on Public Lands: A Strategy for the Future, 5726–6.1

Analyses of DRG Classification and Assignment, 17206–2.18

Analyses of Natural Gases, 1990, 5604–2

Analysis and Evaluation, Federal Juvenile Delinquency Programs, 6064–11

Analysis of a Proposal To Privatize Trust Fund Reserves. Social Security, 26121–397

Analysis of Construction Fatalities—The OSHA Data Base 1985-89, 6608–4

Analysis of Financial Performance of Federal Land Banks, Federal Intermediate Credit Banks, Farm Credit Banks, and Related Associations, 1986-89, 1548–381

Analysis of International Air Travel to and from the U.S. on U.S./Foreign Flag Carriers During 1990: Including a Special Analysis of the Period 1981-90, 2904–13

Analysis of Long-Term Contracts for Imports of Canadian Natural Gas, 3162–4.206

Analysis of Nuclear Power Plant Operating Costs: A 1991 Update, 3168–108

Analysis of Nursing Home Capital Reimbursement Systems, 4652–1.236

Analysis of the Economic and Environmental Effects of Alternative Automotive Fuels, 9196–5

Analysis of the Economic and Environmental Effects of Compressed Natural Gas as a Vehicle Fuel: Volume I, Passenger Cars and Light Trucks, 9196–5.2

Analysis of the Economic and Environmental Effects of Compressed Natural Gas as a Vehicle Fuel: Volume II, Heavy-Duty Vehicles, 9196–5.3

Analysis of the Economic and Environmental Effects of Ethanol as an Automotive Fuel, 9196–5.4

Analysis of the Economic and Environmental Effects of Methanol as an Automotive Fuel, 9196–5.1

Analysis of the President's Budgetary Proposals for FY92, 26304–2

Analysis of the Role of Cancer Prevention and Control Measures in Reducing Cancer Mortality, 4472–1.232

Analysis of the Timber Situation in Alaska: 1970-2010, 1208–367

Analysis of the Timber Situation in the U.S.: 1989-2040, 1208–24.20

Annual Report of the Attorney...

Analytical Report Series. Manufacturing, 2506–16

Analyzing Domestic Mill Consumption of U.S. Upland Cotton, 1561–1.202

Anatomy of the International Debt Crisis, 9292–4.201

Anchor Ice and Bottom-Freezing in High-Latitude Marine Sedimentary Environments: Observations from the Alaskan Beaufort Sea, 2176–1.38

Animal Welfare Enforcement, FY89, Report of the Secretary of Agriculture to the President of the Senate and the Speaker of the House of Representatives, 1394–10

Announcing the Standard for C. Software Standard, 2216–2.199

Annual Distribution of 1990 Marketing Costs. Postal Service, 26119–338

Annual Emergency Room Data, 1990: Statistical Series I. Number 10, 4494–8

Annual Energy Outlook 1991 with Projections to 2010, 3164–75

Annual Energy Review, 1990, 3164–74

Annual Estimates of Nonimmigrant Overstays in the U.S.: 1985-88, 6264–5

Annual Evaluation Report, FY90, 4804–5

Annual Financial Report, FY90, Federal Aviation Administration, 7504–10

Annual Historical Review of FNS Programs, FY89, 1364–9

Annual Housing Survey, Components of Inventory Change: 1973-83, 2485–14

Annual Housing Survey: Supplementary Report. Summary of Housing Characteristics for Selected Metropolitan Areas, 2485–8

Annual Index: Reports Issued in (Year), 26104–17

Annual Input-Output Accounts of the U.S. Economy, 1986, 2702–1.206

Annual Intercensal Estimates of the Resident Population of States: 1981-89, 2324–10

Annual Medical Examiner Data, 1990: Statistical Series I. Number 10, 4494–8

Annual Medicare Program Statistics, 4657–5

Annual Outlook for Oil and Gas, 1991, 3164–89

Annual Outlook for U.S. Coal, 1991, 3164–68

Annual Outlook for U.S. Electric Power 1991, Projections Through 2010, 3164–81

Annual Procurement Report: NASA, 9502–6

Annual Prospects for World Coal Trade, 1991, 3164–77

Annual Report and Summaries of FY91 Activities: Division of Energy Biosciences, 3004–18.4

Annual Report: Budget Review, 1990-91, 9364–10

Annual Report, Navajo and Hopi Relocation Commission, 16004–1

Annual Report of Energy Purchased by REA Borrowers, 1989, 1244–5

Annual Report of Lands Under Control of the U.S. Fish and Wildlife Service, As of Sept. 30, 1990, 5504–8

Annual Report of Lands Under Control of the U.S. Fish and Wildlife Service, As of Sept. 30, 1991, 5504–8

Annual Report of the Architect of the Capitol for the Period Oct. 1, 1987-Sept. 30, 1988, 25944–1

Annual Report of the Attorney General of the U.S. on the Private Counsel Debt Collection Pilot Project for FY89, 6004–20

Annual Report of the Attorney... Index by Titles

Annual Report of the Attorney General of the U.S. on the Private Counsel Debt Collection Pilot Project for FY90, 6004–20

Annual Report of the Board of Trustees of the Federal Hospital Insurance Trust Fund, 1991, 4654–11

Annual Report of the Board of Trustees of the Federal Old-Age and Survivors Insurance and Disability Insurance Trust Funds, 1990, 4704–4

Annual Report of the Board of Trustees of the Federal Old-Age and Survivors Insurance and Disability Insurance Trust Funds, 1991, 4704–4

Annual Report of the Board of Trustees of the Federal Supplementary Medical Insurance Trust Fund, 1991, 4654–12

Annual Report of the Chairman of the Development Coordination Committee, 9904–1

Annual Report of the Code Committee on Military Justice, 3504–3

Annual Report of the Council of Economic Advisers, 204–1

Annual Report of the Department of Justice Asset Forfeiture Program, FY90, 6004–21

Annual Report of the Director of the Administrative Office of the U.S. Courts, 1990, 18204–8

Annual Report of the Director of the U.S. Mint, FY90, 8204–1

Annual Report of the Federal Trade Commission, FY88, 9404–1

Annual Report of the Federal Trade Commission, FY89, 9404–1

Annual Report of the Librarian of Congress, FY90, 26404–1

Annual Report of the Marine Mammal Commission, 1990, 14734–1

Annual Report of the Military Sealift Command, FY90, 3804–14

Annual Report of the Office of Justice Programs, FY90, 6064–18

Annual Report of the Organized Drug Enforcement Task Force Program, 6004–17

Annual Report of the Postmaster General, FY90, 9864–1

Annual Report of the Register of Copyrights, 26404–2

Annual Report of the Rehabilitation Services Administration on Federal Activities Related to the Administration of the Rehabilitation Act of 1973, as Amended, FY90, 4944–1

Annual Report of the Research Grants Program, FY90, 9184–18

Annual Report of the Secretary of Labor Under the Federal Mine Safety and Health Act of 1977, FY89, 6664–6

Annual Report of the Secretary of the Army on Civil Works Activities, 3754–1

Annual Report of the Secretary of Veterans Affairs, FY90, 8604–3

Annual Report of the Surface Air Sampling Program, 3004–31

Annual Report of the U.S. Parole Commission, Oct. 1, 1989-Sept. 30, 1990, 6004–3

Annual Report on Hazardous Materials Transportation, 1989, 7304–4

Annual Report on Low-Level Radioactive Waste Management Progress, 1989, 3354–14

Annual Report on Pipeline Safety, 1989, 7304–5

Annual Report on Sharing of Specialized Medical Resources, Pursuant to the Provisions of 38 U.S.C. Section 5053(e), Secretary of Veterans Affairs, FY90, 8704–5

Annual Report on Strategic Special Nuclear Material Inventory Differences, 3004–32, 3344–2

Annual Report on the Employment of Minorities, Women and People with Disabilities in the Federal Government, FY89, 9244–10

Annual Report on the Impact of the Caribbean Basin Economic Recovery Act on U.S. Industries and Consumers, Sixth Report, 1990, 9884–20

Annual Report on the Status of the Senior Executive Service, 9844–36

Annual Report on Tobacco Statistics, 1989, 1319–1

Annual Report on Tobacco Statistics, 1990, 1319–1

Annual Report Submitted to the Committees on Armed Services of the U.S. Senate and House of Representatives, and to the Secretary of Defense, Secretary of Transportation, and Secretaries of the Army, Navy, and Air Force, Oct. 1, 1989-Sept. 30, 1990, 3504–3

Annual Report to Congress for 1990, Foreign Claims Settlement Commission, 6004–16

Annual Report to Congress: Indian Civil Service Retirement Act, P.L. 96-135, FY89, 4084–6

Annual Report to Congress: Office of Civilian Radioactive Waste Management, 3364–1

Annual Report to Congress on Federal Energy Conservation Programs, 3304–25

Annual Report to Congress on Federal Government Energy Management and Conservation Programs, FY90, 3304–22

Annual Report to Congress on the Community Development Block Grant Program, 1991, 5124–8

Annual Report to Congress on the Federal Equal Opportunity Recruitment Program, 9844–33

Annual Report to Congress on the Urban Development Action Grant Program, 5124–5

Annual Report to Congress 1990: Energy Information Administration, 3164–29

Annual Report to Congress, 1990: Federal Grain Inspection Service, 1294–1

Annual Report to the Congress, FY90, 26354–3

Annual Report to the Congress of the U.S. for the Period Oct. 1, 1989-Sept. 30, 1990, from the Director of the Selective Service System, 9744–1

Annual Report to the Congress of the U.S. on Donation of Surplus Personal Property, 9454–22

Annual Report to the Congress on Community Planning and Development Housing Rehabilitation Programs, FY90, 5124–7

Annual Report to the Congress on the Runaway and Homeless Youth Program, FY88, 4604–3

Annual Report to the Congress on the Runaway and Homeless Youth Program, FY89, 4604–3

Annual Report to the Congress on the Runaway and Homeless Youth Program, FY90, 4604–3

Annual Report to the President and the Congress on the State Energy Conservation Program for Calendar Year 1989, 3304–1

Annual Report to the President, FY90, Information Security Oversight Office, 9454–21

Annual Report, U.S. Department of Education, FY89-90, 4804–6

Annual Report, 1988-89, U.S. National Commission on Libraries and Information Science, 15634–1

Annual Report, 1989-90, U.S. National Commission on Libraries and Information Science, 15634–1

Annual Report—1990, Environmental Monitoring for EG&G Idaho Facilities at the Idaho National Engineering Laboratory, 3354–10

Annual Research Conference, 1989. Mar. 19-22, 1989: Proceedings, 2624–2

Annual Research Conference, 1990. Mar. 18-21, 1990: Proceedings, 2624–2

Annual Research Conference, 1991. Mar. 17-20, 1991: Proceedings, 2624–2

Annual Review of Aircraft Accident Data, U.S. Air Carrier Operations, 1987, 9614–2

Annual Review of Aircraft Accident Data, U.S. General Aviation, 1988, 9614–3

Annual Review of the Chief, National Guard Bureau, FY90, 3504–22

Annual Sales and Year-End Inventories, Purchases, and Gross Margin Estimates of Merchant Wholesalers. 1990 Wholesale Trade. Current Business Reports, 2413–13

Annual Sales, Year-End Inventories, Purchases, Gross Margin, and Accounts Receivable, by Kind of Retail Store. 1989 Retail Trade. Current Business Reports, 2413–5

Annual Status Report on the Uranium Mill Tailings Remedial Action Program, 3354–9

Annual Summary of Births, Marriages, Divorces, and Deaths: U.S., 1990. Monthly Vital Statistics Report, 4144–7

Annual Survey of Manufactures, 1989, 2506–15

Annual Test Report, Department of Defense Dependents Schools, 1990-91, 3504–16

Annual Tropical Cyclone Report, 1990, 3804–8

Annual U.S. Economic Data, 1971-90, 9391–9

Another Look at the Medically Uninsured Using the 1987 Consumer Expenditure Survey, 6886–6.75

Anticipations of Foreign Exchange Volatility and Bid-Ask Spreads, 9366–7.263

Anti-Drug Programs in the Workplace: Are They Here To Stay?, 6722–1.224

Antifriction Bearings, 1990, Current Industrial Report, 2506–12.28

Antimony: Mineral Industry Surveys, 5612–2.1

Antimony: Minerals Yearbook, Volume 1, 1989, 5604–15.5

AOML Annual Report, FY90, 2144–19

Appalachian Highway Program, As Reported by States, 9082–1

Appalachian Highway Program Cumulative Corridor Mileage Summary, 9082–1.3

Appalachian Highway Program Cumulative Mileage Summary, 9082–1.2

Appalachian Highway Program Funding Requirements, 9082–1.1

Index by Titles

Appalachian Regional Commission, 1990 Annual Report, 9084–1

Apparel, Current Industrial Report, 2506–6.1, 2506–6.12

Apparel Expenditures of Older Consumers, 1702–1.202

Apparent Consumption of Industrial Explosives and Blasting Agents in the U.S., 1990. Mineral Industry Surveys, 5614–22

Apple Import Demand: Four Markets for U.S. Fresh Apples, 1568–296

Apples: Certain Conditions of Competition Between the U.S. and Canadian Industries. Report to the Committee on Finance, U.S. Senate, on Investigation No. 332-305 Under Section 332(g) of the Tariff Act of 1930, 9886–4.172

Application of the Leslie Model to Commercial Catch and Effort of the Slipper Lobster, Scyllarides squammosus, Fishery in the Northwestern Hawaiian Islands, 2162–1.203

Applications Received in 1987 and Allowance Rates for Supplemental Security Income, 4742–1.213

Applying Features of Other Countries' Reserves Could Provide Benefits. Army Reserve Forces, 26123–358

Applying Sociotechnical Work System Design Principles in the IRS, 8304–8.1

Apportionments to States from the Land and Water Conservation Fund, FY91, 5544–15

Approval of Awards to Institutions Participating in the College Work-Study, Supplemental Educational Opportunity Grant, and Perkins Loan Programs: Notification to Members of Congress, 4804–17

Aquaculture Situation and Outlook Report, 1561–15

Architect of the Capitol, Annual Report for the Period Oct. 1, 1987-Sept. 30, 1988, 25944–1

Architectural and Transportation Barriers Compliance Board, Annual Report, 17614–1

Arctic Fish Habitat Use Investigations: Nearshore Studies in the Alaskan Beaufort Sea, Summer 1988, 2176–1.37

Are District Presidents More Conservative than Board Governors?, 9373–1.214

Are District Services Jobs Bad Jobs?, 9391–16.205

Are Most-Favored-Nation Exclusions in the Interests of Developing Countries?, 1524–4.2

Are the Preliminary Announcements of Some Macroeconomic Variables Rational?, 9385–8.94

Area Trends, A Supplement to FHA Trends, Section 203 Home Mortgages Insured by FHA, 5142–2

Area Trends in Employment and Unemployment, 6402–1

Area Wage Survey Summary for the Southeast, 1990, 6946–3.21

Area Wage Surveys, 6785–3

Area Wage Surveys: Bull. 3055 Series, 6785–11

Area Wage Surveys: Bull. 3060 Series, 6785–12

Area Wage Surveys, Selected Metropolitan Areas, 1990, 6785–1

Argentina's Experience with Parallel Exchange Markets: 1981-90, 9366–7.261

Arizona Cooperative Snow Survey Data of Federal-State-Private Cooperative Snow Surveys, Water Year 1990, 1264–14.8

Arizona Riparian-Wetland Area Management Strategy, 5726–8.4

Arizona Riparian-Wetland Area Management Strategy, Supplemental Information., 5726–8.4

Arms Control: Intermediate-Range Nuclear Forces Treaty Implementation, 26123–364

Army and Air Force Exchange Service Annual Report, 1988, 3504–21

Army and Air Force Exchange Service Annual Report, 1989, 3504–21

Army Biomedical Research: Concerns About Performance of Brain-Wound Research, 26121–396

Army Logistics: Better Management of the Army's Unserviceable Inventories Could Save Millions, 26123–312

Army Reserve Components: Better Training Could Improve General Support Maintenance Capability, 26123–354

Army Reserve Forces: Applying Features of Other Countries' Reserves Could Provide Benefits, 26123–358

Army Training: Computer Simulations Can Improve Command Training in Large-Scale Exercises, 26123–318

Arsenic in 1990: Mineral Industry Surveys Annual Review, 5614–5.6

Asbestos Issues, 25328–32

Asbestos: Minerals Yearbook, Volume 1, 1990, 5604–20.6

Asbestos Trust Fund, 8102–9.13

ASCS Commodity Fact Sheets, 1806–4

Asian Surimi Industry, 2162–1.202

Aspects of Teacher Supply and Demand in Public School Districts and Private Schools: 1987-88. Schools and Staffing Survey, 4836–3.6

Aspherical Ophthalmoscopy Lenses from Japan. Determination of the Commission in Investigation No. 731-TA-518 (Preliminary) Under the Tariff Act of 1930, Together with the Information Obtained in the Investigation, 9886–14.318

Assessing the Affordability of Private Long-Term Care Insurance, Part 10, 23898–8

Assessment of How Well the CIA Has Estimated the Size of the Economy. Soviet Economy, 26123–365

Assessment of Rules of Origin Under the Caribbean Basin Economic Recovery Act. Report to the President, the Committee on Finance, U.S. Senate, and the Committee on Ways and Means, House of Representatives, on Investigation No. 332-298 Under Section 332 of the Tariff Act of 1930, 9886–4.171

Assessment of the Impact of AID's Participant Training Programs in Nepal, 9916–3.62

Assessment of the Quality of Selected EIA Data Series, 3166–12

Assessment of Wastewater Treatment Facilities in Small Communities, 1588–155

Assets and Liabilities of Insured Domestically Chartered and Foreign Related Banking Institutions, 9365–1

Assistance to Disabled Persons in Developing Countries. Foreign Assistance, 26123–321

Assisted Housing: Utility Allowances Often Fall Short of Actual Utility Expenses, 26113–512

Association Between Exercise and Other Preventive Health Behaviors Among Diabetics, 4042–3.246

Association of Asbestos Exposure with Colorectal Adenomatous Polyps and Cancer, 4472–1.238

Association of Prenatal Nutrition and Educational Services with Low Birth Weight Rates in a Florida Program, 4042–3.235

Association of Sea Turtles with Petroleum Platforms in the North-Central Gulf of Mexico, 5738–26

Association of Selected Cancers with Service in the U.S. Military in Vietnam, Final Report, 4208–33

Assumptions for the Annual Energy Outlook, 1991, 3164–90

Astronomical Almanac for the Year 1991, 3804–7

Astronomical Almanac for the Year 1992, 3804–7

Asymmetric Information, Repeated Lending, and Capital Structure, 9379–14.13

Atlantic Outer Continental Shelf Environmental Support Documents, 5736–6

Atlantis To Boost Fourth NASA Tracking Satellite, 9506–2.143

Atlas of State Profiles Which Estimate Number of Migrant and Seasonal Farmworkers and Members of Their Families, 4108–53

Atlas of U.S. Cancer Mortality Among Nonwhites: 1950-80, 4478–78

Atlas/Data Abstract for the U.S. and Selected Areas, FY89, 3544–29

Atlas/Data Abstract for the U.S. and Selected Areas, FY90, 3544–29

Attorney General's Annual Report on the Justice Assets Forfeiture Fund for FY89, 6004–21

Audit of Testing Laboratory Support to the Environmental Survey Program, 3006–5.21

Audit of the Cost Effectiveness of Contracting for Headquarters Support Services, 3006–5.24

Automated Record Checks of Firearm Purchasers: Issues and Options, 26358–244

Automatic Data Processing Equipment in the U.S. Government: Third and Fourth Quarter, FY90 Summary, 9452–9

Automotive Fuel Economy Program, Fourteenth Annual Report to the Congress, 7764–9

Automotive Products Trade Act of 1965, Twenty-second Annual Report (1987) to the Congress, 2044–35

Automotive Products Trade Act of 1965, Twenty-third Annual Report (1988) to the Congress, 2044–35

Automotive Technology Development Program 12th Annual Report to Congress, 3304–17

Auxiliary Establishments. Enterprise Statistics, 1987, 2329–6

Availability and Distribution of Psychiatric Beds, U.S. and Each State, 1986, 4506–3.41

Availability and Use of Hepatitis B Vaccine in Laboratory and Nursing Schools in the U.S., 4042–3.244

Availability of Census Records About Individuals, 2326–7.81

Availability of Federal Land for Mineral Exploration and Development in Western States, 5606–7

Availability of Federally...

Index by Titles

Availability of Federally Owned Minerals for Exploration and Development in Western States, 5606–7

Availability of Land for Mineral Exploration and Development in Alaska, 5608–152

Availability of Land for Mineral Exploration and Development in Northern Alaska, 1986, 5608–152.6

Availability of Land for Mineral Exploration and Development in Southeastern Alaska, 1984, 5608–152.5

Availability of Primary Nickel in Market-Economy Countries. A Minerals Availability Appraisal, 5606–4.28

Average Annual Pay, 6784–17

Average Annual Pay by State and Industry, 1990, 6784–17.1

Average Annual Pay for the Southeast, 1990, 6946–3.22

Average Annual Pay Levels in Metropolitan Areas, 1990, 6784–17.2

Aviation Noise: Costs of Phasing Out Noisy Aircraft, 26113–534

Aviation Safety: Emergency Revocation Orders of Air Carrier Certificates, 26113–547

Aviation Safety: Limited Success Rebuilding Staff and Finalizing Aging Aircraft Plan, 26113–522

Aviation Safety Statistics, 7502–15

Aviation System Capacity Plan, 1990-91, 7504–43

Aviation System: Capital Investment Plan, 7504–12

Back Injuries in Underground Coal Mining, 5608–166

Background Material and Data on Programs Within the Jurisdiction of the Committee on Ways and Means. Overview of Entitlement Programs. 1991 Green Book, 21784–11

Background Materials on Federal Budget and Tax Policy for FY92 and Beyond, 21788–203

Background Notes on the Countries of the World, 7006–2

Background on Egypt's Cotton Sector, 1561–1.201

Back-to-School Forecast, 1991, 4804–19

Bad News from a Forecasting Model of the U.S. Economy, 9383–6.201

Bail Reform, 25528–114

Balance of Payments and Direct Investment Position Estimates, 1980-86. Foreign Direct Investment in the U.S., 2708–41

Balance Sheets for the U.S. Economy, 1945-90, 9365–4.1

Balances of Budget Authority: Budget of the U.S. Government, FY92, 104–8

Balancing Act: Tax Structure in the Seventh District, 9375–1.211

Balancing Work Responsibilities and Family Needs: The Federal Service Response, 9496–2.7

Ball Bearings, Mounted or Unmounted, and Parts Thereof, from Argentina, Austria, Brazil, Canada, Hong Kong, Hungary, Mexico, the People's Republic of China, Poland, the Republic of Korea, Spain, Taiwan, Turkey and Yugoslavia. Determinations of the Commission in Investigation Nos. 701-TA-307 (Preliminary) and 731-TA-498-511 (Preliminary) Under the Tariff Act of 1930, Together with the Information Obtained in the Investigations, 9886–19.74

Banca Nazionale Del Lavoro Affair and Regulation and Supervision of U.S. Branches and Agencies of Foreign Banks, 21248–155

Bank Cost of Capital and International Competition, 9385–1.203

Bank Credit Commitments, 9381–10.121

Bank Credit "Crumble", 9385–1.208

Bank Failure Contagion in Historical Perspective, 9385–8.99

Bank Holding Companies Securities Subsidiaries' Market Activities Update. Bank Powers, 26119–280

Bank Holding Company Performance, 9381–14.1

Bank Loan Commitments and the Transmission of Monetary Policy, 9385–8.75

Bank Powers: Bank Holding Companies Securities Subsidiaries' Market Activities Update, 26119–280

Bank Structure and Competition, Proceedings of the 26th Annual Conference, May 9-11, 1990, Federal Reserve Bank of Chicago, 9375–7

Bank Supervision: Prompt and Forceful Regulatory Actions Needed, 26119–334

Banking at Credit Unions: An Industry Profile, 9391–16.210

Banking Industry in Turmoil: A Report on the Condition of the U.S. Banking Industry and the Bank Insurance Fund, 21248–147

Banking Review, FDIC, 9292–4

Banking Structure Laws: Current Status and Recommendations for Change, 9381–14.1

Banking Studies, Federal Reserve Bank of Kansas City, 9381–14

Banking Studies, Federal Reserve Bank of Kansas City, 1991 Annual, 9381–14.1

Bargaining Activity in 1992, 6726–1.43

Bargaining Calendar, 1991, 6784–9

Barite: Minerals Yearbook, Volume 1, 1989, 5604–15.7

Barite: Minerals Yearbook, Volume 1, 1990, 5604–20.7

Barter and Monetary Exchange Under Private Information, 9383–20.11

Base Structure Report for FY91, 3504–11

Basin Outlook Reports and Federal-State-Private Cooperative Snow Surveys, 1266–2

BATF: Management Improvements Needed To Handle Increasing Responsibilities, 26119–335

Battleships: Issues Arising from the Explosion Aboard the U.S.S. Iowa, 26123–315

Bauxite, Alumina, and Aluminum: Minerals Yearbook, Volume 1, 1989, 5604–15.8

Bauxite and Alumina: Mineral Industry Surveys, 5612–2.2

Beaches Environmental Assessment, Closure, and Health Act of 1990, 21568–50

Bean Market News, 1311–17

Bean Market Summary, 1990, 1311–18

Beefpacking and Processing Plants: Computer-Assisted Cost Analysis, 1568–301

Beer: Monthly Statistical Release, 8486–1.1

Behavior of Bowhead Whales of the Davis Strait and Bering/Beaufort Stocks vs. Regional Differences in Human Activities, 5738–30

Behavior of Real Rates of Interest in a Small, Opening Economy, 9371–10.56

Behavior of Retail Gasoline Prices: Symmetric or Not?, 9391–1.216

Beige Book: Summary of Commentary on Current Economic Conditions by Federal Reserve District, 9362–8

Benchmark Input-Output Accounts for the U.S. Economy, 1982, 2702–1.213

Beneath the Bottom Line: Agricultural Approaches To Reduce Agrichemical Contamination of Groundwater, 26358–231

Benefits and Beneficiaries Under Public Employee Retirement Systems, FY88, 4742–1.212

Benzyl Paraben from Japan: Determination of the Commission in Investigation No. 731-TA-462 (Final) Under the Tariff Act of 1930, Together with the Information Obtained in the Investigation, 9886–14.303

Bering Sea Phytoplankton Studies, 2176–1.37

Beryllium: Minerals Yearbook, Volume 1, 1990, 5604–20.9

Better Consumer Protection Should Result from 1990 Changes to Baucus Amendment. Medigap Insurance, 26121–410

Better EEOC Guidance and Agency Analysis of Underrepresentation Needed. Federal Affirmative Action, 26119–342

Better Management of the Army's Unserviceable Inventories Could Save Millions. Army Logistics, 26123–312

Better Management of the Military Services' Vehicles Could Save Millions. Motor Vehicles, 26123–344

Better Models Can Reduce Resource Disparities Among Offices. U.S. Attorneys, 26119–323

Better Reporting Needed for Compensation and Assistance Programs. Victims of Crime Act Grants, 26119–348

Better Training Could Improve General Support Maintenance Capability. Army Reserve Components, 26123–354

Beyond Perestroyka: The Soviet Economy in Crisis, 9114–6

Beyond Plain Vanilla: A Taxonomy of Swaps, 9371–1.205

Beyond Rhetoric: A New American Agenda for Children and Families. Final Report, 15528–1

Biannual Water-Resources Review, White Sands Missile Range, New Mexico, 1986-87, 5666–28.7

Bibliography of GAO Documents, 26106–10

Bibliography on Health Indexes, 4122–1

Bid Opening Report: Federal-Aid Highway Construction Contracts, 1990, 7552–12

Bid Opening Report: Federal-Aid Highway Construction Contracts, First Six Months 1991, 7552–12

Biennial Report of the Director, National Institutes of Health, 1989-90, 4434–16

Biennial Report of the National Institutes of Health, 4434–16

Biological Rhythms: Implications for the Worker. New Developments in Neuroscience, 26356–9.3

Biology and Potential Use of Pacific Grenadier, Coryphaenoides acrolepis, Off California, 2162–1.204

Biomass Statistics for Maryland, 1986, 1206–43.3

Biomass Statistics for the Northeastern Region, 1206–43

Biometric Monographs, 9926–1

Biotechnology in a Global Economy, 26358–248

Index by Titles

Bipartisan Commission on Comprehensive Health Care, U.S., Supplement to the Final Report. The Pepper Commission. Call for Action, 23898–5

Bird Populations in Logged and Unlogged Western Larch/Douglas-fir Forest in Northwestern Montana, 1208–372

Birth and Fertility Rates by Education: 1980 and 1985: Vital and Health Statistics Series 21, 4147–21.49

Bismuth in 1990: Mineral Industry Surveys Annual Review, 5614–5.9

Bismuth: Mineral Industry Surveys, 5612–2.3

BJS Data Report, 1989, 6064–25

Black Lung Benefits Act: Annual Report on Administration of the Act During 1989, 6504–3

Black Lung Benefits Act: Annual Report on Administration of the Act During 1990, 6504–3

Black Lung Disability Trust Fund, 8102–9.10

Black Population in the U.S.: March 1989-90, 2546–1.450

Black Women in the Labor Force, 6564–1.2

Black-White Differences in Alcohol Use by Women: Baltimore Survey Findings, 4042–3.212

BLM Adviser: New Mexico, Oklahoma, Texas and Kansas, 1990, 5724–15

BLM Facts and Figures for Utah, 1990, 5724–11.3

BLM Facts: Oregon and Washington, 1990, 5724–11.1

BLM in Wyoming, 1989, 5724–11.5

BLM in Wyoming, 1990, 5724–11.6

BLS Establishment Estimates Revised to March 1990 Benchmarks, 6742–2.204

BLS Regional Reports, Southeast Region, 6946–1

BLS Reports on Survey of Occupational Injuries and Illnesses in 1990, 6844–3

BLS Working Papers, 6886–6

Blue Marlin, Makaira nigricans, Movements in the Western North Atlantic Ocean: Results of a Cooperative Game Fish Tagging Program, 1954-88, 2162–1.203

Board and Care, 4008–112

Board for International Broadcasting, 1991 Annual Report on Radio Free Europe/Radio Liberty, Inc., 10314–1

Board of Governors of the Federal Reserve System Staff Studies, 9366–1

Board of Governors of the Federal Reserve System 77th Annual Report, 1990, 9364–1

Boating Safety Recalls, 7402–5

Boating Statistics, 1990, 7404–1

Bomb Summary, 1990, 6224–5

Bonner Bridge Storm, 2152–8.202

Bonneville Power Administration, Quarterly Report, 3222–2

Bonneville Power Administration, 1990 Annual Report, 3224–1

Boron Hazards to Fish, Wildlife, and Invertebrates: A Synoptic Review, 5506–14.3

Boron: Minerals Yearbook, Volume 1, 1990, 5604–20.10

Both Public and Private Efforts Needed To Reform Health Care, Respondents Say, 9383–19.202

BPA Residential Weatherization Program, 3226–1

Bracket Creep in the Age of Indexing: Have We Solved the Problem?, 9377–9.117

Breast Cancer in Men: Aspects of Familial Aggregation, 4472–1.213

Breast Self-Examination in Relation to the Occurrence of Advanced Breast Cancer, 4472–1.202

Bridge Infrastructure: Matching the Resources to the Need, 26113–539

Brief History of the Farmers Home Administration, 1184–17

British Invasion: Explaining the Strength of UK Acquisitions of U.S. Firms in the Late 1980's, 9385–8.82

Broadcast Station Totals, 9282–4

Broadwoven Fabrics (Gray), Current Industrial Report, 2506–5.11

Broiler Hatchery, 1625–11

Bromine: Minerals Yearbook, Volume 1, 1990, 5604–20.11

Brown Trout Population and Habitat Changes Associated with Increased Minimum Low Flows in Douglas Creek, Wyo., 5508–112

Budget and Forces Summary, 3804–16

Budget Estimates, FY92-93, 9634–9

Budget in Brief, FY92, Department of Transportation, 7304–10

Budget Information for States, FY92, 104–30

Budget of the U.S. Government, FY92, 104–2

Budget of the U.S. Government, FY92, Historical Tables, 104–22

Budgetary and Military Effects of a Treaty Limiting Conventional Forces in Europe, 26306–3.114

Budgetary Treatment of Deposit Insurance: A Framework for Reform, 26308–100

Building a Better Rural Policy: The President's Rural Development Initiative, 1004–16.1

Building Better Communities with Student Volunteers: An Evaluation Report on the Student Community Service Program, 9028–14

Building from Yesterday to Tomorrow: The Continuing Federal Role in Indian Education. Annual Report to the U.S. Congress, 14874–1

Building Skills of Recovering Women Drug Users To Reduce Heterosexual AIDS Transmission, 4042–3.221

Bulgarian Trade Data. International Trade, 26123–323

Bulk Carriers in the World Fleet: Oceangoing Merchant Type Ships of 1,000 Gross Tons and Over (Special Supplement on the U.S.-Flag Great Lakes), 7704–13

Bulk Ibuprofen from India. Determination of the Commission in Investigations Nos. 701-TA-308 (Preliminary) and 731-TA-526 (Preliminary) Under the Tariff Act of 1930, Together with the Information Obtained in the Investigations, 9886–19.77

Bulletin of Hardwood Market Statistics, 1202–4

Burden of Health Care Costs: Business, Households, and Governments, 4652–1.230

Bureau of Census Intercensal Estimates Working Group, Final Report, 2324–10

Bureau of Justice Assistance Discretionary Drug Treatment Programs: The Great Disappearing Act, 21408–120

Bureau of Justice Statistics Annual Report, 6064–21

Bureau of Justice Statistics Bulletin, 6066–25

Bureau of Justice Statistics Special Reports, 6066–19

Cancer. Indian Health...

Bureau of Labor Statistics Press Releases, 6726–1

Bureau of Land Management in Idaho: 1990 Facts Book, 5724–11.4

Bureau of Land Management in Idaho: 1991 Briefing Statements, 5724–11.2

Bureau of Land Management State Offices, Facts and Statistics, 5724–11

Bureau of Prisons Reports, 6242–1

Bureau of Reclamation, 1990 Annual Report, 5824–1

Bureau of the Census Annual Research Conference Proceedings, 2624–2

Burley Quota Underutilization, 1004–16.1

Burley Tobacco, Summary of 1991 Support Program and Related Information: ASCS Commodity Fact Sheet, 1806–4.2

Burley, 1989 Crop. Tobacco Market Review, 1319–5.3

Burley, 1990 Crop. Tobacco Market Review, 1319–5.6

Business America, 2042–24

Business Opportunities in a Changing Europe: A Rhode Island Perspective, 25388–58

Business Outlook Survey, Federal Reserve Bank of Philadelphia, 9387–11

Business Review, Federal Reserve Bank of Philadelphia, 9387–1

Business Volume Sets $77 Billion Record, but Farmer Cooperative Income Declines, 1122–1.211

Cadmium in 1990: Mineral Industry Surveys, Annual Review, 5614–5.11

Cadmium: Mineral Industry Surveys, 5612–2.5

Calcium and Calcium Compounds: Minerals Yearbook, Volume 1, 1990, 5604–20.12

Calibrating Manufacturing Decline in the Midwest: Value Added, Gross State Product, and All Points Between, 9375–13.59

California OCS Phase II Monitoring Program: Year-Three Annual Report, 5734–11

California Water Crisis, 1561–6.202

California's Sweetener Industries—Recent Developments and Prospects, 1561–14.206

California's $7.4 Billion Sales Leads States in Cooperative Business Volume, 1122–1.202

Call for Action. The Pepper Commission: U.S. Bipartisan Commission on Comprehensive Health Care, Supplement to the Final Report, 23898–5

Callable Corporate Bonds: A Vanishing Breed, 9366–6.269

Cambodia: Multilateral Relief Efforts in Border Camps, 26123–313

Can Local Governments Give Citizens What They Want? Referendum Outcomes in Massachusetts, 9373–1.208

Can Losses of Federal Financial Programs Be Reduced?, 9381–1.207

Canada's GRIP Program: A Boon for Canada's Wheat Producers?, 1561–12.202

Canadian Health Insurance: Lessons for the U.S., 26121–424

Canadian Salmon Aquaculture Industry, 2162–1.203

Canadian Sugar and HFCS Industries and U.S. Trade, 1561–14.203

Cancer Incidence in the Families of Children with Ewing's Tumor, 4472–1.214

Cancer. Indian Health Conditions, 4088–2

Cancer Mortality in Cuba and... Index by Titles

Cancer Mortality in Cuba and Among the Cuban-Born in the U.S.: 1979-81, 4042–3.205

Cancer Registry Problems in Classifying Invasive Bladder Cancer, 4472–1.208

Cancer Risk After Iodine-131 Therapy for Hyperthyroidism, 4472–1.218

Cancer Statistics Review, 1973-88, 4474–35

Canned Deciduous Fruit: Semiannual Update, 1925–34.241

Canola: Prospects for an Emerging Market, 1561–3.203

Canola's Growing Importance in North American and Developed East Asian Oilseed Markets, 1524–4.5

Capital Expenditures by Majority-Owned Foreign Affiliates of U.S. Companies, Latest Plans for 1991, 2702–1.207

Capital Expenditures by Majority-Owned Foreign Affiliates of U.S. Companies, Revised Estimates for 1991, 2702–1.222

Capital Expenditures, Depreciable Assets, and Operating Expenditures. 1987 Census of Service Industries. Subject Series., 2393–2

Capital in Banking: Past, Present and Future, 9375–13.61

Capital Punishment, 1990, 6066–25.42

Carbon Cycle Impacts of Future Forest Products Utilization and Recycling Trends, 1004–16.1

Carbon Dioxide and Climate: Summaries of Research in FY90, 3004–18.1

Carbon Dioxide and Climate: Summaries of Research in FY91, 3004–18.7

Carbon Dioxide Effects: Research and Assessment Program, 3006–11

Cardiovascular Disease. Indian Health Conditions, 4088–2

Career of Conceptualizing and Quantifying in Social Science, 1502–3.203

Careers in Teaching: Following Members of the High School Class of 1972 In and Out of Teaching, 4836–1.13

Caribbean Basin Investment Survey, 1990, 2048–141

Carotid Endarterectomy. Health Technology Assessment Report, 1990, 4186–10.2

Carpet and Rugs, 1990, Current Industrial Report, 2506–5.9

Case Management Agency Systems of Administering Long-Term Care: Evidence from the Channeling Demonstration, 4186–7.8

Case Mix, Financial Status, and Capital Investments, 17206–2.19

Case of the Missing Interest Deductions: Will Tax Reform Increase U.S. Saving Rates?, 9377–1.202

Case Studies of Selected Leveraged Buyouts. Leveraged Buyouts, 26119–355

Case-Control Study of Canine Malignant Lymphoma: Positive Association with Dog Owner's Use of 2,4-Dichlorophenoxyacetic Acid Herbicides, 4472–1.220

Caseload Statistics, State Vocational Rehabilitation Agencies, FY90, 4944–5

Case-Mix Specialization in the Market for Hospital Services, 4188–71

Cash Rents for Farms, Cropland, and Pasture, 1960-89, 1548–377

Catalog of Cell Lines, 1990/91: NIGMS Human Genetic Mutant Cell Repository, 4474–23

Catalog of Cell Lines, 1990/91: Supplement, NIGMS Human Genetic Mutant Cell Repository, 4474–23

Catalog of DIOR Reports, 3544–16, 3548–21

Catalog of Federal Domestic Assistance, 1991, 104–5

Catalog of Federal Domestic Assistance, 1991, Update, 104–5

Catalog of Publications of the National Center for Health Statistics, 1990, 4124–1

Catalog of Publications, U.S. Commission on Civil Rights, 11048–188

Catalogue of U.S. Geological Survey Strong-Motion Records, 1988, 5664–14

Catfish, 1631–14

Catfish Industry Perspective, 1004–16.1

Catfish Production, 1631–17, 1631–18

Cattle, 1623–1

Cattle Feeding, 1962-89: Location and Feedlot Size, 1568–300

Cattle on Feed, 1623–2

CBO Papers, 26306–3

CBO Studies, 26306–6

CCC Milk Support Program Activities, 1802–2

CDC's HIV Public Information and Education Programs, 4042–3.256

Celery, 1621–14

Cement in 1990: Mineral Industry Surveys, Advance Summary, 5614–5.21

Cement: Mineral Industry Surveys, 5612–1.2

Cement: Minerals Yearbook, Volume 1, 1989, 5604–15.15

Census Adjustment, 1990: Estimating Census Accuracy---A Complex Task, 26119–327

Census and You: Monthly News from the U.S. Bureau of the Census, 2302–3

Census Bureau Completes Distribution of 1990 Census Information from Summary Tape File 1A, 2328–74

Census Bureau Releases Additional 1990 Census Population and Housing Information for Puerto Rico, 2328–78

Census Bureau Releases Preliminary Coverage Estimates from the Post-Enumeration Survey and Demographic Analysis, 2328–69

Census Bureau Releases Refined Estimates from Post-Enumeration Survey of 1990 Census Coverage, 2328–69

Census Bureau Releases Refined 1990 Census Coverage Estimates from Demographic Analysis, 2328–69

Census Bureau Releases 1990 Census Counts on Hispanic Population Groups, 2328–73

Census Bureau Releases 1990 Census Counts on Specific Racial Groups, 2328–72

Census Bureau Releases 1990 Census Population Counts for Guam, 2328–79

Census Bureau Releases 1990 Census Population Counts for the Virgin Islands, 2328–77

Census Catalog and Guide, 1991, 2304–2

Census Content of Bureau of Economic Analysis Input-Output Data, 9375–13.53

Census Coverage Evaluation Operations, 1990, 21628–96

Census Geography: Concepts and Products, 2326–7.79

Census of Agriculture, 1987. Volume 1. Geographic Area Series, 2331–1

Census of Agriculture, 1987. Volume 4. Census of Horticultural Specialties (1988), 2337–1

Census of Construction Industries, 1987. Industry Series, 2373–1

Census of Governments, 1987. Volume 3. Public Employment. No. 1: Employment of Major Local Governments, 2455–1

Census of Governments, 1987. Volume 3. Public Employment. No. 2: Compendium of Public Employment, 2455–2

Census of Governments, 1987. Volume 3. Public Employment. No. 3: Labor-Management Relations, 2455–3

Census of Governments, 1987. Volume 3. Public Employment. No. 4: Government Costs for Employee Benefits, 2455–4

Census of Governments, 1987. Volume 6. Guide to the 1987 Census of Governments. No. 1: Guide to the 1987 Census of Governments, 2460–1

Census of Horticultural Specialties (1988). 1987 Census of Agriculture. Volume 4, 2337–1

Census of Local Jails, 1988, 6068–144

Census of Local Jails, 1988. Volume I. Selected Findings: Methodology and Summary Tables, 6068–144.1

Census of Local Jails, 1988. Volume II. Data for Individual Jails in the Northeast, 6068–144.2

Census of Local Jails, 1988. Volume III. Data for Individual Jails in the Midwest, 6068–144.3

Census of Local Jails, 1988. Volume IV. Data for Individual Jails in the South, 6068–144.4

Census of Local Jails, 1988. Volume V. Data for Individual Jails in the West, 6068–144.5

Census of Manufacturers, 1987. Subject Series, Manufacturers' Shipments to the Federal Government, 2497–7

Census of Manufactures, 1987. Subject Series. General Summary: Industry, Product Class, and Geographic Area Statistics, 2497–1

Census of Manufactures, 1987. Subject Series. Type of Organization, 2497–5

Census of Mineral Industries, 1987. Geographic Area Series, 2515–1

Census of Mineral Industries, 1987. Subject Series. Fuels and Electric Energy Consumed, 2517–2

Census of Mineral Industries, 1987. Subject Series. General Summary, 2517–1

Census of Population and Housing, 1990: Content Determination Reports, 2626–11

Census of Population and Housing, 1990 P.L. 94-171 Data on CD-ROM, 2551–6

Census of Population and Housing, 1990. P.L. 94-171 Data on CD-ROM, Technical Documentation, 2308–63

Census of Population and Housing, 1990. P.L. 94-171 Higher-Level Geographic Summary Series. State Reports, 2551–5

Census of Population and Housing, 1990. Summary Population and Housing Characteristics, 2551–1

Census of Retail Trade, 1987. Special Report Series. Selected Statistics, 2401–1

Census of Retail Trade, 1987. Subject Series. Measures of Value Produced, Capital Expenditures, Depreciable Assets, and Operating Expenses, 2399–2

Census of Service Industries, 1987. Subject Series. Capital Expenditures, Depreciable Assets, and Operating Expenditures, 2393–2

Census of Service Industries, 1987. Subject Series. Hotels, Motels, and Other Lodging Places, 2393–3

Index by Titles

Census of Service Industries, 1987. Subject Series. Miscellaneous Subjects, 2393–4

Census of Transportation, 1987. Subject Series: Selected Transportation Industries. Miscellaneous Subjects, 2579–1

Census of U.S. Civil Aircraft, 1989, 7504–3

Census of Wholesale Trade, 1987. Subject Series. Measures of Value Produced, Capital Expenditures, Depreciable Assets, and Operating Expenses, 2407–2

Census of Wholesale Trade, 1987. Subject Series. Miscellaneous Subjects, 2407–4

Census Overview and Nomination of Barbara Bryant, 25408–113

Census Profile, 1990, 2326–20

Census, 1990, Showed Gain of 14 Million Housing Units Since 1980, 2328–71

Center for Population Research, National Institute of Child Health and Human Development: 1989 Progress Report, 4474–33

Center for Population Research, National Institute of Child Health and Human Development: 1990 Progress Report, 4474–33

Central Bank Secrecy and Money Surprises: International Evidence, 9393–10.16

Central Liquidity Facility 1990 Annual Report, 9534–5

Central Program Strategy Statement: Bureau for Science and Technology, FY87-91, 9916–12.21

Central-Bank Intervention: Recent Literature, Continuing Controversy, 9377–1.205

Certain Carbon Steel Butt-Weld Pipe Fittings from China and Thailand. Determination of the Commission in Investigations Nos. 731-TA-520 and 521 (Preliminary) Under the Tariff Act of 1930, Together with the Information Obtained in the Investigations, 9886–14.319

Changes in Area and Ownership of Timberland in Western Oregon: 1961-86, 1208–353

Changes in Area of Timberland in the U.S., 1952-2040, By Ownership, Forest Type, Region and State, 1208–357

Changes in Characteristics of Women Who Smoke During Pregnancy: Missouri, 1978-88, 4042–3.203

Changes in Farm Structure, 1004–16.1

Changes in Financial Profile of Cooperatives Handling Grain: First-Handlers with $5 Million or More in Sales, 1983 and 1985, 1128–44.4

Changes in Florida's Industrial Roundwood Products Output, 1977-87, 1208–352

Changes in Hospital Staffing Patterns, 6722–1.217

Changes in Medicare Skilled Nursing Facility Benefit Admissions, 4652–1.222

Changes in Schedule B, Statistical Classification of Domestic and Foreign Commodities Exported from the U.S.: 1990. U.S. Foreign Trade, 2428–5.1

Changes in South Carolina's Industrial Timber Products Output, 1988, 1208–359

Changes in the Cost of Equity Capital for Bank Holding Companies and the Effects on Raising Capital, 9366–6.274

Changes in the Structure of Wages: A Regional Comparison, 9373–1.213

Changes in Unemployment Insurance Legislation During 1990, 6722–1.211

Changes Needed in Loan Servicing Under the Agricultural Credit Act. Farmers Home Administration, 26113–497

Changes to the 1990 Edition of Schedule B, Jan. 1, 1992, 2428–5.1

Changing by Degrees: Steps To Reduce Greenhouse Gases, 26358–233

Changing Chemical Use: The Impact on Producers and Consumers, 1004–16.1

Changing Importance of Large Cattle Feedlots, 1561–7.203

Changing Public Attitudes on Governments and Taxes, 1991, 10044–2

Changing Structure and Cycles in the World Sugar Industry, 1004–16.1

Changing Technology: Pesticide Use and the Environment, 1004–16.1

Changing the Classification of Federal White-Collar Jobs: Potential Management and Budgetary Impacts, 26306–3.119

Characteristics and Financial Circumstances of AFDC Recipients, FY89, 4694–1

Characteristics and Trends of Streamflow and Dissolved Solids in the Upper Colorado River Basin, Arizona, Colorado, New Mexico, Utah, and Wyoming, 5666–27.17

Characteristics of Apartments Completed: 1990. Current Housing Report, 2484–3

Characteristics of Doctoral Scientists and Engineers in the U.S.: 1989, 9627–18

Characteristics of FHA Single-Family Mortgages: Selected Sections of National Housing Act, 1985, 5144–17

Characteristics of FHA Single-Family Mortgages: Selected Sections of National Housing Act, 1986, 5144–17

Characteristics of FHA Single-Family Mortgages: Selected Sections of National Housing Act, 1987, 5144–17

Characteristics of FHA Single-Family Mortgages: Selected Sections of National Housing Act, 1988, 5144–17

Characteristics of FHA Single-Family Mortgages: Selected Sections of National Housing Act, 1989, 5144–17

Characteristics of FHA Single-Family Mortgages: Selected Sections of National Housing Act, 1990, 5144–17

Characteristics of Flue-Cured and Burley Farms Compared, 1561–10.204

Characteristics of Food Stamp Households, Summer 1988, 1364–8

Characteristics of Home Mortgage Debt, 1970-89: Trends and Implications, 9366–6.263

Characteristics of New Housing: 1990. Current Construction Reports, 2384–1

Characteristics of Onion Growers and Farms in 6 Major Onion States, 1561–11.201

Characteristics of Persons Rehabilitated and Reasons for Case Closures in FY84, FY86, and FY88: State-Federal Program of Vocational Rehabilitation, 4944–6

Characteristics of Persons Rehabilitated, State-Federal Program of Vocational Rehabilitation, 4944–6

Characteristics of Persons Served by Private Psychiatric Hospitals, U.S.: 1986, 4506–3.47

Characteristics of Persons With and Without Health Care Coverage: U.S., 1989, 4146–8.203

Characteristics of Physicians, Jan. 1, 1989, 4116–6

Children in Custody: Census...

Characteristics of Science/Engineering Equipment in Academic Settings: 1989-90, 9627–27.4

Characteristics of Social Security Disability Insurance Beneficiaries, 4704–14

Characteristics of Stayers, Movers, and Leavers: Results from the Teacher Followup Survey, 1988-89. Schools and Staffing Survey, 4836–3.5

Characteristics of the 100 Largest Public Elementary and Secondary School Districts in the U.S., 1988-89, 4834–22

Characteristics of U.S. Rice Farms and Operators, 1561–8.205

Characteristics of Working Children. Child Labor, 26121–426

Characterization of Habitat Used by Whooping Cranes During Migration, 5508–111

Characterizing Business Cycles with a Markov Switching Model: Evidence of Multiple Equilibria, 9385–8.96

Cheatgrass Invasion, Shrub Die-off, and Other Aspects of Shrub Biology and Management. Proceedings of the Symposium, 1208–351

Chemical Trade Prospers in the 1980's, 6722–1.229

Chemicals Trade and Production. Statistical Brief, 2326–17.32

Chemistry of Lake Tahoe, California-Nevada, and Nearby Springs, 5666–27.6

Cherokee Indian Agency, 1991 Annual Council Report, 5704–4

Cherry Production, 1621–18.2

Chief, National Guard Bureau Annual Review, 3504–22

Chiefs of State and Cabinet Members of Foreign Governments, 9112–4

Child Abuse and Neglect, 25548–102

Child Abuse Prevention: Status of the Challenge Grant Program, 26121–423

Child Care: Arrangements and Costs, 6722–1.246

Child Day Care Services: An Industry at a Crossroads, 6722–1.202

Child Health USA '90, 4108–49

Child Labor: Characteristics of Working Children, 26121–426

Child Restraint Systems on Aircraft, 21648–61

Child Support and Alimony: 1989, 2546–6.72

Child Support Enforcement, 14th Annual Report to Congress for the Period Ending Sept. 30, 1989, 4694–6

Child Support Received by Teenaged Mothers: 1987, 4698–5

Child Survival in Indonesia, 9916–1.73

Childcare Effects on Social Security Benefits, 2626–10.138

Child-Care Problems: An Obstacle to Work, 6722–1.245

Childhood Injury Prevention in a Suburban Massachusetts Population, 4042–3.236

Childhood Injury: State-by-State Mortality Facts, 4108–54

Childhood Lead Poisoning, New York City, 1988, 4202–7.201

Children and Welfare: Patterns of Multiple Program Participation, 2626–10.133

Children and Youth: The Crisis at Home for American Families, 25548–104

Children in Custody, 6064–5

Children in Custody: Census of Public and Private Juvenile Detention, Correctional and Shelter Facilities, 6064–13

Children in Custody. ...

Index by Titles

Children in Custody. Public Juvenile Facilities, 1989, 6064–5.1

Children in Custody, 1987: A Comparison of Public and Private Juvenile Custody Facilities, 6064–13

Children's Experiences Linked to Various Factors; Better Data Needed. Foster Care, 26121–432

Children's Exposure to Environmental Cigarette Smoke Before and After Birth: Health of Our Nation's Children, 4146–8.204

Children's Well-Being: An International Comparison. Statistical Brief, 2326–17.24

Chilean Fresh Fruit Industry, 1925–34.222

Chile's Salmon Culture Industry, 2162–1.204

Chile's Tomato Processing Industry, 1925–34.211

China: Agriculture and Trade Report, Situation and Outlook Series, 1524–4.3

China's Agricultural Commodity Policies in the 1980's, 1524–4.3

China's Economic Dilemmas in the 1990s: The Problems of Reforms, Modernization, and Interdependence, 23848–155

China's Grain Production Economy: A Review by Regions, 1524–4.3

China's Livestock Feed Industry, 1524–4.3

Chinese Economy in 1990 and 1991: Uncertain Recovery, 9118–9

Chinese Shrimp Culture, 1524–4.3

Chironomidae of the Southeastern U.S.: A Checklist of Species and Notes on Biology, Distribution, and Habitat, 5506–13.3

Chlordane Hazards to Fish, Wildlife, and Invertebrates: A Synoptic Review, 5506–14.1

Choice Beef Prices and Price Spreads Series: Methodology and Revisions, 1568–295

Choices of Health Insurance and the Two-Worker Household. National Medical Expenditure Survey, 4186–8.16

Chrome-Plated Lug Nuts from the People's Republic of China and Taiwan. Determinations of the Commission in Investigations Nos. 731-TA-474-475 (Final) Under the Tariff Act of 1930, Together with the Information Obtained in the Investigations, 9886–14.329

Chromium: Mineral Industry Surveys, 5612–1.3

Chukchi Sea Ice Motions, 1981-82, 2176–1.38

CIR Staff Papers, 2326–18

Circular, Welded, Non-Alloy Steel Pipes and Tubes from Brazil, the Republic of Korea, Mexico, Romania, Taiwan, and Venezuela. Determinations of the Commission in Investigation No. 701-TA-311 (Preliminary) and Nos. 731-TA-532-537 (Preliminary) Under the Tariff Act of 1930, Together with the Information Obtained in the Investigations, 9886–19.81

Cities with Population Greater than 100,000 in 1990, Ranked by Population, 2324–7

Citrus Fruits: 1991 Summary, 1621–18.7

City Employment: 1990, 2466–1.2

City Government Finances: 1988-89, 2466–2.3

Civil Aircraft and Aircraft Engines, Current Industrial Report, 2506–12.24

Civil Service Retirement and Disability Fund, 9844–34

Civil Service Retirement and Disability Fund, A Report Pursuant to Public Law 95-595, Sept. 30, 1989, 9844–34

Civil Service Retirement and Disability Fund, A Report Pursuant to Public Law 95-595, Sept. 30, 1990, 9844–34

Civil Service Work Force as of Sept. 30, 1990, 9504–1

Civilian Manpower Statistics, 3542–16

Civilian Training in High-Altitude Flight Physiology, 7506–10.92

Civilian Use of Military Airfields Has Added Little to System Capacity. Airport Capacity, 26113–524

Clandestine Laboratory Seizures in the U.S., 1990, 6284–3

Class I Freight Railroads, Selected Earnings Data, 9482–2

Classification of Instructional Programs (CIP), 4828–29

Clay Classification Systems of the U.S. Bureau of Mines, Impact on Land Use: Mineral Industry Surveys Annual Advance Clay Summary Supplement, 5614–5.3

Clay Construction Products, Current Industrial Report, 2506–9.2

Clays: Minerals Yearbook, Volume 1, 1989, 5604–15.17

Cleaning Up Our Coastal Waters: An Unfinished Agenda, 9208–131

Clearer Guidance Could Help Focus Services on Those with Severe Disabilities. Vocational Rehabilitation, 26121–438

Clearinghouse Bibliography on Health Indexes, 4122–1

Climate Assessment, a Decadal Review, 1981-90, 2184–9

Climate Assessment, Selected Indicators of Global Climate, 2184–9

Climate Monitoring and Diagnostics Laboratory, No. 18, Summary Report, 1989, 2144–28

Closures for Containers, Current Industrial Report, 2506–11.4

Clothing Expenditures of Single-Parent Households, 1004–16.1

Coal Data: 1983-88. Assessment of the Quality of Selected EIA Data Series, 3166–12.6

Coal Distribution, 3162–8

Coal Mine Subsidence: Several States May Not Meet Federal Insurance Program Objectives, 26113–530

Coal Production, 1990, 3164–25

Coal: Surface Fatalities, First Half 1991, 6662–3.1

Coal: Surface Fatalities, Second Half 1990, 6662–3.1

Coal: Underground Fatalities, First Half 1991, 6662–3.2

Coal: Underground Fatalities, Second Half 1990, 6662–3.2

Coast Guard: Millions in Federal Costs May Not Be Recovered from Exxon Valdez Oil Spill, 26113–510

Coast Guard Publishes New List of Current Boating Safety Recall Campaigns, 7402–5

Coast Guard SAR Statistics, 7404–2

Coastal Environmental Quality in the U.S., 1990: Chemical Contamination in Sediment and Tissues, 2176–3.12

Coastal, Onshore and Stripper Subcategories of the Oil and Gas Extraction Point Source Category: Preliminary Data Summary, 9206–4.12

Coastal Wetlands of the U.S.: An Accounting of a Valuable National Resource, 2178–31

Coated Groundwood Paper from Austria, Belgium, Finland, France, Germany, Italy, the Netherlands, Sweden, and the UK. Determinations of the Commission in Investigations Nos. 731-TA-486-494 (Preliminary) Under the Tariff Act of 1930, Together with the Information Obtained in the Investigations, 9886–14.306

Coated Groundwood Paper from Belgium, Finland, France, Germany, and the UK. Determination of the Commission in Investigations Nos. 731-TA-487, 488, 489, 490, and 494 (Final) Under the Tariff Act of 1930, Together with the Information Obtained in the Investigation, 9886–14.336

Cobalt Availability: A Minerals Availability Appraisal, 5606–4.29

Cobalt: Mineral Industry Surveys, 5612–1.4

Cobalt: Minerals Yearbook, Volume 1, 1989, 5604–15.18

Coca Economy in the Upper Huallaga, 9918–19

Cocoa: Foreign Agricultural Service Circular Series. World Cocoa Situation, 1925–9

Cognitive Impairment and Disruptive Behaviors Among Community-Based Elderly Persons: Implications for Targeting Long-Term Care, 4186–7.10

Cohabitation, Marriage, Marital Dissolution, and Remarriage: U.S., 1988, 4146–8.196

Cohort Study of Fat Intake and Risk of Breast Cancer, 4472–1.204

Coinage Executed During (Month), 8202–1

Cointegration and Transformed Series, 9377–9.104

Cointegration, Exogeneity, and Policy Analysis: An Overview, 9366–7.269

Cointegration: How Short Is the Long Run?, 9381–10.119

Cold Storage, 1631–5

Cold Storage, 1990 Summary, 1631–11

Collective Bargaining During 1991, 6722–1.206

Collective Bargaining in 1990: Search for Solutions Continues, 6722–1.207

College Course Map, Taxonomy and Transcript Data Based on the Postsecondary Records, 1972-84, of the High School Class of 1972, 4888–4

College Library Technology and Cooperation Grants Program, HEA Title II-D: Abstracts and Analysis of Funded Projects 1989, 4874–6

College-Level Remedial Education in the Fall of 1989, 4826–1.30

Colorado River Salinity Control Program, From Inception of Program Through Sept. 30, 1990, 1804–23

Colorado Water Supply Summary, Water Year 1991, 1264–13

Command and Control: Defense's Use of Engineering Contractors for Acquiring Automated Systems, 26125–45

Comment on the Role of Professional Journals in Facilitating Data Access, 1502–3.203

Comments on the Evaluation of Policy Models, 9366–7.267

Commerce Budget in Brief, FY92, 2004–6

Commerce Needs To Improve Fisheries Management in the North Pacific. Fisheries, 26113–523

Commerce Publications Update, 2002–1

Commercial Bank Profitability: Hampered Again by Large Banks' Loan Problems, 9371–1.211

Index by Titles

Commercial Buildings Characteristics, 1989. Commercial Buildings Energy Consumption Survey, 3166–8.9

Commercial Buildings Energy Consumption Survey, 3166–8

Commercial Fertilizers, 9804–30

Commercial Microwave Ovens, Assembled or Unassembled, from Japan. Determination of the Commission in Investigation No. 731-TA-523 (Preliminary) Under the Tariff Act of 1930, Together with the Information Obtained in the Investigation, 9886–14.322

Commercial Nuclear Power, 1991: Prospects for the U.S. and the World, 3164–57

Commercial Use of Space: Many Grantees Making Progress, but NASA Oversight Could Be Improved, 26123–353

Commission on Railroad Retirement Reform: Final Report, 9708–1

Commissioner of Patents and Trademarks, Annual Report, FY90, 2244–1

Commitments and Discharges for the Fiscal Year: Bureau of Prisons, 6242–1.3

Commitments and Discharges for the Month: Bureau of Prisons, 6242–1.2

Commitments of Traders in Commodity Futures, 11922–5

Committee for Purchase from the Blind and Other Severely Handicapped Annual Report, 1990, 11714–1

Commodity Credit Corp. Monthly Sales List, 1802–4

Commodity Credit Corporation Charts: A Summary of Data Through Sept. 30, 1987, 1824–2

Commodity Futures Trading Commission, Annual Report, 1990, 11924–2

Commodity/Country Allocations Under Titles I/III, P.L. 480, 1922–7

Communication Equipment, and Other Electronic Systems and Equipment, 1990, Current Industrial Report, 2506–12.35

Community Development Block Grant Program Directory of Allocations for FY84-91, 5128–17

Community Epidemiology Work Group Proceedings, 4492–5

Community Intervention Trial for Smoking Cessation (COMMIT): Summary of Design and Intervention, 4472–1.231

Community Relations Service, 1990 Annual Report, 6004–9

Companies Participating in the DOD Subcontracting Program, 3542–17

Companies Receiving the Largest Dollar Volume of Prime Contract Awards, FY90, 3544–5

Company Summary. 1987 Enterprise Statistics, 2329–8

Comparative Analysis of Annual Survey and Medicare Cost Report Margin Data, 17206–2.25

Comparative Analysis of Corporate Takeovers, 9385–8.88

Comparative Climatic Data for the U.S., 1990, 2154–8

Comparative International Vital and Health Statistics Reports. Vital and Health Statistics Series 5, 4147–5

Comparing Prices Across Cities: A Hedonic Approach, 6886–6.73

Comparing Serum Ferritin Values from Different Population Surveys. Vital and Health Statistics Series 2, 4147–2.111

Comparing the Cost of Capital in the U.S. and Japan: A Survey of Methods, 9385–1.202

Comparison of Alien Admissions Before and After IRCA, 6266–1.1

Comparison of Alternative Weight Recalibration Methods for Diagnosis-Related Groups, 4652–1.227

Comparison of Behavior of Bowhead Whales of the Davis Strait and Bering/Beaufort Stocks, 5738–29

Comparison of Examination Fees and Availability of Routine Vision Care by Optometrists and Ophthalmologists, 4042–3.238

Comparison of Lower Middle Income Two-Parent and Single-Mother Families, 1702–1.207

Comparison of Medicaid and Non-Medicaid Obstetrical Care in California, 4652–1.241

Comparison of Medicaid Nursing Home Payment Systems, 4652–1.255

Comparison of State Methods for Collecting, Aggregating, and Reporting State Average Daily Attendance (ADA) Totals to the National Center for Education Statistics, 4838–48

Comparison of State Unemployment Insurance Laws, 6402–2

Comparison of Two Methods of Computing Home Health Care Cost Limits. Medicare, 26121–400

Comparison of Urinalysis Technologies for Drug Testing in Criminal Justice, 6066–26.6

Comparison of U.S. and Codex Pesticide Standards. International Food Safety, 26131–88

Comparisons of Diet and Biochemical Characteristics of Stool and Urine Between Chinese Populations with Low and High Colorectal Cancer Rates, 4472–1.201

Compendium of Federal Justice Statistics, 1986, 6064–29

Compendium of HHS Evaluations and Relevant Other Studies, 4004–30

Compendium of Public Employment. 1987 Census of Governments, Volume 3. Public Employment, No. 2, 2455–2

Compensation and Working Conditions, 6782–1

Competing for the Recreational Dollar: An Analysis of the California Commercial Passenger-Carrying Fishing Vessel Industry, 2162–1.202

Competitive Assessment of the U.S. Industrial Air Pollution Control Equipment Industry, 2046–12.45

Competitive Assessment of U.S. Industries, 2046–12

Competitor's View of U.S. Farm Programs, 1004–16.1

Compilations of Advance Data from Vital and Health Statistics. Vital and Health Statistics Series 16, 4147–16

Compilations of Data on Natality, Mortality, Marriage, Divorce, and Induced Terminations of Pregnancy. Vital and Health Statistics Series 24, 4147–24

Complete Catalog, 1991, Cataloging Distribution Service, 26404–6

Composition, Distribution, and Hydrologic Effects of Contaminated Sediments Resulting from the Discharge of Gold Milling Wastes to Whitewood Creek at Lead and Deadwood, South Dakota, 5666–27.13

Composition of Foods, 1356–3

Composition of Foods. Snacks and Sweets: Raw, Processed, Prepared, 1356–3.16

Composition of Foods. 1990 Supplement: Raw, Processed, Prepared, 1356–3.15

Composition of the Active Duty Forces by Race or National Origin Identification and by Gender. Military Personnel, 26123–325

Composition of U.S. Merchandise Trade, 1986-90, Chartbook, 9884–21

Comprehensive and Workable Plan for the Abatement of Lead-Based Paint in Privately Owned Housing, 5188–128

Comprehensive Local Program for the Prevention of Fetal Alcohol Syndrome, 4042–3.239

Comprehensive Precipitation Data Set for Global Land Areas, 3006–11.14

Comprehensive Statement on Postal Operations, 1990, 9864–5

Comptroller General's 1990 Annual Report, 26104–1

Computer Matching Act: Many States Did Not Comply with 30-Day Notice or Data-Verification Provisions, 26121–404

Computer Output Microform (COM) Formats and Reduction Ratios, 16MM and 105MM. Hardware Standard, 2216–2.195

Computer Security and Privacy Plans (CSPP) Review Project, 1989: A First-Year Federal Response to the Computer Security Act of 1987 (Final Report), 2218–85

Computer Simulations Can Improve Command Training in Large-Scale Exercises. Army Training, 26123–318

Computer Use in the U.S.: 1989, 2546–2.158

Concerns About Performance of Brain-Wound Research. Army Biomedical Research, 26121–396

Concerns in the U.S. Real Estate Sector During the 1980s. Foreign Investment, 26123–350

Concordance Between Planned and Approved Visits During Initial Home Care, 4652–1.254

Concordance Between the Standard Industrial Classifications of the U.S. and Canada: 1987 U.S. SIC—1980 Canadian SIC, 2628–31

Concurrent Resolution on the Budget, FY92, 25254–1

Condition of Bilingual Education in the Nation: A Report to the Congress and the President, 4804–14

Condition of Education, 1991, 4824–1

Conduct in a Banking Duopoly, 9387–8.251

Confectionery, 1990, Current Industrial Report, 2506–4.5

Conference Series, Federal Reserve Bank of Boston, 9373–3

Congressional Directory, 1991-92, 102d Congress, 23874–1

Congressional District Population, 1990 and 1980 Censuses: 102nd Congress, 2328–32

Congressional District Ranking by Selected Programs and Commodities, 102nd Congress, 1804–17

Congressional Districts of the U.S.: Federal General Data Standard, Representations and Codes, 2216–2.193

Congressional Election Spending Drops to Low Point, 1990, 9276–1.87

Congressional Presentation for Security Assistance, FY92, 7144–13

Congressional Presentation, FY92, AID. Main Volume, 9904–4.1

Congressional Presentation,... Index by Titles

Congressional Presentation, FY92, AID. Statistical Annex, 9904–4.5

Congressional Presentation, FY92, AID. Summary Tables, 9904–4.4

Congressional Presentation, FY92, U.S. International Development Cooperation Agency, 9904–4

Congressional Presentation, FY92, U.S. International Development Cooperation Agency. International Organizations and Programs, 9904–4.2

Congressional Presentation, FY92, U.S. International Development Cooperation Agency. U.S. Trade and Development Program, 9904–4.3

Congressional Presentation: Peace Corps, FY92, 9654–1

Consequences of the Nuclear Power Plant Accident at Chernobyl, 4042–3.201

Conservation and Environmental Issues in Agriculture: An Economic Evaluation of Policy Options, 1588–153

Conservation and Renewable Energy Schools and Hospitals Program Cycle XII Grants Data: Grants Award Listing, Mar. 19, 1991, 3304–15

Conservation Highlights: Summary of Activities of the Soil Conservation Service for FY90, 1264–2

Conservation Highlights, 1990, 1264–2

Conservation Reserve—Yesterday, Today, and Tomorrow, 1208–360

Consolidated Federal Funds Report, FY90, 2464–3

Consolidated Federal Funds Report, FY90. Volume I: County Areas, 2464–3.1

Consolidated Federal Funds Report, FY90. Volume II: Subcounty Areas, 2464–3.2

Consolidated Financial Statements of the U.S. Government, FY90, 8104–5

Consolidated Financial Statements of the U.S. Government, FY90: Supplemental Analysis and Information, 8104–5

Consolidated Reports of Condition and Income, 9389–18

Constant-Dollar Inventories, Sales, and Inventory-Sales Ratios for Manufacturing and Trade, 2702–1.28

Construction Machinery, 1989, Current Industrial Report, 2506–12.3

Construction Machinery, 1990, Current Industrial Report, 2506–12.3

Construction Market in Mexico, 2042–1.207

Construction of True Cost of Food Indexes from Estimated Engel Curves, 1598–275

Construction Outlook for 1991, 2042–1.201

Construction Programs (C-1), Department of Defense Budget for FY92-93, 3544–39

Construction Review, 2042–1

Consulting Services: Contract Obligations for FY87-89, 26119–343

Consumer Expenditure Survey: Quarterly Data from the Interview Survey, 6762–14

Consumer Expenditure Survey, 1988-89, 6764–5

Consumer Expenditures in 1990, 6726–1.42

Consumer Guide to Uniform Tire Quality Grading, 7764–17

Consumer Income. Current Population Reports. Series P-60, 2546–6

Consumer Installment Credit, 9365–2.6

Consumer Perceptions on Scientific Solutions to Food Safety and Environmental Dilemmas, 1004–16.1

Consumer Price Index, 6762–1

Consumer Price Rise Slows in First Half of 1991, 6722–1.247

Consumer Prices Rise Sharply in 1990, 6722–1.226

Consumer, Scientific, Technical, and Industrial Glassware, 1990, Current Industrial Report, 2506–9.3

Consumer Spending Update, 2322–3

Consumer's Guide to Regional Economic Multipliers, 9391–1.206

Consumption of Energy, 1988. Manufacturing Energy Consumption Survey, 3166–13.5

Consumption on the Cotton System and Stocks, Current Industrial Report, 2506–5.8

Consumption on the Woolen System and Worsted Combing, Current Industrial Report, 2506–5.2

Content Determination Reports. 1990 Census of Population and Housing, 2626–11

Contingent Foreign Liabilities of the U.S. Government, 8002–12

Contraceptive Utilization Among Widowed, Divorced, and Separated Women in the U.S.: 1973 and 1976, 4147–16.4

Contraceptive Utilization in the U.S.: 1973 and 1976, 4147–16.4

Contract Obligations for FY87-89. Consulting Services, 26119–343

Contracting and Market Share Information. ADP Procurement, 26125–41

Contractors Receiving the Largest Dollar Volume of Prime Contract Awards for Research, Development, Test, and Evaluation, FY90, 3544–4

Contracts, Constraints, and Consumption, 9383–20.13

Contracts for Field Projects and Supporting Research on Enhanced Oil Recovery, 3002–14

Contracts for Field Projects and Supporting Research on Enhanced Oil Recovery and Activities of the Oil Implementation Task Force, 3002–14

Controlled Foreign Corporations, 1986, 8302–2.212

Controlling the Risks of Government-Sponsored Enterprises, 26308–99

Convention on International Trade in Endangered Species of Wild Fauna and Flora: 1989 Annual Report, 5504–19

Conventional Home Mortgage Rates, 9442–2

Cooling Season Energy Measurements of Dust and Ventilation Effects on Radiant Barriers, 3308–97

Cooperative Agrichemical and Seed Operations, 1126–1.6

Cooperative Snow Survey Data, 1264–14

Cooperative State-Federal Tuberculosis Eradication Program, Statistical Tables and Status Report, 1394–13

Cooperatives' Growth Slowed Due to Slump in Net Income, 1122–1.209

Co-ops Report Extent of Business Transacted on Noncooperative Basis, 1122–1.203

Co-ops' Share of Grains, Milk, Cotton Up in 1989, 1122–1.204

Copper in the U.S.: Mineral Industry Surveys, 5612–1.6

Copper Industry: Mineral Industry Surveys, 5612–1.6

Copper: Minerals Yearbook, Volume 1, 1989, 5604–15.20

Copyright Infringement Remedies and Nursing Home/Videocassette Copyright, 21528–82

Coral Fishery and Trade of Japan, 2162–1.201

Corn Cleaning Practices of U.S. Commercial Elevators, 1561–4.202

Corporate Foreign Tax Credit, 1986: An Industry Focus, 8302–2.203

Corporate Leverage and Taxes in the U.S. Economy, 9385–8.88

Corporate Leverage and the Consequences of Macroeconomic Instability, 9385–8.78

Corporate Medium-Term Notes, 9366–6.276

Corporation Foreign Tax Credit, 1986, A Geographic Focus, 8302–2.207

Corporation Income Tax Returns, Income Year 1987, 8302–2.204

Corporation Income Tax Returns: Statistics of Income, 1987, 8304–4

Corporation Income Tax Returns, 1988, 8302–2.217

Corporation Statistics, 1988: Data Release, 8302–2.215

Correctional Populations in the U.S., 1988, 6064–26

Correctional Populations in the U.S., 1989, 6064–26

Correlates and Consequences of Alcohol Abuse in the National "Health Care for the Homeless" Client Population, 4488–14

Correlation: Textile and Apparel Categories with the Harmonized Tariff Schedule of the U.S., 2044–31

Cost and Outcome Analysis of Kidney Transplantation. The Implications of Initial Immunosuppressive Protocol and Diabetes, 4658–59

Cost and Quality of Fuels for Electric Utility Plants, 1990, 3164–42

Cost and Revenue Analysis, FY90, Rates and Classification Department, 9864–2

Cost of Capital for Securities Firms in the U.S. and Japan, 9385–1.212

Cost of Environmental Survey Testing, 3006–5.23

Cost of Pipeline and Compressor Station Construction Under Natural Gas Act Section 7(c) for the Years 1983-86, 3084–3

Cost of Pipeline and Compressor Station Construction Under Natural Gas Act Section 7(c) for the Years 1984-87, 3084–3

Cost of Protecting U.S. Interests. Southwest Asia, 26123–360

Cost Savings and BOP's Statutory Authority Need To Be Resolved. Private Prisons, 26119–321

Costs of Phasing Out Noisy Aircraft. Aviation Noise, 26113–534

Costs of Producing and Selling Burley Tobacco: 1989 and Preliminary 1990, 1561–10.201

Costs of Producing and Selling Flue-Cured Tobacco: 1989, 1990, and Preliminary 1991, 1561–10.205

Costs of Producing Oranges and Grapefruit, 1988/89, 1561–6.201

Costs of Providing Screening Mammography, 17266–1.1

Cotton and Wool Situation and Outlook Report, 1561–1

Cotton and Wool Situation and Outlook Yearbook, 1561–1

Cotton: Foreign Agricultural Service Circular Series, 1925–4

Index by Titles

Cotton Ginning Charges, Harvesting Practices, and Selected Marketing Costs, 1990/91 Season, 1564–3

Cotton Ginnings, 1631–19

Cotton Ginnings, By Counties, 2342–2

Cotton Ginnings, By States, 2342–1

Cotton Ginnings in the U.S., Crop of 1990, 2344–1

Cotton in a World of Change, 1004–16.1

Cotton Manufacturers (Customs Value). U.S. General Imports, 2046–9.4

Cotton Manufacturers. U.S. General Imports, 2046–8.1

Cotton or Man-Made Fiber Manufacturers (Customs Value). U.S. General Imports, 2046–9.8

Cotton or Man-Made Fiber Manufacturers. U.S. General Imports, 2046–8.7

Cotton Price Stability and the Outlook for 1991/92, 1004–16.1

Cotton Price Statistics, 1309–1

Cotton Price Statistics, 1990-91, 1309–2

Cotton Production and Water Quality: An Initial Assessment, 1588–151

Cotton Production Estimates: A Historical Review, 1561–1.208

Cotton Quality: Carryover, 1989-90, 1309–8

Cotton Quality: Crop of 1990, 1309–7

Cotton Varieties Planted, 1991 Crop, 1309–6

Cotton, Wool, Man-Made Fiber, and Vegetable Fiber (Except Cotton) and Silk Blend Textiles. U.S. General Imports, 2042–27

Cottonseed Quality, Crop of 1990, 1309–5

Cottonseed Review, 1309–14

Counties with 1990 Population Over 100,000 Ranked by Size, 2328–68

Country and Commodity Allocations Under Public Law 480, Title I/III, 1922–7

Country Development Strategy Statements, 9916–12

Country Exposure Lending Survey, 13002–1

Country Financial Report: Economic Assistance, 9912–4

Country Reports on Economic Policy and Trade Practices, 21384–5

Country Reports on Human Rights Practices for 1990, 21384–3

County and Metropolitan Area Personal Income, 1987-89, 2702–1.209

County Business Patterns, 1988, 2326–6

County Business Patterns, 1989, 2326–8

County Government Employment: 1990, 2466–1.3

County Government Finances: 1988-89, 2466–2.4

Court-Annexed Arbitration in Ten District Courts, 18408–46

Coverage Improves but State Fiscal Problems Jeopardize Continued Progress. Medicaid Expansions, 26121–429

CPI Detailed Report, 6762–2

Crack-Cocaine in Miami, 4498–74

Cranberries, 1621–18.4

Crangonid Shrimp. Species Profiles: Life Histories and Environmental Requirements of Coastal Fishes and Invertebrates (Pacific Northwest), 5506–8.132

Credit Cards and Money Demand: A Cross-Sectional Study, 9379–12.74

Credit Outlook at FmHA, 1004–16.1

Credit Union Directory, 9534–6

Crime and the Nation's Households, 1990, 6066–25.40

Crime in the U.S., 1990. Uniform Crime Reports, 6224–2

Criminal Acts Against Civil Aviation, 1989, 7504–31

Criminal Justice Information Policy: Survey of Criminal History Information Systems, 6068–241

Criminal Victimization in the U.S., 1973-88 Trends, 6066–3.45

Criminal Victimization in the U.S., 1988, 6066–3.42

Criminal Victimization in the U.S., 1989, 6066–3.44

Criminal Victimization, 1989, 6066–25.35

Criminal Victimization, 1990, 6066–25.41

Criteria for a Recommended Standard: Occupational Exposure to Ethylene Glycol Monobutyl Ether and Ethylene Glycol Monobutyl Ether Acetate, 4246–1.98

Critical Evaluation of Exchange Rate Policy in Turkey, 9385–8.112

Crop Production, 1621–1

Crop Sequences Among 1990 Major Field Crops and Associated Farm Program Participation, 1561–16.204

Crop Sugarbeet and Sugarcane Production and Processing Costs, 1989, 1561–14.205

Crop Values, 1990 Summary, 1621–2

Cropping Pattern Comparisons Between 1989 and 1988, 1561–16.201

Crops, Livestock, and Farm Programs: Overlooked Interactions, 1548–375

Cross Sections: A Review of Business and Economic Developments Published Quarterly by the Federal Reserve Bank of Richmond, 9389–16

Cross-Level Inferences of Job Satisfaction in the Prediction of Intent To Leave, 7506–10.94

Crossroads for the Cattle Industry, 9381–1.201

Cross-Sectional Analysis of Mutual Funds' Market Timing and Security Selection Skill, 9385–8.80

Crowded Federal Prisons Can Transfer More Inmates to Halfway Houses. Prison Alternatives, 26119–347

Crushed Stone and Sand and Gravel: Mineral Industry Surveys, 5612–2.20

Crushed Stone, Directory of Principal Producers in the U.S. in 1989: Mineral Industry Surveys Annual Advance Summary Supplement, 5614–5.2

Cumulative Report on Rescissions and Deferrals, 102–2

Current and Forthcoming Publications, 4822–1

Current and Potential Agricultural Trade Between Eastern and Central Europe and Developing Countries, 1524–4.2

Current and Projected Availability of Special Nursing Home Programs for Alzheimer's Disease Patients. National Medical Expenditure Survey, 4186–8.12

Current Business Reports: Advance Monthly Retail Sales, 2413–2

Current Business Reports: Monthly Retail Trade Sales and Inventories, 2413–3

Current Business Reports: Monthly Wholesale Trade Sales and Inventories, 2413–7

Current Business Reports. Motor Freight Transportation and Warehousing Survey, 2413–14

Current Business Reports: Service Annual Survey, 1990, 2413–8

Current Housing Reports,

Current Business Reports: 1989 Retail Trade. Annual Sales, Year-End Inventories, Purchases, Gross Margin, and Accounts Receivable, by Kind of Retail Store, 2413–5

Current Business Reports: 1990 Wholesale Trade. Annual Sales and Year-End Inventories, Purchases, and Gross Margin Estimates of Merchant Wholesalers, 2413–13

Current Construction Reports: Characteristics of New Housing, 1990, 2384–1

Current Construction Reports: Expenditures for Residential Improvements and Repairs, 2382–7

Current Construction Reports: Expenditures for Residential Upkeep and Improvement, 2382–7

Current Construction Reports: Expenditures for Residential Upkeep and Improvement, Annual, 2384–4

Current Construction Reports: Housing Completions, 2382–2

Current Construction Reports: Housing Starts, 2382–1

Current Construction Reports: Housing Units Authorized by Building Permits, 2382–5

Current Construction Reports: Housing Units Authorized by Building Permits, Annual 1990, 2384–2

Current Construction Reports: New One-Family Houses Sold, 2382–3

Current Construction Reports: New One-Family Houses Sold and for Sale, 2382–3

Current Construction Reports: New Residential Construction in Selected Metropolitan Statistical Areas, 2382–9

Current Construction Reports: Price Index of New One-Family Houses Sold, 2382–8

Current Construction Reports: Value of New Construction Put in Place, 2382–4

Current Economic Conditions, 9362–8

Current Efforts To Improve the Soviet Freight Transportation System, 1004–16.1

Current Energy Situation and the National Energy Strategy, 1004–16.1

Current Federal Aid Research Report: Fish, 1990, 5504–23

Current Federal Aid Research Report: Wildlife, 1990, 5504–24

Current Fisheries Statistics, 2166–6

Current Funds Revenues and Expenditures of Institutions of Higher Education, FY80-88, 4844–6

Current Housing Reports. American Housing Survey for Metropolitan Areas, 1988, 2485–6

Current Housing Reports. American Housing Survey for the U.S. in 1989, 2485–12

Current Housing Reports. Annual Housing Survey, Components of Inventory Change: 1973-83, 2485–14

Current Housing Reports. Characteristics of Apartments Completed: 1990, 2484–3

Current Housing Reports. Housing Vacancies and Homeownership, 2482–1

Current Housing Reports. Market Absorption of Apartments, 2482–2

Current Housing Reports. Market Absorption of Apartments: Annual 1990 Absorptions (Apartments Completed in 1989), 2484–2

Current Housing Reports, Series H-111. Housing Vacancies and Homeownership, Annual Statistics: 1990, 2484–1

Current Housing Reports.

Current Housing Reports. Series H-121: Housing Characteristics, 2486–1

Current Housing Reports. Supplement to the American Housing Survey for Selected Metropolitan Areas: 1984, 2485–8

Current Industrial Reports: All Manufacturing Industries, 2506–3

Current Industrial Reports: Apparel, 2506–6

Current Industrial Reports: Chemicals and Petroleum Products; Rubber and Plastics, 2506–8

Current Industrial Reports: Food, 2506–4

Current Industrial Reports: Glass, Clay, and Related Products, 2506–9

Current Industrial Reports: Intermediate Metal Products, 2506–11

Current Industrial Reports: Machinery and Equipment; Electrical and Electronics, 2506–12

Current Industrial Reports: Primary Metals, 2506–10

Current Industrial Reports: Textile Mill Products, 2506–5

Current Industrial Reports: Wood, Paper, and Related Products, 2506–7

Current Information Technology Resource Requirements of the Federal Government: FY91, 104–33

Current International Trade Position of the U.S., 2042–25

Current Population Reports. Series P-20: Population Characteristics, 2546–1

Current Population Reports. Series P-23: Special Studies, 2546–2

Current Population Reports. Series P-25: Population Estimates and Projections, 2546–3

Current Population Reports. Series P-25: Population Estimates and Projections; Estimates of the Population of the U.S. to (Date), 2542–1

Current Population Reports. Series P-60: Consumer Income, 2546–6

Current Population Reports. Series P-70: Household Economic Studies, 2546–20

Current Status of Health Promotion Activities in Four Midwest Cities, 4042–3.223

Current Velocity and Hydrographic Observations in the Southwestern North Atlantic Ocean: Subtropical Atlantic Climate Studies (STACS), 1989, 2146–7.7

Current Wage Developments, 6782–1

Customers Rate Postal Service Performance, 9868–1

Customs Collections Quarterly, 8142–1

Customs Trade Topics, 8142–1

Customs U.S.A., 8144–1

Cyclical Effects of the Unemployment Insurance (UI) Program: Final Report, 6406–6.34

Cyclical Patterns in the Variance of Economic Activity, 9366–6.275

Cyclical Swing or Secular Slide? Why Have New England's Banks Been Losing Money?, 9373–1.220

Cyclicality of Cash Flow and Investment in U.S. Manufacturing, 9375–1.202

Daily Treasury Statement, 8102–4

Dairy Cooperatives: Role and Effects of the Capper-Volstead Antitrust Exemption, 26113–499

Dairy Imports in Sub-Saharan Africa and the Welfare Implications of Import Policies, 1528–321

Index by Titles

Dairy Industry in the 1990's, 1004–16.1

Dairy, Livestock, and Poultry: Foreign Agricultural Service Circular Series, 1925–33

Dairy, Livestock, and Poultry: Foreign Agricultural Service Circular Series. Meat and Dairy Monthly Imports, 1925–31

Dairy, Livestock, and Poultry: U.S. Trade and Prospects. Foreign Agricultural Service Circular Series, 1925–32

Dairy Market Statistics, 1990 Annual Summary, 1317–1

Dairy Monthly Imports: Foreign Agricultural Service Circular Series, 1925–31

Dairy Price Support Program, 1990-91: ASCS Commodity Fact Sheet, 1806–4.5

Dairy Products, 1627–3

Dairy Products, 1990 Summary, 1627–5

Dairy Situation and Outlook Report, 1561–2

Dairy Situation and Outlook Yearbook, 1561–2

Data Book of Child and Adolescent Injury, 4108–56

Data Book, Operating Banks and Branches: Summary of Deposits in All FDIC BIF-Insured Commercial and Savings Banks and U.S. Branches of Foreign Banks, June 30, 1990, 9295–3

Data Collection Organization Effects in the National Medical Expenditure Survey, 4188–68

Data Evaluation and Methods Research. Vital and Health Statistics Series 2, 4147–2

Data from the Drug Abuse Warning Network, Annual Data, 1990, 4494–8

Data from the National Health Interview Survey. Vital and Health Statistics Series 10, 4147–10

Data from the National Vital Statistics System. Vital and Health Statistics Series 20, 4147–20

Data on Health Resources Utilization. Vital and Health Statistics Series 13, 4147–13

Data on Mortality. Vital and Health Statistics Series 20, 4147–20

Data on Natality, Marriage, and Divorce. Vital and Health Statistics Series 21, 4147–21

Data on the Distribution and Abundance of Submersed Aquatic Vegetation in the Tidal Potomac River and Transition Zone of the Potomac Estuary, Maryland, Virginia, and the District of Columbia, 1988, 5666–27.22

De Novo Banking in the Third District, 9387–1.201

Deadliest, Costliest, and Most Intense U.S. Hurricanes of This Century (and Other Frequently Requested Hurricane Facts), 2188–15

Death Investigation in the U.S. and Canada, 1990, 4208–34

Deaths of Hispanic Origin, 15 Reporting States, 1979-81. Vital and Health Statistics Series 20, 4147–20.18

Debits and Deposit Turnover at Commercial Banks, 9365–2.5

Debt Burden Facing College Graduates, 4808–26

Debt Maturity and the Back-to-the-Wall Theory of Corporate Finance, 9366–6.285

Dec. 31, 1990, Federal Civilian Employment by State, Metropolitan Area, Overseas, Citizenship, Major Agency, Pay System Category, and Work Schedule, 9842–1.203

Deciduous Fruit and Table Grape Update: World Apple and Pear Outlook and Southern Hemisphere Focus, 1925–34.207

Decision of the Secretary of Commerce on Whether a Statistical Adjustment of the 1990 Census of Population and Housing Should Be Made for Coverage Deficiencies Resulting in an Overcount or Undercount of the Population, 2008–31

Decline in Establishment Reporting: Impact on CWHS Industrial and Geographic Data, 4742–1.203

Decline in Unemployment Insurance Claims Activity in the 1980s, 6406–6.33

Decline in U.S. Saving and Its Implications for Economic Growth, 9385–1.201

Decline of Corporate Tax Revenues, 25368–173

Defense Environmental Restoration Program Annual Report to Congress for FY90, 3544–36

Defense Inventory: Defense Logistics Agency Customers Order Supplies Uneconomically, 26123–331

Defense Inventory: DOD's Humanitarian Assistance Program, 26123–316

Defense Logistics Agency Customers Order Supplies Uneconomically. Defense Inventory, 26123–331

Defense Personnel: Status of Flag Officers, Selectees, and Billets, 26123–340

Defense Personnel: Status of Implementing Joint Assignments for Military Leaders, 26123–317

Defense Procurement: DOD Purchases of Foreign-Made Machine Tools, 26123–324

Defense Research: Protecting Sensitive Data and Materials at 10 Chemical and Biological Laboratories, 26123–356

Defense '91: Almanac, 3504–13

Defense's Use of Engineering Contractors for Acquiring Automated Systems. Command and Control, 26125–45

Degrees Conferred in Institutions of Higher Education, by Race/Ethnicity and Sex, 4844–17

Delegated Monitoring with Diseconomies of Scale, 9387–8.248

Delivering the Goods: Public Works Technologies, Management, and Finance, 26358–235

Demographic and Behavioral Sciences Branch, Report to National Advisory Child Health and Human Development Council, 4478–194

Demographic Characteristics, Drug Use, and Sexual Behavior of IV Drug Users with AIDS in Bronx, N.Y., 4042–3.206

Demographic Impact of an AIDS Epidemic on an African Country: Application of the iwgAIDS Model, 2326–18.57

Demographic Profiles of the Airway Facilities Work Force, Annual Report, FY89 Year-End Data, 7504–41

Department of Defense Budget for FY92-93. Construction Programs (C-1), 3544–39

Department of Defense Budget for FY92-93. Procurement Programs (P-1), 3544–32

Department of Defense Budget for FY92-93. R, D, T & E Programs (R-1), 3544–33

Department of Defense Inspector General, Semiannual Report to the Congress, Oct. 1, 1989-Mar. 31, 1990, 3542–18

Department of Defense Inspector General, Semiannual Report to the Congress, Apr. 1, 1990-Sept. 30, 1990, 3542–18

Department of Defense Inspector General, Semiannual Report to the Congress, Oct. 1, 1990-Mar. 31, 1991, 3542–18

Index by Titles

Directory of Federally...

Department of Defense Military Functions, Status of Funds, 3542–3

Department of Defense Prime Contract Awards, FY90, 3542–1

Department of Defense Prime Contract Awards, First Half FY91, 3542–1

Department of Defense Real and Personal Property, Sept. 30, 1990, 3544–6

Department of Defense Selected Medical Care Statistics, 3542–15

Department of Education: Annual Evaluation Report, FY90, 4804–5

Department of Energy Annual Procurement and Financial Assistance Report, FY90, 3004–21

Department of Energy Semiannual Report to Congress on Inspector General Audit Reports, 3002–15

Department of Interior News Releases, 5306–4

Department of the Army Historical Summary, FY83, 3704–11

Department of the Treasury News, 8002–7

Department of Veterans Affairs Domiciliary Care for Homeless Veterans Program, Third Progress Report, 8604–10

Department of Veterans Affairs Program for Homeless Chronically Mentally Ill Veterans, Fourth Progress Report, 8604–11

Department Store Inventory Price Indexes, 6762–7

Deposit Growth, Nonperforming Assets, and Return on Assets, by County, 9381–14.1

Deposit Insurance: A Strategy for Reform, 26119–320

Deposit Insurance Reform and Financial Modernization, Volume I, 25248–121

Deposit Insurance Reform and Financial Modernization, Volume II, 25248–122

Deposit Insurance Reform and Financial Modernization, Volume III, 25248–123

Deposit Insurance Reform in the Post-FIRREA Environment: Lessons from the Texas Deposit Market, 9379–14.11

Depreciation of Business-Use Light Trucks, 8006–5.6

Depreciation of Business-Use Passenger Cars, 8006–5.5

Deregulation and the Location of Financial Institution Offices, 9377–1.208

Deregulation, Cost Economies and Allocative Efficiency of Large Commercial Banks, 9375–13.50

Description and Analysis of S. 612 (Savings and Investment Incentive Act of 1991), 25368–175

Description of High-Occupancy Vehicle Facilities in North America, 7888–80

Description of the Physical Environment and Coal-Mining History of West-Central Indiana, with Emphasis on Six Small Watersheds, 5666–27.19

Descriptive Analysis of the Insurance Industry in the U.S., 21248–159

Descriptive Epidemiology of International Cocaine Trafficking, 4498–74

Design of Health Plan Benefits for the Nonelderly, 23898–5

Desk Reference Guide to U.S. Agricultural Trade, 1924–9

Detail Specification for 62.5-um Core Diameter/125-um Cladding Diameter Class Ia Multimode, Graded-Index Optical Waveguide Fibers. Computer-Related Telecommunications Standard, 2216–2.196

Detailed Diagnoses and Procedures, National Hospital Discharge Survey, 1988. Vital and Health Statistics Series 13, 4147–13.105

Detailed Diagnoses and Procedures, National Hospital Discharge Survey, 1989. Vital and Health Statistics Series 13, 4147–13.108

Detecting Level Shifts in Time Series: Misspecification and a Proposed Solution, 9379–12.71

Detentions Have Been Reduced but Better Monitoring Is Needed. Noncriminal Juveniles, 26119–333

Determinants of Genital Human Papillomavirus Infection in Young Women, 4472–1.215

Determinants of the Growth of Foreign Banking Assets in the U.S., 9385–8.108

Determinants of Total Family Charges for Health Care: U.S., 1980, 4146–12.27

Determining Foreign Exchange Risk and Bank Capital Requirements, 9366–7.254

Detroit-Windsor/Port Huron-Sarnia Air Pollution Advisory Board Report to the International Joint Commission, 14648–25

Developing Countries as a Source of U.S. Export Growth, 1524–4.2

Developing Countries' Trade with the European Community, 1524–4.2

Developing Economies: Agriculture and Trade Report, Situation and Outlook Series, 1524–4.2

Development Coordination Committee, Annual Report of the Chairman, 9904–1

Development Impact of Counterpart Funds: A Review of the Literature, 9918–21

Development Impact of U.S. Program Food Assistance: Evidence from the AID Evaluation Literature, 9918–20

Development Issues 1990: U.S. Actions Affecting Developing Countries. 1990 Annual Report of the Chairman of the Development Coordination Committee, 9904–1

Development Issues 1991: U.S. Actions Affecting Developing Countries. 1991 Annual Report of the Chairman of the Development Coordination Committee, 9904–1

Development of Diagnostic Data in the 10-Percent Sample of Disabled SSI Recipients, 4742–1.214

Developmental, Learning, and Emotional Problems: Health of Our Nation's Children, U.S., 1988, 4146–8.193

Developments Affecting U.S. Commercial Relations with the Nonmarket Economy Countries During 1990, 9882–2.203

Developments in Apparel, Textiles, and Fibers Affecting the Consumer, 1702–1.209

Developments in the Middle East, February 1990, 21388–58

Developments in Trade Between the U.S. and the Nonmarket Economy Countries During 1990, 9882–2.202

Diabetes. Indian Health Conditions, 4088–2

Diabetes Mellitus Interagency Coordinating Committee, 17th Annual Report, FY90, 4474–34

Diabetes Surveillance, 1980-87, 4205–41

Diatomite in 1990: Mineral Industry Surveys Annual Report, 5614–5.8

Dicofol (Kelthane) as an Environmental Contaminant: A Review. Fish and Wildlife Technical Report, 5506–12.2

Dictionary of Occupational Titles, Fourth Edition, Revised 1991, 6406–1.1

Dictionary of Occupational Titles, Revised Fourth Edition, 6406–1

Dientamoeba fragilis Detection Methods and Prevalence: A Survey of State Public Health Laboratories, 4042–3.225

Dietary Guidelines for Americans, 1990 Revision, 1004–16.1

Differences Between Oklahoma Indian Infant Mortality and Other Races, 4042–3.209

Differences in Agricultural Research and Productivity Among 26 Countries, 1528–318

Differences in Food Prices Across U.S. Cities: Evidence from CPI Data, 6886–6.78

Differences in Hypertension Prevalence Among U.S. Black and White Women of Childbearing Age, 4042–3.231

Difficult Choices Face the Future of the Recreation Program. Forest Service, 26113–518

Diffusing Innovations: Implementing the Technology Transfer Act of 1986, 26131–85

Diffusion Indexes of Industrial Production, 9362–1.205

Digest of Activities, FY90, U.S. Postal Inspection Service, 9864–9

Digest of Education Statistics, 1990, 4824–2

Digest of Education Statistics, 1991, 4824–2

Digestive System Diseases. Indian Health Conditions, 4088–2

Dimension Stone, Directory of Principal Producers in the U.S. in 1989: Mineral Industry Surveys Annual Advance Summary Supplement, 5614–5.16

Diminishing Role of Commercial Banking in the U.S. Economy, 9375–13.62

Diphtheria, Tetanus, and Pertussis: Recommendations for Vaccine Use and Other Preventive Measures. Recommendations of the Immunization Practices Advisory Committee (ACIP), 4206–2.46

Direct Approach for Estimating Nitrogen, Phosphorus, and Land Demands at the Regional Level, 1588–152

Directorate for Engineering, FY90 Directory of Awards, 9624–24

Director's Report: A Review of the U.S. Marshals Service in FY90, 6294–1

Directory of Awards. Directorate for Science and Engineering Education, 9624–27

Directory of Awards, FY88, Mechanical and Structural Systems, 9626–7.2

Directory of Companies and Plants Producing Salt in the U.S., 1990, 5614–30

Directory of Companies Producing Salt in the U.S., 1989, 5614–30

Directory of Companies Required To File Annual Reports with the Securities and Exchange Commission Under the Securities Exchange Act of 1934, Alphabetically and by Industry Groups, Sept. 30, 1990, 9734–5

Directory of Energy Data Collection Forms, 3164–86

Directory of Energy Information Administration Models, 1991, 3164–87

Directory of Federal Anti-Drug Grants. An Office of National Drug Control Policy White Paper, 236–1.5

Directory of Federally Insured Credit Unions, 9534–6

Directory of Genetic Testing...

Index by Titles

Directory of Genetic Testing Laboratories, 4698–4

Directory of Maternal and Child Health Programs in Major Urban Health Departments, 4108–51

Directory of Members, 1991: Eleventh District—Arizona, California, Nevada, Federal Home Loan Bank of San Francisco, 9304–23

Directory of National Trade Associations, Professional Societies, and Labor Unions of the Construction and Building Materials Industries, 2042–1.202

Directory of Operating Small Business Investment Companies, 9762–4

Directory of Principal Aggregates Producers in the U.S. in 1990: Mineral Industry Surveys Annual Advance Summary Supplement, 5614–5.4

Directory of Principal Crushed Stone Producers in the U.S. in 1989: Mineral Industry Surveys Annual Advance Summary Supplement, 5614–5.2

Directory of Principal Dimension Stone Producers in the U.S. in 1989: Mineral Industry Surveys Annual Advance Summary Supplement, 5614–5.16

Directory of Psychology Staffing and Services in VA Medical Centers, Medical and Regional Office Centers Domiciliary, Outpatient Clinics and Regional Offices with Outpatient Clinics, Seventh Edition, 1991, 8704–2

Directory of Public Elementary and Secondary Education Agencies, 1989-90, 4834–1

Directory of Selected Early Childhood Programs, 1990-91, 4944–10

Directory of U.S. Government Datafiles for Mainframes and Microcomputers, 2224–3

Disability and Health: Characteristics of Persons by Limitation of Activity and Assessed Health Status, U.S., 1984-88, 4146–8.202

Disaggregate Analysis of Discount Window Borrowing, 9385–1.209

Disaster Assistance: Federal, State, and Local Responses to Natural Disasters Need Improvement, 26113–511

Disaster Assistance: Problems in Administering Payments for Nonprogram Crops, 26113–533

Disastrous Floods on the Trinity, Red, and Arkansas Rivers, May 1990. Natural Disaster Survey Report, 2186–6.4

Discrete Time Models of Entry into Marriage Based on Retrospective Marital Histories of Young Adults in the U.S. and the Federal Republic of Germany, 2626–10.143

Discussion of Cooley and Hansen's "Welfare Costs of Moderate Inflations", 9383–20.4

Disposition of Assets by the RTC, 21248–144

Distilled Spirits: Monthly Statistical Release, 8486–1.3

Distribution and Abundance of Fishes and Invertebrates in Central Gulf of Mexico Estuaries, 2176–7.23

Distribution and Abundance of Fishes and Invertebrates in Southeast Estuaries, 2176–7.25

Distribution and Abundance of Fishes and Invertebrates in West Coast Estuaries, Volume II: Species Life History Summaries, 2176–7.24

Distribution and Abundance of Golden Eagles and Other Raptors in Campbell and Converse Counties, Wyoming: Fish and Wildlife Technical Report, 5506–12.1

Distribution and Abundance of Juvenile Salmonids off Oregon and Washington, 1981-85, 2168–123

Distribution of Loans Made by Six Specified Types, By Race or Ethnic Group, 1182–5

Distribution of Obligations By Marital Status, Race, Ethnic Group and Sex, 1182–8

Distribution of Personnel by State and by Selected Locations, Sept. 30, 1990, 3544–7

Distribution of Sexually Immature Components of 10 Northwest Atlantic Groundfish Species Based on Northeast Fisheries Center Bottom Trawl Surveys, 1968-86, 2168–122

Distribution of the American Indian, Eskimo, or Aleut Population, 1990, 2328–76

Distribution of West Indian Manatees (Trichechus manatus) in Puerto Rico: 1988-89, 14738–11

Distributors of TVA Power, Statistics, 9804–19

District Banks in 1990: Bruised, but Not Broken, 9391–16.208

District Forestry Industry: Growing to New Heights?, 9391–16.204

District Real Economy in 1990: Losing Its Fizz, 9391–16.207

District Services: What They Are and Why They Have Grown, 9391–16.203

Diversification of the Agricultural Product Portfolio Through Biotechnology, 1004–16.1

Diversity of Private Schools. Schools and Staffing Survey, 4836–3.7

Divisia Monetary Services Indexes for Switzerland: Are They Useful for Monetary Targeting?, 9391–1.221

Division of Research Resources, Program Highlights, 4434–12

Do Advance Deficiency Payments Affect Credit Markets?, 1541–1.204

Do Bank Holding Companies Act as "Sources of Strength" for Their Bank Subsidiaries?, 9391–1.205

Do Capital Markets Predict Problems in Large Commercial Banks?, 9373–1.210

Do International Reactions of Stock and Bond Markets Reflect Macroeconomic Fundamentals?, 9385–1.211

Do You Know Which Report Contains the Data You Need?, 2308–62

Do You Know Which 1990 Report Is Similar to Your Favorite 1980 Report?, 2308–61

Documentation of the Static World Policy Simulation (SWOPSIM) Modeling Framework, 1528–315

Documents and Committee Reports. Vital and Health Statistics Series 4, 4147–4

DOD Can Improve the Safety of On-Base Track and Equipment. Railroad Safety, 26113–535

DOD Purchases of Foreign-Made Machine Tools. Defense Procurement, 26123–324

DOD Service Academies: Improved Cost and Performance Monitoring Needed, 26123–355

DOD's Humanitarian Assistance Program. Defense Inventory, 26123–316

DOD-Wide Program Is Not Currently Feasible. Lease Refinancing, 26111–75

DOE Needs Better Controls To Identify Contractors Having Foreign Interests. Nuclear Nonproliferation, 26113–520

Does Consumer Sentiment Affect Household Spending? If So, Why?, 9366–6.282

Does Education Pay Off? Statistical Brief, 2326–17.25

Does More Money Mean More Bank Loans?, 9381–1.208

Doing Agricultural Economics, 1502–3.201

Dollar GNP Estimates for China, 2326–18.58

Dollar Summary of Prime Contract Awards by State, Place, and Contractor, FY89, 3544–22

Dollar Summary of Prime Contract Awards by State, Place, and Contractor, FY90, 3544–22

Dollar's Fall Boosts U.S. Machinery Exports, 1985-90, 6722–1.233

Domestic Aviation: Future Challenges. 16th Annual FAA Aviation Forecast Conference Proceedings, 7504–28

Domestic Cannabis Eradication/Suppression Program, 1990, 6284–4

Domestic Corporations Controlled by Foreign Persons, 1988, 8302–2.219

Domestic Natural Gas Reserves and Production Dedicated to Interstate Pipeline Companies, 1990, 3162–4.209

Domestic Offices, Insured Commercial Bank Assets and Liabilities Consolidated Report of Condition, 9365–3

Domestic Oil and Gas Recoverable Resource Base: Supporting Analysis for the National Energy Strategy, 3166–6.51

Domestic Rice Consumption Patterns, 1988/89, 1561–8.204

Domiciliary Care for Homeless Veterans Program Progress Report, 8604–10

Donation of Surplus Personal Property, Annual Report to the Congress of the U.S., 9454–22

Donning Times and Flotation Characteristics of Infant Life Preservers: Four Representative Types, 7506–10.85

DOT Employment Facts, A Report to Management, FY90, 7304–18

Dover and Rock Soles. Species Profiles: Life Histories and Environmental Requirements of Coastal Fishes and Invertebrates (Pacific Northwest), 5506–8.130

Draft Economic Diversity and Dependency Assessment, Rocky Mountain Region, 1208–362

Draft Mission Plan Amendment, 3368–1

Driver Licenses, 1989, 7554–16

Dropout Rates in the U.S.: 1990, 4834–23

Drug Abuse Among Race/Ethnic Minorities, 4498–72

Drug Abuse and Drug Abuse Research, 4008–66, 4498–68

Drug and Alcohol Use at Work: A Survey of Young Workers, 6722–1.237

Drug Control: National Guard Counter-Drug Support to Law Enforcement Agencies, 26123–343

Drug Interdiction: Funding Continues To Increase but Program Effectiveness Is Unknown, 26119–318

Drug Policy and Agriculture: U.S. Trade Impacts of Alternative Crops to Andean Coca, 26123–366

Drug Treatment Services: Funding and Admissions, 4498–73

Drug Use Among American High School Students, College Students and Young Adults, 1975-90, 4494–4

Drug Use and Sexual Behavior of Indigent African American Men, 4042–3.254

Index by Titles

Drug Use, Drinking and Smoking: National Survey Results from High School, College, and Young Adult Populations, 4494–4

Drug Use Forecasting, 6062–3

Drug Use Forecasting (DUF): A Program of the National Institute of Justice Cofunded by the Bureau of Justice Assistance, 6062–3

Drug Utilization in the U.S., 1989: Eleventh Annual Review, 4064–12

Drugs and Crime Facts, 1990, 6064–30

Drugs and Jail Inmates, 1989, 6066–19.63

Drugs and Violence: Causes, Correlates, and Consequences, 4498–70

Drum Reconditioning Industry: Preliminary Data Summary, 9206–4.8

Drunk Driving Facts, 7766–15.3

Duck Stamp Collection, 1991-92, 5504–25

Dwight D. Eisenhower System of Interstate and Defense Highways Status of Development, 7552–5

Dynamics of Hospital Services: Changing Patterns in the Services Provided by Hospitals from 1980 to 1987, 17206–2.22

Early Estimates. Key Statistics for Private Elementary and Secondary Education, 4834–21

Early Estimates. Key Statistics for Public and Private Elementary and Secondary Education, School Year 1990-91, 4834–19

Early Estimates. National Higher Education Statistics: Fall 1990, 4844–14

Early Estimates. National Higher Education Statistics: Fall 1991, 4844–14

Early Estimates. National Postsecondary Statistics, Collegiate and Noncollegiate: Fall 1990, 4844–16

Early Life History of Pacific Herring: 1989 Prince William Sound Herring Egg Incubation Experiment, 2176–1.37

Early Life History of Pacific Herring: 1989 Prince William Sound Herring Larvae Survey, 2176–1.37

Earnings Inequality Accelerates in the 1980's, 6722–1.201

Earth Resources: A Continuing Bibliography with Indexes, 9502–7

Earthquake Hazard Mitigation and Earthquake Insurance, 21248–154

Eastern Europe Business Bulletin, 2042–33

Eastern Europe: Coming Around the First Turn, 9118–13

Eastern Europe: Status of U.S. Assistance Efforts, 26123–319

Eastern Europe: The Impact of Geographic Forces on a Strategic Region, 9118–18

Eastern North Pacific Hurricanes—1990, 2152–8.202

East-West Trade-Statistics Monitoring System: Tenth Annual Analysis of Manufactured Imports from the NMEs, 9882–2.204

Ecology and Management of Walrus Populations: Report of an International Workshop, 26-30 March 1990, Seattle, Wash., U.S.A., 14738–9

Ecology: Community Profiles, 5506–9

Ecology of Wetlands in Big Meadows, Rocky Mountain National Park, Colorado, 5508–113

Econometric Analysis of Borrowing Constraints and Household Debt, 9379–12.73

Econometrics of Elasticities or the Elasticity of Econometrics: An Empirical Analysis of the Behavior of U.S. Imports, 9366–7.250

Economic and Budget Outlook: An Update. A Report to the Senate and House Committees on the Budget, 26304–3.2

Economic and Budget Outlook: FY92-96. A Report to the Senate and House Committees on the Budget, 26304–3.1

Economic and Demographic Systems Analysis: Nome, Alaska, 5736–5.13

Economic and Demographic Systems Analysis: Unalaska and Cold Bay, Alaska, 5736–5.14

Economic and Energy Indicators, 9112–1

Economic Assessment of the Freeze on Program Yields, 1548–376

Economic Censuses of Outlying Areas, 1987. Geographic Area Statistics. Puerto Rico Wholesale Trade, Retail Trade, Service Industries, 2591–1

Economic Censuses of Outlying Areas, 1987. Puerto Rico Subject Statistics: Wholesale Trade, Retail Trade, and Service Industries, 2591–2

Economic Censuses of Outlying Areas, 1987. Puerto Rico, Subject Statistics. Wholesale Trade, Retail Trade, and Service Industries. Part 1: Establishment and Firm Size, Legal Form of Organization, and Corporate Ownership, 2591–2.1

Economic Censuses of Outlying Areas, 1987. Puerto Rico, Subject Statistics. Wholesale Trade, Retail Trade, and Service Industries. Part 2: Miscellaneous Subjects, 2591–2.2

Economic Consequences for Medicaid of Human Immunodeficiency Virus Infection, 4652–1.215

Economic Consequences of Reducing Military Spending, 9391–1.204

Economic Costs of Alcohol and Drug Abuse and Mental Illness: 1985, 4048–35

Economic Development Administration, 1990 Annual Report, 2064–2

Economic Discussion Papers, 6366–3

Economic Effects of Significant U.S. Import Restraints, Phase III: Services, With a Computable General Equilibrium Analysis of Significant U.S. Import Restraints. Report to the Committee on Finance of the U.S. Senate on Investigation No. 332-262 Under Section 332 of the Tariff Act of 1930, 9886–4.173

Economic Growth of OECD Countries, 1980-90, 7144–8

Economic Impact of the Persian Gulf Crisis, 21248–156

Economic Impacts of the S.S. Glacier Bay Oil Spill. Alaska Social and Economic Study, 5736–5.15

Economic Implications of a Ban on EBDC Disease Control Uses in Vegetable Production, 1561–11.204

Economic Implications of Planting Flexibility Provisions for U.S. Upland Cotton Farms, 1561–1.205

Economic Importance of the U.S. Tobacco Industry, 1561–10.203

Economic Indicators, 23842–1

Economic Indicators of the Farm Sector: Costs of Production, 1544–20

Economic Indicators of the Farm Sector: Costs of Production. Major Field Crops, 1989, 1544–20.1

Economic Indicators of the Farm Sector: National Financial Summary, 1989, 1544–16

Economic Indicators of the Farm Sector: National Financial Summary, 1990, 1544–16

Economic Indicators of the Farm Sector: Production and Efficiency Statistics, 1989, 1544–17

Economic Indicators of the Farm Sector: State Financial Summary, 1989, 1544–18

Economic Markets and the Standard Industrial Classification, 6886–6.74

Economic Performance and Policy Adjustment: The Experience of Zimbabwe, 1528–319

Economic Perspectives: Federal Reserve Bank of Chicago, 9375–1

Economic Profile of the Dallas-Fort Worth Metropolitan Area, 1990, 6964–2

Economic Profile of the Houston Metropolitan Area, 1990, 6964–1

Economic Report of the President, Transmitted to the Congress February 1991 Together with the Annual Report of the Council of Economic Advisers, 204–1

Economic Research Service in 1991, 1504–6

Economic Review, Federal Reserve Bank of Atlanta, 9371–1

Economic Review, Federal Reserve Bank of Cleveland, 9377–1

Economic Review, Federal Reserve Bank of Dallas, 9379–1

Economic Review, Federal Reserve Bank of Kansas City, 9381–1

Economic Review, Federal Reserve Bank of Richmond, 9389–1

Economic Review, Federal Reserve Bank of San Francisco, 9393–8

Economic Status of Two-Parent Families with Employed Teens and Young Adults, 1702–1.213

Economic Trends, Federal Reserve Bank of Cleveland, 9377–10

Economic Well-Being of Nonmetro Children, 1598–270

Economics of Energy Futures Markets, 3162–11.201

Economics of Family Disruption. Statistical Brief, 2326–17.27

Economics of Long-Term Global Climate Change: A Preliminary Assessment, 3028–5

Economics Update, Federal Reserve Bank of Atlanta, 9371–15

ECP Monthly Progress Report, By State and Area for Period Ending (Date), 1802–13

Ectopic Pregnancy Surveillance, U.S., 1970-87, 4202–7.202

Edible and Industrial Rapeseed Oils, 1004–16.1

Educating the American Indian/Alaska Native Family: 16th Annual Report to the U.S. Congress, FY89, 14874–1

Education Counts: An Indicator System To Monitor the Nation's Educational Health, 4828–40

Education for Homeless Adults: The First Year, 4804–39.1

Education in Appalachia: Accomplishments and Prospects in a National Context, 9088–36

Education Statistics, A Pocket Digest, 4828–26

Educational and Nonprofit Institutions Receiving Prime Contract Awards for Research, Development, Test, and Evaluation, FY90, 3544–17

Educational Attainment in the... Index by Titles

Educational Attainment in the U.S.: March 1989 and 1988, 2546–1.452

Educational Resources Information Center Annual Report, 4814–3

Education's Library: Actions Needed To Improve Its Usefulness, 26121–414

Effect of Import Competition on Manufacturing Wages, 9385–8.89

Effect of Imports on U.S. Manufacturing Wages, 9385–1.204

Effect of Margins on the Volatility of Stock and Derivative Markets: A Review of the Evidence, 11924–4.2

Effect of Rent Control on Housing Quality Change: A Longitudinal Analysis, 9387–8.246

Effect of Simulated Altitude on the Visual Fields of Glaucoma Patients and the Elderly, 7506–10.80

Effect of the Growing Service Sector on Wages in Texas, 9379–1.210

Effect of the Interim Payment Rate for the Drug Epogen on Medicare Expenditures and Dialysis Facility Operations, 4008–113

Effect of the Medicaid Program on Welfare Participation and Labor Supply, 2626–10.139

Effectiveness of Efforts To Reduce Farm Payments Has Been Limited. Agriculture Payments, 26113–546

Effectiveness of IRS' Return Preparer Penalty Program Is Questionable. Tax Administration, 26119–315

Effectiveness of Law Enforcement Against Financial Crime, Part 2, 21248–142

Effectiveness of Sterilized U.S. Foreign Exchange Intervention: An Empirical Study Based on the Noise Trading Approach, 9385–8.114

Effects of Agricultural Growth in Developing Countries on Agricultural Imports, Particularly from the U.S.: Policy Implications, 1548–372

Effects of Being Uninsured on Health Care Service Use: Estimates from the Survey of Income and Program Participation, 2626–10.120

Effects of Closure Policies on Bank Risk-Taking, 9366–6.272

Effects of Competitive Power Purchases Are Not Yet Certain. Electricity Supply, 26113–498

Effects of Devaluation with a Partial Wage Floor, 9371–10.58

Effects of Domestic Agricultural Policy Reform on Environmental Quality, 1502–3.203

Effects of Exchange Rate and Productivity Changes on U.S. Industrial Output at the State Level, 9387–8.255

Effects of Government Transfer Payments on Charitable Contributions, 6886–6.76

Effects of Greater Economic Integration Within the European Community on the U.S.: Third Followup Report. Investigation No. 332-267, 9886–4.170

Effects of Storm-Water Runoff on Local Ground-Water Quality, Clarksville, Tenn., 5666–27.23

Effects of Surface Coal Mining and Reclamation on the Geohydrology of Six Small Watersheds in West-Central Indiana, 5666–27.20

Effects of the 65 mph Speed Limit Through 1989, Report to Congress, 7764–15

Effects of Utility DSM Programs on Electricity Costs and Prices, 3308–99

Efficient Two-Part Tariffs with Uncertainty and Interdependent Demand, 9387–8.253

Egg Products, 1625–2

Eggs, Chickens, and Turkeys, 1625–1

EIA Publications Directory, 1990, 3168–117

Eighth Report to Congress on the Administration of the Wild Free-Roaming, 5724–8

Eisenhower Mathematics and Science Education Program: An Enabling Resource for Reform. Summary Report, 4808–31

Eisenhower Mathematics and Science Education Program: An Enabling Resource for Reform. Technical Report, 4808–31

Elasmobranchs as Living Resources: Advances in the Biology, Ecology, Systematics, and the Status of the Fisheries, 2168–124

Elder Abuse: A Decade of Shame and Inaction, 21148–62

Electric and Hybrid Vehicles Program, 14th Annual Report to Congress for FY90, 3304–2

Electric Current Abroad, 1991 Edition, 2048–1

Electric Fans from the People's Republic of China. Determination of the Commission in Investigation No. 731-TA-473 (Final) Under the Tariff Act of 1930, Together with the Information Obtained in the Investigation, 9886–14.335

Electric Housewares and Fans, 1990, Current Industrial Report, 2506–12.15

Electric Lamps, Current Industrial Report, 2506–12.13, 2506–12.33

Electric Lighting Fixtures, 1990, Current Industrial Report, 2506–12.19

Electric Plant Cost and Power Production Expenses, 1989, 3164–9

Electric Power Annual, 1989, 3164–11

Electric Power Monthly, 3162–35

Electric Sales and Revenue, 1989, 3164–91

Electric Sales, Revenue, and Bills, 3164–91

Electric Trade in the U.S., 1988, 3164–92

Electrical Work Special Trade Contractors (Industry 1731): 1987 Census of Construction Industries. Industry Series, 2373–1.12

Electricity Sales Statistics, 9802–1

Electricity Sales Statistics, 1990, 9804–14

Electricity Savings Among Participants Three Years After Weatherization in Bonneville's 1986 Residential Weatherization Program, 3226–1.7

Electricity Supply: Supporting Analysis for the National Energy Strategy, 3166–6.49

Electricity Supply: The Effects of Competitive Power Purchases Are Not Yet Certain, 26113–498

Electromedical Equipment and Irradiation Equipment (Including X-Ray), 1990, Current Industrial Report, 2506–12.34

Electronic Data Interchange (EDI). Software Standard, 2216–2.200

Electronic Filing: Who's Participating and Who Isn't, 8304–8.1

Elementary and Secondary Education. The Condition of Education, 1991: Volume 1, 4824–1.1

Elementary and Secondary School Civil Rights Survey: State and National Summaries, 1988, 4804–33

Eleventh Annual Report of the Federal Labor Relations Authority and the Federal Service Impasses Panel, FY89, 13364–1

Eliciting Traders' Knowledge in "Frictionless" Asset Market, 9383–20.14

Emergency Conservation Program (ECP) Monthly Progress Report, By State and Area for Period Ending (Date), 1802–13

Emergency Conservation Program, FY90 Statistical Summary, 1804–22

Emergency Revocation Orders of Air Carrier Certificates. Aviation Safety, 26113–547

Emergency Striped Bass Research Study, Report for 1989, 5504–29

Emigration from the U.S., 6266–2.5

Emission Reductions Possible as Scientific Uncertainties Are Resolved. Global Warming, 26113–495

Emissions and Cost Estimates for Globally Significant Anthropogenic Combustion Sources of NO_x, N_2O, CH_4, CO, and CO_2, 9198–124

EML Surface Air Sampling Program, 1989 Data, 3004–31

Empirical Examination of Government Expenditures and the Ex Ante Crowding Out Effect for the British Economy, 9385–8.83

Empirical Investigation of the Determinants of Discount Window Borrowing: A Disaggregate Analysis, 9385–8.110

Empirical Relationships Between the Total Industrial Production Index and Its Diffusion Indexes, 9366–6.277

Employee Benefits for American Workers, 15496–1.11

Employee Benefits in Small Private Establishments, 1990, 6784–20

Employee Benefits in State and Local Governments Address Family Concerns, 6726–1.41

Employee Drug Testing: Status of Federal Agencies' Programs, 26119–344

Employee Retirement Income Security Act (ERISA), 1989 Report to Congress, 6684–1

Employee Retirement Income Security Act (ERISA), 1990 Report to Congress, 6684–1

Employer Actions To Recruit, Hire, and Retain Eligible Workers Vary. Targeted Jobs Tax Credit, 26121–407

Employer Costs for Employee Compensation in Private Industry, by Establishment Size: March 1990, 6744–22

Employer Sanctions and U.S. Labor Markets: First Report, 6366–5.2

Employer Sanctions and U.S. Labor Markets: Second Report, 6366–5.3

Employer Strategies for a Changing Labor Force: A Primer on Innovative Programs and Policies, 15496–1.12

Employer-Sponsored Prescription Drug Benefits, 6722–1.215

Employment and Earnings, 6742–2

Employment and Earnings Characteristics of Families, 6742–21

Employment and Training Administration Press Releases, 6406–2

Employment and Unemployment: Area Trends, 6402–1

Employment and Wages, Annual Averages, 1990, 6744–16

Employment Cost Index, 6782–5

Employment Data on T.38 Physicians, Dentists and Nurses, 8602–6

Employment Growth in Largest Metropolitan Areas, 1990, 6946–3.20

Employment, Hours, and Earnings, U.S., 1909-90, 6744–4

Index by Titles

Employment in Perspective: Minority Workers, 6742–18

Employment in Perspective: Women in the Labor Force, 6742–17

Employment of Major Local Governments. 1987 Census of Governments, Volume 3. Public Employment, No. 1, 2455–1

Employment of Youth Down This Summer; Unemployment Up, 6744–14

Employment Practices in Selected Large Private Companies. Workforce Issues, 26119–324

Employment Security Administration Account, 8102–9.1

Employment Service: Improved Leadership Needed for Better Performance, 26121–430

Employment Situation, 6742–5

Employment Trends in Farm and Farm-Related Industries, 1975-87, 1598–271

Employment-Unemployment, Monthly Hearings, 23846–4

EMS Interest Rate Differentials and Fiscal Policy: A Model with an Empirical Application to Italy, 9366–7.259

Encouraging Private Investment in Space Activities, 26306–6.154

Endangered and Threatened Species Recovery Program, Report to Congress, 5504–35

End-Stage Renal Disease. Indian Health Conditions, 4088–2

End-Stage Renal Disease, 1988. Health Care Financing Research Report, 4654–16

End-Stage Renal Disease, 1989. Health Care Financing Research Report, 4654–16

Energy Conservation Trends: Understanding the Factors That Affect Conservation Gains in the U.S. Economy, 3308–93

Energy Consumption and Conservation Potential: Supporting Analysis for the National Energy Strategy, 3166–6.48

Energy Dependence and Efficiency, 9375–1.210

Energy Efficiency Improvement Potential of Commercial Aircraft to 2010, 3028–6

Energy Efficiency in the Federal Government: Government by Good Example?, 26358–240

Energy Impact of the Persian Gulf Crisis, 21368–132

Energy in Developing Countries, 26358–232

Energy Information Administration Annual Report to Congress, 1990, 3164–29

Energy Issues for Agriculture: Challenges for Research, 1004–16.1

Energy Management Annual Report, FY89, 9804–26

Energy Management Annual Report, FY90, 9804–26

Energy Policy: Emphasize Conservation, Say District Business Leaders, 9383–19.203

Energy Production and Other Industrial Feed Grain Uses, 1004–16.1

Energy Profiles of Czechoslovakia, Hungary and Poland, and Their Emerging Free-Market Economies, 25318–81

Energy Related Inventions Program, A Joint Program of the Department of Energy and the National Institute of Standards and Technology: Status Report, 2214–5

Energy Resources Performance Report, FY89-90, 3228–11

Energy Security: Impacts of Lifting Alaskan North Slope Oil Exports Ban, 26113–496

Energy Situation Analysis Report, Persian Gulf, 3162–44

Energy Technology Choices: Shaping Our Future, 26358–243

Energy-Related Doctoral Science and Engineering Employment Remains Stable in 1989; R&D Involvement at All-Time High, 3006–8.17

Energy-Related Inventions Program: Commercial Progress of Participants Through 1988, 3308–91

Enforcement Accomplishments Report, FY90, 9184–21

Enforcement of Federal Laws Could Be Strengthened. Wildlife Protection, 26113–525

Engineering Directory of Awards, 9624–24

English Language Programs Division: FY90, 9854–2

Enrollment in Higher Education, Fall 1989, 4844–2

Enterprise Statistics, 1987. Auxiliary Establishments, 2329–6

Enterprise Statistics, 1987. Company Summary, 2329–8

Entry into Marriage and the Transition to Adulthood Among Recent Birth Cohorts of Young Adults in the U.S. and the Federal Republic of Germany, 2626–10.131

Entry Level Jobs: Defining Them and Counting Them, 6742–1.201

Environmental Challenge of the 1990s, Proceedings of the International Conference on Pollution Prevention: Clean Technologies and Clean Products, Washington, D.C., June 10-13, 1990, 9184–22

Environmental Excise Taxes, 1988, 8302–2.202

Environmental Information Handbook Series, 3326–1

Environmental Measurements Laboratory Surface Air Sampling Program, 1989 Data, 3004–31

Environmental Monitoring and Disposal of Radioactive Wastes from U.S. Naval Nuclear-Powered Ships and Their Support Facilities, 1990, 3804–11

Environmental Monitoring for EG&G Idaho Facilities at the Idaho National Engineering Laboratory, Annual Report, 1990, 3354–10

Environmental Quality: The Twenty-first Annual Report of the Council on Environmental Quality Together with the President's Message to Congress, 484–1

Environmental Radiation Data, 9192–5

Environmental Research Laboratories Publication Abstracts, FY90, 2144–25

Environmental Restoration and Waste Management Five-Year Plan, FY93-97, 3024–7

Environmental Tobacco Smoke in the Workplace: Lung Cancer and Other Health Effects, 4248–91

EPA Publications Bibliography, Quarterly Abstract Bulletin, 9182–5

EPA's Toxic Release Inventory Is Useful but Can Be Improved. Toxic Chemicals, 26113–532

Epidemiologic Trends in Drug Abuse. Community Epidemiology Work Group Proceedings, December 1990, 4492–5.1

Epidemiologic Trends in Drug Abuse. Community Epidemiology Work Group Proceedings, June 1991, 4492–5.2

Evaluating Monetary Base...

Epidemiology and Biostatistics Program, FY90 Report, 4474–29

Epidemiology of Cocaine Use and Abuse, 4498–74

Equal Employment: Minority Representation at USDA's National Agricultural Statistics Service, 26119–326

Equity Premium Puzzle, 9387–1.204

Equity Underwriting Risk, 9366–6.260

ERIC Annual Report, 1987, 4814–3

ERIC Annual Report, 1988, 4814–3

ERIC Annual Report, 1989, 4814–3

ERIC Annual Report, 1991, 4814–3

Errata: Evaluation of the State Personal Income Estimates, 2702–1.202

Errata: U.S. Affiliates of Foreign Companies, 2702–1.218

Error-Correction Model of U.S. M2 Demand, 9389–1.202

Escalating Costs of Higher Education, 4808–25

Estimated Female Veteran Population in the U.S., 9924–25

Estimated Oil and Gas Reserves, Gulf of Mexico, Dec. 31, 1989, 5734–6

Estimated Oil and Gas Reserves: Pacific Outer Continental Shelf (as of Dec. 31, 1989), 5734–7

Estimates of Economic Costs of Alcohol and Drug Abuse and Mental Illness, 1985 and 1988, 4042–3.219

Estimates of Employer Contributions for Health Insurance by Worker Characteristics, 2626–10.136

Estimates of Federal Tax Expenditures, FY92-96, 21784–10

Estimates of Households by Age of Householder and Tenure for Counties: July 1, 1985, 2546–3.169

Estimates of Mortgage Originations by State, 1978-89, 5144–21

Estimates of the Resident Population of States, 2324–10

Estimates of the Uninsured Population, 1987. National Medical Expenditure Survey, 4186–8.13

Estimates of U.S. Biofuels Consumption, 1989, 3166–6.56

Estimating Census Accuracy—A Complex Task. 1990 Census Adjustment, 26119–327

Estimating Entry and Exit of U.S. Farms, 1598–269

Estimating Immigrant Assimilation Rates with Synthetic Panel Data, 9385–8.100

Estimating Producer Welfare Effects of the Conservation Reserve Program, 1502–3.202

Estimating the Minimum Risk Maturity Gap, 9371–10.65

Estimation of Flood-Frequency Characteristics and the Effects of Urbanization for Streams in the Philadelphia, Pa. Area, 5666–27.9

Estuaries of the U.S., Vital Statistics of a National Resource Base, 2178–27

Eugene V. Debs: An American Paradox, 6722–1.240

Europe 1992: A Closer Look, 9371–1.210

Europe 1992: An Overview, 9379–1.201

European Court of Justice Orders Equal Treatment in Awarding Pensions to Men and Women, 4742–1.205

European Market for Pistachios, 1925–34.205

European Monetary Union: How Close Is It?, 9371–1.212

Evaluating Monetary Base Targeting Rules, 9379–12.66

Evaluating South Carolina's...

Index by Titles

Evaluating South Carolina's Community Cardiovascular Disease Prevention Project, 4042–3.245

Evaluation of Diagnosis-Related Group Severity and Complexity Refinement, 4652–1.245

Evaluation of "Guia para Dejar de Fumar," a Self-help Guide in Spanish To Quit Smoking, 4042–3.249

Evaluation of New Canal Point Sugarcane Clones, 1990-91 Harvest Season, 1704–2

Evaluation of the Impacts of the Washington Alternative Work Search Experiment, 6406–6.35

Evaluation of the State Personal Income Estimates. Errata, 2702–1.202

Event Risk Premia and Bond Market Incentives for Corporate Leverage, 9385–8.88

Evidence on the Impact of Futures Margin Specifications on the Performance of Futures and Cash Markets, 9375–13.51

Evidence on the Influence of Financial Changes on Interest Rates and Monetary Policy, 9385–8.73

Evolution of Shared ATM Networks, 9387–1.203

Evolving Wine Market in the European Community, 1925–34.232

Examination Customer Satisfaction Survey, 1989, 8304–8.1

Examine Japanese Financial System and Its Effect on Ability of U.S. Firms To Compete, 21248–152

Excess Number of Bladder Cancers in Workers Exposed to Ortho-Toluidine and Aniline, 4472–1.209

Exchange Ideology as a Moderator of the Procedural Justice-Satisfaction Relationship, 7506–10.90

Exchange Rate Rules in Support of Disinflation Programs in Developing Countries, 9366–7.256

Executive Handbook of Selected Data, 4704–12

Exercise of Federal Prosecutorial Authority in a Changing Legal Environment, 21408–123

Expanded, Cointegrated Model of U.S. Trade, 9385–8.117

Expanded Structure Unnecessary and Costly. Navy Homeports, 26123–347

Expectations and the Core Rate of Inflation, 9377–1.201

Expected and Predicted Realignments: The FF/DM Exchange Rate During the EMS, 9366–7.249

Expected Inflation and Real Interest Rates Based on Index-Linked Bond Prices: The UK Experience, 9385–1.214

Expenditure Profiles of Visitors to Southern California Coastal Areas. Public Area Recreation Visitors Survey, 2176–9.6

Expenditures and Sources of Funds for Mental Health Organizations: U.S. and Each State, 1988, 4506–3.45

Expenditures for Residential Improvements and Repairs, Current Construction Reports, 2382–7

Expenditures for Residential Upkeep and Improvement, Annual. Current Construction Reports, 2384–4

Expenditures for Residential Upkeep and Improvement, Current Construction Reports, 2382–7

Expenditures on a Child by Husband-Wife Families: 1990, 1708–87

Expenditures on a Child by Single-Parent Families, 1702–1.203

Expense Preference and the Fed Revisited, 9387–8.245

Experience of France, Germany, and Japan. Health Care Spending Control, 26121–437

Explaining LBOs and Acquisitions, 9385–8.86

Explaining the Postwar Pattern of Personal Saving, 9373–1.219

Explaining the U.S. Export Boom, 9393–8.203

Explaining the Volume of Intraindustry Trade: Are Increasing Returns Necessary?, 9366–7.265

Export Administration Annual Report, FY90, 2024–1

Export Controls: U.S. Controls on Trade with Selected Middle Eastern Countries, 26123–339

Export Demand for U.S. Corn, Soybeans, and Wheat, 1568–297

Export Market Profiles, 1526–6

Export Markets for U.S. Grain and Products, 1925–2.4

Export-Import Bank of the U.S., 1990 Annual Report, 9254–1

Exporting: An Avenue for Dairy Cooperatives, 1128–65

Exports from Manufacturing Establishments: 1987. Analytical Report Series, 2506–16.1

Exposure to Alcoholism in the Family: U.S., 1988, 4146–8.207

Extending Most-Favored-Nation Status for China, 25368–174

External Increasing Returns, Short-Lived Agents and Long-Lived Waste, 9389–19.27

External Quality-Assurance Results for the National Atmospheric Deposition Program and the National Trends Network During 1988, 5664–17

External Quality-Assurance Results for the National Atmospheric Deposition Program and the National Trends Network During 1989, 5664–17

Extra Long Staple Cotton, Summary of 1991 Support Program and Related Information: ASCS Commodity Fact Sheet, 1806–4.10

Extracranial-Intracranial Bypass To Reduce the Risk of Ischemic Stroke. Health Technology Assessment Report, 1990, 4186–10.3

Extramural Trends, FY81-90, 4434–9

Extruded Rubber Thread from Malaysia. Determination of the Commission in Investigations Nos. 303-TA-22 (Preliminary) and 731-TA-527 (Preliminary) Under the Tariff Act of 1930, Together with the Information Obtained in the Investigations, 9886–19.78

FAA Air Traffic Activity, FY90, 7504–27

FAA Altitude Chamber Training Flight Profile: A Survey of Altitude Reactions, 1965-89, 7506–10.78

FAA Aviation Forecast, Annual Conference Proceedings, 7504–28

FAA Aviation Forecasts, 7506–7

FAA Aviation Forecasts: Denver Hub/Other Colorado Airports, 7506–7.39

FAA Aviation Forecasts, FY91-2002, 7504–6

FAA Aviation Forecasts: Las Vegas Hub/Other Nevada Airports, 7506–7.41

FAA Aviation Forecasts: Miami/Ft. Lauderdale, 7506–7.40

FAA Statistical Handbook of Aviation, 1989, 7504–1

Facilities, 1991, Federal Bureau of Prisons, 6244–4

Fact Book: National Cancer Institute, 4474–13

Fact Book of Agriculture, 1990, 1004–14

Fact Sheet, Dept of Defense, Military Strength Worldwide, 3542–9

Fact Sheet for 1990 Decennial Census Counts of Persons in Emergency Shelters for the Homeless and Visible in Street Locations, 2328–70

Factfinder for the Nation, 2326–7

Factor Intensity of U.S. Agricultural Trade, 1548–373

Factors Affecting Reserves of Depository Institutions and Condition Statement of Federal Reserve Banks, 9365–1

Factors Affecting the Competitiveness of Internationally Active Financial Institutions, 9385–1.206

Factors Affecting the International Competitiveness of the U.S., 21788–204

Factors Behind the Shifting Composition of U.S. Manufactured Goods Trade, 9385–8.95

Factors Related to Personnel Attrition in the Selected Reserve. Reserve Components, 26123–329

Factors That Affect Risk of Closure. Rural Hospitals, 26121–392

Facts from the National Center for Statistics and Analysis, 7766–15

Facts on U.S. Working Women, 6564–1

Fall Enrollment in Institutions of Higher Education, 4844–2

Fall Water Supply Summary for the Western U.S., 1991, 1264–4

Falling Behind: The Growing Income Gap in America, 23848–219

Family Disruption and Economic Hardship: The Short-Run Picture for Children, 2546–20.17

Family Economics Review, 1702–1

Family Income and Expenditures of Married-Couple Families When One Spouse Is not Employed, 1702–1.201

Family Structure and Children's Health: U.S., 1988. Vital and Health Statistics Series 10, 4147–10.178

Farm Act and the Budget Reconciliation Act of 1990: How U.S. Farm Policy Mechanisms Will Work Under the New Legislation, 1008–54

Farm Agencies' Field Structure Needs Major Overhaul. U.S. Department of Agriculture, 26113–507

Farm and Housing Activity Report, 1182–1

Farm Bill, 1990, Emphasizes Fruits and Vegetables, 1925–34.208

Farm Credit Administration, Annual Report, 1990, 9264–2

Farm Credit System Annual Information Statement, 9264–5.2

Farm Credit System, Quarterly Information Statement, 9262–2

Farm Employment and Wage Rates, 1910-90, 1618–21

Farm Financial Stress, Farm Exits, and Public Sector Assistance to the Farm Sector in the 1980's, 1598–272

Index by Titles

Farm Labor, 1631–1
Farm Machinery and Lawn and Garden Equipment, 1990, Current Industrial Report, 2506–12.1
Farm Numbers, Land in Farms, 1614–4
Farm Production Expenditures, 1990 Summary, 1614–3
Farm Storage, Drying Equipment, Wet Storage, Forage and Silage, Hay Storage, and Solar Equipment Loans, 1802–9
Farm Storage, Drying Equipment, Wet Storage, Forage and Silage, Hay Storage and Solar Equipment Loans, FY91, 1804–14
Farm Wealth: Its Distribution and Comparison to the Wealth of U.S. Households, 1541–1.207
Farmer Cooperative Statistics, 1989, 1124–1
Farmer Cooperatives, 1122–1
Farmer Cooperatives in the U.S., 1126–1
Farmer Program (CONACT) Property in Inventory, National Summary, 1182–6
Farmer Program Inventory Property, 1182–6
Farmer-Owned Reserve—Old Name, New Game: An Analysis of New Rules and 1990 Wheat Crop Entry, 1561–12.201
Farmers, Cooperatives, and USDA: A History of Agricultural Cooperative Service, 1128–66
Farmers Home Administration: Changes Needed in Loan Servicing Under the Agricultural Credit Act, 26113–497
Farmers Home Administration: Information on Appeals of Farm and Housing Loan Decisions, 26113–516
Farmers Home Administration Report for FY90, 1184–17
Farmers Home Administration: Sales of Farm Inventory Properties, 26113–514
Farmland Values and Japanese Agriculture, 1524–4.5
Farmline, 1502–6
Farm-Raised Salmon: Impacts on U.S. Seafood Trade, 1561–15.201
Fast Response Survey System, 4826–1
Fatal Accident Reporting System, 1989: A Review of Information on Fatal Traffic Crashes in the U.S. in 1989, 7764–10
Fats and Oils: Oilseed Crushings, Current Industrial Report, 2506–4.3
Fats and Oils: Production, Consumption, and Stocks, Current Industrial Report, 2506–4.4
FDA Quarterly Activities Report, 4062–3
FDA's Program and Regulations Need Improvement. Freedom of Information, 26121–436
FDIC Banking Review, 9292–4
Feasibility and Revenue Impact of a Federal Tax Amnesty Program, 21408–125
Feasibility of Collecting Drug Abuse Data by Telephone, 4042–3.230
Feasibility of Linking Research-Related Data Bases to Federal and Non-Federal Medical Administrative Data Bases: Report to Congress, 4188–73
Feasibility Study of the Use of Unemployment Insurance Wage-Record Data as an Evaluation Tool for JTPA, 15496–1.13
FEC Releases Summary of 1989-90 Political Party Finances, 9276–1.88
FEC Releases 1990 Year-End PAC Count, 9276–1.86
FEC Releases 1991 Mid-Year PAC Count, 9276–1.91
Fecundity and Infertility in the U.S., 1965-88, 4146–8.194

Federal Advisory Committees, Nineteenth Annual Report of the President, FY90, 9454–18
Federal Affirmative Action: Better EEOC Guidance and Agency Analysis of Underrepresentation Needed, 26119–342
Federal Agency Use of Nondisclosure Agreements. Information Security, 26123–328
Federal Aid in Fish and Wildlife Restoration, 1988, 5504–1
Federal Aid in Fish and Wildlife Restoration, 1989, 5504–1
Federal Aid in Sport Fish and Wildlife Restoration Funds, 5502–1
Federal Aid: Programs Available to State and Local Governments, 26121–421
Federal and State Endangered Species Expenditures, FY90, 5504–33
Federal Audiovisual Activity, FY89, 9514–1
Federal Audiovisual Activity, FY90, 9514–1
Federal Aviation Administration, Annual Financial Report, FY90, 7504–10
Federal Aviation Noise Policy, 21648–64
Federal Benefit Payments: Agencies Need Death Information from Social Security To Avoid Erroneous Payments, 26121–406
Federal Budget and the Budget Process, An Overview, 21268–43
Federal Capital Improvements Program, National Capital Region, FY91-95, 15454–1
Federal Civil Penalties Inflation Adjustment Act of 1989, 21408–124
Federal Civilian Employment by State, Metropolitan Area, Overseas, Citizenship, Major Agency, Pay System Category, and Work Schedule as of Dec. 31, 1990, 9842–1.203
Federal Civilian Work Years and Personnel Costs in the Executive Branch for FY90, 9842–1.204
Federal Civilian Workforce Statistics: Biennial Report of Employment by Geographic Area, 9844–8
Federal Civilian Workforce Statistics, Employment and Trends, 9842–1
Federal Civilian Workforce Statistics: Pay Structure of the Federal Civil Service, Mar. 31, 1990, 9844–6
Federal Civilian Workforce Statistics: Work Years and Personnel Costs, Executive Branch, U.S. Government, FY89, 9844–31
Federal Coal Management Report, FY90, 5724–10
Federal Construction-Related Expenditures, 1984-92, 2042–1.206
Federal Contracts Are Big Business. Statistical Brief, 2326–17.36
Federal Court Management Statistics, 1991, 18204–3
Federal Credit and Insurance: Information on the Dollar Amount of Direct Loan, Loan Guarantee, and Insurance Programs, 26111–65
Federal Criminal Case Processing, 1980-87: Addendum for 1988 and Preliminary 1989, 6064–31
Federal Criminal Case Processing, 1980-89: With Preliminary Data for 1990, 6064–31
Federal Criminal Justice System: A Model To Estimate System Workload, 26119–340
Federal Dairy Programs: Information on Farm and Retail Milk Prices, 26113–540

Federal Deposit Insurance Corporation 1989 Merger Decisions, 9294–5
Federal Disability Insurance Trust Fund, 8102–9.14
Federal Drug Grants to States. An Office of National Drug Control Policy White Paper, 236–1.4
Federal Efforts Should Target Areas Where Closures Would Threaten Access to Care. Rural Hospitals, 26121–409
Federal Efforts To Combat Fraud, Abuse, and Misconduct in the Nation's S&L's and Banks and To Implement the Criminal and Civil Enforcement Provisions of FIRREA, 21408–119
Federal Election Commission, Annual Report, 1990, 9274–1
Federal Elections 90: Election Results for the U.S. Senate and the U.S. House of Representatives, 9274–5
Federal Emergency Management Agency, Annual Report, 9434–2
Federal Employees' Compensation Act, 6722–1.241
Federal Energy Conservation Programs, Annual Report to Congress, 3304–25
Federal Energy Regulatory Commission: 1990 Annual Report, 3084–9
Federal Expenditures by State for FY90, 2464–2
Federal Financial Institutions Examination Council: Annual Report, 1990, 13004–2
Federal Financing Bank Activity: Federal Financing Bank News, 12802–1
Federal Financing Bank News: Federal Financing Bank Activity, 12802–1
Federal Fiscal Programs, 2702–1.204
Federal Funds for Research and Development: FY89-91, Volume XXXIX, 9627–20
Federal Grain Inspection Service: Annual Report to Congress, 1990, 1294–1
Federal Home Loan Bank of Atlanta, Quarterly Report, 9302–37
Federal Home Loan Bank of Atlanta Review, 9302–2
Federal Home Loan Bank of Atlanta, 1990 Annual Report, 9304–1
Federal Home Loan Bank of Boston, Annual Report, 1990, 9304–2
Federal Home Loan Bank of Boston, First District Facts, 9302–4
Federal Home Loan Bank of Boston Quarterly Report, 9302–35
Federal Home Loan Bank of Chicago, Home Mortgage Commitment Rates in Illinois, 9302–6
Federal Home Loan Bank of Chicago, Home Mortgage Commitment Rates in Wisconsin, 9302–7
Federal Home Loan Bank of Chicago Housing Vacancy Survey, 9304–18
Federal Home Loan Bank of Chicago, Index Report, 9302–30
Federal Home Loan Bank of Chicago, 1990 Annual Report, 9304–4
Federal Home Loan Bank of Cincinnati, 1990 Annual Report, 9304–6
Federal Home Loan Bank of Dallas Quarterly Trends, 9302–31
Federal Home Loan Bank of Dallas, 1990 Annual Report, 9304–11
Federal Home Loan Bank of Des Moines, Quarterly Statistical Report, 9302–9
Federal Home Loan Bank of Des Moines, 1990 Annual Report, 9304–7

Federal Home Loan Bank of Des...

Index by Titles

Federal Home Loan Bank of Des Moines, 1991 Bank Services and Membership Directory, 9304–9

Federal Home Loan Bank of Indianapolis, Annual Report, 1990, 9304–10

Federal Home Loan Bank of Indianapolis Financial Information Report, Monthly, 9302–11

Federal Home Loan Bank of Indianapolis: Possible Adjustable Mortgage Loan Indices, 9302–38

Federal Home Loan Bank of Indianapolis, Quarterly Financial Information Report, 9302–23

Federal Home Loan Bank of New York, Annual Report, 1990, 9304–12

Federal Home Loan Bank of Pittsburgh, 1990 Annual Report, 9304–13

Federal Home Loan Bank of San Francisco, 1990 Annual Report, 9304–14

Federal Home Loan Bank of San Francisco 1991 Directory of Members: Eleventh District—Arizona, California, Nevada, 9304–23

Federal Home Loan Bank of Seattle Housing Vacancy Survey, 9304–21

Federal Home Loan Bank of Seattle, 1990 Annual Report, 9304–15

Federal Home Loan Bank of Topeka, Directory of Members, 9304–17

Federal Home Loan Bank of Topeka Housing Vacancy Survey, 9304–22

Federal Home Loan Bank of Topeka, 1990 Annual Report, 9304–16

Federal Home Loan Bank, Tenth District, Annual Report, 9304–16

Federal Home Loan Banks: Statements of Condition as of (Date), 9442–1

Federal Home Loan Banks 1990 Financial Report, 9444–1

Federal Home Loan Mortgage Corporation Annual Report, 9414–1

Federal Hospital Insurance Trust Fund, 8102–9.15

Federal Hospital Insurance Trust Fund, 1991 Annual Report of the Board of Trustees, 4654–11

Federal Information Processing Standards Publications, 2216–2

Federal Infrastructure Subsidies: Grants or Credits?, 26306–3.113

Federal Job Retention Programs for Distressed Timber Communities, 21728–76

Federal Judicial Workload Statistics, Dec. 31, 1990, 18204–11

Federal Juvenile Delinquency Programs, Analysis and Evaluation, 6064–11

Federal Labor Relations Authority and the Federal Service Impasses Panel, 11th Annual Report, FY89, 13364–1

Federal Lands: Improvements Needed in Managing Concessioners, 26113–531

Federal Maritime Commission 29th Annual Report, FY90, 9334–1

Federal Mediation and Conciliation Service, Annual Report, FY89, 9344–1

Federal Milk Order Market Statistics, 1317–4

Federal Milk Order Market Statistics, 1990 Annual Summary, 1317–3

Federal National Mortgage Association 1987 Report to Congress, 5184–9

Federal National Mortgage Association 1988-89 Report to Congress, 5184–9

Federal Offenders in the U.S. Courts, 1986-90, 18204–1

Federal Offenders in U.S. District Courts, 18204–1

Federal Offshore Statistics: 1989, Leasing, Exploration, Production, and Revenues, 5734–3

Federal Offshore Statistics: 1990, Leasing, Exploration, Production, and Revenues, 5734–3

Federal Old Age and Survivors Insurance Trust Fund, 8102–9.2

Federal Old-Age and Survivors Insurance and Disability Insurance Trust Funds, 1990 Annual Report of the Board of Trustees, 4704–4

Federal Old-Age and Survivors Insurance and Disability Insurance Trust Funds, 1991 Annual Report of the Board of Trustees, 4704–4

Federal Pay: Private Sector Salary Differences by Locality, 26119–332

Federal Personal Property Donations Provide Limited Benefit to the Homeless. Homelessness, 26113–538

Federal Plan for Meteorological Services and Supporting Research, FY92, 2144–2

Federal Prison Industries, Inc., 1990 Annual Report, 6244–3

Federal Recreation Fee Report to Congress, 1990, Including Federal Recreation Visitation and Fee Data with State Park Information Supplement, 5544–14

Federal Reserve Annual Statistical Releases, 9365–5

Federal Reserve Bank of Atlanta Economic Review, 9371–1

Federal Reserve Bank of Atlanta Economics Update, 9371–15

Federal Reserve Bank of Atlanta Regional Update, 9371–14

Federal Reserve Bank of Atlanta Working Paper Series, 9371–10

Federal Reserve Bank of Atlanta, 1990 Annual Report, 9371–4

Federal Reserve Bank of Boston Conference Series, 9373–3

Federal Reserve Bank of Boston, New England Economic Indicators, 9373–2

Federal Reserve Bank of Boston, New England Economic Review, 9373–1

Federal Reserve Bank of Boston Research Reports, 9373–4

Federal Reserve Bank of Boston, 1988 Annual Report, 9373–26

Federal Reserve Bank of Boston, 1989 Annual Report, 9373–26

Federal Reserve Bank of Boston, 1990 Annual Report, 9373–26

Federal Reserve Bank of Chicago Economic Perspectives, 9375–1

Federal Reserve Bank of Chicago Working Paper Series, 9375–13

Federal Reserve Bank of Chicago, 1990 Annual Report, 9375–5

Federal Reserve Bank of Cleveland Economic Review, 9377–1

Federal Reserve Bank of Cleveland Working Papers, 9377–9

Federal Reserve Bank of Cleveland, 1990 Annual Report, 9377–5

Federal Reserve Bank of Dallas Economic Review, 9379–1

Federal Reserve Bank of Dallas Financial Industry Studies, 9379–14

Federal Reserve Bank of Dallas Financial Industry Studies Working Papers, 9379–14

Federal Reserve Bank of Dallas Research Papers, 9379–12

Federal Reserve Bank of Dallas, 1989 Financial Statement, 9379–2

Federal Reserve Bank of Dallas, 1990 Annual Report, 9379–2

Federal Reserve Bank of Kansas City Banking Studies, 9381–14

Federal Reserve Bank of Kansas City Economic Review, 9381–1

Federal Reserve Bank of Kansas City Regional Economic Digest, 9381–16

Federal Reserve Bank of Kansas City Research Working Papers, 9381–10

Federal Reserve Bank of Kansas City, 1990 Annual Report, 9381–3

Federal Reserve Bank of Minneapolis Fedgazette, 9383–19

Federal Reserve Bank of Minneapolis Quarterly Review, 9383–6

Federal Reserve Bank of Minneapolis Staff Reports, 9383–20

Federal Reserve Bank of Minneapolis, 1990 Annual Report, 9383–2

Federal Reserve Bank of New York Quarterly Review, 9385–1

Federal Reserve Bank of New York Research Papers, 9385–8

Federal Reserve Bank of New York, Seventy-sixth Annual Report for the Year Ended Dec. 31, 1990, 9385–2

Federal Reserve Bank of Philadelphia Business Review, 9387–1

Federal Reserve Bank of Philadelphia, Quarterly Regional Economic Report, 9387–10

Federal Reserve Bank of Philadelphia Working Papers, 9387–8

Federal Reserve Bank of Philadelphia, 1990 Annual Report, 9387–3

Federal Reserve Bank of Richmond Economic Review, 9389–1

Federal Reserve Bank of Richmond Working Paper Series, 9389–19

Federal Reserve Bank of Richmond, 1990 Annual Report, 9389–2

Federal Reserve Bank of San Francisco, Annual Report, 1990, 9393–2

Federal Reserve Bank of San Francisco Economic Review, 9393–8

Federal Reserve Bank of San Francisco Working Papers, 9393–10

Federal Reserve Bank of St. Louis Review, 9391–1

Federal Reserve Bank of St. Louis, 1988 Summary Report, 9391–17

Federal Reserve Bank of St. Louis, 1989 Annual Report, 9391–17

Federal Reserve Bank of St. Louis, 1990 Annual Report, 9391–17

Federal Reserve Bulletin, 9362–1

Federal Reserve Monthly Statistical Releases, 9365–2

Federal Reserve Quarterly Statistical Releases, 9365–3

Federal Reserve Semiannual Statistical Releases, 9365–4

Federal Reserve Weekly Statistical Releases, 9365–1

Federal Service Impasses Panel, 11th Annual Report, FY89, 13364–1

Federal, State, and Local Responses to Natural Disasters Need Improvement. Disaster Assistance, 26113–511

Index by Titles

Federal Supplementary Medical Insurance Trust Fund, 8102–9.3
Federal Supplementary Medical Insurance Trust Fund, 1991 Annual Report of the Board of Trustees, 4654–12
Federal Support for Education: FY80-90, 4824–8
Federal Support to the States Has Declined. Refugee Resettlement, 26121–402
Federal Support to Universities, Colleges, and Nonprofit Institutions: FY89, 9627–17
Federal Trade Commission, FY88 Annual Report, 9404–1
Federal Trade Commission, FY89 Annual Report, 9404–1
Federal Trust Fund Reports, 8102–9
Federal Workforce: Inappropriate Use of Experts and Consultants at Selected Civilian Agencies, 26119–354
Federal-Aid Highway Construction Materials Usage Factors, 1988-90, 7554–29
Federally Funded Child Welfare, Foster Care, and Adoption Assistance Programs, 21788–202
Federally Funded Research: Decisions for a Decade, 26358–238
Fedgazette, Federal Reserve Bank of Minneapolis, 9383–19
Feed Grains, Summary of 1991 Support Program and Related Information: ASCS Commodity Fact Sheet, 1806–4.8
Feed Situation and Outlook Report, 1561–4
Feed Situation and Outlook Yearbook, 1561–4
Feldspar: Mineral Industry Survey, 5612–2.18
Feldspar, Nepheline, Syenite, and Aplite: Minerals Yearbook, Volume 1, 1990, 5604–20.19
Felons Sentenced to Probation in State Courts, 1986, 6068–242
Female Victims of Violent Crime, 6068–243
Ferroalloys in 1990: Mineral Industry Surveys Annual Domestic Summary, 5614–5.7
Ferroalloys: Minerals Yearbook, Volume 1, 1989, 5604–15.23
Fertility of American Women: June 1990, 2546–1.455
Fertilizer and Pesticide Use and the Environment, 1004–16.1
Fertilizer Application Timing, 1561–16.204
Fertilizer Materials, Current Industrial Report, 2506–8.2
Fertilizer Materials, 1990, Current Industrial Report, 2506–8.13
Fertilizer Summary Data, 1990, 9804–5
Fertilizer Trends, 9808–66
Few Claims Resolved Through Michigan's Voluntary Arbitration Program. Medical Malpractice, 26121–394
Fewer Older Men in the U.S. Work Force: Technological, Behavioral, and Legislative Contributions to the Decline, 9371–1.202
Fewer Resources, Greater Burdens: Medical Care Coverage for Low-Income Elderly People, 23898–5
FHA Homes, 1987: Data for States and Selected Areas on Characteristics of FHA Operations Under Section 203, 5144–1
FHA Homes, 1988, Section 203(b): Characteristics of FHA Home Mortgage Operations, Total Construction by State, 5144–1
FHA Homes, 1989, Section 203(b): Characteristics of FHA Home Mortgage Operations, Total Construction by State, 5144–1

FHA Homes, 1990, Section 203(b): Characteristics of FHA Home Mortgage Operations, Total Construction by State, 5144–1
FHA Report of Insurance Operations Under Home Mortgage Programs for (Date): FHA Mortgages Insured, 5142–45
FHA Single Family Trends: Statistical Highlights, 5142–44
FHA State Trends of Home Mortgage Characteristics, Section 203b Mortgages Insured, 5144–25
FHA Trends of Home Mortgage Characteristics, Mortgages Insured, Section 203b, 5142–1
FHA Trends of Home Mortgage Characteristics, Section 203b Mortgages Insured, 5144–23
FHA Trends of Home Mortgage Characteristics, Section 203b Mortgages Insured by MSA/PMSA's, 5144–24
FHA Trends of Home Mortgage Characteristics, Section 203b Mortgages Insured by States, 5144–25
FHWA Reports Road Construction Costs, 7552–16
Fiber and Processing Tests, Survey of Leading Cotton Varieties: Crop of 1990, 1309–16
Fiber Deployment Update, End of Year 1990, 9284–18
Field Crops Summary, 1990. Agricultural Chemical Usage, 1616–1.1
Field Observations on Slush Ice Generated During Freezeup in Arctic Coastal Waters, 2176–1.38
Fifteenth Annual Report of the National Advisory Council on Educational Research and Improvement, FY90, 4814–1
Fifteenth Annual Report of the National Commission for Employment Policy, 15494–1
Fifth Annual Research Conference, Mar. 19-22, 1989: Proceedings, 2624–2
Fifty Years of Progress in the Nutrition Field, 1004–16.1
Fifty-first Annual Report of the National Labor Relations Board, FY86, 9584–1
Fifty-fourth Annual Report of the National Labor Relations Board, FY89, 9584–1
Fifty-second Annual Report of the National Labor Relations Board, FY87, 9584–1
Fifty-third Annual Report of the National Labor Relations Board, FY88, 9584–1
Filing Season Statistics, 8302–6
Final Apportionment of Federal Aid in Fish and Wildlife Restoration Funds for FY91, 5502–1
Final Divorce Statistics, 1987, Advance Report, 4147–24.4
Final Divorce Statistics, 1988, Advance Report, 4146–5.121
Final Environmental Report on Proposed Exploratory Drilling Offshore North Carolina, 5738–22
Final Marriage Statistics, 1987, Advance Report, 4147–24.4
Final Marriage Statistics, 1988, Advance Report, 4146–5.122
Final Mortality Statistics, 1987, Advance Report, 4147–24.4
Final Natality Statistics, 1987, Advance Report, 4147–24.4
Final Natality Statistics, 1989, Advance Report, 4146–5.123

Financial Performance of...

Final Report: Longitudinal Study of Structured English Immersion Strategy, Early-Exit and Late-Exit Transitional Bilingual Education Programs for Language-Minority Children, 4808–27
Final Report of the Advisory Committee on the Food and Drug Administration, 4008–115
Final Report of the Director of the Administrative Office of the U.S. Courts on the Demonstration Program of Mandatory Drug Testing of Criminal Defendants, 18208–11
Final Report of the SEC Government-Business Forum on Small Business Capital Formation, 9734–4
Final Report on Residual Tidal Currents and Processing of Pressure and Current Records from the Eastern Bering Sea Shelf, 2176–1.36
Finance and Economics Discussion Series, 9366–6
Finance Companies, 9365–2.7
Finance Outlook: Guarded Optimism, 1004–16.1
Finances of Employee-Retirement Systems of State and Local Governments: 1987-88, 2466–2.1
Finances of Employee-Retirement Systems of State and Local Governments: 1988-89, 2466–2.8
Finances of Selected Public Employee Retirement Systems, 2462–2
Financial Accounting for Pensions: Measures of Funding Status, 9366–6.259
Financial and Compliance Audit, Alaska Power Administration Federal Power Program: Juneau, Alaska, FY90, 3006–5.22
Financial Aspects of Adult Day Care: National Survey Results, 4652–1.234
Financial Assistance by Geographic Area, FY90, 4004–3
Financial Characteristics of Burley Tobacco Farms, 1561–10.202
Financial Characteristics of Dairy Farms, 1989, 1561–2.201
Financial Disclosure: USDA's Systems Limited by Insufficient Top Management Support, 26119–314
Financial Industry Studies: Federal Reserve Bank of Dallas, 9379–14
Financial Industry Studies Working Papers: Federal Reserve Bank of Dallas, 9379–14
Financial Information Report, Monthly, Federal Home Loan Bank of Indianapolis, 9302–11
Financial Information Report, Quarterly, Federal Home Loan Bank of Indianapolis, 9302–23
Financial Institution Performance, 1990, 9381–14.1
Financial Liberalization and Monetary Control in Japan, 9385–1.213
Financial Market Evolution and the Interest Sensitivity of Output, 9385–8.79
Financial Performance in the Social Health Maintenance Organization, 1985-88, 4652–1.202
Financial Performance of Specialized Corn-Soybean Farms, 1987, 1566–8.7
Financial Performance of Specialized Farms, 1566–8
Financial Performance of Specialized Hog Farms, 1987, 1566–8.6

Financial Profiles of... Index by Titles

Financial Profiles of Cooperatives Handling Grain, 1128–44

Financial Reform and Monetary Control in Japan, 9385–8.116

Financial Statistics of Selected Investor-Owned Electric Utilities, 1989, 3164–23

Financial Statistics of Selected Publicly Owned Electric Utilities, 1989, 3164–24

Financial Trends in Federally Insured Credit Unions, Jan. 1-June 30, 1991, 9532–7

Financing Agriculture in the 1990s: Structural Change and Public Policy, Proceedings of the 1990 Meeting of the Federal Reserve Committee on Agriculture and Rural Development, 9368–90

Financing Capital Expenditures in Massachusetts, 9373–1.207, 9373–4.27

Financing Constraints and Investment: New Evidence from the U.S. Hospital Industry, 9387–8.243

Financing Geriatric Programs in Community Health Centers, 4042–3.229

FIP Monthly Progress Report, By State and Area for Period Ending (Date), 1802–11

Fire History and Pattern in a Cascade Range Landscape, 1208–354

Firearm Mortality Among Children, Youth, and Young Adults 1-34 Years of Age, Trends and Current Status: U.S., 1979-88, 4146–5.119

Fire-Cured and Dark Air-Cured, 1989 Crop. Tobacco Market Review, 1319–5.2

Fire-Cured and Dark Air-Cured, 1990 Crop. Tobacco Market Review, 1319–5.5

First Disclosures of National Party "Soft Money" Reported: Records Show Republican Fundraising Lead, 9276–1.94

First District Facts, Federal Home Loan Bank of Boston, 9302–4

First Spacelab Dedicated to Life Sciences Highlights STS-40, 9506–2.142

First 3 Years of the National AIDS Clearinghouse, 4042–3.256

Fiscal Disparities in Chicagoland, 10042–1.203

Fiscal Policy and Trade Adjustment: Are the Deficits Really Twins?, 9371–10.60

Fiscal Policy in the Reagan Years: A Burden on Future Generations?, 9393–8.201

Fiscal Shock: How New England State Budgets Lost Their Balance, 9373–25.202

Fish and Fish Egg Distribution Report of the National Fish Hatchery System, FY90, 5504–10

Fish and Wildlife Plan for Colorado: Program for the Decade, 5726–7.3

Fish and Wildlife Research Reports, 5506–13

Fish and Wildlife Technical Reports, 5506–12

Fish and Wildlife 2000: A Plan for the Future for (State), 5726–7

Fish and Wildlife '90: A Report to the Nation, 5504–20

Fish Kills Caused by Pollution, 1977-87, 9204–3

Fish Kills in Coastal Waters, 1980-89, 2178–32

Fish Meal and Oil, 2162–3

Fish, 1990, Current Federal Aid Research Report, 5504–23

Fisheries and Fish Trade of India, 2162–1.203

Fisheries and Wildlife Research and Development, 5504–20

Fisheries: Commerce Needs To Improve Fisheries Management in the North Pacific, 26113–523

Fisheries Habitat Management on Public Lands: A Strategy for the Future, 5726–6.3

Fisheries Oceanography—A Comprehensive Formulation of Technical Objectives for Offshore Application in the Arctic, 5738–24

Fisheries of Denmark, 2162–1.202

Fisheries of Seychelles, 2162–1.203

Fisheries of the U.S., 1990, 2164–1

Fishermen's Report, Northeast Fisheries Science Center Bottom Trawl Survey, 2164–18

Fishery Market News Reports, 2162–6

Five-Year Plan for Meeting the Automatic Data Processing and Telecommunications Needs of the Federal Government, 104–20

Flat Glass, Current Industrial Report, 2506–9.6

Flight Service Specialist Initial Qualifications Course: Content Validation of FAA Academy Course 50232, 7506–10.83

Floriculture and Environmental Horticulture Products: A Production and Marketing Statistical Review, 1960-88, 1568–293

Floriculture Crops: 1990 Summary, 1631–8

Flour Milling Products, Current Industrial Report, 2506–4.1

Flow of Funds Accounts, Seasonally Adjusted and Unadjusted, 9365–3.3

Flow of Funds Summary Statistics, 9365–3

Flue-Cured Tobacco, Summary of 1991 Support Program and Related Information: ASCS Commodity Fact Sheet, 1806–4.3

Flue-Cured, 1989 Crop. Tobacco Market Review, 1319–5.1

Flue-Cured, 1990 Crop. Tobacco Market Review, 1319–5.4

Fluid Milk Sales by Method of Distribution, 1317–4.201

Fluid Milk Sales by Size and Type of Container, 1317–4.203

Fluid Power Products, Including Aerospace, 1990, Current Industrial Report, 2506–12.31

Flume Studies and Field Observations of the Interaction of Frazil Ice and Anchor Ice with Sediment, 2176–1.38

Fluorescent Lamp Ballasts, Current Industrial Report, 2506–12.14

Fluorspar in 1990: Mineral Industry Surveys, Advance Summary, 5614–5.19

Fluorspar: Mineral Industry Surveys, 5612–2.10

Fluorspar: Minerals Yearbook, Volume 1, 1990, 5604–20.21

Flying Hours: Overview of Navy and Marine Corps Flight Operations, 26123–332

Followup Study of Possible HIV Seropositivity Among Abusers of Parenteral Drugs in 1971-72, 4042–3.237

FOMC in 1990: Onset of Recession, 9391–1.213

Food Aid in the Post-Uruguay Round, 1524–4.2

Food and Agricultural Sciences, 1989 Annual Report from the Secretary of Agriculture to the President and the Congress of the U.S., 1004–19

Food and Agriculture Competitively Awarded Research and Education Grants, FY90, 1764–1

Food Assistance: Information on the Private Sponsors in the 1990 Summer Food Service Program, 26113–541

Food Consumption, Prices, and Expenditures, 1968-89, 1544–4

Food Cost Review, 1990, 1544–9

Food for Peace: 1988 Annual Report on Public Law 480, 1924–7

Food Grain Outlook, 1004–16.1

Food Marketing and New Product Development in Response to Health Concerns, 1004–16.1

Food Review, 1541–7

Food Safety and Quality: Stronger FDA Standards and Oversight Needed for Bottled Water, 26113–519

Food Safety and Quality: Who Does What in the Federal Government, 26113–503

Food Safety and the Environment, 1004–16.1

Food Spending in American Households, 1980-88, 1544–30

Food Stamp Statistical Summary of Project Area Operations Report, January 1990, 1362–6

Food Stamp Statistical Summary of Project Area Operations Report, July 1989, 1362–6

Food Stamp Statistical Summary of Project Area Operations Report, July 1990, 1362–6

Food Trends, 1702–1.212

Footwear, Current Industrial Report, 2506–6.7

Footwear, 1990, Current Industrial Report, 2506–6.8

Forecast Announcements and Locally Persistent Bias, 9387–8.249

Forecast of IFR Aircraft Handled by Air Route Traffic Control Center, FY91-2005, 7504–15

Forecasting Consumer Spending: Should Economists Pay Attention to Consumer Confidence Surveys?, 9381–1.206

Forecasting Season-Average Corn Prices Using Current Futures Prices, 1561–4.201

Forecasting the Louisiana Economy, 9379–1.202

Forecasting U.S. GNP at Monthly Intervals with an Estimated Bivariate Time Series Model, 9371–1.201

Forecasting 1990/91 U.S. Upland Cotton Exports Using Weekly Shipments: An Application of Seasonal Factors, 1561–1.204

Foreign Agricultural Service Circular Series: Cocoa. World Cocoa Situation, 1925–9

Foreign Agricultural Service Circular Series: Cotton, 1925–4

Foreign Agricultural Service Circular Series: Cotton. World Cotton Situation, 1925–4.2

Foreign Agricultural Service Circular Series: Dairy, Livestock, and Poultry, 1925–33

Foreign Agricultural Service Circular Series: Dairy, Livestock, and Poultry. Meat and Dairy Monthly Imports, 1925–31

Foreign Agricultural Service Circular Series: Dairy, Livestock, and Poultry. U.S. Trade and Prospects, 1925–32

Foreign Agricultural Service Circular Series: Dairy, Livestock, and Poultry. World Livestock Situation, 1925–33.2

Foreign Agricultural Service Circular Series: Dairy, Livestock, and Poultry. World Poultry Situation, 1925–33.1

Foreign Agricultural Service Circular Series: Dairy Monthly Imports, 1925–31

Foreign Agricultural Service Circular Series: Grains, 1925–2

Foreign Agricultural Service Circular Series: Horticultural Products Review, 1925–34

Index by Titles

Foreign Agricultural Service Circular Series: Oilseeds, 1925–1

Foreign Agricultural Service Circular Series: Sugar and Honey, 1925–14

Foreign Agricultural Service Circular Series: Tea, Spices and Essential Oils, 1925–15

Foreign Agricultural Service Circular Series: U.S. Seed Exports, 1925–13

Foreign Agricultural Service Circular Series. Wood Products: International Trade and Foreign Markets, 1925–36

Foreign Agricultural Service Circular Series. World Agricultural Production, 1925–28

Foreign Agricultural Service Circular Series: World Coffee Situation, 1925–5

Foreign Agricultural Service Circular Series: World Dairy Situation, 1925–10

Foreign Agricultural Service Circular Series. World Tobacco Situation, 1925–16

Foreign Agricultural Trade of the U.S., 1522–1

Foreign Agricultural Trade of the U.S., FY90 Supplement, 1522–4

Foreign Agricultural Trade of the U.S., CY90 Supplement, 1522–4

Foreign Agricultural Trade of the U.S., 1989: Supplementary Tables, 1524–8

Foreign Agriculture, 1990-91, 1924–12

Foreign Animal Disease Report, 1392–3

Foreign Assistance: AID Can Improve Its Management and Oversight of Host Country Contracts, 26123–342

Foreign Assistance: AID Energy Assistance and Global Warming, 26123–352

Foreign Assistance: Assistance to Disabled Persons in Developing Countries, 26123–321

Foreign Assistance: Funds Obligated Remain Unspent for Years, 26123–327

Foreign Assistance: Obligated but Unspent Funds as of Sept. 30, 1990, 26123–327

Foreign Assistance: Progress in Implementing the Development Fund for Africa, 26123–333

Foreign Claims Settlement Commission. Annual Report to Congress for 1990, 6004–16

Foreign Corporations with Income Effectively Connected with a U.S. Business, 1987, 8302–2.205

Foreign Countries and Plants Certified To Export Meat and Poultry to the U.S., Report of the Secretary of Agriculture to the U.S. Congress, 1374–2

Foreign Currencies Held by the U.S. Government, FY90, 8102–7

Foreign Currencies Held by the U.S. Government, Oct. 1, 1990-Mar. 31, 1991, 8102–7

Foreign Direct Investment in the U.S: Balance of Payments and Direct Investment Position Estimates, 1980-86, 2708–41

Foreign Direct Investment in the U.S.: Detail for Historical-Cost Position and Balance of Payments Flows, 1990, 2702–1.219

Foreign Direct Investment in the U.S.: Operations of U.S. Affiliates of Foreign Companies, Preliminary 1989 Estimates, 2704–4

Foreign Direct Investment in the U.S.: Operations of U.S. Affiliates of Foreign Companies, Revised 1988 Estimates, 2704–4

Foreign Direct Investment in the U.S., Review and Analysis of Current Developments, 2004–9

Foreign Direct Investment in the U.S.: 1989 Transactions, 2044–20

Foreign Direct Investment in U.S. Manufacturing: Effects on the Trade Balance, 9385–8.91

Foreign Economic Trends and Their Implications for the U.S., 2046–4

Foreign Exchange Intervention as a Signal of Monetary Policy, 9373–1.209

Foreign Exchange Rates, 9365–2

Foreign Fishery Information Releases: Supplements to Market News Report, 2162–7

Foreign Flag Merchant Ships Owned by U.S. Parent Companies, As of Jan. 1, 1991, 7702–3

Foreign Interest Rate Disturbance, Financial Flows and Physical Capital Accumulation in a Small Open Economy, 9385–8.102

Foreign Investment: Concerns in the U.S. Real Estate Sector During the 1980s, 26123–350

Foreign Labor Trends, 6366–4

Foreign Markets for U.S. Seafood Products, 2166–19

Foreign Military Sales, Foreign Military Construction Sales and Military Assistance Facts, As of Sept. 30, 1990, 3904–3

Foreign Ownership of U.S. Agricultural Land Through Dec. 31, 1990, 1584–2

Foreign Ownership of U.S. Agricultural Land Through Dec. 31, 1990: County-Level Data, 1584–3

Foreign Recipients of U.S. Income, 1988, 8302–2.206

Foreign Trade Barriers, National Trade Estimate Report, 444–2

Foreign-Trade Zones Board 50th Annual Report to the Congress of the U.S., 2044–30

Forest and Rangeland Resource Interactions: A Supporting Technical Document for the 1989 RPA Assessment, 1208–24.19

Forest Area and Timber Resource Statistics for State and Private Lands in Montana, 1206–25

Forest Insect and Disease Conditions, Intermountain Region, 1986, 1206–11.2

Forest Insect and Disease Conditions, Intermountain Region, 1987, 1206–11.2

Forest Insect and Disease Conditions, Intermountain Region, 1988, 1206–11.2

Forest Insect and Disease Conditions, Intermountain Region, 1989, 1206–11.2

Forest Insect and Disease Conditions, Intermountain Region, 1990, 1206–11.2

Forest Pest Conditions in the Rocky Mountain Region for 1989, 1206–11.1

Forest Pest Conditions in the Rocky Mountain Region for 1990, 1206–11.3

Forest Pest Conditions Reports: USDA Forest Service Regions, 1206–11

Forest Pest Conditions State Reports, 1206–49

Forest Resources of Arizona, 1208–374

Forest Service: Difficult Choices Face the Future of the Recreation Program, 26113–518

Forest Statistics for Alabama, 1206–30

Forest Statistics for Alabama Counties, 1990, 1206–30.10

Forest Statistics for East Oklahoma Counties, 1986, 1206–39.4

Forest Statistics for Kentucky, 1975 and 1988, 1206–12.15

Foster Care, Adoption...

Forest Statistics for Land Outside National Forests in Eastern Montana, 1989, 1206–25.8

Forest Statistics for Land Outside National Forests in Montana, 1206–25

Forest Statistics for Land Outside National Forests in Northwestern Montana, 1989, 1206–25.10

Forest Statistics for Land Outside National Forests in West-Central Montana, 1989, 1206–25.9

Forest Statistics for Land Outside National Forests in Western Montana, 1989, 1206–25.11

Forest Statistics for New Jersey, 1987, 1206–12.14

Forest Statistics for North Carolina, 1206–4

Forest Statistics for North Carolina, 1990, 1206–4.13

Forest Statistics for Oklahoma, 1206–39

Forest Statistics for Southeast Alabama Counties, 1990, 1206–30.9

Forest Statistics for Southwest-South Alabama Counties, 1990, 1206–30.8

Forest Statistics for the Coastal Plain of Virginia, 1991, 1206–6.13

Forest Statistics for the Mountains of North Carolina, 1990, 1206–4.15

Forest Statistics for the Northeast Region, 1206–12

Forest Statistics for the Piedmont of North Carolina, 1990, 1206–4.14

Forest Statistics for Virginia, 1206–6

Forest Statistics for West Virginia, 1975 and 1989, 1206–12.13

Forest Wildlife Habitat Statistics for Maryland and Delaware, 1986, 1206–44.5

Forest Wildlife Habitat Statistics of the Northeastern Region, 1206–44

Forestry Incentives Program (FIP) Monthly Progress Report, By State and Area for Period Ending (Date), 1802–11

Forestry Incentives Program, From Inception of Program Through Sept. 30, 1990, 1804–20

Forestry Issues in the Pacific Northwest, 21168–50

Forestry Wage Surveys, 6787–7

Formerly Utilized MED/AEC Sites Remedial Action Program, 3006–9

Forms 1040, 1040A and 1040EZ by Full-Paid, Other-Than-Full-Paid, Refunds and Electronically-Filed Returns: Projections. 1990-93, Fall Update, 8302–7

Forms 1040, 1040A and 1040EZ by Full-Paid, Other-Than-Full-Paid, Refunds and Electronically-Filed Returns: Projections. 1990-93, Spring Update, 8302–7

Forms 1040, 1040A and 1040EZ by Full-Paid, Other-Than-Full-Paid, Refunds and Electronically-Filed Returns: Projections. 1991-94, Spring Update, 8302–7

Formula Programs: Adjusted Census Data Would Redistribute Small Percentage of Funds to States, 26119–361

Formulation of the 1990 Farm Bill: Part 8 (Wheat, Soybeans, and Feed Grains Programs), 21168–43

Forum on Youth Violence in Minority Communities: Setting the Agenda for Prevention. Summary of the Proceedings, 4042–3.218

Foster Care, Adoption Assistance, and Child Welfare Services, 25368–169

Foster Care:

Foster Care: Children's Experiences Linked to Various Factors; Better Data Needed, 26121–432

Fourteen Co-ops Place on Fortune 500 Corporate List, 1122–1.205

Fourth Progress Report on the Homeless Chronically Mentally Ill Veterans Program, 8604–11

Framework for Limiting the Government's Exposure to Risks. Government-Sponsored Enterprises, 26119–296

Franchise Opportunities Handbook, 2044–27, 2104–7

Freddie Mac, 1990 Annual Report, 9414–1

Free Trade Agreement Bolsters Border Communities, 9383–19.204

Freedom of Information Activities, Annual Report of the Department of Health and Human Services, 1990, 4004–21

Freedom of Information: FDA's Program and Regulations Need Improvement, 26121–436

Freight Trucking: Promising Approach for Predicting Carriers' Safety Risks, 26131–82

Frequency of Cocaine Use and Violence: A Comparison Between Men and Women, 4498–74

Fresh and Chilled Atlantic Salmon from Norway. Determinations of the Commission in Investigation Nos. 701-TA-302 (Final) and 731-TA-454 (Final) Under the Tariff Act of 1930, Together with the Information Obtained in the Investigations, 9886–19.75

Fresh, Chilled, or Frozen Pork from Canada. Views on Second Remand in Investigation No. 701-TA-298 (Final), 9886–15.77

Fresh Fruit and Vegetable Arrival Totals, for 22 Cities, 1311–4.3

Fresh Fruit and Vegetable Arrivals and Shipments, 1990, 1311–4

Fresh Fruit and Vegetable Arrivals in Eastern Cities, by Commodities, States, and Months, 1311–4.1

Fresh Fruit and Vegetable Arrivals in Western Cities, by Commodities, States, and Months, 1311–4.2

Fresh Fruit and Vegetable Prices, 1990: Wholesale Chicago and New York City, F.O.B. Leading Shipping Points, 1311–8

Fresh Fruit and Vegetable Shipments, by Commodities, States, and Months, 1311–4.4

Fresh Fruits, Vegetables and Ornamental Crops. Weekly Summary: Shipments and Arrivals, 1311–3

Fresh Kiwifruit from New Zealand. Determination of the Commission in Investigation No. 731-TA-516 (Preliminary) Under the Tariff Act of 1930, Together with the Information Obtained in the Investigation, 9886–14.316

Frozen Fishery Products, Preliminary, 2162–2

Fruit and Tree Nuts Situation and Outlook Report, 1561–6

Fruit and Tree Nuts Situation and Outlook Yearbook, 1561–6

Fruit and Vegetable Industry Perspective, 1004–16.1

Fruit and Vegetable Truck Cost Report, 1272–1

Fruit and Vegetable Truck Rate and Cost Summary, 1990, 1311–15

Fruits: Production, Use and Value, 1621–18

Fuel Oil and Kerosene Sales, 1989, 3164–94

Fuels and Electric Energy Consumed. 1987 Census of Mineral Industries. Subject Series, 2517–2

Fulbright Program 1990, J. William Fulbright Foreign Scholarship Board, Twenty-seventh Annual Report, 10324–1

Functional Relationship Between Prices and Market Concentration: The Case of the Banking Industry, 9366–6.283

Functionally and Medically Defined Subgroups of Nursing Home Populations, 4652–1.205

Funding Continues To Increase but Program Effectiveness Is Unknown. Drug Interdiction, 26119–318

Funding Fish and Wildlife Projects. National Forests, 26113–529

Funds Obligated Remain Unspent for Years. Foreign Assistance, 26123–327

Further Evidence on Business Cycle Duration Dependence, 9387–8.250

Further Test of a Census Approach to Compiling Data on Fatal Work Injuries, 6722–1.249

Future of Head Start, 23848–217

Future of Social Security: An Update, 9391–1.207

Futures Trading Practices Act of 1989: S. 1729, 25168–77

FY88 Research Proposal and Award Activities by Predominantly Undergraduate Institutions, 9628–85

FY90 Annual Report of the Research Grants Program, 9184–18

FY90 Annual Report on In-house Energy Management, 3004–27

FY90 Guaranteed Student Loan Programs Data Book, 4804–38

FY91 Apportionments to States from the Land and Water Conservation Fund, 5544–15

FY91 Horticultural Exports Set Record, 1925–34.249

FY92 Budget in Brief, Department of Transportation, 7304–10

FY92-93 Military Construction Programs, 3544–15

Gallium in 1990: Mineral Industry Surveys, Annual Review, 5614–5.12

Game Plans for the '90s, 9375–7

Gamma Ray Observatory, Spacewalk Highlight STS-37, 9506–2.141

GAO Bibliographies, 26106–10

GAO Reports and Testimony, 26106–10

Gap Exists Between Need and Provision of Child Care Services, 9383–19.201

Gas Deliverability and Flow Capacity of Surveillance Gas Fields, 3166–10

Gas Mileage Guide, 1992: EPA Fuel Economy Estimates, 3304–11

Gastric Adenocarcinoma and Helicobacter pylori Infection, 4472–1.236

GATT Standards Code Activities of the National Institute of Standards and Technology, 1990, 2214–6

Gem Stone Production in Arizona, Colorado, Idaho, Montana, North Carolina, Oregon, Maine, Utah, Nevada and Tennessee: Mineral Industry Surveys Annual Advance Summary Supplement, 5614–5.10

Gemstones: Minerals Yearbook, Volume 1, 1989, 5604–15.26

Gemstones: Minerals Yearbook, Volume 1, 1990, 5604–20.22

Index by Titles

Gene Amplification Thermal Cyclers and Subassemblies Thereof from the UK. Determination of the Commission in Investigation No. 731-TA-485 (Final) Under the Tariff Act of 1930, Together with the Information Obtained in the Investigation, 9886–14.327

Gene Amplification Thermal Cyclers and Subassemblies Thereof from the UK. Determination of the Commission in Investigation No. 731-TA-485 (Preliminary) Under the Tariff Act of 1930, Together with the Information Obtained in the Investigation, 9886–14.301

Genecology of Longleaf Pine in Georgia and Florida, 1208–345

General Aviation Activity and Avionics Survey, 1989, 7504–29

General Aviation Activity and Avionics Survey, 1990, 7504–29

General Aviation Pilot and Aircraft Activity Survey, 7508–3

General Estimates System 1989: A Review of Information on Police-Reported Traffic Crashes in the U.S., 7764–18

General Services Administration Annual Report, FY90, 9454–1

General Services Administration Semiannual Report to the Congress, Apr. 1-Sept. 30, 1991, 9452–8

General Services Administration Semiannual Report to the Congress, Oct. 1, 1990-Mar. 31, 1991, 9452–8

General Summary: Industry, Product Class, and Geographic Area Statistics. 1987 Census of Manufactures. Subject Series, 2497–1

General Summary. 1987 Census of Mineral Industries. Subject Series, 2517–1

Generally Successful Filing Season in 1991. Tax Administration, 26119–346

Generation and Sales Statistics, FY90, 3222–1

Generation and Sales Statistics, CY90, 3222–1

Generational Accounting: A New Approach for Understanding the Effects of Fiscal Policy on Saving, 9377–9.116

Generational Accounts: A Meaningful Alternative to Deficit Accounting, 9377–9.111

Genetic Monitoring and Screening in the Workplace, 26358–230

Geochemical Relations and Distribution of Selected Trace Elements in Ground Water of the Northern Part of the Western San Joaquin Valley, Calif. Regional Aquifer-System Analysis, 5666–25.11

Geochemistry of Ground Water in Alluvial Basins of Arizona and Adjacent Parts of Nevada, New Mexico, and California. Regional Aquifer-System Analysis, 5666–25.13

Geochemistry of the Cambrian-Ordovician Aquifer System in the Northern Midwest, U.S. Regional Aquifer-System Analysis, 5666–25.10

Geographic Area Series. 1987 Census of Agriculture. Volume 1, 2331–1

Geographic Area Series. 1987 Census of Mineral Industries, 2515–1

Geographic Area Statistics. 1989 Annual Survey of Manufactures, 2506–15.3

Geographic Based Information Management System for Permafrost Prediction in the

Index by Titles

Beaufort and Chukchi Seas. Part I: Submarine Permafrost on the Alaskan Shelf, 2176–1.39

Geographic Based Information Management System for Permafrost Prediction in the Beaufort and Chukchi Seas. Part II: Submarine Permafrost on the Arctic Shelf of Eurasia and the Development of the Arctic in the Pleistocene, 2176–1.39

Geographic Distribution of VA Expenditures, FY90, 8604–6

Geographic Medicare Economic Index: Alternative Approaches, 4658–50

Geographic Notes, 7142–3

Geographic Profile of Employment and Unemployment, 1990, 6744–7

Geographical Distribution of Assets and Liabilities of Major Foreign Branches of U.S. Banks, 9365–3.7

Geohydrology and Water Quality in the Vicinity of the Gettysburg National Military Park and Eisenhower Historic Site, Pennsylvania, 5666–28.8

Geologic Sources, Mobilization, and Transport of Selenium from the California Coast Ranges to the Western San Joaquin Valley: A Reconnaissance Study, 5666–27.10

Geologic Studies in Alaska by the U.S. Geological Survey, 1989, 5664–15

Geophysical Investigations of the Western Ohio-Indiana Region, Annual Report, October 1989-September 1990, 9634–10

Geophysical Monitoring for Climatic Change, No. 17, Summary Report, 1988, 2144–28

Geothermal Progress Monitor, Report No. 12, 3308–87

Germany's Fisheries and Fish Markets, 2162–1.204

Giving Physicians Incentives To Contain Costs Under Medicaid, 4652–1.228

Glass Containers, Current Industrial Report, 2506–9.4

Global Arms Trade: Commerce in Advanced Military Technology and Weapons, 26358–241

Global Climate Trends and Greenhouse Gas Data: Federal Activities in Data Collection, Archiving, and Dissemination, 3028–4

Global Competitiveness of U.S. Advanced-Technology Manufacturing Industries: Communications Technology and Equipment. Report to the Committee on Finance, U.S. Senate, on Investigation No. 332-301 Under Section 332(g) of the Tariff Act of 1930, 9886–4.177

Global Competitiveness of U.S. Advanced-Technology Manufacturing Industries: Communications Technology and Equipment. Summary, 9886–4.177

Global Competitiveness of U.S. Advanced-Technology Manufacturing Industries: Pharmaceuticals. Report to the Committee on Finance, U.S. Senate, on Investigation No. 332-302 Under Section 332(g) of the Tariff Act of 1930, 9886–4.176

Global Competitiveness of U.S. Advanced-Technology Manufacturing Industries: Pharmaceuticals. Summary, 9886–4.176

Global Competitiveness of U.S. Advanced-Technology Manufacturing Industries: Semiconductor Manufacturing and Testing Equipment. Report to the Committee on Finance, U.S. Senate, on

Investigation No. 332-303 Under Section 332(g) of the Tariff Act of 1930, 9886–4.175

Global Competitiveness of U.S. Advanced-Technology Manufacturing Industries: Semiconductor Manufacturing and Testing Equipment. Summary, 9886–4.175

Global Financial Markets: International Coordination Can Help Address Automation Risks, 26125–44

Global Food Assessment Situation and Outlook Report, 1526–8, 1528–313

Global Stock Markets and Links in Real Activity, 9385–8.105

Global Trade Talk: U.S. Customs Service Journal for the International Trade Community, 8142–2

Global Warming: Emission Reductions Possible as Scientific Uncertainties Are Resolved, 26113–495

Globalization of Stock, Futures, and Options Markets, 9371–1.209

Globex Trading System, 9366–6.271

Glossing over the Truth About the Tongass National Forest, 21408–121

Gloves and Mittens, 1990, Current Industrial Report, 2506–6.4

Going Gets Tough: State and Local Governments Confront the Nineties, 9375–1.207

Gold and Silver: Mineral Industry Surveys, 5612–1.10

Gold: Minerals Yearbook, Volume 1, 1989, 5604–15.27

Government Budgets and Property Values, 9379–1.207

Government Costs for Employee Benefits. 1987 Census of Governments. Volume 3. Public Employment, No. 4, 2455–4

Government Employment, 2466–1

Government Finance in a Common Currency Area, 9381–10.120

Government Finances Series, 2466–2

Government Finances: 1988-89, 2466–2.2

Government Finances: 1989-90, Preliminary Report, 2466–2.9

Government Intervention in Latin American Agriculture, 1982-87, 1528–324

Government Intervention in South Korean Agriculture, 1522–3.205

Government Intervention in Soviet Agriculture: Estimates of Consumer and Producer Subsidy Equivalents, 1528–320

Government Life Insurance Program for Veterans and Members of the Services, Annual Report, 1990, 8604–4

Government National Mortgage Association, Financial Statements and Reports on Internal Controls and Compliance with Laws and Regulations, 5144–6

Government National Mortgage Association (GNMA), Annual Report, 1989, 5144–6

Government National Mortgage Association (GNMA), Annual Report, 1990, 5144–6

Government Open Systems Interconnection Profile (GOSIP). Hardware and Software Standards, 2216–2.201

Government Policies and Programs Affecting Tobacco Production and Trade in Major Tobacco Trading Nations, 1561–10.206

Government Purchases and Real Wages, 9379–12.65

Government Shutdown: Permanent Funding Lapse Legislation Needed, 26119–311

Ground-Water Levels in...

Government-Sponsored Enterprises: A Framework for Limiting the Government's Exposure to Risks, 26119–296

Government-Sponsored Enterprises: Safe and Sound?, 9391–16.201

Grain and Feed Market News, Weekly Summary and Statistics, 1313–2

Grain Cooperatives, 1126–1.5

Grain Loan Activity Through (Month), 1802–3

Grain Market News: Quarterly Durum Report, 1313–6

Grain Programs in the 1990 Farm Bill, 1004–16.1

Grain Shipper/Railroad Contract Disclosure: An Experimental Analysis, 1502–3.201

Grain Stocks, 1621–4

Grains: Foreign Agricultural Service Circular Series, 1925–2

Grant Reform Reconsidered, 10042–1.202

Grant-in-Aid for Fisheries: 1989 Annual Report, 2164–3

Grant-in-Aid for Fisheries: 1990 Program Report, 25 Years of the Anadromous Fish Conservation Act, 2164–3

Graphical Kernel System (GKS). Software Standard, 2216–2.197

Graphite in 1990: Mineral Industry Surveys Annual Advance Summary, 5614–5.23

Graphite: Minerals Yearbook, Volume 1, 1989, 5604–15.28

Graphite: Minerals Yearbook, Volume 1, 1990, 5604–20.25

Gray Portland Cement and Cement Clinker from Japan. Determination of the Commission in Investigation No. 731-TA-461 (Final) Under the Tariff Act of 1930, Together with the Information Obtained in the Investigation, 9886–14.309

Gray Portland Cement and Cement Clinker from Venezuela. Determination of the Commission in Investigations Nos. 303-TA-21 (Preliminary) and 731-TA-519 (Preliminary) Under the Tariff Act of 1930, Together with the Information Obtained in the Investigations, 9886–19.76

Grazing Statistical Summary, FY91, 1204–5

Great Lakes, Connecting Channels and St. Lawrence River: Water Levels and Depths, 3752–2

Great Lakes Economy: Looking North and South, 9375–15

Great Lakes Environmental Research Laboratory Annual Report, FY90, 2144–26

Great Lakes Water Levels, 1989, 2174–3

Great Lakes Water Levels, 1990, 2174–3

Green Book, 1991. Overview of Entitlement Programs. Background Material and Data on Programs Within the Jurisdiction of the Committee on Ways and Means, 21784–11

Gross Domestic Product as a Measure of U.S. Production, 2702–1.215

Gross Job Creation, Gross Job Destruction and Employment Reallocation, 9375–13.56

Gross National Product by Industry, 1987-89, 2702–1.208

Gross Product by Industry, 1977-88: Progress Report on Improving the Estimates, 2702–1.201

Ground-Water Data for Michigan, 1988, 5666–28.2

Ground-Water Level Data for North Carolina, 1987, 5666–28.1

Ground-Water Levels in Arkansas, Spring 1990, 5666–28.12

Ground-Water Levels in the...

Index by Titles

Ground-Water Levels in the Alluvial Aquifer in Eastern Arkansas, 1987, 5666–28.6

Ground-Water Levels in Wyoming, 1980 Through September 1989, 5666–28.4

Groundwater Resources, State, Local, and Regional Studies, 5666–28

Groups with Historically High Incidences of Unemployment, 6504–2

Groups with Historically High Incidences of Unemployment: Report to the Congress Required by Section 4(d)(3) of the Fair Labor Standards Act, 6504–4

Growing Use of Computers. Statistical Brief, 2326–17.30

Growth in Japanese Lending and Direct Investment in the U.S.: Are They Related?, 9385–8.97

Growth of Employer-Sponsored Group Life Insurance, 6722–1.248

GSA Travel Services: Small Disadvantaged Businesses Seldom Receive Contracts, 26119–331

Guaranteed Student Loan Programs Data Book, FY90, 4804–38

Guardians of the Eighth Sea, 2152–8.204

Guide for the Management, Analysis, and Interpretation of Occupational Mortality Data, 4248–89

Guide to Agency/Distributor Regulations in Saudi Arabia, 2046–6.9

Guide to Department of Education Programs, 1991, 4804–3

Guide to Foreign Trade Statistics, 1991, 2428–11

Guide to Improving the National Education Data System, 4828–39

Guide to the 1987 Census of Governments. 1987 Census of Governments. Volume 6.

Guide to the 1987 Census of Governments, No. 1, 2460–1

Guideline: American National Dictionary for Information Systems. Software Standard, 2216–2.194

Guidelines for Preventing the Transmission of Tuberculosis in Health-Care Settings, with Special Focus on HIV-Related Issues, 4206–2.35

Guidelines for Prophylaxis Against Pneumocystis carinii Pneumonia for Children Infected with Human Immunodeficiency Virus, 4206–2.38

Gulf of Mexico: Estimated Oil and Gas Reserves, Dec. 31, 1989, 5734–6

Gulf of Mexico Sales 131, 135, and 137: Central, Western, and Eastern Planning Areas. Final Environmental Impact Statement, 5736–1.23

Gypsum in 1990: Mineral Industry Surveys Annual Advance Summary, 5614–5.27

Gypsum: Mineral Industry Surveys, 5612–1.31

Gypsum: Minerals Yearbook, Volume 1, 1989, 5604–15.29

Gypsum Mines and Calcining Plants in the U.S. in 1989: Mineral Industry Surveys Annual Advance Summary Supplement, 5614–5.1

Gypsum Mines and Calcining Plants in the U.S. in 1990: Mineral Industry Surveys Annual Advance Summary Supplement, 5614–5.28

Haemophilus b Conjugate Vaccines for Prevention of Haemophilus Influenzae Type

b Disease Among Infants and Children Two Months of Age and Older: Recommendations of the Immunization Practices Advisory Committee (ACIP), 4206–2.37

Half of the Nation's Population Lives in Large Metropolitan Areas, 2324–8

Handbook of Economic Statistics, 1991, 9114–4

Handbook of Effective Migrant Education Practices, 4808–22

Handbook of Hearing Aid Measurement, 1991, 8704–3

Handling Single Wave Nonresponse in a Panel Survey, 2626–10.117

Hanford Environmental Dose Reconstruction Project, 3356–5

Hanford Environmental Dose Reconstruction Project, Phase I: Air Pathway Report, 3356–5.6

Hanford Environmental Dose Reconstruction Project, Phase I: Columbia River Pathway Report, 3356–5.5

Hanford Environmental Dose Reconstruction Project, Phase I: Summary Report, 3356–5.4

Harbor Maintenance Trust Fund, 8102–9.12

Harbor Seal Trend Count Surveys in Southern Alaska, 1988, 14738–6

Hardwood Plywood, Current Industrial Report, 2506–7.1

Harmonized Tariff Schedule of the U.S. (1992) Annotated for Statistical Reporting Purposes, 9886–13

Harry S. Truman Memorial Scholarship Fund: Status of Account, 14312–1

Harry S. Truman Scholarship Foundation, Annual Report, FY90, 14314–1

Harvest Assessment of Cereal Production, 9918–18

Hatchery Production, 1990 Summary, 1625–8

Have Automobile Weight Reductions Increased Highway Fatalities? Highway Safety, 26131–89

Have Mergers Improved the Financial Performance of Farm Credit Banks?, 1541–1.205

Hay Market News, 1313–5

Hazardous Materials Transportation, 1989 Annual Report, 7304–4

Hazardous Substance Superfund Trust Fund, 8102–9.6

Hazardous Waste: Limited Progress in Closing and Cleaning Up Contaminated Facilities, 26113–528

Hazardous Waste Sites: Descriptions of Sites on Updates to National Priorities List, 9216–3

Hazardous Waste Sites: Descriptions of 6 Sites Placed on the Final National Priorities List in February 1991, 9216–3.25

Hazardous Waste Treatment Industry: Preliminary Data Summary, 9206–4.5

Hazards to Fish, Wildlife, and Invertebrates: Synoptic Reviews, 5506–14

Hazelnut Production, 1621–18.5

HCFA Statistics, 1991, 4654–18

Healing Communities: Progress Report on Domiciliary Care for Homeless Veterans Program, 8604–10

Health and Human Services: Hispanic Representation and Equal Employment Practices in Region VIII, 26121–393

Health Care Cost Containment in the Federal Republic of Germany, 4652–1.238

Health Care Coverage: Findings from the Survey of American Indians and Alaska Natives. National Medical Expenditure Survey, 4186–8.17

Health Care Coverage: U.S., 1976, 4147–16.5

Health Care Financing Program Statistics: Medicare and Medicaid Data Book, 1990, 4654–1

Health Care Financing Review, 4652–1

Health Care Financing Status Report, Research and Demonstrations in Health Care Financing, 4654–10

Health Care Financing System and the Uninsured, 4658–54

Health Care in Rural America: The Frontier Perspective, Part 2, 23898–6

Health Care Spending Control: The Experience of France, Germany, and Japan, 26121–437

Health Effects of Radiation Exposure, 25548–101

Health Information for International Travel, 1991, 4204–11

Health Insurance and Medical Care: Health of Our Nation's Children, U.S., 1988, 4146–8.192

Health Insurance Coverage: A Profile of the Uninsured in Selected States, 26121–403

Health Insurance Coverage Among Disabled Medicare Enrollees, 4652–1.243

Health Maintenance Organizations: Plan Offerings and Enrollments, 6722–1.222

Health Manpower Statistics, FY89, 3544–24

Health of Our Nation's Children. Children's Exposure to Environmental Cigarette Smoke Before and After Birth, 4146–8.204

Health of Our Nation's Children, U.S., 1988. Developmental, Learning, and Emotional Problems, 4146–8.193

Health of Our Nation's Children, U.S., 1988. Health Insurance and Medical Care, 4146–8.192

Health Physics/Radiation Protection Enrollments and Degrees, 1990, 3004–7

Health Status of Minorities and Low Income Groups: Third Edition, 4118–55

Health Status of the Disadvantaged: Chartbook 1990, 4118–56

Health, U.S., and Prevention Profile, 4144–11

Health U.S., 1990, 4144–11

Healthy People 2000: National Health Promotion and Disease Prevention Objectives, 4048–10

Hearing Aids, 8704–3

Heat Burn Injuries, 6846–1.20

Heavy Forged Handtools from the People's Republic of China: Determination of the Commission in Investigation No. 731-TA-457 (Final) Under the Tariff Act of 1930, Together with the Information Obtained in the Investigation, 9886–14.304

Heavy Rail Transit Safety, 1989 Annual Report, 7884–5

Helicobacter pylori Infection in Intestinal- and Diffuse-Type Gastric Adenocarcinomas, 4472–1.211

Helium Resources of the U.S., 1989, 5604–44

Helping Poland Cope with Unemployment, 6722–1.203

Hemoglobin and Selected Iron-Related Findings of Persons 1-74 Years of Age: U.S., 1971-74, 4147–16.5

Hemophilia Pass-Through Payments, 17206–1.10

Index by Titles

Hepatitis Surveillance Report No. 53, 4205–2
Her-2/neu and INT2 Proto-oncogene Amplification in Malignant Breast Tumors in Relation to Reproductive Factors and Exposure to Exogenous Hormones, 4472–1.227
High Technology Employment: Another View, 6722–1.235
Higher Education Act, Title II-B, Abstracts, Library Career Training Program, 4874–1
Higher Education Act, Title II-B, Library Career Training Program, Abstracts of Funded Projects, 1990, 4874–1
Higher World Oil Prices: The Potential for Oil-to-Coal Switching, 3162–37.201
High-Information Content Flat Panel Displays and Display Glass Therefor from Japan. Determination of the Commission in Investigation No. 731-TA-469 (Final) Under the Tariff Act of 1930, Together with the Information Obtained in the Investigation, 9886–14.328
Highlights from the 1989 National Drug and Alcoholism Treatment Unit Survey (NDATUS), 4494–10.1
High-Risk Groups Still Prove Hard To Reach. AIDS-Prevention Programs, 26121–428
High-Tenacity Rayon Filament Yarn from Germany and the Netherlands. Determinations of the Commission in Investigation Nos. 731-TA-530 and 531 (Preliminary) Under the Tariff Act of 1930, Together with the Information Obtained in the Investigations, 9886–14.331
Highway and Motor Vehicle Safety, 1989, 7764–1
Highway Program Consolidation. Transportation Infrastructure, 26113–471
Highway Safety: Have Automobile Weight Reductions Increased Highway Fatalities?, 26131–89
Highway Safety Improvement Programs: 1991 Annual Report of the Secretary of Transportation to the U.S. Congress, 7554–26
Highway Safety: Motorcycle Helmet Laws Save Lives and Reduce Costs to Society, 26113–537
Highway Safety 1989: A Report on Activities Under the Highway Safety Act of 1966, as Amended, 7764–1.1
Highway Statistics, 1990, 7554–1
Highway Taxes and Fees: How They Are Collected and Distributed, 7554–37
Highway Trust Fund, 8102–9.7, 25328–31
Highway Trust Fund: Revenue Sources, Uses, and Spending Controls, 26113–544
Highway Vehicle MPG and Market Shares Report: Model Year 1990, 3302–4
Hispanic Population in the U.S.: March 1990, 2546–1.448
Hispanic Population in the U.S.: March 1991, 2546–1.451
Hispanic Population of the U.S. Southwest Borderland, 2546–2.159
Hispanic Representation and Equal Employment Practices in Region VIII. Health and Human Services, 26121–393
Historical Perspective of the Commercial and Sport Fisheries Offshore California Through 1985, 5738–20
Historical Tables, Budget of the U.S. Government, FY92, 104–22
Historically Black Colleges and Universities of Higher Education, 25258–24

History of the Fisheries of Raritan Bay, New York and New Jersey, 2162–1.205
History of the U.S. Postal Service, Special Supplement, 9864–6
History of the Water Resources Division, USGS, 5668–118
History of the Water Resources Division, USGS: Volume V, July 1, 1947-Apr. 30, 1957, 5668–118.1
HIV Prevalence Estimates and AIDS Case Projections for the U.S.: Report Based upon a Workshop, 4206–2.34
HIV Safety Guidelines and Laboratory Training, 4042–3.256
HIV/AIDS Surveillance, 4202–9
Hog Butchers No Longer: 20 Years of Employment Change in Metropolitan Chicago, 9375–1.204
Hogs and Pigs, 1623–3
Home Blood Pressure Monitoring for Mild Hypertensives, 4042–3.207
Home Equity Loans: Flexible Enough To Withstand a Real Estate Downturn?, 9391–16.206
Home Mortgage Commitment Rates in Illinois, Federal Home Loan Bank of Chicago, 9302–6
Home Mortgage Commitment Rates in Wisconsin, Federal Home Loan Bank of Chicago, 9302–7
Home Mortgage Disclosure Act: Expanded Data on Residential Lending, 9362–1.206
Home Ownership in the 1980's. Statistical Brief, 2326–17.28
Homeless Situation in Michigan, 25418–5
Homeless: What Should Be Done To Meet the Needs of the Homeless in the U.S.? National Debate Topic for High Schools, 1991-92, 25928–9
Homelessness: Federal Personal Property Donations Provide Limited Benefit to the Homeless, 26113–538
Homelessness: McKinney Act Programs and Funding Through FY90, 26104–21
Homework in Macroeconomics: Household Production and Aggregate Fluctuations, 9383–20.5
Honey, 1631–6
Hong Kong's Role in Pacific Rim Agricultural Trade, 1524–4.5
Hop Stocks, 1621–8
Hops Market News, 1313–7
Horticultural Exports Set Record, FY91, 1925–34.249
Horticultural Products Review: Foreign Agricultural Service Circular Series, 1925–34
Horticultural Trade and Outlook for East Asia and Oceania, 1925–34.212
Hospital Back-Up Days: Impact on Joint Medicare and Medicaid Beneficiaries, 4652–1.225
Hospital Cost Variations Under PPS, 17206–2.26
Hospital Experimental Payments Program: 1980-87, 4658–48
Hospital Outpatient Services: Background Report, 17206–1.8
Hospital Studies Program, Hospital Cost and Utilization Project Research Notes, 4186–6
Hospital Studies Program Research Notes, 4186–6
Hospitals Point Source Category: Preliminary Data Summary, 9206–4.3

How Pervasive Is the Product...

Hotels, Motels, and Other Lodging Places. 1987 Census of Service Industries. Subject Series, 2393–3
House Concurrent Resolution on the Budget, FY92, 21264–2
Household and Family Characteristics: March 1990 and 1989, 2546–1.447
Household and Nonhousehold Living Arrangements in Later Life: A Longitudinal Analysis of a Social Process, 2626–10.134
Household Diary Study, FY88, 9864–10
Household Economic Studies. Current Population Reports. Series P-70, 2546–20
Household Wealth and Asset Ownership: 1988, 2546–20.16
House-Poor/House-Rich. Statistical Brief, 2326–17.33
Housing Appraisals and Redlining, 9387–8.242
Housing Completions, Current Construction Reports, 2382–2
Housing Expenditures for Never-Married Men: A Focus on One-Person Consumer Units, 1702–1.208
Housing Finance and the Transmission Mechanism of Monetary Policy, 9385–8.74
Housing for the Elderly: HUD Policy Decisions Delay Section 202 Construction Starts, 26113–506
Housing Highlights, 1990, 2326–21
Housing Starts, Current Construction Reports, 2382–1
Housing Statistics, 2326–7.77
Housing Units Authorized by Building Permits: Annual 1990. Current Construction Reports, 2384–2
Housing Units Authorized by Building Permits, Current Construction Reports, 2382–5
Housing Vacancies and Home Ownership. Current Housing Reports, 2482–1
Housing Vacancies and Homeownership, Annual Statistics: 1990. Current Housing Reports, Series H-111, 2484–1
Housing Vacancy Survey, Federal Home Loan Bank of Chicago, 9304–18
Housing Vacancy Survey, Federal Home Loan Bank of Seattle, 9304–21
Housing Vacancy Survey, Federal Home Loan Bank of Topeka, 9304–22
Housing Voucher Program, 5186–14
HOV Lane Violation Study, 7308–203
How Accurate Are Quality-of-Life Rankings Across Cities?, 9387–1.202
How Are We Doing? An Analysis of Projection Accuracy, 8304–8.1
How Do We Affect Taxpayer Behavior? The Case for Positive Incentives, Assistance or Enforcement. IRS 1990 Research Conference, 8304–25
How Fast Can We Grow?, 9373–1.201
How Federal Milk Order Market Statistics Are Developed and What They Mean, 1317–4.202
How Federal Spending for Infrastructure and Other Public Investments Affects the Economy, 26306–6.158
How Firm Size and Industry Affect Employee Benefits, 6722–1.204
How Long Will It Last?, 9373–25.201
How Much Are We Worth? Household Wealth and Asset Ownership. Statistical Brief, 2326–17.26
How Pervasive Is the Product Cycle? The Empirical Dynamics of American and Japanese Trade Flows, 9366–7.264

How Services and Costs Vary...

Index by Titles

How Services and Costs Vary by Day of Stay for Medicare Hospital Stays, 17208–2

How the CRP Affects Local Economies, 1502–4.203

How Well Do Asset Allocation Managers Allocate Assets?, 9385–8.87

How Will Reform of the Soviet Farm Economy Affect U.S. Agriculture?, 9381–1.210

HUD Policy Decisions Delay Section 202 Construction Starts. Housing for the Elderly, 26113–506

Human Capital and Endogenous Growth: Evidence from Taiwan, 9371–10.55

Human Factors in Aviation Maintenance Phase 1: Progress Report, 7506–10.95

Human Factors in Self-Monitoring of Blood Glucose: Final Report, 4068–71

Human Factors Issues in Aircraft Maintenance and Inspection: "Information Exchange and Communications", 7506–10.77

Human Immunodeficiency Virus (HIV) Infection Codes and New Codes for Kaposi's Sarcoma: Official Authorized Addenda ICD-9-CM (Revision No. 2), Effective Oct. 1, 1991, 4206–2.45

Humanitarian Relief Provided to Evacuees from Kuwait and Iraq. Persian Gulf Crisis, 26123–326

Hurricane Gold. Part I—The Loss, 2152–8.203

Hurricane Gold. Part II—The Find, 2152–8.203

Hurricane Hugo, Sept. 10-22, 1989. Natural Disaster Survey Report, 2186–6.1

Hydroelectric Projects Under License, As of Oct. 24, 1991, 3084–11

Hydrogen Energy Coordinating Committee Annual Report: Summary of DOE Hydrogen Programs for FY90, 3304–18

Hydrologic and Geochemical Monitoring in Long Valley Caldera, Mono County, Calif., 1986, 5666–27.7

Hydrologic Environments and Water-Quality Characteristics at Four Landfills in Mecklenburg County, N.C., 1980-86, 5666–27.11

Hydrology of the Floridan Aquifer System in East-Central Florida. Regional Aquifer-System Analysis, 5666–25.8

Hyperinflation, and Internal Debt Repudiation in Argentina and Brazil: From Expectations Management to the "Bonex" and "Collor" Plans, 9379–12.69

Hypothesis: Nonsteroidal Anti-Inflammatory Drugs Reduce the Incidence of Large-Bowel Cancer, 4472–1.205

Idaho Fish and Wildlife 2000: A Plan for the Future, 5726–7.2

Idaho Forest Pest Conditions and Program Summary, 1989, 1206–49.1

Idaho's Soil and Water: Condition and Trends, 1266–5.1

If the Presidential Election Were Held in 1991, 9276–1.90

IFR Aircraft Handled: Forecast by Air Route Traffic Control Center, 7504–15

IHS and Tribal Hospital Statistics, 4082–1

Immediate Challenges for Public Policy, 9385–2

Immigrant Education: Information on the Emergency Immigrant Education Act Program, 26121–418

Immigrant Links to the Home Country: Empirical Implications for U.S. and Canadian Bilateral Trade Flows, 9379–12.64

Immigrants Admitted by Country or Region, Birth, and Major Occupation Group, 6264–1

Immigrants Admitted by Country or Region of Birth, FY81-90, 6264–4

Immigrants Admitted by Major Occupation Group and Region and Selected Country of Birth, FY90, 6264–1

Immigration and Naturalization Service Bulletins, 6266–2

Immigration Issues, 6266–1

Immigration Management: Strong Leadership and Management Reforms Needed To Address Serious Problems, 26119–317

Immigration Policy and Research Reports, 6366–5

Immigration Reform and Control Act: The President's First Report on the Implementation and Impact of Employer Sanctions, 6264–6

Immigration Reform and Control Act: The President's Second Report on the Implementation and Impact of Employer Sanctions, 6264–6

Immigration Statistics: Advance Report, 6264–4

Impact of Bonneville's Model Conservation Standards on the Energy Efficiency of New Home Construction, 3228–15

Impact of Collection Enforcement Action on Individual Taxpayer Behavior, 8304–8.1

Impact of Domestic Market Structure on Exchange Rate Pass-Through, 9387–8.234

Impact of Elderly In-Migration on Private and Public Economic Development Efforts in Predominantly Rural Areas Along the South Atlantic Coast, 2068–38

Impact of Environmental Safeguards on the Livestock Sector, 1522–3.204

Impact of Higher Patent Fees on Small-Entity and Federal Agency Users. Patent and Trademark Office, 26113–543

Impact of Liabilities for Retiree Health Benefits on Share Prices, 9366–6.270

Impact of Liberalization in the Agricultural Sector. U.S.-Mexico Trade, 26123–335

Impact of Private-Sector Defense Cuts on Regions of the U.S., 9371–1.206

Impact of State Economic Regulation of Motor Carriage on Intrastate and Interstate Commerce, 7308–200

Impact of the Medicare Hospital Prospective Payment System: Report to Congress, 1988 Annual Report, 4654–13

Impact of the Tax Reform Act of 1986: Did It Improve Fairness and Simplicity? IRS 1989 Research Conference, 8304–25

Impact of the U.S. Bureau of Mines Clay Classification Systems on Land Use: Mineral Industry Surveys Annual Advance Clay Summary Supplement, 5614–5.3

Impacts of Lifting Alaskan North Slope Oil Exports Ban. Energy Security, 26113–496

Impacts of U.S. Forest Management Policies on the Carbon Cycle, 1004–16.1

Impairments Due to Injuries: U.S., 1985-87. Vital and Health Statistics Series 10, 4147–10.179

Implantation of the Automatic Cardioverter-Defibrillator. Health Technology Assessment Report, 1990, 4186–10.5

Implementation of Helsinki Final Act, Apr. 1, 1990-Mar. 31, 1991, Twenty-ninth CSCE Report, 7002–1

Implementation of Section 620(s) of the Foreign Assistance Act of 1961, As Amended: A Report to Congress, 1989/90, 9914–1

Implementation of the Compact of 1985, 21448–44

Implementation of the EC Tree Nut Program in Spain and Italy, 1925–34.237

Implementation of the Education of the Handicapped Act, Annual Report to Congress, 4944–4

Implementation of the Individuals with Disabilities Education Act, Thirteenth Annual Report to Congress, 4944–4

Implementation of the Program Fraud Civil Remedies Act of 1986. Program Fraud, 26111–76

Implementing the New Federal Incentives To Deter Prepayments of HUD Mortgages. Rental Housing, 26131–84

Implementing the Technology Transfer Act of 1986. Diffusing Innovations., 26131–85

Implications of a Stricter Qualified Thrift Lender Test. Thrifts and Housing Finance, 26119–337

Implications of Ratifying Montreal Aviation Protocol No. 3. International Aviation, 26113–501

Import Requirements and Restrictions for Tobacco and Tobacco Products in Foreign Markets, 1925–16.207

Important Facts About the Pacific Northwest Region, FY89, 1204–37

Imports and Exports of Fishery Products, Annual Summary, 1990, 2166–6.1

Imports from China and Competitive Conditions in the U.S. Market: Further Examination of Product Groups Identified by the East-West Trade Statistics Monitoring System, 9882–2.201

Improved Cost and Performance Monitoring Needed. DOD Service Academies, 26123–355

Improved Leadership Needed for Better Performance. Employment Service, 26121–430

Improvements Needed in FHWA's Motor Carrier Safety Program. Truck Safety, 26113–505

Improvements Needed in Managing Concessioners. Federal Lands, 26113–531

Improving Drug Abuse Treatment, 4498–73

Improving Operations of Federal Departments and Agencies. Status of Open Recommendations, 26104–5

Improving State Medicaid Programs for Pregnant Women and Children, 4652–1.213

Improving Technology: Modeling Energy Futures for the National Energy Strategy, 3166–6.47

Improving the Quality of Training Under JTPA, 6406–10.1

In Search of the Liquidity Effect, 9366–7.257

Inadequate Oversight Leaves Program Vulnerable to Waste, Abuse, and Mismanagement. Job Training Partnership Act, 26106–8.13

Inadequate Title VI Enforcement by the Office for Civil Rights. Within-School Discrimination, 26121–427

Index by Titles

Inappropriate Use of Experts and Consultants at Selected Civilian Agencies. Federal Workforce, 26119–354

Incidence Rates of Lymphomas and Soft-Tissue Sarcomas and Environmental Measurements of Phenoxy Herbicides, 4472–1.207

Income and Expenditure Patterns of Consumer Units with Reference Person Age 70 to 79 and 80 or Older, 1702–1.204

Income and Expenditures of Families with a Baby, 1702–1.211

Income and Expenditures of Two-Parent Families When One Parent Is Not Employed, 1004–16.1

Income Growth in the Southwest: Implications for Long-Term Development, 9379–1.209

Increased Numbers in Contingent Employment Lack Insurance, Other Benefits. Workers at Risk, 26121–411

Increased Risk of Renal Cell Carcinoma Among Obese Women, 4472–1.230

Increasing the Use of Underutilized Fish and Fishing Opportunities by California Anglers: The Use of Onboard Refrigeration and New Marketing Strategies, 2168–125

Index of Bank Control Share Prices, 9381–14.1

Index of Reports and Testimony: FY90, 26104–17

Index Report, Federal Home Loan Bank of Chicago, 9302–30

Indian Burden of Illness and Future Health Interventions, 4088–2

Indian Business Development Centers and Minority Business Development Centers, Annual Performance Report: Minority Business Development Agency, 2104–6

Indian Civil Service Retirement Act, P.L. 96-135, Annual Report to Congress, FY89, 4084–6

Indian Forests and Woodlands; and the Indian Environmental Regulatory Enhancement Acts, 25418–4

Indian Health Conditions, 4088–2

Indian Health Service: FY90 Hospital Inpatient Workload Summary and Comparison with Previous Year, 4084–4

Indian Health Service: FY90 Outpatient Visit Workload Summary and Comparison with Previous Year, 4084–8

Indian Health Service Nurse Shortage, 25418–6

Indian Health Service: Regional Differences in Indian Health, 1991, 4084–7

Indian Health Service: Trends in Indian Health, 1991, 4084–1

Indian Programs: Tribal Influence in Formulating Budget Priorities Is Limited, 26113–508

Indiana's Timber Resource, 1986: An Analysis, 1208–368

Indicator of Future Inflation Extracted from the Steepness of the Interest Rate Yield Curve Along Its Entire Length, 9385–8.118

Indicators of Comparative East-West Economic Strength, 1989, 7144–11

Indium: Minerals Yearbook, Volume 1, 1989, 5604–15.76

Indium: Minerals Yearbook, Volume 1, 1990, 5604–20.28

Individual Income Tax Rates, 1987, 8302–2.211

Individual Income Tax Returns Data by State, 1986-88, 8302–2.201

Individual Income Tax Returns, Preliminary Data, 1989, 8302–2.209

Individual-Tree Probability of Survival Model for the Northeastern U.S., 1208–369

Indivisibilities, Lotteries, and Sunspot Equilibria, 9383–20.3

Indochinese Refugee Activity and Summary of Refugee Admissions, 7002–4

Indoor Air Quality and Work Environment Study: Library of Congress Madison Building, 4248–92

Indoor Air Quality and Work Environment Study, Library of Congress Madison Building. Volume I: Results of Employee Survey, 4248–92.1

Indoor Air Quality and Work Environment Study, Library of Congress Madison Building. Volume II: Results of Indoor Air Environmental Monitoring, 4248–92.2

Indoor Air Quality and Work Environment Study, Library of Congress Madison Building. Volume III: Association Between Health and Comfort Concerns and Environmental Conditions, 4248–92.3

Indoor Air Quality Environmental Information Handbook: Combustion Sources, 1989 Update, 3008–107, 3326–1.2

Induced Terminations of Pregnancy: Reporting States, 1988, 4146–5.120

Industrial Development in the TVA Area During January-December 1989, 9804–3

Industrial Development in the TVA Area During January-December 1990, 9804–3

Industrial Gases, Current Industrial Report, 2506–8.3

Industrial Gases, 1990, Current Industrial Report, 2506–8.15

Industrial Laundries: Preliminary Data Summary, 9206–4.10

Industrial Minerals in California: Economic Importance, Present Availability, and Future Development, 5668–119

Industrial Production and Capacity Utilization, 9365–2.24

Industry Output and Job Growth Continues Slow into Next Century, 6722–1.253

Industry Perspective, 1004–16.1

Industry Series. 1987 Census of Construction Industries, 2373–1

Industry Wage Survey: Motor Vehicles, June 1989; Motor Vehicle Parts, August 1989, 6787–6.252

Industry Wage Survey: Textile Plants, August 1990, 6787–6.251

Industry Wage Surveys, 6787–6

Infant Mortality. Indian Health Conditions, 4088–2

Infectious Diseases. Indian Health Conditions, 4088–2

Inferring Market Power from Time-Series Data: The Case of the Banking Firm, 9366–6.261

Inflation: Measurement and Policy Issues, 9385–1.207

Inflation, Personal Taxes, and Real Output: A Dynamic Analysis, 9377–9.110

Inflationary Implications of Reducing Market Interest Rates via Alternative Monetary Policy Instruments, 9371–10.59

In-Flight Survey of International Air Travelers: Overseas Travelers to the U.S., January-December 1990, 2904–12

In-Flight Survey of International Air Travelers: Profile of Overseas Travelers to U.S.A. Destinations, 2904–12

Inland Waterways Trust Fund

In-Flight Survey of International Air Travelers: Profile of U.S. Residents Traveling to Overseas Destinations, 2904–14

In-Flight Survey of International Air Travelers: U.S. Travelers to Overseas Countries, January-December 1990, 2904–14

Influence of Housing and Durables on Personal Saving, 9373–1.218

Influence of the Commodity Composition of Trade on Economic Growth, 1502–3.202

Information About the Accuracy of Earnings Records. Social Security, 26121–422

Information and Withholding Documents, 1991-98, Projections, U.S. and Service Centers, 1991 Update, 8304–22

Information Collection Budget of the U.S. Government, 104–19

Information on and Improvements Needed to Surety Bond Guarantee Programs. Small Business, 26113–526

Information on Appeals of Farm and Housing Loan Decisions. Farmers Home Administration, 26113–516

Information on Farm and Retail Milk Prices. Federal Dairy Programs, 26113–540

Information on Federal Single-Family Properties. Property Disposition, 26113–513

Information on Revenue Agent Attrition. Tax Administration, 26119–345

Information on the Administration of Workers' Compensation Programs in Each State and the District of Columbia, 6504–9

Information on the Dollar Amount of Direct Loan, Loan Guarantee, and Insurance Programs. Federal Credit and Insurance, 26111–65

Information on the Emergency Immigrant Education Act Program. Immigrant Education, 26121–418

Information on the Private Sponsors in the 1990 Summer Food Service Program. Food Assistance, 26113–541

Information on Underwriting and Home Loans in the Atlanta Area. Secondary Mortgage Market, 26113–500

Information Resources Management Plan of the Federal Government, 104–19

Information Security: Federal Agency Use of Nondisclosure Agreements, 26123–328

Information Security Oversight Office, Annual Report to the President, FY90, 9454–21

Information-Aggregation Bias, 9389–19.31

Infrastructure and Regional Economic Performance: Comment, 9373–1.217

Inheritance of Nevus Number and Size in Melanoma and Dysplastic Nevus Syndrome Kindreds, 4472–1.235

In-house Energy Management Annual Report, FY90, 3004–27

Initial Results of a National Survey. Off-Label Drugs, 26131–81

Injury Experience in Coal Mining, 1989, 6664–4

Injury Experience in Metallic Mineral Mining, 1989, 6664–3

Injury Experience in Nonmetallic Mineral Mining (Except Stone and Coal), 1989, 6664–1

Injury Experience in Sand and Gravel Mining, 1989, 6664–2

Injury Experience in Stone Mining, 1989, 6664–5

Inland Waterways Trust Fund, 8102–9.8

Inorganic Chemicals, Current... Index by Titles

Inorganic Chemicals, Current Industrial Report, 2506–8.1

Inorganic Chemicals, 1990, Current Industrial Report, 2506–8.14

Inorganic Fertilizer Materials and Related Products, 2506–8.13

Inpatient Summary Data for Indian Health Service and Tribally-Operated Hospitals, 4082–1

Inpatient Summary Data for Indian Health Service Hospitals, 4082–1

Inputs Situation and Outlook Report. Agricultural Resources, 1561–16.201, 1561–16.204

Insect Infestation of Fire-Injured Trees in the Greater Yellowstone Area, 1208–379

Insider's View of the Political Economy of the Too Big To Fail Doctrine, 9377–9.107

Inspection of the Department of Energy's Equal Employment Opportunity Complaint Processing System, 3006–5.25

Inspector General Semiannual Report, Department of Veterans Affairs, Oct. 1, 1990-Mar. 31, 1991, 8602–1

Inspector General Semiannual Report to the Congress, Department of Transportation, Oct. 1, 1990-Mar. 31, 1991, 7302–4

Inspector General's Report to the Congress, Department of Housing and Urban Development. Report No. 25, for the 6-Month Period Ending Mar. 31, 1991, 5002–8

Inspector General's Report to the Congress, Department of Housing and Urban Development. Report No. 26, for the 6-Month Period Ending Sept. 30, 1991, 5002–8

Inspector General's Semiannual Report to the Congress, U.S. Department of Commerce, Oct. 1, 1990-Mar. 31, 1991, 2002–5

Inspector General's Semiannual Report to the Congress, U.S. Department of Commerce, Apr. 1-Sept. 30, 1991, 2002–5

Inspectors General: Work Performed by the Department of Labor Inspector General in 1988 and 1989, 26111–74

Inspectors' Opinions on Improving OSHA Effectiveness. Occupational Safety and Health, 26121–391

Institute of Museum Services, Annual Report, 1990, 9564–7

Instrumentation Awards, FY87-88, Undergraduate, Science, Engineering, and Mathematics Education, 9626–7.4

Insulated Wire and Cable, 1990, Current Industrial Report, 2506–10.8

Insurance Company Failures (Part 3), 21368–133

Insurance Regulation: The Insurance Regulatory Information System Needs Improvement, 26119–316

Insurance Regulatory Information System Needs Improvement. Insurance Regulation, 26119–316

Insurance Report, Federal Employees Health Benefits Program, Retired Federal Employees Health Benefits Program, Federal Employees' Group Life Insurance Program, Sept. 30, 1988, 9844–35

Insurance Report, Federal Employees Health Benefits Program, Retired Federal Employees Health Benefits Program, Federal Employees' Group Life Insurance Program, Sept. 30, 1989, 9844–35

Insured U.S. Commercial Banks with Consolidated Assets of $100 Million or More, Ranked Nationally by Assets, 9362–7

Insuring the Children: A Decade of Change. National Medical Expenditure Survey, 4186–8.14

Integrated Data Base for 1990: U.S. Spent Fuel and Radioactive Waste Inventories, Projections, and Characteristics, 3364–2

Integrated Pest Management (IPM) in the Vegetable Industry During the 1980's, 1568–298

Intensive Studies of Stream Fish Populations in Maine, 9208–130

Inter-American Foundation Annual Report, 1990, 14424–1

Inter-American Foundation in Numbers: 1971-90, 14424–2

Intercity Bus Feeder Project Program Analysis, 7888–79

Interest Rate Expectations and the Slope of the Money Market Yield Curve, 9389–1.201

Interface Between Data Terminal Equipment (DTE) and Data Circuit-Terminating Equipment (DCE) for Operation with Packet-Switched Data Networks (PSDN), or Between Two DTE's, by Dedicated Circuit. Hardware Standard, 2216–2.198

Intergovernmental Perspective, 10042–1

Interior Secretary Awards $34.5 Million in Historic Preservation Grants, 5544–9

Interior Secretary Lujan Announces Disbursement of $19.5 Million to States in 1991 8(g) Payments, 5306–4.9

Interior Secretary Lujan Announces New Wetland Projects, 5306–4.8

Interior Secretary Lujan Awards $19 Million in Urban Park Grants, 5306–4.7

Interjurisdictional Tax and Policy Competition: Good or Bad for the Federal System?, 10048–79

Intermarket Coordination Report, Report to Congress Required by the Market Reform Act of 1990, 11924–4

Intermediate-Range Nuclear Forces Treaty Implementation. Arms Control, 26123–364

Internal Combustion Engines, 1990, Current Industrial Report, 2506–12.6

Internal Revenue Report of Excise Taxes, 8302–1

Internal Revenue Service, 1989 Annual Report, 8304–3

Internal Revenue Service, 1990 Annual Report, 8304–3

International Agreements To Protect the Environment and Wildlife. Report to the Committee on Finance, U.S. Senate, on Investigation No. 332-287 Under Section 332 of the Tariff Act of 1930, 9886–4.169

International Aviation: Implications of Ratifying Montreal Aviation Protocol No. 3, 26113–501

International Comparisons of Hourly Compensation Costs for Production Workers in Manufacturing, 1990, 6822–3

International Coordination Can Help Address Automation Risks. Global Financial Markets, 26125–44

International Economic Competitiveness, Trade Performance and U.S. Living Standards, 21788–204

International Economic Conditions, 9391–7

International Economic Review, 9882–14

International Economic Review Special Edition: Composition of U.S. Merchandise Trade, 1986-90, Chartbook, 9884–21

International Energy Annual, 1989, 3164–50

International Energy Outlook 1991: A Post-War Review of Energy Markets, 3164–84

International Energy Statistical Review, 9112–2

International Evidence on the Historical Properties of Business Cycles, 9383–20.15

International Exchange and Training Programs of the U.S. Government, Annual Report, FY89, 9854–8

International Finance: Annual Report of the Chairman of the National Advisory Council on International Monetary and Financial Policies to the President and to the Congress for FY89, 15344–1

International Finance Corporation, 21248–149

International Finance Discussion Papers, 9366–7

International Finance: The National Advisory Council on International Monetary and Financial Policies Annual Report to the President and to the Congress, 15344–1

International Financing Programs and U.S. International Economic Competitiveness, 2048–152

International Food Safety: Comparison of U.S. and Codex Pesticide Standards, 26131–88

International Investment Position of the U.S. in 1990, 2702–1.212

International Narcotics Control Strategy Report, 7004–17

International Narcotics Control Strategy Report, Mid-Year Update, September 1991, 7004–17.2

International Oil and Gas Exploration and Development Activities, 3162–43

International Organizations and Programs. U.S. International Development Cooperation Agency Congressional Presentation, FY92, 9904–4.2

International Petroleum Statistics Report, 3162–42

International Science and Technology Data Update: 1991, 9627–35

International Strategic Minerals Inventory Summary Reports, 5666–21

International Trade and Foreign Markets. Foreign Agricultural Service Circular Series: Wood Products, 1925–36

International Trade and Payments Data: An Introduction, 9389–1.206

International Trade: Bulgarian Trade Data, 26123–323

International Trade: Iraq's Participation in U.S. Agricultural Export Programs, 26123–314

International Trade: U.S. Business Access to Certain Foreign State-of-the-Art Technology, 26123–361

International Travel To and From the U.S., 1992 Outlook, 2904–9

Internationalization of the Beer Brewing Industry, 9391–1.201

Interpolation, Analysis, and Archival of Data on Sea Ice Trajectories and Ocean Currents Obtained from Satellite-Linked Instruments, 2176–1.38

Interpretive Views on Hispanics' Perinatal Problems of Low Birth Weight and Prenatal Care, 4042–3.234

Index by Titles

Interstate Banking and Competition: Evidence from the Behavior of Stock Returns, 9393–8.205

Interstate Commerce Commission Office of Consumer Protection Annual Performance Reports of Household Goods Carriers Hauling 1,000 or More Shipments for Individual Shippers, 9484–11

Interstate System Status of Development, 7552–5

Intra-North American Trade and Other Trade Issues, 1004–16.1

Introduction to the ITC Computable General Equilibrium Model: Addendum to the Economic Effects of Significant U.S. Import Restraints. Report to the Committee on Finance, U.S. Senate, on Investigation No. 332-262 Under Section 332 of the Tariff Act of 1930, 9886–4.174

Inventories of Steel Producing Mills, Current Industrial Report, 2506–10.3

Inventory and Analysis of Federal Population Research, FY89, 4474–9

Inventory of Agricultural Research, FY90, 1744–2

Inventory of American Intermodal Equipment, 1990, 7704–10

Inventory of Power Plants in the U.S., 1990, 3164–36

Investigating the Banking Consolidation Trend, 9383–6.203

Investigating U.S. Government and Trade Deficits, 9371–1.207

Investigation of Operating Costs for Privately Owned Vehicles, 9454–13

Investment and Market Power, 9375–13.58

Investment and Market Power: Evidence from the U.S. Manufacturing Sector, 9385–8.81

Investment, GNP, and Real Exchange Rates, 9375–1.208

Investment Smoothing with Working Capital: New Evidence on the Impact of Financial Constraints, 9375–13.49

Iodine: Minerals Yearbook, Volume 1, 1990, 5604–20.29

Iraq's Participation in U.S. Agricultural Export Programs. International Trade, 26123–314

Iron and Steel Castings, 1990, Current Industrial Report, 2506–10.1

Iron and Steel: Minerals Yearbook, Volume 1, 1989, 5604–15.34

Iron and Steel Scrap: Mineral Industry Surveys, 5612–1.11

Iron Ore: Mineral Industry Surveys, 5612–1.12

Iron Ore: Minerals Yearbook, Volume 1, 1989, 5604–15.32

Iron Oxide Pigments in 1990: Mineral Industry Surveys, Annual, Preliminary, 5614–5.22

IRS' Administration of the International Boycott Tax Code Provisions. Tax Administration, 26119–349

IRS Annual Report, 1989, 8304–3

IRS Annual Report, 1990, 8304–3

IRS Can Improve Its Program To Find Taxpayers Who Underreport Their Income. Tax Administration, 26119–325

IRS Does Not Investigate Most High-Income Nonfilers. Tax Administration, 26119–322

IRS Needs To Improve Certain Measures of Service Center Quality. Tax Administration, 26119–329

IRS Research Bulletin, 8304–8

IRS 1989 Research Conference, 8304–25

IRS' 1990 Filing Season Performance Continued Recent Positive Trends. Tax Administration, 26119–319

IRS 1990 Research Conference, 8304–25

Is Battered Women's Help Seeking Connected to the Level of Their Abuse?, 4042–3.228

Is There a Shortfall in Public Capital Investment?, 9373–3.34

Is There Any Rationale for Reserve Requirements?, 9377–1.207

Is There Evidence of a Therapy-Related Increase in Germ Cell Mutation Among Childhood Cancer Survivors?, 4472–1.233

Issuance of U.S. Government Securities to Small Investors, 8008–148

Issues Arising from the Explosion Aboard the U.S.S. Iowa. Battleships, 26123–315

Issues in Labor Supply, 9362–1.203

Issues on Relocating Selected Commands from the Washington, D.C., Area. Navy Office Space, 26123–346

Italy-U.S. Fish Trade, 1981-88, 2162–1.201

Jail Inmates, 1990, 6066–25.38

James P. Mitchell: Social Conscience of the Cabinet, 6722–1.239

Japanese Capital Flows in the 1980s, 9393–8.204

Japanese Direct Investment in U.S. Manufacturing, 2048–151

Japanese Imports of Horticultural Products from the U.S. and the World, 1989-90, 1925–34.215

Japanese Overseas Fisheries Aid Told, 2162–1.201

Japan's Corporate Groups, 9375–1.203

Japan's Economic Challenge, 23848–220

Japan's Sablefish Supply and Market, 2162–1.201

Japan's Sea Cucumber Harvest and Market, 2162–1.201

Japan-U.S. Friendship Commission Annual Report, 14694–1

Japan-U.S. Friendship Commission Biennial Report, 1989-90, 14694–1

Japan-Vietnam Fishery Relations, 2162–1.204

Job Displacement, 1979-86: How Blacks Fared Relative to Whites, 6722–1.234

Job Patterns for Minorities and Women in State and Local Government, 1990, 9244–6

Job Task—Competency Linkages for FAA First-Level Supervisors, 7506–10.84

Job Training for the Homeless: Report on Demonstration's First Year, 6406–10.5

Job Training Partnership Act, 26106–8

Job Training Partnership Act: Inadequate Oversight Leaves Program Vulnerable to Waste, Abuse, and Mismanagement, 26106–8.13

Job Training Partnership Act: Racial and Gender Disparities in Services, 26106–8.14

Joint Economic Report, 1991, 23844–2

Joint Statement of Nicholas F. Brady, Secretary of the Treasury, and Richard G. Darman, Director of the Office of Management and Budget on Budget Results for FY91, 8008–153

Journal of Agricultural Economics Research, 1502–3

Journal of the National Cancer Institute, 4472–1

JTPA Staffing and Staff Training at the State and SDA Levels, 6406 10.2

Lands Under Control of the...

Judicial Business of the U.S. Courts, 1991 Annual Report of the Director, 18204–2.1

Justice Expenditure and Employment Extracts: 1984-86, 6064–4

Justice Expenditure and Employment in the U.S., 1988, 6064–9

Juvenile Court Property Cases, 6066–27.5

Juvenile Court Statistics, 1987, 6064–12

Juvenile Court Statistics, 1988, 6064–12

Juvenile Dieting, Unsafe Over-the-Counter Diet Products, and Recent Enforcement Efforts by the Federal Trade Commission, 21728–77

Juvenile Justice Bulletin, 6066–27

Key Financial Measures for 1989 Indicate Improved Co-op Performance, 1122–1.201

Key Statistics for Public and Private Elementary and Secondary Education: Early Estimates, School Year 1990-91, 4834–19

Key Statistics on Public Elementary and Secondary Education. Reported by State and by Regional, Locale, and Wealth Clusters, 1987-88, 4834–20

Key Statistics on Public Elementary and Secondary Education Reported by State and by Regional, Locale, and Wealth Clusters, 1988-89, 4834–20

Knit Fabric Production, 1990, Current Industrial Report, 2506–5.7

Kuwait Reconstruction Exporter Assistance, 2042–1.203

Kyanite and Related Materials: Minerals Yearbook, Volume 1, 1990, 5604–20.34

Labor Agreement Expirations in the Federal Service, 9847–1

Labor and the Supreme Court: Significant Issues of 1990-91, 6722–1.208

Labor Department Announces Public Employment Service Allotments, 6406–2.31

Labor Department Announces $3.2 Million in Grants To Fund Alien Labor Certification Activities, 6406–2.32

Labor Force Projections: The Baby Boom Moves On, 6722–1.252

Labor Market Implications of Unemployment Insurance and Short-Time Compensation, 9383–6.205

Labor Standards and Development in the Global Economy, 6368–9

Labor-Management Relations: Strikes and the Use of Permanent Strike Replacements in the 1970s and 1980s, 26121–405

Labor-Management Relations. 1987 Census of Governments. Volume 3. Public Employment, No. 3., 2455–3

Lake Superior's Wicked November Storms, 2152–8.204

Land Areas of the National Forest System, As of Sept. 30, 1990, 1204–2

Land Use, Water Use, Streamflow Characteristics, and Water-Quality Characteristics of the Charlotte Harbor Inflow Area, Florida, 5666–27.18

Lands Under Control of the U.S. Fish and Wildlife Service, as of Sept. 30, 1990, Annual Report, 5504–8

Lands Under Control of the U.S. Fish and Wildlife Service, as of Sept. 30, 1991, Annual Report, 5504–8

Large Class I Household Goods Carriers Selected Earnings Data, 9482–14
Large Class I Motor Carriers of Passengers Selected Earnings Data, 9482–13
Large Class I Motor Carriers of Property Selected Earnings Data, 9482–5
Large Nondefense R&D Projects in the Budget: 1980-96, 26306–3.116
Large Shocks, Small Shocks, and Economic Fluctuations: Outliers in Macroeconomic Times Series, 9379–12.63
Larval Fish Recruitment and Research in the Americas: Proceedings of the Thirteenth Annual Larval Fish Conference, Merida, Mexico, May 21-26, 1989, 2168–126
Late Expectations: Childbearing Patterns of American Women for the 1990's, 2546–2.162
Law Enforcement Officers Killed and Assaulted, 1990, 6224–3
Layers and Egg Production, 1990 Summary, 1625–7
Lead Industry: Mineral Industry Surveys, 5612–1.13
Lead: Minerals Yearbook, Volume 1, 1989, 5604–15.38
Leaking Underground Storage Tanks Trust Fund, 8102–9.11
Learning Disabled in Employment and Training Programs, 6406–10.4
Learning from One Another: The U.S. and European Banking Experience, 9379–12.70
Learning To Read in Our Nation's Schools. National Assessment of Educational Progress, 1988, 4896–7.2
Learning To Write in Our Nation's Schools. National Assessment of Educational Progress, 1988, 4896–7.1
Lease Refinancing: A DOD-Wide Program Is Not Currently Feasible, 26111–75
Lease Sales: Evaluation of Bidding Results and Competition, 5734–12
Leave Policies in Small Business: Findings from the U.S. Small Business Administration Employee Leave Survey, 9768–21
Legislation To Amend the Lanham Trademark Act Regarding Gray Market Goods, 25528–115
Lender Profitability in the Student Loan Program, 4808–36
Lerner Index, Welfare, and the Structure-Conduct-Performance Linkage, 9387–8.236
Less Developed Countries' Performance in High-Value Agricultural Trade, 1528–316
Less Need for Officers Provides Opportunity for Significant Savings. Reserve Officers' Training Corps, 26123–337
Lessons for the U.S. Canadian Health Insurance, 26121–424
Levels of Mathematics Achievement: Initial Performance Standards for the 1990 NAEP Mathematics Assessment, 4896–8.2
Leverage and Cyclicality, 9385–8.88
Leveraged Buyouts: Case Studies of Selected Leveraged Buyouts, 26119–355
Library of Congress Publications in Print, 1991, 26404–5
Library Programs: College Library Technology and Cooperation Grants Program, HEA Title II-D. Abstracts and Analysis of Funded Projects, 1989, 4874–6
Library Programs: Five-Year Report of Library Services Through Major Urban Resource Libraries (MURLs) and Metropolitan Public Libraries Serving as National or Regional Resource Centers, FY84-88, 4878–4
Library Programs: Library Career Training Program, Abstracts of Funded Projects, 1990, 4874–1
Library Programs: Library Services for Individuals with Limited English Proficiency, FY87, 4874–10
Library Resources for the Blind and Physically Handicapped: A Directory with FY90 Statistics on Readership, Circulation, Budget, Staff, and Collections, 26404–3
Licensed Operating Reactors, Status Summary Report, 9632–1, 9634–12
Licit Importation of Opium, 21528–81
Lifesaving System Threatened by Unreimbursed Costs and Other Factors. Trauma Care, 26121–419
Lifetime Use of Nursing Home Care, 4186–7.9
Light and Shadows on College Athletes, College Transcripts and Labor Market History, 4888–5
Light-Duty Vehicle Summary: First Six Months of Model Year 1991, 3302–4
Lightweight Materials for New Cars: Driving Toward Better Mileage, 5602–4.202
LIHEAP Program Activities, 4694–8.1
Likely Impact on the U.S. of a Free Trade Agreement with Mexico. Report to the Committee on Ways and Means of the U.S. House of Representatives and the Committee on Finance of the U.S. Senate on Investigation No. 332-297 Under Section 332 of the Tariff Act of 1930, 9886–4.168
Lime: Mineral Industry Surveys, 5612–1.15
Lime: Minerals Yearbook, Volume 1, 1989, 5604–15.39
Lime: Minerals Yearbook, Volume 1, 1990, 5604–20.36
Lime, 1990: Mineral Industry Surveys, Advance Summary, 5614–5.18
Limited Partnership Reorganizations, or "Rollups", 25248–124
Limited Progress in Closing and Cleaning Up Contaminated Facilities. Hazardous Waste, 26113–528
Limited Success Rebuilding Staff and Finalizing Aging Aircraft Plan. Aviation Safety, 26113–522
Limits in the Seas, 7006–8
Linking Education and Worksite Training. Transition from School to Work, 26121–431
List of Available Publications of USDA, 1004–13
List of Bureau of Mines Publications and Articles, Jan. 1, 1985-Dec. 31, 1989, with Subject and Author Index, 5608–168
List of Bureau of Mines Publications and Articles, With Subject and Author Index, 5604–40
List of Published Soil Surveys, 1264–11
Listing of Latest Car Theft Rates, 7764–21
Lithium: Minerals Yearbook, Volume 1, 1989, 5604–15.40
Lithium: Minerals Yearbook, Volume 1, 1990, 5604–20.37
Little Is Known About the Effects of Direct-to-Consumer Advertising. Prescription Drugs, 26131–86
Liver Cirrhosis Mortality in the U.S., 1973-87, 4486–1.10
Livestock and Poultry Situation and Outlook Report, 1561–7
Livestock and Poultry Update, 1561–17
Livestock, Meat, and Wool Market News, Weekly Summary and Statistics, 1315–1
Livestock Slaughter, 1623–9
Livestock Slaughter, 1990 Summary, 1623–10
Living Arrangements of Young Adults Living Independently: Evidence from the Luxembourg Income Study, 2546–2.157
Living Benefits: Closing the Gap for LTC Financing, 2626–10.128
Loan Commitments and Bank Risk Exposure, 9377–9.105
Loan Volume Update Guaranteed Student Loan Programs: Stafford, PLUS, SLS Loans, 4802–2
Loans and Securities at All Commercial Banks, 9365–2
Local Area Personal Income, 1984-89, 2704–2
Local Banking Markets and Firm Location, 9377–9.123
Location, Branching, and Bank Portfolio Diversification: The Case of Agricultural Lending, 9393–8.202
Long Staple Cotton Review, 1309–12
Longleaf Pine Resource, 1208–355
Long-Lived Legacy: Managing High-Level and Transuranic Waste at the DOE Nuclear Weapons Complex, 26358–236
Longrun Competitiveness of Australian Agriculture, 1528–311
Longshore and Harbor Workers' Compensation Act: Annual Report on Administration of the Act During FY89, Submitted to Congress 1990, 6504–10
Longshore and Harbor Workers' Compensation Act: Annual Report on Administration of the Act During FY90, Submitted to Congress 1991, 6504–10
Long-Term Care for the Functionally Dependent Elderly. Vital and Health Statistics Series 13, 4147–13.104
Long-Term Care Insurance, 21368–130
Long-Term Care: Projected Needs of the Aging Baby Boom Generation, 26121–433
Long-Term Care Studies Program Research Reports, 4186–7
Looking Back While Going Forward: An Essential for Policy Economists, 1502–3.202
Loss of Medicaid and Access to Health Services, 4652–1.242
Low Calorie Sweeteners Outlook, 1004–16.1
Low Earnings Will Keep Many Children in Poverty. Mother-Only Families, 26121–413
Low Income Home Energy Assistance Program: Report to Congress for FY89, 4694–8
Lower Fat Foods: New Technology, Increased Demand, 1502–4.204
Lower Profits at Tenth District Banks, 9381–16.201
Low-Grade, Latent Prostate Cancer Volume: Predictor of Clinical Cancer Incidence?, 4472–1.221
Low-Income Home Energy Assistance: States Cushioned Funding Cuts but Also Scaled Back Program Benefits, 26121–401
Lumber Production and Mill Stocks, 1990, Current Industrial Report, 2506–7.4
Lung Cancer Incidence Among Patients with Beryllium Disease: A Cohort Mortality Study, 4472–1.224

Index by Titles

Machinery and Equipment; Electrical and Electronics. Current Industrial Reports, 2506–12

Machinery Manufacturing and Rebuilding Industry: Preliminary Data Summary, 9206–4.13

Magnesium and Magnesium Compounds: Minerals Yearbook, Volume 1, 1989, 5604–15.41

Magnesium from Canada and Norway. Determinations of the Commission in Investigation No. 701-TA-309 (Preliminary) and Nos. 731-TA-528 and 529 (Preliminary) Under the Tariff Act of 1930, Together with the Information Obtained in the Investigations, 9886–19.80

Magnesium: Mineral Industry Surveys, 5612–2.12

Magnification Effects and Acyclical Real Wages, 9377–9.114

Mainframe Procurements: Statistics Showing How and What the Government Is Acquiring, 26125–41.8

Maintaining a Trained and Ready Total Force for the 1990s and Beyond. A Statement on the Posture of the U.S. Army, FY92-93, 3704–13

Major Collective Bargaining Settlements in Private Industry, 6782–2

Major Household Appliances, 1990, Current Industrial Report, 2506–12.16

Major Local Smoking Ordinances in the U.S. A Detailed Matrix of the Provisions of Workplace, Restaurant, and Public Places Smoking Ordinances, 4478–196

Major Natural Gas Pipelines, Sept. 30, 1989, 3088–21

Major Nondeposit Funds of Commercial Banks, 9365–2

Major Programs of the Bureau of Labor Statistics, 6728–35

Major Uses of Land in the U.S.: 1987, 1588–48

Major Work Stoppages, 1990, 6784–12

Malaria Surveillance, Annual Summary, 1989, 4205–4

Mammography Screening and Increased Incidence of Breast Cancer in Wisconsin, 4472–1.229

Managed Care in the Military: The Catchment Area Management Demonstrations, 26306–3.117

Management Improvements Needed To Handle Increasing Responsibilities. BATF, 26119–335

Management Information Report: Worker Adjustment Assistance Under the Trade Act of 1974, 6402–13

Management Practices: U.S. Companies Improve Performance Through Quality Efforts, 26123–345

Managing the Nation's Public Lands, FY89, 5724–13

Manatee Grazing Impacts on Seagrasses in Hobe Sound and Jupiter Sound in Southeast Florida During the Winter of 1988-89, 14738–12

Manganese: Mineral Industry Surveys, 5612–1.16

Manganese: Minerals Yearbook, Volume 1, 1989, 5604–15.43

Manganese: Minerals Yearbook, Volume 1, 1990, 5604–20.39

Man-Made Fiber Manufacturers (Customs Value). U.S. General Imports, 2046–9.2

Man-Made Fiber Manufacturers. U.S. General Imports, 2046–8.3

Manpower Assessment Briefs, 3006–8

Manpower Requirements Report, FY92, 3504–1

Manufactured Abrasives: Mineral Industry Surveys, 5612–2.19

Manufactured Housing Construction and Safety Standards, 21248–145

Manufacturers' Pollution Abatement Capital Expenditures and Operating Costs, Advance Report for 1989, Current Industrial Report, 2506–3.6

Manufacturers' Prices and Pharmacists' Charges for Prescription Drugs Used by the Elderly, 4658–56

Manufacturers' Shipments, Inventories, and Orders, Current Industrial Report, 2506–3.1

Manufacturers' Shipments to the Federal Government. 1987 Census of Manufacturers. Subject Series, 2497–7

Manufacturing: Analytical Report Series, 2506–16

Manufacturing Energy Consumption Survey, 3166–13

Manufacturing Fuel Switching Capability, 1988. Manufacturing Energy Consumption Survey, 3166–13.6

Many Deaths and Injuries Caused by Firearms Could Be Prevented. Accidental Shootings, 26131–80

Many Grantees Making Progress, but NASA Oversight Could Be Improved. Commercial Use of Space, 26123–353

Many States Did Not Comply with 30-Day Notice or Data-Verification Provisions. Computer Matching Act, 26121–404

MARAD '90: Annual Report of the Maritime Administration, FY90, 7704–14

Margin Requirements, Speculative Trading and Stock Price Fluctuations: The Case of Japan, 9385–8.72

Marine Accident Report: Grounding of the U.S. Tankship Exxon Valdez on Bligh Reef, Prince William Sound, Near Valdez, Alaska, Mar. 24, 1989, 9618–17

Marine Accident Reports, Brief Format, 9612–4

Marine Fisheries Review, 2162–1

Marine Mammal Commission Annual Report, 1990, 14734–1

Marine Mammal Strandings in the U.S.: Proceedings of the Second Marine Mammal Stranding Workshop, Miami, Florida, Dec. 3-5, 1987, 2168–127

Marine Mammal Strandings: The New England Aquarium Stranding Network, 14738–8

Marine Ranching: Proceedings of the Seventeenth U.S.-Japan Meeting on Aquaculture, Ise, Mie Prefecture, Japan, Oct. 16-18, 1988, 2164–15

Marine Recreational Fishery Statistics Survey, 2166–17

Marine Recreational Fishery Statistics Survey, Atlantic and Gulf Coasts, 1987-89, 2166–17.1

Mariners Weather Log, 2152–8

Marital Status and Living Arrangements: March 1990, 2546–1.449

Market Absorption of Apartments: Annual 1990 Absorptions (Apartments Completed in 1989). Current Housing Reports, 2484–2

Measures of Soviet Gross...

Market Absorption of Apartments. Current Housing Reports, 2482–2

Market Cycles and Their Effect on Real Estate Lending by Credit Unions: Case Study of Region I, 9536–1.6

Market Opportunities in Costa Rica for U.S. Apples, Grapes, and Pears, 1925–34.203

Market Segmentation and 1992: Toward a Theory of Trade in Financial Services, 9366–7.248

Market Share Analysis of Selected Recreation Activities in the Northeastern U.S.: 1979-87, 1208–356

Market Structure and Prospects for U.S. Horticultural Exports to Hong Kong, 1925–34.224

Market Structure Issues and the U.S. Sweetener Industry, 1004–16.1

Market Structures and Prospects for U.S. Horticultural Exports in Singapore and Malaysia, 1925–34.213

Marketable Phosphate Rock: Mineral Industry Surveys, 5612–1.30

Market-Based Deposit Insurance Premiums: An Evaluation, 9366–6.264

Marketing Appalachian District Apples, 1990 Crop, 1311–13

Marketing Florida, Georgia, South Carolina, North Carolina and Appalachian District Peaches, 1990 Crop, 1311–12

Marketing Foreign Raw Cotton to U.S. Mills—Prospects and Costs, 1561–1.206

Marketing in Austria, 2046–6.7

Marketing in Gabon, 2046–6.6

Marketing in Iceland, 2046–6.5

Marketing in Ireland, 2046–6.3

Marketing in Portugal, 2046–6.1

Marketing in Spain, 2046–6.8

Marketing in the Federal Republic of Germany, 2046–6.2

Marketing in Zaire, 2046–6.4

Marketing U.S. Tourism Abroad, A Review of Cooperative Marketing Programs, 2904–11

Markov Model for Nearshore Sea Ice Trajectories, 2176–1.38

Massachusetts in the 1990s: The Role of State Government, 9373–4.27

Massachusetts in the 1990s: The Role of State Government. Overview, 9373–1.202, 9373–4.27

Massive Census Hiring Affected Nonfarm Payroll Employment Picture in 1990, 6742–2.202

Matching the Resources to the Need. Bridge Infrastructure, 26113–539

Materials Shifts in the New Society. New Materials Society: Challenges and Opportunities, Volume 3, 5608–162.3

Maternal Health. Indian Health Conditions, 4088–2

Maternal Mortality Surveillance, U.S., 1979-86, 4202–7.206

MBDA Annual Business Assistance Report for FY90, 2104–6

McKinney Act Programs and Funding Through FY90. Homelessness, 26104–21

Measure of Federal Reserve Credibility, 9387–8.240

Measurement and Efficiency Issues in Commercial Banking, 9366–6.265

Measures of Fit for Calibrated Models, 9375–13.60

Measures of Soviet Gross National Product in 1982 Prices, 23848–223

Measures of Value Produced,... Index by Titles

Measures of Value Produced, Capital Expenditures, Depreciable Assets, and Operating Expenses. 1987 Census of Retail Trade. Subject Series., 2399–2

Measures of Value Produced, Capital Expenditures, Depreciable Assets, and Operating Expenses. 1987 Census of Wholesale Trade. Subject Series., 2407–2

Measuring Cognitive Impairment with Large Data Sets, 4186–7.7

Measuring Geographic Variations in Hospitals' Capital Costs, 4652–1.247

Measuring Hospital Input Price Increases: The Rebased Hospital Market Basket, 4652–1.231

Measuring Input Prices for Physicians: The Revised Medicare Economic Index, 4652–1.246

Measuring Poverty, 23848–221

Measuring State Exports: Is There a Better Way?, 9391–1.219

Measuring the Contribution of Farm Dwellings to Operator Income and Asset Values, 1541–1.211

Measuring the Effect of Benefits and Taxes on Income and Poverty: 1990, 2546–6.69

Meat and Dairy Monthly Imports. Foreign Agricultural Service Circular Series: Dairy, Livestock, and Poultry, 1925–31

Meat and Poultry Inspection, 1990, Report of the Secretary of Agriculture to the U.S. Congress, 1374–1

Meat Animals Production, Disposition and Income, 1990 Summary, 1623–8

Meat Industry Competition and Consolidation in the 1990s, 1004–16.1

Mechanical Properties of Sea Ice and Sea Ice Deformation in the Nearshore Zone, 2176–1.38

Medicaid, 9373–4.27

Medicaid: Alternatives for Improving the Distribution of Funds, 26121–420

Medicaid and Third-Party Liability: Using Information To Achieve Program Goals, 4652–1.212

Medicaid Expansions: Coverage Improves but State Fiscal Problems Jeopardize Continued Progress, 26121–429

Medicaid Home and Community-Based Waivers for Acquired Immunodeficiency Syndrome Patients, 4652–1.216

Medicaid Hospital Payment, 17206–1.11

Medicaid (in Massachusetts), 9373–1.203

Medicaid Mysteries: Transitional Benefits, Medicaid Coverage, and Welfare Exits, 4652–1.217

Medicaid: Oversight of Health Maintenance Organizations in the Chicago Area, 26121–399

Medicaid Payment Policies for Nursing Home Care: A National Survey, 4652–1.253

Medicaid Payment Rates for Nursing Homes, 1979-86, 4652–1.224

Medicaid Prospective Payment: Case-Mix Increase, 4652–1.206

Medicaid Services for Persons with Mental Retardation and Related Conditions, 4658–49

Medicaid Support of Alcohol, Drug Abuse, and Mental Health Services, 4652–1.256

Medicaid, the Uninsured, and National Health Spending: Federal Policy Implications, 4652–1.220

Medicaid-Financed Residential Care for Persons with Mental Retardation, 4652–1.219

Medical Malpractice: Few Claims Resolved Through Michigan's Voluntary Arbitration Program, 26121–394

Medical Monitoring and Screening in the Workplace: Results of a Survey—Background Paper, 26358–250

Medicare and Medicaid Data Book, 1990. Health Care Financing Program Statistics, 4654–1

Medicare and Medicaid's 25th Anniversary: Much Promised, Accomplished, and Left Unfinished, 21148–61

Medicare and the American Health Care System, Report to the Congress, June 1991, 17204–2

Medicare: Comparison of Two Methods of Computing Home Health Care Cost Limits, 26121–400

Medicare Costs Prior to Retirement for Disabled-Worker Beneficiaries, 4742–1.208

Medicare End Stage Renal Disease Population, 1982-87, 4652–1.208

Medicare Expenditures for Physician and Supplier Services, 1970-88, 4652–1.240

Medicare Hospital Mortality Information, 1987-89, 4654–14

Medicare: Payments for Clinical Laboratory Test Services Are Too High, 26121–425

Medicare Prospective Payment and the American Health Care System, Report to the Congress, 17204–2

Medicare Risk Contracting: Determinants of Market Entry, 4652–1.226

Medicare Short-Stay Hospital Services by Diagnosis-Related Groups, 4652–1.250

Medicare Supplement Insurance Policies, 21788–198

Medicare: Variations in Payments to Anesthesiologists Linked to Anesthesia Time, 26121–417

Medicare Volume Performance Standard Rate of Increase for FY91, 17266–1.2

Medicare-Covered Skilled Nursing Facility Services, 1967-88, 4652–1.239

Medicare-Dependent Hospitals Under PPS, 17206–2.16

Medicare's Capital Payment Policy, 17206–1.9

Medigap Insurance: Better Consumer Protection Should Result from 1990 Changes to Baucus Amendment, 26121–410

Medigap Preferred Provider Organizations: Issues, Implications, and Early Experience, 4652–1.248

Mediterranean Citrus Outlook, 1925–34.201

Mediterranean Processed Tomato Product Situation and Outlook, 1925–34.227

Mental Health and Functional Status of Residents of Nursing and Personal Care Homes. National Medical Expenditure Survey, 4186–8.11

Mental Health and Mental Illness. Indian Health Conditions, 4088–2

Mental Health National Statistics: Mental Health Service System Reports, Series CN, 4506–4

Mental Health Service System Reports: Series CN, Mental Health National Statistics, 4506–4

Mental Health Services of the Veterans Administration, U.S., 1986, 4506–3.43

Mental Health Statistical Notes, NIMH Survey and Reports Branch, 4506–3

Mental Illness in Nursing Homes: U.S., 1985. Vital and Health Statistics Series 13, 4147–13.106

Merchant Fleets of the World: Oceangoing Steam and Motor Ships of 1,000 Gross Tons and Over, as of Jan. 1, 1990, 7704–3

Merger Decisions, 1989, Federal Deposit Insurance Corporation, 9294–5

Metal/Nonmetal: Surface Fatalities, First Half 1991, 6662–3.3

Metal/Nonmetal: Surface Fatalities, Second Half 1990, 6662–3.3

Metal/Nonmetal: Underground Fatalities, First Half 1991, 6662–3.4

Metal/Nonmetal: Underground Fatalities, Second Half 1990, 6662–3.4

Metalworking Machinery, Current Industrial Report, 2506–12.12

Methadone Treatment and Drug Addiction, 21968–55

Methamphetamine Abuse: Epidemiologic Issues and Implications, 4498–75

Methamphetamine Abuse in Japan, 4498–75

Methanol as an Alternative Fuel, 9379–12.62

Methanol as an Alternative Fuel: Economic and Health Effects, 9379–1.208

Methodology for Measuring Case-Mix Change: How Much Change in the Case Mix Index Is DRG Creep?, 17206–2.23

Metro/Nonmetro Funding Allocation Under Title II-A, Job Training Partnership Act, 1598–266

Metro/Nonmetro Program Performance Under Title II-A, Job Training Partnership Act, 1598–267

Metropolitan Areas and Cities. 1990 Census Profile, 2326–20.3

Metropolitan Statistical Areas by Population Rank, 2324–8

Mexico's Sugar Industry in Transition—Implications for Sweetener Trade with the U.S., 1561–14.204

Mica in 1990: Mineral Industry Surveys Annual Advance Summary, 5614–5.26

Mica: Minerals Yearbook, Volume 1, 1989, 5604–15.45

Mica: Minerals Yearbook, Volume 1, 1990, 5604–20.40

Michigan Timber Industry: An Assessment of Timber Product Output and Use, 1988, 1206–10.11

Mid-Atlantic Manufacturing Index, 9387–12

Mid-Session Review of the Budget, 104–7

Midsouth Veneer Industry, 1208–43

Midwest Economy: Quantifying Growth and Diversification in the 1980's, 9375–13.63

Military Bases: Observations on the Analyses Supporting Proposed Closures and Realignments, 26123–341

Military Construction Programs, FY92-93, 3544–15

Military Forces in Transition, 1991, 3504–20

Military Manpower Recruiting and Reenlistment Results for the Active Components, 3542–7

Military Manpower Statistics, 3542–14

Military Manpower Training Report for FY92, 3504–5

Military Personnel: Composition of the Active Duty Forces by Race or National Origin Identification and by Gender, 26123–325

Military Presence: U.S. Personnel in the Pacific Theater, 26123–357

Military Sealift Command, FY90 Annual Report, 3804–14

Index by Titles

Military Strength Figures Summarized by DOD, 3542–2

Military Traffic Management Report, 3702–1

Military Women in the Department of Defense: Volume VIII, 3544–26

Milk Production, 1627–1

Milk Production, Disposition and Income, 1990 Summary, 1627–4

Millions in Federal Costs May Not Be Recovered from Exxon Valdez Oil Spill. Coast Guard, 26113–510

Mine Injuries and Worktime, Quarterly, 6662–1

Mine Safety and Health Administration Fatalities Reports, 6662–3

Mineral Commodity Summaries, 1991, 5604–18

Mineral Industries of China, 1989, 5604–38

Mineral Industries of the USSR, 1989, 5604–39

Mineral Industry Surveys: Annual Advance Summaries and Annual Reviews by Commodity, 5614–5

Mineral Industry Surveys: Apparent Consumption of Industrial Explosives and Blasting Agents in the U.S., 1990, 5614–22

Mineral Industry Surveys: Monthly Mineral Surveys, 5612–1

Mineral Industry Surveys: Phosphate Rock 1991 Crop Year, 5614–20

Mineral Industry Surveys: Potash in Crop Year 1990, 5614–19

Mineral Industry Surveys: Quarterly Mineral Surveys, 5612–2

Mineral Investigations in the Juneau Mining District, Alaska, 1984-88, 5608–169

Mineral Revenues: Potential Cost To Repurchase Offshore Oil and Gas Leases, 26113–509

Mineral Revenues 1980-89: Report on Receipts from Federal and Indian Leases, 5738–21

Mineral Revenues 1990: Report on Receipts from Federal and Indian Leases, 5734–2

Minerals Availability Appraisal, 5606–4

Minerals in Hair, Serum, and Urine of Healthy and Anemic Black Children, 4042–3.248

Minerals Today, 5602–4

Minerals Yearbook. Volume 3, Annual Preprints by Country, 5604–17

Minerals Yearbook, 1988. Volume 3. Annual Chapters by Country, 5604–17

Minerals Yearbook, 1989. Volume 1. Annual Chapters by Commodity, 5604–15

Minerals Yearbook, 1989. Volume 2. Annual Chapters by State, 5604–16

Minerals Yearbook, 1989. Volume 2. Area Reports: Domestic, 5604–34

Minerals Yearbook, 1990. Volume 1. Annual Chapters by Commodity, 5604–20

Minimum Wage and Maximum Hours Under the Fair Labor Standards Act, 6504–2

Mining and Quarrying Trends in the Metals and Industrial Minerals Industries: Minerals Yearbook, Volume 1, 1989, 5604–15.1

Mining Machinery and Mineral Processing Equipment, 1990, Current Industrial Report, 2506–12.4

Minivans from Japan. Determination of the Commission in Investigation No. 731-TA-522 (Preliminary) Under the Tariff Act of 1930, Together with the Information Obtained in the Investigation, 9886–14.320

Mink, 1631–7

Minnesota-Wisconsin Manufacturing Grade Milk Price, 1629–6

Minnesota-Wisconsin Manufacturing Grade Milk, Prices Received, 1990 Summary, 1629–2

Minor Oilseeds and the 1990 Farm Bill: Rules, Regulations, and Initial Impacts, 1561–3.202

Minority Business Development Agency Needs To Address Program Weaknesses. Minority Business, 26113–517

Minority Business Enterprise (MBE) Training Program, FY91 Supportive Services Funds Allocation, 7554–40

Minority Business: Minority Business Development Agency Needs To Address Program Weaknesses, 26113–517

Minority Households: A Comparison of Selected Characteristics and Expenditures Contributing to Future Economic Well-Being, 1702–1.206

Minority Participation in Higher Education, 4808–29

Minority Representation at USDA's National Agricultural Statistics Service. Equal Employment, 26119–326

Miscellaneous Subjects. 1987 Census of Service Industries. Subject Series, 2393–4

Miscellaneous Subjects. 1987 Census of Transportation. Subject Series: Selected Transportation Industries, 2579–1

Miscellaneous Subjects. 1987 Census of Wholesale Trade. Subject Series, 2407–4

Mississippi River System and Barge Industry, 9391–16.202

Model To Estimate System Workload. Federal Criminal Justice System, 26119–340

Modeling the Alaskan Continental Shelf Waters, 2176–1.36

Modeling the Effects of Inflation on the Demand for Money, 9379–1.203

Modeling the Liquidity Effect of a Money Shock, 9383–6.202

Modeling Trends in Macroeconomic Time Series, 9379–1.205

Modernizing the Financial System: Recommendations for Safer, More Competitive Banks, 8008–147

Mohair, Summary of 1991 Support Program and Related Information: ASCS Commodity Fact Sheet, 1806–4.13

Molasses Market News, 1311–16

Molasses Market News, Market Summary, 1990, 1311–19

Molybdenum: Mineral Industry Surveys, 5612–1.17

Molybdenum: Minerals Yearbook, Volume 1, 1989, 5604–15.46

Monetary Aggregates as Monetary Targets: A Statistical Investigation, 9371–10.53

Monetary and Exchange Rate Policies in Anticipation of a European Central Bank, 9387–8.238

Monetary Policy and Credit Conditions: Evidence from the Composition of External Finance, 9366–6.268

Monetary Policy and the Farm/Nonfarm Price Ratio: A Comparison of Effects in Alternative Models, 9391–1.217

Monetary Policy Objectives, 1991: Midyear Review of the Federal Reserve Board, 9362–4

Monetary Policy Objectives, 1991: Summary Report of the Federal Reserve Board, 9362–4

Monthly Statistical Release:...

Monetary Policy Objectives, 1991: Testimony of Alan Greenspan, Chairman, Board of Governors of the Federal Reserve System, 9362–4

Monetary Policy Report to Congress Pursuant to the Full Employment and Balanced Growth Act of 1978, 9362–4

Monetary Trends, 9391–2

Money Contributions to Religion, Charity, Education, and Politics, 1702–1.214

Money Demand and Relative Prices in the German Hyperinflation, 9371–10.66

Money Growth, Supply Shocks, and Inflation, 9379–1.204

Money Income of Households, Families, and Persons in the U.S.: 1988-89, 2546–6.68

Money Income of Households, Families, and Persons in the U.S.: 1990, 2546–6.70

Money Laundering: The U.S. Government Is Responding to the Problem, 26123–338

Money Laundering: The Use of Cash Transaction Reports by Federal Law Enforcement Agencies, 26119–356

Money Laundering: Treasury's Financial Crimes Enforcement Network, 26119–330

Money Stock, Liquid Assets, and Debt Measures, 9365–1

Money, Trade Credit and Asset Prices, 9389–19.29

Monitoring of Populations and Productivity of Seabirds at St. George Island, Cape Peirce, and Bluff, Alaska, 1989, 5738–31

Monitoring the Exposure of "America Responds to AIDS" PSA Campaign, 4042–3.256

Montana and the Dakotas Fish and Wildlife 2000: A Plan for the Future, 5726–7.4

Montana Forest Pest Conditions and Program Highlights, 1989, 1206–49.2

Montana's Log Home Industry: Development and Current Status, 1208–370

Monthly and Seasonal Weather Outlook, 2182–1

Monthly Awards for Construction Grants for Wastewater Treatment Works, 9202–3

Monthly Benefit Statistics, 9702–2

Monthly Benefit Statistics, Railroad Retirement and Unemployment Insurance Programs, 9702–2

Monthly Bulletin of Lake Levels for the Great Lakes, 3752–1

Monthly Climatic Data for the World, 2152–4

Monthly Cotton Linters Review, 1309–10

Monthly Energy Review, 3162–24

Monthly Import Detention List, 4062–2

Monthly Labor Review, 6722–1

Monthly Motor Fuel Reported by States, 7552–1

Monthly Product Announcement, 2302–6

Monthly Report on the Status of the Steel Industry: Report to the Subcommittee on Trade, Committee on Ways and Means, on Investigation No. 332-226 Under Section 332 of the Tariff Act of 1930, 9882–13

Monthly Retail Trade, Sales and Inventories, Current Business Reports, 2413–3

Monthly State, Regional and National Heating/Cooling Degree Days Weighted by Population, 2152–13

Monthly Statement of the Public Debt of the U.S., 8242–2

Monthly Statistical Release: Beer, 8486–1.1

Monthly Statistical Release: Distilled Spirits, 8486–1.3

Monthly Statistical Release:...

Index by Titles

Monthly Statistical Release: Tobacco Products, 8486–1.4

Monthly Statistical Release: Wines, 8486–1.2

Monthly Thrift Data, 8432–1

Monthly Traffic Fatality Report, 7762–7

Monthly Treasury Statement of Receipts and Outlays of the U.S. Government, 8102–3

Monthly Vital Statistics Report, Annual Summary of Births, Marriages, Divorces, and Deaths: U.S., 1990, 4144–7

Monthly Vital Statistics Report Provisional Data, 4142–1

Monthly Vital Statistics Report Supplements, 4146–5

Monthly Wholesale Trade: Sales and Inventories, Current Business Reports, 2413–7

Morbidity and Mortality, Weekly Report, 4202–1

Morbidity and Mortality Weekly Report: CDC Surveillance Summaries, 4202–7

Morbidity and Mortality Weekly Report, Recommendations and Reports, 4206–2

More on Money as a Medium of Exchange, 9383–20.10

More on the International Similarity of Interindustry Wage Differentials: Evidence from the Federal Republic of Germany and the U.S., 9366–6.281

Mortality, Cardiovascular Risk Factors, and Diet in China, Finland, and the U.S., 4042–3.202

Mother-Only Families: Low Earnings Will Keep Many Children in Poverty, 26121–413

Motor Freight Transportation and Warehousing Survey, 1989, 2413–14

Motor Gasoline Industry: Past, Present, and Future, 3168–120

Motor Vehicle Safety, 1989: A Report on Activities Under the National Traffic and Motor Vehicle Safety Act of 1966, as Amended, and the Motor Vehicle Information and Cost Savings Act of 1972, as Amended, 7764–1.2

Motor Vehicles: Better Management of the Military Services' Vehicles Could Save Millions, 26123–344

Motor Vehicles, June 1989; Motor Vehicle Parts, August 1989. Industry Wage Survey, 6787–6.252

Motor Vehicles, Model Year 1991, 2702–1.228

Motorcycle Helmet Laws Save Lives and Reduce Costs to Society. Highway Safety, 26113–537

Motorcycle Helmet Use in Texas, 4042–3.251

Mourning Dove Breeding Population Status, 1991, 5504–15

Moveable Capital Cost Weights, Final Report, 17206–2.24

Moving Ahead: 1991 Surface Transportation Legislation, 26358–242

Multifactor Productivity in Farm and Garden Equipment, 6722–1.232

Multifactor Productivity Measures, 1988 and 1989: Private Business, Private Nonfarm Business, and Manufacturing, 6824–2

Multifactor Productivity Measures, 1990: Private Business, Private Nonfarm Business, and Manufacturing, 6824–2

Multi-Jurisdictional Drug Control Task Forces 1988: A Key Program of State Drug Control Strategies, 6068–244

Multilateral Relief Efforts in Border Camps. Cambodia, 26123–313

Multiple Jobholding Unchanged in May 1991, 6726–1.40

Multiplier Approach to the Money Supply Process: A Precautionary Note, 9391–1.218

Multi-Unit Agreements in the Federal Service, 9847–4

Multi-Year Affirmative Action Plan, FY90-92, 7004–21

Municipal Bond Market, Part I: Politics, Taxes, and Yields, 9373–1.215

Musculoskeletal System Diseases. Indian Health Conditions, 4088–2

Mushrooms, 1631–9

NASA ADP Procurement: Contracting and Market Share Information, 21704–1

NASA In-House Commercially Developed Space Facility (CDSF) Study Report: Cost Estimation and Economic Analysis, 21708–129

NASA Is Not Archiving All Potentially Valuable Data. Space Operations, 26125–43

NASA News Press Kits, 9506–2

NASA Office of Inspector General Semiannual Report, Apr. 1-Sept. 30, 1991, 9502–9

NASA Office of Inspector General Semiannual Report, Oct. 1, 1990-Mar. 31, 1991, 9502–9

NASA Personnel: Shortages of Scientists and Engineers Due to Retirements Unlikely in the 1990s, 26123–348

NASA Pocket Statistics, 9504–6

NASA Procurement Report, FY91, 9502–6

NASA Reports Required by Congress, 1989, 21708–129

NASA Reports Required by Congress, 1990, 21704–1

NASA: Space Shuttle Mission STS-37 Press Kit, 9506–2.141

NASA: Space Shuttle Mission STS-39 Press Kit, 9506–2.140

NASA: Space Shuttle Mission STS-40 Press Kit, 9506–2.142

NASA: Space Shuttle Mission STS-43 Press Kit, 9506–2.143

NASA's University Program Active Projects, FY90, 9504–7

National Accident Sampling System: A Report on Traffic Crashes and Injuries in the U.S., 7764–13

National Acid Precipitation Assessment Program, Annual Report and Findings Update, 14354–1

National Advisory Council on Child Nutrition, Biennial Report, 14854–1

National Advisory Council on Educational Research and Improvement 15th Annual Report, FY90, 4814–1

National AIDS Hotline: HIV and AIDS Information Service Through a Toll-Free Telephone System, 4042–3.256

National Air Pollutant Emission Estimates, 1940-89, 9194–13

National Air Quality and Emissions Trends Report, 1989, 9194–1

National Airspace System Plan: Facilities, Equipment, Associated Development and Other Capital Needs, 7504–12

National Airway System, Annual Report, FY89, 7504–37

National Ambulatory Medical Care Survey. 1977 Summary, 4147–16.5

National Ambulatory Medical Care Survey: 1989 Summary, 4146–8.206

National Archives and Records Administration, Annual Report for the Year Ended Sept. 30, 1990, 9514–2

National Assessment of Educational Progress, 1988, 4896–7

National Assessment of Educational Progress, 1990, 4896–8

National Benthic Surveillance Project: Pacific Coast, 2168–121

National Benthic Surveillance Project, Pacific Coast: Part I, Summary and Overview of the Results for Cycles I to III (1984-86), 2168–121.1

National Benthic Surveillance Project, Pacific Coast: Part II, Technical Presentation of the Results for Cycles I to III (1984-86), 2168–121.2

National Cancer Institute Fact Book, 4474–13

National Center for Health Statistics, Catalog of Publications, 1990, 4124–1

National Center for Research Resources, Program Highlights, 1990, 4434–12

National Commission for Employment Policy: Research Report Series, 15496–1

National Commission for Employment Policy: Fifteenth Annual Report, 15494–1

National Committee on Vital and Health Statistics, 1990, 4164–1

National Commuter Transportation Survey, People and Programs, 7888–81

National Corrections Reporting Program, 1985, 6064–33

National Credit Union Administration, Annual Report, 1990, 9534–1

National Credit Union Administration Central Liquidity Facility 1990 Annual Report, 9534–5

National Credit Union Share Insurance Fund, 1990 Annual Report, 9534–7

National Crime Survey, 6066–3

National Debate Topic for High Schools, 1991-92. Homeless: What Should Be Done To Meet the Needs of the Homeless in the U.S.?, 25928–9

National DRG Validation Study, 4006–7

National DRG Validation Study: Short Hospitalizations, 4006–7.4

National Drug and Alcoholism Treatment Unit Survey (NDATUS), 1989, 4494–10

National Drug and Alcoholism Treatment Unit Survey (NDATUS), 1989. Main Findings Report, 4494–10.2

National Drug Control Strategy, 238–1

National Drug Control Strategy, Budget Summary, 238–2

National Economic Trends, 9391–3

National Education Longitudinal Study of 1988, 4826–9

National Education Report: Building a Nation of Learners, 15914–1

National Education Report: Building a Nation of Learners. Executive Summary, 15914–1

National Emission Report: National Emissions Data System, 9194–7

National Endowment for the Arts 1990 Annual Report, 9564–3

National Endowment for the Humanities: Twenty-fifth Anniversary Annual Report, 1990, 9564–2

Index by Titles

National Energy Strategy: Powerful Ideas for America, 3004–34

National Estuarine Eutrophication Project: Workshop Proceedings, 2176–7.22

National Estuarine Inventory Data Atlas, Volume 4: Public Recreation Facilities in Coastal Areas, 2178–29

National Estuarine Inventory: The Quality of Shellfish Growing Waters on the West Coast of the U.S., 2176–7.21

National Food Review, 1541–7

National Forest Fire Report, 1987, 1204–6

National Forest Fire Report, 1988, 1204–6

National Forest Fire Report, 1989, 1204–6

National Forest Statement of Receipts, FY90, 1204–34

National Forests: Funding Fish and Wildlife Projects, 26113–529

National Gazetteer of the U.S.A., 5668–117

National Guard Counter-Drug Support to Law Enforcement Agencies. Drug Control, 26123–343

National Health Expenditures, 1989, 4652–1.221

National Health Expenditures, 1990, 4652–1.252

National Health Interview Survey, 1987, CD-ROM. Vital and Health Statistics Series 10, 4147–10.177

National Heart, Lung, and Blood Institute FY90 Fact Book, 4474–15

National Higher Education Statistics: Early Estimates, Fall 1990, 4844–14

National Higher Education Statistics: Early Estimates, Fall 1991, 4844–14

National Highway Traffic Safety Administration News, 7766–7

National Honey Market News, 1311–2

National Hospital Discharge Survey: Annual Summary, 1988. Vital and Health Statistics Series 13, 4147–13.107

National Hospital Discharge Survey. 1989 Summary, 4146–8.198

National Household Seroprevalence Survey: Feasibility Study Final Report, 4148–30

National Household Survey on Drug Abuse, 4494–5

National Household Survey on Drug Abuse: Highlights, 1988, 4494–5.1

National Household Survey on Drug Abuse: Highlights, 1990, 4494–5.4

National Household Survey on Drug Abuse: Main Findings, 1990, 4494–5.3

National Household Survey on Drug Abuse: Population Estimates, 1990, 4494–5.2

National Housing Production Report, 5184–5

National Institute of Allergy and Infectious Diseases Profile, FY90, 4474–30

National Institute of Child Health and Human Development Reports of Grants and Contracts, 4474–36

National Institute of Dental Research Programs, FY89 Funds, 4474–19

National Institute of Justice AIDS Bulletin, 6066–28

National Institute of Neurological and Communicative Disorders and Stroke Profile, 4474–25

National Institute of Neurological Disorders and Stroke Profile, 4474–25

National Institute of Standards and Technology Publications, 1990 Catalog, 2214–1

National Institute on Drug Abuse Notes, 4492–4

National Institutes of Health Annual Report of International Activities, FY90, 4474–6

National Institutes of Health, Biennial Report of the Director, 4434–16

National Institutes of Health New Grants and Awards: Arranged by State, City and Institution, 4432–1

National Institutes of Health R&D Contracts, Grants for Training, Construction, and Medical Libraries, FY90 Funds, 4434–7.2

National Institutes of Health Research Grants, FY90 Funds, 4434–7.1

National Inventory of Public Outdoor Recreation Facilities in Coastal Areas, 2176–6

National Labor Relations Board: Action Needed To Improve Case-Processing Time at Headquarters, 26121–395

National Labor Relations Board, Fifty-first Annual Report, FY86, 9584–1

National Labor Relations Board, Fifty-second Annual Report, FY87, 9584–1

National Labor Relations Board, Fifty-third Annual Report, FY88, 9584–1

National Labor Relations Board, Fifty-fourth Annual Report, FY89, 9584–1

National Library of Medicine Programs and Services, FY90, 4464–1

National Longitudinal Study, 4836–1

National Marine Fisheries Service Habitat Conservation Efforts in the Southeastern U.S. for 1988, 2162–1.202

National Medical Care Utilization and Expenditure Survey, Series A-C, 4146–12

National Medical Expenditure Survey Methods and Research Findings, 4186–8

National Medicare Competition Evaluation: An Evaluation of the Quality of the Process of Care. Final Analysis Report, 4658–46

National Park Service: Listing of Acreages, 5542–1

National Park Service Monthly Public Use Report, 5542–4

National Park Service: Selected Visitor and Cost Data, 26113–545

National Park Service Statistical Abstract, 1990, 5544–12

National Plan of Integrated Airport Systems (NPIAS), 1990-99: Report of the Secretary of Transportation to the U.S. Congress Pursuant to Section 504(a) of the Airport and Airway Improvement Act of 1982 (P.L. 97-248), 7504–42

National Postsecondary Statistics, Collegiate and Noncollegiate: Early Estimates, Fall 1990, 4844–16

National Poultry Improvement Plan: 1991 Directory of Participants, 1394–15

National Poultry Improvement Plan: 1991 Directory of Participants Handling Egg-Type and Meat-Type Chickens and Turkeys, 1394–15.1

National Poultry Improvement Plan: 1991 Directory of Participants Handling Waterfowl, Exhibition Poultry, and Game Birds, 1394–15.2

National Priorities List, Supplementary Lists and Supporting Materials, 9216–5

National Railroad Passenger Corporation, Annual Report, 1990, 29524–1

National Science Foundation, Annual Report, 1990, 9624–6

National Science Foundation Awards, 9626–7

National Science Foundation Division of Science Resources Studies Publications List, 9627–22

National Science Foundation FY89 Awards by State and Institution, 9624–26

National Security Assessment of the U.S. Gear Industry, 2028–1

National Service: Issues and Options, 26306–3.115

National Severe Storms Laboratory Annual Report, FY90, 2144–20

National Space Science Data Center, 1990 Annual Statistics and Highlights Report, 9504–11

National Status and Trends Program for Marine Environmental Quality, 2176–3

National Study of Guardian Ad Litem Representation, 4608–28

National Survey of Academic Research Instruments and Instrumentation Needs, 9627–27

National Survey of Academic Research Instruments and Instrumentation Needs, Cycle 3: Detailed Analysis Tables, 9627–27.5

National Survey of Family Growth: Design, Estimation, and Inference. Vital and Health Statistics Series 2, 4147–2.112

National Survey of State Maternal and Newborn Drug Testing and Reporting Policies, 4042–3.220

National Toxicology Program, 4044–16

National Toxicology Program: Annual Plan for FY90, 4044–16.2

National Toxicology Program: Review of Current DHHS, DOE, and EPA Research Related to Toxicology, FY90, 4044–16.1

National Trade Data Bank (NTDB): The Export Connection, 2002–6

National Trade Estimate Report on Foreign Trade Barriers, 1991, 444–2

National Transportation Strategic Planning Study, 7308–202

National Urban Mass Transportation Statistics: 1989 Section 15 Annual Report, 7884–4

National Veterinary Services Laboratories Summary of Activities, FY90, 1394–17

National Water Conditions, 5662–3

National Water Summary 1988-89: Hydrologic Events and Floods and Droughts, 5664–12

National Weather Service Offices and Stations, 2184–5

National Wetlands Inventory. Alaska Coastal Wetlands Survey, 5506–11.5

National Wetlands Inventory: Preliminary and Final Reports, 5506–11

National Wetlands Inventory. Preliminary Report of Vermont's Wetland Acreage, 5506–11.3

National Wetlands Inventory. Preliminary Report on Connecticut's Wetland Acreage, 5506–11.4

National Wetlands Inventory. Preliminary Report on Massachusetts' Wetland Acreage, 5506–11.6

National Wetlands Inventory. Wetlands of Delaware, 5506–11.2

National Wetlands Inventory. Wetlands of New Jersey, 5506–11.1

National Wetlands Inventory. Wetlands of Rhode Island, 5506–11.7

National Wool Market Review, Livestock Division, 1315–2

National Workplace Literacy Program, FY90 Project Abstracts, 4804–40

Nationwide Evaluation of Medicaid Competition Demonstrations, 4658–45

Nationwide Food Consumption... Index by Titles

Nationwide Food Consumption Survey, 1987-88. Individual Intake Data, Nonresponse Issues, 1356–1.1

Nationwide Food Consumption Survey, 1987-88: Preliminary Reports, 1356–1

Nationwide Personal Transportation Study, 1990, 7556–6

Nationwide Personal Transportation Study, 1990: Early Results, 7556–6.1

Natural Disaster Survey Reports, 2186–6

Natural Gas Monthly, 3162–4

Natural Gas Productive Capacity for the Lower 48 States, 1980-91, 3164–93

Natural Gas Transportation Services: An Update, 3162–4.204

Natural Ground-Water Quality in Michigan, 1974-87, 5666–28.10

Navajo and Hopi Indian Relocation Commission, Annual Report, 16004–1

Navajo and Hopi Indian Relocation Commission Program Status, 16002–1

Naval Petroleum and Oil Shale Reserves, FY90 Annual Report of Operations, 3334–3

Navarin Basin Oil and Gas Lease Sale 107: Alaska Outer Continental Shelf. Final Environmental Impact Statement, 5736–1.24

Navy Homeports: Expanded Structure Unnecessary and Costly, 26123–347

Navy Military Personnel Statistics, 3802–4

Navy Office Space: Issues on Relocating Selected Commands from the Washington, D.C., Area, 26123–346

Navy Report on Drug or Alcohol Abuse Awareness Education or Rehabilitation Programs, 3802–6

Navy Small and Disadvantaged Business Assistance Directory, 3804–5

Navy's Fleet Modernization Program. Ship Maintenance, 26123–320

NCHS Publication Note: Publications Issued, 4122–2

NCUA Research Studies, 9536–1

NCUA 1990 Yearend Statistics for Federally Insured Credit Unions, 9532–6

NCUA 1991 Midyear Statistics for Federally Insured Credit Unions, 9532–6

NEDS Annual Fuel Summary Report, 9194–14

Needed Repairs and the Financial Condition of the John F. Kennedy Center for the Performing Arts, 21648–62

NEFC Stock Assessment Workshop Report, 2162–9

NEG and NIOSH Basis for an Occupational Health Standard, 4246–4

Nepheline Syenite from Canada. Determination of the Commission in Investigation No. 731-TA-525 (Preliminary) Under the Tariff Act of 1930, Together with the Information Obtained in the Investigation, 9886–14.326

Nested Case-Control Study of Lung Cancer in the Meat Industry, 4472–1.223

Nesting Ecology of Golden Eagles and Other Raptors in Southeastern Montana and Northern Wyoming: Fish and Wildlife Technical Report, 5506–12.1

Net Payments Made to Producers, 1802–10

Nevada Cooperative Snow Survey Data of Federal-State-Private Cooperative Snow Surveys, Water Year 1990, 1264–14.6

Nevada Water Supply Outlook, 1264–8

New BLS Projections: Findings and Implications, 6722–1.250

New Developments in Neuroscience, 26356–9

New Drug Evaluation Statistical Report, 4064–14

New England and New York's Timber Economy: A Review of the Statistics, 1208–375

New England Economic Indicators, 9373–2

New England Economic Review, 9373–1

New England Outlook, 9302–4.201, 9302–4.203

New England's Forests, 1208–363

New Estimates of Hardwood Lumber Exports to Europe and Asia, 1208–373

New Evidence Firms Are Financially Constrained, 9381–1.211

New Evidence on the Relation Between Inflation and Price Dispersion, 6886–6.79

New Immigrant Data for 1989, 6266–2.4

New Immigrant Data for 1990, 6266–2.8

New Jersey Unemployment Insurance Reemployment Demonstration Project Follow-Up Report, 6406–6.32

New Materials Society: Challenges and Opportunities, 5608–162

New Mexico Cooperative Snow Survey Data of Federal-State-Private Cooperative Snow Surveys, Water Year 1990, 1264–14.7

New Mexico Fish and Wildlife 2000: A Plan for the Future, 5726–7.1

New Mexico Riparian-Wetland 2000: A Management Strategy, 5726–8.2

New Nonimmigrant Data for 1990, 6266–2.7

New One-Family Houses Sold and for Sale. Current Construction Reports, 2382–3

New One-Family Houses Sold, Current Construction Reports, 2382–3

New Opportunities for U.S. Universities in Development Assistance: Agriculture, Natural Resources, and Environment, 26358–247

New Private Mortgage Insurance Activity, 5142–38

New Provisions for Upland Cotton Farm Programs, 1561–1.203

New Publications of the Bureau of Mines, 5602–2

New Publications of the U.S. Geological Survey, 5662–1

New Research on Interarea Consumer Price Differences, 6722–1.236

New Residential Construction in Selected Metropolitan Statistical Areas, Current Construction Reports, 2382–9

New Seasonal Adjustment Factors for Household Data Series, 6742–2.205

New Ship Construction, 7704–4

New Survey Data on Pension Benefits, 6722–1.238

New Test for Mean Reversion in Stock Prices, 9366–6.266

New Workload Statistics for 1990 and INS Drug Seizures for 1989, 6266–2.3

New York City Wholesale Fruit and Vegetable Report, 1311–20

New York State's Two-Dose Schedule for Measles Immunization, 4042–3.227

News from the Federal Election Commission, 9276–1

NHTSA Releases Additional 1991 Model Year Crash Test Results, 7766–7.23

NHTSA Releases Final Crash Test Results of 1991 Model Vehicles, 7766–7.28

NHTSA Releases First 1991 Model Year Crash Test Results; Improves Format for Consumers, 7766–7.22

NHTSA Releases Five Additional 1991 Model Year Crash Test Results, 7766–7.26, 7766–7.27

NHTSA Releases Listing of Latest Car Theft Rates, 7764–21

NHTSA Releases Results of Large Car/Small Car Crash Test, 7766–7.25

NHTSA Releases Three Additional 1991 Model Year Crash Test Results, 7766–7.24

Nickel: Mineral Industry Surveys, 5612–1.20

Nickel: Minerals Yearbook, Volume 1, 1989, 5604–15.47

Nickel: Minerals Yearbook, Volume 1, 1990, 5604–20.42

NIDA Notes, 4492–4

NIH Data Book, 1990: Basic Data Relating to the National Institutes of Health, 4434–3

NIH Data Book, 1991: Basic Data Relating to the National Institutes of Health, 4434–3

NIH Grants and Awards, 4434–7

NIH Publications List, 4434–2

NIJ Publications Catalog, 1983-89, 6068–240

Nineteenth Annual Report of the President on Federal Advisory Committees, FY90, 9454–18

Ninth Annual Report of Accomplishments Under the Airport Improvement Program, FY90, 7504–38

NIOH and NIOSH Basis for an Occupational Health Standard, 4246–4

NIOSH Research and Demonstration Grants, FY90, 4244–2

Nitrogen: Minerals Yearbook, Volume 1, 1989, 5604–15.48

NLRB Election Report, 9582–2

NMC Seasonal Performance Summary, 2182–8

NNICC Report, 1990: The Supply of Illicit Drugs to the U.S., 6284–2

No Gift Wasted: Effective Strategies for Educating Highly Able, Disadvantaged Students in Mathematics and Science, 4808–34

NOAA's Estuarine Living Marine Resources Program. Distribution and Abundance of Fishes and Invertebrates in Central Gulf of Mexico Estuaries, 2176–7.23

NOAA's Estuarine Living Marine Resources Program. Distribution and Abundance of Fishes and Invertebrates in Southeast Estuaries, 2176–7.25

NOAA's Estuarine Living Marine Resources Program. Distribution and Abundance of Fishes and Invertebrates in West Coast Estuaries, Volume II: Species Life History Summaries, 2176–7.24

NOAA's Estuarine Living Marine Resources Project. Proposed Estuarine Classification: Analysis of Species Salinity Ranges, 2176–7.20

NOAA's Ocean Fleet Modernization Study, 2148–60

Noise Traders, Excess Volatility, and a Securities Transaction Tax, 9366–6.280

Noise Trading and the Effectiveness of Sterilized Foreign Exchange Intervention, 9385–8.107

Nonagricultural Employment in the Southeast, 6942–7

Non-Certified Hospice Cost Analysis: Final Report, 4658–52

Index by Titles

Noncitrus Fruits and Nuts, 1990 Preliminary, 1621–18.1

Noncitrus Fruits and Nuts: 1990 Summary, 1621–18.3

Noncriminal Juveniles: Detentions Have Been Reduced but Better Monitoring Is Needed, 26119–333

Nonferrous Castings, 1990, Current Industrial Report, 2506–10.5

Nonfuel Minerals Survey Methods, 5604–48

Nonimmigrant Overstays, 6266–2.1

Nonmetro, Metro, and U.S. Bank-Operating Statistics, 1987-89, 1544–29

Nonprofit Charitable Organizations, 1986 and 1987, 8302–2.218

Nonresidential Buildings Energy Consumption Survey, 3166–8

Nonresponse Research for the Survey of Income and Program Participation, 2626–10.118

Nonrubber Footwear Quarterly Statistical Report: Report to the Senate Committee on Finance on Investigation No. 332-191, Under Section 332 of the Tariff Act of 1930, 9882–6

Nonsteroidal Anti-Inflammatory Drugs Reduce the Incidence of Large-Bowel Cancer. A Hypothesis, 4472–1.205

Nonviral Risk Factors for Hepatocellular Carcinoma in a Low-Risk Population, the Non-Asians of Los Angeles County, California, 4472–1.237

North American Fertilizer Capacity Data, 9808–66

North American Free Trade Agreement: Generating Jobs for Americans, 2048–153

North American Free Trade and the Peso: The Case for a North American Currency Area, 9379–12.77

North Atlantic Air Traffic Forecasts for the Years 1991-1996, 2000, 2005, and 2010, 7504–44

North Atlantic Hurricanes, 1990, 2152–8.202

North Coast Navigation, 2152–8.204

North Slope Subsistence Study: Barrow, 1988, 5736–5.12

North Slope Subsistence Study: Barrow, 1988. Alaska Social and Economic Study, 5736–5.12

Northeast Fisheries Center Bottom Trawl Survey Fishermen's Report, Mar. 5-Apr. 16, 1991, Cape Hatteras-Western Scotian Shelf, 2164–18.1

Northeast Fisheries Science Center Bottom Trawl Survey Fishermen's Report, Sept. 9-Oct. 24, 1991, Cape Hatteras-Western Scotian Shelf, 2164–18.3

Northeast Fisheries Science Center Sea Scallop Survey Fishermen's Report, July 29-Aug. 23, 1991, 2164–18.2

Northeast Gulf of Alaska Program, 2176–1.36

Northern Forest Lands: Resident Attitudes and Resource Use, 1208–371

Northern Institutional Profile Analysis: Beaufort Sea. Alaska Social and Economic Study, 5736–5.10

Northern Institutional Profile Analysis: Chukchi Sea. Alaska Social and Economic Study, 5736–5.9

Norway's Salmon Farming Industry, 2162–1.204

Note on Empirical Tests of Separability and the "Approximation" View of Functional Form, 6886–6.77

Note on Labor Contracts with Private Information and Household Production, 9383–20.1

Note on the Value of the Right Data, 1502–3.203

NSF FY89 Awards by State and Institution, 9624–26

NSF's Research Opportunities for Women Program: An Assessment of the First Three Years, 9628–82

NSSDC Data Listing, 9504–10

NTDB: The Export Connection, 2002–6

Nuclear Engineering Enrollments and Degrees, 1990 Appendixes, 3004–5

Nuclear Engineering Undergraduate Enrollments Increased in 1990 While Degrees Decreased. Master's Enrollments and Degrees Decreased and Doctoral Enrollments and Degrees Increased, 3006–8.14

Nuclear Nonproliferation: DOE Needs Better Controls To Identify Contractors Having Foreign Interests, 26113–520

Nuclear Reactors Built, Being Built, or Planned: 1990, 3354–15

Nuclear Safety: Potential Security Weaknesses at Los Alamos and Other DOE Facilities, 26113–493

Nuclear Safety Technical Progress Review, 3352–4

Nuclear Waste: Is There a Need for Federal Interim Storage? Report of the Monitored Retrievable Storage Review Commission, 14818–1

Nuclear Waste: Quarterly Report on DOE's Nuclear Waste Program, as of (Date), 26102–4

Number of Energy-Related Scientists and Engineers To Increase by 10 Percent for 1990-96 Period, 3006–8.16

Number of Paid Fishing and Hunting License Holders, License Sales, and Cost to Anglers and Hunters, FY90, 5504–16

Number of Returns To Be Filed: Projections, CY90-97, Districts, 8304–24

Number of Returns To Be Filed: Projections, CY90-97, U.S., Regions, and Service Centers, 8304–9

Number of Returns To Be Filed, Projections FY91-99: U.S. Spring Update, FY93 Budget Cycle, 8302–4

Nurses' Knowledge, Attitudes, and Beliefs Regarding Organ and Tissue Donation and Transplantation, 4042–3.214

Nutrition Labeling: Current Status and Comparison of Various Proposals, 1004–16.1

OASDI Beneficiaries by State and County, December 1989, 4744–28

OASDI Beneficiaries by State and County, December 1990, 4744–28

Obesity and Colorectal Adenomatous Polyps, 4472–1.206

Object Class Analysis: Budget of the U.S. Government, FY92, 104–9

Obligated but Unspent Funds as of Sept. 30, 1990. Foreign Assistance, 26123–327

Obligations Limitation: Resolution Trust Corporation's Compliance as of (Date), 26102–6

Observations on the Analyses Supporting Proposed Closures and Realignments. Military Bases, 26123–341

Office of Inspector General...

Occupant Protection Facts, 7766–15.2

Occupational Earnings and Wage Trends in Metropolitan Areas, 6785–5

Occupational Earnings in All Metropolitan Areas, August 1990, 6785–9

Occupational Earnings in Selected Areas, 6785–6

Occupational Employment in Manufacturing Industries, 6748–52

Occupational Employment Projections, 6722–1.254

Occupational Exposure: Criteria for a Recommended Standard, 4246–1

Occupational Exposure to Ethylene Glycol Monobutyl Ether and Ethylene Glycol Monobutyl Ether Acetate, 4246–1.98

Occupational Fatalities as Found in Reports of OSHA Fatality/Catastrophe Investigations, 6606–2

Occupational Injuries and Illnesses in the U.S., By Industry, 1989, 6844–1

Occupational Outlook Quarterly, 6742–1

Occupational Radiation Exposure at Commercial Nuclear Power Reactors and Other Facilities, 1987, 9634–3

Occupational Radiation Exposure from U.S. Naval Nuclear Propulsion Plants and Their Support Facilities, 1990, 3804–10

Occupational Safety and Health: Inspectors' Opinions on Improving OSHA Effectiveness, 26121–391

Occupations of Federal White-Collar and Blue-Collar Workers, Federal Civilian Workforce Statistics, 9844–4

Oceanographic Data Exchange, 1989, 2144–15

Oceanographic Monthly Summary, 2182–5

OCS National Compendium: Outer Continental Shelf Oil and Gas Information through October 1990, 5736–3.1

OECD Trade Series, 9116–1

OECD Trade with Asia, 9116–1.7

OECD Trade with Mexico and Central America, 9116–1.2

OECD Trade with South America, 9116–1.4

OECD Trade with Sub-Saharan Africa, 9116–1.6

OECD Trade with the Caribbean, 9116–1.5

OECD Trade with the Middle East, 9116–1.1

OECD Trade with the USSR and Eastern Europe, 9116–1.3

OERI Directory of Computer Data Files, 4868–10

Offenders in Juvenile Court, 1987, 6066–27.6

Office Furniture, 1990, Current Industrial Report, 2506–7.8

Office of Aviation Medicine Reports, 7506–10

Office of Civilian Radioactive Waste Management, Annual Report to Congress, 3364–1

Office of Energy Research Program Summaries, 3004–18

Office of Exploratory Research, Summary of Awards, 9184–18

Office of Federal Contract Compliance Programs, Director's Report, 6508–36

Office of Housing and Urban Programs Annual Report, FY90, 9914–4

Office of Inspector General Semiannual Report to Congress, Department of Agriculture, 1002–4

Office of Inspector General Semiannual Report to Congress, Department of Energy, 3002–12

Office of Inspector General... Index by Titles

Office of Inspector General Semiannual Report to Congress, Department of Health and Human Services, Apr. 1-Sept. 30, 1990, 4002–6

Office of Inspector General Semiannual Report to Congress, Department of Health and Human Services, Apr. 1-Sept. 30, 1990: List of Reports Issued, 4002–6

Office of Inspector General Semiannual Report to Congress, Department of Health and Human Services, Oct. 1, 1990-Mar. 31, 1991, 4002–6

Office of Inspector General Semiannual Report to Congress, Department of Housing and Urban Development, 5002–8

Office of Inspector General Semiannual Report to Congress, Department of Interior, 5302–2

Office of Inspector General Semiannual Report to Congress, Department of State, 7002–6

Office of Inspector General Semiannual Report to Congress, Department of Transportation, 7302–4

Office of Inspector General Semiannual Report to Congress, Department of Veterans Affairs, 8602–1

Office of Inspector General Semiannual Report to Congress, Environmental Protection Agency, 9182–10

Office of Inspector General Semiannual Report to Congress, General Services Administration, 9452–8

Office of Inspector General Semiannual Report to Congress, NASA, 9502–9

Office of Inspector General Semiannual Report to Congress, National Science Foundation, 9622–1

Office of Inspector General Semiannual Report to Congress, Resolution Trust Corporation, 9722–6

Office of Inspector General Semiannual Report to Congress, U.S. Department of Commerce, 2002–5

Office of Inspector General Semiannual Report to Congress, U.S. Department of Education, 4802–1

Office of Inspector General Semiannual Report to Congress, U.S. Department of Labor, 6302–2

Office of Inspector General Semiannual Report to Congress, U.S. Small Business Administration, 9762–5

Office of National Drug Control Policy: Technical Papers, 236–2

Office of National Drug Control Policy: White Papers, 236–1

Office of Navajo and Hopi Indian Relocation, Plan Update, 16008–5

Office of Navajo and Hopi Indian Relocation Program Status, 16002–1

Office of Refugee Resettlement Monthly Data Report, 4692–2

Office of Surface Mining Annual Report, FY90, 5644–1

Office of Technology Assessment, Annual Report to the Congress, FY90, 26354–3

Office of U.S. Foreign Disaster Assistance, Annual Report, FY90, 9914–12

Office Visits by Adolescents, 4146–8.199

Office Visits by Black Patients, National Ambulatory Medical Care Survey: U.S., 1975-76, 4147–16.5

Office Visits for Family Planning, National Ambulatory Medical Care Survey: U.S., 1977, 4147–16.5

Office Visits for Respiratory Conditions, National Ambulatory Medical Care Survey: U.S., 1975-76, 4147–16.5

Office Visits to Cardiovascular Specialists, National Ambulatory Medical Care Survey: U.S., 1975-76, 4147–16.5

Office Visits to Dermatologists: National Ambulatory Medical Care Survey, U.S., 1975-76, 4147–16.4

Office Visits to Ophthalmologists: National Ambulatory Medical Care Survey, U.S., 1976, 4147–16.4

Office Visits to Orthopedic Surgeons, National Ambulatory Medical Care Survey: U.S., 1975-76, 4147–16.4

Office Visits to Otolaryngologists: National Ambulatory Medical Care Survey, U.S.: 1975-76, 4147–16.4

Office Visits to Psychiatrists: National Ambulatory Medical Care Survey, U.S., 1975-76, 4147–16.4

Office Visits to Urologists: National Ambulatory Medical Care Survey, U.S., 1975-76, 4147–16.4

Offices of Drug Evaluation: Statistical Report, 1987-88, 4064–14

Offices of Drug Evaluation: Statistical Report, 1989, 4064–14

Offices of Drug Evaluation: Statistical Report, 1990, 4064–14

Official Guard and Reserve Manpower: Strengths and Statistics, 3542–4

Official Guard and Reserve Manpower Strengths and Statistics, FY90 Summary, 3544–38

Official Summary of Security Transactions and Holdings, 9732–2

Off-Label Drugs: Initial Results of a National Survey, 26131–81

Off-Label Drugs: Reimbursement Policies Constrain Physicians in Their Choice of Cancer Therapies, 26131–81

Offshore Oil Terminals: Potential Role in U.S. Petroleum Distribution, 5738–25

Offshore Scientific and Technical Publications, 1988 Annual, 5734–5

Oil and Gas Field Code Master List, 1990, 3164–70

Oil Crops Situation and Outlook Report, 1561–3

Oil Crops Situation and Outlook Yearbook, 1561–3

Oilseed Outlook, 1004–16.1

Oilseed Provisions in the 1990 Farm Bill, 1004–16.1

Oilseeds: Foreign Agricultural Service Circular Series, 1925–1

Olympia Oyster. Species Profiles: Life Histories and Environmental Requirements of Coastal Fishes and Invertebrates (Pacific Northwest), 5506–8.131

On Flexibility, Capital Structure, and Investment Decisions for the Insured Bank, 9377–9.119

On the Foreign Exchange Risk Premium in a General Equilibrium Model, 9381–10.117

On the Sustainability of International Coordination, 9371–10.61

On the Valuation of Deposit Institutions, 9377–9.112

One-Year Drug Strategy Review, 25528–117

Operation and Effect of the International Boycott Provisions of the Internal Revenue Code, Fifth Annual Report, 8004–13

Operation Desert Shield/Storm: Use of Navy and Marine Corps Reserves, 26123–351

Operation of the Colorado River Basin 1990, Projected Operations 1991: 20th Annual Report, 5824–6

Operation of the Trade Agreements Program, 42nd Report, 1990, 9884–5

Operation of TVA Reservoirs: Annual 1988, 9804–7

Operation of TVA Reservoirs: Annual 1989, 9804–7

Operations, Maintenance, and Replacement: Bonneville Power Administration, 10-Year Plan, 1990-99, 3228–14

Opinion Survey of Taxpayers Contacted by IRS Collection, 8304–8.1

Opportunities Exist To Lower the Cost of Building Federal Prisons. Prison Costs, 26119–341

Optimal Acceptance Policies for Journals, 9387–8.254

Optimal Bank Portfolio Choice Under Fixed-Rate Deposit Insurance, 9377–9.120

Optimal Contingent Bank Liquidation Under Moral Hazard, 9375–13.64

Optimal Monetary Policy Design: Rules vs. Discretion Again, 9385–8.85

Optimality of Nominal Contracts, 9379–12.76

Options in Access to Health Care, Part 9, 23898–7

Oral Diseases. Indian Health Conditions, 4088–2

Orange Import Demand: Four Markets for U.S. Fresh Oranges, 1528–317

Orange Juice Outlook for Selected Countries, 1925–34.214

Orange Juice Situation, 1925–34.231

Oregon Cooperative Snow Survey Data of Federal-State-Private Cooperative Snow Surveys, Water Year 1990, 1264–14.3

Oregon Water Supply Outlook, 1264–9

Oregon-Washington Marine Mammal and Seabird Surveys: Information Synthesis and Hypothesis Formulation, 5738–28

Organizational Structure and Resources of CDC's HIV-AIDS Prevention Program, 4042–3.256

ORS Working Paper Series, 4746–26

Other Tobaccos, Summary of 1991 Support Program: ASCS Commodity Fact Sheet, 1806–4.7

Outer Continental Shelf Environmental Assessment Program: Final Reports of Principal Investigators, 2176–1

Outer Continental Shelf Oil and Gas Activities, 5736–3

Outer Continental Shelf Oil and Gas Leasing and Production Program: Annual Report FY90, 5734–4

Outlook for Agricultural Lenders and Policymakers in the 1990s, 9368–90

Outlook for Cotton, 1004–16.1

Outlook for Dairy, 1004–16.1

Outlook for Farm Commodity Program Spending, FY91-96, 26306–6.160

Outlook for Farm Credit, 1004–16.1

Outlook for Farm Inputs, 1004–16.1

Outlook for Feed Grains, 1004–16.1

Outlook for Floriculture Production and Greenhouse and Nursery Trade, 1990/91, 1004–16.1

Outlook for Food Prices, 1990, 1004–16.1

Outlook for Fruit and Tree Nuts, 1991, 1004–16.1

Index by Titles

Outlook for Natural Gas Imports: Supporting Analysis for the National Energy Strategy, 3166–6.52

Outlook for Natural Gas, 1991, 3162–4.207

Outlook for Oilseeds: Farmer Perspective, 1004–16.1

Outlook for Poultry and Eggs, 1004–16.1

Outlook for Red Meats, 1004–16.1

Outlook for the U.S. Economy, 1991, 1004–16.1

Outlook for Timber Products, 1004–16.1

Outlook for Tobacco, 1004–16.1

Outlook for U.S. Agricultural Exports, 1542–4

Outlook for U.S. Aquaculture, 1004–16.1

Outlook for Vegetables, 1004–16.1

Outlook Mixed for World Grains in 1991/92, 1502–4.202

Outlook '91, Charts: 67th Annual Agricultural Outlook Conference, 1504–9

Outlook '91, Proceedings: 67th Annual Agricultural Outlook Conference, 1004–16

Outpatient Care Programs of Mental Health Organizations, U.S., 1988, 4506–3.46

Outpatient Drug Abuse Treatment Services, 1988: Results of a National Survey, 4498–73

Outpatient Immunosuppressive Drugs Under Medicare, 26358–246

Outpatient Visits by Primary Health Provider, Indian Health Service and Tribally Operated Facilities, FY90, 4084–3

Output and Input Subsidy Policy Options in Bangladesh, 1502–3.203

Over $100 Million Goes to Local Governments for Tax Exempt Lands, 5306–4.10

Overseas Basing: Air Force and Army Processes for Selecting Bases To Close in Europe, 26123–336

Overseas Business Reports: Marketing in Individual Countries, 2046–6

Overseas Private Investment Corporation 1990 Report, 9904–2

Oversight and Reauthorization of McKinney Act Programs, 25408–111

Oversight Hearing on Status of Census Operations in the State of Texas, 21628–92

Oversight Hearing on 1990 Decennial Census Budget, 21628–88

Oversight Hearings on OSHA's Proposed Standard To Protect Health Care Workers Against Blood-Borne Pathogens Including the AIDS and Hepatitis B Viruses, Volume 2, 21348–119

Oversight Hearings on the Condition of the Bank Insurance Fund, 25248–125

Oversight of Health Maintenance Organizations in the Chicago Area. Medicaid, 26121–399

Oversight of "High Risk" Asset Forfeiture Programs at the Justice Department and the Customs Service, 25408–112

Oversight on the Implementation of the Agricultural Credit Act of 1987, 25168–74

Overview of AID Population Assistance, FY90, 9914–13.1

Overview of Entitlement Programs: 1991 Green Book. Background Material and Data on Programs Within the Jurisdiction of the Committee on Ways and Means, 21784–11

Overview of International Egg Production and Trade, 1561–7.204

Overview of Navy and Marine Corps Flight Operations. Flying Hours, 26123–332

Overview of Nursing Home Characteristics: Provisional Data from the 1977 National Nursing Home Survey, 4147–16.4

Overview of Public Social Welfare Expenditures, FY88, 4742–1.202

Overview of Recent Developments in the Underground Storage Market, 3162–4.205

Overview of the Federal Tax System, Including Data on Tax and Revenue Measures Within the Jurisdiction of the Committee on Ways and Means, 21788–197

Overview of the Static World Policy Simulation (SWOPSIM) Modeling Framework, 1528–315

PAC Activity Falls in 1990 Elections, 9276–1.89

Pacific Herring. Species Profiles: Life Histories and Environmental Requirements of Coastal Fishes and Invertebrates (Pacific Northwest), 5506–8.133

Pacific Marine Environmental Laboratory Annual Report, FY90, 2144–21

Pacific Northwest Loads and Resources Study, 1990, 3224–3

Pacific Outer Continental Shelf Region: Production Record by Platform, 1989, 5734–9

Pacific Rim: Agriculture and Trade Report, Situation and Outlook Series, 1524–4.5

Packaged Fluid Milk Sales in Federal Milk Order Markets: By Size and Type of Container and Distribution Method During November 1989, 1317–6

Packers and Stockyards Statistical Report. 1988 Reporting Year, 1384–1

Packers and Stockyards Statistical Report, 1989 Reporting Year, 1384–1

Paid Advertising for AIDS Prevention—Would the Ends Justify the Means?, 4042–3.256

Paint and Allied Products, 1990, Current Industrial Report, 2506–8.16

Paint Formulating Point Source Category: Preliminary Data Summary, 9206–4.7

Paint, Varnish, and Lacquer, Current Industrial Report, 2506–8.4

Panama Canal Commission, Annual Report, Fiscal Year Ended Sept. 30, 1990, 9664–3

Panel Study of the Effects of Leverage on Investment and Employment, 9385–8.77

Parameter Constancy, Mean Square Forecast Errors, and Measuring Forecast Performance: An Exposition, Extensions, and Illustration, 9366–7.266

Paraquat Hazards to Fish, Wildlife, and Invertebrates: A Synoptic Review, 5506–14.2

Parental Drug Abuse and African American Children in Foster Care: Issues and Study Findings, 4008–114

Parks and Recreation: Resource Limitations Affect Condition of Forest Service Recreation Sites, 26113–502

Parolee Data, 6266–2.6

Partnership Returns, 1989, 8302–2.216, 8304–18

Party Spending Limits Set for Off-Year Elections, 1991, 9276–1.92

Passenger Facility Charges, 21648–63

Passengers Could Be Better Informed of Their Rights. Air Travel, 26113–542

Patent and Trademark Office: Impact of Higher Patent Fees on Small-Entity and Federal Agency Users, 26113–543

Performance Profiles of Major...

Patents Issued by the Patent and Trademark Office, 2244–2

Patronage Refunds Boost Income of Local Grain Cooperatives, 1122–1.208

Patterns of Corporate Leverage in Selected Industrialized Countries, 9385–8.103

Patterns of Global Terrorism: 1990, 7004–13

Patterns of Outpatient Prescription Drug Use Among Pennsylvania Elderly, 4652–1.237

Pay Structure of the Federal Civil Service, Mar. 31, 1990, Federal Civilian Workforce Statistics, 9844–6

Payment of Household Debts, 9362–1.201

Payment to Health Maintenance Organizations and the Geographic Factor, 4652–1.203

Payments for Clinical Laboratory Test Services Are Too High. Medicare, 26121–425

Payments in Lieu of Taxes, FY91, 5724–9

Payments to Producers by State and Program During 1990, 1804–12

Payments to States from National Forests Receipts, FY90, 1204–33

PC-GIVE and David Hendry's Econometric Methodology, 9366–7.260

Peace Corps: Congressional Presentation, FY92, 9654–1

Peanut Marketing Summary. 1989 Crop, 1311–5

Peanut Marketing Summary, 1990 Crop, 1311–5

Peanut Report, 1311–1

Peanut Stocks and Processing, 1621–6

Peanuts: Report to the President on Investigation No. 22-52 Under Section 22 of the Agricultural Adjustment Act, As Amended, 9886–10.10

Peat in 1990: Mineral Industry Surveys Annual Advance Summary, 5614–5.24

Peat: Minerals Yearbook, Volume 1, 1989, 5604–15.49

Pedestrian Crash Facts, 1990, 7766–15.5

Pell Grant End of Year Report, 1989-90, 4804–1

Pell Grant Program, End of Year Report, 4804–1

Pelvic Inflammatory Disease: Guidelines for Prevention and Management, 4206–2.41

Pension Benefit Guaranty Corporation: Annual Report, 1990, 9674–1

Pension Plans: Terminations, Asset Reversions, and Replacements Following Leveraged Buyouts, 26121–408

Pension Portability and Labor Mobility: Evidence from the Survey of Income and Program Participation, 2626–10.123

Pensions: Who Is Covered? Statistical Brief, 2326–17.35

Pensions: Worker Coverage and Retirement Benefits, 1987, 2546–20.18

Pepper Commission: U.S. Bipartisan Commission on Comprehensive Health Care, Supplement to the Final Report. Call for Action, 23898–5

Performance and Compatibility Analysis of Oil Weathering and Transport-Related Models for Use in the Environmental Assessment Process, 2176–1.36

Performance Evaluation of the Energy Information Administration, Department of Energy, Report to the President and the Congress, Professional Audit Review Team, 26104–14

Performance Profiles of Major Energy Producers, 1989, 3164–44

Perkins Loan Program,

Perkins Loan Program, Status of Default as of June 30, 1990, 4804–18

Perlite in 1990: Mineral Industry Surveys, Annual Report, 5614–5.14

Permanent and Transient Influences on the Reluctance To Borrow at the Discount Window, 9385–8.111

Permanent Funding Lapse Legislation Needed. Government Shutdown., 26119–311

Persian Gulf Crisis: Humanitarian Relief Provided to Evacuees from Kuwait and Iraq, 26123–326

Persian Gulf Energy Situation Analysis Report, 3162–44

Persistence and Convergence in Relative Regional Incomes, 9387–8.232

Personal Health Practices: Findings from the Survey of American Indians and Alaska Natives. National Medical Expenditure Survey, 4186–8.19

Personal Word Processors from Japan and Singapore. Determinations of the Commission in Investigation Nos. 731-TA-483 and 484 (Preliminary) Under the Tariff Act of 1930, Together with the Information Obtained in the Investigations, 9886–14.302

Personal Word Processors from Japan. Determination of the Commission in Investigation No. 731-TA-483 (Final) Under the Tariff Act of 1930, Together with the Information Obtained in the Investigation, 9886–14.325

Persons Needing Assistance with Everyday Activities. Statistical Brief, 2326–17.22

Peru: An Export Market Profile, 1526–6.14

Pesticide Chemicals Point Source Category: Preliminary Data Summary, 9206–4.2

Pesticide Residues and Food Safety: Aspects of a Changing Structure, 1588–154

Pesticide Review, 1989, For USDA State and County Emergency Records, 1804–5

Pesticide Use by Tillage System, 1988 and 1989 Corn Production, 1561–16.201

Petroleum: An Energy Profile, 3164–95

Petroleum Marketing Monthly, 3162–11

Petroleum Profits in the Fourth Quarter of 1990, 3166–6.46

Petroleum Supply Annual, 1990, 3164–2

Petroleum Supply Monthly, 3162–6

Petroleum Tariffs as a Source of Government Revenue, 9406–1.61

Pharmaceutical Manufacturing Point Source Category: Preliminary Data Summary, 9206–4.4

Pharmaceutical Preparations, Except Biologicals, 1990, Current Industrial Report, 2506–8.5

Philadelphia Research Working Papers, 9387–8

Phosphate Rock: Minerals Yearbook, Volume 1, 1989, 5604–15.51

Phosphate Rock: Minerals Yearbook, Volume 1, 1990, 5604–20.45

Phosphate Rock, 1991 Crop Year, Mineral Industry Surveys, 5614–20

Photovoltaic Energy Program Summary, FY90, 3304–20

Physical Activity and Risk of Developing Colorectal Cancer Among College Alumni, 4472–1.222

Physician Consultative Services Under Medicare: Final Report, 4658–47

Physician Payment Review Commission, Annual Report to Congress, 17264–1

Physician Payment Review Commission: Reports to Congress, 17266–1

Physicians, Nurses, and AIDS: Preliminary Findings from a National Study, 4186–9.11

Pieces of Eight, An Economic Perspective on the 8th District, 9391–16

Pipeline Safety, Annual Report, 7304–5

Pistachio Production Down 59 Percent, 1621–18.6

Pistachio Situation, 1925–34.248

P.L. 94-171 Data on CD-ROM, Technical Documentation. 1990 Census of Population and Housing, 2308–63

P.L. 94-171 Data on CD-ROM. 1990 Census of Population and Housing, 2551–6

P.L. 94-171 Higher-Level Geographic Summary Series. State Reports. 1990 Census of Population and Housing, 2551–5

Plainfield/Crest Hill Tornado, Northern Illinois, Aug. 28, 1990. Natural Disaster Survey Report, 2186–6.3

Plan and Operation of the NHANES I Epidemiologic Followup Study, 1986. Vital and Health Statistics Series 1, 4147–1.26

Plan To Strengthen Public Health in the U.S., 4042–3.255

Plant and Equipment Expenditures and Plans, 2502–2

Planting Flexibility Options for Mississippi River Delta Rice Farms, 1561–8.201

Platinum-Group Metals: Mineral Industry Surveys, 5612–2.14

Playing by the Rules: A Proposal for Federal Budget Reform, 9383–2

Plumbing Fixtures, Current Industrial Report, 2506–11.2

Plywood, Waferboard and Oriented-Strand Board (Formerly "Hardwood Plywood"), 1989—Revised. Current Industrial Report, 2506–7.1

Pocket Projections, 1978-79 to 2000-2001, 4828–27

Point Lay Biographies. Alaska Social and Economic Studies, 5736–5.8

Point Lay Case Study. Alaska Social and Economic Study, 5736–5.8

Policies Toward Corporate Leveraging, 9385–8.88

Policy Choices for Long-Term Care, 26306–6.156

Policy Research Notes, 1542–6

Political and Institutional Independence of U.S. Monetary Policy, 9385–8.106

Polling Place Accessibility in the 1990 General Election, 9274–6

Pollution Abatement and Control Expenditures, 1987-89, 2702–1.229

Polyethylene Terephthalate Film, Sheet, and Strip from Japan and the Republic of Korea. Determinations of the Commission in Investigations Nos. 731-TA-458 and 459 (Final) Under the Tariff Act of 1930, Together with the Information Obtained in the Investigations, 9886–14.313

Population Characteristics. Current Population Reports. Series P-20, 2546–1

Population Characteristics of Humpback Whales in Southeastern Alaska: Summer and Late Season, 1986, 14738–10

Population Ecology, Habitat Requirements, and Conservation of Neotropical Migratory Birds, 1208–382

Population Estimates and Projections. Current Population Reports. Series P-25, 2546–3

Index by Titles

Population Estimates and Projections; Estimates of the Population of the U.S. to (Date). Current Population Reports. Series P-25, 2542–1

Population of Metropolitan Areas by Race and Hispanic Origin: 1990, 2328–75

Population of Metropolitan Areas: 1990 and 1980, by 1990 Population Rank, 2324–8

Population Profile of the U.S., 1991, 2546–2.161

Population Representation in the Military Services: FY90, 3544–41

Population Statistics, 2326–7.78

Population Status and Condition of the Harbor Seal, Phoca vitulina richardsi, in the Waters of the State of Washington: 1975-80, 14738–7

Population Trends and Congressional Apportionment. 1990 Census Profile, 2326–20.1

Population-Based Study of Hospice, Parts I-IV, 4658–53

Port and State Tonnage Ranking Reports, 1989, 3754–7

Portable Electric Typewriters from Singapore. Determination of the Commission in Investigation No. 731-TA-515 (Preliminary) Under the Tariff Act of 1930, Together with the Information Obtained in the Investigation, 9886–14.312

Possible Effects of Electric-Utility DSM Programs, 1990-2010, 3308–98

Postal Service: Annual Distribution of 1990 Marketing Costs, 26119–338

Postmaster General, FY90 Annual Report, 9864–1

Postsecondary Education. The Condition of Education, 1991: Volume 2, 4824–1.2

Postsecondary Faculty, 1988 National Survey, 4846–4

Posture of the U.S. Army, 3704–13

Potash in Crop Year 1990, Mineral Industry Surveys, 5614–19

Potash in 1990: Mineral Industry Surveys, Advance Summary, 5614–5.20

Potato Stocks, 1621–10

Potatoes, 1621–11

Potential Cost To Repurchase Offshore Oil and Gas Leases. Mineral Revenues, 26113–509

Potential Diversification and Bank Acquisition Prices, 9371–10.57

Potential Economic Impacts of Changes in Puerto Rico's Status Under S. 712, 26306–3.112

Potential Effects of Global Climate Change on the U.S., 9188–113

Potential for Coal Liquefaction: Supporting Analysis for the National Energy Strategy, 3166–6.53

Potential Markets for U.S. Textile and Apparel Exports, 2048–155

Potential Security Weaknesses at Los Alamos and Other DOE Facilities. Nuclear Safety, 26113–493

Potential Shortage in National Aircraft Repair Capacity. Aircraft Maintenance, 26113–492

Poultry Market Statistics. 1989 Annual Summary, Federal-State Market News in Cooperation with State Departments of Agriculture, 1317–2

Poultry Market Statistics: 1990 Annual Summary, Federal-State Market News in Cooperation with State Departments of Agriculture, 1317–2

Index by Titles

Poultry Production and Value, 1990 Summary, 1625–5

Poultry Slaughter, 1625–3

Poverty Areas and the 'Underclass': Untangling the Web, 6722–1.219

Poverty in the U.S., 1988-89, 2546–6.67

Poverty in the U.S.: 1990, 2546–6.71

Powerplant and Industrial Fuel Use Act, Annual Report, 3334–1

Practical Guidance for Strengthening Private Industry Councils, 6406–10.3

Pre-Argument Conference Program in the Sixth Circuit Court of Appeals, 18408–45

Precautionary Money Balances with Aggregate Uncertainty, 9366–7.253

Predicting Bank Failures in the 1980s, 9377–1.203

Predicting Employment Tax Compliance: Further Analysis of the SVC-1 Employer Survey, 8304–8.1

Prediction Techniques for Box-Cox Regression Models, 9366–6.262

Predictors of Mortality Among Newly Retired Workers, 4742–1.206

Pregnancy and Childbearing Among Homeless Adolescents: Report of a Workshop, 4108–55

Preliminary Analysis of the Public Costs of Environmental Protection: 1981-2000, 9188–114

Preliminary Apportionment of Federal Aid in Sport Fish and Wildlife Restoration Funds for FY92, 5502–1

Preliminary Data Summary Reports for Industry Point Source Categories, 9206–4

Preliminary Estimates of Age and Sex Compositions of Ducks and Geese Harvested in the 1990 Hunting Season in Comparison with Prior Years, 5504–32

Preliminary Estimates of Waterfowl Harvest and Hunter Activity in the U.S. During the 1990 Hunting Season, 5504–28

Preliminary Estimates on Student Financial Aid Recipients, 1989-90: Report of the 1990 National Postsecondary Student Aid Study, 4846–5.1

Preliminary Indications from the 1990 Census, 21628–91

Preliminary Report on U.S. Production of Selected Synthetic Organic Chemicals, 9882–1

Preliminary 1989 Catch, Value of Middle Atlantic, Chesapeake Fishes Told, 2162–1.204

Preliminary 1989 Catch, Values of New England Fish and Shellfish Noted, 2162–1.204

Premigrational Movements and Behavior of Young Mallards and Wood Ducks in North-Central Minnesota, 5506–13.1

Prepaid Medicaid Chartbook: Selected Enrollment and Utilization Data, 4108–29

Preparation for the 1990 Farm Bill, Part III, 25168–75

Prescription Drugs: Little Is Known About the Effects of Direct-to-Consumer Advertising, 26131–86

President Bush's FY92 Budget, 21268–42

President's Council on Integrity and Efficiency: A Progress Report to the President, FY90, 104–29

President's List of Articles Which May Be Designated or Modified as Eligible Articles for Purposes of the U.S. Generalized System of Preferences: Report to the President on Investigation Nos. TA-131-17, 503(a)-22, and 332-312, 9884–23

Pretrial Release of Felony Defendants, 1988, 6066–25.36

Prevalence, Disability, and Health Care for Psoriasis Among Persons 1-74 Years: U.S., 4147–16.5

Prevalence of Aphakia in the Civil Airman Population, 7506–10.93

Prevalence of Chlamydia trachomatis Infection in Pregnant Patients, 4042–3.240

Prevalence of Chronic Diseases: A Summary of Data from the Survey of American Indians and Alaska Natives. National Medical Expenditure Survey, 4186–8.20

Prevalence of Elevated Serum Cholesterol in Personnel of the U.S. Navy, 4042–3.215

Prevalence, Relation to Crime, and Programs. Rural Drug Abuse, 26131–79

Prevention and Control of Influenza: Recommendations of the Immunization Practices Advisory Committee (ACIP), 4206–2.42

Preventive Health Care for Medicaid Children, 4652–1.214

Preview of the Comprehensive Revision of the National Income and Product Accounts: Definitional and Classificational Changes, 2702–1.221

Preview of the Comprehensive Revision of the National Income and Product Accounts: New and Redesigned Tables, 2702–1.224

Price and Quality in Higher Education, 4888–3

Price Index of New One-Family Houses Sold, Current Construction Reports, 2382–8

Price, Market Security Big Factors in Farmers' Selection of Milk Handler, 1122–1.206

Price Transmission Asymmetry in Pork and Beef Markets, 1502–3.201

Price Trends for Federal-Aid Highway Construction, 7552–7

Prices Received: Minnesota-Wisconsin Manufacturing Grade Milk, 1990 Summary, 1629–2

Primary Care Research: An Agenda for the 90s, 4188–69

Primary Care Research: Theory and Methods. Conference Proceedings, 4184–4

Primary Forest Products Industry and Timber Use, 1206–10

Prime Contract Awards by Region and State, FY88-90, 3544–11

Prime Contract Awards by Service Category and Federal Supply Classification, FY87-90, 3544–18

Prime Contract Awards by State, First Half FY91, 3542–5

Prime Contract Awards, First Half FY91, Department of Defense, 3542–1

Prime Contract Awards, FY90, Department of Defense, 3542–1

Prime Contract Awards in Labor Surplus Areas, FY90, 3542–19

Prime Contract Awards in Labor Surplus Areas, First Half FY91, 3542–19

Prime Contract Awards, Size Distribution, FY90, 3544–19

Primer on Cointegration with an Application to Money and Income, 9391–1.210

Primer on the Arms Trade, 9373–1.221

Principal Deposits of Industrial Minerals in Idaho (Excluding Phosphate), 5606–10.1

Principal Deposits of Industrial Minerals in Selected States, 5606–10

Principal Officers of the Department of State and U.S. Chiefs of Mission, 1778-1990, 7008–1

Procedures Used in...

Principal Ports, 1989 Alphabetic Listing, 3754–7.1

Principal Ports, 1989 by Domestic Tonnage, 3754–7.2

Principal Ports, 1989 by Foreign Tonnage, 3754–7.3

Principal Ports, 1989 by Total Tonnage, 3754–7.4

Principal Threats Facing Communities and Local Emergency Management Coordinators, 9434–6

Principal-Agent Problems in Commercial-Bank Failure Decisions, 9377–9.115

Prior and Concurrent Authorization for Home Health and Skilled Nursing Facility Services, 4658–57

Priority Housing Problems and "Worst Case" Needs in 1989, A Report to Congress, 5184–10

Prison Alternatives: Crowded Federal Prisons Can Transfer More Inmates to Halfway Houses, 26119–347

Prison Costs: Opportunities Exist To Lower the Cost of Building Federal Prisons, 26119–341

Prisoners in 1990, 6066–25.37

Prisoners Under Jurisdiction of State and Federal Correctional Authorities, by Region and State, 6062–4

Private Foundation Returns, 1986 and 1987, 8302–2.210

Private Foundation Statistics for 1988: Data Release, 8302–2.220

Private Organization and Public Agency Partnership in Community Health Education, 4042–3.256

Private Pensions: 1986 Law Will Improve Benefit Equity in Many Small Employers' Plans, 26121–412

Private Prisons: Cost Savings and BOP's Statutory Authority Need To Be Resolved, 26119–321

Private Schools in the U.S.: A Statistical Profile, with Comparisons to Public Schools, 4838–47

Private Sector Salary Differences by Locality. Federal Pay, 26119–332

Private Social Welfare Expenditures, 1972-88, 4742–1.204

Probation and Parole 1989, 6066–25.34

Problems in Administering Payments for Nonprogram Crops. Disaster Assistance, 26113–533

Problems in Estimating the Number of Women in Need of Subsidized Prenatal Care, 4042–3.226

Problems of Drug Dependence, 1988: Proceedings of the 50th Annual Scientific Meeting, The Committee on Problems of Drug Dependence, Inc., 4494–11

Problems of Drug Dependence, 1989: Proceedings of the 51st Annual Scientific Meeting, The Committee on Problems of Drug Dependence, Inc., 4494–11

Problems of Drug Dependence, 1990: Proceeding of the 52nd Annual Scientific Meeting, The Committee on Problems of Drug Dependence, Inc., 4494–11

Procedure Codes: Potential Modifiers of Diagnosis-Related Groups, 4652–1.204

Procedures Used in Establishing 1991/92-Crop Loan Rates for Sugar and Minimum Support Prices for Sugarcane and Sugarbeets, 1561–14.207

Proceedings: Conference on...

Index by Titles

Proceedings: Conference on Bank Structure and Competition, Federal Reserve Bank of Chicago, May 9-11, 1990, 9375–7

Proceedings—Management and Productivity of Western-Montane Forest Soils, 1208–378

Proceedings of Southern Plantation Wood Quality Workshop, 1208–346

Proceedings of the Expert Consultation Meeting on Bald Eagles, 14648–26

Proceedings of the Symposium on Sandalwood in the Pacific, Apr. 9-11, 1990, Honolulu, Hawaii, 1208–366

Proceedings of the Symposium on the Management of Longleaf Pine, 1208–355

Proceedings of the VIIth International Pneumoconioses Conference, Pittsburgh, 1988, 4248–90

Proceedings of the Seventeenth U.S.-Japan Meeting on Aquaculture, Ise, Mie Prefecture, Japan, Oct. 16-18, 1988: Marine Ranching, 2164–15

Proceedings of the 1990 Billings Land Reclamation Symposium on Selenium in Arid and Semiarid Environments, Western U.S., 5668–121

Proceedings of the 1990 Northeastern Recreation Research Symposium, Feb. 25-28, 1990, 1208–356

Proceedings of the 50th Annual Scientific Meeting, The Committee on Problems of Drug Dependence, Inc.: Problems of Drug Dependence, 1988, 4494–11

Proceedings of the 51st Annual Scientific Meeting, The Committee on Problems of Drug Dependence, Inc.: Problems of Drug Dependence, 1989, 4494–11

Proceedings of the 52nd Annual Scientific Meeting, The Committee on Problems of Drug Dependence, Inc.: Problems of Drug Dependence, 1990, 4494–11

Proceedings of 1988 International Symposium on Data on Aging. Vital and Health Statistics Series 5, 4147–5.6

Proceedings—Symposium on Cheatgrass Invasion, Shrub Die-off, and Other Aspects of Shrub Biology and Management, 1208–351

Proceedings: The 26th Annual Conference on Bank Structure and Competition, May 9-11, 1990, Federal Reserve Bank of Chicago, 9375–7

Proceedings: 1988 Southeastern Recreation Research Conference, Volume 10, 1204–38

Proceedings: 1989 Southeastern Recreation Research Conference, Volume 11, 1204–38

Proceedings: 1990 Southeastern Recreation Research Conference, Volume 12, 1204–38

Processed Fishery Products, Annual Summary 1987, 2166–6.2

Processes for Identifying Regional Influences of and Responses to Increasing Atmospheric CO_2 and Climate Change—The MINK Project, 3006–11.15

Procurement Programs (P-1), Department of Defense Budget for FY92-93, 3544–32

Procyclical Labor Productivity, Increasing Returns to Labor, and Labor Hoarding in U.S. Auto Assembly Plant Employment, 6886–6.72

Procyclical Prices: A Demi-Myth?, 9383–6.204

Producer Price Indexes, 6762–5, 6762–6

Producer Price Indexes Supplement, Data for 1990, 6764–2

Product Summary Report. Source: National Electronic Injury Surveillance System, U.S. Consumer Product Safety Commission, National Injury Information Clearinghouse, All Products, 1990, 9164–6

Production and Trade of Fresh Cut Flowers in Selected Countries, 1925–34.210

Production Initiatives in OHA's Region V Comply with Law and Guidelines. Social Security, 26121–398

Production, Prices, Employment, and Trade in Northwest Forest Industries, 1202–3

Production Profile of Sorghum Producers: Government Program Participants vs Nonparticipants, 1541–1.210

Production Sharing: U.S. Imports Under Harmonized Tariff Schedule Subheadings 9802.00.60 and 9802.00.80, 1986-89, 9884–14

Productive Efficiency in Banking, 9375–1.209

Productivity and Costs: Preliminary Statistics, 6822–1

Productivity and Costs, Revised Data for Business, Nonfarm Business, and Manufacturing, and Preliminary Measures for Nonfinancial Corporations, 6822–2

Productivity in Industry and Government, 1989, 6722–1.228

Productivity Measures for Selected Industries and Government Services, 6824–1

Productivity Statistics for Federal Government Functions, FY67-89, 6824–4

Profile, FY90, National Institute of Allergy and Infectious Diseases, 4474–30

Profile of HUD: An Introduction to the Major Programs, Organization, Staffing, and Management Systems of the Department of Housing and Urban Development, 5008–37

Profile of Jail Inmates, 1989, 6066–19.62

Profile of Schools Attended by Eighth Graders in 1988. National Education Longitudinal Study of 1988, 4826–9.10

Profile of Specialized Fruit and Vegetable Farms in 1989, 1541–1.209

Profile of the Foreign-Born Population in the U.S., 2546–2.162

Profile of the "Typical" Federal Civilian Non-Postal Employee, Sept. 30, 1990, 9842–1.201

Profile of the Uninsured in Selected States. Health Insurance Coverage, 26121–403

Profiles in Safety and Health: Eating and Drinking Places, 6722–1.231

Profiles of Faculty in Higher Education Institutions, 1988: 1988 National Survey of Postsecondary Faculty, 4846–4.4

Profiles of Foreign Direct Investment in U.S. Energy, 1989, 3164–80

Profiles of State Programs: Adult Education for the Homeless, 4804–39.2

Profit Sharing Today: Plans and Provisions, 6722–1.223

Program Acquisition Costs by Weapon System: Department of Defense Budget for FY92-93, 3504–2

Program Activities: DOE State and Local Assistance Programs, 3304–21

Program Fraud: Implementation of the Program Fraud Civil Remedies Act of 1986, 26111–76

Program Provisions for Program Crops: A Database for 1961-90, 1568–302

Program Provisions for Rye, Dry Edible Beans, Oil Crops, Tobacco, Sugar, Honey, Wool, Mohair, Gum Naval Stores, and Dairy Products: A Database for 1961-90, 1568–303

Program Summary Book for 1988-89: A Statistical and Historical Reference for OPE Programs, 4804–28

Programs and Activities Authorized by Education for Homeless Children and Youth Program, FY90, Report to Congress, 4804–35

Programs and Collection Procedures. Vital and Health Statistics Series 1, 4147–1

Programs and Plans of the National Center for Education Statistics, 1991 Edition, 4824–7

Programs Available to State and Local Governments. Federal Aid, 26121–421

Progress for Developing Countries in the Uruguay Round, 1524–4.2

Progress in Implementing the Development Fund for Africa. Foreign Assistance, 26123–333

Progress of Research on Outcomes of Health Care Services and Procedures. Report to Congress, 4188–70

Prointegrative Subsidies and Their Effect on Housing Markets: Do Race-Based Loans Work?, 9377–9.108

Project Head Start Statistical Fact Sheet, 4604–8

Projected Needs of the Aging Baby Boom Generation. Long-Term Care, 26121–433

Projections, CY90-97, Number of Returns To Be Filed: Districts, 8304–24

Projections, CY90-97, Number of Returns To Be Filed: U.S., Regions, and Service Centers, 8304–9

Projections: Forms 1040, 1040A and 1040EZ by Full-Paid, Other-Than-Full-Paid, Refunds and Electronically-Filed Returns. 1990-93, Fall Update, 8302–7

Projections: Forms 1040, 1040A and 1040EZ by Full-Paid, Other-Than-Full-Paid, Refunds and Electronically-Filed Returns. 1990-93, Spring Update, 8302–7

Projections: Forms 1040, 1040A and 1040EZ by Full-Paid, Other-Than-Full-Paid, Refunds and Electronically-Filed Returns. 1991-94, Spring Update, 8302–7

Projections FY91-99, Number of Returns To Be Filed: U.S. Spring Update, FY93 Budget Cycle, 8302–4

Projections: Information and Withholding Documents, U.S. and Service Centers, 8304–22

Projections of Health Care Expenditures as a Share of GNP: Actuarial and Economic Approaches, 9366–6.284

Projections of National Health Expenditures Through the Year 2000, 4652–1.251

Projections of Returns To Be Filed in FY91-98, 8302–2.208

Projections of the Incidence of Non-Hodgkin's Lymphoma Related to Acquired Immunodeficiency Syndrome, 4472–1.212

Promising Approach for Predicting Carriers' Safety Risks. Freight Trucking, 26131–82

Promising New Products and Processes from Corn, 1004–16.1

Promoting Heart Health for Southeast Asians: A Database for Planning Interventions, 4042–3.222

Promoting Trade and Investment in Constrained Environments: AID Experience in Latin America and the Caribbean, 9916–3.63

Promotional Activities Under Federal Milk Orders, 1990, 1317–4.204

Index by Titles

Prompt and Forceful Regulatory Actions Needed. Bank Supervision, 26119–334

Property Disposition: Information on Federal Single-Family Properties, 26113–513

Property Taxes, Homeownership Capitalization Rates, and Housing Consumption, 9387–8.252

Proportional Hazards Model of Bank Failure: An Examination of Its Usefulness as an Early Warning Tool, 9377–1.204

Proposal for the Olympic Coast National Marine Sanctuary: Site Evaluation Report, 2178–30

Proposal on the EC Banana Import Regime After 1992, 1925–34.245

Proposals To Reduce Medicare Outlays, 21368–131

Proposed Estuarine Classification: Analysis of Species Salinity Ranges, 2176–7.20

Proposed Outer Continental Shelf Oil and Gas Lease Sales: Final Environmental Impact Statements, 5736–1

Proposed Refugee Admissions for FY92, Report to the Congress, 7004–16

Proposed U.S. Participation in the European Bank for Reconstruction and Development (EBRD), And Update on Exchange Rate Report, 21248–148

Propylene Glycol Ethers and Their Acetates. NEG and NIOSH Basis for an Occupational Health Standard, 4246–4.3

Prospective Payment Assessment Commission: Report and Recommendations to the Congress, Mar. 1, 1991, 17204–1

Prospective Payment Assessment Commission: Report and Recommendations to the Secretary, U.S. Department of Health and Human Services, 17204–1

Prospective Payment Assessment Commission: Reports to Congress, 17206–1

Prospective Payment Assessment Commission: Technical Report Series, 17206–2

Prospective Payment System and Other Effects on Post-Hospital Services, 4652–1.223

Prospective Payments System's Impacts on Rural Hospitals, 4658–51

Prospective Plantings, 1621–22

Prospective Study of Serum Cholesterol Levels and Large-Bowel Cancer, 4472–1.226

Prospects for Energy Supplies, 9371–1.213

Prospects for Japan's Livestock Sector, 1524–4.5

Protecting Sensitive Data and Materials at 10 Chemical and Biological Laboratories. Defense Research, 26123–356

Provisional Legalization Application Statistics, 6262–3

Proximity of Sanitary Landfills to Wetlands and Deepwater Habitats: An Evaluation and Comparison of 1,153 Sanitary Landfills in 11 States, 9188–115

Proxy Reports: Results from a Record Check Study, 2626–10.140

Prudential Margin Policy in a Futures-Style Settlement System, 9366–6.278

Psychiatric Outpatient Care Services in Mental Health Organizations, U.S., 1986, 4506–3.40

Psychometric Report for the NELS:88 Base Year Test Battery. National Education Longitudinal Study of 1988, 4826–9.9

Psychotherapy and Counseling in the Treatment of Drug Abuse, 4498–71

Public Area Recreation Visitors Survey, 2176–9

Public Capital and Private Sector Performance, 9391–1.211

Public Debt News, 8002–7

Public Debts and Deficits in Mexico: A Comment, 9379–12.78

Public Education Finances: 1988-89, 2466–2.5

Public Elementary and Secondary Schools and Agencies in the U.S. and Outlying Areas: School Year 1989-90. Final Tabulations, 4834–17

Public Elementary and Secondary State Aggregate Data, by State, for School Year 1989-90 and FY89, 4834–6

Public Elementary and Secondary State Aggregate Nonfiscal Data, by State, and School Revenues and Current Expenditures, 4834–6

Public Employment. No. 1: Employment of Major Local Governments. 1987 Census of Governments, Volume 3, 2455–1

Public Employment. No. 2: Compendium of Public Employment. 1987 Census of Governments, Volume 3, 2455–2

Public Employment. No. 3: Labor-Management Relations. 1987 Census of Governments. Volume 3, 2455–3

Public Employment. No. 4: Government Costs for Employee Benefits. 1987 Census of Governments. Volume 3, 2455–4

Public Employment: 1990, 2466–1.1

Public Health Implications of Medical Waste: A Report to Congress, 4078–1

Public Health Model of Medicaid Emergency Room Use, 4652–1.232

Public Health Reports, 4042–3

Public Health Service Inter-Agency Guidelines for Screening Donors of Blood, Plasma, Organs, Tissues, and Semen for Evidence of Hepatitis B and Hepatitis C, 4206–2.40

Public Health Service Report on Fluoride Benefits and Risks, 4206–2.43

Public Juvenile Facilities, 1989: Children in Custody, 6064–5.1

Public Land Statistics, 1990, 5724–1

Public Lands Recreation, Volume I. A Management Strategy for Special Recreation Management Areas in Oregon and Washington, 5726–5.3

Public Lands Recreation, Volume II. Special Recreation Management Area Narratives, 5726–5.3

Public Libraries in 50 States and the District of Columbia: 1989, 4824–6

Public Roads, A Journal of Highway Research and Development, 7552–3

Public Social Welfare Expenditures, FY88, 4742–1.209

Public Transportation in the U.S.: Performance and Condition, Report to Congress, 7884–8

Publications Abstracts, FY90, 2804–3

Publications of the National Institute of Standards and Technology, 1990 Catalog, 2214–1

Publications of the National Science Foundation, 9624–16

Publications of the U.S. Geological Survey, 1990, 5664–4

Puerto Rico Subject Statistics: Wholesale Trade, Retail Trade, and Service Industries. 1987 Economic Censuses of Outlying Areas., 2591–2

Quarterly Report on the...

Puerto Rico Wholesale Trade, Retail Trade, Service Industries. 1987 Economic Censuses of Outlying Areas. Geographic Area Statistics, 2591–1

Puerto Rico's Political Status, Part 2, 25368–168

Pulp, Paper and Paperboard Point Source Category: Preliminary Data Summary, 9206–4.1

Pulpwood Prices in the Southeast, 1989, 1204–22

Pulpwood Production in the Northeast, 1989, 1204–18

Pumice and Pumicite in 1990: Mineral Industry Surveys Annual Report, 5614–5.13

Pumpkins: A Commodity Highlight, 1561–11.203

Pumps and Compressors, 1990, Current Industrial Report, 2506–12.8

Purified Protein Derivative (PPD)-Tuberculin Anergy and HIV Infection: Guidelines for Anergy Testing and Management of Anergic Persons at Risk of Tuberculosis, 4206–2.41

Qualifying Facilities Report: A Cumulative List of Filings Made for Small Power Production and Cogeneration Facilities, FY80-90, 3084–13

Quality Control Annual Report: Food Stamp Program, FY89, 1364–15

Quality of Federal Statistics, 23848–218

Quality of Shellfish Growing Waters on the West Coast of the U.S., 2176–7.21

Quality of the Responses of Eighth-Grade Students in NELS:88. National Education Longitudinal Study of 1988, 4826–9.11

Quality of Water from Public-Supply Wells in Principal Aquifers of Illinois, 1984-87, 5666–28.5

Quantity and Quality of Ground-Water Inflow to the San Joaquin River, California, 5666–28.14

Quantity and Quality of Stormwater Runoff Recharged to the Floridan Aquifer System Through Two Drainage Wells in the Orlando, Fla., Area, 5666–27.3

Quarterly Banking Profile, 9292–1

Quarterly Coal Report, 3162–37

Quarterly Financial Information Report, Federal Home Loan Bank of Indianapolis, 9302–23

Quarterly Financial Report for Manufacturing, Mining, and Trade Corporations, 2502–1

Quarterly Industry Review, 7502–16

Quarterly Journal: Comptroller of the Currency, Administrator of National Banks, 8402–3

Quarterly Nonimmigrant Statistics, 6262–2

Quarterly Regional Economic Report, Federal Reserve Bank of Philadelphia, 9387–10

Quarterly Report, Federal Home Loan Bank of Boston, 9302–35

Quarterly Report on DOE's Nuclear Waste Program, as of (Date). Nuclear Waste, 26102–4

Quarterly Report on Program Cost and Schedule, 3362–1

Quarterly Report on the Status of the Steel Industry: Report to the Committee on Ways and Means on Investigation No. 332-226 Under Section 332 of the Tariff Act of 1930, 9882–13

Quarterly Review, Index by Titles

Quarterly Review, Federal Reserve Bank of Minneapolis, 9383–6

Quarterly Review, Federal Reserve Bank of New York, 9385–1

Quarterly Speed Monitoring Summary, 7552–14

Quarterly Speed Summary, 7552–14

Quarterly Statistical Report, Federal Home Loan Bank of Des Moines, 9302–9

Quarterly Summary of Federal, State, and Local Tax Revenue, 2462–3

Quarterly Survey of Agricultural Credit Conditions, Eleventh Federal Reserve District, 9379–11

Quarterly Thrift Industry Statistics, 8432–4

Quarterly Trends, Federal Home Loan Bank of Dallas, 9302–31

Quartz Crystal: Minerals Yearbook, Volume 1, 1990, 5604–20.48

Quartz Crystal, Strontium, Wollastonite, and Zeolites: Minerals Yearbook, Volume 1, 5604–15.78, 5604–15.79

Quasi-Fixed Inputs in the Estimation of Bank Scale Economies, 9371–10.54

Quiet Revolution in the U.S. Food Market, 9381–1.205

R, D, T & E Programs (R-1), Department of Defense Budget for FY92-93, 3544–33

R&D Support and Performance, 9628–83.1

Rabies Prevention—U.S., 1991: Recommendations of the Immunization Practices Advisory Committee (ACIP), 4206–2.39

Race and Ethnic Origin. 1990 Census of Population and Housing: Content Determination Reports, 2626–11.14

Race and Hispanic Origin. 1990 Census Profile, 2326–20.2

Race of Prisoners Admitted to State and Federal Institutions, 1926-86, 6068–245

Race/Ethnicity Trends in Degrees Conferred by Institutions of Higher Education: 1978-79 Through 1988-89, 4844–17

Racial and Ethnic Comparison of Family Formation and Contraceptive Practices Among Low-Income Women, 4042–3.241

Racial and Gender Disparities in Services. Job Training Partnership Act, 26106–8.14

Racial Differences in Health and Health Care Service Utilization: The Effect of Socioeconomic Status, 2626–10.127

Radiation Exposures for DOE and DOE Contractor Employees, 1988: Twenty-first Annual Report, 3324–1

Radio and Television Receivers, Phonographs, and Related Equipment, 1990, Current Industrial Report, 2506–12.20

Radioactive Materials Released from Nuclear Power Plants, Annual Report, 1988, 9634–1

Radium Distribution Map and Radon Potential in the Bonneville Power Administration Service Area, 5668–114

Rail Safety Civil Penalty Cases Closed During FY90, 7604–10

Rail-Highway Crossing Accident/Incident and Inventory Bulletin, No. 12, 1989, 7604–2

Railroad Retirement and Unemployment Insurance Programs. Monthly Benefit Statistics, 9702–2

Railroad Retirement Board, Annual Report FY90, 9704–1

Railroad Safety: DOD Can Improve the Safety of On-Base Track and Equipment, 26113–535

Railroad Safety: Weaknesses Exist in FRA's Enforcement Program, 26113–515

Rainfall and Runoff Quantity and Quality Characteristics of Four Urban Land-Use Catchments in Fresno, Calif., October 1981-April 1983, 5666–27.2

Randolph-Sheppard Vending Facility Program: Annual Report, FY90, 4944–2

Rangewide Plan for Managing Habitat of Desert Bighorn Sheep on Public Lands, 5728–36

Ranitidine Hydrochloride: The Potential Impact on Domestic Competition in the Antiulcer Drug Market of a Temporary Duty Suspension on Imports. Report to the Senate Committee on Finance on Investigation No. 332-300 Under Section 332(g) of the Tariff Act of 1930, 9886–4.167

Ranking of Cities by Population, 2324–7

Rapid Rise in State Per Capita Income Inequality in the 1980's: Sources and Prospects, 1548–379

Rare-Earth Minerals and Metals: Minerals Yearbook, Volume 1, 1989, 5604–15.55

Rational Inflation and Real Internal Debt Bubbles in Argentina and Brazil?, 9379–12.75

RCWP Monthly Progress Report, By State and Area for Period Ending (Date), 1802–14

REA Financed Generating Plants, As of Jan. 1, 1991, 1244–6

Reaching Out Across America: Progress Report on the Homeless Chronically Mentally Ill Veterans Program, 8604–11

Reaction of Interest Rates to the Employment Report: The Role of Policy Anticipations, 9389–1.205

Reaction to Dairy Situation and Outlook, 1004–16.1

Real, Affordable Mortgage, 9373–1.204

Real and Personal Property, Sept. 30, 1990, 3544–6

Real Earnings, 6742–3

Real Estate Asset Inventory. Resolution Trust Corporation, 9722–2

Real Estate Cycle and the Economy: Consequences of the Massachusetts Boom of 1984-87, 9373–1.216

Reapportionment Will Shift 19 Seats in the U.S. House of Representatives. 1990 Census Population for the U.S. Is 249,632,692, 2328–22

Reasons for Closure: Applicants and Extended Evaluation Cases Not Accepted for Vocational Rehabilitation Services, 4944–11

Reasons for the Continuing Growth of Part-Time Employment, 6722–1.218

Reassessment of External Insulin Infusion Pumps. Health Technology Assessment Report, 1990, 4186–10.4

Re-Assessment of the Relationship Between Real Exchange Rates and Real Interest Rates: 1974-90, 9366–7.262

Reauthorization of the Motor Carrier Safety Assistance Program (MCSAP): Options Intended To Improve Highway Safety, 25268–78

Reauthorization of the Older Americans Act, 25248–126

Reauthorizing Programs of the Federal Aviation Administration (Future Airport Capacity Needs and Proposals To Meet Those Needs), 21648–59

Recent Behavior of the Experimental Monetary Aggregate, 9362–6

Recent Developments Affecting the Profitability of Commercial Banks, 9362–1.204

Recent HIV Seroprevalence Levels by Country, 2322–4

Recent Publications of the Department of Education, 4812–1

Recent Trends and Regional Variability in Underground Storage Activities, 3162–4.203

Recent Trends in Capital Formation, 9385–8.92

Recipient Housing in the Housing Voucher and Certificate Programs, 5186–14.4

Reclamation Reform Act of 1982: Annual Report to the Congress, 5824–13

Recommendations for Collection of Laboratory Specimens Associated with Outbreaks of Gastroenteritis, 4206–2.32

Recommendations for Preventing Transmission of Human Immunodeficiency Virus and Hepatitis B Virus to Patients During Exposure-Prone Invasive Procedures, 4206–2.44

Reconnaissance Investigation of Water Quality, Bottom Sediment, and Biota Associated with Irrigation Drainage in and near Stillwater Wildlife Management Area, Churchill County, Nevada, 1986-87, 5666–27.14

Reconnaissance Investigation of Water Quality, Bottom Sediment, and Biota Associated with Irrigation Drainage in the Klamath Basin, California and Oregon, 1988-89, 5666–27.21

Reconnaissance Investigation of Water Quality, Bottom Sediment, and Biota Associated with Irrigation Drainage in the Salton Sea Area, California, 1986-87, 5666–27.4

Reconsideration of the Problem of Social Cost: Free Riders and Monopolists, 9383–20.12

Record Number of Patent Applications in FY90, 2244–2

Recordkeeping Practices Survey, 1989, 2328–67

Recreation Futures for Colorado, 1989. Recreation 2000: A Strategic Plan by State, 5726–5.1

Recreation Use Report 1990, Servicewide by States, 1204–17

Recreation 2000: Strategic Plans for States, 5726–5

Recreational Shellfishing in the U.S., 2178–28

Redesigning Defense: Planning the Transition to the Future U.S. Defense Industrial Base, 26358–245

Redrawing the Poverty Line: Implications for Fighting Hunger and Poverty in America, 21968–56

Reducing Student Loan Defaults: A Plan for Action, 4808–35

Reference Guide on Rice Supply and Distribution for Individual Countries, 1925–2.6

Refined Antimony Trioxide from the People's Republic of China. Determination of the Commission in Investigation No. 731-TA-517 (Preliminary) Under the Tariff Act of 1930, Together with the Information Obtained in the Investigation, 9886–14.317

Index by Titles

Reflections on the Income Estimates from the Initial Panel of the Survey of Income and Program Participation (SIPP), 4746–26.8

Reforming Deposit Insurance When Banks Conduct Loan Workouts and Runs Are Possible, 9387–8.239

Refractories, 1990, Current Industrial Report, 2506–9.1

Refrigeration, Air-Conditioning, and Warm Air Heating Equipment, 1990, Current Industrial Report, 2506–12.7

Refugee Assistance: U.S. Contributions for the 1980s, 26123–334

Refugee Resettlement: Federal Support to the States Has Declined, 26121–402

Refugee Resettlement Program, Report to the Congress, 4694–5

Refund Offset Program Benefits Appear To Exceed Costs. Tax Policy, 26119–339

Region V Head Start: Program Data at a Glance, 4604–12

Regional Aquifer-System Analysis Program, 5666–25

Regional Assessment of Nonpoint-Source Pesticide Residues in Ground Water, San Joaquin Valley, Calif. Regional Aquifer-System Analysis, 5666–25.12

Regional Economic Conditions and the FOMC Votes of District Presidents, 9373–1.205

Regional Economic Digest, Tenth Federal Reserve District, 9381–16

Regional Perspective on the Credit View, 9377–1.206

Regional Review, Federal Reserve Bank of Boston, 9373–25

Regional Tide and Tidal Current Tables, 1992, New York Harbor to Chesapeake Bay, 2174–11

Regional Update, Federal Reserve Bank of Atlanta, 9371–14

Regionally Averaged Diameter Growth in New England Forests, 1208–349

Register of Copyrights 93rd Annual Report, for the Fiscal Year Ending Sept. 30, 1990, 26404–2

Register of Reporting Labor Organizations, 1990, 6468–17

Regulation and Endogenous Contestability, 9387–8.237

Regulation of Underground Petroleum Storage, 3162–6.203

Regulatory Actions Provide Uncertain Protection. Reproductive and Developmental Toxicants, 26131–90

Regulatory Program of the U.S. Government: Apr. 1, 1991-Mar. 31, 1992, 104–28

Rehabilitation Services Administration Annual Report on Federal Activities Related to the Administration of the Rehabilitation Act of 1973, as Amended, FY90, 4944–1

Reimbursement Policies Constrain Physicians in Their Choice of Cancer Therapies. Off-Label Drugs, 26131–81

Relationship Between K-ras Oncogene Activation and Smoking in Adenocarcinoma of the Human Lung, 4472–1.217

Relationships Between Annual Farm Prices and Ending Stocks of Rough Rice, 1561–8.202

Relative Importance of Components in the Consumer Price Indexes, 1990, 6884–1

Relative Price Variability and Inflation: Inter and Intracity Evidence from Brazil in the 1980's, 9379–14.14

Remarriage Among Women in the U.S.: 1985, 2546–2.157

Remote Sensing Data Acquisition, Analysis, and Archival, 2176–1.38

Renewable Energy Excursion: Supporting Analysis for the National Energy Strategy, 3166–6.50

Rental Housing: Implementing the New Federal Incentives To Deter Prepayments of HUD Mortgages, 26131–84

Report and Recommendations to the Congress, Mar. 1, 1991, 17204–1

Report of Mandays for the Month: Bureau of Prisons, 6242–1.4

Report of Railroad Employment, Class I Line-Haul Railroads, 9482–3

Report of the Advisory Committee on the Future of the U.S. Space Program, 9508–38

Report of the Clerk of the House, 21942–1

Report of the Eleventh NEFC Stock Assessment Workshop, Fall 1990, 2162–9

Report of the Epidemiology and Biostatistics Program, FY90, 4474–29

Report of the Forest Service, FY90, 1204–1

Report of the Interdepartment Radio Advisory Committee, Jan. 1-June 30, 1990, 2802–1

Report of the Merit Review Task Force, 9628–84

Report of the Monitored Retrievable Storage Review Commission. Nuclear Waste: Is There a Need for Federal Interim Storage?, 14818–1

Report of the President to the Congress on the Administration of the Federal Railroad Safety Act of 1970, 7604–12

Report of the Proceedings of the Judicial Conference of the U.S., Sept. 12, 1990, 18202–2

Report of the Proceedings of the Judicial Conference of the U.S., Mar. 12, 1991, 18202–2

Report of the Secretary of Agriculture, 1990, 1004–3

Report of the Secretary of Defense to the President and the Congress, 3544–2

Report of the Secretary of the Senate, From Apr. 1-Sept. 30, 1990, 25922–1

Report of the Secretary of the Senate, From Oct. 1, 1990-Mar. 31, 1991, 25922–1

Report of the Secretary of the Treasury on Government Sponsored Enterprises, 8004–15

Report of the Special Interagency Task Force on Western Lending to the Soviet Bloc, 25388–56

Report of the Subcommittee on Financial Institutions Supervision, Regulation and Insurance, Task Force on the International Competitiveness of U.S. Financial Institutions, 21248–153

Report of the Twelfth Northeast Regional Stock Assessment Workshop, Spring 1991, 2162–9

Report of the 1990 National Postsecondary Student Aid Study, 4846–5

Report of the 76th National Conference on Weights and Measures, 1991, 2214–7

Report of Water Masses Receiving Wastes from Ocean Dumping at the 106-Mile Dumpsite, Jan. 1-Dec. 31, 1990, 2164–20

Report on Allied Contributions to the Common Defense, A Report to the U.S. Congress, 3544–28

Report on Applications for Orders Authorizing or Approving the Interception of Wire, Oral,

Report to Congress on the...

or Electronic Communications (Wiretap Report) for the Period Jan. 1-Dec. 31, 1990, 18204–7

Report on Compliance with the Federal Managers' Financial Integrity Act, Department of Housing and Urban Development, 5004–9

Report on Drug or Alcohol Abuse Awareness Education or Rehabilitation Programs, 3802–6

Report on Evaluation of Compliance with On-Site Health and Safety Requirements at Hazardous Waste Incinerators, 6608–5

Report on Pre-Complaint Counseling and Complaint Processing by Federal Agencies for FY89, 9244–11

Report on Quality Changes for 1991 Model Passenger Cars, 6764–3

Report on Survey of U.S. Shipbuilding and Repair Facilities, 1990, 7704–9

Report on Tar, Nicotine, and Carbon Monoxide Content of the Smoke of 475 Varieties of Domestic Cigarettes, 9408–53

Report on the Diet and Health Knowledge Survey, 1004–16.1

Report on the Nation's Renewable Resources, 1208–24

Report on the Organized Crime Drug Enforcement Task Force Program, 1989-90, 6004–17

Report on the Quality of Surgical Care in the Department of Veterans Affairs: The Phase III Report to the Congress of the U.S. Under the Provisions of P.L. 99-166, Section 204, 8704–1

Report on the Western Hemisphere Energy Cooperation Study, 3408–1

Report on the 1987-88 Nationwide Food Consumption Survey, 1004–16.1

Report on U.S. Investment Strategies for Quality Assurance, 2218–84

Report to Congress: Endangered and Threatened Species Recovery Program, 5504–35

Report to Congress from the U.S. Office of Special Counsel, 9494–3

Report to Congress from the U.S. Office of Special Counsel, FY90, 9894–1

Report to Congress: Impact of State Regulation on the Package Express Industry, 7308–201

Report to Congress: Impact of the Changes in the End Stage Renal Disease Composite Rate, 4658–44

Report to Congress: Land and Water Conservation Fund Grants-in-Aid Program, FY90, 5544–18

Report to Congress on Alternative Methods for Funding Public Housing Modernization, 5188–127

Report to Congress on First-Year Operations Under the "Federal Employees Leave Sharing Act of 1988," P.L. 100-566, 9848–40

Report to Congress on Matters Contained in the Helium Act (Public Law 86-777), FY90, 5604–32

Report to Congress on Rent Control, 5188–130

Report to Congress on the Depreciation of Business-Use Light Trucks, 8006–5.6

Report to Congress on the Depreciation of Business-Use Passenger Cars, 8006–5.5

Report to Congress on the Effect of the Full Funding Limit on Pension Benefit Security, 8008–152

Report to Congress on the...

Index by Titles

Report to Congress on the Effects of the 65 mph Speed Limit Through 1989, 7764–15

Report to Congress on the Federal Home Loan Mortgage Corporation, 1989, 5184–8

Report to Congress on the Implementation of the Age Discrimination Act of 1975 During FY90, As Required by Section 308(b) of the Age Discrimination Act of 1975, as Amended, 4004–27

Report to Congress on Voting Practices in the United Nations, 1990, 7004–18

Report to Congress, Programs and Activities Authorized by Education for Homeless Children and Youth Program, FY90, 4804–35

Report to Congress: Progress of Research on Outcomes of Health Care Services and Procedures, 4188–70

Report to Investors of the Farm Credit System, 1990, 9264–5

Report to the Congress and the Trade Policy Committee on Trade Between the U.S. and the Nonmarket Economy Countries, 9882–2

Report to the Congress of the U.S., Utilization and Donation of Federal Personal Property, FY88-90, 9454–22

Report to the Congress on International Economic and Exchange Rate Policy, 8002–14

Report to the Congress on National Defense Stockpile Requirements, 1991, 3544–37

Report to the Congress on Property and Casualty Insurance Company Taxation, 8008–151

Report to the Congress on the Runaway and Homeless Youth Program, 4604–3

Report to the President on Investigations Under Section 22 of the Agricultural Adjustment Act, As Amended, 9886–10

Report to the Senate and House Committees on the Budget, 26304–3

Report: 1990 Survey of Health Occupational Staff, 8604–8

Reported Net Undercount Obscured Magnitude of Error. 1990 Census, 26119–353

Reporting of Communicable Diseases by University Physicians, 4042–3.252

Reports Concerning Significant Actions of the Office of Personnel Management, 9496–2

Reports of the Office of the Inspector General, Department of Energy, 3006–5

Reports of the Proceedings of the Judicial Conference of the U.S., Held in Washington, D.C., Mar. 13, 1990 and Sept. 12, 1990; Annual Report of the Director of the Administrative Office of the U.S. Courts, 1990, 18204–8

Reports to Congress on Depreciable Assets, 8006–5

Reports to Congress: Physician Payment Review Commission, 17266–1

Reports to Congress: Prospective Payment Assessment Commission, 17206–1

Reports to the Congress Required by the Fair Labor Standards Act, 6504–2

Representative Expenditures: Addressing the Neglected Dimension of Fiscal Capacity, 10048–77

Representative U.S. Corn Farms, 1987, 1568–304

Reproductive and Developmental Toxicants: Regulatory Actions Provide Uncertain Protection, 26131–90

Reputation Acquisition, Collateral, and Moral Hazard in Debt Markets, 9387–8.244

Reputation with Multiple Relationships: Reviving Reputation Models of Debt, 9383–20.7

Requiring Formal Training in Preventive Health Practices for Child Day Care Providers, 4042–3.243

Research Agenda for Primary Care: Summary Report of a Conference, 4188–69

Research and Evaluation Report Series, 6406–10

Research in Action, 6066–26

Research Library Trends II: 35 Libraries in the 1970's and Beyond, 4468–4

Research Library Trends, 1951-80 and Beyond: An Update of Purdue's "Past and Likely Future of 58 Research Libraries", 4468–4

Research Papers, Federal Reserve Bank of Dallas, 9379–12

Research Papers, Federal Reserve Bank of New York, 9385–8

Research Proposal and Award Activities by Predominantly Undergraduate Institutions, FY88, 9628–85

Research Reports: Federal Reserve Bank of Boston, 9373–4

Research Working Papers, Federal Reserve Bank of Kansas City, 9381–10

Reserve Component Programs, FY90: Annual Report of the Reserve Forces Policy Board, 3544–31

Reserve Components: Factors Related to Personnel Attrition in the Selected Reserve, 26123–329

Reserve Officers' Training Corps: Less Need for Officers Provides Opportunity for Significant Savings, 26123–337

Residential Energy Uses. Statistical Brief, 2326–17.34

Residential Treatment Centers and Other Organized Mental Health Care for Children and Youth: U.S., 1988, 4506–3.44

Residual Effects of Abused Drugs on Behavior, 4498–69

Resolution Costs of Thrift Failures, 9292–4.202

Resolution Trust Corporation News Release, 9722–1

Resolution Trust Corporation Quarterly Performance Data, 9722–5

Resolution Trust Corporation Real Estate Asset Inventory, 9722–2

Resolution Trust Corporation Semiannual Report, Apr. 1-Sept. 30, 1990, 9722–6

Resolution Trust Corporation Semiannual Report, Oct. 1, 1990-Mar. 31, 1991, 9722–6

Resolution Trust Corporation Semiannual Report, Apr. 1-Sept. 30, 1991, 9722–6

Resolution Trust Corporation, 1989 Annual Report, 9724–1

Resolution Trust Corporation's Compliance as of (Date). Obligations Limitation, 26102–6

Resource Limitations Affect Condition of Forest Service Recreation Sites. Parks and Recreation, 26113–502

Respiratory Diseases. Indian Health Conditions, 4088–2

Response and Procedural Error Variance in Surveys: An Application of Poisson and Neyman Type A Regression, 2626–10.124

Response Capability During Civil Air Carrier Inflight Medical Emergencies, 7506–10.82

Response of Brant and Other Geese to Aircraft Disturbances at Izembek Lagoon, Alaska, 5738–23

Response of the Habitat and Biota of the Inner New York Bight to Abatement of Sewage Sludge Dumping, Third Annual Progress Report, 1989, 2164–19

Resting Pulse Rate of Children and Young Adults Associated with Blood Pressure and Other Cardiovascular Risk Factors, 4042–3.232

Restructuring Health Insurance for Medicare Enrollees, 26306–6.159

Results of Note and Bond Auctions, 8002–7.3

Results of the Preliminary Radiological Survey at the Former Diamond Magnesium Company Site, Luckey, Ohio (DML001), 3006–9.8

Results of the Radiological Survey at 6 Hancock Street, Lodi, N.J. (LJ033), 3006–9.13

Results of the Radiological Survey at 79 Avenue B, Lodi, N.J. (LJ091), 3006–9.9

Results of the Radiological Survey at 90 C Avenue, Lodi, N.J. (LJ079), 3006–9.14

Results of the Radiological Survey at 113 Avenue E, Lodi, N.J. (LJ081), 3006–9.12

Results of the Radiological Survey at 160 Essex Street, Lodi, N.J. (LJ072), 3006–9.11

Results of the Radiological Survey at 174 Essex Street, Lodi, N.J. (LJ073), 3006–9.10

Results of Treasury's [ ]-Day Bill Auction, 8002–7.4

Results of Treasury's Weekly Bill Auctions, 8002–7.1

Results of Treasury's 52-Week Bill Auction, 8002–7.2

Retail Sales Reflect Economic Trends. Statistical Brief, 2326–17.29

Retail Trade, 1989. Annual Sales, Year-End Inventories, Purchases, Gross Margin, and Accounts Receivable, by Kind of Retail Store. Current Business Reports, 2413–5

Retirement Center Bonds Were Risky and Benefited Moderate-Income Elderly. Tax-Exempt Bonds, 26119–328

Return to Profitability: The Performance of Eleventh District Commercial Banks, 9379–1.206

Returns to Cash Rented Farmland and Common Stock, 1940-90, 1561–16.202

Revenue, Pieces and Weight by Classes of Mail and Special Services, 9862–1

Revenue Sources, Uses, and Spending Controls. Highway Trust Fund, 26113–544

Revenues Grow, but Net Income Slumps for Nation's Largest Cooperatives, 1122–1.207

Review Effect on Cost Reports: Impact Smaller than Anticipated, 4652–1.233

Review, Federal Reserve Bank of St. Louis, 9391–1

Review, Fourth District, Federal Home Loan Bank of Atlanta, 9302–2

Review of Corporate Restructuring Activity, 1980-90, 9366–1.161

Review of Final Coverage Improvement Programs and Other Census Operations, 21628–95

Review of Fluoride Benefits and Risks. Report of the Ad Hoc Subcommittee on Fluoride of the Committee To Coordinate Environmental Health and Related Programs, 4048–36

Index by Titles

Review of Internal Revenue Service's Accounts Receivable Inventory, 21788–200

Review of Pretreatment Programs in the Great Lakes Basin, 14648–24

Review of Programs Involving College Students as Tutors or Mentors in Grades K-12, 4808–23

Review of the Implementation of Section 318 of the 1990 Interior Appropriations Act (Old-Growth Forests of the Pacific Northwest), 21168–47

Review of the National Workplace Literacy Program, 4808–37

Review of the South Pacific Tuna Baitfisheries: Small Pelagic Fisheries Associated with Coral Reefs, 2162–1.201

Review of the Use of Food Stamps in Farmers' Markets, 21168–46

Review of 1990 Census Preparations in the Commonwealth of Pennsylvania, 21628–87

Reviewing the Status of Census Operations, 21628–86

Revised Monthly Retail Sales and Inventories: Jan. 1981-Dec. 1990, 2413–3

Revised Monthly Wholesale Trade: Sales and Inventories, 1984-90, Current Business Report, 2413–7

Revision of Seasonally Adjusted Labor Force Series, 6742–2.201

Revision of the U.S. Standard Certificates and Reports, 1989. Vital and Health Statistics Series 4, 4147–4.27

Revisions in Consumption Factors for Pork Consumption Series, 1561–7.201

Rice Market News, 1313–8

Rice Situation and Outlook Report, 1561–8

Rice Situation and Outlook Yearbook, 1561–8

Rice Stocks, 1621–7

Rice, Summary of 1990 Support Program and Related Information: ASCS Commodity Fact Sheet, 1806–4.6

Riparian-Wetland Initiative for the 1990's. Riparian-Wetland Management Strategies, 5726–8.1

Riparian-Wetland Management Strategies, 5726–8

Rise in U.S. Corporate Leveraging in the 1980s, 9385–8.88

Rising Cost of Medical Care and Its Effect on Inflation, 9381–1.212

Rising Demand for Horticultural Products, 1004–16.1

Rising Health Care Costs: Causes, Implications, and Strategies, 26306–6.155

Risk and Failure Among Newly Established Texas Banks, 9379–14.10

Risk Assessment Forum, 9186–9

Risk Aversion Through Nontraditional Export Promotion Programs in Central America, 1528–312

Risk of Bilateral Testicular Germ Cell Cancer in Denmark: 1960-84, 4472–1.225

Risk Premium and the Liquidity Premium in Foreign Exchange Markets, 9381–10.118

Risk Premium in Forward Foreign Exchange Markets and G-3 Central Bank Intervention: Evidence of Daily Effects, 1985-90, 9377–9.118

Risk-Based Capital and Deposit Insurance Reform, 9377–9.109

Robert S. Vance Federal Building, Birmingham, Ala. (H.R. 3961), Federal Courthouse Space and Construction Needs (H.R. 4178), 21648–60

Rocky Mountain Juniper Woodlands: Year-Round Avian Habitat, 1208–364

Rocky Mountain Region Forest Pest Conditions, 1989, 1206–11.1

Rocky Mountain Region Forest Pest Conditions, 1990, 1206–11.3

ROD Annual Report, FY89, 9214–5

Role and Effects of the Capper-Volstead Antitrust Exemption. Dairy Cooperatives, 26113–499

Role of Assistive Technology in Promoting Return to Work for People with Disabilities: The U.S. and Swedish Systems, 4742–1.215

Role of Energy in Real Business Cycle Models, 9375–13.57

Role of Functional Form in Estimating the Effect of a Cash-Only Food Stamp Program, 1502–3.203

Role of Services in New England's Rise and Fall: Engine of Growth or Along for the Ride?, 9373–1.212

Role of the Elderly's Income in Rural Development, 1598–268

Role of Workers' Compensation in Developing Safer Workplaces, 6722–1.243

Rotorcraft Activity Survey, 7508–75

Rounding Errors and Index Numbers, 9375–1.206

RTC Inventory of High Yield Securities, 9722–4

RTC Review, 9722–3

Rubber Mechanical Goods, 1990, Current Industrial Report, 2506–8.17

Rubella Prevention: Recommendations of the Immunization Practices Advisory Committee (ACIP), 4206–2.33

Rules of Origin Issues Related to NAFTA and the North American Automotive Industry. Report to the Committee on Ways and Means, U.S. House of Representatives, on Investigation No. 332-314 Under Section 332 of the Tariff Act of 1930, 9886–4.178

Rum: Annual Report (Covering 1989 and 1990) on Selected Economic Indicators, 9884–15

Runaway and Homeless Youth Program: Annual Report to the Congress, 4604–3

Runaways in Juvenile Courts, 6066–27.4

Rural Clean Water Program (RCWP) Monthly Progress Report, By State and Area for Period Ending (Date), 1802–14

Rural Conditions and Trends, 1502–8

Rural Counties Lead Urban in Education Spending, but Is That Enough?, 1502–7.201

Rural Development Perspectives, 1502–7

Rural Drug Abuse: Prevalence, Relation to Crime, and Programs, 26131–79

Rural Electric Borrowers, 1990 Statistical Report, 1244–1

Rural Electrification Program: Fiscal Year Statistical Summary, 1244–7

Rural Health Care Crisis, 25368–176

Rural Health Care Transition Grant Program, 4658–58

Rural Hospitals: Factors That Affect Risk of Closure, 26121–392

Rural Hospitals: Federal Efforts Should Target Areas Where Closures Would Threaten Access to Care, 26121–409

Rural Hospitals Under Medicare's Prospective Payment System, 17206–1.12

Rural Housing, 21248–143

Rural Telephone Bank 18th Annual Report of the Board of Directors, FY89, 1244–4

Rural Telephone Borrowers, 1990 Statistical Report, 1244–2

Rural Telephone Program: Fiscal Year Statistical Summary, 1244–8

Rye, Summary of 1990 Support Program and Related Information: ASCS Commodity Fact Sheet, 1806–4.1

Rye, Summary of 1991 Support Program and Related Information: ASCS Commodity Fact Sheet, 1806–4.12

Schedule B, Statistical...

Safe Disposal of Radionuclides in Low-Level Radioactive-Waste Repository Sites: Low-Level Radioactive-Waste Disposal Workshop, U.S.G.S., July 11-16, 1987, Big Bear Lake, Calif., Proceedings, 5668–116

Safety Recall Campaigns, 7762–12

Safety Related Recall Campaigns for Motor Vehicles and Motor Vehicle Equipment, Including Tires, 7762–2

Saint Lawrence Seaway Development Corporation, 1989 Annual Report, 7744–1

Salaries of Full-Time Instructional Faculty on 9- and 10-Month Contracts in Institutions of Higher Education, 1979-80 Through 1989-90, 4844–8

Salary and Wage Statistics, Full-Time Employment in Non-Postal Agencies, Mar. 31, 1991, 9842–1.205

Sale of Single Family Housing Inventory, 1182–7

Sales of Farm Inventory Properties. Farmers Home Administration, 26113–514

Salmon Culture in the Faroe Islands, 2162–1.201

Salt: Minerals Yearbook, Volume 1, 1989, 5604–15.56

Sample Design of the 1987 Household Survey. National Medical Expenditure Survey, 4186–8.21

San Andreas Fault System, California, 5668–123

Sand and Gravel: Minerals Yearbook, Volume 1, 1989, 5604–15.57

Sandhill Crane Harvest and Hunter Activity in the Central Flyway During the 1990-91 Hunting Season, 5504–31

Sandia National Laboratories' Final Technical Report. U.S.S. Iowa Explosion, 26123–315

Sanitation Inspections of International Cruise Ships, Summary, 4202–10

SAR Statistics, 1989, U.S. Coast Guard, 7404–2

SAR Statistics, 1990, U.S. Coast Guard, 7404–2

Satellite Situation Report, 9502–2

Saving Effect of Tax-Deferred Retirement Accounts: Evidence from the SIPP, 2626–10.132

Savings and Home Financing Source Book, 1989, 8434–3

Savings and Loan Prosecution Update, 6008–33

Savings Bank Highlights, 9292–5

Savings Estimate for a Medicare Insured Group, 4652–1.244

Savings in Medicaid Costs for Newborns and Their Mothers from Prenatal Participation in the WIC Program, 1368–2

Scale Elasticity and Efficiency for U.S. Banks, 9375–13.66

Schedule B, Statistical Classification of Domestic and Foreign Commodities Exported from the U.S.: 1990. U.S. Foreign Trade, 2428–5

Schedule C, Index by Titles

Schedule C, Classification of Country and Territory Designations for U.S. Foreign Trade Statistics, 2428–3

Schedule C, Classification of Country and Territory Designations for U.S. Foreign Trade Statistics: Jan. 1, 1991, 2428–3.1

Schedule K, Classification of Foreign Ports by Geographic Trade Area and Country: 1991, 2428–12

School Enrollment—Social and Economic Characteristics of Students: October 1989, 2546–1.453

Schools and Hospitals Program Cycle XII Grants Data: Grants Award Listing, Mar. 19, 1991. Conservation and Renewable Energy, 3304–15

Schools and Staffing Survey, 4836–3

Schools and Staffing Survey: 1988 Schools and Staffing Survey Sample Design and Estimation, 4836–3.4

Science and Engineering Degrees: 1966-89, A Source Book, 9627–33

Science and Engineering Doctorates: 1960-90, 9627–30

Science Resources Studies Highlights, 9626–2

Science-Driven Solutions to Food Safety Dilemmas: A Progress Report, 1004–16.1

Scientific Assessment of Stratospheric Ozone, 1989, 9508–37, 21704–1

Scientific Solutions to Food Safety Dilemmas: A Progress Report, 1004–16.1

Scientists and Engineers in Canada and Sweden, 2326–18.63

Scientists and Engineers in Industrialized Societies: An Update for France, West Germany, and the UK, 2326–18.62

Scientists and Engineers in Malaysia, South Korea, and Taiwan, 2326–18.61

Scope Economies: Fixed Costs, Complementarity, and Functional Form, 9389–19.28

Sea Otter (Enhydra lutris): Behavior, Ecology, and Natural History, 5508–109

Sea Otter Symposium: Proceedings of a Symposium To Evaluate the Response Effort on Behalf of Sea Otters After the T/V Exxon Valdez Oil Spill into Prince William Sound, Anchorage, Alaska, 17-19 April 1990, 5508–110

Sea Scallop, Goosefish Landings Set New Records, 2162–1.203

Seam Effect in Panel Surveys, 2626–10.119

Searching for Answers, Annual Report on Drugs and Crime: 1990, 6064–32

SEAS III and Beyond, 2152–8.203

Second Summary of Data on Chemical Contaminants in Sediments from the National Status and Trends Program, 2176–3.13

Secondary Market Prices and Yields and Interest Rates for Home Loans, 5142–20

Secondary Mortgage Market: Information on Underwriting and Home Loans in the Atlanta Area, 26113–500

Secretary of the Army's Report on Civil Works Activities, 3754–1

Secretary of the Army's Report on Civil Works Activities, FY88: Volume 1, 3754–1.1

Secretary's Semiannual Report to the Congress: For the Six Month Period Oct. 1, 1990-Mar. 31, 1991, Pursuant to Section 106 of Public Law 100-504, 5002–11

Secretary's Semiannual Report to the Congress: For the Six Month Period Apr. 1-Sept. 30, 1991, Pursuant to Section 106 of Public Law 100-504, 5002–11

Secretary's Task Force on Competition in the U.S. Domestic Airline Industry, 7308–199

Securities Industry: Strengthening Sales Practice Oversight, 26119–336

Security Assistance, FY92 Congressional Presentation, 7144–13

Sediment-Source Data for Four Basins Tributary to Lake Tahoe, California and Nevada, August 1983-June 1988, 5666–27.12

SEE Directory of Awards, FY89. Directorate for Science and Engineering Education, 9624–27

Seignorage as a Tax: A Quantitative Evaluation, 9383–20.2

Selected Apparel, Current Industrial Report, 2506–6.12

Selected Bibliography on Urbanization in China, 2326–18.60

Selected Borrowings in Immediately Available Funds of Large Member Banks, 9365–1

Selected Compensation and Pension Data, By State of Residence, FY89, 8604–7

Selected Highway Statistics and Charts, 1989, 7554–24

Selected Industrial Air Pollution Control Equipment, 1990, Current Industrial Report, 2506–12.5

Selected Instruments and Related Products, 1989, Current Industrial Report, 2506–12.26

Selected Interest and Exchange Rates: Weekly Series of Charts; and Foreign Exchange Rates, 9365–1.5

Selected Interest Rates, 9365–1, 9365–2.14

Selected Manpower Statistics, FY90, 3544–1

Selected Occupational Fatalities as Found in Reports of OSHA Fatality/Catastrophe Investigations, 6606–2

Selected Occupational Fatalities Related to Vehicle-Mounted Elevating and Rotating Work Platforms as Found in Reports of OSHA Fatality/Catastrophe Investigations, 6606–2.17

Selected Options for Expanding Health Insurance Coverage, 26306–6.157

Selected Publications of the U.S. International Trade Commission, Through December 1990, 9884–12

Selected Spending and Revenue Options, 26306–3.118

Selected Visitor and Cost Data. National Park Service, 26113–545

Selection Criteria for Alcohol Detection Methods, 7506–10.91

Selection of Air Traffic Controllers: Complexity, Requirements, and Public Interest, 7506–10.88

Selection of Air Traffic Controllers for Automated Systems: Applications from Current Research, 7506–10.79

Selective Service System, Annual Report of the Director to the Congress of the U.S., 9744–1

Selenium and Tellurium in 1990: Mineral Industry Surveys Annual Review, 5614–5.25

Self-Employment and the Earnings of Male Immigrants in the U.S., 9385–8.101

Semiannual Appearance of the Resolution Trust Corporation Oversight Board, 21242–1

Semi-Annual Canned Pineapple Situation in Thailand and the Philippines, 1925–34.243

Semiannual NASA Management Report on the Status of Audit Followup, as of Mar. 31, 1990, 21704–1

Semiannual Procurement Report: NASA, 9502–6

Semiannual Report and Appearance by the Oversight Board of the Resolution Trust Corporation, 21242–1

Semiannual Report of the AID Office of Population Subproject Assistance, August 1991, 9914–13.5

Semiannual Report of the Architect of the Capitol, For the Period Apr. 1-Sept. 30, 1990, 25922–2

Semiannual Report of the Architect of the Capitol, For the Period Oct. 1, 1990-Mar. 31, 1991, 25922–2

Semiannual Report of the Inspector General, U.S. Small Business Administration, Covering the Period Apr. 1-Sept. 30, 1990, 9762–5

Semiannual Report of the Inspector General, U.S. Small Business Administration, Covering the Period Oct. 1, 1990-Mar. 31, 1991, 9762–5

Semiannual Report, Office of Inspector General, U.S. Department of Labor, 6302–2

Semiannual Report to Congress on Inspector General Audit Reports, Department of Energy, 3002–15

Semiannual Report to Congress on the Effectiveness of the Civil Aviation Security Program, July 1-Dec. 31, 1989, 7502–5

Semiannual Report to the Congress, VA Office of Inspector General, Apr. 1-Sept. 30, 1991, 8602–1

Semiconductors, Printed Circuit Boards, and Other Electronic Components, 1990, Current Industrial Report, 2506–12.36

Seminar on Quality of Federal Data, 106–4.14

Senate Campaigns, 1992, Spend Over $10 Million, Mid-Year Reports Show, 9276–1.93

Sentencing Guidelines and Policy Statements, 17668–1

Series EE and HH Savings Bonds, Statistical Summary, 8442–1

Serum Selenium Level in Relation to In Situ Cervical Cancer in Australia, 4472–1.203

Service Annual Survey, 1990, Current Business Reports, 2413–8

Service in Vietnam and Risk of Testicular Cancer, 4472–1.228

Service Reports, 3166–6

Servicemen's and Veterans' Group Life Insurance Programs, Twenty-sixth Annual Report, Year Ending June 30, 1991, 8654–1

Seventeenth Annual Report of the Diabetes Mellitus Interagency Coordinating Committee, FY90, 4474–34

Several States May Not Meet Federal Insurance Program Objectives. Coal Mine Subsidence, 26113–530

Sexually Transmitted Disease Statistics, 4204–14

Sexually Transmitted Disease Surveillance, 1989, 4205–42

Sexually Transmitted Disease Surveillance, 1990, 4205–42

Shadyside, Ohio, Flash Floods, June 14, 1990. Natural Disaster Survey Report, 2186–6.2

Index by Titles

SOI Bulletin

Share of Top 100 Earnings Used To Strengthen Member Ownership, 1122–1.210

Shared Training: Learning from Germany, 6722–1.220

Sharing of Specialized Medical Resources, FY90, Secretary of Veterans Affairs Annual Report Pursuant to the Provisions of 38 U.S.C. Section 5053(e), 8704–5

Shark Tagger, 1990 Summary, 2164–21

Sheep and Goat Predator Loss, 1618–20

Sheep and Goats, 1623–4

Sheet Piling from Canada. Determination of the Commission in Investigation No. 731-TA-52 (Final) Under the Tariff Act of 1930, Together with the Information Obtained in the Investigation, 9886–14.311

Sheets, Pillowcases, and Towels, Current Industrial Report, 2506–6.6

Shifting Composition of U.S. Manufactured Goods Trade, 9385–1.205

Shigellosis from Swimming in a Park Pond in Michigan, 4042–3.224

Ship Maintenance: The Navy's Fleet Modernization Program, 26123–320

Shipboard Acoustic Doppler Current Profiler Data Collected During the Subtropical Atlantic Climate Studies (STACS) Project (1983-86), 2146–7.8

Shop Towels from Bangladesh. Determination of the Commission in Investigation No. 731-TA-514 (Preliminary) Under the Tariff Act of 1930, Together with the Information Obtained in the Investigation, 9886–14.310

Shortages of Scientists and Engineers Due to Retirements Unlikely in the 1990s. NASA Personnel, 26123–348

Short-Range Actuarial Projections of the Old-Age, Survivors, and Disability Insurance Program, 1991, 4706–1.105

Short-Run Costs of Disinflation, 9387–8.247

Short-Selling Activity in the Stock Market: The Effects on Small Companies and the Need for Regulation, 21408–122

Short-Term Energy Outlook: Quarterly Projections, 3162–34

Should Government Spending on Capital Goods Be Raised?, 9391–1.208

Significant Features of Fiscal Federalism, 1991 Edition, 10044–1

Significant Incidents of Political Violence Against Americans, 1989, 7004–22

Significant Incidents of Political Violence Against Americans, 1990, 7004–22

Significant Provisions of State Unemployment Insurance Laws, Jan. 6, 1991, 6402–7

Significant Savings but Some Service Quality and Operational Problems. Social Security Downsizing, 26121–415

Silent Killer—Hypothermia, 2152–8.204

Silicon Metal from Argentina. Determination of the Commission in Investigation No. 731-TA-470 (Final) Under the Tariff Act of 1930, Together with the Information Obtained in the Investigation, 9886–14.330

Silicon Metal from Brazil. Determination of the Commission in Investigation No. 731-TA-471 (Final) Under the Tariff Act of 1930, Together with the Information Obtained in the Investigation, 9886–14.321

Silicon Metal from the People's Republic of China. Determination of the Commission in Investigation No. 731-TA-472 (Final) Under the Tariff Act of 1930, Together with the Information Obtained in the Investigation, 9886–14.314

Silicon: Mineral Industry Surveys, 5612–1.34

Silicon: Minerals Yearbook, Volume 1, 1989, 5604–15.58

Silver and Gold: Mineral Industry Surveys, 5612–1.10

Silver: Minerals Yearbook, Volume 1, 1989, 5604–15.59

Simple Estimator of Cointegrating Vectors in Higher Order Integrated Systems, 9375–13.54

Simple Model of Bank Loan Commitments and Monetary Policy, 9385–8.76

Simulation of Rainfall-Runoff Response in Mined and Unmined Watersheds in Coal Areas of West Virginia, 5666–27.1

Singapore: A Growing Market for Fresh Temperate Fruit, 1925–34.229

Single Equation Approach to Estimating Nonstationary Markov Matrices: The Case of U.S. Agriculture, 1974-78, 1548–374

Singular Fact: The Single Audit Program Works, 10042–1.204

SIPP Event History Calendar: Aiding Respondents in the Dating of Longitudinal Processes, 2626–10.135

SIPP Record Check Results: Implications for Measurement Principles and Practice, 2626–10.129

Sixteenth Annual FAA Aviation Forecast Conference Proceedings. Domestic Aviation: Future Challenges, 7504–28

Size and Geographics of U.S. Turkey Growout Operations, 1561–7.202

Slag—Iron and Steel: Minerals Yearbook, Volume 1, 1989, 5604–15.36

Small Business: Information on and Improvements Needed to Surety Bond Guarantee Programs, 26113–526

Small Disadvantaged Businesses Seldom Receive Contracts. GSA Travel Services, 26119–331

Small Farmers Weathered 1980's Financial Stress Better than Large Farmers, 1502–7.202

Small Mammals of a Beaver Pond Ecosystem and Adjacent Riparian Habitat in Idaho, 1208–377

Smoking Initiation in the U.S.: A Role for Worksite and College Smoking Bans, 4472–1.216

Smoking, Tobacco, and Cancer Program, 1985-89 Status Report, 4478–195

Smoking-Attributable Cancer Mortality in 1991: Is Lung Cancer Now the Leading Cause of Death Among Smokers in the U.S.?, 4472–1.219

Snake River Birds of Prey Research Project Annual Report, 1990, 5724–14

Snow Surveys for Alaska, 1266–2.1

Social and Economic Studies, Alaska OCS Region, 5736–5

Social Health Maintenance Organizations' Service Use and Costs, 1985-89, 4652–1.235

Social Security Administration 1991 Annual Report to the Congress, 4704–6

Social Security Administration's 800 Number Telephone Service, 21788–199

Social Security: Analysis of a Proposal To Privatize Trust Fund Reserves, 26121–397

Social Security Bulletin, 4742–1

Social Security Bulletin, Annual Statistical Supplement, 1990, 4744–3

Social Security Downsizing: Significant Savings but Some Service Quality and Operational Problems, 26121–415

Social Security for State-Sector Workers in the PRC: The Reform Decade and Beyond, 4742–1.218

Social Security: Information About the Accuracy of Earnings Records, 26121–422

Social Security: Production Initiatives in OHA's Region V Comply with Law and Guidelines, 26121–398

Social Security Programs in the U.S., 4742–1.217

Social Security Tax Cut, 25368–171

Social Security Technical Panel Report to the 1991 Advisory Council on Social Security: Appendices, 4742–1.201

Social Security: Telephone Access to Local Field Offices, 26121–434

Sociodemographic and Health Characteristics of Persons by Private Health Insurance Coverage and Type of Plan: U.S., 1975, 4147–16.4

Socioeconomic Factors and Cancer Incidence Among Blacks and Whites, 4472–1.210

Socioeconomic Profile of Recreationists at Public Outdoor Recreation Sites in Coastal Areas: Volume 1. Public Area Recreation Visitors Survey, 2176–9.1

Socioeconomic Profile of Recreationists at Public Outdoor Recreation Sites in Coastal Areas: Volume 2. Public Area Recreation Visitors Survey, 2176–9.2

Socioeconomic Profile of Recreationists at Public Outdoor Recreation Sites in Coastal Areas: Volume 3. Public Area Recreation Visitors Survey, 2176–9.3

Socioeconomic Profile of Recreationists at Public Outdoor Recreation Sites in Coastal Areas: Volume 4. Public Area Recreation Visitors Survey, 2176–9.4

Socioeconomic Profile of Recreationists at Public Outdoor Recreation Sites in Coastal Areas: Volume 5. Public Area Recreation Visitors Survey, 2176–9.5

Socioeconomic Profile of Recreationists at Public Outdoor Recreation Sites in Coastal Areas: Volume 6. Public Area Recreation Visitors Survey, 2176–9.7

SOD/SWAMP Cumulative Data Report, 1802–18

Soda Ash and Sodium Sulfate: Mineral Industry Surveys, 5612–1.33

Soda Ash and Sodium Sulfate: Minerals Yearbook, Volume 1, 5604–15.77, 5604–20.54

Soda Ash: Minerals Yearbook, Volume 1, 1989, 5604–15.77

Sodium Sulfate: Minerals Yearbook, Volume 1, 1990, 5604–20.54

Sodium Thiosulfate from the Federal Republic of Germany, the People's Republic of China, and the UK. Determinations of the Commission in Investigations Nos. 731-TA-465, 466, and 468 (Final) Under the Tariff Act of 1930, Together with the Information Obtained in the Investigations, 9886–14.305

Softwood Lumber from Canada. Determination of the Commission in Investigation No. 701-TA-312 (Preliminary) Under Section 703(a) of the Tariff Act of 1930, Together with the Information Obtained in the Investigation, 9886–15.78

Softwood Plywood, Current Industrial Report, 2506–7.2

SOI Bulletin, 8302–2

Soil and Water Conditions and Trends, 1266–5

Soil-Vegetation Correlations in Selected Wetlands and Uplands of North-central Florida, 5506–10.11

Soil-Vegetation Correlations in the Connecticut River Floodplain of Western Massachusetts, 5506–10.12

Soil-Vegetation Correlations in Wetlands and Riparian Areas, 5506–10

Solar Collector Manufacturing Activity, 1989, 3164–62

Sole Proprietorship Returns, 1989, 8302–2.214

Solid Waste: Trade-offs Involved in Beverage Container Deposit Legislation, 26113–494

Solvent Recycling Industry: Preliminary Data Summary, 9206–4.9

Some Evidence on the Impact of Quasi-Fixed Inputs on Bank Scale Economy Estimates, 9371–1.208

Some Issues in Corporate Leveraging: An Overview Essay, 9385–8.88

Some Personality Characteristics of Air Traffic Control Specialist Trainees: Interactions of Personality and Aptitude Test Scores with FAA Academy Success and Career Expectations, 7506–10.87

Some Problems of Infinite Regress in Social-Choice Models: A Category Theory Solution, 9377–9.106

Some Problems with Identification in Parametric Models, 9366–6.258

Sound Medical Evidence: Key to FECA Claims, 6722–1.244

Source Book, Statistics of Income 1988: Corporation Income Tax Returns with Accounting Periods Ended July 1988-June 1989, 8304–21

Source, Extent, and Degradation of Herbicides in a Shallow Aquifer Near Hesston, Kansas, 5666–28.13

Sourcebook of Criminal Justice Statistics, 1990, 6064–6

Sources and Concentrations of Dissolved Solids and Selenium in the San Joaquin River and Its Tributaries, California, October 1985-March 1987, 5666–27.5

Sources of Fluctuations in Long-Term Expected Real Rates of Interest: Evidence from the UK Indexed Bond Market, 9385–8.119

Sources of Revisions to the USDA Income Accounts, 1541–1.202

Sourcing Externalities, 9366–6.267

Southeast Regional Economic Report, Federal Home Loan Bank of Atlanta, 9302–36

Southeast Regional Reports, 6946–1

Southeastern Economy in 1990, 6944–2

Southeastern Interstate Banking and Consolidation: 1984-89, 9371–1.203

Southeastern Power Administration, Annual Report, 1990, 3234–1

Southeastern Regional Office Press Releases, 6946–3

Southern Pulpwood Production, 1988, 1204–23

Southern Pulpwood Production, 1989, 1204–23

Southwest Asia: Cost of Protecting U.S. Interests, 26123–360

Southwest Statistical Summary, 6962–2

Southwestern Power Administration: 1990 Annual Report, 3244–1

Soviet Agriculture and the Outlook for Soviet Purchases of Grain and Oilseeds, 21168–49

Soviet Agriculture System, 1004–16.1

Soviet Economy: Assessment of How Well the CIA Has Estimated the Size of the Economy, 26123–365

Soviet Energy: U.S. Attempts To Aid Oil Production Are Hindered by Many Obstacles, 26123–349

Soviet Military Power, 3504–20

Soviet-American Sail, 1990, 2152–8.202

Space Activities of the U.S., Soviet Union and Other Launching Countries/Organizations, 1957-90, 21704–4

Space Operations: NASA Is Not Archiving All Potentially Valuable Data, 21704–1, 26125–43

Space Station Freedom Capital Development Plan, FY91, 21704–1

Spanish Market for Squid, 2162–1.203

Sparklers from the People's Republic of China. Determination of the Commission in Investigation No. 731-TA-464 (Final) Under the Tariff Act of 1930, Together with the Information Obtained in the Investigation, 9886–14.315

Special Business Problems Confronting Medical Practitioners Resulting from Changes in Medicare Payment Practices, 21728–75

Special Issues Analysis Center: Draft Report on FY89 Title VII Grants as of Sept. 14, 1989, 4808–20.1

Special Issues Analysis Center Reports on Title VII Grants for Limited English Proficiency Students, 4808–20

Special Issues Analysis Center. Special Report A: Types of Services Received by LEP Students, 4808–20.2

Special Issues Analysis Center. Special Report B: Fiscal Resources for Special Services to LEP Students, 4808–20.3

Special Issues Analysis Center. Special Report C: State Activities Related to the Education of LEP Students, 4808–20.4

Special Issues Analysis Center. Special Report D: At-Risk Students—The Special Case of the LEP Students, 4808–20.5

Special Issues Analysis Center. Special Report E: Longitudinal Analysis of Title VII Applicants and Grantees, 4808–20.6

Special Report Series. 1987 Census of Retail Trade, 2401–1

Special Studies. Current Population Reports. Series P-23, 2546–2

Special Supplemental Food Program for Women, Infants and Children. Program Participation and Expenditures, by State, 1362–16

Special Supplemental Food Program for Women, Infants, and Children: Program Participation and Expenditures by State, FY88, 1364–12

Special Supplemental Food Program (WIC) for Women, Infants and Children, Racial Participation, April 1990, 1364–16

Specialty Mental Health Organizations, U.S., 1988. Mental Health Service System Reports, Series CN, 4506–4.14

Species Profiles: Life Histories and Environmental Requirements of Coastal Fishes and Invertebrates, 5506–8

Speculative Effects of Anticipated Trade Policy Under Dual Exchange Rates, 9385–8.104

Spells Without Health Insurance: Distributions of Durations and Their Link to Point-in-Time Estimates of the Uninsured, 2626–10.142

Spells Without Health Insurance: What Affects Spell Duration and Who Are the Chronically Uninsured?, 2626–10.141

Spent Fuel Storage Requirements, 1990-2040, 3354–2

Spent Nuclear Fuel Discharges from U.S. Reactors, 1989, 3166–6.55

Spiral Grain and Annual Ring Width in Natural Unthinned Stands of Lodgepole Pine in North America, 1208–380

Spun Yarn Production, 1990, Current Industrial Report, 2506–5.5

SSA Research and Statistics Publications 1991 Catalog, 4744–12

St. Lawrence Seaway: Traffic Report, 1990 Navigation Season, 7744–2

Stabilization and Financial Sector Reform in Mexico, 9385–8.121

Stable Cartels with a Cournot Fringe, 9387–8.233

Staff Patterns of Epidemiologists in the Health Departments of 12 Southern States, 4042–3.253

Staff Reports, Federal Reserve Bank of Minneapolis, 9383–20

Staff Reports of the Bureau of Economics, 9406–1

Staff Studies, Board of Governors of the Federal Reserve System, 9366–1

Staff Working Papers, 26306–3

Staffing of Mental Health Organizations, U.S., 1986, 4506–3.42

Standardizing Nursing-Home Admission Dates for Short-Term Hospital Stays. National Medical Expenditure Survey, 4186–8.15

START Treaty and Beyond, 26306–6.161

State Administration of the Amended Chapter 1 Program, 4808–32

State and Federal Motor-Fuel Tax Rates by Years, 1980-89, 7554–32

State and Local Government Collective Bargaining Settlements, 1990, 6782–6

State and Local Government Collective Bargaining Settlements, First Six Months, 1991, 6782–6

State and Local Government Employment and Payrolls, 6742–4

State and Local Government Fiscal Position in 1990, 2702–1.205

State and Local Initiatives on Productivity, Technology, and Innovation: Enhancing a National Resource for International Competitiveness, 10048–81

State and Metropolitan Area Data Book, 1991, 2328–54

State and Metropolitan Area Employment and Unemployment, 6742–12

State and Regional Unemployment in 1990, 6726–1.37

State Assistance Programs for SSI Recipients, January 1991, 4704–13

State Catalog of FY90 Low Income Home Energy Assistance Program Characteristics, 4694–9

State Credit Subsidy Programs for Agricultural Producers, 1541–1.201

State Department: Status of the Diplomatic Security Construction Program, 26123–322

State Education Statistics, 4804–32

State Energy Data Report, Consumption Estimates, 1960-89, 3164–39

Index by Titles

State Energy Price and Expenditure Report, 1989, 3164–64

State Energy Price Projections for the Residential Sector, 1990-91, 3166–6.54

State Government Finances: 1990, 2466–2.6

State Government Tax Collections: 1990, 2466–2.7

State Higher Education Profiles, Third Edition: A Comparison of State Higher Education Data for FY87, 4844–13

State Labor Legislation Enacted in 1990, 6722–1.209

State Licensure and Discipline of Health Professionals, 4006–8

State Licensure and Discipline of Podiatrists, 4006–8.4

State Medical Boards and Medical Discipline, 4008–83

State Mineral Summaries, 1991, 5614–6

State of Academic Science and Engineering, 9628–83

State of Mathematics Achievement: NAEP's 1990 Assessment of the Nation and the Trial Assessment of the States. National Assessment of Educational Progress, 1990, 4896–8.1

State of the Bureau of Prisons, 6244–2

State of the Bureau, 1990, 6244–2

State of the World's Children, 25388–57

State Per Capita Personal Income, 1985-90, and State Personal Income, 1988-90: Revised Estimates, 2702–1.216

State Policies and Programs for Encouraging Innovation and Technology Development, 10048–81

State Resources and Services Related to Alcohol and Other Drug Abuse Problems, FY89: An Analysis of State Alcohol and Drug Abuse Profile Data, 4488–15

State Tobacco Prevention and Control Activities: Results of the 1989-90 Association of State and Territorial Health Officials (ASTHO) Survey, Final Report, 4206–2.47

State Trends, a Supplement to FHA Trends, Section 203 Home Mortgages Insured by FHA, 5142–3, 5144–25

State Workers' Compensation: Administration Profiles, 6504–9

State Workers' Compensation Laws, 6502–1

State Workers' Compensation: Legislation Enacted in 1990, 6722–1.210

State-Level Examination of Metro/Nonmetro Per Capita Income Inequality, 1979-87, 1548–380

State-level Income and Balance Sheet Estimates, 1990, 1541–1.212

State-Level Measurement of Performance Outcomes in Postsecondary Vocational Education, 4808–33

State-Level Measurement of Performance Outcomes in Postsecondary Vocational Education. Volume I: Executive Summary, An Overview of State Policies, 4808–33.1

State-Level Measurement of Performance Outcomes in Postsecondary Vocational Education. Volume II: Appendix, Profiles of State Data Collection Activities, 4808–33.2

State-Local Relations Organizations: The ACIR Counterparts, 10048–80

Statement by Dr. Charles H. Bradford Before the National Credit Union Administration Board, Madison, Wisconsin, June 14, 1991, 9538–9

Statement by Dr. Charles H. Bradford Before the National Credit Union Administration Board, Mar. 13, 1991, 9538–8

Statement of Foreign Currencies Purchased with Dollars, FY90, 8102–5

Statement of Foreign Currencies Purchased with Dollars, Oct. 1, 1990-Mar. 31, 1991, 8102–5

Statement of Michael J. Graetz, Deputy Assistant Secretary (Tax Policy), Department of the Treasury, Before the Committee on Ways and Means, U.S. House of Representatives, 8008–149

Statement on the Posture of the U.S. Army, FY92-93: Maintaining a Trained and Ready Total Force for the 1990s and Beyond, 3704–13

States' Activities Report, FY91-92, Charting and Geodetic Services, 2174–10

States Begin JOBS, but Fiscal and Other Problems May Impede Their Progress. Welfare to Work, 26121–435

States Cushioned Funding Cuts but Also Scaled Back Program Benefits. Low-Income Home Energy Assistance, 26121–401

States' Progress in Developing State Revolving Loan Fund Programs. Water Pollution, 26113–521

Stationary Representations, Cointegration, and Rational Expectations with an Application to the Forward Foreign Exchange Market, 9371–10.64

Statistical Abstract of the U.S.: 1991, 2324–1

Statistical Analysis of Fertilizer Application Rate Differences Between 1989 and 1990, 1561–16.201

Statistical Briefs, 2326–17

Statistical Discrepancy in the U.S. International Transactions Accounts: Sources and Suggested Remedies, 9366–7.258

Statistical Estimators for Monitoring Spotted Owls in Oregon and Washington in 1987, 1208–342

Statistical Information on Women in Business. Status Report to Congress, 9768–22

Statistical Notes, NIMH Survey and Reports Branch, 4506–3

Statistical Policy Working Papers, 106–4

Statistical Programs of the U.S. Government, FY92, 104–10

Statistical Releases: Bureau of Alcohol, Tobacco and Firearms, 8486–1

Statistical Report, U.S. Attorney's Office, FY90, 6004–2

Statistical Series G. Semiannual Report Trend Data: Data from the Drug Abuse Warning Network (DAWN), 4492–3

Statistical Series I. Number 9, Annual Data, 1989: Data from the Drug Abuse Warning Network, 4494–8

Statistical Series I. Number 10, Annual Data, 1990: Data from the Drug Abuse Warning Network, 4494–8

Statistical Summary for Fish and Wildlife Restoration, FY90, 5504–13

Statistical Summary of Streamflow Data for Indiana, 5666–27.15

Statistical Summary of VA Activities, 8602–3

Statistical Summary: Series EE and HH Savings Bonds, 8442–1

Statistical Supplement Stockpile Report to Congress, 3902–2

Statistics: Distributors of TVA Power, 9804–19

Status of the Nation's Local...

Statistics for Industry Groups and Industries (Including Capital Expenditures, Inventories, and Supplemental Labor, Fuel, and Electric Energy Costs), 1989 Annual Survey of Manufactures, 2506–15.1

Statistics of Communications Common Carriers, 9284–6

Statistics of Income and Related Administrative Record Research: 1988-89, 8304–17

Statistics of Income Bulletin, 8302–2

Statistics of Income, Corporation Income Tax Returns, 1987, 8304–4

Statistics of Income, Source Book: Active Corporation Income Tax Returns, July 1988-June 1989, 8304–21

Statistics of Interstate Natural Gas Pipeline Companies, 1989, 3164–38

Statistics of Marine Casualties, 1988, 7404–11

Statistics of Publicly Owned Electric Utilities, 3164–24

Statistics on Banking, 1989, 9294–4

Statistics on Race and Ethnicity, 2326–7.80

Statistics Showing How and What the Government Is Acquiring. Mainframe Procurements, 26125–41.8

Status and Trends in Gypsy Moth Defoliation Hazard in Tennessee, 1208–344

Status, Distribution, and Management of Mountain Goats in the Greater Yellowstone Ecosystem, 5548–19

Status of Account: Harry S. Truman Memorial Scholarship Fund, 14312–1

Status of Active Foreign Credits of the U.S. Government: Foreign Credits by U.S. Government Agencies, 8002–6

Status of Biomedical Research Facilities: 1990, 4434–17

Status of Census Operations in State of New York, 21628–90

Status of Census Operations in the State of Pennsylvania, 21628–89

Status of Defense Materials Inventories, 3902–3

Status of Emergency Assistance To Revitalize the Economy. Aid to Panama, 26123–330

Status of Federal Agencies' Programs. Employee Drug Testing, 26119–344

Status of Flag Officers, Selectees, and Billets. Defense Personnel, 26123–340

Status of Foreign Currency Funds Administered by the Agency for International Development, 9912–1

Status of Handicapped Children in Head Start Programs, 4604–1

Status of Implementing Joint Assignments for Military Leaders. Defense Personnel, 26123–317

Status of Loan Agreements, 9912–3

Status of Open Recommendations: Improving Operations of Federal Departments and Agencies, 26104–5

Status of Post-Census Local Review Program, 21628–93

Status of the Challenge Grant Program. Child Abuse Prevention, 26121–423

Status of the Diplomatic Security Construction Program. State Department, 26123–322

Status of the Fishery Resources off the Northeastern U.S. for 1990, 2164–14

Status of the Fishery Resources off the Northeastern U.S. for 1991, 2164–14

Status of the Nation's Local Mass Transportation: Performance and Conditions, 7884–8

Status of the Nonmetro Labor... Index by Titles

Status of the Nonmetro Labor Force, 1987, 1598–264

Status of the Senior Executive Service, 1989, 9844–36

Status of the Senior Executive Service, 1990, 9844–36

Status of the World's Nations. Geographic Notes, 7142–3

Status of U.S. Assistance Efforts. Eastern Europe, 26123–319

Status of U.S. Sugar Import Quotas, 1922–9

Status of U.S. Sugar Tariff-Rate Quota, 1922–9

Status of Waterfowl and Fall Flight Forecast, 1991, 5504–27

Status Report, Education of Homeless Children and Youth Under the Stewart B. McKinney Homeless Assistance Act, 4804–35

Status Report to Congress: Statistical Information on Women in Business, 9768–22

Stealth Budget: Unfunded Liabilities of the Federal Government, 9389–1.204

Steel Industry Annual Report on Competitive Conditions in the Steel Industry and Industry Efforts To Adjust and Modernize, Report to the President on Investigation No. 332-289 Under Section 332 of the Tariff Act of 1930, 9884–24

Steel Mill Products, 1990, Current Industrial Report, 2506–10.2

Steel Shipping Drums and Pails, Current Industrial Report, 2506–11.5

Steel Wire Rope from Argentina and Mexico. Determinations of the Commission in Investigations Nos. 731-TA-476 and 479 (Final) Under the Tariff Act of 1930, Together with the Information Obtained in the Investigations, 9886–14.324

Steel Wire Rope from Argentina, Chile, India, Israel, Mexico, The People's Republic of China, Taiwan, and Thailand. Determinations of the Commission in Investigation Nos. 701-TA-305 and 306 (Preliminary) and 731-TA-476-482 (Preliminary) Under the Tariff Act of 1930, Together with the Information Obtained in the Investigations, 9886–19.73

Steel Wire Rope from Canada. Determination of the Commission in Investigation No. 731-TA-524 (Preliminary) Under the Tariff Act of 1930, Together with the Information Obtained in the Investigation, 9886–14.323

Steel Wire Rope from India, the People's Republic of China, Taiwan, and Thailand. Determinations of the Commission in Investigation No. 701-TA-305 (Final), and Nos. 731-TA-478 and 480-482 (Final) Under the Tariff Act of 1930, Together with the Information Obtained in the Investigations, 9886–19.79

Stochastic Dominance Approach to the Evaluation of Foreign Exchange Forecasts, 9371–10.63

Stochastic Trends and Economic Fluctuations, 9375–13.55

Stock Market Dispersion and Business Cycles, 9375–1.201

Stock Market Efficiency: An Autopsy?, 9373–1.206

Stock Market Volatility in OECD Countries: Recent Trends, Consequences for the Real Economy, and Proposals for Reform, 9366–6.279

Stock Returns and Inflation: Further Tests of the Role of the Central Bank, 9379–14.12

Stocks of Grain, 11922–4

Stocks of Grain at Selected Terminal and Elevator Sites, 1313–4

Stone: Minerals Yearbook, Volume 1, 1989, 5604–15.61

Storage Subsidy Programs, 1548–378

Storm Data, 2152–3

Straight Baseline Claim: Costa Rica. Limits in the Seas, 7006–8.6

Strategic and Critical Materials Report to the Congress: Operations Under the Strategic and Critical Materials Stock Piling Act During the Period April-September 1990, 3542–22

Strategic and Critical Materials Report to the Congress: Operations Under the Strategic and Critical Materials Stock Piling Act During the Period October 1990-March 1991, 3542–22

Strategic Assessment of Near Coastal Waters. National Estuarine Eutrophication Project: Workshop Proceedings, 2176–7.22

Strategic Assessment Reports, 2176–7

Strategic Defense System Tests Highlight STS-39 Mission, 9506–2.140

Strategic Marketing Needed To Lead Agribusiness in International Trade. U.S. Department of Agriculture, 26113–504

Strategic Petroleum Reserve, Quarterly Report, 3002–13

Strategic Plan for California Recreation, 1990-2000. Recreation 2000: A Strategic Plan by State, 5726–5.2

Strategic Special Nuclear Material Inventory Differences, Annual Report, 3004–32, 3344–2

Strategic Targeted Activities for Results System, 9182–11

Strategy for Reform. Deposit Insurance, 26119–320

Strategy for the Future: Habitat Management on Public Lands, 5726–6

Strawberry Trade Situation, 1925–34.218

Streamflow and Stream Quality in the Coal-Mining Region, Patoka River Basin, Southwestern Indiana, 1983-85, 5666–27.8

Strength in Numbers: Your Guide to 1990 Census Redistricting Data from the U.S. Bureau of the Census, 2308–59

Strengthening Sales Practice Oversight. Securities Industry, 26119–336

Strikes and the Use of Permanent Strike Replacements in the 1970s and 1980s. Labor-Management Relations, 26121–405

Strong Leadership and Management Reforms Needed To Address Serious Problems. Immigration Management, 26119–317

Stronger Efforts Needed by EPA To Control Toxic Water Pollution. Water Pollution, 26113–536

Stronger FDA Standards and Oversight Needed for Bottled Water. Food Safety and Quality, 26113–519

Strontium: Minerals Yearbook, Volume 1, 1989, 5604–15.78

Structural Change for Farm Lenders in the 1980s, 9368–90

Structural Change in U.S. Farmland, 1588–150

Structural Unemployment and Public Policy in Interwar Britain: A Review Essay, 9375–13.52

Structure of State Aid to Elementary and Secondary Education, 10048–78

Student Aid and the Cost of Postsecondary Education, 26306–6.153

Studies in American Fertility, 2546–2.162

Studies in Household and Family Formation, 2546–2.157

Studies of Energy Taxes, 3166–6.57

Studies on Corporate Leverage, 9385–8.88

Study Guided by the Health Belief Model of the Predictors of Breast Cancer Screening of Women Ages 40 and Older, 4042–3.233

Study of Academic Instruction for Disadvantaged Students: What Is Taught, and How, to the Children of Poverty. Interim Report from a Two-Year Investigation, 4808–28

Study of Cases Decided by the U.S. Merit Systems Protection Board, FY90, 9494–2

Study of the Cost and Financing of a Commercially Developed Space Facility (CDSF), 21708–129

Study of U.S. Postal Service Productivity and Its Measurement, 9688–6

Study To Evaluate the Use of Mail Service Pharmacies, 4658–60

Subject Index to Current Population Reports, 2546–2.160

Subsea Permafrost: Probing, Thermal Regime, and Data Analyses, 1975-81, 2176–1.39

Subsistence as a Component of the Mixed Economic Base in a Modernizing Community, 1208–350

Substance Abuse Coverage Provided by Employer Medical Plans, 6722–1.221

Substance Abuse. Indian Health Conditions, 4088–2

Substitutability of Crop Rotations for Agrichemicals: Preliminary Results, 1561–16.204

Subtropical Atlantic Climate Study (STACS), 2146–7

Sugar and Honey: Foreign Agricultural Service Circular Series, 1925–14

Sugar and Sweetener Situation and Outlook Report, 1561–14

Sugar and Sweetener Situation and Outlook Yearbook, 1561–14

Sugar Beets and Sugarcane 1990-Crop Sugar Beet and Sugarcane Price Support Program: ASCS Commodity Fact Sheet, 1806–4.4

Sugar Market Statistics, 1621–28

Sugarbeet and Sugarcane Operations, 1989 and Preliminary 1990 Cost of Production Estimates, 1561–14.202

Sugarbeet and Sugarcane Operations, 1990 and Preliminary 1991 Cost of Production Estimates, 1561–14.208

Sulfanilic Acid from the People's Republic of China. Determination of the Commission in Investigation No. 731-TA-538 (Preliminary) Under the Tariff Act of 1930, Together with the Information Obtained in the Investigation, 9886–14.334

Sulfur in 1990: Mineral Industry Surveys Annual Advance Summary, 5614–5.5

Sulfur: Mineral Industry Surveys, 5612–1.23

Sulfur: Minerals Yearbook, Volume 1, 1989, 5604–15.62

Summaries of FY90 Engineering Research, 3004–18.3

Summaries of FY91 Research in the Chemical Sciences, 3004–18.5

Summaries of Physical Research in the Geosciences, 3004–18.2

Index by Titles

Summary and Analysis of International Travel to the U.S., 2902–1

Summary Description of Recent Studies and Publications, 2064–9

Summary of Awards, Division of Mechanics, Structures and Materials Engineering, 9626–7.2

Summary of Awards, FY89, Information, Robotics, and Intelligent Systems, 9626–7.3

Summary of Awards, FY89, Microelectronic Information Processing Systems, 9626–7.1

Summary of Commentary on Current Economic Conditions by Federal Reserve District, 9362–8

Summary of Fatal and Nonfatal Crashes Involving Medium and Heavy Trucks, 7764–20

Summary of Leading Causes for Outpatient Visits, Indian Health Service Direct and Contract Facilities, FY89, 4084–2

Summary of Loan Activity and Operating Results Through (Month), Issued by CCC, 1802–7

Summary of Medical Programs, 8602–4

Summary of Medium and Heavy Truck Crashes in 1989, 7764–20

Summary of Notifiable Diseases, U.S., 1990, 4204–1

Summary of Refugee Admissions, 7002–4

Summary of Selected Characteristics of Large Reservoirs in the U.S. and Puerto Rico, 1988, 5668–120

Summary of Selected Nationwide School Bus Crash Statistics in 1989, 7764–22

Summary of State Appalachian Development Plans and Investment Programs for FY91, 9084–3

Summary of State Chapter 1 Migrant Education Program Participation and Achievement Information, 1987-88, 4808–30

Summary of State Water Quality Laws Affecting Agriculture, 1561–16.203

Summary of the National Atmospheric Deposition Program/National Trends Network Intersite-Comparison Program, Nov. 1978-Nov. 1989, 5668–124

Summary of the 1990 African Tobacco Auctions, 1925–16.205

Summary of VHS&RA Health Services Training by Major Programs for FY89, 8704–4

Summary of VHS&RA Health Services Training by Major Programs for FY90, 8704–4

Summary Population and Housing Characteristics. 1990 Census of Population and Housing., 2551–1

Summary Report of Real Property Leased by the U.S. Throughout the World as of Sept. 30, 1989, 9454–10

Summary Report of Real Property Owned by the U.S. Throughout the World, As of Sept. 30, 1989, 9454–5

Summary Report on Issues in Ecological Risk Assessment, 9186–9.5

Summary Statistics, 1989: Water, Land, and Related Data, 5824–12

Summer Quarter Feed and Residual Use of Wheat, 1561–12.203

Sunflower Acreage Response to Increased Commodity Program Flexibility, 1561–3.201

Sunspots, Asset Bubbles, and the Store of Value Motive in Overlapping Generations Models, 9385–8.90

Supervision of Under-Capitalized Banks: Is There a Case for Change?, 9391–1.212

Supplement to Employment and Earnings, 6744–4.3

Supplement to Producer Price Indexes, Data for 1990, 6764–2

Supplement to the American Housing Survey for Selected Metropolitan Areas: 1984, 2485–8

Supplement to the American Housing Survey for the U.S. in 1985, 2485–13

Supplement to the American Housing Survey for the U.S. in 1987, 2485–13

Supplemental Information to the Arizona Riparian-Wetland Area Management Strategy, 5726–8.4

Supplemental Security Income: State and County Data, December 1989, 4744–27

Supplemental Tidal Predictions: Anchorage, Nikishka, Seldovia, and Valdez, Alaska, 1992, 2174–2.1

Supplements to the Monthly Vital Statistics Report: Advance Reports, 1987. Vital and Health Statistics Series 24, 4147–24.4

Supply of Illicit Drugs to the U.S., the NNICC Report, 1990, 6284–2

Supply Shocks and Household Demand for Motor Fuel, 9371–1.204

Supreme Court for D.C., 21308–27

Surveillance of Communicable Disease in Vermont: Who Reports?, 4042–3.208

Surveillance of Escherichia coli O157 Isolation and Confirmation, U.S., 1988, 4202–7.204

Surveillance of Major Causes of Hospitalization Among the Elderly, 1988, 4202–7.205

Surveillance of Postneonatal Mortality, U.S., 1980-87, 4202–7.208

Survey Designs and Statistical Methods for the Estimation of Avian Population Trends, 5508–108

Survey Evidence of Tighter Credit Conditions: What Does It Mean?, 9389–19.30

Survey Methods and Statistical Summary of Nonfuel Minerals: Minerals Yearbook, Volume 1, 1989, 5604–15.2

Survey Methods and Statistical Summary of Nonfuel Minerals: Minerals Yearbook, Volume 2, 1989, 5604–16.1

Survey Methods and Statistical Summary of Nonfuel Minerals, 1988, 5604–48

Survey of Contracting Statistics, 3804–13

Survey of Current Business, 2702–1

Survey of Federally-Funded Marine Mammal Research and Studies, FY74-90, 14734–2

Survey of Health Occupational Staff, 1990 Report, 8604–8

Survey of Income and Program Participation Selected Papers: 1990 Meeting of the American Statistical Association, 2624–1

Survey of Income and Program Participation Working Paper Series, 2626–10

Survey of Mortgage Lending Activity, 5142–18

Survey of Mortgage Lending Activity, Gross Flows, 5142–30

Survey of Mortgage Lending Activity, State Estimates, 5144–21

Survey of Mortgage-Related Security Holdings of Major Institutions, 5002–12

Survey of Newspaper Coverage of HCFA Hospital Mortality Data, 4042–3.242

Survey of Occupational Injuries and Illnesses, 1989, 6844–7

Tax Amnesty: Improving...

Survey of Payers and Payees with IRS-Identified Invalid TINs, 8304–8.1

Survey of State Public Health Departments on Procedures for Reporting Elder Abuse, 4042–3.213

Survey of Terms of Bank Lending Made During (Latest Survey Date), 9365–3

Survey of the Origins and Purposes of Deposit Protection Programs, 9385–8.93

Survivor Income Benefits Provided by Employers, 6722–1.230

Sustainable Agricultural Development in Ethiopia, 23848–216

Switchgear, Switchboard Apparatus, Relays, and Industrial Controls, 1990, Current Industrial Report, 2506–12.11

Symposium on Effective Highway Accident Countermeasures, 7558–110

Synthesis of Available Biological, Geological, Chemical, Socioeconomic, and Cultural Resource Information for the South Florida Area, 5738–19

Taiwan Market for Building Supplies, 2042–1.205

Take-or-Pay Settlements, 3162–4.202

Tankers in the World Fleet, 7704–17

Target Seedling Symposium: Proceedings, Combined Meeting of the Western Forest Nursery Associations, Aug. 13-17, 1990, Roseburg, Oregon, 1208–376

Targeted Jobs Tax Credit: Employer Actions To Recruit, Hire, and Retain Eligible Workers Vary, 26121–407

Targeting Aid to Distressed Rural Areas: Indicators of Fiscal and Community Well-Being, 1598–265

Tariffs and Trade: U.S. and Mexican Horticultural Products, 1989-90, 1925–34.238

Tart Cherry Juice and Tart Cherry Juice Concentrate from Germany and Yugoslavia. Determination of the Commission in Investigation Nos. 731-TA-512 and 513 (Preliminary) Under the Tariff Act of 1930, Together with the Information Obtained in the Investigations, 9886–14.308

Tastes and Technology in a Two-Country Model of the Business Cycle: Explaining International Co-Movements, 9377–9.113

Tax Administration: A Generally Successful Filing Season in 1991, 26119–346

Tax Administration: Effectiveness of IRS' Return Preparer Penalty Program Is Questionable, 26119–315

Tax Administration: Information on Revenue Agent Attrition, 26119–345

Tax Administration: IRS' Administration of the International Boycott Tax Code Provisions, 26119–349

Tax Administration: IRS Can Improve Its Program To Find Taxpayers Who Underreport Their Income, 26119–325

Tax Administration: IRS Does Not Investigate Most High-Income Nonfilers, 26119–322

Tax Administration: IRS Needs To Improve Certain Measures of Service Center Quality, 26119–329

Tax Administration: IRS' 1990 Filing Season Performance Continued Recent Positive Trends, 26119–319

Tax Amnesty: Improving Compliance?, 8304–8.1

Tax Analysis in a Real... Index by Titles

Tax Analysis in a Real Business Cycle Model: On Measuring Harberger Triangles and Okun Gaps, 9383–20.8

Tax Incentives for Increasing Savings and Investments, 25368–170

Tax Incentives for Rehabilitating Historic Buildings: FY90 Analysis, 5544–17

Tax Increases in the Tenth District: Where Will the Money Come From?, 9381–1.204

Tax Policy: Refund Offset Program Benefits Appear To Exceed Costs, 26119–339

Tax-Exempt Bonds: Retirement Center Bonds Were Risky and Benefited Moderate-Income Elderly, 26119–328

Tea, Spices and Essential Oils: Foreign Agricultural Service Circular Series, 1925–15

Teacher Survey on Safe, Disciplined, and Drug-Free Schools, 4826–1.31

Technical Assistance and Safety Programs: FY90 Project Directory, 7884–1

Technical Report Series: Prospective Payment Assessment Commission, 17206–2

Technology Adoption and Growth, 9383–20.6

Technology Shocks and the Business Cycle, 9375–1.205

Technology Transfer Report, FY90, NASA, 21704–1

Teen Outreach: The Fifth Year of National Replication, Data from the 1988-89 School Year, 25548–104

Teenage Victims, 6066–3.43

Telecommunications: 1991 Survey of Cable Television Rates and Services, 26113–431

Telephone Access to Local Field Offices. Social Security, 26121–434

Telephone Rates Update, 9282–8

Telephone Subscribership in the U.S., 9282–9

Television Channel Utilization, 9282–6

Temperature and Salinity Structure of the Wintertime Bering Sea Marginal Ice Zone, 2176–1.38

Temporal Trends in the Prevalence of Congenital Malformations at Birth Based on the Birth Defects Monitoring Program, U.S., 1979-87, 4202–7.203

Tennessee Valley Authority: Financial Statements for the Fiscal Year Ended Sept. 30, 1989, 9804–32

Tennessee Valley Authority 1990 Annual Report, 9804–1

Tennessee Valley Authority: 1990 Financial Statements, 9804–32

Tenth District Cities: Recent Growth and Prospects for the 1990s, 9381–1.209

Tenth District Economy: Avoiding a Recession?, 9381–1.202

Term Structure of Interest Rates over the Business Cycle, 9366–6.273

Terminal Area Forecasts, FY91-2005, 7504–7

Terminations, Asset Reversions, and Replacements Following Leveraged Buyouts. Pension Plans, 26121–408

Terms of Trade, the Trade Balance, and Stability: The Role of Savings Behavior, 9366–7.251

Terrorism in the U.S., 1990, 6224–6

Tested Achievement: Eighth Grade Class. National Education Longitudinal Study of 1988, 4826–9.8

Testimony of Kenneth W. Gideon, Assistant Secretary (Tax Policy), Department of the Treasury, Before the Committee on Ways and Means, U.S. House of Representatives, 8008–150

Testing a Census Approach to Compiling Data on Fatal Work Injuries, 6722–1.205

Tests of Mean-Variance Efficiency of International Equity Markets, 9381–10.116

Texas Economy: Conditions and Prospects for Recovery, 21248–146

Textile Plant Employment in the Southeast, 6942–1

Textile Plant Employment in the Southeast, 1990, 6944–1

Textile Plants, August 1990, Industry Wage Survey, 6787–6.251

Textural and Mineralogic Analyses of Surficial Sediments Offshore of Myrtle Beach, S.C., 5668–115

Textured Yarn Production, 1990, Current Industrial Report, 2506–5.4

Thailand: Emergence of a Sugar Superpower, 1561–14.201

Thailand's Shrimp Culture Growing, 2162–1.203

Thallium in 1990: Mineral Industry Surveys, Annual Review, 5614–5.17

Theoretical Analysis of Capital Flight from Debtor Nations, 9385–8.109

Third Progress Report on the Domiciliary Care for Homeless Veterans Program, 8604–10

Thirteenth Annual Report to Congress on the Implementation of the Individuals with Disabilities Education Act, 4944–4

Thirty Counties Over 1 Million Population, 1990 Census Shows, 2328–68

Thorium in 1990: Mineral Industry Surveys Annual Review, 5614–5.15

Three Decades of Banking, 9381–14.1

Three-Fifths of the High School Graduates of 1990 Enrolled in College, 6726–1.38

Thrift Delinquency Rates, 9302–4.202

Thrifts and Housing Finance: Implications of a Stricter Qualified Thrift Lender Test, 26119–337

Tidal Current Tables, 2174–1

Tidal Current Tables, 1992: Atlantic Coast of North America, 2174–1.1

Tidal Current Tables, 1992: Pacific Coast of North America and Asia, 2174–1.2

Tidal Salt Marshes of the Southeast Atlantic Coast: A Community Profile, 5506–9.42

Tide Tables 1992, High and Low Water Predictions, 2174–2

Tide Tables 1992, High and Low Water Predictions: Central and Western Pacific Ocean and Indian Ocean, 2174–2.5

Tide Tables 1992, High and Low Water Predictions: East Coast of North and South America Including Greenland, 2174–2.3

Tide Tables 1992, High and Low Water Predictions: Europe and West Coast of Africa Including the Mediterranean Sea, 2174–2.4

Tide Tables 1992, High and Low Water Predictions: West Coast of North and South America Including the Hawaiian Islands, 2174–2.2

TIGER: The Coast-to-Coast Digital Map Data Base, 2628–30

Timber Industries: Northeast Region, 1206–15

Timber Industries of Delaware, 1985, 1206–15.10

Timber Industry Assessments of Timber Product Output and Use, 1206–10

Timber Products Output and Timber Harvests in Alaska: Projections for 1989-2010, 1208–365

Timber Sale Program Annual Report, FY90, 1204–36

Timber Supply Stability Act; Ancient Forest Protection Act of 1990; Community Stability Act of 1990; National Forest Plan Implementation Act of 1990; Development and Consideration of Alternatives for the Conservation of the Northern Spotted Owl; and the Ancient Forest Act of 1990, 21168–45

Timber Value Growth Rates in New England, 1208–348

Time Trends in Incidence of Brain and Central Nervous System Cancers in Connecticut, 4472–1.234

Tin Industry: Mineral Industry Surveys, 5612–1.24

Tin: International Strategic Minerals Inventory Summary Report, 5666–21.10

Tin: Minerals Yearbook, Volume 1, 1989, 5604–15.65

Titanium: Mineral Industry Surveys, 5612–2.16

Titanium: Minerals Yearbook, Volume 1, 1989, 5604–15.66

Title 13, U.S. Code Census, 21628–94

Title 37, U.S. Code: Pay and Allowances of the Uniformed Services (As Amended Through Dec. 31, 1990), 21208–34

To Examine Small Business Trade Opportunities with the Soviet Union and Eastern Europe, 25728–42

Tobacco Advertising in Retail Stores, 4042–3.250

Tobacco Cost of Production, 1004–16.1

Tobacco Market Review, 1319–5

Tobacco Market Review: Burley, 1989 Crop, 1319–5.3

Tobacco Market Review: Burley, 1990 Crop, 1319–5.6

Tobacco Market Review: Fire-Cured and Dark Air-Cured, 1989 Crop, 1319–5.2

Tobacco Market Review: Fire-Cured and Dark Air-Cured, 1990 Crop, 1319–5.5

Tobacco Market Review: Flue-Cured, 1989 Crop, 1319–5.1

Tobacco Market Review: Flue-Cured, 1990 Crop, 1319–5.4

Tobacco Outlook Special Report, 1991, 1925–16.206

Tobacco Products: Monthly Statistical Release, 8486–1.4

Tobacco Situation and Outlook Report, 1561–10

Tobacco Situation: Canada, 1925–16.201

Tobacco Situation: Hong Kong, 1925–16.210

Tobacco Situation: Indonesia, 1925–16.208

Tobacco Situation: Israel, 1925–16.202

Tobacco Situation: Philippines, 1925–16.203

Tobacco Situation: Singapore, 1925–16.212

Tobacco Stocks, 1319–3

Toll Facilities in the U.S.: Bridges, Roads, Tunnels, Ferries, 7554–39

Tomatoes for Processing Up Sharply Again in 1990, 1925–34.202

Top 100 Cooperatives, 1989 Financial Profile, 1124–3

Total Enrollments in Health Physics/Radiation Protection Programs Increased 9 Percent in 1990. Number of Undergraduate Degrees Increased Slightly While Master's and Doctoral Degrees Decreased, 3006–8.15

Total Production Index for Washington, D.C., 9389–1.203

Index by Titles

Toward an Analysis of the Farmers Home Administration's Direct and Guaranteed Farm Loan Programs, 1598–273

Toxic Air Pollutant Emission Factors: A Compilation for Selected Air Toxic Compounds and Sources, Second Edition, 9198–120

Toxic Chemicals: EPA's Toxic Release Inventory Is Useful but Can Be Improved, 26113–532

Tracing the Elderly Through the Health Care System: An Update, 4188–72

Tracking Offenders, 1987, 6066–25.33

Tracking Offenders, 1988, 6066–25.39

Tracking the Economy with the Purchasing Managers Index, 9385–1.215, 9385–8.120

Tracking Wildlife by Satellite: Current Systems and Performance. Fish and Wildlife Technical Report, 5506–12.3

Trade Agreements Program, 1990, Annual Report of the President of the U.S., and 1991 Trade Policy Agenda, 444–1

Trade and Development: Impact of Foreign Aid on U.S. Agriculture, 1548–372

Trade and Employment, 2322–2

Trade and Employment Effects of the Caribbean Basin Economic Recovery Act, 6364–2

Trade Balance Effects of Foreign Direct Investment in U.S. Manufacturing, 9385–1.210

Trade Imbalances and Economic Theory: The Case for a U.S.-Japan Trade Deficit, 9391–1.209

Trade of NATO Countries with China, 1987-90, 7144–14

Trade Patterns of the West, 1989, 7144–10

Trade Policies and Market Opportunities for U.S. Farm Exports: 1990 Annual Report, 1924–8

Trade Policy Agenda, 1991, and 1990 Annual Report of the President of the U.S. on the Trade Agreements Program, 444–1

Trade Restraints and the Competitive Status of the Textile, Apparel, and Nonrubber-Footwear Industries, 26306–6.162

Trade-offs Involved in Beverage Container Deposit Legislation. Solid Waste, 26113–494

Trade-Related Aspects of Intellectual Property Rights: What Is at Stake?, 9391–1.203

Trade-Sensitive U.S. Industries: Employment Trends and Worker Characteristics, 6366–3.27

Trade-Weighted Value of the Dollar, 9379–13

Traffic Fatalities, Semiannual Report, 1990 (January-June), 7762–11

Traffic Fatalities, Preliminary Report, 1990, 7762–11

Traffic Fatality Facts, 1989, 7766–15.1

Traffic Fatality Facts, 1990, 7766–15.4

Traffic Management Progress Report, 3702–1

Traffic Report, 1990 Navigation Season: St. Lawrence Seaway, 7744–2

Traffic Volume Trends, 7552–8

Transition from School to Work: Linking Education and Worksite Training, 26121–431

Transitions in Income and Poverty Status: 1987-88, 2546–20.19

Transport Processes in the North Aleutian Shelf, 2176–1.36

Transport Statistics in the U.S. for the Year Ended Dec. 31, 1989. Part 1: Railroads, 9486–6.1

Transport Statistics in the U.S.: Railroad Companies and Motor Carriers Subject to the Interstate Commerce Act, for the Year Ended Dec. 31, 1989, 9486–6

Transport Statistics in the U.S., Year Ended Dec. 31, 1989. Part 2: Motor Carriers, Release 1, 9486–6.2

Transport Statistics in the U.S., Year Ended Dec. 31, 1989. Part 2: Motor Carriers, Release 2, 9486–6.3

Transportation Accident Fatalities, Preliminary Statistics, 9614–6

Transportation Costs for Forest Products from the Puget Sound Area and Alaska to Pacific Rim Markets, 1208–358

Transportation Energy Data Book: Edition 11, 3304–5

Transportation Equipment Cleaning Industry: Preliminary Data Summary, 9206–4.11

Transportation Infrastructure: Highway Program Consolidation, 26113–471

Transportation Reports and Testimony: January 1989-April 1991, 26106–10.5

Transportation Safety Information Report, 1989 Annual Summary, 7304–19

Transportation, Sorting, and House Values in the Philadelphia Metropolitan Area, 9387–8.231

Trauma Care: Lifesaving System Threatened by Unreimbursed Costs and Other Factors, 26121–419

Treasury Bulletin, 8002–4

Treasury Reporting Rates of Exchange, 8102–6

Treasury's Financial Crimes Enforcement Network. Money Laundering, 26119–330

Treaties in Force: A List of Treaties and Other International Agreements of the U.S. in Force on Jan. 1, 1991, 7004–1

Treatment with Quinidine Gluconate of Persons with Severe Plasmodium falciparum Infection: Discontinuation of Parenteral Quinine from CDC Drug Service, 4206–2.40

Tree Assistance Program, FY89-90 Statistical Summary, 1804–24

Tree Nut Semiannual Situation and Outlook, 1925–34.209

Tree Planting in the U.S., 1990, 1204–7

Tree Value Conversion Standards Revisited, 1208–361

Trend Analyses and Related Statistics, 8304–8

Trends and Patterns in Place of Death for Medicare Enrollees, 4652–1.201

Trends and Patterns of Methamphetamine Abuse in the Republic of Korea, 4498–75

Trends in Academic Progress: Achievement of American Students in Science, 1970-90; Mathematics, 1973-90; Reading, 1971-90; and Writing, 1984-90, 4898–32

Trends in Cocaine Abuse as Reflected in Emergency Room Episodes Reported to DAWN, 4042–3.204

Trends in Contract Coal Transportation, 1979-87, 3168–121

Trends in Costs of Production of Corn, Wheat, and Soybeans, 1975-89, 1541–1.208

Trends in Drug Use and Associated Factors Among American High School Students, College Students, and Young Adults: 1975-89, 4494–4

Trends in Duck Breeding Populations, 1955-91, 5504–30

Tungsten Ore Concentrates...

Trends in Employer-Provided Health Care Benefits, 6722–1.214

Trends in Health Expenditures by Medicare and the Nation, 26308–98

Trends in Housing, 1702–1.205

Trends in Institutional Costs, 4808–24

Trends in LDC External Debt, 1984-90, 9118–11

Trends in Medicaid Payments and Utilization, 1975-89, 4652–1.209

Trends in Resource Protection Policies in Agriculture, 1561–16.203

Trends in Savings, 1702–1.215

Trends in Selected Water-Quality Characteristics, Flathead River at Columbia Falls, British Columbia, and at Columbia Falls, Montana, Water Years 1975-86, 5666–27.16

Trends in Telephone Service, 9282–7

Trends in the International Communications Industry, 1975-89, 9284–17

Trends in the Problem Resolution Program, 8304–8.1

Trends in U.S. Production and Use of Glucose Syrup and Dextrose, 1965-90, and Prospects for the Future, 1561–14.209

Trends in U.S. Soft Drink Consumption—Demand Implications for Low-Calorie and Other Sweeteners, 1561–14.210

Tribal Influence in Formulating Budget Priorities Is Limited. Indian Programs, 26113–508

Triggering Mechanism of Economy-Wide Bank Runs, 9385–8.98

Tri-State Strategy, Volume 1: The Plan. Recreation 2000, 5726–5.5

Tri-State Strategy, Volume 2: Special Recreation Management Areas. Recreation 2000, 5726–5.5

Tri-State Strategy, Volume 3: Background and References. Recreation 2000, 5726–5.5

Troubled Savings and Loan Institutions: Voluntary Restructuring Under Insolvency, 9377–9.121

Trout Production, 1631–16

Truck Safety: Improvements Needed in FHWA's Motor Carrier Safety Program, 26113–505

Truck Trailers, Current Industrial Report, 2506–12.25

Trust Territory of the Pacific Islands, 1990, 7004–6

Tubeless Steel Disc Wheels from Brazil: Determination on Reconsideration of the Commission in Investigation No. 731-TA-335 (Final—Court Remand), Together with the Information Obtained in the Remand Proceeding, 9886–14.333

Tuberculosis Among Foreign-Born Persons Entering the U.S.: Recommendations of the Advisory Committee for Elimination of Tuberculosis, 4206–2.36

Tuberculosis Statistics in the U.S., 1988, 4204–10

Tuberculosis Statistics in the U.S., 1989, 4204–10

Tungsten: Mineral Industry Surveys, 5612–1.25

Tungsten: Minerals Yearbook, Volume 1, 1989, 5604–15.67

Tungsten Ore Concentrates from the People's Republic of China. Determination of the Commission in Investigation No. 731-TA-497 (Final) Under the Tariff Act of 1930, Together with the Information Obtained in the Investigation, 9886–14.332

Tungsten Ore Concentrates...

Index by Titles

Tungsten Ore Concentrates from the People's Republic of China. Determination of the Commission in Investigation No. 731-TA-497 (Preliminary) Under the Tariff Act of 1930, Together with the Information Obtained in the Investigation, 9886–14.307

Turkey Hatchery, 1625–10

Turkeys, 1625–6

Turning Point in the Farm Recovery?, 9381–1.203

Twelfth Annual Report on the Use of Alcohol in Fuels, 3304–9

Twelfth Annual Report to Congress on the Automotive Technology Development Program, 3304–17

Twenty-first Annual Report, Radiation Exposures for DOE and DOE Contractor Employees, 1988, 3324–1

Twenty-ninth CSCE Report, Implementation of Helsinki Final Act, Apr. 1, 1990-Mar. 31, 1991, 7002–1

Twenty-second Annual Report (1987) to the Congress on the Operation of the Automotive Products Trade Act of 1965, 2044–35

Twenty-third Annual Report (1988) to the Congress on the Operation of the Automotive Products Trade Act of 1965, 2044–35

Twenty-two Year Results of a Scots Pine (Pinus sylvestris L.) Provenance Test in North Dakota, 1208–383

Two Notes on Relating the Risk of Disclosure for Microdata and Geographic Area Size, 2626–10.137

Two Studies on Participation in Decision-Making and Equity Among FAA Personnel, 7506–10.89

Type of Organization. Census of Manufactures, 1987. Subject Series, 2497–5

Types of Injuries by Selected Characteristics: U.S., 1985-87. Vital and Health Statistics Series 10, 4147–10.176

UMTA University Research and Training Program FY90 Awards, 7884–7

Underdevelopment and the Enforcement of Laws and Contracts, 9379–12.72

Underrepresentation of Minorities in Supergrade Positions and Above, at the Library of Congress, 21428–9

Understanding International Differences in Leverage Trends, 9385–8.88

Understanding National and Regional Housing Trends, 9387–1.205

Understanding the Factors That Affect Conservation Gains in the U.S. Economy. Energy Conservation Trends, 3308–93

Underwriter Price Support and the IPO Underpricing Puzzle, 9385–8.113

Unemployment Compensation Reform Act of 1990, 21788–201

Unemployment in States and Local Areas, 6742–22

Unemployment Insurance Claims, 6402–15

Unemployment Insurance Occasional Papers, 6406–6

Unemployment Insurance Quality Appraisal Results, FY90, 6404–16

Unemployment Insurance Weekly Claims Report, 6402–14

Unemployment Trust Fund, 8102–9.1

Unemployment Trust Fund Activity Summary, 8102–9.16

UNICOR Federal Prison Industries, Inc.: Annual Report, 6244–3

UNICOR Sales Report, FY89, 6244–5

UNICOR Sales Report, FY90, 6244–5

Uniform Bank Performance Report, State Averages, 13002–3

Uniform Crime Report, January-June, 1991, 6222–1

Uniform Crime Report, 1990 Preliminary Annual Release, 6222–1

Uniform Crime Reports: Crime in the U.S., 1990, 6224–2

Uniform Crime Reports: Law Enforcement Officers Killed and Assaulted, 1990, 6224–3

Uniform Tire Quality Grading, 7764–17

Unintentional Injuries. Indian Health Conditions, 4088–2

Union Members in 1990, 6726–1.36

Union Recognitions and Agreements in the Federal Government. Statistical Report: The Status of Union Representation of Federal Employees Under 5 U.S.C. Chapter 71, 9844–17

University Programs and Facilities in Nuclear Science and Engineering, Seventh Edition, 3008–126

Unlimited Outdoor Adventure, Utah: Volume I, Executive Summary. Recreation 2000: A Revitalized Approach, 5726–5.4

Unlimited Outdoor Adventure, Utah: Volume II, Recreation Management Areas. Recreation 2000: A Revitalized Approach, 5726–5.4

Update on AIDS in Prisons and Jails, 6066–28.1

Update on the Farm Economy, 9362–1.207

Update on U.S. Coalbed Methane Production, 3162–4.201

Update on U.S. Horticultural Imports from Caribbean Basin Initiative Beneficiary Countries, 1925–34.239

Update to the 1991 Catalog of Federal Domestic Assistance, 104–5

Upland Cotton, Summary of 1991 Support Program and Related Information: ASCS Commodity Fact Sheet, 1806–4.9

Uranium Enrichment, Annual Report, 3354–7

Uranium Industry Annual, 1990, 3164–65

Urban Mass Transportation Administration Grants Assistance Programs, Information Summaries, 1990, 7884–10

Urban Population Tops 75% Mark for First Time, Census Bureau Analysis of '90 Data Reveals, 2328–39

Uruguay Round of GATT Trade Negotiations, 9385–8.115

U.S. Advisory Commission on Public Diplomacy, 1991 Report, 17594–1

U.S. Affiliates of Foreign Companies Errata, 2702–1.218

U.S. Affiliates of Foreign Companies: Operations in 1989, 2702–1.214

U.S. Agricultural Trade Goals and Strategy Report, 1991, Message from the President, 21168–44

U.S. Air Carrier Operations, 1987, Annual Review of Aircraft Accident Data, 9614–2

U.S. and District Agricultural Economies: The Expansion Continues, 9391–16.209

U.S. and World Floriculture Continues Up, 1502–4.201

U.S. Apple Exports: Recent Developments, 1925–34.236

U.S. Architectural and Transportation Barriers Compliance Board, FY90 Annual Report, 17614–1

U.S. Army Posture Statement, FY92/93, 3704–13

U.S. Attempts To Aid Oil Production Are Hindered by Many Obstacles. Soviet Energy, 26123–349

U.S. Attorneys: Better Models Can Reduce Resource Disparities Among Offices, 26119–323

U.S. Attorneys' Statistical Report, FY90, 6004–2

U.S. Automobile Industry: Monthly Report on Selected Economic Indicators. Report to the Subcommittee on Trade, Committee on Ways and Means, on Investigation No. 332-207 Under Section 332 of the Tariff Act of 1930, 9882–8

U.S. Automotive Industry: Monthly Report on Selected Economic Indicators. Report to the Subcommittee on Trade, Committee on Ways and Means, on Investigation No. 332-207 Under Section 332 of the Tariff Act of 1930, 9882–8

U.S. Aviation Accidents, Fatalities Down Since '89, 9614–9

U.S. Balance Sheet: What Is It and What Does It Tell Us?, 9391–1.220

U.S. Beef Packing Industry: Changing Market Structure and Performance Implications, 1004–16.1

U.S. Bipartisan Commission on Comprehensive Health Care, Supplement to the Final Report. The Pepper Commission. Call for Action, 23898–5

U.S. Border Patrol Apprehensions, 6266–2.2

U.S. Broiler Exports to the USSR: Temporary Phenomena or Emerging Trend?, 1561–7.205

U.S. Business Access to Certain Foreign State-of-the-Art Technology. International Trade, 26123–361

U.S. Business Enterprises Acquired or Established by Foreign Direct Investors in 1990, 2702–1.210

U.S. Citrus Exports, 1925–34.217

U.S. Civil Airmen Statistics, 1990, 7504–2

U.S. Coast Guard Digest of Law Enforcement Statistics, 7402–4

U.S. Commission on Civil Rights Catalog of Publications, 11048–188

U.S. Companies Improve Performance Through Quality Efforts. Management Practices, 26123–345

U.S. Consumer Product Safety Commission, FY89 Annual Report, 9164–2

U.S. Contributions for the 1980s. Refugee Assistance, 26123–334

U.S. Contributions to International Organizations, 39th Annual Report to the Congress, FY90, 7004–9

U.S. Controls on Trade with Selected Middle Eastern Countries. Export Controls, 26123–339

U.S. Costs in the Persian Gulf Conflict and Foreign Contributions To Offset Such Costs, 102–3

U.S. Cotton Quality Report: Classings Through (Date), 1309–11

U.S. Court of International Trade Annual Report for Fiscal Year Ending September 1991, 18224–2

U.S. Crude Oil, Natural Gas, and Natural Gas Liquids Reserves, 1990 Annual Report, 3164–46

Index by Titles

U.S. Customs—Update 1990, 8144–1

U.S. Dairy Industry at a Crossroad: Biotechnology and Policy Choices, 26358–237

U.S. Department of Agriculture: Farm Agencies' Field Structure Needs Major Overhaul, 26113–507

U.S. Department of Agriculture: Strategic Marketing Needed To Lead Agribusiness in International Trade, 26113–504

U.S. Department of Commerce Annual Report, FY90, 2004–1

U.S. Department of Education, Annual Report, FY89-90, 4804–6

U.S. Department of Energy: Office of Inspector General, Semiannual Report to Congress, 3002–12

U.S. Department of Energy Posture Statement and FY92 Budget Overview, 3024–5

U.S. Department of Housing and Urban Development Annual Report, 1989, 5004–10

U.S. Department of Labor Annual Report for FY90, 6304–1

U.S. Department of State Indexes of Living Costs Abroad, Quarters Allowances, and Hardship Differentials, 6862–1, 7002–7

U.S. Department of State Office of Inspector General: Semiannual Report to the Congress, Oct. 1, 1990-Mar. 31, 1991, 7002–6

U.S. Department of State Office of Inspector General: Semiannual Report to the Congress, Apr. 1-Sept. 30, 1991, 7002–6

U.S. Department of the Interior: Office of Inspector General, Semiannual Report, 5302–2

U.S. Department of Transportation, 22nd Annual Report, FY88, 7304–1

U.S. Direct Investment Abroad: Detail for Historical-Cost Position and Balance of Payments Flows, 1990, 2702–1.220

U.S. Direct Investment Abroad: Operations of U.S. Parent Companies and Their Foreign Affiliates, Revised 1988 Estimates, 2704–5

U.S. Direct Investment Abroad: 1989 Benchmark Survey, Preliminary Results, 2704–5

U.S. Direct Investment Abroad: 1989 Benchmark Survey Results, 2702–1.225

U.S. Earthquakes, 1985, 5664–13

U.S. Economy into the 21st Century, 6722–1.251

U.S. Energy Industry Financial Developments, 3162–38

U.S. Essential Oil Trade, 1925–15.2

U.S. Export Declaration of Foreign Tobacco Content, 1925–16.216

U.S. Export Sales, 1922–3

U.S. Exports, 2424–5

U.S. Exports and Imports by Harmonized Commodity, 6-Digit Harmonized Commodity by Country, 2424–13

U.S. Exports and Imports Transshipped via Canadian Ports, 1989, 7704–11

U.S. Exports: Harmonized Schedule B, Commodity by Country, 2424–10

U.S. Exports of Merchandise, 2422–13

U.S. Exports to Mexico: A State-by-State Overview, 1987-89, 2048–154

U.S. Exports to Mexico: A State-by-State Overview, 1987-90, 2048–154

U.S. Financial Data, 9391–4

U.S. Financial System: A Status Report and a Structural Perspective, 9385–8.84

U.S. Foreign Trade Highlights, 1990, 2044–37

U.S. Foreign Trade in Selected Building Products, 2042–1.204

U.S. Foreign Trade. Schedule B, Statistical Classification of Domestic and Foreign Commodities Exported from the U.S., 2428–5

U.S. Foreign Trade Update: Monthly Analysis for [Date], 2042–34

U.S. Foreign Trade: Waterborne Exports and General Imports. Trade Area, District, Port, Type Service, and U.S. Flag, 2422–7

U.S. Forest Planting Report, 1204–7

U.S. General Aviation, 1988, Annual Review of Aircraft Accident Data, 9614–3

U.S. General Imports, 2424–2

U.S. General Imports: Cotton Manufacturers, 2046–8.1

U.S. General Imports: Cotton or Man-Made Fiber Manufacturers, 2046–8.7

U.S. General Imports: Customs Import Value, 2046–9

U.S. General Imports: Man-Made Fiber Manufacturers, 2046–8.3

U.S. General Imports of Cotton Manufacturers (Customs Value), 2046–9.4

U.S. General Imports of Cotton or Man-Made Fiber Manufacturers (Customs Value), 2046–9.8

U.S. General Imports of Cotton, Wool, Man-Made Fiber, and Vegetable Fiber (Except Cotton) and Silk Blend Textiles, 2042–27

U.S. General Imports of Man-Made Fiber Manufacturers (Customs Value), 2046–9.2

U.S. General Imports of Vegetable Fibers (Except Cotton) and Silk Blend Manufacturers (Customs Value), 2046–9.9

U.S. General Imports of Wool Manufacturers (Customs Value), 2046–9.1

U.S. General Imports: Quantity Totals, 2046–8

U.S. General Imports: Vegetable Fibers Manufacturers, 2046–8.6

U.S. General Imports: Wool Manufacturers, 2046–8.2

U.S. Geological Survey Yearbook, FY90, 5664–8

U.S. Government Annual Report, 1990, 8104–2

U.S. Government Is Responding to the Problem. Money Laundering, 26123–338

U.S. Government Printing Office Annual Report, 1990, 26204–1

U.S. Government Printing Office Sales Publications Pricing Panel Report to the Public Printer, 26208–3

U.S. Grain Exports Quality Report, 1990, 1294–2

U.S. Horticultural Trade with Caribbean Basin Initiative Beneficiary Countries, 1990, 1925–34.230

U.S. Import and Export Price Indexes, 6762–13, 6762–15

U.S. Imports, Exports of Fishery Products, 1989, 2162–1.204

U.S. Imports for Consumption and General Imports: TSUSA Commodity by Country of Origin, 2424–4

U.S. Imports of Fruits and Vegetables Under Plant Quarantine Regulations, FY88, 1524–7

U.S. Imports of Lamb Meat: Final Monitoring Report. Report on Investigation No. 332-264 Under Section 332(g) of the Tariff Act of 1930 As Amended, 9886–4.166

U.S. Imports of Merchandise, 2422–14

U.S. Imports of Textiles and Apparel Under the Multifiber Arrangement: Annual Report for 1990, 9884–18

U.S. Industrial Outlook, 1991, 2044–28

U.S. International Air Travel Statistics, 7302–2

U.S. International Development Cooperation Agency, Congressional Presentation, FY92, 9904–4

U.S. International Development Cooperation Agency, Congressional Presentation, FY92. International Organizations and Programs, 9904–4.2

U.S. International Development Cooperation Agency, Congressional Presentation, FY92. U.S. Trade and Development Program, 9904–4.3

U.S. International Sales and Purchases of Services: U.S. Cross-Border Transactions, 1987-90, and Sales by Affiliates, 1988-89, 2702–1.223

U.S. International Trade Commission, 1990 Annual Report, 9884–1

U.S. International Transactions in 1990, 9362–1.202

U.S. Labor Market Weakened in 1990, 6722–1.212

U.S. Markets for Caribbean Basin Fruits and Vegetables: Selected Characteristics for 17 Fresh and Frozen Imports, 1975-87, 1568–299

U.S. Marshals Service, Director's Report, FY90, 6294–1

U.S. Merchandise Trade: Exports and General Imports by Country, Standard International Trade Classification Revision 3, Country by Commodity, 2424–12

U.S. Merchandise Trade: Exports, General Imports, and Imports for Consumption, Standard International Trade Classification Revision 3, Commodity by Country, 2422–12

U.S. Merchandise Trade Position at Midyear, 2044–38

U.S. Merchant Marine Data Sheet, 7702–1

U.S. Military Strengths Worldwide Fact Sheet, as of (Date), 3542–9

U.S. Milk Markets Under Alternative Federal Order Pricing Policies, 1568–294

U.S. National Commission on Libraries and Information Science Annual Report, 1988-89, 15634–1

U.S. National Commission on Libraries and Information Science Annual Report, 1989-90, 15634–1

U.S. Natural Gas Imports and Exports, 1990, 3162–4.208

U.S. Nuclear Regulatory Commission, 1990 Annual Report, 9634–2

U.S. Oceanborne Foreign Trade Routes, 1988, 7704–2

U.S. Overseas Loans and Grants and Assistance from International Organizations, 9914–5

U.S. Parole Commission Annual Report, 6004–3

U.S. Participation in the UN: Report by the President to the Congress for the Year 1989, 7004–5

U.S. Participation in the UN: Report by the President to the Congress for the Year 1990, 7004–5

U.S. Personnel in the Pacific Theater. Military Presence, 26123–357

U.S. Petroleum Developments:... Index by Titles

U.S. Petroleum Developments: 1990, 3162–6.201

U.S. Petroleum Refining Industry in the 1980's, 3168–119

U.S. Petroleum Supply, 3164–2.1

U.S. Petroleum Trade 1990, 3162–6.202

U.S. Policy in the Bretton Woods Era, 9391–1.214

U.S. Population Up Nearly Two-Thirds in 40 Years; Nevada, California Lead 40-Year Period Growth, 2328–66

U.S. Possessions Corporation Returns, 1987, 8302–2.213

U.S. Postal Inspection Service: Semiannual Report, 9862–2

U.S. Postal Service Cost Segments and Components, FY90, 9864–4

U.S. Potato Statistics, 1949-89, 1568–305

U.S. Quality of Cotton Classed Under Smith-Doxey Act, 1309–15

U.S. Refining Industry, 3164–2.1

U.S. Renal Data System, 1989 Annual Data Report, 4474–37

U.S. Renal Data System, 1990 Annual Data Report, 4474–37

U.S. Renal Data System, 1991 Annual Data Report, 4474–37

U.S. Rice Imports and Domestic Use, 1561–8.206

U.S. Savings Bonds Issued and Redeemed Through (Month), 8242–1

U.S. Secret Service Investigative Activity, FY86-90, 8464–1

U.S. Securities and Exchange Commission Fifty-sixth Annual Report, 1990, 9734–2

U.S. Seed Exports: Foreign Agricultural Service Circular Series, 1925–13

U.S. Sentencing Commission Annual Report, 1990, 17664–1

U.S. Spice Trade, 1925–15.1

U.S. Sugar Statistical Compendium, 1568–306

U.S. Tax Court Analysis of Cases Closed (By Dockets), Oct. 1, 1989-Sept. 30, 1990, 18224–3

U.S. Tax Court, Annual Report, 18224–5

U.S. Tax Court, FY90 Statistical Information, 18224–5

U.S. Telecommunications in a Global Economy: Competitiveness at a Crossroads, 2008–30

U.S. Timber Production, Trade, Consumption, and Price Statistics, 1960-88, 1204–29

U.S. Tobacco Trade, 1983-90, 1925–16.209

U.S. Trade and Development Program. U.S. International Development Cooperation Agency Congressional Presentation, FY92, 9904–4.3

U.S. Trade and Prospects. Foreign Agricultural Service Circular Series: Dairy, Livestock, and Poultry, 1925–32

U.S. Trade Impacts of Alternative Crops to Andean Coca. Drug Policy and Agriculture, 26123–366

U.S. Trade in Tuna for Canning, 1987, 2162–1.202

U.S. Trade Performance, 2044–26

U.S. Trade Remedy Laws: Do They Facilitate or Hinder Free Trade?, 9391–1.215

U.S. Trade Shifts in Selected Commodity Areas, January-June 1990, 9882–9

U.S. Trade Shifts in Selected Commodity Areas, 1990, 9882–9

U.S. Trade with Puerto Rico and U.S. Possessions, 2424–11

U.S. Trade with the European Community, 1958, 1968, 1978, 1980, and 1986-90, 7144–7

U.S. Transportation Deaths Dipped in 1990 for Second Year in a Row, 9614–6

U.S. Underwater Diving Fatality Statistics, 1989, With a Preliminary Assessment of 1990 Fatalities, 2144–5

U.S. Uranium Enrichment, 1990 Report, 3354–7

U.S. Waterborne Exports and General Imports: Trade Area, District, Port, Type Service, and U.S. Flag, 2422–7

U.S. Wholesale Electricity Transactions, 3162–24.201, 3162–35.201

U.S. Worker Rehabilitation in International Perspective, 6722–1.242

U.S.-Canada Free Trade Agreement: Eliminating Barriers to Commerce, 5602–4.201

U.S.-China Agricultural Trade over Two Decades, 1524–4.3

USDA Announces Preliminary Results of 1991 Program Signup, 1004–20.1

USDA Forest Service 25 Percent Payments to States, 1204–33

USDA International Technical Assistance Activities, 1954–2

USDA International Training Activities, 1954–1

USDA Market Development Programs, 1925–34.233

USDA Reports Certificate Exchange Activity Through (Date), 1802–16

USDA's Systems Limited by Insufficient Top Management Support. Financial Disclosure, 26119–314

Use and Cost of Short-Stay Hospital Inpatient Services Under Medicare, 1988, 4652–1.207

Use and Design of Flightcrew Checklists and Manuals, 7506–10.86

Use of Alcohol in Fuels, 12th Annual Report, 3304–9

Use of Cash Transaction Reports by Federal Law Enforcement Agencies. Money Laundering, 26119–356

Use of Family Planning Services by Currently Married Women 15-44 Years of Age: U.S., 1973 and 1976, 4147–16.5

Use of Intrauterine Contraceptive Devices in the U.S., 4147–16.5

Use of Medicare-Covered Home Health Agency Services, 1988, 4652–1.229

Use of Navy and Marine Corps Reserves. Operation Desert Shield/Storm, 26123–351

Use of Selected Medical Device Implants in the U.S., 1988, 4146–8.197

Use of Wilderness for Personal Growth, Therapy, and Education, 1208–347

U.S.-EC Canned Fruit Agreement, 1925–34.223

Used Oil Reclamation and Re-Refining Industry: Preliminary Data Summary, 9206–4.6

Usefulness of P* Measures for Japan and Germany, 9366–7.268

User Friendly Facts: A Resource Book, 1991, 2904–15

User's Guide for the Uniform Bank Performance Report, 13002–3

User's Guide to BEA Information, 2702–1.203, 2708–45

USIA English Language Programs Activities, 9854–2

USIA Office of Cultural Centers and Resources, Annual Library Statistics, FY89, 9854–4

USIA Office of Cultural Centers and Resources, Annual Library Statistics, FY90, 9854–4

Using Econometric Models To Predict Recessions, 9375–1.212

Using External Sustainability To Forecast the Dollar, 9366–7.252

Using Linked Program and Birth Records To Evaluate Coverage and Targeting in Tennessee's WIC Program, 4042–3.216

Using Noisy Indicators To Measure Potential Output, 9375–13.65

Using the Consumer Price Index for Escalation, 6888–34

USITC Investigations Under Section 332 of the Tariff Act of 1930, 9886–4

USITC Investigations Under Section 733(a) and 735(b) of the Tariff Act of 1930, As Amended, 9886–14

USITC Investigations Under Sections 703(a) and 705(b) of the Tariff Act of 1930, As Amended, 9886–15

USITC Investigations Under Sections 703(a), 733(a), 705(b), and 735(b) of the Tariff Act of 1930, As Amended, 9886–19

U.S.-Mexican Horticultural Trade, 1925–34.219

U.S.-Mexican Vegetable Trade, 1561–11.202

U.S.-Mexico Fruit Trade, 1561–6.203

U.S.-Mexico Trade: Impact of Liberalization in the Agricultural Sector, 26123–335

U.S.S. Iowa Explosion: Sandia National Laboratories' Final Technical Report, 26123–315

USSR Agricultural Trade, 1528–322

USSR Agriculture and Trade Report, Situation and Outlook Series, 1524–4.1

USSR: Gross National Products Accounts, 1985, 2326–18.59

Usual Sources of Medical Care and Their Characteristics. National Medical Expenditure Survey, 4186–8.22

Usual Weekly Earnings of Wage and Salary Workers, 6742–20

Utah Cooperative Snow Survey Data of Federal-State-Private Cooperative Snow Surveys, Water Year 1990, 1264–14.2

Utility Allowances Often Fall Short of Actual Utility Expenses. Assisted Housing, 26113–512

Utilization and Donation of Federal Personal Property, FY88-90, Report to the Congress of the U.S., 9454–22

Utilization of Emergency Medical Kits by Air Carriers, 7506–10.81

Utilization of IHS and Tribal Direct and Contract General Hospitals, FY89 and U.S. Non-Federal Short-Stay Hospitals, CY88, 4084–5

Utilization of Indian Health Service and Contract General Hospitals, and U.S. Non-Federal Short-Stay Hospitals, 4084–5

VA Health Care: Alcoholism Screening Procedures Should Be Improved, 26121–416

VA Loan Guaranty Highlights, 8602–2

Valuation of Default-Risky Interest-Rate Swaps, 9371–10.62

Valuation of the U.S. Net International Investment Position, 2702–1.211

Index by Titles

Value of New Construction Put in Place, Current Construction Reports, 2382–4

Value of Product Shipments, 1989 Annual Survey of Manufactures, 2506–15.2

Value-Weighted Quantity Indices of Exports for High-Value Processed Agricultural Products, 1528–323

Vanadium: Mineral Industry Surveys, 5612–1.26

Vanadium: Minerals Yearbook, Volume 1, 1989, 5604–15.68

Vance Federal Building, Birmingham, Ala. (H.R. 3961), Federal Courthouse Space and Construction Needs (H.R. 4178), 21648–60

Variations in Payments to Anesthesiologists Linked to Anesthesia Time. Medicare, 26121–417

Variations in Texas School Quality, 9379–12.67

Various Industries in American Samoa, An Economic Report, 6504–6

Vegetable Fibers (Except Cotton) and Silk Blend Manufacturers (Customs Value). U.S. General Imports, 2046–9.9

Vegetable Fibers Manufacturers. U.S. General Imports, 2046–8.6

Vegetables, 1621–12

Vegetables and Specialties Situation and Outlook Report, 1561–11

Vegetables and Specialties Situation and Outlook Yearbook, 1561–11

Vegetables, Annual Summary, 1621–25

Vegetables Summary, 1990. Agricultural Chemical Usage, 1616–1.2

Vegetables: 1990 Preliminary Acreage, Yield, and Production, 1621–25.1

Vegetables: 1990 Summary, 1621–25.2

Vending Machines (Coin-Operated), 1990, Current Industrial Report, 2506–12.10

Veneer Industry and Timber Use, North Central Region, 1984, 1208–220

Veneer Industry and Timber Use, North Central Region, 1988, 1208–220

Vermiculite in 1990: Mineral Industry Surveys Annual Report, 5614–5.29

Vessel Inventory Report, As of July 1, 1990, 7702–2

Vessel Inventory Report, As of Jan. 1, 1991, 7702–2

Vessel Sanitation Program Operations Manual, 4202–10

Veteran Population, Mar. 31, 1991, 8604–12

Veterans Affairs, Annual Report of the Secretary, FY90, 8604–3

Veterans Benefits Under Current Educational Programs, FY89, 8604–9

Veterans Housing Loan Program Evaluation, Executive Summary, 8608–7

Veterans Housing Loan Program Evaluation, Final Report, 8608–7

Victims of Crime Act Grants: Better Reporting Needed for Compensation and Assistance Programs, 26119–348

View from Another Bridge, 2152–8.201

Violence Against Women: The Increase of Rape in America, 1990, 25528–116

Violence as Regulation and Social Control in the Distribution of Crack, 4498–70

Violence. Indian Health Conditions, 4088–2

Violent Crime in the U.S., 6068–148

Visa Office, 1989 Report, 7184–1

Visitor Fatalities, 1980-90 Inclusive, 5544–6

Vital and Health Statistics Series 1: Program and Collection Procedures, 4147–1

Vital and Health Statistics Series 2: Data Evaluation and Methods Research, 4147–2

Vital and Health Statistics Series 4: Documents and Committee Reports, 4147–4

Vital and Health Statistics Series 5: Comparative International Vital and Health Statistics Reports, 4147–5

Vital and Health Statistics Series 10: Data from the National Health Interview Survey, 4147–10

Vital and Health Statistics Series 13: Data on Health Resources Utilization, 4147–13

Vital and Health Statistics Series 16: Compilations of Advance Data from Vital and Health Statistics, 4147–16

Vital and Health Statistics Series 20: Data from the National Vital Statistics System, 4147–20

Vital and Health Statistics Series 20: Data on Mortality, 4147–20

Vital and Health Statistics Series 21: Data on Natality, Marriage, and Divorce, 4147–21

Vital and Health Statistics Series 24: Compilations of Data on Natality, Mortality, Marriage, Divorce, and Induced Terminations of Pregnancy, 4147–24

Vital Statistics of the U.S., 1986. Volume III: Marriage and Divorce, 4144–4

Vital Statistics of the U.S., 1987. Volume III: Marriage and Divorce, 4144–4

Vital Statistics of the U.S., 1988. Volume II: Mortality, Part A, 4144–2

Vocational Rehabilitation: Clearer Guidance Could Help Focus Services on Those with Severe Disabilities, 26121–438

Volunteers in the U.S.: Who Donates the Time?, 6722–1.213

Voting and Registration in the Election of November 1990, 2546–1.454

Wage Differences Among Metropolitan Areas, 1990, 6785–8

Wage Differences Among Selected Areas, 1990, 6785–13

Wage Differentials and Job Changes, 2626–10.121

Wage Statistics of Class I Railroads in the U.S., 1990, 9484–5

Wages and Compensation: 1990 Negotiated Adjustments, 6722–1.227

Wages and Employment Among the Working Poor: New Evidence from SIPP, 2626–10.122

Wages in the South, 6942–8

Walnut Production, 1621–18.8

Warmwater Fisheries Symposium I, 1991, 1208–381

Washington Cooperative Snow Survey Data of Federal-State-Private Cooperative Snow Surveys, 1264–14.1

Washington's Soil and Water: Condition and Trends, 1982-87, 1266–5.2

Water and Habitat Dynamics of the Mingo Swamp in Southeastern Missouri, 5506–13.2

Water Bank Program: Compilation of Status of Agreements, 1802–5

Water Bank Program: From Inception of Program Through Sept. 30, 1990, 1804–21

Water Level Changes in the High Plains Aquifer Underlying Parts of South Dakota, Wyoming, Nebraska, Colorado, Kansas, New Mexico, Oklahoma, and Texas: Predevelopment Through Nonirrigation Season 1987-88, 5666–28.3

Water-Quality Characteristics...

Water Pollution: States' Progress in Developing State Revolving Loan Fund Programs, 26113–521

Water Pollution: Stronger Efforts Needed by EPA To Control Toxic Water Pollution, 26113–536

Water Quality Protection, 25168–76

Water Resources Activities in Florida, 1989-90, 5666–26.14

Water Resources Activities in Utah by the USGS, Oct. 1, 1988-Sept. 30, 1989, 5666–26.15

Water Resources Activities of the USGS in Kansas, FY87-88, 5666–26.10

Water Resources Activities of the USGS in Montana, Oct. 1987-Sept. 1989, 5666–26.11

Water Resources Activities of the USGS in West Virginia, 1989, 5666–26.12

Water Resources Activities of the USGS: Selected States, 5666–26

Water Resources Data for (State), Water Year 1988, 5666–16

Water Resources Data for (State), Water Year 1989, 5666–12

Water Resources Data for (State), Water Year 1990, 5666–10

Water Resources Development by the U.S. Army Corps of Engineers in (State), 1989, 3756–1

Water Resources Development by the U.S. Army Corps of Engineers in (State), 1991, 3756–2

Water Resources: Local Area Studies, 5666–27

Water Resources of the Fond du Lac Indian Reservation, East-Central Minnesota, 5666–28.9

Water Supply Outlook and Federal-State-Private Cooperative Snow Surveys, 1266–2

Water Supply Outlook and Summary for Oregon, Oct. 1, 1991, 1264–9

Water Supply Outlook for Arizona, 1266–2.2

Water Supply Outlook for Colorado, 1266–2.3

Water Supply Outlook for Idaho, 1266–2.4

Water Supply Outlook for Nevada, 1266–2.6

Water Supply Outlook for New Mexico, 1266–2.11

Water Supply Outlook for Oregon, 1266–2.7

Water Supply Outlook for the Northeastern U.S., 2182–3

Water Supply Outlook for the Western U.S., 1262–1

Water Supply Outlook for Utah, 1266–2.8

Water Supply Outlook for Washington, 1266–2.9

Water Supply Outlook for Wyoming, 1266–2.10

Water Use in South Carolina, 1985, 5666–24.9

Water Use: Selected States, 5666–24

Water Withdrawal and Use in Maryland, 1986, 5666–24.8

Water Year Summary for the Great Basin in Nevada and California, 1991, 1264–8

Waterborne Tonnage by State, 1989, 3754–7.5, 3754–7.6

Waterfowl Habitat Management on Public Lands: A Strategy for the Future, 5726–6.2

Waterfowl Win Big During Migratory Bird Commission Meeting, 5306–4.11

Water-Quality Characteristics of the Columbia Plateau Regional Aquifer System in Parts of Washington, Oregon, and Idaho, 5666–28.11

Water-Quality Data, San...

Water-Quality Data, San Joaquin Valley, Calif., April 1987 to September 1988. Regional Aquifer-System Analysis, 5666–25.9

We Fought Cape Horn . . . and the Horn Won, 2152–8.201

Weaknesses Exist in FRA's Enforcement Program. Railroad Safety., 26113–515

Weather and Soybean Yield: A Regional Analysis, 1561–3.204

Weather, Climate and Variability of U.S. Corn Yield, 1561–4.203

Weekly Climate Bulletin, 2182–6

Weekly Coal Production, 3162–1

Weekly Consolidated Condition Report of Large Commercial Banks in the U.S., 9365–1.3

Weekly Petroleum Status Report, 3162–32

Weekly Weather and Crop Bulletin, 2182–7

Welfare Gains from Wood Preservatives Research, 1502–3.202

Welfare Implications of EPA's New Registration Standard: The Case of Fresh Market Tomatoes, 1588–154

Welfare Participation and Welfare Recidivism: The Role of Family Events, 2626–10.126

Welfare Reform: How Well Is It Working?, 10042–1.201

Welfare to Work: States Begin JOBS, but Fiscal and Other Problems May Impede Their Progress, 26121–435

Welfare-Improving Credit Controls, 9389–19.26

West Germany's Health Care and Health-Insurance System: Combining Universal Access with Cost Control, 23898–5

West Virginia Timber Products Output, 1987, 1206–15.9

Western Area Power Administration, 1990 Annual Report, 3254–1

Western Europe: Agriculture and Trade Report, Situation and Outlook Series, 1524–4.4

Western Gulf of Alaska Tides and Circulation, 2176–1.36

Wetlands Losses in the U.S. 1780's to 1980's, 5508–107

What America's Users Spend on Illegal Drugs. An Office of National Drug Control Policy Technical Paper, 236–2.1

What Do Farmers Consider Important When Making Management Decisions?, 1541–1.206

What Does Performing Linear Regression on Sample Survey Data Mean?, 1502–3.202

What Motivates Oil Producers?: Testing Alternative Hypotheses, 9379–12.68

What Works: 1990 Urban MCH Programs. Directory of Maternal and Child Health Programs in Major Urban Health Departments, 4108–51

Whatever Happened to Child Care in 1989?, 8304–8.1

Wheat Cleaning Practices of U.S. Commercial Elevators, 1561–12.204

Wheat Situation and Outlook Report, 1561–12

Wheat Situation and Outlook Yearbook, 1561–12

Wheat, Summary of 1991 Support Program and Related Information: ASCS Commodity Fact Sheet, 1806–4.11

Which Farmers Will Be Most Affected by Increasing Oil Prices?, 1541–1.203

Index by Titles

White Papers. Office of National Drug Control Policy, 236–1

"Whither New England?", 9373–1.211

Who Are the Self-Employed? Employment Profiles and Recent Trends, 6742–1.202

Who Can Afford To Buy a House?, 2486–1.11

Who Can Afford To Buy a House? Statistical Brief, 2326–17.31

Who Changes the Prime Rate?, 9387–8.235

Who Does What in the Federal Government. Food Safety and Quality, 26113–503

Who Put the Wind Speeds in Admiral Beaufort's Force Scale? Part 2—The New Scales, 2152–8.201

Wholesale Trade, 1990. Annual Sales and Year-End Inventories, Purchases, and Gross Margin Estimates of Merchant Wholesalers. Current Business Reports, 2413–13

Who's Supporting the Kids? Statistical Brief, 2326–17.37

Why Banks Need Commerce Powers, 9393–8.206

Why Is Automobile Insurance in Philadelphia So Damn Expensive?, 9383–20.9

WIC Program Participation—A Marketing Approach, 4042–3.247

Wildlife and Fish Program Status Report, FY89, 5728–37

Wildlife Protection: Enforcement of Federal Laws Could Be Strengthened, 26113–525

Wildlife, 1990, Current Federal Aid Research Report, 5504–24

Will Immigration Reform Affect the Economic Competitiveness of Labor-Intensive Crops?, 1598–276

Wines: Monthly Statistical Release, 8486–1.2

Winter Fuels Report, 3162–45

Winter Wheat and Rye Seedings, 1621–30

Wisconsin Timber Industry: An Assessment of Timber Product Output and Use, 1988, 1206–10.12

Withdrawal and Distribution of Water by Public Water Supplies in Ohio in 1985, 5666–24.7

Within DRG Case Complexity: Change Update and Distributional Differences, 17206–2.21

Within-School Discrimination: Inadequate Title VI Enforcement by the Office for Civil Rights, 26121–427

Wollastonite and Zeolites: Minerals Yearbook, Volume 1, 1989, 5604–15.79

Women at Thirtysomething: Paradoxes of Attainment, 4888–6

Women in Prison, 6066–19.61

Women in the Military: Air Force Revises Job Availability but Entry Screening Needs Review, 26123–359

Women in the Skilled Trades and in Other Manual Occupations, 6564–1.1

Women 65 Years or Older: A Comparison of Economic Well-Being by Living Arrangement, 1702–1.210

Wood Products: Foreign Agricultural Service Circular Series. International Trade and Foreign Markets, 1925–36

Wool and Mohair, 1623–6

Wool Manufacturers (Customs Value). U.S. General Imports, 2046–9.1

Wool Manufacturers. U.S. General Imports, 2046–8.2

Wool Prices Liberalized in International Markets, 1561–1.207

Wool, Summary of 1991 Support Program and Related Information: ASCS Commodity Fact Sheet, 1806–4.14

Work and Poverty in Metro and Nonmetro Areas, 1598–274

Work Experience of the Population in 1990, 6726–1.39

Work Injury Reports, 6846–1

Work Performed by the Department of Labor Inspector General in 1988 and 1989. Inspectors General, 26111–74

Work Years and Personnel Costs, Executive Branch, U.S. Government, FY89. Federal Civilian Workforce Statistics, 9844–31

Worker Debt with Bankruptcy, 9387–8.241

Worker Displacement Still Common in the Late 1980's, 6722–1.225

Workers at Risk: Increased Numbers in Contingent Employment Lack Insurance, Other Benefits, 26121–411

Workers' Compensation and the Distribution of Occupational Injuries, 6886–6.80

Workers' Compensation: Coverage, Benefits, and Costs, 1988, 4742–1.207

Workers with Disabilities in Large and Small Firms: Profiles from the SIPP, 2626–10.130

Workforce Issues: Employment Practices in Selected Large Private Companies, 26119–324

Working Paper Series, Federal Reserve Bank of Atlanta, 9371–10

Working Paper Series, Federal Reserve Bank of Chicago, 9375–13

Working Paper Series, Federal Reserve Bank of Richmond, 9389–19

Working Papers, Federal Reserve Bank of Cleveland, 9377–9

Working Papers, Federal Reserve Bank of San Francisco, 9393–10

Workshop on U.S.-USSR Commercial Relations, Apr. 17, 1989, 25388–56

World Agricultural Production: Foreign Agricultural Service Circular Series, 1925–28

World Agricultural Supply and Demand Estimates, 1522–5

World Agriculture Current Trends and Perspectives, 1522–3

World Agriculture Situation and Outlook Report, 1522–3

World Almond Situation, 1925–34.240

World and U.S. Agricultural Outlook, 1004–16.1

World and U.S. Outlook for Sweeteners, 1004–16.1

World Banana Production and Trade Situation, 1925–34.228

World Canned Pineapple Situation, 1925–34.216

World Cigarette Production and Trade, 1925–16.214

World Citrus Situation, 1925–34.226

World Cocoa Situation. Foreign Agricultural Service Circular Series: Cocoa, 1925–9

World Coffee Situation: Foreign Agricultural Service Circular Series, 1925–5

World Cotton Situation, 1925–4.2

World Dairy Situation: Foreign Agricultural Service Circular Series, 1925–10

World Data Center A, Oceanography: Oceanographic Data Exchange, 1989, 2144–15

World Factbook, 1991, 9114–2

World Fresh Deciduous Fruit Update, 1925–34.244

Index by Titles

World Grain Situation and Outlook, 1925–2.1
World Grain Situation and Outlook: Reference Guide on Rice Supply and Distribution for Individual Countries, 1925–2.6
World Grain Situation and Outlook: World Pulse Trade, 1925–2.5
World Hazelnut Situation, 1925–34.246
World Livestock Situation. Foreign Agricultural Service Circular Series: Dairy, Livestock, and Poultry, 1925–33.2
World Nuclear Fuel Cycle Requirements, 1991, 3164–72
World Oilseed and Products Trade, 1962-88, 1528–314
World Oilseed Situation and Outlook, 1925–1.1
World Outlook for Canned Deciduous Fruit, 1925–34.220
World Poultry Situation. Foreign Agricultural Service Circular Series: Dairy, Livestock, and Poultry, 1925–33.1
World Pulse Trade, 1925–2.5
World Raisin Situation, 1925–34.221, 1925–34.250
World Rice Trade: Prospects and Issues for the Nineties, 1561–8.203
World Squid Supply and Market Study, 2166–19.10
World Sugar Production, Supply, and Distribution, 1974/75-1990/91, 1925–14.1
World Sugar Situation and Outlook, 1925–14.2, 1925–14.3
World Sugar Situation and Outlook. World Sugar Production, Supply, and Distribution, 1974/75-1990/91, 1925–14.1
World Tea Situation, 1925–15.3
World Tobacco Situation: Foreign Agricultural Service Circular Series, 1925–16
World Tobacco Supply and Distribution, 1925–16.213
World Trade in Canned Mushrooms, 1925–34.242
World Unmanufactured Tobacco Production, 1925–16.204, 1925–16.211
World Unmanufactured Tobacco Trade, 1925–16.215
World Walnut Situation, 1925–34.247
World Weather Records, 1971-80, 2156–4
World Wheat Outlook, 1990/91, 1004–16.1
Worldwide Deposition of Strontium-90 Through 1986, 3004–29
Worldwide Manpower Distribution, by Geographical Area, 3542–20
Worldwide Reports on AID Population Programs, FY90, 9914–13
Worldwide U.S. Active Duty Military Personnel Casualties, 3542–21
Worldwide U.S. Active Duty Military Personnel Casualties, Oct. 1, 1988-Sept. 30, 1989, 3544–40
Worldwide U.S. Active Duty Military Personnel Casualties, Oct. 1, 1989-Sept. 30, 1990, 3544–40
Wyoming Cooperative Snow Survey Data of Federal-State-Private Cooperative Snow Surveys, Water Year 1990, 1264–14.5

Year End Asset Sales, Institutions Resolution, Management, and the Strategic Plan, 21248–157
Yearbook of Agriculture, 1990: Americans in Agriculture, 1004–18
Yearbook of Agriculture, 1991: Agriculture and the Environment, 1004–18

Yellowstone Grizzly Bear Investigations, Annual Report of the Interagency Study Team, 1990, 5544–4
Youth and Alcohol, 4006–10
Youth and Alcohol: A National Survey. Do They Know What They're Drinking?, 4006–10.2
Youth and Alcohol: A National Survey. Drinking Habits, Access, Attitudes, and Knowledge, 4006–10.1
Youth and Alcohol: Laws and Enforcement. Compendium of State Laws, 4006–10.3
Youth Deficits: An Emerging Population Problem, 9118–17
Youth Indicators, 1991: Trends in the Well-Being of American Youth, 4818–5
Youth Labor Force Expected To Be Smaller This Summer than Last, 6744–13

Zero Inflation: Transition Costs and Shoe-Leather Benefits, 9377–9.122
Zinc Industry: Mineral Industry Surveys, 5612–1.27
Zinc: Minerals Yearbook, Volume 1, 1989, 5604–15.70
Zirconium and Hafnium: Minerals Yearbook, Volume 1, 1989, 5604–15.71

18th Annual Report of the Board of Directors of the Rural Telephone Bank, FY89, 1244–4
29th Annual Report for FY90, Federal Maritime Commission, 9334–1
33 New Urbanized Areas Reflect Rise of Population Clusters in South, West, 2328–37
50th Annual Report of the Foreign-Trade Zones Board to the Congress of the U.S., For the Fiscal Year Ended Sept. 30, 1988, 2044–30
51st Annual Report of Energy Purchased by REA Borrowers, 1244–5
56th Annual Report of the U.S. Securities and Exchange Commission, FY90, 9734–2
77th Annual Report, 1990, Board of Governors of the Federal Reserve System, 9364–1
93rd Annual Report of the Register of Copyrights, For the Fiscal Year Ending Sept. 30, 1990, 26404–2
100 Companies Receiving the Largest Dollar Volume of Prime Contract Awards, FY90, 3544–5
195 Cities Have Population Over 100,000, New York, First; Los Angeles, Second; San Antonio Joins Top Ten. Mesa, Ariz., Fastest Growing City, 2324–7
500 Contractors Receiving the Largest Dollar Volume of Prime Contract Awards for Research, Development, Test, and Evaluation, FY90, 3544–4

1977 Summary: National Ambulatory Medical Care Survey, 4147–16.5
1984 American Housing Survey for Metropolitan Areas, Supplement, 2485–8
1986 Corporation Foreign Tax Credit, A Geographic Focus, 8302–2.207
1986 Law Will Improve Benefit Equity in Many Small Employers' Plans. Private Pensions, 26121–412

1987 Enterprise Statistics.

1987 Census of Agriculture. Volume 1. Geographic Area Series, State and County Data, 2331–1
1987 Census of Agriculture. Volume 4. Census of Horticultural Specialties (1988), 2337–1
1987 Census of Construction Industries. Industry Series, 2373–1
1987 Census of Governments. Volume 3. Public Employment. No. 1: Employment of Major Local Governments, 2455–1
1987 Census of Governments. Volume 3. Public Employment. No. 2: Compendium of Public Employment, 2455–2
1987 Census of Governments. Volume 3. Public Employment. No. 3: Labor-Management Relations, 2455–3
1987 Census of Governments. Volume 3. Public Employment. No. 4: Government Costs for Employee Benefits, 2455–4
1987 Census of Governments. Volume 6. Guide to the 1987 Census of Governments. No. 1: Guide to the 1987 Census of Governments, 2460–1
1987 Census of Manufacturers. Subject Series. Manufacturers' Shipments to the Federal Government, 2497–7
1987 Census of Manufactures. Subject Series. General Summary: Industry, Product Class, and Geographic Area Statistics, 2497–1
1987 Census of Manufactures. Subject Series. Type of Organization, 2497–5
1987 Census of Mineral Industries. Geographic Area Series, 2515–1
1987 Census of Mineral Industries. Subject Series. Fuels and Electric Energy Consumed, 2517–2
1987 Census of Mineral Industries. Subject Series. General Summary, 2517–1
1987 Census of Retail Trade. Special Report Series. Selected Statistics, 2401–1
1987 Census of Retail Trade. Subject Series. Measures of Value Produced, Capital Expenditures, Depreciable Assets, and Operating Expenses, 2399–2
1987 Census of Service Industries. Subject Series. Capital Expenditures, Depreciable Assets, and Operating Expenditures, 2393–2
1987 Census of Service Industries. Subject Series. Hotels, Motels, and Other Lodging Places, 2393–3
1987 Census of Service Industries. Subject Series. Miscellaneous Subjects, 2393–4
1987 Census of Transportation. Subject Series: Selected Transportation Industries. Miscellaneous Subjects, 2579–1
1987 Census of Wholesale Trade. Subject Series. Measures of Value Produced, Capital Expenditures, Depreciable Assets, and Operating Expenses, 2407–2
1987 Census of Wholesale Trade. Subject Series. Miscellaneous Subjects, 2407–4
1987 Economic Censuses of Outlying Areas. Geographic Area Statistics. Puerto Rico Wholesale Trade, Retail Trade, Service Industries, 2591–1
1987 Economic Censuses of Outlying Areas. Puerto Rico Subject Statistics: Wholesale Trade, Retail Trade, Service Industries, 2591–2
1987 Enterprise Statistics. Auxiliary Establishments, 2329–6
1987 Enterprise Statistics. Company Summary, 2329–8

1987 National Health... Index by Titles

1987 National Health Interview Survey, CD-ROM. Vital and Health Statistics Series 10, 4147–10.177

1987 Report to Congress on the Federal National Mortgage Association, 5184–9

1987-88 Nationwide Food Consumption Survey. Preliminary Reports, 1356–1

1988 American Housing Survey for Metropolitan Areas, 2485–6

1988 Elementary and Secondary School Civil Rights Survey: State and National Summaries, 4804–33

1988 National Survey of Postsecondary Faculty, 4846–4

1988 Schools and Staffing Survey Sample Design and Estimation: Schools and Staffing Survey, 4836–3.4

1988 Summary Report, Federal Reserve Bank of St. Louis, 9391–17

1988 Tuberculosis Statistics in the U.S., 4204–10

1988-89 Report to Congress on the Federal National Mortgage Association, 5184–9

1989 AFDC Recipient Characteristics Study, 4694–1

1989 and Preliminary 1990 Cost of Production Estimates for Sugarbeet and Sugarcane Operations, 1561–14.202

1989 Annual Report on Low-Level Radioactive Waste Management Progress, 3354–14

1989 Annual Report on the Food and Agricultural Sciences, From the Secretary of Agriculture to the President and the Congress of the U.S., 1004–19

1989 Annual Report, Resolution Trust Corporation, 9724–1

1989 Annual Survey of Manufactures, 2506–15

1989 Computer Security and Privacy Plans (CSPP) Review Project: A First-Year Federal Response to the Computer Security Act of 1987 (Final Report), 2218–85

1989 Crop Sugarbeet and Sugarcane Production and Processing Costs, 1561–14.205

1989 Examination Customer Satisfaction Survey, 8304–8.1

1989 Merger Decisions, 9294–5

1989 Motor Freight Transportation and Warehousing Survey, 2413–14

1989 Port and State Tonnage Ranking Reports, 3754–7

1989 Recordkeeping Practices Survey, 2328–67

1989 Report of the President to the Congress on the Administration of the Federal Railroad Safety Act of 1970, 7604–12

1989 Report of the Visa Office, 7184–1

1989 Report to Congress on the Federal Home Loan Mortgage Corporation, 5184–8

1989 SAR Statistics, U.S. Coast Guard, 7404–2

1989 Summary: National Hospital Discharge Survey, 4146–8.198

1989 Summary Statistics: Water, Land, and Related Data, 5824–12

1989 Traffic Fatality Facts, 7766–15.1

1989 Tuberculosis Statistics in the U.S., 4204–10

1989-90 Pell Grant End of Year Report, 4804–1

1990 and Preliminary 1991 Cost of Production Estimates for Sugarbeet and Sugarcane Operations, 1561–14.208

1990 Annual Report, Appalachian Regional Commission, 9084–1

1990 Annual Report, Bureau of Reclamation, 5824–1

1990 Annual Report, Economic Development Administration, 2064–2

1990 Annual Report, Federal Prison Industries, Inc., 6244–3

1990 Annual Report of Foreign Agricultural Research Grants, 1954–3

1990 Annual Report of the Board of Trustees of the Federal Old-Age and Survivors Insurance and Disability Insurance Trust Funds, 4704–4

1990 Annual Report of the Community Relations Service, 6004–9

1990 Annual Report, Office of Housing and Urban Programs, 9914–4

1990 Annual Report on Alaska's Mineral Resources, 5664–11

1990 Annual Report on the Administration of the Radiation Control for Health and Safety Act of 1968, Public Law 90-602, 4064–13

1990 Annual Research Conference, Mar. 18-21, 1990: Proceedings, 2624–2

1990 Annual Statistics and Highlights Report, National Space Science Data Center, 9504–11

1990 Annual Tropical Cyclone Report, 3804–8

1990 BLM Facts and Figures for Utah, 5724–11.3

1990 Caribbean Basin Investment Survey, 2048–141

1990 Census Adjustment: Estimating Census Accuracy—A Complex Task, 26119–327

1990 Census Coverage Evaluation Operations, 21628–96

1990 Census of Population and Housing: Content Determination Reports, 2626–11

1990 Census of Population and Housing, P.L. 94-171 Data on CD-ROM, 2551–6

1990 Census of Population and Housing. P.L. 94-171 Data on CD-ROM, Technical Documentation, 2308–63

1990 Census of Population and Housing. P.L. 94-171 Higher-Level Geographic Summary Series. State Reports, 2551–5

1990 Census of Population and Housing: Summary Population and Housing Characteristics, 2551–1

1990 Census Population for the U.S. Is 249,632,692; Reapportionment Will Shift 19 Seats in the U.S. House of Representatives, 2328–22

1990 Census Profile, 2326–20

1990 Census: Reported Net Undercount Obscured Magnitude of Error, 26119–353

1990 Census Showed Gain of 14 Million Housing Units Since 1980, 2328–71

1990 Congressional Election Spending Drops to Low Point, 9276–1.87

1990 Decennial Census Counts of Persons in Emergency Shelters for the Homeless and Visible in Street Locations. Fact Sheet, 2328–70

1990 Domestic Cannabis Eradication/Suppression Program, 6284–4

1990 Fact Book of Agriculture, 1004–14

1990 Farm Act and the 1990 Budget Reconciliation Act: How U.S. Farm Policy Mechanisms Will Work Under the New Legislation, 1008–54

1990 Farm Bill Emphasizes Fruits and Vegetables, 1925–34.208

1990 Housing Highlights, 2326–21

1990 Nationwide Personal Transportation Study, 7556–6

1990 Nationwide Personal Transportation Study: Early Results, 7556–6.1

1990 Pacific Northwest Loads and Resources Study, 3224–3

1990 Pedestrian Crash Facts, 7766–15.5

1990 Promotional Activities Under Federal Milk Orders, 1317–4.204

1990 Recreation Use Report, Servicewide by States, 1204–17

1990 Report of the Director: Activities of the Administrative Office, 18204–16

1990 Report to Investors of the Farm Credit System, 9264–5

1990 SAR Statistics, U.S. Coast Guard, 7404–2

1990 State-level Income and Balance Sheet Estimates, 1541–1.212

1990 Statistical Report, Rural Electric Borrowers, 1244–1

1990 Statistical Report, Rural Telephone Borrowers, 1244–2

1990 Traffic Fatalities, Preliminary Report, 7762–11

1990 Traffic Fatalities, Semiannual Report, 7762–11

1990 Traffic Fatality Facts, 7766–15.4

1990 Trust Territory of the Pacific Islands, 7004–6

1990 Urban Mass Transportation Administration Grants Assistance Programs, Information Summaries, 7884–10

1990 U.S. Grain Exports: Quality Report, 1294–2

1990 Yearbook of Agriculture: Americans in Agriculture, 1004–18

1990/91 Catalog of Cell Lines: NIGMS Human Genetic Mutant Cell Repository, 4474–23

1990/91 Catalog of Cell Lines: Supplement, NIGMS Human Genetic Mutant Cell Repository, 4474–23

1990/91 Outlook for Floriculture Production and Greenhouse and Nursery Trade, 1004–16.1

1990-91 Aviation System Capacity Plan, 7504–43

1990-91 Dairy Price Support Program: ASCS Commodity Fact Sheet, 1806–4.5

1990-91 Directory of Selected Early Childhood Programs, 4944–10

1991 Annual Report of the Board of Trustees of the Federal Hospital Insurance Trust Fund, 4654–11

1991 Annual Report of the Board of Trustees of the Federal Old-Age and Survivors Insurance and Disability Insurance Trust Funds, 4704–4

1991 Annual Report of the Board of Trustees of the Federal Supplementary Medical Insurance Trust Fund, 4654–12

1991 Annual Report of the Director, 18204–2

1991 Annual Report of the Director: Activities of the Administrative Office of the U.S. Courts, 18204–2.2

1991 Annual Report of the Director: Judicial Business of the U.S. Courts, 18204–2.1

1991 Annual Report on Highway Safety Improvement Programs, Report of the Secretary of Transportation to the U.S. Congress, 7554–26

Index by Titles

1991 Annual Report to Congress on Community Planning and Development Housing Rehabilitation Programs, 5124–7
1991 Annual Research Conference, Mar. 17-20, 1991: Proceedings, 2624–2
1991 Back-to-School Forecast, 4804–19
1991 Catalog of Federal Domestic Assistance, 104–5
1991 Catalog of Federal Domestic Assistance, Update, 104–5
1991 Directory of Members: Eleventh District—Arizona, California, Nevada, Federal Home Loan Bank of San Francisco, 9304–23
1991 Fall Water Supply Summary for the Western U.S., 1264–4
1991 Filing Season Statistics, 8302–6
1991 Green Book. Overview of Entitlement Programs. Background Material and Data on Programs Within the Jurisdiction of the Committee on Ways and Means, 21784–11
1991 Guide to Department of Education Programs, 4804–3
1991 HCFA Statistics, 4654–18
1991 Joint Economic Report, 23844–2
1991 Military Forces in Transition, 3504–20
1991 Monetary Policy Objectives: Midyear Review of the Federal Reserve Board, 9362–4
1991 Monetary Policy Objectives: Summary Report of the Federal Reserve Board, 9362–4
1991 Monetary Policy Objectives: Testimony of Alan Greenspan, Chairman, Board of Governors of the Federal Reserve System, 9362–4
1991 National Trade Estimate Report on Foreign Trade Barriers, 444–2
1991 Outlook for Food Prices, 1004–16.1
1991 Outlook for Fruit and Tree Nuts, 1004–16.1
1991 Outlook for the U.S. Economy, 1004–16.1
1991 Party Spending Limits Set for Off-Year Elections, 9276–1.92
1991 Survey of Cable Television Rates and Services. Telecommunications, 26113–431
1991 Trade Policy Agenda and 1990 Annual Report of the President of the U.S. on the Trade Agreements Program, 444–1
1991 U.S. Industrial Outlook, 2044–28
1991 Water Year Summary for the Great Basin in Nevada and California, 1264–8
1991 Yearbook of Agriculture: Agriculture and the Environment, 1004–18
1991-92 Congressional Directory, 102d Congress, 23874–1
1991-98 Projections: Information and Withholding Documents, U.S. and Service Centers, 1991 Update, 8304–22
1992 Gas Mileage Guide: EPA Fuel Economy Estimates, 3304–11
1992 Outlook: International Travel To and From the U.S., 2904–9
1992 Presidential Candidates Raise $2.7 Million by September 30: Overall Financial Activity Far Below 1988 Campaigns, 9276–1.95
1992 Senate Campaigns Spend Over $10 Million, Mid-Year Reports Show, 9276–1.93

Index by Agency Report Numbers

Index by Agency Report Numbers

Agency report number practices vary from agency to agency, and from publication to publication within an agency. Sometimes a number is noted on the publication, sometimes it is not. In the following list an attempt is made to include every agency report number available in the form in which it appears on the publication.

Those publications covered that did not have identifiable assigned numbers are not included in the list.

EXECUTIVE OFFICE OF THE PRESIDENT

Office of Management and Budget

Stat. Policy Working Paper No. 20 .... 106–4.14

DEPARTMENT OF AGRICULTURE

ACS Res. Rpt. 76 .... 1128–44.4	
ACS Res. Rpt. 95 1128–65	
ACS Service Rpt. 29 1124–1	
AER 617 1588–150	
AER 637 1548–373	
AER 638 1548–375	
AER 641 1568–296	
AER 642 1568–300	
AER 643 1588–48	
AER 644 1528–318	
AER 645 1598–272	
AER 651 1544–9	
AER 655 1528–317	
AFO-(nos.) 1541–1	
Ag 3(10-91) 1631–16	
AgCh 1(91) 1616–1.1	
— 1616–1.2	
Agric. Hndbk. 8,	
1990 Supp 1356–3.15	
Agric. Hndbk. 8-19 .... 1356–3.16	
Agric. Hndbk. 683 1924–9	
Agric. Info. Bull. 578 .... 1566–8.6	
Agric. Info. Bull. 583 .... 1566–8.7	
Agric. Info. Bull. 621 1128–66	
AO-(nos.) 1502–4	
APHIS 91-55-001 .... 1394–15.1	
APHIS 91-55-002 .... 1394–15.2	
Aq 2(date) 1631–18	
AQUA 6.. 1561-15	
AQUA 7 1561–15	
AR-(nos.) 1561–16	
CEP-16R 1802–15	
CEP-18R 1802–13	
CEP-25R 1802–14	
Cooperative Info. Rpt. 1,	
Section 15 .... 1126–1.5	
Cooperative Info. Rpt. 1,	
Section 22 .... 1126–1.6	
CoSt 1(date) 1631–5	
CoSt 1(2-91) 1631–11	
CrPr 2-1(date) 1621–1	
CrPr 2-1(91) 1621–2	
CrPr 2-2(date) 1621–1	
CrPr 2-2(6-91) 1621–23	
CrPr 2-2(9-91) 1621–8	
CrPr 2-3(1-91) 1621–30	

CrPr 2-4(3-91) .... 1621–22 CWS-(nos.) .... 1561–1 Da 1-1(date) .... 1627–1 Da 1-2(91) .... 1627–4 Da 2-1(91) .... 1627–5 Da 2-6(date) .... 1627–3 DS-(nos.) .... 1561–2 ECIFS 9-2 .... 1544–16 ECIFS 9-3 .... 1544–18 ECIFS 9-4 .... 1544–17 ECIFS 9-5 .... 1544–20.1 ECIFS 10-1 .... 1544–16 EMG (nos.) .... 1925–2.4 ERS Staff Rpt. AGES 89-53 .... 1526–6.14 ERS Staff Rpt. AGES 9010 .... 1568–302 ERS Staff Rpt. AGES 9044 .... 1548–372 ERS Staff Rpt. AGES 9066 .... 1548–376 ERS Staff Rpt. AGES 9067 .... 1598–265 ERS Staff Rpt. AGES 9068 .... 1568–294 ERS Staff Rpt. AGES 9071 .... 1598–266 ERS Staff Rpt. AGES 9072 .... 1598–267 ERS Staff Rpt. AGES 9074 .... 1528–312 ERS Staff Rpt. AGES 9075 .... 1548–378 ERS Staff Rpt. AGES 9101 .... 1504–8 ERS Staff Rpt. AGES 9104 .... 1548–379 ERS Staff Rpt. AGES 9105 .... 1588–151 ERS Staff Rpt. AGES 9106 .... 1568–295 ERS Staff Rpt. AGES 9107 .... 1568–298 ERS Staff Rpt. AGES 9108 .... 1548–380 ERS Staff Rpt. AGES 9110 .... 1588–154 ERS Staff Rpt. AGES 9112 .... 1524–8 ERS Staff Rpt. AGES 9114 .... 1528–315 ERS Staff Rpt. AGES 9115 .... 1568–301 ERS Staff Rpt. AGES 9116 .... 1598–273 ERS Staff Rpt. AGES 9117 .... 1548–381 ERS Staff Rpt. AGES 9118 .... 1528–316 ERS Staff Rpt. AGES 9119 .... 1598–269 ERS Staff Rpt. AGES 9120 .... 1584–2 ERS Staff Rpt. AGES 9121 .... 1598–271 ERS Staff Rpt. AGES 9124 .... 1584–3 ERS Staff Rpt. AGES 9126 1598–276

ERS Staff Rpt. AGES 9127 .... 1528–319 ERS Staff Rpt. AGES 9128 .... 1568–303 ERS Staff Rpt. AGES 9134 .... 1588–153 ERS Staff Rpt. AGES 9135 .... 1524–7 ERS Staff Rpt. AGES 9140 .... 1588–155 ERS Staff Rpt. AGES 9142 .... 1528–321 ERS Staff Rpt. AGES 9146 .... 1528–320 ERS Staff Rpt. AGES 9151 .... 1528–315 ERS Staff Rpt. AGES 9152 .... 1528–324 ERS Staff Rpt. AGES 9157 .... 1564–3 FAER 243 .... 1528–311 FC (nos.) .... 1925–4.2 FCB 1-91 .... 1925–9.1 FCB 2-91 .... 1925–9.2 FCOF (nos.).. 1925–5 FD 1-91 .... 1925–10 FD 2-91 .... 1925–10 FD-MI (nos.) .... 1925–31 FDLP (nos.) .... 1925–32 FdS-(nos.) .... 1561–4 FFVS (nos.) .... 1925–13 FG (nos.) .... 1925–2.1 FHORT (nos.) .... 1925–34 FL&P 1-91 .... 1925–33.1 FL&P 2-91 .... 1925–33.2 FL&P 3-91 .... 1925–33.1 FMOS (nos.) .... 1317–4 FOP (nos.) .... 1925–1 FrNt 1-3(91) .... 1621–18.1 — 1621–18.3 FrNt 2-4(6-91) .... 1621–18.2 FrNt 3-1(91) .... 1621–18.7 FrNt 4(8-91) .... 1621–18.4 FrNt 5(8-91) .... 1621–18.5 FrNt 6(9-91) .... 1621–18.8 FrNt 8(8-91) .... 1621–18.6 FS 1-91 .... 1925–14.2 FS 2-91 .... 1925–14.3 FS-383 .... 1204–2 FS Supp. 1-91 .... 1925–14.1 FT (nos.) .... 1925–16 FTEA 1-91 .... 1925–15.1 FTEA 2-91 .... 1925–15.2 FTEA 3-91 .... 1925–15.3 FVAS-1(1990) .... 1311–4.1 FVAS-2(1990) .... 1311–4.2 FVAS-3(1990) .... 1311–4.3 FVAS-4(1990) .... 1311–4.4 Gen. Tech. Rpt. INT-276 .... 1208–351 Gen. Tech. Rpt. INT-280 .... 1208–378 Gen. Tech. Rpt. NE-(nos.) .... 1202–4 Gen. Tech. Rpt. NE-145 .... 1208–356 Gen. Tech. Rpt. PNW-GTR-251 .... 1208–343 Gen. Tech. Rpt. PNW-GTR-254 .... 1208–354 Gen. Tech. Rpt. PNW-GTR-261 .... 1208–365 Gen. Tech. Rpt.

Index by Agency Report Numbers

DEPARTMENT OF AGRICULTURE

PNW-GTR-264	1208–367
Gen. Tech. Rpt. PSW-122	1208–366
Gen. Tech. Rpt. RM-156	1208–24.19
Gen. Tech. Rpt. RM-193	1208–347
Gen. Tech. Rpt. RM-199	1208–24.20
Gen. Tech. Rpt. RM-200	1208–376
Gen. Tech. Rpt. RM-203	1208–360
Gen. Tech. Rpt. RM-205	1208–382
Gen. Tech. Rpt. RM-207	1208–381
Gen. Tech. Rpt. SE-63	1208–346
Gen. Tech. Rpt. SE-64	1208–357
Gen. Tech. Rpt. SE-67	1204–38
Gen. Tech. Rpt. SO-75	1208–355
GFA 1	1528–313
GFA 2	1526–8.1
GrLg 6 (date)	1621–6
GrLg 11-1(date)	1621–4
GrLg 11-3(date)	1621–7
Informational Pub. 200-2	1244–6
List 11	1004–13
LPS-(nos.)	1561–7
LvGn 1(2-91)	1623–4
LvGn 1(4-91)	1618–20
LvGn 2(3-91)	1623–6
LvGn 3(7-91)	1631–7
Misc. Pub. 1063	1004–14
Misc. Pub. 1486	1204–29
Misc. Pub. 1489	1008–54
MtAn 1-1(91)	1623–8
MtAn 1-2(date)	1623–9
MtAn 1-2-1(91)	1623–10
MtAn 2-1(date)	1623–2
MtAn 2-1(2-91)	1631–17
MtAn 2(2-91)	1623–1.1
MtAn 2(7-91)	1623–1.2
MtAn 4(date)	1623–3
NE-INF-91-90	1208–363
NFR-(nos.)	1541–7
OCS-(nos.)	1561–3
P&SA 89-1	1384–1
P&SA 91-1	1384–1
Pot 1-2(date)	1621–10
Pot 6(9-91)	1621–11
Pou 1-1(date)	1625–1
Pou 1-1-1(91)	1625–8
Pou 2-1(date)	1625–3
Pou 2-2	1625–11
Pou 2-4(91)	1625–7
Pou 2-5(date)	1625–2
Pou 3(date)	1625–10
Pou 3-1(91)	1625–5
—	1625–6
PR (nos.)	1922–7
Pr 1(date)	1629–1
Pr 1-3(91)	1629–5
Pr 1-4(91)	1629–2
REA Bull. 201-1	1244–1
REA Elec. Prog. Stat. Bull.	
337	1244–7
REA Info. Pub. 300-4	1244–2
REA Tel. Prog. Stat. Bull.	
T-219	1244–8
Res. Note INT-398	1208–379
Res. Note SE-359	1204–22
Res. Paper INT-440	1208–370
Res. Paper INT-442	1208–372
Res. Paper INT-445	1208–377
Res. Paper INT-449	1208–380
Res. Paper NE-632	1208–348
Res. Paper NE-637	1208–349
Res. Paper NE-638	1208–350
Res. Paper NE-642	1208–369
Res. Paper NE-645	1208–361
Res. Paper NE-652	1208–373
Res. Paper NE-653	1208–371
Res. Paper PNW-RP-420	1208–342
Res. Paper PNW-RP-425	1208–358
Res. Paper RM-296	1208–364
Res. Paper RM-298	1208–383
Res. Paper SE-278	1208–345
Resource Bull. INT-69	1208–374
Resource Bull. INT-71	1206–25.8
Resource Bull. INT-72	1206–25.9
Resource Bull. INT-73	1206–25.10
Resource Bull. INT-74	1206–25.11
Resource Bull. NC-99	1208–220
Resource Bull. NC-113	1208–368
Resource Bull. NC-121	1206–10.11
Resource Bull. NC-124	1206–10.12
Resource Bull. NC-125	1208–220
Resource Bull. NE-110	1206–44.5
Resource Bull. NE-112	1206–12.14
Resource Bull. NE-113	1206–43.3
Resource Bull. NE-114	1206–12.13
Resource Bull. NE-115	1206–15.9
Resource Bull. NE-117	1206–12.15
Resource Bull. NE-118	1206–15.10
Resource Bull. NE-119	1204–18
Resource Bull.	
PNW-RB-170	1208–353
Resource Bull. SE-115	1208–359
Resource Bull. SE-116	1208–352
Resource Bull. SE-117	1206–4.14
Resource Bull. SE-118	1206–4.15
Resource Bull. SE-119	1204–23
Resource Bull. SE-120	1206–4.13
Resource Bull. SE-122	1206–6.13
Resource Bull. SO-121	1206–39.4
Resource Bull. SO-154	1208–43
Resource Bull. SO-155	1206–30.8
Resource Bull. SO-156	1206–30.9
Resource Bull. SO-158	1206–30.10
Resource Bull. SO-159	1204–23
Resource Bull. SO-361	1208–344
Rpt. Code 670	1182–8
Rpt. Code 691	1182–5
Rpt. No. 90-1	1206–49.1
Rpt. No. 90-2	1206–49.2
RS-(nos.)	1561–8
RS-91-1	1524–4.1
RS-91-3	1524–4.3
RS-91-4	1524–4.5
RS-91-5	1524–4.2
RSED-OD-1011	1954–3
Rural Dev. Res. Rpt. 79	1598–264
Rural Dev. Res. Rpt. 80	1598–268
Rural Dev. Res. Rpt. 81	1598–274
Rural Dev. Res. Rpt. 82	1598–270
SeHy 1-3(2-91)	1631–6
SpCr 2(3-91)	1621–8
SpCr 4(date)	1621–28
SpCr 6-1(91)	1631–8
SpCr 8(date)	1631–14
SpSy (date)	1631–1
SpSy 3(7-91)	1614–4
SpSy 5(91)	1614–3
SSR-(v.nos. & nos.)	1561–14
Stat. Bull. 808	1528–322
Stat. Bull. 813	1548–377
Stat. Bull. 817	1568–293
Stat. Bull. 819	1528–314
Stat. Bull. 820	1568–304
Stat. Bull. 821	1568–299
Stat. Bull. 822	1618–21
Stat. Bull. 823	1544–29
Stat. Bull. 824	1544–30
Stat. Bull. 825	1544–4
Stat. Bull. 827	1528–323
Stat. Bull. 828	1317–3
Stat. Bull. 829	1568–305
Stat. Bull. 830	1568–306
Sugar Import Notice	
(nos.-yr.)	1922–9
Supp. 3-91	1925–2.5
Supp. 4-91	1925–2.6
Tech. Bull. 1781	1548–374
Tech. Bull. 1784	1568–297
Tech. Bull. 1786	1588–152
Tech. Bull. 1787	1598–275
TFS-(nos.)	1561–6
TOB-(nos.)	1319–3
TOB-FDA-34	1319–5.5
TOB-FL-33	1319–5.1
TOB-FL-34	1319–5.4
TOB-LA-33	1319–5.2
TOB-LA-34	1319–5.3
—	1319–5.5
TOB-LA-35	1319–5.6
TS-(nos.)	1561–10
TVS-(nos.)	1561–11
Vg 1-1(date)	1621–12
Vg 1-2(91)	1621–25.2
Vg 2-1(date)	1621–12
Vg 2-1-1(date)	1621–14
Vg 2-1-2(8-91)	1631–9
Vg 3-1(date)	1621–12
Vg 3-1(1-91)	1621–25.1
WAP-(nos.)	1925–28
WAS-(nos.)	1522–3
WASDE-(nos.)	1522–5
WIC-2-88	1364–12
WP-(nos.)	1925–36
WS-(nos.)	1561–12
WS-(yr.-nos.)	1311–3

DEPARTMENT OF COMMERCE

Administrative Rpt.

SWR-90-01	2168–125
Census A10:(nos.)	2342–1
Census A20:(nos.)	2342–2
Census A30-90	2344–1
Census AC87-A-55	2331–1.55
Census AC87-A-56	2331–1.56
Census AC87-HOR-1	2337–1
Census AG88-PP-3	2346–1.4
Census AHB-87-9	2485–11.1
Census AHB-87-10	2485–11.2
Census AHB-87-11	2485–11.3
Census AHB-88-1	2485–11.4
Census AHB-88-2	2485–11.6
Census AHB-88-3	2485–11.5
Census AHB-88-5	2485–11.7
Census AHB-88-6	2485–11.8
Census AHB-88-7	2485–11.9
Census AHB-88-9	2485–11.10
Census AHB-88-10	2485–11.11
Census AR87-1	2506–16.1
Census BR-(yr.-nos.)	2413–3
Census BR-89-13	2413–5
Census BR-90-R	2413–3
Census BS-90-1	2413–8
Census BT-89-01	2413–14
Census BW-(yr.-nos.)	2413–7
Census BW-90-A	2413–13
Census BW-90-R	2413–7
Census C20-(yr.-nos.)	2382–1
Census C21-(yr.-nos.)	2382–9
Census C22-(yr.-nos.)	2382–2
Census C25-(yr.-nos.)	2382–3
Census C25-9013	2384–1
Census C27-(yr.-nos.)	2382–8
Census C30-(yr.-nos.)	2382–4
Census C40-(yr.-nos.)	2382–5
Census C40-9013	2384–2
Census C50-(yr.)-Q(nos.)	2382–7
Census CB (yr.-nos.)	2413–2
Census CB90-232	2328–22
Census CB91-07	2328–66
Census CB91-24	2324–7
Census CB91-66	2324–8

Index by Agency Report Numbers

DEPARTMENT OF COMMERCE

Census CB91-101 2328–68
Census CB91-117 2328–70
Census CB91-131 2328–69
Census CB91-155 2328–71
Census CB91-182 2328–32
Census CB91-215 2328–72
Census CB91-216 2328–73
Census CB91-217 2328–74
Census CB91-221 2328–69
Census CB91-222 2328–69
Census CB91-229 2328–75
Census CB91-232 2328–76
Census CB91-259 2328–37
Census CB91-263 2328–77
Census CB91-275 2328–78
Census CB91-276 2328–79
Census CB91-289 2324–10
Census CB91-311 2328–81
Census CB91-334 2328–39
Census CBP-88-1 .... 2326–6.1
Census CBP-89-2 .... 2326–8.2
Census CBP-89-3 .... 2326–8.3
Census CBP-89-4 .... 2326–8.4
Census CBP-89-5 .... 2326–8.5
Census CBP-89-6 .... 2326–8.6
Census CBP-89-7 .... 2326–8.7
Census CBP-89-8 .... 2326–8.8
Census CBP-89-9 .... 2326–8.9
Census CBP-89-10 .... 2326–8.10
Census CBP-89-11 .... 2326–8.11
Census CBP-89-12 .... 2326–8.12
Census CBP-89-13 .... 2326–8.13
Census CBP-89-14 .... 2326–8.14
Census CBP-89-15 .... 2326–8.15
Census CBP-89-16 .... 2326–8.16
Census CBP-89-17 .... 2326–8.17
Census CBP-89-18 .... 2326–8.18
Census CBP-89-19 .... 2326–8.19
Census CBP-89-20 .... 2326–8.20
Census CBP-89-21 .... 2326–8.21
Census CBP-89-22 .... 2326–8.22
Census CBP-89-23 .... 2326–8.23
Census CBP-89-24 .... 2326–8.24
Census CBP-89-25 .... 2326–8.25
Census CBP-89-26 .... 2326–8.26
Census CBP-89-27 .... 2326–8.27
Census CBP-89-28 .... 2326–8.28
Census CBP-89-29 .... 2326–8.29
Census CBP-89-30 .... 2326–8.30
Census CBP-89-31 .... 2326–8.31
Census CBP-89-32 .... 2326–8.32
Census CBP-89-33 .... 2326–8.33
Census CBP-89-34 .... 2326–8.34
Census CBP-89-35 .... 2326–8.35
Census CBP-89-36 .... 2326–8.36
Census CBP-89-37 .... 2326–8.37
Census CBP-89-38 .... 2326–8.38
Census CBP-89-39 .... 2326–8.39
Census CBP-89-40 .... 2326–8.40
Census CBP-89-41 .... 2326–8.41
Census CBP-89-42 .... 2326–8.42
Census CBP-89-43 .... 2326–8.43
Census CBP-89-44 .... 2326–8.44
Census CBP-89-45 .... 2326–8.45
Census CBP-89-46 .... 2326–8.46
Census CBP-89-47 .... 2326–8.47
Census CBP-89-48 .... 2326–8.48
Census CBP-89-49 .... 2326–8.49
Census CBP-89-50 .... 2326–8.50
Census CBP-89-51 .... 2326–8.51
Census CBP-89-52 .... 2326–8.52
Census CBP-89-53 .... 2326–8.53
Census CC87-I-12(Rev.) 2373–1.12
Census CDR-6 .... 2626–11.14
Census CE-376 2322–3
Census CFF No. 1(Rev.) 2326–7.80
Census CFF No. 2(Rev.) 2326–7.81
Census CFF No. 6(Rev.) 2326–7.77
Census CFF No. 7(Rev.) 2326–7.78
Census CFF No. 8(Rev.) 2326–7.79
Census CH-S-1-1 .... 2326–21.1
Census CH-S-1-2 .... 2326–21.2
Census CH-S-1-6 .... 2326–21.6
Census CH-S-1-8 .... 2326–21.8
Census CH-S-1-9 .... 2326–21.9
Census CH-S-1-10 .... 2326–21.10
Census CH-S-1-11 .... 2326–21.11
Census CH-S-1-13 .... 2326–21.13
Census CH-S-1-19 .... 2326–21.19
Census CH-S-1-22 .... 2326–21.22
Census CH-S-1-32 .... 2326–21.32
Census CH-S-1-34 .... 2326–21.34
Census CH-S-1-40 .... 2326–21.40
Census CH-S-1-45 .... 2326–21.45
Census CH-S-1-47 .... 2326–21.47
Census CH-S-1-48 .... 2326–21.48
Census CIR Staff Paper No. 58 .... 2326–18.57
Census CIR Staff Paper No. 59 .... 2326–18.58
Census CIR Staff Paper No. 60 .... 2326–18.59
Census CIR Staff Paper No. 61 .... 2326–18.60
Census CIR Staff Paper No. 62 .... 2326–18.61
Census CIR Staff Paper No. 63 .... 2326–18.62
Census CIR Staff Paper No. 64 .... 2326–18.63
Census CPH-I-1 2308–61
Census CPH-I-2 2308–62
Census ES87-2 2329–6
Census ES87-3 2329–8
Census FT447/1990 2424–10
Census FT895/1989 2424–11
Census FT895/1990 2424–11
Census FT925/(date) 2422–12
Census FT927/1989 2424–12
Census FT927/1990 2424–12
Census FT947/1989 2424–13
Census FT947/1990 2424–13
Census GC87(3)-1 2455–1
Census GC87(3)-2 2455–2
Census GC87(3)-3 2455–3
Census GC87(3)-4 2455–4
Census GC87(6)-1 2460–1
Census GE90-1 .... 2466–1.1
Census GE90-2 .... 2466–1.2
Census GE90-4 .... 2466–1.3
Census GF88-2 .... 2466–2.1
Census GF89-2 .... 2466–2.8
Census GF89-4 .... 2466–2.3
Census GF89-5 .... 2466–2.2
Census GF89-8 .... 2466–2.4
Census GF89-10 .... 2466–2.5
Census GF90-1 .... 2466–2.7
Census GF90-3 .... 2466–2.6
Census GF90-5P 2466–2.9
Census GR (yr.-nos.) 2462–2
Census GT (yr.-nos.) 2462–3
Census H-111-(yr.-nos.) 2482–1
Census H-111-90-A 2484–1
Census H-121-91-1 .... 2486–1.11
Census H-130-(yr.-nos.) 2482–2
Census H-130-90-A 2484–2
Census H-131-90-A 2484–3
Census H-150-89 2485–12
Census H-151-83, No. 1 2485–14
Census H-151-85-1 2485–13
Census H-151-87-1 2485–13
Census H-170-88-8 .... 2485–6.1
Census H-170-88-15 .... 2485–6.5
Census H-170-88-29 .... 2485–6.2
Census H-170-88-45 .... 2485–6.3
Census H-170-88-50 .... 2485–6.4
Census H-170-88-54 .... 2485–6.6
Census H-170-88-56 .... 2485–6.7
Census H-170-88-61 .... 2485–6.8
Census H-171-84 2485–8
Census M3-1(yr.-nos.) 2506–3.1
Census M20 A(yr.-nos.) 2506–4.1
Census M32 G(yr.-nos.) 2506–9.4
Census M33 J(yr.-nos.) 2506–10.3
Census M33 2(yr.-nos.) 2506–10.9
Census M36 D(yr.-nos.) 2506–12.13
Census M37 G(yr.-nos.) 2506–12.24
Census M37 L(yr.-nos.) 2506–12.25
Census M89(AS)-1 .... 2506–15.1
Census M89(AS)-2 .... 2506–15.2
Census M89(AS)-3 .... 2506–15.3
Census MA20 D(90)-1 .... 2506–4.5
Census MA22 F.1(90)-1 .... 2506–5.4
Census MA22 F.2(90)-1 .... 2506–5.5
Census MA22 K(90)-1 .... 2506–5.7
Census MA22 Q(90)-1 .... 2506–5.9
Census MA23 D(90)-1 .... 2506–6.4
Census MA24 F(89)-1(Rev.) 2506–7.1
Census MA24 T(90)-1 .... 2506–7.4
Census MA25 H(90)-1 .... 2506–7.8
Census MA28 A(90)-1 .... 2506–8.14
Census MA28 B(90)-1 .... 2506–8.13
Census MA28 C(90)-1 .... 2506–8.15
Census MA28 F(90)-1 .... 2506–8.16
Census MA28 G(90)-1 .... 2506–8.5
Census MA30 C(90)-1 .... 2506–8.17
Census MA31 A(90)-1 .... 2506–6.8
Census MA32 C(90)-1 .... 2506–9.1
Census MA32 E(90)-1 .... 2506–9.3
Census MA33 A(90)-1 .... 2506–10.1
Census MA33 B(90)-1 .... 2506–10.2
Census MA33 E(90)-1 .... 2506–10.5
Census MA33 L(90)-1 .... 2506–10.8
Census MA35 A(90)-1 .... 2506–12.1
Census MA35 D(90)-1 .... 2506–12.3
Census MA35 F(90)-1 .... 2506–12.4
Census MA35 J(90)-1 .... 2506–12.5
Census MA35 L(90)-1 .... 2506–12.6
Census MA35 M(90)-1 .... 2506–12.7
Census MA35 N(90)-1 .... 2506–12.31
Census MA35 P(90)-1 .... 2506–12.8
Census MA35 Q(90)-1 .... 2506–12.28
Census MA35 U(90)-1 .... 2506–12.10
Census MA36 A(90)-1 .... 2506–12.11
Census MA36 E(90)-1 .... 2506–12.15
Census MA36 F(90)-1 .... 2506–12.16
Census MA36 L(90)-1 .... 2506–12.19
Census MA36 M(90)-1 .... 2506–12.20
Census MA36 P(90)-1 .... 2506–12.35
Census MA36 Q(90)-1 .... 2506–12.36
Census MA36 R(90)-1 .... 2506–12.34
Census MA37 D(90)-1 .... 2506–12.22
Census MA38 B(89)-1 .... 2506–12.26
Census MA200(89)-1 .... 2506–3.6
Census MC87-S-1 2497–1
Census MC87-S-5 2497–5
Census MC87-S-7 2497–7
Census MIC87-A-8 .... 2515–1.8
Census MIC87-S-1 2517–1
Census MIC87-S-2 2517–2
Census MQ20 J(yr.-nos.) 2506–4.3
Census MQ20 K(yr.-nos.) 2506–4.4
Census MQ22 D(yr.-nos.) 2506–5.2
Census MQ22 P(yr.-nos.) 2506–5.8
Census MQ22 T(yr.-nos.) 2506–5.11
Census MQ23 A(yr.-nos.) 2506–6.12
Census MQ23 X(yr.-nos.) 2506–6.6
Census MQ28 A(yr.-nos.) 2506–8.1
Census MQ28 B(yr.-nos.) 2506–8.2
Census MQ28 C(yr.-nos.) 2506–8.3

DEPARTMENT OF COMMERCE

Index by Agency Report Numbers

Census MQ28 F(yr.-nos.) 2506–8.4
Census MQ31 A(yr.-nos.) 2506–6.7
Census MQ32 A(yr.-nos.) 2506–9.6
Census MQ32 D(yr.-nos.) 2506–9.2
Census MQ34 E(yr.-nos.) 2506–11.2
Census MQ34 H(yr.-nos.) 2506–11.4
Census MQ34 K(yr.-nos.) 2506–11.5
Census MQ35 W(yr.-nos.) 2506–12.12
Census MQ36 B(yr.-nos.) 2506–12.33
Census MQ36 C(yr.-nos.) 2506–12.14
Census OA87-E-1 2591–1
Census OA87-E-2 (Pt. 1) 2591–2.1
Census OA87-E-2 (Pt. 2) 2591–2.2
Census P-20, No. 447 .... 2546–1.447
Census P-20, No. 448 .... 2546–1.450
Census P-20, No. 449 .... 2546–1.448
Census P-20, No. 450 .... 2546–1.449
Census P-20, No. 451 .... 2546–1.452
Census P-20, No. 452 .... 2546–1.453
Census P-20, No. 453 .... 2546–1.454
Census P-20, No. 454 .... 2546–1.455
Census P-20, No. 455 .... 2546–1.451
Census P-23, No. 169 .... 2546–2.157
Census P-23, No. 171 .... 2546–2.158
Census P-23, No. 172 .... 2546–2.159
Census P-23, No. 173 .... 2546–2.161
Census P-23, No. 174 .... 2546–2.160
Census P-23, No. 176 .... 2546–2.162
Census P-25, No. 1068 2542–1
Census P-25, No. 1069 2542–1
Census P-25, No.
1070-RD-2 .... 2546–3.169
Census P-25, No. 1071 2542–1
Census P-25, No. 1072 2542–1
Census P-25, No. 1073 2542–1
Census P-25, No. 1074 2542–1
Census P-25, No. 1075 2542–1
Census P-25, No. 1076 2542–1
Census P-25, No. 1077 2542–1
Census P-25, No. 1078 2542–1
Census P-25, No. 1079 2542–1
Census P-60, No. 171 .... 2546–6.67
Census P-60, No. 172 .... 2546–6.68
Census P-60, No. 173 .... 2546–6.72
Census P-60, No. 174 .... 2546–6.70
Census P-60, No. 175 .... 2546–6.71
Census P-60, No. 176-RD 2546–6.69
Census P-70, No. 22 .... 2546–20.16
Census P-70, No. 23 .... 2546–20.17
Census P-70, No. 24 .... 2546–20.19
Census P-70, No. 25 .... 2546–20.18
Census PESVY (yr.-nos.) 2502–2
Census Pub. Bull. B-2 .... 2428–5.1
Census QFR-(yr.-nos.) 2502–1
Census RC87-S-2 2399–2
Census RC87-SP-1 2401–1
Census Res. Notes No. 1 2322–4
Census Res. Notes No. 2 2322–4
Census Res. Notes No. 3 2322–4
Census SB-12-90 .... 2326–17.22
Census SB-13-90 .... 2326–17.23
Census SB-91-1 .... 2326–17.24
Census SB-91-2 .... 2326–17.34
Census SB-91-3 .... 2326–17.29
Census SB-91-4 .... 2326–17.25
Census SB-91-5 .... 2326–17.26
Census SB-91-9 .... 2326–17.28
Census SB-91-10 .... 2326–17.27
Census SB-91-11 .... 2326–17.30
Census SB-91-14 .... 2326–17.31
Census SB-91-18 .... 2326–17.37
Census SB-91-19 .... 2326–17.33
Census SB-91-21 .... 2326–17.35
Census SB-91-22 .... 2326–17.32
Census SB-91-24 .... 2326–17.36
Census SC87-S-2 2393–2
Census SC87-S-3 2393–3

Census SC87-S-4 2393–4
Census SIPP Working
Paper Series, No. 9009 .... 2626–10.117
Census SIPP Working
Paper Series, No. 9010 .... 2626–10.118
Census SIPP Working
Paper Series, No. 9011 .... 2626–10.119
Census SIPP Working
Paper Series, No. 9012 .... 2626–10.120
Census SIPP Working
Paper Series, No. 9013 .... 2626–10.121
Census SIPP Working
Paper Series, No. 9014 .... 2626–10.122
Census SIPP Working
Paper Series, No. 9015 .... 2626–10.123
Census SIPP Working
Paper Series, No. 9016 .... 2626–10.124
Census SIPP Working
Paper Series, No. 9017 .... 2626–10.125
Census SIPP Working
Paper Series, No. 9018 .... 2626–10.126
Census SIPP Working
Paper Series, No. 9019 .... 2626–10.127
Census SIPP Working
Paper Series, No. 9020 .... 2626–10.128
Census SIPP Working
Paper Series, No. 9021 .... 2626–10.129
Census SIPP Working
Paper Series, No. 9022 .... 2626–10.130
Census SIPP Working
Paper Series, No. 9023 .... 2626–10.131
Census SIPP Working
Paper Series, No. 9024 .... 2626–10.132
Census SIPP Working
Paper Series, No. 9025 .... 2626–10.133
Census SIPP Working
Paper Series, No. 9026 .... 2626–10.134
Census SIPP Working
Paper Series, No. 9027 .... 2626–10.135
Census SIPP Working
Paper Series, No. 9028 .... 2626–10.136
Census SIPP Working
Paper Series, No. 9029 .... 2626–10.137
Census SIPP Working
Paper Series, No. 9030 .... 2626–10.138
Census SIPP Working
Paper Series, No. 9031 .... 2626–10.139
Census SIPP Working
Paper Series, No. 9032 .... 2626–10.140
Census SIPP Working
Paper Series, No. 9033 .... 2626–10.141
Census SIPP Working
Paper Series, No. 9034 .... 2626–10.142
Census SIPP Working
Paper Series, No. 9035 .... 2626–10.143
Census TC87-S-1 2579–1
Census TM(yr.-nos.) 2322–2
Census TM985/(yr.-nos.) 2422–7
Census WC87-S-2 2407–2
Census WC87-S-4 2407–4
Census 1990 CPH-1-2 .... 2551–1.2
Census 1990 CPH-1-3 .... 2551–1.3
Census 1990 CPH-1-4 .... 2551–1.4
Census 1990 CPH-1-5 .... 2551–1.5
Census 1990 CPH-1-6 .... 2551–1.6
Census 1990 CPH-1-7 .... 2551–1.7
Census 1990 CPH-1-8 .... 2551–1.8
Census 1990 CPH-1-9 .... 2551–1.9
Census 1990 CPH-1-10 .... 2551–1.10
Census 1990 CPH-1-11 .... 2551–1.11
Census 1990 CPH-1-12 .... 2551–1.12
Census 1990 CPH-1-13 .... 2551–1.13
Census 1990 CPH-1-14 .... 2551–1.14
Census 1990 CPH-1-15 .... 2551–1.15
Census 1990 CPH-1-16 .... 2551–1.16
Census 1990 CPH-1-17 .... 2551–1.17
Census 1990 CPH-1-18 .... 2551–1.18

Census 1990 CPH-1-19 .... 2551–1.19
Census 1990 CPH-1-20 .... 2551–1.20
Census 1990 CPH-1-21 .... 2551–1.21
Census 1990 CPH-1-22 .... 2551–1.22
Census 1990 CPH-1-23 .... 2551–1.23
Census 1990 CPH-1-24 .... 2551–1.24
Census 1990 CPH-1-25 .... 2551–1.25
Census 1990 CPH-1-26 .... 2551–1.26
Census 1990 CPH-1-27 .... 2551–1.27
Census 1990 CPH-1-28 .... 2551–1.28
Census 1990 CPH-1-29 .... 2551–1.29
Census 1990 CPH-1-30 .... 2551–1.30
Census 1990 CPH-1-31 .... 2551–1.31
Census 1990 CPH-1-32 .... 2551–1.32
Census 1990 CPH-1-33 .... 2551–1.33
Census 1990 CPH-1-34 .... 2551–1.34
Census 1990 CPH-1-35 .... 2551–1.35
Census 1990 CPH-1-36 .... 2551–1.36
Census 1990 CPH-1-37 .... 2551–1.37
Census 1990 CPH-1-38 .... 2551–1.38
Census 1990 CPH-1-39 .... 2551–1.39
Census 1990 CPH-1-40 .... 2551–1.40
Census 1990 CPH-1-41 .... 2551–1.41
Census 1990 CPH-1-42 .... 2551–1.42
Census 1990 CPH-1-43 .... 2551–1.43
Census 1990 CPH-1-44 .... 2551–1.44
Census 1990 CPH-1-45 .... 2551–1.45
Census 1990 CPH-1-46 .... 2551–1.46
Census 1990 CPH-1-47 .... 2551–1.47
Census 1990 CPH-1-48 .... 2551–1.48
Census 1990 CPH-1-49 .... 2551–1.49
Census 1990 CPH-1-50 .... 2551–1.50
Census 1990 CPH-1-51 .... 2551–1.51
Census 1990 CPH-1-52 .... 2551–1.52
Census 1990 CPH-1-55 .... 2551–1.55
Census 1990 Profile, No. 1 .... 2326–20.1
Census 1990 Profile, No. 2 .... 2326–20.2
Census 1990 Profile, No. 3 .... 2326–20.3
ELMR Rpt. No. 9 .... 2176–7.25
FCM P1-1991 2144–2
FET 90-85 .... 2046–4.9
FET 90-86 .... 2046–4.10
FET 90-87 .... 2046–4.1
FET 90-88 .... 2046–4.2
FET 90-89 .... 2046–4.3
FET 90-90 .... 2046–4.4
FET 90-91 .... 2046–4.5
FET 90-92 .... 2046–4.6
FET 90-93 .... 2046–4.7
FET 90-94 .... 2046–4.8
FET 91-01 .... 2046–4.11
FET 91-02 .... 2046–4.12
FET 91-03 .... 2046–4.13
FET 91-04 .... 2046–4.23
FET 91-05 .... 2046–4.14
FET 91-06 .... 2046–4.15
FET 91-07 .... 2046–4.16
FET 91-08 .... 2046–4.17
FET 91-09 .... 2046–4.24
FET 91-10 .... 2046–4.18
FET 91-11 .... 2046–4.19
FET 91-12 .... 2046–4.20
FET 91-13 .... 2046–4.21
FET 91-14 .... 2046–4.37
FET 91-15 .... 2046–4.22
FET 91-16 .... 2046–4.25
FET 91-17 .... 2046–4.26
FET 91-18 .... 2046–4.27
FET 91-19 .... 2046–4.28
FET 91-20 .... 2046–4.29
FET 91-21 .... 2046–4.30
FET 91-22 .... 2046–4.31
FET 91-23 .... 2046–4.32
FET 91-24 .... 2046–4.38
FET 91-25 .... 2046–4.33
FET 91-26 .... 2046–4.34
FET 91-27 .... 2046–4.35

Index by Agency Report Numbers

FET 91-28	2046-4.36
FET 91-29	2046-4.39
FET 91-30	2046-4.40
FET 91-31	2046-4.41
FET 91-32	2046-4.42
FET 91-33	2046-4.43
FET 91-34	2046-4.44
FET 91-35	2046-4.45
FET 91-36	2046-4.46
FET 91-37	2046-4.47
FET 91-38	2046-4.48
FET 91-39	2046-4.49
FET 91-40	2046-4.50
FET 91-41	2046-4.51
FET 91-42	2046-4.52
FET 91-43	2046-4.53
FET 91-44	2046-4.54
FET 91-45	2046-4.55
FET 91-46	2046-4.56
FET 91-47	2046-4.57
FET 91-48	2046-4.58
FET 91-49	2046-4.59
FET 91-50	2046-4.60
FET 91-51	2046-4.61
FET 91-52	2046-4.62
FET 91-53	2046-4.63
FET 91-54	2046-4.64
FET 91-55	2046-4.65
FET 91-56	2046-4.66
FET 91-57	2046-4.67
FET 91-58	2046-4.68
FET 91-59	2046-4.69
FET 91-60	2046-4.70
FET 91-61	2046-4.71
FET 91-62	2046-4.72
FET 91-63	2046-4.74
FET 91-64	2046-4.73
FET 91-65	2046-4.75
FET 91-66	2046-4.76
FET 91-67	2046-4.77
FIPS PUB 9-1	2216-2.193
FIPS PUB 11-3	2216-2.194
FIPS PUB 54-1	2216-2.195
FIPS PUB 100-1	2216-2.198
FIPS PUB 120-1	2216-2.197
FIPS PUB 146-1	2216-2.201
FIPS PUB 159	2216-2.196
FIPS PUB 160	2216-2.199
FIPS PUB 161	2216-2.200
Fishery Market News Rpt.	
O-(nos.)	2162-6.3
Fishery Market News Rpt.	
SF-(nos.)	2162-6.5
Fishery Market News Rpt.	
T-(nos.)	2162-6.4
NEFC Ref. Doc. 90-09	2162-9
NEFC Ref. Doc. 91-03	2162-9
NEFSC Ref. Doc. 91-02	2164-20
NIST Spec. Pub. 305,	
Supp. 22	2214-1
NIST Spec. Pub. 816	2214-7
NISTIR 4409	2218-85
NISTIR 4533	2214-5.1
NISTIR 4534	2214-5.2
NISTIR 4559	2214-6
NOAA CFS (nos.) FF	2162-2
NOAA CFS (nos.) FM	2162-3
NOAA CFS 8703	2166-6.2
NOAA CFS 8904	2166-17.1
NOAA CFS 9000	2164-1
NOAA CFS 9002	2166-6.1
NOAA DR ERL	
AOML-18	2146-7.7
NOAA DR ERL	
AOML-20	2146-7.8
NOAA TM	
NMFS-F/NEC-80	2168-122

NOAA TM
NMFS-F/NEC-81 2164-14
NOAA TM
NMFS-F/NEC-82 2164-19
NOAA TM
NMFS-F/NEC-86 2164-14
NOAA TM
NMFS-F/NWC-156 .... 2168-121.1
NOAA TM
NMFS-F/NWC-170 .... 2168-121.2
NOAA TM NOS
OMA 59 .... 2176-3.13
NOAA TM NWS NHC
31 2188-15
NOAA TR NMFS 90 2168-124
NOAA TR NMFS 93 2168-123
NOAA TR NMFS 95 2168-126
NOAA TR NMFS 98 2168-127
NOAA TR NMFS 102 2164-15
OBR 91-01 .... 2046-6.1
OBR 91-02 .... 2046-6.2
OBR 91-03 .... 2046-6.3
OBR 91-04 .... 2046-6.4
OBR 91-05 .... 2046-6.5
OBR 91-06 .... 2046-6.6
OBR 91-07 .... 2046-6.7
OBR 91-08 .... 2046-6.8
OBR 91-09 .... 2046-6.9
PAT 91-1 2244-2
TQ 2200 .... 2046-8.7
TQ 2205 .... 2046-9.8
TQ 2300 .... 2046-8.1
TQ 2305 .... 2046-9.4
TQ 2400 .... 2046-8.2
TQ 2405 .... 2046-9.1
TQ 2496 2042-27
TQ 2600 .... 2046-8.3
TQ 2605 .... 2046-9.2
TQ 2800 .... 2046-8.6
TQ 2805 .... 2046-9.9
URI-SSR-91-22 2144-5
WDCA-OC-90-1 2144-15

DEPARTMENT OF DEFENSE

C-1 3544-39
CRC No. 531-6690 3504-10
F01 3544-6
FAD 748/(yr.) 3542-3
L02 3542-15
L03 3544-29
M01 3544-1
M02 3544-7
M03 3542-14
M04 3542-16
M05 3542-20
M06 3544-24
M07 3544-40
NAVPERS 15658 3802-4
NAVSO P-3523 3804-16
NAVSO P-3675 3804-5
NAVSUP Pub. 561 3804-13
News Release 40-91 3544-15
NT-91-1 3804-11
NT-91-2 3804-10
P01 3544-5
P02 3544-4
P03 3542-1
P04 3544-17
P05 3542-19
P06 3544-11
P07 3544-18
P08 3544-19
P09 3542-5
P14 3542-17
P-1 3544-32
Pub. 91-C-0013 3504-16

DEPARTMENT OF EDUCATION

R-1 3544-33
RCS: DD-RA(M)
1147/1148 3544-38
TR EL-82-4 5506-8

DEPARTMENT OF EDUCATION

AS 91-925 4868-10
Campus-Based Programs
Rpt. No. 92-1 4804-17
Data Series
DR-CCD-88/89-2.2 4834-22
Data Series
DR-CCD-89/90-1.1 4834-17
Data Series
DR-CCD-89/90-2.1 4834-6
Data Series
DR-CCD/SAS-90/91-1.-
1 4834-19
Data Series
DR-IPEDS-87/88-9.1 4844-6
Data Series
DR-IPEDS-88/89-7.1 4844-17
Data Series
DR-IPEDS-89/90 4844-2
Data Series
DR-IPEDS-89/90-6.1 4844-8
Data Series
DR-IPEDS-90/91-1 4844-14
Data Series
DR-IPEDS-90/91-2 4844-16
Data Series
DR-LIB-89/90-1.1 4824-6
Data Series
DR-NPSAS-1990 .... 4846-5.1
Data Series
DR-NSOPF-87/88-1.22 .... 4846-4.4
Data Series
DR-SAS-87/88 .... 4836-3.6
Data Series
DR-SAS-88/89-1.0 .... 4836-3.5
Data Series FF-91-1 4824-8
Data Series FRSS-38 .... 4826-1.30
Data Series FRSS-42 .... 4826-1.31
Data Series NELS
88-88-1.3 .... 4826-9.8
Data Series NELS
88-88-1.4 .... 4826-9.9
Data Series NLS-72 .... 4836-1.13
Data Series
SP-CCD-87/88-7.2 4834-20
Data Series
SP-CCD-88/89-7.2 4834-20
Data Series
SP-PUPR-85-2.2 4838-46
Data Series
SP-SAS-87/88-7.4 .... 4836-3.4
ED/OERI 91-11 4824-1
ED/OERI 91-14 4828-29
ED/OIG 91-7 4802-1
ED/OIG 92-1 4802-1
ED/OPBE 91-12 4808-25
ED/OPBE 91-15 4808-26
ED/OPBE 91-17 .... 4808-33.1
ED/OPBE 91-20 4808-28
ED/OPBE 91-21 4808-29
ED/OPBE 91-23 4808-27
ED/OPBE 91-30 4808-36
ED/OPE 91-19 4804-38
ED/OS 91-4 4804-6
ED/OSERS 91-20 4944-1
LP 91-740 4874-1
LP 91-743 4874-6
LP 91-750 4874-10
NAEP Rpt. No. 21-ST-03 .... 4896-8.1
NAEP Rpt. No. 21-ST-04 .... 4896-8.1
NCES 90-070 4838-46

DEPARTMENT OF EDUCATION

NCES 91-033	4834–17
NCES 91-035	4834–6
NCES 91-039	4834–1
NCES 91-049	4838–48
NCES 91-053	4834–23
NCES 91-054	4838–47
NCES 91-062	4834–22
NCES 91-074	4834–20
NCES 91-076	4834–19
NCES 91-091	4826–1.31
NCES 91-127	4836–3.4
NCES 91-128	4836–3.5
NCES 91-129	4826–9.10
NCES 91-133	4836–3.6
NCES 91-141	4834–20
NCES 91-142	4828–39
NCES 91-191	4826–1.30
NCES 91-212	4844–17
NCES 91-215	4844–16
NCES 91-216	4844–8
NCES 91-217	4844–2
NCES 91-219	4844–6
NCES 91-335	4846–5.1
NCES 91-343	4824–6
NCES 91-369	4844–14
NCES 91-389	4846–4.4
NCES 91-396	4828–29
NCES 91-400	4844–13
NCES 91-460	4826–9.8
NCES 91-468	4826–9.9
NCES 91-470	4836–1.13
NCES 91-487	4826–9.11
NCES 91-631	4824–8
NCES 91-634	4828–40
NCES 91-637	4824–1.1
NCES 91-638	4824–1.2
NCES 91-660	4824–2
NCES 91-661	4828–26
NCES 91-685	4828–27
NCES 91-694	4824–7
NCES 91-697	4824–2
NCES 91-1050	4896–8.1
NCES 91-1259	4896–8.1
NCES 91-1264	4898–32
NCES 92-038	4844–14
NCES 92-082	4836–3.7
No. 19-R-02	4896–7.2
No. 19-W-02	4896–7.1
OR 90-518	4888–3
OR 90-527	4888–4
OR 91-504	4888–5
OR 91-530	4888–6
PIP 91-863	4818–5
RSA-IM-91-08	4944–6
RSA-IM-91-28	4944–5
RSA-IM-91-38	4944–2
RSM-1250	4944–6

DEPARTMENT OF ENERGY

DOE/AD-0010	3004–27
DOE/BC-(yr./nos.)	3002–14
DOE/BP-801	3222–2
DOE/BP-1373	3228–11
DOE/BP-1437	3228–14
DOE/BP-1512	3224–3.1
DOE/BP-1534	3224–1
DOE/BP-1551	3224–3.2
DOE/CE-0019/11	3304–11
DOE/CE-0300 P	3304–17
DOE/CE-0303 T	3308–87
DOE/CE-0305 P	3304–2
DOE/CE-0341	3304–18
DOE/CE-0296P	3304–1
DOE/CH-10093-93	3304–20.1
DOE/CR-0002	3024–5
DOE/EH-0171P	3324–1

DOE/EH-79079-H1	3326–1.2
DOE/EIA-0035(date)	3162–24
DOE/EIA-0095(90)	3164–36
DOE/EIA-0109(yr./nos.)	3162–6
DOE/EIA-0118(90)	3164–25
DOE/EIA-0121(yr./nos.)	3162–37
DOE/EIA-0125(yr./nos.)	3162–8
DOE/EIA-0130(yr./nos.)	3162–4
DOE/EIA-0145(89)	3164–38
DOE/EIA-0149(90)	3168–117
DOE/EIA-0173(90)	3164–29
DOE/EIA-0174(89)	3164–62
DOE/EIA-0191(90)	3164–42
DOE/EIA-0202/(nos.)	3162–34
DOE/EIA-0206(89)	3164–44
DOE/EIA-0208(yr./nos.)	3162–32
DOE/EIA-0214(89)	3164–39
DOE/EIA-0216(90)	3164–46
DOE/EIA-0218(nos.)	3162–1
DOE/EIA-0219(89)	3164–50
DOE/EIA-0226(yr./nos.)	3162–35
DOE/EIA-0246(89)	3166–8.9
DOE/EIA-0249(90)	3164–86
DOE/EIA-0292(89)	3166–12.6
DOE/EIA-0293(91)	3164–87
DOE/EIA-0333(91)	3164–68
DOE/EIA-0340(90)/1	3164–2.1
DOE/EIA-0340(90)/2	3164–2.2
DOE/EIA-0348(89)	3164–11
DOE/EIA-0363(91)	3164–77
DOE/EIA-0370(90)	3164–70
DOE/EIA-0376(89)	3164–64
DOE/EIA-0380(yr./nos.)	3162–11
DOE/EIA-0383(91)	3164–75
DOE/EIA-0384(90)	3164–74
DOE/EIA-0436(91)	3164–72
DOE/EIA-0437(89)/1	3164–23
DOE/EIA-0437(89)/2	3164–24
DOE/EIA-0438(91)	3164–57
DOE/EIA-0455(89)	3164–9
DOE/EIA-0466(89)	3164–80
DOE/EIA-0474(91)	3164–81
DOE/EIA-0478(90)	3164–65
DOE/EIA-0484(91)	3164–84
DOE/EIA-0512(88)	3166–13.5
DOE/EIA-0515(88)	3166–13.6
DOE/EIA-0517(91)	3164–89
DOE/EIA-0520 (yr./nos.)	3162–42
DOE/EIA-0523 (date)	3162–43
DOE/EIA-0527(91)	3164–90
DOE/EIA-0531(88)	3164–92
DOE/EIA-0535(89)	3164–94
DOE/EIA-0536	3168–119
DOE/EIA-0538 (yr./nos.)	3162–45
DOE/EIA-0539	3168–120
DOE/EIA-0540(89)	3164–91
DOE/EIA-0542	3164–93
DOE/EIA-0545(91)	3164–95
DOE/EIA-0547	3168–108
DOE/EIA-0549	3168–121
DOE/EM-0001	3354–9
DOE/EM-0006P	3354–14
DOE/ER-0144/9	3004–18.5
DOE/ER-0474 T	3004–18.2
DOE/ER-0485 P	3004–18.3
DOE/ER-0470T	3004–18.1
DOE/ER-0498T	3004–18.6
DOE/ER-0508T	3004–18.7
DOE/ER-0511P	3004–18.4
DOE/ER-69017T-H1	3006–11.14
DOE/FE-(nos.)	3002–13
DOE/FE-0222P	3334–3
DOE/IE-0019 P	3408–1
DOE/IG-0008/10-11	3002–12
DOE/IG-0008/10-12	3002–12
DOE/IG-0293	3006–5.21
DOE/IG-0295	3006–5.23

Index by Agency Report Numbers

DOE/IG-0297	3006–5.24
DOE/IG-0302	3006–5.25
DOE/OSTI-8200-R54	3354–15
DOE/PE-0092	3308–93
DOE/PE-0094P	3028–4
DOE/PE-0096P	3028–5
DOE/PR-0006	3004–21
DOE/RL-90-44	3354–2
DOE/RL-01830T-H5	3006–11.15
DOE/RL-01830T-H6	3006–11.15
DOE/RL-01830T-H7	3006–11.15
DOE/RL-01830T-H8	3006–11.15
DOE/RL-01830T-H9	3006–11.15
DOE/RL-01830T-H10	3006–11.15
DOE/RL-01830T-H11	3006–11.15
DOE/RL-01830T-H12	3006–11.15
DOE/RW-0006, Rev. 6	3364–2
DOE/RW-0188(nos.)	3362–1
DOE/RW-0299P	3364–1
DOE/RW-0316P	3368–1
DOE/S-0082P	3004–34
DOE/S-0087P	3002–15
DOE/S-0089P FYP	3024–7
DOE/S-0090P Exec.	
Summ	3024–7
DOE/S-0091P	3002–15
DOE/SA-0003P	3344–2
DOE/SWP-9101	3244–1
EGG-2612(90)	3354–10
EML-533	3004–29
EML-541	3004–31
Manpower Assessment	
Brief 14	3006–8.14
Manpower Assessment	
Brief 15	3006–8.15
Manpower Assessment	
Brief 16	3006–8.16
Manpower Assessment	
Brief 17	3006–8.17
ORNL-6622	3028–6
ORNL-6649	3304–5
ORNL-6672	3302–4
ORNL-6672/S1	3302–4
ORNL/CON-271	3308–97
ORNL/CON-301	3308–91
ORNL/CON-305	3226–1.7
ORNL/CON-310	3228–15
ORNL/CON-312	3308–98
ORNL/CON-340	3308–99
ORNL/RASA-88/49	3006–9.11
ORNL/RASA-88/50	3006–9.10
ORNL/RASA-88/53	3006–9.13
ORNL/RASA-88/67	3006–9.14
ORNL/RASA-88/69	3006–9.12
ORNL/RASA-88/79	3006–9.9
ORNL/TM-11182	3006–9.8
PNL-7410 HEDR/Rev. 1	3356–5.4
PNL-7411 HEDR/Rev. 1	3356–5.5
PNL-7412 HEDR/Rev. 1	3356–5.6
SR/CNEAF/91-01	3166–6.5
SR/CNEAF/91-02	3166–6.56
SR/EMEU/91-01	3166–6.54
SR/EMEU/91-02	3166–6.57
SR/NES/90-01	3166–6.47
SR/NES/90-02	3166–6.48
SR/NES/90-03	3166–6.49
SR/NES/90-04	3166–6.50
SR/NES/90-05	3166–6.51
SR/NES/90-06	3166–6.52
SR/NES/90-07	3166–6.53
SR/OA 91-01	3166–6.46
TRO51	3006–11.14
TRO52A	3006–11.15
TRO52B	3006–11.15
TRO52C	3006–11.15
TRO52D	3006–11.15
TRO52E	3006–11.15

Index by Agency Report Numbers

DEPARTMENT OF HEALTH AND HUMAN SERVICES

TRO52F 3006–11.15
TRO52G 3006–11.15
TRO52H 3006–11.15
UC-707 3356–5
UC-731 3344–2
UC-812 3354–2
WR-BC-91-1 .... 3006–5.22

DEPARTMENT OF HEALTH AND HUMAN SERVICES

Actuarial Study No. 104 .... 4706–1.105
ADM (yr.)-151 4482–1
ADM 87-1522 .... 4506–3.42
ADM 89-1605 4494–11
ADM 90-1663 4494–11
ADM 90-1681 .... 4494–5.1
ADM 90-1694 4048–35
ADM 90-1717 4494–8
ADM 90-1839 4494–8
ADM 90-1840 4494–8
ADM 91-319 4044–13
ADM 91-1704 4498–68
ADM 91-1719 4498–69
ADM 91-1720 4498–67
ADM 91-1721 4498–70
ADM 91-1722 4498–71
ADM 91-1729 .... 4494–10.2
ADM 91-1732 .... 4494–5.2
ADM 91-1737 .... 4506–3.41
ADM 91-1738 .... 4506–3.40
ADM 91-1753 4494–11
ADM 91-1754 4498–73
ADM 91-1759 .... 4506–3.42
ADM 91-1773 .... 4492–5.1
ADM 91-1787 4498–74
ADM 91-1788 .... 4494–5.3
ADM 91-1789 .... 4494–5.4
ADM 91-1797 .... 4506–3.43
ADM 91-1813 4494–4
ADM 91-1820 .... 4506–4.14
ADM 91-1828 .... 4506–3.46
ADM 91-1829 .... 4506–3.45
ADM 91-1830 .... 4506–3.47
ADM 91-1835 4494–4
ADM 91-1836 4498–75
ADM 91-1849 .... 4492–5.2
ADM 91-1891 .... 4506–3.44
AHCPR 90-17 4188–69
AHCPR 91-2 .... 4186–8.13
AHCPR 91-8 4188–69
AHCPR 91-10 .... 4186–10.2
AHCPR 91-11 4188–72
AHCPR 91-13 .... 4186–10.3
AHCPR 91-22 .... 4186–6.15
AHCPR 91-24 .... 4186–9.11
AHCPR 91-25 4188–73
AHCPR 91-26 4188–70
AHCPR 91-27 .... 4186–10.4
AHCPR 91-29 .... 4186–8.17
AHCPR 91-31 .... 4186–8.19
AHCPR 91-32 .... 4186–8.20
AHCPR 91-34 4184–4
AHCPR 91-35 .... 4186–8.21
AHCPR 91-36 .... 4186–10.5
AHCPR 91-38 .... 4186–8.22
AHCPR Pub. No. 91-0003 4188–73
AHCPR Pub. No. 91-0004 4188–70
AHCPR Pub. No. 91-0005 .... 4186–7.10
AHCPR Pub. No. 91-0011 4184–4
AHCPR Pub. No. 91-0012 .... 4186–8.16
AHCPR Pub. No. 91-0015 .... 4186–6.15
AHCPR Pub. No. 91-0019 .... 4186–8.15
AHCPR Pub. No. 91-0027 .... 4186–8.17
AHCPR Pub. No. 91-0028 .... 4186–8.18
AHCPR Pub. No. 91-0030 .... 4186–10.4
AHCPR Pub. No. 91-0031 .... 4186–8.20
AHCPR Pub. No. 91-0034 .... 4186–8.19
AHCPR Pub. No. 91-0037 .... 4186–8.21
AHCPR Pub. No. 91-0041 .... 4186–10.5
AHCPR Pub. No. 91-0042 .... 4186–8.22
CDC (yr.)-8017 4202–1
— 4202–7
— 4206–2
CDC 90-8017 4204–1
CDC 90-8322 4204–10
CDC 91-8280 4204–11
CDC 91-8322 4204–10
CIN:A-01-90-00512 4008–113
DHHS (yr.)-1225 4122–1
DHHS 91-20408 .... 4146–12.27
FDA/CDER-90/52 4064–14
FHWA-SA-90-015 7558–110
H. Doc. 101-175 4704–4
HCFA 00720 .... 4654–14.1
HCFA 00721 .... 4654–14.2
HCFA 00722 .... 4654–14.2
HCFA 00723 .... 4654–14.3
HCFA 00724 .... 4654–14.3
HCFA 00725 .... 4654–14.4
HCFA 00726 .... 4654–14.4
HCFA 00727 .... 4654–14.4
HCFA 00728 .... 4654–14.4
HCFA 00729 .... 4654–14.5
HCFA 00730 .... 4654–14.5
HCFA 00731 .... 4654–14.5
HCFA 00732 .... 4654–14.5
HCFA 00733 .... 4654–14.6
HCFA 00734 .... 4654–14.6
HCFA 00735 .... 4654–14.6
HCFA 00736 .... 4654–14.6
HCFA 00737 .... 4654–14.7
HCFA 00738 .... 4654–14.7
HCFA 00739 .... 4654–14.8
HCFA 00740 .... 4654–14.9
HCFA 00741 .... 4654–14.9
HCFA 00742 .... 4654–14.9
HCFA 00743 .... 4654–14.10
HCFA 00744 .... 4654–14.11
HCFA 03285 4658–44
HCFA 03299 4654–16
HCFA 03307 4658–55
HCFA 03308 4658–58
HCFA 03310 4658–57
HCFA 03314 4654–1
HCFA 03315 4654–10
HCFA 03319 4654–16
HCFA 03325 4654–18
Health Technology Assessment Rpt., No. 5 .... 4186–10.2
Health Technology Assessment Rpt., No. 6 .... 4186–10.3
Health Technology Assessment Rpt., No. 9 .... 4186–10.4
Health Technology Assessment Rpt., No. 10 .... 4186–10.5
Hepatitis Surveillance, No. 53 4205–2
HETA 88-364-2102 .... 4248–92.1
HETA 88-364-2103 .... 4248–92.2
HETA 88-364-2104 .... 4248–92.3
HHS-11/8-90(1M600)E 7558–110
HL44 4488–14
Hospital Studies Program Res. Note 15 .... 4186–6.15
HRS-M-CH 90-1 4108–49
HRS-P-DV 90-1 4118–56
LHNCBC 87-2 4468–4
Mental Health Stat. Note No. 183 .... 4506–3.42
Mental Health Stat. Note No. 194 .... 4506–3.40
Mental Health Stat. Note No. 195 .... 4506–3.41
Mental Health Stat. Note No. 196 .... 4506–3.42
Mental Health Stat. Note No. 197 .... 4506–3.43
Mental Health Stat. Note No. 198 .... 4506–3.44
Mental Health Stat. Note No. 199 .... 4506–3.45
Mental Health Stat. Note No. 200 .... 4506–3.46
Mental Health Stat. Note No. 201 .... 4506–3.47
NIDA Res. Mono. 90 4494–11
NIDA Res. Mono. 95 4494–11
NIDA Res. Mono. 101 4498–69
NIDA Res. Mono. 102 4498–67
NIDA Res. Mono. 103 4498–70
NIDA Res. Mono. 104 4498–71
NIDA Res. Mono. 105 4494–11
NIDA Res. Mono. 106 4498–73
NIDA Res. Mono. 110 4498–74
NIDA Res. Mono. 115 4498–75
NIDA Series I, No. 9 4494–8
NIDA Series I, No. 10-A 4494–8
NIDA Series I, No. 10-B 4494–8
NIH (v.nos.&nos.) 4472–1
NIH 90-479 4478–196
NIH 90-1261 4434–3
NIH 90-1582 4478–78
NIH 90-3107 4478–195
NIH 91-7 4434–2
NIH 91-62 4474–6
NIH 91-1042 .... 4434–7.1
NIH 91-1043 .... 4434–7.2
NIH 91-1261 4434–3
NIH 91-2011 4474–23
NIH 91-2309 4434–12
NIH 91-2789 4474–35
NIH 91-2912 4434–16
NIH 91-3176 4474–37
NIH 91-3258 4434–17
NIMH Series CN, No. 14 .... 4506–4.14
NIOSH 54 4248–91
NIOSH 90-108 Pt. I 4248–90
NIOSH 90-108 Pt. II 4248–90
NIOSH 90-115 4248–89
NIOSH 90-118 .... 4246–1.98
NIOSH 91-103 .... 4246–4.3
NIOSH 91-106 4244–2
NLM-LHC-90-01 4468–4
NTP 90-152 .... 4044–16.2
NTP 90-153 .... 4044–16.1
OAI-01-88-00583 .... 4006–8.4
OAI-05-88-00730 .... 4006–7.4
ODAM 11-91 .... 4116–6.1
ODAM 12-91 .... 4116–6.2
ODAM 13-91 .... 4116–6.3
ODAM 14-91 .... 4116–6.4
ODAM 15-91 .... 4116–6.5
ODAM 16-91 .... 4116–6.6
ODAM 17-91 .... 4116–6.7
ODAM 18-91 .... 4116–6.8
ODAM 19-91 .... 4116–6.9
ODAM 20-91 .... 4116–6.10
ODAM 21-91 .... 4116–6.11
ODAM 22-91 .... 4116–6.12
ODAM 23-91 .... 4116–6.13
ODAM 24-91 .... 4116–6.14
ODAM 25-91 .... 4116–6.15
ODAM 26-91 .... 4116–6.16
ODAM 27-91 .... 4116–6.17
ODAM 28-91 .... 4116–6.18
ODAM 29-91 .... 4116–6.19
ODAM 30-91 .... 4116–6.20
ODAM 31-91 .... 4116–6.21
ODAM 32-91 .... 4116–6.22

DEPARTMENT OF HEALTH AND HUMAN SERVICES

ODAM 33-91 .... 4116-6.23	
ODAM 34-91 .... 4116-6.24	
ODAM 35-91 .... 4116-6.25	
ODAM 36-91 .... 4116-6.26	
ODAM 37-91 .... 4116-6.27	
ODAM 38-91 .... 4116-6.28	
ODAM 39-91 .... 4116-6.29	
ODAM 40-91 .... 4116-6.30	
ODAM 41-91 .... 4116-6.31	
ODAM 42-91 .... 4116-6.32	
ODAM 43-91 .... 4116-6.33	
ODAM 44-91 .... 4116-6.34	
ODAM 45-91 .... 4116-6.35	
ODAM 46-91 .... 4116-6.36	
ODAM 47-91 .... 4116-6.37	
ODAM 48-91 .... 4116-6.38	
ODAM 49-91 .... 4116-6.39	
ODAM 50-91 .... 4116-6.40	
ODAM 51-91 .... 4116-6.41	
ODAM 52-91 .... 4116-6.42	
ODAM 53-91 .... 4116-6.43	
ODAM 54-91 .... 4116-6.44	
ODAM 55-91 .... 4116-6.45	
ODAM 56-91 .... 4116-6.46	
ODAM 57-91 .... 4116-6.47	
ODAM 58-91 .... 4116-6.48	
ODAM 59-91 .... 4116-6.49	
ODAM 60-91 .... 4116-6.50	
ODAM 61-91 .... 4116-6.51	
ODAM 62-91 .... 4116-6.52	
ODAM 63-91 .... 4116-6.53	
ODAM 64-91 .... 4116-6.54	
OEI-01-89-00560 .... 4008-83.1	
OEI-01-89-00562 .... 4008-83.2	
OEI-02-89-01860 4008-112	
OEI-09-91-00652 .... 4006-10.1	
OEI-09-91-00653 .... 4006-10.2	
OEI-09-91-00655 .... 4006-10.3	
ORS Working Paper 39 .... 4746-26.8	
OS 90-12 4004-3	
PHS (yr.)-1120 4142-1	
PHS (yr.)-1309-(nos.) 4122-2	
PHS (yr.)-50193 4042-3	
PHS 90-1103 4144-4	
PHS 90-1250, No. 188 .... 4146-8.192	
PHS 90-1307 .... 4147-1.26	
PHS 90-1765 .... 4147-13.104	
PHS 90-1863 .... 4147-16.4	
PHS 90-1954 .... 4147-24.4	
PHS 90-3460 4188-69	
PHS 90-3463 .... 4186-8.12	
PHS 90-3469 .... 4186-8.13	
PHS 90-3470 .... 4186-8.11	
PHS 91-1101 4144-2	
PHS 91-1103 4144-4	
PHS 91-1120,	
Vol. 39, No. 11, Supp 4146-5.119	
PHS 91-1120,	
Vol. 39, No. 12, Supp 4146-5.120	
PHS 91-1120,	
Vol. 39, No. 12, Supp. 2 .... 4146-5.121	
PHS 91-1120,	
Vol. 39, No. 13 4144-7	
PHS 91-1120,	
Vol. 40, No. 4, Supp 4146-5.122	
PHS 91-1205 4164-1	
PHS 91-1232 4144-11	
PHS 91-1250, No. 190 .... 4146-8.193	
PHS 91-1250, No. 191 .... 4146-8.197	
PHS 91-1250, No. 192 .... 4146-8.194	
PHS 91-1250, No. 194 .... 4146-8.196	
PHS 91-1250, No. 195 .... 4146-8.195	
PHS 91-1250, No. 196 .... 4146-8.199	
PHS 91-1250, No. 197 .... 4146-8.202	
PHS 91-1250, No. 198 .... 4146-8.201	
PHS 91-1250, No. 199 .... 4146-8.198	
PHS 91-1250, No. 200 .... 4146-8.200	

PHS 91-1250, No. 201 .... 4146-8.203
PHS 91-1250, No. 202 .... 4146-8.204
PHS 91-1250, No. 203 .... 4146-8.206
PHS 91-1250, No. 204 .... 4146-8.205
PHS 91-1250, No. 205 .... 4146-8.207
PHS 91-1301 4124-1
PHS 91-1385 .... 4147-2.111
PHS 91-1386 .... 4147-2.112
PHS 91-1465 .... 4147-4.27
PHS 91-1482 .... 4147-5.6
PHS 91-1503 .... 4147-10.176
PHS 91-1505 .... 4147-10.179
PHS 91-1506 .... 4147-10.178
PHS 91-1766 .... 4147-13.106
PHS 91-1767 .... 4147-13.107
PHS 91-1768 .... 4147-13.105
PHS 91-1769 .... 4147-13.108
PHS 91-1855 .... 4147-20.18
PHS 91-1864 .... 4147-16.5
PHS 91-1927 .... 4147-21.49
PHS 91-3472 .... 4186-10.2
PHS 91-3473 .... 4186-10.3
PHS 91-50212 4048-10
PHS 92-1120,
Vol. 40, No. 8, Supp 4146-5.123
PHS 92-1250, No. 206 .... 4146-8.208
PHS 92-1250, No. 207 .... 4146-8.209
Series C, Analytical Rpt. 8 .... 4146-12.27
SSA 11-11550 .... 4706-1.105
SSA 13-11700 4742-1
— 4744-3
SSA 13-11786 4704-12
SSA 13-11816 .... 4744-27.1
SSA 13-11817 .... 4744-27.2
SSA 13-11818 .... 4744-27.3
SSA 13-11819 .... 4744-27.4
SSA 13-11820 .... 4744-27.5
SSA 13-11821 .... 4744-27.6
SSA 13-11822 .... 4744-27.7
SSA 13-11823 .... 4744-27.8
SSA 13-11824 .... 4744-27.9
SSA 13-11825 .... 4744-27.10
SSA 13-11925 4744-12
SSA 13-11954 4744-28
SSA 17-002 4704-13
Surveillance Rpt. 15 .... 4486-1.10
Vital and Health Statistics
Series 1, No. 25 .... 4147-1.26
Vital and Health Statistics
Series 2, No. 109 .... 4147-2.112
Vital and Health Statistics
Series 2, No. 111 .... 4147-2.111
Vital and Health Statistics
Series 4, No. 28 .... 4147-4.27
Vital and Health Statistics
Series 5, No. 6 .... 4147-5.6
Vital and Health Statistics
Series 10, CD-ROM
No. 1 .... 4147-10.177
Vital and Health Statistics
Series 10, No. 175 .... 4147-10.176
Vital and Health Statistics
Series 10, No. 177 .... 4147-10.179
Vital and Health Statistics
Series 10, No. 178 .... 4147-10.178
Vital and Health Statistics
Series 13, No. 104 .... 4147-13.104
Vital and Health Statistics
Series 13, No. 105 .... 4147-13.106
Vital and Health Statistics
Series 13, No. 106 .... 4147-13.107
Vital and Health Statistics
Series 13, No. 107 .... 4147-13.105
Vital and Health Statistics
Series 13, No. 108 .... 4147-13.108
Vital and Health Statistics
Series 16, No. 4 .... 4147-16.4

Index by Agency Report Numbers

Vital and Health Statistics
Series 16, No. 5 .... 4147-16.5
Vital and Health Statistics
Series 20, No. 18 .... 4147-20.18
Vital and Health Statistics
Series 21, No. 49 .... 4147-21.49
Vital and Health Statistics
Series 24, No. 4 .... 4147-24.4

DEPARTMENT OF HOUSING AND URBAN DEVELOPMENT

HUD 91-16 5144-21
HUD 329-PA(18) 5004-10
HUD 1256-PDR 5186-14.4
HUD 1270 ADMIN 5008-37
HUD 1285-OS(1) 5002-11
HUD 1285-OS(2) 5002-11
HUD 1296-GNMA 5144-6
HUD 1305-IG 5002-8
HUD 1314-PDR 5184-10
HUD 1333-IG 5002-8
HUD-0005426 5184-9
HUD-0005595 5184-9
HUD-PDR-1295 5188-128
R33SECA 5142-45
RR:250-Areas 5144-24
RR:250 Book (States) 5144-1
RR:250-Sections 5144-17
RR:250-States 5144-25
RR:250-U.S 5144-23
RR:S0101 5144-1
RR:S0102 5144-17

DEPARTMENT OF INTERIOR

Air Pollution and Acid
Rain Rpt. 28 .... 5506-5.26
Biological Rpt. 80(40.28) 5506-5.26
Biological Rpt. 82(11.123) 5506-8.130
Biological Rpt. 82(11.124) 5506-8.131
Biological Rpt. 82(11.125) 5506-8.132
Biological Rpt. 82(11.126) 5506-8.133
Biological Rpt. 85(1.20) 5506-14.3
Biological Rpt. 85(1.21) 5506-14.1
Biological Rpt. 85(1.22) 5506-14.2
Biological Rpt. 85(7.29) 5506-9.42
Biological Rpt. 90(1) 5508-108
Biological Rpt. 90(4) 5508-111
Biological Rpt. 90(6) 5506-10.12
Biological Rpt. 90(9) 5506-10.11
Biological Rpt. 90(11) 5508-112
Biological Rpt. 90(12) 5508-110
Biological Rpt. 90(14) 5508-109
Biological Rpt. 90(15) 5508-113
BLM-AA-GI-90-007-4370 5724-13
BLM-AK-AE-90-041-1737-930 ...... 5726-8.3
BLM-ID-GI-90-024-4830-
91/Rev 5724-11.4
BLM-ID-PT-90-006-4351 .... 5726-7.2
BLM-ID-PT-91-008-4351 5724-14
BLM-MT-PT-90-002-4333 .... 5726-5.5
BLM-MT-PT-90-003-4350 .... 5726-7.4
BLM-NM-GI-89-028-4350 .... 5726-7.1
BLM-NM-GI-90-034-4320 .... 5726-8.2
BLM-NM-GI-91-001-4300 5724-15
BLM-OR-AE-90-16-1792 .... 5724-11.1
BLM-OR-GI-89-12-1792 .... 5726-5.3
BLM-OR-GI-89-13-1792 .... 5726-5.3
BLM-SC-PT-91-006+
1165 5724-1
BLM-UT-PT-90-027-8300 .... 5726-5.4
BLM-WY-AE-90-008-4830 .... 5724-11.5
BLM-WY-AE-91-012-4830 .... 5724-11.6

Index by Agency Report Numbers

DEPARTMENT OF INTERIOR

Bur. Mines IC 9267 5604–44
Bur. Mines IC 9274 5608–167
Bur. Mines IC 9276 .... 5606–4.28
Bur. Mines IC 9286 .... 5606–4.29
Bur. Mines IC 9290 5604–2
Fish and Wildlife Research
No. 5 .... 5506–13.1
Fish and Wildlife Research
No. 6 .... 5506–13.2
Fish and Wildlife Research
No. 7 .... 5506–13.3
Fish and Wildlife Tech.
Rpt. 26 .... 5506–12.1
Fish and Wildlife Tech.
Rpt. 27 .... 5506–12.1
Fish and Wildlife Tech.
Rpt. 29 .... 5506–12.2
Fish and Wildlife Tech.
Rpt. 30 .... 5506–12.3
Fish Distribution Rpt. 25 5504–10
FWS/OMA-91-01 5504–19
FWS/OMA-91-02 5504–19
GS List (nos.) 5662–1
GS Water-Data Rpt.
AL-90-1 .... 5666–10.1
GS Water-Data Rpt.
AR-90-1 .... 5666–10.4
GS Water-Data Rpt.
CA-90-1 .... 5666–10.5
GS Water-Data Rpt.
CA-90-2 .... 5666–10.5
GS Water-Data Rpt.
CA-90-3 .... 5666–10.5
GS Water-Data Rpt.
CA-90-4 .... 5666–10.5
GS Water-Data Rpt.
CA-90-5 .... 5666–10.5
GS Water-Data Rpt.
CO-90-1 .... 5666–10.6
GS Water-Data Rpt.
CO-90-2 .... 5666–10.6
GS Water-Data Rpt.
CT-90-1 .... 5666–10.7
GS Water-Data Rpt.
FL-89-4 .... 5666–12.8
GS Water-Data Rpt.
FL-89-3A 5666–12.8
GS Water-Data Rpt.
FL-90-4 .... 5666–10.8
GS Water-Data Rpt.
FL-90-1A 5666–10.8
GS Water-Data Rpt.
FL-90-1B 5666–10.8
GS Water-Data Rpt.
FL-90-2A 5666–10.8
GS Water-Data Rpt.
FL-90-2B 5666–10.8
GS Water-Data Rpt.
FL-90-3A 5666–10.8
GS Water-Data Rpt.
FL-90-3B 5666–10.8
GS Water-Data Rpt.
GA-90-1 .... 5666–10.9
GS Water-Data Rpt.
HI-89-1 .... 5666–12.10
GS Water-Data Rpt.
IA-90-1 .... 5666–10.14
GS Water-Data Rpt.
ID-90-1 .... 5666–10.11
GS Water-Data Rpt.
IL-90-1 .... 5666–10.12
GS Water-Data Rpt.
IL-90-2 .... 5666–10.12
GS Water-Data Rpt.
IN-90-1 .... 5666–10.13
GS Water-Data Rpt.
KS-90-1 .... 5666–10.15

GS Water-Data Rpt.
KY-90-1 .... 5666–10.16
GS Water-Data Rpt.
LA-90-1 .... 5666–10.17
GS Water-Data Rpt.
MA-RI-89-1 .... 5666–12.20
GS Water-Data Rpt.
MA-RI-90-1 .... 5666–10.20
GS Water-Data Rpt.
MD-DE-90-1 .... 5666–10.19
GS Water-Data Rpt.
MD-DE-90-2 .... 5666–10.19
GS Water-Data Rpt.
ME-90-1 .... 5666–10.18
GS Water-Data Rpt.
MI-90-1 .... 5666–10.21
GS Water-Data Rpt.
MN-89-1 .... 5666–12.22
GS Water-Data Rpt.
MN-89-2 .... 5666–12.22
GS Water-Data Rpt.
MO-90-1 .... 5666–10.24
GS Water-Data Rpt.
MS-90-1 .... 5666–10.23
GS Water-Data Rpt.
MT-90-1 .... 5666–10.25
GS Water-Data Rpt.
NC-90-1 .... 5666–10.32
GS Water-Data Rpt.
NE-90-1 .... 5666–10.26
GS Water-Data Rpt.
NH-VT-90-1 .... 5666–10.28
GS Water-Data Rpt.
NJ-90-1 .... 5666–10.29
GS Water-Data Rpt.
NJ-90-2 .... 5666–10.29
GS Water-Data Rpt.
NM-90-1 .... 5666–10.30
GS Water-Data Rpt.
NV-88-1 .... 5666–16.27
GS Water-Data Rpt.
NY-89-1 .... 5666–12.31
GS Water-Data Rpt.
OH-90-1 .... 5666–10.34
GS Water-Data Rpt.
OH-90-2 .... 5666–10.34
GS Water-Data Rpt.
OK-89-1 .... 5666–12.35
GS Water-Data Rpt.
OR-90-1 .... 5666–10.36
GS Water-Data Rpt.
OR-90-2 .... 5666–10.36
GS Water-Data Rpt.
PA-89-2 .... 5666–12.37
GS Water-Data Rpt.
PR-90-1 .... 5666–10.48
GS Water-Data Rpt.
SC-90-1 .... 5666–10.38
GS Water-Data Rpt.
SD-90-1 .... 5666–10.39
GS Water-Data Rpt.
TN-89-1 .... 5666–12.40
GS Water-Data Rpt.
TN-90-1 .... 5666–10.40
GS Water-Data Rpt.
UT-90-1 .... 5666–10.42
GS Water-Data Rpt.
WA-90-1 .... 5666–10.44
GS Water-Data Rpt.
WV-90-1 .... 5666–10.45
INT-1-06982 .... 5306–4.10
INT. REQ. 2-00185-92 .... 5306–4.11
INT. REQ. 102968 .... 5306–4.7
INT. REQ. 103693 .... 5306–4.9
INT. REQ. 103868 .... 5306–4.8
MMS 88-0042 OCS Study 5738–24
MMS 88-0056 OCS Study 5738–29

MMS 89-0030 OCS Study 5738–28
MMS 89-0073 OCS Study 5738–20
MMS 89-0074 OCS Rpt 5734–6
MMS 89-0077 OCS Study 5736–5.12
MMS 89-0093 OCS Study 5736–5.8
MMS 89-0094 OCS Study 5736–5.8
MMS 90-0014 OCS Rpt 5738–25
MMS 90-0017 OCS Study 5738–27
MMS 90-0019 OCS Study 5738–19
MMS 90-0022 OCS Study 5736–5.9
MMS 90-0023 OCS Study 5736–5.10
MMS 90-0025 OCS Study 5738–26
MMS 90-0042 OCS
EIS/EA 5736–1.23
MMS 90-0046 OCS Study 5738–23
MMS 90-0047 OCS Study 5734–10
MMS 90-0049 OCS Study 5738–31
MMS 90-0063 OCS
EIS/EA 5736–1.22
MMS 90-0065 OCS Study 5736–5.11
MMS 90-0068 OCS Study 5736–5.13
MMS 90-0069 OCS Study 5736–5.14
MMS 90-0071 Stat. Rpt 5734–9
MMS 90-0072 OCS Rpt 5734–3
MMS 90-0081 OCS Study 5736–5.15
MMS 90-0082 OCS Rpt 5734–6
MMS 90-0084 OCS Study 2176–1.36
MMS 90-0086 OCS Rpt 5734–7
MMS 90-0094 OCS Study 2176–1.37
MMS 90-0096 OCS Study 2176–1.38
MMS 91-0008 OCS
EIS/EA 5736–1.24
MMS 91-0013 OCS Rpt 5734–12
MMS 91-0029 OCS Study 5738–30
MMS 91-0032 OCS Info.
Rpt 5736–3.1
MMS 91-0035 OCS Study 2176–1.39
MMS 91-0036 OCS Rpt 5734–5
MMS 91-0041 OCS Rpt 5734–4
MMS 91-0055 OCS Study 5734–10
MMS 91-0068 OCS Rpt 5734–3
MMS Tech. Rpt. 135 .... 5736–5.12
MMS Tech. Rpt. 139 .... 5736–5.8
MMS Tech. Rpt. 140 .... 5736–5.8
MMS Tech. Rpt. 141 .... 5736–5.9
MMS Tech. Rpt. 142 .... 5736–5.10
MMS Tech. Rpt. 143 .... 5736–5.11
MMS Tech. Rpt. 144 .... 5736–5.13
MMS Tech. Rpt. 145 .... 5736–5.14
MMS Tech. Rpt. 146 .... 5736–5.15
USGS Bull. 1946 5664–15
USGS Bull. 1954 5664–13
USGS Bull. 1958 5668–119
USGS Circ. 930-J 5666–21.10
USGS Circ. 1036 5668–116
USGS Circ. 1056 5664–11
USGS Circ. 1057 5664–14
USGS Circ. 1064 5668–121
USGS Open-File Rpt.
88-641 .... 5666–27.6
USGS Open-File Rpt.
89-49 .... 5666–28.7
USGS Open-File Rpt.
89-64 .... 5666–28.6
USGS Open-File Rpt.
89-68 .... 5666–28.1
USGS Open-File Rpt.
89-168 5668–115
USGS Open-File Rpt.
89-259 .... 5666–28.10
USGS Open-File Rpt.
89-340 5668–114
USGS Open-File Rpt.
89-591 .... 5666–26.11
USGS Open-File Rpt.
89-592 .... 5666–26.10
USGS Open-File Rpt.

DEPARTMENT OF INTERIOR

89-597	5666-28.2

USGS Open-File Rpt.

89-618	5666-27.12

USGS Open-File Rpt.

89-4073	5666-28.3

USGS Open-File Rpt.

90-106	5666-28.4

USGS Open-File Rpt.

90-108	5666-25.11

USGS Open-File Rpt.

90-123	5666-27.22

USGS Open-File Rpt.

90-150	5666-26.12

USGS Open-File Rpt.

90-157	5666-26.13

USGS Open-File Rpt.

90-163	5668-120

USGS Open-File Rpt.

90-169	5666-26.14

USGS Open-File Rpt.

90-377	5666-28.12

USGS Open-File Rpt.

90-589	5666-26.15

USGS Open-File Rpt.

91-74	5666-25.9

USGS Professional Paper

1200-US	5668-117

USGS Professional Paper

1403-E	5666-25.8

USGS Professional Paper

1405-D	5666-25.10

USGS Professional Paper

1406-C	5666-25.13

USGS Professional Paper

1493	5668-122

USGS Professional Paper

1515	5668-123

USGS Water-Supply Paper

2298	5666-27.1

USGS Water-Supply Paper

2335	5666-27.2

USGS Water-Supply Paper

2344	5666-27.3

USGS Water-Supply Paper

2358	5666-27.17

USGS Water-Supply Paper

2359-A	5666-27.18

USGS Water-Supply Paper

2368-A	5666-27.19

USGS Water-Supply Paper

2368-B	5666-27.20

USGS Water-Supply Paper

2375	5664-12

USGS/WRD/HD-89/270	5666-16.27
USGS/WRD/HD-90/2/83	5666-12.37
USGS/WRD/HD-90/257	5666-12.40
USGS/WRD/HD-90/266	5666-12.8
USGS/WRD/HD-90/282	5666-12.8
USGS/WRD/HD-90/303	5666-12.22
USGS/WRD/HD-90/304	5666-12.20
USGS/WRD/HD-90/310	5666-12.31
USGS/WRD/HD-90/314	5666-12.10
USGS/WRD/HD-91/233	5666-12.22
USGS/WRD/HD-91/234	5666-10.8
USGS/WRD/HD-91/235	5666-12.35
USGS/WRD/HD-91/237	5666-10.18
USGS/WRD/HD-91/238	5666-10.8
USGS/WRD/HD-91/240	5666-10.25
USGS/WRD/HD-91/241	5666-10.16
USGS/WRD/HD-91/242	5666-10.7
USGS/WRD/HD-91/243	5666-10.8
USGS/WRD/HD-91/244	5666-10.8
USGS/WRD/HD-91/245	5666-10.34
USGS/WRD/HD-91/246	5666-10.34
USGS/WRD/HD-91/249	5666-10.21
USGS/WRD/HD-91/250	5666-10.36
USGS/WRD/HD-91/251	5666-10.19

USGS/WRD/HD-91/252	5666-10.19
USGS/WRD/HD-91/253	5666-10.32
USGS/WRD/HD-91/255	5666-10.45
USGS/WRD/HD-91/256	5666-10.5
USGS/WRD/HD-91/257	5666-10.8
USGS/WRD/HD-91/258	5666-10.48
USGS/WRD/HD-91/260	5666-10.12
USGS/WRD/HD-91/261	5666-10.12
USGS/WRD/HD-91/262	5666-10.1
USGS/WRD/HD-91/263	5666-10.13
USGS/WRD/HD-91/264	5666-10.4
USGS/WRD/HD-91/265	5666-10.20
USGS/WRD/HD-91/266	5666-10.17
USGS/WRD/HD-91/267	5666-10.14
USGS/WRD/HD-91/268	5666-10.11
USGS/WRD/HD-91/269	5666-10.23
USGS/WRD/HD-91/270	5666-10.26
USGS/WRD/HD-91/271	5666-10.9
USGS/WRD/HD-91/272	5666-10.38
USGS/WRD/HD-91/273	5666-10.24
USGS/WRD/HD-91/274	5666-10.15
USGS/WRD/HD-91/275	5666-10.5
USGS/WRD/HD-91/276	5666-10.5
USGS/WRD/HD-91/277	5666-10.42
USGS/WRD/HD-91/278	5666-10.40
USGS/WRD/HD-91/279	5666-10.6
USGS/WRD/HD-91/280	5666-10.6
USGS/WRD/HD-91/281	5666-10.8
USGS/WRD/HD-91/282	5666-10.30
USGS/WRD/HD-91/283	5666-10.5
USGS/WRD/HD-91/285	5666-10.39
USGS/WRD/HD-91/286	5666-10.36
USGS/WRD/HD-91/287	5666-10.8
USGS/WRD/HD-91/288	5666-10.5
USGS/WRD/HD-91/289	5666-10.29
USGS/WRD/HD-91/290	5666-10.29
USGS/WRD/HD-91/295	5666-10.28
USGS/WRD/HD-91/298	5666-10.44

Water-Resources Investigations Rpt.

87-4051	5666-27.13

Water-Resources Investigations Rpt.

87-4194	5666-27.9

Water-Resources Investigations Rpt.

87-4242	5666-28.11

Water-Resources Investigations Rpt.

88-714	5666-24.8

Water-Resources Investigations Rpt.

88-4111	5666-28.5

Water-Resources Investigations Rpt.

88-4114	5666-28.9

Water-Resources Investigations Rpt.

88-4150	5666-27.8

Water-Resources Investigations Rpt.

88-4217	5666-27.5

Water-Resources Investigations Rpt. 89-62 .... 5666-27.15

Water-Resources Investigations Rpt.

89-423	5666-24.7

Water-Resources Investigations Rpt.

89-4033	5666-27.7

Water-Resources Investigations Rpt.

89-4035	5666-27.11

Water-Resources Investigations Rpt.

89-4054	5666-27.16

Water-Resources

Index by Agency Report Numbers

Investigations Rpt.

89-4098	5666-24.9

Water-Resources Investigations Rpt.

89-4102	5666-27.4

Water-Resources Investigations Rpt.

89-4105	5666-27.14

Water-Resources Investigations Rpt.

89-4154	5666-28.8

Water-Resources Investigations Rpt.

90-4019	5666-28.13

Water-Resources Investigations Rpt.

90-4030	5664-17

Water-Resources Investigations Rpt.

90-4044	5666-27.23

Water-Resources Investigations Rpt.

90-4070	5666-27.10

Water-Resources Investigations Rpt.

90-4203	5666-27.21

Water-Resources Investigations Rpt.

91-4019	5666-28.14

Water-Resources Investigations Rpt.

91-4027	5666-25.12

Water-Resources Investigations Rpt.

91-4039	5664-17

Water-Resources Investigations Rpt.

91-4061	5668-124

DEPARTMENT OF JUSTICE

INS Bull. 1	6266-2.1
INS Bull. 2	6266-2.2
INS Bull. 3	6266-2.3
INS Bull. 4	6266-2.4
INS Bull. 5	6266-2.5
INS Bull. 6	6266-2.6
INS Bull. 7	6266-2.7
INS Bull. 8	6266-2.8
NCJ-121514	6064-25
NCJ-122024	6066-3.42
NCJ-123522	6064-33
NCJ-124139	6064-4
NCJ-124280	6064-26
NCJ-124549	6066-28.1
NCJ-124881	6066-27.4
NCJ-124944	6068-242
NCJ-125315	6066-25.33
NCJ-125615	6066-25.35
NCJ-125616	6064-31
NCJ-125617	6064-29
NCJ-125618	6068-245
NCJ-125619	6064-9
NCJ-125620	6068-241
NCJ-125625	6066-27.5
NCJ-125833	6066-25.34
NCJ-126160	6066-27.6
NCJ-126826	6068-243
NCJ-127202	6066-25.36
NCJ-127675	6064-13
NCJ-127855	6068-148
NCJ-127991	6066-19.61
NCJ-127992	6068-144.1
NCJ-128129	6066-3.43
NCJ-128662	6064-30
NCJ-129097	6066-19.62
NCJ-129198	6066-25.37

Index by Agency Report Numbers

DEPARTMENT OF LABOR

NCJ-129292	6066–26.6
NCJ-129391	6066–3.44
NCJ-129392	6066–3.45
NCJ-129756	6066–25.38
NCJ-129861	6066–25.39
NCJ-130234	6066–25.41
NCJ-130302	6066–25.40
NCJ-130445	6064–26
NCJ-130526	6064–31
NCJ-130580	6064–6
NCJ-130759	6068–144.2
NCJ-130760	6068–144.3
NCJ-130761	6068–144.4
NCJ-130762	6068–144.5
NCJ-130836	6066–19.63
NCJ-131648	6066–25.42
Release 91-410	6008–33
Rpt. 1-21	6004–2
Rpt. 91-57	6062–4

DEPARTMENT OF LABOR

BLS Bull. 2358	6846–1.20
BLS Bull. 2370/v.1	6744–4.1
BLS Bull. 2370/v.2	6744–4.2
BLS Bull. 2376	6748–52
BLS Bull. 2377	6784–9
BLS Bull. 2378	6824–1
BLS Bull. 2379	6844–1
BLS Bull. 2380	6884–1
BLS Bull. 2381	6744–7
BLS Bull. 2383	6764–5
BLS Bull. 2384	6787–6.252
BLS Bull. 2386	6787–6.251
BLS Bull. 2388	6784–20
BLS Bull. 2393	6744–16
BLS Bull. 3055-37	6785–11.1
BLS Bull. 3055-38	6785–11.1
BLS Bull. 3055-39	6785–11.2
BLS Bull. 3055-40	6785–11.2
BLS Bull. 3055-41	6785–11.2
BLS Bull. 3055-42	6785–11.2
BLS Bull. 3055-43	6785–11.2
BLS Bull. 3055-44	6785–11.2
BLS Bull. 3055-45	6785–11.2
BLS Bull. 3055-46	6785–11.2
BLS Bull. 3055-47	6785–11.3
BLS Bull. 3055-48	6785–11.3
BLS Bull. 3055-49	6785–11.3
BLS Bull. 3055-50	6785–11.3
BLS Bull. 3055-51	6785–11.3
BLS Bull. 3055-52	6785–11.3
BLS Bull. 3055-53	6785–11.3
BLS Bull. 3055-54	6785–11.3
BLS Bull. 3055-55	6785–11.3
BLS Bull. 3055-56	6785–11.3
BLS Bull. 3055-57	6785–11.4
BLS Bull. 3055-58	6785–11.4
BLS Bull. 3055-59	6785–11.4
BLS Bull. 3055-60	6785–11.4
BLS Bull. 3055-61	6785–1
BLS Bull. 3060-1	6785–12.1
BLS Bull. 3060-2	6785–12.1
BLS Bull. 3060-3	6785–12.2
BLS Bull. 3060-4	6785–12.2
BLS Bull. 3060-5	6785–12.2
BLS Bull. 3060-6	6785–12.2
BLS Bull. 3060-7	6785–12.2
BLS Bull. 3060-8	6785–12.3
BLS Bull. 3060-9	6785–12.3
BLS Bull. 3060-10	6785–12.3
BLS Bull. 3060-11	6785–12.3
BLS Bull. 3060-12	6785–12.3
BLS Bull. 3060-13	6785–12.3
BLS Bull. 3060-14	6785–12.3
BLS Bull. 3060-15	6785–12.4
BLS Bull. 3060-16	6785–12.4
BLS Bull. 3060-17	6785–12.4
BLS Bull. 3060-18	6785–12.5
BLS Bull. 3060-19	6785–12.5
BLS Bull. 3060-20	6785–12.5
BLS Bull. 3060-21	6785–12.5
BLS Bull. 3060-22	6785–12.6
BLS Bull. 3060-23	6785–12.6
BLS Bull. 3060-24	6785–12.6
BLS Bull. 3060-25	6785–12.6
BLS Bull. 3060-26	6785–12.6
BLS Bull. 3060-27	6785–12.7
BLS Bull. 3060-28	6785–12.7
BLS Bull. 3060-29	6785–12.7
BLS Bull. 3060-30	6785–12.7
BLS Rpt. (nos.)	6742–17
BLS Rpt. 761	6888–34
BLS Rpt. 793	6728–35
BLS Rpt. 803	6822–3
BLS Summary 90-14	6785–5.1
BLS Summary 91-1	6844–7
BLS Summary 91-3	6785–5.2
BLS Summary 91-4	6785–6.1
BLS Summary 91-7	6785–13
BLS Summary 91-8	6785–8
BLS Summary 91-9	6785–9
BLS Summary 91-10	6785–6.2
BLS Working Paper 203	6886–6.72
BLS Working Paper 204	6886–6.73
BLS Working Paper 205	6886–6.74
BLS Working Paper 206	6886–6.75
BLS Working Paper 207	6886–6.76
BLS Working Paper 208	6886–6.77
BLS Working Paper 209	6886–6.78
BLS Working Paper 210	6886–6.79
BLS Working Paper 211	6886–6.80
BLS/LAUS/MR(yr./nos.)	6742–22
Econ. Discussion Paper 35	6364–2
Econ. Discussion Paper 36	6366–3.27
Econ. Discussion Paper 37	6364–2
Fact Sheet 90-4	6564–1.2
Fact Sheet 90-5	6564–1.1
FLT 90-52	6366–4.1
FLT 90-53	6366–4.2
FLT 90-54	6366–4.3
FLT 90-55	6366–4.4
FLT 90-56	6366–4.5
FLT 90-57	6366–4.6
FLT 90-58	6366–4.7
FLT 90-59	6366–4.8
FLT 90-60	6366–4.9
FLT 90-61	6366–4.10
FLT 90-62	6366–4.11
FLT 90-63	6366–4.12
FLT 90-64	6366–4.13
FLT 90-65	6366–4.14
FLT 91-01	6366–4.15
FLT 91-02	6366–4.16
FLT 91-03	6366–4.17
FLT 91-04	6366–4.18
FLT 91-05	6366–4.19
FLT 91-06	6366–4.20
FLT 91-07	6366–4.21
FLT 91-08	6366–4.22
FLT 91-09	6366–4.23
FLT 91-10	6366–4.24
FLT 91-11	6366–4.25
FLT 91-12	6366–4.26
FLT 91-13	6366–4.27
FLT 91-14	6366–4.28
FLT 91-15	6366–4.29
FLT 91-16	6366–4.30
FLT 91-17	6366–4.31
FLT 91-18	6366–4.32
FLT 91-19	6366–4.33
FLT 91-20	6366–4.34
FLT 91-21	6366–4.35
FLT 91-22	6366–4.36
FLT 91-23	6366–4.37
FLT 91-24	6366–4.38
FLT 91-25	6366–4.39
FLT 91-26	6366–4.40
FLT 91-27	6366–4.41
FLT 91-28	6366–4.42
FLT 91-29	6366–4.43
FLT 91-30	6366–4.44
FLT 91-31	6366–4.45
FLT 91-32	6366–4.46
FLT 91-33	6366–4.47
FLT 91-34	6366–4.48
FLT 91-35	6366–4.49
FLT 91-36	6366–4.50
FLT 91-37	6366–4.51
FLT 91-38	6366–4.52
FLT 91-39	6366–4.53
FLT 91-40	6366–4.54
FLT 91-41	6366–4.55
FLT 91-42	6366–4.56
FLT 91-43	6366–4.57

Immigration Policy and
Research Rpt. 2 .... 6366–5.2

Immigration Policy and
Research Rpt. 3 .... 6366–5.3

IR 1196	6664–4
IR 1197	6664–3
IR 1198	6664–1
IR 1199	6664–2
IR 1200	6664–5

Research and Evaluation
Rpt. Series 91-A 6406–10.1

Research and Evaluation
Rpt. Series 91-B 6406–10.2

Research and Evaluation
Rpt. Series 91-C 6406–10.3

Research and Evaluation
Rpt. Series 91-E 6406–10.4

Research and Evaluation
Rpt. Series 91-F 6406–10.5

Unemployment Insurance
Occasional Paper No.
91-1 .... 6406–6.32

Unemployment Insurance
Occasional Paper No.
91-2 .... 6406–6.33

Unemployment Insurance
Occasional Paper No.
91-3 .... 6406–6.34

Unemployment Insurance
Occasional Paper No.
91-4 .... 6406–6.35

USDL (yr.-nos.)	6742–3
—	6742–12
—	6742–20
—	6742–21
—	6822–2
USDL 90-573	6764–3
USDL 91-5	6744–22
USDL 91-34	6726–1.36
USDL 91-38	6784–12
USDL 91-74	6726–1.37
USDL 91-79	6782–6
USDL 91-129	6824–2
USDL 91-169	6406–2.31
USDL 91-220	6744–13
USDL 91-264	6726–1.38
USDL 91-390	6784–17.1
USDL 91-393	6782–6
USDL 91-412	6824–2
USDL 91-417	6784–17.2
USDL 91-418	6744–14
USDL 91-447	6726–1.39
USDL 91-500	6406–2.32
USDL 91-547	6726–1.40
USDL 91-549	6726–1.41
USDL 91-600	6844–3

DEPARTMENT OF LABOR

USDL 91-607	6726-1.42
USDL 91-616	6726-1.43

DEPARTMENT OF STATE

IRR 15	7144-11
IRR 21	7144-10
IRR 22	7144-8
IRR 23	7144-7
IRR 30	7144-14
Limits in the Seas, No.	
111	7006-8.6
Pub. 7365	7006-2.50
Pub. 7747	7006-2.21
Pub. 7749	7006-2.9
Pub. 7752	7006-2.23
Pub. 7756	7006-2.4
Pub. 7769	7006-2.24
Pub. 7770	7006-2.12
Pub. 7771	7006-2.35
Pub. 7782	7006-2.34
Pub. 7791	7006-2.51
Pub. 7800	7006-2.30
Pub. 7816	7006-2.18
Pub. 7820	7006-2.46
Pub. 7834	7006-2.36
Pub. 7836	7006-2.7
Pub. 7841	7006-2.33
Pub. 7850	7006-2.22
Pub. 7857	7006-2.10
Pub. 7901	7006-2.47
Pub. 7904	7006-2.15
Pub. 7953	7006-2.32
Pub. 7958	7006-2.28
Pub. 7967	7006-2.25
Pub. 7998	7006-2.14
Pub. 8020	7006-2.37
Pub. 8022	7006-2.27
Pub. 8032	7006-2.52
Pub. 8046	7006-2.16
Pub. 8074	7006-2.41
Pub. 8084	7006-2.45
Pub. 8089	7006-2.40
Pub. 8091	7006-2.6
Pub. 8099	7006-2.3
Pub. 8142	7006-2.11
Pub. 8149	7006-2.38
Pub. 8152	7006-2.19
Pub. 8168	7006-2.31
Pub. 8174	7006-2.43
Pub. 8198	7006-2.20
Pub. 8209	7006-2.13
Pub. 8262	7006-2.1
Pub. 8268	7006-2.54
Pub. 8301	7006-2.26
Pub. 8334	7006-2.42
Pub. 8347	7006-2.5
Pub. 8698	7006-2.8
Pub. 8822	7006-2.17
Pub. 8871	7006-2.49
Pub. 8874	7006-2.26
—	7006-2.53
—	7006-2.54
Pub. 9430	7006-2.39
Pub. 9433	7004-1
Pub. 9542	7006-2.2
Pub. 9767	7004-22
Pub. 9778	7006-2.44
Pub. 9823	7184-1
Pub. 9825	7008-1
Pub. 9836	7004-18
Pub. 9846	7004-6
Pub. 9853-A	7004-17.1
Pub. 9862	7004-13
Pub. 9867	7002-6
Pub. 9869	7004-22
Pub. 9912	7004-9

DEPARTMENT OF TRANSPORTATION

Accident/Incident Bull.

159	7604-1
COMDTPUB P16107.6	7404-2
COMDTPUB P16754.4	7404-1
DOT-FAA (nos.-yr.)	7502-14
DOT-FAA-AM-90-12	7506-10.78
DOT-FAA-AM-90-13	7506-10.79
DOT-FAA-AM-90-14	7506-10.77
DOT-FAA-AM-91-1	7506-10.80
DOT-FAA-AM-91-2	7506-10.81
DOT-FAA-AM-91-3	7506-10.82
DOT-FAA-AM-91-4	7506-10.83
DOT-FAA-AM-91-5	7506-10.84
DOT-FAA-AM-91-6	7506-10.85
DOT-FAA-AM-91-7	7506-10.86
DOT-FAA-AM-91-8	7506-10.87
DOT-FAA-AM-91-9	7506-10.88
DOT-FAA-AM-91-10	7506-10.89
DOT-FAA-AM-91-11	7506-10.90
DOT-FAA-AM-91-12	7506-10.91
DOT-FAA-AM-91-13	7506-10.92
DOT-FAA-AM-91-14	7506-10.93
DOT-FAA-AM-91-15	7506-10.94
DOT-FAA-AM-91-16	7506-10.95
DOT-FAA-APO-89-11	7504-37
DOT-FAA-APO-90-10	7506-7.39
DOT-FAA-APO-90-12	7506-7.40
DOT-FAA-APO-91-1	7504-6
DOT-FAA-APO-91-2	7504-28
DOT-FAA-APO-91-5	7504-7
DOT-FAA-APO-91-7	7506-7.41
DOT-FAA-APO-91-8	7504-15
DOT-FAA-SC-90-1	7504-43
DOT HS (nos.)	7762-2
DOT HS 807 358	7764-17
DOT HS 807 549	7764-17
DOT HS 807 665	7764-18
DOT HS 807 666	7762-11
DOT HS 807 693	7764-10
DOT HS 807 716	7762-11
DOT HS 807 720	7764-1.1
DOT HS 807 721	7764-1.2
DOT HS 807 734	7764-22
DOT HS 807 739	7764-20
DOT HS 807 770	7764-17
DOT-P-16	7308-201
DOT-T-90-12	7308-200
DOT-T-90-19	7888-81
DOT-T-90-22	7308-203
DOT-T-91-03	7888-79
DOT-T-91-05	7888-80
DOT-TSC-UMTA-90-1	7884-5
DOT-VNTSC-RSPA-90-4	7304-19
FHWA-MC-90-018	7554-9
FHWA-PD-91-018	7552-12
FHWA-PD-92-001	7552-12
FHWA-PL-(yr.)-005	7552-8
FHWA-PL-91-001	7554-24
FHWA-PL-91-002	7554-16
FHWA-PL-91-003	7554-1
FHWA-PL-91-009	7554-39
FHWA-PL-91-017	7554-37
FHWA-SA-91-001	7554-26
HFS-30	7554-40
HNG-13	7552-5
—	7554-29
HNG-22	7554-40
HPM-10/7-91(1M525)E	7554-37
MF-205	7554-32
NHTSA 09-91	7766-7.22
NHTSA 11-91	7766-7.23
NHTSA 13-91	7764-21
NHTSA 24-91	7766-7.24
NHTSA 32-91	7766-7.25

Index by Agency Report Numbers

NHTSA 34-91	7766-7.26
NHTSA 38-91	7766-7.27
NHTSA 42-91	7766-7.28
NRM-21	7764-9
UMTA-IT-06-0352-90-1	7884-4
UMTA-MA-06-0194-90-1	7884-5
UMTA-UTS-5-91-1	7884-1

DEPARTMENT OF TREASURY

B(nos.)	8002-7
IR-91-(nos.)	8302-6
IRS Doc. 6149(Rev.11-90)	8304-24
IRS Doc. 6186(Rev.9-90)	8304-9
IRS Doc. 6187(Rev.5-90)	8302-7
IRS Doc. 6187(Rev.5-91)	8302-7
IRS Doc. 6187(Rev.8-90)	8302-7
IRS Doc. 6292(Rev.4-91)	8302-4
IRS Doc. 6961(Rev.4-91)	8304-22
IRS Doc. 7302(Rev.3-90)	8304-25
IRS Doc. 7302(Rev.3-91)	8304-25
IRS Pub. 16(Rev.12-90)	8304-4
IRS Pub. 55(Rev.10-90)	8304-3
IRS Pub. 55(Rev.7-91)	8304-3
IRS Pub. 1053(Rev.6-91)	8304-21
IRS Pub. 1136(date)	8302-2
IRS Pub. 1265(Rev.10-90)	8304-3
IRS Pub. 1299(Rev.12-90)	8304-17
IRS Pub. 1500(Rev.9-91)	8304-8
NB-1336	8008-150
NB-1361	8008-149
NB-1524	8008-153
Rpt. Symbol 76	8486-1.3

DEPARTMENT OF VETERANS AFFAIRS

IB 11-78	8704-3
IB 11-78a	8704-3
RCS 10-0161	8704-4
RCS 50-0568	8602-1
RCS 70-0561	8604-12
Rpt. No. 91-01	8608-7
Semiannual Rpt. 26	8602-1

INDEPENDENT AGENCIES

Central Intelligence Agency

DI EEI (yr.-nos.)	9112-1
DI IESR (yr.-nos.)	9112-2
EA 91-10022	9118-9
LDA CS (yr.-nos.)	9112-4
Ref. Aid CPAS 90-10001	9114-4
Ref. Aid IR 91-10003	9116-1.1
Ref. Aid IR 91-10004	9116-1.3
Ref. Aid IR 91-10005	9116-1.2
Ref. Aid IR 91-10006	9116-1.4
Ref. Aid IR 91-10007	9116-1.5
Ref. Aid IR 91-10008	9116-1.6
Ref. Aid IR 91-10009	9116-1.7
Ref. Aid RTT 91-10021	9116-1.1
Ref. Aid RTT 91-10024	9116-1.3
Ref. Aid RTT 91-10025	9116-1.2
Ref. Aid RTT 91-10026	9116-1.4
Ref. Aid RTT 91-10027	9116-1.5
Ref. Aid RTT 91-10028	9116-1.6
Ref. Aid RTT 91-10029	9116-1.7
RTT 90-10042	9118-11
RTT 90-10012U	9118-17
RTT 91-10064	9118-18

Index by Agency Report Numbers

INDEPENDENT AGENCIES

Environmental Protection Agency

EPA 21E-2002	9184–21
EPA 230/05-89-050	9188–113
EPA 440/1-89-014	9206–4.6
EPA 440/1-89-025	9206–4.1
EPA 440/1-89-050	9206–4.7
EPA 440/1-89-060 E	9206–4.2
EPA 440/1-89-060 N	9206–4.3
EPA 440/1-89-084	9206–4.4
EPA 440/1-89-100	9206–4.5
EPA 440/1-89-101	9206–4.8
EPA 440/1-89-102	9206–4.9
EPA 440/1-89-103	9206–4.10
EPA 440/1-89-104	9206–4.11
EPA 440/1-89-105	9206–4.12
EPA 440/1-89-106	9206–4.13
EPA 450/2-90-011	9198–120
EPA 450/4-91-003	9194–1
EPA 450/4-91-004	9194–13
EPA 520/5-(yr.-nos.)	9192–5
EPA 540/8-90-006	9214–5
EPA 600/3-90-043	9208–130
EPA 600/4-90-012	9188–115
EPA 600/7-90-010	9198–124
EPA 600/8-89-049 F	9198–84.5
EPA 600/9-90-039	9184–22
EPA 625/3-91-018	9186–9.5
EPA GAD-(nos.)	9202–3
EPA No. 9355.6-02	9214–5
HW-8.27	9216–3.25
HW-10.15S	9216–5.3

Federal Deposit Insurance Corp.

P-1400-105-89	9294–4
P-7700-01-91	9295–3.1
P-7700-02-91	9295–3.2
P-7700-03-91	9295–3.3
P-7700-04-91	9295–3.4
P-7700-05-91	9295–3.5
P-7700-06-91	9295–3.6
P-7700-07-91	9295–3.7

Federal Mediation and Conciliation Service

C.2	9365–5.1
C.9	9365–4.1
E.2	9365–3
E.11	9365–3.7
E.15	9365–3.10
E.16	9365–3

Finance and Economics Discussion Series,
No. 144 .... 9366–6.258
Finance and Economics Discussion Series,
No. 145 .... 9366–6.259
Finance and Economics Discussion Series,
No. 146 .... 9366–6.260
Finance and Economics Discussion Series,
No. 147 .... 9366–6.261
Finance and Economics Discussion Series,
No. 148 .... 9366–6.262
Finance and Economics Discussion Series,
No. 149 .... 9366–6.263
Finance and Economics Discussion Series,

No. 150 .... 9366–6.264
Finance and Economics Discussion Series,
No. 151 .... 9366–6.265
Finance and Economics Discussion Series,
No. 152 .... 9366–6.266
Finance and Economics Discussion Series,
No. 153 .... 9366–6.267
Finance and Economics Discussion Series,
No. 154 .... 9366–6.268
Finance and Economics Discussion Series,
No. 155 .... 9366–6.269
Finance and Economics Discussion Series,
No. 156 .... 9366–6.270
Finance and Economics Discussion Series,
No. 157 .... 9366–6.271
Finance and Economics Discussion Series,
No. 158 .... 9366–6.272
Finance and Economics Discussion Series,
No. 159 .... 9366–6.273
Finance and Economics Discussion Series,
No. 160 .... 9366–6.274
Finance and Economics Discussion Series,
No. 161 .... 9366–6.275
Finance and Economics Discussion Series,
No. 162 .... 9366–6.276
Finance and Economics Discussion Series,
No. 163 .... 9366–6.277
Finance and Economics Discussion Series,
No. 164 .... 9366–6.278
Finance and Economics Discussion Series,
No. 165 .... 9366–6.279
Finance and Economics Discussion Series,
No. 166 .... 9366–6.280
Finance and Economics Discussion Series,
No. 167 .... 9366–6.281
Finance and Economics Discussion Series,
No. 168 .... 9366–6.282
Finance and Economics Discussion Series,
No. 169 .... 9366–6.283
Finance and Economics Discussion Series,
No. 170 .... 9366–6.284
Finance and Economics Discussion Series,
No. 171 .... 9366–6.285
FRB 1-2000-0291 C 9364–10
FRB 1-12500-0491 9364–1
G.5 9365–2
G.6 .... 9365–2.5
G.7 9365–2
G.10 9365–2
G.13 .... 9365–2.14
G.17 .... 9365–2.24
G.19 .... 9365–2.6
G.20 .... 9365–2.7
H.3 9365–1
H.5 9365–1
H.6 9365–1

H.8 9365–1
H.10 .... 9365–1.5
H.15 9365–1
H.4.1 9365–1
H.4.2 .... 9365–1.3
Intl. Finance Discussion
Paper 394 .... 9366–7.248
Intl. Finance Discussion
Paper 395 .... 9366–7.249
Intl. Finance Discussion
Paper 396 .... 9366–7.250
Intl. Finance Discussion
Paper 397 .... 9366–7.251
Intl. Finance Discussion
Paper 398 .... 9366–7.252
Intl. Finance Discussion
Paper 399 .... 9366–7.253
Intl. Finance Discussion
Paper 400 .... 9366–7.254
Intl. Finance Discussion
Paper 401 .... 9366–7.255
Intl. Finance Discussion
Paper 402 .... 9366–7.256
Intl. Finance Discussion
Paper 403 .... 9366–7.257
Intl. Finance Discussion
Paper 404 .... 9366–7.258
Intl. Finance Discussion
Paper 405 .... 9366–7.259
Intl. Finance Discussion
Paper 406 .... 9366–7.260
Intl. Finance Discussion
Paper 407 .... 9366–7.261
Intl. Finance Discussion
Paper 408 .... 9366–7.262
Intl. Finance Discussion
Paper 409 .... 9366–7.263
Intl. Finance Discussion
Paper 410 .... 9366–7.264
Intl. Finance Discussion
Paper 411 .... 9366–7.265
Intl. Finance Discussion
Paper 412 .... 9366–7.266
Intl. Finance Discussion
Paper 413 .... 9366–7.267
Intl. Finance Discussion
Paper 414 .... 9366–7.268
Intl. Finance Discussion
Paper 415 .... 9366–7.269
K.7 9366–7
Staff Study 161 .... 9366–1.161
Z.1 .... 9365–3.3
Z.7 9365–3
Z.11 9366–6

Federal Reserve Bank of Atlanta

Working Paper 90-7	9371–10.53
Working Paper 90-8	9371–10.54
Working Paper 90-9	9371–10.55
Working Paper 90-10	9371–10.56
Working Paper 90-11	9371–10.57
Working Paper 90-12	9371–10.58
Working Paper 91-1	9371–10.59
Working Paper 91-2	9371–10.60
Working Paper 91-3	9371–10.61
Working Paper 91-4	9371–10.62
Working Paper 91-5	9371–10.63
Working Paper 91-6	9371–10.64
Working Paper 91-7	9371–10.65
Working Paper 91-8	9371–10.66

INDEPENDENT AGENCIES

Federal Reserve Bank of Boston

Conf. Series No. 34	9373–3.34
Res. Rpt. 72	9373–4.27

Federal Reserve Bank of Chicago

WP-1990-18	9375–13.49
WP-1990-19	9375–13.50
WP-1990-20	9375–13.51
WP-1991-1	9375–13.52
WP-1991-2	9375–13.53
WP-1991-3	9375–13.54
WP-1991-4	9375–13.55
WP-1991-5	9375–13.56
WP-1991-6	9375–13.57
WP-1991-7	9375–13.58
WP-1991-8	9375–13.59
WP-1991-9	9375–13.60
WP-1991-10	9375–13.61
WP-1991-11	9375–13.62
WP-1991-12	9375–13.63
WP-1991-13	9375–13.64
WP-1991-14	9375–13.65
WP-1991-15	9375–13.66

Federal Reserve Bank of Cleveland

Working Paper 9014	9377–9.104
Working Paper 9015	9377–9.105
Working Paper 9016	9377–9.106
Working Paper 9017	9377–9.107
Working Paper 9018	9377–9.108
Working Paper 9019	9377–9.113
Working Paper 9101	9377–9.109
Working Paper 9102	9377–9.110
Working Paper 9103	9377–9.111
Working Paper 9104	9377–9.112
Working Paper 9105	9377–9.114
Working Paper 9106	9377–9.115
Working Paper 9107	9377–9.116
Working Paper 9108	9377–9.117
Working Paper 9109	9377–9.118
Working Paper 9110	9377–9.119
Working Paper 9111	9377–9.120
Working Paper 9112	9377–9.121
Working Paper 9113	9377–9.122
Working Paper 9114	9377–9.123

Federal Reserve Bank of Dallas

FIS 1-91	9379–14.12
FIS 2-91	9379–14.13
FIS 3-91	9379–14.14
FIS 6-90	9379–14.10
FIS 7-90	9379–14.11
Res. Paper 9013	9379–12.62
Res. Paper 9101	9379–12.63
Res. Paper 9102	9379–12.64
Res. Paper 9103	9379–12.65
Res. Paper 9104	9379–12.66
Res. Paper 9105	9379–12.67
Res. Paper 9106	9379–12.68
Res. Paper 9107	9379–12.69
Res. Paper 9108	9379–12.70
Res. Paper 9109	9379–12.71
Res. Paper 9110	9379–12.72
Res. Paper 9111	9379–12.73
Res. Paper 9112	9379–12.74
Res. Paper 9113	9379–12.75

Res. Paper 9114	9379–12.76
Res. Paper 9115	9379–12.77
Res. Paper 9116	9379–12.78
Res. Paper 9117	9379–12.79

Federal Reserve Bank of Kansas City

RWP 90-05	9381–10.116
RWP 90-06	9381–10.117
RWP 90-07	9381–10.118
RWP 90-08	9381–10.119
RWP 90-09	9381–10.120
RWP 90-10	9381–10.121

Federal Reserve Bank of Minneapolis

Staff Rpt. 131	9383–20.1
Staff Rpt. 132	9383–20.2
Staff Rpt. 133	9383–20.3
Staff Rpt. 134	9383–20.4
Staff Rpt. 135	9383–20.5
Staff Rpt. 136	9383–20.6
Staff Rpt. 137	9383–20.7
Staff Rpt. 138	9383–20.8
Staff Rpt. 139	9383–20.9
Staff Rpt. 140	9383–20.10
Staff Rpt. 141	9383–20.11
Staff Rpt. 142	9383–20.12
Staff Rpt. 143	9383–20.13
Staff Rpt. 144	9383–20.14
Staff Rpt. 145	9383–20.15

Federal Reserve Bank of New York

Res. Paper 9006	9385–8.72
Res. Paper 9007	9385–8.73
Res. Paper 9008	9385–8.74
Res. Paper 9009	9385–8.75
Res. Paper 9010	9385–8.76
Res. Paper 9011	9385–8.77
Res. Paper 9012	9385–8.78
Res. Paper 9013	9385–8.79
Res. Paper 9014	9385–8.80
Res. Paper 9015	9385–8.81
Res. Paper 9016	9385–8.82
Res. Paper 9017	9385–8.83
Res. Paper 9018	9385–8.84
Res. Paper 9019	9385–8.85
Res. Paper 9020	9385–8.86
Res. Paper 9021	9385–8.87
Res. Paper 9022-9029	9385–8.88
Res. Paper 9030	9385–8.89
Res. Paper 9031	9385–8.90
Res. Paper 9032	9385–8.91
Res. Paper 9033	9385–8.92
Res. Paper 9034	9385–8.93
Res. Paper 9035	9385–8.94
Res. Paper 9036	9385–8.95
Res. Paper 9037	9385–8.96
Res. Paper 9101	9385–8.97
Res. Paper 9102	9385–8.98
Res. Paper 9103	9385–8.99
Res. Paper 9104	9385–8.100
Res. Paper 9105	9385–8.101
Res. Paper 9106	9385–8.102
Res. Paper 9107	9385–8.103
Res. Paper 9108	9385–8.104
Res. Paper 9109	9385–8.105
Res. Paper 9110	9385–8.106
Res. Paper 9111	9385–8.107
Res. Paper 9112	9385–8.108

Index by Agency Report Numbers

Res. Paper 9113	9385–8.109
Res. Paper 9114	9385–8.110
Res. Paper 9115	9385–8.111
Res. Paper 9116	9385–8.112
Res. Paper 9117	9385–8.113
Res. Paper 9118	9385–8.114
Res. Paper 9119	9385–8.115
Res. Paper 9120	9385–8.116
Res. Paper 9121	9385–8.117
Res. Paper 9122	9385–8.118
Res. Paper 9123	9385–8.119
Res. Paper 9124	9385–8.120
Res. Paper 9125	9385–8.121

Federal Reserve Bank of Philadelphia

Working Paper 90-22	9387–8.231
Working Paper 90-23	9387–8.232
Working Paper 90-24	9387–8.233
Working Paper 90-25	9387–8.234
Working Paper 90-26	9387–8.235
Working Paper 90-27	9387–8.236
Working Paper 90-28	9387–8.237
Working Paper 90-29	9387–8.238
Working Paper 90-30	9387–8.239
Working Paper 91-1	9387–8.240
Working Paper 91-2	9387–8.241
Working Paper 91-3	9387–8.242
Working Paper 91-4	9387–8.243
Working Paper 91-5	9387–8.244
Working Paper 91-6	9387–8.245
Working Paper 91-7	9387–8.246
Working Paper 91-8	9387–8.247
Working Paper 91-9	9387–8.248
Working Paper 91-10	9387–8.249
Working Paper 91-11	9387–8.250
Working Paper 91-12	9387–8.251
Working Paper 91-13	9387–8.252
Working Paper 91-14	9387–8.253
Working Paper 91-15	9387–8.254
Working Paper 91-16	9387–8.255

Federal Reserve Bank of Richmond

Pub. No. P-1	9389–2
Working Paper 91-1	9389–19.26
Working Paper 91-2	9389–19.27
Working Paper 91-3	9389–19.28
Working Paper 91-4	9389–19.29
Working Paper 91-5	9389–19.30
Working Paper 91-6	9389–19.31

Federal Reserve Bank of San Francisco

Working Paper 91-01	9393–10.16

Federal Trade Commission

Pub. 146	9414–1

Foreign Claims Settlement Commission of the U.S.

FEMA 191	9434–6

Index by Agency Report Numbers

INDEPENDENT AGENCIES

Interstate Commerce Commission

Statement A-300	9484–5
Statement M-350	9482–3

National Aeronautics and Space Administration

Global Ozone Research and Monitoring Project Rpt. No. 20	9508–37
NASA SP-7041/(nos.)	9502–7
NASA TM-104231	9504–7
NSSDC/WDC-A-R&S 91-14	9504–11
NSSDC/WDC-A-R&S 91-19	9504–10
Release 91-25	9506–2.140
Release 91-41	9506–2.141
Release 91-69	9506–2.142
Release 91-97	9506–2.143

National Credit Union Administration

NCUA 8060	9532–6
NCUA 8602	9534–6
NCUA Letter No. 127	9532–7
Res. Study 14	9536–1.6

National Labor Relations Board

ER(nos.)	9582–2

National Science Foundation

NSF 88-335	9627–22
NSF 89-72	9626–7.4
NSF 89-96	9626–7.2
NSF 89-114	9626–7.1
NSF 90-2	9624–26
NSF 90-9	9626–7.3
NSF 90-13	9628–82
NSF 90-19	9624–27
NSF 90-35	9628–83
NSF 90-36	9628–85
NSF 90-113	9628–84
NSF 90-119	9624–16
NSF 90-321	9627–13
NSF 90-324	9627–7
NSF 90-327/Final	9627–20
NSF 91-1	9624–6
NSF 91-39	9624–24
NSF 91-304	9627–27.1
NSF 91-305	9627–27.3
NSF 91-309	9627–35
NSF 91-310	9627–30
NSF 91-311	9627–27.2
NSF 91-314	9627–33
NSF 91-315	9627–27.4
NSF 91-316/final	9627–17
NSF 91-317	9627–18

National Transportation Safety Board

NTSB/AAB-(yr.-nos.)	9612–1
NTSB/ARC-90/01	9614–2
NTSB/ARG-91/01	9614–3
NTSB/MAB-(yr.-nos.)	9612–4
NTSB/MAR-90/04	9618–17

SB 91-03	9614–9
SB 91-18	9614–6

Nuclear Regulatory Commission

BNL-NUREG-51581	9634–1
NUREG-0020, Vol. 15	9634–12
NUREG-0713, Vol. 9	9634–3
NUREG-1100, Vol. 7	9634–9
NUREG-1145, Vol. 7	9634–2
NUREG/CR-2907, Vol. 9	9634–1
NUREG/CR-3145, Vol. 9	9634–10

Office of Personnel Management

MW (nos.)	9842–1
MW 56-21	9844–4
OELR 90-3	9847–1
OPM/SASD/OCC-89/1	9844–4
PSOG 89-06	9844–31
PSOG 90-33	9844–6
RI 10-5	9844–35
RI 10-27	9844–34
SES 90-5	9844–36
SES 91-7	9844–36
WPA-IA 5	9844–20

Resolution Trust Corp.

RTC 1400-001-89	9724–1

Tennessee Valley Authority

Bull. Y-209	9804–5
Bull. Y-216	9804–30
Circular Z-290	9808–66.1
Circular Z-305 (Supp.)	9808–66.2
Monthly Rpt. (nos.)	9802–1
Tech. Rpt. No. 29-1-52	9804–7
Tech. Rpt. No. 29-1-53	9804–7
TVA/NFERC-90/9	9804–30
TVA/NFERC-91/2	9808–66.1
TVA/NFERC-91/6	9804–5
TVA/NFERC-91/14	9808–66.2
TVA/P&E/EU&DR-(yr./n-os.)	9802–1
TVA/WR/WRO-90/6	9804–7
TVA/WR/WRO-91/2	9804–7

U.S. Information Agency

Gen. Release No. 28	9868–1

U.S. International Trade Commission

SOC Series C/P (yr.-nos.)	9882–1
USITC Pub. (nos.)	9882–2
—	9882–6
—	9882–13
USITC Pub. 2333	9886–13.1
USITC Pub. 2341	9882–9
USITC Pub. 2343	9886–19.73
USITC Pub. 2344	9886–14.302
USITC Pub. 2345	9886–4.166
USITC Pub. 2346	9886–14.301
USITC Pub. 2349	9884–14
USITC Pub. 2351	9886–4.169
USITC Pub. 2352	9886–4.167
USITC Pub. 2353	9886–4.168
USITC Pub. 2354	9884–1
USITC Pub. 2355	9886–14.303
USITC Pub. 2357	9886–14.304
USITC Pub. 2358	9886–14.305
USITC Pub. 2359	9886–14.306
USITC Pub. 2360	9884–12
USITC Pub. 2362	9886–15.77
USITC Pub. 2365	9884–14
USITC Pub. 2367	9886–14.307
USITC Pub. 2368	9886–4.170
USITC Pub. 2369	9886–10.10
USITC Pub. 2371	9886–19.75
USITC Pub. 2374	9886–19.74
USITC Pub. 2376	9886–14.309
USITC Pub. 2378	9886–14.308
USITC Pub. 2379	9886–14.310
USITC Pub. 2380	9882–9
USITC Pub. 2381	9886–4.171
USITC Pub. 2382	9884–18
USITC Pub. 2383	9886–14.313
USITC Pub. 2384	9886–14.311
USITC Pub. 2385	9886–14.314
USITC Pub. 2387	9886–14.315
USITC Pub. 2388	9886–14.312
USITC Pub. 2394	9886–14.316
USITC Pub. 2395	9886–14.317
USITC Pub. 2396	9886–14.318
USITC Pub. 2398	9884–15
USITC Pub. 2400	9886–19.76
USITC Pub. 2401	9886–14.319
USITC Pub. 2402	9886–14.320
USITC Pub. 2403	9884–5
USITC Pub. 2404	9886–14.321
USITC Pub. 2405	9886–14.322
USITC Pub. 2408	9886–4.172
USITC Pub. 2409	9886–14.323
USITC Pub. 2410	9886–14.324
USITC Pub. 2411	9886–14.325
USITC Pub. 2412	9886–14.327
USITC Pub. 2413	9886–14.328
USITC Pub. 2415	9886–14.326
USITC Pub. 2422	9886–4.173
USITC Pub. 2423	9886–4.174
USITC Pub. 2427	9886–14.329
USITC Pub. 2428	9886–19.77
USITC Pub. 2429	9886–14.330
USITC Pub. 2432	9884–20
USITC Pub. 2434	9886–4.175
USITC Pub. 2435	9886–4.175
USITC Pub. 2436	9884–24
USITC Pub. 2437	9886–4.176
USITC Pub. 2438	9886–4.176
USITC Pub. 2439	9886–4.177
USITC Pub. 2440	9886–4.177
USITC Pub. 2441	9886–19.78
USITC Pub. 2442	9886–19.79
USITC Pub. 2443	9886–19.80
USITC Pub. 2444	9886–14.331
USITC Pub. 2447	9886–14.332
USITC Pub. 2448	9886–14.333
USITC Pub. 2449	9886–13.2
USITC Pub. 2454	9886–19.81
USITC Pub. 2457	9886–14.334
USITC Pub. 2460	9886–4.178
USITC Pub. 2461	9886–14.335
USITC Pub. 2464	9884–23
USITC Pub. 2467	9886–14.336
USITC Pub. 2468	9886–15.78

U.S. Office of Special Counsel

AID Evaluation Special Study No. 68	9916–3.62
AID Evaluation Special Study No. 69	9916–3.63
AID Impact Evaluation Rpt. No. 75	9916–1.73
AID Impact Evaluation	

INDEPENDENT AGENCIES

Rpt. No. 76	9916–1.74

AID Impact Evaluation

Rpt. No. 77	9916–1.75
CONG-R-0105	9914–5
PN-AAV-676	9916–12.21
PN-AAW-904	9916–12.25
PN-AAX-234	9916–3.62
PN-AAX-237	9916–3.63
PN-AAX-238	9916–1.73
PN-AAX-241	9916–1.74
PN-AAX-242	9916–1.75
PN-AAZ-454	9916–12.20
PN-AAZ-481	9916–12.27
PN-AAZ-839	9916–12.28
PN-AAZ-988	9916–12.29
PN-ABB-273	9916–12.31
PN-ABC-465	9916–12.37
PN-ABC-523	9916–12.32
PN-ABC-563	9916–12.30
PN-ABC-805	9916–12.34
PN-ABD-219	9916–12.35
PN-ABD-339	9916–12.38
PN-ABD-343	9916–12.36
PN-ABD-346	9916–12.33
PN-ABD-347	9916–12.39
PN-ABD-390	9916–12.23
PN-ABD-893	9918–20
PN-ABD-895	9918–19
PN-ABE-180	9916–12.40
PN-ABE-258	9916–12.24
PN-ABE-275	9916–12.26
PN-ABE-413	9918–18
PN-ABE-620	9916–12.45
PN-ABE-860	9916–12.43
PN-ABE-881	9916–12.41
PN-ABE-886	9916–12.42
PN-ABE-949	9916–12.44
PN-ABE-950	9916–12.47
PN-ABG-560	9916–12.22
PN-ABH-074	9918–21
PN-ABH-235	9916–12.46
PN-ABH-721	9914–1
W-209	9912–4
W-213	9912–1
W-224	9912–3

SPECIAL BOARDS, COMMITTEES, AND COMMISSIONS

Advisory Commission on Intergovernmental Relations

A-114	10048–81
A-117	10048–80
ACIR Rpt. S-20	10044–2
M-174	10048–77
M-175	10048–78
M-176-II	10044–1.2
M-176	10044–1.1
M-177	10048–79

Federal Financial Institutions Examination Council

Rpt. E.16(126)	13002–1

Federal Labor Relations Authority

FLRA Doc. 1393	13364–1

National Commission for Employment Policy

Res. Rpt. 89-09	15496–1.11
Res. Rpt. 90-01	15496–1.12
Res. Rpt. 90-02	15496–1.13
Rpt. 29	15494–1

Prospective Payment Assessment Commission

C-90-02	17206–1.8
C-91-01	17206–1.9
C-91-02	17206–1.11
C-91-03	17206–1.12
C-91-04	17206–1.10
R-3870-ProPAC	17208–2
Tech. Rpt. E-90-02	17206–2.20
Tech. Rpt. E-90-03	17206–2.21
Tech. Rpt. E-90-04	17206–2.22
Tech. Rpt. E-90-05	17206–2.23
Tech. Rpt. E-90-06	17206–2.24
Tech. Rpt. E-90-08	17206–2.25
Tech. Rpt. E-90-09	17206–2.26
Tech. Rpt. I-90-01	17206–2.16
Tech. Rpt. I-90-02	17206–2.17
Tech. Rpt. I-90-03	17206–2.18
Tech. Rpt. I-90-04	17206–2.19

UNITED STATES COURTS

Federal Judicial Center

FJC-R-90-1	18408–45
FJC-R-90-2	18408–46

CONGRESS

Congressional Committees

H. Doc. 101-253	21168–44
H. Rpt. 101-983	21408–120
H. Rpt. 102-27	23844–2
H. Rpt. 102-32	21264–2
S. Doc. 101-32	25922–2
S. Doc. 101-34, Pt. 1	25922–1.1
S. Doc. 101-34, Pt. 2	25922–1.2
S. Doc. 102-2	25928–9
S. Doc. 102-4, Pt. 1	25922–1.1
S. Doc. 102-4, Pt. 2	25922–1.2
S. Doc. 102-5	25922–2
S. Hrg. 101-151, Pt. 36	23846–4.30
S. Hrg. 101-151, Pt. 37	23846–4.31
S. Hrg. 101-151, Pt. 38	23846–4.32
S. Hrg. 101-151, Pt. 39	23846–4.33
S. Hrg. 101-259, Pt. 3	25168–75
S. Hrg. 101-557, Pt. 2	25368–168
S. Hrg. 101-635, Pt. 3	25728–43
S. Hrg. 101-656	23898–8
S. Hrg. 101-675	25418–5
S. Hrg. 101-691	25728–42
S. Hrg. 101-700	23898–7
S. Hrg. 101-704	25168–74
S. Hrg. 101-720	23848–217
S. Hrg. 101-725	23848–216
S. Hrg. 101-758	25528–114
S. Hrg. 101-774	25418–4
S. Hrg. 101-776	25328–31
S. Hrg. 101-778	25258–24
S. Hrg. 101-792	23848–218
S. Hrg. 101-817	25388–57
S. Hrg. 101-835	25328–32
S. Hrg. 101-838	25548–101
S. Hrg. 101-843	25528–115
S. Hrg. 101-868, Vol. 2	25248–120

Index by Agency Report Numbers

S. Hrg. 101-885	25388–58
S. Hrg. 101-911	25368–171
S. Hrg. 101-918	25368–170
S. Hrg. 101-937, Vol. 2	25248–122
S. Hrg. 101-937, Vol. 3	25248–123
S. Hrg. 101-966	25168–76
S. Hrg. 101-969	23898–6
S. Hrg. 101-971	23848–221
S. Hrg. 101-973, Vol. 1	25248–121
S. Hrg. 101-1000	25408–112
S. Hrg. 101-1004	25418–6
S. Hrg. 101-1031	25408–111
S. Hrg. 101-1032	25408–113
S. Hrg. 101-1051	25548–102
S. Hrg. 101-1052	25168–77
S. Hrg. 101-1065	25368–173
S. Hrg. 101-1080	23848–222
S. Hrg. 101-1102	25248–125
S. Hrg. 101-1149	25368–176
S. Hrg. 101-1206	25528–117
S. Hrg. 101-1207	25368–174
S. Hrg. 101-1217	25548–103
S. Hrg. 102-43	25548–104
S. Hrg. 102-77	25248–124
S. Prt. 101-106	25388–56
S. Prt. 101-115	23898–5
S. Prt. 101-118	25368–169
S. Prt. 101-121	23848–220
S. Prt. 101-123	23848–223
S. Prt. 101-143	25248–126
S. Prt. 102-10	25268–78
S. Prt. 102-21, Vol. 1 & 2	23848–155
S. Prt. 102-34	25318–81
S. Pub. 100-14	25944–1
S. Pub. 102-4	23874–1
S. Rpt. 102-40	25254–1

General Accounting Office

GAO/AFMD-(nos.)	26102–6
GAO/AFMD-91-24	26111–74
GAO/AFMD-91-39	26111–75
GAO/AFMD-91-73	26111–76
GAO/AFMD-91-81 FS	26111–65
GAO/GGD-90-100	26119–314
GAO/GGD-91-10	26119–318
GAO/GGD-91-12	26119–315
GAO/GGD-91-20	26119–316
GAO/GGD-91-21	26119–321
GAO/GGD-91-23	26119–319
GAO/GGD-91-24	26119–337
GAO/GGD-91-26	26119–320
GAO/GGD-91-28	26119–317
GAO/GGD-91-31 BR	26119–326
GAO/GGD-91-36	26119–322
GAO/GGD-91-39	26119–323
GAO/GGD-91-42	26119–327
GAO/GGD-91-47	26119–324
GAO/GGD-91-49	26119–325
GAO/GGD-91-50	26119–328
GAO/GGD-91-52	26119–336
GAO/GGD-91-53	26119–330
GAO/GGD-91-58 BR	26119–331
GAO/GGD-91-62 FS	26119–343
GAO/GGD-91-63 FS	26119–332
GAO/GGD-91-64	26119–339
GAO/GGD-91-65	26119–333
GAO/GGD-91-66	26119–329
GAO/GGD-91-67	26119–335
GAO/GGD-91-69	26119–334
GAO/GGD-91-70	26119–344
GAO/GGD-91-75	26119–340
GAO/GGD-91-76	26119–311
GAO/GGD-91-77 BR	26119–338
GAO/GGD-91-81	26119–345
GAO/GGD-91-86	26119–342
GAO/GGD-91-90	26119–296

Index by Agency Report Numbers

CONGRESS

GAO/GGD-91-98	26119-346	GAO/NSIAD-91-82	26123-321
GAO/GGD-91-99	26119-354	GAO/NSIAD-91-87 FS	26123-316
GAO/GGD-91-105	26119-349	GAO/NSIAD-91-99 FS	26123-313
GAO/GGD-91-107	26119-355	GAO/NSIAD-91-102	26123-337
GAO/GGD-91-113	26119-353	GAO/NSIAD-91-106 FS	26123-328
GAO/GGD-91-125	26119-356	GAO/NSIAD-91-106 FS-S	26123-328
GAO/GGD-91-131	26119-280	GAO/NSIAD-91-107	26123-346
GAO/GGD-92-2	26119-348	GAO/NSIAD-91-108	26123-342
GAO/GGD-92-3	26119-341	GAO/NSIAD-91-110	26123-319
GAO/GGD-92-5	26119-347	GAO/NSIAD-91-113	26123-343
GAO/GGD-92-12	26119-361	GAO/NSIAD-91-123	26123-327
GAO/HRD-90-81	26121-399	GAO/NSIAD-91-127	26123-333
GAO/HRD-90-134	26121-392	GAO/NSIAD-91-130	26123-338
GAO/HRD-90-167	26121-400	GAO/NSIAD-91-132	26123-344
GAO/HRD-91-2	26121-405	GAO/NSIAD-91-134 FS	26123-325
GAO/HRD-91-3	26121-406	GAO/NSIAD-91-135	26123-329
GAO/HRD-91-6	26121-393	GAO/NSIAD-91-137	26123-334
GAO/HRD-91-9 FS	26121-391	GAO/NSIAD-91-140	26123-350
GAO/HRD-91-13	26121-401	GAO/NSIAD-91-142	26123-353
GAO/HRD-91-21	26121-408	GAO/NSIAD-91-143 BR	26123-322
GAO/HRD-91-22	26121-397	GAO/NSIAD-91-150 BR	26123-323
GAO/HRD-91-29	26121-395	GAO/NSIAD-91-155	26123-335
GAO/HRD-91-30	26121-396	GAO/NSIAD-91-158	26123-347
GAO/HRD-91-31 FS	26121-403	GAO/NSIAD-91-160	26123-326
GAO/HRD-91-33	26121-407	GAO/NSIAD-91-168	26123-330
GAO/HRD-91-36 BR	26121-398	GAO/NSIAD-91-185	26123-348
GAO/HRD-91-38	26121-394	GAO/NSIAD-91-190	26123-345
GAO/HRD-91-39	26121-404	GAO/NSIAD-91-192	26123-357
GAO/HRD-91-41	26121-409	GAO/NSIAD-91-193 FS	26123-339
GAO/HRD-91-43	26121-417	GAO/NSIAD-91-195	26123-336
GAO/HRD-91-49	26121-410	GAO/NSIAD-91-199	26123-359
GAO/HRD-91-50	26121-418	GAO/NSIAD-91-203	26123-340
GAO/HRD-91-51	26121-402	GAO/NSIAD-91-214	26123-349
GAO/HRD-91-52	26121-428	GAO/NSIAD-91-219	26123-354
GAO/HRD-91-56	26121-411	GAO/NSIAD-91-221	26123-352
GAO/HRD-91-57	26121-419	GAO/NSIAD-91-224	26123-341
GAO/HRD-91-58	26121-412	GAO/NSIAD-91-238	26123-327
GAO/HRD-91-59	26121-425	GAO/NSIAD-91-239	26123-358
GAO/HRD-91-61	26121-414	GAO/NSIAD-91-244	26123-351
GAO/HRD-91-62	26121-413	GAO/NSIAD-91-250	26123-360
GAO/HRD-91-63	26121-415	GAO/NSIAD-91-262	26123-364
GAO/HRD-91-64	26121-432	GAO/NSIAD-91-274	26123-365
GAO/HRD-91-66 FS	26121-420	GAO/NSIAD-91-278	26123-361
GAO/HRD-91-71	26121-416	GAO/NSIAD-92-12	26123-366
GAO/HRD-91-78	26121-429	GAO/OP-91-1	26104-5
GAO/HRD-91-83 BR	26121-426	GAO/OPA-91-3	26104-17
GAO/HRD-91-85	26121-427	GAO/PART-91-1	26104-14
GAO/HRD-91-86	26121-433	GAO/PEMD-90-24	26131-79
GAO/HRD-91-88	26121-430	GAO/PEMD-91-2	26131-84
GAO/HRD-91-89 FS	26121-422	GAO/PEMD-91-9	26131-80
GAO/HRD-91-90	26121-424	GAO/PEMD-91-12 BR	26131-81
GAO/HRD-91-93 FS	26121-421	GAO/PEMD-91-13	26131-82
GAO/HRD-91-95	26121-423	GAO/PEMD-91-14	26131-81
GAO/HRD-91-97	26106-8.13	GAO/PEMD-91-19	26131-86
GAO/HRD-91-105	26121-431	GAO/PEMD-91-22	26131-88
GAO/HRD-91-106	26121-435	GAO/PEMD-91-23	26131-85
GAO/HRD-91-112	26121-434	GAO/PEMD-92-1	26131-89
GAO/HRD-91-148	26106-8.14	GAO/PEMD-92-3	26131-90
GAO/HRD-92-2	26121-436	GAO/RCED-(date)	26102-4
GAO/HRD-92-9	26121-437	GAO/RCED-90-58	26113-495
GAO/HRD-92-12	26121-438	GAO/RCED-90-169	26113-497
GAO/IMTEC-91-3	26125-43	GAO/RCED-90-182	26113-498
GAO/IMTEC-91-13	26125-41.8	GAO/RCED-90-186	26113-499
GAO/IMTEC-91-19	26125-45	GAO/RCED-91-2	26113-500
GAO/IMTEC-91-62	26125-44	GAO/RCED-91-4	26113-506
GAO/NSIAD-91-4	26123-315	GAO/RCED-91-09	26113-507
GAO/NSIAD-91-20	26123-320	GAO/RCED-91-12	26113-493
GAO/NSIAD-91-23	26123-312	GAO/RCED-91-14	26113-492
GAO/NSIAD-91-39	26123-331	GAO/RCED-91-19 A	26113-503
GAO/NSIAD-91-45	26123-315	GAO/RCED-91-20	26113-508
GAO/NSIAD-91-50 BR	26123-317	GAO/RCED-91-21	26113-496
GAO/NSIAD-91-54	26123-332	GAO/RCED-91-22	26113-504
GAO/NSIAD-91-57	26123-356	GAO/RCED-91-25	26113-494
GAO/NSIAD-91-67	26123-318	GAO/RCED-91-30	26113-505
GAO/NSIAD-91-70	26123-324	GAO/RCED-91-40 A	26113-512.1
GAO/NSIAD-91-76	26123-314	GAO/RCED-91-40 B	26113-512.2
GAO/NSIAD-91-79	26123-355	GAO/RCED-91-43	26113-511

GAO/RCED-91-44	26113-525
GAO/RCED-91-45	26113-501
GAO/RCED-91-48	26113-502
GAO/RCED-91-67	26113-519
GAO/RCED-91-68	26113-510
GAO/RCED-91-69	26113-513
GAO/RCED-91-72	26113-515
GAO/RCED-91-79	26113-528
GAO/RCED-91-83	26113-520
GAO/RCED-91-87	26113-521
GAO/RCED-91-93	26113-509
GAO/RCED-91-96	26113-523
GAO/RCED-91-98	26113-514
GAO/RCED-91-99	26113-526
GAO/RCED-91-106	26113-516
GAO/RCED-91-108	26113-538
GAO/RCED-91-113	26113-529
GAO/RCED-91-114	26113-517
GAO/RCED-91-115	26113-518
GAO/RCED-91-119	26113-522
GAO/RCED-91-121	26113-532
GAO/RCED-91-126	26104-21
GAO/RCED-91-128	26113-534
GAO/RCED-91-130	26113-524
GAO/RCED-91-135	26113-535
GAO/RCED-91-137	26113-533
GAO/RCED-91-140	26113-530
GAO/RCED-91-154	26113-536
GAO/RCED-91-156	26113-542
GAO/RCED-91-163	26113-531
GAO/RCED-91-167	26113-539
GAO/RCED-91-170	26113-537
GAO/RCED-91-182	26106-10.5
GAO/RCED-91-187 FS	26113-540
GAO/RCED-91-195	26113-431
GAO/RCED-91-198	26113-471
GAO/RCED-91-224 BR	26113-541
GAO/RCED-91-247 FS	26113-545
GAO/RCED-92-2	26113-546
GAO/RCED-92-10	26113-547
GAO/RCED-92-19 BR	26113-543
GAO/RCED-92-48 FS	26113-544
GAO/RCED-91-91 A	26113-527.1
GAO/RCED-91-91 B	26113-527.2

Office of Technology Assessment

OTA-A-473	26354-3
OTA-BA-455	26358-230
OTA-BA-463	26356-9.3
OTA-BA-494	26358-248
OTA-BA-495	26358-248
OTA-BP-BA-67	26358-250
OTA-BP-F-71	26358-247
OTA-BP-O-83	26358-236
OTA-E-486	26358-232
OTA-E-492	26358-240
OTA-E-493	26358-243
OTA-F-417	26358-231
OTA-F-418	26358-231
OTA-F-470	26358-237
OTA-F-476	26358-239
OTA-H-452	26358-246
OTA-H-468	26358-234.1
OTA-ISC-460	26358-241
OTA-ISC-461	26358-241
OTA-ISC-500	26358-245
OTA-O-482	26358-233
OTA-O-483	26358-233
OTA-SET-477	26358-235
OTA-SET-478	26358-235
OTA-SET-490	26358-238
OTA-SET-491	26358-238
OTA-SET-496	26358-242
OTA-TCT-497	26358-244

QUASI-OFFICIAL AGENCIES

QUASI-OFFICIAL AGENCIES

American National Red Cross

ARC 501 29254–1

Index by Superintendent of Documents Numbers

Index of Superintendent of Documents Numbers

This index presents, in shelf list order, the Superintendent of Documents (SuDocs) Classification Numbers of publications abstracted by ASI in this Annual, and provides references from SuDoc Numbers to ASI accession numbers.

A1.1:990	1004–3	A13.52/12:990	1206–11.2	A13.88:PNW-GTR-251	1208–343
A1.1/3:991	1002–4	A13.66/13:(date)	1202–3	A13.88:PNW-GTR-254	1208–354
A1.10:990	1004–18	A13.78:INT-440	1208–370	A13.88:PNW-GTR-261	1208–365
A1.10:991	1004–18	A13.78:INT-442	1208–372	A13.88:PNW-GTR-264	1208–367
A1.34:808	1528–322	A13.78:INT-445	1208–377	A13.88:PSW-122	1208–366
A1.34:813	1548–377	A13.78:INT-449	1208–380	A13.88:RM-156	1208–24.19
A1.34:817	1568–293	A13.78:NE-632	1208–348	A13.88:RM-193	1208–347
A1.34:819	1528–314	A13.78:NE-637	1208–349	A13.88:RM-199	1208–24.20
A1.34:820	1568–304	A13.78:NE-638	1208–350	A13.88:RM-200	1208–376
A1.34:821	1568–299	A13.78:NE-642	1208–369	A13.88:RM-203	1208–360
A1.34:822	1618–21	A13.78:NE-645	1208–361	A13.88:RM-205	1208–382
A1.34:823	1544–29	A13.78:NE-652	1208–373	A13.88:RM-207	1208–381
A1.34:824	1544–30	A13.78:NE-653	1208–371	A13.88:SE-63	1208–346
A1.34:827	1528–323	A13.78:PNW-RP-420	1208–342	A13.88:SE-64	1208–357
A1.34:829	1568–305	A13.78:PNW-RP-425	1208–358	A13.88:SE-67	1204–38
A1.34:830	1568–306	A13.78:RM-296	1208–364	A13.88:SO-75	1208–355
A1.34/4:989	1544–4	A13.78:RM-298	1208–383	A13.109:990	1204–7
A1.36:1781	1548–374	A13.78:SE-278	1208–345	A13.113:960-88	1204–29
A1.36:1784	1568–297	A13.79/2:989	1204–22	A13.117:989	1204–37
A1.36:1786	1588–152	A13.79/3:(date)	1202–4	A57.2:Id1/6	1266–5.1
A1.36:1787	1598–275	A13.80:INT-(nos.)	1206–25	A57.9/a:C765/990	1264–2
A1.38/2:990	1004–14	A13.80:INT-69	1208–374	A57.38:list/990	1264–11
A1.47:990	1004–1	A13.80:INT-71	1206–25.8	A57.46:(date)	1266–2.2
A1.75:(nos.)	1566–8	A13.80:INT-72	1206–25.9	A57.46/4:(date)	1266–2.6
A1.75:578	1566–8.6	A13.80:INT-73	1206–25.10	A57.46/5:(date)	1266–2.7
A1.75:583	1566–8.7	A13.80:INT-74	1206–25.11	A57.46/5-3:990	1264–14.3
A1.75:621	1128–66	—	1206–10	A57.46/6:(date)	1266–2.8
A1.76:(nos.)	1356–3	A13.80:NC-(nos.)	1208–220	A57.46/6-3:990	1264–14.2
A1.76:8-19/991	1356–3.16	A13.80:NC-99	1208–368	A57.46/7:(date)	1266–2.9
A1.76:8/990/supp	1356–3.15	A13.80:NC-113	1206–10.11	A57.46/8:991	1264–4
A1.76:683/991	1924–9	A13.80:NC-121	1206–10.12	A57.46/10:(date)	1266–2.10
A1.76/2:(yr.)	1504–3	A13.80:NC-124	1208–220	A57.46/11:(date)	1266–2.4
A1.101:(date)	1802–4	A13.80:NC-125	1206–12	A57.46/12-2:(date/nos.)	1262–1
A1.107:617	1588–150	A13.80:NE-(nos.)	1206–15	A57.46/13:(date)	1266–2.1
A1.107:637	1548–373	—	1206–43	A57.46/14:991	1264–8
A1.107:638	1548–375	—	1206–44	A57.46/18:(date)	1266–2.11
A1.107:641	1568–296	A13.80:NE-110	1206–44.5	A57.46/18-2:990	1264–14.7
A1.107:642	1568–300	A13.80:NE-112	1206–12.14	A57.46/19:(date)	1266–2.3
A1.107:643	1588–48	A13.80:NE-113	1206–43.3	A67.1/2:990-91	1924–12
A1.107:644	1528–318	A13.80:NE-114	1206–12.13	A67.7/3:(v.nos.&nos.)	1922–2
A1.107:645	1598–272	A13.80:NE-115	1206–15.9	A67.18:(ltrs.-nos.)	1925–2
A1.107:655	1528–317	A13.80:NE-117	1206–12.15	A67.18:(nos.)	1925–4
A1.107/2:990	1544–9	A13.80:NE-118	1206–15.10	A67.18:EMG(nos.)	1925–2.4
A1.116:R88/2/989	1244–4	A13.80:PNW-RB-170	1208–353	A67.18:FC(nos.)	1925–4.2
A13.1/3:990	1204–1	A13.80:SE-(nos.)	1206–4	A67.18:FCOF(nos.)	1925–5
A13.2:N42c	1208–363	—	1206–6	A67.18:FD-MI(nos.)	1925–31
A13.2:R59/7/v.(nos.)	1208–362	A13.80:SE-115	1208–359	A67.18:FD1-91	1925–10
A13.2:R59/7/v.1/text	1208–362.1	A13.80:SE-116	1208–352	A67.18:FD2-91	1925–10
A13.2:R59/7/v.2/apps	1208–362.2	A13.80:SE-117	1206–4.14	A67.18:FDLP(nos.)	1925–32
A13.10:990	1204–2	A13.80:SE-118	1206–4.15	A67.18:FFVS(nos.)	1925–13
A13.32/3:987	1204–6	A13.80:SE-120	1206–4.13	A67.18:FG(nos.)	1925–2.1
A13.32/3:988	1204–6	A13.80:SE-122	1206–6.13	A67.18:FHORT(nos.)	1925–34
A13.32/3:989	1204–6	A13.80:SO-(nos.)	1206–30	A67.18:FL&P(nos.)	1925–33
A13.42/2:T48/11	1208–375	—	1206–39	A67.18:FL&P1-91	1925–33.1
A13.52/12:986	1206–11.2	A13.80:SO-121	1206–39.4	A67.18:FL&P2-91	1925–33.2
A13.52/12:987	1206–11.2	A13.80:SO-154	1208–43	A67.18:FL&P3-91	1925–33.1
A13.52/12:988	1206–11.2	A13.80:SO-155	1206–30.8	A67.18:FOP(nos.)	1925–1
A13.52/12:989	1206–11.2	A13.80:SO-156	1206–30.9		1925–1.1
		A13.80:SO-158	1206–30.10	A67.18:FS(nos.)	1925–14
		A13.80:SO-361	1208–344	A67.18:FS1-91	1925–14.2
		A13.80/3:989	1204–18	A67.18:FS1-91/supp	1925–14.1
		A13.80/4:988	1204–23	A67.18:FS2-91	1925–14.3
		A13.80/4:989	1204–23	A67.18:FT(nos.)	1925–16
		A13.83:991	1204–5	A67.18:FTEA(nos.)	1925–15
		A13.88:INT-276	1208–351	A67.18:FTEA1-91	1925–15.1
		A13.88:INT-280	1208–378	A67.18:FTEA2-91	1925–15.2
		A13.88:NE-145	1208–356	A67:FTEA3-91	1925–15.3

A67.18:WAP(nos.)

Index of Superintendent of Documents Numbers

A67.18:WAP(nos.)	1925–28	A88.57:(v.nos.&nos.)	1302–3	A93.17/7-2:990	1522–4
A67.18:WP(nos.)	1925–36	A92.9/4:(date)	1625–2	A93.17/7-3:990	1522–4
A67.18/2:(yr.)	1925–9	A92.9/5:(date)	1625–3	A93.17/7-4:989	1524–8
A67.18/2:991	1925–9.1	A92.9/6:990	1625–8	A93.23/2:(nos.)	1561–3
A67.18/2:991-2	1925–9.2	A92.9/13:990	1625–7	A93.23/2-2:991(yearbook)	1561–3
A67.40:(date)	1922–3	A92.9/15:990	1625–5	A93.24/2:(nos.)	1561–1
A67.40/5:990	1924–8	A92.9/16:(date)	1625–1	A93.25:(nos.)	1561–10
A67.42/2:(nos.)	1922–9	A92.9/17:991	1625–6	A93.26:(v.nos.&nos.)	1502–3
A67.44:988	1924–7	A92.9/17-2:(date)	1625–10	A93.27:243	1528–311
A67.45:(date)	1922–12	A92.10:(date)	1627–1	A93.29/2:(nos.)	1522–3
A68.1/2:990	1244–1	A92.10/2:990	1627–4	A93.29/2-7:990	1524–4.1
A68.1/3:990	1244–2	A92.10/5:990	1627–5	A93.29/2-9:991	1524–4.4
A68.1/4:989	1244–5	A92.10/7:(date)	1627–3	A93.29/2-11:991	1524–4.3
A68.2:P69/990	1244–6	A92.11:(date)	1621–12	A93.29/3:(nos.)	1522–5
A68.13/2:337	1244–7	A92.11/2-2:990	1621–18.1	A93.31/3:(date)	1561–14
A77.245:(date)	1702–1	A92.11/2-3:990	1621–18.3	A93.31/3-2:991(yearbook)	1561–14
A82.2:C76/20/990	1804–17	A92.11/4:988-90	1621–11	A93.33/2:(v.nos.&nos.)	1502–6
A82.76:989	1804–5	A92.11/6:991	1621–18.4	A93.41:79	1598–264
A82.82/2:(CT)	1806–4	A92.11/8:991	1621–18.7	A93.41:80	1598–268
A82.82/2:B92/991	1806–4.2	A92.11/10-2:990	1621–25.2	A93.41:81	1598–274
A82.82/2:D14/990-91/corr. ..	1806–4.5	A92.11/10-4:(date)	1621–14	A93.41:82	1598–270
A82.82/2:F32/991	1806–4.8	A92.11/10-5:991	1631–9	A93.41/2:(v.nos.&nos.)	1502–7
A82.82/2:F67/991	1806–4.3	A92.11/10-6:990	1621–25.1	A93.41/3:(v.nos.&nos.)	1502–8
A82.82/2:M72/991	1806–4.13	A92.11/11:(date)	1621–10	A93.43:(date)	1542–4
A82.82/2:R36/990	1806–4.6	A92.12:(date)	1631–1	A93.44:AGES89-53	1526–6.14
A82.82/2:R98/990	1806–4.1	A92.14:(date)	1621–6	A93.44:AGES9010	1568–302
A82.82/2:R98/991	1806–4.12	A92.15:(date)	1621–4	A93.44:AGES9044	1548–372
A82.82/2:St2/991	1806–4.10	A92.16:(date)	1629–1	A93.44:AGES9066	1548–376
A82.82/2:Su3/2/990	1806–4.4	A92.16/2:990	1629–5	A93.44:AGES9067	1598–265
A82.82/2:T55/991	1806–4.7	A92.16/3:990	1629–2	A93.44:AGES9068	1568–294
A82.82/2:Up4/991	1806–4.9	A92.17:990	1623–8	A93.44:AGES9071	1598–266
A82.82/2:W56/991	1806–4.11	A92.18:990	1623–10	A93.44:AGES9072	1598–267
A82.82/2:W88/991	1806–4.14	A92.18/3:(date)	1623–9	A93.44:AGES9074	1528–312
A82.83/2:(date)	1802–7	A92.18/6:(date)	1623–2	A93.44:AGES9075	1548–378
A82.89/2:990	1804–7	A92.18/6-2:(date)	1623–1	A93.44:AGES9101	1504–8
A82.92:990	1804–20	A92.18/6-2:991	1623–1.1	A93.44:AGES9104	1548–379
A82.93:990	1804–22	A92.18/6-2:991-2	1623–1.2	A93.44:AGES9105	1588–151
A82.94:990	1804–21	A92.18/7:(date)	1623–3	A93.44:AGES9106	1568–295
A82.95:(date)	1802–2	A92.18/8:991	1623–4	A93.44:AGES9107	1568–298
A82.96/2:(date)	1802–16	A92.18/11:991	1631–7	A93.44:AGES9108	1548–380
A82.97:(date)	1802–3	A92.21:(date)	1631–5	A93.44:AGES9110	1588–154
A82.311:987	1824–2	A92.21/2:990	1631–11	A93.44:AGES9114	1528–315
A84.2:H62/991	1184–17	A92.24:(date)	1621–1	A93.44:AGES9115	1568–301
A88.10:(v.nos.&nos.)	1311–1	A92.24/2:991	1621–22	A93.44:AGES9116	1598–273
A88.11:(v.nos.&nos.)	1309–11	A92.24/3:990	1621–2	A93.44:AGES9117	1548–381
A88.11:63/8	1309–8	A92.24/4:990(summary)	1621–1	A93.44:AGES9118	1528–316
A88.11:64/8	1309–7	A92.24/4-2:991	1621–23	A93.44:AGES9119	1598–269
A88.11/3:(v.nos.&nos.)	1309–10	A92.29/5:991	1623–6	A93.44:AGES9120	1584–2
A88.11/9:(v.nos.&nos.)	1309–1	A92.30:991	1621–8	A93.44:AGES9121	1598–271
A88.11/9:72/13	1309–2	A92.30:991-2	1621–8	A93.44:AGES9124	1584–3
A88.11/13:991	1309–6	A92.32:990	1631–8	A93.44:AGES9126	1598–276
A88.11/15:990	1309–5	A92.35/2:991	1614–1	A93.44:AGES9127	1528–319
A88.11/20:(v.nos.&nos.)	1309–12	A92.40:990	1614–3	A93.44:AGES9128	1568–303
A88.11/23:(v.nos.&nos.)	1309–15	A92.41:(date)	1621–28	A93.44:AGES9134	1588–153
A88.12/22:(nos.)	1311–3	A92.43:(date)	1621–7	A93.44:AGES9140	1588–155
A88.12/22-3:990	1311–8	A92.44:(date)	1631–14	A93.44:AGES9142	1528–321
A88.12/31:990	1311–4.1	A92.46:(date)	1625–11	A93.44:AGES9146	1528–320
A88.12/31-2:990	1311–4.2	A92.47:(nos.)	1631–19	A93.44:AGES9151	1528–315
A88.12/31-3:990	1311–4.4	A93.2:Ec7/3/991	1504–6	A93.44:AGES9152	1528–324
A88.14/11:(nos.)	1317–4	A93.2:F22/6	1008–54	A93.44/3:988	1524–7
A88.14/11-2:990	1317–3	A93.9/8:(nos.)	1541–1	A93.44/4:990-91	1564–3
A88.16/4:(v.nos.&nos.)	1315–1	A93.10/2:(nos.)	1502–4	A93.45/3:989	1544–16
A88.18/4-2:(v.nos.&nos.)	1313–2	A93.11:(nos.)	1561–12	A93.45/3:990	1544–16
A88.18/9:(v.nos.&nos.)	1313–8	A93.11/2:(nos.)	1561–4	A93.45/5:989	1544–17
A88.19:(v.nos.&nos.)	1311–2	A93.11/2-2:991(yearbook)	1561–4	A93.45/6:989	1544–18
A88.23:(v.nos.&nos.)	1311–16	A93.11/2-3:991(yearbook)	1561–12	A93.46:(nos.)	1561–7
A88.34:(date)	1319–3	A93.11/3:(nos.)	1561–8	A93.46/2:(date)	1561–17
A88.34/5:989	1319–5.3	A93.12/2:(nos.)	1561–11	A93.47:(nos.)	1561–16
A88.34/5:990	1319–5.6	A93.12/3:(nos.)	1561–6	A94.14:990	1744–2
A88.34/6:989	1319–5.1	A93.12/3-2:991(yearbook)	1561–6	A101.17:(v.nos.&nos.)	1392–3
A88.34/6:990	1319–5.4	A93.13:(nos.)	1561–2	A101.27:990	1394–17
A88.34/8:989	1319–5.2	A93.13/2-2:991(yearbook)	1561–2	A104.1:990	1294–1
A88.34/8:990	1319–5.5	A93.16/3:(nos.)	1541–7	A106.42:990	1764–1
A88.42/3:(v.nos.&nos.)	1309–14	A93.17/7:(date)	1522–1	A107.12:11/991	1004–13

Index of Superintendent of Documents Numbers

C3.204/3-20:989

A108.10:(nos.)	1272–1	—	2506–8
A109.10:(nos.)	1128–44	—	2506–9
A109.10:76	1128–44.4	—	2506–10
A109.10:95	1128–65	—	2506–11
A109.10/2:(nos./sec.)	1126–1	—	2506–12
A109.10/2:1/sec.15/rev	1126–1.5	C3.158:M3-1(yr.-nos.)	2506–3.1
A109.10/2:1/sec.22	1126–1.6	C3.158:M20A(yr.-nos.)	2506–4.1
A109.11:(v.nos.&nos.)	1122–1	C3.158:M32G(yr.-nos.)	2506–9.4
A109.11/2:989	1124–1	C3.158:M33D(yr.-nos.)	2506–10.9
A110.11/2:990	1374–1	C3.158:M33J(yr.-nos.)	2506–10.3
A110.14:989	1374–2	C3.158:M36D(yr.-nos.)	2506–12.13
A110.14:990	1374–2	C3.158:M37G(yr.-nos.)	2506–12.24
AA1.1:990	9024–2	C3.158:M37L(yr.-nos.)	2506–12.25
AA1.2:C73/2	9028–14	C3.158:MA20D(90)-1	2506–4.5
AE1.101:990	9514–2	C3.158:MA22F.1(90)-1	2506–5.4
AE1.110/5:989	9514–1	C3.158:MA22F.2(90)-1	2506–5.5
AE1.110/5:990	9514–1	C3.158:MA22K(90)-1	2506–5.7
C1.1:990	2004–1	C3.158:MA22Q(90)-1	2506–5.9
C1.1/2:991	2002–5	C3.158:MA23A(yr.)-1	2506–6.1
C1.1/2:991-2	2002–5	C3.158:MA23D(90)-1	2506–6.4
C1.1/3:990	2104–6	C3.158:MA24F(89)-1/rev	2506–7.1
C1.24/3:(v.nos.&nos.)	2002–1	C3.158:MA24H(yr.)-1	2506–7.2
C1.39:992	2004–6	C3.158:MA24T(90)-1	2506–7.4
C1.88:(date)	2002–6	C3.158:MA25H(90)-1	2506–7.8
C1.108/2:991	2104–7	C3.158:MA28A(90)-1	2506–8.14
C3.2:Ag8/10	2346–1.4	C3.158:MA28B(90)-1	2506–8.13
C3.2:R24/3	2328–67	C3.158:MA28C(90)-1	2506–8.15
C3.2:R31/9/989	2624–2	C3.158:MA28F(90)-1	2506–8.16
C3.2:R31/9/990	2624–2	C3.158:MA28G(90)-1	2506–8.5
C3.2:R31/9/991	2624–2	C3.158:MA30C(90)-1	2506–8.17
C3.2:Su7/5/990	2624–1	C3.158:MA31A(90)-1	2506–6.8
C3.6/2:F76/991	2428–11	C3.158:MA32C(90)-1	2506–9.1
C3.6/2:St8	2308–59	C3.158:MA32E(90)-1	2506–9.3
C3.20:(nos.)	2342–1	C3.158:MA33A(90)-1	2506–10.1
C3.20/3:(nos.)	2342–2	C3.158:MA33B(90)-1	2506–10.2
C3.24/9-6:989	2506–15.2	C3.158:MA33E(90)-1	2506–10.5
C3.24/9-7:989	2506–15.1	C3.158:MA33L(90)-1	2506–10.8
C3.24/9-9:989	2506–15.3	C3.158:MA35A(90)-1	2506–12.1
C3.24/9-12:(nos.)	2506–16	C3.158:MA35D(89)-1	2506–12.3
C3.24/9-12:87-1	2506–16.1	C3.158:MA35D(90)-1	2506–12.3
C3.24/12:MC87-S-1	2497–1	C3.158:MA35F(90)-1	2506–12.4
C3.24/12:MC87-S-5	2497–5	C3.158:MA35J(90)-1	2506–12.5
C3.24/12:MC87-S-7	2497–7	C3.158:MA35L(90)-1	2506–12.6
C3.31/4:987/v.1/pt.(nos.)	2331–1	C3.158:MA35M(90)-1	2506–12.7
C3.31/4:987/v.1/pt.55	2331–1.55	C3.158:MA35N(90)-1	2506–12.31
C3.31/4:987/v.1/pt.56	2331–1.56	C3.158:MA35P(90)-1	2506–12.8
C3.31/12:987/v.4	2337–1	C3.158:MA35Q(90)-1	2506–12.28
C3.32:990	2344–1	C3.158:MA35U(90)-1	2506–12.10
C3.133:(nos.)	2413–7	C3.158:MA36A(90)-1	2506–12.11
C3.133/2:984-90(summary) ..	2413–7	C3.158:MA36E(90)-1	2506–12.15
C3.133/3:990	2413–13	C3.158:MA36F(90)-1	2506–12.16
C3.134:991	2324–1	C3.158:MA36L(90)-1	2506–12.19
C3.134/5:991	2328–54	C3.158:MA36M(90)-1	2506–12.20
C3.138/3:(nos.)	2413–3	C3.158:MA36P(90)-1	2506–12.35
C3.138/3-2:989	2413–5	C3.158:MA36Q(90)-1	2506–12.36
C3.138/3-3:981-90(summary)	2413–3	C3.158:MA36R(90)-1	2506–12.34
C3.138/3-4:990	2413–8	C3.158:MA37D(90)-1	2506–12.22
C3.138/3-5:989	2413–14	C3.158:MA38B(89)-1	2506–12.26
C3.138/4:(nos.)	2413–2	C3.158:MA200(89)-1/advance	
C3.140/2-3:990	2466–1.2		2506–3.6
C3.140/2-4:990	2466–1.1	C3.158:MQ20J(yr.-nos.)	2506–4.3
C3.140/2-5:990	2466–1.3	C3.158:MQ20K(yr.-nos.)	2506–4.4
C3.145/4:987/v.3/no.1	2455–1	C3.158:MQ22D(yr.-nos.)	2506–5.2
C3.145/4:987/v.3/no.2	2455–2	C3.158:MQ22P(yr.-nos.)	2506–5.8
C3.145/4:987/v.3/no.3	2455–3	C3.158:MQ-22T(yr.-nos.)	2506–5.11
C3.145/4:987/v.3/no.4	2455–4	C3.158:MQ23A(yr.-nos.)	2506–6.12
C3.145/4:987/v.6/no.1	2460–1	C3.158:MQ-23X(yr.-nos.)	2506–6.6
C3.145/6:(date/nos.)	2462–3	C3.158:MQ28A(yr.-nos.)	2506–8.1
C3.150:B/990/rev.2	2428–5.1	C3.158:MQ28B(yr.-nos.)	2506–8.2
C3.158:(ltrs.-nos.)	2506–3	C3.158:MQ28C(yr.-nos.)	2506–8.3
—	2506–4	C3.158:MQ28F(yr.-nos.)	2506–8.4
—	2506–5	C3.158:MQ31A(yr.-nos.)	2506–6.7
—	2506–6	C3.158:MQ-32A(yr.-nos.)	2506–9.6
—	2506–7	C3.158:MQ32D(yr.-nos.)	2506–9.2

C3.158:MQ-34E(yr.-nos.) 2506–11.2
C3.158:MQ-34H(yr.-nos.) 2506–11.4
C3.158:MQ-34K(yr.-nos.) 2506–11.5
C3.158:MQ-35W(yr.-nos.) 2506–12.12
C3.158:MQ-36B(yr.-nos.) 2506–12.33
C3.158:MQ-36C(yr.-nos.) 2506–12.14
C3.163/3:991 2304–2
C3.163/7:(date) 2302–6
C3.164:246/(yr.) 2424–4
C3.164:447/990 2424–10
C3.164:925/(nos.) 2422–12
C3.164:927/989 2424–12
C3.164:927/990 2424–12
C3.164:985-(nos.) 2422–7
C3.164:985/990 2424–11
C3.186:P-20/448 .... 2546–1.450
C3.186:P-23/169 .... 2546–2.157
C3.186:P-23/171 .... 2546–2.158
C3.186:P-23/172 .... 2546–2.159
C3.186:P-23/174 .... 2546–2.160
C3.186:P-23/176 .... 2546–2.162
C3.186:P-25/1070-RD-2 .... 2546–3.169
C3.186:P-60/173 .... 2546–6.72
C3.186:P-60/176-RD 2546–6.69
C3.186:P-70/2/(nos.) 2546–20
C3.186:P-70/2/22 .... 2546–20.16
C3.186:P-70/2/23 .... 2546–20.17
C3.186:P-70/2/24 .... 2546–20.19
C3.186:P-70/2/25 .... 2546–20.18
C3.186/2:988-89 .... 2546–6.68
C3.186/2:990 .... 2546–6.70
C3.186/3-2:990 .... 2546–1.454
C3.186/6:990 .... 2546–1.449
C3.186/7:(nos.) 2542–1
C3.186/8:991 .... 2546–2.161
C3.186/10:990 .... 2546–1.455
C3.186/12:989 .... 2546–1.453
C3.186/14-2:990 .... 2546–1.448
C3.186/14-2:991 .... 2546–1.451
C3.186/17:989-90 .... 2546–1.447
C3.186/22:988-89 .... 2546–6.67
C3.186/22:990 .... 2546–6.71
C3.186/23:988-89 .... 2546–1.452
C3.191/2-2:987-88 .... 2466–2.1
C3.191/2-2:988-89 .... 2466–2.8
C3.191/2-3:990 .... 2466–2.6
C3.191/2-4:988-89 .... 2466–2.2
C3.191/2-4:989-90/prelim 2466–2.9
C3.191/2-5:988-89 .... 2466–2.3
C3.191/2-7:988-89 .... 2466–2.4
C3.191/2-8:990 .... 2466–2.7
C3.191/2-10:988-89 .... 2466–2.5
C3.204/3-(nos.):988 2326–6
C3.204/3-(nos.):989 2326–8
C3.204/3-1:988 .... 2326–6.1
C3.204/3-2:989 .... 2326–8.2
C3.204/3-3:989 .... 2326–8.3
C3.204/3-4:989 .... 2326–8.4
C3.204/3-5:989 .... 2326–8.5
C3.204/3-6:989 .... 2326–8.6
C3.204/3-7:989 .... 2326–8.7
C3.204/3-8:989 .... 2326–8.8
C3.204/3-9:989 .... 2326–8.9
C3.204/3-10:989 .... 2326–8.10
C3.204/3-11:989 .... 2326–8.11
C3.204/3-12:989 .... 2326–8.12
C3.204/3-13:989 .... 2326–8.13
C3.204/3-14:989 .... 2326–8.14
C3.204/3-15:989 .... 2326–8.15
C3.204/3-16:989 .... 2326–8.16
C3.204/3-17:989 .... 2326–8.17
C3.204/3-18:989 .... 2326–8.18
C3.204/3-19:989 .... 2326–8.19
C3.204/3-20:989 .... 2326–8.20

C3.204/3-21:989

Index of Superintendent of Documents Numbers

C3.204/3-21:989	2326-8.21	C3.215/8:(yr.)	2384-4	C3.223/18:990CPH-1-51	2551-1.51
C3.204/3-22:989	2326-8.22	C3.215/8:C50-(nos.)	2382-7	C3.223/18:990CPH-1-52	2551-1.52
C3.204/3-23:989	2326-8.23	C3.215/9:C25-(nos.)	2382-3	C3.223/18:990CPH-1-55	2551-1.55
C3.204/3-24:989	2326-8.24	C3.215/9-2:C27-(nos.)	2382-8	C3.224/3-8:CH-S-1-(nos.)	2326-21
C3.204/3-25:989	2326-8.25	C3.215/9-3:990	2384-1	C3.224/3-8:CH-S-1-1	2326-21.1
C3.204/3-26:989	2326-8.26	C3.215/13:C22-(nos.)	2382-2	C3.224/3-8:CH-S-1-2	2326-21.2
C3.204/3-27:989	2326-8.27	C3.215/15:C21-(nos.)	2382-9	C3.224/3-8:CH-S-1-6	2326-21.6
C3.204/3-28:989	2326-8.28	C3.215/16:984	2485-8	C3.224/3-8:CH-S-1-8	2326-21.8
C3.204/3-29:989	2326-8.29	C3.215/20:88-1	2485-11.4	C3.224/3-8:CH-S-1-9	2326-21.9
C3.204/3-30:989	2326-8.30	C3.215/20:88-2	2485-11.6	C3.224/3-8:CH-S-1-10	2326-21.10
C3.204/3-31:989	2326-8.31	C3.215/20:88-3	2485-11.5	C3.224/3-8:CH-S-1-11	2326-21.11
C3.204/3-32:989	2326-8.32	C3.215/20:88-5	2485-11.7	C3.224/3-8:CH-S-1-13	2326-21.13
C3.204/3-33:989	2326-8.33	C3.215/20:88-6	2485-11.8	C3.224/3-8:CH-S-1-19	2326-21.19
C3.204/3-34:989	2326-8.34	C3.215/20:88-7	2485-11.9	C3.224/3-8:CH-S-1-22	2326-21.22
C3.204/3-35:989	2326-8.35	C3.215/20:88-9	2485-11.10	C3.224/3-8:CH-S-1-32	2326-21.32
C3.204/3-36:989	2326-8.36	C3.215/20:88-10	2485-11.11	C3.224/3-8:CH-S-1-34	2326-21.34
C3.204/3-37:989	2326-8.37	C3.216/2:MIC87-A-(nos.)	2515-1	C3.224/3-8:CH-S-1-40	2326-21.40
C3.204/3-38:989	2326-8.38	C3.216/2:MIC87-A-8	2515-1.8	C3.224/3-8:CH-S-1-45	2326-21.45
C3.204/3-39:989	2326-8.39	C3.216/4:MIC87-S-1	2517-1	C3.224/3-8:CH-S-1-47	2326-21.47
C3.204/3-40:989	2326-8.40	C3.216/4:MIC87-S-2	2517-2	C3.224/3-8:CH-S-1-48	2326-21.48
C3.204/3-41:989	2326-8.41	C3.223/7-5:(nos.)	2326-20	C3.224/11:CDR-(nos.)	2626-11
C3.204/3-42:989	2326-8.42	C3.223/7-5:1	2326-20.1	C3.224/11:CDR-6	2626-11.14
C3.204/3-43:989	2326-8.43	C3.223/7-5:2	2326-20.2	C3.230:ES87-3	2329-8
C3.204/3-44:989	2326-8.44	C3.223/7-5:3	2326-20.3	C3.233/5:TC87-S-1	2579-1
C3.204/3-45:989	2326-8.45	C3.223/18:990CPH-1-(nos.) ..	2551-1	C3.238:(v.nos.& nos.)	2302-3
C3.204/3-46:989	2326-8.46	C3.223/18:990CPH-1-2	2551-1.2	C3.242:(nos.)	2462-2
C3.204/3-47:989	2326-8.47	C3.223/18:990CPH-1-3	2551-1.3	C3.245/3:CC87-I-(nos.)	2373-1
C3.204/3-48:989	2326-8.48	C3.223/18:990CPH-1-4	2551-1.4	C3.245/3:CC87-I-12/rev	2373-1.12
C3.204/3-49:989	2326-8.49	C3.223/18:990CPH-1-5	2551-1.5	C3.252:(nos.)	2326-7
C3.204/3-50:989	2326-8.50	C3.223/18:990CPH-1-6	2551-1.6	C3.252:1/4	2326-7.80
C3.204/3-51:989	2326-8.51	C3.223/18:990CPH-1-7	2551-1.7	C3.252:2/4	2326-7.81
C3.204/3-52:989	2326-8.52	C3.223/18:990CPH-1-8	2551-1.8	C3.252:6/3	2326-7.77
C3.204/3-53:989	2326-8.53	C3.223/18:990CPH-1-9	2551-1.9	C3.252:7/3	2326-7.78
C3.205/8:(nos.-yr.)	2326-17	C3.223/18:990CPH-1-10	2551-1.10	C3.252:8/6	2326-7.79
C3.205/8:12-90	2326-17.22	C3.223/18:990CPH-1-11	2551-1.11	C3.253/2:OA87-E-1	2591-1
C3.205/8:13-90	2326-17.23	C3.223/18:990CPH-1-12	2551-1.12	C3.253/2:OA87-E-2/pt.(nos)...	2591-2
C3.205/8:91-1	2326-17.24	C3.223/18:990CPH-1-13	2551-1.13	C3.253/2:OA87-E-2/pt.1	2591-2.1
C3.205/8:91-2	2326-17.34	C3.223/18:990CPH-1-14	2551-1.14	C3.253/2:OA87-E-2/pt.2	2591-2.2
C3.205/8:91-3	2326-17.29	C3.223/18:990CPH-1-15	2551-1.15	C3.255/3:RC87-S-2	2399-2
C3.205/8:91-4	2326-17.25	C3.223/18:990CPH-1-16	2551-1.16	C3.255/3:RC87-SP-1	2401-1
C3.205/8:91-5	2326-17.26	C3.223/18:990CPH-1-17	2551-1.17	C3.256/3:WC87-S-2	2407-2
C3.205/8:91-9	2326-17.28	C3.223/18:990CPH-1-18	2551-1.18	C3.256/3:WC87-S-4	2407-4
C3.205/8:91-10	2326-17.27	C3.223/18:990CPH-1-19	2551-1.19	C3.257/3:SC87-S-2	2393-2
C3.205/8:91-11	2326-17.30	C3.223/18:990CPH-1-20	2551-1.20	C3.257/3:SC87-S-3	2393-3
C3.205/8:91-14	2326-17.31	C3.223/18:990CPH-1-21	2551-1.21	C3.257/3:SC87-S-4	2393-4
C3.205/8:91-18	2326-17.37	C3.223/18:990CPH-1-22	2551-1.22	C3.266:990	2464-2
C3.205/8:91-19	2326-17.33	C3.223/18:990CPH-1-23	2551-1.23	C3.266/2:990/v.(nos.)	2464-3
C3.205/8:91-21	2326-17.35	C3.223/18:990CPH-1-24	2551-1.24	C3.266/2:990/v.1	2464-3.1
C3.205/8:91-22	2326-17.32	C3.223/18:990CPH-1-25	2551-1.25	C3.266/2:990/v.2	2464-3.2
C3.205/8:91-24	2326-17.36	C3.223/18:990CPH-1-26	2551-1.26	C3.267:(yr.-nos.)	2502-1
C3.215:H-111-(nos.)	2482-1	C3.223/18:990CPH-1-27	2551-1.27	C3.269:TM-(date)	2322-2
C3.215:H-111/90-A	2484-1	C3.223/18:990CPH-1-28	2551-1.28	C3.276:3/1	2322-3
C3.215:H-121-(nos.)	2486-1	C3.223/18:990CPH-1-29	2551-1.29	C3.276:3/2	2322-3
C3.215:H-121-91-1	2486-1.11	C3.223/18:990CPH-1-30	2551-1.30	C3.278:Ex7/(date)	2422-13
C3.215:H-130-(nos.)	2482-2	C3.223/18:990CPH-1-31	2551-1.31	C3.278:Im7/(date)	2422-14
C3.215:H-130/90-A	2484-2	C3.223/18:990CPH-1-32	2551-1.32	C3.281:(CT)/990/CD	2551-6
C3.215:H-131/90-A	2484-3	C3.223/18:990CPH-1-33	2551-1.33	C3.281:Al1b/990/CD/corr ...	2551-6.1
C3.215:H-150/89	2485-12	C3.223/18:990CPH-1-34	2551-1.34	C3.281:Al1s/990/CD	2551-6.2
C3.215:H-151-83-1	2485-14	C3.223/18:990CPH-1-35	2551-1 35	C3.281:Ar4i/990/CD	2551-6.3
C3.215:H-151-85-1	2485-13	C3.223/18:990CPH-1-36	2551-1.36	C3.281:Ar4k/990/CD/corr	2551-6.4
C3.215:H-151-87-1	2485-13	C3.223/18:990CPH-1-37	2551-1.37	C3.281:C12/990/CD	2551-6.5
C3.215:H-170-(yr.-nos.)	2485-6	C3.223/18:990CPH-1-38	2551-1.38	C3.281:C76/990/CD	2551-6.6
C3.215:H-170-88-8	2485-6.1	C3.223/18:990CPH-1-39	2551-1.39	C3.281:F66/990/CD	2551-6.7
C3.215:H-170-88-15	2485-6.5	C3.223/18:990CPH-1-40	2551-1.40	C3.281:H31/990/CD/corr	2551-6.8
C3.215:H-170-88-29	2485-6.2	C3.223/18:990CPH-1-41	2551-1.41	C3.281:Io9/990/CD	2551-6.9
C3.215:H-170-88-45	2485-6.3	C3.223/18:990CPH-1-42	2551-1.42	C3.281:N42j/990/CD	2551-6.10
C3.215:H-170-88-50	2485-6.4	C3.223/18:990CPH-1-43	2551-1.43	C3.281:P81/doc/[notes1-5]...	2308-63
C3.215:H-170-88-54	2485-6.6	C3.223/18:990CPH-1-44	2551-1.44	C13.10:305/supp.22	2214-1
C3.215:H-170-88-56	2485-6.7	C3.223/18:990CPH-1-45	2551-1.45	C13.10/3:991	2214-7
C3.215:H-170-88-61	2485-6.8	C3.223/18:990CPH-1-46	2551-1.46	C13.52:(nos.)	2216-2
C3.215/2:C20-(nos.)	2382-1	C3.223/18:990CPH-1-47	2551-1.47	C13.52:9-1	2216-2.193
C3.215/3:C30-(nos.)	2382-4	C3.223/18:990CPH-1-48	2551-1.48	C13.52:11-3	2216-2.194
C3.215/4:C40-(nos.)	2382-5	C3.223/18:990CPH-1-49	2551-1.49	C13.52:54-1	2216-2.195
C3.215/4:C40-9013	2384-2	C3.223/18:990CPH-1-50	2551-1.50	C13.52:100-1	2216-2.198

Index of Superintendent of Documents Numbers

D1.61/2:(date)

C13.52:120-1	2216-2.197	C55.433:70	2176-1.36	C61.11:N42z/991	2046-4.25
C13.52:146-1	2216-2.201	C55.433:71	2176-1.37	C61.11:N56/991	2046-4.55
C13.52:159	2216-2.196	C55.433:72	2176-1.38	C61.11:N83/991	2046-4.69
C13.52:160	2216-2.199	C55.433:73	2176-1.39	C61.11:Om1/991	2046-4.39
C13.52:161	2216-2.200	C55.438:991-92	2174-10	C61.11:P17/991	2046-4.38
C13.58:4559	2214-6	C55.616:P96/990	2144-25	C61.11:P53/991	2046-4.20
C13.72:(nos.)	2214-5	C59.2:F76/5	2708-41	C61.11:P83/991	2046-4.52
C13.72:4533	2214-5.1	C59.2:F76/6	2004-9	C61.11:Q1/991	2046-4.36
C13.72:4534	2214-5.2	C59.2:In8/4/989/prelim	2704-5	C61.11:Se5/990-2	2046-4.2
C21.1/2:990	2244-1	C59.11:(v.nos.&nos.)	2702-1	C61.11:Si1/991	2046-4.50
C46.1:990	2064-2	C59.18:984-89/v.(nos.)	2704-2	C61.11:Sr3/991	2046-4.11
C46.18:P96/2/991	2064-9	C59.18:984-89/v.1/summ	2704-2.1	C61.11:Su2/991	2046-4.70
C47.2:F91	2904-15	C59.18:984-89/v.2	2704-2.2	C61.11:Sw2/991	2046-4.58
C47.15:(date)	2902-1	C59.18:984-89/v.3	2704-2.3	C61.11:Sw3/991	2046-4.47
C47.20:991-92	2904-11	C59.18:984-89/v.4	2704-2.4	C61.11:Sw6/991	2046-4.33
C51.11/2-2:991	2224-3	C59.18:984-89/v.5	2704-2.5	C61.11:Sw6/991-2	2046-4.65
C55.2:F53/4	2178-32	C59.20:988/rev	2704-4	C61.11:Sy8/991	2046-4.28
C55.2:F62	2148-60.1	C59.20:989/prelim	2704-4	C61.11:T13/990-2	2046-4.8
C55.2:F62/2	2148-60.3	C59.20/2:988/rev	2704-5	C61.11:T15/990	2046-4.6
C55.2:F62/2/highlig	2148-60.4	C60.13:P96/990	2804-3	C61.11:T32/991	2046-4.19
C55.2:Un2/989	2144-5	C60.15:990	2802-1	C61.11:T32/991-2	2046-4.54
C55.13/2:NMFS-F/NEC-81..	2164-14	C61.2:(CT)	2046-12	C61.11:T57/990	2046-4.3
C55.13/2:NMFS-F/NEC-86..	2164-14	C61.2:El2/4	2048-1	C61.11:T83/991	2046-4.27
C55.13/2:NWSNHC31/990 ..	2188-15	C61.2:F49/2	2048-152	C61.11:T83/991-2	2046-4.76
C55.16/2:992	2144-2	C61.2:In2/2	2046-12.45	C61.11:T84/991	2046-4.24
C55.20:F65	2186-6.4	C61.2:J27/2	2048-151	C61.11:Ug1/990	2046-4.9
C55.36:ERLAOML-18	2146-7.7	C61.2:T31/991	2044-31	C61.11:Ug1/991	2046-4.49
C55.36:ERLAOML-20	2146-7.8	C61.2:T31/992	2044-31	C61.11:Un3/991	2046-4.35
C55.102:Of2/990	2184-5	C61.11:Al3/991	2046-4.22	C61.11:Z1/2/991	2046-4.56
C55.109:(v.nos.&nos.)	2182-1	C61.11:Au7/2/991	2046-4.44	C61.11:Z1/991	2046-4.41
C55.113/2:(v.nos.&nos.)	2182-3	C61.11:Au7/991	2046-4.18	C61.11:Z6/991	2046-4.40
C55.123/2:(v.nos.&nos.)	2182-5	C61.11:B14/2/991	2046-4.77	C61.12:(yr.-nos.)	2046-6
C55.129/2:(yr./nos.)	2182-6	C61.11:B22/991	2046-4.73	C61.12:91-01	2046-6.1
C55.196:(date)	2182-8	C61.11:B41/991	2046-4.59	C61.12:91-02	2046-6.2
C55.202:C61/2/990	2154-8	C61.11:B43/990	2046-4.7	C61.12:91-03	2046-6.3
C55.209:(v.nos.&nos.)	2182-7	C61.11:B91/990	2046-4.5	C61.12:91-04	2046-6.4
C55.211:(v.nos.&nos.)	2152-4	C61.11:B92/991	2046-4.14	C61.12:91-05	2046-6.5
C55.212:(v.nos.&nos.)	2152-3	C61.11:B95/991	2046-4.32	C61.12:91-06	2046-6.6
C55.220/3:989	2144-15	C61.11:C14/991	2046-4.57	C61.12:91-07	2046-6.7
C55.281:W89/971-80/v.(nos.)		C61.11:C17/990-2	2046-4.10	C61.12:91-08	2046-6.8
	2156-4	C61.11:C34/991	2046-4.13	C61.12:91-09	2046-6.9
C55.281:W89/971-80/v.1	2156-4.1	C61.11:C76/991	2046-4.66	C61.18:(v.nos.&nos.)	2042-24
C55.281:W89/971-80/v.2	2156-4.2	C61.11:C82/990	2046-4.1	C61.24:990	2024-1
C55.287/60-2:(date)	2152-13.1	C61.11:C99/2/991	2046-4.53	C61.25/2:989	2044-20
C55.287/60-3:(date)	2152-13.2	C61.11:D41/991	2046-4.23	C61.28:(yr.)	2044-26
C55.299/2:(v.nos.&nos.)	2152-8	C61.11:Eg9/991	2046-4.75	C61.28/2:990	2044-37
C55.309/2-2:990	2164-1	C61.11:F47/991	2046-4.67	C61.31:(yr.)	2044-27
C55.309/2-3:987-89	2166-17.1	C61.11:F49/991	2046-4.46	C61.34:991	2044-28
C55.309/2-4:990(summary) ..	2162-2	C61.11:F84/991	2046-4.26	C61.37:(v.nos.&nos.)	2042-1
C55.309/2-7:(nos.)	2162-3	C61.11:F84/991-2	2046-4.64	C61.40:(yr.)	2044-38
C55.309/2-8:(nos.)	2162-2	C61.11:G11/991	2046-4.42	CC1.35:989-90	9284-6
C55.309/2-9:987	2166-6.2	C61.11:G31/991	2046-4.34	CR1.9:C28/991	11048-188
C55.309/2-10:990	2166-6.1	C61.11:G31/991-2	2046-4.71	D1.1:992	3544-2
C55.310:(v.nos.&nos.)	2162-1	C61.11:G34/991	2046-4.51	D1.1/3-2:990	3544-31
C55.318:(date)	2162-6.5	C61.11:G81/991	2046-4.48	D1.19:989-90	3504-3
C55.323:989	2164-3	C61.11:H75/991	2046-4.37	D1.33/4:989	3548-21
C55.323:990	2164-3	C61.11:In2/991	2046-4.31	D1.57:990	3544-5
C55.337:SWR-90-01	2168-125	C61.11:In2/991-2	2046-4.62	D1.57/2:990	3544-4
C55.402:C63	2176-3.12	C61.11:Ir2/991	2046-4.45	D1.57/3:(date)	3542-7
C55.402:Es8/2/v.4	2178-29	C61.11:Is7/991	2046-4.74	D1.57/3:990-2	3542-1
C55.402:Es8/3	2178-27	C61.11:It1/991	2046-4.61	D1.57/3:991	3542-1
C55.402:Es8/4	2176-7.24	C61.11:J76/991	2046-4.29	D1.57/3-5:990	3544-19
C55.402:W53	2178-31	C61.11:K59/991	2046-4.43	D1.57/4:987-90	3544-18
C55.420/2:989	2174-3	C61.11:K84/991	2046-4.21	D1.57/5:988-90	3544-11
C55.420/2:990	2174-3	C61.11:L29/2/991	2046-4.68	D1.57/6:991	3542-5
C55.421:992	2174-2.2	C61.11:L97/991	2046-4.72	D1.57/7:990-2	3542-19
C55.421/2:992	2174-2.3	C61.11:M26/991	2046-4.17	D1.57/7:991	3542-19
C55.421/3:992	2174-2.4	C61.11:M29/2/991	2046-4.15	D1.57/8:990	3544-17
C55.421/4:992	2174-2.5	C61.11:M29/3/991	2046-4.16	D1.57/9:(date)	3542-17
C55.425:992	2174-1.1	C61.11:M44/2/990	2046-4.4	D1.58/2:990	3544-6
C55.425/2:992	2174-1.2	C61.11:M82/991	2046-4.30	D1.58/4:989	3544-29
C55.425/3:992	2174-11	C61.11:M87/991	2046-4.63	D1.58/4:990	3544-29
C55.432:992	2174-2.1	C61.11:N35/991	2046-4.12	D1.61:(date)	3542-14
C55.433:(nos.)	2176-1	C61.11:N38/991	2046-4.60	D1.61/2:(date)	3542-16

D1.61/3:(date)

Index of Superintendent of Documents Numbers

D1.61/3:(date)	3542–20	E2.1:990	3084–9	ED1.2:M58/v.2	4808–22.2
D1.61/4:990	3544–1	E2.12/3:990	3084–13	ED1.10/2:991	4804–3
D1.61/5:990	3544–7	E2.15:G21/989........................	3088–21	ED1.14:92-1	4804–17
D1.61/6:989	3544–40	E3.1:990	3164–29	ED1.18/4:990	4874–1
D1.61/6:990	3544–40	E3.1/2:990	3164–74	ED1.18/8:987..........................	4874–10
D1.62:(date)	3542–15	E3.1/4:991	3164–75	ED1.26:990-2	4802–1
D1.62/2:989	3544–24	E3.1/4-3:991............................	3164–90	ED1.26:991	4802–1
D1.66:990	3904–3	E3.2:As7/3	3166–12.6	ED1.29/2:988-89	4804–28
D1.74:991	3504–20	E3.2:N88/4/update	3168–108	ED1.32:991	4944–4
D1.85:992	7144–13	E3.2:P44/9	3168–119	ED1.32/4:990-91	4944–10
D1.90:990	3544–26	E3.9:(date)...............................	3162–24	ED1.39:990	4804–5
D1.94:990-2	3542–22	E3.11:(yr./nos.)........................	3162–4	ED1.40/4:990	4804–18
D1.94:991	3542–22	E3.11/4:(yr./nos.)....................	3162–1	ED1.102:C56/990	4828–29
D2.15/3:991	3504–13	E3.11/5:(date)..........................	3162–6	ED1.102:M42/v.1	4896–8.2
D12.1:990	3504–22	E3.11/5-5:990/v.(nos.)	3164–2	ED1.102:M42/v.2	4896–8.2
D103.1:(yr.)/v.(nos.)	3754–1	E3.11/5-5:990/v.1	3164–2.1	ED1.102:M74...........................	4828–40
D103.1:988/v.1........................	3754–1.1	E3.11/5-5:990/v.2	3164–2.2	ED1.102:P93/2........................	4838–47
D103.35/(nos.):989	3756–1	E3.11/5-6:(date)	3162–42	ED1.102:P94/4........................	4826–9.10
D103.35/(nos.):991	3756–2	E3.11/7:(date)..........................	3162–8	ED1.102:St9	4826–9.11
D103.35/2:989	3756–1.2	E3.11/7-3:990..........................	3164–25	ED1.102:T72/2.........................	4898–32
D103.35/3:989	3756–1.3	E3.11/7-8:991..........................	3164–68	ED1.108:D26	4828–39
D103.35/6:989	3756–1.6	E3.11/7-9:991..........................	3164–77	ED1.109:991/v.(nos.)..............	4824–1
D103.35/6:991	3756–2.6	E3.11/7-10:991........................	3164–89	ED1.109:991/v.1	4824–1.1
D103.35/7:991	3756–2.7	E3.11/9:(yr./nos.)....................	3162–37	ED1.109:991/v.2	4824–1.2
D103.35/12:989	3756–1.13	E3.11/11-3:989........................	3164–94	ED1.111/2:989-90	4834–1
D103.35/13:989	3756–1.14	E3.11/15-2:990........................	3164–42	ED1.116/3:991	4844–13
D103.35/16:989	3756–1.17	E3.11/17-8:(date)	3162–35	ED1.210:990..............................	4944–1
D103.35/17:991	3756–2.18	E3.11/17-10:989......................	3164–11	ED1.302:C68	4888–5
D103.35/20:989	3756–1.21	E3.11/17-12:988......................	3164–92	ED1.302:El2/989-90	4834–6
D103.35/28:989	3756–1.29	E3.11/20:989	3164–50	ED1.302:L61/3.........................	4878–4
D103.35/37:989	3756–1.38	E3.11/20-3:991........................	3164–84	ED1.302:M42/2	4896–8.1
D103.35/38:989	3756–1.39	E3.11/20-4:(date)	3162–43	ED1.302:M42/2/exec.summ..	4896–8.1
D103.35/45:989	3756–1.46	E3.13/4:(yr./nos.)....................	3162–11	ED1.302:P75/2/991.................	4828–26
D103.35/53:989	3756–1.52	E3.17/4-2:989..........................	3164–9	ED1.302:P75/991.....................	4828–27
D103.116:(date)	3752–1	E3.18/4-2:989..........................	3164–23	ED1.302:P93/4.........................	4888–3
D114.15:983	3704–11	E3.18/4-3:989..........................	3164–24	ED1.302:P93/5.........................	4836–3.7
D201.6/14:990	3804–13	E3.19/2:989	3164–62	ED1.302:P94/5/991.................	4824–7
D208.25:(date)	3802–4	E3.25:989	3164–38	ED1.302:P94/6.........................	4846–4.4
D213.8:991	3804–7	E3.27:990	3168–117	ED1.302:W84	4888–6
D213.8:992	3804–7	E3.29:990	3164–36	ED1.317/2:(yr./nos.)	4812–1
D216.1:990	3804–14	E3.31:(nos.)..............................	3162–34	ED1.326:990	4824–2
D220.11:990	3804–8	E3.32:(date)..............................	3162–32	ED1.326:991	4824–2
D301.73:(v.nos.&nos.)	3602–1	E3.32/3:(yr./nos.)....................	3162–45	ED1.327:991	4818–5
E1.2:St8....................................	3004–34	E3.32/4:(date)..........................	3162–44	ED1.328:C37/988-89..............	4834–22
E1.15/2:991	3344–2	E3.34:990	3164–46	ED1.328:C68/3	4826–1.30
E1.19:(nos.)..............................	3004–18	E3.34/2:990	3164–70	ED1.328:F31/980-90...............	4824–8
E1.19:0144/9	3004–18.5	E3.37:989	3164–44	ED1.328/3:C37/3	4836–3.5
E1.19:0470T	3004–18.1	E3.42:960-89............................	3164–39	ED1.328/3:F96.........................	4844–6
E1.19:0474T	3004–18.2	E3.42/3:989	3164–64	ED1.328/3:H53	4844–2
E1.19:0485P	3004–18.3	E3.43/2:989	3166–8.9	ED1.328/3:H53/2	4844–8
E1.19:0498T	3004–18.6	E3.45:990	3164–86	ED1.328/3:L61.........................	4824–6
E1.19:0508T	3004–18.7	E3.46/4:991	3164–72	ED1.328/3:T22.........................	4836–3.6
E1.19:0511P	3004–18.4	E3.46/5:990	3164–65	ED1.328/3:T22/2.....................	4826–1.31
E1.27:989	3304–1	E3.48:991	3164–87	ED1.328/3:T28.........................	4826–9.8
E1.28:DOE/OSTI-8200-R54	3354–15	E3.50:991	3164–81	ED1.329:990	4834–23
E1.36/2:990	3354–7	E3.51:991	3164–57	ED1.330:C73/991	4868–10
E1.42:988	3324–1	E3.52:989	3164–80	EP1.1/5:991	9182–10
E1.45/2:990	3304–2	E3.54:988	3166–13.5	EP1.1/5:991-2..........................	9182–10
E1.48:0293	3006–5.21	F5 1:990	3224 1	EP1.2:C82/6	9188–114
E1.48:0295	3006–5.23	E5.1/2:(date)............................	3222–2	EP1.21/7:(nos.)........................	9182–5
E1.48:0297	3006–5.24	E5.14:990	3222–1	EP1.23:600/3-90/043	9208–130
E1.48:0302	3006–5.25	E5.14:990-2..............................	3222–1	EP1.23/6:600/9-90/039	9184–22
E1.50/2:990	3004–27	E5.16:989-90............................	3228–11	EP1.23/9:600/8-89/(nos.)......	9198–84
E1.68/2:0299P	3364–1	E6.1:990	3254–1.1	EP1.23/9:600/8-89/049F	9198–84.5
E1.68/2:0316P	3368–1	E6.1:990/app	3254–1.2	EP1.56:(yr.-nos.)......................	9202–3
E1.68/2-6:(date)	3362–1	ED1.1:989-90	4804–6	EP2.2:W29/5	9208–131
E1.84/2:990	3334–3	ED1.2:C43/6	4808–28	EP4.2:T66/3	9198–120
E1.89:0019/11	3304–11	ED1.2:C68	4888–4	EP4.24:940-89	9194–13
E1.89:0303T	3308–87	ED1.2:C68/2/v.1,2	4808–23	EP4.24:989	9194–1
E1.89:0341	3304–18	ED1.2:D35	4808–26	FCA1.1:990................................	9264–2
E1.90/2:(date)..........................	3002–13	ED1.2:G76/2/989-90	4804–1	FEM1.1:(yr.)..............................	9434–2
E1.93:(v.nos.&nos.)	3352–4	ED1.2:H75	4804–39.1	FM1.1:989.................................	9344–1
E1.95:990	3234–1	ED1.2:M58/v.(nos.).................	4808–22	FMC1.1:990	9334–1
E1.95/2:990	3244–1	ED1.2:M58/v.1	4808–22.1	FR1.1:990	9364–1

Index of Superintendent of Documents Numbers

GA1.13:RCED-91-21

Document	Number	Document	Number	Document	Number
FR1.3:(v.nos.&nos.)	9362–1	GA1.13:GGD-91-86	26119–342	GA1.13:NSIAD-91-54............	26123–332
FR1.16:(date)	9365–1.3	GA1.13:GGD-91-90	26119–296	GA1.13:NSIAD-91-57............	26123–356
FR1.17:(date)	9365–2.5	GA1.13:GGD-91-98	26119–346	GA1.13:NSIAD-91-67...........	26123–318
FR1.26:(date)	9365–2.7	GA1.13:GGD-91-99	26119–354	GA1.13:NSIAD-91-70............	26123–324
FR1.32/6:(date)	9365–2.14	GA1.13:GGD-91-105	26119–349	GA1.13:NSIAD-91-76............	26123–314
FR1.36:(date)	9365–2.6	GA1.13:GGD-91-107	26119–355	GA1.13:NSIAD-91-79............	26123–355
FR1.51:(nos.)	9366–1	GA1.13:GGD-91-113	26119–353	GA1.13:NSIAD-91-82............	26123–321
FR1.51:161	9366–1.161	GA1.13:GGD-91-125	26119–356	GA1.13:NSIAD-91-87FS	26123–316
FR1.56:(date)	9365–3.3	GA1.13:GGD-91-131	26119–280	GA1.13:NSIAD-91-99FS	26123–313
FR1.62:(nos.)	9366–7	GA1.13:GGD-92-2	26119–348	GA1.13:NSIAD-91-102..........	26123–337
FR1.62:394	9366–7.248	GA1.13:GGD-92-3	26119–341	GA1.13:NSIAD-91-106FS	26123–328
FR1.62:395	9366–7.249	GA1.13:GGD-92-5	26119–347	GA1.13:NSIAD-91-106FS-S..	26123–328
FR1.62:396	9366–7.250	GA1.13:GGD-92-12	26119–361	GA1.13:NSIAD-91-107..........	26123–346
FR1.62:397	9366–7.251	GA1.13:HRD-(nos.)................	26106–8	GA1.13:NSIAD-91-108..........	26123–342
FR1.62:398	9366–7.252	GA1.13:HRD-90-81................	26121–399	GA1.13:NSIAD-91-110..........	26123–319
FR1.62:399	9366–7.253	GA1.13:HRD-90-134..............	26121–392	GA1.13:NSIAD-91-113..........	26123–343
FR1.62:400	9366–7.254	GA1.13:HRD-90-167..............	26121–400	GA1.13:NSIAD-91-123..........	26123–327
FR1.62:401	9366–7.255	GA1.13:HRD-91-2..................	26121–405	GA1.13:NSIAD-91-127..........	26123–333
FR1.62:402	9366–7.256	GA1.13:HRD-91-3..................	26121–406	GA1.13:NSIAD-91-130..........	26123–338
FR1.62:403	9366–7.257	GA1.13:HRD-91-6..................	26121–393	GA1.13:NSIAD-91-132..........	26123–344
FR1.62:404	9366–7.258	GA1.13:HRD-91-9FS	26121–391	GA1.13:NSIAD-91-134FS	26123–325
FR1.62:405	9366–7.259	GA1.13:HRD-91-13................	26121–401	GA1.13:NSIAD-91-135..........	26123–329
FR1.62:406	9366–7.260	GA1.13:HRD-91-21................	26121–408	GA1.13:NSIAD-91-137..........	26123–334
FR1.62:407	9366–7.261	GA1.13:HRD-91-22................	26121–397	GA1.13:NSIAD-91-140..........	26123–350
FR1.62:408	9366–7.262	GA1.13:HRD-91-29................	26121–395	GA1.13:NSIAD-91-142..........	26123–353
FR1.62:409	9366–7.263	GA1.13:HRD-91-30................	26121–396	GA1.13:NSIAD-91-143BR	26123–322
FR1.62:410	9366–7.264	GA1.13:HRD-91-31FS	26121–403	GA1.13:NSIAD-91-150BR	26123–323
FR1.62:411	9366–7.265	GA1.13:HRD-91-33................	26121–407	GA1.13:NSIAD-91-155..........	26123–335
FR1.62:412	9366–7.266	GA1.13:HRD-91-36BR	26121–398	GA1.13:NSIAD-91-158..........	26123–347
FR1.62:413	9366–7.267	GA1.13:HRD-91-38................	26121–394	GA1.13:NSIAD-91-160..........	26123–326
FR1.62:414	9366–7.268	GA1.13:HRD-91-39................	26121–404	GA1.13:NSIAD-91-168..........	26123–330
FR1.62:415	9366–7.269	GA1.13:HRD-91-41................	26121–409	GA1.13:NSIAD-91-185..........	26123–348
FT1.1:988	9404–1	GA1.13:HRD-91-43................	26121–417	GA1.13:NSIAD-91-190..........	26123–345
FT1.1:989	9404–1	GA1.13:HRD-91-49................	26121–410	GA1.13:NSIAD-91-192..........	26123–357
FT1.2:(CT)	9406–1	GA1.13:HRD-91-50................	26121–418	GA1.13:NSIAD-91-193FS	26123–339
FTZ1.1:988	2044–30	GA1.13:HRD-91-51................	26121–402	GA1.13:NSIAD-91-195..........	26123–336
GA1.1:990................................	26104–1	GA1.13:HRD-91-52................	26121–428	GA1.13:NSIAD-91-199..........	26123–359
GA1.13:(nos.)	26125–41	GA1.13:HRD-91-56................	26121–411	GA1.13:NSIAD-91-203..........	26123–340
GA1.13:AFMD-(nos.)	26102–6	GA1.13:HRD-91-57................	26121–419	GA1.13:NSIAD-91-214..........	26123–349
GA1.13:AFMD-91-24	26111–74	GA1.13:HRD-91-58................	26121–412	GA1.13:NSIAD-91-219..........	26123–354
GA1.13:AFMD-91-39	26111–75	GA1.13:HRD-91-59................	26121–425	GA1.13:NSIAD-91-221..........	26123–352
GA1.13:AFMD-91-73	26111–76	GA1.13:HRD-91-61................	26121–414	GA1.13:NSIAD-91-224..........	26123–341
GA1.13:AFMD-91-81FS........	26111–65	GA1.13:HRD-91-62................	26121–413	GA1.13:NSIAD-91-238..........	26123–327
GA1.13:GGD-90-100	26119–314	GA1.13:HRD-91-63................	26121–415	GA1.13:NSIAD-91-239..........	26123–358
GA1.13:GGD-91-10	26119–318	GA1.13:HRD-91-64................	26121–432	GA1.13:NSIAD-91-244..........	26123–351
GA1.13:GGD-91-12	26119–315	GA1.13:HRD-91-66FS	26121–420	GA1.13:NSIAD-91-250..........	26123–360
GA1.13:GGD-91-20	26119–316	GA1.13:HRD-91-71................	26121–416	GA1.13:NSIAD-91-262..........	26123–364
GA1.13:GGD-91-21	26119–321	GA1.13:HRD-91-78................	26121–429	GA1.13:NSIAD-91-274..........	26123–365
GA1.13:GGD-91-23	26119–319	GA1.13:HRD-91-83BR	26121–426	GA1.13:NSIAD-91-278..........	26123–361
GA1.13:GGD-91-24	26119–337	GA1.13:HRD-91-85................	26121–427	GA1.13:NSIAD-92-12............	26123–366
GA1.13:GGD-91-26	26119–320	GA1.13:HRD-91-86................	26121–433	GA1.13:PART-91-1	26104–14
GA1.13:GGD-91-28	26119–317	GA1.13:HRD-91-88................	26121–430	GA1.13:PEMD-90-24	26131–79
GA1.13:GGD-91-31BR	26119–326	GA1.13:HRD-91-89FS	26121–422	GA1.13:PEMD-91-2	26131–84
GA1.13:GGD-91-36	26119–322	GA1.13:HRD-91-90................	26121–424	GA1.13:PEMD-91-9	26131–80
GA1.13:GGD-91-39	26119–323	GA1.13:HRD-91-93FS	26121–421	GA1.13:PEMD-91-12BR	26131–81
GA1.13:GGD-91-42	26119–327	GA1.13:HRD-91-95................	26121–423	GA1.13:PEMD-91-13	26131–82
GA1.13:GGD-91-47	26119–324	GA1.13:HRD-91-97................	26106–8.13	GA1.13:PEMD-91-14	26131–81
GA1.13:GGD-91-49	26119–325	GA1.13:HRD-91-105..............	26121–431	GA1.13:PEMD-91-19	26131–86
GA1.13:GGD-91-50	26119–328	GA1.13:HRD-91-106..............	26121–435	GA1.13:PEMD-91-22	26131–88
GA1.13:GGD-91-52	26119–336	GA1.13:HRD-91-112..............	26121–434	GA1.13:PEMD-91-23	26131–85
GA1.13:GGD-91-53	26119–330	GA1.13:HRD-91-148..............	26106–8.14	GA1.13:PEMD-92-1	26131–89
GA1.13:GGD-91-58BR..........	26119–331	GA1.13:HRD-92-2..................	26121–436	GA1.13:PEMD-92-3	26131–90
GA1.13:GGD-91-62FS	26119–343	GA1.13:HRD-92-9..................	26121–437	GA1.13:RCED-90-58	26113–495
GA1.13:GGD-91-63FS	26119–332	GA1.13:HRD-92-12................	26121–438	GA1.13:RCED-90-169	26113–497
GA1.13:GGD-91-64	26119–339	GA1.13:IMTEC-91-3..............	26125–43	GA1.13:RCED-90-182	26113–498
GA1.13:GGD-91-65	26119–333	GA1.13:IMTEC-91-13............	26125–41.8	GA1.13:RCED-90-186	26113–499
GA1.13:GGD-91-66	26119–329	GA1.13:IMTEC-91-19............	26125–45	GA1.13:RCED-91-2................	26113–500
GA1.13:GGD-91-67	26119–335	GA1.13:IMTEC-91-62............	26125–44	GA1.13:RCED-91-4................	26113–506
GA1.13:GGD-91-69	26119–334	GA1.13:NSIAD-91-4..............	26123–315	GA1.13:RCED-91-09	26113–507
GA1.13:GGD-91-70	26119–344	GA1.13:NSIAD-91-4S............	26123–315	GA1.13:RCED-91-12	26113–493
GA1.13:GGD-91-75	26119–340	GA1.13:NSIAD-91-20............	26123–320	GA1.13:RCED-91-14	26113–492
GA1.13:GGD-91-76	26119–311	GA1.13:NSIAD-91-23............	26123–312	GA1.13:RCED-91-19A	26113–503
GA1.13:GGD-91-77BR..........	26119–338	GA1.13:NSIAD-91-39............	26123–331	GA1.13:RCED-91-20	26113–508
GA1.13:GGD-91-81	26119–345	GA1.13:NSIAD-91-50BR	26123–317	GA1.13:RCED-91-21	26113–496

GA1.13:RCED-91-22

Index of Superintendent of Documents Numbers

GA1.13:RCED-91-22	26113–504
GA1.13:RCED-91-25	26113–494
GA1.13:RCED-91-30	26113–505
GA1.13:RCED-91-40A	26113–512.1
GA1.13:RCED-91-40B	26113–512.2
GA1.13:RCED-91-43	26113–511
GA1.13:RCED-91-44	26113–525
GA1.13:RCED-91-45	26113–501
GA1.13:RCED-91-48	26113–502
GA1.13:RCED-91-67	26113–519
GA1.13:RCED-91-68	26113–510
GA1.13:RCED-91-69	26113–513
GA1.13:RCED-91-72	26113–515
GA1.13:RCED-91-79	26113–528
GA1.13:RCED-91-83	26113–520
GA1.13:RCED-91-87	26113–521
GA1.13:RCED-91-91A	26113–527.1
GA1.13:RCED-91-91B	26113–527.2
GA1.13:RCED-91-93	26113–509
GA1.13:RCED-91-96	26113–523
GA1.13:RCED-91-98	26113–514
GA1.13:RCED-91-99	26113–526
GA1.13:RCED-91-106	26113–516
GA1.13:RCED-91-108	26113–538
GA1.13:RCED-91-113	26113–529
GA1.13:RCED-91-114	26113–517
GA1.13:RCED-91-115	26113–518
GA1.13:RCED-91-119	26113–522
GA1.13:RCED-91-121	26113–532
GA1.13:RCED-91-126	26104–21
GA1.13:RCED-91-128	26113–534
GA1.13:RCED-91-130	26113–524
GA1.13:RCED-91-135	26113–535
GA1.13:RCED-91-137	26113–533
GA1.13:RCED-91-140	26113–530
GA1.13:RCED-91-154	26113–536
GA1.13:RCED-91-156	26113–542
GA1.13:RCED-91-163	26113–531
GA1.13:RCED-91-167	26113–539
GA1.13:RCED-91-170	26113–537
GA1.13:RCED-91-187FS	26113–540
GA1.13:RCED-91-195	26113–431
GA1.13:RCED-91-198	26113–471
GA1.13:RCED-91-224BR	26113–541
GA1.13:RCED-91-247FS	26113–545
GA1.13:RCED-92-2................	26113–546
GA1.13:RCED-92-10	26113–547
GA1.13:RCED-92-19BR	26113–543
GA1.13:RCED-92-48FS	26113–544
GA1.13/9:RCED-(date)	26102–4
GA1.13/18:991........................	26104–5
GA1.16/3-2:990	26104–17
GP1.1:990	26204–1
GS1.1/3:990-2	9452–8
GS1.1/3:991	9452–8
GS1.15:989	9454–5
GS1.15/2:989	9454–10
GS12.10:990-2	9452–9
H20.7009:v.40/RR-9	4206–2.45
H20.7009:v.40/RR-10	4206–2.46
H20.7009:v.40/RR-11	4206–2.47
HE1.1/2:990-2	4002–6
HE1.1/2:991	4002–6
HE1.2:C73/4/990/v.(nos)	4004–30
HE1.2:C73/4/990/v.1	4004–30.1
HE1.2:C73/4/990/v.2	4004–30.2
HE1.2:F73	4008–115
HE1.57:region(nos.)/990	4004–3
HE1.57:1/990	4004–3.1
HE1.57:2/990	4004–3.2
HE1.57:3/990	4004–3.3
HE1.57:4/990	4004–3.4
HE1.57:5/990	4004–3.5
HE1.57:6/990	4004–3.6

HE1.57:7/990	4004–3.7
HE1.57:8/990	4004–3.8
HE1.57:9/990	4004–3.9
HE1.57:10/990	4004–3.10
HE3.1:991	4704–6
HE3.3:(v.nos.&nos.)	4742–1
HE3.3/3:990	4744–3
HE3.6/3:Ex3/990....................	4704–12
HE3.19:(nos.)	4706–1
HE3.19:104	4706–1.105
HE3.38/5:991	4744–12
HE3.71:989/region(nos.)	4744–27
HE3.71:989/region1	4744–27.1
HE3.71:989/region2................	4744–27.2
HE3.71:989/region3................	4744–27.3
HE3.71:989/region4................	4744–27.4
HE3.71:989/region5................	4744–27.5
HE3.71:989/region6................	4744–27.6
HE3.71:989/region7................	4744–27.7
HE3.71:989/region8................	4744–27.8
HE3.71:989/region9................	4744–27.9
HE3.71:989/region10..............	4744–27.10
HE3.73/2:989	4744–28
HE3.73/2:990	4744–28
HE3.77:991	4704–13
HE3.91:(yr.)	4704–14
HE20.2:D63/8/report	4048–10
HE20.23/2:990	4044–16.2
HE20.30:(v.nos.&nos.)	4042–3
HE20.3001/3:989-90	4434–16
HE20.3009:991	4434–2
HE20.3013/2-2:990/v.(nos.)...	4434–7
HE20.3013/2-2:990/v.1..........	4434–7.1
HE20.3013/2-2:990/v.2..........	4434–7.2
HE20.3033:990	4434–12
HE20.3034:(date)	4432–1
HE20.3041:990	4434–3
HE20.3041:991	4434–3
HE20.3055:981-90	4434–9
HE20.3152:M84/2/950-80/	
rev...	4478–78
HE20.3161:(v.nos.&nos.)	4472–1
HE20.3174:989	4474–13
HE20.3174:990	4474–13
HE20.3178:990	4474–29
HE20.3186:973-88	4474–35
HE20.3216:990	4474–15
HE20.3252:P94/990	4474–30
HE20.3362/2:989	4474–9
HE20.3401/3:989	4474–19
HE20.3464:990-91	4474–23
HE20.3464:990-91/supp	4474–23
HE20.3508:G94/990	4474–25
HE20.3601:990	4464–1
HE20.3602:L61	4468–4
HE20.3701/2:990....................	4474–6
HE20.4017:(nos.)	4062–2
HE20.4033:(nos.)	4062–3
HE20.4202:St2/987-88	4064–14
HE20.4202:St2/989	4064–14
HE20.4202:St2/990	4064–14
HE20.6209:1/(nos.)	4147 1
HE20.6209:1/25	4147–1.26
HE20.6209:2/(nos.)	4147–2
HE20.6209:2/109....................	4147–2.112
HE20.6209:2/111....................	4147–2.111
HE20.6209:4/(nos.)	4147–4
HE20.6209:4/28	4147–4.27
HE20.6209:5/(nos.)	4147–5
HE20.6209:5/6	4147–5.6
HE20.6209:10/175..................	4147–10.176
HE20.6209:10/177..................	4147–10.179
HE20.6209:10/178..................	4147–10.178
HE20.6209:13/104	4147–13.104

HE20.6209:13/105..................	4147–13.106
HE20.6209:16/(nos.)	4147–16
HE20.6209:16/4	4147–16.4
HE20.6209:16/5	4147–16.5
HE20.6209:20/(nos.)	4147–20
HE20.6209:20/18....................	4147–20.18
HE20.6209:21/(nos.)	4147–21
HE20.6209:21/49....................	4147–21.49
HE20.6209:24/(nos.)	4147–24
HE20.6209:24/4	4147–24.4
HE20.6209/3:(nos.)	4146–8
HE20.6209/3:188....................	4146–8.192
HE20.6209/3:190....................	4146–8.193
HE20.6209/3:191....................	4146–8.197
HE20.6209/3:192....................	4146–8.194
HE20.6209/3:194....................	4146–8.196
HE20.6209/3:195....................	4146–8.195
HE20.6209/3:196....................	4146–8.199
HE20.6209/3:197....................	4146–8.202
HE20.6209/3:198....................	4146–8.201
HE20.6209/3:199....................	4146–8.198
HE20.6209/3:200....................	4146–8.200
HE20.6209/3:201....................	4146–8.203
HE20.6209/3:202....................	4146–8.204
HE20.6209/3:203....................	4146–8.206
HE20.6209/3:204....................	4146–8.205
HE20.6209/3:205....................	4146–8.207
HE20.6209/3:206....................	4146–8.208
HE20.6209/3:207....................	4146–8.209
HE20.6209/4-3:10/1/CD	4147–10.177
HE20.6209/7:988	4147–13.107
HE20.6209/9:988	4147–13.105
HE20.6209/9:989	4147–13.108
HE20.6210:987/v.3	4144–4
HE20.6210:988/v.2/pt.A........	4144–2
HE20.6211:990	4164–1
HE20.6216/2-2:(date)	4122–1
HE20.6216/3:(date)	4122–2
HE20.6216/4:990	4124–1
HE20.6217:(v.nos.&nos.)	4142–1
HE20.6217:(v.nos.&nos.)/	
supp..	4146–5
HE20.6217:v.39/11/supp	4146–5.119
HE20.6217:v.39/12/supp	4146–5.120
HE20.6217:v.39/12/supp.2 ...	4146–5.121
HE20.6217:v.39/13	4144–7
HE20.6217:v.40/4/supp	4146–5.122
HE20.6217:v.40/8/supp	4146–5.123
HE20.6223:990	4144–11
HE20.6502:C43/2	4186–8.14
HE20.6502:C65	4186–7.10
HE20.6502:H79/4	4188–71
HE20.6502:R31/3	4188–69
HE20.6502:R31/3/991	4184–4
HE20.6502:R31/5	4188–73
HE20.6512/6:G76/2	4186–9.10
HE20.6514:(nos.)	4186–6
HE20.6514:15	4186–6.15
HE20.6517:H34	4186–8.16
HE20.6517:H81/2	4186–8.21
HE20.6517:Un4	4186–8.13
HE20.6517:7	4186–8.11
HE20.6519:C26	4186–7.8
HE20.6519:C65	4186–7.7
HE20.6617:(CT)/989	4116–6
HE20.6617:Al1b/989..............	4116–6.1
HE20.6617:Al1s/989	4116–6.2
HE20.6617:Ar4i/989	4116–6.3
HE20.6617:Ar4k/989	4116–6.4
HE20.6617:C12/989	4116–6.5
HE20.6617:C71/989	4116–6.6
HE20.6617:C76/989	4116–6.7
HE20.6617:D37/989	4116–6.8
HE20.6617:D63/989	4116–6.9

Index of Superintendent of Documents Numbers

I19.16:1406-C

Document	Number	Document	Number	Document	Number
HE20.6617:F66/989	4116–6.10	HE20.7309:990	4205–42	HE22.34:987-89/reg.6/T31/	
HE20.6617:G29/989	4116–6.11	HE20.7310:988	4204–10	pt.2	4654–14.6
HE20.6617:H31/989	4116–6.12	HE20.7310:989	4204–10	HE22.34:987-89/reg.7/Io9	4654–14.7
HE20.6617:Id1/989	4116–6.13	HE20.7315:991	4204–11	HE22.34:987-89/reg.7/M69 ..	4654–14.7
HE20.6617:Il6/989	4116–6.14	HE20.7502:C16/2	4208–33	HE22.34:987-89/reg.8/C71....	4654–14.8
HE20.6617:In2/989	4116–6.15	HE20.7511:(date)	4202–10	HE22.34:987-89/reg.9/Am3..	4654–14.9
HE20.6617:Io9/989	4116–6.16	HE20.8002:C82	4048–35	HE22.34:987-89/reg.9/C12/	
HE20.6617:K13/989	4116–6.17	HE20.8016:990	4044–13	pt.1	4654–14.9
HE20.6617:K41/989	4116–6.18	HE20.8110/2:CN/(nos.)	4506–4	HE22.34:987-89/reg.9/C12/	
HE20.6617:L93/989	4116–6.19	HE20.8110/2:CN/14	4506–4.14	pt.2	4654–14.9
HE20.6617:M28/989	4116–6.20	HE20.8116:(nos.)	4506–3	HE22.34:987-89/reg.10/All s	4654–14.10
HE20.6617:M36/989	4116–6.21	HE20.8116:183	4506–3.42	HE22.34:987-89/tech.supp	4654–14.11
HE20.6617:M38/989	4116–6.22	HE20.8116:194	4506–3.40	HE22.509:991	4654–18
HE20.6617:M58/989	4116–6.23	HE20.8116:195	4506–3.41	HE23.1002:St2/3/990	4604–8
HE20.6617:M66/989	4116–6.24	HE20.8116:196	4506–3.42	HE23.1012:989	4604–1
HE20.6617:M69i/989	4116–6.25	HE20.8116:197	4506–3.43	HE23.1115:(yrs.)	4604–12
HE20.6617:M69o/989	4116–6.26	HE20.8116:198	4506–3.44	HE23.1301:988	4604–3
HE20.6617:M76/989	4116–6.27	HE20.8116:199	4506–3.45	HE23.1301:989	4604–3
HE20.6617:N27/989	4116–6.28	HE20.8116:200	4506–3.46	HE23.1301:990	4604–3
HE20.6617:N41/989	4116–6.29	HE20.8116:201	4506–3.47	HE24.1:989/v.1,2	4694–6
HE20.6617:N42h/989	4116–6.30	HE20.8202:(CT)	4492–5	HH1.1:989	5004–10
HE20.6617:N42j/989	4116–6.31	—	4494–5	HH1.1/2:991	5002–8
HE20.6617:N42m/989	4116–6.32	HE20.8202:Al1/5	4494–10.2	HH1.1/2:991-2	5002–8
HE20.6617:N42y/989	4116–6.33	HE20.8202:D83/975-89	4494–4	HH1.2:F96/5	5188–127
HE20.6617:N81c/989	4116–6.34	HE20.8202:H81/2/990	4494–5.2	HH1.2:L46/7	5188–128
HE20.6617:N81d/989	4116–6.35	HE20.8202:H81/3	4494–5.1	HH1.2:P94/28	5008–37
HE20.6617:Oh3/989	4116–6.36	HE20.8202:H81/3/990	4494–5.4	HH1.37:989	5144–6
HE20.6617:Ok4/989	4116–6.37	HE20.8202:H81/3/990/main	4494–5.3	HH1.37:990	5144–6
HE20.6617:Or3/989	4116–6.38	HE20.8212/7:(yr.)	4492–3	HH1.79/2:(yr.)	5184–5
HE20.6617:P38/989	4116–6.39	HE20.8212/11:989	4494–8	HH1.99:(date)	5142–18
HE20.6617:R34/989	4116–6.41	HE20.8212/11:990	4494–8	HH1.99/2:(date)	5142–30
HE20.6617:So8c/989	4116–6.42	HE20.8216:101	4498–69	HH1.99/2-2:978-89	5144–21
HE20.6617:So8d/989	4116–6.43	HE20.8216:102	4498–67	HH1.99/3:(date)	5142–20
HE20.6617:T25/989	4116–6.44	HE20.8216:103	4498–70	HH1.99/4-2:(date)	5002–12
HE20.6617:T31/989	4116–6.45	HE20.8216:104	4498–71	HH1.99/8:(date)	5142–38
HE20.6617:Ut1/989	4116–6.46	HE20.8216:106	4498–73	HH2.24:(date)	5142–1
HE20.6617:V59/989	4116–6.47	HE20.8216:110	4498–74	HH2.24/2:(date)	5142–3
HE20.6617:V81/989	4116–6.48	HE20.8216:115	4498–75	HH2.24/3:(date)	5142–2
HE20.6617:W27/989	4116–6.49	HE20.8216/5:988	4494–11	HH2.24/4:987	5144–1
HE20.6617:W52v/989	4116–6.50	HE20.8216/5:989	4494–11	HH2.24/4:988	5144–1
HE20.6617:W75/989	4116–6.51	HE20.8216/5:990	4494–11	HH2.24/4:989	5144–1
HE20.6617:W99/989	4116–6.52	HE20.8217/4:(date)	4492–4	HH2.24/4:990	5144–1
HE20.7009:(v.nos.&nos.)	4202–1	HE20.8219:975-90/v.1,2	4494–4	HH2.24/7:985	5144–17
	4206–2	HE20.8220/2:3	4498–68	HH2.24/7:986	5144–17
HE20.7009:v.39/RR-14	4206–2.32	HE20.8309:(v.nos.&nos.)......	4482–1	HH2.24/7:987	5144–17
HE20.7009:v.39/RR-15	4206–2.33	HE20.8319:989	4488–15	HH2.24/7:988	5144–17
HE20.7009:v.39/RR-16	4206–2.34	HE20.9202:C43/2/990	4108–49	HH2.24/7:989	5144–17
HE20.7009:v.39/RR-17	4206–2.35	HE20.9302:D63/2/990	4118–56	HH2.24/7:990	5144–17
HE20.7009:v.39/RR-18	4206–2.36	HE20.9302:M66/3/991	4118–55	I1.1/7:990-2	5302–2
HE20.7009:v.40/RR-1	4206–2.37	HE20.9402:R26/991	4084–7	I1.1/7:991	5302–2
HE20.7009:v.40/RR-2	4206–2.38	HE20.9414:989	4084–6	I1.96/4:990	5724–10
HE20.7009:v.40/RR-3	4206–2.39	HE20.9421:991	4084–1	I1.98:(CT)	5736–1
HE20.7009:v.40/RR-4	4206–2.40	HE22.2:En2	4658–44	I1.100:990	5724–8
HE20.7009:v.40/RR-5	4206–2.41	HE22.16/2:990	4654–10	I19.1:990	5664–8
HE20.7009:v.40/RR-6	4206–2.42	HE22.18:(v.nos./nos.)	4652–1	I19.2:H62/2/v.5	5668–118.1
HE20.7009:v.40/RR-7	4206–2.43	HE22.18/2:990(supplement)..	4652–1	I19.3:1958	5668–119
HE20.7009:v.40/RR-8	4206–2.44	HE22.19/4-3:990	4654–1	I19.4/2:(nos.)	5666–21
HE20.7009:39/53	4204–1	HE22.21/2:(yr.)	4657–5	I19.4/2:930-J	5666–21.10
HE20.7009/2:(v.nos.&nos.)....	4202–7	HE22.21/2-2:(yr.)	4657–5	I19.4/2:1036	5668–116
HE20.7011/6:53	4205–2	HE22.21/3:988	4654–13	I19.4/2:1064	5668–121
HE20.7011/8:989	4205–4	HE22.26/4:8	4146–12.27	I19.4/3:989	5664–15
HE20.7011/38:(date)	4202–9	HE22.34:987-89/reg.(nos.)/		I19.4/4:990	5664–11
HE20.7102:(CT)	4246–4	(CT)	4654–14	I19.4/6:988	5664–14
HE20.7102:In2/13/v.(nos.)....	4248–92	HE22.34:987-89/reg.1/C76...	4654–14.1	I19.13:2298	5666–27.1
HE20.7102:In2/13/v.1	4248–92.1	HE22.34:987-89/reg.2/N42j..	4654–14.2	I19.13:2358	5666–27.17
HE20.7102:In2/13/v.2	4248–92.2	HE22.34:987-89/reg.2/N42y	4654–14.2	I19.13:2359-A	5666–27.18
HE20.7102:In2/13/v.3	4248–92.3	HE22.34:987-89/reg.3/D37 ..	4654–14.3	I19.13:2368-B	5666–27.20
HE20.7102:N75	4246–4.3	HE22.34:987-89/reg.3/P38....	4654–14.3	I19.13/3:988-89	5664–12
HE20.7102:P74/pts.1,2	4248–90	HE22.34:987-89/reg.5/In2	4654–14.5	I19.14:990	5664–4
HE20.7108:Oc1/3	4248–89	HE22.34:987-89/reg.5/M66 ..	4654–14.5	I19.14/4:(nos.)	5662–1
HE20.7110:(CT)	4246–1	HE22.34:987-89/reg.5/Oh3 ..	4654–14.5	I19.16:1200-US	5668–117
HE20.7110:Et3/3	4246–1.98	HE22.34:987-89/reg.6/Ar4k..	4654–14.6	I19.16:1403-E	5666–25.8
HE20.7126:990	4244–2	HE22.34:987-89/reg.6/L93....	4654–14.6	I19.16:1405-D	5666–25.10
HE20.7309:989	4205–42	HE22.34:987-89/reg.6/T31/		I19.16:1406-C	5666–25.13
		pt.1	4654–14.6		

119.16:1493

Index of Superintendent of Documents Numbers

119.16:1493	5668–122	119.53/2:NJ-90-1	5666–10.29	128.37/a:K98/990....................	5604–20.34
119.16:1515	5668–123	119.53/2:NJ-90-2	5666–10.29	128.37/a:L469/989...................	5604–15.38
119.42:(date)	5662–3	119.53/2:NM-90-1	5666–10.30	128.37/a:L629/989	5604–15.39
119.42/4:(nos.)	5666–24	119.53/2:NV-88-1....................	5666–16.27	128.37/a:L629/990...................	5604–20.36
119.42/4:87-4051	5666–27.13	119.53/2:NY-89-1....................	5666–12.31	128.37/a:L713/989	5604–15.40
119.42/4:87-4194	5666–27.9	119.53/2:OH-90-1....................	5666–10.34	128.37/a:L713/990	5604–20.37
119.42/4:87-4242	5666–28.11	119.53/2:OH-90-2....................	5666–10.34	128.37/a:M274/6/989	5604–15.41
119.42/4:88-714	5666–24.8	119.53/2:OK-89-1....................	5666–12.35	128.37/a:M313/989	5604–15.43
119.42/4:88-4111	5666–28.5	119.53/2:OR-90-1	5666–10.36	128.37/a:M313/990	5604–20.39
119.42/4:88-4114	5666–28.9	119.53/2:OR-90-2....................	5666–10.36	128.37/a:M581/989	5604–15.45
119.42/4:88-4150	5666–27.8	119.53/2:PA-89-2	5666–12.37	128.37/a:M581/990	5604–20.40
119.42/4:88-4217	5666–27.5	119.53/2:PR-90-1	5666–10.48	128.37/a:M664/2/989	5604–15.1
119.42/4:89-62	5666–27.15	119.53/2:SC-90-1	5666–10.38	128.37/a:M739/989	5604–15.46
119.42/4:89-423	5666–24.7	119.53/2:SD-90-1	5666–10.39	128.37/a:N73/988	5604–48
119.42/4:89-4033	5666–27.7	119.53/2:TN-89-1	5666–12.40	128.37/a:N532/989	5604–15.47
119.42/4:89-4035	5666–27.11	119.53/2:TN-90-1	5666–10.40	128.37/a:N532/990	5604–20.42
119.42/4:89-4054	5666–27.16	119.53/2:UT-90-1	5666–10.42	128.37/a:N638/989	5604–15.48
119.42/4:89-4098	5666–24.9	119.53/2:WA-90-1	5666–10.44	128.37/a:P329/989	5604–15.49
119.42/4:89-4102	5666–27.4	119.53/2:WV-90-1	5666–10.45	128.37/a:P566/989	5604–15.51
119.42/4:89-4105	5666–27.14	119.65/2:985	5664–13	128.37/a:P566/990	5604–20.45
119.42/4:89-4154	5666–28.8	119.76:90-163	5668–120	128.37/a:Q28/4/990	5604–20.48
119.42/4:90-4030	5664–17	119.100/3:991	5504–27	128.37/a:R182/989..................	5604–15.55
119.42/4:90-4044	5666–27.23	127.1:990	5824–1	128.37/a:Sa37/989	5604–15.56
119.42/4:90-4070	5666–27.10	127.1/4:989	5824–12	128.37/a:Sa56/989	5604–15.57
119.42/4:90-4203	5666–27.21	127.71:990-91	5824–6	128.37/a:Si34/989	5604–15.58
119.42/4:91-4019	5666–28.14	128.2:C44/2/989......................	5604–38	128.37/a:Si39/3/989	5604–15.59
119.42/4:91-4039	5664–17	128.2:M41/v.(nos.)	5608–162	128.37/a:Sl1/989	5604–15.36
119.42/4:91-4061	5668–124	128.2:M41/v.3.........................	5608–162.3	128.37/a:So16/4/990	5604–20.54
119.53/2:(nos.)	5666–10	128.2:M66/21	5614–6	128.37/a:So16/5/989	5604–15.77
—	5666–12	128.2:M66/22	5606–10.1	128.37/a:St72/2/989	5604–15.61
—	5666–16	128.2:Un3/989	5604–39	128.37/a:St72/3/989	5604–15.61
119.53/2:AL-90-1	5666–10.1	128.5:985-89	5608–168	128.37/a:St89/989	5604–15.78
119.53/2:AR-90-1	5666–10.4	128.5/2:(nos.)	5602–2	128.37/a:Su5/989	5604–15.62
119.53/2:CA-90-1	5666–10.5	128.27:9274	5608–167	128.37/a:Su7/989	5604–15.2
119.53/2:CA-90-2....................	5666–10.5	128.27:9276	5606–4.28	—	5604–16.1
119.53/2:CA-90-3....................	5666–10.5	128.27:9286	5606–4.29	128.37/a:T49/989	5604–15.65
119.53/2:CA-90-4....................	5666–10.5	128.27/2:990	5604–2	128.37/a:T53/989...................	5604–15.66
119.53/2:CA-90-5....................	5666–10.5	128.28/2:(date)	5612–1.15	128.37/a:T834/989	5604–15.67
119.53/2:CO-90-1	5666–10.6	128.28/3:990/advance	5614–5.18	128.37/a:V26/989...................	5604–15.68
119.53/2:CO-90-2....................	5666–10.6	128.29:(date)	5612–1.2	128.37/a:W83/989	5604–15.79
119.53/2:CT-90-1	5666–10.7	128.29/2:990/advance	5614–5.21	128.37/a:Z66/989	5604–15.70
119.53/2:FL-89-3A..................	5666–12.8	128.32:(date)	5612–1.31	128.37/a:Z68/989	5604–15.71
119.53/2:FL-89-4	5666–12.8	128.32/2:990/advance	5614–5.27	128.37/a2:(CT)/988	5604–17
119.53/2:FL-90-1A..................	5666–10.8	128.37:989/v.2	5604–34	128.37/a2:(CT)/989	5604–16
119.53/2:FL-90-1B	5666–10.8	128.37/a:(CT)/989	5604–15	128.37/a2:Af83/11/988	5604–17.80
119.53/2:FL-90-2A..................	5666–10.8	128.37/a:(CT)/990	5604–20	128.37/a2:Al1b/989	5604–16.2
119.53/2:FL-90-2B	5666–10.8	128.37/a:Ab84/989..................	5604–15.3	128.37/a2:Al1s/989	5604–16.3
119.53/2:FL-90-3A..................	5666–10.8	128.37/a:An87/989	5604–15.5	128.37/a2:Ar4i/989	5604–16.4
119.53/2:FL-90-3B	5666–10.8	128.37/a:As15/990..................	5604–20.6	128.37/a2:Ar4k/989	5604–16.5
119.53/2:FL-90-4	5665 10.8	128.37/a:B239/989	5604–15.7	128.37/a2:C12/989	5604–16.6
119.53/2:GA-90-1....................	5666–10.9	128.37/a:B239/990..................	5604–20.7	128.37/a2:C71/989	5604–16.7
119.53/2:HI-89-1	5666–12.10	128.37/a:B329/2/989...............	5604–15.8	128.37/a2:C76/989	5604–16.8
119.53/2:IA-90-1	5666–10.14	128.37/a:B463/990	5604–20.9	128.37/a2:D37/989	5604–16.9
119.53/2:ID-90-1	5666–10.11	128.37/a:B645/990	5604–20.10	128.37/a2:F66/989	5604–16.10
119.53/2:IL-90-1	5666–10.12	128.37/a:B788/990..................	5604–20.11	128.37/a2:G29/989	5604–16.11
119.53/2:IL-90-2......................	5666–10.12	128.37/a:C126/2/990...............	5604–20.12	128.37/a2:H31/989	5604–16.12
119.53/2:IN-90-1	5666–10.13	128.37/a:C332/989	5604–15.15	128.37/a2:Id1/989	5604–16.13
119.53/2:KS-90-1	5666–10.15	128.37/a:C579/989..................	5604–15 17	128.37/a2:Il6/989...................	5604–16.14
119.53/2:KY-90 1	5666–10.16	128.37/a:C632/989..................	5604–15.18	128.37/a2:In2/989	5604–16.15
119.53/2:LA-90-1	5666–10.17	128.37/a:C766/989..................	5604–15.57	128.37/a2:Io9/989	5604–16.16
119.53/2:MA-RI-89-1	5666–12.20	128.37/a:C793/989..................	5604–15.20	128.37/a2:K13/989.................	5604–16.17
119.53/2:MA-RI-90-1	5666–10.20	128.37/a:F333/2/990...............	5604–20.19	128.37/a2:K41/989.................	5604–16.18
119.53/2:MD-DE-90-1............	5666–10.19	128.37/a:F417/989	5604–15.23	128.37/a2:L93/989	5604–16.19
119.53/2:MD-DE-90-2............	5666–10.19	128.37/a:F673/990	5604–20.21	128.37/a2:M28/989	5604–16.20
119.53/2:ME-90-1	5666–10.18	128.37/a:G284/989	5604–15.26	128.37/a2:M36/989	5604–16.21
119.53/2:MI-90-1	5666–10.21	128.37/a:G284/990	5604–20.22	128.37/a2:M38/989	5604–16.22
119.53/2:MN-89-1	5666–12.22	128.37/a:G563/16/989	5604–15.27	128.37/a2:M58/989	5604–16.23
119.53/2:MN-89-2	5666–12.22	128.37/a:G767/989	5604–15.28	128.37/a2:M66/989	5604–16.24
119.53/2:MO-90-1	5666–10.24	128.37/a:G767/990	5604–20.25	128.37/a2:M69i/989...............	5604–16.25
119.53/2:MS-90-1	5666–10.23	128.37/a:G998/989	5604–15.29	128.37/a2:M69o/989	5604–16.26
119.53/2:MT-90-1	5666–10.25	128.37/a:In2/2/989	5604–15.76	128.37/a2:M76/989	5604–16.27
119.53/2:NC-90-1....................	5666–10.32	128.37/a:Io2/990	5604–20.29	128.37/a2:N27/989	5604–16.28
119.53/2:NE-90-1....................	5666–10.26	128.37/a:Ir6/3/989..................	5604–15.32	128.37/a2:N41/989	5604–16.29
119.53/2:NH-VT-90-1	5666–10.28	128.37/a:Ir6/5/989..................	5604–15.34	128.37/a2:N42h/989	5604–16.30

Index of Superintendent of Documents Numbers

ITC1.12:731-TA-471(final)

128.37/a2:N42j/989	5604–16.31	149.77/3:990	5504–35	172.13:990	5734–2
128.37/a2:N42m/989	5604–16.32	149.84:989	5504–12	172.14/2:988	5734–5
128.37/a2:N42y/989	5604–16.33	149.85:989	5504–19	IC1.2:M85/6/990	9484–11
128.37/a2:N81c/989	5604–16.34	149.89/2:80/(40.nos.)	5506–5	IC1.25:989/pt.(nos.)	9486–6
128.37/a2:N81d/989	5604–16.35	149.89/2:80/(40.28)	5506–5.26	IC1.25:989/pt.1	9486–6.1
128.37/a2:Oh3/989	5604–16.36	149.89/2:82/(11.nos.)	5506–8	IC1.25:989/pt.2/release1	9486–6.2
128.37/a2:Ok4/989	5604–16.37	149.89/2:82/(11.123)	5506–8.130	IC1.25:989/pt.2/release2	9486–6.3
128.37/a2:Or3/989	5604–16.38	149.89/2:82/(11.124)	5506–8.131	IC1ste.25/3-2:(date)	9482–3
128.37/a2:P38/989	5604–16.39	149.89/2:82/(11.125.)	5506–8.132	ITC1.1:990	9884–1
128.37/a2:P96r/3/989	5604–16.40	149.89/2:82/(11.126.)	5506–8.133	ITC1.9/3:990	9884–12
128.37/a2:R34/989	5604–16.41	149.89/2:85/(nos.)	5506–9	ITC1.10:(yr.)/[supp. nos.]	9886–13
128.37/a2:So8c/989	5604–16.42	149.89/2:85/(1.nos.)	5506–14	ITC1.10:991/supp.1	9886–13.1
128.37/a2:So8d/989	5604–16.43	149.89/2:85/(1.20)	5506–14.3	ITC1.10:992	9886–13.2
128.37/a2:T25/989	5604–16.44	149.89/2:85/(1.21)	5506–14.1	ITC1.10/3:986-89/prod.	9884–14
128.37/a2:T31/989	5604–16.45	149.89/2:85/(1.22)	5506–14.2	ITC1.12:(nos.)	9886–4
128.37/a2:Ut1/989	5604–16.46	149.89/2:85/(7.29)	5506–9.42	—	9886–10
128.37/a2:V59/989	5604–16.47	149.89/2:90(4)	5508–111	—	9886–14
128.37/a2:V81/989	5604–16.48	149.89/2:90(9)	5506–10.11	—	9886–15
128.37/a2:W27/989	5604–16.49	149.89/2:90(11)	5508–112	—	9886–19
128.53:(date)	5612–1.11	149.89/2:90(12)	5508–110	ITC1.12:TA-131-17,TA-503(a)-	
128.54:(date)	5612–1.16	149.89/2:90(15)	5508–113	22,332-312	9884–23
128.58/2:(date)	5612–1.17	149.92:990	5504–20	ITC1.12:22-52	9886–10.10
128.59/2:(date)	5612–1.6	149.93:991-92	5504–25	ITC1.12:303-TA-21(prelim.),	
128.61/2:(date)	5612–1.10	149.94:990	5504–23	731-TA-519(prelim.)	9886–19.76
128.63:(date)	5612–1.23	149.94/2:990	5504–24	ITC1.12:303-TA-22(prelim.),	
128.63/3:990	5614–5.5	149.99:(nos.)	5506–13	731-TA-527(prelim.)	9886–19.78
128.66:(date)	5612–1.12	149.99:5	5506–13.1	ITC1.12:332-262/addendum..	9886–4.174
128.69:(date)	5612–1.27	149.99:6	5506–13.2	ITC1.12:332-262/services	9886–4.173
128.70:(date)	5612–2.10	149.99:7	5506–13.3	ITC1.12:332-264/final	9886–4.166
128.73:(date)	5612–1.25	149.100:26,27	5506–12.1	ITC1.12:332-267/991	9886–4.170
128.75:(date)	5612–1.34	149.100:29	5506–12.2	ITC1.12:332-287	9886–4.169
128.76:(date)	5612–1.4	149.100:30	5506–12.3	ITC1.12:332-297	9886–4.168
128.77:(date)	5612–2.14	149.102:990	5504–8	ITC1.12:332-298	9886–4.171
128.78:(date)	5612–1.26	149.102:991	5504–8	ITC1.12:332-300	9886–4.167
128.80:(date)	5612–2.2	149.103:989	5504–29	ITC1.12:332-301	9886–4.177
128.82/2:(date)	5612–2.16	153.1/2:990	5724–1	ITC1.12:332-301/summ	9886–4.177
128.84:(date)	5612–1.3	153.2:Al1/8	5728–38	ITC1.12:332-302	9886–4.176
128.85:(date)	5612–1.1	153.2:Ar4/5	5726–8.4	ITC1.12:332-302/summ	9886–4.176
128.87:(date)	5612–1.13	153.2:Ar4/6/supp	5726–8.4	ITC1.12:332-303	9886–4.175
128.92:(date)	5612–1.20	153.2:C71/6	5726–7.3	ITC1.12:332-303/summ	9886–4.175
128.95:(date)	5612–2.1	153.2:F52/3	5726–7.2	ITC1.12:332-305	9886–4.172
128.96:(date)	5612–1.24	153.2:F52/4	5726–7.4	ITC1.12:332-314	9886–4.178
128.101:(date)	5612–2.12	153.2:F52/9	5726–6.1	ITC1.12:701-TA-298(final-	
128.102:(date)	5612–2.5	153.2:R24/5	5726–5.2	second remand)	9886–15.77
128.103:(date)	5612–2.3	153.2:R24/6/v.1	5726–5.5	ITC1.12:701-TA-302(final),	
128.107/2:990/advance	5614–5.24	153.2:R24/6/v.2	5726–5.5	731-TA-454(final)	9886–19.75
128.111/2:(date)	5612–2.18	153.2:R24/6/v.3	5726–5.5	ITC1.12:701-TA-305(final),	
128.112:990	5614–22	153.2:R48/3	5726–8.2	731-TA-478,480-482(final)...	9886–19.79
128.118/2:989	5614–5.2	153.2:R48/4	5726–8.1	ITC1.12:701-TA-305,306(pre-	
128.118/4:(date)	5612–2.20	153.12/2:989	5724–13	lim.),731-TA-476-482(prelim.)	
128.119/2:991	5614–20	153.39:990	5724–14		9886–19.73
128.119/3:(date)	5612–1.30	153.43:990	5724–11.3	ITC1.12:701-TA-307(prelim.)	
128.120/2:990	5614–19	153.43/2:990	5724–11.1	731-TA-498-511(prelim.)..	9886–19.74
128.120/3:990/advance	5614–5.20	153.43/3:989	5724–11.5	ITC1.12:701-TA-308(prelim.)	
128.128/2:990/advance	5614–5.23	153.43/3:990	5724–11.6	731-TA-526(prelim.)	9886–19.77
128.135/2:(date)	5612–1.33	153.43/5:990	5724–15	ITC1.12:701-TA-309(prelim.)	
128.148:991	5604–18	153.48:989	5726–5.1	731-TA-528-529(prelim.)..	9886–19.80
128.149/2:(date)	5602–4	171.1:990	5644–1	ITC1.12:701-TA-311(prelim.)	
128.151:(CT)	5608–152	172.10:989	5734–3	731-TA-532-537(prelim.)..	9886–19.81
128.151:Alls/4	5608–152.6	172.10:990	5734–3	ITC1.12:701-TA-312(prelim.)	9886–15.78
128.151:Alls/7/v.(nos.)	5608–169	172.12/2:89-0093	5736–5.8	ITC1.12:731-TA-52(final)	9886–14.311
128.151:Alls/7/v.1	5608–169.1	172.12/2:90-0019	5738–19	ITC1.12:731-TA-335(final-	
128.151:Alls/7/v.3	5608–169.2	172.12/2:90-0022	5736–5.9	court remand)	9886–14.333
128.167:989	5604–44	172.12/2:90-0023	5736–5.10	ITC1.12:731-TA-457(final)	9886–14.304
128.171:(date)	5612–2.19	172.12/2:90-0025	5738–26	ITC1.12:731-TA-458-459	
129.94:990	5544–4	172.12/2:90-0047	5734–10	(final)	9886–14.313
129.107/2:990	5544–18	172.12/2:90-0065	5736–5.11	ITC1.12:731-TA-461(final)	9886–14.309
129.108:990	5544–14	172.12/2:90-0068	5736–5.13	ITC1.12:731-TA-462(final)	9886–14.303
129.114:990	5544–12	172.12/2:90-0069	5736–5.14	ITC1.12:731-TA-464(final)	9886–14.315
149.6/7:R34	5506–11.7	172.12/2:90-0081	5736–5.15	ITC1.12:731-TA-465,466,468	
149.29/3:988	5504–1	172.12/2:91-0055	5734–10	(final)	9886–14.305
149.29/3:989	5504–1	172.12/3:90-0082	5734–6	ITC1.12:731-TA-469(final)	9886–14.328
149.29/4:990	5504–13	172.12/3-2:990	5734–4	ITC1.12:731-TA-470(final)	9886–14.330
149.69:990	5504–10	172.12/7:P11/989	5734–7	ITC1.12:731-TA-471(final)	9886–14.321

ITC1.12:731-TA-472(final)

Index of Superintendent of Documents Numbers

ITC1.12:731-TA-472(final) ...	9886-14.314	J29.2:V81.................................	6068-148
ITC1.12:731-TA-473(final) ...	9886-14.335	J29.9/2:973-88/trends	6066-3.45
ITC1.12:731-TA-474-475		J29.9/2:988	6066-3.42
(final)...................................	9886-14.329	J29.9/2:989	6066-3.44
ITC1.12:731-TA-476-479		J29.9/6:990	6064-6
(final)...................................	9886-14.324	J29.9/8:H62	6068-241
ITC1.12:731-TA-483(final)	9886-14.325	J29.11/2-2:984-86	6064-4
ITC1.12:731-TA-483,484(pre-		J29.11/2-3:988	6064-9
lim.).....................................	9886-14.302	J29.11/3:990............................	6066-25.42
ITC1.12:731-TA-485(final)	9886-14.327	J29.11/5:990	6066-25.38
ITC1.12:731-TA-485(prelim.)	9886-14.301	J29.11/6:989	6066-25.34
ITC1.12:731-TA-486-494(pre-		J29.11/7:990	6066-25.37
lim.)	9886-14.306	J29.11/8:990	6066-25.40
ITC1.12:731-TA-487-490,494		J29.11/9:987............................	6066-25.33
(final)	9886-14.336	J29.11/9:988	6066-25.39
ITC1.12:731-TA-497(final)	9886-14.332	J29.11/10:989	6066-25.35
ITC1.12:731-TA-497(prelim.)	9886-14.307	J29.11/10:990..........................	6066-25.41
ITC1.12:731-TA-512,513(pre-		J29.11/12:986	6068-242
lim.).....................................	9886-14.308	J29.11/13:985..........................	6064-33
ITC1.12:731-TA-514(prelim.)	9886-14.310	J29.11/14:988	6066-25.36
ITC1.12:731-TA-515(prelim.)	9886-14.312	J29.13:W84	6066-19.61
ITC1.12:731-TA-516(prelim.)	9886-14.316	J29.13/2:989	6066-19.62
ITC1.12:731-TA-517(prelim.)	9886-14.317	J29.13/3:989	6066-19.63
ITC1.12:731-TA-518(prelim.)	9886-14.318	J29.17:988	6064-26
ITC1.12:731-TA-520-521(pre-		J29.17:989	6064-26
lim.)	9886-14.319	J29.19:989	6064-25
ITC1.12:731-TA-522(prelim.)	9886-14.320	J29.20:986	6064-29
ITC1.12:731-TA-523(prelim.)	9886-14.322	J29.21:988/v.(nos.)..................	6068-144
ITC1.12:731-TA-524(prelim.)	9886-14.323	J29.21:988 /v.1........................	6068-144.1
ITC1.12:731-TA-525(prelim.)	9886-14.326	J29.21:988/v.2	6068-144.2
ITC1.12:731-TA-530-531(pre-		J29.21:988/v.3	6068-144.3
lim.)	9886-14.331	J29.21:988/v.4	6068-144.4
ITC1.12:731-TA-538(prelim.)	9886-14.334	J29.21:988/v.5	6068-144.5
ITC1.13:(nos.).........................	9882-2	J29.23:991	6066-3.43
ITC1.14/2:(nos.).....................	9882-1	J31.10:990	6004-2
ITC1.16/3:(date).....................	9882-8	J32.2:C43/5..............................	6064-13
ITC1.21/2:(date).....................	9882-6	J32.10:(CT)	6066-27
ITC1.24:990	9884-5	J32.10:C43/2/989	6064-5.1
ITC1.27:(date).......................	9882-13	J32.10:J98/6	6066-27.6
ITC1.29:(date).......................	9882-14	J32.10:P94...............................	6066-27.5
ITC1.30:990	9884-18	J32.10:R87	6066-27.4
ITC1.31:989-90.......................	9884-15	J32.15:987	6064-12
ITC1.32:990	9884-20	J32.15:988	6064-12
J1.1/6:990	6004-16	Ju10.1/2:990	18204-8
J1.14/7:990	6224-2	Ju10.2:Ac8	18204-16
J1.14/7-2:990/prelim	6222-1	Ju10.10:990-2	18202-2
J1.14/7-2:991	6222-1	Ju10.10:991	18202-2
J1.14/7-6:990	6224-3	Ju10.11:986-90	18204-1
J1.14/7-7:990	6224-5	Ju10.14:991	18204-3
J1.14/22:990	6224-6	Ju10.19:990	18204-7
J1.87:990	6064-18	Ju10.21:990	18204-11
J1.93:989-90	6004-17	Ju13.10:90-1	18408-45
J16.1:990	6244-2	Ju13.10:90-2	18408-46
J16.5:990	6244-3	L1.1:990...................................	6304-1
J21.2/10-2:(date/nos.)	6262-2	L1.74:991	6302-2
J21.22:(nos.)	6266-1	L1.74:991-2	6302-2
J21.22:1	6266-1.1	L1.76:989	6684-1
J23.1:990	6004-9	L1.76:990	6684-1
J24.22:990	6284-2	L1.79:(nos.)	6406-2
J24.25:990	6284-4	L1.79:91-169	6406-2.31
J26.25:(yr.)	6064-11	L1.79:91-500	6406-2.32
J27.1:989-90	6004-3	L1.84:990	6468-17
J28.2:An8/3/990	6064-32	L1.121/32:B86/991	6785-12.6
J28.3/3:Ac7/3.........................	6066-28.1	L2.2:C766/41/991	6888-34
J28.15/2-2:D84/7/990(sum-		L2.2:Su7/2	6844-7
mary)...................................	6062-3	L2.3:2358	6846-1.20
J28.15/2-2:Ur3	6066-26.6	L2.3:2383	6764-5
J28.15/2-3:(yr./nos.)	6062-3	L2.3:2386	6787-6.251
J29.1:(yr.)	6064-21	L2.3:2388	6784-20
J29.2:C26/add........................	6064-31	L2.3/3:M85..............................	6787-6.252
J29.2:C26/980-89	6064-31	L2.3/3-3:F76/2/Wash./990 ..	6787-7.1
J29.2:D84/990	6064-30	L2.3/8:991...............................	6784-9
J29.2:F33/4.............................	6068-243	L2.3/9:990................................	6884-1
J29.2:R11.................................	6068-245	L2.3/11:989	6844-1
		L2.3/12:990	6744-7

L2.3/16:991	6748-52
L2.3/20:991	6824-1
L2.6:(v.nos.&nos.)..................	6722-1
L2.38/3:(date)........................	6762-2
L2.38/3-2:(date)	6762-1
L2.41/2:(v.nos.&nos.)	6742-2
L2.41/2:2370/v.1	6744-4.1
L2.41/2:2370/v.2	6744-4.2
L2.41/2-2:991	6744-4.3
L2.41/4:(date)........................	6742-4
L2.41/9:(yr./nos.)..................	6742-22
L2.41/11:(date).......................	6742-17
L2.41/11-2:(nos.)	6742-18
L2.44:(v.nos.&nos.)	6782-1
L2.45/2:(date)........................	6782-2
L2.45/3:990	6784-12
L2.45/4:990-2.........................	6782-6
L2.45/4:991	6782-6
L2.53/2:(date)........................	6742-5
L2.60/3:(date)........................	6762-13
L2.61:(date)...........................	6762-6
L2.61/10:(date).......................	6762-5
L2.61/11:990/supp.................	6764-2
L2.70/4:(v.nos.&nos.)	6742-1
L2.79:(date)...........................	6762-7
L2.86:(nos.)	6785-5
L2.86:90-14	6785-5.1
L2.86:91-3	6785-5.2
L2.86/5:990	6785-9
L2.104/2:990	6744-16
L2.111/5:(date).......................	6742-12
L2.115:(date)..........................	6742-3
L2.117:(date)..........................	6782-5
L2.118/2:(yr.-nos.)	6742-21
L2.119:(date)..........................	6822-1
—	6822-2
L2.119/2:989	6824-4
L2.120:91-220	6744-13
L2.120:91-264	6726-1.38
L2.120:91-418	6744-14
L2.120:91-447	6726-1.39
L2.120:91-547	6726-1.40
L2.120:91-549	6726-1.41
L2.120/2:990	6726-1.37
L2.120/2-3:990	6784-17.1
L2.120/2-4:990	6784-17.2
L2.120/2-5:990	6726-1.42
L2.120/2-7:991	6764-3
L2.120/2-8:992	6726-1.43
L2.120/2-10:988-89	6824-2
L2.120/2-10:990	6824-2
L2.120/2-11:990	6844-3
L2.120/2-12:990	6726-1.36
L2.121/1:H92/991	6785-12.2
L2.121/3:P56/991	6785-12.4
L2.121/4:L72/991	6785-12.7
L2.121/5:An1/990	6785-11.2
L2.121/5:L89/990	6785-11.3
L2.121/5:Oa4/991	6785-12.2
L2.121/5:R52/991	6785-12.6
L2.121/5:Sa1/991	6785-12.5
L2.121/5:Sa5d/990	6785-11.3
L2.121/5:Sa5f/991	6785-12.2
L2.121/5:Sa5j/991	6785-12.3
L2.121/6:D43/990	6785-11.4
L2.121/9:G12/991	6785-12.5
L2.121/9:M58/990	6785-11.3
L2.121/9:Or5	6785-11.2
L2.121/10:At6/991	6785-12.3
L2.121/10:Au4/991	6785-12.4
L2.121/13:J68/990..................	6785-11.2
L2.121/14:In2/990..................	6785-11.2
L2.121/15:D27/991	6785-12.1
L2.121/18:N42/990	6785-11.2

Index of Superintendent of Documents Numbers

NCU1.21:(nos.)

L2.121/18:Sh8/990	6785–11.3	L2.122/42:C39/991	6785–3.10	L29.16:Z1/990	6366–4.24
L2.121/19:P83/990	6785–11.3	L2.122/43:B38/991	6785–3.6	L29.16:Z6/989-90	6366–4.9
L2.121/21:B65/990	6785–11.1	L2.122/43:El1/991..................	6785–3.5	L29.16:Z6/990-91	6366–4.41
L2.121/22:D48/990.................	6785–11.4	L2.122/43:N81/991................	6785–3.10	L35.2:C76/4	6608–4
L2.121/23:M66/991	6785–12.2	L2.122/43:W11/991	6785–3.8	L36.2:C76/3/991	6508–36
L2.121/24:J13/991..................	6785–12.1	L2.122/43:W63/991	6785–3.5	L36.2:W89/4/991....................	6502–1
L2.121/25:K13/991	6785–12.7	L2.122/46:N76/990	6785–3.1	L36.9:990	6504–2
L2.121/25:Sa2l/991	6785–12.3	L2.122/46:N76/991	6785–3.7	L36.12:(yr.)	6504–4
L2.121/27:Om1/990	6785–11.2	L2.122/47:B75/991	6785–3.4	L36.13:989	6504–3
L2.121/30:B45/990	6785–11.1	L2.122/47:Sp6/991	6785–3.10	L36.13:990	6504–3
L2.121/30:M58/990	6785–11.4	L2.122/47:T11/991	6785–3.5	L36.114/3:(nos.)......................	6564–1
L2.121/30:M75/991	6785–12.3	L2.122/47:Y1/991	6785–3.6	L36.114/3:90-4	6564–1.2
L2.121/30:N42/991................	6785–12.3	L2.122/49:L11/991	6785–3.9	L36.114/3:90-5........................	6564–1.1
L2.121/30:T72/990	6785–11.3	L2.122/53:V81/990	6785–3.2	L37.2:Oc1/2/991/v.(nos.)......	6406–1
L2.121/32:B86/990	6785–11.3	L2.125:991	6728–35	L37.2:Oc1/2/991/v.1	6406–1.1
L2.121/32:N42y/991	6785–12.6	L2.126:(yr.-nos.)	6742–20	L37.2:Oc1/2/991/v.2	6406–1.1
L2.121/33:C38	6785–12.7	L2.130:991	6822–3	L37.2:T68/6	6406–10.1
L2.121/35:C49/991	6785–12.5	L29.15:(nos.)..........................	6366–3	L37.12/2-2:(date)	6402–14
L2.121/35:C59/991	6785–12.7	L29.15:36	6366–3.27	L37.13:(date)..........................	6402–1
L2.121/35:T57/990	6785–11.4	L29.16:(CT)............................	6366–4	L37.20:(nos.)	6406–6
L2.121/38:P53/990	6785–11.3	L29.16:Ar3/990	6366–4.29	L37.20:91-1	6406–6.32
L2.121/38:P68/991	6785–12.2	L29.16:As4	6366–4.17	L37.20:91-2	6406–6.33
L2.121/38:Scr1/991................	6785–12.6	L29.16:Au7/989-90	6366–4.10	L37.20:91-3	6406–6.34
L2.121/39:P28/991	6785–12.6	L29.16:B41/989-90	6366–4.18	L37.20:91-4............................	6406–6.35
L2.121/40:C38	6785–11.2	L29.16:C16/990	6366–4.37	L37.22/2:91-B..........................	6406–10.2
L2.121/43:D16/990................	6785–11.3	L29.16:C19/990-91	6366–4.56	L37.210:991	6402–7
L2.121/43:H81/991	6785–12.3	L29.16:C43/990	6366–4.47	L37.212:991	6402–2
L2.121/44:Sa3/990	6785–11.2	L29.16:C44/989-90	6366–4.25	L37.212:991/rev.1	6402–2
L2.121/46:R41/991	6785–12.5	L29.16:C72/990-91	6366–4.42	L37.213:990	6404–16
L2.121/47:Se1/990	6785–11.3	L29.16:C82/990	6366–4.33	L38.10:1196	6664–4
L2.121/49:M64/991	6785–12.4	L29.16:C99	6366–4.35	L38.10:1197	6664–3
L2.121/51:D63/991	6785–12.3	L29.16:D41/989-90	6366–4.5	L38.10:1198	6664–1
L2.121/54:990	6785–1	L29.16:D71/990-91	6366–4.55	L38.10:1200	6664–5
L2.122/2:Al1s/991..................	6785–3.8	L29.16:Ec9/990	6366–4.49	L38.10/2:989	6664–2
L2.122/4:F77s/991	6785–3.9	L29.16:Egy9/990	6366–4.23	L38.13:989	6664–6
L2.122/5:Sa5b/991	6785–3.6	L29.16:El8/989-90	6366–4.11	L38.16:(date)..........................	6662–1
L2.122/5:St6/991....................	6785–3.6	L29.16:F84/990-91	6366–4.40	L38.19/2:990-2	6662–3.4
L2.122/6:C71/990	6785–3.3	L29.16:G31/989-90	6366–4.3	L38.19/2:991	6662–3.4
L2.122/9:D33/991	6785–3.9	L29.16:G35/990-91	6366–4.44	L38.19/3:990-2	6662–3.3
L2.122/9:J13/990....................	6785–3.4	L29.16:G93/990	6366–4.32	L38.19/3:991	6662–3.3
L2.122/9:M48/991	6785–3.3	L29.16:G99/990......................	6366–4.38	L38.20/2:990-2	6662–3.2
L2.122/9:N81/991	6785–3.5	L29.16:H12/989-90	6366–4.13	L38.20/2:991	6662–3.2
L2.122/10:M23/990	6785–3.2	L29.16:H75/2/989-90	6366–4.4	L38.20/3:990-2	6662–3.1
L2.122/13:P39/991	6785–3.9	L29.16:H75/989	6366–4.14	L38.20/3:991	6662–3.1
L2.122/14:L82/991	6785–3.7	L29.16:In2/2/989-90..............	6366–4.21	LC1.1:990	26404–1
L2.122/15:C32/991	6785–3.7	L29.16:In2/990-91	6366–4.48	LC1.12/2-3:991	26404–5
L2.122/15:D45/991	6785–3.8	L29.16:In8................................	6366–4.53	LC3.1:990	26404–2
L2.122/15:W29/991	6785–3.7	L29.16:Ir2/990-91	6366–4.39	LC19.16:991	26404–3
L2.122/17:L59/991	6785–3.10	L29.16:Is7/988-90	6366–4.8	LC30.27/2:991	26404–6
L2.122/18:A12/991	6785–3.6	L29.16:J27/990........................	6366–4.30	LR1.1:986	9584–1
L2.122/19:M28/990	6785–3.4	L29.16:K42/990	6366–4.46	LR1.1:987	9584–1
L2.122/21:So8/991	6785–3.3	L29.16:K84/990-91	6366–4.28	LR1.1:988	9584–1
L2.122/22:Al7/991	6785–3.8	L29.16:M57/989-90................	6366–4.19	LR1.1:989	9584–1
L2.122/22:An7/990	6785–3.1	L29.16:N38/989-90	6366–4.2	LR1.16:(nos.)	9582–2
L2.122/22:B32/991	6785–3.9	L29.16:N42z/990-91	6366–4.57	MS1.15:990................................	9494–2
L2.122/24:M54/991	6785–3.8	L29.16:N56/990-91	6366–4.54	MS1.16:991	9496–2.7
L2.122/27:G76/991	6785–3.10	L29.16:P17/989-90	6366–4.20	NAS1.2:Oz7/2/v.(nos.)	9508–37
L2.122/28:L33v/990	6785–3.1	L29.16:P43/990-91	6366–4.45	NAS1.2:Oz7/2/v.1..................	9508–37.1
L2.122/32:Al1/990	6785–3.1	L29.16:P53/989-90	6366–4.16	NAS1.2:Oz7/2/v.2..................	9508–37.2
L2.122/32:Al1/990/rev	6785–3.2	L29.16:P83/989-90	6366–4.6	NAS1.2:Sp1/52	9508–38
L2.122/32:N42y/991..............	6785–3.7	L29.16:Si6/990	6366–4.27	NAS1.15:990	9504–7
L2.122/33:As3/991	6785–3.5	L29.16:So8a/990	6366–4.43	NAS1.21:7041/(nos.)..............	9502–7
L2.122/33:F29/991	6785–3.9	L29.16:Sp1/988-90..................	6366–4.15	NAS1.30:991	9502–6
L2.122/33:J13/991..................	6785–3.9	L29.16:Sr3/990........................	6366–4.52	NAS1.30:991-2	9502–6
L2.122/33:R13/991	6785–3.7	L29.16:Sw3/989	6366–4.1	NAS1.40:(v.nos.&nos.)	9502–2
L2.122/34:N81d/991..............	6785–3.9	L29.16:Sw6/989	6366–4.36	NAS1.52:988	9504–9
L2.122/35:D33/990	6785–3.3	L29.16:T13/989	6366–4.7	NAS1.52:989-90......................	9504–9
L2.122/35:L62/991	6785–3.10	L29.16:T32/990-91	6366–4.50	NCU1.1:990	9534–1
L2.122/35:P83/991	6785–3.5	L29.16:T73/990	6366–4.31	NCU1.9/2:990	9532–6
L2.122/35:Sa5/991	6785–3.4	L29.16:T84/990-91	6366–4.51	NCU1.9/3:991	9532–6
L2.122/36:Ok4/991	6785–3.9	L29.16:Un3/2/989..................	6366–4.12	NCU1.16:991	9534–6
L2.122/36:T82/991	6785–3.7	L29.16:Ur8/990	6366–4.22	NCU1.17:990	9534–5
L2.122/37:Eu4/991	6785–3.6	L29.16:V55/989-90	6366–4.26	NCU1.18:990	9534–7
L2.122/41:So8d/991	6785–3.7	L29.16:Y9/990	6366–4.34	NCU1.21:(nos.)........................	9536–1

NCU1.21:14

Index of Superintendent of Documents Numbers

Entry	Number	Entry	Number	Entry	Number
NCU1.21:14	9536–1.6	S1.123:(CT)	7006–2	SE1.27:990	9734–5
NF2.1:990	9564–3	S1.123:Am3	7006–2.53	SE1.35/2:991	9734–4
NF3.1:990	9564–2	S1.123:Ar3/990	7006–2.7	T1.2:F49/8	8008–147
NS1.1:990	9624–6	S1.123:Au7/2/991	7006–2.38	T1.2:G74/991	8004–15
NS1.13:P96/5/978-88/adden-		S1.123:B22/990	7006–2.8	T1.2:Se2/6	8008–148
dum	9627–22	S1.123:B46/990	7006–2.42	T1.45/2:(date)	8002–6
NS1.13/5:991	9624–16	S1.123:B63/991	7006–2.52	T1.45/3:(yr.-nos.)	8002–12
NS1.18:39	9627–20	S1.123:B65/990	7006–2.16	T12.18:(v.nos.&nos.)	8402–3
NS1.22:D65/989	9627–18	S1.123:B73/990	7006–2.4	T17.1:990	8144–1
NS1.22/3:989	9627–13	S1.123:B83/991	7006–2.39	T17.28:(v.nos.&nos.)	8142–2
NS1.22/4:989	9627–7	S1.123:B95/991	7006–2.45	T22.1:989	8304–3
NS1.30/2:989	9627–17	S1.123:C14/990	7006–2.21	T22.1:990	8304–3
NS1.31:(CT)	9626–2	S1.123:C16/991	7006–2.24	T22.2:P94/7/990-97	8304–9
NS1.44:960-90	9627–30	S1.123:C43/990	7006–2.14	T22.2/15:6149	8304–24
NS1.50/2:989	9624–27	S1.123:C89/990	7006–2.5	T22.2/15:6292	8302–4
NS1.52:991	9627–35	S1.123:Ec9/991	7006–2.35	T22.2/15:6961	8304–22
OP1.1:990	9904–2	S1.123:Eg9/990	7006–2.19	T22.2/15:7302/991	8304–25
P1.1:990	9864–1	S1.123:F49/990	7006–2.1	T22.35/4:(v.nos.&nos.)	8302–2
P1.2:H62/991	9864–6	S1.123:F84/990	7006–2.13	T22.35/4a:P25/989	8304–18
P4.6:990	9864–2	S1.123:G31/3	7006–2.36	T22.35/5:987	8304–4
PM1.2:Se5/4	9844–36	S1.123:G34/990	7006–2.40	T22.35/5-2:988	8304–21
PM1.10/2:P29/990	9844–6	S1.123:G81/990	7006–2.20	T22.44/2:1299/990	8304–17
PM1.10/2-2:989	9844–4	S1.123:G86/990	7006–2.17	T22.44/2:1500	8304–8
PM1.10/3:(yr.)	9844–8	S1.123:Is7/991	7006–2.23	T28.1:990	8204–1
PM1.10/4:989	9844–31	S1.123:It1/990	7006–2.2	T28.12:(date)	8202–1
PM1.15:(nos.)	9842–1	S1.123:J27/990	7006–2.12	T34.9:986-90	8464–1
PM1.26:990	9844–20	S1.123:K84/991	7006–2.34	T63.101/2:990	8104–2.2
PM1.42:990	9844–33	S1.123:L29/991	7006–2.26	T63.101/2-2:990/app	8104–2.1
Pr40.10:990	9454–18	S1.123:L49/990	7006–2.18	T63.103/2:(date)	8002–4
Pr41.9:991	204–1	S1.123:L56/990	7006–2.6	T63.113/2:(date)	8102–3
PrEx1.2:(CT)	236–1	S1.123:M57/991	7006–2.50	T63.113/2-2:(date)	8102–4
—	236–2	S1.123:N15/991	7006–2.31	T63.113/3:990	8104–5
PrEx1.2:D84/6	236–1.4	S1.123:N35/990	7006–2.15	T63.113/3:990/supp	8104–5
PrEx1.2:D84/8	236–1.5	S1.123:N38/991	7006–2.25	T63.118/2:990-2	8102–7
PrEx1.2:D84/9	236–2.1	S1.123:N56/2/991	7006–2.32	T63.118/2:991	8102–7
PrEx1.2:D84/991	238–1	S1.123:P75/991	7006–2.37	T63.118/3:990-2	8102–5
PrEx1.2:D84/991/budget	238–2	S1.123:P83/2/990	7006–2.41	T63.118/3:991	8102–5
PrEx2.2:In3/2	104–19	S1.123:Sa6t/991	7006–2.49	T63.121:(date)	8102–6
PrEx2.8:992	104–2	S1.123:Se5/991	7006–2.46	T63.209/8-3:(date)	8242–1
PrEx2.8/8:992	104–22	S1.123:Sp1/991	7006–2.30	T63.215:(date)	8242–2
PrEx2.10/3:992	104–10	S1.123:Su2/991	7006–2.27	T70.9/2:(date)	8486–1.4
PrEx2.12/4:990	104–20	S1.123:Su7/991	7006–2.54	T70.9/3:(date)	8486–1.3
PrEx2.20:991	104–5	S1.123:Sw2/990	7006–2.43	T70.9/4:(date)	8486–1.1
PrEx2.20:991-2	104–5	S1.123:T13/991	7006–2.51	T70.9/5:(date)	8486–1.2
PrEx2.28:(nos.)	106–4	S1.123:T83/990	7006–2.11	T71.7/2:(nos.)	9442–2
PrEx2.28:20	106–4.14	S1.123:T84/991	7006–2.22	T71.17:989	8434–3
PrEx2.30:991-92	104–28	S1.123:Ug1/991	7006–2.28	T71.20:(v.nos.&nos.)	9722–3
PrEx2.31:992	104–7	S1.123:Un34a/2/991	7006–2.47	T71.21:(date)	8432–1
PrEx3.10/7-5:991	9114–4	S1.123:Un34k/990	7006–2.3	TD1.1:988	7304–1
PrEx3.11/2:(nos.)	9112–4	S1.123:Ur8/990	7006–2.10	TD1.1/3:990	7302–4
PrEx3.14:(nos.)	9112–2	S1.123:V37/990	7006–2.44	TD1.2:B85/992	7304–10
PrEx3.14/2:(nos.)	9112–1	S1.123:V55/990	7006–2.9	TD1.2:St8/2	7308–202
PrEx3.15:991	9114–2	S1.123:Z1/991	7006–2.33	TD1.40:(date)	7302–2
PrEx9.10:991	444–2	S1.123/2:991/1	7006–2.29	TD1.40/3:990(summary)	7302–2
PrEx9.11:990-991	444–1	S1.123/2:991/2	7006–2.48	TD1.46:990	7304–18
PrEx14.1:990	484–1	S1.123/2:991/3	7006–2.55	TD1.48:989	7304–19
RR1.1:990	9704–1	S1.138:990	7004–13	TD1.54:(date)	7302–11
RR1.13:(date/nos.)	9702–2	S9.14:991	7004–1	TD1.109/13:(yr.-nos.)	9612–1
S1.1/4:989	7184–1	S18 1/3:989-90	9914 1	TD1.113:988	9614–3
S1.1/8:991	7004–18	S18.2:D49/12	9918–21	TD1.113/5:987	9614–2
S1.2:In2/989	7004–22	S18.2:Ov2/945-90	9914–5	TD2.2:D83/2/989	7554–16
S1.2:In2/990	7004–22	S18.52:(nos.)	9916–1	TD2.2:T57/991	7554–39
S1.2:N16/3/991	7004–17.1	S18.52:75	9916–1.73	TD2.19:(v.nos.&nos.)	7552–3
S1.2:N16/3/991-2	7004–17.2	S18.52:76	9916–1.74	TD2.23:989/charts	7554–24
S1.2:Of2/1778-1990	7008–1	S18.52:77	9916–1.75	TD2.23:990	7554–1
S1.3/5:2/supp.3	7002–1	S18.52/3:(nos.)	9916–3	TD2.30/13:90-015	7558–110
S1.70/7:990	7004–6	S18.52/3:68	9916–3.62	TD2.46/2:(date)	7552–1
S1.70/8:989	7004–5	S18.52/3:69	9916–3.63	TD2.47:990-2	7552–12
S1.70/8:990	7004–5	SBA1.1/3:990-2	9762–5	TD2.47:991	7552–12
S1.70/9:990	7004–9	SBA1.1/3:991	9762–5	TD2.49:(date)	7552–7
S1.76/4:(date)	7002–7	SBA1.2:W84/8	9768–22	TD2.50:(date)	7552–8
S1.119/4:(nos.)	7142–3	SBA1.13/4:Op2/991	9762–4	TD2.58:991	7554–26
S1.119/5:(nos.)	7006–8	SE1.1:990	9734–2	TD2.64:991	7554–37
S1.119/5:111	7006–8.6	SE1.9:(v.nos.&nos.)	9732–2	TD2.310:988	7554–9

Index of Superintendent of Documents Numbers

Y3.T25:13/(nos.)

TD3.103:159	7604-1	TD11.20:(yr.)	7704-13	Y3.F49:1/990	13004-2
TD3.109:989	7604-2	TD11.25:990	7704-9	Y3.F76/4:1/990	10324-1
TD4.2:Av5/2/990	7508-3	TD11.29:(yr.)	7704-17	Y3.In2/10:1/989	14874-1
TD4.2:St2/2/990	7504-2	TD11.31:990	7704-10	Y3.In8/25:1/990	14424-1
TD4.2/10:990	7504-12	VA1.1:990	8604-3	Y3.In8/31:2Ac4/4	14354-1
TD4.14:990	7504-35	VA1.2:H81	8608-7	Y3.J27:1/989-90	14694-1
TD4.18:989	7504-3	VA1.2:H81/summ	8608-7	Y3.L61:1/988-89	15634-1
TD4.19:990	7504-27	VA1.2:L62/12/990	8604-1	Y3.L61:1/989-90	15634-1
TD4.20:989	7504-1	VA1.2:V64/18/991	8604-12	Y3.M33/3:1/990	14734-1
TD4.32/17-2:989	7504-29	VA1.2/11:990	8604-6	Y3.M74/2:2N91	14818-1
TD4.32/17-2:990	7504-29	VA1.22/3:991	8704-3	Y3.N21/16:1/989	15344-1
TD4.33/3:990-99	7504-42	VA1.43/5:(date)	8602-4	Y3.N88:1/990	9634-2
TD4.41:990	7504-10	VA1.46:990	8604-4	Y3.N88:10-2/992-93/v.7	9634-9
TD4.57:91-2	7504-28	VA1.46/2:991	8654-1	Y3.N88:10-5/987	9634-3
TD4.57:91-5	7504-7	VA1.55:25	8602-1	Y3.N88:15/990	9634-12
TD4.57/2:(nos.)	7506-7	VA1.55:26	8602-1	Y3.N88:25-12/988	9634-1
TD4.57/2:90-10	7506-7.39	VA1.67:(nos.)	9926-1	Y3.N88:25/3145/v.9	9634-10
TD4.57/2:90-12	7506-7.40	VA1.75:(date)	8602-6	Y3.P19/2:1/990	9664-3
TD4.57/2:91-7	7506-7.41	VA1.88:989	8604-7	Y3.P29:1/991	17204-1
TD4.57/2:991-2002	7504-6	Y1.1/3:S.pub.100-14	25944-1	Y3.P29:3/991	17204-2
TD4.57/3:989	7504-37	Y1.1/3:101-32	25922-2	Y3.P38/2:1/990	9674-1
TD4.59:(date)	7502-13	Y1.1/3:101-34/pt.1	25922-1.1	Y3.P97:1/990	11714-1
TD4.61:990	7504-38	Y1.1/3:101-34/pt.2	25922-1.2	Y3.R31/2:15/(yr.)/v.(nos.)	9722-2
TD4.65:989	7504-41	Y1.1/3:102-2	25928-9	Y3.R31/2:15/989/v.4	9722-2.1
TD4.210:(yr.-nos.)	7506-10	Y1.1/3:102-4/pt.1	25922-1.1	Y3.R31/2:15/990/v.4/pt.1	9722-2.2
TD4.210:90-12	7506-10.78	Y1.1/3:102-4/pt.2	25922-1.2	Y3.R31/2:15/990/v.4/pt.2	9722-2.3
TD4.210:90-13	7506-10.79	Y1.1/3:102-5	25922-2	Y3.R31/2:15/990-2/v.1	9722-2.4
TD4.210:90-14	7506-10.77	Y1.1/5:102-27	23844-2	Y3.R31/2:15/990-2/v.2/pt.1	9722-2.5
TD4.210:91-1	7506-10.80	Y1.1/5:102-40	25254-1	Y3.R31/2:15/990-2/v.2/pt.2	9722-2.6
TD4.210:91-2	7506-10.81	Y1.1/7:(nos.)	21942-1	Y3.R31/2:15/990-2/v.2/pt.3	9722-2.7
TD4.210:91-3	7506-10.82	Y1.1/7:101-253	21168-44	Y3.R31/2:15/990-2/v.2/pt.4	9722-2.8
TD4.210:91-4	7506-10.83	Y1.1/8:101-983	21408-120	Y3.R31/2:15/990-2/v.3	9722-2.9
TD4.210:91-5	7506-10.84	Y1.1/8:102-32	21264-2	Y3.R31/2:15/991/v.1	9722-2.10
TD4.210:91-6	7506-10.85	Y3.Ad9/8:1/990	10044-3	Y3.R31/2:15/991/v.2/pt.1	9722-2.11
TD4.210:91-7	7506-10.86	Y3.Ad9/8:2Ai2/2	10048-78	Y3.R31/2:15/991/v.2/pt.2	9722-2.12
TD4.210:91-8	7506-10.87	Y3.Ad9/8:2Ex7	10048-77	Y3.R31/2:15/991/v.2/pt.3	9722-2.13
TD4.210:91-9	7506-10.88	Y3.Ad9/8:2In8/5	10048-79	Y3.R31/2:15/991/v.2/pt.4	9722-2.14
TD4.210:91-10	7506-10.89	Y3.Ad9/8:2St2/18	10048-81	Y3.R31/2:15/991/v.3	9722-2.15
TD4.210:91-11	7506-10.90	Y3.Ad9/8:2St2/20	10048-80	Y3.Se4:1/990	9744-1
TD4.210:91-12	7506-10.91	Y3.Ad9/8:11/(v.nos.&nos.)....	10042-1	Y3.Se5:1/990	17664-1
TD4.210:91-13	7506-10.92	Y3.Ad9/8:17/991	10044-2	Y3.Se5:8G94/app.C/991	17668-1.8
TD4.210:91-14	7506-10.93	Y3.Ad9/8:18/991/v.(nos.)	10044-1	Y3.Se5:8G94/991	17668-1.8
TD4.210:91-15	7506-10.94	Y3.Ad9/8:18/991/v.1	10044-1.1	Y3.T22/2:1/990	26354-3
TD4.210:91-16	7506-10.95	Y3.Ad9/8:18/991/v.2	10044-1.2	Y3.T22/2:2Ad7/2/v.(nos.)	26358-234
TD4.810:989-2	7502-5	Y3.Ad9/12:1/991	17594-1	Y3.T22/2:2Ad7/2/v.1	26358-234.1
TD5.11:990	7404-1	Y3.Ap4/2:1/990	9084-1	Y3.T22/2:2Ag8/5	26358-239
TD5.50:989	7404-2	Y3.B27:1/990	17614-1	Y3.T22/2:2Au8/6	26358-244
TD5.50:990	7404-2	Y3.B78:1/991	10314-1	Y3.T22/2:2B43	26358-231
TD6.1:989	7744-1	Y3.C43/2:1/(yr.)	14854-1	Y3.T22/2:2B57/8	26356-9.3
TD7.2:Un3/990	7884-7	Y3.C43/5:2R34	15528-1	Y3.T22/2:2B57/9	26358-248
TD7.9:990	7884-1	Y3.C73/5:1/990	11924-2	Y3.T22/2:2B57/9/summ	26358-248
TD7.11/2:989	7884-4	Y3.C73/5:9-3/(date)	11922-5	Y3.T22/2:2C83	26358-232
TD7.18:990	7884-8	Y3.C73/5:10/(date)	11922-4.3	Y3.T22/2:2D14	26358-237
TD8.8:T51/3	7764-17	Y3.C76/3:1/989	9164-2	Y3.T22/2:2D36/3	26358-233
TD8.9/2:(date)	7762-2	Y3.El2/3:1/990	9274-1	Y3.T22/2:2D36/3/summ	26358-233
TD8.12:989	7764-1.2	Y3.El2/3:2P76/990	9274-6	Y3.T22/2:2D36/4	26358-245
TD8.12/3:989	7764-1.1	Y3.El2/3:16/990	9274-5	Y3.T22/2:2En2/13	26358-240
TD8.26:989	7764-9	Y3.Em7/3:1/15	15494-1	Y3.T22/2:2En2/14	26358-243
TD8.27:989	7764-10	Y3.Em7/3:10/(nos.)	15496-1	Y3.T22/2:2F31/3	26358-238
TD8.32:(yr.)	7764-13	Y3.Em7/3:10/89-09	15496-1.11	Y3.T22/2:2F31/3/summ	26358-238
TD9.15:989	7304-4	Y3.Em7/3:10/90-01	15496-1.12	Y3.T22/2:2G28/5	26358-230
TD10.2:B96	7888-79	Y3.Em7/3:10/90-02	15496-1.13	Y3.T22/2:2G51/2	26358-241
TD10.9/2:(date)	7302-8	Y3.Eq2:12-4/990	9244-6	Y3.T22/2:2G51/2/summ	26358-241
TD10.9/3:(date)	7302-6	Y3.Eq2:12-5/989	9244-10	Y3.T22/2:2G62	26358-235
TD10.9/4:(date)	7302-7	Y3.Ex7/3:1/990	9254-1	Y3.T22/2:2G62/summ	26358-235
TD10.12:989	7304-5	Y3.F31/8:22/990/v.(nos.)	9295-3	Y3.T22/2:2M46/15	26358-250
TD11.1:990	7704-14	Y3.F31/8:22/990/v.1	9295-3.1	Y3.T22/2:2Ou8	26358-246
TD11.10:(date)	7702-1	Y3.F31/8:22/990/v.2	9295-3.2	Y3.T22/2:2T68/7	26358-242
TD11.11:990-2	7702-2	Y3.F31/8:22/990/v.3	9295-3.3	Y3.T22/2:2Un3	26358-247
TD11.11:991	7702-2	Y3.F31/8:22/990/v.4	9295-3.4	Y3.T22/2:2W28/3	26358-236
TD11.13:988	7704-2	Y3.F31/8:22/990/v.5	9295-3.5	Y3.T25:1-3/(yrs.)	9804-19
TD11.14:990	7704-3	Y3.F31/8:22/990/v.6	9295-3.6	Y3.T25:1/990	9804-1
TD11.15:(yr.)	7704-4	Y3.F31/8:22/990/v.7	9295-3.7	Y3.T25:3-2/Y-216	9804-30
TD11.16:991	7702-3	Y3.F31/21-3:1/989	13364-1	Y3.T25:13/(nos.)	9802-1

Y3.T25:13-2/990

Index of Superintendent of Documents Numbers

Y3.T25:13-2/990	9804–14	Y4.F49:S.hrg.101-1149	25368–176	Y10.2:B85/27	26308–100
Y3.T25:30-2/989	9804–3	Y4.F49:S.hrg.101-1207	25368–174	Y10.2:F22/5/991	26306–6.160
Y3.T25:30-2/990	9804–3	Y4.F49:S.prt.101-118............	25368–169	Y10.2:G74/2	26308–99
Y3.T25:70/990	9804–5	Y4.F76/1:C83/3/991..............	21384–5	Y10.2:H34/3	26306–6.155
Y4.Ag4:P39/final/supp	23898–5	Y4.F76/1:M58/20/990	21388–58	Y10.2:H34/4	26306–6.157
Y4.Ag4:P39/pt.2	23898–6	Y4.F76/1-15:990	21384–3	Y10.2:H34/5	26306–6.159
Y4.Ag4:P39/pt.9	23898–7	Y4.F76/2:S.hrg.101-885	25388–58	Y10.2:P75/3	26306–6.156
Y4.Ag4:P39/pt.10	23898–8	Y4.F76/2:S.prt.101-106.........	25388–56	Y10.2:Sp3	26306–6.158
Y4.Ag4:S.prt.101-143..............	25248–126	Y4.G74/7:C49/9	21408–124	Y10.2:St2	26306–6.161
Y4.Ag4/2:El2/51	21148–62	Y4.G74/7:F74	21408–119	Y10.2:T67/2	26306–6.162
Y4.Ag4/2:M46/39	21148–61	Y4.G74/7:P94/20	21408–123	Y10.13:991	26304–3.1
Y4.Ag8/1:101-30/pt.8	21168–43	Y4.G74/7:St6	21408–122	Y10.17:991	26304–3.2
Y4.Ag8/1:101-60	21168–47	Y4.G74/7:T19/14	21408–125	Y10.19:992	26304–2
Y4.Ag8/1:101-68	21168–46	Y4.G74/7:T61	21408–121		
Y4.Ag8/1:101-72	21168–49	Y4.G74/9:S.hrg.101-1000	25408–112		
Y4.Ag8/1:101-73	21168–45	Y4.G74/9:S.hrg.101-1031	25408–111		
Y4.Ag8/1:101-74	21168–50	Y4.G74/9:S.hrg.101-1032	25408–113		
Y4.Ag8/3:S.hrg.101-259/pt.3	25168–75	Y4.H81/3:M66/2	21428–9		
Y4.Ag8/3:S.hrg.101-704	25168–74	Y4.H89:101-24	21968–56		
Y4.Ag8/3:S.hrg.101-966	25168–76	Y4.In2/11:S.hrg.101-774	25418–4		
Y4.Ag8/3:S.hrg.101-1052	25168–77	Y4.In2/11:S.hrg.101-1004.....	25418–6		
Y4.Ar5/2:T53/2/990	21208–34	Y4.In8/14:101-76	21448–44		
Y4.B22/1:F49/21	21248–153	Y4.J89/1:101/89	21528–81		
Y4.B22/1:In7/7/corr	21248–159	Y4.J89/1:101/108	21528–82		
Y4.B22/1:101-107	21248–143	Y4.J89/2:S.hrg.101-758.........	25528–114		
Y4.B22/1:101-111/pt.2	21248–142	Y4.J89/2:S.hrg.101-843.........	25528–115		
Y4.B22/1:101-119	21248–148	Y4.J89/2:S.hrg.101-1206	25528–117		
Y4.B22/1:101-122	21248–144	Y4.J89/2:S.hrg.101-1217.......	25548–103		
Y4.B22/1:101-127	21248–145	Y4.L11/4:S.hrg.101-838	25548–101		
Y4.B22/1:101-128	21248–149	Y4.L11/4:S.hrg.101-1051	25548–102		
Y4.B22/1:101-133	21242–1	Y4.L11/4:S.hrg.102-43	25548–104		
Y4.B22/1:101-137	21248–146	Y4.M53:101-93	21568–50		
Y4.B22/1:101-162	21248–152	Y4.N16:101-2-7	21968–55		
Y4.B22/1:101-168	21248–154	Y4.P84/10:Un3/6/991	21628–94		
Y4.B22/1:101-178	21248–155	Y4.P84/10:101-48	21628–86		
Y4.B22/1:101-180	21248–156	Y4.P84/10:101-55	21628–90		
Y4.B22/1:101-182	21248–157	Y4.P84/10:101-56	21628–87		
Y4.B22/1:102-2	21242–1	Y4.P84/10:101-67	21628–88		
Y4.B22/3:S.hrg.101-675	25418–5	Y4.P84/10:101-72	21628–89		
Y4.B22/3:S.hrg.101-868/v.2 ..	25248–120	Y4.P84/10:101-73	21628–92		
Y4.B22/3:S.hrg.101-973/v.1 ..	25248–121	Y4.P84/10:101-79	21628–96		
Y4.B22/3:S.hrg.101-973/v.2 ..	25248–122	Y4.P84/10:101-85	21628–95		
Y4.B22/3:S.hrg.101-973/v.3 ..	25248–123	Y4.P84/10:101-86	21628–93		
Y4.B22/3:S.hrg.101-1102	25248–125	Y4.P93/1:1/102-4	23874–1		
Y4.B22/3:S.hrg.102-77	25248–124	Y4.P96/10:S.hrg.101-776	25328–31		
Y4.B85/2:S.hrg.101-778	25258–24	Y4.P96/10:S.hrg.101-835	25328–32		
Y4.B85/3:P92/3/992	21268–42	Y4.P96/11:101-37	21648–59		
Y4.C73/7:S.prt.102-10...........	25268–78	Y4.P96/11:101-43	21648–60		
Y4.D63/1:101-3	21308–27	Y4.P96/11:101-54	21648–61		
Y4.Ec7:Ag8/16	23848–216	Y4.P96/11:101-60	21648–63		
Y4.Ec7:C44/11/v.(nos.)	23848–155	Y4.P96/11:101-61	21648–62		
Y4.Ec7:Ec7/(yr.-nos.)	23842–1	Y4.P96/11:101-86	21648–64		
Y4.Ec7:Em7/12/pt.(nos.)	23846–4	Y4.P98/10:101-71	21628–91		
Y4.Ec7:Em7/12/pt.36	23846–4.30	Y4.Sci2:101/0	21708–129		
Y4.Ec7:Em7/12/pt.37	23846–4.31	Y4.Sci2:102/A	21704–1		
Y4.Ec7:Em7/12/pt.38	23846–4.32	Y4.Sci2:102/E	21704–4		
Y4.Ec7:Em7/12/pt.39	23846–4.33	Y4.Sm1:101-69	21728–75		
Y4.Ec7:F31/11	23848–218	Y4.Sm1:101-73	21728–76		
Y4.Ec7:H34/10	23848–217	Y4.Sm1:101-80	21728–77		
Y4.Ec7:J27/16	23848–220	Y4.Sm1/2:S.hrg.101-635/pt.3	25728–43		
Y4.Ec7:P86/2	23848–221	Y4.Sm1/2:S.hrg.101-691	25728–42		
Y4.Ec7:S.hrg.101-1080	23848–222	Y4.T19/4:In8	21788–204		
Y4.Ec7:So8/20	23848–223	Y4.T19/4:Sa9	25368–175		
Y4.Ed8/1:101-84	21348–119	Y4.T19/4-10:992-96	21784–10		
Y4.En2:S.prt.102-34................	25318–81	Y4.W36:WMCP102-4............	21788–203		
Y4.En2/3:101-146	21368–130	Y4.W36:WMCP102-7	21788–197		
Y4.En2/3:101-184	21368–131	Y4.W36:10-4/991	21784–11		
Y4.En2/3:101-204	21368–133	Y4.W36:101-74	21788–198		
Y4.En2/3:101-209	21368–132	Y4.W36:101-83	21788–199		
Y4.F49:S.hrg.101-557/pt.2	25368–168	Y4.W36:101-84	21788–200		
Y4.F49:S.hrg.101-817	25388–57	Y4.W36:101-85	21788–201		
Y4.F49:S.hrg.101-911	25368–171	Y4.W36:101-90	21788–202		
Y4.F49:S.hrg.101-918	25368–170	Y10.2:(CT)	26306–6		
Y4.F49:S.hrg.101-1065	25368–173	Y10.2:Ai2	26306–6.153		

Guide to Selected Standard Classifications

Guide to Selected Standard Classifications
(This guide outlines the major standard classification systems used by various Federal agencies to arrange and present social and economic statistical data.)

Census Regions and Divisions	1023
Outlying Areas of the U.S.	1023
Standard Federal Administrative Regions	1023
Farm Production Regions	1023
Federal Reserve Districts	1024
Federal Home Loan Bank Districts	1024
Bureau of Labor Statistics Regions (and Regional Offices)	1024
Metropolitan Statistical Areas	1025
Consolidated Metropolitan Statistical Areas	1026
Cities with Population over 100,000	1027
Consumer Price Index Cities	1027
Standard Industrial Classification	1028
Standard Occupational Classification	1036
Standard International Trade Classification, Revision 3	1039

Census Regions and Divisions

CENSUS REGIONS SHOWING DIVISIONS INCLUDED IN EACH:

Northeast
New England, Middle Atlantic

Midwest
East North Central, West North Central

South
South Atlantic, East South Central, West South Central

West
Mountain, Pacific

CENSUS DIVISIONS SHOWING STATES INCLUDED IN EACH:

New England
Maine, New Hampshire, Vermont, Massachusetts, Rhode Island, Connecticut

Middle Atlantic
New York, New Jersey, Pennsylvania

East North Central
Ohio, Indiana, Illinois, Michigan, Wisconsin

West North Central
Minnesota, Iowa, Missouri, North Dakota, South Dakota, Nebraska, Kansas

South Atlantic
Delaware, Maryland, District of Columbia, Virginia, West Virginia, North Carolina, South Carolina, Georgia, Florida

East South Central
Kentucky, Tennessee, Alabama, Mississippi

West South Central
Arkansas, Louisiana, Oklahoma, Texas

Mountain
Montana, Idaho, Wyoming, Colorado, New Mexico, Arizona, Utah, Nevada

Pacific
Washington, Oregon, California, Alaska, Hawaii

Outlying Areas of the United States

American Samoa
Guam

Northern Mariana Islands
Puerto Rico

Trust Territory of the Pacific Islands
Virgin Islands

Standard Federal Administrative Regions

Region I
Connecticut, Maine, Massachusetts, New Hampshire, Rhode Island, and Vermont

Region II
New Jersey, New York, Puerto Rico, and the Virgin Islands

Region III
Delaware, District of Columbia, Maryland, Pennsylvania, Virginia, and West Virginia

Region IV
Alabama, Florida, Georgia, Kentucky, Mississippi, North Carolina, South Carolina, and Tennessee

Region V
Illinois, Indiana, Michigan, Minnesota, Ohio, and Wisconsin

Region VI
Arkansas, Louisiana, New Mexico, Oklahoma, and Texas

Region VII
Iowa, Kansas, Missouri, and Nebraska

Region VIII
Colorado, Montana, North Dakota, South Dakota, Utah, and Wyoming

Region IX
American Samoa, Arizona, California, Guam, Hawaii, and Nevada

Region X
Alaska, Idaho, Oregon, and Washington

Farm Production Regions

National agricultural data are frequently grouped into 10 farm production regions, covering the 48 contiguous States. Alaska, Hawaii, and Puerto Rico are each shown separately, if included.

Appalachian
Kentucky, North Carolina, Tennessee, Virginia, West Virginia

Corn Belt
Illinois, Indiana, Iowa, Missouri, Ohio

Delta States
Arkansas, Louisiana, Mississippi

Lake States
Michigan, Minnesota, Wisconsin

Mountain
Arizona, Colorado, Idaho, Montana, Nevada, New Mexico, Utah, Wyoming

Northeast
Connecticut, Delaware, Maine, Maryland, Massachusetts, New Hampshire, New Jersey, New York, Pennsylvania, Rhode Island, Vermont

Northern Plains
Kansas, Nebraska, North Dakota, South Dakota

Pacific
California, Oregon, Washington

Southeast
Alabama, Florida, Georgia, South Carolina

Southern Plains
Oklahoma, Texas

Federal Reserve Districts

District 1 (Boston)
Maine, Massachusetts, New Hampshire, Rhode Island, Vermont; most of Connecticut

District 2 (New York)
New York, Puerto Rico, Virgin Islands; portions of New Jersey; Fairfield Co., Connecticut

District 3 (Philadelphia)
Delaware; portions of New Jersey and Pennsylvania

District 4 (Cleveland)
Ohio; portions of Kentucky, Pennsylvania, West Virginia

District 5 (Richmond)
District of Columbia, Maryland, North & South Carolina, Virginia; portions of West Virginia

District 6 (Atlanta)
Alabama, Florida, Georgia; portions of Louisiana, Mississippi, Tennessee

District 7 (Chicago)
Iowa; portions of Michigan, Illinois, Indiana, Wisconsin

District 8 (St. Louis)
Arkansas; portions of Kentucky, Illinois, Indiana, Mississippi, Missouri, Tennessee

District 9 (Minneapolis)
Minnesota, Montana, North & South Dakota; portions of Michigan and Wisconsin

District 10 (Kansas City)
Colorado, Kansas, Nebraska, Oklahoma Wyoming; portions of Missouri, New Mexico

District 11 (Dallas)
Texas; portions of Louisiana, New Mexico

District 12 (San Francisco)
Alaska, Arizona, California, Guam, Hawaii, Idaho, Nevada, Oregon, Utah, Washington

---

Federal Home Loan Bank Districts

District 1 (Boston)
Connecticut, Maine, Massachusetts, New Hampshire, Rhode Island, and Vermont

District 2 (New York)
New Jersey, New York, Puerto Rico, and Virgin Islands

District 3 (Pittsburgh)
Delaware, Pennsylvania, and West Virginia

District 4 (Atlanta)
Alabama, District of Columbia, Florida, Georgia, Maryland, North Carolina, South Carolina, and Virginia

District 5 (Cincinnati)
Kentucky, Ohio, and Tennessee

District 6 (Indianapolis)
Indiana and Michigan

District 7 (Chicago)
Illinois and Wisconsin

District 8 (Des Moines)
Iowa, Minnesota, Missouri, North Dakota, and South Dakota

District 9 (Dallas)
Arkansas, Louisiana, Mississippi, New Mexico, and Texas

District 10 (Topeka)
Colorado, Kansas, Nebraska, and Oklahoma

District 11 (San Francisco)
Arizona, Nevada, and California

District 12 (Seattle)
Alaska, Hawaii, Guam, Idaho, Montana, Oregon, Utah, Washington, and Wyoming

---

Bureau of Labor Statistics Regions (And Regional Offices)

Region 1: New England (Boston)
Connecticut, Maine, Massachusetts, New Hampshire, Rhode Island, Vermont

Region 2: Middle Atlantic Region (New York)
New Jersey, New York, Puerto Rico, Virgin Islands

Region 3: Mideast Region (Philadelphia)
Delaware, District of Columbia, Maryland, Pennsylvania, Virginia, West Virginia

Region 4: Southeast Region (Atlanta)
Alabama, Florida, Georgia, Kentucky, Mississippi, North Carolina, South Carolina, Tennessee

Region 5: North Central Region (Chicago)
Illinois, Indiana, Michigan, Minnesota, Ohio, Wisconsin

Region 6: Southwest Region (Dallas)
Arkansas, Louisiana, New Mexico, Oklahoma, Texas

Region 7 and 8: Mountain-Plains Region (Kansas City)
Colorado, Iowa, Kansas, Missouri, Montana, Nebraska, North Dakota, South Dakota, Utah, Wyoming

Region 9 and 10: Pacific Region (San Francisco)
Alaska, American Samoa, Arizona, California, Guam, Hawaii, Idaho, Nevada, Oregon, Trust Territory of the Pacific Islands, Washington

Metropolitan Statistical Areas

Metropolitan Statistical Areas (MSAs) were developed to enable all Federal statistical agencies to use the same boundaries in publishing urban data.

As part of the Federal Government's July 1983 revision of its metropolitan area classification, Standard Metropolitan Statistical Areas (SMSAs) were replaced by MSAs and Primary Metropolitan Statistical Areas (PSMAs). In addition, some new areas were designated, and the titles or definitions of several areas were changed. OMB issues supplemental announcements annually to account for new data.

MSAs and PSMAs are listed below. SMSA titles in use through June 1983 are listed in ASI 1983 Annual.

Area Code	Area Title
0040	Abilene, Tex.
0060	Aguadilla, P.R.
0080	Akron, Ohio
0120	Albany, Ga.
0160	Albany-Schenectady-Troy, N.Y.
0200	Albuquerque, N. Mex.
0220	Alexandria, La.
0240	Allentown-Bethlehem-Easton, Pa.-N.J.
0275	Alton-Granite City, Ill.
0280	Altoona, Pa.
0320	Amarillo, Tex.
0360	Anaheim-Santa Ana, Calif.
0380	Anchorage, Alaska
0400	Anderson, Ind.
0405	Anderson, S.C.
0440	Ann Arbor, Mich.
0450	Anniston, Ala.
0460	Appleton-Oshkosh-Neenah, Wis.
0470	Arecibo, P.R.
0480	Asheville, N.C.
0500	Athens, Ga.
0520	Atlanta, Ga.
0560	Atlantic City, N.J.
0600	Augusta, Ga.-S.C.
0620	Aurora-Elgin, Ill.
0640	Austin, Tex.
0680	Bakersfield, Calif.
0720	Baltimore, Md.
0730	Bangor, Maine
0760	Baton Rouge, La.
0780	Battle Creek, Mich.
0840	Beaumont-Port Arthur, Tex.
0845	Beaver County, Pa.
0860	Bellingham, Wash.
0870	Benton Harbor, Mich.
0875	Bergen-Passaic, N.J.
0880	Billings, Mont.
0920	Biloxi-Gulfport, Miss.
0960	Binghamton, N.Y.
1000	Birmingham, Ala.
1010	Bismarck, N.Dak.
1020	Bloomington, Ind.
1040	Bloomington-Normal, Ill.
1080	Boise City, Idaho
1120	Boston, Mass.
1125	Boulder-Longmont, Colo.
1140	Bradenton, Fla.
1145	Brazoria, Tex.
1150	Bremerton, Wash.
1160	Bridgeport-Milford, Conn.
1170	Bristol, Conn.
1200	Brockton, Mass.
1240	Brownsville-Harlingen, Tex.
1260	Bryan-College Station, Tex.
1280	Buffalo, N.Y.
1300	Burlington, N.C.
1305	Burlington, Vt.
1310	Caguas, P.R.
1320	Canton, Ohio
1350	Casper, Wyo.
1360	Cedar Rapids, Iowa
1400	Champaign-Urbana-Rantoul, Ill.
1440	Charleston, S.C.
1480	Charleston, W.Va.
1520	Charlotte-Gastonia-Rock Hill, N.C.-S.C.
1540	Charlottesville, Va.
1560	Chattanooga, Tenn.-Ga.
1580	Cheyenne, Wyo.
1600	Chicago, Ill.
1620	Chico, Calif.
1640	Cincinnati, Ohio-Ky.-Ind.
1660	Clarksville-Hopkinsville, Tenn.-Ky.
1680	Cleveland, Ohio
1720	Colorado Springs, Colo.
1740	Columbia, Mo.
1760	Columbia, S.C.
1800	Columbus, Ga.-Ala.
1840	Columbus, Ohio
1880	Corpus Christi, Tex.
1900	Cumberland, Md.-W.Va.
1920	Dallas, Tex.
1930	Danbury, Conn.
1950	Danville, Va.
1960	Davenport-Rock Island-Moline, Iowa-Ill.
2000	Dayton-Springfield, Ohio
2020	Daytona Beach, Fla.
2040	Decatur, Ill.
2080	Denver, Colo.
2120	Des Moines, Iowa
2160	Detroit, Mich.
2180	Dothan, Ala.
2200	Dubuque, Iowa
2240	Duluth, Minn.-Wis.
2285	East St. Louis-Belleville, Ill.
2290	Eau Claire, Wis.
2320	El Paso, Tex.
2330	Elkhart-Goshen, Ind.
2335	Elmira, N.Y.
2340	Enid, Okla.
2360	Erie, Pa.
2400	Eugene-Springfield, Oreg.
2440	Evansville, Ind.-Ky.
2480	Fall River, Mass.-R.I.
2520	Fargo-Moorhead, N. Dak.-Minn.
2560	Fayetteville, N.C.
2580	Fayetteville-Springdale, Ark.
2600	Fitchburg-Leominster, Mass.
2640	Flint, Mich.
2650	Florence, Ala.
2655	Florence, S.C.
2670	Fort Collins-Loveland, Colo.
2680	Fort Lauderdale-Hollywood-Pompano Beach, Fla.
2700	Fort Myers-Cape Coral, Fla.
2710	Fort Pierce, Fla.
2720	Fort Smith, Ark.-Okla.
2750	Fort Walton Beach, Fla.
2760	Fort Wayne, Ind.
2800	Fort Worth-Arlington, Tex.
2840	Fresno, Calif.
2880	Gadsden, Ala.
2900	Gainesville, Fla.
2920	Galveston-Texas City, Tex.
2960	Gary-Hammond, Ind.
2975	Glens Falls, N.Y.
2985	Grand Forks, N.Dak.
3000	Grand Rapids, Mich.
3040	Great Falls, Mont.
3060	Greeley, Colo.
3080	Green Bay, Wis.
3120	Greensboro-Winston-Salem-High Point, N.C.
3160	Greenville-Spartanburg, S.C.
3180	Hagerstown, Md.
3200	Hamilton-Middletown, Ohio
3240	Harrisburg-Lebanon-Carlisle, Pa.
3280	Hartford, Conn.
3290	Hickory, N.C.
3320	Honolulu, Hawaii
3350	Houma-Thibodaux, La.
3360	Houston, Tex.
3400	Huntington-Ashland, W.Va.-Ky.-Ohio
3440	Huntsville, Ala.
3480	Indianapolis, Ind.
3500	Iowa City, Iowa
3520	Jackson, Mich.
3560	Jackson, Miss.
3580	Jackson, Tenn.
3600	Jacksonville, Fla.
3605	Jacksonville, N.C.
3620	Janesville-Beloit, Wis.
3640	Jersey City, N.J.
3660	Johnson City-Kingsport-Bristol, Tenn.-Va.
3680	Johnstown, Pa.
3690	Joliet, Ill.
3710	Joplin, Mo.
3720	Kalamazoo, Mich.
3740	Kankakee, Ill.
3760	Kansas City, Mo.-Kans.
3800	Kenosha, Wis.
3810	Killeen-Temple, Tex.
3840	Knoxville, Tenn.
3850	Kokomo, Ind.
3870	LaCrosse, Wis.
3880	Lafayette, La.
3920	Lafayette-West Lafayette, Ind.
3960	Lake Charles, La.
3965	Lake County, Ill.
3980	Lakeland-Winter Haven, Fla.
4000	Lancaster, Pa.
4040	Lansing-East Lansing, Mich.
4080	Laredo, Tex.
4100	Las Cruces, N. Mex.
4120	Las Vegas, Nev.
4150	Lawrence, Kans.
4160	Lawrence-Haverhill, Mass.-N.H.
4200	Lawton, Okla.
4240	Lewiston-Auburn, Maine
4280	Lexington-Fayette, Ky.
4320	Lima, Ohio
4360	Lincoln, Nebr.
4400	Little Rock-North Little Rock, Ark.
4420	Longview-Marshall, Tex.
4440	Lorain-Elyria, Ohio
4480	Los Angeles-Long Beach, Calif.
4520	Louisville, Ky.-Ind.
4560	Lowell, Mass.-N.H.
4600	Lubbock, Tex.
4640	Lynchburg, Va.
4680	Macon-Warner Robins, Ga.
4720	Madison, Wis.

Metropolitan Statistical Areas

Guide to Selected Standard Classifications

Code	Area	Code	Area	Code	Area	Code	Area
4760	Manchester, N.H.	5880	Oklahoma City, Okla.	6920	Sacramento, Calif.	8280	Tampa-St. Petersburg-Clearwater, Fla.
4800	Mansfield, Ohio	5910	Olympia, Wash.	6960	Saginaw-Bay City-Midland, Mich.	8320	Terre Haute, Ind.
4840	Mayaguez, P.R.	5920	Omaha, Nebr.-Iowa			8360	Texarkana, Tex.-Ark.
4880	McAllen-Edinburg-Mission, Tex.	5950	Orange County, N.Y.	6980	St. Cloud, Minn.	8400	Toledo, Ohio
		5960	Orlando, Fla.	7000	St. Joseph, Mo.	8440	Topeka, Kans.
4890	Medford, Oreg.	5990	Owensboro, Ky.	7040	St. Louis, Mo.-Ill.	8480	Trenton, N.J.
4900	Melbourne-Titusville-Palm Bay, Fla.	6000	Oxnard-Ventura, Calif.	7080	Salem, Oreg.	8520	Tucson, Ariz.
				7090	Salem-Gloucester, Mass.	8560	Tulsa, Okla.
4920	Memphis, Tenn.-Ark.-Miss.			7120	Salinas-Seaside-Monterey, Calif.	8600	Tuscaloosa, Ala.
5000	Miami-Hialeah, Fla.	6015	Panama City, Fla.			8640	Tyler, Tex.
5015	Middlesex-Somerset-Hunterdon, N.J.	6020	Parkersburg-Marietta, W.Va.-Ohio	7160	Salt Lake City-Ogden, Utah		
		6025	Pascagoula, Miss.	7200	San Angelo, Tex.		
5020	Middletown, Conn.	6060	Pawtucket-Woonsocket-Attleboro, R.I.-Mass.	7240	San Antonio, Tex.	8680	Utica-Rome, N.Y.
5040	Midland, Tex.			7320	San Diego, Calif.		
5080	Milwaukee, Wis.			7360	San Francisco, Calif.		
5120	Minneapolis-St. Paul, Minn.-Wis.	6080	Pensacola, Fla.	7400	San Jose, Calif.	8720	Vallejo-Fairfield-Napa, Calif.
		6120	Peoria, Ill.	7440	San Juan, P.R.	8725	Vancouver, Wash.
5160	Mobile, Ala.	6160	Philadelphia, Pa.-N.J.	7480	Santa Barbara-Santa Maria-Lompoc, Calif.	8750	Victoria, Tex.
5170	Modesto, Calif.	6200	Phoenix, Ariz.			8760	Vineland-Millville-Bridgeton, N.J.
5190	Monmouth-Ocean, N.J.	6240	Pine Bluff, Ark.	7485	Santa Cruz, Calif.	8780	Visalia-Tulare-Porterville, Calif.
5200	Monroe, La.	6280	Pittsburgh, Pa.	7490	Santa Fe, N. Mex.		
5240	Montgomery, Ala.	6320	Pittsfield, Mass.	7500	Santa Rosa-Petaluma, Calif.		
5280	Muncie, Ind.	6360	Ponce, P.R.				
5320	Muskegon, Mich.	6400	Portland, Maine	7510	Sarasota, Fla.		
		6440	Portland, Oreg.	7520	Savannah, Ga.		
5345	Naples, Fla.	6450	Portsmouth-Dover-Rochester, N.H.-Maine	7560	Scranton-Wilkes-Barre, Pa.	8800	Waco, Tex.
5350	Nashua, N.H.			7600	Seattle, Wash.	8840	Washington, D.C.-Md.-Va.
5360	Nashville, Tenn.	6460	Poughkeepsie, N.Y.	7610	Sharon, Pa.	8880	Waterbury, Conn.
5380	Nassau-Suffolk, N.Y.	6480	Providence, R.I.	7620	Sheboygan, Wis.	8920	Waterloo-Cedar Falls, Iowa
5400	New Bedford, Mass.	6520	Provo-Orem, Utah	7640	Sherman-Denison, Tex.		
5440	New Britain, Conn.	6560	Pueblo, Colo.	7680	Shreveport, La.	8940	Wausau, Wis.
5480	New Haven-Meriden, Conn.			7720	Sioux City, Iowa-Nebr.	8960	West Palm Beach-Boca Raton-Delray Beach, Fla.
		6600	Racine, Wis.	7760	Sioux Falls, S.Dak.		
5520	New London-Norwich, Conn.-R.I.	6640	Raleigh-Durham, N.C.	7800	South Bend-Mishawaka, Ind.	9000	Wheeling, W.Va.-Ohio
		6660	Rapid City, S. Dak.			9040	Wichita, Kans.
5560	New Orleans, La.	6680	Reading, Pa.	7840	Spokane, Wash.	9080	Wichita Falls, Tex.
5600	New York, N.Y.	6690	Redding, Calif.	7880	Springfield, Ill.	9140	Williamsport, Pa.
5640	Newark, N.J.	6720	Reno, Nev.	7920	Springfield, Mo.	9160	Wilmington, Del.-N.J.-Md.
5700	Niagara Falls, N.Y.	6740	Richland-Kennewick-Pasco, Wash.	8000	Springfield, Mass.	9200	Wilmington, N.C.
5720	Norfolk-Virginia Beach-Newport News, Va.			8040	Stamford, Conn.	9240	Worcester, Mass.
		6760	Richmond-Petersburg, Va.	8050	State College, Pa.		
5760	Norwalk, Conn.	6780	Riverside-San Bernardino, Calif.	8080	Steubenville-Weirton, Ohio-W. Va.	9260	Yakima, Wash.
				8120	Stockton, Calif.	9280	York, Pa.
		6800	Roanoke, Va.	8160	Syracuse, N.Y.	9320	Youngstown-Warren, Ohio
5775	Oakland, Calif.	6820	Rochester, Minn.	8200	Tacoma, Wash.		
5790	Ocala, Fla.	6840	Rochester, N.Y.	8240	Tallahassee, Fla.	9340	Yuba City, Calif.
5800	Odessa, Tex.	6880	Rockford, Ill.			9360	Yuma, Ariz.

Consolidated Metropolitan Statistical Areas

Consolidated Metropolitan Statistical Areas (CSMAs) consist of component Primary Metropolitan Statistical Areas.

As part of the Federal Government's July 1983 revision of its metropolitan area classification, the term CSMA replaced "Standard Consolidated Statistical Areas." In addition, some new areas were designated, and the titles or definitions of several areas were changed. CSMAs are listed below. Standard Consolidated Statistical Area titles in use through June 1983 are listed in ASI 1983 Annual.

Area Code	Area Title	Code	Area	Code	Area
07	Boston-Lawrence-Salem, Mass.-N.H.	34	Denver-Boulder, Colo.	77	Philadelphia-Wilmington-Trenton, Pa.-Del.-N.J.-Md.
10	Buffalo-Niagara Falls, N.Y.	35	Detroit-Ann Arbor, Mich.	78	Pittsburgh-Beaver Valley, Pa.
14	Chicago-Gary-Lake County, Ill.-Ind.-Wis.	41	Hartford-New Britain-Middletown, Conn.	79	Portland-Vancouver, Oreg.-Wash.
		42	Houston-Galveston-Brazoria, Tex.	80	Providence-Fall River, R.I.-Mass.
21	Cincinnati-Hamilton, Ohio-Ky.-Ind.	49	Los Angeles-Anaheim-Riverside, Calif.	84	San Francisco-Oakland-San Jose, Calif.
28	Cleveland-Akron-Lorain, Ohio	56	Miami-Fort Lauderdale, Fla.	87	San Juan-Caguas, P.R.
31	Dallas-Fort Worth, Tex.	63	Milwaukee-Racine, Wis.	91	Seattle-Tacoma, Wash.
		70	New York-Northern New Jersey-Long Island, N.Y.-N.J.-Conn.		

1026 ASI 1991 Annual

January-December 1991

Cities With Population Over 100,000

1990 Rank and Population

Rank	City	Population
1	New York, NY	7,322,564
2	Los Angeles, CA	3,485,398
3	Chicago, IL	2,783,726
4	Houston, TX	1,630,553
5	Philadelphia, PA	1,585,577
6	San Diego, CA	1,110,549
7	Detroit, MI	1,027,974
8	Dallas, TX	1,006,877
9	Phoenix, AZ	983,403
10	San Antonio, TX	935,933
11	San Jose, CA	782,248
12	Indianapolis, IN	741,952
13	Baltimore, MD	736,014
14	San Francisco, CA	723,959
15	Jacksonville, FL	672,971
16	Columbus, OH	632,910
17	Milwaukee, WI	628,088
18	Memphis, TN	610,337
19	Washington, DC	606,900
20	Boston, MA	574,283
21	Seattle, WA	516,259
22	El Paso, TX	515,342
23	Nashville-Davidson, TN	510,784
24	Cleveland, OH	505,616
25	New Orleans, LA	496,938
26	Denver, CO	467,610
27	Austin, TX	465,622
28	Fort Worth, TX	447,619
29	Oklahoma City, OK	444,719
30	Portland, OR	437,319
31	Kansas City, MO	435,146
32	Long Beach, CA	429,433
33	Tucson, AZ	405,390
34	St. Louis, MO	396,685
35	Charlotte, NC	395,934
36	Atlanta, GA	394,017
37	Virginia Beach, VA	393,069
38	Albuquerque, NM	384,736
39	Oakland, CA	372,242
40	Pittsburgh, PA	369,879
41	Sacramento, CA	369,365
42	Minneapolis, MN	368,383
43	Tulsa, OK	367,302
44	Honolulu, HI	365,272
45	Cincinnati, OH	364,040
46	Miami, FL	358,548
47	Fresno, CA	354,202
48	Omaha, NE	335,795
49	Toledo, OH	332,943
50	Buffalo, NY	328,123
51	Wichita, KS	304,011
52	Santa Ana, CA	293,742
53	Mesa, AZ	288,091
54	Colorado Springs, CO	281,140
55	Tampa, FL	280,015
56	Newark, NJ	275,221
57	St. Paul, MN	272,235
58	Louisville, KY	269,063
59	Anaheim, CA	266,406
60	Birmingham, AL	265,968
61	Arlington, TX	261,721
62	Norfolk, VA	261,229
63	Las Vegas, NV	258,295
64	Corpus Christi, TX	257,453
65	St. Petersburg, FL	238,629
66	Rochester, NY	231,636
67	Jersey City, NJ	228,537
68	Riverside, CA	226,505
69	Anchorage, AK	226,338
70	Lexington-Fayette, KY	225,366
71	Akron, OH	223,019
72	Aurora, CO	222,103
73	Baton Rouge, LA	219,531
74	Stockton, CA	210,943
75	Raleigh, NC	207,951
76	Richmond, VA	203,056
77	Shreveport, LA	198,525
78	Jackson, MS	196,637
79	Mobile, AL	196,278
80	Des Moines, IA	193,187
81	Lincoln, NE	191,972
82	Madison, WI	191,262
83	Grand Rapids, MI	189,126
84	Yonkers, NY	188,082
85	Hialeah, FL	188,004
86	Montgomery, AL	187,106
87	Lubbock, TX	186,206
88	Greensboro, NC	183,521
89	Dayton, OH	182,044
90	Huntington Beach, CA	181,519
91	Garland, TX	180,650
92	Glendale, CA	180,038
93	Columbus, GA	179,278
94	Spokane, WA	177,196
95	Tacoma, WA	176,664
96	Little Rock, AR	175,795
97	Bakersfield, CA	174,820
98	Fremont, CA	173,339
99	Fort Wayne, IN	173,072
100	Newport News, VA	170,045
101	Worcester, MA	169,759
102	Knoxville, TN	165,121
103	Modesto, CA	164,730
104	Orlando, FL	164,693
105	San Bernardino, CA	164,164
106	Syracuse, NY	163,860
107	Providence, RI	160,728
108	Salt Lake City, UT	159,936
109	Huntsville, AL	159,789
110	Amarillo, TX	157,615
111	Springfield, MA	156,983
112	Irving, TX	155,037
113	Chattanooga, TN	152,466
114	Chesapeake, VA	151,976
115	Kansas City, KS	149,767
116	Fort Lauderdale, FL	149,377
117	Glendale, AZ	148,134
118	Warren, MI	144,864
119	Winston-Salem, NC	143,485
120	Garden Grove, CA	143,050
121	Oxnard, CA	142,216
122	Tempe, AZ	141,865
123	Bridgeport, CT	141,686
124	Paterson, NJ	140,891
125	Flint, MI	140,761
126	Springfield, MO	140,494
127	Hartford, CT	139,739
128	Rockford, IL	139,426
129	Savannah, GA	137,560
130	Durham, NC	136,611
131	Chula Vista, CA	135,163
132	Reno, NV	133,850
133	Hampton, VA	133,793
134	Ontario, CA	133,179
135	Torrance, CA	133,107
136	Pomona, CA	131,723
137	Pasadena, CA	131,591
138	New Haven, CT	130,474
139	Scottsdale, AZ	130,069
140	Plano, TX	128,713
141	Oceanside, CA	128,398
142	Lansing, MI	127,321
143	Lakewood, CO	126,481
144	Evansville, IN	126,272
145	Boise, ID	125,738
146	Tallahassee, FL	124,773
147	Laredo, TX	122,899
148	Hollywood, FL	121,697
149	Topeka, KS	119,883
150	Pasadena, TX	119,363
151	Moreno Valley, CA	118,779
152	Sterling Heights, MI	117,810
153	Sunnyvale, CA	117,229
154	Gary, IN	116,646
155	Beaumont, TX	114,323
156	Fullerton, CA	114,144
157	Peoria, IL	113,504
158	Santa Rosa, CA	113,313
159	Eugene, OR	112,669
160	Independence, MO	112,301
161	Overland Park, KS	111,790
162	Hayward, CA	111,498
163	Concord, CA	111,348
164	Alexandria, VA	111,183
165	Orange, CA	110,658
166	Santa Clarita, CA	110,642
167	Irvine, CA	110,330
168	Elizabeth, NJ	110,002
169	Inglewood, CA	109,602
170	Ann Arbor, MI	109,592
171	Vallejo, CA	109,199
172	Waterbury, CT	108,961
173	Salinas, CA	108,777
174	Cedar Rapids, IA	108,751
175	Erie, PA	108,718
176	Escondido, CA	108,635
177	Stamford, CT	108,056
178	Salem, OR	107,786
179	Abilene, TX	106,654
180	Macon, GA	106,612
181	El Monte, CA	106,209
182	South Bend, IN	105,511
183	Springfield, IL	105,227
184	Allentown, PA	105,090
185	Thousand Oaks, CA	104,352
186	Portsmouth, VA	103,907
187	Waco, TX	103,590
188	Lowell, MA	103,439
189	Berkeley, CA	102,724
190	Mesquite, TX	101,484
191	Rancho Cucamonga, CA	101,409
192	Albany, NY	101,082
193	Livonia, MI	100,850
194	Sioux Falls, SD	100,814
195	Simi Valley, CA	100,217

Consumer Price Index Cities

Consumer Price Index data are collected for the following Metropolitan Statistical Areas:

Anchorage, AK
Atlanta, GA
Baltimore, MD
Boston-Lawrence-Salem, MA-NH
Buffalo-Niagara Falls, NY
Chicago-Gary-Lake County, IL-IN-WI
Cincinnati-Hamilton, OH-KY-IN
Cleveland-Akron-Lorain, OH
Dallas-Fort Worth, TX
Denver-Boulder, CO
Detroit-Ann Arbor, MI
Honolulu, HI
Houston-Galveston-Brazoria, TX
Kansas City, MO-KS
Los Angeles-Anaheim-Riverside, CA
Miami-Fort Lauderdale, FL
Milwaukee, WI
Minneapolis-St. Paul, MN-WI
New Orleans, LA
N.Y. Northern N.J.-Long Island, NY-NJ-CT
Phi.-Wilmington-Trenton, PA-NJ-DE-MD
Pittsburgh-Beaver Valley, PA
Portland-Vancouver, OR-WA
St. Louis-East St. Louis, MO-IL
San Diego, CA
San Francisco-Oakland-San Jose, CA
Seattle-Tacoma, WA
Tampa-St. Petersburg-Clearwater, FL
Washington, DC-MD-VA

Standard Industrial Classification

The Standard Industrial Classification (SIC) was developed to classify industrial establishments by the type of activity in which they are engaged, for the purpose of promoting uniformity and comparability of statistical data collected by Federal and State agencies, trade associations, and others. The classification system is at 4 levels: industry divisions, major groups, groups, and individual industries—represented by 1- to 4-digit codes. The following list is taken from the 1987 *Standard Industrial Classification Manual*, which revises the 1972 edition and 1977 supplement. For description of the 1987 Manual, see 108-4 in ASI 1987 Annual.

Group and Industry Code

AGRICULTURE, FORESTRY, AND FISHING

- **01 AGRICULTURAL PRODUCTION—CROPS**
- **011 Cash Grains**
  - 0111 Wheat
  - 0112 Rice
  - 0115 Corn
  - 0116 Soybeans
  - 0119 Cash grains, nec
- **013 Field Crops, Except Cash Grains**
  - 0131 Cotton
  - 0132 Tobacco
  - 0133 Sugarcane and sugar beets
  - 0134 Irish potatoes
  - 0139 Field crops, except cash grains, nec
- **016 Vegetables and Melons**
  - 0161 Vegetables and melons
- **017 Fruits and Tree Nuts**
  - 0171 Berry crops
  - 0172 Grapes
  - 0173 Tree nuts
  - 0174 Citrus fruits
  - 0175 Deciduous tree fruits
  - 0179 Fruits and tree nuts, nec
- **018 Horticultural Specialties**
  - 0181 Ornamental nursery products
  - 0182 Food crops grown under cover
- **019 General Farms, Primarily Crop**
  - 0191 General farms, primarily crop
- **02 AGRICULTURAL PRODUCTION—LIVESTOCK**
- **021 Livestock, Except Dairy and Poultry**
  - 0211 Beef cattle feedlots
  - 0212 Beef cattle, except feedlots
  - 0213 Hogs
  - 0214 Sheep and goats
  - 0219 General livestock, nec
- **024 Dairy Farms**
  - 0241 Dairy farms
- **025 Poultry and Eggs**
  - 0251 Broiler, fryer, and roaster chickens
  - 0252 Chicken eggs
  - 0253 Turkeys and turkey eggs
  - 0254 Poultry hatcheries
  - 0259 Poultry and eggs, nec
- **027 Animal Specialties**
  - 0271 Fur-bearing animals and rabbits
  - 0272 Horses and other equines
  - 0273 Animal aquaculture
  - 0279 Animal specialties, nec
- **029 General Farms, Primarily Animal**
  - 0291 General farms, primarily animal

- **07 AGRICULTURAL SERVICES**
- **071 Soil Preparation Services**
  - 0711 Soil preparation services
- **072 Crop Services**
  - 0721 Crop planting and protecting
  - 0722 Crop harvesting
  - 0723 Crop preparation services for market
  - 0724 Cotton ginning
- **074 Veterinary Services**
  - 0741 Veterinary services for livestock
  - 0742 Veterinary services, specialties
- **075 Animal Services, Except Veterinary**
  - 0751 Livestock services, exc. veterinary
  - 0752 Animal specialty services
- **076 Farm Labor and Management Services**
  - 0761 Farm labor contractors
  - 0762 Farm management services
- **078 Landscape and Horticultural Services**
  - 0781 Landscape counseling and planning
  - 0782 Lawn and garden services
  - 0783 Ornamental shrub and tree services
- **08 FORESTRY**
- **081 Timber Tracts**
  - 0811 Timber tracts
- **083 Forest Products**
  - 0831 Forest products
- **085 Forestry Services**
  - 0851 Forestry services
- **09 FISHING, HUNTING, AND TRAPPING**
- **091 Commercial Fishing**
  - 0912 Finfish
  - 0913 Shellfish
  - 0919 Miscellaneous marine products
- **092 Fish Hatcheries and Preserves**
  - 0921 Fish hatcheries and preserves
- **097 Hunting, Trapping, Game Propagation**
  - 0971 Hunting, trapping, game propagation

MINING

- **10 METAL MINING**
- **101 Iron Ores**
  - 1011 Iron ores
- **102 Copper Ores**
  - 1021 Copper ores
- **103 Lead and Zinc Ores**
  - 1031 Lead and zinc ores
- **104 Gold and Silver Ores**
  - 1041 Gold ores
  - 1044 Silver ores
- **106 Ferroalloy Ores, Except Vanadium**
  - 1061 Ferroalloy ores, except vanadium
- **108 Metal Mining Services**
  - 1081 Metal mining services
- **109 Miscellaneous Metal Ores**
  - 1094 Uranium-radium-vanadium ores
  - 1099 Metal ores, nec
- **12 COAL MINING**
- **122 Bituminous Coal and Lignite Mining**
  - 1221 Bituminous coal and lignite—surface
  - 1222 Bituminous coal—underground
- **123 Anthracite Mining**
  - 1231 Anthracite mining
- **124 Coal Mining Services**
  - 1241 Coal mining services
- **13 OIL AND GAS EXTRACTION**
- **131 Crude Petroleum and Natural Gas**
  - 1311 Crude petroleum and natural gas
- **132 Natural Gas Liquids**
  - 1321 Natural gas liquids
- **138 Oil and Gas Field Services**
  - 1381 Drilling oil and gas wells
  - 1382 Oil and gas exploration services
  - 1389 Oil and gas field services, nec
- **14 NONMETALLIC MINERALS, EXCEPT FUELS**
- **141 Dimension Stone**
  - 1411 Dimension stone
- **142 Crushed and Broken Stone**
  - 1422 Crushed and broken limestone
  - 1423 Crushed and broken granite
  - 1429 Crushed and broken stone, nec
- **144 Sand and Gravel**
  - 1442 Construction sand and gravel
  - 1446 Industrial sand
- **145 Clay, Ceramic, & Refractory Minerals**
  - 1455 Kaolin and ball clay
  - 1459 Clay and related minerals, nec
- **147 Chemical and Fertilizer Minerals**
  - 1474 Potash, soda, and borate minerals
  - 1475 Phosphate rock
  - 1479 Chemical and fertilizer mining, nec
- **148 Nonmetallic Minerals Services**
  - 1481 Nonmetallic minerals services
- **149 Miscellaneous Nonmetallic Minerals**
  - 1499 Miscellaneous nonmetallic minerals

CONSTRUCTION

- **15 GENERAL BUILDING CONTRACTORS**
- **152 Residential Building Construction**
  - 1521 Single-family housing construction
  - 1522 Residential construction, nec
- **153 Operative Builders**
  - 1531 Operative builders
- **154 Nonresidential Building Construction**
  - 1541 Industrial buildings and warehouses
  - 1542 Nonresidential construction, nec
- **16 HEAVY CONSTRUCTION, EX. BUILDING**
- **161 Highway and Street Construction**
  - 1611 Highway and street construction

Guide to Selected Standard Classifications

Standard Industrial Classification

162 Heavy Construction, Except Highway
1622 Bridge, tunnel, & elevated highway
1623 Water, sewer, and utility lines
1629 Heavy construction, nec

17 SPECIAL TRADE CONTRACTORS

171 Plumbing, Heating, Air-Conditioning
1711 Plumbing, heating, air-conditioning

172 Painting and Paper Hanging
1721 Painting and paper hanging

173 Electrical Work
1731 Electrical work

174 Masonry, Stonework, and Plastering
1741 Masonry and other stonework
1742 Plastering, drywall, and insulation
1743 Terrazzo, tile, marble, mosaic work

175 Carpentry and Floor Work
1751 Carpentry work
1752 Floor laying and floor work, nec

176 Roofing, Siding, and Sheet Metal Work
1761 Roofing, siding, and sheet metal work

177 Concrete Work
1771 Concrete work

178 Water Well Drilling
1781 Water well drilling

179 Misc. Special Trade Contractors
1791 Structural steel erection
1793 Glass and glazing work
1794 Excavation work
1795 Wrecking and demolition work
1796 Installing building equipment, nec
1799 Special trade contractors, nec

MANUFACTURING

20 FOOD AND KINDRED PRODUCTS

201 Meat Products
2011 Meat packing plants
2013 Sausages and other prepared meats
2015 Poultry slaughtering and processing

202 Dairy Products
2021 Creamery butter
2022 Cheese, natural and processed
2023 Dry, condensed, evaporated products
2024 Ice cream and frozen desserts
2026 Fluid milk

203 Preserved Fruits and Vegetables
2032 Canned specialties
2033 Canned fruits and vegetables
2034 Dehydrated fruits, vegetables, soups
2035 Pickles, sauces, and salad dressings
2037 Frozen fruits and vegetables
2038 Frozen specialties, nec

204 Grain Mill Products
2041 Flour and other grain mill products
2043 Cereal breakfast foods
2044 Rice milling
2045 Prepared flour mixes and doughs
2046 Wet corn milling
2047 Dog and cat food
2048 Prepared feeds, nec

205 Bakery Products
2051 Bread, cake, and related products
2052 Cookies and crackers
2053 Frozen bakery products, except bread

206 Sugar and Confectionery Products
2061 Raw cane sugar
2062 Cane sugar refining
2063 Beet sugar
2064 Candy & other confectionery products

2066 Chocolate and cocoa products
2067 Chewing gum
2068 Salted and roasted nuts and seeds

207 Fats and Oils
2074 Cottonseed oil mills
2075 Soybean oil mills
2076 Vegetable oil mills, nec
2077 Animal and marine fats and oils
2079 Edible fats and oils, nec

208 Beverages
2082 Malt beverages
2083 Malt
2084 Wines, brandy, and brandy spirits
2085 Distilled and blended liquors
2086 Bottled and canned soft drinks
2087 Flavoring extracts and syrups, nec

209 Misc. Food and Kindred Products
2091 Canned and cured fish and seafoods
2092 Fresh or frozen prepared fish
2095 Roasted coffee
2096 Potato chips and similar snacks
2097 Manufactured ice
2098 Macaroni and spaghetti
2099 Food preparations, nec

21 TOBACCO PRODUCTS

211 Cigarettes
2111 Cigarettes

212 Cigars
2121 Cigars

213 Chewing and Smoking Tobacco
2131 Chewing and smoking tobacco

214 Tobacco Stemming and Redrying
2141 Tobacco stemming and redrying

22 TEXTILE MILL PRODUCTS

221 Broadwoven Fabric Mills, Cotton
2211 Broadwoven fabric mills, cotton

222 Broadwoven Fabric Mills, Manmade
2221 Broadwoven fabric mills, manmade

223 Broadwoven Fabric Mills, Wool
2231 Broadwoven fabric mills, wool

224 Narrow Fabric Mills
2241 Narrow fabric mills

225 Knitting Mills
2251 Women's hosiery, except socks
2252 Hosiery, nec
2253 Knit outerwear mills
2254 Knit underwear mills
2257 Weft knit fabric mills
2258 Lace & warp knit fabric mills
2259 Knitting mills, nec

226 Textile Finishing, Except Wool
2261 Finishing plants, cotton
2262 Finishing plants, manmade
2269 Finishing plants, nec

227 Carpets and Rugs
2273 Carpets and rugs

228 Yarn and Thread Mills
2281 Yarn spinning mills
2282 Throwing and winding mills
2284 Thread mills

229 Miscellaneous Textile Goods
2295 Coated fabrics, not rubberized
2296 Tire cord and fabrics
2297 Nonwoven fabrics
2298 Cordage and twine
2299 Textile goods, nec

23 APPAREL AND OTHER TEXTILE PRODUCTS

231 Men's and Boys' Suits and Coats
2311 Men's and boys' suits and coats

232 Men's and Boys' Furnishings
2321 Men's and boys' shirts
2322 Men's & boys' underwear & nightwear
2323 Men's and boys' neckwear
2325 Men's and boys' trousers and slacks
2326 Men's and boys' work clothing
2329 Men's and boys' clothing, nec

233 Women's and Misses' Outerwear
2331 Women's & misses' blouses & shirts
2335 Women's, juniors', & misses' dresses
2337 Women's and misses' suits and coats
2339 Women's and misses' outerwear, nec

234 Women's and Children's Undergarments
2341 Women's and children's underwear
2342 Bras, girdles, and allied garments

235 Hats, Caps, and Millinery
2353 Hats, caps, and millinery

236 Girls' and Children's Outerwear
2361 Girls' & children's dresses, blouses
2369 Girls' and children's outerwear, nec

237 Fur Goods
2371 Fur goods

238 Miscellaneous Apparel and Accessories
2381 Fabric dress and work gloves
2384 Robes and dressing gowns
2385 Waterproof outerwear
2386 Leather and sheep-lined clothing
2387 Apparel belts
2389 Apparel and accessories, nec

239 Misc. Fabricated Textile Products
2391 Curtains and draperies
2392 Housefurnishings, nec
2393 Textile bags
2394 Canvas and related products
2395 Pleating and stitching
2396 Automotive and apparel trimmings
2397 Schiffli machine embroideries
2399 Fabricated textile products, nec

24 LUMBER AND WOOD PRODUCTS

241 Logging
2411 Logging

242 Sawmills and Planing Mills
2421 Sawmills and planing mills, general
2426 Hardwood dimension & flooring mills
2429 Special product sawmills, nec

243 Millwork, Plywood & Structural Members
2431 Millwork
2434 Wood kitchen cabinets
2435 Hardwood veneer and plywood
2436 Softwood veneer and plywood
2439 Structural wood members, nec

244 Wood Containers
2441 Nailed wood boxes and shook
2448 Wood pallets and skids
2449 Wood containers, nec

245 Wood Buildings and Mobile Homes
2451 Mobile homes
2452 Prefabricated wood buildings

249 Miscellaneous Wood Products
2491 Wood preserving
2493 Reconstituted wood products
2499 Wood products, nec

Standard Industrial Classification

Guide to Selected Standard Classifications

25 FURNITURE AND FIXTURES

251 Household Furniture
- 2511 Wood household furniture
- 2512 Upholstered household furniture
- 2514 Metal household furniture
- 2515 Mattresses and bedsprings
- 2517 Wood TV and radio cabinets
- 2519 Household furniture, nec

252 Office Furniture
- 2521 Wood office furniture
- 2522 Office furniture, except wood

253 Public Building & Related Furniture
- 2531 Public building & related furniture

254 Partitions and Fixtures
- 2541 Wood partitions and fixtures
- 2542 Partitions and fixtures, except wood

259 Miscellaneous Furniture and Fixtures
- 2591 Drapery hardware & blinds & shades
- 2599 Furniture and fixtures, nec

26 PAPER AND ALLIED PRODUCTS

261 Pulp Mills
- 2611 Pulp mills

262 Paper Mills
- 2621 Paper mills

263 Paperboard Mills
- 2631 Paperboard mills

265 Paperboard Containers and Boxes
- 2652 Setup paperboard boxes
- 2653 Corrugated and solid fiber boxes
- 2655 Fiber cans, drums & similar products
- 2656 Sanitary food containers
- 2657 Folding paperboard boxes

267 Misc. Converted Paper Products
- 2671 Paper coated & laminated, packaging
- 2672 Paper coated and laminated, nec
- 2673 Bags: plastics, laminated, & coated
- 2674 Bags: uncoated paper & multiwall
- 2675 Die-cut paper and board
- 2676 Sanitary paper products
- 2677 Envelopes
- 2678 Stationery products
- 2679 Converted paper products, nec

27 PRINTING AND PUBLISHING

271 Newspapers
- 2711 Newspapers

272 Periodicals
- 2721 Periodicals

273 Books
- 2731 Book publishing
- 2732 Book printing

274 Miscellaneous Publishing
- 2741 Miscellaneous publishing

275 Commercial Printing
- 2752 Commercial printing, lithographic
- 2754 Commercial printing, gravure
- 2759 Commercial printing, nec

276 Manifold Business Forms
- 2761 Manifold business forms

277 Greeting Cards
- 2771 Greeting cards

278 Blankbooks and Bookbinding
- 2782 Blankbooks and looseleaf binders
- 2789 Bookbinding and related work

279 Printing Trade Services
- 2791 Typesetting
- 2796 Platemaking services

28 CHEMICALS AND ALLIED PRODUCTS

281 Industrial Inorganic Chemicals
- 2812 Alkalies and chlorine
- 2813 Industrial gases
- 2816 Inorganic pigments
- 2819 Industrial inorganic chemicals, nec

282 Plastics Materials and Synthetics
- 2821 Plastics materials and resins
- 2822 Synthetic rubber
- 2823 Cellulosic manmade fibers
- 2824 Organic fibers, noncellulosic

283 Drugs
- 2833 Medicinals and botanicals
- 2834 Pharmaceutical preparations
- 2835 Diagnostic substances
- 2836 Biological products exc. diagnostic

284 Soap, Cleaners, and Toilet Goods
- 2841 Soap and other detergents
- 2842 Polishes and sanitation goods
- 2843 Surface active agents
- 2844 Toilet preparations

285 Paints and Allied Products
- 2851 Paints and allied products

286 Industrial Organic Chemicals
- 2861 Gum and wood chemicals
- 2865 Cyclic crudes and intermediates
- 2869 Industrial organic chemicals, nec

287 Agricultural Chemicals
- 2873 Nitrogenous fertilizers
- 2874 Phosphatic fertilizers
- 2875 Fertilizers, mixing only
- 2879 Agricultural chemicals, nec

289 Miscellaneous Chemical Products
- 2891 Adhesives and sealants
- 2892 Explosives
- 2893 Printing ink
- 2895 Carbon black
- 2899 Chemical preparations, nec

29 PETROLEUM AND COAL PRODUCTS

291 Petroleum Refining
- 2911 Petroleum refining

295 Asphalt Paving and Roofing Materials
- 2951 Asphalt paving mixtures and blocks
- 2952 Asphalt felts and coatings

299 Misc. Petroleum and Coal Products
- 2992 Lubricating oils and greases
- 2999 Petroleum and coal products, nec

30 RUBBER AND MISC. PLASTICS PRODUCTS

301 Tires and Inner Tubes
- 3011 Tires and inner tubes

302 Rubber and Plastics Footwear
- 3021 Rubber and plastics footwear

305 Hose & Belting & Gaskets & Packing
- 3052 Rubber & plastics hose & belting
- 3053 Gaskets, packing and sealing devices

306 Fabricated Rubber Products, NEC
- 3061 Mechanical rubber goods
- 3069 Fabricated rubber products, nec

308 Miscellaneous Plastics Products, NEC
- 3081 Unsupported plastics film & sheet
- 3082 Unsupported plastics profile shapes
- 3083 Laminated plastics plate & sheet
- 3084 Plastics pipe
- 3085 Plastics bottles
- 3086 Plastics foam products
- 3087 Custom compound purchased resins
- 3088 Plastics plumbing fixtures
- 3089 Plastics products, nec

31 LEATHER AND LEATHER PRODUCTS

311 Leather Tanning and Finishing
- 3111 Leather tanning and finishing

313 Footwear Cut Stock
- 3131 Footwear cut stock

314 Footwear, Except Rubber
- 3142 House slippers
- 3143 Men's footwear, except athletic
- 3144 Women's footwear, except athletic
- 3149 Footwear, except rubber, nec

315 Leather Gloves and Mittens
- 3151 Leather gloves and mittens

316 Luggage
- 3161 Luggage

317 Handbags and Personal Leather Goods
- 3171 Women's handbags and purses
- 3172 Personal leather goods, nec

319 Leather Goods, NEC
- 3199 Leather goods, nec

32 STONE, CLAY, AND GLASS PRODUCTS

321 Flat Glass
- 3211 Flat glass

322 Glass and Glassware, Pressed or Blown
- 3221 Glass containers
- 3229 Pressed and blown glass, nec

323 Products of Purchased Glass
- 3231 Products of purchased glass

324 Cement, Hydraulic
- 3241 Cement, hydraulic

325 Structural Clay Products
- 3251 Brick and structural clay tile
- 3253 Ceramic wall and floor tile
- 3255 Clay refractories
- 3259 Structural clay products, nec

326 Pottery and Related Products
- 3261 Vitreous plumbing fixtures
- 3262 Vitreous china table & kitchenware
- 3263 Semivitreous table & kitchenware
- 3264 Porcelain electrical supplies
- 3269 Pottery products, nec

327 Concrete, Gypsum, and Plaster Products
- 3271 Concrete block and brick
- 3272 Concrete products, nec
- 3273 Ready-mixed concrete
- 3274 Lime
- 3275 Gypsum products

328 Cut Stone and Stone Products
- 3281 Cut stone and stone products

329 Misc. Nonmetallic Mineral Products
- 3291 Abrasive products
- 3292 Asbestos products
- 3295 Minerals, ground or treated
- 3296 Mineral wool
- 3297 Nonclay refractories
- 3299 Nonmetallic mineral products, nec

33 PRIMARY METAL INDUSTRIES

331 Blast Furnace and Basic Steel Products
- 3312 Blast furnaces and steel mills
- 3313 Electrometallurgical products
- 3315 Steel wire and related products
- 3316 Cold finishing of steel shapes
- 3317 Steel pipe and tubes

332 Iron and Steel Foundries
- 3321 Gray and ductile iron foundries
- 3322 Malleable iron foundries
- 3324 Steel investment foundries
- 3325 Steel foundries, nec

Guide to Selected Standard Classifications — Standard Industrial Classification

333 Primary Nonferrous Metals
- 3331 Primary copper
- 3334 Primary aluminum
- 3339 Primary nonferrous metals, nec

334 Secondary Nonferrous Metals
- 3341 Secondary nonferrous metals

335 Nonferrous Rolling and Drawing
- 3351 Copper rolling and drawing
- 3353 Aluminum sheet, plate, and foil
- 3354 Aluminum extruded products
- 3355 Aluminum rolling and drawing, nec
- 3356 Nonferrous rolling and drawing, nec
- 3357 Nonferrous wiredrawing & insulating

336 Nonferrous Foundries (Castings)
- 3363 Aluminum die-castings
- 3364 Nonferrous die-casting exc. aluminum
- 3365 Aluminum foundries
- 3366 Copper foundries
- 3369 Nonferrous foundries, nec

339 Miscellaneous Primary Metal Products
- 3398 Metal heat treating
- 3399 Primary metal products, nec

34 FABRICATED METAL PRODUCTS

341 Metal Cans and Shipping Containers
- 3411 Metal cans
- 3412 Metal barrels, drums, and pails

342 Cutlery, Handtools, and Hardware
- 3421 Cutlery
- 3423 Hand and edge tools, nec
- 3425 Saw blades and handsaws
- 3429 Hardware, nec

343 Plumbing and Heating, Except Electric
- 3431 Metal sanitary ware
- 3432 Plumbing fixture fittings and trim
- 3433 Heating equipment, except electric

344 Fabricated Structural Metal Products
- 3441 Fabricated structural metal
- 3442 Metal doors, sash, and trim
- 3443 Fabricated plate work (boiler shops)
- 3444 Sheet metal work
- 3446 Architectural metal work
- 3448 Prefabricated metal buildings
- 3449 Miscellaneous metal work

345 Screw Machine Products, Bolts, Etc.
- 3451 Screw machine products
- 3452 Bolts, nuts, rivets, and washers

346 Metal Forgings and Stampings
- 3462 Iron and steel forgings
- 3463 Nonferrous forgings
- 3465 Automotive stampings
- 3466 Crowns and closures
- 3469 Metal stampings, nec

347 Metal Services, NEC
- 3471 Plating and polishing
- 3479 Metal coating and allied services

348 Ordnance and Accessories, NEC
- 3482 Small arms ammunition
- 3483 Ammunition, exc. for small arms, nec
- 3484 Small arms
- 3489 Ordnance and accessories, nec

349 Misc. Fabricated Metal Products
- 3491 Industrial valves
- 3492 Fluid power valves & hose fittings
- 3493 Steel springs, except wire
- 3494 Valves and pipe fittings, nec
- 3495 Wire springs
- 3496 Misc. fabricated wire products
- 3497 Metal foil and leaf
- 3498 Fabricated pipe and fittings
- 3499 Fabricated metal products, nec

35 INDUSTRIAL MACHINERY AND EQUIPMENT

351 Engines and Turbines
- 3511 Turbines and turbine generator sets
- 3519 Internal combustion engines, nec

352 Farm and Garden Machinery
- 3523 Farm machinery and equipment
- 3524 Lawn and garden equipment

353 Construction and Related Machinery
- 3531 Construction machinery
- 3532 Mining machinery
- 3533 Oil and gas field machinery
- 3534 Elevators and moving stairways
- 3535 Conveyors and conveying equipment
- 3536 Hoists, cranes, and monorails
- 3537 Industrial trucks and tractors

354 Metalworking Machinery
- 3541 Machine tools, metal cutting types
- 3542 Machine tools, metal forming types
- 3543 Industrial patterns
- 3544 Special dies, tools, jigs & fixtures
- 3545 Machine tool accessories
- 3546 Power-driven handtools
- 3547 Rolling mill machinery
- 3548 Welding apparatus
- 3549 Metalworking machinery, nec

355 Special Industry Machinery
- 3552 Textile machinery
- 3553 Woodworking machinery
- 3554 Paper industries machinery
- 3555 Printing trades machinery
- 3556 Food products machinery
- 3559 Special industry machinery, nec

356 General Industrial Machinery
- 3561 Pumps and pumping equipment
- 3562 Ball and roller bearings
- 3563 Air and gas compressors
- 3564 Blowers and fans
- 3565 Packaging machinery
- 3566 Speed changers, drives, and gears
- 3567 Industrial furnaces and ovens
- 3568 Power transmission equipment, nec
- 3569 General industrial machinery, nec

357 Computer and Office Equipment
- 3571 Electronic computers
- 3572 Computer storage devices
- 3575 Computer terminals
- 3577 Computer peripheral equipment, nec
- 3578 Calculating and accounting equipment
- 3579 Office machines, nec

358 Refrigeration and Service Machinery
- 3581 Automatic vending machines
- 3582 Commercial laundry equipment
- 3585 Refrigeration and heating equipment
- 3586 Measuring and dispensing pumps
- 3589 Service industry machinery, nec

359 Industrial Machinery, NEC
- 3592 Carburetors, pistons, rings, valves
- 3593 Fluid power cylinders & actuators
- 3594 Fluid power pumps and motors
- 3596 Scales and balances, exc. laboratory
- 3599 Industrial machinery, nec

36 ELECTRONIC & OTHER ELECTRIC EQUIPMENT

361 Electric Distribution Equipment
- 3612 Transformers, except electronic
- 3613 Switchgear and switchboard apparatus

362 Electrical Industrial Apparatus
- 3621 Motors and generators

- 3624 Carbon and graphite products
- 3625 Relays and industrial controls
- 3629 Electrical industrial apparatus, nec

363 Household Appliances
- 3631 Household cooking equipment
- 3632 Household refrigerators and freezers
- 3633 Household laundry equipment
- 3634 Electric housewares and fans
- 3635 Household vacuum cleaners
- 3639 Household appliances, nec

364 Electric Lighting and Wiring Equipment
- 3641 Electric lamps
- 3643 Current-carrying wiring devices
- 3644 Noncurrent-carrying wiring devices
- 3645 Residential lighting fixtures
- 3646 Commercial lighting fixtures
- 3647 Vehicular lighting equipment
- 3648 Lighting equipment, nec

365 Household Audio and Video Equipment
- 3651 Household audio and video equipment
- 3652 Prerecorded records and tapes

366 Communications Equipment
- 3661 Telephone and telegraph apparatus
- 3663 Radio & TV communications equipment
- 3669 Communications equipment, nec

367 Electronic Components and Accessories
- 3671 Electron tubes
- 3672 Printed circuit boards
- 3674 Semiconductors and related devices
- 3675 Electronic capacitors
- 3676 Electronic resistors
- 3677 Electronic coils and transformers
- 3678 Electronic connectors
- 3679 Electronic components, nec

369 Misc. Electrical Equipment & Supplies
- 3691 Storage batteries
- 3692 Primary batteries, dry and wet
- 3694 Engine electrical equipment
- 3695 Magnetic and optical recording media
- 3699 Electrical equipment & supplies, nec

37 TRANSPORTATION EQUIPMENT

371 Motor Vehicles and Equipment
- 3711 Motor vehicles and car bodies
- 3713 Truck and bus bodies
- 3714 Motor vehicle parts and accessories
- 3715 Truck trailers
- 3716 Motor homes

372 Aircraft and Parts
- 3721 Aircraft
- 3724 Aircraft engines and engine parts
- 3728 Aircraft parts and equipment, nec

373 Ship and Boat Building and Repairing
- 3731 Ship building and repairing
- 3732 Boat building and repairing

374 Railroad Equipment
- 3743 Railroad equipment

375 Motorcycles, Bicycles, and Parts
- 3751 Motorcycles, bicycles, and parts

376 Guided Missiles, Space Vehicles, Parts
- 3761 Guided missiles and space vehicles
- 3764 Space propulsion units and parts
- 3769 Space vehicle equipment, nec

379 Miscellaneous Transportation Equipment
- 3792 Travel trailers and campers
- 3795 Tanks and tank components
- 3799 Transportation equipment, nec

Standard Industrial Classification

Guide to Selected Standard Classifications

38 INSTRUMENTS AND RELATED PRODUCTS

381 Search and Navigation Equipment
3812 Search and navigation equipment

382 Measuring and Controlling Devices
3821 Laboratory apparatus and furniture
3822 Environmental controls
3823 Process control instruments
3824 Fluid meters and counting devices
3825 Instruments to measure electricity
3826 Analytical instruments
3827 Optical instruments and lenses
3829 Measuring & controlling devices, nec

384 Medical Instruments and Supplies
3841 Surgical and medical instruments
3842 Surgical appliances and supplies
3843 Dental equipment and supplies
3844 X-ray apparatus and tubes
3845 Electromedical equipment

385 Ophthalmic Goods
3851 Ophthalmic goods

386 Photographic Equipment and Supplies
3861 Photographic equipment and supplies

387 Watches, Clocks, Watchcases & Parts
3873 Watches, clocks, watchcases & parts

39 MISCELLANEOUS MANUFACTURING INDUSTRIES

391 Jewelry, Silverware, and Plated Ware
3911 Jewelry, precious metal
3914 Silverware and plated ware
3915 Jewelers' materials & lapidary work

393 Musical Instruments
3931 Musical instruments

394 Toys and Sporting Goods
3942 Dolls and stuffed toys
3944 Games, toys, and children's vehicles
3949 Sporting and athletic goods, nec

395 Pens, Pencils, Office, & Art Supplies
3951 Pens and mechanical pencils
3952 Lead pencils and art goods
3953 Marking devices
3955 Carbon paper and inked ribbons

396 Costume Jewelry and Notions
3961 Costume jewelry
3965 Fasteners, buttons, needles, & pins

399 Miscellaneous Manufactures
3991 Brooms and brushes
3993 Signs and advertising specialities
3995 Burial caskets
3996 Hard surface floor coverings, nec
3999 Manufacturing industries, nec

TRANSPORTATION AND PUBLIC UTILITIES

---

40 RAILROAD TRANSPORTATION

401 Railroads
4011 Railroads, line-haul operating
4013 Switching and terminal services

41 LOCAL AND INTERURBAN PASSENGER TRANSIT

411 Local and Suburban Transportation
4111 Local and suburban transit
4119 Local passenger transportation, nec

412 Taxicabs
4121 Taxicabs

413 Intercity and Rural Bus Transportation
4131 Intercity & rural bus transportation

414 Bus Charter Service
4141 Local bus charter service
4142 Bus charter service, except local

415 School Buses
4151 School buses

417 Bus Terminal and Service Facilities
4173 Bus terminal and service facilities

42 TRUCKING AND WAREHOUSING

421 Trucking & Courier Services, Ex. Air
4212 Local trucking, without storage
4213 Trucking, except local
4214 Local trucking with storage
4215 Courier services, except by air

422 Public Warehousing and Storage
4221 Farm product warehousing and storage
4222 Refrigerated warehousing and storage
4225 General warehousing and storage
4226 Special warehousing and storage, nec

423 Trucking Terminal Facilities
4231 Trucking terminal facilities

43 U.S. POSTAL SERVICE

431 U.S. Postal Service
4311 U.S. Postal Service

44 WATER TRANSPORTATION

441 Deep Sea Foreign Trans. of Freight
4412 Deep sea foreign trans. of freight

442 Deep Sea Domestic Trans. of Freight
4424 Deep sea domestic trans. of freight

443 Freight Trans. on the Great Lakes
4432 Freight trans. on the Great Lakes

444 Water Transportation of Freight, NEC
4449 Water transportation of freight, nec

448 Water Transportation of Passengers
4481 Deep sea passenger trans., ex. ferry
4482 Ferries
4489 Water passenger transportation, nec

449 Water Transportation Services
4491 Marine cargo handling
4492 Towing and tugboat service
4493 Marinas
4499 Water transportation services, nec

45 TRANSPORTATION BY AIR

451 Air Transportation, Scheduled
4512 Air transportation, scheduled
4513 Air courier services

452 Air Transportation, Nonscheduled
4522 Air transportation, nonscheduled

458 Airports, Flying Fields, & Services
4581 Airports, flying fields, & services

46 PIPELINES, EXCEPT NATURAL GAS

461 Pipelines, Except Natural Gas
4612 Crude petroleum pipelines
4613 Refined petroleum pipelines
4619 Pipelines, nec

47 TRANSPORTATION SERVICES

472 Passenger Transportation Arrangement
4724 Travel agencies
4725 Tour operators
4729 Passenger transport arrangement, nec

473 Freight Transportation Arrangement
4731 Freight transportation arrangement

474 Rental of Railroad Cars
4741 Rental of railroad cars

478 Miscellaneous Transportation Services
4783 Packing and crating
4785 Inspection & fixed facilities
4789 Transportation services, nec

48 COMMUNICATIONS

481 Telephone Communications
4812 Radiotelephone communications
4813 Telephone communications, exc. radio

482 Telegraph & Other Communications
4822 Telegraph & other communications

483 Radio and Television Broadcasting
4832 Radio broadcasting stations
4833 Television broadcasting stations

484 Cable and Other Pay TV Services
4841 Cable and other pay TV services

489 Communications Services, NEC
4899 Communications services, nec

49 ELECTRIC, GAS, AND SANITARY SERVICES

491 Electric Services
4911 Electric services

492 Gas Production and Distribution
4922 Natural gas transmission
4923 Gas transmission and distribution
4924 Natural gas distribution
4925 Gas production and/or distribution

493 Combination Utility Services
4931 Electric and other services combined
4932 Gas and other services combined
4939 Combination utilities, nec

494 Water Supply
4941 Water supply

495 Sanitary Services
4952 Sewerage systems
4953 Refuse systems
4959 Sanitary services, nec

496 Steam and Air-Conditioning Supply
4961 Steam and air-conditioning supply

497 Irrigation Systems
4971 Irrigation systems

WHOLESALE TRADE

---

50 WHOLESALE TRADE—DURABLE GOODS

501 Motor Vehicles, Parts, and Supplies
5012 Automobiles and other motor vehicles
5013 Motor vehicle supplies and new parts
5014 Tires and tubes
5015 Motor vehicle parts, used

502 Furniture and Homefurnishings
5021 Furniture
5023 Homefurnishings

503 Lumber and Construction Materials
5031 Lumber, plywood, and millwork
5032 Brick, stone, & related materials
5033 Roofing, siding, & insulation
5039 Construction materials, nec

504 Professional & Commercial Equipment
5043 Photographic equipment and supplies
5044 Office equipment
5045 Computers, peripherals & software

Guide to Selected Standard Classifications

Standard Industrial Classification

5046 Commercial equipment, nec
5047 Medical and hospital equipment
5048 Ophthalmic goods
5049 Professional equipment, nec

505 Metals and Minerals, Except Petroleum
5051 Metals service centers and offices
5052 Coal and other minerals and ores

506 Electrical Goods
5063 Electrical apparatus and equipment
5064 Electrical appliances, TV & radios
5065 Electronic parts and equipment

507 Hardware, Plumbing & Heating Equipment
5072 Hardware
5074 Plumbing & hydronic heating supplies
5075 Warm air heating & air-conditioning
5078 Refrigeration equipment and supplies

508 Machinery, Equipment, and Supplies
5082 Construction and mining machinery
5083 Farm and garden machinery
5084 Industrial machinery and equipment
5085 Industrial supplies
5087 Service establishment equipment
5088 Transportation equipment & supplies

509 Miscellaneous Durable Goods
5091 Sporting & recreational goods
5092 Toys and hobby goods and supplies
5093 Scrap and waste materials
5094 Jewelry & precious stones
5099 Durable goods, nec

51 WHOLESALE TRADE—NONDURABLE GOODS

511 Paper and Paper Products
5111 Printing and writing paper
5112 Stationery and office supplies
5113 Industrial & personal service paper

512 Drugs, Proprietaries, and Sundries
5122 Drugs, proprietaries, and sundries

513 Apparel, Piece Goods, and Notions
5131 Piece goods & notions
5136 Men's and boys' clothing
5137 Women's and children's clothing
5139 Footwear

514 Groceries and Related Products
5141 Groceries, general line
5142 Packaged frozen foods
5143 Dairy products, exc. dried or canned
5144 Poultry and poultry products
5145 Confectionery
5146 Fish and seafoods
5147 Meats and meat products
5148 Fresh fruits and vegetables
5149 Groceries and related products, nec

515 Farm-Product Raw Materials
5153 Grain and field beans
5154 Livestock
5159 Farm-product raw materials, nec

516 Chemicals and Allied Products
5162 Plastics materials & basic shapes
5169 Chemicals & allied products, nec

517 Petroleum and Petroleum Products
5171 Petroleum bulk stations & terminals
5172 Petroleum products, nec

518 Beer, Wine, and Distilled Beverages
5181 Beer and ale
5182 Wine and distilled beverages

519 Misc. Nondurable Goods
5191 Farm supplies

5192 Books, periodicals, & newspapers
5193 Flowers & florists' supplies
5194 Tobacco and tobacco products
5198 Paints, varnishes, and supplies
5199 Nondurable goods, nec

RETAIL TRADE

52 BUILDING MATERIALS & GARDEN SUPPLIES

521 Lumber and Other Building Materials
5211 Lumber and other building materials

523 Paint, Glass, and Wallpaper Stores
5231 Paint, glass, and wallpaper stores

525 Hardware Stores
5251 Hardware stores

526 Retail Nurseries and Garden Stores
5261 Retail nurseries and garden stores

527 Mobile Home Dealers
5271 Mobile home dealers

53 GENERAL MERCHANDISE STORES

531 Department Stores
5311 Department stores

533 Variety Stores
5331 Variety stores

539 Misc. General Merchandise Stores
5399 Misc. general merchandise stores

54 FOOD STORES

541 Grocery Stores
5411 Grocery stores

542 Meat and Fish Markets
5421 Meat and fish markets

543 Fruit and Vegetable Markets
5431 Fruit and vegetable markets

544 Candy, Nut, and Confectionery Stores
5441 Candy, nut, and confectionery stores

545 Dairy Products Stores
5451 Dairy products stores

546 Retail Bakeries
5461 Retail bakeries

549 Miscellaneous Food Stores
5499 Miscellaneous food stores

55 AUTOMOTIVE DEALERS & SERVICE STATIONS

551 New and Used Car Dealers
5511 New and used car dealers

552 Used Car Dealers
5521 Used car dealers

553 Auto and Home Supply Stores
5531 Auto and home supply stores

554 Gasoline Service Stations
5541 Gasoline service stations

555 Boat Dealers
5551 Boat dealers

556 Recreational Vehicle Dealers
5561 Recreational vehicle dealers

557 Motorcycle Dealers
5571 Motorcycle dealers

559 Automotive Dealers, NEC
5599 Automotive dealers, nec

56 APPAREL AND ACCESSORY STORES

561 Men's & Boys' Clothing Stores
5611 Men's & boys' clothing stores

562 Women's Clothing Stores
5621 Women's clothing stores

563 Women's Accessory & Specialty Stores
5632 Women's accessory & specialty stores

564 Children's and Infants' Wear Stores
5641 Children's and infants' wear stores

565 Family Clothing Stores
5651 Family clothing stores

566 Shoe Stores
5661 Shoe stores

569 Misc. Apparel & Accessory Stores
5699 Misc. apparel & accessory stores

57 FURNITURE AND HOMEFURNISHINGS STORES

571 Furniture and Homefurnishings Stores
5712 Furniture stores
5713 Floor covering stores
5714 Drapery and upholstery stores
5719 Misc. homefurnishings stores

572 Household Appliance Stores
5722 Household appliance stores

573 Radio, Television, & Computer Stores
5731 Radio, TV, & electronic stores
5734 Computer and software stores
5735 Record & prerecorded tape stores
5736 Musical instrument stores

58 EATING AND DRINKING PLACES

581 Eating and Drinking Places
5812 Eating places
5813 Drinking places

59 MISCELLANEOUS RETAIL

591 Drug Stores and Proprietary Stores
5912 Drug stores and proprietary stores

592 Liquor Stores
5921 Liquor stores

593 Used Merchandise Stores
5932 Used merchandise stores

594 Miscellaneous Shopping Goods Stores
5941 Sporting goods and bicycle shops
5942 Book stores
5943 Stationery stores
5944 Jewelry stores
5945 Hobby, toy, and game shops
5946 Camera & photographic supply stores
5947 Gift, novelty, and souvenir shops
5948 Luggage and leather goods stores
5949 Sewing, needlework, and piece goods

596 Nonstore Retailers
5961 Catalog and mail-order houses
5962 Merchandising machine operators
5963 Direct selling establishments

598 Fuel Dealers
5983 Fuel oil dealers
5984 Liquefied petroleum gas dealers
5989 Fuel dealers, nec

599 Retail Stores, NEC
5992 Florists
5993 Tobacco stores and stands
5994 News dealers and newsstands
5995 Optical goods stores
5999 Miscellaneous retail stores, nec

FINANCE, INSURANCE, AND REAL ESTATE

60 DEPOSITORY INSTITUTIONS

601 Central Reserve Depositories
6011 Federal reserve banks
6019 Central reserve depository, nec

Standard Industrial Classification

Guide to Selected Standard Classifications

602 Commercial Banks
- 6021 National commercial banks
- 6022 State commercial banks
- 6029 Commercial banks, nec

603 Savings Institutions
- 6035 Federal savings institutions
- 6036 Savings institutions, except federal

606 Credit Unions
- 6061 Federal credit unions
- 6062 State credit unions

608 Foreign Bank & Branches & Agencies
- 6081 Foreign bank & branches & agencies
- 6082 Foreign trade & international banks

609 Functions Closely Related to Banking
- 6091 Nondeposit trust facilities
- 6099 Functions related to deposit banking

61 NONDEPOSITORY INSTITUTIONS

611 Federal & Fed.-Sponsored Credit
- 6111 Federal & fed.-sponsored credit

614 Personal Credit Institutions
- 6141 Personal credit institutions

615 Business Credit Institutions
- 6153 Short-term business credit
- 6159 Misc. business credit institutions

616 Mortgage Bankers and Brokers
- 6162 Mortgage bankers and correspondents
- 6163 Loan brokers

62 SECURITY AND COMMODITY BROKERS

621 Security Brokers and Dealers
- 6211 Security brokers and dealers

622 Commodity Contracts Brokers, Dealers
- 6221 Commodity contracts brokers, dealers

623 Security and Commodity Exchanges
- 6231 Security and commodity exchanges

628 Security and Commodity Services
- 6282 Investment advice
- 6289 Security & commodity services, nec

63 INSURANCE CARRIERS

631 Life Insurance
- 6311 Life insurance

632 Medical Service and Health Insurance
- 6321 Accident and health insurance
- 6324 Hospital and medical service plans

633 Fire, Marine, and Casualty Insurance
- 6331 Fire, marine, and casualty insurance

635 Surety Insurance
- 6351 Surety insurance

636 Title Insurance
- 6361 Title insurance

637 Pension, Health, and Welfare Funds
- 6371 Pension, health, and welfare funds

639 Insurance Carriers, NEC
- 6399 Insurance carriers, nec

64 INSURANCE AGENTS, BROKERS, & SERVICE

641 Insurance Agents, Brokers, & Service
- 6411 Insurance agents, brokers, & service

65 REAL ESTATE

651 Real Estate Operators and Lessors
- 6512 Nonresidential building operators
- 6513 Apartment building operators
- 6514 Dwelling operators, exc. apartments
- 6515 Mobile home site operators
- 6517 Railroad property lessors
- 6519 Real property lessors, nec

653 Real Estate Agents and Managers
- 6531 Real estate agents and managers

654 Title Abstract Offices
- 6541 Title abstract offices

655 Subdividers and Developers
- 6552 Subdividers and developers, nec
- 6553 Cemetery subdividers and developers

67 HOLDING AND OTHER INVESTMENT OFFICES

671 Holding Offices
- 6712 Bank holding companies
- 6719 Holding companies, nec

672 Investment Offices
- 6722 Management investment, open-end
- 6726 Investment offices, nec

673 Trusts
- 6732 Educational, religious, etc. trusts
- 6733 Trusts, nec

679 Miscellaneous Investing
- 6792 Oil royalty traders
- 6794 Patent owners and lessors
- 6798 Real estate investment trusts
- 6799 Investors, nec

SERVICES

70 HOTELS AND OTHER LODGING PLACES

701 Hotels and Motels
- 7011 Hotels and motels

702 Rooming and Boarding Houses
- 7021 Rooming and boarding houses

703 Camps and Recreational Vehicle Parks
- 7032 Sporting and recreational camps
- 7033 Trailer parks and campsites

704 Membership-Basis Organization Hotels
- 7041 Membership-basis organization hotels

72 PERSONAL SERVICES

721 Laundry, Cleaning, & Garment Services
- 7211 Power Laundries, family & commercial
- 7212 Garment pressing & cleaners' agents
- 7213 Linen supply
- 7215 Coin-operated laundries and cleaning
- 7216 Drycleaning plants, except rug
- 7217 Carpet and upholstery cleaning
- 7218 Industrial launderers
- 7219 Laundry and garment services, nec

722 Photographic Studios, Portrait
- 7221 Photographic studios, portrait

723 Beauty Shops
- 7231 Beauty shops

724 Barber Shops
- 7241 Barber shops

725 Shoe Repair and Shoeshine Parlors
- 7251 Shoe repair and shoeshine parlors

726 Funeral Service and Crematories
- 7261 Funeral service and crematories

729 Miscellaneous Personal Services
- 7291 Tax return preparation services
- 7299 Miscellaneous personal services, nec

73 BUSINESS SERVICES

731 Advertising
- 7311 Advertising agencies
- 7312 Outdoor advertising services
- 7313 Radio, TV, publisher representatives
- 7319 Advertising, nec

732 Credit Reporting and Collection
- 7322 Adjustment & collection services
- 7323 Credit reporting services

733 Mailing, Reproduction, Stenographic
- 7331 Direct mail advertising services
- 7334 Photocopying & duplicating services
- 7335 Commercial photography
- 7336 Commercial art and graphic design
- 7338 Secretarial & court reporting

734 Services to Buildings
- 7342 Disinfecting & pest control services
- 7349 Building maintenance services, nec

735 Misc. Equipment Rental & Leasing
- 7352 Medical equipment rental
- 7353 Heavy construction equipment rental
- 7359 Equipment rental & leasing, nec

736 Personnel Supply Services
- 7361 Employment agencies
- 7363 Help supply services

737 Computer and Data Processing Services
- 7371 Computer programming services
- 7372 Prepackaged software
- 7373 Computer integrated systems design
- 7374 Data processing and preparation
- 7375 Information retrieval services
- 7376 Computer facilities management
- 7377 Computer rental & leasing
- 7378 Computer maintenance & repair
- 7379 Computer related services, nec

738 Miscellaneous Business Services
- 7381 Detective & armored car services
- 7382 Security systems services
- 7383 News syndicates
- 7384 Photofinishing laboratories
- 7389 Business services, nec

75 AUTO REPAIR, SERVICES, AND PARKING

751 Automotive Rentals, No Drivers
- 7513 Truck rental and leasing, no drivers
- 7514 Passenger car rental
- 7515 Passenger car leasing
- 7519 Utility trailer rental

752 Automobile Parking
- 7521 Automobile parking

753 Automotive Repair Shops
- 7532 Top & body repair & paint shops
- 7533 Auto exhaust system repair shops
- 7534 Tire retreading and repair shops
- 7536 Automotive glass replacement shops
- 7537 Automotive transmission repair shops
- 7538 General automotive repair shops
- 7539 Automotive repair shops, nec

754 Automotive Services, Except Repair
- 7542 Carwashes
- 7549 Automotive services, nec

76 MISCELLANEOUS REPAIR SERVICES

762 Electrical Repair Shops
- 7622 Radio and television repair
- 7623 Refrigeration service and repair
- 7629 Electrical repair shops, nec

763 Watch, Clock, and Jewelry Repair
- 7631 Watch, clock, and jewelry repair

764 Reupholstery and Furniture Repair
- 7641 Reupholstery and furniture repair

Guide to Selected Standard Classifications

Standard Industrial Classification

769 Miscellaneous Repair Shops
- 7692 Welding repair
- 7694 Armature rewinding shops
- 7699 Repair services, nec

78 MOTION PICTURES

781 Motion Picture Production & Services
- 7812 Motion picture & video production
- 7819 Services allied to motion pictures

782 Motion Picture Distribution & Services
- 7822 Motion picture and tape distribution
- 7829 Motion picture distribution services

783 Motion Picture Theaters
- 7832 Motion picture theaters, ex drive-in
- 7833 Drive-in motion picture theaters

784 Video Tape Rental
- 7841 Video tape rental

79 AMUSEMENT & RECREATION SERVICES

791 Dance Studios, Schools, and Halls
- 7911 Dance studios, schools, and halls

792 Producers, Orchestras, Entertainers
- 7922 Theatrical producers and services
- 7929 Entertainers & entertainment groups

793 Bowling Centers
- 7933 Bowling centers

794 Commercial Sports
- 7941 Sports clubs, managers, & promoters
- 7948 Racing, including track operation

799 Misc. Amusement, Recreation Services
- 7991 Physical fitness facilities
- 7992 Public golf courses
- 7993 Coin-operated amusement devices
- 7996 Amusement parks
- 7997 Membership sports & recreation clubs
- 7999 Amusement and recreation, nec

80 HEALTH SERVICES

801 Offices & Clinics of Medical Doctors
- 8011 Offices & clinics of medical doctors

802 Offices and Clinics of Dentists
- 8021 Offices and clinics of dentists

803 Offices of Osteopathic Physicians
- 8031 Offices of osteopathic physicians

804 Offices of Other Health Practitioners
- 8041 Offices and clinics of chiropractors
- 8042 Offices and clinics of optometrists
- 8043 Offices and clinics of podiatrists
- 8049 Offices of health practitioners, nec

805 Nursing and Personal Care Facilities
- 8051 Skilled nursing care facilities
- 8052 Intermediate care facilities
- 8059 Nursing and personal care, nec

806 Hospitals
- 8062 General medical & surgical hospitals
- 8063 Psychiatric hospitals
- 8069 Specialty hospitals exc. psychiatric

807 Medical and Dental Laboratories
- 8071 Medical laboratories
- 8072 Dental laboratories

808 Home Health Care Services
- 8082 Home health care services

809 Health and Allied Services, NEC
- 8092 Kidney dialysis centers
- 8093 Specialty outpatient clinics, nec
- 8099 Health and allied services, nec

81 LEGAL SERVICES

811 Legal Services
- 8111 Legal services

82 EDUCATIONAL SERVICES

821 Elementary and Secondary Schools
- 8211 Elementary and secondary schools

822 Colleges and Universities
- 8221 Colleges and universities
- 8222 Junior colleges

823 Libraries
- 8231 Libraries

824 Vocational Schools
- 8243 Data processing schools
- 8244 Business and secretarial schools
- 8249 Vocational schools, nec

829 Schools & Educational Services, NEC
- 8299 Schools & educational services, nec

83 SOCIAL SERVICES

832 Individual and Family Services
- 8322 Individual and family services

833 Job Training and Related Services
- 8331 Job training and related services

835 Child Day Care Services
- 8351 Child day care services

836 Residential Care
- 8361 Residential care

839 Social Services, NEC
- 8399 Social services, nec

84 MUSEUMS, BOTANICAL, ZOOLOGICAL GARDENS

841 Museums and Art Galleries
- 8412 Museums and art galleries

842 Botanical and Zoological Gardens
- 8422 Botanical and zoological gardens

86 MEMBERSHIP ORGANIZATIONS

861 Business Associations
- 8611 Business associations

862 Professional Organizations
- 8621 Professional organizations

863 Labor Organizations
- 8631 Labor organizations

864 Civic and Social Associations
- 8641 Civic and social associations

865 Political Organizations
- 8651 Political organizations

866 Religious Organizations
- 8661 Religious organizations

869 Membership Organizations, NEC
- 8699 Membership organizations, nec

87 ENGINEERING & MANAGEMENT SERVICES

871 Engineering & Architectural Services
- 8711 Engineering services
- 8712 Architectural services
- 8713 Surveying services

872 Accounting, Auditing, & Bookkeeping
- 8721 Accounting, auditing, & bookkeeping

873 Research and Testing Services
- 8731 Commercial physical research
- 8732 Commercial nonphysical research
- 8733 Noncommercial research organizations
- 8734 Testing laboratories

874 Management and Public Relations
- 8741 Management services
- 8742 Management consulting services
- 8743 Public relations services
- 8744 Facilities support services
- 8748 Business consulting, nec

88 PRIVATE HOUSEHOLDS

881 Private Households
- 8811 Private households

89 SERVICES, NEC

899 Services, NEC
- 8999 Services, nec

PUBLIC ADMINISTRATION

91 EXECUTIVE, LEGISLATIVE, AND GENERAL

911 Executive Offices
- 9111 Executive offices

912 Legislative Bodies
- 9121 Legislative bodies

913 Executive and Legislative Combined
- 9131 Executive and legislative combined

919 General Government, NEC
- 9199 General government, nec

92 JUSTICE, PUBLIC ORDER, AND SAFETY

921 Courts
- 9211 Courts

922 Public Order and Safety
- 9221 Police protection
- 9222 Legal counsel and prosecution
- 9223 Correctional institutions
- 9224 Fire protection
- 9229 Public order and safety, nec

93 FINANCE, TAXATION, & MONETARY POLICY

931 Finance, Taxation, & Monetary Policy
- 9311 Finance, taxation, & monetary policy

94 ADMINISTRATION OF HUMAN RESOURCES

941 Admin. of Educational Programs
- 9411 Admin. of educational programs

943 Admin. of Public Health Programs
- 9431 Admin. of public health programs

944 Admin. of Social & Manpower Programs
- 9441 Admin. of social & manpower programs

945 Administration of Veterans' Affairs
- 9451 Administration of veterans' affairs

95 ENVIRONMENTAL QUALITY AND HOUSING

951 Environmental Quality
- 9511 Air, water, & solid waste management
- 9512 Land, mineral, wildlife conservation

953 Housing and Urban Development
- 9531 Housing programs
- 9532 Urban and community development

96 ADMINISTRATION OF ECONOMIC PROGRAMS

961 Admin. of General Economic Programs
- 9611 Admin. of general economic programs

962 Regulation, Admin. of Transportation
- 9621 Regulation, admin. of transportation

963 Regulation, Admin. of Utilities
- 9631 Regulation, admin. of utilities

964 Regulation of Agricultural Marketing
- 9641 Regulation of agricultural marketing

965 Regulation Misc. Commercial Sectors
- 9651 Regulation misc. commercial sectors

966 Space Research and Technology
- 9661 Space research and technology

97 NATIONAL SECURITY AND INTL. AFFAIRS

971 National Security
- 9711 National security

972 International Affairs
- 9721 International affairs

NONCLASSIFIABLE ESTABLISHMENTS

99 NONCLASSIFIABLE ESTABLISHMENTS

999 Nonclassifiable Establishments
- 9999 Nonclassifiable establishments

Standard Occupational Classification

The Standard Occupational Classification was developed to provide a standardized system of job descriptions and classification codes for all occupations performed for pay or profit, for use in the presentation and analysis of statistical data about occupations. The classification system is at 4 levels, with division titles, 2- and 3-digit occupation group codes, and 4-digit unit group codes. The classification was used in the 1980 Census of Population and in Labor Department programs.

The classification is presented in the revised 1980 *Standard Occupational Classification Manual*, from which the following list is taken (for description, see ASI 1981 Annual, 2088-2).

Occupation Group Code

EXECUTIVE, ADMINISTRATIVE AND MANAGERIAL OCCUPATIONS

- **11 Officials and Administrators, Public Administration**
  - 111 Legislators
  - 112 Chief Executives and General Administrators
  - 113 Officials and Administrators, Government Agencies

- **12-13 Officials and Administrators, Other**
  - 121 General Managers and Other Top Executives
  - 122 Financial Managers
  - 123 Personnel and Labor Relations Managers
  - 124 Purchasing Managers
  - 125 Managers; Marketing, Advertising, and Public Relations
  - 126 Managers; Engineering, Mathematics, and Natural Sciences
  - 127 Managers; Social Sciences and Related Fields
  - 128 Administrators; Education and Related Fields
  - 131 Managers; Medicine and Health
  - 132 Production Managers, Industrial
  - 133 Construction Managers
  - 134 Public Utilities Managers
  - 135 Managers; Service Organizations
  - 136 Managers; Mining, Quarrying, Well Drilling, and Similar Operations
  - 137 Managers; Administrative Services
  - 139 Officials and Administrators; Other, Not Elsewhere Classified

- **14 Management Related Occupations**
  - 141 Accountants, Auditors, and Other Financial Specialists
  - 142 Management Analysts
  - 143 Personnel, Training, and Labor Relations Specialists
  - 144 Purchasing Agents and Buyers
  - 145 Business and Promotion Agents
  - 147 Inspectors and Compliance Officers
  - 149 Management Related Occupations, Not Elsewhere Classified

ENGINEERS, SURVEYORS AND ARCHITECTS

- **16 Engineers, Surveyors and Architects**
  - 161 Architects
  - 162-3 Engineers
  - 164 Surveyors and Mapping Scientists

NATURAL SCIENTISTS AND MATHEMATICIANS

- **17 Computer, Mathematical, and Operations Research Occupations**
  - 171 Computer Scientists
  - 172 Operations and Systems Researchers and Analysts
  - 173 Mathematical Scientists

- **18 Natural Scientists**
  - 184 Physical Scientists
  - 185 Life Scientists

SOCIAL SCIENTISTS, SOCIAL WORKERS, RELIGIOUS WORKERS, AND LAWYERS

- **19 Social Scientists and Urban Planners**
  - 191 Social Scientists
  - 192 Urban and Regional Planners

- **20 Social, Recreation, and Religious Workers**
  - 203 Social and Recreation Workers
  - 204 Religious Workers

- **21 Lawyers and Judges**
  - 211 Lawyers
  - 212 Judges

TEACHERS, LIBRARIANS, AND COUNSELORS

- **22 Teachers; College, University and Other Postsecondary Institution**

- **23 Teachers, Except Postsecondary Institution**
  - 231 Prekindergarten and Kindergarten Teachers
  - 232 Elementary School Teachers
  - 233 Secondary School Teachers
  - 235 Teachers; Special Education
  - 236 Instructional Coordinators
  - 239 Adult Education and Other Teachers, Not Elsewhere Classified

- **24 Vocational and Educational Counselors**

- **25 Librarians, Archivists, and Curators**
  - 251 Librarians
  - 252 Archivists and Curators

HEALTH DIAGNOSING AND TREATING PRACTITIONERS

- **26 Physicians and Dentists**
  - 261 Physicians
  - 262 Dentists

- **27 Veterinarians**

- **28 Other Health Diagnosing and Treating Practitioners**
  - 281 Optometrists
  - 283 Podiatrists
  - 289 Health Diagnosing and Treating Practitioners, Not Elsewhere Classified

REGISTERED NURSES, PHARMACISTS, DIETITIANS, THERAPISTS, AND PHYSICIAN'S ASSISTANTS

- **29 Registered Nurses**

- **30 Pharmacists, Dietitians, Therapists, and Physician's Assistants**
  - 301 Pharmacists
  - 302 Dietitians
  - 303 Therapists
  - 304 Physician's Assistants

WRITERS, ARTISTS, ENTERTAINERS, AND ATHLETES

- **32 Writers, Artists, Performers, and Related Workers**
  - 321 Authors
  - 322 Designers
  - 323 Musicians and Composers
  - 324 Actors and Directors
  - 325 Painters, Sculptors, Craft-Artists and Artist-Printmakers
  - 326 Photographers
  - 327 Dancers
  - 328 Performers, Not Elsewhere Classified
  - 329 Writers, Artists, and Related Workers; Not Elsewhere Classified

- **33 Editors, Reporters, Public Relations Specialists, and Announcers**
  - 331 Editors and Reporters
  - 332 Public Relations Specialists and Publicity Writers
  - 333 Radio, Television and Other Announcers

- **34 Athletes and Related Workers**

Guide to Selected Standard Classifications

Standard Occupational Classification

HEALTH TECHNOLOGISTS AND TECHNICIANS

36 Health Technologists and Technicians
- 362 Clinical Laboratory Technologists and Technicians
- 363 Dental Hygienists
- 364 Health Record Technologists and Technicians
- 365 Radiologic Technologists and Technicians
- 366 Licensed Practical Nurses
- 369 Health Technologists and Technicians, Not Elsewhere Classified

TECHNOLOGISTS AND TECHNICIANS, EXCEPT HEALTH

37 Engineering and Related Technologists and Technicians
- 371 Engineering Technologists and Technicians
- 372 Drafting Occupations
- 373 Surveying and Mapping Technicians

38 Science Technologists and Technicians
- 382 Biological Technologists and Technicians, Except Health
- 383 Chemical and Nuclear Technologists and Technicians
- 384 Mathematical Technicians
- 389 Science Technologists and Technicians, Not Elsewhere Classified

39 Technicians; Except Health, Engineering, and Science
- 392 Air Traffic Controllers
- 393 Radio and Related Operators
- 396 Legal Technicians
- 397 Programmers
- 398 Technical Writers
- 399 Technicians, Not Elsewhere Classified

MARKETING AND SALES OCCUPATIONS

40 Supervisors; Marketing and Sales Occupations
- 401 Supervisors; Sales Occupations, Insurance, Real Estate, and Business Services
- 402 Supervisors; Sales Occupations, Commodities Except Retail
- 403 Supervisors; Sales Occupations, Retail

41 Insurance, Securities, Real Estate, and Business Service Sales Occupations
- 412 Insurance, Real Estate, and Securities Sales Occupations
- 415 Business Service Sales Occupations

42 Sales Occupations, Commodities Except Retail
- 421 Sales Engineers
- 423 Technical Sales Workers and Service Advisors
- 424 Sales Representatives

43 Sales Occupations, Retail
- 434-5 Salespersons, Commodities
- 436 Sales Occupations; Other

44 Sales Related Occupations
- 444 Appraisers and Related Occupations
- 445 Demonstrators, Promoters, and Models
- 446 Shoppers
- 447 Auctioneers
- 449 Sales Occupations; Other, Not Elsewhere Classified

ADMINISTRATIVE SUPPORT OCCUPATIONS, INCLUDING CLERICAL

45 Supervisors; Administrative Support Occupations, Including Clerical

46-47 Administrative Support Occupations, Including Clerical
- 461 Computer and Peripheral Equipment Operators
- 462 Secretaries, Stenographers and Typists
- 463 General Office Occupations
- 464 Information Clerks
- 466 Correspondence Clerks and Order Clerks
- 469 Record Clerks
- 471 Financial Record Processing Occupations
- 472 Duplicating, Mail and Other Office Machine Operators
- 473 Communications Equipment Operators
- 474 Mail and Message Distributing Occupations
- 475 Material Recording, Scheduling, and Distributing Clerks
- 478 Adjusters, Investigators, and Collectors
- 479 Miscellaneous Administrative Support Occupations, Including Clerical

SERVICE OCCUPATIONS

50 Private Household Occupations
- 502 Day Workers
- 503 Launderers and Ironers
- 504 Cooks, Private Household
- 505 Housekeepers and Butlers
- 506 Child Care Workers, Private Household
- 507 Private Household Cleaners and Servants
- 509 Private Household Occupations, Not Elsewhere Classified

51 Protective Service Occupations
- 511 Supervisors; Service Occupations, Protective
- 512 Firefighting and Fire Prevention Occupations
- 513 Police and Detectives
- 514 Guards

52 Service Occupations, Except Private Household and Protective
- 521 Food and Beverage Preparation and Service Occupations
- 523 Health Service Occupations
- 524 Cleaning and Building Service Occupations, Except Private Household
- 525-6 Personal Service Occupations

AGRICULTURAL, FORESTRY AND FISHING OCCUPATIONS

55 Farm Operators and Managers
- 551 Farmers (Working Proprietors)
- 552 Farm Managers

56 Other Agricultural and Related Occupations
- 561 Farm Occupations, Except Managerial
- 562 Related Agricultural Occupations

57 Forestry and Logging Occupations
- 571 Supervisors; Forestry and Logging Workers
- 572 Forestry Workers, Except Logging
- 573 Timber Cutting and Related Occupations
- 579 Logging Occupations, Not Elsewhere Classified

58 Fishers, Hunters, and Trappers
- 583 Fishers
- 584 Hunters and Trappers

MECHANICS AND REPAIRERS

60 Supervisors; Mechanics and Repairers

61 Mechanics and Repairers
- 611 Vehicle and Mobile Equipment Mechanics and Repairers
- 613 Industrial Machinery Repairers
- 614 Machinery Maintenance Occupations
- 615 Electrical and Electronic Equipment Repairers
- 616 Heating, Air-Conditioning, and Refrigeration Mechanics
- 617 Miscellaneous Mechanics and Repairers

CONSTRUCTION AND EXTRACTIVE OCCUPATIONS

63 Supervisors; Construction and Extractive Occupations
- 631 Supervisors; Construction
- 632 Supervisors; Extractive Occupations

64 Construction Trades
- 641 Brickmasons, Stonemasons, and Hard Tile Setters
- 642 Carpenters and Related Workers
- 643 Electricians and Power Transmission Installers
- 644 Painters, Paperhangers, and Plasterers
- 645 Plumbers, Pipefitters and Steamfitters
- 646-7 Other Construction Trades

65 Extractive Occupations
- 652 Drillers, Oil Well
- 653 Explosive Workers
- 654 Mining Machine Operators
- 656 Extractive Occupations, Not Elsewhere Classified

PRECISION PRODUCTION OCCUPATIONS

67 **Supervisors; Precision Production Occupations**

68 **Precision Production Occupations**
- 681-2 Precision Metal Workers
- 683 Precision Woodworkers
- 684 Precision Printing Occupations
- 685 Precision Textile, Apparel and Furnishings Workers
- 686 Precision Workers; Assorted Materials
- 687 Precision Food Production Occupations
- 688 Precision Inspectors, Testers, and Related Workers

69 **Plant and System Operators**
- 691 Water and Sewage Treatment Plant Operators
- 692 Gas Plant Operators
- 693 Power Plant Operators
- 694 Chemical Plant Operators
- 695 Petroleum Plant Operators
- 696 Miscellaneous Plant or System Operators

PRODUCTION WORKING OCCUPATIONS

71 **Supervisors; Production Occupations**

73-74 **Machine Setup Operators**
- 731-2 Metalworking and Plastic Working Machine Setup Operators
- 733 Metal Fabricating Machine Setup Operators
- 734 Metal and Plastic Processing Machine Setup Operators
- 743 Woodworking Machine Setup Operators
- 744 Printing Machine Setup Operators
- 745 Textile Machine Setup Operators
- 746-7 Assorted Materials: Machine Setup Operators

75-76 **Machine Operators and Tenders**
- 751-2 Metalworking and Plastic Working Machine Operators and Tenders
- 753 Metal Fabricating Machine Operators and Tenders
- 754 Metal and Plastic Processing Machine Operators and Tenders
- 763 Woodworking Machine Operators and Tenders
- 764 Printing Machine Operators and Tenders
- 765 Textile, Apparel and Furnishings Machine Operators and Tenders
- 766-7 Machine Operators and Tenders; Assorted Materials

77 **Fabricators, Assemblers, and Hand Working Occupations**
- 771 Welders and Solderers
- 772 Assemblers
- 774 Fabricators, Not Elsewhere Classified
- 775 Hand Working Occupations

78 **Production Inspectors, Testers, Samplers, and Weighers**
- 782 Production Inspectors, Checkers and Examiners
- 783 Production Testers
- 784 Production Samplers and Weighers
- 785 Graders and Sorters, Except Agricultural
- 787 Production Expediters

TRANSPORTATION AND MATERIAL MOVING OCCUPATIONS

81 **Supervisors; Transportation and Material Moving Occupations**
- 811 Supervisors; Motorized Equipment Operators
- 812 Supervisors; Material Moving Equipment Operators

82 **Transportation Occupations**
- 821 Motor Vehicle Operators
- 823 Rail Transportation Occupations
- 824 Water Transportation Occupations
- 825 Airplane Pilots and Navigators
- 828 Transportation Inspectors

83 **Material Moving Occupations, Except Transportation**
- 831 Material Moving Equipment Operators

HANDLERS, EQUIPMENT CLEANERS, HELPERS AND LABORERS

85 **Supervisors; Handlers, Equipment Cleaners, Helpers, and Laborers**

86 **Helpers**
- 861 Helpers; Machine Operators and Tenders
- 862 Helpers; Fabricators and Inspectors
- 863 Helpers; Mechanics and Repairers
- 864 Helpers; Construction Trades
- 865 Helpers; Extractive Occupations

87 **Handlers, Equipment Cleaners and Laborers**
- 871 Construction Laborers
- 872 Freight, Stock, and Material Movers; Hand
- 873 Garage and Service Station Related Occupations
- 874 Parking Lot Attendants
- 875 Vehicle Washers and Equipment Cleaners
- 876 Miscellaneous Manual Occupations

MILITARY OCCUPATIONS

91 **Military Occupations**

MISCELLANEOUS OCCUPATIONS

99 **Miscellaneous Occupations**

Standard International Trade Classification, Revision 3

The Standard International Trade Classification (SITC) is a statistical classification of commodities in world trade, developed by the United Nations to facilitate international comparison of commodity trade data. The classification is at 5 levels: sections, divisions, groups, subgroups, and items—represented by 1- to 5-digit codes.

SITC Revision 3 was published in 1986. An earlier classification scheme, Revision 2, was published in 1975.

The 1- to 3-digit codes of Revision 3 are listed below. For Revision 2 codes, see ASI 1989 Annual Index volume.

Section, Division, and Group Codes

0 FOOD AND LIVE ANIMALS

00 Live Animals Other Than Animals of Division 03

001 Live animals other than animals of division 03

01 Meat and Meat Preparations

- 011 Meat of bovine animals, fresh, chilled or frozen
- 012 Other meat and edible meat offal, fresh, chilled or frozen (except meat and meat offal unfit or unsuitable for human consumption)
- 016 Meat and edible meat offal, salted, in brine, dried or smoked; edible flours and meals of meat or meat offal
- 017 Meat and edible meat offal, prepared or preserved, n.e.s.

02 Dairy Products and Birds' Eggs

- 022 Milk and cream and milk products other than butter or cheese
- 023 Butter and other fats and oils derived from milk
- 024 Cheese and curd
- 025 Eggs, birds', and egg yolks, fresh, dried or otherwise preserved, sweetened or not; egg albumin

03 Fish (Not Marine Mammals), Crustaceans, Molluscs and Aquatic Invertebrates, and Preparations Thereof

- 034 Fish, fresh (live or dead), chilled or frozen
- 035 Fish, dried, salted or in brine; smoked fish (whether or not cooked before or during the smoking process)
- 036 Crustaceans, molluscs and aquatic invertebrates, whether in shell or not, fresh (live or dead), chilled, frozen, dried, salted or in brine; crustaceans, in shell, cooked by steaming or boiling in water
- 037 Fish, crustaceans, molluscs and other aquatic invertebrates, prepared or preserved, n.e.s.

04 Cereals and Cereal Preparations

- 041 Wheat (including spelt) and meslin, unmilled
- 042 Rice
- 043 Barley, unmilled
- 044 Maize (not including sweet corn) unmilled
- 045 Cereals, unmilled (other than wheat, rice, barley, and maize)
- 046 Meal and flour of wheat and flour of meslin
- 047 Other cereal meals and flours
- 048 Cereal preparations and preparations of flour or starch of fruits or vegetables

05 Vegetables and Fruit

- 054 Vegetables, fresh, chilled, frozen or simply preserved (including dried leguminous vegetables); roots, tubers and other edible vegetable products, n.e.s., fresh or dried
- 056 Vegetables, roots and tubers, prepared or preserved, n.e.s.
- 057 Fruit and nuts (not including oil nuts), fresh or dried
- 058 Fruit, preserved, and fruit preparations (excluding fruit juices)
- 059 Fruit juices (including grape must) and vegetable juices, unfermented and not containing added spirit, whether or not containing added sugar or other sweetening matter

06 Sugars, Sugar Preparations and Honey

- 061 Sugars, molasses and honey
- 062 Sugar confectionery

07 Coffee, Tea, Cocoa, Spices, and Manufactures Thereof

- 071 Coffee and coffee substitutes
- 072 Cocoa
- 073 Chocolate and other food preparations containing cocoa, n.e.s.
- 074 Tea and mate
- 075 Spices

08 Feeding Stuff for Animals (Not Including Unmilled Cereals)

081 Feeding stuff for animals (not including unmilled cereals)

09 Miscellaneous Edible Products and Preparations

- 091 Margarine and shortening
- 098 Edible products and preparations, n.e.s.

1 BEVERAGES AND TOBACCO

11 Beverages

- 111 Non-alcoholic beverages, n.e.s.
- 112 Alcoholic beverages

12 Tobacco and Tobacco Manufactures

- 121 Tobacco, unmanufactured; tobacco refuse
- 122 Tobacco, manufactured (whether or not containing tobacco substitutes)

2 CRUDE MATERIALS, INEDIBLE, EXCEPT FUELS

21 Hides, Skins and Furskins, Raw

- 211 Hides and skins (except furskins), raw
- 212 Furskins, raw (including heads, tails, paws and other pieces or cuttings, suitable for furriers' use), other than hides and skins of group 211

22 Oil Seeds and Oleaginous Fruits

- 222 Oil seeds and oleaginous fruits of a kind used for the extraction of "soft" fixed vegetable oils (excluding flours and meals)
- 223 Oil seeds and oleaginous fruits, whole or broken, of a kind used for the extraction of other fixed vegetable oils (including flours and meals of oil seeds or oleaginous fruit, n.e.s.)

23 Crude Rubber (Including Synthetic and Reclaimed)

- 231 Natural rubber, balata, gutta percha, guayule, chicle and similar natural gums, in primary forms (including latex) or in plates, sheets or strip
- 232 Synthetic rubber; reclaimed rubber; waste, parings and scrap of unhardened rubber

24 Cork and Wood

- 244 Cork, natural, raw and waste (including natural cork in blocks or sheets)
- 245 Fuel wood (excluding wood waste) and wood charcoal
- 246 Wood in chips or particles and wood waste
- 247 Wood in the rough or roughly squared
- 248 Wood, simply worked, and railway sleepers of wood

25 Pulp and Waste Paper

251 Pulp and waste paper

26 Textile Fibres (Other Than Wool Tops and Other Combed Wool) and Their Wastes (Not Manufactured Into Yarn or Fabric)

- 261 Silk
- 263 Cotton
- 264 Jute and other textile bast fibres, n.e.s., raw or processed but not spun; tow and waste of these fibres (including yarn waste and garnetted stock)
- 265 Vegetable textile fibres (other than cotton and jute), raw or processed but not spun; waste of these fibres
- 266 Synthetic fibres suitable for spinning
- 267 Other man-made fibres suitable for spinning and waste of man-made fibres
- 268 Wool and other animal hair (including wool tops)
- 269 Worn clothing and other worn textile articles; rags

SITC, Rev 3

Guide to Selected Standard Classifications

- **27 Crude Fertilizers, Other Than Those of Division 56, and Crude Minerals (Excluding Coal, Petroleum and Precious Stones)**
  - 272 Fertilizers, crude, other than those of division 56
  - 273 Stone, sand and gravel
  - 274 Sulphur and unroasted iron pyrites
  - 277 Natural abrasives, n.e.s. (including industrial diamonds)
  - 278 Other crude minerals
- **28 Metalliferous Ores and Metal Scrap**
  - 281 Iron ore and concentrates
  - 282 Ferrous waste and scrap; remelting ingots of iron or steel
  - 283 Copper ores and concentrates; copper mattes, cement copper
  - 284 Nickel ores and concentrates; nickel mattes, nickel oxide, sinters and other intermediate products of nickel metallurgy
  - 285 Aluminium ores and concentrates (including alumina)
  - 286 Ores and concentrates of uranium or thorium
  - 287 Ores and concentrates of base metals, n.e.s.
  - 288 Non-ferrous base metal waste and scrap, n.e.s.
  - 289 Ores and concentrates of precious metals; waste, scrap and sweepings of precious metals (other than of gold)
- **29 Crude Animal and Vegetable Materials, n.e.s.**
  - 291 Crude animal materials, n.e.s.
  - 292 Crude vegetable materials, n.e.s.

3 MINERAL FUELS, LUBRICANTS AND RELATED MATERIALS

- **32 Coal, Coke and Briquettes**
  - 321 Coal, whether or not pulverized, but not agglomerated
  - 322 Briquettes, lignite and peat
  - 325 Coke and semi-coke (including char) of coal, of lignite or of peat, whether or not agglomerated; retort carbon
- **33 Petroleum, Petroleum Products and Related Materials**
  - 333 Petroleum oils and oils obtained from bituminous minerals, crude
  - 334 Petroleum oils and oils obtained from bituminous minerals (other than crude); preparations, n.e.s., containing by weight 70% or more of petroleum oils or of oils obtained from bituminous minerals, these oils being the basic constituents of the preparations
  - 335 Residual petroleum products, n.e.s. and related materials
- **34 Gas, Natural and Manufactured**
  - 342 Liquefied propane and butane
  - 343 Natural gas, whether or not liquefied
  - 344 Petroleum gases and other gaseous hydrocarbons, n.e.s.
  - 345 Coal gas, water gas, producer gas and similar gases, other than petroleum gases and other gaseous hydrocarbons

- **35 Electric Current**
  - 351 Electric current

4 ANIMAL AND VEGETABLE OILS, FATS AND WAXES

- **41 Animal Oils and Fats**
  - 411 Animal oils and fats
- **42 Fixed Vegetable Fats and Oils, Crude, Refined or Fractionated**
  - 421 Fixed vegetable fats and oils, "soft", crude, refined or fractionated
  - 422 Fixed vegetable fats and oils, crude, refined or fractionated, other than "soft"
- **43 Animal or Vegetable Fats and Oils, Processed; Waxes of Animal or Vegetable Origin; Inedible Mixtures or Preparations of Animal or Vegetable Fats or Oils, n.e.s.**
  - 431 Animal or vegetable fats and oils, processed, waxes, and inedible mixtures or preparations of animal or vegetable fats or oils, n.e.s.

5 CHEMICALS AND RELATED PRODUCTS, N.E.S.

- **51 Organic Chemicals**
  - 511 Hydrocarbons, n.e.s., and their halogenated, sulphonated, nitrated or nitrosated derivatives
  - 512 Alcohols, phenols, phenol-alcohols, and their halogenated, sulphonated, nitrated or nitrosated derivatives
  - 513 Carboxylic acids and their anhydrides, halides, peroxides and peroxyacids; their halogenated, sulphonated, nitrated or nitrosated derivatives
  - 514 Nitrogen-function compounds
  - 515 Organo-inorganic compounds, heterocyclic compounds, nucleic acids and their salts
  - 516 Other organic chemicals
- **52 Inorganic Chemicals**
  - 522 Inorganic chemical elements, oxides and halogen salts
  - 523 Metallic salts and peroxysalts, of inorganic acids
  - 524 Other inorganic chemicals; organic and inorganic compounds of precious metals
  - 525 Radio-active and associated materials
- **53 Dyeing, Tanning and Colouring Materials**
  - 531 Synthetic organic colouring matter and colour lakes, and preparations based thereon
  - 532 Dyeing and tanning extracts, and synthetic tanning materials
  - 533 Pigments, paints, varnishes and related materials
- **54 Medicinal and Pharmaceutical Products**
  - 541 Medicinal and pharmaceutical products, other than medicaments of group 542
  - 542 Medicaments (including veterinary medicaments)

- **55 Essential Oils and Resinoids and Perfume Materials; Toilet, Polishing and Cleansing Preparations**
  - 551 Essential oils, perfume and flavour materials
  - 553 Perfumery, cosmetics or toilet preparations (excluding soaps)
  - 554 Soap, cleansing and polishing preparations
- **56 Fertilizers (Other Than Those of Group 272)**
  - 562 Fertilizers (other than those of group 272)
- **57 Plastics in Primary Forms**
  - 571 Polymers of ethylene, in primary forms
  - 572 Polymers of styrene, in primary forms
  - 573 Polymers of vinyl chloride or of other halogenated olefins, in primary forms
  - 574 Polyacetals, other polyethers and epoxide resins, in primary forms; polycarbonates, alkyd resins and other polyesters, in primary forms
  - 575 Other plastics, in primary forms
  - 579 Waste, parings and scrap, of plastics
- **58 Plastics in Non-primary Forms**
  - 581 Tubes, pipes and hoses of plastics
  - 582 Plates, sheets, film, foil and strip, of plastics
  - 583 Monofilament of which any cross-sectional dimension exceeds 1 mm, rods, sticks and profile shapes, whether or not surface-worked but not otherwise worked, of plastics
- **59 Chemical Materials and Products, n.e.s.**
  - 591 Insecticides, rodenticides, fungicides, herbicides, anti-sprouting products and plant-growth regulators, disinfectants and similar products, put up in forms or packings for retail sale or as preparations or articles (e.g., sulphur-treated bands, wicks and candles, and fly-papers)
  - 592 Starches, inulin and wheat gluten; albuminoidal substances; glues
  - 593 Explosives and pyrotechnic products
  - 597 Prepared additives for mineral oils and the like; prepared liquids for hydraulic transmission; anti-freezing preparations and prepared de-icing fluids; lubricating preparations
  - 598 Miscellaneous chemical products, n.e.s.

6 MANUFACTURED GOODS CLASSIFIED CHIEFLY BY MATERIAL

- **61 Leather, Leather Manufactures, n.e.s., and Dressed Furskins**
  - 611 Leather
  - 612 Manufactures of leather or of composition leather, n.e.s.; saddlery and harness
  - 613 Furskins, tanned or dressed (including heads, tails, paws and

other pieces or cuttings), unassembled, or assembled (without the addition of other materials), other than those of heading 848.3

- **62 Rubber Manufactures, n.e.s.**
  - 621 Materials of rubber (e.g., pastes, plates, sheets, rods, thread, tubes, of rubber)
  - 625 Rubber tyres, interchangeable tyre treads, tyre flaps and inner tubes for wheels of all kinds
  - 629 Articles of rubber, n.e.s.
- **63 Cork and Wood Manufactures (Excluding Furniture)**
  - 633 Cork manufactures
  - 634 Veneers, plywood, particle board, and other wood, worked, n.e.s.
  - 635 Wood manufactures, n.e.s.
- **64 Paper, Paperboard, and Articles of Paper Pulp, of Paper or of Paperboard**
  - 641 Paper and paperboard
  - 642 Paper and paperboard, cut to size or shape, and articles of paper or paperboard
- **65 Textile Yarn, Fabrics, Made-Up Articles, n.e.s., and Related Products**
  - 651 Textile yarn
  - 652 Cotton fabrics, woven (not including narrow or special fabrics)
  - 653 Fabrics, woven, of man-made textile materials (not including narrow or special fabrics)
  - 654 Other textile fabrics, woven
  - 655 Knitted or crocheted fabrics (including tubular knit fabrics, n.e.s., pile fabrics and open-work fabrics), n.e.s.
  - 656 Tulles, lace, embroidery, ribbons, trimmings and other small wares
  - 657 Special yarns, special textile fabrics and related products
  - 658 Made-up articles, wholly or chiefly of textile materials, n.e.s.
  - 659 Floor coverings, etc.
- **66 Non-Metallic Mineral Manufactures, n.e.s.**
  - 661 Lime, cement, and fabricated construction materials (except glass and clay materials)
  - 662 Clay construction materials and refractory construction materials
  - 663 Mineral manufactures, n.e.s.
  - 664 Glass
  - 665 Glassware
  - 666 Pottery
  - 667 Pearls, precious and semi-precious stones, unworked or worked
- **67 Iron and Steel**
  - 671 Pig iron, spiegeleisen, sponge iron, iron or steel granules and powders and ferro-alloys
  - 672 Ingots and other primary forms, of iron or steel; semi-finished products of iron or steel
  - 673 Flat-rolled products, of iron or non-alloy steel, not clad, plated or coated
  - 674 Flat-rolled products of iron or non-alloy steel, clad, plated or coated
  - 675 Flat-rolled products of alloy steel
  - 676 Iron and steel bars, rods, angles, shapes and sections (including sheet piling)
  - 677 Rails and railway track construction material, of iron or steel
  - 678 Wire of iron or steel
  - 679 Tubes, pipes and hollow profiles, and tube or pipe fittings, of iron or steel
- **68 Non-Ferrous Metals**
  - 681 Silver, platinum and other metals of the platinum group
  - 682 Copper
  - 683 Nickel
  - 684 Aluminium
  - 685 Lead
  - 686 Zinc
  - 687 Tin
  - 689 Miscellaneous non-ferrous base metals employed in metallurgy, and cermets
- **69 Manufactures of Metals, n.e.s.**
  - 691 Structures and parts of structures, n.e.s., of iron, steel or aluminium
  - 692 Metal containers for storage or transport
  - 693 Wire products (excluding insulated electrical wiring) and fencing grills
  - 694 Nails, screws, nuts, bolts, rivets and the like, of iron, steel, copper or aluminium
  - 695 Tools for use in the hand or in machines
  - 696 Cutlery
  - 697 Household equipment of base metal, n.e.s.
  - 699 Manufactures of base metal, n.e.s.

7 MACHINERY AND TRANSPORT EQUIPMENT

- **71 Power Generating Machinery and Equipment**
  - 711 Steam or other vapour generating boilers, super-heated water boilers, and auxiliary plant for use therewith; and parts thereof
  - 712 Steam turbines and other vapour turbines, and parts thereof, n.e.s.
  - 713 Internal combustion piston engines, and parts thereof, n.e.s.
  - 714 Engines and motors, non-electric (other than those of groups 712, 713 and 718); parts, n.e.s. of these engines and motors
  - 716 Rotating electric plant and parts thereof, n.e.s.
  - 718 Other power generating machinery and parts thereof, n.e.s.
- **72 Machinery Specialized for Particular Industries**
  - 721 Agricultural machinery (excluding tractors) and parts thereof
  - 722 Tractors (other than those of headings 744.14 and 744.15)
  - 723 Civil engineering and contractors' plant and equipment
  - 724 Textile and leather machinery, and parts thereof, n.e.s.
  - 725 Paper mill and pulp mill machinery, paper cutting machines and other machinery for the manufacture of paper articles; parts thereof
  - 726 Printing and bookbinding machinery, and parts thereof
  - 727 Food-processing machines (excluding domestic)
  - 728 Other machinery and equipment specialized for particular industries, and parts thereof, n.e.s.
- **73 Metalworking Machinery**
  - 731 Machine-tools working by removing metal or other material
  - 733 Machine-tools for working metal, sintered metal carbides or cermets, without removing material
  - 735 Parts, n.e.s., and accessories suitable for use solely or principally with the machines falling within headings 731 and 733 (including work or tool holders, self-opening dieheads, dividing heads and other special attachments for machine-tools); tool holders for any type of tool for working in the hand
  - 737 Metalworking machinery (other than machine-tools), and parts thereof, n.e.s.
- **74 General Industrial Machinery and Equipment, n.e.s., and Machine Parts, n.e.s.**
  - 741 Heating and cooling equipment and parts thereof, n.e.s.
  - 742 Pumps for liquids, whether or not fitted with a measuring device; liquid elevators; parts for such pumps and liquid elevators
  - 743 Pumps (other than pumps for liquids), air or other gas compressors and fans; ventilating or recycling hoods incorporating a fan, whether or not fitted with filters; centrifuges; filtering or purifying apparatus; and parts thereof
  - 744 Mechanical handling equipment, and parts thereof, n.e.s.
  - 745 Other non-electrical machinery, tools and mechanical apparatus, and parts thereof, n.e.s.
  - 746 Ball or roller bearings
  - 747 Taps, cocks, valves and similar appliances, for pipes, boiler shells, tanks, vats and the like (including pressure reducing valves and thermostatically controlled valves)
  - 748 Transmission shafts (including cam shafts and crank shafts) and cranks; bearing housings and plain shaft bearings; gears and gearing; ball screws; gear boxes and other speed changers (including torque converters); flywheels and pulleys (including pulley blocks); clutches and shaft couplings (including universal joints); and parts thereof
  - 749 Non-electric parts and accessories of machinery, n.e.s.
- **75 Office Machines and Automatic Data Processing Machines**
  - 751 Office machines
  - 752 Automatic data processing machines and units thereof; magnetic or optical readers, machines for transcribing data onto data media in coded form and machines for processing such data, n.e.s.
  - 759 Parts and accessories (other than covers, carrying cases and the like) suitable for use solely or principally with machines falling within groups 751 and 752
- **76 Telecommunications and Sound Recording and Reproducing Apparatus and Equipment**
  - 761 Television receivers (including

video monitors and video projectors), whether or not combined, in the same housing, with radio-broadcast receivers or sound or video recording or reproducing apparatus

- 762 Radio-broadcast receivers, whether or not combined, in the same housing, with sound recording or reproducing apparatus or a clock
- 763 Sound recorders or reproducers; television image and sound recorders or reproducers; prepared unrecorded media
- 764 Telecommunications equipment, n.e.s.; and parts, n.e.s., and accessories of apparatus falling within division 76

77 Electrical Machinery, Apparatus and Appliances, n.e.s., and Electrical Parts Thereof (Including Non-Electrical Counterparts, n.e.s. of Electrical Household Type Equipment)

- 771 Electric power machinery (other than rotating electric plant of heading 716), and parts thereof
- 772 Electrical apparatus for switching or protecting electrical circuits or for making connections to or in electrical circuits (e.g., switches, relays, fuses, lightning arresters, voltage limiters, surge suppressors, plugs and sockets, lampholders and junction boxes); electrical resistors (including rheostats and potentiometers), other than heating resistors; printed circuits; boards, panels (including numerical control panels), consoles, desks, cabinets and other bases, equipped with two or more apparatus for switching, protecting or for making connections to or in electrical circuits, for electric control or the distribution of electricity (excluding switching apparatus of heading 764.1)
- 773 Equipment for distributing electricity, n.e.s.
- 774 Electro-diagnostic apparatus for medical, surgical, dental or veterinary sciences and radiological apparatus
- 775 Household type, electrical and non-electrical equipment, n.e.s.
- 776 Thermionic, cold cathode or photo-cathode valves and tubes (e.g., vacuum or vapour or gas filled valves and tubes, mercury arc rectifying valves and tubes, cathode-ray tubes, television camera tubes); diodes, transistors and similar semi-conductor devices; photosensitive semi-conductor devices; light emitting diodes; mounted piezo-electric crystals; electronic integrated circuits and microassemblies; and parts thereof
- 778 Electrical machinery and apparatus, n.e.s.

78 Road Vehicles (Including Air-Cushion Vehicles)

781 Motor cars and other motor vehicles principally designed for the transport of persons (other than public-transport type

vehicles), including station wagons and racing cars

- 782 Motor vehicles for the transport of goods and special purpose motor vehicles
- 783 Road motor vehicles, n.e.s.
- 784 Parts and accessories of the motor vehicles of groups 722, 781, 782 and 783
- 785 Motorcycles (including mopeds) and cycles, motorized and non-motorized; invalid carriages
- 786 Trailers and semi-trailers; other vehicles, not mechanically propelled; specially designed and equipped transport containers

79 Other Transport Equipment

- 791 Railway vehicles (including hovertrains) and associated equipment
- 792 Aircraft and associated equipment; spacecraft (including satellites) and spacecraft launch vehicles; and parts thereof
- 793 Ships, boats (including hovercraft) and floating structures

8 MISCELLANEOUS MANUFACTURED ARTICLES

81 Prefabricated Buildings; Sanitary, Plumbing, Heating and Lighting Fixtures and Fittings, n.e.s.

- 811 Prefabricated buildings
- 812 Sanitary, plumbing and heating fixtures and fittings, n.e.s.
- 813 Lighting fixtures and fittings, n.e.s.

82 Furniture and Parts Thereof; Bedding, Mattresses, Mattress Supports, Cushions and Similar Stuffed Furnishings

821 Furniture and parts thereof; bedding, mattresses, mattress supports, cushions and similar stuffed furnishings

83 Travel Goods, Handbags and Similar Containers

831 Trunks, suit-cases, vanity-cases, executive-cases, brief-cases, school satchels, binocular cases, camera cases, musical instrument cases, spectacle cases, gun cases, holsters and similar containers; travelling bags, toilet bags, rucksacks, handbags, shopping-bags, wallets, purses, map-cases, cigarette-cases, tobacco-pouches, tool bags, sports bags, bottle-cases, jewellery boxes, powder-boxes, cutlery cases and similar containers, of leather or of composition leather, of plastic sheeting, of textile materials, of vulcanized fibre or of paperboard, or wholly or mainly covered with such materials; travel sets for personal toilet, sewing or shoe or clothes cleaning

84 Articles of Apparel and Clothing Accessories

- 841 Men's or boys' coats, jackets, suits, blazers, trousers, shorts, shirts, underwear, knitwear and similar articles of textile fabrics, not knitted or crocheted (other than those of heading 845.2 or 845.6)
- 842 Women's and girls' coats, capes, jackets, suits, blazers, trousers, shorts, shirts, underwear and similar articles of textile fabrics, not knitted or crocheted (other than those of heading 845.2 or 845.6)
- 843 Men's or boys' coats, capes, jackets, suits, blazers, trousers, shorts, shirts, underwear, nightwear and similar articles of textile fabrics, knitted or crocheted (other than those of heading 845.2 or 845.6)
- 844 Women's or girls' coats, capes, jackets, suits, blazers, trousers, shorts, shirts, underwear, nightwear and similar articles of textile fabrics, knitted or crocheted (other than those of heading 845.2 or 845.6)
- 845 Articles of apparel, of textile fabrics, whether or not knitted or crocheted, n.e.s.
- 846 Clothing accessories, of textile fabrics, whether or not knitted or crocheted (other than those for babies)
- 848 Articles of apparel and clothing accessories of other than textile fabrics; headgear of all materials

85 Footwear

851 Footwear

87 Professional, Scientific and Controlling Instruments and Apparatus, n.e.s.

- 871 Optical instruments and apparatus, n.e.s.
- 872 Instruments and appliances, n.e.s., for medical, surgical, dental or veterinary purposes
- 873 Meters and counters, n.e.s.
- 874 Measuring, checking, analysing and controlling instruments and apparatus, n.e.s.

88 Photographic Apparatus, Equipment and Supplies and Optical Goods, n.e.s.; Watches and Clocks

- 881 Photographic apparatus and equipment, n.e.s.
- 882 Photographic and cinematographic supplies
- 883 Cinematograph film, exposed and developed, whether or not incorporating sound track or consisting only of sound track
- 884 Optical goods, n.e.s.
- 885 Watches and clocks

89 Miscellaneous Manufactured Articles, n.e.s.

- 891 Arms and ammunition
- 892 Printed matter
- 893 Articles, n.e.s. of plastics
- 894 Baby carriages, toys, games and sporting goods
- 895 Office and stationery supplies, n.e.s.
- 896 Works of art, collectors' pieces and antiques
- 897 Jewellery, goldsmiths' and silversmiths' wares, and other articles of precious or semi-precious materials, n.e.s.

898 Musical instruments and parts and accessories thereof; records, tapes and other sound or similar recordings (excluding goods of groups 763, 882 and 883)

899 Miscellaneous manufactured articles, n.e.s.

9 COMMODITIES AND TRANSACTIONS NOT CLASSIFIED ELSEWHERE IN THE SITC

- **91 Postal Packages Not Classified According to Kind**
  - 911 Postal packages not classified according to kind
- **93 Special Transactions and Commodities Not Classified According to Kind**
  - 931 Special transactions and commodities not classified according to kind
- **96 Coin (Other Than Gold Coin), Not Being Legal Tender**
  - 961 Coin (other than gold coin), not being legal tender
- **97 Gold, Non-Monetary (Excluding Gold Ores and Concentrates)**
  - 971 Gold, non-monetary (excluding gold ores and concentrates)